MW00717638

Standard & Poor's SmallCap 600 Guide

2000 Edition

Standard & Poor's

McGraw-Hill

New York San Francisco Washington, D.C. Auckland Bogotá
Caracas Lisbon London Madrid Mexico City Milan
Montreal New Delhi San Juan Singapore
Sydney Tokyo Toronto

FOR STANDARD & POOR'S
Vice President, Index Products & Services: Elliott Shurgin
Managing Editor: Shauna Morrison
Publisher: Frank LoVaglio

McGraw-Hill

A Division of The ***McGraw-Hill*** *Companies*

1 2 3 4 5 6 7 8 9 0 AGM/AGM 9 0 9 8 7 6 5 4 3 2 1 0 9

ISBN 0-07-135255-4

The sponsoring editor for this book was Griffin Hansbury, the editing supervisor was Patricia V. Amoroso, and the production supervisor was Modestine Cameron. The front matter and introduction were set by North Market Street Graphics.

Printed and bound by Quebecor/Martinsburg.

This book is printed on acid-free paper.

The companies contained in this handbook represented the components of the S&P SmallCap 600 Index as of October 8, 1999. Additions to and deletions from the Index will cause its composition to change over time. Company additions and company deletions from the Standard & Poor's equity indexes do not in any way reflect an opinion on the investment merits of the company.

ABOUT THE AUTHOR

Standard & Poor's, a division of The McGraw-Hill Companies, Inc., is the nation's leading securities information company. It provides a broad range of financial services, including the respected Standard & Poor's ratings and stock rankings, advisory services, data guides, and the most closely watched and widely reported gauges of stock market activity—the S&P 500, S&P MidCap 400, S&P SmallCap 600, and the S&P Super Composite 1500 stock price indexes. Standard & Poor's products are marketed around the world and used extensively by financial professionals and individual investors.

Introduction

by James M. Nevler, C.F.A.

If you open any copy of *The Wall Street Journal* you will find numerous stock market indexes listed for your reading pleasure and investment research. On January 3, 1995, that list got a new addition, the Standard & Poor's SmallCap 600 Index. You will find it with its older siblings, the S&P 500 and S&P MidCap 400 Stock Indexes, and the S&P Super Composite 1500 Index, which was introduced in May 1995.

The S&P SmallCap 600 is a list of 600 companies which, on average, are considerably smaller than those in the S&P 500 or in the S&P MidCap 400 Index. Since there already were plenty of other stock indexes to follow, it would be logical to ask why the world needed another one. The answer: because institutional investors—the people who manage the funds in corporate retirement plans and mutual funds—asked Standard & Poor's to develop a better way of monitoring the small-company sector of the stock market, as well as provide an index that could be used to build an investment portfolio of small but easily tradable companies.

Few individual investors can afford to build a personal portfolio of 600 common stocks. However, investors who do their own stock picking and understand why all stock portfolios should be diversified will find the SmallCap 600 to be a valuable tool. Research has shown that, over long investment horizons, stocks of smaller companies, as an investment class, will outperform stocks of larger companies. It was not that long ago that Microsoft, Wal-Mart, and COMPAQ Computer were all small companies. It only takes a reasonable number of such winners to turn a well-balanced portfolio of small-company stocks into a highly profitable investment.

However, those same studies of investment results have also shown that, over shorter time horizons, small companies can be much riskier to own than the far larger companies in the S&P 500. Many small companies—whether they are restaurant chains or technology firms—fail every year. Many others mature into solid companies that prosper for decades serving niche markets or loyal local customers. There are many such consistently profitable companies that provide hundreds of well-paying jobs and reliable dividends year in and year out. Yet their common stock prices may languish for years because they are in industries that are out of favor, because Wall Street analysts do not follow them, or because they may have once had financial problems. There is a crucial difference between a great company and a great stock; unfortunately, there is no sure-fire way to determine which is which. With literally thousands of small companies to choose from, the odds that any one of them, selected at random, will become the next Home Depot or Intel are about as long as the odds that any college basketball player, also chosen at random, will become the next Larry Bird or Michael Jordan.

If indeed the next Home Depot and Intel are hidden somewhere in the S&P SmallCap 600, it is not because Standard & Poor's expects them to be superstars. On the contrary, as with all of the Standard & Poor's Indexes, the stocks in the SmallCap 600 are there because they are expected to produce an index whose performance would be *typical* of the market segment from which they were selected. Standard & Poor's mission is not to beat the market, but to define it. Unlike the children in Lake Wobegon, all of the stocks in the S&P SmallCap 600 cannot be above average. As is the case in the S&P 500 and the MidCap 400, some stocks will beat their Index by a wide margin, others will be spectacularly worse, and most will perform somewhere in the middle of the pack. Ironically, however, over the long-term, the average performance of large, medium, and small capitalization stocks, as measured by their respective Standard & Poor's Indices, has proven to be more than good enough to outperform most investment professionals.

Using the Standard & Poor's Indexes to Measure the Market

While each day's trading on the stock market is often described in terms of bulls and bears, most individual common stocks could be described as members in a school of fish. That is because, more often than not, they tend to swim in the same direction as the overall market. Many studies of securities prices, including the theories for which Harry Markowitz and William Sharpe shared the 1990 Nobel Prize in Economic Science, have shown that one of the most important factors in the price performance of virtually any common stock is the overall performance of the stock market—the investment pool from which the school that the stock swims in is drawn.

Of course, some stocks move faster than others and lead the market—whether up or down—while most swim along unnoticed in the middle of the school. Others lag the market, both when prices head upstream and when they head for the bottom of the sea, and some stocks always go their own way. These volatility relationships to the overall market tend to be stable over relatively long periods of time and are measured with a statistic called beta. Betas are derived by running a statistical test called a regression on the performance of a stock against the performance of the overall stock market. However, before you can begin the test, you must first define the "market." The best way to do that is through a stock index. Thanks in large part to the work of Markowitz, Sharpe and their many disciples, the index universally used for that purpose is the Standard and Poor's 500 Index.

By definition, the S&P 500 has a beta of 1.0. A stock that moved in perfect correlation with the S&P 500 also would have a beta of 1.0. A stock with a beta of 1.5 would be expected to gain 1.5% for every 1% gain in the S&P 500, but would lose 1.5% for every 1% drop in the Index. However, as Markowitz pointed out, the performance of a properly diversified collection of smaller, more volatile stocks will not be much more risky than the overall market. Stocks with high betas in that portfolio will be canceled out by the performance of stocks with betas below 1.0 that lag the market, or by stocks with extremely low betas that have almost no response to the market. A stock with a negative beta, if you could find one, would move in the opposite direction to the S&P 500.

Using the Standard & Poor's Indexes for Investment Management

One of the most important purposes of a stock index is to tell investors, in a way, where the fish are and which way the fish are running.

When the S&P 500 was introduced in 1957, all of the fish in its pool were listed on the New York Stock Exchange. The S&P 500 was designed as a sample drawn from that pool to represent the market performance of the leading companies in the leading industries in the U.S.

As both the U.S. economy and the equity markets grew, Standard & Poor's expanded the selection pool for the S&P 500 to include stocks traded on the American Stock Exchange and over the counter on the Nasdaq quotation system. The S&P 500 remains broadly based, containing stocks in approximately 106 different industry groups ranging from aerospace/defense to trucking.

Because of the Index's mandate to select leading stocks in leading industries, the S&P 500 has evolved into a measure of large-capitalization stocks with a distinct, but modest, bias toward growth stocks. The average market capitalization of the companies in the S&P 500 at the end of 1999's second quarter was $22.4 billion, and the median valuation, the point at which the 500 stocks could be split into pools of the 250 largest and 250 smallest companies, was $8.3 billion.

The S&P MidCap 400 Index was created in 1991 to monitor the investment performance of midsized companies. When the MidCap 400 was created, it was drawn from a pool of companies not already in the S&P 500 Index with market capitalizations of between $5.2 billion and $300 million. The average market capitalization of a MidCap 400 stock at the end of the second quarter of 1999 was $2.1 billion.

Together, the S&P 500 and MidCap 400 account for 85% of the stock market's capitalization. However, they still do not track the performance of more than 8000 other common stocks. That is the objective of the S&P SmallCap 600.

SmallCap Stocks

The first question to answer is the obvious one: What exactly is a small-cap stock? There is no obvious answer. Almost every expert has a unique definition. Some well-respected academic studies, for example, included stocks with market values of up to $2 billion. However, the consensus market value range at the end of 1993 appeared to run from $600 million down to $80 million, or from approximately the 50th percentile in market value down to about the 83rd percentile. This percentile range not only was used in developing and testing the SmallCap 600 Index, but it will also be used in screening future candidates for the Index. As overall market capitalizations rise or fall, so will the SmallCap's selection parameters.

As was noted above, potential investment performance is not one of the criteria for membership in any Standard & Poor's equity index. Inclusion in any Standard & Poor's Index—and this also goes for the decision not to select a stock—is not based on the investment merits of the company in question. A good company may pass all of our screens for inclusion but be passed over when a vacancy appears because its industry is already overrepresented in the appropriate index for that stock. Some of the screens are computer-generated, but unlike the Russell 1000 and Russell 2000 indexes, our mechanical market-capitalization screen is only the start of the selection process. The approximately 1850 common stocks that met the SmallCap's capitalization parameters at the end of 1993 were subjected to the following additional requirements:

1. The company must be listed on either the New York Stock Exchange, American Stock Exchange, or Nasdaq Stock Market.
2. The company must have been trading for at least six months in order to be considered, whether it was an initial public offering or a spin-off by an established company.
3. Stocks that did not trade on any three business days during a 12-month period or, in the case of new issues, over the time period they have been public companies, are not considered.
4. Companies with stock prices below $1 are not considered.
5. The annualized share turnover rate must exceed 20% of the common shares outstanding. Standard & Poor's defines share turnover as the trading volume over the previous 12 months divided by the average number of common shares outstanding during that time period.

6. Corporate ownership is reviewed. If 50% or more of the total common shares of a company are owned by another corporation, that company is not eligible because it is considered to be controlled by the other company. Companies in which 60% or more of the common shares are held by insiders, or by insiders in conjunction with another corporation's holdings, also are not eligible.
7. Companies in bankruptcy or in extreme financial distress are not selected for inclusion in the index. Except in rare instances, a filing for bankruptcy by a company in any Standard & Poor's Index will result in its immediate removal. However, as long as it appears to be viable, a company is not removed from an Index just because it is in financial trouble.
8. Finally, the companies that survive the other screens are checked for their bid-ask spreads. The spread is calculated as the average of the percentage of the last sale for 30 consecutive trading days. Only those companies with spreads of 5% or less are considered. For example, if a stock has an average closing price of $5 a share, its closing spread can be no wider than 25 cents (5 bid—5¼ ask). Many Nasdaq stocks have spreads of more than 10%, and 20% to 25% is not unheard of.

The stocks in the candidate pool for the S&P SmallCap 600 are classified into the same economic sectors used in the other Standard & Poor's Indexes. There now are 11 sectors, of which eight are Industrials: Basic Materials, Capital Goods, Communications Services, Consumer Cyclicals, Consumer Staples, Energy, Health Care, and Technology. The other three economic sectors are: Utilities, Transportation, and Financials. As is the case in the S&P 500 and S&P MidCap 400 Indexes, stocks are selected from each sector so that the total S&P SmallCap 600 Index reflects the economic balance of the stocks in the Standard & Poor's internal database. That diversity results in an Index that has a strong family resemblance to its big brothers. As the following table shows, each of Standard & Poor's major industry sectors is well-represented within each Index and across all three Indexes.

Industry Group Representation as of 9/30/99

	S&P 500 Index		S&P MidCap 400		S&P SmallCap 600	
	# of Cos.	% of Respective Index	# of Cos.	% of Respective Index	# of Cos.	% of Respective Index
Industrials	374	74.8	311	77.7	499	83.2
Utilities	41	8.2	40	10.0	27	4.5
Financials	74	14.8	38	9.5	56	9.3
Transportation	11	2.2	11	2.8	18	3.0

Because the stocks in the SmallCap 600 are selected using the same general principles applied to the other Standard & Poor's Indexes, they form a coherent package. In fact, Standard & Poor's has developed a super-composite index that reflects the market-value-weighted performance of all 1500 stocks in the three Indexes. The S&P Super Composite 1500 Index was introduced in May 1995. It consists of a market-value-weighted position in every stock in the S&P 500, S&P MidCap 400, and S&P SmallCap 600 Indexes. Yet, despite their strong family resemblances, the MidCap 400 and SmallCap 600 Indexes are not—like standard and toy poodles—simply scaled-down versions of the S&P 500 Index.

Using the SmallCap 600 for Investment Research

The total market value of the 600 companies in the SmallCap Index at the end of the second quarter of 1999 was $352 billion. That equaled about 2½% of the market value of all the stocks in the Standard & Poor's equity database, or about $478 billion less than the $830 billion combined capitalization of the two largest companies in the S&P 500, General Electric and Microsoft. However, while they are dwarfed by the larger companies in the S&P 500, many of the stocks in the SmallCap 600 Index are large fish in their own small ponds. The Index includes such famous brand names as Chiquita Brands International and Toro Co., as well as companies such as Chemed Corp. (which wholly owns Roto-Rooter) and the Swiss Army Brands (the importer of Swiss Army knives and watches) whose products are household names. Many others have strong positions in important niche markets.

The average market value of a SmallCap company is about $586 million, less than 3% of the average in the S&P 500 and about 28% of the average market value in the MidCap 400. This difference was due both to a smaller number of shares outstanding at most SmallCap companies and to much lower per-share prices. The median share price of an S&P SmallCap stock was $21.25, compared with $27.875 for a MidCap stock and $44.375 for a company in the S&P 500.

The smaller number of shares outstanding and the lower prices at which many SmallCap 600 shares trade are two of the reasons why the stocks in the SmallCap tend to be more volatile than those in the S&P 500 or the MidCap 400. Another, as reflected in the Index's June 1999 average P/E ratio of 32, is their earnings patterns. High P/E ratios (calculated by dividing a company's per share price by its earnings per share) can be generated in two different ways, either by the market paying up for anticipated growth, or by a company's earnings falling short of expectations. Dividend yield is another significant difference between the average SmallCap stock and those in the MidCap 400 or S&P 500. Because many of the industrial companies in the SmallCap are in their expansion phase, they retain earnings to fund their growth and pay no dividends. As a result, the June 1999 dividend yield on the SmallCap 600 was 0.80%, compared with 1.20% on the S&P 500 and 1.10% on the MidCap 400.

Given their increased risk relative to the S&P 500 and the MidCap 400, why should investors own SmallCap stocks? Because, given a long-term time horizon, the SmallCap should outperform both of its larger siblings by a margin that will more than compensate for its higher short-term risks.

It is also possible for an individual investor to construct a well-diversified portfolio of small-cap stocks that will outperform the larger-cap indexes. Many of the 6000 or more small companies to choose from are followed by very few brokerage firm analysts. There are hidden gems out there, not just neglected value stocks, but also classic growth stocks that have yet to develop a following. The problem is finding them, finding out enough about them, and finding their shares trading at a fair bid/ask spread.

Those three problems are minimized if the search begins with the stocks in the SmallCap 600. The stocks have been screened for liquidity, and each is covered by an unbiased Stock Report prepared by an analyst in the Standard & Poor's Equity Research department. Those reports, which make up the remainder of this book, are an excellent place to begin researching a potential investment. Organize your search by first reading the names and the business summaries of each of the 600 companies, making a list as you go along of those that catch your fancy. Next, return to the reports, study those you've selected, and—using the information provided in the reports—pick the ones that you feel deserve serious additional investigation.

We have already prescreened the 600 companies in this book for several of the stock characteristics in which investors generally are most interested, including companies with consistently strong earnings growth, superior dividend payment histories, and those under-followed issues which could include some interesting "hidden values" for those investors willing to accept some degree of incremental risk. At the end of this introduction you will find charts listing companies which score highest on the basis of these criteria. So if you, like most investors, find these characteristics important in potential investments, you might want to turn first to the companies on these lists in your search for attractive investments.

Other Uses of this Book

Given this vast array of data, how might a business person seeking to find out about her competition, a marketing manager looking for clients, or a job seeker use it to best serve their respective purposes?

If you fall into one of these categories—a business person seeking to find out information about her competition, a marketing manager looking for clients, or a job seeker—your task will be arduous to be sure, but this book will provide you with an excellent starting point and your payoff can make it all worthwhile. You will have to go through this book page by page, looking for those companies that are in the industries in which you are interested, that are of the size and financial strength that appeal to you, that are located geographically in your territory or where you're willing to relocate, that have been profitable and growing, and so forth. And then you will have to read about just what's going on at those companies by referring to the appropriate "Business Summary" comments in these reports. But the companies you end up with can be those high-growth entities with the greatest potential.

Of course, this book won't do it all for you. It is, after all, just a starting point, not a conclusive summary of everything you might need to know. It is designed to educate, not to render advice or provide recommendations. But it will get you pointed in the right direction.

How to Read the Reports on the SmallCap 600

In the pages that follow, you will find a wealth of information on each of the 600 companies which comprise the S&P SmallCap 600 Index, information which will allow you to make reasoned investment, business, and personal judgments regarding these companies. But to get the most value from this book, you should take a few moments to familiarize yourself with just what you'll find on these pages.

Following is a glossary of terms and definitions used throughout this book. Please refer to this section as you encounter terms which need further clarification.

Stock Report Terms

Quantitative Evaluations

Standard & Poor's Opinion—Buy, hold or sell recommendations are provided using Standard & Poor's unique STARS (Stock Appreciation Ranking System), which measures short-term (six- to 12-month) appreciation potential of stocks. STARS performance is measured against the performance of the S&P 500 Index.

STARS Rankings are as follows:

- ***** Buy—Expected to be among the best performers over the next 12 months.
- **** Accumulate—Expected to be an above-average performer.
- *** Hold—Expected to be an average performer.
- ** Avoid—Likely to be a below-average performer.
- * Sell—Expected to be a well-below-average performer and fall in price.

Outlook—Using Standard & Poor's exclusive proprietary quantitative model, stocks are ranked in one of five Outlook Groups—ranging from Group 5, listing the most undervalued stocks, to Group 1, the most overvalued issues. Group 5 stocks are expected to generally outperform all others. To identify a stock that is in a strengthening or weakening position, a positive (+) or negative (–) Timing Index is placed next to the Outlook ranking. Using these rankings, here's what action should be taken:

5+ = Buy	2+ = Hold if in portfolio
5 = Hold if in portfolio	2– = Sell
4+ = Hold if in portfolio	1+ = Hold if in portfolio
4– = Sell	1– = Sell
3+ = Hold if in portfolio	
3– = Sell	

The Timing Index helps identify the right time to buy stocks, but its most important function is to indicate when it is time to sell. Because Group 5 stocks have historically produced the best results, Standard & Poor's recommends buying only Group 5 stocks with a positive Timing Index. Then, hold onto each one for as long as it remains in a positive trend (positive Timing Index), even if the ranking falls as the stock appreciates toward overvalued status. This will reduce transaction costs and substantially raise your chances of outperforming the market in the long run. It will also raise the number of transactions which qualify as long-term capital gains for tax purposes.

Fair Value—The price at which a stock should sell today as calculated by Standard & Poor's computers using our quantitative model based on the company's earnings, growth potential, return on equity relative to the S&P 500 and its industry group, price to book ratio history, current yield relative to the S&P 500, and other factors. The current fair price is shown given today's S&P 500 level.

Risk—Rates the volatility of the stock's price over the past year.

Technical Evaluation—In researching the past market history of prices and trading volume for each company, Standard & Poor's computer models apply special technical methods and formulas to identify and project price trends for the stock. They analyze how the price of the stock is moving and evaluate the interrelationships between the moving averages to ultimately determine buy or sell signals—and to decide whether they're bullish, neutral or bearish for the stock. The date the signals were initiated is also provided so you can take advantage of a recent or ongoing uptrend in price, or see how a stock has performed over time since our last technical signal was generated.

Relative Strength Rank—Shows, on a scale of 1 to 99, how the stock has performed compared with all other companies in Standard & Poor's universe of companies on a rolling 13-week basis.

Insider Activity—Gives an insight as to insider sentiment by showing whether directors, officers and key employees—who may have proprietary information not available to the general public—are buying or selling the company's stock during the most recent six months.

Key Stock Statistics

Avg. Daily Vol.—The average daily trading volume of the stock for the past 20 days on a rolling basis, shown in millions.

Market Cap.—The price of the stock multiplied by the number of shares outstanding, shown in billions.

Insider Holdings—The percentage of outstanding shares held by directors, officers and key employees of the company, and others who hold a minimum of 10% of the outstanding shares.

Value of $10,000 Invested 5 years ago—The value today of a $10,000 investment in the stock made five years ago, assuming year-end reinvestment of dividends.

Standard & Poor's Ranking

The investment process involves assessment of various factors—such as products and industry position, company resources and financial policy—with results that make some common stocks more highly esteemed than others. In this assessment, Standard & Poor's believes that earnings and dividend performance is the end result of the interplay of these factors and that, over the long run, the record of this performance has a considerable bearing on relative quality. The rankings, however, do not reflect all of the factors that may bear on stock quality.

Growth and stability of earnings and dividends are the key elements in Standard & Poor's earnings and dividend rankings for common stocks, which are designed to capsulize the nature of this record in a single symbol. It should be noted, however, that the process also takes into consideration certain adjustments and modifications deemed desirable in establishing such rankings.

These rankings are derived by means of a computerized scoring system based on per share earnings and dividend records of the most recent ten years. If a company does not have a ten-year public track record, Standard & Poor's does not rank it. The lack of a Standard & Poor's ranking in no way reflects upon the investment merits of a company. Basic scores are computed for earnings and dividends and then adjusted by a set of predetermined modifiers for growth, stability, and cyclicality. Adjusted scores for earnings and dividends are then combined to yield a final score.

The ranking system also makes allowance for the fact that, in general, corporate size imparts certain recognized advantages from an investment standpoint. Minimum size limits (in terms of corporate sales) are set for the various rankings, but exceptions may be made where a score reflects an outstanding earnings-dividend record.

The final score is then translated into one of the following rankings:

A+ Highest

A High

A− Above Average
B+ Average
B Below Average
B− Lower
C Lowest
D In Reorganization
NR No Ranking

In some instances, rankings may be modified by special considerations, such as natural disasters, massive strikes, or nonrecurring accounting adjustments.

It is important to note that a ranking is not a forecast of future market price performance, but is basically an appraisal of past performance of earnings and dividends and relative current standing. Consequently, rankings should not be used as market recommendations: a high-score stock may at times be so overpriced as to justify its sale while a low-score stock may be attractively priced for purchase. Rankings based upon earnings and dividend records are no substitute for complete analysis. They cannot take into account the potential effects of management changes, internal company policies not yet fully reflected in the earnings and dividend record, public relations standings, recent competitive shifts, and a host of other factors that may be relevant in investment decision making.

Beta

The beta coefficient is a measure of the volatility of a stock's price relative to the S&P 500 Index, which, as we have seen, is the proxy for the overall market. Because calculating a beta requires 60 months of performance data, Standard & Poor's does not calculate betas of stocks that have been trading for less than five years.

Per Share Data ($) Tables

Tangible Book Value; Book Value (See also: "Common Equity" under Industrial)—Indicates the theoretical dollar amount per common share one might expect to receive from a company's tangible "book" assets should liquidation take place. Generally, book value is determined by adding the stated value of the common stock, paid-in capital and retained earnings and then subtracting intangible assets (excess cost over equity of acquired companies, goodwill, and patents), preferred stock at liquidating value and unamortized debt discount. Divide that amount by the outstanding shares to get book value per common share.

Cash Flow—Net income plus depreciation, depletion, and amortization, divided by shares used to calculate earnings per common share. (Also see: "Cash Flow" for Industrial Companies.)

Earnings—The amount a company reports as having been earned for the year on its common stock based on generally accepted accounting standards. Earnings per share are presented on a *"Diluted"* basis pursuant to FASB 128, which became effective December 15, 1997, and are generally reported from continuing operations, before extraordinary items. This reflects a change from previously reported *Primary* earnings per share. INSURANCE companies report *operating earnings* before gains/losses on security transactions and *earnings* after such transactions.

Dividends—Generally total cash payments per share based on the ex-dividend dates over a twelve-month period. May also be reported on a declared basis where this has been established to be a company's payout policy.

Payout Ratio—Indicates the percentage of earnings paid out in dividends. It is calculated by dividing the annual dividend by the earnings. For INSURANCE companies *earnings* after gains/losses on security transactions are used.

Prices High/Low—Shows the calendar year high and low of a stock's market price.

P/E Ratio High/Low—The ratio of market price to earnings—essentially indicates the valuation investors place on a company's earnings. Obtained by dividing the annual earnings into the high and low market price for the year. For INSURANCE companies *operating earnings* before gains/losses on security transactions are used.

Net Asset Value—Appears on investment company reports and reflects the market value of stocks, bonds, and net cash divided by outstanding shares. The % DIFFERENCE indicates the percentage premium or discount of the market price over the net asset value.

Portfolio Turnover—Appears on investment company reports and indicates percentage of total security purchases and sales for the year to overall investment assets. Primarily mirrors trading aggressiveness.

Income/Balance Sheet Data Tables

Banks

Net Interest Income—Interest and dividend income, minus interest expense.

Loan Loss Provision—Amount charged to operating expenses to provide an adequate reserve to cover anticipated losses in the loan portfolio.

Taxable Equivalent Adjustment—Increase to render income from tax-exempt loans and securities comparable to fully taxed income.

Noninterest Income—Service fees, trading and other income, excluding gains/losses on securities transactions.

% Expenses/Op. Revenues—Noninterest expense as a percentage of taxable equivalent net interest income plus noninterest income (before securities gains/losses). A measure of cost control.

Commercial Loans—Commercial, industrial, financial, agricultural loans and leases, gross.

Other Loans—Gross consumer, real estate and foreign loans.

% Loan Loss Reserve—Contra-account to loan assets, built through provisions for loan losses, which serves as a cushion for possible future loan charge-offs.

% Loans/Deposits—Proportion of loans funded by deposits. A measure of liquidity and an indication of bank's ability to write more loans.

Earning Assets—Assets on which interest is earned.

Money Market Assets—Interest-bearing interbank deposits, federal funds sold, trading account securities.

Investment Securities—Federal, state, and local government bonds and other securities.

Gains/Losses on Securities Transactions—Realized losses on sales of securities, usually bonds.

Net Before Taxes—Amount remaining after operating expenses are deducted from income, including gains or losses on security transactions.

Effective Tax Rate—Actual income tax expense divided by net before taxes.

Net Income—The final profit before dividends (common/preferred) from all sources after deduction of expenses, taxes, and fixed charges, but before any discontinued operations or extraordinary items.

Net Interest Margin—A percentage computed by dividing net interest income, on a taxable equivalent basis, by average earning assets. Used as an analytical tool to measure profit margins from providing credit services.

% Return on Revenues—Net income divided by gross revenues.

% Return on Assets—Net income divided by average total assets. An analytical measure of asset-use efficiency and industry comparison.

% Return on Equity—Net income (minus preferred dividend requirements) divided by average common equity. Generally used to measure performance.

Total Assets—Includes interest-earning financial instruments—principally commercial, real estate, consumer loans and leases; investment securities/trading accounts; cash/money market investments; other owned assets.

Cash—Mainly vault cash, interest-bearing deposits placed with banks, reserves required by the Federal Reserve and items in the process of collection—generally referred to as float.

Government Securities—Includes United States Treasury securities and securities of other U.S. government agencies at book or carrying value. A bank's major "liquid asset."

State and Municipal Securities—State and municipal securities owned at book value.

Loans—All domestic and foreign loans (excluding leases), less unearned discount and reserve for possible losses. Generally considered a bank's principal asset.

Deposits—Primarily classified as either *demand* (payable at any time upon demand of depositor) or *time* (not payable within thirty days).

Deposits/Capital Funds—Average deposits divided by average capital funds. Capital funds include capital notes/debentures, other long-term debt, capital stock, surplus, and undivided profits. May be used as a "leverage" measure.

Long-Term Debt—Total borrowings for terms beyond one year including notes payable, mortgages, debentures, term loans, and capitalized lease obligations.

Common Equity—Includes common/capital surplus, undivided profits, reserve for contingencies and other capital reserves.

% Equity to Assets—Average common equity divided by average total assets. Used as a measure of capital adequacy.

% Equity to Loans—Average common equity divided by average loans. Reflects the degree of equity coverage to loans outstanding.

Industrial Companies

Following data is based on Form 10K Annual Report data as filed with SEC.

Revenues—Net sales and other operating revenues. Includes franchise/leased department income for retailers, and royalties for publishers and oil and mining companies. Excludes excise taxes for tobacco, liquor, and oil companies.

Operating Income—Net sales and operating revenues less cost of goods sold and operating expenses (including research and development, profit sharing, exploration and bad debt, but excluding depreciation and amortization).

% Operating Income of Revenues—Net sales and operating revenues divided into operating income. Used as a measure of operating profitability.

Capital Expenditures—The sum of additions at cost to property, plant and equipment and leaseholds, generally excluding amounts arising from acquisitions.

Depreciation—Includes noncash charges for obsolescence, wear on property, current portion of capitalized expenses (intangibles), and depletion charges.

Interest Expense—Includes all interest expense on short/long-term debt, amortization of debt discount/premium and deferred expenses (e.g., financing costs).

Net Before Taxes—Includes operating and nonoperating revenues (including extraordinary items not net of taxes), less all operating and nonoperating expenses, except income taxes and minority interest, but including equity in nonconsolidated subsidiaries.

Effective Tax Rate—Actual income tax charges divided by net before taxes.

Net Income—Profits derived from all sources after deduction of expenses, taxes, and fixed charges, but before any discontinued operations, extraordinary items, and dividends (preferred/common).

% Net Income of Revenues—Net income divided by sales/operating revenues.

Cash Flow—Net income (before extraordinary items and discontinued operations, and after preferred dividends) plus depreciation, depletion, and amortization.

Cash—Includes all cash and government and other marketable securities.

Current Assets—Those assets expected to be realized in cash or used up in the production of revenue within one year.

Current Liabilities—Generally includes all debts/obligations falling due within one year.

Current Ratio—Current assets divided by current liabilities. A measure of liquidity.

Total Assets—Current assets plus net plant and other noncurrent assets (intangibles and deferred items).

% Return on Assets—Net income divided by average total assets on a per common share basis. Used in industry analysis and as a measure of asset-use efficiency.

Long-Term Debt—Debts/obligations due after one year. Includes bonds, notes payable, mortgages, lease obligations, and industrial revenue bonds. Other Long-Term Debt, when reported as a separate account, is excluded. This account generally includes pension and retirement benefits.

Common Equity (See also: "Book Value" under Per Share Data Table)—Common stock plus capital surplus and retained earnings, less any difference between the carrying value and liquidating value of preferred stock.

Total Invested Capital—The sum of stockholders' equity plus long-term debt, capital lease obligations, deferred income taxes, investment credits, and minority interest.

% Long-Term Debt of Invested Capital—Long-term debt divided by total invested capital. Indicates how highly "leveraged" a business might be.

% Return on Equity—Net income less preferred dividend requirements divided by average common shareholders' equity on a per common share basis. Generally used to measure performance and industry comparisons.

Utilities

Operating Revenues—Represents the amount billed to customers by the utility.

Depreciation—Amounts charged to income to compensate for the decline in useful value of plant and equipment.

Maintenance—Amounts spent to keep plants in good operating condition.

Operating Ratio—Ratio of operating costs to operating revenues or the proportion of revenues absorbed by expenses. Obtained by dividing operating expenses including depreciation, maintenance, and taxes by revenues.

Fixed Charges Coverage—The number of times income before interest charges (operating income plus other income) after taxes covers total interest charges and preferred dividend requirements.

Construction Credits—Credits for interest charged to the cost of constructing new plant. A combination of allowance for equity funds used during construction and allowance for borrowed funds used during construction—credit.

Effective Tax Rate—Actual income tax expense divided by the total of net income and actual income tax expense.

Net Income—Amount of earnings for the year which is available for preferred and common dividend payments.

% Return on Revenues—Obtained by dividing net income for the year by revenues.

% Return on Invested Capital—Percentage obtained by dividing income available for fixed charges by average total invested capital.

% Return on Common Equity—Percentage obtained by dividing income available for common stock (net income less preferred dividend requirements) by average common equity.

Gross Property—Includes utility plant at cost, plant work in progress, and nuclear fuel.

Capital Expenditures—Represents the amounts spent on capital improvements to plant and funds for construction programs.

Net Property—Includes items in gross property less provision for depreciation.

% Earned on Net Property—Percentage obtained by dividing operating income by average net property for the year. A measure of plant efficiency.

Total Invested Capital—Sum of total capitalization (common-preferred-debt), accumulated deferred income taxes, accumulated investment tax credits, minority interest, contingency reserves, and contributions in aid of construction.

Total Capitalization—Combined sum of total common equity, preferred stock, and long-term debt.

Long-Term Debt—Debt obligations due beyond one year from balance sheet date.

Capitalization Ratios—Reflect the percentage of each type of debt/equity issues outstanding to total capitalization. % DEBT is obtained by dividing total debt by the sum of debt, preferred, common, paid-in capital and retained earnings. % PREFERRED is obtained by dividing the preferred stocks outstanding by total capitalization. % COMMON, divide the sum of common stocks, paid-in capital and retained earnings by total capitalization.

Finally, at the very bottom of the right-hand page, you'll find general information about the company: its address and telephone number, the names of its senior executive officers and directors (usually including the name of the investor contact), the transfer agent and registrar for the stock, and the state in which the company is incorporated.

HIGH PROJECTED GROWTH AND TRADING BELOW $20

All the issues below meet the following criteria: a projected five-year growth rate of at least 20%; at least a 20% increase in 1999 and2000 estimated earnings; a share price of less than $20; and a P/E ratio of less than 15 based on projected 2000 earnings. The list is sorted by the five-year projected growth rate.

Company (Ticker)	Business	–1999– High	–1999– Low	Recent Price	Fiscal Year End	Earnings Per Share $ 1998 Actual	Earnings Per Share $ 1999 Est.	Earnings Per Share $ 2000 Est.	5-Year Proj. Growth Rate (%)	P/E on 2000 Est.
Apex Inc(APEX)	Mfr/dgn switching systems	35.37	11.00	18.94	Dec	0.75	0.98	1.28	35	14.8
Orthodontic Centers of Amer(OCA)	Manage orthodontic centers	20.12	10.81	15.63	Dec	0.70	0.96	1.25	32	12.5
USA Detergents(USAD)	Mfr laundry/hshld cleaning prd	8.00	4.31	5.13	Dec	0.08	0.54	0.80	32	6.4
Osteotech Inc(OSTE)	Process transplant'n bonetissue	41.12	13.25	13.81	Dec	0.73	0.96	1.27	30	10.9
Pharmaceutical Product Dvlpmt(PPDI)	Product development svcs	38.50	11.56	13.00	Dec	0.85	1.13	1.51	30	8.6
Renal Care Group(RCGI)	Provide nephrology svcs	34.37	14.87	19.88	Dec	0.83	1.12	1.43	28	13.9
Action Performance Cos(ACTN)	Motorsports replicas/merch	48.25	16.25	17.75	Sep	1.48	2.00	2.65	27	6.7
Baker(J.) Inc(JBAK)	Self-svc footwear retailer	9.25	3.62	6.31	Jan	0.14	0.65	0.88	26	7.2
Dura Pharmaceuticals(DURA)	Mkt respiratory ailment drugs	17.68	9.75	12.88	Dec	0.06	0.71	0.92	26	14.0
SLI Inc(SLI)	Mfr miniature light prd	35.00	18.12	19.50	Dec	1.10	1.72	2.16	26	9.0
AmeriCredit Corp(ACF)	Provides used-car financing	17.50	9.81	14.50	Jun	0.76	*1.11	1.43	25	10.1
US Oncology(USON)	Provides managed oncology svcs	15.56	6.43	9.94	Dec	0.61	0.76	0.96	25	10.4
Kroll-O'Gara Co(KROG)	Provide vehicle armoring	41.37	14.00	14.31	Dec	0.69	1.21	1.58	24	9.1
PAREXEL Intl(PRXL)	Pharmaceutical R&D	29.37	8.03	8.44	Jun	0.38	*0.62	0.83	24	10.2
Artesyn Technologies(ATSN)	Dvp/mfr pwr conv eq	26.00	11.81	18.50	Dec	0.67	1.11	1.38	22	13.4
FileNet Corp(FILE)	Document mgmt systems	13.68	6.00	11.94	Dec	0.03	0.54	0.91	21	13.1

*Actual 1999 EPS.

Chart based on September 24, 1999 prices and data.

Note: All earnings estimates are Wall Street consensus projections.

STOCKS OF COMPANIES WITH CONSISTENTLY STRONG EPS GROWTH

These issues have been selected for superior earnings growth. Each company has actual and estimated annual compounded earnings growth rates of 15% or higher. The list is sorted by estimated 2000 P/E.

Company (Ticker)	Business	Fiscal Year End	Earnings Per Share $ 1998 Actual	1999 Est.	2000 Est.	5-Year Proj. Growth Rate (%)	Recent Price	P/E on 2000 Est.
Toll Brothers(TOL)	Luxury single family homes	Oct	2.25	2.70	3.11	15	19.44	6.3
Enhance Financial Svcs Grp(EFS)	Muni/asset-backed debt reinsr	Dec	2.10	2.42	2.81	15	17.88	6.4
Action Performance Cos(ACTN)	Motorsports replicas/merch	Sep	1.48	2.00	2.65	27	17.75	6.7
Tower Automotive(TWR)	Engineered metal stampings	Dec	1.68	2.08	2.48	18	17.81	7.2
Interim Services(IS)	Temporary help services	Dec	1.29	1.55	1.96	21	15.19	7.8
K Swiss Inc 'A'(KSWS)	Dvlp/mkt athletic footwear	Dec	1.10	2.92	3.73	15	32.81	8.8
ADVO Inc(AD)	Direct mail advertis'g svcs	Sep	1.55	1.80	2.09	17	18.63	8.9
JLG Indus(JLG)	Mobile aerial lifts:cranes	Jul	1.05	*1.36	1.67	15	14.94	8.9
SLI Inc(SLI)	Mfr miniature light prd	Dec	1.10	1.72	2.16	26	19.50	9.0
Watsco, Inc(WSO)	Dstrb air cond/heat'g pd	Dec	0.89	1.09	1.27	23	11.50	9.1
Mutual Risk Management(MM)	Provides risk mgmt services	Dec	1.43	1.71	2.02	19	18.94	9.4
Cato Corp'A'(CACOA)	Women's apparel stores	Jan	0.85	1.11	1.36	15	13.56	10.0
AmeriCredit Corp(ACF)	Provides used-car financing	Jun	0.76	*1.11	1.43	25	14.50	10.1
US Oncology(USON)	Provides managed oncology svcs	Dec	0.61	0.76	0.96	25	9.94	10.4
Astec Industries(ASTE)	Asphalt mix plants,pav'g eqp	Dec	1.26	1.67	1.97	18	21.19	10.8
URS Corp(URS)	Engin'g & architectural svcs	Oct	1.43	1.80	2.20	15	23.75	10.8
Men's Wearhouse(SUIT)	Retail off-price men's attire	Jan	1.17	1.51	1.84	22	20.41	11.1
Plantronics Inc(PLT)	Mfr telephone headsets	Mar	3.02	3.60	4.37	16	48.69	11.1
Consolidated Graphics(CGX)	Commercial printing services	Mar	2.28	3.03	3.71	26	41.38	11.2
Quiksilver, Inc(ZQK)	Designs/dstr casual clothing	Oct	0.82	1.13	1.35	22	15.31	11.3
Canandaigua BrandsCl'A'(CBRNA)	Domestic wine producer	Feb	3.30	4.16	4.85	15	57.25	11.8
Inter-Tel Inc(INTL)	Mfr electronic telecommun eqp	Dec	0.32	1.04	1.34	20	16.50	12.3
Orthodontic Centers of Amer(OCA)	Manage orthodontic centers	Dec	0.70	0.96	1.25	32	15.63	12.5
Amer Mgmt Systems(AMSY)	Computer sys mgmt/admin	Dec	1.21	1.57	1.90	23	24.38	12.8

*Actual 1999 EPS.

Chart based on September 24, 1999 prices and data.

Note: All earnings estimates are Wall Street consensus projections.

SMALLCAP 600 - LOW 2000 P/E, HIGH PROJECTED GROWTH RATE

These issues are all members of the Standard & Poor's SmallCap 600 stock price index. Each is expected to show a 20% increase in its 1999 and 2000 earnings. All have a five-year projected earnings growth rate of at least 20% and are currently selling at less than 15 times estimated 2000 earnings. The list is sorted by their 2000 estimated price-to-earnings ratio.

			Earnings Per Share $						
Company (Ticker)	Business	Fiscal Year End	1997 Actual	1998 Actual	1999 Est.	2000 Est.	5-Year Proj. Growth Rate (%)	Recent Price	P/E on 2000 Est.
USA Detergents(USAD)	Mfr laundry/hshld cleaning prd	Dec	-1.53	0.08	0.54	0.80	32	5.13	6.4
Action Performance Cos(ACTN)	Motorsports replicas/merch	Sep	0.69	1.48	2.00	2.65	27	17.75	6.7
Baker(J.) Inc(JBAK)	Self-svc footwear retailer	Jan	0.27	0.14	0.65	0.88	26	6.31	7.2
Interim Services(IS)	Temporary help services	Dec	1.05	1.29	1.55	1.96	21	15.19	7.8
Pharmaceutical Product Dvlpmt(PPDI)	Product development svcs	Dec	0.42	0.85	1.13	1.51	30	13.00	8.6
SLI Inc(SLI)	Mfr miniature light prd	Dec	0.69	1.10	1.72	2.16	26	19.50	9.0
Kroll-O'Gara Co(KROG)	Provide vehicle armoring	Dec	0.09	0.69	1.21	1.58	24	14.31	9.1
Stride Rite(SRR)	Mfr/retail children's shoes	Nov	0.40	0.44	0.61	0.79	20	7.38	9.3
AmeriCredit Corp(ACF)	Provides used-car financing	Jun	0.48	0.76	*1.11	1.43	25	14.50	10.1
PAREXEL Intl(PRXL)	Pharmaceutical R&D	Jun	0.56	0.38	*0.62	0.83	24	8.44	10.2
US Oncology(USON)	Provides managed oncology svcs	Dec	0.48	0.61	0.76	0.96	25	9.94	10.4
Insurance Auto Auctions(IAAI)	Sells insur recovered vehicles	Dec	0.40	0.63	1.10	1.36	20	14.75	10.8
Osteotech Inc(OSTE)	Process transplant'n bonetissu	Dec	0.43	0.73	0.96	1.27	30	13.81	10.9
Men's Wearhouse(SUIT)	Retail off-price men's attire	Jan	0.87	1.17	1.51	1.84	22	20.41	11.1
Consolidated Graphics(CGX)	Commercial printing services	Mar	1.40	2.28	3.03	3.71	26	41.38	11.2
Inter-Tel Inc(INTL)	Mfr electronic telecommun eqp	Dec	0.57	0.32	1.04	1.34	20	16.50	12.3
Orthodontic Centers of Amer(OCA)	Manage orthodontic centers	Dec	0.50	0.70	0.96	1.25	32	15.63	12.5
Amer Mgmt Systems(AMSY)	Computer sys mgmt/admin	Dec	0.74	1.21	1.57	1.90	23	24.38	12.8
FileNet Corp(FILE)	Document mgmt systems	Dec	-0.18	0.03	0.54	0.91	21	11.94	13.1
Artesyn Technologies(ATSN)	Dvp/mfr pwr conv eq	Dec	0.75	0.67	1.11	1.38	22	18.50	13.4
Renal Care Group(RCGI)	Provide nephrology svcs	Dec	0.56	0.83	1.12	1.43	28	19.88	13.9

*Actual 1999 EPS.

Chart based on September 24, 1999 prices and data.

Note: All earnings estimates are Wall Street consensus projections.

COMPANIES THAT HAVE STEADILY INCREASED THEIR DIVIDENDS OVER THE PAST FIVE YEARS

Each of the companies below carries a 5-year compound annual dividend growth rate of at least 10%, has increased its cash payment each year for at least 5 years, has at least a 10% five-year projected earnings growth rate and has a current indicated dividend rate greater than its actual 1998 payment. All of those listed, moreover, are expected to post 10% earnings increases in 1999 and 2000, have a dividend coverage ratio (2000 earnings estimate divided by dividends) of 1.4 or better, and have a 2000 estimated P/E of less than 20. The list is sorted by 5-year dividend growth rate.

Company (Ticker)	Fiscal Year End	Earnings Per Share $ 1998 Actual	1999 Est.	2000 Est.	5-Year Dividend Growth Rate (%)	Recent Price	Indicated Dividend Rate ($)	Yield (%)	P/E on 2000 Est.	5-Year Proj. Growth Rate (%)
Cullen/Frost Bankers(CFR)	Dec	1.38	1.76	1.94	30.9	24.13	0.70	2.9	12.4	13
Roper Industries(ROP)	Oct	1.24	1.54	1.85	29.5	36.50	0.26	0.7	19.7	17
Vital Signs(VITL)	Sep	1.03	1.42	1.63	27.7	19.56	0.16	0.8	12.0	0
Invacare Corp(IVC)	Dec	1.50	1.67	1.88	26.1	18.25	0.05	0.3	9.7	12
Air Express Intl(AEIC)	Dec	1.26	1.44	1.70	23.1	20.75	0.28	1.3	12.2	15
Hudson United Bancorp(HU)	Dec	0.56	2.51	3.02	22.5	28.56	1.00	3.5	9.5	10
Mentor Corp(MNTR)	Mar	0.55	1.09	1.50	21.9	27.69	0.10	0.4	18.5	20
Community First Bankshares(CFBX)	Dec	0.90	1.61	1.80	21.0	16.69	0.56	3.4	9.3	15
Commerce Bancorp(CBH)	Dec	1.98	2.27	2.60	20.8	41.00	0.88	2.1	15.8	13
JLG Indus(JLG)	Jul	1.05	*1.36	1.67	20.6	14.94	0.02	0.1	8.9	15
Hughes Supply(HUG)	Jan	2.55	2.82	3.20	20.0	22.38	0.34	1.5	7.0	15
Henry(Jack) & Assoc(JKHY)	Jun	1.09	*1.50	1.78	19.5	32.88	0.32	1.0	18.5	22
Mutual Risk Management(MM)	Dec	1.43	1.71	2.02	17.4	18.94	0.24	1.3	9.4	19
Banknorth Group(BKNG)	Dec	1.22	2.20	2.46	17.1	29.31	0.72	2.5	11.9	11
ABM Industries Inc(ABM)	Oct	1.44	1.66	1.87	16.8	25.75	0.56	2.2	13.8	16
Myers Indus(MYE)	Dec	1.43	1.64	1.92	16.5	17.50	0.24	1.4	9.1	13
Applebee's Intl(APPB)	Dec	1.67	1.92	2.19	16.1	32.13	0.09	0.3	14.7	15
Rollins Truck Leasing(RLC)	Sep	0.85	0.97	1.09	15.9	10.31	0.20	1.9	9.5	11
OM Group(OMP)	Dec	2.05	2.29	2.62	15.7	36.19	0.40	1.1	13.8	13
Eaton Vance(EV)	Oct	0.81	1.40	2.87	15.3	28.25	0.30	1.1	9.8	0
Cambrex Corp(CBM)	Dec	1.54	1.71	1.99	14.1	26.25	0.12	0.5	13.2	13

*Actual 1999 EPS.

Chart based on September 24, 1999 prices and data.

Note: All earnings estimates are Wall Street consensus projections.

LOW ANALYTICAL COVERAGE, HIGH GROWTH RATE

The companies listed below are covered by three or fewer analysts out of the approximately 2,300 analysts that contribute earnings estimates to S&P. While broader coverage might result in stronger agreement on earnings projections, relative neglect by the financial community often gives purchasers of the stock an advantage. These issues are all expected to have at least a 15% increase in earnings in 1999 and again in 2000. Additionally, their five-year projected growth rate is at least 15%. They are sorted by their five-year projected growth rate.

Company (Ticker)	Business	Fiscal Year End	–1999– High	–1999– Low	Recent Price	Earnings Per Share $ 1998 Actual	Earnings Per Share $ 1999 Est.	Earnings Per Share $ 2000 Est.	5-Yr. Proj. Growth Rate (%)	P/E on 2000 Est.
Vicor Corp(VICR)	Mfr modular pwr converters	Dec	23.75	8.81	19.34	0.37	0.45	0.84	35	23.0
USA Detergents(USAD)	Mfr laundry/hshld cleaning prd	Dec	8.00	4.31	5.13	0.08	0.54	0.80	32	6.4
FactSet Research Systems(FDS)	On-line fin'l database svcs	Aug	59.37	35.56	50.56	0.77	*1.11	1.36	29	37.2
Dendrite International(DRTE)	Manage large sales forces	Dec	50.50	19.75	40.13	0.46	0.80	1.04	28	38.6
Information Resources(IRIC)	Data base prod mktg info svc	Dec	12.12	6.25	10.13	0.13	0.15	0.40	27	25.3
Baker(J.) Inc(JBAK)	Self-svc footwear retailer	Jan	9.25	3.62	6.31	0.14	0.65	0.88	26	7.2
AmeriCredit Corp(ACF)	Provides used-car financing	Jun	17.50	9.81	14.50	0.76	*1.11	1.43	25	10.1
MICROS Systems(MCRS)	Mfr point-of-sale computer sys	Jun	40.00	26.62	37.88	1.20	*1.60	2.02	25	18.8
Rural/Metro Corp(RURL)	Emergency ambulance/fire svcs	Jun	12.00	6.50	6.50	0.54	*1.06	1.24	25	5.2
PAREXEL Intl(PRXL)	Pharmaceutical R&D	Jun	29.37	8.03	8.44	0.38	*0.62	0.83	24	10.2
Henry(Jack) & Assoc(JKHY)	Data process'g svcs to banks	Jun	50.12	26.43	32.88	1.09	*1.50	1.78	22	18.5
CTS Corp(CTS)	Electronic components/subsys	Dec	60.00	20.43	53.00	1.28	1.87	2.29	20	23.1
DeVry Inc(DV)	Tech'l/MBA degree schools	Jun	31.87	18.00	20.31	0.44	*0.55	0.67	20	30.3
Dycom Industries(DY)	Telecommun & electrical svcs	Jul	56.62	29.93	35.94	1.01	*1.55	1.83	20	19.6
Elcor Corp(ELK)	Roofing & industrial products	Jun	30.25	19.18	26.88	0.91	*1.27	1.63	20	16.5
Insurance Auto Auctions(IAAI)	Sells insur recovered vehicles	Dec	19.75	10.00	14.75	0.63	1.10	1.36	20	10.8
Patterson Dental(PDCO)	Dstr dental supplies & equip	Apr	45.75	33.12	45.50	1.23	*1.49	1.86	19	24.5
Zale Corp(ZLC)	Operate jewelry stores	Jul	44.62	30.31	37.75	1.84	*2.21	2.64	18	14.3

*Actual 1999 EPS.

Chart based on September 24, 1999 prices and data.

Note: All earnings estimates are Wall Street consensus projections.

Stock Reports

In using the Stock Reports in this handbook, please pay particular attention to the dates attached to each evaluation, recommendation, or analysis section. Opinions rendered are as of that date and may change often. It is strongly suggested that before investing in any security you should obtain the current analysis on that issue.

To order the latest Standard & Poor's Stock Report on a company, for as little as $3.00 per report, please call:

S&P Reports On-Demand at 1-800-292-0808.

STANDARD & POOR'S STOCK REPORTS

AAR Corp.

NYSE Symbol **AIR**

In S&P SmallCap 600

09-OCT-99

Industry: Aerospace/Defense

Summary: AIR is a leading supplier of products and services for the commercial and military aviation aftermarkets; it also makes containerization products and materials-handling equipment.

Quantitative Evaluations

Outlook (1 Lowest—5 Highest) • **4+**

Fair Value • **27¾**

Risk • **Average**

Earn./Div. Rank • **B+**

Technical Eval. • **Bearish** since 9/99

Rel. Strength Rank (1 Lowest—99 Highest) • **25**

Insider Activity • **NA**

Recent Price • 17⅞

52 Wk Range • 25⅞-14⅝

Yield • 1.9%

12-Mo. P/E • 11.6

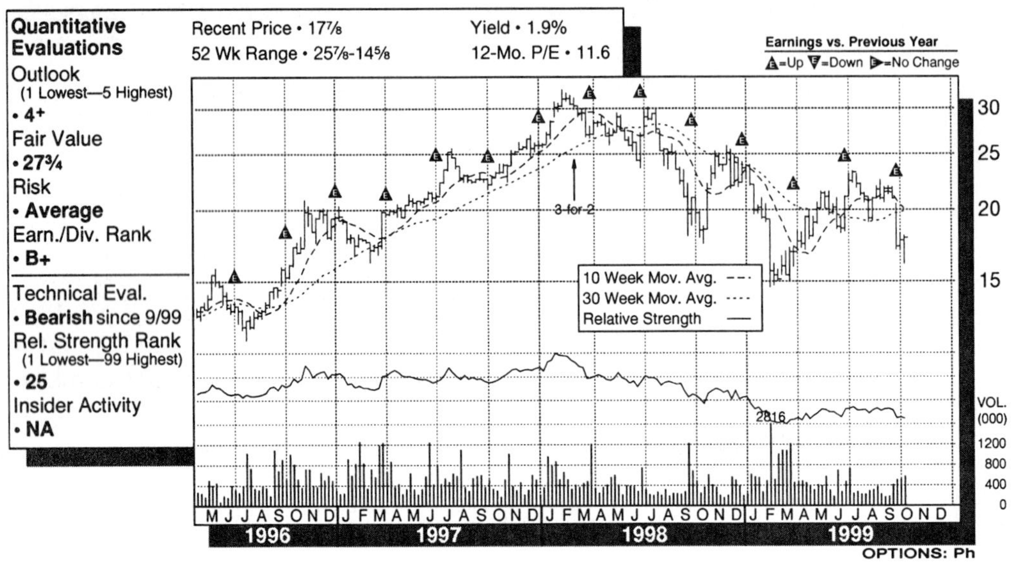

Business Profile - 29-JUN-99

AIR continues to win long-term contracts and grow both through acquisitions and through internal development. In June 1999, the company formed an alliance with Air France Industries to provide full component management support to operators of Airbus A320 aircraft in Central America. AIR has increased the scope of its technical services and manufactured products through additional investment in upgraded facilities, tooling and systems. In November 1998, AIR formed a strategic alliance with Norcross Air Inc. and Puroflow Inc. to provide filtration products. The company continues to buy back stock under a repurchase plan.

Operational Review - 29-JUN-99

Based on a preliminary report, net sales in the fiscal year ended May 31, 1999, advanced 17%, reflecting growth in all three segments; after adjusting for acquisitions, divestitures and joint ventures, sales grew 21%. Gross margins widened, on the greater volume and a more favorable product mix; with well controlled SG&A expense, operating income was up 20%. After higher interest expense, net income was up 17%, to $41,671,000 ($1.49 a share, diluted), from $35,657,000 ($1.27, as adjusted). AIR is continuing to focus on expanding its customer base and broadening its offerings.

Stock Performance - 08-OCT-99

In the past 30 trading days, AIR's shares have declined 15%, compared to a 0.91% fall in the S&P 500. Average trading volume for the past five days was 113,420 shares, compared with the 40-day moving average of 74,846 shares.

Key Stock Statistics

Dividend Rate/Share	0.34	Shareholders	12,000
Shs. outstg. (M)	27.4	Market cap. (B)	$0.490
Avg. daily vol. (M)	0.100	Inst. holdings	81%
Tang. Bk. Value/Share	10.44		
Beta	0.62		

Value of $10,000 invested 5 years ago: $ 20,707

Fiscal Year Ending May 31

	2000	1999	1998	1997	1996	1995
Revenues (Million $)						
1Q	245.9	215.9	170.9	136.0	109.6	97.19
2Q	—	228.8	180.2	135.7	121.3	99.4
3Q	—	227.7	208.5	154.1	136.1	125.2
4Q	—	245.6	222.6	163.5	138.1	129.6
Yr.	—	918.0	782.1	589.3	505.0	451.4
Earnings Per Share ($)						
1Q	**0.39**	**0.34**	0.27	0.20	0.13	0.09
2Q	—	**0.36**	0.31	0.21	0.15	0.09
3Q	—	**0.37**	**0.33**	0.24	0.17	0.12
4Q	—	**0.42**	**0.37**	0.26	0.21	0.15
Yr.	—	**1.49**	**1.27**	**0.91**	**0.66**	0.44

Next earnings report expected: mid December

Dividend Data (Dividends have been paid since 1973.)

Amount ($)	Date Decl.	Ex-Div. Date	Stock of Record	Payment Date
0.085	Oct. 14	Oct. 29	Nov. 02	Dec. 03 '98
0.085	Jan. 11	Jan. 28	Feb. 01	Mar. 03 '99
0.085	Apr. 13	Apr. 29	May. 03	Jun. 03 '99
0.085	Jul. 13	Jul. 29	Aug. 02	Sep. 03 '99

AAR Corp.

Business Summary - 29-JUN-99

This leading provider of aftermarket aviation-related products and services has not been left on the runway during the recent resurgence in the aerospace/aviation industry. Rebounding from the gloomy days of the early 1990s, airlines have continued to experience increased fleet utilization and improved operating earnings.

The rising equipment needs of airlines, particularly startup airlines, and air cargo and small-package carriers, have boosted demand for AIR's aircraft and engines, and airframe and accessories activities. During the past three years, the company has broadened its range of products and services, increased its customer base, and expanded its geographic reach. Aircraft and engines, which accounted for 45% of net sales in FY 99 (May), comprise the sale and lease of aviation products (mainly engines and engine parts) that have been purchased new, used or overhauled. AIR also sells, leases and finances new and used jet aircraft.

Airframe and accessories (41% of FY 99 sales) consist of the sale and lease of airframe parts and accessories, and repair and exchange services. During FY 99, the company acquired Tempco Hydraulics, Inc., a regional aircraft landing gear repair and overhaul business, as part of its strategy to expand service and support capabilities for regional airlines and to become a full line supplier to this growing market. In May 1998, AIR completed a significant expansion of its FAA-licensed Oklahoma airframe maintenance facility, providing 20% more capacity. In late 1997, the company acquired AVSCO Aviation Service Corp. ($80 million in sales), a new parts distributor. This business primarily overhauls, repairs and modifies components for both commercial and military aircraft.

The manufacturing segment (14%) makes and installs cargo handling systems, pallets and containers for airframe manufacturers, commercial and military airlines, and others. In November 1998, AIR sold its PowerBoss industrial products floor cleaning manufacturing unit.

Over the past few years, the number of U.S. military bases both in the U.S. and overseas has been reduced, due to budget cuts and downsizing. With fewer bases, the need for rapid deployment products for moving supplies to hot spots around the world in times of crisis has increased. In response, AIR has stepped up its development and design efforts for such products. The U.S. government accounted for 10.6% of net sales in FY 98, down from 13.9% in FY 97.

Backlog at May 31, 1998, totaled $107.4 million, up from $84.8 million a year earlier. In FY 98, export sales accounted for 26% of total net sales.

Per Share Data ($) (Year Ended May 31)	1999	1998	1997	1996	1995	1994	1993	1992	1991	1990
Tangible Bk. Val.	NA	9.90	9.65	8.29	7.98	7.68	7.66	7.96	7.83	7.55
Cash Flow	NA	1.81	1.41	1.09	0.87	0.70	0.47	0.91	0.97	1.37
Earnings	1.49	1.27	0.92	0.67	0.44	0.40	0.01	0.42	0.62	1.07
Dividends	0.34	0.32	0.32	0.32	0.32	0.32	0.32	0.32	0.32	0.31
Payout Ratio	23%	25%	35%	48%	73%	80%	NM	76%	52%	29%
Cal. Yrs.	1998	1997	1996	1995	1994	1993	1992	1991	1990	1989
Prices - High	32 3/8	27	20 7/8	14 5/8	11 5/8	10	10 5/8	11 1/4	24 5/8	25
- Low	17 3/8	16 1/8	11 7/8	8 1/8	7 7/8	7 5/8	7 1/8	6 1/8	6 1/8	16
P/E Ratio - High	22	21	23	22	26	25	NM	27	40	23
- Low	12	13	13	12	18	19	NM	15	10	15
Income Statement Analysis (Million $)										
Revs.	NA	782	589	505	451	408	383	423	467	445
Oper. Inc.	NA	79.0	55.2	42.6	34.8	29.1	27.2	38.2	42.0	54.0
Depr.	NA	14.3	12.3	10.1	10.3	7.3	10.9	11.6	8.3	7.2
Int. Exp.	NA	14.5	10.8	10.6	10.9	9.6	8.1	8.4	10.1	10.0
Pretax Inc.	NA	51.2	33.0	22.8	14.7	13.7	-1.9	13.6	21.4	38.2
Eff. Tax Rate	NA	30%	30%	30%	29%	31%	NM	26%	31%	33%
Net Inc.	NA	35.7	23.0	16.0	10.5	9.5	0.3	10.0	14.8	25.7
Balance Sheet & Other Fin. Data (Million $)										
Cash	NA	17.2	51.7	33.6	22.5	18.1	2.3	2.3	1.6	4.0
Curr. Assets	NA	468	414	338	322	308	265	290	268	276
Total Assets	NA	671	530	438	426	418	365	395	380	389
Curr. Liab.	NA	149	100	79.4	73.0	68.0	72.0	92.0	79.0	91.0
LT Debt	NA	178	117	118	120	116	66.3	67.3	69.0	72.3
Common Eqty.	NA	301	269	205	197	189	189	197	194	190
Total Cap.	NA	516	419	354	348	344	294	303	301	298
Cap. Exp.	NA	17.5	30.3	7.5	9.1	6.4	8.9	8.2	8.9	10.4
Cash Flow	NA	49.9	35.3	26.1	20.8	16.8	11.2	21.6	23.1	32.8
Curr. Ratio	NA	3.1	4.1	4.3	4.4	4.5	3.7	3.1	3.4	3.0
% LT Debt of Cap.	NA	34.4	27.9	33.3	34.5	33.6	22.6	22.2	22.9	24.3
% Net Inc.of Revs.	NA	4.6	3.9	3.9	2.4	2.3	0.1	2.4	3.2	5.8
% Ret. on Assets	NA	5.9	4.8	3.7	2.5	2.4	0.1	2.6	3.9	6.9
% Ret. on Equity	NA	12.5	9.8	8.0	5.5	5.0	0.1	5.1	7.8	14.2

Data as orig reptd.; bef. results of disc opers/spec. items. Per share data adj. for stk. divs. Bold denotes diluted EPS (FASB 128)-prior periods restated. E-Estimated. NA-Not Available. NM-Not Meaningful. NR-Not Ranked.

Office—One AAR Place, 1100 N. Wood Dale Rd., Wood Dale, IL 60191. **Tel**—(630) 227-2000. **Website**—http://www.aarcorp.com **Chrmn**—I. A. Eichner. **Pres & CEO**—D. P. Storch. **VP, Treas & CFO**—T. J. Romenesko. **VP & Secy**—H. A. Pulsifer. **VP & Investor Contact**—Ann T. Baldwin. **Dirs**—A. R. Abboud, H. B. Bernick, I. A. Eichner, E. D. Jannotta, R. D. Judson, E. E. Schulze, M. Sharp, J. D. Spungin, L. B. Stern, D. P. Storch, R. D. Tabery. **Transfer Agents & Registrars**—First National Bank of Chicago; First Chicago Trust Co. of New York, Jersey City, NJ. **Incorporated**—in Delaware in 1966. **Empl**— 2,700. **S&P Analyst:** Stewart Scharf

STANDARD
&POOR'S
STOCK REPORTS

ABM Industries

NYSE Symbol **ABM**

In S&P SmallCap 600

09-OCT-99

Industry:
Services (Facilities & Environmental)

Summary: ABM, the largest facility services contractor on the NYSE, provides janitorial, air-conditioning, elevator, engineering, lighting, parking and security services.

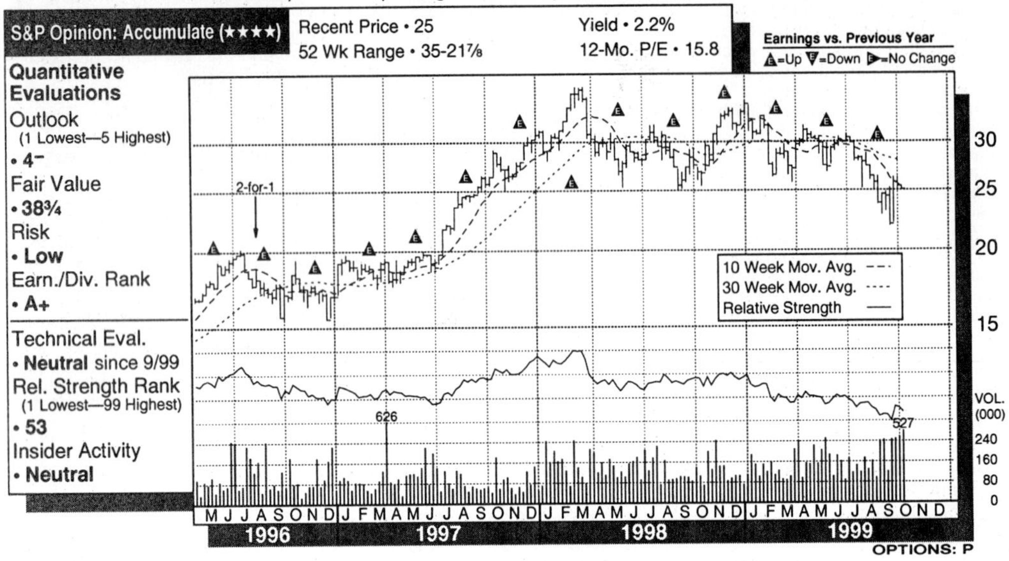

Overview - 21-SEP-99

We expect revenues to increase about 8%-10% through FY 01 (Oct.), driven by the trend toward outsourcing of non-core functions by many U.S. companies, a strong domestic economy and selective acquisitions. With many American firms now focusing the majority of their resources on the design and marketing of their products or services, a growing number of organizations are turning to third parties to handle facility-related work, such as janitorial, security and lighting services. In addition, the top line will benefit from consolidation among client industries, as newly merged firms tend to turn to outsourcing. We see margins widening, reflecting price increases designed to mitigate the effect of wage pressure, as well as SG&A leverage. The bottom line will also be aided by well controlled interest expense. We expect FY 99 EPS to grow 14%, to $1.65, and see FY 00 earnings of $1.86 a share.

Valuation - 21-SEP-99

The shares have fallen thus far in 1999, and were recently trading at 14X our calendar 1999 EPS estimate of $1.68 (12X our calendar 2000 estimate of $1.90), which is at the low end of their historical range and at a significant discount to the P/E multiple of the broader markets. As a result, we continue to recommend investors accumulate the shares. While revenue growth has slowed, and is expected to continue at just a high single digit pace, we feel confident that the company will continue to achieve margin improvement and meet its long term goal of 12%-15% annual EPS increases. ABM offers conservative investors reliable and forecastable growth, solid industry fundamentals and a dividend yield of about 2%. In addition, the company has reduced its debt-to-capital ratio to under 10%, providing it with the flexibility to opportunistically pursue acquisitions.

Key Stock Statistics

S&P EPS Est. 1999	1.65	Tang. Bk. Value/Share	7.26
P/E on S&P Est. 1999	15.2	Beta	0.87
S&P EPS Est. 2000	1.86	Shareholders	6,600
Dividend Rate/Share	0.56	Market cap. (B)	$0.560
Shs. outstg. (M)	22.3	Inst. holdings	66%
Avg. daily vol. (M)	0.080		

Value of $10,000 invested 5 years ago: $ 31,330

Fiscal Year Ending Oct. 31

	1999	1998	1997	1996	1995	1994
Revenues (Million $)						
1Q	391.8	358.8	291.6	254.4	232.1	210.8
2Q	398.3	369.0	294.3	262.1	234.4	215.9
3Q	412.7	381.0	308.5	281.9	245.8	225.0
4Q	—	393.0	358.5	288.6	253.1	233.0
Yr.	—	1,502	1,252	1,087	965.4	884.6
Earnings Per Share ($)						
1Q	**0.29**	**0.25**	**0.22**	0.20	0.17	0.15
2Q	**0.35**	**0.30**	0.26	0.23	0.20	0.18
3Q	**0.46**	**0.40**	0.34	0.29	0.26	0.23
4Q	**E0.55**	**0.49**	0.40	0.33	0.29	0.27
Yr.	**E1.65**	**1.44**	**1.22**	**1.05**	0.92	0.82

Next earnings report expected: mid December

Dividend Data (Dividends have been paid since 1965.)

Amount ($)	Date Decl.	Ex-Div. Date	Stock of Record	Payment Date
0.140	Dec. 15	Jan. 13	Jan. 15	Feb. 03 '99
0.140	Mar. 16	Apr. 13	Apr. 15	May. 05 '99
0.140	Jun. 15	Jul. 13	Jul. 15	Aug. 04 '99
0.140	Sep. 22	Oct. 13	Oct. 15	Nov. 03 '99

A Division of The McGraw-Hill Companies

ABM Industries Incorporated

Business Summary - 21-SEP-99

Over the past few years, companies have increasingly been outsourcing their non-core functions. As a result, companies such as ABM Industries, the largest facility services contractor listed on the New York Stock Exchange, have experienced solid increases in demand. Services provided by ABM to its thousands of commercial, industrial and institutional customers across the U.S. and Canada include air-conditioning, elevator, engineering, janitorial, lighting, parking and security.

Janitorial cleaning services, as well as janitorial supplies and equipment, are provided by ABM's janitorial division (including American Building Maintenance and Easterday Janitorial Supply), which accounted for roughly 56% of revenues in FY 98 (Oct.). Services provided include floor cleaning, dusting and other building cleaning services. This unit operates 79 offices in 37 states, the District of Columbia and one Canadian province. The majority of the division's contracts are for one year, with automatic renewal clauses.

Parking lot and garage operations and commercial security and investigative services are offered by the public service divisions segment (which contributed about 21% of revenues in FY 98). The American Commercial Security Services unit provides security guards, electric monitoring of fire, life and safety devices and security consulting services to a variety of major U.S. cities. The Ampco System Parking division operates roughly 1,500 parking lots and garages. The ABM Facility Services unit provides customers with streamlined centralized control and coordination of multiple facility service needs.

The technical divisions (which offer various elevator, engineering, heating, ventilation and air-conditioning and lighting services) accounted for about 23% of revenues in FY 98. The company believes that the offering of such a wide range of services by an affiliated group provides its customers with an appealing alternative to obtaining the services from a larger number of unrelated individual subcontractors. This unit operates 46 offices in 17 states and the District of Columbia.

Acquisitions have played a major role in ABM's revenue and earnings growth in recent years. FY 98 transactions included the September 1998 purchase of selected assets from Arizona-based Professional Corporate Services; the June 1998 acquisitions of the ongoing business of Lighting Maintenance, Inc. (LMI) and Fecht Electric Co.; and the March 1998 acquisition of certain contracts and assets of Massachusetts-based Maintenance Center Building Services.

Per Share Data ($) (Year Ended Oct. 31)	1998	1997	1996	1995	1994	1993	1992	1991	1990	1989
Tangible Bk. Val.	5.94	4.45	4.51	3.87	3.48	2.98	4.01	3.56	2.95	2.56
Cash Flow	2.29	1.96	1.72	1.52	1.34	1.14	1.11	1.11	1.06	1.00
Earnings	1.44	1.22	1.05	0.93	0.82	0.72	0.71	0.68	0.62	0.56
Dividends	0.48	0.40	0.35	0.30	0.26	0.25	0.24	0.24	0.23	0.23
Payout Ratio	33%	33%	33%	33%	32%	34%	34%	35%	38%	42%
Prices - High	37	31½	20¼	14¼	12	10⅞	10¼	8⅞	10⅜	10
- Low	25	17⅜	13½	10½	8⅝	7¼	7⅞	6⅛	6¼	6⅞
P/E Ratio - High	26	26	19	15	14	15	14	13	17	18
- Low	17	14	13	11	10	10	11	9	10	12
Income Statement Analysis (Million $)										
Revs.	1,502	1,252	1,087	965	885	773	758	739	679	638
Oper. Inc.	80.6	65.8	55.4	46.6	37.8	29.6	26.7	21.4	19.9	23.6
Depr.	19.6	16.1	13.7	11.5	9.3	7.2	6.6	7.0	7.0	6.8
Int. Exp.	3.5	2.7	3.6	3.7	3.5	2.2	2.1	3.1	2.7	2.2
Pretax Inc.	57.5	46.9	38.1	31.4	25.1	20.2	20.4	18.6	10.5	14.6
Eff. Tax Rate	41%	42%	43%	42%	40%	38%	41%	40%	6.60%	40%
Net Inc.	33.9	27.2	21.7	18.2	15.2	12.6	12.0	11.1	9.8	8.7
Balance Sheet & Other Fin. Data (Million $)										
Cash	1.8	1.8	1.6	1.8	7.4	1.7	2.4	2.5	1.6	2.5
Curr. Assets	324	294	234	210	189	167	154	142	132	122
Total Assets	501	467	380	335	299	268	226	212	202	190
Curr. Liab.	158	157	114	114	99	90.3	78.5	80.1	66.5	63.6
LT Debt	33.7	38.4	33.7	22.6	25.3	20.9	15.4	9.5	20.0	20.0
Common Eqty.	238	198	164	142	124	110	101	90.0	79.6	69.4
Total Cap.	271	236	204	171	156	138	116	99	100	89.4
Cap. Exp.	11.7	13.3	10.8	10.2	8.5	6.2	5.2	5.7	6.1	6.0
Cash Flow	53.0	42.8	34.9	29.2	24.0	19.7	18.6	18.1	16.9	15.5
Curr. Ratio	2.1	1.9	2.1	1.8	1.9	1.8	2.0	1.8	2.0	1.9
% LT Debt of Cap.	12.4	16.3	16.5	13.2	16.2	15.2	13.3	9.6	20.1	22.4
% Net Inc.of Revs.	2.3	2.2	2.0	1.9	1.7	1.6	1.6	1.5	1.4	1.4
% Ret. on Assets	7.0	6.4	6.1	5.7	5.3	5.0	5.4	5.3	5.0	4.8
% Ret. on Equity	15.4	15.0	13.9	13.3	12.3	11.7	12.4	13.0	13.1	13.1

Data as orig reptd.; bef. results of disc opers/spec. items. Per share data adj. for stk. divs. Bold denotes diluted EPS (FASB 128)-prior periods restated. E-Estimated. NA-Not Available. NM-Not Meaningful. NR-Not Ranked.

Office—160 Pacific Ave., Suite 222, San Francisco, CA 94111. **Tel**—(415) 733-4000. **Website**—http://www.abm.com **Chrmn**—M. H. Mandles. **Pres & CEO**—W. W. Steele. **VP & Secy**—H. H. Kahn. **VP & CFO**—D. H. Hebble. **Dirs**—M. B. Cattani, L. Chavez, J. F. Egan, L. Helms, C. T. Horngren, H. L. Kotkins, M. H. Mandles, T. Rosenberg, W. W. Steele, W. E. Walsh. **Transfer Agent & Registrar**—ChaseMellon Shareholder Services, San Francisco. **Incorporated**—in California in 1955; reincorporated in Delaware in 1985. **Empl**— 55,000. **S&P Analyst:** Stephen J. Tekirian

STANDARD
&POOR'S
STOCK REPORTS

Action Performance Cos.

NASDAQ Symbol **ACTN**

In S&P SmallCap 600

09-OCT-99

Industry:
Consumer (Jewelry, Novelties & Gifts)

Summary: ACTN designs and markets collectible die-cast and pewter miniature replicas of motorsports vehicles and licensed apparel, souvenirs and other motorsports consumer items.

Quantitative Evaluations

Outlook
(1 Lowest—5 Highest)
• **5**

Fair Value
• **35⅞**

Risk
• **Average**

Earn./Div. Rank
• **NR**

Technical Eval.
• **Bearish** since 7/99

Rel. Strength Rank
(1 Lowest—99 Highest)
• **11**

Insider Activity
• **Favorable**

Recent Price • 21¼
52 Wk Range • 48¼-16¼
Yield • Nil
12-Mo. P/E • 11.6

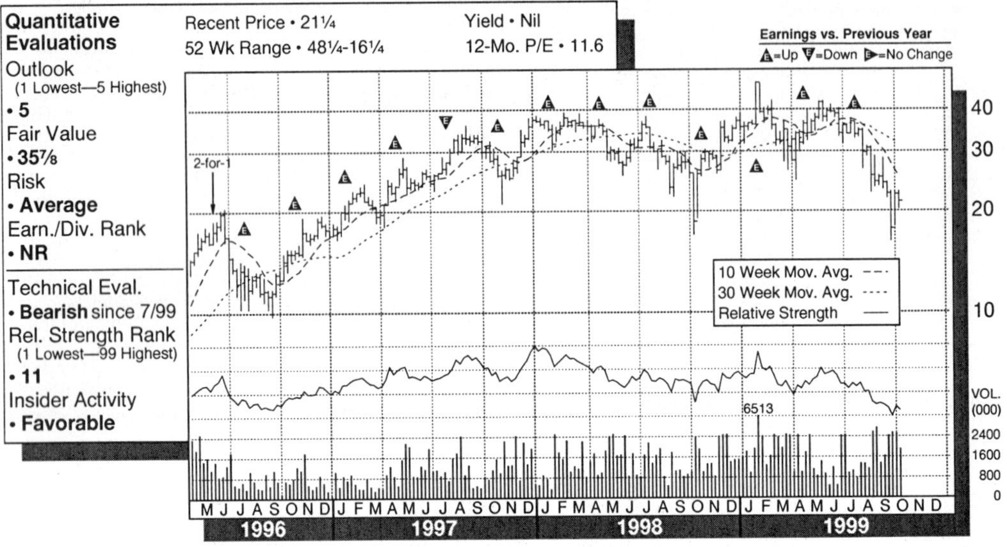

Business Profile - 28-SEP-99

ACTN was pleased with its operating results for the third quarter of FY 99 (Sep.), and stated that it continues to see momentum in motorsports and strong demand for its products. During the quarter the company completed its Star Wars, Wrangler and Superman programs, and management expects to continue to increase its share of the growing domestic market for consumer motorsports products while expanding its revenues by leveraging its expertise against the untapped European motorsports market. In August 1999, the company extended its partnership with Hasbro, Inc. through 2006; ACTN's previously established domestic retail partnership promoting Hasbro's Winner's Circle Brand had resulted in a dramatic increase in sales.

Operational Review - 28-SEP-99

Net sales for the nine months ended June 30, 1999, jumped 46%, year to year, reflecting revenues from recent acquisitions, initial Internet sales, greater sales of die-cast collectible goods, and an increased membership count. Margins widened on the rise in sales of higher margin die-cast collectibles. SG&A expenses expanded 53%, primarily from costs related to the development of the company's Internet site. Pretax income was up 46%. After significantly higher minority interest in earnings, net income advanced 42%, to $22,998,000 ($1.33 a share, on 15% more shares), from $16,240,000 ($0.98).

Stock Performance - 08-OCT-99

In the past 30 trading days, ACTN's shares have declined 13%, compared to a 0.91% fall in the S&P 500. Average trading volume for the past five days was 377,880 shares, compared with the 40-day moving average of 627,544 shares.

Key Stock Statistics

Dividend Rate/Share	Nil	Shareholders	310
Shs. outstg. (M)	16.9	Market cap. (B)	$0.361
Avg. daily vol. (M)	0.602	Inst. holdings	95%
Tang. Bk. Value/Share	3.28		
Beta	1.69		

Value of $10,000 invested 5 years ago: $ 121,782

Fiscal Year Ending Sep. 30

	1999	1998	1997	1996	1995	1994
Revenues (Million $)						
1Q	71.57	42.92	15.18	8.01	4.11	2.70
2Q	78.93	53.16	28.30	9.77	3.67	2.17
3Q	101.5	76.79	39.63	12.28	8.49	6.02
4Q	—	79.00	47.27	14.16	9.87	5.99
Yr.	—	251.9	130.4	44.22	26.13	16.87
Earnings Per Share ($)						
1Q	**0.29**	**0.22**	**0.12**	0.07	0.01	-0.07
2Q	**0.38**	**0.24**	0.17	0.09	0.02	-0.04
3Q	**0.64**	**0.50**	0.08	0.14	0.10	0.08
4Q	—	**0.49**	0.31	0.16	0.12	0.10
Yr.	—	**1.48**	**0.69**	**0.46**	0.27	0.08

Next earnings report expected: mid November

Dividend Data

No cash dividends have been paid.

A Division of The McGraw-Hill Companies

Action Performance Companies, Inc.

Business Summary - 28-SEP-99

Action Performance Companies designs and markets collectible and consumer products that are intended to capitalize on the increasing interest in motorsports.

The company designs and markets collectible die-cast and pewter miniature replicas of motorsports vehicles and designs and markets licensed apparel, souvenirs and other motorsports consumer items, including T-shirts, hats, jackets, mugs, key chains and drink bottles. It also represents popular race car drivers in a broad range of licensing and other revenue-producing opportunities, including product licenses, corporate sponsorships, endorsement contracts and speaking engagements, and develops marketing and product promotional programs for corporate sponsors of motorsports that feature ACTN's die-cast replicas or other products as premium awards intended to increase brand awareness of the products or services of the corporate sponsors. ACTN markets its motorsports collectibles and consumer items under license agreements with popular race drivers, car owners, car sponsors and automobile manufacturers.

Historically, ACTN has designed and marketed die-cast collectibles that mainly feature National Association for Stock Car Auto Racing (NASCAR) drivers and vehicles. In 1995, the company began expanding its lines of die-cast collectibles to include other types of motorsports vehicles, including National Hot Rod Association (NHRA) drag racing, NASCAR's new Super Truck racing series, dirt car racing and sprint car racing.

ACTN focuses on developing long-term relationships with and engages in comprehensive efforts to license the most popular drivers in each top racing category, as well as car owners, car sponsors, car manufacturers and others in these categories. It has license agreements with many of the most popular NASCAR race drivers, including seven-time Winston Cup champion Dale Earnhardt, 1996 Winston Cup champion Terry Labonte and 1995 and 1997 Winston Cup champion Jeff Gordon.

In December 1997, ACTN acquired the U.S. motorsports die-cast collectibles business of Revell-Monogram Inc., a unit of Binney & Smith Inc., for $15 million in cash and a 10-year earn-out for a minimum of an additional $10 million. As part of the agreement, ACTN and Revell-Monogram will form a strategic alliance to develop new product lines in the plastic models and die-cast collectibles businesses.

In April 1999, ACTN announced that it had signed a three-year exclusive licensing and merchandising agreement with Silverstone Circuits Limited, whereby ACTN will obtain the exclusive rights to the British Grand Prix held at Silverstone as well as the rights to market British Grand Prix and Silverstone brand merchandise.

Per Share Data ($) (Year Ended Sep. 30)	1998	1997	1996	1995	1994	1993	1992	1991	1990	1989
Tangible Bk. Val.	1.84	3.56	2.14	1.67	0.87	0.75	NA	NA	NA	NA
Cash Flow	2.19	1.00	0.59	0.36	0.16	0.09	NA	NA	NA	NA
Earnings	1.48	0.69	0.46	0.27	0.08	-0.21	NA	NA	NA	NA
Dividends	Nil	Nil	Nil	Nil	Nil	Nil	NA	NA	NA	NA
Payout Ratio	Nil	Nil	Nil	Nil	Nil	Nil	NA	NA	NA	NA
Prices - High	39¼	38½	20½	9¾	3⅛	3½	NA	NA	NA	NA
- Low	17	16½	6⅜	2⅜	1⅝	1½	NA	NA	NA	NA
P/E Ratio - High	27	56	44	36	38	NM	NA	NA	NA	NA
- Low	11	24	14	9	20	NM	NA	NA	NA	NA
Income Statement Analysis (Million $)										
Revs.	252	130	44.2	26.1	16.9	15.1	NA	NA	NA	NA
Oper. Inc.	56.9	28.0	11.3	5.0	1.3	-0.7	NA	NA	NA	NA
Depr.	11.8	4.5	1.7	0.9	0.7	0.5	NA	NA	NA	NA
Int. Exp.	5.5	2.0	0.1	0.2	0.2	NA	NA	NA	NA	NA
Pretax Inc.	41.2	16.9	9.9	4.2	0.4	-1.2	NA	NA	NA	NA
Eff. Tax Rate	40%	40%	40%	33%	NM	NM	NA	NA	NA	NA
Net Inc.	24.6	10.1	6.0	2.8	0.6	-1.2	NA	NA	NA	NA
Balance Sheet & Other Fin. Data (Million $)										
Cash	60.9	29.3	5.0	6.8	NA	NA	NA	NA	NA	NA
Curr. Assets	144	72.5	22.4	16.1	NA	NA	NA	NA	NA	NA
Total Assets	306	141	31.6	23.4	NA	NA	NA	NA	NA	NA
Curr. Liab.	56.7	15.6	4.3	4.2	NA	NA	NA	NA	NA	NA
LT Debt	112	22.6	0.4	0.3	0.3	NA	NA	NA	NA	NA
Common Eqty.	136	103	27.0	18.9	6.9	5.7	NA	NA	NA	NA
Total Cap.	249	126	27.4	19.2	7.2	NA	NA	NA	NA	NA
Cap. Exp.	21.6	11.2	3.9	3.0	1.7	NA	NA	NA	NA	NA
Cash Flow	36.4	14.6	7.7	3.7	1.3	0.7	NA	NA	NA	NA
Curr. Ratio	2.5	4.7	5.2	3.9	NA	NA	NA	NA	NA	NA
% LT Debt of Cap.	44.9	18.0	1.3	1.5	3.6	NA	NA	NA	NA	NA
% Net Inc.of Revs.	9.8	7.8	13.5	10.6	3.7	NM	NA	NA	NA	NA
% Ret. on Assets	11.0	11.7	21.6	NA	NA	NM	NA	NA	NA	NA
% Ret. on Equity	20.5	15.6	25.9	NA	NA	NM	NA	NA	NA	NA

Data as orig reptd.; bef. results of disc opers/spec. items. Per share data adj. for stk. divs. Bold denotes diluted EPS (FASB 128)-prior periods restated. E-Estimated. NA-Not Available. NM-Not Meaningful. NR-Not Ranked.

Office—4707 East Baseline Rd., Phoenix, AZ 85040. **Tel**—(602) 337-3700. **Fax**—(602) 337-3750. **Website**—http://www.action-performance.com
Chrmn, Pres & CEO—F. W. Wagenhals. **EVP & Secy**—T. J. Wagenhals. **VP, CFO & Treas**—C. S. Besing. **Dirs**—E. J. Bauman, C. S. Besing, J. S. Bickford Sr., P. G. Lang, J. M. Lloyd, G. W. Penske, R. H. Manschot, M. L. Volosin, F. W. Wagenhals, T. J. Wagenhals. **Transfer Agent & Registrar**—American Stock Transfer & Trust Co., NYC. **Incorporated**—in Arizona in 1992. **Empl**— 418. **S&P Analyst:** Matthew C. Hershberg

STANDARD
&POOR'S
STOCK REPORTS

Acxiom Corp.

NASDAQ Symbol **ACXM**

In S&P SmallCap 600

09-OCT-99

Industry: Services (Advertising & Marketing)

Summary: This company provides data products, data integration services and mailing list processing services, as well as data warehousing and decision support services.

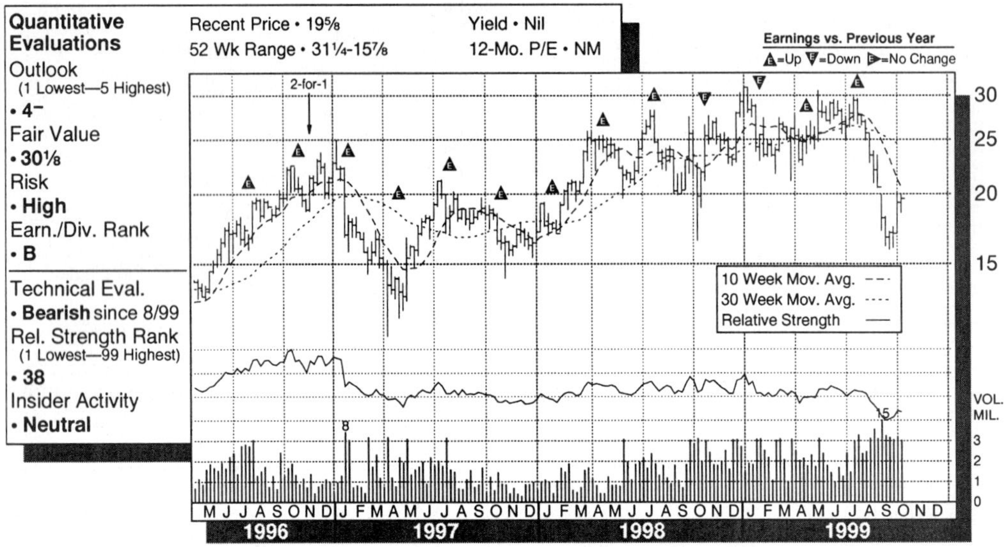

Business Profile - 28-JUN-99

As part of its strategy of growth through acquisition, the company recently made two acquisitions. In June 1999, Acxiom completed the acquisition, for an undisclosed amount, of Computer Graphics, an Arizona-based firm with $25 million in annual revenues that serves the financial services and credit collection industries. In April 1999, ACXM acquired Horizon Systems, a Connecticut-based provider of information management solutions with annual revenues of about $9.1 million. In June 1999, the company announced plans for an offering of 5.5 million shares of ACXM common stock, with 4 million shares to be sold by existing shareholders.

Operational Review - 28-JUN-99

Revenues in the fiscal year ended March 31, 1999, climbed 28%, driven by strong gains in all operating divisions. Despite a larger increase in salaries and benefits expense, margins widened, reflecting well controlled computer and data costs; operating income grew 34%. Results were penalized by charges of $119 million related to a recent acquisition, as well as a rise in interest expense. After taxes of $1,984,000, versus $27,332,000, a net loss of $16,430,000 ($0.22 a share, based on 7.6% fewer shares) contrasted with net income of $46,055,000 ($0.57).

Stock Performance - 08-OCT-99

In the past 30 trading days, ACXM's shares have declined 5%, compared to a 0.91% fall in the S&P 500. Average trading volume for the past five days was 632,660 shares, compared with the 40-day moving average of 1,309,549 shares.

Key Stock Statistics

Dividend Rate/Share	Nil	Shareholders	1,617
Shs. outstg. (M)	84.8	Market cap. (B)	$ 1.7
Avg. daily vol. (M)	0.825	Inst. holdings	62%
Tang. Bk. Value/Share	3.30		
Beta	1.02		

Value of $10,000 invested 5 years ago: $ 36,511

Fiscal Year Ending Mar. 31

	2000	1999	1998	1997	1996	1995
Revenues (Million $)						
1Q	211.5	128.6	100.3	93.95	59.18	46.88
2Q	—	174.4	110.0	97.55	62.38	47.85
3Q	—	187.9	120.7	104.5	71.32	52.74
4Q	—	208.9	134.1	106.0	77.03	54.97
Yr.	—	730.0	465.1	402.0	269.9	202.4
Earnings Per Share ($)						
1Q	**0.18**	**0.12**	0.09	0.07	0.06	0.04
2Q	—	**-0.82**	0.14	0.10	0.08	0.06
3Q	—	**0.17**	**0.19**	0.15	0.11	0.09
4Q	—	**0.23**	**0.18**	0.14	0.10	0.09
Yr.	—	**-0.22**	**0.60**	**0.47**	0.35	0.27

Next earnings report expected: mid October

Dividend Data

No cash dividends have been paid. A shareholder rights plan was adopted in February 1998.

A Division of The McGraw·Hill Companies

Acxiom Corporation

Business Summary - 28-JUN-99

Acxiom Corp. (ACXM) provides comprehensive information management solutions using customer, consumer and business data. Its products and services allow its clients to use information to improve business decision-making and effectively manage customer relationships. Historically, Acxiom's client base has been Fortune 1000 companies in the financial services, insurance information services, publishing, retail and telecommunications industries. However, in recent years, the company has expanded its focus to include the pharmaceuticals/health care, e-commerce, Internet, utilities, automotive, technology, packaged goods and media/entertainment industries. ACXM currently operates through three lines of business: services, data products and information technology management.

Over the past several years, the company's most important initiative has been the development of Acxiom Data Network, which is a Web-enabled technology that allows ACXM to cost effectively provide clients with real-time desktop access to information over the Internet and via private networks. The company believes the Acxiom Data Network will enable it to expand within its existing markets, as well as penetrate smaller businesses that are eager to improve their customer management capabilities.

Acxiom's services division (54% of 1999 revenues) provides solutions that integrate and manage customer, consumer and business data using its information management skills and technology. The unit's services include marketing strategy consulting, data integration, data warehouse management and delivery, customer relationship management applications and list processing.

The company's data product segment (24% of 1999 revenues) focuses on both the consumer and business markets. ACXM Consumer InfoBase contains information on approximately 95% of all U.S. households, including demographic, telephone and lifestyle data for individuals, households and geographic areas. Acxiom's Business InfoBase contains data on approximately 15 million businesses, including information on location, line of business and ownership. ACXM's DataQuick product provides detailed information on over 70 million properties, such as address, ownership, demographics and trend data. The company's List Brokerage service offers clients access to customer lists from consumer products and services firms.

The Information Technology Management division (21% of 1999 revenues) provides data center management, as well as network and client/server management services, 24 hours a day, seven days a week. Services include data center operation, hardware installation and support, technical support and help-desk support.

Per Share Data ($) (Year Ended Mar. 31)	**1999**	**1998**	**1997**	**1996**	**1995**	**1994**	**1993**	**1992**	**1991**	**1990**
Tangible Bk. Val.	2.89	2.79	2.28	2.29	1.96	1.46	1.24	1.13	NA	NA
Cash Flow	0.63	1.28	1.03	0.77	0.69	0.64	0.54	0.29	NA	NA
Earnings	-0.22	0.60	0.47	0.35	0.27	0.19	0.15	0.06	NA	NA
Dividends	Nil	Nil	Nil	Nil	Nil	Nil	Nil	Nil	NA	NA
Payout Ratio	Nil	Nil	Nil	Nil	Nil	Nil	Nil	Nil	NA	NA
Cal. Yrs.	1998	1997	1996	1995	1994	1993	1992	1991	1990	1989
Prices - High	31¼	24	25	16⅛	7½	6⅛	4⅞	2¾	NA	NA
- Low	16½	11⅛	11	6⅞	4⅝	3⅛	1¾	1¼	NA	NA
P/E Ratio - High	NM	40	53	46	28	32	32	50	NA	NA
- Low	NM	19	23	19	17	16	12	23	NA	NA
Income Statement Analysis (Million $)										
Revs.	730	465	402	270	202	152	116	91.0	NA	NA
Oper. Inc.	179	100	84.9	53.3	42.6	34.7	27.8	15.2	NA	NA
Depr.	63.9	40.7	33.2	21.6	19.6	19.4	16.1	9.1	NA	NA
Int. Exp.	17.4	6.0	3.9	1.9	2.4	2.3	2.4	2.2	NA	NA
Pretax Inc.	-14.4	56.5	44.0	29.4	20.1	13.4	10.2	3.2	NA	NA
Eff. Tax Rate	NM	37%	38%	38%	38%	38%	39%	34%	NA	NA
Net Inc.	-16.4	35.6	27.5	18.2	12.4	8.4	6.2	2.1	NA	NA
Balance Sheet & Other Fin. Data (Million $)										
Cash	9.6	5.7	2.7	3.5	3.1	0.5	NA	NA	NA	NA
Curr. Assets	293	115	84.5	54.0	43.5	35.9	36.0	29.9	NA	NA
Total Assets	879	394	300	194	148	123	113	87.0	NA	NA
Curr. Liab.	166	68.3	36.1	31.2	25.0	12.9	14.9	12.5	NA	NA
LT Debt	325	100	87.1	26.9	18.2	35.0	33.2	23.0	NA	NA
Common Eqty.	349	200	156	123	97.2	61.9	52.2	47.4	NA	NA
Total Cap.	713	326	261	161	123	110	93.0	70.0	NA	NA
Cap. Exp.	128	55.8	59.8	39.0	24.4	27.3	28.8	NA	NA	NA
Cash Flow	47.5	76.3	60.7	39.8	32.0	27.8	22.3	11.3	NA	NA
Curr. Ratio	45.6	1.7	2.3	1.7	1.7	2.8	2.4	2.4	NA	NA
% LT Debt of Cap.	1.8	30.6	33.4	16.7	14.9	31.8	35.7	32.7	NA	NA
% Net Inc.of Revs.	NM	7.7	6.8	6.8	6.1	5.5	5.4	2.4	NA	NA
% Ret. on Assets	NM	10.3	11.1	10.6	9.1	7.1	6.2	2.4	NA	NA
% Ret. on Equity	NM	20.0	19.7	16.6	15.6	14.7	12.5	4.7	NA	NA

Data as orig reptd.; bef. results of disc opers/spec. items. Per share data adj. for stk. divs. Bold denotes diluted EPS (FASB 128)-prior periods restated. E-Estimated. NA-Not Available. NM-Not Meaningful. NR-Not Ranked.

Office—1 Information Way, Little Rock, AR 72203-8180. **Tel**—(501) 342-1000. **Website**—http://www.acxiom.com **Chrmn, Pres & CEO**—C. D. Morgan Jr. **EVP, Treas & COO**—R. S. Kline. **CFO & Investor Contact**—Robert S. Bloom. **Secy**—C. L. Hughes. **Dirs**—A. H. Die, W. T. Dillard II, H. C. Gambill, R. S. Kline, M. McLarty, C. D. Morgan, R. A. Pritzker, J. T. Womble. **Transfer Agent & Registrar**—First National Bank of Chicago. **Incorporated** —in Delaware in 1983. **Empl**— 5,260. **S&P Analyst:** Stephen J. Tekirian

STANDARD &POOR'S
STOCK REPORTS

ADAC Laboratories

NASDAQ Symbol **ADAC**

In S&P SmallCap 600

09-OCT-99

Industry: Health Care (Medical Products & Supplies)

Summary: This company provides nuclear medicine and radiation therapy planning systems worldwide, and supplies radiology and cardiology information systems in North America.

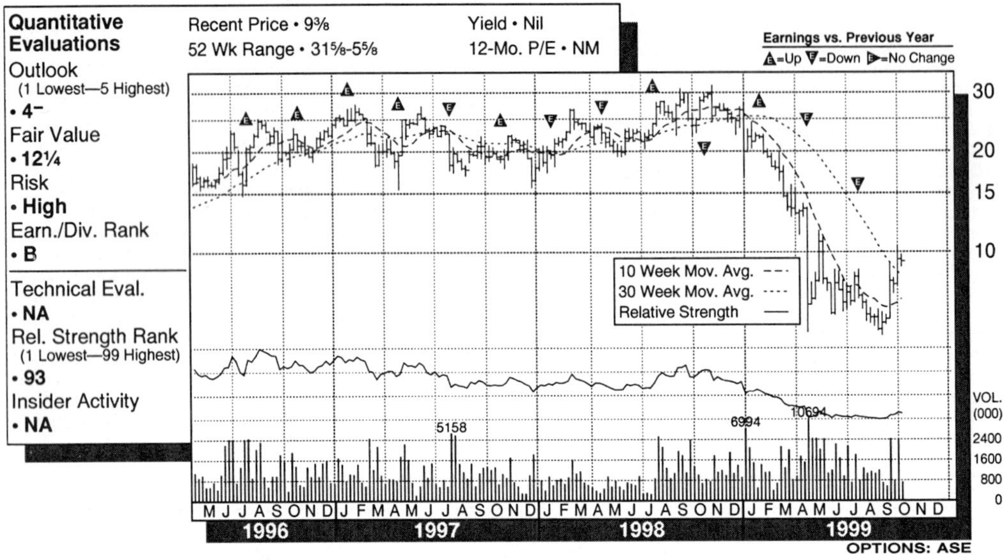

Business Profile - 01-JUL-99

In May 1999, the company said it would delay the release of its FY 99 (Sep.) second quarter results, because of its continuing evaluation of the need for additional reserves and the recording of charges. ADAC believes these actions will have a material adverse effect on its financial performance. In April 1999, ADAC said it expected FY 99 second quarter revenues to be 2% to 8% lower than first quarter revenues, due to delays in recognizing revenue under a revised revenue recognition policy, as well as weakening market demand for its products. In the FY 98 fourth quarter, ADAC decided to restructure its international organizations and discontinue its physician network services business.

Operational Review - 01-JUL-99

Revenues in the three months ended January 3, 1999, were up 40%, year to year, on a 48% increase in product revenue and a 20% rise in service revenue. Gross margins widened, on a more favorable product mix, and the absence of a discontinued product charge. Despite an 82% rise in G&A expenses and a $2.5 million restructuring charge, operating income contrasted with an operating loss. After taxes at 38.0%, versus tax credits of $3.5 million, net income of $3.9 million ($0.18 a share, on 11% more shares) contrasted with a net loss of $5.5 million ($0.29), as restated.

Stock Performance - 08-OCT-99

In the past 30 trading days, ADAC's shares have increased 60%, compared to a 0.91% fall in the S&P 500. Average trading volume for the past five days was 140,840 shares, compared with the 40-day moving average of 252,944 shares.

Key Stock Statistics

Dividend Rate/Share	Nil	Shareholders	2,485
Shs. outstg. (M)	20.5	Market cap. (B)	$0.193
Avg. daily vol. (M)	0.320	Inst. holdings	61%
Tang. Bk. Value/Share	4.08		
Beta	0.50		

Value of $10,000 invested 5 years ago: $ 7,671

Fiscal Year Ending Sep. 30

	1999	1998	1997	1996	1995	1994
Revenues (Million $)						
1Q	94.28	67.44	68.37	54.99	44.23	46.55
2Q	87.39	74.52	69.98	58.44	44.73	47.30
3Q	75.62	69.76	71.51	62.43	45.62	40.08
4Q	—	88.81	72.48	64.93	50.23	42.36
Yr.	—	300.5	282.3	240.8	184.8	176.3
Earnings Per Share ($)						
1Q	**0.18**	**-0.29**	**0.27**	0.20	0.15	0.32
2Q	**-1.02**	**0.27**	0.29	0.22	0.17	0.33
3Q	**-0.64**	**0.17**	0.01	0.24	0.18	0.02
4Q	—	**0.20**	0.31	0.26	0.16	0.39
Yr.	—	**0.36**	**0.69**	0.90	0.65	1.06

Next earnings report expected: early November

Dividend Data

Dividends, suspended in 1990, were resumed in 1992 and omitted in late 1996.

ADAC Laboratories

Business Summary - 01-JUL-99

ADAC Laboratories believes that it is the world market share leader in nuclear medicine and radiation therapy planning systems. The company is also a leading supplier of radiology and cardiology information systems in North America.

ADAC's medical systems (76% and 83% of FY 98 and FY 97 revenues, respectively) include nuclear medicine and radiation therapy planning systems, as well as ADAC Medical Technologies, the company's medical imaging equipment refurbishing business. ADAC also provides customer support and field service for its products.

Nuclear medicine is a diagnostic imaging procedure in which the patient is administered a radiotracer compound, which flows to organs under examination. The patient is then scanned with a gamma camera that detects radiotracer emissions from the organs. The company designs, manufactures and sells a broad line of nuclear medicine cameras and related computer systems, which consist of gamma cameras, computer workstations and clinical software that permits the physician to process the resulting data.

The company's software business (24% and 17% of revenues) includes its Radiation Therapy (RTP) business and its Healthcare Information Systems (HCIS) business. Through its RTP business, ADAC designs, develops and markets radiation therapy planning systems that assist hospitals and cancer treatment centers in planning treatments. RTP's principal product is the Pinnacle (3) radiation treatment planning system, which includes two- and three-dimensional planning capabilities.

HCIS designs, develops, markets, sells and supports integrated solutions consisting of computer equipment and software applications that offer health care providers the necessary tools to process and archive patient clinical information. The company's principal HCIS products are QuadRIS, a radiology information system product and CorCAAT, a cardiology information system product.

On December 29, 1998, the company announced that its financial results for FY 96, FY 97, and the first three quarters of FY 98 would be restated, and previously announced results for the FY 98 fourth quarter would change. The company completed an extensive and critical review of revenue recorded during these periods, and applied a more stringent revenue recognition policy than it had in the past. Items recognized and restated were primarily sales in the Medical Systems unit, where products had been sold and shipped to other than their final installation location. The primary impact was to move revenue and costs forward to future periods, including FY 99.

Per Share Data ($) (Year Ended Sep. 30)	1998	1997	1996	1995	1994	1993	1992	1991	1990	1989
Tangible Bk. Val.	5.51	6.19	4.98	4.20	4.65	3.60	2.76	2.58	2.55	2.52
Cash Flow	0.97	1.42	1.43	1.02	1.41	1.40	0.99	0.27	0.39	1.26
Earnings	0.71	0.86	0.90	0.65	1.06	1.10	0.81	0.06	0.24	1.17
Dividends	Nil	Nil	0.48	0.60	0.48	0.40	0.36	Nil	0.24	0.36
Payout Ratio	Nil	Nil	53%	92%	45%	40%	41%	Nil	102%	30%
Prices - High	31 5/8	27 3/4	25 1/4	13 3/4	14 1/8	16 7/8	15 3/4	7 7/8	18 3/4	18 3/4
- Low	16 7/8	15 3/8	11 5/8	7 1/4	6 1/8	9 1/4	5 1/8	3	2 1/16	12
P/E Ratio - High	45	32	28	21	13	15	19	NM	78	16
- Low	24	18	13	11	6	8	6	NM	9	10
Income Statement Analysis (Million $)										
Revs.	301	282	241	185	176	157	121	101	76.0	98.0
Oper. Inc.	30.1	51.4	39.1	24.8	25.9	24.8	16.4	7.9	5.4	19.4
Depr.	12.4	11.0	9.8	6.4	5.8	5.0	3.0	3.1	2.4	1.5
Int. Exp.	Nil	NA	NA	NA	NA	NA	NA	NA	0.1	0.3
Pretax Inc.	12.1	29.6	25.9	1.7	11.2	19.5	14.2	1.0	3.5	18.1
Eff. Tax Rate	39%	43%	36%	35%	NM	7.50%	9.40%	11%	3.30%	5.20%
Net Inc.	7.4	16.8	16.6	11.1	17.5	18.1	12.9	0.9	3.3	17.1
Balance Sheet & Other Fin. Data (Million $)										
Cash	4.9	5.1	3.1	7.6	7.2	6.7	11.9	5.7	10.6	7.6
Curr. Assets	151	142	135	107	92.1	69.5	54.2	47.7	48.2	52.3
Total Assets	244	207	187	158	122	95.1	77.2	60.1	59.0	60.4
Curr. Liab.	89.8	65.8	80.5	71.3	43.6	39.2	31.8	22.8	21.9	23.9
LT Debt	Nil	Nil	Nil	Nil	Nil	Nil	Nil	Nil	Nil	0.2
Common Eqty.	137	126	100	82.8	74.7	54.7	43.3	37.0	36.5	35.4
Total Cap.	151	137	102	82.8	74.7	54.7	43.3	37.0	36.5	35.6
Cap. Exp.	4.9	6.2	2.8	2.6	4.4	3.0	2.4	2.5	2.0	1.1
Cash Flow	19.8	27.8	26.5	17.5	23.3	23.1	15.9	4.0	5.8	18.6
Curr. Ratio	1.7	2.2	1.7	1.5	2.1	1.8	1.7	2.1	2.2	2.2
% LT Debt of Cap.	Nil	Nil	Nil	Nil	Nil	Nil	Nil	Nil	Nil	0.5
% Net Inc.of Revs.	2.5	5.9	6.9	6.0	9.9	11.5	10.6	0.9	4.4	17.4
% Ret. on Assets	3.3	8.5	9.7	8.0	15.8	20.6	18.5	1.5	5.6	29.9
% Ret. on Equity	5.6	14.8	18.3	14.1	26.5	36.3	31.6	2.4	9.2	59.0

Data as orig reptd.; bef. results of disc opers/spec. items. Per share data adj. for stk. divs. Bold denotes diluted EPS (FASB 128)-prior periods restated. E-Estimated. NA-Not Available. NM-Not Meaningful. NR-Not Ranked.

Office—540 Alder Dr., Milpitas, CA 95035. **Tel**—(408) 321-9100. **Website**—http://www.adaclabs.com **Chrmn & CEO**—R. A. Eckert. **CFO**—R. P. Bunje. **Investor Contact**—Steven R. Polcyn (408 468-3419). **Secy**—K .L. Masterson.**Dirs**—S. D. Czerwinski, R. A. Eckert, G. O. King, D. R. Raney, F. D. Rollo, E. H. Shea Jr. **Transfer Agent & Registrar**—ChaseMellon Shareholder Services, SF. **Incorporated**—in California in 1970. **Empl**—802. **S&P Analyst:** John J. Arege

STANDARD
&POOR'S
STOCK REPORTS

Adaptive Broadband

NASDAQ Symboi **ADAP**

In S&P SmallCap 600

09-OCT-99 **Industry:** Communications Equipment

Summary: ADAP (formerly California Microwave) is the leading U.S. supplier of telecommunications satellite earth stations and microwave radios used in wireless communications.

Quantitative Evaluations

Outlook (1 Lowest—5 Highest)
• **1+**

Fair Value
• **23¾**

Risk
• **Average**

Earn./Div. Rank
• **B**

Technical Eval.
• **Neutral** since 9/99

Rel. Strength Rank (1 Lowest—99 Highest)
• **97**

Insider Activity
• **NA**

Recent Price • 38⅝
52 Wk Range • 40¼-6¾
Yield • Nil
12-Mo. P/E • 49.5

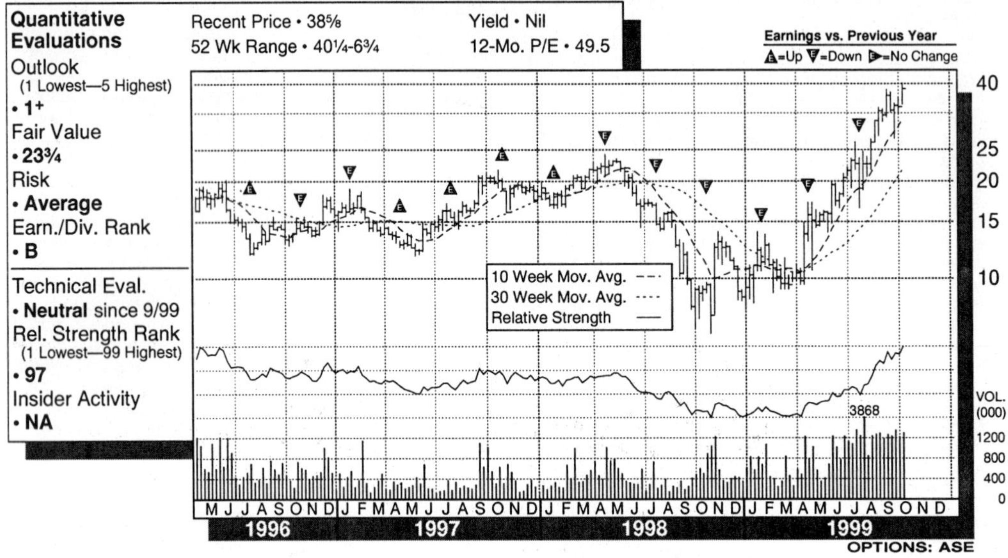

Business Profile - 02-AUG-99

Adaptive Broadband said in July 1999 that in keeping with its strategic plan, announced in April 1998, it has shed non-strategic businesses, building a financial base from which to launch new market initiatives; reorganized into one functional organization; invested in new technologies, through internal development and acquisitions, necessary to address larger market opportunities; strengthened and expanded the life cycles of core product areas with product upgrades and enhancements; and put in place shareholder-friendly corporate governance guidelines. Also in July 1999, ADAP signed a contract, valued initially at $100 million over five years, to sell AB-Access broadband wireless service equipment to I3S, Inc. The present corporate title was adopted in April 1999.

Operational Review - 02-AUG-99

Revenues from continuing operations for FY 99 (Jun.; preliminary) declined 10%, year to year, reflecting weakness in international markets. The lower revenues, higher expenses, and an $11.8 million nonrecurring charge for purchased in-process research and development, led to a widening of the operating loss to $33.0 million, from $642,000. After a 13% rise in interest charges (net) and tax credits in both years, the loss from continuing operations was $26.6 million ($1.79 a share, on 9% fewer shares), against $242,000 ($0.01). Results are before income from discontinued operations of $2.57 a share, versus a loss of $0.46.

Stock Performance - 08-OCT-99

In the past 30 trading days, ADAP's shares have increased 17%, compared to a 0.91% fall in the S&P 500. Average trading volume for the past five days was 459,560 shares, compared with the 40-day moving average of 391,372 shares.

Key Stock Statistics

Dividend Rate/Share	Nil	Shareholders	13,500
Shs. outstg. (M)	14.8	Market cap. (B)	$0.571
Avg. daily vol. (M)	0.396	Inst. holdings	61%
Tang. Bk. Value/Share	3.41		
Beta	1.18		

Value of $10,000 invested 5 years ago: $ 15,927

Fiscal Year Ending Jun. 30

	1999	1998	1997	1996	1995	1994
Revenues (Million $)						
1Q	34.73	64.43	61.78	115.8	115.1	62.52
2Q	43.17	66.55	62.75	116.3	119.1	82.60
3Q	38.55	66.63	58.56	100.1	121.9	104.7
4Q	40.54	71.58	71.07	128.5	111.8	119.2
Yr.	157.0	269.2	254.2	460.6	467.9	369.0
Earnings Per Share ($)						
1Q	**-0.72**	0.14	0.06	0.31	0.32	0.27
2Q	**-0.30**	**0.11**	**-0.18**	0.23	0.37	0.28
3Q	**-0.51**	**0.19**	1.86	0.08	0.37	0.30
4Q	**-0.25**	Nil	0.16	0.10	-1.60	0.35
Yr.	**-1.79**	**0.44**	**0.16**	0.72	-0.51	1.20

Next earnings report expected: late October

Dividend Data

No cash dividends have been paid. A poison pill stock purchase rights plan was adopted in 1989.

Adaptive Broadband Corporation

Business Summary - 02-AUG-99

The strategy of Adaptive Broadband (formerly California Microwave) is to build a strong commercial business in high growth international broadband access markets, and also to continue to reinforce its strong position in its core markets, which include satellite modems, data telemetry and video broadcast radios. The company has stated that it plans to remain in only those markets whose expected growth rates are at least 20% per year.

ADAP is a leading U.S. supplier of satellite earth station and microwave radio infrastructure products, installed in more than 110 countries. In FY 98 (Jun.), the company developed its current strategy and reorganized its operations, selling its Satellite Transmission Systems, Microwave Networks and Services Divisions. ADAP also outsourced some of its manufacturing work, combined its two microwave radio divisions, Microwave Radio Communications and Microwave Data Systems, combined its two government businesses, and decided to sell these government operations. The government division was sold to Northrop Grumman Corp. for $93 million in cash, with proceeds from the sale going to pay for recent acquisitions. Operations as of the first quarter of FY 99 included two divisions, Satellite Communications, and Terrestrial Wireless.

In February 1998, ADAP sold its Satellite Transmission Systems (STS) division to L-3 Communications Corp., for $27 million in cash. The sale was part of a plan to focus resources on maintaining and expanding the company's leading market positions in satellite, terrestrial data radio and other wireless product businesses. In May 1998, ADAP sold its Services division to Telscape International, Inc., for $8.2 million in cash.

In August 1998, the company acquired Adaptive Broadband Ltd., a company that is developing technology that will enable portable, low-cost wireless connections at speeds matching wired network access, for $11 million in cash. In November 1998, ADAP purchased Crown Satellite, a supplier of products and software for the network delivery of internet protocol data and multimedia services, for $7.5 million. The company believes these key acquisitions leverage its background in terrestrial and satellite communications to offer multiple solutions for data transport and internet access needs.

In January 1999, ADAP stated that its broadband strategy is the key to improving its performance. In order to accelerate revenue growth, the company stated that it is investing more in sales and marketing, targeted at domestic telecommunications markets, introducing new product lines obtained through recent acquisitions. It is also focusing on research and development on its selected high-growth, broadband access infrastructure markets. Further, it is implementing the next phase of its strategy by fully consolidating operations.

Per Share Data ($) (Year Ended Jun. 30)	1999	1998	1997	1996	1995	1994	1993	1992	1991	1990
Tangible Bk. Val.	NA	3.69	5.40	7.49	6.47	6.34	7.26	4.57	6.79	5.84
Cash Flow	NA	1.08	0.74	1.69	0.41	1.96	1.65	0.97	1.32	1.26
Earnings	-1.79	0.44	0.16	0.72	-0.51	1.20	0.98	0.56	0.93	0.80
Dividends	Nil	Nil	Nil	Nil	Nil	Nil	Nil	Nil	Nil	Nil
Payout Ratio	Nil	Nil	Nil	Nil	Nil	Nil	Nil	Nil	Nil	Nil
Prices - High	$40\frac{1}{4}$	$24\frac{1}{4}$	$21\frac{3}{4}$	$20\frac{3}{4}$	$39\frac{3}{4}$	$38\frac{1}{4}$	$31\frac{1}{4}$	$19\frac{1}{2}$	25	10
- Low	$8\frac{3}{8}$	$6\frac{3}{4}$	$11\frac{3}{4}$	$11\frac{7}{8}$	$16\frac{1}{4}$	$16\frac{1}{2}$	$12\frac{3}{4}$	$8\frac{3}{4}$	$6\frac{3}{8}$	$5\frac{5}{8}$
P/E Ratio - High	NM	55	NM	29	NM	32	32	35	27	13
- Low	NM	15	NM	16	NM	14	13	16	7	7
Income Statement Analysis (Million $)										
Revs.	NA	269	254	461	468	369	267	199	177	146
Oper. Inc.	NA	20.1	16.5	38.0	31.9	35.8	24.7	13.9	17.1	16.1
Depr.	NA	10.7	9.5	15.7	14.2	9.6	6.7	3.8	3.4	4.0
Int. Exp.	NA	4.5	5.9	4.3	4.8	2.8	2.3	0.9	1.1	1.8
Pretax Inc.	NA	7.5	3.8	18.2	-11.3	23.9	15.9	8.0	12.7	10.5
Eff. Tax Rate	NA	2.45%	33%	36%	NM	37%	37%	36%	37%	37%
Net Inc.	NA	7.3	2.6	11.6	-7.9	15.1	10.0	5.1	8.0	6.6
Balance Sheet & Other Fin. Data (Million $)										
Cash	NA	26.6	5.0	6.1	2.6	13.7	5.4	4.7	4.2	1.7
Curr. Assets	NA	128	184	230	223	193	108	88.3	74.7	67.4
Total Assets	NA	202	266	338	327	294	170	147	98.0	90.0
Curr. Liab.	NA	54.9	72.1	89.2	97.2	81.3	45.1	31.6	28.8	29.0
LT Debt	NA	Nil	72.3	78.8	67.8	70.1	5.3	40.3	2.2	5.2
Common Eqty.	NA	84.6	118	170	154	141	119	75.3	67.5	55.7
Total Cap.	NA	84.6	190	249	222	211	124	116	70.0	61.0
Cap. Exp.	NA	10.4	7.1	27.7	26.8	16.4	10.8	9.6	3.6	3.9
Cash Flow	NA	18.0	12.0	27.3	6.3	24.7	16.7	8.9	11.4	10.6
Curr. Ratio	NA	2.3	2.5	2.6	2.3	2.4	2.4	2.8	2.6	2.3
% LT Debt of Cap.	NA	Nil	38.1	31.6	30.5	33.2	4.2	34.9	3.2	8.6
% Net Inc.of Revs.	NA	2.7	1.0	2.5	NM	4.1	3.7	2.6	4.5	4.6
% Ret. on Assets	NA	3.1	0.9	3.5	NM	6.4	5.5	4.1	8.3	7.5
% Ret. on Equity	NA	7.2	1.8	7.3	NM	11.4	9.2	7.0	12.7	12.7

Data as orig reptd.; bef. results of disc opers/spec. items. Per share data adj. for stk. divs. Bold denotes diluted EPS (FASB 128)-prior periods restated. E-Estimated. NA-Not Available. NM-Not Meaningful. NR-Not Ranked.

Office—1143 Borregas Avenue, Sunnyvale, CA 94089. **Tel**—(408) 732-4000. **Website**—http://www.adaptivebroadband.com **Chrmn, Pres & CEO**—F. D. Lawrence. **COO**—L F. Blachowicz. **EVP & CFO**—D. S. Birks. **VP & Investor Contact**—Stephanie M. Day. **Dirs**—L. G. Denend, A. M. Gray, A. H. Hausman, G. A. Joulwan, F. D. Lawrence, W. B Marx, T. W. Ward, K. J. Wees, F. W. Whitridge, Jr. **Transfer Agent & Registrar**—First National Bank of Boston. **Incorporated**—in California in 1968; reincorporated in Delaware in 1987. **Empl**— 1,528. **S&P Analyst:** N.J.D.

STANDARD
&POOR'S
STOCK REPORTS

Advanced Tissue Sciences

NASDAQ Symbol **ATIS**

In S&P SmallCap 600

09-OCT-99

Industry:
Biotechnology

Summary: This company is engaged in the development and manufacture of human-based tissue products for therapeutic applications.

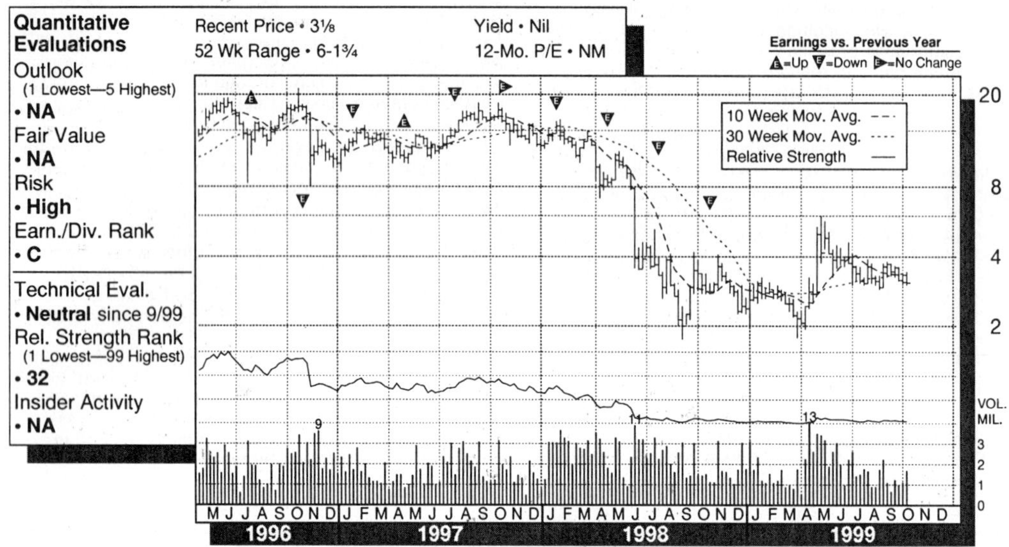

Business Profile - 01-SEP-99

In May 1999, the company and INAMED Corp. formed an alliance to develop and market human-based, tissue engineered products for aesthetic and reconstructive applications. Also in May, ATIS was issued a U.S. patent covering three-dimensional cartilage compositions and methods of growing living cartilage in vitro. Smith & Nephew plc, ATIS's partner in its Dermagraft and cartilage joint ventures, increased its equity position in ATIS to 8% in June 1999 by converting a $10 million loan it provided to ATIS into 2.8 million shares of ATIS common stock. In July 1999, ATIS filed a registration statement for an offering of five million shares of its common stock, which the company intends to offer directly.

Operational Review - 01-SEP-99

Total revenues for the six months ended June 30, 1999, advanced 126%, year to year, driven by higher sales of both TransCyte and Dermagraft, as well as $15.3 million in joint venture-related contracts and fees, versus $4.7 million. Total costs and expenses declined 8.5%, reflecting a 25% decrease in SG&A costs, primarily related to the transfer of sales and marketing activities to the Dermagraft joint venture, and lower cost of goods sold. After $10,455,000 of equity in losses of joint ventures, versus $8,889,000, and lower interest expense, the net loss narrowed to $10.2 million ($0.25 a share, after initial preferred dividends), from $22.9 million ($0.59).

Stock Performance - 08-OCT-99

In the past 30 trading days, ATIS's shares have declined 15%, compared to a 0.91% fall in the S&P 500. Average trading volume for the past five days was 332,540 shares, compared with the 40-day moving average of 270,603 shares.

Key Stock Statistics

Dividend Rate/Share	Nil	Shareholders	1,441
Shs. outstg. (M)	52.4	Market cap. (B)	$0.161
Avg. daily vol. (M)	0.246	Inst. holdings	17%
Tang. Bk. Value/Share	NM		
Beta	1.17		

Value of $10,000 invested 5 years ago: $ 3,730

Fiscal Year Ending Dec. 31

	1999	1998	1997	1996	1995	1994
Revenues (Million $)						
1Q	10.87	5.31	2.65	1.23	1.11	0.66
2Q	11.12	4.43	3.62	11.86	1.10	0.61
3Q	—	4.46	3.27	2.10	1.24	0.98
4Q	—	—	3.61	1.77	1.30	0.97
Yr.	—	20.48	13.15	16.96	4.75	3.22
Earnings Per Share ($)						
1Q	**-0.14**	**-0.28**	-0.20	-0.21	-0.18	-0.19
2Q	**-0.11**	**-0.30**	-0.22	0.05	-0.19	-0.19
3Q	—	**-0.30**	-0.24	-0.24	-0.16	-0.20
4Q	—	—	-0.30	-0.21	-0.19	-0.17
Yr.	—	**-1.11**	**-0.96**	**-0.61**	**-0.72**	**-0.75**

Next earnings report expected: mid November

Dividend Data

No cash dividends have been paid.

Advanced Tissue Sciences, Inc.

Business Summary - 01-SEP-99

Advanced Tissue Sciences, Inc.'s strategy is to apply its proprietary tissue-engineering technology to the development, manufacturing, and marketing of human-based tissue products for tissue repair and transplantation. This technology utilizes the scientific disciplines of cell biology, bioengineering, biochemistry, and polymer science to cultivate living human cells in vivo or ex vivo through a methodology permitting cells to develop and assemble into functioning three-dimensional tissue. ATIS is focusing its commercialization efforts on cost-effective products for skin, cartilage, and cardiovascular medical applications.

The company's two commercial products, TransCyte and Dermagraft, are therapeutic skin substitutes, designed as temporary or permanent replacements for human dermis (the inner skin layer) that has been injured or destroyed. TransCyte, a temporary skin covering for full-thickness and partial-thickness burns, was approved by the FDA in March 1997 for third-degree burns, and in October 1997 for second-degree burns. In March 1999, ATIS announced results of a study showing TransCyte reduced the required hospital stay and related costs for some patients treated with TransCyte, relative to standard care. This product is marketed worldwide through the company's Dermagraft joint venture, a 50-50 partnership between ATIS and Smith & Nephew plc.

Dermagraft is a living human dermal replacement for diabetic foot ulcers. In January 1998, an FDA advisory panel recommended the FDA grant pre-market approval (PMA) to Dermagraft. In June 1998, the FDA stated the PMA application was not approvable without supportive data from additional clinical trials. ATIS is conducting trials to potentially obtain supportive information. In August 1997, the company received approval to market Dermagraft in Canada. In October 1997, Dermagraft was launched in the U.K. through the Dermagraft joint venture. In March 1999, ATIS initiated a pilot clinical trial on Dermagraft for treating venous ulcers.

The Dermagraft joint venture was initiated in 1996 to develop, manufacture, and commercialize wound treatment therapies. Dermagraft was the first product marketed through this venture. In January 1998, the partnership was expanded to include venous ulcers, pressure sores, burns, and other skin tissue wounds. In August 1998, the agreement was amended to include the selling and marketing of TransCyte, with U.S. sales commencing in October 1998. As of 1999, year-end, ATIS was eligible to receive up to $136 million in payments from Smith & Nephew, contingent upon certain milestones being achieved.

In May 1999, ATIS and INAMED Corp. entered into a strategic partnership, whereby INAMED licensed rights to further develop, manufacture, and sell tissue-engineered products for use in cosmetic surgery, cartilage for plastic and reconstructive surgery, and extracellular matrix for use in breast reconstruction.

Per Share Data ($) (Year Ended Dec. 31)	1998	1997	1996	1995	1994	1993	1992	1991	1990	1989
Tangible Bk. Val.	NM	0.33	1.26	0.73	0.90	0.89	1.57	NA	NA	NA
Cash Flow	-0.99	-0.90	-0.56	-0.67	-0.72	NA	NA	NA	NA	NA
Earnings	-1.11	-0.96	-0.61	-0.72	-0.75	-0.67	-1.40	NA	NA	NA
Dividends	Nil	Nil	Nil	Nil	Nil	Nil	Nil	NA	NA	NA
Payout Ratio	Nil	Nil	Nil	Nil	Nil	Nil	Nil	NA	NA	NA
Prices - High	$15\frac{5}{8}$	$18\frac{1}{2}$	$21\frac{1}{4}$	15	$9\frac{1}{2}$	14	$19\frac{1}{4}$	NA	NA	NA
- Low	$1\frac{3}{4}$	$9\frac{7}{8}$	8	$5\frac{1}{2}$	$4\frac{1}{4}$	$6\frac{1}{2}$	$7\frac{3}{8}$	NA	NA	NA
P/E Ratio - High	NM	NM	NM	NM	NM	NM	NM	NA	NA	NA
- Low	NM	NM	NM	NM	NM	NM	NM	NA	NA	NA
Income Statement Analysis (Million $)										
Revs.	21.8	13.2	14.6	3.6	2.0	4.9	0.8	NA	NA	NA
Oper. Inc.	-18.6	-21.1	-22.9	-22.9	-24.0	-18.5	-11.9	NA	NA	NA
Depr.	4.8	2.1	1.8	1.4	1.1	0.9	0.6	NA	NA	NA
Int. Exp.	2.3	0.9	0.0	0.0	0.0	NM	0.2	NA	NA	NA
Pretax Inc.	-43.3	-36.1	-22.4	-23.1	-22.8	-17.7	-32.0	NA	NA	NA
Eff. Tax Rate	NM	NM	NM	Nil	Nil	Nil	Nil	NA	NA	NA
Net Inc.	-43.3	-36.1	-22.4	-23.1	-22.8	-17.7	-32.0	NA	NA	NA
Balance Sheet & Other Fin. Data (Million $)										
Cash	16.6	15.1	40.2	18.9	22.0	21.7	NA	NA	NA	NA
Curr. Assets	28.8	23.1	44.0	21.0	24.1	23.0	NA	NA	NA	NA
Total Assets	54.0	50.5	56.5	31.1	33.4	30.4	NA	NA	NA	NA
Curr. Liab.	8.4	9.9	8.0	5.2	5.0	5.5	NA	NA	NA	NA
LT Debt	27.3	26.2	0.1	0.0	0.0	0.1	NA	NA	NA	NA
Common Eqty.	12.0	14.0	43.4	25.9	28.4	24.9	NA	NA	NA	NA
Total Cap.	45.0	40.4	43.4	25.9	28.4	24.9	NA	NA	NA	NA
Cap. Exp.	3.7	15.6	3.1	1.5	3.1	4.3	0.8	NA	NA	NA
Cash Flow	-39.1	-34.0	-20.6	-21.7	-21.7	16.8	-31.4	NA	NA	NA
Curr. Ratio	3.4	2.3	5.5	4.0	4.8	4.2	NA	NA	NA	NA
% LT Debt of Cap.	60.5	64.8	Nil	0.1	0.1	0.2	NA	NA	NA	NA
% Net Inc.of Revs.	NM	NM	NM	NM	NM	NA	NM	NA	NA	NA
% Ret. on Assets	NM	NM	NM	NM	NM	NM	NA	NA	NA	NA
% Ret. on Equity	NM	NM	NM	NM	NM	NM	NA	NA	NA	NA

Data as orig. reptd.; bef. results of disc. opers. and/or spec. items. Per share data adj. for stk. divs. as of ex-div. date. Revs. in Income Statement tbl. do not incl. int. inc. E-Estimated. NA-Not Available. NM-Not Meaningful. NR-Not Ranked.

Office—10933 N. Torrey Pines Rd., La Jolla, CA 92037. **Tel**—(858) 713-7300. **Website**—http://www.advancedtissue.com **Chrmn & CEO**—A. J. Benvenuto. **Pres & COO**—G. K. Naughton. **VP-Fin & CFO**—M. V. Swanson. **Dirs**—A. J. Benvenuto, J. E. Groopman, J. L. Heckel, G. K. Naughton, R. L. Nelson, D. Ogden, D. S. Tappan, G. R. Wilensky. **Transfer Agent**—ChaseMellon Shareholder Services, Ridgefield Park, NJ. **Incorporated**—in Delaware in 1987. **Empl**— 207. **S&P Analyst:** Frank DiLorenzo

STANDARD
&POOR'S
STOCK REPORTS

ADVO, Inc.

NYSE Symbol **AD**

In S&P SmallCap 600

09-OCT-99

Industry: Services (Advertising & Marketing)

Summary: ADVO is the largest direct-mail marketing company in the U.S. It specializes in shared and solo direct mail services.

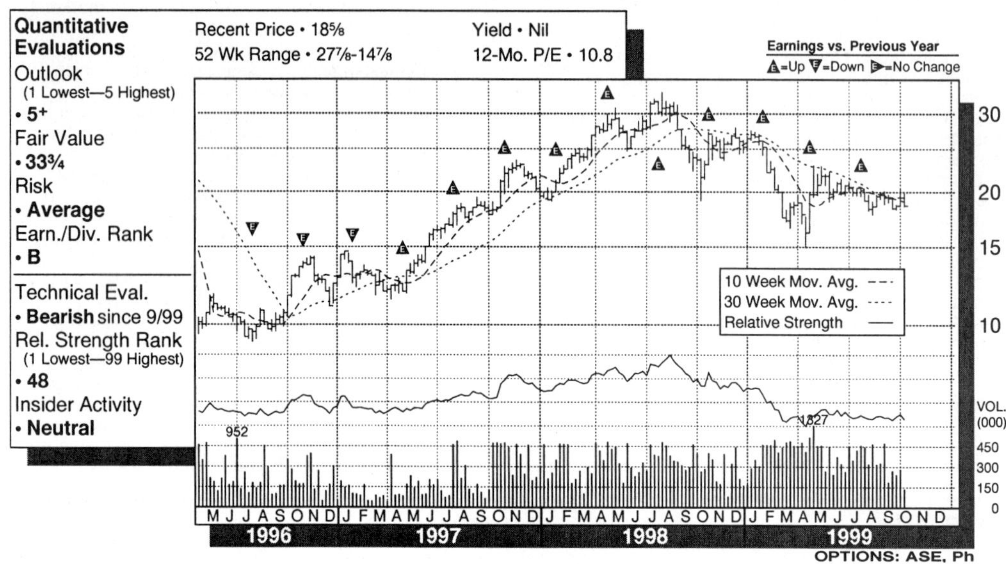

Business Profile - 26-JUL-99

Essentially flat revenues in the first three quarters of FY 99 (Sep.) reflected the company's trend away from heavier, less profitable products. In the third quarter, packages distributed were down 0.1%, to 768.1 million. Pieces per package were also down 4.4%, but revenue per thousand pieces rose 0.9%. Despite the short term revenue impact realized in the third quarter, management expects to deliver EPS growth in line with current expectations for FY 99 and FY 00. At the time of the announcement, the approximate EPS consensus estimate for FY 99 and FY 00 was $1.81 and $2.09, respectively. In the third quarter of FY 99 AD repurchased about 550,000 of its shares.

Operational Review - 26-JUL-99

Revenues in the nine months ended June 26, 1999, were essentially unchanged, year to year. Despite higher selling, general and administrative expenses, profitability improved on wider gross margins; operating profit climbed 8.5%. Following higher net interest and other expense, after taxes at 38.5%, versus 39.0%, net income advanced 11%, to $28.7 million ($1.30 a share, on 4.5% fewer shares), from $26.0 million ($1.12).

Stock Performance - 08-OCT-99

In the past 30 trading days, AD's shares have declined 6%, compared to a 0.91% fall in the S&P 500. Average trading volume for the past five days was 26,560 shares, compared with the 40-day moving average of 62,841 shares.

Key Stock Statistics

Dividend Rate/Share	Nil	Shareholders	831
Shs. outstg. (M)	21.2	Market cap. (B)	$0.395
Avg. daily vol. (M)	0.046	Inst. holdings	87%
Tang. Bk. Value/Share	NM		
Beta	0.93		

Value of $10,000 invested 5 years ago: $ 17,923

Fiscal Year Ending Sep. 30

	1999	1998	1997	1996	1995	1994
Revenues (Million $)						
1Q	268.6	262.1	255.1	256.5	248.1	246.8
2Q	253.5	253.2	242.5	232.0	239.6	229.7
3Q	262.1	269.0	258.2	245.7	256.7	256.1
4Q	—	262.1	260.6	251.9	267.5	242.9
Yr.	—	1,047	1,016	986.2	1,012	975.5
Earnings Per Share ($)						
1Q	**0.45**	**0.36**	**0.25**	0.29	0.44	0.29
2Q	**0.28**	**0.24**	0.11	-0.32	0.12	0.10
3Q	**0.58**	**0.52**	0.38	0.18	0.39	0.38
4Q	—	**0.42**	0.35	0.29	0.33	0.28
Yr.	—	**1.55**	**1.09**	0.47	1.33	1.05

Next earnings report expected: late October

Dividend Data

A special cash dividend of $10 a share was paid in March 1996.

ADVO, Inc.

Business Summary - 26-JUL-99

If you have a mailing address, chances are you have received one of ADVO's shared mail or solo mail packages. Established in 1929, this direct mail marketer is the U.S. Post Office's largest customer. ADVO, Inc. (AD) delivers more than 27 billion pieces of advertising annually to over 60 million households.

ADVO's direct mail marketing products and services primarily include shared mail and solo mail. The shared mail program, called Marriage Mail, involves the combination of several advertisers in a single mail package. Packages are assembled for distribution by ZIP code and, in most instances, each household within the ZIP code will receive a mail package. Customers can designate all or only a part of a ZIP code they wish to target, based on shared demographic characteristics and proximity to key retail shopping areas. Some larger businesses will provide ADVO with their own preprinted advertising materials, while smaller businesses may select one of several turnkey advertising products. ADVO believes that its shared mail programs are the largest of their kind and provide weekly distribution to approximately 120 markets.

The company's shared mail programs offer significant cost reduction when compared to mailing on an individual basis. However, some customers may decide to maintain an exclusive image and complete control over the timing and target of their mailings and may prefer to use ADVO's solo mail. The service includes addressing and processing brochures and circulars for individual distribution. Each customer bears the full cost of postage and handling for each mailing and may elect to use ADVO's mailing list or its own.

Customers' advertising circulars are processed by approximately 2,400 production employees who work at 19 mail processing facilities located throughout the U.S.

ADVO maintains a computerized mailing list with over 116 million delivery points. Management believes that this is the largest residential/household mailing list in the country and was used by the U.S. Census Bureau as a base for developing the mailing list for its 1980 and 1990 census questionnaire mailings. The list is updated bimonthly and is thought to be nearly 100% accurate. Portions of the list are rented to organizations interested in distributing their own mailings.

Additionally, ADVO offers coordination and production of custom promotional magazines and circulars. In February 1998, the company acquired The Mailhouse, Inc., a franchise-based cooperative that creates and distributes targeted coupons in an envelope format for local merchants. At the end of FY 98 (Sep.), there were approximately 300 franchise units in 26 states.

Per Share Data ($) (Year Ended Sep. 30)	1998	1997	1996	1995	1994	1993	1992	1991	1990	1989
Tangible Bk. Val.	NM	NM	NM	6.26	4.60	4.72	5.13	4.64	3.56	2.59
Cash Flow	2.61	1.82	1.10	1.89	1.51	0.57	1.21	1.18	1.05	0.52
Earnings	1.55	1.09	0.47	1.33	1.05	0.21	0.89	0.85	0.76	0.27
Dividends	Nil	Nil	10.03	0.13	0.10	0.06	Nil	Nil	Nil	Nil
Payout Ratio	Nil	Nil	NM	9%	9%	29%	Nil	Nil	Nil	Nil
Prices - High	$33\frac{5}{8}$	$23\frac{5}{8}$	$26\frac{1}{8}$	$27\frac{1}{2}$	20	$24\frac{3}{4}$	$22\frac{1}{4}$	$18\frac{7}{8}$	10	$8\frac{7}{8}$
- Low	19	$11\frac{3}{8}$	$9\frac{1}{8}$	$16\frac{1}{2}$	15	$14\frac{1}{4}$	$12\frac{3}{8}$	9	$6\frac{3}{4}$	$3\frac{3}{4}$
P/E Ratio - High	22	22	56	21	19	118	25	22	13	33
- Low	12	10	19	12	14	68	14	11	9	14
Income Statement Analysis (Million $)										
Revs.	1,047	1,016	986	1,012	975	911	788	697	655	618
Oper. Inc.	96.7	76.8	52.0	59.2	51.6	41.8	36.2	33.0	28.7	12.7
Depr.	24.6	18.2	15.2	13.0	11.0	9.2	7.6	7.3	6.2	5.9
Int. Exp.	14.0	14.8	9.7	NA	NA	0.2	Nil	Nil	Nil	Nil
Pretax Inc.	58.4	43.7	18.5	50.5	41.3	8.1	30.1	28.3	24.8	7.7
Eff. Tax Rate	39%	39%	40%	39%	39%	34%	32%	32%	34%	31%
Net Inc.	35.6	26.8	11.3	30.9	25.2	5.4	20.5	19.3	16.4	5.3
Balance Sheet & Other Fin. Data (Million $)										
Cash	8.7	26.0	13.3	54.5	71.1	71.4	65.7	52.6	41.6	22.2
Curr. Assets	111	116	104	156	151	151	129	104	88.0	62.0
Total Assets	219	209	209	234	226	227	190	156	133	108
Curr. Liab.	111	116	102	97.0	104	91.3	72.7	56.6	55.7	49.2
LT Debt	168	141	161	Nil	Nil	Nil	Nil	Nil	Nil	Nil
Common Eqty.	-74.9	-59.9	-85.2	130	108	118	95.7	78.1	56.3	40.5
Total Cap.	105	90.3	82.5	136	112	118	116	98.0	76.0	59.0
Cap. Exp.	29.3	28.6	17.8	20.3	13.3	14.2	11.2	7.8	6.8	5.3
Cash Flow	60.2	45.0	26.5	43.9	36.1	14.6	28.1	26.6	22.5	11.2
Curr. Ratio	1.0	1.0	1.0	1.6	1.4	1.7	1.8	1.8	1.6	1.3
% LT Debt of Cap.	159.9	155.7	195.0	Nil	Nil	Nil	Nil	Nil	Nil	Nil
% Net Inc.of Revs.	3.4	2.6	1.1	3.0	2.6	0.6	2.6	2.8	2.5	0.9
% Ret. on Assets	16.7	13.6	5.4	13.4	11.5	2.2	11.7	13.1	13.5	5.1
% Ret. on Equity	NM	NM	0.5	25.9	23.0	4.4	23.3	28.3	33.6	12.7

Data as orig. reptd.; bef. results of disc. opers. and/or spec. items. Per share data adj. for stk. divs. as of ex-div. date. Divs. for FY 96 incl. $10 spec. div. Bold denotes diluted EPS (FASB 128). E-Estimated. NA-Not Available. NM-Not Meaningful. NR-Not Ranked.

Office—One Univac Lane, Windsor, CT 06095. **Tel**—(860) 285-6100. **Website**—http://www.advo.com **Chrmn & CEO**—G. M. Mulloy. **SVP, CFO & Investor Contact**—Donald McCombs (860-285-6391). **Dirs**—B. Crawford, D. F. Dyer, J. W. Fritz, G. M. Mulloy, H. H. Newman, J. R. Rockwell, J. L. Vogelstein. **Transfer Agent & Registrar**—ChaseMellon Shareholder Services, East Hartford, CT. **Incorporated**—in Delaware in 1971. **Empl**—4,600. **S&P Analyst:** Jordan Horoschak

Agribrands International

STANDARD & POOR'S
STOCK REPORTS

NYSE Symbol **AGX**
In S&P SmallCap 600

09-OCT-99 **Industry:** Foods

Summary: AGX, spun off by Ralston Purina Co. in April 1998, is an international producer and marketer of formula animal feeds and other agricultural products.

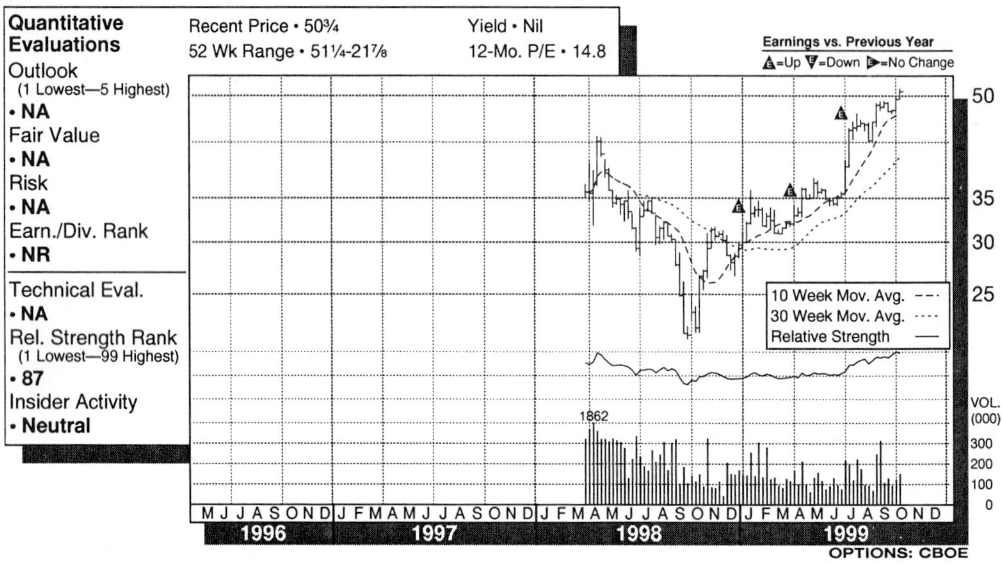

Business Profile - 01-JUN-99

Operating profit in the first half of FY 99 (Aug.) increased 30%, year to year, reflecting larger profits in Venezuela, as well as broad-based gains in Europe. In the same period, cash flow from operations totaled $47.2 million, compared to a negative cash flow of $16.6 million in the first six months of FY 98. The improvement reflected increased earnings and changes in levels of inventory and receivables. In recent periods, price declines for animal feed have been less drastic than the sharp drop in ingredient costs. AGX believes that once commodity prices stabilize, industry margins should return to normal. In September 1998, directors authorized the repurchase of up to 2,000,000 shares of the company's common stock.

Operational Review - 01-JUN-99

Net sales in the six months ended February 28, 1999, declined 9.1%, year to year, primarily reflecting lower animal feed prices and lower volume in Europe. Results benefited from improved margins in the Americas and Europe due to lower commodity prices, partly offset by flat profits in Asia from less favorable currency translations; pretax income advanced 149%. After taxes at 45.8%, versus 57.1%, net income more than tripled to $18.9 million ($1.76 a share), from $6.0 million ($0.56).

Stock Performance - 08-OCT-99

In the past 30 trading days, AGX's shares have increased 5%, compared to a 0.91% fall in the S&P 500. Average trading volume for the past five days was 29,620 shares, compared with the 40-day moving average of 34,121 shares.

Key Stock Statistics

Dividend Rate/Share	Nil	Shareholders	18,148
Shs. outstg. (M)	10.5	Market cap. (B)	$0.532
Avg. daily vol. (M)	0.024	Inst. holdings	66%
Tang. Bk. Value/Share	35.00		
Beta	NA		

Value of $10,000 invested 5 years ago: NA

Fiscal Year Ending Aug. 31

	1999	1998	1997	1996	1995	1994
Revenues (Million $)						
1Q	332.4	374.8	—	—	—	—
2Q	310.7	333.0	—	—	—	—
3Q	311.8	351.1	—	—	—	—
4Q	—	351.2	—	—	—	—
Yr.	—	1,410	1,528	—	—	—
Earnings Per Share ($)						
1Q	**1.03**	**0.37**	—	—	—	—
2Q	**0.72**	**0.19**	—	—	—	—
3Q	**1.27**	**0.32**	—	—	—	—
4Q	—	**0.41**	—	—	—	—
Yr.	—	**1.29**	0.77	—	—	—

Next earnings report expected: late October

Dividend Data

No dividends have been paid, and the company does not intend to pay any in the foreseeable future.

Agribrands International, Inc.

Business Summary - 01-JUN-99

Operating its business almost exclusively outside of the U.S., Agribrands International, Inc. (AGX) is a leading international producer and marketer of formula animal feeds and other agricultural products. With a worldwide network of approximately 3,200 independent dealers, as well as independent and direct sales forces, AGX and its subsidiaries market a broad line of animal feeds and nutrition products, including feeds for hogs, dairy cows, cattle, poultry (broilers and layers), rabbits, horses, shrimp and fish. The company and its subsidiaries and joint venture partners operate 74 manufacturing plants in 16 countries on four continents. Formerly a subsidiary of Ralston Purina Co. (RAL), AGX was spun off to RAL shareholders on April 1, 1998, with one AGX common share distributed for every 10 RAL common shares held.

The company's products are generally marketed under the widely recognized brand names Purina and Chow and the Checkerboard logo, and under product names such as Omolene and Hi-Octane.

AGX's objective is to enhance growth and profitability by delivering premium quality products and services to its dealers and customers, expanding its strong market positions into new growing agricultural markets, maintaining effective cost control programs, and developing and implementing methods for more efficient manufacturing and distribution operations, while at the same time, maintaining aggressive pricing and promotion of its products.

The company intends to increase sales through further penetration of existing markets and expansion into broader geographic markets. It has established fast-growing operations in the People's Republic of China, Southeast Asia and Eastern Europe, and believes that, despite current economic crises in Asia Pacific markets, each of these regions presents significant opportunities for expansion and growth on a profitable basis. AGX will also continue to pursue acquisitions to expand or complement market areas and product lines, and to strategically invest in the development of new products.

AGX plans to embark on cost-saving and productivity programs as part of its strategy to maximize operating efficiencies. Since 1995, the Agribrands business has restructured or divested underperforming assets, and is actively reviewing measures to reduce excess capacity and exit unprofitable markets.

In FY 98 (Aug.), the Americas (excluding the U.S.) contributed 44% of sales and 46% of operating profit, Europe 28% and 16%, and Asia Pacific 28% and 38%.

In September 1998, directors approved the repurchase of up to 2 million AGX common shares.

Per Share Data ($) (Year Ended Aug. 31)	1998	1997	1996	1995	1994	1993	1992	1991	1990	1989
Tangible Bk. Val.	51.18	NA	NA	NA	NA	NA	NA	NA	NA	NA
Cash Flow	3.28	NA	NA	NA	NA	NA	NA	NA	NA	NA
Earnings	1.29	0.77	NA	NA	NA	NA	NA	NA	NA	NA
Dividends	Nil	NA	NA	NA	NA	NA	NA	NA	NA	NA
Payout Ratio	Nil	NA	NA	NA	NA	NA	NA	NA	NA	NA
Prices - High	43⅜	NA	NA	NA	NA	NA	NA	NA	NA	NA
- Low	21⅜	NA	NA	NA	NA	NA	NA	NA	NA	NA
P/E Ratio - High	34	NA	NA	NA	NA	NA	NA	NA	NA	NA
- Low	17	NA	NA	NA	NA	NA	NA	NA	NA	NA
Income Statement Analysis (Million $)										
Revs.	1,410	1,528	NA	NA	NA	NA	NA	NA	NA	NA
Oper. Inc.	80.5	NA	NA	NA	NA	NA	NA	NA	NA	NA
Depr.	21.2	NA	NA	NA	NA	NA	NA	NA	NA	NA
Int. Exp.	12.0	9.5	NA	NA	NA	NA	NA	NA	NA	NA
Pretax Inc.	34.2	29.3	NA	NA	NA	NA	NA	NA	NA	NA
Eff. Tax Rate	60%	73%	73%	NA	NA	NA	NA	NA	NA	NA
Net Inc.	13.8	7.9	NA	NA	NA	NA	NA	NA	NA	NA
Balance Sheet & Other Fin. Data (Million $)										
Cash	138	100	NA	NA	NA	NA	NA	NA	NA	NA
Curr. Assets	351	333	NA	NA	NA	NA	NA	NA	NA	NA
Total Assets	578	531	NA	NA	NA	NA	NA	NA	NA	NA
Curr. Liab.	197	221	NA	NA	NA	NA	NA	NA	NA	NA
LT Debt	14.2	19.3	NA	NA	NA	NA	NA	NA	NA	NA
Common Eqty.	339	255	NA	NA	NA	NA	NA	NA	NA	NA
Total Cap.	359	285	NA	NA	NA	NA	NA	NA	NA	NA
Cap. Exp.	44.6	NA	NA	NA	NA	NA	NA	NA	NA	NA
Cash Flow	35.0	NA	NA	NA	NA	NA	NA	NA	NA	NA
Curr. Ratio	1.8	1.5	NA	NA	NA	NA	NA	NA	NA	NA
% LT Debt of Cap.	4.0	6.8	NA	NA	NA	NA	NA	NA	NA	NA
% Net Inc.of Revs.	1.0	0.5	0.5	NA	NA	NA	NA	NA	NA	NA
% Ret. on Assets	2.5	NA	NA	NA	NA	NA	NA	NA	NA	NA
% Ret. on Equity	4.6	NA	NA	NA	NA	NA	NA	NA	NA	NA

Data as orig. reptd.; bef. results of disc. opers. and/or spec. items. Data for 1997 pro forma; bal. sh. & bk. val. as of Nov. 30, 1997. Per share data adj. for stk. divs. as of ex-div. date. Bold denotes diluted EPS (FASB 128). E-Estimated. NA-Not Available. NM-Not Meaningful. NR-Not Ranked.

Office—9811 South Forty Drive, St. Louis, MO 63124. **Tel**—(314) 812-0500. **Chrmn, Pres & CEO**—W. P. Stiritz. **CFO**—D. R. Wenzel. **Treas**—R. W. Rickert Jr. **Secy**—M. J. Costello. **Dirs**—D. R. Banks, J. W. Brown, M. D. Ingram, H. D. McCarty, J. R. Micheletto, M. K. Sneider, W. P. Stiritz. **Transfer Agent**—Continental Stock Transfer & Trust Co., NYC. **Incorporated**—in Missouri in 1997. **Empl**— 5,781. **S&P Analyst:** S.A.H.

STANDARD
&POOR'S
STOCK REPORTS

Air Express International

Nasdaq Symbol **AEIC**

In S&P SmallCap 600

09-OCT-99 **Industry:** Air Freight

Summary: This company provides air and ocean freight forwarding and customs brokerage services. Foreign markets contribute a majority of revenues.

S&P Opinion: Hold (★★★)

Recent Price • 26 | Yield • 1.1%
52 Wk Range • 30-14⅛ | 12-Mo. P/E • 18.8

Quantitative Evaluations

Outlook
(1 Lowest—5 Highest)
• **4+**

Fair Value
• **29⅛**

Risk
• **Average**

Earn./Div. Rank
• **B+**

Technical Eval.
• **Bearish** since 8/99

Rel. Strength Rank
(1 Lowest—99 Highest)
• **84**

Insider Activity
• **NA**

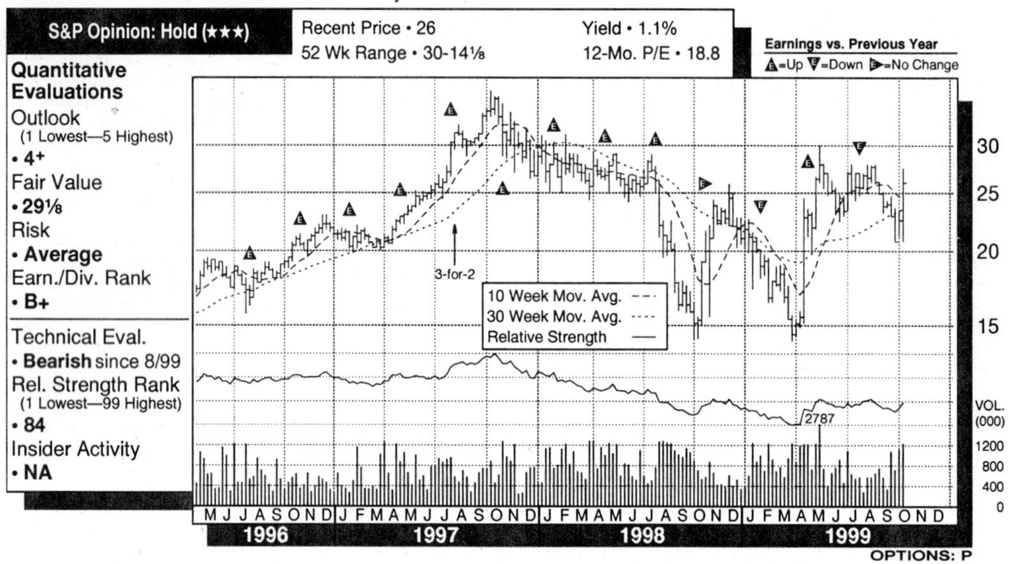

OPTIONS: P

Overview - 05-OCT-99

Net revenues could grow 2.6% in 1999, after 1998's gain of 0.5%. AEIC's fastest growing segment in 1999 will be its customs brokerage, reflecting expansion of services in the U.S., and the acquisition of Gulf Coast Drawback Services. Revenue growth will be aided by acquisitions of existing company agents, including Aero Expreso Internacional and Associated Customhouse. AEIC's warehousing and distribution business may be flat. Air freight forwarding volumes may be flat, as improvement in Asia is offset by continued weakness in the U.S. and Europe. While transportation costs will ease, margins could narrow, as cargo rates drop. Ocean forwarding will show good gains, reflecting a recovery in Asian markets, and acquisitions. Overall improvement will be restricted by higher terminal and administrative costs. Net income will be bolstered by securities gains, and comparisons will reflect the absence of a charge for contract concessions.

Valuation - 05-OCT-99

The shares of this forwarder have pulled back somewhat, after rallying sharply through mid-1999. The charge into AEIC reflected investor expectations that the worst is over in Asia. Although we concur with this view, we doubt that the turnaround will be as dramatic as share price gains would indicate. Also buoying the shares have been rumors that United Parcel Service is on the prowl for an international forwarding company. We think 1998 demonstrated that international air and ocean freight forwarding markets are mature and vulnerable to the business cycle. Consequently, AEIC no longer deserves the growth stock P/E multiple that it carried in the past. Compared to that of its peers, AEIC's P/E, price to EBITDA, and price to sales ratios indicate that the stock is generously priced. For the near term, we rate AEIC an average performer.

Key Stock Statistics

S&P EPS Est. 1999	1.50	Tang. Bk. Value/Share	6.33
P/E on S&P Est. 1999	17.3	Beta	1.23
S&P EPS Est. 2000	1.70	Shareholders	832
Dividend Rate/Share	0.28	Market cap. (B)	$0.872
Shs. outstg. (M)	33.5	Inst. holdings	67%
Avg. daily vol. (M)	0.218		

Value of $10,000 invested 5 years ago: $ 30,875

Fiscal Year Ending Dec. 31

	1999	1998	1997	1996	1995	1994
Revenues (Million $)						
1Q	354.7	372.4	351.2	294.8	280.0	204.8
2Q	373.3	378.5	386.6	320.7	299.4	238.0
3Q	—	373.0	395.4	340.9	314.3	258.1
4Q	—	389.4	412.6	379.1	328.6	296.4
Yr.	—	1,513	1,546	1,335	1,222	997.4
Earnings Per Share ($)						
1Q	**0.40**	**0.28**	**0.25**	**0.21**	0.19	0.13
2Q	**0.38**	**0.39**	**0.37**	**0.30**	0.28	0.24
3Q	**E0.40**	**0.38**	**0.38**	**0.31**	0.26	0.24
4Q	**E0.32**	**0.22**	**0.41**	**0.35**	0.32	0.25
Yr.	**E1.50**	**1.26**	**1.41**	**1.16**	**0.99**	**0.81**

Next earnings report expected: late October

Dividend Data (Dividends have been paid since 1991.)

Amount ($)	Date Decl.	Ex-Div. Date	Stock of Record	Payment Date
0.060	Oct. 21	Jan. 07	Jan. 08	Jan. 29 '99
0.060	Jan. 15	Mar. 30	Apr. 02	Apr. 23 '99
0.070	Jun. 17	Jul. 07	Jul. 09	Jul. 30 '99
0.070	Sep. 10	Oct. 06	Oct. 08	Oct. 29 '99

Air Express International Corporation

Business Summary - 05-OCT-99

Air Express International primarily provides services that facilitate the movement of freight across international markers. The company's core business, air and ocean freight forwarding, involves purchasing transportation services in bulk from air and ocean carriers at wholesale rates, and profiting from the spread by offering consolidation services at retail rates. Because freight forwarders face less competition from integrated air carriers in international markets, AEIC has focused on foreign markets (60% of 1998 total revenues).

The company is the oldest and largest U.S. air freight forwarder, based on gross revenues. Air freight forwarding generated 62% of net revenues in 1998. An air forwarder consolidates shipments bound for common destinations, and delivers them in bulk to air carriers for transportation to various distribution points. Company employees or agents distribute individual parcels to their final destinations. As a forwarder, AEIC neither owns nor operates aircraft, but is fully liable for lost or damaged shipments.

AEIC provides air freight services to 3,000 cities in more than 200 nations through a network of 705 offices. It owns and operates 44% of these facilities. In recent years, the company has sought greater control over its agents by making equity investments or full purchase. It believes tighter control, coupled with integration of operating systems, lets it deliver a higher and more consistent level of service. Accordingly, in 1998, AEIC bought out its Rochester, NY, agent, Associated Customhouse Brokers; its Argentine agent, Aero Expreso Internacional; and its Korean agent, Korea Air Freight Ltd.

Ocean forwarding generated 13% of net revenues in 1998. As an ocean forwarder, AEIC provides consolidation services similar to those of its air operation, buying bulk space on container ships. In 1998, it handled 148,000 container loads, up from 122,000 loads in 1997. In December 1998 AEIC entered an agreement with FastShip Inc., which is developing containerships capable of speeds twice those of conventional vessels; the company would guarantee FastShip 15,000 containers annually. Initial Trans-Atlantic service is expected to begin in 2003.

Customs brokerage services (23% of net revenues) form an integral part of AEIC's service. A customs broker prepares and assembles the required documents needed to move cargo through international gateways. AEIC also pays customs duties, arranges for transportation after clearance has been obtained and recovers excess duty payments (drawback). Customs brokerage has been the company's fastest growing segment in recent years, aided by acquisitions.

Logistics, which includes warehousing and distribution services, accounted for 2% of net revenues in 1998. AEIC owns or operates warehousing facilities in 10 nations.

Per Share Data ($) (Year Ended Dec. 31)	1998	1997	1996	1995	1994	1993	1992	1991	1990	1989
Tangible Bk. Val.	6.01	6.04	4.90	2.47	1.81	1.57	1.54	1.46	0.91	0.35
Cash Flow	1.76	1.86	1.60	1.41	1.15	0.90	0.99	0.75	0.66	0.50
Earnings	1.26	1.41	1.21	1.05	0.85	0.66	0.72	0.53	0.44	0.34
Dividends	0.22	0.19	0.19	0.09	0.12	0.08	0.05	0.02	Nil	Nil
Payout Ratio	17%	13%	15%	9%	14%	11%	8%	4%	Nil	Nil
Prices - High	31 3/8	37 1/8	23	17 5/8	13 3/8	13 1/8	12 1/4	6 3/8	3 3/4	3 7/8
- Low	14 1/4	19 7/8	13 3/8	12 3/8	8 1/8	8	5 7/8	2 7/8	2 1/8	2 3/4
P/E Ratio - High	25	26	19	17	16	20	17	12	8	11
- Low	11	14	11	12	10	12	8	5	5	8
Income Statement Analysis (Million $)										
Revs.	1,513	1,546	1,335	1,222	997	726	672	602	568	514
Oper. Inc.	79.5	86.8	71.4	59.3	45.9	37.7	39.0	30.2	27.6	21.2
Depr.	17.4	15.8	12.7	9.8	7.6	6.3	7.0	5.5	5.3	4.2
Int. Exp.	Nil	1.0	1.3	3.3	3.2	3.7	2.2	2.6	3.8	5.3
Pretax Inc.	69.5	79.1	62.1	47.6	36.8	28.0	29.9	23.0	19.2	14.9
Eff. Tax Rate	37%	38%	38%	39%	39%	38%	38%	40%	42%	43%
Net Inc.	43.8	49.5	38.5	29.0	22.6	17.3	18.6	13.8	11.1	8.5
Balance Sheet & Other Fin. Data (Million $)										
Cash	67.4	67.6	46.5	54.5	44.2	65.2	14.1	27.9	19.9	14.1
Curr. Assets	441	442	399	328	253	219	147	151	138	128
Total Assets	675	638	581	487	381	296	208	208	193	180
Curr. Liab.	312	307	299	251	194	139	136	118	112	107
LT Debt	42.6	31.0	16.6	82.8	84.0	78.5	7.1	24.9	28.4	32.3
Common Eqty.	311	292	259	148	99	78.1	65.4	65.3	52.4	40.5
Total Cap.	353	323	276	230	185	158	72.5	90.2	80.9	72.8
Cap. Exp.	36.0	18.7	13.8	20.4	12.1	4.9	15.2	6.8	6.4	3.0
Cash Flow	61.2	65.3	51.2	38.8	30.3	23.6	25.7	19.3	16.3	12.7
Curr. Ratio	1.4	1.4	1.3	1.3	1.3	1.6	1.1	1.3	1.2	1.2
% LT Debt of Cap.	12.0	9.6	6.0	36.0	45.4	49.8	9.8	27.6	35.2	44.4
% Net Inc.of Revs.	2.9	3.2	2.9	2.4	2.3	2.4	2.8	2.3	1.9	1.7
% Ret. on Assets	6.7	8.1	7.2	6.7	6.7	6.9	8.8	6.9	5.9	4.6
% Ret. on Equity	14.5	18.0	18.9	23.6	25.4	24.2	28.2	23.3	23.5	22.8

Data as orig reptd.; bef. results of disc opers/spec. items. Per share data adj. for stk. divs. Bold denotes diluted EPS (FASB 128)-prior periods restated. E-Estimated. NA-Not Available. NM-Not Meaningful. NR-Not Ranked.

Registrar & Transfer Agent—Chemical Mellon Shareholder Services, NYC. **Office**—120 Tokeneke Rd., Darien, CT 06820. **Tel**—(203) 655-7900. **Website**—http://www.aeilogistics.com **Chrmn**—H. J. Hartong Jr. **Pres & CEO**—G. Rohrmann. **EVP, CFO & Investor Contact**—Dennis M. Dolan (203-655-5713). **VP & Secy**—D. J. McCauley. **Dirs**—J. M. Fowler, H. J. Hartong Jr., D. J. Keller, A. L. Lewis IV, R. T. Niner, J. Radziwill, G. Rohrmann, N. E. Vargas. **Transfer Agent & Registrar**—ChaseMellon Shareholder Services, NYC. **Incorporated**—in Illinois in 1946; reincorporated in Delaware in 1982. **Empl**— 7,423. **S&P Analyst:** Stephen R. Klein

STANDARD
&POOR'S
STOCK REPORTS

Allen Telecom

NYSE Symbol **ALN**

In S&P SmallCap 600

09-OCT-99

Industry:
Communications
Equipment

Summary: This company (formerly Allen Group) primarily supplies equipment and services to the two-way wireless communications marketplace.

Quantitative Evaluations

Outlook
(1 Lowest—5 Highest)
• 3

Fair Value
• 10⅝

Risk
• High

Earn./Div. Rank
• B

Technical Eval.
• **Bullish** since 9/99

Rel. Strength Rank
(1 Lowest—99 Highest)
• 87

Insider Activity
• NA

Recent Price • 10⅛
52 Wk Range • 11⅞-4½
Yield • Nil
12-Mo. P/E • NM

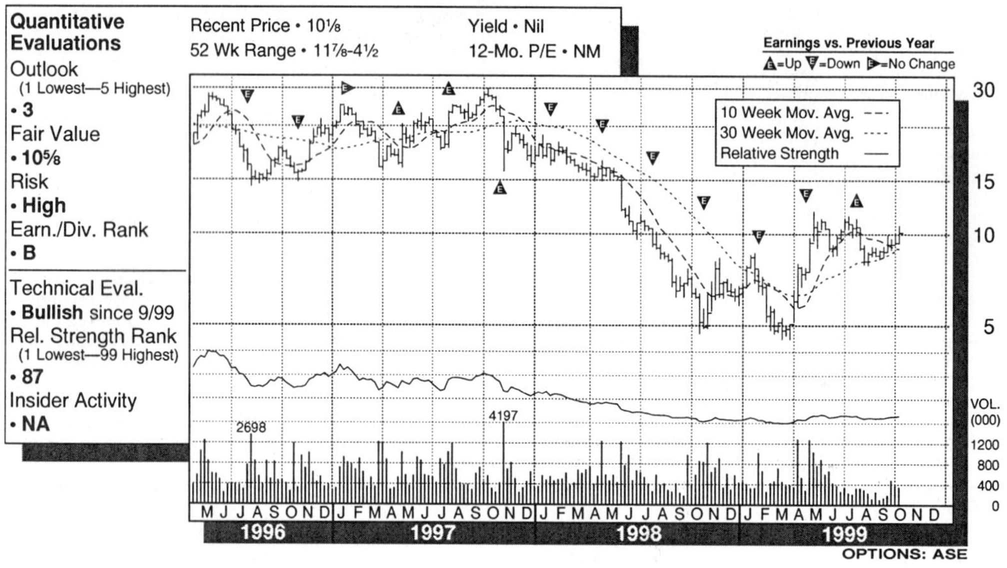

OPTIONS: ASE

Business Profile - 15-SEP-99

Allen Telecom said recently that it is increasingly confident about the remainder of 1999, due to strengthened financial ratios, an increase in its backlog, and discussions with customers that suggest growth in sales and earnings for the balance of the year. Backlog at June 30, 1999, was $70.1 million, up 37% from the level at December 31, 1998. Although the company reported a sales increase in the second quarter of 1999 versus the first quarter, the growth was somewhat less than ALN had expected. In March 1999, the company sold its Marta Technologies subsidiary to Environmental Systems Products. A $1.4 million gain was recorded on the sale in the first quarter.

Operational Review - 15-SEP-99

Sales in the first half of 1999 fell 27%, year to year, reflecting a global decline in demand for wireless communications products, with all geographic areas showing declines. Margins widened, despite the lower volume, due to an improved product mix and a focus on cost containment that led to lower SG&A expenses and R&D costs. Despite higher interest expense and a lower income tax benefit, the loss from continuing operations narrowed to $1,419,000 ($0.05 a share, before a gain of $0.08 on the sale of the emissions testing business) from $4,796,000 ($0.18).

Stock Performance - 08-OCT-99

In the past 30 trading days, ALN's shares have increased 19%, compared to a 0.91% fall in the S&P 500. Average trading volume for the past five days was 67,680 shares, compared with the 40-day moving average of 49,500 shares.

Key Stock Statistics

Dividend Rate/Share	Nil	Shareholders	1,745
Shs. outstg. (M)	27.6	Market cap. (B)	$0.280
Avg. daily vol. (M)	0.068	Inst. holdings	75%
Tang. Bk. Value/Share	4.12		
Beta	2.19		

Value of $10,000 invested 5 years ago: NA

Fiscal Year Ending Dec. 31

	1999	1998	1997	1996	1995	1994
Revenues (Million $)						
1Q	75.91	113.4	102.5	84.47	59.27	76.94
2Q	77.50	98.01	108.9	88.46	83.88	81.77
3Q	—	90.96	111.4	95.01	88.30	84.48
4Q	—	85.67	109.8	101.6	83.93	88.16
Yr.	—	388.0	432.5	369.5	315.4	331.4
Earnings Per Share ($)						
1Q	**-0.05**	**0.23**	**0.26**	**0.18**	0.27	0.21
2Q	Nil	**-0.41**	**0.25**	**0.21**	0.35	0.25
3Q	—	**0.10**	**0.29**	**0.13**	0.35	0.33
4Q	—	**-0.12**	**0.08**	**0.25**	0.25	0.33
Yr.	—	**-0.21**	**0.88**	**0.76**	**1.02**	**0.76**

Next earnings report expected: late October

Dividend Data

Dividends, omitted in 1987 and resumed in 1991, were omitted again in September 1996. A poison pill stock purchase rights plan was adopted in 1988.

Allen Telecom Inc.

Business Summary - 15-SEP-99

This leading supplier of equipment and services to the worldwide two-way wireless communications market intends to use the Allen Telecom name to unify its offerings of a broad range of products with strong brand names. In September 1995, ALN completed the spinoff of its entire truck products segment into a new entity, TransPro. In March 1999, the company sold its automotive emissions testing business, which had been classified as discontinued since 1996.

Products sold include system expansion, site management, and mobile and base station antennas for the worldwide wireless communications market. Demand for the company's equipment is a function of the development of wireless communications systems around the world, together with ALN's ability to develop new products and technologies related to system coverage and capacity and components for other manufacturers' wireless systems.

ALN's systems products support both coverage and capacity enhancement for GSM, TDMA, CDMA and analog wireless carriers. Products include low and high power repeaters to fill coverage gaps caused by obstructions, such as mountains, tunnels and buildings; and fiber optic-based radio frequency distribution systems. In addition, the company sells indoor coverage systems and a rage of test equipment and software to test and optimize wireless networks.

Through its site management division, ALN is the world's largest supplier of cell site subsystems. Site management products include sophisticated filters, which ensure that incoming signals are received and outgoing signals are transmitted clearly; duplexers, which allow one antenna to be used for both transmission and reception; and low noise, tower mounted multi-carrier and power amplifiers, which enhance the reception of weak signals and boost outgoing signals.

The company is also a leading North American supplier of base station antennas, including analog as well as newer digital and PCS antennas. In addition, ALN supplies mobile automobile antennas, as well as antennas for Global Positioning System (GPS) mapping.

International sales have increased steadily over the years, accounting for 61% of sales in 1998. ALN continues to see significant growth in international markets in the future as existing cellular systems are expanded and new cellular licenses are granted, and as other parts of the world begin to install advanced wireless systems. Export sales from the U.S. are primarily to major wireless telephone companies. European sales are primarily to major European original equipment manufacturers and cellular or PCS operators. Four major telecommunications equipment companies together accounted for 30% of sales in 1998.

Per Share Data ($) (Year Ended Dec. 31)	1998	1997	1996	1995	1994	1993	1992	1991	1990	1989
Tangible Bk. Val.	4.30	4.91	5.60	5.35	6.30	7.52	1.97	4.46	3.77	4.04
Cash Flow	0.70	1.47	1.28	1.63	1.47	1.56	1.19	1.01	0.08	0.82
Earnings	-0.21	0.88	0.76	1.22	1.12	1.19	0.81	0.68	-0.28	0.34
Dividends	Nil	Nil	Nil	0.20	0.17	0.22	0.10	0.05	Nil	Nil
Payout Ratio	Nil	Nil	Nil	16%	15%	18%	13%	7%	Nil	Nil
Prices - High	21 1/8	30	28 7/8	39 3/8	25 5/8	29 1/4	15	10 1/8	9 1/8	7 5/8
- Low	4 5/8	16	14 1/4	21 1/4	13 1/2	13	9 1/2	4 1/2	4 1/2	4 1/8
P/E Ratio - High	NM	34	38	32	23	25	19	15	NM	23
- Low	NM	18	19	17	12	11	12	7	NM	12
Income Statement Analysis (Million $)										
Revs.	388	433	369	315	331	280	296	262	352	362
Oper. Inc.	16.8	66.0	66.1	60.7	56.8	44.1	41.5	33.0	38.7	34.1
Depr.	24.6	16.2	14.1	11.1	9.2	8.3	7.4	6.3	6.7	8.7
Int. Exp.	8.3	4.5	3.8	3.2	4.4	3.2	6.8	7.0	11.2	10.4
Pretax Inc.	-8.6	46.7	46.5	47.8	46.9	33.0	23.7	18.4	3.0	15.0
Eff. Tax Rate	NM	38%	42%	40%	38%	11%	16%	9.40%	142%	32%
Net Inc.	-5.5	24.0	20.6	32.6	29.2	29.5	19.9	16.6	-1.3	10.2
Balance Sheet & Other Fin. Data (Million $)										
Cash	19.9	30.8	23.9	15.7	55.2	11.2	4.4	7.5	0.8	22.7
Curr. Assets	203	242	199	178	178	131	164	159	179	186
Total Assets	466	514	411	364	358	325	388	308	330	318
Curr. Liab.	69.5	131	105	84.4	70.0	59.0	NA	NA	70.0	73.0
LT Debt	129	97.9	50.0	47.0	45.0	52.0	131	93.0	114	101
Common Eqty.	250	261	226	210	224	195	102	84.0	71.0	74.0
Total Cap.	385	366	295	257	271	247	291	236	242	233
Cap. Exp.	18.1	22.2	17.5	16.8	8.9	11.4	6.7	5.0	6.6	7.4
Cash Flow	19.1	40.2	34.7	43.7	38.4	35.7	23.3	18.9	1.4	14.9
Curr. Ratio	2.9	1.8	1.9	2.1	2.5	2.2	NA	NA	2.5	2.6
% LT Debt of Cap.	33.4	26.8	16.9	18.3	16.6	21.0	45.1	39.5	47.1	43.2
% Net Inc.of Revs.	NM	5.5	5.6	10.4	8.8	10.5	6.7	6.3	NM	2.8
% Ret. on Assets	NM	5.2	5.3	9.1	8.5	7.1	5.6	5.2	NM	3.1
% Ret. on Equity	NM	9.9	9.4	15.1	13.9	16.7	16.6	16.2	NM	9.2

Data as orig reptd.; bef. results of disc opers/spec. items. Per share data adj. for stk. divs. Bold denotes diluted EPS (FASB 128)-prior periods restated. E-Estimated. NA-Not Available. NM-Not Meaningful. NR-Not Ranked.

Office—25101 Chagrin Blvd., Suite 350, Beachwood, OH 44122. **Tel**—(216) 765-5818. **Website**—http://www.allentelecom.com **Chrmn**—P. W. Colburn. **Pres & CEO**—R. G. Paul. **EVP & CFO**—R. A. Youdelman. **VP, Treas & Contr**—J. L. LePorte III. **VP & Secy**—M. P. Folan, III. **Investor Contact**—Dianne B. McCormick. **Dirs**—P. W. Colburn, J. K. Conway, J. C. Lyons, J. F. McNiff, R. G. Paul, C. W. Robinson, M. F. Roetter, G. B. Smith. **Transfer Agent & Registrar**—Harris Trust Co. of New York, Cleveland. **Incorporated**—in Michigan in 1928; reincorporated in Delaware in 1969. **Empl**— 2,300. **S&P Analyst:** Jim Corridore

STANDARD & POOR'S
STOCK REPORTS

Alliance Pharmaceutical

NASDAQ Symbol **ALLP**

In S&P SmallCap 600

23-OCT-99

Industry: Biotechnology

Summary: Thi biotechnology firm is developing products based on its expertise in perfluorochemicals, surfactants, and pharmaceutical manufacturing processes.

Quantitative Evaluations

Outlook (1 Lowest—5 Highest)
• NA

Fair Value
• NA

Risk
• High

Earn./Div. Rank
• C

Technical Eval.
• NA

Rel. Strength Rank (1 Lowest—99 Highest)
• 81

Insider Activity
• NA

Recent Price • 5
52 Wk Range • 7-2¼
Yield • Nil
12-Mo. P/E • NM

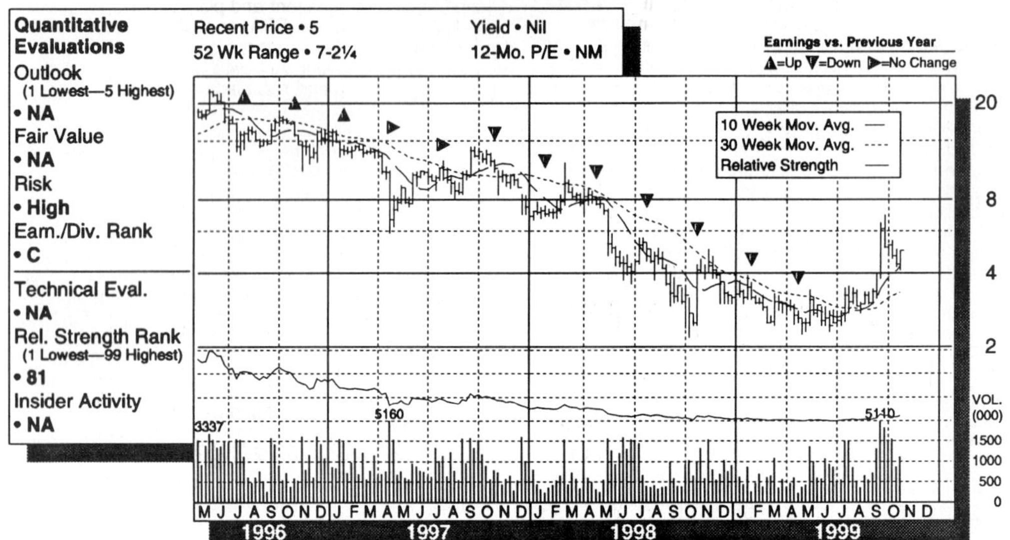

Business Profile - 13-OCT-99

In September 1999, ALLP reached an agreement with the FDA on the design of a Phase III study for Oxygent, an intravascular blood substitute designed to reduce the need for donor blood transfusions in surgical patients. Also in September, the company and Hoechst Marion Roussell (HMR) reached an agreement whereby HMR may sell up to $3 million in raw materials to ALLP for use in its LiquiVent and Oxygent Products. In May 1999, ALLP announced results of two Phase III studies on Imagent, an ultrasound enhancement powder, that showed Imagent provided clearer ultrasound images of the heart. As of mid-year 1999, the company expected research revenue to decrease in 2000 compared to 1999, as a result of reduced revenue from its agreement with Schering AG.

Operational Review - 13-OCT-99

Revenues declined 61% in FY 99 (Jun.), mainly reflecting decreased research revenue from Ortho Biotech, Inc. Total operating expenses rose 19%, on higher clinical trial and product development expenditures, increases in staffing and depreciation costs, and a rise in professional fees. Following sharply lower net investment and other income, due to a lower average cash balance, the net loss widened to $60.8 million ($1.89 a share, after preferred dividends), from $33.0 ($1.04). Cash and cash equivalents totaled $19.1 million on June 30, 1999.

Stock Performance - 22-OCT-99

In the past 30 trading days, ALLP's shares have increased 9%, compared to a 4% fall in the S&P 500. Average trading volume for the past five days was 407,780 shares, compared with the 40-day moving average of 414,926 shares.

Key Stock Statistics

Dividend Rate/Share	Nil	Shareholders	1,700
Shs. outstg. (M)	43.5	Market cap. (B)	$0.190
Avg. daily vol. (M)	0.283	Inst. holdings	34%
Tang. Bk. Value/Share	0.97		
Beta	0.70		

Value of $10,000 invested 5 years ago: $ 5,468

Fiscal Year Ending Jun. 30

	1999	1998	1997	1996	1995	1994
Revenues (Million $)						
1Q	5.10	6.54	5.75	2.15	5.18	0.15
2Q	1.05	5.27	22.13	2.04	2.03	0.10
3Q	1.02	4.33	6.84	7.23	2.48	0.12
4Q	—	5.07	9.87	5.91	2.13	0.04
Yr.	8.25	21.21	44.58	17.32	11.82	0.41
Earnings Per Share ($)						
1Q	**-0.33**	**-0.20**	-0.15	-0.31	-0.38	-0.41
2Q	**-0.53**	**-0.24**	**-0.18**	-0.29	-0.34	-0.52
3Q	**-0.48**	**-0.32**	-0.15	-0.15	-0.31	-0.38
4Q	—	**-0.28**	-0.16	-0.16	-0.40	-0.52
Yr.	**-1.89**	**-1.04**	**-0.63**	-0.91	-1.35	-1.83

Next earnings report expected: mid November

Dividend Data

No cash has been paid.

Alliance Pharmaceutical Corp.

23-OCT-99

Business Summary - 13-OCT-99

Alliance Pharmaceutical is focused on transforming scientific innovations into novel therapeutics that may be licensed to major pharmaceutical firms. ALLP's strategy is to identify product candidates through alliances with researchers and clinicians in medical centers and universities and to advance and commercialize these products with the aid of collaborative agreements.

ALLP's products are based on its expertise with perfluorochemicals, inert biochemical agents with a high solubility for physiological gases; and surfactants, compounds with the ability to bind dissimilar substances. As of mid-year 1999, ALLP had three products in Phase III human clinical trials.

Oxygent (perflubron emulsion) is an intravascular oxygen carrier (blood substitute) designed to maintain tissue oxygenation during surgery. In September 1999, ALLP and the FDA agreed to key design parameters for a Phase III clinical study in patients undergoing coronary artery bypass surgery. A Phase III trial in general surgery patients was also ongoing. In May 1998, ALLP restructured its agreement with partner Ortho Biotech, Inc. and is now solely responsible for the costs and further development of Oxygent.

LiquiVent (neat perflubron) is being developed as an intrapulmonary oxygen-carrying agent to reduce a patient's exposure to the harmful effects of mechanical ventilation. ALLP initiated a Phase II/III clinical study for LiquiVent in November, 1998 in patients with acute lung injury and acute respiratory distress syndrome. The FDA has granted LiquiVent "fast track" status.

Imagent is an intravenous contrast agent for the enhancement of ultrasound images that assess cardiac function. As of mid-year 1999, ALLP had completed two Phase III trials with Imagent and planned to file a New Drug Application with the FDA, as well as an application with EU authorities. Imagent is being developed with Germany's Schering AG, with Schering receiving worldwide marketing and manufacturing rights in exchange for milestone payments and royalties.

In November 1996, ALLP acquired MDV Technologies Inc., and its thermo-reversible gel product, FloGel, a potential anti-adhesion treatment for persons undergoing abdominal or pelvic surgeries. As of mid-year 1999, ALLP was analyzing data on FloGel from a recently completed pilot clinical study.

Other products in development include: PulmoSpheres, a novel pulmonary drug delivery adjuvant that utilizes liquid-based spheres to encapsulate drug compounds; and RODA, a minimally invasive device for the real-time monitoring of oxygenation and cardiovascular dynamics of surgical and post-surgical patients.

In June 1999, ALLP received proceeds of $23,275,000 through the sale of 9,500,000 common shares at $2.45 per share. In the company's audited 1999 financial statements, the auditors noted that, without additional financing, ALLP lacks sufficient working capital to fund operations beyond December 1999. As of June 30, 1999 ALLP's acc umulated deficit was $326.7 million.

Per Share Data ($) (Year Ended Jun. 30)	1999	1998	1997	1996	1995	1994	1993	1992	1991	1990
Tangible Bk. Val.	0.97	2.07	2.93	3.38	1.32	2.33	2.68	3.99	0.91	1.93
Cash Flow	-1.65	-0.88	-0.50	-0.79	-1.22	-1.67	-1.24	-1.09	-1.02	-0.82
Earnings	-1.89	-1.04	-0.63	-0.91	-1.35	-1.83	-1.39	-1.25	-1.24	-0.94
Dividends	Nil	Nil	Nil	Nil	Nil	Nil	Nil	Nil	Nil	Nil
Payout Ratio	Nil	Nil	Nil	Nil	Nil	Nil	Nil	Nil	Nil	Nil
Prices - High	7	11 3/8	15 3/4	22 7/8	14 1/4	12 1/4	15	44	32 1/4	12 1/2
- Low	2 1/4	2 9/16	5 7/8	10 1/2	4 1/4	5 5/8	7 1/4	8 1/4	9	5 1/4
P/E Ratio - High	NM	NM	NM	NM	NM	NM	NM	NM	NM	NM
- Low	NM	NM	NM	NM	NM	NM	NM	NM	NA	NA
Income Statement Analysis (Million $)										
Revs.	8.3	21.2	44.6	17.3	11.8	0.4	2.4	1.8	1.6	1.7
Oper. Inc.	-54.4	-31.7	2.6	-20.5	-27.5	-35.4	-25.8	-19.8	-15.4	-12.8
Depr.	6.3	5.1	4.0	3.1	2.9	3.1	3.0	2.8	3.1	1.6
Int. Exp.	Nil	Nil	Nil	Nil	NM	NM	0.0	0.3	0.9	0.9
Pretax Inc.	-60.8	-33.0	-19.0	-22.2	-29.1	-36.9	26.4	-21.8	-17.7	-12.5
Eff. Tax Rate	NM	NM	NM	NM	NM	NM	NM	Nil	Nil	Nil
Net Inc.	-60.8	-33.0	-19.0	-22.2	-29.1	-36.9	-26.4	-21.8	-17.7	-12.5
Balance Sheet & Other Fin. Data (Million $)										
Cash	19.1	11.8	71.6	71.4	23.4	21.1	39.5	66.4	16.8	30.6
Curr. Assets	24.4	57.4	80.0	79.0	27.5	22.4	42.7	68.2	17.7	32.0
Total Assets	66.0	93.7	112	108	56.0	53.1	72.5	98.0	44.8	59.5
Curr. Liab.	13.4	8.7	17.8	5.7	5.1	3.0	3.0	2.7	2.0	2.1
LT Debt	10.5	8.9	2.7	0.9	Nil	Nil	Nil	0.2	8.3	8.5
Common Eqty.	42.1	76.1	91.3	101	50.1	49.8	69.1	94.6	33.9	48.8
Total Cap.	52.6	85.0	94.1	102	50.1	49.8	69.1	94.8	42.2	57.3
Cap. Exp.	6.2	10.1	6.8	4.0	1.3	1.9	2.5	3.6	1.3	3.0
Cash Flow	-54.5	-27.9	-15.0	-20.1	-26.9	-33.9	-23.4	-19.0	-14.6	-10.9
Curr. Ratio	1.8	6.6	4.5	13.8	5.4	7.6	14.5	25.6	8.7	15.0
% LT Debt of Cap.	20.0	10.5	2.9	1.0	Nil	Nil	Nil	0.2	19.8	14.8
% Net Inc.of Revs.	NM	NM	NM	NM	NM	NM	NM	NM	NM	NM
% Ret. on Assets	NM	NM	NM	NM	NM	NM	NM	NM	NM	NM
% Ret. on Equity	NM	NM	NM	NM	NM	NM	NM	NM	NM	NM

Data as orig reptd.; bef. results of disc opers/spec. items. Per share data adj. for stk. divs. Bold denotes diluted EPS (FASB 128)-prior periods restated. E-Estimated. NA-Not Available. NM-Not Meaningful. NR-Not Ranked.

Office—3040 Science Park Rd., San Diego, CA 92121. **Tel**—(858) 410-5200. **Website**—http://www.allp.com **Chrmn & CEO**—D. J. Roth. **Pres & COO**—T. D. Roth. **CFO & Treas**—T. T. Hart. **Dirs**— P. Cuatrecasas, C. O. Johnson, S. M. McGrath, D. E. O'Neill, H. M. Ranney, J. G. Riess, D. J. Roth, T. D. Roth, T. F. Zuck. **Transfer Agent & Registrar**—American Stock Transfer Co., NYC. **Incorporated**—in New York in 1983. **Empl**— 221. **S&P Analyst:** Frank DiLorenzo

STANDARD
&POOR'S
STOCK REPORTS

Alliant Techsystems

NYSE Symbol **ATK**

In S&P SmallCap 600

09-OCT-99

Industry: Aerospace/Defense

Summary: ATK, the largest supplier of weapons ammunition to the U.S. military, is also a major global maker of rocket engines.

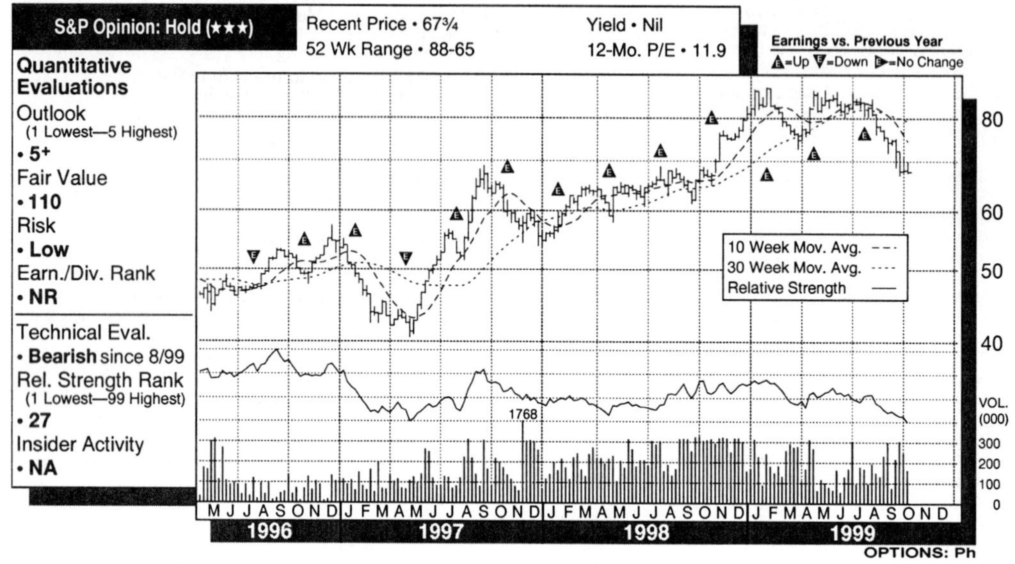

Quantitative Evaluations

Outlook
(1 Lowest—5 Highest)
• **5+**

Fair Value
• **110**

Risk
• **Low**

Earn./Div. Rank
• **NR**

Technical Eval.
• **Bearish** since 8/99

Rel. Strength Rank
(1 Lowest—99 Highest)
• **27**

Insider Activity
• **NA**

Overview - 23-SEP-99

Record FY 99 backlog of $2.5 billion should help drive near-term mid-single-digit revenue growth, which in turn should propel near-term operating profit margins to over 10% of revenues, with returns on equity (ROE) in the respectable 13-15% range. Near-term profitability should also be spurred by recent organizational changes, including flattening ATK's organizational structure to place more responsibility for segment performance and accountability on divisional presidents. Longer term, ATK's sales and earnings growth prospects are bolstered by accelerating U.S. and European demand for precision missiles. As one of the leading global makers of precision ammunition, as well as missile and rocket motors, ATK is well positioned to capitalize on the potential for seismic changes in global military procurement needs. ATK also plans to augment earnings growth by boosting international sales from 6% to 10% of revenues, as well as by making complementary acquisitions.

Valuation - 23-SEP-99

From 1991 through 1998, ATK shares solidly outpaced the broad market, rising at a seven-year annual rate of 21%, versus 17% for the S&P 500. The shares rose especially sharply in 1994, when management began consolidating operations and improving profitability. In 1994, operating profit margins stood at only 2.2%; now, ATK posts profit margins of 10%. Although we expect the overall global defense industry to grow at sluggish rates at best, we believe the relatively faster growing precision missiles and electronics segments will help ATK grow earnings at an average annual rate of 10%, with average ROE of 15%. However, we believe much of ATK's favorable prospects are already reflected in the company's current stock price.

Key Stock Statistics

S&P EPS Est. 2000	6.25	Tang. Bk. Value/Share	0.27
P/E on S&P Est. 2000	10.8	Beta	0.19
Dividend Rate/Share	Nil	Shareholders	12,006
Shs. outstg. (M)	10.3	Market cap. (B)	$0.694
Avg. daily vol. (M)	0.048	Inst. holdings	81%

Value of $10,000 invested 5 years ago: $ 22,869

Fiscal Year Ending Mar. 31

	2000	1999	1998	1997	1996	1995
Revenues (Million $)						
1Q	272.7	256.3	251.6	230.2	292.9	168.9
2Q	—	259.0	266.9	247.7	267.6	137.2
3Q	—	274.4	269.2	300.8	298.2	173.2
4Q	—	300.7	287.7	310.8	335.0	309.7
Yr.	—	1,090	1,076	1,089	1,194	789.1
Earnings Per Share ($)						
1Q	**1.39**	**1.21**	**1.10**	**0.74**	0.78	0.68
2Q	**E1.40**	**1.30**	**1.18**	**0.96**	0.86	-1.44
3Q	**E1.61**	**1.45**	**1.33**	**1.28**	1.10	0.37
4Q	**E1.85**	**1.59**	**1.45**	**1.43**	1.69	-6.45
Yr.	**E6.25**	**5.52**	**5.08**	**2.73**	**3.61**	**-7.27**

Next earnings report expected: late October

Dividend Data

No cash dividends have been paid on the common stock since its distribution in October 1990. "Poison pill" stock purchase rights were distributed with the common stock.

Alliant Techsystems Inc.

Business Summary - 23-SEP-99

As one of the world's largest makers of ammunition, and missile and rocket motors, ATK is well positioned to capitalize on growing global military demand for precision weapons and defense electronics, the only relatively fast growing segments of the otherwise sluggish global defense industry.

Since the end of the Cold War, U.S. military procurement requirements have changed radically. With the implosion of once-enormous Soviet military forces, the Pentagon no longer needs to purchase large amounts of traditional weaponry such as tanks, warplanes and naval vessels. However, new global threats, such as potentially destabilizing regional conflicts, the proliferation of long-range missiles and international terrorism, are forcing global military establishments to rely increasingly on precision weapons, guidance systems and surveillance equipment to prevent, contain or win conflicts anywhere in the world.

ATK's strategy to boost earnings growth and returns includes expanding internally generated sales (by increasing ATK's presence in the faster growing precision missile/defense electronics markets, and boosting international sales from 6% to 10% of revenues). ATK's growth strategy also includes making complementary acquisitions.

Sales to the U.S. government, and to defense contractors such as Lockheed Martin, Boeing and Raytheon, constitute about 75% of total revenues. In the past three fiscal years, company-funded research & development expenses averaged 1.2% of revenues.

ATK's Conventional Munitions segment (44% of FY 99 (Mar.) revenues) primarily makes tank ammunition, missile engines and warheads. The segment is the largest supplier of ammunition to the U.S. military. Other major customers inculde Raytheon, the world's largest defense electronics and missile maker. In FY 99, segment profit margins and capital expenditures were 4.0% and 2.9%, respectively, of sales.

Alliant's Aerospace segment (36% of FY 99 revenues) mostly makes engines for satellite-carrying rockets, such as Boeing's Delta, Lockheed Martin's Titan and Orbital Sciences' Pegasus rockets. Other major rocket engine makers include the Thiokol division of Cordant Technologies, CSD, the Aerojet division of Gencorp Inc., and the ARC division of Sequa Corp. In FY 99, segment profit margins and capital expenditures were 10% and 6.1%, respectively, of sales.

ATK's Defense Systems segment (20% of FY 99 revenues) primarily makes tank and demolition systems, and precision-guided munitions. In FY 99, segment profit margins and capital expenditures were 1.7% and 1.5%, respectively, of sales.

Per Share Data ($) (Year Ended Mar. 31)	1999	1998	1997	1996	1995	1994	1993	1992	1991	1990
Tangible Bk. Val.	NM	6.92	7.11	NM	5.51	6.44	5.21	16.92	NA	13.06
Cash Flow	9.27	8.63	6.67	9.08	-4.74	5.23	-2.03	7.50	NA	6.08
Earnings	5.52	5.08	2.73	4.43	-7.22	3.21	-4.68	4.57	NA	2.55
Dividends	Nil	Nil	Nil	Nil	Nil	Nil	Nil	Nil	NA	Nil
Payout Ratio	Nil	Nil	Nil	Nil	Nil	Nil	Nil	Nil	NA	Nil
Cal. Yrs.	1998	1997	1996	1995	1994	1993	1992	1991	1990	1989
Prices - High	83	69	57 3/8	53	40 5/8	31	28 5/8	29 1/4	15 1/4	NA
- Low	55	40 1/2	43 3/4	34 7/8	21 3/4	22	19 1/8	13	8 5/8	NA
P/E Ratio - High	15	14	21	12	NM	10	NM	6	6	NA
- Low	10	8	16	8	NM	7	NM	3	3	NA
Income Statement Analysis (Million $)										
Revs.	1,090	1,076	1,089	1,194	789	775	1,005	1,187	NA	1,248
Oper. Inc.	149	140	123	177	42.6	60.0	86.0	120	NA	118
Depr.	45.9	47.5	52.7	62.4	25.0	20.5	26.9	29.2	NA	33.7
Int. Exp.	24.7	27.6	35.1	45.1	11.4	8.2	22.7	16.2	NA	10.8
Pretax Inc.	79.5	67.9	36.7	76.4	-72.6	32.5	-70.3	74.2	NA	33.6
Eff. Tax Rate	15%	NM	NM	22%	NM	Nil	NM	38%	NA	27%
Net Inc.	67.6	67.9	36.7	59.6	-72.6	32.5	-45.2	45.7	NA	24.4
Balance Sheet & Other Fin. Data (Million $)										
Cash	21.1	69.0	123	45.4	26.5	50.9	81.3	74.5	NA	13.9
Curr. Assets	343	373	425	425	464	287	350	345	NA	344
Total Assets	894	932	1,010	1,017	1,052	438	457	522	NA	507
Curr. Liab.	286	277	331	367	336	255	229	209	NA	225
LT Debt	306	181	237	350	395	Nil	65.0	108	NA	136
Common Eqty.	119	221	219	157	140	92.0	66.0	178	NA	132
Total Cap.	425	402	456	507	539	109	141	298	NA	271
Cap. Exp.	43.7	20.4	28.5	28.0	19.3	20.7	11.3	19.5	NA	31.6
Cash Flow	114	115	89.4	122	-47.6	53.0	-18.3	74.9	NA	58.1
Curr. Ratio	1.2	1.3	1.3	1.2	1.4	1.1	1.5	1.7	NA	1.5
% LT Debt of Cap.	72.0	45.0	52.0	69.0	73.3	Nil	46.5	36.0	NA	50.4
% Net Inc.of Revs.	6.2	6.3	3.4	5.0	NM	4.2	NM	3.9	NA	2.0
% Ret. on Assets	7.4	7.0	3.6	5.8	NM	7.2	NM	8.8	NA	NA
% Ret. on Equity	35.2	30.9	19.5	40.0	NM	41.1	NM	29.2	NA	NA

Data as orig. reptd.; bef. results of disc. opers. and/or spec. items. Per share data adj. for stk. divs. as of ex-div. date. Prior to 1992, yr. ended Dec. 31. Results in FY 95, FY 93 include substantial restructuring charges. Bold denotes diluted EPS (FASB 128). E-Estimated. NA-Not Available. NM-Not Meaningful. NR-Not Ranked.

Office—600 Second St., N.E., Hopkins, MN 55343-8384. **Tel**—(612) 931-6000. **E-mail**—alliant_corporate@atk.com **Website**—http://www.atk.com **Chrmn & CEO**—P. D. Miller. **Pres**—P. A. Bukowick. **CFO & Treas**—S. S. Meyers. **Secy**—C. H. Gauck. **VP & Investor Contact**—Richard N. Jowett (612-931-6080). **Dirs**—P. A. Bukowick, G. F. Decker, T. L. Gossage, J. M. Greenblatt, J. G. Guss, D. E. Jeremiah, G. N. Kelley, J. F. Mazzella, P. D. Miller, D. L. Nir, M.T. Smith. **Transfer Agent & Registrar**—ChaseMellon Shareholder Services, NYC. **Incorporated**—in Delaware in 1990. **Empl**—6,110. **S&P Analyst:** Robert E. Friedman, CPA

STANDARD
&POOR'S
STOCK REPORTS

Alpha Industries

NASDAQ Symbol **AHAA**

In S&P SmallCap 600

09-OCT-99

Industry: Electronics (Instrumentation)

Summary: This company manufactures products used in radio and microwave applications for communications, defense and other markets.

Quantitative Evaluations

Outlook (1 Lowest—5 Highest) • **1⁻**

Fair Value • **46⅝**

Risk • **NA**

Earn./Div. Rank • **B-**

Technical Eval. • **Bullish** since 8/99

Rel. Strength Rank (1 Lowest—99 Highest) • **80**

Insider Activity • **NA**

Recent Price • 54⅝

52 Wk Range • 59¾-6⅝

Yield • Nil

12-Mo. P/E • 41.7

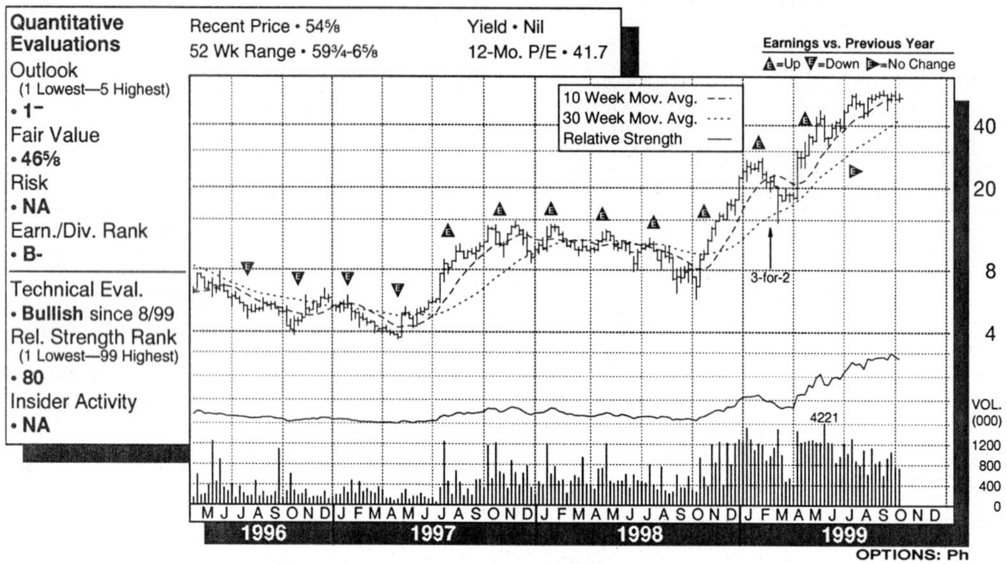

Business Profile - 03-AUG-99

In May 1999, the company sold publicly 3 million common shares at $35 each. Net proceeds were earmarked for working capital and other general corporate purposes, which may include purchase of equipment, expansion of facilities, and potential acquisitions. AHAA has said that its markets are strong, and it has been winning new orders from a wide range of customers. The company is increasing its penetration of major wireless equipment OEMs, and sees continued strength in the wireless telephony markets.

Operational Review - 03-AUG-99

Net sales in the three months ended June 27, 1999, advanced 29%, year to year, reflecting strength in the company's major markets, particularly wireless semiconductors, which recorded a 70% sales gain. Profitability benefited from the increased sales, and from greater operating efficiencies; pretax income soared 55%. After taxes at 36.0%, versus 10.0% (reflecting utilization of net operating loss carryforwards), net income was up 10%, to $4,389,000 ($0.25 a share, on 11% more shares), from $3,974,000 ($0.25, as adjusted).

Stock Performance - 08-OCT-99

In the past 30 trading days, AHAA's shares have declined 2%, compared to a 0.91% fall in the S&P 500. Average trading volume for the past five days was 145,780 shares, compared with the 40-day moving average of 175,564 shares.

Key Stock Statistics

Dividend Rate/Share	Nil	Shareholders	1,000
Shs. outstg. (M)	19.4	Market cap. (B)	$ 1.1
Avg. daily vol. (M)	0.173	Inst. holdings	77%
Tang. Bk. Value/Share	10.05		
Beta	2.42		

Value of $10,000 invested 5 years ago: $ 198,636

Fiscal Year Ending Mar. 31

	2000	1999	1998	1997	1996	1995
Revenues (Million $)						
1Q	38.61	29.96	25.71	20.07	22.43	18.68
2Q	—	29.63	28.57	20.14	23.73	18.25
3Q	—	32.49	30.75	22.29	25.24	19.36
4Q	—	34.27	31.85	22.76	25.49	21.97
Yr.	—	126.3	116.9	85.23	96.89	78.25
Earnings Per Share ($)						
1Q	**0.25**	**0.25**	0.07	-0.23	0.09	0.05
2Q	—	**0.26**	0.15	-0.32	0.09	0.05
3Q	—	**0.29**	**0.21**	-0.14	0.11	0.07
4Q	—	**0.51**	**0.23**	-0.36	0.01	0.07
Yr.	—	**1.31**	**0.65**	**-1.05**	**0.29**	0.24

Next earnings report expected: mid October

Dividend Data

Amount ($)	Date Decl.	Ex-Div. Date	Stock of Record	Payment Date
3-for-2	Jan. 28	Feb. 19	Feb. 08	Feb. 18 '99

A Division of The McGraw-Hill Companies

Alpha Industries, Inc.

Business Summary - 03-AUG-99

Alpha Industries, Inc. designs and manufactures a broad range of monolithic integrated circuits, ceramic products, discrete semiconductors and subsystems for microwave, millimeter wave and radio frequency wireless communications applications. During FY 99 (Mar.), 83% of sales were to manufacturers of commercial products, primarily in the wireless communications markets, and included components for products such as wireless telephones and base stations in addition to motion detectors and sensors. The remaining 17% of sales were for use in a wide variety of defense-related systems.

Wireless semiconductor products accounted for about 52% of sales and 38% of operating income in FY 99, application specific products 28% and 52%, and ceramic products 20% and 10%.

The company's wireless semiconductor products group supplies GaAs (gallium arsenide) integrated circuits and discrete semiconductors in high volume for wireless telephone handsets and wireless data applications.

The application specific products group supplies radio frequency, microwave frequency and millimeter wave frequency GaAs integrated circuits, and discrete semiconductors and components for customized products in the satellite communications, broadband data and defense markets.

The ceramics products group uses electrical ceramic and ferrite technologies to supply resonators and filters, mainly for wireless base station equipment.

Company-sponsored R&D spending in FY 99 totaled $12.9 million (10% of sales), versus $10.0 million (9%) in FY 99. About 75% of R&D expenditures are currently earmarked for the development of processes and applications related to high volume products in the wireless semiconductor products group, which target the fast-growing wireless markets.

Customers include leading OEMs in the wireless communications industry and their principal suppliers. Sales to the 15 largest customers accounted for 64% of sales in FY 99; Motorola provided 28%. About 17% of sales were to the U.S. government and its prime contractors and subcontractors. In FY 99, 6% of sales were made to customers in Europe.

In FY 99, AHAA's capital expenditures totaled $17.7 million, with $14.3 million related to the wireless semiconductor products group, mainly for the expansion of the GaAs fabrication facility, estimated to cost a total of $18 million, and scheduled to be completed in the summer of 1999. This expansion is expected to increase capacity significantly.

Per Share Data ($)										
(Year Ended Mar. 31)	1999	1998	1997	1996	1995	1994	1993	1992	1991	1990
Tangible Bk. Val.	5.07	3.56	2.90	3.86	2.39	2.15	3.17	3.44	3.43	3.34
Cash Flow	1.80	1.08	-0.65	0.64	0.59	-0.62	0.15	0.45	0.59	-0.91
Earnings	1.31	0.65	-1.05	0.29	0.24	-1.02	-0.27	0.01	0.12	-1.40
Dividends	Nil	Nil	Nil	Nil	Nil	Nil	Nil	Nil	Nil	Nil
Payout Ratio	Nil	Nil	Nil	Nil	Nil	Nil	NM	Nil	Nil	Nil
Cal. Yrs.	1998	1997	1996	1995	1994	1993	1992	1991	1990	1989
Prices - High	24 7/8	13 3/4	9 1/4	13 1/8	4 7/8	4 1/4	2 5/8	2 7/8	2 1/2	3 5/8
- Low	5 3/4	3 5/8	3 7/8	4 1/4	2	1 3/4	1 5/16	1 1/16	1 1/2	2 3/16
P/E Ratio - High	19	21	NM	46	20	NM	NM	NM	21	NM
- Low	4	6	NM	15	8	NM	NM	NM	13	NM
Income Statement Analysis (Million $)										
Revs.	126	117	85.3	96.9	78.3	70.1	69.5	71.0	66.3	64.7
Oper. Inc.	27.0	18.4	-7.4	9.2	8.1	0.4	4.2	6.0	9.4	2.8
Depr.	7.9	6.7	5.9	4.6	4.1	4.5	4.7	4.8	5.1	5.3
Int. Exp.	0.3	0.5	0.6	0.7	0.7	0.8	0.9	0.7	0.7	0.6
Pretax Inc.	20.2	11.4	-15.6	4.5	3.3	-11.2	-2.8	0.2	2.2	-15.9
Eff. Tax Rate	NM	10%	NM	15%	15%	NM	NM	41%	42%	NM
Net Inc.	21.5	10.3	-15.6	3.8	2.9	-11.5	-3.0	0.1	1.3	-15.1
Balance Sheet & Other Fin. Data (Million $)										
Cash	14.0	14.4	7.0	15.5	3.5	1.7	3.4	2.2	1.7	4.9
Curr. Assets	62.8	43.2	35.2	46.6	27.2	23.0	28.3	27.2	27.5	26.7
Total Assets	107	76.9	65.3	75.4	50.2	44.4	53.8	53.2	57.1	59.4
Curr. Liab.	20.1	17.1	16.8	13.9	16.2	14.1	12.5	9.4	13.1	17.3
LT Debt	0.7	1.6	3.6	3.1	5.5	5.7	5.2	5.0	5.3	5.7
Common Eqty.	81.0	55.8	43.4	57.5	27.7	24.3	35.6	38.5	38.2	35.9
Total Cap.	84.9	57.4	47.0	60.7	33.2	30.0	40.8	43.5	43.6	41.6
Cap. Exp.	17.7	11.0	8.0	12.0	4.9	2.9	4.1	1.3	2.2	4.8
Cash Flow	29.4	17.0	-9.7	8.4	7.0	-7.0	1.7	5.0	6.4	-9.8
Curr. Ratio	3.1	2.5	2.1	3.4	1.7	1.6	2.3	2.9	2.1	1.5
% LT Debt of Cap.	1.0	2.8	7.7	5.2	16.6	19.1	12.8	11.6	12.3	13.6
% Net Inc.of Revs.	17.1	8.8	NM	3.9	3.6	NM	NM	0.2	2.0	NM
% Ret. on Assets	23.4	14.5	NM	6.0	6.0	NM	NM	0.2	2.2	NM
% Ret. on Equity	31.4	20.8	NM	8.9	11.0	NM	NM	0.3	3.5	NM

Data as orig reptd.; bef. results of disc opers/spec. items. Per share data adj. for stk. divs. Bold denotes diluted EPS (FASB 128)-prior periods restated. E-Estimated. NA-Not Available. NM-Not Meaningful. NR-Not Ranked.

Office—20 Sylvan Rd., Woburn, MA 01801. **Tel**—(781) 935-5150. **Website**—http://www.alphaind.com **Chrmn**—G. S. Kariotis. **Pres & CEO**—T. C. Leonard. **VP & CFO**—P. E. Vincent. **Secy & Investor Contact**—James C. Nemiah (617-824-4426). **Dirs**—T. R. Furey, J. W. Henderson, G. S. Kariotis, T. C. Leonard, A. Pappas, S. Topol. **Transfer Agent & Registrar**—American Stock Transfer & Trust Co. **Incorporated**—in Delaware in 1962. **Empl**— 940. **S&P Analyst:** J.J.S.

STANDARD
&POOR'S
STOCK REPORTS

ALPHARMA INC.

NYSE Symbol **ALO**

In S&P SmallCap 600

09-OCT-99

Industry:
Health Care (Drugs - Generic & Other)

Summary: This company develops, manufactures, and markets specialty generic and proprietary human pharmaceuticals and animal health products.

Quantitative Evaluations

Outlook
(1 Lowest—5 Highest)
• **3⁻**

Fair Value
• **39⅛**

Risk
• **High**

Earn./Div. Rank
• **B-**

Technical Eval.
• **Bullish** since 9/99

Rel. Strength Rank
(1 Lowest—99 Highest)
• **35**

Insider Activity
• **Neutral**

Recent Price • 32¼
52 Wk Range • 43⅜-22½
Yield • 0.6%
12-Mo. P/E • 27.6

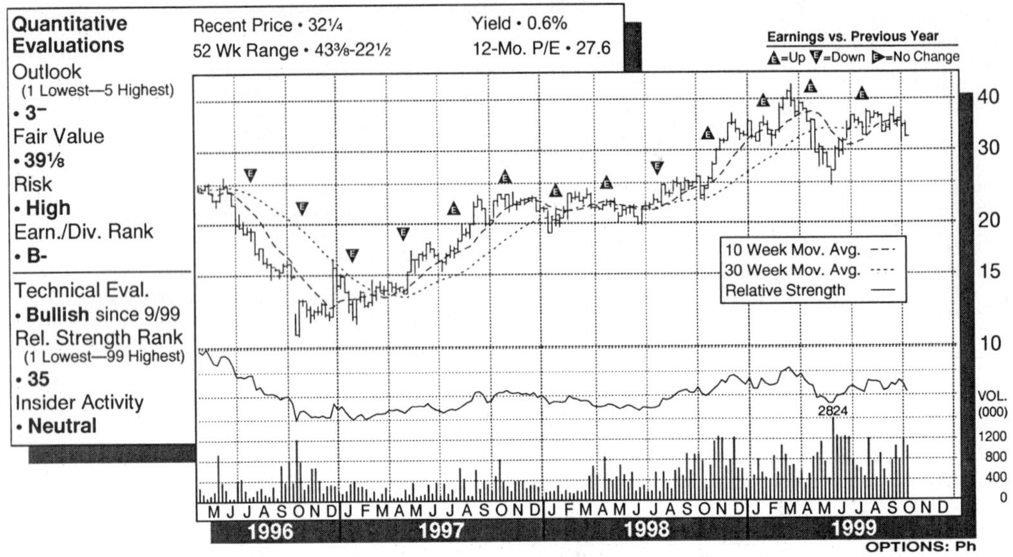

OPTIONS: Ph

Business Profile - 08-SEP-99

In August 1999, ALO received tentative FDA approval to manufacture and market Minoxidil Topical Solution USP 5% for Men, a treatment for hair loss. In July 1999, ALO announced that a strategic alliance between the company and Ascent Pediatrics, Inc. was approved by Ascent shareholders. ALO will provide $40 million in financing and has an option to acquire Ascent in 2002. In June 1999, ALO acquired Isis Pharma Group, the German generic drug business of Schwarz Pharma, for about $150 million. Also in June, ALO issued $170 million in 3% convertible senior subordinated notes maturing in 2006. During 1999's second quarter, the company received 70 new product, market and manufacturing approvals worldwide.

Operational Review - 08-SEP-99

Total revenue in the six months ended June 30, 1999, advanced 20%, year to year, mainly reflecting acquisitions in the International Pharmaceuticals Division, sales volume growth in certain areas, and new product introductions. Margins widened due to acquisitions, higher volumes, and manufacturing efficiencies. Comparisons also benefited from the absence of acquisition charges of $3.6 million ($0.12 a share) recorded in 1998; pretax income rose 72%. After taxes at 36.6%, versus 44.7%, net income nearly doubled to $15.2 million ($0.55 a share, on 7.8% more shares), from $7.7 million ($0.30).

Stock Performance - 08-OCT-99

In the past 30 trading days, ALO's shares have declined 3%, compared to a 0.91% fall in the S&P 500. Average trading volume for the past five days was 207,900 shares, compared with the 40-day moving average of 171,503 shares.

Key Stock Statistics

Dividend Rate/Share	0.18	Shareholders	1,000
Shs. outstg. (M)	27.5	Market cap. (B)	$0.583
Avg. daily vol. (M)	0.205	Inst. holdings	0%
Tang. Bk. Value/Share	NM		
Beta	0.26		

Value of $10,000 invested 5 years ago: $ 24,186

Fiscal Year Ending Dec. 31

	1999	1998	1997	1996	1995	1994
Revenues (Million $)						
1Q	156.8	126.6	121.4	127.8	126.1	107.4
2Q	163.8	139.5	119.0	121.2	123.8	111.0
3Q	—	164.3	125.2	122.4	132.4	117.4
4Q	—	174.2	134.6	114.7	138.6	133.5
Yr.	—	604.6	500.3	486.2	520.9	469.3
Earnings Per Share ($)						
1Q	**0.27**	**0.21**	**0.10**	**0.21**	0.18	0.16
2Q	**0.28**	**0.09**	**0.16**	**-0.21**	0.14	0.13
3Q	—	**0.28**	**0.22**	Nil	0.29	0.19
4Q	—	**0.32**	**0.26**	**-0.54**	0.26	-0.56
Yr.	—	**0.92**	**0.76**	**-0.53**	**0.87**	**-0.08**

Next earnings report expected: late October

Dividend Data (Dividends have been paid since 1984.)

Amount ($)	Date Decl.	Ex-Div. Date	Stock of Record	Payment Date
0.045	Dec. 09	Jan. 06	Jan. 08	Jan. 22 '99
0.045	Mar. 19	Apr. 07	Apr. 09	Apr. 23 '99
0.045	Jun. 11	Jul. 07	Jul. 09	Jul. 23 '99
0.045	Oct. 04	Oct. 06	Oct. 08	Oct. 22 '99

A Division of The McGraw-Hill Companies

ALPHARMA INC.

Business Summary - 08-SEP-99

This multinational pharmaceutical firm's strategy is to strengthen its market leadership positions, expand its geographic presence, and develop and/or acquire critical mass in key markets and technologies. Alpharma is the largest manufacturer of generic liquid and topical pharmaceuticals in the U.S., is a leading maker of specialty antibiotics, and has an established and growing market position in finished pharmaceuticals in Europe and the Far East.

ALO's organizational structure consists of five divisions: U.S. Pharmaceuticals ($178.8 million in 1998 revenues), International Pharmaceuticals ($193.1 million), Fine Chemicals ($53.0 million), Animal Health ($166.3 million), and Aquatic Animal Health ($19.0 million).

The U.S. Pharmaceuticals Division develops, manufactures, and markets generic prescription and over-the-counter (OTC) pharmaceuticals under the Alpharma, Barre, and NMC labels, as well as private labels. This division produces approximately 170 products in the following categories: liquid pharmaceuticals, including cough and cold remedies; creams, lotions, and ointments; and suppositories, aerosols, and other specialty generic products.

The International Pharmaceuticals Division produces and sells approximately 290 prescription and OTC products in tablet, ointment, cream, liquid, suppository, and injectable dosage formulations. This business unit has a strong marketing presence in the Nordic countries, the U.K., the Netherlands, and Indonesia. In June 1999, the company expanded into the German market with the acquisition of Isis Pharma Group, the generic drug division of Schwarz Pharma. In April 1999, ALO moved into the French market by purchasing the generic pharmaceutical business of Jumer Laboratories.

The Fine Chemicals Division develops, produces, and sells bulk antibiotics to the pharmaceutical industry for use in finished dose products sold throughout the world. This division also manufactures active ingredients for use in human and veterinary pharmaceuticals produced by third parties.

ALO's Animal Health Division is a leading worldwide supplier of feed additives to the poultry and swine industries. The Aquatic Animal Health Division is a leader in the manufacture and marketing of vaccines for use in immunizing farmed fish.

In July 1999, shareholders of Ascent Pediatrics approved an alliance with Alpharma, whereby ALO would provide Ascent with financing and would also have an option to acquire Ascent in the first-half of 2002. This transaction provides ALO with a branded pediatric product line for its U.S. Pharmaceuticals unit.

Norway-based A.L. Industrier (ALI) owns all of ALO's Class B common stock, or 35.2% of the company's total common stock outstanding. The Class B shares give ALI the right to elect a majority of ALO's directors and to cast a majority of the proxy votes.

Per Share Data ($) (Year Ended Dec. 31)	1998	1997	1996	1995	1994	1993	1992	1991	1990	1989
Tangible Bk. Val.	NM	3.50	3.04	3.55	2.43	3.22	4.07	1.49	2.26	1.63
Cash Flow	2.37	2.12	0.92	2.29	0.77	0.93	1.16	0.85	1.33	1.09
Earnings	0.92	0.76	-0.53	0.86	-0.08	0.40	0.62	0.30	0.84	0.71
Dividends	0.18	0.18	0.18	0.18	0.18	0.18	0.17	0.16	0.11	0.09
Payout Ratio	20%	24%	NM	21%	NM	45%	34%	54%	13%	12%
Prices - High	36 7/8	23 7/8	27 3/8	26 3/8	20 5/8	29 3/8	28 1/2	24 3/4	17	12 1/4
- Low	18 7/8	11 3/8	10 5/8	16 1/2	12 5/8	12 3/4	18	14 3/8	11 1/4	8 5/8
P/E Ratio - High	40	31	NM	31	NM	73	46	83	20	17
- Low	21	15	NM	19	NM	32	29	48	13	12
Income Statement Analysis (Million $)										
Revs.	605	500	486	521	469	338	295	291	275	266
Oper. Inc.	103	77.8	35.4	83.5	34.3	32.4	38.3	24.3	41.9	37.5
Depr.	38.1	30.9	31.5	31.0	18.3	11.5	9.8	9.2	8.3	6.4
Int. Exp.	25.6	18.6	20.0	22.0	16.1	6.9	10.3	12.3	11.9	11.7
Pretax Inc.	39.0	27.8	-16.3	30.2	1.7	14.8	17.6	7.7	22.7	20.5
Eff. Tax Rate	38%	37%	NM	38%	198%	42%	35%	34%	38%	42%
Net Inc.	24.2	17.4	-11.5	18.8	-1.7	8.6	11.4	5.1	14.1	11.8
Balance Sheet & Other Fin. Data (Million $)										
Cash	14.4	11.0	15.9	18.4	15.5	8.4	5.6	4.2	8.5	2.8
Curr. Assets	335	274	275	283	250	176	155	160	148	126
Total Assets	909	632	613	635	592	423	372	359	328	290
Curr. Liab.	170	134	156	169	155	125	87.0	106	96.0	78.0
LT Debt	429	224	234	220	220	82.0	74.0	119	101	102
Common Eqty.	267	238	186	205	181	185	184	114	111	93.0
Total Cap.	728	489	450	456	429	290	281	250	230	210
Cap. Exp.	31.3	27.8	30.9	24.8	44.3	20.6	16.9	10.5	13.2	18.0
Cash Flow	62.3	48.3	20.0	49.8	16.6	20.1	21.1	14.3	22.4	18.2
Curr. Ratio	2.0	2.0	1.8	1.7	1.6	1.4	1.8	1.5	1.5	1.6
% LT Debt of Cap.	58.9	45.8	52.0	48.2	51.3	28.2	26.2	47.8	44.1	48.3
% Net Inc.of Revs.	4.0	3.5	NM	3.6	NM	2.5	3.9	1.7	5.1	4.4
% Ret. on Assets	3.1	2.8	NM	5.7	NM	2.2	2.8	1.5	4.6	4.3
% Ret. on Equity	9.6	8.2	NM	9.7	NM	4.7	6.9	4.5	13.8	13.5

Data as orig reptd.; bef. results of disc opers/spec. items. Per share data adj. for stk. divs. Bold denotes diluted EPS (FASB 128)-prior periods restated. E-Estimated. NA-Not Available. NM-Not Meaningful. NR-Not Ranked.

Office—One Executive Drive, Fort Lee, NJ 07024. **Reincorporated**—in Delaware in 1983. **Tel**—(201) 947-7774. **Website**—http://www.alpharma.com **Chrmn**—E. W. Sissener. **Pres & CEO**—G. W. Munthe. **VP-Fin & CFO**—J. E. Smith. **Secy**—B. P. Hecht. **Treas**—A. N. Marchio, II. **VP & Investor Contact**—Diane M. Cady. **Dirs**—O. A. Broymer, I. R. Cohen, T. G. Gibian, G. E. Hess, E. Hornnaess, G.W. Munthe, E. W. Sissener, E. G. Tandberg, P. G. Tombros.**Transfer Agent & Registrar**—First National Bank of Boston. **Incorporated**—in Delaware in 1983; predecessor incorporated in New Jersey in 1975. **Empl**— 3,000. **S&P Analyst:** Frank DiLorenzo

STANDARD &POOR'S
STOCK REPORTS

Amcast Industrial

NYSE Symbol **AIZ**

In S&P SmallCap 600

09-OCT-99

Industry: Manufacturing (Diversified)

Summary: Amcast is a leading manufacturer of technology-intensive metal products, mainly flow control products and engineered components.

Quantitative Evaluations

Outlook (1 Lowest—5 Highest)
• **4+**

Fair Value
• **17¾**

Risk
• **Average**

Earn./Div. Rank
• **B**

Technical Eval.
• **Bearish** since 8/99

Rel. Strength Rank (1 Lowest—99 Highest)
• **18**

Insider Activity
• **NA**

Recent Price • 13¼ | 52 Wk Range • 22-12¾ | Yield • 4.2% | 12-Mo. P/E • 6.4

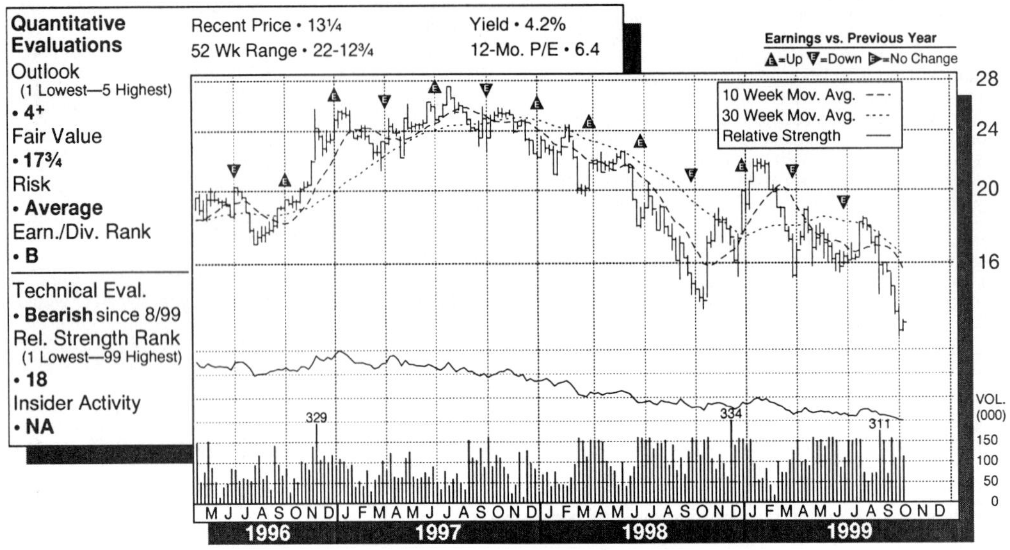

Business Profile - 29-JUL-99

Demand for the company's products in both its flow control and engineered components segments remained strong in the FY 99 (Aug.) third quarter. However, production costs increased due to operating inefficiencies caused by high turnover of skilled labor in two Midwest plants, as well as the launch of new suspension products at the company's newest plant in Ohio. While there will be some continuing impact in the fourth quarter, AIZ is optimistic about resuming the upward trend in profitability of the engineered components segment. In October 1998, the company sold its Superior Valve Co. unit. In December 1998, directors approved the repurchase of up to 750,000 company common shares.

Operational Review - 29-JUL-99

Net sales in the first nine months of FY 99 (Aug.) rose 1.9%, year to year, reflecting strong markets for the company's copper and brass plumbing fittings, aluminum automobile wheels, and performance-critical aluminum automotive components. Gross margins widened slightly on operating efficiencies and improvements; in the absence of a $9.8 million restructuring charge, pretax income climbed 35%. After taxes at 38.8%, versus 28.3%, net income was up 15%, to $18,270,000 ($1.98 a share), from $15,853,000 ($1.71, before a charge of $0.93 for the cumulative effect of an accounting change).

Stock Performance - 08-OCT-99

In the past 30 trading days, AIZ's shares have declined 16%, compared to a 0.91% fall in the S&P 500. Average trading volume for the past five days was 22,320 shares, compared with the 40-day moving average of 30,844 shares.

Key Stock Statistics

Dividend Rate/Share	0.56	Shareholders	6,819
Shs. outstg. (M)	9.1	Market cap. (B)	$0.121
Avg. daily vol. (M)	0.030	Inst. holdings	48%
Tang. Bk. Value/Share	12.30		
Beta	0.66		

Value of $10,000 invested 5 years ago: $ 7,387

Fiscal Year Ending Aug. 31

	1999	1998	1997	1996	1995	1994
Revenues (Million $)						
1Q	146.0	141.0	90.79	86.47	77.00	60.33
2Q	141.7	137.0	91.33	81.80	81.76	67.70
3Q	157.8	159.3	106.2	87.57	86.40	70.90
4Q	—	137.2	98.71	88.11	83.08	72.93
Yr.	—	574.4	387.1	343.9	328.2	271.9
Earnings Per Share ($)						
1Q	**1.09**	**0.49**	0.48	0.47	0.43	0.32
2Q	**0.49**	**0.61**	0.24	0.46	0.50	0.42
3Q	**0.41**	**0.61**	0.50	0.34	0.55	0.51
4Q	—	**0.10**	0.28	0.58	0.54	0.47
Yr.	—	**1.81**	**1.48**	1.85	2.02	1.72

Next earnings report expected: mid October

Dividend Data (Dividends have been paid since 1936.)

Amount ($)	Date Decl.	Ex-Div. Date	Stock of Record	Payment Date
0.140	Oct. 21	Nov. 27	Dec. 01	Dec. 16 '98
0.140	Feb. 25	Mar. 09	Mar. 11	Mar. 26 '99
0.140	May. 26	Jun. 08	Jun. 10	Jun. 25 '99
0.140	Aug. 26	Sep. 08	Sep. 10	Sep. 27 '99

A Division of The McGraw-Hill Companies

STANDARD
&POOR'S
STOCK REPORTS

Amcast Industrial Corporation

09-OCT-99

Business Summary - 29-JUL-99

Amcast (AIZ) is a leading manufacturer of technology-intensive metal products. It has two business segments: brand name flow control products marketed through national distribution channels; and engineered components for original equipment manufacturers. Sales in FY 98 (Aug.) were obtained as follows: flow control products, 32%; engineered components (U.S.), 39%; and engineered components (foreign), 29%.

Amcast serves three major sectors of the economy: automotive (68%), construction (25%), and industrial (7%).

The company's flow control business is a leading supplier of pipe fittings for the industrial, commercial, and residential construction markets. These products are sold through distributors and wholesalers. Shipments are primarily made by truck from company locations directly to customers.

The engineered components segment produces cast and fabricated metal products principally for sale to original equipment manufacturers in the transportation, construction, air conditioning, refrigeration and aerospace industries. Products made by the North American operations include castings for suspension, air conditioning and anti-lock braking systems, master cylinders, differential carriers, brake calipers and cast aluminum wheels for use on automobiles and light trucks, and parts for use in heating and air conditioning systems.

The August 1997 and April 1998 acquisitions of Speedline and Lee Brass Co. significantly contributed to sales and earnings. Sales from the two companies boosted total sales 53% in the third quarter and 45% in the first nine months of FY 98. The acquisition of Speedline significantly broadened AIZ's line of aluminum wheel products, and established a European launching pad for its aluminum automotive underbody components. Speedline makes light-alloy wheels for Audi, Fiat, Mercedes-Benz, Rolls-Royce, and other European automakers.

Sales to GM accounted for 26% of total sales in FY 98, versus 36% in FY 97.

In October 1998, Amcast sold Superior Valve Co., which produces specialty valves for compressed gas and commercial refrigeration markets, for $35.6 million in cash. The unit had been part of the company's flow control business, and had FY 98 sales of $42 million. A $9 million gain was realized on the transaction.

Per Share Data ($) (Year Ended Aug. 31)	1998	1997	1996	1995	1994	1993	1992	1991	1990	1989
Tangible Bk. Val.	10.67	13.23	15.80	14.52	12.70	11.46	11.01	10.33	8.93	10.88
Cash Flow	5.28	3.86	3.88	3.71	3.24	2.88	3.55	2.90	-0.20	2.58
Earnings	1.81	1.50	1.85	2.02	1.72	1.44	1.66	1.04	-1.97	1.12
Dividends	0.56	0.42	0.56	0.54	0.49	0.48	0.48	0.48	0.48	0.47
Payout Ratio	31%	28%	30%	27%	28%	33%	29%	46%	NM	42%
Prices - High	24½	27½	25¾	22¼	25⅞	22½	25	21¾	12½	13⅝
- Low	13⅞	21¼	16⅜	16¾	19⅜	15½	11⅝	6	6¼	10⅞
P/E Ratio - High	14	18	14	11	15	16	15	21	NM	12
- Low	8	14	9	8	11	11	7	6	NM	10
Income Statement Analysis (Million $)										
Revs.	574	387	344	328	272	223	237	271	274	329
Oper. Inc.	67.8	47.7	44.8	41.4	36.0	30.9	34.9	27.2	22.0	30.4
Depr.	32.1	20.5	17.4	14.4	12.8	12.0	13.6	12.1	12.0	10.5
Int. Exp.	15.0	5.1	2.4	1.4	1.6	2.1	3.3	4.7	4.7	5.1
Pretax Inc.	23.0	20.0	24.7	26.1	22.1	18.8	18.7	10.9	-19.8	12.4
Eff. Tax Rate	27%	35%	36%	34%	35%	36%	36%	38%	NM	35%
Net Inc.	16.8	13.0	15.9	17.2	14.5	12.1	12.0	6.7	-13.4	8.0
Balance Sheet & Other Fin. Data (Million $)										
Cash	7.0	9.6	5.4	1.3	15.4	2.3	3.1	1.6	1.7	1.0
Curr. Assets	223	203	109	103	97.0	75.0	74.0	91.0	94.0	101
Total Assets	563	509	509	229	194	177	174	179	185	195
Curr. Liab.	136	177	425	55.2	48.8	38.8	41.2	46.4	53.1	54.2
LT Debt	218	145	58.8	29.7	13.9	17.9	22.3	40.4	41.2	33.0
Common Eqty.	161	158	136	124	110	99	94.4	69.3	67.4	90.0
Total Cap.	404	303	207	161	128	119	117	116	113	134
Cap. Exp.	46.8	40.3	48.6	41.7	15.6	14.0	23.8	9.9	16.7	17.6
Cash Flow	48.9	33.4	33.4	31.6	27.3	24.1	25.6	18.8	-1.4	18.6
Curr. Ratio	1.6	1.1	2.1	1.9	2.0	1.9	1.8	2.0	1.8	1.9
% LT Debt of Cap.	53.9	47.8	28.4	18.4	10.9	15.1	19.0	34.9	36.5	24.7
% Net Inc.of Revs.	2.9	3.4	4.6	5.2	5.3	5.4	5.1	2.5	NM	2.4
% Ret. on Assets	3.1	3.3	6.4	8.1	7.8	6.9	5.9	3.8	NM	4.2
% Ret. on Equity	10.5	8.8	12.2	14.7	13.8	12.4	13.0	10.0	NM	9.0

Data as orig reptd.; bef. results of disc opers/spec. items. Per share data adj. for stk. divs. Bold denotes diluted EPS (FASB 128)-prior periods restated. E-Estimated. NA-Not Available. NM-Not Meaningful. NR-Not Ranked.

Office—7887 Washington Village Dr., Dayton, OH 45459. **Tel**—(937) 291-7000. **Website**—http://www.amcast.com **Chrmn, Pres & CEO**—J. H. Shuey. **VP-Fin**—D. D. Watts. **VP & Secy**—D. G. Daly. **Investor Contact**—Michael Higgins (937-291-7015). **Dirs**—J. K. Baker, W. E. Blankley, P. H. Forster, I. W. Gorr, L. W. Ladehoff, E. T. O'Loughlin, W. G. Roth, J. H. Shuey, R. W. Van Sant. **Transfer Agent & Registrar**—First Chicago Trust Co. **Incorporated**—in Ohio in 1869. **Empl**— 5,000. **S&P Analyst:** P.D.W

STANDARD
&POOR'S
STOCK REPORTS

AMCOL International

NYSE Symbol **ACO**

In S&P SmallCap 600

09-OCT-99

Industry: Manufacturing (Diversified)

Summary: This company is a specialty chemical and mineral producer that primarily makes liquid-absorbing products.

Quantitative Evaluations

Outlook (1 Lowest—5 Highest)
• **4+**

Fair Value
• **19¼**

Risk
• **NA**

Earn./Div. Rank
• **A**

Technical Eval.
• **Bearish** since 9/99

Rel. Strength Rank (1 Lowest—99 Highest)
• **64**

Insider Activity
• **NA**

Recent Price • 14⅛
52 Wk Range • 15⅜-8
Yield • 2.0%
12-Mo. P/E • 14.7

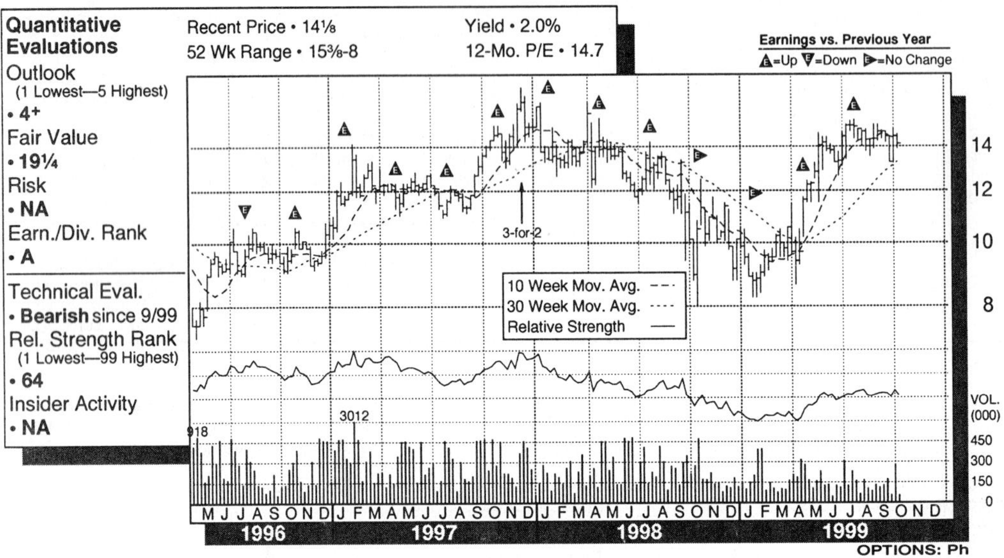

Business Profile - 13-JUL-99

In May 1999, AMCOL reported that it has positive prospects for the remainder of 1999 and expects both sales growth and profit improvement in the absorbent polymers, minerals and environmental segments. For 1999, AMCOL anticipates approximately 7% sales growth, 22% growth in operating profit and about 25% growth in net income. In May 1999, AMCOL acquired a 20% interest in the Indian company, Ashapura Minechem, Ltd. Terms were not disclosed, but ACO noted that Ashapura's high-quality mineral deposits, strategic location and technological expertise provide a strong foundation for future growth.

Operational Review - 13-JUL-99

Net sales for the three months ended March 31, 1999, increased 6.1%, year to year, due to higher sales in the absorbent polymers, environmental and transportation segments, partially offset by lower sales in the minerals division. Profitability benefited from lower raw material costs in the absorbent polymers segment, the sale of the U.S. Fuller's Earth business in 1998 and divestiture of two underperforming facilities and favorable weather in the environmental segment. Operating income advanced 24%. Following 11% lower interest expense (net), net income rose 66%, to $5.7 million ($0.21 a share), from $3.5 million ($0.12).

Stock Performance - 08-OCT-99

In the past 30 trading days, ACO's shares have declined 2%, compared to a 0.91% fall in the S&P 500. Average trading volume for the past five days was 10,720 shares, compared with the 40-day moving average of 25,849 shares.

Key Stock Statistics

Dividend Rate/Share	0.28	Shareholders	3,515
Shs. outstg. (M)	26.7	Market cap. (B)	$0.378
Avg. daily vol. (M)	0.028	Inst. holdings	37%
Tang. Bk. Value/Share	6.17		
Beta	0.20		

Value of $10,000 invested 5 years ago: $ 10,282

Fiscal Year Ending Dec. 31

	1999	1998	1997	1996	1995	1994
Revenues (Million $)						
1Q	129.0	121.6	107.9	85.54	78.75	57.85
2Q	141.9	125.6	113.5	96.76	83.66	64.01
3Q	—	137.4	126.1	109.5	92.98	71.98
4Q	—	136.9	129.5	113.5	92.30	71.61
Yr.	—	521.5	477.1	405.4	347.7	265.4
Earnings Per Share ($)						
1Q	**0.21**	**0.12**	**0.11**	0.04	0.13	0.09
2Q	**0.29**	**0.20**	**0.15**	0.10	0.16	0.11
3Q	—	**0.24**	**0.24**	0.20	0.17	0.15
4Q	—	**0.23**	**0.23**	0.18	0.15	0.17
Yr.	—	**0.78**	**0.72**	**0.52**	**0.60**	0.52

Next earnings report expected: mid October

Dividend Data (Dividends have been paid since 1937.)

Amount ($)	Date Decl.	Ex-Div. Date	Stock of Record	Payment Date
0.060	Nov. 06	Dec. 03	Dec. 07	Jan. 04 '99
0.060	Feb. 04	Feb. 18	Feb. 22	Mar. 05 '99
0.070	May. 11	May. 20	May. 24	Jun. 07 '99
0.070	Aug. 11	Aug. 19	Aug. 23	Sep. 07 '99

A Division of The McGraw-Hill Companies

AMCOL International Corp.

Business Summary - 13-JUL-99

AMCOL International Corp., produces and markets a range of specialty minerals and chemicals used for industrial, environmental and consumer-related applications.

In February 1999, the company reported that it intends to focus on research and development, improved resource management, operational efficiency and global penetration. ACO pointed out that cost control is a top priority for its global operations. As part of this effort, it intends to monitor its operations in order to identify cost reduction opportunities and adopt effective practices for use in other locations. The company also indicated that it will grow revenues by enlarging operations in Southeast Asia, Latin America and Europe. ACO believes that it can capitalize on low costs associated with these regions and enjoy greater returns as global economies recover.

Net sales by operating segment in 1998 were divided: absorbent polymers, 42%; minerals, 32%; environmental, 20%; and transportation, 6.0%.

The absorbent polymers segment produces superabsorbent polymers (SAP), a category of polymers known for extremely high water absorbency. SAPs, which are composed of acrylic acid, potassium, sodium alkalis and catalysts, are produced in the company's U.S. and U.K. facilities. Most SAP sales are for use as an absorbent in personal care products, such as diapers and feminine hygiene products.

The minerals segment produces two types of bentonite (a montmorillonite clay), sodium bentonite and calcium bentonite. Sodium bentonite is commonly called western bentonite, due to its occurrence in the Western U.S., and calcium bentonite is also known as Fuller's Earth. Uses for bentonite include: metalcasting molds, well drilling stabilizers, cat litter products, cosmetic and pharmaceutical applications and livestock feed agents. At 1998 consumption rates and product mix, ACO estimates its proven reserves of commercially usable sodium bentonite at 30 years and its proven calcium bentonite reserves at 20 years.

The environmental segment sells sodium bentonite and other products for use in environmental and construction applications. Uses include: lining and capping landfills and containment in tank farms, waste lagoons, leach pads, slurry walls and wetlands reclamation projects.

ACO's transportation segment operates a long-haul trucking business and freight brokerage business, primarily for delivery of the company's products in the U.S. After dropping off ACO's products, the transportation segment offers to haul third party products on return trips.

In January 1999, ACO reported that it is confident that its nanocomposites business, which is not yet reporting as a separate segment, will contribute to the company's future growth as it develops ways to enhance plastics by using additive minerals.

Per Share Data ($) (Year Ended Dec. 31)	1998	1997	1996	1995	1994	1993	1992	1991	1990	1989
Tangible Bk. Val.	5.77	5.53	5.13	4.69	4.47	4.31	2.13	2.09	1.96	1.85
Cash Flow	1.94	1.82	1.47	1.32	0.99	0.91	0.74	0.55	0.49	0.55
Earnings	0.78	0.72	0.52	0.60	0.52	0.51	0.34	0.17	0.10	0.21
Dividends	0.23	0.21	0.19	0.17	0.16	0.13	0.11	0.10	0.10	0.10
Payout Ratio	29%	29%	36%	29%	31%	26%	30%	57%	97%	45%
Prices - High	$16\frac{3}{8}$	$17\frac{1}{4}$	$11\frac{3}{8}$	$12\frac{1}{8}$	$16\frac{7}{8}$	22	$6\frac{1}{4}$	$2\frac{7}{8}$	3	$3\frac{1}{2}$
- Low	8	$10\frac{1}{8}$	$7\frac{1}{8}$	$7\frac{7}{8}$	7	6	$2\frac{5}{8}$	$1\frac{5}{8}$	$1\frac{15}{16}$	$2\frac{1}{8}$
P/E Ratio - High	21	24	22	20	32	43	19	17	29	16
- Low	10	14	14	13	13	12	8	10	19	10
Income Statement Analysis (Million $)										
Revs.	522	477	405	348	265	219	183	149	132	125
Oper. Inc.	75.3	73.4	60.2	53.7	37.6	31.6	26.3	18.8	17.3	18.7
Depr.	33.1	31.9	27.9	21.3	13.6	10.5	9.8	9.2	9.1	8.1
Int. Exp.	7.9	8.6	8.4	6.7	3.0	3.0	3.5	4.4	4.8	4.5
Pretax Inc.	34.4	32.4	23.2	26.9	22.2	18.8	12.7	5.5	3.3	7.1
Eff. Tax Rate	36%	35%	34%	34%	31%	30%	32%	26%	28%	29%
Net Inc.	22.1	21.0	15.2	17.8	15.3	13.1	8.5	4.0	2.4	5.0
Balance Sheet & Other Fin. Data (Million $)										
Cash	2.8	3.1	3.0	1.9	10.4	20.5	3.5	2.9	2.9	2.4
Curr. Assets	164	150	148	126	106	93.0	60.2	60.1	54.2	51.5
Total Assets	358	351	351	322	261	181	127	127	125	121
Curr. Liab.	74.1	67.2	51.9	35.9	36.6	27.4	21.1	20.8	14.2	16.0
LT Debt	96.3	94.4	119	117	71.5	16.7	38.3	43.8	47.8	43.7
Common Eqty.	173	176	167	155	141	125	55.6	54.4	52.7	51.2
Total Cap.	277	277	293	279	218	147	99	100	103	98.0
Cap. Exp.	37.7	32.7	34.3	62.8	81.0	32.1	11.3	7.9	8.5	14.4
Cash Flow	55.2	53.0	43.1	39.1	28.9	23.7	18.3	13.2	11.4	13.2
Curr. Ratio	2.2	2.2	2.9	3.5	2.9	3.4	2.9	2.9	3.8	3.2
% LT Debt of Cap.	34.8	34.1	40.6	41.9	32.8	11.3	38.6	43.9	46.4	44.7
% Net Inc.of Revs.	4.2	4.4	3.8	5.1	5.8	6.0	4.7	2.7	1.8	4.0
% Ret. on Assets	6.2	6.0	4.5	6.1	6.9	7.9	6.7	3.2	1.9	4.3
% Ret. on Equity	12.7	12.3	9.4	11.9	11.4	13.7	15.4	7.5	4.5	10.1

Data as orig reptd.; bef. results of disc opers/spec. items. Per share data adj. for stk. divs. Bold denotes diluted EPS (FASB 128)-prior periods restated. E-Estimated. NA-Not Available. NM-Not Meaningful. NR-Not Ranked.

Office—One North Arlington, 1500 W. Shure Dr., Suite 500, Arlington Heights, IL 60004-7803. **Tel**—(847) 394-8730. **Fax**—(847) 506-6199. **Website**—http://www.amcol.com **Email**—invest@amcol.com **Chrmn & CEO**—J. Hughes. **Pres & COO**—L. E. Washow. **SVP & CFO**—P. G. Shelton. **Secy**—C. O. Redman. **Investor Contact**—Jodi Warner. **Dirs**—A. Brown, R. E. Driscoll III, J. Hughes, J. A. McClung, J. D. Proops, C. E. Ray, C. O. Redman, P. G. Shelton, D. E. Stahl, L. E. Washow, A. L.Weaver, P. C. Weaver. **Transfer Agent**—Harris Trust & Savings Bank, Chicago, Illinois. **Incorporated**—in Delaware in 1959. **Empl**— 1,625. **S&P Analyst:** J. F.

STANDARD
&POOR'S
STOCK REPORTS

American Freightways

Nasdaq Symbol **AFWY**

In S&P SmallCap 600

09-OCT-99 **Industry:** Truckers

Summary: This non-union less-than-truckload (LTL) motor carrier provides all-points regional and interregional service in 32 states, Canada, Mexico and Latin America.

S&P Opinion: Accumulate (★★★★)

Recent Price • 15⅝
52 Wk Range • 24⅜-6½
Yield • Nil
12-Mo. P/E • 13.7

Quantitative Evaluations

Outlook (1 Lowest—5 Highest)
• **5**

Fair Value
• **28¼**

Risk
• **Average**

Earn./Div. Rank
• **B**

Technical Eval.
• **Bearish** since 9/99

Rel. Strength Rank (1 Lowest—99 Highest)
• **12**

Insider Activity
• **Unfavorable**

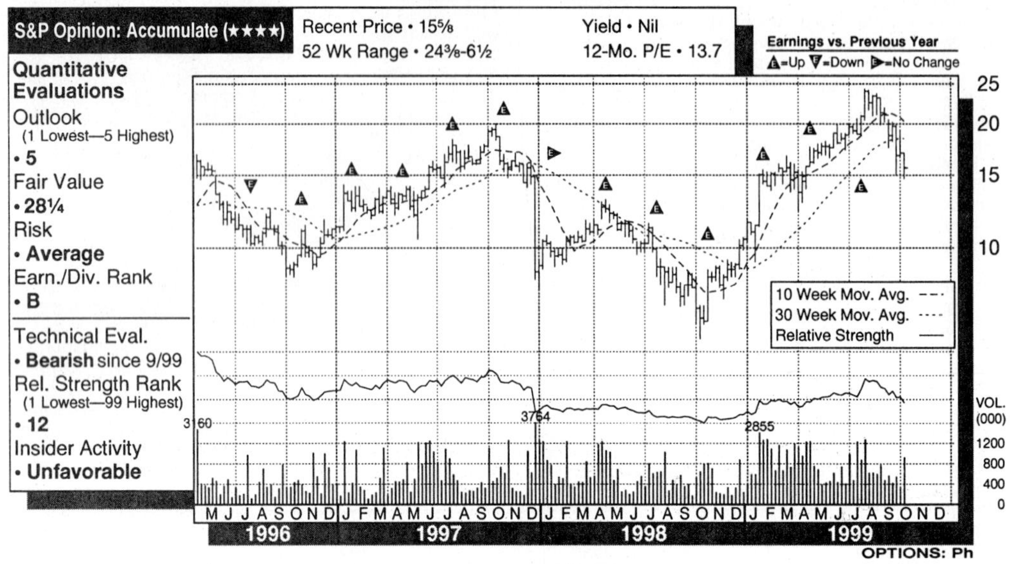

OPTIONS: Ph

Overview - 07-SEP-99

Revenue growth in 1999 is projected at 14%, slightly faster than 1998's 13.3% pace. Total tonnage handled is projected to rise about 10%, somewhat faster than 1998's 9.2%, and well above industry trends. AFWY will benefit from the April 1999 start of all-points service to New Jersey and Pennsylvania. AFWY also is adding North and South Dakota in October 1999. In 1998, the company launched service to Michigan, and, through affiliated carriers, to Hawaii and Alaska; Central and South America were added in June 1999. Operating margins should widen. Unit labor costs will ease, as recently implemented cost cutting programs provide productivity gains. Operating taxes, communications and utilities will grow in line with revenues. Depreciation charges will increase less rapidly, as AFWY acquires more equipment through lease. Insurance costs are seen increasing more rapidly. Fuel prices will be higher in 1999. Rates will remain firm in 1999, with AFWY realizing a 4% net price increase.

Valuation - 07-SEP-99

The shares of this regional LTL carrier have climbed sharply since late 1998, outperforming most of its peers. AFWY was hammered by investors who apparently anticipated a recession in 1999 stemming from problems in Asia and Russia. AFWY's P/E multiple has expanded, as the company ramps up its expansion program after slowing its growth between 1996 and 1998, when costs spun out of control. Service is being added to four new states in 1999. While the shares were recently sporting a P/E multiple about 25% above that accorded the stock of other truckers, its price to EBITDA was less than a 10% premium. Moreover, AFWY's price to growth rate (0.87) is at a 20% discount to other truckers. We think the stock is attractively priced, and merits accumulation.

Key Stock Statistics

S&P EPS Est. 1999	1.35	Tang. Bk. Value/Share	8.72
P/E on S&P Est. 1999	11.6	Beta	0.79
S&P EPS Est. 2000	1.50	Shareholders	3,184
Dividend Rate/Share	Nil	Market cap. (B)	$0.499
Shs. outstg. (M)	31.9	Inst. holdings	41%
Avg. daily vol. (M)	0.109		

Value of $10,000 invested 5 years ago: $ 7,911

Fiscal Year Ending Dec. 31

	1999	1998	1997	1996	1995	1994
Revenues (Million $)						
1Q	265.4	230.7	193.1	166.2	132.5	99.3
2Q	291.2	246.4	219.1	181.1	142.0	123.7
3Q	—	254.1	233.8	192.5	149.4	124.1
4Q	—	255.2	224.4	189.3	148.2	118.5
Yr.	—	986.3	870.3	729.0	572.1	465.6
Earnings Per Share ($)						
1Q	**0.21**	**0.10**	**0.05**	**0.02**	0.20	0.14
2Q	**0.40**	**0.24**	**0.22**	**0.09**	0.26	0.32
3Q	**E0.35**	**0.26**	**0.25**	**0.10**	0.08	0.25
4Q	**E0.39**	**0.27**	**0.05**	**0.05**	-0.12	0.19
Yr.	**E1.35**	**0.87**	**0.56**	**0.25**	**0.42**	**0.89**

Next earnings report expected: early October

Dividend Data

The company has not paid cash dividends in the past and does not intend to pay any in the foreseeable future. A shareholder rights plan was adopted in August 1998.

American Freightways Corporation

09-OCT-99

Business Summary - 07-SEP-99

American Freightways is one of the fastest growing truckers serving the less-than-truckload (LTL) segment. It was the seventh largest LTL carrier in 1998, based on revenue. AFWY is stepping up its expansion program in 1999 after deliberately slowing its for several years, in order to get profits back on track. Growth has been aided by a high level of service, and all-points coverage in states served.

AFWY, formed in 1982, is one of the few successful LTL carriers launched in the post-deregulation environment. With April 1999 expansion into New Jersey and Pennsylvania, AFWY now offers service to 32 states, primarily in the Midwest, South, Mid-Atlantic and Southwest. AFWY moves into North and South Dakota in October 1999. Service is also provided to Canada, Mexico, Puerto Rico, Alaska, Hawaii, Guam, and, since June 1999, to Central and South America, through alliances with forwarders and motor carriers.

AFWY is accelerating is growth in 1999 with the addition of all-point service to New Jersey, Pennsylvania, North and South Dakota. Its goal is eventually to offer full service to all 48 continental states. AFWY deliberately slowed its expansion in 1997 and 1998 to one state per year, after adding five states in 1996, in order to build freight densities and improve profit margins. Operating margins, which deteriorated in 1996 to 3.7%, from 10.7% in 1994, recovered to 6.1% in 1998. AFWY aims for a 10% operating margin.

AFWY restructured its linehaul process in 1996. This cut the amount of freight sent from satellite terminals to central consolidation facilities. With freight moving directly from originating service center to destination terminal, more shipments can be upgraded to next day service. Costs are also cut, as decreased handling reduced potential damage, and requires fewer dock workers.

The restructuring of the linehaul system was undertaken to help AFWY gain a larger share of short-haul regional LTL freight. and reduce transit times for more distant routes. AFWY's new, faster service, dubbed American Flyer, was formally unveiled in 1999. In 1998, 46% of shipments were next day (regional) and 40% second day. With American Flyer, AFWY hopes to boost second-day deliveries to 49% of the total. American Flyer commits AFWY to second-day delivery on routes of up to 1,500 miles. The program is unique in the LTL industry, in that the company is using a single system to handle intrastate, regional, interregional, and long-haul shipments.

AFWY differentiates itself from other carriers by offering total coverage to all points in states where it operates. To provide shippers with shipment tracing services, AFWY has installed equipment at its service centers to scan freight information as shipments are handled. Information about shipment location is fed to AFWY's network via mobile communications equipment, and accessed by shippers through AFWY's website.

At March 11, 1999, 34% of the common shares were held by members of the Garrison family.

Per Share Data ($) (Year Ended Dec. 31)	**1998**	**1997**	**1996**	**1995**	**1994**	**1993**	**1992**	**1991**	**1990**	**1989**
Tangible Bk. Val.	8.08	7.20	6.60	6.32	5.81	3.91	3.24	2.80	NA	NA
Cash Flow	2.63	2.22	1.75	1.62	1.81	1.34	1.10	0.81	NA	NA
Earnings	0.87	0.56	0.25	0.42	0.89	0.59	0.50	0.31	NA	NA
Dividends	Nil	Nil	Nil	Nil	Nil	Nil	Nil	Nil	NA	NA
Payout Ratio	Nil	Nil	Nil	Nil	Nil	Nil	Nil	Nil	NA	NA
Prices - High	13 1/8	20	16 7/8	24 1/4	24 7/8	20 1/2	12	9 3/4	NA	NA
- Low	6	7 7/8	8 1/2	9 7/8	15 1/2	11 3/8	6 3/4	4 3/4	NA	NA
P/E Ratio - High	15	36	67	58	28	35	24	32	NA	NA
- Low	7	14	34	24	17	19	14	16	NA	NA
Income Statement Analysis (Million $)										
Revs.	986	870	729	572	466	328	262	198	NA	NA
Oper. Inc.	116	97.9	74.0	69.1	77.6	52.4	43.4	30.4	NA	NA
Depr.	55.7	52.6	46.9	37.6	27.9	21.5	17.1	14.5	NA	NA
Int. Exp.	15.5	16.3	14.7	10.2	7.8	5.8	5.4	5.1	NA	NA
Pretax Inc.	46.3	29.3	12.8	21.3	43.6	27.0	22.0	12.6	NA	NA
Eff. Tax Rate	41%	39%	39%	39%	38%	38%	37%	36%	NA	NA
Net Inc.	27.5	17.8	7.9	13.1	27.0	16.8	13.9	8.0	NA	NA
Balance Sheet & Other Fin. Data (Million $)										
Cash	3.3	1.8	4.4	2.6	4.0	0.2	NA	NA	NA	NA
Curr. Assets	135	105	92.0	77.2	54.2	37.7	NA	NA	NA	NA
Total Assets	642	576	550	478	355	251	NA	NA	NA	NA
Curr. Liab.	107	78.5	66.2	52.5	44.4	35.1	NA	NA	NA	NA
LT Debt	206	210	227	189	105	89.0	NA	NA	NA	NA
Common Eqty.	256	227	206	195	177	109	NA	NA	NA	NA
Total Cap.	535	497	484	425	311	216	NA	NA	NA	NA
Cap. Exp.	94.4	67.9	107	138	116	95.0	49.0	35.0	NA	NA
Cash Flow	83.2	70.4	54.8	50.7	54.9	38.3	31.0	22.6	NA	NA
Curr. Ratio	1.3	1.3	1.4	1.5	1.2	1.1	NA	NA	NA	NA
% LT Debt of Cap.	38.5	42.3	46.9	44.5	33.7	41.2	NA	NA	NA	NA
% Net Inc.of Revs.	2.8	2.0	10.8	2.3	5.7	5.1	5.3	4.1	NA	NA
% Ret. on Assets	4.5	3.2	1.5	3.2	8.9	7.9	NA	NA	NA	NA
% Ret. on Equity	11.4	8.2	3.9	3.6	18.9	16.8	NA	NA	NA	NA

Data as orig reptd.; bef. results of disc opers/spec. items. Per share data adj. for stk. divs. Bold denotes diluted EPS (FASB 128)-prior periods restated. E-Estimated. NA-Not Available. NM-Not Meaningful. NR-Not Ranked.

Office— 2200 Forward Drive, Harrison, AR 72601.**Tel**—(870) 741-9000. **Website**—http://www.arfw.com **Chrmn**—F. S. Garrison. **Pres & CEO**—T. Garrison. **VP, Secy & Treas**—W. Garrison. **EVP, CFO & Investor Contact**—Frank Conner. **Dirs**—F. Conner, F. S. Garrison, T. Garrison, W. Garrison, J. P. Hammerschmidt, T. J. Jones, K. Reeves, W. P. Stiritz, D. Z. Williams. **Transfer Agent**—Wachovia Shareholder Services, Boston. **Incorporated**—in Arkansas in 1985. **Empl**— 13,200. **S&P Analyst:** Stephen R. Klein

STANDARD
&POOR'S
STOCK REPORTS

American Management Systems

Nasdaq Symbol **AMSY**

In S&P SmallCap 600

09-OCT-99

Industry:
Computer (Software & Services)

Summary: This company offers business and information technology consulting and systems integration services.

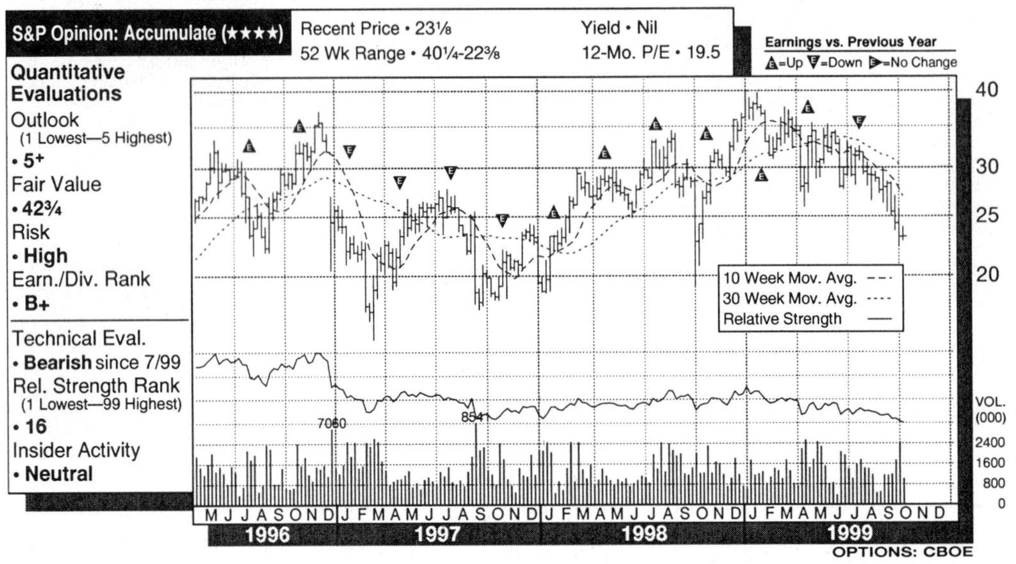

Overview - 19-JUL-99

Revenues are expected to increase nearly 20% in 1999, spurred by continued strong demand for the company's information technology services. Telecommunications revenues should rebound in 1999, following disappointing results in 1998, after a reorganization as a result of the cancellation of a major contract. Revenues in the financial services segment remain weak, but growth across all other segments should continue to be strong. The state and local government business has been particularly robust in recent quarters. International operations weakened in 1997 and in 1998, but are expected to improve in 1999. Margins should also continue to expand in 1999. Pretax margins widened more than expected in the first half of the year. EPS for the 1999 second quarter included a charge of $0.27 for an after tax reserve to cover an ongoing contract dispute.

Valuation - 19-JUL-99

Excluding a charge for a reserve related to an ongoing contract dispute, results for the second quarter would have met analyst expectations. Results in recent quarters have been boosted by strength at the state and local government business, as well as by a rebound at the telecommunications unit. The company is focusing more on electronic commerce business opportunities, which have been growing rapidly. AMSY expects its e-commerce and Internet-related revenues to double in 1999, to approximately $400 million. We expect the company to build on its historical record of growth. Much of the company's success can be attributed to AMSY's repeat business, which accounts for 85% to 90% of total revenues. With the shares recently trading at a significant discount to the P/E of the overall market, we recommend accumulating the stock.

Key Stock Statistics

S&P EPS Est. 1999	1.56	Tang. Bk. Value/Share	7.18
P/E on S&P Est. 1999	14.9	Beta	0.85
S&P EPS Est. 2000	1.90	Shareholders	1,430
Dividend Rate/Share	Nil	Market cap. (B)	$0.975
Shs. outstg. (M)	42.0	Inst. holdings	62%
Avg. daily vol. (M)	0.338		

Value of $10,000 invested 5 years ago: $ 26,415

Fiscal Year Ending Dec. 31

	1999	1998	1997	1996	1995	1994
Revenues (Million $)						
1Q	290.9	223.0	196.3	181.4	135.8	100.3
2Q	305.3	250.7	220.9	188.8	157.5	109.8
3Q	—	282.2	225.5	217.5	162.7	119.1
4Q	—	301.9	229.6	224.5	176.5	130.7
Yr.	—	1,058	872.3	812.2	632.4	459.9
Earnings Per Share ($)						
1Q	**0.37**	**0.21**	**0.14**	**0.16**	0.12	0.12
2Q	**0.10**	**0.28**	**0.18**	**0.20**	0.16	0.15
3Q	—	**0.34**	**0.11**	**0.25**	0.19	0.15
4Q	—	**0.38**	**0.31**	**-0.24**	0.25	0.18
Yr.	—	**1.21**	**0.74**	**0.37**	**0.72**	**0.60**

Next earnings report expected: mid October

Dividend Data

No cash dividends have been paid. Three-for-two stock splits were effected five times since 1985.

A Division of The McGraw-Hill Companies

American Management Systems, Incorporated

Business Summary - 19-JUL-99

American Management Systems attempts to partner with clients to achieve breakthrough performance through the intelligent use of information technology.

Through 57 offices worldwide, AMSY helps clients use information technology to improve the performance of their organizations, targeting businesses and governmental units in selected markets where the potential benefits of a technology-based solution are greatest. The company develops and integrates information systems for clients, and it develops and licenses proprietary software products.

Target markets include telecommunications (24% of 1998 services and products revenues, down from 30% in 1997), financial services (21%, 25%), state and local governments and education (27%, 20%) and the federal government (23%, 22%). Telecommunication revenues declined in 1997 and 1998, due to the cancellation of a major Swiss contract. However, revenues in the segment rose sequentially in the last three quarters of 1998.

AMSY assists telecommunications clients with order processing, billing and collections, and it helps financial institutions develop systems for risk management, credit collections and loan originations. In its government and education markets, AMSY provides services and software products for financial and revenue management and other functions.

In 1998, the company initiated a cross-target market practice that will deliver customer facing web solutions, including eBill, eCare and eMarketing. These services are intended to help clients in financial services, telecommunications, government and utilities achieve greater cost savings, improve customer service, and leverage cross-selling and up-selling opportunities.

AMSY considers its long-term relationships with clients and its development of specialized areas of expertise to be among its greatest strengths. Each year, approximately 85% to 90% of the company's business comes from clients with which AMSY had worked the year before. AMSY believes it has established a leadership position in the state and local government market by performing successfully under contracts with state taxation departments that link its own compensation with enhanced revenue collections for the state.

International business accounted for 28% of total revenues in 1997, down from 34% in 1996, due to the canceled Swiss telecom contract.

Per Share Data ($) (Year Ended Dec. 31)	1998	1997	1996	1995	1994	1993	1992	1991	1990	1989
Tangible Bk. Val.	6.84	5.60	4.81	4.21	3.33	2.65	2.35	1.96	1.54	1.32
Cash Flow	2.11	1.56	1.31	1.46	1.13	0.69	0.67	0.53	0.48	0.32
Earnings	1.21	0.74	0.37	0.72	0.60	0.46	0.45	0.33	0.31	0.16
Dividends	Nil	Nil	Nil	Nil	Nil	Nil	Nil	Nil	Nil	Nil
Payout Ratio	Nil	Nil	Nil	Nil	Nil	Nil	Nil	Nil	Nil	Nil
Prices - High	40¼	27¾	37⅛	21⅛	12⅞	10½	10½	8½	5⅞	5½
- Low	18¾	15¾	18¼	11	8	6⅝	5⅜	4⅞	3⅛	3⅛
P/E Ratio - High	33	37	46	29	21	23	23	25	19	33
- Low	15	21	23	15	13	14	12	15	10	19
Income Statement Analysis (Million $)										
Revs.	1,058	872	812	632	460	364	333	285	262	225
Oper. Inc.	129	89.0	66.9	80.9	61.0	39.0	37.1	28.0	25.2	14.8
Depr.	38.6	34.7	39.3	30.2	20.7	8.3	7.7	7.1	6.0	5.4
Int. Exp.	4.2	5.8	3.2	2.3	1.4	0.7	1.0	1.5	1.7	2.2
Pretax Inc.	87.3	51.4	26.2	49.8	39.5	30.7	29.4	21.0	19.2	9.5
Eff. Tax Rate	41%	39%	41%	41%	41%	42%	41%	38%	38%	34%
Net Inc.	51.8	31.2	15.5	29.2	23.4	17.8	17.5	13.1	12.0	6.2
Balance Sheet & Other Fin. Data (Million $)										
Cash	119	49.6	62.8	35.8	34.2	15.6	32.5	28.4	25.4	19.0
Curr. Assets	388	299	324	251	182	125	123	104	95.0	91.0
Total Assets	538	421	424	338	252	185	166	146	134	124
Curr. Liab.	181	130	199	135	92.5	57.9	50.3	47.9	47.3	41.6
LT Debt	22.7	27.9	13.7	20.4	12.9	11.0	4.4	10.0	12.3	14.0
Common Eqty.	292	239	203	176	138	99	85.5	68.9	53.5	47.5
Total Cap.	336	282	224	202	159	126	115	97.0	85.0	81.0
Cap. Exp.	10.6	15.9	27.5	22.5	17.0	13.3	7.6	9.4	6.8	7.4
Cash Flow	90.4	65.9	54.8	59.4	43.8	25.2	23.7	18.6	16.5	11.2
Curr. Ratio	2.1	2.3	1.6	1.9	2.0	2.2	2.4	2.2	2.0	2.2
% LT Debt of Cap.	6.8	9.9	6.1	10.1	8.1	8.7	3.8	10.3	14.5	17.4
% Net Inc.of Revs.	4.9	3.6	1.9	4.6	5.1	4.9	5.3	4.6	4.6	2.8
% Ret. on Assets	10.8	7.4	4.1	9.9	10.3	10.0	11.0	9.2	9.4	5.5
% Ret. on Equity	19.5	14.1	8.2	18.6	18.8	18.2	20.2	18.7	20.9	12.6

Data as orig reptd.; bef. results of disc opers/spec. items. Per share data adj. for stk. divs. Bold denotes diluted EPS (FASB 128)-prior periods restated. E-Estimated. NA-Not Available. NM-Not Meaningful. NR-Not Ranked.

Office—4050 Legato Rd., Fairfax, VA 22033. **Tel**—(703) 267-8000. **Website**—http://www.amsinc.com **Chrmn & CEO**—P. A. Brands. **EVP & CFO**—R. L. Schillereff. **Investor Contact**—Rafael Dominguez (703 267-5493).**Dirs**—D. J. Altobello, P. A. Brands, J. J. Forese, P. W. Gross, D. Leonard, W. Lewis, F. V. Malek, F. A. Nicolai, A. G Spoon. **Transfer Agent & Registrar**—ChaseMellon Shareholder Services.**Incorporated**—in Delaware in 1970. **Empl**— 8,200. **S&P Analyst:** Brian Goodstadt

American States Water

NYSE Symbol **AWR**

In S&P SmallCap 600

09-OCT-99

Industry:
Water Utilities

Summary: This water supply company serves customers in areas of southern, northern and coastal California, and provides electric service to a small section of San Bernardino County.

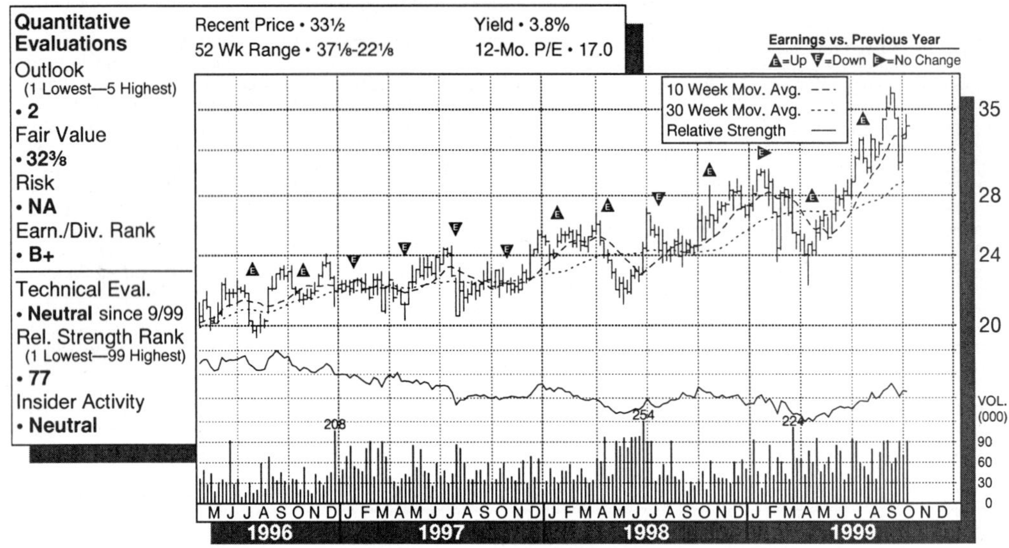

Business Profile - 07-SEP-99

In March 1999, AWR signed a three-year utility services agreement with an Arizona water utility. Also in March, the company filed applications to increase rates in four additional water rate making districts, effective January 2000. In September, AWR stated it had agreed to terms with public utility commission staff regarding its four proposed rate increases and anticipates a final decision in December. In January 1999, American States implemented increased water rates in six rate making districts covering approximately 65% of its water customers. In January 1999, the company issued $40 million of medium term notes to repay bank debt, which funded capital expenditures. Directors increased the quarterly cash dividend 1.6%, to $0.32 a share from $0.315, with the March 1, 1999, payment.

Operational Review - 07-SEP-99

Operating revenues for the six months ended June 30, 1999, rose 20%, year to year, reflecting increased water sales volumes, primarily due to much drier and warmer weather, and general rate increases. Profitability benefited from the growth in revenues and smaller increases in water purchased expenses and the cost of power purchased for pumping. Following 9.0% higher interest charges, net income climbed 60%, to $7,383,000 ($0.82 a share, after preferred dividends) from $4,610,000 ($0.51).

Stock Performance - 08-OCT-99

In the past 30 trading days, AWR's shares have declined 2%, compared to a 0.91% fall in the S&P 500. Average trading volume for the past five days was 19,380 shares, compared with the 40-day moving average of 17,226 shares.

Key Stock Statistics

Dividend Rate/Share	1.28	Shareholders	3,874
Shs. outstg. (M)	9.0	Market cap. (B)	$0.300
Avg. daily vol. (M)	0.016	Inst. holdings	26%
Tang. Bk. Value/Share	21.30		
Beta	0.48		

Value of $10,000 invested 5 years ago: $ 20,687

Fiscal Year Ending Dec. 31

	1999	1998	1997	1996	1995	1994
Revenues (Million $)						
1Q	36.13	29.96	32.21	30.40	24.95	24.18
2Q	42.12	35.00	39.34	39.89	32.37	30.49
3Q	—	47.00	45.70	45.22	39.53	38.69
4Q	—	36.10	36.51	36.02	32.93	29.31
Yr.	—	148.1	153.8	151.5	129.8	122.7
Earnings Per Share ($)						
1Q	**0.33**	**0.20**	**0.14**	**0.27**	0.14	0.15
2Q	**0.49**	**0.31**	**0.34**	**0.52**	0.38	0.29
3Q	—	**0.71**	**0.67**	**0.68**	0.67	0.66
4Q	—	**0.40**	**0.40**	**0.22**	0.34	0.33
Yr.	—	**1.62**	**1.56**	**1.69**	**1.54**	1.43

Next earnings report expected: late October

Dividend Data (Dividends have been paid since 1931.)

Amount ($)	Date Decl.	Ex-Div. Date	Stock of Record	Payment Date
0.315	Oct. 27	Nov. 05	Nov. 09	Dec. 01 '98
0.320	Jan. 26	Feb. 04	Feb. 08	Mar. 01 '99
0.320	Apr. 26	May. 06	May. 10	Jun. 01 '99
0.320	Jul. 26	Aug. 05	Aug. 09	Sep. 01 '99

STANDARD
&POOR'S
STOCK REPORTS

American States Water Company

Business Summary - 07-SEP-99

Unlike utilities in the electric, gas and telecommunications fields, water companies are expected to retain, at least for the near term, their monopoly status, and to remain for the most part under traditional cost-of-service regulation. During 1998, American States Water Co. (AWR) moved to take advantage of long-term opportunities in unregulated business lines by adopting a holding company structure and forming American States Utility Services, Inc. (ASUS) to provide unregulated water and wastewater services.

AWR's primary operating subsidiary is Southern California Water Co. (SCW), which served 242,634 water customers and 20,865 electric customers as of the end of 1998. SCW's customer base covers 75 communities in 10 counties throughout California. AWR provides water to three regions and 21 territories. Region I covers 7 customer service areas in northern and central California. Region II, representing about 73% of SCW's water customers, covers 6 areas in Los Angeles and Orange counties. Region III covers 8 water customer service areas and the southern California Bear Valley electric customer service area.

AWR buys, produces, distributes and sells water (91% of revenues in 1998). Approximately 39% of the company's water supply is purchased from wholesalers of imported water, with the remainder produced from owned wells. The company's new unregulated ASUS unit contracts to lease, operate and maintain governmentally owned water and wastewater systems and to provide other services to local governments to assist them in the operation and maintenance of their water and wastewater systems. In March 1999, ASUS also signed a utility service agreement to provide billing, cash processing and call handling services for the 7,500 customers served by Brooke Utilities of Arizona.

Population growth, increases in customer water usage, and water wells taken out of service due to water quality problems have created ongoing water supply concerns. A poor water supply can increase costs and hurt margins by requiring capital expenditures for new water pipelines and by requiring the company to increasingly rely on more expensive purchased water. Heavier than normal rainfall in the 1997-1998 winter brought most of California's reservoirs to near capacity and AWR stated in February 1999 that it had made significant operating progress in dealing with water supply problems that plagued earnings during most of 1997.

SCW has a gross construction budget of $46.5 million for 1999. In January 1999, the company issued $40 million of 6.59% medium term notes due 2029 in order to repay bank debt, which funded previous capital expenditures. AWR's dividend increase announced in January 1999 continues a trend of annual dividend hikes dating back to 1953.

Per Share Data ($) (Year Ended Dec. 31)	1998	1997	1996	1995	1994	1993	1992	1991	1990	1989
Tangible Bk. Val.	21.30	20.04	19.69	19.03	18.42	14.92	13.28	12.59	11.31	10.96
Earnings	1.62	1.56	1.69	1.54	1.43	1.66	1.81	2.34	1.41	1.38
Dividends	1.26	1.25	1.23	1.21	1.20	1.19	1.15	1.10	1.08	1.03
Payout Ratio	78%	80%	72%	78%	84%	125%	63%	47%	77%	75%
Prices - High	29 1/4	25 5/8	24 1/8	21	22	24 3/8	20 5/8	17 7/8	15 3/4	15 3/8
- Low	21 1/8	20 1/4	18 3/4	15 3/4	15 1/4	19 5/8	16	13 5/8	12 5/8	12 1/8
P/E Ratio - High	18	16	14	14	15	15	11	8	11	11
- Low	13	13	11	10	11	12	9	6	9	9

Income Statement Analysis (Million $)	1998	1997	1996	1995	1994	1993	1992	1991	1990	1989
Revs.	148	154	152	130	123	109	101	90.7	90.4	85.6
Depr.	12.5	11.0	10.1	8.5	8.1	7.4	6.5	6.0	5.2	4.7
Maint.	7.3	7.3	7.8	5.8	6.9	6.5	5.1	5.2	5.0	4.6
Fxd. Chgs. Cov.	3.1	3.9	3.2	3.2	3.5	3.0	3.5	3.0	2.4	2.1
Constr. Credits	Nil	Nil	Nil	Nil	Nil	Nil	Nil	Nil	Nil	Nil
Eff. Tax Rate	39%	42%	43%	42%	45%	24%	41%	36%	42%	38%
Net Inc.	14.6	14.1	13.5	12.2	11.3	12.0	12.1	15.4	8.9	8.7

Balance Sheet & Other Fin. Data (Million $)	1998	1997	1996	1995	1994	1993	1992	1991	1990	1989
Gross Prop.	554	510	472	438	408	380	355	331	300	275
Cap. Exp.	41.8	34.7	32.0	25.8	30.9	28.1	28.2	32.5	27.1	25.7
Net Prop.	416	385	358	335	315	295	278	259	236	214
Capitalization:										
LT Debt	121	115	107	107	92.9	84.3	84.2	82.6	67.3	67.8
% LT Debt	44	43	42	47	43	42	48	49	48	49
Pfd.	2.0	2.0	2.1	2.1	2.2	2.2	2.2	2.3	2.3	2.4
% Pfd.	0.72	0.80	0.80	0.90	1.00	1.10	1.30	1.40	1.60	1.70
Common	154	151	147	122	119	117	88.2	83.2	71.1	68.6
% Common	56	56	57	53	56	57	51	50	51	50
Total Cap.	341	NA	327	300	279	267	214	206	171	170
% Oper. Ratio	82.5	85.0	84.5	83.5	84.6	81.5	81.0	81.4	83.7	82.7
% Earn. on Net Prop.	6.3	6.3	6.8	6.6	6.2	7.0	7.1	6.8	6.5	6.9
% Return On Revs.	9.9	9.1	8.9	9.4	9.2	11.1	12.1	16.9	9.9	10.2
% Return On Invest. Capital	10.8	10.3	7.6	10.5	7.0	8.5	9.5	12.2	9.0	9.6
% Return On Com. Equity	9.5	9.4	9.7	10.0	9.5	11.7	14.1	19.9	12.6	12.8

Data as orig reptd.; bef. results of disc opers/spec. items. Per share data adj. for stk. divs. Bold denotes diluted EPS (FASB 128)-prior periods restated. E-Estimated. NA-Not Available. NM-Not Meaningful. NR-Not Ranked.

Office—630 East Foothill Blvd., San Dimas, CA 91773. **Tel**—(909) 394-3600. **Website**—http://www.aswater.com **Chrmn**—L. E. Ross. **Pres & CEO**—F. E. Wicks. **VP-Fin, CFO, Treas, Secy & Investor Contact**—McClellan Harris III. **Dirs**—J. L. Anderson, J. E. Auer, N. P. Dodge Jr., A. M. Holloway, R. F. Kathol, L. E. Ross, F. E. Wicks. **Transfer Agent & Registrar**—ChaseMellon Shareholder Services, LA. **Incorporated**—in California in 1998. **Empl**— 470. **S&P Analyst:** Craig K. Shere, CFA

STANDARD
&POOR'S
STOCK REPORTS

AmeriCredit Corp.

NYSE Symbol **ACF**

In S&P SmallCap 600

09-OCT-99

Industry: Consumer Finance

Summary: This consumer finance company specializes in financing automobile sales contracts and also purchases and sells home equity loans.

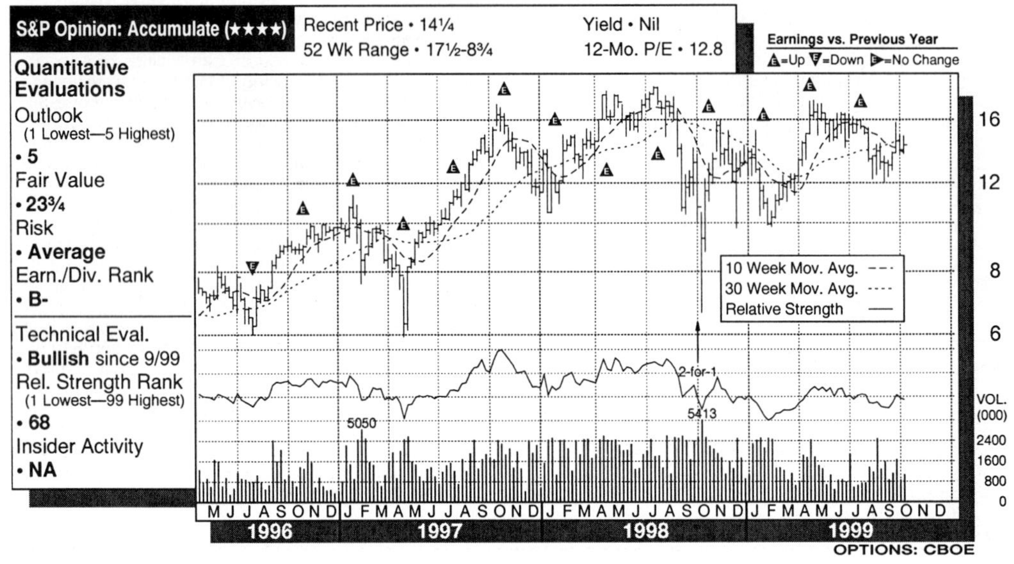

Overview - 10-AUG-99

Strong consumer spending, especially for automobiles, has shown few signs of slowing down in a healthy economy, implying that ACF should continue to enjoy substantial growth prospects. At June 30, 1999, auto loan purchases and managed auto receivables were up 66% and 78%, respectively, from a year earlier. With its proprietary credit-scoring model enabling ACF to improve its loan delinquency rate and net chargeoffs, ACF is considered the industry leader in sub-prime auto lending. Net charge-offs fell to 4.7%, from 5.1%, of average managed auto receivables for FY 99 (Jun.). We expect this percentage to continue to improve over the remainder of calendar year 1999. Due to an accounting change for securitization revenue recognition, ACF restated the first quarter of FY 99, as well as fiscal years 98, 97, and 96.

Valuation - 10-AUG-99

The stock was up 16% for the first half of 1999, after having traded down as much as 20% during the year. ACF continues to grow at a brisk pace, as liquidity returned to the asset backed security market. We see potential illiquidity for securitization as the one significant threat to ACF's continued strong growth. However, due to ACF's strong reputation in the marketplace, its credit scoring model, and the fact that ACF's paper is backed by an insurance policy provided by Financial Security Assurance, we remain optimistic about the company's future. As a leader in its industry with a significant competitive advantage, ACF warrants a higher price to earnings multiple than its current level. With projected 3-5 year earnings growth around 22%, and trading at around 10X our upwardly revised $1.38 FY 00 EPS estimate, ACF is attractive for capital appreciation.

Key Stock Statistics

S&P EPS Est. 2000	1.38	Tang. Bk. Value/Share	6.23
P/E on S&P Est. 2000	10.3	Beta	1.13
Dividend Rate/Share	Nil	Shareholders	300
Shs. outstg. (M)	72.0	Market cap. (B)	$ 1.0
Avg. daily vol. (M)	0.232	Inst. holdings	77%

Value of $10,000 invested 5 years ago: $ 36,774

Fiscal Year Ending Jun. 30

	1999	1998	1997	1996	1995	1994
Revenues (Million $)						
1Q	69.77	44.47	25.00	13.92	4.83	3.70
2Q	78.32	49.25	27.76	19.70	6.78	3.98
3Q	85.07	54.46	33.09	22.00	8.97	3.91
4Q	102.3	61.16	37.51	24.01	11.68	4.29
Yr.	335.5	209.3	123.4	79.63	33.08	15.88
Earnings Per Share ($)						
1Q	**0.23**	**0.16**	**0.10**	0.04	0.03	0.02
2Q	**0.26**	**0.18**	**0.11**	0.09	0.04	0.02
3Q	**0.29**	**0.20**	**0.13**	0.10	0.05	0.02
4Q	**0.33**	**0.21**	**0.14**	0.11	0.36	0.02
Yr.	**1.11**	**0.76**	**0.48**	**0.34**	0.48	0.08

Next earnings report expected: mid October

Dividend Data

No cash dividends have been paid. The shares were split three for two in 1990.

A Division of The McGraw-Hill Companies

AmeriCredit Corp.

Business Summary - 10-AUG-99

AmeriCredit Corp. is a consumer finance company that specializes in purchasing, securitizing, and servicing auto loans and originating and selling mortgage loans. As of June 1998, it had 120 branch offices in 36 states.

Total revenues have changed composition in recent fiscal years (Jun.) as gains on the sale of receivables have increased to 54% of revenues in FY 98, up from 28% in FY 96, and servicing fee income has risen to 19% of revenues in FY 98, up from 5% in FY 96. Finance charge income made up 24% of total revenues in FY 98, down from 64% in FY 96. Investment and other income remained steady at 3% of revenues throughout the period.

Through its AmeriCredit Financial Services (AFS) branch network, ACF purchases loans, acting as a funding source for franchised and independent dealers to finance customer purchases, primarily of used cars. Target customers typically are unable to obtain financing from traditional sources. They may have had financial difficulties and are attempting to re-establish credit or may not have sufficient credit history.

Through its AmeriCredit Mortgage Services operation, ACF originates and sells mortgage loans in the wholesale market. It originated and sold $137.2 million in loans in FY 98 and recently opened offices in Cincinnati and Fort Worth.

Average managed auto receivables grew 108% in FY 98, due to higher loan purchase volume. This growth was the result of expansion and same store increases.

As auto dealers are a significant loan source, it is imperative that ACF have positive, productive relationships with them. As evidence of ACF's growing endorsement by auto dealers, its loans purchased from auto dealers increased 68% in FY 98 from the previous year.

The most cost effective source of funds for continued loan purchases has been through securitization. The company uses net proceeds from the sale of these loans to pay down borrowings, thus increasing availability for future purchases. Revenue is recognized as a gain on the sale of receivables, which represents net proceeds (minus the carrying value of the receivables), plus an estimate of the present value of all future excess cash flows above those obligated to investors. Unfortunately, any future losses or prepayments that exceed the company's estimates would be charged against earnings. Through June 30, 1998, ACF had securitized about $1.6 billion in loans, with no such charges having been made.

ACF incorporates certain technologies to support its decision making process. Underwriters have on hand a credit scoring model which allows them to quickly assess the credit risk of borrowers. Risk-based pricing tools help price loans for sale and statistically based behavioral assessment models aid collectors in focusing on the highest risk accounts.

ACF opened 44 branches and expanded 3 in FY 98. It is also now licensed to purchase auto loans in all 50 states and plans to open 45 more branches in 1999.

Per Share Data ($) (Year Ended Jun. 30)	1999	1998	1997	1996	1995	1994	1993	1992	1991	1990
Tangible Bk. Val.	NA	4.58	3.57	2.86	2.56	2.08	2.11	2.35	2.74	3.31
Earnings	1.11	0.76	0.63	0.35	0.47	0.08	-0.33	-0.39	-0.57	0.34
Dividends	Nil	Nil	Nil	Nil	Nil	Nil	Nil	Nil	Nil	Nil
Payout Ratio	Nil	Nil	Nil	Nil	Nil	Nil	Nil	Nil	Nil	Nil
Prices - High	17 1/2	18 5/8	17 1/4	10	5 3/4	4 1/8	2 3/8	2 3/8	2 7/8	11 1/2
- Low	9 3/4	6 5/8	6	5 1/4	2 5/8	2 5/8	1 1/16	1 1/16	1 1/16	1 11/16
P/E Ratio - High	16	25	27	28	12	51	NM	NM	NM	34
- Low	9	9	9	15	6	32	NM	NM	NM	5
Income Statement Analysis (Million $)										
Total Revs.	NA	209	138	81.0	33.1	15.9	24.9	74.2	190	164
Int. Exp.	NA	27.1	16.3	13.1	4.0	0.2	0.2	0.3	2.5	2.0
Exp./Op. Revs.	NA	58%	54%	58%	70%	68%	178%	131%	125%	85%
Pretax Inc.	NA	80.2	62.9	34.3	10.0	5.1	-19.4	-23.3	-47.2	24.1
Eff. Tax Rate	NA	38%	39%	37%	NM	Nil	Nil	NM	NM	34%
Net Inc.	NA	49.3	38.7	21.6	28.9	5.1	-19.4	-24.2	-36.2	15.8
Balance Sheet & Other Fin. Data (Million $)										
Cash & Secs.	NA	188	80.4	24.0	33.6	42.3	68.4	39.3	14.3	71.9
Loans	NA	343	267	251	222	72.2	43.9	69.5	115	112
Total Assets	NA	714	493	330	286	122	131	154	181	223
ST Debt	NA	171	16.6	30.4	70.5	0.2	0.4	0.5	1.6	0.4
Capitalization:										
Debt	NA	176	132	37.8	64.7	0.2	0.9	1.3	1.3	2.4
Equity	NA	288	217	163	147	120	123	147	172	208
Total	NA	495	349	201	212	120	124	149	173	211
Price Times Bk. Val.: High	NA	4.1	4.2	3.5	2.2	2.0	1.1	1.0	1.0	3.5
Price Times Bk. Val.: Low	NA	2.1	1.7	1.8	1.0	1.2	0.5	0.5	0.4	0.5
% Return On Revs.	NA	23.6	28.1	26.7	87.3	31.9	NM	NM	NM	9.6
% Ret. on Assets	NA	8.2	9.4	7.0	14.2	4.0	NM	NM	NM	11.7
% Ret. on Equity	NA	19.5	20.4	13.9	21.7	4.2	NM	NM	NM	13.7
Loans/Equity	NA	122.9	136.2	152.2	110.2	47.9	42.0	57.9	59.9	60.1

Data as orig reptd.; bef. results of disc opers/spec. items. Per share data adj. for stk. divs. Bold denotes diluted EPS (FASB 128)-prior periods restated. E-Estimated. NA-Not Available. NM-Not Meaningful. NR-Not Ranked.

Office—801 Cherry St., Suite 3900, Fort Worth, TX 76102. **Tel**—(817) 302-7000. **Website**—http://www.americredit.com **Chrmn & CEO**—C. H. Morris Jr. **Pres & COO**—M. R. Barrington. **Vice Chrmn & CFO**—D. E. Berce. **SVP & Secy**—C. A. Choate. **Investor Contact**—Kim Welch (817-302-7009). **Dirs**—M. R. Barrington, D. E. Berce, A. R. Dike, E. H. Esstman, J. H. Greer, D. K. Higgins, K. H. Jones Jr., C. H. Morris Jr. **Transfer Agent & Registrar**—Chasemellon Shareholder Services, Dallas. **Incorporated**—in Texas in 1988. **Empl**— 2,300. **S&P Analyst:** Jonathan Rudy

STANDARD
&POOR'S
STOCK REPORTS

Ames Department Stores

Nasdaq Symbol **AMES**

In S&P SmallCap 600

09-OCT-99 **Industry:** Retail (Discounters)

Summary: Ames is the largest regional full-line discount retailer in the U.S., with 450 stores in 19 states and the District of Columbia.

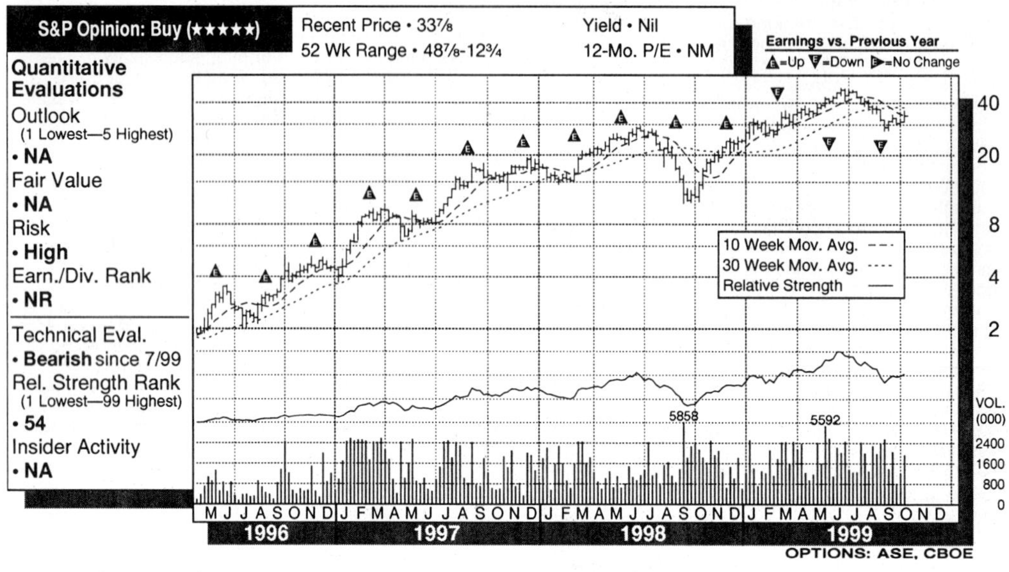

Overview - 31-AUG-99

Ames dramatically increased its store base with the late 1998 acquisition of Hills Stores. The company is completing the remodeling and remerchandising of the former Hills locations, as well as several acquired former Caldor locations. The last group of these stores is slated to reopen in late September. In the six months ended July 31, 1999, total sales increased 63%, year to year, and sales at units open more than a year rose 9.3%. This was above the rate of growth in U.S. consumer spending. In the second half of FY 00 (Jan.) and in FY 01, we have assumed lower same-store sales gains, of about 4%. Excluding operations of the Hills stores prior to their conversion to Ames locations, margins are expected to widen, as overhead, advertising and other expenses are leveraged over the larger store base. Not accounting for the Hills-related expenses, we estimate that EPS will rise to $1.93 in FY 00, with a further gain, to $3.05, in FY 01.

Valuation - 31-AUG-99

After more than quadrupling this spring from its late 1998 low price, the stock has undergone a seasonal correction, which is typical for retail stocks. This year, the summer swoon in the sector has been exacerbated by concerns regarding a slowdown in consumer spending, in light of higher interest rates. We think that these fears will prove to be largely unfounded. The Federal Reserve enjoys a high degree of confidence that it can control inflation without pushing the economy into recession. Jobs are expected to remain plentiful, with productivity gains fueling higher wages. With the share price having corrected this summer by about 40% from its high, we view AMES as a strong buy, and expect the shares to sharply outperform the market over the next six to 12 months.

Key Stock Statistics

S&P EPS Est. 2000	2.00	Tang. Bk. Value/Share	1.45
P/E on S&P Est. 2000	16.9	Beta	2.38
S&P EPS Est. 2001	3.12	Shareholders	8,274
Dividend Rate/Share	Nil	Market cap. (B)	$0.988
Shs. outstg. (M)	29.2	Inst. holdings	82%
Avg. daily vol. (M)	0.298		

Value of $10,000 invested 5 years ago: $ 150,555

Fiscal Year Ending Jan. 31

	2000	1999	1998	1997	1996	1995
Revenues (Million $)						
1Q	829.1	499.0	432.6	438.7	441.7	435.8
2Q	856.2	536.3	503.6	499.1	504.2	491.3
3Q	—	599.2	527.6	516.9	505.9	511.3
4Q	—	872.7	769.4	707.0	669.0	704.5
Yr.	—	2,507	2,233	2,162	2,121	2,143
Earnings Per Share ($)						
1Q	**-1.10**	**-0.09**	**-0.28**	-0.34	-0.55	-0.68
2Q	**-0.80**	**0.35**	**0.31**	0.21	0.15	0.31
3Q	—	**0.26**	**0.15**	0.02	-0.24	-0.25
4Q	—	**0.87**	**1.23**	0.93	0.54	1.44
Yr.	—	**1.40**	**1.46**	**0.85**	**-0.08**	0.86

Next earnings report expected: mid November

Dividend Data

No cash dividends have been paid. Dividends cannot be declared under the terms of the company's revolving credit facility. In 1994, the company adopted a stock purchase rights plan.

A Division of The McGraw-Hill Companies

Ames Department Stores, Inc.

Business Summary - 31-AUG-99

Ames Department Stores is the largest regional full-line discount retailer in the U.S., with stores in 19 states and the District of Columbia. The December 1998 acquisition of the Hills Stores Company discount chain increased the store base by 50% from 300 to 450.

The remodeling, remerchandising and reopening of nearly all the 155 Hills stores is being completed in three phases, with the simultaneous grand opening of 50 stores in April 1999, 54 in July 1999, and 47 planned for September 1999. Four of the stores that were in markets with existing Ames stores, as well as seven underperforming Ames stores in markets where the company acquired a Hills location, were closed. In 1999, the company also acquired 10 former Caldor locations and one store that was part of the former Jamesway chain.

In FY 99 (Jan.), home lines accounted for 39% of sales, softlines 30%, and hardlines 27%. Women's apparel alone accounted for 13% of sales. Shoe departments in all the stores that are operated by a licensee accounted for 4% of total sales.

Ames primarily targets working women with families and senior citizens with an average annual household income between $25,000 and $35,000. An everyday value pricing strategy is emphasized, augmented by weekly newspaper circulars.

Stores range from 38,000 to 70,000 sq. ft., of selling area. Stores are located in rural communities (some of which are not served by other large retail stores), high-traffic suburban sites, small cities and several major metropolitan areas.

Merchandise is purchased centrally and shipped by vendors either directly to individual stores or to Ames's distribution centers in Massachusetts and Pennsylvania. A distribution center in Columbus, Ohio, was acquired as part of the Hills purchase, and a distribution center in Westfield, MA, was acquired from Caldor in March 1999.

The acquisition of Hills Stores was completed on December 31, 1998. Pursuant to a tender offer, cash consideration of $130 million was paid for a majority of Hills stock and senior notes, with the remaining stock acquired by subsequent merger. Liabilities assumed totaled approximately $200 million, including $51 million of the senior notes that were not tendered and $148 million of capitalized leasehold and financing obligations. Ames paid for the acquisition with cash from operations and funding provided under a new revolving credit facility for up to $650 million. Borrowings under the facility were subsequently reduced with proceeds from the April 1999 sale of $200 million principal amount of 10% senior notes and the May 1999 secondary offering of 5.1 million shares of Ames common stock at a price of $38.75 each.

Per Share Data ($) (Year Ended Jan. 31)	1999	1998	1997	1996	1995	1994	1993	1992	1991	1990
Tangible Bk. Val.	1.45	7.70	5.28	4.01	4.22	2.66	1.68	NA	NA	NA
Cash Flow	2.04	2.06	1.43	0.53	1.11	0.57	-1.19	NA	NA	NA
Earnings	1.40	1.46	0.82	-0.08	0.86	0.47	-1.19	NA	NA	NA
Dividends	Nil	Nil	Nil	Nil	Nil	Nil	Nil	NA	NA	NA
Payout Ratio	Nil	Nil	Nil	Nil	Nil	Nil	Nil	NA	NA	NA
Cal. Yrs.	1998	1997	1996	1995	1994	1993	1992	1991	1990	1989
Prices - High	29 5/8	19 5/8	5 1/4	3 3/4	6 1/2	4 7/8	2	NA	NA	NA
- Low	10 1/2	3 5/8	1 3/16	1 1/8	1 7/8	1	1 3/4	NA	NA	NA
P/E Ratio - High	21	13	6	NM	8	10	NM	NA	NA	NA
- Low	8	3	1	NM	2	2	NM	NA	NA	NA
Income Statement Analysis (Million $)										
Revs.	2,507	2,233	2,162	2,121	2,143	2,124	142	NA	NA	NA
Oper. Inc.	61.4	47.8	29.4	10.6	2.0	-0.1	-24.9	NA	NA	NA
Depr.	15.5	14.3	12.5	12.4	5.3	2.1	NM	NA	NA	NA
Int. Exp.	15.3	11.6	19.0	24.1	26.5	28.9	1.9	NA	NA	NA
Pretax Inc.	52.6	53.6	26.8	-1.6	26.8	13.2	-23.9	NA	NA	NA
Eff. Tax Rate	36%	36%	30%	NM	31%	25%	Nil	NA	NA	NA
Net Inc.	33.8	34.5	18.7	-1.6	18.5	9.9	-23.9	NA	NA	NA
Balance Sheet & Other Fin. Data (Million $)										
Cash	35.7	57.8	46.2	14.2	30.4	72.4	NA	NA	NA	NA
Curr. Assets	704	513	468	444	486	543	NA	NA	NA	NA
Total Assets	1,483	610	537	506	533	567	NA	NA	NA	NA
Curr. Liab.	715	344	330	303	294	323	NA	NA	NA	NA
LT Debt	288	35.7	38.2	53.7	77.1	93.3	NA	NA	NA	NA
Common Eqty.	324	173	108	83.3	84.9	60.4	NA	NA	NA	NA
Total Cap.	612	209	146	137	162	154	NA	NA	NA	NA
Cap. Exp.	51.6	32.9	19.8	27.2	24.5	20.2	3.5	NA	NA	NA
Cash Flow	49.3	48.8	31.2	10.7	23.8	12.0	-23.9	NA	NA	NA
Curr. Ratio	1.0	1.5	1.4	1.5	1.7	1.7	NA	NA	NA	NA
% LT Debt of Cap.	47.1	17.1	26.2	39.2	47.6	60.7	NA	NA	NA	NA
% Net Inc.of Revs.	1.3	1.6	0.9	NM	0.9	0.5	NM	NA	NA	NA
% Ret. on Assets	3.2	6.0	3.6	NM	3.4	NA	NA	NA	NA	NA
% Ret. on Equity	13.6	24.6	19.6	NM	25.5	NA	NA	NA	NA	NA

Data as orig reptd.; bef. results of disc opers/spec. items. Per share data adj. for stk. divs. Bold denotes diluted EPS (FASB 128)-prior periods restated. E-Estimated. NA-Not Available. NM-Not Meaningful. NR-Not Ranked.

Office—2418 Main St., Rocky Hill, CT 06067. **Tel**—(860) 257-2000. **Website**—http://www.AmesStores.com **Pres & CEO**—J. R. Ettore.**EVP & COO**—D. T. Lemire. **EVP & CFO**—R. de Aguiar. **Investor Contact**—C. Skahill (860-257-5078). **Dirs**—F. X. Basile, P. M. Buxbaum, A. Cohen, J. R. Ettore, R. M. Felner, S. S. Pearlman. **Transfer Agent & Registrar**—ChaseMellon Shareholder Services, LLC., NYC. **Incorporated**—In Delaware in 1962; reorganized in 1992. **Empl**— 36,400. **S&P Analyst:** Mark S. Basham

STANDARD
&POOR'S
STOCK REPORTS

AMRESCO, INC.

NASDAQ Symbol **AMMB**

In S&P SmallCap 600

09-OCT-99 **Industry:** Financial (Diversified)

Summary: This diversified financial services company specializes in commercial and residential real estate lending, asset management workout services and commercial finance.

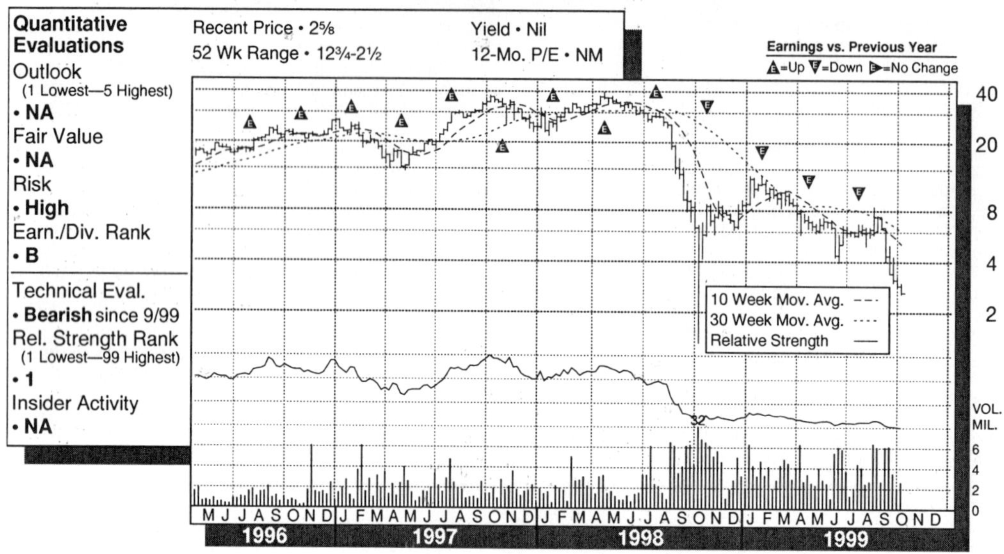

Business Profile - 30-SEP-99

In September 1999, AMRESCO entered an exclusive dealing agreement with Lend Lease Corp., a global real estate and financial services company, related to the potential sale of AMMB's asset management, commercial mortgage banking and servicing, and real estate structured finance business platforms. In July 1999, AMMB formed Finance America, LLC, a joint venture with Lehman ALI, Inc., to originate, purchase, sell and securitize sub-prime residential and home equity loans. In April 1999, AMMB announced the restructuring of its earnout agreement related to its 1998 acquisition of Mortgage Investors Corp., allowing it to make the entire $105 million payment in cash rather than the previously agreed upon 18% cash and 82% shares.

Operational Review - 30-SEP-99

Revenues in the six months ended June 30, 1999, rose 5.8%, year to year, as gains on the securitizations of small business loans and gains on the sale of residential mortgage banking loans from a newly acquired subsidiary outweighed the effects of the discontinuance of the company's capital markets operation in late 1998. After 14% higher expenses, resulting from an expansion of commercial finance operations and the newly added residential business, pretax income was down 31%. After taxes at 41.5%, versus 38.9%, net income fell 34%, to $22,342,000 ($0.41 a share, on 30% more shares), from $33,709,000 ($0.80).

Stock Performance - 08-OCT-99

In the past 30 trading days, AMMB's shares have declined 65%, compared to a 0.91% fall in the S&P 500. Average trading volume for the past five days was 517,740 shares, compared with the 40-day moving average of 1,040,141 shares.

Key Stock Statistics

Dividend Rate/Share	Nil	Shareholders	2,699
Shs. outstg. (M)	48.8	Market cap. (B)	$0.128
Avg. daily vol. (M)	0.748	Inst. holdings	29%
Tang. Bk. Value/Share	6.82		
Beta	1.69		

Value of $10,000 invested 5 years ago: $ 3,786

Fiscal Year Ending Dec. 31

	1999	1998	1997	1996	1995	1994
Revenues (Million $)						
1Q	170.3	143.1	74.84	36.90	20.18	40.56
2Q	164.1	177.9	103.9	46.81	23.48	40.46
3Q	—	177.8	112.8	45.49	25.42	46.78
4Q	—	30.80	132.3	70.87	41.41	29.38
Yr.	—	526.8	423.8	200.1	110.5	157.2
Earnings Per Share ($)						
1Q	**0.21**	**0.35**	**0.25**	**0.17**	0.13	0.23
2Q	**0.20**	**0.45**	**0.34**	**0.25**	0.17	0.23
3Q	—	**0.02**	**0.41**	**0.29**	0.21	0.37
4Q	—	**-2.27**	**0.53**	**0.34**	0.25	0.05
Yr.	—	**-1.61**	**1.53**	**1.06**	**0.75**	**0.88**

Next earnings report expected: late October

Dividend Data (Dividends have been paid since 1998.)

Dividends, which were omitted in 1989 and reinstated in 1993, were again omitted in 1995. A stockholder rights plan was adopted in May 1997 and March 1999.

A Division of The McGraw-Hill Companies

Business Summary - 30-SEP-99

In 1994, Dallas-based AMRESCO, Inc., began a diversification process, building business units that could use the company's core real estate management and lending expertise to pursue growth in markets that it felt were underserved by traditional lenders. AMMB now operates in five lines of business, after its entry into the businesses of commercial mortgage banking, commercial finance, residential mortgage lending and loan servicing. AMMB also oriented its asset management activities toward direct investments in asset portfolios and the special servicing of large portfolios of asset-backed securities.

Asset management accounted for 21% of AMMB's total revenues in 1998 (25% the year before). The company's asset management business manages and resolves portfolios of performing, underperforming and nonperforming loans and provides special servicing for nonperforming or underperforming loans in commercial mortgage-backed bond trusts and similar securitized commercial asset-backed loan portfolios.

AMRESCO's commercial mortgage banking business (13% of 1998 revenues; 23% of 1997's), involves fee based origination and servicing of commercial real estate mortgages and commercial real estate brokerage. AMMB's commercial mortgage banking services are performed through Holliday Fenoglio Fowler, AMRESCO Capital and AMRESCO Services.

AMMB's home equity lending business consists of originating, selling and servicing nonconforming first mortgage loans. Home equity lending comprised 28% of revenues in 1998, compared to 40% in 1997. Loan production decreased to $3.5 billion in 1998, from $3.6 billion in the prior year, as the company suffered significant losses related to home equity loans accumulated and held for subsequent securitization. As a result, AMMB discontinued its bulk purchase of home equity loans and origination of loans through correspondent channels. AMMB has repostured its home equity lending business. After February 1999 alliances formed with LaSalle National Bank and Morgan Stanley Dean Witter, AMMB will now originate and service commercial mortgage loans funded by LaSalle, and sell them to the two partners, who will take on the risk of securitization.

In 1996, AMMB organized the Commercial Finance Group to provide financing to commercial borrowers in various targeted markets. This business unit focuses on loans to franchisees of nationally recognized restaurant, hospitality and service organizations, small business owners, real estate structured finance activities, communications finance, and single family residential construction lending. The residential mortgage banking business, consisting of the newly (August 1998) acquired operations of Mortgage Investors Corp., originates and sells Veterans Administration streamlined refinanced loans.

Per Share Data ($) (Year Ended Dec. 31)	1998	1997	1996	1995	1994	1993	1992	1991	1990	1989
Tangible Bk. Val.	5.69	8.07	6.35	4.09	4.81	3.65	2.41	3.05	3.10	2.24
Earnings	-1.61	1.53	1.12	0.76	0.88	2.15	0.50	0.33	0.20	-0.75
Dividends	Nil	Nil	Nil	0.10	0.20	0.15	Nil	Nil	Nil	0.18
Payout Ratio	Nil	Nil	Nil	13%	23%	7%	Nil	Nil	Nil	NM
Prices - High	39¾	37⅞	27⅜	13½	9¼	7½	4½	5	3⅜	5½
- Low	1 5/16	13½	11¾	5⅞	5½	3¾	2⅜	2½	2	2⅛
P/E Ratio - High	NM	25	24	18	11	3	9	15	17	NM
- Low	NM	9	10	8	6	2	5	8	10	NM
Income Statement Analysis (Million $)										
Premium Inc.	Nil	Nil	Nil	Nil	NA	NA	NA	NA	NA	NA
Invest. Inc.	398	204	104	40.1	13.1	2.6	NA	NA	NA	NA
Oth. Revs.	129	220	96.5	70.4	NA	NA	NA	NA	NA	NA
Total Revs.	527	424	200	111	157	177	47.2	40.7	37.5	25.4
Int. Exp.	232	102	36.8	6.9	1.8	0.8	0.1	0.2	0.8	1.3
Exp./Op. Revs.	487%	79%	75%	73%	77%	77%	NA	NA	NA	NA
Pretax Inc.	-101	92.1	50.5	30.3	35.7	40.2	5.4	3.6	2.2	-7.0
Eff. Tax Rate	NM	39%	38%	38%	41%	40%	21%	6.20%	13%	NM
Net Inc.	-69.2	56.2	31.3	18.7	20.9	24.2	5.3	3.3	1.9	-7.0
Balance Sheet & Other Fin. Data (Million $)										
Receivables	20.7	19.2	12.2	20.2	20.7	39.4	NA	NA	NA	NA
Cash & Invest.	605	25.9	63.2	38.0	20.4	43.4	3.5	2.0	1.0	1.2
Loans	943	1,979	417	299	30.9	33.8	NA	NA	NA	NA
Total Assets	2,919	2,634	1,076	522	172	164	44.3	50.6	49.6	57.7
Capitalization:										
Debt	1,335	839	375	173	16.5	28.1	0.3	0.2	1.6	9.2
Equity	585	409	302	161	114	91.7	35.7	43.8	38.5	33.5
Total	1,920	1,248	677	334	130	120	36.0	45.1	40.1	42.7
Price Times Bk. Val.: High	7.0	4.7	4.3	3.3	1.9	2.1	1.9	1.6	1.1	2.5
Price Times Bk. Val.: Low	0.2	1.7	1.9	1.4	1.1	1.0	1.0	0.8	0.6	0.9
% Return On Revs.	NM	13.3	15.6	16.9	13.3	13.7	11.2	8.2	5.2	NM
% Ret. on Assets	NM	3.0	3.9	5.4	12.5	23.3	13.0	6.7	3.6	NM
% Ret. on Equity	NM	18.8	13.5	13.5	20.4	43.4	16.3	8.1	5.4	NM
Loans/Equity	1.6	372.4	138.1	217.9	31.5	30.6	NA	NA	NA	NA

Data as orig reptd.; bef. results of disc opers/spec. items. Per share data adj. for stk. divs. Bold denotes diluted EPS (FASB 128)-prior periods restated. E-Estimated. NA-Not Available. NM-Not Meaningful. NR-Not Ranked.

Office—700 N. Pearl St., Suite 2400, LB 342, Dallas, TX 75201-7424**Tel**—(214) 953-7700. **Website**—http://www.amresco.com **Chrmn & CEO**—R. H. Lutz, Jr. **Pres & COO**—R. L. Adair III. **EVP & CFO**—B. L. Edwards. **SVP & Secy**—L. K. Blackwell. **Investor Contact**—Natalie Johnson (214-953-7881). **Dirs**—R. L. Adair III, J. P. Cotton, Jr., R. L. Cravey, G. E. Eickhoff, S. E. Harris, A. J. Jorgensen, R. H. Lutz, Jr., B. W. Schnitzer. **Transfer Agent & Registrar**—The Bank of New York, NYC. **Incorporated**—in Delaware in 1977. **Empl**— 3,693. **S&P Analyst:** Markos N. Kaminis

STANDARD
&POOR'S
STOCK REPORTS

Analogic Corp.

NASDAQ Symbol **ALOG**

In S&P SmallCap 600

09-OCT-99

Industry: Electronics (Instrumentation)

Summary: ALOG designs and makes high-technology, high-precision analog/digital signal processing equipment for the worldwide medical, industrial and scientific industries.

Quantitative Evaluations

Outlook
(1 Lowest—5 Highest)
• 3

Fair Value
• 33¾

Risk
• Average

Earn./Div. Rank
• B+

Technical Eval.
• Bearish since 9/99

Rel. Strength Rank
(1 Lowest—99 Highest)
• 12

Insider Activity
• NA

Recent Price • 26⅝
52 Wk Range • 40½-26⅝
Yield • 1.1%
12-Mo. P/E • 14.9

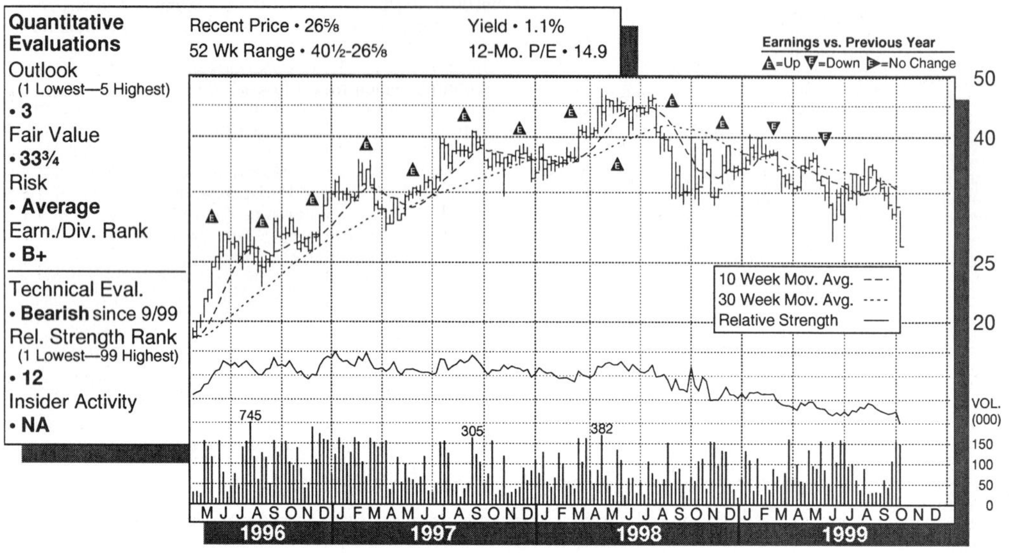

Business Profile - 03-AUG-99

In June 1999, Analogic acquired the assets of Noranda Advanced Materials' medical detectors and pure metals business. These are now part of ANRAD, a new, wholly owned subsidiary formed by Analogic to develop and manufacture selenium-based flat panel X-ray detectors for the medical and industrial market. Softness in the Asian and South American markets has adversely affected Analogic's product revenues during FY 99 (Jul.). As of April 30, 1999, the company had repurchased 10,000 shares at an aggregate cost of $345,000, as part of a plan, announced on March 16, 1999, to purchase, a number of its shares from time to time in the open market.

Operational Review - 03-AUG-99

Total revenues in the first nine months of FY 99 declined 1.1%, year to year, as increased sales of medical technology products were more than offset by lower signal processing technology and industrial technology products sales. Profitability was adversely affected by softness in the Asian and South American markets, expenses related to new engineering and production start-up programs, and additional costs associated with making the company's systems Year 2000 compliant. Pretax income fell 17%. After taxes at 25.9%, versus 33.8%, and minority interest, net income was down 6.2%, to $15,652,000 ($1.23 a share), from $16,678,000 ($1.31).

Stock Performance - 08-OCT-99

In the past 30 trading days, ALOG's shares have declined 22%, compared to a 0.91% fall in the S&P 500. Average trading volume for the past five days was 29,660 shares, compared with the 40-day moving average of 16,464 shares.

Key Stock Statistics

Dividend Rate/Share	0.28	Shareholders	911
Shs. outstg. (M)	12.7	Market cap. (B)	$0.338
Avg. daily vol. (M)	0.025	Inst. holdings	46%
Tang. Bk. Value/Share	20.92		
Beta	0.49		

Value of $10,000 invested 5 years ago: $ 17,492

Fiscal Year Ending Jul. 31

	1999	1998	1997	1996	1995	1994
Revenues (Million $)						
1Q	67.17	63.93	59.47	46.48	50.93	46.11
2Q	72.69	71.65	61.73	53.15	52.54	49.59
3Q	70.86	77.38	64.17	60.49	49.10	47.13
4Q	—	81.52	71.36	70.35	56.25	50.93
Yr.	—	294.5	256.7	230.5	208.8	193.8
Earnings Per Share ($)						
1Q	**0.37**	**0.36**	**0.31**	0.11	0.28	0.26
2Q	**0.44**	**0.45**	**0.36**	0.16	0.25	0.30
3Q	**0.42**	**0.50**	**0.41**	0.30	0.15	0.29
4Q	—	**0.56**	**0.50**	0.47	0.34	0.33
Yr.	—	**1.87**	**1.58**	**1.04**	**1.02**	**1.18**

Next earnings report expected: NA

Dividend Data (Dividends have been paid since 1995.)

Amount ($)	Date Decl.	Ex-Div. Date	Stock of Record	Payment Date
0.070	Jan. 22	Feb. 03	Feb. 05	Feb. 19 '99
0.070	Mar. 11	Mar. 24	Mar. 26	Apr. 09 '99
0.070	Jun. 11	Jun. 23	Jun. 25	Jul. 09 '99
0.070	Oct. 07	Oct. 19	Oct. 21	Nov. 04 '99

STANDARD
&POOR'S
STOCK REPORTS

Analogic Corporation

09-OCT-99

Business Summary - 03-AUG-99

Analogic Corporation designs, makes and sells standard and customized high-precision data acquisition, conversion and signal processing equipment, which is primarily incorporated by OEMs into systems used in medical, industrial and scientific applications.

The medical technology product group accounted for about 74% of revenues in FY 98 (Jul.), signal processing technology 19%, and industrial technology 7%.

Product, service, engineering and licensing export revenue from foreign companies accounted for 33% of sales in FY 98 and 34% in FY 97.

Medical Technology products, primarily medical imaging data acquisition systems, are used in advanced X-ray equipment known as computer-assisted tomography (CAT) scanners. Analogic also makes CAT scanners using proprietary technology, electronic equipment for diagnostic image printers, ultrasound imaging equipment and systems, magnetic resonance imaging equipment, and fetal monitoring products. Camtronics Ltd. (77% owned) designs and makes medical image processing equipment.

Signal Processing Technology products consist of analog-to-digital (A/D) and digital-to-analog (D/A) converters and supporting modules. A/D devices convert continuously varying analog signals into the numerical digital form required by computers, while D/A converters transform computer output in digital form into analog signals required by process control equipment. The group also produces interconnecting and supporting modules for the A/D and D/A converters, high-speed digital signal processors, such as Array Processors, and image processing equipment.

Industrial Technology products include digital panel instruments, which measure analog inputs and display the results in numerical (digital) form. They are incorporated in precision thermometers, blood analyzers and automatic test equipment. The group also produces industrial data acquisition and conversion systems, test and measurement devices and automation systems.

The three largest customers in FY 98, Phillips, GE and Imation, accounted for 16.1%, 7.7% and 7.2% of total revenues, respectively.

Capital expenditures totaled about $9.9 million for the nine months ended April 30, 1999, compared with $9.7 million in the year-earlier period.

As of April 30, 1999, Analogic had repurchased 10,000 common shares at an aggregate cost of $345,000, as part of a plan, announced on March 16, 1999, to purchase a number of its shares from time to time in the open market.

Per Share Data ($) (Year Ended Jul. 31)	1998	1997	1996	1995	1994	1993	1992	1991	1990	1989
Tangible Bk. Val.	19.89	18.15	17.03	16.22	14.97	13.53	12.76	11.97	10.86	9.99
Cash Flow	2.49	2.00	1.54	1.51	1.69	1.67	1.47	1.49	1.38	1.44
Earnings	1.87	1.58	1.04	1.02	1.18	1.01	0.78	0.91	0.85	0.97
Dividends	0.23	0.20	0.18	0.08	Nil	Nil	Nil	Nil	Nil	Nil
Payout Ratio	12%	13%	17%	8%	Nil	Nil	Nil	Nil	Nil	Nil
Prices - High	48	41	33½	21¾	20	16¾	13⅛	14¾	10⅛	11⅛
- Low	31	28⅛	17¼	16	14⅝	12¾	10¼	8	8	8⅜
P/E Ratio - High	26	26	32	21	17	17	17	16	12	11
- Low	17	18	17	16	12	13	13	9	9	9
Income Statement Analysis (Million $)										
Revs.	289	251	224	204	189	174	145	137	138	133
Oper. Inc.	42.5	31.4	17.1	17.7	21.1	22.8	14.1	21.0	20.1	16.0
Depr.	7.9	5.4	6.2	6.5	6.4	8.1	8.8	7.8	7.8	7.0
Int. Exp.	0.5	0.6	0.8	0.8	1.3	1.1	1.6	1.0	1.0	1.1
Pretax Inc.	37.0	28.0	16.2	16.9	19.6	18.6	13.3	17.0	17.9	21.3
Eff. Tax Rate	32%	24%	26%	22%	16%	30%	19%	24%	26%	32%
Net Inc.	23.9	20.1	13.1	12.7	14.7	12.4	9.9	12.2	12.4	14.5
Balance Sheet & Other Fin. Data (Million $)										
Cash	27.6	114	101	100	94.4	87.8	72.4	82.2	77.2	65.5
Curr. Assets	237	222	202	196	177	165	138	145	142	132
Total Assets	303	282	265	260	240	223	197	190	185	181
Curr. Liab.	36.7	35.5	33.5	30.6	26.2	25.6	19.1	16.5	17.4	18.2
LT Debt	7.7	8.6	9.5	10.2	11.0	13.2	16.5	13.0	11.2	11.6
Common Eqty.	251	228	212	201	184	169	156	157	154	147
Total Cap.	266	246	230	228	212	196	178	174	168	162
Cap. Exp.	14.6	6.3	6.2	8.2	7.3	4.4	4.5	7.7	5.7	4.4
Cash Flow	31.8	25.5	19.3	18.9	21.1	20.5	18.7	20.1	20.3	21.5
Curr. Ratio	6.5	6.3	6.0	6.4	6.8	6.4	7.2	8.8	8.1	7.3
% LT Debt of Cap.	2.9	3.5	4.1	4.4	5.2	6.7	9.3	7.5	6.7	7.1
% Net Inc.of Revs.	8.3	8.0	5.8	6.2	7.8	7.2	6.8	8.9	9.0	10.9
% Ret. on Assets	8.2	7.3	5.0	5.0	6.2	5.9	5.3	6.7	6.9	8.4
% Ret. on Equity	10.0	9.2	6.4	6.5	8.3	7.6	6.6	8.2	8.5	10.5

Data as orig. reptd.; bef. results of disc. opers. and/or spec. items. Per share data adj. for stk. divs. as of ex-div. date. Quarterly revenues table includes interest and dividend income. Bold denotes diluted EPS (FASB 128). E-Estimated. NA-Not Available. NM-Not Meaningful. NR-Not Ranked.

Office—8 Centennial Drive, Peabody, MA 01960. **Tel**—(978) 977-3000. **Website**—http://www.analogic.com **Chrmn & CEO**—B. M. Gordon. **SVP, Treas & Investor Contact**—John A. Tarello. **Dirs**—M. R. Brown, B. M. Gordon, B. W. Steinhauer, J. A. Tarello, E. F. Voboril, G. L. Wilson. **Transfer Agent**—Boston EquiServe, L.P. **Incorporated**—in Massachusetts in 1967. **Empl**— 1,650. **S&P Analyst:** J.J.S.

STANDARD
&POOR'S
STOCK REPORTS

Analysts International

NASDAQ Symbol **ANLY**

In S&P SmallCap 600

09-OCT-99

Industry:
Services (Computer Systems)

Summary: This company provides contract programming and related software services through its branch and field offices to users and manufacturers of computers.

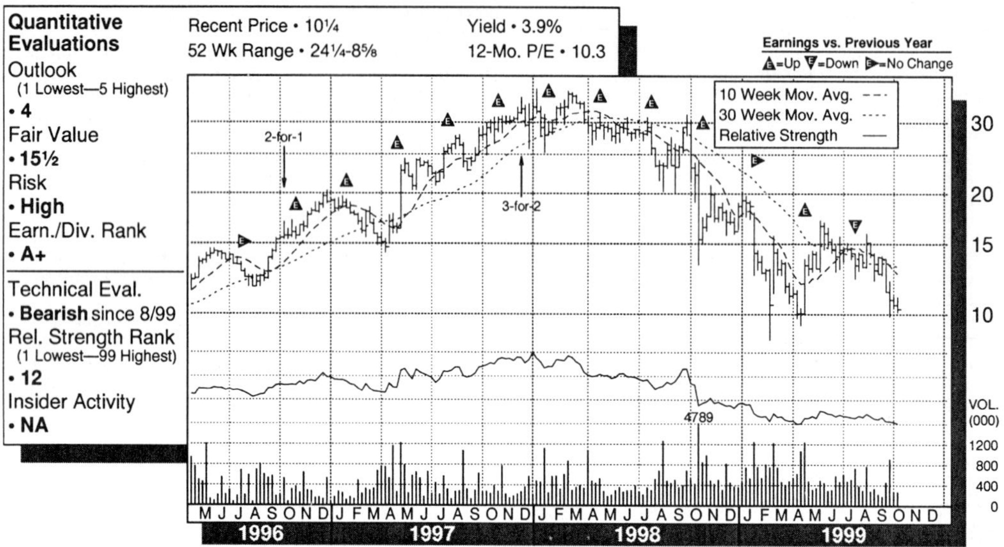

Business Profile - 23-JUN-99

ANLY believes that in 1999, its clients have been focusing on Year 2000 problem testing and compliance. As a result, new application implementations have been postponed and the demand for normal services has been slow at the same time that Year 2000 business has been phasing out. This paradox has affected stock prices in ANLY's sector. However, the company believes that next year, demand for its services should be strong and that growth will return to a rate comparable to that before the Year 2000 diversion. In May 1999, ANLY announced that it was awarded contracts from the states of Iowa and Kentucky.

Operational Review - 23-JUN-99

For the nine months ended March 31, 1999, total revenues rose 9.2%, year to year, reflecting increases in hourly rates for professional services provided directly and in billable hours provided through sub-suppliers. Gross and operating margins narrowed, reflecting increased idle time and labor costs. Pretax income was up 4.2%. After taxes at 39.3%, versus 40.0%, net income rose 5.4%, to $16,792,000 ($0.74 per share), from $15,939,000 ($0.70).

Stock Performance - 08-OCT-99

In the past 30 trading days, ANLY's shares have declined 20%, compared to a 0.91% fall in the S&P 500. Average trading volume for the past five days was 53,020 shares, compared with the 40-day moving average of 73,795 shares.

Key Stock Statistics

Dividend Rate/Share	0.40	Shareholders	8,500
Shs. outstg. (M)	22.6	Market cap. (B)	$0.233
Avg. daily vol. (M)	0.094	Inst. holdings	52%
Tang. Bk. Value/Share	3.54		
Beta	0.76		

Value of $10,000 invested 5 years ago: $ 19,289

Fiscal Year Ending Jun. 30

	1999	1998	1997	1996	1995	1994
Revenues (Million $)						
1Q	158.5	135.2	98.02	73.07	48.40	41.74
2Q	153.0	141.3	101.8	78.79	50.72	42.86
3Q	154.1	150.0	113.7	85.98	55.22	45.05
4Q	154.6	161.0	126.0	91.71	64.09	46.33
Yr.	620.2	587.4	439.6	329.5	218.4	176.0
Earnings Per Share ($)						
1Q	**0.27**	0.23	0.17	0.13	0.11	0.09
2Q	**0.22**	**0.22**	0.17	0.13	0.12	0.09
3Q	**0.25**	**0.24**	0.19	0.15	0.13	0.08
4Q	**0.26**	**0.29**	0.19	0.15	0.15	0.10
Yr.	**1.00**	**0.99**	**0.73**	0.56	0.51	0.37

Next earnings report expected: mid October

Dividend Data (Dividends have been paid since 1988.)

Amount ($)	Date Decl.	Ex-Div. Date	Stock of Record	Payment Date
0.100	Dec. 17	Jan. 27	Jan. 29	Feb. 12 '99
0.100	Feb. 18	Apr. 28	Apr. 30	May. 14 '99
0.100	Jun. 24	Jul. 28	Jul. 30	Aug. 13 '99
0.100	Aug. 19	Oct. 27	Oct. 29	Nov. 15 '99

A Division of The McGraw-Hill Companies

Analysts International Corporation

Business Summary - 23-JUN-99

Analysts International Corp. provides a full range of computer software services to computer users, computer manufacturers and software developers throughout the U.S., Canada and the U.K. ANLY offers a wide range of service offerings, sometimes referred to by others in the industry as "solutions," including custom software development under company project management, Year 2000 assessment and remediation services, supplemental information technology (IT) and software engineering staffing, maintenance of legacy systems, help-desk services and single-source staffing of programmers and other software professionals through the company's TechWest division.

The company provides its services to a variety of industry segments, ranging from manufacturing to food. In FY 98 (Jun.), customers in the telecommunications, electronics, manufacturing and services sectors provided 25%, 22%, 12% and 10% of total revenues, respectively.

ANLY provided services to approximately 900 clients during FY 98. ANLY's two biggest customers, U S WEST and IBM, provide a relatively large percentage of total revenues. ANLY's TechWest division supplies technical personnel who serve U S WEST's information technology and software engineering needs. Revenues from U S WEST accounted for about 22% of total revenues during FY 97 and FY 98, and the company expects it to contribute the same percentage of FY 99 revenues. ANLY provides technical services to IBM and its customers. Revenues from IBM accounted for about 16% to 21% of total revenues during the last three fiscal years. In December 1997, the company renewed its contract with IBM for three more years.

Out of the company's 5,300 employees at June 30, 1998, approximately 4,500 were systems analysts, computer programmers and other technical personnel whose services are billable to clients. Several years of programming experience is generally a prerequisite to employment with ANLY.

In 1996, the company formed a business unit to assist companies in solving the Year 2000 problem. The unit consists of consultants with expertise in the problem which acts as a central resource to other consultants in the field. In 1997, the company formed an alliance with Viasoft Inc., whereby ANLY will license Viasoft's Year 2000 services and technology in providing Year 2000 solutions.

In December 1998, ANLY announced the acquisition of the information technology consulting and services business of Enterprise Solutions Inc., which specializes in data warehouse and decision support solutions. Terms of the deal were not disclosed. In February 1999, ANLY acquired Real World Training Systems LLC, a provider of software services.

Per Share Data ($) (Year Ended Jun. 30)	1999	1998	1997	1996	1995	1994	1993	1992	1991	1990
Tangible Bk. Val.	NA	3.54	2.79	2.44	2.07	1.71	1.50	1.23	1.09	0.95
Cash Flow	NA	1.15	0.85	0.66	0.60	0.44	0.45	0.31	0.30	0.31
Earnings	1.00	0.99	0.73	0.56	0.52	0.37	0.38	0.25	0.26	0.29
Dividends	0.38	0.36	0.29	0.24	0.17	0.15	0.13	0.12	0.12	0.11
Payout Ratio	38%	36%	40%	43%	33%	41%	29%	49%	45%	31%
Prices - High	19 3/4	36	28	20 3/8	11	6 7/8	8	5 3/4	4	5 1/4
- Low	8 5/8	13 1/4	36 1/2	9 1/8	6 5/8	4 7/8	5	3 1/2	2 5/8	2 1/4
P/E Ratio - High	20	36	50	26	21	19	21	23	15	18
- Low	9	13	19	16	13	13	13	14	10	8
Income Statement Analysis (Million $)										
Revs.	NA	587	440	330	218	176	160	130	117	108
Oper. Inc.	NA	40.1	29.0	21.9	19.6	14.2	14.4	9.3	9.0	9.7
Depr.	NA	3.7	2.8	2.2	1.8	1.7	1.4	1.1	0.7	0.5
Int. Exp.	NA	Nil	Nil	Nil	Nil	Nil	Nil	Nil	Nil	Nil
Pretax Inc.	NA	37.7	27.2	20.7	18.5	12.8	13.5	8.7	8.9	9.9
Eff. Tax Rate	NA	40%	40%	40%	39%	38%	39%	38%	38%	39%
Net Inc.	NA	22.6	16.4	12.4	11.3	8.0	8.3	5.4	5.6	6.0
Balance Sheet & Other Fin. Data (Million $)										
Cash	NA	11.9	17.9	17.0	12.6	10.7	9.9	7.4	7.0	5.3
Curr. Assets	NA	110	87.8	69.0	56.8	41.3	35.0	29.1	23.8	23.1
Total Assets	NA	133	105	81.4	67.5	51.2	44.9	38.1	32.1	29.3
Curr. Liab.	NA	42.5	32.8	22.0	17.0	9.8	8.9	8.6	6.8	7.4
LT Debt	NA	Nil	Nil	Nil	Nil	Nil	Nil	Nil	Nil	Nil
Common Eqty.	NA	90.2	66.1	53.7	45.1	36.6	31.7	25.8	22.7	19.6
Total Cap.	NA	90.2	72.5	53.7	45.1	36.6	31.7	25.8	22.7	19.6
Cap. Exp.	NA	7.7	3.0	2.9	1.9	1.3	1.6	2.2	2.1	1.6
Cash Flow	NA	26.3	19.2	14.6	13.0	9.6	9.7	6.5	6.3	6.5
Curr. Ratio	NA	2.6	2.7	3.1	3.3	4.2	3.9	3.4	3.5	3.1
% LT Debt of Cap.	NA	Nil	NM	Nil	Nil	Nil	Nil	Nil	Nil	Nil
% Net Inc.of Revs.	NA	3.8	3.7	3.8	5.1	4.5	5.2	4.1	4.8	5.6
% Ret. on Assets	NA	19.0	17.5	16.7	18.9	16.5	19.8	15.2	18.1	21.7
% Ret. on Equity	NA	27.8	24.8	25.1	27.5	23.2	28.6	22.1	26.3	34.0

Data as orig reptd.; bef. results of disc opers/spec. items. Per share data adj. for stk. divs. Bold denotes diluted EPS (FASB 128)-prior periods restated. E-Estimated. NA-Not Available. NM-Not Meaningful. NR-Not Ranked.

Office—3601 West 76th St., Minneapolis, MN 55435.**Tel**—(612) 835-5900. **Website**—http://www.analysts.com **Chrmn & CEO**—F. W. Lang. **Pres & COO**—V. C. Benda. **VP-Fin & Treas**—G. M. McGrath. **Secy**—T. R. Mahler. **Investor Contact**—George Zak (847) 619-4673. **Dirs**—V. C. Benda, W. K. Drake, F. W. Lang, M. A. Loftus, E. M. Mahoney, R. Prince. **Transfer Agent**—State Street Bank & Trust Co., Boston. **Incorporated**—in Minnesota in 1966. **Empl**— 5,300. **S&P Analyst:** Scott H. Kessler

STANDARD
&POOR'S
STOCK REPORTS

Anchor BanCorp Wisconsin

NASDAQ Symbol **ABCW**

In S&P SmallCap 600

09-OCT-99

Industry: Savings & Loan Companies

Summary: This company's main subsidiary is AnchorBank, a savings and loan with nearly 50 full-service offices located in Wisconsin.

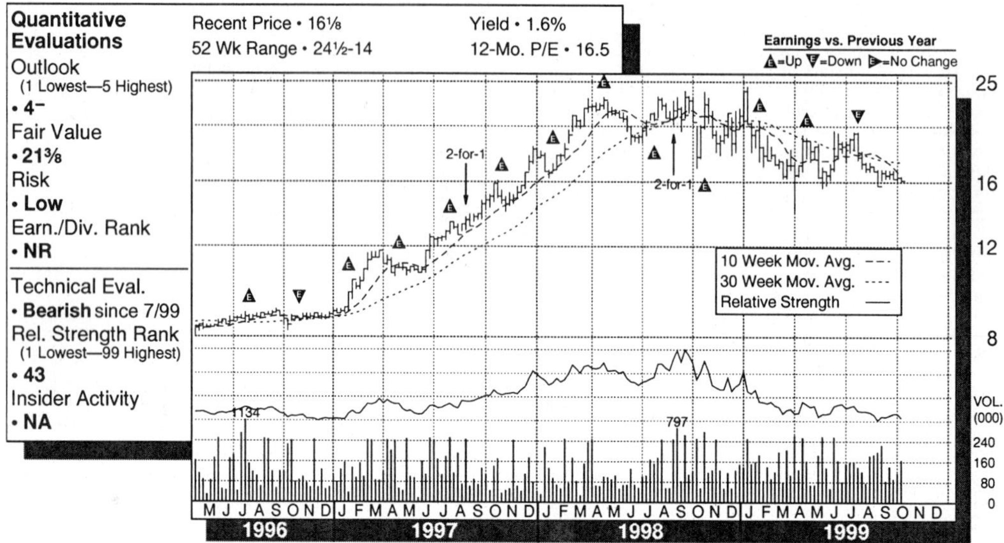

Business Profile - 10-AUG-99

In June 1999, ABCW acquired FCB Financial Corp. for about 7.45 million common shares. FCB is the parent company of Fox Cities Bank, a $535 million federally chartered savings association, with 13 offices in eight Wisconsin cities. Following the acquisition, Anchor was operating a total of 48 full-service offices and two lending only facilities. The transaction is expected to have no effect on ABCW's earnings per share in FY 00 (Mar.) and to be 1%-2% accretive in FY 01. Management believes that the acquisition gives it a presence in two of the healthiest areas in Wisconsin - Duane County and the Fox River Valley.

Operational Review - 10-AUG-99

Net interest income for the three months ended June 30, 1999, rose 3.5%, year to year. However, the provision for loan losses tripled, noninterest income fell 33% and noninterest expense increased 83% mainly reflecting $8.5 million of expenses related to the acquisition of FCB Financial Corp., and a $1.8 million writeoff of goodwill. Pretax income fell 94%. After taxes at 78.2%, versus 38.1%, net income was down 98%, to $157,000 ($0.01 a share) from $7,858,000 ($0.31). Results for the FY 99 period were restated to reflect the FCB Financial Corp. acquisition.

Stock Performance - 08-OCT-99

In the past 30 trading days, ABCW's shares have increased 2%, compared to a 0.91% fall in the S&P 500. Average trading volume for the past five days was 32,980 shares, compared with the 40-day moving average of 30,641 shares.

Key Stock Statistics

Dividend Rate/Share	0.26	Shareholders	2,200
Shs. outstg. (M)	25.4	Market cap. (B)	$0.409
Avg. daily vol. (M)	0.025	Inst. holdings	28%
Tang. Bk. Value/Share	9.29		
Beta	0.33		

Value of $10,000 invested 5 years ago: $ 35,505

Fiscal Year Ending Mar. 31

	2000	1999	1998	1997	1996	1995
Revenues (Million $)						
1Q	52.11	42.93	39.05	38.26	30.78	—
2Q	—	44.73	39.86	40.35	34.10	—
3Q	—	43.51	41.34	40.64	34.69	—
4Q	—	42.83	40.93	—	35.41	26.40
Yr.	—	174.0	161.2	157.8	135.0	112.4
Earnings Per Share ($)						
1Q	**0.01**	**0.33**	**0.24**	**0.23**	0.17	—
2Q	—	**0.33**	**0.26**	**0.01**	0.16	—
3Q	—	**0.32**	**0.29**	**0.24**	0.16	—
4Q	—	**0.30**	**0.27**	**0.24**	0.18	—
Yr.	—	**1.28**	**1.06**	**0.71**	0.68	0.67

Next earnings report expected: late October

Dividend Data (Dividends have been paid since 1993.)

Amount ($)	Date Decl.	Ex-Div. Date	Stock of Record	Payment Date
0.050	Oct. 20	Oct. 28	Oct. 30	Nov. 13 '98
0.050	Jan. 21	Jan. 28	Feb. 01	Feb. 15 '99
0.050	Apr. 20	Apr. 28	May. 01	May. 15 '99
0.065	Jul. 20	Jul. 28	Jul. 30	Aug. 13 '99

A Division of The McGraw-Hill Companies

Anchor BanCorp Wisconsin, Inc.

Business Summary - 10-AUG-99

With its main subsidiary, AnchorBank, organized in 1919, Anchor BanCorp Wisconsin operates a savings and loan business in Wisconsin. As of March 31, 1999, its operations were mainly in the metropolitan area of Madison, WI, the suburban communities of Dane County, WI, and southern Wisconsin, as well as contiguous counties in Iowa and Illinois. In addition to its main office in Madison, the bank was operating 35 full-service offices and two loan origination offices.

The company expanded its operations through the June 1999 acquisition of FCB Financial Corp. for about 7.45 million common shares. FCB is the parent company of Fox Cities Bank, a $535 million federally chartered savings association which has 13 offices located in Appleton, Berlin, Darboy, Menasha, Neenah, Oshkosh, Ripon, Wautoma and Winneconne. All of the Fox Cities Bank offices will operate as AnchorBank branch offices. Following the acquisition, the company was operating 48 full service offices and two lending only facilities, and had assets of about $2.6 billion.

Lending efforts are focused on the origination of single-family residential loans secured by properties located mainly in Wisconsin. Adjustable-rate loans are generally being originated for inclusion in the bank's loan portfolio, and fixed-rate loans are generally being originated for sale into the secondary market.

Gross loans receivable totaled $1.83 billion at the end of FY 99 (Mar.) and were divided as follows: single-family residential mortgages 46%, multi-family residential mortgages 12%, commercial real estate mortgages 12%, construction loans 9%, land loans 1%, consumer loans 18%, and commercial business loans 2%.

As of March 31, 1999, the allowance for loan and foreclosure losses totaled $20,208,000 (1.11% of loans outstanding), compared with $21,833,000 (1.30%) a year earlier. Net chargeoffs totaled $2,240,000 (0.13% of average loans) in FY 99, versus $1,217,000 (0.08%) a year earlier. As of March 31, 1999, total nonperforming assets aggregated $5,132,000 (0.24% of total assets), compared with $12,863,000 (0.64%) a year earlier.

In FY 99, the average yield on total interest-earning assets was 7.71% (7.99% in FY 98), while the average rate paid on total interest-bearing liabilities was 4.84% (4.99%), for a net interest rate spread of 2.87% (3.00%).

Interest on loans accounted for about 80% of total income in FY 99, interest on mortgage-related securities 7%, interest on investment securities 3%, gains on sale of loans 4%, and other noninterest income 6%.

Total deposits of $1.50 billion at the end of FY 99 were divided: NOW accounts 12%, money market accounts 16%, passbook accounts 7% and certificates of deposit 65%.

Per Share Data ($)

(Year Ended Mar. 31)	1999	1998	1997	1996	1995	1994	1993	1992	1991	1990
Tangible Bk. Val.	7.88	14.28	6.43	6.00	5.49	4.87	4.29	NA	NA	NA
Earnings	1.28	1.06	0.71	0.68	0.66	0.58	NA	NA	NA	NA
Dividends	0.18	0.23	0.14	0.10	0.08	0.05	0.05	NA	NA	NA
Payout Ratio	14%	22%	20%	15%	11%	9%	NA	NA	NA	NA
Cal. Yrs.	1998	1997	1996	1995	1994	1993	1992	1991	1990	1989
Prices - High	$24\frac{1}{8}$	$18\frac{3}{4}$	$9\frac{1}{8}$	$9\frac{1}{8}$	$6\frac{3}{8}$	$5\frac{1}{4}$	$3\frac{5}{8}$	NA	NA	NA
- Low	$16\frac{1}{4}$	$8\frac{7}{8}$	$7\frac{1}{2}$	$5\frac{7}{8}$	$4\frac{3}{8}$	$3\frac{3}{8}$	$2\frac{3}{8}$	NA	NA	NA
P/E Ratio - High	19	18	12	13	9	9	8	NA	NA	NA
- Low	13	8	10	8	6	5	5	NA	NA	NA

Income Statement Analysis (Million $)

	1999	1998	1997	1996	1995	1994	1993	1992	1991	1990
Net Int. Inc.	62.4	59.4	55.5	50.7	50.6	47.8	47.9	37.4	NA	NA
Loan Loss Prov.	0.8	0.3	0.5	0.5	1.6	4.3	7.4	7.8	NA	NA
Non Int. Inc.	18.0	12.2	17.2	9.0	7.6	11.0	11.6	8.9	NA	NA
Non Int. Exp.	41.4	38.3	47.4	37.1	33.0	32.8	NA	NA	NA	NA
Pretax Inc.	38.2	33.0	21.5	22.5	23.5	21.7	17.8	8.9	NA	NA
Eff. Tax Rate	38%	38%	35%	35%	39%	38%	39%	35%	NA	NA
Net Inc.	23.5	20.5	13.9	14.5	14.4	13.5	10.9	5.8	NA	NA
% Net Int. Marg.	3.08	3.18	3.14	3.18	NA	NA	NA	NA	NA	NA

Balance Sheet & Other Fin. Data (Million $)

	1999	1998	1997	1996	1995	1994	1993	1992	1991	1990
Total Assets	2,142	1,999	1,885	1,755	1,511	1,380	1,297	1,265	NA	NA
Loans	1,724	1,591	1,627	1,486	1,358	1,220	NA	NA	NA	NA
Deposits	1,506	1,392	1,312	1,241	1,098	1,066	NA	NA	NA	NA
Capitalization:										
Debt	428	412	392	317	275	187	NA	NA	NA	NA
Equity	142	128	118	118	111	105	NA	NA	NA	NA
Total	571	540	510	435	386	292	NA	NA	NA	NA
% Ret. on Assets	1.1	1.1	0.8	0.9	1.0	1.0	0.8	NA	NA	NA
% Ret. on Equity	17.4	16.7	11.8	12.6	13.3	13.0	14.1	NA	NA	NA
% Loan Loss Resv.	1.2	1.4	1.5	1.6	1.8	2.0	1.9	1.6	NA	NA
% Risk Based Capital	10.1	10.2	10.7	NA	NA	NA	NA	NA	NA	NA
Price Times Book Value:										
Hi	3.1	2.7	1.4	1.5	1.2	1.1	0.9	NA	NA	NA
Low	1.8	1.3	1.2	1.0	0.8	0.7	0.6	NA	NA	NA

Data as orig reptd.; bef. results of disc opers/spec. items. Per share data adj. for stk. divs. Bold denotes diluted EPS (FASB 128)-prior periods restated. E-Estimated. NA-Not Available. NM-Not Meaningful. NR-Not Ranked.

Office—25 West Main St., Madison, WI 53703. **Tel**—(608) 252-8700. **Website**—http://www.anchorbank.com **Chrmn, Pres & CEO**—D. J. Timmerman. **CFO & Treas**—M. W. Helser. **VP-Secy**—J. A. Cattelino**Dirs**—R. A. Bergstrom, H. C. Berkenstadt, R. D Kropidlowski, G. M. Larson, D. D. Parker, P Richter, B. A. Robertson, D. J. Timmerman. **Transfer Agent & Registrar**—Firstar Trust, Milwaukee. **Incorporated**—in Wisconsin in 1992. **Empl**— 711. **S&P Analyst:** J.J.S.

STANDARD
&POOR'S
STOCK REPORTS

Anchor Gaming

NASDAQ Symbol **SLOT**

In S&P SmallCap 600

09-OCT-99

Industry: Gaming, Lottery & Pari-mutuel Cos.

Summary: This diversified gaming company operates two casinos in Colorado, develops proprietary games, and operates a gaming machine route.

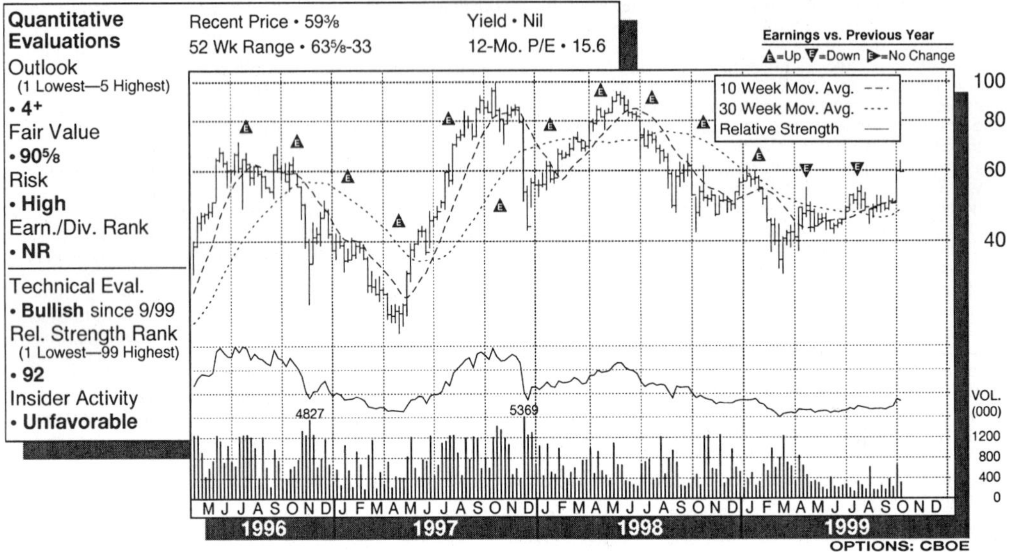

Business Profile - 29-SEP-99

On June 29, 1999, Anchor Gaming acquired Powerhouse Technologies, Inc. (PTI) for approximately $289 million. PTI is one of the leading suppliers of system software, equipment and related services for on-line lotteries, video lotteries, and pari-mutuel systems throughout the world, and is a manufacturer and distributor of gaming devices for casinos. The combined entity will have annualized revenues of roughly $450 million. The company repurchased 165,000 shares of its common stock during the fourth quarter of FY 99 (Jun.) for approximately $7.5 million or an average price of $45.20 per share. As of June 30, 1999 there were 369,700 shares authorized for repurchase under SLOT's previously announced repurchase program.

Operational Review - 29-SEP-99

Total revenues (preliminary) in FY 99 (Jun.) rose 7.3%, year to year, driven by an 8.8% advance in proprietary games operations and a 12% increase in route operations. Margins narrowed, reflecting increased costs of proprietary games, casino and route operations, and with higher depreciation and amortization charges and a $17.5 million charge for acquired R&D in the current period; income from operations fell 21%. Other income was down 3.0%, and after taxes at 45.3%, versus 37.5%, net income declined 31%, to $47,507,000 ($3.82 a share, based on 5.6% fewer shares), from $68,400,000 ($5.20).

Stock Performance - 08-OCT-99

In the past 30 trading days, SLOT's shares have increased 21%, compared to a 0.91% fall in the S&P 500. Average trading volume for the past five days was 61,140 shares, compared with the 40-day moving average of 58,000 shares.

Key Stock Statistics

Dividend Rate/Share	Nil	Shareholders	10,000
Shs. outstg. (M)	11.9	Market cap. (B)	$0.706
Avg. daily vol. (M)	0.077	Inst. holdings	40%
Tang. Bk. Value/Share	16.43		
Beta	1.50		

Value of $10,000 invested 5 years ago: NA

Fiscal Year Ending Jun. 30

	1999	1998	1997	1996	1995	1994
Revenues (Million $)						
1Q	64.60	54.48	35.18	27.82	23.58	8.07
2Q	61.84	53.51	35.66	27.24	22.57	8.40
3Q	59.82	59.18	36.79	29.05	23.96	17.71
4Q	62.67	64.76	46.12	32.36	27.30	20.59
Yr.	248.9	231.9	153.8	116.5	97.41	54.77
Earnings Per Share ($)						
1Q	**1.48**	1.23	0.60	0.43	0.33	0.20
2Q	**1.34**	**1.20**	**0.60**	0.40	0.32	0.16
3Q	**1.18**	**1.33**	0.63	0.46	0.34	0.32
4Q	**-0.22**	**1.42**	0.78	0.54	0.42	0.30
Yr.	**3.82**	**5.20**	**2.63**	1.84	1.40	1.03

Next earnings report expected: late October

Dividend Data

No cash dividends have been paid, and the company has said it does not intend to pay any for the foreseeable future. A shareholder rights plan was authorized in 1997.

A Division of The McGraw-Hill Companies

STANDARD
&POOR'S
STOCK REPORTS

Anchor Gaming

Business Summary - 29-SEP-99

This Colorado casino operator has hit the jackpot as a developer of proprietary games, whose revenue contribution burst from less than 1% in FY 93 (Jun.) to 49% in FY 98; Anchor Gaming also operates a gaming machine route in Nevada. In March 1999, the company announced the acquisition, for approximately $280 million of cash, of Powerhouse Technologies (Nasdaq: PWRH). Powerhouse is a leading global supplier of software, equipment and related services for on-line lotteries, video lotteries and pari-mutual systems. The combined entity will have annualized revenues of roughly $450 million. In FY 98, casino operations contributed 35% of revenues (45% in FY 97), proprietary games 49% (32%), route operations 15% (22%), and food and beverage 1% (1%).

In Colorado, the company operates two casinos, both of which emphasize gaming machine play. Its Colorado Central Station Casino is located in Black Hawk, CO, and features about 700 gaming machines, 10 blackjack tables, and nine poker tables; it is the highest revenue earning casino in the state of Colorado. The Colorado Grande Casino, in Cripple Creek, CO, features about 210 gaming machines, 44 adjacent parking spaces, and a full service restaurant and bar. Black Hawk and Central City are contiguous, located approximately 40 miles from Denver and 10 miles from Interstate 70. Cripple Creek is located about 45 miles from Colorado Springs.

The company develops proprietary games, which it markets to casinos and uses in its own gaming operations. These games are developed mainly in-house, manufactured by major gaming companies, and then modified by SLOT. The company's strategy is to develop games that provide casinos with a higher win per machine than their existing gaming devices while generating recurring revenues to the company from royalty, revenue participation, fixed daily rental fees, or other similar arrangements. Proprietary games may be played on gaming machines or at gaming tables, depending on the particular game. The company's proprietary games include Double Down Stud (its first internally developed proprietary game), Silver Strike, Clear Winner (introduced in the FY 95 fourth quarter), Wheel of Gold (FY 96), CashBall (FY 98), Crazy Joker Poker (FY 98), and SafeBuster (FY 98).

SLOT's gaming machine route operations in Nevada consist of about 840 gaming machines at 60 locations. Gaming machine route operations involve the installation, operation and service of gaming machines (primarily video poker machines) under space leases with retail chains and under participation arrangements with local taverns and other retailers, mainly in the Las Vegas area.

Per Share Data ($) (Year Ended Jun. 30)	1999	1998	1997	1996	1995	1994	1993	1992	1991	1990
Tangible Bk. Val.	NA	16.43	12.96	10.86	5.52	NA	NA	NA	NA	NA
Cash Flow	NA	6.16	3.25	2.16	1.69	1.29	NA	NA	NA	NA
Earnings	3.82	5.20	2.61	1.84	1.40	1.03	0.71	0.43	NA	NA
Dividends	Nil	Nil	Nil	Nil	Nil	Nil	NA	NA	NA	NA
Payout Ratio	Nil	Nil	Nil	Nil	Nil	Nil	NA	NA	NA	NA
Prices - High	63⅝	94¾	99½	71	26½	19½	NA	NA	NA	NA
- Low	33	42	23½	21½	15¼	10½	NA	NA	NA	NA
P/E Ratio - High	17	18	38	39	19	19	NA	NA	NA	NA
- Low	9	8	9	12	11	10	NA	NA	NA	NA
Income Statement Analysis (Million $)										
Revs.	NA	232	154	116	97.0	55.0	29.0	26.0	NA	NA
Oper. Inc.	NA	119	64.1	38.0	28.1	17.0	NA	NA	NA	NA
Depr.	NA	12.7	8.8	4.1	3.3	2.3	NA	NA	NA	NA
Int. Exp.	NA	0.2	0.3	0.4	0.7	1.3	0.9	1.4	NA	NA
Pretax Inc.	NA	110	57.0	35.5	25.5	13.4	7.0	4.2	NA	NA
Eff. Tax Rate	NA	37%	37%	37%	37%	35%	34%	34%	NA	NA
Net Inc.	NA	68.4	35.7	22.3	16.0	8.7	4.6	2.8	NA	NA
Balance Sheet & Other Fin. Data (Million $)										
Cash	NA	73.2	66.4	78.1	26.1	10.5	3.9	2.1	NA	NA
Curr. Assets	NA	88.0	78.3	89.0	34.2	NA	NA	NA	NA	NA
Total Assets	NA	245	189	162	79.0	58.9	22.6	17.9	NA	NA
Curr. Liab.	NA	33.6	13.6	11.0	7.7	NA	NA	NA	NA	NA
LT Debt	NA	Nil	2.8	3.6	6.0	6.9	17.2	11.6	NA	NA
Common Eqty.	NA	210	171	146	65.0	47.0	3.8	1.5	NA	NA
Total Cap.	NA	212	174	150	71.5	54.2	21.4	13.3	NA	NA
Cap. Exp.	NA	22.5	38.1	27.9	7.8	14.4	NA	NA	NA	NA
Cash Flow	NA	81.1	44.5	26.4	19.3	NA	NA	NA	NA	NA
Curr. Ratio	NA	2.6	5.7	8.1	4.4	NA	NA	NA	NA	NA
% LT Debt of Cap.	NA	Nil	1.6	2.4	8.4	12.7	80.4	87.2	NA	NA
% Net Inc.of Revs.	NA	29.5	23.2	19.2	16.5	15.8	15.9	10.8	NA	NA
% Ret. on Assets	NA	31.5	20.3	18.5	23.2	21.3	22.4	NA	NA	NA
% Ret. on Equity	NA	35.8	22.5	21.1	28.6	NA	NA	NA	NA	NA

Data as orig reptd.; bef. results of disc opers/spec. items. Per share data adj. for stk. divs. Bold denotes diluted EPS (FASB 128)-prior periods restated. E-Estimated. NA-Not Available. NM-Not Meaningful. NR-Not Ranked.

Office—815 Pilot Rd., Las Vegas, Suite G, NV 89119. **Tel**—(702) 896-7568. **Chrmn**—S. E. Fulton. **CEO & Pres.**—M. D. Rumbolz. **EVP & Secy**—T. J. Matthews. **CFO & Investor Contact**—Geoffrey A. Sage. **Dirs**—S. D. Beath, M. B. Fulton, S. E. Fulton, G. J. Hettinger. E. F. Jones, M. D. Rumbolz. **Transfer Agent & Registrar**—ChaseMellon Shareholder Services, Encino, CA. **Incorporated**—in Nevada in 1993. **Empl**— 920. **S&P Analyst:** Stephen J. Tekirian

STANDARD
&POOR'S
STOCK REPORTS

Angelica Corp.

NYSE Symbol **AGL**

In S&P SmallCap 600

09-OCT-99

Industry:
Services (Commercial & Consumer)

Summary: AGL provides textile rental and laundry services to health care institutions, manufactures uniforms, and operates a national chain of specialty retail stores.

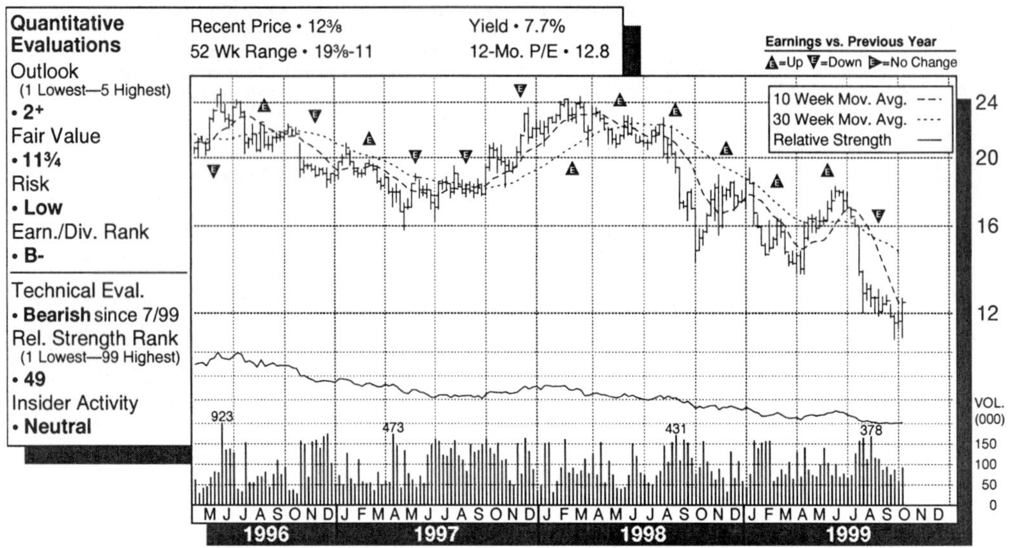

Business Profile - 15-JUL-99

In May 1999, AGL noted that while results for the first quarter of FY 00 (Jan.) were better than expected on a per share basis, the company did not feel that it was adding to sales and textile service revenues as quickly as needed to add value to the company. AGL believes it needs to increase the amount of new business being generated at textile services; add more sales representatives at manufacturing and marketing; and increase same-store sales at Life Uniform more consistently, and reduce cost of goods for this segment as well. At textile services, AGL has established goals to reduce labor and utility costs by 20% over the next three-year planning period. At Life Retail, the company is evaluating additional distribution channels, and intends to be more aggressive in closing down those stores with continuing operating losses.

Operational Review - 15-JUL-99

Total revenues in the three months ended May 1, 1999, declined 5.9%, year to year, as a 6.4% increase in Life Retail store sales was more than outweighed by a 2.0% decrease in textile service revenues and a 16% drop in manufacturing and marketing sales. Margins widened, largely on improvements at the textile services and manufacturing and marketing businesses. After taxes at 38.0% in both periods, net income edged up 2.6%, to $2,491,000 ($0.29 a share, on 5.9% fewer shares) from $2,428,000 ($0.26).

Stock Performance - 08-OCT-99

In the past 30 trading days, AGL's shares have increased 3%, compared to a 0.91% fall in the S&P 500. Average trading volume for the past five days was 18,340 shares, compared with the 40-day moving average of 18,251 shares.

Key Stock Statistics

Dividend Rate/Share	0.96	Shareholders	1,408
Shs. outstg. (M)	8.7	Market cap. (B)	$0.108
Avg. daily vol. (M)	0.015	Inst. holdings	65%
Tang. Bk. Value/Share	18.33		
Beta	0.59		

Value of $10,000 invested 5 years ago: $ 5,905

Fiscal Year Ending Jan. 31

	2000	1999	1998	1997	1996	1995
Revenues (Million $)						
1Q	121.1	128.7	127.4	121.6	123.8	117.0
2Q	115.8	123.2	129.2	122.6	121.9	118.2
3Q	—	121.6	132.8	124.3	123.6	120.1
4Q	—	118.2	137.2	120.7	117.7	117.5
Yr.	—	491.6	526.5	489.2	487.0	472.8
Earnings Per Share ($)						
1Q	**0.29**	**0.26**	**0.22**	0.33	0.38	0.35
2Q	**0.15**	**0.20**	**0.14**	0.30	0.29	0.35
3Q	—	**0.31**	**-1.29**	0.20	0.31	0.46
4Q	—	**0.22**	**0.18**	0.05	-0.85	0.28
Yr.	—	**0.99**	**-0.75**	**0.88**	0.13	1.44

Next earnings report expected: mid November

Dividend Data (Dividends have been paid since 1954.)

Amount ($)	Date Decl.	Ex-Div. Date	Stock of Record	Payment Date
0.240	Nov. 25	Dec. 11	Dec. 15	Jan. 01 '99
0.240	Feb. 24	Mar. 11	Mar. 15	Apr. 01 '99
0.240	May. 25	Jun. 11	Jun. 15	Jul. 01 '99
0.240	Sep. 01	Sep. 13	Sep. 15	Oct. 01 '99

A Division of The McGraw-Hill Companies

Angelica Corporation

Business Summary - 15-JUL-99

Since 1878, Angelica Corp. (AGL) has provided products and services to a variety of institutions and individuals in the health services, hospitality and other service industries.

The textiles services division has 30 laundry plants generally in or near various major metropolitan areas in the U.S. principally providing textile rental and laundry services for health care institutions. This segment also provides general linen services in selected areas, principally to hotels, motels and restaurants. The markets in which the textile services division operates are very competitive, being characterized generally by a large number of independent, privately owned competitors. While industry statistics are not available, the company believes that its textile services division constitutes the largest supplier of textile rental and laundry services to health care institutions in the U.S.

AGL's manufacturing and marketing operations consist of Angelica Image Apparel in the U.S. and two smaller operations in Canada, collectively engaged in the manufacture and sale of uniforms and business career apparel for a wide variety of institutions and businesses. The raw materials used by Angelica Image Apparel in the conduct of its business consist principally of textile piece goods, thread and trimmings such as buttons, zippers and labels. The company purchases piece goods from most major U.S. manufacturers of textile products. Recently, AGL has been closing some of its domestic manufacturing plants and sourcing more of its image apparel from domestic and foreign contractors and other foreign suppliers. At the end of FY 99 (Jan.), foreign suppliers accounted for slightly more than 40% of this segment's products. The company believes that it is one of the leading suppliers of garments to hospitals, hotels and motels, food service establishments, and textile service suppliers in the U.S.

The retail sales segment is a specialty retailer offering uniforms and shoes primarily for nurses and other health care professionals through a nationwide chain of retail stores under the name Life Uniform and Shoe Shops, located primarily in malls and strip shopping centers. AGL believes there are about 2,000 specialty retail stores in the U.S., primarily privately owned, offering merchandise comparable to that offered by its retail sales segment. In addition, such merchandise is also offered by others, including some large chain apparel retailers. AGL believes its retail sales segment is the largest U.S. specialty retailer offering uniforms and shoes to nurses and other health care professionals.

Per Share Data ($) (Year Ended Jan. 31)	1999	1998	1997	1996	1995	1994	1993	1992	1991	1990
Tangible Bk. Val.	18.30	18.15	19.86	19.82	20.77	20.49	20.87	20.43	18.92	17.01
Cash Flow	2.91	0.75	2.34	1.63	2.90	2.64	2.86	3.68	3.47	3.08
Earnings	0.99	-0.75	0.88	0.13	1.44	1.23	1.50	2.43	2.37	2.06
Dividends	0.96	0.96	0.96	0.95	0.94	0.93	0.92	0.89	0.84	0.77
Payout Ratio	97%	NM	109%	NM	65%	76%	60%	37%	35%	37%
Cal. Yrs.	1998	1997	1996	1995	1994	1993	1992	1991	1990	1989
Prices - High	24 1/2	23 5/8	25 1/8	27 1/2	29 1/2	28 3/8	40	40 1/4	33 7/8	30 3/8
- Low	14 1/8	15 3/4	18 1/8	19 3/8	24 1/2	22 1/2	22 1/4	29 5/8	27	22
P/E Ratio - High	25	NM	29	NM	20	23	27	17	14	15
- Low	14	NM	21	NM	17	18	15	12	11	11
Income Statement Analysis (Million $)										
Revs.	492	527	489	487	473	427	431	434	414	369
Oper. Inc.	43.9	30.8	38.5	42.0	45.5	41.9	45.0	57.2	53.4	45.6
Depr.	17.3	13.7	13.4	13.8	13.3	12.9	12.6	11.7	10.3	9.4
Int. Exp.	9.7	10.7	9.6	9.1	7.9	7.4	7.5	7.0	6.3	5.1
Pretax Inc.	14.3	-11.1	12.9	1.9	21.3	18.1	22.3	36.5	35.9	31.2
Eff. Tax Rate	38%	NM	38%	39%	39%	38%	38%	38%	39%	39%
Net Inc.	8.9	-6.9	8.0	1.1	13.1	11.2	13.8	22.7	22.1	19.2
Balance Sheet & Other Fin. Data (Million $)										
Cash	6.9	2.8	2.1	11.0	2.2	2.0	2.7	6.1	2.0	6.9
Curr. Assets	197	229	232	227	220	210	205	211	205	184
Total Assets	339	379	374	353	354	333	327	335	316	279
Curr. Liab.	61.3	87.4	69.4	69.4	69.2	53.1	43.7	50.4	70.4	53.7
LT Debt	90.9	96.7	97.4	100	69.7	72.3	78.2	80.5	57.8	50.6
Common Eqty.	166	174	189	190	197	192	189	190	176	161
Total Cap.	264	276	291	293	270	269	273	275	238	218
Cap. Exp.	8.7	21.3	23.6	8.8	11.5	12.2	11.8	13.3	14.1	13.6
Cash Flow	26.2	6.8	21.4	14.9	26.4	24.0	26.4	34.4	32.4	28.6
Curr. Ratio	3.2	2.6	3.3	5.0	3.2	4.0	4.7	4.2	2.9	3.4
% LT Debt of Cap.	34.5	35.0	33.5	34.2	25.8	26.9	28.7	29.3	24.3	23.2
% Net Inc.of Revs.	1.8	NM	1.7	NM	2.8	2.6	3.2	5.2	5.3	5.2
% Ret. on Assets	2.5	NM	2.2	NM	3.8	3.4	4.2	6.9	7.4	7.5
% Ret. on Equity	5.2	NM	4.3	NM	6.7	5.8	7.4	12.4	13.1	12.4

Data as orig reptd.; bef. results of disc opers/spec. items. Per share data adj. for stk. divs. Bold denotes diluted EPS (FASB 128)-prior periods restated. E-Estimated. NA-Not Available. NM-Not Meaningful. NR-Not Ranked.

Office—424 S. Woods Mill Rd., Chesterfield, MO 63017-3406. **Tel**—(314) 854-3800. **Website**—http://www.angelica-corp.com**Chrmn, Pres & CEO**—D. W. Hubble. **SVP-Fin, CFO & Investor Contact**—Theodore M. Armstrong. **Treas & Secy**—T. M. Degnan. **Dirs**—D. A. Abrahamson, S. S. Elliot, E. H. Harbison Jr., D. H. Hubble, L. F. Loewe, C. W. Mueller, W. A. Peck, W. P. Stiritz, H. E. Trusheim. **Transfer Agent & Registrar**—Boatmen's Trust Co., St. Louis. **Incorporated**—in Missouri in 1904; reincorporated in Missouri in 1968. **Empl**— 8,600. **S&P Analyst:** M.I.

STANDARD
&POOR'S
STOCK REPORTS

Anixter International

NYSE Symbol **AXE**
In S&P SmallCap 600

09-OCT-99

Industry:
Communications Equipment

Summary: This company distributes wiring systems for voice, data and video networks and electrical power applications in North America, Europe, Asia and Latin America.

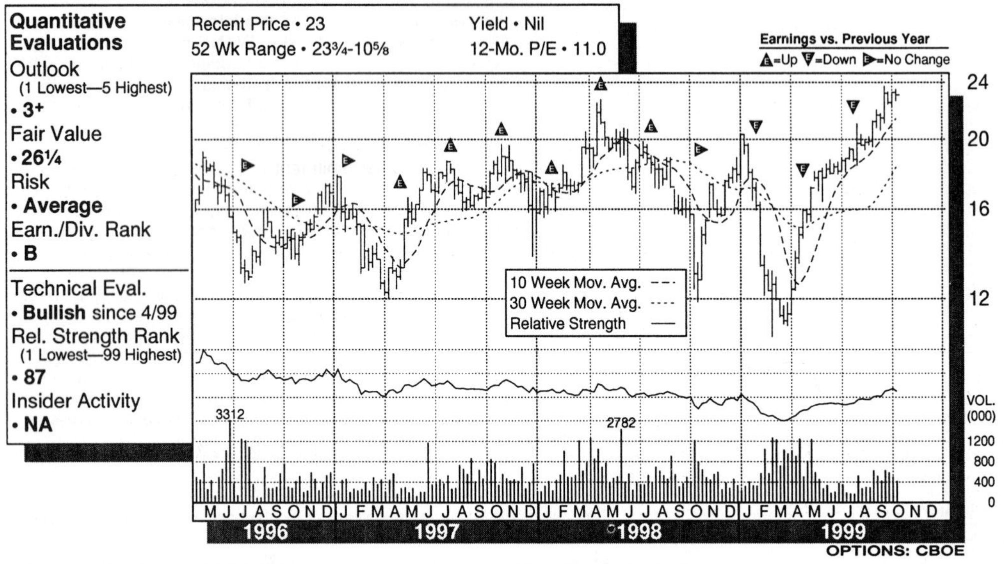

Business Profile - 25-AUG-99

Anixter's goal for 1999 is to achieve double-digit sales growth and improve operating margins. Based upon the positive trends in late second quarter bookings, AXE believes that its sales momentum will continue. However, AXE remains cautious about the possibility of short term sales disruptions in 1999, as customers deal with Y2K issues. In April 1999, AXE sold its North American Network Integration business to Ameritech (NYSE: AIT) for about $216 million in cash. AXE said this will allow it to focus entirely on expanding its distribution business. By devoting all of its efforts to distributing communications and wire and cable products, the company believes it can profitably build on its position as the leading global distributor.

Operational Review - 25-AUG-99

Total revenues from continuing operations in the six months ended July 2, 1999, rose 9.3%, year to year, reflecting increases of 13% and 2.0% in North America and Europe, respectively. Gross margins narrowed, but operating expenses grew less rapidly than revenues, and operating profit was up 11%, to $50.5 million, from $45.7 million. Absent a gain of $24.3 million from an investment in the year-earlier period, and after taxes at 42.0%, versus 41.7%, income from continuing operations declined 38%, to $19.9 million ($0.51 a share, on 17% fewer shares), from $32.2 million ($0.68). Results exclude income from discontinued operations of $1.15 and $0.34 a share in the respective periods.

Stock Performance - 08-OCT-99

In the past 30 trading days, AXE's shares have increased 9%, compared to a 0.91% fall in the S&P 500. Average trading volume for the past five days was 81,840 shares, compared with the 40-day moving average of 100,687 shares.

Key Stock Statistics

Dividend Rate/Share	Nil	Shareholders	5,420
Shs. outstg. (M)	36.0	Market cap. (B)	$0.830
Avg. daily vol. (M)	0.105	Inst. holdings	54%
Tang. Bk. Value/Share	4.62		
Beta	0.81		

Value of $10,000 invested 5 years ago: $ 16,472

Fiscal Year Ending Dec. 31

	1999	1998	1997	1996	1995	1994
Revenues (Million $)						
1Q	595.1	748.5	658.7	567.4	502.9	362.8
2Q	658.5	783.4	682.6	611.8	542.0	423.0
3Q	—	804.5	726.5	631.5	571.1	456.3
4Q	—	584.5	737.4	664.6	578.8	490.6
Yr.	—	2,349	2,805	2,475	2,195	1,733
Earnings Per Share ($)						
1Q	**0.19**	**0.35**	**0.23**	**0.20**	0.19	0.04
2Q	**0.33**	**0.46**	**0.22**	**0.16**	0.16	0.26
3Q	—	**0.24**	**0.24**	**0.17**	0.17	0.17
4Q	—	**0.07**	**0.26**	**0.19**	0.19	0.26
Yr.	—	**0.99**	**0.95**	**0.72**	**0.70**	**0.72**

Next earnings report expected: late October

Dividend Data

Common dividends were last paid in 1979. A two-for-one stock split was effected in 1995.

A Division of The McGraw-Hill Companies

Anixter International Inc.

Business Summary - 25-AUG-99

In April 1999, Anixter sold its North American Network Integration business. It had sold its European Network Integration business in the 1998 fourth quarter. As a result, the company is no longer in the business of providing services for the design, deployment and support of network infrastructures.

In keeping with its exit from the design, deployment and support of network infrastructures, AXE sold its remaining 7.1 million ANTEC Corp. shares in the first half of 1998, resulting in net after-tax proceeds of about $100 million. ANTEC is a communications technology company that specializes in design and engineering of hybrid fiber/coax broadband networks and the manufacturing, materials management and distribution of products for these networks.

Following its recent divestitures, the company is a leading distributor of wiring systems for voice, data and video networks and electrical power applications in North America, Europe, Asia and Latin America. It stocks and/or sells a full line of these products from a network of 98 locations in the U.S., 18 in Canada, 11 in the U.K., 26 in Europe, 18 in Latin America, 4 in Australia, and 14 in Asia. AXE sells about 54,000 products to 80,000 active customers.

Products distributed by AXE include communication (voice, data and video) products used to connect personal computers, peripheral equipment, mainframe equipment and various networks to each other. The products include an assortment of transmission media (copper and fiber optic cable) and components, as well as active data components for networking applications. The company sells products that are incorporated in local area networks (LANs), the internetworking of LANs to form wide area networks (WANs) and enterprise networks. AXE's products also include electrical wiring system products used for the transmission of electrical energy and control/monitoring of industrial processes.

Prior to 1989, the company's operations were primarily limited to North America and the U.K. In 1989, AXE made a major commitment to expand its operations into the international voice, data and video communications markets. Since then, it has opened businesses throughout Western and Central Europe and in significant markets in the Pacific Rim (other than Japan) and Latin America.

An important element of the company's business strategy is to develop and maintain close relationships with key suppliers, including the world's leading manufacturers of networking, communications cabling and electrical wiring systems products. These relationships stress joint product planning, inventory management, technical support, advertising and marketing. AXE does not compete with its suppliers in product design or manufacturing activities. About 44% of the purchases in 1998 were from the five largest suppliers.

Per Share Data ($)										
(Year Ended Dec. 31)	**1998**	**1997**	**1996**	**1995**	**1994**	**1993**	**1992**	**1991**	**1990**	**1989**
Tangible Bk. Val.	4.24	10.09	5.26	5.07	6.05	-0.20	-2.74	2.02	2.49	4.21
Cash Flow	1.58	1.62	1.27	1.10	0.97	1.57	0.17	-0.20	0.53	1.62
Earnings	0.99	0.95	0.73	0.71	0.72	0.21	-1.13	-1.21	-0.41	0.23
Dividends	Nil	Nil	Nil	Nil	Nil	Nil	Nil	Nil	Nil	Nil
Payout Ratio	Nil	Nil	Nil	Nil	Nil	Nil	Nil	Nil	Nil	Nil
Prices - High	22¾	19⅝	20	22⅛	18⅛	16⅞	12¼	10⅛	12	14½
- Low	11⅞	12	12⅝	16⅝	11⅜	10⅛	8	4⅞	3⅞	9
P/E Ratio - High	23	21	27	31	25	78	NM	NM	NM	61
- Low	12	13	17	23	16	47	NM	NM	NM	38
Income Statement Analysis (Million $)										
Revs.	2,349	2,805	2,475	2,195	1,733	1,909	1,682	1,689	1,977	2,121
Oper. Inc.	114	143	115	121	86.0	240	234	253	286	491
Depr.	26.8	31.9	26.9	21.7	16.0	82.0	76.0	69.0	89.0	139
Int. Exp.	31.7	33.5	29.9	24.8	NA	NA	190	207	236	299
Pretax Inc.	76.5	79.6	64.8	74.4	70.0	45.8	-79.8	-83.6	-39.7	71.1
Eff. Tax Rate	42%	43%	44%	48%	34%	65%	NM	NM	NM	58%
Net Inc.	44.7	45.3	36.1	39.1	46.2	16.1	-59.8	-77.0	-32.8	29.9
Balance Sheet & Other Fin. Data (Million $)										
Cash	20.5	10.6	18.2	10.5	14.0	53.0	45.0	29.0	56.0	28.0
Curr. Assets	907	1,014	869	781	621	681	564	607	742	681
Total Assets	1,322	1,441	1,261	1,185	1,111	2,494	2,641	2,752	3,443	4,126
Curr. Liab.	341	448	314	332	267	365	412	617	498	520
LT Debt	544	469	468	334	281	1,514	1,738	1,568	2,142	2,717
Common Eqty.	412	477	436	449	544	405	284	431	541	749
Total Cap.	973	979	934	818	833	2,117	2,190	2,081	2,766	3,563
Cap. Exp.	26.4	27.8	32.9	31.3	17.0	13.0	17.0	81.0	82.0	296
Cash Flow	71.5	77.2	63.0	60.8	62.0	95.0	10.0	-14.0	50.0	163
Curr. Ratio	2.7	2.3	2.8	2.4	2.3	1.9	1.4	1.0	1.5	1.3
% LT Debt of Cap.	55.9	47.9	50.2	40.9	33.7	71.5	79.4	75.3	77.4	76.3
% Net Inc.of Revs.	1.9	1.6	1.5	1.8	2.7	0.8	NM	NM	NM	1.4
% Ret. on Assets	3.2	3.4	2.9	3.4	2.8	0.6	NM	NM	NM	0.7
% Ret. on Equity	10.1	9.9	8.2	7.9	10.2	3.5	NM	NM	NM	3.3

Data as orig reptd.; bef. results of disc opers/spec. items. Per share data adj. for stk. divs. Bold denotes diluted EPS (FASB 128)-prior periods restated. E-Estimated. NA-Not Available. NM-Not Meaningful. NR-Not Ranked.

Office—4711 Golf Rd., Skokie, IL 60076. **Tel**—(847) 677-2600. **Website**—www.anixter.com **Chrmn**—S. Zell. **Pres & CEO**—R. F. Dammeyer. **SVP-Fin & CFO**—D. J. Letham. **SVP & Secy**—J. E. Knox. **SVP & Investor Contact**—Kirk E. Brewer (312-466-4042). **Dirs**—Sir J. Blyth, R.L. Crandall, R. F. Dammeyer, R. E. Fowler Jr., R. W. Grubbs Jr., F. P. Handy, M. N. Klein, J. R. Petty, S. Z. Rosenberg, S. M. Sloan, T. C. Theobald, S. Zell. **Transfer Agent & Registrar**—ChaseMellon Shareholder Services, Ridgefield Park, NJ. **Incorporated**— in Delaware in 1967. **Empl**— 4,800. **S&P Analyst:** J.J.A.

STANDARD
&POOR'S
STOCK REPORTS

AnnTaylor Stores

NYSE Symbol **ANN**

In S&P SmallCap 600

09-OCT-99

Industry: Retail (Specialty-Apparel)

Summary: This leading specialty retailer of women's better-quality apparel, shoes and accessories operates more than 385 stores in 41 states and the District of Columbia.

Quantitative Evaluations

Outlook (1 Lowest—5 Highest) • **2-**

Fair Value • **41**

Risk • **Average**

Earn./Div. Rank • **B-**

Technical Eval. • **Bullish** since 9/99

Rel. Strength Rank (1 Lowest—99 Highest) • **66**

Insider Activity • **NA**

Recent Price • 40¼

52 Wk Range • 53-21⅜

Yield • Nil

12-Mo. P/E • 21.9

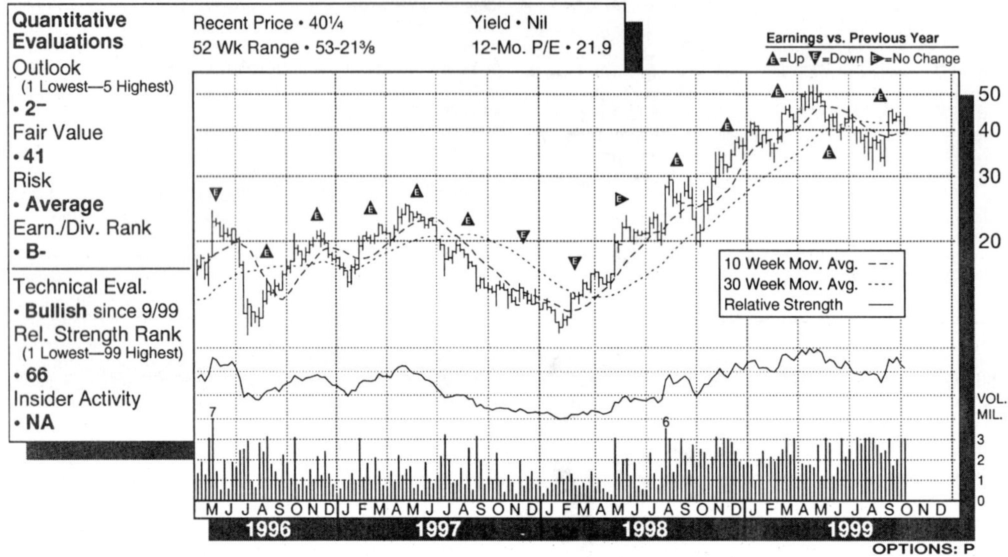

OPTIONS: P

Business Profile - 06-JUL-99

In June 1999, ANN announced its intention to raise at least $100 million through the sale of discounted convertible bonds, due in 2019. ANN plans to use the proceeds to refinance its current 8.75% Subordinated Notes due in 2000. As of June 11, 1999, ANN operated 383 stores in 42 states and the District of Columbia. For the quarter ending May 1, 1999, merchandise inventories were approximately $137 million. Cash and equivalents were over $65 million.

Operational Review - 06-JUL-99

Net sales for the three months ended May 1, 1999, were up 26%, year to year, the result of a 17% increase in comparable store sales and a higher store count. Gross margins widened, as the company benefited from selling a greater amount of products at full prices. SG&A expense rose less rapidly than sales, aided by better leverage of fixed expenses from the comparable store sales increase. After an 8.6% drop in interest expense, and taxes at 44.2%, versus 48.8%, net income was up sharply, to $14,755,000 ($0.51 a share), from $6,419,000 ($0.25).

Stock Performance - 08-OCT-99

In the past 30 trading days, ANN's shares have increased 20%, compared to a 0.91% fall in the S&P 500. Average trading volume for the past five days was 657,120 shares, compared with the 40-day moving average of 541,549 shares.

Key Stock Statistics

Dividend Rate/Share	Nil	Shareholders	730
Shs. outstg. (M)	31.5	Market cap. (B)	$ 1.3
Avg. daily vol. (M)	0.519	Inst. holdings	0%
Tang. Bk. Value/Share	7.80		
Beta	1.01		

Value of $10,000 invested 5 years ago: $ 16,262

Fiscal Year Ending Jan. 31

	2000	1999	1998	1997	1996	1995
Revenues (Million $)						
1Q	249.4	198.2	197.1	184.5	168.3	145.0
2Q	265.8	223.4	185.0	187.9	183.7	159.9
3Q	—	227.5	187.2	212.7	212.7	164.6
4Q	—	262.8	211.8	213.1	200.6	188.9
Yr.	—	911.9	781.0	798.1	731.1	658.8
Earnings Per Share ($)						
1Q	**0.51**	**0.25**	0.25	0.08	0.15	0.36
2Q	**0.42**	**0.27**	0.04	0.03	-0.13	0.34
3Q	—	**0.50**	0.08	0.13	0.03	0.35
4Q	—	**0.42**	**0.09**	0.12	-0.05	-1.05
Yr.	—	**1.44**	**0.47**	**0.36**	-0.04	1.40

Next earnings report expected: mid November

Dividend Data

No dividends have been paid.

A Division of The McGraw-Hill Companies

AnnTaylor Stores Corporation

Business Summary - 06-JUL-99

Long known as a leading specialty retailer of women's better-quality apparel, shoes and accessories, AnnTaylor Stores offers its customers a distinct fashion point of view. The company believes that its customer base is made up primarily of relatively affluent, fashion-conscious women who prefer classic styles, updated to reflect current fashion trends. ANN stores offer a collection of career and casual separates, weekend wear, dresses, tops, accessories, and shoes. As of January 30, 1999, the company operated 365 stores in 41 states and the District of Columbia. Of these stores, 306 were Ann Taylor stores, 46 were Ann Taylor Loft stores, and 13 were Ann Taylor Factory Stores.

The company emphasizes a total wardrobing strategy, whereby it trains its sales associates to assist customers in coordinating their wardrobe, helping them to achieve the Ann Taylor look, while reflecting each customer's personal style. The company believes that its customer base consists of women between 25 and 55 years old, and have limited time to shop. Stores offer a variety of coordinated apparel and an assortment of shoes and accessories to enable customers to assemble complete outfits. New moderate-priced stores are also being operated under the name AnnTaylor Loft. Merchandise is designed uniquely for these stores and is sold under the Ann Taylor Loft label.

AnnTaylor stores are located primarily in malls and upscale specialty retail centers, with the balance located in downtown and village locations.

Substantially all of the merchandise offered at the stores is developed by ANN's in-house product design and development teams, which design merchandise only for the company. The company's merchandising groups determine inventory needs for the upcoming season, edit the assortments developed by the design teams, plan monthly merchandise flows, and arrange for the production of merchandise either through ANN's sourcing division, or with manufacturers who are private label specialists. The company sources merchandise from about 235 manufacturers and vendors, none of which accounted for more than 9% of ANN's merchandise purchases in FY 99 (Jan.). Merchandise is manufactured in over 20 countries, with approximately 10% made in Hong Kong, and 35% made in China.

ANN's expansion strategy includes opening new stores in markets that it believes have the sufficient concentration of target customers. The company also plans to add stores, or expand the size of existing stores, in markets where it already has a presence.

Per Share Data ($)										
(Year Ended Jan. 31)	**1999**	**1998**	**1997**	**1996**	**1995**	**1994**	**1993**	**1992**	**1991**	**1990**
Tangible Bk. Val.	4.24	2.03	1.02	0.36	0.13	-3.42	-4.69	-6.24	-21.14	-21.91
Cash Flow	2.55	1.98	1.82	1.18	2.32	1.47	1.08	0.87	1.08	0.26
Earnings	1.44	0.47	0.36	-0.04	1.40	0.66	0.28	0.05	0.08	-0.91
Dividends	Nil	Nil	Nil	Nil	Nil	Nil	Nil	Nil	Nil	Nil
Payout Ratio	Nil	Nil	Nil	Nil	Nil	Nil	Nil	Nil	Nil	Nil
Cal. Yrs.	1998	1997	1996	1995	1994	1993	1992	1991	1990	1989
Prices - High	40¼	25¼	24¼	38	44⅞	30	25	36½	NA	NA
- Low	11¼	13	9¼	9⅞	20½	17½	14½	12	NA	NA
P/E Ratio - High	28	54	67	NM	32	45	89	NM	NA	NA
- Low	8	28	26	NM	15	27	52	NA	NA	NA
Income Statement Analysis (Million $)										
Revs.	912	781	798	731	666	508	474	444	411	354
Oper. Inc.	135	88.8	89.9	53.6	99	69.0	59.5	58.9	72.2	60.0
Depr.	39.8	38.8	36.3	28.3	21.3	18.0	17.0	15.7	14.2	14.7
Int. Exp.	18.1	20.0	24.4	21.0	14.2	17.7	21.3	34.0	50.1	55.9
Pretax Inc.	72.9	29.5	21.6	4.3	62.9	31.5	17.1	8.7	7.8	-10.6
Eff. Tax Rate	46%	59%	60%	1.21%	48%	55%	65%	88%	86%	NM
Net Inc.	39.3	12.0	8.7	-0.9	32.6	14.3	5.9	1.0	1.1	-11.2
Balance Sheet & Other Fin. Data (Million $)										
Cash	67.0	31.4	7.0	1.3	1.6	0.3	0.2	0.2	0.1	0.1
Curr. Assets	298	210	197	199	168	121	108	99	104	82.0
Total Assets	775	684	688	679	598	513	488	492	511	493
Curr. Liab.	130	87.9	78.0	112	65.9	68.1	78.5	72.4	61.9	58.3
LT Debt	201	105	131	232	200	180	158	186	367	356
Common Eqty.	433	384	371	326	326	259	245	229	58.0	58.0
Total Cap.	633	489	598	559	526	440	404	415	446	433
Cap. Exp.	45.1	22.9	16.1	78.4	61.3	25.1	4.3	10.0	11.8	6.1
Cash Flow	79.1	50.8	45.0	27.4	53.9	32.3	22.9	16.7	15.2	3.5
Curr. Ratio	2.3	2.4	2.5	1.8	2.6	1.8	1.4	1.4	1.7	1.4
% LT Debt of Cap.	31.7	21.5	21.9	41.5	38.0	41.0	39.2	44.8	82.4	82.1
% Net Inc.of Revs.	4.3	1.5	1.1	NM	4.9	2.8	1.2	0.2	0.3	NM
% Ret. on Assets	5.4	1.7	1.3	NM	5.7	2.8	1.2	0.1	0.2	NM
% Ret. on Equity	9.6	3.2	2.5	NM	10.8	5.6	2.4	0.6	2.1	NM

Data as orig. reptd.; bef. results of disc. opers. and/or spec. items. Per share data adj. for stk. divs. as of ex-div. date. Bold denotes diluted EPS (FASB 128). E-Estimated. NA-Not Available. NM-Not Meaningful. NR-Not Ranked.

Office—142 W. 57th St., New York, NY 10019.**Tel**—(212) 541-3300. **Chrmn & CEO**—J. P. Spainhour. **Pres & COO**—P. DeRosa. **EVP, CFO & Treas**—B. Erdos. **Dirs**—G. S. Armstrong, J. J. Burke Jr., W. E. Cantrell, P. DeRosa, R. C. Grayson, R. W. Hovsepian, R. B. Lazarus, H. M. Merriman, J. P. Spainhour. **Transfer Agent & Registrar**—Continental Stock Transfer & Trust Co., NYC. **Incorporated**—in Delaware in 1988. **Empl**— 7,300. **S&P Analyst:** Matthew C. Hershberg

STANDARD
&POOR'S
STOCK REPORTS

APEX Inc.

NASDAQ Symbol **APEX**

In S&P SmallCap 600

09-OCT-99

Industry: Computers (Networking)

Summary: APEX manufactures server management products, including console switching systems, remote server management products and integrated server cabinet solutions.

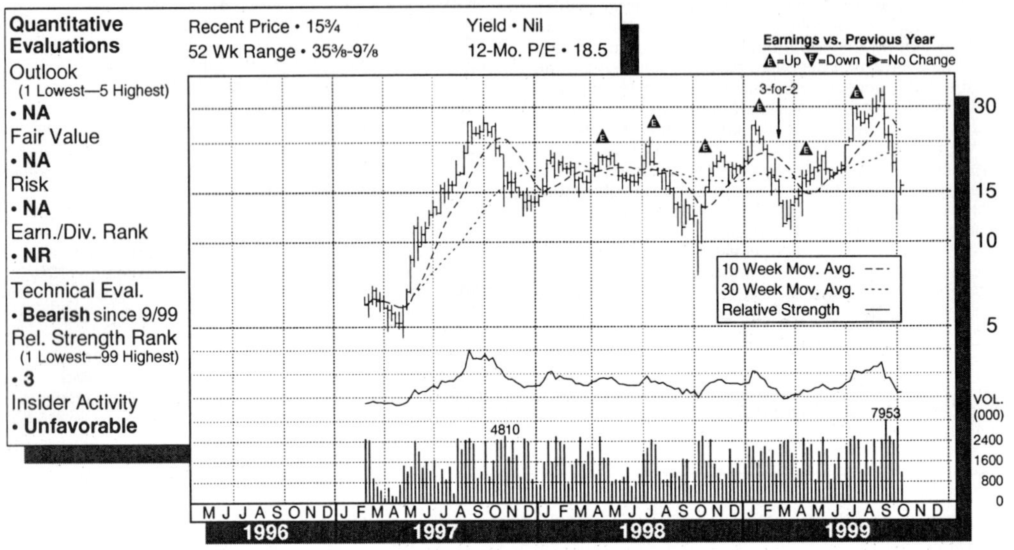

Business Profile - 20-JUL-99

APEX said that the strength in sales activity early in 1999's second quarter continued through June, concurrent with the company's move to a new facility in Redmond, WA. Second quarter 1999 operating expenses include moving costs of about $300,000 ($0.01 per share). A 3-for-2 stock split was distributed in March 1999. The present corporate title was adopted in mid-1999, reflecting APEX's predominance in the server management and console switching area.

Operational Review - 20-JUL-99

Net sales for the six months ended July 2, 1999, advanced 39%, year to year, mainly reflecting increased demand for private-label products. Profitability was restricted by a sharp rise in research and development expenses and by an increase in lower-margin private-label OEM sales as a percentage of total sales. Pretax income was up 32%. After taxes at 34.4%, versus 33.5%, net income rose 30%, to $9,041,000 ($0.43 a share) from $6,944,000 ($0.33, adjusted).

Stock Performance - 08-OCT-99

In the past 30 trading days, APEX's shares have declined 48%, compared to a 0.91% fall in the S&P 500. Average trading volume for the past five days was 229,680 shares, compared with the 40-day moving average of 739,790 shares.

Key Stock Statistics

Dividend Rate/Share	Nil	Shareholders	53
Shs. outstg. (M)	20.6	Market cap. (B)	$0.324
Avg. daily vol. (M)	0.721	Inst. holdings	62%
Tang. Bk. Value/Share	3.88		
Beta	NA		

Value of $10,000 invested 5 years ago: NA

Fiscal Year Ending Dec. 31

	1999	1998	1997	1996	1995	1994
Revenues (Million $)						
1Q	20.68	15.70	11.59	—	—	—
2Q	26.58	18.30	12.09	—	—	—
3Q	—	18.14	15.28	—	—	—
4Q	—	23.49	16.43	—	—	—
Yr.	—	75.64	55.39	33.62	19.67	—
Earnings Per Share ($)						
1Q	**0.19**	**0.16**	0.12	—	—	—
2Q	**0.24**	**0.17**	0.11	—	—	—
3Q	—	**0.19**	0.15	—	—	—
4Q	—	**0.23**	**0.16**	—	—	—
Yr.	—	**0.75**	**0.55**	**0.29**	**0.19**	—

Next earnings report expected: mid October

Dividend Data

Amount ($)	Date Decl.	Ex-Div. Date	Stock of Record	Payment Date
3-for-2	Jan. 28	Mar. 04	Feb. 10	Mar. 03 '99

APEX Inc.

Business Summary - 20-JUL-99

APEX Inc. (formerly APEX PC Solutions, Inc.) manufactures stand-alone switching systems and integrated server cabinet solutions for the client/server computing market.

Originally a division of Apex Computer Co., the company became a separate entity through a spinoff in February 1993. Throughout 1993, APEX derived revenues mainly from the provision of computer maintenance services to Microsoft Corp. In May 1994, the company began selling stand-alone switching systems to Compaq Computer Corp. for integration into server cabinets. In June 1994, it discontinued its computer maintenance service business and decided to concentrate on sales of stand-alone switching products and server cabinets, including server cabinets with integrated switching systems. The present corporate title was adopted in mid-1999 to reflect the company's focus in the server management and console switching area.

The company's switching systems enable client/server network administrators to manage multiple servers from a single keyboard video monitor and mouse configuration (a "console"). Specifically APEX's products reduce personnel, space, energy, depreciation and maintenance costs that organizations increasingly face when adopting client/server architecture. Its switching and integrated server cabinet solutions enable network administrators to more efficiently manage their organizations' complex and growing server populations.

APEX provides "plug and play" switching systems and integrated server cabinet solutions for many of the network administration, management and storage problems faced by organizations using client/server architecture. Its switching products, including Outlook, Outlook (4), Viewpoint and Emerge, enable network administrators to access multiple servers from one or more centralized consoles, consolidate hardware requirements, and provide direct hardwired connections between the switch and the attached servers which facilitate access to servers even when the network is down.

The company markets and sells its products through a direct sales force and various distribution channels. A substantial portion of its sales are concentrated among a limited number of original equipment manufacturers (OEMs) that purchase its switching systems on a private-label basis. Sales to OEM customers represented about 60% of net sales in 1998, versus 65% the year before; sales of APEX-branded products represented about 40% and 35%, respectively.

APEX supplies stand-alone switching systems to Compaq Computer Corp. and Hewlett-Packard Co. under private-label arrangements for integration into their product offerings. Sales to Compaq Computer accounted for about 43% of sales in 1998, versus 51% the year before.

Engineering and product development expenditures totaled $3.2 million in 1998, compared with $2.0 million the year before.

Per Share Data ($) (Year Ended Dec. 31)	1998	1997	1996	1995	1994	1993	1992	1991	1990	1989
Tangible Bk. Val.	3.42	2.62	NM	NA	NA	NA	NA	NA	NA	NA
Cash Flow	0.76	0.56	0.40	NA	NA	NA	NA	NA	NA	NA
Earnings	0.75	0.55	0.29	NA	NA	NA	NA	NA	NA	NA
Dividends	Nil	Nil	Nil	NA	NA	NA	NA	NA	NA	NA
Payout Ratio	Nil	Nil	Nil	NA	NA	NA	NA	NA	NA	NA
Prices - High	23½	27⅞	NA	NA	NA	NA	NA	NA	NA	NA
- Low	7⅝	4⅝	NA	NA	NA	NA	NA	NA	NA	NA
P/E Ratio - High	31	52	NA	NA	NA	NA	NA	NA	NA	NA
- Low	10	8	NA	NA	NA	NA	NA	NA	NA	NA
Income Statement Analysis (Million $)										
Revs.	75.6	55.4	33.6	NA	NA	NA	NA	NA	NA	NA
Oper. Inc.	21.3	14.9	7.5	NA	NA	NA	NA	NA	NA	NA
Depr.	0.3	0.2	0.2	NA	NA	NA	NA	NA	NA	NA
Int. Exp.	Nil	Nil	1.9	NA	NA	NA	NA	NA	NA	NA
Pretax Inc.	23.6	15.6	5.5	NA	NA	NA	NA	NA	NA	NA
Eff. Tax Rate	34%	33%	34%	NA	NA	NA	NA	NA	NA	NA
Net Inc.	15.7	10.5	3.6	NA	NA	NA	NA	NA	NA	NA
Balance Sheet & Other Fin. Data (Million $)										
Cash	51.9	39.7	2.1	NA	NA	NA	NA	NA	NA	NA
Curr. Assets	71.3	53.6	10.9	NA	NA	NA	NA	NA	NA	NA
Total Assets	73.4	55.3	12.0	NA	NA	NA	NA	NA	NA	NA
Curr. Liab.	4.0	2.5	2.5	NA	NA	NA	NA	NA	NA	NA
LT Debt	Nil	Nil	25.1	NA	NA	NA	NA	NA	NA	NA
Common Eqty.	69.4	52.7	-18.9	NA	NA	NA	NA	NA	NA	NA
Total Cap.	69.4	52.7	9.4	NA	NA	NA	NA	NA	NA	NA
Cap. Exp.	0.1	0.1	0.0	NA	NA	NA	NA	NA	NA	NA
Cash Flow	16.1	10.7	3.8	NA	NA	NA	NA	NA	NA	NA
Curr. Ratio	18.0	21.5	4.3	NA	NA	NA	NA	NA	NA	NA
% LT Debt of Cap.	Nil	Nil	267.0	NA	NA	NA	NA	NA	NA	NA
% Net Inc.of Revs.	20.8	18.9	10.7	NA	NA	NA	NA	NA	NA	NA
% Ret. on Assets	24.4	31.1	NA	NA	NA	NA	NA	NA	NA	NA
% Ret. on Equity	25.7	61.8	NA	NA	NA	NA	NA	NA	NA	NA

Data as orig reptd.; bef. results of disc opers/spec. items. Per share data adj. for stk. divs. Bold denotes diluted EPS (FASB 128)-prior periods restated. E-Estimated. NA-Not Available. NM-Not Meaningful. NR-Not Ranked.

Office—9911 Willows Road N.E., Redmond, WA 98052. **Tel**—(425) 861-5858. **Website**—http://www.apex.com **Email**—info@apexpc.com **Pres & CEO**—K. J. Hafer. **VP-CFO & Treas**—B. L. Harmon. **Secy**—S. F. Saracino. **Dirs**—F. Fichtner, K. J. Hafer, E. L. Harper, W. McAleer. **Transfer Agent & Registrar**—ChaseMellon Shareholder Services, Seattle, WA. **Incorporated**—in Washington in 1992. **Empl**— 82. **S&P Analyst:** J. J. Schemitsch

STANDARD &POOR'S
STOCK REPORTS

Apogee Enterprises

NASDAQ Symbol **APOG**

In S&P SmallCap 600

09-OCT-99

Industry: Building Materials

Summary: This leading supplier of glass technologies and services recently discontinued its auto glass and building products divisions.

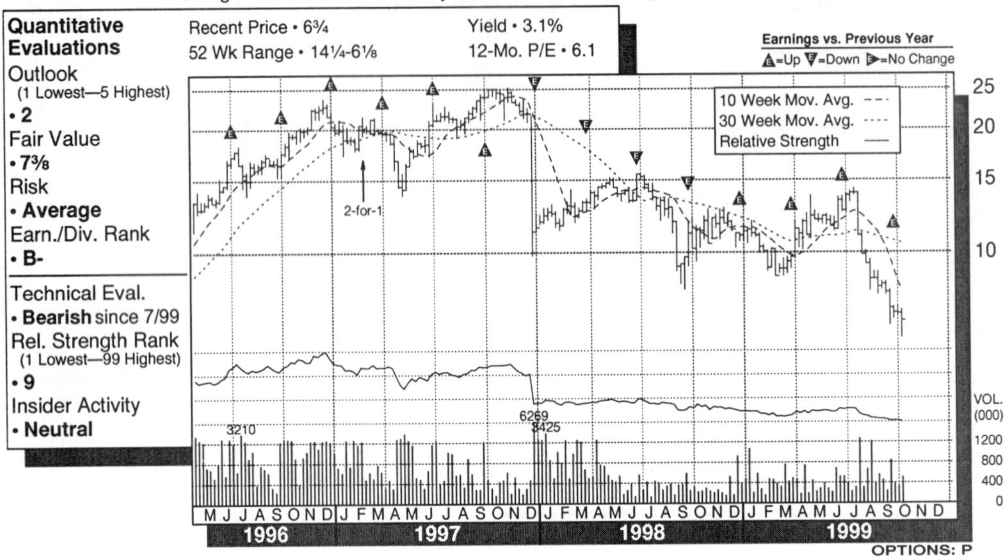

Business Profile - 05-JUL-99

Apogee continues to focus on its glass technologies and glass services businesses, recently selling its large-scale domestic curtainwall business, Harmon Ltd. This sale, along with last year's exiting of its international curtainwall operations and the sale of its detention and security unit, effectively eliminates APOG's curtainwall and construction businesses. The company believes its new direction will provide greater opportunities for growth. In February, APOG sold all eight of its Midas Muffler franchises, which were previously part of APOG's now discontinued auto glass segment. The company has more than 400 retail and wholesale auto glass locations in the U.S. The dividend was boosted 6% in late 1998.

Operational Review - 05-JUL-99

Net sales from continuing operations in the three months ended May 29, 1999, advanced 11%, year to year, reflecting higher sales in both the glass technologies and glass services segments. Profitability benefited from strength in glass services, which outweighed higher expenses for glass technologies, and operating income was up 14%. Following a rise in depreciation and amortization charges, income from continuing operations rose 7.8%, to $4,515,000 ($0.16 a diluted share), from $4,188,000 ($0.15). Per share results exclude a $0.01 loss from discontinued operations in the prior year period. APOG expects further growth in glass technologies in FY 00, with overall margins aided by increased fixed-cost absorption in the second half.

Stock Performance - 08-OCT-99

In the past 30 trading days, APOG's shares have declined 17%, compared to a 0.91% fall in the S&P 500. Average trading volume for the past five days was 99,760 shares, compared with the 40-day moving average of 93,469 shares.

Key Stock Statistics

Dividend Rate/Share	0.21	Shareholders	7,300
Shs. outstg. (M)	27.8	Market cap. (B)	$0.190
Avg. daily vol. (M)	0.101	Inst. holdings	52%
Tang. Bk. Value/Share	2.74		
Beta	1.03		

Value of $10,000 invested 5 years ago: $ 9,422

Fiscal Year Ending Feb. 28

	2000	1999	1998	1997	1996	1995
Revenues (Million $)						
1Q	211.1	233.1	223.9	228.6	219.0	179.0
2Q	218.4	250.9	246.0	253.2	222.2	186.0
3Q	—	236.0	235.0	228.8	215.5	186.3
4Q	—	201.3	208.0	240.2	214.4	205.4
Yr.	—	792.5	912.8	950.8	871.1	756.5
Earnings Per Share ($)						
1Q	**0.16**	**0.14**	0.24	0.18	0.13	0.10
2Q	**0.51**	**0.33**	0.34	0.28	0.20	0.16
3Q	—	**0.26**	-0.37	0.27	0.19	0.14
4Q	—	**0.18**	**-2.06**	0.20	0.13	0.09
Yr.	—	**0.71**	**-0.71**	**0.93**	**0.65**	**0.48**

Next earnings report expected: mid December

Dividend Data (Dividends have been paid since 1974.)

Amount ($)	Date Decl.	Ex-Div. Date	Stock of Record	Payment Date
0.053	Oct. 12	Oct. 23	Oct. 27	Nov. 11 '98
0.053	Jan. 11	Jan. 22	Jan. 26	Feb. 11 '99
0.053	Apr. 16	Apr. 29	May. 03	May. 18 '99
0.053	Jul. 28	Aug. 12	Aug. 16	Aug. 31 '99

A Division of The McGraw-Hill Companies

Apogee Enterprises, Inc.

Business Summary - 05-JUL-99

In April 1999, Apogee Enterprises, Inc. (APOG) said it would modify its business structure into two segments: glass technologies and glass services. Glass technologies includes its current operations plus the Wausau Architectural Products Group, which produces windows with glass fabricated by Viracon. The new glass services segment consists of auto glass businesses and Harmon Inc., a leading provider of building glass services. As of February 1999, the glass services segment had 76 wholesale locations and 341 service centers. The company has discontinued its detention/security systems and curtainwall contracting businesses. Glass technologies accounted for 41% of revenues and 50% of operating profits in FY 99 (Feb.), while glass services contributed 59% and 50%.

The discontinued building products and services segment's operating units consist of nonresidential construction and architectural metals. In May 1999, APOG sold Harmon Ltd. ($85 million in sales in FY 99), one of the largest designers of curtainwall and window systems for nonresidential construction in the U.S., to CH Holdings, Inc., a privately held St. Louis-based curtainwall construction company. In FY 98, APOG decided to exit its European and Asian international curtainwall operations. The architectural products unit operates under the name Wausau Metals, which fabricates high-quality aluminum window and curtainwall systems.

The glass technologies unit consists of Viracon and Tru Vue, and the Viratec Thin Films joint venture (spun out of the former glass fabrication division). The unit produces flat laminated safety glass, architectural glass, coated glass for computer anti-glare screens, and picture framing glass. A new Optium facility for the cathode ray tube business began operating in late 1998. A new Viracon facility in Statesboro, GA (commenced production in March 1999), and the planned expansion at the Owatonna facility, are expected to add over 60% of production capacity over the next two fiscal years.

The discontinued automotive glass segment was engaged in the replacement and repair business through its Harmon Glass service centers (retail), Glass Depot distribution centers (wholesale) and Curvlite fabrication center.

In late 1998, the company sold its detention and security unit to CompuDyne Corp. for about $23 million.

Export sales accounted for 5% of the FY 99 total. Backlog at February 27, 1999, was up 10%, year to year, to $148.4 million.

Per Share Data ($) (Year Ended Feb. 28)	1999	1998	1997	1996	1995	1994	1993	1992	1991	1990
Tangible Bk. Val.	2.74	2.15	4.29	4.75	4.33	4.21	4.08	4.02	3.86	3.36
Cash Flow	1.64	-0.97	1.66	1.26	1.04	0.71	0.74	0.92	1.11	0.96
Earnings	0.91	-1.84	0.93	0.66	0.48	0.13	0.17	0.32	0.63	0.52
Dividends	0.20	0.19	0.35	0.17	0.16	0.15	0.14	0.13	0.12	0.10
Payout Ratio	22%	NM	38%	26%	34%	121%	84%	41%	19%	19%
Cal. Yrs.	1998	1997	1996	1995	1994	1993	1992	1991	1990	1989
Prices - High	15½	25¼	23¾	9⅛	9¼	8⅞	7	9	10⅛	9⅜
- Low	8⅛	9¾	8⅛	6½	5¾	4⅞	4⅛	4¾	6⅞	6
P/E Ratio - High	17	NM	26	14	19	71	41	29	16	18
- Low	9	NM	9	10	12	39	24	15	11	11
Income Statement Analysis (Million $)										
Revs.	793	913	951	871	757	688	572	596	600	590
Oper. Inc.	68.1	64.9	67.0	49.0	39.5	28.0	21.5	41.4	46.6	44.2
Depr.	25.9	24.0	20.5	16.5	15.2	15.7	15.1	16.3	13.3	12.1
Int. Exp.	11.5	9.4	8.1	7.0	5.0	3.6	3.0	2.9	3.8	6.2
Pretax Inc.	31.2	-63.5	40.0	27.1	20.9	6.6	6.5	15.8	28.8	23.4
Eff. Tax Rate	38%	NM	35%	36%	39%	40%	30%	46%	41%	40%
Net Inc.	19.7	-51.1	26.2	17.8	13.1	3.3	4.5	8.5	17.0	14.1
Balance Sheet & Other Fin. Data (Million $)										
Cash	1.3	7.9	4.1	7.4	2.9	10.8	8.9	18.7	20.5	12.2
Curr. Assets	205	262	305	259	257	221	169	166	163	155
Total Assets	471	464	501	386	362	306	251	250	250	244
Curr. Liab.	115	178	177	142	136	141	100	101	102	95.0
LT Debt	165	152	128	79.1	80.6	35.7	28.4	25.3	29.4	41.4
Common Eqty.	131	110	172	139	125	114	112	114	109	96.0
Total Cap.	296	262	300	219	207	151	141	141	142	144
Cap. Exp.	77.7	38.2	35.6	22.6	25.0	15.2	9.3	15.9	17.2	18.1
Cash Flow	45.6	-27.1	46.7	34.4	28.2	19.0	19.6	24.8	30.3	26.2
Curr. Ratio	1.8	1.5	1.7	1.8	1.9	1.6	1.7	1.6	1.6	1.6
% LT Debt of Cap.	55.8	58.1	42.6	36.0	39.0	23.6	20.2	17.9	20.7	28.8
% Net Inc.of Revs.	2.5	NM	2.8	2.0	1.7	0.5	0.8	1.4	2.8	2.4
% Ret. on Assets	4.2	NM	6.0	4.8	3.9	1.2	1.8	3.4	6.9	6.2
% Ret. on Equity	16.4	NM	16.9	13.5	10.9	2.9	4.0	7.6	16.6	15.7

Data as orig reptd.; bef. results of disc opers/spec. items. Per share data adj. for stk. divs. Bold denotes diluted EPS (FASB 128)-prior periods restated. E-Estimated. NA-Not Available. NM-Not Meaningful. NR-Not Ranked.

Office—7900 Xerxes Ave. South, Minneapolis, MN 55431. **Tel**—(612) 835-1874. **Chrmn, Pres & CEO**—R. Huffer. **EVP**—J. L. Martineau. **VP-Fin, CFO & Investor Contact**—R. G. Barbieri. **Treas**—M. A. Bevilacqua. **Secy**—M. L. Richards. **Dirs**—J. B. Cohen, D. W. Goldfus, B. B. Grogan, H. A. Hammerly, J. P. Horner, R. Huffer, J. L. Martineau, S. C. Mitchell, L. J. Niederhofer, D. E. Nugent, M. E. Shannon. **Transfer Agent & Registrar**—American Stock Transfer & Trust Co., NYC. **Incorporated**—in Minnesota in 1949. **Empl**— 6,367. **S&P Analyst:** Stewart Scharf

STANDARD
&POOR'S
STOCK REPORTS

Applebee's International

Nasdaq Symbol **APPB**

In S&P SmallCap 600

09-OCT-99

Industry: Restaurants

Summary: This company develops, franchises and operates a growing chain of more than 1,080 full-service Applebee's restaurants and 65 restaurants in the Rio Bravo group.

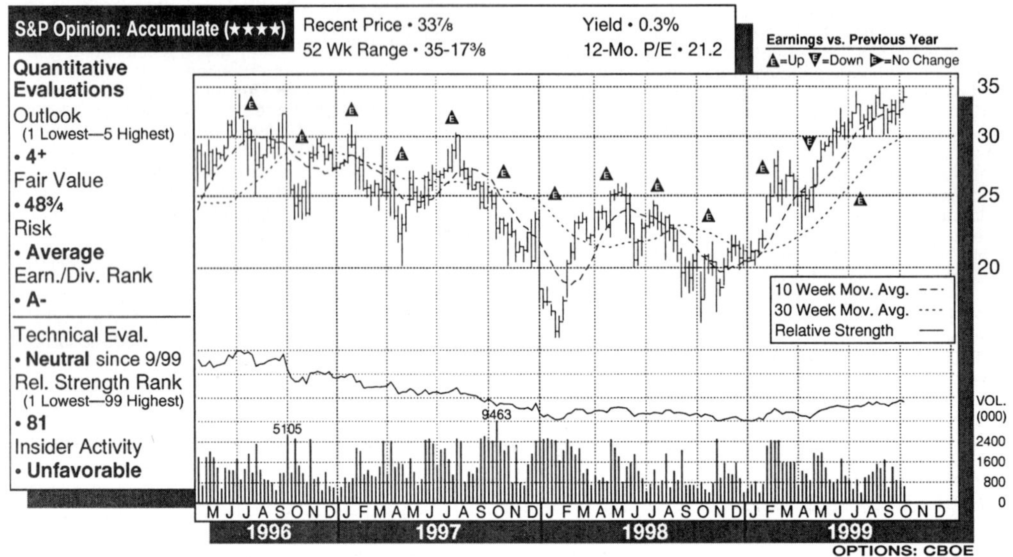

Overview - 08-SEP-99

Operating revenues should increase about 13% in 1999, primarily as a result of new openings of about 105 Applebee's restaurants. Comparable- unit sales should increase of 1.0% to 1.5%, as many restaurants are already operating near sales capacity. Food and beverage prices should remain tame. Cost of sales should increase slightly as a percentage of company restaurant sales, mainly due to higher occupancy costs and higher labor costs. General and administrative costs should increase slightly, with higher bonus accruals. Interest expense should remain about level. In February 1999, APPB sold its weak performing Rio Bravo division, for $65 million; the transaction resulted in a pretax loss of $9.3 million in the first quarter. Excluding the sale, APPB earned $0.44 in the first quarter of 1999. APPB aims to deliver 15% annual earnings gains over the next five years. The company believes there is ample room for 1,800 Applebee's restaurants in the U.S.

Valuation - 08-SEP-99

The shares have continued to rise with solid gains in same-store sales. We have retained our accumulate recommendation on the stock. Same-store sales rose 3.6% in the second quarter; operating earnings increased 7%. With a 24% decline in interest expense, earnings rose 16%. We believe that Applebee's units remain on track for solid operating earnings. An upbeat outlook for the casual dining segment and the stock's current modest valuation give us cause for optimism in coming months. The company has lowered its capital expenditure program to $60-$65 million for 1999, from $78 million in 1998. Free cash flow from operations will be used to fund the company's $100 million share purchase program over the next two years.

Key Stock Statistics

S&P EPS Est. 1999	1.71	Tang. Bk. Value/Share	6.58
P/E on S&P Est. 1999	19.8	Beta	0.88
S&P EPS Est. 2000	2.20	Shareholders	1,282
Dividend Rate/Share	0.09	Market cap. (B)	$0.966
Shs. outstg. (M)	28.5	Inst. holdings	69%
Avg. daily vol. (M)	0.185		

Value of $10,000 invested 5 years ago: $ 15,418

Fiscal Year Ending Dec. 31

	1999	1998	1997	1996	1995	1994
Revenues (Million $)						
1Q	179.3	146.6	116.3	95.04	75.44	45.63
2Q	164.0	166.4	130.7	104.6	83.80	49.70
3Q	—	168.7	133.9	107.1	88.08	54.88
4Q	—	165.9	135.0	106.4	96.24	58.32
Yr.	—	647.6	515.8	413.1	343.6	208.5
Earnings Per Share ($)						
1Q	**0.25**	**0.39**	**0.34**	**0.29**	0.15	0.11
2Q	**0.51**	**0.44**	**0.39**	**0.35**	0.24	0.14
3Q	**E0.50**	**0.45**	**0.39**	**0.30**	0.28	0.19
4Q	**E0.45**	**0.39**	**0.31**	**0.27**	0.26	0.18
Yr.	**E1.71**	**1.67**	**1.43**	**1.21**	**0.92**	**0.63**

Next earnings report expected: early November

Dividend Data (Dividends have been paid since 1991.)

Amount ($)	Date Decl.	Ex-Div. Date	Stock of Record	Payment Date
0.090	Nov. 19	Dec. 14	Dec. 16	Jan. 21 '99

Applebee's International, Inc.

Business Summary - 08-SEP-99

Applebee's restaurants are a fixture in suburban shopping districts and shopping malls across the U.S. Applebee's International, Inc. is one of the fastest growing U.S. restaurant companies. It is the second largest company (in terms of revenues) in the dinnerhouse segment of the restaurant industry. As of December 27, 1998, there were 1,064 Applebee's Neighborhood Grill & Bar restaurants, of which 817 were operated by franchisees and 247 by the company, with the greatest concentration in the Southeast. The company sold its Rio Bravo Cantina chain of 66 restaurants and four specialty restaurants in April 1999 for $68 million.

The first Applebee's restaurant opened in 1986 and initially developed and operated six restaurants as a franchisee of the Applebee's Neighborhood Grill & Bar division of Creative Food 'N Fun Co., an indirect subsidiary of W. R. Grace & Co. In March 1988, substantially all assets of the Applebee's division were purchased for about $21 million. At that time, the division operated 13 restaurants (excluding one not acquired), and there were 41 franchised units (including the company's six restaurants).

Each Applebee's restaurant offers an extensive selection of moderately priced high-quality food and beverage items appealing both to families and adults. Systemwide sales totaled $2.06 billion in 1998, an increase of 14% from 1997. Systemwide sales include franchisee sales and company-owned and operated sales. Weighted average weekly sales at company-owned restaurants decreased 1.2% in 1998, to about $40,664. This reflected the fact that many Applebee's company-owned restaurants operate near sales capacity, and various markets continue to experience competitive pressures. Although market share increases with the opening of multiple restaurants within a market, decreases in same-unit sales may result.

While continuing to penetrate established markets, the company launched a new prototype for smaller, less competitive markets with populations under 25,000. These units are designed with a lower cost of entry, lower menu prices and lower cost of operations than traditional units. The company opened two prototypes in 1998 and plans 150 of these units of part of its 1,800 unit potential.

Growth of the Applebee's chain since March 1988 has reflected active franchising efforts. APPB has also begun pursuing international franchising of the Applebee's concept, initially focusing on major cities in Canada, Mexico, the U.K., Central America, the Middle East and Europe. At the end of 1998, the company operated 18 restaurants internationally.

In February 1999, directors approved plans to repurchase $100 million common shares over a two year period. This follows a $50 million share repurchase program in 1998.

Per Share Data ($) (Year Ended Dec. 31)	1998	1997	1996	1995	1994	1993	1992	1991	1990	1989
Tangible Bk. Val.	6.52	7.55	6.93	5.56	2.82	2.38	2.42	1.00	0.73	0.57
Cash Flow	2.81	2.19	1.72	1.42	1.01	0.67	0.41	0.39	0.29	0.19
Earnings	1.67	1.43	1.22	0.94	0.62	0.44	0.27	0.22	0.13	Nil
Dividends	0.07	0.07	0.07	0.06	0.05	0.04	0.03	0.02	0.01	Nil
Payout Ratio	4%	5%	6%	6%	8%	9%	12%	9%	10%	Nil
Prices - High	26	31 1/8	34 1/4	31 3/4	25 1/4	22 1/2	9 5/8	5 1/8	7 1/4	5 3/8
- Low	16 1/8	17 3/4	17 3/4	13 3/8	11	7 3/8	4 3/4	2 5/16	2	4 1/4
P/E Ratio - High	16	22	28	34	41	51	35	23	57	NM
- Low	10	12	15	14	18	17	17	10	16	NM
Income Statement Analysis (Million $)										
Revs.	648	516	413	344	209	117	56.5	45.1	38.2	29.9
Oper. Inc.	124	96.6	80.1	62.6	36.0	19.0	9.4	6.3	5.0	3.7
Depr.	34.7	24.1	15.7	14.3	8.7	5.1	2.6	2.4	2.3	2.2
Int. Exp.	9.9	1.7	1.6	2.5	1.2	0.2	Nil	Nil	Nil	1.7
Pretax Inc.	80.4	71.8	60.7	47.8	25.6	15.4	8.3	5.0	2.9	-0.1
Eff. Tax Rate	37%	37%	37%	37%	34%	39%	39%	39%	39%	Nil
Net Inc.	50.7	45.1	38.0	27.4	16.9	9.5	5.1	3.1	1.8	-0.1
Balance Sheet & Other Fin. Data (Million $)										
Cash	1.8	19.8	57.4	52.0	17.2	16.2	22.8	9.7	2.4	2.2
Curr. Assets	34.9	44.0	84.0	74.6	31.6	24.4	28.2	12.1	5.0	4.3
Total Assets	511	377	314	271	152	104	68.1	30.0	26.2	22.6
Curr. Liab.	66.0	62.5	42.0	38.4	27.9	19.2	8.0	6.2	5.4	2.8
LT Debt	146	22.6	24.6	25.8	23.7	2.2	0.1	Nil	Nil	Nil
Common Eqty.	296	290	245	204	96.7	79.2	58.6	23.2	20.4	19.3
Total Cap.	443	313	270	230	122	82.5	59.1	23.2	20.4	19.3
Cap. Exp.	77.7	90.5	65.7	51.8	40.4	37.8	9.2	1.3	4.7	1.6
Cash Flow	85.3	69.2	53.7	41.8	25.6	14.6	7.8	5.4	4.1	1.9
Curr. Ratio	0.5	0.7	2.0	1.9	1.1	1.3	3.5	1.9	0.9	1.5
% LT Debt of Cap.	32.9	7.2	9.1	12.6	19.4	2.6	0.1	Nil	Nil	Nil
% Net Inc.of Revs.	7.8	8.7	9.2	8.0	8.1	8.1	9.1	6.8	4.7	NM
% Ret. on Assets	11.4	13.0	13.0	12.2	12.4	10.7	9.1	11.0	7.4	NM
% Ret. on Equity	17.3	16.8	16.9	17.5	18.0	13.3	11.1	14.2	9.1	NM

Data as orig. reptd.; bef. results of disc. opers. and/or spec. items. Per share data adj. for stk. divs. as of ex-div. date. Bold denotes diluted EPS (FASB 128). E-Estimated. NA-Not Available. NM-Not Meaningful. NR-Not Ranked.

Office—4551 W. 107th Street, Suite 100, Overland Park, KS 66207. **Tel**—(913) 967-4000. **Chrmn & Co-CEO**—A. J. Gustin Jr. **Pres, Co-CEO & COO**—L. L. Hill. **EVP, CFO & Treas**—G. D. Shadid. **VP & Secy**—R. T. Steinkamp. **Dirs**—E. Belton, D. P. Curran, A. J. Gustin Jr., E. Hansen, M. S. Hansen, J. P. Helms, K. D. Hill, L. L. Hill, R. A. Martin, B. Sack. **Transfer Agent & Registrar**—American Stock Transfer & Trust Co., NYC. **Incorporated**—in Delaware in 1988. **Empl**— 20,300. **S&P Analyst:** Karen J. Sack, CFA

Applied Industrial Technologies

NYSE Symbol **APZ**

In S&P SmallCap 600

09-OCT-99

Industry:
Auto Parts & Equipment

Summary: This company distributes bearings, mechanical and electrical drive systems, industrial rubber products, fluid power components and specialty maintenance and repair products.

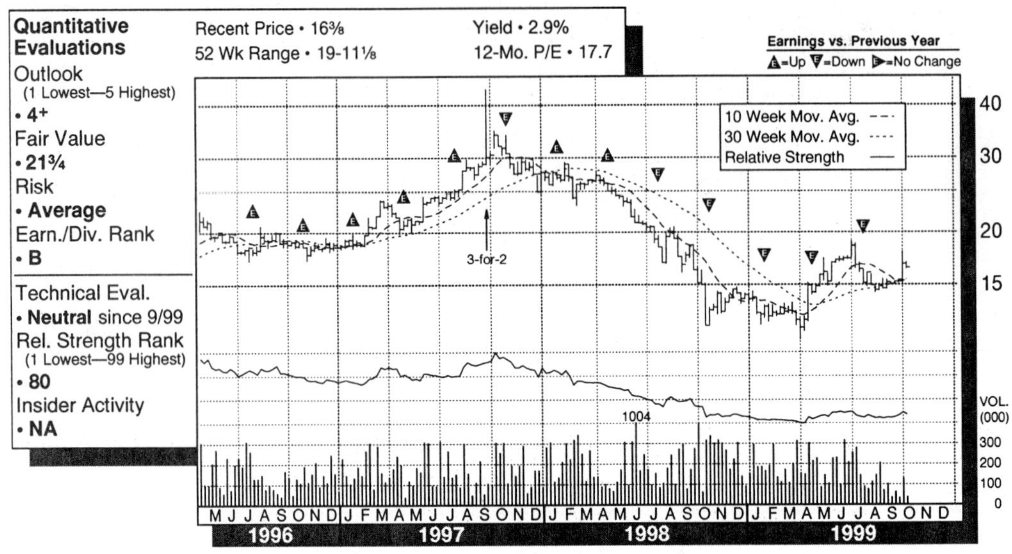

Business Profile - 17-JUN-99

The company has moved away from its historical focus on the industrial bearings markets, and toward non-bearing, high-growth technologies and the provision of total system solutions, rather than only distribution. As part of its change of focus, APZ has embarked on an aggressive acquisition program. Most recently, it acquired three distributors of industrial products, including bearings and mechanical and electrical drive systems, with combined annual sales of $15 million. In FY 98 (Jun.), the company acquired Invetech Co., a distributor of industrial components, and completed six additional acquisitions. APZ repurchased 1,284,000 shares in the first nine months of FY 99. As of April 15, 1999, it was authorized to purchase up to 1 million more shares.

Operational Review - 17-JUN-99

Net sales in the nine months ended March 31, 1999, rose 2.7%, year to year, aided by the inclusion of Invetech and several other acquisitions. Gross margins narrowed to 25.0% of sales, from 25.8%, on lower discounts and allowances, and the absence of favorable cost adjustments. With selling, distribution and administrative expenses up 4.8%, operating income dropped 32%. After higher net interest expense, and taxes at 41.1%, versus 38.9%, net income fell 43%, to $12,118,000 ($0.56 a share), from $21,326,000 ($0.98).

Stock Performance - 08-OCT-99

In the past 30 trading days, APZ's shares have increased 12%, compared to a 0.91% fall in the S&P 500. Average trading volume for the past five days was 7,320 shares, compared with the 40-day moving average of 17,133 shares.

Key Stock Statistics

Dividend Rate/Share	0.48	Shareholders	2,741
Shs. outstg. (M)	24.1	Market cap. (B)	$0.396
Avg. daily vol. (M)	0.013	Inst. holdings	52%
Tang. Bk. Value/Share	9.60		
Beta	-0.02		

Value of $10,000 invested 5 years ago: $ 14,954

Fiscal Year Ending Jun. 30

	1999	1998	1997	1996	1995	1994
Revenues (Million $)						
1Q	379.2	344.7	282.3	277.1	247.6	222.7
2Q	371.4	368.6	275.0	275.1	249.9	226.3
3Q	386.6	393.9	297.2	296.1	277.0	239.7
4Q	390.7	384.2	305.8	295.5	280.3	247.5
Yr.	1,528	1,491	1,160	1,144	1,055	936.3
Earnings Per Share ($)						
1Q	**0.06**	0.22	0.29	0.25	0.18	0.14
2Q	**0.20**	**0.35**	0.32	0.28	0.20	0.14
3Q	**0.30**	**0.41**	0.37	0.33	0.25	0.17
4Q	**0.37**	**0.40**	0.48	0.41	0.36	0.30
Yr.	**0.93**	**1.38**	**1.44**	**1.25**	0.98	0.75

Next earnings report expected: mid October

Dividend Data (Dividends have been paid since 1957.)

Amount ($)	Date Decl.	Ex-Div. Date	Stock of Record	Payment Date
0.120	Oct. 20	Nov. 12	Nov. 16	Nov. 30 '98
0.120	Jan. 21	Feb. 10	Feb. 15	Feb. 26 '99
0.120	Apr. 15	May. 12	May. 14	May. 28 '99
0.120	Jul. 15	Aug. 12	Aug. 16	Aug. 31 '99

Applied Industrial Technologies, Inc.

Business Summary - 17-JUN-99

Applied Industrial Technologies Inc. (formerly Bearings Inc.) distributes bearings, mechanical and electrical drive systems, industrial rubber products, fluid power products and systems, linear motion products and general maintenance and specialty repair items through eight distribution centers, 34 mechanical, rubber and fluid power shops, and more than 380 branches in 45 states.

The company distributes and sells ball, roller, mounted and plane bearings, mechanical and electrical drive systems, industrial rubber products, fluid power transmission components, linear motion and position control products and general maintenance and specialty items used in connection with the foregoing such as seals, sealants, fluid sealing, O rings, retaining rings, adhesives, lubricants, maintenance tools and equipment, and safety and hygiene products.

Distribution is conducted on a nonexclusive basis for many manufacturers. Although APZ does not generally manufacture products sold, it does assemble filter carts and fluid power units. It also rebuilds precision machine spindles, assembles speed reducers, pumps, valves, cylinders and hydraulic motors, provides custom machining, assembles fluid power systems, operates rubber shops that modify conveyor belts and provides hose assemblies. Products are purchased from more than 100 major suppliers, and resold to a wide range of industries, including industrial machinery, forest products, automotive, primary metals, agriculture and food processing, chemical processing, transportation, mining, textiles and utilities. No single customer accounts for more than 2% of net sales.

In July 1997, in the largest acquisition in its history, the company acquired Invetech Co., a distributor of industrial components based in Detroit, MI, for $22.9 million in cash, and 2.1 million common shares. The acquisition expanded the company's geographic reach into Michigan and Colorado, and added substantial expertise in serving the automotive industry.

In February 1996, APZ acquired Engineered Sales, Inc., an applied technology distributor. In August 1996, it signed an agreement to become the primary supplier for Electronic Data Systems Corp.'s new integrated supply service.

Per Share Data ($) (Year Ended Jun. 30)	1999	1998	1997	1996	1995	1994	1993	1992	1991	1990
Tangible Bk. Val.	9.60	10.91	10.87	9.91	9.44	8.86	7.83	7.64	8.00	8.32
Cash Flow	1.76	2.13	2.13	1.95	1.73	1.55	1.33	0.68	0.97	1.26
Earnings	0.93	1.38	1.46	1.27	0.98	0.75	0.55	-0.11	0.27	0.76
Dividends	0.48	0.47	0.41	0.36	0.31	0.28	0.28	0.28	0.28	0.28
Payout Ratio	52%	34%	28%	28%	32%	38%	52%	NM	105%	37%
Prices - High	19	29 1/4	43 5/8	22 1/2	19 3/4	16 5/8	13 7/8	10 3/8	10 1/2	12 5/8
- Low	11 1/8	12	18 1/4	16	12 1/4	12 3/8	9 1/8	7 1/2	7	6
P/E Ratio - High	20	21	30	18	20	22	25	NM	39	17
- Low	12	9	12	13	12	17	17	NM	26	8
Income Statement Analysis (Million $)										
Revs.	1,528	1,491	1,160	1,144	1,055	936	831	818	814	651
Oper. Inc.	59.8	74.9	64.2	62.8	50.2	41.4	33.3	25.1	28.3	37.4
Depr.	17.3	16.4	13.6	13.5	13.3	13.6	12.8	12.6	11.1	8.2
Int. Exp.	10.1	9.5	6.5	9.0	7.7	6.4	5.5	7.0	10.3	5.4
Pretax Inc.	32.6	49.8	45.1	40.8	29.7	21.7	15.5	-1.9	7.5	20.3
Eff. Tax Rate	39%	40%	40%	43%	43%	41%	42%	NM	43%	40%
Net Inc.	19.9	30.1	27.1	23.3	16.9	12.7	8.9	-1.7	4.3	12.2
Balance Sheet & Other Fin. Data (Million $)										
Cash	19.2	9.3	22.4	9.2	4.8	10.9	4.6	9.3	8.4	5.7
Curr. Assets	389	415	285	295	265	249	221	234	235	300
Total Assets	574	606	394	404	359	344	316	331	328	380
Curr. Liab.	132	193	121	143	112	105	90.0	192	181	236
LT Debt	126	90.0	51.4	62.9	74.0	80.0	80.0	Nil	Nil	Nil
Common Eqty.	294	295	208	189	165	150	135	129	134	135
Total Cap.	420	385	259	252	241	234	221	134	139	140
Cap. Exp.	13.5	33.8	21.6	23.5	15.1	16.6	13.6	20.4	21.1	17.5
Cash Flow	37.2	46.6	40.7	36.8	30.2	26.3	21.7	10.9	15.4	20.4
Curr. Ratio	2.9	2.1	2.4	2.1	2.4	2.4	2.4	1.2	1.3	1.3
% LT Debt of Cap.	30.0	23.3	19.9	24.9	30.9	34.2	36.3	Nil	Nil	Nil
% Net Inc.of Revs.	1.3	2.0	2.3	2.0	1.6	1.4	1.1	NM	0.5	1.9
% Ret. on Assets	3.4	6.0	6.8	6.1	4.7	3.8	2.7	NM	1.2	3.9
% Ret. on Equity	6.8	12.0	13.7	13.2	10.7	8.9	6.7	NM	3.2	9.2

Data as orig reptd.; bef. results of disc opers/spec. items. Per share data adj. for stk. divs. Bold denotes diluted EPS (FASB 128)-prior periods restated. E-Estimated. NA-Not Available. NM-Not Meaningful. NR-Not Ranked.

Office—One Applied Plaza, Cleveland, OH 44115. **Tel**—(216) 426-4000. **Fax**—(216) 426-4845. **Website**—http://appliedindustrial.com **Chrmn & CEO**—J. C. Dannemiller. **Pres & COO**—D. L. Pugh. **VP, CFO, Treas & Investor Contact**—John R. Whitten. **VP & Secy**—R. C. Stinson. **Dirs**—W. G. Bares, R.D. Blackwell, W. E. Butler, T. A. Commes, J. C. Dannemiller, R. B. Every, R. R. Gifford, L. T. Hiltz, J. J. Kahl, J. M. Moore, J. S. Thornton. **Transfer Agent & Registrar**—Harris Trust and Savings Bank, Chicago. **Incorporated**—in Delaware in 1928; reincorporated in Ohio in 1988. **Empl**— 5,061. **S&P Analyst:** C.C.P.

STANDARD
&POOR'S
STOCK REPORTS

Applied Power

NYSE Symbol **APW**

In S&P SmallCap 600

09-OCT-99 **Industry:** Machinery (Diversified)

Summary: This diversified manufacturer makes hydraulic tools, hydraulic components, and technical office furniture.

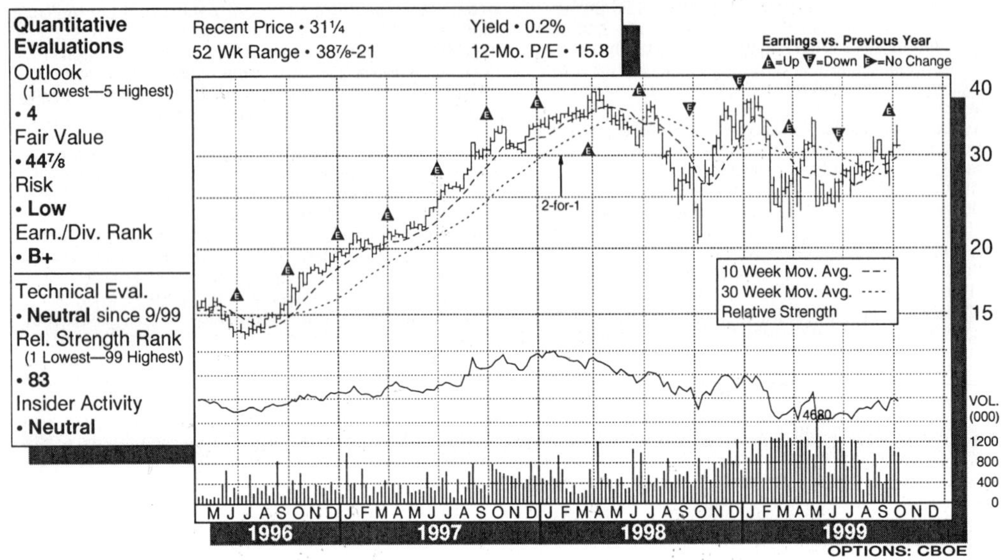

Business Profile - 26-AUG-99

APW believes that the information age is just getting started, and that the electronic enclosure systems market will have above-average growth for many years to come. As a result, over the past few years, the company has been focusing on the electronic enclosure systems market. Applied Power expects FY 99 (Aug.) sales to be about $1.8 billion, or $25-$30 million lower than originally forecast, and EPS in the $2.05-$2.15 range, as a result of the strengthening U.S. dollar, versus European currencies, and lower product volumes by a major customer. During the second half of FY 99, management expects all of its businesses will enjoy improved sales growth and margins, aided by cost reduction initiatives begun in the fourth quarter of FY 98.

Operational Review - 26-AUG-99

Revenues in the first nine months of FY 99 (Aug.) advanced 51%, year to year, primarily due to the acquisitions of AA Manufacturing, PMP, PTI, Premier, Brown, Vero and Rubicon, all in the Enclosure Products & Systems group (EPS). Gross margins narrowed on the rapid expansion of lower margin enclosure businesses in the EPS group. However, aggressive management of engineering, selling and administrative expenses resulted in a 55% rise in operating income. Following a significant rise in net financing costs, reflecting borrowings to finance the Vero and Rubicon acquisitions, net income declined 3.1%, to $56.2 million ($1.40 a share), from $58.0 million ($1.44).

Stock Performance - 08-OCT-99

In the past 30 trading days, APW's shares have increased 2%, compared to a 0.91% fall in the S&P 500. Average trading volume for the past five days was 195,420 shares, compared with the 40-day moving average of 152,764 shares.

Key Stock Statistics

Dividend Rate/Share	0.06	Shareholders	4,865
Shs. outstg. (M)	38.9	Market cap. (B)	$ 1.2
Avg. daily vol. (M)	0.181	Inst. holdings	76%
Tang. Bk. Value/Share	NM		
Beta	1.01		

Value of $10,000 invested 5 years ago: $ 39,101

Fiscal Year Ending Aug. 31

	1999	1998	1997	1996	1995	1994
Revenues (Million $)						
1Q	435.7	275.4	153.1	139.3	125.8	103.6
2Q	422.0	279.4	157.2	137.1	124.5	101.9
3Q	440.5	303.9	173.8	147.6	139.3	111.3
4Q	452.9	372.0	188.2	147.3	137.4	116.8
Yr.	1,751	1,231	672.3	571.2	527.1	433.6
Earnings Per Share ($)						
1Q	**0.41**	**0.48**	0.34	0.28	0.20	0.11
2Q	**0.48**	**0.41**	0.33	0.28	0.17	0.13
3Q	**0.51**	**0.55**	0.39	0.33	0.27	0.20
4Q	**0.58**	**-0.78**	0.41	0.33	0.28	0.20
Yr.	**1.98**	**0.66**	**1.47**	1.21	0.91	0.64

Next earnings report expected: mid December

Dividend Data (Dividends have been paid since 1987.)

Amount ($)	Date Decl.	Ex-Div. Date	Stock of Record	Payment Date
0.015	Nov. 03	Nov. 13	Nov. 17	Nov. 30 '98
0.015	Jan. 12	Feb. 05	Feb. 09	Feb. 26 '99
0.015	May. 11	May. 19	May. 21	Jun. 01 '99
0.015	Aug. 03	Aug. 13	Aug. 17	Aug. 31 '99

Applied Power Inc.

Business Summary - 26-AUG-99

Applied Power Inc. is a global company comprised of three business segments. It derives nearly 40% of revenues from sales of technical office workstations and cabinets, 35% from sales of custom systems, and 26% from sales of hydraulic tools to the general industrial and construction markets.

The company has a healthy international presence, although the strong U.S. economy and recent acquisitions have increased the North American percentage of revenue. In FY 98 (Aug.), 23%, 3% and 1% of total revenues came from sales to Europe, Asia and Latin America, respectively.

APW's higher-margin Enclosure Products & Systems group (EPS, formerly Technical Environments and Enclosures) makes a broad line of technical furniture and electrical and electronic cabinet enclosure systems for various electronic and other technical equipment. EPS also makes custom workstations for computer-oriented offices. The company is targeting the fast-growing local area network (LAN) office, media production, telecom and laboratory markets. APW has been augmenting EPS's growth by purchasing other technical office furniture manufacturers. EPS's largest customer, IBM, is expected to account for just under 10% of total EPS sales in FY 99.

The Engineered Solutions (ESG) segment provides customized solutions to OEM customers in the truck, aerospace, automotive, recreational vehicle, and electrical/electronic enclosure markets. ESG possesses particular competence in hydraulic, electromechanical, rubber molding, magnetic, thermal systems and electronic control techniques. ESG also produces hydraulics for medical equipment manufacturers. In addition, the group makes devices that reduce vibration, shock and noise. ESG primarily sells its vibration reduction devices to aircraft manufacturers, airlines and medical instrument makers.

Tools and Supplies (T&S) provides industrial and electrical tools and accessories through various distributor and retail channels worldwide. It primarily makes hydraulic tools for industrial and construction customers. T&S sells its products (more than 10,000 SKUs) through 2,500 independent distributors worldwide. This segment also makes electrical products for electrical contractors and the do-it-yourself market. It sells its products to about 4,000 wholesale distributors, as well as to retail home centers such as Home Depot, Ace Hardware and Sears.

In July 1998, APW acquired ZERO Corp. for 11.2 million shares (valued at $386 million). ZERO's primary business is protecting electronics; its system packaging, thermal management and engineered cases serve the telecommunications, instrumentation and data-processing markets.

Per Share Data ($) (Year Ended Aug. 31)	1999	1998	1997	1996	1995	1994	1993	1992	1991	1990
Tangible Bk. Val.	NA	NM	4.65	2.81	2.38	1.48	0.79	0.99	0.70	0.44
Cash Flow	NA	1.84	4.57	1.96	1.58	1.36	0.94	0.93	1.06	1.49
Earnings	1.98	0.66	1.47	1.21	0.91	0.64	0.33	0.36	0.30	0.74
Dividends	0.06	0.08	0.12	0.06	0.06	0.06	0.06	0.06	0.06	0.06
Payout Ratio	3%	11%	8%	5%	7%	9%	18%	16%	20%	8%
Prices - High	38 7/8	40 1/8	35 1/8	20	17 5/8	12 5/8	9 1/4	10	10	13 5/8
- Low	21 3/8	20 3/8	19 1/4	13 3/8	11 3/8	8 1/8	7 1/4	6 3/4	5 1/4	6 1/4
P/E Ratio - High	20	61	24	17	19	20	28	27	33	18
- Low	11	31	13	11	12	13	22	18	18	8
Income Statement Analysis (Million $)										
Revs.	NA	1,231	672	571	527	433	360	357	434	445
Oper. Inc.	NA	153	96.5	78.5	67.3	61.6	46.6	50.7	62.7	75.0
Depr.	NA	47.6	23.7	21.1	18.5	19.4	15.8	14.8	19.9	19.9
Int. Exp.	NA	NA	12.0	8.5	10.3	11.4	11.7	14.6	19.8	20.4
Pretax Inc.	NA	57.4	62.7	49.2	29.5	25.3	13.4	15.9	16.9	34.4
Eff. Tax Rate	NA	54%	33%	32%	32%	33%	35%	40%	54%	43%
Net Inc.	NA	26.7	42.0	34.0	25.0	16.9	8.7	9.5	7.8	19.6
Balance Sheet & Other Fin. Data (Million $)										
Cash	NA	6.3	5.8	1.0	0.9	1.9	0.9	3.0	3.6	6.5
Curr. Assets	NA	365	226	207	190	175	162	156	144	191
Total Assets	NA	1,175	464	381	333	317	291	289	326	394
Curr. Liab.	NA	261	128	108	97.4	102	93.0	79.0	86.0	127
LT Debt	NA	513	102	76.5	74.2	78.0	87.0	105	114	142
Common Eqty.	NA	342	204	168	132	107	88.0	97.0	117	115
Total Cap.	NA	878	320	260	222	185	175	202	231	257
Cap. Exp.	NA	56.8	22.7	23.0	16.0	12.7	11.5	9.3	12.6	16.8
Cash Flow	NA	74.3	65.7	54.8	43.5	36.3	24.5	24.3	27.8	39.5
Curr. Ratio	NA	1.4	1.8	1.9	2.0	1.7	1.7	2.0	1.7	1.5
% LT Debt of Cap.	NA	58.4	31.7	29.4	33.3	42.2	49.6	52.1	49.5	55.1
% Net Inc.of Revs.	NA	2.2	6.3	5.9	4.7	3.9	2.4	2.7	1.8	4.4
% Ret. on Assets	NA	2.9	10.0	9.5	6.7	5.6	3.0	3.1	2.2	5.1
% Ret. on Equity	NA	8.2	22.6	22.5	2.1	17.3	9.4	8.9	6.7	19.3

Data as orig reptd.; bef. results of disc opers/spec. items. Per share data adj. for stk. divs. Bold denotes diluted EPS (FASB 128)-prior periods restated. E-Estimated. NA-Not Available. NM-Not Meaningful. NR-Not Ranked.

Office—N22 W23685 Ridgeview Pkwy, Waukesha, WI 53188-1013**Tel**—(414) 523-7600.**Website**—http://www.apw-inc.com**Chrmn, Pres & CEO**—R. G. Sim. **SVP-CFO & Investor Contact**—Robert C. Arzbaecher. **Treas**—R. Rohr-Dralle.**Secy**—A. W. Asmuth. **Dirs**—H. R. Crowther, J. L. Heckel, R. A. Kashnow, L. D. Kozlowski, J. J. McDonough, R. G. Sim. **Transfer Agent & Registrar**—First Trust Co., Milwaukee. **Incorporated**—in Wisconsin in 1910. **Empl**— 11,350. **S&P Analyst:** John A. Massey

STANDARD
&POOR'S
STOCK REPORTS

AptarGroup, Inc.

NYSE Symbol **ATR**

In S&P SmallCap 600

09-OCT-99

Industry: Manufacturing (Specialized)

Summary: ATR is a leading manufacturer of pumps, dispensing closures and aerosol valves for fragrance/cosmetics, personal care, pharmaceutical, household/industrial and food products.

Quantitative Evaluations

Outlook
(1 Lowest—5 Highest)
• **2-**

Fair Value
• **26**

Risk
• **Low**

Earn./Div. Rank
• **NR**

Technical Eval.
• **Bearish** since 7/99

Rel. Strength Rank
(1 Lowest—99 Highest)
• **57**

Insider Activity
• **NA**

Recent Price • 25¾
52 Wk Range • 31½-20⅞
Yield • 0.8%
12-Mo. P/E • 15.0

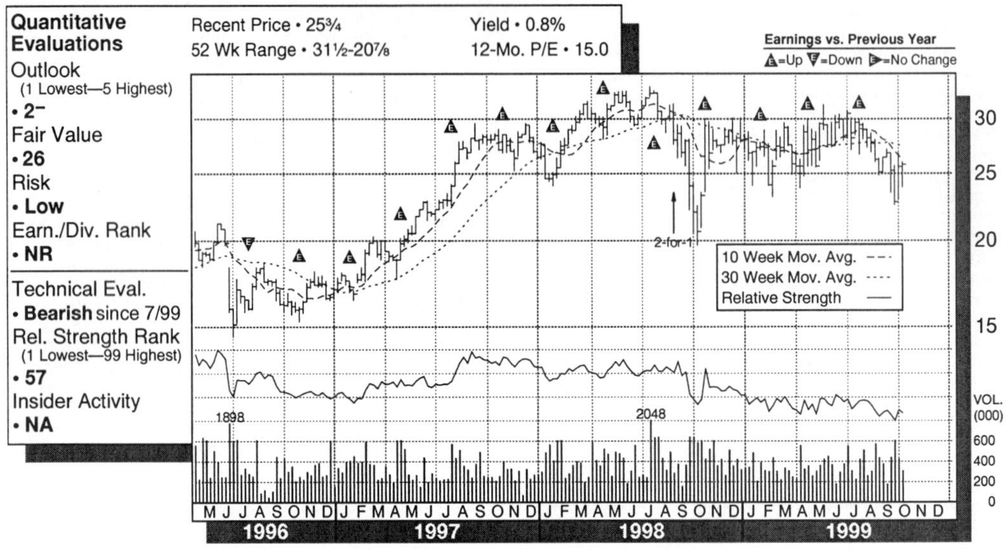

Business Profile - 14-SEP-99

In July 1999, ATR said it expected demand for pumps for cosmetic applications to strengthen, and demand for pumps for fragrance applications to improve modestly. Sales of dispensing closures to the personal care, household and food markets were also expected to increase. Demand for standard aerosol valves was seen weakening, but demand for pumps and metered dose aerosol valves by the pharmaceutical market was expected to remain strong. In February 1999, the company acquired privately held Emson Research Inc., a leading supplier of perfume pumps in the North American market, with a growing presence in selected international markets. Emson's 1998 sales were about $85 million. The dividend was boosted 25% with the August 1999 payment.

Operational Review - 14-SEP-99

Net sales in the six months ended June 30, 1999, advanced 15%, year to year, reflecting acquisitions. Gross margins widened slightly, and operating expenses rose less rapidly than revenues. However, with depreciation and amortization charges up 27%, and interest expense up sharply, as a result of debt related to recent acquisitions, pretax income was up only 2.4%. After taxes at 35.3%, versus 40.3%, net income gained 11%, to $30,449,000 ($0.82 a share), from $27,445,000 ($0.75, as adjusted).

Stock Performance - 08-OCT-99

In the past 30 trading days, ATR's shares have increased 2%, compared to a 0.91% fall in the S&P 500. Average trading volume for the past five days was 61,200 shares, compared with the 40-day moving average of 85,921 shares.

Key Stock Statistics

Dividend Rate/Share	0.20	Shareholders	900
Shs. outstg. (M)	36.4	Market cap. (B)	$0.938
Avg. daily vol. (M)	0.090	Inst. holdings	76%
Tang. Bk. Value/Share	11.27		
Beta	0.39		

Value of $10,000 invested 5 years ago: $ 25,804

Fiscal Year Ending Dec. 31

	1999	1998	1997	1996	1995	1994
Revenues (Million $)						
1Q	198.2	170.9	158.3	152.9	135.6	117.2
2Q	208.9	181.8	171.8	151.1	142.4	118.2
3Q	—	182.7	163.5	155.9	140.6	120.0
4Q	—	178.1	161.8	155.9	138.8	118.9
Yr.	—	713.5	655.4	615.8	557.5	474.3
Earnings Per Share ($)						
1Q	**0.39**	**0.36**	**0.32**	**0.29**	0.27	0.23
2Q	**0.44**	**0.39**	**0.33**	**0.24**	0.28	0.23
3Q	—	**0.39**	**0.34**	**0.24**	0.23	0.20
4Q	—	**0.51**	**0.29**	**0.24**	0.21	0.17
Yr.	—	**1.65**	**1.27**	**1.02**	**0.99**	0.82

Next earnings report expected: late October

Dividend Data (Dividends have been paid since 1993.)

Amount ($)	Date Decl.	Ex-Div. Date	Stock of Record	Payment Date
0.040	Oct. 23	Oct. 30	Nov. 03	Nov. 24 '98
0.040	Jan. 21	Feb. 01	Feb. 03	Feb. 25 '99
0.040	Apr. 22	May. 03	May. 05	May. 26 '99
0.050	Jul. 22	Jul. 30	Aug. 03	Aug. 24 '99

AptarGroup, Inc.

Business Summary - 14-SEP-99

From humble beginnings in the late 1940s as a U.S. manufacturer of aerosol valves through its SeaquistPerfect Dispensing division, AptarGroup has grown to become a multinational supplier of a broad line of dispensing packaging systems. The business, which was acquired by Pittway Corp. in 1964, became an independent publicly owned corporation upon its spinoff from Pittway in April 1993. ATR has grown primarily by acquiring relatively small companies, and via internal expansion.

ATR designs, manufactures and sells consumer product dispensing systems, focusing on providing value-added components to global consumer product marketers in the fragrance/cosmetics, personal care, pharmaceutical, household products and food industries. Value-added packaging allows consumers to conveniently dispense a product in an aesthetic looking package that consistently meets basic dosage characteristics as required. The company believes it is the largest supplier of pharmaceutical, fragrance/cosmetics and personal care fine mist pumps worldwide and the largest supplier of dispensing closures and aerosol valves in North America. It has manufacturing facilities throughout the world, but primarily in North America, Europe and Asia, serving more than 1,000 customers.

The company's pumps (60% of sales in 1998) are finger-driven dispensing systems that disperse a spray or lotion from non-pressurized containers. The style of pump depends on the product being dispensed, with smaller, fine mist pumps used for perfumes, for instance, and less dainty high-output trigger pumps employed to squirt out household cleaners. Dispensing closures (22%) are plastic caps used mainly for squeezable containers which allow a product to be dispensed without removing the cap. ATR sees future growth opportunities as consumer marketers continue to convert non-dispensing closures (such as twist-off caps for shampoo bottles) to dispensing closures.

Aerosol valves (16%) are mechanisms that dispense products from pressurized containers. The company's continuous spray valves are often used with hair spray, spray paint, and certain household and automotive products. A second type of valve, the metered aerosol valve, is sold mainly to the pharmaceutical market for lung and heart medications that need to be dispensed in precise amounts.

A significant portion of operations is located in Europe; sales there accounted for 57% of ATR's total in 1998.

Per Share Data ($) (Year Ended Dec. 31)	1998	1997	1996	1995	1994	1993	1992	1991	1990	1989
Tangible Bk. Val.	10.13	8.37	8.05	7.37	7.55	5.92	4.39	NA	NA	NA
Cash Flow	3.13	2.64	2.38	2.21	1.99	1.61	1.69	NA	NA	NA
Earnings	1.65	1.27	1.04	0.99	0.82	0.67	0.59	NA	NA	NA
Dividends	0.16	0.15	0.14	0.13	0.12	0.05	NA	NA	NA	NA
Payout Ratio	10%	12%	13%	13%	14%	8%	NA	NA	NA	NA
Prices - High	33½	29⅝	21⅝	19⅛	14½	11	NA	NA	NA	NA
- Low	19⅝	16⅜	14½	12⅜	10⅛	8	NA	NA	NA	NA
P/E Ratio - High	20	23	21	19	18	17	NA	NA	NA	NA
- Low	12	13	14	12	12	12	NA	NA	NA	NA
Income Statement Analysis (Million $)										
Revs.	714	655	616	557	474	412	445	NA	NA	NA
Oper. Inc.	150	129	112	103	87.0	71.3	72.8	NA	NA	NA
Depr.	54.4	49.9	47.9	43.5	38.4	30.3	35.3	NA	NA	NA
Int. Exp.	6.5	5.3	6.3	5.9	8.2	10.2	14.7	NA	NA	NA
Pretax Inc.	100	78.9	60.5	57.6	43.2	35.5	29.2	NA	NA	NA
Eff. Tax Rate	39%	41%	37%	38%	37%	37%	35%	NA	NA	NA
Net Inc.	60.8	46.5	37.5	35.7	27.3	21.6	19.0	NA	NA	NA
Balance Sheet & Other Fin. Data (Million $)										
Cash	25.2	17.7	16.4	17.3	20.1	16.4	12.2	NA	NA	NA
Curr. Assets	317	256	237	224	184	158	167	NA	NA	NA
Total Assets	715	585	576	559	465	408	420	NA	NA	NA
Curr. Liab.	167	125	116	123	106	153	160	NA	NA	NA
LT Debt	80.9	70.7	76.6	80.7	53.8	41.3	47.6	NA	NA	NA
Common Eqty.	416	342	336	312	271	190	180	NA	NA	NA
Total Cap.	526	439	440	416	345	247	246	NA	NA	NA
Cap. Exp.	79.8	71.2	62.8	55.5	42.0	112	45.6	NA	NA	NA
Cash Flow	115	96.4	85.4	79.2	65.6	51.8	54.3	NA	NA	NA
Curr. Ratio	1.9	2.0	2.0	1.8	1.7	1.0	1.0	NA	NA	NA
% LT Debt of Cap.	15.4	16.1	17.4	19.4	15.6	16.7	19.3	NA	NA	NA
% Net Inc.of Revs.	8.5	7.1	6.1	6.4	5.7	5.2	4.3	NA	NA	NA
% Ret. on Assets	9.4	8.0	6.6	7.0	5.9	NM	NA	NA	NA	NA
% Ret. on Equity	16.1	13.7	11.6	12.3	11.3	NM	NA	NA	NA	NA

Data as orig reptd.; bef. results of disc opers/spec. items. Per share data adj. for stk. divs. Bold denotes diluted EPS (FASB 128)-prior periods restated. E-Estimated. NA-Not Available. NM-Not Meaningful. NR-Not Ranked.

Office—475 West Terra Cotta Ave., Suite E, Crystal Lake, IL 60014. **Tel**—(815) 477-0424. **Website**—http://www.aptargroup.com **Chrmn**—K. Harris. **Pres & CEO**—C. A. Siebel. **EVP, CFO, Secy & Treas**—S. J. Hagge. **Investor Contact**—Ralph Poltermann. **Dirs**—E. L. Barnett, R. Barrows, R. Gruska, L. A. Guthart, K. Harris, A. Pilz, P. Pfeiffer, C. A. Siebel, J. C. Smith. **Transfer Agent & Registrar**—ChaseMellon Shareholder Services, Ridgefield Park, NJ. **Incorporated**—in Delaware in 1992. **Empl**— 5,700. **S&P Analyst:** C.C.P.

STANDARD & POOR'S
STOCK REPORTS

Aquarion Co.

NYSE Symbol **WTR**

In S&P SmallCap 600

23-OCT-99

Industry: Water Utilities

Summary: Aquarion has agreed to be acquired by Kelda Group plc for $37.05 a share in cash. The transaction is expected to be completed in early 2000.

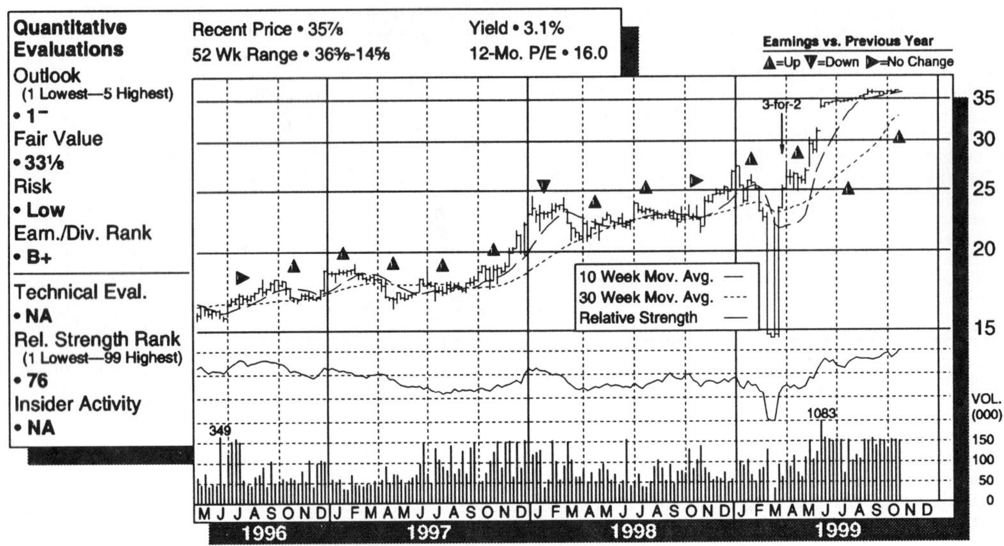

Business Profile - 14-OCT-99

On June 1, 1999, Aquarion agreed to be acquired by Kelda Group plc (formerly Yorkshire Water plc) for $37.05 a share in cash, in a transaction valued at approximately $600 million, including the assumption of $155 million in debt. The transaction was approved by WTR shareholders in late September. It is subject to regulatory approval and is expected to be completed in early 2000. Based in Leeds, England, Kelda has annual revenues of $1.1 billion and provides water, sewage, and environmental services in the U.K. and Europe.

Operational Review - 14-OCT-99

Operating revenues for the six months ended June 30, 1999, rose 2.1%, year to year, reflecting increased weather-related water sales, a March 1999 increase in WTR's BHC Western Division water rates, and increased sales volume at the company's Timco lumber division. Profitability benefited from improved results from water utility and lumber operations and a 6.4% decrease in interest expense. Pretax income advanced 3.0%. After taxes at 39.4%, versus 44.4%, net income was up 12%, to $7,918,000 ($0.67 a share), from $7,043,000 ($0.62, adjusted).

Stock Performance - 22-OCT-99

In the past 30 trading days, WTR's shares have increased 0.52%, compared to a 4% fall in the S&P 500. Average trading volume for the past five days was 40,040 shares, compared with the 40-day moving average of 36,523 shares.

Key Stock Statistics

Dividend Rate/Share	1.12	Shareholders	8,138
Shs. outstg. (M)	11.4	Market cap. (B)	$0.413
Avg. daily vol. (M)	0.035	Inst. holdings	23%
Tang. Bk. Value/Share	13.27		
Beta	0.17		

Value of $10,000 invested 5 years ago: $ 25,473

Fiscal Year Ending Dec. 31

	1999	1998	1997	1996	1995	1994
Revenues (Million $)						
1Q	25.72	25.38	23.39	20.99	25.60	25.85
2Q	27.56	26.83	26.52	23.01	28.41	29.62
3Q	43.90	29.97	29.23	25.50	30.00	29.65
4Q	—	33.49	27.97	25.30	34.19	36.86
Yr.	—	115.7	107.1	94.80	118.2	122.0
Earnings Per Share ($)						
1Q	**0.29**	**0.27**	0.23	0.20	0.23	0.27
2Q	**0.38**	**0.35**	0.33	0.31	0.31	0.37
3Q	**0.97**	**0.53**	0.53	0.40	0.32	0.35
4Q	—	**0.59**	**0.31**	0.43	0.41	0.27
Yr.	—	**1.74**	**1.39**	**1.32**	**1.30**	1.25

Next earnings report expected: NA

Dividend Data (Dividends have been paid since 1890.)

Amount ($)	Date Decl.	Ex-Div. Date	Stock of Record	Payment Date
3-for-2	Feb. 16	Mar. 23	Mar. 01	Mar. 22 '99
0.278	Mar. 23	Apr. 07	Apr. 09	Apr. 30 '99
0.278	Jun. 15	Jul. 07	Jul. 09	Jul. 30 '99
0.280	Sep. 21	Oct. 06	Oct. 08	Oct. 29 '99

Business Summary - 14-OCT-99

Aquarion's strategy consists of several elements, the first of which is to grow internally through capital additions, and externally through acquisitions. Second, the company intends to bolster earnings and asset utilization through the sale of surplus land. Third, Aquarion is pursuing opportunities in contract management operations. Lastly, WTR plans to enhance earnings and return on equity through aggressive cost containment.

WTR is a holding company whose subsidiaries are involved in the regulated business of public water supply as well as various nonutility businesses. The company's utility subsidiaries, BHC Co. and Sea Cliff Water Co., collect, treat, and distribute water to residential, commercial, and industrial customers, to other utilities for resale, and for private and municipal fire protection. These utilities provide water to customers in Connecticut, and Long Island, NY. In 1998, the utilities drew 63% from residential customers, 16% from commercial customers, 3% from industrial customers, 13% from fire protection customers and 5% from other sources. In addition, BHC sold 436 acres of land in 1998, including 401 acres of surplus, off-watershed land to the city of Shelton, CT. In September 1999, the company completed the sale of a 640-acre tract of land for $12.4 million to a local land trust. The utility division has budgeted $27 million for capital expenditures in 1999.

Aquarion's non-utility subsidiaries include Timco, Aquarion Management Services (AMS) and Main Street South. Timco processes timber through a sawmill complex located in New Hampshire. Lumber manufactured by Timco is used in the remodeling and do it yourself markets and, to a lesser degree, in the construction of new homes. AMS provides customers with a variety of utility management services, including contract management and operations, information services and collections, as well as various engineering, operations and management consulting services. In January 1999, AMS began a five-year, $2.5 million contract to operate a water treatment plant in New Castle, NY. To gain experience in wastewater operations and benefit from the growing trend toward public-partnerships in the utility sector, AMS obtained a small contract from the town of Sharon, CT. Main Street is the company's utility subsidiary created to assist BHC in marketing surplus land.

The company's operations are divided into four industry groups. In 1998, operating revenues were derived 78% from public water supply, 12% from timber processing, 9% from real estate, including both Main Street South and surplus utility land sales, and 1% from utility management services.

Per Share Data ($) (Year Ended Dec. 31)	1998	1997	1996	1995	1994	1993	1992	1991	1990	1989
Tangible Bk. Val.	16.42	14.99	13.90	13.15	12.76	12.43	11.81	11.25	11.56	14.86
Earnings	1.74	1.39	1.33	1.27	1.25	1.17	1.01	-1.17	0.99	1.40
Dividends	1.10	1.08	1.08	0.81	1.35	1.08	1.08	1.08	1.07	1.05
Payout Ratio	63%	78%	81%	64%	108%	92%	107%	NM	108%	75%
Prices - High	27⅜	24⅝	18⅞	17⅜	18⅝	19½	17	18⅛	17¼	19¾
- Low	20¾	16¼	15⅝	14⅜	14⅜	16⅜	13⅜	13¼	12⅝	16¼
P/E Ratio - High	16	18	14	14	15	17	17	NM	17	14
- Low	12	12	11	11	11	14	13	NM	13	12
Income Statement Analysis (Million $)										
Revs.	116	107	94.8	118	122	107	104	100	77.8	78.3
Depr.	14.5	13.4	13.8	13.0	11.6	10.6	9.5	8.9	7.6	6.8
Maint.	NA	NA	NA	NA	NA	NA	NA	NA	NA	NA
Fxd. Chgs. Cov.	4.2	3.3	3.4	3.4	3.7	2.8	2.5	0.4	2.2	3.4
Constr. Credits	0.2	0.8	1.1	0.9	0.6	0.6	0.7	0.4	0.8	0.5
Eff. Tax Rate	41%	44%	40%	44%	46%	38%	40%	NM	22%	43%
Net Inc.	20.0	15.0	13.8	12.9	12.2	11.0	8.6	-8.5	7.1	10.0
Balance Sheet & Other Fin. Data (Million $)										
Gross Prop.	493	482	455	432	379	368	352	327	311	289
Cap. Exp.	21.2	28.7	38.6	41.6	19.8	17.9	25.4	17.9	19.1	20.1
Net Prop.	347	340	323	296	256	250	243	227	219	206
Capitalization:										
LT Debt	141	151	148	132	115	116	106	95.3	100	68.2
% LT Debt	49	53	55	52	51	51	52	55	52	42
Pfd.	Nil	Nil	Nil	0.3	0.3	0.4	0.4	2.2	2.5	3.2
% Pfd.	Nil	Nil	Nil	0.10	0.20	0.20	0.20	1.20	1.30	2.00
Common	147	134	123	122	112	111	97.2	75.5	90.5	90.3
% Common	51	47	45	48	49	49	48	44	47	56
Total Cap.	352	356	344	325	319	317	285	212	229	195
% Oper. Ratio	73.8	76.2	76.8	82.0	83.6	81.7	83.2	84.1	81.1	78.0
% Earn. on Net Prop.	17.1	15.3	14.6	7.7	7.9	8.0	7.4	7.1	6.9	8.6
% Return On Revs.	17.3	14.0	14.6	10.9	10.0	10.2	8.3	NM	9.1	12.7
% Return On Invest. Capital	12.6	10.7	9.4	7.1	6.3	5.9	7.3	0.6	6.9	9.0
% Return On Com. Equity	14.2	11.7	11.3	10.9	10.8	10.6	9.1	NM	7.8	11.3

Data as orig reptd.; bef. results of disc opers/spec. items. Per share data adj. for stk. divs. Bold denotes diluted EPS (FASB 128)-prior periods restated. E-Estimated. NA-Not Available. NM-Not Meaningful. NR-Not Ranked.

Office—835 Main St., Bridgeport, CT 06604. **Tel**—(203) 335-2333. **Website**—http://www.aquarion.com**Chrmn**—G.W. Edwards, Jr. **Pres & CEO**—R. K. Schmidt. **EVP, CFO & Treas**—J. M. Hansen. **VP, Secy & Investor Contact**—Larry L. Bingaman (203-336-7626). **Dirs**—G. W. Edwards Jr., G. Etherington, J. D. Greenwood, D. M. Halsted, Jr., E. G. Hotard, J. E. McGregor, G. J. Ratcliffe, R. K. Schmidt, J. A. Urquhart. **Transfer Agent & Registrar**—ChaseMellon Securities Trust Co., Ridgefield Park, NJ. **Incorporated**—in Connecticut in 1857; reincorporated in Delaware in 1968. **Empl**— 384. **S&P Analyst:** Craig K. Shere, CFA

STANDARD
&POOR'S
STOCK REPORTS

Arctic Cat

NASDAQ Symbol **ACAT**

In S&P SmallCap 600

09-OCT-99

Industry: Leisure Time (Products)

Summary: This company designs, makes and markets snowmobiles, personal watercraft, all-terrain vehicles, and related parts, garments and accessories.

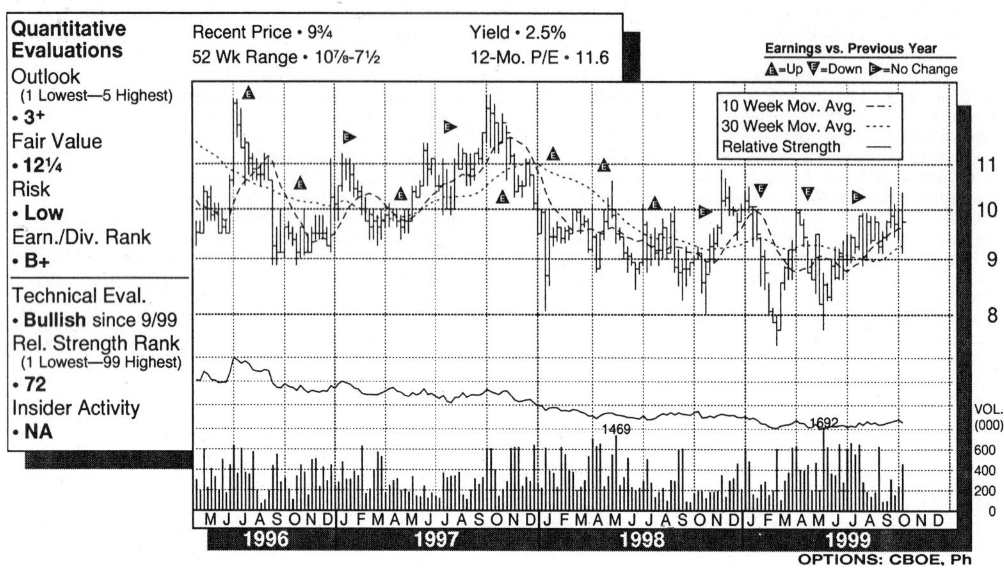

Business Profile - 14-JUL-99

After two years of little snow and warmer than normal winter weather, industry-wide snowmobile retail sales declined again in FY 99 (Mar.). The company believes that growth in all-terrain vehicle and personal watercraft sales will offset the expected decline in snowmobile sales in FY 00, leading to revenues similar to those of FY 99. Meanwhile, the company intends to work aggressively on implementing operating improvements, lowering product and operating costs, and reducing inventories. Suzuki Motor Co., which owns all of the Class B common shares, is the largest stockholder.

Operational Review - 14-JUL-99

Net sales in FY 99 (Mar.) fell 4.7% from those of the prior year, as increased sales of all-terrain vehicles were outweighed by lower snowmobile and personal watercraft unit volume, primarily reflecting reduced dealer orders. Gross margins narrowed on a less favorable product mix and higher warranty expense. Despite a 7.7% reduction in SG&A expenses and 60% higher interest income, net income declined 9.2%, to $23,115,000 ($0.84 a share, on 4.8% fewer shares), from $25,449,000 ($0.88).

Stock Performance - 08-OCT-99

In the past 30 trading days, ACAT's shares have increased 5%, compared to a 0.91% fall in the S&P 500. Average trading volume for the past five days was 90,860 shares, compared with the 40-day moving average of 61,367 shares.

Key Stock Statistics

Dividend Rate/Share	0.24	Shareholders	800
Shs. outstg. (M)	25.8	Market cap. (B)	$0.178
Avg. daily vol. (M)	0.057	Inst. holdings	37%
Tang. Bk. Value/Share	6.59		
Beta	0.46		

Value of $10,000 invested 5 years ago: $ 6,856

Fiscal Year Ending Mar. 31

	2000	1999	1998	1997	1996	1995
Revenues (Million $)						
1Q	86.83	88.65	85.47	89.13	61.70	56.00
2Q	—	193.4	196.8	177.9	166.1	149.2
3Q	—	109.8	139.8	133.9	123.6	112.8
4Q	—	88.57	82.09	67.66	53.56	49.10
Yr.	—	480.4	504.2	468.6	404.9	367.1
Earnings Per Share ($)						
1Q	**0.05**	**0.05**	0.03	0.03	-0.14	0.12
2Q	—	**0.68**	0.68	0.63	0.60	0.64
3Q	—	**0.16**	**0.21**	0.20	0.20	0.36
4Q	—	**-0.06**	**-0.05**	-0.08	-0.10	Nil
Yr.	—	**0.84**	**0.88**	**0.78**	0.56	1.13

Next earnings report expected: early November

Dividend Data (Dividends have been paid since 1992.)

Amount ($)	Date Decl.	Ex-Div. Date	Stock of Record	Payment Date
0.060	Oct. 29	Nov. 13	Nov. 17	Dec. 02 '98
0.060	Jan. 27	Feb. 12	Feb. 17	Mar. 02 '99
0.060	May. 03	May. 12	May. 14	Jun. 01 '99
0.060	Jul. 28	Aug. 16	Aug. 18	Sep. 01 '99

A Division of The McGraw-Hill Companies

Arctic Cat Inc.

Business Summary - 14-JUL-99

One of only four major participants in the snowmobile industry, and operating under a brand name that has existed for more than three decades, Arctic Cat Inc. (formerly Arctco, Inc.) designs, engineers, makes and markets a full line of snowmobiles, as well as all-terrain vehicles (ATVs) under the Arctic Cat name, personal watercraft under the Tigershark name, and related parts, garments and accessories.

The company produces a full line of snowmobiles, which accounted for 56% of total net sales in FY 99 (Mar.). There were 32 basic models at the end of FY 99, all marketed under the Arctic Cat brand name. Snowmobiles, with suggested retail prices ranging from $3,599 to $9,999 (except for a children's model with a suggested price of $1,349), are sold in the U.S., Canada, Scandinavia, and other international markets. In FY 99, about 85% of the company's snowmobile sales were from models or model variations not available three years earlier.

ACAT began shipping all-terrain vehicles (ATVs; 23% of total net sales), also marketed under the Arctic Cat name, in December 1995, with the Bearcat 454 4x4. Since then, the company's ATV line has grown to include six models (ranging in price from $4,399 to $6,449), all of which are designed for the utility, farming/ranching, and hunting/fishing markets. ACAT believes that continued increases in its ATV sales in FY 99 reflected favorable dealer and consumer reception of the Arctic Cat product and growth in the ATV market.

The company's personal watercraft (4%), sold under the Tigershark brand name, combine performance, durability and style. The seven models offered are sold at prices ranging from $4,899 to $8,299. The company attributed lower personal watercraft unit sales volume in FY 99 to an industry-wide softening in consumer demand.

Parts, garments and accessories (17%) include replacement parts, upgrades, maintenance supplies, and suits, jackets, pants and other accessories.

ACAT sells its products through an extensive network of independent dealers located throughout the contiguous U.S. and Canada, and through distributors representing dealers in Alaska, Europe, the Middle East, Asia, and other international markets. Sales to foreign customers accounted for 21% of the total in FY 99.

During FY 99, the company spent $18.5 million to repurchase 2,049,114 of its common shares under stock repurchase programs. In April 1999, directors authorized the repurchase of an additional $30 million of common stock.

Per Share Data ($) (Year Ended Mar. 31)	1999	1998	1997	1996	1995	1994	1993	1992	1991	1990
Tangible Bk. Val.	6.65	6.25	5.73	5.27	4.96	4.02	3.23	2.73	2.41	NA
Cash Flow	1.29	1.34	0.83	0.82	1.32	1.10	0.74	NA	NA	NA
Earnings	0.84	0.88	0.78	0.56	1.13	0.94	0.62	0.46	0.49	NA
Dividends	0.24	0.24	0.24	0.24	0.21	0.15	0.12	0.03	Nil	NA
Payout Ratio	29%	27%	31%	43%	19%	16%	19%	7%	Nil	NA
Cal. Yrs.	1998	1997	1996	1995	1994	1993	1992	1991	1990	1989
Prices - High	$10\frac{7}{8}$	$12\frac{3}{4}$	$13\frac{1}{8}$	$19\frac{1}{2}$	$21\frac{3}{4}$	$18\frac{1}{8}$	$9\frac{1}{8}$	NA	NA	NA
- Low	8	$9\frac{1}{4}$	$8\frac{7}{8}$	$10\frac{3}{8}$	$13\frac{3}{8}$	$8\frac{1}{8}$	$4\frac{1}{2}$	NA	NA	NA
P/E Ratio - High	13	14	17	35	19	19	15	NA	NA	NA
- Low	10	11	11	19	12	9	7	NA	NA	NA
Income Statement Analysis (Million $)										
Revs.	480	504	469	405	367	268	185	148	152	NA
Oper. Inc.	45.4	51.0	45.4	31.2	54.4	44.8	29.2	NA	NA	NA
Depr.	12.5	13.4	11.4	7.7	5.5	4.6	3.6	NA	NA	NA
Int. Exp.	0.0	0.1	0.1	Nil	0.0	0.1	0.2	0.3	0.6	NA
Pretax Inc.	35.8	39.5	35.8	25.8	51.4	41.7	26.9	19.6	20.3	NA
Eff. Tax Rate	35%	36%	36%	36%	35%	34%	33%	33%	34%	NA
Net Inc.	23.1	25.4	23.0	16.6	33.4	27.5	18.0	13.2	13.4	NA
Balance Sheet & Other Fin. Data (Million $)										
Cash	51.4	24.8	50.7	44.0	65.2	59.9	54.8	59.6	42.9	NA
Curr. Assets	202	190	178	178	164	140	NA	NA	NA	NA
Total Assets	240	230	218	208	184	155	122	104	91.0	NA
Curr. Liab.	60.2	47.6	46.9	48.3	35.1	35.2	NA	NA	NA	NA
LT Debt	Nil	Nil	Nil	Nil	Nil	Nil	0.6	1.3	2.1	NA
Common Eqty.	175	178	167	156	147	118	94.0	79.0	66.0	NA
Total Cap.	180	182	171	160	149	120	94.9	80.7	68.5	NA
Cap. Exp.	10.5	13.7	21.2	17.2	10.7	6.7	5.8	NA	NA	NA
Cash Flow	35.6	38.8	34.4	24.3	38.8	32.1	21.6	NA	NA	NA
Curr. Ratio	3.4	4.0	3.8	3.7	4.7	4.0	NA	NA	NA	NA
% LT Debt of Cap.	Nil	Nil	Nil	Nil	Nil	Nil	0.6	1.7	3.0	NA
% Net Inc.of Revs.	4.8	5.0	4.9	4.1	9.1	10.3	0.7	8.9	8.9	NA
% Ret. on Assets	9.8	11.4	10.8	8.5	19.7	19.9	15.9	13.7	18.3	NA
% Ret. on Equity	13.1	14.8	14.2	10.9	25.2	25.9	20.7	18.4	26.5	NA

Data as orig reptd.; bef. results of disc opers/spec. items. Per share data adj. for stk. divs. Bold denotes diluted EPS (FASB 128)-prior periods restated. E-Estimated. NA-Not Available. NM-Not Meaningful. NR-Not Ranked.

Office—601 Brooks Ave. South, Thief River Falls, MN 56701. **Tel**—(218) 681-8558. **Website**—http://www.arctic-cat.com **Chrmn**—W. G. Ness. **Pres & CEO**—C. A. Twomey. **CFO & Secy**—T. C. Delmore. **Dirs**—R. J. Dondelinger, W. I. Hagen, J. C. Heinmiller, T. Kaito, W. G. Ness, G. A. Ostrander, K.J. Roering, C. A. Twomey. **Transfer Agent & Registrar**—Norwest Bank Minnesota, South St. Paul. **Incorporated**—in Minnesota in 1982. **Empl**— 1,685. **S&P Analyst:** S.R.B.

STANDARD
&POOR'S
STOCK REPORTS

Arkansas Best

NASDAQ Symbol **ABFS**

In S&P SmallCap 600

09-OCT-99 **Industry:** Truckers

Summary: ABFS is mainly engaged in the motor carrier and freight forwarding business. It also has truck tire retreading and sales operations.

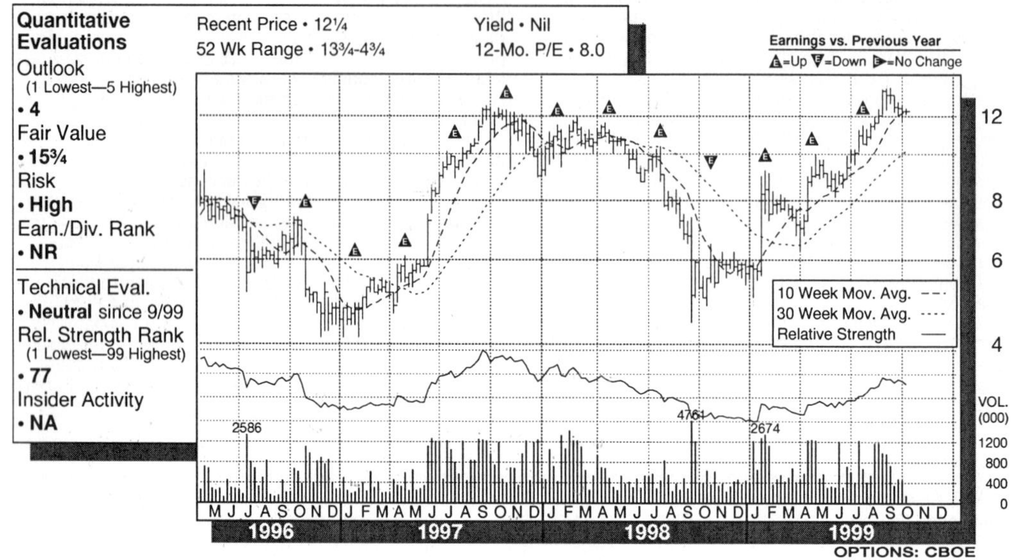

Business Profile - 01-JUL-99

Arkansas Best said in April 1999 that it has introduced changes in its freight-handling network that reduces, by one-third, the cycle time of shipments moving through its distribution centers. At G.I. Trucking, ABFS expected to continue to place emphasis on margin improvement. Although steps taken to exit unprofitable freight lanes at Clipper Domestic have initially resulted in lower revenue, ABFS was looking for long-term profitability to improve. In April 1999, ABFS sold its Clipper International operations to an investor group. The transaction did not result in a significant gain or loss for ABFS. ABFS kept its Clipper domestic operations.

Operational Review - 01-JUL-99

Revenues from continuing operations for the first quarter of 1999 rose 4.6%, year to year. Operating margins at both ABF Freight Systems and at G.I. Trucking improved, and there were smaller operating losses at both Clipper Domestic and Treadco. Overall operating profit soared 56%. After a 1.9% decline in other expenses (net), pretax income more than doubled. Following taxes at 42.0%, versus 41.3%, income from continuing operations was up 99%, to $7.5 million ($0.32 a share, after preferred dividends and on 17% more shares) from $3.8 million ($0.14). Results were before losses from discontinued operations of $0.03 a share, versus $0.01.

Stock Performance - 08-OCT-99

In the past 30 trading days, ABFS's shares have declined 9%, compared to a 0.91% fall in the S&P 500. Average trading volume for the past five days was 27,920 shares, compared with the 40-day moving average of 133,444 shares.

Key Stock Statistics

Dividend Rate/Share	Nil	Shareholders	800
Shs. outstg. (M)	19.7	Market cap. (B)	$0.242
Avg. daily vol. (M)	0.069	Inst. holdings	46%
Tang. Bk. Value/Share	3.99		
Beta	0.87		

Value of $10,000 invested 5 years ago: $ 7,963

Fiscal Year Ending Dec. 31

	1999	1998	1997	1996	1995	1994
Revenues (Million $)						
1Q	394.4	387.9	406.8	401.4	311.2	265.0
2Q	418.9	416.9	435.8	414.5	312.1	210.8
3Q	—	431.5	425.3	428.5	398.6	294.3
4Q	—	415.2	400.1	414.8	415.4	328.4
Yr.	—	1,651	1,644	1,659	1,437	1,098
Earnings Per Share ($)						
1Q	**0.32**	**0.13**	-0.07	-0.54	0.21	0.23
2Q	**0.47**	**0.31**	0.20	-0.51	0.03	-0.23
3Q	—	**0.34**	0.41	-0.49	-0.73	0.42
4Q	—	**0.41**	**0.19**	-0.56	-1.41	0.32
Yr.	—	**1.21**	**0.84**	**-1.98**	**-1.80**	0.74

Next earnings report expected: mid October

Dividend Data

The quarterly cash dividend was omitted in May 1996.

A Division of The McGraw-Hill Companies

Arkansas Best Corporation

Business Summary - 01-JUL-99

From a humble beginning as Arkansas Motor Freight with 10 employees over 60 years ago, Arkansas Best has grown into a diversified holding company engaged through its subsidiaries primarily in motor carrier transportation operations, intermodal and ocean transportation operations, and truck tire retreading and new tire sales. Principal subsidiaries, as of year-end 1998, were ABF Freight System; Treadco; Clipper Exxpress and related companies (Clipper Domestic); and G.I. Trucking.

Less-than-truckload (LTL) motor carrier operations are conductedthrough ABF Freight System, ABF Freight System (B.C.), ABF Freight System Canada, ABF Cartage, Land-Marine Cargo, and G.I. Trucking.

ABF Freight System (71% of 1998 revenue), the largest subsidiary of the company, is the fourth largest U.S. LTL motor carrier. It provides direct service to about 99% of U.S. cities with a population of 25,000 or more. ABF Freight System provides interstate and intrastate direct service to more than 43,000 points through 310 terminals in all 50 states, Canada and Puerto Rico.

ABF Freight System concentrates on long-haul transportation of general commodities freight, food, textiles, apparel, furniture, appliances, chemicals, non-bulk petroleum products, rubber, plastics, metal and metal products, wood, glass, automotive parts, and machinery.

G.I. Trucking (8%) is a non-union regionalLTL motor carrier, offering one to three-day regional servicethrough 75 service centers in 15 western states including Hawaii and Alaska. G.I. Trucking accounted for 8% of ABFS's consolidated1998 revenues.

Clipper Domestic (7%), consisting of Clipper LTL and Clipper Freight Management, offers domestic intermodal freight services, utilizing rail, over-the-road, and air transportation modes. Clipper LTL's collection and distribution network consists of 24 service centers geographically dispersed throughout the United States. Clipper Freight provides intermodal and truck brokerage, warehousing, consolidation, transloading, and repacking services.

Treadco (11%) is the largest independent U.S. tire retreader for the trucking industry and the fourth largest commercial truck tire dealer. It has 56 locations in the U.S., primarily in the South, Southwest, lower Midwest and West.

In April 1999, ABFS sold its Clipper International operations to an investor group led by Clipper International's management. Terms were not disclosed.

In April 1999, ABFS acquired that portion of Treadco, Inc. that it did not already own through a cash tender. ABFS purchased about 2.5 million Treadco common shares at $9 each. ABFS had previously owned about 49% of Treadco.

Per Share Data ($) (Year Ended Dec. 31)	1998	1997	1996	1995	1994	1993	1992	1991	1990	1989
Tangible Bk. Val.	2.49	0.93	NM	1.68	3.31	5.00	NA	NA	NA	NA
Cash Flow	3.45	3.52	1.25	0.97	2.60	2.73	2.95	2.66	NA	NA
Earnings	1.21	0.84	-2.10	-1.90	0.74	0.89	0.99	0.61	NA	NA
Dividends	Nil	Nil	0.01	0.04	0.04	0.04	0.02	Nil	NA	NA
Payout Ratio	Nil	Nil	NM	NM	5%	4%	2%	Nil	NA	NA
Prices - High	11 7/8	12 5/8	9 3/8	13 3/8	15 3/4	17	17 1/8	NA	NA	NA
- Low	4 3/8	4 1/8	4 1/8	6 5/8	10 1/8	8 1/8	8 7/8	NA	NA	NA
P/E Ratio - High	10	15	NM	NM	21	19	17	NA	NA	NA
- Low	4	5	NM	NM	14	9	9	NA	NA	NA
Income Statement Analysis (Million $)										
Revs.	1,651	1,644	1,659	1,437	1,098	1,010	960	884	NA	NA
Oper. Inc.	112	112	38.7	28.3	79.7	82.7	94.8	85.9	NA	NA
Depr.	45.2	48.9	61.0	51.8	31.6	31.3	37.5	42.8	NA	NA
Int. Exp.	18.4	23.9	31.9	17.3	7.6	7.2	17.3	34.4	NA	NA
Pretax Inc.	53.8	40.4	-58.5	-47.0	36.6	40.3	35.6	15.5	NA	NA
Eff. Tax Rate	41%	48%	NM	NM	49%	48%	47%	50%	NA	NA
Net Inc.	28.7	20.9	-36.6	-32.8	18.7	21.0	18.8	7.8	NA	NA
Balance Sheet & Other Fin. Data (Million $)										
Cash	4.5	7.2	1.8	16.9	3.5	7.0	NA	NA	NA	NA
Curr. Assets	230	237	259	322	186	151	NA	NA	NA	NA
Total Assets	711	698	843	986	569	448	NA	NA	NA	NA
Curr. Liab.	264	268	301	303	223	140	NA	NA	NA	NA
LT Debt	196	203	327	399	59.3	43.7	NA	NA	NA	NA
Common Eqty.	174	149	137	178	217	202	NA	NA	NA	NA
Total Cap.	426	408	498	564	340	304	NA	NA	NA	NA
Cap. Exp.	60.9	11.6	27.7	49.7	47.3	13.7	21.1	19.4	NA	NA
Cash Flow	69.6	69.8	24.4	19.0	50.3	52.3	56.3	50.6	NA	NA
Curr. Ratio	0.9	0.9	0.9	1.1	0.8	1.1	NA	NA	NA	NA
% LT Debt of Cap.	46.0	49.6	65.6	70.8	17.5	14.4	NA	NA	NA	NA
% Net Inc.of Revs.	1.7	12.7	NM	NM	1.7	2.1	2.0	0.9	NA	NA
% Ret. on Assets	4.1	2.7	NM	NM	3.7	4.8	NA	NA	NA	NA
% Ret. on Equity	15.3	14.6	NM	NM	8.9	12.5	NA	NA	NA	NA

Data as orig reptd.; bef. results of disc opers/spec. items. Per share data adj. for stk. divs. Bold denotes diluted EPS (FASB 128)-prior periods restated. E-Estimated. NA-Not Available. NM-Not Meaningful. NR-Not Ranked.

Office—3801 Old Greenwood Rd., Fort Smith, AR 72903. **Tel**—(501) 785-6000. **Website**—http://www.arkbest.com **Chrmn**—W. A. Marquard. **Pres & CEO**—R. A. Young III. **VP, CFO & Treas**—D. E. Loeffler. **Investor Contact**—David Humphrey (501-785-6200).**Dirs**—F. Edelstein, A. J. Fritz, W. A. Marquard, J. H. Morris, R. A. Young III, A. J. Zakon. **Transfer Agent & Registrar**—Harris Trust & Savings Bank, Chicago. **Incorporated**—in Delaware in 1988. **Empl**— 14,829. **S&P Analyst:** N.J.D.

STANDARD
&POOR'S
STOCK REPORTS

Artesyn Technologies

NASDAQ Symbol **ATSN**

In S&P SmallCap 600

09-OCT-99

Industry: Electrical Equipment

Summary: This company is a leading provider of power conversion equipment, real-time systems and logistics management for the communications industry.

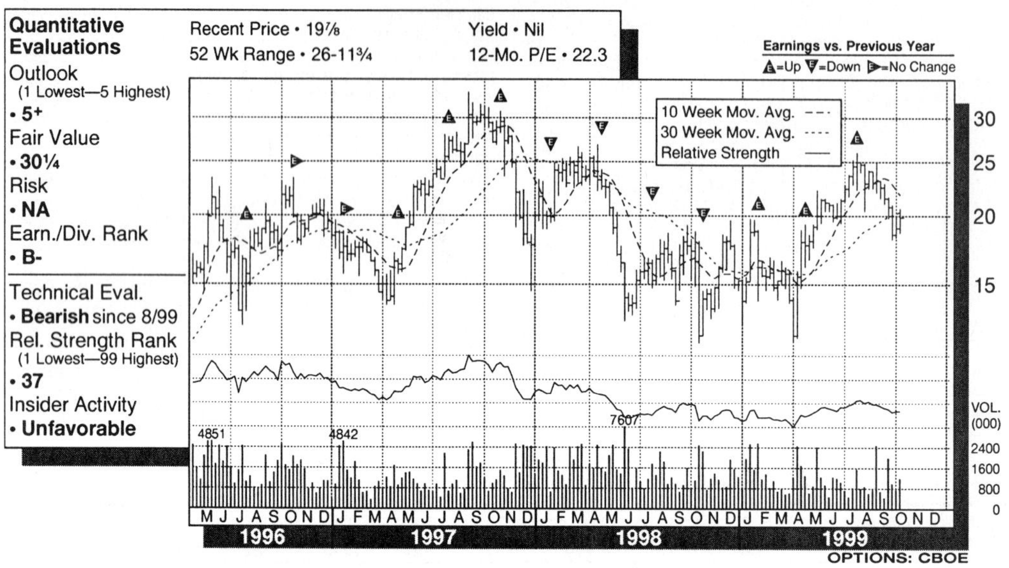

Business Profile - 05-OCT-99

The company believes that the timely introduction of new technology and products is an important component of its competitive strategy and anticipates that future research and development spending will not differ significantly from the historical norm of about 6%-8% of sales. In August 1999, Artesyn said it expects its gross margins to increase modestly for the remainder of 1999 due to a more favorable sales and product mix and improved cost of purchased materials. Through July 20, 1999, the company had repurchased about 2.5 million shares of its common stock for a total of $38.6 million.

Operational Review - 05-OCT-99

Sales in the 26 weeks ended July 2, 1999, rose 6.1%, year to year, reflecting higher than anticipated shipments to major OEM customers in the networking and computing market sectors. Margins narrowed, hurt by new product start-up costs and a less favorable sales mix. SG&A costs declined 8.0% on efficiencies from the Zytec Corp. merger, partially offset by higher information technology outlays. In the absence of a $7.2 million restructuring charge in 1998, pretax income surged 84%. After taxes at 32.3%, versus 34.0%, net income advanced 88%, to $17,721,000 ($0.45 a share, based on 5.6% fewer shares), from $9,411,000 ($0.23).

Stock Performance - 08-OCT-99

In the past 30 trading days, ATSN's shares have declined 14%, compared to a 0.91% fall in the S&P 500. Average trading volume for the past five days was 234,040 shares, compared with the 40-day moving average of 252,282 shares.

Key Stock Statistics

Dividend Rate/Share	Nil	Shareholders	20,701
Shs. outstg. (M)	37.5	Market cap. (B)	$0.744
Avg. daily vol. (M)	0.242	Inst. holdings	72%
Tang. Bk. Value/Share	3.94		
Beta	0.70		

Value of $10,000 invested 5 years ago: $ 85,964

Fiscal Year Ending Dec. 31

	1999	1998	1997	1996	1995	1994
Revenues (Million $)						
1Q	135.1	147.2	114.5	50.44	44.30	37.66
2Q	150.4	121.8	130.9	51.67	47.32	38.39
3Q	—	124.6	133.7	57.76	46.91	36.94
4Q	—	138.8	148.2	62.62	52.86	41.80
Yr.	—	532.4	527.2	222.5	191.4	154.8
Earnings Per Share ($)						
1Q	**0.19**	**0.08**	**0.19**	**0.17**	0.09	0.06
2Q	**0.27**	**0.15**	**0.26**	**0.24**	0.12	0.07
3Q	—	**0.20**	**0.25**	**0.18**	0.18	0.07
4Q	—	**0.24**	**0.10**	**0.20**	0.20	0.09
Yr.	—	**0.67**	**0.80**	**0.78**	**0.49**	**0.23**

Next earnings report expected: mid October

Dividend Data

No cash has been paid.

A Division of The McGraw-Hill Companies

Artesyn Technologies, Inc.

Business Summary - 05-OCT-99

Artesyn Technologies, Inc. (ATSN; formerly Computer Products, Inc.) is a manufacturer of standard and custom-designed electronic products and subsystems for the communications industry and other real-time systems applications. The company is one of the leading suppliers of power supplies, power converters and distributed power systems to the communications industry. ATSN ranks among the top 10 independent power supply manufacturers in sales volume worldwide.

The company currently offers standard power products in over 1,000 configurations and accommodates a broad range of client applications. Artesyn also targets the custom power supply business because it capitalizes on the company's strengths in the fields of sophisticated design, volume manufacturing and customer service.

Power conversion products include AC-to-DC power supplies and modular DC-to-DC converters that focus on the worldwide communications market, including networking, data communications, telecommunications and wireless infrastructure. Computer, industrial and instrumentation markets are also served. AC-to-DC power supplies are used to convert alternating electric current (the form in which virtually all electric current is delivered by utility companies) to a precisely controlled direct current. Direct current is required to operate virtually all solid-state electronic equipment. DC-to-DC converters are used to convert a particular direct current voltage into another (higher or lower) direct current voltage that is required by the electronic device to which it is connected.

Artesyn's communications products are designed around and incorporate industry standards that permit easy portability to a variety of applications. The technology relies on powerful microprocessors from sources such as Motorola, Intel and MIPS. The primary product line combines both the worldwide industry standard VMEbus, which defines physical board size and signal characteristics for the interconnection of microprocessors. Application requirements for these products usually include environments requiring rapid computer response time with high-quality processing capabilities.

In 1998, three customers accounted for 17%, 11% and 10% of aggregate sales, respectively.

On December 29, 1997, ATSN merged with Zytec Corp., another leading provider of power supplies and systems to the communications market, forming a $530 million concern with a focus on data networking. In May 1998, the company changed its name from Computer Products, Inc., to Artesyn Technologies, Inc.

Per Share Data ($) (Year Ended Dec. 31)	1998	1997	1996	1995	1994	1993	1992	1991	1990	1989
Tangible Bk. Val.	3.72	3.18	2.68	2.08	1.23	0.81	0.59	0.42	1.28	1.65
Cash Flow	1.08	1.12	1.07	0.84	0.53	0.26	0.30	-0.05	0.42	0.38
Earnings	0.67	0.80	0.80	0.61	0.29	0.03	0.10	-0.21	0.20	0.20
Dividends	Nil	Nil	Nil	Nil	Nil	Nil	Nil	Nil	Nil	Nil
Payout Ratio	Nil	Nil	Nil	Nil	Nil	Nil	Nil	Nil	Nil	Nil
Prices - High	26 7/8	33 3/8	23 3/8	13 3/4	3 5/8	3 1/2	5 1/4	3 1/8	3 3/8	3 1/2
- Low	11 3/4	13 3/4	8 7/8	3 1/8	2 1/8	2	2	1 1/2	1 7/16	2
P/E Ratio - High	40	42	29	23	12	NM	53	NM	17	18
- Low	18	17	11	5	7	NM	21	NM	7	10
Income Statement Analysis (Million $)										
Revs.	532	527	222	191	155	124	115	83.0	107	120
Oper. Inc.	66.1	69.0	35.6	27.0	17.5	11.7	11.2	7.8	13.4	14.1
Depr.	16.9	13.6	6.7	5.3	5.1	4.8	4.4	3.1	4.5	3.6
Int. Exp.	4.0	4.9	2.7	3.3	3.8	3.7	4.3	4.7	6.8	6.0
Pretax Inc.	40.4	49.4	26.5	19.6	9.2	1.0	3.5	-4.1	5.2	7.6
Eff. Tax Rate	33%	36%	26%	28%	34%	40%	43%	NM	22%	47%
Net Inc.	27.0	31.9	19.6	14.1	6.1	0.6	2.0	-4.2	4.1	4.1
Balance Sheet & Other Fin. Data (Million $)										
Cash	41.5	55.4	26.1	26.7	20.2	10.1	15.6	27.2	35.7	25.0
Curr. Assets	205	213	102	90.9	67.6	54.5	54.9	58.1	67.8	63.4
Total Assets	325	322	154	136	114	101	103	105	115	114
Curr. Liab.	84.4	97.5	40.4	38.9	27.3	23.4	25.4	22.6	17.2	18.9
LT Debt	50.3	52.9	23.5	30.0	47.2	45.2	46.5	53.0	58.0	62.1
Common Eqty.	181	163	84.0	61.5	40.0	32.8	30.8	28.5	40.2	33.0
Total Cap.	236	219	113	97.6	87.0	78.0	77.0	82.0	98.0	95.0
Cap. Exp.	26.8	22.2	6.9	7.4	4.7	3.4	8.1	1.5	1.3	2.0
Cash Flow	43.9	45.5	26.2	19.4	11.1	5.4	6.4	-1.1	8.5	7.7
Curr. Ratio	2.4	2.2	2.5	2.3	2.5	2.3	2.2	2.6	4.0	3.4
% LT Debt of Cap.	21.3	24.2	25.9	36.9	54.1	58.0	60.1	65.0	59.1	65.3
% Net Inc.of Revs.	5.1	6.1	8.8	7.4	3.9	0.5	1.7	NM	3.8	3.4
% Ret. on Assets	8.4	13.4	13.5	11.3	5.6	0.6	1.9	NM	3.5	3.6
% Ret. on Equity	15.6	25.9	26.9	27.8	16.6	1.9	6.7	NM	11.1	13.8

Data as orig reptd.; bef. results of disc opers/spec. items. Per share data adj. for stk. divs. Bold denotes diluted EPS (FASB 128)-prior periods restated. E-Estimated. NA-Not Available. NM-Not Meaningful. NR-Not Ranked.

Office—7900 Glades Rd., Suite 500, Boca Raton, FL 33434-4105. **Tel**—(561) 451-1000. **Website**—http://www.artesyn.com **Co-Chrmn, Pres & CEO**—J. M. O'Donnell. **VP-Fin, CFO & Secy**—R. J. Thompson. **Dirs**—E. S. Croft III, F. C. Lee, L. J. Matthews, J. M. O'Donnell, S. A. Ollendorff, P. A. O'Reilly, B. Sager, A. E. Sapp Jr., R. D. Schmidt, L. Solomon. **Transfer Agent & Registrar**—Bank of New York, NYC. **Incorporated**—in Florida in 1968. **Empl**— 6,600. **S&P Analyst:** P.L.H.

Ashworth Inc.

NASDAQ Symbol **ASHW**

In S&P SmallCap 600

09-OCT-99

Industry:
Textiles (Apparel)

Summary: This company designs and manufactures golf-inspired lifestyle sportswear.

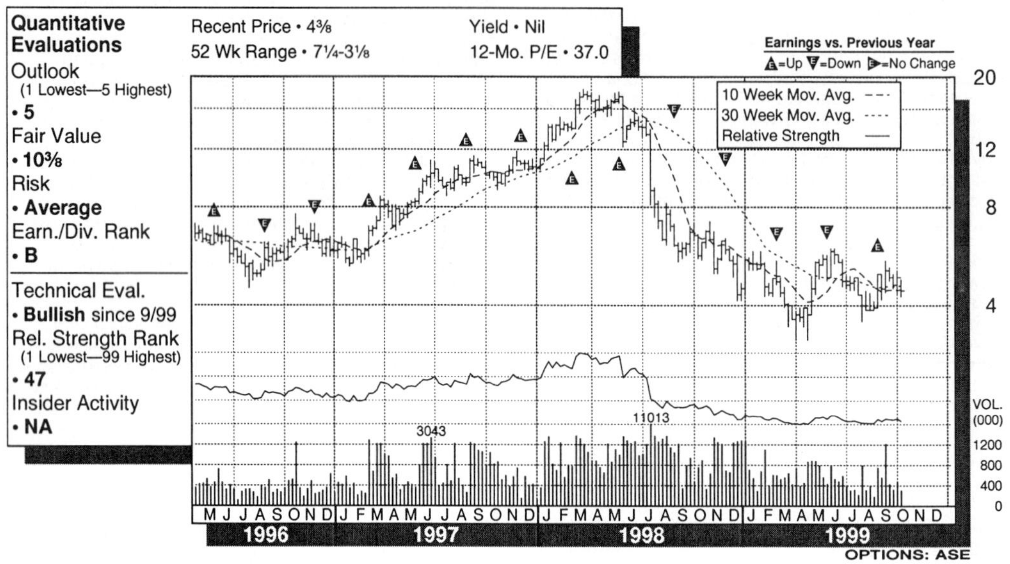

Business Profile - 19-JUL-99

Aided by certain initiatives begun in the first half of FY 99 (Oct.), results returned to profitability in the second quarter, and ASHW significantly reduced its inventory and trade receivables level. Inventory at April 30, 1999, was down 13% and 7.4% from the level at October 31, 1998, and April 30, 1998, respectively. The inventory level at the end of the second quarter of FY 99 was ASHW's lowest since the third quarter of FY 97. In looking forward to the balance of FY 99, the company anticipates positive sales results versus the FY 98 period, and said it will continue to emphasize cost efficient practices and improving inventory turns, while enhancing its overall marketing efforts.

Operational Review - 19-JUL-99

Net sales in the first half of FY 99 fell 11%, year to year, reflecting a 5.9% dip in domestic sales, as well as a 32% decline in foreign sales. Gross margins narrowed, on higher per unit costs resulting from increased domestic sourcing as well as higher discount and allowance expense. SG&A expenses rose 9.5%, on the additions of the Canadian, women's, and corporate divisions following the second quarter of FY 98, as well as increased costs of distribution. After higher other expenses, and taxes at 39.1% in each period, net income plunged 71%, to $1,841,000 ($0.13 a share, on 5.0% fewer shares), from $6,379,000 ($0.43).

Stock Performance - 08-OCT-99

In the past 30 trading days, ASHW's shares have declined 11%, compared to a 0.91% fall in the S&P 500. Average trading volume for the past five days was 59,680 shares, compared with the 40-day moving average of 109,597 shares.

Key Stock Statistics

Dividend Rate/Share	Nil	Shareholders	10,000
Shs. outstg. (M)	14.1	Market cap. (B)	$0.062
Avg. daily vol. (M)	0.075	Inst. holdings	23%
Tang. Bk. Value/Share	4.98		
Beta	1.11		

Value of $10,000 invested 5 years ago: $ 4,127

Fiscal Year Ending Oct. 31

	1999	1998	1997	1996	1995	1994
Revenues (Million $)						
1Q	19.66	24.03	19.84	17.07	14.59	11.04
2Q	35.69	38.06	30.62	26.36	26.44	21.27
3Q	30.07	25.60	21.70	17.88	20.38	16.96
4Q	—	19.66	16.99	14.10	13.11	11.57
Yr.	—	107.3	89.15	75.41	74.52	60.84
Earnings Per Share ($)						
1Q	**-0.03**	**0.13**	0.10	0.07	0.07	0.06
2Q	**0.17**	**0.30**	0.23	0.21	0.15	0.20
3Q	**0.11**	**0.05**	0.06	0.02	0.07	0.13
4Q	—	**-0.13**	Nil	-0.18	-0.17	0.01
Yr.	—	**0.36**	**0.38**	**0.12**	0.12	0.40

Next earnings report expected: mid December

Dividend Data

No cash dividends have been paid. A stockholder rights plans was adopted in September 1998.

Ashworth, Inc.

Business Summary - 19-JUL-99

Ashworth Inc. (ASHW) designs, markets and distributes a full line of sports apparel, headwear, and accessories under the Ashworth label. The Ashworth products have been retailed in golf pro shops, resorts, at better department and specialty retail stores, and in selected international markets.

At its inception, the company designed and marketed classically styled, natural fiber golfwear and distributed it in the U.S. under the Ashworth brand exclusively to golf pro shops and resorts. ASHW has been credited with developing the new look in golfwear over the past 10 years, using natural fibers and a loose relaxed fit emphasizing quality in product and presentation, which are now industry standards. Its men's and women's golf lifestyle apparel is aimed predominately at the younger active male and female consumers in the middle/upper middle income range and is priced in the middle to upper middle price range for golf apparel. For the past few years, the company has been a leading golf apparel line sold at pro shops in the U.S. ASHW also sells lifestyle products including home office and home theatre furnishings, bathroom accessories and small gift items through its concept retail store opened in October 1997.

ASHW's men's division designs 11 collections per year, each consisting of about 30 to 40 styles. Product design is largely one of classic, timeless designs with an emphasis on quality and natural fibers.

The Ashworth men's collections consists of knit and woven shirts, pullovers, sweaters, vests, pants, shorts, hats, and accessories. The company also designs a Weather Systems collection made largely of technical fabrics and produced for a variety of weather conditions including cold and rainy as well as hot and humid. In 1996, ASHW introduced a Basics line of shirts, pants and shorts in popular styles and colors that do not change significantly from season to season.

In 1998, ASHW introduced its new women's line. The women's division designs eight collections per year, each consisting of about 20 to 30 styles. Product design incorporates casual elegance and timeless simplicity with an emphasis on quality.

In 1998, the company expanded its in-store shop program and now has a presence in about 600 locations throughout the U.S. It plans to continue marketing the shop program to current customers and new accounts.

Per Share Data ($) (Year Ended Oct. 31)	1998	1997	1996	1995	1994	1993	1992	1991	1990	1989
Tangible Bk. Val.	4.77	3.95	3.20	3.06	2.84	2.31	1.87	0.73	0.50	0.03
Cash Flow	0.51	0.53	0.31	0.32	0.55	0.42	0.24	0.16	0.05	0.01
Earnings	0.36	0.37	0.12	0.12	0.40	0.34	0.19	0.13	0.04	-0.01
Dividends	Nil	Nil	Nil	Nil	Nil	Nil	Nil	Nil	Nil	Nil
Payout Ratio	Nil	Nil	Nil	Nil	Nil	Nil	Nil	Nil	Nil	Nil
Prices - High	18 3/8	11 7/8	7 3/4	10 7/8	13 1/4	12	9	7 1/4	4 1/8	NA
- Low	4 1/8	5 1/4	4 1/2	5	7 3/8	6 1/4	4 3/8	2 3/16	1	NA
P/E Ratio - High	51	32	65	91	33	35	47	56	NM	NA
- Low	11	14	37	42	18	18	23	17	NM	NA
Income Statement Analysis (Million $)										
Revs.	107	89.1	75.4	74.5	60.8	45.8	28.6	17.0	7.5	2.1
Oper. Inc.	11.1	11.0	5.6	6.0	10.2	7.7	4.1	2.6	0.7	0.1
Depr.	2.2	2.1	2.3	2.5	1.9	1.1	0.6	0.3	0.1	0.1
Int. Exp.	0.5	0.6	1.1	1.1	0.6	0.3	0.3	0.2	0.1	0.1
Pretax Inc.	8.7	7.9	2.4	2.4	8.1	6.5	3.4	2.1	0.5	0.0
Eff. Tax Rate	39%	39%	41%	42%	40%	40%	40%	42%	45%	NM
Net Inc.	5.3	4.8	1.4	1.4	4.9	4.0	2.0	1.2	0.3	0.0
Balance Sheet & Other Fin. Data (Million $)										
Cash	4.8	3.8	1.9	1.6	5.3	7.7	5.8	0.6	1.4	0.0
Curr. Assets	66.2	55.0	41.7	45.2	34.6	26.5	21.2	8.4	4.9	1.3
Total Assets	81.6	68.8	54.9	58.1	47.3	33.5	25.7	10.1	5.4	1.6
Curr. Liab.	9.9	10.1	10.2	16.0	8.6	4.6	3.8	3.0	1.4	0.8
LT Debt	3.4	4.3	5.3	5.2	5.8	2.9	1.7	0.7	0.3	0.6
Common Eqty.	67.1	53.0	38.9	36.4	32.9	26.1	20.2	6.4	3.8	0.1
Total Cap.	71.2	58.0	44.8	42.1	38.7	28.9	21.9	7.2	4.1	0.7
Cap. Exp.	2.4	2.0	2.5	2.1	6.8	2.7	1.6	0.4	0.2	0.1
Cash Flow	7.5	7.0	3.7	3.9	6.7	5.0	2.6	1.5	0.4	0.0
Curr. Ratio	6.7	5.4	4.1	2.8	4.0	5.8	5.6	2.8	3.6	1.5
% LT Debt of Cap.	4.8	7.5	11.9	12.4	14.9	10.0	7.8	10.4	6.8	86.2
% Net Inc.of Revs.	4.9	5.4	1.9	1.9	8.0	8.6	7.1	7.3	3.4	NM
% Ret. on Assets	7.0	7.8	2.5	2.6	11.9	13.1	10.6	15.1	5.9	NM
% Ret. on Equity	8.8	10.5	3.7	4.0	16.3	16.7	14.4	22.9	12.8	NM

Data as orig reptd.; bef. results of disc opers/spec. items. Per share data adj. for stk. divs. Bold denotes diluted EPS (FASB 128)-prior periods restated. E-Estimated. NA-Not Available. NM-Not Meaningful. NR-Not Ranked.

Office—2791 Loker Avenue West, Carlsbad, CA 92008. **Tel**—(760) 438-6610. **Website**—http://www.ashworthInc.com**Pres & CEO**—R. L. Herrel. **VP-Fin, CFO & Treas**—A. J. Newman. **Dirs**—S. Bartolin, Jr., S. G. Carpenter, A. P. Gambucci, J. M. Hanson, H. M. Hecht, R. L. Herrel Sr., J. W. Nantz. **Transfer Agent & Registrar**—American Securities Transfer, Inc., Denver. **Incorporated**—in Delaware in 1987. **Empl**— 461. **S&P Analyst:** M.I.

STANDARD
&POOR'S
STOCK REPORTS

Aspect Telecommunications

Nasdaq Symbol **ASPT**

In S&P SmallCap 600

09-OCT-99

Industry: Communications Equipment

Summary: Aspect is a leading supplier of customer relationship solutions that enable companies to provide best-of-class services to their customers.

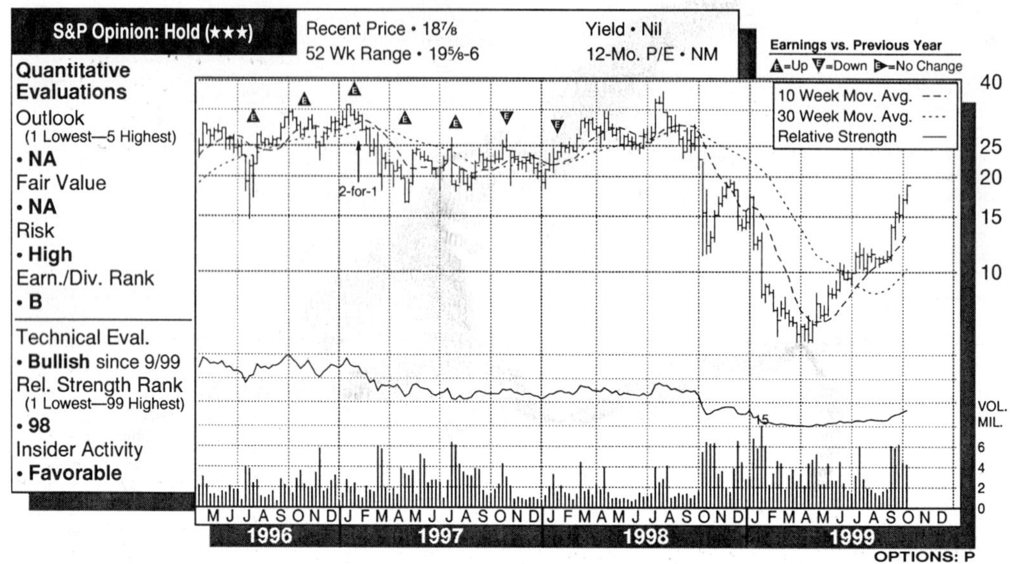

Overview - 26-JUL-99

ASPT is beginning a transition to an enterprise software company from a communications equipment company specializing in call centers. The company will provide both packaged applications and middleware to help manage customer relationships. Management believes that there will be solid demand for these new products over time. However, the shift will depress near-term results as the sales organization becomes accustomed to the new products. We now expect sales to drop by about 12% in 1999 with gross margins falling by about 600 basis points in light of the transition. For next year, we expect sales to grow by 19% as the transition to a software company is completed. Overall margins should improve as high-margin software begins to dominate the sales mix. We see profitability being reached by the end of fourth quarter.

Valuation - 26-JUL-99

We continue to rate the shares a hold. Shares of ASPT have plummeted in reaction to the company's transformation to an enterprise software firm. The company's second quarter results highlight the difficulties that ASPT is likely to face until the switchover is completed. Sales fell 11% in the quarter, and we expect that sales of the company's hardware equipment, which is being deemphasized, will continue to fall. In light of the difficult transition period, we expect that near-term results for the company, as well as the stock, are likely to be relatively unpredictable. The company appears to have a solid enough balance sheet to withstand this transition and we do believe that there is suitable market demand for ASPT's software. Still, we would only hold the shares for now, given the significant risks involved with the change in strategy.

Key Stock Statistics

S&P EPS Est. 1999	-0.88	Tang. Bk. Value/Share	3.07
P/E on S&P Est. 1999	NM	Beta	0.39
S&P EPS Est. 2000	-0.10	Shareholders	790
Dividend Rate/Share	Nil	Market cap. (B)	$0.895
Shs. outstg. (M)	47.5	Inst. holdings	53%
Avg. daily vol. (M)	1.121		

Value of $10,000 invested 5 years ago: $ 17,840

Fiscal Year Ending Dec. 31

	1999	1998	1997	1996	1995	1994
Revenues (Million $)						
1Q	100.1	113.5	91.62	67.30	42.73	32.89
2Q	112.2	126.1	93.54	72.91	46.23	35.12
3Q	—	137.9	99.2	80.22	49.30	38.17
4Q	—	134.8	106.3	88.55	60.72	41.06
Yr.	—	512.3	390.6	308.7	199.0	147.2
Earnings Per Share ($)						
1Q	**-0.27**	—	0.21	0.18	0.12	0.09
2Q	**-0.26**	—	0.24	0.20	0.14	0.10
3Q	**E-0.20**	—	0.13	0.20	0.14	0.10
4Q	**E-0.15**	—	**0.08**	0.20	0.15	0.11
Yr.	**E-0.88**	**0.61**	**0.67**	0.79	**0.52**	0.41

Next earnings report expected: mid October

Dividend Data

No cash dividends have been paid.

Aspect Telecommunications Corporation

Business Summary - 26-JUL-99

Following the release of its 1998 fourth quarter earnings, the company announced a change in strategy and focus. ASPT is beginning a transition to an enterprise software company focused on customer relationship solutions from a communications equipment company specializing in call centers. The company will provide both packaged applications and middleware to help manage customer relationships.

Aspect now offers integrated software suites designed to enable companies to deliver responsive and cost-effective customer service using call center solutions to interact with their customers via voice, video, data, the Internet, and e-mail. ASPT also consults, trains, and delivers system integration services to help organizations effectively plan, integrate and manage call centers. As the company's products are considered by customers to be mission-critical systems in front-office applications, ASPT provides 24-hour a day, 7-day a week support.

Historically, the company's core product offering has been a highly scaleable, mission-critical family of digital automatic call distributor systems known as the Aspect ACD System. Introduced in 1987, this product line has accounted for the majority of the company's sales volume to date. The system, which integrates call processing, voice processing and data processing technologies, is designed to provide benefits in four key areas: intelligent call management, staff productivity, management information and system availability. The system offers several features, including the ability to dynamically change the routing of calls, the summary and detailed views of calling volumes, call handling efficiencies, trends, and other information about each business application, and the ability to control redundancy, which reduces the risk of downtime due to component failure.

In order to complement the hardware, Aspect has developed software to perform various functions. The company's InterQueue software is designed to provide a real-time coordinated load-balancing and resource allocation that allows large call centers to be implemented as a single system over a large geographic area. Aspect also offers a suite of management software applications enabling direct access and centralized control of a call center system.

In May 1998, Aspect announced the acquisition of privately held Voicetek Corp., a provider of software platforms and application solutions for interactive voice response (IVR) and network-deployed enhanced services solutions. Voicetek's products and partnerships will complement and enhance Aspect's set of integrated call center solutions. The purchase price consisted of approximately $72 million in cash for all Voicetek common and preferred shares outstanding; in addition, all outstanding Voicetek options were converted into approximately 450,000 Aspect options, and Aspect assumed certain operating assets and liabilities of Voicetek. The transaction was accounted for as a purchase and resulted in a one-time charge of $10 million in the second quarter of 1998.

Per Share Data ($) (Year Ended Dec. 31)	1998	1997	1996	1995	1994	1993	1992	1991	1990	1989
Tangible Bk. Val.	3.63	4.50	3.90	1.94	1.99	1.58	1.26	1.13	1.17	-1.27
Cash Flow	1.28	1.00	1.02	0.75	0.58	0.38	0.19	0.06	0.17	0.08
Earnings	0.61	0.67	0.79	0.55	0.41	0.27	0.10	-0.04	0.09	0.03
Dividends	Nil	Nil	Nil	Nil	Nil	Nil	Nil	Nil	Nil	Nil
Payout Ratio	Nil	Nil	Nil	Nil	Nil	Nil	Nil	NM	Nil	Nil
Prices - High	$37\frac{7}{8}$	$33\frac{5}{8}$	$32\frac{3}{4}$	$19\frac{5}{8}$	$11\frac{1}{2}$	$10\frac{7}{8}$	$3\frac{3}{4}$	$2\frac{3}{4}$	6	NA
- Low	$11\frac{1}{4}$	$16\frac{1}{2}$	$14\frac{5}{8}$	$7\frac{3}{4}$	6	$3\frac{1}{2}$	$1\frac{3}{4}$	$1\frac{7}{16}$	$1\frac{1}{2}$	NA
P/E Ratio - High	61	50	41	36	28	40	38	NM	64	NA
- Low	18	25	19	14	15	13	17	NM	16	NA
Income Statement Analysis (Million $)										
Revs.	512	391	309	199	147	106	71.0	44.2	47.9	30.6
Oper. Inc.	102	69.8	74.0	44.3	35.2	22.6	8.8	0.5	6.8	3.3
Depr.	35.6	17.2	16.3	8.7	7.1	4.5	3.5	3.9	2.8	1.4
Int. Exp.	4.3	0.3	2.8	3.2	3.2	0.9	0.2	0.3	0.4	0.3
Pretax Inc.	59.2	60.3	59.8	38.1	28.3	18.8	6.6	-1.7	5.7	2.3
Eff. Tax Rate	45%	42%	37%	37%	38%	39%	38%	Nil	39%	55%
Net Inc.	32.5	35.2	37.6	24.0	17.6	11.5	4.1	-1.7	3.5	1.0
Balance Sheet & Other Fin. Data (Million $)										
Cash	67.1	106	116	93.6	103	93.1	36.2	32.8	32.3	8.7
Curr. Assets	363	266	199	153	143	123	55.5	48.2	44.9	15.7
Total Assets	561	370	283	216	166	138	64.6	57.0	54.5	20.8
Curr. Liab.	104	96.0	59.1	44.0	30.2	18.9	14.2	10.6	6.1	6.8
LT Debt	154	6.5	4.5	59.5	55.0	55.0	0.1	0.7	1.5	1.2
Common Eqty.	298	268	219	112	80.8	64.3	50.2	45.6	46.7	12.6
Total Cap.	456	274	224	172	136	119	50.2	46.3	48.2	13.8
Cap. Exp.	28.9	24.9	33.2	16.6	13.1	8.8	4.5	3.0	5.6	2.9
Cash Flow	68.1	52.4	53.9	32.7	24.6	16.0	7.6	2.2	6.3	2.5
Curr. Ratio	3.5	2.8	3.4	3.5	4.7	6.5	3.9	4.6	7.3	2.3
% LT Debt of Cap.	33.7	2.4	2.0	34.6	40.5	46.1	0.1	1.5	3.0	8.8
% Net Inc.of Revs.	6.3	9.0	12.2	12.1	11.9	10.8	5.8	NM	7.2	3.3
% Ret. on Assets	7.0	10.8	15.1	12.6	11.5	11.2	6.8	NM	4.3	6.6
% Ret. on Equity	11.5	14.4	22.7	24.8	24.2	19.9	8.6	NM	NM	11.8

Data as orig reptd.; bef. results of disc opers/spec. items. Per share data adj. for stk. divs. Bold denotes diluted EPS (FASB 128)-prior periods restated. E-Estimated. NA-Not Available. NM-Not Meaningful. NR-Not Ranked.

Office—1730 Fox Dr., San Jose, CA 95131-2312. **Tel**—(408) 325-2200. **Website**—http://www.aspect.com **Chrmn, Pres & CEO**—J. R. Carreker. **VP-Fin & CFO**—E. J. Keller. **Dirs**—J. R. Carreker, D. J. Engel, N. A. Fogelsong, J. L. Patterson, J. W. Peth.**Transfer Agent & Registrar**—First National Bank of Boston. **Incorporated**—in California in 1985. **Empl**— 2,200. **S&P Analyst:** Mark Cavallone

STANDARD
&POOR'S
STOCK REPORTS

Aspen Technology

NASDAQ Symbol **AZPN**

In S&P SmallCap 600

09-OCT-99

Industry:
Computer (Software & Services)

Summary: Aspen supplies integrated software and service solutions used by companies in the process industries for manufacturing enterprise optimization.

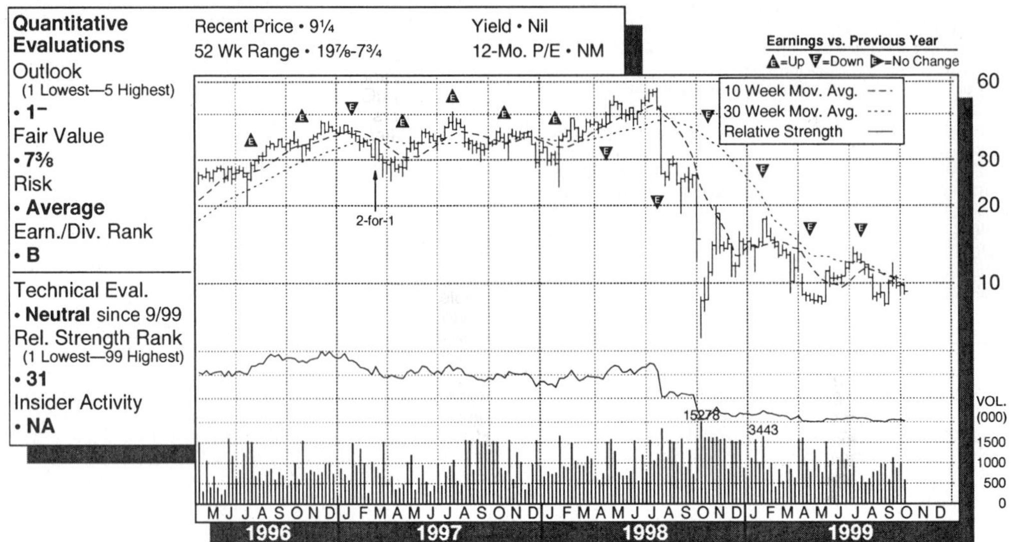

Business Profile - 18-AUG-99

Aspen believes that the actions it took at the start of the fourth quarter of FY 99 (Jun.) to streamline its organization, reduce headcount and eliminate other nonessential operating expenses will substantially lower its costs in FY 00. Related restructuring and other charges totaling $17.9 million were recorded in FY 99's fourth quarter. The company believes that the most significant transaction in the fourth quarter was an agreement with Equistar Chemicals, LP and Lyondell Chemical to expand their initial, single-site enterprise optimization implementation to standardize on its integrated, plantwide Plantelligence solution at all of its processing plants worldwide.

Operational Review - 18-AUG-99

Total revenues for the fiscal year ended June 30, 1999 (preliminary) declined 13% from those of FY 98, as a 34% decrease in software licenses revenues more than offset higher revenues from maintenance and other services. Results were penalized by the lower software licenses revenues, increased selling and marketing and R&D expenses, and a fourth quarter $17.9 million restructuring charge. Following tax credits of $16,111,000, versus taxes at 49.0%, a net loss of $25,735,000 ($1.04 a share) contrasted with net income of $14,636,000 ($0.59).

Stock Performance - 08-OCT-99

In the past 30 trading days, AZPN's shares have increased 1%, compared to a 0.91% fall in the S&P 500. Average trading volume for the past five days was 114,600 shares, compared with the 40-day moving average of 175,395 shares.

Key Stock Statistics

Dividend Rate/Share	Nil	Shareholders	1,172
Shs. outstg. (M)	24.9	Market cap. (B)	$0.231
Avg. daily vol. (M)	0.178	Inst. holdings	66%
Tang. Bk. Value/Share	6.17		
Beta	NA		

Value of $10,000 invested 5 years ago: NA

Fiscal Year Ending Jun. 30

	1999	1998	1997	1996	1995	1994
Revenues (Million $)						
1Q	46.71	44.29	34.87	13.27	9.70	—
2Q	61.66	56.47	44.20	17.94	13.95	—
3Q	54.19	63.72	47.98	31.09	15.17	—
4Q	57.04	74.51	53.25	41.31	18.68	—
Yr.	219.6	252.6	180.3	103.6	57.50	37.23
Earnings Per Share ($)						
1Q	**-0.26**	0.08	0.07	0.03	0.02	—
2Q	**0.02**	**0.31**	-0.10	0.13	0.09	—
3Q	**-0.23**	Nil	0.27	-1.40	0.10	—
4Q	**-0.56**	**0.18**	0.38	0.24	0.14	—
Yr.	**-1.04**	**0.59**	**0.63**	-0.96	0.35	—

Next earnings report expected: NA

Dividend Data

No cash dividends have been paid. The company currently intends to retain all of its earnings, if any, to use in its business and does not anticipate paying any cash dividends for the foreseeable future.

A Division of The McGraw-Hill Companies

Aspen Technology, Inc.

Business Summary - 18-AUG-99

Aspen Technology, Inc. is the leading supplier of software and service solutions used by companies in the process industries to design, operate and manage their manufacturing processes. The company's goal is to enable process manufacturers to improve their profitability and competitive position by designing, operating and managing their enterprises closer to their true potential.

The process industries include manufacturers of chemicals, petrochemicals, petroleum products, pharmaceuticals, pulp and paper, electric power, food and beverages, consumer products, and metals and minerals. AZPN offers a comprehensive, integrated suite of process manufacturing optimization solutions that help process manufacturers enhance profitability by improving efficiency, productivity, capacity utilization, safety and environmental compliance throughout the entire manufacturing life-cycle, from research and development to engineering, planning and scheduling, procurement, production and distribution.

In addition to its software solutions, the company offers systems implementation, advanced process control, real-time optimization and other consulting services through its staff of 481 project engineers. As part of its strategy to offer the broadest, most integrated suite of process manufacturing optimization solutions, Aspen has acquired businesses from time to time to obtain technologies and expertise that complement or enhance its core solutions. The company has more than 750 customers worldwide, including 44 of the 50 largest chemical companies, 17 of the 20 largest petroleum refiners, and 16 of the 20 largest pharmaceutical companies.

The company offers the following principal process design software solutions: Aspen Plus, DynaPlus/SPEEDUP, Batch Plus, and Aspen Zyqad, AZPN offers the following principal process operation software solutions: Aspen RT-Opt, DMCplus, and OTISS. Principal management software solutions offered by the company are: InfoPlus 21, MIMI, Aspen PIMS, Aspen ADVISOR and 1stQuality.

AZPN offers implementation, advanced process control, real-time optimization and other consulting services in order to provide its customers with complete solutions.

The company typically combines acquired technologies with its pre-existing products in order to offer solutions that include the best features and functionality of both. Through the end of FY 98 (Jun.), the company had completed 15 acquisitions which have provided it with, or significantly enhanced its capabilities in the areas of process information management, advanced process control and optimization, advanced planning and scheduling, and supply management.

Aspen derived about 45% of its FY 98 revenues from customers outside the U.S., and it expects international operations to continue to account for a major portion of its revenues in the future.

Per Share Data ($) (Year Ended Jun. 30)	1999	1998	1997	1996	1995	1994	1993	1992	1991	1990
Tangible Bk. Val.	NA	6.21	NA	4.73	2.75	2.40	NA	NA	NA	NA
Cash Flow	NA	1.16	NA	-1.20	1.05	0.75	NA	NA	NA	NA
Earnings	-1.04	0.59	0.63	-0.96	0.35	NA	NA	NA	NA	NA
Dividends	Nil	Nil	Nil	Nil	Nil	NA	NA	NA	NA	NA
Payout Ratio	Nil	Nil	Nil	Nil	Nil	NA	NA	NA	NA	NA
Prices - High	18 1/8	56 7/8	46 1/4	42 1/2	18 1/2	10 1/8	NA	NA	NA	NA
- Low	8 1/8	6 1/8	24 3/4	15 3/4	8 1/2	6 1/2	NA	NA	NA	NA
P/E Ratio - High	NM	96	73	NM	52	46	NA	NA	NA	NA
- Low	NM	10	39	NM	24	29	NA	NA	NA	NA
Income Statement Analysis (Million $)										
Revs.	NA	253	180	104	57.5	37.2	NA	NA	NA	NA
Oper. Inc.	NA	42.9	29.1	-6.1	10.2	4.7	NA	NA	NA	NA
Depr.	NA	14.1	11.3	5.6	2.7	1.9	NA	NA	NA	NA
Int. Exp.	NA	0.4	0.2	1.3	0.6	0.5	NA	NA	NA	NA
Pretax Inc.	NA	28.7	22.8	-9.6	9.1	4.0	NA	NA	NA	NA
Eff. Tax Rate	NA	49%	42%	NM	41%	37%	NA	NA	NA	NA
Net Inc.	NA	14.6	13.2	-15.2	5.4	2.5	NA	NA	NA	NA
Balance Sheet & Other Fin. Data (Million $)										
Cash	NA	78.7	16.1	9.0	4.2	2.5	NA	NA	NA	NA
Curr. Assets	NA	238	115	112	46.1	20.8	NA	NA	NA	NA
Total Assets	NA	343	192	160	75.7	39.5	NA	NA	NA	NA
Curr. Liab.	NA	65.2	44.0	43.2	18.5	13.7	NA	NA	NA	NA
LT Debt	NA	90.6	NA	NA	NA	NA	NA	NA	NA	NA
Common Eqty.	NA	165	131	100	41.8	15.5	NA	NA	NA	NA
Total Cap.	NA	262	NA	NA	NA	NA	NA	NA	NA	NA
Cap. Exp.	NA	19.4	NA	NA	NA	NA	NA	NA	NA	NA
Cash Flow	NA	28.8	24.5	-9.5	8.2	4.4	NA	NA	NA	NA
Curr. Ratio	NA	3.7	2.6	2.6	2.5	1.5	NA	NA	NA	NA
% LT Debt of Cap.	NA	34.6	NA	NA	NA	NA	NA	NA	NA	NA
% Net Inc.of Revs.	NA	5.8	7.3	NM	9.4	6.8	NA	NA	NA	NA
% Ret. on Assets	NA	5.5	7.5	NM	9.4	NA	NA	NA	NA	NA
% Ret. on Equity	NA	9.9	11.4	NM	18.9	NA	NA	NA	NA	NA

Data as orig reptd.; bef. results of disc opers/spec. items. Per share data adj. for stk. divs. Bold denotes diluted EPS (FASB 128)-prior periods restated. E-Estimated. NA-Not Available. NM-Not Meaningful. NR-Not Ranked.

Office—Ten Canal Park, Cambridge, MA 02141. **Tel**—(617) 949-1000. **Website**—http://www.aspentech.com **Chrmn & CEO**—L. B. Evans. **Pres**—J. F. Boston. **SVP-CFO**—L. W. Zappala. **SVP-Secy**—S. J. Doyle. **Investor Contact**—Josh Young (617-949-1274). **Dirs**—J. F. Boston, G. T. Brebach Jr., D. R. Brown, L. B. Evans, J. C, McArdle, A. Ross. **Transfer Agent & Registrar**—Boston EquiServe, L.P., Boston, MA. **Incorporated**—in Delaware in 1981. **Empl**— 1,518. **S&P Analyst:** J. J. Schemitsch

STANDARD
&POOR'S
STOCK REPORTS

Astec Industries

NASDAQ Symbol **ASTE**

In S&P SmallCap 600

09-OCT-99

Industry:
Manufacturing (Specialized)

Summary: This company manufactures equipment and components used in the production and application of hot-mix asphalt and other construction aggregates.

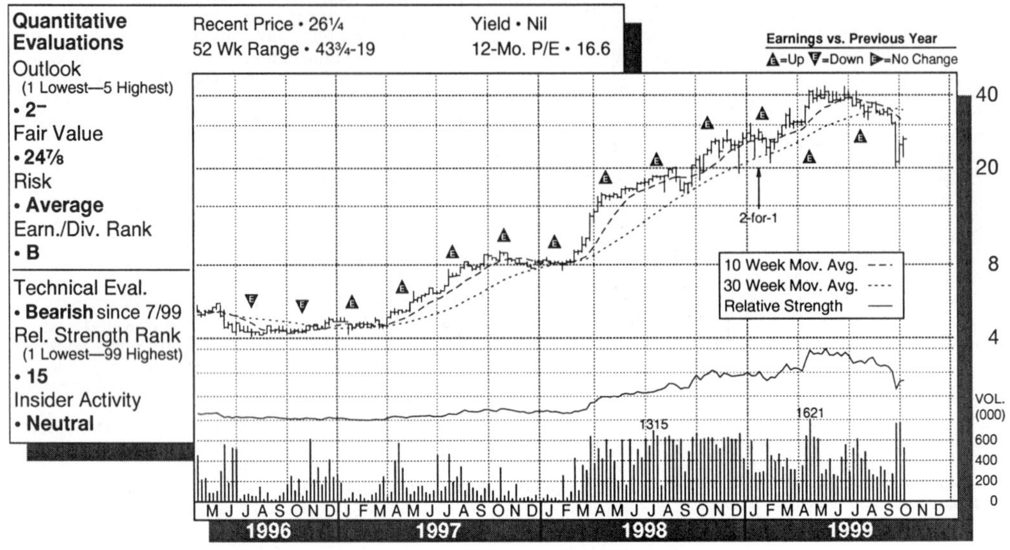

Business Profile - 26-MAY-99

Astec Industries reported in April 1999 that it had a record backlog of orders at the end of the first quarter of 1999, up 24% from the previous year, and the company is increasing capacity to meet demand. Astec said that if recent strong trends continue, it expects 1999 to be an excellent year. The company noted in February 1999 that about half of 1998's growth was attributable to the Kolberg-Pioneer acquisition in December 1997. Astec made two additional acquisitions in 1998 in order to expand the aggregate processing equipment line and to help meet demand for asphalt plant products and services.

Operational Review - 26-MAY-99

For the three months ended March 31, 1999, net sales increased 28%, year to year, aided by the Johnson Crushers acquisition and increased sales of road paving equipment, asphalt plants and related components. Margins widened on the higher volume and good control over selling, general and administrative expenses; operating income rose 46%. Aided by sharply higher other income (net), pretax income was up 51%. After taxes at 38.9%, against 39.9%, net income advanced 54%, to $8.6 million ($0.43 a share), from $5.6 million ($0.29, as adjusted for the January 1999 2-for-1 stock split).

Stock Performance - 08-OCT-99

In the past 30 trading days, ASTE's shares have declined 21%, compared to a 0.91% fall in the S&P 500. Average trading volume for the past five days was 104,340 shares, compared with the 40-day moving average of 124,205 shares.

Key Stock Statistics

Dividend Rate/Share	Nil	Shareholders	600
Shs. outstg. (M)	19.1	Market cap. (B)	$0.502
Avg. daily vol. (M)	0.192	Inst. holdings	53%
Tang. Bk. Value/Share	8.03		
Beta	0.83		

Value of $10,000 invested 5 years ago: $ 34,186

Fiscal Year Ending Dec. 31

	1999	1998	1997	1996	1995	1994
Revenues (Million $)						
1Q	112.5	88.16	62.98	59.57	57.54	46.23
2Q	120.0	108.1	73.16	63.21	70.37	62.69
3Q	—	88.80	65.04	47.18	65.02	49.02
4Q	—	78.86	64.19	51.45	49.67	55.87
Yr.	—	363.9	265.4	221.4	242.6	213.8
Earnings Per Share ($)						
1Q	**0.43**	**0.29**	**0.17**	**0.14**	0.13	0.14
2Q	**0.55**	**0.38**	**0.24**	**0.11**	0.23	0.27
3Q	—	**0.29**	**0.15**	**0.05**	0.14	0.16
4Q	—	**0.29**	**0.15**	**-0.09**	-0.27	0.61
Yr.	—	**1.26**	**0.71**	**0.21**	**0.23**	**1.18**

Next earnings report expected: mid October

Dividend Data

Amount ($)	Date Decl.	Ex-Div. Date	Stock of Record	Payment Date
2-for-1	Dec. 10	Jan. 19	Dec. 31	Jan. 18 '99

Astec Industries, Inc.

Business Summary - 26-MAY-99

Astec Industries, Inc. (ASTE), which produces building and infrastructure equipment, stated in March 1999 that its strategy is to become the low-cost producer in each of its product lines, while also developing new products and providing quality customer service. In addition, ASTE intends to evaluate possible acquisitions that would complement or expand its businesses or customer relationships. Astec believes it offers the broadest and most technically advanced collection of equipment in the infrastructure equipment industry. It believes that it is well situated to take advantage of increased spending for road related equipment, stemming from a Federal highway construction bill, TEA21.

In 1998, the U.S. accounted for 80.9% of net sales. International sales represented 19.1% of sales and included sales in Canada, Latin America, Europe, Asia, Australia and Africa.

ASTE manufactures and finances (for customers who purchase equipment) over 150 different products related to road building, construction, environmental remediation and heat transfer testing. The company's business units (10 subsidiaries and a joint venture) have separate management teams and offer different products and services. Astec's three business segments are: hot-mix asphalt plant, related heat transfer equipment and mobile construction equipment.

Astec's products include: hot-mix asphalt plants, soil purification equipment, thermal oil heaters, mixing equipment, agitating and storage tanks, aggregate processing equipment, gravel and asphalt vibrating screens, recycling equipment for asphalt and concrete, asphalt paving equipment, material transfer vehicles, chain and wheel trenching equipment, as well as sampling and testing equipment. Astec also sells replacement parts for its equipment.

In December 1997, Astec acquired Kolberg-Pioneer, Inc., a manufacturer and distributor of an extensive line of aggregate processing equipment for the sand and gravel, mining, quarry and concrete recycle markets.

In November, 1998, Astec acquired Johnson Crushers International, Inc. Astec believes this acquisition will both expand and enhance its product lines and market penetration in the aggregate processing equipment area. The company expects the acquisition to add about $25 million to sales volume and be accretive to earnings in 1999.

Also in 1998, Astec acquired EssTee Manufacturing to aid Astec in meeting record demand for asphalt plant products and services. The company reported in February 1999, that it would focus EssTee's production on hot-mix asphalt storage bins for new asphalt plants, which constitute an important part of Astec's strategy.

Per Share Data ($)										
(Year Ended Dec. 31)	1998	1997	1996	1995	1994	1993	1992	1991	1990	1989
Tangible Bk. Val.	6.33	5.22	4.69	4.55	4.10	3.17	1.77	1.35	1.10	2.21
Cash Flow	1.68	1.09	0.51	0.51	1.39	0.71	0.64	0.26	-0.65	-0.02
Earnings	1.26	0.71	0.21	0.23	1.19	0.54	0.41	0.04	-0.93	-0.27
Dividends	Nil	Nil	Nil	Nil	Nil	Nil	Nil	Nil	Nil	Nil
Payout Ratio	Nil	Nil	Nil	Nil	Nil	Nil	Nil	Nil	Nil	Nil
Prices - High	28 3/4	9 1/4	5 5/8	7 1/8	10 1/8	7 7/8	5 1/8	1 13/16	2 5/8	4 3/8
- Low	7 5/8	4 1/8	4 1/8	4 7/8	5 7/8	4 1/4	1 3/8	13/16	1/2	2 1/16
P/E Ratio - High	23	13	26	32	8	15	13	48	NM	NM
- Low	6	6	19	22	5	8	3	21	NM	NM
Income Statement Analysis (Million $)										
Revs.	364	265	221	243	214	173	149	135	135	189
Oper. Inc.	48.6	31.6	14.1	16.0	17.7	13.5	11.1	9.6	4.2	3.6
Depr.	8.1	6.9	5.8	5.7	3.9	3.1	3.5	3.3	4.1	3.8
Int. Exp.	2.7	2.4	1.7	2.1	0.7	1.8	3.2	4.6	6.3	6.8
Pretax Inc.	39.6	23.0	7.0	6.1	25.7	9.8	6.4	0.6	-13.1	-4.3
Eff. Tax Rate	38%	40%	39%	26%	8.90%	4.40%	6.60%	10%	NM	NM
Net Inc.	24.4	13.8	4.3	4.6	23.4	9.3	6.0	0.5	-13.5	-4.0
Balance Sheet & Other Fin. Data (Million $)										
Cash	5.4	2.9	3.4	3.1	10.5	15.8	13.8	13.7	8.6	0.8
Curr. Assets	145	119	104	96.6	102	76.5	67.8	68.0	90.3	96.2
Total Assets	249	192	168	154	156	103	88.0	91.0	112	128
Curr. Liab.	63.0	47.2	34.4	38.6	49.1	35.7	34.1	36.8	40.5	36.0
LT Debt	47.2	35.2	36.5	17.1	16.2	Nil	22.7	29.4	50.3	53.6
Common Eqty.	133	106	99	95.9	90.4	64.1	27.6	21.3	17.2	33.4
Total Cap.	184	144	133	113	107	64.1	50.3	50.7	67.5	87.0
Cap. Exp.	46.5	25.3	8.7	15.1	21.9	8.8	2.5	2.1	1.8	6.1
Cash Flow	32.6	20.8	10.2	10.2	27.4	12.4	9.5	3.8	-9.3	-0.3
Curr. Ratio	2.3	2.5	3.0	2.5	2.1	2.1	2.0	1.8	2.2	2.7
% LT Debt of Cap.	25.7	24.4	23.0	15.1	15.2	Nil	45.1	58.0	74.5	61.5
% Net Inc.of Revs.	6.7	5.2	2.0	1.9	11.0	5.4	4.0	0.4	NM	NM
% Ret. on Assets	11.1	7.7	4.8	2.9	18.0	8.5	6.7	0.5	NM	NM
% Ret. on Equity	20.5	13.5	4.5	0.8	30.1	18.5	24.4	2.7	NM	NM

Data as orig reptd.; bef. results of disc opers/spec. items. Per share data adj. for stk. divs. Bold denotes diluted EPS (FASB 128)-prior periods restated. E-Estimated. NA-Not Available. NM-Not Meaningful. NR-Not Ranked.

Office—4101 Jerome Ave. (P.O. Box 72787), Chattanooga, TN 37407. **Tel**—(423) 867-4210. **Fax**—(423) 867-4127. **Website**—http://www.astecindustries.com **Chrmn & Pres**—J. D. Brock. **VP-Secy & Investor Contact**—R. W. Bethea, Jr. **VP-CFO & Treas**—F. M. Hall **Dirs**—J. D. Brock, G. C. Dillon, R. Dressler, R. W. Dunmire, D. K. Frierson, W. D. Gehl, A. E. Guth, W. B. Sansom, E. D. Sloan Jr., W. N. Smith, R. G. Stafford. **Transfer Agent & Registrar**—ChaseMellon Shareholder Services, Ridgefield Park, NJ. **Incorporated**—in Tennessee in 1972. **Empl**— 2,285. **S&P Analyst:** J. Friendly

STANDARD
&POOR'S
STOCK REPORTS

Atlantic Coast Airlines Holdings

NASDAQ Symbol **ACAI**

In S&P SmallCap 600

09-OCT-99

Industry:
Airlines

Summary: This company operates a regional airline serving destinations in 24 states in the Eastern and Midwestern U.S.

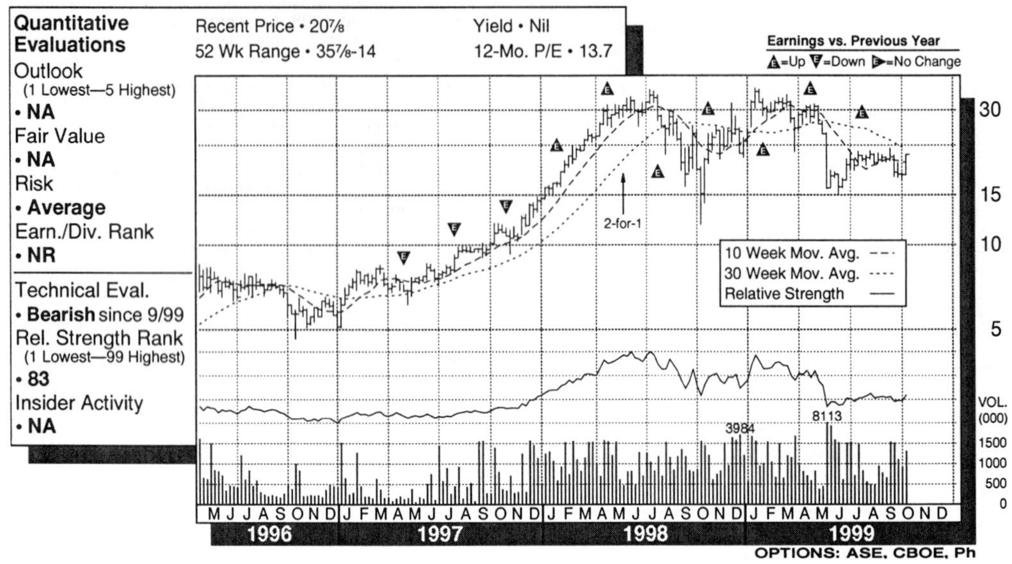

Business Profile - 22-JUL-99

The company's long-term growth objective calls for promoting its code-sharing relationship with United Airlines, and implementing its regional jet fleet strategy, under which it intends to initiate service to markets beyond the economic operating range of turboprop aircraft. As of mid-May 1999, the company's fleet consisted of 20 regional jets and 60 turboprop aircraft, and it had firm orders for an additional 23 regional jets with deliveries through 2001. The introduction of new regional jets is intended to expand business into new markets and increase capacity in existing markets. In April 1999, directors authorized the repurchase of about 5% of the company's outstanding common shares in the open market.

Operational Review - 22-JUL-99

Operating revenues in the first quarter of 1999 advanced 26%, year to year, reflecting an increase in available seat miles following a service expansion, as well as a higher load factor. Total expenses were up 29%, attributable to additional flight crews and other costs to support an increased level of operations, and pretax income rose 7.6%. After taxes at 32.0%, versus 42.0%, net income climbed 26%, to $3,763,000 ($0.18 a share) from $2,983,000 ($0.16). Results in the 1999 period exclude a charge of $0.04 a share from the cumulative effect of an accounting change.

Stock Performance - 08-OCT-99

In the past 30 trading days, ACAI's shares have increased 2%, compared to a 0.91% fall in the S&P 500. Average trading volume for the past five days was 259,820 shares, compared with the 40-day moving average of 232,328 shares.

Key Stock Statistics

Dividend Rate/Share	Nil	Shareholders	109
Shs. outstg. (M)	18.7	Market cap. (B)	$0.389
Avg. daily vol. (M)	0.242	Inst. holdings	74%
Tang. Bk. Value/Share	5.62		
Beta	1.67		

Value of $10,000 invested 5 years ago: $ 51,308

Fiscal Year Ending Dec. 31

	1999	1998	1997	1996	1995	1994
Revenues (Million $)						
1Q	73.00	58.06	41.11	37.86	30.68	—
2Q	92.40	75.76	53.22	50.37	41.40	—
3Q	—	78.10	54.86	49.54	43.96	—
4Q	—	78.03	56.25	44.72	40.92	—
Yr.	—	289.9	205.4	182.5	157.0	159.0
Earnings Per Share ($)						
1Q	0.18	0.16	0.04	0.05	—	-0.61
2Q	0.51	0.42	0.34	0.48	—	-0.59
3Q	—	0.49	0.29	0.41	—	-0.43
4Q	—	0.36	0.17	0.15	—	-0.20
Yr.	—	1.42	0.80	1.08	0.69	-1.83

Next earnings report expected: late October

Dividend Data

No cash dividends have been paid. The company intends to retain its earnings to finance the growth of its operations and does not anticipate paying cash dividends in the foreseeable future.

A Division of The McGraw-Hill Companies

Atlantic Coast Airlines Holdings, Inc.

Business Summary - 22-JUL-99

With 530 scheduled non-stop flights every weekday, Atlantic Coast Airlines Holdings operates as a large regional airline serving 51 destinations in 24 states in the Eastern and Midwestern U.S. Marketing as United Express, the only code-sharing regional airline for United Airlines, Inc., the company serves primarily business travelers through its main operations at Washington-Dulles International Airport, which serves the Northern Virginia and Washington, D.C. markets.

The company coordinates its schedules with United Airlines, particularly at Washington-Dulles, where United operates 75 daily departures to 32 destinations in the U.S., Europe and Latin America, and at Chicago's O'Hare International Airport, where United has 519 daily departures to 105 destinations in the U.S., Europe, Asia and Latin America. Atlantic Coast's code-sharing arrangement with United allows the company to list its flights under United's two letter flight designator code in airline computer reservation systems and to award United's Mileage Plus frequent flyer miles to its passengers. The company also participates with United in cooperative advertising and marketing agreements. Under the agreement, the company pays United monthly fees based on the total number of revenue passengers boarded on its flights.

Together with United, the company generated about 57% of passenger traffic at Washington-Dulles in 1998. As of March 1999, the company scheduled 232 non-stop flights from Washington-Dulles. Based on the frequency of operations, the company's top four airports are Washington-Dulles, Chicago O'Hare, New York-JFK and Newark. During 1998, the company added new routes from Washington-Dulles and began operations at Chicago-O'Hare.

Atlantic Coast operates a fleet of 75 aircraft, consisting of 15 Canadair Regional Jets and 60 turboprops (32 British Aerospace Jetstream-41 and 28 British Aerospace Jetstream-32). As of March 1999, the company had 28 regional jets on order from Bombardier. As part of a long term strategy, the company intends to continue to expand its jet fleet by initiating service to markets beyond the economic operating range of turboprop aircraft. It plans to selectively deploy regional jets to its existing turboprop routes in the short-haul, high-density East Coast markets. This has provided additional connecting passengers to the company's turboprop flights and to United's jets flying from Washington-Dulles.

In 1998, the company recorded 170,116 departures (146,069 in 1997), 2,534,077 revenue passengers carried (1,666,975), 792,934 revenue passenger miles (419,977), and a passenger load factor of 56.2% (48.8%). The average fare in 1998 was $113, down from $122 in 1997.

Per Share Data ($) (Year Ended Dec. 31)	1998	1997	1996	1995	1994	1993	1992	1991	1990	1989
Tangible Bk. Val.	5.41	2.22	1.87	0.70	NA	0.69	NA	NA	NA	NA
Cash Flow	1.66	0.93	1.23	0.84	-1.66	0.27	NA	NA	NA	NA
Earnings	1.42	0.80	1.08	0.69	-1.83	0.01	NA	NA	NA	NA
Dividends	Nil	Nil	Nil	Nil	Nil	Nil	NA	NA	NA	NA
Payout Ratio	Nil	Nil	Nil	Nil	Nil	Nil	NA	NA	NA	NA
Prices - High	35½	16	8⅝	5¾	4⅜	8½	NA	NA	NA	NA
- Low	11¾	6	3¾	⅞	¾	3¾	NA	NA	NA	NA
P/E Ratio - High	25	20	8	8	NM	1700	NA	NA	NA	NA
- Low	8	7	3	1	NM	750	NA	NA	NA	NA
Income Statement Analysis (Million $)										
Revs.	290	205	182	157	159	149	NA	NA	NA	NA
Oper. Inc.	59.2	32.5	22.7	14.6	-6.8	4.2	NA	NA	NA	NA
Depr.	6.5	3.6	2.8	2.2	2.3	2.0	NA	NA	NA	NA
Int. Exp.	5.6	3.5	1.0	1.8	2.2	2.0	NA	NA	NA	NA
Pretax Inc.	51.5	26.8	19.6	11.3	-25.1	0.1	NA	NA	NA	NA
Eff. Tax Rate	41%	46%	2.29%	NM	NM	64%	NA	NA	NA	NA
Net Inc.	30.4	14.5	19.2	12.5	-25.1	0.0	NA	NA	NA	NA
Balance Sheet & Other Fin. Data (Million $)										
Cash	64.5	39.2	21.5	8.4	2.3	2.6	NA	NA	NA	NA
Curr. Assets	105	76.9	41.7	26.6	23.2	22.6	NA	NA	NA	NA
Total Assets	228	149	64.8	47.5	40.1	52.4	NA	NA	NA	NA
Curr. Liab.	36.4	31.7	24.0	22.1	27.7	26.5	NA	NA	NA	NA
LT Debt	64.7	76.1	5.7	NA	NA	NA	NA	NA	NA	NA
Common Eqty.	110	34.8	34.6	14.6	1.9	19.6	NA	NA	NA	NA
Total Cap.	181	NA	40.3	NA	NA	NA	NA	NA	NA	NA
Cap. Exp.	51.0	26.0	2.1	4.3	1.5	NA	NA	NA	NA	NA
Cash Flow	36.9	18.1	22.0	14.7	-22.8	2.0	NA	NA	NA	NA
Curr. Ratio	2.9	2.4	1.7	1.2	0.8	0.9	NA	NA	NA	NA
% LT Debt of Cap.	35.7	68.7	14.2	NA	NA	NA	NA	NA	NA	NA
% Net Inc.of Revs.	10.5	7.1	10.5	8.0	NM	0.0	NA	NA	NA	NA
% Ret. on Assets	16.2	13.6	34.1	28.5	NM	NA	NA	NA	NA	NA
% Ret. on Equity	41.9	41.8	77.9	151.7	NM	NA	NA	NA	NA	NA

Data as orig reptd.; bef. results of disc opers/spec. items. Per share data adj. for stk. divs. Bold denotes diluted EPS (FASB 128)-prior periods restated. E-Estimated. NA-Not Available. NM-Not Meaningful. NR-Not Ranked.

Office—515-A Shaw Rd., Dulles, VA 20166. **Tel**—(703) 925-6000. **Website**—http://www.atlanticcoast.com **Chrmn**—C. E. Acker. **Pres & CEO**—K. B. Skeen. **EVP & COO**—T. J. Moore. **SVP, CFO & Treas**—P. H. Tate. **Dirs**—C. E. Acker, R. Buchanan, S. M. Coughlin, J. Elsbury, J. Kerley, J. Miller, K. B. Skeen, J. Sullivan, T. J. Moore. **Transfer Agent & Registrar**—Continental Stock Transfer & Trust Co., NYC. **Incorporated**—in Delaware in 1991. **Empl**— 2,214. **S&P Analyst:** Stephen R. Biggar

STANDARD
&POOR'S
STOCK REPORTS

Atmos Energy

NYSE Symbol **ATO**

In S&P SmallCap 600

09-OCT-99 **Industry:** Natural Gas

Summary: This company distributes natural gas and propane to more than one million customers in 13 states.

Quantitative Evaluations

Outlook
(1 Lowest—5 Highest)
• **2-**

Fair Value
• **24⅛**

Risk
• **Low**

Earn./Div. Rank
• **B+**

Technical Eval.
• **Bearish** since 9/99

Rel. Strength Rank
(1 Lowest—99 Highest)
• **56**

Insider Activity
• **NA**

Recent Price • 24⅜
52 Wk Range • 33-22¾
Yield • 4.5%
12-Mo. P/E • 21.6

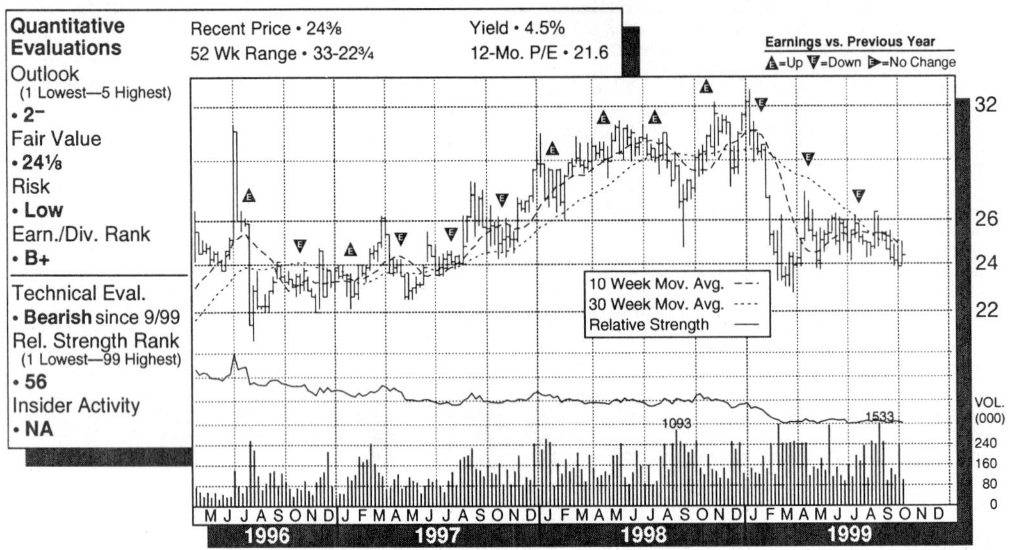

Business Profile - 21-SEP-99

In order to mitigate the impact of weather on the company's various service areas, ATO has filed requests for rate increases in several states. The combined rate proceedings, which state authorities will respond to by late 1999 or early 2000, will affect about 568,000 customers (54% of total customers). In March 1999, Atmos agreed to pay $3.5 million to settle a lawsuit related to lost profits incurred as a result of a subsidiary's alleged delays in repairing a gas leak. This company expects to achieve $375 million of long-term cost savings following the successful integration of United Cities Gas Co. (UCG), which was acquired in 1997.

Operational Review - 21-SEP-99

Operating revenues in the nine months ended June 30, 1999, fell 19%, year to year, reflecting lower gas throughput on 12% warmer weather, and reduced sales to irrigation customers due to heavier rainfall in the West Texas region; gross profit declined 8.5%. Operating expenses rose 5.5%, resulting from lower cost savings from the UCG integration, higher depreciation and amortization charges and costs related to a litigation settlement. Net income declined 34%, to $38.9 million ($1.27 a share, diluted, on 2.5% more shares), from $59.2 million ($1.98).

Stock Performance - 08-OCT-99

In the past 30 trading days, ATO's shares have declined 4%, compared to a 0.91% fall in the S&P 500. Average trading volume for the past five days was 19,660 shares, compared with the 40-day moving average of 71,174 shares.

Key Stock Statistics

Dividend Rate/Share	1.10	Shareholders	29,867
Shs. outstg. (M)	31.1	Market cap. (B)	$0.757
Avg. daily vol. (M)	0.029	Inst. holdings	34%
Tang. Bk. Value/Share	12.21		
Beta	0.19		

Value of $10,000 invested 5 years ago: $ 16,650

Fiscal Year Ending Sep. 30

	1999	1998	1997	1996	1995	1994
Revenues (Million $)						
1Q	210.2	295.3	280.6	130.5	117.8	145.5
2Q	261.4	288.6	362.6	191.1	157.3	186.9
3Q	109.6	137.3	143.7	93.57	84.69	90.01
4Q	—	127.0	119.9	68.60	75.99	77.35
Yr.	—	848.2	906.8	483.7	435.8	499.8
Earnings Per Share ($)						
1Q	**0.50**	**0.68**	0.62	0.59	0.42	0.47
2Q	**0.94**	**1.25**	1.04	1.15	0.91	0.87
3Q	**-0.17**	**0.06**	-0.10	0.02	0.01	-0.08
4Q	—	**-0.13**	-0.74	-0.25	-0.11	-0.29
Yr.	—	**1.84**	**0.81**	**1.42**	**1.06**	**1.05**

Next earnings report expected: mid November

Dividend Data (Dividends have been paid since 1984.)

Amount ($)	Date Decl.	Ex-Div. Date	Stock of Record	Payment Date
0.275	Nov. 11	Nov. 23	Nov. 25	Dec. 10 '98
0.275	Feb. 10	Feb. 23	Feb. 25	Mar. 10 '99
0.275	May. 12	May. 21	May. 25	Jun. 10 '99
0.275	Aug. 11	Aug. 23	Aug. 25	Sep. 10 '99

A Division of The McGraw·Hill Companies

STANDARD
&POOR'S
STOCK REPORTS

Atmos Energy Corporation

09-OCT-99

Business Summary - 21-SEP-99

Atmos Energy Corp. distributes and sells natural gas and propane to approximately 1,058,000 residential, commercial, industrial, agricultural and other customers. It sells natural gas through about 1,020,000 meters in 802 cities, towns and communities located in Texas, Louisiana, Kentucky, Colorado, Kansas, Illinois, Tennessee, Iowa, Virginia, Georgia, South Carolina and Missouri. ATO also transports gas for others through parts of its distribution system. The company's utility divisions are Energas Co., Greeley Gas Co., Trans Louisiana Gas Co., United Cities Gas Co. (UCG) and Western Kentucky Gas Co.

The natural gas industry is subject to a number of factors, including a continuing need to obtain adequate and timely rate relief from regulatory authorities; inherent seasonality of the business; competition with alternate fuels; competition with other gas sources for industrial customers; and possible volatility in the supply and price of natural gas. Due to its diverse geographic expansions, Atmos believes that it is somewhat hedged against exposure to weather patterns, economic conditions and regulatory climates. About 88% of revenues in FY 98 (Sep.) came from sales at rates set by or subject to approval by local or state authorities.

ATO also operates certain non-utility businesses through wholly owned subsidiaries. UCG Storage Co. provides natural gas storage services, and owns natural gas storage fields in Kentucky and Kansas. UCG Energy Corp. leases appliances, real estate and equipment, and vehicles, owns a small interest in a partnership engaged in exploration and production, and has a 45% interest in a gas marketing business. Atmos Propane Inc., a subsidiary of UCG Energy, is engaged in the retail distribution and wholesale supply of propane. At September 30, 1998, Atmos Propane served 37,400 customers.

During FY 98, ATO sold 138,550 MMcf of gas, at an average price of $4.87 per Mcf and an average cost of $3.24 per Mcf. This compared with 147,244 MMcf sold in FY 97, at an average price and cost of $5.11 per Mcf and $3.51 per Mcf, respectively. The company transported 56,224 MMcf and 48,000 MMcf in 1998 and 1997, respectively; the average transportation revenue per Mcf was $0.43 and $0.41. Storage and energy services volumes totaled 20,823 MMcf and 16,964 MMcf. Propane sales in FY 98 and FY 97 totaled 33.7 million gallons and 33.0 million gallons, respectively. Heating degree days (the number of degrees each day that the average temperature is below 65 degrees; the greater the number of degree days, the colder the climate) totaled 3,799 in FY 98, equal to 95% of normal, versus 3,909 days, or 98% of normal, in FY 97.

The dividend increase in late 1998 marked the 11th consecutive annual increase.

Per Share Data ($) (Year Ended Sep. 30)	1998	1997	1996	1995	1994	1993	1992	1991	1990	1989
Tangible Bk. Val.	12.21	11.04	10.75	10.20	9.78	10.39	9.17	8.88	8.71	8.51
Earnings	1.84	0.81	1.51	1.22	0.97	1.45	0.97	0.80	0.98	0.89
Dividends	1.06	1.01	0.96	0.92	0.88	0.85	0.83	0.80	0.77	0.75
Payout Ratio	58%	125%	64%	75%	91%	59%	85%	100%	79%	84%
Prices - High	32 1/4	27 7/8	31	23	20 1/4	21 1/8	15 7/8	15 3/8	12 1/2	12
- Low	24 3/4	22 1/8	20 7/8	16 1/8	15 7/8	15 1/8	12 5/8	10 1/2	10 3/8	9 3/4
P/E Ratio - High	18	34	21	19	21	15	16	19	13	14
- Low	13	27	14	13	16	10	13	13	11	11
Income Statement Analysis (Million $)										
Revs.	848	907	484	436	500	388	340	336	352	342
Depr.	47.6	45.3	20.8	20.7	18.8	13.6	13.6	12.6	13.5	12.7
Maint.	10.3	12.0	4.2	4.3	5.9	3.8	3.3	3.9	4.3	5.8
Fxd. Chgs. Cov.	3.5	2.1	3.5	3.1	2.9	3.5	2.4	2.1	2.2	2.2
Constr. Credits	NA	NA	NA	NA	NA	NA	NA	NA	NA	NA
Eff. Tax Rate	37%	37%	36%	34%	36%	37%	33%	28%	32%	31%
Net Inc.	55.3	23.8	23.9	18.9	14.7	15.7	10.0	7.9	9.0	8.1
Balance Sheet & Other Fin. Data (Million $)										
Gross Prop.	1,446	1,333	666	595	544	399	364	333	307	300
Cap. Exp.	135	122	77.6	62.9	50.4	38.4	33.3	30.2	25.3	21.6
Net Prop.	918	849	414	363	327	241	219	206	195	195
Capitalization:										
LT Debt	399	303	122	131	138	85.3	91.3	95.6	81.8	91.9
% LT Debt	52	48	42	45	48	42	49	51	51	54
Pfd.	Nil	Nil	Nil	Nil	Nil	Nil	Nil	Nil	Nil	Nil
% Pfd.	Nil	Nil	Nil	Nil	Nil	Nil	Nil	Nil	Nil	Nil
Common	371	327	172	158	150	118	96.0	90.3	79.8	77.7
% Common	48	52	59	55	52	58	51	49	49	46
Total Cap.	850	718	334	323	318	232	214	212	189	195
% Oper. Ratio	89.2	94.2	91.9	92.5	94.7	93.3	94.0	94.6	94.5	94.9
% Earn. on Net Prop.	9.2	8.3	10.0	9.3	8.4	11.3	9.6	9.0	9.9	9.1
% Return On Revs.	6.5	2.6	5.0	4.3	2.9	4.0	2.9	2.4	2.5	2.4
% Return On Invest. Capital	7.1	8.2	11.8	10.1	9.1	11.6	9.7	9.0	10.4	9.6
% Return On Com. Equity	15.8	9.5	14.5	12.2	10.2	14.7	10.8	9.3	11.4	10.5

Data as orig reptd.; bef. results of disc opers/spec. items. Per share data adj. for stk. divs. Bold denotes diluted EPS (FASB 128)-prior periods restated. E-Estimated. NA-Not Available. NM-Not Meaningful. NR-Not Ranked.

Office—Three Lincoln Centre, Suite 1800, 5430 LBJ Freeway, Dallas, TX 75240. **Tel**—(972) 934-9227. **Website**—http://www.atmosenergy.com **Chrmn, Pres & CEO**—R. W. Best. **EVP & CFO**—L. J. Dagley. **Secy**—G. A. Blanscet. **VP & Investor Contact**—Lynn Hord (972-855-3729). **Dirs**—T. W. Bain II, R. W. Best, D. Busbee, R.W. Cardin, T. J. Garland, G. C. Koonce, V. J. Lewis, T. C. Meredith, P. E. Nichol, C. S. Quinn, L. Schlessman, C. K. Vaughan, R. Ware II. **Transfer Agent & Registrar**—Boston EquiServe, L.P. **Organized**—in Texas in 1983. **Empl**— 2,193. **S&P Analyst:** Ephraim Juskowicz

STANDARD
&POOR'S
STOCK REPORTS

Auspex Systems

NASDAQ Symbol **ASPX**

In S&P SmallCap 600

09-OCT-99 **Industry:** Computers (Hardware) **Summary:** ASPX is a leading provider of network data-access solutions.

Quantitative Evaluations

Outlook (1 Lowest—5 Highest) • **NA**

Fair Value • **NA**

Risk • **High**

Earn./Div. Rank • **B-**

Technical Eval. • **Bearish** since 9/99

Rel. Strength Rank (1 Lowest—99 Highest) • **22**

Insider Activity • **Neutral**

Recent Price • 8⅞

52 Wk Range • 13¼-1¹¹⁄₁₆

Yield • Nil

12-Mo. P/E • NM

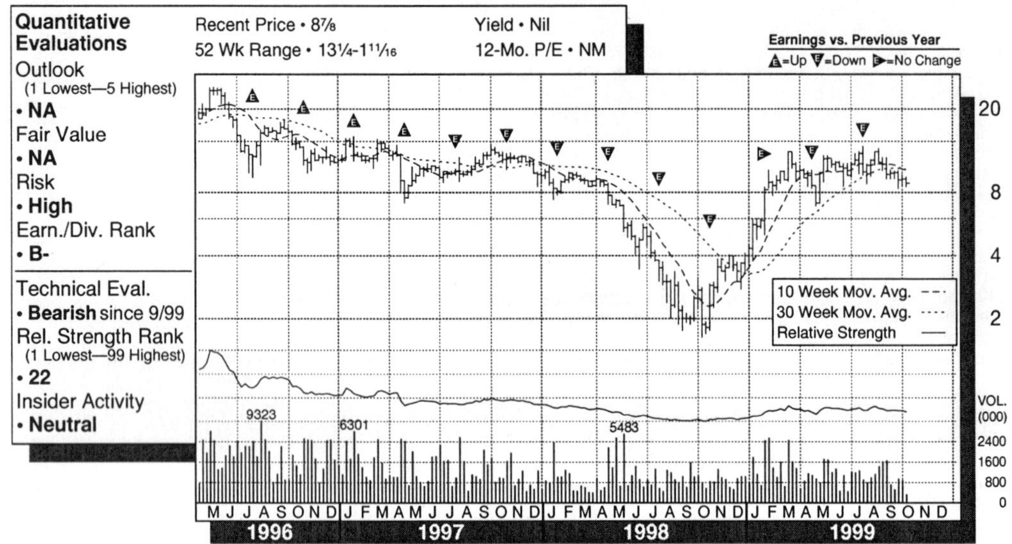

Business Profile - 20-JUL-99

The company plans to continue to introduce new products and upgrades to existing products on an ongoing basis. In July 1999, ASPX announced the immediate availability of NeTservices 2.0 software for its flagship 4Front NS2000 Enterprise system. The software allows both UNIX and Windows NT data to be consolidated and managed on the same NS2000 platform. In June, the company entered into a strategic partnership with Legato Systems, to focus on the development of high-performance data management applications and expansion of the Network Data Management Protocol. The balance sheet remains strong, with $45.5 million in cash and short term investments, and no long term debt, at March 31, 1999.

Operational Review - 20-JUL-99

Total revenues in the nine months ended March 31, 1999, fell 34%, year to year, reflecting the timing of new product introductions, as well as increased competitive pressures. Results were penalized by the volume decline, lower pricing on system sales, which are entering end of life cycle, and continued development costs of the Auspex 4Front series of products; the pretax loss widened. After taxes of $107,000, versus tax benefits of $4,371,000, the net loss increased to $25,535,000 ($0.99 a share), from $8,119,000 ($0.32).

Stock Performance - 08-OCT-99

In the past 30 trading days, ASPX's shares have declined 19%, compared to a 0.91% fall in the S&P 500. Average trading volume for the past five days was 62,480 shares, compared with the 40-day moving average of 204,285 shares.

Key Stock Statistics

Dividend Rate/Share	Nil	Shareholders	667
Shs. outstg. (M)	26.3	Market cap. (B)	$0.233
Avg. daily vol. (M)	0.130	Inst. holdings	66%
Tang. Bk. Value/Share	4.48		
Beta	1.42		

Value of $10,000 invested 5 years ago: $ 9,309

Fiscal Year Ending Jun. 30

	1999	1998	1997	1996	1995	1994
Revenues (Million $)						
1Q	30.06	48.59	43.01	33.54	23.87	20.40
2Q	30.56	43.44	49.08	38.00	26.44	20.38
3Q	26.77	40.39	55.61	43.33	30.03	21.44
4Q	26.09	36.50	54.79	47.77	35.28	21.09
Yr.	113.5	168.9	202.5	162.6	115.6	83.28
Earnings Per Share ($)						
1Q	**-0.26**	0.07	0.17	0.14	0.09	0.10
2Q	**-0.30**	**-0.30**	**0.19**	0.18	0.11	0.09
3Q	**-0.42**	**-0.09**	0.25	0.21	0.14	0.09
4Q	**-0.51**	**-0.36**	-0.09	0.24	0.18	0.07
Yr.	**-1.50**	**-0.69**	**0.52**	**0.77**	**0.51**	**0.34**

Next earnings report expected: late October

Dividend Data

No cash dividends have been paid. A poison pill stock purchase rights plan was adopted in 1995.

A Division of The McGraw-Hill Companies

Auspex Systems, Inc.

Business Summary - 20-JUL-99

As the data explosion continues, companies are making more information available to a growing and diverse constituency of employees, vendors, customers and shareholders, and it must be available 24 hours a day, seven days a week. Auspex Systems has responded to this daunting challenge with a unique family of high-performance, network data-serving solutions, including a full line of network data servers, high-availability software products and data storage management solutions, each designed to meet the needs of businesses for fast, reliable and continuously available access to information.

The traditional approach to moving data, using multiple general purpose servers that are designed to perform computing tasks such as transaction processing and applications, typically results in degraded performance when the amount of network traffic increases. ASPX's unique family of high-performance network data-serving solutions offers a fundamentally different approach to delivering immediate and secure access to information. The company's NetServer is based on a patented system to "serve" large amounts of data quickly and reliably to the desktop.

In 1995, the company began shipping its first software product, DataGuard, which allows users to continuously access their data in the event of a disruption associated with the UNIX host operating system. In March 1996, ASPX began shipping its second software product, ServerGuard. ServerGuard operates between multiple Auspex servers providing the industry's first local and wide area network-based fail-over and disaster recovery system for uninterrupted service. In FY 97 (Jun.), the company introduced FastBackup, a software product that enables a customer to achieve DLT-based backup and restore throughput of up to 100 gigabytes per hour cost effectively. ASPX also introduced DriveGuard, a solution for high-availability data protection, in FY 97. DriveGuard provides mission-critical data security, at a significantly lower cost than that of mirrored configurations. In FY 98, the company introduced NeTservices, a software product that allows UNIX and Windows NT clients to share files on the same platform with reliability, performance and scalability.

In January 1999, ASPX introduced a next generation platform that incorporates its strategic initiatives for UNIX, Windows NT and Network Data Management solutions. It believes that by leveraging its proven software-based FMP architecture onto commodity hardware, it can improve price/performance at the high end in markets already served, and reduce the cost of entry-level products to expand mid-range opportunities.

Per Share Data ($) (Year Ended Jun. 30)	1999	1998	1997	1996	1995	1994	1993	1992	1991	1990
Tangible Bk. Val.	NA	4.48	5.13	4.51	3.46	2.91	2.66	4.20	NA	NA
Cash Flow	NA	-0.12	1.01	1.12	0.84	0.64	0.59	0.38	NA	NA
Earnings	-1.50	-0.69	0.52	0.77	0.51	0.34	0.36	0.25	NA	NA
Dividends	Nil	Nil	Nil	Nil	Nil	Nil	Nil	Nil	NA	NA
Payout Ratio	Nil	Nil	Nil	Nil	Nil	Nil	Nil	Nil	NA	NA
Prices - High	13¼	10¾	14⅞	25½	18¾	10	15½	NA	NA	NA
- Low	3¾	1⅝	7⅛	9⅜	6½	3⅞	7½	NA	NA	NA
P/E Ratio - High	NM	NM	29	33	37	29	43	NA	NA	NA
- Low	NM	NM	14	12	13	11	22	NA	NA	NA
Income Statement Analysis (Million $)										
Revs.	NA	169	202	163	116	83.3	73.5	51.5	NA	NA
Oper. Inc.	NA	-14.0	41.7	36.6	21.9	15.8	14.5	8.0	NA	NA
Depr.	NA	14.4	12.4	8.9	8.0	7.5	5.0	2.6	NA	NA
Int. Exp.	NA	0.0	0.0	0.1	0.1	0.1	0.1	0.1	NA	NA
Pretax Inc.	NA	-26.7	24.4	29.6	15.9	9.8	10.0	5.6	NA	NA
Eff. Tax Rate	NA	NM	45%	33%	22%	15%	19%	12%	NA	NA
Net Inc.	NA	-17.3	13.4	19.8	12.4	8.3	8.1	4.9	NA	NA
Balance Sheet & Other Fin. Data (Million $)										
Cash	NA	23.3	25.1	50.5	44.6	42.1	49.8	16.3	NA	NA
Curr. Assets	NA	111	134	117	93.6	75.8	68.2	27.4	NA	NA
Total Assets	NA	147	157	136	107	85.4	76.7	33.0	NA	NA
Curr. Liab.	NA	32.0	28.8	26.0	25.7	18.3	14.4	9.8	NA	NA
LT Debt	NA	Nil	0.0	0.0	0.2	0.4	0.8	0.7	NA	NA
Common Eqty.	NA	115	128	110	80.7	66.6	61.6	21.0	NA	NA
Total Cap.	NA	115	128	110	80.9	67.0	62.4	21.7	NA	NA
Cap. Exp.	NA	28.9	16.4	15.4	8.1	7.9	7.0	5.1	NA	NA
Cash Flow	NA	-3.0	25.9	28.7	20.4	15.8	13.1	7.5	NA	NA
Curr. Ratio	NA	3.5	4.7	4.5	3.6	4.1	4.7	2.8	NA	NA
% LT Debt of Cap.	NA	Nil	NM	NM	0.2	0.6	1.3	3.1	NA	NA
% Net Inc.of Revs.	NA	NM	6.6	12.2	10.7	10.0	11.1	9.5	NA	NA
% Ret. on Assets	NA	NM	9.2	16.3	12.9	10.3	7.1	22.2	NA	NA
% Ret. on Equity	NA	NM	11.3	20.8	16.8	13.0	10.2	39.8	NA	NA

Data as orig reptd.; bef. results of disc opers/spec. items. Per share data adj. for stk. divs. Bold denotes diluted EPS (FASB 128)-prior periods restated. E-Estimated. NA-Not Available. NM-Not Meaningful. NR-Not Ranked.

Office—2300 Central Expy., Santa Clara, CA 95050. **Tel**—(408) 566-2000. **Website**—http://www.auspex.com **Pres & CEO**—B. N. Moore. **VP-Fin & CFO**—R. M. Case. **Investor Contact**—Sharon Travers (408-566-2213). **Dirs**—R. S. Cheheyl, W. F. King, B. N. Moore. **Transfer Agent & Registrar**—Boston EquiServe, L.P. **Incorporated**—in California in 1987; reincorporated in Delaware in 1991. **Empl**— 612. **S&P Analyst:** P.L.H.

Authentic Fitness

NYSE Symbol **ASM**

In S&P SmallCap 600

09-OCT-99 **Industry:** Textiles (Apparel)

Summary: This company designs, manufactures and sells swimwear, swimwear accessories and active fitness apparel.

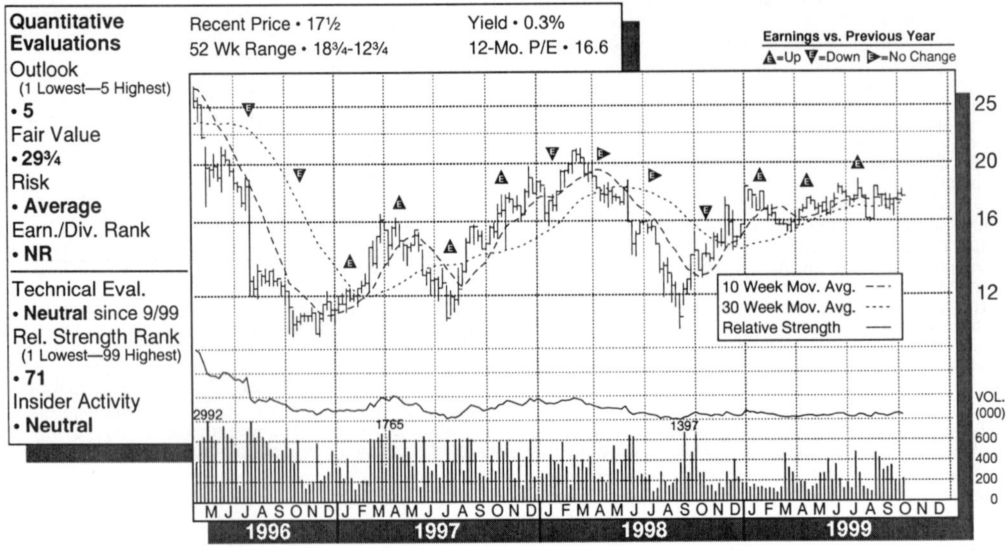

Business Profile - 01-JUL-99

In October 1998, ASM announced plans to discontinue sourcing products from KT West, Inc. at the company's owned Checotah, OK, facility. The company also announced plans to consolidate sourcing from its leased Montebello, CA, facility into its Commerce, CA, facility. These decisions were part of ASM's continued strategy to develop a more efficient method of sourcing of its products. As a result, the company recorded a charge of approximately $2 million, net of tax benefits, in the first quarter of FY 99 (Jun.). ASM also noted that results for the first nine months of FY 98 included charges related to the write-off of assets and other costs related to the closing of the company's Bally's Fitness Center stores, as well as a consolidation of its manufacturing facilities.

Operational Review - 01-JUL-99

Net revenues for the nine months ended April 3, 1999, increased 10%, year to year, reflecting higher sales in the Speedo division, the Kid's swim division, and the men's swim division, partially offset by slower growth at the company's retail stores and designer swimwear division. Gross margins narrowed, hurt by the absence of insurance proceeds, and despite well-controlled operating expenses and lower interest expense, net income fell 2.1%, to $10,536,000 ($0.51 a share, on 7.5% fewer shares), from $10,762,000 ($0.48). Results in the 1999 period exclude the negative effect of an accounting change of $2.5 million ($0.12 a share).

Stock Performance - 08-OCT-99

In the past 30 trading days, ASM's shares have declined 0.36%, compared to a 0.91% fall in the S&P 500. Average trading volume for the past five days was 42,500 shares, compared with the 40-day moving average of 62,462 shares.

Key Stock Statistics

Dividend Rate/Share	0.05	Shareholders	141
Shs. outstg. (M)	23.0	Market cap. (B)	$0.404
Avg. daily vol. (M)	0.047	Inst. holdings	40%
Tang. Bk. Value/Share	3.47		
Beta	0.31		

Value of $10,000 invested 5 years ago: $ 12,652

Fiscal Year Ending Jun. 30

	1999	1998	1997	1996	1995	1994
Revenues (Million $)						
1Q	39.62	36.97	38.67	42.91	37.60	28.61
2Q	78.04	72.65	70.44	77.30	56.32	36.82
3Q	144.3	127.9	105.0	98.86	74.85	53.30
4Q	148.9	129.9	109.0	90.54	97.37	59.83
Yr.	410.8	367.5	323.1	309.6	266.1	178.6
Earnings Per Share ($)						
1Q	**-0.34**	**-0.31**	**-0.52**	0.10	0.10	0.10
2Q	**0.20**	**0.16**	**0.21**	-0.06	0.21	-0.04
3Q	**0.69**	**0.62**	**0.62**	-0.27	0.28	0.20
4Q	**0.69**	**0.53**	**0.53**	-1.78	0.32	0.20
Yr.	**1.06**	**1.01**	**0.85**	**-2.00**	0.90	0.49

Next earnings report expected: late October

Dividend Data (Dividends have been paid since 1995.)

Amount ($)	Date Decl.	Ex-Div. Date	Stock of Record	Payment Date
0.013	Nov. 23	Dec. 02	Dec. 04	Jan. 05 '99
0.013	Mar. 03	Mar. 09	Mar. 11	Apr. 08 '99
0.013	May. 07	Jun. 10	Jun. 14	Jul. 08 '99
0.013	Aug. 20	Aug. 31	Sep. 02	Oct. 07 '99

Authentic Fitness Corporation

09-OCT-99

Business Summary - 01-JUL-99

When we go for a swim, we probably have used the products of Authentic Fitness. Organized in 1990, Authentic Fitness Corporation designs, manufactures and markets swimwear, accessories, and active fitness apparel. The company's sports brand names such as Speedo, Speedo Authentic Fitness, Catalina, Anne Cole, Cole of California, Sunset Beach, Sandcastle, Sporting Life and Oscar de la Renta, and White Stag. ASM also operates Authentic Fitness retail stores, which sell active fitness apparel under the Speedo and Speedo Authentic Fitness names. In FY 98 (Jun.), 54% of revenues were derived from the Speedo division, 27% from the Designer Swimwear division, 15% from the Retail division, and 2% from the White Stag divisions. Consistent with its intention to focus on core Speedo businesses, ASM exited the skiwear and outlet store businesses in May 1996.

The Speedo division's product lines consist of women's and men's competition swimwear and swimwear accessories, men's swimwear and coordinating T-shirts, women's fitness swimwear and Speedo Authentic Fitness activewear and children's swimwear. The Speedo brand name is prominent in the competition swimwear market, and is the dominant brand in that market in the U.S. and Canada (over 60% market share in 1998). The majority of its sales are to repeat customers in a fairly constant core group of basic body styles. Speedo accessories include swim goggles, swimming caps, nose clips, masks, snorkels, ear plugs, kickboards, floatation devices, and aquatic exercise gear.

In December, 1998, ASM was operating a total of 140 Authentic Fitness retail stores, which offer a complete line of Speedo and Speedo Authentic Fitness products and average approximately 1,100 sq. ft. in size.

The Designer Swimwear division markets women's swimwear under the brandnames Catalina, Anne Cole, Cole of California, Oscar de la Renta, Sandcastle, Sunset Beach, White Stag and Sporting Life. Anne Cole and Oscar de la Renta are designer brands, Cole of California, Sandcastle and Sporting Life are missy brands, and Sunset is a junior brand. The Catalina and White Stag brands are targeted to the mass merchandise market. During the 1997 selling season, three of ASM's designer brands were among the top 10 sellers at retail. Anne Cole was the fourth best selling missy brand, Cole of California was the eighth best selling missy brand, and Sunset Beach was the third best selling junior brand.

As of May 15, 1998, ASM had repurchased 385,700 shares at an average price of about $16 per share, under an authorized $20 million repurchase announcement made in May 1997.

In December 1998, ASM launched a new Speedo internet shopping site that will allow consumers a fast and convenient way to purchase Speedo swimwear and work-out wear.

Per Share Data ($) (Year Ended Jun. 30)	1999	1998	1997	1996	1995	1994	1993	1992	1991	1990
Tangible Bk. Val.	NA	3.47	2.58	2.11	3.45	2.63	0.64	-0.14	-0.30	NA
Cash Flow	NA	1.47	1.28	-1.22	1.20	0.70	0.72	0.58	0.39	NA
Earnings	1.06	1.01	0.85	-2.00	0.90	0.49	0.56	0.42	0.23	NA
Dividends	0.05	0.05	0.05	0.05	Nil	Nil	Nil	Nil	NA	NA
Payout Ratio	5%	5%	6%	NM	Nil	Nil	Nil	Nil	NA	NA
Prices - High	18 3/4	21 1/4	19 3/4	29	23 3/8	16	16	11 7/8	NA	NA
- Low	15 1/4	10 1/2	10 7/8	10 3/8	11 7/8	10 7/8	8 1/2	6 1/8	NA	NA
P/E Ratio - High	18	21	19	NM	26	33	29	28	NA	NA
- Low	14	10	13	NM	13	22	15	14	NA	NA
Income Statement Analysis (Million $)										
Revs.	NA	367	323	310	266	179	133	101	86.0	NA
Oper. Inc.	NA	61.5	55.8	-16.3	45.1	30.8	22.3	19.9	14.0	NA
Depr.	NA	10.4	9.8	15.5	6.5	4.3	2.8	2.7	2.8	NA
Int. Exp.	NA	14.3	13.6	11.5	7.0	4.4	4.3	3.8	5.0	NA
Pretax Inc.	NA	35.5	29.1	-57.0	31.6	16.4	15.2	13.3	6.2	NA
Eff. Tax Rate	NA	36%	35%	NM	38%	42%	36%	44%	36%	NA
Net Inc.	NA	22.8	19.0	-39.4	19.5	9.6	9.8	7.4	4.0	NA
Balance Sheet & Other Fin. Data (Million $)										
Cash	NA	0.6	1.2	1.5	0.8	1.1	0.1	0.4	0.1	NA
Curr. Assets	NA	195	194	165	163	104	65.2	44.9	55.8	NA
Total Assets	NA	316	322	281	278	198	118	98.0	109	NA
Curr. Liab.	NA	125	140	112	96.5	49.8	37.9	24.2	35.5	NA
LT Debt	NA	33.1	42.7	51.9	32.4	19.2	21.5	26.0	27.6	NA
Common Eqty.	NA	151	134	117	142	122	57.0	47.8	44.2	NA
Total Cap.	NA	191	181	169	182	148	80.2	73.8	73.7	NA
Cap. Exp.	NA	6.7	16.9	12.7	19.3	13.9	1.8	0.8	NA	NA
Cash Flow	NA	33.1	28.9	-23.9	26.0	13.9	12.6	10.2	6.8	NA
Curr. Ratio	NA	1.6	1.4	1.5	1.7	2.1	1.7	1.9	1.6	NA
% LT Debt of Cap.	NA	17.3	23.5	30.7	17.8	12.9	26.8	35.2	37.4	NA
% Net Inc.of Revs.	NA	6.2	5.9	NM	7.3	5.3	7.4	6.3	4.6	NA
% Ret. on Assets	NA	7.1	6.3	NM	8.2	6.0	7.5	NA	NA	NA
% Ret. on Equity	NA	16.0	15.2	NM	14.8	10.7	18.4	NA	NA	NA

Data as orig reptd.; bef. results of disc opers/spec. items. Per share data adj. for stk. divs. Bold denotes diluted EPS (FASB 128)-prior periods restated. E-Estimated. NA-Not Available. NM-Not Meaningful. NR-Not Ranked.

Office—6040 Bandini Blvd., Commerce, CA 90040. **Tel**—(323) 726-1262. **Chrmn & CEO**—L. J. Wachner. **Pres & COO**—C. G. Staff. **SVP & CFO**—M. P. McHugh **VP-Fin & Secy**—W. W. Chan. **Dirs**—S. S. Arkin, S. D. Buchalter, J. A. Califano Jr., W. S. Finkelstein, L. J. Wachner, R. D. Walter. **Transfer Agent**—Bank of New York, NYC.**Incorporated**—in Delaware in 1990. **Empl**— 1,293. **S&P Analyst:** Matthew C. Hershberg

STANDARD &POOR'S STOCK REPORTS

Aviation Sales

NYSE Symbol AVS
In S&P SmallCap 600

23-OCT-99

Industry: Aerospace/Defense

Summary: This company is a leading distributor of aircraft spare parts to major commercial passenger airlines, air cargo carriers, and maintenance and repair facilities.

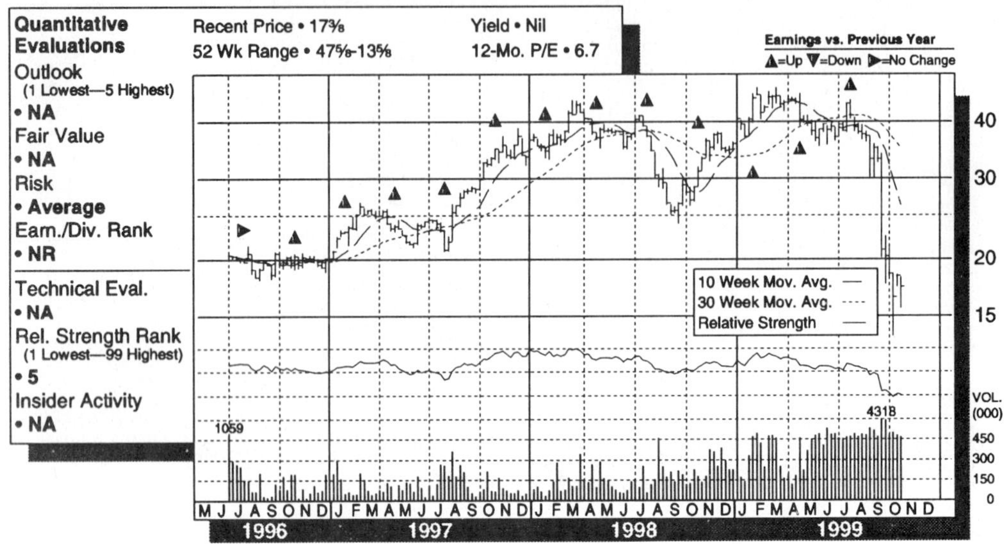

Business Profile - 14-OCT-99

In September 1999, AVS said it anticipates 1999 per share earnings growth of 15% to 17%, and that based on this level of growth, it expects fully diluted earnings per share to be between $0.48 and $0.50 on revenue of some $170 million in the third quarter of 1999 and $2.30 to $2.35 on revenues of about $718 million for the full year. AVS added that results in its manufacturing and flight surfaces repair operations will not meet its plans, citing Boeing's order cancellations and delivery push-outs during the third quarter and higher expense levels in new facilities and equipment. Other factors contributing to the shortfall include delays in lease transactions and higher interest costs.

Operational Review - 14-OCT-99

Operating revenues for the six months ended June 30, 1999, rose 74%, year to year, as restated, aided by acquisitions, increased sales from investments in additional inventories and improved capacity utilization. Gross margins narrowed, due to a less favorable sales mix; however, with operating expenses up just 35%, operating profits improved 85%, to $44.3 million from $23.9 million. Following sharply higher interest and other expenses, and taxes at 39.1%, versus 38.9%, income was up 75%, to $17,421,000 ($1.32 a share, on 4.7% more shares) from $9,947,000 ($0.79, before a charge of $0.05 for early extinguishment of debt).

Stock Performance - 22-OCT-99

In the past 30 trading days, AVS's shares have declined 45%, compared to a 4% fall in the S&P 500. Average trading volume for the past five days was 256,880 shares, compared with the 40-day moving average of 413,574 shares.

Key Stock Statistics

Dividend Rate/Share	Nil	Shareholders	318
Shs. outstg. (M)	15.0	Market cap. (B)	$0.276
Avg. daily vol. (M)	0.184	Inst. holdings	66%
Tang. Bk. Value/Share	5.14		
Beta	NA		

Value of $10,000 invested 5 years ago: NA

Fiscal Year Ending Dec. 31

	1999	1998	1997	1996	1995	1994
Revenues (Million $)						
1Q	178.0	82.46	54.85	35.55	—	—
2Q	179.3	91.12	58.12	36.16	—	—
3Q	—	127.5	67.10	41.18	—	—
4Q	—	163.8	76.82	49.05	—	—
Yr.	—	500.8	256.9	161.9	113.8	—
Earnings Per Share ($)						
1Q	0.61	0.45	0.32	0.26	0.38	—
2Q	0.71	0.50	0.45	0.30	0.30	—
3Q	—	0.63	0.47	0.27	0.18	—
4Q	—	0.64	0.53	0.24	0.14	—
Yr.	—	2.06	1.77	1.32	1.00	—

Next earnings report expected: early November

Dividend Data

No cash dividends have been paid, and the company does not intend to pay any for the foreseeable future.

Aviation Sales Company

Business Summary - 14-OCT-99

Aviation Sales Co. (AVS) is a leading provider of fully integrated aviation inventory and maintenance, repair and overhaul services. The company believes it is the largest independent provider of heavy maintenance services for aircraft in North America and the largest redistributor of aircraft parts in the world. AVS sells aircraft spare parts and provides inventory management services and maintenance, repair and overhaul (MRO) services to commercial passenger airlines, air cargo carriers, maintenance and repair facilities and other redistributors throughout the world.

The company believes the July 1998 acquisition of Whitehall Corp., for 2,844,079 common shares, provides it with a substantial foothold in the $27 billion worldwide MRO market. AVS expects Whitehall, combined with its other recently acquired maintenance and repair operations, to significantly expand its capabilities in the MRO market and allow it to provide its airline customers "nose to tail" maintenance, repair and inventory management solutions.

Parts sold by the company include airframe and engine components for commercial airplanes, including Boeing, McDonnell Douglas, Lockheed and Airbus aircraft and Pratt & Whitney, General Electric and Rolls Royce jet engines. MRO services offered by the company through its six FAA-licensed repair stations include aircraft heavy maintenance and modification and repair and overhaul on a wide range of aircraft and aircraft components. Inventory management services offered by the company include purchasing services, repair management, warehouse management, aircraft disassembly services, and consignment and leasing of inventories of aircraft parts and engines. AVS also makes certain aircraft parts for sale to original equipment manufacturers, including precision engine parts.

The company believes the annual worldwide market for aircraft spare parts is approximately $11.0 billion, of which approximately $1.3 billion reflects annual sales of aircraft spare parts in the redistribution market. AVS believes the market for spare parts and the redistribution market in particular are growing due to (i) the increasing size and the age of the worldwide airline fleet (the worldwide fleet of commercial airplanes is expected to more than double from 1997 to 2017) and (ii) increased outsourcing by airlines of inventory management functions in response to cost control pressures. These pressures have also contributed to a reduction in the number of approved vendors utilized by airlines and maintenance and repair facilities, which in turn has led to consolidation in the redistribution market.

In September 1998, AVS acquired Triad International Maintenance Co. (TIMCO), an operator of an FAA licensed repair station with $113 million in sales, from Primark Corp. (PMK; NYSE) for $70 million. AVS expects the acquisition to add $0.10 to $0.15 to diluted EPS in 1999. In July 1998, AVS acquired Whitehall Corp., a leader in the maintenance, r epair and overhaul of aircraft.

Per Share Data ($)										
(Year Ended Dec. 31)	**1998**	**1997**	**1996**	**1995**	**1994**	**1993**	**1992**	**1991**	**1990**	**1989**
Tangible Bk. Val.	5.14	8.28	9.47	0.03	NA	NA	NA	NA	NA	NA
Cash Flow	3.48	2.22	2.92	1.45	NA	NA	NA	NA	NA	NA
Earnings	2.06	1.77	1.48	1.26	NA	NA	NA	NA	NA	NA
Dividends	Nil	Nil	Nil	Nil	NA	NA	NA	NA	NA	NA
Payout Ratio	Nil	Nil	Nil	Nil	NA	NA	NA	NA	NA	NA
Prices - High	44⁵/₈	38⁷/₈	21¹/₂	NA	NA	NA	NA	NA	NA	NA
- Low	24	20¹/₂	18	NA	NA	NA	NA	NA	NA	NA
P/E Ratio - High	22	22	15	NA	NA	NA	NA	NA	NA	NA
- Low	12	12	12	NA	NA	NA	NA	NA	NA	NA
Income Statement Analysis (Million $)										
Revs.	501	257	162	114	NA	NA	NA	NA	NA	NA
Oper. Inc.	72.7	39.3	25.2	20.0	NA	NA	NA	NA	NA	NA
Depr.	11.3	4.3	2.9	1.5	NA	NA	NA	NA	NA	NA
Int. Exp.	21.3	7.4	5.3	2.6	NA	NA	NA	NA	NA	NA
Pretax Inc.	41.6	27.6	16.9	16.0	NA	NA	NA	NA	NA	NA
Eff. Tax Rate	37%	39%	NM	39%	NA	NA	NA	NA	NA	NA
Net Inc.	26.1	16.8	17.4	9.7	NA	NA	NA	NA	NA	NA
Balance Sheet & Other Fin. Data (Million $)										
Cash	10.5	5.0	1.3	0.3	NA	NA	NA	NA	NA	NA
Curr. Assets	426	216	117	80.2	NA	NA	NA	NA	NA	NA
Total Assets	599	285	145	102	NA	NA	NA	NA	NA	NA
Curr. Liab.	256	133	48.4	32.8	NA	NA	NA	NA	NA	NA
LT Debt	187	52.6	14.9	20.0	NA	NA	NA	NA	NA	NA
Common Eqty.	154	98.2	81.1	65.0	NA	NA	NA	NA	NA	NA
Total Cap.	341	151	95.9	85.0	NA	NA	NA	NA	NA	NA
Cap. Exp.	16.6	4.4	1.1	0.9	NA	NA	NA	NA	NA	NA
Cash Flow	37.4	21.1	20.3	11.2	NA	NA	NA	NA	NA	NA
Curr. Ratio	1.7	1.6	2.4	2.4	NA	NA	NA	NA	NA	NA
% LT Debt of Cap.	54.8	34.9	15.6	23.5	NA	NA	NA	NA	NA	NA
% Net Inc.of Revs.	5.2	6.5	10.8	8.5	NA	NA	NA	NA	NA	NA
% Ret. on Assets	5.9	7.8	14.6	NA	NA	NA	NA	NA	NA	NA
% Ret. on Equity	20.7	18.7	NM	NA	NA	NA	NA	NA	NA	NA

Data as orig reptd.; bef. results of disc opers/spec. items. Per share data adj. for stk. divs. Bold denotes diluted EPS (FASB 128)-prior periods restated. E-Estimated. NA-Not Available. NM-Not Meaningful. NR-Not Ranked.

Office—6905 N.W. 25th St., Miami, FL 33122.**Tel**—(305) 592-4055. **Website**—http://www.avsales.com **Chrmn, Pres & CEO**—D. S. Baker. **VP & Treas**—G. Braithwaite. **Dirs**—R. Alpert, G. F. Baker III, D. S. Baker, J. N. Greenblatt, S. Humphreys, P. B. Schwartz, H. M. Woody. **Transfer Agent & Registrar**—Continental Stock Transfer & Trust Co. **Incorporated**—in Delaware in 1996.**Empl**— 3,800. **S&P Analyst:** P.L.H.

Avid Technology

NASDAQ Symbol **AVID**

In S&P SmallCap 600

09-OCT-99

Industry:
Computer (Software & Services)

Summary: This company develops, markets, sells and supports a wide range of disk-based systems for capturing, editing and distributing digital media.

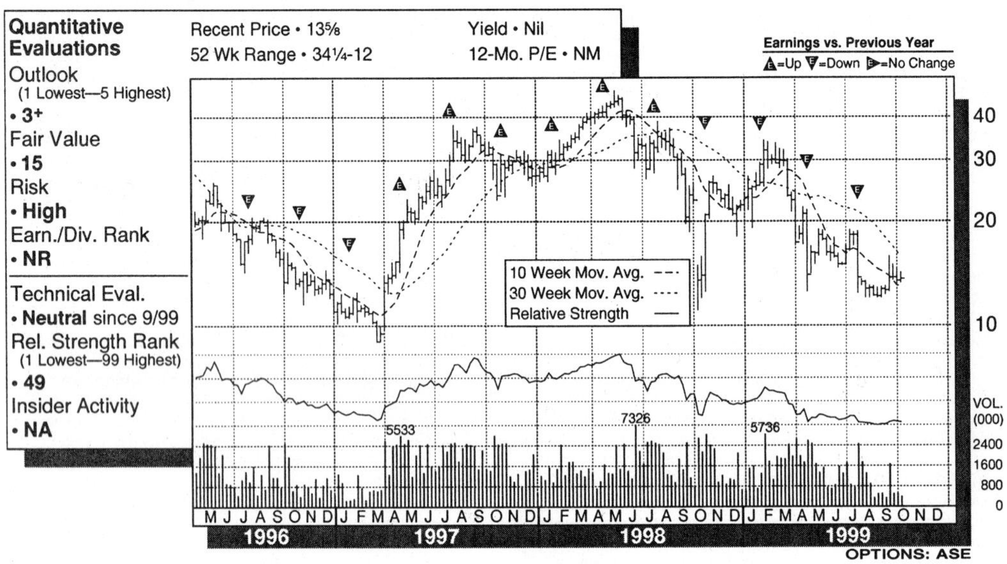

Business Profile - 21-JUL-99

As part of its operational strategy, AVID intends to focus on digital products for individuals who want tools for editing home video productions, as well as creators of web-based video. In June 1999, AVID announced the release of its Avid Cinema product for Windows 1.5, the latest version of its PC video editing and publishing product, which provides storyboard templates developed by professional screenwriters to help users script their own movies for home, school, or office use. The company noted that over 250,000 people currently use its Avid Cinema product.

Operational Review - 21-JUL-99

Net revenues for the quarter ended March 31, 1999, edged up 2.3%, year to year, reflecting increased sales of Softimage and digital audio products, partially offset by lower sales of Media Composer and related products. Gross margins widened on lower material costs, improved manufacturing efficiencies, and a more favorable product mix. Following substantially higher R&D and marketing and selling expenses, a $20.5 million amortization charge for the purchase of Softimage, and 76% lower interest income, a net loss of $11,454,000 ($0.47 a share) contrasted with a net income of $7,705,000 ($0.31).

Stock Performance - 08-OCT-99

In the past 30 trading days, AVID's shares have increased 12%, compared to a 0.91% fall in the S&P 500. Average trading volume for the past five days was 76,520 shares, compared with the 40-day moving average of 119,228 shares.

Key Stock Statistics

Dividend Rate/Share	Nil	Shareholders	602
Shs. outstg. (M)	23.7	Market cap. (B)	$0.323
Avg. daily vol. (M)	0.150	Inst. holdings	52%
Tang. Bk. Value/Share	5.76		
Beta	1.16		

Value of $10,000 invested 5 years ago: $ 6,374

Fiscal Year Ending Dec. 31

	1999	1998	1997	1996	1995	1994
Revenues (Million $)						
1Q	111.3	108.7	108.2	92.04	83.89	37.50
2Q	116.3	112.8	122.9	109.1	98.45	45.10
3Q	—	116.2	116.5	114.7	114.4	54.00
4Q	—	144.6	123.7	113.2	109.9	67.00
Yr.	—	482.4	471.3	429.0	406.6	203.7
Earnings Per Share ($)						
1Q	**-0.47**	**0.31**	**0.08**	**-1.08**	-0.05	0.11
2Q	**-0.34**	**0.37**	**0.27**	**-0.17**	0.31	0.26
3Q	—	**-0.89**	**0.34**	**-0.32**	0.43	0.33
4Q	—	**0.04**	**0.37**	**-0.23**	0.07	0.40
Yr.	—	**-0.15**	**1.08**	**-1.80**	**0.77**	**0.99**

Next earnings report expected: late October

Dividend Data

No cash dividends have been paid. The company intends to retain earnings for use in the operation of its business and does not expect to pay cash dividends in the foreseeable future. A shareholder rights plan was adopted in 1996.

Avid Technology, Inc.

Business Summary - 21-JUL-99

Avid Technology develops, markets, sells and supports a wide range of disk-based systems for creating and manipulating digital media content. Its digital, non-linear video and film editing systems are designed to improve the productivity of video and film editors by permitting them to edit moving pictures and sound in a faster, easier, more creative and more cost-effective manner than traditional analog systems.

Products are divided into the following categories: editing, audio, digital news gathering, newsroom computer systems, graphics and special effects products, and storage systems. Editing products include the Media Composer, a nonlinear editing system designed for professional film and video editors; the Film Composer, a 24-frames-per-second editing system for projects that originate and finish on film; Avid Cinema, a desktop editing product for people with no previous editing experience; and MCXpress, a video editing system for CD-ROM and Internet distribution.

Audio products consist of two audio workstations for professional use: Pro Tools and ProControl, for the radio and music markets, and AudioVision, for post-production work with film and video.

Digital news gathering products include NewsCutter, which enables broadcast news editors to quickly edit hard news, features and news series; MediaServer, a workgroup video production server; Avid Cinema, a desktop editing product for people who have little or no previous digital video editing experience

Graphics and special effects products include Media Illusion, a digital compositioning, layering and special effects software solution; Matador, a two-dimensional post-production paint software system; Elastic Reality, which provides animation, warping and morphing of shapes and images; and Marquee, a title-animation software package for Silicon Graphics and Windows NT workstations.

Storage systems are offered for all of Avid's systems and are used to add media editing or playback capacity, improve image quality, support media sharing and protect media from loss due to hardware failure.

Sales outside of North America accounted for 49% of net revenues in 1998 (49% in 1997).

In August 1998, AVID acquired Softimage from Microsoft for $79 million in cash and a package of notes, additional AVID shares, and options to Softimage employees.

In October 1998, AVID formed a strategic alliance with Tektronix, Inc. On January 27, 1999, both companies organized a joint venture, dedicated to providing the next generation of digital news production products by combining each companies' newsroom computer systems and certain personnel.

Per Share Data ($) (Year Ended Dec. 31)	1998	1997	1996	1995	1994	1993	1992	1991	1990	1989
Tangible Bk. Val.	11.90	10.42	10.00	11.84	9.90	7.89	7.11	NA	NA	NA
Cash Flow	2.21	2.13	-0.40	1.73	1.97	0.88	0.41	NA	NA	NA
Earnings	-0.15	1.08	-1.80	0.77	1.10	0.38	0.29	-0.27	-0.84	NA
Dividends	NA	Nil	Nil	Nil	Nil	Nil	Nil	Nil	Nil	NA
Payout Ratio	Nil	Nil	Nil	Nil	Nil	Nil	Nil	Nil	Nil	NA
Prices - High	47¾	38	26	49¼	43¾	27½	NA	NA	NA	NA
- Low	11	9	10⅛	16¾	20½	16	NA	NA	NA	NA
P/E Ratio - High	NM	35	NM	64	40	72	NA	NA	NA	NA
- Low	NM	8	NM	22	19	42	NA	NA	NA	NA
Income Statement Analysis (Million $)										
Revs.	482	471	429	407	204	113	52.0	NA	NA	NA
Oper. Inc.	71.2	55.5	-0.8	47.6	27.2	7.9	5.2	NA	NA	NA
Depr.	55.9	25.4	29.6	19.5	10.4	4.9	1.6	NA	NA	NA
Int. Exp.	0.3	0.2	0.4	0.8	0.1	0.1	0.1	NA	NA	NA
Pretax Inc.	-4.4	38.2	-55.9	24.0	17.7	4.6	3.5	NA	NA	NA
Eff. Tax Rate	NM	31%	NM	36%	27%	19%	54%	NA	NA	NA
Net Inc.	-3.6	26.4	-38.0	15.4	13.0	3.7	2.3	NA	NA	NA
Balance Sheet & Other Fin. Data (Million $)										
Cash	112	108	93.0	32.8	28.3	38.9	NA	NA	NA	NA
Curr. Assets	242	301	232	243	121	91.0	NA	NA	NA	NA
Total Assets	487	357	301	332	148	105	NA	NA	NA	NA
Curr. Liab.	123	115	86.3	81.0	48.4	23.3	NA	NA	NA	NA
LT Debt	13.3	0.4	1.2	3.0	2.4	0.6	NA	NA	NA	NA
Common Eqty.	290	242	213	248	97.8	81.5	NA	NA	NA	NA
Total Cap.	304	242	215	251	100	82.0	NA	NA	NA	NA
Cap. Exp.	15.9	15.7	28.2	42.4	22.5	11.9	6.4	NA	NA	NA
Cash Flow	52.3	51.8	-8.4	35.0	23.4	8.6	3.1	NA	NA	NA
Curr. Ratio	2.0	2.6	2.7	3.0	2.5	3.9	NA	NA	NA	NA
% LT Debt of Cap.	4.4	0.0	0.6	1.8	2.4	0.7	NA	NA	NA	NA
% Net Inc.of Revs.	NM	5.6	NM	3.8	6.4	3.3	4.5	NA	NA	NA
% Ret. on Assets	NM	8.0	NM	6.0	10.3	5.3	NA	NA	NA	NA
% Ret. on Equity	NM	11.6	NM	8.2	14.5	9.7	NA	NA	NA	NA

Data as orig reptd.; bef. results of disc opers/spec. items. Per share data adj. for stk. divs. Bold denotes diluted EPS (FASB 128)-prior periods restated. E-Estimated. NA-Not Available. NM-Not Meaningful. NR-Not Ranked.

Office—One Park West, Avid Technology Park, Tewksbury, MA 01876. **Tel**—(978) 640-6789. **Website**—http://www.avid.com **Chrmn & CEO**—W. J. Miller. **Pres & COO**—C. A. Jenks. **SVP-Fin & CFO**—W. L. Flaherty. **Investor Contact**—Rick Gaisser (978) 640-3563.**Dirs**—C. T. Brumback, P. C. Gotcher, R. M. Halperin, N. Hawthorne, R. J. Heinen Jr., D. Langlois, W. J. Miller, L. S. Salhany, W. J. Warner. **Transfer Agent & Registrar**—Boston EquiServe, L.P., Canton, MA. **Incorporated**—in Delaware in 1987. **Empl**— 1,929. **S&P Analyst:** Matthew C. Hershberg

Aztar Corp.

NYSE Symbol **AZR**

In S&P SmallCap 600

09-OCT-99

Industry: Gaming, Lottery & Pari-mutuel Cos.

Summary: AZR operates casino/hotels in Atlantic City and Nevada, as well as casino boats in Evansville, IN, and Caruthersville, MO.

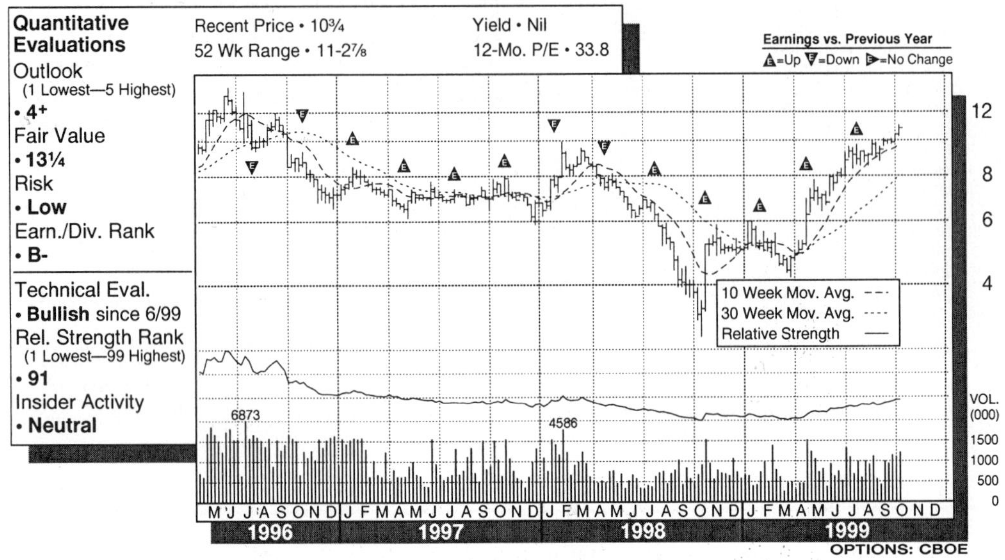

Business Profile - 23-JUL-99

In February 1999, AZR extended its option to purchase its partner's interest in the Tropicana Las Vegas through February 2002. With the opening of many destination resorts on the famed Las Vegas Strip, AZR expects a revitalization of the Las Vegas market. As the current wave of new mega-resorts comes on line, and the market eventually absorbs this capacity, the company believes the development potential of the Tropicana site will become more focused. With regard to its East Coast operations, AZR said the Atlantic City market continued to show strong momentum in the 1999 second quarter, giving the company the opportunity to use its large room base to capitalize on strong and growing consumer demand for casino entertainment in the booming Northeast gaming market.

Operational Review - 23-JUL-99

Revenues in the six months ended June 30, 1999, slid fractionally, year to year, as a 3.4% drop in casino revenues outweighed gains in room, food and beverage, and other revenues. Margins widened slightly; operating income advanced 10%. With a 3.2% drop in net interest expense, after taxes at 38.0%, versus 39.5%, income more than doubled, to $8,765,000 ($0.18 a share), from $4,337,000 ($0.09). Results exclude charges for early retirement of debt of $0.09 and $0.03 a share in the respective periods.

Stock Performance - 08-OCT-99

In the past 30 trading days, AZR's shares have increased 18%, compared to a 0.91% fall in the S&P 500. Average trading volume for the past five days was 240,540 shares, compared with the 40-day moving average of 190,518 shares.

Key Stock Statistics

Dividend Rate/Share	Nil	Shareholders	10,600
Shs. outstg. (M)	44.6	Market cap. (B)	$0.482
Avg. daily vol. (M)	0.219	Inst. holdings	53%
Tang. Bk. Value/Share	9.80		
Beta	1.10		

Value of $10,000 invested 5 years ago: $ 16,320

Fiscal Year Ending Dec. 31

	1999	1998	1997	1996	1995	1994
Revenues (Million $)						
1Q	190.5	196.8	189.8	180.2	135.6	130.6
2Q	206.7	203.2	200.4	189.5	145.4	135.8
3Q	—	210.1	201.9	204.3	154.9	146.8
4Q	—	196.1	190.3	203.5	137.0	128.3
Yr.	—	806.1	782.4	777.5	572.9	541.4
Earnings Per Share ($)						
1Q	**0.06**	**0.01**	**0.05**	**0.02**	0.05	0.11
2Q	**0.13**	**0.08**	**0.07**	Nil	0.01	0.17
3Q	—	**0.12**	**0.07**	Nil	0.11	0.19
4Q	—	**0.02**	**-0.11**	**0.42**	-0.31	-0.05
Yr.	—	**0.23**	**0.08**	**0.46**	**-0.15**	0.42

Next earnings report expected: late October

Dividend Data

Initiation of common share dividends is not expected.

Aztar Corporation

Business Summary - 23-JUL-99

Although Aztar operates five casinos in four states, this gaming company is sometimes overshadowed by its larger competitors. AZR's earnings record is lackluster, but the company is sometimes seen as a candidate to be acquired in a consolidating industry. In addition, its Las Vegas casino/hotel site may be redeveloped.

The five gaming projects operated by the company include over 300,000 sq. ft. of casino space, 8,750 slot machines, 325 table games, and about 5,250 hotel rooms.

Like many other gaming companies, AZR has looked to newly legalized casino markets for expansion opportunities. In Indiana, a casino boat that opened in December 1995 has been generating more than 30% of AZR's operating profit. However, a competing casino boat was recently launched, closer to potential customers in the Louisville, KY, area. Since AZR's casino debut in Evansville, IN, it has opened other facilities there, including a 250-room hotel and a parking garage. In Caruthersville, MO, AZR opened a smaller-scale casino boat in April 1995. This casino's relatively remote location, plus the existence of loss limits ($500 per customer) in Missouri, have contributed to lackluster results.

Much of the company's operating profit is generated by its largest casino/hotel, the renamed Tropicana in Atlantic City. Following a 1996 expansion, the Tropicana is one of Atlantic City's biggest casino/hotels, with 1,624 hotel rooms, and about 124,000 sq. ft. of casino space. However, most visitors to Atlantic City are day-trippers, whose per capita spending is relatively small. Atlantic City has 12 casino/hotels, and has yet to approach Las Vegas as an overnight destination market.

In the glitter of Las Vegas, AZR's Tropicana casino/hotel is at the southern end of the famous Strip. The age and island motif of the Tropicana may pale in comparison to neighbors like the castle-themed Excalibur or recently opened New York, New York casino/hotel, but the company is considering a major redevelopment at its increasingly prime Las Vegas location. The Tropicana site and facility are leased by AZR from an unconsolidated partnership in which AZR has a 50% interest. AZR has an option to acquire the other 50% interest. In recent times, the Las Vegas Tropicana, which has 1,875 hotel rooms and about 100,000 sq. ft. of casino space, has been providing AZR with no more than a modest profit.

In Laughlin, NV, about 85 miles south of Las Vegas, AZR operates the Ramada Express, which has a Victorian-era railroad theme, including a train that runs on the property. The facility includes about 1,500 guest rooms, and a 50,000 sq. ft. casino.

Per Share Data ($)										
(Year Ended Dec. 31)	**1998**	**1997**	**1996**	**1995**	**1994**	**1993**	**1992**	**1991**	**1990**	**1989**
Tangible Bk. Val.	9.80	NM	3.46	9.40	9.52	9.13	8.84	8.21	8.05	8.28
Cash Flow	1.38	1.18	1.64	0.88	1.39	1.10	1.14	0.76	0.24	0.05
Earnings	0.23	0.08	0.47	-0.14	0.42	0.28	0.41	0.05	-0.42	-1.18
Dividends	Nil	Nil	Nil	Nil	Nil	Nil	Nil	Nil	Nil	Nil
Payout Ratio	Nil	Nil	Nil	Nil	Nil	Nil	Nil	Nil	Nil	Nil
Prices - High	9 7/8	8 1/2	14 1/8	10 1/2	7 7/8	10 1/8	7 5/8	7 5/8	8 1/4	9
- Low	2 7/8	5 7/8	6 1/2	5 5/8	5 3/8	6	4 5/8	2 3/4	2 3/8	6 1/2
P/E Ratio - High	43	NM	30	NM	19	36	19	NM	NM	NM
- Low	12	NM	14	NM	13	21	11	NM	NM	NM
Income Statement Analysis (Million $)										
Revs.	806	782	777	573	541	519	512	481	508	522
Oper. Inc.	135	119	111	82.0	106	66.2	54.7	35.6	45.1	1.4
Depr.	53.5	51.5	49.4	39.5	37.0	31.6	27.6	27.0	26.5	34.2
Int. Exp.	59.6	62.5	63.1	56.3	52.4	48.9	32.2	32.4	33.4	43.7
Pretax Inc.	19.9	2.3	-2.1	-10.2	18.7	12.4	26.0	2.8	-14.0	-62.2
Eff. Tax Rate	42%	NM	NM	NM	10%	8.30%	37%	2.20%	NM	NM
Net Inc.	11.5	4.4	20.6	-5.0	16.8	11.4	16.4	2.7	-15.9	-47.7
Balance Sheet & Other Fin. Data (Million $)										
Cash	58.6	46.1	44.1	26.5	52.0	40.0	100	82.2	74.1	99
Curr. Assets	122	119	113	73.0	94.0	82.0	158	121	116	149
Total Assets	1,078	1,091	1,120	1,013	915	877	850	638	642	678
Curr. Liab.	100	125	120	102	73.0	74.0	77.0	93.0	94.0	106
LT Debt	488	492	527	496	430	404	378	177	180	181
Common Eqty.	454	444	439	360	357	341	327	311	304	339
Total Cap.	954	943	972	880	821	781	749	520	521	545
Cap. Exp.	25.1	25.1	120	136	54.0	78.0	24.0	22.0	24.0	116
Cash Flow	64.4	55.3	69.3	34.5	53.2	42.3	43.4	28.9	9.7	2.1
Curr. Ratio	1.2	1.0	0.9	0.7	1.3	1.1	2.0	1.3	1.2	1.4
% LT Debt of Cap.	51.1	52.2	54.2	56.4	52.4	51.7	50.5	34.0	34.6	33.2
% Net Inc.of Revs.	1.4	0.6	2.7	NM	3.1	2.2	3.2	0.6	NM	NM
% Ret. on Assets	1.1	0.4	1.9	NM	1.9	1.3	2.2	0.4	NM	NM
% Ret. on Equity	2.4	0.9	5.2	NM	4.6	3.2	5.0	0.6	NM	NM

Data as orig reptd.; bef. results of disc opers/spec. items. Per share data adj. for stk. divs. Bold denotes diluted EPS (FASB 128)-prior periods restated. E-Estimated. NA-Not Available. NM-Not Meaningful. NR-Not Ranked.

Office—2390 E. Camelback Rd., Suite 400, Phoenix, AZ 85016-3452. **Tel**—(602) 381-4100. **Chrmn, Pres & CEO**—P. E. Rubeli. **EVP & CFO**—R. M. Haddock. **Treas**—N. A. Ciarfalia. **VP & Secy**—N. W. Armstrong Jr. **VP & Investor Contact**—Joe C. Cole. **Dirs**—J. B. Bohle, G. M. Burns, E. M. Carson, L. C. Faiss, R. M. Haddock, J. M. Kunkel, J. R. Norton III, R. S. Rosow, P. E. Rubeli, R. Snell, T. W. Thomas. **Transfer Agent & Registrar**—ChaseMellon Shareholder Services, LA. **Incorporated**—in Delaware in 1989. **Empl**— 10,800. **S&P Analyst:** M.I.

STANDARD
&POOR'S
STOCK REPORTS

Baker (J.) Inc.

NASDAQ Symbol **JBAK**

In S&P SmallCap 600

09-OCT-99 **Industry:** Retail (Specialty)

Summary: J. Baker operates specialty apparel store chains and licensed discount footwear departments.

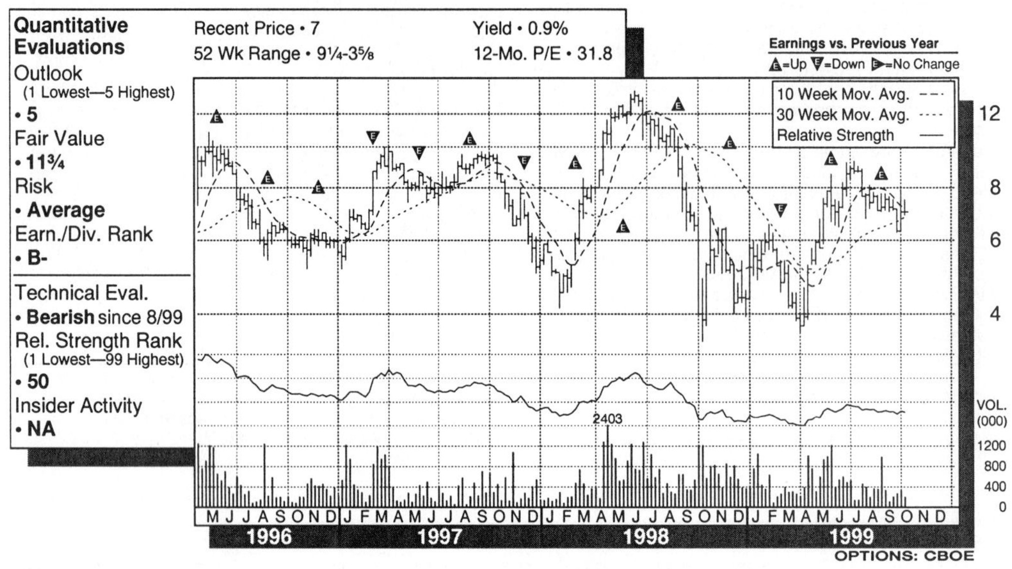

Business Profile - 28-SEP-99

J. Baker recently said that its financial momentum continued in the second quarter of FY 00 (Jan.), aided by the integration of the Repp operations into the company's big and tall business. JBAK recently began remodeling the Repp Big and Tall stores and will be introducing new upscale merchandise at 40-50 Repp Premier locations, 10 of which will be new stores. The company is optimistic about the upcoming Fall selling season, as it begins to transition its stores toward Fall merchandise assortments. In addition, JBAK will be expanding Repp by Mail's e-commerce site in the fourth quarter, which management now believes has the necessary distribution capabilities to successfully execute its Internet strategy.

Operational Review - 28-SEP-99

Net sales for the six months ended July 31, 1999, rose 9.3%, year to year, mainly on initial sales from the acquisition of Repp Ltd. Big and Tall and a 4.7% comparable store sales increase. Margins widened on well-contained cost of sales and SG&A expenses. Operating income advanced 17%. Following smaller increases in depreciation and amortization and interest expenses, pretax income rose 33%. After taxes at 36.0%, versus 39.0%, net income was up 40%, to $4,354,018 ($0.30 a share), from $3,110,508 ($0.22).

Stock Performance - 08-OCT-99

In the past 30 trading days, JBAK's shares have declined 3%, compared to a 0.91% fall in the S&P 500. Average trading volume for the past five days was 39,140 shares, compared with the 40-day moving average of 70,182 shares.

Key Stock Statistics

Dividend Rate/Share	0.06	Shareholders	728
Shs. outstg. (M)	14.1	Market cap. (B)	$0.098
Avg. daily vol. (M)	0.049	Inst. holdings	72%
Tang. Bk. Value/Share	6.07		
Beta	1.25		

Value of $10,000 invested 5 years ago: $ 4,226

Fiscal Year Ending Jan. 31

	2000	1999	1998	1997	1996	1995
Revenues (Million $)						
1Q	129.2	126.6	137.3	195.5	231.4	221.0
2Q	169.3	146.5	143.9	231.8	272.5	256.3
3Q	—	138.3	139.2	222.8	245.3	262.0
4Q	—	172.9	171.7	247.4	271.3	303.3
Yr.	—	584.3	592.1	897.5	1,020	1,043
Earnings Per Share ($)						
1Q	**0.07**	**0.04**	**0.02**	**0.06**	0.05	0.23
2Q	**0.23**	**0.18**	**0.14**	**0.11**	0.10	0.52
3Q	—	**0.05**	**-0.10**	**0.10**	-2.98	0.47
4Q	—	**-0.13**	**0.22**	**-8.29**	0.05	0.49
Yr.	—	**0.14**	**0.27**	**-8.02**	**-2.79**	**1.46**

Next earnings report expected: late November

Dividend Data (Dividends have been paid since 1987.)

Amount ($)	Date Decl.	Ex-Div. Date	Stock of Record	Payment Date
0.015	Dec. 09	Jan. 15	Jan. 20	Jan. 29 '99
0.015	Mar. 30	Apr. 16	Apr. 20	Apr. 30 '99
0.015	Jun. 02	Jul. 16	Jul. 20	Jul. 30 '99
0.015	Sep. 16	Oct. 18	Oct. 20	Oct. 29 '99

J. Baker, Inc.

Business Summary - 28-SEP-99

J. Baker is focused on the retail sale of apparel and footwear sales in three niche markets: big and tall men's apparel and shoes; workwear and uniforms for industry and services businesses; and health care apparel. The company sells footwear through self-service licensed footwear departments in discount department stores.

As of August 1999, the company was operating 452 Casual Male Big & Tall stores, 132 Repp Big and Tall stores, 63 Work 'n Gear stores and 2 Rx stores.

Casual Male Big & Tall is the company's chain of big and tall apparel stores providing fashion, casual and dress clothing and footwear for big and tall men. The chain specializes in a wide range of high quality apparel and accessories for men with waist sizes between 40" and 66" and who are 6'2" or taller. These stores offer private label and brand name casual sportswear and dresswear such as sport coats, dress pants, dress shirts, a wide variety of casual clothing, and shoes. The stores target the middle income male, and limits the amount of high-fashion-oriented and low-turnover tailored clothing offered, and focuses on basic items and classic fashion sportswear, thereby minimizing fashion risk and markdowns.

The Repp Big & Tall stores and the Repp Ltd. By Mail catalog business. were acquired for about $26.2 million in May 1999. These operations had sales of about $18.4 million in the three months ended July 31, 1999.

The Work 'n Gear division is focused entirely on utility workwear, uniforms, health care apparel and footwear. The chain carries a wide variety of workwear products, including rugged specialty outerwear, work shirts and pants, cold weather accessories, and a complete line of health care apparel and uniforms for industry and service businesses. Work 'n Gear stores are generally located in strip shopping centers or are free standing.

The licensed discount shoe division enters into licensing agreements to exclusively operate shoe departments for department stores. Under these agreements, JBAK operates under the store name and pays a licensing fee based on a percentage of sales. This division sells a wide variety of family footwear, including men's, women's and children's dress, casual and athletic footwear, work shoes, boots and slippers. Most of its licensed footwear departments are operated on a self-service basis.

During the past several years, the company has restructured its footwear operations in order to focus its efforts on the development and growth of its Casual Male Big and Tall and Work 'n Gear apparel business. In connection with the restructuring, the company completed the sale of its SCOA and Parade of Shoes businesses in March 1997.

Per Share Data ($)										
(Year Ended Jan. 31)	**1999**	**1998**	**1997**	**1996**	**1995**	**1994**	**1993**	**1992**	**1991**	**1990**
Tangible Bk. Val.	5.56	5.41	5.05	12.36	16.13	14.51	12.81	9.88	9.05	8.40
Cash Flow	1.26	1.35	-5.87	-0.45	3.08	2.74	2.13	1.63	1.45	2.00
Earnings	0.14	0.27	-8.02	-2.79	1.71	1.70	1.25	0.78	0.73	1.46
Dividends	0.06	0.06	0.06	0.06	0.06	0.06	0.06	0.06	0.06	0.06
Payout Ratio	43%	22%	NM	NM	4%	4%	6%	8%	8%	5%
Cal. Yrs.	1998	1997	1996	1995	1994	1993	1992	1991	1990	1989
Prices - High	13⅝	10⅛	10⅞	15⅞	22⅜	25⅞	21¼	14⅛	22⅛	22⅜
- Low	3⅜	5	4	5⅜	14½	15⅜	9⅛	3	3¼	9⅞
P/E Ratio - High	97	37	NM	NM	13	15	17	18	30	15
- Low	25	19	NM	NM	8	9	7	4	4	7
Income Statement Analysis (Million $)										
Revs.	584	592	898	1,020	1,043	919	532	494	421	399
Oper. Inc.	33.5	38.2	7.3	47.8	65.0	58.0	38.6	32.0	29.0	33.7
Depr.	15.8	15.1	29.4	32.4	19.0	14.2	9.4	8.8	7.4	4.9
Int. Exp.	14.7	13.5	13.1	11.0	9.7	8.1	8.2	10.4	10.4	8.9
Pretax Inc.	3.2	6.3	-157	-64.2	36.9	36.4	21.1	12.9	11.3	20.1
Eff. Tax Rate	36%	39%	NM	NM	36%	36%	37%	38%	35%	35%
Net Inc.	2.0	3.8	-110	-38.6	23.6	23.3	13.3	8.0	7.4	13.1
Balance Sheet & Other Fin. Data (Million $)										
Cash	3.7	4.0	4.0	3.3	4.9	3.6	6.4	2.5	4.5	4.5
Curr. Assets	189	192	272	337	374	322	279	198	191	161
Total Assets	324	335	382	526	579	502	432	297	283	237
Curr. Liab.	68.5	69.3	90.2	132	138	135	140	99	81.0	88.0
LT Debt	175	186	214	207	205	155	95.9	79.5	97.5	58.4
Common Eqty.	78.2	75.3	72.0	184	223	200	173	105	92.0	85.0
Total Cap.	253	261	286	391	434	355	271	193	196	149
Cap. Exp.	9.9	8.8	16.4	28.1	44.5	24.1	11.2	5.5	15.0	16.9
Cash Flow	17.8	18.9	-81.6	-6.2	42.6	37.5	22.6	16.8	14.8	18.1
Curr. Ratio	2.8	2.8	3.0	2.5	2.7	2.4	2.0	2.0	2.4	1.8
% LT Debt of Cap.	69.1	71.2	74.8	5.3	47.1	43.6	35.4	41.1	49.7	39.3
% Net Inc.of Revs.	0.3	0.6	NM	NM	2.3	2.5	2.5	1.6	1.8	3.3
% Ret. on Assets	0.6	1.1	NM	NM	4.4	4.9	3.3	2.7	2.8	7.0
% Ret. on Equity	2.7	5.2	NM	NM	11.1	12.4	8.7	8.0	8.3	20.0

Data as orig reptd.; bef. results of disc opers/spec. items. Per share data adj. for stk. divs. Bold denotes diluted EPS (FASB 128)-prior periods restated. E-Estimated. NA-Not Available. NM-Not Meaningful. NR-Not Ranked.

Office—555 Turnpike St., Canton, MA 02021. **Tel**—(781) 828-9300. **Website**—http://www.thinkbig.com**Chrmn**—S. N. Baker. **Pres & CEO**—A. I. Weinstein.**EVP, CFO & Treas**—P. G. Rosenberg.**Clerk**—M. T. Beaudouin.**Dirs**—S. N. Baker, J. C. Clifford, D. J. Kahn, H. Leppo, D. Pulver, T. M. Ronick, M. M. Rosenblatt, N. Ryan, A. I. Weinstein.**Transfer Agent & Registrar**—Fleet National Bank, Providence, RI. **Incorporated**—in Massachusetts in 1985. **Empl**— 6,154. **S&P Analyst:** Matthew C. Hershberg

STANDARD &POOR'S
STOCK REPORTS

Baldor Electric

NYSE Symbol **BEZ**

In S&P SmallCap 600

09-OCT-99

Industry: Electrical Equipment

Summary: Baldor designs, makes and sells a diverse line of industrial electric motors and variable-speed drives.

Quantitative Evaluations

Outlook (1 Lowest—5 Highest)
• **3-**

Fair Value
• **21¾**

Risk
• **Low**

Earn./Div. Rank
• **A**

Technical Eval.
• **Bearish** since 7/99

Rel. Strength Rank (1 Lowest—99 Highest)
• **79**

Insider Activity
• **NA**

Recent Price • 19⅛
52 Wk Range • 22-17¼
Yield • 2.3%
12-Mo. P/E • 16.7

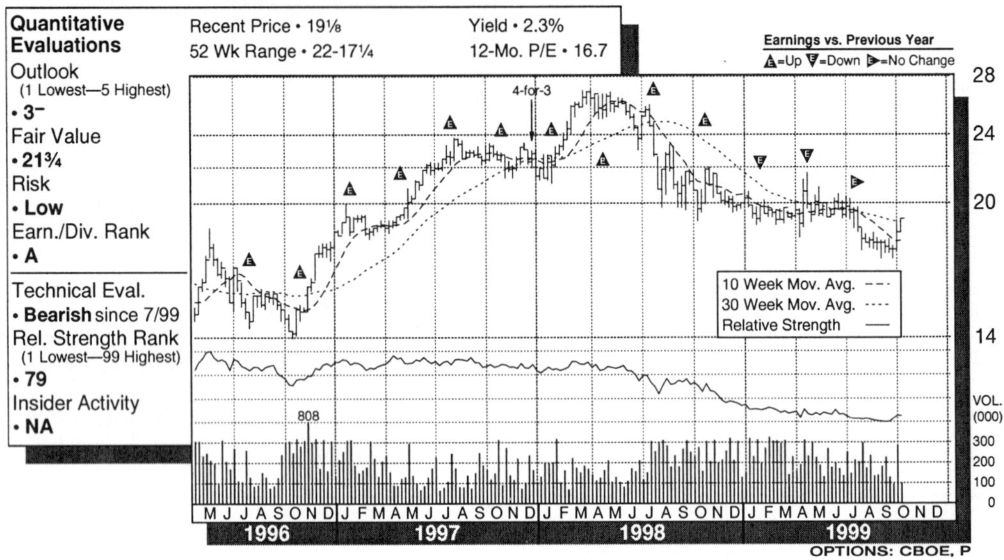

OPTIONS: CBOE, P

Business Profile - 03-JUN-99

This leading manufacturer of industrial electric motors and drives for a wide variety of markets recorded seven consecutive years of rising sales and earnings through 1998. Contributing to Baldor's strong performance were improved productivity, reduced manufacturing costs and successful new product introductions. In September 1998, directors authorized a stock buyback program for up to 1,500,000 common shares; as of early February 1999, over 870,000 shares had been repurchased under the program.

Operational Review - 03-JUN-99

Sales declined 7.8%, year to year, in the three months ended March 31, 1999, reflecting decreased volume. Compared to the fourth quarter of 1998, sales were up 4.7%. Gross margins improved slightly, and pretax income was down 7.3%. After taxes at 38.0% in each quarter, net earnings also fell 7.3%, to $10,731,000 ($0.29 a share), from $11,580,000 ($0.31).

Stock Performance - 08-OCT-99

In the past 30 trading days, BEZ's shares have increased 7%, compared to a 0.91% fall in the S&P 500. Average trading volume for the past five days was 19,500 shares, compared with the 40-day moving average of 32,446 shares.

Key Stock Statistics

Dividend Rate/Share	0.44	Shareholders	5,400
Shs. outstg. (M)	38.6	Market cap. (B)	$0.740
Avg. daily vol. (M)	0.030	Inst. holdings	30%
Tang. Bk. Value/Share	6.88		
Beta	0.52		

Value of $10,000 invested 5 years ago: $ 17,845

Fiscal Year Ending Dec. 31

	1999	1998	1997	1996	1995	1994
Revenues (Million $)						
1Q	142.1	154.2	129.9	121.5	114.6	97.48
2Q	152.1	152.1	141.9	129.9	121.8	104.8
3Q	—	147.4	142.5	125.1	120.0	105.4
4Q	—	135.8	143.6	126.3	116.6	110.4
Yr.	—	589.4	557.9	502.9	473.1	418.1
Earnings Per Share ($)						
1Q	**0.29**	**0.31**	**0.26**	**0.22**	0.20	0.15
2Q	**0.30**	**0.30**	**0.28**	**0.25**	0.21	0.17
3Q	—	**0.29**	**0.27**	**0.25**	0.22	0.18
4Q	—	**0.27**	**0.28**	**0.25**	0.21	0.19
Yr.	—	**1.17**	**1.09**	**0.97**	**0.84**	0.69

Next earnings report expected: mid October

Dividend Data (Dividends have been paid since 1938.)

Amount ($)	Date Decl.	Ex-Div. Date	Stock of Record	Payment Date
0.100	Nov. 02	Dec. 10	Dec. 14	Jan. 04 '99
0.110	Feb. 09	Mar. 08	Mar. 10	Mar. 31 '99
0.110	May. 03	Jun. 14	Jun. 16	Jun. 30 '99
0.110	Aug. 03	Sep. 07	Sep. 09	Sep. 30 '99

A Division of The McGraw-Hill Companies

Baldor Electric Company

Business Summary - 03-JUN-99

Baldor Electric designs, manufactures and markets electric motors and drives. Its products also include speed reducers, industrial grinders, buffers, polishing lathes, stampings and repair parts. The company has made several small acquisitions, but the bulk of its growth has come internally from broadening its markets and product lines. New products introduced in the past five years accounted for 30% of total sales in 1998. Sales of industrial electric motors generated 76% of the total in 1998, while sales of industrial controls (drives) contributed the remaining 23%.

The AC (alternating current) motor product line ranges in size from 1/50 through 1,000 horsepower, and the DC (direct current) motor product line ranges from 1/50 through 700 horsepower. Industrial control products include servo products, brushless DC and SCR controls, and inverter and vector drives.

Motors and drives are manufactured for general-purpose uses (stock products) and for individual customer requirements and specifications (custom products). Stock product sales account for about 63% of the company's business, with most going to customers that place orders for immediate shipment.

Marketing of products is conducted throughout the U.S. and in more than 60 other countries. The field sales organization consists of more than 50 independent manufacturers' representative groups, including 37 in the U.S., with the remainder in Canada, Europe, Latin America, Australia and the Far East. Export and international sales provided 15% of total revenues in 1998 and in the prior two years.

Custom products are sold directly to original equipment manufacturers (OEMs). Stock products are sold to independent distributors for resale, often as replacement components in industrial machinery that is being modernized or upgraded for improved performance.

Many components used in the company's products are manufactured by Baldor itself, including laminations, motor hardware and aluminum die castings. Manufacturing its own components permits the company to achieve a high degree of control over cost, quality and availability. Baldor's motor manufacturing operations also include machining, welding, winding, assembly and finishing operations.

In April 1997, the company acquired Optimised Control Ltd. for a combination of cash and common stock.

Per Share Data ($) (Year Ended Dec. 31)	1998	1997	1996	1995	1994	1993	1992	1991	1990	1989
Tangible Bk. Val.	7.21	6.76	5.73	5.69	5.03	4.47	4.08	3.80	3.57	3.29
Cash Flow	1.71	1.61	1.45	1.25	1.04	0.81	0.71	0.64	0.72	0.64
Earnings	1.17	1.09	0.97	0.84	0.69	0.52	0.42	0.33	0.40	0.38
Dividends	0.40	0.36	0.30	0.25	0.21	0.16	0.14	0.13	0.13	0.12
Payout Ratio	34%	33%	31%	29%	30%	31%	34%	39%	33%	31%
Prices - High	27 1/8	23 7/8	18 3/4	19 7/8	13 3/4	12 3/8	9 3/8	7	6 1/8	6 3/4
- Low	19	18 1/4	13 7/8	13	10 5/8	8 1/8	6 1/8	4 3/8	4 1/2	4 1/4
P/E Ratio - High	23	22	19	24	20	24	23	21	15	18
- Low	16	17	14	15	15	16	15	13	11	11
Income Statement Analysis (Million $)										
Revs.	589	558	503	473	418	357	319	286	294	281
Oper. Inc.	92.2	85.3	74.6	67.2	55.9	42.6	35.9	30.9	34.1	31.5
Depr.	20.5	19.3	17.3	15.5	13.1	10.7	10.8	10.9	10.4	9.3
Int. Exp.	1.7	2.1	2.7	1.3	1.3	1.0	0.9	1.3	1.2	1.4
Pretax Inc.	72.0	65.6	57.2	52.9	43.2	32.4	25.0	19.4	23.2	21.5
Eff. Tax Rate	38%	39%	39%	39%	39%	40%	39%	39%	39%	39%
Net Inc.	44.6	40.4	35.2	32.3	26.4	19.4	15.3	11.9	14.1	13.1
Balance Sheet & Other Fin. Data (Million $)										
Cash	38.8	9.6	25.8	34.8	34.8	30.2	22.7	12.0	7.7	6.8
Curr. Assets	256	219	218	212	181	152	129	117	113	104
Total Assets	412	356	325	313	283	238	212	203	201	186
Curr. Liab.	80.4	78.2	71.2	67.0	62.6	43.4	32.0	32.4	38.0	33.9
LT Debt	57.0	27.9	45.0	25.2	26.3	22.5	23.2	24.4	25.3	22.5
Common Eqty.	264	243	200	211	184	161	145	134	124	115
Total Cap.	332	278	254	246	221	195	180	171	163	152
Cap. Exp.	38.2	26.9	23.2	23.1	22.1	15.0	11.6	9.8	13.7	14.9
Cash Flow	65.1	59.7	52.5	47.9	39.5	30.1	26.0	22.8	24.6	22.4
Curr. Ratio	3.2	2.8	3.1	3.2	2.9	3.5	4.0	3.6	3.0	3.1
% LT Debt of Cap.	17.2	10.0	17.7	10.2	11.9	11.6	12.9	14.3	15.5	14.8
% Net Inc.of Revs.	7.6	7.2	7.0	6.8	6.3	5.4	4.8	4.2	4.8	4.7
% Ret. on Assets	11.6	11.8	11.0	10.8	10.0	8.6	7.3	5.9	7.3	7.4
% Ret. on Equity	17.6	18.2	17.1	16.3	15.2	12.6	10.9	9.2	11.8	11.9

Data as orig. reptd.; bef. results of disc. opers. and/or spec. items. Per share data adj. for stk. divs. as of ex-div. date. Bold denotes diluted EPS (FASB 128). E-Estimated. NA-Not Available. NM-Not Meaningful. NR-Not Ranked.

Office—5711 R.S. Boreham Jr. St., Fort Smith, AR 72908. **Tel**—(501) 646-4711. **Website**—http://www.baldor.com **Chrmn**—R. S. Boreham Jr. **Vice Chrmn**—R. L. Qualls. **Pres & Investor Contact**—John A. McFarland. **EVP-Fin, CFO, Secy & Treas**—L. G. Davis. **Dirs**—J. W. Asher Jr., F. C. Ballman, O. A. Baumann, R. S. Boreham Jr., R. E. Jaudes, J. A. McFarland, R. J. Messey, R. L. Proost, R. L. Qualls. **Transfer Agent & Registrar**—Continental Stock Transfer & Trust Company, NYC. **Incorporated**—in Missouri in 1920. **Empl**— 3,865. **S&P Analyst:** S.A.H.

STANDARD
&POOR'S
STOCK REPORTS

Bangor Hydro-Electric

NYSE Symbol **BGR**

In S&P SmallCap 600

09-OCT-99

Industry:
Electric Companies

Summary: BGR, Maine's second largest electric utility, serves more than 100,000 customers in the eastern and east coastal parts of the state.

Quantitative Evaluations

Outlook (1 Lowest—5 Highest) • **NA**

Fair Value • **NA**

Risk • **Average**

Earn./Div. Rank • **B**

Technical Eval. • **Bullish** since 6/99

Rel. Strength Rank (1 Lowest—99 Highest) • **71**

Insider Activity • **Neutral**

Recent Price • 16½
52 Wk Range • 16⅞-9⅛
Yield • 3.6%
12-Mo. P/E • 9.2

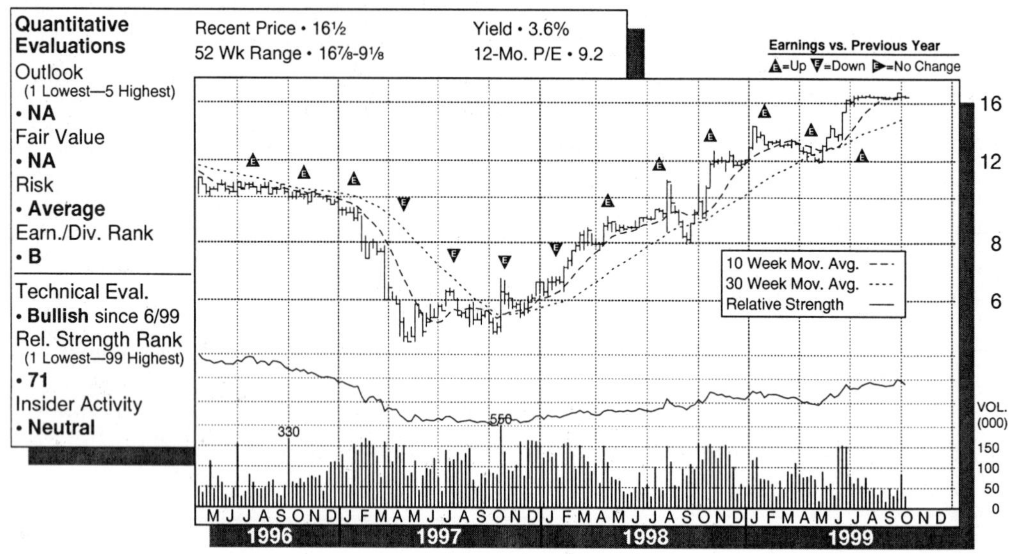

Business Profile - 07-JUN-99

On May 27, 1999, the company sold most of its hydroelectric assets, its interest in an oil-fired generation facility, and certain transmission rights to PP&L Resources, Inc., for $79 million. The transaction reflected a Maine electric utility restructuring law, enacted in 1997, requiring all investor-owned electric utilities to divest their non-nuclear generation assets and generation-related businesses before March 1, 2000. Also in May, the Maine Public Utilities Commission (MPUC) approved a 1.36% increase in the standard tariff charged by BGR to its customers. Results in the last several quarters have benefited from a February 1998 rate increase that boosted annual revenues by $13.2 million.

Operational Review - 07-JUN-99

Revenues in the first three months of 1999 advanced 2.3%, year to year, reflecting increased revenues authorized by the MPUC, as well as a 3.4% increase in kilowatt hour sales. Aided by savings from the restructuring of a major power purchase contract in mid-1998, reduced oil-related and purchased power costs (reflecting a decline in the price of residual oil), and lower expenses associated with the permanent shutdown of the Maine Yankee nuclear plant, operating income climbed 18%. With lower interest expense, net income soared 75%, to $4,212,000 ($0.47 a share, after preferred dividends), from $2,408,000 ($0.28).

Stock Performance - 08-OCT-99

In the past 30 trading days, BGR's shares were unchanged, compared to a 0.91% fall in the S&P 500. Average trading volume for the past five days was 5,800 shares, compared with the 40-day moving average of 8,359 shares.

Key Stock Statistics

Dividend Rate/Share	0.60	Shareholders	7,700
Shs. outstg. (M)	7.4	Market cap. (B)	$0.122
Avg. daily vol. (M)	0.009	Inst. holdings	36%
Tang. Bk. Value/Share	16.14		
Beta	0.63		

Value of $10,000 invested 5 years ago: $ 12,684

Fiscal Year Ending Dec. 31

	1999	1998	1997	1996	1995	1994
Revenues (Million $)						
1Q	50.22	1.33	48.18	48.16	48.30	46.40
2Q	47.30	46.60	42.24	43.15	43.70	39.70
3Q	—	49.16	47.56	47.35	46.02	42.60
4Q	—	50.29	49.36	48.71	46.93	45.50
Yr.	—	195.1	187.3	187.4	184.9	174.1
Earnings Per Share ($)						
1Q	**0.47**	**0.28**	**0.05**	**0.51**	0.40	0.11
2Q	**0.43**	**0.27**	**-0.19**	**0.32**	-0.29	0.22
3Q	—	**0.36**	**-0.07**	**0.26**	0.05	0.37
4Q	—	**0.48**	**-0.47**	**0.24**	0.20	0.12
Yr.	—	**1.33**	**-0.24**	**1.33**	**0.36**	**0.84**

Next earnings report expected: mid October

Dividend Data (Dividends have been paid since 1999.)

Amount ($)	Date Decl.	Ex-Div. Date	Stock of Record	Payment Date
0.150	Jun. 16	Jun. 28	Jun. 30	Jul. 20 '99
0.150	Sep. 15	Sep. 28	Sep. 30	Oct. 20 '99

Bangor Hydro-Electric Company

Business Summary - 07-JUN-99

Despite its name, this electric utility company (the second largest in Maine) obtained only 15% of its electric generation in 1998 from hydroelectric sources. About three-quarters of its power requirements are purchased from the New England Power Pool and others. BGR hasn't used a nuclear power source since December 1996, when the Maine Yankee nuclear plant, in which it had a 7% ownership interest, was shut down due to safety and other concerns.

BGR serves some 106,000 customers in a 5,275 sq. mi. area in eastern and east coastal Maine. Counties served include Penobscot, Hancock, Washington, Waldo, Piscataquis and Aroostook. BGR also sells energy to other utilities for resale.

In 1998, 30% of the company's kilowatt hour (kwh) sales were to residential customers, 31% to commercial customers, and 39% to industrial customers. The maximum peak electric demand experienced during the 1998-98 winter was about 277 megawatts (mw), on December 14, 1998. At that time, BGR had about 339 mw of generating capacity and firm purchased power, comprised of 101 mw from company-owned generating units, 9.6 mw from Hydro Quebec, 53.4 mw from non-utility power producers and 175 mw from short-term economy purchases.

In May 1999, BGR sold substantially all of its hydro-electric generating assets, as well as its interest in an oil-fired generation facility and certain transmission rights, to PP&L Resources, Inc., for $79 million. The sale was in accordance with a Maine law aimed at promoting customer choice in the supply of electricity. The law requires all investor-owned electric utilities to divest their non-nuclear generation assets by March 1, 2000.

On February 9, 1998, the Maine Public Utilities Commission (MPUC) issued a final order on a company request filed in March 1997, to increase its rates. Of the $22 million increase in annual revenues requested, the MPUC authorized an increase of $13.2 million annually. The MPUC order is based upon a determination that BGR should earn an annual return of 12.75% on common equity. It also includes an alternative rate plan under which company rates are subject to certain reconciliations based upon actual expenditures and an annual adjustment beginning May 1, 1999, to account for inflation. On February 16, 1999, BGR filed a request for a rate increase of 2.0% under the alternative rate plan. In May 1999, the MPUC approved an increase of 1.36%.

In August 1997, directors of the Maine Yankee nuclear plant in Wiscasset, ME, voted to cease operations at the plant permanently. Maine Yankee had experienced a number of operational and regulatory problems, and was shut down at the end of 1996.

Per Share Data ($)										
(Year Ended Dec. 31)	**1998**	**1997**	**1996**	**1995**	**1994**	**1993**	**1992**	**1991**	**1990**	**1989**
Tangible Bk. Val.	16.14	14.34	14.71	14.13	14.50	15.09	15.17	14.86	15.16	14.89
Earnings	1.33	-0.24	1.33	0.36	0.84	0.63	1.60	1.33	1.52	1.91
Dividends	Nil	Nil	0.72	0.87	1.32	1.32	1.32	1.29	1.25	1.18
Payout Ratio	Nil	Nil	54%	NM	163%	223%	83%	105%	82%	62%
Prices - High	$12\frac{3}{4}$	$9\frac{1}{2}$	$12\frac{1}{2}$	$12\frac{7}{8}$	19	$24\frac{1}{8}$	$20\frac{1}{4}$	$18\frac{1}{8}$	$16\frac{3}{4}$	$16\frac{3}{4}$
- Low	$6\frac{1}{8}$	$4\frac{7}{8}$	$9\frac{1}{4}$	$9\frac{1}{8}$	$9\frac{3}{8}$	$17\frac{7}{8}$	$16\frac{3}{4}$	$14\frac{1}{4}$	$13\frac{7}{8}$	$13\frac{1}{2}$
P/E Ratio - High	9	NM	9	36	23	38	13	14	11	9
- Low	4	NM	7	25	11	28	10	11	9	7
Income Statement Analysis (Million $)										
Revs.	195	187	187	185	174	178	177	147	134	121
Depr.	11.4	11.9	7.4	6.5	5.4	4.8	4.1	3.8	4.2	4.3
Maint.	NA	32.5	32.4	35.7	33.5	29.5	27.0	25.3	23.9	22.4
Fxd. Chgs. Cov.	NA	0.9	1.5	1.2	1.7	1.4	2.3	NA	NA	NA
Constr. Credits	1.1	0.8	1.1	1.3	2.6	5.3	2.4	NA	NA	NA
Eff. Tax Rate	37%	NM	30%	29%	33%	28%	37%	32%	36%	36%
Net Inc.	11.5	-0.4	11.3	4.3	7.5	5.3	10.3	8.2	8.4	8.8
Balance Sheet & Other Fin. Data (Million $)										
Gross Prop.	367	353	342	324	304	282	256	232	210	188
Cap. Exp.	18.2	17.5	18.8	19.5	21.5	37.6	24.3	NA	NA	NA
Net Prop.	265	256	254	242	228	210	188	166	146	127
Capitalization:										
LT Debt	263	222	274	288	116	119	101	82.0	99	67.0
% LT Debt	67	65	69	71	48	51	50	45	53	44
Pfd.	12.3	13.9	15.4	16.8	18.5	19.9	19.8	19.8	19.8	19.7
% Pfd.	3.13	4.00	3.90	4.20	7.70	8.60	9.80	11	11	13
Common	119	107	108	103	106	94.0	82.0	80.0	68.0	66.0
% Common	30	31	27	25	44	40	40	44	36	43
Total Cap.	475	414	472	480	311	301	245	225	216	187
% Oper. Ratio	71.8	75.3	80.7	87.2	90.1	90.6	89.5	NA	NA	NA
% Earn. on Net Prop.	13.5	9.4	14.7	10.1	7.9	8.4	10.5	NA	NA	NA
% Return On Revs.	5.9	NM	6.1	2.4	4.3	3.0	5.8	5.6	6.2	7.3
% Return On Invest. Capital	19.3	5.1	9.1	7.6	6.1	5.2	8.6	NA	NA	NA
% Return On Com. Equity	9.1	NM	9.1	2.5	5.5	3.9	10.6	8.2	10.1	13.1

Data as orig reptd.; bef. results of disc opers/spec. items. Per share data adj. for stk. divs. Bold denotes diluted EPS (FASB 128)-prior periods restated. E-Estimated. NA-Not Available. NM-Not Meaningful. NR-Not Ranked.

Office—33 State St. (P.O. Box 932), Bangor, ME 04402-0932. **Tel**—(207) 945-5621. **Fax**—(207) 990-6954. **Chrmn, Pres & CEO**—R. S. Briggs. **SVP & COO**—C. R. Lee. **VP-Fin, Treas & Investor Contact**—Frederick S. Samp. **Secy**—A. Landry. **Dirs**—R. S. Briggs, W. C. Bullock Jr., J. J. Bush, D. M. Carlisle, J. H. Cyr, M. M. Kane, N. A. Ledwin, C. R. Lee, J. E. Rier, Jr. **Transfer Agent & Registrar**—ChaseMellon Shareholder Services, Ridgefield Park, NJ. **Incorporated**—in Maine in 1924. **Empl**— 434. **S&P Analyst:** S.A.H.

STANDARD &POOR'S
STOCK REPORTS

Banknorth Group

NASDAQ Symbol **BKNG**

In S&P SmallCap 600

09-OCT-99

Industry:
Banks (Regional)

Summary: This New England-based multibank holding company recently agreed to be acquired by Peoples Heritage Financial Group in a transaction valued at $781 million.

Quantitative Evaluations

Outlook (1 Lowest—5 Highest) • **2-**

Fair Value • **29¼**

Risk • **Low**

Earn./Div. Rank • **B**

Technical Eval. • **Bearish** since 8/99

Rel. Strength Rank (1 Lowest—99 Highest) • **73**

Insider Activity • **Neutral**

Recent Price • 31
52 Wk Range • 37⅞-24¾
Yield • 2.3%
12-Mo. P/E • 20.7

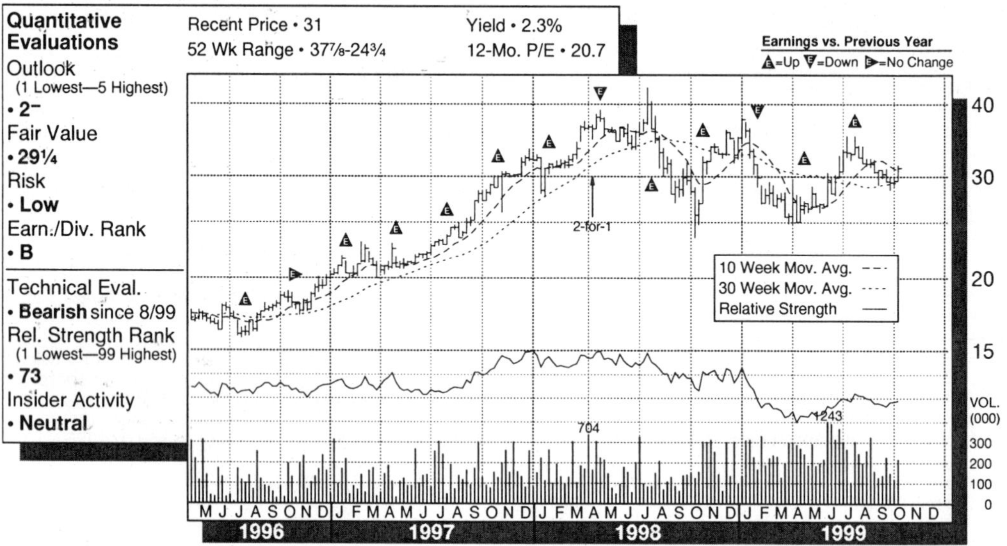

Business Profile - 12-JUL-99

In June 1999, Banknorth agreed to be acquired by Peoples Heritage Financial Group, Inc. (Nasdaq: PHBK) in a transaction valued at $780.7 million. The acquisition will create a $17 billion multi-state banking and financial services company. Shareholders of BKNG will receive 1.825 shares of Peoples Heritage common stock for each whole share of BKNG, plus cash in lieu of any fractional share interest. The transaction is subject to approval by shareholders of both companies and regulatory approvals and is expected to close by year-end 1999, with the operational conversion expected to be completed during the second quarter of 2000. Peoples Heritage will take on the Banknorth name.

Operational Review - 12-JUL-99

Net interest income for the three months ended March 31, 1999, advanced 7.0%, year to year, as an increase in average earning assets was partially offset by a narrowing of the net interest margin. Noninterest income increased 67%, on higher ATM, mortgage banking, and investment management income, as well as a $2.6 million gain from the curtailment of the Evergreen pension plan. Noninterest expenses rose 12%, including merger related expenses of $1.2 million. After taxes at 31.6%, versus 30.8%, net income rose 36%, to $13.5 million ($0.57 a share), from $9.9 million ($0.42).

Stock Performance - 08-OCT-99

In the past 30 trading days, BKNG's shares have increased 2%, compared to a 0.91% fall in the S&P 500. Average trading volume for the past five days was 43,160 shares, compared with the 40-day moving average of 44,256 shares.

Key Stock Statistics

Dividend Rate/Share	0.72	Shareholders	4,184
Shs. outstg. (M)	23.3	Market cap. (B)	$0.722
Avg. daily vol. (M)	0.035	Inst. holdings	46%
Tang. Bk. Value/Share	10.17		
Beta	0.93		

Value of $10,000 invested 5 years ago: $ 36,148

Fiscal Year Ending Dec. 31

	1999	1998	1997	1996	1995	1994
Revenues (Million $)						
1Q	92.69	63.18	57.61	49.02	41.84	32.75
2Q	92.91	65.53	60.89	53.91	43.26	34.41
3Q	—	66.45	64.32	55.63	44.37	36.62
4Q	—	90.30	67.01	56.75	44.06	40.61
Yr.	—	350.2	249.8	215.3	173.5	144.4
Earnings Per Share ($)						
1Q	**0.57**	**0.44**	0.45	0.32	0.39	0.17
2Q	**0.60**	**0.53**	0.45	0.43	0.40	0.25
3Q	—	**0.58**	0.48	0.43	0.43	0.33
4Q	—	**-0.19**	**0.55**	0.45	0.43	0.42
Yr.	—	**1.22**	**1.93**	**1.64**	**1.64**	**1.18**

Next earnings report expected: mid October

Dividend Data (Dividends have been paid since 1993.)

Amount ($)	Date Decl.	Ex-Div. Date	Stock of Record	Payment Date
0.160	Nov. 05	Nov. 18	Nov. 20	Dec. 04 '98
0.180	Jan. 26	Feb. 17	Feb. 19	Mar. 05 '99
0.180	Mar. 25	May. 19	May. 21	Jun. 04 '99
0.180	Aug. 09	Aug. 18	Aug. 20	Sep. 03 '99

A Division of The McGraw-Hill Companies

Banknorth Group, Inc.

Business Summary - 12-JUL-99

In June 1999, Banknorth Group agreed to be acquired by Peoples Heritage Financial Group, Inc. (Nasdaq: PHBK) in a transaction valued at $780.7 million. Shareholders of Banknorth will receive 1.825 shares of Peoples Heritage for each whole share of BKNG, plus cash for any fractional shares. The transaction is subject to approval by shareholders of both companies and regulatory approvals and is expected to close by year-end 1999, with operational integration expected to be completed during the second quarter of 2000.

Through internal growth and acquisitions, BKNG has become the largest multibank holding company in Vermont, operating 101 branch offices through eight community banks in New York, Massachusetts, New Hampshire and Vermont. In addition, the bank offers mortgage banking services and investment and asset management.

Interest on loans contributes the majority of income to the bank. Loans outstanding totaled $2.8 billion at December 31, 1998. Loans at the end of recent years were divided as follows: residential real estate 37% (41% in 1997), commercial, financial, and agricultural 24% (22%), commercial real estate 22% (21%), installment 12% (11%), lease and credit card receivables 4% (4%), and construction and development 1% (1%).

Banks must regularly reserve against potential losses. Banknorth's allowance for possible loan losses represented 1.6% of total loans at 1998 year-end, up from 1.5% a year earlier. Asset quality has improved over the past several years, as nonperforming assets declined to 0.55% of total assets in 1998, from 0.59% in 1997, and net chargeoffs declined to 0.21% of average total loans, from 0.26%, over the same period.

Deposits represent the main (and most cost effective) source of funds to the bank. At year-end 1998, total deposits were $3.6 billion, and were apportioned: noninterest bearing demand 15%, NOW accounts and money market savings 41%, regular savings 9%, time deposits under $100,000 28%, and time deposits $100,000 and greater 7%.

Lending profitability, commonly measured by the yield on a bank's average earning assets, or the net interest margin, is affected by changes in the mix and volume of assets and liabilities, as well as changes in interest rates. During 1998, Banknorth saw a narrowing of its net interest margin, to 4.34%, from 4.58% in 1997, as lower yields on average earning assets combined with a higher cost of funds.

In November 1998, BKNG purchased ten full-service branches from BankBoston, representing $291.5 million in deposits. These branches became part of First Massachusetts Bank, a subsidiary bank of Banknorth. In December 1998, BKNG acquired Evergreen Bank, which had $1.1 billion in assets at year-end 1998.

Per Share Data ($) (Year Ended Dec. 31)	1998	1997	1996	1995	1994	1993	1992	1991	1990	1989
Tangible Bk. Val.	10.17	12.84	10.90	10.88	9.04	9.73	9.36	9.21	9.46	9.47
Earnings	1.22	1.93	1.65	1.65	1.17	0.84	0.16	-0.27	0.55	1.31
Dividends	0.64	0.58	0.50	0.46	0.30	0.20	Nil	Nil	0.54	0.49
Payout Ratio	52%	30%	30%	28%	26%	24%	Nil	Nil	99%	37%
Prices - High	42¾	33½	20¾	19¾	13	10¾	7¾	5¾	9⅝	12
- Low	23½	20	15¾	10⅞	8⅞	6⅞	4⅛	2⅝	4⅛	7¾
P/E Ratio - High	35	17	13	12	11	13	48	NM	18	9
- Low	19	10	10	7	8	8	25	NM	8	6
Income Statement Analysis (Million $)										
Net Int. Inc.	164	119	109	84.6	74.8	68.5	65.1	70.3	70.0	72.4
Tax Equiv. Adj.	1.6	0.6	0.6	0.7	0.5	0.6	0.9	1.3	2.0	2.3
Non Int. Inc.	41.0	31.1	25.3	21.3	22.2	23.6	23.6	19.5	23.8	21.4
Loan Loss Prov.	9.3	7.7	5.6	4.4	3.1	4.0	13.1	29.3	20.2	7.2
Exp./Op. Revs.	74%	65%	68%	66%	72%	78%	82%	76%	67%	64%
Pretax Inc.	43.4	45.3	37.4	30.6	21.6	16.7	2.3	-8.8	9.4	25.8
Eff. Tax Rate	33%	33%	32%	27%	27%	31%	7.00%	NM	21%	31%
Net Inc.	28.9	30.5	25.4	22.4	15.9	11.5	2.2	-3.7	7.4	17.8
% Net Int. Marg.	4.34	4.57	4.86	4.79	4.65	4.68	4.52	4.73	4.75	4.81
Balance Sheet & Other Fin. Data (Million $)										
Money Mkt. Assets	NA	85.8	92.0	90.0	86.0	70.0	108	85.0	108	115
Inv. Securities	1,148	734	565	409	436	403	292	337	266	235
Com'l Loans	1,306	332	301	628	588	553	543	554	653	635
Other Loans	1,531	1,628	1,547	723	708	566	538	613	581	639
Total Assets	4,403	2,923	2,601	1,910	1,874	1,662	1,562	1,660	1,654	1,627
Demand Deposits	546	324	288	402	428	363	381	741	715	709
Time Deposits	3,093	1,876	1,778	1,159	1,015	900	957	684	746	710
LT Debt	104	16.5	26.0	56.0	122	96.8	17.6	14.0	NM	0.5
Common Eqty.	321	230	207	160	136	132	127	125	129	124
% Ret. on Assets	0.8	1.1	1.1	1.2	0.9	0.7	0.1	NM	0.5	1.1
% Ret. on Equity	10.5	14.0	13.8	15.1	12.1	8.9	1.7	NM	5.7	14.3
% Loan Loss Resv.	1.6	1.3	1.3	1.6	1.7	1.9	2.0	1.9	2.0	1.2
% Loans/Deposits	78.0	88.4	89.4	86.6	89.7	88.6	80.8	80.4	82.7	87.3
% Equity to Assets	7.5	7.9	8.1	7.8	7.6	8.1	7.8	7.8	8.0	7.6

Data as orig. reptd.; bef. results of disc opers. and/or spec. items. Per share data adj. for stk. divs. as of ex-div. date. Bold denotes diluted EPS (FASB 128). E-Estimated. NA-Not Available. NM-Not Meaningful. NR-Not Ranked.

Office—300 Financial Plaza, P.O. Box 5420, Burlington, VT 05401. **Tel**—(802) 658-9959. **Website**—http://www.banknorth.com **Chrmn**—A. P. Pizzagalli. **Pres & CEO**—W. H. Chadwick. **EVP, CFO & Investor Contact**—Thomas J. Pruitt (802-860-5558). **Treas**—N. E. Robinson. **Secy**—T. M. Dowling. **Dirs**—T. J. Amidon, J. D. Arthur, R. A. Carrara, W. H. Chadwick, S. C. Crampton, G. W. Dougan, R. F. Flacke, L. F. Hackett, K. Hoisington, D. G. Hyde, A. J. Mashuta, A. P. Pizzagalli, J. B. Packard, T. P. Salmon, P. E. Welch. **Transfer Agent & Registrar**—Registrar and Transfer Co., Cranford, NJ. **Incorporated**—in Delaware in 1989. **Empl**— 1,153. **S&P Analyst:** J. Rudy

STANDARD &POOR'S
STOCK REPORTS

Barnes Group

NYSE Symbol **B**

In S&P SmallCap 600

09-OCT-99

Industry: Manufacturing (Diversified)

Summary: Barnes is a diversified maker of precision springs and complex aerospace components, and a major direct-to-user distributor of industrial maintenance and repair products.

Quantitative Evaluations

Outlook (1 Lowest—5 Highest)
• **NA**

Fair Value
• **NA**

Risk
• **Low**

Earn./Div. Rank
• **B+**

Technical Eval.
• **Bullish** since 9/99

Rel. Strength Rank (1 Lowest—99 Highest)
• **62**

Insider Activity
• **NA**

Recent Price • 21⅛
52 Wk Range • 31⅞-15⅞
Yield • 3.6%
12-Mo. P/E • 11.8

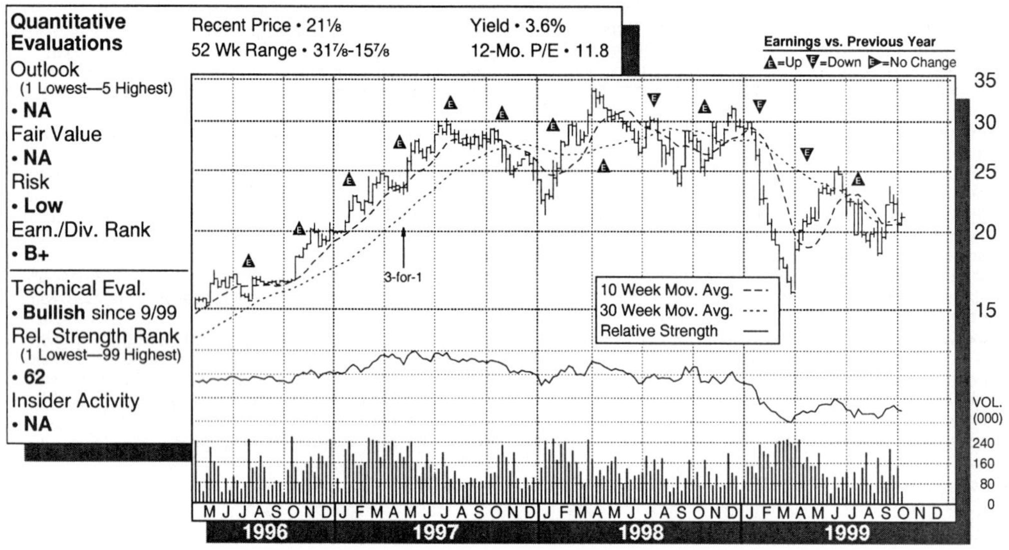

Business Profile - 29-SEP-99

Barnes said in July 1999 that while second quarter 1999 results were disappointing, it continued to remain committed to achieving balanced, sustainable, and profitable growth. In spite of the overall flattening of business in the aerospace market, B has aggressive plans in place to broaden its customer base and develop new business. The company's Associated Spring unit recently sold its Arden, NC, facility, and consolidated its operations into Milwaukee, WI, and Mexico facilities. B acquired the nitrogen gas springs business of Teledyne Fluid Systems for $89.7 million in August, 1999.

Operational Review - 29-SEP-99

Net sales for the first half of 1999 declined 5.8%, year to year, reflecting decreases in all segments. However, higher profits at Associated Spring and absence of prior-year costs related to a former CEO retirement package outweighed lower earnings for Bowman Distribution and Barnes Aerospace. Following higher other income and slightly lower interest expense, pretax income was up 8.3%. After taxes at 36.5%, versus 37.5%, net income moved ahead 10%, to $18.1 million ($0.91 a share), from $16.5 million ($0.81).

Stock Performance - 08-OCT-99

In the past 30 trading days, B's shares have increased 14%, compared to a 0.91% fall in the S&P 500. Average trading volume for the past five days was 9,460 shares, compared with the 40-day moving average of 23,813 shares.

Key Stock Statistics

Dividend Rate/Share	0.76	Shareholders	2,985
Shs. outstg. (M)	19.4	Market cap. (B)	$0.409
Avg. daily vol. (M)	0.026	Inst. holdings	49%
Tang. Bk. Value/Share	8.89		
Beta	0.75		

Value of $10,000 invested 5 years ago: $ 24,482

Fiscal Year Ending Dec. 31

	1999	1998	1997	1996	1995	1994
Revenues (Million $)						
1Q	162.3	168.9	158.1	150.1	158.6	142.1
2Q	156.3	169.2	165.9	152.6	151.0	143.2
3Q	—	158.3	158.5	147.1	141.7	140.3
4Q	—	154.9	160.1	145.2	141.2	143.7
Yr.	—	651.2	642.7	595.0	592.5	569.2
Earnings Per Share ($)						
1Q	**0.50**	**0.58**	**0.49**	**0.33**	0.43	0.26
2Q	**0.41**	**0.23**	**0.52**	**0.43**	0.37	0.29
3Q	—	**0.52**	**0.49**	**0.43**	0.32	0.28
4Q	—	**0.36**	**0.46**	**0.42**	0.28	0.24
Yr.	—	**1.69**	**1.96**	**1.63**	**1.38**	1.07

Next earnings report expected: mid October

Dividend Data (Dividends have been paid since 1934.)

Amount ($)	Date Decl.	Ex-Div. Date	Stock of Record	Payment Date
0.180	Oct. 16	Nov. 27	Dec. 01	Dec. 10 '98
0.180	Feb. 19	Feb. 25	Mar. 01	Mar. 10 '99
0.190	Apr. 14	May. 27	Jun. 01	Jun. 10 '99
0.190	Jul. 16	Aug. 27	Aug. 31	Sep. 10 '99

Barnes Group Inc.

Business Summary - 29-SEP-99

Barnes Group Inc. is a diversified international manufacturer and distributor, serving a range of industrial and transportation markets with precision metal parts and industrial supplies. The company, which is headquartered in Bristol, CT, was founded in 1857.

Profits by business segment were obtained as follows in 1998: Associated Spring 32%, Bowman Distribution 47%, and Barnes Aerospace 20%. International operations accounted for 21% of sales.

Associated Spring makes a wide range of custom metal parts for mechanical purposes. It is equipped to produce nearly every type of spring requiring precision engineering, as well as an extensive line of precision metal components and assemblies. Its products range in size from fine hairsprings for instruments to large springs for heavy machinery, and its output of a given metal part may vary in amount from a few units to several million. The unit does not produce leaf springs or bed springs.

The automotive and automotive parts industries constitute Associated's largest single custom metal parts market. Other important outlets include manufacturers of industrial and textile machinery, motors, generators, electronic equipment, aircraft, diesel and other internal combustion engines, household appliances and fixtures, hardware, office equipment, agricultural equipment, railroad equipment, general machinery and scientific instruments.

Bowman Distribution markets a variety of replacement parts and other products, including fasteners and special purpose hardware, general purpose electric and gas welding supplies, and industrial maintenance supplies. It is also engaged in the distribution of die springs which are sold under the company's Raymond trademark and certain standard parts consisting primarily of coil and flat springs (which are made primarily by the Associated Spring unit).

Sales by Bowman Distribution in the U.S. and Canada are primarily to industrial and food processing plants, chemical and petrochemical process industries, contractors, new-car dealers, garages, service stations, operators of vehicle fleets, railroads, electric utilities and airline ground maintenance facilities.

Barnes Aerospace is engaged in the advanced fabrication and precision machining of components for jet engines and airframes, the repair and overhaul of jet engine components, the manufacture of machined and fabricated parts and assemblies, the refurbishing of jet engine components, and the hot forming and fabrication of titanium and other high-temperature alloys for use in precision details and assemblies for aircraft engine and airframe applications.

Per Share Data ($) (Year Ended Dec. 31)	1998	1997	1996	1995	1994	1993	1992	1991	1990	1989
Tangible Bk. Val.	8.59	8.04	6.89	5.53	4.49	3.74	3.85	6.21	5.58	4.83
Cash Flow	3.13	3.39	2.97	2.76	2.31	1.47	1.59	1.94	1.88	1.61
Earnings	1.69	2.00	1.63	1.40	1.07	0.23	0.31	0.87	0.92	0.65
Dividends	0.69	0.65	0.60	0.53	0.48	0.47	0.47	0.47	0.47	0.47
Payout Ratio	41%	33%	37%	38%	45%	NM	149%	54%	51%	76%
Prices - High	34	30$^{3}/_{8}$	20$^{5}/_{8}$	15$^{1}/_{4}$	13$^{1}/_{4}$	11	12	12$^{5}/_{8}$	10$^{1}/_{2}$	12$^{7}/_{8}$
- Low	21$^{1}/_{4}$	19$^{3}/_{4}$	11$^{5}/_{8}$	12	9$^{7}/_{8}$	10	9$^{3}/_{8}$	8$^{5}/_{8}$	8	9$^{5}/_{8}$
P/E Ratio - High	20	15	13	11	12	47	38	15	11	20
- Low	13	10	7	9	9	43	30	10	9	15
Income Statement Analysis (Million $)										
Revs.	651	643	595	593	569	502	529	536	546	511
Oper. Inc.	83.7	93.9	81.9	75.6	60.4	40.5	48.8	57.8	58.7	57.1
Depr.	28.4	28.1	26.6	26.8	23.7	23.1	23.7	19.8	17.5	16.6
Int. Exp.	4.1	4.9	5.0	5.3	5.1	5.2	6.6	8.9	10.2	10.2
Pretax Inc.	54.7	64.5	52.3	45.5	33.9	8.4	7.7	28.8	30.0	23.1
Eff. Tax Rate	37%	37%	38%	39%	40%	48%	24%	45%	44%	47%
Net Inc.	34.5	40.4	32.6	27.5	20.3	4.4	5.8	15.9	16.8	12.4
Balance Sheet & Other Fin. Data (Million $)										
Cash	42.8	32.5	24.0	17.7	22.0	24.1	39.1	21.4	17.0	18.0
Curr. Assets	207	203	190	173	176	169	186	191	193	189
Total Assets	419	408	390	362	352	333	348	342	342	328
Curr. Liab.	100	89.9	80.1	77.5	87.0	82.0	93.0	88.0	102	100
LT Debt	51.0	62.0	75.0	77.5	79.8	82.0	84.0	94.3	96.3	98.3
Common Eqty.	189	181	157	129	107	92.0	94.0	139	126	113
Total Cap.	240	243	232	206	190	177	180	246	233	219
Cap. Exp.	35.5	33.3	33.9	35.9	31.8	22.2	10.2	19.1	21.6	18.2
Cash Flow	62.9	68.5	59.2	54.2	44.0	27.5	29.6	39.1	34.3	27.7
Curr. Ratio	2.1	2.3	2.4	2.2	2.0	2.1	2.0	2.2	1.9	1.9
% LT Debt of Cap.	21.3	25.5	32.3	37.6	42.1	46.4	46.6	38.4	41.3	44.8
% Net Inc.of Revs.	5.3	6.3	5.5	4.6	3.6	0.9	1.1	3.0	3.1	2.4
% Ret. on Assets	8.3	10.1	8.7	7.7	5.9	1.3	1.7	4.6	5.0	3.7
% Ret. on Equity	18.7	23.9	22.8	23.2	20.2	4.7	5.0	11.9	14.0	9.4

Data as orig reptd.; bef. results of disc opers/spec. items. Per share data adj. for stk. divs. Bold denotes diluted EPS (FASB 128)-prior periods restated. E-Estimated. NA-Not Available. NM-Not Meaningful. NR-Not Ranked.

Office—123 Main St., Bristol, CT 06011-0489. **Tel**—(860) 583-7070. **Website**—http://www.barnesgroupinc.com **Chrmn**—T. O. Barnes. **Pres & CEO**—E. M. Carpenter. **VP & Treas**—J. J. Locher. **VP & Secy**—W. V. Grickis Jr. **Investor Contact**—Robert D. LiPira. **Dirs**—T. O. Barnes, G. G. Benanav, W. S. Bristow Jr., R. J. Callander, E. M. Carpenter, G. T. Carpenter, D. R. Ecton, R. W. Fiondella, F. E. Grzelecki, M. P. Joseph. **Transfer Agent & Registrar**—ChaseMellon Shareholder Services, Ridgefield Park, NJ. **Incorporated**—in Delaware in 1925. **Empl**— 3,847. **S&P Analyst:** NJD

STANDARD
&POOR'S
STOCK REPORTS

Barr Laboratories

NYSE Symbol **BRL**

In S&P SmallCap 600

09-OCT-99

Industry:
Health Care (Drugs - Generic & Other)

Summary: This leading generic pharmaceutical manufacturer is also developing and commercializing its own line of proprietary drug products.

Quantitative Evaluations

Outlook
(1 Lowest—5 Highest)
• **5**

Fair Value
• **55⅞**

Risk
• **High**

Earn./Div. Rank
• **B**

Technical Eval.
• **Bearish** since 8/99

Rel. Strength Rank
(1 Lowest—99 Highest)
• **18**

Insider Activity
• **NA**

Recent Price • 29
52 Wk Range • 49¾-28¼
Yield • Nil
12-Mo. P/E • 13.9

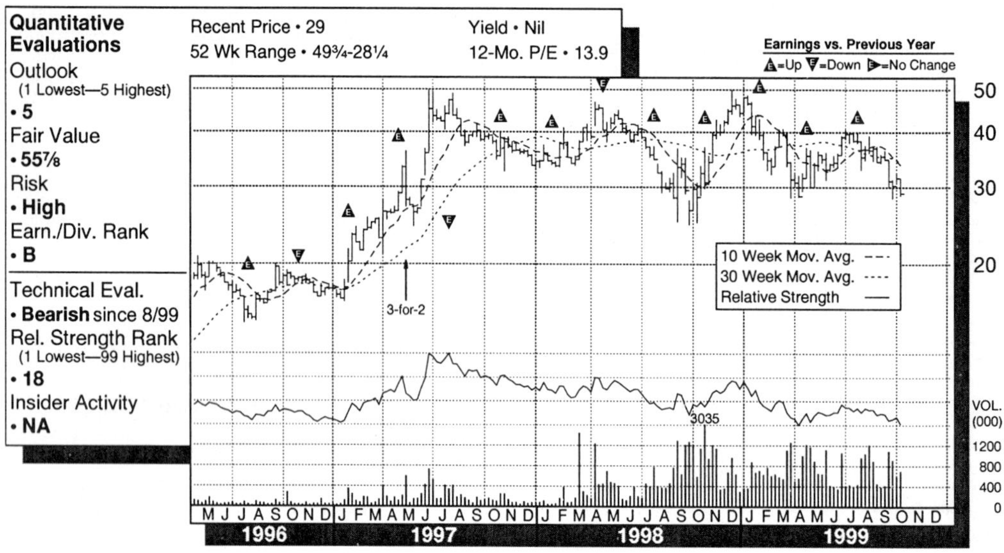

Business Profile - 05-OCT-99

In September 1999, BRL received approval from the FDA to initiate clinical trials on a proprietary drug candidate designed to treat symptoms related to prostate cancer therapy. The company planned to begin testing on its product by year-end 1999. BRL also expected to file an Investigational New Drug application with the FDA for its Seasonale oral contraceptive in the third quarter of FY 00 (Jun.). The company planned to spend between $40 and $45 million on research and development in FY 00. In June 1999, BRL received FDA approval to market Cefadroxil 500 mg capsules, a generic version of Bristol-Myers Squibb's Duricef capsules, which are used in treating certain urinary tract and skin infections.

Operational Review - 05-OCT-99

Total revenues advanced 18% in FY 99 (Jun.), as growth in generic product sales was partially offset by lower proceeds from supply agreements. Gross margins widened on a more favorable product mix, and following well-controlled SG&A costs, net income rose 47%, to $49,250,000 ($2.09 a share), from $33,510,000 ($1.45). Results in 1998 exclude a $0.04 a share loss for the early extinguishment of debt. Cash, cash equivalents, and marketable securities totaled $103 million on June 30, 1999.

Stock Performance - 08-OCT-99

In the past 30 trading days, BRL's shares have declined 15%, compared to a 0.91% fall in the S&P 500. Average trading volume for the past five days was 138,380 shares, compared with the 40-day moving average of 137,869 shares.

Key Stock Statistics

Dividend Rate/Share	Nil	Shareholders	665
Shs. outstg. (M)	22.8	Market cap. (B)	$0.662
Avg. daily vol. (M)	0.163	Inst. holdings	34%
Tang. Bk. Value/Share	6.99		
Beta	1.37		

Value of $10,000 invested 5 years ago: $ 33,108

Fiscal Year Ending Jun. 30

	1999	1998	1997	1996	1995	1994
Revenues (Million $)						
1Q	97.15	96.27	64.23	54.18	44.05	13.20
2Q	109.2	92.33	67.34	57.47	50.88	25.62
3Q	122.6	96.39	84.71	60.09	49.29	29.68
4Q	115.1	92.32	68.21	60.50	55.51	40.64
Yr.	444.0	377.3	284.5	232.2	199.7	109.1
Earnings Per Share ($)						
1Q	**0.48**	0.45	0.08	0.10	0.09	Nil
2Q	**0.52**	**0.31**	**0.10**	0.09	0.11	0.01
3Q	**0.54**	**0.31**	0.67	0.06	0.05	0.03
4Q	**0.56**	**0.38**	0.02	0.07	0.06	0.08
Yr.	**2.09**	**1.45**	**0.87**	0.33	0.32	0.12

Next earnings report expected: late October

Dividend Data

The company paid a three-for-two stock split on May 7, 1997.

Barr Laboratories, Inc.

Business Summary - 23-SEP-99

Founded in 1970, Barr Laboratories, Inc. is a leading developer, producer, and marketer of generic pharmaceuticals, with a product focus on the following six core therapeutic areas: oncology, female healthcare, cardiovascular, anti-infective, pain management, and psychotherapeutics.

BRL's three-pronged business strategy consists of the following elements: the development and marketing of generic pharmaceuticals with certain barriers to entry; challenging potentially weak patents covering select branded pharmaceuticals; and the development and commercialization of proprietary drug products.

As of FY 99 (Jun.), BRL marketed 70 generic and proprietary therapeutics, with Tamoxifen Citrate and Warfarin Sodium being the company's two largest selling products. Tamoxifen (66% of 1999 product sales), a generic version of Nolvadex, is used for treating advanced breast cancer and to impede the recurrence of tumors following surgery. In October 1998, the FDA also approved Tamoxifen for the prevention of breast cancer in women at high risk to develop the disease.

Warfarin Sodium (15% of 1999 product sales) is a generic version of DuPont's anticoagulant Coumadin. During FY 99, BRL became the first company to market Warfarin in all nine available oral dosage strengths. Additional generic products sold by BRL include Naltrexone for treating alcohol dependence; Dyazide for the treatment of hypertension; and Oxycodone/APAP, a narcotic analgesic. As of September 1999, the company also had eight Abbreviated New Drug Applications (ANDA) pending with the FDA for generic drugs.

In September 1998, Preven Emergency Contraceptive Kit became the firm's first proprietary drug to gain FDA approval. Co-developed with marketing partner, Gynetics, Inc., Preven is the first FDA approved product designed to prevent pregnancy if taken within 72 hours of unprotected intercourse. As of September 1999, BRL had ten additional proprietary compounds in development, which included four cancer products, three oral contraceptives, one hormonal product, an anti-viral therapy, and a psycho-therapeutic product.

As of September 1999, the company was challenging a patent on Eli Lilly's drug Prozac. In addition, BRL was challenging a patent on Ortho Pharmaceutical's Ortho-Novum 7/7/7 oral contraceptive. If BRL is successful at challenging a patent, it will develop and file for approval of a generic version of the product.

In January 1997, BRL successfully challenged Bayer AG's patent for the antibiotic Ciprofloxacin (generic for Cipro). The company received rights to market generic Ciprofloxacin, manufactured by Bayer. Bayer has the option to, and currently does, make payments to BRL, to keep the company from selling generic Cipro.

BRL markets its products in the U.S. and Puerto Rico by utilizing a small integrated sales and marketing force. Through FY 99, BRL had 140 direct purchase customers and 105 indirect customers, with the company's largest customer, McK esson Drug Co., accounting for about 14% of net product sales in FY 99.

Per Share Data ($) (Year Ended Jun. 30)	1999	1998	1997	1996	1995	1994	1993	1992	1991	1990
Tangible Bk. Val.	NA	6.99	4.79	3.81	3.44	2.80	2.65	2.27	2.26	1.82
Cash Flow	NA	1.68	1.09	0.55	0.54	0.29	0.57	0.06	0.40	0.21
Earnings	2.09	1.45	0.87	0.32	0.32	0.12	0.40	-0.10	0.25	0.06
Dividends	Nil	Nil	Nil	Nil	Nil	Nil	Nil	Nil	Nil	Nil
Payout Ratio	Nil	Nil	Nil	Nil	Nil	Nil	Nil	Nil	Nil	Nil
Prices - High	48 1/2	49 3/4	49 7/8	20 7/8	13 5/8	11 7/8	11 5/8	10 1/8	16 5/8	4 1/8
- Low	28 1/4	24 5/8	16 3/8	11 3/8	7 1/2	6 5/8	3 1/4	2 5/8	3 1/2	2 3/16
P/E Ratio - High	23	34	57	65	43	NM	29	NM	66	67
- Low	14	17	19	36	24	NM	8	NM	14	35
Income Statement Analysis (Million $)										
Revs.	NA	377	284	232	200	109	58.0	101	94.0	70.0
Oper. Inc.	NA	58.9	35.4	14.8	15.2	8.8	-2.3	1.7	11.4	7.3
Depr.	NA	5.5	5.0	4.9	4.4	3.6	3.3	3.0	2.6	2.5
Int. Exp.	NA	0.9	0.9	1.8	2.5	3.1	3.1	2.2	1.7	1.9
Pretax Inc.	NA	54.7	32.1	11.5	10.2	3.7	12.8	-3.5	7.1	1.5
Eff. Tax Rate	NA	39%	39%	38%	38%	39%	39%	NM	36%	30%
Net Inc.	NA	33.5	19.4	7.1	6.4	2.3	7.8	-1.9	4.5	1.1
Balance Sheet & Other Fin. Data (Million $)										
Cash	NA	73.0	31.9	44.9	53.0	36.5	25.0	11.7	17.4	0.5
Curr. Assets	NA	217	127	123	121	91.7	60.0	53.2	66.6	40.8
Total Assets	NA	311	204	169	156	126	93.5	87.3	95.1	64.5
Curr. Liab.	NA	122	85.3	69.8	62.1	38.5	8.6	41.0	19.7	21.9
LT Debt	NA	32.2	14.9	17.7	20.4	30.4	30.5	0.5	31.0	9.0
Common Eqty.	NA	156	102	80.0	72.0	55.0	51.5	42.8	41.9	31.1
Total Cap.	NA	189	118	99	93.6	87.2	84.6	46.3	75.4	42.5
Cap. Exp.	NA	20.4	35.1	16.1	6.3	4.8	4.4	9.3	5.9	2.5
Cash Flow	NA	39.0	24.4	12.1	10.8	5.9	11.0	1.1	7.2	3.6
Curr. Ratio	NA	1.8	1.5	1.8	1.9	2.4	6.9	0.2	3.4	1.9
% LT Debt of Cap.	NA	17.0	12.6	17.9	21.7	34.9	36.1	1.2	41.1	21.0
% Net Inc.of Revs.	NA	8.9	6.8	3.1	3.1	2.1	13.4	NM	4.8	1.5
% Ret. on Assets	NA	13.0	10.4	4.4	4.5	2.1	8.6	NM	5.5	1.7
% Ret. on Equity	NA	26.0	21.3	9.4	10.0	4.3	16.5	NM	12.0	3.5

Data as orig reptd.; bef. results of disc opers/spec. items. Per share data adj. for stk. divs. Bold denotes diluted EPS (FASB 128)-prior periods restated. E-Estimated. NA-Not Available. NM-Not Meaningful. NR-Not Ranked.

Office—Two Quaker Rd., P. O. Box 2900, Pomona, NY 10970-0519. **Tel**—(914) 362-1100. **Website**—http://www.barrlabs.com **Chrmn, CEO & Pres**—B. L. Downey. **Vice Chrmn**—E. A. Cohen. **SVP, CFO & Treas**—W. T. McKee. **SVP & Secy**—P. M. Bisaro. **Dirs**—P. M. Bisaro, R. J. Bolger, E. A. Cohen, B. L. Downey, M. F. Florence, J. M. Kay, B. C. Sherman, G. P. Stephan. **Transfer Agent**—Continental Stock Transfer & Trust Co., NYC. **Incorporated**—in New York in 1970. **Empl**— 574. **S&P Analyst:** Frank DiLorenzo

STANDARD
&POOR'S
STOCK REPORTS

Barrett Resources

NYSE Symbol **BRR**

In S&P SmallCap 600

23-OCT-99

Industry:
Oil & Gas (Exploration & Production)

Summary: This independent natural gas and oil exploration and production company is also involved in gas gathering, marketing and trading activities.

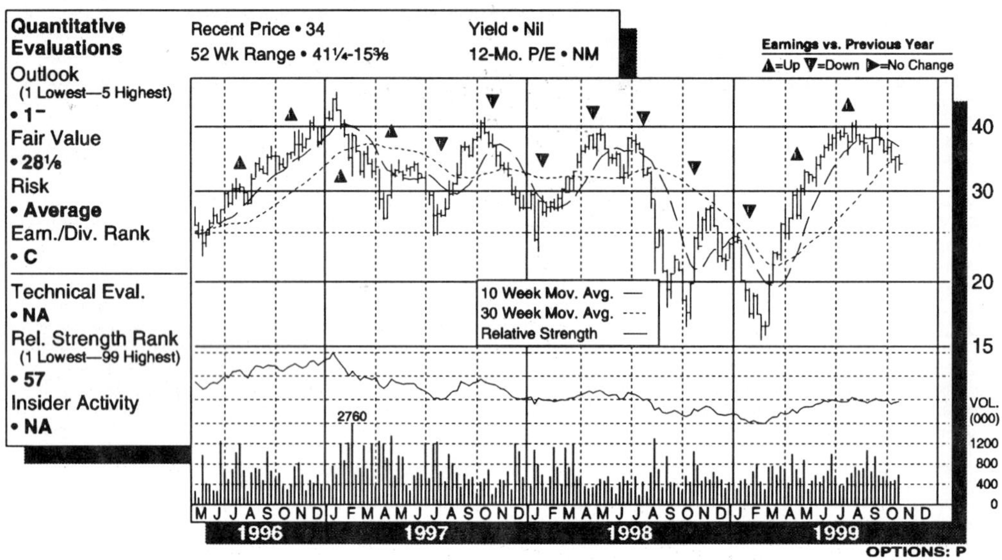

Business Profile - 15-OCT-99

Due to unsatisfactory bids, the company has rescinded its decision to divest its Gulf of Mexico properties. However, Barrett will continue to focus on its core Rocky Mountain asset base. With the recovery of commodity prices, the 1999 capital expenditure budget was recently raised from $111 million to $130 million. The majority of spending (85%) will be directed toward the Rocky Mountain region; most of the remainder will focus on the company's Piceance, Wind River and Powder River coal bed methane projects. A bill signed into law in October 1998 let BRR resume drilling of coal bed methane wells located on fee leases in the Powder River Basin.

Operational Review - 15-OCT-99

Revenues in the six months ended June 30, 1999, advanced 70%, year to year, on increased trading activities. The associated rise in trading costs led to a 72% hike in overall operating expenses. Net income rose 40%, to $11.8 million ($0.36 a share, diluted), from $8.8 million ($0.27). Barrett expects cash flow from producing properties and borrowing capacity to be sufficient to fund its anticipated capital and operating requirements.

Stock Performance - 22-OCT-99

In the past 30 trading days, BRR's shares have declined 12%, compared to a 4% fall in the S&P 500. Average trading volume for the past five days was 92,640 shares, compared with the 40-day moving average of 140,656 shares.

Key Stock Statistics

Dividend Rate/Share	Nil	Shareholders	3,587
Shs. outstg. (M)	32.5	Market cap. (B)	$ 1.1
Avg. daily vol. (M)	0.102	Inst. holdings	73%
Tang. Bk. Value/Share	10.77		
Beta	0.96		

Value of $10,000 invested 5 years ago: $ 33,794

Fiscal Year Ending Dec. 31

	1999	1998	1997	1996	1995	1994
Revenues (Million $)						
1Q	221.2	131.7	76.55	41.98	33.06	9.37
2Q	226.3	131.9	71.22	46.91	31.28	9.72
3Q	—	146.7	89.17	46.06	27.22	11.61
4Q	—	215.0	145.7	66.30	35.07	14.88
Yr.	—	625.4	382.6	201.3	126.6	--
Earnings Per Share ($)						
1Q	0.24	0.19	0.31	0.14	0.11	0.14
2Q	0.13	0.08	0.14	0.25	0.13	0.07
3Q	—	0.06	0.14	0.22	-0.47	0.07
4Q	—	-3.28	0.32	0.39	0.14	0.02
Yr.	—	-2.95	0.92	1.02	-0.09	0.46

Next earnings report expected: early November

Dividend Data

No cash dividends have been paid. Barrett anticipates that all earnings will be retained for the development of its business and that no cash dividends will be declared for the foreseeable future.

A Division of The McGraw-Hill Companies

Barrett Resources Corporation

Business Summary - 15-OCT-99

Denver-based Barrett Resources Corp. is an independent oil and natural gas exploration and production company. Significant producing regions include the Rocky Mountain Region of Colorado, Wyoming and Utah; the Mid-Continent Region of Kansas, Oklahoma, New Mexico and Texas; and the Gulf of Mexico region offshore Texas and Louisiana. BRR has a 70% working interest in an exploratory prospect in Peru; although three test wells in Peru indicated a significant presence of heavy oil, the wells were temporarily abandoned until the company deems development economic. Its initial interest in the region stemmed from geological similarities between Peru and the Rockies.

Barrett markets all of its own gas and oil production from wells that it operates. In addition, the company engages in natural gas trading activities, which involves purchasing gas from third parties and selling it to others at a profit. According to BRR, the experience gained from these trading activities enables the company to better market its own production.

Total proved reserves as of December 31, 1998, were 912.4 Bcf of natural gas and 9,650 MBbls. of crude oil and condensate, or 970.3 Bcf of gas equivalent (Bcfe), comprised of 94% and 6% natural gas and oil, respectively. Total proved reserves at year-end 1997 were 851.2 Bcf of natural gas, and 18,651 MBbls. of crude oil and condensate, or 963.2 Bcfe, comprised of 88% and 12% natural gas and oil, respectively. Proved developed reserves represented 60% and 64% of total reserves at the end of 1998 and 1997, respectively. The company replaced 107% of total 1998 production -- 96% through extensions, discoveries and revisions, and 4% through acquisitions. Estimated pretax future net revenues, discounted at 10%, amounted to $627.8 million, versus $745 million. The drop reflects lower prices for oil and gas: $2.01 per Mcf and $9.35 per bbl., respectively, versus $2.19 per Mcf and $15.52 per bbl.

Gas and oil production in 1998 totaled 94.9 Bcf and 2.0 MMBbl., respectively. This compared with 76.6 Bcf of gas and 2.2 MMBbl. of oil in 1997. The average price realization for gas during the two respective years was $1.92 and $2.18 per Mcf; oil averaged $11.42 and $17.69 per bbl. Average production costs per Mcf of natural gas equivalent was $0.55 in 1998 and $0.64 in 1997.

During 1998, the company drilled 397 gross (200.1 net) development wells, of which 380 (191.5) were productive, and 27 gross (15.9) exploratory wells, 21 (12.3) of which were successful. Barrett owned interests in 705,513 gross (414,159 net) developed acres and 3,698,160 gross (2,233,592) undeveloped acres.

Per Share Data ($) (Year Ended Dec. 31)	1998	1997	1996	1995	1994	1993	1992	1991	1990	1989
Tangible Bk. Val.	10.41	13.13	12.06	7.64	6.15	5.82	4.49	4.25	4.09	2.89
Cash Flow	0.26	3.18	2.61	1.25	0.95	1.08	0.43	0.42	0.43	0.43
Earnings	-2.95	0.92	1.02	-0.09	0.37	0.53	0.09	0.17	0.19	0.14
Dividends	Nil	Nil	Nil	Nil	Nil	Nil	Nil	Nil	Nil	Nil
Payout Ratio	Nil	Nil	Nil	Nil	Nil	Nil	Nil	Nil	Nil	Nil
Prices - High	39⅝	46⅞	43	30⅝	22¾	16	10¾	6½	8¾	7
- Low	16⅜	24⅝	22	16⅞	10⅜	8⅜	3⅛	3¼	5⅛	2⅞
P/E Ratio - High	NM	51	42	NM	61	30	NM	38	46	50
- Low	NM	27	22	NM	28	16	NM	19	27	21
Income Statement Analysis (Million $)										
Revs.	618	378	201	127	40.3	41.6	23.6	13.9	7.5	6.0
Oper. Inc.	137	130	92.6	51.1	10.4	10.9	3.6	3.0	2.8	2.5
Depr. Depl. & Amort.	102	72.4	45.8	33.5	6.9	6.1	3.3	2.4	1.9	1.7
Int. Exp.	20.9	13.2	3.7	5.0	0.0	0.0	0.0	0.0	0.1	0.0
Pretax Inc.	-149	47.2	44.5	-0.4	4.5	5.9	0.9	1.9	1.8	1.2
Eff. Tax Rate	NM	38%	34%	NM	1.50%	2.60%	1.90%	7.80%	18%	24%
Net Inc.	-93.7	29.3	29.5	-2.2	4.4	5.8	0.9	1.7	1.5	0.9
Balance Sheet & Other Fin. Data (Million $)										
Cash	14.3	14.5	14.5	7.5	9.7	35.2	11.3	18.9	19.9	5.3
Curr. Assets	153	122	89.7	39.7	28.8	53.3	19.9	24.4	28.6	8.6
Total Assets	839	873	577	340	106	91.0	57.0	55.0	51.0	26.0
Curr. Liab.	158	125	78.3	36.1	33.0	22.5	13.3	12.9	10.9	8.1
LT Debt	334	266	70.0	89.0	Nil	Nil	Nil	Nil	Nil	0.1
Common Eqty.	333	412	378	192	72.9	68.2	43.3	42.0	40.4	17.6
Total Cap.	681	748	499	304	72.9	68.2	43.3	42.6	40.4	17.7
Cap. Exp.	203	341	203	82.8	47.8	21.4	9.9	10.9	8.1	4.6
Cash Flow	8.4	102	75.3	31.2	11.3	11.8	4.2	4.1	3.4	2.6
Curr. Ratio	1.0	1.0	1.1	1.1	0.9	2.4	1.5	1.9	2.6	1.1
% LT Debt of Cap.	49.1	35.7	14.0	29.2	Nil	Nil	Nil	Nil	Nil	0.5
% Ret. on Assets	NM	4.0	6.4	NM	4.5	7.2	1.7	3.2	3.1	3.7
% Ret. on Equity	NM	7.4	10.4	NM	6.3	9.5	2.2	4.2	4.3	5.2

Data as orig. reptd.; bef. results of disc. opers. and/or spec. items. Per share data adj. for stk. divs. as of ex-div. date. Prior to 1995, year ended Sep. 30. E-Estimated. NA-Not Available. NM-Not Meaningful. NR-Not Ranked.

Office—1515 Arapahoe St., Tower 3, Suite 1000, Denver, CO 80202. **Tel**—(303) 572-3900. **Website**—http://www.brr.com **Chrmn & CEO**—W. J. Barrett. **Pres & COO**—A. R. Reed. **EVP & CFO**—J. Frank. Keller. **SVP, Treas & Investor Contact**—Robert Howard. **Dirs**—W. J. Barrett, C. R. Buford, D. Cody, J. M. Fitzgibbons, W. W. Grant III, J. F. Keller, A. R. Reed, J. T. Rodgers, P. S. E. Schreiber. **Transfer Agent & Registrar**—Bank Boston, N. A., Boston, MA **Incorporated**—in Delaware in 1987. **Empl**— 196. **S&P Analyst:** Ephraim Juskowicz

STANDARD &POOR'S

STOCK REPORTS

Bassett Furniture Industries

NASDAQ Symbol **BSET**

In S&P SmallCap 600

09-OCT-99

Industry: Household Furnishings & Appliances

Summary: Bassett is a leading producer of wood furniture for bedroom, dining room, living room and nursery use, as well as upholstered furniture and other related products.

Quantitative Evaluations

Outlook (1 Lowest—5 Highest)
• 3+

Fair Value
• 23¼

Risk
• Low

Earn./Div. Rank
• B-

Technical Eval.
• **Bearish** since 8/99

Rel. Strength Rank (1 Lowest—99 Highest)
• 35

Insider Activity
• **Unfavorable**

Recent Price • 18⅞
52 Wk Range • 27-15⅜
Yield • 4.2%
12-Mo. P/E • 12.7

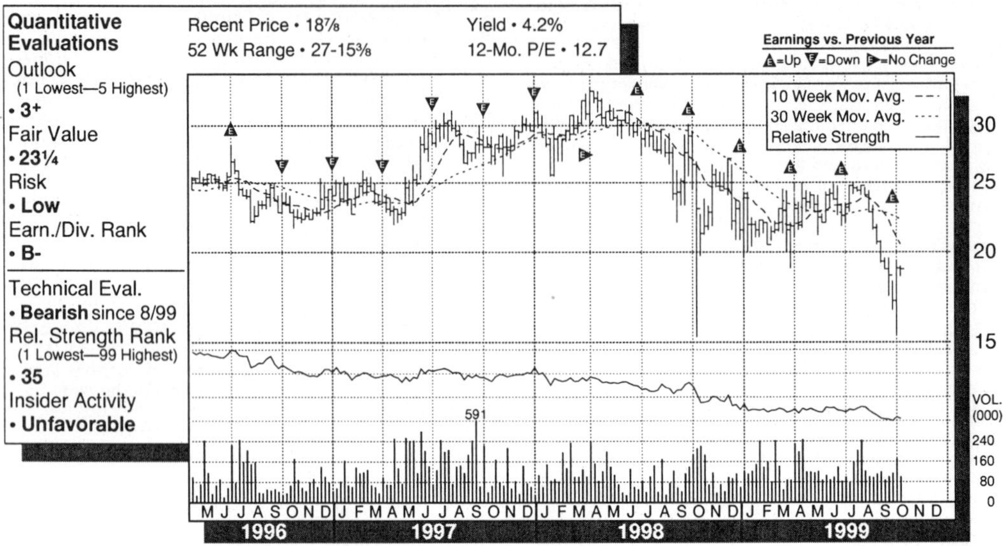

Business Profile - 08-OCT-99

The company sold its bedding division to LIS Corp. for $8.2 million in the third quarter of FY 99 (Nov.). The Bassett Furniture Direct (BFD) retail program has grown from 30 stores in mid-1998 to 44 stores at the end of August 1999, contributing to sales growth. BFD accounted for 20% of sales in the first nine months of FY 99, up from 14% in FY 98. The company plans to open six to 11 additional stores by the end of 1999. BSET is also focusing on improving its gross profit margins.

Operational Review - 08-OCT-99

Net sales in the nine months ended August 28, 1999, declined 1.0%, year to year, reflecting the absence of bedding revenues since April 1999, partly offset by higher sales from the expanding Bassett Furniture Direct (retail outlet) program. Gross margins widened, on a more favorable product mix, price increases, and higher production levels. SG&A expenses rose 11%, reflecting increased spending on marketing, retail store expansion, and plant startup costs. After a 32% rise in other income, pretax income advanced 47%. After taxes at 31.8%, versus 24.2%, net income was up 32%, to $13,879,000 ($1.10 a share), from $10,521,000 ($0.81).

Stock Performance - 08-OCT-99

In the past 30 trading days, BSET's shares have declined 8%, compared to a 0.91% fall in the S&P 500. Average trading volume for the past five days was 19,620 shares, compared with the 40-day moving average of 22,721 shares.

Key Stock Statistics

Dividend Rate/Share	0.80	Shareholders	1,752
Shs. outstg. (M)	12.5	Market cap. (B)	$0.237
Avg. daily vol. (M)	0.024	Inst. holdings	50%
Tang. Bk. Value/Share	20.90		
Beta	0.75		

Value of $10,000 invested 5 years ago: $ 6,611

Fiscal Year Ending Nov. 30

	1999	1998	1997	1996	1995	1994
Revenues (Million $)						
1Q	99.8	98.33	109.8	112.0	123.5	121.7
2Q	103.7	98.34	113.2	111.3	119.0	134.6
3Q	88.80	98.09	110.3	109.0	119.2	125.0
4Q	—	102.8	113.6	118.5	129.1	129.3
Yr.	—	397.6	446.9	450.7	490.8	510.6
Earnings Per Share ($)						
1Q	**0.34**	**0.26**	0.26	0.35	0.35	0.33
2Q	**0.40**	**0.30**	-1.07	0.37	0.35	0.53
3Q	**0.36**	**0.24**	-0.39	0.36	0.41	0.32
4Q	—	**0.40**	-0.30	0.31	0.52	0.57
Yr.	—	**1.20**	**-1.50**	**1.39**	1.63	1.75

Next earnings report expected: mid January

Dividend Data (Dividends have been paid since 1935.)

Amount ($)	Date Decl.	Ex-Div. Date	Stock of Record	Payment Date
0.200	Feb. 11	Feb. 19	Feb. 23	Mar. 02 '99
0.200	Mar. 30	May. 13	May. 17	Jun. 01 '99
0.200	Jun. 29	Aug. 13	Aug. 17	Sep. 01 '99
0.200	Sep. 28	Nov. 12	Nov. 16	Nov. 30 '99

A Division of The McGraw-Hill Companies

Bassett Furniture Industries, Incorporated

Business Summary - 08-OCT-99

Bassett Furniture Industries, one of the largest U.S. furniture manufacturers, has been refocusing its product mix and improving operating efficiencies. In FY 98 (Nov.), the company achieved most of the objectives established in a 1997 restructuring plan. The plan called for BSET to focus on its core Bassett line, eliminate three product lines (National/Mt. Airy, Impact and veneer production), close 14 manufacturing facilities, and lay off approximately 1,000 employees.

The company manufactures and sells a full line of furniture, including bedroom and dining suites and accent pieces, occasional tables, wall and entertainment units, home office systems and computer workstations, upholstered sofas, love seats, and chairs (both motion and stationary), recliners, and mattresses and box springs. The three main product lines are wood (60% of FY 98 sales), upholstery (30%), and bedding (10%). Almost all sourcing is done domestically.

Raw materials used by BSET are generally available from many domestic sources. The company did not experience significant raw materials cost pressures in 1998.

Products are distributed through a large number of retailers, including mass merchandisers, department stores, independent furniture stores, chain furniture stores, decorator showrooms, warehouse showrooms, specialty stores and rent-to-own stores. Distribution channels also include proprietary retail outlets, known as Bassett Furniture Direct; and the Bassett Gallery stores and warehouse stores called Bassett Direct Plus. Sales to J.C. Penney Co. accounted for 15% of revenues in FY 98. International sales accounted for 3.6% of sales in FY 98

Although the furniture industry is highly competitive, with many domestic and foreign manufacturers, BSET believes it has been one of the largest domestic furniture retailers, for a number of reasons. The company believes it offers its customers a product with superior quality and styling at attractive prices. BSET also feels that its prompt delivery and courteous service have been significant factors in its success. With consumer tastes constantly changing, the company is continuously involved in the development of new designs and products.

The company believes its trademark Bassett and the names of its marketing divisions and products are important, due to customer recognition of the names, and identification with the company's broad range of products. BSET also owns certain patents and licenses that it considers significant in the conduct of business.

The company sold its bedding division to LIS Corp. for $8.2 million in the third quarter of FY 99 (Nov.).

Per Share Data ($)										
(Year Ended Nov. 30)	**1998**	**1997**	**1996**	**1995**	**1994**	**1993**	**1992**	**1991**	**1990**	**1989**
Tangible Bk. Val.	20.56	20.01	22.29	21.88	20.95	19.99	18.99	17.72	16.89	17.29
Cash Flow	1.73	-1.03	1.85	2.24	2.36	2.41	2.50	1.92	0.88	1.76
Earnings	1.20	-1.50	1.39	1.63	1.75	1.79	1.90	1.37	0.34	1.22
Dividends	0.80	0.80	0.80	1.00	0.80	0.78	0.64	0.53	0.67	1.07
Payout Ratio	67%	NM	58%	61%	46%	44%	33%	39%	187%	85%
Prices - High	34	31½	28¼	30¼	37¼	44	35¼	21¼	20¼	21¼
- Low	15¼	21⅞	21⅝	20⅛	25¼	27½	19½	16⅞	15⅛	18½
P/E Ratio - High	28	NM	20	19	21	25	18	15	58	17
- Low	13	NM	16	12	14	15	10	12	43	15
Income Statement Analysis (Million $)										
Revs.	398	447	451	491	511	504	473	402	436	460
Oper. Inc.	16.5	-28.5	13.6	25.7	33.9	36.2	36.7	22.7	23.5	25.5
Depr.	6.9	6.2	6.3	8.6	8.8	9.0	8.5	7.9	7.9	8.3
Int. Exp.	Nil	Nil	Nil	Nil	Nil	Nil	Nil	Nil	Nil	Nil
Pretax Inc.	21.1	-42.0	22.3	30.1	34.8	36.5	39.3	26.9	6.9	26.7
Eff. Tax Rate	25%	NM	17%	24%	28%	29%	30%	26%	25%	29%
Net Inc.	15.7	-19.6	18.5	22.9	25.0	25.9	27.5	19.8	5.1	19.0
Balance Sheet & Other Fin. Data (Million $)										
Cash	65.2	29.6	57.3	51.3	42.3	53.0	50.2	74.0	57.6	76.4
Curr. Assets	144	200	195	205	199	202	193	202	183	212
Total Assets	322	320	335	347	340	331	319	291	271	305
Curr. Liab.	44.7	47.9	30.3	35.4	35.0	33.2	36.9	29.0	20.1	42.2
LT Debt	Nil	Nil	Nil	Nil	Nil	Nil	Nil	Nil	Nil	Nil
Common Eqty.	265	261	291	299	295	289	274	255	244	263
Total Cap.	266	261	294	301	296	289	274	255	244	263
Cap. Exp.	22.6	10.8	9.6	7.2	10.0	6.2	9.9	7.9	9.1	8.2
Cash Flow	22.6	-13.4	24.8	31.5	33.8	34.9	36.0	27.7	13.0	27.3
Curr. Ratio	3.2	4.2	6.4	5.8	5.7	6.1	5.2	7.0	9.1	5.0
% LT Debt of Cap.	Nil	Nil	Nil	0.7	Nil	Nil	Nil	Nil	Nil	Nil
% Net Inc.of Revs.	4.0	NM	4.1	4.7	4.9	5.1	5.8	4.9	1.2	4.1
% Ret. on Assets	4.9	NM	5.4	6.7	7.5	8.0	9.0	7.1	1.8	6.2
% Ret. on Equity	6.0	NM	6.3	7.7	8.7	9.2	10.4	8.0	2.1	7.2

Data as orig reptd.; bef. results of disc opers/spec. items. Per share data adj. for stk. divs. Bold denotes diluted EPS (FASB 128)-prior periods restated. E-Estimated. NA-Not Available. NM-Not Meaningful. NR-Not Ranked.

Office—P.O. Box 626, Bassett, VA 24055. **Tel**—(540) 629-6000. **Website**—http://www.bassettfurniture.com **Chrmn & CEO**—P. Fulton. **Pres & COO**—R. H. Spilman, Jr. **VP-Fin & Investor Contact**—G. S. Elliot. **VP & Secy**—J. R. Hervey. **Dirs**—A. W. Brinkley, P. W. Brown, T. E. Capps, W. D. Davis, A. T. Dickson, P. Fulton, W. H. Goodwin Jr., H. H. Haworth, M. E. Murphy, A. F. Sloan, R. H. Spilman, Jr. **Transfer Agent & Registrar**—Co.'s office. **Incorporated**—in Virginia in 1930. **Empl**— 5,400. **S&P Analyst:** Howard Choe

STANDARD
&POOR'S
STOCK REPORTS

BE Aerospace

NASDAQ Symbol **BEAV**

In S&P SmallCap 600

09-OCT-99

Industry:
Aerospace/Defense

Summary: BEAV makes cabin interior products for commercial aircraft, including seating, passenger entertainment and service systems, and galley structures and inserts.

Quantitative Evaluations

Outlook
(1 Lowest—5 Highest)
• **5**

Fair Value
• **23¼**

Risk
• **Average**

Earn./Div. Rank
• **C**

Technical Eval.
• **Bearish** since 8/99

Rel. Strength Rank
(1 Lowest—99 Highest)
• **5**

Insider Activity
• **NA**

Recent Price • 11⅜
52 Wk Range • 27¼-11⅜
Yield • Nil
12-Mo. P/E • 81.7

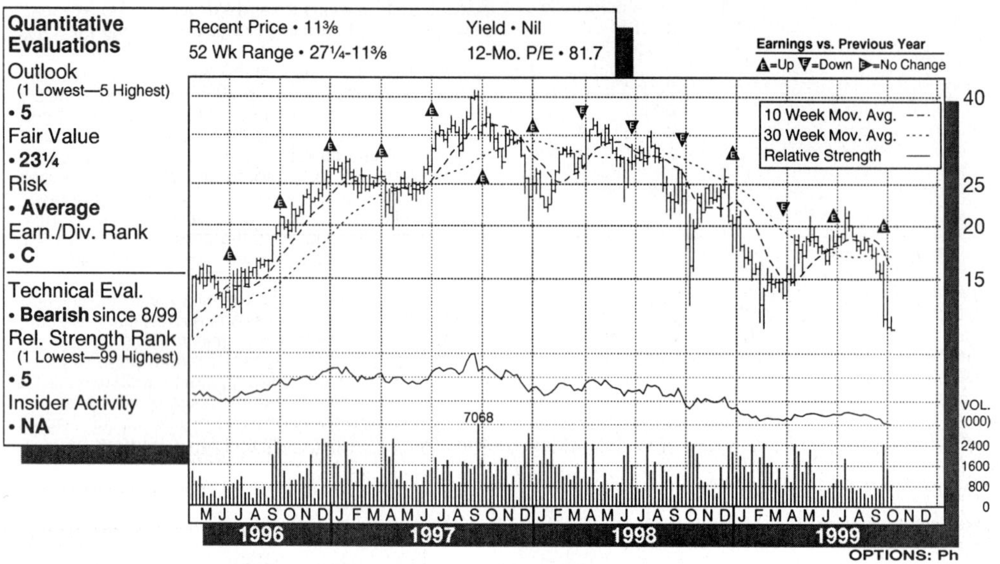

Business Profile - 18-AUG-99

BE Aerospace has been growing both internally and through acquisitions. During FY 2000 (Feb.), the company expects to complete the integration of recently acquired businesses, as it consolidates its facilities, reduces its work force, and implements new information technology tools. Pretax charges of $88 million were incurred in the FY 99 fourth quarter for an 8% work force reduction, the closing of seven facilities, and new product introductions. BEAV expects restructuring and integration activities to significantly lower its cost structure and improve productivity. In February 1999, the company sold a 51% stake in its in-flight entertainment business to Sextant Avionique S.A., a supplier of avionics systems, for about $62 million.

Operational Review - 18-AUG-99

Net sales in the three months ended May 29, 1999, advanced 32%, year to year, reflecting strong aftermarket sales for aircraft cabin refurbishment and business jets due to acquisitions; sales were up 14% on a pro forma basis. Gross margins narrowed on learning curve inefficiencies related to new product introductions and a new information technology system. With well controlled SG&A and R&D expenses, and in the absence of $32 million of acquisition-related expenses, net income of $11,415,000 ($0.46 a share, diluted) contrasted with a net loss of $23,875,000 ($1.03). On a pro forma basis, net income rose 35%.

Stock Performance - 08-OCT-99

In the past 30 trading days, BEAV's shares have declined 36%, compared to a 0.91% fall in the S&P 500. Average trading volume for the past five days was 165,020 shares, compared with the 40-day moving average of 191,779 shares.

Key Stock Statistics

Dividend Rate/Share	Nil	Shareholders	14,300
Shs. outstg. (M)	24.8	Market cap. (B)	$0.284
Avg. daily vol. (M)	0.274	Inst. holdings	56%
Tang. Bk. Value/Share	NM		
Beta	1.16		

Value of $10,000 invested 5 years ago: $ 11,295

Fiscal Year Ending Feb. 28

	2000	1999	1998	1997	1996	1995
Revenues (Million $)						
1Q	185.0	140.0	113.8	97.30	55.59	57.57
2Q	191.9	156.3	119.8	103.0	57.45	55.20
3Q	—	195.8	129.0	107.8	55.19	57.28
4Q	—	209.2	125.3	104.2	64.35	59.30
Yr.	—	701.3	488.0	412.4	232.6	229.3
Earnings Per Share ($)						
1Q	**0.46**	**-1.03**	0.30	0.08	Nil	0.07
2Q	**0.55**	**-1.44**	0.35	0.11	-0.02	0.06
3Q	—	**0.59**	0.40	0.23	-0.21	-0.90
4Q	—	**-1.65**	**0.26**	0.29	-1.92	0.03
Yr.	—	**-3.36**	**1.30**	**0.72**	-3.71	-0.75

Next earnings report expected: late December

Dividend Data

The company has not paid cash dividends, and it does not intend to pay any in the immediate future.

A Division of The McGraw-Hill Companies

BE Aerospace, Inc.

Business Summary - 18-AUG-99

BE Aerospace, Inc. (formerly BE Avionics) is the world's largest manufacturer of commercial aircraft cabin interior products, serving virtually all major airlines. It also offers upgrade, maintenance and repair services. Having achieved leading global market share in each of its major product categories, BEAV's strategy is to maintain its leadership position through various initiatives, including new product development and acquisitions.

Revenues come mainly from refurbishment or upgrade programs for airlines' existing aircraft fleet and new aircraft deliveries. BEAV believes that its large installed base of products gives it significant advantage over competitors in obtaining orders for refurbishment programs, since airlines typically purchase equipment from original suppliers.

Major product lines include first, business, tourist class and commuter seats; a broad range of galley products such as coffee and beverage makers, ovens, liquid containers, refrigeration equipment and galley structures; and in-flight entertainment products including an interactive video system.

In FY 99 (Feb.), seating products accounted for 42% of revenues, interior systems 20% and entertainment systems 11%. Approximately 27% of BEAV's revenues are derived from flight structures and integration services, business jet and VIP products, and service revenues. Refurbishment and retrofit programs, along with spares revenues, generated 56% of the company's total revenues in FY 99. The company believes it has benefited from three major trends in the aerospace industry: an increase in refurbishment and upgrade orders; expansion of worldwide fleet and shift toward wide-body aircraft; and business jet and VIP aircraft fleet expansion and related retrofit opportunities. BEAV noted that the aftermarket is expected to provide 60% of its revenues during FY 00, up from 53% in FY 94. The company expects this to grow to 70% within 10 years.

BEAV has a leading share of the market for passenger control units as well as related wiring and harness assemblies. It also makes an individual interactive seat video system, MDDS (multimedia digital distribution system), with features such as video games, pay-per-view and shopping, advanced multiplexer systems, hard-wired distribution systems (also sold to rail and bus lines) and other passenger entertainment and service products.

During FY 99, the company completed four acquisitions for $354 million, including the August 1998 purchase of SMR Aerospace, Inc., a provider of cabin services, for $142 million. Since 1989, BEAV has acquired 15 companies for an aggregate purchase price of $680 million.

In February 1998, BEAV sold $250 million of subordinated notes. In March 1998, it redeemed its $125 million of 9.75% senior notes.

Per Share Data ($) (Year Ended Feb. 28)	1999	1998	1997	1996	1995	1994	1993	1992	1991	1990
Tangible Bk. Val.	NM	8.60	7.57	2.69	7.79	8.38	7.39	5.42	3.18	2.36
Cash Flow	-1.72	2.33	1.98	-2.60	0.25	1.20	1.70	0.24	0.88	0.78
Earnings	-3.36	1.30	0.72	-3.71	-0.75	0.35	1.03	-0.18	0.65	0.43
Dividends	Nil	Nil	Nil	Nil	Nil	Nil	Nil	Nil	Nil	Nil
Payout Ratio	Nil	Nil	Nil	Nil	Nil	Nil	Nil	Nil	Nil	Nil
Cal. Yrs.	1998	1997	1996	1995	1994	1993	1992	1991	1990	1989
Prices - High	35¾	41½	28⅜	11¼	11¾	15¼	15¾	16¾	10¾	NA
- Low	13	19½	9⅞	5¼	7	8¾	9⅞	7½	4¾	NA
P/E Ratio - High	NM	32	39	NM	NM	44	15	NM	17	NA
- Low	NM	15	14	NM	NM	25	10	NM	7	NA
Income Statement Analysis (Million $)										
Revs.	701	488	412	233	229	203	198	12.0	24.0	23.0
Oper. Inc.	56.8	82.8	66.5	-23.0	36.0	34.5	30.8	0.7	8.7	6.8
Depr.	40.7	24.2	24.1	18.4	16.1	13.1	8.0	4.0	1.7	1.9
Int. Exp.	41.7	22.8	27.1	18.6	15.0	14.1	4.0	NM	0.1	1.6
Pretax Inc.	-79.5	35.9	15.2	-60.0	-18.9	8.8	18.8	-2.6	7.2	3.3
Eff. Tax Rate	NM	15%	10%	NM	NM	39%	36%	NM	35%	30%
Net Inc.	-83.4	30.5	13.7	-60.0	-12.1	5.4	12.2	-1.7	4.7	2.3
Balance Sheet & Other Fin. Data (Million $)										
Cash	39.5	165	44.1	15.4	8.3	13.7	14.3	7.2	6.3	3.5
Curr. Assets	314	382	213	150	143	136	205	57.0	17.0	11.0
Total Assets	904	682	491	434	380	375	314	135	26.0	21.0
Curr. Liab.	170	120	91.1	108	66.0	59.5	71.0	30.0	3.4	3.5
LT Debt	584	350	225	273	173	159	128	41.0	Nil	2.0
Common Eqty.	116	197	166	44.2	125	134	108	57.0	22.0	16.0
Total Cap.	700	548	391	319	309	311	239	100	23.0	18.0
Cap. Exp.	37.5	28.9	14.4	13.7	12.2	11.0	7.3	1.1	0.4	0.4
Cash Flow	-42.7	54.7	37.8	-41.6	4.1	18.5	20.1	2.3	6.4	4.2
Curr. Ratio	1.8	3.2	2.3	1.4	2.2	2.3	2.9	1.9	5.0	3.1
% LT Debt of Cap.	83.4	63.8	57.5	85.7	55.8	51.2	53.6	40.6	Nil	9.1
% Net Inc.of Revs.	NM	6.3	3.3	NM	NM	2.6	6.1	NM	19.4	10.1
% Ret. on Assets	NM	5.2	2.9	NM	NM	1.5	6.6	NM	19.6	14.4
% Ret. on Equity	NM	16.8	13.0	NM	NM	4.2	15.7	NM	24.0	22.6

Data as orig reptd.; bef. results of disc opers/spec. items. Per share data adj. for stk. divs. Bold denotes diluted EPS (FASB 128)-prior periods restated. E-Estimated. NA-Not Available. NM-Not Meaningful. NR-Not Ranked.

Office—1400 Corporate Center Way, Wellington, FL 33414. **Tel**—(561) 791-5000. **Fax**—(561) 791-7900. **Chrmn**—A. J. Khoury. **Vice Chrmn & CEO**—R. J. Khoury. **Pres & COO**—P. E. Fulchino. **SVP & CFO**—T. P. McCaffrey. **Treas**—J. P. Holtzman. **Secy**—E. J. Moriarty. **Investor Contact**—Jay Jacobson (914-722-2737). **Dirs**—J. C. Cowart, P. E. Fulchino, R. G. Hamermesh, A. J. Khoury, R. J. Khoury, B. H. Rowe, H. Wyss. **Transfer Agent & Registrar**—BankBoston, N.A. **Incorporated**—in Delaware in 1987. **Empl**— 5,600. **S&P Analyst:** Stewart Scharf

STANDARD &POOR'S
STOCK REPORTS

Belden Inc.

NYSE Symbol **BWC**
In S&P SmallCap 600

09-OCT-99

Industry: Electrical Equipment

Summary: Belden manufactures wire, cable and cord products for the electronics and electrical markets.

Quantitative Evaluations

Outlook (1 Lowest—5 Highest)
• **4+**

Fair Value
• **28⅛**

Risk
• **Low**

Earn./Div. Rank
• **NR**

Technical Eval.
• **Bearish** since 9/99

Rel. Strength Rank (1 Lowest—99 Highest)
• **37**

Insider Activity
• **NA**

Recent Price • 21
52 Wk Range • 25½-11⅜
Yield • 1.0%
12-Mo. P/E • 33.9

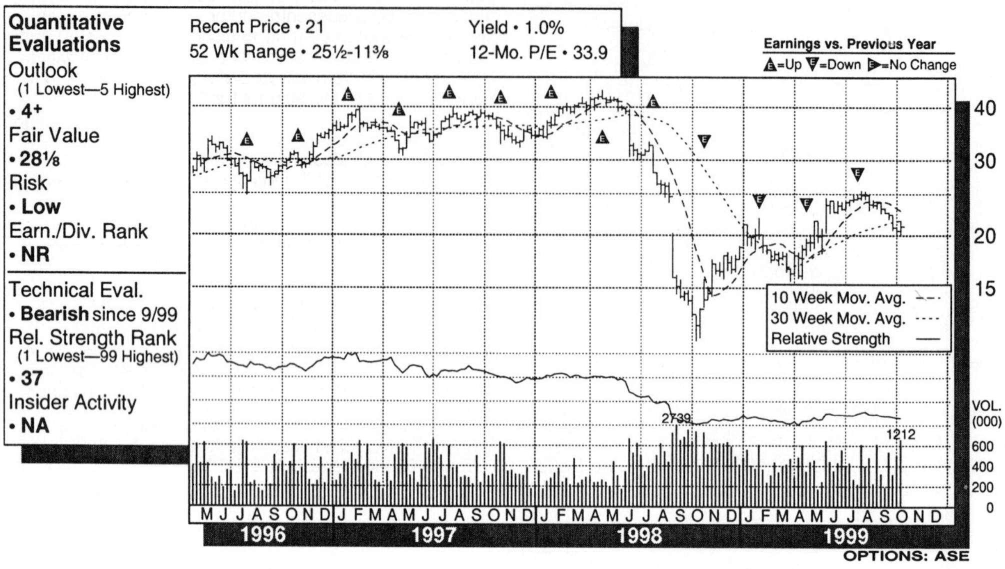

OPTIONS: ASE

Business Profile - 27-JUL-99

In late-June 1999, BWC acquired Cable Systems Holding Co. (CSHC) and its subsidiary, Cable Systems International Inc. (CSI). CSI is a leading manufacturer of copper cable products primarily for telecommunications applications. CSI had revenues for the latest twelve months ended June 30, 1999, of about $290 million. In April, BWC noted that it planned to divest its cord products division and signed a letter of intent with Volex Group p.l.c. to sell the business for cash. BWC decided to divest the segment in order to concentrate on its electronic and specialty electrical wire and cable businesses.

Operational Review - 27-JUL-99

Revenues in the first half of 1999 were down 8.1%, year to year. Gross margins narrowed sharply, on manufacturing inefficiencies due to lower production levels and lower prices; operating income fell 46%. With increased interest expense and after taxes at 37.7%, versus 38.7%, income from continuing operations fell 49%, to $15,465,000 ($0.63 a share), from $30,316,000 ($1.15). Per share results in the 1999 period exclude a loss from discontinued operations of $0.20, while results in the 1998 period exclude income from discontinued operations of $0.01.

Stock Performance - 08-OCT-99

In the past 30 trading days, BWC's shares have declined 12%, compared to a 0.91% fall in the S&P 500. Average trading volume for the past five days was 242,300 shares, compared with the 40-day moving average of 100,974 shares.

Key Stock Statistics

Dividend Rate/Share	0.20	Shareholders	1,000
Shs. outstg. (M)	24.4	Market cap. (B)	$0.512
Avg. daily vol. (M)	0.127	Inst. holdings	79%
Tang. Bk. Value/Share	5.71		
Beta	1.26		

Value of $10,000 invested 5 years ago: $ 11,787

Fiscal Year Ending Dec. 31

	1999	1998	1997	1996	1995	1994
Revenues (Million $)						
1Q	159.6	190.4	176.0	169.3	114.1	99.9
2Q	166.2	196.3	192.6	167.7	160.0	103.4
3Q	—	164.3	183.7	159.0	156.7	110.0
4Q	—	172.6	194.9	171.4	177.8	126.4
Yr.	—	723.6	747.2	667.4	608.6	439.7
Earnings Per Share ($)						
1Q	**0.26**	**0.59**	**0.53**	**0.48**	0.37	0.31
2Q	**0.38**	**0.58**	**0.55**	**0.51**	0.41	0.33
3Q	—	**0.10**	**0.55**	**0.51**	0.43	0.37
4Q	—	**0.06**	**0.68**	**0.61**	0.55	0.46
Yr.	—	**1.35**	**2.30**	**2.11**	**1.76**	1.46

Next earnings report expected: late October

Dividend Data (Dividends have been paid since 1994.)

Amount ($)	Date Decl.	Ex-Div. Date	Stock of Record	Payment Date
0.050	Nov. 19	Dec. 07	Dec. 09	Jan. 05 '99
0.050	Feb. 18	Feb. 25	Mar. 01	Apr. 02 '99
0.050	May. 06	May. 27	Jun. 01	Jul. 02 '99
0.050	Aug. 20	Sep. 01	Sep. 03	Oct. 04 '99

STANDARD
&POOR'S
STOCK REPORTS

Belden Inc.

Business Summary - 27-JUL-99

Belden Inc. is a leader in the design, manufacture and marketing of specialty wire, cable and cord products. It serves many major growing and competitive markets, such as computer networking and computer equipment; broadcast, entertainment and cable TV; industrial instrumentation and control; and electrical equipment, including power tools, floor care equipment, home appliances and motor and test apparatus. Belden's products are positioned at the upper end of the value-added range used for electrical signal transmission in broadcast, data and industrial automation applications.

In 1998, computer products provided 41% of revenues; audio/visual 20%; industrial 20%; and electrical 19%.

Sales to several business units of Anixter International Inc. accounted for 17% of the total in 1998, versus 16% in 1997 and 17% in 1996. Sales in Europe accounted for 16% of the total in 1998, Canada 6%, and exports (largely to the Pacific Rim) 10%.

Belden meets the demands of its markets with various product configurations, which include, for the electronic markets, multiconductor products, coaxial cable, fiber optic cables, heat-shrinkable tubing and wire management products; and for the electrical markets, cords and lead, hook-up and other wire.

A multiconductor cable consists of two or more insulated conductors that are cabled together. Major end-uses for multiconductor cable include computer networking and computer equipment, as well as various applications within the industrial signal, instrumentation and control market.

Coaxial cable consists of a central inner conductor surrounded by a concentric outer conductor or shield. Primary applications are in audio/video markets, such as broadcast and entertainment (which use broadcast cables to distribute audio and video signals for the TV, music and other entertainment industries) and cable TV.

Fiber optic cables are used to transmit light signals through glass or plastic fibers. The principal application is premises data distribution systems using multimode fiber.

A cord is a two-or three-conductor cable with a molded plug on one or both ends. Most cords are sold directly to OEMs for incorporation in portable electric power tools, floor care equipment and home appliances. Cord products are marketed through distributors and appliance wholesalers. Lead, hook-up and other wire consists of single-conductor wire that is used for electrical leads in motors, internal wiring and test equipment.

In April 1999, BWC noted that it planned to divest its cord products division and signed a letter of intent with Volex Group p.l.c. to sell the business for cash. BWC decided to divest the division in order to concentrate on its electronic and specialty electrical wire and cable businesses.

Per Share Data ($)										
(Year Ended Dec. 31)	**1998**	**1997**	**1996**	**1995**	**1994**	**1993**	**1992**	**1991**	**1990**	**1989**
Tangible Bk. Val.	5.16	5.49	5.79	4.44	3.15	1.85	1.27	NA	NA	NA
Cash Flow	2.30	3.06	2.78	2.39	1.92	1.72	1.55	NA	NA	NA
Earnings	1.35	2.30	2.11	1.76	1.46	1.21	1.05	NA	NA	NA
Dividends	0.20	0.20	0.20	0.20	0.20	Nil	NA	NA	NA	NA
Payout Ratio	15%	9%	9%	11%	14%	Nil	NA	NA	NA	NA
Prices - High	43⅞	39⅞	37	29⅞	22½	18⅝	NA	NA	NA	NA
- Low	11¼	30⅝	24⅛	19¾	16⅛	14¼	NA	NA	NA	NA
P/E Ratio - High	32	17	18	17	15	15	NA	NA	NA	NA
- Low	8	13	11	11	11	12	NA	NA	NA	NA
Income Statement Analysis (Million $)										
Revs.	724	747	667	609	440	384	366	NA	NA	NA
Oper. Inc.	99	127	112	95.5	77.3	68.7	62.2	NA	NA	NA
Depr.	24.3	19.8	17.6	15.9	12.0	12.0	13.0	NA	NA	NA
Int. Exp.	7.7	7.0	3.5	3.9	2.6	2.7	3.2	NA	NA	NA
Pretax Inc.	56.3	99	90.8	75.7	62.7	53.9	44.2	NA	NA	NA
Eff. Tax Rate	39%	39%	39%	39%	39%	39%	38%	NA	NA	NA
Net Inc.	34.5	60.7	55.2	46.2	38.1	32.7	27.2	NA	NA	NA
Balance Sheet & Other Fin. Data (Million $)										
Cash	3.3	0.9	1.8	0.8	4.7	2.4	0.2	NA	NA	NA
Curr. Assets	215	237	191	173	110	102	100	NA	NA	NA
Total Assets	506	475	372	333	204	197	192	NA	NA	NA
Curr. Liab.	79.4	83.1	82.7	83.2	45.7	40.6	40.7	NA	NA	NA
LT Debt	163	124	71.6	81.5	37.3	68.0	78.4	NA	NA	NA
Common Eqty.	220	229	180	132	93.6	60.5	45.2	NA	NA	NA
Total Cap.	397	366	262	221	138	136	130	NA	NA	NA
Cap. Exp.	40.8	28.7	26.1	21.8	13.3	16.6	NA	NA	NA	NA
Cash Flow	58.9	80.5	72.8	62.1	50.1	44.8	40.2	NA	NA	NA
Curr. Ratio	2.7	2.9	2.3	2.1	2.4	2.5	2.5	NA	NA	NA
% LT Debt of Cap.	41.1	33.9	27.4	36.8	26.9	50.1	60.1	NA	NA	NA
% Net Inc.of Revs.	4.8	8.1	8.3	7.6	8.7	8.5	7.4	NA	NA	NA
% Ret. on Assets	7.0	14.3	15.7	17.2	19.0	NM	NA	NA	NA	NA
% Ret. on Equity	15.4	29.7	35.5	40.9	49.4	NA	NA	NA	NA	NA

Data as orig reptd.; bef. results of disc opers/spec. items. Per share data adj. for stk. divs. Bold denotes diluted EPS (FASB 128)-prior periods restated. E-Estimated. NA-Not Available. NM-Not Meaningful. NR-Not Ranked.

Office—7701 Forsyth Blvd., Suite 800, St. Louis, MO 63105. **Tel**—(314) 854-8000. **Fax**—(314) 854-8001. **Website**—http://www.belden.com **Chrmn, CEO & Pres**—C. B. Cunningham. **VP, CFO, Treas & Investor Contact**—Richard K. Reece. **VP & Secy**—K. L. Bloomfield. **Dirs**—L. D. Bain, C. I. Byrnes, J. R. Coppola, C. B. Cunningham, J. R. Dallepezze, A. E. Riedel, B. G. Rethore. **Transfer Agent & Registrar**—Boatmen's Trust Co., St. Louis. **Incorporated**—in Delaware in 1993. **Empl**— 4,700. **S&P Analyst:** M.I.

Benchmark Electronics

NYSE Symbol **BHE**

In S&P SmallCap 600

09-OCT-99 **Industry:** Electrical Equipment

Summary: BHE provides contract manufacturing and engineering services to original equipment manufacturers in various industries.

Quantitative Evaluations

Outlook
(1 Lowest—5 Highest)
• 5

Fair Value
• 57¾

Risk
• **Average**

Earn./Div. Rank
• **B+**

Technical Eval.
• **Neutral** since 9/99

Rel. Strength Rank
(1 Lowest—99 Highest)
• **71**

Insider Activity
• **NA**

Recent Price • 36¾
52 Wk Range • 43¾-17⅞
Yield • Nil
12-Mo. P/E • 23.9

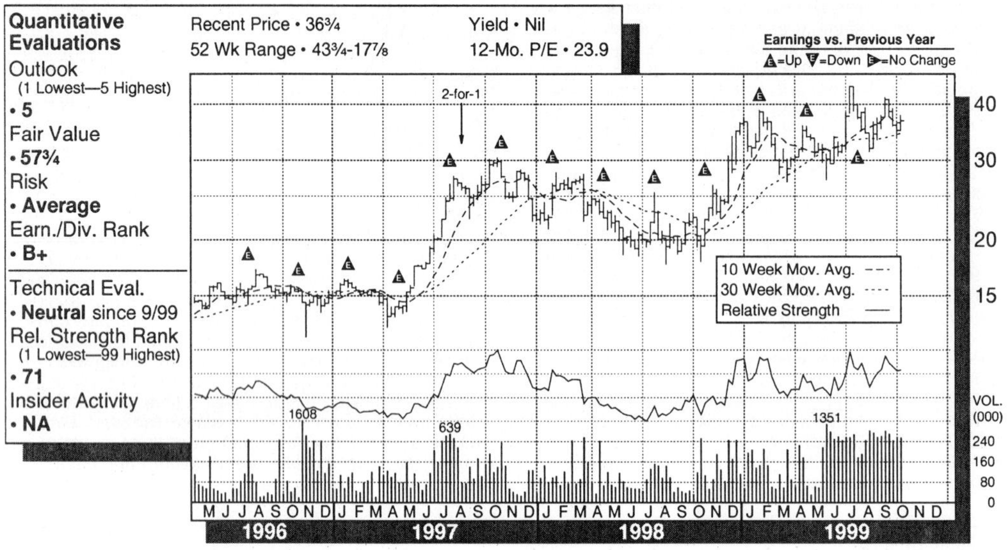

Business Profile - 14-JUL-99

The company seeks to grow by acquiring additional facilities or businesses, and by achieving additional operating efficiencies in existing operations. The scope of operations was expanded through the February 1998 acquisition of Lockheed Martin's commercial electronics unit (LCEC), one of New England's largest electronics manufacturing services companies, for $70 million. In July 1999, BHE entered into a definitive agreement to buy AVEX Electronics from J.M. Huber Corp., for $255 million in cash and 1 million common shares. AVEX, with 1998 revenues of $841 million, provides contract electronics design, manufacturing and testing services to original equipment manufacturers primarily in the telecommunications industry. The transaction is expected to close by early August 1999.

Operational Review - 14-JUL-99

Sales in the three months ended March 31, 1999, advanced 36%, year to year, aided by the LCEC acquisition (February 1998). Margins narrowed, as SG&A expenses rose 40%, and amortization and goodwill charges increased 56%; the gain in operating income was held to 30%. With interest expense up 25%, after taxes at 36.4%, versus 38.7%, net income climbed 35%, to $5,037,000 ($0.40 a share, on 3.8% more share), from $3,742,000 ($0.31).

Stock Performance - 08-OCT-99

In the past 30 trading days, BHE's shares have increased 1%, compared to a 0.91% fall in the S&P 500. Average trading volume for the past five days was 80,420 shares, compared with the 40-day moving average of 106,823 shares.

Key Stock Statistics

Dividend Rate/Share	Nil	Shareholders	124
Shs. outstg. (M)	15.2	Market cap. (B)	$0.559
Avg. daily vol. (M)	0.086	Inst. holdings	70%
Tang. Bk. Value/Share	7.66		
Beta	1.17		

Value of $10,000 invested 5 years ago: $ 30,785

Fiscal Year Ending Dec. 31

	1999	1998	1997	1996	1995	1994
Revenues (Million $)						
1Q	146.6	108.0	75.72	30.38	23.12	24.28
2Q	162.6	132.6	78.16	33.50	23.65	25.05
3Q	—	139.7	83.18	62.30	24.39	25.10
4Q	—	143.7	88.17	75.11	26.20	23.75
Yr.	—	524.1	325.2	201.3	97.35	98.17
Earnings Per Share ($)						
1Q	**0.40**	**0.31**	**0.28**	**0.22**	0.19	0.17
2Q	**0.41**	**0.31**	**0.30**	**0.24**	0.20	0.17
3Q	—	**0.35**	**0.33**	**0.26**	0.19	0.18
4Q	—	**0.38**	**0.35**	**0.24**	0.17	0.20
Yr.	—	**1.35**	**1.25**	**0.96**	**0.75**	**0.71**

Next earnings report expected: mid October

Dividend Data

The company has never paid a cash dividend. A two-for-one stock split was effected in August 1997. A shareholder rights plan was adopted in December 1998.

Benchmark Electronics, Inc.

Business Summary - 14-JUL-99

Benchmark Electronics provides contract electronics manufacturing and design services to original equipment manufacturers (OEMs) in industries that include medical devices, communications equipment, industrial and business computers, testing instrumentation and industrial controls. The company specializes in manufacturing high quality, technologically complex printed circuit board (PCB) assemblies for customers that require low to medium volume production runs.

The basis for the development of the contract manufacturing industry in recent years has been increasing reliance by OEMs on contract manufacturers such as BHE to make PCB board assemblies. As a result of outsourcing manufacturing services, the contract manufacturing industry in the U.S. grew at a compound annual rate of 21% from 1994 through 1998, according to industry sources. A 1997 industry study forecast that the contract manufacturing industry would grow at an approximate compound annual rate of 20% through 2000, as OEMs continue to outsource manufacturing requirements and look to contract manufacturers to provide additional services.

Substantially all of the company's manufacturing services are provided on a turnkey basis, whereby BHE purchases customer-specified components from its network of suppliers, assembles the components on finished PCBs, performs post-production testing, and provides the customer with production process and testing documentation. The company offers customers flexible, just-in-time delivery programs, allowing product shipments to be closely coordinated with customer inventory requirements.

In 1996, BHE acquired EMD Technologies, Inc. The acquisition moved the company into the top tier of electronic manufacturing services industry (EMSI) providers. With the acquisition of EMD, BHE can offer product software and circuit design, bare PCB layout, mechanical product design, and test fixture/software development all under one roof. In February 1998, BHE acquired Lockheed Commercial Electronics Co. (LCEC) from Lockheed Martin, for $70 million in cash. LCEC is one of New England's largest electronics manufacturing services companies. It provides a broad range of services, including PCB assembly and test, system assembly and test, prototyping, depot repair, and engineering support services.

On March 1, 1999, the company acquired certain assets from Stratus Computer Ireland, a wholly owned subsidiary of Ascend Communications, Inc., for $48 million, subject to adjustment. In connection with the transaction, BHE entered into a three-year supply agreement to provide system integration services to Ascend and Stratus Holding Ltd., and also hired 260 employees.

Per Share Data ($) (Year Ended Dec. 31)	1998	1997	1996	1995	1994	1993	1992	1991	1990	1989
Tangible Bk. Val.	7.66	8.48	7.03	5.80	5.00	4.29	3.71	2.55	2.22	0.84
Cash Flow	2.45	2.09	1.66	1.00	0.94	0.72	0.57	0.46	0.46	0.36
Earnings	1.35	1.25	0.96	0.75	0.70	0.55	0.41	0.33	0.38	0.33
Dividends	Nil	Nil	Nil	Nil	Nil	Nil	Nil	Nil	Nil	Nil
Payout Ratio	Nil	Nil	Nil	Nil	Nil	Nil	Nil	Nil	Nil	Nil
Prices - High	37 1/2	30 1/2	17 1/4	16	14	12	8 7/8	6 1/8	4 3/8	NA
- Low	17 5/8	12 3/4	12 1/8	10 1/8	11 1/4	7 1/2	5 1/4	2 5/16	1 13/16	NA
P/E Ratio - High	28	24	18	21	20	22	21	19	12	NA
- Low	13	10	13	13	16	14	13	7	5	NA
Income Statement Analysis (Million $)										
Revs.	524	325	201	97.4	98.2	75.9	50.6	33.3	21.3	18.1
Oper. Inc.	44.0	35.3	21.8	11.3	10.7	8.0	5.4	3.8	3.0	2.0
Depr.	13.3	10.2	6.4	2.1	1.9	1.4	1.1	0.8	0.4	0.2
Int. Exp.	4.4	2.5	1.4	Nil	Nil	Nil	Nil	Nil	0.1	0.1
Pretax Inc.	26.9	24.0	14.4	9.5	9.0	6.9	4.8	3.3	3.1	1.9
Eff. Tax Rate	39%	37%	39%	36%	36%	36%	34%	36%	35%	29%
Net Inc.	16.4	15.1	8.9	6.2	5.8	4.5	3.1	2.1	2.0	1.4
Balance Sheet & Other Fin. Data (Million $)										
Cash	23.1	21.0	13.8	2.8	8.4	10.1	13.3	3.1	7.1	0.1
Curr. Assets	139	125	103	47.0	38.5	42.0	30.3	15.6	15.7	5.1
Total Assets	242	190	168	57.0	48.2	47.4	34.4	20.0	17.4	6.6
Curr. Liab.	53.2	37.3	30.7	9.7	7.6	12.9	4.5	3.3	2.8	2.3
LT Debt	46.1	30.3	30.4	Nil	Nil	Nil	Nil	Nil	Nil	0.1
Common Eqty.	138	121	105	46.6	40.1	34.2	29.6	16.3	14.2	3.5
Total Cap.	189	153	137	47.4	40.7	34.6	29.8	16.5	14.3	3.7
Cap. Exp.	12.2	10.4	8.7	2.3	6.3	2.8	0.9	7.2	0.5	1.3
Cash Flow	29.7	25.2	15.2	8.2	7.7	5.9	4.3	2.9	2.4	1.5
Curr. Ratio	2.6	3.4	3.4	4.9	5.1	3.3	6.8	4.7	5.6	2.2
% LT Debt of Cap.	24.4	19.8	22.2	Nil	Nil	Nil	Nil	Nil	Nil	2.4
% Net Inc.of Revs.	3.1	4.6	4.4	6.4	5.9	5.9	6.2	6.3	9.4	7.6
% Ret. on Assets	7.6	8.4	7.9	11.7	12.0	10.9	10.6	11.3	14.6	26.1
% Ret. on Equity	12.6	13.4	11.7	14.2	15.5	14.0	12.5	13.8	20.6	50.3

Data as orig reptd.; bef. results of disc opers/spec. items. Per share data adj. for stk. divs. Bold denotes diluted EPS (FASB 128)-prior periods restated. E-Estimated. NA-Not Available. NM-Not Meaningful. NR-Not Ranked.

Office—3000 Technology Dr., Angleton, TX 77515. **Tel**—(409) 849-6550. **Fax**—(409) 848-5271 **Website**—http://www.bench.com **Chrmn**—J. C. Custer. **Pres & CEO**—D. E. Nigbor. **EVP**—Cary T. Fu. **Secy**—L. A. Gurton. **Dirs**—D. H. Arnold, S. A. Barton, G. W. Bodzy, J. C. Custer, P. G. Dorflinger, C. T. Fu, D. E. Nigbor. **Transfer Agent & Registrar**—Harris Trust & Savings Bank, c/o Harris Trust Co. of New York, NYC. **Incorporated**—in Texas in 1981. **Empl**— 2,280. **S&P Analyst:** C.C.P.

STANDARD
&POOR'S
STOCK REPORTS

Benton Oil & Gas

NYSE Symbol **BNO**

In S&P SmallCap 600

09-OCT-99

Industry:
Oil & Gas (Exploration & Production)

Summary: This independent oil and gas exploration and production company has operations mainly in western Siberia (Russia) and eastern Venezuela.

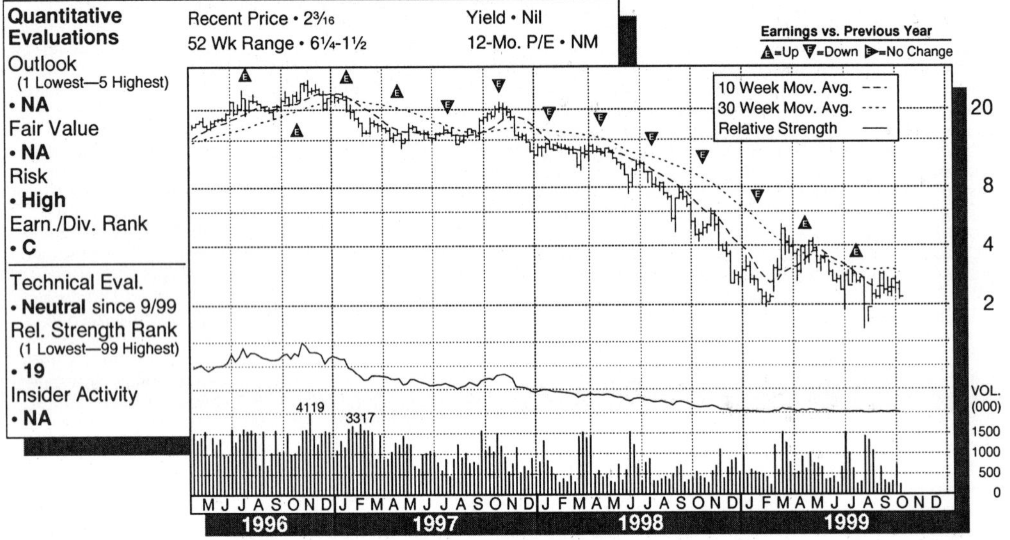

Business Profile - 21-JUN-99

Reduced revenues in the 1999 first quarter reflected lower production volumes and significantly reduced oil price realizations associated with a prevailing weak commodity environment earlier in the year. Average production of 33,166 bbl. of oil per day was down 21% from the 1998 first quarter average of 41,891 bbl. per day. On June 1, 1999, the company announced that the first exploratory well on the Qingshui Block in China had proved unsuccessful. In early May, BNO reported that the first exploratory well on the Delta Centro block in Venezuela had proved unsuccessful. The company and its partners are re-evaluating the future potential of the block. BNO's net share of costs associated with this well is expected to total $6 million to $7 million.

Operational Review - 21-JUN-99

Revenues in the three months ended March 31, 1999, fell 34%, year to year, as decreased oil sales revenue in Venezuela reflected declines in world crude oil prices and lower sales quantities. However, in the absence of a $17.5 million writedown of oil and gas properties, the net loss narrowed to $8,663,000 ($0.29 a share) from $20,986,000 ($0.71).

Stock Performance - 08-OCT-99

In the past 30 trading days, BNO's shares were unchanged, compared to a 0.91% fall in the S&P 500. Average trading volume for the past five days was 47,640 shares, compared with the 40-day moving average of 97,395 shares.

Key Stock Statistics

Dividend Rate/Share	Nil	Shareholders	1,064
Shs. outstg. (M)	29.6	Market cap. (B)	$0.065
Avg. daily vol. (M)	0.076	Inst. holdings	35%
Tang. Bk. Value/Share	NM		
Beta	0.24		

Value of $10,000 invested 5 years ago: $ 3,364

Fiscal Year Ending Dec. 31

	1999	1998	1997	1996	1995	1994
Revenues (Million $)						
1Q	22.04	33.26	46.30	32.94	12.66	3.76
2Q	25.75	28.21	40.98	41.89	13.21	8.48
3Q	—	23.88	45.19	40.90	18.29	9.57
4Q	—	26.80	46.56	49.34	20.91	12.90
Yr.	—	112.2	179.0	165.1	65.07	34.70
Earnings Per Share ($)						
1Q	**-0.29**	**-0.71**	**0.28**	**0.22**	0.08	-0.05
2Q	**-0.26**	**-1.69**	**0.15**	**0.47**	0.04	0.05
3Q	—	**-0.27**	**0.09**	**0.29**	0.11	0.07
4Q	—	**-3.54**	**0.07**	**0.30**	0.17	0.05
Yr.	—	**-6.21**	**0.59**	**1.29**	**0.40**	**0.12**

Next earnings report expected: mid November

Dividend Data

No cash dividends have been paid. A poison pill stockholder rights plan was adopted in 1995. Two-for-one stock splits were effected in 1990 and 1991.

Benton Oil and Gas Company

Business Summary - 21-JUN-99

Benton Oil & Gas, is an independent energy company that began operations in 1989. Originally active only in the U.S., it has developed significant interests in oil and gas properties in Venezuela and Russia, and has recently certain acquired interests in China, Jordan, Senegal, and the U.S. Operations are currently conducted mainly through an 80%-owned Venezuelan subsidiary, Benton-Vinncler, C.A., which operates the South Monagas Unit in Venezuela, and a 34%-owned Russian joint venture, GEOILBENT, which operates the North Gubkinskoye Field in West Siberia, Russia.

BNO has recently expanded into projects that involve exploration components: in Venezuela through participation in the Delta Centro exploration block; in Santa Barbara County, CA, through the acquisition of a participation interest in three state offshore oil and gas leases; and in China through a farmout agreement with Shell Exploration (China) Ltd. and the acquisition of the WAB-21 Exploration block.

In the three years through 1998, the company expanded its reserves, with proved reserves increasing from 109,620 bbl. of oil equivalent (BOE) in 1996 to 168,888 MBOE in 1998. However, average daily production fell to 35,879 BOE, from 36,648 BOE.

BNO seeks to identify and exploit new oil and gas reserves primarily in under-developed but proven hydrocarbon regions thereby seeking to minimize the associated risk of such activities. The company plans to minimize risk by employing the following strategies in its business activities: (i) seeking new reserves primarily in areas of low geologic risk; (ii) using proven advanced technology in both exploration and development to maximize recovery, including the exploration of higher risk, higher potential areas; (iii) establishing a local presence through joint venture partners and the use of local personnel; (iv) committing capital in a phased manner to limit total commitments at any one time; and (v) reducing foreign exchange risks through receipt of revenues in U.S. currency.

The company has used its experience to seek and develop new reserves in countries where perceived potential political and operating difficulties have sometimes discouraged other energy companies from competing. As a result, it has established operations in Venezuela and Russia with significant reserves that have been acquired and developed at relatively low costs. BNO is seeking similar opportunities in other countries and areas that it believes have high potential.

Per Share Data ($) (Year Ended Dec. 31)	1998	1997	1996	1995	1994	1993	1992	1991	1990	1989
Tangible Bk. Val.	0.44	6.71	6.05	4.06	3.54	3.40	2.89	1.96	1.17	0.57
Cash Flow	-5.01	2.13	2.46	1.05	0.53	-0.12	0.01	0.28	0.12	-0.10
Earnings	-6.21	0.59	1.30	0.40	0.12	-0.26	-0.22	0.03	0.01	-0.13
Dividends	Nil	Nil	Nil	Nil	Nil	Nil	Nil	Nil	Nil	Nil
Payout Ratio	Nil	Nil	Nil	Nil	Nil	NM	NM	Nil	Nil	Nil
Prices - High	13⅝	24¾	28⅝	16⅛	9⅛	10¼	11⅛	18¾	8⅜	2⅝
- Low	2 7/16	11¼	11¼	8⅝	4¼	3⅞	5	6⅛	2	1¼
P/E Ratio - High	NM	42	22	40	76	NM	NM	NM	NM	NM
- Low	NM	19	9	22	35	NM	NM	NA	NA	NA
Income Statement Analysis (Million $)										
Revs.	90.3	164	148	62.2	32.1	7.4	8.4	11.2	4.4	0.3
Oper. Inc.	20.0	99	104	42.0	17.3	-0.5	1.7	4.9	1.0	-0.4
Depr. Depl. & Amort.	35.6	47.6	34.5	17.4	10.3	2.6	3.0	3.0	0.8	0.1
Int. Exp.	32.9	24.2	16.1	7.5	3.9	2.0	1.8	1.7	0.3	0.1
Pretax Inc.	-230	41.9	68.8	18.4	5.8	-4.8	-2.9	0.5	0.2	-0.5
Eff. Tax Rate	NM	42%	30%	14%	12%	NM	NM	34%	26%	NM
Net Inc.	-183	18.0	38.4	10.6	3.0	-4.8	-2.9	0.3	0.1	-0.5
Balance Sheet & Other Fin. Data (Million $)										
Cash	125	86.3	88.9	26.5	33.7	36.3	13.7	3.7	5.1	1.5
Curr. Assets	92.8	224	151	51.6	62.4	39.5	14.8	7.0	8.1	2.2
Total Assets	339	584	436	215	163	109	68.2	49.4	27.3	4.5
Curr. Liab.	36.9	58.4	52.1	54.5	40.6	12.8	4.3	21.8	9.9	1.5
LT Debt	288	280	175	49.5	31.9	11.8	11.3	7.4	7.3	0.4
Common Eqty.	13.0	198	175	104	88.3	84.0	50.5	20.2	10.1	2.6
Total Cap.	302	526	384	160	122	95.8	63.9	27.6	17.3	3.0
Cap. Exp.	120	110	95.5	68.3	38.4	26.1	17.0	25.4	22.6	4.8
Cash Flow	-147	65.6	72.8	28.0	13.3	-2.2	0.1	3.4	1.0	-0.4
Curr. Ratio	2.5	3.8	2.9	0.9	1.5	3.1	3.4	0.3	0.8	1.5
% LT Debt of Cap.	95.5	53.2	45.6	30.9	26.2	12.3	17.7	26.9	41.9	13.9
% Ret. on Assets	NM	3.5	12.0	5.6	2.2	NM	NM	0.8	0.7	NM
% Ret. on Equity	NM	9.7	27.5	11.0	3.4	NM	NM	2.1	1.6	NM

Data as orig reptd.; bef. results of disc opers/spec. items. Per share data adj. for stk. divs. Bold denotes diluted EPS (FASB 128)-prior periods restated. E-Estimated. NA-Not Available. NM-Not Meaningful. NR-Not Ranked.

Office—6267 Carpinteria Avenue, Suite 200, Carpinteria, CA 93013. **Tel**—(805) 566-5600. **Chrmn, CEO & COO**—A. E. Benton. **SVP, CFO & Treas**—J. M. Whipkey. **VP & Contr**—C. C. Hickok. **Dirs**—A. E. Benton, R. W. Fetzner, G. A. Garrettson, B. M. McIntyre, M. B. Wray. **Transfer Agent & Registrar**—ChaseMellon Shareholder Services, LA. **Incorporated**—in Delaware in 1988. **Empl**— 240. **S&P Analyst:** C.C.P.

STANDARD
&POOR'S
STOCK REPORTS

Billing Concepts

NASDAQ Symbol **BILL**

In S&P SmallCap 600

09-OCT-99

Industry: Services (Data Processing)

Summary: This third-party billing clearinghouse and information management services provider to the telecommunications industry plans to split into two separate public companies.

Quantitative Evaluations

Outlook (1 Lowest—5 Highest) • **5**

Fair Value • **9½**

Risk • **NA**

Earn./Div. Rank • **NR**

Technical Eval. • **Bearish** since 6/99

Rel. Strength Rank (1 Lowest—99 Highest) • **10**

Insider Activity • **Favorable**

Recent Price • 5⅛
52 Wk Range • 17¼-4⅛
Yield • Nil
12-Mo. P/E • 9.2

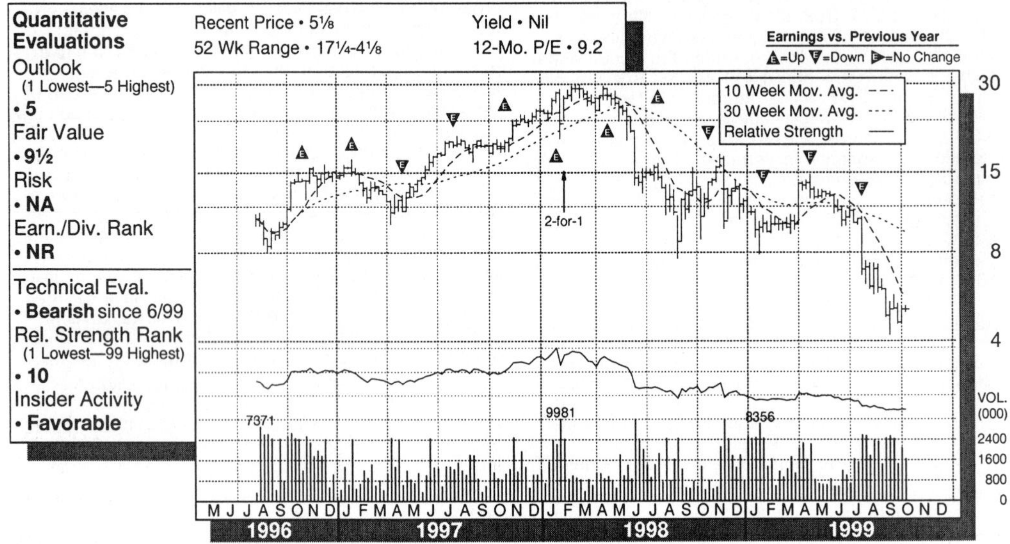

Business Profile - 11-JUN-99

In April 1999, the company disclosed its intention to split its business into two separate public companies. The systems and software unit will operate under an undetermined corporate name, while the local exchange carrier (LEC) billing division will function under the name Billing Concepts Corporation. Management believes the separation will benefit both units, as they will each be able to pursue their distinct missions and leverage their different operating and financial characteristics. As a result of this decision, results of the local exchange carrier division have been classified as discontinued operations.

Operational Review - 11-JUN-99

Revenues from continuing systems group operations in the six months ended March 31, 1999, nearly doubled, year to year, to $22,765,000. Margins widened, reflecting a more favorable sales mix and less rapid increases in SG&A and R&D expenditures; operating income advanced to $2,464,000, from $108,000. The loss from continuing operations narrowed to $281,000 ($0.01 a share, based on 4.5% more shares), from $725,000 ($0.02). Results exclude income from discontinued operations of $0.36 and $0.43 a share in the respective periods.

Stock Performance - 08-OCT-99

In the past 30 trading days, BILL's shares have declined 15%, compared to a 0.91% fall in the S&P 500. Average trading volume for the past five days was 325,920 shares, compared with the 40-day moving average of 468,721 shares.

Key Stock Statistics

Dividend Rate/Share	Nil	Shareholders	476
Shs. outstg. (M)	37.4	Market cap. (B)	$0.191
Avg. daily vol. (M)	0.386	Inst. holdings	54%
Tang. Bk. Value/Share	2.98		
Beta	NA		

Value of $10,000 invested 5 years ago: NA

Fiscal Year Ending Sep. 30

	1999	1998	1997	1996	1995	1994
Revenues (Million $)						
1Q	47.92	38.25	27.82	23.35	17.01	—
2Q	10.93	41.01	27.38	26.95	17.93	—
3Q	11.30	40.41	31.89	25.73	21.37	—
4Q	—	41.09	35.74	27.85	24.54	—
Yr.	—	160.8	122.8	103.9	80.85	57.75
Earnings Per Share ($)						
1Q	**0.19**	**0.20**	**0.15**	0.14	0.10	—
2Q	**-0.01**	**0.21**	0.16	0.17	0.10	—
3Q	**-0.02**	**0.20**	-0.41	0.14	0.14	—
4Q	—	**0.14**	0.18	0.14	0.14	—
Yr.	—	**0.74**	**0.11**	0.58	0.48	0.30

Next earnings report expected: mid November

Dividend Data

No cash dividends have been paid. The company presently intends to retain all earnings for the operation and development of its business and does not anticipate paying any cash dividends on the common stock for the foreseeable future.

A Division of The McGraw-Hill Companies

Billing Concepts Corp.

Business Summary - 11-JUN-99

Billing Concepts Corp. (formerly Billing Information Concepts Corp.), spun off by U.S. Long Distance Corp. to its shareholders in August 1996, is one of the largest U.S. third-party providers of billing clearinghouse and information services to the telecommunications industry. In April 1999, the company disclosed its intention to split its business into two separate public companies. The systems and software segment will operate under an undetermined corporate name, while the local exchange carrier (LEC) billing division will function under the name Billing Concepts Corp.

Customers include direct dial long distance telephone companies, operator services providers, information providers, telecommunications equipment suppliers, local exchange companies, Internet service providers, data services providers and integrated communications services providers. BILL maintains contractual billing arrangements with more than 1,300 local telephone companies that provide access lines to, and collect for services from, end-users of telecommunication services.

BILL direct dial long distance customers use the company as a billing clearinghouse for processing and collecting call records generated by their end users. Although these clients can bill end users directly, BILL provides these carriers with a cost-effective means of billing and collecting residential and small commercial accounts through the local telephone companies.

The company acts as an aggregator of telephone call records and other transactions from various sources. Due to its large volume, it receives discounted billing costs with local telephone companies, and can pass on these discounts to its clients. Moreover, BILL can provide services to long distance carriers and operator services providers that would otherwise be unable to make the substantial investments in billing and collection agreements with local telephone companies.

BILL expects the Telecommunications Act to create new opportunities for third-party clearinghouses. The Telecommunications Act requires that the Regional Bell Operating Companies use separate subsidiaries to provide services not related to their existing regulated local services. BILL has contracted with two Regional Bell Operating Companies (RBOCs) to provide long distance billing services and is currently negotiating with several other RBOCs to provide both in-territory and out-of-territory billing for their long distance services.

In December 1998, the company acquired, in exchange for 2,492,759 common shares, Communications Software Consultants Inc. (CommSoft), a privately held software development and consulting firm that specializes in the telecommunications industry. CommSoft had estimated 1998 revenues of approximately $18 million. In September 1998, BILL acquired for $10 million a 22% stake in Princeton TeleCom Corp. (PTC). PTC is a New Jersey-based, privately held company that specializes in electronic bill publishing over the Internet , and in advanced payment solutions.

Per Share Data ($) (Year Ended Sep. 30)	1998	1997	1996	1995	1994	1993	1992	1991	1990	1989
Tangible Bk. Val.	2.70	3.01	0.75	NA	NA	NA	NA	NA	NA	NA
Cash Flow	0.93	0.46	NA	NA	NA	NA	NA	NA	NA	NA
Earnings	0.74	0.12	0.58	0.48	0.30	NA	NA	NA	NA	NA
Dividends	Nil	Nil	Nil	NA	NA	NA	NA	NA	NA	NA
Payout Ratio	Nil	Nil	Nil	NA	NA	NA	NA	NA	NA	NA
Prices - High	30	23¾	16⅛	NA	NA	NA	NA	NA	NA	NA
- Low	7⅝	10	8	NA	NA	NA	NA	NA	NA	NA
P/E Ratio - High	41	NM	28	NA	NA	NA	NA	NA	NA	NA
- Low	10	NM	14	NA	NA	NA	NA	NA	NA	NA
Income Statement Analysis (Million $)										
Revs.	161	123	104	80.8	57.7	46.5	33.2	NA	NA	NA
Oper. Inc.	47.5	38.5	30.8	23.5	14.3	NA	NA	NA	NA	NA
Depr.	6.5	3.8	2.1	1.2	0.9	NA	NA	NA	NA	NA
Int. Exp.	0.2	0.5	0.3	0.2	0.1	NA	NA	NA	NA	NA
Pretax Inc.	43.5	14.0	28.8	22.8	13.6	NA	NA	NA	NA	NA
Eff. Tax Rate	40%	74%	38%	38%	37%	NA	NA	NA	NA	NA
Net Inc.	25.9	3.7	17.9	14.1	8.6	6.4	5.8	NA	NA	NA
Balance Sheet & Other Fin. Data (Million $)										
Cash	118	41.4	34.1	26.8	NA	NA	NA	NA	NA	NA
Curr. Assets	220	141	124	101	NA	NA	NA	NA	NA	NA
Total Assets	259	167	138	107	89.7	74.7	63.6	NA	NA	NA
Curr. Liab.	162	113	110	83.4	NA	NA	NA	NA	NA	NA
LT Debt	1.7	2.6	5.0	2.2	0.8	0.4	0.3	NA	NA	NA
Common Eqty.	92.3	48.7	22.6	Nil	NA	NA	NA	NA	NA	NA
Total Cap.	96.6	53.3	27.7	23.4	NA	NA	NA	NA	NA	NA
Cap. Exp.	11.3	17.6	15.7	1.9	6.1	NA	NA	NA	NA	NA
Cash Flow	32.4	7.5	20.0	15.3	9.5	NA	NA	NA	NA	NA
Curr. Ratio	1.4	1.2	1.1	1.2	NA	NA	NA	NA	NA	NA
% LT Debt of Cap.	1.8	4.9	18.1	9.4	NA	NA	NA	NA	NA	NA
% Net Inc.of Revs.	16.1	3.0	17.2	17.5	14.8	13.9	17.5	NA	NA	NA
% Ret. on Assets	12.2	2.4	14.6	14.3	10.4	9.3	NA	NA	NA	NA
% Ret. on Equity	36.8	10.4	NA	NA	NA	NA	NA	NA	NA	NA

Data as orig reptd.; bef. results of disc opers/spec. items. Per share data adj. for stk. divs. Bold denotes diluted EPS (FASB 128)-prior periods restated. E-Estimated. NA-Not Available. NM-Not Meaningful. NR-Not Ranked.

Office—7411 John Smith Drive, San Antonio, TX 78229. **Tel**—(210) 949-7000. **Website**—http://www.billingconcepts.com **Chrmn & CEO**—P. H. Holmes Jr. **Pres & COO**—A. W. Saltzman. **SVP, CFO & Secy**—K. E. Simmons. **Dirs**—L. Cooke, P. H. Holmes Jr., T. G. Loeffler, A. W. Saltzman, J. E. Sowell. **Transfer Agent & Registrar**—Montreal Trust Co., Montreal. **Incorporated**—Delaware in 1996. **Empl**— 730. **S&P Analyst:** Stephen J. Tekirian

STANDARD & POOR'S
STOCK REPORTS

Bindley Western Industries

NYSE Symbol **BDY**

In S&P SmallCap 600

09-OCT-99

Industry: Distributors (Food & Health)

Summary: BDY is one of the largest U.S. drug wholesalers, specializing in the distribution of prescription drugs and related products.

Quantitative Evaluations

Outlook (1 Lowest—5 Highest) • **4-**

Fair Value • **20¾**

Risk • **Low**

Earn./Div. Rank • **B+**

Technical Eval. • **Bearish** since 7/99

Rel. Strength Rank (1 Lowest—99 Highest) • **7**

Insider Activity • **Unfavorable**

Recent Price • 13

52 Wk Range • 37-12¼

Yield • 0.5%

12-Mo. P/E • 20.6

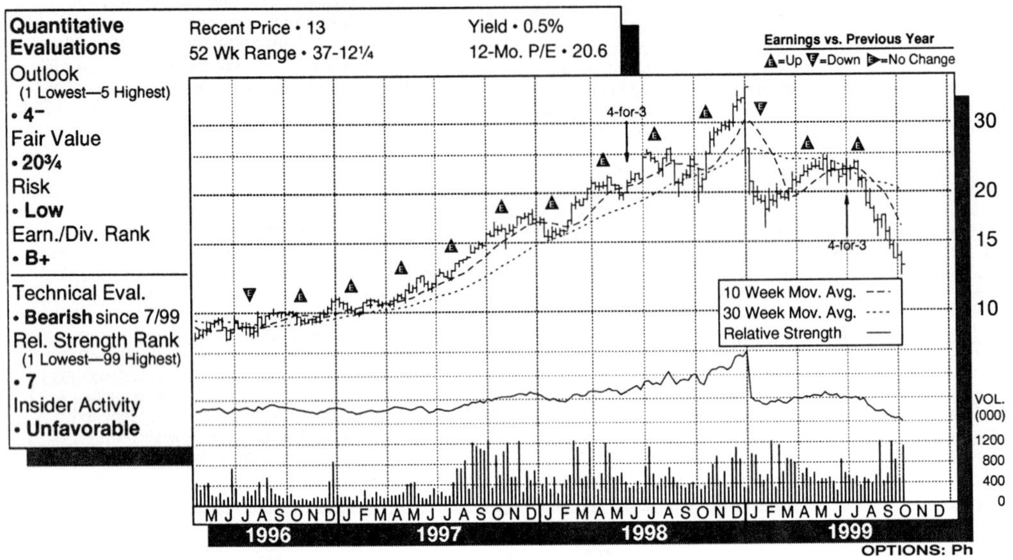

Business Profile - 02-SEP-99

In August 1999, the company acquired Central Pharmacy Services, Inc. (CPSI), for about $55 million in stock. CPSI, headquartered in Atlanta, operates specialized nuclear pharmacies that prepare and deliver unit dose radiopharmaceuticals for use in nuclear imaging procedures in hospitals and clinics; it had 1998 sales of $33 million. During the first week of May 1999, BDY began servicing more than 350 new locations. A new distribution facility is scheduled to open in Colorado in October, filling a void in the company's distribution network. BDY expects to expand its managed care business through new contracts and growth from customers such as Express Scripts, CVS and Eckerd.

Operational Review - 02-SEP-99

Total revenues in the six months ended June 30, 1999, rose 5.5%, year to year, as higher net sales from stock outweighed a decline in net brokerage sales. With well controlled selling, general and administrative expenses, operating income climbed 12%. Despite higher interest expense, with a smaller rise in depreciation and amortization charges, after taxes at 39.7% in each period, net income gained 14%, to $17.9 million ($0.54 a share, on 13% more shares), from $15.7 million ($0.54, as adjusted).

Stock Performance - 08-OCT-99

In the past 30 trading days, BDY's shares have declined 23%, compared to a 0.91% fall in the S&P 500. Average trading volume for the past five days was 222,600 shares, compared with the 40-day moving average of 163,403 shares.

Key Stock Statistics

Dividend Rate/Share	0.06	Shareholders	1,000
Shs. outstg. (M)	30.6	Market cap. (B)	$0.397
Avg. daily vol. (M)	0.180	Inst. holdings	66%
Tang. Bk. Value/Share	10.80		
Beta	1.07		

Value of $10,000 invested 5 years ago: NA

Fiscal Year Ending Dec. 31

	1999	1998	1997	1996	1995	1994
Revenues (Million $)						
1Q	1,975	1,962	1,635	1,189	1,114	917.0
2Q	2,045	1,848	1,811	1,218	1,126	987.0
3Q	—	1,814	1,813	1,336	1,122	1,013
4Q	—	1,998	2,053	1,576	1,309	1,118
Yr.	—	7,623	7,312	5,319	4,670	4,034
Earnings Per Share ($)						
1Q	**0.27**	**0.26**	**0.23**	**0.20**	0.19	0.17
2Q	**0.27**	**0.26**	**0.22**	**0.17**	0.19	0.17
3Q	—	**0.26**	**0.21**	**0.18**	0.16	0.16
4Q	—	**-0.16**	**0.24**	**0.21**	0.20	0.18
Yr.	—	**0.63**	**0.89**	**0.77**	**0.72**	**0.68**

Next earnings report expected: late October

Dividend Data (Dividends have been paid since 1990.)

Amount ($)	Date Decl.	Ex-Div. Date	Stock of Record	Payment Date
0.020	Mar. 03	Mar. 08	Mar. 12	Mar. 23 '99
4-for-3	May. 21	Jun. 28	Jun. 11	Jun. 25 '99
0.015	May. 26	Jul. 07	Jul. 09	Jul. 16 '99
0.015	Sep. 13	Sep. 16	Sep. 20	Sep. 30 '99

Bindley Western Industries, Inc.

Business Summary - 02-SEP-99

Bindley Western Industries is the fifth largest U.S. wholesale distributor of pharmaceuticals and related healthcare products. In 1998, the company operated in two segments, BWI and Priority Healthcare Corp. On December 31, 1998, BDY spun off Priority to shareholders; for each BDY share, shareholders received 0.448 of a Priority Class A common share.

It is estimated that about 80% of pharmaceutical sales are currently distributed through wholesalers, versus under 47% in 1970. Outsourcing distribution allows manufacturers to better allocate their resources to R&D and manufacturing. During 1998, it is estimated that the five largest national wholesalers had a combined U.S. market share of 80% for the distribution of prescription drugs.

BWI product lines include ethical pharmaceuticals (prescription drugs), dialysis supplies, health and beauty care products, and home health care merchandise. The company's wholesale drug customer base includes chain drug companies that operate their own warehouses, individual drug stores, chain and independent supermarkets, mass retailers with their own pharmacies, hospitals, clinics, HMOs, state and federal government agencies, and other health care providers. In 1998, BWI served four of the 10 leading U.S. chain drug companies. About 49% of 1998 net sales came from chain drug warehouse customers, with Eckerd and CVS accounting for 18% and 17%, respectively. The BWI drug wholesaling operation serves customers in 37 states and Puerto Rico, from 14 distribution centers located in 13 states. A 15th distribution center is expected to open in Colorado in October 1999.

In each of the last five years, about 85% (based on sales volume) of sales were provided by ethical pharmaceutical products. Of the thousands of prescription drugs carried in inventory, a comparatively small number account for a disproportionately large share of the total dollar volume of products sold. The company's five largest suppliers in 1998 were Astra Pharmaceutical, Bristol-Myers Squibb, Pfizer, Eli Lilly, and SmithKline Beecham. No single vendor accounted for over 10% of net sales.

Priority Healthcare Corp. (82% owned, prior to its spinoff to shareholders on December 31, 1998) is a national distributor of specialty pharmaceuticals and related medical supplies to the alternate site healthcare market, and also provides patient-specific, self-injectable biopharmaceuticals and disease treatment programs to individuals with chronic diseases. It sells more than 3,500 SKUs of specialty pharmaceutical and medical supplies to outpatient rental care centers and office-based physicians in the oncology and infectious disease markets. During 1998, 27% of Priority's revenues were derived from sales of erythropoietin (EPO) to the renal care market.

Per Share Data ($) (Year Ended Dec. 31)	1998	1997	1996	1995	1994	1993	1992	1991	1990	1989
Tangible Bk. Val.	10.40	14.78	9.03	8.60	7.93	7.25	6.95	6.69	5.92	NA
Cash Flow	0.91	1.45	1.17	1.11	1.05	0.79	0.83	0.84	0.84	NA
Earnings	0.63	0.89	0.85	0.80	0.75	0.49	0.57	0.91	0.56	NA
Dividends	0.06	0.05	0.05	0.05	0.05	0.04	0.03	0.03	0.02	NA
Payout Ratio	9%	5%	5%	6%	6%	8%	6%	4%	3%	NA
Prices - High	37	18 1/4	11 7/8	11	8 3/4	8 1/8	11 5/8	10 1/4	8	NA
- Low	15 1/4	9 3/4	8 1/2	7 5/8	6 1/4	5 3/8	6 1/2	6 3/8	4 7/8	NA
P/E Ratio - High	59	20	14	14	12	16	20	11	14	NA
- Low	24	11	10	10	8	11	11	7	9	NA
Income Statement Analysis (Million $)										
Revs.	7,621	7,310	5,318	4,670	4,034	3,426	2,911	2,393	2,042	NA
Oper. Inc.	83.7	61.6	49.9	41.8	38.7	32.7	30.2	30.7	21.8	NA
Depr.	8.4	7.4	6.7	6.3	5.8	5.7	4.7	3.8	3.3	NA
Int. Exp.	18.5	15.9	13.0	10.1	11.2	8.1	8.4	13.4	13.1	NA
Pretax Inc.	39.7	39.8	30.9	28.0	25.0	16.4	16.0	17.7	10.3	NA
Eff. Tax Rate	47%	40%	42%	41%	41%	42%	35%	36%	36%	NA
Net Inc.	19.1	23.7	18.0	16.4	14.7	9.6	10.4	11.4	6.7	NA
Balance Sheet & Other Fin. Data (Million $)										
Cash	43.0	42.9	63.7	34.8	40.9	38.3	NA	NA	NA	NA
Curr. Assets	1,176	1,185	851	773	736	665	NA	NA	NA	NA
Total Assets	1,287	1,291	941	844	803	732	680	NA	NA	NA
Curr. Liab.	949	898	616	569	547	490	NA	NA	NA	NA
LT Debt	0.6	32.1	100	69.5	69.5	69.7	70.2	NA	NA	NA
Common Eqty.	333	346	222	201	180	166	157	NA	NA	NA
Total Cap.	337	393	325	275	256	242	230	NA	NA	NA
Cap. Exp.	33.5	22.6	15.6	7.9	3.6	5.7	22.1	NA	NA	NA
Cash Flow	27.6	31.2	24.7	22.7	20.6	15.2	15.1	15.1	9.9	NA
Curr. Ratio	1.2	1.3	1.4	1.4	1.3	1.4	NA	NA	NA	NA
% LT Debt of Cap.	0.2	8.1	30.8	25.3	27.1	28.8	30.5	NA	NA	NA
% Net Inc.of Revs.	0.3	0.3	0.3	0.0	0.4	0.3	0.4	0.5	0.3	NA
% Ret. on Assets	1.5	2.1	2.0	2.0	1.9	1.4	NA	NA	NA	NA
% Ret. on Equity	5.6	8.4	8.5	8.6	8.5	5.9	8.5	NA	NA	NA

Data as orig reptd.; bef. results of disc opers/spec. items. Per share data adj. for stk. divs. Bold denotes diluted EPS (FASB 128)-prior periods restated. E-Estimated. NA-Not Available. NM-Not Meaningful. NR-Not Ranked.

Office—8909 Purdue Rd., Indianapolis, IN 46268. **Tel**—(317) 704-4000. **Website**—http://www.bindley.com **Chrmn, Pres & CEO**—W. E. Bindley. **EVP & Secy**—M. D. McCormick. **EVP & CFO**—T. J. Salentine. **Treas**—M. L. Shinn. **Dirs**—W. E. Bindley, W. F. Bindley II, K. W. Burks, S. B. Harris, R. L. Koch II, M. D. McCormick, J. T. McGinley, J. K. Risk III, T. J. Salentine, K. C. Smith, C. Woo. **Transfer Agent & Registrar**—Harris Trust & Savings Bank, Chicago.**Incorporated**—in Indiana in 1983. **Empl**— 1,254. **S&P Analyst:** J.W.H.

STANDARD &POOR'S

STOCK REPORTS

Bio-Technology General

NASDAQ Symbol **BTGC**

In S&P SmallCap 600

09-OCT-99

Industry: Biotechnology

Summary: This company develops, manufactures and markets pharmaceuticals and biotechnology products for human health care, with a focus on treatments for growth and weight disorders.

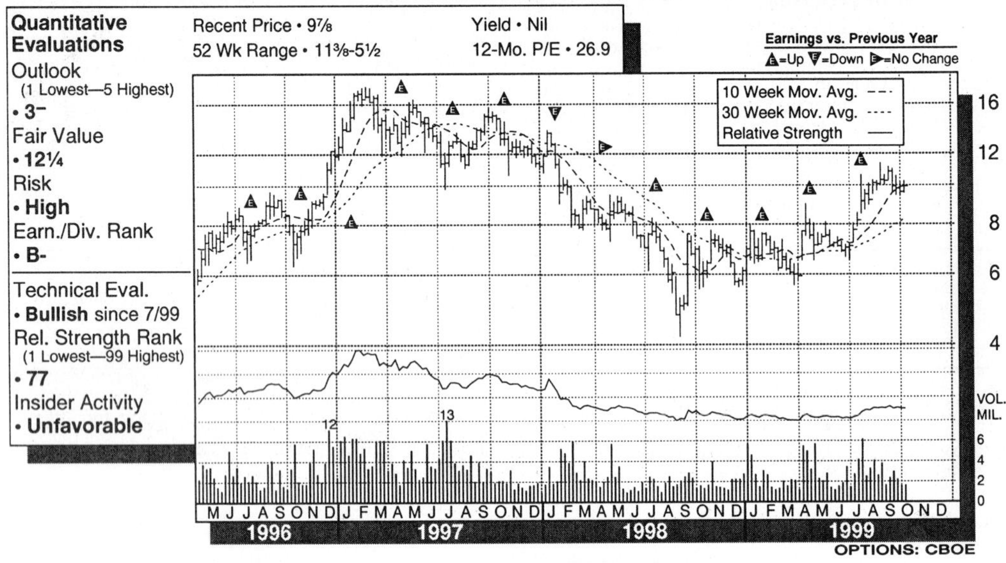

Business Profile - 02-JUN-99

The company currently has five products that have received regulatory approval and are being marketed for conditions such as involuntary weight loss, hypogonadism, growth hormone deficiency in children, and to protect the corneal endothelium during ophthalmic surgery. BTGC focuses on increasing market penetration of its existing products, expanding into new markets, and commercializing additional products. In November 1998, BTGC's opthalmic surgical aid, BioLon, was launched in the U.S. by marketing partner Akorn, Inc. In April 1999, the distributor for BTGC's Oxandrin product (to prevent weight loss) said it would adjust inventory levels to reflect a recent decline in the drug's sales growth rate. BTGC believes Oxandrin's growth should pick up following the publication by JAMA, a prominent medical journal, of an article noting the beneficial effects of the drug in HIV patients.

Operational Review - 02-JUN-99

Revenues in the first three months of 1999 rose 16%, year to year, on higher contract fee revenue and greater interest and other income. Declines in R&D spending and cost of product sales were outweighed by a sharp increase in SG&A, reflecting higher legal fees and increased promotional and marketing activities; total expenses were up 14%. After taxes at 31.0%, versus 30.2%, net income increased 19%, to $4,006,000 ($0.08 a share, on 3.4% more shares), from $3,365,000 ($0.07).

Stock Performance - 08-OCT-99

In the past 30 trading days, BTGC's shares have declined 4%, compared to a 0.91% fall in the S&P 500. Average trading volume for the past five days was 314,820 shares, compared with the 40-day moving average of 472,600 shares.

Key Stock Statistics

Dividend Rate/Share	Nil	Shareholders	1,700
Shs. outstg. (M)	52.5	Market cap. (B)	$0.522
Avg. daily vol. (M)	0.410	Inst. holdings	16%
Tang. Bk. Value/Share	2.49		
Beta	1.29		

Value of $10,000 invested 5 years ago: $ 18,927

Fiscal Year Ending Dec. 31

	1999	1998	1997	1996	1995	1994
Revenues (Million $)						
1Q	20.23	17.44	14.77	10.71	5.75	5.68
2Q	22.88	18.65	15.69	12.19	7.29	7.76
3Q	—	19.57	17.92	12.13	5.06	1.90
4Q	—	21.20	15.24	12.67	9.86	2.10
Yr.	—	76.86	63.62	47.74	27.96	17.44
Earnings Per Share ($)						
1Q	**0.08**	**0.07**	0.07	0.02	0.01	-0.02
2Q	**0.10**	**0.09**	0.08	0.06	0.01	0.01
3Q	—	**0.10**	0.09	0.07	-0.02	-0.12
4Q	—	**0.10**	**0.05**	0.32	0.08	-0.10
Yr.	—	**0.36**	**0.28**	**0.47**	**0.08**	-0.23

Next earnings report expected: mid October

Dividend Data

The company has never paid a cash dividend.

A Division of The McGraw-Hill Companies

Bio-Technology General Corporation

Business Summary - 02-JUN-99

With strong demand for its human growth hormone and weight gain products bulking up its bottom line, Bio-Technology General (BTGC) is one of the few profitable biotechnology concerns. Its genetically engineered products address conditions such as endocrinology and metabolic disorders, cardio/pulmonary diseases, and ophthalmic and skin disorders.

The company's best selling product, Oxandrin, was launched in late 1995, to treat involuntary weight loss. Oxandrin is an oral anabolic agent used to promote weight gain after weight loss following extensive surgery, chronic infections and severe trauma. The company is currently conducting Phase III and IV (post approval) clinical studies to further support the role of Oxandrin in the treatment of many of these conditions. BTGC is also pursuing expanded use of the drug in patients with chronic obstructive pulminary disease, inoperable non-small cell lung cancer, and in patients who have undergone liver transplants. The drug accounted for 59% of 1998 product sales, up from 52% in 1997.

BTGC's other lead drug, Bio-Tropin, an authentic human growth hormone (hGh), is used in the treatment of short stature and growth disorders. Bio-Tropin is marketed in Europe through licensee Ferring Group and in Japan and China through JCR Pharmaceuticals. After the company received FDA approval to market Bio-Tropin, a preliminary injunction was issued prohibiting its sale in the U.S. The action resulted from a motion filed by Genentech claiming patent infringement on one of its own growth hormone drugs. Bio-Tropin accounted for 25% of product revenues in 1998, down from 31% in 1997.

The company also markets BioLon (sodium hyaluronate) for the protection of the corneal endothelium during intraocular surgery. In 1998, the product provided 10% of revenues, down from 13% in 1997. Other products include Delatestryl, injectable testosterone to treat hypogonadism; Mircette, an oral contraceptive; and Silkis, a vitamin D derivative for the topical treatment of recalcitrant psoriasis and other skin disorders.

The research pipeline includes Bio-Hep-B, a vaccine against hepatitis B virus; OxSODrol, recombinant superoxide dismutase for the prevention of bronchopulmonary dysplasia (a chronic lung disease that affects premature infants); recombinant insulin for diabetes; and Fibrimage, a thrombus imaging agent.

In January 1999, the company licensed its human insulin technology to subsidiaries of Azko Nobel for worldwide manufacturing and marketing. BTGC will receive license fees, milestone payments, and royalties on all commercial sales of the insulin product. In April 1999, BTGC announced two major anti-cancer research collaborations, with Massachusetts General Hospital and Israel's Weizmann Institute of Science.

Per Share Data ($) (Year Ended Dec. 31)	1998	1997	1996	1995	1994	1993	1992	1991	1990	1989
Tangible Bk. Val.	NA	1.69	1.31	0.47	0.41	0.38	0.65	1.05	0.42	-0.01
Cash Flow	NA	0.33	0.53	0.14	-0.16	-0.53	-0.30	-0.30	-0.30	-0.93
Earnings	0.36	0.28	0.47	0.08	-0.23	-0.63	-0.38	-0.38	-0.40	-1.17
Dividends	Nil	Nil	Nil	Nil	Nil	Nil	Nil	Nil	Nil	Nil
Payout Ratio	Nil	Nil	Nil	Nil	Nil	Nil	Nil	Nil	Nil	Nil
Prices - High	13¾	17¾	13¼	5	5⅞	6¾	11⅝	10½	4⅜	3
- Low	4⅛	9⅞	4½	2	1½	4½	4⅜	1 5/16	1	1
P/E Ratio - High	38	63	28	62	NM	NM	NM	NM	NM	NM
- Low	12	35	10	25	NM	NM	NM	NM	NA	NA
Income Statement Analysis (Million $)										
Revs.	NA	63.6	46.6	27.2	16.9	13.3	4.9	4.7	2.6	3.2
Oper. Inc.	NA	22.4	14.1	6.2	-6.3	-7.8	-8.4	-6.6	-6.4	-5.2
Depr.	NA	2.6	2.8	2.6	2.9	3.6	2.0	1.6	1.6	1.6
Int. Exp.	NA	0.3	0.2	0.2	0.3	0.4	0.5	0.2	0.1	2.0
Pretax Inc.	NA	21.2	10.9	3.4	-8.9	22.8	-9.8	-7.9	-6.2	-8.0
Eff. Tax Rate	NA	32%	NM	NM	NM	NM	NM	Nil	Nil	Nil
Net Inc.	NA	14.5	22.9	3.4	-8.9	-22.8	-9.8	-7.9	-6.2	-8.0
Balance Sheet & Other Fin. Data (Million $)										
Cash	NA	9.3	19.8	6.9	16.9	16.1	18.4	24.0	8.1	5.2
Curr. Assets	NA	76.9	49.7	20.6	21.4	19.6	20.4	26.2	9.4	6.2
Total Assets	NA	95.4	73.6	31.7	32.3	31.1	32.9	36.1	16.7	14.6
Curr. Liab.	NA	8.6	9.1	5.4	7.8	7.4	2.9	2.1	1.5	1.7
LT Debt	NA	Nil	0.3	0.7	1.3	3.5	5.8	3.6	4.8	8.1
Common Eqty.	NA	82.9	60.6	25.7	23.2	20.1	24.1	29.9	8.2	0.3
Total Cap.	NA	82.9	60.8	26.4	24.5	23.6	29.8	33.5	13.0	8.4
Cap. Exp.	NA	3.1	3.0	1.6	1.8	1.6	1.5	0.6	0.3	0.3
Cash Flow	NA	17.1	25.7	6.0	-6.1	-19.2	-7.7	-6.3	-4.6	-6.4
Curr. Ratio	NA	9.0	5.5	3.8	2.8	2.7	7.0	12.4	6.4	3.6
% LT Debt of Cap.	NA	Nil	0.5	2.5	5.2	14.8	19.4	10.8	37.1	96.1
% Net Inc.of Revs.	NA	22.8	49.1	12.2	NM	NM	NM	NM	NM	NM
% Ret. on Assets	NA	17.1	42.7	10.7	NM	NM	NM	NM	NM	NM
% Ret. on Equity	NA	20.2	53.1	14.0	NM	NM	NM	NM	NM	NM

Data as orig reptd.; bef. results of disc opers/spec. items. Per share data adj. for stk. divs. Bold denotes diluted EPS (FASB 128)-prior periods restated. E-Estimated. NA-Not Available. NM-Not Meaningful. NR-Not Ranked.

Office—70 Wood Ave. South, Iselin, NJ 08830.**Tel**—(732) 632-8800. **Chrmn & CEO**—S. Fass. **Pres & COO**—V. Thompson. **VP-Fin & CFO**—Y. Sternlicht. **Dirs**—H. J. Conrad, S. Fass, C. Kaplan, M. Marx, A. Rosenfield, D. Tendler, V. Thompson, D. Tolkowsky, F. Wattleton, H. Weissbach. **Transfer Agent & Registrar**—American Stock Transfer & Trust Co., NYC. **Incorporated**—in Delaware in 1980. **Empl**— 271. **S&P Analyst:** David Moskowitz

STANDARD
&POOR'S
STOCK REPORTS

Biomatrix, Inc.

NYSE Symbol **BXM**

In S&P SmallCap 600

09-OCT-99

Industry:
Biotechnology

Summary: BXM develops, manufactures and commercializes elastoviscous products made from proprietary biological polymers, used in therapeutic medical applications and in skin care products.

Quantitative Evaluations

Outlook
(1 Lowest—5 Highest)
• 5

Fair Value
• 38¼

Risk
• NA

Earn./Div. Rank
• B-

Technical Eval.
• **Neutral** since 9/99

Rel. Strength Rank
(1 Lowest—99 Highest)
• 91

Insider Activity
• NA

Recent Price • 26
52 Wk Range • 45-15¼

Yield • Nil
12-Mo. P/E • 29.5

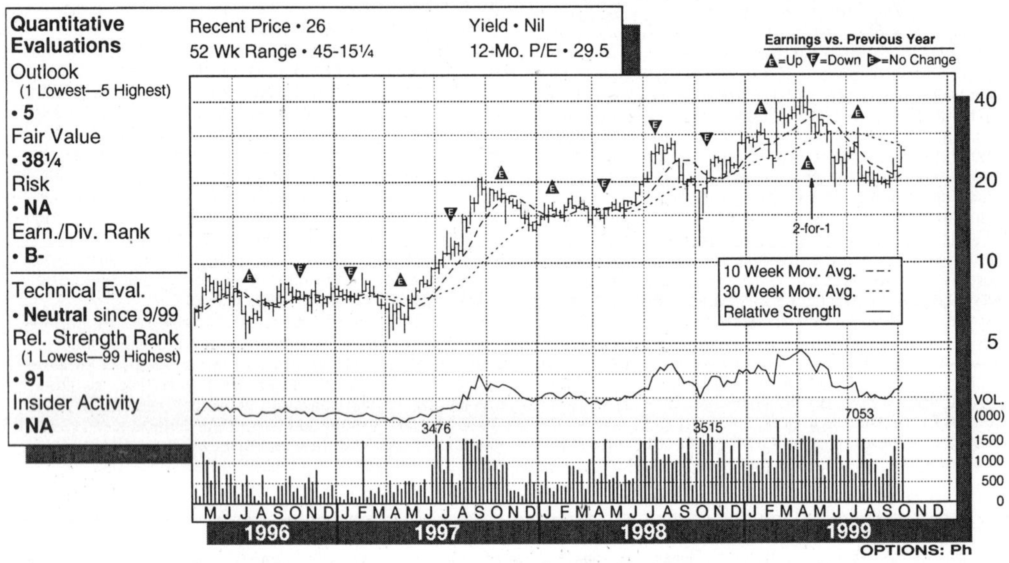

Business Profile - 02-JUL-99

In May 1999, Biomatrix announced plans to launch Synvisc, its product for the treatment of pain in osteoarthritis of the knee, in Mexico and Peru through marketing partner, Novartis Pharma AG. BXM has approvals for Synvisc in 38 countries, has launched Synvisc in 21 of those countries, and has filed for approvals in about 55 additional countries. During the first quarter of 1999, the company's newly constructed U.S. manufacturing plant received FDA approval and it began shipping to its marketing partners. BXM believes that the investment in 1998 in its two manufacturing plants will ensure that it can meet increased demand for its two leading products, Synvisc and Hylaform.

Operational Review - 02-JUL-99

Total revenues for the three months ended March 31, 1999, more than doubled, year to year, as product sales rose to $16.5 million from $4.6 million, mainly reflecting increased market penetration of Synvisc, the company's treatment for osteoarthritis of the knee, in the U.S., Europe and several newly launched international markets. Profitability benefited from the strong growth in product sales, and pretax income increased to $5.5 million from $1.2 million. After taxes at 40.0%, versus 33.3%, net income rose to $3.3 million from $0.8 million. Earnings per share were $0.14 based on 5.5% more average shares, versus $0.04, both adjusted for the April 1999 2-for-1 stock split.

Stock Performance - 08-OCT-99

In the past 30 trading days, BXM's shares have increased 31%, compared to a 0.91% fall in the S&P 500. Average trading volume for the past five days was 287,540 shares, compared with the 40-day moving average of 187,136 shares.

Key Stock Statistics

Dividend Rate/Share	Nil	Shareholders	241
Shs. outstg. (M)	23.0	Market cap. (B)	$0.597
Avg. daily vol. (M)	0.217	Inst. holdings	48%
Tang. Bk. Value/Share	2.76		
Beta	0.35		

Value of $10,000 invested 5 years ago: $ 63,030

Fiscal Year Ending Dec. 31

	1999	1998	1997	1996	1995	1994
Revenues (Million $)						
1Q	16.60	7.50	6.04	1.74	1.10	0.98
2Q	25.20	9.68	4.98	8.54	1.49	6.10
3Q	—	11.63	13.87	2.47	4.67	0.89
4Q	—	18.80	7.69	2.83	3.81	0.94
Yr.	—	47.60	32.56	15.58	11.07	8.91
Earnings Per Share ($)						
1Q	**0.14**	**0.04**	0.12	-0.06	-0.10	-0.10
2Q	**0.31**	**0.05**	0.06	0.25	-0.09	0.08
3Q	—	**0.12**	0.42	-0.03	0.12	-0.10
4Q	—	**0.30**	**0.09**	-0.03	0.06	-0.10
Yr.	—	**0.51**	**0.69**	**0.13**	**-0.01**	**-0.23**

Next earnings report expected: mid October

Dividend Data

Amount ($)	Date Decl.	Ex-Div. Date	Stock of Record	Payment Date
2-for-1	Apr. 06	Apr. 26	Apr. 16	Apr. 23 '99

Biomatrix, Inc.

Business Summary - 02-JUL-99

Biomatrix, Inc. develops, manufactures, markets and sells a series of proprietary viscoelastic products made of biological polymers called hylans for use in therapeutic medical applications and skin care. Hylans are chemically modified forms of the naturally occurring hyaluronan (also known as hyaluronic acid or sodium hyaluronate). Hylans are the second generation of viscoelastics used in medicine, and are characterized by significantly enhanced physical (rheological) properties (elasticity, viscosity and pseudoplasticity), as compared to naturally occurring hyaluronan, from which the first generation viscoelastics are made. The discovery of hylans has allowed Biomatrix to develop a range of patented products with superior viscoelastic properties in the forms of fluids, gels and solids.

BXM believes that it is distinguished from other companies in the field by its association with Dr. Endre A Balazs, a co-founder and current chief executive officer and chief scientific officer of the company; he invented the use of hyaluronan in medicine and developed the first generation hyaluronan based viscoelastics used in medicine worldwide.

To date, the company has developed and commercialized four medical therapeutic products: Synvisc, Hylaform, Hylashield and Gelvisc Vet.

Synvisc is a viscoelastic device made of patented hylan biopolymers. It is used for the treatment of osteoarthritis to reduce pain and improve joint mobility. Synvisc treatment involves a series of injections into the affected joint. It supplements the elastoviscosity of the synovial fluid of the arthritic joint, and is regarded as a liquid prosthesis for the joint because it replaces the pathologically low estoviscous fluid with a supplement of fluid with enhanced elastoviscous properties. This medical treatment modality is called visco supplementation. Synvisc is administered over a two-week period and involves a series of three injections into the arthritic joint.

Biomatrix has FDA clearance to market Synvisc in the U.S. and approval to market it in countries of the European Union, and certain countries in South America and Asia. Through marketing and distribution agreements with a number of large multi-national pharmaceutical companies, and through its wholly-owned subsidiaries, BXM has contracts to market Synvisc in approximately 90 countries.

BXM's other viscoelastic products include: Hylaform for the correction of facial wrinkles and depressed scars, which is marketed in 23 countries by Collagen Corp.; Gelvisc Vet for the treatment of arthritis in animals; two Hylashield products for the protection of the surface of the eye from noxious environmental conditions; and several polymers for the skin care industry.

Per Share Data ($) **(Year Ended Dec. 31)**	**1998**	**1997**	**1996**	**1995**	**1994**	**1993**	**1992**	**1991**	**1990**	**1989**
Tangible Bk. Val.	2.26	1.58	0.83	0.69	NA	NA	NA	NA	NA	NA
Cash Flow	0.58	0.73	0.15	0.02	NA	NA	NA	NA	-0.32	NA
Earnings	0.51	0.69	0.13	-0.01	NA	NA	NA	NA	NA	NA
Dividends	Nil	Nil	Nil	Nil	Nil	Nil	NA	NA	NA	NA
Payout Ratio	Nil	Nil	Nil	Nil	Nil	Nil	NA	NA	NA	NA
Prices - High	30½	21	10½	8⅝	NA	NA	NA	NA	NA	NA
- Low	11⅝	5¼	5⅛	1½	NA	NA	NA	NA	NA	NA
P/E Ratio - High	60	30	84	NM	NA	NM	NA	NA	NA	NA
- Low	23	8	41	NM	NA	NM	NA	NA	NA	NA
Income Statement Analysis (Million $)										
Revs.	47.6	32.6	15.6	11.1	8.9	3.5	3.1	2.7	2.6	NA
Oper. Inc.	15.3	15.9	2.8	-0.4	NA	-8.4	-7.3	-3.8	-2.0	NA
Depr.	1.6	0.7	0.6	0.5	NA	0.6	0.4	0.2	0.2	NA
Int. Exp.	1.0	0.1	0.1	0.1	NA	0.1	0.0	0.3	0.3	NA
Pretax Inc.	14.1	16.3	2.9	-0.2	-4.2	-8.9	-6.6	-3.9	-2.7	NA
Eff. Tax Rate	14%	3.29%	4.60%	NM	NM	NM	NM	NM	NA	NA
Net Inc.	12.1	15.7	2.8	-0.2	-4.4	-8.9	-6.6	-3.9	-2.7	NA
Balance Sheet & Other Fin. Data (Million $)										
Cash	16.5	17.4	13.6	8.9	NA	5.0	9.3	25.4	0.2	NA
Curr. Assets	41.3	25.9	16.3	12.6	NA	11.4	19.1	26.2	0.7	NA
Total Assets	83.3	44.2	26.0	17.4	7.8	16.9	24.8	29.3	1.6	NA
Curr. Liab.	14.3	4.0	2.5	2.5	NA	2.6	2.4	2.0	2.8	NA
LT Debt	17.6	5.6	5.8	0.7	1.5	NA	NA	NA	NA	NA
Common Eqty.	51.4	34.6	17.7	14.1	10.2	11.0	20.0	26.9	-4.4	NA
Total Cap.	69.0	40.2	23.5	14.8	11.7	NA	NA	NA	NA	NA
Cap. Exp.	19.5	NA	0.8	0.3	NA	NA	NA	NA	NA	NA
Cash Flow	13.7	16.5	3.4	0.3	NA	-8.3	NA	NA	-2.6	NA
Curr. Ratio	2.9	6.5	6.5	5.0	NA	4.5	7.8	13.3	0.3	NA
% LT Debt of Cap.	25.5	13.9	24.6	4.9	12.8	NA	NA	NA	NA	NA
% Net Inc.of Revs.	25.4	48.3	17.9	NM	NM	NM	NM	NM	NA	NA
% Ret. on Assets	19.0	44.8	13.0	NM	NM	NM	NM	NM	NA	NA
% Ret. on Equity	28.1	60.2	17.6	NM	NM	NM	NM	NM	NA	NA

Data as orig reptd.; bef. results of disc opers/spec. items. Per share data adj. for stk. divs. Bold denotes diluted EPS (FASB 128)-prior periods restated. E-Estimated. NA-Not Available. NM-Not Meaningful. NR-Not Ranked.

Office—65 Railroad Ave., Ridgefield, NJ 07657. **Tel**—(201) 945-9550. **Fax**—(201) 945-0363. **Website**—http://www.biomatrix.com **CEO**—E. A. Balazs. **Pres**—R. B. Riggs. **VP-Fin & CFO**—M. Seifert. **Investor Contact**—Anne Marie Fields (201-945-9550 ext. 267). **Dirs**—E. A. Balazs, H. S. Campbell, J. L. Denlinger, K. Mark, J. P. Morreale, R. B. Riggs, J. A. Vida. **Transfer Agent & Registrar**—State Street Bank & Trust Co., Quincy, MA. **Incorporated**—in Delaware in 1981. **Empl**— 369. **S&P Analyst:** J.J.S.

STANDARD &POOR'S STOCK REPORTS

Birmingham Steel

NYSE Symbol **BIR**

In S&P SmallCap 600

09-OCT-99

Industry: Iron & Steel

Summary: This company operates mini-mills that produce rebar and merchant products. It also specializes in making high-quality rod and wire at its American Steel & Wire subsidiary.

S&P Opinion: Accumulate (★★★★) | Recent Price • 7¼ | 52 Wk Range • 9-3½ | Yield • 1.4% | 12-Mo. P/E • NM

Quantitative Evaluations

Outlook (1 Lowest—5 Highest)
• **4**

Fair Value
• **11¼**

Risk
• **Average**

Earn./Div. Rank
• **B-**

Technical Eval.
• **Bullish** since 9/99

Rel. Strength Rank (1 Lowest—99 Highest)
• **72**

Insider Activity
• **NA**

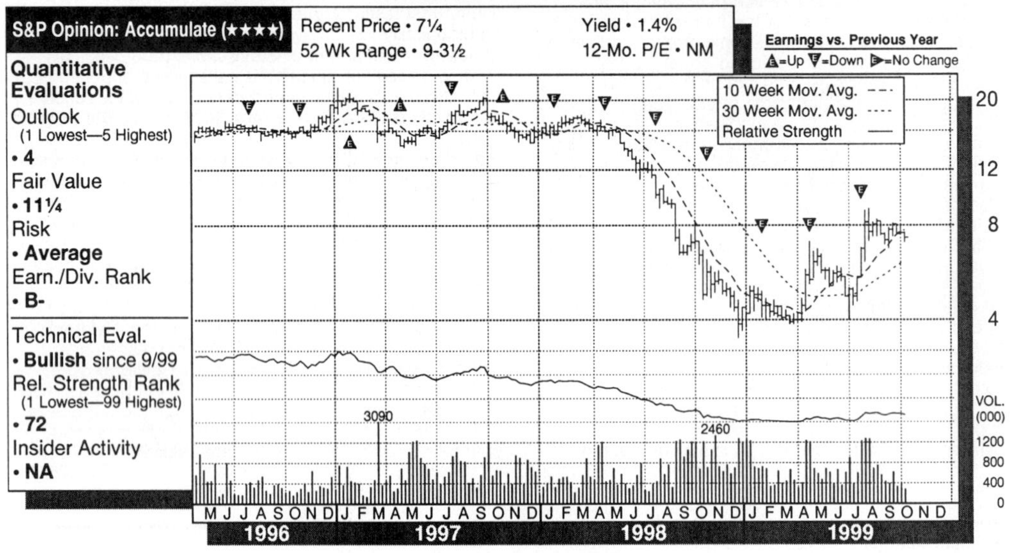

Overview - 24-AUG-99

On August 18, 1999, the company announced that it would sell its special quality bar unit and its 50% stake in American Iron Reduction. BIR is also exploring options with regard to its 50% stake in Pacific Coast Recycling. It said the restructuring was part of a strategy to focus on core minimill and scrap operations. Earlier, on August 2, an investor group led by former Nucor Corp. (NYSE: NUE) CEO John Correnti and James Todd, former BIR chairman and CEO, announced its intention to launch a proxy fight to replace BIR's directors and install Mr. Correnti as chairman and CEO. The group holds a 7.8% stake in BIR. Assuming continued economic growth in the U.S., a lower level of imports, and rebuilding of distributor inventories, shipments from continuing operations should rebound and prices stabilize in FY 2000 (Jun.). In the absence of losses from divested businesses, and with lower interest expense, BIR should return to profitability in FY 2000.

Valuation - 24-AUG-99

Following news of BIR's restructuring, we are maintaining our accumulate rating, even though the shares were recently up 60% since April 15, 1999, when we upgraded them to accumulate. While the restructuring will likely result in a large fourth quarter charge, we believe the market has begun to value BIR based on FY 2000 prospects. The decision to divest the special bar quality (sbq) unit and focus on core minimill units is good news. The sbq unit has been incurring losses for some time, and its disposal will relieve a drag on EPS. Another positive factor is that FY 2000 cash flow should rise dramatically, with much lower capital spending. The increase in cash flow will let BIR pay down debt and strengthen the balance sheet. Finally, the prospect of a proxy fight gives current management a powerful incentive to increase shareholder value.

Key Stock Statistics

S&P EPS Est. 2000	0.60	Tang. Bk. Value/Share	13.97
P/E on S&P Est. 2000	12.2	Beta	0.33
Dividend Rate/Share	0.10	Shareholders	1,477
Shs. outstg. (M)	29.6	Market cap. (B)	$0.217
Avg. daily vol. (M)	0.079	Inst. holdings	36%

Value of $10,000 invested 5 years ago: $ 3,145

Fiscal Year Ending Jun. 30

	1999	1998	1997	1996	1995	1994
Revenues (Million $)						
1Q	271.0	287.6	233.4	207.3	220.6	127.6
2Q	226.8	267.4	210.1	197.4	203.2	146.8
3Q	224.5	298.2	257.9	197.1	236.9	204.2
4Q	184.0	282.8	277.5	230.8	224.8	224.3
Yr.	709.9	1,136	979.0	832.5	885.5	702.9
Earnings Per Share ($)						
1Q	**0.03**	0.24	0.22	0.29	0.42	0.15
2Q	**-0.17**	**0.09**	0.21	0.02	0.42	0.17
3Q	**-0.53**	**-0.14**	0.02	-0.51	0.45	0.20
4Q	**-0.59**	**-0.14**	0.05	0.12	0.45	0.31
Yr.	**-0.11**	**0.05**	**0.50**	-0.08	1.74	0.86

Next earnings report expected: late January

Dividend Data (Dividends have been paid since 1988.)

Amount ($)	Date Decl.	Ex-Div. Date	Stock of Record	Payment Date
0.025	Oct. 13	Oct. 21	Oct. 23	Nov. 03 '98
0.025	Jan. 19	Jan. 27	Jan. 29	Feb. 08 '99
0.025	Apr. 20	Apr. 28	Apr. 30	May. 10 '99
0.025	Jul. 20	Jul. 28	Jul. 30	Aug. 09 '99

Birmingham Steel Corporation

Business Summary - 24-AUG-99

On August 18, 1999, Birmingham Steel said it would sell its special quality bar unit and its 50% stake in American Iron Reduction. BIR is also exploring options with regard to its 50% stake in Pacific Coast Recycling. The company said the restructuring was part of a strategy to focus on core minimill and scrap operations. Earlier, on August 2, 1999, an investor group led by former Nucor Corp. CEO John Correnti and James Todd, former BIR chairman and CEO, announced that it intended to launch a proxy fight to replace BIR's directors and install Mr. Correnti as chairman and CEO. The group holds a 7.8% stake in BIR.

BIR's main products are steel reinforcing bar (rebar) used in the construction industry, and merchant steel products sold to distributors and to fabricators and OEMs for conversion into finished goods. Through American Steel & Wire (ASW), it makes steel rod and wire primarily for the automotive, fastener, welding, appliance and aerospace industries.

In May 1996, BIR began the startup of its $115 million high-quality bar mill in Cleveland. The addition of this mill nearly doubled ASW's annual rolling capacity, to 1.1 million tons, and will let ASW make larger, higher-margin bar products. The mill will help achieve BIR's long-term goal of improving the product mix by increasing shipments of rod/bar relative to rebar.

In August 1996, BIR began construction of a $200 million Memphis melt shop. The shop will supply one million tons of high-quality billets (pieces of semi-finished steel) annually to the Cleveland bar mill and end the current practice of purchasing high-cost billets from outside vendors. The melt shop began startup in November 1997.

In addition to reducing its dependence on outside sources of billets, BIR formed a joint venture with GS Industries to build a direct reduced iron (DRI) plant to cut scrap costs. DRI is a scrap substitute manufactured from virgin iron ore. The use of DRI in its electric arc furnaces will enable the company to substantially reduce its dependence on expensive low-residual scrap. BIR and GS will each receive half of the plant's minimum annual production of 1.2 million metric tons of DRI. Startup began in January 1998.

BIR shipped 3,329,000 tons in FY 98, versus 2,835,731 tons in FY 97 and 2,402,697 tons in FY 96, Of total tonnage shipped in FY 98, 43% (46% in FY 97) was rebar, 28% (25%) merchant products, 20% (23%) rod/bar, and 9% (6%) was semi-finished billet. Upon completion of its capital program in late 1999, BIR's shipment capacity will be about 4.0 million tons annually.

BIR's main competitors in rebar and merchant steel are Bayou Steel, Chaparral Steel, Co-Steel Inc., Commercial Metals Co., and Nucor Corp.

Per Share Data ($) (Year Ended Jun. 30)	1999	1998	1997	1996	1995	1994	1993	1992	1991	1990
Tangible Bk. Val.	NA	14.07	14.20	14.06	15.00	14.21	10.36	10.03	7.80	8.13
Cash Flow	NA	1.92	2.07	1.14	2.85	1.99	1.41	2.04	0.83	1.62
Earnings	-0.11	0.05	0.50	-0.08	1.74	0.86	0.60	1.11	NM	0.89
Dividends	0.08	0.40	0.40	0.40	0.40	0.75	0.37	0.33	0.33	0.33
Payout Ratio	NM	NM	80%	NM	23%	29%	61%	35%	NM	37%
Prices - High	9	18	22	19 3/8	22 3/4	32 5/8	20 3/4	25 3/4	15 5/8	18 3/4
- Low	3 7/8	3 1/2	14 1/8	14 1/2	14	18 3/4	15 3/4	13 5/8	8 3/8	7
P/E Ratio - High	NM	NM	44	NM	13	38	46	23	NM	21
- Low	NM	70	28	NM	8	22	30	12	NM	8
Income Statement Analysis (Million $)										
Revs.	NA	1,136	979	832	885	703	442	418	408	443
Oper. Inc.	NA	124	95.4	64.3	119	69.9	42.7	55.0	36.5	57.6
Depr.	NA	58.3	45.8	34.7	32.3	27.7	17.3	16.8	14.0	13.4
Int. Exp.	NA	35.5	29.0	18.5	8.8	11.1	8.7	9.9	9.1	9.7
Pretax Inc.	NA	4.4	22.4	-2.4	86.0	35.8	21.3	32.2	1.0	26.4
Eff. Tax Rate	NA	26%	46%	NM	41%	41%	40%	38%	98%	38%
Net Inc.	NA	1.6	14.4	-2.2	50.6	21.2	12.8	19.9	NM	16.3
Balance Sheet & Other Fin. Data (Million $)										
Cash	NA	0.9	1.0	6.7	4.3	28.9	0.3	0.5	0.5	0.1
Curr. Assets	NA	394	367	328	303	276	147	128	127	136
Total Assets	NA	1,245	1,211	928	757	690	456	388	345	314
Curr. Liab.	NA	156	138	116	96.0	62.7	114	54.0	92.0	114
LT Debt	NA	559	526	307	143	143	90.1	93.7	98.4	27.2
Common Eqty.	NA	461	472	448	460	439	223	215	134	151
Total Cap.	NA	1,081	1,067	806	513	623	339	331	250	197
Cap. Exp.	NA	147	197	172	76.1	40.4	76.0	56.1	69.8	35.4
Cash Flow	NA	56.9	603	32.5	82.9	48.9	30.1	36.7	14.5	29.7
Curr. Ratio	NA	2.5	2.7	2.7	3.1	4.4	1.3	2.4	1.4	1.2
% LT Debt of Cap.	NA	51.7	49.3	38.2	27.9	22.9	26.6	28.3	39.3	13.8
% Net Inc.of Revs.	NA	0.1	1.5	NM	5.7	3.0	2.9	4.8	NM	3.7
% Ret. on Assets	NA	0.1	1.3	NM	17.4	3.7	3.0	4.8	NM	5.3
% Ret. on Equity	NA	0.3	3.1	NM	11.2	6.4	5.8	10.4	NM	11.1

Data as orig reptd.; bef. results of disc opers/spec. items. Per share data adj. for stk. divs. Bold denotes diluted EPS (FASB 128)-prior periods restated. E-Estimated. NA-Not Available. NM-Not Meaningful. NR-Not Ranked.

Office—1000 Urban Center Parkway, Suite 300, Birmingham, AL 35242-2516. **Tel**—(205) 970-1200. **Website**—http://www.birsteel.com **Chrmn & CEO**—R. A. Garvey. **EVP & CFO**—K. E. Walsh. **VP & Investor Contact**—J. Daniel Garrett. **Secy**—C. W. Pecher. **Dirs**—W. J. Cabaniss Jr., C. S. Clegg, E. M. de Windt, R. A. Garvey, E. B. Jones, R. H. Jones, R. D. Kennedy, R. de J. Osborne, J. H. Roberts, G. A. Stinson. **Transfer Agent & Registrar**—First Union National Bank, Charlotte, NC. **Incorporated**—in Delaware in 1983. **Empl**— 1,789. **S&P Analyst:** Leo Larkin

STANDARD
&POOR'S
STOCK REPORTS

BISYS Group

NASDAQ Symbol **BSYS**

In S&P SmallCap 600

09-OCT-99

Industry: Services (Data Processing)

Summary: This company is a leading U.S. third-party provider of data processing and related services to financial institutions.

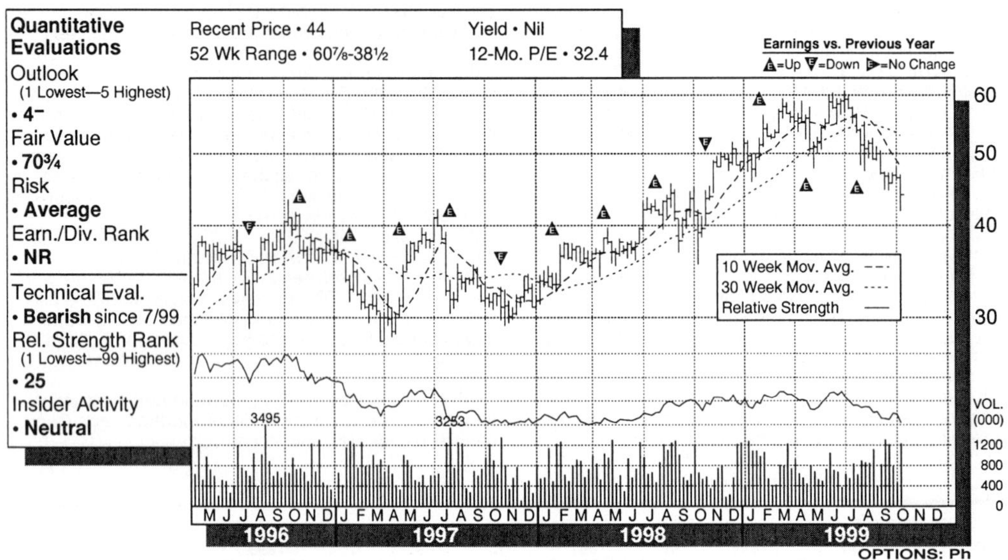

Business Profile - 29-JUN-99

In June 1999, BISYS announced the acquisition of Dover International, a leading provider of professional certification training, continuing education and other support services for the financial services industry. Dover provides Internet and instructor-led training and outsourcing of various compliance, professional licensing and other support functions for investment advisors, broker-dealers and insurance agencies. In May 1999, BISYS announced that it completed multi-year outsourcing agreements with 14 newly chartered banks within the previous six months.

Operational Review - 29-JUN-99

For the nine months ended March 31, 1999, revenues rose 19%, year to year, as new client growth and cross-selling activities more than offset lost business. Profitability was penalized by $19 million in acquired in-process R&D and much lower interest income. Pretax income was up 8.1%. After taxes at 56.9%, versus 40.1%, net income fell 22%, to $19,410,000 ($0.70 per share), from $24,969,000 ($0.92). The company noted that excluding the $19 million in-process R&D charge, net income for the FY 99 period would have totaled $38,650,000 ($1.39).

Stock Performance - 08-OCT-99

In the past 30 trading days, BSYS's shares have declined 12%, compared to a 0.91% fall in the S&P 500. Average trading volume for the past five days was 280,900 shares, compared with the 40-day moving average of 218,690 shares.

Key Stock Statistics

Dividend Rate/Share	Nil	Shareholders	3,845
Shs. outstg. (M)	27.0	Market cap. (B)	$ 1.2
Avg. daily vol. (M)	0.194	Inst. holdings	86%
Tang. Bk. Value/Share	5.10		
Beta	0.52		

Value of $10,000 invested 5 years ago: $ 25,507

Fiscal Year Ending Jun. 30

	1999	1998	1997	1996	1995	1994
Revenues (Million $)						
1Q	101.9	91.46	72.40	52.27	37.46	25.21
2Q	112.0	91.43	74.80	55.94	39.59	35.33
3Q	121.3	98.95	83.96	65.92	49.06	36.72
4Q	137.5	104.5	87.84	72.92	54.70	39.40
Yr.	472.7	386.3	319.0	247.1	200.5	136.7
Earnings Per Share ($)						
1Q	**-0.35**	**0.06**	**0.29**	0.22	0.17	0.16
2Q	**0.44**	**0.37**	**0.34**	0.28	0.17	0.21
3Q	**0.58**	**0.49**	**0.42**	0.38	-0.62	0.25
4Q	**0.66**	**0.55**	**0.50**	-0.50	0.03	0.25
Yr.	**1.36**	**1.46**	**1.55**	**0.72**	-0.27	0.86

Next earnings report expected: late October

Dividend Data

No cash dividends have been paid on the common shares. The company does not intend to pay cash dividends in the foreseeable future.

A Division of The McGraw-Hill Companies

The BISYS Group, Inc.

Business Summary - 29-JUN-99

An outsourcing pioneer, The BISYS Group performs many functions for its financial services clients. The company supports over 9,000 financial institutions and corporate clients. BISYS provides technology outsourcing, check imaging applications and brokerage services to more than 1,000 financial institutions nationwide; distributes and administers over 60 families of mutual funds consisting of more than 900 portfolios; provides retirement plan record keeping services to over 6,900 companies in partnership with 30 of the nation's leading bank and investment management companies; and provides insurance distribution solutions, Internet/telephone marketing, enterprise-wide networking services, and loan/deposit product pricing research.

BISYS aims to be the single source of all relevant outsourcing solutions for its clients and improve their performance, profitability and competitive position. The company strives to expand the scope of its services through focused account management, emphasizing services with recurring revenues and long-term contracts.

The TOTALPLUS product line provides bank-wide automation which enables community banks to compete with super-regionals, and non-bank competitors. TOTALPLUS supports virtually all aspects of a banking institution's automation requirements related to its operation, customer management and product distribution functions, proprietary central site and client site computing solutions. Capabilities include deposit and loan requirements and general financial management of the institution, transaction and data management, electronic banking and customer information management. During FY 98 (Jun.), BISYS launched the banking industry's first true client/server outsourcing alternative based on an open computing environment, as well as full-service Internet banking.

BISYS Investment Services provides distribution, administration, fund accounting and transfer agency services to over 60 mutual fund complexes encompassing more than 900 individual portfolios with a market value exceeding $200 billion in assets. BISYS also provides 401(k) plan marketing support, administration and recordkeeping services to 30 of the nation's leading bank and investment management companies.

BISYS also provides outsourcing services for the distribution and administration of insurance, and uses alliances with major insurance companies and national producer groups to provide a full range of outsourcing services for insurance product distribution. BISYS services a network of, and markets products and services through, more than 60,000 insurance agents and brokers nationwide.

In December 1998, BISYS announced that it launched its TotalCS outsourcing solution with 10 new community banks. In January 1999, the company announced a new $100 million stock buy-back program.

Per Share Data ($) (Year Ended Jun. 30)	1999	1998	1997	1996	1995	1994	1993	1992	1991	1990
Tangible Bk. Val.	NA	5.10	4.61	2.52	1.30	-0.30	3.99	1.09	-0.24	NA
Cash Flow	NA	2.01	1.99	1.12	0.21	1.28	0.53	-0.33	0.74	0.26
Earnings	1.36	1.46	1.55	0.72	-0.27	0.86	0.23	-2.64	-3.01	-4.32
Dividends	Nil	Nil	Nil	Nil	Nil	Nil	Nil	Nil	Nil	Nil
Payout Ratio	Nil	Nil	Nil	Nil	Nil	Nil	Nil	Nil	Nil	Nil
Prices - High	60 7/8	52 1/4	42 1/8	43 3/8	31 1/8	22 3/8	24 1/2	20	NA	NA
- Low	41 3/4	32 1/2	27 7/8	27 1/4	17 1/2	17	16 1/2	9 7/8	NA	NA
P/E Ratio - High	45	36	27	60	NM	26	NM	NM	NM	NM
- Low	31	22	18	38	NM	20	NM	NA	NA	NA
Income Statement Analysis (Million $)										
Revs.	NA	386	319	247	201	137	88.3	74.5	62.9	54.7
Oper. Inc.	NA	-88.7	79.0	62.1	16.0	26.0	20.2	12.4	13.1	10.2
Depr.	NA	14.8	11.8	10.0	11.0	6.6	4.4	20.2	23.4	22.6
Int. Exp.	NA	Nil	Nil	Nil	0.7	1.0	0.3	4.8	7.0	7.4
Pretax Inc.	NA	66.8	67.9	30.3	-4.0	18.4	7.4	-21.9	-17.3	-19.7
Eff. Tax Rate	NA	40%	40%	41%	NM	25%	54%	Nil	Nil	Nil
Net Inc.	NA	40.0	40.8	18.0	-6.4	13.8	3.4	-21.9	-17.3	-19.7
Balance Sheet & Other Fin. Data (Million $)										
Cash	NA	93.4	80.0	39.3	7.2	5.9	40.2	6.4	0.2	Nil
Curr. Assets	NA	180	152	104	54.9	28.8	55.3	17.7	11.6	9.3
Total Assets	NA	334	265	215	165	139	85.1	37.3	56.8	74.1
Curr. Liab.	NA	82.4	64.4	64.0	50.0	25.0	13.1	14.0	14.3	10.7
LT Debt	NA	1.6	1.6	1.7	Nil	27.4	0.1	6.2	50.6	54.4
Common Eqty.	NA	238	192	143	115	84.8	70.1	13.6	-28.7	-9.9
Total Cap.	NA	250	200	150	115	112	70.3	19.8	42.0	63.1
Cap. Exp.	NA	16.9	16.0	12.7	9.2	6.8	4.3	1.5	2.7	1.9
Cash Flow	NA	54.9	52.5	28.0	5.0	20.4	7.8	-2.9	4.6	1.3
Curr. Ratio	NA	2.2	2.4	1.6	0.9	1.2	4.2	1.3	0.8	0.9
% LT Debt of Cap.	NA	0.6	0.8	1.2	Nil	24.4	0.2	31.3	120.4	86.1
% Net Inc.of Revs.	NA	10.4	12.8	7.3	NM	10.1	3.8	NM	NM	NM
% Ret. on Assets	NA	13.4	17.0	9.5	NM	12.2	5.2	NM	NM	NM
% Ret. on Equity	NA	18.6	24.3	14.0	NM	17.7	7.8	NM	NM	NM

Data as orig reptd.; bef. results of disc opers/spec. items. Per share data adj. for stk. divs. Bold denotes diluted EPS (FASB 128)-prior periods restated. E-Estimated. NA-Not Available. NM-Not Meaningful. NR-Not Ranked.

Office—150 Clove Rd., Little Falls, NJ 07424. **Tel**—(973) 812-8600. **Website**—http://www.bisys.com **Chrm & CEO**—L. J. Mangum. **Pres & COO**—P. H. Bourke. **EVP & CFO**—D. R. Sheehan. **Secy**—K. J. Dell.**Dirs**—R. J. Casale, T. A. Cooper, J. W. DeDapper, J. J. Lyons, L. J. Mangum, T. E. McInerney. **Transfer Agent & Registrar**—Bank of New York, NYC. **Incorporated**—in Delaware in 1989. **Empl**— 2,200. **S&P Analyst:** Scott H. Kessler

STANDARD
&POOR'S
STOCK REPORTS

Black Box

Nasdaq Symbol **BBOX**

In S&P SmallCap 600

09-OCT-99 **Industry:** Electrical Equipment

Summary: This company provides a broad range of networking products, as well as on-site technical support.

S&P Opinion: Buy (★★★★★) Recent Price • 49¼ 52 Wk Range • 58½-24 Yield • Nil 12-Mo. P/E • 22.4

Quantitative Evaluations
Outlook (1 Lowest—5 Highest) • **4−**
Fair Value • **64¾**
Risk • **High**
Earn./Div. Rank • **NR**

Technical Eval. • **Bullish** since 9/99
Rel. Strength Rank (1 Lowest—99 Highest) • **57**
Insider Activity • **Neutral**

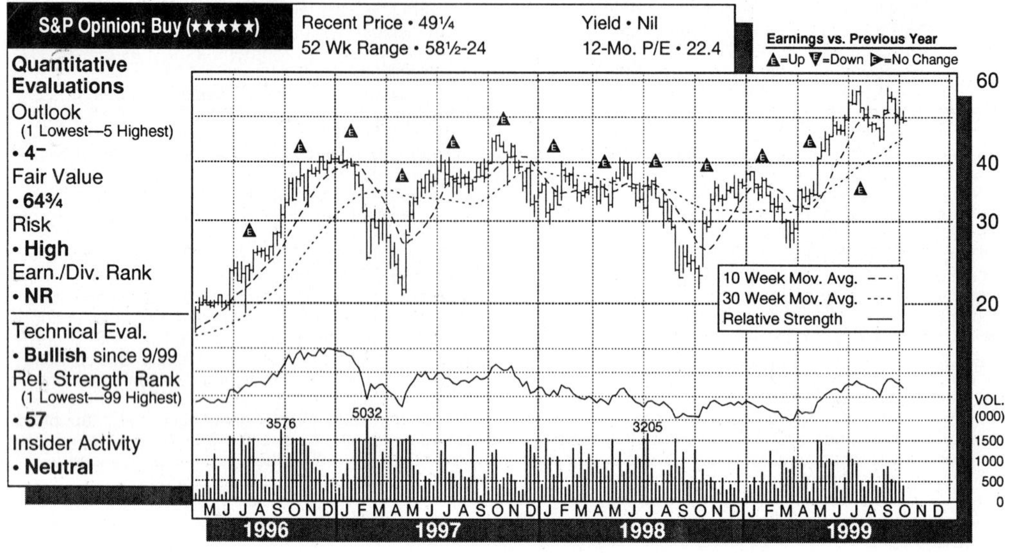

Overview - 20-JUL-99

We expect revenues to grow about 30% in FY 2000 (Mar.), driven both by internal growth, which is benefiting from strengthening performance across all geographies; and by acquisitions, fueled by rapid expansion of BBOX's on-site technical services unit, which should generate in excess of $125 million in annualized revenues in FY 2000. We expect margins to narrow somewhat, reflecting the rising proportion of on-site service business, which generates lower margins than the catalog unit. This gross margin pressure should be partly offset by acquisition synergies and cross-selling opportunities. We are also encouraged by BBOX's growth prospects in its Latin American operations, as the achievement of critical mass in that region will result in contributions to the bottom line. EPS comparisons will also benefit from ongoing share repurchases. We currently see FY 2000 EPS rising about 23%, to $2.53.

Valuation - 20-JUL-99

The shares have risen since sharply since early April 1999, and were recently trading at 22X our upward revised calendar 1999 EPS estimate of $2.46 (19X our calendar 2000 estimate of $2.90), still representing a discount to the P/E of the overall market. As a result, we continue to recommend that investors buy the stock. We look favorably on the company's core networking product business, as the telecommunications industry remains healthy. In addition, we are encouraged by BBOX's aggressive penetration of the on-site technical support business, which represents an industry with solid organic growth prospects and ample consolidation opportunities, both domestically and abroad. Moreover, the shares should be supported by a healthy balance sheet, minimal capital expenditure requirements, and strong free cash flow.

Key Stock Statistics

S&P EPS Est. 2000	2.55	Tang. Bk. Value/Share	3.53
P/E on S&P Est. 2000	19.3	Beta	1.25
S&P EPS Est. 2001	3.01	Shareholders	137
Dividend Rate/Share	Nil	Market cap. (B)	$0.920
Shs. outstg. (M)	18.7	Inst. holdings	86%
Avg. daily vol. (M)	0.097		

Value of $10,000 invested 5 years ago: $ 23,176

Fiscal Year Ending Mar. 31

	2000	1999	1998	1997	1996	1995
Revenues (Million $)						
1Q	97.52	73.10	64.20	52.86	44.48	37.30
2Q	—	79.13	68.93	56.17	46.46	40.15
3Q	—	84.79	74.64	57.66	47.24	40.60
4Q	—	92.96	76.14	62.87	55.25	46.72
Yr.	—	330.0	279.8	232.2	193.4	164.8
Earnings Per Share ($)						
1Q	**0.57**	**0.46**	0.39	0.31	0.24	0.20
2Q	**E0.62**	**0.49**	0.42	0.34	0.26	0.22
3Q	**E0.65**	**0.53**	**0.44**	0.35	0.27	0.22
4Q	**E0.71**	**0.62**	**0.49**	0.41	0.34	0.25
Yr.	**E2.55**	**2.09**	**1.75**	**1.40**	**1.10**	**0.89**

Next earnings report expected: mid October

Dividend Data

No dividends have been paid.

A Division of The McGraw-Hill Companies

Black Box Corporation

Business Summary - 20-JUL-99

Black Box is a leading worldwide direct marketer and technical service provider of computer communications and networking equipment and services. The company provides expert technical support 24 hours a day, seven days a week, and also provides on-site installation services in selected markets. Through its Black Box Catalog, available in eight languages, the company offers more than 12,000 products, 90% of which are BBOX-labeled. While Black Box sells its products to businesses of all sizes, including many of the Fortune 1000 companies in the U.S., the majority of active customers are small and mid-size businesses. The company is represented in 77 countries and operates 28 subsidiaries in five continents.

During FY 99 (Mar.), the company significantly expanded its technical services offering to include on-site services. BBOX believes the on-site offering will allow it to further penetrate the telecommunications market. The company has expanded this business primarily through aggressive acquisition activity. As of July 1999, BBOX had announced 17 acquisitions in the on-site technical support industry since January 1998, including three in FY 2000. BBOX's stated goal is to achieve annualized on-site revenues of $125 million by the end of FY 2000.

In FY 99, 44% of revenues were generated from outside the U.S. and Canada, reflecting increased utilization of computer systems and networks on a worldwide basis. The company operates subsidiaries in 16 countries, including the U.K., France, Japan and Brazil. In addition, BBOX has distributor agreements in 61 other countries.

BBOX's primary marketing tool is its targeted mailing of a comprehensive, fully illustrated color catalog, as well as other direct promotional material mailed to systems design decision-makers. The company's catalogs present a wide choice of items, using a combination of product features and benefits, photographs, product descriptions, product specifications, compatibility charts, potential applications, and other helpful technical information.

The company differentiates itself from other direct marketers and distributors through its private label brand, and through its technical support. Black Box complements its products with more than 600 technical support professionals, available by phone, free of charge, seven days a week, 24 hours a day, and via fee-based on-site cabling and installation services. In addition, BBOX's MIS and inventory management systems enable it to ship 95% of orders on the day that the orders are received.

Per Share Data ($) (Year Ended Mar. 31)	1999	1998	1997	1996	1995	1994	1993	1992	1991	1990
Tangible Bk. Val.	4.87	3.32	1.11	NM	NM	0.25	NA	NA	NA	NA
Cash Flow	2.50	2.11	1.75	1.46	1.31	1.42	NA	NA	NA	NA
Earnings	2.09	1.75	1.40	1.10	0.89	0.71	0.47	NA	NA	NA
Dividends	Nil	Nil	Nil	Nil	Nil	Nil	NA	NA	NA	NA
Payout Ratio	Nil	Nil	Nil	Nil	Nil	Nil	NA	NA	NA	NA
Cal. Yrs.	1998	1997	1996	1995	1994	1993	1992	1991	1990	1989
Prices - High	41	46	41½	19¾	22½	21¼	15¾	NA	NA	NA
- Low	21½	20¾	13¼	12⅝	8⅝	11¼	13¼	NA	NA	NA
P/E Ratio - High	20	26	29	18	25	19	33	NA	NA	NA
- Low	10	12	9	11	9	10	28	NA	NA	NA
Income Statement Analysis (Million $)										
Revs.	330	280	232	193	165	142	NA	NA	NA	NA
Oper. Inc.	71.0	60.7	51.9	44.1	39.6	38.7	NA	NA	NA	NA
Depr.	7.6	6.3	6.2	6.1	6.8	11.3	NA	NA	NA	NA
Int. Exp.	0.6	2.7	3.6	5.8	NA	NA	NA	NA	NA	NA
Pretax Inc.	63.0	52.1	41.9	32.6	25.6	20.7	NA	NA	NA	NA
Eff. Tax Rate	40%	41%	42%	44%	43%	45%	NA	NA	NA	NA
Net Inc.	38.1	30.9	24.3	18.3	14.5	11.4	NA	NA	NA	NA
Balance Sheet & Other Fin. Data (Million $)										
Cash	5.9	10.6	1.4	1.9	2.5	2.2	NA	NA	NA	NA
Curr. Assets	117	100	83.9	62.8	54.2	52.9	NA	NA	NA	NA
Total Assets	246	185	173	156	152	186	NA	NA	NA	NA
Curr. Liab.	44.0	38.3	45.7	32.8	31.2	18.7	NA	NA	NA	NA
LT Debt	0.2	8.0	21.2	41.4	56.9	80.5	NA	NA	NA	NA
Common Eqty.	193	128	94.3	67.1	47.1	65.3	NA	NA	NA	NA
Total Cap.	202	147	128	123	121	168	NA	NA	NA	NA
Cap. Exp.	9.4	2.3	2.8	2.5	3.5	NA	NA	NA	NA	NA
Cash Flow	45.7	37.2	30.5	24.3	21.3	22.8	NA	NA	NA	NA
Curr. Ratio	2.7	2.6	1.8	1.9	1.7	2.8	NA	NA	NA	NA
% LT Debt of Cap.	0.1	5.4	16.6	33.7	47.1	47.9	NA	NA	NA	NA
% Net Inc.of Revs.	11.6	11.0	10.5	9.4	8.8	8.1	NA	NA	NA	NA
% Ret. on Assets	17.7	17.2	14.8	11.9	8.6	6.0	NA	NA	NA	NA
% Ret. on Equity	23.8	27.8	30.2	32.1	25.9	19.9	NA	NA	NA	NA

Data as orig reptd.; bef. results of disc opers/spec. items. Per share data adj. for stk. divs. Bold denotes diluted EPS (FASB 128)-prior periods restated. E-Estimated. NA-Not Available. NM-Not Meaningful. NR-Not Ranked.

Office—1000 Park Dr., Lawrence, PA 15055. **Tel**—(724) 746-5500. **Fax**—(724) 746-0746. **Website**—www.blackbox.com **Chrmn, Pres, CEO, COO & Secy**—F. C. Young. **VP, CFO & Treas**—A. M. Baird. **Dirs**—W. F. Andrews, W. R. Newlin, B. D. Young, F. C. Young. **Transfer Agent & Registrar**—American Stock Transfer & Trust Co., NYC. **Incorporated**—in California in 1973; reincorporated in Delaware in 1989. **Empl**— 1,200. **S&P Analyst:** Stephen J. Tekirian

BMC Industries

NYSE Symbol **BMC**

In S&P SmallCap 600

09-OCT-99

Industry:
Manufacturing (Specialized)

Summary: One of the world's largest makers of aperture masks for color TV tubes and computer monitors, BMC is also a leading producer of polycarbonate, glass and plastic eyewear lenses.

Quantitative Evaluations

Outlook (1 Lowest—5 Highest) • **4−**

Fair Value • **15⅞**

Risk • **Average**

Earn./Div. Rank • **B+**

Technical Eval. • **Neutral** since 9/99

Rel. Strength Rank (1 Lowest—99 Highest) • **76**

Insider Activity • **Favorable**

Recent Price • 12⅛

52 Wk Range • 13⅜-3⅞

Yield • 0.5%

12-Mo. P/E • 29.7

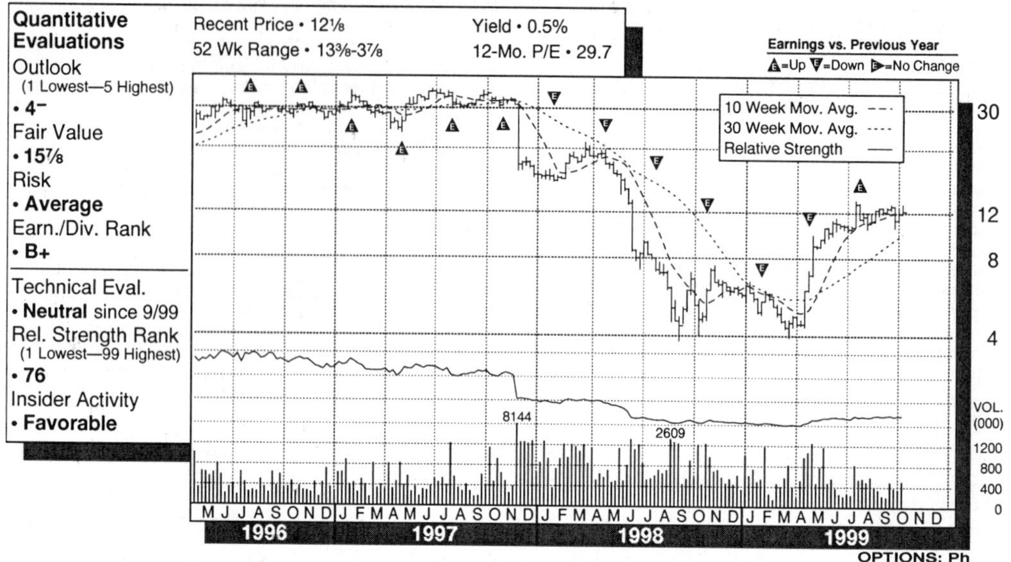

Business Profile - 08-JUN-99

BMC's strategy is based on continuous process improvement and the expansion of operations through capacity upgrades. The VisionEase subsidiary launched a new polycarbonate progressive lens during the 1998 fourth quarter in response to significant demand for high-quality polycarbonate progressive lenses. Initial orders were received during the fourth quarter of 1998 and significant sales and margin contributions are expected by the middle of 1999. The company believes that its positive first quarter results in 1999 reflect the benefits from the integration of the Orcolite acquisition (in May 1998) and the progress BMC has made in returning the mask business to profitability.

Operational Review - 08-JUN-99

Revenues for the three months ended March 31, 1999, rose 5.7%, year to year, as 40% higher sales from the optical products segment, due mainly to the acquisition of Orcolite in May 1998, was partially offset by 10% lower sales from the precision imaged products (PIP) segment, which reflected a temporary slowdown at one of PIP's units and decreased sales of AK steel entertainment masks. Gross margins widened on a more favorable product mix, but selling expenses were up 33%, and operating income gained 14%. Following sharply higher interest expenses, and after taxes at 34.9%, versus 30.9%, net income fell 16%, to $3,191,000 ($0.12 a share) from $3,809,000 ($0.14).

Stock Performance - 08-OCT-99

In the past 30 trading days, BMC's shares have declined 3%, compared to a 0.91% fall in the S&P 500. Average trading volume for the past five days was 99,640 shares, compared with the 40-day moving average of 72,438 shares.

Key Stock Statistics

Dividend Rate/Share	0.06	Shareholders	1,001
Shs. outstg. (M)	27.4	Market cap. (B)	$0.333
Avg. daily vol. (M)	0.085	Inst. holdings	47%
Tang. Bk. Value/Share	2.41		
Beta	1.32		

Value of $10,000 invested 5 years ago: $ 23,591

Fiscal Year Ending Dec. 31

	1999	1998	1997	1996	1995	1994
Revenues (Million $)						
1Q	84.65	80.08	77.13	68.30	61.33	52.41
2Q	93.34	84.94	80.26	68.17	69.65	57.31
3Q	—	88.58	79.09	68.16	59.20	53.98
4Q	—	81.53	76.07	75.86	65.17	56.28
Yr.	—	335.1	312.5	280.5	255.4	220.0
Earnings Per Share ($)						
1Q	**0.12**	**0.14**	**0.28**	**0.22**	0.17	0.10
2Q	**0.18**	**-1.42**	**0.42**	**0.35**	0.27	0.17
3Q	—	**-0.07**	**0.31**	**0.25**	0.16	0.08
4Q	—	**0.17**	**0.24**	**0.42**	0.28	0.19
Yr.	—	**-1.13**	**1.25**	1.24	**0.87**	**0.42**

Next earnings report expected: late October

Dividend Data (Dividends have been paid since 1994.)

Amount ($)	Date Decl.	Ex-Div. Date	Stock of Record	Payment Date
0.015	Dec. 11	Dec. 21	Dec. 23	Jan. 06 '99
0.015	Mar. 11	Mar. 22	Mar. 24	Apr. 07 '99
0.015	Jun. 10	Jun. 21	Jun. 23	Jul. 07 '99
0.015	Sep. 08	Sep. 20	Sep. 22	Oct. 06 '99

BMC Industries, Inc.

Business Summary - 08-JUN-99

BMC Industries (BMC), which dates back to 1907, consists of two product groups: Precision Imaged Products and Optical Products. Precision Imaged Products is comprised of two units: mask operations, producing aperture masks, an integral component of every color television and computer monitor picture tube; and Buckbee-Mears St. Paul (BMSP), a leading domestic producer of precision photo-etched parts. The Optical Products group makes and markets polycarbonate, glass and hard-resin plastic ophthalmic lenses

The principal business of the Precision Imaged Products group is the manufacture of aperture masks, which accounted for 54% of BMC's 1998 revenues. BMC is the sole independent manufacturer of aperture masks outside of Asia. As such, the company is a principal supplier to virtually every non-Japanese picture tube manufacturer. BMC is also engaged in ongoing efforts to develop the manufacturing and technical expertise necessary to produce a variety of new products, including high definition television (HDTV), multimedia and pure flat mask products. The company has delivered limited quantities of these masks and believes these efforts will leave the company well positioned for future growth in these segments. The company has also continued its efforts to leverage BMSP's capabilities to attract large end-product manufacturers for joint venture projects. BMSP achieved ISO 9002 certification in 1998, which it believes is critical for supplying a broad base of customers.

The Optical Products group, which operates under the Vision-Ease Lens trade name, is a leading designer and manufacturer of polycarbonate, glass and hard-resin plastic ophthalmic lenses. Vision-Ease supplies lenses to ophthalmic laboratories and retail dispensers throughout the world, offering a full line of lenses in each material. Bifocal and other multifocal lenses account for the majority of Vision-Ease's sales. With double-digit worldwide market growth, polycarbonate lenses continue to be an area of growth and strategic focus for Vision-Ease. Polycarbonate lenses are lighter in weight and can be made thinner, and thus more cosmetically appealing, than glass and traditional hard-resin plastic lenses. Moreover, polycarbonate lenses absorb harmful ultraviolet rays and are the most shatterproof lenses available.

In May 1998, BMC acquired the Monsanto Co.'s Orcolite operations, based in Azusa, CA, for $100 million. Orcolite, a producer of polycarbonate and hard-resin plastic ophthalmic lenses, will be managed as part of BMC's Vision-Ease Lens subsidiary. The acquisition is expected to solidify the company's position as the leading supplier of polycarbonate lenses.

The company markets its lenses to more than 750 wholesalers and retailers in the United States and to more than 60 wholesalers and retailers internationally. One customer, Precision LensCrafters, accounted for 13% of Vision-Ease's total revenues in 1998.

Per Share Data ($) (Year Ended Dec. 31)	1998	1997	1996	1995	1994	1993	1992	1991	1990	1989
Tangible Bk. Val.	2.21	6.43	5.26	4.01	3.06	2.57	1.70	1.42	1.02	0.82
Cash Flow	-0.36	1.72	1.60	1.16	0.85	0.73	0.65	0.71	0.40	0.49
Earnings	-1.13	1.25	1.24	0.87	0.55	0.42	0.30	0.37	0.09	0.24
Dividends	0.06	0.06	0.05	0.07	0.02	Nil	Nil	Nil	Nil	Nil
Payout Ratio	NM	5%	4%	8%	4%	Nil	Nil	Nil	Nil	Nil
Prices - High	$22\frac{1}{4}$	$35\frac{5}{8}$	$32\frac{3}{8}$	$23\frac{5}{8}$	$8\frac{3}{8}$	$5\frac{3}{8}$	3	$2\frac{3}{8}$	$2\frac{7}{8}$	$2\frac{5}{8}$
- Low	$3\frac{3}{4}$	$15\frac{3}{4}$	$19\frac{3}{4}$	$7\frac{3}{4}$	$4\frac{7}{8}$	$2\frac{5}{16}$	$1\frac{5}{8}$	$\frac{13}{16}$	$\frac{13}{16}$	$1\frac{11}{16}$
P/E Ratio - High	NM	28	26	27	15	13	10	6	33	11
- Low	NM	13	16	9	9	6	5	2	9	7
Income Statement Analysis (Million $)										
Revs.	335	313	280	255	220	195	181	203	175	164
Oper. Inc.	37.5	65.4	62.6	46.9	35.0	27.7	21.5	26.5	18.5	19.0
Depr.	21.0	13.3	10.2	8.3	8.3	7.8	8.0	7.6	6.9	5.6
Int. Exp.	13.5	1.3	0.5	0.6	3.1	5.1	6.7	8.2	7.8	7.5
Pretax Inc.	-48.7	51.2	52.4	38.9	24.3	15.2	7.7	10.0	3.9	6.6
Eff. Tax Rate	NM	30%	33%	37%	38%	32%	9.20%	18%	53%	18%
Net Inc.	-30.6	35.7	35.1	24.5	15.0	10.4	7.0	8.2	1.9	5.4
Balance Sheet & Other Fin. Data (Million $)										
Cash	1.0	2.4	2.5	15.9	14.3	10.9	9.4	12.2	1.9	10.9
Curr. Assets	152	122	91.7	83.4	78.8	72.0	68.0	70.0	74.0	68.0
Total Assets	339	319	233	182	139	130	119	125	128	116
Curr. Liab.	57.0	46.9	50.3	50.6	40.0	37.0	33.0	35.0	39.0	29.0
LT Debt	187	73.4	16.6	Nil	Nil	18.3	35.4	46.4	56.4	61.7
Common Eqty.	133	179	144	108	81.8	58.9	37.5	30.9	22.4	17.9
Total Cap.	324	255	163	110	82.8	78.0	74.0	79.0	81.0	81.0
Cap. Exp.	21.4	75.1	54.7	39.2	13.5	7.9	6.8	6.3	10.1	15.6
Cash Flow	-9.6	49.1	45.3	32.8	23.3	18.2	15.1	15.8	8.7	11.0
Curr. Ratio	2.7	2.6	1.8	1.6	2.0	1.9	2.1	2.0	1.9	2.4
% LT Debt of Cap.	57.8	28.7	10.2	Nil	0.1	23.5	47.8	58.8	70.0	76.2
% Net Inc.of Revs.	NM	11.4	12.5	9.6	6.8	5.3	3.9	4.1	1.1	3.3
% Ret. on Assets	NM	12.9	16.9	15.3	10.3	8.2	5.7	6.5	1.5	4.7
% Ret. on Equity	NM	22.1	27.9	25.8	19.8	21.2	20.4	30.8	9.1	34.5

Data as orig reptd.; bef. results of disc opers/spec. items. Per share data adj. for stk. divs. Bold denotes diluted EPS (FASB 128)-prior periods restated. E-Estimated. NA-Not Available. NM-Not Meaningful. NR-Not Ranked.

Office—One Meridian Crossings, Suite 850, Minneapolis, MN 55423. **Tel**—(612) 851-6000. **Fax**—(612) 851-6050. **Website**—http://www.bmcind.com**Chrmn, Pres & CEO**—P. B. Burke. **VP-Fin & CFO**—J. J. Hattara.**Investor Contact**—Bradley J. Schumacher (612-851-6017).**Dirs**—L. D. Altman, P. B. Burke, J. W. Castro, H. T. Davis, J. E. Davis, H. A. Hammerly, J. Ramich.**Transfer Agent & Registrar**—Norwest Bank Minnesota, South St. Paul. **Incorporated**—in Minnesota in 1907. **Empl**— 3,141. **S&P Analyst:** C.C.P.

STANDARD
&POOR'S
STOCK REPORTS

Bombay Co.

NYSE Symbol **BBA**

In S&P SmallCap 600

09-OCT-99

Industry:
Retail (Specialty)

Summary: This specialty retailer markets traditionally styled furniture, prints and accessories through a chain of more than 400 Bombay Company stores in the U.S. and Canada.

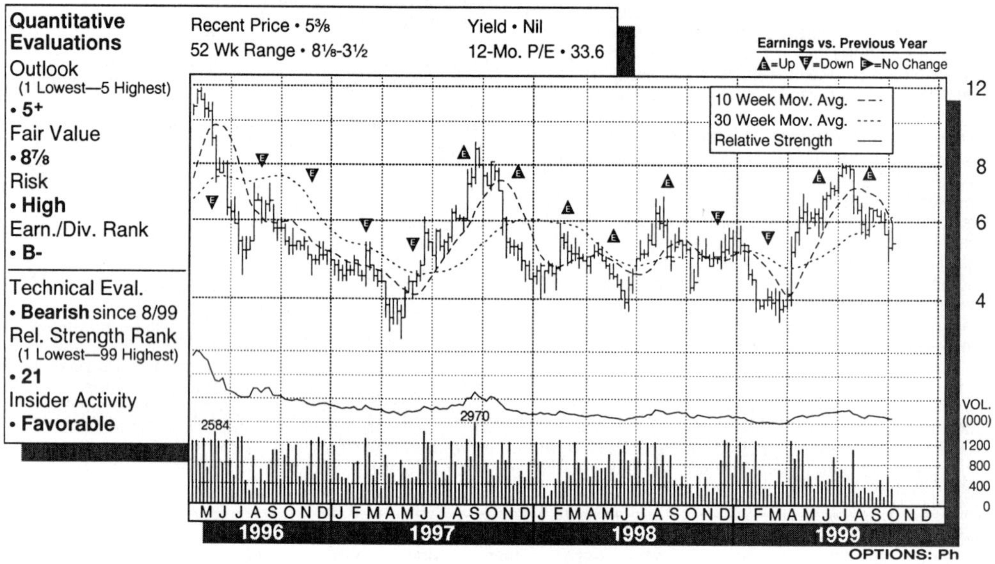

Business Profile - 10-JUN-99

As of June 1999, Bombay Company sold its products through a network of 421 stores. The company also offers purchases through its mail order operations in the U.S. and Canada, as well as over the Internet at www.bombayco.com. BBA announced that in the first quarter of FY 00 (Jan.), over 95% of the increase in sales came from growth in the accessories area. The company said that a focus on smaller, "take-with" items resulted in more customers buying in the company's stores, as the transaction count increased almost 20%. BBA also stated that its product margin improved through the introduction of fashion-right products and more selective promotions. Management stated that it expects current trends to continue into the second quarter, as it relies on selective promotions and special purchases to maintain the company's momentum, and said that it is looking forward to showing a profit in the second quarter.

Operational Review - 10-JUN-99

Net sales for the three months ended May 1, 1999, grew 10%, year to year. Same-store sales increased about 6%. Gross margins widened, aided by the introduction of fashion-right product and more selective promotions. With only a 5.6% rise in SG&A expenses, the net loss narrowed to $2,431,000 ($0.07 a share, on 3.6% fewer shares), from $3,881,000 ($0.10).

Stock Performance - 08-OCT-99

In the past 30 trading days, BBA's shares have declined 16%, compared to a 0.91% fall in the S&P 500. Average trading volume for the past five days was 64,040 shares, compared with the 40-day moving average of 65,672 shares.

Key Stock Statistics

Dividend Rate/Share	Nil	Shareholders	2,500
Shs. outstg. (M)	36.3	Market cap. (B)	$0.195
Avg. daily vol. (M)	0.077	Inst. holdings	66%
Tang. Bk. Value/Share	4.14		
Beta	1.04		

Value of $10,000 invested 5 years ago: $ 1,791

Fiscal Year Ending Jan. 31

	2000	1999	1998	1997	1996	1995
Revenues (Million $)						
1Q	75.29	68.34	67.23	68.08	77.94	64.34
2Q	90.76	82.01	68.74	71.20	69.67	78.20
3Q	—	75.88	71.33	72.82	70.42	77.47
4Q	—	130.5	126.3	124.2	127.4	142.9
Yr.	—	356.7	332.6	336.3	345.4	362.9
Earnings Per Share ($)						
1Q	**-0.07**	**-0.10**	**-0.12**	-0.08	0.05	0.06
2Q	**0.01**	**-0.01**	**-0.03**	-0.06	0.01	0.06
3Q	—	**-0.07**	**-0.05**	-0.16	-0.04	0.01
4Q	—	**0.30**	**0.31**	0.23	0.32	-0.38
Yr.	—	**0.11**	**0.12**	**-0.07**	**0.33**	-0.25

Next earnings report expected: mid November

Dividend Data

A three-for-two stock split was effected in December 1993, following similar splits in July 1993, December 1992, March 1992 and October 1987. The most recent cash payment was in 1983. Tandy Brands Accessories Inc. was spun off in December 1990.

The Bombay Company, Inc.

Business Summary - 10-JUN-99

The Bombay Company is a leading specialty retailer that markets traditional and classic furniture. As of January 30, 1999, it was operating 361 Bombay stores in 42 states and 51 stores in nine Canadian Provinces. During FY 99 (Jan.), BBA added 15 new stores, relocated or enlarged 16 stores, and closed 18 stores. In FY 99, the company had an assortment of about 3,500 stock keeping units (SKUs), of which 2,200 were introduced in FY 99, up from 1,200 SKU introductions in FY 98.

Furniture represented 49% of total sales for each of the past three fiscal years. This category includes both wood and metal ready-to-assemble furniture focusing on the bedroom, living room, dining room, and home office. BBA's furniture is manufactured by contractors located mainly in China, Taiwan, Malaysia, Mexico, Indonesia, India, and the U.S.

Accessories are the broadest category offered by the company, and represented 27% and 26% of total sales in FY 99 and FY 98, respectively. This category includes functional and decorative accessories including jewelry and memorabilia boxes, baskets, candles and scents, crystal, ceramics, frames and desktop products, textiles, and floral and holiday products. These items are imported from 14 countries in Asia, North America, and Europe.

Wall decor represented 15% and 17% of total sales in FY 99 and FY 98, respectively. Products include prints, mirrors and sconces. This merchandise is primarily sourced from the U.S., Canada, Italy and Korea.

Lamps and other items accounted for 9% and 8% of total sales in FY 99 and FY 98, respectively. These products are sourced mainly from China, Taiwan, and the U.S.

Merchandise is manufactured to company specifications through a network of manufacturers located principally in Asia and North America. Internally designed or styled products account for about 95% of Bombay's products. Approximately 60% of production needs are satisfied through overseas sources, and about 70% of the company's merchandise requirements are provided from 35 contractors in eight countries.

During FY 99, BBA's store openings included five outlet stores which were typically located in traditional outlet malls. The company views the use of outlets as an opportunity to increase sales to a different customer base, to assist in the orderly clearance of merchandise, and to further capitalize on its strength in designing and sourcing proprietary products. BBA's store opening plans for FY 00 include five to eight outlet locations.

Total sales for the four week period ended May 29, 1999, were up 19%, year to year. Comparable-store sales were up 14%.

Per Share Data ($) (Year Ended Jan. 31)	1999	1998	1997	1996	1995	1994	1993	1992	1991	1990
Tangible Bk. Val.	4.21	4.14	4.04	4.07	3.66	4.02	3.21	1.81	1.48	1.69
Cash Flow	0.38	0.38	0.22	0.65	-0.21	0.83	0.42	0.46	0.35	0.33
Earnings	0.11	0.12	-0.07	0.33	-0.39	0.60	0.23	0.29	0.18	0.21
Dividends	Nil	Nil	Nil	Nil	Nil	Nil	Nil	Nil	Nil	Nil
Payout Ratio	Nil	Nil	Nil	Nil	Nil	Nil	Nil	Nil	Nil	Nil
Cal. Yrs.	1998	1997	1996	1995	1994	1993	1992	1991	1990	1989
Prices - High	$6\frac{3}{4}$	9	$11\frac{7}{8}$	11	$32\frac{3}{4}$	$32\frac{7}{8}$	$16\frac{1}{4}$	$5\frac{1}{4}$	$5\frac{1}{2}$	$5\frac{1}{2}$
- Low	$3\frac{3}{4}$	$3\frac{1}{4}$	$4\frac{1}{2}$	$4\frac{3}{4}$	$8\frac{3}{4}$	$12\frac{5}{8}$	$4\frac{1}{2}$	$1\frac{15}{16}$	$1\frac{7}{8}$	$2\frac{3}{16}$
P/E Ratio - High	62	75	NM	33	55	NM	56	29	27	22
- Low	34	27	NM	14	15	NM	15	10	9	9

Income Statement Analysis (Million $)										
Revs.	357	333	336	345	241	317	232	176	139	112
Oper. Inc.	15.3	14.8	6.2	25.5	23.7	45.7	32.7	21.5	15.2	13.5
Depr.	10.3	9.9	11.2	11.9	6.8	8.9	6.7	5.7	5.2	3.6
Int. Exp.	Nil	Nil	Nil	0.1	0.4	0.1	0.2	0.5	0.6	0.9
Pretax Inc.	6.8	7.3	-4.4	20.4	-24.3	37.6	13.4	15.7	9.8	9.5
Eff. Tax Rate	41%	39%	NM	39%	NM	39%	39%	39%	41%	38%
Net Inc.	4.0	4.5	-2.8	12.4	-14.7	22.9	8.2	9.6	5.9	5.9

Balance Sheet & Other Fin. Data (Million $)										
Cash	52.8	56.1	63.1	24.1	30.7	20.4	42.8	10.1	1.0	3.3
Curr. Assets	137	149	145	133	128	119	111	45.0	34.2	27.7
Total Assets	194	195	195	191	190	181	143	79.2	66.2	69.2
Curr. Liab.	30.3	30.4	35.1	31.7	50.1	29.3	24.1	17.4	14.5	11.8
LT Debt	Nil	Nil	Nil	Nil	Nil	Nil	Nil	Nil	2.5	2.5
Common Eqty.	156	158	154	152	135	147	116	59.1	47.3	53.6
Total Cap.	156	158	154	152	135	147	116	59.1	49.7	56.1
Cap. Exp.	17.3	4.0	4.4	5.9	22.1	35.3	15.0	7.5	8.9	11.6
Cash Flow	14.4	14.3	8.3	24.3	-7.9	31.8	14.9	15.3	11.0	9.5
Curr. Ratio	4.5	4.9	4.1	4.2	2.5	4.1	4.6	2.6	2.4	2.4
% LT Debt of Cap.	Nil	Nil	Nil	Nil	Nil	Nil	Nil	Nil	5.0	4.4
% Net Inc.of Revs.	1.1	1.3	NM	3.6	NM	7.2	3.5	5.5	4.2	5.3
% Ret. on Assets	2.1	2.3	NM	6.6	NM	14.0	7.1	13.1	8.6	8.1
% Ret. on Equity	2.6	2.9	NM	8.7	NM	17.3	9.0	17.9	11.6	12.0

Data as orig. reptd.; bef. results of disc. opers. and/or spec. items. Per share data adj. for stk. divs. as of ex-div. date. Yrs. ended Jun. 30 prior to 1995; data for FY 95 in Per Share Data & Income Statement tbls. for seven mos. ended Jan. E-Estimated. NA-Not Available. NM-Not Meaningful. NR-Not Ranked.

Office—550 Bailey Ave., Fort Worth, TX 76107. **Tel**—(817) 347-8200. **Website**—http://www.bombayco.com **Chrmn & CEO**—R. S. Jackson. **Pres & COO**—C. Mehrlander. **VP & Secy**—M. J. Veitenheimer. **VP-Fin & Treas**—E. D. Crowley. **Dirs**—B. Bass, G. B. Cobbe, E. H. Damon, G. E. Hemmerle, A. R. Megarry, C. Mehrlander, R. E. Runice, C. R. Thompson. **Transfer Agent & Registrar**—Boston EquiServe, Canton, MA. **Incorporated**—in Delaware in 1975. **Empl**— 5,000. **S&P Analyst:** Matthew C. Hershberg

STANDARD
&POOR'S
STOCK REPORTS

Books-A-Million

NASDAQ Symbol **BAMM**

In S&P SmallCap 600

09-OCT-99

Industry:
Retail (Specialty)

Summary: This leading book retailer operates 178 stores in 17 states (mainly in the Southeast), selling books, magazines, newspapers, collectibles, greeting cards and gifts.

Quantitative Evaluations

Outlook
(1 Lowest—5 Highest)
• **2-**

Fair Value
• **8½**

Risk
• **Average**

Earn./Div. Rank
• **B**

Technical Eval.
• **Bearish** since 8/99

Rel. Strength Rank
(1 Lowest—99 Highest)
• **76**

Insider Activity
• **NA**

Recent Price • 9⅜
52 Wk Range • 47-2⅝
Yield • Nil
12-Mo. P/E • 30.2

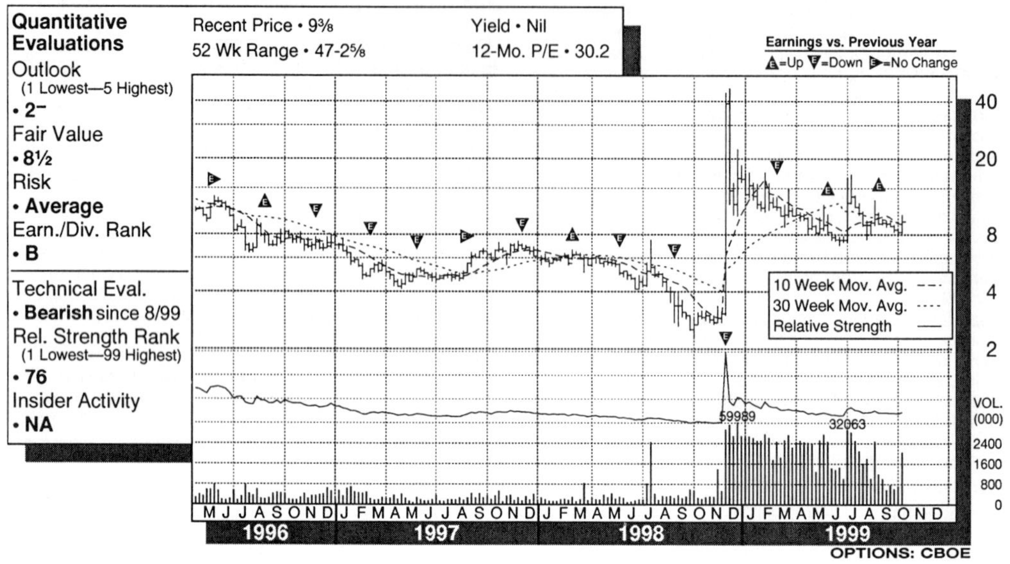

Business Profile - 31-AUG-99

Books-A-Million's strategy has been to take advantage of the environment of each particular area by opening bookstores in three different formats, including large superstores operating under the names Books-A-Million and Books & Co., and combination book and greeting cards stores, operating under the name Bookland. Recently, BAMM forged a strategic alliance with Wal-Mart Stores, Inc., the world's largest retailer, which makes the company the exclusive provider and distributor of books and related products to Wal-Mart's online customers. In November 1998, the company began selling books at its website--www.booksamillion.com.

Operational Review - 31-AUG-99

Net sales in the first half of FY 00 (Jan.) rose 15%, year to year, reflecting strong performance across a broad range of merchandise categories; comparable store sales were up 5.1%. Earnings before interest, taxes and depreciation advanced 21%, to $9.4 million from $7.8 million. Net income of $329,000 ($0.02 a share) contrasted with a loss of $504,000 ($0.03).

Stock Performance - 08-OCT-99

In the past 30 trading days, BAMM's shares have increased 3%, compared to a 0.91% fall in the S&P 500. Average trading volume for the past five days was 407,460 shares, compared with the 40-day moving average of 254,367 shares.

Key Stock Statistics

Dividend Rate/Share	Nil	Shareholders	6,180
Shs. outstg. (M)	18.0	Market cap. (B)	$0.169
Avg. daily vol. (M)	0.204	Inst. holdings	20%
Tang. Bk. Value/Share	6.34		
Beta	NA		

Value of $10,000 invested 5 years ago: $ 8,620

Fiscal Year Ending Jan. 31

	2000	1999	1998	1997	1996	1995
Revenues (Million $)						
1Q	85.13	74.47	68.24	56.59	44.01	30.94
2Q	89.88	77.96	71.87	60.46	52.03	37.28
3Q	—	78.96	71.61	64.51	48.77	37.19
4Q	—	116.5	113.0	97.06	84.99	66.96
Yr.	—	347.9	324.8	278.6	229.8	172.4
Earnings Per Share ($)						
1Q	**0.02**	Nil	0.02	0.06	0.06	0.05
2Q	Nil	**-0.03**	0.03	0.03	-0.02	0.07
3Q	—	**-0.08**	-0.02	Nil	0.04	0.03
4Q	—	**0.36**	**0.37**	0.25	0.35	0.32
Yr.	—	**0.26**	**0.40**	**0.33**	**0.42**	0.47

Next earnings report expected: mid November

Dividend Data

No cash dividends have been paid.

A Division of The McGraw-Hill Companies

Books-A-Million, Inc.

Business Summary - 31-AUG-99

From its humble beginnings in 1917 as a single store made out of old piano crates, Books-A-Million has grown to 178 stores in 17 southeastern states. The company's current growth strategy is focused on opening superstores and combination stores in new and existing market areas. It also is continuing to review profitability trends and prospects of existing stores and closing or relocating underperforming stores or converting stores to different formats.

BAMM has developed three distinct store formats to address the various market areas it serves -- superstores, combination and traditional.

Superstores, first opened in 1988, average about 20,000 sq. ft. and operate under the name Books-A-Million. BAMM developed its superstores to capitalize on the growing consumer demand for the convenience, selection and value associated with the superstore retailing format. Each superstore is designed to be a receptive and open environment conducive to browsing and reading and includes ample space for promotional events open to the public, including book autograph sessions and children's storytelling. The company operated 124 Books-A-Million superstores as of January 30, 1999.

Combination stores average about 4,500 sq. ft. and carry a broad selection of best sellers and other hardcover and paperback books, bargain books, magazines, gifts and greeting cards. As a result of the increased customer traffic it generates, the combination store format has been particularly successful in smaller market areas that do not readily sustain stand-alone book and greeting card stores. BAMM had 27 combination stores as of January 30, 1999.

The company's traditional bookstores average about 3,500sq. ft. and offer a wide selection of best sellers and other hardcover and paperback books, magazines and newspapers. Traditional bookstores are located in multiple types of market areas, but are generally located in market areas that are larger than those in which combination stores are located. There were 22 traditional bookstores in operation as of January 30, 1999.

Since November 1998, BAMM has been selling a broad range of products over the Internet at its website-- www.booksamillion.com. Products sold by booksamillion.com are similar to those sold in the company's Books-A-Million superstores and include a wide selection of books, magazines and gift items. Booksamillion.com also operates an online cafe on its website under the name joemuggs.com. Joemuggs.com offers a wide selection of whole bean coffee, confections and related gift items for purchase over the Internet. In January of 1999, BAMM acquired NetCentral, Inc., an Internet development company, to assist it in its Internet development efforts.

Per Share Data ($) (Year Ended Jan. 31)	**1999**	**1998**	**1997**	**1996**	**1995**	**1994**	**1993**	**1992**	**1991**	**1990**
Tangible Bk. Val.	6.33	5.85	5.45	5.11	4.66	4.29	2.61	NA	NA	NA
Cash Flow	1.00	1.06	0.88	0.82	0.71	0.56	0.55	0.40	0.29	NA
Earnings	0.26	0.40	0.33	0.43	0.47	0.37	0.32	0.21	0.13	NA
Dividends	Nil	Nil	Nil	Nil	Nil	Nil	Nil	Nil	Nil	NA
Payout Ratio	Nil	Nil	Nil	Nil	Nil	Nil	Nil	Nil	Nil	NA
Cal. Yrs.	1998	1997	1996	1995	1994	1993	1992	1991	1990	1989
Prices - High	47	$7\frac{5}{8}$	$12\frac{7}{8}$	$18\frac{5}{8}$	$17\frac{3}{4}$	$12\frac{7}{8}$	$9\frac{1}{8}$	NA	NA	NA
- Low	$2\frac{1}{4}$	$4\frac{1}{8}$	$6\frac{3}{8}$	$12\frac{3}{8}$	$9\frac{1}{4}$	$5\frac{7}{8}$	$6\frac{1}{2}$	NA	NA	NA
P/E Ratio - High	NM	19	39	43	28	35	28	NA	NA	NA
- Low	NM	10	19	29	20	16	20	NA	NA	NA
Income Statement Analysis (Million $)										
Revs.	348	325	279	230	172	123	95.0	73.0	65.0	NA
Oper. Inc.	24.7	27.2	21.7	22.1	16.7	11.7	8.4	6.1	5.0	NA
Depr.	13.0	11.6	9.5	6.8	4.3	3.0	2.4	1.7	1.5	NA
Int. Exp.	4.4	4.3	2.8	0.7	0.0	Nil	0.7	1.3	1.6	NA
Pretax Inc.	7.3	11.2	9.3	11.9	13.0	9.1	5.4	3.0	1.9	NA
Eff. Tax Rate	38%	38%	38%	37%	38%	38%	38%	37%	37%	NA
Net Inc.	4.5	7.0	5.8	7.5	8.1	5.6	3.3	1.9	1.2	NA
Balance Sheet & Other Fin. Data (Million $)										
Cash	4.3	3.9	4.8	1.9	21.5	35.4	NA	NA	NA	NA
Curr. Assets	202	178	169	140	120	99	NA	NA	NA	NA
Total Assets	272	246	234	191	158	115	68.0	41.0	NA	NA
Curr. Liab.	118	95.7	98.1	85.3	70.3	40.2	NA	NA	NA	NA
LT Debt	36.9	45.2	37.6	14.1	4.6	Nil	Nil	3.8	NA	NA
Common Eqty.	115	103	96.4	90.5	82.4	74.2	37.7	8.1	NA	NA
Total Cap.	153	150	135	106	87.8	74.8	37.7	11.9	NA	NA
Cap. Exp.	15.7	14.4	23.7	23.9	24.4	8.3	6.7	NA	NA	NA
Cash Flow	17.5	18.6	15.3	14.3	12.3	8.6	5.7	3.7	2.7	NA
Curr. Ratio	1.7	1.9	1.7	1.6	1.7	2.5	1.6	NA	NA	NA
% LT Debt of Cap.	24.1	30.1	27.8	13.3	5.2	Nil	Nil	31.6	NA	NA
% Net Inc.of Revs.	1.3	2.1	2.1	3.3	4.7	4.6	3.5	2.6	1.8	NA
% Ret. on Assets	1.7	2.9	2.7	4.2	5.9	6.2	6.2	5.0	NA	NA
% Ret. on Equity	4.1	7.0	6.2	8.6	10.3	10.1	14.6	26.8	NA	NA

Data as orig reptd.; bef. results of disc opers/spec. items. Per share data adj. for stk. divs. Bold denotes diluted EPS (FASB 128)-prior periods restated. E-Estimated. NA-Not Available. NM-Not Meaningful. NR-Not Ranked.

Office—402 Industrial Lane, Birmingham AL 35211. **Tel**—(205) 942-3737. **Website**—http://www.booksamillion.com. **Chrmn**—C. C. Anderson. **Pres & CEO**—C. B. Anderson. **EVP, CFO & Secy**—Sandra B. Cochran. **Dirs**—C. B. Anderson, C. C. Anderson, T. C. Anderson, R. G. Bruno, J. B. Mason.**Transfer Agent & Registrar**—AmSouth Bank, Birmingham. **Incorporated**—in Alabama in 1964; reincorporated in Delaware in 1992. **Empl**— 4,500. **S&P Analyst:** M.I.

STANDARD
&POOR'S
STOCK REPORTS

Bowne & Co.

NYSE Symbol **BNE**

In S&P SmallCap 600

09-OCT-99 **Industry:** Specialty Printing

Summary: This company is the world's largest financial printer. It also provides localization services to the software industry and Internet business services.

Quantitative Evaluations

Outlook (1 Lowest—5 Highest)
• **5**

Fair Value
• **20⅛**

Risk
• **Average**

Earn./Div. Rank
• **B+**

Technical Eval.
• **Bearish** since 9/99

Rel. Strength Rank (1 Lowest—99 Highest)
• **18**

Insider Activity
• **NA**

Recent Price • 11½
52 Wk Range • 19½-10⅛
Yield • 1.9%
12-Mo. P/E • 31.2

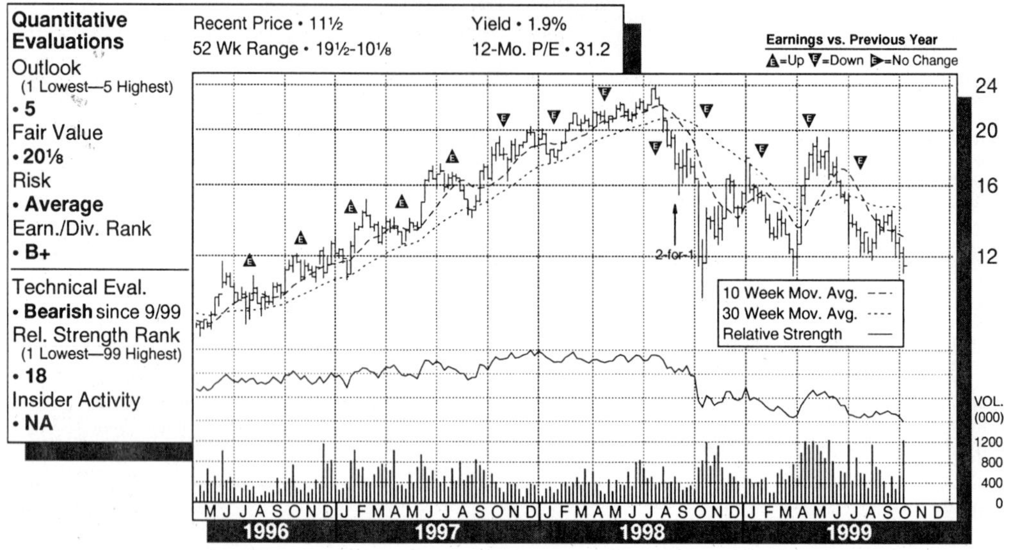

Business Profile - 10-JUN-99

Bowne & Co said in May 1999, that the rebound of the financial markets enabled it to experience robust financial printing activity in March and thereafter. Inventories for financial printing increased to $30.9 million at March 31, 1999, from $19.4 million at year-end 1998. BNE expected these higher inventory levels to benefit revenue in the next few months, as is typical in the financial print industry. In addition, BNE said that it saw several developments in financial services that it believes will continue to drive growth in the financial printing business, including demutualization of the insurance sector. Moreover, the trend of improving newer business solution offerings was expected to continue. Trading in Bowne's shares shifted to the NYSE from the ASE in July, 1999.

Operational Review - 10-JUN-99

Net sales for the first quarter of 1999 advanced 13%, year to year, due to acquisitions, partially offset by lower demand for transactional printing. However, profitability was hurt by a greater proportion of sales from both lower margin products within financial printing and from lower margin segments; 60% larger depreciation/amortization, attributed to new businesses, expanded facilities, and equipment acquisitions; and a substantial jump in interest expenses. After taxes at 62.1%, versus 41.1%, net income dropped 87%, to $1.7 million ($0.05 a share) from $13.0 million ($0.34, adjusted).

Stock Performance - 08-OCT-99

In the past 30 trading days, BNE's shares have declined 14%, compared to a 0.91% fall in the S&P 500. Average trading volume for the past five days was 292,660 shares, compared with the 40-day moving average of 122,013 shares.

Key Stock Statistics

Dividend Rate/Share	0.22	Shareholders	1,400
Shs. outstg. (M)	36.9	Market cap. (B)	$0.427
Avg. daily vol. (M)	0.140	Inst. holdings	67%
Tang. Bk. Value/Share	5.55		
Beta	1.20		

Value of $10,000 invested 5 years ago: $ 11,569

Fiscal Year Ending Dec. 31

	1999	1998	1997	1996	1995	1994
Revenues (Million $)						
1Q	218.7	194.3	153.7	90.73	76.81	82.08
2Q	272.5	219.3	193.8	136.4	102.5	119.2
3Q	—	225.4	177.7	134.2	103.1	95.59
4Q	—	208.5	191.5	140.1	110.3	83.80
Yr.	—	847.6	716.6	501.4	392.7	380.6
Earnings Per Share ($)						
1Q	**0.05**	**0.34**	**0.83**	0.10	0.06	0.19
2Q	**0.35**	**0.41**	**0.41**	0.35	0.17	0.43
3Q	—	**0.04**	**0.28**	0.38	0.20	0.17
4Q	—	**-0.07**	**0.34**	0.38	0.24	0.10
Yr.	—	**0.72**	**1.99**	1.21	0.67	0.90

Next earnings report expected: mid November

Dividend Data (Dividends have been paid since 1941.)

Amount ($)	Date Decl.	Ex-Div. Date	Stock of Record	Payment Date
0.055	Oct. 28	Nov. 10	Nov. 13	Nov. 25 '98
0.055	Jan. 27	Feb. 10	Feb. 12	Feb. 24 '99
0.055	Apr. 28	May. 12	May. 14	May. 26 '99
0.055	Jul. 28	Aug. 11	Aug. 13	Aug. 25 '99

Bowne & Co., Inc.

Business Summary - 10-JUN-99

Prior to several years ago, Bowne & Co.'s focus was principally on financial printing and certain types of commercial printing. Since then, BNE has been making a transition that it believes will allow it to leverage document management and information management technologies it has traditionally employed into a variety of new business solutions for customers. The transition has involved a re-focusing on what Bowne calls empowering information, the management, repurposing and distribution of a client's information to any audience, through any medium, in any language, anywhere in the world.

Bowne manages documents on the clients' site or at its own facilities; and provides business services and solutions for transactional financial, corporate reporting, and mutual fund printing, as well as providing digital data management, integrated Internet applications, localization, translation and document management outsourcing.

Transactional financial printing accounted for 42% of total revenues in 1998, corporate reporting printing 14%, mutual fund printing 12%, commercial printing 10%, digital printing and other 4%, outsourcing 10%, internet consulting and development 2%, and localization 6%.

Financial printing consists of transactional financial, corporate reporting, mutual fund, commercial and digital printing. Outsourcing involves document management solutions primarily for the legal and financial communities. Internet consulting and development involves providing integrated Internet applications primarily for the financial sector. Localization consists of translation and reengineering of software products.

Transactional financial printing includes registration statements, tax-exempt offering circulars, prospectuses, debt agreements, special proxy statements, tender offer materials and other documents related to corporate financings, acquisitions and mergers. Corporate reporting includes interim reports and regular proxy materials prepared by corporations for distribution to stockholders, Securities and Exchange Commission reports on Form 10-K and other forms, and stock exchange listing applications.

Mutual fund printing includes regulatory and stockholder communications such as annual or interim reports, prospectuses, information statements, and marketing-related materials. BNE receives its clients' information in myriad formats and repurposes it for distribution typically in print or digitally via EDGAR or Internet formats.

Digital data management provides customers' individual clients with high-speed, customized periodic statements or other on-demand printing. Such customers include mutual funds, stock brokers, investment banks, retail banks and other financial institutions.

Per Share Data ($) (Year Ended Dec. 31)	1998	1997	1996	1995	1994	1993	1992	1991	1990	1989
Tangible Bk. Val.	5.17	8.06	7.54	6.53	6.41	5.68	4.86	4.23	3.90	3.29
Cash Flow	1.84	2.67	1.81	1.19	1.33	1.35	1.15	0.74	0.56	0.52
Earnings	0.72	1.99	1.21	0.67	0.90	1.02	0.82	0.42	0.24	0.23
Dividends	0.20	0.18	0.18	0.18	0.16	0.15	0.13	0.13	0.13	0.13
Payout Ratio	28%	9%	15%	27%	18%	12%	16%	30%	51%	53%
Prices - High	23 7/8	20 3/8	13	10 1/2	14 1/4	10 7/8	9 1/4	8 1/4	7 1/2	7 1/4
- Low	10 1/8	10 7/8	8 5/8	7 3/4	7 3/4	7 3/8	6 5/8	4 7/8	4	5 1/4
P/E Ratio - High	33	10	11	16	16	11	11	20	31	32
- Low	14	5	7	11	9	7	8	11	16	23
Income Statement Analysis (Million $)										
Revs.	848	717	501	393	381	333	282	236	201	190
Oper. Inc.	108	114	92.0	56.8	65.3	68.4	57.0	35.7	24.7	23.0
Depr.	41.9	29.7	21.2	17.9	15.2	11.4	10.9	10.8	10.8	10.2
Int. Exp.	5.5	1.6	0.7	0.9	1.1	2.3	2.9	3.5	3.4	3.5
Pretax Inc.	54.4	121	75.0	41.8	54.2	59.0	47.0	25.1	14.5	15.9
Eff. Tax Rate	50%	42%	43%	44%	42%	40%	40%	43%	42%	50%
Net Inc.	27.1	69.5	42.5	23.3	31.2	35.3	28.3	14.3	8.4	8.2
Balance Sheet & Other Fin. Data (Million $)										
Cash	24.2	40.6	36.5	36.6	38.5	33.1	55.7	30.8	29.7	37.8
Curr. Assets	276	286	235	184	158	153	131	113	93.0	100
Total Assets	642	501	386	326	292	284	244	226	204	205
Curr. Liab.	163	121	87.5	107	51.3	64.7	42.7	38.7	26.6	28.5
LT Debt	74.9	2.5	2.5	2.8	3.2	8.8	22.3	30.8	34.2	34.4
Common Eqty.	379	377	281	242	223	197	167	144	132	131
Total Cap.	454	361	284	244	226	206	189	175	167	166
Cap. Exp.	50.2	35.2	44.5	20.0	27.2	24.5	17.5	9.3	13.8	12.0
Cash Flow	69.1	99	63.8	41.2	46.4	46.7	39.2	25.1	19.2	18.3
Curr. Ratio	1.7	2.4	2.7	2.7	3.1	2.4	3.1	2.9	3.5	3.5
% LT Debt of Cap.	16.5	0.7	0.9	1.1	1.4	4.3	11.8	17.6	20.6	20.7
% Net Inc.of Revs.	3.2	9.7	8.5	5.9	8.2	10.6	10.0	6.1	4.2	4.3
% Ret. on Assets	4.7	15.7	11.9	7.6	10.8	13.3	12.0	6.6	4.1	4.0
% Ret. on Equity	7.2	20.7	16.3	10.0	14.9	19.4	18.1	10.3	6.4	6.2

Data as orig. reptd.; bef. results of disc. opers. and/or spec. items. Per share data adj. for stk. divs. as of ex-div. date. Prior to 1998, yrs. ended Oct. 31. E-Estimated. NA-Not Available. NM-Not Meaningful. NR-Not Ranked.

Office—345 Hudson St., New York, NY 10014. **Tel**—(212) 924-5500. **Website**—http://www.bowne.com **Chrmn & CEO**—R. M. Johnson. **Pres & COO**—J. P. O'Neil. **EVP**—C. J. Crosetto. **SVP & CFO**—D. K. Fletcher. **Counsel &Secy**—D. F. Bauer. **Treas & Investor Contact**—William J. Coote (212) 886-0614; bill.coote@bowne.com.**Dirs**—R. M. Conway, R. M. Johnson, J. P. O'Neil, H. M. Schwarz, W. M. Smith, L. A. Stanley, V. Tese, H. Wallaesa, R. R. West. **Transfer Agent & Registrar**—Bank of New York, NYC. **Incorporated**—established in 1775 in New York; incorporated in 1909; reincorporated in 1968 in New York,; reincorporated again in 1998 in Delaware. **Empl**— 7,200. **S&P Analyst:** N.J.D.

Brady Corp.

NYSE Symbol **BRC**

In S&P SmallCap 600

26-OCT-99

Industry: Manufacturing (Specialized)

Summary: This company is an international manufacturer and marketer of safety, graphics, specialty tape, and industrial identification products.

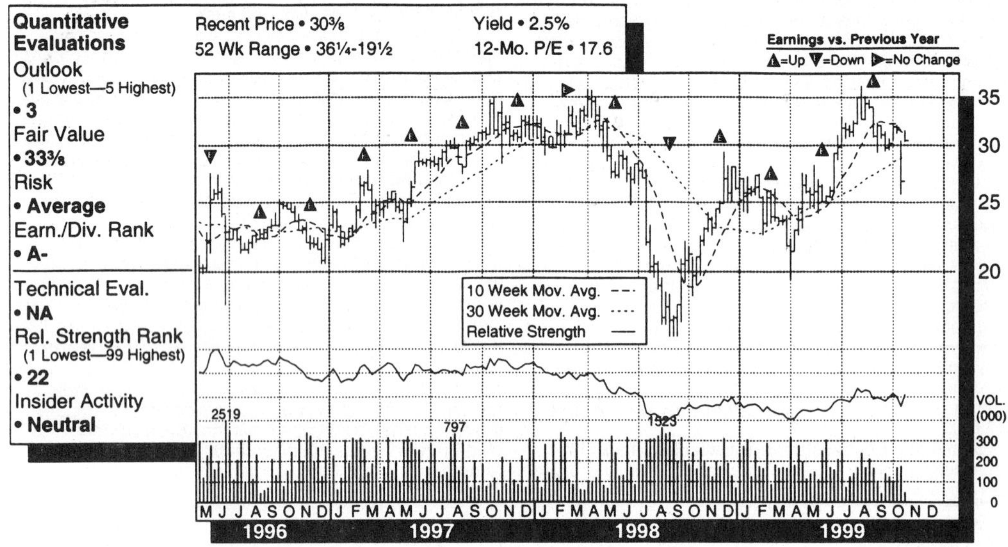

Business Profile - 25-OCT-99

In September 1999, the company reported growth despite the impact of the Asian economic crisis on its industrial markets during the year. In FY 00 (Jul.), BRC targets sales growth of 6% to 9%, with additional growth if it is successful in making new acquisitions. In August 1999, BRC announced it will begin manufacturing high-performance labels and precision die-cut materials in the Jiangsu Province, China later this year. Also, in August 1999, BRC acquired the graphics division of SOFT S.A. (annual sales of approximately $10 million), a European printing system business. In July 1999, the company acquired the Holman Groupe S.A., a French automatic identification and data collection company (about $6 million in annual sales).

Operational Review - 25-OCT-99

Based on a preliminary report, net sales for the FY 00 (Jul.), advanced 3.5%, from the previous year, reflecting strong international growth. Gross margins improved on a favorable product mix, including proprietary printing systems, software and high-performance materials, as well as cost control and productivity initiatives. Following a non-recurring operating credit of $611,000 versus a charge of $5.4 million (related to a workforce reduction and the discontinuation of product lines), and the doubling of investment income, net income climbed 41%, to $39.6 million ($1.73 per class A share), from $28.0 million ($1.23).

Stock Performance - 22-OCT-99

In the past 30 trading days, BRC's shares have declined 14%, compared to a 4% fall in the S&P 500. Average trading volume for the past five days was 33,440 shares, compared with the 40-day moving average of 26,736 shares.

Key Stock Statistics

Dividend Rate/Share	0.68	Shareholders	500
Shs. outstg. (M)	22.6	Market cap. (B)	$0.552
Avg. daily vol. (M)	0.026	Inst. holdings	56%
Tang. Bk. Value/Share	9.33		
Beta	1.00		

Value of $10,000 invested 5 years ago: $ 20,761

Fiscal Year Ending Jul. 31

	1999	1998	1997	1996	1995	1994
Revenues (Million $)						
1Q	116.8	115.3	97.22	79.22	69.04	59.64
2Q	112.3	107.2	109.9	87.82	78.86	64.11
3Q	121.5	118.8	108.3	94.65	83.32	65.89
4Q	102.3	113.9	110.7	97.85	83.14	66.21
Yr.	470.9	455.1	426.1	359.5	314.4	255.8
Earnings Per Share ($)						
1Q	**0.38**	0.37	0.30	0.30	0.23	0.20
2Q	**0.35**	**0.31**	0.31	0.26	0.28	0.18
3Q	**0.57**	**0.44**	0.43	0.36	0.43	0.25
4Q	**0.43**	**0.11**	0.40	0.36	0.33	0.22
Yr.	**1.73**	**1.23**	**1.43**	1.27	1.28	0.85

Next earnings report expected: mid November

Dividend Data (Dividends have been paid since 1984.)

Amount ($)	Date Decl.	Ex-Div. Date	Stock of Record	Payment Date
0.160	Nov. 23	Jan. 06	Jan. 08	Jan. 31 '99
0.160	Feb. 23	Apr. 07	Apr. 09	Apr. 30 '99
0.160	May. 10	Jul. 07	Jul. 09	Jul. 30 '99
0.170	Sep. 14	Oct. 06	Oct. 08	Oct. 31 '99

Brady Corporation

Business Summary - 25-OCT-99

Founded in 1914 by W.H. Brady, BRC is a leading manufacturer of high performance identification products and materials worldwide, and believes it is the world leader in complete idéntification solutions. The company is committed to new product development, leveraging distribution channels and sales efforts to increase market penetration, pursuing significant growth opportunities in international markets. As part of this strategy, BRC is pursuing acquisitions and forming joint ventures.

In February 1999, the company stated that its long-term performance goal is to grow sales at a compound annual growth rate of at least 15% on a rolling five-year basis and to grow net income at a faster rate.

In November 1998, BRC acquired VEB Sistemas de Etiquetas Ltda., an industrial label manufacturer in Brazil, and opened a sales office in the Philippines. In August 1999, BRC announced it will begin manufacturing high-performance labels and precision die-cut materials in the Jiangsu Province, China later this year. Also, in August 1999, the company acquired the graphics division of SOFT S.A., a European printing system business. In July 1999, the company acquired the Holman Groupe S.A., a French automatic identification and data collection company.

BRC operates 18 manufacturing facilities around the world, and also sells through subsidiaries or sales offices in the U.S. (57% of FY 98 (Jul.) net sales), Europe (30%), Asia/Pacific (8%) and other (5%).

The company's sales are driven by the push of industries worldwide to improve productivity and safety. BRC makes over 30,000 stock and custom items, produces identification, safety and graphics products that help customers create safer work environments for their employees and keep better track of their non-human assets. BRC's products are divided into three main categories: Industrial Identification and Data-Collection Products (wire and cable markers, high performance labels, stand-alone printing systems, and automatic identification and data-collection systems); Safety and Facility Identification Products (signs, pipe and valve markers, storage markers, asset identification markers, lockout/tagout products, traffic control products and other); and OEM Components (specialty tapes, die-cut materials, graphics products and other).

The company believes that it is the leading domestic producer of self-adhesive wire markers, pipe markers, audio and video leader and splicing tapes and reinforcing rings for floppy disks and believes that it is a leading domestic producer of safety signs.

As of July 31, 1998, the amount of the company's backlog was approximately $20.4 million, compared to $19.9 million in the previous year.

Per Share Data ($) (Year Ended Jul. 31)	1999	1998	1997	1996	1995	1994	1993	1992	1991	1990
Tangible Bk. Val.	NA	9.33	7.63	6.95	7.69	6.54	5.78	5.42	5.22	4.69
Cash Flow	NA	1.84	2.08	1.77	1.70	1.27	1.23	0.77	1.04	0.98
Earnings	1.73	1.23	1.44	1.27	1.28	0.85	0.78	0.38	0.71	0.70
Dividends	0.64	0.60	0.52	0.40	0.32	0.23	0.20	0.19	0.16	0.13
Payout Ratio	37%	49%	36%	31%	25%	27%	26%	49%	23%	19%
Prices - High	36¼	35¾	35	27½	24½	16⅜	14⅜	12½	14	12⅛
- Low	19½	16¼	21⅝	18	15⅝	14⅛	11⅜	10	8½	6½
P/E Ratio - High	21	29	24	22	19	19	16	33	20	18
- Low	11	13	15	14	12	17	15	27	12	9
Income Statement Analysis (Million $)										
Revs.	NA	455	426	360	314	256	243	236	211	191
Oper. Inc.	NA	64.6	64.5	51.7	49.7	38.8	33.9	30.4	27.4	28.5
Depr.	NA	13.3	14.2	10.6	9.2	9.3	9.8	8.4	7.2	6.3
Int. Exp.	NA	0.4	0.3	0.3	0.6	0.4	0.1	0.2	0.6	0.7
Pretax Inc.	NA	46.2	51.3	45.4	44.6	29.9	25.8	15.4	22.5	25.6
Eff. Tax Rate	NA	39%	38%	38%	38%	38%	35%	45%	31%	41%
Net Inc.	NA	28.0	31.7	28.0	27.9	18.5	16.9	8.4	15.4	15.0
Balance Sheet & Other Fin. Data (Million $)										
Cash	NA	65.6	65.3	49.2	89.1	66.1	42.4	28.5	36.0	38.4
Curr. Assets	NA	184	188	156	164	132	188	94.6	96.1	94.0
Total Assets	NA	312	292	262	230	203	180	173	157	147
Curr. Liab.	NA	58.7	57.2	46.4	34.5	31.7	27.7	28.5	25.2	26.2
LT Debt	NA	3.7	3.9	1.8	1.9	1.9	2.0	2.5	2.0	3.3
Common Eqty.	NA	231	204	186	168	142	125	117	112	101
Total Cap.	NA	207	211	190	173	147	130	122	117	107
Cap. Exp.	NA	17.2	6.7	10.4	8.1	6.5	12.3	24.1	15.1	13.4
Cash Flow	NA	41.1	45.6	38.6	37.1	27.6	26.4	16.6	22.4	21.0
Curr. Ratio	NA	3.1	3.3	3.4	4.8	4.2	3.8	3.3	3.8	3.6
% LT Debt of Cap.	NA	1.6	1.8	0.9	1.1	1.3	1.5	2.1	1.7	3.1
% Net Inc.of Revs.	NA	6.2	7.4	7.8	8.9	7.2	6.9	3.6	7.3	7.9
% Ret. on Assets	NA	9.3	11.5	11.4	12.9	9.7	9.5	5.1	10.1	10.8
% Ret. on Equity	NA	12.8	16.1	15.8	17.8	13.7	13.7	7.1	14.2	15.8

Data as orig reptd.; bef. results of disc opers/spec. items. Per share data adj. for stk. divs. Bold denotes diluted EPS (FASB 128)-prior periods restated. E-Estimated. NA-Not Available. NM-Not Meaningful. NR-Not Ranked.

Office—Post Office Box 571, Milwaukee, WI 53201-0571. **Tel**—(414) 358-6600. **Website**—http://www.bradycorp.com **Pres & CEO**—K.M. Hudson. **VP & CFO**—F.M. Jaehnert. **Investor Contact**—Laurie Bernardy (414) 438-6880. **Dirs**—R.A. Bemis, R.C. Buchanan, F.W. Harris, K.M. Hudson, P.J. Lettenberger, G.E. Nei, R.D. Peirce. **Transfer Agent**—Firstar Trust Co., Milwaukee. **Incorporated**—in 1939. **Empl**— 2,700. **S&P Analyst:** T. Vital

STANDARD &POOR'S
STOCK REPORTS

Brightpoint, Inc.

NASDAQ Symbol **CELL**

In S&P SmallCap 600

09-OCT-99

Industry: Communications Equipment

Summary: This leading worldwide distributor of wireless communications products also provides logistics services such as inventory management and packaging.

Quantitative Evaluations

Outlook (1 Lowest—5 Highest)
• **5**

Fair Value
• **14¼**

Risk
• **High**

Earn./Div. Rank
• **B+**

Technical Eval.
• **Bullish** since 9/99

Rel. Strength Rank (1 Lowest—99 Highest)
• **96**

Insider Activity
• **Neutral**

Recent Price • 7⅜
52 Wk Range • 19⅞-3½
Yield • Nil
12-Mo. P/E • NM

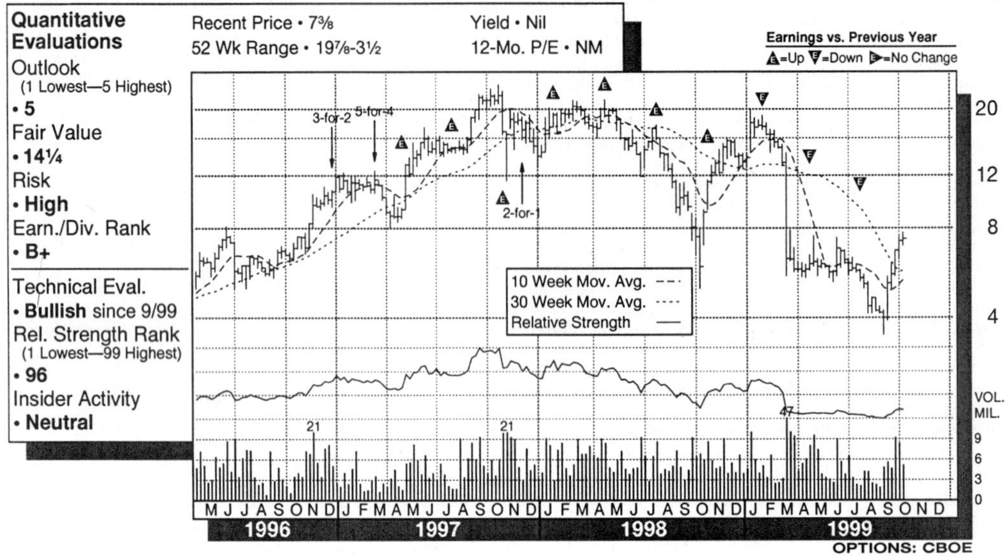

Business Profile - 06-JUL-99

In June 1999, the company announced a restructuring plan that will result in a 1999 second quarter charge of about $75 million to $90 million ($1.40 to $1.65 a share). Major elements of the plan include disposal of U.K. operations; exiting two joint operations in China; and elimination or restructuring of other business activities, including the sale of a 67% interest in a Hong Kong-based accessories company, and disposal of operations in Argentina and Poland. CELL expects the plan to result in a headcount reduction of about 350 employees, and a quarterly reduction in selling, general and administrative expenses of about $6 million, beginning in the 1999 fourth quarter.

Operational Review - 06-JUL-99

Net sales in the three months ended March 31, 1999, advanced 8.6%, year to year. Results were hurt by an inadequate supply of desired product for sale through CELL's distribution services (specifically in the China and Taiwan markets), devaluation of the Brazilian currency, and the absence of revenues from the trading business, which the company exited in the 1998 fourth quarter. A loss of $1,212,000 ($0.02 a share) contrasted with income of $8,843,000 ($0.17). Results in the 1999 period exclude a charge of $0.27 a share from the cumulative effect of an accounting change.

Stock Performance - 08-OCT-99

In the past 30 trading days, CELL's shares have increased 77%, compared to a 0.91% fall in the S&P 500. Average trading volume for the past five days was 1,015,600 shares, compared with the 40-day moving average of 1,099,967 shares.

Key Stock Statistics

Dividend Rate/Share	Nil	Shareholders	438
Shs. outstg. (M)	53.4	Market cap. (B)	$0.393
Avg. daily vol. (M)	1.430	Inst. holdings	33%
Tang. Bk. Value/Share	1.42		
Beta	1.62		

Value of $10,000 invested 5 years ago: NA

Fiscal Year Ending Dec. 31

	1999	1998	1997	1996	1995	1994
Revenues (Million $)						
1Q	372.7	343.3	199.2	113.0	—	—
2Q	414.0	329.8	220.0	119.9	—	—
3Q	—	445.8	243.2	145.3	—	—
4Q	—	509.7	373.2	211.6	—	—
Yr.	—	1,629	1,036	589.7	419.0	309.0
Earnings Per Share ($)						
1Q	**-0.02**	**0.17**	**0.12**	**0.06**	—	—
2Q	**-1.70**	**0.17**	**0.10**	**0.06**	—	—
3Q	—	**0.18**	**0.12**	**0.08**	—	—
4Q	—	**-0.14**	**0.18**	**0.10**	—	—
Yr.	—	**0.38**	**0.53**	NA	**0.21**	0.16

Next earnings report expected: late October

Dividend Data

The company has not paid any cash dividends on its common stock. A two-for-one stock split was effected in November 1997.

A Division of The McGraw-Hill Companies

Brightpoint, Inc.

Business Summary - 06-JUL-99

Brightpoint, a distributor of wireless communications products, announced a broad restructuring plan on June 30, 1999. The primary goal of the plan is to better position the company for the long term by eliminating or restructuring identified nonperforming business activities and improving its cost structure. The company expects the plan to result in a nonrecurring charge of about $75 million to $90 million ($1.40 to $1.65 a share) in the 1999 second quarter. CELL believes the successful execution of the plan will improve profitability significantly.

Major components of the plan include the complete disposal of U.K. operations, including the sale of the airtime reselling business, completed in June 1999; the company's exit from its two joint operations in China, which were hurt by CELL's difficulties in obtaining adequate product supply; elimination or restructuring of other business activities, including the sale of a 67% interest in a Hong Kong-based accessories company, and disposal of operations in Argentina and Poland. The plan also includes steps to improve the cost structure, not only through the elimination and restructuring of nonperforming business activities, but also through additional selective cost reductions.

CELL believes it is well positioned to benefit from recent trends in the wireless communications industry. Markets for wireless products and services have grown substantially in recent years. From 1997 to 1998, the number of worldwide wireless subscribers increased by 75 million, or 36%, to about 286 million. Nonetheless, at the end of 1998, wireless penetration was estimated at only 24% of the U.S. population, and, on average, at less than 5% of the world population, indicating significant worldwide opportunities for growth in the wireless communications industry.

The company's distribution services include purchasing, marketing, selling, warehousing and shipping a broad selection of wireless communications products from leading manufacturers. Products distributed by CELL include handsets designed to work on substantially all operating platforms (including analog and digital platforms) and feature prominent brand names such as Nokia, Ericsson, Motorola, Kyocera, Siemens, Sony and Samsung. Handset sales accounted for 82% of 1998 revenues.

In addition, CELL distributes handset accessories, such as batteries, chargers, cases, hands-free kits, and other items. Sales of accessories accounted for 9% of revenues in 1998. Logistics services, such as support for prepaid programs, inventory management, procurement and product fulfillment, provided 9% of revenues in 1998.

About 29% of 1998 revenues were derived from North America, 12% from Latin America, 27% from Asia-Pacific, and 32% from Europe, the Middle East and Africa.

Per Share Data ($) (Year Ended Dec. 31)	1998	1997	1996	1995	1994	1993	1992	1991	1990	1989
Tangible Bk. Val.	2.96	3.34	2.19	1.63	NA	NA	NA	NA	NA	NA
Cash Flow	0.59	0.61	0.27	0.21	0.17	NA	NA	NA	NA	NA
Earnings	0.38	0.53	0.24	0.21	0.16	NA	NA	NA	NA	NA
Dividends	Nil	Nil	Nil	Nil	Nil	NA	NA	NA	NA	NA
Payout Ratio	Nil	Nil	Nil	Nil	Nil	NA	NA	NA	NA	NA
Prices - High	21 5/8	24 1/4	12 1/8	5 1/2	3 1/2	NA	NA	NA	NA	NA
- Low	5	8	3 5/8	2 7/8	1 1/4	NA	NA	NA	NA	NA
P/E Ratio - High	57	46	49	26	22	NA	NA	NA	NA	NA
- Low	13	15	15	14	8	NA	NA	NA	NA	NA
Income Statement Analysis (Million $)										
Revs.	NA	1,036	590	419	309	NA	NA	NA	NA	NA
Oper. Inc.	NA	45.9	26.1	13.6	7.8	NA	NA	NA	NA	NA
Depr.	11.3	4.0	1.1	0.2	0.1	NA	NA	NA	NA	NA
Int. Exp.	12.5	6.4	2.1	1.4	0.2	NA	NA	NA	NA	NA
Pretax Inc.	31.2	12.0	20.1	12.0	7.5	NA	NA	NA	NA	NA
Eff. Tax Rate	36%	32%	39%	39%	39%	NA	NA	NA	NA	NA
Net Inc.	20.2	25.5	10.6	7.3	4.6	NA	NA	NA	NA	NA
Balance Sheet & Other Fin. Data (Million $)										
Cash	49.5	6.4	32.3	0.7	NA	NA	NA	NA	NA	NA
Curr. Assets	549	392	267	117	NA	NA	NA	NA	NA	NA
Total Assets	714	457	299	120	NA	NA	NA	NA	NA	NA
Curr. Liab.	188	110	123	54.3	NA	NA	NA	NA	NA	NA
LT Debt	287	147	79.6	0.6	NA	NA	NA	NA	NA	NA
Common Eqty.	240	199	95.0	64.9	NA	NA	NA	NA	NA	NA
Total Cap.	527	347	176	65.5	NA	NA	NA	NA	NA	NA
Cap. Exp.	30.1	18.1	6.0	2.5	4.5	NA	NA	NA	NA	NA
Cash Flow	31.5	29.5	11.7	7.5	4.7	NA	NA	NA	NA	NA
Curr. Ratio	2.9	3.4	2.2	2.2	NA	NA	NA	NA	NA	NA
% LT Debt of Cap.	54.5	42.3	45.2	0.8	NA	NA	NA	NA	NA	NA
% Net Inc.of Revs.	1.2	2.5	1.8	1.7	NA	NA	NA	NA	NA	NA
% Ret. on Assets	3.5	6.8	5.1	NA	NA	NA	NA	NA	NA	NA
% Ret. on Equity	9.2	17.3	13.3	NA	NA	NA	NA	NA	NA	NA

Data as orig reptd.; bef. results of disc opers/spec. items. Per share data adj. for stk. divs. Bold denotes diluted EPS (FASB 128)-prior periods restated. E-Estimated. NA-Not Available. NM-Not Meaningful. NR-Not Ranked.

Office—6402 Corporate Dr., Indianapolis, IN 46278. **Tel**—(317) 297-6100. **Website**—http://www.brightpoint.com **Chrmn & CEO**—R. J. Laikin. **Pres**—J. M. Howell. **EVP & COO**—T. Kapostasy. **EVP-Fin, CFO & Treas**—P. A. Bounsall. **EVP & Secy**—S. E. Fivel. **Dirs**—J. W. Adams, R. M. Dick, T. S. Housefield, J. M. Howell, R. J. Laikin, S. B. Sands, S. H. Simon, T. H. Stuart, R. F. Wagner. **Transfer Agent & Registrar**—Continental Stock Transfer & Trust Co. NYC. **Incorporated**—in Delaware in 1994; previously incorporated in Indiana in 1989. **Empl**— 1,500. **S&P Analyst:** J.J.S.

STANDARD &POOR'S
STOCK REPORTS

Brown Shoe

NYSE Symbol **BWS**

In S&P SmallCap 600

09-OCT-99

Industry: Footwear

Summary: This company (formerly Brown Group) manufactures, imports and retails a wide variety of women's, men's and children's shoes.

Quantitative Evaluations

Outlook
(1 Lowest—5 Highest)
• **4-**

Fair Value
• **25⅝**

Risk
• **Average**

Earn./Div. Rank
• **B-**

Technical Eval.
• **Bearish** since 9/99

Rel. Strength Rank
(1 Lowest—99 Highest)
• **83**

Insider Activity
• **NA**

Recent Price • 19½
52 Wk Range • 21¾-12¾
Yield • 2.1%
12-Mo. P/E • 10.9

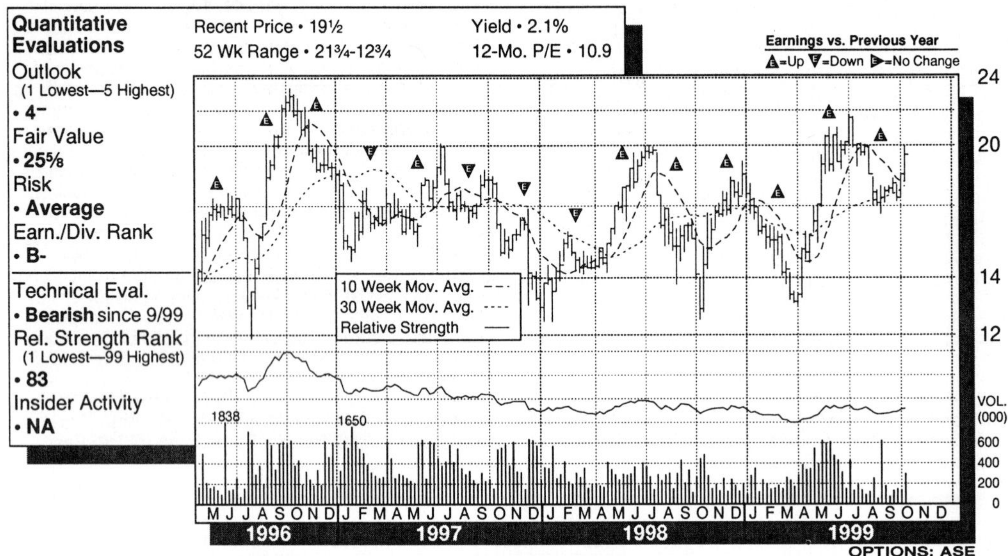

Business Profile - 09-JUL-99

In May 1999, BWS changed its name from Brown Group Inc. to Brown Shoe Company to more accurately reflect the company's business focus. The company's strategy has been to transform itself back to a company dedicated to operating and growing its footwear businesses. BWS believes that oversupply and excess retail space is creating pressure for industry consolidation. With a strengthened balance sheet and improved operations, the company believes that it is in a strong position to capture market share. The company expects its businesses to grow in 1999 and a more aggressive rate of store openings for the Famous Footwear and the roll-out of its repositioned Naturalsport brand are planned. The company also expects the Naturalizer, Life Stride brands and the Pogoda operations to contribute to growth.

Operational Review - 09-JUL-99

Net sales in the 13 weeks ended May 1, 1999, declined 1.4%, year to year, reflecting lower sales in the wholesale division and from the Naturalizer retail operations. However, gross margins widened due to a favorable product mix and profitability also benefited from 17% lower interest expenses; pretax income jumped 46%. After taxes at 38.0% versus 44.4%, net income surged 63% to $6,316,000 ($0.35 a share) from $3,871,000 ($0.22).

Stock Performance - 08-OCT-99

In the past 30 trading days, BWS's shares have increased 12%, compared to a 0.91% fall in the S&P 500. Average trading volume for the past five days was 58,820 shares, compared with the 40-day moving average of 47,015 shares.

Key Stock Statistics

Dividend Rate/Share	0.40	Shareholders	6,700
Shs. outstg. (M)	18.2	Market cap. (B)	$0.356
Avg. daily vol. (M)	0.035	Inst. holdings	62%
Tang. Bk. Value/Share	12.71		
Beta	0.79		

Value of $10,000 invested 5 years ago: $ 7,714

Fiscal Year Ending Jan. 31

	2000	1999	1998	1997	1996	1995
Revenues (Million $)						
1Q	396.8	402.3	391.8	355.8	357.4	369.5
2Q	410.1	383.6	378.8	390.0	342.9	353.0
3Q	—	412.0	433.9	420.4	406.9	406.9
4Q	—	340.6	362.7	358.9	348.7	322.2
Yr.	—	1,539	1,567	1,525	1,456	1,462
Earnings Per Share ($)						
1Q	**0.35**	**0.22**	0.09	0.03	-0.25	0.42
2Q	**0.58**	**0.24**	0.20	0.31	-0.48	0.43
3Q	—	**0.72**	-0.75	0.73	0.55	0.85
4Q	—	**0.14**	**-0.72**	0.08	0.21	0.21
Yr.	—	**1.32**	**-1.19**	**1.15**	0.04	1.91

Next earnings report expected: mid November

Dividend Data (Dividends have been paid since 1923.)

Amount ($)	Date Decl.	Ex-Div. Date	Stock of Record	Payment Date
0.100	Dec. 03	Dec. 10	Dec. 14	Jan. 02 '99
0.100	Mar. 04	Mar. 11	Mar. 15	Apr. 01 '99
0.100	May. 27	Jun. 03	Jun. 07	Jul. 01 '99
0.100	Sep. 09	Sep. 16	Sep. 20	Oct. 01 '99

STANDARD
&POOR'S
STOCK REPORTS

Brown Shoe Company, Inc.

09-OCT-99

Business Summary - 09-JUL-99

Founded in 1878, Brown Shoe Company, a footwear manufacturer and retailer, believes that it can capture marketshare amid a consolidating industry. The company's wholesale operation distributes shoes to about 2,800 retailers, including department stores, mass merchandisers and independent retailers. Retail operations include 1,289 shoe stores (as of January 30, 1999) in the U.S. and Canada, under the names, Famous Footwear, Naturalizer and F.X. LaSalle. In FY 99 (Jan.), about 68% of footwear sales were made at retail, up from 66% in FY 98. The composition of footwear sales was: 59% women's; 25% men's; and 16% children's.

Famous Footwear is America's largest retailer of branded footwear for the entire family. Founded over 30 years ago, Famous Footwear was purchased in 1981 as a 32 store chain and has since grown to 827 stores in the U.S. at the end of FY 99. Naturalizer stores are showcases for the company's flagship brand of women's shoes. BWS operates 331 Naturalizer stores in the U.S. and Canada, with a target customer between 40 and 60 years of age. The typical Naturalizer store product is priced between $50 and $85 per pair. At the end of FY 99, the Canadian retailing division operated 16 F. X. LaSalle stores, which sell better grade men's and women's footwear in the $100 to $250 range.

Footwear is distributed by the company's Brown Branded, Pagoda and Canada Wholesale divisions to retailers in the U.S., Canada and to affiliates. The Branded Marketing division designs and markets many of the company's brands, including Naturalizer, Life Stride, LS Studio and Night Life. These shoes are sold to nearly all major U.S. department stores. Each brand is targeted to a specific customer segment. The Pagoda division sources and markets private brand footwear for many of the nation's retailers, including Dillard's, Edison Brothers, Famous Footwear, Kmart, Mercantile, Payless Shoe Source, Sears, Target and Wal-Mart. It provided wholesale customers with 45 million pairs of shoes in FY 99, up from 43 million in FY 98. The Brown Shoe Sourcing division (formerly known as Pagoda Trading) sources substantially all of the footwear globally for the retail and wholesale divisions. In FY 99, this division sourced 58.8 million pairs of shoes, with over three quarters of the amount originating from China.

Due to excessive inventories and declining performance, the company withdrew (excluding Canada) from international distribution and marketing of footwear by reducing its investment in its Pagoda International division in FY 98.

In May 1999, BWS changed its name from Brown Group Inc. to Brown Shoe Company to more accurately reflect the company's business focus on footwear.

Per Share Data ($)										
(Year Ended Jan. 31)	**1999**	**1998**	**1997**	**1996**	**1995**	**1994**	**1993**	**1992**	**1991**	**1990**
Tangible Bk. Val.	11.95	11.04	13.19	12.92	13.90	13.27	16.69	18.10	19.47	19.39
Cash Flow	2.82	0.33	2.61	1.39	3.17	3.17	1.93	2.68	3.52	3.39
Earnings	1.32	-1.19	1.15	0.04	1.91	-0.39	0.27	0.92	1.85	1.78
Dividends	0.10	0.85	1.00	1.30	1.60	1.60	1.60	1.60	1.60	1.60
Payout Ratio	8%	NM	87%	NM	84%	NM	594%	176%	87%	91%
Cal. Yrs.	1998	1997	1996	1995	1994	1993	1992	1991	1990	1989
Prices - High	20	20 1/8	23 3/8	33 3/8	38 7/8	35 7/8	29	28 3/8	30	35 1/2
- Low	12 3/8	12 3/8	11 7/8	12 1/2	30 5/8	28 3/8	21	21 5/8	19 3/4	26 3/4
P/E Ratio - High	15	NM	20	NM	20	NM	NM	31	16	20
- Low	9	NM	10	NM	16	NM	NM	24	11	15
Income Statement Analysis (Million $)										
Revs.	1,539	1,567	1,525	1,456	1,465	1,598	1,791	1,728	1,764	1,821
Oper. Inc.	88.4	45.8	71.1	37.0	89.0	74.0	59.0	65.0	91.0	91.0
Depr.	26.9	26.7	25.9	23.8	22.1	22.8	28.4	30.1	28.6	28.0
Int. Exp.	19.4	21.8	19.3	16.0	15.8	17.6	16.8	16.0	18.2	20.7
Pretax Inc.	37.6	-2.2	27.2	-5.0	60.0	-11.8	5.0	22.0	49.0	47.0
Eff. Tax Rate	37%	NM	25%	NM	44%	NM	8.50%	30%	35%	34%
Net Inc.	23.7	-20.9	20.3	0.7	33.6	-6.7	4.7	15.7	31.8	30.8
Balance Sheet & Other Fin. Data (Million $)										
Cash	45.5	50.1	38.7	35.1	18.9	16.9	21.6	18.7	16.3	22.3
Curr. Assets	497	539	565	505	479	612	580	514	536	531
Total Assets	655	695	722	661	637	772	760	705	737	713
Curr. Liab.	246	278	264	296	220	371	318	217	250	225
LT Debt	172	197	197	105	133	135	123	145	129	132
Common Eqty.	221	199	237	232	250	234	289	313	336	339
Total Cap.	399	403	443	348	396	376	419	468	483	485
Cap. Exp.	22.7	21.7	21.0	26.9	32.5	30.2	24.3	24.7	32.6	31.3
Cash Flow	50.6	5.8	46.2	24.5	55.7	16.1	33.1	45.8	60.4	58.8
Curr. Ratio	2.0	1.9	2.1	1.7	2.2	1.6	1.8	2.4	2.1	2.4
% LT Debt of Cap.	43.1	48.9	44.5	30.2	33.7	36.0	29.4	30.9	26.6	27.3
% Net Inc.of Revs.	1.5	NM	1.3	0.1	2.3	NM	0.3	0.9	1.8	1.7
% Ret. on Assets	3.5	NM	2.9	0.1	4.7	NM	0.6	2.2	4.4	4.3
% Ret. on Equity	10.8	NM	8.7	0.3	13.8	NM	1.5	4.8	9.5	9.2

Data as orig reptd.; bef. results of disc opers/spec. items. Per share data adj. for stk. divs. Bold denotes diluted EPS (FASB 128)-prior periods restated. E-Estimated. NA-Not Available. NM-Not Meaningful. NR-Not Ranked.

Office—8300 Maryland Ave., St. Louis, MO 63105. **Tel**—(314) 854-4000. **Website**—http://www.brownshoe.com **Chrmn, Pres & CEO**—R. A. Fromm. **EVP, CFO & Investor Contact**—H. E. Rich. **VP & Secy**—R. D. Pickle. **Dirs**—J. L. Bower, J. C. Esrey, R. A. Fromm, R. A. Liddy, J. P. MacCarthy, P. G. McGinnis, H. E. Rich, J. E. Ritter. **Transfer Agent & Registrar**—First Chicago Trust Co. of New York. **Incorporated**—in New York in 1913. **Empl**— 11,000. **S&P Analyst:** Howard Choe

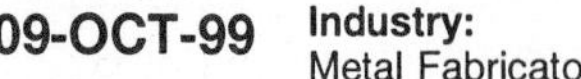

Brush Wellman

NYSE Symbol **BW**

In S&P SmallCap 600

09-OCT-99

Industry: Metal Fabricators

Summary: This company is a worldwide supplier of beryllium alloy and specialty engineered products.

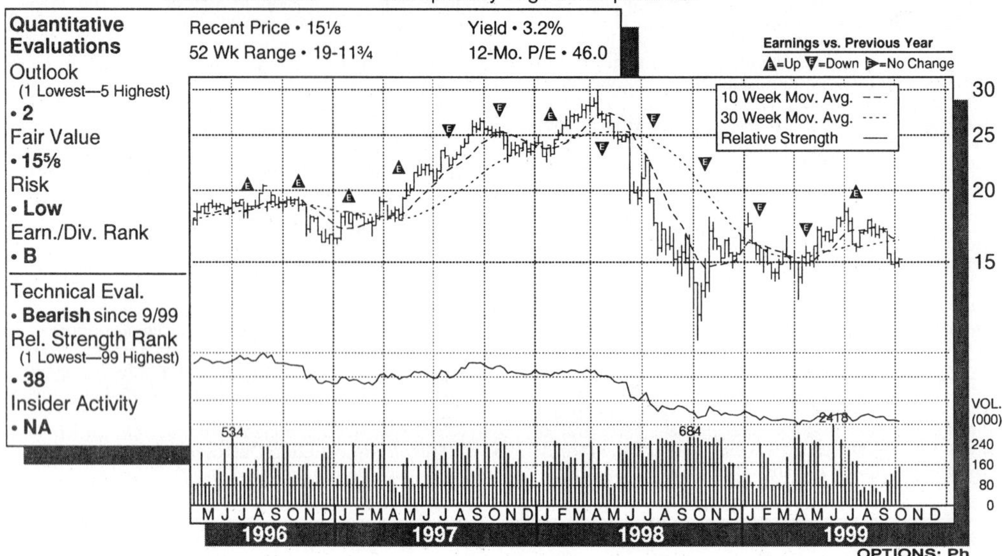

Business Profile - 10-MAY-99

In April 1999, BW reported that the company is making progress on the completion and start up of a $117 million alloy expansion project, and that demand for alloy strip is strong. The company believes that newly developed alloys and other products, in conjunction with its new manufacturing capabilities, offer opportunities for growth. BW intends to adhere to its long-term strategy of improving its base business and being a global leader in nonferrous speciality alloys and also building a microelectronics business. In February 1999, BW expanded an Arizona metal plant with new production capacity and research and development facilities, as part of the company's strategy to strengthen operations in the metal matrix composite market.

Operational Review - 10-MAY-99

For the three months ended March 31, 1999, net sales decreased fractionally, year to year, with lower sales in the Metal Systems Group as well as the Ceramic Products and Circuits Processing divisions, outweighing higher sales in the Williams Advanced Materials segment. Margins were hurt by a 7.1% rise in SG&A expenses, higher product costs, capacity constraints and increased fixed costs associated with the alloy expansion project. Operating income was down 31%. Following sharply higher interest expense and flat depreciation and amortization expense, pretax income fell 60%. After taxes at 26.8%, versus 28.0%, net income also declined 60%, to $2.5 million ($0.15 a share), from $6.2 million ($0.37).

Stock Performance - 08-OCT-99

In the past 30 trading days, BW's shares have declined 9%, compared to a 0.91% fall in the S&P 500. Average trading volume for the past five days was 30,060 shares, compared with the 40-day moving average of 18,479 shares.

Key Stock Statistics

Dividend Rate/Share	0.48	Shareholders	2,329
Shs. outstg. (M)	16.3	Market cap. (B)	$0.248
Avg. daily vol. (M)	0.025	Inst. holdings	61%
Tang. Bk. Value/Share	13.68		
Beta	0.68		

Value of $10,000 invested 5 years ago: $ 12,184

Fiscal Year Ending Dec. 31

	1999	1998	1997	1996	1995	1994
Revenues (Million $)						
1Q	113.2	114.2	99.7	93.80	98.91	84.79
2Q	108.7	103.0	113.4	104.3	97.28	86.56
3Q	—	96.24	109.1	88.31	89.36	86.73
4Q	—	96.48	111.7	89.82	84.06	87.79
Yr.	—	409.9	433.8	376.3	369.6	345.9
Earnings Per Share ($)						
1Q	**0.15**	**0.37**	**0.40**	**0.32**	0.42	0.35
2Q	**0.20**	**-0.80**	**0.46**	**0.51**	0.40	0.36
3Q	—	**0.01**	**0.24**	**0.29**	0.20	0.15
4Q	—	**-0.02**	**0.46**	**0.41**	0.24	0.28
Yr.	—	**-0.44**	**1.56**	**1.53**	**1.27**	**1.15**

Next earnings report expected: late October

Dividend Data (Dividends have been paid since 1972.)

Amount ($)	Date Decl.	Ex-Div. Date	Stock of Record	Payment Date
0.120	Dec. 01	Dec. 16	Dec. 18	Jan. 04 '99
0.120	Mar. 02	Mar. 17	Mar. 19	Apr. 05 '99
0.120	May. 04	Jun. 16	Jun. 18	Jul. 05 '99
0.120	Sep. 15	Sep. 23	Sep. 27	Oct. 04 '99

A Division of The McGraw-Hill Companies

Brush Wellman Inc.

Business Summary - 10-MAY-99

Brush Wellman, a leading producer of engineered materials and an integrated supplier of beryllium and beryllium alloys, reported in March 1999 that it is seeking to improve its base business, become a global leader in nonferrous speciality alloys, and to build a microelectronics business. BW stated that a $117 million effort to expand and upgrade alloy and strips capacity encountered difficulties in 1998. The company expects the expansion to be fully operational in the second half of 1999, and generate improved product quality and reduced cost. BW considers growth opportunities for its alloy products to be very attractive. The company anticipates that as a result of its expanded manufacturing capabilities, new products and organizational improvements, the year 1999 should show expanded sales, greater productivity and higher earnings.

BW operates two primary business segments, the Metal Systems Group and the Microelectronics Group. Metal Systems is composed of alloy products (primarily copper beryllium), beryllium products and engineered materials systems, which are produced by the company's wholly owned subsidiary, Technical Materials, Inc. The Microelectronics Group is comprised of Williams Advanced Materials, Inc. (WAM), Ceramic Products and Circuits Processing Technology, Inc.

In 1998, 72% of the company's sales were from the Metal Systems Group and 26% of sales stemmed from the Microelectronics segment. In 1997, Metal Systems represented 70% of sales and Microelectronics accounted for 29%.

The Metal Systems Group produces beryllium and copper beryllium alloy. Beryllium is extracted from bertrandite and imported beryl ore. BW owns mineral rights and mines for bertrandite in Utah. Copper beryllium, which is an alloy sold by BW in strip and bulk form, offers high electrical and thermal conductivities, high strength and hardness, good formability and resistance to corrosion wear and fatigue. Copper beryllium find uses in computers, telecommunications, automotive electronics, energy systems and plastic molds. BW also manufactures combinations of precious and non-precious metals in continuous strip form that are used in complex electronic and electrical telecommunications, automobiles and computers.

The Microelectronics Group, through its WAM unit, produces precious metal and specialty metal products for the hybrid microelectronics, semiconductors, optical media, electron tube, magnetic head materials, and other applications. WAM's products, which are fabricated for high reliability applications, include, vapor deposition materials, braze materials, ultra fine wire, sealing lids and dental alloys. The Ceramic Products segment makes beryllium ceramics, powder metallurgy and component assemblies. These products are used in wireless communications, automotive, medical and aerospace applications.

Per Share Data ($) (Year Ended Dec. 31)	1998	1997	1996	1995	1994	1993	1992	1991	1990	1989
Tangible Bk. Val.	13.61	14.45	13.46	12.46	11.59	10.70	10.49	10.10	13.43	13.10
Cash Flow	0.89	2.70	2.67	2.36	2.35	1.75	1.90	-0.30	2.58	2.35
Earnings	-0.44	1.56	1.52	1.26	1.14	0.40	0.65	-1.72	1.09	1.10
Dividends	0.48	0.46	0.42	0.36	0.26	0.20	0.26	0.59	0.71	0.67
Payout Ratio	NM	29%	28%	29%	23%	50%	40%	NM	65%	58%
Prices - High	30	26¾	20½	23⅝	18⅝	17½	19	20	25¼	30¼
- Low	10⅞	16⅛	16⅛	14½	13⅜	11	12¼	9½	11½	20¼
P/E Ratio - High	NM	17	13	19	16	44	29	NM	23	28
- Low	NM	10	11	12	12	28	19	NM	11	18
Income Statement Analysis (Million $)										
Revs.	410	434	376	370	346	295	265	267	297	318
Oper. Inc.	33.0	55.0	53.8	48.4	47.3	34.6	38.4	44.8	52.9	61.1
Depr.	21.5	18.7	18.5	18.0	19.6	21.7	20.2	34.9	23.2	23.2
Int. Exp.	1.2	0.6	1.1	1.6	2.4	3.2	3.8	4.4	3.9	3.6
Pretax Inc.	-11.6	35.5	33.2	27.4	23.0	7.7	13.7	-36.2	24.8	26.3
Eff. Tax Rate	NM	28%	26%	25%	19%	16%	24%	NM	29%	30%
Net Inc.	-7.1	25.6	24.5	20.7	18.6	6.5	10.5	-27.5	17.6	18.5
Balance Sheet & Other Fin. Data (Million $)										
Cash	1.9	7.2	31.7	29.6	20.4	7.7	4.2	1.7	1.9	5.2
Curr. Assets	195	179	197	192	181	156	148	145	152	150
Total Assets	404	384	356	332	317	293	310	307	339	338
Curr. Liab.	93.5	78.3	69.1	66.6	65.9	51.0	59.9	64.7	62.8	71.6
LT Debt	32.1	17.9	18.9	17.0	18.5	24.0	33.8	34.9	26.7	21.1
Common Eqty.	222	237	219	200	187	172	169	162	216	212
Total Cap.	260	255	239	220	209	202	210	205	267	258
Cap. Exp.	36.7	53.1	26.8	25.0	17.8	12.7	14.5	20.0	21.9	20.1
Cash Flow	14.4	44.3	43.0	38.7	38.2	28.2	30.7	-4.8	41.6	39.7
Curr. Ratio	2.1	2.3	2.9	2.9	2.7	3.1	2.5	2.2	2.4	2.1
% LT Debt of Cap.	12.3	7.0	7.9	7.8	8.9	11.9	16.1	17.1	10.0	8.2
% Net Inc.of Revs.	NM	5.9	6.6	5.6	5.4	2.2	4.0	NM	5.9	5.8
% Ret. on Assets	NM	6.9	7.2	6.4	6.1	2.1	3.4	NM	5.2	5.5
% Ret. on Equity	NM	11.2	11.7	10.7	10.3	3.8	6.3	NM	8.2	8.6

Data as orig reptd.; bef. results of disc opers/spec. items. Per share data adj. for stk. divs. Bold denotes diluted EPS (FASB 128)-prior periods restated. E-Estimated. NA-Not Available. NM-Not Meaningful. NR-Not Ranked.

Office—17876 St. Clair Ave., Cleveland, OH 44110.**Tel**—(216) 486-4200. **Fax**—(216) 383-4091. **Website**—http://www.brushwellman.com. **Chrmn, Pres, & CEO**—G. D. Harnett. **Treas & Secy & Investor Contact**—Michael C. Hasychak (216) 383-6823. **Dirs**—A. C. Bersticker, C. F. Brush III, D. L. Burner, G. D. Harnett, D. H. Hoag, J. P. Keithley, W. P. Madar, R. M. McInnes, W. R. Robertson, J. Sherwin, Jr. **Transfer Agent & Registrar**—National City Bank, Cleveland, OH. (800) 622-6757. **Incorporated**—in Ohio in 1931. **Empl**— 2,187. **S&P Analyst:** J. Friendly

Buckeye Technologies

NYSE Symbol **BKI**

In S&P SmallCap 600

09-OCT-99

Industry:
Paper & Forest Products

Summary: Buckeye is a manufacturer and marketer of specialty cellulose and absorbent products.

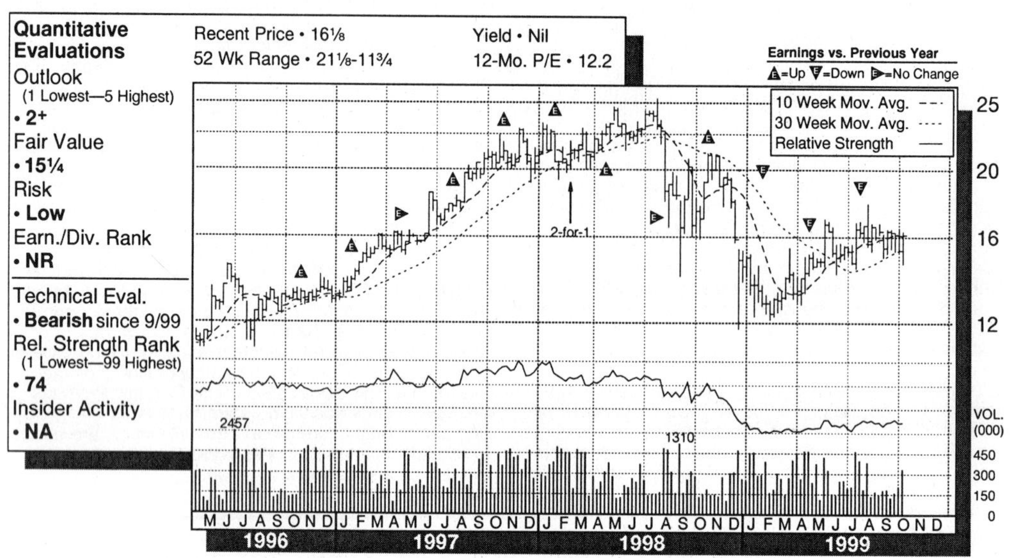

Business Profile - 20-AUG-99

Buckeye Technologies said, in August 1999, that over the past several months, it has put in place a number of key building blocks that should provide the basis for substantial future growth. The combination of the planned acquisition of UPM-Kymmene's Walkisoft business and Buckeye's large, new airlaid machine for North America, will triple the size of Buckeye's nonwovens business. In addition, Buckeye's new cellulosic fibers and airlaid nonwovens products were described as being well received in the marketplace. The company expected these initiatives, coupled with an intense focus on cost reduction, to fuel its future sales and earnings growth. In July 1999, Buckeye and UPM-Kymmene signed a letter of intent for Buckeye to acquire essentially all of the assets of Walkisoft, UPM's nonwovens business, for about $120 million.

Operational Review - 20-AUG-99

Net sales for FY 99 (Jun.; preliminary) slid 2.0%, year to year, reflecting weak markets in Europe, Asia, and South America. Margins narrowed on the lower sales, and operating profit decreased 7.7%. After 7.2% higher interest expense, pretax income fell 16%. Following taxes at 31.7%, versus 34.1%, net income dropped 13%, to $48.0 million ($1.32 a share, on 4.5% fewer average shares outstanding), from $55.3 million ($1.45).

Stock Performance - 08-OCT-99

In the past 30 trading days, BKI's shares have declined 1%, compared to a 0.91% fall in the S&P 500. Average trading volume for the past five days was 66,520 shares, compared with the 40-day moving average of 38,141 shares.

Key Stock Statistics

Dividend Rate/Share	Nil	Shareholders	5,500
Shs. outstg. (M)	35.4	Market cap. (B)	$0.571
Avg. daily vol. (M)	0.041	Inst. holdings	42%
Tang. Bk. Value/Share	1.41		
Beta	NA		

Value of $10,000 invested 5 years ago: NA

Fiscal Year Ending Jun. 30

	1999	1998	1997	1996	1995	1994
Revenues (Million $)						
1Q	156.2	153.3	126.5	108.6	--	—
2Q	147.3	153.6	143.0	117.0	--	—
3Q	155.9	162.5	139.5	113.3	--	—
4Q	158.4	160.8	149.9	132.2	--	—
Yr.	617.7	630.2	558.9	471.0	464.2	—
Earnings Per Share ($)						
1Q	**0.36**	0.34	**0.31**	0.18	--	—
2Q	**0.30**	**0.34**	**0.33**	0.23	--	—
3Q	**0.32**	**0.37**	**0.36**	0.36	--	—
4Q	**0.34**	**0.38**	**0.38**	0.34	--	—
Yr.	**1.32**	**1.45**	**1.38**	1.11	0.83	—

Next earnings report expected: mid October

Dividend Data

No cash dividends have been paid, and the company intends for the foreseeable future to retain earnings to finance the development of its business and for the repayment of debt.

Buckeye Technologies Corporation

Business Summary - 20-AUG-99

Following its May 1997 acquisition of Merfin International Inc., Buckeye Technologies (formerly Buckeye Cellulose Corp.) reorganized into two divisions: the Specialty Cellulose division, supplying the chemical, textile fibers and specialty paper industries; and the Absorbent Products division, supplying consumer product companies that market absorbent and hygienic brands. BKI is a leading manufacturer and worldwide marketer of high-quality, value-added specialty cellulose pulps and, through Merfin, is a leading manufacturer of air-laid fabrics used in feminine hygiene and adult incontinence products. The company believes it is the world's only manufacturer of both wood-based and cotton linter-based specialty cellulose pulps, and that it produces the broadest range of specialty pulps in the industry.

The cellulose pulp market can be divided into two categories: commodity pulps and specialty cellulose pulps. BKI participates exclusively in the estimated $7 billion annual specialty cellulose pulp market, which accounts for about 3% of the total cellulose pulp market. Specialty cellulose pulps are used to impart unique chemical or physical characteristics to a broad and diverse range of specialty end-products. Specialty pulps generally command higher prices and tend to be less cyclical than commodity pulps. The more demanding performance requirements for specialty pulps limit customer ability to substitute other products.

The company's specialty pulps can be broadly grouped into three categories: chemical cellulose pulps, which accounted for 39% of FY 98 (Jun.) gross sales; absorbent pulps (39%); and customized paper pulps (22%).

About 31% of FY 98 sales were derived from the U.S., 38% from Europe, 17% from Asia, and 14% from other regions. Procter & Gamble, the world's largest diaper manufacturer, is the company's largest single customer, accounting for 31% of FY 98 net sales. Under a long-term agreement, Procter & Gamble is required to purchase a specified tonnage of BKI's fluff pulp through 2002.

In May 1997, the company acquired Merfin International Inc., for about U.S.$200 million, including assumption of debt. Funding came from borrowings from a $275 million credit facility. Merfin is a leading manufacturer of air-laid fabrics used as ultra-thin absorbent cores in feminine hygiene and adult incontinence products, as well as in hot towels, baby wipes, table top products and a variety of industrial wipes.

Net sales in FY 98 were up 13%, reflecting the Merfin acquisition and the late 1996 acquisition of Alpha Cellulose Holdings, a specialty cellulose facility in Lumberton, NC. After acquisition-related interest expense and debt amortization costs, the gain in net income was restricted to 5.7%, to $55.3 million.

Per Share Data ($) (Year Ended Jun. 30)	1999	1998	1997	1996	1995	1994	1993	1992	1991	1990
Tangible Bk. Val.	NA	0.63	NM	3.13	1.85	NA	NA	NA	NA	NA
Cash Flow	NA	2.60	2.35	1.75	NA	NA	NA	NA	NA	NA
Earnings	1.32	1.45	1.40	1.11	0.83	NA	NA	NA	NA	NA
Dividends	Nil	Nil	Nil	Nil	NA	NA	NA	NA	NA	NA
Payout Ratio	Nil	Nil	Nil	Nil	NA	NA	NA	NA	NA	NA
Prices - High	17 7/8	25 3/8	23 3/8	14 5/8	11 1/2	NA	NA	NA	NA	NA
- Low	12 1/8	11 3/4	12 7/8	10 5/8	9 1/4	NA	NA	NA	NA	NA
P/E Ratio - High	14	18	17	13	14	NA	NA	NA	NA	NA
- Low	9	8	9	10	11	NA	NA	NA	NA	NA
Income Statement Analysis (Million $)										
Revs.	NA	630	559	471	464	NA	NA	NA	NA	NA
Oper. Inc.	NA	166	145	135	NA	NA	NA	NA	NA	NA
Depr.	NA	44.0	36.1	26.7	NA	NA	NA	NA	NA	NA
Int. Exp.	NA	36.8	28.7	18.1	22.3	NA	NA	NA	NA	NA
Pretax Inc.	NA	83.9	80.2	72.5	56.5	NA	NA	NA	NA	NA
Eff. Tax Rate	NA	34%	34%	35%	37%	NA	NA	NA	NA	NA
Net Inc.	NA	55.3	53.3	47.0	35.6	NA	NA	NA	NA	NA
Balance Sheet & Other Fin. Data (Million $)										
Cash	NA	1.5	8.1	2.9	3.7	NA	NA	NA	NA	NA
Curr. Assets	NA	204	201	179	142	NA	NA	NA	NA	NA
Total Assets	NA	752	737	453	413	NA	NA	NA	NA	NA
Curr. Liab.	NA	76.0	83.0	61.4	43.3	NA	NA	NA	NA	NA
LT Debt	NA	456	475	218	242	NA	NA	NA	NA	NA
Common Eqty.	NA	156	128	141	99	NA	NA	NA	NA	NA
Total Cap.	NA	647	633	374	353	NA	NA	NA	NA	NA
Cap. Exp.	NA	66.7	42.8	34.8	NA	NA	NA	NA	NA	NA
Cash Flow	NA	99	89.4	73.7	NA	NA	NA	NA	NA	NA
Curr. Ratio	NA	2.7	2.4	2.9	3.3	NA	NA	NA	NA	NA
% LT Debt of Cap.	NA	70.6	75.0	58.3	68.7	NA	NA	NA	NA	NA
% Net Inc.of Revs.	NA	8.8	9.5	10.0	7.7	NA	NA	NA	NA	NA
% Ret. on Assets	NA	7.4	9.0	11.3	NA	NA	NA	NA	NA	NA
% Ret. on Equity	NA	38.9	39.6	41.7	NA	NA	NA	NA	NA	NA

Data as orig reptd.; bef. results of disc opers/spec. items. Per share data adj. for stk. divs. Bold denotes diluted EPS (FASB 128)-prior periods restated. E-Estimated. NA-Not Available. NM-Not Meaningful. NR-Not Ranked.

Office—1001 Tillman St., Memphis, TN 38112. **Tel**—(901) 320-8100. **Website**—http://www.bkitech.com **Chrmn & CEO**—R. E. Cannon. **Pres & COO**—D. B. Ferraro. **Investor Contact**—Frank A. McGrew IV (901-320-8100). **Dirs**—R. E. Cannon, R. H. Cannon, R. Cavaney, D. B. Ferraro, H. F. Frigon, S. M. Mencoff, H. J. Phillips Sr. **Transfer Agent & Registrar**—Union Planters National Bank. **Incorporated**—in Delaware in 1992. **Empl**—1,800. **S&P Analyst:** N.J.D.

STANDARD &POOR'S
STOCK REPORTS

Building Materials Holding Corp.

NASDAQ Symbol **BMHC**

In S&P SmallCap 600

09-OCT-99

Industry: Retail (Building Supplies)

Summary: BMHC is the holding company for BMC West Corp, a regional distributor and retailer of building materials, operating 55 centers in 18 distinct regional markets in 10 western states.

Quantitative Evaluations

Outlook (1 Lowest—5 Highest)
• **5**

Fair Value
• **15½**

Risk
• **Average**

Earn./Div. Rank
• **NR**

Technical Eval.
• **Bearish** since 8/99

Rel. Strength Rank (1 Lowest—99 Highest)
• **27**

Insider Activity
• **Neutral**

Recent Price • 9⅞
52 Wk Range • 13½-9
Yield • Nil
12-Mo. P/E • 6.6

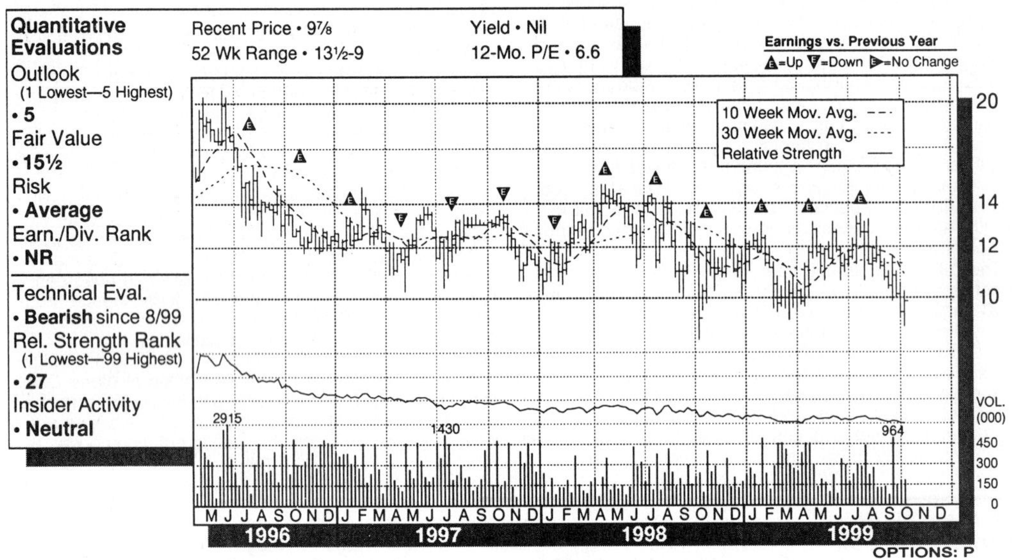

Business Profile - 28-JUN-99

In April 1999, the company announced that results for the quarter ended March 31, 1999, were aided by a focus on increasing the availability of value-added products, which enhanced same-store sales and gross margins. As a result, BMHC was able to gain market share as well as higher total sales per building permit. In May 1999, BMHC acquired, for $28 million, a 49% interest in Knipp Brothers, a framing company with operations in Phoenix and Tucson, AZ, and Las Vegas, NV. Management expects this purchase to enhance BMHC's market penetration in the Phoenix area, and allow BMHC to take advantage of the strong Las Vegas housing market, an area where it currently has no operations.

Operational Review - 28-JUN-99

Net sales for the three months ended March 31, 1999, advanced 17%, year to year, reflecting 12% higher same store sales, aided by wood product price inflation, and acquisitions,. Gross margins widened, mainly due to BMHC's efforts to increase sales from value- added products. SG&A expense rose 19%, on higher product costs and as well as the expenses of integrating newly acquired businesses. Net income was up sharply, to $2,521,000 ($0.20 a share), from $850,000 ($0.07).

Stock Performance - 08-OCT-99

In the past 30 trading days, BMHC's shares have declined 12%, compared to a 0.91% fall in the S&P 500. Average trading volume for the past five days was 35,720 shares, compared with the 40-day moving average of 49,323 shares.

Key Stock Statistics

Dividend Rate/Share	Nil	Shareholders	5,909
Shs. outstg. (M)	12.7	Market cap. (B)	$0.125
Avg. daily vol. (M)	0.073	Inst. holdings	68%
Tang. Bk. Value/Share	11.52		
Beta	1.02		

Value of $10,000 invested 5 years ago: $ 4,937

Fiscal Year Ending Dec. 31

	1999	1998	1997	1996	1995	1994
Revenues (Million $)						
1Q	215.6	183.6	146.8	147.6	120.5	112.1
2Q	256.0	226.0	190.6	193.0	166.2	141.8
3Q	—	249.8	201.9	206.5	178.5	157.8
4Q	—	217.9	188.7	170.9	165.0	135.3
Yr.	—	877.3	728.1	718.0	630.2	547.1
Earnings Per Share ($)						
1Q	**0.20**	**0.07**	**0.04**	**0.08**	0.05	0.26
2Q	**0.55**	**0.38**	**0.29**	**0.38**	0.25	0.54
3Q	—	**0.53**	**0.35**	**0.38**	0.35	0.55
4Q	—	**0.22**	**0.11**	**0.15**	0.14	0.27
Yr.	—	**1.20**	**0.78**	**1.00**	**0.79**	**1.62**

Next earnings report expected: late October

Dividend Data

No cash dividends have been paid on the common stock. A three-for-two stock split was effected March 4, 1994. A shareholder rights plan was adopted in July 1993.

A Division of The McGraw-Hill Companies

Building Materials Holding Corporation

Business Summary - 28-JUN-99

Building Materials Holding Corp. is a holding corporation for BMC West Corp., a leading distributor and retailer of building materials in the western U.S. In recent years, the company has increased its focus on selling higher margin value-added products customized to customer specifications. These products include pre-hung doors, millwork, and roof trusses. BMC West targets professional contractors, who tend to be large volume, repeat customers, requiring a high degree of certainty regarding product availability and delivery, as well as a number of specialized services not offered by home center retailers. The company also targets the repair and remodel market, generally consisting of project-oriented consumers and contractors hired by them, for projects such as room additions, kitchen and bathroom remodeling, and fence and deck installations.

As of December 31, 1998, the company was operating 58 building materials centers in Arizona, California, Colorado, Idaho, Montana, Nevada, Oregon, Texas, Utah, and Washington. Each of the company's building material centers tailors its product and service mix to meet the demands of the particular local market in which it serves. Products include lumber, panel products, roofing materials, pre-hung doors, millwork, roof trusses, pre-assembled windows, cabinets, hardware, paint and tools, which are mainly used for new residential construction, light commercial construction, and repair and remodeling projects. The products are sold by experienced professionals including field and facility-based sales personnel, as well as support personnel.

The company offers various services, including assistance with project design and materials specifications, coordination of delivery orders to job sites, provision of credit to pre-approved contractors, and the referral of retail customers to pre-qualified contractors. Complete home packages, which are delivered to the sites of building customers according to their particular construction schedules, account for a significant percentage of total sales. In each of the last three years, professional contractors accounted for about 77% to 81% of net sales, and project oriented consumers or the contractors hired by them accounted for 18% to 22% of net sales.

BMHC's acquisition strategy includes seeking building materials centers and value-added facilities that serve the professional contractor and the project-oriented consumer in new and existing markets in the U.S. The industry's fragmented nature presents BMHC opportunities to acquire other multi-center distributors that could be acquired as new stand-alone subsidiaries.

Per Share Data ($) (Year Ended Dec. 31)	1998	1997	1996	1995	1994	1993	1992	1991	1990	1989
Tangible Bk. Val.	10.70	9.85	10.48	7.92	9.43	6.17	4.57	3.71	2.81	1.93
Cash Flow	2.22	1.69	1.93	1.83	2.25	1.53	1.09	0.78	1.62	1.09
Earnings	1.20	0.78	1.00	0.79	1.62	1.13	0.62	0.21	0.82	0.39
Dividends	Nil	Nil	Nil	Nil	Nil	Nil	Nil	Nil	Nil	Nil
Payout Ratio	Nil	Nil	Nil	Nil	Nil	Nil	Nil	Nil	Nil	Nil
Prices - High	15	14 7/8	21	17 1/4	30 1/2	21 1/2	7 1/2	6 7/8	NA	NA
- Low	8 5/8	10 1/8	11 3/4	11 1/4	12	5 7/8	5 3/8	3 7/8	NA	NA
P/E Ratio - High	12	19	21	22	19	19	12	33	NA	NA
- Low	7	13	12	14	7	5	9	19	NA	NA
Income Statement Analysis (Million $)										
Revs.	877	728	718	630	547	400	291	219	224	196
Oper. Inc.	47.0	33.5	37.5	31.0	33.5	21.3	12.1	7.5	9.5	6.6
Depr.	13.0	11.0	10.3	9.2	5.5	3.0	2.6	2.2	2.4	2.1
Int. Exp.	10.2	8.7	10.4	10.7	6.5	4.5	5.0	5.3	5.8	5.3
Pretax Inc.	24.9	15.7	17.9	12.7	23.0	14.7	4.9	0.9	2.6	1.2
Eff. Tax Rate	39%	40%	39%	39%	38%	40%	27%	12%	4.90%	Nil
Net Inc.	15.1	9.5	11.0	7.8	14.3	8.8	3.6	0.8	2.5	1.2
Balance Sheet & Other Fin. Data (Million $)										
Cash	8.3	8.2	7.1	6.0	5.2	1.6	0.7	0.6	0.4	0.8
Curr. Assets	184	177	157	141	128	94.0	59.8	46.1	43.8	40.1
Total Assets	374	340	288	265	222	142	92.0	73.5	68.1	57.8
Curr. Liab.	67.2	58.2	46.8	41.0	51.4	33.7	20.9	16.2	15.0	14.1
LT Debt	118	113	90.2	121	76.4	53.3	32.3	32.9	40.2	33.2
Common Eqty.	180	161	145	96.0	85.9	48.4	33.8	19.4	8.2	5.7
Total Cap.	303	279	235	220	170	108	71.1	57.3	53.2	43.7
Cap. Exp.	19.6	13.3	14.4	16.9	15.1	15.5	7.6	4.8	6.3	1.9
Cash Flow	28.1	20.5	21.3	17.0	19.8	11.8	6.2	3.0	4.9	3.3
Curr. Ratio	2.7	3.0	3.4	3.4	2.5	2.8	2.9	2.8	2.9	2.8
% LT Debt of Cap.	38.8	40.7	38.4	55.0	45.0	49.5	45.5	57.4	75.6	76.0
% Net Inc.of Revs.	1.7	1.3	1.5	1.2	2.6	2.2	1.2	0.4	1.1	0.6
% Ret. on Assets	4.2	3.0	7.4	3.2	7.4	7.3	3.7	0.8	4.0	2.2
% Ret. on Equity	8.9	6.2	9.1	8.5	20.0	20.8	11.6	4.7	35.5	22.9

Data as orig reptd.; bef. results of disc opers/spec. items. Per share data adj. for stk. divs. Bold denotes diluted EPS (FASB 128)-prior periods restated. E-Estimated. NA-Not Available. NM-Not Meaningful. NR-Not Ranked.

Office—One Market Plaza, Steuart Tower, Ste. 2650, San Francisco, CA 94105.**Tel**—(415) 227-1650. **Chrmn**—G. E. McCown. **Pres & CEO**—R. E. Mellor. **SVP-Fin, Treas & Investor Contact**—Ellis C. Goebel. **Dirs**—A. F. Beck, H. J. Brown, W. J. Fix, R. V. Hansberger, D. S. Hendrickson, G. O. Mabry, G. E. McCown, R. E. Mellor, P. S. O'Neill. **Transfer Agent & Registrar**—American Stock Transfer & Trust Co., NYC. **Incorporated**—in Delaware in 1987. **Empl**— 4,100. **S&P Analyst:** Matthew C. Hershberg

STANDARD
&POOR'S
STOCK REPORTS

Burr-Brown Corp.

NASDAQ Symbol **BBRC**

In S&P SmallCap 600

09-OCT-99

Industry:
Electronics (Semiconductors)

Summary: This company makes high-performance analog and mixed-signal integrated circuits used in the processing of electronic signals.

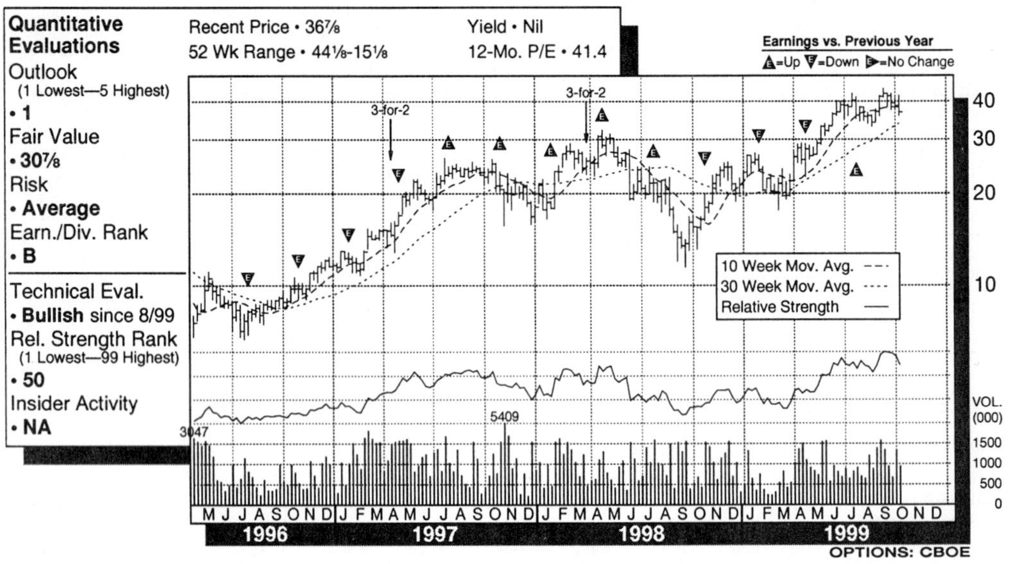

Business Profile - 09-SEP-99

In July 1999, the company said it expected solid sequential and earnings growth in each of the remaining quarters of 1999. BBRC emphasizes the introduction of new products; in 1998, the company introduced a record number of new products, for the fourth consecutive year. BBRC believed that, as a result of this record, as well as continued R&D efforts, it was well positioned for 1999. In August 1999, the company announced the development of its first direct stream digital audio digital-to-analog converter, used in a variety of Sony products. In July 1999, BBRC announced what it called the fastest analog front end chip available for high-bit-rate digital subscriber line communications systems.

Operational Review - 09-SEP-99

Net revenues in the six months ended July 3, 1999, slid 4.4%, year to year, as lower revenues in Europe and the Far East outweighed small gains in North America and strength in the communications sector. Profits were restricted by narrowing of gross margins and increased R&D spending; pretax income dropped 11%. After taxes at 27.0%, versus 28.5%, net income was down 9.3%, to $17,769,000 ($0.46 a share), from $19,600,000 ($0.51).

Stock Performance - 08-OCT-99

In the past 30 trading days, BBRC's shares have declined 0.34%, compared to a 0.91% fall in the S&P 500. Average trading volume for the past five days was 185,720 shares, compared with the 40-day moving average of 250,923 shares.

Key Stock Statistics

Dividend Rate/Share	Nil	Shareholders	6,100
Shs. outstg. (M)	36.9	Market cap. (B)	$ 1.4
Avg. daily vol. (M)	0.192	Inst. holdings	61%
Tang. Bk. Value/Share	7.87		
Beta	1.84		

Value of $10,000 invested 5 years ago: $ 191,466

Fiscal Year Ending Dec. 31

	1999	1998	1997	1996	1995	1994
Revenues (Million $)						
1Q	61.01	68.69	54.77	61.17	59.55	47.36
2Q	68.21	66.52	62.51	58.18	69.59	47.61
3Q	—	61.16	65.93	50.11	70.22	49.22
4Q	—	61.73	68.90	50.53	69.80	50.02
Yr.	—	258.1	252.1	220.0	269.2	194.2
Earnings Per Share ($)						
1Q	**0.20**	**0.27**	**0.17**	**0.30**	0.14	0.05
2Q	**0.27**	**0.25**	**0.20**	**0.18**	0.20	0.06
3Q	—	**0.20**	**0.22**	**0.15**	0.24	0.05
4Q	—	**0.23**	**0.26**	**0.16**	0.24	0.03
Yr.	—	**0.94**	**0.86**	**0.79**	**0.83**	**0.20**

Next earnings report expected: late October

Dividend Data

BBRC has never paid cash dividends on its common stock. It is the current policy of directors to retain earnings to finance expansion of the company's operations, and BBRC does not expect to pay dividends in the foreseeable future.

Burr-Brown Corporation

Business Summary - 09-SEP-99

Traditionally a well-diversified manufacturer of high-performance analog and mixed-signal integrated circuits (ICs), Burr-Brown has been increasingly penetrating the fast-growing communications market. In 1998, BBRC derived for the first time more than 50% of revenues from its newer-served communications, consumer and computing markets. Communications applications revenues accounted for 23% of total revenues in 1998, up from 6% in 1994. The company continues to target these markets and the industrial segment.

The company's product strategy has been to concentrate on proprietary high-precision or high-performance products. Burr-Brown identifies specific high-volume markets in which its enhanced high-performance products are required. It then develops and supplies as complete a function as possible, often becoming a customer's sole source for particular components. Its strategy has generally enabled it to avoid direct competition with major semiconductor manufacturers, which typically focus on low-cost, high-volume products.

Analog signal-processing ICs are used to process and transmit analog data signals prior to their conversion to digital signals. Burr-Brown's analog circuits include operational amplifiers, instrumentation amplifiers, programmable gain amplifiers, isolation amplifiers, current transmitters, and other analog signal-processing components.

Data conversion components are IC devices used to convert analog signals to digital form (A/D converters) and vice-versa (D/A converters). Such conversion is necessary in virtually all applications in which digital computers or processors measure and control the analog signals from a physical condition.

Through majority-owned Intelligent Instrumentation Inc., the company also manufactures and markets a line of data acquisition products, including plug-in boards, portable data acquisition systems, microterminals, and supporting software for IBM-compatible PCs, as well as signal conditioning accessories for such systems, and signal processing software and hardware products designed to run on IBM-compatible PCs.

BBRC introduced a record 87 new products in 1998. Many of these products are standard linear integrated circuits (SLICs), and an increasing number of products are application specific standard products (ASSPs) which target large and rapidly emerging applications within communications, consumer, industrial and computing markets. Examples include highly-integrated ASSPs developed for broadband communications, CT scanners, digital camcorders, digital still cameras and scanners. New products introduced in the past five years are now the source of half of BBRC's annual revenue.

Per Share Data ($) (Year Ended Dec. 31)	1998	1997	1996	1995	1994	1993	1992	1991	1990	1989
Tangible Bk. Val.	7.44	6.47	8.37	4.89	2.71	2.47	2.48	2.50	2.81	2.62
Cash Flow	1.38	1.23	1.14	1.19	0.52	0.40	0.37	0.09	0.49	0.61
Earnings	0.94	0.86	0.79	0.83	0.20	0.09	0.03	-0.30	0.13	0.27
Dividends	Nil	Nil	Nil	Nil	Nil	Nil	Nil	Nil	Nil	Nil
Payout Ratio	Nil	Nil	Nil	Nil	Nil	Nil	Nil	Nil	Nil	Nil
Prices - High	32¼	26⅛	14	18⅜	4⅝	2⅞	2½	3	3⅜	4¼
- Low	11⅜	10¾	6½	3	1 11/16	1 7/16	1¼	1 9/16	1 11/16	2 1/16
P/E Ratio - High	34	30	18	22	23	34	85	NM	26	16
- Low	12	13	8	4	9	16	41	NM	13	8
Income Statement Analysis (Million $)										
Revs.	258	252	220	269	194	169	163	179	177	169
Oper. Inc.	61.6	57.4	43.4	53.2	21.1	17.9	18.0	24.1	22.6	30.7
Depr.	16.9	13.8	13.3	12.7	10.6	10.1	11.0	12.8	11.7	11.1
Int. Exp.	0.5	0.4	0.7	1.1	1.7	2.3	3.8	4.3	3.6	4.6
Pretax Inc.	48.5	46.7	39.8	40.0	8.3	4.5	1.7	-9.4	7.8	15.4
Eff. Tax Rate	26%	30%	26%	27%	22%	38%	42%	NM	45%	44%
Net Inc.	35.9	32.7	29.7	29.2	6.5	2.8	1.0	-9.7	4.3	8.7
Balance Sheet & Other Fin. Data (Million $)										
Cash	72.4	54.3	52.8	86.2	9.9	13.1	9.5	3.3	3.1	2.4
Curr. Assets	199	173	154	196	92.0	95.0	90.0	101	93.0	89.0
Total Assets	339	299	262	252	143	142	141	163	164	161
Curr. Liab.	58.1	58.5	55.6	66.0	46.5	44.5	37.1	43.1	40.1	46.0
LT Debt	2.9	1.5	1.8	1.8	1.8	8.8	11.7	33.7	27.5	24.4
Common Eqty.	274	235	199	179	87.6	79.6	80.0	80.8	90.4	84.4
Total Cap.	280	240	203	181	91.0	90.0	95.0	118	122	114
Cap. Exp.	26.5	25.6	31.9	17.6	12.1	7.1	5.6	11.9	14.1	28.0
Cash Flow	52.8	46.5	43.0	41.9	17.1	12.9	12.0	3.1	16.0	19.8
Curr. Ratio	3.4	2.9	2.8	3.0	2.0	2.1	2.4	2.4	2.3	1.9
% LT Debt of Cap.	1.0	0.6	0.9	1.0	2.0	9.8	12.3	28.5	22.5	21.5
% Net Inc.of Revs.	13.9	13.0	13.5	10.9	3.3	1.7	0.6	NM	2.4	5.1
% Ret. on Assets	11.2	11.6	11.6	14.8	4.5	2.0	0.7	NM	2.6	5.9
% Ret. on Equity	14.1	15.0	15.7	21.9	7.7	3.5	1.2	NM	4.9	10.8

Data as orig reptd.; bef. results of disc opers/spec. items. Per share data adj. for stk. divs. Bold denotes diluted EPS (FASB 128)-prior periods restated. E-Estimated. NA-Not Available. NM-Not Meaningful. NR-Not Ranked.

Office—6730 S. Tucson Blvd., Tucson, AZ 85706. **Tel**—(520) 746-1111. **Website**—http://www.burr-brown.com **Chrmn, Pres & CEO**—S. P. Madavi. **Secy**—B. S. Paulson. **CFO**—J. S. Blouin. **Dirs**—F. J. Aguilar, J. S. Anderegg Jr., T. R. Brown Jr., M. A. Gumucio, S. P. Madavi. **Transfer Agent & Registrar**—Harris Trust & Savings Bank, Chicago. **Incorporated**—in Arizona in 1956; reincorporated in Delaware in 1983. **Empl**— 1,324. **S&P Analyst:** Scott H. Kessler

Butler Manufacturing

NYSE Symbol **BBR**

In S&P SmallCap 600

09-OCT-99

Industry: Engineering & Construction

Summary: This company is a leading supplier of pre-fab buildings and related products, and construction services for the commercial construction market.

Quantitative Evaluations

Outlook
(1 Lowest—5 Highest)
• **4+**

Fair Value
• **40⅛**

Risk
• **Low**

Earn./Div. Rank
• **B**

Technical Eval.
• **Bearish** since 9/99

Rel. Strength Rank
(1 Lowest—99 Highest)
• **35**

Insider Activity
• **Neutral**

Recent Price • 25½
52 Wk Range • 29⅞-20
Yield • 2.5%
12-Mo. P/E • 24.6

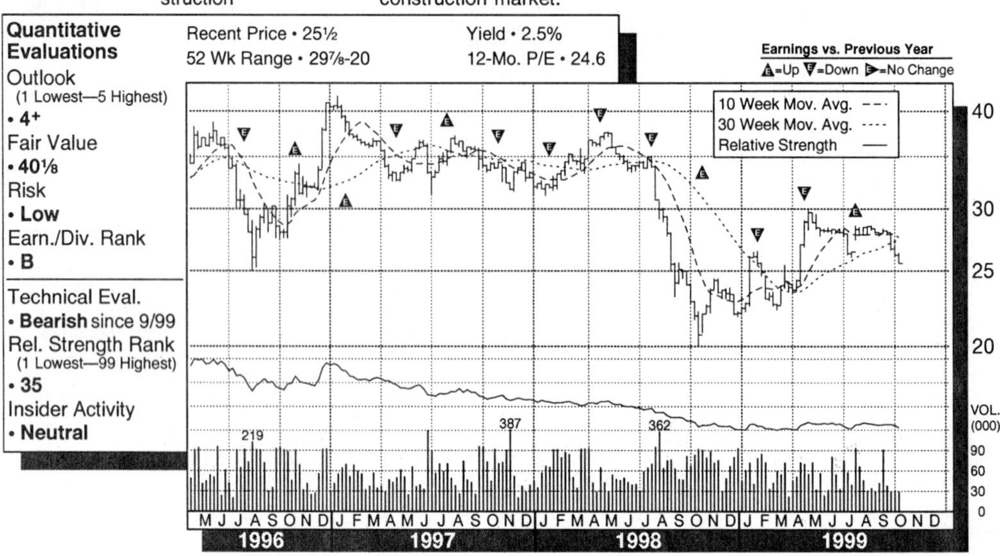

Business Profile - 15-JUL-99

The company's international metal building systems business posted mixed results in 1998. China operations were profitable in the second half, but in Brazil, BBR decided to close down manufacturing operations, reflecting that country's economic turmoil and currency devaluation. In Europe, the company is addressing cost and currency problems by moving its U.K. operations to Hungary; this was expected to be completed by mid-1999. Assuming a reasonable domestic economy and the repositioning of BBR's international business, the company expects to show substantial improvement in profitabability. In early 1999, directors authorized the repurchase of 800,000 shares; during the first quarter, the company purchased 151,000 shares.

Operational Review - 15-JUL-99

Revenues in the 1999 first quarter rose 5.0%, year to year, on higher sales in the Vistawall group, China metal buildings subsidiary, and Real Estate and Construction operations, partly offset by lower U.S. Building Systems sales and disappointing European results. Margins were stable, aided by slightly lower cost of goods sold as a percentage of sales. Results were penalized by a restructuring charge of $1.5 million for the discontinuation of Brazilian operations, and higher interest expense; net income fell 77%, to $264,000 ($0.04 a share, on 5.7% fewer shares), from $1,159,000 ($0.15). Backlog at March 31, 1999, stood at $315 million, up 2% from the level a year earlier.

Stock Performance - 08-OCT-99

In the past 30 trading days, BBR's shares have declined 9%, compared to a 0.91% fall in the S&P 500. Average trading volume for the past five days was 5,700 shares, compared with the 40-day moving average of 8,328 shares.

Key Stock Statistics

Dividend Rate/Share	0.64	Shareholders	2,310
Shs. outstg. (M)	7.1	Market cap. (B)	$0.183
Avg. daily vol. (M)	0.006	Inst. holdings	46%
Tang. Bk. Value/Share	21.00		
Beta	0.65		

Value of $10,000 invested 5 years ago: $ 15,403

Fiscal Year Ending Dec. 31

	1999	1998	1997	1996	1995	1994
Revenues (Million $)						
1Q	203.4	193.8	188.1	175.7	194.8	117.0
2Q	248.7	238.5	241.1	193.4	206.8	175.0
3Q	—	268.1	241.0	229.0	206.6	190.0
4Q	—	261.8	254.4	272.0	218.3	210.0
Yr.	—	962.2	924.6	870.2	826.5	692.0
Earnings Per Share ($)						
1Q	**0.04**	**0.15**	**0.25**	**0.42**	0.48	-0.19
2Q	**0.89**	**0.64**	**2.46**	**0.75**	0.81	0.69
3Q	—	**0.88**	**0.86**	**1.14**	1.00	0.89
4Q	—	**-0.79**	**0.86**	**1.04**	0.78	0.67
Yr.	—	**0.92**	**4.43**	**3.35**	**3.07**	2.09

Next earnings report expected: mid October

Dividend Data (Dividends have been paid since 1994.)

Amount ($)	Date Decl.	Ex-Div. Date	Stock of Record	Payment Date
0.150	Dec. 15	Dec. 23	Dec. 28	Jan. 12 '99
0.150	Jan. 19	Mar. 18	Mar. 22	Apr. 06 '99
0.150	Jun. 15	Jun. 23	Jun. 25	Jul. 13 '99
0.160	Sep. 22	Sep. 29	Oct. 01	Oct. 15 '99

Butler Manufacturing Company

Business Summary - 15-JUL-99

Butler Manufacturing believes it is the largest U.S. maker of pre-fab steel buildings, and the second largest maker of wood frame buildings. In recent years, the company has been focusing on expanding its overseas presence, and now has wholly owned subsidiaries in the U.K., France, Germany, China, and Brazil, as well as a 90%-owned joint venture in Hungary and a 30%-owned joint venture in Saudi Arabia.

The company consists of four business segments: Building Systems, which designs, produces and markets custom designed pre-fabricated commercial, industrial and agricultural buildings; Construction Services, which provides construction management services for purchasers of large, complex or multiple site building projects; Architectural Products, which makes curtain wall and storefront systems, custom window systems, skylights and roof vents for non-residential buildings; and Real Estate, which offers build-to-suit-to-lease development services for corporations who prefer to lease rather than own their facilities.

The building systems segment (65% of sales in 1998) consists primarily of one- to five-story steel and one- to two-story wood framed buildings for use as office buildings, manufacturing, facilities, warehouses, schools, shopping centers, livestock and farm buildings.

In December 1998, the company restructured its international building systems operations. The restructuring led to the closing of BBR's U.K. and Brazilian pre-engineering steel frame building manufacturing plants. In addition, European operations were to move to an expanded facility in Hungary during 1999. U.S. exports are focused on Central America, the Caribbean, and certain Latin American countries (including Brazil).

Through the Vistawall group, the architectural products segment (18%) segment makes aluminum curtain wall systems for mid and high-rise office markets, entry doors, custom architectural window systems, translucent roof and wall systems, skylights, and other storefront products for low-rise retail and commercial markets.

The construction services segment (14%), through BUCON, Inc., provides a full range of construction management services to major purchasers of construction. Butler Heavy Structures, a unit of BUCON, serves large complex building designs using heavy fabricated mill steel in combination with Butler's pre-fab products. Revenues are derived primarily from general contracting.

The real estate segment (3%) obtains lease commitment from third-parties, and then develops and constructs the facilities to be leased through BBR's building system dealers. After a project has been occupied by lessees, the company sells the project to investors.

Per Share Data ($) (Year Ended Dec. 31)	1998	1997	1996	1995	1994	1993	1992	1991	1990	1989
Tangible Bk. Val.	20.63	20.50	16.46	13.54	10.47	8.28	5.76	5.46	7.15	6.06
Cash Flow	2.88	6.04	4.61	4.19	2.99	3.65	1.39	-0.29	2.77	3.02
Earnings	0.92	4.43	3.35	3.07	2.09	2.56	0.17	-1.74	1.21	1.43
Dividends	0.57	0.52	0.44	0.37	0.13	Nil	Nil	Nil	Nil	13.80
Payout Ratio	62%	12%	13%	12%	6%	Nil	Nil	Nil	Nil	NM
Prices - High	37 5/8	41 7/8	41	40 1/2	23 5/8	21	10 1/8	13 1/2	12 1/2	30 7/8
- Low	20	31 1/4	25	19 7/8	14 3/8	9	7	6 1/8	8 1/2	11 1/8
P/E Ratio - High	41	9	12	13	11	8	59	NM	10	22
- Low	22	7	7	6	7	4	40	NM	7	8
Income Statement Analysis (Million $)										
Revs.	962	925	870	827	692	576	500	461	564	580
Oper. Inc.	51.5	54.2	59.2	56.6	40.1	23.6	18.8	10.6	38.5	35.7
Depr.	14.9	12.5	9.7	8.9	6.7	7.7	8.4	4.9	10.7	15.4
Int. Exp.	5.7	5.1	4.3	4.1	3.9	4.6	6.0	9.9	10.6	8.0
Pretax Inc.	17.7	59.8	46.0	42.3	28.7	29.8	2.4	-13.7	16.0	19.2
Eff. Tax Rate	61%	43%	44%	45%	46%	39%	53%	NM	49%	49%
Net Inc.	7.0	34.4	25.8	23.4	15.1	18.1	1.1	-11.9	8.2	9.8
Balance Sheet & Other Fin. Data (Million $)										
Cash	10.3	5.5	2.0	7.3	5.3	14.9	7.7	6.2	10.5	2.2
Curr. Assets	254	233	222	187	189	128	120	115	132	145
Total Assets	394	375	337	283	271	205	200	203	226	241
Curr. Liab.	161	165	161	126	136	98.0	73.0	85.0	88.0	77.0
LT Debt	62.9	33.9	38.4	43.0	40.0	30.0	67.0	68.0	71.0	105
Common Eqty.	150	157	124	102	79.0	62.0	42.0	39.0	50.0	42.0
Total Cap.	217	194	167	148	124	97.0	116	114	130	158
Cap. Exp.	14.8	30.2	22.7	22.7	13.7	6.5	5.0	5.7	8.0	9.1
Cash Flow	21.9	46.9	35.5	32.0	22.0	25.8	9.5	-2.0	18.9	20.7
Curr. Ratio	1.6	1.4	1.4	1.5	1.4	1.3	1.6	1.3	1.5	1.9
% LT Debt of Cap.	29.0	17.5	23.0	28.9	32.5	31.4	58.0	59.4	54.5	66.6
% Net Inc.of Revs.	0.7	3.7	3.0	2.8	2.2	3.1	0.2	NM	1.4	1.7
% Ret. on Assets	1.8	9.7	8.3	8.4	6.4	8.8	0.6	NM	3.5	3.9
% Ret. on Equity	4.6	24.5	22.7	25.9	21.5	34.4	2.8	NM	17.7	11.8

Data as orig reptd.; bef. results of disc opers/spec. items. Per share data adj. for stk. divs. Bold denotes diluted EPS (FASB 128)-prior periods restated. E-Estimated. NA-Not Available. NM-Not Meaningful. NR-Not Ranked.

Office—BMA Tower - Penn Valley Park, P.O. Box 419917-0917, Kansas City, MO 64141-0917. **Reincorporated**—in Delaware in 1969. **Tel**—(816) 968-3000. **Chrmn**—D. H. Pratt. **Pres & CEO**—J. J. Holland. **VP & Secy**—R. O. Ballentine. **VP-Fin & CFO**—L. C. Miller. **EVP & Investor Contact**—John J. Holland. **Dirs**—H. G. Bernthal, K. D.Brooksher, G M. Christensen, A. M. Hallene, C. L. W. Haw, R. J. Novello, D. H. Pratt, R. J. Reintjes, J. A. Rogala, G. L. Tapella, R. H. West. **Transfer Agent & Registrar**—UMB Bank, Kansas City. **Incorporated**— in Missouri in 1902; reincorporated in Delaware in 1969. **Empl**— 5,171. **S&P Analyst:** John A. Massey

STANDARD &POOR'S STOCK REPORTS

C&D Technologies

NYSE Symbol **CHP**

In S&P SmallCap 600

09-OCT-99

Industry: Electrical Equipment

Summary: CHP (formerly Charter Power Systems) produces and markets electrical power storage and conversion products used in telecommunications, computers and office equipment.

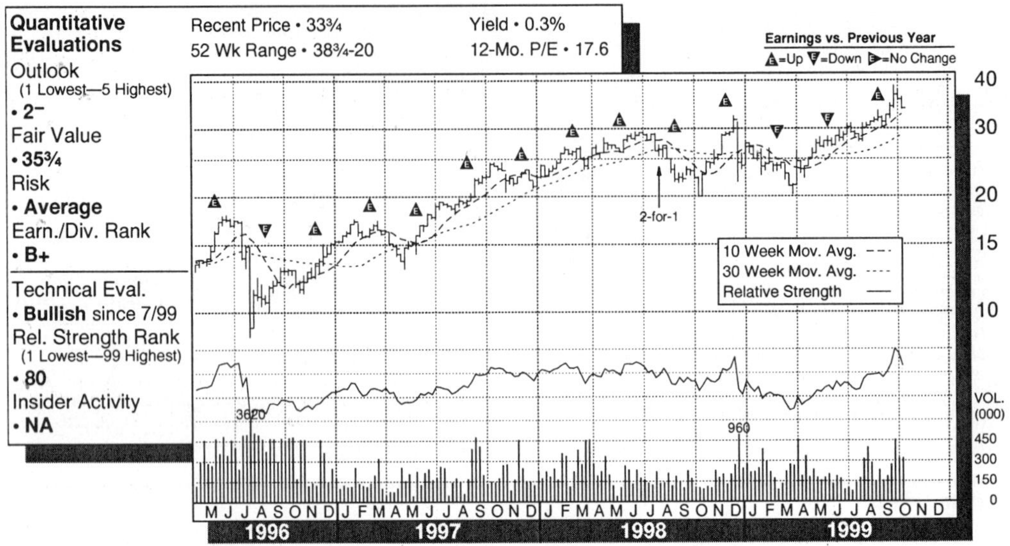

Business Profile - 05-OCT-99

In March 1999, the company acquired the North American and European specialty battery operations of Johnson Controls. The specialty battery division (now the Dynasty division) produces and markets industrial batteries under the Dynasty brand name for the uninterruptible power supply (UPS), telecommunications and broadband cable markets, primarily in North America, with approximately 20% of sales in Europe and Asia. In August, the remaining joint venture interest in a battery business based in Shanghai was acquired from Johnson Controls, and the battery division now has manufacturing facilities in Shanghai as well as Milwaukee, WI.

Operational Review - 05-OCT-99

Net sales in the six months ended July 31, 1999, climbed 33%, year to year, mainly reflecting the recently acquired Dynasty division and increased sales from the Powercom division, partially offset by lower sales from the Power Electronics division. Margins narrowed on 47% higher SG&A expenses, and the gain in operating income was held to 22%. With interest expense of $3.4 million, against $76,000, and after taxes at 36.0%, versus 36.5%, net income was up 5.3%, to $12,380,000 ($0.96 a share) from $11,756,000 ($0.92).

Stock Performance - 08-OCT-99

In the past 30 trading days, CHP's shares have increased 6%, compared to a 0.91% fall in the S&P 500. Average trading volume for the past five days was 63,320 shares, compared with the 40-day moving average of 53,190 shares.

Key Stock Statistics

Dividend Rate/Share	0.11	Shareholders	2,256
Shs. outstg. (M)	12.8	Market cap. (B)	$0.434
Avg. daily vol. (M)	0.068	Inst. holdings	92%
Tang. Bk. Value/Share	9.10		
Beta	0.93		

Value of $10,000 invested 5 years ago: $ 56,399

Fiscal Year Ending Jan. 31

	2000	1999	1998	1997	1996	1995
Revenues (Million $)						
1Q	99.6	78.91	73.35	62.43	58.78	42.60
2Q	111.8	80.07	75.38	71.75	63.38	47.62
3Q	—	81.60	81.38	76.58	61.46	54.62
4Q	—	73.39	77.95	76.15	58.81	55.13
Yr.	—	314.0	308.1	286.9	242.4	200.0
Earnings Per Share ($)						
1Q	**0.42**	**0.45**	**0.33**	**0.28**	0.25	0.17
2Q	**0.54**	**0.47**	**0.38**	**0.20**	0.30	0.17
3Q	—	**0.53**	**0.42**	**0.33**	0.30	0.22
4Q	—	**0.43**	**0.43**	**0.36**	0.23	0.19
Yr.	—	**1.88**	**1.56**	**1.16**	**1.09**	**0.76**

Next earnings report expected: late November

Dividend Data (Dividends have been paid since 1987.)

Amount ($)	Date Decl.	Ex-Div. Date	Stock of Record	Payment Date
0.028	Jan. 26	Feb. 10	Feb. 12	Feb. 26 '99
0.028	Apr. 27	May. 06	May. 10	May. 24 '99
0.028	Jun. 29	Jul. 07	Jul. 09	Jul. 23 '99
0.028	Sep. 28	Oct. 13	Oct. 15	Oct. 29 '99

A Division of The McGraw-Hill Companies

C&D Technologies, Inc.

Business Summary - 05-OCT-99

C&D Technologies, Inc. (formerly Charter Power Systems, Inc.) was organized in November 1985, to acquire all the assets of the 80 year old C&D Power Systems division of Allied Corp. The company is a leading North American producer of integrated reserve power systems for telecommunications, electronic information, and industrial applications. It is also a leading producer of embedded high-frequency switching power supplies used in telecommunications equipment, advanced office electronics, and sophisticated computer systems, and of motive power systems for electric industrial vehicles. CHP's integrated reserve power systems consist of industrial lead-acid batteries, as well as power rectifiers, power control and distribution equipment and related accessories.

The company operates through three segments: the powercom division, which accounted for 56% of total sales in FY 99 (Jan.), versus 52% in FY 98; the motor power division 23% (22%); and the power electronics division 21% (25%).

The powercom division makes and markets integrated reserve power systems and components for the standby power market which includes telecommunications, uninterruptible power supplies and utilities and controls. Integrated reserve power systems monitor and regulate electric power flow and provide backup power in the event of a primary power loss or interruption. The division also produces the individual components of the systems, including power rectifiers, system monitors, power boards, chargers and reserve batteries.

The motive power division produces complete systems and individual components (including power electronics and batteries) to power, monitor, charge and test the batteries used in electronic industrial vehicles, including fork-lift trucks, automated guided vehicles and airline ground support equipment. Products are marketed to end users in a broad array of industries, dealers of fork-lift trucks and other material handling vehicles, and, to a lesser extent, original equipment manufacturers.

The power electronics division makes and markets custom, standard and modified standard electronic power supply systems for large OEMs of telecommunications equipment, office products, computers and workstations. The division also manufactures cellular phone battery chargers.

The company continues to develop new products in all areas of its business. CHP spent $8.3 million on research and development in FY 99, $8.8 million FY 98, and $8.1 million FY 97. During FY 99, the company's powercom division introduced the Orion battery, a competitively priced valve-regulated battery designed primarily for the telecommunications markets. During FY 98, CHP's motive power division introduced the low maintenance Liberty Eclipse battery and charger, dramatically reducing customer cost of operation.

Per Share Data ($) (Year Ended Jan. 31)	1999	1998	1997	1996	1995	1994	1993	1992	1991	1990
Tangible Bk. Val.	9.10	14.06	5.18	5.28	3.67	-0.86	2.62	2.78	2.52	2.04
Cash Flow	2.79	4.99	1.82	1.56	1.28	2.31	0.43	0.72	0.98	0.74
Earnings	1.88	1.56	1.16	1.09	0.75	0.54	-0.06	0.25	0.53	0.33
Dividends	0.06	0.06	0.06	0.06	0.06	0.06	0.04	0.06	0.06	0.06
Payout Ratio	3%	4%	5%	5%	7%	10%	NM	22%	11%	17%
Cal. Yrs.	1998	1997	1996	1995	1994	1993	1992	1991	1990	1989
Prices - High	$32\frac{3}{8}$	$24\frac{5}{8}$	18	$15\frac{7}{8}$	$9\frac{1}{4}$	$7\frac{1}{4}$	5	$6\frac{3}{4}$	$4\frac{1}{4}$	$3\frac{1}{2}$
- Low	$19\frac{7}{8}$	13	$8\frac{5}{8}$	$8\frac{3}{4}$	$4\frac{7}{8}$	$2\frac{5}{16}$	$2\frac{1}{8}$	3	$2\frac{1}{4}$	$2\frac{5}{16}$
P/E Ratio - High	17	16	16	15	12	13	NM	27	8	11
- Low	11	8	7	8	6	4	NM	12	4	7
Income Statement Analysis (Million $)										
Revs.	314	308	287	242	200	377	134	151	165	158
Oper. Inc.	48.9	45.1	32.9	28.7	22.1	-0.5	10.0	18.6	20.0	17.0
Depr.	11.3	11.8	8.5	6.1	6.6	16.8	5.7	5.6	5.2	4.7
Int. Exp.	0.1	1.1	NA	1.4	1.3	5.4	1.1	2.3	4.3	6.3
Pretax Inc.	37.7	31.0	23.1	21.2	13.9	23.0	-0.3	5.2	10.2	4.8
Eff. Tax Rate	35%	37%	35%	34%	33%	9.90%	NM	43%	42%	22%
Net Inc.	24.5	19.7	14.9	14.0	9.4	20.2	-0.6	2.9	6.0	3.8
Balance Sheet & Other Fin. Data (Million $)										
Cash	5.0	1.2	0.9	10.9	1.2	15.5	1.8	1.6	1.5	1.4
Curr. Assets	109	93.4	89.3	85.6	64.1	50.0	51.0	42.3	48.7	54.3
Total Assets	186	166	160	131	112	230	98.0	87.0	98.0	105
Curr. Liab.	45.0	46.1	43.9	35.3	36.3	52.0	35.3	22.9	28.6	26.9
LT Debt	1.8	10.3	29.4	15.4	14.2	12.4	20.6	25.2	30.6	46.3
Common Eqty.	124	97.3	74.9	68.9	51.7	-10.0	33.1	35.2	31.9	26.5
Total Cap.	128	110	108	87.1	69.5	88.0	57.7	61.2	66.0	75.9
Cap. Exp.	15.8	13.6	16.3	7.9	7.7	5.9	7.3	5.2	4.9	6.6
Cash Flow	35.8	31.5	23.4	20.0	16.0	32.1	5.0	8.5	11.2	8.5
Curr. Ratio	2.4	2.0	2.0	2.4	1.8	1.0	1.4	1.8	1.7	2.0
% LT Debt of Cap.	1.4	9.3	18.1	17.7	20.4	14.0	35.8	41.3	46.4	61.0
% Net Inc.of Revs.	7.8	6.4	5.2	5.8	4.7	5.3	NM	1.9	3.6	2.4
% Ret. on Assets	13.9	12.1	10.3	11.6	9.0	8.1	NM	3.2	5.9	3.6
% Ret. on Equity	22.2	22.9	20.8	23.3	20.0	NM	NM	8.7	20.4	14.9

Data as orig reptd.; bef. results of disc opers/spec. items. Per share data adj. for stk. divs. Bold denotes diluted EPS (FASB 128)-prior periods restated. E-Estimated. NA-Not Available. NM-Not Meaningful. NR-Not Ranked.

Office—1400 Union Meeting Rd., Blue Bell, PA 19422. **Tel**—(215) 619-2700. **Chrmn**—W. Harral III. **Pres & CEO**—W. H. Roberts, Jr.**VP-Fin & CFO**—S. E. Markert Jr. **Secy**—G. M. Feit. **Dirs**—K. P. Dowd, G. M. Feit, W. Harral III, P. S. Lewis, G. MacKenzie, W. H. Roberts, Jr., J. A. H. Shober. **Transfer Agent**—Trust Co. of New Jersey, Jersey City. **Incorporated**—in Delaware in 1985. **Empl**— 2,446. **S&P Analyst:** C.C.P.

C-COR.net

NASDAQ Symbol **CCBL**

In S&P SmallCap 600

09-OCT-99

Industry:
Electrical Equipment

Summary: C-COR.net Corp. (formerly C-Cor Electronics Inc.) designs and manufactures electronic equipment used in various communication networks worldwide.

Quantitative Evaluations

Outlook
(1 Lowest—5 Highest)
• **3+**
Fair Value
• **35¼**
Risk
• **High**
Earn./Div. Rank
• **B**

Technical Eval.
• **Bullish** since 9/99
Rel. Strength Rank
(1 Lowest—99 Highest)
• **94**
Insider Activity
• **NA**

Recent Price • 35½
52 Wk Range • 39½-10
Yield • Nil
12-Mo. P/E • 31.2

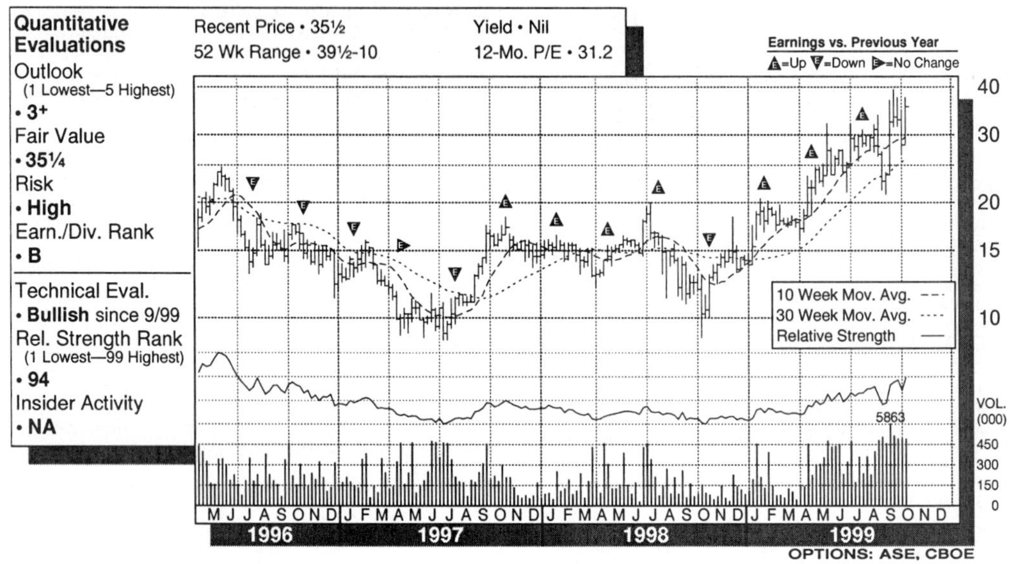

Business Profile - 30-AUG-99

The previously announced acquisition of Convergence.com Corp. closed on July 9, 1999, while the Silicon Valley Communications, Inc. acquisition is expected to close in the first quarter of FY 2000 (Jun.). Both mergers will be accounted for on a pooling of interests basis. In FY 99, both Convergence.com and Silicon Valley Communications incurred costs in excess of their revenues from investing in technology and infrastructure. In the first quarter of FY 2000, CCBL will record a one-time charge related to the business combinations of $3.5 - $4.5 million.

Operational Review - 30-AUG-99

Based on a preliminary report of audited results, net sales rose 13% in the fiscal year ended June 25, 1999. Despite higher research and product development costs, profitability improved on wider gross margins and well controlled selling and administrative expenses; operating profit climbed 37%. With lower other expenses and in the absence of a $625,000 restructuring charge, after taxes at 35.4%, versus 32.0%, net income jumped 43%, to $10,455,000 ($1.10 a share), from $7,317,000 ($0.78). Results exclude gains on the disposal of discontinued operations of $0.04 and $0.10 a share in the respective years.

Stock Performance - 08-OCT-99

In the past 30 trading days, CCBL's shares have increased 56%, compared to a 0.91% fall in the S&P 500. Average trading volume for the past five days was 186,300 shares, compared with the 40-day moving average of 347,800 shares.

Key Stock Statistics

Dividend Rate/Share	Nil	Shareholders	599
Shs. outstg. (M)	9.2	Market cap. (B)	$0.326
Avg. daily vol. (M)	0.246	Inst. holdings	59%
Tang. Bk. Value/Share	5.34		
Beta	0.76		

Value of $10,000 invested 5 years ago: $ 39,513

Fiscal Year Ending Jun. 30

	1999	1998	1997	1996	1995	1994
Revenues (Million $)						
1Q	33.22	37.07	31.84	39.64	27.55	15.72
2Q	36.85	37.19	30.70	35.66	29.73	15.60
3Q	44.14	40.25	32.80	36.90	29.99	17.83
4Q	57.07	37.65	36.60	36.70	50.17	25.90
Yr.	171.3	152.1	131.9	148.9	137.4	75.05
Earnings Per Share ($)						
1Q	**0.15**	**0.20**	**0.16**	0.27	0.23	0.13
2Q	**0.20**	**0.17**	**0.06**	0.07	0.20	0.10
3Q	**0.30**	**0.20**	**0.14**	0.14	0.07	0.05
4Q	**0.45**	**0.21**	**0.09**	0.12	0.35	0.15
Yr.	**1.10**	**0.78**	**0.44**	**0.91**	0.84	0.43

Next earnings report expected: mid October

Dividend Data

No cash dividends have been paid. A two-for-one stock split was effected in 1994. A "poison pill" shareholder rights plan was adopted in 1999.

C-COR.net Corp.

Business Summary - 30-AUG-99

For more than 40 years, C-COR.net Corp. (formerly C-Cor Electronics Inc.) has designed and manufactured electronic equipment used in a variety of communications networks that affect daily life. The company's radio frequency (RF) and fiber-optic products and services support and maintain the transmission of voice, video and data communications in such common activities as watching cable television and making telephone calls. CCBL is a global player, with 21% of FY 98 (Jun.) net sales generated from international operations, primarily in Canada, Asia, Europe and Latin America. Time-Warner Cable and Rogers Cablesystems each accounted for 18% of net sales in FY 98.

A restructuring plan aimed at increasing gross margins has led to improved profitability, generated from economies of scale from higher production volumes, a more favorable product mix, and lower manufacturing costs. In July 1997, CCBL said it was discontinuing its digital fiber optic business, located in Fremont, CA. In addition, during FY 97, the company transferred certain manufacturing operations to Mexico, reconfigured its worldwide sales territories, and consolidated its sales force. In June 1998, the company decided to close its Reedsville, PA, manufacturing plant and to terminate approximately 143 employees.

C-COR.net's RF amplifiers, under the FlexNet series name, allow for the delivery of both analog and digital channels. During FY 98, CCBL introduced a new line of AM fiber optic headend and node products for use in HFC applications. These products were expected to be available for shipment beginning in FY 99. Under the trade name NAVICOR, the products transmit and receive voice, video and data signals.

C-COR.net's manufacturing facilities have been approved for ISO 9001 registration, a comprehensive series of requirements that include quality assurance in design, development, production, installation and servicing. This designation, it is believed, will benefit the company's strategy of competing on the basis of premium quality.

C-COR.net's ability to compete successfully depends largely on whether it can adapt to rapid changes in technology. Consequently, the company invests significantly in research and development. In FY 98 and FY 97, R&D expenditures were roughly $7.5 million and $5.7 million, respectively, primarily aimed at developing NAVICOR, fiber optic technology, new RF products and optical lid upgrades.

In July 1999, CCBL acquired Convergence.com Corp., a provider of Internet-enabling technical services, in exchange for about 1.45 million common shares. Upon completion of the acquisition, CCBL changed its name from C-Cor Electronics Inc. to C-COR.net Corp., and Convergence.com began operating under the name Broadband Management Services. Convergence.com has annual revenues of $2.7 million.

Per Share Data ($) (Year Ended Jun. 30)	1999	1998	1997	1996	1995	1994	1993	1992	1991	1990
Tangible Bk. Val.	NA	5.34	4.56	5.47	4.63	3.54	3.00	2.54	2.25	2.95
Cash Flow	NA	1.43	0.96	1.08	1.24	0.68	0.58	0.44	-0.20	0.73
Earnings	1.10	0.78	0.45	0.60	0.84	0.43	0.37	0.25	-0.39	0.64
Dividends	Nil	Nil	Nil	Nil	Nil	Nil	Nil	Nil	Nil	Nil
Payout Ratio	Nil	Nil	Nil	Nil	Nil	Nil	Nil	Nil	Nil	Nil
Prices - High	$39\frac{1}{2}$	20	$18\frac{3}{8}$	$24\frac{3}{4}$	$36\frac{1}{2}$	$36\frac{1}{2}$	10	$7\frac{3}{4}$	$5\frac{1}{8}$	$7\frac{1}{2}$
- Low	$13\frac{3}{4}$	$8\frac{7}{8}$	$8\frac{3}{4}$	$11\frac{1}{4}$	$16\frac{3}{4}$	$6\frac{3}{4}$	$5\frac{3}{8}$	$4\frac{1}{4}$	$1\frac{11}{16}$	$1\frac{5}{8}$
P/E Ratio - High	36	26	41	41	43	85	27	31	NM	12
- Low	13	11	19	19	20	16	15	17	NM	3
Income Statement Analysis (Million $)										
Revs.	NA	152	132	149	137	75.0	56.0	52.2	32.7	60.3
Oper. Inc.	NA	18.2	10.7	14.0	16.7	8.1	7.0	5.2	-4.5	8.9
Depr.	NA	6.1	4.9	4.7	3.9	2.4	1.9	1.8	1.6	0.9
Int. Exp.	NA	0.3	0.3	1.0	0.7	0.0	0.0	0.1	0.2	0.1
Pretax Inc.	NA	10.8	5.7	8.7	12.4	6.0	5.0	3.4	-5.8	8.9
Eff. Tax Rate	NA	32%	25%	32%	33%	33%	33%	33%	NM	38%
Net Inc.	NA	7.3	4.3	5.9	8.3	4.0	3.4	2.3	-3.5	5.5
Balance Sheet & Other Fin. Data (Million $)										
Cash	NA	2.3	0.8	1.8	1.9	5.1	9.7	4.6	4.3	3.6
Curr. Assets	NA	44.7	43.8	51.5	64.1	39.2	28.9	25.8	21.4	27.8
Total Assets	NA	75.5	71.1	78.4	87.7	49.5	37.3	33.9	30.2	32.6
Curr. Liab.	NA	17.4	21.0	16.0	39.7	14.2	6.8	6.9	5.8	6.8
LT Debt	NA	5.5	6.4	7.2	2.0	0.4	0.5	0.7	0.8	0.4
Common Eqty.	NA	50.2	41.7	53.3	44.7	34.1	29.5	25.7	23.4	25.4
Total Cap.	NA	57.1	49.4	61.9	47.6	35.0	30.1	26.7	24.3	25.8
Cap. Exp.	NA	8.8	5.9	8.0	15.4	4.1	1.9	0.6	1.9	1.9
Cash Flow	NA	13.4	9.2	10.6	12.2	6.4	5.3	4.0	-1.8	6.4
Curr. Ratio	NA	2.6	2.1	3.2	1.6	2.8	4.2	3.7	3.7	4.1
% LT Debt of Cap.	NA	9.7	12.9	11.6	4.3	1.3	1.7	2.7	3.3	1.6
% Net Inc.of Revs.	NA	4.8	3.2	4.0	6.0	5.4	6.1	4.4	NM	9.2
% Ret. on Assets	NA	10.0	5.7	7.1	12.0	9.3	9.5	7.1	NM	18.1
% Ret. on Equity	NA	15.9	9.0	12.0	20.8	12.6	12.2	9.3	NM	24.3

Data as orig reptd.; bef. results of disc opers/spec. items. Per share data adj. for stk. divs. Bold denotes diluted EPS (FASB 128)-prior periods restated. E-Estimated. NA-Not Available. NM-Not Meaningful. NR-Not Ranked.

Office—60 Decibel Rd., State College, PA 16801. **Tel**—(814) 238-2461. **Website**—http://www.c-cor.com **Chrmn**—R. E. Perry. **Pres & CEO**—D. A. Woodle. **VP-Fin, Treas & Secy**—C. A. Miller. **Investor Contact**—Sally O. Thiel. **Dirs**—D. M. Cook Jr., I. N. R. Harper Jr., J. K. Hassan, A. P. Jones, J. J. Omlor, R. E. Perry, F. Rusinko Jr., J. J. Tietjen, D. A. Woodle. **Transfer Agent & Registrar**—American Stock Transfer & Trust Co., NYC. **Incorporated**—in Pennsylvania in 1953. **Empl**— 1,200. **S&P Analyst:** Jordan Horoschak

STANDARD
&POOR'S
STOCK REPORTS

C-Cube Microsystems

NASDAQ Symbol **CUBE**

In S&P SmallCap 600

09-OCT-99

Industry:
Communications Equipment

Summary: C-Cube is a leading provider of integrated circuits and software that implement international standards for the compression of digital images and video.

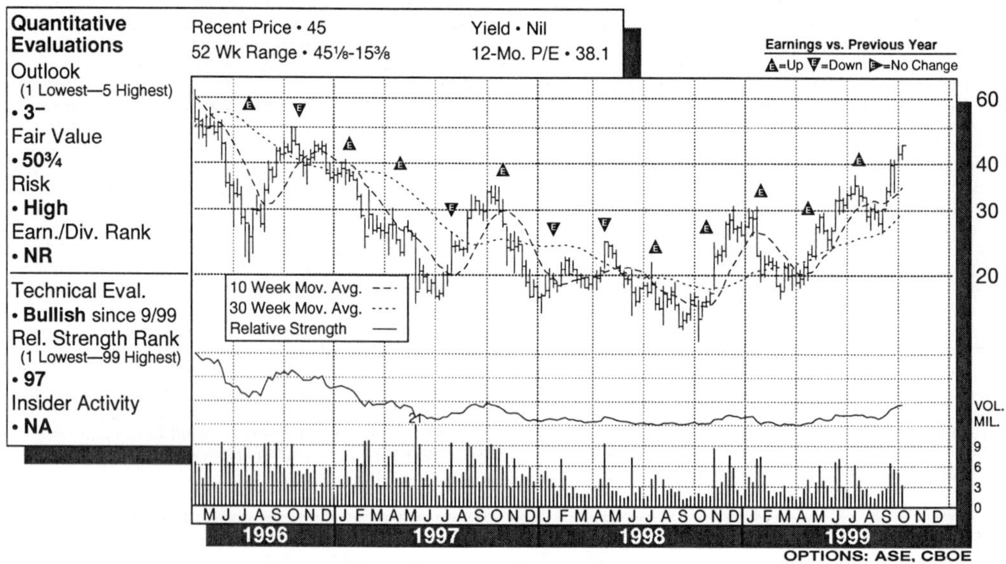

Business Profile - 27-AUG-99

CUBE, which offers highly integrated, standards-based digital video compression solutions, has been focusing R&D efforts on developing chips for use in digital video disc (DVD) systems, which make use of a new format for recording data. In July 1999, CUBE said that according to industry analysts at Dataquest and Cahners In-Stat, it was leading the world in delivery of MPEG silicon. In August 1999, CUBE's DiviCom subsidiary announced that it had been selected to implement the first direct broadcast satellite service in China. In July 1999, DiviCom was selected to supply the first multi-channel/multi-point distribution system (MMDS, also known as wireless cable) digital head-end in Puerto Rico.

Operational Review - 27-AUG-99

In the six months ended June 30, 1999, net revenues rose 12%, year to year, led by growth in sales of DiviCom's encoder products, attributable to design improvements and feature and quality enhancements, and strength in international markets. Gross margins widened, aided by a more favorable product mix and operating efficiencies; income from operations climbed 15%. Other income was up sharply, and income before special items advanced 25%, to $24,592,000 ($0.59 a share, on 2.0% more shares), from $19,709,000 ($0.52). Results exclude a special credit of $0.03 a share in 1998.

Stock Performance - 08-OCT-99

In the past 30 trading days, CUBE's shares have increased 63%, compared to a 0.91% fall in the S&P 500. Average trading volume for the past five days was 642,260 shares, compared with the 40-day moving average of 733,046 shares.

Key Stock Statistics

Dividend Rate/Share	Nil	Shareholders	1,044
Shs. outstg. (M)	39.9	Market cap. (B)	$ 1.8
Avg. daily vol. (M)	1.014	Inst. holdings	46%
Tang. Bk. Value/Share	5.88		
Beta	1.43		

Value of $10,000 invested 5 years ago: NA

Fiscal Year Ending Dec. 31

	1999	1998	1997	1996	1995	1994
Revenues (Million $)						
1Q	96.46	87.32	94.13	68.10	17.11	8.50
2Q	94.10	82.52	71.10	72.96	21.61	10.00
3Q	—	86.16	81.72	83.18	35.32	12.31
4Q	—	95.80	90.07	95.22	50.55	14.15
Yr.	—	351.8	337.0	319.8	124.6	45.02
Earnings Per Share ($)						
1Q	**0.32**	**0.27**	0.41	0.38	0.10	0.02
2Q	**0.28**	**0.25**	0.20	0.39	0.12	0.03
3Q	—	**0.28**	0.25	-3.46	0.24	0.04
4Q	—	**0.31**	**0.30**	0.45	0.26	0.06
Yr.	—	**1.11**	**1.15**	**-2.15**	**0.74**	**0.16**

Next earnings report expected: mid October

Dividend Data

No cash dividends have been paid. The company intends to retain earnings to finance its business and does not expect to pay cash dividends in the foreseeable future.

C-Cube Microsystems Inc.

Business Summary - 27-AUG-99

C-Cube Microsystems Inc. designs, manufactures and sells semiconductors and systems for digital video applications. CUBE seeks to benefit from a continuing transition from analog to digital video formats, using its digital compression technology. Digital video offers a number of fundamental advantages over analog video, including the ability to be compressed to gain efficiencies in transmission and storage, transmitted and reproduced without perceptible image degradation, as well as random accessing and nonlinear editing capabilities. Digital video compression has enabled the development of a significant number of consumer electronics technologies, including video compact disc (VideoCD).

In the consumer market, CUBE is focused on VideoCD, playback and recordable digital video disc (DVD) and digital VCR players. CUBE's communications segment targets interactive set-top boxes, broadcast encoders and emerging applications in non-linear editing, time shift and Internet television boxes. Typical customers for CUBE's consumer electronics semiconductors include Acer, Dell, Gateway, Hitachi, JVC, LG Electronics, Samsung, Sony and Toshiba. CUBE's core businesses (the Semiconductor division) accounted for 59% and 65% of net revenues in 1998 and 1997, respectively.

CUBE is also a leading provider of digital video communication systems through its DiviCom subsidiary (41% and 35%). Acquired by CUBE in 1996 for $65.7 million in cash and some 2.3 million CUBE common shares, the unit designs, manufactures and sells products and systems that enable the transmission of digital video, audio and data over a variety of networks including satellite, wireless, terrestrial, fiber and cable. DiviCom's DiviSys technology integration group provides consulting and implementation services to the segment's customers.

In 1998 and 1997, international revenues accounted for some 62% and 65%, respectively, of CUBE's net revenues, and the company believes international revenues will continue to account for a significant portion of net revenues. During 1998, no customer accounted for 10% or more of net revenues. Sales to Sinorex, a distributor, accounted for 20% and 12% of CUBE's net revenues during 1997 and 1996, respectively.

The company believes that the introduction of new products in target markets is essential to its growth. R&D spending in 1998 totaled $74.0 million (21% of sales), up from $64.2 million (19%) in 1997.

In January 1999, CUBE announced the acquisition of communication technology, patents and personnel from TV/Com International, materially strengthening CUBE's already strong commitment to the digital video communications segment and complementing the company's MPEG set-top product portfolio.

Per Share Data ($) **(Year Ended Dec. 31)**	**1998**	**1997**	**1996**	**1995**	**1994**	**1993**	**1992**	**1991**	**1990**	**1989**
Tangible Bk. Val.	5.88	4.02	1.96	2.55	1.67	1.52	NA	NA	NA	NA
Cash Flow	1.60	1.48	-1.93	0.81	0.23	0.04	NA	NA	NA	NA
Earnings	1.11	1.15	-2.15	0.72	0.16	-0.02	NA	NA	NA	NA
Dividends	Nil	Nil	Nil	Nil	Nil	Nil	NA	NA	NA	NA
Payout Ratio	Nil	Nil	Nil	Nil	Nil	Nil	NA	NA	NA	NA
Prices - High	30 7/8	41	73 1/2	65	12 3/8	NA	NA	NA	NA	NA
- Low	13 1/4	15 3/4	21 1/2	7 1/2	7 1/2	NA	NA	NA	NA	NA
P/E Ratio - High	28	36	NM	90	77	NM	NA	NA	NA	NA
- Low	12	14	NM	10	47	NM	NA	NA	NA	NA
Income Statement Analysis (Million $)										
Revs.	352	337	320	125	45.0	23.7	NA	NA	NA	NA
Oper. Inc.	79.0	86.1	32.0	31.0	6.5	1.3	NA	NA	NA	NA
Depr.	22.6	17.4	7.7	3.1	2.1	1.4	NA	NA	NA	NA
Int. Exp.	4.3	6.0	6.0	1.6	NA	0.6	NA	NA	NA	NA
Pretax Inc.	60.7	67.0	-39.8	29.8	5.1	-0.4	NA	NA	NA	NA
Eff. Tax Rate	30%	34%	NM	16%	1.40%	NM	NA	NA	NA	NA
Net Inc.	42.8	44.3	-73.0	24.9	5.0	-0.5	NA	NA	NA	NA
Balance Sheet & Other Fin. Data (Million $)										
Cash	108	145	82.0	144	43.8	39.2	NA	NA	NA	NA
Curr. Assets	292	248	193	186	61.0	NA	NA	NA	NA	NA
Total Assets	343	304	280	204	67.9	56.6	NA	NA	NA	NA
Curr. Liab.	71.6	40.0	68.2	27.6	12.3	NA	NA	NA	NA	NA
LT Debt	23.6	87.5	87.7	88.0	2.1	2.6	NA	NA	NA	NA
Common Eqty.	243	175	119	87.5	53.5	43.1	NA	NA	NA	NA
Total Cap.	272	264	211	176	55.6	45.7	NA	NA	NA	NA
Cap. Exp.	20.0	13.6	17.1	5.4	1.5	1.5	NA	NA	NA	NA
Cash Flow	65.4	61.7	-65.3	27.9	7.1	1.0	NA	NA	NA	NA
Curr. Ratio	4.1	6.2	2.8	14.8	5.0	NA	NA	NA	NA	NA
% LT Debt of Cap.	8.7	33.2	41.6	50.0	3.7	5.7	NA	NA	NA	NA
% Net Inc.of Revs.	12.2	13.2	NM	19.9	11.1	NM	NA	NA	NA	NA
% Ret. on Assets	13.2	15.2	NM	18.3	10.1	NM	NA	NA	NA	NA
% Ret. on Equity	20.4	30.2	NM	17.6	14.9	NM	NA	NA	NA	NA

Data as orig. reptd.; bef. results of disc. opers. and/or spec. items. Per share data adj. for stk. divs. as of ex-div. date. Bold denotes diluted EPS (FASB 128). E-Estimated. NA-Not Available. NM-Not Meaningful. NR-Not Ranked.

Office—1778 McCarthy Blvd., Milpitas, CA 95035. **Tel**—(408) 490-8000. **Website**—http://www.c-cube.com **Chrmn**—D. T. Valentine. **Pres & CEO**—A. A. Balkanski. **VP-Fin, CFO & Investor Contact**—W. Walczykowski. **Secy**—R. Foreman. **Dirs**—A. A. Balkanski, B. S. Futa, D. McKinney, G. Reyes, T. J. Rodgers, D. T. Valentine. **Transfer Agent & Registrar**—First National Bank of Boston. **Incorporated**—in California in 1988; reincorporated in Delaware in 1994. **Empl**— 929. **S&P Analyst:** Scott H. Kessler

STANDARD & POOR'S STOCK REPORTS

Cable Design Technologies

NYSE Symbol **CDT**

In S&P SmallCap 600

09-OCT-99

Industry: Communications Equipment

Summary: CDT designs and manufactures technologically advanced electronic data transmission cables for various applications.

Quantitative Evaluations

Outlook (1 Lowest—5 Highest)
• **4+**

Fair Value
• **30**

Risk
• **High**

Earn./Div. Rank
• **NR**

Technical Eval.
• **Bullish** since 8/99

Rel. Strength Rank (1 Lowest—99 Highest)
• **88**

Insider Activity
• **NA**

Recent Price • 22⅞
52 Wk Range • 24⅞-10¾
Yield • Nil
12-Mo. P/E • 16.9

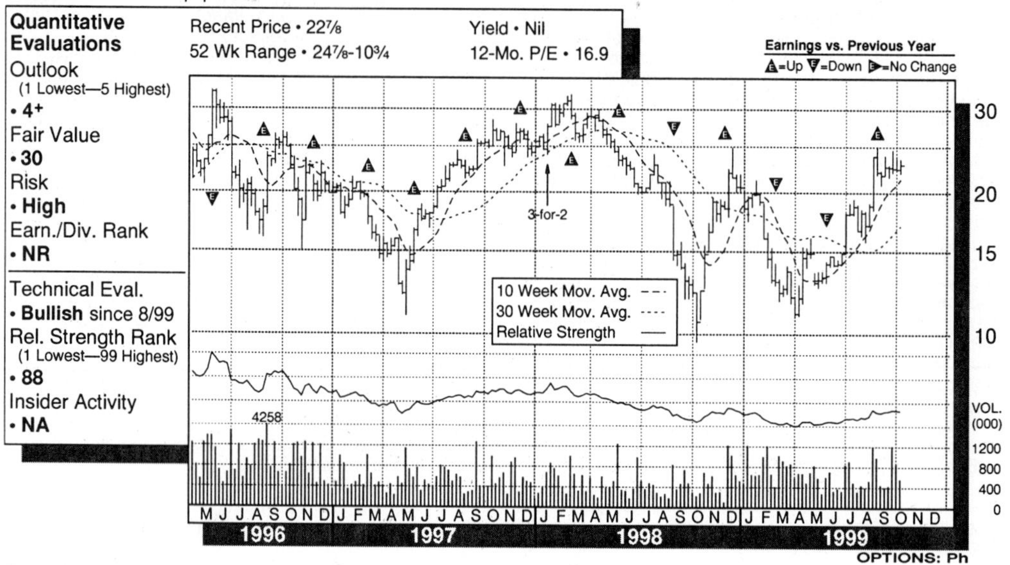

Business Profile - 13-JUL-99

The company attributed lower year-to-year sales and earnings in the third quarter of FY 99 (Jul.) to less than anticipated sales of communication cable in the U.S. market and a slow February, as well as less favorable foreign currency translation and a decline in the average price of copper. CDT believes it remains a prime beneficiary of Internet growth, the investment in high bandwidth technologies and worldwide demand for faster transmission speeds. Markets for the company's coaxial cable products include automation and process control, multi-media, broadcast, and potential CATV applications. Officers and directors own more than 20% of the outstanding shares.

Operational Review - 13-JUL-99

Net sales for the first nine months of FY 99 (Jul.) rose 3.0%, year to year, as sales from recently acquired businesses were partially offset by less favorable foreign currency translations and a decline in the average price of copper on communication cable sales. Gross margins widened on an improved product mix and less product outsourcing. Following $5.2 million of non-recurring expenses (a $6.3 million charge for a December 1998 share repurchase plan offset by a $1.1 million gain on the sale of assets) and 60% higher interest expense, pretax income declined 16%. After taxes at 40.4%, versus 38.1%, net income was down 19%, to $26,053,000 ($0.89 a share, on 6.8% fewer shares) from $32,034,000 ($1.02).

Stock Performance - 08-OCT-99

In the past 30 trading days, CDT's shares have increased 4%, compared to a 0.91% fall in the S&P 500. Average trading volume for the past five days was 110,840 shares, compared with the 40-day moving average of 155,033 shares.

Key Stock Statistics

Dividend Rate/Share	Nil	Shareholders	153
Shs. outstg. (M)	28.2	Market cap. (B)	$0.646
Avg. daily vol. (M)	0.153	Inst. holdings	63%
Tang. Bk. Value/Share	6.15		
Beta	1.84		

Value of $10,000 invested 5 years ago: $ 49,150

Fiscal Year Ending Jul. 31

	1999	1998	1997	1996	1995	1994
Revenues (Million $)						
1Q	173.6	162.1	116.0	65.05	44.92	34.65
2Q	160.9	155.6	114.0	67.24	44.39	33.30
3Q	165.6	167.7	130.0	112.2	47.94	38.12
4Q	183.9	166.2	157.1	112.8	51.70	39.32
Yr.	684.0	651.7	517.0	357.4	188.9	145.4
Earnings Per Share ($)						
1Q	**0.41**	0.37	0.27	0.22	0.13	0.12
2Q	**0.16**	**0.32**	0.26	0.21	0.12	0.10
3Q	**0.31**	**0.34**	0.30	-0.13	0.15	0.10
4Q	**0.48**	**0.27**	0.35	0.27	0.18	0.12
Yr.	**1.36**	**1.29**	**1.17**	0.57	0.57	0.44

Next earnings report expected: early December

Dividend Data

No cash dividends have been paid. A 3-for-2 stock split was effected in January 1998.

A Division of The McGraw-Hill Companies

Cable Design Technologies Corporation

Business Summary - 13-JUL-99

Cable Design Technologies Corp. is a designer and manufacturer of specialty electronic data transmission cables and network structured wiring systems. CDT products include high performance copper, fiber optic, and composite cable constructions, connectors and component assemblies that are used in network, communication, computer interconnect, wireless, commercial aviation, automotive, automation & process control, and other applications.

Sales contributions by product line in FY 98 (Jul.) were: network 42% (48% in FY 97), communication 19% (19%), automation & process control 22% (21%), specialty 16% (10%) and non-cable 1% (2%).

The network product line encompasses the cable and the components, including connectors, wiring racks and panels, outlets and interconnecting hardware, to complete the end-to-end network structured wiring system requirements of LANS (local area networks) and WANS (wide area networks).

Communications products consist primarily of outside communication, switchboard and equipment cable mainly manufactured by the company's NORCOM/CDT facility in Kingston, Ontario, which is the largest communication cable operation in Canada.

The automation & process control product line encompasses four applications for data and signal transmission cables. Automation applications include climate control, premise video distribution and sophisticated security and signal systems involving motion detection, electronic card and video surveillance technologies. Process control applications include remote signaling and electronic monitoring systems. Sound applications include voice activation, evacuation and other similar systems. Safety applications refer to certain attributes of data transmission cable that improve the safety and performance of such cable under hazardous conditions, particularly in buildings for advanced fire alarm and safety systems.

Specialty products refers to a family of highly engineered wire and cable products for a variety of specialized applications and niche markets, including commercial aviation and marine, automotive electronics, broadcast, wireless component assemblies, CATV, microwave antenna, medical electronics, electronic testing equipment, robotics, electronically controlled factory equipment, copiers, home entertainment and appliances.

Non-cable manufacturing activities unrelated to the company's core business consists primarily of precision tire molds and sheet metal products.

Per Share Data ($) (Year Ended Jul. 31)	1999	1998	1997	1996	1995	1994	1993	1992	1991	1990
Tangible Bk. Val.	NA	5.93	5.41	5.33	0.83	0.12	0.55	NM	NA	NA
Cash Flow	NA	1.74	1.49	0.79	0.72	0.58	0.46	0.37	NA	NA
Earnings	1.36	1.29	1.17	0.57	0.57	0.43	0.30	0.23	NA	NA
Dividends	Nil	Nil	Nil	Nil	Nil	Nil	Nil	Nil	NA	NA
Payout Ratio	Nil	Nil	Nil	Nil	Nil	Nil	Nil	Nil	NA	NA
Prices - High	$24\frac{7}{8}$	$32\frac{1}{4}$	$28\frac{1}{2}$	34	$21\frac{5}{8}$	$8\frac{3}{4}$	5	5	NA	NA
- Low	$10\frac{7}{8}$	$9\frac{5}{8}$	$10\frac{7}{8}$	$14\frac{3}{4}$	$6\frac{3}{8}$	$4\frac{3}{8}$	$4\frac{3}{8}$	$4\frac{3}{8}$	NA	NA
P/E Ratio - High	18	25	24	60	38	20	17	21	NA	NA
- Low	8	7	9	32	11	10	14	19	NA	NA
Income Statement Analysis (Million $)										
Revs.	NA	652	517	357	189	145	127	127	NA	NA
Oper. Inc.	NA	93.6	72.7	54.2	33.4	25.2	22.5	20.5	NA	NA
Depr.	NA	14.0	10.1	6.0	3.8	3.4	3.1	2.8	NA	NA
Int. Exp.	NA	8.6	5.3	5.4	5.1	5.3	8.4	10.4	NA	NA
Pretax Inc.	NA	65.8	57.3	25.9	24.5	16.9	10.5	8.0	NA	NA
Eff. Tax Rate	NA	38%	37%	39%	40%	40%	43%	42%	NA	NA
Net Inc.	NA	40.5	36.0	15.3	14.7	10.1	6.0	4.7	NA	NA
Balance Sheet & Other Fin. Data (Million $)										
Cash	NA	11.1	9.0	16.1	2.2	2.2	0.3	NA	NA	NA
Curr. Assets	NA	277	248	208	74.3	60.6	46.9	NA	NA	NA
Total Assets	NA	504	429	320	119	103	83.7	NA	NA	NA
Curr. Liab.	NA	102	85.5	72.7	30.9	21.4	21.7	NA	NA	NA
LT Debt	NA	136	127	73.1	52.7	63.8	77.5	NA	NA	NA
Common Eqty.	NA	245	205	165	31.9	16.2	-16.3	-21.4	NA	NA
Total Cap.	NA	NA	338	243	395	81.4	62.1	NA	NA	NA
Cap. Exp.	NA	49.2	26.7	15.9	5.7	4.0	2.5	1.6	NA	NA
Cash Flow	NA	54.5	46.1	21.9	18.5	13.5	9.1	7.4	NA	NA
Curr. Ratio	NA	2.7	2.9	2.9	2.4	2.8	2.2	NA	NA	NA
% LT Debt of Cap.	NA	34.4	37.4	30.1	59.8	78.4	124.8	NA	NA	NA
% Net Inc.of Revs.	NA	6.2	7.0	4.3	7.8	7.0	4.7	3.9	NA	NA
% Ret. on Assets	NA	8.7	9.6	7.0	13.2	10.9	8.0	NA	NA	NA
% Ret. on Equity	NA	18.0	19.4	15.5	61.0	NM	NM	NM	NA	NA

Data as orig reptd.; bef. results of disc opers/spec. items. Per share data adj. for stk. divs. Bold denotes diluted EPS (FASB 128)-prior periods restated. E-Estimated. NA-Not Available. NM-Not Meaningful. NR-Not Ranked.

Office—Foster Plaza 7, 661 Andersen Drive, Pittsburgh, PA 15220. **Tel**—(412) 937-2300. **Fax**—(412) 937-9690. **Website**—http://www.cdtc.com **Chrmn**—B. C. Cressey. **Pres & CEO**—P. M. Olson. **VP-CFO & Secy**—K. O. Hale. **Dirs**—B. C. Cressey, M. S. Gelbach Jr., G. Graeber, M. F. O. Harris, G. Kalnasy, P. M. Olson, R. C. Tuttle. **Transfer Agent & Registrar**—Bank of Boston. **Incorporated**—in Delaware in 1988. **Empl**— 3,200. **S&P Analyst:** S.R.B.

STANDARD
&POOR'S
STOCK REPORTS

Cabot Oil & Gas

NYSE Symbol **COG**

In S&P SmallCap 600

09-OCT-99

Industry:
Oil & Gas (Exploration & Production)

Summary: This company explores for, produces, purchases and markets natural gas and, to a lesser extent, produces and sells crude oil.

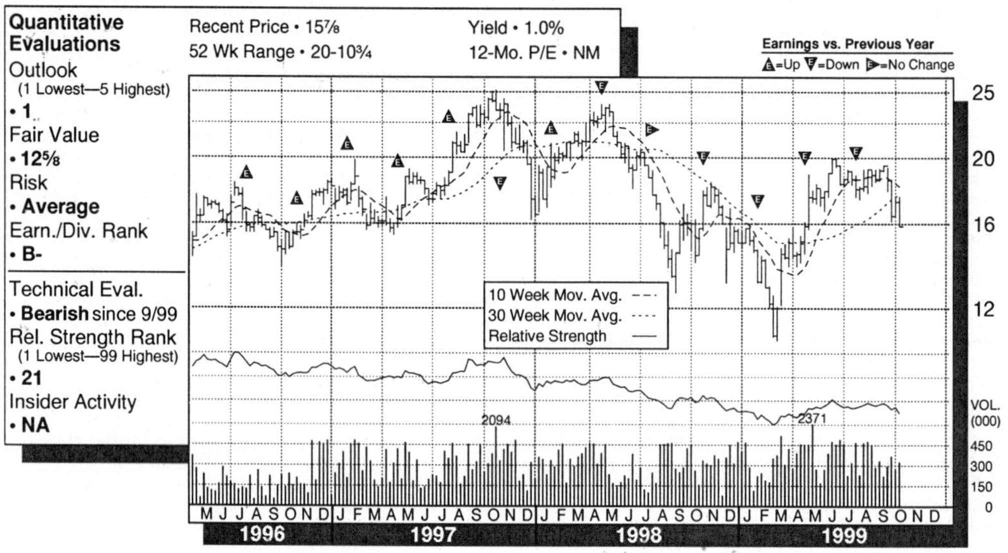

Business Profile - 06-JUL-99

In April 1999, Cabot said that although first quarter 1999 results fell short of its financial objectives, the operational turnaround in the Gulf Coast exceeded its expectations. New production from the Kacee field and the Oryx properties brought production to record levels in this region. The company also believes workover and drilling opportunities from the Oryx acquisition and the UPR joint venture initiated in February 1998 offer even greater upside growth potential. COG plans to sell certain non-strategic properties during 1999, to reduce long term debt. It expects a late 1998 reorganization that reduced employment levels about 6% to result in annual savings of $1.5 million.

Operational Review - 06-JUL-99

Revenues in the three months ended March 31, 1999, declined 14%, year to year, as a 16% drop in realized natural gas prices and 23% lower oil prices outweighed the impact of higher production. Results were hurt by lower natural gas and oil prices, 36% higher depreciation, depletion and amortization charges, and a 58% increase in interest expense; a pretax loss of $3,874,000 contrasted with pretax income of $6,459,000. After tax credits of $1,432,000, versus taxes at 40.5%, a net loss of $2,442,000 ($0.13 a share, after preferred dividends) contrasted with net income of $3,843,000 ($0.12).

Stock Performance - 08-OCT-99

In the past 30 trading days, COG's shares have declined 14%, compared to a 0.91% fall in the S&P 500. Average trading volume for the past five days was 64,460 shares, compared with the 40-day moving average of 65,021 shares.

Key Stock Statistics

Dividend Rate/Share	0.16	Shareholders	1,500
Shs. outstg. (M)	24.7	Market cap. (B)	$0.393
Avg. daily vol. (M)	0.062	Inst. holdings	83%
Tang. Bk. Value/Share	7.41		
Beta	1.10		

Value of $10,000 invested 5 years ago: $ 7,959

Fiscal Year Ending Dec. 31

	1999	1998	1997	1996	1995	1994
Revenues (Million $)						
1Q	35.28	40.79	52.79	41.20	58.12	65.84
2Q	41.06	41.67	39.41	37.35	51.35	56.45
3Q	—	37.39	40.77	35.50	47.98	55.76
4Q	—	39.76	52.16	49.02	56.47	59.02
Yr.	—	159.6	185.1	163.1	213.9	237.1
Earnings Per Share ($)						
1Q	**-0.13**	**0.12**	**0.42**	**0.23**	-0.36	0.23
2Q	Nil	**0.09**	**0.09**	**0.04**	-0.23	-0.11
3Q	—	**-0.10**	**0.10**	**0.13**	-3.22	-0.20
4Q	—	**-0.03**	**0.38**	**0.27**	-0.24	-0.14
Yr.	—	**0.08**	**0.97**	**0.66**	**-4.05**	-0.25

Next earnings report expected: late October

Dividend Data (Dividends have been paid since 1990.)

Amount ($)	Date Decl.	Ex-Div. Date	Stock of Record	Payment Date
0.040	Nov. 03	Nov. 10	Nov. 13	Nov. 27 '98
0.040	Jan. 29	Feb. 10	Feb. 12	Feb. 26 '99
0.040	May. 11	May. 19	May. 21	May. 28 '99
0.040	Aug. 04	Aug. 11	Aug. 13	Aug. 27 '99

A Division of The McGraw-Hill Companies

STANDARD &POOR'S
STOCK REPORTS

Cabot Oil & Gas Corporation

09-OCT-99

Business Summary - 06-JUL-99

A domestic independent natural gas producer and marketer, Cabot Oil & Gas Corp. (COG) is continuing to focus on its strategies designed to grow through the drill bit, acquisitions, and greater emphasis on marketing. In addition, the company plans to continue to capitalize on opportunities provided by its expanded exploration efforts.

The success of COG's strategies can be measured by the achievement of three goals. The first is to increase cash flow from both increased production and reduced costs. Although 1998 production rose only slightly, Cabot expects newly acquired Gulf Coast properties to boost 1999 production by about 5 Bcfe. It expects the benefits of the 1998 reorganization to help lower costs in 1999 and beyond.

The company's second goal is to maintain reserves per share while increasing production to protect long-term shareholder value. Excluding revisions, reserve additions from the 1998 drilling program replaced 146% of production. In addition, COG acquired reserves during 1998 through asset purchases. Most significantly, it purchased about 72 Bcfe of proved reserves from Oryx Energy Co. in December 1998. As a result, proved reserve levels increased in 1998 to 1.04 Tcfe, the highest level in the company's history.

Cabot's third goal is to strive to reduce debt as a percentage of total capitalization, without diluting shareholder value.

The company explores for, develops, produces, stores, transports, purchases and markets natural gas and, to a lesser extent, produces and sells crude oil. Its core areas are concentrated in three regions: (1) the Appalachian region of West Virginia and Pennsylvania; (2) the western region, with operations in the Anadarko area of Kansas, Oklahoma and the Texas Panhandle, and the Green River Basin of Wyoming; and (3) the Gulf Coast region, including south Texas and south Louisiana. At December 31, 1998, estimated proved reserves aggregated 1,042.8 Bcfe, of which 96% was natural gas.

COG is one of the largest producers of natural gas in the Appalachian Basin, where it has conducted operations for more than a century. The company acquired its operations in the Rocky Mountains and the Gulf Coast through the 1994 merger with Washington Energy Resources. Cabot has maintained its reserve base through low-risk development drilling and strategic acquisitions.

While continuing its strong development drilling program, Cabot has significantly expanded its exploration program in the past three years. It experienced a 69% gross success rate for its exploratory drilling program in 1998, based on participation in 39 exploratory wells. A large part of the exploration activity has been focused in the Gulf Coast region.

Through marketing activities, the company provides a wide array of services, including gas supply and transportation management, short- and long-term supply contracts, capacity brokering, and risk management alternatives.

Per Share Data ($) (Year Ended Dec. 31)	1998	1997	1996	1995	1994	1993	1992	1991	1990	1989
Tangible Bk. Val.	7.41	7.46	7.03	6.48	10.67	5.61	5.78	5.83	5.62	4.67
Cash Flow	1.74	2.74	2.54	-1.73	2.23	1.78	1.65	1.34	1.84	1.82
Earnings	0.08	1.00	0.67	-4.05	-0.25	0.10	0.11	0.01	0.57	0.02
Dividends	0.16	0.16	0.16	0.16	0.16	0.16	0.16	0.16	0.12	NA
Payout Ratio	NM	16%	24%	NM	NM	160%	147%	430%	21%	NA
Prices - High	24	$25\frac{1}{8}$	$18\frac{1}{2}$	17	$23\frac{3}{4}$	27	20	$18\frac{1}{8}$	$18\frac{1}{2}$	NA
- Low	$12\frac{5}{8}$	$15\frac{3}{8}$	$13\frac{1}{8}$	$12\frac{3}{8}$	$13\frac{3}{8}$	$15\frac{3}{8}$	$10\frac{1}{4}$	$11\frac{1}{4}$	14	NA
P/E Ratio - High	NM	25	28	NM	NM	NM	NM	NM	32	NA
- Low	NM	15	20	NM	NM	NM	NM	NM	25	NA
Income Statement Analysis (Million $)										
Revs.	160	185	163	214	237	164	148	140	128	132
Oper. Inc.	26.9	63.8	47.0	-115	69.5	54.0	48.9	44.8	38.8	42.9
Depr. Depl. & Amort.	41.2	40.6	42.7	47.2	54.6	34.5	31.5	27.2	23.1	36.0
Int. Exp.	18.6	18.0	17.4	24.9	16.7	10.3	9.8	9.4	5.4	9.3
Pretax Inc.	8.8	45.9	31.4	-141	-1.6	9.7	8.2	6.1	22.6	-2.2
Eff. Tax Rate	40%	38%	34%	NM	NM	64%	73%	79%	36%	NM
Net Inc.	5.3	28.3	20.8	-86.6	-1.0	3.5	2.2	1.3	14.6	0.4
Balance Sheet & Other Fin. Data (Million $)										
Cash	2.2	1.8	1.4	3.0	3.8	2.9	1.1	2.2	2.0	0.6
Curr. Assets	71.1	70.5	79.6	52.3	52.0	44.6	41.7	32.9	25.2	25.3
Total Assets	704	542	561	528	688	445	349	334	302	289
Curr. Liab.	99	85.9	72.6	60.9	53.7	37.3	32.8	35.9	33.6	38.5
LT Debt	327	183	248	249	268	169	120	105	80.0	92.0
Common Eqty.	183	184	161	148	243	115	118	119	115	93.0
Total Cap.	596	447	478	460	629	401	310	296	260	247
Cap. Exp.	204	73.5	60.7	25.7	73.0	129	37.0	46.1	39.5	NA
Cash Flow	43.1	63.8	57.9	-39.4	49.2	36.5	33.8	27.4	37.7	36.4
Curr. Ratio	0.7	0.8	1.1	0.9	1.0	1.2	1.3	0.9	0.8	0.7
% LT Debt of Cap.	54.9	40.9	51.9	54.2	42.6	42.1	38.7	35.5	30.8	37.1
% Ret. on Assets	0.9	5.1	3.8	NM	NM	0.9	0.7	0.4	4.9	NA
% Ret. on Equity	1.0	13.5	9.9	NM	NM	1.8	1.9	0.2	9.7	NA

Data as orig reptd.; bef. results of disc opers/spec. items. Per share data adj. for stk. divs. Bold denotes diluted EPS (FASB 128)-prior periods restated. E-Estimated. NA-Not Available. NM-Not Meaningful. NR-Not Ranked.

Office—15375 Memorial Dr., Houston, TX 77079. **Tel**—(281) 589-4600. **Website**—http://www.cabotog.com **Chrmn, Pres & CEO**—R. R. Seegmiller. **VP-Fin**—P. F. Boling. **Secy**—Lisa A. Machesney. **VP, Treas & Investor Contact**—Scott C. Schroeder (281-589-4993). **Dirs**—R. F. Bailey, S. W. Bodman, H. O. Boswell, J. G. L. Cabot, W. E. Esler, W. H. Knoell, C. W. Nance, P. D. Peacock, R. R. Seegmiller, C. P. Siess Jr., W. P. Vititoe. **Transfer Agent & Registrar**—Boston EquiServe, L.P. **Incorporated**—in Delaware in 1989. **Empl**— 365. **S&P Analyst:** J.J.S.

STANDARD &POOR'S
STOCK REPORTS

Cambrex Corp.

NYSE Symbol **CBM**
In S&P SmallCap 600

23-OCT-99 **Industry:** Chemicals (Specialty)

Summary: This company produces and sells biotechnology products, chemical intermediates and specialty chemicals.

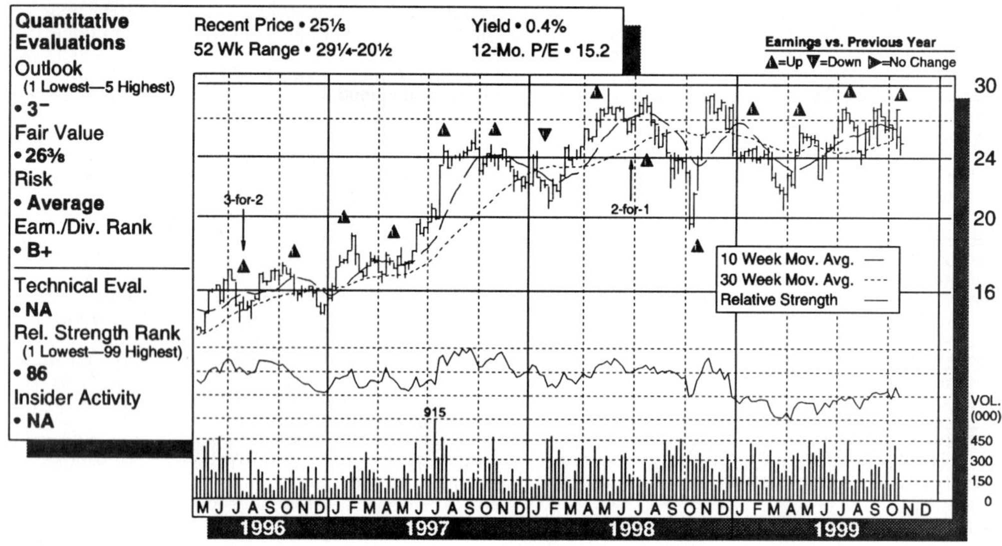

Business Profile - 21-OCT-99

In October 1999, CBM reported that in the third quarter human health sales were up 24% due to sales of generic pharmaceuticals, new product sales and the March 1999 acquisition of Irotec, a manufacturer of active pharmaceutical ingredients. Biotechnology sales increased 45% from shipments of cell culture, endotoxin detection products and the July 1999 acquisition of BioWhittaker Molecular Applications (formerly the BioProducts Division of FMC Corp.). Animal health/agriculture products decreased 16% due to reduced shipments of Vitamin B3 to animal feed markets. And the specialty business sales decreased 6%, reflecting lower sales of polymers and specialty castor oils. Royalty income ended in December 1998 with the termination of the exclusion portion of a license agreement with Mylan Laboratories.

Operational Review - 21-OCT-99

Gross sales in the nine months ended September 30, 1999, grew 7.6%, year to year, benefiting from both acquisition and internal growth in the human health and biotechnology product segments. Gross margins narrowed on the absence of royalties (ended in December 1998), as well as start-up and validation costs for a new large-scale cGMP plant in Ireland. After taxes at 32.4%, versus 41.1%, net income advanced 10%, to $31.8 million ($1.25 per share), from $28.9 million ($1.14).

Stock Performance - 22-OCT-99

In the past 30 trading days, CBM's shares have declined 0.22%, compared to a 4% fall in the S&P 500. Average trading volume for the past five days was 25,160 shares, compared with the 40-day moving average of 40,577 shares.

Key Stock Statistics

Dividend Rate/Share	0.12	Shareholders	4,372
Shs. outstg. (M)	24.6	Market cap. (B)	$0.685
Avg. daily vol. (M)	0.052	Inst. holdings	71%
Tang. Bk. Value/Share	6.15		
Beta	0.83		

Value of $10,000 invested 5 years ago: $ 43,072

Fiscal Year Ending Dec. 31

	1999	1998	1997	1996	1995	1994
Revenues (Million $)						
1Q	117.5	113.6	91.89	93.93	93.39	51.05
2Q	122.7	123.5	98.26	90.27	88.22	58.22
3Q	118.6	108.0	80.71	86.05	87.39	57.61
4Q	—	112.2	101.5	89.15	88.19	74.76
Yr.	—	457.2	371.3	359.4	357.2	241.6
Earnings Per Share ($)						
1Q	0.40	0.36	0.31	0.26	0.25	0.13
2Q	0.47	0.43	0.37	0.32	0.29	0.20
3Q	0.38	0.35	0.30	0.26	0.23	0.14
4Q	—	0.40	-0.26	0.35	0.22	0.18
Yr.	—	1.54	0.73	1.19	0.98	0.66

Next earnings report expected: late January

Dividend Data (Dividends have been paid since 1989.)

Amount ($)	Date Decl.	Ex-Div. Date	Stock of Record	Payment Date
0.030	Oct. 22	Nov. 04	Nov. 06	Nov. 20 '98
0.030	Jan. 28	Feb. 10	Feb. 12	Feb. 26 '99
0.030	Apr. 22	May. 05	May. 07	May. 21 '99
0.030	Jul. 23	Aug. 04	Aug. 06	Aug. 20 '99

Cambrex Corporation

Business Summary - 21-OCT-99

Cambrex Corporation provides products and services to the life sciences industries. The company has four distinct segments: human health (44% of 1998 gross sales), biotechnology (15%), animal health/agriculture (13%) and specialty business (28%). CBM exports products (15%) to various areas, primarily Western Europe, Asia and Latin America. Sales from international operations accounted for approximately 35% of 1998 gross sales.

CBM has focused on niche markets that have global opportunities, building on strong customer relations to enhance its new product pipeline, and supporting technology, while being a leader in environmental, health and safety performance. CBM has expanded operations through internal growth and through strategic acquisitions of product lines, technology and firms that aid its position in niche markets. In 1999 through October, the company acquired Irotec Laboratories, Ltd., a manufacturer of active pharmaceutical ingredients, which included a new cGMP pharmaceutical manufacturing plant; FMC Corporation's BioProducts business; and Poietic Technologies, Inc., the leading supplier of normal human cells of hemotopoietic origin.

The human health segment has eight principal product groups: active pharmaceutical ingredients (27% of 1998 gross sales), pharmaceutical intermediates (6%), imaging chemicals (3%), personal care ingredients (4%), biomedicals (1%), catalysts (2%), chiral technology (1%) and nutraceuticals (0.2%).

The biotechnology segment consists of cell culture products (10% of 1998 gross sales), including living cell cultures, cell culture media supplements; endotoxin detection products (4%) supplied to the biotechnology and pharmaceutical industries; and other (1%).

The animal health/agriculture segment consists of three product groups: Vitamin B3 (3% of 1998 gross sales), used in feed additives and for veterinary products; animal health products (4%) used in disease prevention; and agricultural intermediates (6%) used in crop protection.

The specialty business segment consists of two product groups: performance enhancing chemicals (18% of 1998 gross sales), which are designed to impart special properties when small quantities are included in the formulation of specific products; and polymer systems (10%), which include monomers or two component polymer systems for use in high volume, high performance applications.

In August 1999, CBM's BioWhittaker subsidiary completed a marketing and supply agreement with Osiris Therapeutics, Inc. covering adult stem cells, the progenitors of structural and connective tissues. And CBM's CasChem subsidiary began producing and marketing sebacic acid using a continuous process, also producing 2-octanone and 2-octanol with higher purity than currently available.

Per Share Data ($)										
(Year Ended Dec. 31)	**1998**	**1997**	**1996**	**1995**	**1994**	**1993**	**1992**	**1991**	**1990**	**1989**
Tangible Bk. Val.	6.12	4.13	7.66	6.14	6.39	5.62	5.21	4.88	4.97	5.19
Cash Flow	3.12	2.00	2.38	2.22	1.48	1.22	1.06	0.49	0.10	0.49
Earnings	1.54	0.73	1.19	0.98	0.65	0.55	0.42	0.00	-0.35	0.18
Dividends	0.11	0.10	0.08	0.07	0.07	0.07	0.07	0.07	0.07	0.02
Payout Ratio	7%	14%	7%	7%	10%	12%	15%	NM	NM	9%
Prices - High	29¾	26¼	17½	14½	9⅛	7⅛	6⅛	3⅜	4⅜	5¾
- Low	19¼	16	12⅞	8⅞	6⅝	5⅝	2¾	1 5/16	1⅜	4⅛
P/E Ratio - High	19	36	15	15	14	13	14	NM	NM	31
- Low	13	22	11	9	10	10	7	NM	NM	22
Income Statement Analysis (Million $)										
Revs.	457	374	359	357	242	197	179	145	134	131
Oper. Inc.	113	81.8	74.8	69.5	35.0	28.4	24.9	7.2	12.3	13.4
Depr.	40.1	31.1	28.4	25.0	14.0	10.7	9.3	6.9	6.5	6.8
Int. Exp.	10.5	5.6	6.2	11.1	4.7	2.8	2.5	2.7	2.2	1.4
Pretax Inc.	61.7	32.6	40.7	31.2	16.9	13.4	10.3	0.1	-4.3	5.1
Eff. Tax Rate	37%	45%	31%	37%	34%	36%	40%	40%	NM	40%
Net Inc.	39.1	17.8	28.2	19.7	11.1	8.6	6.2	0.0	-5.1	3.1
Balance Sheet & Other Fin. Data (Million $)										
Cash	48.5	21.5	7.3	4.8	9.1	0.2	0.6	0.1	2.2	0.8
Curr. Assets	232	185	137	144	131	66.8	59.4	48.2	54.3	59.7
Total Assets	617	552	404	403	360	167	148	112	110	129
Curr. Liab.	75.2	67.9	73.9	74.3	111	28.3	23.5	16.9	14.9	12.9
LT Debt	191	194	60.1	100	116	36.3	39.8	19.0	18.5	22.2
Common Eqty.	277	226	229	189	102	87.6	75.2	68.7	69.2	87.0
Total Cap.	520	464	311	309	232	130	118	91.0	91.0	116
Cap. Exp.	43.0	35.9	32.3	46.4	20.8	15.8	9.1	16.1	6.3	7.7
Cash Flow	79.2	48.9	56.7	44.6	25.1	19.4	15.6	6.9	1.4	9.9
Curr. Ratio	3.1	2.7	1.9	1.9	1.2	2.4	2.5	2.9	3.6	4.6
% LT Debt of Cap.	36.8	41.8	19.3	32.2	49.9	27.9	33.7	20.9	20.2	19.2
% Net Inc.of Revs.	8.6	4.8	7.8	5.5	4.6	4.4	3.5	NM	NM	2.3
% Ret. on Assets	6.7	3.7	7.0	5.2	4.2	5.3	4.7	NM	NM	2.5
% Ret. on Equity	15.6	7.8	13.5	13.5	11.6	10.2	8.6	NM	NM	3.6

Data as orig. reptd.; bef. results of disc. opers. and/or spec. items. Per share data adj. for stk. divs. as of ex-div. date. Bk. Val. figs. in Per Share Data incl. intangibles. Bold denotes diluted EPS (FASB 128). E-Estimated. NA-Not Available. NM-Not Meaningful. NR-Not Ranked.

Office—One Meadowlands Plaza, East Rutherford, NJ 07073. **Tel**—(201) 804-3000. **Fax**—(201) 804-9852. **Website**—http://www.cambrex.com **Chrmn**—C.C. Baldwin Jr. **Pres & CEO**—J.A. Mack. **VP, CFO & Investor Contact**—Douglas H. MacMillan (201) 804-3025. **Dirs**—C.C. Baldwin Jr., R.B. Dixon, G.J.W. Goodman, R.W. Haley, K.R. Harrigan, L.J. Hendrix, I. Kaufthal, W.B. Korb, R. LeBuhn, J.A. Mack, J.R. Miller, D.P. Phypers. **Transfer Agent & Registrar**—American Stock Transfer & Trust Co., NYC. **Incorporated**—in Delaware in 1983. **Empl**— 1,750. **S&P Analyst:** T.J. Vital

STANDARD &POOR'S
STOCK REPORTS

Canandaigua Brands

Nasdaq Symbol **CBRNA**

In S&P SmallCap 600

09-OCT-99

Industry: Beverages (Alcoholic)

Summary: This leading U.S. producer and marketer of alcoholic beverages (formerly Canandaigua Wine Co.) has grown rapidly in recent years, primarily through acquisitions.

S&P Opinion: Buy (★★★★★)

Recent Price • 58½
52 Wk Range • 61½-40
Yield • Nil
12-Mo. P/E • 16.9

Quantitative Evaluations
Outlook
(1 Lowest—5 Highest)
• **4**
Fair Value
• **84¼**
Risk
• **Average**
Earn./Div. Rank
• **B+**

Technical Eval.
• **Bullish** since 8/99
Rel. Strength Rank
(1 Lowest—99 Highest)
• **79**
Insider Activity
• **NA**

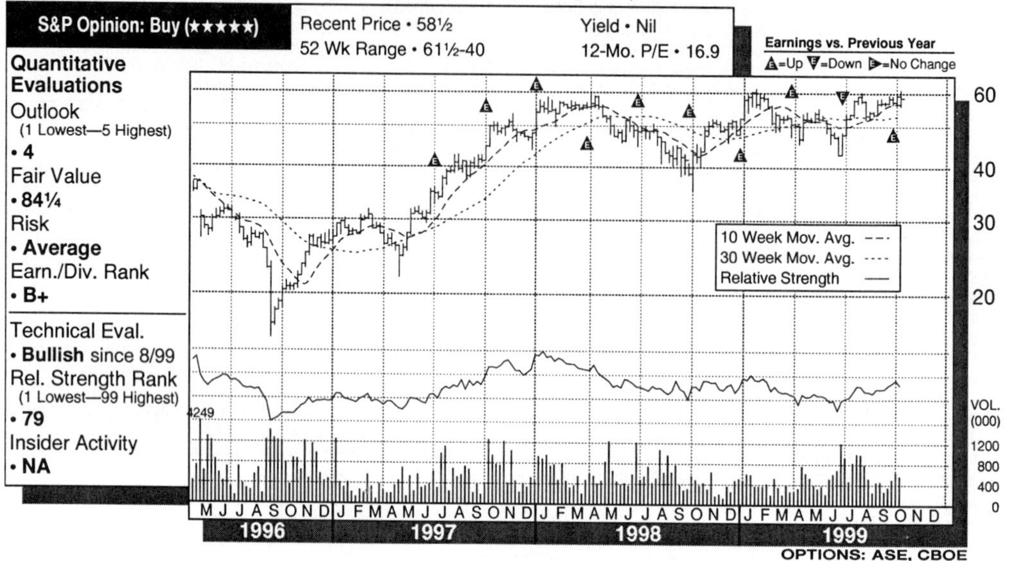

OPTIONS: ASE, CBOE

Overview - 04-OCT-99

Net sales (after excise taxes) are projected to rise at least 50% in FY 2000 (Feb.), reflecting contributions from several acquisitions, 16% to 18% unit volume growth for imported beers, and solid unit volume gains in other product segments. The company has made several acquisitions in the past year, including the December 1998 buyout of U.K.-based Matthew Clark plc, the April purchase of several Canadian whiskey brands from Diageo plc., and the recent acquisitions of Simi Winery and Franciscan Estates. Cost structure improvements and increasing emphasis on more profitable premium wines should help to offset the addition of lower margin sales from the Matthew Clark acquisition. Assuming a 2% to 3% reduction in the number of shares outstanding, EPS before special items should advance to $4.25 in FY 2000, from FY 99's $3.38.

Valuation - 04-OCT-99

The shares have rebounded from their summer lows, as the earnings outlook continues to improve, on strong volume gains across the company's beverage segments. Volume shipments of imported beers continue to exceed expectations, while wine volumes are showing solid gains, on strong new product growth and favorable consumption trends. The recent acquisitions of Franciscan Estates and Simi Winery positioned CBRNA as a major player in the fast growing, highly profitable premium wine segment. CBRNA has moved to reduce interest costs, converting a substantial portion of floating rate debt to fixed rate debt. Results should also benefit from cost reduction efforts, and EPS comparisons will be aided by aggressive share repurchases. We continue to rate the shares buy, at a recent level of only 14X our estimated FY 2000 EPS, a sharp discount to the P/Es of the S&P 500 and CBRNA's peers, and to the company's EPS growth rate.

Key Stock Statistics

S&P EPS Est. 2000	4.25	Tang. Bk. Value/Share	NM
P/E on S&P Est. 2000	13.8	Beta	0.99
S&P EPS Est. 2001	4.90	Shareholders	1,700
Dividend Rate/Share	Nil	Market cap. (B)	$0.866
Shs. outstg. (M)	18.0	Inst. holdings	61%
Avg. daily vol. (M)	0.101		

Value of $10,000 invested 5 years ago: $ 18,571

Fiscal Year Ending Feb. 28

	2000	1999	1998	1997	1996	1995
Revenues (Million $)						
1Q	530.2	312.9	306.0	276.5	—	243.5
2Q	621.6	349.4	301.5	279.2	—	210.9
3Q	—	375.6	322.7	317.7	—	222.8
4Q	—	459.4	282.6	261.6	—	229.3
Yr.	—	1,497	1,213	1,135	535.0	906.5
Earnings Per Share ($)						
1Q	**0.59**	**0.70**	**0.53**	**0.43**	—	0.61
2Q	**1.14**	**0.83**	**0.65**	**0.25**	—	0.50
3Q	—	**1.07**	**0.92**	**0.43**	—	0.53
4Q	—	**0.65**	**0.53**	**0.31**	—	0.50
Yr.	—	**3.30**	**2.62**	**1.42**	0.17	2.14

Next earnings report expected: late December

Dividend Data

No cash dividends have been paid. The Class A and Class B shares were split three for two in 1991 and 1992.

Canandaigua Brands, Inc.

Business Summary - 04-OCT-99

Through an aggressive acquisition policy over the past few years, Canandaigua Brands, Inc. (formerly Canandaigua Wine Co.) has become the second largest U.S. supplier of wines, the second largest importer of beers, and the fourth largest supplier of distilled spirits. The December 1998 acquisition of Matthew Clark plc established the company as a leading alcoholic beverage producer and wholesaler in the U.K. CBRNA markets more than 180 brands, including imported beers, wines, spirits, cider and bottled water.

The Canandaigua Wine division produces, bottles, imports and markets table wine, dessert wine, sparkling wine and brandy in the U.S. Leading brands include Inglenook, Almaden, Paul Masson, Arbor Mist, Manischewitz, Taylor, Marcus James, Estate Cellars, Vina Santa Carolina, Dunnwood, Mystic Cliffs, Cook's J. Roget, Richards Wild Irish Rose, and Paul Masson Grande Amber Brandy. Most of the wine is marketed in the popularly priced segment of the market. As a related part of its wine business, the company is one of the leading U.S. producers of grape juice concentrate.

The Barton division produces, bottles, imports and markets a diversified line of beer and distilled spirits. Barton distributes five of the 25 leading imported beer brands in the U.S.: Corona Extra, Modelo Especial, Corona Light, Pacifico and St. Pauli Girl. Other imported beer brands include Negra Modelo, Tsingtao, Peroni, Double Diamond, and Tetleys English Ale. Principle distilled spirits brands include Black Velvet, Fleischmann's, Mr. Boston, Canadian LTD, Chi-Chi's prepared cocktails, Ten High, Montezuma, Barton, Inver House, and Monte Alban distilled spirits.

CBRNA is working to reposition its portfolio of brands to benefit from growth trends in the alcoholic beverage industry. To achieve these goals, the company intends to adjust the price/volume relationships of certain brands; develop new brands, and introduce line extensions; expand geographic distribution; and acquire businesses that meet its strategic and financial objectives. The December 1998 acquisition of U.K.-based Matthew Clark plc provided a presence in the U.K., and a platform for growth in the European market. Matthew Clark brings a number of leading market positions in the U.K., including positions as leading producer of branded boxed wine, leading branded producer of fortified British wine, leading branded bottler of sparkling water, and second leading producer of cider.

In April 1999, furthering its expansion, CBRNA acquired several Canadian whiskey brands, including Black Velvet, from Diageo plc, for $185.5 million. In June 1999, the company completed the purchase of Franciscan Vineyards, Inc. and Simi Winery, Inc., positioning itself as a major player in the premium wine market.

Per Share Data ($) (Year Ended Feb. 28)	1999	1998	1997	1996	1995	1994	1993	1992	1991	1990
Tangible Bk. Val.	NM	9.29	19.32	18.17	17.97	12.76	9.92	8.21	5.76	4.90
Cash Flow	5.35	4.36	3.03	0.86	3.22	1.41	1.92	1.66	1.38	0.98
Earnings	3.30	2.62	1.41	0.17	2.14	0.74	1.30	1.08	0.84	0.46
Dividends	Nil	Nil	Nil	Nil	Nil	Nil	Nil	Nil	Nil	Nil
Payout Ratio	Nil	Nil	Nil	Nil	Nil	Nil	Nil	Nil	Nil	Nil
Cal. Yrs.	1998	1997	1996	1995	1994	1993	1992	1991	1990	1989
Prices - High	59 3/4	57 5/8	39 1/2	53	53	38 1/2	32	17	12	6 1/4
- Low	35 1/4	21 7/8	15 3/4	29 3/4	29 3/4	20 1/4	13 1/2	10 1/2	5 1/4	4 1/8
P/E Ratio - High	18	22	28	NM	25	52	25	16	14	14
- Low	11	8	11	NM	14	27	10	10	6	9
Income Statement Analysis (Million $)										
Revs.	1,497	1,213	1,135	535	907	630	306	245	177	180
Oper. Inc.	187	150	113	40.4	114	71.5	38.8	30.1	20.3	15.2
Depr.	38.6	33.2	31.9	14.0	20.7	10.5	7.4	6.1	5.0	5.0
Int. Exp.	41.5	32.2	34.1	17.4	25.1	18.4	6.3	6.5	4.6	4.6
Pretax Inc.	104	84.9	47.8	6.7	66.7	18.9	25.3	17.9	11.7	6.4
Eff. Tax Rate	59%	41%	42%	50%	39%	38%	38%	37%	34%	31%
Net Inc.	61.9	50.1	27.8	3.3	41.0	11.7	15.6	11.4	7.7	4.4
Balance Sheet & Other Fin. Data (Million $)										
Cash	27.6	1.2	10.0	3.3	4.2	1.5	3.7	2.2	28.6	26.3
Curr. Assets	856	564	501	518	402	454	244	134	98.0	91.0
Total Assets	1,794	1,073	1,020	1,055	786	827	355	218	147	143
Curr. Liab.	832	283	247	300	175	238	96.8	52.2	24.6	23.8
LT Debt	415	309	339	328	199	289	108	61.9	62.3	63.1
Common Eqty.	435	415	365	357	352	204	126	95.5	52.0	47.2
Total Cap.	1,355	783	765	742	600	537	255	165	122	118
Cap. Exp.	49.9	31.2	31.6	16.1	37.0	141	20.3	38.1	4.4	4.1
Cash Flow	101	83.2	59.7	17.3	61.7	22.3	23.0	17.4	12.7	9.4
Curr. Ratio	1.0	2.0	2.0	1.7	2.3	1.9	2.5	2.6	4.0	3.8
% LT Debt of Cap.	30.6	39.5	44.3	44.2	33.2	53.8	42.5	37.5	51.0	53.3
% Net Inc.of Revs.	4.1	4.1	2.4	0.6	4.6	1.9	5.1	4.6	4.4	2.5
% Ret. on Assets	4.3	4.8	2.7	NA	5.1	1.8	5.3	5.6	5.5	3.1
% Ret. on Equity	14.6	12.8	7.7	NA	14.8	6.5	13.5	14.0	16.0	9.9

Data as orig. reptd.; bef. results of disc. opers. and/or spec. items. Per share data adj. for stk. divs. as of ex-div. date. E-Estimated. NA-Not Available. NM-Not Meaningful. NR-Not Ranked. Yrs. ended Aug. 31 prior to 1996; FY 96 revs., EPS and inc. data are for six mos.

Office—235 N. Bloomfield Rd., Canandaigua, NY 14424. **Tel**—(716) 393-4130. **Fax**—(716) 394-6017. **Chrmn & CEO**—Richard Sands. **EVP & Secy**—Robert Sands. **SVP & CFO**—T. Summer. **VP & Investor Contact**—Kristen Jenks. **Dirs**—G. Bresler, J. A. Locke, T. C. McDermott, M. Sands, Richard Sands, Robert Sands, P. L. Smith. **Transfer Agent & Registrar**—Bank of Boston. **Incorporated**—in Delaware in 1972. **Empl**— 4,230. **S&P Analyst:** Richard Joy

Capital Re

NYSE Symbol **KRE**

In S&P SmallCap 600

09-OCT-99 **Industry:** Insurance (Property-Casualty)

Summary: This specialty reinsurance company has agreed to be acquired by ACE Limited (NYSE: ACL).

Quantitative Evaluations

Outlook (1 Lowest—5 Highest)
• **5**

Fair Value
• **17½**

Risk
• **Average**

Earn./Div. Rank
• **B+**

Technical Eval.
• **Bearish** since 6/99

Rel. Strength Rank (1 Lowest—99 Highest)
• **76**

Insider Activity
• **NA**

Recent Price • 13
52 Wk Range • 22⅝-9⅜
Yield • 1.2%
12-Mo. P/E • NM

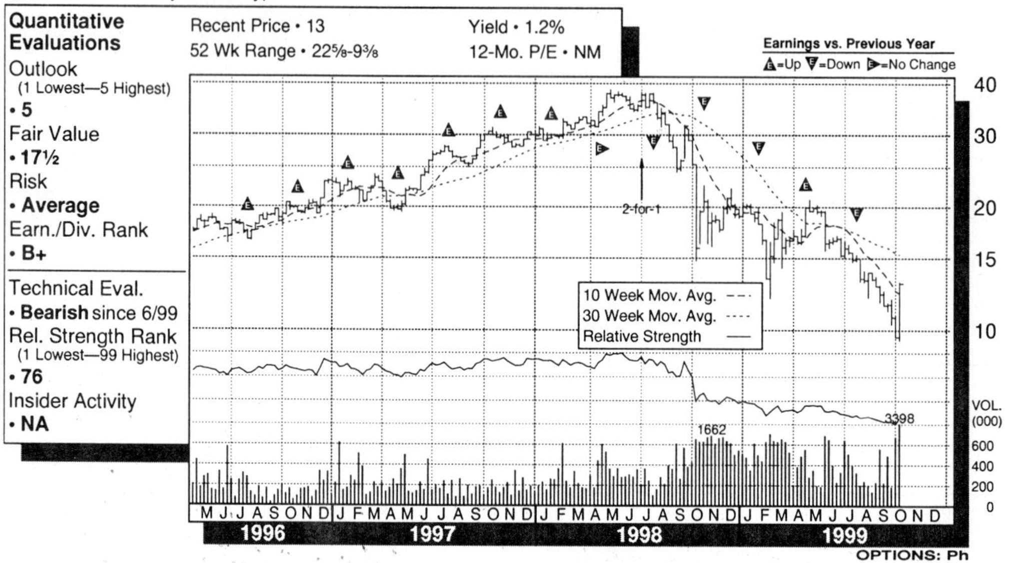

OPTIONS: Ph

Business Profile - 02-JUN-99

On May 27, 1999, Capital Re announced it had executed a binding letter of intent to merge with Bermuda-based insurer ACE Limited (NYSE: ACL). If closed as expected in the third quarter of 1999, KRE shareholders would receive 0.6 shares of ACL for each share of KRE at closing, subject to a maximum value of $22 per share. Based on ACL's closing price of May 26, 1999, the merger transaction value of KRE shares would be $18.90 per share. The acquisition news was accompanied by notice that KRE has a $67 million exposure to transactions with International Financial Services Life Insurance Co. that are under investigation by Missouri and Mississippi authorities. KRE's results in recent quarters have been hurt by other portfolio losses. In February 1999, a subsidiary of ACL agreed to invest $75 million in KRE through a common stock purchase; final regulatory approval is expected soon.

Operational Review - 02-JUN-99

In the first three months of 1999, total revenues increased 1.0%, year to year (as restated), as higher investment income and income from an affiliate outweighed lower net premiums earned. Total expenses rose 7.9%, sending pretax income down 7.3%. After taxes at 24.9%, versus 27.1%, net income fell 4.4%, to $19,379,000 ($0.60 a share), from $20,276,000 ($0.62, as restated). Results exclude losses from discontinued operations of $0.20 and $0.01 a share in the respective interims.

Stock Performance - 08-OCT-99

In the past 30 trading days, KRE's shares have increased 1%, compared to a 0.91% fall in the S&P 500. Average trading volume for the past five days was 679,520 shares, compared with the 40-day moving average of 171,436 shares.

Key Stock Statistics

Dividend Rate/Share	0.16	Shareholders	36
Shs. outstg. (M)	36.5	Market cap. (B)	$0.475
Avg. daily vol. (M)	0.278	Inst. holdings	39%
Tang. Bk. Value/Share	15.37		
Beta	0.53		

Value of $10,000 invested 5 years ago: $ 10,522

Fiscal Year Ending Dec. 31

	1999	1998	1997	1996	1995	1994
Revenues (Million $)						
1Q	61.35	70.73	—	32.54	25.57	27.46
2Q	59.30	70.49	—	35.34	28.10	27.00
3Q	—	64.80	—	34.81	24.90	23.02
4Q	—	57.56	—	41.93	28.51	23.97
Yr.	—	234.9	201.7	146.4	107.1	101.5
Earnings Per Share ($)						
1Q	**0.60**	**0.53**	**0.53**	0.42	**0.38**	0.35
2Q	**-2.79**	**0.49**	**0.49**	**0.42**	**0.38**	0.35
3Q	—	**0.44**	**0.56**	0.44	**0.38**	0.33
4Q	—	**-0.31**	**59.00**	0.52	**0.40**	0.32
Yr.	—	**1.35**	**2.18**	1.80	**1.52**	**1.33**

Next earnings report expected: early November

Dividend Data (Dividends have been paid since 1992.)

Amount ($)	Date Decl.	Ex-Div. Date	Stock of Record	Payment Date
0.040	Dec. 10	Dec. 18	Dec. 22	Dec. 29 '98
0.040	Mar. 10	Mar. 18	Mar. 22	Mar. 29 '99
0.040	May. 20	Jun. 15	Jun. 17	Jun. 24 '99
0.040	Aug. 23	Sep. 20	Sep. 22	Sep. 29 '99

Capital Re Corporation

Business Summary - 02-JUN-99

Capital Re Corp. is an insurance holding company for a group of reinsurance companies. Operations are pursued through two principal divisions: financial guaranty insurance (municipal and non-municipal reinsurance and credit default swaps); and financial risks (mortgage guaranty reinsurance, trade credit reinsurance, title reinsurance, and financial solutions).

On May 27, 1999, KRE announced it had executed a binding letter of intent to merge with ACE Limited (NYSE: ACL), a Bermuda-based insurer. Terms call for KRE shareholders to receive 0.6 shares of ACL for each share of KRE at closing, which is expected in the third quarter of 1999, subject to a maximum value of $22 per share. The company also has a pending agreement with ACL whereby a subsidiary of ACL is to invest $75 million in KRE through a common stock purchase; this investment is expected to proceed shortly after final regulatory approval is received.

Gross premiums written in 1998 totaled $213.9 million ($169.9 million in 1997), and broke out by business line as follows: municipal 26% (31%), non-municipal 19% (10%), mortgage 31% (42%), credit 16% (14%), title 3% (2%), and financial solutions 5% (1%). The geographic diversification of gross premiums written was 79.3% (76.7%) U.S. and 20.7% (23.3%) non-U.S.

In all of its principal areas of specialization, KRE seeks to provide innovative reinsurance solutions to satisfy the diverse risk and financial management demands of its primary clients. These solutions often take the form of complex reinsurance arrangements that provide value other than pure risk management, such as financial statement benefit, regulatory relief, and rating agency qualified capital.

As of year-end 1998, Capital Re was providing its reinsurance products through five subsidiaries: Capital Reinsurance Co., KRE Reinsurance Ltd., Capital Credit Reinsurance Co. Ltd., Capital Mortgage Reinsurance Co., and Capital Title Reinsurance Co.

Capital Reinsurance is engaged in the business of financial guaranty reinsurance, primarily the reinsurance of municipal and non-municipal bond insurance obligations. KRE Reinsurance Ltd. also assumes financial guaranty risk, both as a retrocessionaire of Capital Reinsurance and as a direct reinsurer of third party primary insurers.

Capital Credit Reinsurance writes trade credit reinsurance in the U.S. and Europe. Capital Mortgage Reinsurance reinsures residential mortgage guaranty insurance obligations. Capital Title Reinsurance reinsures title insurance policies.

Per Share Data ($) (Year Ended Dec. 31)	1998	1997	1996	1995	1994	1993	1992	1991	1990	1989
Tangible Bk. Val.	19.39	17.71	15.18	14.09	11.01	10.83	9.36	8.19	7.11	NA
Oper. Earnings	1.38	NA	NA	NA	1.30	1.20	0.95	1.00	NA	NA
Earnings	1.35	2.15	1.80	1.54	1.34	1.22	1.08	1.07	0.97	NA
Dividends	0.16	0.14	0.13	0.10	0.10	0.10	0.08	NA	NA	NA
Payout Ratio	12%	7%	7%	7%	7%	8%	7%	NA	NA	NA
Prices - High	38¾	31½	23⅜	15⅞	13¾	14½	12⅛	NA	NA	NA
- Low	14¾	19⅜	14¼	11	9¼	10¼	8⅝	NA	NA	NA
P/E Ratio - High	29	15	13	10	10	12	11	NA	NA	NA
- Low	11	9	8	7	7	8	8	NA	NA	NA
Income Statement Analysis (Million $)										
Premium Inc.	168	134	92.4	60.1	58.9	44.9	27.8	19.7	13.8	10.3
Net Invest. Inc.	64.9	56.6	51.6	46.7	40.1	32.1	23.8	16.5	15.5	14.6
Oth. Revs.	1.7	11.4	2.4	2.0	2.5	2.4	6.9	5.0	1.8	1.3
Total Revs.	235	202	146	107	102	79.5	58.4	41.3	31.0	26.2
Pretax Inc.	60.6	102	77.2	60.1	53.1	49.9	39.6	28.6	22.7	20.0
Net Oper. Inc.	45.1	NA	NA	NA	38.7	35.8	26.6	20.7	16.4	12.7
Net Inc.	44.2	70.1	56.5	45.5	39.8	36.4	30.2	22.2	16.9	13.5
Balance Sheet & Other Fin. Data (Million $)										
Cash & Equiv.	25.3	18.9	27.6	14.0	13.5	10.0	8.3	5.5	4.3	6.0
Premiums Due	17.1	27.6	5.8	17.9	4.0	3.1	13.2	9.8	9.6	4.3
Invest. Assets: Bonds	1,087	1,011	901	772	574	514	416	238	180	NA
Invest. Assets: Stocks	Nil	Nil	Nil	Nil	Nil	Nil	Nil	Nil	Nil	NA
Invest. Assets: Loans	Nil	Nil	Nil	Nil	Nil	Nil	Nil	Nil	Nil	NA
Invest. Assets: Total	1,190	101	901	772	637	552	444	273	203	181
Deferred Policy Costs	135	135	111	102	90.6	75.5	53.9	40.9	28.2	19.7
Total Assets	1,509	1,388	1,156	982	810	712	538	339	254	212
Debt	150	175	100	90.7	90.7	90.7	74.6	2.3	Nil	NA
Common Eqty.	611	569	489	412	326	324	280	190	145	122
Prop. & Cas. Loss Ratio	51.4	13.6	NA	NA	NA	NA	NA	NA	NA	NA
Prop. & Cas. Expense Ratio	47.8	47.6	NA	NA	NA	NA	NA	NA	NA	NA
Prop. & Cas. Combined Ratio	99.2	61.2	NA	NA	NA	NA	NA	NA	NA	NA
% Return On Revs.	18.8	48.6	38.6	42.6	39.2	45.7	51.6	53.6	54.4	51.7
% Ret. on Equity	7.5	13.2	12.5	5.1	12.2	12.3	12.8	14.3	12.7	11.7

Data as orig reptd.; bef. results of disc opers/spec. items. Per share data adj. for stk. divs. Bold denotes diluted EPS (FASB 128)-prior periods restated. E-Estimated. NA-Not Available. NM-Not Meaningful. NR-Not Ranked.

Office—1325 Ave. of the Americas, 18th Fl., New York, NY 10019. **Tel**—(212) 974-0100. **Chrmn & CEO**—J. F. Jurschak. **Pres & COO**—J. W. Swain. **EVP & CFO**—D. A. Buzen. **SVP & Secy**—A. S. Roseman. **Investor Contact**—Cathy C. Bailey. **Dirs**—H. W. Conrad Jr., D. J. Frederico, R. L. Huber, S. D. Kesler, J. F. Jurschak, J. R. Respess, P. H. Robinson, E. L. Russell, B. D. Stewart, J. F. Stuermer, J. W. Swain. **Transfer Agent & Registrar**—Registrar & Transfer Co., Cranford, NJ. **Incorporated**—in Delaware in 1991. **Empl**— 67. **S&P Analyst:** T. W. Smith, CFA

STANDARD
&POOR'S
STOCK REPORTS

Caraustar Industries

NASDAQ Symbol **CSAR**

In S&P SmallCap 600

09-OCT-99

Industry: Paper & Forest Products

Summary: This major manufacturer of recycled paperboard and converted paperboard products operates 51 converting facilities and 25 recycling and waste collection facilities.

Quantitative Evaluations

Outlook
(1 Lowest—5 Highest)
• **2+**

Fair Value
• **24½**

Risk
• **Average**

Earn./Div. Rank
• **A-**

Technical Eval.
• **Bearish** since 9/99

Rel. Strength Rank
(1 Lowest—99 Highest)
• **76**

Insider Activity
• **Neutral**

Recent Price • 24⅞
52 Wk Range • 30¼-19¾
Yield • 2.9%
12-Mo. P/E • 13.3

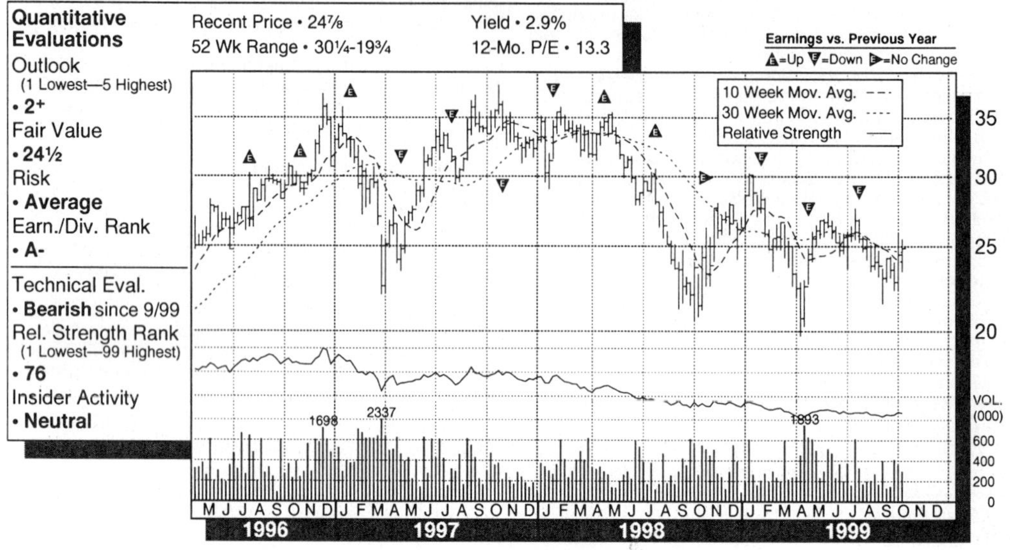

Business Profile - 10-AUG-99

This company, which initiated an operating cost reduction plan during 1998, is seeking to expand its presence in the markets for more sophisticated tubes and cores, which require stronger paper grades and new converting technology. CSAR believes that these markets, which include the yarn carrier and plastic film sectors, offer significant growth potential and potentially higher operating margins. In April 1999, CSAR acquired International Paper's recycled boxboard mill in Sprague, CT. Also in the second quarter, the company acquired Tenneco's folding carton business ($106 million in sales), and sold publicly $200 million of notes. The company also will continue to buy back stock.

Operational Review - 10-AUG-99

Net sales in the first half of 1999 advanced 9.1%, year to year, reflecting higher mill and converting unit volume due to acquisitions. Gross margins narrowed on higher operating costs due to weak production in basic manufacturing sectors, and with higher SG&A expenses and a rise in interest expense offsetting increased equity in income of affiliates, net income fell 18%, to $21,731,000 ($0.87 a share, diluted, on 2.0% fewer shares), from $26,508,000 ($1.04). CSAR expects earnings to improve during the balance of the year , with recent price increases and the integration of acquired businesses leading to sharply better results for 2000.

Stock Performance - 08-OCT-99

In the past 30 trading days, CSAR's shares have increased 5%, compared to a 0.91% fall in the S&P 500. Average trading volume for the past five days was 58,580 shares, compared with the 40-day moving average of 55,062 shares.

Key Stock Statistics

Dividend Rate/Share	0.72	Shareholders	4,500
Shs. outstg. (M)	25.0	Market cap. (B)	$0.622
Avg. daily vol. (M)	0.060	Inst. holdings	56%
Tang. Bk. Value/Share	4.88		
Beta	0.45		

Value of $10,000 invested 5 years ago: $ 16,712

Fiscal Year Ending Dec. 31

	1999	1998	1997	1996	1995	1994
Revenues (Million $)						
1Q	187.6	176.9	157.6	144.5	130.4	97.00
2Q	212.5	189.7	160.8	140.4	139.7	102.7
3Q	—	188.5	173.7	158.2	138.0	112.4
4Q	—	181.8	176.0	159.6	136.6	119.1
Yr.	—	736.9	668.1	602.7	544.6	431.2
Earnings Per Share ($)						
1Q	**0.46**	**0.52**	**0.47**	**0.53**	0.35	0.29
2Q	**0.41**	**0.52**	**0.51**	**0.61**	0.40	0.31
3Q	—	**0.50**	**0.50**	**0.58**	0.40	0.36
4Q	—	**0.50**	**0.55**	**0.56**	0.51	0.42
Yr.	—	**2.04**	**2.03**	**2.28**	**1.66**	1.38

Next earnings report expected: mid October

Dividend Data (Dividends have been paid since 1993.)

Amount ($)	Date Decl.	Ex-Div. Date	Stock of Record	Payment Date
0.180	Oct. 26	Dec. 15	Dec. 17	Jan. 07 '99
0.180	Feb. 16	Mar. 17	Mar. 19	Apr. 06 '99
0.180	Apr. 27	Jun. 16	Jun. 18	Jul. 06 '99
0.180	Jul. 20	Sep. 15	Sep. 17	Oct. 05 '99

A Division of The McGraw-Hill Companies

Business Summary - 10-AUG-99

Caraustar Industries, Inc. (CSAR) continues to grow by acquiring companies that can aid its principal operations and closing those that are not a strategic fit. The company manufactures recycled paperboard and converted paperboard products through 91 facilities in the U.S., Canada, Mexico and the U.K. It makes its products primarily from recovered fiber, which is derived from recycled wastepaper. CSAR also has an equity interest in a gypsum wallboard manufacturing plant, a specialty paperboard converting plant and two tube plants.

The company's primary manufacturing activity is the production of uncoated recycled paperboard. In this process, wastepaper is reduced to pulp, cleaned and refined and then processed into various grades of paperboard for internal consumption or sale in four principal markets: tubes, cores and composite containers; folding cartons; gypsum wallboard facing paper; and other specialty and converted products. CSAR is the only major producer of recycled paperboard products operating in all four of these markets. The company operates 15 recycled paperboard mills in 12 states. In 1998, 36% of the recycled paperboard sold by its paperboard mills was consumed internally by CSAR converting facilities; the remaining 64% was sold to manufacturers in various industries. External sales of unconverted paperboard accounted for 37% of 1998 net sales.

CSAR derived 34% of net sales (17% of operating income) in 1998 from sales of tubes, cores and composite containers; 42% (75%) from paperboard; and 24% (8%) from carton and custom packaging.

The company's tube and core converting plants obtain most of their recycled paperboard from its paperboard mills. Because of the relatively high cost of shipping tubes and cores, facilities generally serve customers within a relatively small geographic area. During the five years through December 31, 1998, the company spent an average of $33 million annually for capital expenditures. CSAR anticipates capital expenditures of $38 million in 1999.

During 1998, the company continued to expand in its primary markets through acquisitions. In June 1998, the company acquired Tenneco Packaging's 20% stake in the CPI joint venture for $27 million, increasing CSAR's interest in the CPI operations to 100%. In March 1998, CSAR acquired Chesapeake Paperboard Co. ($42 million in revenues) for $21 million (including $8.2 million of assumed debt), expanding its annual recycled paperboard capacity to over 1,050,000 tons. In August 1997, the company acquired Oak Tree Packaging Corp. ($44 million in annual revenues; three folding carton facilities) for $16.9 million in equity and the assumption of $17 million in debt and preferred stock.

During 1998, CSAR repurchased 1,043,000 of its shares for $25 million.

Per Share Data ($) (Year Ended Dec. 31)	1998	1997	1996	1995	1994	1993	1992	1991	1990	1989
Tangible Bk. Val.	4.59	4.32	3.57	4.73	3.76	2.86	1.93	-3.89	NA	NA
Cash Flow	3.56	3.37	3.31	2.34	1.95	1.57	1.74	1.68	NA	NA
Earnings	2.04	2.03	2.28	1.66	1.38	1.08	1.26	1.19	NA	NA
Dividends	0.64	0.58	0.50	0.43	0.38	0.33	0.08	Nil	NA	NA
Payout Ratio	31%	29%	22%	26%	27%	30%	8%	Nil	NA	NA
Prices - High	36	38 1/8	37 1/4	23	22 1/2	20 1/4	20 1/4	NA	NA	NA
- Low	20 1/2	22	18 5/8	15 3/4	15	13 1/4	14 7/8	NA	NA	NA
P/E Ratio - High	18	19	16	14	16	19	16	NA	NA	NA
- Low	10	11	8	9	11	12	12	NA	NA	NA
Income Statement Analysis (Million $)										
Revs.	737	668	603	545	456	365	309	276	NA	NA
Oper. Inc.	134	130	125	93.0	78.9	61.0	61.7	59.1	NA	NA
Depr.	38.7	34.0	26.3	17.7	14.5	12.5	9.5	8.5	NA	NA
Int. Exp.	16.1	14.0	10.6	7.0	6.9	6.8	12.3	16.4	NA	NA
Pretax Inc.	83.0	81.7	95.2	69.1	57.6	42.5	39.9	34.2	NA	NA
Eff. Tax Rate	37%	38%	38%	38%	38%	36%	38%	38%	NA	NA
Net Inc.	51.8	51.1	57.9	43.0	35.5	27.3	24.9	21.2	NA	NA
Balance Sheet & Other Fin. Data (Million $)										
Cash	2.6	1.4	11.9	8.8	12.5	14.4	23.7	3.1	NA	NA
Curr. Assets	155	141	127	114	101	82.6	75.1	48.8	NA	NA
Total Assets	619	550	476	322	267	221	184	134	NA	NA
Curr. Liab.	103	69.3	74.7	67.1	52.3	39.6	28.6	47.4	NA	NA
LT Debt	82.9	83.1	83.2	83.4	83.0	84.0	83.0	126	NA	NA
Common Eqty.	233	214	171	139	102	74.4	47.6	-68.7	NA	NA
Total Cap.	360	343	292	245	204	171	146	71.0	NA	NA
Cap. Exp.	40.7	36.2	32.0	28.0	29.3	21.3	16.6	10.6	NA	NA
Cash Flow	90.5	85.1	84.2	60.7	50.0	39.8	34.4	29.8	NA	NA
Curr. Ratio	1.5	2.0	1.7	1.7	1.9	2.1	2.6	1.0	NA	NA
% LT Debt of Cap.	23.0	24.2	28.4	34.0	41.0	48.9	57.3	176.7	NA	NA
% Net Inc.of Revs.	7.0	7.6	9.6	7.9	7.8	7.5	8.1	7.7	NA	NA
% Ret. on Assets	8.9	9.9	14.5	14.6	14.5	13.4	13.5	NA	NA	NA
% Ret. on Equity	23.0	26.5	37.3	35.7	39.9	44.6	NM	NA	NA	NA

Data as orig. reptd.; bef. results of disc. opers. and/or spec. items. Per share data adj. for stk. divs. as of ex-div. date. Bold denotes diluted EPS (FASB 128). E-Estimated. NA-Not Available. NM-Not Meaningful. NR-Not Ranked.

Office—3100 Washington St., Austell, GA 30001. **Tel**—(770) 948-3101. **Chrmn**—R. M. Robinson II. **Pres & CEO**—T. V. Brown. **VP, CFO & Investor Contact**—H. Lee Thrash III. **Secy**—M. R. Mays. **Dirs**—T. V. Brown, J. H. Hance Jr., R. M. Holt Jr., D. M. Love, J. D. Munford, B. M. Prillaman, R. M. Robinson II, J. E. Rogers, H. L. Thrash III. **Transfer Agent & Registrar**—First Union National Bank of North Carolina, Charlotte. **Incorporated**—in North Carolina in 1980. **Empl**— 5,063. **S&P Analyst:** Stewart Scharf

Carmike Cinemas

NYSE Symbol **CKE**

In S&P SmallCap 600

09-OCT-99

Industry: Entertainment

Summary: This company is the largest U.S. motion picture exhibitor in terms of total theatres operated.

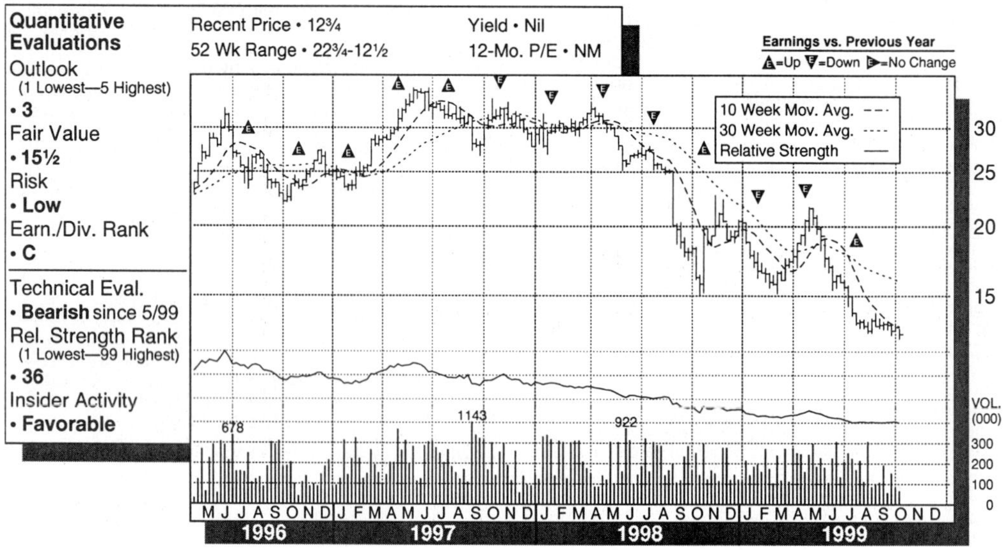

Business Profile - 08-JUL-99

The company attributed disappointing first quarter theatre attendance to the lack of blockbuster movies (such as Titanic in the 1998 period). To help bolster earnings, CKE has been focusing on cost cutting and cost controls. In the second quarter, the company intended to open five new complexes, with 79 screens, and to reopen 53 screens that were closed in the first quarter for stadium retro-fits. In the first quarter, CKE placed privately $200 million of senior subordinated notes due 2009, amended its revolving credit facility, and obtained a $75 million term loan.

Operational Review - 08-JUL-99

Total revenues in the three months ended March 31, 1999, declined 17%, as decreased attendance reflected the absence of blockbuster films. Results were hurt by the combination of fixed costs with lower revenues; operating income fell 39%. With higher interest expense and depreciation charges, after tax benefits of $3.7 million, versus taxes at 38.0%, a loss of $2.3 million ($0.27 a share, after preferred dividends) contrasted with income of $3.8 million ($0.33). Results in 1999 exclude a charge of $0.56 a share related to debt restructuring.

Stock Performance - 08-OCT-99

In the past 30 trading days, CKE's shares have declined 3%, compared to a 0.91% fall in the S&P 500. Average trading volume for the past five days was 12,860 shares, compared with the 40-day moving average of 21,087 shares.

Key Stock Statistics

Dividend Rate/Share	Nil	Shareholders	800
Shs. outstg. (M)	11.4	Market cap. (B)	$0.128
Avg. daily vol. (M)	0.017	Inst. holdings	63%
Tang. Bk. Value/Share	9.59		
Beta	0.72		

Value of $10,000 invested 5 years ago: $ 7,117

Fiscal Year Ending Dec. 31

	1999	1998	1997	1996	1995	1994
Revenues (Million $)						
1Q	97.72	117.1	108.5	92.16	63.90	67.43
2Q	125.3	110.7	110.1	104.7	91.23	68.09
3Q	—	134.7	128.7	121.1	112.4	109.0
4Q	—	119.0	111.3	108.8	97.20	83.10
Yr.	—	481.6	458.6	426.7	364.8	327.6
Earnings Per Share ($)						
1Q	-0.27	**0.33**	**0.35**	**-2.30**	-0.18	0.20
2Q	**0.28**	**0.03**	**0.53**	**0.43**	0.37	0.20
3Q	—	**0.77**	**0.72**	**0.85**	0.70	1.25
4Q	—	**-3.87**	**0.18**	**0.37**	0.28	0.36
Yr.	—	-2.73	**1.78**	**-0.65**	1.16	2.00

Next earnings report expected: mid November

Dividend Data

No dividends have been paid since the company's initial public stock offering. Carmike's loan agreement prohibits the payment of cash dividends.

Carmike Cinemas, Inc.

Business Summary - 08-JUL-99

Carmike is the largest U.S. motion picture exhibitor, in terms of the number of theatres operated, and the third largest, in terms of the number of screens operated. The company did not reach this position by chance. Its growth strategy includes acquiring theatre chains, and building its own theatres and screens in markets with little or no competition.

As of March 31, 1999, the company was operating 2,653 screens at 463 locations in 36 states. Theatres are principally in smaller communities, with populations ranging from 7,700 to 456,000, and where CKE is the sole or leading exhibitor.

In 1998, CKE increased its screens per theatre to 5.7 from 5.2, building multiplex theatres with 12 to 20 screens each. An increase in the number of screens per theatre boosts profit margins, as infrastructure, such as box office and concession stands, is leveraged over more movie selections and seats. Most company theatres principally exhibit first-run films, but CKE also converts marginally profitable theatres to Discount Theatres that exhibit films formerly shown on a first-run basis. At the end of 1998, there were 64 Discount Theatres (250 screens).

The company is positioning itself for long-term growth by closing older and underperforming theatre locations. In December 1998, directors approved a restructuring plan involving the closure or disposition of 28 theatres (116 screens) in underperforming markets. As a result of the restructuring, CKE recognized a charge of $34.7 million in the 1998 fourth quarter.

CKE is expanding and improving its theatre base, adding and retrofitting new stadium seating auditoriums and digital stereo surround sound to existing facilities. At the end of 1998, the company had 303 screens with stadium seating, and it planned to provide stadium seating in another 465 auditoriums during 1999. CKE also upgraded 114 facilities in 1998, and added 16 auditoriums to existing theatres. It plans to expand into new markets, while adhering strictly to its secondary market niche. At the end of 1998, the company had 152 screens under construction, and intended to develop approximately 382 screens during 1999.

Since 1997, the company has opened five family entertainment centers under the name Hollywood Connection, including three developed by an equally owned joint venture with Wal-Mart Stores. The centers include multi-screen theatres, and entertainment amenities such as indoor roller skating rinks, themed putting golf courses, bumper car attractions, state-of-the-art games arcades, restaurants, and laser tag arenas. CKE continues to evaluate this concept, and is exploring alternate revenue sources.

Per Share Data ($) (Year Ended Dec. 31)	1998	1997	1996	1995	1994	1993	1992	1991	1990	1989
Tangible Bk. Val.	10.06	11.88	10.32	11.27	11.54	7.94	8.51	8.63	7.85	5.60
Cash Flow	0.57	4.72	1.89	3.58	4.66	3.55	2.25	1.95	1.83	2.23
Earnings	-2.73	1.78	-0.65	1.16	2.00	1.50	0.80	0.75	0.84	1.22
Dividends	Nil	Nil	Nil	Nil	Nil	Nil	Nil	Nil	Nil	Nil
Payout Ratio	Nil	Nil	Nil	Nil	Nil	Nil	Nil	Nil	Nil	Nil
Prices - High	33 1/8	35 3/8	32 1/2	25 1/2	24 3/8	20 3/4	17	17 1/4	16 3/8	13 7/8
- Low	15	23 1/8	20 1/4	18 3/4	16 3/8	12 7/8	10 1/2	9	7 1/4	7 3/4
P/E Ratio - High	NM	20	NM	22	12	14	21	23	19	11
- Low	NM	13	NM	16	8	9	13	12	9	6
Income Statement Analysis (Million $)										
Revs.	482	459	427	365	328	242	172	146	127	99
Oper. Inc.	NA	89.1	82.4	65.0	67.8	50.3	32.9	28.8	26.0	22.6
Depr.	37.5	33.4	28.4	27.2	22.5	16.3	11.1	9.2	7.4	5.2
Int. Exp.	27.2	23.1	21.4	16.8	17.4	14.8	11.8	10.2	8.3	7.4
Pretax Inc.	-48.8	32.6	-11.7	21.7	28.2	19.8	10.1	9.6	10.5	10.5
Eff. Tax Rate	NM	38%	NM	40%	40%	40%	40%	41%	40%	41%
Net Inc.	-30.6	20.2	-7.3	13.1	17.0	11.9	6.1	5.7	6.3	6.2
Balance Sheet & Other Fin. Data (Million $)										
Cash	17.8	16.5	12.3	18.8	22.7	32.7	32.1	24.0	30.4	15.2
Curr. Assets	28.8	31.0	26.1	39.6	33.5	42.2	39.0	32.7	40.2	20.1
Total Assets	698	620	489	478	378	327	230	184	179	135
Curr. Liab.	84.7	63.0	53.7	56.2	44.2	37.2	27.3	17.0	15.8	12.5
LT Debt	350	342	253	218	144	181	120	91.6	94.0	85.1
Common Eqty.	226	203	178	185	172	93.9	75.7	69.2	63.3	32.8
Total Cap.	577	557	436	422	333	290	203	167	163	122
Cap. Exp.	147	126	71.0	58.0	29.1	33.5	13.3	22.7	34.1	31.0
Cash Flow	6.5	53.6	21.1	40.3	39.5	28.1	17.2	14.9	13.7	11.4
Curr. Ratio	0.3	0.5	0.5	0.7	0.8	1.1	1.4	1.9	2.5	1.6
% LT Debt of Cap.	60.8	61.4	58.1	51.8	43.2	62.3	59.2	54.8	57.7	69.5
% Net Inc.of Revs.	NM	4.4	NM	3.6	5.2	4.9	3.6	3.9	4.9	6.3
% Ret. on Assets	NM	3.6	NM	3.1	4.1	4.2	2.9	3.1	3.3	5.0
% Ret. on Equity	NM	10.6	NM	7.3	11.2	13.6	8.4	8.6	11.3	21.2

Data as orig reptd.; bef. results of disc opers/spec. items. Per share data adj. for stk. divs. Bold denotes diluted EPS (FASB 128)-prior periods restated. E-Estimated. NA-Not Available. NM-Not Meaningful. NR-Not Ranked.

Office—1301 First Ave., Columbus, GA 31901. **Tel**—(706) 576-3400. **Website**—http://www.carmike.com **Chrmn**—C. L. Patrick. **Pres & CEO**—M. W. Patrick. **Investor Contact**—Phil Smitley (706-576-2836). **SVP & Secy**—F. L. Champion, III. **Dirs**—J. W. Jordan II, C. L. Patrick, C. L. Patrick, Jr., M. W. Patrick, C. E. Sanders, D. W. Zalaznick. **Transfer Agent & Registrar**—Synovus Trust Co., Columbus, GA. **Incorporated**— in Delaware in 1982. **Empl**— 10,500. **S&P Analyst:** A. Bensinger

STANDARD
&POOR'S
STOCK REPORTS

Carolina First

NASDAQ Symbol **CAFC**

In S&P SmallCap 600

09-OCT-99

Industry:
Banks (Regional)

Summary: This bank holding company owns Carolina First Bank and Citrus Bank, with about 84 branch offices and $3.1 billion in assets.

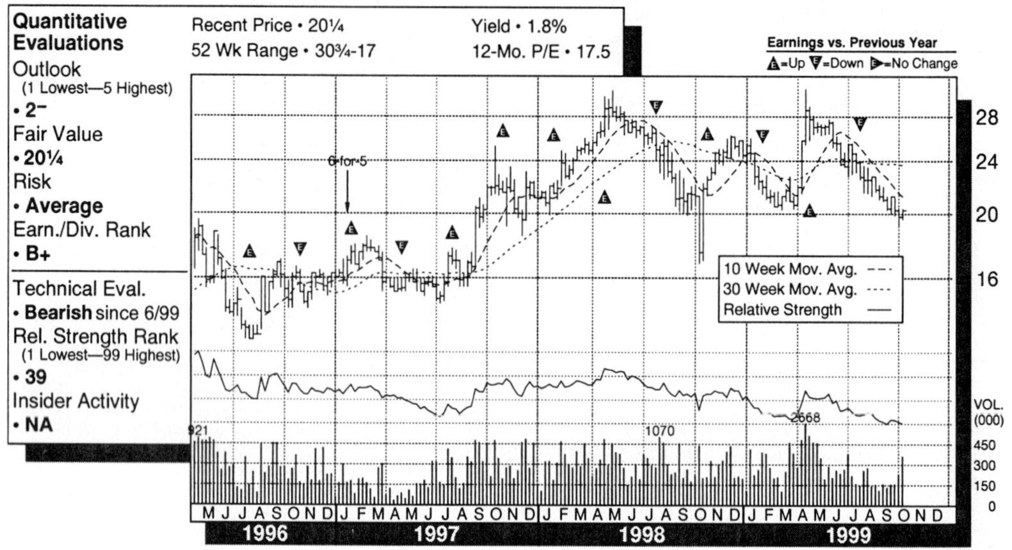

Business Profile - 28-JUL-99

In July 1999, Carolina First completed the acquisition of Citrus Bank for approximately 3.1 million common shares, valued at approximately $74 million. As of July 1, 1999, Citrus Bank had assets of $275 million with 8 branch locations in the Orlando and central FL area. In April 1999, CAFC acquired Citizens First National Bank, which had assets of approximately $59 million and 4 branch locations in northern FL, for about $14.1 million. Citizens First and Citrus Bank, as well as a Citizens First de novo branch in Jacksonville, FL, will operate in FL under the Citrus Bank name with assets of around $330 million and 13 branches.

Operational Review - 28-JUL-99

Net interest income in the six months ended June 30, 1999, advanced 28%, as growth in average earning assets combined with a wider net interest margin (4.50% versus 4.21%). The provision for loan losses rose 22%, to $6.8 million from $5.6 million. Noninterest income more than tripled to $30.1 million, mainly due to gains on the disposition of equity investments and the sale of CAFC's credit card portfolio. Noninterest expenses increased 96%, primarily due to a charitable contribution to the Carolina First Foundation, as well as merger and Y2K expenses. Net income increased 24%, to $12.6 million ($0.56 a share, on 28% more shares), from $10.2 million ($0.59).

Stock Performance - 08-OCT-99

In the past 30 trading days, CAFC's shares have declined 5%, compared to a 0.91% fall in the S&P 500. Average trading volume for the past five days was 71,960 shares, compared with the 40-day moving average of 36,992 shares.

Key Stock Statistics

Dividend Rate/Share	0.36	Shareholders	3,200
Shs. outstg. (M)	25.7	Market cap. (B)	$0.520
Avg. daily vol. (M)	0.045	Inst. holdings	17%
Tang. Bk. Value/Share	10.40		
Beta	0.97		

Value of $10,000 invested 5 years ago: $ 22,424

Fiscal Year Ending Dec. 31

	1999	1998	1997	1996	1995	1994
Revenues (Million $)						
1Q	69.98	46.74	33.48	32.39	28.07	15.69
2Q	59.84	48.59	38.55	32.15	27.64	18.84
3Q	—	51.39	40.45	38.68	30.24	21.40
4Q	—	56.69	42.85	35.00	33.12	23.51
Yr.	—	203.4	155.3	138.2	119.1	79.46
Earnings Per Share ($)						
1Q	**0.29**	**0.28**	**0.15**	**0.20**	0.20	0.21
2Q	**0.28**	**0.31**	**0.41**	**0.23**	0.20	0.20
3Q	—	**0.31**	**0.30**	**0.21**	0.23	0.22
4Q	—	**0.30**	**0.32**	**0.28**	0.23	-1.37
Yr.	—	**1.19**	**1.18**	**0.92**	**0.84**	-0.75

Next earnings report expected: late October

Dividend Data (Dividends have been paid since 1994.)

Amount ($)	Date Decl.	Ex-Div. Date	Stock of Record	Payment Date
0.090	Dec. 16	Jan. 13	Jan. 15	Feb. 01 '99
0.090	Feb. 17	Apr. 15	Apr. 19	May. 01 '99
0.090	May. 19	Jul. 13	Jul. 15	Aug. 01 '99
0.090	Aug. 18	Oct. 13	Oct. 15	Nov. 01 '99

A Division of The McGraw-Hill Companies

Business Summary - 28-JUL-99

An important part of Carolina First Corporation's growth strategy is to target markets where banking relationships are in a state of flux due to bank mergers. The company is expanding into northern and central Florida. This represents an extension of CAFC's existing strategy, which has proven to be successful in South Carolina, to another southeastern market with similar conditions.

Through its 71 banking offices in South Carolina and 13 offices in Florida with $3.1 billion in assets as of June 30, 1999, the company strives to be a "super community bank," serving individuals and small-to-midsize companies. Subsidiaries also include Carolina First Bank, F.S.B. (a federal savings bank), Citrus Bank (a state-chartered bank), Carolina First Mortgage Co., Carolina First Investment Co., Blue Ridge Finance Co. (a consumer finance company), and Resource Processing Group (a credit card servicing company).

Interest on loans provides the majority of total income. Totaling $1.9 billion at year-end 1998, net loans broke down as follows in recent years: commercial, financial and agricultural 15% (up from 14% in 1997), real estate mortgage and construction 63% (55%), consumer and credit cards 14% (12%), and other 8% (19%).

Banks must regularly provision against possible losses. CAFC's allowance for loan losses covered nonperforming loans by over 8.6 times at year-end 1998, up from around 6.6 times a year earlier. Asset quality declined slightly during the year, as nonperforming assets rose to 0.28% of total loans, from 0.23%.

Deposits are the largest (and most cost effective) source of funds to the bank. At December 31, 1998, deposits totaled approximately $2.1 billion, and were apportioned 14% non interest-bearing demand, 23% interest-bearing demand, 8% money market, 4% savings, and 51% time.

Lending profitability, commonly measured by the yield on a bank's average earning assets, or net interest margin, is affected by changes in the volume and mix of assets and liabilities, as well as changes in interest rates. During 1998, Carolina First's net interest margin declined to 4.24%, from 4.36%, which resulted from lower earning asset yields and slightly higher deposit costs.

As of March 31, 1999, CAFC owned 2.5 million common shares and warrants to purchase another 3.5 million shares (a 17% ownership stake) in Affinity Technology Group, a Columbia, SC, enterprise that is developing a new generation of bank machines. It has also invested in NET.B@nk, Inc., formerly Atlanta Internet Bank, F.S.B., a de novo banking operation formed to provide banking services on the Internet, introduced in October 1996. Following the initial public offering of Net.B@nk, Inc. stock in July 1997, CAFC, as of March 31, 1999, owned 805,000 shares or a 9.4% stake in the operation.

In April 1999, CAFC sold $112 million of credit card receivables to First USA, N.A.

Per Share Data ($) (Year Ended Dec. 31)	1998	1997	1996	1995	1994	1993	1992	1991	1990	1989
Tangible Bk. Val.	9.72	9.75	7.79	5.27	6.81	5.17	6.60	6.79	7.33	7.08
Earnings	1.19	1.18	0.96	0.87	-0.75	0.72	0.45	0.41	0.26	0.23
Dividends	0.32	0.28	0.23	0.19	0.16	Nil	Nil	Nil	Nil	Nil
Payout Ratio	27%	24%	24%	22%	NM	Nil	Nil	Nil	Nil	Nil
Prices - High	30 5/8	25 1/4	20 1/2	16 1/8	12 1/2	11 1/8	9 1/2	6 3/4	9 5/8	9 5/8
- Low	16 3/4	14 5/8	12 7/8	10 1/8	9 1/8	8 1/4	5 5/8	5 1/4	6	7 1/8
P/E Ratio - High	26	21	21	19	NM	16	21	16	38	43
- Low	14	12	13	12	NM	11	13	13	23	32
Income Statement Analysis (Million $)										
Net Int. Inc.	89.1	66.7	57.1	50.8	41.6	26.9	17.8	12.9	10.2	8.0
Loan Loss Prov.	11.1	11.6	10.3	6.8	0.9	0.9	1.4	1.4	0.8	0.9
Non Int. Inc.	21.9	16.6	21.3	17.3	7.9	6.3	3.1	1.6	1.1	1.0
Non Int. Exp.	64.8	52.2	51.7	46.9	50.5	25.2	16.1	11.6	8.9	NA
Pretax Inc.	35.6	22.4	16.4	14.4	-1.9	7.1	3.7	2.1	1.6	NA
Eff. Tax Rate	37%	36%	36%	35%	NM	31%	32%	21%	36%	NA
Net Inc.	22.4	14.3	10.5	9.4	-1.9	4.9	2.5	1.7	1.1	0.9
% Net Int. Marg.	4.24	4.36	4.35	4.54	4.89	4.31	4.06	3.63	3.37	3.00
Balance Sheet & Other Fin. Data (Million $)										
Total Assets	2,726	2,156	1,574	1,415	1,120	816	529	447	346	326
Loans	1,867	1,351	1,113	1,054	795	559	392	335	273	231
Deposits	2,125	1,747	1,281	1,095	925	725	476	407	300	288
Capitalization:										
Debt	63.1	39.1	26.4	26.3	1.2	1.2	1.3	1.3	NA	NA
Equity	344	202	104	62.0	42.0	47.2	33.9	31.9	30.2	28.8
Total	408	241	131	121	80.2	64.1	45.5	33.2	NA	NA
% Ret. on Assets	0.9	0.8	0.7	0.7	NM	0.7	0.5	0.4	0.3	0.3
% Ret. on Equity	8.2	9.4	12.7	11.9	NM	8.5	6.3	5.4	3.5	3.3
% Loan Loss Resv.	1.0	1.2	1.0	0.8	0.6	1.0	1.1	1.1	0.9	0.9
% Risk Based Capital	12.9	11.2	10.4	10.2	8.4	9.4	11.6	NA	NA	NA
Price Times Book Value:										
Hi	3.2	2.6	2.6	3.1	1.8	2.2	1.4	1.0	NA	NA
Low	1.7	1.5	1.7	1.9	1.3	1.6	0.9	0.8	NA	NA

Data as orig reptd.; bef. results of disc opers/spec. items. Per share data adj. for stk. divs. Bold denotes diluted EPS (FASB 128)-prior periods restated. E-Estimated. NA-Not Available. NM-Not Meaningful. NR-Not Ranked.

Office—102 S. Main St., Greenville, SC 29601. **Tel**—(864) 255-7900. **Website**—http://www.carolinafirst.com **Chrmn**—W. R. Timmons Jr. **Pres & CEO**—M. I. Whittle Jr. **EVP, CFO, Secy & Investor Contact**—William S. Hummers III. **Dirs**—J. B. Farr, C. C. Grimes Jr., M. D. Hagy, W. S. Hummers III, V. E. Merchant, Jr., H. E. Russell, Jr., C. B. Schooler, E. P. Stall, E. E. Stone IV, W. R. Timmons Jr., D. C. Wakefield III, M. I. Whittle Jr. **Transfer Agent & Registrar**—Reliance Trust Co., Atlanta. **Incorporated**—in South Carolina in 1986. **Empl**— 847. **S&P Analyst:** J. Rudy

STANDARD &POOR'S STOCK REPORTS

Cascade Natural Gas

NYSE Symbol **CGC**

In S&P SmallCap 600

09-OCT-99 **Industry:** Natural Gas

Summary: CGC is a natural gas distributor serving communities in Washington and Oregon.

Quantitative Evaluations

Outlook (1 Lowest—5 Highest) • **2**

Fair Value • **17⅞**

Risk • **Low**

Earn./Div. Rank • **B**

Technical Eval. • **Bullish** since 8/99

Rel. Strength Rank (1 Lowest—99 Highest) • **70**

Insider Activity • **NA**

Recent Price • 17⅞ | Yield • 5.4%

52 Wk Range • 19¾-14⅜ | 12-Mo. P/E • 14.9

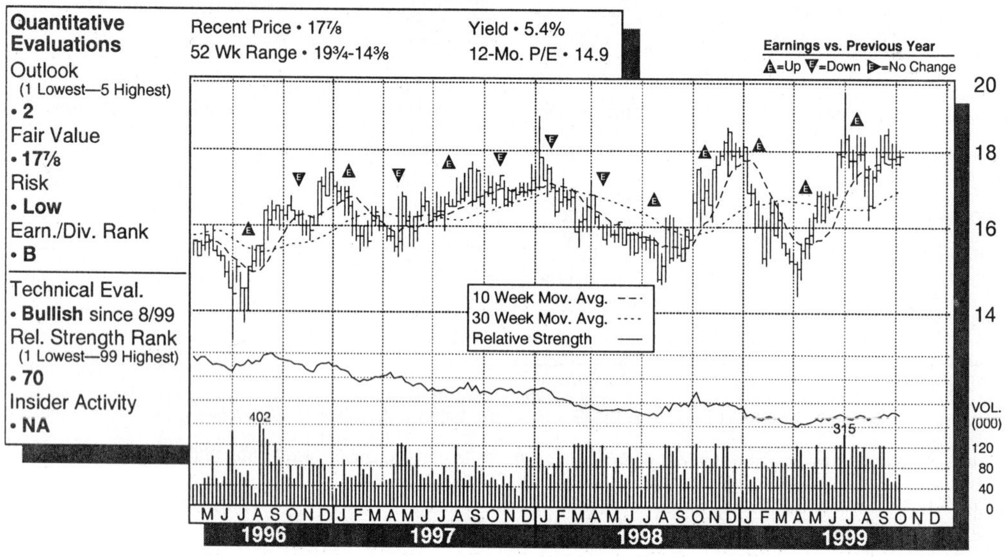

Business Profile - 01-JUN-99

CGC reported in October 1998 that several changes in its operations in FY 98 should facilitate earnings growth in the future, reflecting its continued rapid customer growth. Regulatory changes in Washington State contracts now require appliances that make it possible for the company to manage new customer additions for profitability. Further, capital expenditures for structural reinforcements to reflect growth will be greatly reduced in the future; they are estimated at $300,000 for FY 99, down from several million dollars in recent years. In addition, in September 1998, Cascade announced an adjustment in depreciation rates that will cut reported expenses by approximately $2 million annually.

Operational Review - 01-JUN-99

Revenues for the six months ended March 31, 1999, rose 5.9%, year to year. The operating margin improved, reflecting new customers and increased residential consumption per customer; with the cost of operations down 2.8%, reflecting CGC's increased focus on achieving cost reductions and efficiencies, as well as lower depreciation and amortization charges, operating income gained 19%. With interest and other expenses up 6.3%, and after taxes at 37.5% in both periods, net income advanced 23%, to $14,773,000 ($1.32 a share) from $12,051,000 ($1.07).

Stock Performance - 08-OCT-99

In the past 30 trading days, CGC's shares have increased 2%, compared to a 0.91% fall in the S&P 500. Average trading volume for the past five days was 13,220 shares, compared with the 40-day moving average of 18,110 shares.

Key Stock Statistics

Dividend Rate/Share	0.96	Shareholders	10,000
Shs. outstg. (M)	11.0	Market cap. (B)	$0.197
Avg. daily vol. (M)	0.011	Inst. holdings	29%
Tang. Bk. Value/Share	10.75		
Beta	0.02		

Value of $10,000 invested 5 years ago: $ 14,108

Fiscal Year Ending Sep. 30

	1999	1998	1997	1996	1995	1994
Revenues (Million $)						
1Q	62.93	60.98	64.97	56.91	64.61	64.75
2Q	71.12	65.55	71.17	67.62	34.71	36.26
3Q	42.87	37.00	33.73	33.46	26.51	28.87
4Q	—	26.13	25.91	26.58	56.91	62.53
Yr.	—	189.7	195.8	184.6	182.7	192.4
Earnings Per Share ($)						
1Q	**0.60**	**0.51**	**0.59**	0.56	0.63	0.54
2Q	**0.72**	**0.57**	0.69	0.72	-0.11	-0.16
3Q	**0.06**	**-0.07**	-0.10	-0.20	-0.27	-0.28
4Q	—	**-0.18**	-0.23	-0.22	0.56	0.50
Yr.	—	**0.82**	**0.93**	0.84	0.80	0.60

Next earnings report expected: early November

Dividend Data (Dividends have been paid since 1964.)

Amount ($)	Date Decl.	Ex-Div. Date	Stock of Record	Payment Date
0.240	Dec. 15	Jan. 13	Jan. 15	Feb. 15 '99
0.240	Mar. 16	Apr. 13	Apr. 15	May. 14 '99
0.240	Jun. 16	Jul. 13	Jul. 15	Aug. 13 '99
0.240	Sep. 16	Oct. 13	Oct. 15	Nov. 15 '99

A Division of The McGraw-Hill Companies

Cascade Natural Gas Corporation

Business Summary - 01-JUN-99

Supported by diverse local economies and robust population growth, Cascade continued to be one of the fastest growing gas distribution companies in the U.S. during FY 98 (Sep.). The company serves Washington and Oregon communities with a total population of approximately 780,000. Roughly 82% of gas distribution revenues are from Washington, and the remainder from Oregon. At the end of FY 98, the company's core customer base included 142,645 residential customers, 25,415 commercial customers, 436 industrial customers and 20 traditional interruptible customers. CGC also has 177 non-core customers.

The residential and commercial markets, which principally use natural gas for space and water heating, represent less than 20% of total gas deliveries, but provide over 60% of Cascade's operating margin. The use of gas for space heating is very weather-sensitive and the company has pursued a marketing strategy to encourage installation of gas water heaters in an effort to mitigate the seasonality of its residential and commercial revenues.

The industrial base in Cascade's service area ranges from producers of paper, chemicals and textiles to processors of vegetables, fish and milk. Electric generation companies represent a significant portion of the company's industrial revenues. Diminished availability of hydroelectric generation, due to lower snowfall in the northwest, increased industrial demand for natural gas in FY 98. Non-core customers are generally large industrial and institutional customers who have chosen "unbundled" service, meaning that they select from among several supply and upstream pipeline transportation options, independent of Cascade's distribution service. The company's margin from non-core customers is generally limited to this distribution service.

It is to CGC's benefit to maintain predictable natural gas prices because costs above projections filed with state regulators cannot be entirely passed on to consumers. Accordingly, during 1998 Cascade purchased approximately 79% of its gas supples through firm gas supply contracts and only 21% via 30-day spot market contracts. A small profit from prices paid for natural gas in FY 98 contrasted with losses in FY 97, resulting from an abnormal spike in natural gas prices during the heating season.

FY 98 results were adversely affected by weather that was 9% warmer than FY 97 and 11% warmer than normal. The company estimated that the divergence from normal weather affected earnings by $0.17 a share for the fiscal year.

Per Share Data ($) (Year Ended Sep. 30)	1998	1997	1996	1995	1994	1993	1992	1991	1990	1989
Tangible Bk. Val.	10.09	10.18	10.12	9.79	9.84	10.00	9.05	8.59	8.33	7.91
Earnings	0.82	0.93	0.84	0.80	0.60	1.05	0.63	1.14	1.26	1.29
Dividends	0.96	0.96	0.96	0.96	0.96	0.94	0.93	0.90	0.87	0.85
Payout Ratio	117%	103%	114%	120%	160%	90%	146%	79%	69%	66%
Prices - High	18 5/8	19	17 1/2	17 1/2	18 1/8	19 1/2	17	16 7/8	12 5/8	13 3/4
- Low	14 5/8	15 1/4	13 3/8	13	12 3/4	15 1/2	13 5/8	11 1/8	10 1/8	9 3/8
P/E Ratio - High	23	20	21	22	30	18	27	15	10	11
- Low	18	16	16	16	21	14	21	10	8	7
Income Statement Analysis (Million $)										
Revs.	190	196	185	183	192	187	152	154	161	174
Depr.	13.5	13.4	12.4	11.7	10.1	9.2	8.4	7.7	7.3	6.8
Maint.	NA	NA	NA	NA	NA	NA	NA	NA	NA	NA
Fxd. Chgs. Cov.	2.3	2.5	1.8	2.0	2.0	2.5	1.9	2.4	2.5	2.6
Constr. Credits	0.6	0.5	0.6	0.4	0.2	0.3	0.2	0.2	0.1	0.1
Eff. Tax Rate	37%	37%	34%	37%	35%	37%	37%	36%	35%	38%
Net Inc.	9.5	10.6	8.2	7.7	5.8	8.9	4.8	7.7	8.4	8.5
Balance Sheet & Other Fin. Data (Million $)										
Gross Prop.	434	426	403	378	342	315	284	249	231	217
Cap. Exp.	25.6	29.2	41.1	37.6	27.0	33.0	35.3	19.7	16.4	12.9
Net Prop.	266	265	256	239	214	197	175	148	137	129
Capitalization:										
LT Debt	111	121	102	102	100	87.0	74.7	57.1	60.8	60.1
% LT Debt	49	51	47	51	45	48	49	47	51	52
Pfd.	6.4	6.6	6.8	6.8	7.2	7.5	8.0	8.3	2.4	2.9
% Pfd.	2.80	2.80	3.20	3.50	3.70	4.20	5.20	6.70	2.10	2.50
Common	111	112	109	89.5	87.7	85.7	69.2	57.2	54.9	51.7
% Common	49	47	50	45	45	48	46	47	47	45
Total Cap.	249	256	237	218	214	198	168	137	132	129
% Oper. Ratio	89.8	90.0	90.2	90.5	92.6	91.4	92.0	90.8	89.8	90.2
% Earn. on Net Prop.	9.6	7.6	7.3	9.6	7.0	8.7	7.5	9.9	12.2	13.5
% Return On Revs.	5.0	5.4	4.4	4.2	3.0	4.7	3.2	5.0	5.2	4.9
% Return On Invest. Capital	10.0	8.1	8.0	10.4	6.9	8.8	8.2	11.6	13.0	13.0
% Return On Com. Equity	8.1	9.2	7.7	8.1	6.0	11.0	6.7	13.4	15.4	16.6

Data as orig. reptd.; bef. results of disc. opers. and/or spec. items. Per share data adj. for stk. divs. as of ex-div. date. Yrs. ended Dec. 31 prior to 1996. Bold denotes diluted EPS (FASB 128). E-Estimated. NA-Not Available. NM-Not Meaningful. NR-Not Ranked.

Office—222 Fairview Ave. North, Seattle, WA 98109. **Tel**—(206) 624-3900. **Chrmn, Pres & CEO**—W. B. Matsuyama. **VP-Fin, CFO & Investor Contact**—J. D. Wessling. **Contr**—J. E. Haug. **Dirs**— C. Burnham, Jr., M. C. Clapp, T.E. Cronin, D. A. Ederer, H. L. Hubbard, W. B. Matsuyama, L. L. Pinnt, B. G. Ragen, M. A. Williams. **Transfer Agent & Registrar**—Bank of New York, NYC. **Incorporated**—in Washington in 1953. **Empl**— 484. **S&P Analyst:** C.C.P.

STANDARD &POOR'S STOCK REPORTS

Casey's General Stores

NASDAQ Symbol **CASY**

In S&P SmallCap 600

09-OCT-99

Industry: Retail (Specialty)

Summary: This company operates 1,183 convenience stores in nine midwestern states, selling a broad selection of food, beverage, health and automotive products.

Quantitative Evaluations

Outlook (1 Lowest—5 Highest) • **5**

Fair Value • **20⅞**

Risk • **Low**

Earn./Div. Rank • **A+**

Technical Eval. • **Bearish** since 9/99

Rel. Strength Rank (1 Lowest—99 Highest) • **43**

Insider Activity • **NA**

Recent Price • 13⅛

52 Wk Range • 16¾-12¼

Yield • 0.5%

12-Mo. P/E • 16.4

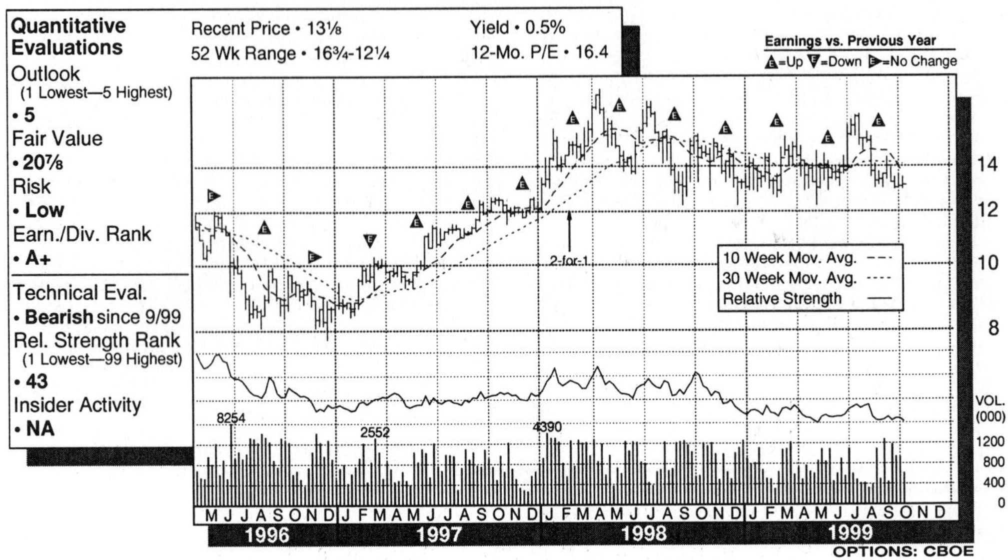

Business Profile - 28-JUL-99

CASY's continues to achieve record sales and earnings through a combination of new store openings and additional sales of gasoline and prepared foods at its retail convenience stores. For FY 99 (Apr.), the company added 80 new stores, and plans to increase the number of stores by about 8% annually over the next several years, including a target of 85 new stores in FY 00 and 90 new stores in FY 01. Given the company's accelerating construction plan, capital expenditures have been running higher than cash flow from operations. In April 1999, CASY issued $50 million of Senior Notes to pay down debt and for new store construction.

Operational Review - 28-JUL-99

Based on a preliminary report, total revenues in FY 99 (Apr.) were up 5.4% from those of the prior year, on higher sales of gasoline, groceries, prepared foods and fountain sodas, coupled with an increased store count. Gross margins widened on increased gas margins, higher cigarette prices and substantially greater pizza sales. Operating expenses rose 10%, and despite 12% higher depreciation expense and a 19% rise in interest costs, net income jumped 20%, to $40,237,000 ($0.76 a share), from $33,467,000 ($0.63).

Stock Performance - 08-OCT-99

In the past 30 trading days, CASY's shares have declined 2%, compared to a 0.91% fall in the S&P 500. Average trading volume for the past five days was 120,960 shares, compared with the 40-day moving average of 195,913 shares.

Key Stock Statistics

Dividend Rate/Share	0.06	Shareholders	3,057
Shs. outstg. (M)	52.7	Market cap. (B)	$0.692
Avg. daily vol. (M)	0.181	Inst. holdings	57%
Tang. Bk. Value/Share	5.73		
Beta	0.64		

Value of $10,000 invested 5 years ago: $ 22,039

Fiscal Year Ending Apr. 30

	2000	1999	1998	1997	1996	1995
Revenues (Million $)						
1Q	387.2	332.4	320.6	286.9	253.0	221.3
2Q	—	322.3	317.4	286.3	244.6	223.7
3Q	—	291.6	276.9	273.3	221.6	199.4
4Q	—	304.7	271.0	262.5	236.9	204.5
Yr.	—	1,251	1,187	1,109	954.8	848.8
Earnings Per Share ($)						
1Q	**0.28**	**0.24**	0.20	0.17	0.15	0.13
2Q	—	**0.24**	0.20	0.17	0.17	0.14
3Q	—	**0.17**	**0.14**	0.10	0.13	0.11
4Q	—	**0.12**	**0.09**	0.07	0.06	0.06
Yr.	—	**0.76**	**0.63**	**0.51**	**0.51**	0.44

Next earnings report expected: early December

Dividend Data (Dividends have been paid since 1990.)

Amount ($)	Date Decl.	Ex-Div. Date	Stock of Record	Payment Date
0.015	Nov. 30	Jan. 28	Feb. 01	Feb. 15 '99
0.015	Mar. 02	Apr. 29	May. 03	May. 17 '99
0.015	Jun. 15	Jul. 29	Aug. 02	Aug. 16 '99
0.015	Aug. 31	Oct. 28	Nov. 01	Nov. 15 '99

Casey's General Stores, Inc.

Business Summary - 28-JUL-99

One company has found a way to make a big business out of small towns. Casey's General Stores, Inc. (CASY) has left the city behind and caters to the needs of many of the small towns in the Midwest. Casey's, through its company stores and franchises, operated 1,183 convenience stores as of June 15, 1999 that serve gasoline and freshly prepared food. Approximately 70% of all Casey's General Stores are located in areas with populations of fewer than 5,000 persons.

Casey's revenue is derived from the sale of food, and beverages and non-food products such as health and beauty aids, tobacco products, automotive products and gasoline by company stores and from the wholesale sale of merchandise items and gasoline to franchised stores. The company also generates revenues from continuing monthly royalties based on sales by franchised stores.

Casey's, headquartered in Ankeny, IA, was incorporated in 1967 and began marketing made-from-scratch pizza, its most popular prepared food product, in 1984, offering it to 93% of its stores by 1997. The company tries to define the space between the convenience store and the traditional small town general store. It experiments with additions to the company's product line and each Casey's General Store typically carries approximately 1,800 food and non-food items. Each store also sells gasoline or gasohol and may sell hardware, ammunition and pet supplies.

The company makes substantial capital investments in its stores. During the first nine months of FY 99 (Apr), it spent $55,368,000 for property and equipment, primarily for the construction and remodeling of company stores, compared with $50,304,000 in the same period in the prior year. In FY 98, capital expenditures totaled over $85 million.

Including company stores and franchises, Casey's as of April 1998 was operating 317 stores in Iowa, 283 in Illinois, 238 in Missouri, 95 in Kansas, 67 in Minnesota, 54 in Nebraska, 20 in South Dakota, 19 in Indiana, and 16 in Wisconsin. The company intends to continue to increase the number of the profitable company stores. Casey's derives approximately 95% of its gross profits from retail sales by company-owned stores. For the near term, Casey's will limit its expansion to small communities in its current market before pursuing expansion in other territories.

Per Share Data ($)										
(Year Ended Apr. 30)	**1999**	**1998**	**1997**	**1996**	**1995**	**1994**	**1993**	**1992**	**1991**	**1990**
Tangible Bk. Val.	5.73	5.01	4.42	3.93	3.46	3.06	2.44	2.16	1.93	1.74
Cash Flow	1.41	1.21	1.02	0.98	0.86	0.77	0.65	0.56	0.47	0.40
Earnings	0.76	0.63	0.52	0.51	0.44	0.36	0.30	0.26	0.20	0.18
Dividends	0.06	0.10	0.05	0.05	0.05	0.04	0.03	0.03	0.03	Nil
Payout Ratio	8%	17%	10%	10%	11%	10%	10%	12%	12%	Nil
Cal. Yrs.	1998	1997	1996	1995	1994	1993	1992	1991	1990	1989
Prices - High	18¼	12⅞	12½	12¾	7¾	6¼	4⅞	4¼	2⅞	3⅝
- Low	12¼	8⅜	7¾	7¼	5¼	3¾	3⅛	1⁵⁄₁₆	1¼	1¹⁵⁄₁₆
P/E Ratio - High	24	20	24	25	17	17	16	16	14	20
- Low	16	13	15	14	12	10	11	6	6	11
Income Statement Analysis (Million $)										
Revs.	1,256	1,192	1,114	960	854	615	578	525	519	456
Oper. Inc.	105	89.8	76.1	73.4	65.2	51.9	42.2	36.6	31.3	27.4
Depr.	33.9	30.4	26.9	24.7	22.2	18.4	15.5	13.3	12.2	10.1
Int. Exp.	7.6	6.6	7.9	7.2	6.4	8.0	6.2	5.4	5.4	5.4
Pretax Inc.	64.4	53.5	43.2	43.0	37.4	27.0	21.5	18.5	14.4	13.3
Eff. Tax Rate	37%	38%	38%	38%	39%	39%	38%	38%	37%	37%
Net Inc.	40.2	33.5	27.0	26.8	22.9	16.6	13.3	11.5	9.0	8.4
Balance Sheet & Other Fin. Data (Million $)										
Cash	5.9	4.0	10.0	26.6	6.8	11.9	18.1	8.8	8.9	7.7
Curr. Assets	70.2	52.5	54.8	70.0	43.2	41.4	46.5	33.0	31.6	30.5
Total Assets	563	480	427	405	345	318	281	219	198	185
Curr. Liab.	83.8	90.0	73.8	83.0	77.0	75.5	55.5	46.6	35.8	29.9
LT Debt	123	79.1	79.7	81.0	60.0	61.4	99	61.4	63.8	64.5
Common Eqty.	302	266	232	206	180	158	108	95.9	84.8	79.5
Total Cap.	476	387	352	320	267	242	224	172	161	155
Cap. Exp.	97.7	85.3	66.7	60.4	52.6	67.1	51.4	35.4	22.7	35.2
Cash Flow	74.2	63.8	53.9	51.4	45.1	35.0	28.8	24.8	21.3	18.5
Curr. Ratio	0.8	0.6	0.7	0.8	0.5	0.5	0.8	0.7	0.9	1.0
% LT Debt of Cap.	25.7	20.4	22.6	25.4	22.5	25.4	44.1	35.7	39.5	41.6
% Net Inc.of Revs.	3.2	2.8	2.4	2.8	2.7	2.7	2.3	2.2	1.7	1.8
% Ret. on Assets	7.7	7.4	6.5	7.2	6.9	5.1	5.3	5.5	4.8	4.8
% Ret. on Equity	14.2	13.4	12.3	13.9	13.5	11.6	13.1	12.7	11.2	11.1

Data as orig reptd.; bef. results of disc opers/spec. items. Per share data adj. for stk. divs. Bold denotes diluted EPS (FASB 128)-prior periods restated. E-Estimated. NA-Not Available. NM-Not Meaningful. NR-Not Ranked.

Office—One Convenience Blvd., Ankeny, IA 50021. **Tel**—(515) 965-6100. **Chrmn & CEO**—D. F. Lamberti. **Pres & COO**—R. M. Lamb. **Secy**—J. G. Harmon. **CFO, Treas & Investor Contact**—Douglas K. Shull. **Dirs**—J. R. Fitzgibbon, J. G. Harmon, K. H. Haynie, R. M. Lamb, D. F. Lamberti, P. C. Sullivan, J. P. Taylor. **Transfer Agent & Registrar**—United Missouri Bank of Kansas City. **Incorporated**—in Iowa in 1967. **Empl**— 10,366. **S&P Analyst:** Matthew C. Hershberg

STANDARD &POOR'S
STOCK REPORTS

Cash America International

NYSE Symbol **PWN**

In S&P SmallCap 600

09-OCT-99

Industry: Consumer Finance

Summary: Cash America International is a leading pawn shop operator, with more than 450 locations. It also provides check cashing services.

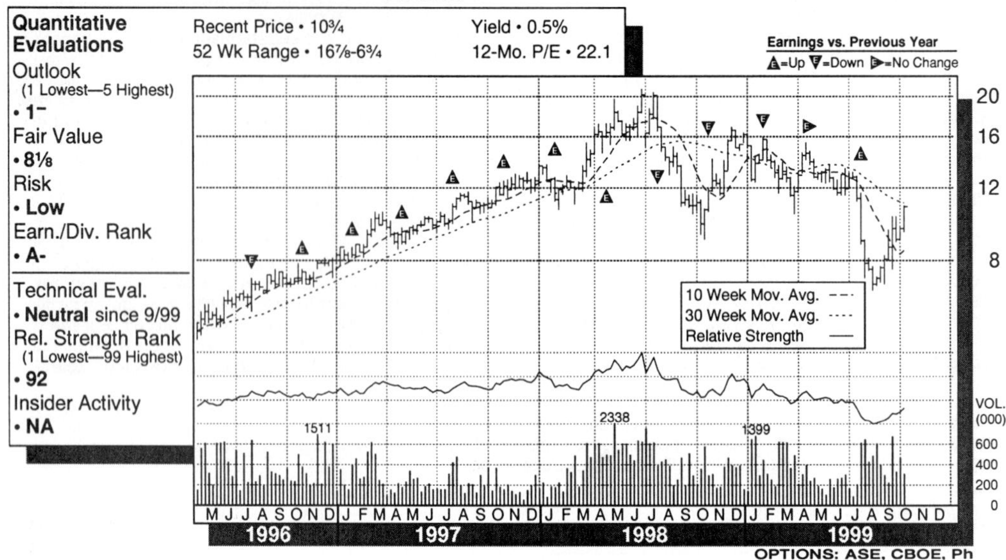

Business Profile - 15-JUL-99

In March 1999, PWN's subsidiary, Mr. Payroll Corp., announced the completion of a capital transaction with Wells Fargo Bank N.A. Wells Fargo is to contribute $21 million in equity capital and the assets of an existing network of 200 ATM's, worth roughly $6 million, to Mr. Payroll, in exchange for a 45% interest in that subsidiary. The capital will be used for the development and distribution of a new fully automated check cashing and financial services machine. PWN and Wells Fargo will be equal partners in Mr. Payroll, with Mr. Payroll's management team controlling the remaining interest. PWN will retain sole ownership of Mr. Payroll's manned check cashing operation. In January 1999, Mr. Payroll agreed with H-E-B Grocery Co. to deploy check cashing machines in 10 H-E-B Houston area stores.

Operational Review - 15-JUL-99

Total revenues for the three months ended March 31, 1999, rose 14%, year to year, primarily due to the contributions of finance and service charges and proceeds from the disposition of merchandise resulting from the net addition of 46 lending locations since March 31, 1998. Profitability was restrained by an increase in the cost of disposed merchandise, and 17% higher total operating expenses. After a gain from the issuance of subsidiary stock in 1999 only, and taxes at 34.2%, versus 37.4%, net income was up 5.9%, to $4,800,000 ($0.18 a share, based on 3.1% more average shares), from $4,534,000 ($0.18).

Stock Performance - 08-OCT-99

In the past 30 trading days, PWN's shares have increased 41%, compared to a 0.91% fall in the S&P 500. Average trading volume for the past five days was 60,760 shares, compared with the 40-day moving average of 101,246 shares.

Key Stock Statistics

Dividend Rate/Share	0.05	Shareholders	972
Shs. outstg. (M)	25.6	Market cap. (B)	$0.277
Avg. daily vol. (M)	0.122	Inst. holdings	76%
Tang. Bk. Value/Share	4.00		
Beta	0.99		

Value of $10,000 invested 5 years ago: $ 11,890

Fiscal Year Ending Dec. 31

	1999	1998	1997	1996	1995	1994
Revenues (Million $)						
1Q	95.69	84.19	76.52	68.54	60.27	55.31
2Q	86.34	78.25	69.42	65.93	60.10	57.20
3Q	—	80.51	70.31	64.67	57.64	63.26
4Q	—	56.41	87.12	81.83	75.58	86.33
Yr.	—	342.9	303.4	281.0	253.6	262.1
Earnings Per Share ($)						
1Q	**0.18**	**0.18**	0.15	0.11	0.09	0.10
2Q	**0.07**	**0.06**	0.12	0.10	0.11	0.11
3Q	—	**0.08**	0.14	0.12	0.06	0.15
4Q	—	**0.17**	**0.25**	0.21	0.19	0.18
Yr.	—	**0.48**	**0.66**	**0.54**	**0.45**	0.54

Next earnings report expected: late October

Dividend Data (Dividends have been paid since 1988.)

Amount ($)	Date Decl.	Ex-Div. Date	Stock of Record	Payment Date
0.013	Oct. 21	Oct. 30	Nov. 03	Nov. 17 '98
0.013	Jan. 27	Jan. 29	Feb. 02	Feb. 16 '99
0.013	Apr. 21	Apr. 30	May. 04	May. 18 '99
0.013	Jul. 20	Jul. 29	Aug. 02	Aug. 16 '99

A Division of The McGraw-Hill Companies

Business Summary - 15-JUL-99

Cash America International is a leading provider of secured, non-recourse loans to individuals, commonly referred to as pawn loans. The company caters to a growing niche of an estimated 70 million consumers who are either unable or unwilling to transact with traditional financial institutions. At December 31, 1998, Cash America operated through 414 domestic shops, 39 in the United Kingdom and 11 in Sweden. PWN also provides check cashing services in 20 states through its subsidiary, Mr. Payroll Corp., and rental of tires and wheels through its subsidiary, Rent-A-Tire, Inc.

A pawn loan transaction consists of a short-term loan, typically 90 days or less in the U.S., which is secured by an item of the borrower's. The loan may be repaid and the collateral redeemed at any time. In the event the borrower does not repay the loan, the collateral becomes property of PWN and is available for disposition. Collateral forfeited in the U.K. and Sweden is sold through public auctions. During 1998, lending net revenue was comprised of finance and service charges on loans (60%) and net proceeds earned on the disposition of merchandise (39%).

In 1998, outstanding loans rose 15%, to $129 million and included approximately 1.3 million individual lending arrangements. Loan growth was partially driven by the addition of 68 lending locations through various acquisitions and internal development. PWN plans to increase its domestic presence beyond the 16 states in which it currently operates and into new foreign markets as well.

Cash America employs a proprietary loan and inventory tracking system that links its domestic locations and efficiently manages loans and inventory. PWN believes this system effectively processes unredeemed collateral and quickens the pace of inventory turnover.

In March 1999, PWN completed a strategic partnership with Wells Fargo Bank, in which the bank contributed approximately $27 million in cash and assets in exchange for a 45% equity stake in Mr. Payroll Corp. At year-end 1998, Mr. Payroll, PWN's check cashing subsidiary, had a network of 127 manned check cashing centers, 10 of which were company owned and the rest operated by independent franchisees.

Since deploying its first automated check cashing machine in June 1997, Mr. Payroll had established 91 machines in 19 states by year-end 1998. Thirty-eight of its outstanding machines were company owned, with the remainder sold to a variety of end users, including financial institutions and retailers. Mr. Payroll contracts with the end users to offer check cashing services for fees equaling a portion of income earned.

Rent-A-Tire, PWN's wholly owned subsidiary, is an operator of four tire and wheel rental stores and manager of 14 additional stores located in Texas. The subsidiary contributed $2.5 million to net revenue in 1998.

Per Share Data ($) (Year Ended Dec. 31)	1998	1997	1996	1995	1994	1993	1992	1991	1990	1989
Tangible Bk. Val.	3.95	4.23	3.63	3.92	4.17	3.77	3.58	2.74	2.50	2.22
Cash Flow	1.17	1.29	1.10	0.97	0.34	0.71	0.70	0.63	0.52	0.42
Earnings	0.48	0.66	0.54	0.45	0.54	0.48	0.45	0.43	0.37	0.30
Dividends	0.10	0.05	0.05	0.05	0.05	0.05	0.05	0.04	0.03	0.02
Payout Ratio	20%	8%	9%	11%	9%	10%	10%	9%	7%	7%
Prices - High	20 7/8	13 3/4	8 1/2	9 3/4	10 1/8	11	12 7/8	9 3/4	10 1/4	7 5/8
- Low	9	8	4 3/4	4 5/8	7 1/2	6 3/8	7 1/4	6	5 3/4	3 1/4
P/E Ratio - High	43	21	16	22	19	23	29	23	28	26
- Low	19	12	9	10	14	13	16	14	16	11
Income Statement Analysis (Million $)										
Revs.	343	303	281	254	262	225	186	138	116	87.0
Oper. Inc.	51.9	54.2	51.4	46.8	40.2	31.9	28.7	22.0	19.1	14.2
Depr.	18.1	15.9	16.1	15.3	8.8	6.7	7.0	4.7	3.9	3.1
Int. Exp.	13.6	11.6	9.4	10.4	6.3	3.8	1.6	1.8	1.5	0.5
Pretax Inc.	20.4	26.2	25.1	20.6	25.0	21.8	20.3	17.5	13.7	11.1
Eff. Tax Rate	38%	37%	38%	38%	38%	36%	36%	40%	37%	37%
Net Inc.	12.6	16.6	15.7	12.8	15.5	13.8	13.0	10.5	8.7	7.0
Balance Sheet & Other Fin. Data (Million $)										
Cash	4.4	1.1	1.3	3.4	4.8	2.2	4.2	1.4	3.0	3.8
Curr. Assets	244	202	190	178	189	132	122	77.8	66.5	53.0
Total Assets	411	341	325	315	324	245	216	138	117	98.0
Curr. Liab.	30.8	26.8	25.0	16.0	21.0	14.2	12.5	7.1	6.9	6.7
LT Debt	189	146	146	123	120	64.0	50.0	30.5	20.1	9.6
Common Eqty.	187	168	154	176	183	167	154	100	89.9	81.6
Total Cap.	380	314	300	299	303	231	204	131	110	91.0
Cap. Exp.	22.4	16.4	7.2	13.5	22.8	16.7	19.6	7.7	5.8	5.2
Cash Flow	30.7	32.5	31.8	28.1	24.3	20.5	20.0	15.3	12.6	10.1
Curr. Ratio	7.9	7.5	7.6	11.1	9.0	9.3	9.8	11.0	9.6	7.9
% LT Debt of Cap.	49.8	46.5	48.7	41.2	39.5	27.7	24.5	23.4	18.2	10.5
% Net Inc.of Revs.	3.7	5.5	5.6	5.1	5.9	6.2	7.0	7.6	7.5	8.0
% Ret. on Assets	3.4	5.0	4.9	4.0	5.4	6.0	6.8	8.3	8.0	7.7
% Ret. on Equity	7.1	10.3	9.5	7.1	8.8	8.6	9.5	11.1	10.1	8.9

Data as orig reptd.; bef. results of disc opers/spec. items. Per share data adj. for stk. divs. Bold denotes diluted EPS (FASB 128)-prior periods restated. E-Estimated. NA-Not Available. NM-Not Meaningful. NR-Not Ranked.

Office—1600 W. 7th St., Fort Worth, TX 76102-2599. **Tel**—(817) 335-1100. **Chrmn & CEO**—J. R. Daugherty. **Pres & COO**—D. R. Feehan. **EVP & CFO**—T. A. Bessant, Jr.**EVP & Secy**—H. A. Simpson.**Dirs**—J. R. Daugherty, A. R. Dike, D. R. Feehan, J. H. Graves, B. D. Hunter, T. J. McKibben, A. M. Micallef, C. H. Morris, Jr., C. P. Motheral, S. W. Rizzo, R. Rogers. **Transfer Agent & Registrar**—ChaseMellon Shareholder Services, Dallas, TX. **Incorporated**—in Texas in 1984. **Empl**— 3,035. **S&P Analyst:** Markos N. Kaminis

Castle (A.M.)

ASE Symbol **CAS**

In S&P SmallCap 600

11-OCT-99 **Industry:** Iron & Steel

Summary: This independent metals service center company provides a complete range of inventories and preprocessing services; it also distributes a broad range of industrial plastics.

Quantitative Evaluations

Outlook (1 Lowest—5 Highest)
• **4**

Fair Value
• **19⅜**

Risk
• **Average**

Earn./Div. Rank
• **B**

Technical Eval.
• **Bearish** since 8/99

Rel. Strength Rank (1 Lowest—99 Highest)
• **28**

Insider Activity
• **NA**

Recent Price • 13
52 Wk Range • 19⅜-12
Yield • 6.0%
12-Mo. P/E • 16.7

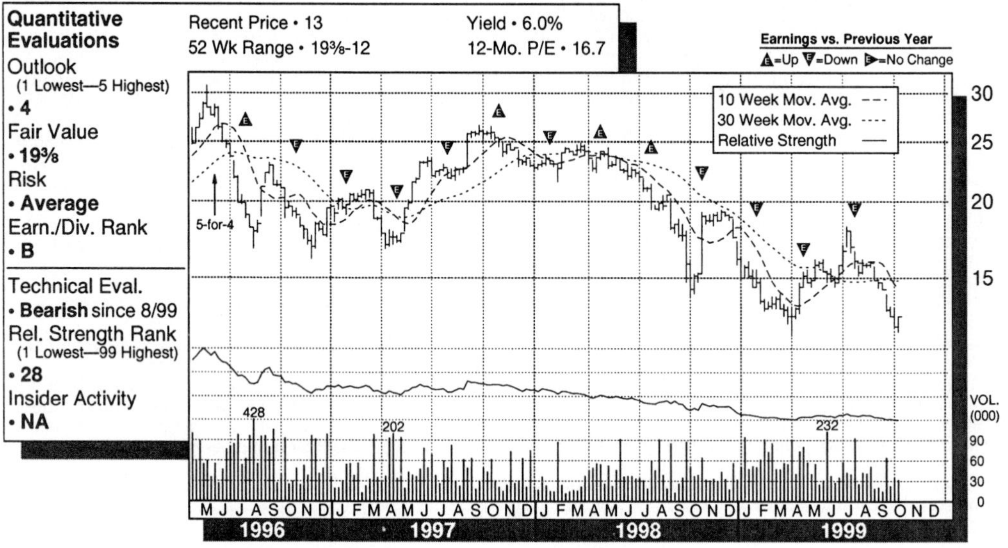

Business Profile - 11-OCT-99

Through the first half of 1999, the company's results have been adversely affected by a combination of excess inventory in the overall market and pricing pressures. Although gross margins have improved, reflecting the company's expansion of value added and processing capabilities, operating costs have risen due to recent acquisitions. Results were also hurt by significantly higher interest costs, which resulted from higher borrowing levels that were used to finance the company's growth and acquisition strategy. As of June 30, 1999, total debt was $28 million higher than the level at June 30, 1998 and the debt to capital ratio stood at 53.6%, which is over the target range of 45%.

Operational Review - 11-OCT-99

Net sales in the six months ended June 30, 1999, fell 13%, year to year, reflecting a decrease in tons sold, coupled with a reduction in average selling prices and a shift in sales mix. Gross margins widened on the company's expansion of value-added services and processing capabilities; however, with higher operating expenses, a rise in depreciation and amortization charges, and significantly higher net interest expense, and after taxes at 40.8%, versus 39.8%, net income plunged 56%, to $5,889,000 ($0.42 a share), from $13,452,000 ($0.96).

Stock Performance - 08-OCT-99

In the past 30 trading days, CAS's shares have declined 13%, compared to a 0.91% fall in the S&P 500. Average trading volume for the past five days was 6,300 shares, compared with the 40-day moving average of 6,521 shares.

Key Stock Statistics

Dividend Rate/Share	0.78	Shareholders	1,699
Shs. outstg. (M)	14.0	Market cap. (B)	$0.183
Avg. daily vol. (M)	0.008	Inst. holdings	52%
Tang. Bk. Value/Share	8.66		
Beta	0.61		

Value of $10,000 invested 5 years ago: $ 17,143

Fiscal Year Ending Dec. 31

	1999	1998	1997	1996	1995	1994
Revenues (Million $)						
1Q	183.5	211.7	177.3	175.1	169.1	133.8
2Q	180.0	205.1	188.0	174.8	163.1	131.8
3Q	—	195.5	192.7	162.3	149.0	132.2
4Q	—	180.5	196.8	160.4	146.7	138.7
Yr.	—	792.9	754.9	672.6	627.8	536.6
Earnings Per Share ($)						
1Q	**0.20**	**0.51**	**0.44**	**0.54**	0.59	0.27
2Q	**0.22**	**0.45**	**0.44**	**0.50**	0.50	0.24
3Q	—	**0.27**	**0.41**	**0.37**	0.38	0.27
4Q	—	**0.09**	**0.41**	**0.44**	0.46	0.34
Yr.	—	**1.32**	**1.69**	**1.86**	**1.93**	1.12

Next earnings report expected: mid October

Dividend Data (Dividends have been paid since 1934.)

Amount ($)	Date Decl.	Ex-Div. Date	Stock of Record	Payment Date
0.195	Oct. 22	Nov. 04	Nov. 06	Nov. 13 '98
0.195	Jan. 28	Feb. 03	Feb. 05	Feb. 19 '99
0.195	Apr. 22	May. 05	May. 07	May. 18 '99
0.195	Jul. 22	Aug. 04	Aug. 06	Aug. 13 '99

A.M. Castle & Co.

Business Summary - 11-OCT-99

A.M. Castle & Co. (CAS) is one of North America's largest, independent metals service center companies.

The company, founded in 1890, provides highly engineered materials and value-added processing services to a wide range of industrial companies within the $700 billion producer durable equipment sector of the economy. The customer base includes many Fortune 500 companies as well as thousands of medium and smaller sized ones spread across the entire spectrum of metals using industries. The company feels that one of its strengths lies in its market diversification, with no single industry accounting for more than 6% of its total business and no one customer more than 2%. The company's coast-to-coast network of metals service centers provides next day delivery to over 90% of the markets it serves, and two day delivery to virtually all of the rest.

The company noted that 1998 was a challenging year as market conditions for highly engineered metals weakened during the second half and the company's customers, North America's durable equipment makers, became increasingly cautious with their purchases. This environment continued into the fall reflecting the difficulties in Asia and its effect on some of the company's customers' key markets.

Net income decreased 22% in 1998, reflecting higher interest, depreciation and amortization expenses associated with the unprecedented level of investment during the 1995 through 1998 period. Looking ahead, the company expects capital expenditures to moderate, resulting in stronger cash flow performance as its markets move off the low point of this cycle. Management believes that the investments and infrastructure it has put into place will allow the company to grow to $1.5 billion in revenues within the next five years.

The company's market diversification strategy is intended to mitigating the impact of the business cycle on CAS's performance and use of capital. The company's long-term financial goals are: to achieve a 15% return on opening equity at the bottom of the cycle, and a 21% or better return at the top. In 1998, the company's most difficult year since the early 1990s, its return on equity was 13.2%, sightly below its target. Management is hopeful that 1999 will see a correction in the current imbalance between supply and demand, together with a move towards a more stable balance between domestic and import sources.

Per Share Data ($) (Year Ended Dec. 31)	1998	1997	1996	1995	1994	1993	1992	1991	1990	1989
Tangible Bk. Val.	8.66	10.36	9.30	7.81	5.88	5.04	4.74	4.67	4.94	5.15
Cash Flow	1.92	2.14	2.22	2.25	1.45	0.86	0.60	0.40	0.61	0.97
Earnings	1.32	1.70	1.86	1.93	1.12	0.51	0.25	0.02	0.23	0.64
Dividends	0.76	0.66	0.57	0.43	0.26	0.21	0.21	0.29	0.36	0.34
Payout Ratio	57%	39%	31%	22%	24%	42%	86%	955%	158%	54%
Prices - High	24 7/8	26 5/8	30 7/8	22 5/8	13 1/8	9 1/4	6 7/8	7 5/8	7 1/2	8 7/8
- Low	14	16 3/4	16 1/8	9 3/4	8 7/8	6	5 5/8	5 1/4	5 1/8	6 5/8
P/E Ratio - High	19	16	17	12	12	18	28	NM	33	14
- Low	11	10	9	5	8	12	22	NM	22	10
Income Statement Analysis (Million $)										
Revs.	793	755	673	628	537	474	424	436	479	501
Oper. Inc.	48.7	49.9	51.0	51.7	33.1	20.2	15.3	12.5	17.8	23.8
Depr.	8.5	6.2	5.0	4.5	4.6	4.8	4.9	5.3	5.2	4.4
Int. Exp.	9.5	4.4	3.2	3.0	3.3	3.9	4.4	7.0	6.9	5.3
Pretax Inc.	30.7	39.5	43.1	44.3	25.3	11.6	6.1	0.4	5.8	14.3
Eff. Tax Rate	40%	40%	40%	40%	39%	41%	44%	47%	46%	39%
Net Inc.	18.5	23.8	26.1	26.8	15.4	6.9	3.4	0.2	3.1	8.7
Balance Sheet & Other Fin. Data (Million $)										
Cash	3.0	2.8	1.8	0.7	1.0	1.5	0.7	0.3	0.3	1.8
Curr. Assets	306	243	164	162	158	152	142	133	163	149
Total Assets	460	366	261	223	213	204	195	190	227	202
Curr. Liab.	125	124	84.0	77.5	82.1	66.1	66.7	53.5	73.3	73.4
LT Debt	172	90.7	40.9	28.0	38.5	58.0	53.0	63.3	76.7	51.0
Common Eqty.	144	137	122	103	82.2	69.5	65.5	64.7	68.3	69.7
Total Cap.	331	240	174	142	128	136	126	137	153	129
Cap. Exp.	30.2	16.2	22.5	11.8	7.9	4.6	1.8	3.3	13.4	10.4
Cash Flow	27.0	30.1	31.1	31.3	20.0	11.7	8.3	5.5	8.3	13.0
Curr. Ratio	2.5	2.0	2.0	2.1	1.9	2.3	2.1	2.5	2.2	2.0
% LT Debt of Cap.	52.0	37.8	23.5	19.7	30.0	42.8	42.0	46.2	50.0	39.6
% Net Inc.of Revs.	2.3	3.2	3.9	4.3	2.9	1.5	0.8	NM	0.7	1.7
% Ret. on Assets	4.5	7.6	10.8	12.3	7.3	3.5	1.8	0.1	1.5	4.2
% Ret. on Equity	13.2	18.4	23.2	28.9	20.2	10.2	5.2	0.3	4.5	12.8

Data as orig reptd.; bef. results of disc opers/spec. items. Per share data adj. for stk. divs. Bold denotes diluted EPS (FASB 128)-prior periods restated. E-Estimated. NA-Not Available. NM-Not Meaningful. NR-Not Ranked.

Office—3400 N. Wolf Rd., Franklin Park, IL 60131. **Reincorporated**—in Delaware in 1967. **Tel**—(847) 455-7111. **Fax**—(847) 455-7136. **Website**—http://www.amcastle.com**Chrmn**—M. Simpson. **Pres & CEO**—R. G. Mork. **EVP & COO**—A. Raney. **VP & CFO**—E. F. Culliton. **Treas & Contr**—J. A. Podojil. **Secy**—J. M. Aufox. **Investor Contact**—Debra Davis (312-266-7800). **Dirs**—D. T. Carroll, E. F. Culliton, W. K. Hall, R. S. Hamada, P. J. Herbert III, J. P. Keller, J. W. McCarter, Jr., J. McCartney, R. G. Mork, J.W. Puth, M. Simpson. **Transfer Agent & Registrar**—American Stock Transfer & Trust Co., NYC. **Empl**— 1,900. **S&P Analyst:** C.C.P.

Catalina Marketing

NYSE Symbol **POS**

In S&P SmallCap 600

09-OCT-99

Industry:
Services (Advertising & Marketing)

Summary: This leader in point-of-scan electronic marketing delivers customized checkout coupons for manufacturers' products to customers targeted on the basis of their purchases.

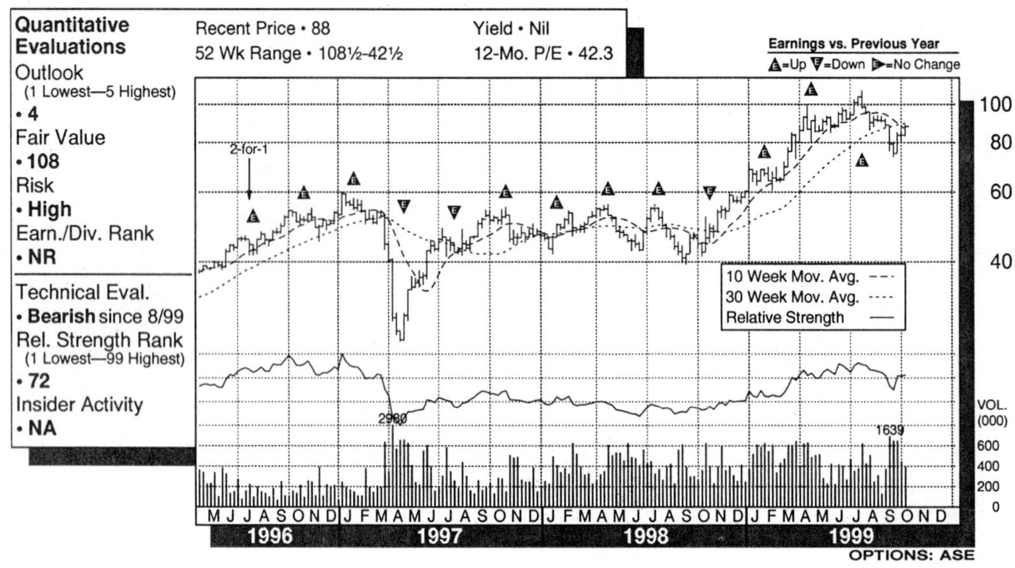

Business Profile - 26-JUL-99

The company added 165 net domestic store installations in the first quarter of FY 2000 (Mar.), resulting in a 7.2% increase, to 12,257 installed stores, as of June 30, 1999. The international installed store base increased 54%, year to year. During the first quarter, POS reached an agreement to install the Health Resource Network in more than 2,500 Walgreens stores. Upon completion of the Walgreens installations, as well as ongoing Rite Aid installations, Health Resource Network will have an installed base of more than 10,000 retail pharmacies, versus 4,000 current outlets. The ValuPage online program averaged more than 2.8 million visitors a month in the first three months of FY 2000. In April 1999, POS acquired CompuScan Marketing, Inc., an in-store promotional company.

Operational Review - 26-JUL-99

Revenue in the three months ended June 30, 1999, climbed 28%, year to year, reflecting an increase in the installed store base. With higher selling, general and administrative expenses, the gain in operating income was held to 26%. Net income soared 29%, to $8,703,000 ($0.45 a share, on 2.4% more shares), from $6,738,000 ($0.35).

Stock Performance - 08-OCT-99

In the past 30 trading days, POS's shares have declined 3%, compared to a 0.91% fall in the S&P 500. Average trading volume for the past five days was 77,420 shares, compared with the 40-day moving average of 141,208 shares.

Key Stock Statistics

Dividend Rate/Share	Nil	Shareholders	533
Shs. outstg. (M)	18.5	Market cap. (B)	$ 1.6
Avg. daily vol. (M)	0.153	Inst. holdings	84%
Tang. Bk. Value/Share	5.21		
Beta	0.95		

Value of $10,000 invested 5 years ago: $ 35,200

Fiscal Year Ending Mar. 31

	2000	1999	1998	1997	1996	1995
Revenues (Million $)						
1Q	72.61	56.83	46.66	38.13	30.61	27.45
2Q	—	64.45	52.73	41.62	30.94	24.75
3Q	—	67.60	63.70	46.34	36.55	30.27
4Q	—	75.90	54.06	46.05	36.05	30.78
Yr.	—	264.8	217.2	172.1	134.2	113.3
Earnings Per Share ($)						
1Q	**0.45**	**0.35**	0.30	0.31	0.26	0.23
2Q	—	**0.34**	0.43	0.35	0.27	0.21
3Q	—	**0.64**	**0.57**	0.40	0.30	0.23
4Q	—	**0.65**	**0.43**	0.27	0.28	0.18
Yr.	—	**1.98**	**1.73**	**1.33**	1.10	0.85

Next earnings report expected: mid October

Dividend Data

Catalina does not expect to pay cash dividends in the forseeable future.

Catalina Marketing Corporation

Business Summary - 26-JUL-99

Most supermarket shoppers give their coupons to the cashier at the checkout, but customers targeted by the strategic marketing of Catalina Marketing are given coupons by the cashier. The company provides manufacturers of consumer and pharmaceutical products and retailers with a cost-effective method to deliver advertising messages and promotional incentives directly to targeted customers, based on their purchasing behavior.

The company has developed an electronic network designed to employ the Universal Product Code (UPC) labeling standard, which enjoys widespread use in retail stores. POS's system links software, personal computers, databases, and specially designed printers to point-of-scan controllers. When a shopper makes a purchase, the system evaluates the product's UPC data, matches it with manufacturer or retailer programmed promotions, and directs the printer located near the register to print the appropriate message or coupon. Printing takes place throughout the checkout process, and coupons are handed directly to the customer at the conclusion of the transaction. The company's U.S. Checkout Coupon programs generated 80% and 83% of total revenues in FY 99 (Mar.) and FY 98, respectively.

POS offers manufacturers 13 four-week cycles annually for more than 500 product categories. These categories are typically based on standard industry classifications of household and consumer products sold in supermarkets, such as coffee, baby foods and frozen dinners.

POS receives a fee for each promotion printed and pays a distribution fee to the retailer based on the number of manufacturer promotions printed. The retailer pays a one-time fee for each installation, and generally agrees to use the network in its store for a minimum of five years.

At June 30, 1999, the company's network was installed in 12,257 stores in the U.S., reaching about 161 million shoppers weekly. Outside the U.S., the network was installed in 2,249 stores.

In the first quarter of FY 2000, POS agreed to install its Health Resource Network in more than 2,500 Walgreens stores. The agreement, together with an August 1997 Rite-Aid agreement, will result in an installed base of more than 10,000 retail pharmacies. As of June 30, 1999, the Health Resource system was installed in 4,152 pharmacy outlets.

A developing product line includes SuperMarkets Online, which provides the industry's only online secure coupon format through ValuPage. Although the operation is still operating at a loss, ValuPage averaged more than 2.8 million visitors a month in the first three months of FY 2000.

Per Share Data ($) (Year Ended Mar. 31)	1999	1998	1997	1996	1995	1994	1993	1992	1991	1990
Tangible Bk. Val.	4.64	3.86	3.99	3.65	2.83	2.27	1.54	1.02	0.93	NA
Cash Flow	3.42	2.97	2.21	1.82	1.60	1.18	0.86	0.67	0.34	NA
Earnings	1.98	1.73	1.33	1.10	0.85	0.62	0.41	0.26	0.08	NA
Dividends	Nil	Nil	Nil	Nil	Nil	Nil	Nil	Nil	NA	NA
Payout Ratio	Nil	Nil	Nil	Nil	Nil	Nil	Nil	Nil	NA	NA
Cal. Yrs.	1998	1997	1996	1995	1994	1993	1992	1991	1990	1989
Prices - High	70½	60	55½	32½	28⅛	25⅛	19⅝	NA	NA	NA
- Low	39⅜	25⅛	29¼	20	20⅝	14¼	10	NA	NA	NA
P/E Ratio - High	36	35	42	29	33	41	49	NA	NA	NA
- Low	20	15	22	18	24	23	25	NA	NA	NA
Income Statement Analysis (Million $)										
Revs.	265	217	172	134	113	91.4	71.9	51.7	33.1	24.6
Oper. Inc.	95.3	76.6	61.3	49.1	42.9	29.8	25.5	14.1	5.8	2.7
Depr.	27.3	23.7	17.9	14.5	15.1	11.4	9.3	7.8	4.9	2.4
Int. Exp.	Nil	Nil	Nil	Nil	Nil	Nil	0.1	0.3	0.3	0.3
Pretax Inc.	65.6	51.9	45.1	36.2	27.9	19.2	13.3	6.7	1.8	0.7
Eff. Tax Rate	43%	37%	40%	41%	40%	40%	38%	29%	20%	15%
Net Inc.	37.6	32.9	27.2	22.0	17.2	12.7	8.2	4.8	1.4	0.6
Balance Sheet & Other Fin. Data (Million $)										
Cash	13.9	18.4	13.7	25.8	30.7	26.9	25.6	6.5	4.2	NA
Curr. Assets	95.5	63.6	61.7	65.3	60.2	51.2	39.9	25.8	12.5	NA
Total Assets	221	157	155	114	99	85.5	61.2	44.5	31.1	NA
Curr. Liab.	93.8	61.5	53.5	40.5	42.7	40.2	31.9	23.3	18.1	NA
LT Debt	0.6	0.4	0.9	Nil	Nil	Nil	Nil	2.4	2.5	NA
Common Eqty.	121	90.0	96.9	71.2	55.5	44.9	29.3	18.8	10.5	NA
Total Cap.	127	95.5	97.8	73.7	56.6	45.3	29.3	21.2	13.0	NA
Cap. Exp.	40.0	24.2	34.7	23.6	20.3	25.2	12.2	11.6	9.8	3.7
Cash Flow	65.0	56.6	45.2	36.4	32.3	24.1	17.5	12.6	6.3	3.0
Curr. Ratio	1.0	1.0	1.2	1.6	1.4	1.3	1.3	1.1	0.7	NA
% LT Debt of Cap.	0.5	0.5	1.0	Nil	Nil	Nil	Nil	11.2	19.3	NA
% Net Inc.of Revs.	14.2	15.1	15.9	16.4	15.2	13.9	11.4	9.2	4.3	2.3
% Ret. on Assets	19.9	21.1	20.3	20.9	18.7	17.0	15.4	13.2	NA	NA
% Ret. on Equity	35.7	35.2	32.4	34.8	34.4	33.7	33.8	36.9	NA	NA

Data as orig reptd.; bef. results of disc opers/spec. items. Per share data adj. for stk. divs. Bold denotes diluted EPS (FASB 128)-prior periods restated. E-Estimated. NA-Not Available. NM-Not Meaningful. NR-Not Ranked.

Office—11300 Ninth St. North, St. Petersburg, FL 33716-2329. **Tel**—(813) 579-5000. **Website**—http://www.catalinamktg.com **Chrmn**—G. W. Off. **Pres & CEO**—D. D. Granger. **CFO**—J. Post. **Dirs**—F. H. Barker, F. W. Beinecke, P. W. Collins, S. I. D'Agostino, D. D. Granger, T. D. Greer, G. W. Off, T. W. Smith, M. B. Wilson. **Transfer Agent & Registrar**—ChaseMellon Shareholder Services, LA. **Incorporated**—in Delaware in 1992. **Empl**—1,001. **S&P Analyst:** Jordan Horoschak

STANDARD
&POOR'S
STOCK REPORTS

Cato Corp.

NASDAQ Symbol **CACOA**

In S&P SmallCap 600

09-OCT-99

Industry: Retail (Specialty-Apparel)

Summary: This long-established retailer operates more than 750 stores in 21 states, offering women's popular-priced apparel for fashion-conscious junior, missy and large-size customers.

Quantitative Evaluations

Outlook
(1 Lowest—5 Highest)
• **4+**

Fair Value
• **18¾**

Risk
• **Average**

Earn./Div. Rank
• **B**

Technical Eval.
• **Bullish** since 8/99

Rel. Strength Rank
(1 Lowest—99 Highest)
• **83**

Insider Activity
• **NA**

Recent Price • 14¼
52 Wk Range • 15⅝-7½
Yield • 2.1%
12-Mo. P/E • 12.6

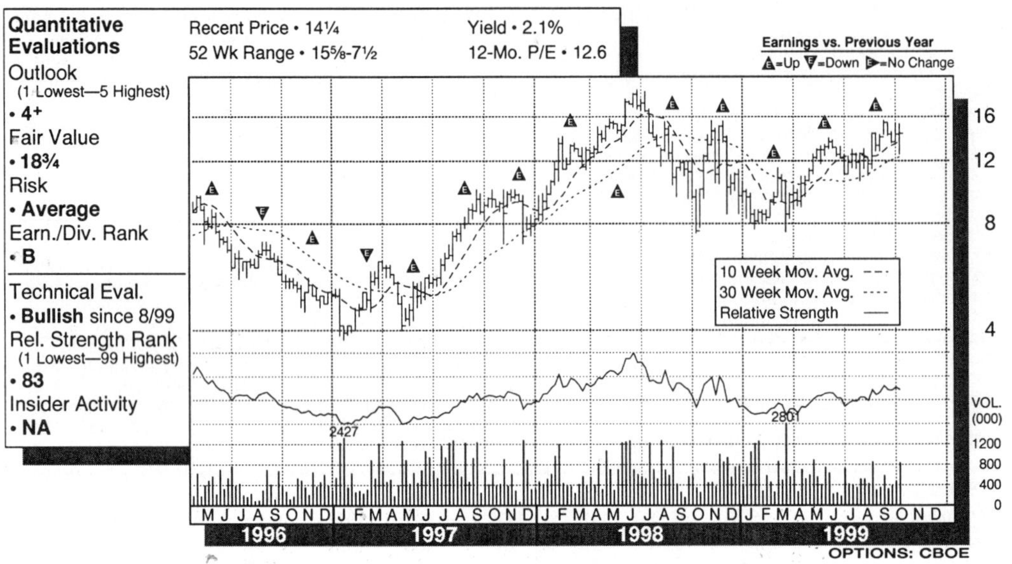

Business Profile - 30-JUN-99

Cato Corporation operated 756 stores as of May 29, 1999, offering everyday low prices, without the need for special sales. The first quarter of FY 00 (Jan.) marked the ninth consecutive quarter of year over year earnings increases. Results in the first quarter benefitted from improved gross margins and lower than expected SG&A expenses. The company recently said its store development pace is on target. Cato opened 21 new stores in the quarter and relocated six stores in the same period. Cato's plans are to open a total of 75 new stores in FY 00.

Operational Review - 30-JUN-99

Total revenues for the three months ended May 1, 1999, rose 12%, year to year, reflecting 7% higher same-store sales, an increased store count, and improved merchandise offerings. Cost of sales rose 12%, the result of markdowns on slow moving merchandise, which helped to enhance inventory flow. SG&A expense increased only 5.5%, and after taxes at 35.0%, versus 34.0%, net income rose 24%, to $13,738,000 ($0.51 a share), from $11,117,000 ($0.39).

Stock Performance - 08-OCT-99

In the past 30 trading days, CACOA's shares have increased 8%, compared to a 0.91% fall in the S&P 500. Average trading volume for the past five days was 165,400 shares, compared with the 40-day moving average of 103,749 shares.

Key Stock Statistics

Dividend Rate/Share	0.30	Shareholders	4,700
Shs. outstg. (M)	26.5	Market cap. (B)	$0.304
Avg. daily vol. (M)	0.099	Inst. holdings	47%
Tang. Bk. Value/Share	7.08		
Beta	0.40		

Value of $10,000 invested 5 years ago: $ 8,095

Fiscal Year Ending Jan. 31

	2000	1999	1998	1997	1996	1995
Revenues (Million $)						
1Q	158.3	141.0	127.5	123.5	117.8	113.1
2Q	153.5	132.6	124.5	116.0	117.8	113.3
3Q	—	118.6	113.7	111.5	109.3	112.2
4Q	—	146.8	146.8	140.5	145.1	137.6
Yr.	—	543.7	512.5	491.5	490.0	476.2
Earnings Per Share ($)						
1Q	**0.51**	**0.39**	**0.28**	**0.27**	0.26	0.28
2Q	**0.37**	**0.20**	**0.13**	**0.08**	0.10	0.15
3Q	—	**0.10**	**0.05**	**-0.03**	-0.05	0.10
4Q	—	**0.16**	**0.15**	**-0.07**	0.11	0.10
Yr.	—	**0.85**	**0.62**	**0.25**	**0.42**	**0.63**

Next earnings report expected: mid November

Dividend Data (Dividends have been paid since 1992.)

Amount ($)	Date Decl.	Ex-Div. Date	Stock of Record	Payment Date
0.050	Dec. 03	Dec. 17	Dec. 21	Jan. 04 '99
0.055	Mar. 04	Mar. 11	Mar. 15	Mar. 29 '99
0.075	May. 24	Jun. 03	Jun. 07	Jun. 21 '99
0.075	Aug. 26	Sep. 09	Sep. 13	Sep. 27 '99

A Division of The McGraw-Hill Companies

The Cato Corporation

Business Summary - 30-JUN-99

More than 50 years old, Cato (CACOA) continues to sell apparel and related accessories to women and girls, catering to smaller populations at its Cato, Cato Plus and It's Fashion! stores in 21 states throughout the South and Midwest. CACOA is headquartered in Charlotte, NC.

Cato operated 732 women's specialty stores as of January 30, 1999, up from 693 a year earlier. The company intends to open about 75 stores in FY 00 (Jan.). Most stores range in size from 3,000 to 6,000 square feet, with the average store at about 4,300 square feet. The stores are mainly located in strip shopping centers that are anchored by a national discount store.

The company offers its own credit card and layaway plan. Credit and layaway sales represented 21% of retail sales in FY 99, with credit card sales alone accounting for 16%. The company's net bad debt expense was 4.3% of sales in FY 99.

The target customer for Cato is the fashion-oriented woman, in the low-to-middle income range. Its merchandising strategy is to provide quality, affordably priced apparel and accessories for the fashion-conscious junior, missy or large-size customer. In addition, the company offers clothing and accessories for girls 7-16 years old in selected locations. The stores feature a broad assortment of apparel and accessories, including casual and dressy sportswear, dresses, careerwear, coats, hosiery, shoes, costume jewelry, handbags, and millinery. A large portion of the company's merchandise is sold under private labels and is produced by various vendors to meet Cato's particular product specifications.

The company's main objective is to be the leading specialty apparel retailer for women. A key element of Cato's business strategy is to offer a wide assortment of merchandise in terms of apparel, accessories, color, selection, and sizes. Cato also strives to offer merchandise that is priced below department stores and higher-end specialty chains, while also selling more fashionable clothing than what is offered at discount stores.

Most of Cato's stores are located in the Southeast in small to medium sized towns, with populations ranging from 10,000 to 50,000.

Sales for the 17-week period ended May 29, 1999, rose 13%, year to year. Same-store sales rose 7% over the same period.

Per Share Data ($)										
(Year Ended Jan. 31)	**1999**	**1998**	**1997**	**1996**	**1995**	**1994**	**1993**	**1992**	**1991**	**1990**
Tangible Bk. Val.	6.39	5.75	5.34	5.27	4.98	4.50	2.94	1.37	0.91	1.37
Cash Flow	1.12	0.89	0.54	0.69	0.86	1.02	0.89	0.63	-0.23	-0.04
Earnings	0.85	0.62	0.25	0.42	0.62	0.84	0.74	0.43	-0.45	-0.24
Dividends	0.18	0.16	0.16	0.16	0.14	0.09	0.04	Nil	0.01	0.05
Payout Ratio	21%	26%	64%	38%	23%	10%	5%	Nil	Nil	NM
Cal. Yrs.	1998	1997	1996	1995	1994	1993	1992	1991	1990	1989
Prices - High	19 1/8	10	10 1/8	8 7/8	21 1/2	24 3/4	16 5/8	10 1/8	2 7/16	3 1/2
- Low	7 1/2	3 3/4	4 1/2	5	5 1/2	14 3/4	7 1/8	3/8	3/8	2 3/16
P/E Ratio - High	22	16	40	21	35	29	23	23	NM	NM
- Low	9	6	18	12	9	18	10	1	NM	NM
Income Statement Analysis (Million $)										
Revs.	524	497	492	490	476	420	341	274	238	257
Oper. Inc.	25.4	17.8	10.5	12.8	35.7	44.0	35.1	22.7	7.5	7.6
Depr.	7.6	7.7	8.3	7.8	6.8	5.5	4.2	4.3	4.9	4.5
Int. Exp.	0.2	0.3	0.3	0.3	0.4	0.3	1.2	3.3	3.4	3.6
Pretax Inc.	36.8	25.4	10.9	18.0	28.5	38.3	29.7	15.1	-15.0	-10.4
Eff. Tax Rate	35%	32%	36%	34%	37%	35%	36%	37%	NM	NM
Net Inc.	23.9	17.4	7.0	12.0	18.1	24.8	19.1	9.5	-10.0	-5.3
Balance Sheet & Other Fin. Data (Million $)										
Cash	44.1	41.6	16.6	26.1	46.2	42.6	29.7	16.6	3.0	5.1
Curr. Assets	198	186	161	150	143	139	94.2	69.5	55.3	60.2
Total Assets	259	241	218	210	201	179	122	95.0	83.0	97.0
Curr. Liab.	73.6	72.2	56.1	48.2	48.9	47.2	40.4	36.3	29.9	26.6
LT Debt	Nil	Nil	Nil	Nil	Nil	Nil	Nil	24.9	29.4	34.0
Common Eqty.	172	158	152	150	142	128	78.2	30.5	20.0	30.3
Total Cap.	178	163	156	154	146	131	80.9	56.2	49.4	69.3
Cap. Exp.	13.5	7.4	8.4	9.4	25.5	17.2	7.6	1.7	1.8	4.3
Cash Flow	31.6	25.1	15.4	19.8	24.9	30.3	23.3	13.9	-5.1	-0.9
Curr. Ratio	2.7	2.6	2.9	3.1	2.9	2.9	2.3	1.9	1.8	2.3
% LT Debt of Cap.	Nil	Nil	Nil	Nil	Nil	Nil	Nil	44.3	59.6	49.0
% Net Inc.of Revs.	4.6	3.5	1.4	2.4	3.8	5.9	5.6	3.5	NM	NM
% Ret. on Assets	9.6	7.6	3.3	5.8	9.5	16.1	16.2	10.6	NM	NM
% Ret. on Equity	14.5	11.2	4.7	8.2	13.4	23.5	33.3	37.6	NM	NM

Data as orig. reptd.; bef. results of disc. opers. and/or spec. items. Per share data adj. for stk. divs. as of ex-div. date. Bold denotes diluted EPS (FASB 128). E-Estimated. NA-Not Available. NM-Not Meaningful. NR-Not Ranked.

Office—8100 Denmark Rd., Charlotte, NC 28273-5975. **Tel**—(704) 554-8510. **Chrmn**—W. H. Cato Jr. **Vice Chrmn, Pres & CEO**—J. P. D. Cato. **EVP, CFO & Secy & Investor Contact**—Michael O. Moore (704-551-7201). **Dirs**—R. W. Bradshaw Jr., E. T. Cato, J. P. D. Cato, T. E. Cato, W. H. Cato Jr., G. S. Currin, P. Fulton, C. Cato Goodyear, G. Hamrick, H. A. Severson, J. H. Shaw, A. F. Sloan. **Transfer Agent & Registrar**—First Union National Bank, Charlotte, NC. **Incorporated**—in Delaware in 1946. **Empl**— 7,000. **S&P Analyst:** Matthew C. Hershberg

STANDARD
&POOR'S
STOCK REPORTS

CDI Corp.

NYSE Symbol **CDI**
In S&P SmallCap 600

09-OCT-99 **Industry:** Services (Employment)

Summary: CDI provides technical and engineering services and temporary office support and executive recruitment services.

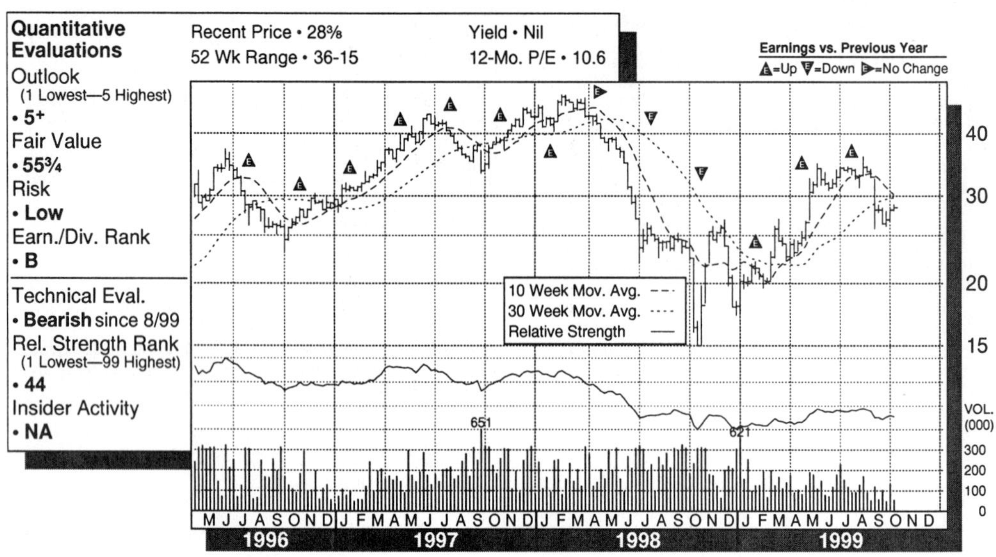

Business Profile - 05-MAY-99

Results in recent periods reflect CDI's focus on improving the profitability of its existing businesses and targeting new growth to higher margin opportunities. Since a reorganization in the second half of 1998, the technical services and information technology services business units have stabilized, focusing on higher margin opportunities, and are showing sustained improvement. In the 1999 first quarter, CDI's Todays Staffing segment acquired Chicago-based Staffing Consultants Inc. Chicago represents the largest U.S. market for temporary staffing. In August 1998, directors authorized the repurchase of up to 5% of the common shares; through December 31, 1998, 889,700 shares had been acquired.

Operational Review - 05-MAY-99

Revenues in the first three months of 1999 advanced 2.7%, year to year, as higher revenues in the information technology and Todays Staffing segments outweighed lower revenues at the management recruiters international segment. Gross margins widened, and operating income gained 14%. After taxes at 39.4%, versus 39.0%, net income was up 9.6%, to $11,733,000 ($0.62 a share, on 4.6% fewer shares), from $10,709,000 ($0.54).

Stock Performance - 08-OCT-99

In the past 30 trading days, CDI's shares have declined 13%, compared to a 0.91% fall in the S&P 500. Average trading volume for the past five days was 10,580 shares, compared with the 40-day moving average of 16,572 shares.

Key Stock Statistics

Dividend Rate/Share	Nil	Shareholders	8,000
Shs. outstg. (M)	19.1	Market cap. (B)	$0.542
Avg. daily vol. (M)	0.017	Inst. holdings	40%
Tang. Bk. Value/Share	10.70		
Beta	0.34		

Value of $10,000 invested 5 years ago: $ 22,749

Fiscal Year Ending Dec. 31

	1999	1998	1997	1996	1995	1994
Revenues (Million $)						
1Q	389.1	379.0	360.5	330.8	292.4	249.2
2Q	407.6	388.9	378.1	338.9	312.5	264.9
3Q	—	389.5	383.1	353.8	331.5	288.7
4Q	—	383.4	375.1	351.4	334.0	294.8
Yr.	—	1,541	1,497	1,375	1,270	1,098
Earnings Per Share ($)						
1Q	**0.62**	**0.54**	**0.54**	**0.44**	0.32	0.20
2Q	**0.65**	**0.47**	**0.60**	**0.53**	0.40	0.23
3Q	—	**0.63**	**0.69**	**0.65**	0.45	0.34
4Q	—	**0.62**	**0.53**	**0.52**	0.38	0.37
Yr.	—	**2.25**	**2.36**	**2.14**	**1.57**	**0.89**

Next earnings report expected: late October

Dividend Data

No cash dividends have been paid since 1970.

CDI Corp.

Business Summary - 05-MAY-99

CDI Corporation (CDI) is a leading provider of technical and temporary personnel and is also a top management recruiter. The Technical Services division accounted for 58% of 1998 revenues; Information Technology 21%; Todays Staffing 14%; and Management Recruitment 7%.

Technical Services, believed to be the largest operation of its kind in the U.S., provides staffing, outsourcing, and consulting services in the fields of engineering, technical and other fields. Customers use CDI for expansion programs, to staff special projects, and to meet peak period personnel needs. Services include project planning and feasibility studies, conceptual engineering, detail engineering and design, procurement and project management. The division serves about 3,000 customers, mainly in the aircraft, aerospace, automotive, chemicals, construction, electronics, industrial equipment, marine, power/energy, and telecommunications fields.

The Information Technology Services segment provides staffing and outsourcing services in the information technology field. In staffing, the division manages a customer's entire information technology contract staffing needs. In outsourcing, it focuses on application development and maintenance, distributed systems management, and help desk services. In 1998, a single company provided 30% of the division's revenues.

The Todays Staffing segment offers clerical, secretarial, office support, legal, financial staffing, and other temporary personnel; the division, with more than 10,000 customers, operates through a network of 126 offices in the U.S. and Canada.

Management Recruiters searches for and recruits management, technical, sales, clerical, and other personnel for permanent employment positions in numerous fields including accounting, finance, administrative, information technology, managerial, personnel, production, research and development, sales, supervision, and technical. Management Recruiters has 733 franchised offices and 46 company-owned offices throughout North America, providing services to both large and small employers.

CDI's is seeking growth by designing an incentive program to accelerate cross-selling of services across its core businesses; implementing several initiatives at Management Recruiters International and Todays Staffing to position these businesses for increased revenues and profitability; and winning new contracts with existing customers.

Per Share Data ($) (Year Ended Dec. 31)	1998	1997	1996	1995	1994	1993	1992	1991	1990	1989
Tangible Bk. Val.	8.66	10.02	8.14	6.50	5.93	4.70	4.17	4.08	4.85	4.38
Cash Flow	2.98	2.96	2.70	2.17	1.85	1.17	0.95	0.45	1.36	1.66
Earnings	2.25	2.36	2.14	1.55	1.13	0.40	0.17	-0.39	0.61	1.05
Dividends	Nil	Nil	Nil	Nil	Nil	Nil	Nil	Nil	Nil	Nil
Payout Ratio	Nil	Nil	Nil	Nil	Nil	Nil	Nil	Nil	Nil	Nil
Prices - High	47 7/8	45 3/4	37 1/4	26 5/8	19 7/8	13 1/8	10 3/8	9 3/4	15 5/8	18 1/2
- Low	15	27 3/4	18	13 1/2	10 1/4	6 7/8	6	5 3/4	5 5/8	9 7/8
P/E Ratio - High	21	19	17	17	18	33	61	NM	26	18
- Low	7	12	8	9	9	17	35	NM	9	9
Income Statement Analysis (Million $)										
Revs.	1,541	1,497	1,375	1,270	1,098	921	855	768	921	887
Oper. Inc.	90.6	91.3	84.7	68.3	55.1	31.7	25.2	16.6	42.8	52.9
Depr.	14.5	12.1	11.2	12.4	14.2	15.3	15.2	16.6	14.7	12.0
Int. Exp.	1.4	2.3	3.5	4.5	4.1	3.7	4.1	4.7	7.7	6.7
Pretax Inc.	74.7	76.8	70.2	51.4	36.8	12.6	5.9	-9.2	20.3	34.1
Eff. Tax Rate	39%	37%	39%	40%	39%	38%	43%	NM	40%	41%
Net Inc.	44.2	46.9	42.5	30.7	22.4	7.8	3.4	-7.6	12.0	20.7
Balance Sheet & Other Fin. Data (Million $)										
Cash	7.0	7.0	6.1	4.5	5.2	20.4	2.5	3.3	4.3	4.0
Curr. Assets	333	290	288	272	224	193	172	157	174	195
Total Assets	436	349	340	329	298	267	244	228	255	274
Curr. Liab.	146	121	107	110	96.2	85.1	56.8	49.5	73.0	71.7
LT Debt	35.1	Nil	48.9	67.9	58.8	62.0	72.2	67.1	61.2	90.9
Common Eqty.	241	226	17.0	145	139	117	109	105	113	102
Total Cap.	279	217	226	213	198	179	185	176	179	199
Cap. Exp.	23.1	11.9	13.5	16.7	14.0	11.2	8.8	4.1	17.3	24.6
Cash Flow	58.7	59.1	53.7	43.1	36.5	23.2	18.7	8.9	26.8	32.7
Curr. Ratio	2.3	2.4	2.7	2.5	2.3	2.3	3.0	3.2	2.4	2.7
% LT Debt of Cap.	12.6	NM	21.6	31.8	29.7	34.7	39.0	38.1	34.1	45.6
% Net Inc.of Revs.	2.9	3.1	3.1	2.4	2.0	0.8	0.4	NM	1.3	2.3
% Ret. on Assets	11.3	13.6	12.8	10.0	7.9	3.1	1.5	NM	4.6	8.7
% Ret. on Equity	18.5	22.9	26.5	21.6	17.5	7.0	3.2	NM	11.2	22.5

Data as orig reptd.; bef. results of disc opers/spec. items. Per share data adj. for stk. divs. Bold denotes diluted EPS (FASB 128)-prior periods restated. E-Estimated. NA-Not Available. NM-Not Meaningful. NR-Not Ranked.

Office—1717 Arch St., 35th Fl., Philadelphia, PA 19103-2768. **Tel**—(215) 569-2200. **Fax**—(215) 496-0799. **Website**—www.cdicorp.com **Pres & CEO**—M. Wienick. **EVP & CFO**—J. D. Sanford. **EVP & COO**—R. J. Mannarino. **SVP & Secy**—J. R. Seiders. **Dirs**—W. E. Blankley, J. M. Coleman, W. R. Garrison, K. H. Harrell, L. C. Karlson, A. M. Levantin, A. B. Miller, M. Wienick, B. J. Winokur. **Transfer Agent & Registrar**—ChaseMellon Shareholder Services, Ridgefield Park, NJ. **Incorporated**—in Pennsylvania in 1950. **Empl**— 31,000. **S&P Analyst:** M.I.

STANDARD &POOR'S
STOCK REPORTS

CEC Entertainment

NYSE Symbol **CEC**

In S&P SmallCap 600

09-OCT-99

Industry: Restaurants

Summary: This family restaurant/entertainment center company operates or franchises more than 300 Chuck E. Cheese's restaurants in 44 states.

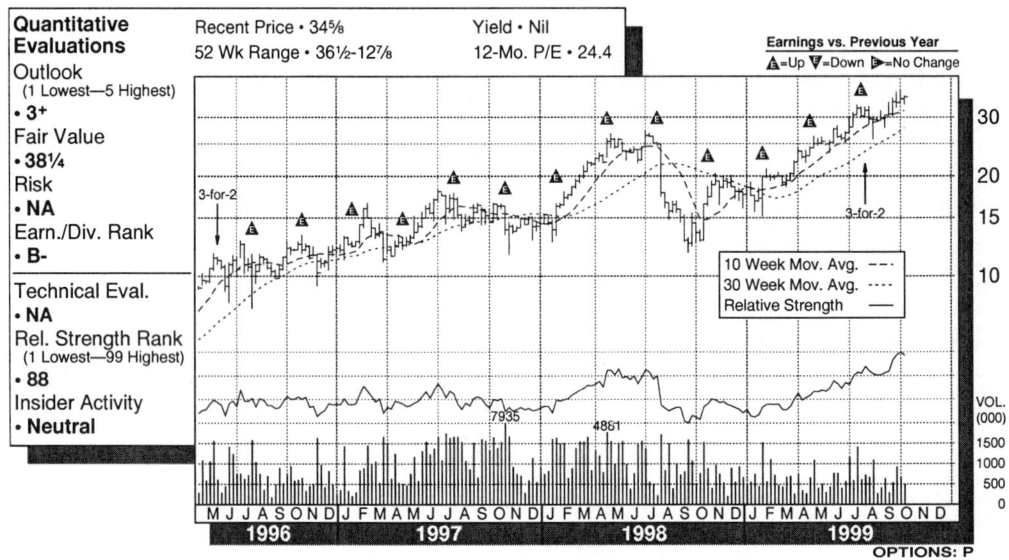

Business Profile - 23-JUN-99

In 1998, the company opened 22 new stores, followed by six more in the first quarter of 1999. CEC has a stated goal of opening 25 new units for all of 1999. In addition, the company expects to complete its Phase II restaurant renovations by the end of the second quarter of 1999. In 1998, CEC upgraded 117 restaurants. In the first quarter of 1999, revenues jumped nearly 9%, paced by a 33% increase in food and beverage revenues. In July 1998, the company changed its name from ShowBiz Pizza Time (SHBZ) to CEC Entertainment (CEC), and the shares began trading on the NYSE.

Operational Review - 23-JUN-99

Revenues in the three months ended April 4, 1999, rose 8.9%, year to year, driven by solid increases in both games and merchandise revenues and food and beverage sales. Margins widened, reflecting smaller increases in direct costs, partially offset by a rise in SG&A expenses; operating income grew 16%. Results benefited from just a 12% increase in depreciation and amortization charges, as well as a decline in interest expense. After taxes at 39.2% in both periods, net income advanced 23%, to $14,381,000 ($0.78 a share), from $11,683,000 ($0.63).

Stock Performance - 08-OCT-99

In the past 30 trading days, CEC's shares have increased 17%, compared to a 0.91% fall in the S&P 500. Average trading volume for the past five days was 98,060 shares, compared with the 40-day moving average of 106,508 shares.

Key Stock Statistics

Dividend Rate/Share	Nil	Shareholders	2,967
Shs. outstg. (M)	32.0	Market cap. (B)	$ 1.1
Avg. daily vol. (M)	0.129	Inst. holdings	79%
Tang. Bk. Value/Share	6.61		
Beta	1.20		

Value of $10,000 invested 5 years ago: $ 58,797

Fiscal Year Ending Dec. 31

	1999	1998	1997	1996	1995	1994
Revenues (Million $)						
1Q	118.4	105.0	91.59	78.45	72.75	76.37
2Q	398.8	88.90	84.03	69.85	62.64	64.02
3Q	—	98.11	85.60	74.78	66.98	68.29
4Q	—	87.37	89.04	70.91	61.41	59.15
Yr.	—	379.4	350.3	292.9	263.8	267.8
Earnings Per Share ($)						
1Q	**0.52**	**0.42**	**0.28**	**0.19**	0.09	0.12
2Q	**0.59**	**0.26**	**0.21**	**0.08**	-0.04	0.04
3Q	—	**0.31**	**0.21**	**0.13**	Nil	0.04
4Q	—	**0.22**	**0.20**	**0.08**	-0.05	-0.19
Yr.	—	**1.20**	**0.89**	**0.47**	**-0.01**	**0.01**

Next earnings report expected: mid October

Dividend Data

Amount ($)	Date Decl.	Ex-Div. Date	Stock of Record	Payment Date
3-for-2	Jun. 24	Jul. 26	Jul. 01	Jul. 23 '99

CEC Entertainment, Inc.

Business Summary - 23-JUN-99

Mention the name Chuck E. Cheese to kids just about anywhere in the U.S. and they'll jump up and down and beg to be taken there for food and fun. The popular restaurant chain is operated by CEC Entertainment (formerly ShowBiz Pizza Time), which owns or franchises 330 Chuck E. Cheese's restaurants in 44 states and Canada. In addition to pizza, salads, sandwiches and desserts, the combo restaurant/entertainment centers offer family-oriented games, rides, arcade activities, computer-controlled robots, and musical and comic entertainment. The restaurants, which cater to children ages two to 12, are especially popular for birthday parties.

The company opened its first Chuck E. Cheese's restaurant in March 1980. The restaurants, typically located in shopping centers or in free-standing buildings nearby, are big, ranging in size from 8,000 to 14,000 sq. ft.; 40% of the space is devoted to the family-oriented playroom. The fun room includes coin and token operated attractions, arcade-style games, kiddie rides, video games, skill oriented games, and other attractions such as "Sky Tubes" suspended from or reaching to the ceiling.

Each Chuck E. Cheese's restaurant typically employs a general manager, one or two managers, an electronic specialist responsible for maintenance of robotic characters and between 45 and 75 food preparation and service employees, most of whom work on a part-time basis.

The company believes its success is highly dependent on maintaining a unique and exciting environment in its restaurants. As a result, CEC believes it is essential to reinvest capital through the evolution of its games, rides and entertainment packages, as well as enhancement of its facilities. In 1994, the company undertook a repositioning program designed to expand and improve its Chuck E. Cheese's restaurants. Between March 1994 and September 1997, the company remodeled all of its restaurants. In 1997, CEC initiated Phase II of its program, which included a new game package, enhanced prize and merchandise offerings and improved product presentation and service. The company completed Phase II upgrades of 107 locations in 1997 and 117 restaurants in 1998. CEC expects to upgrade the remaining 25 units by the end of the second quarter of 1999. The company has also expanded the size of a number of its restaurants, typically by 1,000 to 4,000 square feet.

In 1998, the company opened 14 new restaurants, not including locations that were acquired by franchisees. CEC expects to open approximately 25 restaurants in 1999 through a combination of new restaurants and acquisition of existing units.

Per Share Data ($)										
(Year Ended Dec. 31)	**1998**	**1997**	**1996**	**1995**	**1994**	**1993**	**1992**	**1991**	**1990**	**1989**
Tangible Bk. Val.	6.80	5.75	5.12	4.60	4.55	4.59	4.31	3.75	3.34	NA
Cash Flow	2.20	1.80	1.37	0.85	0.97	1.15	1.13	0.73	0.58	NA
Earnings	1.20	0.89	0.47	-0.01	0.01	0.38	0.49	0.57	0.27	NA
Dividends	Nil	Nil	Nil	Nil	Nil	Nil	Nil	Nil	Nil	NA
Payout Ratio	Nil	Nil	Nil	Nil	Nil	Nil	Nil	Nil	Nil	NA
Prices - High	27 1/2	18 1/4	13 3/8	6 1/8	6 7/8	15 3/4	15 3/8	11 3/8	7 3/4	NA
- Low	11 3/4	11	5 3/8	3 1/4	3 1/4	5 1/2	8 7/8	4 1/4	2 5/16	NA
P/E Ratio - High	23	20	29	NM	NM	41	31	31	20	NA
- Low	10	12	11	NM	NM	14	18	12	9	NA
Income Statement Analysis (Million $)										
Revs.	379	349	293	263	268	272	253	208	182	NA
Oper. Inc.	84.8	69.9	50.0	25.9	27.7	42.4	46.4	37.3	30.4	NA
Depr.	27.6	25.5	25.1	23.2	26.0	23.1	19.2	16.1	13.1	NA
Int. Exp.	2.7	2.9	3.5	3.1	1.9	0.8	NA	NA	NA	NA
Pretax Inc.	55.0	42.7	22.2	0.4	3.1	18.2	25.2	19.0	13.9	NA
Eff. Tax Rate	39%	40%	41%	83%	78%	35%	39%	5.50%	4.90%	NA
Net Inc.	33.7	25.5	13.2	0.1	0.7	11.9	15.5	17.9	13.2	NA
Balance Sheet & Other Fin. Data (Million $)										
Cash	3.2	7.3	3.4	5.6	2.4	4.5	NA	NA	NA	NA
Curr. Assets	17.8	25.3	27.6	20.0	15.9	20.4	NA	NA	NA	NA
Total Assets	252	226	217	199	188	194	173	158	NA	NA
Curr. Liab.	41.8	39.0	33.6	29.9	36.6	24.8	NA	NA	NA	NA
LT Debt	18.9	23.8	34.7	35.8	19.9	26.8	27.7	21.4	NA	NA
Common Eqty.	184	156	141	128	126	137	132	116	NA	NA
Total Cap.	205	182	178	167	148	166	150	137	NA	NA
Cap. Exp.	66.7	48.5	51.7	28.3	29.4	44.6	33.9	25.1	21.5	NA
Cash Flow	61.1	50.8	38.1	23.0	26.5	34.7	34.5	34.0	26.3	NA
Curr. Ratio	0.4	0.6	0.8	0.7	0.4	0.8	NA	NA	NA	NA
% LT Debt of Cap.	9.2	13.1	19.5	21.4	13.4	16.2	11.8	15.6	NA	NA
% Net Inc.of Revs.	8.9	7.3	4.5	NM	0.3	4.4	6.1	8.6	7.2	NA
% Ret. on Assets	14.1	11.5	6.4	NM	0.4	6.1	8.4	7.6	NA	NA
% Ret. on Equity	19.7	17.0	9.8	NM	0.3	8.5	12.3	10.5	NA	NA

Data as orig reptd.; bef. results of disc opers/spec. items. Per share data adj. for stk. divs. Bold denotes diluted EPS (FASB 128)-prior periods restated. E-Estimated. NA-Not Available. NM-Not Meaningful. NR-Not Ranked.

Office—4441 West Airport Freeway, P. O. Box 152077, Irving, TX 75015. **Tel**—(972) 258-8507. **Website**—http://www.chuckecheese.com **Chrmn & CEO**—R. M. Frank. **Pres**—M. H. Magusiak. **EVP, CFO & Treas**—L. Page. **Dirs**—R. M. Frank, R. T. Huston, M. H. Magusiak, T. T. Morris, L. P. Neeb, C. I. Pharr, W. Tyree, R. E. Woolridge. **Transfer Agent & Registrar**—First National Bank of Boston, Canton, MA. **Incorporated**—in Kansas in 1980. **Empl**— 13,800. **S&P Analyst:** Stephen J. Tekirian

STANDARD
&POOR'S
STOCK REPORTS

Centigram Communications

NASDAQ Symbol **CGRM**

In S&P SmallCap 600

09-OCT-99

Industry:
Computers (Peripherals)

Summary: This company develops and markets voice, data and fax communications server products for telephones and personal computers.

Quantitative Evaluations

Outlook
(1 Lowest—5 Highest)
• **1+**

Fair Value
• **10**

Risk
• **Average**

Earn./Div. Rank
• **C**

Technical Eval.
• **Bullish** since 8/99

Rel. Strength Rank
(1 Lowest—99 Highest)
• **66**

Insider Activity
• **NA**

Recent Price • 10¼
52 Wk Range • 13⅛-5
Yield • Nil
12-Mo. P/E • NM

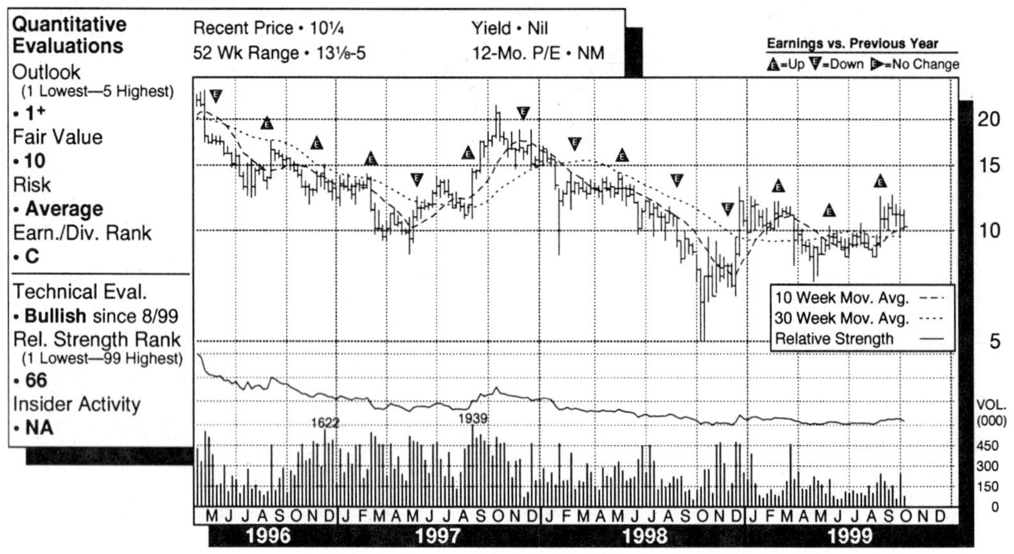

Business Profile - 01-SEP-99

Since the May 1998 sale of its computer premises equipment (CPE) division, the company has focused on providers of telecommunications services. In recent months, it has concentrated on extending its product offerings from messaging to unified communications, including links to the Internet and advanced networking capabilities. CGRM recently reached an agreement with Boston Communications Group (BCC) under which its Series 6 platform will be integrated with BCC's prepaid system and distributed as a jointly branded product to international markets. This will enable CGRM to bring its product to market more quickly, and to devote greater resources to other development projects.

Operational Review - 01-SEP-99

Net revenue in the nine months ended July 31, 1999, increased 8.0%, year to year, as higher large system sales outweighed declines in smaller system products, primarily reflecting the sale of the CPE division in May 1998. Gross margins widened. With significantly lower SG&A and R&D spending, and in the absence of $10.6 million charges, the operating loss was cut to $2.6 million, from $26.9 million. With much lower other income, in the absence of a $16.4 million gain on the sale of CPE, the net loss narrowed to $1,046,000 ($0.17 a share, on 9.2% fewer shares), from $10,850,000 ($1.56).

Stock Performance - 08-OCT-99

In the past 30 trading days, CGRM's shares have declined 5%, compared to a 0.91% fall in the S&P 500. Average trading volume for the past five days was 15,440 shares, compared with the 40-day moving average of 32,167 shares.

Key Stock Statistics

Dividend Rate/Share	Nil	Shareholders	300
Shs. outstg. (M)	6.0	Market cap. (B)	$0.061
Avg. daily vol. (M)	0.026	Inst. holdings	66%
Tang. Bk. Value/Share	8.70		
Beta	0.50		

Value of $10,000 invested 5 years ago: $ 2,887

Fiscal Year Ending Oct. 31

	1999	1998	1997	1996	1995	1994
Revenues (Million $)						
1Q	20.23	18.16	27.91	24.01	14.91	17.00
2Q	20.84	21.20	24.90	24.53	16.45	17.92
3Q	21.02	18.14	27.01	26.50	17.57	19.50
4Q	—	20.08	29.01	29.28	20.44	21.61
Yr.	—	77.59	108.8	104.3	69.37	79.20
Earnings Per Share ($)						
1Q	**-0.10**	**-0.85**	0.10	0.07	-0.12	0.15
2Q	**-0.03**	**-0.66**	-0.90	-0.19	-0.05	0.11
3Q	**-0.03**	**-0.45**	0.45	0.10	-0.26	0.11
4Q	—	**-0.20**	0.11	0.16	-0.21	0.46
Yr.	—	**-1.77**	**-0.24**	0.14	-0.63	1.18

Next earnings report expected: early December

Dividend Data

No cash dividends have been paid. Terms of a credit facility restrict payments.

A Division of The **McGraw·Hill** *Companies*

Centigram Communications Corporation

Business Summary - 01-SEP-99

Since the May 1998 sale of its customer premises equipment (CPE) division to Mitel Corp., for $26.8 million in cash, Centigram Communications has focused on providing revenue-generating integrated enhanced services to service providers in emerging markets. It had provided integrated messaging systems to both the CPE and service provider marketplaces since 1984. Headquartered in San Jose, CA, CGRM has sales and support offices in North America, Asia, Europe, Latin America and Australia.

As of the end of January 1999, the company had an installed base of nearly 2,500 revenue producing systems, providing message management services for telephone companies, cellular providers, paging companies, and service bureaus. In June 1998, the company acquired Telephone Connections (TTC), a developer of enhanced telecommunications services, for $11.6 million. In January 1999, the company said TTC was expected to provide it with a broader portfolio of competitive new products for the service provider market.

CGRM's communications products provide call management, voice messaging, paging, and text transmission for use with telephones, cellular phones, and computers. Products include VoiceMemo, which provides voice messaging and call processing capabilities; Telephone Answering, which automatically answers a busy telephone and records a voice message; and Automated Attendant, which answers incoming calls and allows callers to direct calls to extensions without the aid of a human operator. The company generally has no long-term order commitments for its products, and a significant portion of bookings and shipments have historically occurred near the end of a quarter. Accordingly, revenues are difficult to predict, and quarterly operating performance can fluctuate substantially.

In January 1999, the company said it had increased its focus on international sales in recent periods. Export sales accounted for 46%, 44%, and 30% of net revenue in FY 98 (Oct.), FY 97 and FY 96, respectively.

In March 1999, the company announced its selection by Cable & Wireless as a global supplier of messaging platforms, and a $2.4 million order from Korea's second largest cellular phone carrier to provide additional messaging services. In October 1998, Centigram signed an intellectual property cross-licensing agreement with Lucent Technologies and paid Lucent $9.2 million, in order to settle a patent infringement dispute.

Per Share Data ($) (Year Ended Oct. 31)	1998	1997	1996	1995	1994	1993	1992	1991	1990	1989
Tangible Bk. Val.	8.91	11.60	11.78	11.59	12.82	NA	NA	NA	NA	NA
Cash Flow	-0.73	1.02	1.24	0.20	1.72	1.48	NA	NA	NA	NA
Earnings	-1.77	-0.24	0.14	-0.63	1.18	1.00	0.49	0.67	NA	NA
Dividends	Nil	Nil	Nil	Nil	Nil	NA	NA	NA	NA	NA
Payout Ratio	Nil	Nil	Nil	Nil	Nil	NA	NA	NA	NA	NA
Prices - High	16⅞	21⅞	24⅛	25⅛	43	39¾	14¼	NA	NA	NA
- Low	5	8⅝	11⅝	12¼	10	11¼	3¾	NA	NA	NA
P/E Ratio - High	NM	NM	NM	NM	36	40	NA	NA	NA	NA
- Low	NM	NM	NM	NM	8	11	NA	NA	NA	NA
Income Statement Analysis (Million $)										
Revs.	77.6	109	104	69.4	79.2	60.0	44.7	36.0	NA	NA
Oper. Inc.	-11.2	5.0	6.5	-0.3	12.7	9.5	NA	NA	NA	NA
Depr.	7.2	8.7	7.7	5.4	3.5	2.5	NA	NA	NA	NA
Int. Exp.	0.1	0.1	0.1	0.1	0.2	0.4	NA	NA	NA	NA
Pretax Inc.	-11.8	-0.8	1.1	-4.1	10.8	7.3	NA	NA	NA	NA
Eff. Tax Rate	NM	NM	0.06%	NM	28%	29%	NA	NA	NA	NA
Net Inc.	-12.2	-1.7	1.0	-4.1	7.7	5.2	2.3	2.3	NA	NA
Balance Sheet & Other Fin. Data (Million $)										
Cash	23.4	19.8	42.1	55.7	60.4	NA	NA	NA	NA	NA
Curr. Assets	78.8	85.1	85.6	83.5	91.1	NA	NA	NA	NA	NA
Total Assets	96.0	100	104	99	102	48.0	34.0	21.0	NA	NA
Curr. Liab.	30.8	18.3	20.6	19.0	18.7	NA	NA	NA	NA	NA
LT Debt	Nil	Nil	0.1	0.2	0.4	0.8	1.1	1.6	NA	NA
Common Eqty.	65.2	81.6	83.4	79.8	83.2	32.0	24.0	11.0	NA	NA
Total Cap.	65.2	81.6	83.5	80.0	83.6	32.8	25.1	12.6	NA	NA
Cap. Exp.	3.0	6.2	10.6	8.0	7.2	3.2	NA	NA	NA	NA
Cash Flow	-5.0	7.1	8.7	1.3	11.3	7.7	NA	NA	NA	NA
Curr. Ratio	2.6	4.7	4.2	4.4	4.9	NA	NA	NA	NA	NA
% LT Debt of Cap.	Nil	Nil	0.1	0.3	0.5	2.5	4.4	12.4	NA	NA
% Net Inc.of Revs.	NM	NM	1.0	NM	9.8	8.7	NA	NA	NA	NA
% Ret. on Assets	NM	NM	1.0	NM	10.3	12.8	8.4	NA	NA	NA
% Ret. on Equity	NM	NM	1.2	NM	13.4	18.5	13.1	NA	NA	NA

Data as orig. reptd.; yr. ended Sep. prior to 1995; bef. results of disc. opers. and/or spec. items. Per share data adj. for stk. divs. as of ex-div. date. E-Estimated. NA-Not Available. NM-Not Meaningful. NR-Not Ranked.

Office—91 E. Tasman Dr., San Jose, CA 95134. **Tel**—(408) 944-0250. **Fax**—(408) 428-3732. **Website**—http://www.centigram.com **Email**—dan.spalding@centigram.com **Pres & CEO**—R. L. Puette. **SVP & CFO**—D. P. Wolf. **VP & Contr**—T. E. Brunton. **Secy**—L. W. Sonsini. **Investor Contact**—Dan Spalding (408-428-3559). **Dirs**—J. H. Boyle, D. Chance, J. F. Gibbons, E. R. Kozel, D. S. Lee, D. O. Morton, R. L. Puette. **Transfer Agent & Registrar**—First National Bank of Boston. **Incorporated**—in California in 1980; reincorporated in Delaware in 1991. **Empl**— 325. **S&P Analyst:** C.K.S.

STANDARD
&POOR'S
STOCK REPORTS

Central Hudson Gas & Electric

NYSE Symbol **CNH**

In S&P SmallCap 600

23-OCT-99

Industry: Electric Companies

Summary: This medium-sized utility provides electric and, to a lesser extent, gas service to a large area of New York's mid-Hudson River Valley.

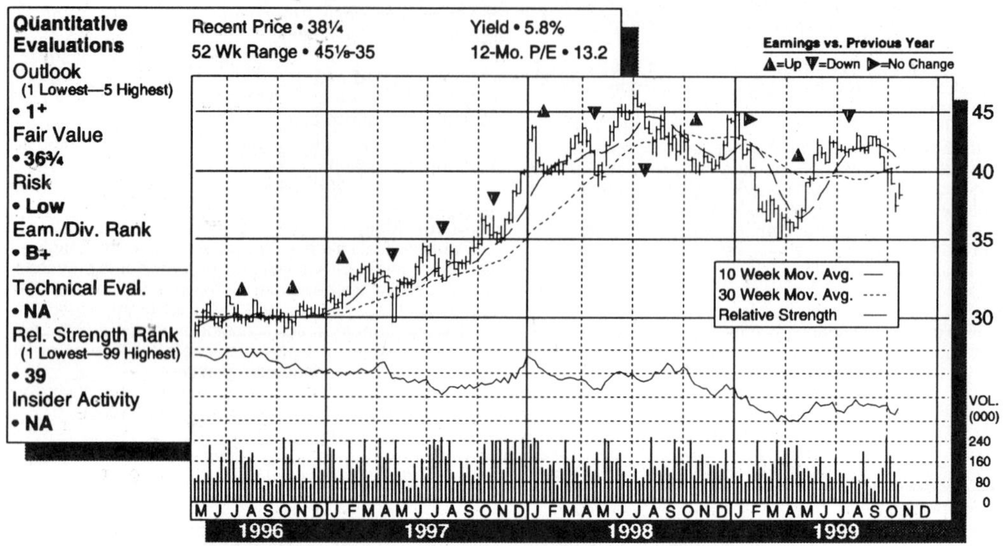

Business Profile - 14-OCT-99

In response to the deregulation of New York's electricity market, the company plans to focus on increasing efficiency and improving effectiveness. In addition, Central Hudson plans to use capital from the divestiture of its generating plants to develop successful utility businesses in the northeastern U.S. Lastly, CH Energy Group, a holding company for regulated and unregulated activities, will be formed in late 1999. The company's costs associated with Tropical Storm Floyd, which caused more damage in CNH's service territory than any other region in the state, totaled $8 million. The storm will not result in higher customer bills because of Central Hudson's agreement with state regulators to freeze electric rates.

Operational Review - 14-OCT-99

Revenues in the six months ended June 30, 1999, climbed 2.9%, year to year, reflecting higher electric sales. Operating expenses rose 3.0%, due to increased costs for fuel used in electricity generation, purchased natural gas and maintenance. With lower other income and higher interest expense, net income was down 2.7%, to $27.0 million ($1.59 a share, after preferred dividends), from $27.6 million ($1.61).

Stock Performance - 22-OCT-99

In the past 30 trading days, CNH's shares have declined 12%, compared to a 4% fall in the S&P 500. Average trading volume for the past five days was 36,800 shares, compared with the 40-day moving average of 33,115 shares.

Key Stock Statistics

Dividend Rate/Share	2.16	Shareholders	24,200
Shs. outstg. (M)	16.9	Market cap. (B)	$0.631
Avg. daily vol. (M)	0.042	Inst. holdings	35%
Tang. Bk. Value/Share	27.70		
Beta	0.15		

Value of $10,000 invested 5 years ago: $ 17,599

Fiscal Year Ending Dec. 31

	1999	1998	1997	1996	1995	1994
Revenues (Million $)						
1Q	146.5	143.9	151.9	153.8	144.7	162.8
2Q	177.0	112.1	118.6	117.0	118.6	117.2
3Q	134.3	125.7	123.5	117.7	127.5	116.1
4Q	—	121.8	126.3	125.5	121.4	119.5
Yr.	—	503.5	520.3	514.0	512.2	515.7
Earnings Per Share ($)						
1Q	1.09	1.06	1.18	1.20	1.06	1.22
2Q	0.51	0.54	0.55	0.58	0.55	0.45
3Q	—	0.77	0.72	0.73	0.70	0.65
4Q	—	0.52	0.52	0.48	0.43	0.36
Yr.	—	2.90	2.97	2.99	2.74	2.68

Next earnings report expected: early February

Dividend Data (Dividends have been paid since 1903.)

Amount ($)	Date Decl.	Ex-Div. Date	Stock of Record	Payment Date
0.540	Dec. 18	Jan. 07	Jan. 11	Feb. 01 '99
0.540	Mar. 26	Apr. 07	Apr. 09	May. 01 '99
0.540	Jun. 25	Jul. 07	Jul. 09	Aug. 02 '99
0.540	Sep. 24	Oct. 06	Oct. 11	Nov. 01 '99

A Division of The McGraw-Hill Companies

STANDARD &POOR'S STOCK REPORTS

Central Hudson Gas & Electric Corporation

23-OCT-99

Business Summary - 14-OCT-99

Central Hudson Gas & Electric generates, purchases and distributes electricity to 267,000 customers, and purchases and distributes gas to 61,000 customers. The company's 2,600 square mile service area extends about 85 miles along and 25 to 40 miles east and west of the Hudson River. The southern end of the territory is about 25 miles north of New York City, and the northern end 10 miles south of Albany, NY. Electric service is available throughout the territory; natural gas is provided in and around Poughkeepsie, Beacon, Newburgh and Kingston, NY.

The regulatory framework under which utilities operate is undergoing significant changes. The Public Service Commission of the State of New York (PSC) and the Federal Energy Regulatory Commission (FERC), which regulate CNH's retail and wholesale rates, respectively, have adopted policies to promote competition in the gas and electric markets that allow customers to choose alternate power suppliers.

Under an agreement with the PSC approved in 1998, the company agreed to freeze electric rates through June 2001, while phasing in a retail choice program for all of its customers. The agreement also required a 5% rate reduction for large industrial customers and a 10.6% cap on equity return. Consistent with the agreement's provisions, CH Energy Group was formed as a holding company for regulated and for unregulated activities. Regulated activities will continue to be conducted through Central Hudson Gas & Electric Corp. Unregulated affiliates include CH Resources, Inc. and Central Hudson Enterprises Corp. CH Resources was established to hold real property for generating electricity. Central Hudson Enterprises is engaged in marketing electric, gas and oil related services. Although similar deregulation efforts in the gas industry were previously instituted for large users, recent legislation requires that small users be given the opportunity to combine their power needs and buy from alternate suppliers.

CNH's two primary fossil fuel-fired electric generating stations are the Roseton and the Danskammer Point plants. Electric revenues generally peak in the summer, due to increased air conditioner use. Electric sales in the company's territory in 1998 and 1997 were 4,536 million kwh and 4,490 million kwh, respectively. The average price of electricity for customers in 1998 was 8.45 cents per kwh, a 1.2% decrease from the 1997 average. The primary sources of generation were coal (40%), purchased power (23%), and oil (19%); nuclear, gas and hydroelectric constituted the remainder. The company's gas system consists of 161 miles and 986 miles of transmission and distribution pipelines, respectively. Natural gas firm sales, which peak in the winter, due to heating requirements, totaled 9,001 MMcf in 1998.

Per Share Data ($)										
(Year Ended Dec. 31)	1998	1997	1996	1995	1994	1993	1992	1991	1990	1989
Tangible Bk. Val.	27.70	27.29	26.48	24.82	22.46	21.91	22.69	21.96	21.76	21.11
Earnings	2.90	2.97	2.99	2.74	2.68	2.68	2.65	2.40	2.38	2.28
Dividends	2.15	2.13	2.11	2.10	2.07	2.03	1.96	1.88	1.80	1.76
Payout Ratio	74%	72%	71%	77%	77%	77%	74%	78%	76%	77%
Prices - High	47	43 7/8	31 1/2	31 7/8	30 3/8	35 3/4	31 1/4	29	24 7/8	24 1/8
- Low	38 7/8	29 3/4	28 3/4	25 3/8	22 7/8	28 3/8	25 7/8	22 5/8	20	20 3/8
P/E Ratio - High	16	15	11	12	11	13	12	12	10	11
- Low	13	10	10	9	9	11	10	9	8	9
Income Statement Analysis (Million $)										
Revs.	503	520	514	512	516	517	524	495	504	470
Depr.	45.6	43.9	42.6	41.5	40.4	39.7	39.6	37.2	36.1	35.3
Maint.	26.9	27.6	28.9	29.4	32.7	34.5	34.2	31.5	30.4	23.9
Fxd. Chgs. Cov.	3.5	3.6	3.7	3.2	3.6	3.4	2.7	2.4	2.2	2.1
Constr. Credits	0.9	0.7	1.0	1.5	1.4	1.5	1.5	2.2	1.7	0.9
Eff. Tax Rate	35%	32%	36%	35%	35%	35%	34%	33%	33%	33%
Net Inc.	52.5	55.1	56.1	52.7	50.9	50.4	47.7	42.9	41.0	39.1
Balance Sheet & Other Fin. Data (Million $)										
Gross Prop.	1,580	1,474	1,442	1,405	1,359	1,329	1,302	1,272	1,212	1,173
Cap. Exp.	45.7	43.9	49.9	50.3	58.0	54.0	62.0	71.0	51.0	42.0
Net Prop.	947	971	940	937	931	915	905	885	855	848
Capitalization:										
LT Debt	357	362	362	389	389	392	441	416	408	447
% LT Debt	40	40	41	43	43	44	49	49	50	53
Pfd.	56.0	56.0	56.0	56.0	81.0	81.0	80.2	81.0	81.0	81.0
% Pfd.	6.30	6.30	6.30	6.20	8.90	7.20	8.90	9.50	9.90	9.50
Common	472	477	472	454	437	418	378	360	334	321
% Common	53	53	53	51	48	37	42	42	41	38
Total Cap.	1,088	1,100	1,087	1,089	1,146	1,122	1,012	962	913	931
% Oper. Ratio	80.3	86.5	85.2	86.2	85.8	85.6	85.8	84.7	84.5	83.7
% Earn. on Net Prop.	7.4	7.5	8.1	7.6	7.9	8.2	8.3	8.7	9.1	9.0
% Return On Revs.	10.4	10.6	10.9	10.3	9.9	9.7	9.1	8.7	8.1	8.3
% Return On Invest. Capital	7.3	7.4	7.7	7.5	7.2	7.5	8.1	8.4	8.9	8.8
% Return On Com. Equity	10.4	10.9	11.3	10.7	10.7	11.3	10.8	10.6	10.8	10.1

Data as orig reptd.; bef. results of disc opers/spec. items. Per share data adj. for stk. divs. Bold denotes diluted EPS (FASB 128)-prior periods restated. E-Estimated. NA-Not Available. NM-Not Meaningful. NR-Not Ranked.

Office—284 South Ave, Poughkeepsie, NY 12601-4879. **Tel**—(914) 452-2000. **Website**—http://www.cenhud.com **Chrmn & CEO**—P. J. Ganci. **Pres & COO**—C. E. Meyer. **CFO, Treas, Secy & Investor Contact**—Steven V. Lant (914-486-5254). **Dirs**—J. Effron, F. D. Fergusson, H. K. Fridrich, E. F. X. Gallagher, P. J. Ganci, S. J. Grubel, C. LaForge, J. E. Mack III, E. P. Swyer. **Transfer Agent & Registrar**—First Chicago Trust Co. of New York, Jersey City, NJ. **Incorporated**—in New York in 1926. **Empl**— 1,149. **S&P Analyst:** Ephraim Juskowicz

STANDARD
&POOR'S
STOCK REPORTS

Central Parking

NYSE Symbol **CPC**

In S&P SmallCap 600

09-OCT-99

Industry: Services (Commercial & Consumer)

Summary: CPC is a leading U.S. provider of parking services.

Quantitative Evaluations

Outlook (1 Lowest—5 Highest) • **5**

Fair Value • **48**

Risk • **Low**

Earn./Div. Rank • **NR**

Technical Eval. • **Bearish** since 8/99

Rel. Strength Rank (1 Lowest—99 Highest) • **29**

Insider Activity • **Neutral**

Recent Price • 28¼

52 Wk Range • 44⅝-25⅜

Yield • 0.2%

12-Mo. P/E • 50.4

Earnings vs. Previous Year
▲=Up ▼=Down ▶=No Change

10 Week Mov. Avg.
30 Week Mov. Avg.
Relative Strength

3-for-2

4842

1068

50
40
30
20

VOL. (000)
450
300
150
0

M J J A S O N D J F M A M J J A S O N D J F M A M J J A S O N D J F M A M J J A S O N D
1996 1997 1998 1999

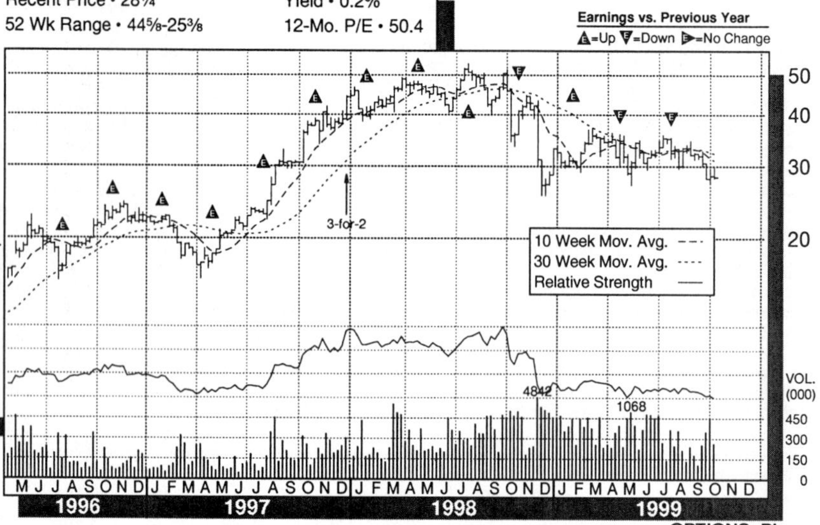

OPTIONS: Ph

Business Profile - 12-AUG-99

The company seeks to add local parking facilities. It also targets real estate managers and developers with a national presence, pursues acquisitions of other parking service operators, and aims to expand its international presence. In March 1999, CPC acquired Allright Holdings, a Houston-based provider of parking services with annual revenues of about $216 million, versus the company's $383 million. The merger was accounted for as a pooling of interests, and results for prior periods were restated. In August 1999, CPC said it was in the process of divesting certain facilities, as part of an agreement with the U.S. Department of Justice in connection with the Allright transaction. The company is also continuing to integrate Allright. Since the merger was completed, CPC has integrated information systems in 32 of the 81 cities where Allright is established.

Operational Review - 12-AUG-99

Revenues in the nine months ended June 30, 1999, advanced 29%, year to year. After merger and integration related expenses of $32.8 million, and an extraordinary item, net income fell 70%, to $5.8 million ($0.16 a share, on 6.6% fewer shares), from $19.3 million ($0.56), as restated.

Stock Performance - 08-OCT-99

In the past 30 trading days, CPC's shares have declined 12%, compared to a 0.91% fall in the S&P 500. Average trading volume for the past five days was 52,340 shares, compared with the 40-day moving average of 51,159 shares.

Key Stock Statistics

Dividend Rate/Share	0.06	Shareholders	7,000
Shs. outstg. (M)	36.7	Market cap. (B)	$ 1.0
Avg. daily vol. (M)	0.067	Inst. holdings	31%
Tang. Bk. Value/Share	NM		
Beta	NA		

Value of $10,000 invested 5 years ago: NA

Fiscal Year Ending Sep. 30

	1999	1998	1997	1996	1995	1994
Revenues (Million $)						
1Q	114.8	71.19	41.42	33.30	29.90	26.70
2Q	183.2	91.22	55.92	35.68	31.20	27.20
3Q	190.7	112.2	60.03	37.50	32.40	29.80
4Q	—	112.0	65.60	36.88	32.70	28.50
Yr.	—	383.2	223.0	143.3	126.2	112.2
Earnings Per Share ($)						
1Q	**0.30**	**0.21**	0.15	0.13	0.11	0.08
2Q	**-0.36**	**0.23**	0.17	0.13	0.10	0.07
3Q	**0.23**	**0.27**	0.20	0.14	0.11	0.16
4Q	—	**0.23**	0.25	0.13	0.10	0.07
Yr.	—	**0.94**	**0.77**	**0.53**	0.43	0.37

Next earnings report expected: early December

Dividend Data (Dividends have been paid since 1996.)

Amount ($)	Date Decl.	Ex-Div. Date	Stock of Record	Payment Date
0.015	Dec. 11	Dec. 29	Dec. 31	Jan. 14 '99
0.015	Mar. 05	Mar. 29	Mar. 31	Apr. 14 '99
0.015	Jun. 15	Jun. 28	Jun. 30	Jul. 14 '99
0.015	Sep. 17	Sep. 28	Sep. 30	Oct. 14 '99

Central Parking Corporation

Business Summary - 12-AUG-99

A leading provider of parking services in the U.S., Central Parking Corp. (CPC) substantially expanded the total size of its system with the March 1999 acquisition of Allright Holdings, a Houston-based provider of parking services operating 2,315 facilities in more than 100 cities in the U.S. and Canada. Including Allright, CPC operates 4,755 parking facilities containing more than 1.5 million spaces at locations in 40 states, the District of Columbia, Canada, Puerto Rico, the U.K., Ireland, Spain, Germany, Malaysia, Chile and Mexico.

The company provides parking management services at multi-level parking facilities and surface lots. It also provides parking consulting, shuttle, valet, parking meter enforcement, and billing and collection services. CPC operates parking facilities under management contracts, leases and fee ownership. The March 1999 acquisition of Allright nearly doubled the number of locations, and increased the number of parking spaces by more than 50%. As of May 1999, CPC operated 4,850 parking facilities, containing more than 1.6 million spaces.

The company's responsibilities under a management contract include hiring, training and staffing parking personnel and providing collection, accounting, marketing and other services. CPC generally receives a base monthly fee for managing the facilities, plus additional fees for ancillary services, and it often receives a percentage of facility revenues above a base amount. A typical management contract is for a term of one to three years.

Lease arrangements are typically for three to 10 years, and provide for a contractually established payment to the facility owner regardless of the operating earnings of the parking facility. Rent can be a flat annual amount, a percentage of gross revenues, or a combination of both. Leased facilities require a longer commitment and a larger capital investment by the company but provide a more stable source of revenue and greater opportunity for long-term revenue growth.

Ownership of parking facilities, either independently or through joint ventures, typically requires a larger capital investment than managed or leased facilities but provides maximum control over operations, and all growth in revenues flows directly to the company.

In connection with the Allright Holdings acquisition in March 1999, the company issued 7.5 million common shares, and assumed $254 million of debt. Allright had revenues of about $216 million in its most recent fiscal year.

Per Share Data ($) (Year Ended Sep. 30)	1998	1997	1996	1995	1994	1993	1992	1991	1990	1989
Tangible Bk. Val.	NM	2.28	2.71	1.51	1.98	NA	NA	NA	NA	NA
Cash Flow	1.38	0.95	0.57	0.52	0.49	0.31	0.29	NA	NA	NA
Earnings	0.94	0.77	0.53	0.43	0.37	0.21	0.22	0.11	NA	NA
Dividends	0.06	0.06	0.05	NA	NA	NA	NA	NA	NA	NA
Payout Ratio	6%	8%	10%	NA	NA	NA	NA	NA	NA	NA
Prices - High	53$^{3}/_{8}$	46$^{3}/_{4}$	24$^{5}/_{8}$	13$^{1}/_{8}$	NA	NA	NA	NA	NA	NA
- Low	25$^{3}/_{8}$	15$^{7}/_{8}$	12	8	NA	NA	NA	NA	NA	NA
P/E Ratio - High	57	61	47	30	NA	NA	NA	NA	NA	NA
- Low	27	21	23	18	NA	NA	NA	NA	NA	NA
Income Statement Analysis (Million $)										
Revs.	383	223	143	126	112	95.0	46.0	31.0	NA	NA
Oper. Inc.	59.5	32.8	19.4	16.5	13.8	10.1	7.6	5.2	NA	NA
Depr.	12.6	5.0	2.5	2.9	2.6	2.3	1.4	1.1	NA	NA
Int. Exp.	7.4	4.6	Nil	Nil	0.0	0.2	0.2	NA	NA	NA
Pretax Inc.	44.2	32.4	21.7	15.5	14.1	8.7	8.4	4.2	NA	NA
Eff. Tax Rate	40%	38%	33%	36%	37%	40%	36%	36%	NA	NA
Net Inc.	26.6	20.2	13.7	9.9	9.0	5.2	5.4	2.7	NA	NA
Balance Sheet & Other Fin. Data (Million $)										
Cash	19.8	10.0	28.6	10.2	NA	NA	NA	NA	NA	NA
Curr. Assets	68.6	39.6	45.2	26.5	NA	NA	NA	NA	NA	NA
Total Assets	545	234	107	70.4	NA	NA	NA	NA	NA	NA
Curr. Liab.	92.7	48.8	25.7	23.8	NA	NA	NA	NA	NA	NA
LT Debt	60.7	73.3	Nil	Nil	Nil	NA	NA	NA	NA	NA
Common Eqty.	260	100	76.8	41.3	57.3	NA	NA	NA	NA	NA
Total Cap.	429	177	78.4	41.9	NA	NA	NA	NA	NA	NA
Cap. Exp.	25.6	6.3	16.7	5.4	4.3	2.6	6.7	NA	NA	NA
Cash Flow	39.2	25.2	15.2	12.0	11.3	7.3	6.5	NA	NA	NA
Curr. Ratio	0.7	0.8	1.8	1.1	NA	NA	NA	NA	NA	NA
% LT Debt of Cap.	14.2	41.4	Nil	Nil	NA	NA	NA	NA	NA	NA
% Net Inc.of Revs.	6.9	9.1	9.5	7.9	8.0	5.5	11.7	8.8	NA	NA
% Ret. on Assets	6.8	11.8	15.4	15.2	NA	NA	NA	NA	NA	NA
% Ret. on Equity	14.8	22.5	23.2	25.9	NA	NA	NA	NA	NA	NA

Data as orig reptd.; bef. results of disc opers/spec. items. Per share data adj. for stk. divs. Bold denotes diluted EPS (FASB 128)-prior periods restated. E-Estimated. NA-Not Available. NM-Not Meaningful. NR-Not Ranked.

Office—2401 21st Ave. South, Suite 200, Nashville, TN 37212. **Tel**—(615) 297-4255. **Chrmn & CEO**—M. J. Carell, Jr. **Pres & COO**—J. H. Bond. **CFO**—S. A. Tisdell. **VP & Secy**—H. J. Abbott. **Dirs**—J. H. Bond, M. J. Carell, Jr., C. Conlee, J. Eakin, L. Harwood, L. Katz, E. Nelson, W. C. O'Neil, Jr., P. E. Sadler, J. C. Stadler. **Transfer Agent & Registrar**—SunTrust Bank of Atlanta. **Incorporated**—in Tennessee in 1968. **Empl**— 12,000. **S&P Analyst:** JJA

STANDARD &POOR'S
STOCK REPORTS

Central Vermont Public Service

NYSE Symbol **CV**

In S&P SmallCap 600

09-OCT-99

Industry: Electric Companies

Summary: This small electric utility serves a large portion of Vermont and parts of New Hampshire.

Quantitative Evaluations
Outlook
(1 Lowest—5 Highest)
• **NA**
Fair Value
• **NA**
Risk
• **Low**
Earn./Div. Rank
• **B**

Technical Eval.
• **Bullish** since 8/99
Rel. Strength Rank
(1 Lowest—99 Highest)
• **64**
Insider Activity
• **NA**

Recent Price • 13¼
52 Wk Range • 14⅜-9½
Yield • 6.6%
12-Mo. P/E • 13.4

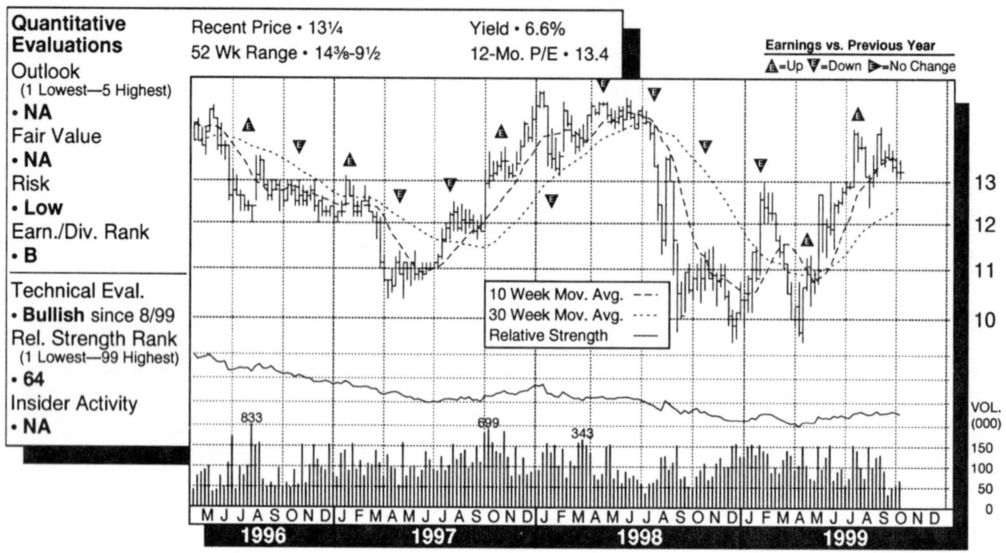

Business Profile - 06-OCT-99

In July 1999, CV sold $75 million of 8 1/8% second mortgage bonds priced at 99.915%. The bonds were sold in accordance with the Securities and Exchange Commission Rule 144A and are due in 2004. The proceeds were used to repay $15 million of outstanding loans under the company's revolving credit facility. Funds will also be used for general corporate purposes relative to CV's utility business. Additionally, the company canceled its $40 million revolving credit facility.

Operational Review - 06-OCT-99

Operating revenues in the six months ended June 30, 1999, advanced 28%, year to year, on a 6.7% increase in total retail sales, and a sharp rise in total resale sales, mainly reflecting an alliance with Virginia Power to supply wholesale power in New England. Total operating expenses rose less rapidly; operating income soared to $24.1 million from $15.1 million. After declines in both net other income and interest expense, income almost tripled to $13,146,000 ($1.07 a share, after preferred dividends), from $4,812,000 ($0.26). Results in the 1998 period exclude an extraordinary gain of $0.08 a share.

Stock Performance - 08-OCT-99

In the past 30 trading days, CV's shares have declined 7%, compared to a 0.91% fall in the S&P 500. Average trading volume for the past five days was 13,300 shares, compared with the 40-day moving average of 16,472 shares.

Key Stock Statistics

Dividend Rate/Share	0.88	Shareholders	13,700
Shs. outstg. (M)	11.5	Market cap. (B)	$0.152
Avg. daily vol. (M)	0.010	Inst. holdings	30%
Tang. Bk. Value/Share	16.48		
Beta	0.82		

Value of $10,000 invested 5 years ago: $ 9,675

Fiscal Year Ending Dec. 31

	1999	1998	1997	1996	1995	1994
Revenues (Million $)						
1Q	98.64	83.96	88.49	84.25	86.86	83.89
2Q	93.14	66.41	65.44	61.39	62.85	57.68
3Q	—	69.52	67.99	63.83	60.31	59.03
4Q	—	83.95	82.81	81.33	78.25	76.56
Yr.	—	303.8	304.7	290.8	288.3	277.2
Earnings Per Share ($)						
1Q	**1.07**	**0.78**	1.20	1.23	1.13	1.04
2Q	Nil	**-0.52**	-0.21	-0.08	-0.13	-0.22
3Q	—	**-0.06**	0.14	-0.11	0.11	-0.11
4Q	—	**-0.03**	**0.19**	0.47	0.42	0.38
Yr.	—	**0.18**	**1.32**	**1.51**	**1.53**	1.08

Next earnings report expected: early November

Dividend Data (Dividends have been paid since 1944.)

Amount ($)	Date Decl.	Ex-Div. Date	Stock of Record	Payment Date
0.220	Dec. 07	Jan. 27	Jan. 31	Feb. 15 '99
0.220	Apr. 12	Apr. 28	Apr. 30	May. 14 '99
0.220	Jul. 19	Jul. 28	Jul. 30	Aug. 13 '99
0.220	Sep. 20	Oct. 27	Oct. 29	Nov. 15 '99

A Division of The McGraw-Hill Companies

Central Vermont Public Service Corporation

Business Summary - 06-OCT-99

CV is a significant player in the utility market in the northern New England territory. Central Vermont Public Service and its Connecticut Valley Electric unit supply electricity to customers in nearly three-quarters of Vermont's towns, villages and cities and to parts of New Hampshire bordering the Connecticut River. About half of Vermont's residents receive service from the company, as do 10,000 customers in 13 New Hampshire towns.

In 1998, residential customers accounted for 46% of total retail sales (45% in 1997), commercial customers 40% (41%), industrial customers 13% (13%), and other retail customers 1% (1%).

Power sources in 1998 were: nuclear 33%; coal 2%; company-owned hydro 6%; jointly owned units 3%; small power producers 6%; other 22%; 28% of the power supply was imported from Canada. Peak load in 1998 was 420.6 mw.

CV's nuclear power is derived primarily from its 31.3% (160-mw entitlement) interest in the Vermont Yankee plant. The company also has interests in the Maine Yankee nuclear plant (2.0%, 16.9 mw), Connecticut Yankee (2.0%, 11.6 mw) and Yankee Atomic (3.5%). In early 1992, Yankee Atomic decided to permanently discontinue operation of its plant. CV's share of the remaining shutdown cost is about $4.8 million, which it believes will be recovered through the regulatory process.

In an effort to mitigate eroding earnings and cash flow prospects during the Vermont Supreme Court review process related to a rate case, in June 1998, the company filed with the Vermont Public Service Board (PSB) a request for a 10.7% rate increase ($24.9 million of annualized revenues) effective March 1, 1999. The rate case proceeding supplanted a 6.6% rate increase request filed in September 1997 that is now stayed pending review. On October 27, 1998, the company reached agreement with the Vermont Department of Public Service regarding the 10.7% rate increase request. The agreement, which was approved by the PSB on December 11, 1998, provided for a temporary rate increase in Vermont retail rates of 4.7%, or $10.9 million on an annualized basis, beginning January 1, 1999.

Wholly owned Catamount Energy Corp. invests in nonregulated energy-related projects. It currently has interests in five operating independent power projects, following the recent sale of its interest in its Williams Lake facility. CV's nonutility subsidiary, SmartEnergy Services, Inc., provides reliable energy-efficient products and services, including the rental of electric water heaters. In August 1996, Catamount purchased a 10% interest in a $107 million biomass power generating station in Thetford, England, from Fibrowatt Ltd.

Per Share Data ($) **(Year Ended Dec. 31)**	**1998**	**1997**	**1996**	**1995**	**1994**	**1993**	**1992**	**1991**	**1990**	**1989**
Tangible Bk. Val.	15.64	16.38	16.19	15.51	14.56	15.03	14.21	14.03	13.68	13.36
Earnings	0.18	1.32	1.51	1.53	1.08	1.64	1.71	1.65	1.62	1.73
Dividends	0.88	0.88	0.84	0.80	1.42	1.42	1.39	1.39	1.37	1.34
Payout Ratio	NM	67%	56%	52%	131%	87%	81%	84%	85%	78%
Prices - High	$15\frac{3}{8}$	$15\frac{3}{8}$	$15\frac{1}{8}$	$14\frac{3}{8}$	22	$25\frac{3}{4}$	25	$22\frac{7}{8}$	$19\frac{5}{8}$	$19\frac{3}{8}$
- Low	$9\frac{1}{2}$	$10\frac{3}{8}$	12	$13\frac{1}{4}$	$12\frac{1}{8}$	$20\frac{1}{8}$	$19\frac{1}{2}$	17	$14\frac{5}{8}$	$14\frac{3}{4}$
P/E Ratio - High	86	12	10	9	20	16	15	14	12	11
- Low	53	8	8	9	11	12	11	10	9	9
Income Statement Analysis (Million $)										
Revs.	304	305	291	288	277	279	275	233	232	227
Depr.	16.7	16.9	18.0	17.3	16.5	15.4	14.4	12.4	11.2	10.2
Maint.	15.6	15.3	14.9	12.9	12.2	11.7	11.9	11.2	12.6	10.8
Fxd. Chgs. Cov.	0.9	2.8	3.0	3.0	3.6	3.7	3.0	2.6	2.6	3.1
Constr. Credits	0.0	0.1	0.5	3.5	0.4	0.1	0.4	0.7	0.1	0.9
Eff. Tax Rate	3.47%	35%	34%	36%	45%	38%	37%	25%	31%	40%
Net Inc.	4.0	17.2	19.4	19.9	14.8	21.3	21.4	18.6	17.5	18.2
Balance Sheet & Other Fin. Data (Million $)										
Gross Prop.	519	507	471	463	450	432	419	401	386	339
Cap. Exp.	16.0	14.0	19.0	21.3	22.6	20.5	20.5	19.0	21.2	28.0
Net Prop.	359	355	325	327	325	319	316	312	306	268
Capitalization:										
LT Debt	106	110	136	139	141	144	131	154	154	115
% LT Debt	34	34	39	40	41	41	40	45	50	43
Pfd.	26.1	27.1	28.1	28.0	28.1	35.1	35.1	35.1	15.1	15.1
% Pfd.	8.37	8.40	8.00	8.10	8.30	9.90	11	10	4.90	5.70
Common	179	187	186	180	171	174	159	152	142	135
% Common	58	58	53	52	50	49	49	45	46	51
Total Cap.	366	385	415	412	401	414	361	374	346	301
% Oper. Ratio	97.5	89.4	92.0	91.6	92.4	90.7	89.5	88.4	88.9	87.7
% Earn. on Net Prop.	2.2	5.2	7.1	7.4	6.6	8.2	9.2	8.8	8.9	10.7
% Return On Revs.	1.3	5.6	6.7	6.9	5.3	7.6	7.8	8.0	7.6	8.0
% Return On Invest. Capital	5.1	5.9	4.7	7.4	6.1	7.8	9.3	8.8	9.7	10.6
% Return On Com. Equity	1.1	8.1	9.5	10.2	7.2	11.0	11.8	11.8	12.0	13.0

Data as orig reptd.; bef. results of disc opers/spec. items. Per share data adj. for stk. divs. Bold denotes diluted EPS (FASB 128)-prior periods restated. E-Estimated. NA-Not Available. NM-Not Meaningful. NR-Not Ranked.

Office—77 Grove St., Rutland, VT 05701. **Tel**—(802) 773-2711. **Chrmn**—F. H. Bertrand. **Pres & CEO**—R. H. Young Jr. **SVP, Treas & CFO**—F. J. Boyle. **VP & Secy**—J. M. Kraus. **Dirs**—R.L. Barnett, F. H. Bertrand, R. L. Brooks, R. G. Clarke, L. F. Hackett, P. J. Martin, M. A. McKenzie, J. L. Scites, R. H. Young. **Transfer Agents & Registrars**—Co.'s office; First National Bank of Boston. **Incorporated**—in Vermont in 1929. **Empl**— 532. **S&P Analyst:** V.G.P.

STANDARD
&POOR'S
STOCK REPORTS

Centura Banks

NYSE Symbol **CBC**

In S&P SmallCap 600

09-OCT-99

Industry:
Banks (Regional)

Summary: This bank holding company provides banking, insurance and investment services to individuals and businesses in North Carolina, South Carolina and Hampton Roads, VA.

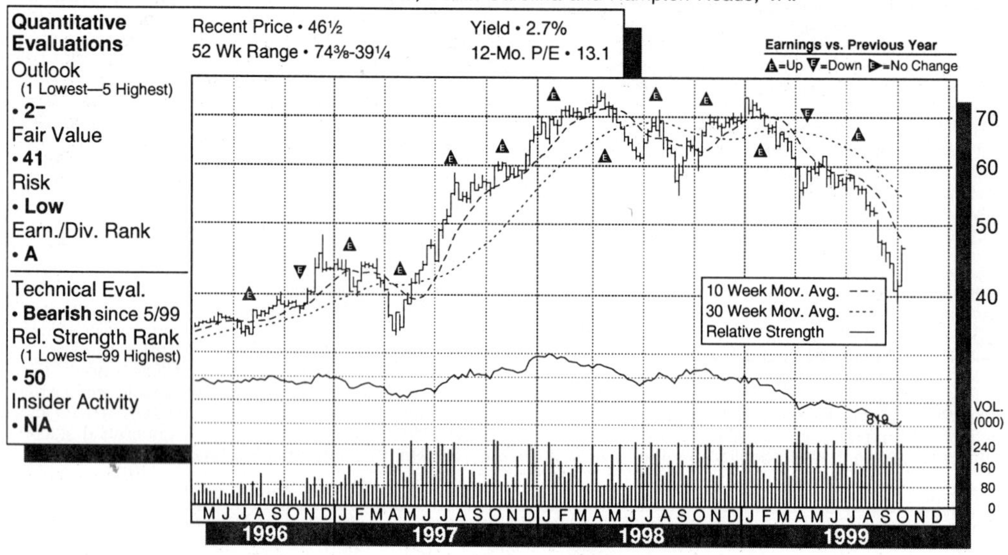

Business Profile - 16-SEP-99

In August 1999, the company announced the development of Internet services, including banking, investment and insurance, with rollout expected in the third quarter. Also in August, CBC agreed to acquire Triangle Bancorp Inc., a $2 billion asset North Carolina bank, through an exchange of stock valued at about $608 million. The company expects to incur $60 million in pretax charges upon closing, and to realize annualized cost savings of $32 million beginning in 2001. In March 1999, CBC acquired First Coastal Bankshares, Inc., adding $578 million in assets, and an increased presence in the Hampton Roads region of Virginia.

Operational Review - 16-SEP-99

Net interest income in the six months ended June 30, 1999, rose 7.8%, year to year, as increased average earning assets outweighed a 10 basis point narrowing of the net interest margin, to 4.24%. The provision for loan losses increased 80%, to $12,677,000, reflecting increased loans, higher nonperforming assets, and a post-merger realignment of the allowance for loan losses. Noninterest income increased 15%, reflecting greater mortgage income, and higher service charges on deposit accounts after a restructuring of fee accumulation. Noninterest expense was up 11%, on acquisition-related increases in personnel expense, and $6.9 million in merger-related charges. After taxes at 33.7%, versus 34.0%, net income was up 1.6%, to $49,366,000 ($1.71 a share), from $48,570,000 ($1.70).

Stock Performance - 08-OCT-99

In the past 30 trading days, CBC's shares have declined 2%, compared to a 0.91% fall in the S&P 500. Average trading volume for the past five days was 70,320 shares, compared with the 40-day moving average of 70,000 shares.

Key Stock Statistics

Dividend Rate/Share	1.28	Shareholders	13,500
Shs. outstg. (M)	28.5	Market cap. (B)	$ 1.3
Avg. daily vol. (M)	0.054	Inst. holdings	25%
Tang. Bk. Value/Share	24.16		
Beta	0.94		

Value of $10,000 invested 5 years ago: $ 26,425

Fiscal Year Ending Dec. 31

	1999	1998	1997	1996	1995	1994
Revenues (Million $)						
1Q	195.8	168.3	145.8	137.9	96.25	80.34
2Q	196.7	177.5	153.5	138.2	105.9	82.52
3Q	203.9	182.8	161.8	144.1	116.8	87.79
4Q	—	183.5	171.3	150.4	120.6	91.06
Yr.	—	712.1	632.3	570.6	439.6	341.7
Earnings Per Share ($)						
1Q	**0.71**	**0.85**	**0.68**	**0.67**	0.67	0.50
2Q	**1.00**	**0.89**	**0.76**	**0.66**	0.63	0.57
3Q	**0.86**	**0.93**	**0.82**	**0.57**	0.66	0.63
4Q	—	**0.93**	**0.89**	**0.70**	0.68	0.65
Yr.	—	**3.60**	**3.15**	**2.60**	**2.45**	**2.19**

Next earnings report expected: NA

Dividend Data (Dividends have been paid since 1990.)

Amount ($)	Date Decl.	Ex-Div. Date	Stock of Record	Payment Date
0.290	Jan. 11	Feb. 24	Feb. 26	Mar. 16 '99
0.320	Apr. 21	May. 26	May. 28	Jun. 15 '99
0.320	Aug. 19	Aug. 27	Aug. 31	Sep. 15 '99
0.320	Oct. 05	Nov. 26	Nov. 30	Dec. 15 '99

A Division of The McGraw-Hill Companies

Centura Banks, Inc.

Business Summary - 16-SEP-99

Centura Banks, based in Rocky Mount, NC, aims to become the primary financial services provider for each of its customers by offering a full line of services. With $8.2 billion in assets at year-end 1998, the company's financial services offerings included full-service commercial and consumer banking; retail securities brokerage; insurance brokerage covering various consumer and commercial lines; commercial and retail leasing; asset management; and mortgage banking.

The company's customer driven strategy includes the provision of services through convenient delivery channels. At year-end 1998, the bank operated 210 financial stores, including 32 in supermarkets. CBC offers Centura Highway, a direct telephone banking center that handles a broad range of financial services. The bank also serves customers through its Internet home page and a telephone network operated by a third party and connected to personal computers of customers.

Through its customer database and sales tracking system that combines financial, demographic, behavioral and psychographic data, CBC gains in-depth knowledge of its customers. This supports decision-making about services offered, delivery channels, locations, staffing and marketing. However, the company believes information alone is not sufficient to understand customer needs; financial services officers are encouraged to visit the bank's best customers.

In 1994, CBC became the first U.S. bank to adopt an Economic Value Added (EVA) management system. It uses EVA to evaluate business performance and link it to incentive rewards for employees, after the shareholder receives a fair return. CBC is diversifying its revenue sources, generating a larger portion from noninterest sources. After generating 31% of revenues from fee income in 1998, CBC has targeted 50% for the future. Its asset management business pretax income increased 58%, to $4.1 million, in 1998.

The company made four acquisitions in 1998, adding $164 million in assets. The January 1998 acquisition of Moore & Johnson, Inc. of Raleigh, NC, aided the development of Centura Insurance Services, Inc., as one of the largest independent insurance brokers in North Carolina. In March 1998, CBC purchased Pee Dee Bankshares, Inc., a $138 million asset bank in Timmonsville, SC. During 1998, the company opened or acquired 11 offices in Hannaford and Kroger supermarkets in North Carolina and the Hampton Roads region of Virginia. In January 1999, it acquired Capital Advisors, a private commercial mortgage banking company that provides long-term real estate financing in the Southeast. CBC added $61 million in assets through the February 1999 acquisition of Scotland Bancorp of Laurinburg, NC.

Per Share Data ($) (Year Ended Dec. 31)	1998	1997	1996	1995	1994	1993	1992	1991	1990	1989
Tangible Bk. Val.	23.66	20.82	18.51	18.13	15.79	14.98	13.36	12.29	12.45	11.78
Earnings	3.60	3.15	2.60	2.64	2.35	2.14	1.70	0.62	1.27	1.70
Dividends	1.14	1.06	1.00	0.85	0.74	0.69	0.63	0.60	0.15	NA
Payout Ratio	32%	34%	38%	32%	31%	32%	37%	98%	NM	NA
Prices - High	76	69	48¼	35½	25¼	24⅝	20½	16	13¾	NA
- Low	54¾	35¼	33¾	22½	18	19¼	12½	11⅝	12⅜	NA
P/E Ratio - High	21	22	18	13	11	12	12	26	11	NA
- Low	15	11	13	9	8	9	7	19	10	NA
Income Statement Analysis (Million $)										
Net Int. Inc.	299	268	250	204	182	153	125	105	108	102
Tax Equiv. Adj.	7.3	7.7	6.0	5.2	5.7	6.1	6.1	6.7	6.1	NA
Non Int. Inc.	136	110	92.9	59.8	48.6	51.1	36.3	29.1	37.8	28.1
Loan Loss Prov.	15.1	13.4	9.6	7.4	6.7	8.5	15.1	20.8	10.0	6.1
Exp./Op. Revs.	121%	65%	66%	62%	62%	64%	65%	72%	72%	69%
Pretax Inc.	147	125	107	90.0	77.4	62.2	39.9	11.5	26.2	34.2
Eff. Tax Rate	34%	34%	37%	36%	36%	34%	33%	24%	32%	31%
Net Inc.	96.9	83.1	68.2	58.0	49.6	41.1	26.9	8.8	17.7	23.7
% Net Int. Marg.	4.45	4.56	4.66	4.76	4.96	4.81	4.87	4.80	4.80	NA
Balance Sheet & Other Fin. Data (Million $)										
Money Mkt. Assets	39.3	44.0	33.0	40.0	376	521	63.1	28.2	20.2	38.0
Inv. Securities	2,075	1,829	1,578	1,259	539	668	566	530	504	465
Com'l Loans	1,089	846	743	3,018	2,950	2,579	441	413	636	1,684
Other Loans	4,314	3,741	3,366	30.2	NA	NA	1,675	1,386	1,168	NA
Total Assets	8,236	7,125	6,294	5,326	4,240	4,139	3,029	2,612	2,605	2,434
Demand Deposits	947	816	721	607	536	507	397	324	344	361
Time Deposits	4,734	4,549	2,945	2,475	2,934	3,103	2,259	1,993	1,960	1,766
LT Debt	555	382	311	227	109	44.9	45.9	16.4	22.4	17.4
Common Eqty.	630	538	475	391	324	311	211	182	174	164
% Ret. on Assets	1.3	1.2	1.1	1.2	1.2	1.1	0.9	0.3	0.7	1.0
% Ret. on Equity	16.6	16.4	14.8	16.2	15.6	15.6	13.3	5.0	10.5	15.2
% Loan Loss Resv.	1.2	1.4	1.4	1.4	1.5	1.6	1.5	1.5	1.1	1.1
% Loans/Deposits	95.1	85.5	86.1	86.5	85.0	71.5	79.7	77.6	78.3	79.2
% Equity to Assets	7.6	7.6	7.6	7.5	7.8	7.3	7.0	7.0	6.7	6.7

Data as orig reptd.; bef. results of disc opers/spec. items. Per share data adj. for stk. divs. Bold denotes diluted EPS (FASB 128)-prior periods restated. E-Estimated. NA-Not Available. NM-Not Meaningful. NR-Not Ranked.

Office—134 North Church St., Rocky Mount, NC 27804. **Tel**—(252) 454-4400. **Website**—http://www.centura.com **Chrmn & CEO**—C. W. Sewell, Jr. **Vice Chrmn & Investor Contact**—Frank L. Pattillo (252-454-8341). **Pres**—W. H. Wilkerson. **CFO**—S. J. Goldstein. **Dirs**—R. H. Barnhardt, C. W. Beasley, T. A. Betts, Jr., H. T. Bowers, E. L. Evans, B. W. Franklin, S. E. Gravely, J. H. High, M. K. Hooker, R. L. Hubbard, W. H. Kincheloe, C. T. Lane, —J. H. Nelson, D. E. Painter, Jr., O. T. Parks, III, F. L. Pattillo, W. H. Redding, Jr., C. M. Reeves, III, C. W. Sewell, Jr., G. T. Stronach, III, A. P. Thorpe, III, W. H. Wilkerson. C. P. Wilkins. **Transfer Agent & Registrar**—Registrar & Transfer Co., Cranford, NJ. **Incorporated**—in North Carolina in 1990. **Empl**— 2,940. **S&P Analyst:** Markos N. Kaminis

STANDARD &POOR'S
STOCK REPORTS

Cephalon, Inc.

NASDAQ Symbol **CEPH**

In S&P SmallCap 600

09-OCT-99

Industry: Biotechnology

Summary: This neuroscience company is developing therapeutic products to treat neurodegenerative diseases, such as ALS (Lou Gehrig's disease), Alzheimer's, and head and spinal injuries.

Quantitative Evaluations

Outlook (1 Lowest—5 Highest)
• **NA**

Fair Value
• **NA**

Risk
• **High**

Earn./Div. Rank
• **C**

Technical Eval.
• **Bullish** since 8/99

Rel. Strength Rank (1 Lowest—99 Highest)
• **44**

Insider Activity
• **NA**

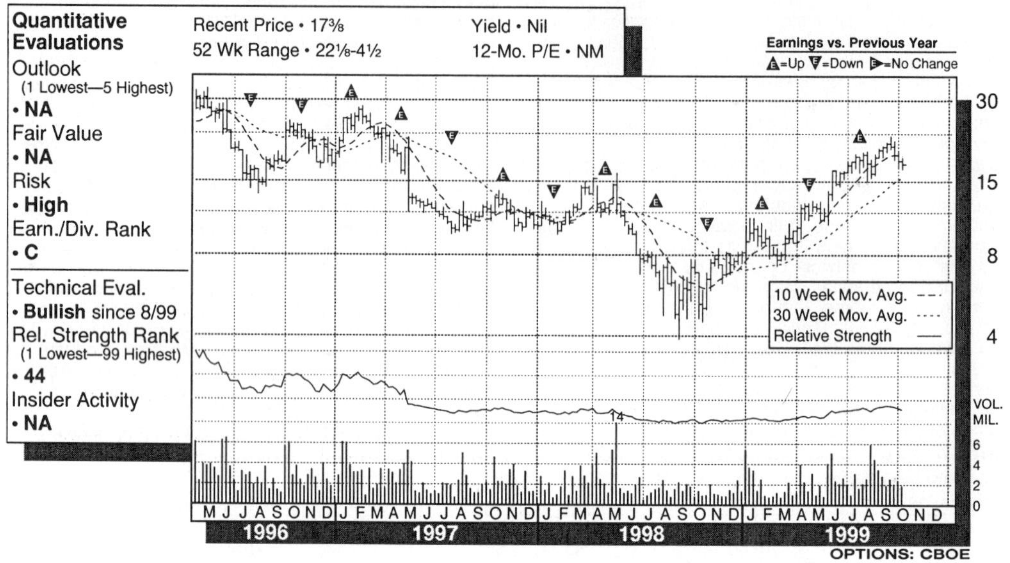

Business Profile - 13-AUG-99

In August 1999, CEPH announced plans to raise $100 million in a convertible preferred stock offering. In July 1999, CEPH and H. Lundbeck A/S initiated Phase I trials on CEP-1347 for treating neurodegenerative diseases. In June 1999, CEPH and Abbott Labs signed an agreement to market and further develop Gabitril, one of Abbott's anti-epileptic drugs, in the U.S. Also in June, CEPH agreed to settle on securities litigation related to Myotrophin for $17 million. In December 1998, CEPH received FDA approval for Provigil as a treatment for excessive daytime sleepiness. CEPH began marketing Provigil in the U.S. and Ireland in February 1999, and in the U.K. in March 1998.

Operational Review - 13-AUG-99

Revenues in the first six months of 1999 more than doubled to $15.0 million, from $7.0 million, primarily due to the initiation of sales for Provigil in 1999. Following cost of product sales of $839,000 for 1999 only, due to Provigil costs, 9.7% lower R&D spending, and significantly higher SG&A expenses, related to the marketing of Provigil and a $4.3 million charge for securities litigation, total costs and expenses rose 24%. After net interest expense of $1,650,000, contrasted with net interest income of $1,969,000, the net loss widened to $31.4 million ($1.09 a share), from $27.2 million ($0.97). Cash and investments totaled $85.6 million at June 30, 1999.

Stock Performance - 08-OCT-99

In the past 30 trading days, CEPH's shares have declined 11%, compared to a 0.91% fall in the S&P 500. Average trading volume for the past five days was 366,000 shares, compared with the 40-day moving average of 542,810 shares.

Key Stock Statistics

Dividend Rate/Share	Nil	Shareholders	757
Shs. outstg. (M)	30.8	Market cap. (B)	$0.535
Avg. daily vol. (M)	0.435	Inst. holdings	50%
Tang. Bk. Value/Share	1.60		
Beta	1.61		

Value of $10,000 invested 5 years ago: $ 10,610

Fiscal Year Ending Dec. 31

	1999	1998	1997	1996	1995	1994
Revenues (Million $)						
1Q	4.23	3.57	5.63	3.73	2.63	3.14
2Q	10.75	3.41	3.89	4.06	14.91	7.41
3Q	—	2.77	4.60	3.62	19.17	5.21
4Q	—	5.90	9.02	9.96	10.29	5.92
Yr.	—	15.66	23.14	21.37	47.00	21.68
Earnings Per Share ($)						
1Q	**-0.69**	**-0.53**	-0.61	-0.62	-0.69	-0.81
2Q	**-0.40**	**-0.44**	-0.76	-0.70	-0.22	-0.39
3Q	—	**-0.48**	-0.47	-0.68	-0.22	-0.42
4Q	—	**-0.50**	**-0.52**	-0.20	-0.51	-0.54
Yr.	—	**-1.95**	**-2.36**	**-2.19**	**-1.63**	**-2.13**

Next earnings report expected: early November

Dividend Data

Cash dividends have never been paid. Cephalon intends to retain any earnings to finance growth. A "poison pill" stock purchase rights plan was adopted in 1993.

Cephalon, Inc.

Business Summary - 13-AUG-99

Cephalon's strategy is to discover, develop, and market novel therapeutics to treat neurological disorders, sleep disorders, and cancer. The firm's research is focused on comprehending the cellular mechanisms of cell survival and cell death as a pathway for discovering and creating compounds that may destroy or inhibit diseased cells. This research employs the following four technology disciplines: neurotrophic factors, gene transcription regulators, signal transduction modulators, and protease inhibitors.

In December 1998, the FDA approved CEPH's lead product, Provigil (modafinil) tablets, as a treatment for excessive daytime sleepiness due to narcolepsy. Narcolepsy is a chronic, lifelong sleep disorder that affects about 125,000 people in the U.S. In February 1999, CEPH began marketing Provigil in the U.S. through its own sales force. The company's U.K. sales organization commenced U.K. marketing of Provigil in March 1998 and marketing in Ireland in February 1999. In May 1999, CEPH initiated sales in Austria. CEPH was also attempting to gain approval in Mexico and Switzerland. Azwell Pharmaceuticals was granted rights from CEPH to develop and commercialize Provigil in Japan, while Dompe SpA was granted rights for Italy.

As of mid-1999, CEPH was conducting clinical trials to ascertain the potential use of Provigil as a treatment for excessive daytime sleepiness unrelated to narcolepsy, such as sleep disorders resulting from sleep apnea and multiple sclerosis.

As of mid-1999, CEPH was collaborating with Chiron Corp. for the commercialization of Myotrophin in the U.S. as a treatment for amyotrophic lateral sclerosis (ALS). ALS is a neurological disorder characterized by the chronic degeneration of motor neurons, leading to muscle function loss and death. CEPH filed for marketing approval in the U.S. in February 1997. In May 1998, the FDA said the application for Myotrophin was potentially approvable, contingent upon the submission of additional data. CEPH planned to submit supplementary data to the FDA in an attempt to obtain approval, which remains very uncertain. In September 1998, CEPH and Chiron withdrew their European marketing application due to concerns Myotrophin would not be approved.

CEPH has conducted pilot studies exploring the utility of Myotrophin in other indications, such as multiple sclerosis and peripheral neuropathies. Further development will be contingent upon the outcome of Myotrophin's pending FDA application.

The company is collaborating with H. Lundbeck A/S on treatments for neurodegenerative disorders. The lead compound in this program, CEP-1347, began Phase I studies in July 1999 for treating Parkinson's disease. As of mid-1999, CEPH was also working with TAP Holdings Inc. on the clinical development of a compound for treating prostate cancer.

In June 1999, the company agreed to settle securities litigation filed in 1996 alleging clinical studies of Myotrophin were misleading. CEPH will pay a total of $17.0 million in full settlement.

Per Share Data ($) (Year Ended Dec. 31)	1998	1997	1996	1995	1994	1993	1992	1991	1990	1989
Tangible Bk. Val.	2.00	3.66	5.58	7.56	6.17	5.28	6.25	6.91	1.90	1.12
Cash Flow	-1.87	-2.27	-2.02	-1.34	-1.74	-1.28	-0.55	-0.18	-0.54	-0.35
Earnings	-1.95	-2.36	-2.19	-1.63	-2.13	-1.77	-0.80	-0.26	-0.59	-0.39
Dividends	Nil	Nil	Nil	Nil	Nil	Nil	Nil	Nil	Nil	Nil
Payout Ratio	Nil	Nil	Nil	Nil	Nil	Nil	Nil	Nil	Nil	Nil
Prices - High	16 1/8	28 1/2	40 7/8	41 1/2	19 1/2	18 3/4	16 3/4	19 1/2	NA	NA
- Low	3 7/8	9 1/2	13 3/8	5 3/4	7 1/2	8 1/2	7	11	NA	NA
P/E Ratio - High	NM	NM	NM	NM	NM	NM	NM	NM	NM	NM
- Low	NM	NM	NM	NM	NM	NM	NM	NA	NA	NA
Income Statement Analysis (Million $)										
Revs.	15.7	23.1	21.4	47.0	21.7	16.9	9.1	5.0	0.1	0.1
Oper. Inc.	-56.6	-62.9	-65.1	-36.9	-28.3	-14.6	-8.0	-4.0	-3.0	-1.8
Depr.	2.3	2.2	4.2	5.8	6.7	5.3	2.2	0.6	0.3	0.1
Int. Exp.	1.9	3.2	2.3	3.1	1.4	0.8	0.2	0.0	0.0	0.0
Pretax Inc.	-55.4	-60.4	-53.3	-33.0	-36.1	-19.2	-7.2	-2.0	-3.0	-1.6
Eff. Tax Rate	NM	NM	NM	NM	NM	NM	NM	Nil	Nil	Nil
Net Inc.	-55.4	-60.4	-53.3	-33.0	-36.1	-19.2	-7.2	-2.0	-3.0	-1.6
Balance Sheet & Other Fin. Data (Million $)										
Cash	4.0	10.3	147	178	105	49.4	33.8	24.4	9.7	4.7
Curr. Assets	72.6	127	155	188	113	51.7	37.3	25.0	10.0	4.9
Total Assets	94.7	151	178	221	140	78.1	71.1	61.7	10.9	5.6
Curr. Liab.	18.5	20.5	21.6	18.4	10.8	3.4	2.3	0.8	0.7	0.4
LT Debt	15.1	27.6	17.0	21.7	16.1	11.6	12.0	Nil	0.4	0.4
Common Eqty.	57.6	100	137	180	113	63.1	56.7	60.9	9.7	4.8
Total Cap.	72.7	100	154	202	129	74.7	68.7	60.9	10.2	5.2
Cap. Exp.	0.6	0.8	2.1	17.5	10.5	6.8	4.7	1.2	0.1	0.1
Cash Flow	-53.1	-58.2	-49.1	-27.2	-29.4	-13.9	-4.9	-1.4	-2.8	-1.5
Curr. Ratio	3.9	6.2	3.8	10.2	10.4	15.1	16.1	30.0	14.2	12.4
% LT Debt of Cap.	20.8	21.6	11.0	10.7	12.5	15.5	17.5	Nil	4.3	7.8
% Net Inc.of Revs.	NM	NM	NM	NM	NM	NM	NM	NM	NM	NM
% Ret. on Assets	NM	NM	NM	NM	NM	NM	NM	NM	NM	NM
% Ret. on Equity	NM	NM	NM	NM	NM	NM	NM	NM	NM	NM

Data as orig reptd.; bef. results of disc opers/spec. items. Per share data adj. for stk. divs. Bold denotes diluted EPS (FASB 128)-prior periods restated. E-Estimated. NA-Not Available. NM-Not Meaningful. NR-Not Ranked.

Office—145 Brandywine Pkwy., West Chester, PA 19380. **Tel**—(610) 344-0200. **Website**—http://www.cephalon.com **Pres & CEO**—F. Baldino Jr. **SVP-Fin & CFO**—J. K. Buchi. **Dirs**—F. Baldino Jr., W. P. Egan, R. J. Feeney, M. D. Greenacre, K. E. Moley, H. Witzel. **Transfer Agent & Registrar**—American Stock Transfer & Trust Co., NYC. **Incorporated**—In Delaware in 1987. **Empl**— 295. **S&P Analyst:** Frank DiLorenzo

STANDARD
&POOR'S
STOCK REPORTS

Cerner Corp.

NASDAQ Symbol **CERN**

In S&P SmallCap 600

09-OCT-99

Industry:
Services (Commercial & Consumer)

Summary: CERN provides health care organizations with health information systems that allow information to be shared among clinical disciplines and across multiple facilities.

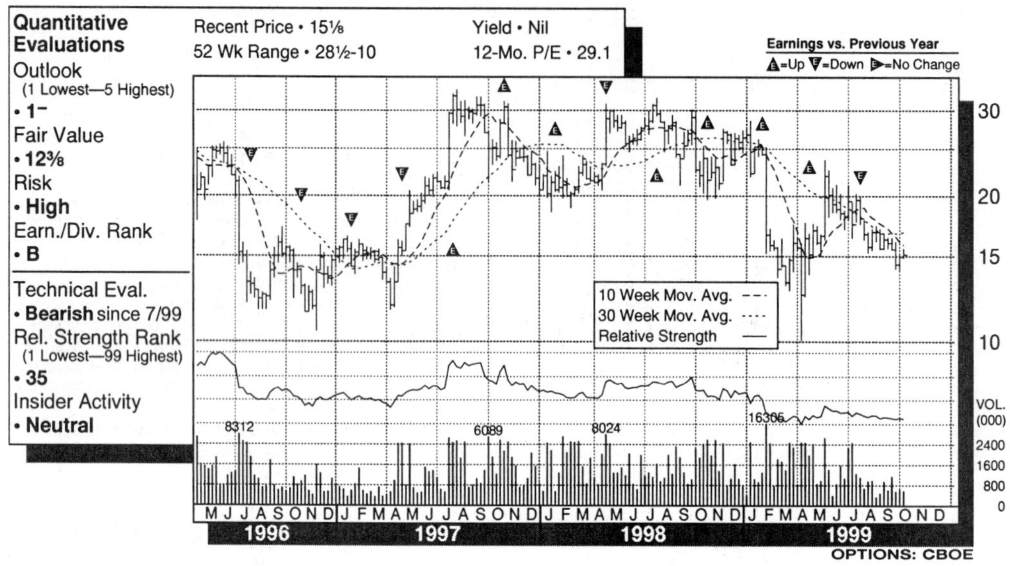

Business Profile - 14-JUN-99

Earnings in the 1999 first quarter came in below analyst estimates, as uncertainties surrounding the Y2K issue led prospective clients to delay certain software purchasing decisions. In May 1999, the company announced an agreement with Dragon Systems to integrate Dragon's speech recognition technology into CERN's HNA Millennium product. In April 1999, the company completed a $100 million private placement of debt. Proceeds were to be used to retire CERN's existing $30 million of debt, fund proposed capital improvements, and strengthen the company's cash position.

Operational Review - 14-JUN-99

Revenues in the three months ended April 3, 1999, rose 18%, year to year, driven by a 24% increase in support and maintenance, as well as a 14% rise in system sales. Margins narrowed, reflecting more rapid increases in costs of client services and software development; operating income was up 4.9%. In the absence of in-process R&D writeoffs, after taxes at 38.0%, versus 39.3%, net income surged 320%, to $2,817,000 ($0.08 a share, on 1.7% more shares), from $671,000 ($0.02).

Stock Performance - 08-OCT-99

In the past 30 trading days, CERN's shares have declined 3%, compared to a 0.91% fall in the S&P 500. Average trading volume for the past five days was 111,280 shares, compared with the 40-day moving average of 131,495 shares.

Key Stock Statistics

Dividend Rate/Share	Nil	Shareholders	1,300
Shs. outstg. (M)	33.6	Market cap. (B)	$0.509
Avg. daily vol. (M)	0.141	Inst. holdings	43%
Tang. Bk. Value/Share	9.06		
Beta	1.83		

Value of $10,000 invested 5 years ago: $ 6,954

Fiscal Year Ending Dec. 31

	1999	1998	1997	1996	1995	1994
Revenues (Million $)						
1Q	86.74	73.67	51.12	52.58	43.20	30.50
2Q	82.78	79.15	63.32	46.71	49.00	39.80
3Q	—	82.83	60.78	43.40	41.72	40.90
4Q	—	95.24	69.38	46.42	53.02	44.70
Yr.	—	330.9	245.1	189.1	186.9	155.9
Earnings Per Share ($)						
1Q	**0.08**	**0.02**	**0.06**	**0.13**	0.15	0.10
2Q	**0.01**	**0.16**	**0.10**	**0.05**	0.21	0.17
3Q	—	**0.19**	**0.13**	**0.02**	0.11	0.17
4Q	—	**0.24**	**0.16**	**0.05**	0.25	0.22
Yr.	—	**0.61**	**0.45**	**0.25**	**0.72**	**0.66**

Next earnings report expected: late October

Dividend Data

No cash dividends have been paid. The company intends to retain its earnings for use in its business and does not anticipate paying cash dividends in the foreseeable future. The common stock was split two for one in May 1992, March 1993, and August 1995.

A Division of The McGraw-Hill Companies

Business Summary - 14-JUN-99

As the health care industry continues to consolidate, and becomes increasingly interconnected, there is a need for information systems that link all parties. Cerner Corp. (CERN) provides clinical and management information systems for all points in the health care process. The company's interrelated systems are designed to automate the health care process by accumulating data on care provided to members/patients, maintaining such data in a database repository and providing access to this data for users of clinical information across a health care system, including the home, physicians' offices, and ambulatory, inpatient and intensive care settings.

CERN's systems are designed around its Health Network Architecture (HNA), a single unified system. HNA allows each participating facility in an integrated health care enterprise to access an individual's clinical record at the point of care, to organize it for specific needs of the physician, nurse, laboratory technician or other care provider on a real-time basis, and to use the information in management decisions. HNA Millennium, the company's fifth generation of HNA, uses a three-tier client/server technology, and features Windows 95 and Windows NT graphical desktops that can be personalized for specific needs, scaleability, point-of-care interfaces, and data analysis capabilities.

The HNA Millennium system provides healthcare organizations with a single system based on a fully integrated common architecture and data structure. HNA Millennium provides real time access to all information across multiple applications, such as laboratory, pharmacy, nursing and physicians, to all of those needing those services, regardless of location.

The company believes a new center of health care is emerging: the Integrated Health Organization (IHO), a combination of payers, physicians and institutional providers affiliated to service a community or defined member population. The focus of the IHO is to be accountable for the health status of a defined population, with substantial financial incentives to manage health on a preventative or wellness basis and reduce costs. CERN anticipates that many large IHOs will emerge in the U.S. in the next decade. These IHOs will need to implement information systems that manage the delivery of care across an entire community while simultaneously managing the business side of health management.

Key elements of CERN's business strategy include penetrating the integrated health care market; penetrating the physician market as physicians combine to form organizations such as independent practice associations and preferred provider organizations; and expanding core businesses such as clinical domain systems.

Total revenue backlog was $470.9 million ($315.0 million in contract backlog and $230.5 million in support backlog) at April 4, 1999.

Per Share Data ($) (Year Ended Dec. 31)	1998	1997	1996	1995	1994	1993	1992	1991	1990	1989
Tangible Bk. Val.	7.84	6.97	6.90	6.68	2.84	2.05	1.51	1.09	0.96	0.97
Cash Flow	1.37	0.99	0.71	1.10	0.86	0.63	0.44	0.25	0.12	0.17
Earnings	0.61	0.45	0.25	0.72	0.66	0.50	0.35	0.18	0.06	0.12
Dividends	Nil	Nil	Nil	Nil	Nil	Nil	Nil	Nil	Nil	Nil
Payout Ratio	Nil	Nil	Nil	Nil	Nil	Nil	Nil	Nil	Nil	Nil
Prices - High	31⅞	33⅛	26¾	36	24¾	22⅞	14⅛	3¼	1¾	2
- Low	18½	11⅝	10½	20	11¾	7⅞	2⅞	1⅛	⅝	1 3/16
P/E Ratio - High	46	74	107	50	38	46	41	18	31	17
- Low	26	26	42	28	18	16	8	7	14	10
Income Statement Analysis (Million $)										
Revs.	331	245	189	187	156	121	101	77.0	51.0	57.0
Oper. Inc.	64.0	40.2	26.1	49.5	39.9	28.1	19.3	10.0	4.2	7.2
Depr.	25.4	18.1	15.5	12.2	6.1	3.8	2.8	1.9	1.6	1.5
Int. Exp.	2.5	2.4	2.5	2.4	1.9	0.7	0.7	0.9	0.7	0.6
Pretax Inc.	33.3	24.5	10.6	37.2	32.5	24.1	16.3	7.6	2.5	5.6
Eff. Tax Rate	38%	38%	36%	40%	40%	40%	39%	38%	37%	36%
Net Inc.	20.6	15.1	8.3	22.5	19.5	14.6	9.9	4.7	1.6	3.6
Balance Sheet & Other Fin. Data (Million $)										
Cash	42.7	7.5	111	112	15.3	16.8	13.7	8.7	7.1	7.4
Curr. Assets	217	208	212	217	83.7	67.2	45.9	39.7	38.6	45.2
Total Assets	436	332	315	304	156	105	67.0	56.0	52.0	55.0
Curr. Liab.	98.2	51.5	41.2	42.8	31.3	24.6	15.4	17.1	17.8	23.3
LT Debt	25.0	30.0	30.0	30.1	30.2	10.4	8.3	8.0	7.7	1.6
Common Eqty.	271	234	231	221	85.8	64.2	38.6	27.5	24.1	28.1
Total Cap.	318	280	274	261	125	80.0	51.0	39.0	35.0	32.0
Cap. Exp.	23.6	14.8	15.3	18.9	32.2	7.1	4.7	1.8	3.2	1.3
Cash Flow	46.0	33.2	23.8	34.7	25.6	18.3	12.7	6.6	3.2	5.0
Curr. Ratio	2.2	4.0	5.1	5.1	2.7	2.7	3.0	2.3	2.2	1.9
% LT Debt of Cap.	7.9	10.7	11.0	11.5	24.2	12.9	16.2	20.5	22.4	5.1
% Net Inc.of Revs.	6.2	6.2	4.4	12.0	12.5	12.1	9.8	6.1	3.0	6.3
% Ret. on Assets	5.4	4.7	2.7	13.6	14.8	16.6	16.1	8.6	3.1	7.0
% Ret. on Equity	8.2	6.5	3.7	14.7	25.7	27.7	29.8	18.1	6.4	13.6

Data as orig reptd.; bef. results of disc opers/spec. items. Per share data adj. for stk. divs. Bold denotes diluted EPS (FASB 128)-prior periods restated. E-Estimated. NA-Not Available. NM-Not Meaningful. NR-Not Ranked.

Office—2800 Rockcreek Pky., Suite 601, Kansas City, MO 64117. **Tel**—(816) 221-1024. **Website**—http://www.cerner.com **Chrmn & CEO**—N. L. Patterson. **Vice Chrmn**—C. W. Illig. **EVP & COO**—G.P. Tobin. **VP & CFO**—M. G. Naughton. **Dirs**—J. C. Danforth, M. E. Herman, C. W. Illig, T. A. McDonnell, N. L. Patterson, III, T. C. Tinstman. **Transfer Agent & Registrar**—Securities Transfer Division, UMB Bank, Kansas City, MO. **Incorporated**—in Missouri in 1980. **Empl**— 2,600. **S&P Analyst:** Stephen J. Tekirian

STANDARD
&POOR'S
STOCK REPORTS

Champion Enterprises

NYSE Symbol **CHB**

In S&P SmallCap 600

09-OCT-99 **Industry:** Homebuilding

Summary: This Michigan-based company is the leading U.S. producer and third largest retailer of manufactured homes.

Quantitative Evaluations

Outlook (1 Lowest—5 Highest)
• **5**

Fair Value
• **20¼**

Risk
• **Average**

Earn./Div. Rank
• **B**

Technical Eval.
• **Neutral** since 9/99

Rel. Strength Rank (1 Lowest—99 Highest)
• **6**

Insider Activity
• **Neutral**

Recent Price • 8⅝
52 Wk Range • 27⅜-8⅛
Yield • Nil
12-Mo. P/E • 4.2

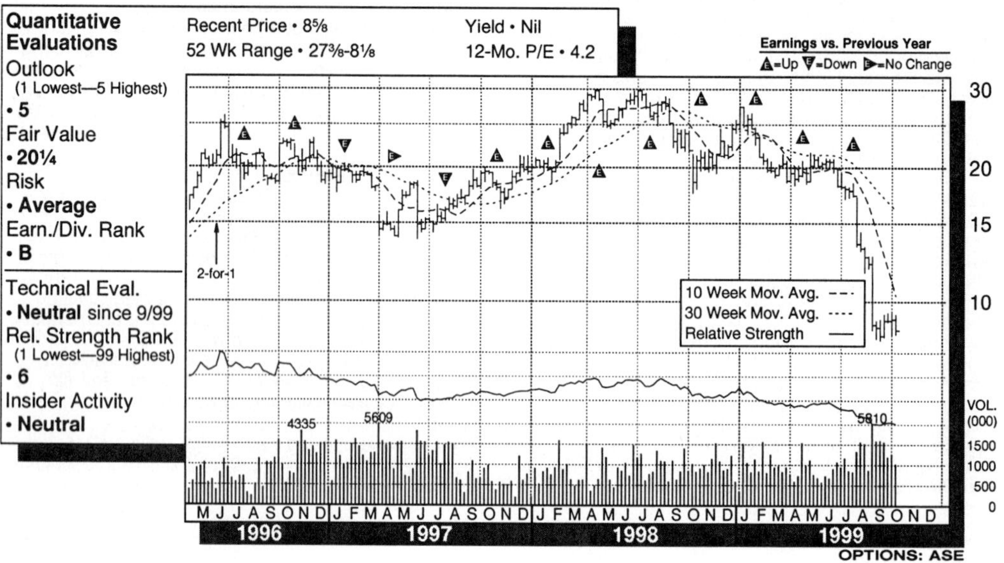

Business Profile - 14-SEP-99

The company expects earnings for the second half of 1999 to be down 40% from last year's $1.03 a share, reflecting excess retail inventory and competitive market conditions. The projection, which is well below the earlier consensus estimate of $0.94, excludes a $0.41 third quarter charge related to the July 1999 bankruptcy filing of CHB's largest independent retail customer. As a result, CHB has consolidated its manufacturing operations in North Carolina. The company plans to continue to expand its retail operations, which will experience margin pressure from start-up expenses. Through August 5, 1999, CHB had repurchased 743,000 of its shares for $13 million under a 3.0 million share buyback authorization. After the sale of $200 million of notes in May 1999, CHB's debt-to-capital at July 3, 1999, was 45%, up from 39% at the end of 1998.

Operational Review - 14-SEP-99

Revenues in the first half of 1999 advanced 23%, year to year, primarily reflecting retail acquisitions and, to a lesser extent, higher wholesale manufacturing volume of multi-section homes. Gross margins widened on the greater volume, improved manufacturing margins and expanded retail operations, and operating income rose 26%. However, with acquisition-related costs and sharply higher interest expense, the gain in net income was held to 16%, to $50,379,000 ($1.02 a share, diluted), from $43,447,000 ($0.88).

Stock Performance - 08-OCT-99

In the past 30 trading days, CHB's shares have declined 3%, compared to a 0.91% fall in the S&P 500. Average trading volume for the past five days was 202,920 shares, compared with the 40-day moving average of 438,379 shares.

Key Stock Statistics

Dividend Rate/Share	Nil	Shareholders	19,000
Shs. outstg. (M)	48.3	Market cap. (B)	$0.417
Avg. daily vol. (M)	0.276	Inst. holdings	74%
Tang. Bk. Value/Share	NM		
Beta	1.24		

Value of $10,000 invested 5 years ago: $ 19,574

Fiscal Year Ending Dec. 31

	1999	1998	1997	1996	1995	1994
Revenues (Million $)						
1Q	624.6	463.0	378.9	342.8	170.3	125.0
2Q	664.6	582.5	456.0	428.6	206.6	157.1
3Q	—	615.0	455.1	447.1	215.1	168.8
4Q	—	593.8	429.7	425.6	205.8	164.8
Yr.	—	2,254	1,675	1,644	797.9	615.7
Earnings Per Share ($)						
1Q	**0.43**	**0.36**	0.28	0.28	0.18	0.16
2Q	**0.59**	**0.52**	0.37	0.39	0.28	0.26
3Q	—	**0.57**	0.42	0.41	0.30	0.26
4Q	—	**0.46**	**0.39**	0.01	0.24	0.14
Yr.	—	**1.91**	**1.45**	**1.06**	**1.10**	0.81

Next earnings report expected: late October

Dividend Data

No cash dividends have been paid since July 1974.

Champion Enterprises, Inc.

Business Summary - 14-SEP-99

Champion Enterprises (CHB), formerly Champion Home Builders, is the leader in wholesale sales of mobile and modular (manufactured) homes in the U.S. CHB homes include Champion, Chandeleur, Crest Ridge, Dutch Housing, Grand Manor, Homes of Legend, Lamplighter, Moduline International, Redman, Western Homes and Moduline Industries (Canada).

During the past five years, CHB has significantly expanded its manufactured housing operations through acquisitions, internal growth and, in October 1996, a pooling-of-interests merger with Redman Industries, then the third largest manufactured home producer, based in Dallas, TX.

The company's strategy is twofold: to expand current operations to take advantage of the growing market, and to continue to seek acquisitions that provide further growth and strong returns. In January 1999, CHB acquired Homes of Merit ($130 million in revenues), a maker of mid- to high-level homes, and Heartland Homes ($55 million), an operator of nine Texas housing retail centers. During 1998, CHB acquired 13 manufacturing retailers operating 165 home centers for $277 million in cash and $12 million in stock. In July 1998, CHB acquired ICA Group, operator of 23 housing retail locations. In April 1998, CHB acquired Homes America Group ($65 million in sales; 25 retail housing sales centers) and four manufactured housing retailers in Louisiana. CHB's U.S. manufacturing market share grew to 18.3% in 1998, from 17.7% in 1997. As of May 1999, the company had 65 homebuilding facilities in 18 states and western Canada, with four additional facilities to be constructed during 1999. CHB had opened 40 new stores through internal expansion during 1998 and was operating 268 home centers in 28 states.

The company has 3,500 home dealerships strategically located in the U.S. and Canada. It maintains a regional focus, with the ability to respond quickly to local changes in customer demands and expectations. A June 1996 survey revealed that customers have an average income of $35,000 and are typically 40 years old, with a household of three or more.

In its manufacturing operations, CHB sold 70,359 homes in 1998, up from 64,285 homes in 1997, a 9% increase. The average home price was $27,000, up from $25,700 in 1997. CHB's share of the U.S. wholesale market in 1998 (based on homes sold) was 18.3%, up from 17.7% in 1997. New retail homes sold totaled 11,738 in 1998, up significantly from 983 in 1997. The company's average retail sales price for new homes sold in 1998 was $45,075, down from $60,367 in 1997.

According to the U.S. Department of Commerce, manufactured housing wholesale shipments accounted for 23% of all single-family housing starts and 30% of all new single-family homes sold in 1998. The market for manufactured housing is affected by several factors, including consumer confidence, job creation, and general economic growth. In addition, demographic trends, such as changes in population growth, and competition affec t the demand for housing products.

Per Share Data ($) (Year Ended Dec. 31)	1998	1997	1996	1995	1994	1993	1992	1991	1990	1989
Tangible Bk. Val.	NM	3.45	2.14	1.02	1.40	1.59	1.22	1.16	0.89	0.88
Cash Flow	2.46	1.80	1.39	1.21	0.94	0.46	0.23	0.06	0.10	-0.41
Earnings	1.91	1.45	1.09	1.01	0.81	0.39	0.17	-0.02	0.01	-0.49
Dividends	Nil	Nil	Nil	Nil	Nil	Nil	Nil	Nil	Nil	Nil
Payout Ratio	Nil	Nil	Nil	Nil	Nil	Nil	Nil	Nil	Nil	Nil
Prices - High	30	$21\frac{1}{4}$	$26\frac{1}{8}$	$15\frac{1}{2}$	$10\frac{1}{8}$	5	$2\frac{3}{4}$	$1\frac{1}{2}$	1	$1\frac{1}{4}$
- Low	$17\frac{1}{2}$	$13\frac{3}{4}$	$11\frac{7}{8}$	$6\frac{3}{4}$	$4\frac{3}{8}$	$2\frac{5}{16}$	$\frac{3}{4}$	$\frac{5}{8}$	$\frac{1}{2}$	$\frac{9}{16}$
P/E Ratio - High	16	15	24	15	12	13	16	NM	80	NM
- Low	9	9	11	7	5	6	4	NM	38	NM
Income Statement Analysis (Million $)										
Revs.	2,254	1,675	1,644	798	616	342	235	270	288	313
Oper. Inc.	197	134	131	61.1	40.6	13.8	7.2	1.4	4.7	-8.8
Depr.	26.9	17.1	14.9	6.2	3.9	2.2	1.6	2.2	2.3	2.4
Int. Exp.	15.8	1.2	2.3	2.3	0.8	0.5	0.7	1.1	1.4	1.8
Pretax Inc.	157	117	94.2	53.5	34.1	12.6	6.0	0.1	1.4	-13.1
Eff. Tax Rate	40%	40%	43%	40%	26%	11%	19%	NM	75%	NM
Net Inc.	94.2	70.8	53.6	32.3	25.2	11.2	4.8	-0.6	0.3	-13.9
Balance Sheet & Other Fin. Data (Million $)										
Cash	23.8	60.3	19.0	15.0	73.0	34.4	20.7	15.1	10.9	7.8
Curr. Assets	386	230	217	108	97.8	74.4	58.5	56.7	48.0	51.9
Total Assets	1,022	501	501	236	171	98.0	81.0	81.0	77.0	83.0
Curr. Liab.	394	183	195	104	79.1	42.5	36.6	39.2	40.5	45.1
LT Debt	118	1.8	1.2	Nil	Nil	2.8	3.8	4.5	5.4	6.5
Common Eqty.	405	280	227	113	79.3	45.9	34.0	31.4	24.1	23.3
Total Cap.	523	282	228	113	79.3	48.7	37.8	35.8	29.5	30.0
Cap. Exp.	49.1	38.3	50.7	9.0	10.6	6.6	2.8	2.3	1.7	5.1
Cash Flow	121	87.9	68.5	38.4	29.1	13.4	6.5	1.5	2.6	-11.5
Curr. Ratio	1.0	1.3	1.1	1.0	1.2	1.8	1.6	1.4	1.2	1.2
% LT Debt of Cap.	22.6	0.7	0.5	Nil	Nil	5.8	10.1	12.5	18.4	21.8
% Net Inc.of Revs.	4.2	4.2	3.2	4.0	4.1	3.3	2.0	NM	0.1	NM
% Ret. on Assets	12.4	14.5	12.6	15.8	18.4	12.3	5.9	NM	0.4	NM
% Ret. on Equity	27.5	27.9	26.6	33.5	39.5	27.6	14.5	NM	1.4	NM

Data as orig reptd.; bef. results of disc opers/spec. items. Per share data adj. for stk. divs. Bold denotes diluted EPS (FASB 128)-prior periods restated. E-Estimated. NA-Not Available. NM-Not Meaningful. NR-Not Ranked.

Office—2701 University Dr., Suite 320, Auburn Hills, MI 48326. **Tel**—(810) 340-9090. **Website**—www.champent.com **Chrmn & Pres**—W. R. Young, Jr. **EVP & CFO**—J. H. Stegmayer. **COO**—P. C. Surles. **VP & Secy**—J. J. Collins, Jr. **Dirs**—R. W. Anestis, S. Isakow, B. D. Jellison, E. R. Levine, G. R. Mrkonic, R. L. Stark, C. S. Valdiserri, W. R. Young, Jr. **Transfer Agent & Registrar**—Harris Trust and Savings Bank, Chicago. **Incorporated**—in Michigan in 1953; reincorporated in Delaware in 1987. **Empl**— 15,000. **S&P Analyst:** Stewart Scharf

STANDARD
&POOR'S
STOCK REPORTS

Checkpoint Systems

NYSE Symbol **CKP**

In S&P SmallCap 600

09-OCT-99

Industry:
Electrical Equipment

Summary: Checkpoint makes electronic article merchandising systems used by retailers to prevent theft, and electronic access control systems used to restrict access to areas or buildings.

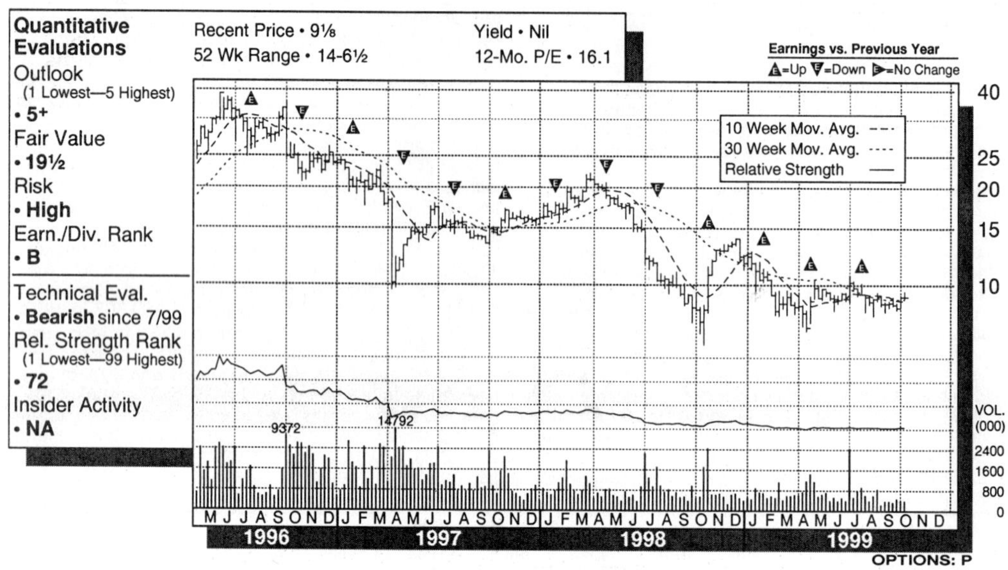

Business Profile - 22-JUN-99

The company has achieved substantial growth in the past five years through internal expansion as well as acquisitions. More than 350,000 Checkpoint electronic article surveillance (EAS) systems have now been installed worldwide. Demand for the company's products has been bolstered by the increasing use of source tagging, whereby an electronic tag is inserted into a product at the time of manufacture. The company intends to continue to expand its presence in the supermarket industry, as part of efforts to further penetrate the worldwide security market.

Operational Review - 22-JUN-99

In the first quarter of 1999, revenues rose 2.4%, year to year, reflecting increased international sales of the company's EAS systems, partly offset by lower CCTV and electronic access control sales. Gross margins narrowed, but SG&A expenses were well controlled due to the effects of a recent restructuring and headcount reduction; operating profit was up 5.5%. Following lower depreciation and amortization charges, which were mostly offset by a foreign currency exchange loss, net income advanced 9.3%, to $1,392,000 ($0.05 a share, on 12% fewer shares) from $1,273,000 ($0.04).

Stock Performance - 08-OCT-99

In the past 30 trading days, CKP's shares have increased 5%, compared to a 0.91% fall in the S&P 500. Average trading volume for the past five days was 72,760 shares, compared with the 40-day moving average of 83,810 shares.

Key Stock Statistics

Dividend Rate/Share	Nil	Shareholders	1,487
Shs. outstg. (M)	30.2	Market cap. (B)	$0.277
Avg. daily vol. (M)	0.076	Inst. holdings	59%
Tang. Bk. Value/Share	5.71		
Beta	0.66		

Value of $10,000 invested 5 years ago: $ 16,708

Fiscal Year Ending Dec. 31

	1999	1998	1997	1996	1995	1994
Revenues (Million $)						
1Q	81.75	79.86	68.18	66.99	37.36	26.22
2Q	87.31	90.58	81.04	74.79	49.74	28.66
3Q	—	94.04	87.96	73.77	52.80	33.93
4Q	—	97.93	98.79	76.22	64.84	39.52
Yr.	—	362.4	336.0	291.8	204.7	128.3
Earnings Per Share ($)						
1Q	**0.05**	**0.04**	**0.07**	**0.10**	0.01	0.03
2Q	**0.14**	**0.11**	**0.14**	**0.18**	0.13	0.05
3Q	—	**0.20**	**0.17**	**0.15**	0.16	0.10
4Q	—	**0.19**	**-0.15**	**0.16**	0.11	0.12
Yr.	—	**0.53**	**0.23**	**0.60**	**0.42**	**0.29**

Next earnings report expected: late October

Dividend Data

No regular cash dividends have been paid.

Checkpoint Systems, Inc.

Business Summary - 22-JUN-99

Checkpoint Systems (CKP) designs and manufactures integrated electronic security systems aimed primarily at helping retailers prevent the theft of merchandise. The company's systems include electronic article surveillance (EAS), closed-circuit television (CCTV), point-of-sale (POS) monitoring and electronic access control (EAC) systems. Industry sources estimate that up to 360,000 major retail location in the U.S. alone would benefit from installation of an EAS system. Of these, only one-third have installed EAS systems.

EAS systems generally consist of three components: circuits embedded in tags or labels, called tags, which can be detected and are placed in the items to be protected; sensors that detect the tags when they enter a detection area, such as the doorway of a store; and deactivation equipment, which disarms the tag when items are properly paid for. CKP's principal products are the components of its EAS system, which includes various sensors and a variety of patented targets. Depending on their product mix, customers can choose from a wide variety of targets, including disposable paper tags and reusable hard plastic tags (used primarily in the apparel market). In 1998, sales of EAS sensors accounted for 22% of total revenues (26% in 1997), EAS deactivation units 11% (12%) and EAS tags 32% (32%).

CCTV systems and monitoring services include a full line of camera, monitoring, perimeter protection and fire/intrusion alarm equipment, as well as POS monitoring systems that record and store on videotape every transaction at each check-out: both visual and individual transaction data. in 1998, about 19% of total revenues was derived from CCTV systems, versus 16% in 1997.

Electronic access controls utilize an electronic key, such as a card with a magnetic strip, and a card reader to restrict access to certain areas to authorized individuals. The most advanced EAC systems use plastic cards containing an encoded digital integrated circuit that can be coded with specific information, such as cardholder identity and security clearance/access level, and can record that information along with time of entry and exit. Electronic access control systems accounted for 3% of total revenues in 1998 and 1997.

The remaining revenues are derived from service, replacement parts and other activities.

CKP markets its products primarily to retailers in the hard goods (supermarkets, drug stores, mass merchandisers and music/electronics); soft goods (department stores, apparel stores); specialty stores and sporting goods segments. The company also sells its products to libraries. Revenues outside of North America accounted for about 50% of the total in 1998.

Per Share Data ($) (Year Ended Dec. 31)	1998	1997	1996	1995	1994	1993	1992	1991	1990	1989
Tangible Bk. Val.	5.93	5.77	6.18	2.16	2.92	2.64	2.55	1.99	2.03	1.59
Cash Flow	1.30	0.90	1.14	0.86	0.66	0.34	0.41	0.18	0.47	0.40
Earnings	0.53	0.23	0.60	0.42	0.29	0.08	0.23	0.03	0.36	0.30
Dividends	Nil	Nil	Nil	Nil	Nil	Nil	Nil	Nil	Nil	Nil
Payout Ratio	Nil	Nil	Nil	Nil	Nil	Nil	Nil	Nil	Nil	Nil
Prices - High	22 1/8	24 3/4	39	19 1/2	10 3/4	10 1/8	9 1/8	5 7/8	8	6 1/4
- Low	6 1/2	9 5/8	17 7/8	8	5 3/8	4 1/8	4	3 3/8	3 1/8	3 1/4
P/E Ratio - High	42	NM	65	48	37	NM	40	NM	22	20
- Low	12	NM	30	19	19	NM	18	NM	9	10
Income Statement Analysis (Million $)										
Revs.	362	336	292	205	128	93.0	72.2	52.9	56.7	50.8
Oper. Inc.	55.7	43.2	48.4	31.2	19.8	4.9	8.9	3.8	9.4	8.3
Depr.	25.7	23.5	18.3	12.2	8.0	5.5	3.8	3.0	2.2	1.8
Int. Exp.	9.6	9.6	9.6	5.0	3.1	0.9	0.4	0.3	0.2	0.2
Pretax Inc.	26.2	13.6	29.9	16.6	8.4	2.1	4.9	0.6	6.7	6.9
Eff. Tax Rate	32%	40%	32%	31%	25%	22%	9.50%	20%	NM	19%
Net Inc.	17.7	8.2	20.4	11.4	6.3	1.6	4.4	0.5	6.9	5.6
Balance Sheet & Other Fin. Data (Million $)										
Cash	35.9	64.1	186	77.5	0.9	Nil	2.3	1.3	3.0	4.5
Curr. Assets	265	298	348	215	69.2	54.9	39.7	29.1	29.7	29.3
Total Assets	508	516	522	362	128	105	74.3	57.7	53.1	44.4
Curr. Liab.	78.6	86.1	62.4	66.6	29.8	26.9	14.0	14.8	11.8	10.6
LT Debt	166	151	153	156	35.6	24.3	9.3	0.8	Nil	1.2
Common Eqty.	262	278	301	138	61.3	53.8	51.1	42.1	41.3	32.6
Total Cap.	429	430	459	296	98.1	78.1	60.4	42.9	41.3	33.8
Cap. Exp.	12.3	26.7	10.5	9.4	4.5	12.0	7.7	6.9	10.0	6.7
Cash Flow	43.4	31.8	38.7	23.6	14.3	7.1	8.2	3.5	9.1	7.4
Curr. Ratio	3.4	3.5	5.6	3.2	2.3	2.0	2.8	2.0	2.5	2.8
% LT Debt of Cap.	38.7	35.1	33.3	52.7	36.2	31.1	15.4	1.8	Nil	3.5
% Net Inc.of Revs.	4.9	2.4	7.0	5.6	4.9	1.7	6.1	1.0	12.2	11.0
% Ret. on Assets	3.5	1.6	4.6	4.7	5.3	1.8	6.5	0.9	14.1	13.6
% Ret. on Equity	6.6	2.8	9.2	11.5	10.8	3.1	9.3	1.2	18.6	19.0

Data as orig reptd.; bef. results of disc opers/spec. items. Per share data adj. for stk. divs. Bold denotes diluted EPS (FASB 128)-prior periods restated. E-Estimated. NA-Not Available. NM-Not Meaningful. NR-Not Ranked.

Office—101 Wolf Dr., P.O. Box 188, Thorofare, NJ 08086. **Tel**—1 800 257-5540. **Website**—http://www.checkpointsystems.com **Chrmn**—D. W. Clark Jr. **Pres & CEO**—K. P. Dowd. **SVP, CFO & Treas**—J. A. Reinhold. **VP & Secy**—N. D. Austin. **Investor Relations**—1-800-257-5540. **Dirs**—R. D. Blackwell, R. J. Censits, D. W. Clark Jr., K. P. Dowd, A. R. Hirsig, W. P. Lyons, Jr., E. Margaona, R. E. Martino, A. E. Wolf. **Transfer Agent**—American Stock Transfer & Trust Co., NYC. **Incorporated**—in Pennsylvania in 1969. **Empl**— 3,044. **S&P Analyst:** Jim Corridore

STANDARD
&POOR'S
STOCK REPORTS

Cheesecake Factory

NASDAQ Symbol **CAKE**

In S&P SmallCap 600

09-OCT-99 **Industry:** Restaurants

Summary: This company operates 30 upscale, moderately priced, casual dining restaurants under The Cheesecake Factory name, offering an extensive menu of more than 200 items.

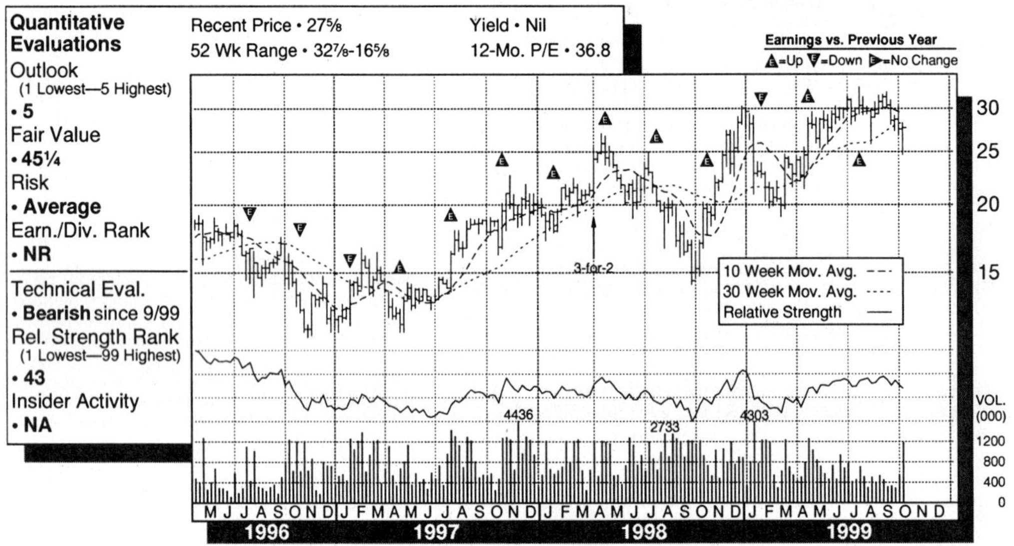

Business Profile - 04-AUG-99

The company set a goal of increasing total restaurant sq. ft. by 25% or more in each of 1999 and 2000. It opened its 30th Cheesecake Factory Restaurant, in Columbus, OH, in July 1999; its second Cheesecake Factory Express, at the DisneyQuest family entertainment center in Chicago, in June; and its first Grand Lux Cafe, at the Venetian Resort-Hotel-Casino in Las Vegas, in May. Two additional Cheesecake Factory restaurants, in Boulder, CO, and Providence, RI, are scheduled to open in September 1999. CAKE has moved to boost margins with initiatives aimed at achieving sustained pretax margins of 10% or better by the end of 2000.

Operational Review - 04-AUG-99

Total revenues in the six months ended June 30, 1999, climbed 30%, year to year, reflecting the opening of new restaurants, and a 4.0% increase in comparable-restaurant sales. Margins widened, aided by measures to reduce costs and improve productivity; operating income advanced 36%. With lower net interest income, after taxes at 36.5%, versus 34.4%, the gain in income was held to 25%, to $8,891,000 ($0.42 a share), from $7,119,000 ($0.35, before a charge of $0.31 for the cumulative effect of an accounting change).

Stock Performance - 08-OCT-99

In the past 30 trading days, CAKE's shares have declined 11%, compared to a 0.91% fall in the S&P 500. Average trading volume for the past five days was 232,940 shares, compared with the 40-day moving average of 102,441 shares.

Key Stock Statistics

Dividend Rate/Share	Nil	Shareholders	8,600
Shs. outstg. (M)	20.1	Market cap. (B)	$0.556
Avg. daily vol. (M)	0.116	Inst. holdings	78%
Tang. Bk. Value/Share	8.42		
Beta	1.57		

Value of $10,000 invested 5 years ago: $ 18,147

Fiscal Year Ending Dec. 31

	1999	1998	1997	1996	1995	1994
Revenues (Million $)						
1Q	74.82	59.50	45.23	35.38	24.97	18.75
2Q	85.77	64.27	51.00	39.21	28.50	20.43
3Q	—	68.58	53.55	42.20	29.37	22.20
4Q	—	72.87	58.81	43.52	34.33	24.21
Yr.	—	265.2	208.6	160.3	117.2	85.59
Earnings Per Share ($)						
1Q	**0.18**	**0.15**	**0.11**	**0.10**	0.11	0.09
2Q	**0.25**	**0.17**	**0.15**	**0.13**	0.15	0.12
3Q	—	**0.19**	**0.17**	**0.11**	0.15	0.13
4Q	—	**0.15**	**0.16**	**0.03**	0.13	0.13
Yr.	—	**0.68**	**0.58**	**0.35**	**0.52**	**0.45**

Next earnings report expected: late October

Dividend Data

No cash dividends have been paid. The company intends to retain its earnings to finance the growth and development of its business and does not anticipate paying cash dividends on the common stock for the foreseeable future.

The Cheesecake Factory Incorporated

Business Summary - 04-AUG-99

The Cheesecake Factory (CAKE) has given new meaning to the word diversification; it makes and sells about 40 varieties of cheesecake, including chocolate chip cookie dough, double-chocolate upside-down Jack Daniel's, Adam's peanut butter cup fudge ripple, pumpkin, and white chocolate raspberry truffle. The company sells these creamy confections, as well as a variety of other food items, through a chain of Cheesecake Factory restaurants throughout the U.S. It also sells its bakery products to grocery stores, other restaurants and chains, food-service facilities, and through mail order.

The company, founded in 1972 as a retail and wholesale bakery, opened its first restaurant in Beverly Hills in 1978. As of July 22, 1999, CAKE was operating 30 Cheesecake restaurants in 12 states and Washington, DC. It also had two Cheesecake Factory Express limited menu foodservice operations in two states, and one Grand Lux Cafe, CAKE's new upscale casual dining concept, at a hotel-casino in Las Vegas. It had opened several new restaurants thus far in 1999.

The core Cheesecake Factory Restaurants have an upscale decor combined with moderate prices (average check per person was $14.60 in 1998), and offer more than 200 items, including hamburgers, chicken, omelets, pasta, pizza, salads, sandwiches, seafood, steaks, and desserts.

The company has created a new restaurant concept, a bakery cafe under The Cheesecake Factory brand name. The cafes are designed to emphasize the company's distinctive desserts, accompanied by beverages, sandwiches, and salads in a self-service format. The first bakery cafe opened in July 1997. As of March 23, 1999, CAKE was operating three bakery cafes, ranging in size from 250 sq. ft. to 850 sq. ft.

At its bakery production facility in Calabasas Hills, CA, the company produces approximately 50 varieties of cheesecake and other baked desserts based on proprietary recipes. CAKE markets its cheesecakes on a wholesale basis to grocery and retail outlets, other restaurant operators and foodservice distributors.

In October 1997, the company agreed to be the exclusive foodservice operator for Disney's new DisneyQuest concept, which was launched in June 1998. A Cheesecake Factory Express opened at DisneyQuest in mid-July 1999. In June 1997, CAKE agreed to develop and operate a casual dining concept in the Venetian Resort-Hotel-Casino in Las Vegas, under The Grand Lux Cafe name. The unit opened in May 1999.

In 1998, restaurant sales contributed 88% of total revenues, down from 90% in 1997. Bakery sales accounted for the remaining 12% and 10% of revenues in 1998 and 1997, respectively.

Per Share Data ($) (Year Ended Dec. 31)	1998	1997	1996	1995	1994	1993	1992	1991	1990	1989
Tangible Bk. Val.	7.97	7.60	5.09	4.68	4.04	2.05	NA	NA	NA	NA
Cash Flow	1.10	1.36	0.35	1.12	0.69	0.50	NA	NA	NA	NA
Earnings	0.68	0.58	0.35	0.52	0.46	0.34	NA	NA	NA	NA
Dividends	Nil	Nil	Nil	Nil	Nil	Nil	NA	NA	NA	NA
Payout Ratio	Nil	Nil	Nil	Nil	Nil	Nil	NA	NA	NA	NA
Prices - High	30 3/8	22 5/8	19 1/8	20 1/8	16 1/2	15 7/8	NA	NA	NA	NA
- Low	14 1/4	11 5/8	11 3/8	9 1/8	9	9 1/4	NA	NA	NA	NA
P/E Ratio - High	45	39	54	39	36	47	NA	NA	NA	NA
- Low	21	20	32	18	20	27	NA	NA	NA	NA
Income Statement Analysis (Million $)										
Revs.	265	209	160	117	86.0	67.0	52.0	NA	NA	NA
Oper. Inc.	26.3	27.6	19.5	16.2	12.6	9.1	5.7	NA	NA	NA
Depr.	8.5	13.3	10.7	5.8	3.6	2.3	1.4	NA	NA	NA
Int. Exp.	Nil	NA	Nil	Nil	0.0	0.0	0.3	NA	NA	NA
Pretax Inc.	21.1	15.2	8.9	11.7	10.7	7.6	4.2	NA	NA	NA
Eff. Tax Rate	34%	34%	34%	26%	32%	37%	NM	NA	NA	NA
Net Inc.	14.0	9.9	5.9	8.6	7.3	4.8	4.2	NA	NA	NA
Balance Sheet & Other Fin. Data (Million $)										
Cash	31.1	43.5	10.3	14.2	9.5	NA	NA	NA	NA	NA
Curr. Assets	54.7	78.0	27.4	29.6	21.0	NA	NA	NA	NA	NA
Total Assets	185	180	108	91.8	73.2	34.7	27.5	NA	NA	NA
Curr. Liab.	24.4	27.4	18.6	15.7	8.9	NA	NA	NA	NA	NA
LT Debt	Nil	Nil	6.0	Nil	Nil	0.3	4.5	NA	NA	NA
Common Eqty.	160	153	83.5	76.2	64.3	23.1	3.0	NA	NA	NA
Total Cap.	161	153	89.5	76.2	64.3	23.5	7.5	NA	NA	NA
Cap. Exp.	28.0	21.7	23.2	29.5	13.1	7.5	NA	NA	NA	NA
Cash Flow	22.6	23.3	16.6	14.5	10.9	7.0	5.6	NA	NA	NA
Curr. Ratio	2.2	2.8	1.5	1.9	2.4	NA	NA	NA	NA	NA
% LT Debt of Cap.	Nil	Nil	6.7	Nil	Nil	1.4	60.1	NA	NA	NA
% Net Inc.of Revs.	5.3	4.8	3.7	7.4	8.4	7.1	8.1	NA	NA	NA
% Ret. on Assets	7.7	6.9	5.9	10.4	13.3	15.5	NA	NA	NA	NA
% Ret. on Equity	9.0	8.4	7.4	12.3	15.5	18.6	NA	NA	NA	NA

Data as orig reptd.; bef. results of disc opers/spec. items. Per share data adj. for stk. divs. Bold denotes diluted EPS (FASB 128)-prior periods restated. E-Estimated. NA-Not Available. NM-Not Meaningful. NR-Not Ranked.

Office—26950 Agoura Rd., Calabasas Hills, CA 91301. **Tel**—(818) 871-3000. **Website**—http://www.thecheesecakefactory.com **Chrmn, Pres & CEO**—D. Overton. **EVP & CFO**—G. W. Deitchle. **Dirs**—T. L. Gregory, J. I. Kransdorf, D. Overton, W. H. White. **Transfer Agent & Registrar**—U. S. Stock Transfer Co., Glendale, CA. **Incorporated**—in Delaware in 1992. **Empl**— 6,714. **S&P Analyst:** S.A.H.

STANDARD
&POOR'S
STOCK REPORTS

Chemed Corp.

NYSE Symbol **CHE**

In S&P SmallCap 600

09-OCT-99

Industry:
Services (Commercial & Consumer)

Summary: CHE owns Roto-Rooter, a plumbing and drain cleaning company, and has interests in home health care and appliance and air-conditioning repair businesses.

Quantitative Evaluations

Outlook
(1 Lowest—5 Highest)
• **4–**

Fair Value
• **43**

Risk
• **Low**

Earn./Div. Rank
• **B**

Technical Eval.
• **Bearish** since 8/99

Rel. Strength Rank
(1 Lowest—99 Highest)
• **51**

Insider Activity
• **Neutral**

Recent Price • 29¾
52 Wk Range • 35⅛-25¾
Yield • 7.1%
12-Mo. P/E • 16.5

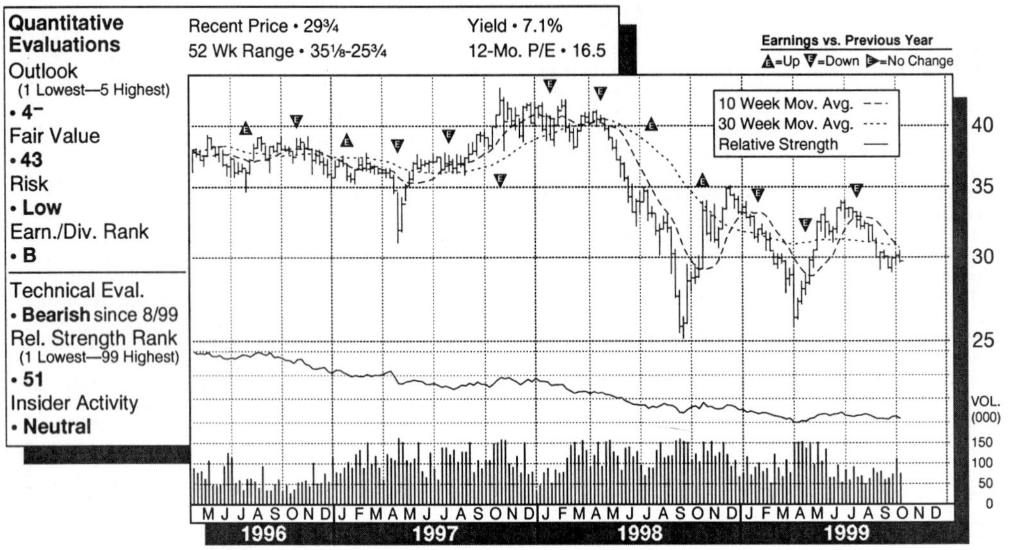

Business Profile - 30-SEP-99

Chemed's guiding philosophy is to invest in businesses that are marketing and service oriented, recession resistant, and net cash generators. CHE also remains committed to its long-term strategy of expanding Roto-Rooter's service offerings to both commercial and residential customers. The company intends to continue to capitalize on the Roto-Rooter brand image, acquire strategically positioned Roto-Rooter franchise locations, and acquire local and regional service companies that complement its existing network of Roto-Rooter branch locations. In August 1999, CHE's Service America subsidiary acquired Tucson, AZ-based Action Service Inc., a provider of heating and air-conditioning sales and service, with revenues of $1.8 million in 1998.

Operational Review - 30-SEP-99

Revenues for the six months ended June 30, 1999, advanced 16%, year to year, reflecting internal growth and acquisitions. All business groups posted revenues gains, with the 29% increase at Roto-Rooter being the most notable. Margins widened, and operating income was up 24%. However, with a 40% drop in other income (net), primarily the result of lower investment gains, and after taxes at 39.3%, versus 38.9%, net income slipped 11%, to $10,469,000 ($1.00 a share, on 4.5% more shares), from $11,817,000 ($1.17).

Stock Performance - 08-OCT-99

In the past 30 trading days, CHE's shares have declined 0.83%, compared to a 0.91% fall in the S&P 500. Average trading volume for the past five days was 14,800 shares, compared with the 40-day moving average of 15,877 shares.

Key Stock Statistics

Dividend Rate/Share	2.12	Shareholders	5,167
Shs. outstg. (M)	10.4	Market cap. (B)	$0.311
Avg. daily vol. (M)	0.016	Inst. holdings	36%
Tang. Bk. Value/Share	3.88		
Beta	0.36		

Value of $10,000 invested 5 years ago: $ 13,554

Fiscal Year Ending Dec. 31

	1999	1998	1997	1996	1995	1994
Revenues (Million $)						
1Q	104.1	88.41	77.66	167.5	169.9	152.1
2Q	109.4	94.94	86.02	170.5	177.3	161.4
3Q	—	96.52	87.43	173.7	177.6	166.1
4Q	—	101.4	90.62	172.2	174.4	165.5
Yr.	—	381.3	341.7	683.8	699.2	645.0
Earnings Per Share ($)						
1Q	**0.51**	**0.62**	0.74	1.24	0.55	0.33
2Q	**0.49**	**0.55**	0.39	0.58	0.54	0.45
3Q	—	**0.47**	0.21	0.39	0.58	0.33
4Q	—	**0.33**	**0.36**	1.01	0.41	0.37
Yr.	—	**1.97**	**1.71**	3.23	2.07	1.47

Next earnings report expected: mid October

Dividend Data (Dividends have been paid since 1971.)

Amount ($)	Date Decl.	Ex-Div. Date	Stock of Record	Payment Date
0.530	Nov. 05	Nov. 18	Nov. 20	Dec. 10 '98
0.530	Feb. 04	Feb. 17	Feb. 19	Mar. 10 '99
0.530	May. 18	May. 28	Jun. 02	Jun. 16 '99
0.530	Aug. 05	Aug. 18	Aug. 20	Sep. 10 '99

A Division of The McGraw-Hill Companies

Chemed Corporation

Business Summary - 30-SEP-99

Chemed Corp. provides the following services to home owners, families and businesses: plumbing and drain cleaning (Roto-Rooter); home health care (Patient Care); and residential appliance and air-conditioning repair (Service America). It also has an investment portfolio.

Operating profits by business segment in 1998 were derived: Roto-Rooter 69%, Patient Care 18%, and Service America 13%.

The Roto-Rooter segment consists of the combined operations of the Roto-Rooter Group, a group of wholly owned businesses that provide repair and maintenance services to residential and commercial accounts. Services consist primarily of sewer, drain, and pipe cleaning, plumbing and HVAC (heating, ventilating, and air conditioning) services. These services are delivered through company-owned, contractor-operated and franchised locations. Roto-Rooter also manufactures and sells certain products and equipment used to provide such services.

The Patient Care segment consists of the consolidated operations of the wholly owned businesses comprising the company's Patient Care Group. This group offers complete, professional home-healthcare services primarily in the New York-New Jersey-Connecticut area. Services provided to patients at home consist primarily of skilled nursing; home health aid; physical, speech, respiratory, and occupational therapies; medical social work; and nutrition. About 37% of Patient Care's net revenues in 1998 were derived from services provided to patients with coverage under various Medicare and Medicaid programs.

The Service America segment consists of the consolidated operations of the wholly owned businesses comprising the company's Service America Systems Group. This group provides HVAC and appliance repair and maintenance services primarily to residential customers through service contracts and retail sales. In addition, Service America sells air conditioning equipment and duct cleaning services.

The company's earnings during the past several years have been augmented by its portfolio of private and publicly traded investments. Among CHE's more prominent publicly traded holdings are Omnicare Inc. and XL Capital Ltd.

During 1998, the company made 16 acquisitions within the Patient Care, Roto-Rooter and Service America segments for a total cost of $18.6 million in cash and deferred payments. In addition, two pooling-of-interests business combinations were completed within the Roto-Rooter unit. In 1997, CHE made 12 acquisitions for a total cost of $12.7 million in cash.

Per Share Data ($) (Year Ended Dec. 31)	1998	1997	1996	1995	1994	1993	1992	1991	1990	1989
Tangible Bk. Val.	5.23	7.09	1.37	7.21	5.24	2.05	5.65	7.58	11.04	11.77
Cash Flow	3.68	3.22	5.14	3.92	3.08	3.10	2.40	1.90	3.82	4.77
Earnings	1.97	1.71	3.23	2.07	1.47	1.75	1.45	1.10	1.60	2.54
Dividends	2.12	2.09	2.08	2.06	2.04	2.01	2.00	1.97	1.96	1.84
Payout Ratio	108%	122%	64%	100%	139%	115%	138%	179%	123%	72%
Prices - High	42⅜	43½	40⅛	40¼	36⅛	32¾	32⅜	28¼	36¾	38¾
- Low	25⅛	31	34⅝	30⅜	30¼	25½	24¼	17¼	18	32½
P/E Ratio - High	21	25	12	19	25	19	22	26	23	15
- Low	13	18	11	15	21	15	17	16	11	12
Income Statement Analysis (Million $)										
Revs.	381	342	684	699	645	525	401	352	599	592
Oper. Inc.	37.4	34.6	50.2	51.2	44.9	36.3	24.4	17.6	57.7	71.2
Depr.	17.3	15.2	18.8	18.2	15.8	13.1	9.2	8.1	23.1	21.7
Int. Exp.	6.8	10.6	9.0	8.5	8.8	8.9	5.7	5.7	7.6	8.9
Pretax Inc.	32.1	27.9	57.4	41.0	29.8	30.2	23.9	19.2	29.7	44.3
Eff. Tax Rate	38%	39%	38%	38%	37%	31%	27%	28%	35%	34%
Net Inc.	19.9	17.1	31.7	20.4	14.5	17.1	14.3	11.0	16.6	26.2
Balance Sheet & Other Fin. Data (Million $)										
Cash	41.4	71.0	11.9	19.2	24.2	15.8	47.7	83.0	1.4	6.5
Curr. Assets	125	177	192	219	183	145	162	163	144	150
Total Assets	430	449	559	532	505	430	405	364	328	335
Curr. Liab.	91.1	94.4	125	145	143	128	104	84.7	94.0	88.0
LT Debt	80.4	83.7	158	85.4	92.1	98.1	104	77.9	82.1	86.0
Common Eqty.	223	228	218	209	186	137	134	139	113	121
Total Cap.	304	312	394	351	322	267	266	245	227	242
Cap. Exp.	22.0	20.1	19.0	15.4	18.4	13.9	8.2	11.4	13.0	14.1
Cash Flow	37.2	32.2	50.6	38.6	30.3	30.3	23.4	19.1	39.6	47.9
Curr. Ratio	1.4	1.9	1.5	1.5	1.3	1.1	1.6	1.9	1.5	1.7
% LT Debt of Cap.	26.5	26.8	40.1	24.3	28.6	36.7	39.0	31.8	36.2	35.5
% Net Inc.of Revs.	5.2	5.0	4.6	2.9	2.3	3.3	3.6	3.1	2.8	4.4
% Ret. on Assets	4.5	3.4	5.8	3.9	3.1	4.1	3.7	3.5	5.0	7.6
% Ret. on Equity	8.8	7.7	14.9	10.3	9.0	12.6	10.5	9.0	14.2	21.6

Data as orig reptd.; bef. results of disc opers/spec. items. Per share data adj. for stk. divs. Bold denotes diluted EPS (FASB 128)-prior periods restated. E-Estimated. NA-Not Available. NM-Not Meaningful. NR-Not Ranked.

Office—2600 Chemed Center, 255 E. Fifth St, Cincinnati, OH 45202.**Tel**—(513) 762-6900. **Website**—http://www.chemed.com **Chrmn & CEO**—E. L. Hutton. **Pres**—K. J. McNamara. **EVP, Treas & Investor Contact**—Timothy S. O'Toole. **VP & Secy**—N. C. Dallob. **Dirs**—R.L. Arquilla, J. H. Devlin, C. H. Erhart Jr., J. F. Gemunder, P. P. Grace, E. L. Hutton, T. C. Hutton, W. L. Krebs, S. E. Laney, S. S. Lee, K. J. McNamara, J. M. Mount, T. S. O'Toole, D. E. Saunders, P. C. Voet, G. J. Walsh III. **Transfer Agent & Registrar**—Norwest Bank Minnesota N.A., South St. Paul, Minnesota. **Incorporated**—in Delaware in 1970. **Empl**— 7,671. **S&P Analyst:** M.I.

STANDARD &POOR'S
STOCK REPORTS

ChemFirst

NYSE Symbol **CEM**

In S&P SmallCap 600

23-OCT-99 **Industry:** Chemicals

Summary: This company consists of the former industrial specialty chemicals businesses of First Mississippi Corp.

Quantitative Evaluations

Recent Price • 27 | 52 Wk Range • 28-17¾ | Yield • 1.5% | 12-Mo. P/E • 25.0

Outlook (1 Lowest—5 Highest) • 2+

Fair Value • 27⅜

Risk • NA

Earn./Div. Rank • NR

Technical Eval. • NA

Rel. Strength Rank (1 Lowest—99 Highest) • 78

Insider Activity • NA

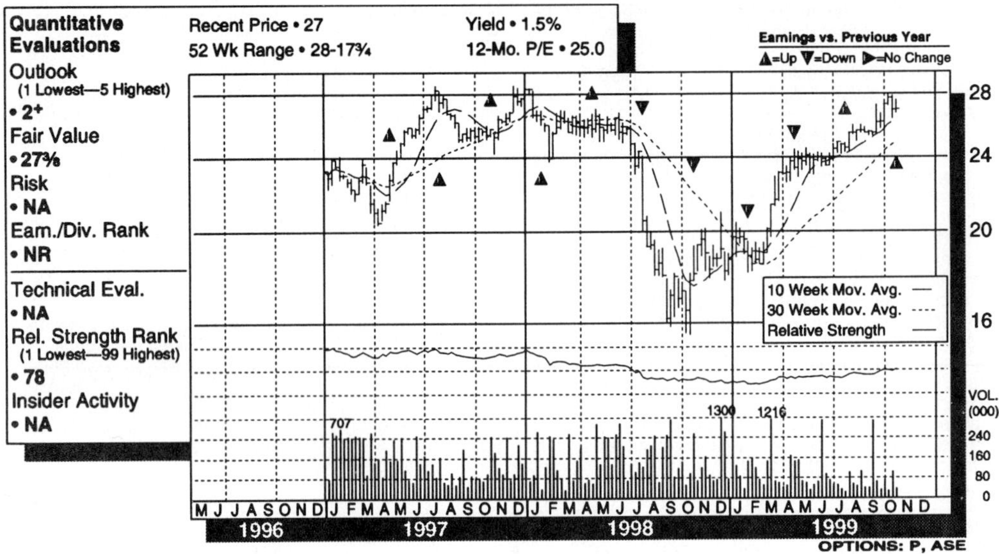

Business Profile - 22-OCT-99

In October 1999, the company reported that third quarter earnings improved on continuing strong aniline demand, and expected further improvement in the fourth quarter aided by better results from electronic chemicals. In the third quarter of 1999, the company discontinued its Steel and Engineered Products and Services operations. As of the end of the third quarter, operations were winding down at FirstMiss Steel, with the focus on liquidation of inventories and collection of receivables. The company was in discussions with buyers interested in Engineered Products and Services.

Operational Review - 22-OCT-99

Net sales in the nine months ended September 30, 1999, advanced 4.1%, year to year, on higher sales of polyurethane chemicals. Margins improved on higher sales from the strong demand for aniline (used to make polyurethane), additional production from the new Baytown, TX aniline facility, and higher production and lower costs at the Pascagoula, MS aniline plant. However, in the absence of $8 million in other income, income from continuing operations declined 12.7%, to $16.1 million ($0.87 per share), from $18.4 million ($0.94). Results for 1998 exclude losses from discontinued operations of $436,000 ($0.02) and disposal of businesses of $12 million ($0.61).

Stock Performance - 22-OCT-99

In the past 30 trading days, CEM's shares have increased 6%, compared to a 4% fall in the S&P 500. Average trading volume for the past five days was 6,120 shares, compared with the 40-day moving average of 38,628 shares.

Key Stock Statistics

Dividend Rate/Share	0.40	Shareholders	4,330
Shs. outstg. (M)	18.1	Market cap. (B)	$0.488
Avg. daily vol. (M)	0.012	Inst. holdings	50%
Tang. Bk. Value/Share	15.67		
Beta	0.94		

Value of $10,000 invested 5 years ago: NA

Fiscal Year Ending Dec. 31

	1999	1998	1997	1996	1995	1994
Revenues (Million $)						
1Q	69.84	74.20	113.1	97.14	—	—
2Q	81.36	78.10	111.2	98.07	—	—
3Q	79.28	74.80	106.1	95.43	—	—
4Q	—	78.08	117.8	93.00	—	—
Yr.	—	305.1	445.8	383.6	353.0	—
Earnings Per Share ($)						
1Q	0.25	0.47	0.39	0.11	—	—
2Q	0.30	0.19	0.38	-0.51	—	—
3Q	0.33	0.27	0.33	0.20	—	—
4Q	—	0.33	0.78	-0.30	—	—
Yr.	—	1.27	1.86	-0.50	0.46	—

Next earnings report expected: late October

Dividend Data (Dividends have been paid since 1997.)

Amount ($)	Date Decl.	Ex-Div. Date	Stock of Record	Payment Date
0.100	Nov. 25	Dec. 08	Dec. 10	Dec. 28 '98
0.100	Feb. 24	Mar. 08	Mar. 10	Mar. 25 '99
0.100	May. 25	Jun. 08	Jun. 10	Jun. 25 '99
0.100	Aug. 24	Sep. 07	Sep. 09	Sep. 24 '99

Business Summary - 22-OCT-99

ChemFirst Inc. was formed in December 1996, through the spinoff of the chemicals and technology businesses of First Mississippi Corp., which than merged its remaining business, fertilizers, with Mississippi Chemical Group. CEM operates in two segments, electronic and other specialty chemicals (59% of 1998 revenues), and polyurethane chemicals (41%). In late 1999, the company reclassified the engineered products and services, and the steel operation, as discontinued operations pending disposition. Generally, CEM's core chemicals are not seasonal and working capital requirements do not vary significantly from period to period.

The electronic and other specialty chemicals segment produces specialty chemicals for use by others in electronic, agricultural, pharmaceutical, polymer and photosensitive applications. These products are sold both on specification and performance and must typically be qualified for use by the customer in addition to meeting certain specifications. CEM is one of the largest producers of post-metal cleaning solutions for semiconductor production. Although there are approximately 12 companies in this market worldwide, only CEM and three others have significant market share for advanced and post-metal cleaning solutions required by the current state-of-the-art semiconductor industry.

The polyurethane chemicals segment produces aniline and nitrobenzene. Aniline is CEM's largest volume product, and the company is one of the five major U.S. producers of aniline, with approximately 25% of domestic capacity and an estimated 7.5% of world capacity. Most of the aniline is used to produce MDI, a primary ingredient in polyurethane foam, widely used in residential and commercial construction. Typically these chemicals are more sensitive to the business cycle and the cost of raw materials than are most electronic and specialty chemicals, although CEM's sales contracts provide protection from fluctuation in raw material price for most of the aniline sold.

The discontinued engineered products and services business consists of Callidus Technologies, which makes industrial burners, flares, and incinerators, and thermal plasma energy systems and equipment. Callidus had 1998 sales of $68 million, and a net loss of $1.7 million. CEM also plans to sell FirstMiss Steel (sales of $55 million; classified as discontinued operations in 1998), which operates a steel melting and casting facility.

During the third quarter of 1999, 38,700 shares of CEM stock were acquired at a cost of $1 million. As of October 1999, CEM had repurchased more than 3.1 million shares, for $71.8 million, since starting a stock buyback program in January 1997, including 1.8 million shares for $42.6 million in 1998. Approximately $38 million remains authorized for repurchase.

Per Share Data ($) (Year Ended Dec. 31)	1998	1997	1996	1995	1994	1993	1992	1991	1990	1989
Tangible Bk. Val.	15.48	15.15	14.42	NA	NA	NA	NA	NA	NA	NA
Cash Flow	2.48	2.85	0.37	NA	NA	NA	NA	NA	NA	NA
Earnings	1.27	1.86	-0.50	NA	NA	NA	NA	NA	NA	NA
Dividends	0.40	0.40	Nil	NA	NA	NA	NA	NA	NA	NA
Payout Ratio	31%	22%	Nil	NA	NA	NA	NA	NA	NA	NA
Prices - High	28⅜	28⅝	23¼	NA	NA	NA	NA	NA	NA	NA
- Low	15½	20⅝	22¼	NA	NA	NA	NA	NA	NA	NA
P/E Ratio - High	22	15	NM	NA	NA	NA	NA	NA	NA	NA
- Low	12	11	NM	NA	NA	NA	NA	NA	NA	NA
Income Statement Analysis (Million $)										
Revs.	305	446	384	353	NA	NA	NA	NA	NA	NA
Oper. Inc.	49.3	59.0	NA	NA	NA	NA	NA	NA	NA	NA
Depr.	23.7	20.6	NA	NA	NA	NA	NA	NA	NA	NA
Int. Exp.	2.0	0.4	NA	NA	NA	NA	NA	NA	NA	NA
Pretax Inc.	40.1	62.7	NA	NA	NA	NA	NA	NA	NA	NA
Eff. Tax Rate	39%	38%	NM	NA	NA	NA	NA	NA	NA	NA
Net Inc.	24.7	38.9	-10.4	9.5	NA	NA	NA	NA	NA	NA
Balance Sheet & Other Fin. Data (Million $)										
Cash	11.2	7.8	NA	NA	NA	NA	NA	NA	NA	NA
Curr. Assets	161	173	NA	NA	NA	NA	NA	NA	NA	NA
Total Assets	443	459	NA	NA	NA	NA	NA	NA	NA	NA
Curr. Liab.	44.0	95.4	NA	NA	NA	NA	NA	NA	NA	NA
LT Debt	65.0	4.9	NA	NA	NA	NA	NA	NA	NA	NA
Common Eqty.	285	322	NA	NA	NA	NA	NA	NA	NA	NA
Total Cap.	365	345	NA	NA	NA	NA	NA	NA	NA	NA
Cap. Exp.	43.8	95.6	NA	NA	NA	NA	NA	NA	NA	NA
Cash Flow	48.3	59.5	NA	NA	NA	NA	NA	NA	NA	NA
Curr. Ratio	3.7	1.8	NA	NA	NA	NA	NA	NA	NA	NA
% LT Debt of Cap.	17.8	1.4	NA	NA	NA	NA	NA	NA	NA	NA
% Net Inc.of Revs.	8.1	8.7	NM	NA	NA	NA	NA	NA	NA	NA
% Ret. on Assets	5.5	8.9	NM	NA	NA	NA	NA	NA	NA	NA
% Ret. on Equity	8.1	14.1	NM	NA	NA	NA	NA	NA	NA	NA

Data as orig. reptd.; pro forma; bef. results of disc. opers. and/or spec. items. Per share data adj. for stk. divs. as of ex-div. date. Prior to 1997, fiscal year ended June 30. E-Estimated. NA-Not Available. NM-Not Meaningful. NR-Not Ranked.

Office—Post Office Box 1249, Jackson, MS 39215-1249. **Registrars**—Bank of New York, NYC; Deposit Guaranty National Bank, Jackson, MS. **Transfer Agents**—Bank of New York, NYC; Co.'s office. **Tel**—(601) 948-7550. **Fax**—(601) 949-0228. **Website**—http://www.chemfirst.com **Chrmn & CEO**—J.K. Williams. **Pres**—R.M. Summerford. **Secy & Investor Contact**—James L. McArthur (601) 949-0285. **Dirs**—R.P. Anderson, P.A. Becker, J.W. Crook, M.J. Ferris, J.E. Fligg, R.P. Guyton, P.W. Murrill, W.A. Percy II, D.F. Smith, L.R. Speed, R.G. Turner, J.K. Williams. **Incorporated**—in Mississippi in 1957. **Empl**— 1,087. **S&P Analyst:** T.J. Vital

STANDARD
&POOR'S
STOCK REPORTS

Chiquita Brands International

NYSE Symbol **CQB**

In S&P SmallCap 600

09-OCT-99

Industry:
Foods

Summary: This company is a leading producer, processor and distributor of fresh fruits and vegetables and prepared food products marketed under the Chiquita and other brand names.

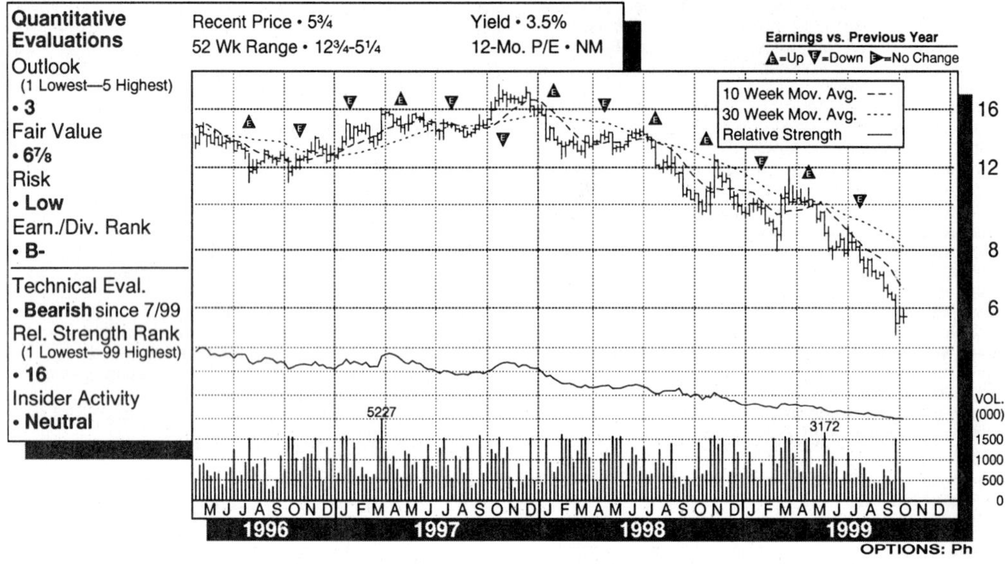

Business Profile - 24-AUG-99

CQB attributes the weak results in recent years to a quota system policy imposed by the European Union (EU) on the Latin American banana industry. A revised EU trading arrangement is currently being ruled on by the World Trade Organization (WTO). Effective March 3, 1999, the U.S. conditionally imposed prohibitive duties on selected EU products, but announced that it would refrain from collecting the higher duties until the WTO has ruled in the arbitration. In June 1999, the company issued $200 million of 10% senior notes; net proceeds of $195 million were used to repay indebtedness. In April 1999, CQB acquired certain canning assets in Oregon for $20 million. During the first half of 1999, CQB spent approximately $40 million to rehabilitate its Honduras operations, after Hurricane Mitch significantly damaged its plantations in October 1998.

Operational Review - 24-AUG-99

Net sales for the six months ended June 30, 1999, declined 6.3%, reflecting a 7.9% drop in fresh produce, primarily due to lower banana pricing. Margins were hurt by reduced earnings in the fresh produce business. Operating income was down 17%. After sharply lower other income, and taxes at 13.2% versus 8.3%, net income fell 40%, to $56.0 million ($0.69 a share), from $93.9 million ($1.17).

Stock Performance - 08-OCT-99

In the past 30 trading days, CQB's shares have declined 19%, compared to a 0.91% fall in the S&P 500. Average trading volume for the past five days was 85,340 shares, compared with the 40-day moving average of 140,062 shares.

Key Stock Statistics

Dividend Rate/Share	0.20	Shareholders	6,500
Shs. outstg. (M)	65.8	Market cap. (B)	$0.378
Avg. daily vol. (M)	0.164	Inst. holdings	64%
Tang. Bk. Value/Share	5.94		
Beta	0.55		

Value of $10,000 invested 5 years ago: $ 5,543

Fiscal Year Ending Dec. 31

	1999	1998	1997	1996	1995	1994
Revenues (Million $)						
1Q	693.0	717.2	631.4	624.8	674.3	1,056
2Q	676.9	744.2	646.2	713.7	727.5	1,007
3Q	—	632.1	556.3	541.6	569.0	900.9
4Q	—	626.8	599.8	555.2	595.2	997.4
Yr.	—	2,720	2,434	2,435	2,566	3,962
Earnings Per Share ($)						
1Q	**0.60**	**0.52**	**0.69**	**0.38**	0.55	0.62
2Q	**0.05**	**0.66**	**0.57**	**0.68**	0.52	0.51
3Q	—	**-0.23**	**-0.57**	**-0.20**	-0.19	-1.59
4Q	—	**-1.62**	**-1.01**	**-1.65**	-0.58	-0.70
Yr.	—	**-0.55**	**-0.29**	**-0.72**	**0.37**	-1.07

Next earnings report expected: mid October

Dividend Data (Dividends have been paid since 1985.)

Amount ($)	Date Decl.	Ex-Div. Date	Stock of Record	Payment Date
0.050	Oct. 21	Nov. 18	Nov. 21	Dec. 07 '98
0.050	Jan. 21	Feb. 17	Feb. 21	Mar. 07 '99
0.050	Apr. 22	May. 19	May. 21	Jun. 07 '99
0.050	Jul. 22	Aug. 18	Aug. 21	Sep. 07 '99

Chiquita Brands International, Inc.

Business Summary - 24-AUG-99

Chiquita Brands International is focusing on building value from its internationally-recognized leading brand name. The company plans to expand the marketing and distribution of its fresh produce and increasing its processed foods.

The fresh foods segment (82% of total net sales in 1998) features a full line of fresh fruits and vegetables sold under the Chiquita and other brand names. In recent years, the company has been focusing on increasing the product base with additional fresh fruits and vegetables. The core of the the fresh food segment is the marketing, distribution and sourcing of bananas, which accounted for approximately 70% of segment sales over the past three years. Bananas are grown by subsidiaries or purchased from suppliers in areas that include Costa Rica, Colombia, Panama, Ecuador, Guatemala, and Honduras.

The processed foods segment (18%) include private-label and branded canned vegetables, fruit and vegetable juices and processed bananas sold under the Chiquita brand. In early 1998, CQB expanded the capacity, product lines and geographic coverage of its vegetable canning operations by acquiring Stokely USA, Inc., a vegetable canning company with annual net sales of $150 million. Sales of canned vegetables accounted for 81% of processed food sales in 1998.

Principal production and processing operations are conducted in the U.S. and Central and South America. In 1998, approximately half of fresh produce sales were in North America with the remainder in Europe and other international markets.

In February 1996, Ecuador, the world's largest exporter of bananas, joined the U.S. and several Latin American governments in an international trade challenge against the European Union (EU) quota policy, using procedures of the World Trade Organization (WTO). The WTO ruled that the banana import policy violated world trade rules, and the EU adopted a revised trade policy that was implemented in January 1999. However, the opposing governments disapproved of the revised EU trading policy, and the WTO arbitration panel announced that it will rule on the acceptability of the revised policy. Effective March 3, 1999, the U.S. conditionally imposed prohibitive duties on selected EU products, but announced that it would refrain from collecting the higher duties until the WTO has ruled in the arbitration.

In September 1998, the Enquirer, a 500,000-circulation paper owned by Gannet Co. Inc., agreed to pay Chiquita more than $10 million in damages, following the guilty plea of a former Enquirer reporter to illegally tapping into CQB's voice mail system.

In June 1998, CQB acquired Campbell Mushroom Pty Limited, which had annual sales of $30 million, for $12 million in common stock and $5 million in cash. In December 1998, CQB sold its Central American plastic products operation for $18 million.

Per Share Data ($)										
(Year Ended Dec. 31)	**1998**	**1997**	**1996**	**1995**	**1994**	**1993**	**1992**	**1991**	**1990**	**1989**
Tangible Bk. Val.	5.21	5.75	5.25	6.38	5.63	7.77	9.01	15.38	11.53	8.84
Cash Flow	0.98	1.31	1.03	2.33	1.07	0.92	-2.73	3.87	3.43	2.81
Earnings	-0.55	-0.29	-0.72	0.37	-1.07	-0.99	-4.28	2.55	2.23	1.70
Dividends	0.20	0.20	0.20	0.20	0.20	0.44	0.66	0.55	0.35	0.20
Payout Ratio	NM	NM	NM	54%	NM	NM	NM	21%	17%	11%
Prices - High	16¼	18⅛	16½	18⅛	19⅜	17¾	40⅛	50¾	32⅛	17⅝
- Low	9¼	12⅝	11⅛	12⅛	11¼	10	15¼	29⅜	16	12⅞
P/E Ratio - High	NM	NM	NM	49	NM	NM	NM	20	14	10
- Low	NM	NM	NM	33	NM	NM	NM	12	7	8
Income Statement Analysis (Million $)										
Revs.	2,720	2,434	2,435	2,566	3,962	2,533	2,723	4,627	4,273	3,823
Oper. Inc.	178	192	181	280	283	206	45.1	293	224	190
Depr.	99	91.6	96.5	105	116	103	80.4	66.7	50.4	44.0
Int. Exp.	109	109	130	164	174	178	176	117	71.0	62.0
Pretax Inc.	-9.9	8.5	-16.7	41.9	-35.0	-39.0	-216	183	152	111
Eff. Tax Rate	NM	96%	NM	33%	NM	NM	NM	30%	38%	39%
Net Inc.	-18.4	0.3	-27.7	28.0	-49.0	-51.0	-221	128	94.0	68.0
Balance Sheet & Other Fin. Data (Million $)										
Cash	88.9	126	286	271	179	151	413	830	349	289
Curr. Assets	840	783	844	877	918	770	1,071	1,682	1,136	918
Total Assets	2,509	2,402	2,467	2,624	2,902	2,741	2,881	3,143	2,174	1,613
Curr. Liab.	531	483	464	510	651	504	588	698	698	499
LT Debt	1,003	962	1,079	1,242	1,365	1,438	1,411	1,227	522	417
Common Eqty.	541	527	460	528	443	544	617	968	688	464
Total Cap.	1,797	1,742	1,804	1,914	2,010	2,040	2,086	2,195	1,210	881
Cap. Exp.	118	76.2	74.6	64.6	149	197	410	411	323	131
Cash Flow	63.6	75.0	56.8	124	56.0	47.0	-140	195	144	112
Curr. Ratio	1.6	1.6	1.8	1.7	1.4	1.5	1.8	2.4	1.6	1.8
% LT Debt of Cap.	55.8	55.2	59.8	64.9	67.9	70.5	67.7	55.9	43.1	47.3
% Net Inc.of Revs.	NM	0.0	NM	1.1	NM	NM	NM	2.8	2.2	1.8
% Ret. on Assets	NM	0.0	NM	0.6	NM	NM	NM	4.6	4.6	4.4
% Ret. on Equity	NM	NM	NM	4.0	NM	NM	NM	14.9	15.3	15.6

Data as orig reptd.; bef. results of disc opers/spec. items. Per share data adj. for stk. divs. Bold denotes diluted EPS (FASB 128)-prior periods restated. E-Estimated. NA-Not Available. NM-Not Meaningful. NR-Not Ranked.

Office—250 East Fifth St., Cincinnati, OH 45202. **Tel**—(513) 784-8000. **Website**—http://www.chiquita.com **Chrmn & CEO**—C. H. Lindner. **Vice Chrmn**—K. E. Lindner. **Pres & COO**—S. G. Warshaw. **SVP & CFO**—W. J. Ligan. **VP & Secy**—R. W. Olson. **Investor Contact**—Joseph W. Hagin. **Dirs**—C. H. Lindner, K. E. Lindner, F. J. Runk, J. H. Sisco, W. W. Verity, O. W. Waddell, S. G. Warshaw. **Transfer Agent & Registrar**—Securities Transfer Co., Cincinnati, OH**Incorporated**—in New Jersey in 1899 as United Fruit Co. **Empl**— 37,000. **S&P Analyst:** A. Bensinger

STANDARD
&POOR'S
STOCK REPORTS

Chittenden Corp.

NYSE Symbol **CHZ**

In S&P SmallCap 600

09-OCT-99

Industry:
Banks (Regional)

Summary: This Vermont-based bank holding company, with assets of $4.1 billion, acquired Vermont Financial Services for $387 million in stock in May 1999.

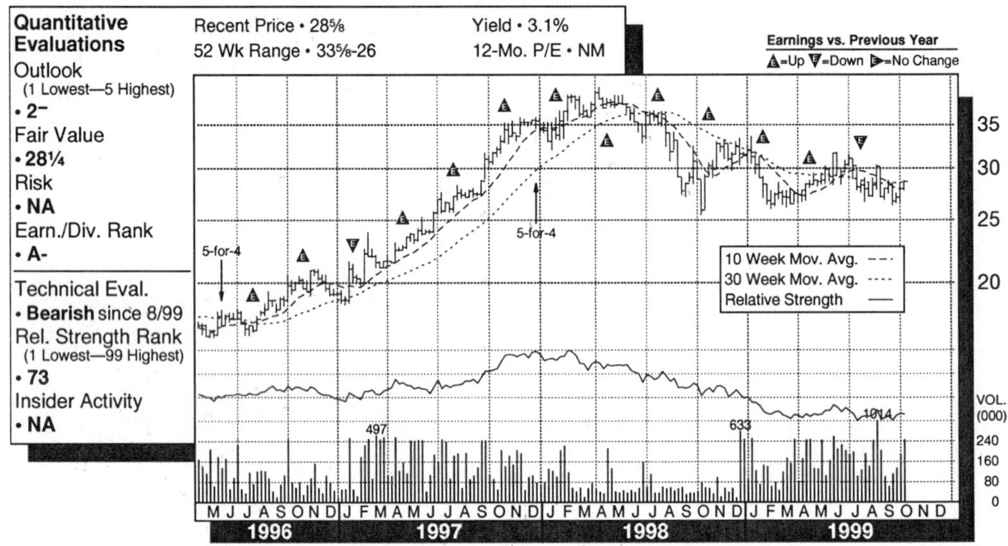

Business Profile - 26-AUG-99

In late May 1999, the company acquired Vermont Financial Services Corp., a bank holding company with assets of $2.1 billion, in a stock-for-stock merger valued at some $387 million. CHZ issued about 14 million common shares in the transaction. Management believes the acquisition will provide an entry into the southern New Hampshire market while offering additional opportunities in its existing Vermont and Massachusetts markets.

Operational Review - 26-AUG-99

Net interest income for the six months ended June 30, 1999, rose 0.9%, year to year, as restated, reflecting a higher level of average interest-earning assets. The yield on earning assets was 4.61%, down from 4.76%, with the decline attributed to increased liquidity in CHZ's mix of investments and loans caused by deposit growth outpacing loan growth. The provision for loan losses was down 7.6%, to $4.4 million. Noninterest income decreased 1.2%, and noninterest expense advanced 96% on $71 million of special charges; a pretax loss contrasted with pretax income. After an income tax benefit, versus taxes at 37.8%, the net loss was $32,484,000 ($1.16 a share), against net income of $24,255,000 ($0.83).

Stock Performance - 08-OCT-99

In the past 30 trading days, CHZ's shares have increased 6%, compared to a 0.91% fall in the S&P 500. Average trading volume for the past five days was 57,880 shares, compared with the 40-day moving average of 53,751 shares.

Key Stock Statistics

Dividend Rate/Share	0.88	Shareholders	2,877
Shs. outstg. (M)	28.2	Market cap. (B)	$0.807
Avg. daily vol. (M)	0.036	Inst. holdings	38%
Tang. Bk. Value/Share	10.54		
Beta	0.79		

Value of $10,000 invested 5 years ago: $ 35,130

Fiscal Year Ending Dec. 31

	1999	1998	1997	1996	1995	1994
Revenues (Million $)						
1Q	44.64	45.42	42.59	43.48	31.73	24.90
2Q	88.28	46.37	44.72	44.98	36.79	26.45
3Q	—	46.45	45.33	—	38.10	27.49
4Q	—	46.06	45.77	—	38.61	29.62
Yr.	—	176.8	178.4	167.5	145.2	108.5
Earnings Per Share ($)						
1Q	**0.52**	**0.50**	**0.44**	**0.39**	0.38	—
2Q	**-1.58**	**0.53**	**0.49**	**0.43**	0.38	—
3Q	—	**0.53**	**0.50**	**0.44**	0.44	—
4Q	—	**0.54**	**0.50**	**0.40**	0.41	—
Yr.	—	**2.09**	**1.94**	**1.75**	**1.47**	1.26

Next earnings report expected: late October

Dividend Data (Dividends have been paid since 1992.)

Amount ($)	Date Decl.	Ex-Div. Date	Stock of Record	Payment Date
0.200	Oct. 21	Oct. 28	Oct. 30	Nov. 13 '98
0.200	Jan. 21	Feb. 03	Feb. 05	Feb. 19 '99
0.220	Apr. 21	May. 05	May. 07	May. 21 '99
0.220	Jul. 22	Aug. 04	Aug. 06	Aug. 20 '99

A Division of The McGraw-Hill Companies

Chittenden Corporation

Business Summary - 26-AUG-99

Headquartered in Burlington, VT, Chittenden Corp. (CHZ) is the holding company for Chittenden Trust Co., Flagship Bank and Trust Co., The Bank of Western Massachusetts, and Chittenden Connecticut Corp., a non-bank mortgage company.

On May 28, 1999, the company completed the acquisition of Vermont Financial Services Corp. in a stock-for-stock merger. Vermont Financial was the parent company of Vermont National Bank, headquartered in Brattleboro, VT, and United Bank, headquartered in Greenfield, MA. Approximately 14 million shares of the company's common stock were issued in the transaction, which brought the total number of Chittenden shares outstanding to 28 million.

Through its subsidiaries, the company offers a variety of lending services, with loans totaling $2.9 billion at June 30, 1999. As of year-end 1998, the largest loan category was commercial loans, including those secured by commercial real estate, and others made to a variety of businesses, including retail concerns, small manufacturing businesses, larger corporations, other commercial banks, and to political subdivisions in the U.S. Commercial loans amounted to 50% of the total loans outstanding at December 31, 1998.

Through its subsidiaries, CHZ offers various lending services. The largest loan category is commercial loans (comprising 40% of total loans outstanding as of June 30, 1999). Commercial loans include those secured by commercial real estate, and others made to various businesses, including retail concerns, small manufacturing businesses, larger corporations, other commercial banks, and to political subdivisions in the U.S.

Loans secured by residential properties, including closed-ended home equity loans, accounted for 38% of loans outstanding as of June 30, 1999. The company underwrites substantially all of its residential mortgages based on secondary market standards and sells substantially all of its fixed-rate residential mortgage loans on a servicing-retained basis. Variable or adjusted rate mortgage loans are typically held in the portfolio.

Consumer loans (17%) include direct and indirect installment loans, auto leases, and revolving credit.

As of year-end 1998, the company's lending activities were conducted primarily in Vermont and Massachusetts, with additional activity related to nearby market areas in Quebec, New York, New Hampshire, Maine and Connecticut.

Per Share Data ($) (Year Ended Dec. 31)	1998	1997	1996	1995	1994	1993	1992	1991	1990	1989
Tangible Bk. Val.	11.47	11.25	10.69	9.68	8.51	8.05	7.27	6.57	5.83	NA
Earnings	2.09	1.94	1.75	1.47	1.26	0.91	NA	NA	NA	NA
Dividends	0.78	1.29	0.57	0.32	0.22	0.10	0.07	Nil	0.21	0.25
Payout Ratio	37%	66%	33%	20%	17%	11%	NA	NA	NA	NA
Prices - High	40	36	21	20½	11¼	9¾	6¾	5½	4⅞	7⅝
- Low	25⅜	18½	15⅜	10½	9	6	3⅜	1½	1 13/16	4⅜
P/E Ratio - High	19	19	12	14	8	10	10	12	NM	20
- Low	12	10	9	7	7	6	5	3	NM	11
Income Statement Analysis (Million $)										
Net Int. Inc.	91.0	90.6	84.0	65.4	53.9	50.2	41.2	38.5	39.3	42.8
Tax Equiv. Adj.	2.2	7.5	7.6	NA	NA	NA	NA	NA	NA	NA
Non Int. Inc.	32.4	28.2	25.0	29.8	24.0	24.2	19.7	17.7	15.5	16.6
Loan Loss Prov.	5.1	4.0	4.2	4.0	4.3	6.6	7.1	8.2	11.9	10.7
Exp./Op. Revs.	57%	59%	59%	64%	64%	69%	73%	74%	85%	73%
Pretax Inc.	46.5	44.7	40.2	30.6	23.3	16.8	9.6	6.3	-3.9	5.1
Eff. Tax Rate	34%	34%	33%	32%	33%	31%	25%	22%	NA	14%
Net Inc.	30.7	29.4	26.7	20.9	15.5	11.6	7.1	4.9	-1.5	4.3
% Net Int. Marg.	4.94	5.11	4.99	NA	NA	NA	NA	NA	NA	NA
Balance Sheet & Other Fin. Data (Million $)										
Money Mkt. Assets	NA	5.6	5.6	NA	NA	NA	NA	NA	NA	NA
Inv. Securities	509	363	305	NA	NA	NA	NA	NA	NA	NA
Com'l Loans	481	774	692	NA	NA	NA	NA	NA	NA	NA
Other Loans	919	625	653	653	NA	NA	NA	NA	NA	NA
Total Assets	2,122	1,977	1,989	1,521	1,214	1,231	1,121	1,130	1,066	1,027
Demand Deposits	321	303	286	NA	NA	NA	NA	NA	NA	NA
Time Deposits	1,570	1,455	1,476	NA	NA	NA	NA	NA	NA	NA
LT Debt	0.3	2.2	2.5	2.5	1.5	4.4	NA	NA	NA	NA
Common Eqty.	175	162	174	137	98.3	97.7	82.1	74.6	67.0	71.8
% Ret. on Assets	1.5	1.5	1.5	1.5	1.3	1.0	0.6	0.4	NA	0.4
% Ret. on Equity	18.2	17.5	17.2	17.8	15.9	12.9	9.1	6.9	NA	6.0
% Loan Loss Resv.	1.8	1.9	2.2	2.4	2.2	2.2	1.9	1.7	1.6	1.6
% Loans/Deposits	74.0	79.6	73.6	77.8	81.6	82.2	84.2	81.5	84.1	87.8
% Equity to Assets	8.2	8.5	8.9	8.6	8.0	7.6	7.0	6.4	6.6	7.0

Data as orig reptd.; bef. results of disc opers/spec. items. Per share data adj. for stk. divs. Bold denotes diluted EPS (FASB 128)-prior periods restated. E-Estimated. NA-Not Available. NM-Not Meaningful. NR-Not Ranked.

Office—Two Burlington Square, Burlington, VT 05401. **Tel**—(802) 658-4000. **Website**—http://www.chittenden.com **Email**—info@chittenden.com **Chrmn, Pres & CEO**—P. A. Perrault. **EVP-CFO, Treas & Investor Contact**—Kurk W. Walters (802 660-1561). **Dirs**—F. H. Bertrand, D. M. Boardman, P. J. Carrara, W. P. Cody, S. W. Crawford, R. D. Driscoll, P. M. Drumheller, J. K. Dwight, L. Hutton, P. A. Kolvoord, S. A. Morse, J. C. Pizzagalli, E. A. Pomerleau, M. W. Richards, P. D. Spera, M. D. Wilson Jr. **Transfer Agent & Registrar**—Boston EquiServe, L.P. **Incorporated**—in Vermont in 1971. **Empl**— 1,046. **S&P Analyst:** C.C.P.

STANDARD
&POOR'S
STOCK REPORTS

ChoicePoint Inc.

NYSE Symbol **CPS**

In S&P SmallCap 600

09-OCT-99

Industry:
Services (Commercial & Consumer)

Summary: CPS is a leading provider of risk management and fraud prevention information and related technology solutions to the insurance industry.

Quantitative Evaluations

Outlook
(1 Lowest—5 Highest)
• **NA**

Fair Value
• **NA**

Risk
• **Low**

Earn./Div. Rank
• **NR**

Technical Eval.
• **Neutral** since 9/99

Rel. Strength Rank
(1 Lowest—99 Highest)
• **70**

Insider Activity
• **Neutral**

Recent Price • 65⅝
52 Wk Range • 71¼-41⅞
Yield • Nil
12-Mo. P/E • 26.0

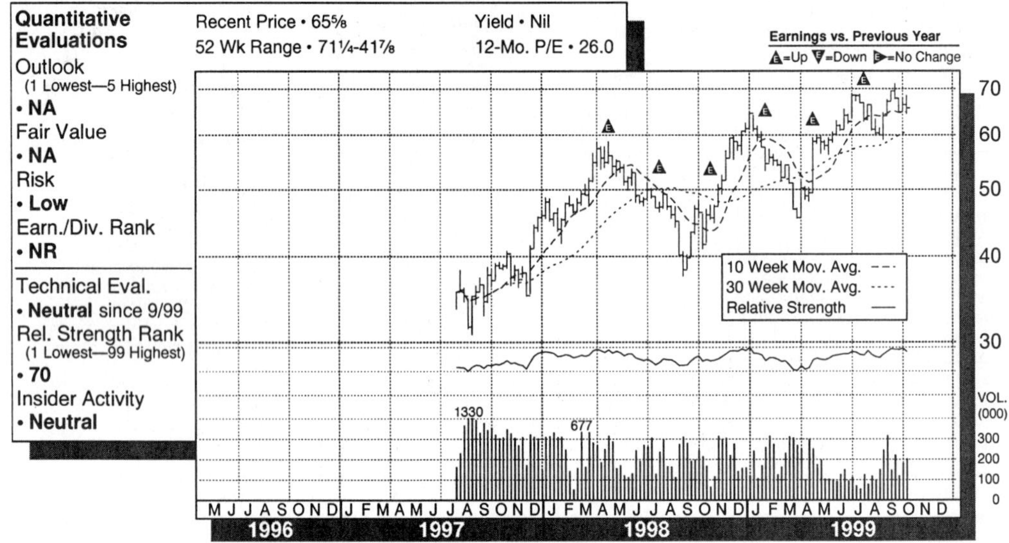

Business Profile - 30-AUG-99

During 1998, CPS acquired six companies, established several strategic alliances, and completed a major divestiture. In 1999, the company planned to shift its focus primarily to integration and value creation from these transactions. In December 1998, CPS sold its life and health insurance field underwriting services and insurance claim investigation services. This transaction, together with the December 1997 divestiture of the paramedical services group, completed the company's exit from the field-based life and health insurance information services business. A reduction of labor-intensive offerings, while enhancing data and technology capabilities, is consistent with CPS's ongoing business strategy.

Operational Review - 30-AUG-99

Operating revenue in the six months ended June 30, 1999, rose 3.2%, year to year, as strong revenue performance in automated products and acquisitions outweighed the absence of revenue from certain field businesses sold in December 1998. A 1.5% decline in the cost of services outweighed 9.1% higher SG&A expenses and $1.6 million of unusual charges; operating income gained 11%. A $2.5 million gain on business sales in the current period outweighed higher interest expense; after taxes at 43.3% in each period, net income advanced 14%, to $18,159,000 ($1.21 a share), from $15,890,000 ($1.05).

Stock Performance - 08-OCT-99

In the past 30 trading days, CPS's shares have increased 3%, compared to a 0.91% fall in the S&P 500. Average trading volume for the past five days was 40,180 shares, compared with the 40-day moving average of 44,613 shares.

Key Stock Statistics

Dividend Rate/Share	Nil	Shareholders	5,486
Shs. outstg. (M)	14.7	Market cap. (B)	$0.967
Avg. daily vol. (M)	0.036	Inst. holdings	67%
Tang. Bk. Value/Share	NM		
Beta	NA		

Value of $10,000 invested 5 years ago: NA

Fiscal Year Ending Dec. 31

	1999	1998	1997	1996	1995	1994
Revenues (Million $)						
1Q	99.7	94.55	102.9	—	—	—
2Q	108.0	106.7	108.6	—	—	—
3Q	—	101.9	106.5	—	—	—
4Q	—	103.3	99.4	—	—	—
Yr.	—	406.5	417.3	389.3	—	—
Earnings Per Share ($)						
1Q	**0.60**	**0.50**	0.36	—	—	—
2Q	**0.61**	**0.55**	0.48	—	—	—
3Q	—	**0.55**	0.52	—	—	—
4Q	—	**0.76**	**0.56**	—	—	—
Yr.	—	**2.36**	**1.92**	1.41	—	—

Next earnings report expected: late October

Dividend Data

No cash dividends have been paid, and the company does not anticipate paying any cash dividends in the foreseeable future. The company currently intends to retain future earnings to finance operations and the expansion of its business.

A Division of The McGraw-Hill Companies

ChoicePoint Incorporated

Business Summary - 30-AUG-99

ChoicePoint (CPS) began operations as the Insurance Services Group of Equifax Inc. The two companies came to a parting of the ways when Equifax spun off CPS to its shareholders in August 1997. The company is now a leading provider of risk management and fraud prevention information and related technology solutions to the insurance industry, and also offers risk management and fraud prevention solutions to organizations in other industries.

Since January 1, 1999, the company has operated through two primary service groups: Insurance Services, and Business & Government Services.

CPS provides underwriting information to property and casualty insurance companies in the U. S. and the U. K. Personal lines property and casualty insurance services include automated direct marketing, underwriting and claims information, such as motor vehicle reports, the company's Comprehensive Loss Underwriting Exchange database services, vehicle registration services, credit reports, modeling services, and driver's license information. CPS also provides laboratory information services and related technology offerings to major U.S. life and health insurance companies.

In addition to personal lines underwriting information, the company provides services to the commercial property and casualty insurance market, including commercial inspections for underwriting purposes, workers compensation audits of commercial properties, and development of high-end customized application rating and issuance software for commercial customers.

Through its Business & Government Services group, CPS provides risk management and fraud prevention services and related technology solutions, asset recovery services and database marketing services to Fortune 1000 corporations, asset-based lenders, legal and professional service providers, health care service providers, and local, state and federal government agencies, as well as to the insurance markets.

The company also provides enhanced information services to government agencies, such as uncovering ownership of hidden assets; locating individuals and providing leads for criminal and civil investigations; providing parent locator services, which locate for the public sector individuals who are in violation of court mandates; and screening of certain Medicare and Medicaid providers and provider applicants to assist in identifying and reducing health care fraud. In connection with its business and government services, CPS provides automated and in-demand searches and filings of public business records, including Uniform Commercial Code searches and filings, bankruptcy, lien and judgment searches, searches of partnership and corporation filing records, and criminal record searches to assist organizations and lending institutions in managing potential risk exposure.

Per Share Data ($) (Year Ended Dec. 31)	1998	1997	1996	1995	1994	1993	1992	1991	1990	1989
Tangible Bk. Val.	NM	NM	NM	NA	NA	NA	NA	NA	NA	NA
Cash Flow	4.43	3.86	NA	NA	NA	NA	NA	NA	NA	NA
Earnings	2.36	1.92	1.41	NA	NA	NA	NA	NA	NA	NA
Dividends	Nil	Nil	NA	NA	NA	NA	NA	NA	NA	NA
Payout Ratio	Nil	Nil	NA	NA	NA	NA	NA	NA	NA	NA
Prices - High	64½	33	NA	NA	NA	NA	NA	NA	NA	NA
- Low	37⅜	30¾	NA	NA	NA	NA	NA	NA	NA	NA
P/E Ratio - High	27	25	NA	NA	NA	NA	NA	NA	NA	NA
- Low	16	16	NA	NA	NA	NA	NA	NA	NA	NA
Income Statement Analysis (Million $)										
Revs.	406	417	389	NA	NA	NA	NA	NA	NA	NA
Oper. Inc.	96.2	79.9	50.0	NA	NA	NA	NA	NA	NA	NA
Depr.	31.0	27.6	NA	NA	NA	NA	NA	NA	NA	NA
Int. Exp.	7.7	6.6	7.4	NA	NA	NA	NA	NA	NA	NA
Pretax Inc.	62.5	53.5	37.2	NA	NA	NA	NA	NA	NA	NA
Eff. Tax Rate	43%	46%	44%	NA	NA	NA	NA	NA	NA	NA
Net Inc.	35.4	28.9	21.0	NA	NA	NA	NA	NA	NA	NA
Balance Sheet & Other Fin. Data (Million $)										
Cash	18.9	26.9	4.5	NA	NA	NA	NA	NA	NA	NA
Curr. Assets	144	146	109	NA	NA	NA	NA	NA	NA	NA
Total Assets	534	360	319	NA	NA	NA	NA	NA	NA	NA
Curr. Liab.	125	77.2	48.3	NA	NA	NA	NA	NA	NA	NA
LT Debt	192	95.5	116	NA	NA	NA	NA	NA	NA	NA
Common Eqty.	160	128	95.4	NA	NA	NA	NA	NA	NA	NA
Total Cap.	351	223	211	NA	NA	NA	NA	NA	NA	NA
Cap. Exp.	13.6	20.0	NA	NA	NA	NA	NA	NA	NA	NA
Cash Flow	66.5	56.6	NA	NA	NA	NA	NA	NA	NA	NA
Curr. Ratio	1.1	1.9	2.3	NA	NA	NA	NA	NA	NA	NA
% LT Debt of Cap.	54.6	42.8	55.0	NA	NA	NA	NA	NA	NA	NA
% Net Inc.of Revs.	8.7	6.9	5.4	NA	NA	NA	NA	NA	NA	NA
% Ret. on Assets	7.9	8.7	NA	NA	NA	NA	NA	NA	NA	NA
% Ret. on Equity	24.7	45.3	NA	NA	NA	NA	NA	NA	NA	NA

Data as orig reptd.; bef. results of disc opers/spec. items. Per share data adj. for stk. divs. Bold denotes diluted EPS (FASB 128)-prior periods restated. E-Estimated. NA-Not Available. NM-Not Meaningful. NR-Not Ranked.

Office—1000 Alderman Dr., Alpharetta, GA 30005. **Tel**—(770) 752-6000. **Website**—http://www.choicepointinc.com **Chrmn**—C. B. Rogers Jr. **Pres & CEO**—D. V. Smith. **EVP, CFO & Treas**—D. C. Curling. **Dirs**—R. V. Barbaro, J. M. Denny, T. H. Irvin, N. C. Lautenbach, J. B. North, C. B. Rogers Jr., D. V. Smith, C. I. Story. **Transfer Agent & Registrar**—SunTrust Bank, Atlanta, GA. **Incorporated**—in Georgia in 1997. **Empl**— 3,500. **S&P Analyst:** C.C.P.

STANDARD &POOR'S
STOCK REPORTS

CIBER, Inc.

NYSE Symbol **CBR**
In S&P SmallCap 600

09-OCT-99 **Industry:** Services (Computer Systems) **Summary:** CBR provides information technology consulting services.

S&P Opinion: Accumulate (★★★★) Recent Price • 14⅞ 52 Wk Range • 29½-13¾ Yield • Nil 12-Mo. P/E • 15.7

Quantitative Evaluations
Outlook
(1 Lowest—5 Highest)
• **5**
Fair Value
• **27¼**
Risk
• **High**
Earn./Div. Rank
• **B+**

Technical Eval.
• **Bearish** since 9/99
Rel. Strength Rank
(1 Lowest—99 Highest)
• **17**
Insider Activity
• **Neutral**

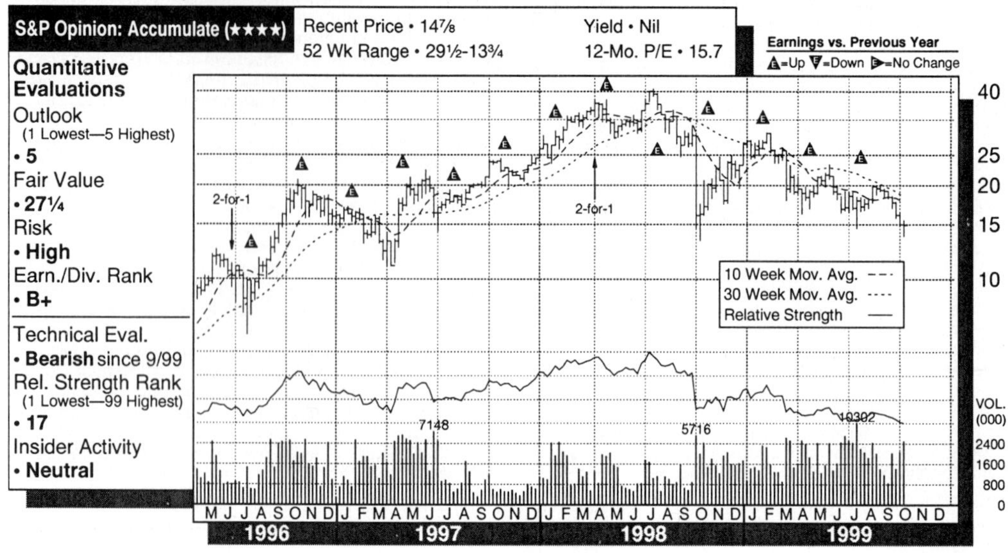

Overview - 24-AUG-99

We expect revenues to increase at a 25%-30% rate through FY 00 (Jun.), driven by both internal growth and acquisitions. Organic growth should be fueled by demand for integration services related to enterprise resource planning (ERP) software, particularly in the areas of sales force automation and supply chain management applications. In addition, Ciber is well positioned to benefit from the recent surge in the market for Web-enabled and "e-commerce" solutions. We expect CBR to continue its acquisition strategy, with the company focusing on its most promising service markets and international expansion opportunities. We see margins narrowing a bit in the foreseeable future, reflecting near-term investments designed to position CBR for long-term growth. Following an increase in shares outstanding, reflecting recent acquisitions, we expect FY 00 operating EPS to grow 14%, to $1.12.

Valuation - 24-AUG-99

Shares of CBR have fallen thus far in 1999, due to challenges facing the information technology services industry. As a result, the stock is currently trading at 19 times our calendar 1999 EPS estimate of $1.03 (15X our calendar 2000 estimate of $1.25), which represents a substantial discount to Ciber's long-term growth rate and the P/E multiple of the broader markets. Consequently, we have reiterated our accumulate recommendation on the stock. The technology services sector has been hurt by a deceleration of client spending in 1999, as a result of budgetary resources being dedicated to Year 2000 issues. However, we expect this market to improve in the first half of calendar 2000, as customers resume their robust spending on information technology. An area of particular strength should be Internet-related solutions, reflecting the emergence of the Web as a primary vehicle of business communications.

Key Stock Statistics

S&P EPS Est. 2000	1.12	Tang. Bk. Value/Share	2.54
P/E on S&P Est. 2000	13.3	Beta	1.36
Dividend Rate/Share	Nil	Shareholders	15,000
Shs. outstg. (M)	58.4	Market cap. (B)	$0.873
Avg. daily vol. (M)	0.441	Inst. holdings	42%

Value of $10,000 invested 5 years ago: NA

Fiscal Year Ending Jun. 30

	1999	1998	1997	1996	1995	1994
Revenues (Million $)						
1Q	165.7	123.2	54.03	31.55	26.66	—
2Q	174.1	135.3	59.72	32.40	27.91	—
3Q	190.0	141.6	69.65	36.70	31.82	—
4Q	195.1	150.2	78.87	45.26	33.76	—
Yr.	719.7	550.4	262.3	156.9	120.2	79.80
Earnings Per Share ($)						
1Q	**0.20**	**0.12**	0.07	0.06	0.04	—
2Q	**0.26**	**0.13**	0.07	0.05	0.03	—
3Q	**0.24**	**0.20**	0.12	0.07	0.05	—
4Q	**0.24**	**0.20**	0.14	0.07	0.03	—
Yr.	**0.95**	**0.65**	**0.40**	0.24	0.14	0.09

Next earnings report expected: mid October

Dividend Data

No cash dividends have been paid.

CIBER, Inc.

Business Summary - 24-AUG-99

CIBER, Inc., founded in 1974 and public since 1994, provides system integration consulting services. The company offers services in four principal areas: management consulting of business/IT solutions, Enterprise Resource Planning (ERP) implementation services, information technology consulting services, and network technology design/integration consulting.

Revenues are generated from two areas: the CIBER Information Services (CIS) division; and CIBER Solutions. The CIS division provides application software development and maintenance services and, through its CIBR2000 division, millennium date change solutions. CIBER Solutions consists of the following wholly owned subsidiaries: Spectrum Technology Group (Spectrum), Business Information Technology (BIT), The Summit Group (acquired in 1998), and CIBER Network Services (CNSI).

Spectrum provides information technology consulting solutions to business problems, specifically in the areas of data warehousing, data modeling and enterprise architecture, as well as project management and systems integration services. BIT specializes in the implementation and integration of human resource and financial software application products, plus workflow automation and manufacturing/distribution software systems, primarily for client/server networks. A substantial portion of BIT's revenues is derived from assisting clients implementing PeopleSoft, Inc. software. Summit is a leading provider of enterprise resource solutions (ERS). CNSI provides a wide range of local-area and wide-area network solutions, from design and procurement to installation and maintenance with services including Internet and intranet connectivity.

With a network of about 80 offices in more than 20 states and Canada, CBR has many long-term clients, including American Express, AT&T, Fidelity Investments, Ford Motor, GTE, IBM, MCI Telecommunications, Monsanto, U S West Communications, and Xerox.

The company has expanded its geographic breadth, diversified its technical expertise, expanded its client base, and believes it has achieved other competitive advantages through ongoing business combinations. In 1998, CBR acquired six different organizations, for a total of approximately $224 million.

Per Share Data ($) (Year Ended Jun. 30)	1999	1998	1997	1996	1995	1994	1993	1992	1991	1990
Tangible Bk. Val.	NA	2.54	1.72	1.25	0.40	0.30	0.62	NA	NA	NA
Cash Flow	NA	0.90	0.47	0.32	0.19	NA	NA	NA	NA	NA
Earnings	0.95	0.65	0.39	0.24	0.14	0.09	0.06	0.04	NA	NA
Dividends	Nil	Nil	Nil	Nil	Nil	Nil	NA	NA	NA	NA
Payout Ratio	Nil	Nil	Nil	Nil	Nil	Nil	NA	NA	NA	NA
Prices - High	$29\frac{1}{2}$	$40\frac{7}{8}$	29	$20\frac{7}{8}$	$8\frac{1}{2}$	$2\frac{3}{4}$	NA	NA	NA	NA
- Low	$13\frac{3}{4}$	$13\frac{1}{4}$	11	$4\frac{3}{4}$	$2\frac{1}{4}$	$1\frac{15}{16}$	NA	NA	NA	NA
P/E Ratio - High	31	63	74	85	63	33	NA	NA	NA	NA
- Low	14	20	28	20	17	23	NA	NA	NA	NA
Income Statement Analysis (Million $)										
Revs.	NA	550	262	157	120	79.8	63.1	51.3	NA	NA
Oper. Inc.	NA	71.7	31.5	16.8	10.3	NA	NA	NA	NA	NA
Depr.	NA	9.4	4.5	2.5	1.9	NA	NA	NA	NA	NA
Int. Exp.	NA	0.2	Nil	0.2	0.3	NA	NA	NA	NA	NA
Pretax Inc.	NA	59.3	26.7	13.8	7.2	NA	NA	NA	NA	NA
Eff. Tax Rate	NA	38%	45%	44%	44%	36%	NA	NA	NA	NA
Net Inc.	NA	36.5	14.6	8.5	4.3	2.3	1.4	1.0	NA	NA
Balance Sheet & Other Fin. Data (Million $)										
Cash	NA	37.4	23.0	16.6	2.1	NA	NA	NA	NA	NA
Curr. Assets	NA	161	80.8	48.4	26.1	NA	NA	NA	NA	NA
Total Assets	NA	216	123	64.6	40.8	30.8	15.7	12.7	NA	NA
Curr. Liab.	NA	53.1	20.1	9.2	16.4	NA	NA	NA	NA	NA
LT Debt	NA	Nil	Nil	0.2	0.3	NA	NA	NA	NA	NA
Common Eqty.	NA	163	103	55.2	24.0	19.1	5.4	3.9	NA	NA
Total Cap.	NA	163	103	55.4	24.3	NA	NA	NA	NA	NA
Cap. Exp.	NA	11.6	3.1	1.5	0.8	NA	NA	NA	NA	NA
Cash Flow	NA	46.0	19.2	11.0	6.1	NA	NA	NA	NA	NA
Curr. Ratio	NA	3.0	4.0	5.3	1.6	NA	NA	NA	NA	NA
% LT Debt of Cap.	NA	Nil	Nil	0.1	0.1	NA	NA	NA	NA	NA
% Net Inc.of Revs.	NA	6.6	5.6	5.4	3.6	NA	NA	NA	NA	NA
% Ret. on Assets	NA	21.5	15.0	16.2	11.9	9.6	9.6	NA	NA	NA
% Ret. on Equity	NA	27.4	18.1	21.5	20.0	18.8	30.9	NA	NA	NA

Data as orig reptd.; bef. results of disc opers/spec. items. Per share data adj. for stk. divs. Bold denotes diluted EPS (FASB 128)-prior periods restated. E-Estimated. NA-Not Available. NM-Not Meaningful. NR-Not Ranked.

Office—5251 DTC Parkway, Suite 1400, Englewood, CO 80111. **Tel**—(303) 220-0100. **Website**—http://www.ciber.com **Chrmn**—B. G. Stevenson. **Pres, CEO & Secy**—M. J. Slingerlend. **VP, CFO & Treas**—M. J. Slingerlend. **Dirs**—R. L. Burger, J. G. Brocksmith, A. McGill, R. A. Montoni, J. A. Rutherford, M. J. Slingerlend, J. C. Spira, B. G. Stevenson. **Transfer Agent & Registrar**—American Securities Transfer, Inc., Denver. **Incorporated**—in Delaware in 1994. **Empl**— 5,700. **S&P Analyst:** Stephen J. Tekirian

STANDARD
&POOR'S
STOCK REPORTS

CILCORP Inc.

NYSE Symbol **CER**

In S&P SmallCap 600

09-OCT-99 **Industry:** Electric Companies

Summary: CILCORP, which supplies electricity and gas to central and east central Illinois, agreed in November 1998 to be acquired by The AES Corp.

Quantitative Evaluations

Outlook (1 Lowest—5 Highest) • **2**

Fair Value • **65¼**

Risk • **Low**

Earn./Div. Rank • **B**

Technical Eval. • **Bullish** since 2/99

Rel. Strength Rank (1 Lowest—99 Highest) • **70**

Insider Activity • **NA**

Recent Price • 64¾ · 52 Wk Range • 65-50⅝ · Yield • 3.8% · 12-Mo. P/E • 39.5

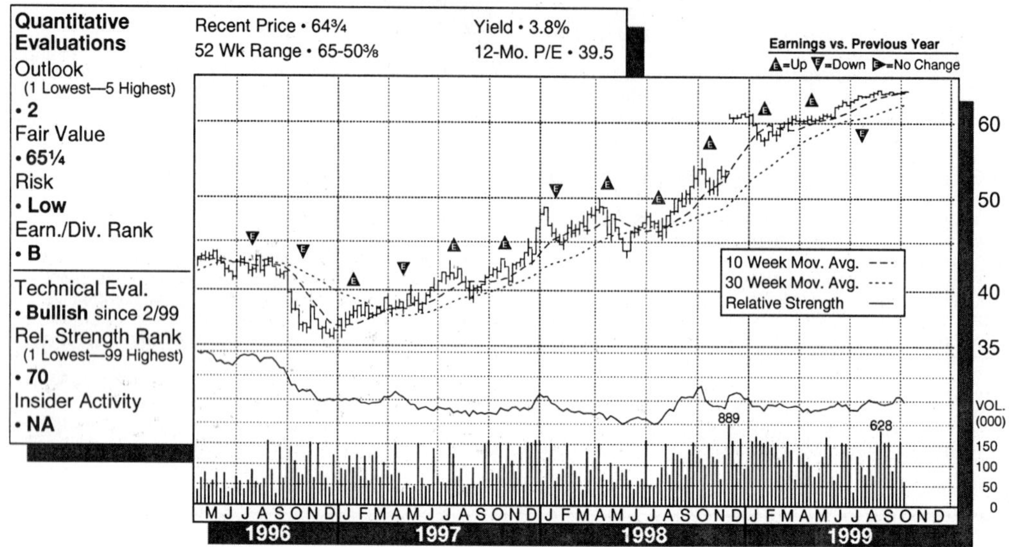

Business Profile - 06-JUL-99

In November 1998, The AES Corp. (AES) and CILCORP signed an agreement under which AES would acquire CER for $65 a share in cash, or about $885 million. The transaction has been approved by U.S. Federal Energy Regulatory Commission, the Federal Trade Commission, the Illinois Commerce Commission, and CER shareholders. Still pending, as of late June 1999, was an AES request before the Securities and Exchange Commission for an exemption under the Public Utility Holding Company Act of 1935. CER expected a decision on the exemption in time to allow for a third quarter 1999 closing. AES, based in Arlington, Virginia, is a global power company that owns or has an interest in more than 90 power facilities, totaling over 27,000 MW. In 1998, AES recorded net income of $311 million on revenues of $2.4 billion.

Operational Review - 06-JUL-99

Revenues for the first quarter of 1999 advanced 9.0%, year to year. Income from continuing operations was up 11%, to $12.6 million ($0.92 a share) from $11.3 million ($0.83, before $0.27 loss from discontinued operations). Results benefited from the fourth quarter 1998 discontinuation of the QST Enterprises subsidiary, higher earnings at CER's ongoing non-utility subsidiaries, and a slight improvement in profits from Central Illinois Light Co. due to higher natural gas margins.

Stock Performance - 08-OCT-99

In the past 30 trading days, CER's shares have increased 0.68%, compared to a 0.91% fall in the S&P 500. Average trading volume for the past five days was 11,860 shares, compared with the 40-day moving average of 44,128 shares.

Key Stock Statistics

Dividend Rate/Share	2.46	Shareholders	12,873
Shs. outstg. (M)	13.6	Market cap. (B)	$0.882
Avg. daily vol. (M)	0.025	Inst. holdings	28%
Tang. Bk. Value/Share	24.60		
Beta	0.19		

Value of $10,000 invested 5 years ago: $ 23,607

Fiscal Year Ending Dec. 31

	1999	1998	1997	1996	1995	1994
Revenues (Million $)						
1Q	168.2	154.3	192.2	178.0	170.6	177.0
2Q	120.3	121.4	173.1	129.7	132.5	137.0
3Q	—	141.1	228.5	138.6	157.6	146.0
4Q	—	142.2	382.7	182.1	154.1	144.7
Yr.	—	559.0	976.5	628.4	614.7	605.1
Earnings Per Share ($)						
1Q	**0.92**	**0.83**	**0.72**	**0.79**	0.88	0.75
2Q	**0.05**	**0.56**	**0.41**	**0.20**	0.43	0.53
3Q	—	**1.32**	**0.95**	**0.93**	1.47	0.73
4Q	—	**0.08**	**-1.37**	**0.19**	0.15	0.49
Yr.	—	**2.79**	**0.71**	**2.07**	**2.93**	**2.50**

Next earnings report expected: late October

Dividend Data (Dividends have been paid since 1921.)

Amount ($)	Date Decl.	Ex-Div. Date	Stock of Record	Payment Date
0.615	Oct. 27	Nov. 18	Nov. 20	Dec. 18 '98
0.615	Jan. 26	Feb. 17	Feb. 19	Mar. 19 '99
0.615	Apr. 27	May. 19	May. 21	Jun. 18 '99
0.615	Jun. 24	Aug. 25	Aug. 27	Sep. 20 '99

CILCORP Inc.

Business Summary - 06-JUL-99

CILCORP is a holding company whose operations primarily reflect the operations of Central Illinois Light Co. (CILCO). The company also has two first-tier subsidiaries, CILCORP InvestmentManagement Inc. (CIM) and CILCORP Ventures Inc. (CVI). QSTEnterprises Inc. (QST) was classified as a discontinued operation for accounting purposes in early 1999.

CILCO is primarily engaged in the generation, transmission, distribution and sale of electric energy in an area of approximately 3,700 square miles in central and east-central Illinois; and thepurchase, distribution, transportation and sale of natural gas inan area of approximately 4,500 square miles in central and east-central Illinois.

CILCO has two wholly-owned subsidiaries, CILCO Exploration andDevelopment Co. (CEDCO) and CILCO Energy Corp. (CECO). CEDCO was formed to engage in the exploration and development ofgas, oil, coal and other mineral resources. CECO was formed toresearch and develop new sources of energy, including theconversion of coal and other minerals into gas. The operationsof these subsidiaries were not significant as of year-end 1998.

CIM, which manages the company's investment portfolio, holds eight leveraged lease investments through three wholly-ownedsubsidiaries: CILCORP Lease Management Inc., formed in1985; and CIM Leasing Inc. and CIM Air Leasing Inc., both formed in 1993. CIM's other wholly-owned subsidiary is CIM Energy Investments Inc., formed in 1989 to invest in non-regulated, independent power production facilities. CIM also directly owns limited partnershipinterests in affordable housing portfolios.

CVI, which primarily invests in ventures in energy-related products and services, has an 80% interest in the Agricultural Researchand Development Corp. and has one wholly-owned subsidiary,CILCORP Energy Services Inc. (CESI). CESI was formed to pursue energy-related opportunities in the non-regulated market. Its primary business is the sale of gas management services (including commodity purchasing). During the three years through 1998, CESI provided certain energy-related services to Caterpillar Inc.

Discontinued QST operations provided energy and energy-related services through its QST Energy subsidiary. QST Energy's QST Energy Trading subsidiary purchased and sold energy in the wholesale market. In August 1998, QST sold QST Communications, which provided fiber optic telecommunications services. In the fourth quarter of 1998, QST decided to discontinue its energy business and report those results as discontinued operations. In late June 1999, CER sold its environmental and engineering services subsidiary, QST Environmental, for $18 million.

Per Share Data ($) (Year Ended Dec. 31)	1998	1997	1996	1995	1994	1993	1992	1991	1990	1989
Tangible Bk. Val.	24.60	25.85	25.30	25.30	24.50	24.41	24.22	24.19	23.23	25.77
Earnings	2.79	0.90	2.07	2.93	2.50	2.60	2.48	3.14	2.69	3.58
Dividends	2.46	2.46	2.46	2.46	2.46	2.46	2.46	2.46	2.46	2.46
Payout Ratio	346%	346%	119%	84%	98%	95%	99%	80%	90%	69%
Prices - High	61½	49	45⅛	44¾	37½	43¾	40⅝	38¼	38⅝	39¼
- Low	43¼	35⅝	35½	31⅞	28¾	35¾	33⅝	31	29¾	31⅝
P/E Ratio - High	22	69	22	15	15	17	16	12	14	11
- Low	16	50	17	11	12	14	14	10	11	9
Income Statement Analysis (Million $)										
Revs.	559	976	628	615	605	585	581	590	537	459
Depr.	66.2	66.7	65.7	63.3	61.1	60.0	57.7	55.4	52.9	48.3
Maint.	NA	NA	NA	NA	NA	25.6	24.3	25.3	23.8	22.2
Fxd. Chgs. Cov.	2.8	2.8	2.6	3.2	2.8	2.5	2.6	2.6	2.7	2.8
Constr. Credits	0.0	0.1	0.1	-0.5	1.0	0.2	0.3	0.5	0.3	0.2
Eff. Tax Rate	34%	61%	34%	38%	36%	35%	39%	42%	40%	36%
Net Inc.	38.2	9.6	27.9	38.6	32.6	37.6	36.5	44.9	40.8	52.8
Balance Sheet & Other Fin. Data (Million $)										
Gross Prop.	1,686	1,659	1,579	1,523	1,448	1,417	1,370	1,329	1,287	1,250
Cap. Exp.	67.1	61.2	46.7	74.0	95.8	78.3	69.1	63.7	84.7	52.0
Net Prop.	873	889	855	840	794	798	778	770	764	750
Capitalization:										
LT Debt	352	299	321	344	327	326	308	325	298	301
% LT Debt	51	42	43	45	44	44	43	44	44	42
Pfd.	Nil	66.1	66.1	66.1	66.1	66.1	64.6	64.6	64.6	64.6
% Pfd.	Nil	9.20	8.70	8.60	9.00	9.00	9.10	9.00	9.50	9.10
Common	336	353	368	362	345	342	339	341	320	348
% Common	49	49	49	47	47	47	48	47	47	49
Total Cap.	946	979	1,013	1,038	1,010	991	1,034	1,053	1,043	1,037
% Oper. Ratio	87.1	93.4	88.0	84.5	86.8	88.9	88.6	89.4	87.1	83.6
% Earn. on Net Prop.	10.4	6.4	8.9	19.6	7.7	7.6	7.5	7.9	8.0	8.1
% Return On Revs.	6.8	1.0	4.4	6.3	5.4	6.4	6.3	7.6	7.6	11.5
% Return On Invest. Capital	11.1	1.2	7.3	9.2	6.1	8.1	8.0	9.6	9.4	10.4
% Return On Com. Equity	11.1	2.7	7.7	10.9	9.5	10.0	9.5	11.8	10.7	14.2

Data as orig reptd.; bef. results of disc opers/spec. items. Per share data adj. for stk. divs. Bold denotes diluted EPS (FASB 128)-prior periods restated. E-Estimated. NA-Not Available. NM-Not Meaningful. NR-Not Ranked.

Office—300 Hamilton Blvd., Suite 300, Peoria, IL 61602. **Registrars**—First of America Trust Co., Peoria; Continental Stock Transfer & Trust Co., NYC. **Tel**—(309) 675-8810. **Fax**—(309) 675-8800. **Website**—http://www.cilco.com **Pres & CEO**—R. O. Viets. **EVP**—W. M. Shay. **VP, Secy & Treas**—J. G. Sahn. **Treas**—M. P. Austin. **Dirs**—M. Alexis, J. R. Brazil, W. Bunn III, J. D. Caulder, H. J. Holland, K. E. Smith, R. O. Viets, M. M. Yeomans. **Transfer Agents**—Continental Stock Transfer & Trust Co., NYC; Co.'s office. **Incorporated**—in Illinois in 1913. **Empl**— 1,274. **S&P Analyst:** N.J.D.

STANDARD
&POOR'S
STOCK REPORTS

CKE Restaurants

NYSE Symbol **CKR**
In S&P SmallCap 600

09-OCT-99

Industry:
Restaurants

Summary: This restaurant company owns, franchises, and licenses nearly 3,800 restaurants under the brand names Hardee's, Carl's Jr. and Taco Bueno.

Quantitative Evaluations

Outlook
(1 Lowest—5 Highest)
• **NA**
Fair Value
• **NA**
Risk
• **High**
Earn./Div. Rank
• **B**

Technical Eval.
• **Bearish** since 7/99
Rel. Strength Rank
(1 Lowest—99 Highest)
• **4**
Insider Activity
• **Unfavorable**

Recent Price • 6⅞
52 Wk Range • 30¼-6⅜
Yield • 1.2%
12-Mo. P/E • 6.3

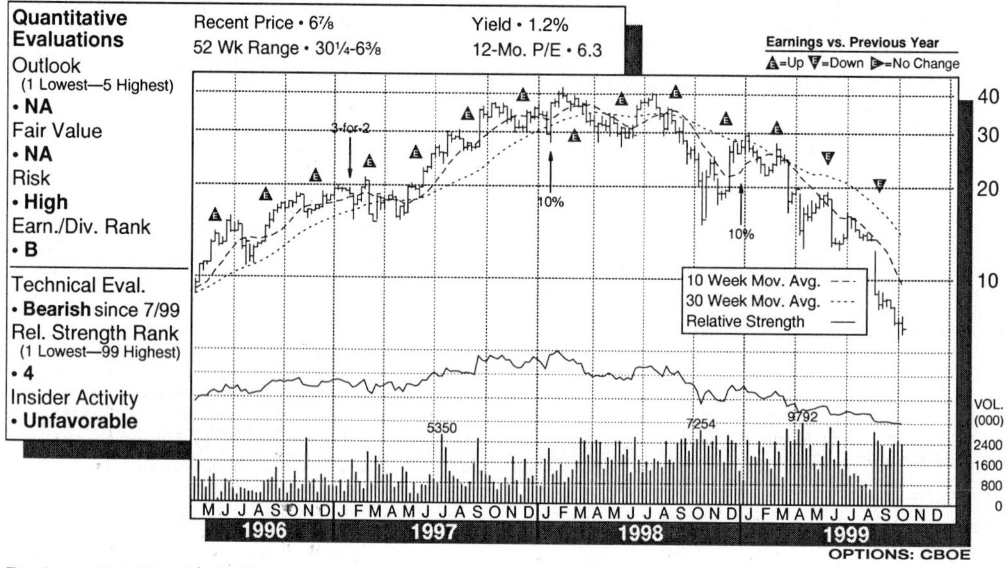

Business Profile - 03-AUG-99

To improve the Hardee's menu and reach a broader target market, CKE is repositioning and remodeling the entire Hardee's system to "Star Hardee's". The Star Hardee's brand combines aspects of the Carl's Jr. restaurant concept with the traditional Hardee's concept. As of the first quarter of FY 00 (Jan.), the company and its franchisors have remodeled approximately 325 Hardee's restaurant units into the new concept, with plans to remodel 400 to 600 restaurants in FY 00. CKE also plans on an aggressive expansion strategy for its Taco Bueno and Carl's Jr. restaurants. To finance its expansion plans, in March 1999, CKE issued $200 million of senior subordinated notes, with proceeds used to repay a portion of its senior credit facility.

Operational Review - 03-AUG-99

Total revenues for the sixteen weeks ended May 17, 1998, rose 13%, reflecting revenues from additional Hardee's restaurants acquired early in 1998, Hardee's-to-Carl's Jr. conversions and strong results at the Taco Bueno restaurants. However, profitability was hurt by higher occupancy and advertising expenses, a substantial rise in depreciation and amortization, and a 70% jump in interest expense on increased borrowing levels. Net income declined 16%, to $19.1 million ($0.36 a share), from $22.7 million ($0.43). Results in FY 00 exclude a $0.3 million ($0.01) extraordinary gain from the early retirement of debt.

Stock Performance - 08-OCT-99

In the past 30 trading days, CKR's shares have declined 17%, compared to a 0.91% fall in the S&P 500. Average trading volume for the past five days was 499,260 shares, compared with the 40-day moving average of 658,944 shares.

Key Stock Statistics

Dividend Rate/Share	0.08	Shareholders	1,800
Shs. outstg. (M)	52.1	Market cap. (B)	$0.361
Avg. daily vol. (M)	0.542	Inst. holdings	69%
Tang. Bk. Value/Share	7.00		
Beta	0.68		

Value of $10,000 invested 5 years ago: $ 12,302

Fiscal Year Ending Jan. 31

	2000	1999	1998	1997	1996	1995
Revenues (Million $)						
1Q	595.7	528.2	235.4	152.9	137.6	135.0
2Q	465.3	474.8	242.1	128.1	108.0	105.3
3Q	—	457.6	347.5	162.3	113.1	103.8
4Q	—	431.4	324.8	170.7	106.7	99.6
Yr.	—	1,892	1,150	614.1	465.4	443.8
Earnings Per Share ($)						
1Q	**0.36**	**0.43**	**0.25**	**0.15**	0.06	0.02
2Q	**0.20**	**0.42**	**0.23**	**0.15**	0.08	0.03
3Q	—	**0.31**	**0.25**	**0.15**	0.09	0.01
4Q	—	**0.25**	**0.24**	**0.15**	0.09	-0.02
Yr.	—	**1.39**	**0.97**	**0.61**	0.32	0.04

Next earnings report expected: early December

Dividend Data (Dividends have been paid since 1988.)

Amount ($)	Date Decl.	Ex-Div. Date	Stock of Record	Payment Date
0.040	Sep. 23	Oct. 02	Oct. 06	Oct. 30 '98
10%	Dec. 17	Dec. 23	Dec. 28	Jan. 11 '99
0.040	Mar. 17	Apr. 07	Apr. 09	Apr. 30 '99
0.040	Sep. 29	Sep. 30	Oct. 04	Oct. 28 '99

A Division of The McGraw-Hill Companies

CKE Restaurants, Inc.

Business Summary - 03-AUG-99

CKE Restaurants, a leading owner, operator and franchisor of nearly 3,800 quick-service restaurants, continues to focus on improving the operations of underperforming restaurant assets. The company's strategy includes revitalizing its Hardee's brand, expanding its Carl's Jr. and Taco Bueno chains, and pursuing strategic joint venture agreements.

At May 1999, the company operated 2,784 Hardee's restaurants in 34 states and 10 foreign countries, 878 Carl's Jr. restaurants, and 112 Taco Bueno restaurants in Texas and Oklahoma.

In an effort to revitalize same store sales of its Hardee's brand, CKE is repositioning and remodeling the entire Hardee's system to "Star Hardee's". The Star Hardee's brand will combine the Hardee's name and Carl's Jr.'s star on the signs and packaging. It will also incorporate the Carl Jr.'s charbroiling cooking process of burgers and chicken sandwiches alongside favorites from the Hardee's menu. As of May 1999, the company and its franchisors have remodeled approximately 325 Hardee's restaurant units into the new concept, with plans to remodel an additional 400 to 600 restaurants during FY 00 (Jan.).

Hardee's, founded in 1961, was acquired by the company in July 1997; based on domestic system-wide sales, it is the fourth largest U.S. quick-service hamburger chain. The restaurants have a leading market presence in the Southeast and Midwest. Generating 30% of overall sales, the chain's strength is its breakfast menu. On April 1, 1998, CKE acquired Flagstar Enterprises, Inc. for $380 million and the assumption of $45.6 million in capital lease obligations. Flagstar was the largest franchisee in the Hardee's system, operating 557 Hardee's restaurants.

Based on domestic system-wide sales, Carl's Jr. is the seventh largest U.S. quick-service hamburger restaurant chain. Restaurants are mainly located on the West Coast, with a leading market presence in California. In FY 00, CKE plans to open 75-100 new Carl's Jr. units.

In May 1995, CKE entered into an agreement with Santa Barbara Restaurant Group (SRBG) to offer the Green Burrito menu at selected Carl's Jr. locations. Under the agreement, the company must provide a total of 192 dual-brand Carl's Jr./Green Burrito restaurants by 2002. In September 1998, CKE sold its JB's restaurants and Galaxy Diner concepts to SRBG. CKE owns about 11% of SRBG.

The Taco Bueno concept is a quick-service chain of Mexican restaurants located in Texas and Oklahoma. CKE plans to aggressively expand the Taco Bueno brand, with plans to open 15 new units in FY 00.

As of May 1999, CKE had repurchased $38 million of its convertible subordinated notes, out of a $50 million buyback program.

Per Share Data ($) (Year Ended Jan. 31)	1999	1998	1997	1996	1995	1994	1993	1992	1991	1990
Tangible Bk. Val.	6.45	7.87	5.35	3.01	2.67	2.72	2.58	2.75	2.41	2.05
Cash Flow	2.67	1.94	1.34	0.95	0.71	0.82	0.68	1.20	1.16	0.82
Earnings	1.39	0.97	0.60	0.33	0.04	0.13	-0.09	0.40	0.40	0.17
Dividends	0.07	0.06	0.04	0.04	0.04	0.04	0.04	0.04	0.04	0.04
Payout Ratio	5%	7%	7%	14%	114%	33%	NM	11%	11%	26%
Cal. Yrs.	1998	1997	1996	1995	1994	1993	1992	1991	1990	1989
Prices - High	42	37½	20	9⅞	7⅞	5⅞	6⅛	5½	7	9¾
- Low	15	15⅛	8	3½	3⅝	3¾	3¾	3⅛	3	6¼
P/E Ratio - High	30	39	33	31	NM	44	NM	14	18	59
- Low	11	16	13	11	NM	28	NM	8	8	37
Income Statement Analysis (Million $)										
Revs.	1,892	1,150	614	465	444	460	503	532	520	510
Oper. Inc.	245	133	69.1	47.1	31.4	38.0	29.0	44.5	55.8	53.3
Depr.	77.1	46.4	73.6	21.4	22.8	22.8	25.2	26.6	25.3	22.3
Int. Exp.	43.5	16.9	9.9	10.0	9.2	10.4	13.7	16.9	18.7	19.3
Pretax Inc.	124	76.6	36.7	18.0	2.4	6.3	-7.3	18.9	18.8	7.5
Eff. Tax Rate	40%	39%	39%	39%	47%	29%	NM	31%	31%	26%
Net Inc.	74.5	46.8	22.3	11.0	1.3	4.4	-3.1	13.0	13.0	5.6
Balance Sheet & Other Fin. Data (Million $)										
Cash	40.3	30.4	39.8	25.9	18.2	32.9	44.4	36.7	31.6	34.6
Curr. Assets	134	92.2	72.9	57.0	57.0	69.0	91.0	84.0	81.0	82.0
Total Assets	1,497	957	401	247	244	242	269	293	305	307
Curr. Liab.	202	176	83.9	61.0	72.0	67.0	91.0	92.0	105	110
LT Debt	613	196	81.9	71.0	70.0	63.0	80.0	102	117	125
Common Eqty.	587	499	215	101	88.0	92.0	85.0	90.0	79.0	67.0
Total Cap.	1,215	695	297	172	158	155	165	192	196	192
Cap. Exp.	10.7	89.2	47.9	27.0	40.0	22.0	12.9	31.6	34.1	45.4
Cash Flow	152	93.2	49.4	32.0	24.0	27.3	22.1	39.6	38.3	27.8
Curr. Ratio	0.7	0.5	0.9	0.9	0.8	1.0	1.0	0.9	0.8	0.7
% LT Debt of Cap.	50.5	28.2	27.6	41.3	44.1	40.7	48.6	53.2	59.8	65.3
% Net Inc.of Revs.	3.9	4.1	3.7	2.4	0.3	1.0	NM	2.5	2.5	1.1
% Ret. on Assets	6.1	6.9	6.9	4.5	0.5	1.7	NM	4.4	4.2	1.9
% Ret. on Equity	13.7	13.1	14.2	11.6	1.4	4.9	NM	15.5	17.9	8.6

Data as orig reptd.; bef. results of disc opers/spec. items. Per share data adj. for stk. divs. Bold denotes diluted EPS (FASB 128)-prior periods restated. E-Estimated. NA-Not Available. NM-Not Meaningful. NR-Not Ranked.

Office—1200 North Harbor Blvd., Anaheim, CA 92801. **Organized**—in California in 1966. **Tel**—(714) 774-5796. **Website**—http://www.ckr.com **Chrmn & CEO**—W. P. Foley II. **Pres & COO**—C. T. Thompson. **EVP & CFO**—C. A. Strunk. **SVP & Investor Contact**—Loren C. Pannier. **EVP & Secy**—A. F. Puzder. **Dirs**—B. Allumbaugh, P. Churm, W. P. Foley II, C. L. Karcher, C. N. Karcher, D. D. Lane, W. H. Lester, F. P. Willey. **Transfer Agent & Registrar**—ChaseMellon Shareholder Services, Los Angeles. **Incorporated**—Delaware; organized in California in 1966. **Empl**— 67,000. **S&P Analyst:** A. Bensinger

STANDARD &POOR'S
STOCK REPORTS

CLARCOR Inc.

NYSE Symbol **CLC**
In S&P SmallCap 600

09-OCT-99

Industry: Manufacturing (Diversified)

Summary: CLC is a diversified marketer and manufacturer of mobile and environmental filtration products and consumer and industrial packaging products.

Quantitative Evaluations

Outlook (1 Lowest—5 Highest)
• **3+**
Fair Value
• **21⅝**
Risk
• **Low**
Earn./Div. Rank
• **A-**

Technical Eval.
• **Bearish** since 8/99
Rel. Strength Rank (1 Lowest—99 Highest)
• **35**
Insider Activity
• **NA**

Recent Price • 16¾
52 Wk Range • 21⅜-14¼
Yield • 2.7%
12-Mo. P/E • 11.8

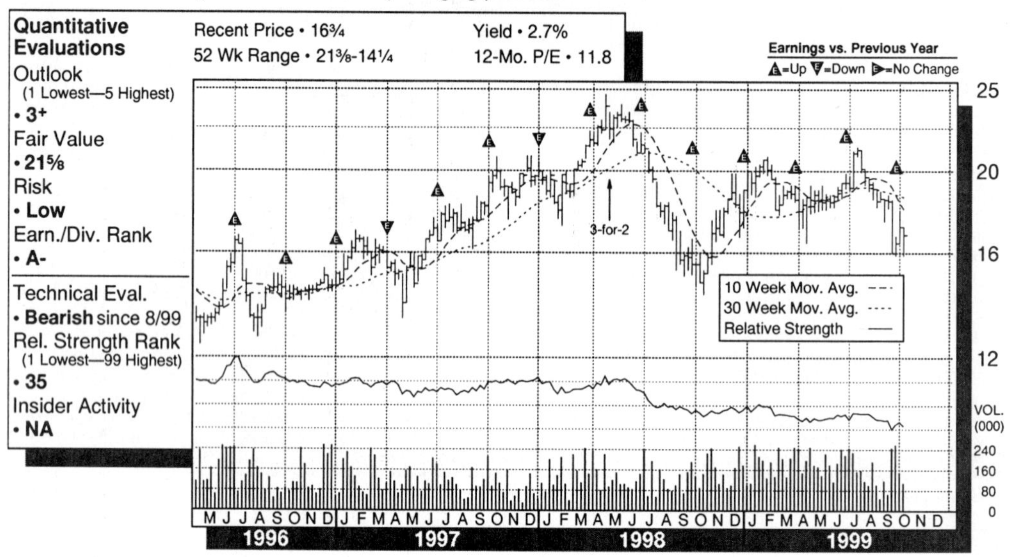

Business Profile - 07-JUL-99

CLARCOR's share earnings have increased for six consecutive years through FY 98 (Nov.). CLC seeks growth through acquisitions and internal expansion, with emphasis on entry into new markets and product development. In June 1999, the company said it expected sales to grow faster as FY 99 progresses, leading to another record year in sales and profits. Aided by continued reduced discretionary spending, CLC anticipated that engine/mobile filtration margins would be maintained and that industrial/environmental filtration margins would improve. Better results were anticipated at United Air Specialists, reflecting several management and administrative changes. The J.L. Clark packaging unit was expected to benefit from a new strategic focus as FY 99 progresses.

Operational Review - 07-JUL-99

Net sales for the first half of FY 99 (Nov.) rose 2.2%, year to year, reflecting sales gains of 5.0% for engine/mobile filtration and 4.2% for industrial/environmental filtration, which outweighed an 11% drop for packaging. Profits were up 15% for engine/mobile filtration; and down 7.0% for industrial/environmental filtration and 33% for packaging. Overall operating profit increased 7.1%. After a 54% drop in total other expenses (net), and taxes at 36.6% versus 37.3%, net income moved ahead 11%, to $14.9 million ($0.61 a share, on 1.3% fewer shares), from $13.4 million ($0.54).

Stock Performance - 08-OCT-99

In the past 30 trading days, CLC's shares have declined 9%, compared to a 0.91% fall in the S&P 500. Average trading volume for the past five days was 21,480 shares, compared with the 40-day moving average of 33,274 shares.

Key Stock Statistics

Dividend Rate/Share	0.46	Shareholders	6,000
Shs. outstg. (M)	24.0	Market cap. (B)	$0.403
Avg. daily vol. (M)	0.049	Inst. holdings	57%
Tang. Bk. Value/Share	7.27		
Beta	0.84		

Value of $10,000 invested 5 years ago: $ 13,985

Fiscal Year Ending Nov. 30

	1999	1998	1997	1996	1995	1994
Revenues (Million $)						
1Q	99.2	97.79	86.96	72.08	62.14	55.89
2Q	110.5	107.3	96.68	81.57	70.48	65.13
3Q	112.1	110.1	104.6	88.93	71.83	67.72
4Q	—	111.7	106.0	90.81	85.75	81.38
Yr.	—	426.8	394.3	333.4	290.2	270.1
Earnings Per Share ($)						
1Q	**0.25**	**0.21**	0.13	0.18	0.18	0.15
2Q	**0.36**	**0.32**	0.29	0.26	0.22	0.19
3Q	**0.40**	**0.35**	0.33	0.29	0.27	0.27
4Q	—	**0.41**	0.36	0.39	0.32	0.32
Yr.	—	**1.30**	**1.11**	1.12	0.99	0.93

Next earnings report expected: mid January

Dividend Data (Dividends have been paid since 1921.)

Amount ($)	Date Decl.	Ex-Div. Date	Stock of Record	Payment Date
0.113	Dec. 16	Jan. 13	Jan. 15	Jan. 29 '99
0.113	Mar. 23	Apr. 14	Apr. 16	Apr. 30 '99
0.113	Jun. 21	Jul. 14	Jul. 16	Jul. 30 '99
0.115	Sep. 21	Oct. 13	Oct. 15	Oct. 29 '99

A Division of The McGraw-Hill Companies

CLARCOR Inc.

Business Summary - 07-JUL-99

If you have ever gone to a store and purchased tea, potato chips, cosmetics or pharmaceuticals, there is a reasonable chance that the packaging was made by CLARCOR. However, the bulk of the company's business is not derived from packaging, but from the marketing and manufacturing of mobile and environmental filtration products.

CLARCOR conducted business in three principal industry segments in FY 98 (Nov.): engine/mobile filtration, (52% of FY 98 sales, and 75% of operating profits); industrial/environmental filtration (32%, and 14%); and packaging (16%, and 11%; formerly referred to as consumer packaging).

The engine/mobile filtration segment markets a full line of oil, air, fuel, coolant and hydraulic fluid filters. The filters are used in a wide variety of applications including engines and industrial equipment and in processes where filter efficiency, reliability and durability are essential.

Impure air or fluid flows through semi-porous paper, cotton, synthetic, chemical or membrane filter media with high-efficiency filtration characteristics. The impurities on the media are disposed of when the filter is changed. The filters are sold throughout the United States, Canada and worldwide, primarily in the replacement market for trucks, automobiles, locomotives, marine, construction, industrial and agricultural equipment. In addition, some first-fit filters are sold to the original equipment market.

The industrial/environmental filtration segment markets commercial and industrial air filters and systems, electrostatic contamination control equipment and electrostatic high precision spraying equipment. The air filters and systems remove contaminants from recirculated indoor air and from process air which is exhausted outdoors. The products represent a complete line of air cleaners with a wide range of uses for maintaining high quality standards in interior air and exterior pollution control. These products are sold throughout the United States, Canada, and worldwide.

The packaging segment manufactures a wide variety of different types and sizes of containers and metal packaging specialties. Metal, plastic and paper containers, combination metal/plastic containers and plastic closures are used in packaging a wide variety of dry and paste form products, such as food specialties (tea, spices, dry bakery products, potato chips, pretzels, candy and other confections); beverages and juices; cosmetics and toiletries; drugs and pharmaceuticals; and chemical specialties (hand cleaners, soaps and special cleaning compounds).

Metal packaging specialties include shells for dry batteries, film canisters, dispensers for razor blades, candles, spools for insulated and fine wire, and custom decorated flat steel sheets.

Per Share Data ($) (Year Ended Nov. 30)	1998	1997	1996	1995	1994	1993	1992	1991	1990	1989
Tangible Bk. Val.	6.90	6.41	5.87	5.21	4.62	4.00	3.86	3.35	2.75	2.22
Cash Flow	1.80	1.60	1.56	1.36	1.25	1.06	0.97	1.16	1.27	0.59
Earnings	1.30	1.11	1.12	0.99	0.93	0.77	0.73	0.83	0.91	0.31
Dividends	0.44	0.43	0.43	0.42	0.41	0.41	0.40	0.37	0.35	0.32
Payout Ratio	34%	39%	38%	43%	45%	52%	55%	44%	38%	91%
Prices - High	24 5/8	20 7/8	16 3/4	18	14 7/8	14 1/8	15	15 1/8	11 7/8	12 5/8
- Low	14 1/4	13 3/8	12 3/8	12 3/8	10 5/8	10 5/8	10	9 3/8	7 7/8	7 7/8
P/E Ratio - High	19	19	15	18	16	18	20	18	13	40
- Low	11	12	11	13	11	14	14	11	9	25

Income Statement Analysis (Million $)	1998	1997	1996	1995	1994	1993	1992	1991	1990	1989
Revs.	427	394	333	290	270	225	180	180	215	204
Oper. Inc.	64.0	59.0	50.3	43.6	39.7	35.4	32.0	38.2	41.6	35.8
Depr.	12.4	11.6	9.8	8.2	7.3	6.3	5.4	7.3	7.8	7.1
Int. Exp.	2.3	2.8	3.2	2.7	2.8	3.5	3.8	3.7	3.7	1.4
Pretax Inc.	51.3	44.2	40.0	34.1	32.6	27.1	25.3	28.5	32.6	19.0
Eff. Tax Rate	38%	39%	37%	36%	37%	36%	35%	35%	37%	58%
Net Inc.	32.1	26.9	25.0	22.0	20.6	17.3	16.5	18.5	20.4	7.9

Balance Sheet & Other Fin. Data (Million $)	1998	1997	1996	1995	1994	1993	1992	1991	1990	1989
Cash	33.3	30.3	17.4	18.8	19.6	13.8	15.1	9.6	14.8	4.8
Curr. Assets	168	161	125	118	99	86.2	93.6	75.2	72.6	58.0
Total Assets	306	283	244	223	188	170	161	158	144	131
Curr. Liab.	61.2	54.2	45.0	42.5	39.5	23.3	25.3	20.6	20.8	21.4
LT Debt	36.4	37.7	35.5	34.4	17.0	24.6	29.3	35.8	35.8	32.6
Common Eqty.	187	171	146	131	117	105	100	96.0	83.0	73.0
Total Cap.	233	219	191	171	140	133	132	137	123	110
Cap. Exp.	15.8	11.3	21.7	13.9	11.4	17.9	6.6	8.1	8.6	8.3
Cash Flow	44.5	38.5	34.8	30.2	27.9	23.5	21.9	25.8	28.2	15.1
Curr. Ratio	2.7	3.0	2.8	2.8	2.5	2.6	3.7	3.7	3.5	2.7
% LT Debt of Cap.	15.6	17.2	18.7	20.1	12.1	18.4	22.1	26.1	29.0	29.8
% Net Inc.of Revs.	7.5	6.8	7.5	7.6	7.6	7.7	8.8	10.3	9.5	3.9
% Ret. on Assets	10.9	10.2	10.7	10.7	11.5	10.5	10.3	12.2	14.9	6.3
% Ret. on Equity	17.9	17.0	18.0	17.7	18.6	17.0	16.9	20.7	26.4	8.9

Data as orig reptd.; bef. results of disc opers/spec. items. Per share data adj. for stk. divs. Bold denotes diluted EPS (FASB 128)-prior periods restated. E-Estimated. NA-Not Available. NM-Not Meaningful. NR-Not Ranked.

Office—2323 Sixth St., P.O. Box 7007, Rockford, IL 61125. **Tel**—(815) 962-8867. **Website**—http://www.clarcor.com **Chrmn, CEO & Investor Contact**—Lawrence E. Gloyd. **Pres & COO**—N. E. Johnson. **VP-Fin & CFO**—B. A. Klein. **VP & Secy**—M. S. Blaylock. **Dirs**—J. M. Adam, M. R. Brown, C. J. Dargene, L. E. Gloyd, R. H. Jenkins, N. E. Johnson, P. R. Lochner Jr, J. L. Packard, S. K. Smith Jr., D. A. Wolf. **Transfer Agent & Registrar**—First Chicago Trust Co. of New York, Jersey City, NJ. **Incorporated**—in Delaware in 1969. **Empl**— 3,096. **S&P Analyst:** N.J. D.

STANDARD
&POOR'S
STOCK REPORTS

Clarify, Inc.

NASDAQ Symbol **CLFY**

In S&P SmallCap 600

09-OCT-99

Industry:
Computer (Software & Services)

Summary: Clarify develops and provides enterprise-scale, Internet-ready front office applications for management of customer relationships over their lifetime.

Quantitative Evaluations
Outlook
(1 Lowest—5 Highest)
• **5**
Fair Value
• **88¾**
Risk
• **High**
Earn./Div. Rank
• **NR**

Technical Eval.
• **Bullish** since 8/99
Rel. Strength Rank
(1 Lowest—99 Highest)
• **85**
Insider Activity
• **Unfavorable**

Recent Price • 45⅞
52 Wk Range • 50½-7½
Yield • Nil
12-Mo. P/E • 93.6

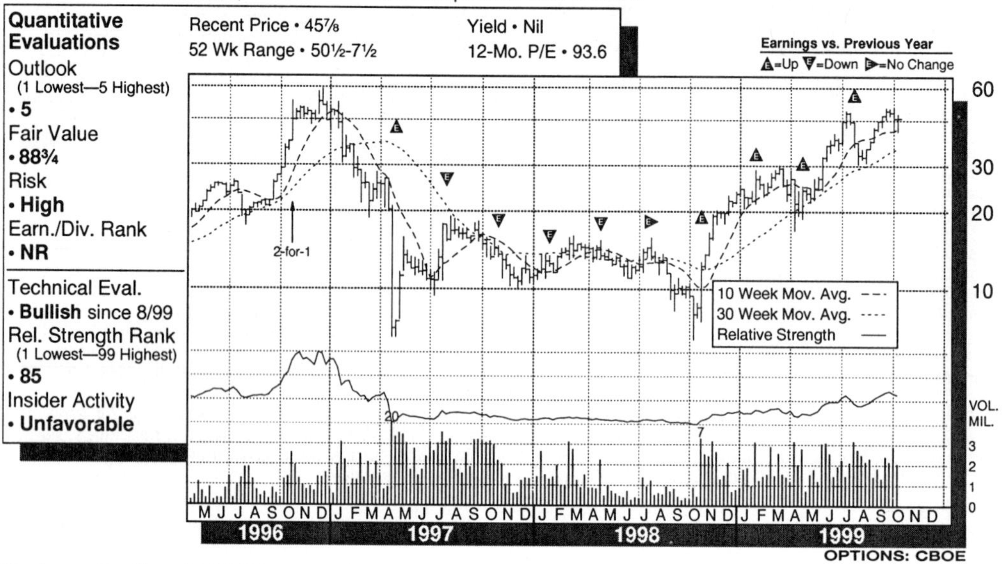

Business Profile - 05-AUG-99

During the second quarter of 1999, Clarify experienced a record number of million-dollar-plus wins, including Ascend Communications, diAX Telecom and Sprint Spectrum. In addition to its success in the telecom market, the company closed contracts with American Express Financial Corp., Anheuser-Busch and H&R Block. In addition to its own direct sales efforts, the company is experiencing steady increases in business led by system integrator partners both in Europe and the United States. One of CLFY's key initiatives for 1999 and beyond is to continue to accelerate these partnership programs at it seeks additional ways to gain leverage from its business model.

Operational Review - 05-AUG-99

Total revenues for the six months ended June 30, 1999, advanced 75%, year to year, on a 48% gain in license fees and 126% higher services revenues. The increase in license fees stemmed from further market acceptance of the company's existing products, continued enhancement of those products, and increased breadth of the product offerings. Services revenues were bolstered mainly by an increase in maintenance and consulting. Profitability benefited considerably from the strong growth in revenues, and pretax income increased to $10,022,000 from $2,858,000. After taxes at 39.0%, versus 37.0%, net income rose to $6,114,000 ($0.25 a share, based on 11% more average shares) from $1,801,000 ($0.08).

Stock Performance - 08-OCT-99

In the past 30 trading days, CLFY's shares have increased 10%, compared to a 0.91% fall in the S&P 500. Average trading volume for the past five days was 405,380 shares, compared with the 40-day moving average of 415,208 shares.

Key Stock Statistics

Dividend Rate/Share	Nil	Shareholders	219
Shs. outstg. (M)	23.2	Market cap. (B)	$ 1.1
Avg. daily vol. (M)	0.471	Inst. holdings	81%
Tang. Bk. Value/Share	3.73		
Beta	NA		

Value of $10,000 invested 5 years ago: NA

Fiscal Year Ending Dec. 31

	1999	1998	1997	1996	1995	1994
Revenues (Million $)						
1Q	43.36	24.90	19.36	7.78	—	—
2Q	52.30	29.83	19.43	11.14	—	—
3Q	—	34.46	21.89	17.00	—	—
4Q	—	41.33	27.54	19.23	7.01	—
Yr.	—	130.5	88.22	56.32	20.95	10.18
Earnings Per Share ($)						
1Q	0.11	0.03	0.09	0.04	—	—
2Q	0.14	0.05	0.05	0.06	—	—
3Q	—	0.09	0.01	0.15	—	—
4Q	—	0.15	0.03	0.13	—	—
Yr.	—	0.32	0.18	0.38	0.09	-0.07

Next earnings report expected: late October

Dividend Data

No cash dividends have been paid and the company does not expect to pay any cash dividends for the foreseeable future.

A Division of The McGraw-Hill Companies

Clarify, Inc.

Business Summary - 05-AUG-99

A growing number of companies have been turning to Clarify, Inc. in order to attract, acquire and retain customers at significantly reduced costs. Founded in 1990 in San Jose, CA, the heart of Silicon Valley, Clarify is a leading developer and provider of enterprise-scale, Internet-ready front office applications for managing the quality and life of customer relationships. CLFY helps companies build service into every customer interaction across a variety of media with integrated solutions that automate call center, sales and marketing, technical support, field service and logistics, quality assurance, and help desk processes.

CLFY's business solutions are designed for enterprises that place a premium on customer relationships. Its solutions enable a company's customer-facing organizations to work together to provide superior customer service. For example, because of the power of its workflow management engine, Clarify customers can make commitments to certain business standards via Clarify business rules, such as responding to customer requests within 24 hours. Accountable managers are automatically notified when commitments are not met.

A key initiative in 1998 was Clarify's announcement of a major new release of its integrated suite of sales and service applications, Clarify FrontOffice 98, which serves as the front line for customer interactions as well as the centralized resource for all customer information. Clarify FrontOffice 98 does this by integrating the efforts of business's customer-facing organizations and unifying information about customers in a central database that is updated in real time.

Clarify's Call Center Solution, Sales and Marketing Solution, Customer Service Solution, Field Service Solution, and Help Desk Solution leverage the latest database, Web, mobile, and intelligent software agent technology to help businesses make customer interaction consistent, knowledge-based, personalized, and shared across organizations.

CLFY's solution for the telecommunications marketplace, Clarify CommCenter, is an enterprise-scale, Internet-ready suite of operations support systems (OSS) applications. Clarify CommCenter links the sales and service sides of the telecommunications business. Within the same application, providers can create orders, answer questions, process trouble tickets, and update the status as problems move toward resolutions. The company entered the telecommunications market in 1996, and telecommunications currently comprises about 25% of Clarify's total global business.

The company markets its software and services primarily through its direct sales organization. Clarify maintains sales and support offices throughout North America, Europe, and the Asia/Pacific region. International revenues accounted for 25% of total revenues in 1998, up from 14% the year before. A variety of industries employ CLFY's solutions, including telecommunications, high technology, financial services, healthcare, con sumer products, and travel and entertainment.

Per Share Data ($) (Year Ended Dec. 31)	1998	1997	1996	1995	1994	1993	1992	1991	1990	1989
Tangible Bk. Val.	3.22	2.68	2.28	1.58	NA	NA	NA	NA	NA	NA
Cash Flow	0.58	0.39	0.46	0.28	-0.54	NA	NA	NA	NA	NA
Earnings	0.32	0.18	0.38	0.09	NA	NA	NA	NA	NA	NA
Dividends	Nil	Nil	Nil	Nil	NA	NA	NA	NA	NA	NA
Payout Ratio	Nil	Nil	Nil	Nil	NA	NA	NA	NA	NA	NA
Prices - High	25	52¾	59¼	16⅜	NA	NA	NA	NA	NA	NA
- Low	6⅜	6½	11⅛	6½	NA	NA	NA	NA	NA	NA
P/E Ratio - High	78	NM	155	181	NA	NA	NA	NA	NA	NA
- Low	20	NM	29	72	NA	NA	NA	NA	NA	NA
Income Statement Analysis (Million $)										
Revs.	131	88.2	56.3	20.9	10.2	NA	NA	NA	NA	NA
Oper. Inc.	15.8	9.6	10.3	2.3	-0.8	NA	NA	NA	NA	NA
Depr.	5.7	4.7	1.8	0.7	0.4	NA	NA	NA	NA	NA
Int. Exp.	0.0	Nil	Nil	0.2	0.1	NA	NA	NA	NA	NA
Pretax Inc.	11.6	6.2	9.1	1.7	-1.3	NA	NA	NA	NA	NA
Eff. Tax Rate	37%	37%	10%	7.56%	NM	NA	NA	NA	NA	NA
Net Inc.	7.3	3.9	8.2	1.6	-1.3	NA	NA	NA	NA	NA
Balance Sheet & Other Fin. Data (Million $)										
Cash	31.3	20.7	34.5	31.6	3.2	NA	NA	NA	NA	NA
Curr. Assets	110	72.2	59.3	38.4	7.6	NA	NA	NA	NA	NA
Total Assets	123	86.8	70.7	40.6	8.5	NA	NA	NA	NA	NA
Curr. Liab.	51.3	29.7	23.7	8.5	4.2	NA	NA	NA	NA	NA
LT Debt	Nil	Nil	Nil	Nil	NA	NA	NA	NA	NA	NA
Common Eqty.	71.3	57.1	46.9	32.1	3.6	NA	NA	NA	NA	NA
Total Cap.	71.3	57.1	46.9	32.0	NA	NA	NA	NA	NA	NA
Cap. Exp.	5.5	5.1	8.0	2.0	NA	NA	NA	NA	NA	NA
Cash Flow	13.0	8.6	10.0	2.3	-0.9	NA	NA	NA	NA	NA
Curr. Ratio	2.1	2.4	2.5	4.5	1.8	NA	NA	NA	NA	NA
% LT Debt of Cap.	Nil	Nil	Nil	Nil	NA	NA	NA	NA	NA	NA
% Net Inc.of Revs.	5.6	4.5	14.6	7.5	NM	NA	NA	NA	NA	NA
% Ret. on Assets	7.0	5.0	14.7	6.4	NM	NA	NA	NA	NA	NA
% Ret. on Equity	11.4	7.6	20.8	8.8	NM	NA	NA	NA	NA	NA

Data as orig reptd.; bef. results of disc opers/spec. items. Per share data adj. for stk. divs. Bold denotes diluted EPS (FASB 128)-prior periods restated. E-Estimated. NA-Not Available. NM-Not Meaningful. NR-Not Ranked.

Office—2560 Orchard Parkway, San Jose, CA 95131**Tel**—(408) 573-3000.**Website**—http://www.clarify.com**EMail**—info@clarify.com**Pres & CEO**—A. Zingale.**Chrmn**—D. A. Stamm.**VP-CFO**—J. A. Praisner.**Dirs**—T. H. Bredt, J. A. Costello, C. H. Greendale, D. A. Stamm, A. Zingale.**Transfer Agent & Registrar**—Harris Trust Co. of California, Los Angeles.**Incorporated**—in Delaware in 1990.**Empl**— 630. **S&P Analyst:** J. J. Schemitsch

STANDARD
&POOR'S
STOCK REPORTS

Coachmen Industries

NYSE Symbol **COA**
In S&P SmallCap 600

23-OCT-99

Industry: Leisure Time (Products)

Summary: This leading manufacturer of recreational vehicles has related interests in parts and supplies, and is the largest U.S. modular home producer.

Quantitative Evaluations

Outlook (1 Lowest—5 Highest)
• **NA**
Fair Value
• **NA**
Risk
• **Average**
Earn./Div. Rank
• **B**

Technical Eval.
• **NA**
Rel. Strength Rank (1 Lowest—99 Highest)
• **17**
Insider Activity
• **Neutral**

Recent Price • 15¼
52 Wk Range • 26⅞-13⅝
Yield • 1.4%
12-Mo. P/E • 7.5

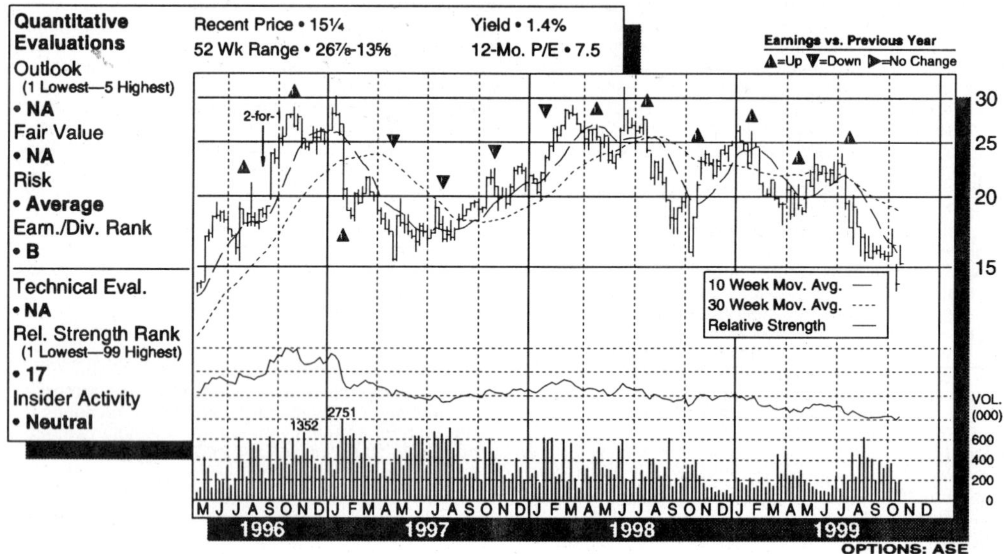

Business Profile - 15-OCT-99

In August 1999, the company and Walt Disney World Resort announced a strategic alliance to cross market products. Disney has designated Coachmen as the official recreational vehicle at two of its resorts and will prominently display COA vehicles at the sites. The company will in turn offer two free weeks of camping at the Disney resorts with the purchase of a Coachmen motorhome, travel trailer or fifth wheel. As a demonstration of confidence in the future prospects of the RV market and the company, COA opened its largest plant (92,599 sq. ft.), in Middlebury, Indiana, in early August 1999. The company continues to be optimistic about demand for both recreational vehicles and modular housing, citing a vibrant economy, attractive interest rates, strong consumer confidence, and favorable demographics.

Operational Review - 15-OCT-99

Net sales in the six months ended June 30, 1999, advanced 10%, year to year, reflecting increased sales of RVs and modular housing units. Gross margins narrowed mainly due to software implementation and material shortage problems in the RV segment. Profitability was helped by well controlled operating expenses and a gain on sale of properties; pretax income rose 9%. After taxes, net income climbed 8.1%, to $16,886,000 ($1.01 a share, on fewer shares), from $15,622,000 ($0.89).

Stock Performance - 22-OCT-99

In the past 30 trading days, COA's shares have declined 13%, compared to a 4% fall in the S&P 500. Average trading volume for the past five days was 73,900 shares, compared with the 40-day moving average of 86,264 shares.

Key Stock Statistics

Dividend Rate/Share	0.20	Shareholders	1,718
Shs. outstg. (M)	16.7	Market cap. (B)	$0.234
Avg. daily vol. (M)	0.056	Inst. holdings	77%
Tang. Bk. Value/Share	13.02		
Beta	0.51		

Value of $10,000 invested 5 years ago: $ 18,337

Fiscal Year Ending Dec. 31

	1999	1998	1997	1996	1995	1994
Revenues (Million $)						
1Q	211.0	175.6	158.1	148.6	131.8	93.64
2Q	203.2	201.1	169.4	166.7	128.2	100.3
3Q	—	202.6	174.9	154.2	131.0	103.0
4Q	—	176.7	159.2	136.9	124.9	97.09
Yr.	—	756.0	661.6	606.5	515.9	394.0
Earnings Per Share ($)						
1Q	**0.43**	**0.36**	**0.25**	**0.26**	0.22	0.18
2Q	**0.58**	**0.53**	**0.37**	**0.57**	0.28	0.28
3Q	—	**0.59**	**0.44**	**0.54**	0.31	0.26
4Q	—	**0.43**	**0.36**	**0.39**	0.37	0.28
Yr.	—	**1.92**	**1.42**	**1.76**	**1.17**	**1.00**

Next earnings report expected: NA

Dividend Data (Dividends have been paid since 1982.)

Amount ($)	Date Decl.	Ex-Div. Date	Stock of Record	Payment Date
0.050	Oct. 28	Nov. 05	Nov. 09	Nov. 30 '98
0.050	Feb. 09	Feb. 16	Feb. 18	Mar. 11 '99
0.050	May. 05	May. 18	May. 20	Jun. 10 '99
0.050	Aug. 10	Aug. 20	Aug. 24	Sep. 14 '99

A Division of The McGraw-Hill Companies

Coachmen Industries, Inc.

Business Summary - 15-OCT-99

Coachmen Industries is one of the largest full-line manufacturers of recreational vehicles (RVs), and is the largest builder of modular homes in the U.S.

Motorhomes, travel trailers and modular homes accounted for 53%, 20% and 17%, respectively, of sales in 1998.

In 1998, the company derived 76% of its pretax profits from the vehicle segment and 24% from housing operations.

A motorhome is a self-powered mobile dwelling built on a special heavy-duty chassis. A travel trailer is a mobile dwelling designed to be towed behind another vehicle. Camping trailers are smaller towed units constructed with sidewalls that may be raised up and folded out. Truck campers are designed to be mounted on the bed of a pickup truck.

The company manufactures and sells a wide array of RVs, including Class A and C motorhomes, travel trailers, fifth-wheel trailers, camping trailers, truck campers, van campers, van and truck conversions and related parts and supplies. COA's RVs are sold under brand names that include Coachmen, Shasta and Viking. Vehicles are sold through more than 1,300 independent and nine company-owned dealers throughout the U.S.

COA produces RVs on an assembly line basis, with components primarily purchased from outside sources. However, for some items (such as cushions, fiberglass products and furniture) where it is profitable for the company to do so, or where it has experienced shortages of supplies, the company has undertaken to manufacture its own supplies. Vehicles generally are produced against orders received from dealers. The highest level of sales occurs during the spring and summer months. COA does not finance retail consumer purchases of its products, nor does it generally guarantee consumer financing. The company considers itself customer driven, and sales and service representatives regularly visit dealers and respond quickly to questions and suggestions. Open forum meetings with owners are held at campouts.

The company sold a total of 625,748 vehicles in 1998, up from 547,541 in 1997 and 507,717 in 1996.

The company's housing division, which has plant locations in Indiana, Iowa, North Carolina, Ohio and Tennessee, supplies modular housing to more than 300 builder/developers in 19 states. Modular homes are built to the same local building codes as site-built homes in factories where building occurs unaffected by weather conditions. An average two-module home can be made in a few days.

Per Share Data ($) (Year Ended Dec. 31)	1998	1997	1996	1995	1994	1993	1992	1991	1990	1989
Tangible Bk. Val.	12.11	10.71	9.46	5.75	5.03	4.14	3.33	2.79	3.73	4.56
Cash Flow	2.38	1.82	2.16	1.46	1.22	1.06	0.76	-0.73	-0.56	0.07
Earnings	1.92	1.42	1.79	1.18	1.00	0.87	0.56	-0.94	-0.78	-0.15
Dividends	0.20	0.20	0.19	0.14	0.12	0.10	0.04	0.04	0.14	0.20
Payout Ratio	10%	14%	10%	12%	12%	11%	7%	NM	NM	NM
Prices - High	31 1/2	30 3/8	29	11 7/8	9 1/4	10 3/8	8 7/8	4	4 1/4	5 1/2
- Low	15 5/8	15 3/8	9 1/2	6 3/4	5 7/8	5 5/8	2 3/4	1 13/16	1 3/4	3 1/4
P/E Ratio - High	16	21	16	10	9	12	16	NM	NM	NM
- Low	8	11	5	6	6	6	5	NM	NM	NM
Income Statement Analysis (Million $)										
Revs.	756	662	606	516	394	330	293	231	272	314
Oper. Inc.	53.9	42.1	45.3	30.8	25.6	15.5	10.0	-7.8	-6.6	-2.7
Depr.	7.9	6.8	5.6	4.1	3.1	2.9	2.8	2.8	3.3	3.4
Int. Exp.	1.7	2.5	1.6	3.1	1.5	2.0	2.9	3.6	3.5	3.4
Pretax Inc.	50.3	38.8	41.5	28.0	22.8	12.7	8.3	-13.3	-12.6	-3.7
Eff. Tax Rate	34%	36%	34%	37%	35%	Nil	1.50%	NM	NM	NM
Net Inc.	33.1	24.8	27.3	17.5	14.8	12.7	8.1	-13.4	-11.5	-2.3
Balance Sheet & Other Fin. Data (Million $)										
Cash	23.0	71.4	66.9	17.5	20.3	4.4	3.3	1.3	2.2	3.7
Curr. Assets	185	190	164	102	89.2	62.6	55.6	49.8	61.9	77.8
Total Assets	268	259	227	150	125	95.0	89.0	86.0	105	122
Curr. Liab.	45.7	49.7	38.5	41.0	37.8	24.4	29.5	33.7	38.9	41.1
LT Debt	10.2	12.6	14.8	12.1	7.0	3.8	5.3	6.8	7.8	7.4
Common Eqty.	205	190	168	91.0	74.8	61.0	48.6	40.5	54.4	69.5
Total Cap.	216	203	182	103	81.8	64.8	53.9	47.3	62.2	77.6
Cap. Exp.	22.2	14.2	14.9	15.2	5.1	NA	NA	3.3	4.2	4.4
Cash Flow	41.0	31.6	33.0	21.7	17.9	15.6	10.9	-10.7	-8.2	1.0
Curr. Ratio	4.1	3.8	4.3	2.5	2.4	2.6	1.9	1.5	1.6	1.9
% LT Debt of Cap.	4.7	6.2	8.1	11.7	8.6	5.8	9.9	14.4	12.6	9.5
% Net Inc.of Revs.	4.4	3.7	4.5	3.4	3.8	3.9	2.8	NM	NM	NM
% Ret. on Assets	12.5	10.2	14.5	12.8	13.4	13.8	9.2	NM	NM	NM
% Ret. on Equity	16.7	13.8	21.1	21.2	21.7	23.1	18.2	NM	NM	NM

Data as orig reptd.; bef. results of disc opers/spec. items. Per share data adj. for stk. divs. Bold denotes diluted EPS (FASB 128)-prior periods restated. E-Estimated. NA-Not Available. NM-Not Meaningful. NR-Not Ranked.

Office—2831 Dexter Drive, P.O. Box 3300, Elkhart, IN 46515. **Tel**—(219) 262-0123. **Fax**—(219) 262-8823. **Website**—http://www.coachmen.com **Chrmn & CEO**—C. C. Skinner. **Pres & COO**—K. D. Corson. **EVP & CFO**—J. E. Jack. **Treas & Investor Contact**—Donald P. Rockwell. **Dirs**— K. D. Corson, T. H. Corson, R. J. Deputy, W. P. Johnson, P. G. Lux, E. W. Miller, F. M. Miller, C. C. Skinner. **Transfer Agent & Registrar**—First Chicago Trust Co. of New York, NYC. **Incorporated**—in Indiana in 1964. **Empl**— 4,690. **S&P Analyst:** Howard Choe

STANDARD &POOR'S
STOCK REPORTS

Coca-Cola Bottling Co. Consol.

NASDAQ Symbol **COKE**

In S&P SmallCap 600

09-OCT-99

Industry: Beverages (Non-Alcoholic)

Summary: This company is engaged in bottling, canning and marketing carbonated soft drinks, primarily products of The Coca-Cola Co., in the Southeast.

Quantitative Evaluations

Outlook (1 Lowest—5 Highest) • **NA**

Fair Value • **NA**

Risk • **Low**

Earn./Div. Rank • **B**

Technical Eval. • **Bearish** since 9/99

Rel. Strength Rank (1 Lowest—99 Highest) • **43**

Insider Activity • **NA**

Recent Price • 54⅝ | Yield • 1.8%

52 Wk Range • 62-52⅞ | 12-Mo. P/E • 48.3

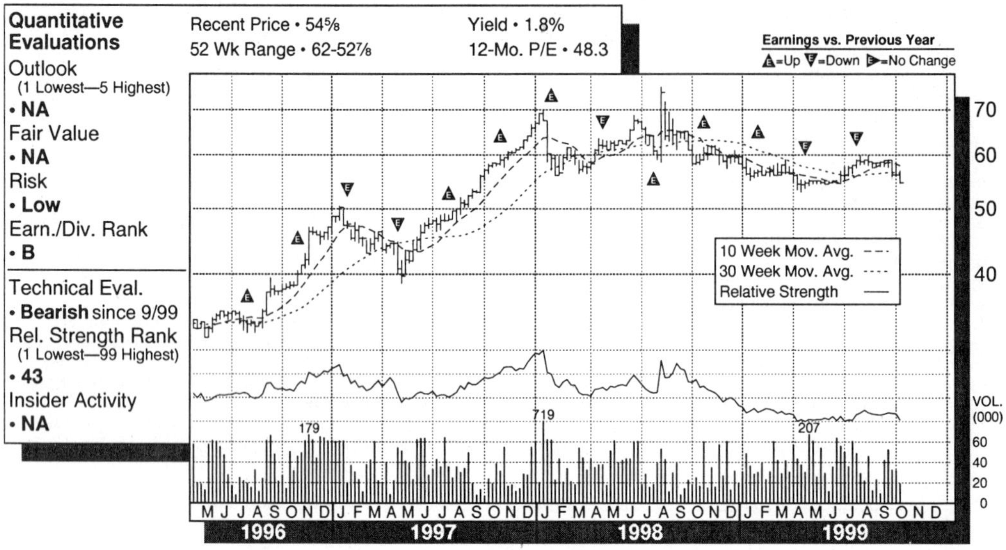

Business Profile - 28-SEP-99

COKE's volume growth continues to significantly exceed the U.S. soft drink industry average. Recent short-term operating results have been adversely affected by substantial strategic investments in the company's infrastructure to support accelerated growth. In April 1999, COKE issued $250 million of 10-year 6.375% debentures, with part of the proceeds used to finance a $155 million buyout of equipment that had previously been leased. The company has been aggressively expanding through acquisitions of other Coca-Cola bottlers. In May 1999, the company acquired the Carolina Coca-Cola Bottling Co., a South Carolina bottler, for $36.6 million. In August 1999, COKE agreed to acquire Virginia-based Lynchburg Coca-Cola Bottling Co.

Operational Review - 28-SEP-99

Net sales in the six months ended July 4, 1999, advanced 8.2%, year to year, reflecting solid volume growth and higher selling prices. However, results were hurt by the continued investment in the infrastructure to support accelerated growth, particularly higher depreciation and interest expenses related to the purchase of assets that were previously leased. Pretax income declined 76%. After taxes at 35.0%, versus 37.1%, net income also fell 76%, to $1.7 million ($0.20 a share), from $6.9 million ($0.82).

Stock Performance - 08-OCT-99

In the past 30 trading days, COKE's shares have declined 7%, compared to a 0.91% fall in the S&P 500. Average trading volume for the past five days was 3,740 shares, compared with the 40-day moving average of 5,656 shares.

Key Stock Statistics

Dividend Rate/Share	1.00	Shareholders	2,400
Shs. outstg. (M)	8.7	Market cap. (B)	$0.349
Avg. daily vol. (M)	0.007	Inst. holdings	25%
Tang. Bk. Value/Share	NM		
Beta	0.15		

Value of $10,000 invested 5 years ago: $ 17,056

Fiscal Year Ending Dec. 31

	1999	1998	1997	1996	1995	1994
Revenues (Million $)						
1Q	220.3	203.3	178.4	172.0	171.0	163.8
2Q	261.0	241.4	208.2	213.6	207.9	200.7
3Q	—	248.5	219.1	204.6	203.6	188.4
4Q	—	235.2	196.5	183.6	179.5	171.0
Yr.	—	928.5	802.1	773.8	761.9	723.9
Earnings Per Share ($)						
1Q	**-0.53**	**-0.29**	**0.01**	**10.00**	0.21	0.16
2Q	**0.71**	**1.11**	**1.08**	**1.02**	0.87	0.72
3Q	—	**0.82**	**0.78**	**0.69**	0.50	0.53
4Q	—	**0.11**	**-0.07**	**-0.09**	0.09	0.11
Yr.	—	**1.75**	**1.79**	**1.73**	**1.67**	**1.52**

Next earnings report expected: late October

Dividend Data (Dividends have been paid since 1967.)

Amount ($)	Date Decl.	Ex-Div. Date	Stock of Record	Payment Date
0.250	Nov. 03	Nov. 18	Nov. 20	Dec. 04 '98
0.250	Feb. 02	Feb. 17	Feb. 19	Mar. 05 '99
0.250	May. 04	May. 19	May. 21	Jun. 04 '99
0.250	Aug. 03	Aug. 18	Aug. 20	Sep. 03 '99

Coca-Cola Bottling Co. Consolidated

Business Summary - 28-SEP-99

Coca-Cola Bottling Co. Consolidated (COKE) is the second largest Coca-Cola bottler in the nation. COKE holds franchises under which it bottles, cans and markets carbonated soft drinks, primarily products of The Coca-Cola Co. Prior to 1984, the company's business was concentrated in North Carolina, but, through a major expansion program, its operating territory has been extended to a 12-state area in the Southeast, covering a franchise territory of approximately 12.4 million people. Major markets include North Carolina, south Alabama, south Georgia, middle Tennessee, western Virginia, and West Virginia. In addition, South Carolina is covered through a joint venture.

COKE's franchises from The Coca-Cola Co. allow it to produce and market Coca-Cola Co. soft drinks in bottles, cans and five gallon, pressurized, pre-mix containers. Products under franchise from The Coca-Cola Co. include Coca-Cola classic, caffeine free Coca-Cola classic, diet Coke, caffeine free diet Coke, Cherry Coke, TAB, diet Mello Yellow, Mr. PiBB, Barq's Root Beer, Fresca, Minute Maid orange and diet Minute Maid orange sodas. Also, in most of its regions, the company produces and markets Dr Pepper. Products in the citrus category include Sprite, diet Sprite, and Mello Yellow. In the first quarter of 1998, the company introduced a new citrus brand named Surge. In addition, the company also distributes and markets POWERaDE, Cool from Nestea, Fruitopia, and Minute Maid Juices To Go in certain of its markets. In April 1999, the company began distributing Dasani bottled water, another Coca-Cola Co. product.

In 1998, products of The Coca-Cola Co. accounted for 89% of soft drink sales. A majority of total sales are through the "take-home market" (supermarkets, convenience stores and other retail outlets); the remaining sales were made in the "cold drink market" (primarily vending machines).

Piedmont Coca-Cola Bottling Partnership (formed in 1993) is an equally owned joint venture with Coca-Cola Co. It produces and sells soft drink products in certain North and South Carolina bottling territories. COKE provides a majority of the soft drink products to Piedmont and receives a fee for managing the business.

During the past several years, COKE has attempted to concentrate its soft drink production into fewer facilities for efficiency and to meet changing market conditions. At the end of 1998, COKE had four production facilities and 56 distribution centers.

COKE continues to focus on strategic acquisitions, particularly in the Southeast. In January 1998, the company acquired the assets of a Coca-Cola bottler in Florence, Alabama for $33.6 million. In June 1998, the company acquired St. Paul Coca-Cola Bottling Company Inc., a small Coca-Cola bottler in southwestern Virginia. In May 1999, the company acquired Carolina Coca-Cola Bottling Company, a South Carolina bottler, for $36.6 million.

Per Share Data ($) (Year Ended Dec. 31)	1998	1997	1996	1995	1994	1993	1992	1991	1990	1989
Tangible Bk. Val.	NM	NA	NM	NM	-31.61	-33.39	-56.60	-40.28	-12.94	-10.26
Cash Flow	7.64	7.20	6.13	5.87	5.45	5.71	4.19	3.47	3.19	2.70
Earnings	1.75	1.79	1.74	1.67	1.52	1.60	-0.23	0.24	-0.02	-0.32
Dividends	1.00	1.00	1.00	1.00	1.00	0.88	0.88	0.88	0.88	0.88
Payout Ratio	57%	56%	57%	60%	66%	55%	NM	366%	NM	NM
Prices - High	75¾	69	48¾	35⅞	37¼	41½	20¾	26½	25	32½
- Low	56	38¾	31½	26	24	17	15¼	16¼	15	22
P/E Ratio - High	43	39	28	21	25	26	NM	NM	NM	NM
- Low	32	22	18	16	16	11	NM	NM	NM	NM
Income Statement Analysis (Million $)										
Revs.	929	802	774	762	724	687	656	465	431	384
Oper. Inc.	117	109	101	101	92.2	95.3	84.4	56.6	59.3	51.3
Depr.	50.0	46.0	40.8	39.0	36.5	38.1	40.5	29.7	29.5	27.5
Int. Exp.	39.9	37.5	30.4	33.1	31.4	31.0	36.9	21.6	24.1	24.7
Pretax Inc.	23.2	24.3	26.0	25.2	24.4	24.0	4.9	3.0	2.2	-2.5
Eff. Tax Rate	36%	37%	37%	38%	42%	38%	57%	0.70%	90%	NM
Net Inc.	14.9	15.3	16.2	15.5	14.1	14.8	2.1	2.9	0.2	-2.9
Balance Sheet & Other Fin. Data (Million $)										
Cash	6.7	4.4	2.9	2.4	1.8	1.3	1.4	1.0	3.2	3.4
Curr. Assets	139	127	111	70.3	59.6	58.4	49.2	59.5	35.5	36.9
Total Assets	825	778	702	677	664	648	786	785	468	449
Curr. Liab.	134	107	76.7	89.6	78.2	81.9	66.1	72.6	46.8	39.6
LT Debt	491	494	439	420	433	434	555	479	238	230
Common Eqty.	15.8	9.3	22.3	39.0	34.0	30.0	26.0	155	161	167
Total Cap.	628	615	570	556	556	544	691	696	409	400
Cap. Exp.	46.8	100	30.0	37.0	49.0	29.0	33.0	24.0	16.0	26.0
Cash Flow	64.9	61.3	56.9	54.5	50.6	52.9	38.4	31.9	29.3	24.6
Curr. Ratio	1.0	1.2	1.4	0.9	0.8	0.7	0.7	0.8	0.8	0.9
% LT Debt of Cap.	78.3	80.3	77.1	75.5	77.8	79.8	80.4	68.9	58.0	57.5
% Net Inc.of Revs.	1.6	1.9	2.1	2.0	2.0	2.2	0.3	0.6	0.1	NM
% Ret. on Assets	1.9	2.1	2.3	2.3	2.2	2.1	0.3	0.5	0.1	NM
% Ret. on Equity	118.7	96.8	52.8	42.7	44.5	53.2	NM	1.4	NM	NM

Data as orig reptd.; bef. results of disc opers/spec. items. Per share data adj. for stk. divs. Bold denotes diluted EPS (FASB 128)-prior periods restated. E-Estimated. NA-Not Available. NM-Not Meaningful. NR-Not Ranked.

Reincorporated—in Delaware in 1980. **Office**—1900 Rexford Rd., Charlotte, NC 28211. **Tel**—(704) 551-4400. **Chrmn & CEO**—J. F. Harrison III. **Vice-Chrmn**—R. M. Henson. **Pres & COO**—J. L. Moore, Jr. **VP-CFO & Investor Contact**—D. V. Singer. **VP & Treas**—J. W. Albright. **Secy**—J. F. Henry, Jr. **Dirs**—H. W. M. Belk, J. M. Belk, J. F. Harrison III, J. F. Harrison Jr., R. M. Henson, E. Holyfield, H. R. Jones, Jr., N. McWherter, J. L. Moore, J. W. Murrey III, C. L. Wallace. **Transfer Agent**—First Union National Bank, Charlotte. **Incorporated**—in Delaware in 1980. **Empl**— 6,000. **S&P Analyst:** A. Bensinger

STANDARD
&POOR'S
STOCK REPORTS

Coeur d'Alene Mines

NYSE Symbol **CDE**

In S&P SmallCap 600

09-OCT-99

Industry: Gold & Precious Metals Mining

Summary: Based in Coeur d'Alene, Idaho, this company is the largest U.S. primary silver producer. It also mines and explores for gold.

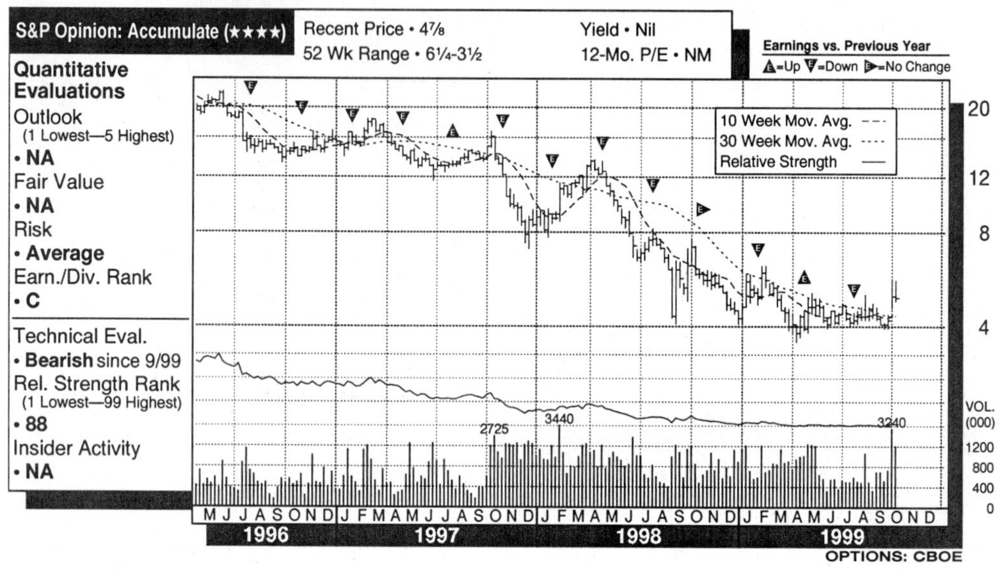

Overview - 16-AUG-99

On May 13, 1999, CDE and Asarco Inc. (NYSE; AR) agreed to a transaction in which Asarco will acquire a 19.3% fully diluted common stock interest in CDE in exchange for most of AR's silver mining assets. Additionally, AR will nominate two directors to CDE's board of directors. CDE will issue 7.125 million new CDE common shares in exchange for AR's 50% interest in Silver Valley Resources, an advanced Bolivian silver exploration project, and shares and warrants representing a 5% interest in Pan American Silver Corp. (NASDAQ; PAAS) and a 20% net profit interest in the Quiruvilca silver mine in Peru. Based on the closing price of CDE on May 13, 1999, the purchase price is about $33.4 million. The transaction will add some 132 million oz. of silver to CDE's reserves and resources. Subject to various conditions, the deal will close in September 1999.

Valuation - 16-AUG-99

We are maintaining our accumulate rating on CDE, following 1999's second quarter results. Our rating reflects our favorable view of silver market fundamentals.Fabrication demand has exceeded mine production and scrap recovery since 1989. Since 1993, the metal has been in an erratic uptrend. Silver declined 15% in 1998, to $5.02/oz. from $5.99/oz. at 1997's year end. However, the average price was $5.54/oz. in 1998, versus $4.88/oz. in 1997 and $5.18/oz. in 1996. In contrast to gold, silver remained well above its 21-year closing low of $3.51/oz. in 1991. With its pact with AR, CDE has broken the logjam in its production and reserve profile, albeit at the cost of dilution. At any rate, the deal solidifies CDE as the leading U.S. primary silver producer and positions it for the eventual upturn in silver prices.

Key Stock Statistics

S&P EPS Est. 1999	-1.45	Tang. Bk. Value/Share	2.31
P/E on S&P Est. 1999	NM	Beta	1.58
S&P EPS Est. 2000	-0.80	Shareholders	7,378
Dividend Rate/Share	Nil	Market cap. (B)	$0.108
Shs. outstg. (M)	21.9	Inst. holdings	24%
Avg. daily vol. (M)	0.286		

Value of $10,000 invested 5 years ago: $ 2,360

Fiscal Year Ending Dec. 31

	1999	1998	1997	1996	1995	1994
Revenues (Million $)						
1Q	18.26	21.17	24.67	22.61	17.89	22.90
2Q	21.68	32.26	33.66	18.75	23.62	22.29
3Q	—	23.89	38.63	21.56	24.80	23.53
4Q	—	25.19	42.28	29.81	22.93	22.31
Yr.	—	102.5	139.0	92.73	89.24	91.02
Earnings Per Share ($)						
1Q	**-0.45**	**-2.77**	**-0.20**	**-0.02**	-0.21	-0.17
2Q	**-0.44**	**-0.36**	**-0.13**	**-2.75**	0.08	-0.09
3Q	**E-0.31**	**-0.41**	**-0.41**	**-0.03**	0.13	0.11
4Q	**E-0.25**	**-0.41**	**-0.39**	**-0.11**	-0.08	-0.11
Yr.	**E-1.45**	**-11.73**	**-1.12**	**-2.93**	**-0.07**	**-0.26**

Next earnings report expected: mid November

Dividend Data

Cash dividends, initiated in 1988 and paid annually, were omitted in March 1997. A "poison pill" stock purchase rights plan was adopted in 1989.

Coeur d'Alene Mines Corporation

Business Summary - 16-AUG-99

Coeur d'Alene, the largest primary silver producer in the U.S., also mines and explores for gold. CDE's main strategy for achieving reserve and production growth is to seek exploration and acquisition opportunities in politically stable countries having mining traditions.

On May 13, 1999, CDE and Asarco Inc, (NYSE; AR) agreed to a transaction whereby AR will acquire a 19.3% fully diluted common stock interest in CDE in exchange for most of AR's silver mining assets. Additionally, AR will nominate two directors to CDE's board of directors. CDE will issue 7.125 million new CDE common shares in exchange for AR's 50% interest in Silver Valley Resources, an advanced Bolivian silver exploration project, and shares and warrants representing a 5% interest in Pan American Silver Corp. (NASDAQ: PAAS) and a 20% net profit interest in the Quiruvilca silver mine in Peru. Based on the closing price of CDE on May 13, 1999, the purchase price is about $33.4 million. The transaction will add some 132 million oz. of silver to CDE's reserves and resources.

Silver production totaled 10.7 million oz. in 1998, versus 11.0 million oz. in 1997 and 9.5 million oz. in 1996. Silver reserves were 79.8 million oz. at year end 1998, versus 99.0 million at 1997's year end and 109.0 million at 1996's year end. Gold production totaled 209,959 oz. in 1998, versus 290,962 oz. in 1997 and 214,130 oz. in 1996. Gold reserves totaled 2.8 million oz. at the end of 1998, 3.1 million oz. at the end of 1997 and 3.4 million oz. at the end of 1996.

CDE's wholly owned Rochester silver-gold mine in Nevada is one of North America's largest and lowest cost silver producing mines. Silver production totaled 7.23 million oz. in 1998, versus 6.69 million oz. in 1997, and 6.25 million oz. in 1996; gold production was 88,165 oz. in 1998, versus 90,019 oz. in 1997, and 74,293 oz. in 1996. Cash costs at Rochester declined to $4.07/oz in 1998 from $4.36/oz. in 1997; total costs declined to $4.67/oz. from $5.03/oz.

CDE's 80%-owned Golden Cross mine (New Zealand) produced 15,858 oz. of gold and 49,536 oz. of silver in 1998, versus 83,110 oz. of gold and 217,776 oz. of silver in 1997, and 64,365 oz. of gold and 205,070 oz. of silver in 1996. Production at Golden Cross ceased in 1998's third quarter.

In January 1995, CDE, ASARCO Inc. and Callahan Mining formed Silver Valley Resources by combining their interests in the Galena and Coeur mines. Operations began in May 1996 and output totaled 833,267 oz. of silver at a $3.18/oz. cash cost. Production at the two mines totaled 1,760,815 oz. in 1998 versus 1,717,357 oz. in 1997.

CDE's Fachinal mine (Chile) became operational in November 1995. Fachinal mined 28,358 oz. of gold and 1,597,676 oz. of silver in 1998, versus 30,601 oz. of gold and 2,243,761 oz. of silver in 1997.

Per Share Data ($) (Year Ended Dec. 31)	1998	1997	1996	1995	1994	1993	1992	1991	1990	1989
Tangible Bk. Val.	2.89	13.99	15.31	11.49	10.29	11.14	11.81	12.01	13.86	12.04
Cash Flow	-10.32	0.50	-2.31	0.98	0.90	-0.03	0.30	-0.48	0.50	1.94
Earnings	-11.73	-1.12	-2.93	-0.08	-0.26	-0.87	-0.05	-0.94	-0.17	0.94
Dividends	Nil	Nil	0.15	0.15	0.15	0.15	0.15	0.15	0.15	0.15
Payout Ratio	Nil	Nil	NM	NM	NM	NM	NM	NM	NM	16%
Prices - High	13 5/8	18 3/8	25 3/4	21 5/8	23 1/2	24 5/8	18 3/8	23	31	24 1/8
- Low	4	7	13 1/4	14 1/2	14 3/8	9 7/8	10 7/8	13 3/8	13 3/8	15 1/2
P/E Ratio - High	NM	NM	NM	NM	NM	NM	NM	NM	NM	26
- Low	NM	NM	NM	NM	NM	NM	NM	NM	NM	16
Income Statement Analysis (Million $)										
Revs.	103	139	93.0	89.0	91.0	78.2	51.5	59.2	52.1	69.3
Oper. Inc.	13.2	10.7	2.5	16.1	13.5	5.4	-2.9	-1.3	5.6	15.9
Depr.	31.0	35.6	13.4	16.9	17.8	12.9	5.4	7.0	7.0	10.0
Int. Exp.	13.7	10.3	3.6	9.7	15.6	9.3	4.1	3.9	4.0	4.3
Pretax Inc.	-244	-14.3	-55.8	-1.1	-3.7	-16.7	-4.5	-15.0	-2.7	10.7
Eff. Tax Rate	NM	NM	NM	NM	NM	NM	NM	NM	NM	12%
Net Inc.	-245	-14.1	-54.6	-1.3	-3.9	-13.3	-0.8	-14.4	-1.7	9.4
Balance Sheet & Other Fin. Data (Million $)										
Cash	127	114	168	81.8	143	85.0	156	111	105	80.0
Curr. Assets	184	260	211	127	192	129	192	145	138	102
Total Assets	366	661	580	446	413	326	325	262	239	196
Curr. Liab.	30.6	38.5	32.0	21.0	18.5	21.6	9.8	14.2	9.9	9.5
LT Debt	246	290	190	174	227	129	131	58.0	60.0	61.0
Common Eqty.	70.0	315	339	240	160	171	181	184	166	120
Total Cap.	324	615	406	415	389	302	315	246	229	186
Cap. Exp.	3.2	2.9	4.8	44.9	33.3	68.6	21.5	16.7	17.9	12.7
Cash Flow	-225	11.0	-49.6	15.6	13.9	-0.4	4.7	-7.4	5.2	19.4
Curr. Ratio	6.0	6.8	6.6	6.0	10.4	6.0	19.5	10.3	13.9	10.8
% LT Debt of Cap.	76.2	47.2	46.8	42.0	58.4	42.8	41.6	23.5	26.0	33.0
% Net Inc.of Revs.	NM	NM	NM	NM	NM	NM	NM	NM	NM	13.6
% Ret. on Assets	NM	NM	NM	NM	NM	NM	NM	NM	NM	4.9
% Ret. on Equity	NM	NM	NM	NM	NM	NM	NM	NM	NM	8.1

Data as orig reptd.; bef. results of disc opers/spec. items. Per share data adj. for stk. divs. Bold denotes diluted EPS (FASB 128)-prior periods restated. E-Estimated. NA-Not Available. NM-Not Meaningful. NR-Not Ranked.

Office—P.O. Box I, Coeur d'Alene, ID 83816-0316. **Tel**—(208) 667-3511. **Fax**—(208) 667-2213. **Website**—http://www.coeur.com **Chrmn, Pres & CEO**—D. E. Wheeler. **SVP & COO**—M. L. Clark. **VP, CFO & Treas**—K. L. Packard. **Secy**—R. Gardner. **VP & Investor Contact**—Gordon Bigler. **Dirs**—C. D. Andrus, J. C. Bennett, J. J. Curran, D. B. Hagadone, J. A. McClure, J. H. Robinson, D. E. Wheeler. **Transfer Agent & Registrar**—ChaseMellon Shareholder Services, L.L.C., Ridgefield Park, NJ. **Incorporated**—in Idaho in 1928. **Empl**— 949. **S&P Analyst:** Leo J. Larkin

STANDARD
&POOR'S
STOCK REPORTS

Cognex Corp.

Nasdaq Symbol **CGNX**

In S&P SmallCap 600

09-OCT-99

Industry: Manufacturing (Specialized)

Summary: This company designs, develops, manufactures and markets machine vision systems used to gauge, guide, inspect and identify products in manufacturing operations.

S&P Opinion: Accumulate (★★★★) Recent Price • 30⅛ | 52 Wk Range • 35⅞-10¾ | Yield • Nil | 12-Mo. P/E • NM

Quantitative Evaluations

Outlook (1 Lowest—5 Highest) • 3

Fair Value • 31⅞

Risk • **Average**

Earn./Div. Rank • **B+**

Technical Eval. • **Bullish** since 9/99

Rel. Strength Rank (1 Lowest—99 Highest) • **49**

Insider Activity • **Neutral**

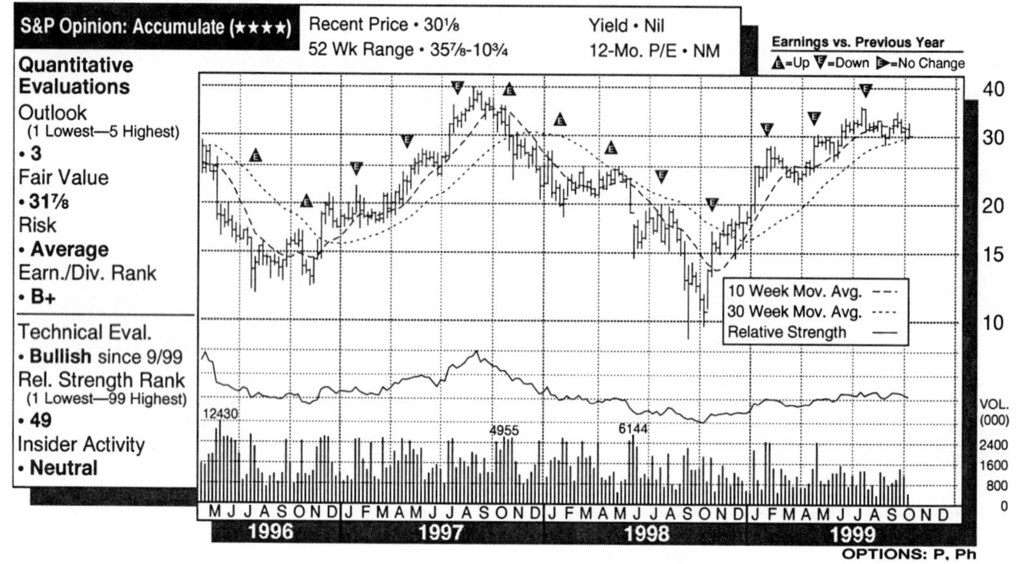

OPTIONS: P, Ph

Overview - 06-OCT-99

Look for the 1999 third quarter to keep up the year-over-year growth that resumed in the second quarter. In comparison to the third quarter of 1998, we expect revenues to rise more than 60%. Asia's recovery appears to be solid, and Japanese officials have expressed a commitment to see that the rebound in their economy does not stall. For all of 1999, we think revenues will increase 20% over 1998. This is higher than the 15% we were looking for at mid-year, reflecting our increasing optimism. We think strong growth will continue in 2000, with revenues rising 30%-35%. Margins are likely to continue to improve to the historical pre-1998 range of 24%-26%. We have raised our EPS estimates sharply in line with our growing confidence in the global economic recovery.

Valuation - 06-OCT-99

We rate the shares accumulate. The semiconductor and electronics industries, the two biggest sources of demand for Cognex, are experiencing robust growth after a difficult two years precipitated by the Asian economic crisis. This in turn is leading to increased capital spending on new equipment. Whereas in the first half of 1999, US. demand was the primary catalyst for the resumption in sales momentum for Cognex, foreign demand particularly throughout Asia is now augmenting domestic growth. The global recovery increasingly appears sustainable, despite continuing worries about weakness of the dollar and higher interest rates. Also, a weaker dollar generally makes U.S. goods more competitive overseas, and results in sales in foreign currencies being translated into more dollars. We think the stock can return to levels that reflect its historical premium valuation relative to the market, and retest its $40 all-time high in 1997.

Key Stock Statistics

S&P EPS Est. 1999	0.57	Tang. Bk. Value/Share	5.84
P/E on S&P Est. 1999	52.9	Beta	1.81
S&P EPS Est. 2000	1.15	Shareholders	17,000
Dividend Rate/Share	Nil	Market cap. (B)	$ 1.2
Shs. outstg. (M)	41.0	Inst. holdings	71%
Avg. daily vol. (M)	0.197		

Value of $10,000 invested 5 years ago: $ 40,847

Fiscal Year Ending Dec. 31

	1999	1998	1997	1996	1995	1994
Revenues (Million $)						
1Q	27.49	40.06	28.14	34.89	19.40	12.80
2Q	35.27	32.04	36.27	34.95	23.70	15.00
3Q	—	24.66	43.94	26.54	29.78	16.60
4Q	—	25.09	46.99	26.47	31.60	18.10
Yr.	—	121.8	155.3	122.8	104.5	62.50
Earnings Per Share ($)						
1Q	**0.07**	**0.24**	**0.15**	**0.25**	0.14	0.09
2Q	**0.14**	**0.15**	**0.21**	**0.23**	0.18	0.10
3Q	**E0.17**	**0.02**	**0.24**	**0.08**	-0.02	0.12
4Q	**E0.19**	**0.05**	**0.31**	**0.14**	0.25	0.13
Yr.	**E0.57**	**0.47**	**0.91**	**0.69**	**0.65**	**0.43**

Next earnings report expected: late October

Dividend Data

No cash dividends have been paid. The company intends to retain its earnings to finance the development and expansion of its business and does not anticipate paying cash dividends in the foreseeable future.

A Division of The McGraw-Hill Companies

Cognex Corporation

Business Summary - 06-OCT-99

Large scale manufacturing routinely involves repetitive tasks that are costly or time consuming for human beings to perform. Tasks as simple as determining if a label is affixed properly, or as complex as aligning a semiconductor, would require vast amounts of labor if performed manually. Cognex Corp. designs, develops, manufactures and markets a family of machine vision systems that replace human vision in a wide range of manufacturing processes. These systems use specialized cameras to capture an image of an object during the manufacturing process. Sophisticated image analysis software then extracts information about the object, such as "what is it?" or "where is it?"

The company's strategy is to expand its position as a leading worldwide supplier of machine vision systems for factory automation. Cognex believes this market offers the greatest opportunity for selling high value-added products in large volumes. In July 1998, Cognex took a major step to increase its share of the global machine vision market by acquiring for cash certain technologies of the Allen Bradley machine vision business of Rockwell Automation, one of its largest competitors. The company also entered into a global relationship with Rockwell Automation under which it is the preferred supplier of machine vision products to Rockwell's customers worldwide.

The company's machine vision systems consist of hardware and software designed to give customers the flexibility to easily configure complete vision solutions without requiring extensive in-house expertise in image processing or analysis. Prior to 1998, all Cognex machine vision systems ran on proprietary hardware systems, but in 1998, the company introduced the MVS-8000 family of systems, based on Intel microprocessors. Among recent advances in software, PatMax pattern location software has been enthusiastically received by customers in many industries, notably for robotic guidance applications, a relatively new area for Cognex.

Machine vision systems sold by the company are defined as either general-purpose or application-specific products. General-purpose machine vision products let customers solve a wide range of problems. Customers select the tools necessary to solve their vision problem from the company's vision software library, and configure their solutions either by writing a C-language program or by using a graphical user interface. Application-specific machine vision products are packaged combinations of software and hardware, designed to solve targeted problems without customization by the company or its customers.

Principal customers are original equipment manufacturers in the electronics and semiconductor industries; system integrators that create complete, automated inspection systems for end users on the factory floor; and the end users themselves -- companies that manufacture a diverse array of products such as radios, phones and ball-point pens. International sales, mostly to Japan and Europe, accounted for 63% of total revenues in 1998 (62% in 1997).

Per Share Data ($) (Year Ended Dec. 31)	1998	1997	1996	1995	1994	1993	1992	1991	1990	1989
Tangible Bk. Val.	5.55	5.66	4.47	3.85	2.77	1.62	1.24	1.08	0.73	0.47
Cash Flow	0.63	1.04	0.81	0.63	0.48	0.35	0.20	0.29	0.20	0.14
Earnings	0.47	0.91	0.69	0.55	0.43	0.32	0.17	0.27	0.19	0.13
Dividends	Nil	Nil	Nil	Nil	Nil	Nil	Nil	Nil	Nil	Nil
Payout Ratio	Nil	Nil	Nil	Nil	Nil	Nil	Nil	Nil	Nil	Nil
Prices - High	$27\frac{3}{8}$	$39\frac{7}{8}$	35	$38\frac{1}{2}$	14	$8\frac{7}{8}$	$7\frac{1}{2}$	$8\frac{1}{4}$	$4\frac{1}{4}$	$2\frac{5}{8}$
- Low	9	$17\frac{1}{4}$	$11\frac{3}{4}$	$10\frac{1}{2}$	$5\frac{7}{8}$	$4\frac{5}{8}$	$2\frac{3}{8}$	$3\frac{1}{4}$	$1\frac{11}{16}$	$1\frac{1}{4}$
P/E Ratio - High	58	44	51	70	32	28	43	31	22	22
- Low	19	19	17	19	14	15	14	12	9	10
Income Statement Analysis (Million $)										
Revs.	122	155	123	105	62.5	43.4	28.6	31.5	23.6	15.9
Oper. Inc.	27.0	60.6	43.4	48.0	23.6	16.0	8.2	13.3	9.2	5.0
Depr.	7.2	5.8	5.1	3.2	1.8	1.3	0.9	0.7	0.5	0.4
Int. Exp.	Nil	Nil	Nil	Nil	Nil	Nil	Nil	Nil	Nil	Nil
Pretax Inc.	27.3	58.3	43.7	37.6	23.3	16.0	8.4	14.0	10.0	5.2
Eff. Tax Rate	26%	31%	31%	39%	31%	30%	28%	32%	35%	28%
Net Inc.	20.2	40.5	30.4	23.0	16.1	11.1	6.1	9.5	6.5	3.7
Balance Sheet & Other Fin. Data (Million $)										
Cash	158	178	134	90.6	81.5	44.6	37.5	33.5	20.7	14.1
Curr. Assets	207	224	169	136	97.7	57.4	45.0	39.4	25.2	16.9
Total Assets	248	262	201	162	113	61.0	48.0	42.0	28.0	18.0
Curr. Liab.	22.9	24.4	17.0	16.4	9.2	5.8	6.9	5.3	3.9	3.8
LT Debt	Nil	Nil	Nil	Nil	Nil	Nil	Nil	Nil	Nil	Nil
Common Eqty.	223	236	183	144	104	55.0	41.0	36.0	24.0	14.0
Total Cap.	223	236	183	144	104	55.0	41.0	36.0	24.0	14.0
Cap. Exp.	7.2	10.9	10.2	10.5	13.1	1.8	1.5	1.1	1.1	1.0
Cash Flow	27.4	46.3	35.5	26.2	17.8	12.4	7.0	10.2	7.0	4.1
Curr. Ratio	9.0	9.2	9.9	8.3	10.6	10.0	6.5	7.5	6.5	4.5
% LT Debt of Cap.	Nil	Nil	Nil	Nil	NM	NM	NM	NM	NM	NM
% Net Inc.of Revs.	16.6	26.1	24.7	22.0	25.7	25.7	21.3	30.1	27.7	23.4
% Ret. on Assets	7.9	17.5	16.7	16.7	17.9	20.3	13.7	26.9	27.6	NA
% Ret. on Equity	8.8	19.3	18.6	18.6	19.6	23.0	15.8	31.1	33.3	NA

Data as orig reptd.; bef. results of disc opers/spec. items. Per share data adj. for stk. divs. Bold denotes diluted EPS (FASB 128)-prior periods restated. E-Estimated. NA-Not Available. NM-Not Meaningful. NR-Not Ranked.

Office—One Vision Dr., Natick, MA 01760-2059. **Tel**—(508) 650-3000. **Website**—http://www.cognex.com **Chrmn, Pres & CEO**—R. J. Shillman. **CFO**—R. A. Morin. **EVP**—P. Alias. **Dirs**—J. G. Fishman, W. A. Krivsky, R. J. Shillman, A. Sun, R. Wasserman. **Transfer Agent**—Bank Boston, N.A. **Incorporated**—in Massachusetts in 1981. **Empl**— 575. **S&P Analyst:** Mark Basham

STANDARD
&POOR'S
STOCK REPORTS

Coherent, Inc.

Nasdaq Symbol **COHR**

In S&P SmallCap 600

09-OCT-99

Industry:
Electronics (Instrumentation)

Summary: This company is a leading manufacturer of products based on laser, optics and microelectronic technologies for medical, scientific and telecommunications markets.

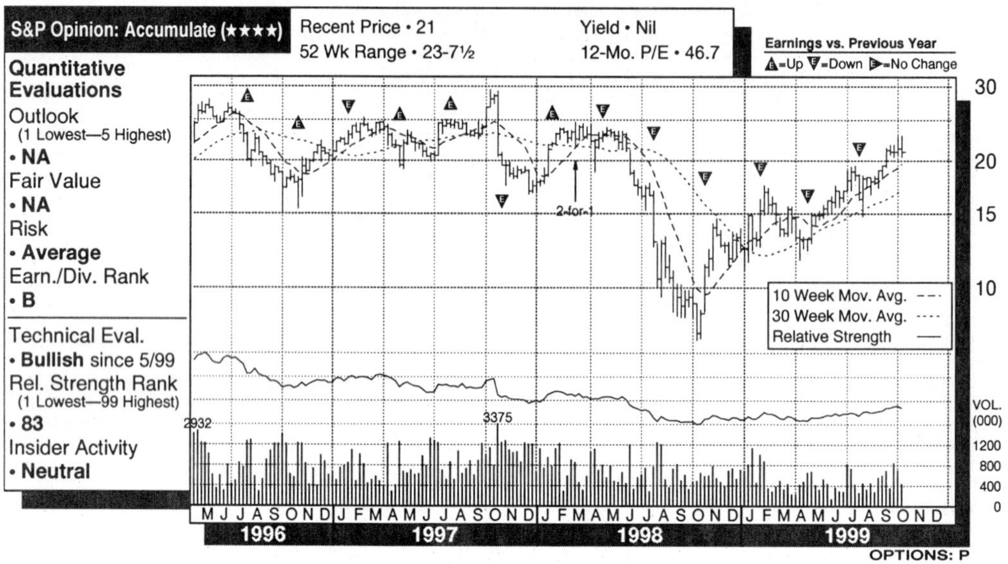

Overview - 28-JUL-99

We expect revenues to grow at a 15%-17% pace for the foreseeable future, driven by strength in the hair removal business, which reflects the April 1999 acquisition of Star Medical Technologies. In addition, a rebound in the global semiconductor industry is expected to fuel strong growth in COHR's semiconductor-related products. Margins should widen, reflecting SG&A expense leverage, well controlled R&D spending and an anticipated return to profitability in the medical segment. The company's medical division, which has performed poorly for several quarters, is expected to slowly show signs of improvement, aided by the recent hiring of a unit president. We currently see FY 99 (Sep.) operating earnings rising 29%, to $0.88, from 1998's $0.68 (excludes a special gain of $0.11). We expect EPS to jump 23%, to $1.08, in FY 00.

Valuation - 28-JUL-99

The shares have rebounded since October 1998, reflecting an improved earnings outlook, and were recently trading at about 17X our calendar 1999 EPS estimate of $0.95 (14X our calendar 2000 estimate of $1.13), representing a discount to the P/E multiple of the broader markets. As a result, we continue to recommend that investors accumulate the shares. After a poor performance in the third quarter of FY 98, COHR has since posted solid results, fueled by cost controls, a rebound in the semiconductor market and efforts to improve its ailing medical segment. We are very encouraged by the results at recently acquired Star Medical Technologies, which should provide a major stimulus to the top line. In addition, we expect COHR to improve its already healthy balance sheet through increased focus on cash collections.

Key Stock Statistics

S&P EPS Est. 1999	0.88	Tang. Bk. Value/Share	9.40
P/E on S&P Est. 1999	23.9	Beta	1.49
S&P EPS Est. 2000	1.08	Shareholders	2,118
Dividend Rate/Share	Nil	Market cap. (B)	$0.505
Shs. outstg. (M)	24.1	Inst. holdings	67%
Avg. daily vol. (M)	0.116		

Value of $10,000 invested 5 years ago: $ 32,941

Fiscal Year Ending Sep. 30

	1999	1998	1997	1996	1995	1994
Revenues (Million $)						
1Q	105.6	101.4	93.89	83.68	58.58	47.03
2Q	116.5	105.9	90.99	90.55	66.46	55.22
3Q	115.0	98.55	102.3	89.33	76.25	55.26
4Q	—	104.7	103.8	100.9	84.21	57.87
Yr.	—	410.4	391.0	364.4	285.5	215.4
Earnings Per Share ($)						
1Q	**0.18**	**0.32**	-0.03	0.28	0.17	0.07
2Q	**0.22**	**0.29**	0.38	0.32	0.20	0.14
3Q	**-0.24**	**-0.07**	0.48	0.34	0.23	0.14
4Q	—	**0.26**	0.28	0.37	0.28	0.14
Yr.	—	**0.79**	**1.12**	**1.31**	0.88	0.50

Next earnings report expected: late October

Dividend Data

The company does not expect to pay cash dividends.

Coherent, Inc.

Business Summary - 28-JUL-99

Coherent (COHR) is a leading maker of electro-optical systems and medical instruments using laser, precision optic and microelectronic technologies, is focused on laser product innovations. For the past several years, the company has committed from 10% to 11% of annual revenues to R&D efforts, and today has about 200 U.S. patents in force. International sales accounted for 55% of the total in each of the last two fiscal years (Sep.).

The company currently produces more than 150 lasers, laser systems, precision optics and component products. Medical products range in price from $25,000 to $500,000. Scientific products range from $10,000 to $450,000. Component products sell for between $500 and $50,000, and include semiconductor lasers, precision optics, thin film coatings, accessories, laser measurement and testing instruments.

COHR operates through two key product segments: electro-optical products and medical products. Electro-optical products (62% of FY 98 revenues) include lasers and laser systems for scientific, medical research, micromachining, commercial applications, semiconductor inspection, precision optics and related accessories. These lasers have a broad range of power and operate in the visible (V), ultraviolet (UV) and infrared (IR) portions of the electromagnetic spectrum. Coherent's optics and optical products include special-purpose lenses, mirrors and advanced optical coatings.

Medical products (38% of revenues) consist of a broad line of surgical laser systems used in ophthalmology, gynecology, urology, dermatology, plastic surgery, aesthetic surgery, orthopedic surgery and many other medical specialties. These lasers are designed to improve the quality of patient care, frequently decreasing overall treatment costs compared with conventional procedures. Most of the products also make it possible to perform treatments in a doctor's office, a surgery center, or an outpatient center in a hospital, instead of requiring inpatient hospitalization.

In FY 97, COHR entered the telecommunications market and expanded its semiconductor laser capabilities with the acquisition of Micracor, Inc., and the purchase of an 80% interest in Tutcore, OY, Ltd. It expanded its precision optics capability and enhanced its product line with the acquisition of Ealing Electro-Optics. It also entered the laser hair removal market through a partnering agreement with Palomar Medical Technologies. In April 1999, the company completed the acquisition of Palomar's Star Medical Technologies unit for $65 million in cash. Star is the only company with FDA approval for a diode-based laser hair removal product. The company expects to record a charge of $0.44 a share in the FY 99 (Sep.) third quarter related to the acquisition.

Per Share Data ($) (Year Ended Sep. 30)	1998	1997	1996	1995	1994	1993	1992	1991	1990	1989
Tangible Bk. Val.	10.58	9.51	8.34	6.95	6.21	5.66	5.11	4.95	5.00	4.86
Cash Flow	1.52	1.75	1.94	1.28	0.88	0.82	0.55	0.45	0.40	0.87
Earnings	0.79	1.12	1.31	0.88	0.50	0.47	0.14	0.01	-0.03	0.47
Dividends	Nil	Nil	Nil	Nil	Nil	Nil	Nil	Nil	Nil	Nil
Payout Ratio	Nil	Nil	Nil	Nil	Nil	Nil	Nil	Nil	Nil	Nil
Prices - High	$24\frac{3}{4}$	$29\frac{1}{2}$	28	$22\frac{1}{4}$	$8\frac{3}{4}$	$8\frac{1}{8}$	$8\frac{1}{4}$	$8\frac{3}{4}$	$7\frac{1}{2}$	$9\frac{7}{8}$
- Low	$7\frac{1}{2}$	$16\frac{5}{8}$	$15\frac{1}{8}$	$8\frac{1}{4}$	$5\frac{3}{4}$	$5\frac{1}{8}$	$3\frac{7}{8}$	$4\frac{1}{4}$	$3\frac{5}{8}$	$4\frac{7}{8}$
P/E Ratio - High	31	26	21	25	18	17	59	NM	NM	21
- Low	9	15	11	9	11	11	28	NM	NM	10
Income Statement Analysis (Million $)										
Revs.	410	391	364	285	215	197	215	208	191	202
Oper. Inc.	41.3	56.9	57.1	38.9	24.2	21.2	13.3	10.2	10.7	19.7
Depr.	17.2	14.6	12.4	9.0	7.9	7.3	7.9	8.2	7.7	7.3
Int. Exp.	1.2	1.2	Nil	1.1	1.9	2.0	1.8	1.3	1.2	1.4
Pretax Inc.	24.6	48.1	50.1	32.1	16.9	13.9	5.9	3.5	4.6	18.4
Eff. Tax Rate	20%	43%	39%	39%	38%	35%	47%	82%	91%	48%
Net Inc.	18.8	26.3	30.3	19.3	10.3	9.3	2.6	0.2	-0.4	8.6
Balance Sheet & Other Fin. Data (Million $)										
Cash	15.9	21.5	34.6	44.7	43.8	37.1	29.7	16.3	24.2	21.6
Curr. Assets	273	255	218	185	156	144	141	130	123	121
Total Assets	391	362	231	256	212	194	188	169	164	162
Curr. Liab.	99	102	94.9	78.2	58.6	56.0	62.9	55.5	52.3	51.9
LT Debt	12.8	9.7	3.9	5.1	8.9	14.1	15.6	6.6	7.0	6.3
Common Eqty.	263	231	198	161	133	117	103	97.0	96.0	95.0
Total Cap.	279	249	202	173	148	136	125	112	110	108
Cap. Exp.	22.4	24.9	24.9	8.4	10.7	12.7	15.7	7.0	6.9	6.1
Cash Flow	36.0	40.9	42.7	28.3	18.2	16.6	10.6	8.4	7.2	15.8
Curr. Ratio	2.8	2.5	2.3	2.4	2.7	2.6	2.2	2.3	2.3	2.3
% LT Debt of Cap.	4.6	3.9	2.0	3.0	6.0	10.3	12.4	5.9	6.3	5.8
% Net Inc.of Revs.	4.6	6.7	8.3	6.8	4.8	4.7	1.2	0.1	NM	4.2
% Ret. on Assets	5.0	7.8	10.7	8.3	5.1	4.8	1.5	0.1	NM	5.3
% Ret. on Equity	7.6	12.3	16.9	13.1	8.1	8.3	2.6	0.2	NM	9.4

Data as orig reptd.; bef. results of disc opers/spec. items. Per share data adj. for stk. divs. Bold denotes diluted EPS (FASB 128)-prior periods restated. E-Estimated. NA-Not Available. NM-Not Meaningful. NR-Not Ranked.

Office—5100 Patrick Henry Dr., Santa Clara, CA 95054. **Tel**—(408) 764-4000. **Fax**—(408) 764-4800. **Website**—http://www.cohr.com **Chrmn**—H. E. Gauthier. **Pres & CEO**—B. J. Couillaud. **EVP-CFO**—Robert J. Quillinan. **Treas**—D. C. Bucek. **Secy**—L. W. Sonsini. **Investor Contact**—Peter Schuman (408-764-4174). **Dirs**—C. W. Cantoni, F. Carrubba, B. J. Couillaud, H. E. Gauthier, T. S. Nelsen, J. E. Robertson. **Transfer Agent & Registrar**—EquiServe, Boston, MA.**Incorporated**—in California in 1966; reincorporated in Delaware in 1990. **Empl**— 2,396. **S&P Analyst:** Stephen J. Tekirian

STANDARD
&POOR'S
STOCK REPORTS

Commerce Bancorp (N.J.)

NYSE Symbol **CBH**

In S&P SmallCap 600

09-OCT-99

Industry: Banks (Regional)

Summary: This multibank holding company operates a network of branch offices serving New Jersey, Southeastern Philadelphia and Delaware.

Quantitative Evaluations

Outlook (1 Lowest—5 Highest)
• **1-**

Fair Value
• **39⅜**

Risk
• **Low**

Earn./Div. Rank
• **A**

Technical Eval.
• **Bearish** since 9/99

Rel. Strength Rank (1 Lowest—99 Highest)
• **65**

Insider Activity
• **Unfavorable**

Recent Price • 42½
52 Wk Range • 50½-34¼
Yield • 2.1%
12-Mo. P/E • 19.9

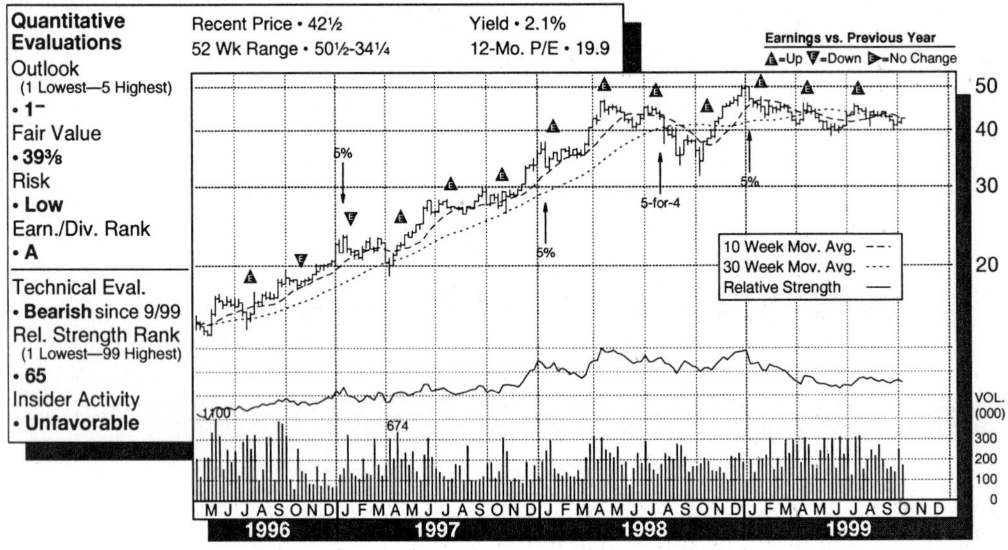

Business Profile - 16-JUN-99

In March 1999, CBH stated that its goals for 1999 included: construction of 25 to 30 new offices in New Jersey and southeastern Pennsylvania, expansion into Delaware, and growth targets of 15% for earnings and 20% for total assets. CBH also noted that its goals over the next five years are to grow assets to $11 billion, to increase the number of banking offices from 100 to 200, to achieve an increase of 15% annually in net income per share, and to increase its return on equity to 20%. In January 1999, CBH acquired New Jersey-based Prestige State Bank, with $328 million in assets and seven branches, and New Jersey-based Tinton Falls State Bank, with $201 million in assets and six branches.

Operational Review - 16-JUN-99

Net interest income advanced 24% in the three months ended March 31, 1999, year to year, mainly attributable to volume increases in the loan and investment portfolios. While non-interest income increased 29%, reflecting higher revenue from service charges on deposits and CBH's insurance and capital markets subsidiaries, non-interest expense rose 28%, due mainly to new branch activity and the expansion of CBH's insurance and capital markets subsidiaries. After taxes at 33.4%, versus 35.3%, net income climbed 21% to $15.5 million ($0.54 per share), from $12.8 million ($0.46).

Stock Performance - 08-OCT-99

In the past 30 trading days, CBH's shares have declined 1%, compared to a 0.91% fall in the S&P 500. Average trading volume for the past five days was 33,940 shares, compared with the 40-day moving average of 39,641 shares.

Key Stock Statistics

Dividend Rate/Share	0.88	Shareholders	15,000
Shs. outstg. (M)	27.8	Market cap. (B)	$ 1.2
Avg. daily vol. (M)	0.036	Inst. holdings	32%
Tang. Bk. Value/Share	12.50		
Beta	1.01		

Value of $10,000 invested 5 years ago: $ 50,857

Fiscal Year Ending Dec. 31

	1999	1998	1997	1996	1995	1994
Revenues (Million $)						
1Q	114.9	87.78	68.29	48.33	45.01	38.74
2Q	121.0	92.27	72.72	50.08	46.41	40.78
3Q	—	97.25	79.69	52.79	47.04	43.33
4Q	—	100.9	80.85	58.18	48.55	42.68
Yr.	—	378.2	301.6	209.4	187.0	165.5
Earnings Per Share ($)						
1Q	**0.54**	**0.46**	**0.40**	**0.34**	0.34	0.35
2Q	**0.56**	**0.49**	**0.43**	**0.35**	0.35	0.40
3Q	—	**0.50**	**0.44**	**0.33**	0.36	0.41
4Q	—	**0.52**	**0.44**	**0.28**	0.36	0.34
Yr.	—	**1.98**	**1.71**	**1.30**	**1.28**	**1.20**

Next earnings report expected: mid October

Dividend Data (Dividends have been paid since 1984.)

Amount ($)	Date Decl.	Ex-Div. Date	Stock of Record	Payment Date
5%	Dec. 16	Jan. 05	Jan. 07	Jan. 21 '99
0.220	Jun. 22	Jul. 07	Jul. 09	Jul. 20 '99
0.220	Sep. 21	Oct. 04	Oct. 06	Oct. 20 '99

Commerce Bancorp, Inc. (N.J.)

Business Summary - 16-JUN-99

Commerce Bancorp celebrated its 25th anniversary in 1998. Through acquisitions and internal growth, this $5.6 billion New Jersey-based bank holding company continues toward its goal of 200 offices and $11.0 billion in assets by the end of 2003. At year-end 1998, Commerce Bancorp operated 96 offices through four banking subsidiaries: Commerce NJ ($3.0 billion in assets, 43 offices), Commerce Shore ($512.1 million, 13 offices), Commerce PA ($806.9 million, 18 offices) and Commerce North ($600.3 million, 10 offices). A fifth subsidiary, Commerce Central, was created in early 1999 in conjunction with the acquisition of Prestige State Bank, which operated seven branches. Additionally, the company provides regional insurance brokerage through Commerce Insurance and securities dealer services through Commerce Capital Markets.

Traditionally, banks derive the majority of their revenue from interest on loans. CBH's loan portfolio, totaling $1.93 billion at year-end 1998, was divided in recent years: commercial real estate 37% (down from 40% in 1997), commercial 19% (18%), residential 16% (12%), and consumer 28% (30%).

At year-end 1998, Commerce's allowance for loan losses represented 1.37% of loans outstanding, down from 1.51% a year earlier. Net charge-offs fell to only 0.04% of average loans in 1998, versus 0.10% a year earlier.

Recent performance has been aided by strong growth in deposits, which are the main (and most cost effective) source of funds to the bank. Averaging $3.9 billion during 1998 ($3.2 billion in 1997), total deposits were apportioned: interest-bearing demand 33%, non-interest-bearing demand 21%, savings 20% and time 26%.

Lending profitability, commonly measured by the yield on a bank's average earning assets, or the net interest margin, is affected by changes in the volume and mix of assets and liabilities, as well as changes in interest rates. CBH's net interest margin narrowed to 4.33% in 1998, from 4.51% a year earlier, as a drop in lending yields more than offset a slight decline in the cost of funds.

In 1997, Commerce continued to grow through acquisitions, adding Independence Bancorp in northern New Jersey and announcing an agreement to acquire A. H. Williams & Co., a Philadelphia-based public finance company (completed in 1998).

In January 1999, Commerce continued its acquisition strategy, acquiring New Jersey-based Tinton Falls Savings Bank, with $201 million in assets and six branches and Prestige State Bank, with $328 million in assets and seven branches.

Per Share Data ($) (Year Ended Dec. 31)	1998	1997	1996	1995	1994	1993	1992	1991	1990	1989
Tangible Bk. Val.	12.50	11.31	9.86	9.27	7.24	6.31	6.86	6.60	7.09	7.31
Earnings	1.98	1.71	1.51	1.40	1.50	1.14	0.89	0.58	0.38	0.85
Dividends	0.92	0.61	0.48	0.43	0.39	0.30	0.26	0.24	0.46	0.41
Payout Ratio	46%	34%	32%	30%	26%	26%	29%	41%	123%	47%
Prices - High	50½	37⅝	23	16⅞	14⅞	11¼	8¾	5⅝	7	8⅝
- Low	31⅝	19	13⅞	10¼	9¼	8½	5	2⅞	3¼	5⅝
P/E Ratio - High	25	21	15	12	10	10	10	10	19	10
- Low	16	11	9	7	6	7	6	5	9	7
Income Statement Analysis (Million $)										
Net Int. Inc.	174	147	109	95.3	90.5	69.7	51.5	38.4	36.0	32.3
Tax Equiv. Adj.	2.4	1.4	0.9	0.4	0.4	0.5	0.6	0.8	1.2	1.6
Non Int. Inc.	86.0	55.1	30.0	21.4	16.9	14.4	12.1	10.0	8.7	6.5
Loan Loss Prov.	5.9	4.7	3.0	2.2	4.2	6.0	6.3	5.5	5.1	1.4
Exp./Op. Revs.	69%	68%	70%	66%	67%	68%	67%	79%	76%	75%
Pretax Inc.	74.8	61.9	41.5	36.9	32.0	23.2	14.4	8.0	5.3	7.8
Eff. Tax Rate	34%	35%	36%	36%	36%	37%	31%	25%	19%	17%
Net Inc.	49.3	40.3	26.6	23.5	20.4	14.6	10.0	6.0	4.3	6.5
% Net Int. Marg.	4.38	4.55	4.63	4.49	4.40	4.40	4.50	4.40	5.10	5.30
Balance Sheet & Other Fin. Data (Million $)										
Money Mkt. Assets	85.4	168	173	177	129	106	137	88.0	147	86.0
Inv. Securities	2,411	2,197	1,449	1,203	1,264	1,091	603	343	187	140
Com'l Loans	367	254	661	572	514	469	419	391	333	304
Other Loans	1,564	1,157	435	336	288	232	202	188	221	212
Total Assets	4,894	3,939	2,862	2,416	2,291	2,033	1,426	1,058	934	786
Demand Deposits	1,037	763	1,303	1,097	878	763	550	451	420	343
Time Deposits	3,398	2,607	1,271	1,128	957	982	786	536	447	381
LT Debt	80.5	23.0	26.3	27.4	28.4	29.0	6.5	7.3	8.2	0.7
Common Eqty.	302	248	181	162	104	78.2	81.9	58.2	54.3	55.9
% Ret. on Assets	1.1	1.2	1.0	1.0	0.9	0.8	0.8	0.6	0.5	0.9
% Ret. on Equity	17.9	18.6	15.5	16.7	19.4	16.5	14.4	11.0	7.7	15.2
% Loan Loss Resv.	1.4	1.5	1.4	1.5	1.5	1.4	1.4	1.5	1.2	0.7
% Loans/Deposits	43.5	39.9	42.1	40.8	42.0	40.2	46.5	58.6	63.9	71.3
% Equity to Assets	6.2	6.3	6.5	5.8	4.9	4.0	5.6	5.5	6.7	5.9

Data as orig reptd.; bef. results of disc opers/spec. items. Per share data adj. for stk. divs. Bold denotes diluted EPS (FASB 128)-prior periods restated. E-Estimated. NA-Not Available. NM-Not Meaningful. NR-Not Ranked.

Office—Commerce Atrium, 1701 Route 70 East, Cherry Hill, NJ 08034-5400. **Tel**—(609) 751-9000. **Website**—www.commerceonline.com **Chrmn & Pres**—V. W. Hill II. **EVP & Investor Contact**—C. Edward Jordan, Jr. **CFO**—T. J. Sukay. **Secy**—R. C. Beck. **Dirs**—D. Baird IV, R. C. Beck, J. R. Bershad, J. Buckelew, V. W. Hill II, C. E. Jordan, Jr., M. N. Kerr, S. M. Lewis, D. J. Ragone, W. A. Schwartz, Jr., J. T. Tarquini, Jr., F. C. Videon, Sr. **Transfer Agent & Registrar**—ChaseMellon Shareholder Services, Ridgefield Park, NJ. **Incorporated**—in New Jersey in 1982. **Empl**— 2,777. **S&P Analyst:** J. Rudy

Commercial Federal

NYSE Symbol **CFB**

In S&P SmallCap 600

09-OCT-99

Industry: Banks (Regional)

Summary: Through its principal subsidiary, Commercial Federal Bank, this company conducts banking operations primarily in Iowa, Kansas, Nebraska and Colorado.

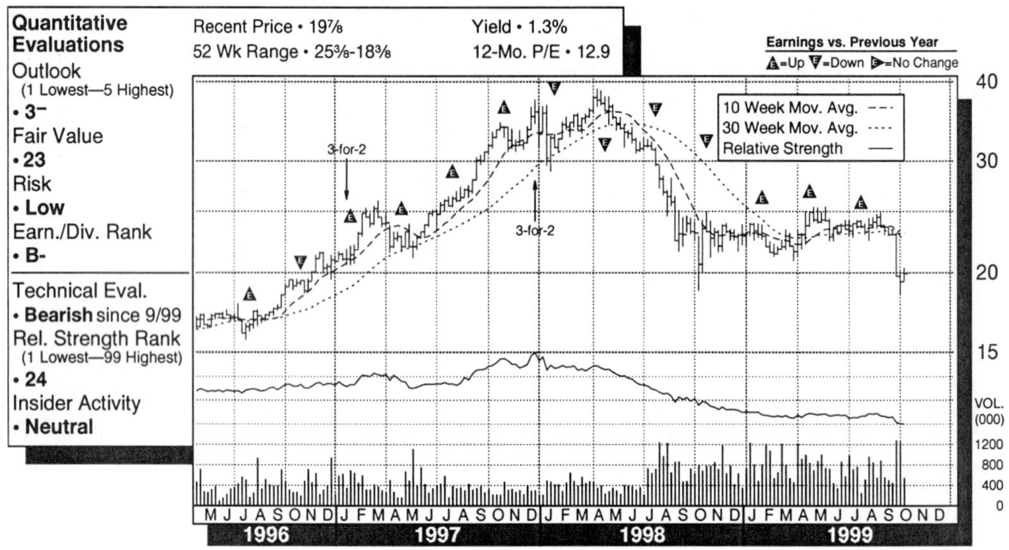

Business Profile - 15-SEP-99

In April 1999, CFB stated that it was positioned to re-emphasize building its fee income and evaluating its operating expenses now that the company has consolidated seven companies and installed its Y2K platform computer systems. CFB also announced in April 1999 a stock repurchase program of up to 5% of the company's stock over the next 18 months. In March 1999, Commercial Federal acquired Midland First Financial Corp., a Missouri-based commercial bank with $413 million in assets and eight branches. The total purchase consideration was $83 million in cash, which included $17 million to pay off certain Midland debt.

Operational Review - 15-SEP-99

Based on a brief preliminary report, net interest income for FY 99 (Jun.) rose 20% from that of the prior year, due to growth in interest-earning assets resulting from recent acquisitions. Following $27.1 million in after-tax merger-related and other charges, net income increased 5.7%, to $92.4 million ($1.54 a share), from $87.4 million ($1.52).

Stock Performance - 08-OCT-99

In the past 30 trading days, CFB's shares have declined 16%, compared to a 0.91% fall in the S&P 500. Average trading volume for the past five days was 107,460 shares, compared with the 40-day moving average of 185,308 shares.

Key Stock Statistics

Dividend Rate/Share	0.26	Shareholders	2,700
Shs. outstg. (M)	60.6	Market cap. (B)	$ 1.2
Avg. daily vol. (M)	0.239	Inst. holdings	58%
Tang. Bk. Value/Share	13.54		
Beta	1.00		

Value of $10,000 invested 5 years ago: $ 23,457

Fiscal Year Ending Jun. 30

	1999	1998	1997	1996	1995	1994
Revenues (Million $)						
1Q	225.8	148.5	136.4	120.6	106.1	97.36
2Q	231.7	151.3	142.5	134.3	111.4	90.47
3Q	239.7	174.2	148.5	135.6	113.7	99.2
4Q	—	262.0	144.4	150.2	118.3	93.53
Yr.	—	735.9	563.5	540.7	449.5	397.8
Earnings Per Share ($)						
1Q	**0.25**	**0.51**	-0.12	0.34	0.02	0.29
2Q	**0.52**	**0.47**	0.47	0.36	0.04	0.31
3Q	**0.27**	**0.21**	0.49	0.48	0.46	0.33
4Q	**0.49**	**0.43**	0.52	0.46	0.42	-1.13
Yr.	**1.54**	**1.62**	**1.35**	**1.59**	0.94	-0.20

Next earnings report expected: late October

Dividend Data (Dividends have been paid since 1995.)

Amount ($)	Date Decl.	Ex-Div. Date	Stock of Record	Payment Date
0.065	Nov. 17	Dec. 28	Dec. 30	Jan. 14 '99
0.065	Feb. 10	Mar. 26	Mar. 30	Apr. 14 '99
0.065	Jun. 09	Jun. 24	Jun. 28	Jul. 14 '99
0.065	Sep. 15	Sep. 27	Sep. 29	Oct. 14 '99

A Division of The McGraw-Hill Companies

Commercial Federal Corporation

Business Summary - 15-SEP-99

Nebraska-based Commercial Federal Corporation, a bank holding company, was incorporated in 1983. At March 31, 1999, the corporation had assets of $12.9 billion. CFB operated 254 branches in Iowa, Kansas, Nebraska, Colorado, Oklahoma, Missouri, Arizona, Minnesota, and South Dakota.

CFB's primary subsidiary is Commercial Federal Bank, a federal savings bank originally chartered in 1887 and which converted from mutual to stock ownership in December 1994. Mainly through acquisitions, the bank has been evolving from a thrift institution into a community banking institution offering a wide array of services. In January 1998, the company acquired First National Bank Shares, Ltd. of Great Bend, Kansas with seven branches and $148 million in assets. In February 1998, CFB acquired Iowa-based Liberty Financial Corp. with 45 branches and $658 million in assets. Also in February 1998, the company acquired Kansas-based Mid Continent Bancshares, Inc. with ten branches and $406 million in assets. In May 1998, the company acquired Iowa-based Perpetual Midwest Financial, Inc. with five branches and $412 million in assets. These acquisitions have allowed the bank to offer commercial and agricultural loans, business checking, equipment leasing, mortgage banking, trust and investment services. Not only has CFB added to traditional services but to locations as well. The company has established branches in non-traditional locations such as supermarkets and convenience stores. To offer more conveniences to retail customers, CFB has also installed more ATM outlets and expanded services in telephone and PC banking. All mortgage banking is handled by Commercial Federal Mortgage Corporation, a wholly owned subsidiary, and through a nationwide correspondent network of mortgage loan originators

CFB's strategy for growth emphasizes both external and internal growth. The company's retail strategy is to market its multiple products and services to new and existing customers. In tandem, CFB plans to expand its existing branches and open new ones. In fiscal 1998, CFB acquired four institutions, continuing its strategy of external growth through selective acquisitions. The company selects acquisition candidates based on the extent to which they can enhance CFB's retail presence in both new and underserved markets.

Apart from CFB's efforts to diversify, loans and leases remained as the company's main revenue source at 72% of total income for the fiscal year ended June 1998. General and administrative expenses were up sharply at 22% (before Federal deposit insurance special assessment in FY 1997) due to acquisition related costs.

In July 1998, CFB acquired Iowa-based Amerus Bank, with $1.3 billion in assets. In August 1998, CFB acquired Colorado-based First Colorado Bancorp, a unitary savings and loan company with $1.6 billion in assets.

Per Share Data ($) (Year Ended Jun. 30)	1999	1998	1997	1996	1995	1994	1993	1992	1991	1990
Tangible Bk. Val.	NA	13.54	12.67	10.97	9.49	7.38	6.68	5.73	3.45	1.22
Earnings	1.54	1.62	1.36	1.66	0.94	-0.20	1.08	2.24	0.53	-2.05
Dividends	0.25	0.21	0.19	0.18	Nil	Nil	Nil	Nil	Nil	Nil
Payout Ratio	16%	13%	14%	11%	Nil	Nil	Nil	Nil	Nil	Nil
Prices - High	25 3/8	39	37 1/2	21 1/2	17	12 3/8	12 5/8	8 1/8	2 3/4	1 3/4
- Low	18 3/8	18 3/4	20 5/8	15 3/8	9	7 3/4	7 1/4	2 1/4	1	3/4
P/E Ratio - High	17	24	28	13	18	NM	12	4	5	NM
- Low	12	12	15	9	10	NM	7	1	2	NM
Income Statement Analysis (Million $)										
Net Int. Inc.	NA	230	168	163	134	126	116	85.0	55.1	61.0
Loan Loss Prov.	NA	15.3	8.1	6.1	6.0	6.0	5.7	7.4	9.1	27.6
Non Int. Inc.	NA	85.8	58.5	49.6	37.6	32.3	23.3	68.5	52.8	20.2
Non Int. Exp.	NA	195	150	124	117	143	83.2	78.8	74.4	83.2
Pretax Inc.	NA	108	68.5	82.3	48.3	8.6	50.6	67.4	24.4	-29.6
Eff. Tax Rate	NA	38%	35%	33%	43%	NM	39%	37%	63%	NM
Net Inc.	NA	67.3	44.7	55.3	27.5	-5.6	30.8	42.3	9.1	-31.9
% Net Int. Marg.	NA	2.59	2.60	2.60	2.40	2.30	2.53	1.98	1.42	1.50
Balance Sheet & Other Fin. Data (Million $)										
Total Assets	NA	8,853	7,097	6,608	5,954	5,521	4,871	4,641	5,078	5,619
Loans	NA	6,413	5,190	4,724	5,323	4,898	4,231	3,860	4,074	4,630
Deposits	NA	5,363	4,379	4,305	3,591	3,356	2,391	2,301	2,249	2,405
Capitalization:										
Debt	NA	2,272	2,184	1,790	1,712	1,584	1,924	1,509	1,414	1,317
Equity	NA	643	426	413	310	279	278	237	166	141
Total	NA	2,915	2,610	2,203	2,022	1,863	2,202	1,746	1,580	1,457
% Ret. on Assets	NA	0.8	0.7	0.8	0.4	NM	0.7	0.9	0.2	NM
% Ret. on Equity	NA	12.6	11.0	14.7	9.3	NM	12.0	21.0	6.0	NM
% Loan Loss Resv.	NA	0.9	0.9	1.0	0.9	1.2	1.3	1.2	1.3	0.5
% Risk Based Capital	NA	13.8	13.8	13.6	13.5	13.1	12.8	8.9	6.6	6.3
Price Times Book Value:										
Hi	NA	2.9	2.2	1.6	1.8	1.7	1.9	1.2	0.8	1.4
Low	NA	2.0	1.6	1.1	1.0	1.1	1.1	0.4	0.3	0.6

Data as orig reptd.; bef. results of disc opers/spec. items. Per share data adj. for stk. divs. Bold denotes diluted EPS (FASB 128)-prior periods restated. E-Estimated. NA-Not Available. NM-Not Meaningful. NR-Not Ranked.

Organized—in Nebraska in 1887. **Office**—2120 S. 72nd St., Omaha, NE 68124. **Tel**—(402) 554-9200. **Website**—http://www.comfedbank.com **Chrmn & CEO**—W. A. Fitzgerald. **Pres & COO**—J. A. Laphen. **EVP & Secy**—G. L. Matter. **Fin VP & Investor Contact**—Larry R. Goddard (402-390-6553). **Dirs**—T. A. Anderson, W. A. Fitzgerald, M. P. Glinsky, R. F. Krohn, C. G. Mammel, S.G. Marvin, R. S. Milligan, J. P. O'Donnell, M. T. O'Niel, R. D. Taylor, A. J. Tesi.**Transfer Agent**—Shareowner Services. **Empl**— 3,481. **S&P Analyst:** J. Rudy

STANDARD &POOR'S
STOCK REPORTS

Commercial Metals

NYSE Symbol **CMC**

In S&P SmallCap 600

09-OCT-99

Industry: Iron & Steel

Summary: This company manufactures, recycles and markets steel, metal products and other materials, and provides related services.

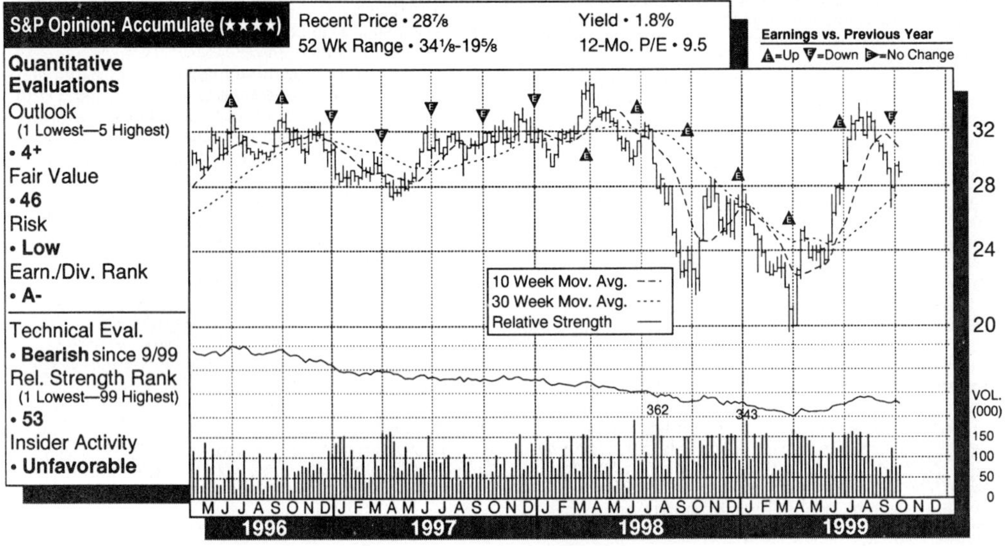

Overview - 18-JUN-99

We project 7.0% sales growth in FY 00 (Aug.), reflecting gains in all three segments. Steel manufacturing should experience a strong rebound as imports decline and production constraints tied to the start-up of two new plants abates. Underlying demand for steel is expected to stay firm in FY 00 and the steel unit will be better able to capitalize on this trend. Sales and profits for marketing/trading should increase from FY 99 on improved conditions in Asia. Finally, ferrous and non ferrous scrap appear to have troughed, likely reflecting a recovery in global metal consumption. Accordingly, recycling's losses should narrow in FY 00. Partly offsetting these factors are a decline in lifo credits and the absence of a gain from a litigation settlement. Lifo contributed $0.45 to EPS for FY 99's first three quarters. EPS, excluding such items, should post a sizable gain in FY 00.

Valuation - 18-JUN-99

On June 7, 1999 we upgraded CMC to buy from accumulate based on our expectation that the stock would begin to trade on FY 00 EPS. Currently trading at 9.5 times our FY 00 estimate, CMC is one of the most attractively valued metals companies we cover. While there are no other companies that can be directly compared to CMC on account of its diverse business profile, the average P/E for the integrated steel companies we follow is 15 times 1999's EPS. Given that CMC enjoys far greater EPS consistency and has much lower financial leverage vis a vis the integrated steels, CMC is undervalued at current levels. Additionally, capital spending should decline substantially in FY 00 and this will lead to a significant improvement in free cash flow per share. We anticipate that free cash flow will total $2.35 in FY 00 versus FY 99's negative $4.12. This turnaround should enable CMC to repurchase shares and reduce debt.

Key Stock Statistics

S&P EPS Est. 1999	2.80	Tang. Bk. Value/Share	26.18
P/E on S&P Est. 1999	10.3	Beta	0.67
S&P EPS Est. 2000	2.85	Shareholders	2,634
Dividend Rate/Share	0.52	Market cap. (B)	$0.415
Shs. outstg. (M)	14.3	Inst. holdings	48%
Avg. daily vol. (M)	0.017		

Value of $10,000 invested 5 years ago: $ 11,435

Fiscal Year Ending Aug. 31

	1999	1998	1997	1996	1995	1994
Revenues (Million $)						
1Q	549.4	550.5	531.0	590.2	413.7	380.0
2Q	550.5	568.2	525.8	518.2	533.0	389.9
3Q	582.1	606.0	589.6	639.1	574.2	440.6
4Q	—	642.8	612.0	574.8	595.9	447.2
Yr.	—	2,368	2,258	2,322	2,117	1,658
Earnings Per Share ($)						
1Q	**0.75**	0.54	0.60	0.70	0.44	0.38
2Q	**0.57**	**0.56**	0.47	0.67	0.67	0.28
3Q	**0.76**	**0.75**	0.63	0.79	0.73	0.48
4Q	**E0.72**	**1.00**	0.85	0.86	0.66	0.63
Yr.	**E2.80**	**2.82**	**2.54**	3.01	2.52	1.75

Next earnings report expected: mid October

Dividend Data (Dividends have been paid since 1964.)

Amount ($)	Date Decl.	Ex-Div. Date	Stock of Record	Payment Date
0.130	Dec. 14	Jan. 06	Jan. 08	Jan. 28 '99
0.130	Mar. 15	Apr. 07	Apr. 09	Apr. 23 '99
0.130	Jun. 21	Jul. 07	Jul. 09	Jul. 23 '99
0.130	Sep. 27	Oct. 06	Oct. 08	Oct. 22 '99

Commercial Metals Company

Business Summary - 18-JUN-99

Commercial Metals engages in raw material and industrial product-related activities, including worldwide marketing and trading, manufacturing and fabrication of steel, copper tube production, and metals recycling. Segment contributions (profits in millions) in FY 98 (Aug.) were:

	Sales	Profits
Manufacturing	52%	$74.8
Marketing and trading	32%	$20.6
Recycling	16%	-1.4

International sales accounted for 32% of total revenues in FY 98, versus 33% in FY 97, 39% in FY 96, and 35% in FY 95.

The manufacturing group includes the CMC Steel Group, Howell Metal Company, and a railroad salvage company. CMC Steel is engaged in minimill steel production, steel fabricating, steel joist manufacturing, fence post manufacturing and railcar rebuilding. The steel minimills manufacture reinforcing bar, angles, rounds, channels, flats and special sections used in highways, concrete structures and general manufacturing. Minimill shipments totaled 2,008,000 tons in FY 98, versus 1,926,000 tons in FY 97 and 1,730,000 tons in FY 96. Steel processing entails fabrication of reinforcing and structural steel used primarily in construction of commercial and non-commercial businesses.

CMC's principal competitors in the minimill industry are Bayou Steel, Birmingham Steel, Co-Steel and Nucor Corp.

Howell Metal manufactures copper water, air conditioning and refrigeration tubing for use in commercial, industrial and residential construction.

The railroad salvage company dismantles and recovers steel rail, track components and other materials from obsolete or abandoned railroads.

Through a network of trading offices around the world, CMC markets and trades primary and secondary metals, steel, ores and concentrates, industrial minerals, ferroalloys, chemicals, and other materials used by a variety of industries. The marketing and trading segment also provides services including market and technical information, financing, transportation and shipping, storage, insurance and hedging.

The recycling segment processes ferrous and nonferrous scrap metals for further recycling into new metal products, which are sold to steel mills and foundries, aluminum sheet and ingot manufacturers, specialty steel mills and other industrial manufacturers. Shipments for this segment totaled 1,469,0000 tons in FY 98 (1,367,000 tons in FY 97), with ferrous metals accounting for 1,280,000 tons (1,155,000 tons) and nonferrous metals 188,055 tons (212,000 tons). Ferrous scrap is the primary raw material for minimills such as those operated by CMC and its competitors.

Per Share Data ($) (Year Ended Aug. 31)	1998	1997	1996	1995	1994	1993	1992	1991	1990	1989
Tangible Bk. Val.	26.18	24.04	22.20	19.72	17.01	15.96	14.92	14.43	13.97	12.69
Cash Flow	5.96	5.41	5.73	5.04	3.77	3.31	2.64	2.49	3.16	3.15
Earnings	2.82	2.53	3.01	2.52	1.75	1.46	0.87	0.84	1.70	1.84
Dividends	0.52	0.52	0.48	0.48	0.46	0.39	0.39	0.39	0.38	0.31
Payout Ratio	18%	21%	16%	19%	26%	27%	44%	46%	21%	17%
Prices - High	36	33 7/8	33 1/2	29	29 1/8	30	20 1/8	16 3/4	16 3/4	17 7/8
- Low	21 1/2	27 1/8	24 3/8	23	21	19 3/8	14 1/8	12 1/4	12 1/8	14 7/8
P/E Ratio - High	13	13	11	12	17	21	23	20	10	10
- Low	8	11	8	9	12	13	16	15	7	8
Income Statement Analysis (Million $)										
Revs.	2,368	2,248	2,310	2,107	1,666	1,569	1,166	1,161	1,137	1,309
Oper. Inc.	134	109	118	109	80.3	71.8	55.9	50.5	70.6	73.8
Depr.	47.5	43.7	41.6	38.1	30.1	27.4	25.6	23.6	22.2	20.2
Int. Exp.	18.1	14.6	16.1	15.4	10.4	9.8	10.1	9.6	8.8	10.8
Pretax Inc.	68.1	61.0	72.9	58.0	40.9	35.1	20.3	18.3	39.8	43.4
Eff. Tax Rate	37%	37%	37%	34%	36%	38%	38%	35%	35%	34%
Net Inc.	42.7	38.6	46.0	38.2	26.2	21.7	12.5	12.0	25.9	28.5
Balance Sheet & Other Fin. Data (Million $)										
Cash	31.0	33.0	24.3	21.0	38.3	47.4	47.4	33.2	38.6	65.6
Curr. Assets	674	585	539	534	446	398	378	319	289	315
Total Assets	1,003	839	767	748	605	542	516	461	416	419
Curr. Liab.	426	278	264	268	271	215	204	199	149	155
LT Debt	174	185	147	158	72.1	76.7	87.2	45.5	54.4	60.5
Common Eqty.	381	355	335	303	243	235	212	204	200	191
Total Cap.	577	561	503	480	334	327	312	262	267	264
Cap. Exp.	120	71.0	48.0	39.3	48.2	37.6	24.5	42.7	43.7	26.4
Cash Flow	90.2	82.3	87.6	76.3	56.3	49.0	38.1	35.6	48.1	48.6
Curr. Ratio	1.6	2.1	2.0	2.0	1.6	1.9	1.9	1.6	1.9	2.0
% LT Debt of Cap.	30.1	33.1	29.2	32.9	21.6	23.5	28.0	17.4	20.4	23.0
% Net Inc.of Revs.	1.8	1.7	2.0	1.8	1.6	1.4	1.1	1.0	2.3	2.2
% Ret. on Assets	4.6	4.8	6.1	5.6	4.6	4.0	2.6	2.8	6.4	7.5
% Ret. on Equity	11.6	11.2	14.5	14.0	11.1	9.5	6.0	6.0	13.6	15.9

Data as orig. reptd.; bef. results of disc. opers. and/or spec. items. Per share data adj. for stk. divs. as of ex-div. date. Revs. in quarterly table incl. other inc. Bold denotes diluted EPS (FASB 128). E-Estimated. NA-Not Available. NM-Not Meaningful. NR-Not Ranked.

Office—7800 Stemmons Freeway, P.O. Box 1046, Dallas, TX 75221. **Tel**—(214) 689-4300. **Website**—http://www.commercialmetals.com **Pres & CEO**—S. A. Rabin. **VP & Secy**—D. M. Sudbury. **VP-CFO**—W. B. Larson.**Investor Contact**—Debbie Okle (214-689-4354). **Dirs**—A. A. Eisenstat, M. Feldman, A. L. Howell, W. F. Kammann, R. E. Loewenberg, A. A. Massaro, D. G. Owen, C. B. Peterson, S. A. Rabin, M. Selig, R. R. Womack. **Transfer Agent & Registrar**—ChaseMellon Shareholder Services, LLC. Ridgefield Park, NJ. **Incorporated**—in Delaware in 1946. **Empl**— 7,350. **S&P Analyst:** Leo J. Larkin

STANDARD
&POOR'S
STOCK REPORTS

Commonwealth Industries

Nasdaq Symbol **CMIN**

In S&P SmallCap 600

09-OCT-99 **Industry:** Aluminum

Summary: CMIN is a leading manufacturer of aluminum sheet for the transportation, construction and consumer durables markets.

S&P Opinion: Hold (★★★)

Recent Price • 13
52 Wk Range • 18⅜-6⅜
Yield • 1.5%
12-Mo. P/E • 23.6

Quantitative Evaluations

Outlook (1 Lowest—5 Highest)
• **5**

Fair Value
• **18¼**

Risk
• **Average**

Earn./Div. Rank
• **NR**

Technical Eval.
• **Bearish** since 9/99

Rel. Strength Rank (1 Lowest—99 Highest)
• **30**

Insider Activity
• **NA**

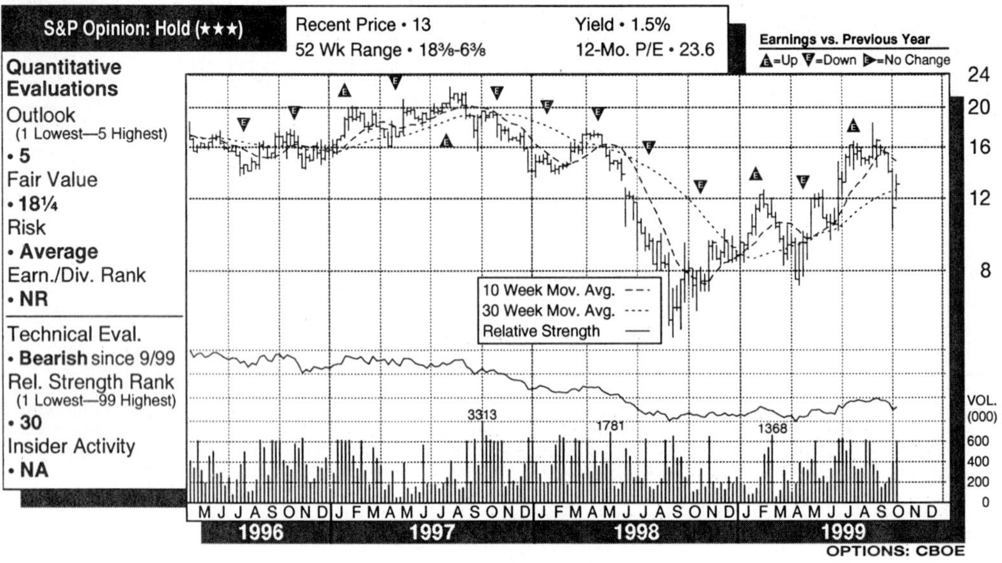

Overview - 08-OCT-99

On September 30, 1999, CMIN said it expected earnings for the 1999 third quarter to fall short of analyst estimates of $0.44 a share. The company anticipates that actual results will be $0.28 to $0.32 below the analyst projection; it expects to report third quarter EPS on October 18, 1999. CMIN said the EPS shortfall was mostly the result of reduced metal margins in the aluminum business unit. Margin erosion occurred as a result of the impact of adopting the last-in, first out (LIFO) method of inventory accounting during the recent period of increasing metal prices. The adoption of LIFO in a period of rising prices increases the cost of goods sold. Assuming a less rapid increase in metal prices in 2000, and therefore less LIFO impact, sales and EPS should rise in 2000.

Valuation - 08-OCT-99

Despite CMIN's announcement of an EPS shortfall for the 1999 third quarter, we have elected to maintain our hold rating on the shares. We believe the disappointing third quarter performance is a temporary setback, caused by a lag between rising costs and the company's ability to recover those costs by increasing its product prices. We expect cost increases to moderate; this will enable CMIN to get profits back on track. At this juncture, the shares should be valued on projected EPS for 2000, rather than for 1999. AT a recent level of about 11.4X our 2000 EPS estimate, versus 17.5X for the aluminum group, the stock is undervalued, in light of the fact that CMIN has less financial and operating leverage than its integrated rivals, However, its much smaller size and short history as a public company are weighing on the P/E multiple. CMIN has excellent long-term potential, but we think it will take time for the company to gain recognition. Current holders can maintain existing positions.

Key Stock Statistics

S&P EPS Est. 1999	0.90	Tang. Bk. Value/Share	10.48
P/E on S&P Est. 1999	14.4	Beta	NA
S&P EPS Est. 2000	1.10	Shareholders	4,800
Dividend Rate/Share	0.20	Market cap. (B)	$0.207
Shs. outstg. (M)	15.9	Inst. holdings	71%
Avg. daily vol. (M)	0.072		

Value of $10,000 invested 5 years ago: NA

Fiscal Year Ending Dec. 31

	1999	1998	1997	1996	1995	1994
Revenues (Million $)						
1Q	238.8	248.9	272.2	167.5	173.9	104.2
2Q	271.5	258.4	287.2	159.7	192.2	121.4
3Q	—	231.3	271.2	170.1	160.3	137.0
4Q	—	229.3	260.2	241.9	145.1	134.0
Yr.	—	968.0	1,091	739.2	671.5	496.5
Earnings Per Share ($)						
1Q	**0.14**	**0.18**	**0.21**	**0.23**	0.85	—
2Q	**0.41**	**-0.17**	**0.41**	**0.21**	1.27	—
3Q	**E0.15**	**-0.13**	**0.15**	**0.45**	0.75	—
4Q	**E0.20**	**0.13**	**0.08**	**0.55**	0.45	—
Yr.	**E0.90**	**-0.01**	**0.78**	**1.45**	**3.31**	—

Next earnings report expected: mid October

Dividend Data (Dividends have been paid since 1995.)

Amount ($)	Date Decl.	Ex-Div. Date	Stock of Record	Payment Date
0.050	Oct. 15	Oct. 22	Oct. 26	Nov. 09 '98
0.050	Dec. 16	Jan. 28	Feb. 01	Feb. 15 '99
0.050	Apr. 22	Apr. 29	May. 03	May. 17 '99
0.050	Jul. 26	Aug. 05	Aug. 09	Aug. 23 '99

A Division of The McGraw-Hill Companies

Business Summary - 08-OCT-99

Commonwealth Industries Inc., (formerly Commonwealth Aluminum) is a leading manufacturer of aluminum sheet for the transportation, construction and consumer durables end-use markets. The company owns and operates at Lewisport, KY, one of the largest multi-purpose aluminum rolling mills in North America.

Following its acquisition of CasTech Aluminum Group Inc. in September 1996, CMIN's shipment capability increased to over 1.0 billion lbs. of aluminum sheet. The acquisition also included Alflex, a maker of flexible conduit, aluminum armored cable, and related products for construction applications. Aflex produces various electrical products, including non-metallic conduit and plastic jacketed steel flexible conduit for wet, harsh or corrosive applications. It also makes armored cable. Sales totaled of $121.3 million in 1998, or 12.5% of CMIN's total sales for the year (11.6% in 1997). Alflex was expanding its capacity for producing cable products by 50% with the construction of a new plant located in Rocky Mountain, NC, with startup scheduled for the 1999 second quarter.

Aluminum sheet products manufactured by the company are generally referred to as common alloy products. They are sold to distributors and end-users, principally for use in transportation equipment such as truck trailers and bodies and automotive parts; building and construction products such as roofing, siding, windows and gutters; beverage cans and consumer durables such as cookware and appliances.

Unlike integrated producers, CMIN relies on scrap and purchased aluminum ingot as its basic raw material. It melts scrap or ingot in a furnace, and transforms the molten metal into a finished aluminum sheet product. It does not own or mine bauxite or make alumina. CMIN's capital costs are substantially lower than those of its integrated rivals, because it does not require mining, material handling, smelters and other equipment needed to transform bauxite into ingot and finished aluminum products. As a result, its operating leverage and earnings are less volatile than those of integrated companies. However, the scrap based method used by CMIN and other minimills cannot produce a high quality product that can compete with top of the line sheet produced via the integrated process that uses bauxite and alumina as raw materials.

CMIN's principal integrated rivals are Alcoa, Alcan, Kaiser Aluminum, and Reynolds Metals. The company's minimill rivals are Quanex Corp.'s Nichols Homeshield subsidiary and Century Aluminum.

Aluminum shipments totaled 884.2 million lbs. in 1998, versus 990.2 million lbs. in 1997 and 712.5 million lbs. in 1996. Shipments of electrical wiring products totaled 517.4 million sq. ft., versus 521.7 million sq. ft., in 1997 and 137 million sq. ft. in 1996. Shipments by market in 1998 were: building and construction, 39%; can stock, 8%; consumer durables and other, 11%; distribution, 30%; and transportation, 12%

Per Share Data ($) (Year Ended Dec. 31)	1998	1997	1996	1995	1994	1993	1992	1991	1990	1989
Tangible Bk. Val.	9.88	9.84	5.11	20.90	17.86	NA	NA	NA	NA	NA
Cash Flow	2.19	3.74	3.65	5.14	NA	NA	NA	NA	NA	NA
Earnings	-0.01	0.78	1.44	3.32	NA	NA	NA	NA	NA	NA
Dividends	0.20	0.20	0.20	0.15	Nil	NA	NA	NA	NA	NA
Payout Ratio	NM	26%	14%	5%	Nil	NA	NA	NA	NA	NA
Prices - High	17¾	22½	18⅞	24⅞	NA	NA	NA	NA	NA	NA
- Low	5½	13½	13⅝	14	NA	NA	NA	NA	NA	NA
P/E Ratio - High	NM	29	13	7	NA	NA	NA	NA	NA	NA
- Low	NM	17	9	4	NA	NA	NA	NA	NA	NA
Income Statement Analysis (Million $)										
Revs.	968	1,091	739	672	497	NA	NA	NA	NA	NA
Oper. Inc.	56.1	76.3	41.7	60.8	37.7	NA	NA	NA	NA	NA
Depr.	34.7	34.7	22.5	18.6	17.4	NA	NA	NA	NA	NA
Int. Exp.	22.2	30.5	9.9	3.5	0.1	NA	NA	NA	NA	NA
Pretax Inc.	-0.4	11.5	9.5	43.1	22.8	NA	NA	NA	NA	NA
Eff. Tax Rate	NM	21%	NM	22%	3.10%	NA	NA	NA	NA	NA
Net Inc.	0.1	9.1	14.8	33.8	22.1	NA	NA	NA	NA	NA
Balance Sheet & Other Fin. Data (Million $)										
Cash	0.0	Nil	1.9	2.7	Nil	NA	NA	NA	NA	NA
Curr. Assets	201	217	332	227	236	NA	NA	NA	NA	NA
Total Assets	648	667	795	421	439	NA	NA	NA	NA	NA
Curr. Liab.	85.4	104	125	73.9	102	NA	NA	NA	NA	NA
LT Debt	125	126	336	37.4	6.5	NA	NA	NA	NA	NA
Common Eqty.	327	330	227	213	243	NA	NA	NA	NA	NA
Total Cap.	452	456	563	250	250	NA	NA	NA	NA	NA
Cap. Exp.	33.6	21.7	14.8	15.2	19.7	NA	NA	NA	NA	NA
Cash Flow	34.9	43.8	37.2	52.4	39.5	NA	NA	NA	NA	NA
Curr. Ratio	2.3	2.1	2.7	3.1	2.3	NA	NA	NA	NA	NA
% LT Debt of Cap.	27.7	27.6	59.7	15.0	2.6	NA	NA	NA	NA	NA
% Net Inc.of Revs.	NM	0.8	2.0	5.0	4.4	NA	NA	NA	NA	NA
% Ret. on Assets	NM	1.2	2.4	7.9	NA	NA	NA	NA	NA	NA
% Ret. on Equity	NM	3.3	6.7	14.8	NA	NA	NA	NA	NA	NA

Data as orig. reptd.; bef. results of disc. opers. and/or spec. items. Per share data adj. for stk. divs. as of ex-div. date. Bold denotes diluted EPS (FASB 128). E-Estimated. NA-Not Available. NM-Not Meaningful. NR-Not Ranked.

Office—500 West Jefferson St., 19th floor, Louisville, KY 40202-2823. **Tel**—(502) 589-8100. **Fax**—(502) 589-8158. **Website**—http://www.cacky.com **Chrmn**—P. E. Lego. **Pres & CEO**—M. V. Kaminski. **EVP, CFO & Secy**—D. L. Marsh, Jr. **VP & Investor Contact**—William G. Toler (502-589-8138). **Dirs**—C. G. Burke, C. F. Fetterholf, M. V. Kaminski, P. E. Lego, J. E. Merow, V. Torasso. **Transfer Agent**—National City Bank, Cleveland. **Incorporated**—in Delaware in 1984. **Empl**— 2,173. **S&P Analyst:** Leo J. Larkin

STANDARD &POOR'S
STOCK REPORTS

CommScope, Inc.

NYSE Symbol **CTV**

In S&P SmallCap 600

09-OCT-99

Industry: Communications Equipment

Summary: CommScope is the world's largest manufacturer of coaxial cable, and a leading supplier of high-performance cables for LAN and other applications.

Quantitative Evaluations

Outlook (1 Lowest—5 Highest)
• **NA**

Fair Value
• **NA**

Risk
• **Low**

Earn./Div. Rank
• **NR**

Technical Eval.
• **Neutral** since 9/99

Rel. Strength Rank (1 Lowest—99 Highest)
• **75**

Insider Activity
• **NA**

Recent Price • 34⅝
52 Wk Range • 40-9⅜

Yield • Nil
12-Mo. P/E • 33.7

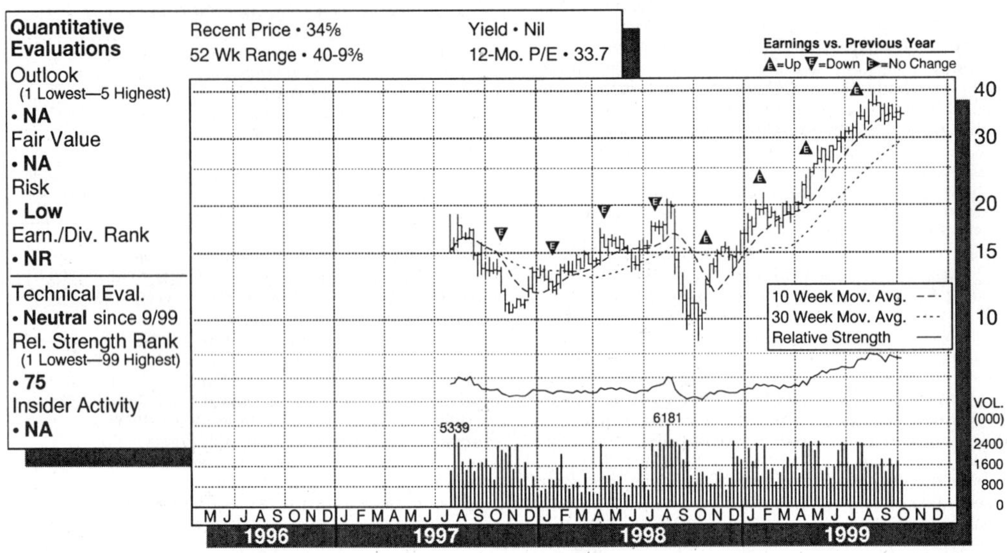

Business Profile - 12-JUL-99

Orders booked in the 1999 first quarter totaled $159.1 million, up from $131.8 million in the 1998 period. In January 1999, the company acquired Alcatel's Belgian coaxial cable operations; the business, with annual sales of $35 million, is the largest European manufacturer of CATV coaxial cable. The acquired business achieved breakeven results for the 1999 first quarter, and CTV believes it provides an excellent platform for growth in Europe. In February 1999, the company acquired the clad wire fabrication equipment and technology of Texas Instruments' materials and controls business; terms were not disclosed. CTV expects the acquisition to allow it to further vertically integrate its processes, resulting in greater efficiencies.

Operational Review - 12-JUL-99

Net sales in the three months ended March 31, 1999, advanced 11%, year to year, mainly reflecting strengthening worldwide coaxial cable sales. International sales climbed 41%. Profitability benefited from the higher sales, cost reduction initiatives, and a 33% decrease in interest expense; pretax income soared 68%. After taxes at 36.3%, versus 37.1%, net income surged 70%, to $10,760,000 ($0.21 a share, on 3.9% more shares), from $6,332,000 ($0.13).

Stock Performance - 08-OCT-99

In the past 30 trading days, CTV's shares have declined 6%, compared to a 0.91% fall in the S&P 500. Average trading volume for the past five days was 194,380 shares, compared with the 40-day moving average of 316,282 shares.

Key Stock Statistics

Dividend Rate/Share	Nil	Shareholders	860
Shs. outstg. (M)	50.7	Market cap. (B)	$ 1.8
Avg. daily vol. (M)	0.306	Inst. holdings	81%
Tang. Bk. Value/Share	1.06		
Beta	NA		

Value of $10,000 invested 5 years ago: NA

Fiscal Year Ending Dec. 31

	1999	1998	1997	1996	1995	1994
Revenues (Million $)						
1Q	148.1	133.6	147.9	130.9	—	—
2Q	186.9	141.9	159.3	142.0	—	—
3Q	—	150.1	147.3	148.6	—	—
4Q	—	146.2	144.8	150.7	—	—
Yr.	—	571.7	599.2	572.2	—	—
Earnings Per Share ($)						
1Q	**0.21**	**0.13**	**0.26**	**0.23**	—	—
2Q	**0.33**	**0.17**	**0.24**	**0.24**	—	—
3Q	—	**0.23**	**0.14**	**0.29**	—	—
4Q	—	**0.26**	**0.06**	**0.30**	—	—
Yr.	—	**0.79**	**0.70**	**1.06**	—	—

Next earnings report expected: late October

Dividend Data

No dividends have been paid.

CommScope, Inc.

Business Summary - 12-JUL-99

CommScope, Inc., spun off by General Instrument (now known as General Semiconductor) in July 1997, believes it is the world's most technologically advanced, low-cost provider of coaxial cable.

As a result of the company's leading product offerings, cost efficient manufacturing processes, and economies of scale resulting from its leading market share, CTV believes it is well positioned to capitalize on the opportunity provided by the convergence of video, voice and data, and the resulting demand for bandwidth and high-speed access. The company also believes several industry trends will drive demand for its products. These trends include the endorsement of hybrid fiber coaxial (HFC) cable systems by major cable, telephone and technology companies; increasing use of the Internet; growing demand for high-speed local area network (LAN) access; and continuing rapid deployment of wireless communications systems worldwide.

CTV has adopted a growth strategy to expand, strengthen and expand its current market position as the leading supply of coaxial cable for broadband communications. The principal elements of its strategy are to capitalize on the HFC shift; develop proprietary products and expand market opportunities; improve operating efficiencies; and leverage its global platform.

The company is a leading worldwide manufacturer of a broad line of coaxial cables and other high-performance electronic and fiber optic cable products primarily for communications applications including cable television, telephony and Internet access. It is the largest manufacturer and supplier of coaxial cable for HFC cable systems in the U.S., with over 50% market share in 1998 (based on sales volume), and is a leading supplier of coaxial cable for video distribution applications, such as satellite television and security surveillance.

CTV is also a leading provider of high-performance premise wiring for LANs and it believes that it has developed a next generation wireless antenna cable. The company sells its products to about 2,400 customers in more than 85 countries. It expanded its global presence through the early 1999 acquisition of Alcatel's cable television (CATV) coaxial cable business, Europe's largest manufacturer of CATV coaxial cable.

About 80% of the company's revenues in 1998 were from the cable television and video distribution markets, 13% LAN applications, and 7% other high-performance cable markets, including cable for wireless applications, industrial and other wiring applications. About 24% of 1998 revenues were from international customers. CTV believes continued growth in international markets, including developing markets in Asia, the Middle East and Latin America, and the expected privatization of the telecommunications structure in many European countries, represent significant future opportunities.

Per Share Data ($) (Year Ended Dec. 31)	1998	1997	1996	1995	1994	1993	1992	1991	1990	1989
Tangible Bk. Val.	0.41	NM	NM	NA	NA	NA	NA	NA	NA	NA
Cash Flow	1.29	1.20	NA	NA	NA	NA	NA	NA	NA	NA
Earnings	0.79	0.70	1.12	NA	NA	NA	NA	NA	NA	NA
Dividends	Nil	Nil	Nil	NA	NA	NA	NA	NA	NA	NA
Payout Ratio	Nil	Nil	Nil	NA	NA	NA	NA	NA	NA	NA
Prices - High	20¾	19	NA	NA	NA	NA	NA	NA	NA	NA
- Low	8¾	10⅝	NA	NA	NA	NA	NA	NA	NA	NA
P/E Ratio - High	26	27	NA	NA	NA	NA	NA	NA	NA	NA
- Low	11	15	NA	NA	NA	NA	NA	NA	NA	NA
Income Statement Analysis (Million $)										
Revs.	572	599	572	NA	NA	NA	NA	NA	NA	NA
Oper. Inc.	95.6	101	NA	NA	NA	NA	NA	NA	NA	NA
Depr.	24.6	21.7	NA	NA	NA	NA	NA	NA	NA	NA
Int. Exp.	15.4	13.7	NA	NA	NA	NA	NA	NA	NA	NA
Pretax Inc.	60.2	61.5	84.4	NA	NA	NA	NA	NA	NA	NA
Eff. Tax Rate	35%	39%	38%	NA	NA	NA	NA	NA	NA	NA
Net Inc.	39.2	37.5	52.4	NA	NA	NA	NA	NA	NA	NA
Balance Sheet & Other Fin. Data (Million $)										
Cash	4.1	3.3	NA	NA	NA	NA	NA	NA	NA	NA
Curr. Assets	144	156	171	NA	NA	NA	NA	NA	NA	NA
Total Assets	465	484	493	NA	NA	NA	NA	NA	NA	NA
Curr. Liab.	50.4	43.0	58.0	NA	NA	NA	NA	NA	NA	NA
LT Debt	182	266	275	NA	NA	NA	NA	NA	NA	NA
Common Eqty.	204	150	135	NA	NA	NA	NA	NA	NA	NA
Total Cap.	403	431	426	NA	NA	NA	NA	NA	NA	NA
Cap. Exp.	22.8	29.9	NA	NA	NA	NA	NA	NA	NA	NA
Cash Flow	63.9	59.1	NA	NA	NA	NA	NA	NA	NA	NA
Curr. Ratio	2.9	3.6	2.9	NA	NA	NA	NA	NA	NA	NA
% LT Debt of Cap.	45.1	61.7	64.6	NA	NA	NA	NA	NA	NA	NA
% Net Inc.of Revs.	6.9	6.3	9.2	NA	NA	NA	NA	NA	NA	NA
% Ret. on Assets	8.3	7.8	NA	NA	NA	NA	NA	NA	NA	NA
% Ret. on Equity	22.2	13.8	NA	NA	NA	NA	NA	NA	NA	NA

Data as orig. reptd. (pro forma in 1996; bal. sheet as of Mar. 31, 1997); bef. results of disc. opers. and/or spec. items. Per share data adj. for stk. divs. as of ex-div. date. Bold denotes diluted EPS (FASB 128). E-Estimated. NA-Not Available. NM-Not Meaningful. NR-Not Ranked.

Office—1375 Lenoir Rhyne Blvd., P.O. Box 1729, Hickory, NC 28603. **Tel**—(828) 324-2200. **Website**—http://www.commscope.com **Chrmn & CEO**—F. M. Drendel. **Pres & COO**—B. D. Garrett. **EVP & CFO**—J. L. Leonhardt. **VP & Secy**—F. B. Wyatt II. **Investor Contact**—Phil Armstrong (828-323-4848).**Dirs**—E. D. Breen, F. M. Drendel, L. Faircloth, B. L. George, G. N. Hutton Jr., J. N. Whitson. **Transfer Agent & Registrar**—ChaseMellon Shareholder Services, Ridgefield Park, NJ. **Incorporated**—in Delaware in 1997. **Empl**— 2,600. **S&P Analyst:** J.J.S.

STANDARD
&POOR'S
STOCK REPORTS

Community First Bankshares

NASDAQ Symbol **CFBX**

In S&P SmallCap 600

09-OCT-99

Industry:
Banks (Regional)

Summary: This multi-bank holding company operates in more than 150 communities in several Southwestern, Midwestern and Rocky Mountain states.

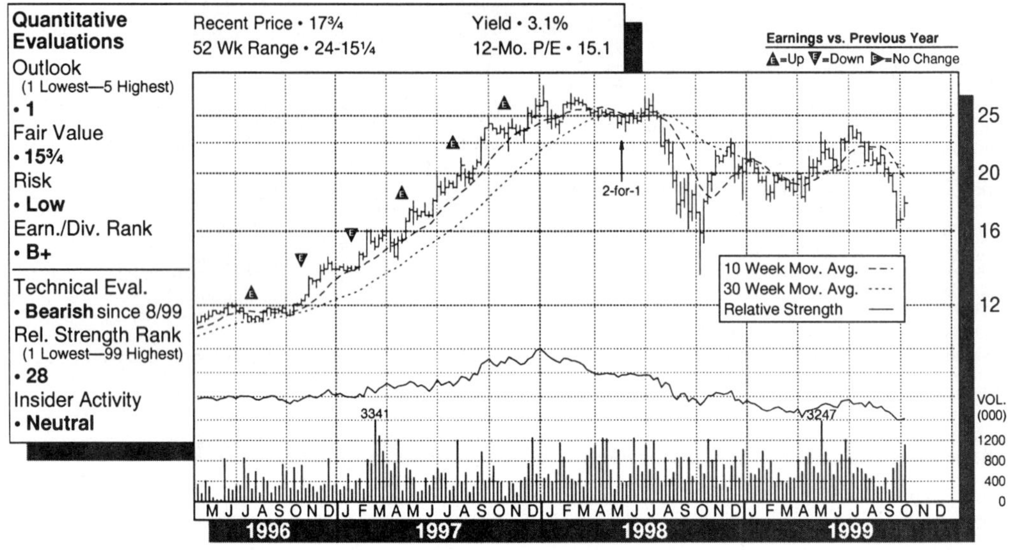

Business Profile - 18-AUG-99

Community First has been an aggressive acquirer, adding banks and bank branches in 50 communities during 1998. Its acquisition strategy has focused on banks generally with between $20 million and $150 million in assets. In July 1999, the company signed a definitive agreement to acquire River Bancorp of Ramsey, MN (assets of $36 million), in a stock transaction. Earlier, in May 1999, a definitive agreement was signed to acquire Valley National Corp. of El Cajon, CA (assets of $241 million). In May 1999, Community First completed the disposal of its sub-prime lending portfolio acquired through a merger in 1996, noting that it intends to focus on community banking.

Operational Review - 18-AUG-99

Net interest income in the first half of 1999 rose 6.6%, year to year, aided by an increase in the level of interest earning assets. The provision for loan losses was 84% higher, at $11.0 million, in connection with a decision to exit sub-prime lending activities. Noninterest income increased 11% on growth in insurance commissions and service charges and greater gains on the sale of investment securities. Following 9.2% lower noninterest expense, mainly related to cost reduction initiatives, pretax income climbed 46%. After taxes at 33.6%, versus 27.5%, income from continuing operations was up 33%, to $36,064,000 ($0.76 a share) from $27,050,000 ($0.56). Results exclude an $0.08 a share loss from discontinued operations in 1998.

Stock Performance - 08-OCT-99

In the past 30 trading days, CFBX's shares have declined 17%, compared to a 0.91% fall in the S&P 500. Average trading volume for the past five days was 221,540 shares, compared with the 40-day moving average of 117,677 shares.

Key Stock Statistics

Dividend Rate/Share	0.56	Shareholders	1,314
Shs. outstg. (M)	47.0	Market cap. (B)	$0.838
Avg. daily vol. (M)	0.167	Inst. holdings	44%
Tang. Bk. Value/Share	5.40		
Beta	0.99		

Value of $10,000 invested 5 years ago: $ 33,166

Fiscal Year Ending Dec. 31

	1999	1998	1997	1996	1995	1994
Revenues (Million $)						
1Q	125.8	118.3	70.31	59.60	34.77	23.43
2Q	129.4	128.0	76.56	62.24	40.97	26.97
3Q	—	133.9	93.68	65.21	48.05	28.52
4Q	—	129.3	91.00	69.65	49.63	29.49
Yr.	—	509.5	331.6	256.8	179.9	108.7
Earnings Per Share ($)						
1Q	**0.37**	**0.35**	0.30	0.25	0.20	—
2Q	**0.39**	**0.21**	0.29	0.27	0.20	—
3Q	—	**0.28**	0.33	0.24	0.27	—
4Q	—	**0.14**	—	0.17	0.27	—
Yr.	—	**0.98**	**1.20**	**0.90**	**0.88**	**0.71**

Next earnings report expected: mid October

Dividend Data (Dividends have been paid since 1991.)

Amount ($)	Date Decl.	Ex-Div. Date	Stock of Record	Payment Date
0.110	Oct. 26	Nov. 27	Dec. 01	Dec. 15 '98
0.140	Feb. 03	Feb. 25	Mar. 01	Mar. 15 '99
0.140	May. 05	May. 27	Jun. 01	Jun. 15 '99
0.140	Aug. 03	Aug. 30	Sep. 01	Sep. 15 '99

Business Summary - 18-AUG-99

Having acquired banks and bank branches in 50 communities in 1998, Community First Bankshares now operates in more than 150 communities in Arizona, Colorado, Iowa, Minnesota, Nebraska, New Mexico, North Dakota, South Dakota, Utah, Wisconsin and Wyoming. Its strategy is to operate and continue to acquire banks and bank branches in these states, as well as Kansas, California, Idaho, Illinois, Missouri, Nevada, Oklahoma and Texas.

Community banks operated by the company provide a full range of commercial and consumer banking services mainly to individuals and businesses in small and medium-sized communities and the surrounding market areas. The company also owns and operates insurance agencies in 32 communities served by the banks. These agencies primarily sell property and casualty insurance and other types of insurance including life, accident, and crop and hail insurance.

At the end of 1998, average earning assets, from which interest income is derived, totaled $5.3 billion and consisted mainly of loans (61%) and investment securities (37%). Sources of funds, generally used in the lending business, included time deposits (36%), savings deposits (18%), interest-bearing checking (14%), demand deposits (14%), short-term borrowings (6%), long-term debt (2%), shareholders' equity (7%) and other (3%).

Total loans of $3.4 billion at the end of 1998 were divided: real estate 36%, commercial 27%, consumer and other 18%, real estate construction 10% and agricultural 9%.

At 1998 year end, nonperforming assets, consisting of nonaccrual loans, restructured loans and other real estate, amounted to $26.3 million (0.78% of total loans and related assets), up from $19.1 million (0.63%) a year earlier. The allowance for loan losses, which is set aside for possible loan defaults, was $50.2 million (1.48% of total loans) at 1998 year end, up from $40.0 million (1.32%) a year earlier. Net charge-offs, or the amount of loans deemed uncollectible, were $14.3 million (0.44% of average loans) in 1998, versus $6.3 million (0.24%) in 1997.

Interest income on loans provided 63% of total income in 1998, interest income on investment securities 24%, other interest income 1%, service charges on deposit accounts 6%, insurance commissions 1%, and other noninterest income 5%.

Per Share Data ($) (Year Ended Dec. 31)	1998	1997	1996	1995	1994	1993	1992	1991	1990	1989
Tangible Bk. Val.	5.77	5.96	5.32	4.83	5.28	5.09	4.53	4.40	4.38	NA
Earnings	0.98	1.20	0.90	0.88	NA	NA	NA	NA	NA	NA
Dividends	0.44	0.35	0.29	0.24	0.22	0.20	0.17	0.04	NA	NA
Payout Ratio	40%	29%	31%	27%	NA	NA	NA	NA	NA	NA
Prices - High	27 1/4	28 1/8	14 1/2	11 5/8	8 1/4	7 1/2	7 1/4	6 3/4	NA	NA
- Low	13 1/2	13 5/8	10	6 5/8	6 1/8	5 5/8	5 3/8	5 1/4	NA	NA
P/E Ratio - High	25	23	15	12	10	10	12	11	NA	NA
- Low	12	11	10	7	7	7	9	8	NA	NA
Income Statement Analysis (Million $)										
Net Int. Inc.	261	161	134	88.1	58.4	49.3	43.1	31.7	21.4	NA
Tax Equiv. Adj.	NA	NA	NA	NA	NA	NA	NA	NA	NA	NA
Non Int. Inc.	58.5	36.1	27.3	17.7	12.0	10.3	8.4	4.6	3.2	NA
Loan Loss Prov.	22.5	5.4	6.8	2.4	1.8	1.5	1.7	2.3	1.6	NA
Exp./Op. Revs.	72%	63%	65%	64%	65%	67%	65%	62%	59%	NA
Pretax Inc.	68.4	67.4	50.5	35.5	23.0	19.3	17.0	11.6	8.6	NA
Eff. Tax Rate	31%	32%	36%	36%	39%	37%	36%	33%	32%	NA
Net Inc.	47.0	45.9	32.5	22.8	13.2	11.2	9.7	6.8	5.1	NA
% Net Int. Marg.	5.09	NA	NA	NA	NA	NA	NA	NA	NA	NA
Balance Sheet & Other Fin. Data (Million $)										
Money Mkt. Assets	5.2	NA	NA	NA	NA	NA	NA	NA	NA	NA
Inv. Securities	2,050	NA	NA	NA	NA	NA	NA	NA	NA	NA
Com'l Loans	904	NA	NA	NA	NA	NA	NA	NA	NA	NA
Other Loans	2,482	NA	NA	NA	NA	NA	NA	NA	NA	NA
Total Assets	6,003	4,856	3,116	2,327	1,466	1,266	1,087	826	543	NA
Demand Deposits	548	NA	NA	NA	NA	NA	NA	NA	NA	NA
Time Deposits	4,337	NA	NA	NA	NA	NA	NA	NA	NA	NA
LT Debt	213	NA	NA	NA	NA	NA	NA	NA	NA	NA
Common Eqty.	405	339	222	133	81.8	77.6	69.0	52.6	29.0	NA
% Ret. on Assets	0.9	1.2	1.2	1.2	1.0	1.0	1.0	1.0	NA	NA
% Ret. on Equity	12.6	16.3	17.4	19.7	15.2	15.3	15.9	15.0	NA	NA
% Loan Loss Resv.	1.5	1.0	1.3	1.3	1.3	1.4	1.4	1.5	1.7	NA
% Loans/Deposits	69.3	72.6	81.3	75.2	75.7	64.9	61.2	52.7	54.0	NA
% Equity to Assets	6.9	7.0	6.5	5.7	5.8	6.2	6.4	6.0	NA	NA

Data as orig reptd.; bef. results of disc opers/spec. items. Per share data adj. for stk. divs. Bold denotes diluted EPS (FASB 128)-prior periods restated. E-Estimated. NA-Not Available. NM-Not Meaningful. NR-Not Ranked.

Office—520 Main Ave., Fargo, ND 58124. **Tel**—(888) CFB-BEST. **Website**—http://www.cfbx.com **Chrmn, Pres & CEO**—D. R. Mengedoth. **CFO, Treas & Secy**—M. A. Anderson. **Investor Contact**—Carol Renner (701-298-5709). **Dirs**—J. T. Anderson, P. E. Benedict, P. Delaney, J. H. Flittie, D. G. Knudson, D. M. Mathisen, D. R. Mengedoth, M. R. Seymann, T. C. Wold, H. L. Wollman. **Transfer Agent & Registrar**—Norwest Bank Minnesota, N.A., South St. Paul. **Incorporated**—in Delaware in 1987. **Empl**— 2,600. **S&P Analyst:** Stephen. R. Biggar

STANDARD &POOR'S
STOCK REPORTS

Computer Task Group

NYSE Symbol **TSK**

In S&P SmallCap 600

09-OCT-99

Industry: Services (Computer Systems)

Summary: This information technology services company focuses on organizations with large, complex information and data processing requirements.

Quantitative Evaluations

Outlook (1 Lowest—5 Highest) • **4**

Fair Value • **22**

Risk • **Average**

Earn./Div. Rank • **B+**

Technical Eval. • **Bearish** since 9/99

Rel. Strength Rank (1 Lowest—99 Highest) • **35**

Insider Activity • **Neutral**

Recent Price • 15 | Yield • 0.3%

52 Wk Range • 34½-13⅛ | 12-Mo. P/E • 10.4

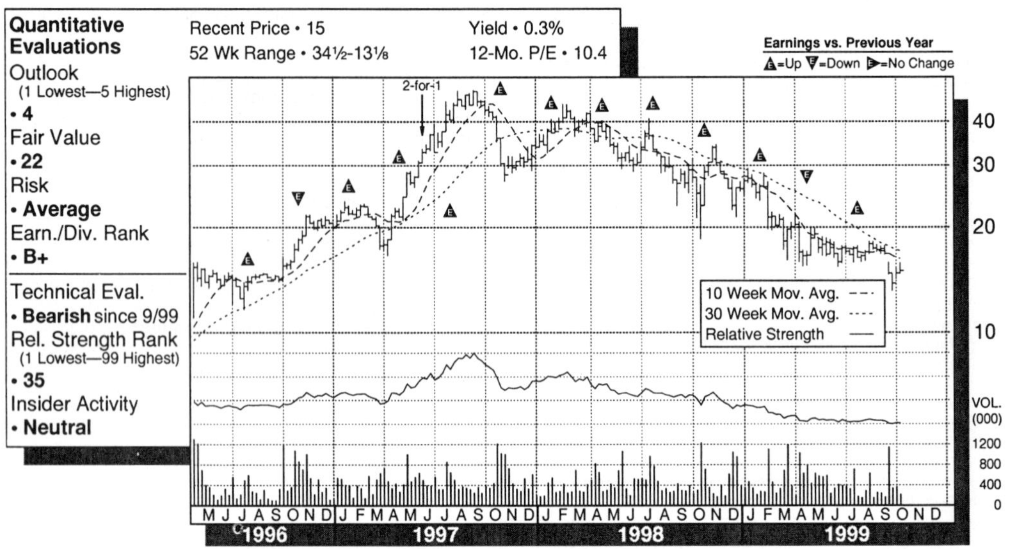

Business Profile - 23-JUN-99

The company focuses on building business relationships with key clients, or those companies that present a significant opportunity for a long-term, high value business relationship. TSK aims to make these key clients into strategic partners, or to accept responsibility for a defined deliverable, service level, or management process for them. Contracts were signed in the 1999 first quarter with a large European financial services company, a national textile company, a large metropolitan area health care provider, and a large retail grocery chain.

Operational Review - 23-JUN-99

Revenues in the three months ended March 26, 1999, advanced 6.3%, year to year, reflecting an acquisition and the provision of higher-value services to customers, partly offset by weaker revenues from oil and gas clients and IBM. Results were restricted by costs of continued investment in sales and marketing, recruiting and training programs, and by a $1.5 million charge to provide for a preliminary arbitration award related to a contract dispute; net income fell 7.4%, to $4,699,000 ($0.28 a share), from $5,077,000 ($0.30).

Stock Performance - 08-OCT-99

In the past 30 trading days, TSK's shares have declined 13%, compared to a 0.91% fall in the S&P 500. Average trading volume for the past five days was 42,000 shares, compared with the 40-day moving average of 72,515 shares.

Key Stock Statistics

Dividend Rate/Share	0.05	Shareholders	3,512
Shs. outstg. (M)	20.9	Market cap. (B)	$0.313
Avg. daily vol. (M)	0.102	Inst. holdings	58%
Tang. Bk. Value/Share	0.43		
Beta	1.69		

Value of $10,000 invested 5 years ago: $ 43,948

Fiscal Year Ending Dec. 31

	1999	1998	1997	1996	1995	1994
Revenues (Million $)						
1Q	116.6	109.7	94.94	90.01	82.23	77.01
2Q	125.5	117.7	100.1	91.32	84.61	77.95
3Q	—	116.2	101.1	89.41	85.61	69.00
4Q	—	124.4	111.4	94.34	86.96	77.61
Yr.	—	467.8	407.6	365.1	339.4	301.6
Earnings Per Share ($)						
1Q	**0.28**	**0.30**	**0.21**	**0.13**	0.10	0.06
2Q	**0.38**	**0.34**	**0.26**	**0.15**	0.11	0.07
3Q	—	**0.37**	**0.26**	**0.17**	0.29	0.07
4Q	—	**0.41**	**0.29**	**0.18**	0.12	0.08
Yr.	—	**1.42**	**1.01**	**0.63**	**0.62**	**0.26**

Next earnings report expected: mid October

Dividend Data (Dividends have been paid since 1976.)

Amount ($)	Date Decl.	Ex-Div. Date	Stock of Record	Payment Date
0.050	Apr. 28	May. 06	May. 10	May. 28 '99

A Division of The McGraw-Hill Companies

Computer Task Group, Incorporated

Business Summary - 23-JUN-99

Computer Task Group is an information technology (IT) services company that provides IT solutions to the largest U.S. corporations and others through strategic partnerships. A typical customer is an organization with large, complex information and data processing requirements. Services provided typically encompass the information technology business solution life cycle, including phases for planning, development and managing and maintaining the IT solution. A portion of IT services provided (less than 15% of revenues in the 1999 first quarter) involves Y2K assessment, planning, remediation, testing, and contingency planning services. In 1998, TSK derived 85% of operating profits from domestic operations, with the balance obtained overseas.

The company works with customers to develop effective business solutions through information systems and technology. TSK's professional staff may support a customer's software development team on a specific application or project, or may manage the project entirely for the customer. The range of services extends from flexible staffing provided on a per diem basis to managing multimillion-dollar technology projects. Most services are provided on-site at customer facilities. A network of offices provides wide geographical coverage with the capability of servicing large companies with multiple locations.

IBM is the company's largest customer, accounting for 32% of 1998 revenues. TSK expects to continue to derive a significant portion of its business from IBM in 1999 and future years, and to actively pursue new business with IBM. While a significant decline in revenue from IBM would have a material adverse impact, the company believes the loss of all IBM business is unlikely, due to the recent renewal of a national contract, the number of contracts in existence with IBM, the diversity of the projects performed for IBM, and the number of locations and divisions involved.

Most companies follow a continuous process to create IT business solutions. The IT business solution life cycle begins with planning, as companies design strategies to meet overall business objectives by utilizing IT. Planning is followed by development, in which companies develop and implement IT solutions using their newly devised plans, Finally, these solutions must be managed and maintained to ensure systems and technologies are supported to preserve their effectiveness. TSK provides services in each of these three areas.

The company has developed a professional staff resource database, CTG-Smartsource, used to screen and qualify individuals who are available to work on client information technology needs. The database has more than 190,000 candidates available for assignments.

Per Share Data ($) (Year Ended Dec. 31)	1998	1997	1996	1995	1994	1993	1992	1991	1990	1989
Tangible Bk. Val.	3.89	2.33	6.48	2.71	2.54	3.33	3.07	2.77	5.47	5.05
Cash Flow	1.65	1.32	2.11	0.97	0.57	-0.94	0.63	0.35	0.63	-0.20
Earnings	1.42	1.01	0.63	0.61	0.26	-1.31	0.28	0.05	0.39	-0.44
Dividends	0.05	0.05	0.05	0.05	0.05	0.05	0.03	0.03	0.03	0.03
Payout Ratio	4%	5%	8%	8%	19%	NM	8%	50%	6%	NM
Prices - High	45	49 3/8	21 3/4	11	5 1/4	4 1/2	5	5 5/8	6 1/8	7 7/8
- Low	18 1/2	16 5/8	8 3/8	4 1/8	3 3/8	3	3 1/2	3 1/2	3 3/8	4 1/4
P/E Ratio - High	32	49	35	18	20	NM	18	NM	16	NM
- Low	13	16	13	7	13	NM	13	NM	9	NM
Income Statement Analysis (Million $)										
Revs.	468	408	365	339	302	295	303	285	244	233
Oper. Inc.	44.9	34.4	26.2	18.9	6.2	12.7	17.6	8.8	15.9	7.7
Depr.	5.0	5.4	7.7	6.2	5.9	7.9	7.0	5.7	4.6	4.3
Int. Exp.	0.5	0.8	0.8	1.3	1.2	1.1	1.4	2.0	0.7	2.0
Pretax Inc.	40.8	30.3	18.5	12.0	8.1	-30.7	10.1	1.6	12.6	-11.6
Eff. Tax Rate	41%	41%	40%	11%	41%	NM	45%	43%	43%	NM
Net Inc.	24.0	17.9	11.1	10.8	4.8	-27.7	5.6	0.9	7.2	-7.8
Balance Sheet & Other Fin. Data (Million $)										
Cash	57.7	25.0	41.5	16.5	5.1	11.8	13.3	10.6	14.6	19.6
Curr. Assets	137	88.9	101	78.8	68.2	78.8	75.8	71.1	68.5	67.1
Total Assets	157	108	121	105	95.0	109	138	139	134	107
Curr. Liab.	62.5	41.8	39.7	29.3	29.3	27.5	28.1	30.3	33.0	15.7
LT Debt	Nil	Nil	Nil	3.6	6.1	8.4	10.5	13.8	11.6	1.4
Common Eqty.	83.4	65.1	71.5	61.5	50.7	62.5	92.6	87.2	83.3	83.6
Total Cap.	83.4	55.3	71.5	65.1	57.0	71.0	105	103	97.0	87.0
Cap. Exp.	5.1	4.8	3.6	5.4	4.2	5.4	4.3	7.6	5.8	3.2
Cash Flow	29.0	23.3	18.7	16.9	10.7	-19.9	12.5	6.5	11.8	-3.5
Curr. Ratio	2.2	2.1	2.5	2.7	2.3	2.9	2.7	2.3	2.1	4.3
% LT Debt of Cap.	Nil	Nil	Nil	5.6	10.8	11.9	10.1	13.4	12.0	1.6
% Net Inc.of Revs.	5.1	4.4	3.1	3.2	1.6	NM	1.9	0.3	3.0	NM
% Ret. on Assets	18.2	15.6	9.8	10.8	4.5	NM	3.9	0.6	6.2	NM
% Ret. on Equity	32.4	24.6	16.7	19.3	8.1	NM	5.9	0.9	8.9	NM

Data as orig reptd.; bef. results of disc opers/spec. items. Per share data adj. for stk. divs. Bold denotes diluted EPS (FASB 128)-prior periods restated. E-Estimated. NA-Not Available. NM-Not Meaningful. NR-Not Ranked.

Office—800 Delaware Ave., Buffalo, NY 14209. **Tel**—(716) 882-8000. **Fax**—(716) 887-7456. **Website**—http://www.ctg.com **Chrmn & CEO**—G. S. Fitzgerald. **VP & Secy**—J. G. Makowski. **VP-Fin, CFO, Secy & Investor Contact**—James R. Boldt. **Dirs**—G. B. Beitzel, R. L. Crandall, R. K. Elliott, G. S. Fitzgerald, R. A. Marks, B. Z. Shattuck. **Transfer Agent & Registrar**—First National Bank of Boston. **Incorporated**—in New York in 1966. **Empl**— 6,000. **S&P Analyst:** P.L.H.

STANDARD
&POOR'S
STOCK REPORTS

Concord Communications

NASDAQ Symbol **CCRD**

In S&P SmallCap 600

27-OCT-99

Industry: Computer (Software & Services)

Summary: Concord develops and supports turnkey, automated, scalable, web-based performance analysis and reporting solutions for the management of computer networks.

Quantitative Evaluations

Outlook
(1 Lowest—5 Highest)
• **NA**
Fair Value
• **NA**
Risk
• **NA**
Earn./Div. Rank
• **NR**

Technical Eval.
• **Neutral** since 10/99
Rel. Strength Rank
(1 Lowest—99 Highest)
• **89**
Insider Activity
• **Unfavorable**

Recent Price • 40⅜
52 Wk Range • 69¾-29⅝
Yield • Nil
12-Mo. P/E • 41.2

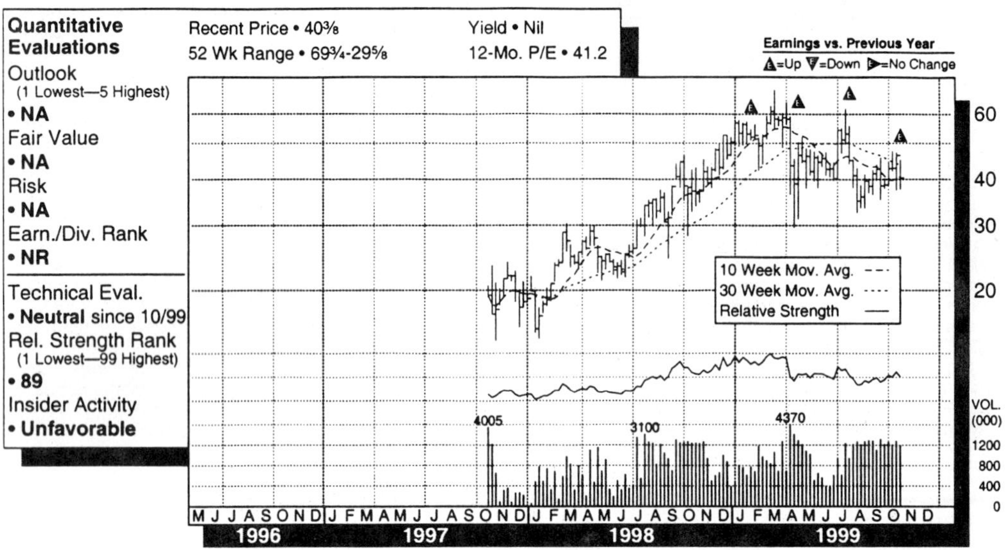

Business Profile - 27-OCT-99

In October 1999, the company agreed to acquire, in exchange for about 815,248 common shares, Empire Technologies, a privately held provider of solutions for proactive self-management of UNIX and Windows NT systems, as well as mission-critical applications. The transaction, which has been approved by directors of each company, is subject to certain closing conditions. CCRD believe the acquisition marks its first step in delivering on its strategy of consolidating "best of breed" solutions to enable more effective e-business.

Operational Review - 27-OCT-99

Revenues in the nine months ended September 30, 1999, advanced 74%, year to year. License revenues were bolstered by increased sales to new customers, and additional sales to existing customers for new products and upgrades of existing licenses. Service revenues benefited from an increase in maintenance contracts, training and professional services for new and existing customers. Profitability improved considerably; pretax income more than doubled, to $13,666,000, from $5,642,000. After taxes at 38.0%, versus 3.8%, net income was up 56%, to $8,470,000 ($0.59 a share), from $5,428,000 ($0.39).

Stock Performance - 22-OCT-99

In the past 30 trading days, CCRD's shares have increased 9%, compared to a 4% fall in the S&P 500. Average trading volume for the past five days was 251,400 shares, compared with the 40-day moving average of 367,938 shares.

Key Stock Statistics

Dividend Rate/Share	Nil	Shareholders	233
Shs. outstg. (M)	13.5	Market cap. (B)	$0.644
Avg. daily vol. (M)	0.303	Inst. holdings	92%
Tang. Bk. Value/Share	4.06		
Beta	NA		

Value of $10,000 invested 5 years ago: NA

Fiscal Year Ending Dec. 31

	1999	1998	1997	1996	1995	1994
Revenues (Million $)						
1Q	13.53	7.06	—	—	—	—
2Q	15.06	8.54	—	—	—	—
3Q	17.02	10.60	5.26	—	—	—
4Q	—	13.29	6.61	—	—	—
Yr.	—	39.48	19.57	9.01	—	—
Earnings Per Share ($)						
1Q	**0.17**	**0.08**	—	—	—	—
2Q	**0.19**	**0.13**	—	—	—	—
3Q	**0.23**	**0.12**	—	—	—	—
4Q	—	**0.17**	**0.07**	—	—	—
Yr.	—	**0.64**	**0.01**	**-0.57**	**-0.84**	—

Next earnings report expected: late January

Dividend Data

No cash dividends have been paid. The company currently expects to retain all future earnings for use in its business, and does not anticipate paying cash dividends for the foreseeable future.

Concord Communications, Inc.

Business Summary - 27-OCT-99

Concord Communications, Inc. develops, markets and supports a family of turnkey, automated, scalable, web-based performance analysis and reporting solutions for the management of computer networks. By providing a global view of network performance, the company's products permit the effective and efficient management of large and medium-size multi-vendor networks, both by end users and network service providers, including telecommunications carriers, Internet Service Providers (ISPs), systems integrators and outsourcers.

Substantially all revenues are derived from the company's Network Health product family, which began shipping in the first quarter of 1995. Network Health retrieves and compiles vital network statistics, performs extensive analyses of the statistics, and provides intuitive, informative, user-friendly graphical reports. Concord's products can simultaneously poll, analyze and report on 10,000 to 20,000 elements per workstation.

Concord's Network Health product family provides organizations with the following benefits: capacity planning: providing information to support business decisions relating to network utilization and future capacity requirements; reduction in data communication expenses: identifying excess capacity on each WAN, leased line or frame relay circuit; effective allocation of resources: allowing management to effectively deploy networking resources and personnel; and service level monitoring: assisting managers in making network resource allocation decisions within an organization and assisting both network service providers and end users in monitoring the availability of negotiated service level agreements.

In providing these benefits, the Network Health product family incorporates the following features: fully automated, turnkey implementation; scalable, software-only solution; multi-level reporting; and technology and vendor independence.

Concord markets its products in the U.S. to organizations with large and medium-size networks, as well as network service providers which include telecommunications carriers, ISPs, systems integrators and outsourcers primarily through a direct sales force, sales agents and through value-added resellers (VARs).

Internationally, the company markets exclusively through distributors. Revenues from international locations (primarily Europe) accounted for about 18% of revenues in 1998, up from 12% in 1997. A continuing increase in revenues from international locations as a percentage of total revenues mainly reflects the company's expansion of its operations outside the U.S., including both the hiring of additional personnel and the establishment of additional reseller agreements.

Per Share Data ($) (Year Ended Dec. 31)	1998	1997	1996	1995	1994	1993	1992	1991	1990	1989
Tangible Bk. Val.	3.51	2.87	NM	NA	NA	NA	NA	NA	NA	NA
Cash Flow	0.71	0.06	-0.41	NA	NA	NA	NA	NA	NA	NA
Earnings	0.64	0.01	-0.57	NA	NA	NA	NA	NA	NA	NA
Dividends	Nil	Nil	Nil	NA	NA	NA	NA	NA	NA	NA
Payout Ratio	Nil	Nil	Nil	NA	NA	NA	NA	NA	NA	NA
Prices - High	57 3/8	23 7/8	NA	NA	NA	NA	NA	NA	NA	NA
- Low	14 3/4	14	NA	NA	NA	NA	NA	NA	NA	NA
P/E Ratio - High	90	NM	NM	NA	NA	NA	NA	NA	NA	NA
- Low	23	NM	NM	NA	NA	NA	NA	NA	NA	NA
Income Statement Analysis (Million $)										
Revs.	39.5	19.6	9.0	NA	NA	NA	NA	NA	NA	NA
Oper. Inc.	8.2	0.4	-4.7	NA	NA	NA	NA	NA	NA	NA
Depr.	0.9	0.6	0.4	NA	NA	NA	NA	NA	NA	NA
Int. Exp.	Nil	0.1	Nil	NA	NA	NA	NA	NA	NA	NA
Pretax Inc.	9.6	0.1	-5.1	NA	NA	NA	NA	NA	NA	NA
Eff. Tax Rate	5.54%	NM	NM	NA	NA	NA	NA	NA	NA	NA
Net Inc.	9.1	0.1	-5.1	NA	NA	NA	NA	NA	NA	NA
Balance Sheet & Other Fin. Data (Million $)										
Cash	50.4	36.5	1.7	NA	NA	NA	NA	NA	NA	NA
Curr. Assets	56.0	39.9	4.1	NA	NA	NA	NA	NA	NA	NA
Total Assets	58.7	41.9	5.6	NA	NA	NA	NA	NA	NA	NA
Curr. Liab.	12.9	7.4	5.5	NA	NA	NA	NA	NA	NA	NA
LT Debt	Nil	Nil	0.7	NA	NA	NA	NA	NA	NA	NA
Common Eqty.	45.7	34.5	-15.0	NA	NA	NA	NA	NA	NA	NA
Total Cap.	45.7	34.5	0.1	NA	NA	NA	NA	NA	NA	NA
Cap. Exp.	1.9	1.1	0.7	NA	NA	NA	NA	NA	NA	NA
Cash Flow	10.0	0.7	-4.7	NA	NA	NA	NA	NA	NA	NA
Curr. Ratio	4.3	5.4	0.8	NA	NA	NA	NA	NA	NA	NA
% LT Debt of Cap.	Nil	Nil	NM	NA	NA	NA	NA	NA	NA	NA
% Net Inc.of Revs.	23.0	0.7	NM	NA	NA	NA	NA	NA	NA	NA
% Ret. on Assets	18.1	NM	NM	NA	NA	NA	NA	NA	NA	NA
% Ret. on Equity	22.6	NM	NM	NA	NA	NA	NA	NA	NA	NA

Data as orig reptd.; bef. results of disc opers/spec. items. Per share data adj. for stk. divs. Bold denotes diluted EPS (FASB 128)-prior periods restated. E-Estimated. NA-Not Available. NM-Not Meaningful. NR-Not Ranked.

Office—600 Nickerson Road, Marlboro, MA 01752. **Tel**—(508) 460-4646. **Website**—http://www.concord.com **Pres & CEO**—J. A. Blaeser. **VP-CFO, Treas & Clerk**—G. E. Haroian. **Dirs**—J. A. Blaesser, F. W. W. Bolander, R. M. Burnes Jr., R. C. Hawk, J. R. Held, D. Kamra, R. M. Wadsworth. **Transfer Agent & Registrar**—Boston EquiServe, L.P., Canton, MA. **Incorporated**—in Massachusetts in 1980. **Empl**— 173. **S&P Analyst:** J. J. Schemitsch

STANDARD
&POOR'S
STOCK REPORTS

Cone Mills

NYSE Symbol **COE**

In S&P SmallCap 600

09-OCT-99

Industry:
Textiles (Specialty)

Summary: The world's largest producer of denim fabrics, Cone also makes a variety of other apparel fabrics and sells decorative fabrics to home furnishings markets.

Quantitative Evaluations

Outlook
(1 Lowest—5 Highest)
• **NA**

Fair Value
• **NA**

Risk
• **Low**

Earn./Div. Rank
• **NR**

Technical Eval.
• **Bearish** since 8/99

Rel. Strength Rank
(1 Lowest—99 Highest)
• **15**

Insider Activity
• **Favorable**

Recent Price • 4⅝

52 Wk Range • 7⅛-3¾

Yield • Nil

12-Mo. P/E • NM

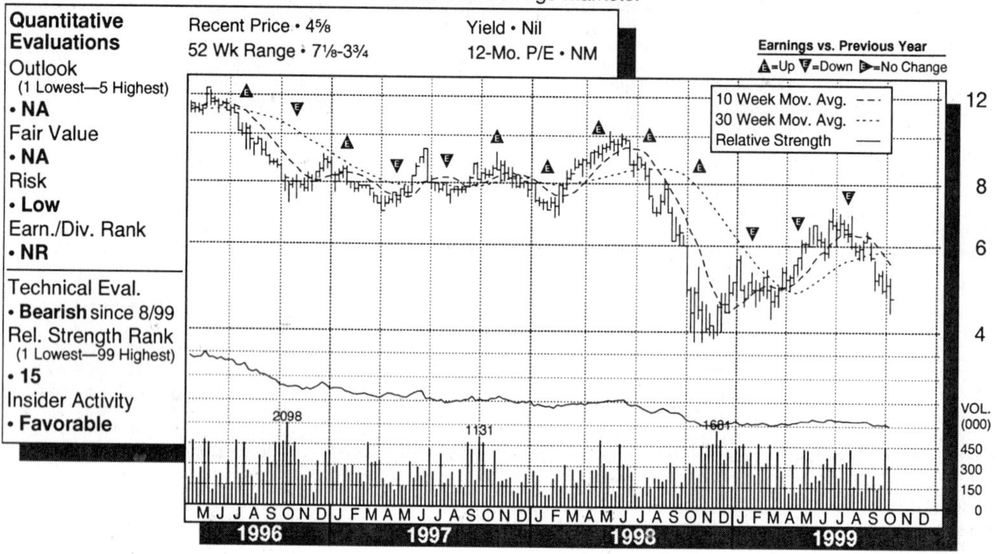

Business Profile - 06-OCT-99

In line with the company's strategy to form alliances that provide apparel manufacturing services in different platforms throughout the world, the company announced an alliance with Deborah/Starlite of Mexico in June 1999. The company has also formed a strategic alliance with Guatemala-based Koramsa, an apparel manufacturer, to market apparel sourcing capabilities. In conjunction with the company's restructuring plan, Cone Mills announced in August 1999, that it would reduce the work force at its Carlisle plant in South Carolina by 25%. In September 1999, an investor group increased its stake in COE to about 12.6% and was seeking board representation.

Operational Review - 06-OCT-99

Net sales in the six months ended July 4, 1999, declined 14%, year to year, reflecting weaker consumer demand for denim products. Gross margins narrowed, mainly due to lower unit sales and pricing. Operating expenses (including a $12.9 million restructuring charge) exceeded gross profit, and after interest expense, a $14.6 million pretax loss compared with pretax income of $3.1 million. After a tax credit, versus taxes at 33.0%, and equity in earnings of unconsolidated affiliate of $2.0 million versus $2.5 million, a loss of $7,718,000 ($0.36 a share, after preferred dividends) contrasted with income of $4,595,000 ($0.12). Results in 1999 exclude a $0.04 a share charge for the cumulative effect of accounting charge.

Stock Performance - 08-OCT-99

In the past 30 trading days, COE's shares have declined 25%, compared to a 0.91% fall in the S&P 500. Average trading volume for the past five days was 62,640 shares, compared with the 40-day moving average of 47,915 shares.

Key Stock Statistics

Dividend Rate/Share	Nil	Shareholders	500
Shs. outstg. (M)	25.5	Market cap. (B)	$0.119
Avg. daily vol. (M)	0.054	Inst. holdings	29%
Tang. Bk. Value/Share	5.19		
Beta	0.18		

Value of $10,000 invested 5 years ago: $ 2,777

Fiscal Year Ending Dec. 31

	1999	1998	1997	1996	1995	1994
Revenues (Million $)						
1Q	157.3	190.2	174.7	199.3	226.2	195.9
2Q	174.5	197.3	185.8	208.1	232.9	201.7
3Q	—	187.4	185.5	180.8	231.7	203.5
4Q	—	153.8	170.8	157.7	219.4	205.1
Yr.	—	728.6	716.9	745.9	910.2	806.2
Earnings Per Share ($)						
1Q	**-0.36**	**0.03**	**-0.10**	**0.24**	0.11	0.34
2Q	Nil	**0.09**	**-0.07**	**0.11**	-0.06	0.33
3Q	—	**0.08**	**-0.08**	**-0.11**	0.19	0.28
4Q	—	**-0.58**	**-0.22**	**-0.44**	-0.46	0.24
Yr.	—	**-0.37**	**-0.47**	**-0.19**	**-0.22**	1.19

Next earnings report expected: mid October

Dividend Data

No cash has been paid.

Business Summary - 06-OCT-99

Founded in 1891, Cone Mills is the largest producer of denim fabrics in the world and the largest commission printer of home furnishings fabrics in North America. The company operates in four principal business segments: denim and khaki; yard-dyed products; commission finishing; and decorative fabrics.

The company's denim products are primarily designed for use in garments targeted for the upper-end market, where styling and quality generally command premium fabric prices. The company categorizes the market into heavyweight denim and speciality weight denims. Heavyweight denim is used primarily in jeans and is by far the largest segment of the denim market. Within the heavyweight market, the company further classifies its denims as "value-added" and "basic." Valued-added denims are distinguished by fabric construction, yarn variations, finishes and new product introductions. Basic denims are less differentiated by styling with competition being primarily on the basis of price, quality and service. Cone's valued-added denims are sold principally to brand name apparel companies (such as Levi Strauss, which accounted for 32% of COE's revenues in 1998), specialty retailers and brand name garment producers.

Commission finishing, consisting of the Carlisle and Raytex plants, is the largest commission printer of decorative fabrics in the U.S. and provides custom printing and plainshade dyeing services to leading home furnishing stylists and distributors. The home furnishing fabrics processed at the Carlisle facility are generally used for upholstery and drapery prints. COE also provides fabric printing and plainshade dyeing services to converters of fashion apparel fabrics.

The decorative fabrics unit includes John Wolf and Cone Jacquards. John Wolf is a "converter" of printed and solid woven fabrics for upholstery, draperies and bedspreads. A converter designs and distributes fabrics, which are made and printed for the converter by others. Cone Jacquards, a modern 138,000 sq. ft. facility with wide weaving machines, produces broadloom and jacquard fabrics for furniture makers, fabric distributors, retailers, converters and specialty product manufacturers.

The company is engaged in denim production in Mexico through a joint venture facility with Compania Industrial de Parras, S. A. This facility has been producing basic denims and yarn since late 1995. In August 1998, the company formed an alliance with Ashima Group of India, under which it markets Ashima denim and sportswear products outside the Indian sub-continent.

In January 1999, the company announced a comprehensive restructuring plan which entailed: closing the Salisbury plant; consolidating the denim and sportswear fabrics businesses; discontinuing yarn production at its North Carolina plants; restructuring the Carlisle plant; and downsizing administrative staff.

Per Share Data ($) **(Year Ended Dec. 31)**	**1998**	**1997**	**1996**	**1995**	**1994**	**1993**	**1992**	**1991**	**1990**	**1989**
Tangible Bk. Val.	4.48	4.82	5.22	5.28	5.84	6.19	4.52	3.35	NA	NA
Cash Flow	0.70	0.52	0.80	0.91	2.02	2.43	2.50	1.07	NA	NA
Earnings	-0.37	-0.47	-0.19	-0.22	1.19	1.68	1.67	0.29	NA	NA
Dividends	Nil	Nil	Nil	Nil	Nil	Nil	Nil	NA	NA	NA
Payout Ratio	Nil	Nil	Nil	Nil	Nil	Nil	Nil	NA	NA	NA
Prices - High	10¼	9⅜	12⅜	14⅜	17¼	19⅝	16	NA	NA	NA
- Low	3¾	7	7¼	10⅝	11⅛	13⅜	10	NA	NA	NA
P/E Ratio - High	NM	NM	NM	NM	14	12	10	NA	NA	NA
- Low	NM	NM	NM	NM	9	8	6	NA	NA	NA
Income Statement Analysis (Million $)										
Revs.	729	717	746	910	806	769	705	633	NA	NA
Oper. Inc.	37.2	22.8	44.9	63.7	86.0	107	98.0	56.0	NA	NA
Depr.	27.7	25.9	26.9	28.3	23.3	21.0	20.0	20.4	NA	NA
Int. Exp.	14.9	14.2	15.5	15.1	7.9	7.0	10.9	19.0	NA	NA
Pretax Inc.	-14.6	-17.4	-4.5	20.9	55.5	79.5	70.2	19.8	NA	NA
Eff. Tax Rate	NM	NM	NM	35%	36%	38%	35%	38%	NA	NA
Net Inc.	-6.7	-9.4	-2.2	-3.3	35.8	49.6	45.4	12.2	NA	NA
Balance Sheet & Other Fin. Data (Million $)										
Cash	0.6	0.9	1.0	0.3	1.2	0.5	7.3	6.4	NA	NA
Curr. Assets	168	180	204	234	213	202	216	259	NA	NA
Total Assets	489	507	530	584	524	432	402	443	NA	NA
Curr. Liab.	104	121	120	151	118	104	121	127	NA	NA
LT Debt	161	140	150	162	126	77.0	77.0	138	NA	NA
Common Eqty.	144	158	210	184	198	172	125	135	NA	NA
Total Cap.	373	336	400	425	400	324	277	312	NA	NA
Cap. Exp.	32.8	36.2	36.2	61.7	37.5	38.7	25.4	NA	NA	NA
Cash Flow	18.0	13.7	21.7	25.0	56.3	67.8	60.8	28.0	NA	NA
Curr. Ratio	1.6	1.5	1.7	1.6	1.8	1.9	1.8	2.0	NA	NA
% LT Debt of Cap.	43.2	41.7	37.5	38.1	31.5	23.8	27.6	44.1	NA	NA
% Net Inc.of Revs.	NM	NM	NM	NM	4.4	6.4	6.4	1.9	NA	NA
% Ret. on Assets	NM	NM	NM	NM	7.5	11.9	6.3	NA	NA	NA
% Ret. on Equity	NM	NM	NM	NM	18.0	31.5	49.3	NA	NA	NA

Data as orig reptd.; bef. results of disc opers/spec. items. Per share data adj. for stk. divs. Bold denotes diluted EPS (FASB 128)-prior periods restated. E-Estimated. NA-Not Available. NM-Not Meaningful. NR-Not Ranked.

Office—3101 N. Elm St., Greensboro, NC 27408. **Tel**—(336) 379-6220. **Website**—http://www.cone.com. **Chrmn**—D. L. Trogdon. **Pres & CEO**—J. L. Bakane. **EVP & CFO**—A. L. Furr. **Treas & Investor Contact**—David E. Bray. **VP & Secy**—N. W. Kooce.**Dirs**—J. L. Bakane, D. R. Bray, J. C. Kimmel, D. T. Kollat, C. M. Reid, J. W. Rosenblum, N. Shreiber, D. L. Trogdon, C. C. Wilson. **Transfer Agent & Registrar**—First Union National Bank of North Carolina, Charlotte. **Incorporated**—in North Carolina. **Empl**— 6,100. **S&P Analyst:** Howard Choe

STANDARD
&POOR'S
STOCK REPORTS

Connecticut Energy

NYSE Symbol **CNE**

In S&P SmallCap 600

09-OCT-99

Industry:
Natural Gas

Summary: This holding company, whose principal subsidiary provides natural gas in three counties in Connecticut, has agreed to be acquired by Energy East Corp.

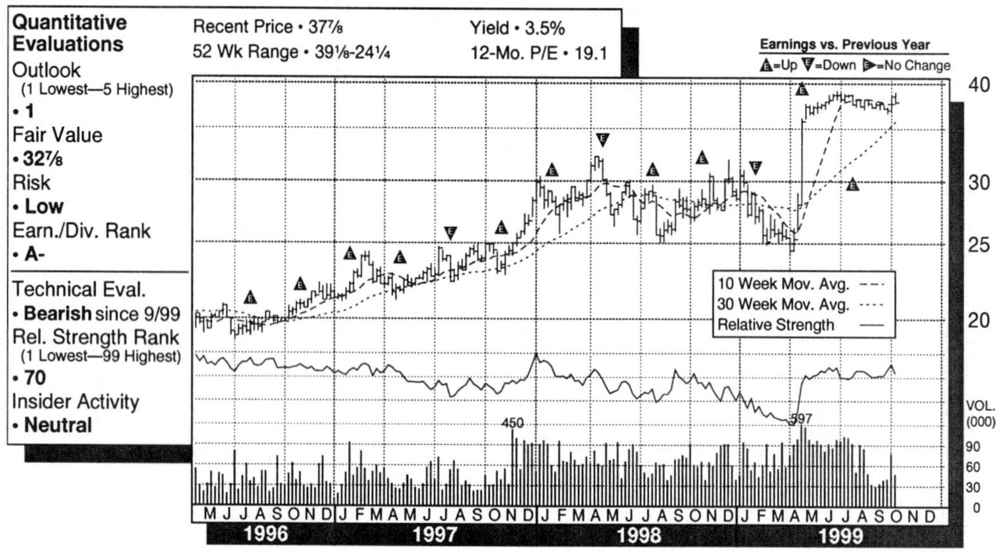

Business Profile - 20-AUG-99

On April 23, 1999, the company signed a definitive agreement to be acquired by Energy East Corp. in a transaction valued at $617 million. Under the agreement, shareholders would receive $42 a share, 50% in stock and 50% in cash. Shareholders will have a choice of receiving stock or cash, subject to pro-ration. The transaction is subject to approval from regulatory authorities and CNE stockholders. Earlier Connecticut Energy said that although it expects to continue to focus on expanding its utility customer base as the deregulation of the gas utility industry continues, it anticipates that an increasing portion of earnings will come from unregulated operations.

Operational Review - 20-AUG-99

Revenues in the nine months ended June 30, 1999, declined 5.6%, year to year, on lower interruptible volumes, partly offset by increased firm volumes. Gross margins widened, and, with operating expenses up 2.9%, operating profit gained 16%. After merger related expenses of $1.5 million, net income rose 8.2%, to $22,075,000 ($2.13 a share, on 3.0% more shares), from $20,397,000 ($2.03).

Stock Performance - 08-OCT-99

In the past 30 trading days, CNE's shares have increased 2%, compared to a 0.91% fall in the S&P 500. Average trading volume for the past five days was 9,400 shares, compared with the 40-day moving average of 8,782 shares.

Key Stock Statistics

Dividend Rate/Share	1.34	Shareholders	9,770
Shs. outstg. (M)	10.4	Market cap. (B)	$0.393
Avg. daily vol. (M)	0.010	Inst. holdings	39%
Tang. Bk. Value/Share	16.16		
Beta	0.31		

Value of $10,000 invested 5 years ago: $ 20,410

Fiscal Year Ending Sep. 30

	1999	1998	1997	1996	1995	1994
Revenues (Million $)						
1Q	61.59	76.51	74.87	69.78	65.52	66.71
2Q	106.2	100.8	106.9	120.2	103.3	111.8
3Q	35.38	38.00	44.03	43.95	39.76	36.84
4Q	—	27.15	26.24	27.18	23.53	25.49
Yr.	—	242.4	252.0	261.1	232.1	240.9
Earnings Per Share ($)						
1Q	**0.59**	**0.64**	0.60	0.57	0.57	0.67
2Q	**1.62**	**1.49**	1.67	1.64	1.79	1.77
3Q	**-0.07**	**-0.10**	-0.13	-0.08	-0.23	-0.16
4Q	—	**-0.13**	-0.32	-0.42	-0.52	-0.53
Yr.	—	**1.88**	**1.81**	1.70	1.60	1.58

Next earnings report expected: early November

Dividend Data (Dividends have been paid since 1850.)

Amount ($)	Date Decl.	Ex-Div. Date	Stock of Record	Payment Date
0.335	Nov. 24	Dec. 03	Dec. 07	Dec. 31 '98
0.335	Jan. 26	Mar. 17	Mar. 19	Mar. 31 '99
0.335	May. 25	Jun. 16	Jun. 18	Jun. 30 '99
0.335	Jul. 27	Sep. 15	Sep. 17	Sep. 30 '99

A Division of The McGraw-Hill Companies

Connecticut Energy Corporation

Business Summary - 20-AUG-99

Connecticut Energy Corp. is a utility holding company that, through its predecessor companies, has compiled the longest consecutive dividend payment record of any nonfinancial company listed on the New York Stock Exchange. Cash dividends have been paid on the common stock since 1850.

Through wholly owned Southern Connecticut Gas Co. (Southern), CNE delivers natural gas in 22 Connecticut communities to more than 158,000 customers. The service area consists of towns along the southern Connecticut coast from Westport to Old Saybrook; the service area also includes the urban communities of Bridgeport and New Haven.

Southern provides three types of gas service: firm sales, firm transportation, and interruptible.

Firm service is provided to residential, commercial and industrial customers who require a continuous gas supply throughout the year. Southern serves about 181,000 firm residential units. Firm transportation is available to commercial and industrial customers who have secured their own gas supply and require that Southern transport this supply on its distribution system. Interruptible service is available to those commercial and industrial customers and multifamily residential dwellings that have dual fuel capabilities, allowing them to alternate between natural gas and another fuel source.

From FY 92 (Sep.) to FY 98, the average number of on-system customers served by Southern grew from about 152,100 to 157,800, with residential customers accounting for 58.9% of FY 98 revenues; commercial firm, 17.7%; industrial firm, 3.9%; and interruptible and other, 19.5%.

Southern concentrates on customer additions that are the most cost-effective to achieve. Over the past several years, Southern has focused on adding load along its existing mains, which generally requires a lower capital outlay. About 59% of the residences along Southern's mains heat with natural gas. The conversion of these homes from an alternative fuel to natural gas heat has been a major factor in increased load growth.

In an effort to capture new markets, CNE has been expanding its two unregulated subsidiaries, CNE Energy Services Group and CNE Development, both formed in FY 95. It has also developed a third unregulated subsidiary, CNE Venture-Tech. Energy Services provides various energy products and services to commercial and industrial customers throughout New England, from installation and maintenance of equipment to procuring the most cost-effective energy commodity. CNE Development participates in a natural gas purchasing cooperative. Venture-Tech seeks investment opportunities in information technology related to utility operations.

Per Share Data ($)										
(Year Ended Sep. 30)	**1998**	**1997**	**1996**	**1995**	**1994**	**1993**	**1992**	**1991**	**1990**	**1989**
Tangible Bk. Val.	16.16	15.10	15.31	14.15	13.72	12.47	11.91	12.36	11.74	11.98
Earnings	1.88	1.81	1.70	1.60	1.58	1.50	1.43	1.38	1.12	1.28
Dividends	1.33	1.32	1.31	1.30	1.29	1.28	1.26	1.24	1.23	1.20
Payout Ratio	71%	73%	77%	81%	82%	85%	88%	90%	110%	94%
Prices - High	32 1/4	30 3/8	22 1/4	22 3/8	25	26 1/2	24 3/4	20 3/8	18	18 7/8
- Low	25	21	18 5/8	18 1/2	18 5/8	22 1/2	18 7/8	14 1/4	14 1/2	14
P/E Ratio - High	17	17	13	14	16	18	17	15	16	15
- Low	13	12	11	12	12	15	13	10	13	11
Income Statement Analysis (Million $)										
Revs.	242	252	261	232	241	213	203	179	174	171
Depr.	16.9	15.8	14.8	14.1	13.0	12.1	11.3	10.5	10.7	10.3
Maint.	3.7	3.6	3.8	3.7	4.0	3.7	3.6	3.6	4.0	3.9
Fxd. Chgs. Cov.	2.9	2.9	2.8	2.8	2.6	2.3	2.2	2.4	2.2	2.4
Constr. Credits	Nil	Nil	Nil	Nil	Nil	Nil	Nil	Nil	Nil	Nil
Eff. Tax Rate	25%	35%	33%	35%	30%	26%	24%	39%	41%	43%
Net Inc.	19.0	16.4	15.2	14.1	12.8	11.1	10.2	9.0	6.9	7.8
Balance Sheet & Other Fin. Data (Million $)										
Gross Prop.	417	403	376	355	332	314	294	274	255	242
Cap. Exp.	24.7	28.5	25.3	27.6	26.7	26.1	22.8	20.4	23.4	23.7
Net Prop.	280	272	258	248	234	222	210	199	189	181
Capitalization:										
LT Debt	150	134	139	119	120	121	94.1	87.4	91.5	79.7
% LT Debt	46	48	50	48	49	55	50	49	55	51
Pfd.	NA	NA	NA	NA	NA	0.6	0.7	0.7	0.8	0.8
% Pfd.	NA	NA	NA	NA	NA	0.30	0.40	0.40	0.50	0.60
Common	177	145	138	136	126	100	92.6	88.6	74.4	75.0
% Common	54	52	50	52	51	45	49	50	45	48
Total Cap.	403	279	277	251	301	239	205	194	182	170
% Oper. Ratio	86.2	88.5	89.1	88.4	89.6	89.1	89.0	88.9	90.3	80.8
% Earn. on Net Prop.	10.8	10.8	11.4	11.2	11.0	10.7	10.9	10.2	9.1	9.9
% Return On Revs.	7.8	6.5	5.8	6.1	5.3	5.2	5.0	5.0	4.0	4.6
% Return On Invest. Capital	8.5	4.8	8.7	8.6	9.1	10.2	10.9	10.4	9.7	10.1
% Return On Com. Equity	11.8	11.6	11.9	10.9	11.4	11.5	11.3	11.0	9.3	10.6

Data as orig reptd.; bef. results of disc opers/spec. items. Per share data adj. for stk. divs. Bold denotes diluted EPS (FASB 128)-prior periods restated. E-Estimated. NA-Not Available. NM-Not Meaningful. NR-Not Ranked.

Office—855 Main St., Bridgeport, CT 06604. **Tel**—(800) 760-7776. **Website**—www.connenergy.com **Chrmn, Pres & CEO**—J. R. Crespo. **VP, CFO & Treas**—C. A. Forest. **VP & Secy**—S. W. Bowlby. **Investor Contact**—Judith E. Falango (203-382-8156). **Dirs**—H. Chauncey Jr., J. P. Comer, J. R. Crespo, R. F. Freeman, R. M. Hoyt, N. M. Marsilius III, S. M. Sugden, C. D. Turner. **Transfer Agent & Registrar**—Boston EquiServe. **Incorporated**—in Connecticut in 1967; reincorporated in Connecticut in 1979. **Empl**— 488. **S&P Analyst:** C.C.P.

STANDARD
&POOR'S
STOCK REPORTS

Consolidated Graphics

NYSE Symbol **CGX**

In S&P SmallCap 600

09-OCT-99

Industry: Specialty Printing

Summary: This company provides general commercial printing services through 46 printing companies in the U.S.

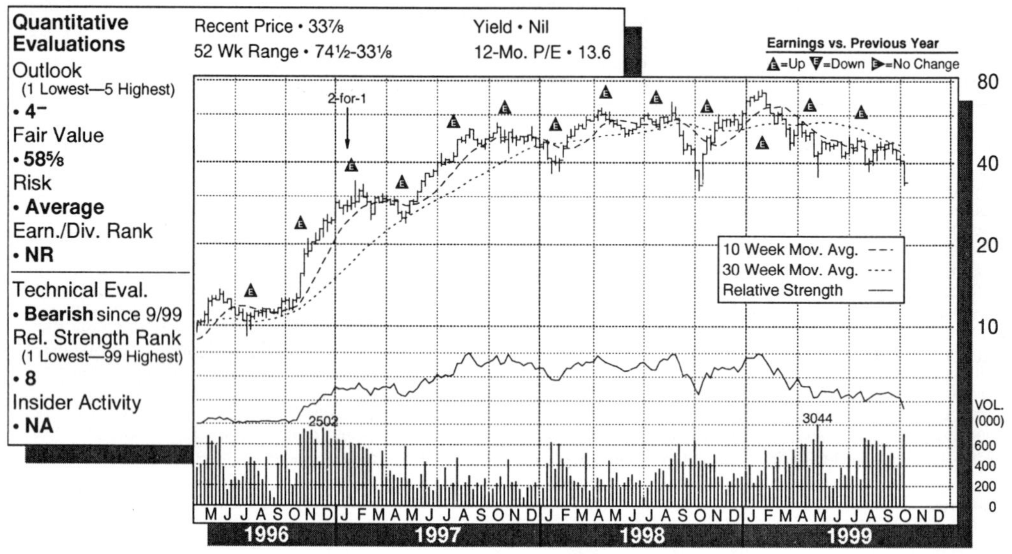

Business Profile - 11-JUN-99

Consolidated Graphics plans to continue growing its companies while making acquisitions in FY 00 (Mar.). In April 1999, CGX announced that it had acquired 54 printing companies with over $280 million in revenue. The company noted that, consistent with its history, it has substantially improved the profitability of these companies by investing in advanced technology and through the introduction of CGX's management techniques. CGX believes that it adds value to its acquired companies through synergies resulting from purchasing economies and the centralization of certain administrative functions. The company believes that its ability to invest in printing technology is an important strength that should substantially improve production quality and capacity while reducing costs.

Operational Review - 11-JUN-99

Based on a preliminary report, sales for the year ended March 31, 1999, rose 88% from those of the prior year, mainly reflecting sales from acquired companies. Gross margins narrowed slightly. Selling expense and G&A expense both increased 91%, and following a more than doubling of interest expense, net income rose 76%, to $32,275,000 ($2.28 a share, on 7.7% more shares), from $18,390,000 ($1.40).

Stock Performance - 08-OCT-99

In the past 30 trading days, CGX's shares have declined 26%, compared to a 0.91% fall in the S&P 500. Average trading volume for the past five days was 33,680 shares, compared with the 40-day moving average of 44,867 shares.

Key Stock Statistics

Dividend Rate/Share	Nil	Shareholders	100
Shs. outstg. (M)	15.7	Market cap. (B)	$0.534
Avg. daily vol. (M)	0.160	Inst. holdings	64%
Tang. Bk. Value/Share	6.70		
Beta	1.38		

Value of $10,000 invested 5 years ago: NA

Fiscal Year Ending Mar. 31

	2000	1999	1998	1997	1996	1995
Revenues (Million $)						
1Q	145.8	85.10	50.68	28.26	19.48	11.53
2Q	—	103.3	53.36	34.45	19.31	10.79
3Q	—	118.3	60.98	38.19	22.26	16.33
4Q	—	129.3	66.27	43.19	24.09	18.52
Yr.	—	436.0	231.3	144.1	85.13	57.17
Earnings Per Share ($)						
1Q	**0.70**	**0.48**	0.30	0.14	0.10	0.15
2Q	—	**0.54**	0.33	0.20	0.13	0.10
3Q	—	**0.60**	**0.37**	0.22	0.03	0.09
4Q	—	**0.65**	**0.41**	0.25	0.10	0.13
Yr.	—	**2.28**	**1.40**	**0.81**	0.36	0.46

Next earnings report expected: late October

Dividend Data

No cash dividends have been paid. A two-for-one split was effected in 1997.

Consolidated Graphics, Inc.

Business Summary - 11-JUN-99

As a result of an ongoing acquisition program, this provider of general commercial printing services in the U.S. has expanded its network of printing companies through acquisitions. In April 1999, the company said that upon the completion of all pending acquisitions, CGX will have 55 companies with annualized revenues of more than $605 million.

Management believes that an abundance of acquisition opportunities exist, because of the fragmented nature of the U.S. general commercial printing industry. The commercial printing business is composed of a large number of locally oriented, family-owned businesses, many of which tend to be viable acquisition targets. The owners are eager to expand by becoming part of a larger organization and, in some instances, wish to retire from the business. Because there are relatively few buyers with adequate financing and management expertise attempting to acquire these local printing companies, CGX has been and expects to continue to be able to implement its acquisition strategy at attractive prices.

CGX's strategy is to grow through acquisitions of smaller, locally oriented printing companies (generally having $2 million to $20 million in annual sales), to enhance the acquired company's competitiveness and profitability, and develop a group of companies in individual geographic markets.

Each of the company's operations provides general commercial printing services relating to the production of annual reports, training manuals, product and capability brochures, direct mail pieces, catalogs and other promotional material, all of which tend to be recurring in nature. One of its printing companies also provides transaction-oriented financial printing services, including the printing of registration and information statements filed with the SEC.

CGX's commercial printing focuses on the production of promotional, investor relations and other sales materials for various customers including corporations, mutual fund companies, advertising agencies, graphic design firms and direct mail and catalog retailers. The company's customer list includes major corporations headquartered in the markets in which the company operates. It believes it is one of the leading general commercial printers in the Houston and Denver markets.

In April 1999, Consolidated Graphics announced the acquisition of 21 printing companies representing over $280 million in revenue. Through these acquisitions, CGX has acquired companies in Baltimore, Bloomington and Ft. Wayne, IN; Boston; Chicago; Cleveland; Columbia, SC; Memphis, TN; Milwaukee; Philadelphia; San Francisco; Washington, D.C.; and Wichita, KS.

Per Share Data ($) (Year Ended Mar. 31)	1999	1998	1997	1996	1995	1994	1993	1992	1991	1990
Tangible Bk. Val.	6.33	5.95	4.85	3.78	3.49	1.61	1.06	NA	NA	NA
Cash Flow	3.72	2.17	1.28	0.70	0.88	0.82	0.48	0.23	0.24	NA
Earnings	2.28	1.40	0.81	0.36	0.46	0.53	0.37	0.14	0.17	NA
Dividends	Nil	Nil	Nil	Nil	Nil	Nil	Nil	Nil	Nil	NA
Payout Ratio	Nil	Nil	Nil	Nil	Nil	Nil	Nil	Nil	Nil	NA
Cal. Yrs.	1998	1997	1996	1995	1994	1993	1992	1991	1990	1989
Prices - High	67⅝	56⅛	29	13⅛	11¼	NA	NA	NA	NA	NA
- Low	31½	23⅞	8⅛	4¾	4⅞	NA	NA	NA	NA	NA
P/E Ratio - High	30	40	36	36	24	NA	NA	NA	NA	NA
- Low	14	17	10	13	11	NA	NA	NA	NA	NA
Income Statement Analysis (Million $)										
Revs.	436	231	144	85.1	57.2	48.6	28.9	20.5	14.9	NA
Oper. Inc.	80.9	43.4	24.1	12.3	11.4	7.9	4.7	2.9	1.9	NA
Depr.	20.2	10.0	5.8	3.8	4.1	1.6	0.6	0.5	0.4	NA
Int. Exp.	7.8	3.8	2.3	0.9	0.4	1.1	0.7	0.6	0.5	NA
Pretax Inc.	52.9	29.7	16.0	6.1	6.9	5.3	3.3	1.8	1.5	NA
Eff. Tax Rate	39%	38%	37%	35%	35%	34%	37%	38%	34%	NA
Net Inc.	32.3	18.4	10.1	4.0	4.5	3.5	2.1	0.8	0.9	NA
Balance Sheet & Other Fin. Data (Million $)										
Cash	6.5	5.3	3.6	3.1	1.7	2.1	NA	NA	NA	NA
Curr. Assets	131	71.7	43.1	31.5	24.3	16.6	NA	NA	NA	NA
Total Assets	490	238	136	87.8	60.3	36.8	34.7	13.6	12.4	NA
Curr. Liab.	80.8	43.6	21.0	12.6	10.5	8.7	NA	NA	NA	NA
LT Debt	171	73.0	39.3	20.1	8.8	13.5	13.8	4.1	4.0	NA
Common Eqty.	214	105	66.4	49.9	38.2	9.0	6.0	3.6	2.8	NA
Total Cap.	409	194	115	75.2	49.8	25.8	22.9	7.7	6.9	NA
Cap. Exp.	30.4	10.6	10.2	6.0	2.4	3.4	NA	NA	NA	NA
Cash Flow	52.5	28.4	15.9	7.8	8.5	4.5	2.7	1.3	1.3	NA
Curr. Ratio	1.6	1.6	2.0	2.5	2.3	1.9	NA	NA	NA	NA
% LT Debt of Cap.	41.7	37.6	34.2	26.7	17.7	52.2	60.3	53.0	58.9	NA
% Net Inc.of Revs.	7.4	8.0	7.1	4.7	7.8	7.2	7.3	3.8	6.3	NA
% Ret. on Assets	8.9	9.9	9.1	5.4	9.2	9.8	8.7	6.0	7.4	NA
% Ret. on Equity	20.2	21.4	17.4	9.1	18.8	39.4	42.8	24.4	32.8	NA

Data as orig. reptd.; bef. results of disc. opers. and/or spec. items. Per share data adj. for stk. divs. as of ex-div. date. Bold denotes diluted EPS (FASB 128). E-Estimated. NA-Not Available. NM-Not Meaningful. NR-Not Ranked.

Office—5858 Westheimer Road, Ste. 200, Houston, TX 77057. **Tel**—(713) 787-0977. **Website**—www.consolidatedgraphics.com. **Pres & CEO**—J. R. Davis. **VP & CFO**—G. C. Colville. **VP, Treas & Investor Contact**—Ronald E. Hale Jr. **Dirs**—L. J. Alexander, B. F. Carruth, C. C. Comer, J. R. Davis, G. L. Forbes, W. D. Hawkins, J. H. Limmer, T. E. Smith, H. N. West. **Transfer Agent & Registrar**—American Stock Transfer & Trust Co., NYC. **Incorporated**—in Texas in 1985. **Empl**— 1,417. **S&P Analyst:** Matthew C. Hershberg

STANDARD &POOR'S STOCK REPORTS

Consolidated Products

NYSE Symbol **COP**

In S&P SmallCap 600

09-OCT-99 **Industry:** Restaurants

Summary: This growing restaurant operator has more than 260 units in the Midwest and Southeast, operating mainly under the Steak n Shake name.

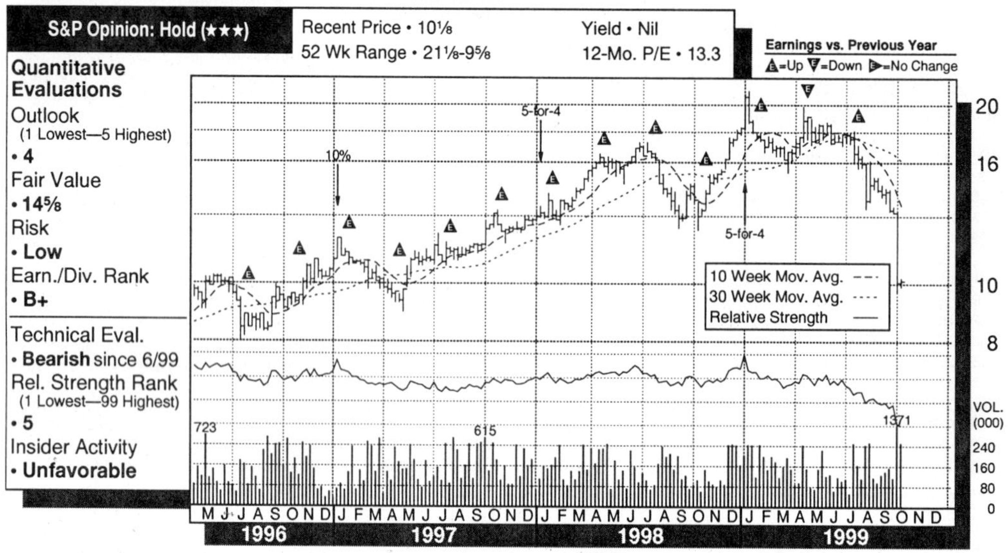

Overview - 29-SEP-99

Sales should rise about 20% in the remainder of FY 99 (Sep.), fueled by expansion of the Steak n Shake chain. COP plans to open about 20 company-operated units in the fourth quarter of FY 99, bringing the full year total to nearly 40 new company-owned stores. We expect revenues to advance roughly 17% in FY 00, which is below our previous top-line growth estimates of nearly 22%. The deceleration of sales growth reflects the company's inability to adequately control costs amid its aggressive store opening program. Operating margins are likely to narrow, reflecting wage pressures resulting from a tight labor market and a manager recruitment and training initiative, partly offset by menu price increases and improving food costs. We have lowered our FY 99 EPS estimate by $0.02, to $0.82, and have reduced our FY 00 earnings estimate to $0.91, from $1.00.

Valuation - 29-SEP-99

Shares of COP have trended lower in recent months, culminating in a sharp decline in late September 1999, as a result of the company's announcement that earnings in the fourth quarter of FY 99 would fall short of analysts' expectations. Consequently, the shares were recently trading at 14X our downwardly revised FY 00 EPS estimate of $0.91. Management attributed the shortfall to higher labor costs and delays in new store openings. In addition, the company said it expected to open only 40 locations in FY 00, which is 20% below previous new store guidance. As a result of COP's narrowing margins and less aggressive expansion strategy, we have downgraded the shares to neutral, from accumulate. Despite continued strength in same-store sales, two earnings preannouncements over the last three quarters have led us to question management's ability to deliver consistent EPS growth.

Key Stock Statistics

S&P EPS Est. 1999	0.82	Tang. Bk. Value/Share	4.98
P/E on S&P Est. 1999	12.3	Beta	0.99
S&P EPS Est. 2000	0.91	Shareholders	7,922
Dividend Rate/Share	Nil	Market cap. (B)	$0.269
Shs. outstg. (M)	26.6	Inst. holdings	38%
Avg. daily vol. (M)	0.099		

Value of $10,000 invested 5 years ago: $ 23,162

Fiscal Year Ending Sep. 30

	1999	1998	1997	1996	1995	1994
Revenues (Million $)						
1Q	79.01	63.42	54.34	47.01	39.63	33.66
2Q	104.0	91.14	78.24	65.02	54.71	45.69
3Q	88.48	72.53	65.73	56.44	45.39	38.86
4Q	—	84.00	67.07	56.92	47.01	40.43
Yr.	—	312.6	262.7	224.2	186.7	158.6
Earnings Per Share ($)						
1Q	**0.18**	**0.15**	0.13	0.12	0.13	0.11
2Q	**0.15**	**0.18**	0.15	0.12	0.12	0.09
3Q	**0.23**	**0.20**	0.19	0.15	0.12	0.13
4Q	—	**0.21**	0.18	0.15	0.13	0.14
Yr.	—	**0.74**	**0.65**	0.54	0.50	0.47

Next earnings report expected: late November

Dividend Data

No cash dividends have been paid. The common stock was split five for four in December 1997 and again in December 1998.

Consolidated Products, Inc.

Business Summary - 29-SEP-99

Despite an increasingly competitive restaurant environment over the past few years, revenues and earnings have sizzled at this operator of Steak n Shake restaurants, which has been aggressively expanding its restaurant base. Founded in 1934, Consolidated Products (formerly Steak n Shake, Inc.) primarily operates and franchises 284 (233 company-owned and 51 franchised units) Steak n Shake restaurants in 14 states in the Midwest and Southeast. It also operates 11 specialty restaurants in Indiana and Illinois, primarily under the Colorado Steakhouse name.

In FY 98 (Sep.), the company opened 33 new units and repurchased eight restaurants from franchisees. COP's five-year expansion plan calls for an annual increase of at least 20% in the number of company-operated Steak n Shake units. Growth is expected to be funded by cash flow from operations, capital raised through sale and leaseback transactions, bank borrowings, and the issuance of debt and equity securities.

The 284 Steak n Shake restaurants at September 30, 1998, were in Indiana (56 units), Illinois (53), Missouri (52), Florida (48), Georgia (19), Ohio (15), Kentucky (12), Tennessee (11), Michigan (10), Arkansas, Iowa and Kansas (two each), and North Carolina and Mississippi (one each).

Steak n Shake caters to a distinct niche in the mid-scale, casual dining segment of the restaurant industry by offering counter, dining room, drive-through and carry-out service. The units feature steakburgers, french fries, and hand-dipped milk shakes, as well as grilled chicken breast sandwiches, beef or chicken taco salads, homestyle soups and a variety of salads. The restaurants serve a complete breakfast, and most operate 24 hours a day.

Most Steak n Shake restaurants are freestanding units with adequate parking. Unlike fast-food restaurants, Steak n Shake's food is freshly prepared, cooked in view of the customer and served by a friendly staff. In FY 98, the average customer check was $5.25 per person; however, the average check was approximately $5.50 and $5.75 during peak lunch and dinner hours, respectively.

The 11 specialty restaurants, in Indiana and Illinois, consisted primarily of Colorado Steakhouse units with a western theme reminiscent of a Colorado log cabin. The menu features steak and prime rib with limited non-beef choices such as salmon, chicken and pork. Average check at the specialty restaurants generally approximates $15.

Per Share Data ($) (Year Ended Sep. 30)	1998	1997	1996	1995	1994	1993	1992	1991	1990	1989
Tangible Bk. Val.	19.25	2.87	2.65	2.01	1.31	0.77	0.14	-0.37	1.92	1.55
Cash Flow	1.23	0.86	0.89	0.94	0.85	0.75	0.73	0.67	0.81	0.73
Earnings	0.74	0.65	0.54	0.50	0.47	0.36	0.32	0.27	0.42	0.38
Dividends	Nil	Nil	Nil	Nil	Nil	Nil	Nil	1.54	0.07	0.05
Payout Ratio	Nil	Nil	Nil	Nil	Nil	Nil	Nil	NM	16%	14%
Prices - High	20 5/8	13 1/2	11 3/8	8 7/8	5 5/8	4 3/4	3 7/8	2 1/8	4 3/4	4 1/8
- Low	12 1/4	9	7	4 3/4	4 1/8	3	1 7/8	1 1/16	3/4	2 5/8
P/E Ratio - High	28	21	21	18	12	13	12	8	11	11
- Low	17	14	13	10	9	9	6	4	2	7
Income Statement Analysis (Million $)										
Revs.	307	263	224	187	160	133	127	116	106	99
Oper. Inc.	40.0	34.3	27.4	23.0	20.5	18.2	17.1	14.7	13.7	12.3
Depr.	13.0	10.7	8.6	7.0	5.9	5.6	5.3	4.9	4.5	4.1
Int. Exp.	2.5	3.6	3.8	3.8	4.6	5.1	5.6	5.5	1.9	2.1
Pretax Inc.	30.9	25.6	20.9	16.1	11.3	8.4	7.0	5.4	8.3	7.2
Eff. Tax Rate	36%	37%	38%	38%	37%	38%	41%	40%	40%	40%
Net Inc.	19.7	16.1	13.0	10.0	7.2	5.2	4.2	3.3	5.0	4.3
Balance Sheet & Other Fin. Data (Million $)										
Cash	14.0	2.7	0.6	1.4	10.3	8.8	12.6	8.3	0.6	2.8
Curr. Assets	40.0	20.0	15.1	14.5	19.4	16.3	19.4	13.1	5.7	7.6
Total Assets	190	167	131	100	80.3	70.6	67.1	64.1	55.8	50.0
Curr. Liab.	40.0	38.5	37.3	28.9	24.5	18.5	19.5	17.2	17.2	13.7
LT Debt	31.2	34.6	32.0	28.3	36.1	41.0	45.7	51.2	16.0	18.1
Common Eqty.	115	93.0	57.8	42.6	19.7	11.0	1.8	-4.4	22.5	18.0
Total Cap.	150	129	90.1	70.9	55.8	52.1	47.5	46.9	38.6	36.3
Cap. Exp.	51.4	52.2	46.2	42.9	20.6	15.2	6.8	8.1	13.8	10.3
Cash Flow	32.7	26.8	21.6	17.0	13.1	10.8	9.4	8.2	9.4	8.4
Curr. Ratio	1.0	0.5	0.4	0.5	0.8	0.9	1.0	0.8	0.3	0.6
% LT Debt of Cap.	20.8	26.9	35.5	39.9	64.7	78.7	96.3	109.2	41.4	49.8
% Net Inc.of Revs.	6.4	6.1	5.8	5.4	4.5	3.9	3.3	2.8	4.7	4.4
% Ret. on Assets	11.0	10.8	11.3	11.2	9.3	7.0	6.3	5.4	9.3	8.8
% Ret. on Equity	18.9	21.4	25.7	32.2	45.8	78.9	NM	NM	24.4	26.8

Data as orig reptd.; bef. results of disc opers/spec. items. Per share data adj. for stk. divs. Bold denotes diluted EPS (FASB 128)-prior periods restated. E-Estimated. NA-Not Available. NM-Not Meaningful. NR-Not Ranked.

Office—500 Century Bldg., 36 S. Pennsylvania St., Indianapolis, IN 46204. **Tel**—(317) 633-4100. **Chrmn**—E. W. Kelley. **Vice Chrmn & Secy**—S. S. Aramian. **Pres & CEO**—A. B. Gilman. **SVP, Treas & Investor Contact**—James W. Bear. **VP & Secy**—C. J. Wendling. **Dirs**—S. S. Aramian, A. T. Bonda, N. Gilliatt, A. B. Gilman, E. W. Kelley, C. E. Lanham, J. F. Risk, J. Williamson Jr. **Transfer Agent & Registrar**—Harris Trust & Savings Bank, Chicago. **Incorporated**—in Delaware in 1951; reincorporated in Indiana in 1977. **Empl**— 14,000. **S&P Analyst:** Stephen J. Tekirian

STANDARD
&POOR'S
STOCK REPORTS

Cooper Companies

NYSE Symbol **COO**

In S&P SmallCap 600

09-OCT-99

Industry: Health Care (Medical Products & Supplies)

Summary: COO develops, manufactures and markets proprietary specialty health care products for eye care and gynecology.

Quantitative Evaluations

Outlook (1 Lowest—5 Highest) • **4+**

Fair Value • **47¾**

Risk • **Average**

Earn./Div. Rank • **B-**

Technical Eval. • **Bullish** since 8/99

Rel. Strength Rank (1 Lowest—99 Highest) • **94**

Insider Activity • **NA**

Recent Price • 30⅞

52 Wk Range • 31⅞-11¾

Yield • 0.3%

12-Mo. P/E • 13.8

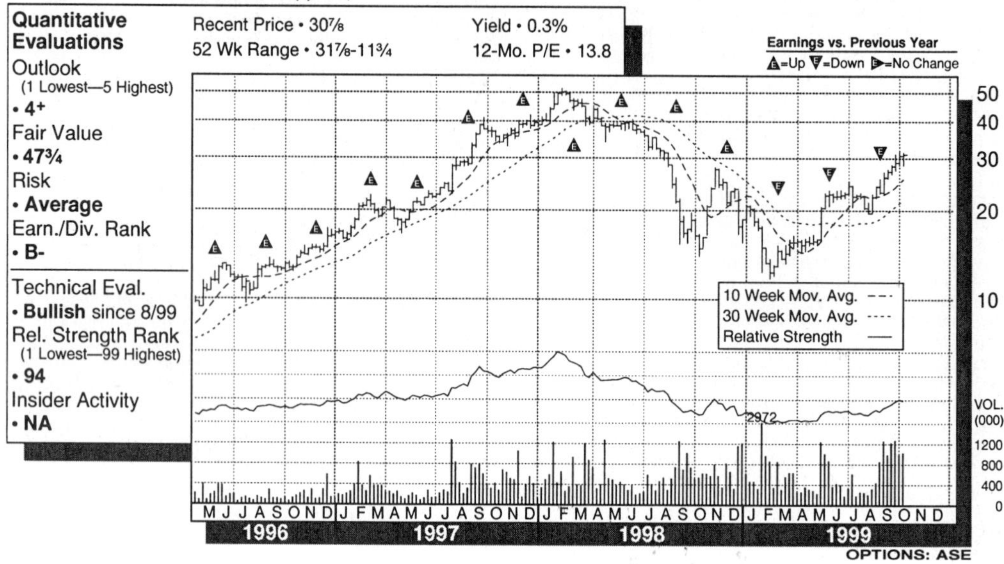

Business Profile - 15-SEP-99

The company has three major business objectives: to increase revenue and earnings 20% a year for the next five years; to become the global leader in the toric soft contact lens market within the next two years (over 27% of the market at the end of the FY 99 (Oct.) third quarter); and to expand the CooperSurgical division from a current level of $30 million to $100 million in revenue in five years, through continued internal growth, including recently introduced products and selective acquisitions. COO expects its CooperVision division to achieve 15% to 20% annual growth over the next five years, with 30 new contact lens product introductions scheduled. In April 1999, the company sold its Hospital Group of America psychiatric services business for $27 million in cash, plus an additional $3 million if certain contingencies are met.

Operational Review - 15-SEP-99

Net sales in the nine months ended July 31, 1999, gained 13%, year to year. Gross margins widened. After a 14% increase in SG&A expenses and lower R&D expense, operating profit was up 14%. After higher interest expense, lower other income, and taxes at 33.0%, versus tax benefits of $1,864,000, income from continuing operations fell 31%, to $14,481,000 ($1.01 a share, on 6.9% fewer shares), from $21,060,000 ($1.37). Results exclude income from discontinued operations of $0.22 and $0.23 a share in the respective periods.

Stock Performance - 08-OCT-99

In the past 30 trading days, COO's shares have increased 34%, compared to a 0.91% fall in the S&P 500. Average trading volume for the past five days was 202,920 shares, compared with the 40-day moving average of 240,262 shares.

Key Stock Statistics

Dividend Rate/Share	0.08	Shareholders	2,579
Shs. outstg. (M)	14.0	Market cap. (B)	$0.434
Avg. daily vol. (M)	0.266	Inst. holdings	48%
Tang. Bk. Value/Share	5.32		
Beta	0.83		

Value of $10,000 invested 5 years ago: $ 150,285

Fiscal Year Ending Oct. 31

	1999	1998	1997	1996	1995	1994
Revenues (Million $)						
1Q	34.96	42.84	28.38	22.25	23.21	22.91
2Q	41.74	51.76	33.66	26.78	23.79	24.46
3Q	43.40	54.18	38.95	28.87	25.25	23.90
4Q	—	40.65	40.49	31.24	24.84	24.38
Yr.	—	147.2	141.5	109.1	97.09	95.65
Earnings Per Share ($)						
1Q	**0.18**	**0.39**	0.28	0.06	0.03	-0.51
2Q	**0.38**	**0.55**	0.44	0.24	0.06	-0.39
3Q	**0.46**	**0.66**	0.55	0.40	0.24	0.27
4Q	—	**2.45**	2.14	0.72	-0.31	0.12
Yr.	—	**3.79**	**3.33**	**1.32**	0.01	-0.45

Next earnings report expected: mid December

Dividend Data (Dividends have been paid since 1999.)

Amount ($)	Date Decl.	Ex-Div. Date	Stock of Record	Payment Date
0.020	May. 20	Jun. 11	Jun. 15	Jul. 05 '99
0.020	Sep. 03	Sep. 13	Sep. 15	Oct. 05 '99

The Cooper Companies, Inc.

Business Summary - 15-SEP-99

The Cooper Companies, Inc. provides underserved niches in the health care market with proprietary products and services, such as specialty contact lenses, diagnostic and surgical instruments for women's health care, and treatment for various mental illnesses. Operations consist of two main units: CooperVision, Inc. (CVI) and CooperSurgical, Inc. (CSI).

CooperVision (81% of FY 98 (Oct.) revenues from continuing operations) makes contact lenses that correct visual defects. It specializes in soft toric lenses that correct astigmatism, an irregularity in the shape of the cornea. Instead of competing in the lower margin market for lenses to correct more common cases of nearsightedness, CVI focuses on higher margin, technologically advanced specialty lenses for patients whose vision is more difficult to correct. Major brand names include Hydrasoft, Preference, Vantage, Permaflex and Cooper Clear.

In February 1998, COO introduced Frequency 55 disposable replacement sphere contact lenses in the U.S. Replacement spherical lenses are the largest contact lens U.S. market segment. In May 1998, COO introduced two new toric products: Hydrasoft Toric Options, a custom replacement lens for astigmatic patients with complex correction requirements; and Frequency 55 Toric, for replacement at two-week or monthly intervals.

CooperVision is expected to grow 15% to 20% a year over the next five years. Its new product program has four major components. The first is to complete the worldwide roll out of the existing CooperVision toric lens line, first in Europe, then in Japan and Australia during 1999. Second, it plans to launch a new cast molded toric lens in the Frequency line in late 1999. Third is the Frequency AB, a spherical lens that features a design that can improve visual acuity for many contact lens patients who wear disposable lenses. Initial marketing in Europe will continue through 1999; a North American launch date has not been set. A fourth new product, the Frequency UV, featuring an ultraviolet light blocking agent in the lens material, is available in smaller markets outside the U.S., and was to be launched in major European markets in 1999.

In December 1997, COO acquired Aspect Vision Care, a U.K.-based maker of contact lenses, for about $51 million.

CooperSurgical (19%) supplies products related to women's health care, including proprietary gynecological and surgical instruments, accessories and related devices. In May 1998, it introduced the Cerveillance Scope, which uses digital imaging and proprietary software to provide enhanced visualization and documentation in cervix examinations. COO also introduced the FemExam'r' pH and Amines TestCard, designed for use in physicians' offices to rapidly and economically screen and diagnose common vaginal infections.

Per Share Data ($) (Year Ended Oct. 31)	1998	1997	1996	1995	1994	1993	1992	1991	1990	1989
Tangible Bk. Val.	4.22	5.06	-0.53	NM	-1.68	-1.59	2.10	0.39	3.12	-0.93
Cash Flow	4.33	4.06	1.63	0.26	-0.09	-3.06	-1.71	-2.91	-0.60	-3.39
Earnings	3.79	3.70	1.41	0.01	-0.45	-3.39	-1.92	-3.15	-0.78	-3.66
Dividends	Nil	Nil	Nil	Nil	Nil	Nil	Nil	Nil	Nil	Nil
Payout Ratio	Nil	Nil	Nil	Nil	Nil	Nil	Nil	Nil	Nil	Nil
Prices - High	51 5/8	42	17	11 1/4	10 1/2	3 3/4	13 1/8	18 3/8	14 5/8	16 1/8
- Low	14	15 7/8	6 3/8	5 1/4	1 5/16	13/16	2 5/8	9	7 1/2	6 3/8
P/E Ratio - High	14	11	12	NM	NM	NM	NM	NM	NM	NM
- Low	4	4	5	NM	NM	NM	NM	NM	NM	NM
Income Statement Analysis (Million $)										
Revs.	147	142	109	97.0	96.0	93.0	63.1	36.0	48.0	53.0
Oper. Inc.	37.9	30.5	20.7	13.0	4.1	17.6	-63.3	-28.3	-11.9	-16.9
Depr.	8.2	4.7	2.6	2.7	3.7	3.4	2.3	2.0	1.4	2.1
Int. Exp.	6.3	4.2	5.3	4.7	4.5	6.1	6.7	7.1	9.0	22.4
Pretax Inc.	23.1	21.8	12.1	0.2	-9.0	-34.0	-16.0	-25.0	-4.0	-18.0
Eff. Tax Rate	NM	NM	NM	50%	NM	NM	NM	NM	NM	NM
Net Inc.	57.8	48.4	16.6	0.1	-5.0	-34.0	-0.2	-25.0	-1.0	-16.0
Balance Sheet & Other Fin. Data (Million $)										
Cash	7.3	18.2	6.8	11.2	10.0	17.0	75.0	144	173	230
Curr. Assets	116	68.6	42.4	41.2	44.0	52.0	120	174	197	277
Total Assets	296	175	103	92.0	95.0	110	174	188	217	288
Curr. Liab.	46.7	33.6	33.3	39.6	42.0	38.0	54.0	52.0	45.0	64.0
LT Debt	78.7	9.1	47.9	43.5	46.0	48.0	59.0	49.0	71.0	103
Common Eqty.	145	112	15.3	-1.7	-4.0	Nil	31.0	12.0	33.0	-7.0
Total Cap.	224	142	69.6	52.4	43.0	49.0	120	136	172	224
Cap. Exp.	19.6	7.7	3.2	3.0	0.9	1.8	3.7	1.5	0.5	20.9
Cash Flow	66.0	53.1	19.2	2.8	-1.0	-31.0	-16.0	-25.0	-5.0	-26.0
Curr. Ratio	2.5	2.0	1.3	1.0	1.0	1.4	2.2	3.4	4.4	4.3
% LT Debt of Cap.	35.1	6.4	68.8	83.0	108.6	99.1	48.8	35.8	41.1	46.0
% Net Inc.of Revs.	39.3	34.1	15.2	NM	NM	NM	NM	NM	NM	NM
% Ret. on Assets	24.5	34.8	16.9	NM	NM	NM	NM	NM	NM	NM
% Ret. on Equity	45.0	76.3	1.2	NM	NM	NM	NM	NM	NM	NM

Data as orig reptd.; bef. results of disc opers/spec. items. Per share data adj. for stk. divs. Bold denotes diluted EPS (FASB 128)-prior periods restated. E-Estimated. NA-Not Available. NM-Not Meaningful. NR-Not Ranked.

Office—6140 Stoneridge Mall Rd., Suite 590, Pleasanton, CA 94588. **Tel**—(510) 460-3600. **Website**—http://www.coopercos.com **Chrmn**—A. E. Rubenstein. **Pres & CEO**—A. T. Bender. **EVP, CFO & Treas**—R. S. Weiss. **Secy**—C.R. Kaufman. **Investor Contact**—B. Norris Battin (888-822-2660). **Dirs**—A. T. Bender, M. H. Kalkstein, M. Marx, D. Press, S. Rosenberg, A. E. Rubenstein, R. S. Weiss, S. Zinberg. **Transfer Agent & Registrar**—American Stock Transfer & Trust Co., NYC. **Incorporated**—in Delaware in 1980. **Empl**— 1,900. **S&P Analyst:** John J. Arege

STANDARD
&POOR'S
STOCK REPORTS

COR Therapeutics

NASDAQ Symbol **CORR**

In S&P SmallCap 600

09-OCT-99

Industry: Biotechnology

Summary: This company is engaged in the discovery, development and commercialization of biopharmaceutical products to treat and prevent severe cardiovascular diseases.

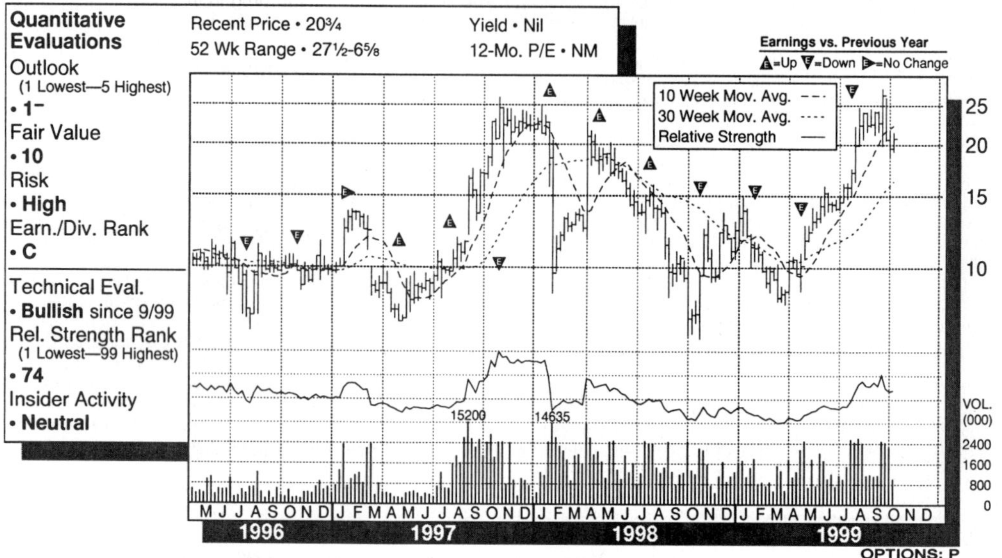

Business Profile - 28-SEP-99

In May 1998, CORR received FDA marketing approval for its first commercialized product, Integrilin, to treat acute coronary syndromes (ACS) and to prevent abrupt arterial closure following angioplasty. In July 1999, Integrilin received marketing authorization in the European Union (EU) for ACS; CORR received a $12 million milestone payment from partner Schering-Plough in August 1999 as a result of Integrilin's EU marketing authorization. In September 1999, the company announced plans to offer $100 million of convertible subordinated notes, with conversion options yet to be determined. CORR reported favorable Phase I and early Phase II results for its oral formulation of Integrilin to prevent ACS and stroke in March 1999.

Operational Review - 28-SEP-99

Total revenues in the six months ended June 30, 1999 declined 50%, year to year, as initial revenue from Integrilin sales and higher development and other contract revenue were more than offset by the absence of $32 million in milestone payments from Schering-Plough. Total expenses rose 28%, mainly reflecting copromotion costs of $7.2 million in 1999 only. Following 25% lower net interest income, a net loss of $21.5 million ($0.88 a share) contrasted with net income of $4.0 million ($0.16). Cash, cash equivalents, and short-term investments totaled $54.0 million as of June 30, 1999.

Stock Performance - 08-OCT-99

In the past 30 trading days, CORR's shares have declined 8%, compared to a 0.91% fall in the S&P 500. Average trading volume for the past five days was 199,920 shares, compared with the 40-day moving average of 351,031 shares.

Key Stock Statistics

Dividend Rate/Share	Nil	Shareholders	350
Shs. outstg. (M)	24.6	Market cap. (B)	$0.511
Avg. daily vol. (M)	0.459	Inst. holdings	50%
Tang. Bk. Value/Share	2.23		
Beta	0.92		

Value of $10,000 invested 5 years ago: $ 13,719

Fiscal Year Ending Dec. 31

	1999	1998	1997	1996	1995	1994
Revenues (Million $)						
1Q	7.52	8.41	6.33	2.53	0.00	0.02
2Q	9.01	24.51	6.58	4.79	21.05	Nil
3Q	—	2.85	2.91	6.54	7.85	Nil
4Q	—	6.19	6.37	4.89	2.95	0.50
Yr.	—	41.96	22.19	18.76	31.85	0.52
Earnings Per Share ($)						
1Q	**-0.48**	**-0.22**	-0.38	-0.59	-0.45	-0.28
2Q	**-0.39**	**0.36**	-0.45	-0.48	0.57	-0.57
3Q	—	**-0.67**	-0.54	-0.30	-0.05	-0.68
4Q	—	**-0.63**	**-0.26**	-0.49	-0.49	-0.53
Yr.	—	**-1.14**	**-1.60**	**-1.86**	**-0.39**	**-2.07**

Next earnings report expected: late October

Dividend Data

No cash dividends have been paid. In 1995, the company adopted a shareholder rights plan.

A Division of The McGraw-Hill Companies

COR Therapeutics, Inc.

Business Summary - 28-SEP-99

Each year about one million people in the U.S. die as a result of heart attacks, strokes and related cardiovascular diseases. COR Therapeutics (CORR) focuses on the discovery, development and commercialization of pharmaceutical products to prevent and treat severe cardiovascular diseases.

CORR is concentrating on the development of products to treat unstable angina, acute myocardial infarction, venous thrombosis, and restenosis (a renarrowing of blood vessels following angioplasty). Integrilin, the company's first commercialized product, received FDA approval in May 1998 for the treatment of acute coronary syndrome (ACS) and as an adjunct to percutaneous coronary intervention (PCI). ACS encompasses unstable angina and non-Q wave myocardial infarction. The product blocks the platelet receptor, GP IIb/IIIa, inhibiting platelet aggregation and helping to prevent thrombus formations that can lead to heart attack or death in ACS patients and patients undergoing PCI (angioplasty) procedures. Integrilin has the broadest range of indications among GP IIb/IIIa inhibitors approved in the U.S.

In April 1995, the company signed a worldwide collaborative agreement with Schering-Plough to develop and commercialize Integrilin. Schering paid CORR a $20 million licensing fee, and agreed to additional milestone payments (up to $100 million) upon reaching certain performance goals. An $8 million payment was made in 1998's first quarter, after Integrilin was accepted for review by European regulatory authorities, and a $24 million payment was made in the second quarter of 1998, after Integrilin received FDA approval. CORR and Schering co-promote the drug in the U.S. and share any profits or losses. In March 1999, the European Committee for Proprietary Medicinal Products issued a positive opinion recommending the approval of Integrilin in Europe.

The company's second product, cromafiban, is an oral GP IIb/IIIa inhibitor in Phase II clinical trials to treat patients with a history of acute coronary syndromes and cerebrovascular accidents. Over six million people in the U.S. have a history of heart attack, stroke or transient ischemic attack. Cromafiban may prove useful in preventing these catastrophic events.

The company also has six compounds in early research and preclinical development for the treatment of various cardiovascular conditions. CORR has a collaboration with Kyowa Hakko Kogyo, Ltd. to discover and develop drugs that prevent restenosis following angioplasty. The agreement has been extended until November 1999.

The company's strategy is centered around four key areas: maximizing the revenue potential of Integrilin, maintaining a cardiovascular disease focus, maximizing the value of strategic collaborations, and continuing to build relationships with clinicians and scientists.

Per Share Data ($) (Year Ended Dec. 31)	1998	1997	1996	1995	1994	1993	1992	1991	1990	1989
Tangible Bk. Val.	2.23	3.30	2.52	4.23	4.51	6.44	4.09	4.99	-9.10	NM
Cash Flow	-1.00	-1.43	-1.68	-0.21	-1.96	-1.16	-0.79	-0.52	-0.81	-0.45
Earnings	-1.14	-1.60	-1.86	-0.39	-2.07	-1.27	-0.86	-0.62	-0.93	-0.51
Dividends	Nil	Nil	Nil	Nil	Nil	Nil	Nil	Nil	Nil	Nil
Payout Ratio	Nil	Nil	Nil	Nil	Nil	Nil	Nil	Nil	Nil	Nil
Prices - High	24 7/8	26 1/8	12 1/2	19 1/2	17 1/4	19 1/4	18	22	NA	NA
- Low	6 5/8	7 3/8	7	7 3/4	9	8 1/2	9	7 1/2	NA	NA
P/E Ratio - High	NM	NM	NM	NM	NM	NM	NM	NM	NM	NM
- Low	NM	NM	NM	NM	NM	NM	NM	NA	NA	NA
Income Statement Analysis (Million $)										
Revs.	42.0	22.2	18.8	31.9	0.5	2.5	1.7	2.4	0.5	0.4
Oper. Inc.	-27.9	-32.2	-35.7	-8.0	-42.1	-21.2	-11.6	-5.0	-5.0	-2.7
Depr.	3.4	3.5	3.6	3.5	2.1	1.7	0.9	0.9	0.8	0.3
Int. Exp.	0.7	0.6	0.8	0.8	0.2	0.3	0.2	0.3	0.3	0.2
Pretax Inc.	-27.6	-33.5	-36.5	-7.5	-39.5	-19.7	-10.2	-5.1	-5.8	-2.7
Eff. Tax Rate	NM	NM	NM	NM	NM	NM	NM	Nil	Nil	Nil
Net Inc.	-27.6	-33.5	-36.5	-7.5	-39.5	-19.7	-10.2	-5.1	-5.8	-2.7
Balance Sheet & Other Fin. Data (Million $)										
Cash	10.5	22.2	53.1	84.8	94.0	122	49.1	58.7	4.3	5.6
Curr. Assets	97.7	90.0	64.2	92.8	97.0	124	50.1	59.2	4.4	6.1
Total Assets	103	95.4	71.2	101	106	130	53.8	61.0	6.7	8.2
Curr. Liab.	45.2	14.2	17.4	14.1	15.0	8.1	4.4	1.7	0.9	0.8
LT Debt	3.3	2.8	3.4	4.6	4.7	3.1	0.8	0.8	1.3	1.1
Common Eqty.	54.6	78.4	50.4	82.2	87.0	119	48.6	58.4	-9.4	-3.7
Total Cap.	57.9	81.2	53.2	86.8	91.0	122	49.4	59.2	5.7	7.5
Cap. Exp.	3.4	1.9	2.6	2.7	6.7	4.4	2.8	0.3	0.9	1.4
Cash Flow	-24.3	-29.9	-33.0	-4.0	-37.4	-18.0	-9.3	-4.3	-5.0	-2.4
Curr. Ratio	2.2	6.3	3.7	6.6	6.5	15.3	11.3	34.4	4.7	7.8
% LT Debt of Cap.	5.6	3.5	6.3	5.3	5.1	2.5	1.7	1.4	23.0	15.3
% Net Inc.of Revs.	NM	NM	NM	NM	NM	NM	NM	NM	NM	NM
% Ret. on Assets	NM	NM	NM	NM	NM	NM	NM	NM	NM	NM
% Ret. on Equity	NM	NM	NM	NM	NM	NM	NM	NM	NM	NM

Data as orig. reptd.; bef. results of disc. opers. and/or spec. items. Per share data adj. for stk. divs. as of ex-div. date. Bold denotes diluted EPS (FASB 128). E-Estimated. NA-Not Available. NM-Not Meaningful. NR-Not Ranked.

Office—256 E. Grand Ave., South San Francisco, CA 94080.**Tel**—(650) 244-6800. **Fax**—(650) 244-9208. **Website**—http://www.corr.com **Pres & CEO**—V. M. Kailian. **VP & Secy**—R. L. Douglas Jr. **Dirs**—S. R. Coughlin, J. T. Doluisio, C. J. Homcy, J. T. Jackson, V. M. Kailian, E. Mario, R. R. Momsen, L. H. Smith Jr.**Transfer Agent & Registrar**—ChaseMellon Shareholder Services, San Francisco. **Incorporated**—in Delaware in 1988. **Empl**— 321. **S&P Analyst:** Frank DiLorenzo

STANDARD
&POOR'S
STOCK REPORTS

Corn Products International

NYSE Symbol **CPO**

In S&P SmallCap 600

09-OCT-99

Industry: Agricultural Products

Summary: This company, which was spun off by Bestfoods in late 1997, is one of the world's largest corn refiners.

S&P Opinion: Accumulate (★★★★)

Recent Price • 29⅜ | Yield • 1.4%
52 Wk Range • 35¼-21½ | 12-Mo. P/E • 17.6

Quantitative Evaluations

Outlook (1 Lowest—5 Highest)
• NA
Fair Value
• NA
Risk
• NA
Earn./Div. Rank
• NR

Technical Eval.
• NA
Rel. Strength Rank (1 Lowest—99 Highest)
• 36
Insider Activity
• NA

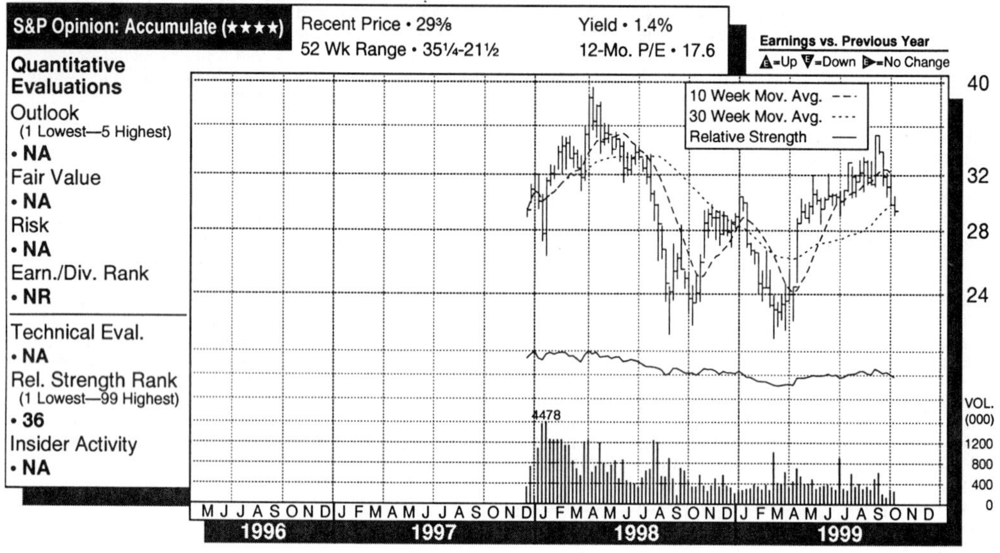

Overview - 23-JUL-99

We expect sales for the balance of 1999 to rise 18% to 20%, supported by contributions from acquisitions in Mexico and South Korea, but restricted somewhat by continuing soft market conditions in Latin America. Because the company holds leading market positions in Chile, Brazil, Colombia and Mexico, international operations will remain a key component of CPO's future success. Margins should show significant improvement, reflecting increased prices for high fructose corn syrup (HFCS), as well as lower raw material costs stemming from a large corn harvest. In addition, if the company's recently underperforming dextrose business improves, it is likely that margins could experience greater improvement than anticipated. Results should also benefit from a continuing decline in interest costs related to acquisition financing. We expect earnings in 1999 to grow to $2.00 a share, up 68% from 1998's $1.19. We see a further gain, to $2.60, for 2000.

Valuation - 23-JUL-99

We continue to rate the stock accumulate. The shares have climbed sharply in recent weeks, reflecting the company's improved earnings outlook. The profitability picture for 1999 and 2000 is extremely positive, in light of CPO's recent business expansion in Mexico, an acquisition in South Korea, and margin expansion resulting from lower raw material prices and stronger prices for HFCS. With the possibility of additional HFCS consolidation and removal of industry capacity, coupled with increasing domestic demand, prices could strengthen further. We continue to view the shares, recently trading at only 13X our 2000 EPS estimate, as attractive for long-term capital appreciation.

Key Stock Statistics

S&P EPS Est. 1999	2.00	Tang. Bk. Value/Share	22.55
P/E on S&P Est. 1999	14.7	Beta	NA
S&P EPS Est. 2000	2.60	Shareholders	NA
Dividend Rate/Share	0.40	Market cap. (B)	$ 1.1
Shs. outstg. (M)	37.2	Inst. holdings	65%
Avg. daily vol. (M)	0.043		

Value of $10,000 invested 5 years ago: NA

Fiscal Year Ending Dec. 31

	1999	1998	1997	1996	1995	1994
Revenues (Million $)						
1Q	396.6	339.0	—	—	—	—
2Q	441.3	366.8	—	—	—	—
3Q	—	359.5	—	—	—	—
4Q	—	382.7	—	—	—	—
Yr.	—	1,448	1,418	1,524	—	—
Earnings Per Share ($)						
1Q	**0.42**	**0.21**	—	—	—	—
2Q	**0.58**	**0.30**	—	—	—	—
3Q	**E0.52**	**0.35**	—	—	—	—
4Q	**E0.48**	**0.32**	—	—	—	—
Yr.	**E2.00**	**1.19**	**-2.02**	**0.64**	**3.79**	—

Next earnings report expected: late October

Dividend Data (Dividends have been paid since 1998.)

Amount ($)	Date Decl.	Ex-Div. Date	Stock of Record	Payment Date
0.080	Nov. 20	Dec. 30	Jan. 04	Jan. 25 '99
0.080	Mar. 17	Mar. 29	Mar. 31	Apr. 23 '99
0.080	May. 19	Jun. 28	Jun. 30	Jul. 23 '99
0.100	Sep. 22	Sep. 28	Sep. 30	Oct. 15 '99

A Division of The McGraw-Hill Companies

Corn Products International, Inc.

Business Summary - 23-JUL-99

Corn Products International, Inc., spun off from CPC International (renamed Bestfoods) in late 1997, is one of the word's largest corn refiners. It produces a wide variety of food ingredients and industrial products derived from the wet milling of corn and other farinaceous materials, for use in more than 60 industries. After seeing profits decline markedly in 1996 and 1997, due to an expansion of high fructose corn syrup capacity that led to a supply/demand imbalance and falling prices, the company spent 1998 focusing on improving prices, volume, profit margins, and efficiencies by striving for optimal product selection and production capacity usage, and for cost reductions in purchasing and manufacturing.

The corn refining business supplies customers with value-added products processed from starch and commodity products. The company's most important customers are in the food and beverage, pharmaceuticals, paper products, corrugated and laminated paper, textiles and brewing industries, and in the animal feed markets. Corn refining involves the wet milling and processing of corn. During front end grind, corn is steeped in water and separated into starch and co-products such as animal feed and germ. The starch is then either dried for sale or further modified or refined through various processes to make products designed to serve the particular needs of various industries. The germ is refined to produce corn oil.

Products are largely divided into sweeteners (50% of net sales in 1998), starch (25%), and co-products (25%). Sweeteners include high fructose corn syrup used in soft drinks and other beverages and foods; glucose corn syrups used throughout the food industry; high maltose corn syrups with a unique carbohydrate profile; maltodextin used in applications including dry mixes, sports drinks, baked products and confection; and dextrose, both monohydrate and anhydrous, used in the food industry.

Starch products include mainly corn starch used as a component in the production of paper, corrugated containers, construction materials and textiles, as well as numerous food applications as a thickener and binder. Co-products include corn oil used as cooking oil and in the production of margarine, salad dressings, shortening, mayonnaise and other foods, and corn gluten feed sold as animal feed and corn gluten meal sold as a feed protein, primarily to the poultry industry.

Products are sold directly to manufacturers and distributors by the company's own sales personnel. CPO's operations include 41 plants in 22 countries, including subsidiaries, joint ventures and alliances in Latin America, Asia, Africa, Australia and New Zealand. About 63% of net sales in 1998 were generated in North America.

Per Share Data ($) (Year Ended Dec. 31)	1998	1997	1996	1995	1994	1993	1992	1991	1990	1989
Tangible Bk. Val.	24.60	27.70	NA	NA	NA	NA	NA	NA	NA	NA
Cash Flow	3.82	0.87	3.16	NA	NA	NA	NA	NA	NA	NA
Earnings	1.19	-2.02	0.72	NA	NA	NA	NA	NA	NA	NA
Dividends	0.08	Nil	NA	NA	NA	NA	NA	NA	NA	NA
Payout Ratio	7%	Nil	NA	NA	NA	NA	NA	NA	NA	NA
Prices - High	39 1/2	32	NA	NA	NA	NA	NA	NA	NA	NA
- Low	21 3/4	28 7/8	NA	NA	NA	NA	NA	NA	NA	NA
P/E Ratio - High	33	NM	NA	NA	NA	NA	NA	NA	NA	NA
- Low	18	NM	NA	NA	NA	NA	NA	NA	NA	NA
Income Statement Analysis (Million $)										
Revs.	1,448	1,418	1,524	NA	NA	NA	NA	NA	NA	NA
Oper. Inc.	165	151	143	NA	NA	NA	NA	NA	NA	NA
Depr.	95.0	103	88.0	NA	NA	NA	NA	NA	NA	NA
Int. Exp.	13.0	28.0	28.0	NA	NA	NA	NA	NA	NA	NA
Pretax Inc.	71.0	-89.0	37.0	NA	NA	NA	NA	NA	NA	NA
Eff. Tax Rate	35%	NM	32%	NA	NA	NA	NA	NA	NA	NA
Net Inc.	43.0	-72.0	23.0	NA	NA	NA	NA	NA	NA	NA
Balance Sheet & Other Fin. Data (Million $)										
Cash	36.0	85.0	32.0	NA	NA	NA	NA	NA	NA	NA
Curr. Assets	465	423	434	NA	NA	NA	NA	NA	NA	NA
Total Assets	1,946	1,666	1,663	NA	NA	NA	NA	NA	NA	NA
Curr. Liab.	405	496	287	NA	NA	NA	NA	NA	NA	NA
LT Debt	154	13.0	350	NA	NA	NA	NA	NA	NA	NA
Common Eqty.	1,053	986	1,025	NA	NA	NA	NA	NA	NA	NA
Total Cap.	1,478	1,133	1,439	NA	NA	NA	NA	NA	NA	NA
Cap. Exp.	91.0	116	NA	NA	NA	NA	NA	NA	NA	NA
Cash Flow	138	31.0	111	NA	NA	NA	NA	NA	NA	NA
Curr. Ratio	1.1	0.9	1.5	NA	NA	NA	NA	NA	NA	NA
% LT Debt of Cap.	10.4	1.1	24.3	NA	NA	NA	NA	NA	NA	NA
% Net Inc.of Revs.	3.0	NM	1.5	NA	NA	NA	NA	NA	NA	NA
% Ret. on Assets	2.4	NM	NA	NA	NA	NA	NA	NA	NA	NA
% Ret. on Equity	4.2	NM	NA	NA	NA	NA	NA	NA	NA	NA

Data as orig. reptd.; bef. results of disc. opers. and/or spec. items. Pro forma in 1996, balance sheet as of Jun. 30, 1997. Per share data adj. for stk. divs. as of ex-div. date. Bold denotes diluted EPS (FASB 128). E-Estimated. NA-Not Available. NM-Not Meaningful. NR-Not Ranked.

Office—6500 South Archer Rd., Bedford Park, IL 60501. **Tel**—(708) 563-2400. **Website**—http://www.cornproducts.com **Chrmn & CEO**—K. Schlatter. **Pres**—S. C. Scott. **VP & Secy**—M. E. Doane. **VP-Fin & CFO**—J. W. Ripley. **Investor Contact**—Richard Vandervoort (708 563-5824).**Dirs**—I. Aranguren-Castiello, A. C. DeCrane, Jr., W. C. Ferguson, G. E. Greiner, R. M. Gross, R. G. Holder, B. H. Kastory, W. S. Norman, K. Schlatter, S. C. Scott, C. B. Storms. **Transfer Agent & Registrar**—First Chicago Trust Co. of New York, Jersey City, NJ. **Incorporated**—in Delaware in 1997. **Empl**— 5,550. **S&P Analyst:** Maureen C. Carini

STANDARD
&POOR'S
STOCK REPORTS

Coventry Health Care

Nasdaq Symbol **CVTY**

In S&P SmallCap 600

09-OCT-99

Industry: Health Care (Managed Care)

Summary: This company provides a wide range of managed health care benefits and services to nearly 1.4 million members in 12 states.

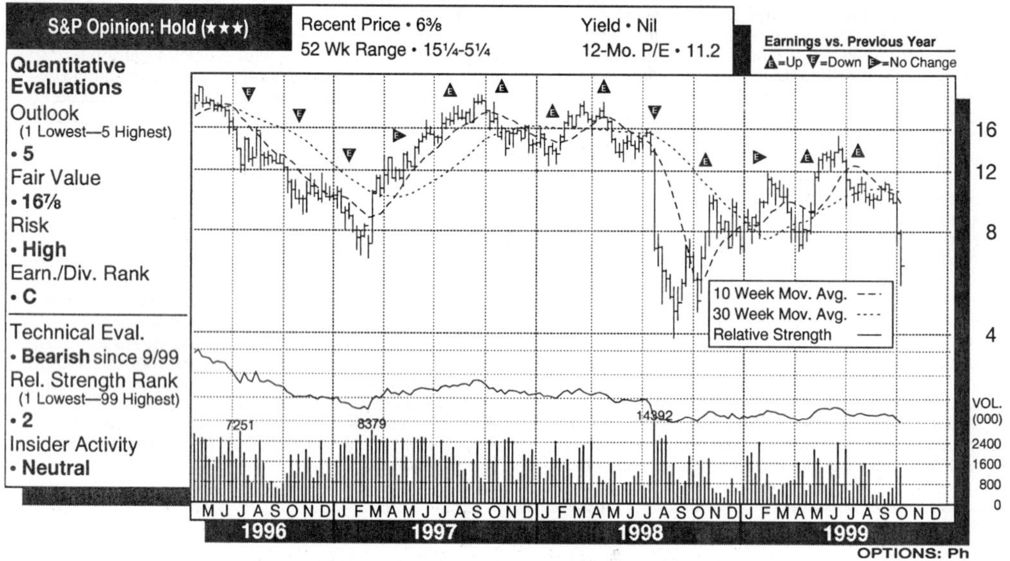

OPTIONS: Ph

Overview - 13-SEP-99

Premium revenues in 1999 should reach $2.5 billion, assuming commercial rate hikes of 8% to 10%, and slight membership growth. In January 1999, CVTY implemented commercial rate increases (about 50% of total membership) of 8%, and the pricing environment remains favorable for the remainder of 1999. The medical loss ratio in the 1999 second quarter rose sequentially to 85.9%, from 85.4%, reflecting higher patient utilization. CVTY has largely completed recontracting with providers, following the July 1998 bankruptcy of Allegheny Health, Education & Research Foundation (AHERF), one of CVTY's largest health care providers. In the 1998 second quarter, CVTY established a $55 million reserve, which it believes is sufficient to cover health care costs for members under the old AHERF agreement. We look for a medical loss ratio of about 85.5% for 1999, aided by commercial rate hikes, lower patient utilization, and pharmacy benefit initiatives, along with improved operating margins. We see 1999 EPS reaching $0.62, and 2000 EPS at $0.75.

Valuation - 13-SEP-99

We are maintaining our hold rating on the stock. The company has made significant progress in its operational turnaround efforts, and expects to complete a consolidation of its service center operations from 20 to three, and to move its entire membership to a single platform by 1999 year end. This could result in some operating uncertainty in the near term. However, 1999 second quarter revenues and earnings met our expectations, reflecting rate increases in excess of 10%, and lower SG&A expenses as a percentage of revenues. Nevertheless, despite a more favorable outlook, with the shares recently trading at 14X our 2000 EPS estimate, the stock is fairly priced relative to that of CVTY's managed care peers.

Key Stock Statistics

S&P EPS Est. 1999	0.62	Tang. Bk. Value/Share	3.16
P/E on S&P Est. 1999	10.3	Beta	1.16
S&P EPS Est. 2000	0.75	Shareholders	7,500
Dividend Rate/Share	Nil	Market cap. (B)	$0.377
Shs. outstg. (M)	59.1	Inst. holdings	37%
Avg. daily vol. (M)	0.197		

Value of $10,000 invested 5 years ago: $ 3,000

Fiscal Year Ending Dec. 31

	1999	1998	1997	1996	1995	1994
Revenues (Million $)						
1Q	527.9	330.2	299.4	236.9	209.7	184.8
2Q	531.8	583.8	301.1	257.7	208.9	185.8
3Q	—	593.3	306.7	272.9	211.1	188.8
4Q	—	603.1	321.2	289.6	222.7	187.9
Yr.	—	2,110	1,228	1,057	852.4	747.3
Earnings Per Share ($)						
1Q	**0.14**	**0.13**	**-0.03**	**-0.03**	0.30	0.24
2Q	**0.15**	**-0.47**	**0.20**	**-0.26**	0.07	0.27
3Q	**E0.16**	**0.09**	**0.08**	**0.01**	0.05	0.27
4Q	**E0.17**	**0.11**	**0.11**	**-1.58**	-0.42	0.20
Yr.	**E0.62**	**-0.22**	**0.36**	**-1.87**	Nil	**0.93**

Next earnings report expected: late October

Dividend Data

No cash dividends have been paid.

A Division of The McGraw-Hill Companies

Coventry Health Care, Inc.

Business Summary - 13-SEP-99

Following the April 1998 merger of Coventry Corp. and the health care unit of The Principal Financial Group, Coventry Health Care ranks among the largest U.S. managed health care providers. It provides a full range of managed care products including health maintenance organization (HMO), preferred provider organization (PPO), point-of-service (POS), Medicare Risk and Medicaid plans. At June 30, 1999, the company had 1,394,568 members in 12 states. Geographically, the primary emphasis is on Pennsylvania and Missouri, where about 63% of the at-risk members are located. CVTY divested its Illinois (58,817 members) and Florida markets (161,162) in 1998.

Health care services provided by the company's HMOs include ambulatory and inpatient physician care, hospitalization, pharmacy, dental, optical, mental health, ancillary diagnostic and therapeutic services. In general, a fixed monthly enrollment fee covers all HMO services, although some plans require co-payments or deductibles in addition to the basic premium. A primary care physician assumes overall responsibility for member care, including preventive and routine medical care and specialist or consulting physician referrals.

CVTY also offers fully insured flexible products, including PPO and POS plans, which permit enrollees to join an HMO but allow them to utilize non-network providers in return for higher levels of deductibles and co-payments.

The company offers a Medicare risk product, under which it receives a fixed premium per member which is set annually by the Health Care Financing Administration (HCFA). It also offers a Medicare cost product which allows for reimbursement by HCFA only for the cost of services rendered, including services provided at the health plan's medical offices and a portion of administrative expenses. Under a Medicare supplement product, members enroll individually and pay a monthly premium for health services not covered under Medicare.

CVTY also offers health care coverage to Medicaid recipients, where it receives a monthly premium, set by individual state regulators, based on the age and sex of the recipients enrolled in its health plans.

The company's health plans offer an administrative services only (ASO, or non-risk) product to large employers who are self-insured. Under ASO contracts, employers who fund their own health plans receive the benefit of provider pricing arrangements from the health plan, and the health plan also provides a variety of administrative services such as claims processing, utilization review and quality assurance for the employers. CVTY receives a fee for such services.

Officers and directors own about 17% of the shares outstanding.

Per Share Data ($) (Year Ended Dec. 31)	1998	1997	1996	1995	1994	1993	1992	1991	1990	1989
Tangible Bk. Val.	2.39	0.28	NM	1.30	0.60	0.53	-0.17	-0.78	-1.39	NA
Cash Flow	0.27	0.72	-0.56	0.46	1.28	1.07	0.78	0.65	0.96	0.94
Earnings	-0.22	0.36	-1.86	Nil	0.96	0.80	0.56	0.40	0.59	0.58
Dividends	Nil	Nil	Nil	Nil	Nil	Nil	Nil	Nil	Nil	Nil
Payout Ratio	Nil	Nil	Nil	Nil	Nil	Nil	Nil	Nil	Nil	Nil
Prices - High	19¼	20⅛	21⅜	31	26¾	22⅛	12⅜	9½	NA	NA
- Low	3⅞	6⅝	8⅞	11	15¾	8¾	5¼	3½	NA	NA
P/E Ratio - High	NM	56	NM	NM	28	28	22	24	NA	NA
- Low	NM	18	NM	NM	16	11	9	9	NA	NA
Income Statement Analysis (Million $)										
Revs.	2,110	1,228	1,057	852	747	583	430	340	394	218
Oper. Inc.	51.1	18.5	-38.7	16.0	66.5	48.2	33.5	24.1	28.0	21.1
Depr.	25.8	12.7	42.9	14.7	9.2	7.1	5.3	5.7	6.3	3.6
Int. Exp.	8.6	10.3	6.3	4.9	2.7	2.7	3.7	5.6	9.9	7.6
Pretax Inc.	-17.5	20.3	-84.2	1.5	56.0	40.3	25.9	16.0	15.9	13.7
Eff. Tax Rate	NM	41%	NM	99%	44%	40%	41%	38%	37%	33%
Net Inc.	-11.7	11.9	-61.3	Nil	28.1	20.3	13.8	8.7	10.0	9.1
Balance Sheet & Other Fin. Data (Million $)										
Cash	409	154	98.0	85.8	75.4	71.3	55.3	23.3	43.5	31.6
Curr. Assets	591	237	208	143	114	100	78.2	43.4	90.0	56.3
Total Assets	1,091	469	449	386	332	243	193	164	269	180
Curr. Liab.	566	261	282	156	132	107	75.9	53.6	97.5	51.0
LT Debt	46.4	85.7	57.3	65.6	65.1	37.3	47.4	54.2	80.0	60.5
Common Eqty.	437	118	100	154	131	87.9	62.4	47.3	64.4	51.5
Total Cap.	483	204	158	222	196	134	114	105	157	119
Cap. Exp.	3.2	7.2	12.7	16.3	21.3	12.8	4.4	3.1	4.0	3.3
Cash Flow	14.1	24.6	-18.4	14.7	37.3	27.4	19.1	14.4	16.3	12.7
Curr. Ratio	1.0	0.9	0.7	0.9	0.9	0.9	1.0	0.8	0.9	1.1
% LT Debt of Cap.	9.6	42.1	36.3	29.6	33.2	27.9	41.5	51.8	51.1	51.0
% Net Inc.of Revs.	NM	1.0	NM	NM	3.8	3.5	3.2	2.6	2.5	4.2
% Ret. on Assets	NM	2.6	NM	NM	9.4	9.1	7.8	0.8	4.5	5.0
% Ret. on Equity	NM	10.9	NM	NM	24.5	26.6	25.2	3.4	17.3	21.6

Data as orig. reptd.; bef. results of disc. opers. and/or spec. items. Per share data adj. for stk. divs. as of ex-div. date. Bold denotes diluted EPS (FASB 128). E-Estimated. NA-Not Available. NM-Not Meaningful. NR-Not Ranked.

Office— 6705 Rockledge Blvd., Suite 900, Bethesda, MD 20817. **Tel**—(301) 581-0600. **Chrmn**—J. H. Austin. **Pres & CEO**—A. F. Wise. **EVP, Treas & CFO**—D. B. Wolf. **EVP** —T. P. McDonough. **VP & Secy**—S. R. Smith. **Investor Contact**—Lisa Toews-Daugherty (301-581-2778). **Dirs**—J. H. Austin, T. L. Blair, D. J. Drury, E. D. Farley Jr., T. J. Graf, P. T. Hackett, L. Kugelman, R. W. Moorhead III, E. Tallett, A. F. Wise. **Transfer Agent**—ChaseMellon Shareholder Services, Pittsburgh. **Incorporated**—in Delaware in 1986. **Empl**— 3,050. **S&P Analyst:** John J. Arege

STANDARD
&POOR'S
STOCK REPORTS

CPI Corp.

NYSE Symbol **CPY**

In S&P SmallCap 600

09-OCT-99

Industry:
Services (Commercial & Consumer)

Summary: This company, which primarily operates photographic studios as a licensee of Sears, has agreed to be acquired by American Securities Capital Partners, L.P.

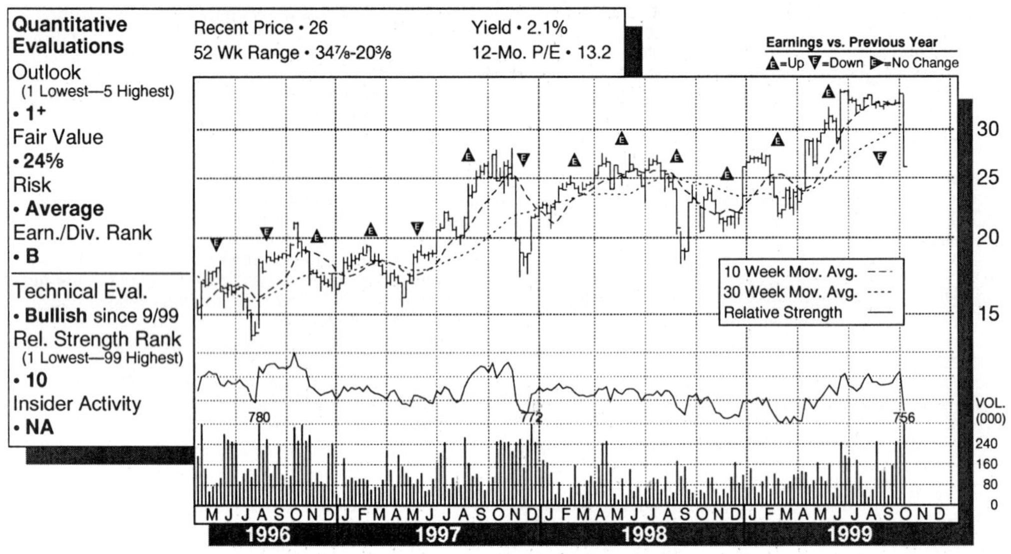

Business Profile - 19-JUL-99

In June 1999, CPY and American Securities Capital Partners, L.P. (ASCP) entered into a definitive merger agreement under which entities controlled by affiliates of ASCP and CPY's management will acquire CPY for $37.00 per share in cash. CPY's directors have unanimously approved the agreement, and the company will solicit proxies from its shareholders to approve the merger agreement at a meeting later in the summer. If the transaction is approved, each share of common stock will be converted into the right to receive $37.00 in cash.

Operational Review - 19-JUL-99

Net sales in the 12 weeks ended May 1, 1999, advanced 5.9%, year to year, as an 8.2% increase in sales for portrait studios more than outweighed a 4.7% drop in wall decor sales. Gross margins widened on the increased volume; operating income was up 19%. After taxes at 35.1%, versus a tax benefit of $272,000, net income was $74,000 ($0.01 a share, on 2.5% more shares), against a net loss of $506,000 ($0.05).

Stock Performance - 08-OCT-99

In the past 30 trading days, CPY's shares have declined 20%, compared to a 0.91% fall in the S&P 500. Average trading volume for the past five days was 151,280 shares, compared with the 40-day moving average of 54,205 shares.

Key Stock Statistics

Dividend Rate/Share	0.56	Shareholders	2,458
Shs. outstg. (M)	9.1	Market cap. (B)	$0.238
Avg. daily vol. (M)	0.075	Inst. holdings	72%
Tang. Bk. Value/Share	12.48		
Beta	0.70		

Value of $10,000 invested 5 years ago: $ 17,720

Fiscal Year Ending Jan. 31

	2000	1999	1998	1997	1996	1995
Revenues (Million $)						
1Q	77.66	73.35	70.17	104.7	103.4	100.1
2Q	71.23	71.00	68.49	105.4	107.1	104.7
3Q	—	124.0	108.2	145.4	166.2	175.4
4Q	—	121.2	119.9	111.5	150.0	153.0
Yr.	—	389.5	366.7	467.0	526.6	533.1
Earnings Per Share ($)						
1Q	**0.01**	**-0.05**	-0.20	-0.15	-0.03	-0.17
2Q	**-0.10**	**0.13**	0.12	-0.06	0.18	0.11
3Q	—	**0.59**	-0.06	0.36	0.24	0.28
4Q	—	**1.48**	1.22	0.91	0.88	0.86
Yr.	—	**2.15**	**1.07**	**1.06**	1.26	1.05

Next earnings report expected: mid December

Dividend Data (Dividends have been paid since 1985.)

Amount ($)	Date Decl.	Ex-Div. Date	Stock of Record	Payment Date
0.140	Nov. 05	Nov. 12	Nov. 16	Nov. 23 '98
0.140	Feb. 11	Feb. 18	Feb. 22	Mar. 01 '99
0.140	May. 06	May. 13	May. 17	May. 24 '99
0.140	Aug. 05	Aug. 12	Aug. 16	Aug. 23 '99

A Division of The McGraw-Hill Companies

Business Summary - 19-JUL-99

Founded in 1942, CPI Corp. (CPY) operates professional portrait studios throughout the U.S., Canada and Puerto Rico and poster, print and framing outlets throughout the U.S.

In FY 99 (Jan.), about 84% of CPY's net sales and substantially all of its operating earnings (before deduction of general corporate expenses, net interest income (expense), other income and income tax expense) were derived from its Sears Portrait Studio business. The company has operated portrait studios as a Sears, Roebuck and Co. licensee since 1961, when it was one of more than 15 Sears portrait photography licensees. Today, CPY is the only operator of Sears Portrait Studios in the U.S., Canada and Puerto Rico. As of June 1999, CPY operated its 1,029 Sears Portrait Studio locations under multiple license agreements.

In the U.S., CPY and Sears have entered into three license agreements for fixed location studios as of January 1, 1999. These agreements expire on December 31, 2003. The Sears store and Puerto Rico agreements provide for the company to pay Sears a license fee of 15% of total annual net sales for studios located in a Sears store. The Off-Mall agreement provides for the company to pay Sears a license fee of 7.5% of total annual net sales for studios not located in a Sears store but located in retail locations where Sears does not otherwise have a presence. Net sales for all agreements are defined as gross sales less customer returns, allowances and sales taxes. CPY provides all studio furniture, equipment, fixtures and leasehold improvements and conducts advertising at its own expense, and is responsible for hiring, training and compensating its employees and must indemnify Sears against all claims.

In addition, since the 1993 acquisition of Prints Plus, Inc., the company has operated a wall decor business. Prints Plus is a poster, print and custom framing retail chain with 152 stores located in malls throughout the U.S. as of June 1999.

In June 1999, CPY and American Securities Capital Partners, L.P. (ASCP) entered into a definitive merger agreement under which entities controlled by affiliates of ASCP and CPY's management will acquire CPY for $37.00 per share in cash. CPY's directors have unanimously approved the agreement, and the company will solicit proxies from its shareholders to approve the merger agreement at a meeting later in the summer. If the transaction is approved, each share of common stock will be converted into the right to receive $37.00 in cash.

Per Share Data ($) (Year Ended Jan. 31)	1999	1998	1997	1996	1995	1994	1993	1992	1991	1990
Tangible Bk. Val.	11.81	10.26	11.90	8.88	7.93	7.84	7.33	7.09	9.66	8.17
Cash Flow	5.06	3.60	3.86	4.19	3.63	2.95	3.42	3.46	3.66	3.32
Earnings	2.15	1.07	1.06	1.26	1.05	0.76	1.54	1.80	2.19	1.97
Dividends	0.56	0.56	0.56	0.56	0.56	0.56	0.56	0.56	0.50	0.42
Payout Ratio	26%	52%	53%	44%	53%	74%	36%	30%	22%	21%
Cal. Yrs.	1998	1997	1996	1995	1994	1993	1992	1991	1990	1989
Prices - High	27 3/8	28	21 1/4	22 1/8	21 7/8	20 7/8	27 1/8	34 3/4	34 3/8	33 7/8
- Low	18 1/8	15 5/8	13 5/8	13 3/4	14	13 3/4	14 7/8	21 3/4	23 1/2	19 3/4
P/E Ratio - High	13	26	20	18	21	27	18	19	16	17
- Low	8	14	13	11	13	18	10	12	11	10
Income Statement Analysis (Million $)										
Revs.	390	367	467	527	533	476	449	415	374	351
Oper. Inc.	59.1	58.2	58.3	72.7	63.8	50.9	62.4	64.4	69.6	66.8
Depr.	29.8	30.0	37.9	41.0	36.4	32.1	27.5	26.5	22.6	21.3
Int. Exp.	4.6	4.5	5.1	5.1	5.3	2.0	0.2	0.1	0.1	0.1
Pretax Inc.	33.8	20.9	22.8	27.6	23.5	18.5	36.5	43.3	53.5	48.3
Eff. Tax Rate	35%	39%	37%	36%	37%	40%	38%	37%	37%	36%
Net Inc.	21.9	12.7	14.3	17.7	14.8	11.1	22.6	27.1	33.6	30.9
Balance Sheet & Other Fin. Data (Million $)										
Cash	76.0	1.2	21.9	8.3	14.4	66.4	21.0	31.2	88.3	70.0
Curr. Assets	114	94.4	63.7	72.8	82.0	128	73.0	84.0	130	106
Total Assets	235	229	247	300	300	306	238	239	219	196
Curr. Liab.	35.8	47.4	50.8	64.0	69.8	65.2	56.8	67.1	51.4	47.8
LT Debt	59.6	59.5	44.9	54.8	59.7	59.8	0.3	0.6	0.5	0.3
Common Eqty.	117	102	140	174	166	176	172	160	152	133
Total Cap.	184	164	191	231	226	236	175	165	159	141
Cap. Exp.	15.0	21.7	35.0	48.8	77.1	45.4	13.3	40.6	20.3	25.6
Cash Flow	51.7	42.7	52.2	58.7	51.2	43.3	50.1	53.6	56.2	52.2
Curr. Ratio	3.2	2.0	1.3	1.1	1.2	2.0	1.3	1.2	2.5	2.2
% LT Debt of Cap.	32.3	36.3	23.5	23.7	26.4	25.4	0.2	0.3	0.3	0.2
% Net Inc.of Revs.	5.6	3.5	3.1	3.4	2.8	2.3	5.0	6.5	9.0	8.8
% Ret. on Assets	9.5	5.3	5.2	5.9	5.0	4.1	9.5	12.0	16.4	16.2
% Ret. on Equity	20.1	10.5	9.1	10.4	8.9	6.4	13.6	17.6	23.8	23.6

Data as orig reptd.; bef. results of disc opers/spec. items. Per share data adj. for stk. divs. Bold denotes diluted EPS (FASB 128)-prior periods restated. E-Estimated. NA-Not Available. NM-Not Meaningful. NR-Not Ranked.

Office—1706 Washington Ave., St. Louis, MO 63103-1790. **Tel**—(314) 231-1575. **Website**—http://www.cpicorp.com **Chrmn & CEO**—A. V. Essman. **Pres**—R. Isaak. **EVP, CFO & Treas**—B. C. Arthur. **Secy**—J. E. Nelson. **Dirs**—M. Bohm, A. V. Essman, R. Isaak, M. A. Krey, L. M. Liberman, P. J. Morris, N. L. Reding, M. Sneider, R. L. Virgil. **Transfer Agent & Registrar**—Boatmen's Trust Co., St. Louis. **Incorporated**—in Delaware in 1982. **Empl**— 8,178. **S&P Analyst:** M.I.

STANDARD & POOR'S
STOCK REPORTS

Cross (A.T.) Co.

ASE Symbol **ATX**

In S&P SmallCap 600

09-OCT-99

Industry: Consumer (Jewelry, Novelties & Gifts)

Summary: This leading maker of fine writing instruments recently entered the personal digital products market.

Quantitative Evaluations

Outlook (1 Lowest—5 Highest)
• **NA**

Fair Value
• **NA**

Risk
• **NA**

Earn./Div. Rank
• **C**

Technical Eval.
• **Bearish** since 9/99

Rel. Strength Rank (1 Lowest—99 Highest)
• **20**

Insider Activity
• **Favorable**

Recent Price • 4¼ | 52 Wk Range • 8⅝-3⅞ | Yield • Nil | 12-Mo. P/E • NM

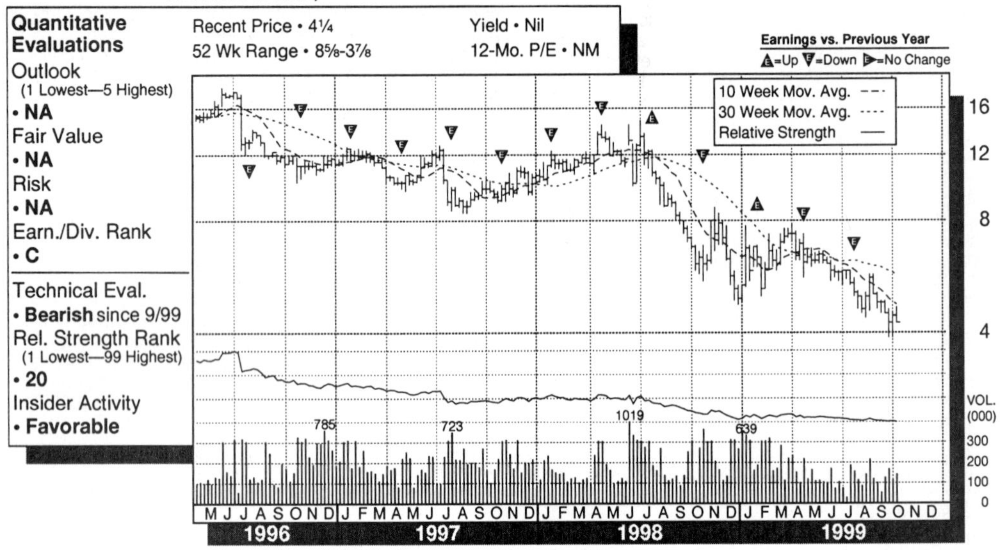

Business Profile - 27-JUL-99

Domestic writing instrument sales continued to slump in the second quarter of 1999, falling 14% in the first half of the year. In an attempt to gain market share, the Pen Computing Group made price reductions in the first quarter and incurred a first half pre-tax loss of $12.5 million, compared to $3.0 million in the year-ago period. As a result, management is reviewing the possible sale or discontinuance of the product line. Higher spending levels are anticipated to support other new product efforts, such as e-commerce capabilities and the testing of Cross product kiosks in five U.S. shopping malls. In July 1999, as part of a strategy to leverage itself as an OEM supplier of writing instruments, ATX acquired C&J Jewelry Company, Inc., a manufacturer of writing instruments for a luxury goods retailer.

Operational Review - 27-JUL-99

Net sales in the six months ended July 3, 1999, fell 17%, year to year, on decreases in the domestic writing instrument unit and the Pen Computing Group. Profitability declined on a less rapid decline in cost of goods sold and higher selling, general and administrative expenses; the operating loss widened significantly. With lower interest income, and tax benefits of $3.3 million, versus $620,000, the loss from continuing operations widened to $9.4 million ($0.56 a share), from $1.3 million ($0.08). Results in the 1999 and 1998 periods exclude income from discontinued operations of $0.09 and $0.10 a share, respectively.

Stock Performance - 08-OCT-99

In the past 30 trading days, ATX's shares have declined 16%, compared to a 0.91% fall in the S&P 500. Average trading volume for the past five days was 28,060 shares, compared with the 40-day moving average of 26,274 shares.

Key Stock Statistics

Dividend Rate/Share	Nil	Shareholders	1,900
Shs. outstg. (M)	16.7	Market cap. (B)	$0.063
Avg. daily vol. (M)	0.027	Inst. holdings	25%
Tang. Bk. Value/Share	5.76		
Beta	0.56		

Value of $10,000 invested 5 years ago: $ 3,590

Fiscal Year Ending Dec. 31

	1999	1998	1997	1996	1995	1994
Revenues (Million $)						
1Q	28.52	31.53	36.80	36.05	35.41	35.19
2Q	26.76	34.69	31.12	41.52	44.88	40.62
3Q	—	33.85	36.63	43.05	44.86	45.93
4Q	—	53.66	53.28	58.57	65.94	55.40
Yr.	—	153.7	154.7	179.2	191.1	177.1
Earnings Per Share ($)						
1Q	**-0.16**	**-0.08**	0.05	**0.09**	0.09	0.08
2Q	**-0.40**	Nil	-0.16	**0.05**	0.10	0.04
3Q	—	**-0.27**	-0.04	**0.09**	0.17	0.16
4Q	—	**-0.08**	**-0.11**	**0.13**	0.45	0.34
Yr.	—	**-0.43**	**-0.26**	**0.36**	**0.76**	**0.55**

Next earnings report expected: late October

Dividend Data (Dividends have been paid since 1952.)

Amount ($)	Date Decl.	Ex-Div. Date	Stock of Record	Payment Date
0.080	Oct. 20	Oct. 30	Nov. 03	Nov. 17 '98

A.T. Cross Company

Business Summary - 27-JUL-99

In 1877, Alonzo Cross was granted his first patent for a stylographic pen with an ink reservoir and a pencil-like tip, a design that proved to be extremely popular in coming years. The ball point pen that is synonymous with the name A.T. Cross was first introduced by the company in 1952. The new ball point pen and matching mechanical pencil were successfully marketed to businesses over the next two decades. In 1971, ATX made its IPO, using the proceeds to launch a global expansion. The company is now a major international manufacturer of fine writing instruments. Foreign sales accounted for 43% of total revenues in 1998.

The company has experienced disappointing sales and earnings in recent years, reflecting lower sales in U.S. and Asia. In 1998, results were restricted by costs of investment in the Pen Computing Group and timepiece business. To stimulate revenue growth, ATX has broadened its product line with the addition of watches and the Pen Computing Group.

ATX's writing instruments include ball point pens, mechanical pencils, rolling/porous-point pens and fountain pens. The company offers six styles, primarily priced from $10 to $50, including Century, Century II, Radiance, Solo and Metropolis. Metropolis failed to meet expectations, and is being phased out as of early 1999. ATX entered the premium end of the market ($55 to $400) with the release of the wider girth Townsend line in 1993, and the Pinnacle line in 1997. Writing instruments are sold throughout the U.S. to about 6,300 active retail and wholesale accounts.

Watch sales climbed 50% in 1998, the second year of test marketing, but overall results were below management's expectations. Discussions are underway with several potential licensees, as part of a broader strategic effort.

The Pen Computing Group designs, manufactures and markets electronic pen products. The CrossPad was jointly developed by IBM and ATX, and was introduced in the spring of 1998. The product enables users to write in ink on standard paper, and then to transfer their handwriting directly to a PC. Once in the PC, the handwriting can be filed, edited, faxed, e-mailed, printed out in handwritten form, or converted to ASCII text.

In December 1998, the common stock dividend was eliminated, to let the company concentrate its funds on the investment requirements of the Pen Computing Group.

Per Share Data ($)										
(Year Ended Dec. 31)	**1998**	**1997**	**1996**	**1995**	**1994**	**1993**	**1992**	**1991**	**1990**	**1989**
Tangible Bk. Val.	6.30	6.84	7.69	7.96	7.79	7.72	8.64	9.33	9.60	9.20
Cash Flow	0.08	0.23	0.85	1.23	1.00	0.40	0.98	1.58	1.93	2.64
Earnings	-0.43	-0.26	0.40	0.81	0.62	0.03	0.64	1.26	1.62	2.15
Dividends	0.32	0.48	0.64	0.64	0.64	0.96	1.28	1.28	1.25	1.18
Payout Ratio	NM	NM	160%	79%	103%	NM	200%	102%	77%	55%
Prices - High	$14\frac{7}{8}$	$12\frac{3}{4}$	$18\frac{1}{4}$	$17\frac{1}{2}$	$17\frac{5}{8}$	$20\frac{1}{4}$	$27\frac{5}{8}$	$28\frac{1}{8}$	36	41
- Low	$4\frac{3}{4}$	$8\frac{3}{8}$	$10\frac{1}{8}$	$12\frac{7}{8}$	$12\frac{1}{2}$	$12\frac{3}{8}$	17	$21\frac{1}{2}$	20	32
P/E Ratio - High	NM	NM	46	22	28	NM	43	22	22	19
- Low	NM	NM	25	16	20	NM	27	17	12	15
Income Statement Analysis (Million $)										
Revs.	154	155	179	191	177	165	200	217	223	247
Oper. Inc.	-5.1	-0.4	14.8	23.6	21.4	16.3	20.7	29.9	38.5	53.7
Depr.	8.4	8.2	7.5	7.0	6.3	6.2	5.7	5.5	5.2	5.2
Int. Exp.	Nil	Nil	Nil	Nil	Nil	Nil	Nil	Nil	Nil	Nil
Pretax Inc.	-10.9	-6.7	9.4	20.0	19.0	1.6	16.0	29.6	38.4	53.7
Eff. Tax Rate	NM	NM	30%	34%	45%	68%	32%	29%	29%	33%
Net Inc.	-7.1	-4.4	6.6	13.4	10.5	0.5	10.8	21.2	27.2	36.0
Balance Sheet & Other Fin. Data (Million $)										
Cash	22.8	25.8	43.5	54.0	72.0	71.1	65.2	65.9	70.4	64.5
Curr. Assets	106	110	119	135	131	130	144	157	158	149
Total Assets	156	158	175	189	180	179	194	208	207	196
Curr. Liab.	46.3	39.3	42.9	52.4	46.8	40.2	39.8	42.7	41.5	38.4
LT Debt	Nil	Nil	Nil	Nil	Nil	Nil	Nil	Nil	Nil	Nil
Common Eqty.	104	113	127	132	129	134	151	162	162	154
Total Cap.	104	113	127	132	129	134	151	162	162	154
Cap. Exp.	6.5	7.5	9.1	10.8	7.7	8.5	5.4	8.4	5.9	9.8
Cash Flow	1.3	3.9	14.1	20.4	16.9	6.7	16.6	26.7	32.4	41.2
Curr. Ratio	2.3	2.8	2.8	2.6	2.8	3.2	3.6	3.7	3.8	3.9
% LT Debt of Cap.	Nil	Nil	Nil	Nil	Nil	Nil	Nil	Nil	Nil	Nil
% Net Inc.of Revs.	NM	NM	3.7	7.0	5.9	0.3	5.4	9.8	12.2	14.6
% Ret. on Assets	NM	NM	3.6	7.3	5.9	0.3	5.4	10.2	13.5	19.3
% Ret. on Equity	NM	NM	5.1	10.3	8.1	0.4	6.9	13.1	17.2	24.7

Data as orig reptd.; bef. results of disc opers/spec. items. Per share data adj. for stk. divs. Bold denotes diluted EPS (FASB 128)-prior periods restated. E-Estimated. NA-Not Available. NM-Not Meaningful. NR-Not Ranked.

Office—One Albion Rd., Lincoln, RI 02865. **Registrar**—Citizens Trust Co., Providence. **Tel**—(401) 333-1200. **Website**—http://www.crossusa.com **Chrmn**—B. R. Boss. **Pres & CEO**—R. A. Boss. **EVP & COO**—J. E. Buckley. **SVP, Treas & CFO**—J. T. Ruggieri. **VP & Secy**—T. C. Benik. **Dirs**—B. R. Boss, R. A. Boss, J. E. Buckley, B. V. Buonanno, Jr., H. F. Krimendahl II, T. Murray, J. C. Tappan, E. G. Torrance, A. Van Dam. **Transfer Agent & Registrar**—Fleet National Bank of Rhode Island, Providence. **Incorporated**—in Rhode Island in 1916. **Empl**— 1,000. **S&P Analyst:** Jordan Horoschak

STANDARD
&POOR'S
STOCK REPORTS

Cross Timbers Oil

NYSE Symbol **XTO**

In S&P SmallCap 600

09-OCT-99

Industry:
Oil & Gas (Exploration & Production)

Summary: This oil and gas production and transportation company has properties in Texas, Oklahoma, Kansas, New Mexico, Wyoming and Alaska.

Quantitative Evaluations

Outlook
(1 Lowest—5 Highest)
• **1**

Fair Value
• **10¾**

Risk
• **Average**

Earn./Div. Rank
• **NR**

Technical Eval.
• **Neutral** since 9/99

Rel. Strength Rank
(1 Lowest—99 Highest)
• **36**

Insider Activity
• **NA**

Recent Price • 11⅝
52 Wk Range • 16½-4½

Yield • 0.3%
12-Mo. P/E • NM

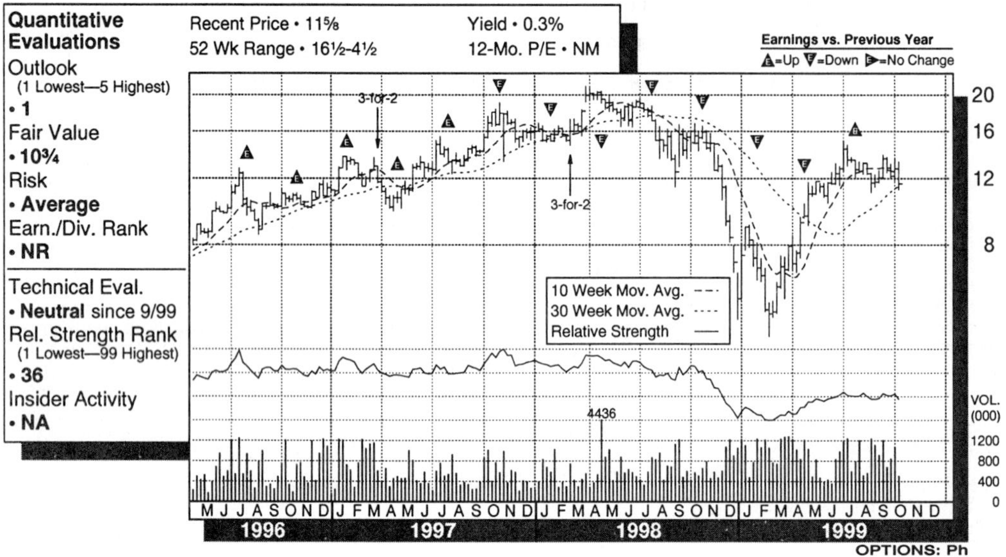

Business Profile - 30-JUN-99

The company's business strategy is focused on acquiring long-lived, operating oil and gas properties and increasing production and reserves through development, exploitation and exploration activities. Management's goal during 1999 is to reduce debt by as much as $300 million and to achieve debt levels of 40 to 45 cents per Mcfe. The company plans to reduce debt through the sale of Hugoton Royalty Trust units, completed in April 1999, and the dedication of cash flow above development costs.

Operational Review - 30-JUN-99

Revenues in the first quarter of 1999 advanced 39%, year to year, as oil and gas production gains following property acquisitions and development activity outweighed lower average sales prices. Expenses increased 47%, mainly due to the acquisitions and development activity, and with a 38% rise in interest expense a net loss of $1,462,000 ($0.04 a share, after preferred dividends) contrasted with net income of $261,000 (Nil).

Stock Performance - 08-OCT-99

In the past 30 trading days, XTO's shares have declined 1%, compared to a 0.91% fall in the S&P 500. Average trading volume for the past five days was 99,680 shares, compared with the 40-day moving average of 203,305 shares.

Key Stock Statistics

Dividend Rate/Share	0.04	Shareholders	320
Shs. outstg. (M)	48.8	Market cap. (B)	$0.567
Avg. daily vol. (M)	0.153	Inst. holdings	61%
Tang. Bk. Value/Share	NM		
Beta	1.18		

Value of $10,000 invested 5 years ago: $ 19,755

Fiscal Year Ending Dec. 31

	1999	1998	1997	1996	1995	1994
Revenues (Million $)						
1Q	69.51	50.62	53.49	36.08	24.22	22.61
2Q	65.50	67.53	45.97	36.74	27.94	24.02
3Q	—	67.04	44.09	39.20	28.07	25.29
4Q	—	70.82	57.12	49.37	32.68	24.36
Yr.	—	249.5	200.7	161.4	112.9	96.28
Earnings Per Share ($)						
1Q	**-0.04**	Nil	**0.26**	0.11	0.04	-0.01
2Q	**0.61**	**0.02**	**0.09**	0.04	0.03	0.02
3Q	—	**-0.69**	**0.07**	0.12	0.03	0.04
4Q	—	**-0.90**	**0.17**	0.23	-0.36	0.04
Yr.	—	**-1.65**	**0.59**	**0.48**	**-0.29**	0.08

Next earnings report expected: late October

Dividend Data (Dividends have been paid since 1993.)

Amount ($)	Date Decl.	Ex-Div. Date	Stock of Record	Payment Date
0.040	Nov. 18	Dec. 29	Dec. 31	Jan. 15 '99
0.010	Feb. 17	Mar. 29	Mar. 31	Apr. 15 '99
0.010	May. 18	Jun. 28	Jun. 30	Jul. 15 '99
0.010	Aug. 24	Sep. 28	Sep. 30	Oct. 15 '99

A Division of The McGraw-Hill Companies

Cross Timbers Oil Company

Business Summary - 30-JUN-99

This oil and gas company combines an aggressive capital structure with a relatively low-risk operating strategy to increase reserves and earnings. With several acquisitions of gas production properties in recent years, Cross Timbers Oil Co. (XTO) has effected a shift toward natural gas production.

The company ended 1998 with proved oil reserves of 54.5 million bbl., up 14% from the level a year earlier, and proved reserves of natural gas of 1.2 billion cubic feet, up 47%. Growth in proved reserves resulted from acquisition of gas-producing properties, as well as development and exploitation activities. Daily oil and gas production in 1998 averaged 12,598 bbl. and 229,717 Mcf, respectively. Oil and gas accounted respectively for 23% and 73% of revenues in 1998. XTO also has gas gathering, processing and marketing operations, which accounted for 4% of revenues.

During 1998, the company received sales prices of $12.21 per bbl. of oil ($18.90 in 1997) and $2.07 per Mcf of natural gas ($2.20). It also drilled 193 gross (77.5 net) development wells and five gross (4.0 net) exploratory wells. XTO has generated a substantial inventory of about 1,075 potential development drilling locations in its existing properties, to support future net reserve additions.

XTO has grown mainly through acquisitions of proved oil and gas reserves, followed by development and strategic acquisitions of additional interests. In 1998, the company began to emphasize exploration of unproved reserves as part of its business strategy. XTO has allocated less than 5% of its $60 million development budget for exploration activities in 1999.

The company's proved reserves are mainly located in relatively long-lived fields with well established production histories, concentrated in western Oklahoma, the East Texas Basin, the Permian Basin of West Texas and New Mexico, the Hugoton Field of Oklahoma and Kansas, the San Juan Basin of northwestern New Mexico (acquired in December 1997), the Green River Basin of Wyoming, and the Middle Ground Shoal Field of Alaska's Cook Inlet.

In December 1998, the company formed the Hugoton Royalty Trust by conveying an 80% net profits interest in properties located in the Hugoton area of Kansas and Oklahoma, the Anadarko Basin of Oklahoma and the Green River Basin of Wyoming. These properties represent about 30% of the company's existing reserve base. In April 1999, XTO offered 17,004,000 Hugoton Royalty Trust units (including overallotment) at $9.50 per unit. Proceeds were to be used to reduce debt under a senior credit facility.

In May 1998, XTO announced plans to make strategic acquisitions totaling $150 million between May 1998 and the end of 1999. In February 1999, directors approved a development budget of $60 million for 1999. The company expects to drill or participate in the drilling of about 100 wells and plans to implement about 240 workover and recompletion activities. It plans to fund the budget through int ernally generated sources. The development budget may be revised, depending on commodity prices.

Per Share Data ($) (Year Ended Dec. 31)	1998	1997	1996	1995	1994	1993	1992	1991	1990	1989
Tangible Bk. Val.	3.33	3.59	2.97	3.16	3.16	3.21	3.25	NA	NA	NA
Cash Flow	0.28	1.78	1.45	0.68	0.97	0.63	0.85	NA	NA	NA
Earnings	-1.65	0.59	0.49	-0.29	0.08	-0.12	0.20	NA	NA	NA
Dividends	0.08	0.15	0.13	0.13	0.13	0.10	NA	NA	NA	NA
Payout Ratio	NM	25%	27%	NM	158%	NM	NA	NA	NA	NA
Prices - High	21 1/8	19 1/8	12 3/4	8	7 3/8	8 3/8	NA	NA	NA	NA
- Low	5	9 7/8	7	5 7/8	5 1/2	5 3/4	NA	NA	NA	NA
P/E Ratio - High	NM	32	26	NM	87	NM	NA	NA	NA	NA
- Low	NM	17	14	NM	66	NM	NA	NA	NA	NA
Income Statement Analysis (Million $)										
Revs.	249	201	161	113	96.0	78.1	107	NA	NA	NA
Oper. Inc.	124	114	85.9	52.7	44.2	29.7	39.4	NA	NA	NA
Depr. Depl. & Amort.	83.6	47.7	37.9	36.9	31.7	24.6	23.7	NA	NA	NA
Int. Exp.	52.1	26.7	17.2	12.9	8.3	5.6	4.7	NA	NA	NA
Pretax Inc.	-105	39.2	31.0	-0.2	4.8	-0.4	11.0	NA	NA	NA
Eff. Tax Rate	NM	34%	34%	NM	36%	NM	34%	NA	NA	NA
Net Inc.	-69.8	25.7	20.3	-11.2	3.0	-4.0	7.2	NA	NA	NA
Balance Sheet & Other Fin. Data (Million $)										
Cash	12.3	3.8	3.9	2.2	7.8	2.1	4.3	NA	NA	NA
Curr. Assets	138	52.2	51.8	32.7	26.9	22.8	21.8	NA	NA	NA
Total Assets	1,208	788	523	403	292	258	220	NA	NA	NA
Curr. Liab.	100	54.9	52.0	31.1	28.5	25.3	15.9	NA	NA	NA
LT Debt	921	539	315	238	143	112	79.9	NA	NA	NA
Common Eqty.	149	142	114	131	113	115	120	NA	NA	NA
Total Cap.	1,105	730	468	372	264	233	204	NA	NA	NA
Cap. Exp.	296	257	114	171	30.0	105	NA	NA	NA	NA
Cash Flow	12.0	71.6	57.6	25.7	34.8	20.6	31.0	NA	NA	NA
Curr. Ratio	1.4	1.0	1.0	1.1	0.9	0.9	1.4	NA	NA	NA
% LT Debt of Cap.	83.3	73.8	67.3	64.0	54.1	48.1	39.1	NA	NA	NA
% Ret. on Assets	NM	3.9	4.4	NM	1.1	NM	NA	NA	NA	NA
% Ret. on Equity	NM	18.7	16.2	NM	2.7	NM	NA	NA	NA	NA

Data as orig reptd.; bef. results of disc opers/spec. items. Per share data adj. for stk. divs. Bold denotes diluted EPS (FASB 128)-prior periods restated. E-Estimated. NA-Not Available. NM-Not Meaningful. NR-Not Ranked.

Office—810 Houston St., Suite 2000, Fort Worth, TX 76102. **Organized**—in Delaware in 1990. **Tel**—(817) 870-2800. **Website**—http://www.crosstimbers.com **Chrmn & CEO**—B. R. Simpson. **Vice Chrmn & Pres**—S. E. Palko. **SVP, CFO & Investor Contact**—Louis G. Baldwin. **Dirs**—J. L. King Jr., S. E. Palko, J. P. Randall, S. G. Sherman, B. R. Simpson. **Transfer Agent & Registrar**—ChaseMellon Shareholder Services, Dallas. **Incorporated**—in Delaware in 1990. **Empl**— 521. **S&P Analyst:** SRB

STANDARD
&POOR'S
STOCK REPORTS

CTS Corp.

NYSE Symbol **CTS**

In S&P SmallCap 600

09-OCT-99 **Industry:** Manufacturing (Specialized) **Summary:** CTS manufactures and sells a broad line of passive electronic components and electronic assemblies.

Quantitative Evaluations
Outlook
(1 Lowest—5 Highest)
• **2**
Fair Value
• **54⅜**
Risk
• **Low**
Earn./Div. Rank
• **B+**

Technical Eval.
• **Bullish** since 4/99
Rel. Strength Rank
(1 Lowest—99 Highest)
• **92**
Insider Activity
• **NA**

Recent Price • 56
52 Wk Range • 60½-12
Yield • 0.2%
12-Mo. P/E • 44.8

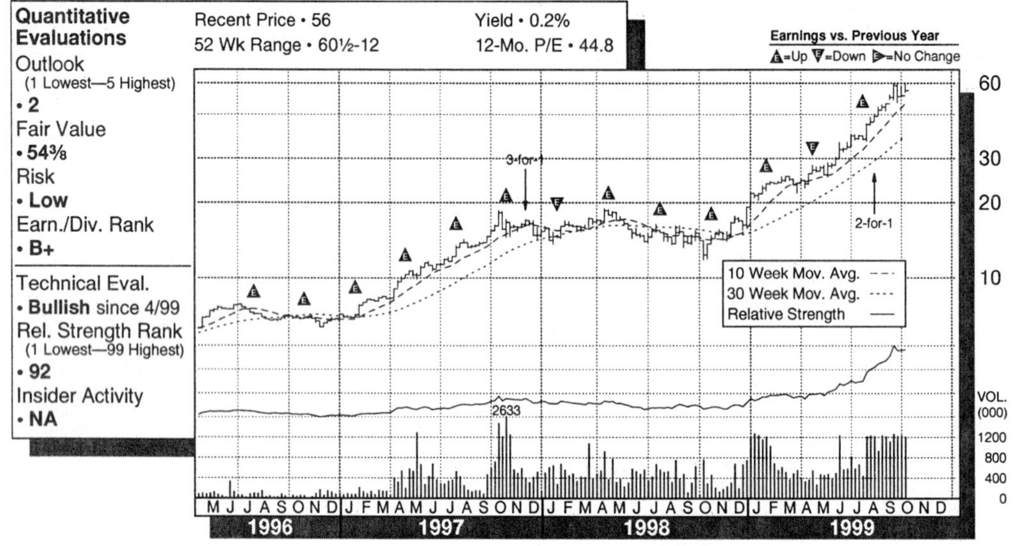

Business Profile - 26-AUG-99

In February 1999, the company acquired the components product division of Motorola, Inc., which makes ceramics, quartz, ocscillators, lead zirconate titanate and other products primarily for the wireless communications industry, for $145 million, including the assumption of debt, plus contingent payments over five years of up to $100 million. The acquired business had earnings before interest, taxes, depreciation and amortization of $23 million in 1998 on revenues of $315 million. Management, which expects revenues of about $240 million from the business in 1999, believes the deal will immediately add to earnings, and, moreover, that it can achieve $3 million to $5 million in annual cost savings over the next three years. In addition, CTS is soliciting buyers for the remaining non-strategic businesses of Dynamics Corp of America.

Operational Review - 26-AUG-99

Net sales in the six months ended July 4, 1999, surged 54%, year to year, reflecting the acquisition of CTS wireless components. After a one-time $12.9 million ($0.30 after tax) non-cash writeoff of acquired in process research and development, operating profit rose just 14%. Interest expense rose sharply on higher debt. After taxes at 31.0%, vs. 33.0%, income from continuing operations rose 2.3% to $16,653,000 ($0.58 a share, as adjusted, on 5.1% fewer shares), from $16,278,000 ($0.54, excluding income from discontinued operations of $0.07).

Stock Performance - 08-OCT-99

In the past 30 trading days, CTS's shares have increased 16%, compared to a 0.91% fall in the S&P 500. Average trading volume for the past five days was 242,960 shares, compared with the 40-day moving average of 278,833 shares.

Key Stock Statistics

Dividend Rate/Share	0.12	Shareholders	1,435
Shs. outstg. (M)	27.6	Market cap. (B)	$ 1.5
Avg. daily vol. (M)	0.299	Inst. holdings	65%
Tang. Bk. Value/Share	3.82		
Beta	0.68		

Value of $10,000 invested 5 years ago: $ 180,742

Fiscal Year Ending Dec. 31

	1999	1998	1997	1996	1995	1994
Revenues (Million $)						
1Q	120.3	94.00	91.27	80.19	75.98	64.36
2Q	177.8	99.3	107.5	83.82	76.41	70.62
3Q	—	83.80	89.98	76.46	73.89	65.95
4Q	—	93.30	126.4	80.83	73.88	67.78
Yr.	—	370.4	415.1	321.3	300.2	268.7
Earnings Per Share ($)						
1Q	**0.08**	**0.23**	**0.22**	**0.14**	0.10	0.08
2Q	**0.51**	**0.30**	**0.27**	**0.17**	0.15	0.13
3Q	—	**0.28**	**0.24**	**0.16**	0.14	0.10
4Q	—	**0.35**	**-0.01**	**0.20**	0.16	0.15
Yr.	—	**1.17**	**0.71**	**0.67**	**0.55**	**0.45**

Next earnings report expected: mid October

Dividend Data (Dividends have been paid since 1930.)

Amount ($)	Date Decl.	Ex-Div. Date	Stock of Record	Payment Date
0.060	Feb. 19	Mar. 29	Mar. 31	Apr. 30 '99
0.060	Apr. 30	Jun. 28	Jun. 30	Jul. 30 '99
2-for-1	Jun. 24	Aug. 13	Jul. 12	Aug. 12 '99
.q03	Aug. 20	Sep. 28	Sep. 30	Oct. 29 '99

A Division of The McGraw-Hill Companies

CTS Corporation

Business Summary - 26-AUG-99

CTS designs, makes, assembles and sells a broad line of passive electronic components and electronic assemblies, serving the electronic needs of original equipment manufacturers worldwide in the computer equipment, automotive, communications equipment and other markets. In February 1999, operations were considerably expanded with the purchase of the component products division of Motorola for some $145 million, not including possible contingent payments.

In 1998, electronic components represented 67% of revenues and 85% of operating profits. Electronic assemblies contributed the remaining 33% and 15% of revenues and operating profit, respectively.

International sales were 40% of the total, with sales in the United Kingdom accounting for 62% of overseas business.

Electronic components consist principally of automotive sensors used in commercial or consumer vehicles, frequency control devices such as crystals and clocks, loudspeakers, resistor networks, switches and variable resistors.

Electronic assemblies are assemblies of electronic or electronic and mechanical products, which, apart from the assembly, may themselves be marketed as separate stand-alone products. These products consist mainly of flex cable assemblies used in the disk drive market, hybrid microcircuits used in the health care market, cursor controls for computers and interconnect products such as backpedal and connectors used in the telecommunications industry.

Within the two business segments, the company's products are principally sold into four primary original equipment manufacturer (OEM) markets including computer equipment, automotive, communications equipment and other. Other markets include OEMs for consumer electronics, instruments and controls and defense and aerospace equipment. Sales of electronic components to the automotive industry accounted for 32% of total sales, while sales of electronic assemblies to computer equipment makers constituted 23% of overall revenues.

The company believes that it competes most effectively in custom products manufactured to meet specific applications of OEMs. CTS believes it has certain advantages over some of its competitors, including the ability to apply a broad range of technologies and material capabilities; the capability to sell a wide range of products made to consistent standards of quality and delivery; and the fact that it is one of the largest manufacturers of automatic throttle position sensors in the world.

Raw materials used in CTS products include steel, brass, aluminum, precious metals, resistive and conductive inks, passive electronic components and semiconductors; ceramic materials used in resistor networks and hybrid microcircuits; synthetic quartz for use in frequency control devices; and molding compounds for sensors, loudspeakers and other products.

Per Share Data ($) (Year Ended Dec. 31)	1998	1997	1996	1995	1994	1993	1992	1991	1990	1989
Tangible Bk. Val.	4.54	4.86	5.17	4.53	4.08	3.67	3.65	3.74	3.72	3.54
Cash Flow	1.82	1.25	1.07	0.92	0.81	0.60	0.44	0.56	0.66	0.84
Earnings	1.17	0.71	0.67	0.55	0.45	0.21	0.06	0.14	0.24	0.43
Dividends	0.12	0.12	0.12	0.10	0.08	0.07	0.11	0.13	0.13	0.10
Payout Ratio	10%	17%	17%	18%	17%	31%	180%	91%	52%	24%
Prices - High	22	18 5/8	7 7/8	6 1/4	5 1/8	3 5/8	4 1/8	4	4	4 1/4
- Low	11 7/8	6 7/8	6	4 5/8	3 1/4	2 7/8	2 7/8	2 3/4	2 5/8	3 3/4
P/E Ratio - High	19	26	12	11	11	17	66	29	17	10
- Low	10	10	9	8	7	13	46	20	11	9
Income Statement Analysis (Million $)										
Revs.	370	415	321	300	269	237	227	230	251	262
Oper. Inc.	68.8	68.3	45.9	39.2	31.9	23.2	14.9	17.5	23.9	29.4
Depr.	19.2	17.0	12.5	11.7	11.2	12.1	11.7	13.1	13.1	13.4
Int. Exp.	2.2	2.9	1.4	1.8	0.7	1.0	1.3	1.3	1.4	1.6
Pretax Inc.	49.4	35.1	33.6	27.7	21.5	10.3	3.8	6.2	9.5	17.4
Eff. Tax Rate	31%	35%	37%	38%	35%	36%	50%	33%	23%	18%
Net Inc.	34.1	22.8	21.2	17.2	14.0	6.6	1.9	4.2	7.3	14.3
Balance Sheet & Other Fin. Data (Million $)										
Cash	16.3	39.8	45.0	37.3	2.9	23.5	18.5	18.1	13.4	13.3
Curr. Assets	119	186	138	126	111	97.0	87.0	91.0	91.0	95.0
Total Assets	293	330	249	227	207	185	171	176	173	177
Curr. Liab.	82.4	92.4	51.4	51.0	44.8	49.9	37.3	39.6	39.1	37.9
LT Debt	55.6	63.5	11.2	13.7	15.6	4.8	9.7	9.3	6.0	8.3
Common Eqty.	124	147	166	146	132	119	119	122	122	125
Total Cap.	207	233	194	172	157	129	132	135	131	135
Cap. Exp.	21.3	22.4	17.2	11.0	10.0	11.7	8.8	16.0	11.8	10.8
Cash Flow	53.2	39.8	33.7	28.8	25.2	18.7	13.6	17.3	20.4	27.6
Curr. Ratio	1.4	2.0	2.7	2.5	2.5	1.9	2.3	2.3	2.3	2.5
% LT Debt of Cap.	26.9	27.3	5.8	8.0	10.0	3.7	7.4	6.9	4.6	6.1
% Net Inc.of Revs.	9.2	5.5	6.6	5.7	5.2	2.8	0.8	1.8	2.9	5.4
% Ret. on Assets	10.9	7.9	8.9	7.9	7.1	3.7	1.1	2.4	4.3	7.8
% Ret. on Equity	25.1	14.5	13.5	12.3	11.1	5.5	1.6	3.4	6.1	11.9

Data as orig reptd.; bef. results of disc opers/spec. items. Per share data adj. for stk. divs. Bold denotes diluted EPS (FASB 128)-prior periods restated. E-Estimated. NA-Not Available. NM-Not Meaningful. NR-Not Ranked.

Office—905 West Blvd. North, Elkhart, IN 46514. **Tel**—(219) 293-7511. **Fax**—(219) 293-6146. **Website**—http://www.ctscorp.com **Chrmn, Pres & CEO**—J. P. Walker. **EVP, Gen Counsel & Secy**—J. M. Davis. **Investor Contact**—Timothy J. Cunningham. **Dirs**—L. J. Ciancia, T. G. Cody, G. H. Frieling Jr., R. A. Profusek, J. P. Walker, R. J. Weisenburger. **Transfer Agent & Registrar**—EquiServe, Canton, MA. **Incorporated**—in Indiana in 1929. **Empl**— 8,425. **S&P Analyst:** E.P.L.

STANDARD &POOR'S STOCK REPORTS

Cullen/Frost Bankers

NYSE Symbol **CFR**

In S&P SmallCap 600

09-OCT-99

Industry: Banks (Regional)

Summary: The largest multibank holding company headquartered in Texas, Cullen/Frost owns two subsidiary banks with 79 offices in various cities in the state.

Quantitative Evaluations

Outlook (1 Lowest—5 Highest) • **3**

Fair Value • **26⅛**

Risk • **Low**

Earn./Div. Rank • **B**

Technical Eval. • **Bearish** since 9/99

Rel. Strength Rank (1 Lowest—99 Highest) • **76**

Insider Activity • **Neutral**

Recent Price • 26¼ | Yield • 2.7%

52 Wk Range • 28⅞-22¾ | 12-Mo. P/E • 15.5

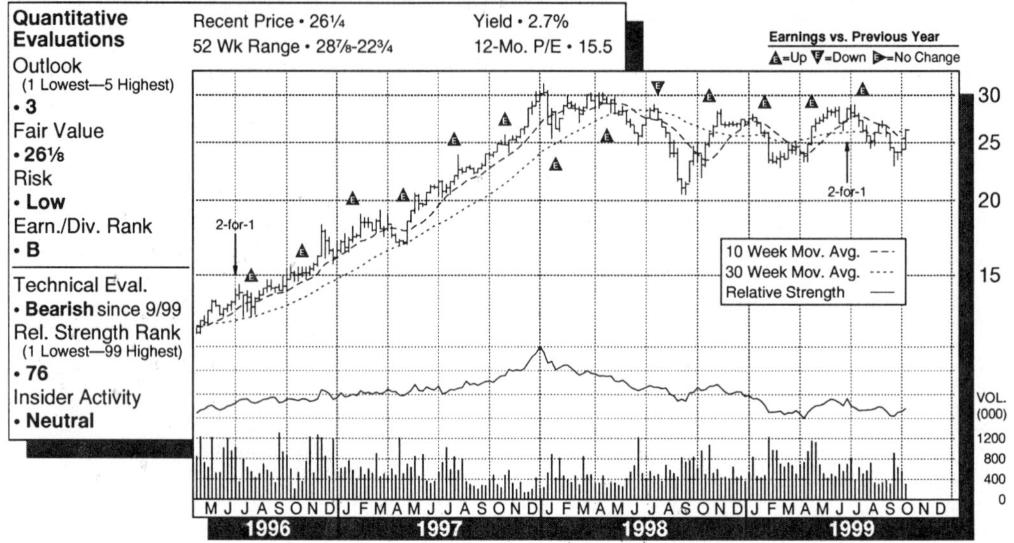

Business Profile - 21-MAY-99

In March 1999, Frost Insurance Agency, a subsidiary of Frost National Bank, signed a letter of intent to acquire Professional Insurance Agents, Inc. (PIA), a mid-sized independent insurance agency based in Victoria, TX. Terms of the transaction, expected to close in the second quarter, were not disclosed. In May 1999, CFR acquired Commerce Financial Corp., the parent company of Bank of Commerce, with assets of $181 million. In January 1999, CFR sought approval from the Federal Reserve to form a Section 20 investment banking subsidiary, expected to be operational in July 1999. In April 1999, CFR increased the cash dividend, announced a two-for-one stock split, and also announced a two-year stock repurchase program of up to $100 million.

Operational Review - 21-MAY-99

Net Interest Income in 1998 advanced 14% from the prior year, primarily due to loan growth generated internally and through acquisitions, as well as lower deposit costs. The net interest margin increased to 4.93%, from 4.87%. The provision for possible loan losses rose 13% to $10.4 million. Noninterest income increased 14%, mainly due to growth in trust income and certain service charges. Noninterest expenses rose 18%, reflecting a $12.2 million merger related charge, and 13% higher salaries and wages. After taxes at 35.8%, versus 35.2%, net income increased 3.7%, to $75,645,000 ($2.77 a share), from $72,967,000 ($2.67).

Stock Performance - 08-OCT-99

In the past 30 trading days, CFR's shares have declined 2%, compared to a 0.91% fall in the S&P 500. Average trading volume for the past five days was 59,740 shares, compared with the 40-day moving average of 94,377 shares.

Key Stock Statistics

Dividend Rate/Share	0.70	Shareholders	2,647
Shs. outstg. (M)	53.5	Market cap. (B)	$ 1.4
Avg. daily vol. (M)	0.119	Inst. holdings	57%
Tang. Bk. Value/Share	9.55		
Beta	1.00		

Value of $10,000 invested 5 years ago: $ 33,693

Fiscal Year Ending Dec. 31

	1999	1998	1997	1996	1995	1994
Revenues (Million $)						
1Q	147.5	117.8	101.8	92.99	79.41	67.08
2Q	147.3	141.2	109.4	96.77	86.66	68.99
3Q	—	143.9	110.3	96.42	87.48	74.12
4Q	—	163.9	112.6	98.87	88.80	72.14
Yr.	—	566.8	505.8	385.1	343.8	282.3
Earnings Per Share ($)						
1Q	**0.45**	**0.36**	**0.33**	**0.28**	0.23	0.20
2Q	**0.44**	**0.21**	**0.34**	**0.29**	0.25	0.20
3Q	—	**0.40**	**0.35**	**0.30**	0.26	0.21
4Q	—	**0.41**	**0.36**	**0.32**	0.27	0.21
Yr.	—	**1.38**	**1.37**	**1.20**	**1.02**	**0.83**

Next earnings report expected: mid October

Dividend Data (Dividends have been paid since 1993.)

Amount ($)	Date Decl.	Ex-Div. Date	Stock of Record	Payment Date
0.300	Jan. 26	Feb. 24	Feb. 26	Mar. 15 '99
0.350	Apr. 27	May. 27	Jun. 01	Jun. 15 '99
2-for-1	Apr. 27	Jun. 23	Jun. 01	Jun. 02 '99
0.175	Jul. 27	Aug. 30	Sep. 01	Sep. 15 '99

A Division of The McGraw-Hill Companies

Cullen/Frost Bankers, Inc.

Business Summary - 21-MAY-99

This Texas bank holding company, with $6.9 billion in assets (primarily loans and investments) at year-end 1998, is one of the few companies that can boast of providing financial services for 130 years under one name. Cullen/Frost Bankers operated a total of 79 financial centers (at 1998 year end) in eight Texas banking markets: San Antonio, Houston/Galveston, Fort Worth/Dallas, Austin, Corpus Christi, San Marcos, McAllen. and New Braunfels. CFR is the largest bank headquartered in San Antonio and South Texas.

CFR derives the majority of its income from lending activities, which have benefited from the strong regional economies in its Texas markets. Loans, at December 31, 1998, totaled $3.65 billion (up 17% from $3.12 billion at the end of 1997). Loans were divided in 1998 and 1997, respectively, as follows: real estate, 47%, 43%; commercial and industrial, 33%, 30%; consumer, 17%, 23%; international (mostly Mexican), 1%, 3%; other, 2%, 1%.

Cullen/Frost also has strong fee-based revenue, which is not dependent on demand for loans. Accounting for about 34% of overall net revenue in 1998, noninterest income growth was largely driven by trust income (CFR ranks among the 60 largest trust banks in the U.S.) and service charges on deposit accounts.

The net interest margin (the amount of interest income earned in loans less what the bank pays to acquire those funds, as a percent of average earning assets) for 1998 was 4.93%, up from 4.74% in 1997, as the bank's cost of funds declined slightly.

CFR continues to have high asset quality. The ratio of nonperforming assets (loans where principal and interest payments are not being received as per original terms) to total assets at the end of 1998 was 0.25%, down from 0.30% a year earlier. Additionally, the level of net chargeoffs (amount of loans written off as bad debt expense, less any recoveries) represented 0.18% of average net loans, down from the year-earlier level of 0.21%.

Total deposits grew 1.5% in 1998, to $5.8 billion. International deposits, principally from Mexico, averaged $642.8 million, or 12% of average total deposits.

In January 1999, CFR acquired Keller State Bank, which had assets of $73.5 million and deposits of $64.6 million.

Per Share Data ($) (Year Ended Dec. 31)	1998	1997	1996	1995	1994	1993	1992	1991	1990	1989
Tangible Bk. Val.	9.60	9.17	8.43	7.62	6.64	6.21	4.95	4.39	4.45	4.73
Earnings	1.39	1.38	1.20	1.02	0.83	0.87	0.41	0.01	-0.21	0.07
Dividends	0.57	0.48	0.41	0.28	0.17	0.04	Nil	Nil	Nil	Nil
Payout Ratio	42%	35%	34%	28%	20%	4%	Nil	Nil	Nil	Nil
Prices - High	30 5/8	31 3/8	18 1/4	12 7/8	9 7/8	10 1/8	7 1/8	3 1/2	2 5/8	4 1/4
- Low	20 1/2	16 3/8	11 3/4	7 1/2	7 1/8	6 3/4	3 1/8	1 7/16	1 3/16	2 5/16
P/E Ratio - High	22	23	15	13	12	12	17	NM	NM	59
- Low	15	12	10	7	9	8	7	NM	NM	33
Income Statement Analysis (Million $)										
Net Int. Inc.	268	197	179	152	136	128	117	109	110	107
Tax Equiv. Adj.	2.8	1.1	1.0	0.9	0.6	0.9	1.1	2.1	2.9	3.6
Non Int. Inc.	138	109	95.5	89.1	80.9	74.8	62.1	55.5	50.5	50.0
Loan Loss Prov.	10.4	7.9	7.3	6.3	Nil	-6.1	NM	10.0	32.0	28.9
Exp./Op. Revs.	68%	65%	66%	67%	71%	85%	85%	93%	84%	78%
Pretax Inc.	118	99	85.7	71.3	57.6	38.1	25.8	0.8	-8.0	2.9
Eff. Tax Rate	36%	36%	36%	35%	35%	NM	32%	76%	NM	7.00%
Net Inc.	75.6	63.5	55.0	46.3	37.4	38.8	17.6	0.2	-8.2	2.7
% Net Int. Marg.	4.04	4.74	4.76	4.56	4.40	4.29	4.47	4.13	3.93	3.60
Balance Sheet & Other Fin. Data (Million $)										
Money Mkt. Assets	103	190	53.0	101	168	250	283	99	276	449
Inv. Securities	2,092	1,492	1,476	1,537	1,594	1,612	1,414	1,439	1,237	1,257
Com'l Loans	346	804	650	509	383	312	268	301	377	462
Other Loans	3,300	1,842	1,602	1,309	1,099	944	756	787	908	922
Total Assets	6,870	5,231	4,888	4,200	3,794	3,639	3,151	3,079	3,255	3,505
Demand Deposits	1,843	1,339	1,331	992	832	881	766	669	656	647
Time Deposits	4,002	3,145	2,911	2,654	2,256	2,268	2,003	2,097	2,222	2,333
LT Debt	98.5	98.4	Nil	Nil	Nil	Nil	13.4	14.7	16.3	17.5
Common Eqty.	513	408	379	341	293	274	206	176	173	179
% Ret. on Assets	1.3	1.3	1.2	1.2	1.0	1.1	0.6	0.0	NM	0.1
% Ret. on Equity	16.4	16.1	15.3	14.3	13.0	15.6	9.2	0.1	NM	1.5
% Loan Loss Resv.	1.5	1.6	1.6	1.7	1.7	2.1	3.1	4.0	3.6	3.1
% Loans/Deposits	62.4	56.1	53.1	49.8	47.7	39.6	36.5	38.8	44.1	46.0
% Equity to Assets	7.6	7.8	7.9	8.0	7.8	7.1	6.3	5.7	5.4	5.1

Data as orig. reptd.; bef. results of disc. opers. and/or spec. items. Per share data adj. for stk. divs. as of ex-div. date. Bold denotes diluted EPS (FASB 128). E-Estimated. NA-Not Available. NM-Not Meaningful. NR-Not Ranked.

Office—P.O. Box 1600, 100 W. Houston St., San Antonio, TX 78205. **Organized**—in 1966. **Tel**—(210) 220-4011. **Sr Chrmn**—T. C. Frost. **Chrmn & CEO**—R. W. Evans Jr. **Pres**—R. S. McClane. **EVP & CFO**—P. D. Green. **Secy**—D. M. Jack. **Investor Contact**—Bart R. Vincent (210-220-4878). **Dirs**—R. D. Alexander, I. Arnold Jr., R. S. Caldwell, R. R. Cardenas, H. E. Catto, B. W. Coleman, H. H. Cullen, R. H. Cullen, E. H. Dawson, C. Edwards, R. M. Escobedo, R. W. Evans Jr., W. N. Finnegan III, T. C. Frost, P. B. Frost, J. Fulton,—J.W. Gorman Jr., J.L. Hayne Jr., R. M. Kleberg III, R.S. McClane Jr., I.C. Steen, C.V. Vaughan, H. Wilkins, M.B. Williamson.**Transfer Agent & Registrar**—Frost National Bank, San Antonio. **Empl**— 3,095. **S&P Analyst:** J. Rudy.

STANDARD &POOR'S
STOCK REPORTS

Curative Health Services

NASDAQ Symbol **CURE**

In S&P SmallCap 600

09-OCT-99

Industry: Health Care (Specialized Services)

Summary: This company manages a nationwide network of wound care centers that offer patients comprehensive, multidisciplinary wound treatment programs.

Quantitative Evaluations

Outlook
(1 Lowest—5 Highest)
• **NA**

Fair Value
• **NA**

Risk
• **Average**

Earn./Div. Rank
• **B-**

Technical Eval.
• **Bearish** since 6/99

Rel. Strength Rank
(1 Lowest—99 Highest)
• **44**

Insider Activity
• **NA**

Recent Price • 5¼
52 Wk Range • 35-3⅜
Yield • Nil
12-Mo. P/E • 4.2

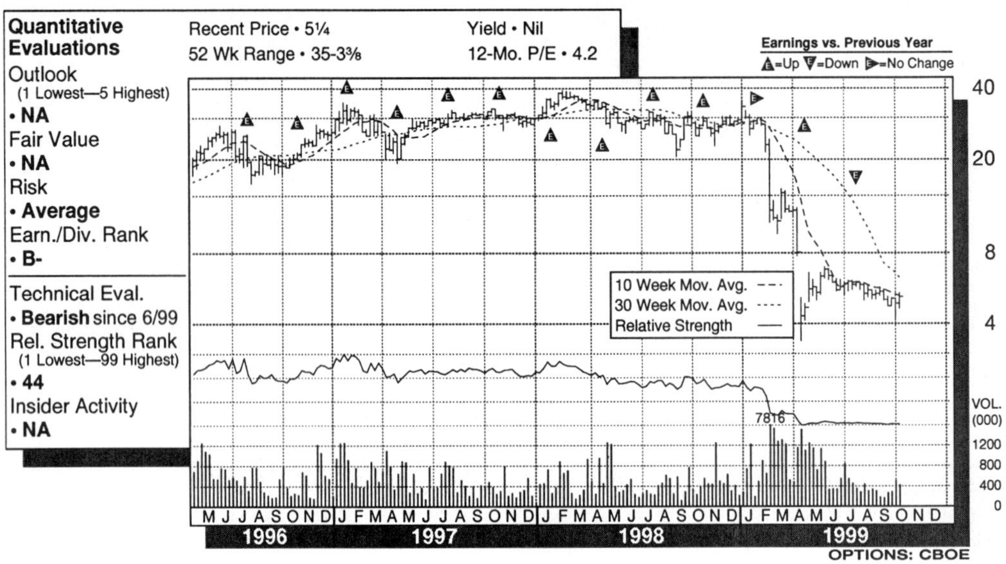

Business Profile - 01-SEP-99

In August 1999, Curative Health Services stated that legal actions taken by the U.S. Department of Justice (DOJ) against the company had resulted in unanticipated expenses, contract terminations, and decreased sales development. In April 1999, the DOJ alleged CURE made improper charges to certain hospitals. Subsequent to these allegations, a number of lawsuits were initiated against CURE charging the company with improper Medicare billings. In March 1999, the company announced that it had completed the repurchase of 2 million of its common shares, and subsequently reported that its directors authorized the repurchase of up to 1.5 million more shares.

Operational Review - 01-SEP-99

Revenues in the six months ended June 30, 1999, increased fractionally, year to year, primarily reflecting higher total new patient volumes offset by contract terminations and lower revenues from the company's Procuren therapy. Profitability was penalized by an increase in cost of sales and services, related to additional staffing and $1.1 million in operating expenses for new facilities, and higher SG&A costs, attributable to legal expenses. After lower interest income, net income declined 24%, to $6,131,000 ($0.55 a share, on 15% fewer shares), from $8,073,000 ($0.61). Cash and marketable securities totaled $38.9 million on June 30, 1999.

Stock Performance - 08-OCT-99

In the past 30 trading days, CURE's shares have declined 3%, compared to a 0.91% fall in the S&P 500. Average trading volume for the past five days was 83,360 shares, compared with the 40-day moving average of 62,723 shares.

Key Stock Statistics

Dividend Rate/Share	Nil	Shareholders	214
Shs. outstg. (M)	10.1	Market cap. (B)	$0.053
Avg. daily vol. (M)	0.073	Inst. holdings	36%
Tang. Bk. Value/Share	6.66		
Beta	1.32		

Value of $10,000 invested 5 years ago: $ 8,186

Fiscal Year Ending Dec. 31

	1999	1998	1997	1996	1995	1994
Revenues (Million $)						
1Q	25.24	24.51	19.65	14.92	12.01	8.89
2Q	25.62	26.04	21.69	16.39	12.92	9.57
3Q	—	26.72	22.71	17.46	13.32	10.54
4Q	—	26.72	23.86	18.63	14.19	11.58
Yr.	—	104.0	87.91	67.40	52.44	40.57
Earnings Per Share ($)						
1Q	**0.31**	**0.29**	0.28	0.17	0.05	-0.09
2Q	**0.23**	**0.32**	0.30	0.21	0.08	-0.23
3Q	—	**0.34**	0.33	0.24	0.12	0.02
4Q	—	**0.35**	**0.35**	0.28	0.14	0.03
Yr.	—	**1.30**	**1.27**	**0.90**	0.39	-0.27

Next earnings report expected: late October

Dividend Data

No cash dividends have been paid. The company intends to retain earnings for use in the development of its business and does not expect to pay cash dividends in the foreseeable future.

A Division of The McGraw-Hill Companies

Curative Health Services, Inc.

Business Summary - 01-SEP-99

Curative Health Services, Inc.'s strategy is to expand its presence in the chronic wound care market by improving its wound management program and broadening its delivery models to encompass all aspects of care for wound management. The company manages, on behalf of hospital clients, a nationwide network of wound care centers that offer a wide range of services, which allows the company to provide customized wound care.

Chronic wounds are common in patients with diabetes and venous stasis disease, as well as in patients who are immobilized and afflicted with pressure sores. CURE's wound management program consists of diagnostic and therapeutic treatment regimens designed to meet each patient's specific wound care needs on a cost effective basis. As of June 30, 1999, the company's wound care center network consisted of over 160 outpatient clinics generally located on or near campuses of acute care hospitals in 34 states.

It is CURE's contention that the high degree of specialization and expertise offered by its wound care centers provides many benefits: to patients through superior wound care, enhancing quality of life and, in many cases, allowing them to avoid amputation; to affiliated hospitals by enabling them to differentiate themselves from competitors through better wound care treatment outcomes and to reduce costs by decreasing inpatient lengths of stay; to affiliated physicians by providing greater access to patients; and to insurers and managed care providers by offering a cost effective alternative to traditional wound care. Related to these factors, the company believes its program provides a better approach to chronic wound management than the traditional approach, which CURE feels lacks comprehensive wound programs, effective technology, positive outcomes, and cost efficiency.

The company's wound healing agent, Procuren, is a naturally occurring complex mixture of growth factors that promotes the growth of human skin, soft tissue, and blood vessels. Procuren is produced by stimulating the release of growth factors from platelets contained in the patient's own blood. As of 1998 year-end, it has been used to treat over 50,000 patients as part of a comprehensive treatment program.

As of 1998 year-end CURE planned to further penetrate its position in disease and wound care management in the following ways: continue to develop the company's nationwide network of outpatient wound care centers; develop new service models to enhance market penetration; provide a comprehensive managed care product; enhance the company's wound management program; and expand into other disease management areas.

In April 1999, the company received a document subpoena from the U.S. Department of Health and Human Services directing CURE to produce a broad range of documents. Subsequently in April, the U.S. Department of Justice alleged CURE made improper charges to Colombia/HCA hospitals and other hospitals. A number of lawsuits have since been filed against the company.

Per Share Data ($) (Year Ended Dec. 31)	1998	1997	1996	1995	1994	1993	1992	1991	1990	1989
Tangible Bk. Val.	7.04	5.72	4.05	1.42	0.85	1.70	2.17	2.54	-10.43	NA
Cash Flow	1.52	1.43	0.99	0.48	-0.17	-0.36	-0.31	-0.13	-0.62	NA
Earnings	1.30	1.27	0.90	0.39	-0.27	-0.44	-0.37	-0.20	-0.67	NA
Dividends	Nil	Nil	Nil	Nil	Nil	Nil	Nil	Nil	Nil	NA
Payout Ratio	Nil	Nil	Nil	Nil	Nil	Nil	Nil	Nil	Nil	NA
Prices - High	39 1/4	35	28 1/4	17	6 1/2	8	21 1/2	23	NA	NA
- Low	20 1/2	19 1/4	13 1/4	3 3/8	1 5/8	3 7/8	4 1/2	7 1/2	NA	NA
P/E Ratio - High	30	28	31	44	NM	NM	NM	NM	NA	NA
- Low	16	15	15	9	NM	NM	NA	NA	NA	NA
Income Statement Analysis (Million $)										
Revs.	104	87.9	67.4	52.4	40.6	31.3	26.8	19.5	10.2	NA
Oper. Inc.	27.4	19.1	11.5	4.9	-0.5	-4.5	-4.2	-2.1	-4.2	NA
Depr.	2.8	2.0	1.2	1.0	1.0	0.8	0.6	0.5	0.3	NA
Int. Exp.	Nil	NA	Nil	Nil	Nil	NA	0.1	0.1	0.1	NA
Pretax Inc.	27.3	19.8	11.7	4.4	-3.0	-4.7	-3.8	-1.9	-4.2	NA
Eff. Tax Rate	37%	17%	8.60%	4.90%	NM	NM	NM	NM	NM	NA
Net Inc.	17.0	16.5	10.7	4.2	-2.7	-4.4	-3.6	-1.6	-4.2	NA
Balance Sheet & Other Fin. Data (Million $)										
Cash	70.1	39.7	43.1	12.2	7.3	9.5	18.5	24.9	1.9	NA
Curr. Assets	92.1	74.9	56.4	20.8	14.8	19.4	25.5	30.2	5.0	NA
Total Assets	109	84.9	84.9	25.0	18.6	25.3	29.1	32.5	7.4	NA
Curr. Liab.	15.7	12.3	10.6	8.2	7.6	7.7	6.4	5.8	3.2	NA
LT Debt	Nil	0.0	1.0	1.2	1.3	0.5	0.2	0.3	0.4	NA
Common Eqty.	93.4	72.6	50.3	15.6	9.8	16.8	21.4	25.1	-16.6	NA
Total Cap.	93.4	72.6	51.3	16.8	11.0	17.6	22.2	26.2	4.3	NA
Cap. Exp.	6.8	6.5	2.5	2.0	0.6	0.9	1.6	0.9	0.1	NA
Cash Flow	19.8	18.5	11.9	5.2	-1.7	-3.6	-3.1	-1.1	-3.9	NA
Curr. Ratio	5.9	6.1	5.3	2.5	2.0	2.5	4.0	5.2	1.6	NA
% LT Debt of Cap.	Nil	NM	2.0	7.1	11.4	2.9	0.9	1.3	10.2	NA
% Net Inc.of Revs.	16.4	18.7	15.9	8.0	NM	NM	NM	NM	NM	NA
% Ret. on Assets	17.6	22.4	24.6	19.3	NM	NM	NM	NM	NM	NA
% Ret. on Equity	20.5	26.8	32.4	33.2	NM	NM	NM	NM	NM	NA

Data as orig reptd.; bef. results of disc opers/spec. items. Per share data adj. for stk. divs. Bold denotes diluted EPS (FASB 128)-prior periods restated. E-Estimated. NA-Not Available. NM-Not Meaningful. NR-Not Ranked.

Office—150 Motor Parkway, Hauppauge, NY 11788-5108. **Tel**—(516) 232-7000. **Website**—http://www.curative.com **Chrmn**—L. J. Stuesser. **Pres & CEO**—J. Vakoutis. **VP-Fin, CFO & Secy**—J. C. Prior. **Dirs**—G. Canet, D. Gregorie, L. Hoff, T. Maudlin, G. Moufflet, L. J. Stuesser, J. Vakoutis. **Transfer Agent**—Norwest Bank Minnesota, South St. Paul. **Incorporated**—in Minnesota in 1984. **Empl**— 731. **S&P Analyst:** Frank DiLorenzo

STANDARD
&POOR'S
STOCK REPORTS

Cygnus, Inc.

NASDAQ Symbol **CYGN**

In S&P SmallCap 600

09-OCT-99

Industry:
Health Care (Drugs - Generic & Other)

Summary: This company focuses primarily on developing a painless, continuous glucose monitoring device, transdermal drug delivery systems, and mucosal drug delivery systems.

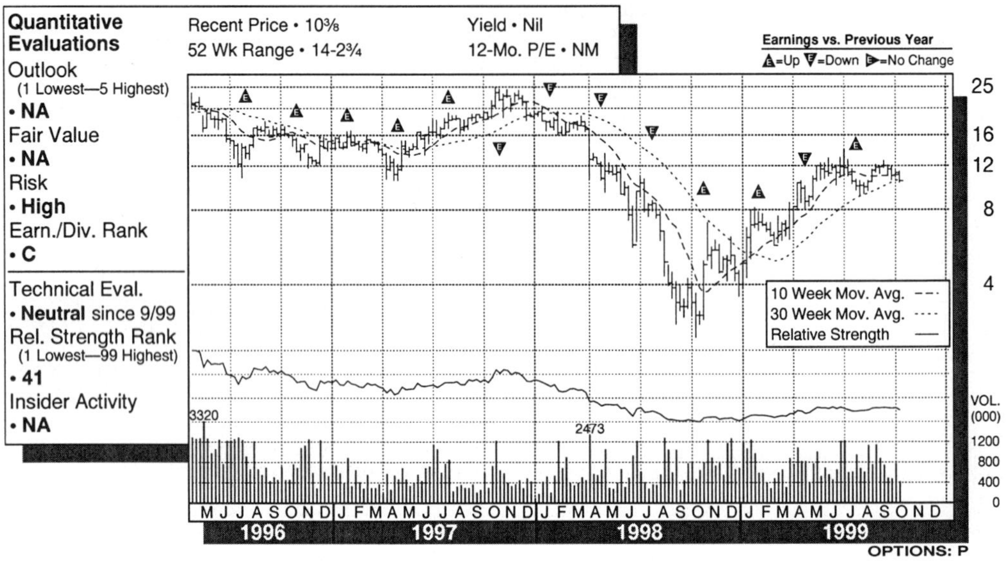

Business Profile - 11-MAY-99

Revenues have decreased in recent quarters, reflecting a lack of sales of FemPatch, an estrogen transdermal patch. FemPatch, CYGN's second commercial product, was launched in 1997. In November 1998, Warner-Lambert, sublicensee of FemPatch marketing rights, terminated its supply agreement with the company. CYGN does not expect further product revenues until new products are commercialized. In December 1998, CYGN submitted a new drug application to the FDA for its seven-day estrogen transdermal hormone replacement therapy patch, the E2III. Operations have consumed substantial amounts of cash, mostly for research and development, and future capital requirements will depend on product development, the time required to file for regulatory approvals, the ability to obtain licensing arrangements, and the demand for products.

Operational Review - 11-MAY-99

Total revenues in the three months ended March 31, 1999, fell 16%, year to year, reflecting the absence of FemPatch system sales, and a 5.8% drop in contract revenues. After a 30% increase in R&D expenses, the operating loss widened to $6.4 million, from $5.5 million. After interest expense, versus interest income, the net loss increased to $6.8 million ($0.31 per share, on 9.5% more shares), from $5.5 million ($0.28).

Stock Performance - 08-OCT-99

In the past 30 trading days, CYGN's shares have declined 12%, compared to a 0.91% fall in the S&P 500. Average trading volume for the past five days was 81,260 shares, compared with the 40-day moving average of 143,067 shares.

Key Stock Statistics

Dividend Rate/Share	Nil	Shareholders	542
Shs. outstg. (M)	24.1	Market cap. (B)	$0.252
Avg. daily vol. (M)	0.105	Inst. holdings	42%
Tang. Bk. Value/Share	NM		
Beta	1.99		

Value of $10,000 invested 5 years ago: $ 9,277

Fiscal Year Ending Dec. 31

	1999	1998	1997	1996	1995	1994
Revenues (Million $)						
1Q	2.92	3.46	9.29	3.76	5.40	5.53
2Q	4.06	2.88	8.24	8.99	4.77	5.41
3Q	—	2.78	5.44	10.81	3.87	4.73
4Q	—	2.53	6.53	12.64	4.97	5.59
Yr.	—	11.66	29.50	36.20	19.01	21.27
Earnings Per Share ($)						
1Q	**-0.31**	**-0.28**	-0.02	-0.23	-0.18	-0.07
2Q	**-0.22**	**-0.48**	-0.02	-0.17	-0.19	-0.13
3Q	—	**-0.48**	-2.36	-0.15	-0.28	-0.24
4Q	—	**-0.21**	**-0.27**	-0.05	-0.15	-0.79
Yr.	—	**-1.95**	**-2.67**	**-0.60**	-0.79	-1.24

Next earnings report expected: late October

Dividend Data

No cash dividends have been paid, and the company does not expect to pay any in the foreseeable future.

Cygnus, Inc.

Business Summary - 11-MAY-99

Cygnus, best known for its Nicotrol transdermal patch, which helps people quit smoking, is involved in the development of diagnostic and drug delivery systems. Its current focus is on the development of a painless, continuous glucose monitoring device and transdermal drug delivery systems.

CYGN has developed a continuous glucose monitoring device called the GlucoWatch, which is worn like a wristwatch and is designed to extract and measure glucose levels automatically and frequently through intact skin, and to display and store blood glucose levels and trends. The extracted glucose is collected in the GlucoPad, a transdermal patch that is changed daily.

In December 1998, the company said it had begun FDA submission-directed studies for its GlucoWatch monitor for adults with diabetes. It intends to submit a pre-market approval application (PMA) to the FDA by June 1999. CYGN said that the FDA indicated the application was appropriate for expedited review.

In January 1999, CYGN said it had submitted the first part of its pre-market approval application for the GlucoWatch Automatic Glucose Biographer (GAGB). The GAGB is designed to take frequent measurements of the glucose level to provide an abundance of data to potentially better control fluctuating glucose levels.

In 1998, the company entered into long term agreements with E.I. du Pont de Nemours & Company for the development and supply of thick film materials for the GlucoWatch monitor. A key component of the GlucoWatch monitor is the sensor, which CYGN developed with Dupont materials. The agreement calls for continued cooperation for future sensor technology developments and continued supply of materials.

Transdermal delivery systems provide for the controlled release of drugs directly into the bloodstream through intact skin by means of a small adhesive patch. By delivering a steady flow of drugs over an extended period of time, transdermal systems can enable more controlled, effective treatment. CYGN's transdermal product line currently focuses on smoking cessation, hormone replacement therapy and contraception. Its two most commercially advanced products are the Nicotrol nicotine patch, which is currently being marketed (licensed in the U.S. by Johnson & Johnson, and worldwide by Pharmacia & Upjohn); and the FemPatch estrogen replacement patch, approved by the FDA in December 1996.

In November 1998, the company said it would receive $2.7 million from Pharmacia & Upjohn (NYSE: PNU) as a result of an arbitration proceeding filed in 1997 related to Nicotrol. In March 1997, PNU had exercised its option to purchase the U.S. manufacturing rights for Nicotrol. The agreement provided for PNU to pay CYGN for existing inventory costs, and for certain purchase order commitments. CYGN had been unable to reach an agreement with PNU on these matters.

Per Share Data ($) (Year Ended Dec. 31)	1998	1997	1996	1995	1994	1993	1992	1991	1990	1989
Tangible Bk. Val.	NM	NA	1.67	2.10	1.16	1.89	2.64	NA	NA	NA
Cash Flow	-1.85	-2.52	-0.44	-0.62	-1.08	-0.61	-1.21	NA	NA	NA
Earnings	-1.95	-2.67	-0.60	-0.79	-1.24	-0.77	-1.36	-0.64	-0.43	NA
Dividends	Nil	Nil	Nil	Nil	Nil	Nil	Nil	Nil	Nil	NA
Payout Ratio	Nil	Nil	Nil	Nil	Nil	Nil	Nil	Nil	Nil	NA
Prices - High	21	25	25 7/8	23 5/8	12 7/8	12 1/2	32 1/4	NA	NA	NA
- Low	2 7/16	10 1/2	10 3/4	5 5/8	5 1/2	5 1/2	8	NA	NA	NA
P/E Ratio - High	NM	NM	NM	NM	NM	NM	NM	NA	NA	NA
- Low	NM	NM	NM	NM	NM	NM	NM	NA	NA	NA
Income Statement Analysis (Million $)										
Revs.	11.7	29.5	36.2	19.0	21.3	17.5	25.6	5.1	5.9	NA
Oper. Inc.	-33.8	-9.2	-10.1	-10.5	-15.7	-9.4	-16.7	NA	NA	NA
Depr.	1.9	2.7	2.8	2.7	2.4	2.2	2.0	NA	NA	NA
Int. Exp.	9.7	1.8	1.0	0.8	0.3	0.5	0.3	NA	NA	NA
Pretax Inc.	-39.4	-50.5	-11.1	-12.8	-17.4	-10.6	-17.5	-7.1	-3.4	NA
Eff. Tax Rate	NM	NM	NM	NM	Nil	Nil	Nil	Nil	NA	NA
Net Inc.	-39.4	-50.5	-11.1	-12.8	-17.4	-10.6	-17.5	-7.1	NA	NA
Balance Sheet & Other Fin. Data (Million $)										
Cash	10.2	20.7	49.4	46.5	28.1	28.2	NA	NA	NA	NA
Curr. Assets	27.5	39.8	60.5	49.8	30.6	38.2	NA	NA	NA	NA
Total Assets	43.5	49.3	68.8	57.9	38.6	46.9	52.7	32.2	9.7	NA
Curr. Liab.	16.0	29.8	24.1	11.3	12.6	14.1	NA	NA	NA	NA
LT Debt	31.4	27.2	7.5	2.7	2.8	2.6	NA	NA	NA	NA
Common Eqty.	-32.8	-13.8	31.2	38.3	18.1	26.2	36.2	27.3	5.9	NA
Total Cap.	-1.4	13.4	38.7	40.2	20.9	28.8	NA	NA	NA	NA
Cap. Exp.	3.4	3.1	1.5	2.4	2.7	1.4	4.5	NA	NA	NA
Cash Flow	-37.5	-47.7	-8.3	-10.2	-15.0	-8.4	15.5	NA	NA	NA
Curr. Ratio	NM	1.3	2.5	4.4	2.4	2.7	NA	NA	NA	NA
% LT Debt of Cap.	-2290.0	203.0	19.4	6.7	13.6	9.0	NA	NA	NA	NA
% Net Inc.of Revs.	NM	NM	NM	NM	NM	NM	NM	NM	NM	NA
% Ret. on Assets	NM	NM	NM	NM	NM	NM	NM	NM	NM	NA
% Ret. on Equity	NM	NM	NM	NM	NM	NM	NM	NM	NM	NA

Data as orig reptd.; bef. results of disc opers/spec. items. Per share data adj. for stk. divs. Bold denotes diluted EPS (FASB 128)-prior periods restated. E-Estimated. NA-Not Available. NM-Not Meaningful. NR-Not Ranked.

Office—400 Penobscot Dr., Redwood City, CA 94063-4719. **Tel**—(650) 369-4300. **Website**—http://www.cygn.com **Chrmn, Pres & CEO** —J. C. Hodgman. **Vice Chrmn**—A.F. Marion. **SVP-Fin, CFO & Investor Contact**—Craig W. Carlson. **Secy** —B. G. McClung. **Dirs**—F. T. Cary, J. C. Hodgman, A. F. Marion, R. G. Rogers, W. B. Wriston. **Transfer Agent & Registrar**—ChaseMellon Shareholder Services, San Francisco. **Incorporated**—in California in 1985; reincorporated in Delaware in 1995. **Empl**— 130. **S&P Analyst:** John J. Arege

Cyrk, Inc.

NASDAQ Symbol **CYRK**

In S&P SmallCap 600

09-OCT-99 **Industry:** Consumer (Jewelry, Novelties & Gifts)

Summary: This full-service promotional marketing company designs and manufactures high-impact promotional products and programs.

Quantitative Evaluations

Outlook (1 Lowest—5 Highest) • **NA**

Fair Value • **NA**

Risk • **Average**

Earn./Div. Rank • **NR**

Technical Eval. • **Bullish** since 9/99

Rel. Strength Rank (1 Lowest—99 Highest) • **79**

Insider Activity • **NA**

Recent Price • 6 | Yield • Nil

52 Wk Range • 10¼-4⅝ | 12-Mo. P/E • 13.4

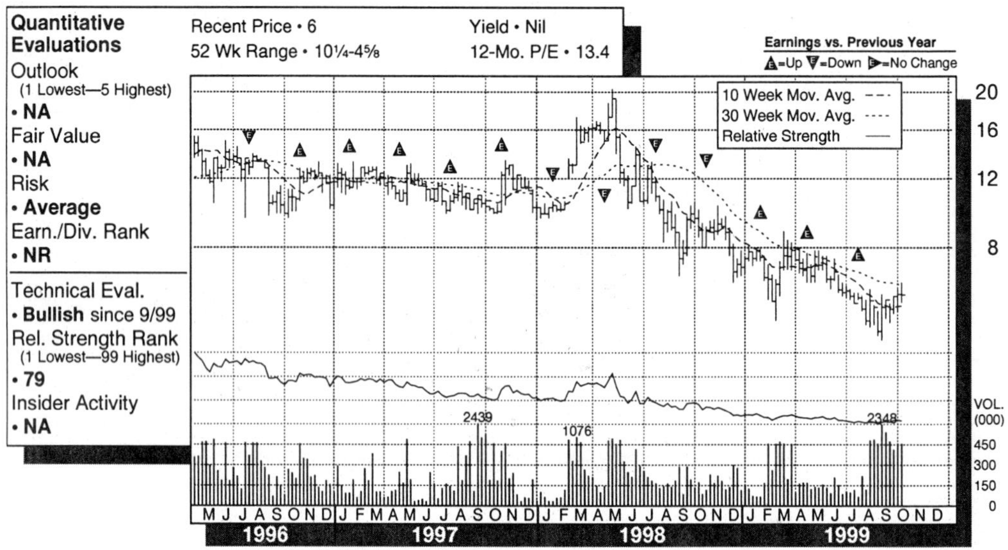

Business Profile - 28-JUL-99

This full-service integrated provider of marketing and promotional products and services derives the majority of its revenues from the sale of promotional products to consumer products companies. In 1998, CYRK reorganized, achieved profitability sooner than anticipated, and bolstered its position as a global leader in the promotional marketing industry. The company's 1999 business plan targets EPS of $0.40 to $0.48. With revenue from certain major accounts coming in the later quarters of 1999, a loss was posted in the first quarter, but CYRK remained confident that it would achieve its plan, producing the highest EPS in four years.

Operational Review - 28-JUL-99

Net sales in the three months ended March 31, 1999, declined 6.0%, year to year, reflecting reduced sales to Pepsi-Cola, and a decrease in sales associated with discontinued operations. Gross margins widened, on more favorable margins associated with the company's focus on the promotional marketing industry; although SG&A expenses rose 12%, in the absence of $15.5 million of restructuring expense, the operating loss narrowed. The net loss was cut to $3,223,000 ($0.21 a share, on 8.2% more shares), from $9,851,000 ($0.69).

Stock Performance - 08-OCT-99

In the past 30 trading days, CYRK's shares have increased 24%, compared to a 0.91% fall in the S&P 500. Average trading volume for the past five days was 96,840 shares, compared with the 40-day moving average of 187,805 shares.

Key Stock Statistics

Dividend Rate/Share	Nil	Shareholders	2,700
Shs. outstg. (M)	15.7	Market cap. (B)	$0.095
Avg. daily vol. (M)	0.104	Inst. holdings	35%
Tang. Bk. Value/Share	6.18		
Beta	0.66		

Value of $10,000 invested 5 years ago: $ 2,629

Fiscal Year Ending Dec. 31

	1999	1998	1997	1996	1995	1994
Revenues (Million $)						
1Q	159.1	169.1	97.19	65.10	44.00	76.00
2Q	313.5	212.6	106.6	44.14	34.00	142.0
3Q	—	163.7	170.8	55.56	26.00	114.0
4Q	—	212.4	184.1	86.10	31.00	70.00
Yr.	—	757.9	558.6	250.9	136.0	402.0
Earnings Per Share ($)						
1Q	**-0.21**	**-0.69**	0.21	**0.15**	0.05	0.65
2Q	**0.15**	**-0.03**	0.05	**-0.09**	0.01	1.18
3Q	—	**-0.02**	0.01	**-0.05**	-0.14	0.88
4Q	—	**0.46**	**0.02**	**0.03**	-0.14	0.47
Yr.	—	**-0.20**	**0.25**	**0.04**	**-0.22**	3.20

Next earnings report expected: mid November

Dividend Data

No cash dividends have been paid. The company intends to retain earnings to finance growth and does not expect to pay cash dividends for the foreseeable future.

Cyrk, Inc.

Business Summary - 28-JUL-99

Cyrk is interested in promoting its clients, rather than itself. The company designs, develops, manufactures and distributes products for promotional programs such as McDonald's Happy Meal and Pepsi-Cola's Pepsi Stuff. CYRK focuses its sales efforts on large consumer products and services companies seeking to promote their brand names and corporate identities and build brand loyalty.

Many of the company's large-scale consumer promotions include custom products conceived, designed and produced by CYRK's Custom Product and Licensing group. The group has custom designed and developed proprietary products including toys, apparel and accessories for McDonald's and other consumer promotional programs, including the Marlboro Gear and Pepsi Stuff promotions. The company expanded its licensing activities in 1998, and entered into licensing agreements with customers such as Ty, Inc. and Mars, Inc.

Historically, the company's business has been heavily concentrated with two customers, Philip Morris and Pepsi-Cola. As part a continuing plan to diversify its customer base and broaden its capability, the company made two key acquisitions in 1997: the April 1997 purchase of Tonkin, Inc., a provider of custom promotional programs and licensed promotional products; and the June 1997 acquisition of Simon Marketing, Inc., a global promotion agency. Simon's business is heavily concentrated with McDonald's, which accounted for 57% of CYRK's net sales in 1998, up from 36% in 1997.

CYRK has been making an effort to reduce its dependence on promotional products of Philip Morris (a business affected by new FDA regulation of tobacco products). Philip Morris accounted for 11% of net sales in 1998, down from 16% in 1997. In addition, CYRK's agreements with Pepsi were terminated in December 1997, and its sales to Pepsi were minimal in 1998.

Through a licensing agreement with Ty, the company has the exclusive right to develop and market licensed Beanie Babies products. During 1998, it created and marketed the premier edition of the Beanie Babies Official Club, a consumer membership kit that included authentic Beanie Babies merchandise, and marketed other Beanie Babies licensed products. Sales of Beanie Babies related products accounted for 7% of net sales for 1998, and 1999 revenues and profitability were expected to benefit significantly from the sale of Beanie Babies products, with the majority in the second half of the year.

International sales accounted for 36%, 27% and 7% of net sales in 1998, 1997 and 1996, respectively. International sales are currently made through company account representatives in the U.S., as well as through the company's German, U.K. and Hong Kong subsidiaries.

Per Share Data ($) (Year Ended Dec. 31)	1998	1997	1996	1995	1994	1993	1992	1991	1990	1989
Tangible Bk. Val.	6.14	6.03	11.52	11.54	11.74	3.34	NA	NA	NA	NA
Cash Flow	0.40	0.74	0.30	-0.04	3.28	NA	NA	NA	NA	NA
Earnings	-0.20	0.25	0.04	-0.22	3.20	1.18	0.44	NA	NA	NA
Dividends	Nil	Nil	Nil	Nil	Nil	Nil	Nil	NA	NA	NA
Payout Ratio	Nil	Nil	Nil	Nil	Nil	Nil	Nil	NA	NA	NA
Prices - High	20 3/8	13 3/8	18 1/8	41 1/4	44 3/4	23	NA	NA	NA	NA
- Low	6 1/2	9 1/2	9 1/2	7	20 1/2	10	NA	NA	NA	NA
P/E Ratio - High	NM	53	NM	NM	14	19	NA	NA	NA	NA
- Low	NM	38	NM	NM	6	8	NA	NA	NA	NA
Income Statement Analysis (Million $)										
Revs.	758	559	251	136	402	166	53.0	NA	NA	NA
Oper. Inc.	11.4	15.6	2.8	-4.3	53.8	15.9	5.6	NA	NA	NA
Depr.	9.0	6.4	2.9	2.0	0.8	0.4	0.2	NA	NA	NA
Int. Exp.	2.6	2.1	Nil	Nil	1.2	0.7	0.6	NA	NA	NA
Pretax Inc.	-5.2	8.1	1.3	-3.5	51.7	14.7	4.8	NA	NA	NA
Eff. Tax Rate	NM	60%	65%	NM	41%	41%	40%	NA	NA	NA
Net Inc.	-3.0	3.2	0.4	-2.3	30.4	8.7	2.9	NA	NA	NA
Balance Sheet & Other Fin. Data (Million $)										
Cash	75.8	42.5	46.6	62.2	33.9	10.4	NA	NA	NA	NA
Curr. Assets	235	205	167	120	137	65.0	NA	NA	NA	NA
Total Assets	337	314	190	138	147	67.0	NA	NA	NA	NA
Curr. Liab.	147	144	65.1	13.4	20.8	39.5	NA	NA	NA	NA
LT Debt	12.1	9.6	Nil	Nil	0.0	0.1	NA	NA	NA	NA
Common Eqty.	178	160	124	124	126	28.0	NA	NA	NA	NA
Total Cap.	190	170	125	124	126	28.0	NA	NA	NA	NA
Cap. Exp.	5.3	6.0	3.4	3.9	5.8	2.0	0.4	NA	NA	NA
Cash Flow	6.0	9.7	3.3	-0.4	31.2	9.1	12.2	NA	NA	NA
Curr. Ratio	1.6	1.4	2.6	8.9	6.6	1.6	NA	NA	NA	NA
% LT Debt of Cap.	6.4	5.6	Nil	Nil	NM	0.2	NA	NA	NA	NA
% Net Inc.of Revs.	NM	0.6	0.2	NM	7.6	5.5	5.2	NA	NA	NA
% Ret. on Assets	NM	1.3	0.2	NM	28.4	NM	NA	NA	NA	NA
% Ret. on Equity	NM	2.3	0.3	NM	39.5	NM	NA	NA	NA	NA

Data as orig. reptd.; bef. results of disc. opers. and/or spec. items. Per share data adj. for stk. divs. as of ex-div. date. Data for 1993 and 1992 pro forma. Bold denotes diluted EPS (FASB 128). E-Estimated. NA-Not Available. NM-Not Meaningful. NR-Not Ranked.

Office—3 Pond Rd., Gloucester, MA 01930. **Tel**—(978) 283-5800. **Website**—http://www.cyrk.com **Pres, CEO & COO**—P. D. Brady. **EVP, CFO & Investor Contact**—Dominic F. Mammola. **Dirs**—T. L. Axelrod, J. W. Bartlett, P. D. Brady, J. A. Kouba, D. F. Mammola, G. P. Shlopak. **Transfer Agent & Registrar**—First National Bank of Boston. **Incorporated**—in Delaware in 1990. **Empl**— 1,300. **S&P Analyst:** C.C.P.

STANDARD
&POOR'S
STOCK REPORTS

D. R. Horton

NYSE Symbol **DHI**
In S&P SmallCap 600

09-OCT-99 **Industry:** Homebuilding

Summary: This company primarily builds and sells single-family homes in most regions of the U.S.

Quantitative Evaluations

Outlook
(1 Lowest—5 Highest)
• **5**

Fair Value
• **31⅝**

Risk
• **Average**

Earn./Div. Rank
• **NR**

Technical Eval.
• **Bearish** since 7/99

Rel. Strength Rank
(1 Lowest—99 Highest)
• **13**

Insider Activity
• **NA**

Recent Price • 12
52 Wk Range • 23-11⅞
Yield • 1.0%
12-Mo. P/E • 5.2

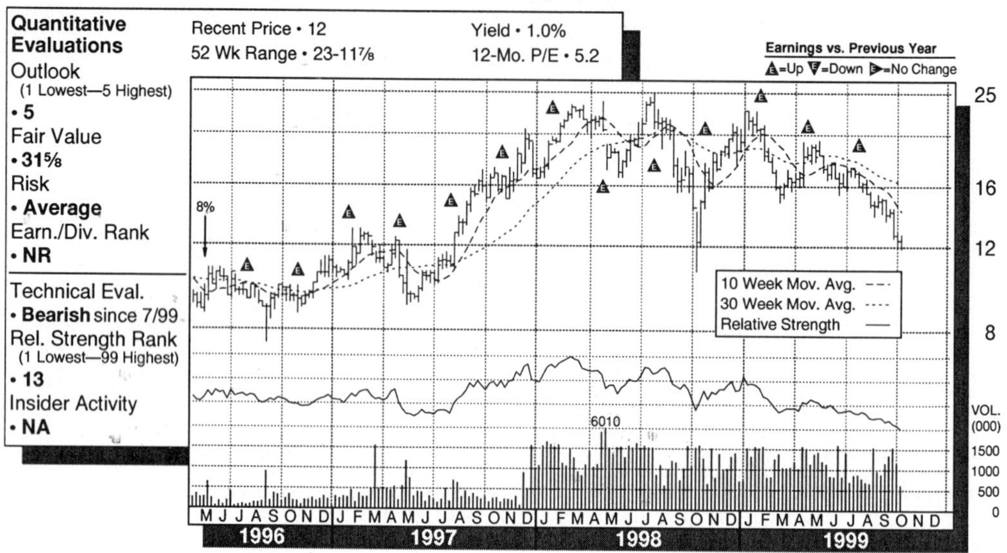

Business Profile - 02-JUL-99

DHI, one of the most geographically diversified homebuilders, with activities in 23 states and 40 markets, positions itself between large-volume and local custom homebuilders, and sells its single-family homes to the entry-level and move-up market segments. The company's strategy is to continue to enter new markets, primarily through acquisitions of existing homebuilders, as shown by the early 1999 purchase of Cambridge Homes of Chicago for $153 million. The company believes existing homebuilders have benefits not found in startup operations, such as brand name recognition, proven product acceptance, and local industry relationships. In late 1998, directors approved stock and debt repurchase programs for up to $100 million each.

Operational Review - 02-JUL-99

Total sales in the first half of FY 99 (Sep.) climbed 55%, year to year, due to the strong housing demand in all of DHI's markets, entry into new geographical markets, higher average home prices sold, and several acquisitions. Operating margins widened, on the larger revenue base and cost containment efforts. With a greater contribution from financial services operations, net income soared 75%, to $66.1 million ($1.05 a share, on 1.2% more shares), from $37.8 million ($0.64). At March 31, 1999, the backlog of sales contracts stood at $1,369 million (7,952 homes), up 34% from $1,022 million (6,032 homes) at December 31, 1998.

Stock Performance - 08-OCT-99

In the past 30 trading days, DHI's shares have declined 20%, compared to a 0.91% fall in the S&P 500. Average trading volume for the past five days was 122,380 shares, compared with the 40-day moving average of 252,631 shares.

Key Stock Statistics

Dividend Rate/Share	0.12	Shareholders	286
Shs. outstg. (M)	64.2	Market cap. (B)	$0.771
Avg. daily vol. (M)	0.250	Inst. holdings	63%
Tang. Bk. Value/Share	9.59		
Beta	1.31		

Value of $10,000 invested 5 years ago: $ 12,202

Fiscal Year Ending Sep. 30

	1999	1998	1997	1996	1995	1994
Revenues (Million $)						
1Q	652.8	423.2	144.4	121.1	168.9	78.90
2Q	690.6	453.0	159.6	114.0	87.08	82.61
3Q	833.1	613.9	250.1	143.3	120.5	107.8
4Q	—	686.9	283.2	168.9	132.8	124.0
Yr.	—	2,177	837.3	547.3	437.4	393.3
Earnings Per Share ($)						
1Q	**0.52**	**0.28**	**0.21**	0.19	0.14	0.13
2Q	**0.52**	**0.36**	0.20	0.16	0.15	0.13
3Q	**0.68**	**0.39**	0.26	0.23	0.22	0.17
4Q	—	**0.53**	0.34	0.29	0.24	0.21
Yr.	—	**1.56**	**1.15**	0.87	0.74	0.64

Next earnings report expected: early November

Dividend Data (Dividends have been paid since 1997.)

Amount ($)	Date Decl.	Ex-Div. Date	Stock of Record	Payment Date
0.030	Jan. 20	Feb. 02	Feb. 04	Feb. 16 '99
0.030	Apr. 22	May. 04	May. 06	May. 14 '99
0.030	Jul. 26	Aug. 09	Aug. 11	Aug. 25 '99
0.030	Oct. 04	Oct. 19	Oct. 21	Oct. 28 '99

A Division of The McGraw-Hill Companies

Business Summary - 02-JUL-99

With operating divisions in 24 states and 41 markets, D. R. Horton is one of the most geographically diversified homebuilders in the U.S. The company positions itself between large-volume and local custom homebuilders and sells its single-family homes to the entry-level and move-up market segments. DHI believes it is able to offer a broader selection of homes than high-volume homebuilders and at lower prices than local homebuilders. The revenue breakdown (restated for the April 1998 acquisition of Continental Homes) by geographic region in recent fiscal years (Sep.) was:

	FY 98	FY 97	FY 96
Mid-Atlantic	17%	12%	10%
Midwest	6%	6%	8%
Southeast	18%	16%	10%
Southwest	37%	44%	55%
West	22%	22%	17%

In April 1998, Horton acquired Continental Homes, in exchange for about 15.5 million shares. Continental is a diversified homebuilder focused on the Southwest market, with FY 97 (May) sales of $726 million. Like DHI, Continental targets entry-level and first-time move-up homebuyers. Management believed the acquisition would help secure a leading share of important homebuilding markets, and increase DHI's financial strength.

Although management believes there are significant growth opportunities in DHI's existing markets, the company intends to continue entering new markets, primarily through acquisitions of existing homebuilders. DHI believes its diversification strategy reduces its exposure to market volatility. Management seeks to purchase existing operations that possess established land positions, as well as pre-existing relationships with land owners, developers, subcontractors and suppliers. The company will typically refrain from making material investments in land, homes and overhead until its targeted markets demonstrate significant growth potential. Management attempts to reduce risk by acquiring approved building lots through options.

DHI residences generally range in size from 1,000 sq. ft. to 5,000 sq. ft., and in price from $80,000 to $600,000. The company generally offers between five and 10 home designs per subdivision, but is prepared to customize its designs to the homebuyer's individual taste. DHI primarily uses model and speculative homes to market its units and typically sells homes through commissioned employees and independent real estate brokers.

DHI's activities are conducted through 53 decentralized operation divisions. Management believes its decentralized structure gives more operating flexibility to its local managers. Each operating division is responsible for site selections, contract negotiations and property development.

Per Share Data ($) (Year Ended Sep. 30)	1998	1997	1996	1995	1994	1993	1992	1991	1990	1989
Tangible Bk. Val.	8.82	6.28	5.36	3.75	3.03	2.43	2.09	0.85	NA	NA
Cash Flow	1.66	1.13	0.95	0.81	0.68	0.33	0.39	0.41	NA	NA
Earnings	1.56	1.01	0.87	0.74	0.64	0.32	0.38	0.40	NA	NA
Dividends	0.09	0.06	Nil	Nil	Nil	Nil	Nil	Nil	NA	NA
Payout Ratio	6%	6%	Nil	Nil	Nil	Nil	Nil	Nil	NA	NA
Prices - High	24 7/8	21	11 7/8	11	11 1/4	10 1/4	6 1/2	NA	NA	NA
- Low	10 5/8	9	7 1/2	5 1/4	5 3/8	5 1/2	4	NA	NA	NA
P/E Ratio - High	16	21	14	15	18	32	17	NA	NA	NA
- Low	7	9	9	7	8	17	10	NA	NA	NA
Income Statement Analysis (Million $)										
Revs.	2,177	837	547	437	393	190	183	124	NA	NA
Oper. Inc.	189	66.9	47.0	35.1	29.3	14.1	14.6	10.9	NA	NA
Depr.	9.8	4.4	2.6	2.0	1.2	0.4	0.3	0.2	NA	NA
Int. Exp.	16.2	5.2	14.8	13.5	7.3	2.5	2.0	2.9	NA	NA
Pretax Inc.	159	59.9	44.4	32.6	28.6	13.9	14.2	8.0	NA	NA
Eff. Tax Rate	41%	40%	38%	37%	38%	36%	35%	Nil	NA	NA
Net Inc.	93.4	36.2	36.2	20.5	17.7	8.8	9.2	8.0	NA	NA
Balance Sheet & Other Fin. Data (Million $)										
Cash	76.8	44.0	32.5	16.7	11.2	19.9	8.5	14.4	NA	NA
Curr. Assets	NA	NA	NA	NA	NA	NA	NA	NA	NA	NA
Total Assets	1,668	720	403	319	231	159	104	60.0	NA	NA
Curr. Liab.	NA	NA	NA	NA	NA	NA	NA	NA	NA	NA
LT Debt	855	355	159	135	8.2	13.1	4.0	0.1	NA	NA
Common Eqty.	549	263	159	106	84.6	65.9	55.9	16.5	NA	NA
Total Cap.	1,407	618	336	241	92.7	78.9	59.9	16.5	NA	NA
Cap. Exp.	11.6	5.3	2.7	2.4	2.6	1.5	1.4	0.6	NA	NA
Cash Flow	103	40.6	30.0	22.6	18.9	9.2	9.5	8.2	NA	NA
Curr. Ratio	NA	NA	NA	NA	NA	NA	NA	NA	NA	NA
% LT Debt of Cap.	60.8	57.5	47.2	55.9	8.8	16.5	6.6	0.4	NA	NA
% Net Inc.of Revs.	4.3	4.3	5.0	4.7	4.5	4.7	5.0	6.5	NA	NA
% Ret. on Assets	7.8	6.4	7.6	7.5	9.0	6.7	9.8	NA	NA	NA
% Ret. on Equity	23.0	16.4	19.0	21.5	23.4	14.5	23.4	NA	NA	NA

Data as orig reptd.; bef. results of disc opers/spec. items. Per share data adj. for stk. divs. Bold denotes diluted EPS (FASB 128)-prior periods restated. E-Estimated. NA-Not Available. NM-Not Meaningful. NR-Not Ranked.

Office—1901 Ascension Blvd., Suite 100, Arlington, TX 76006. **Tel**—(817) 856-8200. **Website**—www.DRHorton.com **Chrmn**—D. R. Horton. **Vice Chrmn & CEO**—D. J. Tomnitz. **Pres**—R. Beckwitt. **EVP, CFO, Treas & Investor Contact**—David J. Keller. **Dirs**—B. S. Anderson, R. Beckwitt, R. I. Galland, D. R. Horton, R. L. Horton, T. J. Horton, D. J. Keller, F. I. Neff, S. J. Stone, D. J. Tomnitz. **Transfer Agent & Registrar**—KeyCorp Shareholder Services, Cleveland. **Incorporated**—in Delaware in 1991. **Empl**— 2,465. **S&P Analyst:** John A. Massey

STANDARD
&POOR'S
STOCK REPORTS

Dain Rauscher

NYSE Symbol **DRC**
In S&P SmallCap 600

09-OCT-99 **Industry:** Investment Banking/ Brokerage

Summary: This holding company is one of the largest U.S. regional full-service brokers and investment bankers.

Quantitative Evaluations
Outlook (1 Lowest—5 Highest) • **2**
Fair Value • **49¼**
Risk • **NA**
Earn./Div. Rank • **B**

Technical Eval. • **Bearish** since 8/99
Rel. Strength Rank (1 Lowest—99 Highest) • **63**
Insider Activity • **Neutral**

Recent Price • 49⅛
52 Wk Range • 59⅛-27¾
Yield • 1.8%
12-Mo. P/E • 17.4

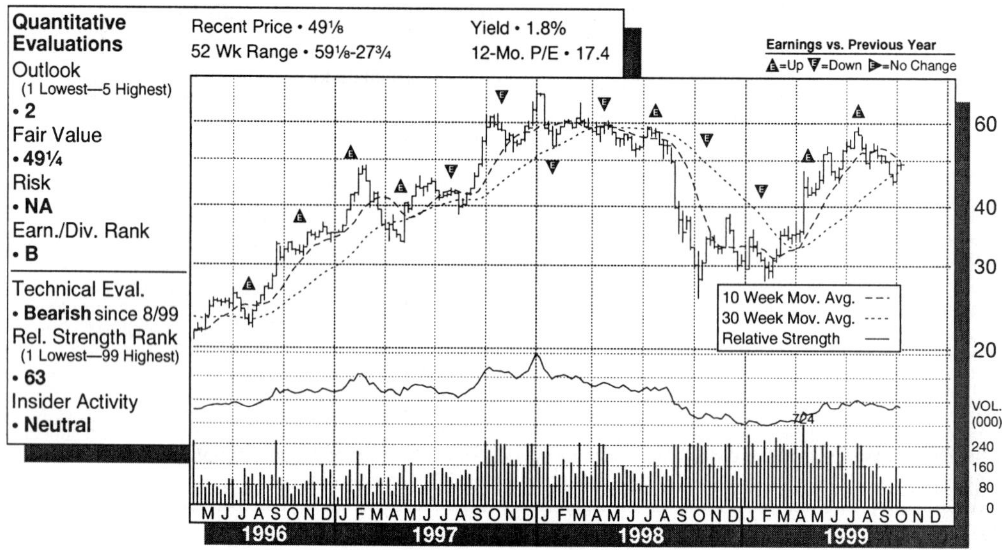

Business Profile - 19-JUL-99

In January 1999, Dain Rauscher acquired the national public finance practice of Artemis Capital Group, which was then integrated into DRC's Fixed Income Capital Markets Group. The company stated that, as a result of this acquisition, it will be able to offer investors a significantly expanded range of municipal new issues from a diverse array of major issuers across the nation. During the fourth quarter of 1998, DRC recorded $23.8 million (pretax) in litigation expenses to settle several lawsuits regarding the company's alleged involvement in the bankruptcy of Orange County, CA, and the failure of a former subsidiary, Midwest Life Insurance Company.

Operational Review - 19-JUL-99

Total revenues in the three months ended March 31, 1999, were up 26%, year to year, primarily due to a $15.4 million pretax gain on the sale of an equity investment, as well as a strong increase in investment banking and underwriting revenue. Results also benefited from the absence of $20 million in pretax merger and restructuring charges related to the acquisition of Wessels, Arnold, & Henderson, LLC.; pretax income compared to a pretax loss. After taxes at 37.5%, versus a tax credit of $1.1 million, net income of $22.6 million ($1.70 a share) contrasted with a net loss of $2.0 million ($0.16).

Stock Performance - 08-OCT-99

In the past 30 trading days, DRC's shares have declined 4%, compared to a 0.91% fall in the S&P 500. Average trading volume for the past five days was 22,300 shares, compared with the 40-day moving average of 24,046 shares.

Key Stock Statistics

Dividend Rate/Share	0.88	Shareholders	6,500
Shs. outstg. (M)	12.4	Market cap. (B)	$0.611
Avg. daily vol. (M)	0.022	Inst. holdings	36%
Tang. Bk. Value/Share	19.53		
Beta	1.35		

Value of $10,000 invested 5 years ago: $ 29,552

Fiscal Year Ending Dec. 31

	1999	1998	1997	1996	1995	1994
Revenues (Million $)						
1Q	220.7	188.0	180.1	170.8	134.0	131.1
2Q	251.6	208.5	168.5	167.6	147.2	117.6
3Q	—	200.8	196.6	165.5	160.2	118.2
4Q	—	214.3	205.5	179.5	165.3	129.4
Yr.	—	820.3	750.7	683.3	606.8	496.3
Earnings Per Share ($)						
1Q	**1.70**	**-0.16**	**1.22**	**1.21**	0.45	0.80
2Q	**1.26**	**0.90**	**0.86**	**1.04**	0.69	0.47
3Q	—	**0.27**	**0.54**	**1.02**	0.86	0.47
4Q	—	**-0.43**	**1.16**	**1.23**	0.86	0.29
Yr.	—	**0.61**	**3.77**	**4.49**	**2.85**	**2.03**

Next earnings report expected: mid October

Dividend Data (Dividends have been paid since 1992.)

Amount ($)	Date Decl.	Ex-Div. Date	Stock of Record	Payment Date
0.220	Oct. 28	Nov. 06	Nov. 11	Nov. 25 '98
0.220	Feb. 03	Feb. 12	Feb. 17	Mar. 03 '99
0.220	Apr. 27	May. 07	May. 11	May. 25 '99
0.220	Aug. 06	Aug. 18	Aug. 20	Sep. 03 '99

A Division of The McGraw-Hill Companies

Dain Rauscher Corporation

Business Summary - 19-JUL-99

In 1998, this holding company combined its main broker-dealer subsidiaries Dain Bosworth Inc. and Rauscher Pierce Refsnes, Inc. into one firm (Dain Rauscher Inc.) and changed its name to Dain Rauscher Corporation (DRC) from Interra Financial Inc.

With roots firmly planted in the North and the Southwest, Dain Rauscher is one of the largest U.S. regional brokerage and investment banking companies. The company offers securities broker-dealer and investment banking services to individual, institutional, corporate and governmental clients, mainly in the western half of the U.S. DRC's three major business segments are: Private Client Group, Equity Capital Markets, and Fixed Income Capital Markets. Other subsidiaries include: Insight Investment Management, and Dain Rauscher Lending Services.

Net revenue, which increased 8.3% in 1998, to $749.4 million, consisted of the following in recent years: Private Client Group 71% in 1998 (71% in 1997), Equity Capital Markets 12% (14%), Fixed Income 15% (12%), and gain on sale of investment securities/corporate 2% (3%).

Net revenue for the Equity Capital Markets Group decreased 4% in 1998, to $93.3 million. This segment was negatively affected by the changes required to merge Dain Bosworth and Rauscher Pierce Refsnes, as well as the acquisition of Wessels, Arnold and Henderson. Equity Capital Markets includes investment banking (other than municipal finance), mergers and acquisitions, institutional equity sales and trading activities.

The Private Client Group generates revenue primarily from commissions earned by investment executives on individual (retail) investor activity. Additional sources of revenue include asset management fees paid to the group by Insight Investment Management, and fees paid by customers for DRC to manage or arrange to manage their portfolios. Because they are based on a percentage of assets under management, fees are less volatile than commissions, which fluctuate with changes in trading volumes.

Fixed Income Capital Markets' revenue comes from municipal fixed income underwriting fees, as well as taxable and tax-exempt fixed income securities sales and trading. DRC experienced a significant increase in municipal and other tax-exempt underwriting fees in 1998, primarily due to low interest rates.

In March 1998, DRC acquired Wessels, Arnold, and Henderson, a privately held investment banking, institutional equity sales and trading firm, for $150 million, including $120 million in cash and $30 million in five-year subordinated debentures. As a result, DRC recorded a pretax merger charge of $20 million in the first quarter of 1998. Wessels was integrated into the Equity Capital Markets Group.

Per Share Data ($) (Year Ended Dec. 31)	1998	1997	1996	1995	1994	1993	1992	1991	1990	1989
Tangible Bk. Val.	16.59	26.00	22.66	18.44	16.20	14.57	10.89	8.37	6.13	5.01
Cash Flow	2.06	4.67	NA	NA	NA	NA	NA	NA	NA	NA
Earnings	0.61	3.77	4.46	2.86	2.03	3.78	2.69	1.67	0.11	0.23
Dividends	0.88	0.72	0.56	0.43	0.37	0.19	0.08	Nil	Nil	Nil
Payout Ratio	144%	19%	13%	15%	18%	5%	3%	Nil	Nil	Nil
Prices - High	69	70 1/4	36 7/8	27 1/8	21 3/4	22 5/8	13	11 7/8	5 5/8	7 1/8
- Low	25 1/2	33 3/8	20 1/2	14 7/8	13 3/8	11 7/8	8 3/4	3 3/8	3 1/4	4 5/8
P/E Ratio - High	NM	19	8	9	11	6	5	7	53	31
- Low	NM	9	5	5	7	3	3	2	30	21
Income Statement Analysis (Million $)										
Commissions	300	275	223	176	131	139	119	98.0	81.0	82.0
Int. Inc.	129	122	111	109	75.2	54.9	55.5	74.7	88.4	95.6
Total Revs.	820	751	683	607	496	512	438	378	313	320
Int. Exp.	71.0	58.6	57.6	64.8	38.9	28.7	32.4	55.7	73.2	83.4
Pretax Inc.	12.5	76.8	87.4	56.3	39.8	77.4	53.7	33.0	1.6	3.9
Eff. Tax Rate	36%	36%	35%	36%	36%	38%	36%	36%	18%	26%
Net Inc.	8.0	49.3	56.8	35.9	25.5	47.6	34.5	21.1	1.3	2.9
Balance Sheet & Other Fin. Data (Million $)										
Total Assets	2,466	2,304	1,827	2,022	1,953	1,786	1,271	1,461	1,368	1,520
Cash Items	47.3	35.9	49.4	437	361	595	536	625	649	724
Receivables	1,545	1,480	1,238	1,022	917	710	479	502	304	363
Secs. Owned	380	542	289	323	319	271	141	214	204	218
Sec. Borrowed	279	179	25.0	97.0	150	124	19.0	62.0	96.0	117
Due Brokers & Cust.	1,385	1,400	1,169	1,287	1,117	1,149	923	1,047	883	997
Other Liabs.	473	226	330	374	444	314	181	221	268	282
Capitalization:										
Debt	113	366	27.3	41.0	47.0	22.0	16.0	27.0	45.0	62.0
Equity	330	319	276	222	195	178	132	103	74.0	59.0
Total	442	335	303	263	242	200	148	131	121	124
% Return On Revs.	1.5	6.6	8.3	5.9	5.1	9.3	7.9	5.6	0.4	0.9
% Ret. on Assets	0.3	2.4	3.0	1.8	1.3	3.1	2.5	1.5	0.1	0.2
% Ret. on Equity	2.5	16.6	19.3	17.2	13.6	30.7	29.4	23.7	1.7	4.9

Data as orig reptd.; bef. results of disc opers/spec. items. Per share data adj. for stk. divs. Bold denotes diluted EPS (FASB 128)-prior periods restated. E-Estimated. NA-Not Available. NM-Not Meaningful. NR-Not Ranked.

Office—Dain Rauscher Plaza, 60 S. Sixth St., Minneapolis, MN 55402-4422. **Tel**—(612) 371-7750. **Website**—http://www.dainrauscher.com **Chrmn, Pres & CEO**—I. Weiser. **Vice Chrmn & CFO**—J. C. Appel. **SVP & Secy**—C. J. Smith. **SVP & CIO**—D. J. Strachan. **Investor Contact**—Jennifer Driscoll (612-373-1647). **Dirs**—J. C. Appel, J. E. Attwell, S. S. Boren, F. G. Fitz-Gerald, W. F. Mondale, C. A. Rundell Jr., R. L. Ryan, A. R. Schulze Jr., I. Weiser, K. J. Wessels. **Transfer Agent & Registrar**—Norwest Bank Minnesota, Minneapolis. **Incorporated**—in Delaware in 1973. **Empl**— 3,600. **S&P Analyst:** J. Rudy

STANDARD
&POOR'S
STOCK REPORTS

Dallas Semiconductor

NYSE Symbol **DS**

In S&P SmallCap 600

09-OCT-99

Industry: Electronics (Semiconductors)

Summary: Dallas Semiconductor makes high-performance CMOS integrated circuits and semiconductor-based systems for numerous specialized applications.

Quantitative Evaluations

Outlook
(1 Lowest—5 Highest)
• **3−**

Fair Value
• **62¼**

Risk
• **Average**

Earn./Div. Rank
• **B+**

Technical Eval.
• **Neutral** since 9/99

Rel. Strength Rank
(1 Lowest—99 Highest)
• **72**

Insider Activity
• **Unfavorable**

Recent Price • 52⅜
52 Wk Range • 57-24⅝
Yield • 0.4%
12-Mo. P/E • 26.9

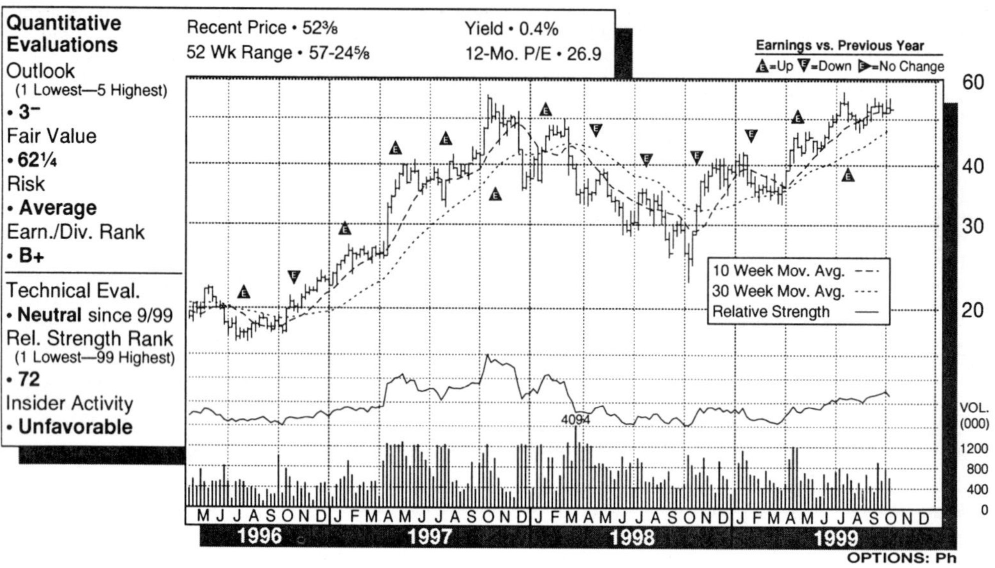

OPTIONS: Ph

Business Profile - 24-SEP-99

In the 1999 second quarter, the company expanded its line of communication products with new Quad Transceivers, which offer greater density and lower cost to help increase the speed of data transmission across wireline and wireless applications. DS is expanding its use of subcontractors located in the Philippines, and, for the third quarter, the company expects up to 25% of final test and module assembly operations will be performed at subcontractor facilities in the Philippines. DS expects to realize cost savings from the new assembly locations in late 1999. It also anticipates that improved yields and sales of new products will boost gross margins. In September 1999, DS adopted a stockholders' rights plan.

Operational Review - 24-SEP-99

Net sales in the six months ended July 4, 1999, rose 4.6%, year to year, on gains in the communications and timekeeping product categories. Despite narrower margins for new products, with lower R&D and SG&A expense, operating income increased 12%. After higher interest income, and taxes at 31.2%, versus 32.0%, net income advanced 13%, to $31.2 million ($1.02 a share, on 2.2% more shares), from $27.5 million ($0.92).

Stock Performance - 08-OCT-99

In the past 30 trading days, DS's shares have increased 1%, compared to a 0.91% fall in the S&P 500. Average trading volume for the past five days was 119,520 shares, compared with the 40-day moving average of 117,695 shares.

Key Stock Statistics

Dividend Rate/Share	0.20	Shareholders	573
Shs. outstg. (M)	28.9	Market cap. (B)	$ 1.5
Avg. daily vol. (M)	0.140	Inst. holdings	74%
Tang. Bk. Value/Share	15.56		
Beta	0.88		

Value of $10,000 invested 5 years ago: $ 34,521

Fiscal Year Ending Dec. 31

	1999	1998	1997	1996	1995	1994
Revenues (Million $)						
1Q	88.56	87.45	88.70	65.58	52.04	43.18
2Q	94.02	87.03	91.04	70.36	57.04	45.04
3Q	—	83.10	93.07	72.02	60.51	45.20
4Q	—	85.03	95.40	80.39	63.69	48.01
Yr.	—	342.6	368.2	288.4	233.3	181.4
Earnings Per Share ($)						
1Q	**0.50**	**0.45**	**0.50**	**0.30**	0.30	0.27
2Q	**0.52**	**0.47**	**0.52**	**0.36**	0.32	0.27
3Q	—	**0.45**	**0.57**	**0.28**	0.34	0.27
4Q	—	**0.48**	**0.60**	**0.37**	0.36	0.28
Yr.	—	**1.85**	**2.19**	**1.37**	**1.32**	**1.09**

Next earnings report expected: early October

Dividend Data (Dividends have been paid since 1995.)

Amount ($)	Date Decl.	Ex-Div. Date	Stock of Record	Payment Date
0.040	Oct. 23	Nov. 10	Nov. 13	Dec. 01 '98
0.050	Jan. 27	Feb. 10	Feb. 15	Mar. 01 '99
0.050	Apr. 22	May. 12	May. 14	Jun. 01 '99
0.050	Jul. 26	Aug. 11	Aug. 13	Sep. 01 '99

A Division of The **McGraw·Hill** *Companies*

Dallas Semiconductor Corporation

Business Summary - 24-SEP-99

Dallas Semiconductor, which designs, manufactures and markets electronic chips and chip-based subsystems, uses customer problems as an entry point to develop products with widespread applications. Founded in 1984, the company has developed 326 proprietary base products with more than 2,000 variations, and remains committed to new product development as a means to increase future revenues and diversify markets, product offerings and customers.

The company uses advanced technologies to gain a competitive edge over traditional approaches to semiconductors. Combining lithium power cells with low-power CMOS chips can power the chips for the useful life of the equipment in which they are used. Products are organized around categories sharing common technologies, markets or applications.

Communications products are offered for high capacity voice, data and video transmission and address the requirements of high capacity digital link protocols. DS's transmission line terminators quiet transmission lines between computers and peripherals such as disk drives, permitting high speed, high integrity data transmission.

DS's system extension business provides complete solutions to common problems facing many systems designers, such as managing thermal problems resulting from the continuous process of putting more power into smaller chips. For example, the system monitors the power supply voltages in a system and issues a warning if any fall below a critical value.

Computer Timekeeping devices remain in demand in the dynamic communications, consumer, industrial and medical markets. Commercial Timekeeping products provide advanced features such as clock-calendar display, talk-time, re-dial timing, and power management for digital cellular phones, and are used in data communications network routers, hubs and bridges to monitor communications traffic and store network configuration data.

The automatic information division designs products that can be attached to an object, or carried by a person, identifying the user and holding relevant information. Unlike bar codes, there is no need to refer to a remote database to decipher the code: information is available in the device itself. These read/write products can also be updated through a computer while affixed to an object. Automatic information chips can facilitate automation by tracking a work piece as it travels along an assembly line, or can identify people for access to secure areas.

Microcontroller products combine a central processing unit, data memory, program memory and input-output devices on a single chip in order to control a wide variety of electronic systems.

Per Share Data ($) **(Year Ended Dec. 31)**	**1998**	**1997**	**1996**	**1995**	**1994**	**1993**	**1992**	**1991**	**1990**	**1989**
Tangible Bk. Val.	14.69	12.74	10.25	8.92	7.66	6.53	5.47	4.69	4.08	3.53
Cash Flow	3.31	3.41	2.39	1.10	1.65	1.47	1.21	1.08	0.99	0.79
Earnings	1.85	2.19	1.37	1.32	1.09	0.95	0.71	0.58	0.56	0.45
Dividends	0.16	0.14	0.12	0.10	Nil	Nil	Nil	Nil	Nil	Nil
Payout Ratio	9%	6%	9%	8%	Nil	Nil	Nil	Nil	Nil	Nil
Prices - High	50	56	24	24 7/8	20 1/8	19	14 1/2	12 3/8	9 5/8	8 5/8
- Low	22 5/8	22 3/8	17	15	13 3/8	11 3/4	7	5 3/8	4 1/8	5 3/4
P/E Ratio - High	27	26	18	19	18	20	20	21	17	19
- Low	12	10	12	11	12	12	10	9	7	13
Income Statement Analysis (Million $)										
Revs.	343	368	288	233	181	157	120	104	100	82.0
Oper. Inc.	120	126	83.0	66.0	57.2	50.8	39.5	33.4	29.0	21.0
Depr.	43.7	35.8	28.4	14.0	15.3	13.9	13.1	12.9	10.9	8.5
Int. Exp.	NA	Nil	NA	NA	0.0	0.1	0.3	0.9	1.3	1.4
Pretax Inc.	81.3	94.5	57.1	54.9	45.1	39.7	29.0	23.0	20.4	14.8
Eff. Tax Rate	32%	32%	33%	33%	34%	36%	36%	36%	32%	25%
Net Inc.	55.4	64.6	38.4	36.7	29.7	25.6	18.6	14.7	13.8	11.1
Balance Sheet & Other Fin. Data (Million $)										
Cash	128	115	70.3	69.3	17.5	32.3	21.8	45.8	45.9	38.8
Curr. Assets	264	250	170	162	92.6	91.2	68.0	80.4	78.8	69.3
Total Assets	461	417	314	272	221	187	156	129	120	106
Curr. Liab.	46.3	66.1	41.1	37.0	26.5	21.0	20.6	11.5	15.2	14.0
LT Debt	Nil	Nil	Nil	Nil	Nil	Nil	Nil	4.3	7.7	8.8
Common Eqty.	415	351	273	235	195	166	136	113	97.0	83.0
Total Cap.	415	351	273	235	195	166	136	118	105	92.0
Cap. Exp.	76.0	58.6	60.5	49.3	44.7	21.1	15.8	13.1	15.7	16.9
Cash Flow	99	100	66.8	29.8	45.0	39.5	31.7	27.6	24.8	19.6
Curr. Ratio	5.7	3.8	4.1	4.4	3.5	4.3	3.3	7.0	5.2	4.9
% LT Debt of Cap.	Nil	Nil	Nil	Nil	Nil	Nil	Nil	3.6	7.3	9.6
% Net Inc.of Revs.	16.2	17.5	13.3	15.8	16.4	16.3	15.4	14.2	13.8	13.5
% Ret. on Assets	12.6	17.7	13.1	14.9	14.6	14.8	12.8	11.7	12.2	11.2
% Ret. on Equity	14.5	20.6	15.1	17.1	16.5	16.8	14.7	13.9	15.3	14.3

Data as orig reptd.; bef. results of disc opers/spec. items. Per share data adj. for stk. divs. Bold denotes diluted EPS (FASB 128)-prior periods restated. E-Estimated. NA-Not Available. NM-Not Meaningful. NR-Not Ranked.

Office—4401 S. Beltwood Parkway, Dallas, TX 75244-3292. **Tel**—(972) 371-4000. **Website**—http://www.dalsemi.com **Chrmn, CEO & Pres**—C. V. Prothro. **VP-Fin & Investor Contact**—Alan P. Hale. **Secy**—M. K. Suggs. **Dirs**—M. L. Bolan, R. L. King, C. C. Mai, C. V. Prothro, M. D. Sampels, C. J. Santoro, E. R. Zumwalt Jr. **Transfer Agent & Registrar**—ChaseMellon Shareholder Services, Ridgefield Park, NJ. **Incorporated**—in Delaware in 1984. **Empl**— 1,530. **S&P Analyst:** J.W.H.

STANDARD &POOR'S
STOCK REPORTS

DAMARK International

NASDAQ Symbol **DMRK**

In S&P SmallCap 600

09-OCT-99 **Industry:** Retail (Home Shopping)

Summary: In addition to being a catalog retailer, DAMARK provides marketing services to list-owning companies.

Quantitative Evaluations

Outlook
(1 Lowest—5 Highest)
• 1+

Fair Value
• 7⅛

Risk
• High

Earn./Div. Rank
• C

Technical Eval.
• Bullish since 9/99

Rel. Strength Rank
(1 Lowest—99 Highest)
• 91

Insider Activity
• NA

Recent Price • 10
52 Wk Range • 12¼-5⅜
Yield • Nil
12-Mo. P/E • NM

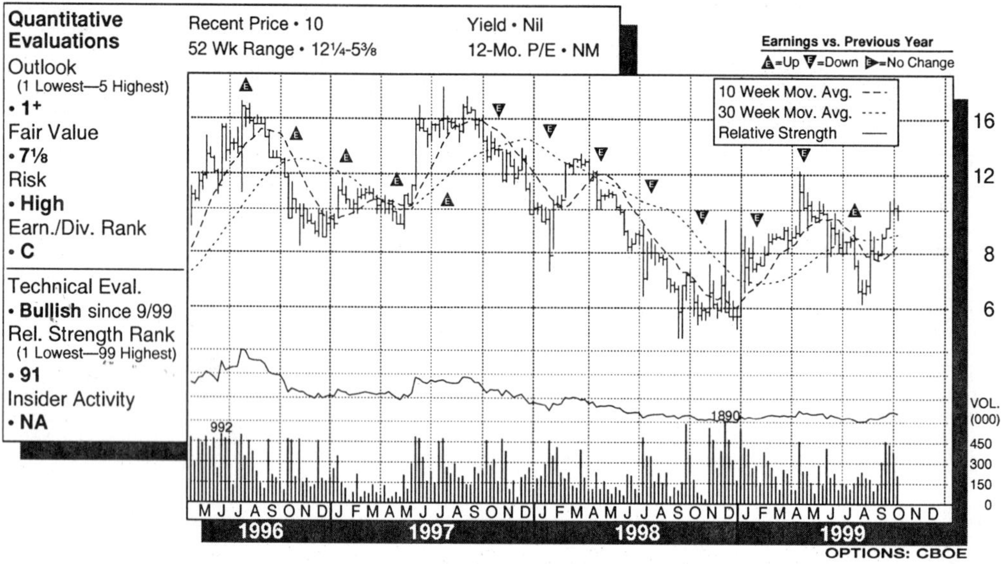

Business Profile - 09-AUG-99

For 1999, the company is focusing on three operating priorities: aggressively expanding its position in the membership services industry by increasing revenues, programs, client relationships and the share of clients served; improving the economic model of the catalog business to position it for profitable growth in new customer segments and channels; and providing high-impact member and client service in all activities. In the first half of 1999, DAMARK added 1,281,000 new members, compared with 750,000 in the first half of 1998. As of June 30, 1999, the company was virtually debt free for the first time since the second quarter of 1996.

Operational Review - 09-AUG-99

Net revenues in the first half of 1999 declined 12%, reflecting 23% lower catalog revenues, stemming from changes in promotional strategies and continued soft customer response rates; membership and related revenues were up 50%. Results were aided by the changes in promotional strategies, a decrease in computer sales (which carry lower gross margins), and 67% lower interest expense. There was a pretax loss of $3,999,000, down from $6,774,000. After tax credits in both periods, the net loss totaled $2,639,000 ($0.44 a share, based on 22% fewer average shares), down from $4,471,000 ($0.58). Results exclude an extraordinary credit of $0.05 a share in the 1999 period.

Stock Performance - 08-OCT-99

In the past 30 trading days, DMRK's shares have increased 25%, compared to a 0.91% fall in the S&P 500. Average trading volume for the past five days was 41,100 shares, compared with the 40-day moving average of 57,100 shares.

Key Stock Statistics

Dividend Rate/Share	Nil	Shareholders	643
Shs. outstg. (M)	6.0	Market cap. (B)	$0.060
Avg. daily vol. (M)	0.075	Inst. holdings	52%
Tang. Bk. Value/Share	5.11		
Beta	0.45		

Value of $10,000 invested 5 years ago: $ 4,395

Fiscal Year Ending Dec. 31

	1999	1998	1997	1996	1995	1994
Revenues (Million $)						
1Q	109.4	135.1	128.6	116.9	128.3	114.0
2Q	112.3	115.7	147.5	124.1	111.7	93.75
3Q	—	93.96	134.8	112.2	112.1	102.3
4Q	—	139.7	183.7	160.5	148.0	167.3
Yr.	—	484.4	594.6	513.7	500.0	477.4
Earnings Per Share ($)						
1Q	**-0.15**	**0.02**	**0.05**	-0.02	-0.12	0.14
2Q	**-0.29**	**-0.62**	**0.25**	0.17	-0.30	-0.09
3Q	—	**-0.77**	**0.09**	0.18	0.02	0.12
4Q	—	**-1.50**	**0.35**	0.37	0.20	0.42
Yr.	—	**-2.71**	**0.74**	**0.70**	**-0.20**	**0.59**

Next earnings report expected: mid October

Dividend Data

The company has never paid a cash dividend on its common stock. DAMARK intends to retain earnings for use in the operation and expansion of its business and does not expect to pay any cash dividends in the foreseeable future. In addition, a bank credit agreement restricts the payment of dividends.

DAMARK International, Inc.

Business Summary - 09-AUG-99

DAMARK International (DMRK) has been undergoing a business transformation. The primary driver of this major strategic change was the recognition that its core catalog formula was likely to come under extreme competitive pressure. Consequently, management began to re-deploy the direct marketing expertise gained in the catalog retail business in what it believes to be an under-penetrated growth industry - membership services. In this area, in addition to serving its own customers, the company serves large list-owning companies by creating membership and merchandising offers targeted to their customers using their brand names.

The catalog business accounted for about 82% of revenues and a $31.0 million operating loss in 1998; membership services provided 18% of revenues and an operating profit of $16.2 million.

Most of the catalogs produced by the company are 64 to 79 pages in length and contain about 300 to 350 product advertisements. Periodically, the company develops certain specialty catalogs, generally 48 pages, which feature single categories such as electronics, home decor, home office, or refurbished merchandise. In addition, DAMARK produces its "Big Book," a 160 to 172 page general merchandise catalog. The company's toll-free lines are answered 24 hours per day, seven days a week.

Sales by product category in 1998 were as follows: 27% computer, 19% consumer electronics, 14% home office, 18% home improvement, 16% home decor and 6% sports/fitness. In addition to product sales, the company generates revenues and fees from shipping, handling and order precessing charges, extended warranty sales, list rentals and co-marketing arrangements.

DAMARK has differed from most catalog retailers by targeting well-educated males with above average income and a propensity to shop by direct response. During 1998, the company introduced a new catalog title directed at a consumer segment with different demographics. In general, this formula is targeted to appeal to consumers with median household incomes of $30,000 to $35,000 and less available credit. The response rate in 1998 on front-end prospects (new customers) was 1.48% and 2.69% on back-end prospects (previous customers or repeat business), while the average order was $132 for front-end prospects and $191 for back-end customers.

In its membership services operations, the company develops, markets and manages fee-based programs that provide purchase price discount and other benefits related to consumer needs in the areas of shopping, travel, hospitality, entertainment, health/fitness and household financial management.

Per Share Data ($) (Year Ended Dec. 31)	1998	1997	1996	1995	1994	1993	1992	1991	1990	1989
Tangible Bk. Val.	5.57	8.56	7.77	7.30	6.82	6.78	3.80	NA	NA	NA
Cash Flow	0.12	1.77	1.48	0.35	0.95	0.93	0.54	NA	NA	NA
Earnings	-2.71	0.74	0.70	-0.20	0.59	0.67	0.21	NA	NA	NA
Dividends	Nil	Nil	Nil	Nil	Nil	Nil	Nil	NA	NA	NA
Payout Ratio	Nil	Nil	Nil	Nil	Nil	Nil	Nil	NA	NA	NA
Prices - High	13 3/8	18 7/8	17 1/2	9	31	23 3/4	14 1/4	NA	NA	NA
- Low	5 1/8	9	6	5 1/2	5 3/4	4 3/4	3 3/4	NA	NA	NA
P/E Ratio - High	NM	26	25	NM	53	35	68	NA	NA	NA
- Low	NM	12	9	NM	10	7	18	NA	NA	NA
Income Statement Analysis (Million $)										
Revs.	484	595	514	500	477	364	270	NA	NA	NA
Oper. Inc.	-5.5	20.1	16.1	3.2	12.9	11.7	6.7	NA	NA	NA
Depr.	20.5	8.7	6.9	5.1	3.6	2.2	2.4	NA	NA	NA
Int. Exp.	3.2	1.8	0.1	0.2	0.2	0.2	1.6	NA	NA	NA
Pretax Inc.	-29.7	9.6	9.1	-2.8	8.3	8.8	2.4	NA	NA	NA
Eff. Tax Rate	NM	34%	34%	NM	29%	34%	35%	NA	NA	NA
Net Inc.	-19.6	6.3	6.1	-1.9	5.9	5.8	1.6	NA	NA	NA
Balance Sheet & Other Fin. Data (Million $)										
Cash	0.0	0.5	NM	8.7	7.2	24.7	NA	NA	NA	NA
Curr. Assets	107	160	98.4	100	117	123	NA	NA	NA	NA
Total Assets	140	206	143	142	156	147	74.0	NA	NA	NA
Curr. Liab.	106	136	78.8	75.4	81.5	79.7	NA	NA	NA	NA
LT Debt	Nil	Nil	Nil	Nil	0.3	0.5	NA	NA	NA	NA
Common Eqty.	34.1	68.7	62.5	64.9	72.0	64.3	29.5	NA	NA	NA
Total Cap.	34.1	70.2	63.9	66.3	74.0	67.0	NA	NA	NA	NA
Cap. Exp.	7.7	10.0	8.6	NA	19.1	6.1	3.0	NA	NA	NA
Cash Flow	0.9	15.0	12.9	3.2	9.5	8.0	4.0	NA	NA	NA
Curr. Ratio	1.0	1.2	1.3	1.3	1.4	1.5	NA	NA	NA	NA
% LT Debt of Cap.	Nil	Nil	Nil	Nil	0.3	0.7	NA	NA	NA	NA
% Net Inc.of Revs.	NM	1.1	1.2	NM	1.2	1.6	0.6	NA	NA	NA
% Ret. on Assets	NM	3.6	4.3	NM	3.9	5.2	2.3	NA	NA	NA
% Ret. on Equity	NM	9.6	9.5	NM	8.6	12.3	7.7	NA	NA	NA

Data as orig reptd.; bef. results of disc opers/spec. items. Per share data adj. for stk. divs. Bold denotes diluted EPS (FASB 128)-prior periods restated. E-Estimated. NA-Not Available. NM-Not Meaningful. NR-Not Ranked.

Office—7101 Winnetka Ave. North, Minneapolis, MN 55428. **Tel**—(612) 531-0066. **Website**—http://www.damark.com **Chrmn & CEO**—M. A. Cohn. **Investor Contact**—investor.relations@damark.com **Dirs**—M. A. Cohn, T. A. Cusick, J. W. Eugster, S. J. Hemsley, H. Roitenberg, R. Strangis, J. N. Waller. **Transfer Agent & Registrar**—Norwest Bank Minnesota, Minneapolis. **Incorporated**—in Minnesota in 1986. **Empl**— 1,945. **S&P Analyst:** J.J.S.

STANDARD &POOR'S STOCK REPORTS

Datascope Corp.

NASDAQ Symbol **DSCP**

In S&P SmallCap 600

09-OCT-99

Industry: Health Care (Medical Products & Supplies)

Summary: This company makes products for clinical health care markets in interventional cardiology, critical care and cardiovascular and vascular surgery.

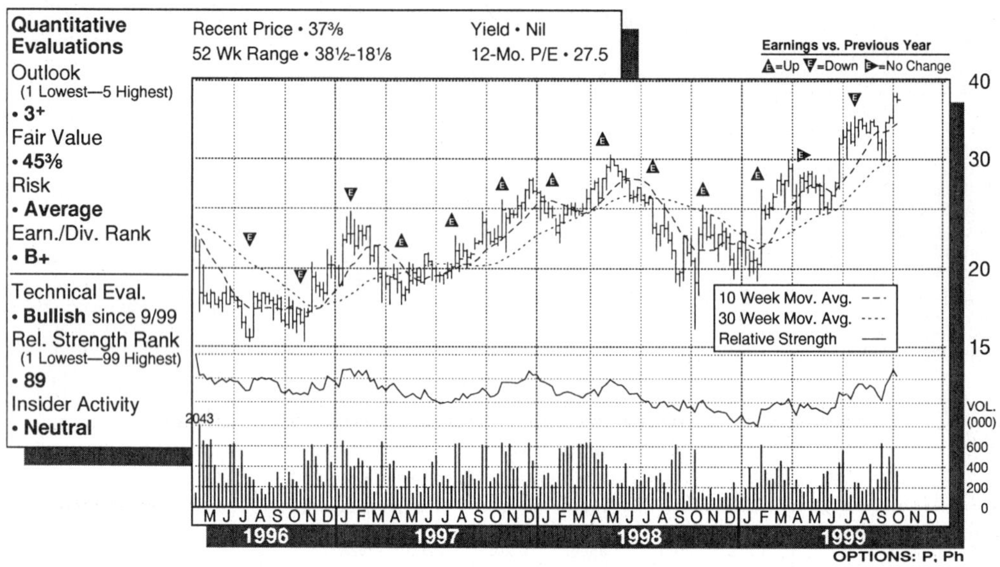

Business Profile - 20-JUL-99

During the FY 99 (Jun.) third quarter, DSCP recorded a $864,000 pretax restructuring charge, related to cost reduction initiatives. The charge included the cost of employee severance and related termination expenses for approximately 40 employees (4% of the domestic work force). The restructuring is expected to provide annual savings of about $2.5 million. In April 1999, DSCP began U.S. clinical trials of its third generation VasoSeal product. In March 1999, the company announced the receipt of approval to market its System 98 intra-aortic balloon pump and its Profile 8 Fr. balloon catheter in Japan. The Profile 8 Fr. balloon catheter was launched in the U.S. in the FY 98 fourth quarter.

Operational Review - 20-JUL-99

Net sales in the nine months ended March 31, 1999, rose 8.8%, year to year, reflecting a 43% increase in sales of VasoSeal, as well as higher patient monitoring and cardiac assist product sales. Gross margins widened, on higher selling prices for VasoSeal and cost reductions. Despite an 11% rise in SG&A expense, and an $864,000 pretax restructuring charge, operating profits were up 9.6%. After lower interest income, and taxes at 30.2% in each period, net income was up only fractionally, to $14,533,000 ($0.93 a share, on 4.6% fewer shares), from $14,521,000 ($0.88).

Stock Performance - 08-OCT-99

In the past 30 trading days, DSCP's shares have increased 10%, compared to a 0.91% fall in the S&P 500. Average trading volume for the past five days was 71,720 shares, compared with the 40-day moving average of 93,285 shares.

Key Stock Statistics

Dividend Rate/Share	Nil	Shareholders	930
Shs. outstg. (M)	15.2	Market cap. (B)	$0.569
Avg. daily vol. (M)	0.090	Inst. holdings	66%
Tang. Bk. Value/Share	12.91		
Beta	0.53		

Value of $10,000 invested 5 years ago: $ 26,696

Fiscal Year Ending Jun. 30

	1999	1998	1997	1996	1995	1994
Revenues (Million $)						
1Q	55.70	54.30	47.60	45.90	41.60	38.10
2Q	66.70	62.70	57.60	52.30	48.40	45.20
3Q	70.50	60.30	57.90	54.60	50.50	47.30
4Q	76.20	65.10	62.50	58.50	55.20	52.20
Yr.	269.1	242.4	225.6	211.3	195.7	182.8
Earnings Per Share ($)						
1Q	**0.17**	**0.16**	**-0.20**	0.19	0.17	0.15
2Q	**0.38**	**0.34**	**0.31**	0.76	0.27	0.24
3Q	**0.38**	**0.38**	**0.35**	0.33	0.28	0.26
4Q	**0.43**	**0.44**	**0.40**	-0.05	0.35	0.32
Yr.	**1.36**	**1.32**	**0.86**	**1.24**	**1.07**	**0.97**

Next earnings report expected: late October

Dividend Data

No cash has been paid.

Datascope Corp.

Business Summary - 20-JUL-99

DSCP manufactures products for clinical health care markets in cardiology, anesthesiology, cardiovascular and vascular surgery, and for use in emergency medicine and critical care.

Intra-aortic balloon pumping (IABP) systems produced by DSCP's cardiac assist business provided 42% of sales in FY 98 (Jun.). The systems increase the supply of oxygen-rich blood to the heart, while reducing its demand for oxygen. As a pioneer in IABP systems, the company introduced the first balloon catheter capable of percutaneous insertion (by arterial puncture through the skin), an innovation which eliminated the need for surgical insertion and expanded the market for IABP products from cardiac surgery to the interventional cardiology market. In May 1998, DSCP received FDA approval to market its 8Fr. Co-Lumen intra-aortic balloon catheter, which has the smallest profile of any balloon catheter.

Patient monitoring products (38% of sales) measure a broad range of physiological data designed to provide for patient safety and management of patient care. The company's monitors are capable of continuous and simultaneous measurement of multiple parameters, and are used in operating rooms, emergency rooms, critical care units, post-anesthesia care units and recover rooms, intensive care units, and labor and delivery rooms. The PASSPORT monitor is a portable, battery-powered, patient monitor that offers the features of a traditional bedside monitor in a transportable unit that can move with the patient to different settings in the hospital.

DSCP's Collagen Products division (12%) manufactures and sells two principal product lines: the VasoSeal VHD device, which can rapidly seal femoral arterial punctures after catheterization procedures, including balloon angioplasty and diagnostic angiography; and other hemostatic products that are used during surgery. In August 1998, the company received CE mark approval for a second generation arterial puncture and sealing device, known as VasoSeal ES, allowing its sale throughout the European Union.

The InterVascular, Inc. subsidiary makes a line of knitted and woven polyester vascular grafts (8%) and patches for reconstructive vascular and cardiovascular surgery. The company also manufactures the InterGard, its collagen-coated vascular grafts that are implanted surgically to replace diseased arteries. The approval of the coated InterGard range of products in both the U.S. and Japan led to significant sales increases to DSCP's distributors in FY 98.

In December 1998, DSCP announced the receipt of FDA approval to market its second generation arterial puncture sealing device, VasoSeal ES, allowing sale throughout the U.S.

Per Share Data ($)										
(Year Ended Jun. 30)	1999	1998	1997	1996	1995	1994	1993	1992	1991	1990
Tangible Bk. Val.	NA	12.91	11.84	11.15	10.16	8.98	7.97	7.01	6.46	5.99
Cash Flow	NA	1.91	1.45	1.76	1.57	1.36	1.31	0.76	0.82	0.98
Earnings	1.36	1.32	0.86	1.24	1.07	0.97	0.97	0.47	0.55	0.60
Dividends	Nil	Nil	Nil	Nil	Nil	Nil	Nil	Nil	Nil	Nil
Payout Ratio	Nil	Nil	Nil	Nil	Nil	Nil	Nil	Nil	Nil	Nil
Prices - High	38 1/2	30 1/2	28	25 1/2	27 1/4	19 3/4	26 1/2	41 3/4	39 1/8	11 1/4
- Low	19 1/8	16	17 1/2	15 1/4	15 1/2	12	11 3/4	17 3/4	9 1/2	6 1/4
P/E Ratio - High	28	23	33	21	25	20	27	89	71	19
- Low	14	12	20	12	14	12	12	38	17	10
Income Statement Analysis (Million $)										
Revs.	NA	242	226	211	196	183	166	157	135	120
Oper. Inc.	NA	34.7	31.6	21.4	30.7	27.1	23.6	20.9	13.6	12.4
Depr.	NA	9.8	9.6	8.6	8.2	6.3	5.5	4.8	4.3	5.9
Int. Exp.	NA	0.0	0.0	0.1	0.1	0.0	0.0	0.2	0.2	0.2
Pretax Inc.	NA	29.7	17.8	26.8	25.0	22.1	22.1	10.6	12.5	14.1
Eff. Tax Rate	NA	27%	21%	24%	30%	29%	29%	28%	31%	34%
Net Inc.	NA	21.6	14.1	20.4	17.3	15.7	15.7	7.7	8.6	9.3
Balance Sheet & Other Fin. Data (Million $)										
Cash	NA	37.7	59.9	67.4	56.2	45.4	45.2	32.1	28.7	19.3
Curr. Assets	NA	155	156	163	144	138	122	110	98.0	92.0
Total Assets	NA	253	238	234	207	185	158	141	128	124
Curr. Liab.	NA	37.3	32.5	42.0	33.4	33.3	23.2	25.5	23.9	27.0
LT Debt	NA	Nil	Nil	Nil	Nil	Nil	Nil	Nil	Nil	0.1
Common Eqty.	NA	201	192	182	163	144	128	110	100	92.0
Total Cap.	NA	201	192	182	163	144	128	110	100	93.0
Cap. Exp.	NA	7.8	5.3	13.0	15.3	19.0	11.2	5.3	4.2	9.3
Cash Flow	NA	31.4	23.7	29.0	25.5	21.9	21.3	12.5	12.9	15.2
Curr. Ratio	NA	4.2	4.8	3.9	4.3	4.2	5.2	4.3	4.1	3.4
% LT Debt of Cap.	NA	Nil	Nil	Nil	Nil	Nil	Nil	Nil	Nil	0.1
% Net Inc.of Revs.	NA	8.9	6.3	9.7	8.8	8.6	9.5	4.9	6.4	7.7
% Ret. on Assets	NA	8.8	6.0	9.3	8.8	9.1	10.4	5.7	6.8	8.2
% Ret. on Equity	NA	11.0	7.5	11.8	11.3	11.5	13.1	7.3	8.9	10.7

Data as orig reptd.; bef. results of disc opers/spec. items. Per share data adj. for stk. divs. Bold denotes diluted EPS (FASB 128)-prior periods restated. E-Estimated. NA-Not Available. NM-Not Meaningful. NR-Not Ranked.

Office—14 Philips Pkwy., Montvale, NJ 07645-9998. **Tel**—(201) 391-8100. **Fax**—(201) 307-5400. **Chrmn, Pres & CEO**—L. Saper. **SVP & Secy**—M. Pitkowsky. **VP, CFO & Investor Contact**—Leonard S. Goodman (201-307-5317). **Dirs**—A. Abramson, D. Altschiller, W. L. Asmundson, J. Grayzel, G. Heller, A. Nash, L. Saper. **Transfer Agent**—Continental Stock Transfer & Trust Co., NYC. **Incorporated**—in New York in 1964, reincorporated in Delaware in 1989. **Empl**— 1,300. **S&P Analyst:** John J. Arege

DBT Online

NYSE Symbol **DBT**

In S&P SmallCap 600

09-OCT-99

Industry: Services (Data Processing)

Summary: DBT provides online investigative information services to law enforcement, legal, insurance and other clients.

Quantitative Evaluations

Outlook (1 Lowest—5 Highest) • **NA**

Fair Value • **NA**

Risk • **NA**

Earn./Div. Rank • **NR**

Technical Eval. • **Bearish** since 9/99

Rel. Strength Rank (1 Lowest—99 Highest) • **25**

Insider Activity • **NA**

Recent Price • 25⅝

52 Wk Range • 39⅞-12¾

Yield • Nil

12-Mo. P/E • 71.2

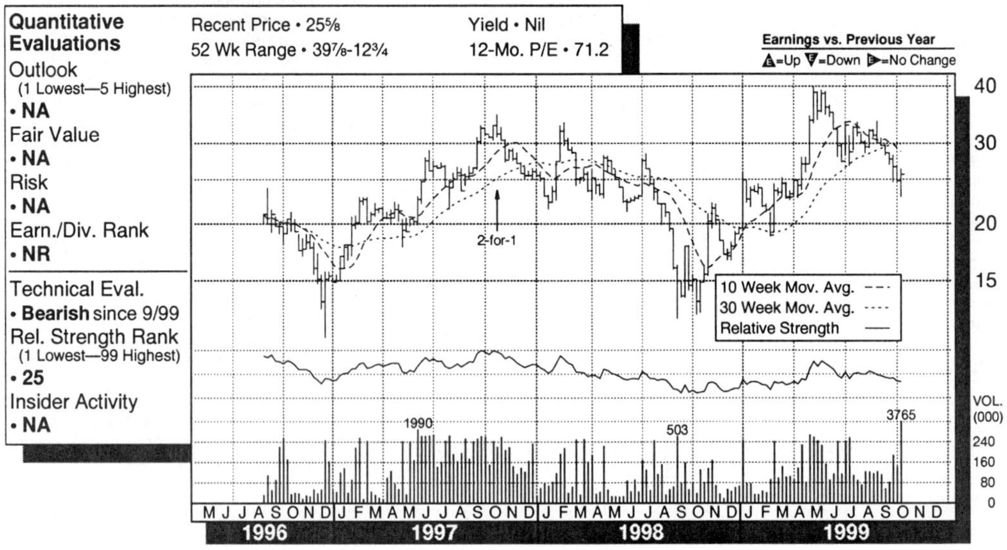

Business Profile - 28-JUN-99

The company seeks increased penetration of current sectors; the signing of large, national contracts with key government and corporate clients; and the launching new products and services built on the AutoTrack XP platform. As 1999 progresses, DBT expects revenues to continue to grow, while expenses drop as a percentage of revenues, leading to wider operating margins. In 1998, customers for the company's online investigative services and products increased 46%, to a record 14,000, with 60% of online revenues generated outside of DBT's original Florida base. In May 1999, DBT acquired I.R.S.C., Inc., a leading provider of court records and other public record information for pre-employment screening.

Operational Review - 28-JUN-99

Total revenues and royalties in the first quarter of 1999 advanced 32%, year to year, reflecting gains in the electronic information division due to the addition of new subscribers and increased usage by existing subscribers to its AutoTrack on line information service. Gross margins widened on well controlled operating costs, but with higher sales and marketing expenses, and a rise in R&D expenditures outweighing well controlled general and administrative expenses, the gain in net income was held to 19%, to $1,870,800 ($0.10 a share, diluted), from $1,568,100 ($0.08).

Stock Performance - 08-OCT-99

In the past 30 trading days, DBT's shares have declined 15%, compared to a 0.91% fall in the S&P 500. Average trading volume for the past five days was 753,020 shares, compared with the 40-day moving average of 117,282 shares.

Key Stock Statistics

Dividend Rate/Share	Nil	Shareholders	522
Shs. outstg. (M)	19.0	Market cap. (B)	$0.487
Avg. daily vol. (M)	0.209	Inst. holdings	30%
Tang. Bk. Value/Share	4.42		
Beta	NA		

Value of $10,000 invested 5 years ago: NA

Fiscal Year Ending Dec. 31

	1999	1998	1997	1996	1995	1994
Revenues (Million $)						
1Q	14.79	12.42	7.60	—	—	—
2Q	18.06	13.05	8.84	—	—	—
3Q	—	13.57	10.13	—	—	—
4Q	—	14.51	10.98	—	—	—
Yr.	—	53.55	37.55	18.70	8.10	—
Earnings Per Share ($)						
1Q	**0.10**	**0.08**	**0.05**	—	—	—
2Q	**0.08**	**0.09**	**0.08**	—	—	—
3Q	—	**0.09**	**0.08**	—	—	—
4Q	—	**0.09**	**0.11**	0.01	—	—
Yr.	—	**0.35**	**0.33**	**0.04**	-0.13	—

Next earnings report expected: late October

Dividend Data

No cash dividends have been paid. A two-for-one common stock split was effected in October 1997.

A Division of The McGraw-Hill Companies

DBT Online, Inc.

Business Summary - 28-JUN-99

In August 1996, the former shareholders of Patlex (whose chairman and CEO was former astronaut and Eastern Airlines chief Frank Borman) approved adoption of a holding company structure, and each share of Patlex was converted into a DBT Online share. At the same time, the company merged with Database Technologies, Inc., with the former shareholders of Database Technologies owning 67% of the new company.

DBT Online is a holding company with businesses that serve the electronic information (88% of 1998 revenues and 56% of operating profit) and patent enforcement (12% and 44%) industries. Its electronic information businesses are on-line providers of integrated database services and related reports primarily to law enforcement and other governmental agencies, law firms, insurance companies and licensed investigation companies. Its patent enforcement business is engaged in the exploitation and enforcement of two laser patents and generates its revenues through patent royalties.

The Electronic Information Group (EIG) consists of Database Technologies, Inc. and The Information Connectivity Group, Inc., (acquired in 1997). It is a national provider of on-line integrated database services and related reports to law enforcement and other governmental agencies, law firms, insurance companies and licensed investigation companies. The EIG has developed proprietary software which contains unique algorithms and utilizes advanced microprocessor-based technology to locate, cross reference and retrieve public records from multiple data sources. The EIG allows its restricted customer base to access its system from desktop computers and generate reports which are delivered in an organized, comprehensive and easy to read format. The system simultaneously accesses a multitude of data sources containing billions of records as if they were part of a single database in preparing the computer-generated reports. EIG has increased its customer base rapidly over the past four years, from about 1,000 active customers in December 1994 to approximately 14,000 active customers in December 1998, and 15,500 customers at March 31, 1999.

Products include AutoTrack, which provides online access to over four billion public records and information, and AutoTrack XP, a new Windows compatible product that allows access to EIG's database warehouse using Web browser technology.

Patlex, which has been engaged in the patent exploitation and enforcement business since late 1979, owns a 64% interest in the royalty income from, and a 42.86% ownership interest in, the Laser Patents, which derive from patent applications originally filed by Dr. Gordon Gould in 1959. Patlex is also the exclusive licensing agent for the Laser Patents. The patent enforcement business includes the identification of laser products and laser applications which infringe the Laser Patents and the execution of licensing agreements through normal commercial negotiations or pursuant to settlements of litigation brought against infringers of the Laser Patents.

Per Share Data ($) (Year Ended Dec. 31)	1998	1997	1996	1995	1994	1993	1992	1991	1990	1989
Tangible Bk. Val.	3.70	3.19	0.32	NA	NA	NA	NA	NA	NA	NA
Cash Flow	0.76	0.64	0.28	-0.03	NA	NA	NA	NA	NA	NA
Earnings	0.35	0.33	0.04	-0.13	NA	NA	NA	NA	NA	NA
Dividends	Nil	Nil	Nil	Nil	NA	NA	NA	NA	NA	NA
Payout Ratio	Nil	Nil	Nil	Nil	NA	NA	NA	NA	NA	NA
Prices - High	33 3/8	34 3/4	24	NA	NA	NA	NA	NA	NA	NA
- Low	12 3/8	14 7/8	11 1/4	NA	NA	NA	NA	NA	NA	NA
P/E Ratio - High	95	NM	600	NA	NA	NA	NA	NA	NA	NA
- Low	35	NM	281	NA	NA	NA	NA	NA	NA	NA
Income Statement Analysis (Million $)										
Revs.	53.5	37.5	18.7	8.1	NA	NA	NA	NA	NA	NA
Oper. Inc.	15.1	13.2	3.9	1.7	NA	NA	NA	NA	NA	NA
Depr.	7.7	5.6	3.0	0.9	NA	NA	NA	NA	NA	NA
Int. Exp.	Nil	0.0	0.2	0.1	NA	NA	NA	NA	NA	NA
Pretax Inc.	9.7	9.1	0.8	-1.0	NA	NA	NA	NA	NA	NA
Eff. Tax Rate	31%	34%	31%	NM	NA	NA	NA	NA	NA	NA
Net Inc.	6.7	6.0	0.5	-1.2	NA	NA	NA	NA	NA	NA
Balance Sheet & Other Fin. Data (Million $)										
Cash	21.3	7.7	7.0	1.6	NA	NA	NA	NA	NA	NA
Curr. Assets	57.7	58.2	9.8	2.9	NA	NA	NA	NA	NA	NA
Total Assets	90.5	84.6	29.6	6.6	NA	NA	NA	NA	NA	NA
Curr. Liab.	4.3	4.8	5.6	2.4	NA	NA	NA	NA	NA	NA
LT Debt	Nil	Nil	1.4	1.5	NA	NA	NA	NA	NA	NA
Common Eqty.	82.8	75.6	18.2	2.6	NA	NA	NA	NA	NA	NA
Total Cap.	86.2	79.8	23.9	4.1	NA	NA	NA	NA	NA	NA
Cap. Exp.	14.4	6.4	5.3	3.1	NA	NA	NA	NA	NA	NA
Cash Flow	14.4	11.6	3.5	-0.3	NA	NA	NA	NA	NA	NA
Curr. Ratio	13.4	12.2	1.8	1.2	NA	NA	NA	NA	NA	NA
% LT Debt of Cap.	Nil	Nil	5.9	36.6	NA	NA	NA	NA	NA	NA
% Net Inc.of Revs.	12.5	16.0	2.8	NM	NA	NA	NA	NA	NA	NA
% Ret. on Assets	7.7	10.5	2.8	NM	NA	NA	NA	NA	NA	NA
% Ret. on Equity	8.5	12.8	5.0	NM	NA	NA	NA	NA	NA	NA

Data as orig reptd.; bef. results of disc opers/spec. items. Per share data adj. for stk. divs. Bold denotes diluted EPS (FASB 128)-prior periods restated. E-Estimated. NA-Not Available. NM-Not Meaningful. NR-Not Ranked.

Office—5550 W. Flamingo Road, Suite B-5, Las Vegas, NV 89103. **Tel**—(702) 257-1112. **Chrmn**—F. Borman. **Pres & CEO**—C. A. Lieppe. **VP-Fin, Treas, CFO & Investor Contact**—T. M. Leonard. **VP & Secy**—J. H. Muetterties. **Dirs**—G. Betty, F. Borman, G. E. Erlbaum, J. E. Glassman, J. Hight, K. G. Langone, C. A. Lieppe, B. Marcus, A. E. Pearson, T. J. Quarles, E. L. Step, S. Zalcberg. **Transfer Agent & Registrar**—LaSalle National Trust, Chicago. **Incorporated**—in Pennsylvania in 1996. **Empl**— 247. **S&P Analyst:** S.S.

STANDARD &POOR'S
STOCK REPORTS

Delphi Financial Group

NYSE Symbol **DFG**

In S&P SmallCap 600

09-OCT-99

Industry: Insurance (Life & Health)

Summary: Through subsidiaries, Delphi provides a diverse portfolio of employee benefit products to customers across the U.S.

Quantitative Evaluations

Outlook
(1 Lowest—5 Highest)
• **4+**

Fair Value
• **39**

Risk
• **Average**

Earn./Div. Rank
• **B+**

Technical Eval.
• **Bearish** since 8/99

Rel. Strength Rank
(1 Lowest—99 Highest)
• **27**

Insider Activity
• **NA**

Recent Price • 30⅝
52 Wk Range • 56⅞-27
Yield • Nil
12-Mo. P/E • 13.3

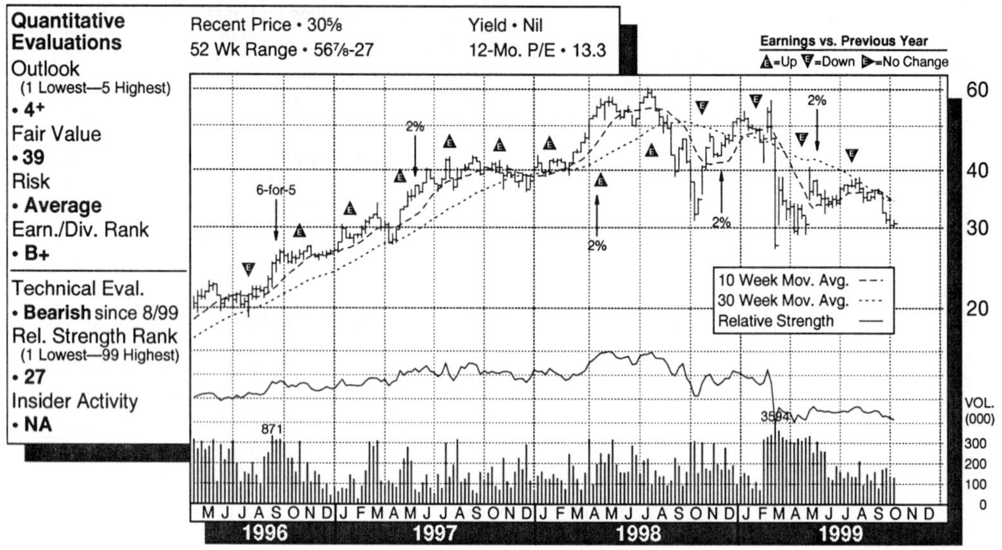

Business Profile - 09-SEP-99

Effective April 30, 1999, Delphi completed the disposition of its Unicover Managers, Inc. subsidiary. Unicover is a reinsurance-underwriting manager, specializing in workers' compensation. DFG purchased the subsidiary in late 1998 for $22 million, plus a contingent consideration of cash and stock. DFG sold the subsidiary to certain former owners of Unicover, and estimated that the net effect of its investment in and subsequent disposal of Unicover, from a cash flow standpoint, would be neutral. The sale came after a disclosure by Cologne Life Reinsurance Company, pertaining to an anticipated loss in a reinsurance pool managed by Unicover. DFG believes with the finalization of the sale, it has distanced itself from any potential related liability.

Operational Review - 09-SEP-99

Total revenues for the six months ended June 30, 1999, rose 12.5%, year to year, primarily reflecting higher premium and fee income resulting from strong growth in most of its employee benefit products. However, business growth also caused a 34% increase in benefits and expenses, overshadowing a lower combined ratio; operating income decreased 35%. After interest expense and taxes at 30.9%, versus 33.2%, income from continuing operations fell 37%, to $39,760,000 ($1.72 a share, after dividends on Capital Securities), from $63,009,000 ($2.82, adjusted). Results in the 1999 period exclude a loss of $13.8 million ($0.65) for the disposal of discontinued operations.

Stock Performance - 08-OCT-99

In the past 30 trading days, DFG's shares have declined 13%, compared to a 0.91% fall in the S&P 500. Average trading volume for the past five days was 25,820 shares, compared with the 40-day moving average of 28,200 shares.

Key Stock Statistics

Dividend Rate/Share	Nil	Shareholders	1,700
Shs. outstg. (M)	20.2	Market cap. (B)	$0.457
Avg. daily vol. (M)	0.030	Inst. holdings	36%
Tang. Bk. Value/Share	22.22		
Beta	0.53		

Value of $10,000 invested 5 years ago: $ 16,072

Fiscal Year Ending Dec. 31

	1999	1998	1997	1996	1995	1994
Revenues (Million $)						
1Q	211.4	171.2	139.1	102.2	86.95	88.77
2Q	171.0	152.4	127.6	120.7	96.80	93.23
3Q	—	125.9	135.5	128.7	92.66	93.30
4Q	—	177.1	133.4	136.0	103.4	90.00
Yr.	—	626.6	535.6	487.3	379.8	365.3
Earnings Per Share ($)						
1Q	**0.95**	**1.80**	**0.97**	0.57	0.22	0.32
2Q	**0.76**	**1.02**	**0.76**	0.62	0.62	0.40
3Q	—	**0.49**	**0.95**	0.68	0.53	0.66
4Q	—	**0.75**	**0.90**	0.75	0.56	0.26
Yr.	—	**4.05**	**3.59**	**2.69**	**2.11**	**1.67**

Next earnings report expected: late October

Dividend Data

Amount ($)	Date Decl.	Ex-Div. Date	Stock of Record	Payment Date
2%	Nov. 19	Nov. 27	Dec. 01	Dec. 15 '98
2%	May. 12	May. 21	May. 25	Jun. 08 '99

Delphi Financial Group, Inc.

Business Summary - 09-SEP-99

With a focus on small to mid-sized customers, Delphi Financial Group, Inc., offers a diverse portfolio of group employee benefit products across the U.S. Delphi is a holding company, providing services through its subsidiaries, Delphi Capital Management, Inc., Reliance Standard Life Insurance Co., Safety National Casualty Corp. and Matrix Absence Management, Inc. DFG's offerings include life, disability, workers' compensation, dental and personal accident insurance, as well as reinsurance underwriting and integrated disability and absence management services. Premiums generated from group employee benefit products totaled $416.4 million in 1998, compared to $355.9 million a year earlier.

The company also offers asset accumulation products, consisting mostly of annuities, that are offered to both individuals and groups. Income generated by asset accumulation products totaled $2.6 million in 1998, versus $3.1 million in 1997, reflecting a decline in the demand for fixed annuity products due to the low interest rate environment.

DFG's operating strategy is to offer financial products and services that have the potential for significant growth or that require expertise to meet the specialized needs of its customers. By concentrating its offerings to small to mid-size employers, DFG believes it has targeted a group responsible for nearly all of the employment growth in the American economy over the past few years.

Delphi markets its group products to employer-employee groups and associations in a variety of industries, insuring groups ranging from 10 to more than 1,000 individuals. The average size of DFG's insured groups ranges from 100 to 300 employees.

Delphi's investment portfolio is an important component of its profitability. Net investment income accounted for 27% of total revenue in 1998. The company manages the portfolio with an emphasis on liquidity and yield, while managing the duration of its interest sensitive assets and liabilities and minimizing risks associated with interest rate fluctuations. The weighted average annual yield on DFG's investment portfolio was 8.1%, compared with 7.9% in 1997.

In June 1998, DFG acquired Matrix Absence Management, a leading provider of integrated disability services to the employee benefits market, for $35 million in stock, cash and notes.

As of March 19, 1999, 49.9% of the voting power of the common stock was controlled by one man, by means of beneficial ownership of the corporate general partner of Rosenkranz & Company.

Per Share Data ($) (Year Ended Dec. 31)	1998	1997	1996	1995	1994	1993	1992	1991	1990	1989
Tangible Bk. Val.	22.22	20.62	13.92	8.38	3.71	5.96	10.31	9.22	7.88	NA
Oper. Earnings	3.80	3.13	NA	NA	NA	NA	NA	NA	NA	NA
Earnings	4.05	3.59	2.66	1.94	1.65	3.36	1.83	1.09	1.25	1.64
Dividends	Nil	Nil	Nil	Nil	Nil	Nil	Nil	Nil	Nil	Nil
Payout Ratio	Nil	Nil	Nil	Nil	Nil	Nil	Nil	Nil	Nil	Nil
Prices - High	60½	43	27⅞	18¼	19½	19⅞	11½	7¾	12½	NA
- Low	31	27⅛	16¼	12⅜	12¾	10⅝	4⅜	4¾	6⅛	NA
P/E Ratio - High	15	12	10	9	12	6	6	7	10	NA
- Low	8	8	6	6	8	3	2	4	5	NA
Income Statement Analysis (Million $)										
Life Ins. In Force	68,353	57.0	51,625	43,468	45.6	39.7	33.1	26.0	20.6	13.7
Prem. Inc.: Life	174	146	147	129	129	126	107	88.0	75.0	73.0
Prem. Inc.: A & H	166	161	187	130	118	103	92.7	83.9	77.7	81.7
Net Invest. Inc.	169	160	155	117	107	177	134	133	149	136
Total Revs.	627	536	487	380	365	426	356	333	304	296
Pretax Inc.	132	113	81.3	47.4	37.4	72.9	37.2	24.0	24.4	28.0
Net Oper. Inc.	NA	NA	NA	NA	NA	NA	NA	NA	NA	NA
Net Inc.	87.0	75.0	53.8	30.5	25.8	46.8	24.6	16.8	18.8	20.2
Balance Sheet & Other Fin. Data (Million $)										
Cash & Equiv.	372	50.6	89.7	16.7	1.0	94.0	107	76.0	123	NA
Premiums Due	356	235	215	183	181	39.0	Nil	Nil	Nil	Nil
Invest. Assets: Bonds	1,890	2,165	1,892	1,554	1,671	1,483	1,369	1,319	1,333	NA
Invest. Assets: Stocks	Nil	Nil	74.0	127	156	225	167	218	164	NA
Invest. Assets: Loans	Nil	Nil	Nil	Nil	Nil	Nil	Nil	Nil	Nil	Nil
Invest. Assets: Total	2,061	2,430	2,295	1,775	1,964	1,948	1,775	1,711	1,898	1,386
Deferred Policy Costs	NA	NA	94.5	94.4	114	112	Nil	Nil	Nil	Nil
Total Assets	3,396	3,204	2,858	2,327	2,474	2,344	2,184	2,005	2,197	1,541
Debt	365	480	950	336	360	310	164	173	187	205
Common Eqty.	566	509	367	223	170	201	129	114	98.0	51.0
% Return On Revs.	13.9	14.0	11.0	8.0	7.1	11.0	6.9	5.0	6.2	6.8
% Ret. on Assets	2.6	2.5	2.1	1.3	1.1	2.1	1.2	0.8	1.0	1.4
% Ret. on Equity	16.2	17.1	18.2	15.5	13.9	28.3	20.2	15.8	25.2	49.3
% Invest. Yield	7.5	6.7	7.6	6.6	5.4	9.5	7.7	8.1	10.6	11.2

Data as orig. reptd.; bef. results of disc. opers. and/or spec. items. Per share data adj. for stk. divs. as of ex-div. date. Bold denotes diluted EPS (FASB 128). E-Estimated. NA-Not Available. NM-Not Meaningful. NR-Not Ranked.

Office—1105 N. Market St., Suite 1230, Wilmington, DE 19899. **Tel**—(302) 478-5142. **Chrmn, Pres & CEO**—R. Rosenkranz. **Secy**—L. Eike. **VP & Treas**—L. E. Daurelle. **Investor Contact**—(215) 787-3943. **Dirs**—E. A. Fox, C. P. O'Brien, L. S. Ranieri, R. Rosenkranz, T. L. Rhodes, R. M. Smith, Jr., B. K. Werner. **Transfer Agent**—First Union National Bank, Charlotte, NC. **Incorporated**—in Delaware in 1987. **Empl**— 725. **S&P Analyst:** Markos N. Kaminis

STANDARD
&POOR'S
STOCK REPORTS

Delta and Pine Land

NYSE Symbol **DLP**

In S&P SmallCap 600

09-OCT-99

Industry: Agricultural Products

Summary: In May 1998, DLP, the largest U.S. commercial breeder, producer and marketer of cotton planting seed, agreed to be acquired by Monsanto Co.

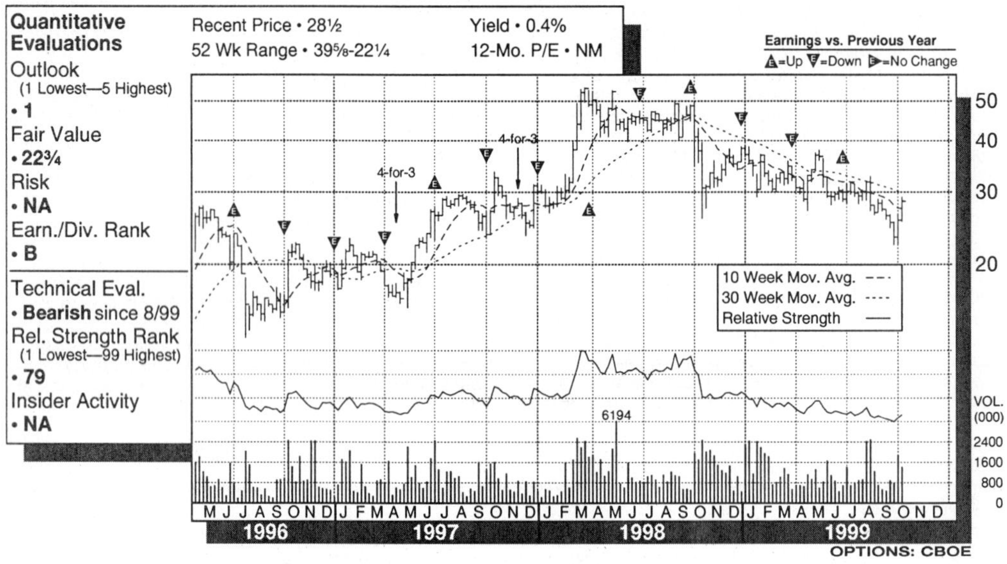

Business Profile - 23-SEP-99

In May 1998, the company agreed to be acquired by Monsanto Co. (NYSE: MTC), with each DLP common share to be exchanged for 0.8625 of a MTC share (recent price about $37). The agreement has been approved by shareholders, but in August 1999, DLP and MTC received civil investigative demands from the U.S. Department of Justice, seeking information to determine whether there have been any exchanges of information between MTC or DLP, or any acquisitions likely to have substantially lessened competition in the sale or development of cottonseed or cottonseed genetic traits. MTC and DLP have said they intend to cooperate with the investigation.

Operational Review - 23-SEP-99

Net sales and licensing fees in the nine months ended May 31, 1999, increased 14%, year to year, on higher sales of cottonseed. Despite well controlled selling, general and administrative expenses, with a less favorable product mix and higher R&D costs, the gain in operating income was held to 11%. With a $5.6 million increase in merger charges, higher interest expense, and a greater loss on the sale of assets, after taxes at 39.1%, versus 39.5%, net income fell 13%, to $16.7 million ($0.41 a share, after preferred dividends), from $19.1 million ($0.47).

Stock Performance - 08-OCT-99

In the past 30 trading days, DLP's shares have increased 1%, compared to a 0.91% fall in the S&P 500. Average trading volume for the past five days was 280,180 shares, compared with the 40-day moving average of 200,236 shares.

Key Stock Statistics

Dividend Rate/Share	0.12	Shareholders	400
Shs. outstg. (M)	38.5	Market cap. (B)	$ 1.1
Avg. daily vol. (M)	0.246	Inst. holdings	54%
Tang. Bk. Value/Share	2.29		
Beta	0.96		

Value of $10,000 invested 5 years ago: $ 60,044

Fiscal Year Ending Aug. 31

	1999	1998	1997	1996	1995	1994
Revenues (Million $)						
1Q	7.20	5.34	6.32	5.33	1.50	0.70
2Q	72.80	77.25	66.43	63.40	40.40	30.00
3Q	158.6	126.0	116.4	82.65	36.00	36.70
4Q	—	-15.13	—	1.89	0.70	0.10
Yr.	—	192.3	183.3	153.3	78.70	67.50
Earnings Per Share ($)						
1Q	**-0.17**	-0.12	-0.12	-0.10	-0.07	-0.06
2Q	**0.06**	**0.24**	0.23	0.27	0.23	0.11
3Q	**0.51**	**0.34**	0.51	0.34	0.20	0.24
4Q	—	**-0.45**	-0.49	-0.13	-0.06	-0.06
Yr.	—	**0.04**	**0.17**	0.40	0.29	0.23

Next earnings report expected: late October

Dividend Data (Dividends have been paid since 1993.)

Amount ($)	Date Decl.	Ex-Div. Date	Stock of Record	Payment Date
0.030	Nov. 23	Nov. 25	Nov. 30	Dec. 11 '98
0.030	Feb. 12	Feb. 24	Feb. 26	Mar. 15 '99
0.030	May. 05	May. 26	May. 31	Jun. 14 '99
0.030	Aug. 04	Aug. 27	Aug. 31	Sep. 17 '99

A Division of The McGraw-Hill Companies

Delta and Pine Land Company

Business Summary - 23-SEP-99

Since 1915, Mississippi-based Delta and Pine Land Co. has been breeding, producing and marketing cotton planting seed for varieties of the crop that are grown primarily east of Texas and in Arizona. DLP may hark back to the waning days of the Old South, but its business approach is thoroughly modern. In May 1998, the company agreed to be acquired by Monsanto Co. (NYSE: MTC), with each DLP common share to be exchanged for 0.8625 of a MTC share. The agreement has been approved by shareholders, but is subject to regulatory approval. In October 1998, Monsanto and American Home Products terminated a merger agreement.

DLP is now the largest U.S. commercial breeder, producer and marketer of cotton planting seed. It has used its extensive classical plant breeding programs to develop a gene pool necessary for producing cotton varieties with improved agronomic traits important to farmers, such as crop yield, and to textile manufacturers, such as enhanced fiber characteristics. Its cotton varieties are produced under the brand names Deltapine, Paymaster, Sure Grow and Supima. In 1980, DLP added soybean seed to its product line, and in 1988 it added hybrid sorghum seed.

The company has annual agreements with certain growers to produce seed for cotton and soybeans. The growers plant seed purchased from DLP, and, if the seed meets company standards upon harvest, DLP is obligated to purchase specified minimum quantities of seed at prices equal to the commodity market price of the seed, plus a grower premium. DLP then conditions the seed for sale.

DLP has a collaborative licensing agreement with Monsanto that provides for commercialization of Monsanto's Bollgard technology in DLP's NuCOTN cotton varieties. Bollgard is toxic to certain lepidopteran larvae, the principal cotton pests in many cotton growing areas. Since 1997, the company has marketed in the U.S. genetically modified cotton planting seed providing tolerance to glyphosate-based herbicides.

Domestically, DLP promotes its cottonseed directly to farmers and sells cottonseed through distributors and dealers. During the 1980s, the company began to market its products, primarily cottonseed, internationally. Over a period of years, DLP has strengthened and expanded its international staff in order to support its expanding joint venture activities. The company believes it has an attractive opportunity to penetrate foreign markets because of its widely adaptable, superior cotton varieties, technological know-how in producing and conditioning seed, and brand name recognition.

Per Share Data ($) (Year Ended Aug. 31)	1998	1997	1996	1995	1994	1993	1992	1991	1990	1989
Tangible Bk. Val.	1.89	1.71	1.63	1.13	0.81	0.81	NA	NA	NA	NA
Cash Flow	0.21	0.31	0.50	0.37	0.29	0.33	NA	NA	NA	NA
Earnings	0.04	0.17	0.39	0.29	0.23	0.26	0.25	NA	NA	NA
Dividends	0.12	0.08	0.06	0.05	0.05	0.02	NA	NA	NA	NA
Payout Ratio	NM	47%	16%	16%	20%	4%	NA	NA	NA	NA
Prices - High	54	33⅝	27⅞	14	5⅜	5⅛	NA	NA	NA	NA
- Low	25⅞	15⅝	13⅛	4¾	3½	3⅜	NA	NA	NA	NA
P/E Ratio - High	NM	NM	71	48	24	20	NA	NA	NA	NA
- Low	NM	NM	33	17	15	13	NA	NA	NA	NA
Income Statement Analysis (Million $)										
Revs.	192	183	153	78.7	67.5	66.1	68.4	63.2	NA	NA
Oper. Inc.	35.6	37.2	31.2	20.1	14.9	17.1	NA	NA	NA	NA
Depr.	6.7	5.1	4.0	2.7	2.2	2.0	NA	NA	NA	NA
Int. Exp.	3.2	2.2	2.4	1.8	1.2	2.1	NA	NA	NA	NA
Pretax Inc.	3.2	9.7	23.7	16.0	12.0	13.4	12.5	9.6	NA	NA
Eff. Tax Rate	41%	29%	36%	37%	36%	38%	NA	NA	NA	NA
Net Inc.	1.9	6.9	15.3	10.1	7.7	8.3	7.9	6.1	NA	NA
Balance Sheet & Other Fin. Data (Million $)										
Cash	8.1	1.9	0.6	5.6	1.1	NA	NA	NA	NA	NA
Curr. Assets	175	145	112	29.8	24.8	20.9	24.1	16.7	NA	NA
Total Assets	252	221	180	75.8	63.6	43.9	43.6	35.2	NA	NA
Curr. Liab.	116	113	76.0	19.3	15.8	15.2	20.2	15.2	NA	NA
LT Debt	47.1	30.5	31.5	11.3	12.0	Nil	13.8	3.6	NA	NA
Common Eqty.	80.6	72.5	69.3	43.4	34.4	28.1	11.2	16.1	NA	NA
Total Cap.	136	103	104	56.5	47.8	NA	NA	NA	NA	NA
Cap. Exp.	10.2	17.1	16.0	8.8	3.2	2.3	NA	NA	NA	NA
Cash Flow	8.4	11.9	19.3	12.8	9.9	10.3	NA	NA	NA	NA
Curr. Ratio	1.5	1.3	1.5	1.5	1.6	1.4	1.2	1.1	NA	NA
% LT Debt of Cap.	34.6	29.6	30.4	20.0	25.1	NA	NA	NA	NA	NA
% Net Inc.of Revs.	1.0	3.8	10.0	12.8	11.4	12.6	11.5	9.7	NA	NA
% Ret. on Assets	0.8	3.5	11.4	14.5	14.3	19.0	20.0	NA	NA	NA
% Ret. on Equity	2.3	9.7	26.0	26.0	24.6	42.2	57.9	NA	NA	NA

Data as orig reptd.; bef. results of disc opers/spec. items. Per share data adj. for stk. divs. Bold denotes diluted EPS (FASB 128)-prior periods restated. E-Estimated. NA-Not Available. NM-Not Meaningful. NR-Not Ranked.

Office—One Cotton Row, Scott, MI 38772. **Tel**—(601) 742-4500. **Chrmn & CEO**—R. D. Malkin. **VP-Fin & Treas**—W. T. Jagodinski. **Dirs**—N. Chua, J. E. M. Jacoby, R. Malkin, J. M. Murphy, S. P. Roth, R. E. Scheidt. **Transfer Agent & Registrar**—Harris Trust and Savings Bank, Chicago. **Incorporated**—in Delaware in 1978.**Empl**— 581. **S&P Analyst:** J.W.H.

STANDARD &POOR'S STOCK REPORTS

Delta Woodside Industries

NYSE Symbol **DLW**

In S&P SmallCap 600

09-OCT-99

Industry: Textiles (Specialty)

Summary: This company manufactures and sells a wide variety of textile and apparel products.

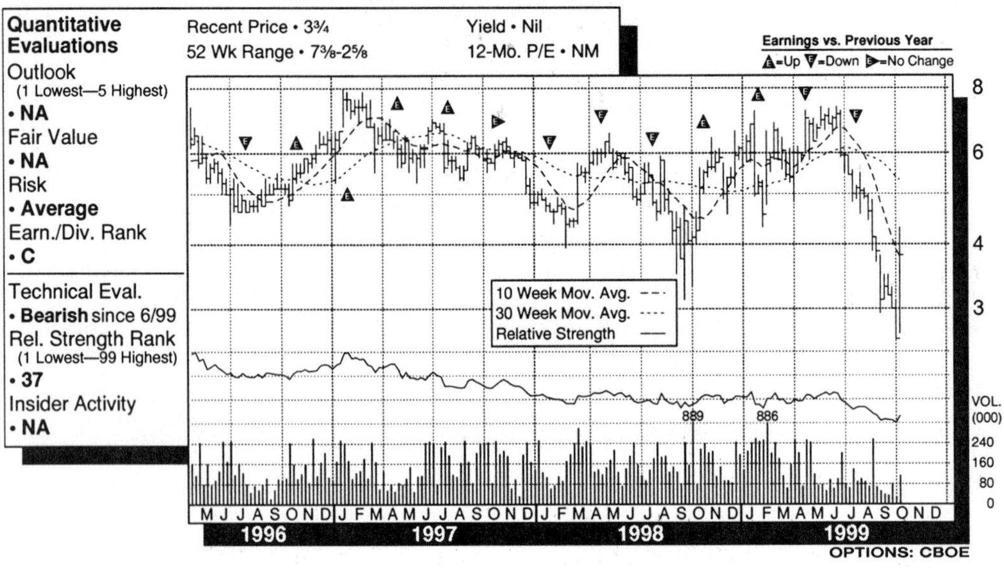

Business Profile - 15-SEP-99

In August 1999, the company announced that it will not go forth with reorganization/spinoff plans that were previously announced in June 1999. Because of weakness in the bond market, DLW said it will not spin off its two apparel operating companies, Delta Apparel and Duck Head Apparel. Furthermore, because the company believes that shareholders will be best served by separating the operating companies, Delta Mills (its textile subsidiary) will not acquire the two apparel divisions. The company continues to explore strategic alternatives to accomplish the separation of its operating companies. Also in August, the company announced that it will suspend quarterly dividends until operating results improve. Order backlog from continuing operations was off 38% from a year earlier as of July 3, 1999.

Operational Review - 15-SEP-99

Based on a preliminary report, net sales fell 7.9% in FY 99 (Jun.), despite an extra week of operation. Following goodwill writeoffs and inventory writedowns totaling $31.8 million, versus an $8.9 million goodwill writeoff in FY 98, a loss from continuing operations of $32,489,000 ($1.35 a share) contrasted with income of $2,616,000 ($0.11). Results exclude losses from discontinued operations of $0.28 and $1.89 a share in the respective years.

Stock Performance - 08-OCT-99

In the past 30 trading days, DLW's shares have declined 2%, compared to a 0.91% fall in the S&P 500. Average trading volume for the past five days was 22,200 shares, compared with the 40-day moving average of 21,287 shares.

Key Stock Statistics

Dividend Rate/Share	Nil	Shareholders	1,857
Shs. outstg. (M)	23.7	Market cap. (B)	$0.090
Avg. daily vol. (M)	0.013	Inst. holdings	44%
Tang. Bk. Value/Share	6.54		
Beta	0.66		

Value of $10,000 invested 5 years ago: $ 3,973

Fiscal Year Ending Jun. 30

	1999	1998	1997	1996	1995	1994
Revenues (Million $)						
1Q	130.6	139.1	144.5	141.0	141.3	146.4
2Q	113.8	124.9	162.7	150.6	142.5	149.3
3Q	109.5	121.5	163.9	143.3	150.9	155.2
4Q	139.1	149.9	180.8	165.3	162.8	162.8
Yr.	493.0	535.5	651.8	600.2	597.5	613.8
Earnings Per Share ($)						
1Q	**0.33**	**0.14**	**0.14**	0.05	0.17	0.07
2Q	**0.03**	**-0.02**	**0.14**	0.02	0.02	-1.31
3Q	**-0.18**	**-0.17**	**0.18**	-0.35	0.04	0.27
4Q	**-1.55**	**0.07**	**0.14**	-2.28	0.19	0.26
Yr.	**-1.35**	**0.11**	**0.60**	**-0.95**	0.42	-0.70

Next earnings report expected: mid October

Dividend Data (Dividends have been paid since 1988.)

Amount ($)	Date Decl.	Ex-Div. Date	Stock of Record	Payment Date
0.025	Nov. 06	Nov. 18	Nov. 20	Dec. 07 '98
0.025	Feb. 04	Feb. 17	Feb. 19	Mar. 05 '99
0.025	May. 06	May. 19	May. 21	Jun. 07 '99

Delta Woodside Industries, Inc.

Business Summary - 15-SEP-99

Hurt by years of weak results, this manufacturer of apparel and textiles has been shedding unprofitable businesses and, after scrapping a recapitalization/spinoff proposal in August 1999, is continuing to explore strategic alternatives to separate its operating companies. In 1998, DLW closed its Stevcoknit division, and in early 1999 sold its Nautilus International fitness equipment business. As of August 1999, the company operated 15 plants and 24 garment outlet stores located in 12 states, Costa Rica and Honduras.

The Delta Mills Inc. unit, through its Delta Mills Marketing Co. subsidiary, the largest of DLW's businesses, sells a variety of cotton, synthetic and blended finished and unfinished woven products which are sold for the ultimate production of apparel, home furnishings and other products. Delta Mills is a leading producer of cotton pants-weight woven fabric used in the manufacture of casual slacks. Other apparel items manufactured with the company's woven fabric include women's chinos pants, women's blazers, career apparel (uniforms) and battle dress camouflage military uniforms. Generally, profitability of this unit is enhanced by increases in the use of its manufacturing capacity and is affected by the relative mix of more or less profitable goods being produced and the cost and availability of raw materials.

Duck Head Apparel sells men's and boys' casual wear, including the "Duck Head" line, in major department stores, mostly in the southeastern U.S., and through 24 Duck Head outlet stores in 12 states. At the end of FY 98, there were over 500 men's and 200 boys' Duck Head shops in department stores.

Through Delta Apparel, the company manufactures and sells knitted T-shirts, fleece goods and sportswear, such as polo-type shirts and sweatshirts. It markets its products primarily to companies that screen print shirts for resale and to distributors.

In August 1999, the company said it had decided not to go forth with reorganization plans that were announced in June 1999. Due to weakness in the bond market, DLW said it would not spin off its two operating companies, Delta Apparel and Duck Head Apparel. Furthermore, because the company believes that shareholders will be best served by separating the operating companies, its Delta Mills textile subsidiary will not acquire the two apparel divisions.

Per Share Data ($) (Year Ended Jun. 30)	1999	1998	1997	1996	1995	1994	1993	1992	1991	1990
Tangible Bk. Val.	NA	6.54	8.16	7.80	10.64	11.75	12.72	12.08	8.17	6.76
Cash Flow	NA	1.08	1.54	-1.35	1.43	0.16	1.71	2.18	1.99	0.97
Earnings	-1.35	0.11	0.30	-2.56	0.42	-0.70	1.07	1.62	1.27	0.32
Dividends	0.10	0.10	Nil	0.30	0.40	0.40	0.40	0.35	0.30	0.30
Payout Ratio	NM	91%	Nil	NM	95%	NM	37%	23%	26%	95%
Prices - High	7 3/8	6 5/8	8	8	11 3/8	12 1/2	16 1/4	22	25 1/4	11 1/2
- Low	2 5/8	3 1/8	4 5/8	4 3/8	7 1/2	9 3/4	10 1/4	11 1/2	5	3 5/8
P/E Ratio - High	NM	60	27	NM	27	NM	15	14	20	36
- Low	NM	28	15	NM	18	NM	10	7	4	11
Income Statement Analysis (Million $)										
Revs.	NA	535	652	600	598	614	686	705	590	501
Oper. Inc.	NA	59.3	60.3	-24.4	46.0	38.1	65.6	90.7	72.6	44.1
Depr.	NA	23.9	30.3	29.5	24.6	21.3	17.1	13.7	13.6	12.3
Int. Exp.	NA	23.4	23.7	19.0	13.6	8.6	8.0	11.8	22.2	25.8
Pretax Inc.	NA	3.5	9.4	-83.6	17.8	-25.9	45.2	65.8	37.6	8.0
Eff. Tax Rate	NA	25%	21%	NM	43%	NM	38%	39%	36%	25%
Net Inc.	NA	2.6	7.4	-62.6	10.1	-17.3	28.2	40.0	24.0	6.0
Balance Sheet & Other Fin. Data (Million $)										
Cash	NA	2.8	2.7	6.3	0.7	2.1	3.7	0.8	0.4	1.6
Curr. Assets	NA	266	312	280	363	337	346	344	282	258
Total Assets	NA	474	558	538	610	567	574	525	434	414
Curr. Liab.	NA	94.8	82.4	312	76.2	95.0	84.0	78.0	176	191
LT Debt	NA	184	228	0.3	219	162	130	110	71.2	85.7
Common Eqty.	NA	180	225	217	286	285	336	319	173	127
Total Cap.	NA	567	467	218	527	466	484	443	255	222
Cap. Exp.	NA	14.6	23.2	67.4	32.2	29.9	55.7	42.9	15.9	21.7
Cash Flow	NA	26.5	37.7	-33.1	34.7	4.0	45.3	53.7	37.5	18.2
Curr. Ratio	NA	2.8	3.8	0.9	4.8	3.5	4.1	4.4	1.6	1.4
% LT Debt of Cap.	NA	50.0	48.8	Nil	41.6	34.8	26.9	24.9	27.9	38.6
% Net Inc.of Revs.	NA	0.5	1.1	NM	1.7	NM	4.1	5.7	4.1	1.2
% Ret. on Assets	NA	1.0	1.3	NM	1.7	NM	5.1	7.5	5.3	1.6
% Ret. on Equity	NA	1.3	3.3	NM	3.5	NM	8.6	15.0	15.2	4.7

Data as orig reptd.; bef. results of disc opers/spec. items. Per share data adj. for stk. divs. Bold denotes diluted EPS (FASB 128)-prior periods restated. E-Estimated. NA-Not Available. NM-Not Meaningful. NR-Not Ranked.

Office—233 North Main St., Hammond Square, Suite 200, Greenville, SC 29601. **Tel**—(864) 232-8301. **Website**—http://www.deltaapparel.com **Pres & CEO**—E. E. Maddrey II. **EVP, Treas & CFO**—B. C. Rainsford. **VP, Secy & Investor Contact**—Jane H. Greer. **Dirs**—C. C. Guy, J. F. Kane, M. Lennon, E. E. Maddrey II, B. A. Mickel, B. C. Rainsford. **Transfer Agent**—First Union National Bank of North Carolina, Charlotte. **Incorporated**—in South Carolina in 1972. **Empl**— 5,000. **S&P Analyst:** Howard Choe

STANDARD
&POOR'S
STOCK REPORTS

Dendrite International

NASDAQ Symbol **DRTE**

In S&P SmallCap 600

09-OCT-99

Industry:
Computer (Software & Services)

Summary: This company provides sales force effectiveness solutions to manage, coordinate and control the activities of large sales forces, mainly within the pharmaceutical industry.

Quantitative Evaluations

Outlook
(1 Lowest—5 Highest)
• **4⁻**

Fair Value
• **39¾**

Risk
• **High**

Earn./Div. Rank
• **NR**

Technical Eval.
• **Bullish** since 8/99

Rel. Strength Rank
(1 Lowest—99 Highest)
• **90**

Insider Activity
• **Unfavorable**

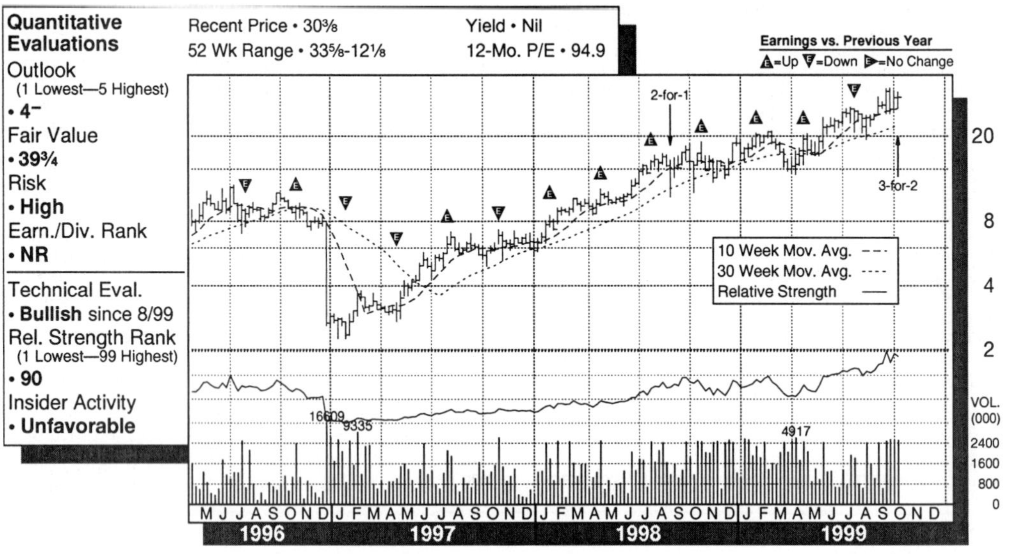

Business Profile - 21-SEP-99

The company attributed improved earnings in the second quarter of 1999 to continued strength in its U.S. pharmaceutical business, strong momentum at the SalesPlus CorNet Americas division, successful wins by SalesPlus Europe, and rapid growth in Japan. Dendrite now expects to exceed analyst earnings estimates for the third quarter of 1999 by $0.01 to $0.02 a share. In May 1999, the company acquired CorNet International Ltd., a provider of sales force effectiveness solutions for the U.S. pharmaceutical, consumer and business to business markets, in exchange for 1.5 million common shares. In June 1999, it purchased substantially all of Marketing Management International, Inc., which offers palmtop software and paper-based sales force effectiveness solutions and consulting services, for $7.3 million in cash and $3.4 million in stock.

Operational Review - 21-SEP-99

Revenues in the first half of 1999 advanced 34%, year to year, aided by increased license fees from pharmaceutical customers, and higher service revenues, due to an expanded installed base of sales force software products. Gross margins widened, on greater operating efficiencies; despite $3.5 million of merger and acquisition expense, pretax income climbed 27%. After taxes at 43.8%, versus 38.5%, net income was up 16%, to $6,225,000 ($0.23 a share), from $5,371,000 ($0.21).

Stock Performance - 08-OCT-99

In the past 30 trading days, DRTE's shares have increased 20%, compared to a 0.91% fall in the S&P 500. Average trading volume for the past five days was 723,870 shares, compared with the 40-day moving average of 512,315 shares.

Key Stock Statistics

Dividend Rate/Share	Nil	Shareholders	91
Shs. outstg. (M)	38.8	Market cap. (B)	$ 1.2
Avg. daily vol. (M)	0.714	Inst. holdings	81%
Tang. Bk. Value/Share	1.77		
Beta	NA		

Value of $10,000 invested 5 years ago: NA

Fiscal Year Ending Dec. 31

	1999	1998	1997	1996	1995	1994
Revenues (Million $)						
1Q	32.40	22.63	16.64	14.22	—	—
2Q	41.85	28.33	18.07	17.26	12.60	—
3Q	—	30.47	20.37	18.60	14.38	—
4Q	—	31.10	23.37	16.17	15.97	—
Yr.	—	112.5	78.45	66.25	54.12	39.43
Earnings Per Share ($)						
1Q	**0.10**	**0.05**	**-0.01**	**0.03**	—	—
2Q	**0.05**	**0.07**	**0.02**	**-0.04**	0.03	—
3Q	—	**0.07**	**0.05**	**0.05**	0.04	—
4Q	—	**0.12**	**0.08**	**-0.10**	0.06	—
Yr.	—	**0.31**	**0.13**	**-0.06**	**0.15**	—

Next earnings report expected: late October

Dividend Data

No cash dividends have been paid. The company does not anticipate paying cash dividends in the foreseeable future.

Dendrite International, Inc.

Business Summary - 21-SEP-99

Originally founded to provide solutions that enable companies to manage, coordinate and control large sales force activities, Dendrite International is now a leading worldwide supplier of a comprehensive range of sale force software products and support services to the pharmaceutical industry. It also supplies solutions to manufacturers of consumer packaged goods.

The company's sales force effectiveness solutions are designed to help customers increase sales and improve the profitability of their operations by allowing them to improve the use of sales, customer and market information; and to manage, coordinate and control their sales activities more efficiently in complex selling environments. Sales force solutions enable customers to realign sales territories, reallocate sales personnel on a customer or formulary basis, and redeploy sales and marketing resources more rapidly and precisely.

Pharmaceutical sales force software products consist mainly of ForcePharma, SalesPlus and J Force. ForcePharma, which is targeted at large multinational pharmaceutical customers, has functions that include customer management, customer targeting, planning, sample management, meetings and synchronization of multiple databases. SalesPlus, acquired from a Belgium-based company in July 1998, is offered to prescription-only pharmaceutical customers with business needs that do not require all of the features of the ForcePharma product. J Force is a sales force effectiveness product developed specifically for the Japanese market, to address the unique characteristics of the Japanese prescription-only pharmaceutical market. The company also offers the ForceCompanion product, a Windows-based palmtop solution for remote use by pharmaceutical company sales representatives.

For the consumer packaged goods (CPG) market, DRTE offers ForceOne, which contains most of the basic features as ForcePharma, as well as features specifically created for the CPG industry.

The company also offers certain analytical software and reporting tools under the ForceMultiplieRx and ForceAnalyzeRx product names. These products let users analyze data such as prescription trends, and produce reports based on the results of these analyses.

Support services (89% of 1998 revenues), which are typically provided under multi-year agreements, include software implementation, technical and hardware support, and sales force support. Implementation services include project management, data modeling, configuration, database modeling, remote computer hardware preparation and training. Technical and hardware support services include project management, software customization, database maintenance, software code maintenance, server support, asset management, business interruption services and Y2K compliance testing. Sales force support services include project management, retraining, territory realignment, telephone support, and data analysis.

Per Share Data ($) (Year Ended Dec. 31)	1998	1997	1996	1995	1994	1993	1992	1991	1990	1989
Tangible Bk. Val.	1.57	1.13	1.03	1.01	NA	NA	NA	NA	NA	NA
Cash Flow	0.39	0.21	0.00	0.20	NA	NA	NA	NA	NA	NA
Earnings	0.31	0.13	-0.06	0.15	NA	NA	NA	NA	NA	NA
Dividends	Nil	Nil	Nil	Nil	NA	NA	NA	NA	NA	NA
Payout Ratio	Nil	Nil	Nil	Nil	NA	NA	NA	NA	NA	NA
Prices - High	19 5/8	7 3/8	11 7/8	7 5/8	NA	NA	NA	NA	NA	NA
- Low	6 1/4	2 1/4	2 5/8	4 1/2	NA	NA	NA	NA	NA	NA
P/E Ratio - High	64	NM	NM	50	NA	NA	NA	NA	NA	NA
- Low	21	NM	NM	30	NA	NA	NA	NA	NA	NA
Income Statement Analysis (Million $)										
Revs.	113	78.4	66.2	54.1	NA	NA	NA	NA	NA	NA
Oper. Inc.	22.1	10.0	2.6	8.7	NA	NA	NA	NA	NA	NA
Depr.	3.0	2.7	2.0	1.5	NA	NA	NA	NA	NA	NA
Int. Exp.	Nil	NM	NM	NM	NA	NA	NA	NA	NA	NA
Pretax Inc.	18.6	7.5	-1.3	7.7	NA	NA	NA	NA	NA	NA
Eff. Tax Rate	40%	39%	NM	39%	NA	NA	NA	NA	NA	NA
Net Inc.	11.3	4.6	-1.9	4.7	NA	NA	NA	NA	NA	NA
Balance Sheet & Other Fin. Data (Million $)										
Cash	31.3	15.9	10.9	11.5	NA	NA	NA	NA	NA	NA
Curr. Assets	62.5	46.3	42.2	39.6	NA	NA	NA	NA	NA	NA
Total Assets	74.8	53.0	49.2	45.3	NA	NA	NA	NA	NA	NA
Curr. Liab.	14.5	12.3	11.8	11.0	NA	NA	NA	NA	NA	NA
LT Debt	0.4	Nil	Nil	Nil	NA	NA	NA	NA	NA	NA
Common Eqty.	56.7	38.2	35.2	32.3	NA	NA	NA	NA	NA	NA
Total Cap.	59.9	40.2	36.7	33.8	NA	NA	NA	NA	NA	NA
Cap. Exp.	2.0	1.3	0.8	1.5	NA	NA	NA	NA	NA	NA
Cash Flow	14.3	7.3	0.1	6.2	NA	NA	NA	NA	NA	NA
Curr. Ratio	4.3	3.8	3.6	3.6	NA	NA	NA	NA	NA	NA
% LT Debt of Cap.	0.6	Nil	Nil	Nil	NA	NA	NA	NA	NA	NA
% Net Inc.of Revs.	10.0	5.9	NM	8.7	NA	NA	NA	NA	NA	NA
% Ret. on Assets	17.6	9.0	NM	NA	NA	NA	NA	NA	NA	NA
% Ret. on Equity	23.8	12.6	NM	NA	NA	NA	NA	NA	NA	NA

Data as orig reptd.; bef. results of disc opers/spec. items. Per share data adj. for stk. divs. Bold denotes diluted EPS (FASB 128)-prior periods restated. E-Estimated. NA-Not Available. NM-Not Meaningful. NR-Not Ranked.

Office—1200 Mount Kemble Ave., Morristown, NJ 07960. **Tel**—(973) 425-1200. **Website**—http://www.drte.com **Pres & CEO**—J. E. Bailye. **EVP & CFO**—G. T. Robson. **Dirs**—J. E. Bailye, B. M. Goldsmith, E. J. Kfoury, P. A. Margolis, J. H. Martinson, T. H. Osbourne. **Transfer Agent & Registrar**—Continental Stock Transfer & Trust Co., NYC. **Incorporated**—in New Jersey in 1987. **Empl**— 1,100. **S&P Analyst:** Stephen R. Biggar

Department 56

NYSE Symbol **DFS**

In S&P SmallCap 600

09-OCT-99

Industry:
Consumer (Jewelry, Novelties & Gifts)

Summary: DFS designs collectibles and other specialty giftware products sold through gift and home accessories retailers.

Quantitative Evaluations

Outlook (1 Lowest—5 Highest) • 5+

Fair Value • 46¾

Risk • Average

Earn./Div. Rank • NR

Technical Eval. • Bearish since 8/99

Rel. Strength Rank (1 Lowest—99 Highest) • 23

Insider Activity • NA

Recent Price • 23½

52 Wk Range • 37⅞-22⅞

Yield • Nil

12-Mo. P/E • 9.8

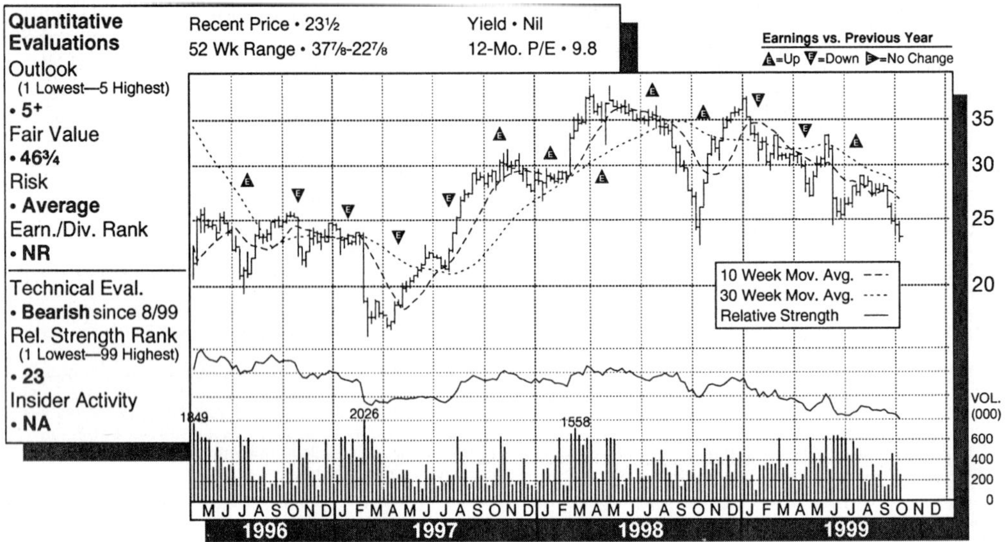

Business Profile - 01-SEP-99

In July 1999, DFS said that through the second quarter, customer orders rose about 3%, to $230 million from $224 million a year earlier. Management was encouraged by the strong demand for its core Village products, including its new Seasons Bay and Monopoly lines, its first new continuity gift lines in five years. It expects sales and earnings for 1999 to be higher than than those of 1998. In 1999's second quarter, DFS repurchased 617,000 common shares at an average price of $29 per share under its share repurchase program. Since the end of the quarter through July 27, 1999, it repurchased another 301,000 shares at an average price of $27 each, bringing the total number of shares repurchased since the start of 1999 to 1.0 million shares. .

Operational Review - 01-SEP-99

Net sales for the 26 weeks ended July 2, 1999, fell 2.2%, year to year, mainly due to delays resulting from the integration of the new computer system. Profitability was penalized by the reduced sales volume. an increase in showroom expenses, higher amortization, and greater marketing and distribution expenses. After taxes at 38.0%, versus 39.5%, net income dropped 10%, to $22,082,000 ($1.22 a share, on 7.1% fewer shares), from $24,609,000 ($1.26).

Stock Performance - 08-OCT-99

In the past 30 trading days, DFS's shares have declined 15%, compared to a 0.91% fall in the S&P 500. Average trading volume for the past five days was 49,880 shares, compared with the 40-day moving average of 56,141 shares.

Key Stock Statistics

Dividend Rate/Share	Nil	Shareholders	913
Shs. outstg. (M)	17.4	Market cap. (B)	$0.409
Avg. daily vol. (M)	0.061	Inst. holdings	89%
Tang. Bk. Value/Share	1.48		
Beta	0.40		

Value of $10,000 invested 5 years ago: $ 8,726

Fiscal Year Ending Dec. 31

	1999	1998	1997	1996	1995	1994
Revenues (Million $)						
1Q	33.65	49.03	45.73	59.00	53.05	45.50
2Q	82.72	69.92	58.56	75.28	74.76	64.42
3Q	—	71.51	61.60	60.21	77.03	66.37
4Q	—	52.91	53.60	34.29	47.21	41.60
Yr.	—	243.4	219.5	228.8	252.1	217.9
Earnings Per Share ($)						
1Q	**0.18**	**0.47**	**0.40**	**0.56**	0.46	0.33
2Q	**1.04**	**0.80**	**0.59**	**0.79**	0.73	0.56
3Q	—	**0.81**	**0.63**	**0.57**	0.84	0.59
4Q	—	**0.38**	**0.42**	**0.19**	0.25	0.19
Yr.	—	**2.45**	**2.05**	**2.11**	**2.28**	1.67

Next earnings report expected: late October

Dividend Data

The company has said it does not expect to pay cash dividends in the foreseeable future. A shareholder rights plan was adopted in April 1997.

Department 56, Inc.

Business Summary - 01-SEP-99

Best known for its Village Series of collectible, handcrafted ceramic and porcelain houses, Department 56, Inc. (DFS) is a leading designer, importer and distributor of fine-quality collectibles and other specialty giftware products sold through gift, home accessory and specialty retailers. The company is also known for its extensive line of holiday and home decorative accessories, including its Snowbabies collectible porcelain and pewter handpainted figurines.

The company's Village Series products consist of several series of collectible, handcrafted lit ceramic and porcelain houses, buildings and related accessories that depict nostalgic winter scenes. DFS introduces new lit pieces, limited edition pieces, figurines and other accessories each year to complement the collections. To allow for these new introductions and keep each series appropriately balanced, the company has traditionally retired a number of existing pieces from production each year. The decision to retire a product is based on management's judgement of consumer demand, whether a piece continues to fit the evolving design characteristics of a series, manufacturing considerations and other marketing factors.

Village Series products consist of two broad collections: The Original Snow Village Collection, and The Heritage Village Collection. The Original Snow Village Collection consists of lit ceramic houses and accessories designed around a single "Main Street U.S.A." theme. The Heritage Village Collection consists of porcelain houses and accessories designed around several different village themes.

Village accessories, including figurines, vehicles and other decorative items, are also sold to collectors, allowing them to refresh their collections by changing displays and creating personalized settings. A wide range of other decorative giftware is also offered, including Snowbabies and Snowbunnies figurines, Christmas, Easter, and non-seasonal decorative items, tableware, decorative tins, acrylics, gift bags, "teddy bears" and other "plush" items.

DFS's principal customers are about 20,000 independent gift retailers (accounting for about 90% of sales) across the U.S., including about 1,500 independently owned Gold Key and Showcase Dealers. About 10% of DFS sales are made to department stores and mail-order houses.

As part of the company's strategy of selective distribution, only about 5,900 retailers receive the Village Series and/or Snowbabies products. Some of DFS's Village Series products and porcelain Snowbabies figurines have been sold on allocation for each of the last 11 and eight years, respectively. The company periodically evaluates and adjusts its distribution network, and reviews its policies with a view of optimizing both its distribution strategy and the store-level operations of its independent dealers.

Per Share Data ($) (Year Ended Dec. 31)	1998	1997	1996	1995	1994	1993	1992	1991	1990	1989
Tangible Bk. Val.	1.18	1.27	1.54	NM	-3.37	-5.42	-6.62	NA	NA	NA
Cash Flow	2.84	2.36	2.40	2.56	1.94	1.42	0.96	NA	NA	NA
Earnings	2.45	2.05	2.11	2.28	1.67	1.16	0.70	NA	NA	NA
Dividends	Nil	Nil	Nil	Nil	Nil	Nil	NA	NA	NA	NA
Payout Ratio	Nil	Nil	Nil	Nil	Nil	Nil	NA	NA	NA	NA
Prices - High	$39\frac{1}{4}$	$31\frac{3}{4}$	$41\frac{7}{8}$	48	40	$29\frac{7}{8}$	NA	NA	NA	NA
- Low	$22\frac{7}{8}$	$16\frac{7}{8}$	$19\frac{1}{2}$	$32\frac{5}{8}$	26	18	NA	NA	NA	NA
P/E Ratio - High	16	15	20	21	24	26	NA	NA	NA	NA
- Low	9	8	9	14	16	16	NA	NA	NA	NA
Income Statement Analysis (Million $)										
Revs.	243	219	229	252	218	184	151	NA	NA	NA
Oper. Inc.	88.3	77.3	87.0	95.8	78.9	63.4	47.2	NA	NA	NA
Depr.	7.3	6.6	6.3	6.2	5.9	5.6	5.6	NA	NA	NA
Int. Exp.	4.8	4.4	6.1	9.6	12.6	16.1	16.3	NA	NA	NA
Pretax Inc.	76.6	70.7	75.7	83.3	61.2	42.7	26.3	NA	NA	NA
Eff. Tax Rate	39%	40%	39%	41%	41%	41%	42%	NA	NA	NA
Net Inc.	46.5	42.8	45.9	49.6	36.1	25.0	15.2	NA	NA	NA
Balance Sheet & Other Fin. Data (Million $)										
Cash	2.8	37.4	46.4	7.8	2.2	7.4	48.2	NA	NA	NA
Curr. Assets	57.9	87.7	109	77.7	52.4	44.6	80.2	NA	NA	NA
Total Assets	233	260	286	259	240	235	275	NA	NA	NA
Curr. Liab.	28.6	46.9	41.3	41.7	39.0	18.2	18.3	NA	NA	NA
LT Debt	20.0	20.0	40.0	60.0	93.0	148	213	NA	NA	NA
Common Eqty.	179	187	197	150	100	61.7	37.2	NA	NA	NA
Total Cap.	205	213	244	217	201	217	257	NA	NA	NA
Cap. Exp.	NA	7.8	1.5	1.6	2.6	1.3	NA	NA	NA	NA
Cash Flow	53.8	49.4	52.2	55.8	42.0	30.6	20.8	NA	NA	NA
Curr. Ratio	2.0	1.9	2.6	1.9	1.3	2.5	4.4	NA	NA	NA
% LT Debt of Cap.	9.8	9.4	16.4	27.6	46.3	68.3	82.9	NA	NA	NA
% Net Inc.of Revs.	19.1	19.5	20.1	19.7	16.6	13.6	10.1	NA	NA	NA
% Ret. on Assets	18.9	15.7	16.9	19.9	15.2	0.1	NA	NA	NA	NA
% Ret. on Equity	25.5	22.3	26.5	39.6	44.5	0.4	NA	NA	NA	NA

Data as orig reptd.; bef. results of disc opers/spec. items. Per share data adj. for stk. divs. Bold denotes diluted EPS (FASB 128)-prior periods restated. E-Estimated. NA-Not Available. NM-Not Meaningful. NR-Not Ranked.

Office—One Village Place, 6436 City West Parkway, Eden Prairie, MN 55344. **Tel**—(612) 944-5600. **Website**—http://www.department56.com. **Chrmn & CEO**—S. E. Engel. **SVP & CFO**—P. C. Tomlinson Jr.**SVP & Secy**—D. H. Weiser. **VP-Fin**— T. J. Schugel. **Dirs**—J. Chiat, M. Clark, S. Engel, W. B. Little, G. S. Mathews, S. G. Rothmeier, V. Weber. **Transfer Agent & Registrar**—ChaseMellon Shareholder Services, NYC. **Incorporated**—in Delaware in 1992. **Empl**— 268. **S&P Analyst:** Matthew C. Hershberg

DeVry Inc.

NYSE Symbol **DV**

In S&P SmallCap 600

09-OCT-99

Industry: Services (Commercial & Consumer)

Summary: DeVry owns and operates the DeVry Institutes, the Keller Graduate School of Management, Corporate Educational Services, and Becker CPA Review.

Quantitative Evaluations

Outlook (1 Lowest—5 Highest) • **4**

Fair Value • **27½**

Risk • **Average**

Earn./Div. Rank • **B**

Technical Eval. • **Bearish** since 9/99

Rel. Strength Rank (1 Lowest—99 Highest) • **15**

Insider Activity • **Neutral**

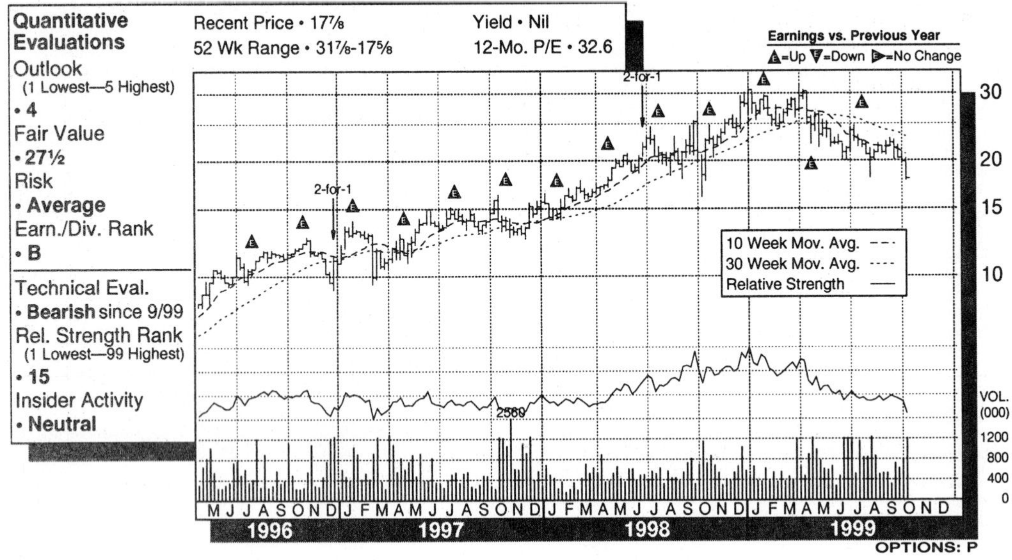

Business Profile - 10-AUG-99

The summer of 1999 marked the 26th consecutive term of year to year increases in student enrollment. In July 1999, DV acquired Denver Technical College (DTC), the first acquisition for the DeVry Institutes division. DTC, which has more than 1,700 students, offers undergraduate and graduate degree programs. Also in July, Becker CPA review acquired Conviser Duffy CPA Review, which serves 12,000 students annually, at more than 200 locations. Both the DTC and Conviser acquisitions are expected to be accretive to earnings. DV's third Los Angeles-area school will open in the fall of 1999, and its third Chicago-area campus will open in the summer of 2000. In 1998, DV established seven new DeVry and Keller Graduate School sites, and also acquired Fox Geanty CPA Review.

Operational Review - 10-AUG-99

Based on a preliminary report, revenues advanced 19% in the fiscal year ended June 30, 1999, on greater student enrollments, and the opening of new DeVry Institute campuses and new Keller Graduate School of Management centers. Results benefited from the greater volume; net income climbed 26%, to $38.8 million ($0.55 a share), from $30.7 million ($0.44, as adjusted).

Stock Performance - 08-OCT-99

In the past 30 trading days, DV's shares have declined 15%, compared to a 0.91% fall in the S&P 500. Average trading volume for the past five days was 251,320 shares, compared with the 40-day moving average of 133,741 shares.

Key Stock Statistics

Dividend Rate/Share	Nil	Shareholders	571
Shs. outstg. (M)	69.4	Market cap. (B)	$ 1.2
Avg. daily vol. (M)	0.168	Inst. holdings	69%
Tang. Bk. Value/Share	1.42		
Beta	1.14		

Value of $10,000 invested 5 years ago: $ 51,248

Fiscal Year Ending Jun. 30

	1999	1998	1997	1996	1995	1994
Revenues (Million $)						
1Q	93.86	80.42	69.25	59.84	51.96	49.75
2Q	107.8	90.34	81.26	66.94	59.30	55.00
3Q	110.2	92.85	81.13	68.41	59.74	55.13
4Q	108.7	89.85	76.68	64.82	57.60	51.55
Yr.	420.6	353.5	308.3	260.0	228.6	211.4
Earnings Per Share ($)						
1Q	**0.11**	**0.09**	**0.07**	0.06	0.05	0.04
2Q	**0.15**	**0.12**	**0.10**	0.08	0.07	0.06
3Q	**0.15**	**0.12**	**0.10**	0.08	0.06	0.05
4Q	**0.14**	**0.11**	**0.09**	0.07	0.05	0.04
Yr.	**0.55**	**0.44**	**0.35**	**0.29**	0.22	0.18

Next earnings report expected: mid October

Dividend Data

No cash dividends have been paid. A two-for-one common stock split was effected in June 1998.

DeVry Inc.

Business Summary - 10-AUG-99

DeVry Inc. is capitalizing on a continuing increase in the number of people seeking higher education. The company, one of the leading private-sector higher education providers through its DeVry Institutes and Keller Graduate School of Management, has benefited from a number of trends, including a widely held belief that a high school education is no longer sufficient preparation for the modern job market. Today's student population is older, and has a unique set of needs, including increased scheduling convenience, affordability, and the availability of more career-oriented courses.

A key element of DV's strategy is providing much sought after technology-based training. Over the past two decades, corporate America has been restructuring work to improve quality, productivity and profitability by investing heavily in new computer, network and telecommunications technologies. The company believes each year of formal schooling after high school can add from 5% to 25% to annual earnings. Moreover, holders of technology-oriented degrees, such as engineering and computer science degrees, can earn some of the highest salaries.

The company expects changing demographics to continue to benefit the DeVry Institutes' future enrollment. After a period of nearly two decades during which the number of graduating high school seniors declined 25%, to 2.4 million, 1995 marked the beginning of a rise in the number of high school graduates. The National Center for Education Statistics forecasts an increase to 3.1 million graduates by 2005, rivaling the peak of 3.1 million in the late 1970s. DV believes these statistics will translate into an increase in potential DeVry Institute students.

Founded in 1931, DeVry Institutes operates 12 campuses in the U.S. and three in Canada. For the 1998 summer semester, enrollment totaled more than 33,088 full and part-time students, up 12.1%, year to year. DeVry Institutes offer associate and bachelors degree programs in electronics, engineering, computer information systems, telecommunications, accounting, business administration and technical management. DeVry Institutes operations accounted for 87% of company revenues in FY 98 (Jun.).

The Keller Graduate School of Management offers graduate degrees in business administration and project and human resource management. More than 3,857 students registered for the 1998 summer semester, up 23% from the 1997 level.

In 1996, DV acquired Becker CPA Review, the leading international training firm preparing students to take the Certified Public Accountant exam. More than one-third of all students passing the CPA exam are Becker students at one of the 190 class locations worldwide. Becker CPA Review alumni now number more than 200,000 since the course was founded in 1957.

Per Share Data ($)										
(Year Ended Jun. 30)	1999	1998	1997	1996	1995	1994	1993	1992	1991	1990
Tangible Bk. Val.	NA	1.42	0.98	0.29	0.54	0.32	0.13	-0.02	-0.44	-7.20
Cash Flow	NA	0.64	0.52	0.40	0.32	0.29	0.24	0.20	0.52	1.45
Earnings	0.55	0.44	0.35	0.28	0.22	0.18	0.14	0.09	-0.35	-0.64
Dividends	Nil	Nil	Nil	Nil	Nil	Nil	Nil	Nil	Nil	NA
Payout Ratio	Nil	Nil	Nil	Nil	Nil	Nil	Nil	Nil	Nil	NA
Prices - High	31 7/8	30 5/8	16 1/2	12 3/4	7	4 1/4	3 3/4	2 3/4	2 1/16	NA
- Low	17 3/4	14	9 1/2	6 1/2	3 7/8	3	2 7/16	1 11/16	1 1/8	NA
P/E Ratio - High	58	70	46	44	32	23	26	29	NM	NA
- Low	32	32	27	23	17	16	17	18	NM	NA
Income Statement Analysis (Million $)										
Revs.	NA	352	307	259	227	211	192	179	162	156
Oper. Inc.	NA	63.8	53.0	40.3	33.8	32.1	28.8	28.3	25.9	27.7
Depr.	NA	14.0	11.3	7.6	6.2	7.1	6.7	7.1	8.6	19.2
Int. Exp.	NA	0.9	2.9	1.1	3.1	4.6	6.8	9.7	13.8	16.0
Pretax Inc.	NA	50.5	39.9	32.7	25.8	21.0	15.6	9.9	-3.7	-6.3
Eff. Tax Rate	NA	39%	39%	41%	42%	42%	40%	40%	NM	NM
Net Inc.	NA	30.7	24.2	19.2	14.9	12.2	9.4	5.9	-3.5	-5.9
Balance Sheet & Other Fin. Data (Million $)										
Cash	NA	48.8	51.0	46.5	46.4	33.8	22.9	25.4	20.5	18.4
Curr. Assets	NA	69.7	70.5	61.6	58.0	48.9	37.7	42.9	32.3	30.8
Total Assets	NA	224	207	178	127	107	99	112	96.0	109
Curr. Liab.	NA	66.0	58.3	52.5	48.9	40.2	44.4	41.6	34.5	37.0
LT Debt	NA	10.0	33.0	61.5	33.0	40.0	42.0	67.0	83.0	112
Common Eqty.	NA	136	105	57.3	38.0	23.0	11.0	1.3	-23.1	-53.0
Total Cap.	NA	150	141	121	71.0	62.9	53.5	70.2	60.7	71.6
Cap. Exp.	NA	31.8	28.8	18.4	14.6	6.3	5.1	3.9	2.1	2.3
Cash Flow	NA	44.7	35.4	26.8	21.1	19.3	16.2	13.0	5.1	13.3
Curr. Ratio	NA	1.1	1.2	1.2	1.2	1.2	0.8	1.0	0.9	0.8
% LT Debt of Cap.	NA	6.7	23.3	50.8	46.5	63.1	79.4	95.8	137.3	156.9
% Net Inc.of Revs.	NA	8.7	7.9	7.4	6.6	5.8	4.9	3.3	NM	NM
% Ret. on Assets	NA	14.3	12.6	12.6	11.8	11.9	8.8	5.4	NM	NM
% Ret. on Equity	NA	25.4	29.8	40.4	48.9	71.9	152.5	NM	NM	NM

Data as orig reptd.; bef. results of disc opers/spec. items. Per share data adj. for stk. divs. Bold denotes diluted EPS (FASB 128)-prior periods restated. E-Estimated. NA-Not Available. NM-Not Meaningful. NR-Not Ranked.

Office—One Tower Lane,Suite 1000, Oakbrook Terrace, IL 60181-4624. **Tel**—(630) 571-7700. **Website**—http://www.devry.com **Chrmn & CEO**—D. J. Keller. **Pres & COO**—R. L. Taylor. **VP-Fin, CFO & Contr**—N. M. Levine. **SVP & Secy**—M. J. Cason. **Investor Contact**—Diane Salucci (630-574-1931). **Dirs**—E. M. Akin, C. A. Bowsher, D. S. Brown, A. I. Gannon, D. J. Keller, R. E. King, F.A. Krehbiel, T. E. Manning, R. C. McCormack, J. A. McGee, H. J. Melvoin, R. L. Taylor. **Transfer Agent**—Harris Trust & Savings Bank, Chicago. **Incorporated**—in Delaware in 1987. **Empl**— 2,850. **S&P Analyst:** Jordan Horoschak

STANDARD
&POOR'S
STOCK REPORTS

Diagnostic Products

NYSE Symbol **DP**

In S&P SmallCap 600

09-OCT-99

Industry:
Health Care (Medical Products & Supplies)

Summary: This company is the world's leading independent producer of immunodiagnostic test kits and related instrumentation.

Quantitative Evaluations
Outlook
(1 Lowest—5 Highest)
• **4**
Fair Value
• **42¼**
Risk
• **Average**
Earn./Div. Rank
• **B+**

Technical Eval.
• **Bearish** since 9/99
Rel. Strength Rank
(1 Lowest—99 Highest)
• **79**
Insider Activity
• **Neutral**

Recent Price • 27⅞
52 Wk Range • 35¼-20⅜
Yield • 1.7%
12-Mo. P/E • 18.8

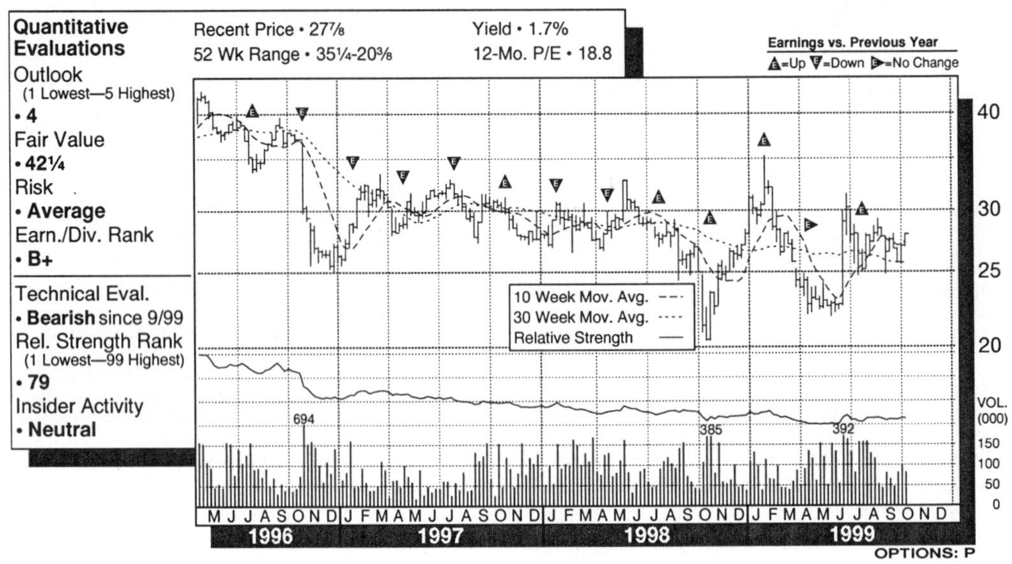

Business Profile - 13-SEP-99

Sales of the company's IMMULITE automated immunoassay systems increased 20% in the 1999 first half, reaching $16.1 million. DP shipped 216 IMMULITE systems in the second quarter, bringing the total number of IMMULITE systems shipped worldwide to about 4,400. Sales of IMMULITE assays and instruments accounted for 67% of 1999 sales through June 30. As expected, radioimmunoassay (RIA) business continued to decrease, with RIA sales accounting for under 20% of total revenues through the 1999 first half. With 9.9% of first quarter RIA sales to Brazil, the recent currency devaluation in Brazil resulted in an after-tax foreign exchange loss of $0.03 a share. The company continues to experience solid growth in IMMULITE reagent sales.

Operational Review - 13-SEP-99

Net sales in the six months ended June 30, 1999, rose 10%, year to year, as higher IMMULITE system sales outweighed lower RIA product sales. Gross margins narrowed, reflecting a less favorable product mix. Selling expenses rose less rapidly than revenues, but general and administrative expenses increased 12%, in part due to a $536,000 ($0.03 a share) pretax foreign exchange loss; pretax income was up 2.6%. After taxes at 29.1%, versus 29.6%, net income rose 3.4%, to $9,612,000 ($0.70 a share), from $9,298,000 ($0.67).

Stock Performance - 08-OCT-99

In the past 30 trading days, DP's shares have increased 0.67%, compared to a 0.91% fall in the S&P 500. Average trading volume for the past five days was 16,220 shares, compared with the 40-day moving average of 13,969 shares.

Key Stock Statistics

Dividend Rate/Share	0.48	Shareholders	428
Shs. outstg. (M)	13.7	Market cap. (B)	$0.382
Avg. daily vol. (M)	0.015	Inst. holdings	33%
Tang. Bk. Value/Share	13.55		
Beta	0.61		

Value of $10,000 invested 5 years ago: $ 16,495

Fiscal Year Ending Dec. 31

	1999	1998	1997	1996	1995	1994
Revenues (Million $)						
1Q	50.47	46.10	44.40	43.25	39.20	27.77
2Q	54.59	49.28	46.76	43.37	38.53	30.13
3Q	—	48.77	46.40	43.36	40.53	30.64
4Q	—	52.49	48.70	46.86	41.38	37.91
Yr.	—	196.6	186.3	176.8	159.7	126.5
Earnings Per Share ($)						
1Q	**0.30**	**0.30**	**0.34**	**0.47**	0.42	0.26
2Q	**0.40**	**0.37**	**0.35**	**0.47**	0.44	0.29
3Q	—	**0.39**	**0.37**	**0.31**	0.43	0.32
4Q	—	**0.40**	**0.26**	**0.40**	0.46	0.37
Yr.	—	**1.46**	**1.32**	**1.65**	**1.75**	**1.20**

Next earnings report expected: late October

Dividend Data (Dividends have been paid since 1988.)

Amount ($)	Date Decl.	Ex-Div. Date	Stock of Record	Payment Date
0.120	Jan. 04	Feb. 01	Feb. 03	Feb. 17 '99
0.120	Apr. 02	May. 03	May. 05	May. 19 '99
0.120	Jul. 01	Aug. 02	Aug. 04	Aug. 18 '99
0.120	Oct. 01	Nov. 01	Nov. 03	Nov. 17 '99

Business Summary - 13-SEP-99

Since its founding in 1971, Diagnostic Products (DP) has become the world's leading developer, producer and seller of medical immunodiagnostic test kits and related instrumentation that use state-of-the-art technology derived from immunology and molecular biology. Immulite assays and instruments provided 64% and 54% of sales in 1998 and 1997, respectively, and the company expects the percentage to continue to rise.

DP's kits are used by hospitals, clinical, veterinary, research and forensic laboratories, and doctors' offices to obtain precise and rapid identification and measurement of hormones, drugs, viruses, bacteria and other substances present in body fluids and tissues at infinitesimal concentrations.

Principal clinical applications of the company's more than 400 assays are for diagnosis of thyroid conditions and anemia; testing for pregnancy, fertility and fetal well-being; management of diabetes and certain types of cancer; drug abuse testing; rapid diagnosis of infectious diseases (including sexually transmitted diseases); allergy testing; and diagnosis of disorders due to hormone and steroid imbalances. DP believes it is the market leader in fertility testing, with the most comprehensive line of kits currently available. Its kits are used for in-vitro (outside the body) testing, typically in a test tube.

With the 1992 acquisition of Cirrus Diagnostics Inc., DP entered the market for fully automated, non-isotopic diagnostic instrumentation systems, the fastest growing segment of the immunoassay market. The IMMULITE system, developed by Cirrus, is a fully automated, random-access instrument that performs immunoassays using chemiluminescent technology, and can process up to 120 samples per hour.

As of December 31, 1998, the company had 85 IMMULITE assays available in the international markets, including 53 approved by the FDA for U.S. marketing. DP has focused on offering the most complete panel of tests for specific disease states, including thyroid, fertility and cancer testing. Since its introduction in 1992, more than 4,000 IMMULITE systems were shipped through March 31, 1999.

Prior to 1992, DP concentrated on radioimmunoassay (RIA), which utilizes radioisotopes to achieve high levels of test specificity and sensitivity. RIA tests are labor intensive and must be performed by skilled technicians. In the 1980s, the immunodiagnostic market began to shift away from RIA, reflecting concerns regarding the disposal of radioactive materials used in RIA tests and demand for labor-saving, automated immunodiagnostic systems that use nonisotopic tests. As a result, sales of RIA products have decreased from over 50% of sales in 1995 to 22% in 1998.

In the 1998 first quarter, DP began shipping the IMMULITE 2000, a high speed continuous random access analyzer with a throughput of up to 200 tests per hour, as well as advanced features such as primary tube sampling and proprietary auto-dilution capability.

Per Share Data ($) (Year Ended Dec. 31)	1998	1997	1996	1995	1994	1993	1992	1991	1990	1989
Tangible Bk. Val.	13.62	12.56	12.32	10.87	9.36	8.30	7.92	7.38	6.51	5.40
Cash Flow	2.85	2.42	2.69	1.49	1.67	1.35	1.60	1.79	1.64	1.42
Earnings	1.46	1.32	1.65	1.75	1.24	1.04	1.26	1.49	1.35	1.20
Dividends	0.48	0.48	0.48	0.46	0.40	0.30	0.32	0.32	0.24	0.20
Payout Ratio	33%	36%	29%	26%	32%	29%	24%	20%	17%	16%
Prices - High	32 7/8	33 1/2	42 7/8	44 7/8	26 5/8	30 3/4	44	53 3/4	44	38
- Low	20 3/8	25 1/2	25	24 1/4	17 3/4	17 1/8	20 1/8	28 1/4	22 1/4	19 1/4
P/E Ratio - High	23	25	26	26	21	30	35	36	33	32
- Low	14	19	15	14	14	16	16	19	16	16
Income Statement Analysis (Million $)										
Revs.	197	186	177	160	126	107	103	90.1	75.9	60.3
Oper. Inc.	46.0	39.0	43.1	35.0	26.3	22.3	26.6	26.2	23.1	20.1
Depr.	19.4	15.3	14.4	6.1	5.9	4.2	4.7	4.0	3.8	2.7
Int. Exp.	Nil	Nil	Nil	Nil	Nil	Nil	Nil	Nil	Nil	Nil
Pretax Inc.	28.2	25.7	31.7	19.9	22.6	19.9	23.7	27.9	24.5	22.1
Eff. Tax Rate	28%	29%	28%	29%	26%	29%	27%	31%	30%	31%
Net Inc.	20.2	18.2	22.9	14.2	16.7	14.2	17.3	19.3	17.3	15.2
Balance Sheet & Other Fin. Data (Million $)										
Cash	18.6	20.4	13.8	16.5	14.8	12.9	22.7	30.2	24.3	20.3
Curr. Assets	127	119	106	96.6	78.3	68.9	70.3	76.3	64.3	53.4
Total Assets	246	222	207	189	153	137	134	131	102	84.0
Curr. Liab.	46.1	35.9	24.7	26.1	17.6	13.9	14.8	23.9	15.4	12.4
LT Debt	Nil	Nil	Nil	Nil	Nil	Nil	Nil	Nil	Nil	Nil
Common Eqty.	200	186	182	163	135	123	120	107	87.0	71.2
Total Cap.	200	186	182	163	135	123	120	107	87.0	71.2
Cap. Exp.	11.2	10.5	8.0	7.6	8.5	7.7	15.1	9.5	6.0	6.0
Cash Flow	39.6	33.5	37.4	20.3	22.6	18.4	22.0	23.3	21.1	17.9
Curr. Ratio	2.8	3.3	4.3	3.7	4.4	5.0	4.8	3.2	4.2	4.3
% LT Debt of Cap.	Nil	Nil	Nil	Nil	Nil	Nil	Nil	Nil	Nil	Nil
% Net Inc.of Revs.	10.3	9.8	13.0	8.9	13.2	13.3	16.7	21.5	22.8	25.2
% Ret. on Assets	8.6	8.5	12.3	8.3	11.6	10.5	12.6	16.5	18.5	20.3
% Ret. on Equity	10.5	9.9	13.3	9.5	13.0	11.7	14.8	19.8	21.7	23.5

Data as orig reptd.; bef. results of disc opers/spec. items. Per share data adj. for stk. divs. Bold denotes diluted EPS (FASB 128)-prior periods restated. E-Estimated. NA-Not Available. NM-Not Meaningful. NR-Not Ranked.

Office—5700 W. 96th St., Los Angeles, CA 90045-5597. **Tel**—(310) 645-8200. **Website**—http://www.dpcweb.com **Chrmn & CEO** —M. H. Salter. **Pres & COO**—Michael Ziering. **VP-Fin & CFO**—J. Brill. **Secy**—Marilyn Ziering. **Dirs**—S. A. Aroesty, F. Frank, M. H. Salter, J. D. Watson, Michael Ziering, S. Ziering. **Transfer Agent & Registrar**—ChaseMellon Shaerholder Services, LA. **Incorporated**—in California in 1971. **Empl**— 1,601. **S&P Analyst:** John J. Arege

STANDARD
&POOR'S
STOCK REPORTS

Digi International

NASDAQ Symbol **DGII**

In S&P SmallCap 600

09-OCT-99

Industry:
Computers (Networking)

Summary: Digi is a leading producer of data communications hardware and software products that permit microcomputers to function as multiuser and networked computer systems.

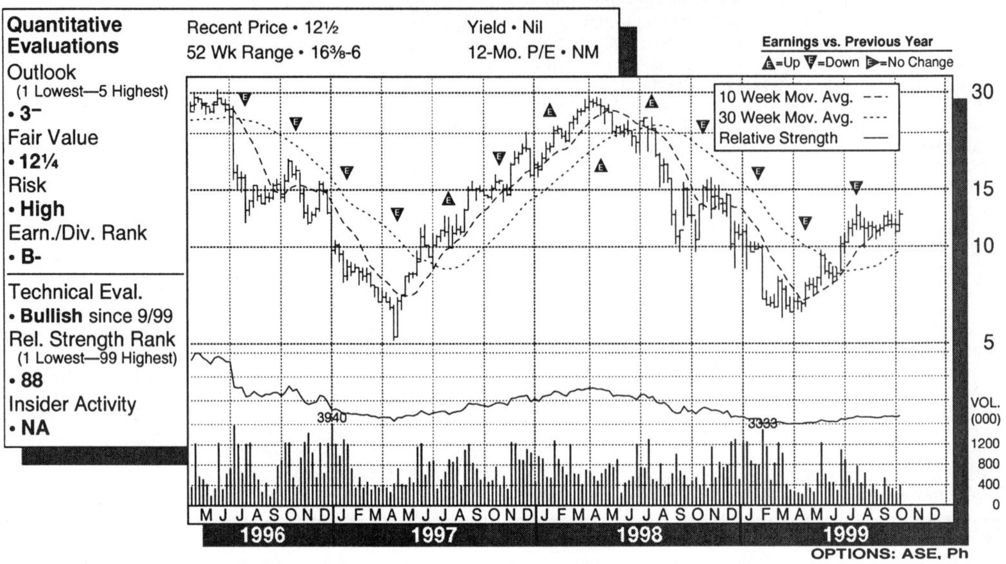

Business Profile - 27-JUL-99

In response to comments by the SEC regarding Digi's acquisition of ITK International and Central Data Corp., the company elected to restate its financial statements to reduce the amount allocated to in-process R&D from $39.2 million to $16.1 million. As a result, the amount allocated to intangible assets and goodwill increased by $23.1 million. This amount will be amortized over the next five to seven years. In the second quarter of FY 99 (Sep.), the company discontinued several modem products, wrote down inventories, reorganized its sales organization, and instituted a channel inventory management program. The company hopes to increase profitability through revenue growth while maintaining controls on operating expenses.

Operational Review - 27-JUL-99

In the first nine months of FY 99 (Sep). as restated for change in treatment of in-process R&D charges, revenues advanced 8.3%, year to year, reflecting acquisitions, partly offset by reduced physical layer product sales and lower sales to distribution markets. Gross margins narrowed due to a less favorable product mix. Results were adversely affected by sharply higher SG&A expenses and R&D costs, increased depreciation and amortization charges, and a $1.5 million restructuring charge. Net income declined 97%, to $481,147 ($0.03 a share, based on 3.9% more shares) from $14,918,582 ($1.05).

Stock Performance - 08-OCT-99

In the past 30 trading days, DGII's shares have increased 13%, compared to a 0.91% fall in the S&P 500. Average trading volume for the past five days was 76,720 shares, compared with the 40-day moving average of 69,923 shares.

Key Stock Statistics

Dividend Rate/Share	Nil	Shareholders	8,900
Shs. outstg. (M)	14.9	Market cap. (B)	$0.187
Avg. daily vol. (M)	0.065	Inst. holdings	36%
Tang. Bk. Value/Share	4.86		
Beta	1.68		

Value of $10,000 invested 5 years ago: $ 5,645

Fiscal Year Ending Sep. 30

	1999	1998	1997	1996	1995	1994
Revenues (Million $)						
1Q	51.40	42.59	42.24	43.87	37.88	25.99
2Q	42.63	45.06	40.39	48.50	40.08	31.65
3Q	51.15	46.45	40.84	50.32	41.18	35.19
4Q	—	48.83	42.13	53.15	45.84	38.12
Yr.	—	182.9	165.6	195.8	165.0	130.9
Earnings Per Share ($)						
1Q	**0.09**	**0.27**	-0.19	0.33	0.32	0.28
2Q	**-0.17**	**0.33**	-0.70	0.34	0.33	0.28
3Q	**0.15**	**0.45**	0.01	Nil	0.35	0.29
4Q	—	**-2.62**	-0.29	0.02	0.38	0.31
Yr.	—	**-1.65**	**-1.18**	**0.68**	1.38	1.15

Next earnings report expected: mid November

Dividend Data

No cash dividends have been paid. A two-for-one stock split was effected in 1991 and a three-for-two stock split was effected in 1992.

Digi International Inc.

Business Summary - 27-JUL-99

Formed in 1985, Digi International Inc. (DGII) is a leading producer of data communications hardware and software products that deliver connectivity solutions for multiuser environments, remote access markets (LAN and WAN) and the LAN connect market. Minnesota-based DGII believes it is the market leader in the multiuser segment of the computer industry and in the server centric portion of the remote access market.

DGII's communications interface cards (80% of FY 98 (Sep.) sales) are used for multiuser and remote access environments. The core multiport access products connect terminals, PCs running on terminal emulation software and other serial devices to a PC-based host. These products can be used for point-of-sale applications, on-line transaction processing, factory automation, dial-in/dial-out connections and data dissemination. In addition, DGII's server-based remote access products address the need for high-performance, dial-in/dial-out connections for wide area networking, including accessing the Internet. These products connect telecommuters, mobile workers and branch offices to corporate LANs, or branch offices to other branches, and are also used to make connections to the Internet.

DGII entered the LAN connect market with the 1993 acquisition of MiLAN Technology Corp. DGII's LAN connect group provides Ethernet, Fast Ethernet Gigabit Ethernet and ATM networking products.

In July 1998, the company entered the Internet telephony market with the acquisition of ITK International for 615,000 common shares and $12.5 million in cash. ITK products incorporate Voice over Internet Protocol (VoIP) technology, which converts voice signals to TCP/IP packets and routes them over IP networks such as the Internet and company intranets. ITK's VoIP technology is still under development.

Also in July 1998, the company expanded its product line through the acquisition of Central Data Corp., a provider of remote access solutions, for 220,000 common shares and $13.5 million in cash. In connection with both the ITK and Central Data acquisitions, a $39.2 million charge was taken in the fourth quarter of FY 98 for acquired in-process research and development.

Digi markets its products to a broad range of customers, including major domestic and international distributors, system integrators, value-added resellers, and original equipment manufacturers (OEMs). Products are sold through a network of more than 185 distributors in the U.S., Canada and 65 countries worldwide, as well as through OEM contracts. International customers, mainly in Europe, accounted for 21% of net sales in FY 98 and 24% of net sales in FY 97. In FY 98, Ingram Micro and Tech Data accounted for 16% and 14% of net sales, respectively.

Per Share Data ($) (Year Ended Sep. 30)	1998	1997	1996	1995	1994	1993	1992	1991	1990	1989
Tangible Bk. Val.	4.36	6.58	7.43	6.96	6.64	5.68	4.62	3.77	1.72	0.70
Cash Flow	-1.09	-0.68	1.16	1.62	1.25	1.14	0.94	0.75	0.44	0.33
Earnings	-1.65	-1.18	0.69	1.38	1.15	1.02	0.82	0.65	0.41	0.31
Dividends	Nil	Nil	Nil	Nil	Nil	Nil	Nil	Nil	Nil	Nil
Payout Ratio	Nil	Nil	Nil	Nil	Nil	Nil	Nil	Nil	Nil	Nil
Prices - High	29½	22¾	30¾	30¼	22½	26¼	24¼	20½	7⅜	3⅞
- Low	8½	5⅛	8⅝	17⅛	11¼	16	11	5⅞	2⅞	3
P/E Ratio - High	NM	NM	45	22	20	26	30	32	18	13
- Low	NM	NM	12	12	10	16	13	9	7	9
Income Statement Analysis (Million $)										
Revs.	183	166	196	165	131	93.4	57.8	40.8	23.2	14.6
Oper. Inc.	31.9	12.8	26.4	30.8	25.8	23.1	16.7	12.3	6.8	4.2
Depr.	7.7	6.7	6.4	3.4	1.5	1.9	1.7	1.3	0.4	0.2
Int. Exp.	Nil	Nil	Nil	Nil	Nil	Nil	Nil	Nil	Nil	Nil
Pretax Inc.	-12.9	-15.7	16.8	29.4	25.4	22.5	16.6	11.9	7.4	4.2
Eff. Tax Rate	NM	NM	45%	34%	34%	34%	31%	33%	32%	32%
Net Inc.	-22.7	-15.8	9.3	19.3	16.7	14.8	11.4	8.0	5.0	2.8
Balance Sheet & Other Fin. Data (Million $)										
Cash	10.4	31.3	8.9	28.0	37.3	51.5	40.3	34.6	12.7	2.5
Curr. Assets	92.4	84.8	89.7	94.3	84.3	78.0	59.4	45.9	18.9	6.5
Total Assets	161	118	130	126	103	88.9	66.5	53.2	21.4	7.5
Curr. Liab.	54.5	22.8	20.0	20.2	11.6	8.4	4.0	2.4	1.0	1.6
LT Debt	Nil	Nil	Nil	Nil	Nil	Nil	Nil	Nil	Nil	Nil
Common Eqty.	94.8	95.5	110	106	91.1	80.5	62.5	50.9	20.4	5.8
Total Cap.	106	95.5	110	106	91.1	80.5	62.5	50.9	20.4	5.8
Cap. Exp.	5.8	8.8	12.9	9.6	3.9	4.2	1.2	2.2	0.7	0.5
Cash Flow	-14.9	-9.1	15.6	22.8	18.2	16.6	13.2	9.3	5.4	3.0
Curr. Ratio	1.7	3.7	4.5	4.7	7.2	9.3	15.0	19.5	18.5	4.0
% LT Debt of Cap.	10.5	Nil	Nil	Nil	Nil	Nil	Nil	Nil	Nil	Nil
% Net Inc.of Revs.	NM	NM	4.7	11.7	12.8	15.8	19.8	19.5	21.7	19.3
% Ret. on Assets	NM	NM	7.3	16.9	17.7	18.7	19.1	20.6	31.5	47.6
% Ret. on Equity	NM	NM	8.6	19.6	19.8	20.3	20.2	21.5	35.2	64.5

Data as orig reptd.; bef. results of disc opers/spec. items. Per share data adj. for stk. divs. Bold denotes diluted EPS (FASB 128)-prior periods restated. E-Estimated. NA-Not Available. NM-Not Meaningful. NR-Not Ranked.

Office—11001 Bren Rd. East, Minnetonka, MN 55344. **Tel**—(612) 912-3444. **Website**—http://www.dgii.com **Chrmn, Interim Pres & Interim CEO**—J. P. Schinas. **EVP & COO**—D. J. Glader. **SVP & CFO**—S. A. Wehrwein. **Secy**—J. E. Nicholson. **Dirs**—W. K. Drake, R. E. Eichhorn, R. S. Moe, M. Moroz, J. P. Schinas, D. Stanley. **Transfer Agent & Registrar**—Norwest Bank Minnesota, South St. Paul. **Incorporated**—in Delaware in 1989. **Empl**— 703. **S&P Analyst:** Jim Corridore

STANDARD
&POOR'S
STOCK REPORTS

Digital Microwave

NASDAQ Symbol **DMIC**

In S&P SmallCap 600

09-OCT-99

Industry: Communications Equipment

Summary: DMIC makes advanced, high-performance, short-haul digital microwave radio communication products.

Quantitative Evaluations

Outlook
(1 Lowest—5 Highest)
• **1⁻**

Fair Value
• **11⅞**

Risk
• **High**

Earn./Div. Rank
• **B**

Technical Eval.
• **Bullish** since 8/99

Rel. Strength Rank
(1 Lowest—99 Highest)
• **95**

Insider Activity
• **Unfavorable**

Recent Price • 17¼
52 Wk Range • 18⅛-2¾
Yield • Nil
12-Mo. P/E • NM

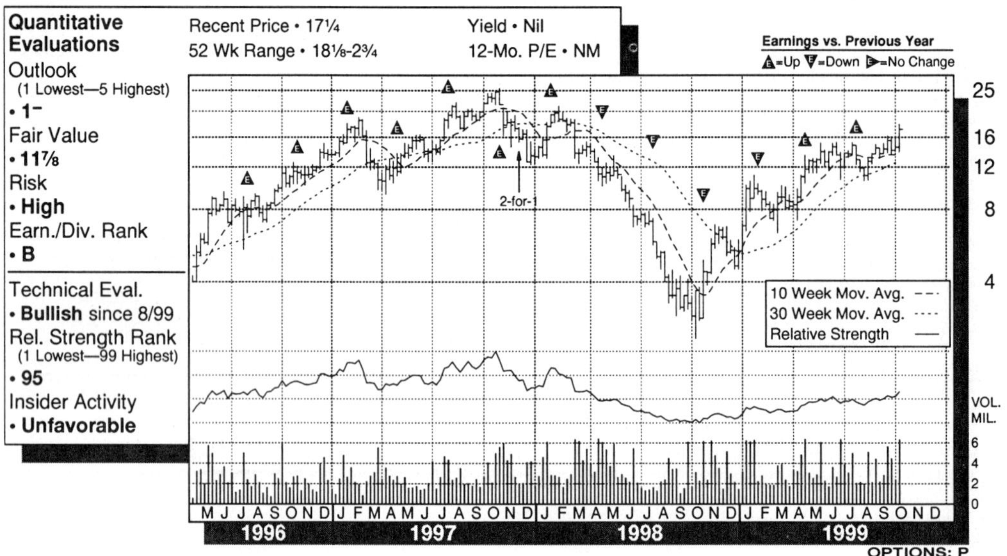

Business Profile - 23-JUL-99

During the first quarter of FY 00 (Mar.), the company received $67.8 million in new orders, up from $54.3 million in the year-earlier period. The backlog at June 30, 1999, was $65.7 million. In July 1999, DMIC received orders totaling $10.4 million from China United Telecommunications Corp. in the People's Republic of China. In October 1998, the company acquired Innova Corp., a provider of wireless products and services, for about 14.7 million common shares. DMIC incurred one-time restructuring charges of $67.7 million in FY 99, which contributed to a large net loss for the full year.

Operational Review - 23-JUL-99

Net sales for the three months ended June 30, 1999, rose 4.3%, year to year. Profit comparisons benefited from the absence of prior-year merger and restructuring charges of $7.2 million and from a 29% decrease in selling, general and administrative expenses. Net income of $160,000 (less than $0.01 a share, based on 11% more average shares) contrasted with a net loss of $15,482,000 ($0.25). Results for the FY 99 period were restated to reflect the pooling-of-interests acquisition of Innova Corp. on October 8, 1998.

Stock Performance - 08-OCT-99

In the past 30 trading days, DMIC's shares have increased 19%, compared to a 0.91% fall in the S&P 500. Average trading volume for the past five days was 1,898,740 shares, compared with the 40-day moving average of 852,105 shares.

Key Stock Statistics

Dividend Rate/Share	Nil	Shareholders	199
Shs. outstg. (M)	63.9	Market cap. (B)	$ 1.1
Avg. daily vol. (M)	1.091	Inst. holdings	63%
Tang. Bk. Value/Share	2.09		
Beta	2.64		

Value of $10,000 invested 5 years ago: $ 11,596

Fiscal Year Ending Mar. 31

	2000	1999	1998	1997	1996	1995
Revenues (Million $)						
1Q	65.95	53.00	56.73	36.81	39.69	34.28
2Q	—	49.61	67.11	41.53	41.79	37.09
3Q	—	58.28	71.95	47.76	32.70	48.92
4Q	—	59.73	81.87	52.25	36.24	33.36
Yr.	—	236.5	310.5	178.3	150.4	153.7
Earnings Per Share ($)						
1Q	Nil	**-0.30**	0.15	0.04	0.01	0.07
2Q	—	**-0.15**	0.18	0.07	0.01	0.09
3Q	—	**-1.09**	**0.22**	0.12	-0.21	0.10
4Q	—	**-0.04**	**-0.13**	0.13	0.01	-0.18
Yr.	—	**-1.57**	**0.42**	**0.35**	-0.20	0.07

Next earnings report expected: mid October

Dividend Data

A two-for-one common stock split was effected in November 1997.

A Division of The McGraw-Hill Companies

Digital Microwave Corporation

Business Summary - 23-JUL-99

A manufacturer of advanced wireless microwave radio communications products, Digital Microwave Corp. incurred one-time charges in FY 99 (Mar.) for staff reductions, facility consolidations, organizational restructuring, and charges related to the October 1998 acquisition of Innova Corp. These restructuring charges totaled $67.7 million and led to a net loss for FY 99 of $96.7 million ($1.57 a share). In response to the significant impact of the weak Asian economic climate in FY 99, the company focused on reducing expenses and initiated a proactive restructuring and acquisition strategy.

DMIC manufactures and markets advanced wireless solutions for worldwide telephone network interconnection and access. The company offers a broad line of products, operating using a variety of transmission frequencies (0.3 to 38 GigaHertz) and transmission capacities (64 Kilobits to 45 Megabits per second), allowing it to market and sell its products to service providers in many locations worldwide with varying interconnection and access requirements.

The company believes that it is well positioned to address the worldwide market for wireless infrastructure suppliers, and its current strategy calls for building on the strength of its current products, which offer point-to-point solutions, and its strong global sales, service and support organization to become a leading worldwide supplier of wireless network connectivity products. In particular, it believes that there are substantial telecommunications infrastructures being built for the first time in many Asian countries, infrastructures are being expanded in Europe, and personal communications services (PCS) interconnect networks are being constructed in the U.S.

The company intends to focus significant resources on product development to maintain competitiveness and support entry into new wireless opportunities including wireless data transport and alternative local telephone facilities access.

Products are marketed directly to service providers, which incorporate products into their telecommunications networks to deliver services directly to consumers, and through relationships with original equipment manufacturers, such as Motorola, Siemens and Northern Telecom, which provide and install integrated systems to service providers. The company has developed a global sales, service and support organization, with offices in North America, South America, Europe, the Middle East, Asia, Africa, New Zealand and Australia.

In October 1998, the company acquired Innova Corp., a provider of wireless products and services, for about 14.7 million common shares. The basis for this acquisition was Innova's low-cost technology for its low-to-medium capacity products and minimal overlap in the customer bases of the two companies.

Per Share Data ($)										
(Year Ended Mar. 31)	**1999**	**1998**	**1997**	**1996**	**1995**	**1994**	**1993**	**1992**	**1991**	**1990**
Tangible Bk. Val.	2.11	3.58	3.17	1.57	1.28	1.11	1.91	2.21	3.04	2.85
Cash Flow	-1.15	0.69	0.52	0.02	0.30	-0.65	0.04	-0.52	0.39	0.66
Earnings	-1.57	0.42	0.34	-0.20	0.07	-0.91	-0.28	-0.82	0.15	0.54
Dividends	Nil	Nil	Nil	Nil	Nil	Nil	Nil	Nil	Nil	Nil
Payout Ratio	Nil	Nil	Nil	Nil	Nil	Nil	Nil	Nil	Nil	Nil
Cal. Yrs.	1998	1997	1996	1995	1994	1993	1992	1991	1990	1989
Prices - High	21 5/8	25 5/8	15 1/8	10 3/8	14 3/4	15	6 1/4	10 1/8	17 1/4	17 1/8
- Low	2 5/16	9 1/4	4	4 3/4	4 1/4	2 5/8	2 1/4	3 1/4	5 1/2	9 7/8
P/E Ratio - High	NM	61	44	NM	NM	NM	NM	NM	NM	32
- Low	NM	22	12	NM	NM	NM	NM	NM	NM	18
Income Statement Analysis (Million $)										
Revs.	236	310	178	150	154	116	108	90.0	136	111
Oper. Inc.	-40.3	48.4	19.7	-1.7	9.1	10.9	0.3	-11.2	18.6	23.6
Depr.	25.9	12.9	5.8	6.3	6.4	6.5	7.7	7.2	5.7	3.1
Int. Exp.	0.5	0.3	1.0	1.9	0.5	0.6	1.1	1.3	1.5	0.6
Pretax Inc.	-96.1	23.7	13.0	-7.9	2.2	-21.4	-6.7	-23.9	5.0	20.0
Eff. Tax Rate	NM	16%	10%	NM	10%	NM	NM	NM	25%	34%
Net Inc.	-96.7	19.9	11.7	-6.0	2.0	-22.5	-6.7	-19.7	3.8	13.2
Balance Sheet & Other Fin. Data (Million $)										
Cash	21.5	25.1	58.3	9.0	3.0	4.7	5.4	2.3	3.7	0.1
Curr. Assets	154	192	152	80.7	88.6	72.6	61.9	72.8	90.8	81.8
Total Assets	202	240	170	96.0	103	84.0	73.0	87.0	108	94.0
Curr. Liab.	68.7	61.7	52.5	43.3	61.6	54.6	26.5	33.6	35.0	26.5
LT Debt	2.2	0.2	0.2	2.8	6.4	0.5	0.2	0.6	0.9	0.1
Common Eqty.	131	178	118	49.7	34.6	28.6	46.3	53.0	72.6	67.7
Total Cap.	133	179	118	52.5	41.0	29.1	46.5	53.6	73.5	67.7
Cap. Exp.	24.7	22.6	8.5	4.5	8.1	5.9	4.5	3.7	9.6	8.1
Cash Flow	-70.8	32.7	17.5	0.4	8.3	-16.0	1.0	-12.4	9.5	16.3
Curr. Ratio	2.2	3.1	2.9	1.9	1.4	1.3	2.3	2.2	2.6	3.1
% LT Debt of Cap.	1.7	0.1	0.1	5.3	15.5	1.6	0.4	1.2	1.3	0.1
% Net Inc.of Revs.	NM	6.4	6.6	NM	1.3	NM	NM	NM	2.8	11.9
% Ret. on Assets	NM	9.7	8.8	NM	2.1	NM	NM	NM	3.7	16.0
% Ret. on Equity	NM	13.4	13.9	NM	6.1	NM	NM	NM	5.4	21.9

Data as orig reptd.; bef. results of disc opers/spec. items. Per share data adj. for stk. divs. Bold denotes diluted EPS (FASB 128)-prior periods restated. E-Estimated. NA-Not Available. NM-Not Meaningful. NR-Not Ranked.

Office—170 Rose Orchard Way, San Jose, CA 95134. **Reincorporated**—in Delaware in 1987. **Tel**—(408) 943-0777. **Website**—www.dmcwave.com **Chrmn & CEO**—C. D. Kissner. **SVP, CFO & Secy**—C. A. Thomsen. **Investor Contact**—Rebecca Wallo. **Dirs**—R. C. Alberding, P. S. Bachow, J. W. Combs, C. D. Kissner, V. F. Mendicino, J. D. Meindl, H. Oringer. **Transfer Agent**—ChaseMellon Shareholder Services, SF. **Empl**— 873. **S&P Analyst:** J.J.S.

DIMON Inc.

NYSE Symbol **DMN**

In S&P SmallCap 600

09-OCT-99

Industry:
Agricultural Products

Summary: DIMON is the world's second largest leaf tobacco dealer, with operation in more than 30 countries.

Quantitative Evaluations

Outlook
(1 Lowest—5 Highest)
• 5

Fair Value
• 7⅞

Risk
• **Average**

Earn./Div. Rank
• **NR**

Technical Eval.
• **Bearish** since 8/99

Rel. Strength Rank
(1 Lowest—99 Highest)
• 18

Insider Activity
• NA

Recent Price • 3⅞
52 Wk Range • 13½-3¼

Yield • 5.2%
12-Mo. P/E • NM

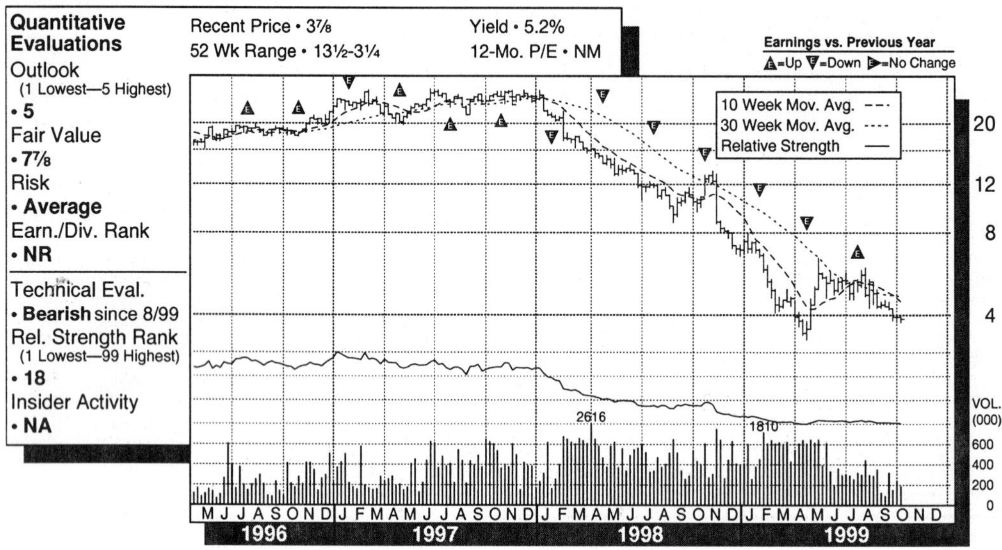

Business Profile - 07-JUL-99

As a result of a continuing difficult leaf-trading environment, DIMON has undertaken cost efficiency restructuring programs and debt reduction actions to enhance the company's operations and financial condition. DIMON plans on closing its processing plant in Kinston, NC, reducing staff at its processing facility in Farmville, NC, and substantially downsizing its leaf tobacco buying department in the U.S. The company also plans on closing a processing facility in Germany and a sales office in Brazil. DIMON has significantly lowered its debt through the sale of its flower business and through inventory and receivable liquidation efforts.

Operational Review - 07-JUL-99

Sales and other operating revenues from continuing operations for the nine months ended March 31, 1999, declined 12%, reflecting decreases in tobacco quantity and prices due to global demand pressures. Margins narrowed, hurt by the liquidation of old crop tobaccos during a period of depressed leaf prices, and after a $23.1 million restructuring charge, a loss from continuing operations of $40.3 million ($0.90 a share, on 9.3% fewer shares) contrasted with income of $39.7 million ($0.88). Results exclude income and disposal gains from discontinued operations of $0.51 a share and $0.05 a share in the respective periods.

Stock Performance - 08-OCT-99

In the past 30 trading days, DMN's shares have declined 10%, compared to a 0.91% fall in the S&P 500. Average trading volume for the past five days was 36,540 shares, compared with the 40-day moving average of 44,249 shares.

Key Stock Statistics

Dividend Rate/Share	0.20	Shareholders	4,576
Shs. outstg. (M)	44.5	Market cap. (B)	$0.173
Avg. daily vol. (M)	0.044	Inst. holdings	55%
Tang. Bk. Value/Share	4.77		
Beta	0.36		

Value of $10,000 invested 5 years ago: NA

Fiscal Year Ending Jun. 30

	1999	1998	1997	1996	1995	1994
Revenues (Million $)						
1Q	384.2	513.1	410.7	339.7	272.9	–
2Q	595.1	688.5	771.3	763.4	631.5	—
3Q	485.4	744.6	668.1	577.1	644.1	—
4Q	350.6	513.1	663.0	487.3	380.2	—
Yr.	1,815	2,172	2,513	2,167	1,928	1,447
Earnings Per Share ($)						
1Q	**-0.19**	**0.44**	0.36	0.16	-0.04	–
2Q	**-0.20**	**0.25**	**0.40**	0.48	0.10	—
3Q	**-0.52**	**0.22**	0.44	0.16	0.20	—
4Q	**0.27**	**0.05**	0.58	0.21	-1.05	—
Yr.	**-0.63**	**0.94**	**1.67**	**0.92**	-0.79	-0.17

Next earnings report expected: mid November

Dividend Data (Dividends have been paid since 1995.)

Amount ($)	Date Decl.	Ex-Div. Date	Stock of Record	Payment Date
0.090	Nov. 13	Nov. 27	Dec. 01	Dec. 15 '98
0.090	Feb. 26	Mar. 04	Mar. 08	Mar. 15 '99
0.050	May. 25	Jun. 02	Jun. 05	Jun. 15 '99
0.050	Aug. 27	Sep. 03	Sep. 08	Sep. 15 '99

A Division of The McGraw-Hill Companies

DIMON Incorporated

Business Summary - 07-JUL-99

In April 1997, DIMON completed the largest acquisition in the history of the tobacco leaf industry when it purchased Intabex Holdings Worldwide S.A. (Intabex), the world's fourth largest leaf tobacco dealer with annual sales of about $700 million, in a transaction valued at approximately $264 million. The acquisition made DIMON the world's second largest tobacco leaf dealer and increased its tobacco-related revenues in FY 97 (Jun.) by 20%. The acquisition also boosted its approximate market share in the established worldwide leaf tobacco market from 30% to 37% on a pro forma basis. In addition, DMN strengthened its presence in several important tobacco growing regions, including Brazil, Argentina, Malawi, Thailand and Zimbabwe.

As one of the world's largest leaf tobacco merchants, DIMON selects, purchases, processes, stores, packs, ships, and in some markets provides agronomy expertise and financing for growing leaf tobacco. The company processes tobacco to meet each customer's specifications as to quality, yield, chemistry, particle size, moisture, content, and other characteristics. DIMON purchases tobacco in about 32 countries and sells it to manufacturers of cigarettes including Philip Morris, RJR Nabisco, Japan Tobacco, and other consumer tobacco product companies, in about 60 countries throughout the world.

The company's primary business objective is to capitalize on growth in worldwide consumption of American blend cigarettes by becoming the low-cost preferred supplier of leaf tobacco to the large multinational manufacturers of American blend cigarettes. Strategies to achieve this goal include increasing the company's operations in low-cost tobacco growing regions, capitalizing on outsourcing trends, improving efficiency while reducing operating costs, and expanding operations in new markets.

In FY 98, DIMON delivered approximately 28% of its tobacco sales to customers in the United States, approximately 37% to customers in Europe, and the remainder to customers located in Asia, South America and elsewhere. DIMON plans on expanding its operations in South America, Africa and China, the largest production areas of flue-cured and burley tobacco outside the U.S.

On October 5, 1998, DIMON announced the completion of the sale of its flower import and export business, Florimex Worldwide, to USA Floral Products, Inc. for $90 million.

In May 1999, DIMON resolved a prior purchase price adjustment dispute with former Intabex shareholders. As a result, DIMON will cancel $50 million in convertible subordinated debentures that were issued as part of the purchase price of Intabex.

Per Share Data ($) (Year Ended Jun. 30)	1999	1998	1997	1996	1995	1994	1993	1992	1991	1990
Tangible Bk. Val.	NA	4.77	4.46	6.03	4.52	5.85	NA	NA	NA	NA
Cash Flow	NA	1.91	2.65	1.86	0.04	0.58	2.47	2.25	NA	NA
Earnings	-0.63	0.94	1.79	1.00	-0.79	-0.17	1.81	1.57	NA	NA
Dividends	0.19	0.66	0.58	0.54	Nil	NA	NA	NA	NA	NA
Payout Ratio	NM	70%	33%	54%	Nil	NA	NA	NA	NA	NA
Prices - High	7⅞	26¼	26¾	23¼	18⅝	NA	NA	NA	NA	NA
- Low	3¼	6½	19¾	16	13¾	NA	NA	NA	NA	NA
P/E Ratio - High	NM	28	15	23	NM	NA	NA	NA	NA	NA
- Low	NM	7	11	16	NM	NA	NA	NA	NA	NA
Income Statement Analysis (Million $)										
Revs.	NA	2,172	2,513	2,167	1,928	1,447	1,677	1,698	NA	NA
Oper. Inc.	NA	183	218	164	69.3	49.0	138	135	NA	NA
Depr.	NA	43.5	37.2	33.8	31.9	28.8	24.5	24.0	NA	NA
Int. Exp.	NA	83.8	53.0	46.9	45.2	35.1	38.1	42.8	NA	NA
Pretax Inc.	NA	56.6	124	67.2	-24.0	-1.4	94.5	79.3	NA	NA
Eff. Tax Rate	NA	26%	38%	40%	NM	NM	29%	30%	NA	NA
Net Inc.	NA	41.8	77.2	39.9	-30.2	-6.6	67.0	54.1	NA	NA
Balance Sheet & Other Fin. Data (Million $)										
Cash	NA	18.7	107	53.8	42.3	22.7	NA	NA	NA	NA
Curr. Assets	NA	1,209	1,371	669	731	938	NA	NA	NA	NA
Total Assets	NA	1,797	1,988	1,020	1,094	1,307	NA	NA	NA	NA
Curr. Liab.	NA	503	671	246	454	741	NA	NA	NA	NA
LT Debt	NA	797	826	391	344	245	NA	NA	NA	NA
Common Eqty.	NA	422	408	316	239	277	NA	NA	NA	NA
Total Cap.	NA	1,256	1,272	729	640	566	NA	NA	NA	NA
Cap. Exp.	NA	61.2	60.9	41.3	27.0	NA	NA	NA	NA	NA
Cash Flow	NA	85.3	114	73.7	1.7	22.3	91.5	79.5	NA	NA
Curr. Ratio	NA	2.4	2.0	2.7	1.6	1.3	NA	NA	NA	NA
% LT Debt of Cap.	NA	63.4	64.9	53.6	54.5	43.3	NA	NA	NA	NA
% Net Inc.of Revs.	NA	1.9	3.1	1.8	NM	NM	4.0	3.2	NA	NA
% Ret. on Assets	NA	2.2	5.1	3.8	NM	NA	NA	NA	NA	NA
% Ret. on Equity	NA	10.1	21.3	21.3	NM	NA	NA	NA	NA	NA

Data as orig. reptd.; bef. results of disc. opers. and/or spec. items. Data for 1994-1992 pro forma. Per share data adj. for stk. divs. as of ex-div. date. Bold denotes diluted EPS (FASB 128). E-Estimated. NA-Not Available. NM-Not Meaningful. NR-Not Ranked.

Office—512 Bridge St., Danville, VA 24543-0681. **Tel**—(804) 792-7511. **Website**—http://www.dimon-inc.com **Chrmn**—J. L. Lanier Jr.**Vice-Chrmn**—A. C. Monk III. **Pres & CEO**—B. J. Harker. **SVP-CFO**—J. A. Cooley. **VP & Secy**—J. O. Hunnicutt III. **SVP-Treas & Investor Contact**—R. L. Bond.**Dirs**—L. N. Dibrell III, R. S. Dickson, H. F. Frigon, J. M. Hines, J. E. Johnson, Jr., T. F. Keller, J. L. Lanier, Jr., A. C. Monk III, R. T. Monk, Jr., W. R. Slee, Jr, N. A. Scher. **Transfer Agent & Registrar**—First Union National Bank, Charlotte, NC. **Incorporated**—Virginia in 1995.**Empl**— 4,000. **S&P Analyst:** A. Bensinger

STANDARD &POOR'S
STOCK REPORTS

Dionex Corp.

NASDAQ Symbol **DNEX**

In S&P SmallCap 600

09-OCT-99

Industry: Manufacturing (Specialized)

Summary: This company makes chromatography systems and related products that isolate and identify the components of chemical mixtures.

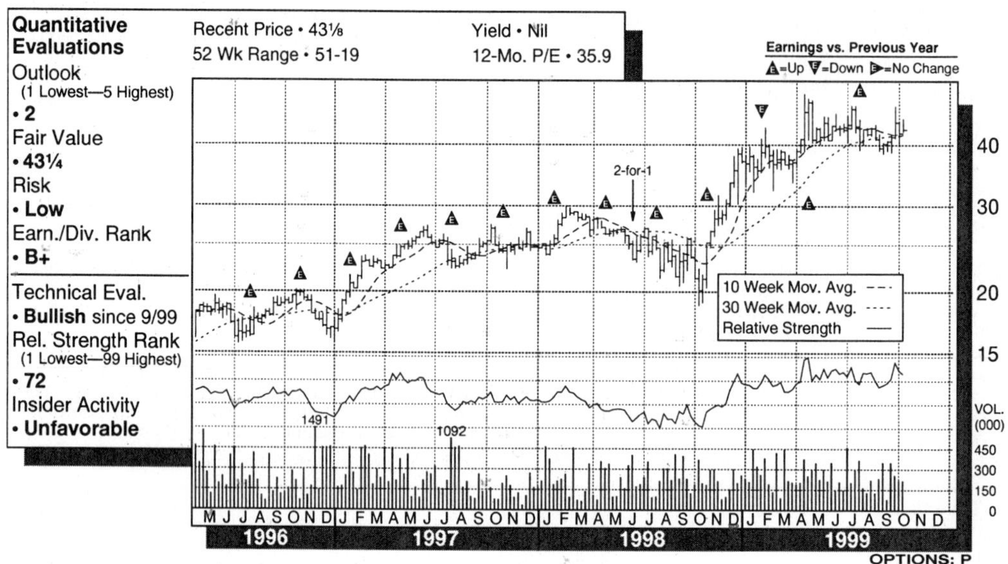

Business Profile - 23-SEP-99

In July 1999, the company said that during FY 99 (Jun.) it introduced several new products and applications that enhanced its core ion chromatography and extraction businesses. It also acquired (in October 1998) Softron GmbH, a privately held German company that specializes in high performance liquid chromatography (HPLC) systems, with annual revenues of about $10 million. The acquisition has enabled DNEX to offer a broader range of HPLC systems and automation products, and strengthens its presence in Europe, where most of Softron's business is conducted.

Operational Review - 23-SEP-99

Net sales (preliminary) in the fiscal year ended June 30, 1999, advanced 15%, year to year. Gross margins narrowed reflecting a revaluation of acquired inventory in connection with the Softron acquisition. SG&A expenses rose less rapidly than revenues and R&D expenses were up 12%. However, after a $4,991,000 write-off of in-process R&D and lower interest income, pretax income fell 1.8%. After taxes at 33.2%, versus 34.0%, net income declined 0.6% to $28,474,000 ($1.20 a share, based on fewer shares), from $28,650,000 ($1.18).

Stock Performance - 08-OCT-99

In the past 30 trading days, DNEX's shares have increased 9%, compared to a 0.91% fall in the S&P 500. Average trading volume for the past five days was 42,460 shares, compared with the 40-day moving average of 46,085 shares.

Key Stock Statistics

Dividend Rate/Share	Nil	Shareholders	1,700
Shs. outstg. (M)	22.3	Market cap. (B)	$0.962
Avg. daily vol. (M)	0.051	Inst. holdings	66%
Tang. Bk. Value/Share	3.85		
Beta	0.57		

Value of $10,000 invested 5 years ago: $ 53,867

Fiscal Year Ending Jun. 30

	1999	1998	1997	1996	1995	1994
Revenues (Million $)						
1Q	34.85	33.93	31.51	30.06	27.04	25.46
2Q	44.51	39.42	36.60	34.01	30.62	28.13
3Q	47.07	38.40	36.65	34.03	30.58	27.72
4Q	46.52	38.76	37.30	34.91	31.78	28.22
Yr.	172.9	150.5	142.1	133.0	120.0	109.5
Earnings Per Share ($)						
1Q	**0.26**	0.23	0.20	0.16	0.14	0.11
2Q	**0.17**	**0.32**	0.27	0.21	0.17	0.14
3Q	**0.38**	**0.31**	0.28	0.26	0.18	0.15
4Q	**0.39**	**0.32**	0.28	0.24	0.19	0.15
Yr.	**1.20**	**1.18**	**1.03**	0.88	0.67	0.55

Next earnings report expected: mid October

Dividend Data

No cash has been paid. A number of stock splits have been effected, the most recent being a two-for-one stock split distributed in June 1998.

Dionex Corporation

Business Summary - 23-SEP-99

Dionex Corp. (DNEX) pioneered ion chromatography more than 20 years ago, providing chemists with a powerful new tool for analyzing the components of a wide range of samples. In 1995, the company introduced accelerated solvent extraction (ASE), a new technique for extracting compounds from solid materials such as soil and plastic prior to analysis. DNEX has also been extending the utility of high performance liquid chromatography (HPLC), another key technology, for biological and environmental applications. For example, the company is working with regulatory agencies in the U.S. and abroad to develop effective methods for analyzing organic contaminants that plague the environment.

The company's chromatography systems and its product development efforts are focused on these three technologies, led by ion chromatography (IC), a technique that separates ions, or charged molecules, and typically identifies them based on their electrical conductivity. The sale of IC systems and related products accounts for a majority of revenues. HPLC separates biological molecules such as proteins and pharmaceuticals and identifies them by measuring the amount of light they absorb or emit. DNEX's ASE 200 system, based on the company's new ASE technology, extracts solid samples using common solvents.

The company's chromatography systems and related products are used extensively in environmental analysis and by a broad range of industries to isolate and identify the individual components of complex chemical mixtures. In its important environmental market, DNEX's methods and instrumentation are used worldwide to analyze drinking water, waste water and air in accordance with governmental regulatory procedures. In addition, the company's ASE technology offers rapid extraction of difficult environmental samples such as soil and sludge.

DNEX's products are also used by industry to ensure the quality of their products and processes. DNEX's systems provide detailed information about chemical processes for customers in the chemical and petrochemical industries, for instance, and allow plant managers to monitor problematic contaminants in feedstocks, equipment and finished products. In semiconductor fabrication, where water purity is critical, the company's IC technology, which can detect and identify ions at part-per-trillion concentration levels, is used to monitor water for trace-level contaminants. DNEX also serves customers in the pharmaceutical, life science, biotechnology and power generation industries.

Net sales grew 6%, to $151 million, in FY 98 (Jun.), reflecting improved demand for DNEX's systems in North America and Europe. However, problems associated with Asian economies limited revenue growth in that region.

Per Share Data ($) (Year Ended Jun. 30)	1999	1998	1997	1996	1995	1994	1993	1992	1991	1990
Tangible Bk. Val.	NA	3.17	7.10	3.33	3.79	3.67	3.12	2.96	2.42	2.19
Cash Flow	NA	1.28	1.13	0.98	0.76	0.63	0.57	0.50	0.47	0.41
Earnings	1.20	1.18	1.03	0.88	0.67	0.55	0.51	0.45	0.42	0.36
Dividends	Nil	Nil	Nil	Nil	Nil	Nil	Nil	Nil	Nil	Nil
Payout Ratio	Nil	Nil	Nil	Nil	Nil	Nil	Nil	Nil	Nil	Nil
Prices - High	51	39 5/8	27 1/2	20 1/4	14 5/8	9 3/4	11 1/8	10 1/4	8 1/2	7
- Low	32	18 3/4	17 1/4	13 7/8	9 1/4	7 7/8	7 3/4	6 1/4	4 5/8	3 5/8
P/E Ratio - High	42	34	27	23	22	18	22	23	20	19
- Low	27	16	17	16	14	14	15	14	11	10
Income Statement Analysis (Million $)										
Revs.	NA	151	142	133	120	110	106	96.4	89.3	80.6
Oper. Inc.	NA	44.7	43.3	36.6	30.3	27.4	25.8	22.4	20.7	18.7
Depr.	NA	2.5	2.6	2.9	2.6	2.5	2.0	1.9	1.8	1.9
Int. Exp.	NA	0.1	0.1	0.1	0.1	0.3	0.5	0.7	0.6	0.3
Pretax Inc.	NA	43.4	40.0	36.7	31.7	26.1	24.9	22.5	21.8	19.9
Eff. Tax Rate	NA	34%	34%	35%	38%	35%	35%	35%	35%	35%
Net Inc.	NA	28.6	26.2	24.0	19.8	17.0	16.3	14.7	14.2	13.0
Balance Sheet & Other Fin. Data (Million $)										
Cash	NA	13.2	24.6	33.6	49.5	51.3	42.5	49.5	48.3	50.8
Curr. Assets	NA	69.4	79.8	77.8	93.5	92.5	82.9	84.7	80.6	80.4
Total Assets	NA	107	118	113	132	133	118	120	109	106
Curr. Liab.	NA	33.6	31.6	29.9	26.2	21.1	22.1	23.8	23.2	21.8
LT Debt	NA	Nil	Nil	Nil	0.1	0.1	0.1	0.1	0.1	0.2
Common Eqty.	NA	70.7	84.2	82.0	104	111	94.9	94.9	85.3	83.7
Total Cap.	NA	73.6	86.5	83.0	106	112	96.0	96.2	86.2	84.5
Cap. Exp.	NA	2.5	2.6	3.0	2.0	7.8	1.2	8.5	4.5	3.8
Cash Flow	NA	31.2	28.8	26.8	22.4	19.5	18.3	16.7	15.9	14.8
Curr. Ratio	NA	2.1	2.5	2.6	3.6	4.4	3.8	3.6	3.5	3.7
% LT Debt of Cap.	NA	Nil	Nil	Nil	0.1	0.1	0.1	0.1	0.2	0.2
% Net Inc.of Revs.	NA	19.0	18.5	18.1	16.5	15.6	15.4	15.3	15.9	16.1
% Ret. on Assets	NA	25.4	22.7	19.6	14.9	13.6	14.1	13.0	13.1	13.0
% Ret. on Equity	NA	37.0	31.5	25.8	18.4	16.6	17.6	16.6	16.8	16.1

Data as orig reptd.; bef. results of disc opers/spec. items. Per share data adj. for stk. divs. Bold denotes diluted EPS (FASB 128)-prior periods restated. E-Estimated. NA-Not Available. NM-Not Meaningful. NR-Not Ranked.

Office—1228 Titan Way, Sunnyvale, CA 94086. **Tel**—(408) 737-0700. **Pres & CEO**—A. B. Bowman. **Secy**—J. C. Gaither. **VP, CFO & Investor Contact**—Michael W. Pope. **Dirs**—D. L. Anderson, J. F. Battey, A. B. Bowman, B. J. Moore, R. Pigliucci. **Transfer Agent & Registrar**—Boston EquiServe. **Incorporated**—in California in 1980; reincorporated in Delaware in 1986. **Empl**— 685. **S&P Analyst:** P.L.H.

STANDARD
&POOR'S
STOCK REPORTS

Discount Auto Parts

NYSE Symbol **DAP**
In S&P SmallCap 600

09-OCT-99 **Industry:** Retail (Specialty)

Summary: DAP operates more than 500 stores in the Southeast, selling automotive replacement parts and maintenance items to the do-it-yourself customer.

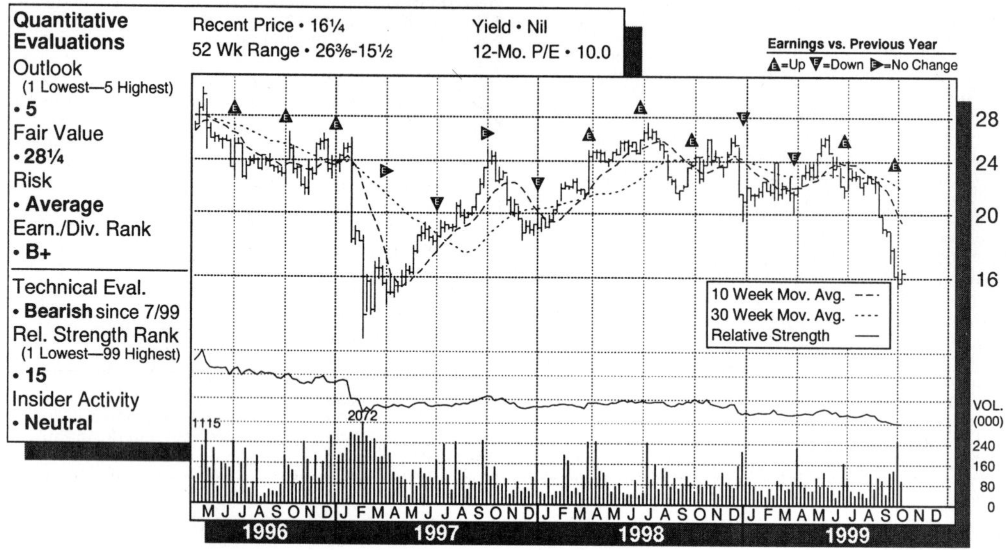

Business Profile - 19-MAY-99

Discount Auto Parts, a traditional Do-It-Yourself (DIY) auto parts store, has continued to achieve strong operating results in the automotive part aftermarket. During the third quarter of FY 99 (May), the company added 19 mini-depot stores, making a total of 537 stores (24 depot and 513 mini-depot) as of March 2, 1999. For FY 99, DAP expects to add about 105 stores, of which 85 were added through the third quarter. For FY 00, the company expects to add approximately 80 to 90 stores. In September 1998, DAP announced that it had acquired Rose Auto Parts, a subsidiary of National Auto Parts, which added 39 retail locations and a warehouse.

Operational Review - 19-MAY-99

Net sales rose for the thirty-nine weeks ended March 2, 1999, rose 14%, year to year, reflecting a higher store count, the acquisition of Rose Auto Parts, and a 2% increase in comparable store sales. Gross margins widened on lower product costs, a more favorable product mix, and vendor incentive programs. SG&A costs increased 23%, mainly due to expenses related to the company's commercial delivery program and a shift in advertising credits. Despite the absence of an acquisition termination fee, and 24% higher interest expense, net income rose 1.8%, to $19,865,000 ($1.18 a share), from $19,510,000 ($1.17).

Stock Performance - 08-OCT-99

In the past 30 trading days, DAP's shares have declined 18%, compared to a 0.91% fall in the S&P 500. Average trading volume for the past five days was 19,120 shares, compared with the 40-day moving average of 26,195 shares.

Key Stock Statistics

Dividend Rate/Share	Nil	Shareholders	630
Shs. outstg. (M)	16.7	Market cap. (B)	$0.272
Avg. daily vol. (M)	0.036	Inst. holdings	47%
Tang. Bk. Value/Share	16.58		
Beta	0.83		

Value of $10,000 invested 5 years ago: $ 5,931

Fiscal Year Ending May 31

	2000	1999	1998	1997	1996	1995
Revenues (Million $)						
1Q	143.6	123.0	109.7	90.10	71.35	57.81
2Q	—	120.3	105.2	105.8	73.77	59.97
3Q	—	127.4	110.3	101.9	75.43	63.92
4Q	—	140.8	122.2	107.4	86.93	72.00
Yr.	—	511.5	447.5	405.2	307.5	253.7
Earnings Per Share ($)						
1Q	**0.44**	**0.42**	0.39	0.39	0.34	0.52
2Q	—	**0.33**	0.37	0.42	0.36	0.29
3Q	—	**0.39**	**0.42**	0.34	0.34	0.31
4Q	—	**0.47**	**0.46**	-0.37	0.40	0.36
Yr.	—	**1.61**	**1.63**	**0.77**	1.44	1.48

Next earnings report expected: mid December

Dividend Data

No dividends have been paid, and the company has no plans to pay any, as it intends to retain all earnings for future operations and expansion of its business.

A Division of The McGraw-Hill Companies

Discount Auto Parts, Inc.

Business Summary - 19-MAY-99

Discount Auto Parts (DAP) is now one of the Southeast's leading retailers of replacement parts, maintenance items, and accessories serving the car owner. The company was started as a single store in 1971 by the Fontaine family in Eloise, FL, and, as of March 2, 1999, supported 537 stores throughout Florida, Georgia, Alabama, South Carolina and Mississippi, up from 400 stores at the end of FY 97 (May) and 314 at the end of FY 96.

DAP attributes its continuing growth to its employee-centered management and team-building. DAP continues to meet its goal of being the market leader in its existing markets. DAP now has a highly focused store concept that continually strives to improve merchandising concepts. In February 1998, DAP began the rollout of a company delivery program, whereby auto service centers and commercial mechanics can maintain an account with DAP and order parts for delivery from nearby stores. As of August 1998, the program had been rolled out to 45 DAP stores.

The company's stores use two different formats: mini-depot and depot. The smaller standard-format stores have been phased out. Mini-depot stores (513 as of March 2, 1999) under DAP's new standardized format have had an average of approximately 4,800 sq. ft. of selling space and 15,400 stock-keeping units (SKUs); depot stores (24) will average 10,000 sq. ft. of space and 20,000 SKUs. Although brandname products are emphasized, a number of private-label products are also carried under the Discount Auto and Power Pak names.

In September 1998, DAP acquired Rose Auto Parts, a subsidiary of National Auto Parts, which added 39 retail locations, primarily in Southeast Florida, and a warehouse facility in Miami. This acquisition should help DAP to effectively service its expanding commercial delivery service. As of March 2, 1999, DAP had already opened 85 new stores, leaving 20 additional stores left to be added for the company to reach its goal of 105 new stores by the end of FY 99.

Discount Auto relies on its parts management strategies, low operating costs, and increased direct importing to give it a competitive advantage. The company also plans to place emphasis on further expansion in Florida and neighboring states, due to the states fast growing climate.

Per Share Data ($) (Year Ended May 31)	1999	1998	1997	1996	1995	1994	1993	1992	1991	1990
Tangible Bk. Val.	NA	15.45	13.80	13.04	8.47	6.99	5.96	4.84	NA	NA
Cash Flow	NA	2.52	1.52	2.07	2.00	1.39	1.39	0.95	NA	NA
Earnings	1.61	1.63	0.77	1.44	1.48	1.03	0.89	0.66	NA	NA
Dividends	Nil	Nil	Nil	Nil	Nil	Nil	Nil	NA	NA	NA
Payout Ratio	Nil	Nil	Nil	Nil	Nil	Nil	Nil	NA	NA	NA
Cal. Yrs.	1998	1997	1996	1995	1994	1993	1992	1991	1990	1989
Prices - High	$27\frac{1}{2}$	26	$31\frac{1}{8}$	$33\frac{7}{8}$	$27\frac{5}{8}$	$31\frac{1}{8}$	$28\frac{1}{8}$	NA	NA	NA
- Low	19	$12\frac{7}{8}$	$21\frac{1}{4}$	$17\frac{3}{4}$	$13\frac{7}{8}$	$20\frac{5}{8}$	18	NA	NA	NA
P/E Ratio - High	17	16	40	24	19	30	32	NA	NA	NA
- Low	12	8	28	12	9	20	28	NA	NA	NA
Income Statement Analysis (Million $)										
Revs.	NA	447	405	307	254	208	177	141	NA	NA
Oper. Inc.	NA	67.0	59.7	50.4	38.1	31.1	26.4	20.3	NA	NA
Depr.	NA	15.0	12.5	9.9	7.2	5.0	4.7	3.9	NA	NA
Int. Exp.	NA	10.2	6.1	5.1	6.3	5.1	3.6	2.9	NA	NA
Pretax Inc.	NA	44.2	20.7	36.6	30.6	23.3	18.9	14.0	NA	NA
Eff. Tax Rate	NA	38%	39%	39%	33%	39%	28%	37%	NA	NA
Net Inc.	NA	27.2	12.7	22.5	20.6	14.3	13.6	8.9	NA	NA
Balance Sheet & Other Fin. Data (Million $)										
Cash	NA	5.1	6.4	4.6	4.6	16.3	14.4	NA	NA	NA
Curr. Assets	NA	195	177	125	104	80.4	68.1	NA	NA	NA
Total Assets	NA	512	443	334	271	214	159	131	NA	NA
Curr. Liab.	NA	89.1	96.1	65.4	57.2	46.4	34.2	NA	NA	NA
LT Debt	NA	161	114	50.4	94.6	70.1	42.0	37.3	NA	NA
Common Eqty.	NA	257	229	216	118	97.2	82.8	65.8	NA	NA
Total Cap.	NA	423	347	269	214	167	125	103	NA	NA
Cap. Exp.	NA	64.6	70.2	58.2	42.3	47.9	22.5	NA	NA	NA
Cash Flow	NA	42.2	25.2	32.4	27.8	19.3	18.3	12.8	NA	NA
Curr. Ratio	NA	2.2	1.8	1.9	1.8	1.7	2.0	NA	NA	NA
% LT Debt of Cap.	NA	38.0	32.9	18.8	44.3	41.9	33.7	36.1	NA	NA
% Net Inc.of Revs.	NA	6.1	3.1	7.3	8.1	6.9	7.7	6.3	NA	NA
% Ret. on Assets	NA	5.7	3.3	7.5	8.5	7.7	8.2	NA	NA	NA
% Ret. on Equity	NA	11.2	5.7	13.5	19.2	15.9	20.6	NA	NA	NA

Data as orig reptd.; bef. results of disc opers/spec. items. Per share data adj. for stk. divs. Bold denotes diluted EPS (FASB 128)-prior periods restated. E-Estimated. NA-Not Available. NM-Not Meaningful. NR-Not Ranked.

Office—4900 Frontage Road South, Lakeland, FL 33815. **Tel**—(941) 687-9226.**CEO**—P. J. Fontaine. **Pres & COO**—W. C. Perkins.**CFO, Secy & Investor Contact**—C. Michael Moore (941-284-2010). **Dirs**—P. J. Fontaine, W. C. Perkins, W. Shatzer, A. G. Tunstall, D. P. Walling, E. E. Wardlow.**Transfer Agent & Registrar**—ChaseMellon Shareholder Services, Ridgefield Park, NJ. **Incorporated**—in Florida in 1972. **Empl**— 4,350.
S&P Analyst: Matthew C. Hershberg

STANDARD
&POOR'S
STOCK REPORTS

Dixie Group

NASDAQ Symbol **DXYN**

In S&P SmallCap 600

23-OCT-99 **Industry:** Textiles (Specialty)

Summary: Dixie Group is a leading carpet and rug manufacturer.

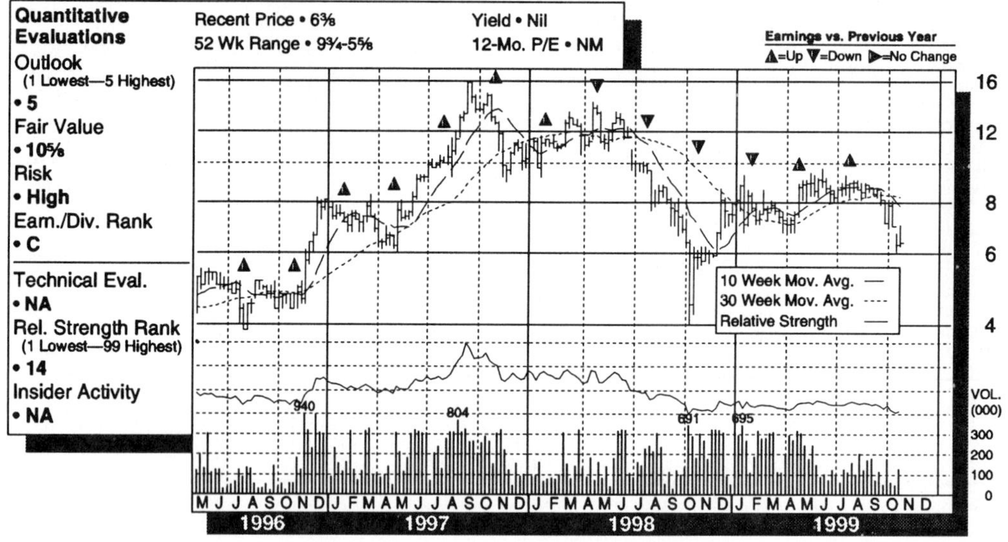

Business Profile - 13-OCT-99

Dixie is exiting textile markets to focus exclusively on its more profitable and growing floorcovering business. In 1999's second quarter, the company completed the disposal of its textile products business (discontinued in 1998), generating total proceeds of approximately $47.4 million. Following the company's purchase of Multitex Corporation of America, a carpet producer, in early 1999 for $30.4 million, it sold Multitex's carpet yarn spinning facility in Ulmer, SC, to Mohawk Industries for approximately $10 million in July. DXYN believes that market conditions will be favorable for the balance of the year.

Operational Review - 13-OCT-99

Revenues from continuing operations in the six months ended June 26, 1999, increased 18%, year to year, reflecting the acquisition of Globaltex Carpets in January 1999. Gross margins widened and pretax income climbed 22%. After taxes at 39.3%, versus 37.9%, income from continuing operations rose 19%, to $6,640,000 ($0.57 a share), from $5,588,000 ($0.47). Results exclude a loss from discontinued operations of $0.04 a share in 1998 and income from disposal of discontinued operations of $0.39 in 1999 and a loss of $1.31 in 1998.

Stock Performance - 22-OCT-99

In the past 30 trading days, DXYN's shares have declined 27%, compared to a 4% fall in the S&P 500. Average trading volume for the past five days was 12,560 shares, compared with the 40-day moving average of 24,408 shares.

Key Stock Statistics

Dividend Rate/Share	Nil	Shareholders	4,500
Shs. outstg. (M)	11.4	Market cap. (B)	$0.067
Avg. daily vol. (M)	0.021	Inst. holdings	50%
Tang. Bk. Value/Share	5.21		
Beta	0.61		

Value of $10,000 invested 5 years ago: $ 6,297

Fiscal Year Ending Dec. 31

	1999	1998	1997	1996	1995	1994
Revenues (Million $)						
1Q	141.2	118.6	162.4	161.5	181.7	164.8
2Q	152.1	130.5	169.2	168.0	177.8	178.3
3Q	—	120.4	159.9	145.4	161.3	173.9
4Q	—	126.9	170.4	140.2	150.1	171.5
Yr.	—	496.4	661.8	615.1	670.8	688.5
Earnings Per Share ($)						
1Q	**0.22**	**0.19**	**0.26**	**-0.09**	0.06	-0.33
2Q	**0.35**	**0.28**	**0.29**	**0.12**	0.03	0.01
3Q	—	**0.14**	**0.25**	**0.18**	-0.53	0.04
4Q	—	**0.16**	**0.19**	**-1.21**	-4.24	0.04
Yr.	—	**0.77**	**0.99**	**-1.00**	**-4.44**	**-0.26**

Next earnings report expected: late October

Dividend Data (Dividends have been paid since 1998.)

Cash dividends were paid each year from 1954 to 1994. Three $0.05 payments were made in 1998.

The Dixie Group, Inc.

Business Summary - 13-OCT-99

From 1993 through 1998, the company sold or closed the majority of its textile related operations. During 1998, the company made the decision to exit and hold for sale its remaining textile operations considered to have limited shareholder return potential. During the same period of textile related asset divestiture, the company acquired numerous carpet makers, including Carriage Carpets, Bretlin Carpets and Masland Carpets in 1993, Patrick Carpet Mills in 1994, Danube Carpet Mills and certain carpet assets of General Felt in 1997, Ideal Fibers in late 1998, and Multitex Corporation of America in early 1999. Carpet manufacturing accounted for 81% of sales and 89% of profits from continuing operations in 1998, with floorcovering base materials contributing the rest.

Masland Carpets makes specialty carpets and rugs for the high-end residential and commercial marketplaces. Its products are marketed to the architectural and interior design community and select specialty floorcovering showrooms. Masland's business includes a product line designed to cater to value oriented commercial customers where style, design and quality are required.

Carriage Carpets supplies tufted broadloom carpet for customers of the factory built housing, recreational vehicle, van conversion and exposition trade show industries.

Bretlin is a manufacturer of indoor/outdoor needlebond carpet and runners, floormats, decorative accent rugs, commercial/industrial polypropylene needlebond carpet and synthetic fiber cushion. Its products are marketed to home centers, mass merchants, floorcovering groups or co-ops, distributors and independent floorcovering retailers.

The floorcovering base materials segment, which includes Candlewick Yarns and the filament yarn extrusion assets of Ideal Fibers, produces yarns for the carpet industry and are sold for applications in residential and commercial carpet, bath and decorative accent rugs, and automotive floorcovering. A substantial majority of the production volume is utilized in the company's carpet making operation. As a vertically integrated supplier, this group focuses on the development and production of low cost yarn through extrusion, spinning and finishing. Its mission is to satisfy the internal needs of the carpet making group at a competitive cost and to supply external customers with innovative products, the production of which has the effect of lowering the company's total unit cost of production.

In 1999's second quarter, the company completed the disposal of its textile products business (discontinued in 1998), generating total proceeds of approximately $47.4 million. Following the company's purchase of Multitex Corporation of America, a carpet producer, in early 1999 for $30.4 million, it sold Multitex's carpet yarn spinning facility in Ulmer, SC, to Mohawk Industries for approximately $10 million in July.

Per Share Data ($) (Year Ended Dec. 31)	1998	1997	1996	1995	1994	1993	1992	1991	1990	1989
Tangible Bk. Val.	4.19	5.09	6.87	7.37	9.53	10.06	12.46	11.91	15.20	14.70
Cash Flow	2.35	3.07	1.52	1.38	2.41	2.96	3.26	-0.43	2.71	2.71
Earnings	0.77	0.99	-1.00	-4.44	-0.24	0.41	0.65	-2.88	0.71	1.13
Dividends	0.15	Nil	Nil	Nil	0.20	0.20	0.20	0.42	0.68	0.68
Payout Ratio	19%	Nil	Nil	Nil	NM	49%	31%	NM	96%	57%
Prices - High	14¼	16	8¼	7⅜	11¼	16¾	14¼	15¼	16¼	22½
- Low	4	6	3¾	3⅜	6¾	8¾	8¾	7½	7⅞	14
P/E Ratio - High	19	16	NM	NM	NM	41	22	NM	23	20
- Low	5	6	NM	NM	NM	21	13	NM	11	12
Income Statement Analysis (Million $)										
Revs.	496	662	615	671	689	595	470	492	556	571
Oper. Inc.	47.0	58.6	54.0	51.4	41.3	36.8	44.5	28.7	45.2	46.0
Depr.	18.7	24.5	28.2	36.0	35.2	29.2	22.9	21.6	19.2	16.3
Int. Exp.	10.3	12.6	13.0	15.6	13.7	12.8	10.8	12.2	10.8	7.6
Pretax Inc.	14.7	18.8	-15.5	-64.7	-11.9	9.0	11.3	-31.6	12.7	24.1
Eff. Tax Rate	38%	38%	NM	NM	NM	48%	50%	NM	46%	52%
Net Inc.	9.1	11.6	-11.2	-52.2	-3.2	4.7	5.7	-25.4	6.8	11.7
Balance Sheet & Other Fin. Data (Million $)										
Cash	2.8	1.8	2.0	3.4	1.9	4.0	1.4	2.3	2.0	3.4
Curr. Assets	166	136	131	157	153	148	128	136	141	139
Total Assets	375	387	328	397	488	497	372	347	359	347
Curr. Liab.	85.6	67.9	58.5	46.0	63.8	59.2	45.0	37.0	43.8	37.8
LT Debt	154	161	129	192	182	182	165	154	126	111
Common Eqty.	100	121	109	118	171	176	145	141	174	185
Total Cap.	277	309	260	340	413	424	324	306	314	307
Cap. Exp.	33.4	26.5	17.6	30.0	36.0	116	26.0	38.0	31.0	33.0
Cash Flow	27.8	36.1	17.0	-16.2	32.0	33.9	28.5	-3.8	26.0	28.1
Curr. Ratio	1.9	2.0	2.2	3.4	2.4	2.5	2.9	3.7	3.2	3.7
% LT Debt of Cap.	55.6	52.1	49.5	56.6	44.0	43.0	50.9	50.3	40.1	36.1
% Net Inc.of Revs.	1.8	1.8	NM	NM	NM	0.8	1.2	NM	1.2	2.1
% Ret. on Assets	2.4	3.3	NM	NM	NM	1.0	1.6	NM	2.0	3.6
% Ret. on Equity	8.2	10.1	NM	NM	NM	2.6	3.9	NM	4.0	6.4

Data as orig reptd.; bef. results of disc opers/spec. items. Per share data adj. for stk. divs. Bold denotes diluted EPS (FASB 128)-prior periods restated. E-Estimated. NA-Not Available. NM-Not Meaningful. NR-Not Ranked.

Office—1100 S. Watkins St., Chattanooga, TN 37404. **Tel**—(423) 698-2501. **Website**—http://www.thedixiegroup.com. **Chrmn & CEO**—D. K. Frierson. **Pres & COO**—W. N. Fry IV. **Treas**—G. A. Harmon. **Secy**—S. T. Klein. **Dirs**—J. D. Brock, P. K. Brock, L. A. Brooks, Jr., D. K. Frierson, P. K. Frierson, W. N. Fry IV, J. W. Murrey III, P. L. Smith, R. J. Sudderth, Jr. **Transfer Agent**—SunTrust Bank, Atlanta. **Incorporated**—in Tennessee in 1920. **Empl**— 3,100. **S&P Analyst:** Howard Choe

STANDARD
&POOR'S
STOCK REPORTS

Downey Financial Corp.

NYSE Symbol **DSL**

In S&P SmallCap 600

09-OCT-99

Industry:
Savings & Loan Companies

Summary: This company, through its Downey Savings and Loan subsidiary (with assets of $6.6 billion), provides diversified savings and loan services in northern and southern California.

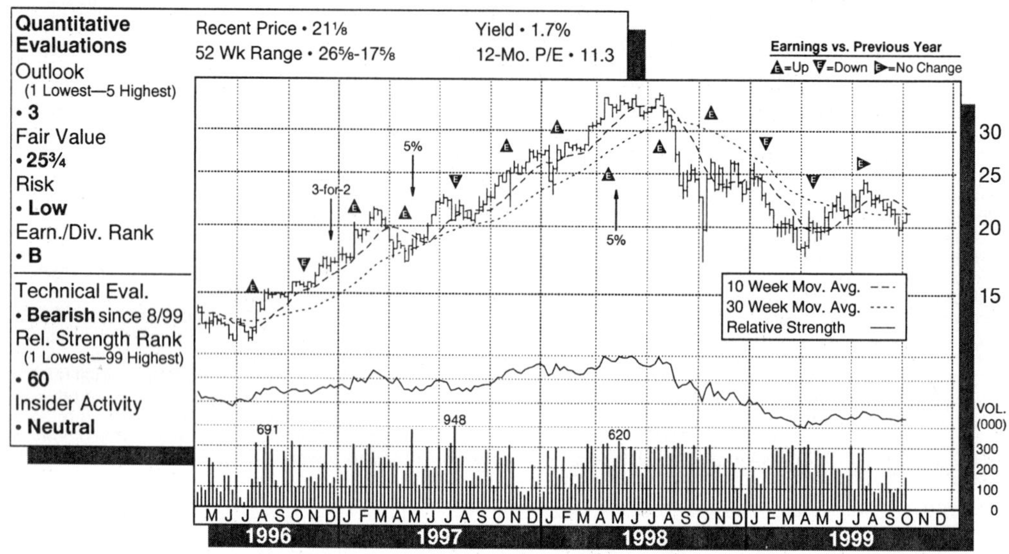

Business Profile - 02-JUL-99

In the first quarter of 1999, Downey opened five new in-store branches and closed one traditional branch, bringing total branches at the end of the quarter to 95, including 33 which are in-store. Recent expansion, particularly into supermarket banking, has boosted the company's retail deposit franchise. In 1999's first quarter, single family loan originations totaled $1.43 billion, more than triple the $453 million originated in 1998's first quarter. Of the 1999 first quarter total, $647 million represented originations of loans for sale and $189 million represented originations for portfolio of subprime credits as part of Downey's strategy to enhance the portfolio's net yield.

Operational Review - 02-JUL-99

Net interest income in the three months ended March 31, 1999, advanced 15%, year to year, reflecting an increase of 7.8% in average earning assets and a higher effective interest rate spread. The provision for loan losses rose to $2,381,000 from $272,000. Total other income fell 24%, in the absence of prior-year gains of $5.4 million from the sale of joint venture investments. Following 37% higher noninterest expense, pretax income fell 30%. After taxes at 42.5%, versus 42.8%, net income also was down 30%, to $12,348,000 ($0.44 a share) from $17,565,000 ($0.62).

Stock Performance - 08-OCT-99

In the past 30 trading days, DSL's shares have declined 2%, compared to a 0.91% fall in the S&P 500. Average trading volume for the past five days was 30,940 shares, compared with the 40-day moving average of 23,792 shares.

Key Stock Statistics

Dividend Rate/Share	0.36	Shareholders	1,078
Shs. outstg. (M)	28.1	Market cap. (B)	$0.596
Avg. daily vol. (M)	0.022	Inst. holdings	38%
Tang. Bk. Value/Share	17.83		
Beta	0.90		

Value of $10,000 invested 5 years ago: $ 20,535

Fiscal Year Ending Dec. 31

	1999	1998	1997	1996	1995	1994
Revenues (Million $)						
1Q	125.2	124.7	108.6	92.16	79.91	54.71
2Q	135.5	121.7	108.6	87.15	84.24	58.76
3Q	—	118.7	117.1	93.12	85.67	62.24
4Q	—	122.7	121.3	99.1	89.60	70.99
Yr.	—	487.8	455.6	371.6	339.5	246.7
Earnings Per Share ($)						
1Q	**0.44**	**0.62**	**0.44**	0.37	0.12	0.21
2Q	**0.53**	**0.53**	**0.30**	**0.37**	0.15	0.23
3Q	—	**0.45**	**0.37**	**-0.23**	0.19	0.20
4Q	—	**0.45**	**0.50**	**0.30**	0.30	0.20
Yr.	—	**2.05**	**1.61**	**0.73**	**0.75**	**0.84**

Next earnings report expected: mid October

Dividend Data (Dividends have been paid since 1986.)

Amount ($)	Date Decl.	Ex-Div. Date	Stock of Record	Payment Date
0.080	Oct. 28	Nov. 09	Nov. 12	Nov. 30 '98
0.080	Jan. 27	Feb. 08	Feb. 10	Feb. 26 '99
0.090	Apr. 28	May. 10	May. 12	May. 27 '99
0.090	Jul. 28	Aug. 09	Aug. 11	Aug. 26 '99

A Division of The McGraw-Hill Companies

Downey Financial Corporation

Business Summary - 02-JUL-99

Downey Financial Corp. is a $6.6 billion asset savings and loan institution operating primarily in California; it has nearly 100 branches throughout that state. Historically, Downey has focused its lending activities on the origination of first mortgage loans secured by residential property and retail neighborhood shopping centers. To a lesser degree, it has also concentrated on originating real estate loans secured by multi-family and commercial and industrial properties, including office buildings, land and other properties with income producing capabilities.

In addition, Downey has provided construction loan financing for residential (both single family and multi-family) and commercial retail neighborhood shopping center projects, including loans to joint ventures where DSL Service Co. or the bank was a participant.

Downey also originates loans to businesses through its commercial banking operations and loans on new and used automobiles through the purchase of motor vehicle sales contracts from auto dealers in California and other western states. The thrift's indirect auto lending program is in addition to automobile loans originated directly through Downey's branch network.

During 1999, Downey's primary focus will continue to be the origination of adjustable rate single family mortgage loans, particularly subprime loans which carry higher interest rates, and consumer loans. In addition, management expects to continue its secondary marketing activities of selling its production of certain fixed rate single family loans as well as certain adjustable rate mortgage (ARM) loan products. In view of the current low interest rate environment and customer preference for fixed rate loans, Downey said that it may originate more single family loans for sale in the secondary market than for its portfolio during 1999 as was the case in 1998.

The allowance for loan losses totaled $31,517,000 (0.58% of loans outstanding) at the end of 1998, versus $32,092,000 (0.60%) a year earlier. Net loan charge-offs amounted to $4,474,000 (0.09% of average loans) in 1998, compared with $6,642,000 (0.13%) a year earlier.

As of December 31, 1998, gross nonperforming assets (consisting of nonaccrual loans, real estate acquired in settlement of loans and repossessed automobiles) totaled $27.4 million (0.44% of total assets), compared with $52.1 million (0.89%) a year earlier.

The average yield on total interest-earning assets was 7.78% in 1998 (7.72% in 1997), while the average rate paid on total interest-bearing liabilities was 4.93% (5.09%), for an interest-rate spread of 2.85% (2.63%).

Interest on loans accounted for 87% of total income in 1998, other interest income 4%, loan and deposit-related fees 3%, income from real estate and joint ventures held for investment 5%, and other noninterest income 1%.

Per Share Data ($) (Year Ended Dec. 31)	1998	1997	1996	1995	1994	1993	1992	1991	1990	1989
Tangible Bk. Val.	16.64	15.33	13.75	13.47	12.81	12.21	10.89	9.53	8.81	7.46
Earnings	2.05	1.61	0.73	0.75	0.84	1.01	1.49	0.89	1.50	0.10
Dividends	0.32	0.30	0.29	0.28	0.28	0.20	0.18	0.18	0.16	0.16
Payout Ratio	15%	19%	40%	37%	33%	20%	12%	20%	11%	159%
Prices - High	35¼	27¾	18¼	14¾	12½	16	10⅜	10⅝	11⅜	13⅞
- Low	17¼	17	12¼	8⅝	8⅛	8¼	6½	6⅛	5⅞	5⅞
P/E Ratio - High	17	17	25	20	15	16	7	12	8	NM
- Low	8	11	17	11	10	8	4	7	4	NM
Income Statement Analysis (Million $)										
Net Int. Inc.	174	154	135	105	106	112	116	115	86.0	54.0
Loan Loss Prov.	3.9	8.6	9.1	9.0	4.2	1.1	9.0	5.7	3.8	7.0
Non Int. Inc.	47.3	35.2	19.7	20.4	17.6	14.1	15.3	-11.4	30.0	11.0
Non Int. Exp.	117	101	114	79.2	79.7	76.4	73.2	67.3	68.5	65.7
Pretax Inc.	101	79.4	36.5	36.7	40.2	48.4	49.5	30.8	44.1	-7.7
Eff. Tax Rate	43%	43%	36%	43%	42%	41%	16%	19%	4.70%	NM
Net Inc.	58.0	45.2	20.7	21.1	23.5	28.6	41.9	24.9	42.0	2.7
% Net Int. Marg.	3.08	2.83	2.96	2.33	2.99	3.44	3.53	3.11	2.39	2.10
Balance Sheet & Other Fin. Data (Million $)										
Total Assets	6,270	5,836	5,198	4,656	4,651	3,467	3,478	3,778	4,168	4,099
Loans	5,309	5,282	4,747	4,184	4,189	2,917	2,766	3,254	3,002	2,713
Deposits	5,040	4,870	4,173	3,790	3,557	3,069	3,108	3,355	3,361	3,511
Capitalization:										
Debt	538	365	397	240	477	13.7	15.0	97.0	262	22.0
Equity	481	430	392	384	366	351	313	277	257	219
Total	1,018	795	789	624	843	365	328	373	519	241
% Ret. on Assets	1.0	0.8	0.4	0.5	0.6	0.8	1.2	0.6	1.0	0.1
% Ret. on Equity	12.7	11.0	5.3	5.6	6.6	8.6	14.2	9.3	17.6	1.3
% Loan Loss Resv.	0.6	0.6	0.6	0.7	0.6	0.9	1.0	0.6	0.6	0.6
% Risk Based Capital	12.9	12.6	NA	14.3	14.2	16.9	14.4	12.1	11.1	9.4
Price Times Book Value:										
Hi	2.1	1.7	1.3	1.1	1.0	1.3	1.0	1.1	1.3	1.9
Low	1.0	1.1	0.9	0.6	0.6	0.7	0.6	0.6	0.7	0.8

Data as orig reptd.; bef. results of disc opers/spec. items. Per share data adj. for stk. divs. Bold denotes diluted EPS (FASB 128)-prior periods restated. E-Estimated. NA-Not Available. NM-Not Meaningful. NR-Not Ranked.

Office—3501 Jamboree Rd., Newport Beach, CA 92660. **Tel**—(949) 854-0300. **Chrmn**—M. L. McAlister. **Vice-Chrmn**—C. E. Olson.**Pres & CEO**—D. D. Rosenthal.**EVP-Secy**—D. E. Royer.**EVP, CFO & Investor Contact**—Thomas E. Prince. **Dirs**—M. Abrahams, P. Kouri, M. L. McAlister, B. McQuarrie, C. E. Olson, D. E. Rosenthal, L. C. Smull, S. Yellen. **Transfer Agent & Registrar**—American Stock Transfer & Trust Co. **Incorporated**—in California in 1957; reincorporated in Delaware in 1994. **Empl**— 1,270. **S&P Analyst:** J.J.S.

Dress Barn

NASDAQ Symbol **DBRN**

In S&P SmallCap 600

09-OCT-99

Industry:
Retail (Discounters)

Summary: This retailer operates a chain of women's apparel stores, mainly in the East, offering moderate- to better-quality brand name merchandise at discount prices.

Quantitative Evaluations

Outlook
(1 Lowest—5 Highest)
• **4+**

Fair Value
• **23¼**

Risk
• **Average**

Earn./Div. Rank
• **B+**

Technical Eval.
• **Bullish** since 9/99

Rel. Strength Rank
(1 Lowest—99 Highest)
• **88**

Insider Activity
• **NA**

Recent Price • 18
52 Wk Range • 19⅝-11¼

Yield • Nil
12-Mo. P/E • 11.8

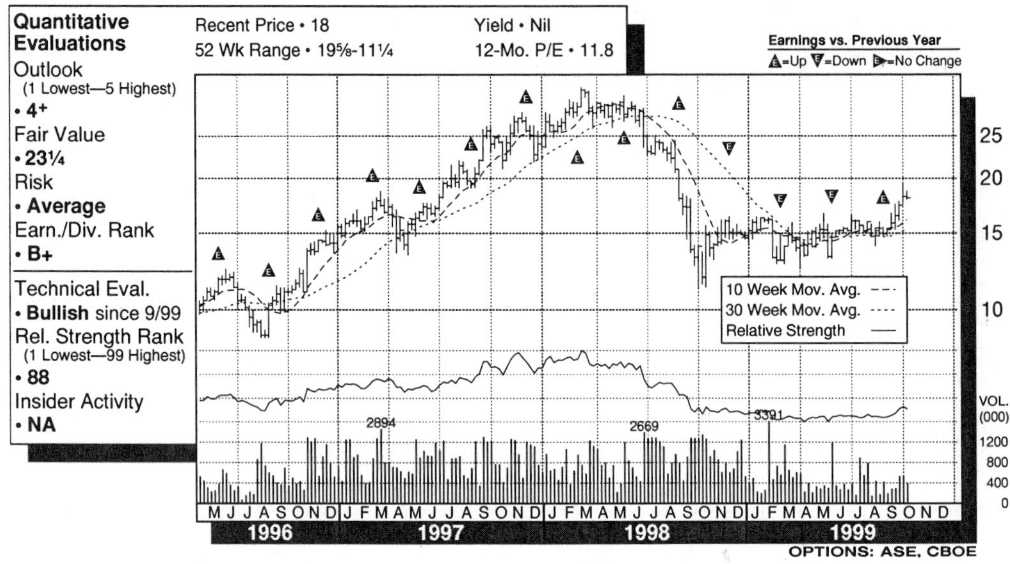

OPTIONS: ASE, CBOE

Business Profile - 15-SEP-99

Dress Barn said that total sales for the four-week period ended August 28, 1999, were $44.5 million, an increase of about 5% versus the same period last year. During the same period, same store sales decreased about 1%. As the working woman continues to "dress down," DBRN will intensify its efforts to build and expand the casual career merchandise offered at its stores. The company's primary strategy for the remainder of FY 99 (Jul.) is to continue opening primarily combo stores, which offer Dress Barn and Dress Barn Woman merchandise, while converting existing single-format stores into combo stores, while continuing to close underperforming locations. As of August 28, 1999, the company operated 679 stores in 43 states.

Operational Review - 15-SEP-99

Net sales for the 39 weeks ended April 24, 1999, rose 1.0%, year to year, reflecting an approximate 6% increase in total square footage, partially offset by a 4% drop in comparable store sales. Margins narrowed on higher cost of sales and SG&A expenses. Operating income declined 17%. Following 16% higher depreciation and amortization expense, and taxes at 36.5% in both periods, net income dropped 24%, to $21,870,000 ($0.98 a share, on 5.9% fewer shares), from $28,900,000 ($1.22).

Stock Performance - 08-OCT-99

In the past 30 trading days, DBRN's shares have increased 21%, compared to a 0.91% fall in the S&P 500. Average trading volume for the past five days was 77,260 shares, compared with the 40-day moving average of 71,010 shares.

Key Stock Statistics

Dividend Rate/Share	Nil	Shareholders	2,000
Shs. outstg. (M)	19.9	Market cap. (B)	$0.359
Avg. daily vol. (M)	0.087	Inst. holdings	66%
Tang. Bk. Value/Share	12.13		
Beta	1.12		

Value of $10,000 invested 5 years ago: $ 13,761

Fiscal Year Ending Jul. 31

	1999	1998	1997	1996	1995	1994
Revenues (Million $)						
1Q	158.8	156.2	142.8	137.3	130.1	119.7
2Q	146.2	144.2	131.5	119.1	116.7	106.6
3Q	144.3	144.3	134.1	125.2	123.5	112.9
4Q	166.7	153.1	146.5	133.9	130.0	118.2
Yr.	616.0	598.2	554.8	515.5	500.8	457.3
Earnings Per Share ($)						
1Q	**0.39**	0.47	0.35	0.27	0.29	0.29
2Q	**0.27**	**0.34**	0.23	0.08	0.11	0.10
3Q	**0.31**	**0.41**	0.32	0.23	0.22	0.19
4Q	**0.56**	**0.48**	0.47	0.27	0.20	0.15
Yr.	**1.53**	**1.70**	**1.33**	0.84	0.82	0.73

Next earnings report expected: late November

Dividend Data

No cash has been paid.

The Dress Barn, Inc.

Business Summary - 15-SEP-99

For the price-conscious working woman, Dress Barn, Inc. (DBRN) is there to offer moderate to better quality in-season apparel and accessories. DBRN also offers a broad assortment of casual wear to suit its customers' total lifestyle needs. In the past several years, the company has evolved from an off-price chain to a value-priced specialty retailer. DBRN attempts to distinguish itself from other off-price retailers by offering a carefully edited selection of first-quality merchandise and service-oriented salespeople, combined with a comfortable shopping environment and convenient locations. As part of its continuous focus on its target customer, the company has developed its own line of private label brands, which accounted for about 65% of net sales in FY 98 (Jul.).

DBRN's stores operate primarily under the Dress Barn and Dress Barn Woman names, with the latter featuring larger sizes of styles found in the regular Dress Barn stores. As of August 28, 1999, the company operated 679 stores in 43 states, both regular Dress Barn stores and Combo stores. The Combo stores carry merchandise from both of DBRN's stores in one location. The Dress Barn and Dress Barn Woman stores average approximately 4,500 and 4,000 square feet, respectively, and the Combo stores average about 9,000 square feet. Based on the success of its Combo stores, DBRN is focusing its expansion strategy on opening new Combo stores and converting existing stores to the combination format. The company plans to open approximately 60 additional Combo stores by the end of FY 99. As part of its strategy, DBRN expects to close about 40 underperforming locations in FY 99, compared with 60 in FY 98.

All aspects of DBRN's business are designed to be responsive to the company's targeted customer. Since 1962, the company has consistently targeted price-conscious, fashion-minded working women. The convenient locations of DBRN's stores, mainly in strip and outlet centers, carefully selected merchandise, comfortable store environment and friendly service embody the company's strong focus on its customers. DBRN believes that it enhances its customers shopping experience by avoiding aggressive sales tactics that often result from a commission-based compensation structure.

The company continually seeks to reduce costs in all aspects of its operations, and seeks to create cost awareness at all levels. DBRN believes that its highly liquid balance sheet and internally generated funds from its operations provide the company with an advantage that enables it to pursue its long-term strategies regarding the opening of new stores, capital expenditures and acquisitions.

Per Share Data ($) (Year Ended Jul. 31)	1999	1998	1997	1996	1995	1994	1993	1992	1991	1990
Tangible Bk. Val.	NA	11.63	10.24	8.82	8.02	7.15	6.42	5.51	4.74	4.11
Cash Flow	NA	2.45	2.04	1.55	1.44	1.27	1.31	1.12	0.99	0.87
Earnings	1.53	1.70	1.35	0.84	0.82	0.73	0.86	0.74	0.68	0.64
Dividends	Nil	Nil	Nil	0.68	Nil	Nil	Nil	Nil	Nil	Nil
Payout Ratio	Nil	Nil	Nil	47%	Nil	Nil	Nil	Nil	Nil	Nil
Prices - High	19 5/8	32 3/8	28 3/8	15 3/4	11	14	23 1/2	20 1/8	15 1/2	12 3/4
- Low	12 3/8	11 1/4	13 3/8	8 5/8	8 1/4	8 1/4	10 1/4	7 3/4	6	4 3/4
P/E Ratio - High	13	19	21	19	13	19	27	27	23	20
- Low	8	7	10	10	10	11	12	10	9	7
Income Statement Analysis (Million $)										
Revs.	NA	598	555	516	501	457	420	363	325	284
Oper. Inc.	NA	74.7	61.4	45.3	40.1	35.9	37.3	30.1	27.5	25.4
Depr.	NA	17.8	16.1	15.8	14.0	12.0	9.8	8.1	6.8	5.2
Int. Exp.	NA	NA	Nil	Nil	Nil	Nil	Nil	Nil	Nil	Nil
Pretax Inc.	NA	63.4	50.0	30.0	29.0	25.6	29.7	25.0	23.7	22.8
Eff. Tax Rate	NA	37%	37%	37%	37%	37%	36%	35%	37%	37%
Net Inc.	NA	40.2	31.8	18.9	18.3	16.2	19.0	16.2	15.0	14.4
Balance Sheet & Other Fin. Data (Million $)										
Cash	NA	3.0	1.1	91.3	72.0	62.0	61.1	50.7	39.1	35.2
Curr. Assets	NA	250	226	184	163	146	143	125	95.0	86.0
Total Assets	NA	345	310	266	244	218	202	173	138	125
Curr. Liab.	NA	79.5	72.7	61.1	60.0	56.8	59.1	51.0	32.6	30.2
LT Debt	NA	Nil	3.5	3.5	3.5	Nil	Nil	Nil	Nil	Nil
Common Eqty.	NA	266	233	199	179	159	142	120	103	93.0
Total Cap.	NA	266	237	205	184	161	143	122	105	95.0
Cap. Exp.	NA	21.7	16.5	17.1	22.0	25.5	21.9	14.9	10.1	14.5
Cash Flow	NA	58.0	47.9	34.7	32.0	28.1	28.9	24.3	21.7	19.6
Curr. Ratio	NA	3.1	3.1	3.0	2.7	2.6	2.4	2.4	2.9	2.8
% LT Debt of Cap.	NA	NM	1.5	1.7	1.9	Nil	Nil	Nil	Nil	Nil
% Net Inc.of Revs.	NA	6.7	5.7	3.7	3.7	3.5	4.5	4.5	4.6	5.1
% Ret. on Assets	NA	12.3	11.0	7.4	8.0	7.7	10.1	10.4	11.6	12.6
% Ret. on Equity	NA	16.1	14.7	10.0	10.9	10.7	14.4	14.5	15.6	16.9

Data as orig reptd.; bef. results of disc opers/spec. items. Per share data adj. for stk. divs. Bold denotes diluted EPS (FASB 128)-prior periods restated. E-Estimated. NA-Not Available. NM-Not Meaningful. NR-Not Ranked.

Office—30 Dunnigan Drive, Suffern, NY 10901. **Tel**—(914) 369-4500. **Website**—http://www.dress-barn.com **Chrmn & CEO**—E. S. Jaffe. **Pres & COO**—B. Steinberg. **SVP, CFO & Investor Contact**—Armand Correia. **Secy & Treas**—Roslyn S. Jaffe. **Dirs**—K. Eppler, M. S. Handler, E. S. Jaffe, R. S. Jaffe, D. Jonas, E. D. Solomon, B. Steinberg. **Transfer Agent & Registrar**—First City Transfer Co., Iselin, NJ. **Incorporated**—in Connecticut in 1966. **Empl**— 7,000. **S&P Analyst:** Matthew C. Hershberg

STANDARD
&POOR'S
STOCK REPORTS

Dril-Quip, Inc.

NYSE Symbol **DRQ**

In S&P SmallCap 600

09-OCT-99

Industry: Oil & Gas (Drilling & Equipment)

Summary: This company is a leading maker of highly engineered offshore drilling and production equipment.

Quantitative Evaluations

Outlook (1 Lowest—5 Highest)
• **NA**

Fair Value
• **NA**

Risk
• **NA**

Earn./Div. Rank
• **NR**

Technical Eval.
• **NA**

Rel. Strength Rank (1 Lowest—99 Highest)
• **22**

Insider Activity
• **Neutral**

Recent Price • 22⅜
52 Wk Range • 30½-11¾
Yield • Nil
12-Mo. P/E • 26.1

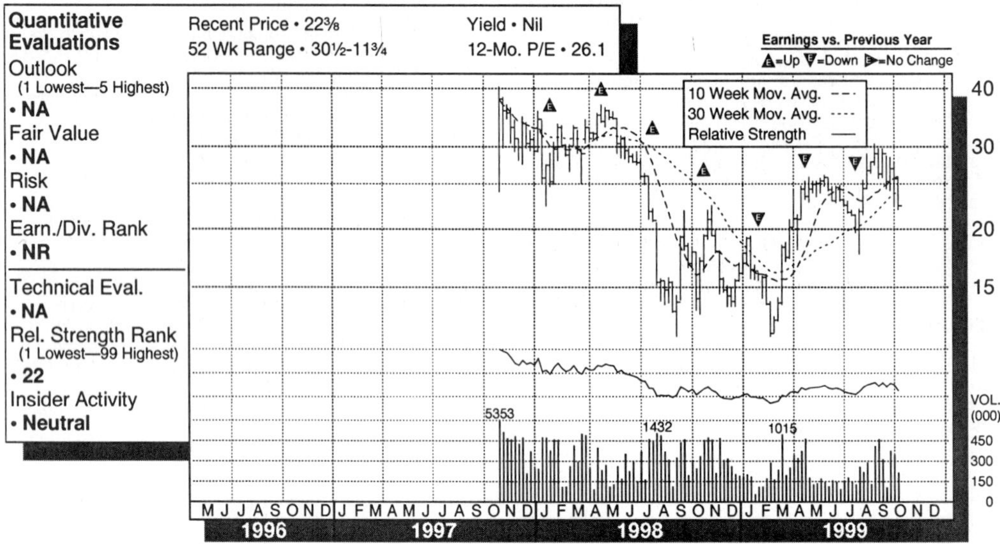

Business Profile - 22-JUN-99

Depressed oil prices, which have led to worldwide exploration and production budget cuts by most major oil companies, resulted in pricing pressure and lower demand for the company's products in the first quarter of 1999. Dril-Quip has noted that it may see a reduction in orders for 1999, which could continue to adversely affect revenues and earnings. Elements of the company's strategy include continuing to develop new products, increasing manufacturing capacity to maintain and improve market share, reducing costs and increasing operational efficiencies, and expanding into selected international markets.

Operational Review - 22-JUN-99

Revenues in the first quarter of 1999 declined 3.0%, year to year, reflecting lower export sales from the U.S. and reduced sales in the Asia-Pacific area due to depressed oil prices. Gross margins were relatively flat, but with higher operating expenses related to an increase in personnel to support greater sales efforts and development testing of new products, pretax income fell 23%. After taxes at 34.9%, versus 34.5%, net income was down 24%, to $3,142,000 ($0.18 a share) from $4,129,000 ($0.24).

Stock Performance - 08-OCT-99

In the past 30 trading days, DRQ's shares have declined 23%, compared to a 0.91% fall in the S&P 500. Average trading volume for the past five days was 42,320 shares, compared with the 40-day moving average of 61,218 shares.

Key Stock Statistics

Dividend Rate/Share	Nil	Shareholders	43
Shs. outstg. (M)	17.2	Market cap. (B)	$0.387
Avg. daily vol. (M)	0.051	Inst. holdings	27%
Tang. Bk. Value/Share	8.45		
Beta	NA		

Value of $10,000 invested 5 years ago: NA

Fiscal Year Ending Dec. 31

	1999	1998	1997	1996	1995	1994
Revenues (Million $)						
1Q	39.58	40.82	34.22	—	—	—
2Q	39.90	44.89	34.45	—	—	—
3Q	—	47.13	38.00	—	—	—
4Q	—	44.81	40.15	—	—	—
Yr.	—	177.6	146.8	115.9	108.4	80.55
Earnings Per Share ($)						
1Q	**0.18**	**0.24**	**0.16**	**0.12**	—	—
2Q	**0.17**	**0.26**	**0.20**	**0.16**	—	—
3Q	—	**0.26**	**0.24**	**0.14**	—	—
4Q	—	**0.25**	**0.26**	**0.21**	—	—
Yr.	—	**1.01**	**0.87**	**0.63**	**0.46**	**0.09**

Next earnings report expected: late October

Dividend Data

No cash dividends have been paid. The company intends to retain its earnings for the operation and development of its business and does not anticipate paying cash dividends in the foreseeable future.

A Division of The McGraw-Hill Companies

Dril-Quip, Inc.

Business Summary - 22-JUN-99

Dril-Quip, Inc. is one of the world's leading manufacturers of highly engineered offshore drilling and production equipment for use in deepwater, harsh environment and severe service applications. It also provides installation and reconditioning services and rents running tools for use in connection with the installation and retrieval of its products. Revenues are derived from product sales (88% of revenues in 1998) and services (12%).

The company designs and manufactures subsea equipment, surface equipment and offshore rig equipment for use by major integrated, large independent and foreign national oil and gas concerns in offshore areas throughout the world. Principal products include subsea and surface wellheads, subsea and surface production trees (used to control the flow of oil and gas from a production well), mudline hanger systems (to support the weight of multiple casing strings at the ocean floor while drilling a well), specialty connectors and associated pipe, drilling and production riser systems (to provide the vertical conduit between the floating drilling vessel and the subsea wellhead), wellhead connectors and diverters (to divert gases off the rig during the drilling operation to protect against shallow gas blowouts).

Products are used to explore for oil and gas on offshore drilling rigs, such as floating rigs and jack-ups, and for drilling and production of oil and gas wells on offshore platforms, tension leg platforms (floating production platforms connected to the ocean floor by vertical mooring tethers), Spars (a floating cylindrical structure anchored in place) and moored vessels.

Products are marketed through major international energy markets worldwide. Principal customers are major integrated oil and gas companies, large independent oil and gas companies and foreign national oil and gas companies, as well as offshore drilling contractors and engineering and construction companies. About 62% of revenues in 1998 were derived from foreign markets.

The company's service group provides field installation services, reconditioning of customer-owned products, and rental of running tools for installation and retrieval of its products.

In October 1997, Dril-Quip completed its initial public offering of 5,750,000 common shares at $24 a share. Of the shares, 2,875,000 were sold by the company and 2,875,000 by selling shareholders. Net proceeds of about $63.4 million were used to increase manufacturing capacity, improve and expand facilities, and manufacture additional running tools for rental.

Per Share Data ($)										
(Year Ended Dec. 31)	**1998**	**1997**	**1996**	**1995**	**1994**	**1993**	**1992**	**1991**	**1990**	**1989**
Tangible Bk. Val.	8.23	7.20	3.54	2.75	2.29	2.11	1.95	NA	NA	NA
Cash Flow	1.34	1.20	0.94	0.78	0.36	0.43	0.36	NA	NA	NA
Earnings	1.01	0.87	0.63	0.46	0.09	0.17	0.12	NA	NA	NA
Dividends	Nil	Nil	NA	NA	NA	NA	NA	NA	NA	NA
Payout Ratio	Nil	Nil	NA	NA	NA	NA	NA	NA	NA	NA
Prices - High	37	40⅜	NA	NA	NA	NA	NA	NA	NA	NA
- Low	11¾	24	NA	NA	NA	NA	NA	NA	NA	NA
P/E Ratio - High	37	46	NA	NA	NA	NA	NA	NA	NA	NA
- Low	12	28	NA	NA	NA	NA	NA	NA	NA	NA
Income Statement Analysis (Million $)										
Revs.	178	147	116	108	80.5	82.6	65.2	NA	NA	NA
Oper. Inc.	31.1	26.5	20.4	17.2	8.1	8.6	8.1	NA	NA	NA
Depr.	5.7	5.0	4.4	4.7	3.9	3.8	3.6	NA	NA	NA
Int. Exp.	0.0	2.0	2.6	2.9	2.3	1.5	1.9	NA	NA	NA
Pretax Inc.	26.7	19.5	13.4	9.6	1.9	3.3	2.6	NA	NA	NA
Eff. Tax Rate	35%	34%	32%	32%	33%	27%	36%	NA	NA	NA
Net Inc.	17.4	12.9	9.1	6.6	1.3	2.4	1.6	NA	NA	NA
Balance Sheet & Other Fin. Data (Million $)										
Cash	11.9	32.6	1.4	2.6	NA	NA	NA	NA	NA	NA
Curr. Assets	117	117	83.0	65.1	NA	NA	NA	NA	NA	NA
Total Assets	177	153	115	93.2	79.2	70.3	65.7	NA	NA	NA
Curr. Liab.	33.6	27.4	33.5	24.4	NA	NA	NA	NA	NA	NA
LT Debt	0.1	0.3	29.0	28.0	NA	NA	NA	NA	NA	NA
Common Eqty.	142	124	50.9	39.5	32.9	30.3	28.0	NA	NA	NA
Total Cap.	144	126	81.3	68.8	NA	NA	NA	NA	NA	NA
Cap. Exp.	29.6	10.4	7.2	6.2	4.6	6.6	4.3	NA	NA	NA
Cash Flow	23.1	17.9	13.5	11.2	5.2	6.2	5.2	NA	NA	NA
Curr. Ratio	3.5	4.3	2.5	2.7	NA	NA	NA	NA	NA	NA
% LT Debt of Cap.	0.1	0.2	31.7	40.7	NA	NA	NA	NA	NA	NA
% Net Inc.of Revs.	9.8	8.8	7.9	6.1	1.6	2.9	2.5	NA	NA	NA
% Ret. on Assets	10.6	9.7	8.8	7.6	1.7	3.5	NA	NA	NA	NA
% Ret. on Equity	13.1	14.8	20.2	18.2	4.1	8.3	NA	NA	NA	NA

Data as orig reptd.; bef. results of disc opers/spec. items. Per share data adj. for stk. divs. Bold denotes diluted EPS (FASB 128)-prior periods restated. E-Estimated. NA-Not Available. NM-Not Meaningful. NR-Not Ranked.

Office—13550 Hempstead Highway, Houston, TX 77040. **Tel**—(713) 939-7711. **Co-Chrmn & Co-CEO**—L. E. Reimert, G. D. Smith, J. M. Walker. **CFO**—J. M. Brooks. **Dirs**—J. M. Alexander, G. W. Loveless, L. E. Reimert, G. D. Smith, J. M. Walker. **Transfer Agent & Registrar**—ChaseMellon Shareholder Services. **Incorporated**—in Delaware in 1997. **Empl**— 1,169. **S&P Analyst:** S.R.B.

STANDARD
&POOR'S
STOCK REPORTS

DSP Communications

NYSE Symbol **DSP**

In S&P SmallCap 600

09-OCT-99

Industry:
Communications
Equipment

Summary: DSP is a leading developer of chip sets and products for the cellular, personal communication services, and wireless local loop markets.

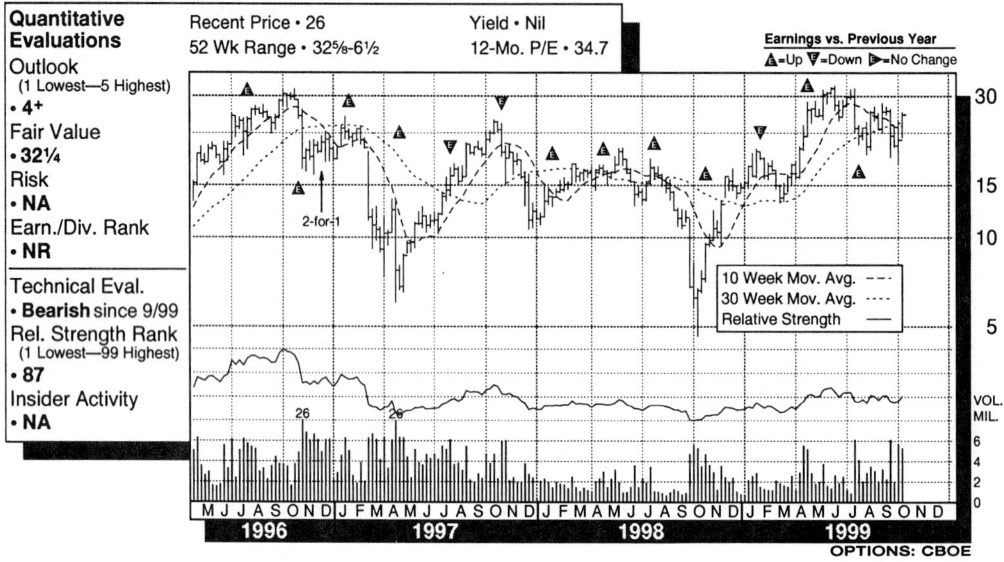

Business Profile - 20-JUL-99

In January 1999, the company said worldwide handset sales were continuing to grow rapidly, adding that it saw increasing opportunities to expand its product offerings in 1999 in the U.S., Japan, South Korea, and Latin America. In December 1998, DSP acquired privately held, Calgary, Canada-based Isotel Research Ltd., a developer of call processing software and Java-based products and services for wireless standards, including TDMA, CDMA, and third generation standards. By bundling its own chip sets and reference design with Isotel's software technology, DSP expected to provide cellular phone manufacturers with a one-stop, integrated solution for wireless technology. In the 1999 first quarter, the company repurchased about 644,100 common shares, for $9.5 million.

Operational Review - 20-JUL-99

Revenues in the six months ended June 30, 1999, advanced 45%, year to year, reflecting strong demand for the company's PDC chip sets and volume sales of CDMA chip sets, which began in the 1998 second quarter. However, profitability was restricted by changes in the customer and product mix, and by sharply higher sales and marketing expenses. After taxes at 11.0%, versus 10.5%, net income was up 18%, to $17,472,000 ($0.40 a share, on 2.4% more shares), from $14,838,000 ($0.35).

Stock Performance - 08-OCT-99

In the past 30 trading days, DSP's shares have increased 12%, compared to a 0.91% fall in the S&P 500. Average trading volume for the past five days was 1,054,200 shares, compared with the 40-day moving average of 773,687 shares.

Key Stock Statistics

Dividend Rate/Share	Nil	Shareholders	10,000
Shs. outstg. (M)	41.0	Market cap. (B)	$ 1.1
Avg. daily vol. (M)	0.987	Inst. holdings	84%
Tang. Bk. Value/Share	3.21		
Beta	NA		

Value of $10,000 invested 5 years ago: NA

Fiscal Year Ending Dec. 31

	1999	1998	1997	1996	1995	1994
Revenues (Million $)						
1Q	35.92	23.09	20.30	17.32	4.26	—
2Q	41.87	30.47	8.69	20.33	8.02	—
3Q	—	34.86	20.47	23.40	12.84	—
4Q	—	42.68	32.03	27.85	15.75	—
Yr.	—	131.1	81.50	88.90	40.87	15.97
Earnings Per Share ($)						
1Q	**0.19**	**0.16**	**0.13**	0.09	0.02	—
2Q	**0.22**	**0.19**	**0.02**	0.13	0.04	—
3Q	—	**0.21**	**0.14**	0.16	0.07	—
4Q	—	**0.14**	**0.20**	0.10	-0.19	—
Yr.	—	**0.70**	**0.48**	**0.48**	**-0.08**	**0.09**

Next earnings report expected: mid October

Dividend Data

No cash dividends have been paid, and the company does not intend to pay any in the foreseeable future.

A Division of The McGraw-Hill Companies

DSP Communications, Inc.

Business Summary - 20-JUL-99

DSP Communications was founded in 1987 to create new technologies for the emerging cellular market. The company is continuing to develop its own technologies and products that combine leading-edge algorithm and system design expertise with proprietary VLSI design.

Demand for wireless personal communications services has grown rapidly in recent years, as cellular, paging and other emerging wireless personal communications services have become widely available and increasingly affordable to growing numbers of consumers and businesses. Changes in telecommunications regulations and allocations of additional radio spectrum frequencies have further stimulated growth of both wireless voice and data communications.

The company entered the Japanese market in 1991, and quickly became a major supplier to the cellular telephone industry. By 1995, DSP had a share of about 25% of the Japanese digital cellular market. In 1997, the company announced several new customer agreements, with Fujitsu, Kenwood and Siemens, among others. DSP also completed the development of baseband chip sets jointly with NEC Electronics, supporting both voice and data capabilities, for use in the TDMA (Time Division Multiple Access) market, and began commercial shipments during the second half of 1997. In addition, the company has developed baseband chip sets for use in the CDMA (Code Division Multiple Access) market. In the 1997 fourth quarter, DSP made shipments of operational samples of its CDMA chip set; in the first quarter of 1998, it began commercial volume production of the CDMA chip sets.

Digital Signal Processing (DSP) technology converts light, sound and other naturally occurring analog wave forms into a stream of digital values (i.e., ones and zeros). Electronic systems can process, manipulate, exchange or store these values, which are reconverted to analog format for playback. Unlike analog technology and regular, non-DSP microprocessors, DSP microprocessors are capable of manipulating audio and speech by multiplying and processing millions of instructions per second in one cycle. Non-DSP microprocessors require multiple cycles for the same task and also work at a slower rate. The company's expertise in digital signal processing and wireless technologies includes proprietary algorithms and software, vocoder technology, system design and VLSI circuit design.

All of the company's integrated circuits are currently fabricated by independent third parties, and DSP intends to continue to use independent foundries in the future.

DSP sells a majority of its products and provides technology development services to OEMs located outside of the U.S., primarily in Japan. Revenues from Japan accounted for 74% of total revenues in 1998, versus 80% in 1997.

Per Share Data ($) (Year Ended Dec. 31)	1998	1997	1996	1995	1994	1993	1992	1991	1990	1989
Tangible Bk. Val.	2.76	2.81	3.03	0.89	0.82	0.16	0.07	NA	NA	NA
Cash Flow	0.76	0.53	0.52	-0.12	0.08	-0.07	-0.21	NA	NA	NA
Earnings	0.70	0.48	0.48	-0.08	0.09	-0.08	-0.23	NA	NA	NA
Dividends	Nil	Nil	Nil	Nil	Nil	Nil	Nil	NA	NA	NA
Payout Ratio	Nil	Nil	Nil	Nil	Nil	Nil	Nil	NA	NA	NA
Prices - High	20	25⅝	31¾	12¼	NA	NA	NA	NA	NA	NA
- Low	4⅝	6	7½	2½	NA	NA	NA	NA	NA	NA
P/E Ratio - High	29	53	66	NM	NA	NA	NA	NA	NA	NA
- Low	7	12	15	NM	NA	NA	NA	NA	NA	NA
Income Statement Analysis (Million $)										
Revs.	131	81.5	88.9	40.9	15.6	4.1	2.6	NA	NA	NA
Oper. Inc.	34.3	20.0	21.8	9.0	3.0	-0.9	-2.3	NA	NA	NA
Depr.	2.7	2.3	1.8	0.6	0.3	0.2	0.1	NA	NA	NA
Int. Exp.	Nil	Nil	Nil	0.1	0.1	0.1	0.1	NA	NA	NA
Pretax Inc.	33.5	24.0	24.9	-1.2	2.3	-1.0	-2.6	NA	NA	NA
Eff. Tax Rate	12%	11%	13%	NM	4.69%	NM	NM	NA	NA	NA
Net Inc.	29.4	21.4	21.8	-2.4	2.2	-1.0	-2.6	NA	NA	NA
Balance Sheet & Other Fin. Data (Million $)										
Cash	66.8	82.0	77.8	10.3	8.1	3.6	2.5	NA	NA	NA
Curr. Assets	129	135	147	38.3	9.8	NA	NA	NA	NA	NA
Total Assets	145	143	155	44.1	11.0	6.4	3.8	NA	NA	NA
Curr. Liab.	33.9	27.0	18.0	9.1	4.4	NA	NA	NA	NA	NA
LT Debt	Nil	Nil	Nil	0.2	0.1	0.2	Nil	NA	NA	NA
Common Eqty.	111	116	137	34.9	6.5	4.1	2.1	NA	NA	NA
Total Cap.	111	116	137	35.0	6.7	4.3	2.1	NA	NA	NA
Cap. Exp.	3.0	2.1	2.7	1.2	0.3	NA	NA	NA	NA	NA
Cash Flow	32.1	23.7	23.5	-1.8	2.6	-0.8	-2.5	NA	NA	NA
Curr. Ratio	3.8	5.0	8.2	4.2	2.3	NA	NA	NA	NA	NA
% LT Debt of Cap.	Nil	Nil	Nil	0.3	2.0	4.4	Nil	NA	NA	NA
% Net Inc.of Revs.	22.4	26.2	24.5	NM	14.3	NM	NM	NA	NA	NA
% Ret. on Assets	20.4	14.4	21.8	NM	25.6	NM	NM	NA	NA	NA
% Ret. on Equity	25.8	17.0	25.3	NM	41.9	NM	NM	NA	NA	NA

Data as orig reptd.; bef. results of disc opers/spec. items. Per share data adj. for stk. divs. Bold denotes diluted EPS (FASB 128)-prior periods restated. E-Estimated. NA-Not Available. NM-Not Meaningful. NR-Not Ranked.

Office—20300 Stevens Creek Blvd., Cupertino, CA 95014. **Tel**—(408) 777-2700. **Website**—http://www.dspc.com **Chrmn**—D. Gilo. **Pres & CEO**—J. Perl.**VP-Fin & CFO**—D. Aber. **Secy**—S. P. Pezzola. **Investor Relations**—(408-777-2720). **Dirs**—L. Broad, N. Brownstein, A. Fischer, D. Gilo, S. Iwamoto, A. Schonzeit. **Transfer Agent**—ChaseMellon Shareholder Services, SF. **Incorporated**—in Delaware in 1994. **Empl**— 230. **S&P Analyst:** J.J.S.

STANDARD & POOR'S
STOCK REPORTS

Dura Pharmaceuticals

Nasdaq Symbol **DURA**

In S&P SmallCap 600

09-OCT-99

Industry: Health Care (Drugs - Generic & Other)

Summary: Dura Pharmaceuticals is a developer and marketer of prescription pharmaceutical products for the treatment of allergies, asthma and related respiratory conditions.

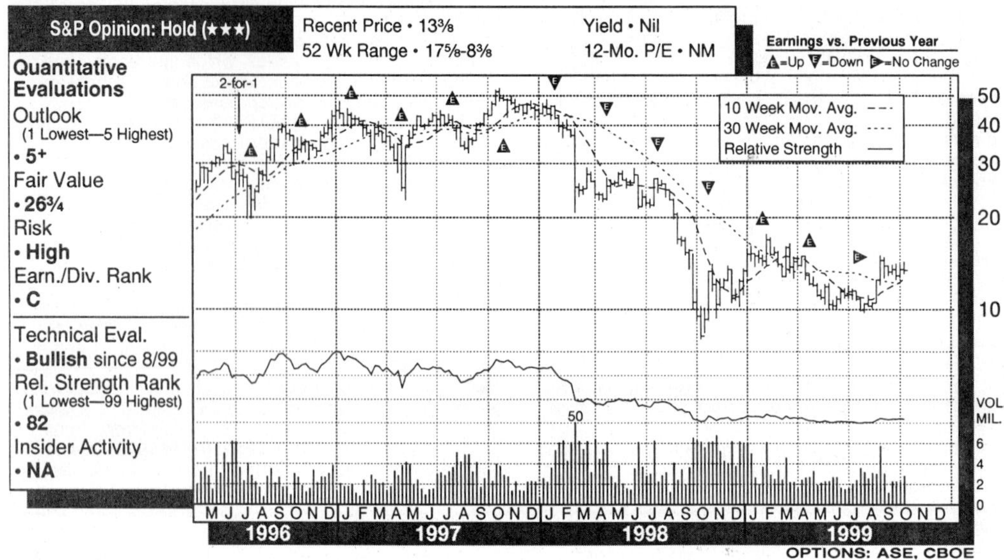

Overview - 20-JUL-99

Revenues are projected at about $300 million in 1999, up from 1998's $199 million. The gain should reflect about $65 million in sales from two intravenous antibiotics -- Maxipime and Azactam -- acquired from Bristol-Myers Squibb in December 1998. Volume gains are also projected for Ceclor CD oral antibiotic and Nasarel and Nasalide allergy drugs, aided by an enlarged sales force. Contract revenues are expected to rise by about 30%, boosted by increased payments from Spiros Corp. II for work on Spiros dry powder inhaler products and payments from Lilly & Co. for the development of inhaled insulin products. Gains are also indicated for the Health Script mail order pharmacy business. EPS from operations are estimated at $0.72, with further progress to the $0.92 area seen for 2000.

Valuation - 20-JUL-99

After a bounce in late 1998 and early 1999, the shares resumed their downtrend, and remain sharply below the highs of past years. The stock fell sharply during 1998, reflecting several quarterly earnings disappointments and a non-approvable letter from the FDA on Dura's Albuterol Spiros product. More recently, the shares have been under pressure from investor concern over proposed new FASB accounting standards that would disallow off balance sheet funding vehicles such as those used by Dura. Nevertheless, Dura's prospects should improve in coming quarters. New drugs acquired from Bristol-Myers Squibb in late 1998, coupled with growth in existing lines and a beefed up sales force, should lead to improved EPS growth over the coming years. Significant potential is still seen for Dura's new Spiros dry powder inhalation products once they obtain FDA approval. The depressed shares, which trade well below the average drug stock multiple, merit retention.

Key Stock Statistics

S&P EPS Est. 1999	0.72	Tang. Bk. Value/Share	0.79
P/E on S&P Est. 1999	18.7	Beta	0.70
S&P EPS Est. 2000	0.92	Shareholders	450
Dividend Rate/Share	Nil	Market cap. (B)	$0.593
Shs. outstg. (M)	44.1	Inst. holdings	65%
Avg. daily vol. (M)	0.469		

Value of $10,000 invested 5 years ago: $ 37,067

Fiscal Year Ending Dec. 31

	1999	1998	1997	1996	1995	1994
Revenues (Million $)						
1Q	55.08	48.77	40.89	18.59	7.40	—
2Q	68.01	51.94	43.63	18.80	11.39	—
3Q	—	43.36	43.34	26.02	11.45	—
4Q	—	55.09	53.46	40.82	13.24	—
Yr.	—	199.2	181.3	104.1	43.49	32.70
Earnings Per Share ($)						
1Q	**0.17**	**0.15**	**0.19**	**0.11**	0.04	0.01
2Q	**0.17**	**0.17**	**0.20**	**0.12**	0.07	0.02
3Q	**E0.13**	**0.05**	**0.24**	**0.14**	0.06	0.03
4Q	**E0.25**	**-0.33**	**-2.57**	**0.22**	-1.44	0.04
Yr.	**E0.72**	**0.06**	**-1.93**	**0.60**	**-1.53**	0.10

Next earnings report expected: mid October

Dividend Data

No cash dividends have been paid on the public shares.

Dura Pharmaceuticals, Inc.

Business Summary - 20-JUL-99

Dura Pharmaceuticals is a specialty pharmaceutical company that develops and markets prescription pharmaceutical products for the treatment of asthma, hay fever, chronic obstructive pulmonary disease and related respiratory ailments. Dura also operates a mail order prescription drug pharmacy.

The company currently markets some 35 prescription products, including 25 that are off patent. The principal product is Ceclor CD, an antibiotic that was acquired from Eli Lilly & Co. in September 1996. Other important products include antibiotics such as Keftab (also acquired from Eli Lilly) and Capastat/Seromycin; cough/cold/allergy products, including Nasarel and Nasalide (acquired from Syntex in May 1997), Dura-Vent, Dura-Gest, Rondec and Entex; and asthma treatments such as Tornalate. In July 1998, Dura acquired the single-source tuberculosis drug Myambutol from American Home Products for $33.5 million. In late 1998, the company expanded into intravenous antibiotics through the acquisition of Maxipime and Azactam from Bristol-Myers Squibb for $130 million.

Dura employs a dual marketing strategy, utilizing its focused field sales force of over 400 people, and a dedicated managed care sales staff of about 15 representatives who cover managed care organizations and retail pharmacy chains. The field sales force targets a physician base that includes approximately 90,000 U.S. allergists, ear, nose and throat specialists, pulmonologists, and a selected subset of pediatricians and generalist physicians, believed by the company to write collectively approximately 85% of respiratory pharmaceutical prescriptions.

Through its Health Script mail service pharmacy, Dura delivers to patients nationwide more than 100 prescription respiratory products manufactured by other pharmaceutical companies. This business is primarily focused on providing long-term medication for patients with chronic respiratory conditions.

An important component of Dura's strategy for future growth comprises its new Spiros pulmonary drug delivery system, which has been designed to aerosolize pharmaceuticals in dry powder formulations for delivery to the lungs. The Spiros system provides more consistent dosing than conventional inhalers, and does not require chlorofluorocarbon (CFC) propellants that are used in currently marketed inhalers. Despite a recent setback, Dura plans to resubmit to the FDA new clinical data on Spiros Albuterol, an inhaler that delivers a powder aerosol formulation of albuterol (a leading generic asthma medication). Additional Spiros products incorporating aerosol formulations of other asthma drugs such as beclomethasone, as well as an inhaled insuling product are also in the development stage. All of these products are being developed in conjunction with Spiros Corp. II, an R&D firm that raised $101 million from a public equity offering in December 1997.

Per Share Data ($) (Year Ended Dec. 31)	1998	1997	1996	1995	1994	1993	1992	1991	1990	1989
Tangible Bk. Val.	0.79	3.73	5.79	2.03	NA	NA	NA	NA	NA	NA
Cash Flow	0.48	-1.59	0.76	-2.89	0.26	-0.95	-0.86	-0.68	-1.46	NA
Earnings	0.06	-1.93	0.60	-1.53	0.10	-0.55	-0.47	NA	NA	NA
Dividends	Nil	Nil	Nil	Nil	Nil	Nil	NA	NA	NA	NA
Payout Ratio	Nil	Nil	Nil	Nil	Nil	Nil	NA	NA	NA	NA
Prices - High	48 5/8	53	47 7/8	17 3/4	7 1/4	3 7/8	NA	NA	NA	NA
- Low	8	22 3/4	16 3/8	5 3/4	3 1/8	2	NA	NA	NA	NA
P/E Ratio - High	NM	NM	80	NM	73	NM	NA	NA	NA	NA
- Low	NM	NM	31	NM	NA	NM	NA	NA	NA	NA
Income Statement Analysis (Million $)										
Revs.	199	181	104	43.5	23.5	15.8	9.6	5.5	3.8	NA
Oper. Inc.	42.4	74.8	28.0	-8.5	2.1	-4.9	-6.5	-2.2	-4.3	NA
Depr.	20.5	15.2	6.3	2.0	0.7	1.0	0.5	1.1	2.5	NA
Int. Exp.	12.1	5.8	0.7	0.9	0.2	0.3	0.2	1.3	1.5	NA
Pretax Inc.	1.8	-65.9	27.9	-35.4	1.9	-8.2	-6.8	-4.4	-8.8	NA
Eff. Tax Rate	NM	NM	13%	NM	1.70%	NA	NA	NA	NA	NA
Net Inc.	2.7	-84.7	24.3	-35.8	1.9	-8.2	-6.8	-4.4	-8.8	NA
Balance Sheet & Other Fin. Data (Million $)										
Cash	31.1	72.0	131	25.6	33.5	4.0	8.2	2.1	1.5	NA
Curr. Assets	303	441	272	78.5	41.0	9.6	16.4	3.3	2.8	NA
Total Assets	825	775	505	144	56.1	20.0	26.3	5.3	5.5	NA
Curr. Liab.	62.2	48.5	52.1	18.7	4.5	2.8	3.4	1.3	2.0	NA
LT Debt	353	297	6.7	15.4	2.8	4.7	4.6	NA	NA	NA
Common Eqty.	410	429	444	109	48.5	12.6	18.3	-14.1	-41.9	NA
Total Cap.	763	726	450	125	51.0	17.0	23.0	NA	NA	NA
Cap. Exp.	42.2	24.1	12.8	7.8	2.8	NA	NA	NA	NA	NA
Cash Flow	23.2	-69.5	30.6	-33.8	2.6	-7.1	-6.3	-3.2	-6.3	NA
Curr. Ratio	4.9	9.1	5.2	4.2	9.0	3.5	4.8	2.5	1.4	NA
% LT Debt of Cap.	46.2	40.9	1.5	12.3	5.4	27.3	20.2	NA	NA	NA
% Net Inc.of Revs.	1.4	NM	23.4	NM	8.2	NM	NM	NA	NA	NA
% Ret. on Assets	0.3	NM	7.5	NM	5.1	NM	NA	NA	NA	NA
% Ret. on Equity	0.7	NM	8.8	NM	6.3	NM	NA	NA	NA	NA

Data as orig reptd.; bef. results of disc opers/spec. items. Per share data adj. for stk. divs. Bold denotes diluted EPS (FASB 128)-prior periods restated. E-Estimated. NA-Not Available. NM-Not Meaningful. NR-Not Ranked.

Office—7475 Lusk Blvd., San Diego, CA 92121. **Tel**—(619) 457-2553. **Website**—http://www.durapharm.com **Chrmn & CEO**—C. L. Garner. **SVP & CFO**—M. T. Borer. **VP & Secy**—J. R. Cook. **Investor Contact**—Karen Lundstedt. **Dirs**—J. C. Blair, H. J. Conrad, J. C. Cook Jr., C. L. Garner, D. F. Hale, D. S. Kabakoff, G. V. Ramseier, C. G. Smith. **Transfer Agent & Registrar**—ChaseMellon Shareholder Services, LA. **Incorporated**—in California in 1981; reincorporated in Delaware in 1997. **Empl**— 942. **S&P Analyst:** Herman Saftlas

STANDARD
&POOR'S
STOCK REPORTS

Dycom Industries

NYSE Symbol **DY**

In S&P SmallCap 600

09-OCT-99 **Industry:** Engineering & Construction

Summary: DY is a leading provider of engineering, construction, and maintenance services to telecommunications providers throughout the U.S.

Quantitative Evaluations

Outlook
(1 Lowest—5 Highest)
• **3⁻**

Fair Value
• **46¾**

Risk
• **High**

Earn./Div. Rank
• **B**

Technical Eval.
• **Bearish** since 8/99

Rel. Strength Rank
(1 Lowest—99 Highest)
• **59**

Insider Activity
• **Neutral**

Recent Price • 40⅞
52 Wk Range • 56⅝-20¼
Yield • Nil
12-Mo. P/E • 26.4

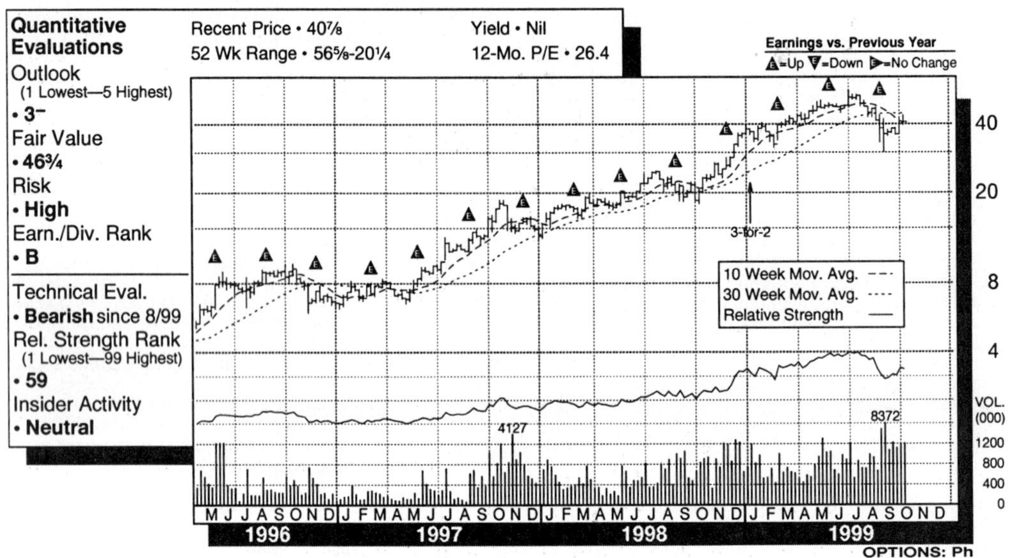

Business Profile - 09-JUL-99

Underwriters offered 2,700,000 Dycom common shares at $48.50 a share in May 1999, with 2,500,000 shares sold on behalf of Dycom. About $33.7 million of company net proceeds were used to repay debt and the remaining proceeds were earmarked to fund DY's growth strategy, including acquisitions, working capital and capital expenditures, and for other general corporate purposes. In April 1999, Dycom acquired for 516,128 common shares Apex Digital TV, Inc., a provider of installation and maintenance services to direct broadcast satellite providers. In March 1999, the company acquired for $21.8 million in cash and 258,066 common shares Ervin Cable Construction Inc., which constructs and installs new cable television systems.

Operational Review - 09-JUL-99

Total revenues for the nine months ended April 30, 1999, advanced 22%, year to year. The gain primarily reflected strong growth in telecommunications services revenues, which stemmed from increased volume of projects and activities related to cable television construction services, geographic expansion, and increased services to existing customers. Profitability improved and pretax income rose 55%. After taxes at 39.7%, versus 34.8%, net income was up 44%, to $22,911,000 ($1.01 a share) from $15,947,000 ($0.69, adjusted).

Stock Performance - 08-OCT-99

In the past 30 trading days, DY's shares have increased 7%, compared to a 0.91% fall in the S&P 500. Average trading volume for the past five days was 245,000 shares, compared with the 40-day moving average of 541,967 shares.

Key Stock Statistics

Dividend Rate/Share	Nil	Shareholders	618
Shs. outstg. (M)	25.6	Market cap. (B)	$ 1.0
Avg. daily vol. (M)	0.250	Inst. holdings	73%
Tang. Bk. Value/Share	4.25		
Beta	1.16		

Value of $10,000 invested 5 years ago: $ 175,178

Fiscal Year Ending Jul. 31

	1999	1998	1997	1996	1995	1994
Revenues (Million $)						
1Q	109.3	91.43	56.41	37.61	36.42	32.02
2Q	97.46	81.46	57.28	32.83	33.79	26.99
3Q	122.4	96.87	63.18	35.39	36.53	31.52
4Q	144.3	101.6	67.05	39.31	38.54	31.96
Yr.	473.4	371.4	243.9	145.1	145.3	122.5
Earnings Per Share ($)						
1Q	**0.33**	**0.25**	**0.15**	0.07	0.07	-0.04
2Q	**0.29**	**0.20**	**0.13**	0.08	0.09	-0.34
3Q	**0.38**	**0.24**	**0.19**	0.13	0.08	0.02
4Q	**0.53**	**0.31**	**0.25**	0.21	0.11	-0.25
Yr.	**1.55**	**1.01**	**0.73**	**0.49**	0.35	-0.61

Next earnings report expected: late November

Dividend Data

Amount ($)	Date Decl.	Ex-Div. Date	Stock of Record	Payment Date
3-for-2	Dec. 14	Jan. 05	Dec. 23	Jan. 04 '99

Dycom Industries, Inc.

Business Summary - 09-JUL-99

Dycom Industries, Inc. (DY), founded in 1969, is one of North America's largest telecommunications and electrical services companies, providing engineering, design, construction, maintenance and facilities locating services to the telecommunications, cable television, and electrical utility industries.

Operations are concentrated in three areas: cable placement, maintenance, and engineering services for the telecommunications and cable television industries; installation of integrated voice, data, and video communications infrastructure within buildings; and utilities mapping and locating services, and electrical utility contracting including the installation, upgrading, and maintenance of high voltage power grids.

The majority of DY's business is derived from companies that are engaged in transmitting information using video, voice or data networks. Its customers consist primarily of large, blue-chip telecommunications and utilities corporations, which engage the company through multi-year master service agreements. Under master service agreements, DY agrees to provide, for a period of several years, all specified service requirements to its customer within a given geographical territory.

Telecommunications services, which accounted for 90% of revenues in FY 98 (Jun.), involve the design of aerial, buried and underground fiber optic and copper cable systems from the telephone central office to the ultimate consumer's home or business. This segment also includes premise wiring services to a variety of large corporations and government agencies; and the placement and splicing of cable, excavation of trenches in which to place the cable, placement of related structures, and maintenance and removal of these facilities.

Utility locating services (5%) involve identification of the exact location of underground utilities such as telephone, cable television, power and gas. These services are performed under contracts with utility companies for the benefit of parties excavating in an area where underground utilities are located.

Electrical services (5%) include installing and maintaining electrical transmission and distribution lines, setting utility poles and stringing electrical lines above ground, and constructing substation facilities and switchyards.

The company's customer base has broadened in recent years, but the customer base remains highly concentrated. In FY 98, Dycom's five leading customers accounted for 65% of its total contract revenues. Approximately 24% of total revenues were derived from Comcast Cable Communications, and 22% were from BellSouth Telecommunications.

In April 1998, DY acquired Installation Technicians, Inc. (ITI) and CableCom Inc., in exchange for 600,000 and 1,200,000 common shares, respectively. CableCom provides construction services to cable television multiple system operators throughout the U.S. ITI provides construction and engineering services to local and long distance tele phone companies throughout the U.S.

Per Share Data ($) (Year Ended Jul. 31)	1999	1998	1997	1996	1995	1994	1993	1992	1991	1990
Tangible Bk. Val.	NA	6.37	1.78	1.00	0.49	0.12	0.57	1.00	1.29	2.06
Cash Flow	NA	2.55	1.21	0.91	0.81	-0.03	-1.62	0.25	0.42	1.11
Earnings	1.55	1.01	0.68	0.49	0.35	-0.61	-2.27	-0.36	-0.13	0.73
Dividends	Nil	Nil	Nil	Nil	Nil	Nil	Nil	Nil	Nil	Nil
Payout Ratio	Nil	Nil	Nil	Nil	Nil	Nil	Nil	Nil	Nil	Nil
Prices - High	56 5/8	39 1/2	18 5/8	9 7/8	5 5/8	2 3/4	3 7/8	7 3/8	11 1/8	9 3/8
- Low	29 7/8	14 1/8	6 1/8	3 1/4	1 11/16	1 5/16	1 5/16	2 5/16	4 5/8	4 1/2
P/E Ratio - High	37	39	27	20	16	NM	NM	NM	NM	13
- Low	19	14	9	7	5	NM	NM	NM	NM	6
Income Statement Analysis (Million $)										
Revs.	NA	369	243	144	145	122	137	134	149	165
Oper. Inc.	NA	46.9	28.7	15.1	14.0	1.9	0.7	4.4	7.8	18.6
Depr.	NA	13.5	8.7	5.7	5.9	7.3	8.4	7.8	7.2	4.9
Int. Exp.	NA	NA	1.9	1.5	2.0	1.7	1.8	2.1	3.1	2.3
Pretax Inc.	NA	36.1	19.0	9.1	4.4	-7.5	-32.5	-5.4	-0.4	12.8
Eff. Tax Rate	NA	36%	41%	30%	NM	NM	NM	NM	NM	25%
Net Inc.	NA	23.0	11.2	6.4	4.4	-7.8	-29.2	-4.6	-1.7	9.6
Balance Sheet & Other Fin. Data (Million $)										
Cash	NA	35.9	6.6	3.8	4.3	2.6	4.4	6.3	6.2	4.6
Curr. Assets	NA	118	55.2	26.8	27.6	23.2	28.5	35.9	36.9	46.0
Total Assets	NA	166	88.2	52.1	52.0	49.0	60.0	95.0	97.0	101
Curr. Liab.	NA	37.0	39.0	17.8	20.1	36.6	17.6	21.9	21.0	17.3
LT Debt	NA	13.4	9.0	9.5	13.9	Nil	23.2	23.5	25.4	25.9
Common Eqty.	NA	98.4	33.8	17.8	11.2	6.7	14.2	45.3	50.2	57.8
Total Cap.	NA	112	42.8	27.2	25.1	6.9	38.4	68.8	75.7	83.7
Cap. Exp.	NA	21.5	12.1	7.6	6.0	5.0	6.9	5.1	13.5	4.8
Cash Flow	NA	36.5	19.9	12.1	10.3	-0.4	-20.8	3.2	5.5	14.5
Curr. Ratio	NA	3.2	1.4	1.5	1.4	0.6	1.6	1.6	1.8	2.7
% LT Debt of Cap.	NA	12.0	21.1	34.7	55.4	Nil	60.4	34.2	33.6	30.9
% Net Inc.of Revs.	NA	6.2	4.6	4.4	3.0	NM	NM	NM	NM	5.8
% Ret. on Assets	NA	18.1	14.5	12.3	8.9	NM	NM	NM	NM	12.0
% Ret. on Equity	NA	34.9	40.8	44.1	49.6	NM	NM	NM	NM	19.4

Data as orig reptd.; bef. results of disc opers/spec. items. Per share data adj. for stk. divs. Bold denotes diluted EPS (FASB 128)-prior periods restated. E-Estimated. NA-Not Available. NM-Not Meaningful. NR-Not Ranked.

Office—4440 PGA Blvd., Suite 600, Palm Beach Gardens, FL 33410. **Tel**—(561) 627-7171. **Website**—http://www.dycomind.com **Chrmn**—T. R. Pledger. **Pres & CEO**—S. E. Nielsen. **SVP**—K. G. Geraghty. **Secy**—P. B. Frazier. **Dirs**—L. W. Adams, Jr., S. E. Nielsen, T. R. Pledger, W. L. Revell, R. P. Younkin. **Transfer Agent & Registrar**—First Union National Bank of North Carolina, Charlotte. **Incorporated**—in Florida in 1969. **Empl**— 3,834. **S&P Analyst:** J.J.S.

STANDARD &POOR'S
STOCK REPORTS

E. W. Blanch Holdings

NYSE Symbol **EWB**

In S&P SmallCap 600

23-OCT-99

Industry: Insurance Brokers

Summary: This company is a leading provider of integrated risk management services, primarily including reinsurance brokerage and consulting services.

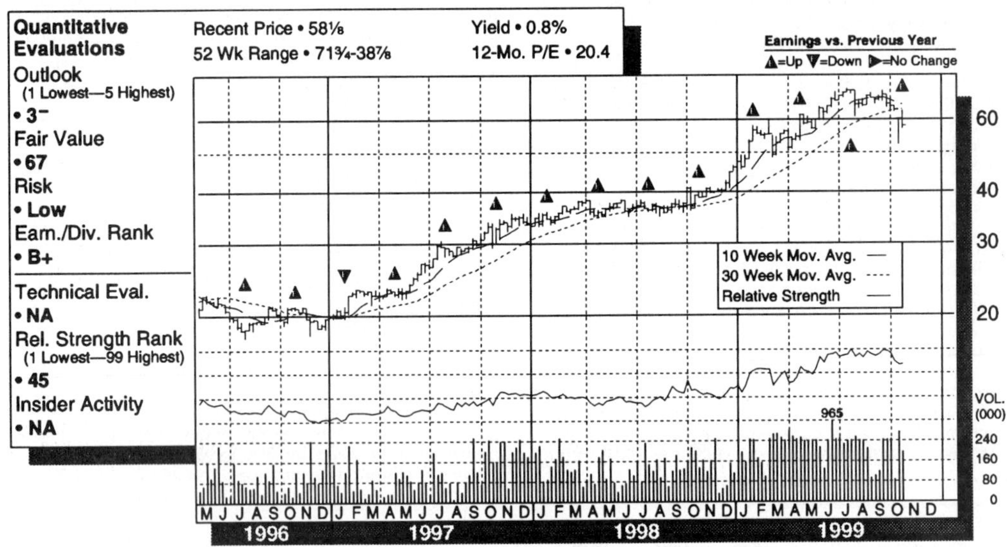

Business Profile - 21-OCT-99

The company has been developing significant new business and expanding relationships with existing clients, while at the same time developing a leadership position in the emerging businesses and technologies affecting its industry. In early October 1999, EWB acquired the 30% of its international joint venture Swire Blanch Insurance (Holdings), Ltd., it did not previously own, from Hong Kong based conglomerate Swire Pacific Ltd. Swire Blanch Insurance (Holdings), Ltd. is now a wholly owned subsidiary of EWB renamed E.W. Blanch (Holdings), Ltd. Swire Pacific will continue to use the services of EWB as its preferred insurance broker.

Operational Review - 21-OCT-99

Revenues in the nine months ended September 30, 1999, climbed 21%, year to year. Total expenses were well controlled, advancing 11%, and with higher net interest income, pretax income was up 45%, to $57.3 million. However, after taxes at 40.8%, versus 38.5%, lower minority interest, and a 131% surge in equity in net loss of unconsolidated subsidiaries, net income was up 32%, to $28,120,000 ($2.05 a share), from $21,302,000 ($1.62).

Stock Performance - 22-OCT-99

In the past 30 trading days, EWB's shares have declined 11%, compared to a 4% fall in the S&P 500. Average trading volume for the past five days was 17,500 shares, compared with the 40-day moving average of 39,618 shares.

Key Stock Statistics

Dividend Rate/Share	0.48	Shareholders	288
Shs. outstg. (M)	13.1	Market cap. (B)	$0.790
Avg. daily vol. (M)	0.060	Inst. holdings	65%
Tang. Bk. Value/Share	7.66		
Beta	0.47		

Value of $10,000 invested 5 years ago: $ 36,305

Fiscal Year Ending Dec. 31

	1999	1998	1997	1996	1995	1994
Revenues (Million $)						
1Q	62.01	46.95	37.03	25.88	26.83	21.71
2Q	58.39	47.37	40.06	22.87	20.44	17.17
3Q	59.00	55.04	45.37	29.83	27.20	22.57
4Q	—	63.36	44.33	30.46	20.46	19.27
Yr.	—	203.6	166.8	109.0	94.94	80.72
Earnings Per Share ($)						
1Q	**0.70**	**0.57**	**0.50**	**0.39**	0.44	0.40
2Q	**0.58**	**0.46**	**0.38**	**0.22**	0.20	0.21
3Q	**0.78**	**0.76**	**0.62**	**0.52**	0.49	0.46
4Q	—	**0.79**	**0.49**	**-0.65**	0.21	0.14
Yr.	—	**2.42**	**1.99**	**0.48**	**1.34**	**1.22**

Next earnings report expected: late January

Dividend Data (Dividends have been paid since 1993.)

Amount ($)	Date Decl.	Ex-Div. Date	Stock of Record	Payment Date
0.120	Oct. 19	Nov. 05	Nov. 09	Dec. 01 '98
0.120	Jan. 28	Feb. 05	Feb. 09	Mar. 02 '99
0.120	Apr. 26	Apr. 29	May. 03	Jun. 01 '99
0.120	Jul. 28	Jul. 29	Aug. 02	Sep. 01 '99

E. W. Blanch Holdings, Inc.

Business Summary - 21-OCT-99

E. W. Blanch Holdings, Inc. (EWB) is a leading provider of integrated risk management services, primarily reinsurance brokerage and consulting services. Reinsurance is the process by which insurance companies purchase insurance themselves to manage their exposure to risks and catastrophic events. EWB acts as the intermediary, or broker, in these transactions.

EWB earns revenues from the structuring, placement and servicing of reinsurance, primarily on a treaty basis. The company is a significant intermediary in the property catastrophe and casualty reinsurance markets. Catastrophe reinsurance indemnifies a ceding company against a catastrophic loss resulting from a single event such as a hurricane, earthquake or tornado. Casualty reinsurance indemnifies a ceding company for a specified loss caused by injuries to third parties including resulting legal liability. EWB's activities in the casualty reinsurance arena relate primarily to professional liability, workers' compensation, and specialized casualty exposures underwritten by excess and surplus lines insurance carriers. Revenues increased from $109 million in 1996 to $204 million in 1998. In the past several years, EWB has expanded its operations in the international area through joint venture agreements and acquisitions.

In April 1998, the company consolidated its headquarters in Dallas, Texas, but the focus for EWB is increasingly becoming international. In 1998, 23.5% of revenues came from foreign operations, up from 22.7% in 1997. In 1996, foreign operations produced less than 1% of total revenues. Through E.W. Blanch (Holdings), Ltd., formerly Swire Blanch Insurance (Holdings), Ltd., a wholly owned subsidiary, the company significantly increased its activities outside of its traditional United States territory. The company now has offices in the United Kingdom, Copenhagen, Hong Kong, Singapore, Australia, Mexico, Brazil, Argentina and Chile. The company plans even further overseas development in the future. Although EWB's foreign operations do not currently benefit from the higher profit margins of their domestic operations, the firm seeks to grow international profitability through increased revenue production and processing efficiencies.

EWB's customer base is well diversified both domestically and internationally. During 1998, no domestic or foreign client accounted for more than 10% of consolidated revenues.

In addition to the reinsurance business, EWB provides risk management consulting and administration services to insurance and reinsurance companies. The company licenses a reinsurance software system to interested parties, which serves to supplement EWB's core reinsurance business. Other consultation services involve the financial industry where the firm provides advice on financial control of employee benefits packages and pension fund administration.

Per Share Data ($) (Year Ended Dec. 31)	1998	1997	1996	1995	1994	1993	1992	1991	1990	1989
Tangible Bk. Val.	6.25	3.28	3.84	2.10	1.40	3.38	2.88	NA	NA	NA
Cash Flow	3.34	2.66	0.94	1.72	1.42	1.11	0.88	0.58	0.38	NA
Earnings	2.42	1.99	0.48	1.34	1.22	0.97	0.75	0.50	0.37	0.26
Dividends	0.46	0.40	0.40	0.40	0.32	0.08	NA	NA	NA	NA
Payout Ratio	19%	20%	83%	30%	26%	8%	NA	NA	NA	NA
Prices - High	48¼	35⅝	25½	23⅜	23	23½	NA	NA	NA	NA
- Low	33	19¾	17¾	16½	15¾	16½	NA	NA	NA	NA
P/E Ratio - High	20	18	53	17	19	24	NA	NA	NA	NA
- Low	14	10	37	12	13	17	NA	NA	NA	NA
Income Statement Analysis (Million $)										
Revs.	204	167	109	94.9	80.7	64.7	54.7	44.0	43.0	37.8
Oper. Inc.	66.0	53.2	39.3	35.3	31.9	24.0	16.8	10.0	8.3	NA
Depr.	12.1	8.7	6.1	5.1	2.9	1.9	1.6	1.0	0.8	NA
Int. Exp.	1.7	1.3	0.2	0.4	0.4	0.4	0.7	0.2	0.2	0.2
Pretax Inc.	57.5	43.2	10.3	29.8	28.7	21.6	15.3	9.7	7.1	5.1
Eff. Tax Rate	43%	39%	39%	39%	41%	40%	40%	37%	36%	38%
Net Inc.	31.8	25.7	6.3	18.2	17.1	13.0	9.2	6.2	4.6	3.2
Balance Sheet & Other Fin. Data (Million $)										
Cash	0.7	11.6	1.1	5.0	1.3	7.9	NA	NA	NA	NA
Curr. Assets	62.2	51.4	35.8	25.0	17.8	12.0	47.9	NA	NA	NA
Total Assets	933	920	515	497	530	432	NA	NA	NA	NA
Curr. Liab.	48.3	37.0	13.2	13.6	21.1	5.3	NA	NA	NA	NA
LT Debt	0.6	13.7	1.2	0.3	0.7	0.9	2.7	NA	NA	NA
Common Eqty.	111	76.5	68.5	66.7	60.7	58.3	51.8	NA	NA	NA
Total Cap.	115	91.7	69.6	68.3	62.5	59.8	54.5	NA	NA	NA
Cap. Exp.	19.5	12.9	4.7	3.9	2.8	2.6	1.0	0.7	1.5	NA
Cash Flow	43.9	34.4	12.4	23.3	19.9	14.9	10.9	7.1	4.7	NA
Curr. Ratio	1.3	1.4	2.7	1.8	0.8	2.3	NA	NA	NA	NA
% LT Debt of Cap.	0.5	14.9	1.7	0.5	1.1	1.6	5.0	NA	NA	NA
% Net Inc.of Revs.	15.6	15.4	5.8	19.2	21.1	20.1	16.9	14.0	10.6	8.4
% Ret. on Assets	3.4	3.6	1.3	3.5	3.5	3.1	NA	NA	NA	NA
% Ret. on Equity	34.0	35.5	9.4	28.6	28.7	35.2	NA	NA	NA	NA

Data as orig reptd.; bef. results of disc opers/spec. items. Per share data adj. for stk. divs. Bold denotes diluted EPS (FASB 128)-prior periods restated. E-Estimated. NA-Not Available. NM-Not Meaningful. NR-Not Ranked.

Office—500 North Akard, Suite 4500, Dallas, TX 75201. **Tel**—(214) 756-7000. **Website**—http://www.ewb.com **Chrmn & CEO**—E. W. Blanch Jr. **Pres & COO**—C. L. Walker. **EVP & CFO**—I. D. Packer. **SVP & Secy**—D. P. O'Keefe. **Investor Contact**—Kristina Hallam. **Dirs**—E. W. Blanch Jr., R. R. Fox, P. B. Ingrey, J. N. Land Jr., W. B. Madden, S. G. Rothmeier, J. D. Sargent, C. L. Walker, F. S. Wilkinson Jr. **Transfer Agent & Registrar**—Norwest Bank Minnesota, South St. Paul. **Incorporated**—in Delaware in 1993. **Empl**— 1,164. **S&P Analyst:** M.I.

STANDARD
&POOR'S
STOCK REPORTS

Earthgrains Company

NYSE Symbol **EGR**

In S&P SmallCap 600

09-OCT-99 **Industry:** Foods

Summary: EGR produces and distributes fresh baked goods and refrigerated dough products in the U.S. and Europe.

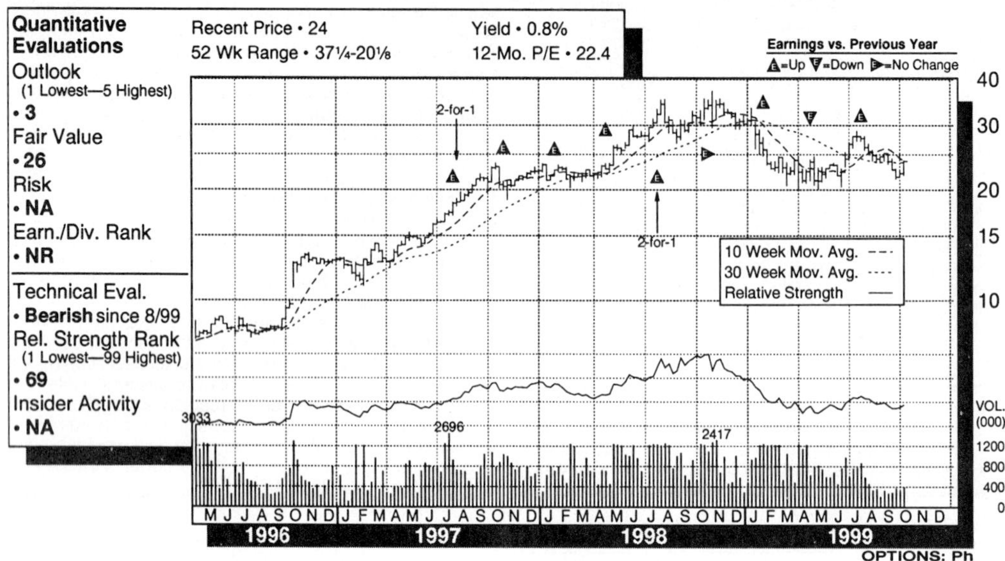

Business Profile - 04-OCT-99

The company is focusing on reducing costs, improving margins, rationalizing capacity, and seeking to provide value to customers. Plans call for continuing to drive margin improvement through brand building, customer partnering, cost reduction, and consolidation and acquisition moves. EGR's acquisition strategy consists primarily of eliminating redundancies, expanding customer partnerships, leveraging investments in information technology and new products, and expanding markets for existing products, such as Earth Grains brand breads and bagels. In June 1999, the company acquired Patrick Raulet, S.A., a leading French producer of refrigerated dough products. This acquisition complements EGR's existing business, making it the largest refrigerated dough supplier in France.

Operational Review - 04-OCT-99

Net sales in the 12 weeks ended June 22, 1999, advanced 3.8%, year to year, as acquisition contributions and new supply agreements were partially offset by divestitures and a decline in refrigerated dough product revenues. International sales were impacted by a $0.6 million unfavorable foreign currency exchange rate impact. Margins widened, due to enhanced operating efficiencies, price and mix improvement, acquisition benefits and lower raw material costs. After taxes at 37.6%, versus 40.1%, net income gained 15%, to $12.5 million ($0.30 a share, on 0.9% fewer shares), from $10.9 million ($0.26).

Stock Performance - 08-OCT-99

In the past 30 trading days, EGR's shares have declined 3%, compared to a 0.91% fall in the S&P 500. Average trading volume for the past five days was 77,380 shares, compared with the 40-day moving average of 62,990 shares.

Key Stock Statistics

Dividend Rate/Share	0.20	Shareholders	35,000
Shs. outstg. (M)	42.7	Market cap. (B)	$ 1.0
Avg. daily vol. (M)	0.067	Inst. holdings	64%
Tang. Bk. Value/Share	5.71		
Beta	NA		

Value of $10,000 invested 5 years ago: NA

Fiscal Year Ending Mar. 31

	2000	1999	1998	1997	1996	1995
Revenues (Million $)						
1Q	449.6	433.0	377.4	370.5	—	—
2Q	469.4	442.4	382.5	381.8	—	—
3Q	—	609.2	514.7	522.7	—	—
4Q	—	440.6	444.4	387.6	—	—
Yr.	—	1,925	1,719	1,663	1,665	—
Earnings Per Share ($)						
1Q	**0.30**	**0.26**	0.17	0.02	—	—
2Q	**0.37**	**0.23**	0.23	0.11	—	—
3Q	—	**0.40**	**0.33**	0.23	—	—
4Q	—	Nil	**0.17**	0.05	—	—
Yr.	—	**0.89**	**0.89**	**0.40**	-0.63	—

Next earnings report expected: late January

Dividend Data (Dividends have been paid since 1996.)

Amount ($)	Date Decl.	Ex-Div. Date	Stock of Record	Payment Date
0.040	Jan. 22	Feb. 10	Feb. 12	Feb. 28 '99
0.040	Apr. 29	May. 12	May. 14	May. 31 '99
0.050	Jul. 16	Aug. 11	Aug. 13	Aug. 31 '99
0.050	Oct. 01	Nov. 09	Nov. 12	Nov. 30 '99

A Division of The McGraw-Hill Companies

The Earthgrains Company

Business Summary - 04-OCT-99

Earthgrains is the third largest U.S. bread and baked goods producer. In FY 97 (Mar.), its first full fiscal year as an independent company, EGR was able to effect a significant turnaround, following a large loss in the preceding year. The company improved revenue and profit margins in each of its businesses, and a continued focus on cost effectiveness (including a restructuring and consolidation program that involved plant consolidations and staff reorganization) resulted in lower costs of products sold and reduced operating expenses. Earnings continued to advance in FY 98 and FY 99.

EGR is a leading producer and distributor of packaged bakery products for sale to retail grocers and food service companies in the U.S. and Europe. Its product lines include fresh, refrigerated and frozen baked goods, refrigerated and frozen dough products, and shelf stable toaster pastries.

Sales in Europe accounted for 16% of FY 99 sales, and 19% of FY 98 sales.

In the U.S., the company's fresh-baked goods are produced at 45 manufacturing facilities in 17 states, and are sold in 28 states in the Southeast, South, Southwest, Midwest and Northern and Central California. Its principal fresh baked goods are baked bread, rolls, cookies, snack cakes and other sweet goods. The majority of EGR's fresh baked goods are sold under the Colonial, Rainbo, Iron Kids, Heiner's, Grant's Farm, and Earth Grains brand names; snack cakes and other sweet goods are sold principally under the Bread Cake and Merico brand names. This segment also produces fresh baked goods for sale under the brand names of its customers. EGR also supplies specialty rolls, sandwich buns, and other products to fast-food chains such as Burger King, Pizza Hut, Waffle House and Jack in the Box. The company operates approximately 275 retail thrift stores that sell certain returned products.

In addition to its leading position in the fresh-baked segment, EGR is the second largest maker of refrigerated and frozen dough products, which include biscuits, dinner rolls, sweet rolls, danish, cookies, crescent rolls and breadsticks. EGR is the only U.S. manufacturer of store-brand refrigerated dough products, which are sold nationwide under more than 100 store brands.

Outside the U.S., EGR was operating, as of March 1999, 10 bakeries in Spain, one bakery in northern Portugal and three refrigerated dough plants in France. EGR sells refrigerated dough products throughout Europe.

Per Share Data ($) (Year Ended Mar. 31)	1999	1998	1997	1996	1995	1994	1993	1992	1991	1990
Tangible Bk. Val.	5.71	6.93	10.26	10.89	NA	NA	NA	NA	NA	NA
Cash Flow	3.29	5.77	2.49	1.32	NA	NA	NA	NA	NA	NA
Earnings	0.89	0.89	0.40	-0.63	NA	NA	NA	NA	NA	NA
Dividends	0.13	0.10	0.04	Nil	NA	NA	NA	NA	NA	NA
Payout Ratio	15%	11%	9%	Nil	NA	NA	NA	NA	NA	NA
Cal. Yrs.	1998	1997	1996	1995	1994	1993	1992	1991	1990	1989
Prices - High	37¼	23¾	13½	NA	NA	NA	NA	NA	NA	NA
- Low	20¼	11	6⅜	NA	NA	NA	NA	NA	NA	NA
P/E Ratio - High	42	27	34	NA	NA	NA	NA	NA	NA	NA
- Low	23	12	16	NA	NA	NA	NA	NA	NA	NA
Income Statement Analysis (Million $)										
Revs.	1,925	1,719	1,663	1,665	NA	NA	NA	NA	NA	NA
Oper. Inc.	204	152	112	48.3	NA	NA	NA	NA	NA	NA
Depr.	102	85.0	84.5	79.5	NA	NA	NA	NA	NA	NA
Int. Exp.	19.5	8.2	6.3	7.3	NA	NA	NA	NA	NA	NA
Pretax Inc.	59.9	62.0	22.7	-33.8	NA	NA	NA	NA	NA	NA
Eff. Tax Rate	37%	39%	29%	NM	NA	NA	NA	NA	NA	NA
Net Inc.	38.0	37.8	16.2	-25.7	NA	NA	NA	NA	NA	NA
Balance Sheet & Other Fin. Data (Million $)										
Cash	53.1	43.7	43.1	33.4	NA	NA	NA	NA	NA	NA
Curr. Assets	385	326	297	256	NA	NA	NA	NA	NA	NA
Total Assets	1,592	1,394	1,172	1,130	NA	NA	NA	NA	NA	NA
Curr. Liab.	283	234	216	198	NA	NA	NA	NA	NA	NA
LT Debt	379	267	103	81.5	NA	NA	NA	NA	NA	NA
Common Eqty.	639	607	582	574	NA	NA	NA	NA	NA	NA
Total Cap.	1,121	974	789	655	NA	NA	NA	NA	NA	NA
Cap. Exp.	86.5	79.6	71.2	109	NA	NA	NA	NA	NA	NA
Cash Flow	140	122	101	53.8	NA	NA	NA	NA	NA	NA
Curr. Ratio	1.4	1.4	1.4	1.3	NA	NA	NA	NA	NA	NA
% LT Debt of Cap.	33.8	27.4	13.1	12.4	NA	NA	NA	NA	NA	NA
% Net Inc.of Revs.	2.0	2.2	1.0	NM	NA	NA	NA	NA	NA	NA
% Ret. on Assets	2.5	2.9	1.4	NA	NA	NA	NA	NA	NA	NA
% Ret. on Equity	6.1	6.4	NA	NA	NA	NA	NA	NA	NA	NA

Data as orig. reptd.; bef. results of disc. opers. and/or spec. items. Per share data adj. for stk. divs. as of ex-div. date. Data for FY 96 refer to yr. ended December 31, 1995. Yr. end changed in 1996 from December 31 to March 31. Bold denotes diluted EPS (FASB 128). .NA-Not Available. NM-Not Meaningful. NR-Not Ranked.

Office—8400 Maryland Ave., St. Louis, MO 63105. **Tel**—314-259-7000.**Website**—http://www.earthgrains.com **Chrmn & CEO**—B. H. Beracha. **VP & CFO**—M. H. Krieger. **VP & Secy**—J. M. Noelker. **VP & Investor Contact**—Molly Salky (314-259-7018). **Dirs**—J. J. Adorjan, P. F. Benoist, B. H. Beracha, M. K. Clark, J. Iglesias, J. E. Ritter, W. E. Stevens. **Transfer Agent & Registrar**—ChaseMellon Shareholder Services. **Incorporated**—in Delaware. **Empl**— 19,400. **S&P Analyst:** Richard Joy

STANDARD &POOR'S
STOCK REPORTS

Eastern Utilities Associates

NYSE Symbol **EUA**

In S&P SmallCap 600

09-OCT-99

Industry: Electric Companies

Summary: This Boston-based holding company, which operates utilities in southeastern Massachusetts and Rhode Island, has agreed to merge with New England Electric System.

S&P Opinion: Hold (★★★)

Recent Price • 29⅞
52 Wk Range • 31⅝-24½
Yield • 5.5%
12-Mo. P/E • 41.6

Quantitative Evaluations

Outlook (1 Lowest—5 Highest) • **1**

Fair Value • **24⅛**

Risk • **Low**

Earn./Div. Rank • **B**

Technical Eval. • **Neutral** since 8/99

Rel. Strength Rank (1 Lowest—99 Highest) • **68**

Insider Activity • **NA**

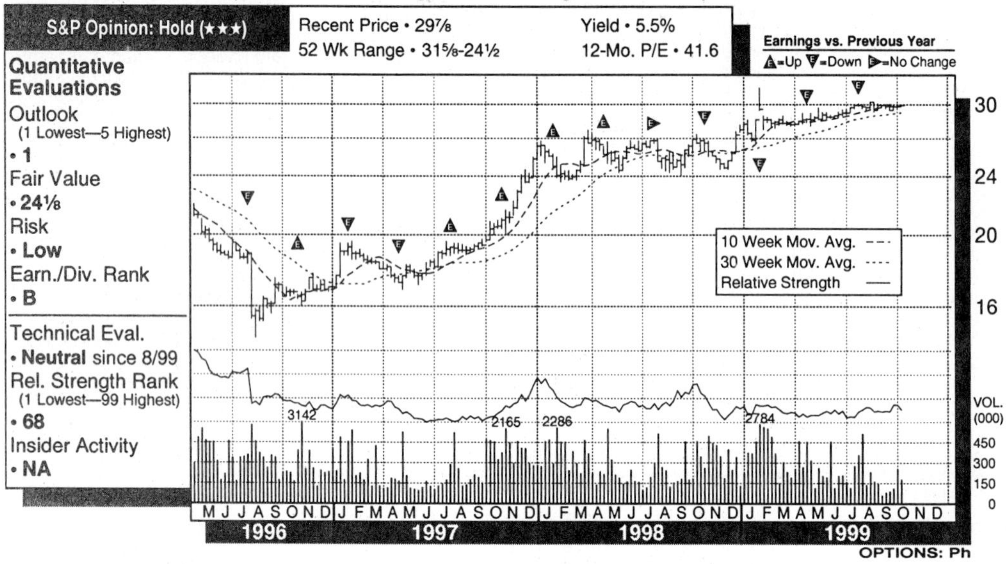

OPTIONS: Ph

Overview - 02-SEP-99

We expect EUA's planned merger with New England Electric System (NES) to be completed by early 2000. The merger (which is not contingent upon the completion of a merger between NES and U.K.-based National Grid Group) would combine the two lowest cost, major electric companies in the region, and would have more electric customers in both Massachusetts and Rhode Island than any other utility. We expect EPS to decline in 1999, primarily reflecting a second quarter charge of $0.77 related to the discontinuance of several energy related businesses. In 1998 earnings declined $0.16, due to nonrecurring charges and a 10% rate reduction that went into effect with the March 1, 1998 implementation of full customer choice in Massachusetts. As part of a settlement agreement in December 1997 (that granted EUA the full recovery of its stranded costs), EUA sold (for nearly twice their respective book values) its Canal Station interest and its Somerset plant.

Valuation - 02-SEP-99

We would continue to hold EUA shares. Under terms of the merger agreement with NES, EUA shareholders will receive $31 a share in cash, with the payment increased by $0.003 per day if the merger is not completed on or before the six month following shareholder approval on May 17, 1999. The shares are up 5.5% year to date (compared to a 8.2% decline for the S&P Index of Electric Companies). After a 51% gain in 1997, the shares were up just 7.6% in 1998 (versus a 10.2% increase for the Index). The exceptional strength in 1997 reflected legislation permitting the full recovery of EUA's stranded costs. Barring unanticipated problems with the planned merger, we would expect the shares to gradually approach the $31 level. We also expect the dividend (yielding about 5.6%) to be maintained at its current level until the closing of the merger.

Key Stock Statistics

S&P EPS Est. 1999	0.90	Tang. Bk. Value/Share	17.34
P/E on S&P Est. 1999	33.3	Beta	0.48
S&P EPS Est. 2000	1.55	Shareholders	11,130
Dividend Rate/Share	1.66	Market cap. (B)	$0.612
Shs. outstg. (M)	20.4	Inst. holdings	51%
Avg. daily vol. (M)	0.031		

Value of $10,000 invested 5 years ago: $ 15,652

Fiscal Year Ending Dec. 31

	1999	1998	1997	1996	1995	1994
Revenues (Million $)						
1Q	138.9	139.3	141.8	134.8	138.0	150.2
2Q	133.4	130.1	138.9	122.8	146.1	137.3
3Q	—	136.0	142.0	131.1	143.9	143.9
4Q	—	133.4	145.9	138.4	135.3	132.9
Yr.	—	538.8	568.5	527.1	563.4	564.3
Earnings Per Share ($)						
1Q	**0.27**	**0.54**	**0.51**	**0.56**	0.57	0.80
2Q	**-0.42**	**0.29**	**0.29**	**0.13**	0.38	0.52
3Q	**E0.54**	**0.45**	**0.54**	**0.43**	0.15	0.67
4Q	**E0.51**	**0.42**	**0.52**	**0.38**	0.51	0.42
Yr.	**E0.90**	**1.70**	**1.86**	**1.50**	**1.61**	2.41

Next earnings report expected: late October

Dividend Data (Dividends have been paid since 1928.)

Amount ($)	Date Decl.	Ex-Div. Date	Stock of Record	Payment Date
0.415	Oct. 15	Oct. 29	Nov. 02	Nov. 16 '98
0.415	Jan. 19	Jan. 28	Feb. 01	Feb. 16 '99
0.415	Apr. 19	Apr. 28	Apr. 30	May. 15 '99
0.415	Jul. 19	Jul. 29	Aug. 02	Aug. 16 '99

Eastern Utilities Associates

Business Summary - 02-SEP-99

On February 1, 1999, Eastern Utilities Associates (EUA) agreed to be acquired by New England Electric System for $31 a share, with the price subject to upward adjustment. The proposed merger is expected to close in early 2000.

With legislation in Massachusetts and Rhode Island having removed many of the uncertainties related to the restructuring and consolidation of the utility industry, the combined company will be well positioned for an era of competitive electricity markets.

EUA supplies electricity to around 305,000 retail customers in southeastern Massachusetts and in Rhode Island. The core electric business (which accounted for 89% of revenues and more than 100% of EUA's operating income in 1998) consists of Montaup, a wholesale electric subsidiary that (following the sale of its generation facilities) will continue to transmit electricity to EUA's three wholly-owned electric utilities: Blackstone, Eastern Edison and Newport.

Electric revenues by customer class in 1998 were: residential, 43% (42% in 1997); commercial, 36% (35%); industrial, 17% (17%); and other, 4% (6%).

Power sources in 1998 were: oil 26% (31% in 1997), natural gas 29% (28%), coal 17% (18%), nuclear 23% (17%), and other 6% (6%).

In November 1997, Massachusetts passed legislation requiring, effective March 1, 1998, the states electric utilities to reduce rates by 10% (with an additional 5% reduction to be implemented on September 1, 1999) and to provide choice of supplier to all customers. The legislation also provided for the full recovery of stranded costs and called for the divestiture of Montaup's generation facilities, with the proceeds used to mitigate stranded cost recovery.

In August 1996, Rhode Island passed the Utility Restructuring Act of 1996 (URA). The legislation provided for unbundling of electric service into generation, transmission and distribution functions; the phasing in of choice of electricity supplier for all customer classes by July 1, 1998 (later moved up to January 1, 1998); and the full recovery of stranded costs through a non-bypassable transition charge.

EUA's nonregulated subsidiaries recorded an operating loss of $0.04 a share in 1998, with losses at the investment ($0.26 a share), energy services ($0.01) and telecommunications units ($0.01) more than offsetting earnings of $0.20 at EUA Ocean State (which owns a 29.9% interest in non-utility generating units) and $0.04 at EUA Cogenex (which provides energy efficiency products and energy management services).

In April 1999, EUA's Montaup subsidiary completed the sale of its Somerset generating facility to NRG Energy, for $55 million. Earlier, in December 1998, the subsidiary sold its 50% interest in Unit 2 of the Canal Generating Station in Sandwich, Massachusetts to Southern Energy, for $75 million.

Per Share Data ($)										
(Year Ended Dec. 31)	**1998**	**1997**	**1996**	**1995**	**1994**	**1993**	**1992**	**1991**	**1990**	**1989**
Tangible Bk. Val.	18.29	17.73	17.60	17.72	17.62	17.46	14.91	14.05	13.75	23.37
Earnings	1.70	1.86	1.50	1.61	2.41	2.44	2.00	1.58	-8.21	2.95
Dividends	1.66	1.66	1.65	1.58	1.51	1.42	1.36	1.45	2.58	2.48
Payout Ratio	98%	89%	110%	98%	63%	58%	68%	92%	NM	84%
Prices - High	28³/₈	26³/₄	24¹/₂	25¹/₄	27³/₄	29⁷/₈	25¹/₄	25	41¹/₂	41³/₄
- Low	23¹/₂	16⁷/₈	14¹/₂	21¹/₄	21¹/₈	23⁵/₈	20³/₈	15³/₄	20³/₄	30³/₈
P/E Ratio - High	17	14	16	16	12	12	13	16	NM	14
- Low	14	9	10	13	9	10	10	10	NM	10
Income Statement Analysis (Million $)										
Revs.	539	569	527	563	564	566	526	524	452	409
Depr.	52.9	49.5	45.5	45.5	46.5	44.7	41.3	40.6	37.5	25.9
Maint.	20.1	30.4	25.0	23.5	23.5	25.1	20.0	20.9	22.5	18.3
Fxd. Chgs. Cov.	NA	2.1	1.8	1.9	2.1	1.9	1.9	1.7	NM	3.3
Constr. Credits	0.8	1.0	2.2	3.2	2.1	2.4	2.0	2.5	55.6	85.4
Eff. Tax Rate	35%	27%	25%	30%	29%	27%	32%	33%	NM	32%
Net Inc.	34.7	38.0	30.6	32.6	47.4	44.9	34.1	26.3	-130	40.9
Balance Sheet & Other Fin. Data (Million $)										
Gross Prop.	1,061	1,156	1,071	1,045	1,029	1,025	1,008	998	992	1,363
Cap. Exp.	51.2	76.1	62.7	78.0	51.0	61.0	42.0	52.0	60.0	161
Net Prop.	707	780	720	721	725	728	733	746	751	1,159
Capitalization:										
LT Debt	345	333	406	435	455	497	463	488	444	606
% LT Debt	48	45	50	52	53	58	60	62	61	59
Pfd.	NA	34.5	33.9	33.2	32.3	32.0	44.3	45.8	50.4	49.7
% Pfd.	NA	4.70	4.20	3.90	3.80	3.70	5.70	5.80	6.90	4.80
Common	374	373	372	375	365	333	267	249	237	375
% Common	52	50	46	45	43	39	35	32	32	36
Total Cap.	861	904	981	984	991	999	935	928	871	1,202
% Oper. Ratio	89.0	90.1	89.4	87.3	87.0	86.7	87.8	87.6	87.7	85.7
% Earn. on Net Prop.	8.3	7.5	7.8	9.9	10.1	10.3	8.7	8.7	5.8	5.4
% Return On Revs.	6.4	6.7	5.8	5.8	8.4	7.9	6.5	5.0	NM	10.0
% Return On Invest. Capital	12.3	8.9	7.4	7.7	9.3	9.8	9.5	8.6	NM	5.9
% Return On Com. Equity	9.3	10.2	8.2	8.8	13.6	15.0	13.2	10.8	NM	12.1

Data as orig reptd.; bef. results of disc opers/spec. items. Per share data adj. for stk. divs. Bold denotes diluted EPS (FASB 128)-prior periods restated. E-Estimated. NA-Not Available. NM-Not Meaningful. NR-Not Ranked.

Office—One Liberty Square, Boston, MA 02109. **Organized**—in Massachusetts in 1928. **Tel**—(617) 357-9590. **Website**—http://www.eua.com **Chrmn & CEO**—D. G. Pardus. **Pres & COO**—J. R. Stevens. **Treas, Secy & Investor Contact**—Clifford J. Hebert Jr. **Trustees**—R. A. Boss, P. J. Choquette Jr., P. S. Damon, P. B. Freeman, L. A. Liebenow, J. Makowski, W. W. Marple Jr., D. G. Pardus, M. M. Stapleton, J. R. Stevens, W. N. Thorndike. **Transfer Agent & Registrar**—BankBoston, N.A., c/o EquiServe. **Empl**— 950. **S&P Analyst:** Justin McCann

Eaton Vance

NYSE Symbol **EV**

In S&P SmallCap 600

09-OCT-99

Industry:
Investment Management

Summary: This Boston-based holding company is primarily engaged in investment management.

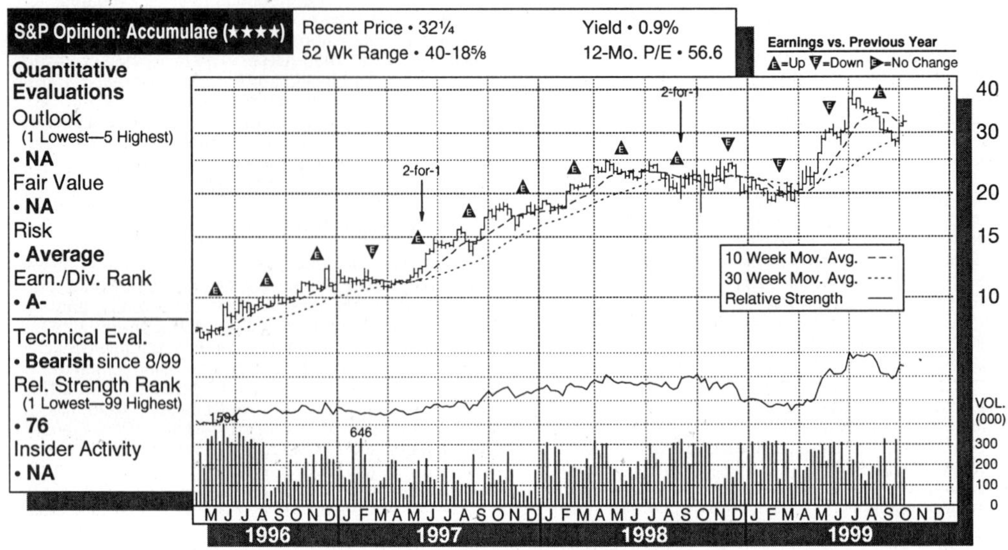

Overview - 08-JUL-99

Net sales of EV-managed funds increased 100% in the first half of FY 99 (Oct.), to $5.2 billion from $2.6 billion in the first six months of FY 98. This contributed to a 45% increase in managed assets as of April 30, 1999, to $37.0 billion from $25.5 billion a year earlier. With the start of the FY 99 third quarter (May 1), the company resumed capitalizing and amortizing sales commissions for certain of its funds. The SEC had ruled in 1998 that these commissions had to be expensed as start-up costs. We have increased our earnings estimates to reflect the change. In FY 99, when we are projecting revenues will approach $350 million, the change in accounting will only affect the second half of the year, and we have upped our estimate from $1.50 to $1.60. In FY 00, we expect revenues will approach $430 million, and have sharply raised our EPS estimate from $1.80 to $3.00.

Valuation - 08-JUL-99

The change in accounting for sales commissions for certain of EV's funds will result in a better match of expenses with revenues. Reported profits will also more closely track cash flow from operations. Under the rules in place from July 1998 to April 1999, reported earnings were very volatile, while cash flow remained largely unaffected. While we continued to recommend purchase of the shares during this period, the market largely ignored the stock, but it now seems to be highly pleased with the sharp increase in reported earnings that will result from the accounting change, as the shares have skyrocketed since May. Although EV is now much closer to full value, the shares still merit accumulation as the outlook for continued growth in managed assets remains positive.

Key Stock Statistics

S&P EPS Est. 1999	2.40	Tang. Bk. Value/Share	5.03
P/E on S&P Est. 1999	13.4	Beta	0.67
S&P EPS Est. 2000	3.00	Shareholders	951
Dividend Rate/Share	0.30	Market cap. (B)	$ 1.2
Shs. outstg. (M)	35.9	Inst. holdings	33%
Avg. daily vol. (M)	0.049		

Value of $10,000 invested 5 years ago: NA

Fiscal Year Ending Oct. 31

	1999	1998	1997	1996	1995	1994
Revenues (Million $)						
1Q	75.48	55.27	47.81	44.50	41.54	53.89
2Q	84.32	59.99	47.44	45.46	40.73	54.25
3Q	91.05	67.00	47.74	45.06	42.69	54.81
4Q	—	67.72	53.86	46.34	42.96	55.83
Yr.	—	250.0	200.9	181.4	167.9	218.0
Earnings Per Share ($)						
1Q	**-0.27**	**0.29**	0.26	0.26	0.15	0.17
2Q	**0.27**	**0.30**	0.24	0.23	0.16	0.20
3Q	**0.70**	**0.36**	0.28	0.24	0.23	0.16
4Q	—	**-0.15**	0.27	0.20	0.18	0.22
Yr.	—	**0.81**	**1.04**	**0.94**	0.72	0.75

Next earnings report expected: late November

Dividend Data (Dividends have been paid since 1976.)

Amount ($)	Date Decl.	Ex-Div. Date	Stock of Record	Payment Date
0.075	Oct. 15	Oct. 28	Oct. 30	Nov. 09 '98
0.075	Jan. 21	Jan. 28	Feb. 01	Feb. 08 '99
0.075	Apr. 21	Apr. 29	May. 03	May. 10 '99
0.075	Jul. 14	Jul. 28	Jul. 30	Aug. 09 '99

Business Summary - 08-JUL-99

Eaton Vance Corp. is a Boston-based investment advisory company. Historically, it has focused on offering products in the fixed-income sector, with particular emphasis on tax-free municipal bonds. However, with industry dynamics pushing an increasing number of investors into the stock market for superior investment returns, EV has targeted its equity business as a growth area. This was a primary driver in the 33% increase in total assets under management to $28.4 billion at the end of FY 98 (Oct.), from $21.3 billion at October 31, 1997.

Reflecting this strategy, the trend in recent years has been for equities to account for a higher percentage of fund assets, while non-taxable fixed income assets have declined as a percentage of assets under management. Managed assets at the end of fiscal 1998 were divided: equities 34%, non-taxable fixed income 26%, bank loans 22%, taxable fixed income 8%, money market 1%, and separately managed accounts 9%. This compares to fiscal 1997 end when assets were: equities 25%, non-taxable fixed income 35%, bank loans 18%, taxable fixed income 10%, money market 1%, and separately managed accounts 11%.

The company derives the vast majority of its revenue from investment advisory and administration fees and distribution income received from the Eaton Vance funds and separately managed accounts. These fees are calculated as a percentage of assets under management, and as such, the company's operating results are largely dependent on its ability to attract and retain funds, and on the overall health of the securities markets.

Net fund sales were $5.6 billion in FY 98, a four-fold increase from the $1.4 billion in FY 97, reflecting strong equity fund sales before the July 1998 market peak and strong sales of bank loan funds in the latter part of the year. Eaton Vance employs two separate mutual fund sales teams that operate through different distribution channels. The company uses targeted marketing to push its funds through a wide variety of national and regional broker/dealers, independent broker/dealers and banks. To further improve distribution, EV has recently begun marketing its products through independent fee-based advisers.

Eaton Vance has committed to sell most of the assets of Northeast Properties, a real estate subsidiary with 662,000 sq. ft. of properties in Massachusetts, New Hampshire and New York. In FY 98, a $2.6 million charge was recorded to reduce the value of certain of the properties to net realizable value.

In addition to steadily increasing its cash dividend over the past decade, Eaton Vance has used its significant cash reserves to repurchase stock. In FY 98, it bought back 2,099,000 shares of its non-voting common stock.

Per Share Data ($) (Year Ended Oct. 31)	1998	1997	1996	1995	1994	1993	1992	1991	1990	1989
Tangible Bk. Val.	5.91	6.04	5.54	5.17	4.49	3.89	2.51	1.94	1.56	1.41
Cash Flow	0.90	1.10	1.00	0.79	2.24	2.03	1.65	1.31	0.95	0.63
Earnings	0.81	1.04	0.94	0.72	0.75	0.77	0.62	0.44	0.26	0.25
Dividends	0.26	0.21	0.18	0.16	0.15	0.12	0.09	0.07	0.06	0.05
Payout Ratio	31%	20%	19%	22%	20%	16%	14%	17%	23%	21%
Prices - High	25 1/8	19 1/8	12 1/2	9 7/8	9 3/8	10 3/8	7 5/8	4 1/8	3 1/2	3 1/2
- Low	17 1/2	10 1/2	6 1/2	6 7/8	6 1/8	7 1/4	3 7/8	2	1 13/16	2 3/4
P/E Ratio - High	31	18	13	14	13	13	12	9	14	14
- Low	22	10	7	9	8	9	6	5	7	11
Income Statement Analysis (Million $)										
Commissions	152	118	100	85.4	85.8	75.2	69.5	61.5	55.1	NA
Int. Inc.	5.6	3.6	3.7	2.6	4.9	4.6	3.7	3.7	2.7	3.3
Total Revs.	250	201	181	168	218	189	153	120	94.0	64.0
Int. Exp.	3.8	4.0	3.7	4.7	5.3	4.9	3.3	3.1	3.6	NA
Pretax Inc.	50.0	67.5	59.9	46.1	47.7	47.0	33.1	21.1	16.4	13.5
Eff. Tax Rate	39%	40%	40%	38%	40%	42%	42%	40%	53%	46%
Net Inc.	30.5	40.2	35.8	30.4	28.5	27.3	19.3	12.7	7.7	7.3
Balance Sheet & Other Fin. Data (Million $)										
Total Assets	380	387	360	358	456	426	318	278	224	242
Cash Items	54.4	141	116	79.0	34.0	28.7	25.5	17.1	15.7	91.0
Receivables	11.2	13.1	7.7	1.6	13.1	11.6	10.5	7.2	4.1	3.5
Secs. Owned	NA	NA	NA	NA	88.3	80.2	64.0	50.8	36.1	NA
Sec. Borrowed	NA	NA	NA	Nil	Nil	Nil	Nil	Nil	Nil	NA
Due Brokers & Cust.	NA	NA	NA	Nil	Nil	Nil	Nil	Nil	Nil	NA
Other Liabs.	2.1	121	125	138	226	205	162	153	124	NA
Capitalization:										
Debt	53.0	50.9	54.5	56.1	60.3	73.2	78.4	64.0	50.6	14.2
Equity	212	226	211	195	166	145	77.5	59.6	47.9	43.9
Total	212	347	336	333	229	221	156	125	100	58.0
% Return On Revs.	12.2	20.0	19.8	16.1	13.1	14.5	12.6	10.6	8.2	11.4
% Ret. on Assets	8.0	10.8	10.0	6.6	6.5	7.4	6.4	5.1	3.3	3.6
% Ret. on Equity	13.9	18.4	17.7	15.0	18.3	24.7	28.0	23.5	16.9	17.9

Data as orig reptd.; bef. results of disc opers/spec. items. Per share data adj. for stk. divs. Bold denotes diluted EPS (FASB 128)-prior periods restated. E-Estimated. NA-Not Available. NM-Not Meaningful. NR-Not Ranked.

Office—24 Federal St., Boston, MA 02110. **Tel**—(617) 482-8260. **Website**—http://www.eatonvance.com **Chrmn, Pres & CEO**—J. B. Hawkes. **VP & Secy**—T. Otis. **VP, CFO & Investor Contact**—William M. Steul. **Dirs**—J. G. L. Cabot, J. B. Hawkes, J. M. Nelson, V. M. O'Reilly, B. A. Rowland, Jr., R. Z. Sorenson. **Transfer Agent & Registrar**—BostonEquiserve. **Incorporated**—in Maryland in 1959. **Empl**— 367. **S&P Analyst:** Mark S. Basham

STANDARD & POOR'S STOCK REPORTS

Elcor Corp.

NYSE Symbol **ELK**

In S&P SmallCap 600

09-OCT-99

Industry: Building Materials

Summary: ELK produces and markets roofing materials, manufactures industrial products, and provides consulting and technology licensing services.

Quantitative Evaluations

Outlook (1 Lowest—5 Highest) • **3+**

Fair Value • **29⅞**

Risk • **Low**

Earn./Div. Rank • **B**

Technical Eval. • **Bullish** since 9/99

Rel. Strength Rank (1 Lowest—99 Highest) • **69**

Insider Activity • **Favorable**

Recent Price • 25⅛

52 Wk Range • 30¼-13¼

Yield • 0.8%

12-Mo. P/E • 19.8

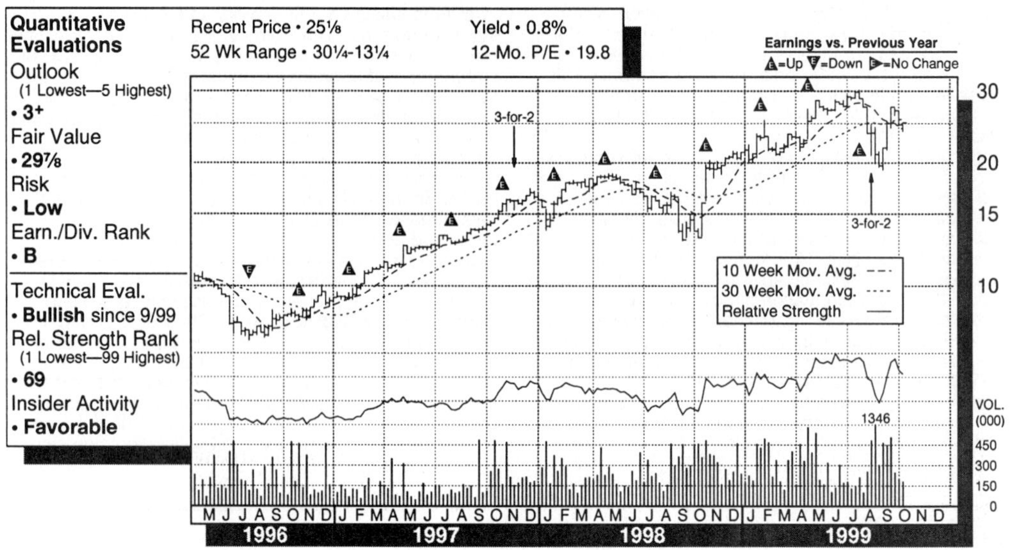

Business Profile - 05-AUG-99

Recent results have been aided by strong demand in the residential roofing replacement market and a continued high level of new construction. The third expansion of ELK's conductive coatings facilities was completed during FY 99's second quarter as ELK ramps up production of wireless digital cellular phone components to meet soaring demand. Longer term, the company believes it has the potential to more than double earnings over the next three years. The common stock was split 3-for-2 and the dividend raised 7% in August 1999.

Operational Review - 05-AUG-99

Sales for the nine months ended March 31, 1999, rose 18%, year to year, primarily reflecting increased production, a record level of shipments of the company's laminated fiberglass asphalt shingles, and accelerating demand for products used in digital wireless cellular phones. Gross margins widened, and with well controlled SG&A expense, operating profit advanced 44%. With lower interest expense, and after taxes at 37.8%, versus 36.5%, net income was up 48%, to $17,319,000 ($1.30 a share) from $11,711,000 ($0.87). Results in the FY 99 period exclude a $0.32 a share charge for the cumulative effect of an accounting change.

Stock Performance - 08-OCT-99

In the past 30 trading days, ELK's shares have increased 28%, compared to a 0.91% fall in the S&P 500. Average trading volume for the past five days was 35,660 shares, compared with the 40-day moving average of 109,682 shares.

Key Stock Statistics

Dividend Rate/Share	0.20	Shareholders	992
Shs. outstg. (M)	19.5	Market cap. (B)	$0.491
Avg. daily vol. (M)	0.079	Inst. holdings	67%
Tang. Bk. Value/Share	7.03		
Beta	0.75		

Value of $10,000 invested 5 years ago: $ 31,742

Fiscal Year Ending Jun. 30

	1999	1998	1997	1996	1995	1994
Revenues (Million $)						
1Q	85.87	73.52	64.54	48.53	38.48	42.85
2Q	71.20	60.96	26.00	45.36	35.97	36.97
3Q	70.74	59.23	57.12	50.05	37.82	37.96
4Q	90.07	74.47	58.46	52.52	46.79	39.26
Yr.	317.9	268.2	206.1	196.5	159.1	157.0
Earnings Per Share ($)						
1Q	**0.37**	0.27	0.19	0.18	0.16	0.22
2Q	**0.23**	**0.15**	0.12	0.11	0.06	0.14
3Q	**0.25**	**0.17**	0.13	0.12	0.08	0.17
4Q	**0.40**	**0.33**	0.21	0.11	0.18	0.24
Yr.	**1.27**	**0.91**	**0.61**	0.52	0.48	0.78

Next earnings report expected: mid October

Dividend Data (Dividends have been paid since 1995.)

Amount ($)	Date Decl.	Ex-Div. Date	Stock of Record	Payment Date
0.070	Mar. 29	Apr. 13	Apr. 15	May. 12 '99
0.075	Jun. 28	Jul. 13	Jul. 15	Aug. 11 '99
3-for-2	Jun. 28	Aug. 12	Jul. 15	Aug. 11 '99
0.050	Sep. 27	Oct. 12	Oct. 14	Nov. 10 '99

A Division of The McGraw-Hill Companies

Elcor Corporation

Business Summary - 05-AUG-99

Elcor Corp., through subsidiaries, makes roofing and industrial products. It also provides technology licensing and engineering support services. In FY 98 (Jun.), roofing products contributed 86% of sales and 70% of profits, and industrial products 14% and 30%, respectively.

Major roofing products are premium laminated fiberglass asphalt roofing shingles sold under the names Prestique, Raised Profile, Capstone and others. The company also makes nonwoven fiberglass roofing mat, used primarily in the manufacture of asphalt shingles and nonwoven mats used in other industrial applications.

Premium laminated asphalt shingles account for about 30% of the residential sloped asphalt shingle roofing market. About 80% of asphalt shingles are used in reroofing and remodeling, and 20% are used in new construction. Homes are reroofed about every 17 years, and the national housing stock grows each year, as the number of newly constructed homes exceeds the number of homes removed from the stock. In recent years, many homeowners concerned with the potential fire hazard associated with wood shingled roofs, have turned to premium laminated fiberglass asphalt shingles, which carry the highest rating for resisting flame spread awarded by Underwriters Laboratory.

The Chromium subsidiary is engaged in the remanufacture of diesel engine cylinder liners, and tin plating of pistons, primarily for the railroad, marine and stationary power industries; and the remanufacture of hard chrome plating of original equipment cylinder liners and tin plating of pistons for major domestic locomotive manufacturers and stationary power equipment manufacturers. In addition, Chromium performs electroless shielding of plastic enclosures for telecommunications, medical electronic and other electronic equipment, designed to provide electromagnetic and radio frequency interference protection.

The Ortloff Engineers subsidiary provides technology licensing and engineering support services, and engineering consulting services to the oil and gas production, gas processing and sulfur recovery industries.

During the past five years, the company's subsidiaries have invested more than $125 million to expand production capacity, reduce manufacturing costs, improve quality and productivity, and ensure safety of the workplace and protection of the environment. These investments included construction of the new Shafter, CA, laminated asphalt shingle manufacturing plant, the new Ennis, TX, nonwoven fiberglass roofing mat facility, and improvements at other sites.

Per Share Data ($) (Year Ended Jun. 30)	1999	1998	1997	1996	1995	1994	1993	1992	1991	1990
Tangible Bk. Val.	NA	9.52	5.70	5.18	4.77	4.31	3.57	1.24	0.72	1.72
Cash Flow	NA	2.17	1.08	0.76	0.66	1.00	1.11	0.54	-0.25	0.54
Earnings	1.27	0.91	0.65	0.52	0.48	0.78	0.85	0.26	-0.53	0.12
Dividends	0.18	0.16	0.12	0.08	Nil	Nil	Nil	Nil	0.10	0.10
Payout Ratio	14%	18%	18%	16%	Nil	Nil	Nil	Nil	NM	87%
Prices - High	30 1/4	21 7/8	17 3/8	11 3/8	10 5/8	11 1/2	16 1/4	8 5/8	4 1/4	5 5/8
- Low	19 1/8	12 7/8	9 1/4	7 3/8	5 3/4	6 1/4	7 1/2	3 1/2	1 13/16	2
P/E Ratio - High	24	24	27	22	22	15	19	33	NM	49
- Low	15	14	14	14	12	8	9	13	NM	17
Income Statement Analysis (Million $)										
Revs.	NA	268	231	197	159	157	173	149	129	151
Oper. Inc.	NA	41.6	30.2	21.4	19.0	28.9	29.8	13.9	-0.8	11.4
Depr.	NA	11.1	8.7	4.7	3.6	4.4	4.5	4.5	4.6	6.8
Int. Exp.	NA	2.6	1.1	0.4	0.1	0.2	1.4	3.1	3.6	3.9
Pretax Inc.	NA	28.5	20.6	16.5	15.3	24.9	23.9	6.5	-8.7	2.7
Eff. Tax Rate	NA	36%	37%	38%	38%	38%	38%	33%	NM	34%
Net Inc.	NA	18.3	13.0	10.3	9.6	15.6	14.8	4.3	-8.7	1.8
Balance Sheet & Other Fin. Data (Million $)										
Cash	NA	5.2	3.6	3.7	3.7	5.9	18.5	2.7	5.4	2.8
Curr. Assets	NA	94.5	86.3	77.7	53.4	61.2	62.6	42.8	45.3	54.0
Total Assets	NA	217	207	192	137	108	91.0	72.0	77.0	96.0
Curr. Liab.	NA	27.2	28.3	28.6	21.3	21.7	21.5	27.8	24.1	22.0
LT Debt	NA	48.0	52.6	53.0	18.4	Nil	Nil	23.3	40.8	46.5
Common Eqty.	NA	126	113	102	93.6	85.2	69.7	20.6	11.8	27.7
Total Cap.	NA	190	179	164	116	86.6	69.7	43.8	52.6	74.2
Cap. Exp.	NA	14.3	15.8	40.7	42.4	17.3	3.3	2.0	3.8	4.3
Cash Flow	NA	29.4	21.7	15.0	13.1	20.0	19.2	8.9	-4.1	8.6
Curr. Ratio	NA	3.5	3.1	2.7	2.5	2.8	2.9	1.5	1.9	2.4
% LT Debt of Cap.	NA	25.3	29.4	32.4	15.9	Nil	Nil	53.0	77.6	62.6
% Net Inc.of Revs.	NA	6.8	5.6	5.2	6.0	9.9	8.5	2.9	NM	1.2
% Ret. on Assets	NA	8.6	6.5	6.3	7.7	15.5	16.8	5.8	NM	1.9
% Ret. on Equity	NA	15.4	12.1	10.6	10.6	20.0	31.4	26.7	NM	6.7

Data as orig reptd.; bef. results of disc opers/spec. items. Per share data adj. for stk. divs. Bold denotes diluted EPS (FASB 128)-prior periods restated. E-Estimated. NA-Not Available. NM-Not Meaningful. NR-Not Ranked.

Office—14643 Dallas Parkway, Suite 1000, Wellington Centre, Dallas, TX 75240-8871. **Tel**—(972) 851-0500. **Website**—http://www.elcor.com **Chrmn, Pres & CEO**—H. K. Work. **Vice Chrmn, Treas & Investor Contact**—Richard J. Rosebery. **VP & Secy**—D. G. Sisler. **Dirs**—J. E. Hall, T. D. Karol, D. V. Kesler, W. F. Ortloff, D. W. Quinn, R. J. Rosebery, H. Work. **Transfer Agent & Registrar**—ChaseMellon Shareholder Services, Ridgefield Park, NJ. **Incorporated**—in Delaware in 1965. **Empl**— 867. **S&P Analyst:** C.C.P.

STANDARD
&POOR'S
STOCK REPORTS

Electro Scientific Industries

NASDAQ Symbol **ESIO**

In S&P SmallCap 600

09-OCT-99

Industry:
Electrical Equipment

Summary: ESIO makes products used in electronics manufacturing, including laser production systems, production and test equipment, laser trim systems and laser and drilling systems.

Quantitative Evaluations

Outlook
(1 Lowest—5 Highest)
• **2-**

Fair Value
• **52**

Risk
• **Average**

Earn./Div. Rank
• **B-**

Technical Eval.
• **Bullish** since 8/99

Rel. Strength Rank
(1 Lowest—99 Highest)
• **89**

Insider Activity
• **NA**

Recent Price • 50¼
52 Wk Range • 56½-14⅜

Yield • Nil
12-Mo. P/E • 59.8

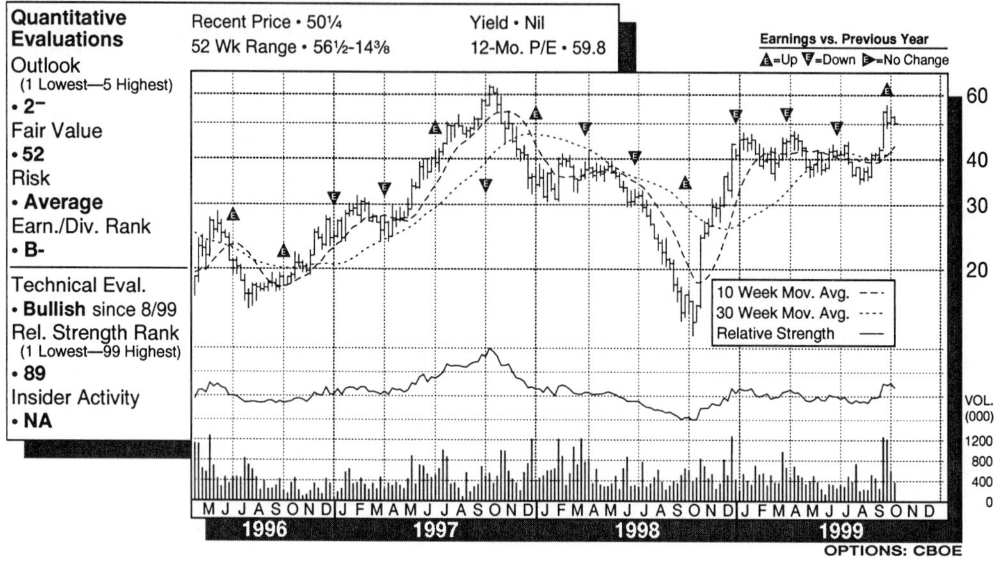

Business Profile - 27-AUG-99

The company's business depends in large part on capital spending by manufacturers of electronic devices. In FY 99 (May), ESIO's memory yield improvement business increased 6%, while the overall industry was down. In addition, the company expanded its market position in machine vision and electronic component systems, with the integration of the recently acquired MicroVision and Testec businesses. New products introduced included the Model 9800, a semiconductor yield improvement system for next-generation production of semiconductor products; and Models 5150 and 5200, systems that provide enabling technology for advanced integrated circuit packages and printed wiring board production. Backlog stood at $23 million at May 31, 1999, down from $25 million at May 31, 1998.

Operational Review - 27-AUG-99

Net sales fell 20% in FY 99, on lower sales of electronic component systems, machine vision equipment, and circuit fine tuning equipment. Gross margins narrowed, on a less favorable product mix. SG&A expense declined 6.9%; despite a drop in non-recurring operating expenses to $4.2 million, from $14.6 million, operating profits plunged 68%. After taxes at 31.4%, versus 30.8%, net income was down 66%, to $7,528,000 ($0.57 a share), from $22,347,000 ($1.71) as restated.

Stock Performance - 08-OCT-99

In the past 30 trading days, ESIO's shares have increased 22%, compared to a 0.91% fall in the S&P 500. Average trading volume for the past five days was 73,500 shares, compared with the 40-day moving average of 142,756 shares.

Key Stock Statistics

Dividend Rate/Share	Nil	Shareholders	624
Shs. outstg. (M)	13.0	Market cap. (B)	$0.656
Avg. daily vol. (M)	0.207	Inst. holdings	68%
Tang. Bk. Value/Share	15.43		
Beta	2.12		

Value of $10,000 invested 5 years ago: $ 32,682

Fiscal Year Ending May 31

	2000	1999	1998	1997	1996	1995
Revenues (Million $)						
1Q	58.97	48.42	48.36	34.86	35.97	21.01
2Q	—	49.04	59.87	35.10	40.84	24.80
3Q	—	51.51	57.59	37.20	41.63	29.40
4Q	—	57.28	55.03	43.00	41.27	33.00
Yr.	—	206.2	229.6	150.2	159.7	108.2
Earnings Per Share ($)						
1Q	**0.36**	**0.09**	**-0.17**	**0.36**	0.06	0.33
2Q	—	**0.19**	**0.70**	**0.21**	0.57	0.36
3Q	—	**0.07**	**0.40**	**0.55**	0.61	0.39
4Q	—	**0.22**	**0.54**	**0.67**	0.63	0.43
Yr.	—	**0.57**	**1.47**	2.19	**1.79**	**1.90**

Next earnings report expected: late December

Dividend Data

No cash dividends have been paid.

A Division of The McGraw-Hill Companies

Electro Scientific Industries, Inc.

Business Summary - 27-AUG-99

Electro Scientific Industries provides electronics manufacturers with equipment necessary to produce key components in wireless telecommunications, computers, automotive electronics and many other electronic products. The company believes it is the leading supplier of advanced laser systems used to fine tune electronic circuitry, to improve the yield of semiconductor memory devices, and of high-speed test and termination equipment used in the high-volume production of miniature capacitors. In addition, ESIO produces a family of mechanical and laser drilling systems for production of printed wiring boards for manufacturers of semiconductors, electronics and other products.

ESIO's memory yield improvement product line is designed and developed to cost-effectively meet memory production challenges associated with shrinking geometries, material changes, and increased wafer sizes, and offers enabling technology for next generation devices.

The company's test and production systems for miniature capacitors consist of automated test, production and handling equipment for the manufacture of miniature multi-layer ceramic capacitors (MLCCs) used in electronic circuits. Large numbers of MLCCs are used in circuits that process analog signals or operate at high frequencies such as in video products (VCRs and camcorders), voice communication products, wireless telecommunication products and computers.

ESIO's fine-tuning systems are used to tune the precise frequency of electronic circuits that receive and transmit signals in pagers, cellular telephones and other wireless devices. Laser trimming systems are also used to tune automotive electronic assemblies such as engine control circuits.

The company's vision systems combine advanced computer technology, proprietary software and optical equipment to reduce application development time and provide machine vision inspection that facilitates quality products and fast throughput. ESIO's advanced laser technology provides a cost effective method for forming electrical connections between layers, called vias, in a multiple layer substrate.

Research and development spending in FY 99 (May) and FY 98 totaled $30.3 million (14.7% of sales) and $34.8 million (13.5%), respectively.

International sales accounted for 56% of the total in FY 99, versus 59% in FY 98.

Per Share Data ($) (Year Ended May 31)	1999	1998	1997	1996	1995	1994	1993	1992	1991	1990
Tangible Bk. Val.	15.43	16.04	15.42	13.28	11.28	8.34	7.11	6.79	7.74	7.58
Cash Flow	1.08	1.94	2.54	2.19	1.88	1.58	0.77	-0.56	0.64	-0.07
Earnings	0.57	1.47	2.19	1.87	1.53	1.23	0.37	-1.00	0.20	-0.52
Dividends	Nil	Nil	Nil	Nil	Nil	Nil	Nil	Nil	Nil	Nil
Payout Ratio	Nil	Nil	Nil	Nil	Nil	Nil	Nil	Nil	Nil	Nil
Cal. Yrs.	1998	1997	1996	1995	1994	1993	1992	1991	1990	1989
Prices - High	45 3/8	63 3/4	29	41 1/2	21 5/8	17	5 1/2	7	9	14 1/2
- Low	13 1/8	23 3/4	15 1/2	17 1/2	8 5/8	5	2 1/2	2 3/4	3 1/8	7
P/E Ratio - High	80	43	13	22	14	14	15	NM	45	NM
- Low	23	16	7	9	6	4	7	NM	16	NM
Income Statement Analysis (Million $)										
Revs.	206	230	150	160	108	72.6	67.9	58.2	66.7	73.9
Oper. Inc.	20.7	44.7	30.4	33.6	18.7	10.7	5.6	-2.7	4.0	-0.7
Depr.	6.8	5.5	3.1	2.8	2.6	2.3	2.5	2.7	2.7	2.7
Int. Exp.	Nil	Nil	Nil	Nil	NA	0.6	0.8	1.0	1.3	1.2
Pretax Inc.	11.0	26.9	28.7	25.3	16.5	10.0	2.6	-6.9	1.6	-4.3
Eff. Tax Rate	31%	37%	34%	37%	30%	21%	14%	NM	23%	NM
Net Inc.	7.5	16.9	18.9	16.1	11.5	7.9	2.2	-6.1	1.2	-3.2
Balance Sheet & Other Fin. Data (Million $)										
Cash	7.8	9.8	43.2	37.0	28.4	8.2	2.8	3.4	5.5	10.3
Curr. Assets	174	159	127	112	91.2	44.3	40.5	35.3	45.0	47.9
Total Assets	222	199	149	133	111	62.4	61.2	58.5	68.7	72.0
Curr. Liab.	13.5	17.2	13.7	17.6	15.1	8.1	11.6	11.5	11.9	16.0
LT Debt	Nil	Nil	Nil	Nil	Nil	Nil	4.8	5.0	7.6	8.4
Common Eqty.	201	182	135	115	94.4	53.5	44.0	41.5	47.3	46.1
Total Cap.	201	182	135	115	94.4	53.5	48.8	46.5	56.4	56.0
Cap. Exp.	8.5	12.5	3.4	3.6	3.0	2.1	0.8	2.8	2.5	3.0
Cash Flow	14.3	22.4	22.0	18.8	14.1	10.1	4.7	-3.4	3.9	-0.4
Curr. Ratio	12.8	9.3	9.3	6.4	6.0	5.5	3.5	3.1	3.8	3.0
% LT Debt of Cap.	Nil	Nil	Nil	Nil	Nil	Nil	9.9	10.7	13.4	15.1
% Net Inc.of Revs.	3.7	7.4	12.6	10.1	10.6	10.9	3.3	NM	1.8	NM
% Ret. on Assets	3.6	9.7	13.4	13.2	12.0	12.5	3.7	NM	1.7	NM
% Ret. on Equity	3.9	10.6	15.1	9.9	14.0	15.9	5.2	NM	2.6	NM

Data as orig reptd.; bef. results of disc opers/spec. items. Per share data adj. for stk. divs. Bold denotes diluted EPS (FASB 128)-prior periods restated. E-Estimated. NA-Not Available. NM-Not Meaningful. NR-Not Ranked.

Office—13900 N.W. Science Park Dr., Portland, OR 97229-5497. **Tel**—(503) 641-4141. **Fax**—(503) 643-4873. **Website**—http://www.elcsci.com **Chrmn**—D. F. Bolender. **Pres & CEO**—D. R. VanLuvanee. **SVP-Fin & CFO**—J.C. Howell. **VP & Secy**—J.L. Reinhart. **Dirs**—D. F. Bolender, L. L. Hansen, W. A. Porter, V. B. Ryles Jr., G.F. Taylor, K. Thomson, J. D. Tompkins D. R. VanLuvanee. **Transfer Agent & Registrar**—First Chicago Trust Co. of New York, NYC. **Incorporated**—in Oregon in 1953. **Empl**— 875. **S&P Analyst:** J.J.A.

Electroglas, Inc.

Nasdaq Symbol **EGLS**

In S&P SmallCap 600

09-OCT-99

Industry:
Equipment (Semiconductor)

Summary: This company is a leader in the development, manufacture, marketing and servicing of automatic wafer probing equipment for use in the testing of integrated circuit (IC) devices.

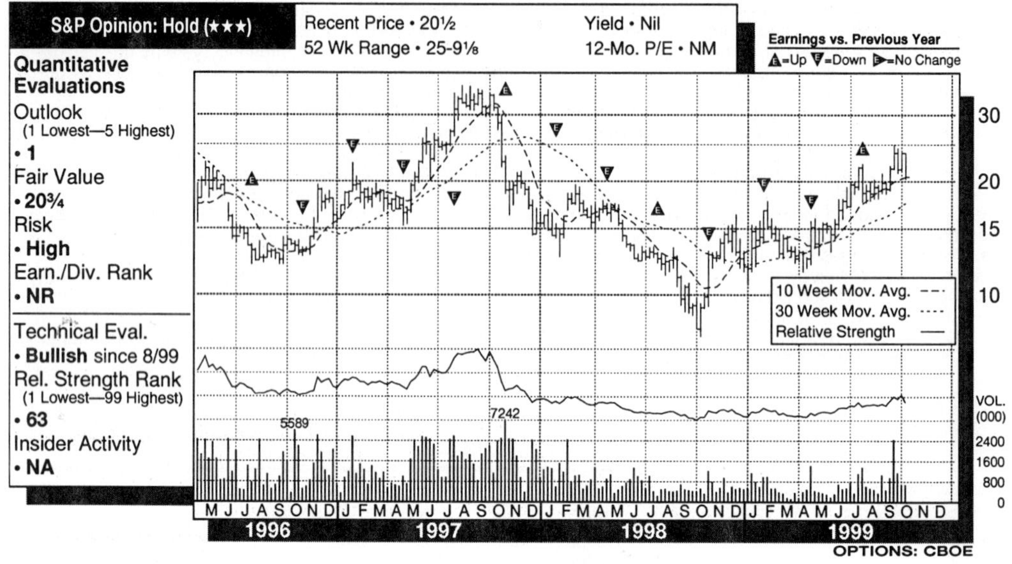

Overview - 09-AUG-99

In 1999, we expect sales to be up about 15% from those of the prior year, as the semiconductor equipment market recovers from a tumultuous 1998. In the first half of 1999, bookings were up roughly 25%, setting the stage for positive growth over the remainder of this year and into 2000. We expect gross margins to improve on a sequential basis from current low levels, aided by higher volume and a more favorable product mix. Profitability will also benefit from the company's leaner cost structure; current prober headcount is roughly 30% below the peak level. Interest income generated from the company's healthy cash balances will help buffer the bottom line as well. Overall, we look for a loss of $0.08 a share for 1999, a decent improvement from 1998's loss of $0.69 a share (before charges). We expect EGLS to return to profitability in 2000, with EPS approximating $0.65.

Valuation - 09-AUG-99

The shares of this chip equipment maker have recovered sharply from last October's low, reflecting improved semiconductor industry conditions. Although we expect operating results to improve over the next few quarters, we are maintaining our neutral rating on the shares, as a result of the limited visibility of earnings. On a positive note, EGLS is one of only three wafer-prober suppliers in the world, and maintains a strong position in a long-term growth market. As semiconductor complexity increases, longer test times per die are required, and therefore more probers are needed to maintain the same throughput. Given these positive dynamics, we believe the shares are a solid holding, at 2.3X book value.

Key Stock Statistics

S&P EPS Est. 1999	-0.08	Tang. Bk. Value/Share	8.19
P/E on S&P Est. 1999	NM	Beta	2.14
S&P EPS Est. 2000	0.65	Shareholders	10,350
Dividend Rate/Share	Nil	Market cap. (B)	$0.407
Shs. outstg. (M)	19.8	Inst. holdings	64%
Avg. daily vol. (M)	0.259		

Value of $10,000 invested 5 years ago: $ 25,702

Fiscal Year Ending Dec. 31

	1999	1998	1997	1996	1995	1994
Revenues (Million $)						
1Q	17.33	36.87	25.55	51.84	33.92	24.63
2Q	29.76	27.54	36.08	48.87	39.40	27.58
3Q	—	22.50	44.26	31.47	45.34	29.36
4Q	—	14.70	44.15	19.78	50.58	30.74
Yr.	—	101.6	150.0	151.9	169.2	112.3
Earnings Per Share ($)						
1Q	**-0.30**	**-0.02**	Nil	**0.62**	0.39	0.28
2Q	**0.05**	**-0.26**	**-1.14**	**0.50**	0.48	0.32
3Q	—	**-0.30**	**0.29**	**0.24**	0.54	0.37
4Q	—	**-1.04**	**-0.05**	Nil	0.64	0.34
Yr.	—	**-1.62**	**-0.86**	**1.36**	**2.05**	**1.31**

Next earnings report expected: late October

Dividend Data

EGLS intends to retain earnings for use in its business and does not expect to pay cash dividends in the foreseeable future. A two-for-one stock split was effected in December 1995.

Electroglas, Inc.

Business Summary - 09-AUG-99

Electroglas, Inc. operates in a niche market in the rapidly growing semiconductor equipment industry: the manufacturing of automatic wafer probing equipment. While the total worldwide market for wafer probing equipment is small, it is expected to show strong growth over the next several years. In addition, the company has only two major competitors: Tokyo Electron Labs and Tokyo Seimitsu.

There are several elements to the company's strategy. These include a focus on technological innovation, as EGLS has invested heavily in engineering, research and development to add features and functionality to its products. The company also seeks to maintain strong customer relationships, working closely with customers to determine their needs and specifications. To enhance its future growth, EGLS plans to increase its focus on the Japanese market, which has been difficult for the company to penetrate. In addition, EGLS seeks to expand its product offerings through new internally developed products and strategic alliances and acquisitions.

Semiconductor devices are fabricated by repeating a complex series of process steps on a wafer substrate, usually made of silicon and measuring three to eight inches in diameter. A wafer prober successfully positions each integrated circuit on a wafer so that the electrical contact points on the finished wafer align under and make contact with the probe pins, which are located on a probe card mounted on the wafer prober.

Parametric testing is performed during the wafer fabrication process ("in-line"), at the completion of the wafer fabrication process while the individual ICs are still intact on the wafer ("end-of-line"), and after the completion of the cutting and packaging of individual ICs ("wafer sort"), to identify ICs that do not conform to specifications. EGLS's probers are used for in-line and end-of-line testing.

The company's primary product lines are the 2000 series and Horizon 4000 wafer probers. The older 2000 Series products are used primarily for wafers whose diameters are six inches and less. The Horizon 4000 Series products, used primarily for eight inch wafers, consist of four models: the Horizon 4060X, which features wafer sizing, noncontact wafer realign, single wafer load and quick load stations and a robotic transfer mechanism; the Horizon 4080X Automatic Prober, targeted at high-volume semiconductor production lines of eight-inch wafers; and the Horizon 4085X Automatic Prober, developed to meet the exacting standards required for probing high-pin-count advanced logic devices; and the Horizon 4090, which was introduced in 1996.

EGLS is developing a range of software products, named SORTnet, to be used for the management and control of data gained during the test process.

Per Share Data ($) (Year Ended Dec. 31)	1998	1997	1996	1995	1994	1993	1992	1991	1990	1989
Tangible Bk. Val.	8.42	9.48	9.91	8.74	6.35	2.90	0.77	NA	NA	NA
Cash Flow	-1.07	-0.43	1.59	2.16	1.39	1.16	0.39	NA	NA	NA
Earnings	-1.62	-0.86	1.36	2.05	1.31	1.07	0.32	NA	NA	NA
Dividends	Nil	Nil	Nil	Nil	Nil	Nil	Nil	NA	NA	NA
Payout Ratio	Nil	Nil	Nil	Nil	Nil	Nil	Nil	NA	NA	NA
Prices - High	19 5/8	35 7/8	25 3/4	40 1/4	25 1/4	14 3/8	NA	NA	NA	NA
- Low	7 3/4	14 3/8	12	13 5/8	11 1/2	6 7/8	NA	NA	NA	NA
P/E Ratio - High	NM	NM	19	20	19	13	NA	NA	NA	NA
- Low	NM	NM	9	7	9	6	NA	NA	NA	NA
Income Statement Analysis (Million $)										
Revs.	102	150	152	169	112	79.0	55.0	59.8	64.8	64.5
Oper. Inc.	-19.3	17.2	32.9	55.5	33.7	17.8	7.5	11.6	14.9	NA
Depr.	10.8	8.0	4.1	2.0	1.3	1.2	1.0	1.0	0.8	NA
Int. Exp.	NA	Nil	Nil	Nil	Nil	Nil	Nil	Nil	Nil	Nil
Pretax Inc.	-34.2	-13.0	33.7	57.5	35.4	17.1	7.0	11.3	14.1	16.1
Eff. Tax Rate	NM	NM	27%	36%	37%	14%	37%	39%	37%	38%
Net Inc.	-31.6	-15.9	24.5	37.1	22.3	14.7	4.3	6.9	8.9	10.0
Balance Sheet & Other Fin. Data (Million $)										
Cash	30.7	20.3	129	118	79.2	21.7	0.0	NM	NA	NA
Curr. Assets	153	199	184	182	118	43.0	17.6	18.6	NA	NA
Total Assets	184	230	198	192	132	53.0	20.0	21.4	21.0	18.8
Curr. Liab.	16.5	26.6	24.2	34.0	21.1	13.5	9.6	11.6	NA	NA
LT Debt	NA	Nil	Nil	Nil	Nil	Nil	Nil	Nil	Nil	Nil
Common Eqty.	168	200	174	157	111	39.0	10.5	9.7	10.5	10.5
Total Cap.	168	204	174	157	111	39.0	10.5	9.7	10.5	10.5
Cap. Exp.	3.0	10.7	8.0	3.5	2.1	0.7	0.7	0.7	1.2	NA
Cash Flow	-20.8	-7.9	28.6	39.1	23.6	15.8	5.3	7.9	9.7	NA
Curr. Ratio	9.3	7.5	7.6	5.4	5.6	3.2	1.8	1.6	NA	NA
% LT Debt of Cap.	NA	Nil	Nil	Nil	Nil	Nil	Nil	Nil	Nil	Nil
% Net Inc.of Revs.	NM	NM	16.1	22.0	19.9	18.5	8.0	11.6	13.7	15.5
% Ret. on Assets	NM	NM	12.6	22.9	22.4	NM	20.7	16.3	44.5	50.0
% Ret. on Equity	NM	NM	14.8	27.7	27.7	NM	NM	NM	NM	NM

Data as orig reptd.; bef. results of disc opers/spec. items. Per share data adj. for stk. divs. Bold denotes diluted EPS (FASB 128)-prior periods restated. E-Estimated. NA-Not Available. NM-Not Meaningful. NR-Not Ranked.

Office—2901 Coronado Dr., Santa Clara, CA 95054. **Tel**—(408) 727-6500. **Website**—http://www.electroglas.com **Chrmn & CEO**—C. S. Wozniak. **VP-Fin, CFO, Treas, Secy & Investor Contact**—Armand J. Stegall. **Dirs**—N. R. Bonke, J. Dox, R. D. Emerick, R. J. Frankenberg, C. Wozniak. **Transfer Agent & Registrar**—Boston EquiServe LP. **Incorporated**—in Delaware in 1993. **Empl**— 593. **S&P Analyst:** B. McGovern

STANDARD
&POOR'S
STOCK REPORTS

Energen Corp.

NYSE Symbol **EGN**

In S&P SmallCap 600

09-OCT-99 **Industry:** Natural Gas

Summary: This diversified energy company is involved in natural gas distribution, and oil and gas exploration and production.

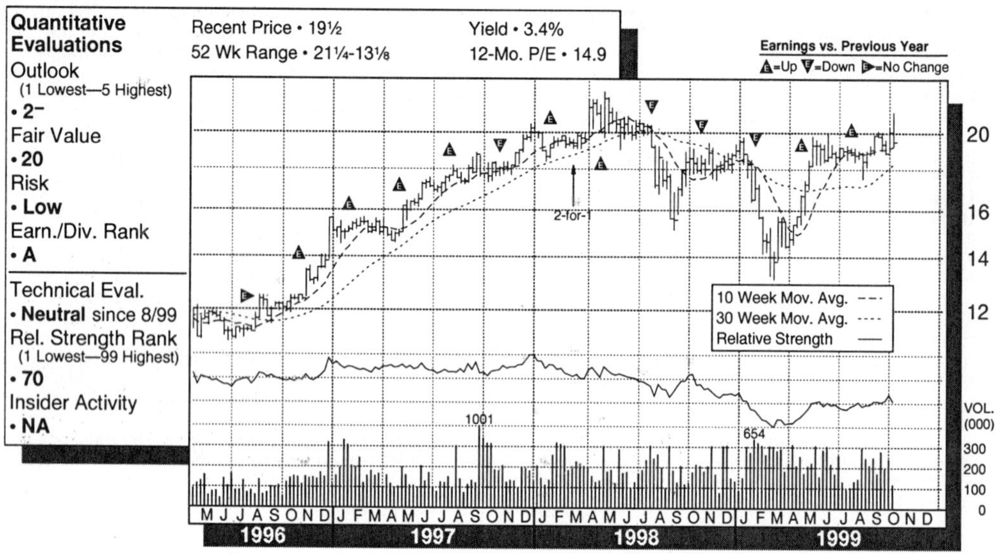

Business Profile - 08-SEP-99

In July 1999, Energen stated that it expected EPS to exceed $1.30 for FY 99 (Sep.) and $1.40 for FY 00. Also in July, EGN sold interests in 33 federal Gulf of Mexico blocks for $17 million. The company has an aggressive growth strategy calling for significant capital investment in oil and gas properties. Including the October 1998 acquisition of TOTAL Minatome, EGN spent $177 million for the acquisition and development of oil and gas properties during the first three quarters of FY 99 (Sep). Over the five years ending in FY 03, the company anticipates spending approximately $1 billion in the acquisition, development, and exploration of producing properties.

Operational Review - 08-SEP-99

Operating revenues for the nine months ended June 30, 1999, declined 3.2%, year to year, as decreased natural gas distribution, due to lower weather related demand, and weak fuel prices offset greater oil and gas production and increased gains from the sale of properties. Operating expenses fell 7.3%, with a significant decrease in the cost of gas for distribution offsetting higher operations and maintenance expense, the latter due largely to the October 1998 acquisition of TOTAL Minatome Corporation. After 26% higher interest expense, also resulting from the TOTAL acquisition, and taxes at 0.5%, versus a tax benefit of $2,599,000, net income rose 7.3%, to $49,724,000 ($1.66 a share) from $46,334,000 ($1.58).

Stock Performance - 08-OCT-99

In the past 30 trading days, EGN's shares have increased 2%, compared to a 0.91% fall in the S&P 500. Average trading volume for the past five days was 22,980 shares, compared with the 40-day moving average of 43,408 shares.

Key Stock Statistics

Dividend Rate/Share	0.66	Shareholders	9,140
Shs. outstg. (M)	29.8	Market cap. (B)	$0.582
Avg. daily vol. (M)	0.041	Inst. holdings	46%
Tang. Bk. Value/Share	12.55		
Beta	0.62		

Value of $10,000 invested 5 years ago: $ 22,599

Fiscal Year Ending Sep. 30

	1999	1998	1997	1996	1995	1994
Revenues (Million $)						
1Q	114.0	125.9	97.00	78.82	73.48	87.92
2Q	188.4	198.0	182.9	171.0	140.8	168.1
3Q	108.5	93.91	90.88	87.13	61.53	73.13
4Q	—	78.05	77.41	62.50	45.37	47.94
Yr.	—	502.6	448.2	399.4	321.2	377.1
Earnings Per Share ($)						
1Q	**0.13**	**0.21**	**0.14**	0.10	0.13	0.11
2Q	**1.42**	**1.37**	1.21	1.06	0.99	1.01
3Q	**0.12**	Nil	0.12	0.05	0.05	0.18
4Q	—	**-0.34**	-0.29	-0.23	-0.29	-0.21
Yr.	—	**1.23**	**1.14**	0.97	0.89	1.09

Next earnings report expected: late October

Dividend Data (Dividends have been paid since 1943.)

Amount ($)	Date Decl.	Ex-Div. Date	Stock of Record	Payment Date
0.160	Oct. 28	Nov. 10	Nov. 13	Dec. 01 '98
0.160	Jan. 27	Feb. 10	Feb. 12	Mar. 01 '99
0.160	Apr. 28	May. 12	May. 14	Jun. 01 '99
0.165	Jul. 28	Aug. 11	Aug. 13	Sep. 01 '99

Energen Corporation

Business Summary - 08-SEP-99

Energen (EGN) is a diversified energy holding company engaged in natural gas distribution and oil and natural gas exploration and production; its two major subsidiaries are Alabama Gas Corp. (Alagasco) and Energen Resource Corp., (formerly Taurus Exploration Inc.). While Alagasco earns within its allowed range of return of equity, the company's five-year plan, spanning through FY 00 (Sep.), calls for Energen to invest, through Energen Resources, $400 million in the acquisition of producing properties with development potential, and $100 million in offshore Gulf of Mexico exploration and development.

Alagasco, Alabama's largest gas distribution utility, purchases gas through interstate and intrastate marketers and suppliers and distributes the purchased gas through its distribution facilities for sale to end-users of natural gas. Alagasco also provides transportation services to industrial and commercial customers located on its distribution system. These customers purchase gas directly from producers, marketers or suppliers and arrange for delivery of the gas into the Alagasco distribution system; Alagasco charges a fee to transport the gas through its distribution system to the customer's facility. In FY 98, Alagasco served an average of 423,602 residential customers, 34,733 small commercial and industrial customers, and 49 large commercial and industrial transportation customers. Deliveries of sales and transportation gas totaled 115,347 million cubic feet (MMcf) in FY 98.

The Alagasco distribution system includes approximately 9,060 miles of main and more than 9,800 miles of service lines, odorization and regulation facilities, and customer meters. Alagasco also operates two liquefied natural gas facilities, which it uses to meet peak demand. Alagasco's distribution system is connected to and has firm transportation contracts with two major interstate pipeline systems: Southern and Transcontinental Gas Pipe Line Corp.

Energen Resources is involved in the exploration and production of natural gas and oil in the Gulf of Mexico, and through coalbed methane projects in Alabama's Black Warrior Coal Basin. At the end of FY 98, Energen Resources' remaining recoverable reserves totaled 764.9 billion cubic feet equivalent (Bcfe), and were located primarily in Alabama, New Mexico, Texas, Mississippi, Louisiana and the Gulf of Mexico. Natural gas represents over 70% of Energen Resources' reserves with oil and natural gas liquids constituting the balance. In October 1998, Energen Resources acquired TOTAL Minatome Corp. and then sold 31% of TOTAL Minatome to Westport Oil and Gas Company, Inc. Energen paid about $135 million for TOTAL Minatome, raising EGN's proved oil and natural gas reserves to nearly one trillion cubic feet equivalent.

Per Share Data ($) (Year Ended Sep. 30)	1998	1997	1996	1995	1994	1993	1992	1991	1990	1989
Tangible Bk. Val.	23.98	10.46	8.44	7.97	7.65	6.80	6.38	6.04	6.11	5.84
Earnings	1.23	1.16	0.97	0.89	1.09	0.89	0.77	0.71	0.68	0.59
Dividends	0.94	0.60	0.58	0.56	0.55	0.53	0.51	0.48	0.45	0.43
Payout Ratio	76%	52%	60%	64%	50%	59%	66%	67%	66%	72%
Prices - High	22 1/2	20 5/8	15 5/8	12 5/8	12	13 3/8	9 5/8	9 1/2	10 1/4	12 1/4
- Low	15 1/8	14 1/2	10 7/8	10 1/8	9 5/8	9 1/8	7 1/2	8	8	7 3/4
P/E Ratio - High	18	18	16	14	11	15	13	13	15	20
- Low	12	13	11	11	9	10	10	11	12	13
Income Statement Analysis (Million $)										
Revs.	503	448	399	321	377	357	332	326	325	309
Depr.	81.0	59.7	41.1	29.6	28.0	25.3	26.3	24.1	23.0	22.4
Maint.	NA	11.1	11.1	9.8	9.5	9.2	9.1	8.2	8.4	6.8
Fxd. Chgs. Cov.	2.1	2.4	2.9	3.0	3.5	3.0	2.5	2.5	2.5	2.6
Constr. Credits	NA	NA	NA	NA	NA	NA	NA	NA	NA	NA
Eff. Tax Rate	NA	9.65%	19%	16%	22%	16%	2.40%	2.50%	8.90%	8.60%
Net Inc.	36.2	29.0	21.5	19.3	23.8	18.1	15.7	14.1	13.2	11.1
Balance Sheet & Other Fin. Data (Million $)										
Gross Prop.	1,152	1,042	545	504	465	429	411	393	377	357
Cap. Exp.	175	283	168	68.9	45.5	43.7	22.5	46.9	41.9	59.5
Net Prop.	756	667	277	256	233	213	208	206	205	203
Capitalization:										
LT Debt	373	280	196	132	118	85.9	90.6	77.7	82.8	86.2
% LT Debt	53	48	51	43	42	38	41	39	40	43
Pfd.	Nil	Nil	Nil	Nil	Nil	Nil	1.8	1.8	1.8	2.5
% Pfd.	Nil	Nil	Nil	Nil	Nil	Nil	0.80	0.90	0.90	1.20
Common	329	301	188	174	167	140	130	122	121	113
% Common	47	52	49	57	59	62	58	61	59	56
Total Cap.	702	581	385	312	292	232	230	225	236	236
% Oper. Ratio	87.3	89.1	91.6	90.0	92.2	92.5	93.2	92.9	93.0	94.1
% Earn. on Net Prop.	8.6	9.4	12.7	13.2	13.1	12.7	10.8	11.2	11.9	9.6
% Return On Revs.	7.2	6.5	5.4	6.0	6.3	5.1	4.7	4.3	4.1	3.6
% Return On Invest. Capital	5.6	6.1	10.2	11.5	13.4	12.5	11.5	10.7	10.3	8.9
% Return On Com. Equity	11.5	11.8	11.9	11.3	15.5	13.4	12.5	12.0	11.3	11.0

Data as orig reptd.; bef. results of disc opers/spec. items. Per share data adj. for stk. divs. Bold denotes diluted EPS (FASB 128)-prior periods restated. E-Estimated. NA-Not Available. NM-Not Meaningful. NR-Not Ranked.

Office—605 21st Street North, Birmingham, AL 35203. **Tel**—(205) 326-2700. **Website**—http://www.energen.com **Chrmn, Pres & CEO**—W. M. Warren Jr. **EVP-Fin, Treas & CFO**—G. C. Ketcham. **Secy**—D. C. Reynolds. **Investor Contact**—Julie S. Ryland (205-326-8421). **Dirs**—S. D. Ban, J. W. Banton, R. D. Cash, J. M. Davis Jr., J. S. M. French, R. J. Lysinger, W. M. Warren Jr. **Transfer Agent & Registrar**—First Chicago Trust Company of New York. **Incorporated**—in Alabama in 1929. **Empl**— 1,421. **S&P Analyst:** Craig K. Shere, CFA

STANDARD
&POOR'S
STOCK REPORTS

Enesco Group

NYSE Symbol **ENC**

In S&P SmallCap 600

09-OCT-99

Industry: Consumer (Jewelry, Novelties & Gifts)

Summary: This company (formerly Stanhome Inc.) is a global marketer of branded gifts and collectibles.

Quantitative Evaluations

Outlook
(1 Lowest—5 Highest)
• **NA**

Fair Value
• **NA**

Risk
• **NA**

Earn./Div. Rank
• **B-**

Technical Eval.
• **Bearish** since 7/99

Rel. Strength Rank
(1 Lowest—99 Highest)
• **19**

Insider Activity
• **NA**

Recent Price • 15⅝
52 Wk Range • 26-12⅞
Yield • 7.2%
12-Mo. P/E • NM

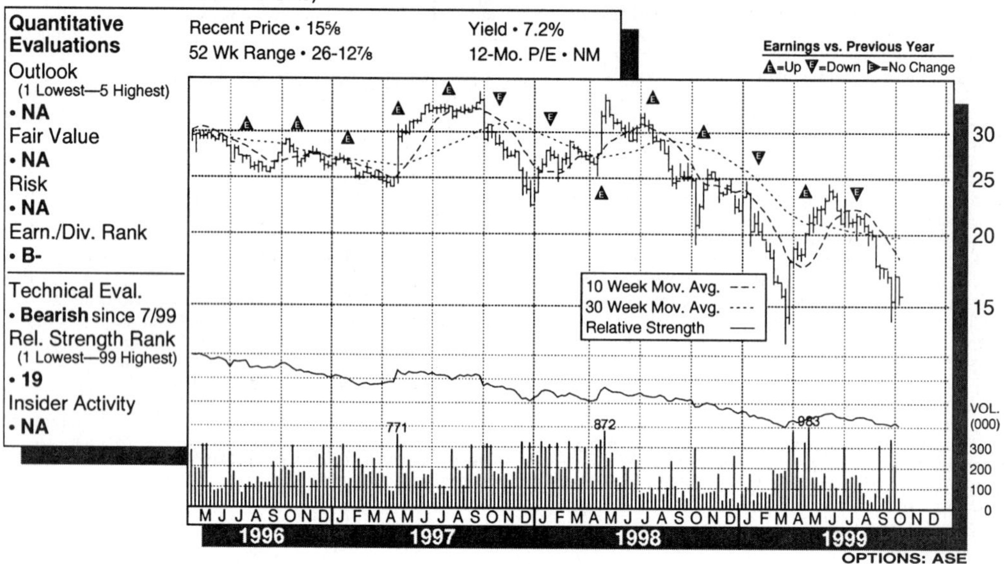

Business Profile - 26-AUG-99

ENC is analyzing all of its product lines, seeking to improve efficiency, and to phase out product lines that do not have adequate return. While the company said it was disappointed in the slower than expected recovery of second quarter 1999 sales, it remains confident and fully committed to its strategic plans and initiatives. Comparable unfilled orders continue to be up over those of 1998, and new order intake year-to-date (excluding close-outs) is running only 6% behind comparable 1998 figures despite fewer stock keeping units (SKUs) and continued tight credit controls. To further improve gross margins and reduce fixed costs and inventories, the company in July 1999 sold its assembly and packaging subsidiary in Mexico for about book value. ENC has repurchased 2.1 million shares of its common stock under its repurchase program, with another 1.4 million shares authorized for purchase.

Operational Review - 26-AUG-99

Net sales in the first half of 1999 declined 23%, year to year, reflecting fewer SKUs, programmed inventory reductions, and tighter credit controls in the U.S. Gross margins widened, aided by the elimination of unprofitable lines. Following a 16% drop in selling, distribution, general and administrative expenses, operating profit was down 38%. After sharply lower net other expense, and taxes at 40.0%, versus 43.0%, net income decreased 35%, to $9,958,000 ($0.66 a share, on 9.1% fewer shares), from $15,270,000 ($0.92).

Stock Performance - 08-OCT-99

In the past 30 trading days, ENC's shares have declined 12%, compared to a 0.91% fall in the S&P 500. Average trading volume for the past five days was 10,780 shares, compared with the 40-day moving average of 40,767 shares.

Key Stock Statistics

Dividend Rate/Share	1.12	Shareholders	3,162
Shs. outstg. (M)	13.8	Market cap. (B)	$0.216
Avg. daily vol. (M)	0.050	Inst. holdings	77%
Tang. Bk. Value/Share	6.93		
Beta	0.72		

Value of $10,000 invested 5 years ago: $ 6,018

Fiscal Year Ending Dec. 31

	1999	1998	1997	1996	1995	1994
Revenues (Million $)						
1Q	93.93	108.2	102.1	183.0	184.9	171.8
2Q	94.93	137.2	137.0	217.7	209.5	188.6
3Q	—	110.2	128.3	209.9	205.7	193.3
4Q	—	95.48	108.9	234.3	230.1	236.6
Yr.	—	451.0	476.2	845.0	830.2	790.2
Earnings Per Share ($)						
1Q	**0.28**	**0.21**	**0.12**	**0.10**	**0.24**	0.41
2Q	**0.39**	**0.72**	**0.55**	**0.51**	**0.46**	0.59
3Q	—	**0.39**	**-0.16**	**0.68**	**0.64**	0.67
4Q	—	**-2.77**	**0.07**	**0.52**	**0.47**	0.58
Yr.	—	**-1.38**	**0.60**	**1.80**	**1.81**	2.26

Next earnings report expected: late October

Dividend Data (Dividends have been paid since 1943.)

Amount ($)	Date Decl.	Ex-Div. Date	Stock of Record	Payment Date
0.280	Dec. 02	Dec. 14	Dec. 16	Jan. 01 '99
0.280	Mar. 03	Mar. 15	Mar. 17	Apr. 01 '99
0.280	Jun. 02	Jun. 14	Jun. 16	Jul. 01 '99
0.280	Sep. 01	Sep. 13	Sep. 15	Oct. 01 '99

Enesco Group, Inc.

Business Summary - 26-AUG-99

As part of a program to enhance shareholder value, Enesco Group, Inc. (formerly Stanhope Inc.) sold its Hamilton Direct Response and Stanhome Direct Selling groups in 1997. Following the sales, the company's business consisted of its Enesco Giftware operation. ENC has relocated its principal executive offices to Itasca, IL, and is completing a transformation to focus on the design and marketing of branded gifts, collectibles and decorative accents.

The company is a leading importer and distributor of creatively designed giftware items, including proprietary and licensed lines of collectibles. Products include a diverse line of branded porcelain bisque, cold cast and resin figurines, cottages, musicals, music boxes, ornaments, waterballs, miniatures, tableware, sculpture, general home accessories and other giftware primarily produced by independent manufacturers in the Far East. In some instances, a manufacturer's total production capacity is exclusively devoted to Enesco products.

Well known licensed lines include Precious Moments, Cherished Teddies, Barbie, Mickey & Co., Mickey Unlimited, Coca Cola, and McDonald's. The Precious Moments line accounted for 38% of revenue from continuing operations in 1998; Cherished Teddies accounted for 20%. International sales accounted for 19% of total sales in 1998.

In May 1997, ENC sold its Hamilton Direct Response business to the Bradford Group for $48.3 million, including the repayment of $30.8 million of intercompany debt. The sale agreement also provided for two license agreements under which Bradford would sell certain propriety products and licensed lines of products for an initial five-year period. In December 1997, the company sold its home care and cosmetics business to Yves Rocher, for $68.4 million in cash; the transaction included the sale of the Stanhome name. ENC incurred an after tax charge of $6.0 million ($0.34 a share) in the 1997 fourth quarter, to write down assets that were not part of the sale. In the third quarter of 1997, ENC incurred an $18 million pretax charge to downsize and move its headquarters. The loss that was posted in 1998 reflected the writedown of goodwill of some $46 million related to the acquisition of two UK companies in 1994.

As of the 1998 year-end, Enesco was analyzing the economic return for all its product lines in the U.S., with the objective of improving the supply process and phasing out those lines that do not provide adequate returns. ENC planned to extend this review to its international operations in 1999. The company also slowed new product introductions for its Precious Moments and Cherished Teddies lines in order to assist retailers in moving inventories. Sales declined in 1998 and in the first half of 1999 due to the product line eliminations and other cost reduction measures. ENC does not expect to see sales increases until the second half of 1999.

Per Share Data ($) (Year Ended Dec. 31)	1998	1997	1996	1995	1994	1993	1992	1991	1990	1989
Tangible Bk. Val.	6.93	8.10	8.64	8.02	7.72	10.88	10.96	10.20	9.14	7.07
Cash Flow	-1.03	0.92	2.65	2.92	2.79	2.18	2.80	2.67	2.98	2.60
Earnings	-1.38	0.60	2.12	2.22	2.26	1.68	2.32	2.22	2.55	2.23
Dividends	1.12	1.12	1.09	1.06	1.03	1.00	0.96	0.92	0.83	0.71
Payout Ratio	NM	187%	51%	48%	46%	60%	41%	40%	32%	31%
Prices - High	35	35¼	32⅝	33⅜	37	34¾	41⅝	44¾	35¼	35½
- Low	19⅛	22¼	25⅜	26⅞	28¾	25⅞	30⅛	30¾	25⅝	18⅜
P/E Ratio - High	NM	59	15	15	16	21	18	20	14	16
- Low	NM	37	12	12	13	15	13	14	10	8
Income Statement Analysis (Million $)										
Revs.	451	476	845	830	790	751	744	710	676	571
Oper. Inc.	54.8	36.3	90.9	100	88.2	90.1	91.0	86.4	94.3	86.2
Depr.	5.7	5.7	9.5	13.1	10.4	9.8	9.8	9.2	7.7	6.7
Int. Exp.	3.6	6.8	8.7	7.8	2.0	2.0	3.4	5.0	5.4	6.0
Pretax Inc.	-3.3	20.8	69.3	76.3	80.7	66.1	87.0	81.1	90.3	79.7
Eff. Tax Rate	NM	49%	44%	45%	45%	50%	46%	45%	43%	44%
Net Inc.	-22.4	10.5	38.4	41.9	44.1	33.1	46.7	45.1	51.1	44.6
Balance Sheet & Other Fin. Data (Million $)										
Cash	17.9	35.7	27.5	23.1	19.4	60.7	42.3	52.2	51.8	43.8
Curr. Assets	206	248	357	342	323	314	298	294	271	219
Total Assets	320	400	555	534	512	430	416	419	392	335
Curr. Liab.	130	150	249	242	220	155	143	159	162	150
LT Debt	Nil	Nil	Nil	Nil	Nil	Nil	0.9	1.2	1.4	1.4
Common Eqty.	151	229	279	267	269	254	257	241	211	170
Total Cap.	158	229	279	267	269	254	258	242	213	172
Cap. Exp.	4.5	4.9	9.3	13.5	16.8	6.5	6.9	7.8	10.9	5.1
Cash Flow	-16.8	16.2	47.9	55.0	54.5	43.0	56.5	54.3	59.6	52.4
Curr. Ratio	1.6	1.6	1.4	1.4	1.5	2.0	2.1	1.8	1.7	1.5
% LT Debt of Cap.	Nil	Nil	Nil	Nil	Nil	Nil	0.4	0.5	0.7	0.8
% Net Inc.of Revs.	NM	2.2	4.5	5.1	5.6	4.4	6.3	6.3	7.6	7.8
% Ret. on Assets	NM	2.2	6.9	8.0	9.4	7.9	11.2	11.0	14.0	14.8
% Ret. on Equity	NM	4.2	14.1	15.7	16.9	13.1	18.8	19.8	26.6	27.6

Data as orig reptd.; bef. results of disc opers/spec. items. Per share data adj. for stk. divs. Bold denotes diluted EPS (FASB 128)-prior periods restated. E-Estimated. NA-Not Available. NM-Not Meaningful. NR-Not Ranked.

Office—225 Windsor Dr., Itasca, IL 60143. **Tel**—(630) 875-5300. **Chrmn**—J. F. Cauley. **CEO**—J. A. Hutsell. **VP & CFO**—A. G. Keirstead. **Treas**—J. W. Lemajeur. **VP & Secy**—P. R. Johnson. **Dirs**— J. F. Cauley Jr., C. W. Elliott, E. Freedman, J. R. Haberkorn, T. R. Horton, J. Hutsell, A. G. Keirstead, H. G. Perkins, H. L. Tower, A. L. Verville. **Transfer Agent & Registrar**—ChaseMellon Shareholder Services, Ridgefield Park, NJ. **Incorporated**—in Massachusetts in 1931. **Empl**— 1,750. **S&P Analyst:** P.L.H.

STANDARD & POOR'S
STOCK REPORTS

Enhance Financial Services

NYSE Symbol **EFS**
In S&P SmallCap 600

09-OCT-99

Industry: Insurance (Property-Casualty)

Summary: This company provides financial guaranty insurance and reinsurance and other products and services utilizing its credit-related analytical skills.

S&P Opinion: Accumulate (★★★★)

Recent Price • 18⅝
52 Wk Range • 30⅜-16¾
Yield • 1.3%
12-Mo. P/E • 8.6

Quantitative Evaluations

Outlook (1 Lowest—5 Highest) • **5**
Fair Value • **28⅝**
Risk • **Low**
Earn./Div. Rank • **B+**

Technical Eval. • **Bearish** since 9/99
Rel. Strength Rank (1 Lowest—99 Highest) • **45**
Insider Activity • **Neutral**

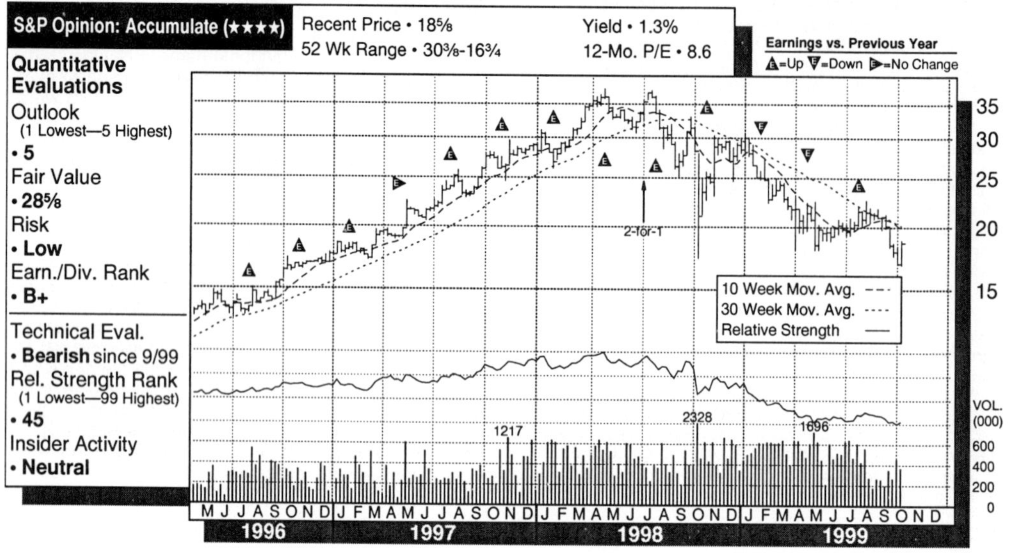

Overview - 11-AUG-99

Enhance's leading market share position in the financial guaranty reinsurance industry, with 23.6% of total gross premiums ceded in 1998, leaves EFS well-positioned to generate premium earned growth of approximately 8% through 2000. C-BASS, which also enjoys a market leadership position, tripled EPS over the first six months of 1998, and is developing a consistent and potentially self-funding earnings stream. Singer Asset Finance lost $0.08 during the first half of 1999, but management told analysts that it had reduced expenses significantly, and believed the opening of the Florida and Texas lottery assignment markets could lead to a $0.05 profit in full-year 1999. The April 1999 acquisition of a portfolio of residential mortgage-backed securities should reduce EFS's effective operating tax rate to about 8.5% and aid EPS expansion of 17% through 2001.

Valuation - 11-AUG-99

EFS shares have decreased nearly 29% year to date, while the S&P SmallCap 600 was unchanged. A credit rating agency's review of Enhance Reinsurance's triple A financial strength rating has been a drag to the stock, but two other rating agencies have maintained the top grade. EFS believes any downside related to a downgrade would be offset by opportunities in other insurance lines. In light of Singer's recent efforts, we expect that business to turn around in the second half of 1999. It is likely that time-tested evidence of successful diversification will be a necessity before the shares are awarded any multiple expansion. Even maintaining current multiples however, EPS growth of 17% would enable the achievement of EFS's goal of 15% ROE by 2001 and imply healthy capital appreciation. With EFS shares currently trading at a significant discount to their long-term operating EPS growth rate and only 1.2 times book value, we feel they have superior upside potential.

Key Stock Statistics

S&P EPS Est. 1999	2.46	Tang. Bk. Value/Share	17.92
P/E on S&P Est. 1999	7.6	Beta	0.83
S&P EPS Est. 2000	2.87	Shareholders	115
Dividend Rate/Share	0.24	Market cap. (B)	$0.708
Shs. outstg. (M)	38.0	Inst. holdings	70%
Avg. daily vol. (M)	0.071		

Value of $10,000 invested 5 years ago: $ 20,177

Fiscal Year Ending Dec. 31

	1999	1998	1997	1996	1995	1994
Revenues (Million $)						
1Q	44.44	48.31	32.48	32.62	25.54	24.21
2Q	51.62	51.42	45.16	28.91	26.30	22.81
3Q	—	59.18	42.08	31.93	27.57	26.04
4Q	—	48.58	50.68	38.84	33.35	23.38
Yr.	—	207.5	170.4	132.3	112.5	96.44
Earnings Per Share ($)						
1Q	**0.46**	**0.49**	**0.37**	**0.37**	0.30	0.29
2Q	**0.60**	**0.52**	**0.44**	**0.33**	0.32	0.23
3Q	—	**0.58**	**0.45**	**0.38**	0.34	0.24
4Q	—	**0.51**	**0.53**	**0.45**	0.41	-0.02
Yr.	—	**2.10**	**1.78**	**1.52**	**1.36**	**0.74**

Next earnings report expected: early November

Dividend Data (Dividends have been paid since 1992.)

Amount ($)	Date Decl.	Ex-Div. Date	Stock of Record	Payment Date
0.060	Dec. 09	Dec. 17	Dec. 21	Dec. 28 '98
0.060	Mar. 25	Mar. 31	Apr. 05	Apr. 09 '99
0.060	Jun. 03	Jun. 10	Jun. 14	Jun. 18 '99
0.060	Sep. 23	Sep. 30	Oct. 04	Oct. 08 '99

A Division of The McGraw-Hill Companies

Enhance Financial Services Group Inc.

Business Summary - 11-AUG-99

Enhance Financial Services Group is transforming itself from a company that primarily offers financial guarantee reinsurance into a provider of diversified financial services. Enhance is leveraging its credit-related analytical skills to create new higher-return businesses. Management anticipates that a significant portion of the company's future growth will come from these asset-based and non-financial guaranty businesses.

EFS's primary business remains the reinsurance of financial guaranties of municipal and asset-backed debt obligations issued by monoline financial guaranty insurers. The reinsurance of financial guaranty insurance is a commitment to reimburse another insurance company for a specified portion of the insurance risk underwritten for debt holders. This business accounted for nearly 62% of EFS's gross premiums written in 1998. During 1998, EFS received a leading market share of about 25% of the total reinsurance premiums ceded by all monoline financial guaranty insurers.

Enhance's other insurance businesses include direct financial guaranty insurance of smaller debt obligations, trade credit reinsurance and excess-SIPC/excess-ICS and similar types of bonds. These businesses accounted for 38% of gross premiums written in 1998.

In 1996, Enhance formed Credit-Based Asset Servicing and Securitization LLC ("C-BASS"), a joint venture with MGIC Investment, a leading provider of private mortgage insurance. C-BASS purchases, services and securitizes single-family residential sub-performing, non-performing and seller-financed mortgage loans and real estate and subordinated residential mortgage-backed securities. In December 1998, EFS and MGIC formed a second venture, Sherman Financial Group LLC. Sherman was organized to purchase, service and securitize delinquent consumer assets, including charged-off credit card receivables.

Wholly owned Singer Asset Finance Company, L.L.C. purchases state lottery prizes, structured settlement payment rights and other long-term payment streams. Singer then securitizes these assets and sells pools of them in the securities market. In August 1998, EFS formed Enhance Consumer Services, LLC to purchase or create loans secured by life insurance policies from customers living with terminal illness. The company then markets and securitizes those payment streams.

In late 1997, EFS and Swiss Re each acquired a 25% interest in SBF, one of Brazil's largest surety companies. The remaining interest in SBF is held by Banco Pactual, S.A., one of Brazil's largest investment banks. Terms of the joint venture call for the expansion of SBF in the Latin American insurance and other credit-related markets. In July 1998, EFS formed AGS Financial LLC, a venture which holds an 80% interest focused on structured finance, asset servicing and specialized investment banking services in Latin American markets.

Per Share Data ($) (Year Ended Dec. 31)	1998	1997	1996	1995	1994	1993	1992	1991	1990	1989
Tangible Bk. Val.	17.50	15.03	13.52	12.29	10.22	10.07	9.14	8.23	7.23	6.33
Oper. Earnings	2.10	1.77	1.45	1.29	NA	NA	NA	NA	NA	NA
Earnings	2.10	1.78	1.56	1.36	0.74	1.04	1.03	0.93	0.80	0.78
Dividends	0.23	0.22	0.20	0.18	0.16	0.14	0.12	NA	NA	NA
Payout Ratio	11%	12%	13%	13%	21%	13%	12%	NA	NA	NA
Prices - High	37 5/8	31 1/8	18 1/4	13 1/2	10 3/8	12 1/2	10 5/8	NA	NA	NA
- Low	17 1/4	17 1/8	11 5/8	8	7 3/4	8 3/4	7 3/4	NA	NA	NA
P/E Ratio - High	18	17	12	10	14	12	10	NA	NA	NA
- Low	8	10	7	6	10	8	7	NA	NA	NA
Income Statement Analysis (Million $)										
Premium Inc.	129	85.5	77.4	63.0	61.8	59.6	45.6	35.9	24.8	19.8
Net Invest. Inc.	53.4	50.6	48.1	44.2	39.0	32.8	30.3	27.2	22.6	17.5
Oth. Revs.	24.8	34.3	6.7	5.3	-4.3	17.9	9.3	6.7	0.4	0.5
Total Revs.	207	170	132	113	96.4	110	85.2	69.8	47.8	37.8
Pretax Inc.	113	94.0	76.4	63.8	32.7	50.3	49.4	40.9	32.2	28.3
Net Oper. Inc.	80.1	68.4	51.7	44.7	NA	NA	NA	NA	NA	NA
Net Inc.	82.5	68.8	55.7	47.3	26.6	38.0	37.6	32.4	25.1	23.0
Balance Sheet & Other Fin. Data (Million $)										
Cash & Equiv.	5.5	5.7	5.4	19.5	39.1	20.4	21.5	13.3	10.5	9.0
Premiums Due	36.0	30.0	22.5	21.2	9.8	10.5	8.0	9.7	8.4	3.6
Invest. Assets: Bonds	891	819	758	696	620	622	487	428	352	258
Invest. Assets: Stocks	0.8	0.8	0.9	0.7	0.7	0.5	0.5	0.4	1.6	2.1
Invest. Assets: Loans	Nil	Nil	Nil	Nil	Nil	Nil	Nil	Nil	Nil	Nil
Invest. Assets: Total	1,040	938	815	748	651	624	488	429	360	279
Deferred Policy Costs	104	95.6	87.3	81.0	74.0	66.2	54.6	48.4	41.4	34.5
Total Assets	1,336	1,148	983	881	765	735	584	509	430	330
Debt	75.0	75.0	75.0	78.4	79.8	81.2	7.6	9.0	Nil	Nil
Common Eqty.	663	581	488	424	360	364	332	288	253	189
Prop. & Cas. Loss Ratio	10.1	11.4	11.9	15.1	37.0	37.0	20.4	14.2	9.1	0.1
Prop. & Cas. Expense Ratio	48.6	50.3	52.6	54.2	56.7	54.9	57.6	65.8	55.6	57.2
Prop. & Cas. Combined Ratio	58.7	61.7	64.5	69.3	93.7	91.9	78.0	80.0	64.7	57.3
% Return On Revs.	39.7	40.4	42.1	42.1	27.5	34.4	44.2	46.4	52.5	60.9
% Ret. on Equity	13.3	12.9	29.0	12.1	7.3	10.9	12.1	12.0	11.3	13.0

Data as orig reptd.; bef. results of disc opers/spec. items. Per share data adj. for stk. divs. Bold denotes diluted EPS (FASB 128)-prior periods restated. E-Estimated. NA-Not Available. NM-Not Meaningful. NR-Not Ranked.

Office—335 Madison Ave., New York, NY 10017. **Tel**—(212) 983-3100. **Website**—http://www.efsgroup.com **Chrmn**—A. R. Tessler. **Vice Chrmn**—W. O. Sellers. **Pres & CEO**—D. Gross. **EVP & CFO**—A. Dubroff. **EVP & Secy**—S. Bergman. **VP & Investor Contact**—Bernard J. Kilkelly (212 984-9259). **Dirs**—D. Gross, B. W. Harries, D. R. Markin, J. A. Novik, R. P. Saltzman, W. O. Sellers, R. J. Shima, S. R. Stuart, A. R. Tessler, F. K. Wallison, J. Wind. **Transfer Agent & Registrar**—First Chicago Trust Company, a division of Equiserve, Jersey City, NJ. **Incorporated**—in New York in 1985. **Empl**— 260. **S&P Analyst:** Markos N. Kaminis

STANDARD
&POOR'S
STOCK REPORTS

Enzo Biochem

ASE Symbol **ENZ**
In S&P SmallCap 600

11-OCT-99 **Industry:** Biotechnology

Summary: This biotechnology company is engaged in research, manufacturing and marketing of diagnostic and research products based on molecular biology and genetic engineering.

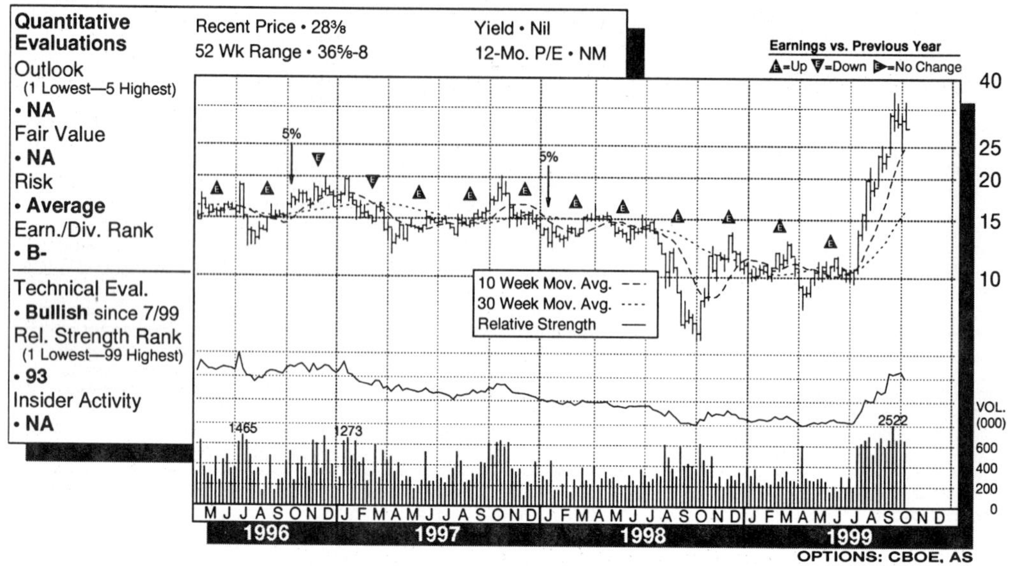

Business Profile - 11-OCT-99

In October 1999, Enzo Biochem, Inc. reported findings showing that its gene transfer vector, HGTV43, was capable of achieving greater levels of stable gene transfer to specific target cells, relative to certain other genetic delivery systems. In September 1999, the U.S. Court of Appeals for the Federal Circuit rejected an attempt by Calgene, Inc. to invalidate an ENZ patent for genetic antisense technology. In July 1999, the company initiated a human clinical trial on its novel hepatitis B treatment. In May 1999, ENZ announced favorable preclinical results for this treatment, which is designed to mitigate immune responses that may cause serious liver damage. As of mid-year 1999, ENZ's HIV treatment was in Phase I clinical testing.

Operational Review - 11-OCT-99

Operating revenues in the nine months ended April 30, 1999 (latest available) increased 11%, year to year, mainly due to higher research product sales and an increase in screening test prices. Total costs and expenses rose only 5.7%, as well-controlled general and administrative and clinical lab costs offset double digit increases in both product costs and R&D spending. Net income surged 87%, to $3,705,000 ($0.15 a share), from $1,984,000 ($0.08). Cash and cash equivalents totaled $41.9 million as of April 30, 1999.

Stock Performance - 08-OCT-99

In the past 30 trading days, ENZ's shares have increased 27%, compared to a 0.91% fall in the S&P 500. Average trading volume for the past five days was 243,880 shares, compared with the 40-day moving average of 273,344 shares.

Key Stock Statistics

Dividend Rate/Share	Nil	Shareholders	1,433
Shs. outstg. (M)	24.9	Market cap. (B)	$0.707
Avg. daily vol. (M)	0.314	Inst. holdings	12%
Tang. Bk. Value/Share	2.22		
Beta	0.93		

Value of $10,000 invested 5 years ago: $ 20,691

Fiscal Year Ending Jul. 31

	1999	1998	1997	1996	1995	1994
Revenues (Million $)						
1Q	10.52	9.81	8.01	8.56	8.03	5.18
2Q	11.00	10.33	7.73	8.01	7.04	4.48
3Q	12.19	10.70	8.89	8.55	8.22	4.88
4Q	—	10.08	10.32	9.37	8.41	8.27
Yr.	—	40.42	34.94	34.49	31.70	22.80
Earnings Per Share ($)						
1Q	**0.03**	0.02	0.01	0.04	0.78	0.03
2Q	**0.05**	**0.02**	**0.01**	0.02	0.03	-0.03
3Q	**0.07**	**0.04**	0.03	0.02	Nil	-0.01
4Q	—	**0.06**	0.02	-0.41	-0.57	0.22
Yr.	—	**0.13**	**0.06**	-0.32	0.24	0.22

Next earnings report expected: early November

Dividend Data

No cash dividends have been paid.

Enzo Biochem, Inc.

Business Summary - 11-OCT-99

Enzo Biochem Inc. (ENZ) researches, develops, manufactures and markets innovative health care products based on molecular biology and genetic engineering techniques, and also provides diagnostic services to the medical community. It currently focuses on development of products based on gene labeling and gene regulation.

ENZ has three subsidiaries, each of which performs one of the company's three business activities: diagnostic and research product development; therapeutic product research and development; and the operation of a clinical reference laboratory. In FY 98 (Jul.), 31% of revenues came from product sales, and 69% from clinical reference laboratory services. In FY 97, 38% of revenues came from product sales, and 62% from clinical reference laboratory services.

Enzo Diagnostics Inc. develops and markets biomedical products used largely to detect viral infections, using DNA probes. Its product development focuses on Bioprobe nucleic acid probes to detect sexually transmitted and other infectious diseases, such as AIDS, herpes, chlamydia, tuberculosis, hepatitis and cytomegalovirus. It has distribution agreements with Boehringer Mannheim, Amersham International, Sigma Chemical, Dako O/S, and Ortho Diagnostic Systems. Boehringer Mannheim represented approximately 21% and 25% of the company's consolidated operating revenues in FY 98 and FY 97, respectively

Enzo markets two BioProbe products: PathoGene DNA probe kits to detect a variety of specific viruses, and BioPap DNA probe kits to detect certain types of human papillomavirus (HPV) in pap smear samples. It also markets two Microplate Hybridization Assays (MHAs) to detect HIV-1 virus causing AIDS and a bacteria that causes tuberculosis. MHAs to detect HIV-2 and hepatitis B and C viruses are also available.

Enzo Therapeutics, Inc. is applying its technological capabilities for manipulating genetic material to the development of therapeutic treatments. In the third quarter of FY 97, a patent covering ENZ's genetic antisense technology was issued in Japan and upheld in Europe. This technology enables the regulation of gene function. During FY 98, the company improved its GenSert Universal System, designed to universally deliver any gene into any cell. ENZ's drug development program is utilizing the GenSert system in combination with the company's antisense technology to develop medicines for a variety of cancers, infections and other conditions.

Enzo Clinical Labs, Inc. operates a clinical reference laboratory offering diagnostic services to the greater New York medical community. The services include a variety of tests to detect precancerous conditions, cervical cancers and sexually transmitted diseases.

In January 1998, ENZ entered into a licensing agreement with Japan Tobacco, Inc., for use of the company's patented genetic antisense technology in Japan. This agreement is the first agricultural licensing agreement involving Enzo's proprietary technology and involves upfront fees, commercialization payments plus royalties.

Per Share Data ($) (Year Ended Jul. 31)	1998	1997	1996	1995	1994	1993	1992	1991	1990	1989
Tangible Bk. Val.	2.22	2.04	1.79	1.96	1.78	1.00	1.05	-0.82	0.03	0.19
Cash Flow	0.18	0.10	-0.28	0.28	0.26	-0.26	-0.01	-0.75	-0.25	-0.28
Earnings	0.13	0.06	-0.32	0.24	0.22	-0.31	-0.08	-0.82	-0.31	-0.32
Dividends	Nil	Nil	Nil	Nil	Nil	Nil	Nil	Nil	Nil	Nil
Payout Ratio	Nil	Nil	Nil	Nil	Nil	Nil	Nil	Nil	Nil	Nil
Prices - High	16 1/2	20 1/4	20	22 1/4	17 1/8	18 3/4	6 5/8	7 3/8	4	4 3/8
- Low	6 3/8	11 5/8	12 1/4	8 1/4	6 5/8	5 1/4	2 3/4	1/2	1 1/2	2 1/4
P/E Ratio - High	NM	NM	NM	93	79	NM	NM	NM	NM	NM
- Low	NM	NM	NM	35	30	NM	NA	NA	NA	NA
Income Statement Analysis (Million $)										
Revs.	40.4	34.9	34.5	31.7	22.8	20.0	20.5	19.8	19.4	12.1
Oper. Inc.	1.9	1.0	0.3	-0.4	-2.7	-1.7	1.8	-1.6	-0.8	-1.5
Depr.	1.2	1.3	1.3	1.2	1.1	1.2	1.1	0.9	0.8	0.5
Int. Exp.	Nil	Nil	0.0	0.1	0.1	0.3	2.3	5.2	5.4	4.9
Pretax Inc.	2.6	1.6	-7.5	9.7	2.2	-6.3	-1.1	-10.8	-3.9	-4.0
Eff. Tax Rate	NM	7.10%	NM	42%	NM	NM	NM	NM	NM	NM
Net Inc.	3.4	1.4	-7.7	5.6	5.1	-6.4	-1.2	-10.8	-4.1	-4.1
Balance Sheet & Other Fin. Data (Million $)										
Cash	33.5	25.3	17.8	11.1	4.2	0.7	0.8	0.6	7.9	30.4
Curr. Assets	55.4	45.6	35.9	30.3	25.7	7.9	9.4	9.7	16.2	36.7
Total Assets	72.2	67.4	62.8	72.5	65.0	47.6	49.8	49.3	66.5	74.6
Curr. Liab.	2.4	2.4	6.5	5.8	8.6	10.3	12.1	43.4	5.6	5.5
LT Debt	Nil	0.1	0.1	4.7	4.4	4.2	4.2	4.5	48.1	53.9
Common Eqty.	68.8	64.0	55.3	61.1	51.2	32.4	33.0	1.1	12.7	15.1
Total Cap.	68.8	64.1	55.4	65.8	55.8	36.8	37.4	5.8	60.9	69.1
Cap. Exp.	0.6	0.7	0.7	1.0	1.8	3.5	2.4	9.0	8.2	4.2
Cash Flow	4.6	2.7	-6.4	6.8	6.2	-5.2	-0.2	-9.9	-3.3	-3.7
Curr. Ratio	22.9	19.2	5.6	5.2	3.0	0.8	0.8	0.2	2.9	6.7
% LT Debt of Cap.	Nil	Nil	0.2	7.1	7.8	11.3	11.2	78.6	78.9	78.0
% Net Inc.of Revs.	8.4	4.2	NM	17.7	22.4	NM	NM	NM	NM	NM
% Ret. on Assets	4.9	2.2	NM	8.2	8.7	NM	NM	NM	NM	NM
% Ret. on Equity	5.1	2.4	NM	10.0	11.8	NM	NM	NM	NM	NM

Data as orig reptd.; bef. results of disc opers/spec. items. Per share data adj. for stk. divs. Bold denotes diluted EPS (FASB 128)-prior periods restated. E-Estimated. NA-Not Available. NM-Not Meaningful. NR-Not Ranked.

Office—60 Executive Blvd., Farmingdale, NY 11735 **Tel**—(516) 755-5500. **Website**—http://www.enzobio.com **Chrmn & CEO**—E. Rabbani. **Pres**—B. W. Weiner. **COO & Secy**—S. K. Rabbani. **Dirs**—J. J. Delucca, E. Rabbani, S. K. Rabbani, J. B. Sias, B. W. Weiner. **Transfer Agent**—Continental Stock Transfer & Trust Co., NYC. **Incorporated**—in New York in 1976. **Empl**—189. **S&P Analyst:** Frank DiLorenzo

Epicor Software

NASDAQ Symbol **EPIC**

In S&P SmallCap 600

09-OCT-99

Industry:
Computer (Software & Services)

Summary: Epicor (formerly Platinum Software) is the largest enterprise software supplier focused exclusively on the requirements of midmarket companies

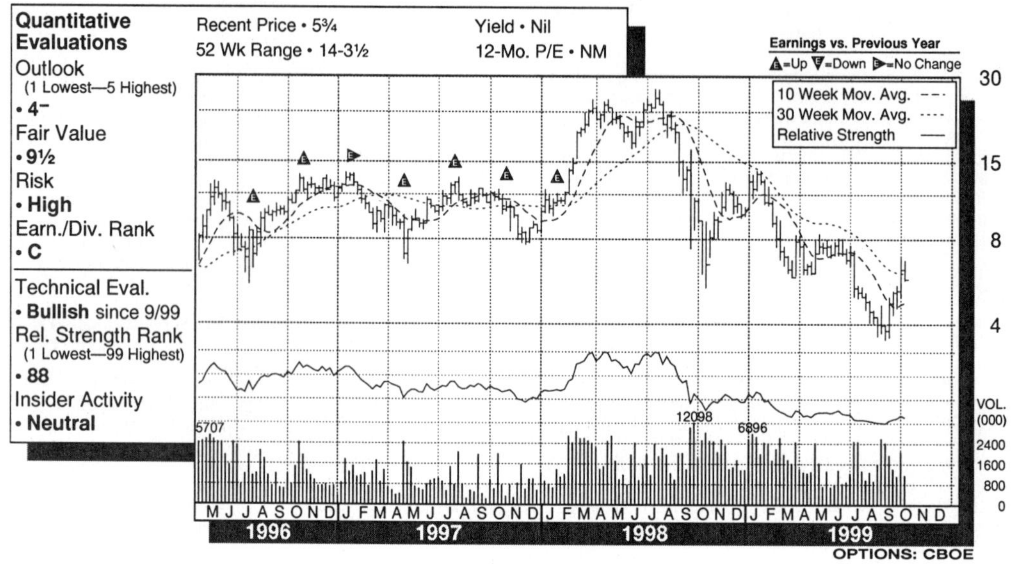

Business Profile - 20-JUL-99

In July 1999, the company said that for 1999's second quarter it expects to report total revenues slightly below those of its first quarter with earnings per share at or near breakeven. Management believes the company's revenues and earnings growth were adversely affected by several factors, including continuing merger-related sale performance issues and a general industry-wide slowdown in the demand for ERP software. Second quarter results were also impacted by the reclassification of DataWorks Impresa for Backoffice operation to an on-going entity from an asset held for sale. EPIC added it expected revenue levels in the third and fourth quarters of 1999 to be similar to those of the second quarter, principally due to an industry-wide slowdown.

Operational Review - 20-JUL-99

Revenues in the three months ended March 31, 1999, amounted to $66.1 million. Cost of revenues was $28.0 million, and gross profit totaled $38.1 million. Operating expenses were $36.7 million, other income was $1.1 million, and pretax income $2.4 million. After taxes at 15.0%, income was $2.1 million ($0.05 a share). Year over year comparison are not reflected since the quarter ended March 31, 1999 represents the first quarter where results of operations for the combined entities of Platinum Software and DataWorks are presented.

Stock Performance - 08-OCT-99

In the past 30 trading days, EPIC's shares have increased 45%, compared to a 0.91% fall in the S&P 500. Average trading volume for the past five days was 230,060 shares, compared with the 40-day moving average of 423,079 shares.

Key Stock Statistics

Dividend Rate/Share	Nil	Shareholders	1,600
Shs. outstg. (M)	40.8	Market cap. (B)	$0.235
Avg. daily vol. (M)	0.286	Inst. holdings	35%
Tang. Bk. Value/Share	0.54		
Beta	1.80		

Value of $10,000 invested 5 years ago: $ 2,283

Fiscal Year Ending Dec. 31

	1999	1998	1997	1996	1995	1994
Revenues (Million $)						
1Q	66.11	—	18.26	10.86	12.60	14.60
2Q	65.16	—	21.65	12.68	10.16	13.30
3Q	—	30.33	26.37	14.01	8.36	13.40
4Q	—	33.39	32.20	16.71	9.40	14.90
Yr.	—	63.72	122.3	58.10	40.56	56.20
Earnings Per Share ($)						
1Q	**0.05**	—	0.05	-0.11	-0.32	Nil
2Q	**0.01**	—	**0.07**	-0.03	-0.82	-0.22
3Q	—	0.16	**0.15**	0.03	-0.97	-0.15
4Q	—	-0.24	**0.19**	-0.18	-0.18	-0.08
Yr.	—	**-0.07**	**0.27**	**-0.20**	-2.23	-0.44

Next earnings report expected: late October

Dividend Data

No cash dividends have been paid. The company plans for the foreseeable future to retain any earnings for use in the business.

Epicor Software Corporation

Business Summary - 20-JUL-99

Epicor Software (formerly Platinum Software) designs, develop, markets and supports enterprise resource planning software solutions for use by mid-sized companies as well as divisions and subsidiaries of larger corporations worldwide. Effective December 31, 1998, operations were considerably expanded through the purchase of DataWorks Corp., a provider of enterprise resource planning software, for 11.7 million shares of the company's stock. Revenues in the six months ended December 31, 1998 were obtained as follows: license fees 52%, services 48%, and royalties nil.

Following the merger, the company has three primary areas of focus for its software products: front office applications, which include its Clientele and Platinum ERA Front Office sales force automation and customer service and support applications which provide growing and mid-sized companies with comprehensive customer relationship management fuctionality; General Services applications, which include Platinum ERA Financials, Platinum ERA Distribution and Platinum for Windows; and Manufacturing applications, which include Platinum ERA Manufacturing, Avante (average price of about $175,000), an ERP suite designed to meet the needs of rapidly growing manufacturers of discrete, highly engineered products. The company's software products incorporate a significant number of internationalized features to address global market opportunities, including support for national languages, multiple currencies and accounting for value-added taxation. EPIC also offers consulting, training and support services to supplement the use of its software products by customers.

Operating income or loss in the six months ended December 31, 1998, by region: the U. S. -$2,207,000, Australasia -$1,366,000, Europe -$200,000, Canada $163,000, and Latin America $1,513,000.

The company's client/server enterprise business targets the middle market, comprised of enterprises with revenues of between $50 million and $500 million. Customers in this market segment require proven client/server software solutions that are easy to install, manage and use, but flexible enough to address the challenges of a specific organization. Mid-sized enterprises also lack dedicated information technology management resources and need solutions that do not require a high level of ongoing maintenance and support for their continued operation. Increasingly, customers in this segment are looking for Microsoft SQL Server based solutions and the company believes its Platinum ERA product line is well positioned to address this requirement.

On December 31, 1998, EPIC acquired DataWorks Corp., a publicly traded provider of enterprise resource planning software. As consideration for the acquisition, Epicor issued 11,739,459 shares of common stock in exchange for all of DataWorks' shares.

Per Share Data ($) (Year Ended Dec. 31)	1998	1997	1996	1995	1994	1993	1992	1991	1990	1989
Tangible Bk. Val.	1.95	0.43	NM	NM	NM	4.13	4.67	2.00	NA	NA
Cash Flow	0.05	0.62	0.05	-1.81	-0.02	-4.35	-1.52	NA	NA	NA
Earnings	-0.07	0.27	-0.25	-2.23	-0.44	-4.80	-1.68	0.11	NA	NA
Dividends	Nil	Nil	Nil	Nil	Nil	Nil	Nil	Nil	NA	NA
Payout Ratio	Nil	Nil	Nil	Nil	Nil	Nil	Nil	Nil	NA	NA
Prices - High	27¼	27¼	13¾	13½	16⅞	25¼	39¾	19⅞	NA	NA
- Low	5⅜	5⅜	6½	3⅛	4¾	3½	13½	9⅜	NA	NA
P/E Ratio - High	NM	NM	NM	NM	NM	NM	NM	NM	NA	NA
- Low	NM	NM	NM	NM	NA	NA	NA	NA	NA	NA
Income Statement Analysis (Million $)										
Revs.	63.7	98.5	58.1	40.6	56.2	53.4	28.1	NA	NA	NA
Oper. Inc.	13.5	16.6	1.7	-21.1	-0.3	-23.8	-4.0	NA	NA	NA
Depr.	3.5	5.1	5.8	6.2	5.5	5.5	1.7	NA	NA	NA
Int. Exp.	0.1	0.0	0.1	1.3	0.7	0.0	0.1	NA	NA	NA
Pretax Inc.	-1.9	13.3	-4.9	-32.9	-5.7	-59.3	-17.2	NA	NA	NA
Eff. Tax Rate	NM	NM	NM	NM	NM	NM	NM	NA	NA	NA
Net Inc.	-2.1	13.3	-4.9	-32.9	-5.7	-59.5	-17.2	NA	NA	NA
Balance Sheet & Other Fin. Data (Million $)										
Cash	22.2	11.3	6.3	16.5	26.8	8.8	47.2	NA	NA	NA
Curr. Assets	152	55.4	29.8	27.3	44.4	26.7	64.4	NA	NA	NA
Total Assets	212	68.0	41.8	40.0	65.8	48.1	80.6	NA	NA	NA
Curr. Liab.	93.2	33.0	27.1	23.8	20.1	36.9	22.2	NA	NA	NA
LT Debt	Nil	Nil	Nil	Nil	15.8	10.0	Nil	NA	NA	NA
Common Eqty.	110	14.2	-15.8	-15.8	-2.0	1.2	58.4	NA	NA	NA
Total Cap.	110	15.6	-15.8	-15.8	45.8	11.2	58.4	NA	NA	NA
Cap. Exp.	3.7	4.1	3.0	2.5	NA	10.4	6.3	NA	NA	NA
Cash Flow	1.4	18.5	0.9	-26.7	-0.2	-54.0	-15.5	NA	NA	NA
Curr. Ratio	1.6	1.7	1.1	1.1	2.2	0.7	0.3	NA	NA	NA
% LT Debt of Cap.	Nil	Nil	Nil	NM	34.5	89.3	NM	NA	NA	NA
% Net Inc.of Revs.	NM	13.6	NM	NM	NM	NM	NM	NA	NA	NA
% Ret. on Assets	NM	24.3	NM	NM	NM	NM	NM	NA	NA	NA
% Ret. on Equity	NM	NM	NM	NM	NM	NM	NM	NA	NA	NA

Data as orig reptd.; bef. results of disc opers/spec. items. Per share data adj. for stk. divs. Bold denotes diluted EPS (FASB 128)-prior periods restated. Data for 1998 represents six mos. end Dec. 31; prior to 1998, yrs. ended Jun. 30 of fol. cal. yr. E-Estimated. NA-Not Available. NM-Not Meaningful. NR-Not Ranked.

Office—195 Technology Dr., Irvine, CA 92618-2402. **Tel**—(949) 585-4000. **Website**—http://www.epicor.com **Chrmn, Pres & CEO**—L. G. Klaus. **Investor Contact**—Valerie Brodie. **Dirs**—S. W. Clifton, D. R. Dixon, L. J. Doerr, L. G. Klaus, A. J. Marks. **Transfer Agent & Registrar**—ChaseMellon Shareholder Services, LA. **Incorporated**—in Delaware in 1984. **Empl**— 1,690. **S&P Analyst:** P.L.H.

STANDARD
&POOR'S
STOCK REPORTS

Esterline Technologies

NYSE Symbol **ESL**

In S&P SmallCap 600

09-OCT-99

Industry: Manufacturing (Diversified)

Summary: This company makes equipment used for production of printed circuit boards, metal fabrication, instrumentation, power measurement, process control and engineered products.

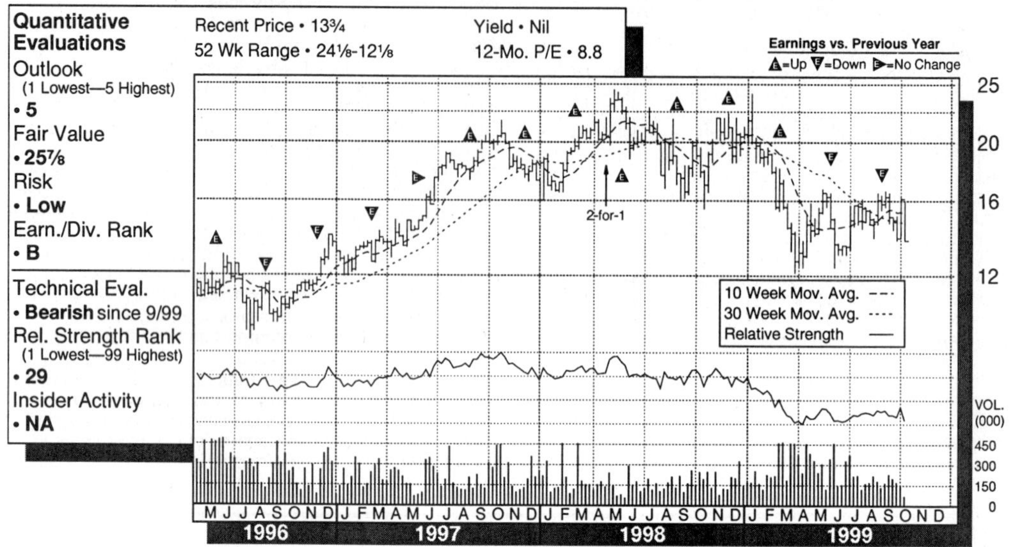

Business Profile - 11-MAY-99

The acquisition of Kirkhill Rubber Co. by the aerospace and defense group accounted for much of the revenue growth in the first quarter of FY 99 (Oct.). Even before acquisitions, the aerospace and defense segment experienced sales growth of 15%. Automation group sales were down 22% in the quarter due to a depressed worldwide market for printed circuit board manufacturing equipment and the continued Asian economic crisis. On March 1, 1999, following a late February announcement, ESL was added to the Standard and Poor's SmallCap 600 Index. Company-wide backlog at January 31, 1999, was $164 million, compared with $171 million at January 31, 1998. The reduction was due to an order rate decline for capital equipment.

Operational Review - 11-MAY-99

Net sales in the three months ended January 31, 1999, rose 14%, year to year, as revenue gains in aerospace and defense outweighed a decrease in automation sales. Despite narrowing margins in the automation group, profitability improved on well controlled selling, general and administrative expenses; operating income climbed 22%. Following depreciation and amortization charges, sharply higher net interest expense, and taxes at 36.6%, versus 34.2%, net income advanced 4.6%, to $5,057,000 ($0.29 a share), from $4,836,000 ($0.27, adjusted).

Stock Performance - 08-OCT-99

In the past 30 trading days, ESL's shares have declined 13%, compared to a 0.91% fall in the S&P 500. Average trading volume for the past five days was 13,380 shares, compared with the 40-day moving average of 32,572 shares.

Key Stock Statistics

Dividend Rate/Share	Nil	Shareholders	853
Shs. outstg. (M)	17.3	Market cap. (B)	$0.238
Avg. daily vol. (M)	0.029	Inst. holdings	61%
Tang. Bk. Value/Share	6.69		
Beta	0.69		

Value of $10,000 invested 5 years ago: $ 36,065

Fiscal Year Ending Oct. 31

	1999	1998	1997	1996	1995	1994
Revenues (Million $)						
1Q	108.7	95.73	82.20	84.00	83.33	57.87
2Q	116.1	114.5	97.95	88.98	84.81	70.87
3Q	112.8	110.9	102.1	81.73	87.32	71.68
4Q	—	132.7	108.7	98.14	96.44	93.63
Yr.	—	453.9	391.0	352.8	351.9	294.0
Earnings Per Share ($)						
1Q	**0.29**	**0.28**	**0.21**	0.24	0.16	-0.03
2Q	**0.40**	**0.45**	0.38	0.38	0.22	0.09
3Q	**0.34**	**0.45**	0.40	0.29	0.47	0.12
4Q	—	**0.52**	0.46	0.39	0.42	0.40
Yr.	—	**1.70**	**1.44**	**1.31**	1.26	0.57

Next earnings report expected: NA

Dividend Data

Dividends were omitted in 1986, after having been paid since 1969. A shareholder rights plan was adopted in 1992.

Esterline Technologies Corporation

Business Summary - 11-MAY-99

Esterline Technologies (formerly Esterline Corp.) believes participation in several markets and industries helps generate consistent and sustainable total performance. ESL is a manufacturer with operations in electronic equipment, metal fabrication, commercial aerospace and defense. The company conducts its operations through three business segments: automation, aerospace/defense and instrumentation.

Foreign sales accounted for 16% of revenues and 2% of operating earnings in FY 98 (Oct.)

Automation consists of three operations: Excellon, Equipment Sales Co. and Whitney, accounting for 32% of FY 98 sales. Excellon manufacturers highly efficient automated drilling systems for the printed circuit board industry. Laser technology is expected to improve drilling systems in the near future. Whitney designs and builds highly productive automated machine tools for cutting and punching plate and structural steel for construction, transportation, agricultural and mining equipment manufacturers and independent steel fabrication centers. Whitney recently introduced laser technology into its line of products.

Aerospace/defense consists of seven operations: Armtec, Auxitrol, Hytek, Kirkhill, Mason, Midcon and TA Mfg., which accounted for 42% of FY 98 sales. Armtec manufacturers molded fiber cartridge cases, mortar increments, igniter tubes and other combustible ammunition components for the U.S. Armed Forces. Technology is also licensed to foreign defense contractors and governments. Armtec is currently the only U.S. supplier of combustible casings utilized by the U.S. Army. Auxitrol is a French manufacturer of high precision temperature and pressure sensing devices, and hydraulic controls used primarily in aerospace applications. Kirkhill and TA Mfg. manufacture clamps, seals, tubing and coverings for the aerospace market. Other operations in aerospace/defense segment include metal finishing and inspection services.

Instrumentation includes Korry Electronics (information and control components, and integrated thin-panel data systems); and Federal Products (high-precision analog and digital dimensional and surface measurement and inspection instruments and systems). The Angus Electronics subsidiary (recording instruments, together with other analytical, process and environmental monitoring instrumentation) was sold in May 1997. Instrumentation contributed 26% of FY 98 revenues.

Research and development programs increased in 1998 to $20.3 million, compared to $17.6 million in 1997 and $15.4 million in 1996.

The company focused its efforts on growth through acquisitions, product development and manufacturing facility expansion during FY 98. Seven acquisitions were completed during the year, as were two new facilities and expansions of two other facilities.

Per Share Data ($) (Year Ended Oct. 31)	1998	1997	1996	1995	1994	1993	1992	1991	1990	1989
Tangible Bk. Val.	5.60	9.59	8.37	6.30	5.03	4.25	2.99	2.25	1.48	0.48
Cash Flow	2.73	2.43	2.30	2.58	1.82	-0.91	1.87	2.02	1.49	0.91
Earnings	1.70	1.44	1.30	1.26	0.57	-1.95	0.38	0.56	0.54	0.47
Dividends	Nil	Nil	Nil	Nil	Nil	Nil	Nil	Nil	Nil	Nil
Payout Ratio	Nil	Nil	Nil	Nil	Nil	Nil	Nil	Nil	Nil	Nil
Prices - High	24½	21¾	14	15¼	7⅞	6½	8¾	8½	6¼	7¾
- Low	15½	12	9⅜	6¼	3¼	3⅝	3¾	3⅛	2¾	5
P/E Ratio - High	14	15	11	12	13	NM	23	15	12	16
- Low	9	8	7	5	6	NM	10	5	5	11
Income Statement Analysis (Million $)										
Revs.	454	391	353	352	294	285	305	351	389	284
Oper. Inc.	67.5	56.7	50.7	25.5	31.2	22.7	35.2	43.8	41.7	24.5
Depr.	18.3	17.4	16.3	19.3	16.4	13.8	19.8	19.1	12.4	7.3
Int. Exp.	3.8	3.6	4.3	5.6	6.0	6.3	7.2	12.7	17.4	3.5
Pretax Inc.	46.9	38.1	32.1	26.5	8.8	-38.0	8.1	12.0	11.9	13.7
Eff. Tax Rate	36%	34%	33%	34%	14%	NM	38%	39%	41%	43%
Net Inc.	30.1	25.3	21.3	17.4	7.6	-25.6	5.1	7.3	7.1	7.9
Balance Sheet & Other Fin. Data (Million $)										
Cash	8.9	56.0	46.4	22.1	9.1	3.2	3.1	2.3	1.1	1.7
Curr. Assets	178	194	179	142	119	97.0	98.0	109	132	143
Total Assets	387	290	277	226	216	206	232	256	290	304
Curr. Liab.	108	101	106	106	109	88.0	77.0	88.0	116	131
LT Debt	74.0	23.2	29.0	36.0	42.0	62.0	69.0	87.0	99	110
Common Eqty.	196	166	142	84.0	65.0	55.0	83.0	77.0	71.0	63.0
Total Cap.	279	189	171	119	107	118	155	168	173	173
Cap. Exp.	29.8	17.4	17.2	Nil	11.3	9.6	10.8	6.9	13.5	9.2
Cash Flow	48.4	42.7	37.6	33.9	24.0	-11.9	24.9	26.5	19.5	15.2
Curr. Ratio	1.6	1.9	1.7	1.3	1.1	1.1	1.3	1.2	1.1	1.1
% LT Debt of Cap.	26.5	12.3	17.0	30.3	38.9	53.0	44.1	51.7	57.3	63.7
% Net Inc.of Revs.	6.6	6.5	6.0	4.9	2.6	NM	1.7	2.1	1.8	2.8
% Ret. on Assets	8.9	8.9	8.5	7.8	3.6	NM	2.1	2.7	2.4	3.7
% Ret. on Equity	16.6	16.4	18.8	23.3	12.5	NM	6.4	9.8	10.5	12.5

Data as orig reptd.; bef. results of disc opers/spec. items. Per share data adj. for stk. divs. Bold denotes diluted EPS (FASB 128)-prior periods restated. E-Estimated. NA-Not Available. NM-Not Meaningful. NR-Not Ranked.

Office—10800 NE 8th St., Suite 600, Bellevue, WA 98004. **Tel**—(425) 453-9400. **Chrmn**—W. P. Hurlbut. **Pres & CEO**—R. W. Cremin. **CFO & Secy**—R. D. George. **Investor Contact**—Brian D. Keogh. **Dirs**—R. R. Albrecht, G. W. Anderson, J. F. Clearman, R. S. Cline, R. W. Cremin, E. J. Finn, R. F. Goldhammer, W. P. Hurlbut, J. D. Leitman, P. G. Schloemer, M. T. Stamper. **Transfer Agent & Registrar**—ChaseMellon Shareholder Services, NYC. **Incorporated**—in Delaware in 1967. **Empl**— 4,200. **S&P Analyst:** J.W.H.

Etec Systems

Nasdaq Symbol **ETEC**

In S&P SmallCap 600

09-OCT-99

Industry: Equipment (Semiconductor)

Summary: Etec is the leading producer of mask pattern generation equipment for the semiconductor industry.

S&P Opinion: Accumulate (★★★★) Recent Price • 35¾ | 52 Wk Range • 55-20¾ | Yield • Nil | 12-Mo. P/E • NM

Quantitative Evaluations

Outlook (1 Lowest—5 Highest) • **4+**

Fair Value • **56¼**

Risk • **NA**

Earn./Div. Rank • **NR**

Technical Eval. • **Neutral** since 9/99

Rel. Strength Rank (1 Lowest—99 Highest) • **30**

Insider Activity • **NA**

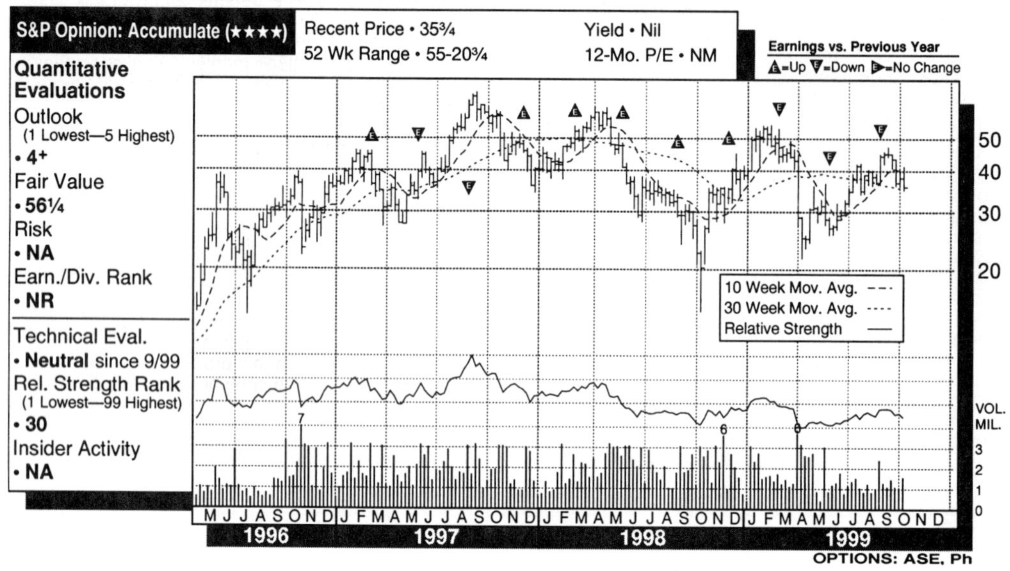

OPTIONS: ASE, Ph

Overview - 30-AUG-99

Following a drop of 18% in FY 99 (Oct.), sales should rebound by a similar amount in FY 00, as the semiconductor industry recovery extends to the photomask sector. Last year, overcapacity and delays in the semiconductor design cycle resulted in a weak environment for mask writing equipment. In recent quarters, however, the mask industry has shown signs of improvement, as evidenced by stronger operating results for Photronics and DuPont Photomask, two of ETEC's largest customers. Rapid adoption of 0.25 micron and below processing technology for chipmakers will likely result in stronger demand for advanced photomasks. This, in turn, should alleviate the overcapacity situation and prompt additional investment in mask-making equipment. We expect substantial margin improvement as fixed costs are spread over a larger sales base. As a result, EPS should improve to $0.80 in FY 00, from the $0.41 recorded for FY 99 (before charges).

Valuation - 30-AUG-99

We have upgraded our opinion on ETEC to accumulate from hold, reflecting prospects for strong sales and earnings growth next year. The photomask sector appears to have reached a cyclical trough, and is likely to show strong growth over the next several quarters. As the dominant supplier of mask pattern generation equipment, ETEC is well positioned to benefit from this trend. We believe that the mask industry's recent under-investment in leading edge capability could result in a shortage of high-end photomasks over the next 12 to 18 months, prompting strong demand for ETEC's products. Given these positive trends, we believe the shares are attractively valued for aggressive investors, at 3.7X our FY 00 (Oct.) sales estimate.

Key Stock Statistics

S&P EPS Est. 2000	0.80	Tang. Bk. Value/Share	11.21
P/E on S&P Est. 2000	44.7	Beta	NA
Dividend Rate/Share	Nil	Shareholders	248
Shs. outstg. (M)	21.4	Market cap. (B)	$0.765
Avg. daily vol. (M)	0.255	Inst. holdings	84%

Value of $10,000 invested 5 years ago: NA

Fiscal Year Ending Jul. 31

	1999	1998	1997	1996	1995	1994
Revenues (Million $)						
1Q	78.90	68.37	44.89	24.70	19.50	—
2Q	53.04	62.17	53.68	31.60	19.80	—
3Q	57.19	70.03	69.70	41.70	21.70	—
4Q	48.05	87.77	72.65	47.60	21.90	—
Yr.	237.2	288.3	240.9	145.6	82.90	68.70
Earnings Per Share ($)						
1Q	**0.43**	0.41	0.33	—	—	—
2Q	**0.08**	**0.38**	**0.35**	0.20	—	—
3Q	**-0.29**	**0.47**	0.34	0.80	—	—
4Q	**-0.18**	**0.80**	0.54	0.78	—	—
Yr.	**0.05**	**2.05**	**1.57**	2.07	0.31	0.12

Next earnings report expected: mid November

Dividend Data

No cash dividends have been paid, and the company does not anticipate paying any for the foreseeable future. It currently intends to retain its earnings for the development of its business. A shareholder rights plan was adopted in 1997.

Etec Systems, Inc.

Business Summary - 30-AUG-99

As the leading supplier of photomask pattern generation equipment, Etec Systems plays a crucial role in the drive to extend semiconductor manufacturing capability. The company's products enable the production of photomasks, which are quartz plates used as masters to transfer semiconductor circuit patterns onto silicon wafers. In turn, these semiconductor chips are used in a variety of electronic products, including personal computers, cell phones, telecommunications equipment and automobiles, to control, manage and manipulate data.

The company's pattern generation equipment transforms electronic design data into complex master patterns or masks, similar to a photographic negative, which are then used many times to create chips. Each chip needs an average of 16 to 24 different masks in the manufacturing process to create a unique electronic function. Semiconductor manufacturers use ETEC's products to help meet the challenge of shrinking feature sizes, increasing device complexity, and providing better accuracy and throughput.

ETEC is the technology leader in the global semiconductor mask pattern generation market, holding a market share of more than 75%. The company is the only mask PG supplier with a dual technology strategy offering both electron-beam and laser-beam based systems. The different characteristics of these systems suit different segments of the mask pattern generation market. Electron beam systems have a much smaller beam spot size than laser beam systems and are best suited for leading-edge market segments that require the highest resolution and accuracy.

Most revenues are derived from the sale of a relatively small number of systems at prices ranging from about $6.0 million to $13.0 million. Consequently, results for any given period could be adversely affected by any delay in the recognition of revenue for a single system or upgrade. ETEC also derives significant revenues from service and support of its installed base of systems. Sales outside of the U.S. comprised about 74% and 72% of revenues in FY 98 (Jul.) and FY 97, respectively.

ETEC also manufactures and sells the DigiRite 2000 laser direct imaging system through its Interconnect Products Group. The system allows printed circuit board manufacturers to transfer computer generated patterns directly to the printed circuit boards, eliminating the intermediate steps associated with printing patterns on masks. Revenue from this product was immaterial in FY 98, but is expected to contribute over the course of FY 99.

Per Share Data ($) (Year Ended Jul. 31)	1999	1998	1997	1996	1995	1994	1993	1992	1991	1990
Tangible Bk. Val.	NA	11.22	9.12	5.91	NM	NM	NM	NA	NA	NA
Cash Flow	NA	2.45	1.78	2.10	0.30	0.18	-0.49	NA	NA	NA
Earnings	0.05	2.05	1.57	2.07	0.31	0.12	-0.94	-2.86	-0.23	NA
Dividends	Nil	Nil	Nil	Nil	Nil	Nil	Nil	Nil	Nil	NA
Payout Ratio	Nil	Nil	Nil	Nil	Nil	Nil	Nil	Nil	Nil	NA
Prices - High	55	62 3/8	69 1/8	39 1/2	14 1/4	NA	NA	NA	NA	NA
- Low	21 5/8	14 7/8	27	7 3/4	9 1/8	NA	NA	NA	NA	NA
P/E Ratio - High	NM	30	44	19	46	NA	NA	NA	NA	NA
- Low	NM	7	17	4	29	NA	NA	NA	NA	NA
Income Statement Analysis (Million $)										
Revs.	NA	288	241	146	83.0	69.0	59.0	NA	NA	NA
Oper. Inc.	NA	76.1	58.9	28.5	14.4	13.4	0.2	NA	NA	NA
Depr.	NA	9.0	4.6	1.6	3.0	3.8	4.6	NA	NA	NA
Int. Exp.	NA	0.8	1.0	1.8	4.2	5.1	5.9	NA	NA	NA
Pretax Inc.	NA	70.9	53.3	21.3	6.8	3.9	-12.9	NA	NA	NA
Eff. Tax Rate	NA	34%	35%	NM	34%	59%	NM	NA	NA	NA
Net Inc.	NA	46.8	34.4	37.8	4.5	1.6	-11.4	NA	NA	NA
Balance Sheet & Other Fin. Data (Million $)										
Cash	NA	63.6	56.0	68.6	23.6	6.6	NA	NA	NA	NA
Curr. Assets	NA	301	238	186	75.0	50.5	NA	NA	NA	NA
Total Assets	NA	359	285	209	86.0	63.0	NA	NA	NA	NA
Curr. Liab.	NA	105	82.2	74.4	52.1	44.3	NA	NA	NA	NA
LT Debt	NA	Nil	Nil	6.7	16.9	31.3	NA	NA	NA	NA
Common Eqty.	NA	247	198	116	-67.0	-76.0	NA	NA	NA	NA
Total Cap.	NA	247	198	121	25.8	-45.0	NA	NA	NA	NA
Cap. Exp.	NA	26.8	27.1	11.7	2.9	2.0	0.7	NA	NA	NA
Cash Flow	NA	55.8	39.1	38.3	4.4	2.5	-6.8	NA	NA	NA
Curr. Ratio	NA	2.9	2.9	2.5	1.4	1.1	NA	NA	NA	NA
% LT Debt of Cap.	NA	Nil	Nil	5.5	65.3	NM	NA	NA	NA	NA
% Net Inc.of Revs.	NA	16.2	14.3	25.9	5.4	2.3	NM	NA	NA	NA
% Ret. on Assets	NA	14.5	14.0	25.6	6.0	NM	NA	NA	NA	NA
% Ret. on Equity	NA	21.1	22.0	157.7	NM	NM	NA	NA	NA	NA

Data as orig reptd.; bef. results of disc opers/spec. items. Per share data adj. for stk. divs. Bold denotes diluted EPS (FASB 128)-prior periods restated. E-Estimated. NA-Not Available. NM-Not Meaningful. NR-Not Ranked.

Office—26460 Corporate Ave., Hayward, CA 94545. **Tel**—(510) 783-9210. **Website**—http://www.etec.com **Chrmn, Pres & CEO**—S. E. Cooper. **VP & CFO**—W. Snyder. **Dirs**—S. E. Cooper, E. J. Gelbach, J. B. McBennett, W. Ryan, W. Siegle, T. Suzuki, T. M. Trent, R. L. Wehrli. **Transfer Agent & Registrar**—Bank of Boston. **Incorporated**—in Nevada in 1989. **Empl**— 1,119. **S&P Analyst:** B. McGovern

STANDARD
&POOR'S
STOCK REPORTS

Ethan Allen Interiors

NYSE Symbol **ETH**

In S&P SmallCap 600

09-OCT-99

Industry:
Household Furnishings & Appliances

Summary: This home furnishings manufacturer sells its products through Ethan Allen Galleries, most of which are owned by independent dealers.

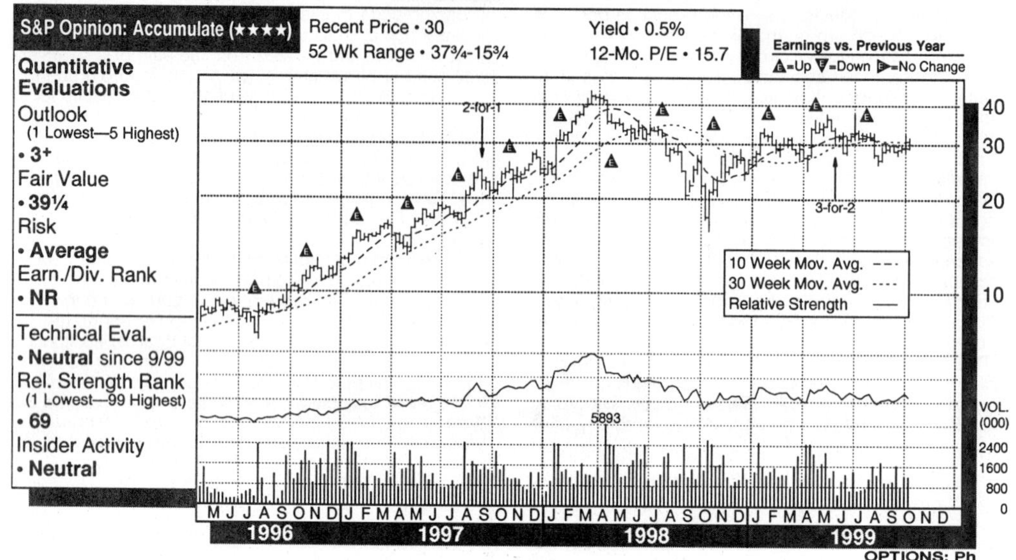

OPTIONS: Ph

Overview - 30-AUG-99

Sales should rise at a low double digit pace in FY 00 (Jun.), reflecting additional units in operation, higher same-store sales and a new e-commerce initiative. Comparable-store sales should benefit from a repositioning of the product mix to appeal to a broader consumer base, a program to renovate or relocate existing stores, and more frequent advertising and promotional campaigns. In addition, sales should benefit from favorable trends, including high housing activity, low interest and unemployment rates and baby boomers in their peak remodeling years. Margins should be aided by manufacturing efficiencies, lower interest expense, and a strengthening of the upholstery and accessory lines. We see EPS rising 13%, to $2.17 in FY 00 (Jun.), from FY 99's $1.92. ETH is pursuing an aggressive growth strategy, including investments in technology, employee training and new stores.

Valuation - 30-AUG-99

The shares of this well-managed company have advanced more than 300% since early 1996. More recently, the shares have fallen from their 1999 peak on fears that the recent rise in mortgage interest rates would hurt demand for furnishings. We believe these fears are overblown, as overall economic and demographic trends remain favorable, with high housing activity and consumer confidence, a rising stock market, and baby boomers entering their peak years of spending on household furnishings. Since 1996, returns on sales, assets and equity have been trending upward on higher margins that reflect management's attention to all facets of the business. Improving cash flow has allowed ETH to significantly reduce long term debt. At just 13 times our FY 00 EPS estimate, and 15 times our FY 00 free cash flow forecast, the shares merit accumulation.

Key Stock Statistics

S&P EPS Est. 2000	2.17	Tang. Bk. Value/Share	6.16
P/E on S&P Est. 2000	13.9	Beta	0.84
Dividend Rate/Share	0.16	Shareholders	413
Shs. outstg. (M)	40.9	Market cap. (B)	$ 1.2
Avg. daily vol. (M)	0.238	Inst. holdings	73%

Value of $10,000 invested 5 years ago: $ 29,222

Fiscal Year Ending Jun. 30

	1999	1998	1997	1996	1995	1994
Revenues (Million $)						
1Q	166.2	152.5	132.4	116.9	113.5	96.77
2Q	193.7	172.7	138.3	127.2	125.7	108.3
3Q	194.6	171.4	144.7	134.6	123.6	115.9
4Q	207.8	182.7	156.4	131.0	113.2	116.3
Yr.	762.2	679.3	571.8	509.8	476.1	437.3
Earnings Per Share ($)						
1Q	**0.38**	0.32	0.20	0.10	0.13	0.10
2Q	**0.50**	**0.43**	0.28	0.18	0.16	0.13
3Q	**0.51**	**0.43**	0.29	0.19	0.16	0.14
4Q	**0.54**	**0.45**	0.34	0.17	0.07	0.14
Yr.	**1.92**	**1.63**	**1.11**	0.64	0.52	0.51

Next earnings report expected: mid October

Dividend Data (Dividends have been paid since 1996.)

Amount ($)	Date Decl.	Ex-Div. Date	Stock of Record	Payment Date
0.040	Jan. 27	Apr. 07	Apr. 09	Apr. 23 '99
3-for-2	Apr. 28	May. 24	May. 07	May. 21 '99
0.040	Apr. 28	Jul. 07	Jul. 09	Jul. 23 '99
0.040	Aug. 05	Oct. 06	Oct. 08	Oct. 22 '99

A Division of The McGraw-Hill Companies

Ethan Allen Interiors Inc.

Business Summary - 30-AUG-99

Ethan Allen Interiors (ETH) focuses its growth strategy on realizing greater potential from its existing stores, opening new stores domestically and abroad, and improving service levels through a strengthened vertically integrated manufacturing and distribution system. In addition to new eye-catching store fronts, innovative products, such as ETH's new EA Organizer modular home office collection, and expanded spending on national television advertising campaigns, have increased the pace of sales.

The state of the housing industry is a significant factor affecting furniture sales. Also impacting shipments is the level of interest rates and the pace of economic activity. Given the lag in housing sales to furniture purchases, the strong housing activity in 1997 and 1998 bodes well for furniture sales into 2000.

Ethan Allen Interiors, through wholly owned Ethan Allen Inc., is a leading manufacturer and retailer of home furnishings. One of the 10 largest U.S. manufacturers of household furniture, ETH produces or assembles about 90% of its products at 21 manufacturing facilities and three saw mills, thereby maintaining greater control over cost, quality and service to its customers. The company has 10 regional distribution centers located throughout the U.S.

As of early August 1999, ETH's products were being sold through a network of 314 Ethan Allen Galleries. The galleries exclusively sell Ethan Allen products. The company owned and operated 72 galleries, while independent dealers owned and operated 242 galleries in North America and abroad. Sales to independent dealer-owned stores accounted for 63% of net sales in FY 98 (Jun.).

The company's products are positioned in terms of selection, quality and value in what it considers to be the four currently most important style categories in home furnishings: Formal, American Country, Casual Contemporary and Classic Elegance. ETH has grouped its products into collections within these categories. Each collection includes case goods (58% of FY 98 sales), consisting primarily of wood furnishings such as bedroom and dining room furniture, wall units and tables; upholstered products (28%), consisting largely of sofas, loveseats, chairs, recliners and swivel rockers; home furnishing accessories (13%), including carpeting and area rugs, lighting products, clocks, wall decor, bedding ensembles, draperies and decorative accessories; and indoor/outdoor furniture (1%).

The company employs a showcase gallery concept: products are displayed in complete room ensembles, including furnishings, wall decor, window treatments, floor coverings, accents and accessories. ETH believes that the gallery concept results in higher sales, as it encourages customers to buy a complete home collection, including case goods, upholstery and accessories, and provides designers an opportunity to offer additional service. While the average gallery is 15,000 sq. ft., in May 1997, the company opened a three-stores-in-on e 30,000 sq. ft. prototype store in Stamford, CT.

Per Share Data ($) (Year Ended Jun. 30)	1999	1998	1997	1996	1995	1994	1993	1992	1991	1990
Tangible Bk. Val.	NA	6.16	4.90	3.83	3.15	3.99	3.00	1.20	NA	NA
Cash Flow	NA	1.99	1.49	1.04	0.91	0.83	0.28	0.47	NA	NA
Earnings	1.92	1.63	1.11	0.64	0.52	0.51	-0.07	-0.08	NA	NA
Dividends	0.13	0.08	0.05	Nil	Nil	Nil	Nil	NA	NA	NA
Payout Ratio	7%	5%	5%	Nil	Nil	Nil	Nil	NA	NA	NA
Prices - High	37¾	44⅜	28⅝	13	8⅜	10⅝	10½	NA	NA	NA
- Low	24⅝	15¾	12⅜	6½	5¾	6½	5⅜	NA	NA	NA
P/E Ratio - High	20	27	26	20	16	21	NM	NA	NA	NA
- Low	13	10	11	10	11	13	NM	NA	NA	NA
Income Statement Analysis (Million $)										
Revs.	NA	679	572	510	476	437	384	351	NA	NA
Oper. Inc.	NA	136	102	73.1	64.9	62.8	50.7	32.5	NA	NA
Depr.	NA	15.9	16.4	17.5	17.2	13.3	13.8	19.6	NA	NA
Int. Exp.	NA	4.6	5.9	8.9	10.8	13.3	41.8	13.2	NA	NA
Pretax Inc.	NA	119	80.7	47.0	36.0	38.6	-3.4	1.1	NA	NA
Eff. Tax Rate	NA	39%	40%	40%	37%	42%	NM	69%	NA	NA
Net Inc.	NA	71.9	48.7	28.1	22.7	22.6	-2.3	0.3	NA	NA
Balance Sheet & Other Fin. Data (Million $)										
Cash	NA	19.4	39.8	9.1	7.5	6.7	4.8	4.6	NA	NA
Curr. Assets	NA	188	195	168	176	167	148	142	NA	NA
Total Assets	NA	433	428	396	408	413	396	391	NA	NA
Curr. Liab.	NA	73.6	63.3	59.1	53.5	64.4	57.4	48.5	NA	NA
LT Debt	NA	12.5	66.8	82.7	127	139	154	161	NA	NA
Common Eqty.	NA	314	265	220	193	171	116	95.2	NA	NA
Total Cap.	NA	359	365	336	354	347	337	340	NA	NA
Cap. Exp.	NA	29.7	23.4	13.3	11.2	12.2	7.7	NA	NA	NA
Cash Flow	NA	87.8	65.2	45.6	40.0	35.2	11.0	16.8	NA	NA
Curr. Ratio	NA	2.6	3.1	2.8	3.3	2.6	2.6	2.9	NA	NA
% LT Debt of Cap.	NA	35.0	18.3	24.6	35.9	40.1	45.6	47.6	NA	NA
% Net Inc.of Revs.	NA	10.6	8.5	5.5	4.8	5.2	NM	0.1	NA	NA
% Ret. on Assets	NA	16.7	11.8	7.0	5.5	5.3	NM	NA	NA	NA
% Ret. on Equity	NA	24.8	20.1	13.6	12.5	14.6	NM	NA	NA	NA

Data as orig reptd.; bef. results of disc opers/spec. items. Per share data adj. for stk. divs. Bold denotes diluted EPS (FASB 128)-prior periods restated. E-Estimated. NA-Not Available. NM-Not Meaningful. NR-Not Ranked.

Office—Ethan Allen Drive, Danbury, CT 06811. **Tel**—(203) 743-8000. **Website**—http://www.ethanallen.com **Chrmn, Pres & CEO**—M. F. Kathwari. **VP & Investor Contact**—Margaret W. Lupton (203-743-8234).**Secy**—R. Khazarian.**Dirs**—C. A. Clark, K. Gamble, M. F. Kathwari, H. G. McDonell, E. H. Meyer, W. W. Sprague. **Transfer Agent & Registrar**—Harris Trust Co. of Chicago. **Empl**— 7,018. **S&P Analyst:** Efraim Levy

STANDARD &POOR'S
STOCK REPORTS

Exabyte Corp.

NASDAQ Symbol **EXBT**

In S&P SmallCap 600

09-OCT-99

Industry: Computers (Peripherals)

Summary: Exabyte designs, develops, makes and markets high-capacity 8mm cartridge and other tape subsystems for cost-effective data storage solutions.

Quantitative Evaluations

Outlook (1 Lowest—5 Highest) • **2-**

Fair Value • **4½**

Risk • **Average**

Earn./Div. Rank • **C**

Technical Eval. • **Bullish** since 9/99

Rel. Strength Rank (1 Lowest—99 Highest) • **91**

Insider Activity • **NA**

Recent Price • 4¾

52 Wk Range • 9-3⅜

Yield • Nil

12-Mo. P/E • NM

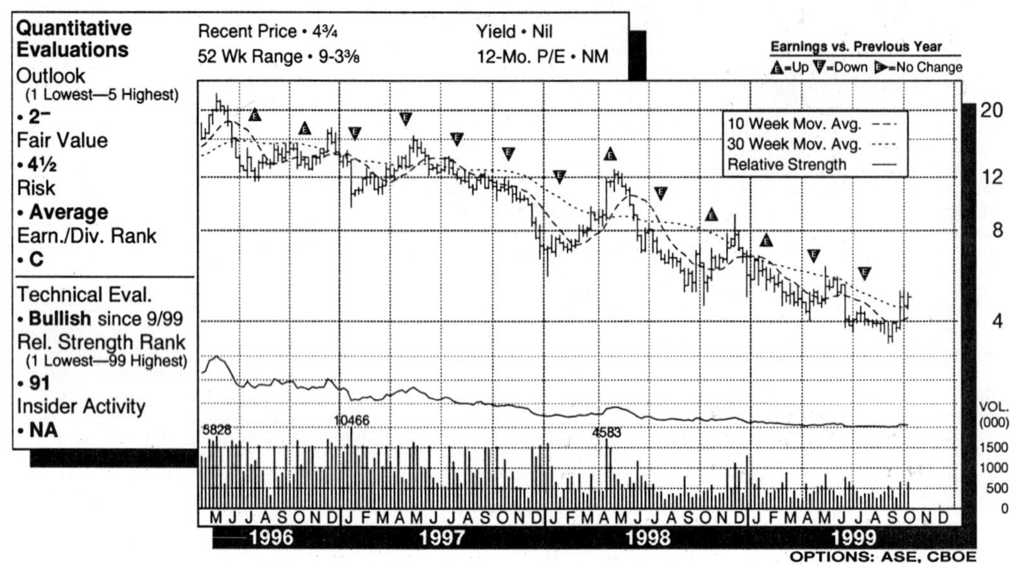

OPTIONS: ASE, CBOE

Business Profile - 30-AUG-99

On August 19, 1999, the company said it plans to cut nearly 16% of its global staff by year-end as part of a previously announced restructuring that is intended to cut costs and capacity by merging several operational and marketing businesses under common management. The reductions are expected to save about $12 million annually. Also, a one-time charge for severance costs, benefits extensions and outplacement services of about $2.8 million will be incurred during the third quarter. In March 1999, Exabyte expanded its family of tape drives by introducing the Mammoth-LT tape drive, a price performance tape drive for small to medium size business customers.

Operational Review - 30-AUG-99

Net sales for the six months ended July 3, 1999, declined 26%, year to year, reflecting decreased sales of end of life drives, Eliant 820 drives and 8mm libraries. Gross margins narrowed on the lower sales volume and lower pricing, and with SG&A expenses down fractionally and research & development expenses up 25%, an operating loss contrasted with operating income. After an income tax benefit, versus taxes at 34.0%, the net loss was $20,371,000 ($0.92 a share), against net income of $2,180,000 ($0.10).

Stock Performance - 08-OCT-99

In the past 30 trading days, EXBT's shares have increased 20%, compared to a 0.91% fall in the S&P 500. Average trading volume for the past five days was 128,000 shares, compared with the 40-day moving average of 95,072 shares.

Key Stock Statistics

Dividend Rate/Share	Nil	Shareholders	662
Shs. outstg. (M)	22.3	Market cap. (B)	$0.107
Avg. daily vol. (M)	0.099	Inst. holdings	64%
Tang. Bk. Value/Share	6.45		
Beta	0.25		

Value of $10,000 invested 5 years ago: $ 2,730

Fiscal Year Ending Dec. 31

	1999	1998	1997	1996	1995	1994
Revenues (Million $)						
1Q	62.65	80.75	85.43	93.82	96.19	86.89
2Q	48.52	69.75	97.14	90.46	96.98	92.68
3Q	—	72.81	78.47	92.74	84.10	99.0
4Q	—	63.20	74.64	85.87	96.87	103.3
Yr.	—	286.5	335.7	362.9	374.1	381.8
Earnings Per Share ($)						
1Q	**-0.16**	**0.09**	**0.05**	0.15	0.34	0.32
2Q	**-0.76**	**0.01**	**0.05**	0.16	0.08	0.34
3Q	—	**0.02**	**-0.68**	0.17	-1.13	0.40
4Q	—	**-0.24**	**-0.79**	-0.09	0.15	0.41
Yr.	—	**-0.12**	**-1.38**	**0.39**	**-0.57**	1.48

Next earnings report expected: mid October

Dividend Data

The company has never paid cash dividends on its common stock. A shareholder rights plan was adopted in 1991.

Exabyte Corporation

Business Summary - 30-AUG-99

Exabyte was formed in 1985 to capitalize on its proprietary adaptation to the computer industry of 8mm helical scan recording technology, originally developed for video applications in the 1950s. EXBT is currently the world's largest company devoted solely to the design, manufacture and marketing of tape storage products. The company's products include cartridge tape subsystems based on 8mm helical scan and quarter-inch technologies and robotic tape libraries. Exabyte derives its name from the mathematical term "exa" (the largest named number) and "byte" (the memory space needed to store one character of computer information).

The company's strategic focus is the information storage and retrieval tape drive market for workstations, mid-range computer systems and networks, primarily for data backup and archival applications. Computer manufacturers and resellers require a variety of storage products that vary in price, performance, capacity and form-factor characteristics as their needs for data backup and archival storage increase. Exabyte's current strategy is to offer a number of products to address a broad range of these requirements.

The company's operations are segmented into three divisions, each responsible for a specific line of products or services. They include the Drives & Media division; the Storage Automation Solutions division; and the Worldwide Quality and Customer Services division.

The Drives & Media division manufactures 8mm tape drive products and media that address the mid-range markets, including UNIX and NT server markets. These products are sold primarily to Exabyte's reseller and original equipment manufacturer (OEM) customers. Additionally, all of the company's 8mm tape drives can be incorporated into one or more of its 8mm robotic tape library offerings. In 1998, sales of 8mm tape drive products represented 53% of revenue.

The company's robotic tape libraries, systems offerings and associated products are the responsibility of the Storage Automation Solutions division. Exabyte offers a family of robotic tape libraries that automate the storage and retrieval of substantial amounts of data. Each library incorporates one or more tape drives and multiple media cartridges. The primary sales channels for the company's robotic tape libraries are OEMs and resellers. The libraries are targeted for use in applications ranging from small department networks to large application servers. In 1998, revenues from library sales were 20% of total revenue.

Exabyte's Worldwide Quality and Customer Services division provides a full range of warranty and post-warranty support services for the company's library, tape drive and media products. These services, which are delivered through a worldwide network of service centers and authorized service providers, support the company's OEM, reseller and end-user customers in the deployment, operation and maintenance of Exabyte products. In 1998, revenue from servi ce and support programs accounted for 7% of total revenue.

Per Share Data ($) (Year Ended Dec. 31)	1998	1997	1996	1995	1994	1993	1992	1991	1990	1989
Tangible Bk. Val.	7.49	7.61	9.02	8.54	9.10	7.49	6.70	5.51	3.80	2.38
Cash Flow	0.62	-0.50	1.15	0.22	2.07	1.36	1.36	1.78	1.47	0.73
Earnings	-0.12	-1.38	0.39	-0.57	1.48	0.76	0.95	1.51	1.32	0.65
Dividends	Nil	Nil	Nil	Nil	Nil	Nil	Nil	Nil	Nil	Nil
Payout Ratio	Nil	Nil	Nil	Nil	Nil	Nil	Nil	Nil	Nil	Nil
Prices - High	12¾	16½	22¾	21⅝	24	18¾	40⅝	31⅝	25⅜	13⅛
- Low	4½	5⅝	11⅝	10	14	7¼	12	13⅛	6⅝	10
P/E Ratio - High	NM	NM	58	NM	16	25	43	21	19	20
- Low	NM	NM	30	NM	9	10	13	9	5	15
Income Statement Analysis (Million $)										
Revs.	287	336	363	374	382	310	287	234	170	89.0
Oper. Inc.	8.7	-32.7	28.6	-7.4	61.3	35.3	59.4	54.2	43.7	19.2
Depr.	16.6	19.7	17.1	17.1	13.0	12.9	9.0	5.7	3.2	1.4
Int. Exp.	0.6	0.6	0.5	0.3	0.2	0.2	0.1	0.1	0.1	0.1
Pretax Inc.	-6.1	-53.1	12.7	-23.0	47.8	23.9	38.9	50.2	42.9	19.4
Eff. Tax Rate	NM	NM	32%	NM	32%	32%	47%	36%	36%	36%
Net Inc.	-2.8	-30.8	8.6	-12.4	32.4	16.2	20.5	32.2	27.6	12.4
Balance Sheet & Other Fin. Data (Million $)										
Cash	56.6	47.0	66.8	68.8	80.3	66.0	51.2	55.6	28.8	30.1
Curr. Assets	156	176	196	197	204	168	155	135	89.0	58.0
Total Assets	208	221	256	250	243	197	183	150	101	62.0
Curr. Liab.	34.1	47.6	52.7	60.0	45.6	38.3	42.3	37.7	25.5	16.5
LT Debt	7.5	3.0	3.5	4.2	0.2	0.5	0.5	0.1	0.2	0.2
Common Eqty.	166	171	200	186	197	159	140	112	75.0	46.0
Total Cap.	174	174	203	190	197	159	141	112	75.0	46.0
Cap. Exp.	9.4	11.8	19.3	23.4	13.6	8.0	17.8	6.8	9.3	2.9
Cash Flow	13.9	-11.1	25.7	4.7	45.4	29.0	29.5	37.9	30.8	13.7
Curr. Ratio	4.6	3.7	3.7	3.3	4.5	4.4	3.7	3.6	3.5	3.5
% LT Debt of Cap.	4.3	1.7	1.7	2.2	0.1	0.3	0.4	0.1	0.3	0.4
% Net Inc.of Revs.	NM	NM	2.3	NM	8.5	5.2	7.1	13.8	16.2	13.9
% Ret. on Assets	NM	NM	3.4	NM	14.6	8.5	12.1	25.4	33.4	30.9
% Ret. on Equity	NM	NM	4.5	NM	18.1	10.8	16.0	34.0	45.2	43.9

Data as orig reptd.; bef. results of disc opers/spec. items. Per share data adj. for stk. divs. Bold denotes diluted EPS (FASB 128)-prior periods restated. E-Estimated. NA-Not Available. NM-Not Meaningful. NR-Not Ranked.

Office—1685 38th St., Boulder, CO 80301-9803. **Tel**—(303) 442-4333. **Website**—http://www.exabyte.com **Chrmn, Pres & CEO**—W. L. Marriner. **VP, CFO & Secy**—S. F. Smith. **Dirs**—P. D. Behrendt, S. C. Johnson, A. L. Jones, W. L. Marriner, T. E. Pardun, M. W. Perry, R. Z. Sorenson. **Transfer Agent & Registrar**—First National Bank of Boston. **Incorporated**—in Delaware in 1985. **Empl**— 1,212. **S&P Analyst:** C.C.P.

STANDARD
&POOR'S
STOCK REPORTS

Expeditors International

NASDAQ Symbol **EXPD**

In S&P SmallCap 600

09-OCT-99 **Industry:** Air Freight

Summary: This company is a global air and ocean freight forwarder and customs broker.

Quantitative Evaluations

Outlook (1 Lowest—5 Highest) • **2⁻**

Fair Value • **34⅜**

Risk • **Average**

Earn./Div. Rank • **B+**

Technical Eval. • **Bullish** since 7/99

Rel. Strength Rank (1 Lowest—99 Highest) • **75**

Insider Activity • **Neutral**

Recent Price • 34¼ | 52 Wk Range • 37¾-14⅛ | Yield • 0.3% | 12-Mo. P/E • 36.1

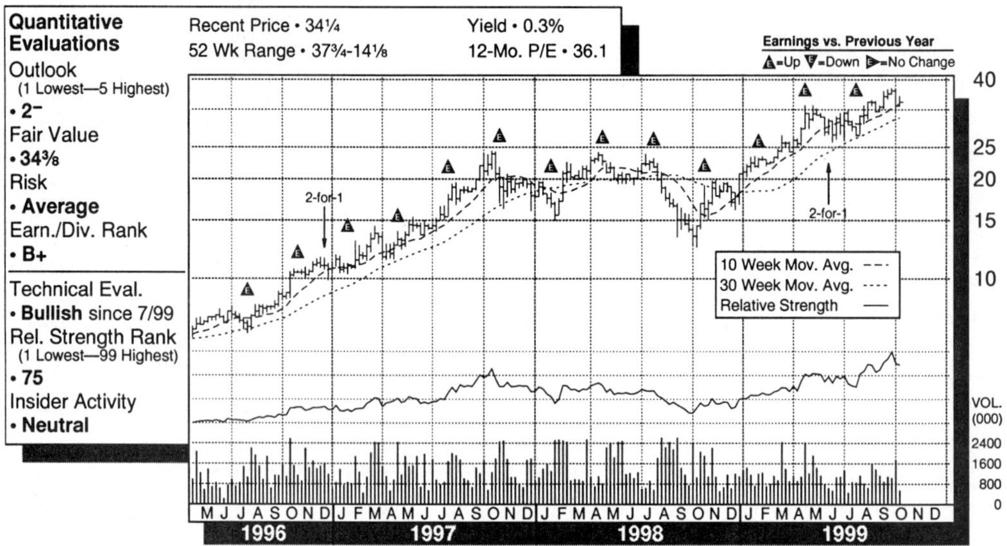

Business Profile - 28-JUN-99

Expeditors International provides logistics services worldwide through a network of 145 offices. The company pursues a strategy of organic growth, supplemented by certain strategic acquisitions, where economic benefits significantly exceed premiums. In the first quarter of 1999, EXPD opened seven new offices – in Athens, Greece; Ankara, Istanbul, Izmir and Mersin, Turkey; East Midlands, U.K.; and Nogales, Mexico. Historically, the company has been subject to seasonal trends, with the first quarter the weakest and the third quarter generally the strongest, ahead of the holiday season. Same-store revenue and operating income increased 21% and 14%, respectively, in the first quarter.

Operational Review - 28-JUN-99

Net revenues (excluding carrier charges) in the first quarter of 1999 advanced 25%, year to year, primarily due to increased airfreight tonnage handled, resulting from economic improvements in Far Eastern countries, and aggressive marketing of ocean freight rates for eastbound cargo from the Far East. Operating profit margins narrowed slightly on higher staffing levels following 1998's peak season (second half of the year). After taxes at 37.0%, versus 38.3%, net income rose 19%, to $9,521,000 ($0.18 a share), from $8,034,000 ($0.15). Per share results have been adjusted for a 2-for-1 stock split on May 31, 1999.

Stock Performance - 08-OCT-99

In the past 30 trading days, EXPD's shares have increased 7%, compared to a 0.91% fall in the S&P 500. Average trading volume for the past five days was 105,560 shares, compared with the 40-day moving average of 236,751 shares.

Key Stock Statistics

Dividend Rate/Share	0.10	Shareholders	8,953
Shs. outstg. (M)	50.2	Market cap. (B)	$ 1.7
Avg. daily vol. (M)	0.216	Inst. holdings	64%
Tang. Bk. Value/Share	4.85		
Beta	1.61		

Value of $10,000 invested 5 years ago: $ 93,180

Fiscal Year Ending Dec. 31

	1999	1998	1997	1996	1995	1994
Revenues (Million $)						
1Q	283.7	223.3	196.0	137.7	122.9	93.09
2Q	332.0	242.0	225.6	166.2	141.5	106.1
3Q	—	289.7	262.3	204.9	159.2	123.8
4Q	—	308.7	270.1	221.3	161.1	127.6
Yr.	—	1,064	954.0	730.1	584.7	450.6
Earnings Per Share ($)						
1Q	**0.18**	**0.15**	**0.10**	**0.08**	0.07	0.05
2Q	**0.25**	**0.21**	**0.15**	**0.10**	0.08	0.07
3Q	—	**0.27**	**0.22**	**0.15**	0.10	0.08
4Q	—	**0.27**	**0.24**	**0.14**	0.10	0.08
Yr.	—	**0.89**	**0.73**	**0.47**	**0.34**	**0.27**

Next earnings report expected: early November

Dividend Data (Dividends have been paid since 1993.)

Amount ($)	Date Decl.	Ex-Div. Date	Stock of Record	Payment Date
0.070	Nov. 19	Nov. 27	Dec. 01	Dec. 15 '98
0.050	May. 06	May. 21	Jun. 01	Jun. 15 '99
2-for-1	May. 06	Jun. 01	May. 17	May. 31 '99

A Division of The McGraw-Hill Companies

Expeditors International of Washington, Inc.

Business Summary - 28-JUN-99

Seattle-based Expeditors International's original focus was on air freight shipments from the Far East to the U.S. Today, the company's capabilities include worldwide air freight, ocean freight and distribution services, with a complete range of global services through an integrated information management system. Services include freight forwarding, vendor consolidation, customs clearance, marine insurance, distribution and other international services.

Shipments of computer components, other electronic equipment, housewares, sporting goods, machine parts and toys comprise a significant percentage of the company's business. Typical import customers include computer retailers and distributors of consumer electronics, department store chains, clothing and shoe wholesalers, manufacturers and catalogue stores.

Air freight services accounted for 41% of net revenues in 1998. The company typically acts either as a freight consolidator (purchasing cargo space on airlines and reselling it to customers at lower rates than the airline would charge customers directly) or as an agent for the airlines (receiving shipments from suppliers, consolidating and forwarding them to the airlines). Because of the high cost of air freight, shipments are usually characterized by a high value-to-weight ratio, such as computer components, and time sensitivity. EXPD also performs breakbulk services, breaking down consolidated shipments and distributing each lot to its final destination.

In the Customs Brokerage and Import Services division, which accounted for 40% of the company's net revenues in 1998, EXPD assists importers in clearing shipments through customs by preparing documentation, calculating and providing payment of duties, and arranging government inspections. Domestic services also include temporary warehousing, inland transportation, inventory management, cargo insurance and distribution. Ocean Freight Services accounted for 19% of net revenues in 1998. Revenue comes from commissions paid by carriers and fees charged to customers for added services, including preparing documentation, procuring insurance, arranging packing and crating, and providing consultation. Expeditors Cargo Management Systems (ECMS) supplies a sophisticated ocean consolidation service to large volume customers that have signed service agreements with ocean carriers. Utilizing ECMS, the company obtains less than container load shipments and consolidates them into full container loads. ECMS customers pay a fee for access to the data and handling charges for shipments.

The company staffs its offices largely with managers and other key personnel who are citizens of the nations in which they operate and who have extensive experience in global logistics. Marketing and customer service staffs are responsible for marketing directly to local shippers and traffic managers.

Per Share Data ($) (Year Ended Dec. 31)	1998	1997	1996	1995	1994	1993	1992	1991	1990	1989
Tangible Bk. Val.	4.40	3.46	2.89	2.44	2.12	1.83	1.64	1.40	1.17	0.94
Cash Flow	1.18	0.94	0.63	0.48	0.38	0.29	0.30	0.27	0.25	0.24
Earnings	0.89	0.73	0.47	0.34	0.27	0.21	0.23	0.22	0.21	0.20
Dividends	0.07	0.05	0.04	0.03	0.03	0.03	Nil	Nil	Nil	Nil
Payout Ratio	8%	7%	8%	9%	9%	12%	Nil	Nil	Nil	Nil
Prices - High	24 1/8	24 3/8	11 5/8	7 1/8	5 7/8	4 3/8	4 1/2	4	3 1/2	3 5/8
- Low	12 1/2	10 3/8	5 3/4	5	3 3/4	3 1/8	3 1/2	2 1/16	1 3/4	1 15/16
P/E Ratio - High	27	33	24	20	22	21	19	18	17	18
- Low	14	14	12	14	14	15	15	10	8	10
Income Statement Analysis (Million $)										
Revs.	1,064	954	730	585	451	361	333	254	207	194
Oper. Inc.	88.9	71.1	45.6	33.5	26.5	21.1	17.7	14.9	13.0	12.5
Depr.	15.5	11.2	8.1	6.6	5.2	3.9	3.2	2.4	1.8	1.9
Int. Exp.	0.5	0.4	0.2	0.3	0.2	0.3	0.2	0.2	0.2	0.2
Pretax Inc.	75.6	62.6	39.6	28.4	22.4	17.1	15.7	14.3	13.5	12.3
Eff. Tax Rate	37%	39%	39%	39%	41%	40%	28%	28%	28%	24%
Net Inc.	47.3	38.4	24.3	17.4	13.2	10.2	11.3	10.2	9.7	9.3
Balance Sheet & Other Fin. Data (Million $)										
Cash	49.4	42.1	37.3	36.6	18.4	28.5	28.1	27.6	26.0	20.5
Curr. Assets	284	260	215	168	126	118	92.5	86.8	72.1	53.2
Total Assets	407	342	272	204	157	145	118	107	91.0	65.0
Curr. Liab.	189	172	132	86.9	56.2	57.3	38.2	39.4	35.4	18.7
LT Debt	Nil	Nil	Nil	Nil	Nil	Nil	0.8	0.9	1.0	1.7
Common Eqty.	217	170	140	117	101	87.6	79.0	66.4	55.0	44.5
Total Cap.	217	170	140	117	101	87.6	79.8	67.3	56.1	46.2
Cap. Exp.	52.5	36.0	20.8	9.3	8.6	5.7	10.5	2.6	8.2	3.2
Cash Flow	62.8	49.6	32.4	24.0	18.4	14.0	14.5	12.6	11.5	11.2
Curr. Ratio	1.5	1.5	1.6	1.9	2.2	2.1	2.4	2.2	2.0	2.8
% LT Debt of Cap.	Nil	Nil	Nil	Nil	Nil	Nil	1.0	1.3	1.8	3.7
% Net Inc.of Revs.	4.4	4.0	3.3	3.0	2.9	2.8	3.4	4.0	4.7	4.8
% Ret. on Assets	12.6	12.5	10.2	9.5	8.7	7.7	10.0	10.3	12.4	15.8
% Ret. on Equity	24.4	24.8	18.9	16.0	13.9	12.2	15.4	16.7	19.5	23.5

Data as orig reptd.; bef. results of disc opers/spec. items. Per share data adj. for stk. divs. Bold denotes diluted EPS (FASB 128)-prior periods restated. E-Estimated. NA-Not Available. NM-Not Meaningful. NR-Not Ranked.

Office—1015 Third Ave., Seattle, WA 98104. **Tel**—(206) 674-3400. **Website**—www.expd.com **Chrmn & CEO**—P. J. Rose. **Pres & COO**—K. M. Walsh. **SVP, CFO, Treas & Investor Contact**—R. Jordan Gates. **SVP, Gen Counsel & Secy**—J. J. King. **Dirs**—J. J. Casey, D. Kourkoumelis, J. W. Meisenbach, P. J. Rose, K. M. Walsh, J. K. Wang. **Transfer Agent & Registrar**—ChaseMellon Shareholder Services, Seattle. **Incorporated**—in Washington in 1979. **Empl**— 5,300. **S&P Analyst:** John A. Massey

Express Scripts

Nasdaq Symbol **ESRX**

In S&P SmallCap 600

09-OCT-99

Industry: Health Care (Managed Care)

Summary: This company offers prescription benefits, eyecare, infusion therapy and disease state management services.

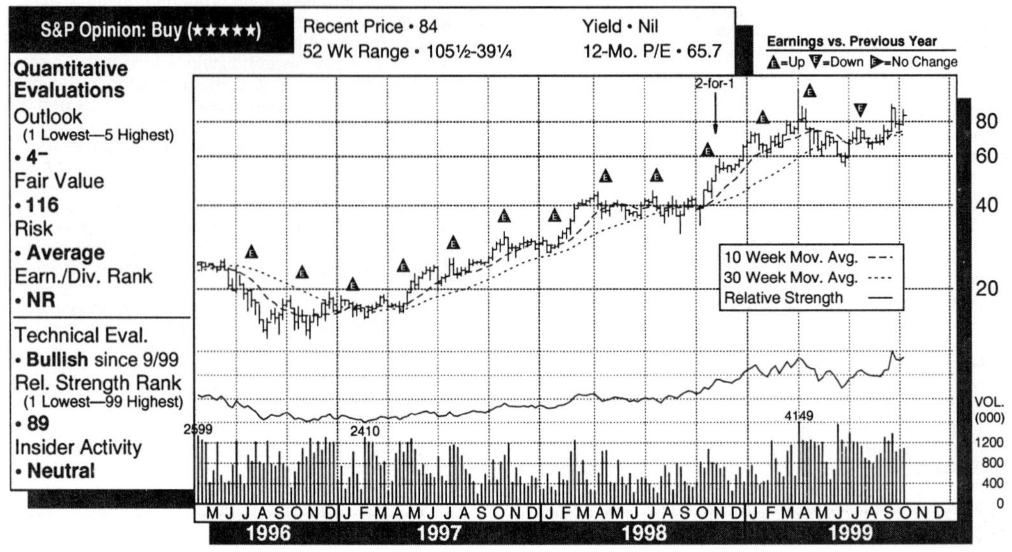

Overview - 10-JUN-99

Aided by the inclusion of Diversified Pharmaceutical Services Inc. (DPS), expanding demand from existing customers, new customer additions, and greater service offerings, we look for 1999 revenues of about $4.0 billion, up over 40% from 1998's $2.8 billion. Gross margins will suffer, as increased usage of the company's own pharmacy network requires that these drug ingredient costs be included in the cost of goods sold, but manufacturing efficiencies should allow gross margins to stabilize at around 8% in 1999. Operating margins will benefit from increased sales to large employer markets and rising mail order volumes, particularly following the launch of the company's Internet site by mid-1999. We currently look for 1999 EPS of $1.73, with an advance in 2000 to $2.20.

Valuation - 10-JUN-99

Moving in sympathy with the drug distribution group, the stock has lagged the performance of the S&P 500 Index during the first half of 1999. However, we are maintaining a strong buy rating, and believe ESRX will continue to benefit from its focus on value-added service offerings, broad pharmacy networks, and Internet strategies. With surging demand from commercial customers, and the prospect of Medicare utilizing pharmacy benefits managers in order to extend drug benefits to beneficiaries, the company should generate explosive revenue and earnings growth, and is attractive as the largest pure play in the pharmacy benefits management (PBM) industry. In an industry where size is critical, ESRX's operational efficiencies provide a significant competitive advantage, and we expect surging revenues to allow for strong EPS growth for the foreseeable future. With the shares trading well below 1X estimated 1999 sales, we look for substantial price appreciation.

Key Stock Statistics

S&P EPS Est. 1999	1.75	Tang. Bk. Value/Share	NM
P/E on S&P Est. 1999	48.0	Beta	1.26
S&P EPS Est. 2000	2.30	Shareholders	200
Dividend Rate/Share	Nil	Market cap. (B)	$ 2.0
Shs. outstg. (M)	38.5	Inst. holdings	50%
Avg. daily vol. (M)	0.297		

Value of $10,000 invested 5 years ago: $ 71,542

Fiscal Year Ending Dec. 31

	1999	1998	1997	1996	1995	1994
Revenues (Million $)						
1Q	899.1	371.4	262.0	168.4	118.0	83.08
2Q	996.8	807.4	300.5	184.7	135.2	89.97
3Q	—	807.3	319.9	194.3	138.5	100.7
4Q	—	838.8	348.2	226.2	152.8	110.8
Yr.	—	2,825	1,231	773.6	544.5	384.5
Earnings Per Share ($)						
1Q	**0.39**	**0.29**	**0.23**	**0.18**	0.14	0.09
2Q	**0.20**	**0.28**	**0.25**	**0.20**	0.15	0.10
3Q	**E0.46**	**0.34**	**0.26**	**0.21**	0.15	0.11
4Q	**E0.48**	**0.35**	**0.27**	**0.21**	0.15	0.12
Yr.	**E1.75**	**1.27**	**1.01**	**0.80**	**0.60**	**0.42**

Next earnings report expected: late October

Dividend Data

Amount ($)	Date Decl.	Ex-Div. Date	Stock of Record	Payment Date
2-for-1	Oct. 12	Nov. 02	Oct. 20	Oct. 30 '98

Express Scripts, Inc.

Business Summary - 10-JUN-99

Express Scripts ranks as the third largest pharmacy benefits manager (PBM) in the U.S., trailing only Rite-Aid PCS and Merck-Medco. At 1998 year-end, programs were provided to nearly 23 million individuals. During the year, the company managed drug expenditures totaling $4.6 billion, processed 113.2 million claims through its pharmacy networks, and filled 7.4 million mail pharmacy prescriptions. ESRX is a major provider of PBM services to the managed care industry; it has contracts with Aetna U.S. Healthcare, United HealthCare and Oxford Health Plans.

The company's PBM services (98% of 1998 revenues) involve the management of outpatient prescription drug usage through the application of managed care principles and advanced information technologies. Core services include retail pharmacy network administration, mail pharmacy services, benefit plan design consultation, formulary administration, electronic point-of-sale claims processing and drug utilization review. Advanced PBM services include the development of formulary compliance and therapeutic substitution programs, therapy management services such as prior authorization, therapy guidelines, step therapy protocols and formulary interventions, management information reporting and analytic capabilities, provider profiling, and outcomes assessments.

ESRX's PBM net revenues generally include administrative fees, dispensing fees and ingredient costs of pharmaceuticals dispensed from retail pharmacies included in one of its networks or from one of its mail pharmacies. The company then records the associated costs in the cost of revenues. Where ESRX only administers the contracts between its clients and the clients' retail pharmacy networks, net revenues include only the administrative fees.

Non-PBM services (2% of 1998 revenues) include outpatient infusion therapy, specialty distribution and vision care services.

In April 1999, ESRX purchased the Diversified Pharmaceutical Services (DPS) unit of SmithKline Beecham, for about $700 million in cash. Giving effect to the DPS transaction on a pro forma basis, ESRX provided PBM services to 46,400 individuals, with $9.9 billion of annual drug spending, processed 275,534 pharmacy network claims and filled 8,514 mail pharmacy prescriptions in 1998.

The company intends to launch two Internet sites by mid-1999. YourPharmacy.com will serve as an online drug store, and will offer both prescription and OTC medications, vitamins, herbs and health and beauty aids. DrugDigest.org will provide fact-based information on a variety of medications, vitamins and herbs.

Per Share Data ($)										
(Year Ended Dec. 31)	**1998**	**1997**	**1996**	**1995**	**1994**	**1993**	**1992**	**1991**	**1990**	**1989**
Tangible Bk. Val.	NM	6.17	5.04	2.58	1.78	1.30	1.02	0.17	NA	NA
Cash Flow	2.07	1.33	1.00	0.74	0.53	0.34	0.22	0.17	NA	NA
Earnings	1.27	1.01	0.80	0.60	0.42	0.28	0.18	0.14	NA	NA
Dividends	Nil	Nil	Nil	Nil	Nil	Nil	Nil	Nil	NA	NA
Payout Ratio	Nil	Nil	Nil	Nil	Nil	Nil	Nil	Nil	NA	NA
Prices - High	69	32 3/8	29	27 1/2	19 1/8	11 3/4	8 1/4	NA	NA	NA
- Low	27	15 5/8	13 1/4	12 1/2	11	4 3/4	3 1/8	NA	NA	NA
P/E Ratio - High	54	32	36	46	46	43	46	NA	NA	NA
- Low	21	15	17	21	26	17	17	NA	NA	NA
Income Statement Analysis (Million $)										
Revs.	2,825	1,231	774	544	385	120	71.0	47.0	NA	NA
Oper. Inc.	116	59.3	46.3	33.3	23.8	14.8	8.3	5.3	NA	NA
Depr.	27.0	10.5	6.7	4.4	3.3	1.9	1.0	0.7	NA	NA
Int. Exp.	20.2	0.2	0.1	0.1	0.1	0.1	0.1	0.1	NA	NA
Pretax Inc.	76.2	54.7	43.1	29.6	20.8	13.0	7.4	4.7	NA	NA
Eff. Tax Rate	44%	39%	39%	38%	39%	38%	37%	38%	NA	NA
Net Inc.	42.7	33.4	26.1	18.3	17.7	8.1	4.6	2.9	NA	NA
Balance Sheet & Other Fin. Data (Million $)										
Cash	123	64.2	79.6	11.5	5.7	2.0	11.8	3.5	NA	NA
Curr. Assets	657	364	263	144	92.8	63.3	40.1	16.6	NA	NA
Total Assets	1,095	403	300	164	108	75.4	45.4	20.2	NA	NA
Curr. Liab.	539	198	135	86.0	55.9	37.1	15.7	16.8	NA	NA
LT Debt	306	Nil	Nil	Nil	Nil	Nil	Nil	Nil	NA	NA
Common Eqty.	250	204	164	77.4	52.5	38.3	29.7	3.4	NA	NA
Total Cap.	556	204	166	78.3	52.5	38.3	29.7	3.4	NA	NA
Cap. Exp.	23.9	13.0	9.5	8.1	6.3	7.1	2.5	1.8	NA	NA
Cash Flow	69.7	43.9	32.9	22.7	16.0	10.0	5.6	3.6	NA	NA
Curr. Ratio	1.2	1.8	2.0	1.7	1.7	1.7	2.6	1.0	NA	NA
% LT Debt of Cap.	55.1	Nil	Nil	Nil	Nil	Nil	Nil	Nil	NA	NA
% Net Inc.of Revs.	1.5	2.7	3.4	3.4	3.3	6.7	6.5	6.1	NA	NA
% Ret. on Assets	5.7	9.5	11.3	13.4	13.8	13.3	12.6	NA	NA	NA
% Ret. on Equity	18.8	18.2	21.7	28.2	28.0	23.7	26.9	NA	NA	NA

Data as orig reptd.; bef. results of disc opers/spec. items. Per share data adj. for stk. divs. Bold denotes diluted EPS (FASB 128)-prior periods restated. E-Estimated. NA-Not Available. NM-Not Meaningful. NR-Not Ranked.

Office—14000 Riverport Dr., Maryland Heights, MO 63043. **Tel**—(314) 770-1666. **Website**—http://www.express-scripts.com **Chrmn**—H. L. Waltman. **Pres & CEO**—B. A. Toan. **EVP**—S. L. Bascomb. **SVP & CFO**—G. Paz. **Dirs**—H. Atkins, J. E. Campbell, R. M. Kernan Jr., R. A. Norling, F. J. Sievert, N. Steinig, S. Sternberg, B. A. Toan, H. L. Waltman, N. Zachary. **Transfer Agent & Registrar**—American Stock Transfer & Trust Co., NYC. **Incorporated**—in Missouri in 1986; reincorporated in Delaware in 1992. **Empl**— 3,354. **S&P Analyst:** Robert M. Gold

STANDARD
&POOR'S
STOCK REPORTS

FactSet Research Systems

NYSE Symbol **FDS**

In S&P SmallCap 600

09-OCT-99

Industry:
Services (Data Processing)

Summary: FDS provides on-line integrated database services to the financial community.

Quantitative Evaluations

Outlook
(1 Lowest—5 Highest)
• **4−**

Fair Value
• **77¼**

Risk
• **Average**

Earn./Div. Rank
• **NR**

Technical Eval.
• **Bullish** since 9/99

Rel. Strength Rank
(1 Lowest—99 Highest)
• **85**

Insider Activity
• **NA**

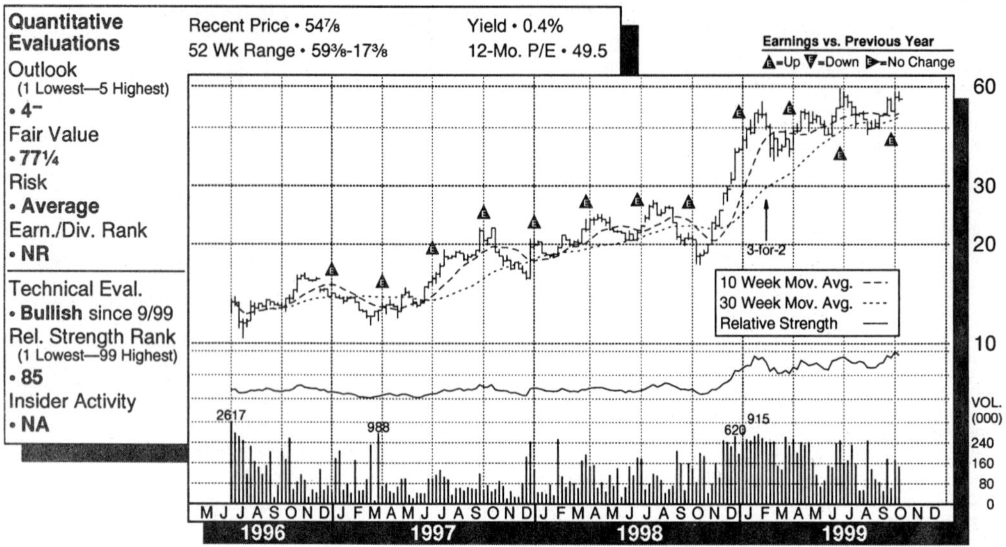

Business Profile - 15-JUN-99

Earnings have advanced rapidly in recent years, with return on equity above 25% since FY 95 (Aug.), and no long term debt on the company's balance sheet. FDS has been developing a new feature for its system called Directions. Directions, designed to be an easier-to-use system that FDS expects will help broaden its potential user base, is to be released in FY 99. Average client commitments -- forward-looking annual revenues for all services being supplied -- totaled $103.2 million as of February 28, 1999, a year-to-year gain of 31%. Commitments have risen in virtually every month in the company's 20-year history. Officers and directors control more than 35% of the stock.

Operational Review - 15-JUN-99

Total revenues for the six months ended February 28, 1999, climbed 34%, year to year, reflecting new clients, expansion in the number of user passwords, and new services and databases. Margins widened on the higher sales, and operating profit moved ahead 43%. Following other income, and taxes at 39.0% versus 44.1%, net income increased 55%, to $8.8 million from $5.7 million. Share earnings (adjusted for the February 1999 3-for-2 split) were $0.53, against $0.36.

Stock Performance - 08-OCT-99

In the past 30 trading days, FDS's shares have increased 21%, compared to a 0.91% fall in the S&P 500. Average trading volume for the past five days was 29,200 shares, compared with the 40-day moving average of 23,426 shares.

Key Stock Statistics

Dividend Rate/Share	0.20	Shareholders	1,500
Shs. outstg. (M)	15.6	Market cap. (B)	$0.860
Avg. daily vol. (M)	0.028	Inst. holdings	39%
Tang. Bk. Value/Share	4.74		
Beta	NA		

Value of $10,000 invested 5 years ago: NA

Fiscal Year Ending Aug. 31

	1999	1998	1997	1996	1995	1994
Revenues (Million $)						
1Q	23.83	17.49	12.82	10.14	—	—
2Q	25.24	19.06	13.99	10.56	—	—
3Q	26.45	20.20	15.10	11.44	—	—
4Q	28.32	22.16	16.45	12.21	—	—
Yr.	103.8	78.91	58.36	44.35	36.19	29.00
Earnings Per Share ($)						
1Q	**0.26**	0.17	0.12	0.09	—	—
2Q	**0.27**	**0.18**	0.13	0.09	—	—
3Q	**0.28**	**0.20**	0.15	0.11	—	—
4Q	**0.29**	**0.22**	0.15	0.11	—	—
Yr.	**1.11**	**0.77**	**0.55**	0.40	0.32	0.14

Next earnings report expected: mid December

Dividend Data (Dividends have been paid since 1999.)

Amount ($)	Date Decl.	Ex-Div. Date	Stock of Record	Payment Date
3-for-2	Jan. 08	Feb. 08	Jan. 22	Feb. 05 '99
0.179	Jan. 08	Feb. 24	Feb. 26	Mar. 22 '99
0.050	Mar. 16	May. 26	May. 31	Jun. 21 '99
0.050	Jun. 15	Aug. 27	Aug. 31	Sep. 20 '99

A Division of The McGraw-Hill Companies

FactSet Research Systems Inc.

Business Summary - 15-JUN-99

FactSet Research Systems Inc. is a provider of online integrated database services to the global financial community. The company provides a comprehensive, one-stop source of financial information and analytics for investment managers, investment bankers, and other financial professionals. FactSet combines more than 100 databases into a single mainframe information system that is accessible by clients through their personal computers.

The company acquires financial information from over 30 database vendors and, when possible, strives to maintain contractual relationships with a minimum of two database providers for each type of financial data. Database vendor charges may be billed directly to FactSet or its clients. Data charges to the company are on a fixed or royalty (per client) fee basis, with contracts generally renewable annually and cancelable on one year's notice.

FactSet's proprietary communication and software tools enable users to access the company's mainframe centers and its integrated data library in order to create investment analyses using Windows-based programs. Wide area network connections are designed to provide a direct, high-speed data transmission link between FactSet's mainframes and the client's network. Through the company's proprietary software tools, clients can download, screen, manipulate and analyze data in numerous formats, allowing for custom reports and charts designed by and for the user. By charging annual flat fees, clients are encouraged to make full use of the FactSet system.

The company believes that an integral part of its service is its superior consulting and training services. FactSet also believes that its client support consultants create lasting and profitable client relationships by providing hands-on training and continuous technical support to clients. Clients can gain a stronger understanding of FactSet's system by working with client support consultants in developing custom applications and spreadsheets that meet their information needs.

Due to the vast array of financial data that financial service professionals depend on, the company believes that it has become increasingly important for financial service firms to integrate different types of financial information from multiple databases in order to reach their investment decisions. Without being able to integrate financial data from many different sources, individual users must access and retrieve data from different sources, often in varied formats, and manually integrate the data to complete their objective.

Direct competitors include online and CD-ROM database suppliers and integrators such as OneSource Inc., COMPUSTAT PC Plus, Baseline Inc., StockVal Inc., Disclosure Inc. and IDD Information Services primarily in the United States; and Datastream and Randall-Helms primarily in international markets.

Per Share Data ($) (Year Ended Aug. 31)	1999	1998	1997	1996	1995	1994	1993	1992	1991	1990
Tangible Bk. Val.	NA	3.52	2.62	1.97	1.51	1.15	NA	NA	NA	NA
Cash Flow	NA	1.16	0.84	0.59	0.48	0.29	0.42	NA	NA	NA
Earnings	1.11	0.77	0.55	0.40	0.32	0.14	0.21	NA	NA	NA
Dividends	0.15	Nil	Nil	Nil	NA	NA	NA	NA	NA	NA
Payout Ratio	14%	Nil	Nil	Nil	NA	NA	NA	NA	NA	NA
Prices - High	59 3/8	42 3/8	22 3/8	16 3/8	NA	NA	NA	NA	NA	NA
- Low	35 1/2	17 3/8	11 3/8	10 3/8	NA	NA	NA	NA	NA	NA
P/E Ratio - High	53	55	41	41	NA	NA	NA	NA	NA	NA
- Low	32	23	21	26	NA	NA	NA	NA	NA	NA
Income Statement Analysis (Million $)										
Revs.	NA	45.3	58.4	44.3	36.2	29.0	23.9	19.3	16.4	NA
Oper. Inc.	NA	27.4	19.6	13.7	10.5	5.6	6.8	NA	NA	NA
Depr.	NA	6.6	4.7	3.0	2.4	2.2	1.8	NA	NA	NA
Int. Exp.	NA	NA	Nil	Nil	Nil	Nil	Nil	Nil	Nil	NA
Pretax Inc.	NA	22.4	15.7	11.4	8.7	3.7	5.2	4.3	3.8	NA
Eff. Tax Rate	NA	44%	43%	43%	43%	47%	44%	45%	44%	NA
Net Inc.	NA	12.6	8.9	6.5	4.9	1.9	2.9	2.3	2.1	NA
Balance Sheet & Other Fin. Data (Million $)										
Cash	NA	37.6	26.8	17.0	12.7	7.5	6.2	7.5	5.3	NA
Curr. Assets	NA	54.2	40.0	26.8	22.7	16.6	NA	NA	NA	NA
Total Assets	NA	70.6	50.8	36.5	28.7	22.3	20.4	13.7	11.4	NA
Curr. Liab.	NA	19.1	12.9	7.8	6.8	5.8	NA	NA	NA	NA
LT Debt	NA	Nil	Nil	Nil	Nil	Nil	Nil	Nil	Nil	NA
Common Eqty.	NA	51.0	37.6	28.2	21.4	16.0	13.8	10.9	8.7	NA
Total Cap.	NA	51.0	37.7	28.2	21.4	16.0	13.8	10.9	8.7	NA
Cap. Exp.	NA	12.0	5.8	6.4	2.3	2.5	3.0	NA	NA	NA
Cash Flow	NA	19.2	13.7	9.5	7.4	4.2	5.9	NA	NA	NA
Curr. Ratio	NA	2.8	3.1	3.4	3.3	2.9	NA	NA	NA	NA
% LT Debt of Cap.	NA	Nil	Nil	Nil	Nil	Nil	Nil	Nil	Nil	NA
% Net Inc.of Revs.	NA	27.8	15.3	14.6	13.6	6.7	12.0	12.1	12.8	NA
% Ret. on Assets	NA	20.8	20.5	19.9	19.4	9.1	16.9	18.6	NA	NA
% Ret. on Equity	NA	28.4	27.1	26.1	26.4	13.1	23.3	23.9	NA	NA

Data as orig reptd.; bef. results of disc opers/spec. items. Per share data adj. for stk. divs. Bold denotes diluted EPS (FASB 128)-prior periods restated. E-Estimated. NA-Not Available. NM-Not Meaningful. NR-Not Ranked.

Office—One Greenwich Plaza, Greenwich, CT 06830. **Tel**—(203) 863-1500. **Fax**—(203) 863-1501. **Website**—http://www.factset.com **Chrmn & CEO**—H. E. Wille. **Pres**—C. J. Snyder. **SVP, CFO & Secy**—E. S. Wong. **Dirs**—J. D. Connolly, D. Korus, J. E. Laird, Jr., J. C. Mickle, W. F. Siebecker, C. J. Snyder, H. E. Wille. **Transfer Agent & Registrar**—Bank of New York, NYC. **Incorporated**—in Delaware; business founded in 1978. **Empl**— 265. **S&P Analyst:** M.C.

STANDARD
&POOR'S
STOCK REPORTS

Fair, Isaac & Co.

NYSE Symbol **FIC**

In S&P SmallCap 600

09-OCT-99

Industry:
Computer (Software & Services)

Summary: FIC is a leading developer of predictive models, software systems, and marketing database management and decision services used in the credit, insurance and marketing industries.

Quantitative Evaluations

Outlook
(1 Lowest—5 Highest)
• **3**

Fair Value
• **31⅜**

Risk
• **Average**

Earn./Div. Rank
• **A-**

Technical Eval.
• **Neutral** since 9/99

Rel. Strength Rank
(1 Lowest—99 Highest)
• **47**

Insider Activity
• **NA**

Recent Price • 29¾
52 Wk Range • 54½-26¼
Yield • 0.3%
12-Mo. P/E • 14.4

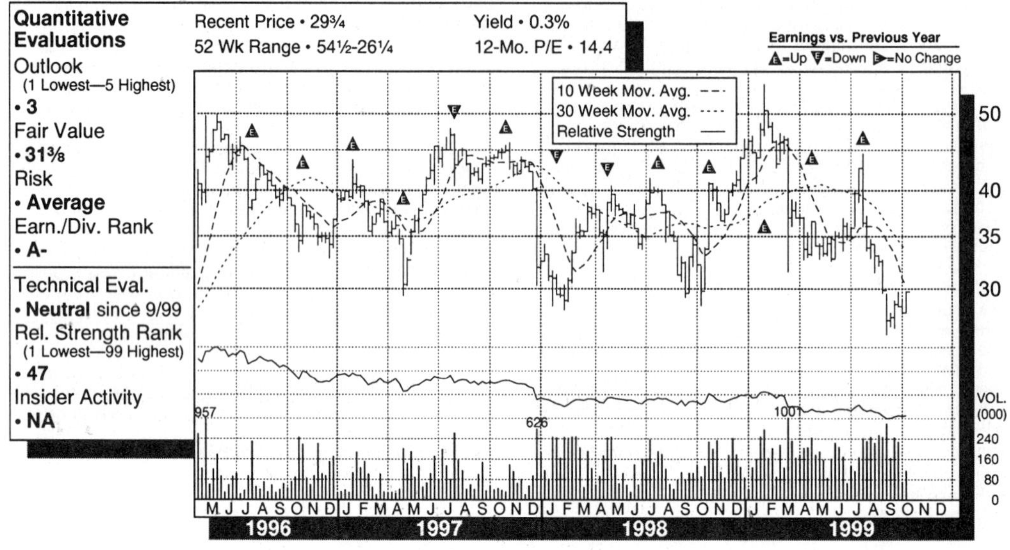

Business Profile - 08-JUN-99

In April 1999, FIC said that its market environment continues to be difficult - clients' Year 2000 issues, consolidation in the financial services industry, and turmoil in international markets have slowed the company's growth. FIC also said that big increases in R&D spending in FY 97 (Oct.) and FY 98 have resulted in an extensive list of new and enhanced products and services that have been or will be introduced in FY 99. In March 1999, FIC announced that it approved a stock repurchase program under which it will begin purchasing up to one million shares of company common stock.

Operational Review - 08-JUN-99

Revenues in the six months ended March 31, 1999, rose 21%, year to year, mainly reflecting increased revenues from CRMA (Credit Risk & Management Associates) and sales of credit applications scorecards and processing software; growth in usage of FIC scoring services and the number of FIC-managed bankcard accounts; and a 42% jump in DynaMark revenues. Profitability was aided by the reassignment of personnel and related costs and decreased expenses for media advertising. After taxes at 42.0%, versus 41.2%, net income rose 53%, to $14,512,000 ($1.00 per share), from $9,455,000 ($0.66).

Stock Performance - 08-OCT-99

In the past 30 trading days, FIC's shares have declined 0.42%, compared to a 0.91% fall in the S&P 500. Average trading volume for the past five days was 22,720 shares, compared with the 40-day moving average of 60,767 shares.

Key Stock Statistics

Dividend Rate/Share	0.08	Shareholders	312
Shs. outstg. (M)	14.0	Market cap. (B)	$0.417
Avg. daily vol. (M)	0.035	Inst. holdings	38%
Tang. Bk. Value/Share	9.83		
Beta	1.00		

Value of $10,000 invested 5 years ago: $ 26,805

Fiscal Year Ending Sep. 30

	1999	1998	1997	1996	1995	1994
Revenues (Million $)						
1Q	67.98	53.51	41.53	32.63	25.63	21.02
2Q	68.87	59.66	46.46	35.28	26.38	21.00
3Q	67.24	64.64	49.04	37.12	28.67	22.64
4Q	—	67.74	56.23	43.73	33.19	25.51
Yr.	—	245.6	199.0	148.8	113.9	90.28
Earnings Per Share ($)						
1Q	**0.49**	**0.28**	0.35	0.28	0.22	0.18
2Q	**0.51**	**0.38**	0.39	0.34	0.23	0.17
3Q	**0.49**	**0.45**	0.32	0.34	0.25	0.20
4Q	—	**0.59**	0.44	0.31	0.30	0.24
Yr.	—	**1.68**	**1.46**	1.27	1.00	0.80

Next earnings report expected: late October

Dividend Data (Dividends have been paid since 1989.)

Amount ($)	Date Decl.	Ex-Div. Date	Stock of Record	Payment Date
0.020	Nov. 25	Dec. 03	Dec. 07	Dec. 22 '98
0.020	Feb. 02	Feb. 17	Feb. 19	Mar. 05 '99
0.020	May. 18	May. 27	Jun. 01	Jun. 21 '99
0.020	Aug. 17	Aug. 26	Aug. 30	Sep. 17 '99

Fair, Isaac and Company, Incorporated

Business Summary - 08-JUN-99

Fair, Isaac and Co. (FIC) has been a pioneer in the development of statistical tools, called scoring algorithms, which are routinely employed in all phases of the credit account cycle: direct mail solicitation, application processing, card reissuance, on-line credit authorization, and collection. The company also produces software systems and components for the implementation of its scoring algorithms and credit and risk management consulting services (provided by FIC's subsidiary, Credit & Risk Management Associates, Inc.).

The company's best-known product, the Credit Application Scoring Algorithm, is used to calculate the risk of lending to individual credit applicants. The company's user base of over 600 companies includes about 75 of the 100 largest banks in the U.S., some 40 banks in the U.K., more than 70 retailers, seven oil companies, and major travel and entertainment card companies. Products and services sold to the consumer credit industry have traditionally accounted for most of Fair, Isaac's revenues, but the company is actively marketing its products and services to other segments of the credit industry, including mortgage and small business lending and non-credit industries, such as personal lines insurance, direct marketing, telecommunications and health care. Consumer credit and direct marketing accounted for 73% and 20% of FY 98 (Sep.) revenues, respectively, and 77% and 15% of FY 97 revenues.

DynaMark Inc., acquired in 1992, provides a variety of data processing and database management services to companies and organizations in the direct marketing industry. The subsidiary offers several proprietary tools in connection with such services. Dynalink, gives financial institutions and other users remote computer access to their warehoused customer account files or marketing databases. DynaMatch uses a unique scoring system to identify matching or duplicate records that most standard systems would overlook.

Other key products include: Behavior Scoring Algorithms, which enable companies to define rules for treating existing credit customers on an ongoing basis; PreScore Algorithms, used for screening mailings that solicit credit applications; and Automated Strategic Application Processing systems, which are stand-alone assemblies of hardware and software that automate the processing of credit applications.

The company's most advanced product is the Adaptive Control System, marketed under the name TRIAD. An Adaptive Control System is a complex of behavior scoring algorithms, computer software and account management strategy focused on one or more aspects of the management of a consumer credit or similar portfolio.

The percentage of revenues derived from customers outside the U.S. has been remarkably consistent over recent years -- 17% in FY 98, FY 97 and FY 96.

Per Share Data ($)										
(Year Ended Sep. 30)	**1998**	**1997**	**1996**	**1995**	**1994**	**1993**	**1992**	**1991**	**1990**	**1989**
Tangible Bk. Val.	8.80	7.05	5.48	4.20	3.31	2.50	2.37	2.02	1.80	1.69
Cash Flow	2.72	2.28	1.88	1.50	1.15	0.69	0.41	0.32	0.21	0.23
Earnings	1.68	1.46	1.27	1.00	0.81	0.43	0.33	0.24	0.14	0.17
Dividends	0.08	0.08	0.08	0.08	0.07	0.07	0.07	0.05	0.05	0.05
Payout Ratio	5%	5%	6%	8%	9%	16%	20%	21%	35%	28%
Prices - High	46½	47⅞	50	30¾	28⅝	11¼	8	6	3⅜	4½
- Low	28⅛	29⅜	21½	17	10½	5⅞	4¾	2⅜	2¼	2½
P/E Ratio - High	28	33	39	31	36	26	24	26	24	26
- Low	17	20	17	17	13	14	14	10	16	15
Income Statement Analysis (Million $)										
Revs.	246	199	149	114	90.3	66.7	42.6	31.8	25.5	23.2
Oper. Inc.	55.4	49.5	35.8	26.0	20.1	12.2	6.6	4.0	1.7	2.4
Depr.	14.9	11.8	7.9	6.2	4.3	3.1	1.0	0.9	0.8	0.6
Int. Exp.	0.8	0.3	0.1	0.2	0.2	0.3	NM	Nil	Nil	Nil
Pretax Inc.	42.1	35.5	27.2	21.4	16.6	8.7	6.7	4.4	2.4	3.2
Eff. Tax Rate	42%	42%	41%	41%	39%	39%	41%	37%	33%	38%
Net Inc.	24.3	20.7	16.2	12.7	10.0	5.3	3.9	2.8	1.6	2.0
Balance Sheet & Other Fin. Data (Million $)										
Cash	14.2	13.2	15.7	8.3	14.9	10.7	12.1	16.3	17.2	13.5
Curr. Assets	103	81.8	61.5	47.8	38.3	32.0	24.7	24.6	24.4	20.8
Total Assets	190	145	113	88.3	70.9	54.2	41.9	31.4	27.6	25.9
Curr. Liab.	47.8	34.1	28.2	23.4	21.8	17.3	11.4	8.1	7.3	5.7
LT Debt	0.8	1.2	1.6	1.9	2.3	2.7	2.7	Nil	Nil	Nil
Common Eqty.	133	103	78.3	56.1	42.9	31.5	26.6	22.3	19.7	18.4
Total Cap.	134	104	80.9	64.9	45.3	34.2	29.3	22.3	20.1	19.8
Cap. Exp.	15.7	21.7	1.7	10.7	5.3	5.7	6.2	1.0	1.0	1.3
Cash Flow	39.3	32.4	24.0	18.9	14.3	8.4	4.9	3.6	2.4	2.6
Curr. Ratio	2.1	2.4	2.2	2.0	1.8	1.8	2.2	3.0	3.3	3.6
% LT Debt of Cap.	0.6	1.1	2.0	2.9	5.2	8.0	9.1	Nil	Nil	Nil
% Net Inc.of Revs.	9.9	10.4	10.9	11.2	11.1	7.9	9.2	8.7	6.1	8.5
% Ret. on Assets	14.5	16.0	16.1	16.0	15.8	10.8	10.6	9.3	5.8	7.8
% Ret. on Equity	20.6	22.8	24.1	25.7	26.6	17.9	15.9	13.1	8.2	11.2

Data as orig reptd.; bef. results of disc opers/spec. items. Per share data adj. for stk. divs. Bold denotes diluted EPS (FASB 128)-prior periods restated. E-Estimated. NA-Not Available. NM-Not Meaningful. NR-Not Ranked.

Office—120 N. Redwood Dr., San Rafael, CA 94903-1996. **Tel**—(415) 472-2211. **Website**—http://www.fairisaac.com **Chrmn**—R. M. Oliver. **Pres & CEO**—L. E. Rosenberger. **EVP & COO**—J. D. Woldrich. **SVP, CFO & Treas**—P. Cole. **SVP, Secy & Genl Counsel**—P. L. McCorkell. **Dirs**—A. G. Battle, B. J. Brooks Jr., H. R. Heller, G. R. Henshaw, D. S. P. Hopkins, R. M. Oliver, L. E. Rosenberger, R. D. Sanderson, J. D. Woldrich. **Transfer Agent & Registrar**—ChaseMellon Shareholder Services, SF. **Incorporated**—in Delaware in 1987. **Empl**— 1,487. **S&P Analyst:** Scott H. Kessler

Fedders Corp.

NYSE Symbol **FJC**

In S&P SmallCap 600

09-OCT-99

Industry:
Household Furnishings & Appliances

Summary: This manufacturer of room air conditioners has the largest share of the U.S. room air conditioner market.

Quantitative Evaluations

Outlook
(1 Lowest—5 Highest)
• NA

Fair Value
• NA

Risk
• Low

Earn./Div. Rank
• B-

Technical Eval.
• Bearish since 9/99

Rel. Strength Rank
(1 Lowest—99 Highest)
• 49

Insider Activity
• NA

Recent Price • 6
52 Wk Range • 7-4

Yield • 2.0%
12-Mo. P/E • 11.3

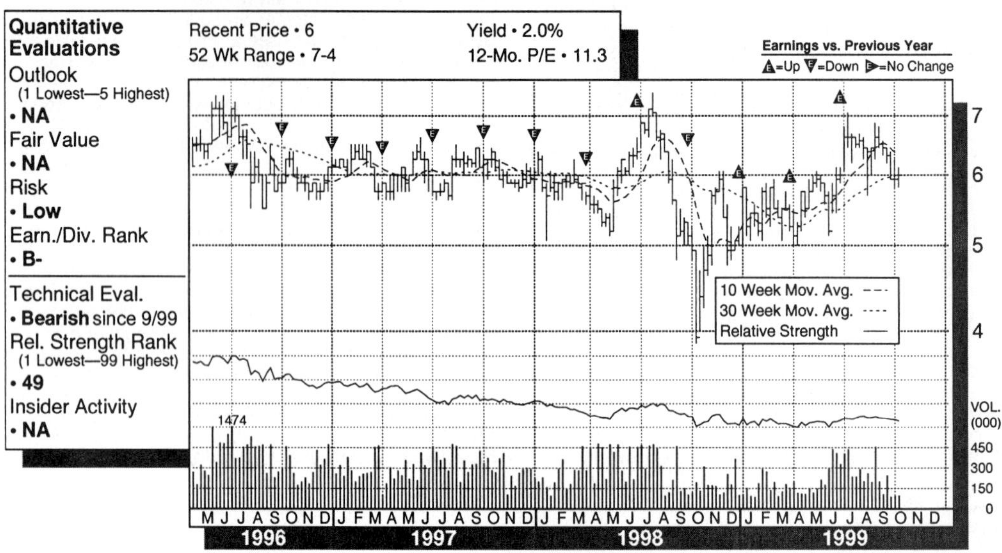

Business Profile - 19-AUG-99

In August 1999, the company completed its cash tender offer for all the outstanding shares of Trion, Inc. for $5.50 a share, or a total of some $35.1 million. Trion, a world leader in the indoor air quality industry, makes and sells a broad line of products that improve air quality in cleanrooms, industrial/commercial and residential environments. Trion's product line is complementary to Fedders' existing line of air conditioners and dehumidifiers, and many of its products, including air cleaners and humidifiers, are counter-seasonal to air conditioner and dehumidifier sales.

Operational Review - 19-AUG-99

Sales in the first nine months of FY 99 (Aug.) climbed 13%, year to year, reflecting a more pronounced seasonal shift in domestic sales in the second half of the fiscal year, primarily because major retailers that continue to gain market share require delivery closer to the air conditioning season. Results benefited from the higher volume and the absence of a $16.8 million restructuring charge in 1998, partially offset by higher net interest expense. Pretax income of $23.6 million contrasted with a pretax loss of $2.5 million. After taxes at 32.5%, versus tax credits of $863,000, income was $15,950,000 ($0.42 a share), against a loss of $1,605,000 million ($0.04).

Stock Performance - 08-OCT-99

In the past 30 trading days, FJC's shares have declined 9%, compared to a 0.91% fall in the S&P 500. Average trading volume for the past five days was 18,380 shares, compared with the 40-day moving average of 38,497 shares.

Key Stock Statistics

Dividend Rate/Share	0.12	Shareholders	8,700
Shs. outstg. (M)	36.0	Market cap. (B)	$0.097
Avg. daily vol. (M)	0.026	Inst. holdings	20%
Tang. Bk. Value/Share	1.45		
Beta	0.54		

Value of $10,000 invested 5 years ago: $ 18,756

Fiscal Year Ending Aug. 31

	1999	1998	1997	1996	1995	1994
Revenues (Million $)						
1Q	25.70	25.49	33.09	27.81	20.13	10.53
2Q	58.89	33.58	60.59	88.33	72.36	36.96
3Q	175.6	172.1	143.8	173.9	145.9	95.81
4Q	—	90.99	76.64	81.77	78.14	88.27
Yr.	—	322.1	314.1	371.8	316.5	231.6
Earnings Per Share ($)						
1Q	**-0.08**	-0.09	-0.05	0.01	-0.03	-0.10
2Q	**0.02**	**-0.32**	0.04	0.15	0.14	0.03
3Q	**0.48**	**0.37**	0.30	0.42	0.44	0.30
4Q	—	**0.11**	0.12	0.16	0.18	0.26
Yr.	—	**0.07**	**0.39**	0.74	0.72	0.49

Next earnings report expected: mid October

Dividend Data (Dividends have been paid since 1995.)

Amount ($)	Date Decl.	Ex-Div. Date	Stock of Record	Payment Date
0.025	Oct. 27	Nov. 10	Nov. 13	Dec. 01 '98
0.025	Dec. 22	Feb. 10	Feb. 12	Mar. 02 '99
0.025	Feb. 23	May. 12	May. 14	Jun. 01 '99
0.030	Jun. 22	Aug. 18	Aug. 20	Sep. 01 '99

Fedders Corporation

Business Summary - 19-AUG-99

Although earnings growth of this room air conditioner manufacturer cooled off in FY 97 (Aug.) and FY 98, the company plans to heat up international growth in the next century. Fedders (FJC), the largest U.S. manufacturer of room air conditioners, holds about a 30% domestic market share. However, the U.S. air conditioner market is a slow growing, mature industry, and the company's international subsidiary is investing much of its planning and resources in penetrating the much larger and faster-growing international market. FJC believes the market for room air conditioners outside of North America, in units, is about five times the size of the U.S. market. Demand for air conditioners outside of North America accelerated in recent years, and continues to grow rapidly, with increased disposable income in populous nations in hot weather climates.

Worldwide growth in demand is the cornerstone of FJC's long-term strategy. In November 1995, the company entered into a joint venture in China with the Ningbo General Air Conditioner Factory, in which FJC has a 60% interest. Also in June 1998, the company entered into a joint venture in Spain with Bosch-Siemens Hausgerate GmbH, to make air conditioners in Spain and for the European market and for export. With its entry into these new markets, FJC expects to obtain 50% of its revenues internationally by 2001.

In August 1996, FJC acquired Rotorex, a manufacturer of heating and cooling systems parts. The company believed that there was a worldwide shortage of compressors, a crucial part of air conditioners and the company's expansion plans, and that by acquiring Rotorex, it would lock in a supply of compressors.

Air conditioners are manufactured in models ranging in capacity from 5,000 BTUs to 32,000 BTUs. Products are sold under the brand names Fedders, Airtemp and Emerson Quiet Kool, as well as under private labels, primarily to retail chains and buying groups. Rotorex manufactures and markets a broad line of rotary compressors, primarily for use in Fedders room air conditioners. FJC's Melcor unit manufactures solid-state heat pump modules, selling them under the trademarks MELCOR and FRIGICHIP.

FJC has several significantly larger competitors, including Frigidaire, Whirlpool, Matsushita and Mitsubishi, which sell a broad line of products. However, after 50 years of producing its narrow product line, the company believes it is the lowest-cost producer of room air conditioners.

In June 1998, the company announced plans to spin off its Melcor subsidiary; however, in December 1998, it cancelled the spinoff, saying it was in the best interests of stockholders to retain the subsidiary and diversify its revenues and profits.

Per Share Data ($) **(Year Ended Aug. 31)**	**1998**	**1997**	**1996**	**1995**	**1994**	**1993**	**1992**	**1991**	**1990**	**1989**
Tangible Bk. Val.	1.29	2.40	2.23	1.90	1.08	0.45	-0.44	0.14	0.77	0.93
Cash Flow	0.29	0.70	0.90	0.90	0.61	0.09	-0.32	-0.02	-0.02	0.92
Earnings	0.07	0.40	0.74	0.72	0.49	-0.05	-0.70	-0.32	-0.45	0.64
Dividends	0.09	0.08	0.08	0.02	Nil	Nil	Nil	0.19	0.26	0.21
Payout Ratio	121%	20%	11%	3%	Nil	Nil	Nil	NM	NM	34%
Prices - High	$7\frac{3}{8}$	$6\frac{5}{8}$	$7\frac{3}{8}$	$7\frac{7}{8}$	$4\frac{3}{4}$	$4\frac{1}{8}$	$5\frac{3}{8}$	$5\frac{3}{4}$	$9\frac{1}{4}$	$9\frac{3}{4}$
- Low	$3\frac{7}{8}$	$5\frac{5}{8}$	$5\frac{1}{2}$	$4\frac{3}{4}$	$3\frac{3}{8}$	$2\frac{5}{16}$	$1\frac{13}{16}$	$3\frac{3}{8}$	$2\frac{5}{8}$	$6\frac{3}{8}$
P/E Ratio - High	NM	17	10	11	10	NM	NM	NM	NM	15
- Low	NM	14	7	7	7	NM	NM	NM	NM	10
Income Statement Analysis (Million $)										
Revs.	322	314	372	316	232	159	192	191	241	368
Oper. Inc.	38.8	41.7	57.6	45.2	28.7	6.9	7.5	8.7	28.0	50.8
Depr.	9.3	9.9	6.6	7.5	4.8	5.0	13.6	10.6	15.1	9.2
Int. Exp.	11.2	4.3	2.4	2.7	4.1	4.2	15.6	11.8	12.6	6.2
Pretax Inc.	4.2	28.3	50.3	35.7	19.8	-2.3	-25.0	13.7	-17.0	35.8
Eff. Tax Rate	38%	36%	38%	17%	3.00%	NM	NM	NM	NM	38%
Net Inc.	3.0	18.8	31.2	29.5	19.2	-1.8	-24.9	-11.2	-15.6	22.1
Balance Sheet & Other Fin. Data (Million $)										
Cash	91.0	110	90.3	57.7	34.9	8.6	8.7	2.9	Nil	Nil
Curr. Assets	168	195	159	99	66.0	42.0	78.0	88.0	114	163
Total Assets	305	329	290	137	101	81.0	179	197	215	281
Curr. Liab.	74.3	53.6	72.0	43.0	28.0	25.0	106	95.0	56.0	108
LT Debt	109	113	38.5	4.5	17.3	23.4	45.0	49.0	88.4	81.6
Common Eqty.	389	139	152	82.5	49.3	24.2	19.0	44.2	61.5	82.6
Total Cap.	218	264	204	87.0	68.0	54.0	70.0	98.0	156	168
Cap. Exp.	8.5	9.2	7.0	9.0	3.6	2.7	3.7	3.6	7.1	8.9
Cash Flow	12.3	28.7	37.7	37.0	24.0	3.2	-11.3	-0.6	-0.5	30.6
Curr. Ratio	2.3	3.6	2.2	2.3	2.4	1.7	0.7	0.9	2.1	1.5
% LT Debt of Cap.	49.9	43.0	18.9	5.1	25.5	43.6	64.4	50.2	56.8	48.5
% Net Inc.of Revs.	0.9	6.0	8.4	9.3	8.3	NM	NM	NM	NM	6.0
% Ret. on Assets	0.9	6.1	14.6	24.8	20.6	NM	NM	NM	NM	9.3
% Ret. on Equity	1.1	12.9	25.8	44.7	51.4	NM	NM	NM	NM	34.3

Data as orig reptd.; bef. results of disc opers/spec. items. Per share data adj. for stk. divs. Bold denotes diluted EPS (FASB 128)-prior periods restated. E-Estimated. NA-Not Available. NM-Not Meaningful. NR-Not Ranked.

Office—Westgate Corporate Center, 505 Martinsville Rd., P.O. Box 813, Liberty Corner, NJ 07938. **Tel**—(908) 604-8686. **Website**—http://www.fedders.com **Chrmn**—S. Giordano. **Vice Chrmn, Pres & CEO**—S. Giordano Jr. **SVP & Secy**—K. E. Hansen. **VP & CFO**—M. Giordano. **Investor Contact**—Judy Katz. **Dirs**—W. J. Brennan, D. C. Chang, J. Giordano, S. Giordano, S. Giordano Jr., C. A. Keen, H. S. Modlin, C. R. Moll, S. A. Muscarnera, A. E. Puleo. **Transfer Agent & Registrar**—American Stock & Transfer Co.**Incorporated**—in New York in 1913; reincorporated in Delaware in 1984. **Empl**— 2,700. **S&P Analyst:** P.L.H.

Fidelity National Financial

NYSE Symbol **FNF**

In S&P SmallCap 600

09-OCT-99

Industry: Insurance (Property-Casualty)

Summary: Through subsidiaries, FNF is one of the largest U.S. title insurance underwriters, engaged in the business of issuing title insurance and providing other title-related services.

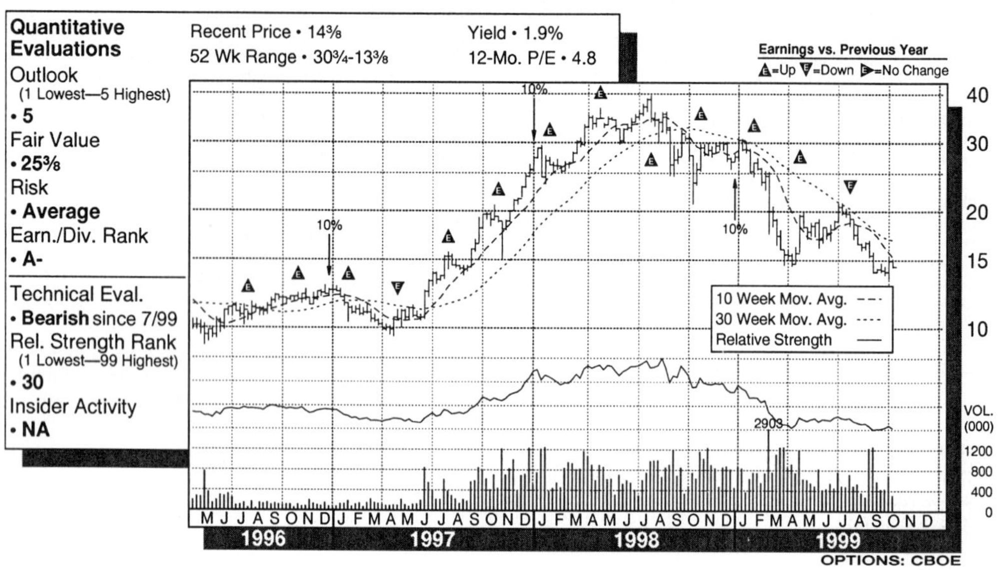

Business Profile - 14-SEP-99

In August 1999, FNF agreed to purchase Chicago Title Corp. (NYSE: CTZ), a leading national provider of real estate services, for $1.2 billion in cash and stock. The allocation between cash and stock will be adjusted so CTZ stockholders will receive more than 50% of the outstanding stock of the new company. The transaction, expected to close in the first quarter of 1999, is subject to approval by stockholders of both companies and the requisite regulatory authorities. FNF aims to maximize operating profits by increasing its share of the title insurance business in markets it serves; managing operating expenses effectively through the real estate cycle; minimize net claim payments; and continuing to implement a value-added acquisition and diversification program.

Operational Review - 14-SEP-99

In the first half of 1999, revenues advanced 20%, year to year, as a result of a 21% rise in title premiums reflecting favorable market conditions and higher escrow and other fees, partly offset by lower interest and investment income. Costs and expenses rose more rapidly than revenues on significantly higher other operating expenses and agent commissions; pretax income fell 15%. After taxes at 41.0% versus 41.9%, net income was down 13% to $43,508,000 ($1.35 a share), from $50,119,000 ($1.55, adjusted).

Stock Performance - 08-OCT-99

In the past 30 trading days, FNF's shares have declined 6%, compared to a 0.91% fall in the S&P 500. Average trading volume for the past five days was 59,820 shares, compared with the 40-day moving average of 152,695 shares.

Key Stock Statistics

Dividend Rate/Share	0.28	Shareholders	900
Shs. outstg. (M)	30.5	Market cap. (B)	$0.440
Avg. daily vol. (M)	0.091	Inst. holdings	47%
Tang. Bk. Value/Share	11.72		
Beta	1.56		

Value of $10,000 invested 5 years ago: $ 8,592

Fiscal Year Ending Dec. 31

	1999	1998	1997	1996	1995	1994
Revenues (Million $)						
1Q	344.3	262.2	153.2	126.4	83.06	143.6
2Q	357.8	321.4	178.5	171.6	95.49	129.4
3Q	—	329.4	197.9	166.7	113.5	113.3
4Q	—	375.4	217.2	172.2	117.8	106.4
Yr.	—	1,288	746.7	636.9	409.9	492.8
Earnings Per Share ($)						
1Q	**0.60**	**0.53**	**0.16**	**0.26**	**-0.14**	0.29
2Q	**0.75**	**1.02**	**0.44**	**0.35**	**0.05**	0.16
3Q	—	**0.82**	**0.71**	**0.32**	**0.30**	0.11
4Q	—	**0.87**	**0.56**	**0.30**	**0.18**	-0.15
Yr.	—	**3.23**	**1.89**	**1.22**	**0.45**	0.44

Next earnings report expected: late October

Dividend Data (Dividends have been paid since 1987.)

Amount ($)	Date Decl.	Ex-Div. Date	Stock of Record	Payment Date
0.070	Dec. 15	Jan. 22	Jan. 26	Feb. 09 '99
0.070	Mar. 17	Apr. 07	Apr. 09	May. 28 '99
0.070	Jun. 14	Jul. 07	Jul. 09	Jul. 22 '99
0.070	Sep. 30	Oct. 08	Oct. 13	Oct. 27 '99

Fidelity National Financial, Inc.

Business Summary - 14-SEP-99

Fidelity National Financial, Inc. (FNF), headquartered in Irvine, CA, is one of the largest underwriters of title insurance policies in the U.S. and also performs other title-related services. Title insurance revenue is closely related to the level of real estate activity and the average price of real estate sales. The overall strong economy, stable mortgage interest rates and strength in the real estate market, especially in California and on the West Coast, contributed to very favorable conditions for the industry from 1996 through 1998.

FNF operates through a number of subsidiaries currently licensed to issue title insurance policies through direct operations and approximately 2,900 independent agents in all states (except Iowa) and the District of Columbia, the Bahamas, the Virgin Islands and Puerto Rico. For the entire industry, 12 states accounted for 72% of title premiums written in the U.S. in 1997, and California, the largest contributor, accounted for 18%.

Title insurance premiums accounted for 70.6% of FNF's revenues in 1998, with about 38% of the insurance premium revenue coming from California.

FNF also provides other title-related services such as escrow, collection and trust activities, real estate information services, trustee sale guarantees, credit reporting, attorney services, flood certification, tax monitoring, reconveyances, recordings, foreclosure publishing and posting services and exchange intermediary services in connection with real estate transactions.

In 1998, 57% of total title-related revenue was generated from direct operations (57% in 1997), while 43% was generated from agency operations (43%). In 1998, direct operations opened 987,000 orders (621,000 in 1997) and closed 670,000 orders (436,000).

On August 20, 1998, the company acquired Alamo Title Holding Co. for about 2.1 million FNF shares. Earlier, In February, FNF completed the acquisition of Granite Financial, Inc., which conducts an equipment leasing business, for some 4.5 million shares.

Per Share Data ($) (Year Ended Dec. 31)	1998	1997	1996	1995	1994	1993	1992	1991	1990	1989
Tangible Bk. Val.	11.72	8.34	5.74	4.53	5.27	4.96	3.00	2.07	1.67	1.47
Oper. Earnings	NA	NA	NA	NA	NA	NA	NA	NA	NA	0.29
Earnings	3.23	2.37	1.41	0.44	0.44	1.62	0.80	0.40	0.33	0.30
Dividends	0.25	0.25	0.23	0.19	0.19	0.15	0.12	0.10	0.09	0.06
Payout Ratio	8%	11%	16%	43%	43%	10%	15%	26%	27%	21%
Prices - High	39 5/8	28 5/8	13 1/2	13	18 3/8	18 5/8	8 3/8	4 1/8	2 1/2	2 1/8
- Low	20 7/8	9 1/2	9	6 3/4	6 5/8	7 5/8	4	1 3/4	1 11/16	1 1/4
P/E Ratio - High	12	12	10	29	41	11	11	10	8	7
- Low	6	4	6	15	15	5	5	4	5	4
Income Statement Analysis (Million $)										
Premium Inc.	910	533	476	286	369	430	289	163	132	122
Net Invest. Inc.	39.6	33.5	8.3	8.4	3.3	12.1	4.3	2.3	2.2	2.0
Oth. Revs.	339	99	143	107	112	131	89.1	55.5	49.2	39.7
Total Revs.	1,288	747	637	410	493	575	382	221	183	163
Pretax Inc.	175	73.4	40.6	9.5	12.3	52.5	8.0	10.0	8.2	8.5
Net Oper. Inc.	NA	NA	NA	NA	NA	NA	NA	NA	NA	4.9
Net Inc.	106	41.5	24.3	7.6	9.7	36.3	5.2	6.2	5.2	5.0
Balance Sheet & Other Fin. Data (Million $)										
Cash & Equiv.	51.3	54.0	64.0	47.4	34.7	42.7	48.5	21.0	11.3	10.1
Premiums Due	NA	61.5	65.7	55.7	41.6	28.5	15.7	15.2	11.9	13.1
Invest. Assets: Bonds	330	217	166	129	176	212	84.1	3.6	5.2	4.0
Invest. Assets: Stocks	50.2	70.4	43.6	31.4	15.5	6.3	2.8	7.0	0.7	1.9
Invest. Assets: Loans	Nil	Nil	Nil	Nil	Nil	Nil	Nil	Nil	Nil	Nil
Invest. Assets: Total	511	326	228	180	218	226	94.1	10.9	5.9	5.9
Deferred Policy Costs	NA	Nil	Nil	Nil	Nil	Nil	Nil	Nil	Nil	Nil
Total Assets	969	601	509	405	418	396	249	125	106	90.1
Debt	179	123	149	136	142	52.8	26.1	30.3	24.5	14.7
Common Eqty.	397	196	110	77.9	74.0	115	62.4	38.2	28.7	27.8
Prop. & Cas. Loss Ratio	NA	6.6	7.8	9.2	6.3	4.2	7.2	6.0	5.2	4.5
Prop. & Cas. Expense Ratio	NA	NA	NA	NA	NA	NA	NA	NA	NA	NA
Prop. & Cas. Combined Ratio	NA	NA	NA	NA	NA	NA	NA	NA	NA	NA
% Return On Revs.	8.2	5.6	3.8	1.9	2.0	6.3	4.0	2.8	2.8	3.1
% Ret. on Equity	35.6	27.1	25.9	10.0	10.3	40.3	30.0	18.6	18.5	18.5

Data as orig reptd.; bef. results of disc opers/spec. items. Per share data adj. for stk. divs. Bold denotes diluted EPS (FASB 128)-prior periods restated. E-Estimated. NA-Not Available. NM-Not Meaningful. NR-Not Ranked.

Office—17911 Von Karman Ave., Irvine, CA 92614. **Reincorporated**—in Delaware in 1986. **Tel**—(949) 622-5000. **Chrmn & CEO**—W.P. Foley II. **Pres**—F. P. Willey. **EVP, CFO & Treas**—C. A. Strunk. **SVP & Secy**—M. Jones Kane. **VP & Investor Contact**—Jo Etta Bandy. **Dirs**—W. P. Foley II, W. A. Imparato, D. M. Koll, D. D. Lane, S. C. Mahood, J. T. Talbot, C. H. Thompson, F. P. Willey. **Transfer Agent & Registrar**—Continental Stock Transfer & Trust Co., NYC. **Empl**— 7,400. **S&P Analyst:** S.A.H.

FileNET Corp.

Nasdaq Symbol **FILE**

In S&P SmallCap 600

09-OCT-99

Industry:
Computer (Software & Services)

Summary: This company specializes in imaging and business process automation solutions that electronically capture, store, retrieve, transmit and manage document images, data and text.

S&P Opinion: Hold (★★★)

Recent Price • 11⅝
52 Wk Range • 13⅝-4⅝
Yield • Nil
12-Mo. P/E • NM

Quantitative Evaluations

Outlook (1 Lowest—5 Highest) • **5**

Fair Value • **19½**

Risk • **High**

Earn./Div. Rank • **B-**

Technical Eval. • **Bullish** since 8/99

Rel. Strength Rank (1 Lowest—99 Highest) • **86**

Insider Activity • **NA**

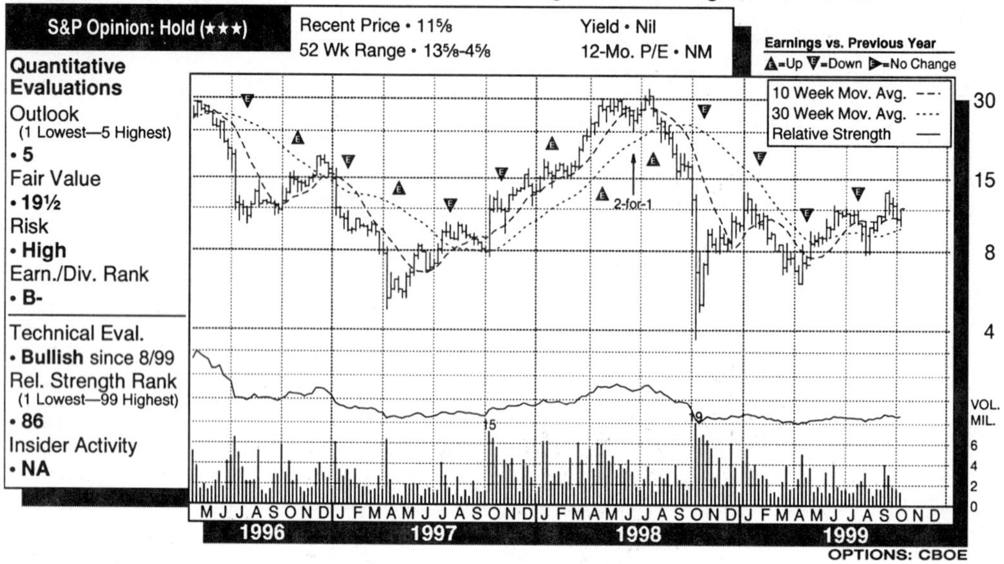

Overview - 28-JUL-99

We expect FileNET's revenues to increase 20% in 1999, fueled by strength in the company's services business, which we believe will post 24% revenue growth this year. The company's software segment has been weak in 1999, but we believe the May 1999 new system release of its flagship Panagon product, which includes added document management and Internet functionality, will likely accelerate software sales growth. Nevertheless, as the year 2000 approaches, companies will be less inclined to purchase and deploy enterprise software solutions for fear of complicating Y2K fixes. As a result, we believe that purchases of FileNET's software during the second half of 1999 will be adversely affected. However, because the company's services business contributes significantly to total revenues and its software is generally less expensive than that of other enterprise software firms, FileNET may fare better than many of its peers.

Valuation - 28-JUL-99

Immediately following the disclosure of a disappointing loss for the third quarter of 1998, we downgraded shares of FILE from accumulate to hold. Although the shares fell sharply from their summer 1998 high, we believe FILE will need some time to recover from the problems that plagued it in 1998, especially as it faces a possible slowdown in product demand for the second half of 1999. These factors, along with the resulting poor earnings visibility, suggest that the stock's appreciation will be hampered. Nevertheless, as of June 1999, FILE had a strong balance sheet with $2.21 per share in cash and no long-term debt, which may appeal to some value investors. However, until FileNET proves it can deliver consistent revenue and earnings growth across all its businesses, we see the stock as a market performer.

Key Stock Statistics

S&P EPS Est. 1999	0.59	Tang. Bk. Value/Share	4.17
P/E on S&P Est. 1999	19.8	Beta	1.13
S&P EPS Est. 2000	0.90	Shareholders	860
Dividend Rate/Share	Nil	Market cap. (B)	$0.377
Shs. outstg. (M)	32.3	Inst. holdings	34%
Avg. daily vol. (M)	0.379		

Value of $10,000 invested 5 years ago: $ 10,871

Fiscal Year Ending Dec. 31

	1999	1998	1997	1996	1995	1994
Revenues (Million $)						
1Q	81.44	73.61	47.56	66.74	45.06	38.75
2Q	86.09	80.37	62.45	65.00	53.29	44.90
3Q	—	71.15	65.01	64.62	53.55	42.59
4Q	—	85.10	76.40	72.55	63.58	53.45
Yr.	—	310.2	251.4	268.9	215.5	179.7
Earnings Per Share ($)						
1Q	**0.06**	**0.08**	**-0.32**	**-0.40**	0.12	0.10
2Q	**0.12**	**0.14**	**-0.13**	**0.08**	0.11	0.17
3Q	**E0.15**	**-0.18**	**0.06**	**0.11**	0.01	0.17
4Q	**E0.25**	**-0.01**	**0.18**	**0.10**	0.29	0.24
Yr.	**E0.59**	**0.03**	**-0.18**	**-0.09**	**0.26**	**0.47**

Next earnings report expected: mid October

Dividend Data

The company has never paid a dividend on its common stock and does not expect to pay any cash dividends in the foreseeable future. A "poison pill" stock purchase rights plan was adopted in 1988.

FileNET Corporation

Business Summary - 28-JUL-99

According to FileNET Corp., 80% of the information needed to run a business is not located in a database, but scattered across hard drives, on Web pages, in file drawers, and in piles of paper. FileNET believes that with its software and services, it can help organize and provide access to this information.

FileNET develops, markets and supports integrated document management (IDM) software products that provide solutions for managing unstructured information, thereby enhancing an enterprise's productivity. Stamford, CT-based research firm GartnerGroup believes that the IDM software market will grow from an estimated $660 million in 1998, to $1.6 billion by 2001.

FILE also provides services related to the implementation of its software products. The company's Panagon software allows users to access, edit, process, organize, secure, store and archive documents in client/server and Web-based environments. FILE also manufactures and sells a line of 12-inch optical storage and retrieval libraries

Revenues for 1998 and 1997, respectively, were derived from the sale of: software (55% and 53%), services (37% and 35%), and hardware (8% and 12%). International sales have historically amounted to 33% of total revenues, comprising 32% in 1998. At the end of 1998, FILE had customers in over 70 countries.

The Panagon family of IDM software (introduced in February, 1998) allows users to capture any type of document electronically, then access, manage, publish and integrate the information with their existing business applications throughout the enterprise. Using Microsoft's Windows Explorer or Netscape's Navigator Internet browser software, customers can search the enterprise network for information, retrieve all types of documents, work with the information, and then route it as needed for further review, processing, or decision making. The Panagon IDM Desktop products are built around Microsoft's component software architecture and allow applications to be developed and tailored to meet an organization's requirements.

Users of FILE's products include companies that possess large, active document files in businesses such as: financial services (banking, mortgage and securities organizations), insurance (life, health, property, and casualty insurance organizations), and manufacturing (discrete and process manufacturers).

In November 1998, FILE announced a limited restructuring, impacting sales and marketing operations. Staff was reduced by some 100 employees and contractors, 5% of its workforce. In the fourth quarter of 1998, the company took a related $2 million charge for severance package costs and the consolidation of functions and facilities.

Per Share Data ($) (Year Ended Dec. 31)	1998	1997	1996	1995	1994	1993	1992	1991	1990	1989
Tangible Bk. Val.	4.09	3.92	4.42	5.17	4.71	3.85	3.44	3.79	3.38	3.21
Cash Flow	0.49	0.26	0.30	0.89	1.03	0.66	-0.07	0.65	0.50	0.38
Earnings	0.03	-0.18	-0.09	0.54	0.69	0.35	-0.38	0.38	0.18	0.14
Dividends	Nil	Nil	Nil	Nil	Nil	Nil	Nil	Nil	Nil	Nil
Payout Ratio	Nil	Nil	Nil	Nil	Nil	Nil	Nil	Nil	Nil	Nil
Prices - High	32 7/8	16 3/8	33 1/2	25 1/2	14 5/8	11 1/2	18 3/4	12 1/2	10 3/4	6 7/8
- Low	3 5/8	4 3/4	10	12 5/8	7 1/8	4 3/8	5 1/4	3 3/8	2 1/2	3 3/4
P/E Ratio - High	NM	NM	NM	48	21	32	NM	33	58	47
- Low	NM	NM	NM	24	10	12	NM	9	14	26
Income Statement Analysis (Million $)										
Revs.	310	251	269	215	180	159	138	122	103	83.0
Oper. Inc.	14.9	8.4	26.8	36.1	27.7	18.7	6.3	17.5	11.7	9.6
Depr.	15.4	13.3	11.8	9.6	8.1	6.6	6.5	5.8	6.5	4.8
Int. Exp.	Nil	Nil	Nil	Nil	0.1	0.4	0.6	0.4	0.4	0.3
Pretax Inc.	1.3	-7.7	1.8	22.9	21.4	12.5	-9.8	12.5	5.1	3.9
Eff. Tax Rate	29%	NM	245%	35%	25%	38%	NM	35%	27%	23%
Net Inc.	1.0	-5.5	-2.6	14.8	16.1	7.8	-8.0	8.1	3.8	3.0
Balance Sheet & Other Fin. Data (Million $)										
Cash	71.3	37.3	50.5	68.8	41.0	43.5	29.3	32.8	22.3	19.7
Curr. Assets	144	144	149	138	95.1	96.3	77.2	76.3	66.7	62.5
Total Assets	207	180	196	182	142	123	102	104	91.0	82.0
Curr. Liab.	76.5	60.6	59.4	46.7	34.7	37.6	28.9	23.6	22.8	18.6
LT Debt	Nil	Nil	Nil	0.1	Nil	0.2	0.1	0.2	0.3	0.6
Common Eqty.	130	119	133	134	104	82.8	72.7	78.2	67.5	63.1
Total Cap.	130	119	136	136	107	85.1	73.5	80.2	67.8	63.7
Cap. Exp.	32.5	14.2	17.8	12.5	10.7	6.7	10.6	6.3	8.2	7.5
Cash Flow	16.3	7.8	9.2	24.5	24.2	14.4	-1.5	13.9	10.3	7.7
Curr. Ratio	1.9	2.4	2.5	3.0	2.7	2.6	2.7	3.2	2.9	3.4
% LT Debt of Cap.	Nil	Nil	Nil	0.1	Nil	0.2	0.1	0.3	0.4	0.9
% Net Inc.of Revs.	0.3	NM	NM	6.9	8.9	4.9	NM	6.6	3.7	3.6
% Ret. on Assets	0.5	NM	NM	9.1	12.0	6.9	NM	8.2	4.3	3.9
% Ret. on Equity	0.8	NM	NM	12.8	16.9	9.9	NM	11.0	5.7	4.8

Data as orig reptd.; bef. results of disc opers/spec. items. Per share data adj. for stk. divs. Bold denotes diluted EPS (FASB 128)-prior periods restated. E-Estimated. NA-Not Available. NM-Not Meaningful. NR-Not Ranked.

Office—3565 Harbor Blvd., Costa Mesa, CA 92626. **Tel**—(714) 966-3400. **Website**—http://www.filenet.com. **Chrmn** —T. J. Smith. **Pres, CEO & COO**—L. D. Roberts. **SVP-Secy**—M. K. Carrington. **SVP-Fin, CFO & Investor Contact**—Mark S. St. Clare. **Dirs**—W. P. Lyons, L. G. Klaus, L. D. Roberts, J. C. Savage, R. S. Siboni, T. J. Smith, C. M. Ticknor. **Transfer Agent & Registrar**—Boston EquiServe, Boston. **Incorporated**—in California in 1982; reincorporated in Delaware in 1987. **Empl**— 1,666. **S&P Analyst:** Scott H. Kessler

STANDARD &POOR'S
STOCK REPORTS

First American Financial

NYSE Symbol **FAF**

In S&P SmallCap 600

09-OCT-99 **Industry:** Insurance (Property-Casualty)

Summary: First American Financial is a leading provider of title insurance and real estate information services.

Quantitative Evaluations

Outlook (1 Lowest—5 Highest) • **3-**

Fair Value • **14¼**

Risk • **Average**

Earn./Div. Rank • **B+**

Technical Eval. • **Bearish** since 7/99

Rel. Strength Rank (1 Lowest—99 Highest) • **21**

Insider Activity • **NA**

Recent Price • 12⅝ | 52 Wk Range • 37-11¾ | Yield • 1.9% | 12-Mo. P/E • 4.9

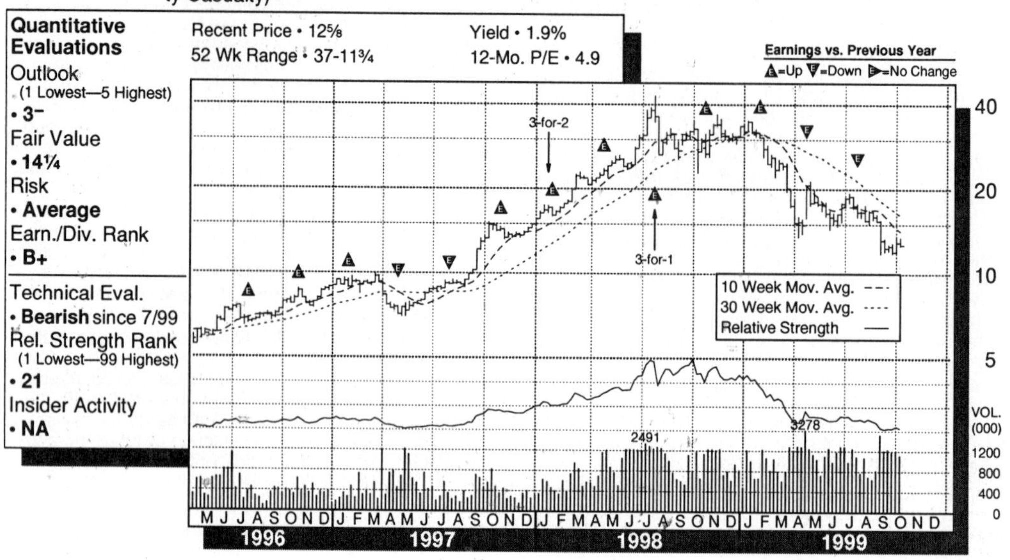

Business Profile - 14-SEP-99

In the first half of 1999, FAF acquired 12 companies, including title insurers and real estate and consumer information providers, for a total of $30.4 million in cash, $4.2 million in notes, and 1,119,321 common shares. In May 1999, the company acquired San Francisco-based National Information Group, a provider of specialized information services and related insurance products, in exchange for about three million common shares. In June 1999, FAF and Freddie Mac completed a pilot program for FAF's FAST-AU (First American Software Technologies for Automated Underwriting), which, using the Internet as a conduit, provides mortgage brokers with an electronic point-of-sale access channel to automated underwriting systems.

Operational Review - 14-SEP-99

Revenues in the six months ended June 30, 1999, rose 10%, year to year, as a healthy real estate market drove strong growth of title closures. However, after 18% higher total expenses, reflecting volume driven increases in salary and personnel costs and premiums retained by agents, as well as acquisition costs, pretax income fell 43%. After taxes at 34.8%, versus 35.7%, and lower minority interest expense, net income declined 42%, to $53,099,000 ($0.80 a share, on 10% more shares, as adjusted), from $91,433,000 ($1.51), as restated. A change in the revenue recognition policy for tax service contracts resulted in an after tax EPS decrease of $0.22 in the 1999 period.

Stock Performance - 08-OCT-99

In the past 30 trading days, FAF's shares have declined 18%, compared to a 0.91% fall in the S&P 500. Average trading volume for the past five days was 221,040 shares, compared with the 40-day moving average of 275,446 shares.

Key Stock Statistics

Dividend Rate/Share	0.24	Shareholders	3,033
Shs. outstg. (M)	65.2	Market cap. (B)	$0.827
Avg. daily vol. (M)	0.250	Inst. holdings	49%
Tang. Bk. Value/Share	9.71		
Beta	0.90		

Value of $10,000 invested 5 years ago: $ 18,160

Fiscal Year Ending Dec. 31

	1999	1998	1997	1996	1995	1994
Revenues (Million $)						
1Q	706.9	605.0	382.9	347.4	261.1	372.4
2Q	770.4	704.3	450.4	413.4	293.2	369.0
3Q	—	753.3	501.9	411.3	331.3	334.9
4Q	—	797.3	552.4	425.5	364.5	300.1
Yr.	—	2,877	1,887	1,598	1,250	1,376
Earnings Per Share ($)						
1Q	0.40	0.83	0.05	0.17	-0.25	0.18
2Q	0.44	0.80	0.35	0.38	0.02	0.15
3Q	—	0.93	0.39	0.26	0.18	0.09
4Q	—	0.85	0.42	0.22	0.19	-0.06
Yr.	—	3.32	1.21	1.03	0.15	0.37

Next earnings report expected: mid October

Dividend Data (Dividends have been paid since 1909.)

Amount ($)	Date Decl.	Ex-Div. Date	Stock of Record	Payment Date
0.060	Dec. 16	Dec. 29	Dec. 31	Jan. 15 '99
0.060	Feb. 26	Mar. 29	Mar. 31	Apr. 15 '99
0.060	Jun. 25	Jul. 01	Jul. 06	Jul. 15 '99
0.060	Aug. 27	Sep. 28	Sep. 30	Oct. 15 '99

The First American Financial Corporation

Business Summary - 14-SEP-99

With operations throughout the U.S. and abroad, First American Financial seeks to provide all of the information products required to close a real estate transaction. Its growth has been achieved primarily through an active acquisition strategy that has emphasized geographic expansion and the development of new products and markets. By acquiring companies, rather than forming strategic alliances, FAF can control the delivery of products. Management believes marketing multiple products to the real estate industry provides opportunities to gain new customers and boost market share.

In 1998, title insurance operations accounted for 74% of operating revenues and 63% of pretax profits. Title insurance protects lenders against challenges to the title claim of a property, and policyholders against loss from a prior occurrence, such as a forged deed somewhere in the chain of title. According to American Land Title Association statistics, FAF held a leading 22% share of the title insurance market in 1998. It had the largest or second largest share of the market in 30 states and the District of Columbia. In 1998, FAF added 44 title offices and it planned to accelerate its expansion. For the past decade, the company has emphasized its wider profit margin, commercial sales program. FAF believes title insurance is gaining acceptance in international markets, leading it to devote sales efforts to Canada, the U.K., and Australia.

In 1998, low mortgage interest rates and an improved national real estate economy helped produce high volumes of new home sales and residential resales. Combined with higher refinance and home equity transactions, FAF's title insurance segment produced pretax profits of $227.9 million in 1998 ($79.6 million in 1997), on revenues of $2.06 billion ($1.5 billion).

The real estate information business generated the bulk of remaining revenues (21%) and profits (28%) in 1998. The segment provides services such as real estate tax monitoring, mortgage credit reporting and flood zone certification, mortgage loan origination and servicing systems, mortgage document preparation and other property information services. FAF is the industry leader in gathering, packaging and distributing real estate related information.

In a diversification effort, FAF initiated a consumer risk management division in 1998. The segment markets services that include automotive credit reporting, direct-to-consumer credit reporting, multifamily resident screening and pre-employment screening. FAF aimed to expand opportunities for revenue consistency, not tied to the real estate industry.

FAF also has trust operations, with $1.8 billion of personal and institutional assets under administration, and a thrift business with $67.4 million of demand deposits and $72.0 million of loans extended at year-end 1998.

Per Share Data ($) (Year Ended Dec. 31)	1998	1997	1996	1995	1994	1993	1992	1991	1990	1989
Tangible Bk. Val.	9.28	5.35	5.10	4.50	4.50	4.49	3.20	2.07	2.73	2.74
Oper. Earnings	NA	NA	NA	0.13	0.38	1.21	NA	NA	NA	NA
Earnings	3.32	1.21	1.04	0.15	0.37	1.22	1.01	0.07	0.07	0.29
Dividends	0.20	0.17	0.15	0.13	0.13	0.11	0.09	0.09	0.09	0.08
Payout Ratio	6%	14%	15%	90%	36%	9%	9%	120%	117%	27%
Prices - High	43	16 5/8	9 1/8	6 1/8	8 3/8	8 3/4	6	2 7/8	3 1/8	3 3/4
- Low	15 7/8	7	5 1/2	3 5/8	3 1/2	5	2 5/8	1 3/8	1 7/16	2 7/16
P/E Ratio - High	13	14	9	41	23	7	6	40	43	13
- Low	5	6	5	25	10	4	3	20	20	9
Income Statement Analysis (Million $)										
Premium Inc.	2,802	1,860	1,268	1,035	1,222	1,249	998	738	688	681
Net Invest. Inc.	31.1	27.3	26.4	23.0	19.4	19.9	13.1	19.2	19.7	16.0
Oth. Revs.	44.0	Nil	303	192	135	129	0.1	Nil	Nil	2.0
Total Revs.	2,877	1,887	1,598	1,250	1,376	1,398	1,115	757	708	699
Pretax Inc.	361	106	89.2	13.8	32.0	104	71.5	6.1	-6.1	20.7
Net Oper. Inc.	NA	NA	NA	6.6	19.3	61.8	NA	NA	NA	NA
Net Inc.	199	64.7	53.6	7.6	18.9	62.1	43.3	3.0	3.3	13.5
Balance Sheet & Other Fin. Data (Million $)										
Cash & Equiv.	375	182	173	146	154	130	120	77.4	67.2	72.8
Premiums Due	191	128	89.4	75.1	47.1	64.6	48.2	38.5	27.1	35.8
Invest. Assets: Bonds	228	152	131	129	149	166	138	68.1	81.6	72.8
Invest. Assets: Stocks	27.3	13.9	8.5	21.4	21.8	21.1	7.6	2.7	8.0	10.1
Invest. Assets: Loans	72.0	63.4	54.3	46.1	40.5	33.3	30.8	26.8	15.0	NA
Invest. Assets: Total	423	293	245	240	255	262	219	136	138	144
Deferred Policy Costs	NA	25.0	24.8	24.3	26.6	23.5	18.4	Nil	Nil	Nil
Total Assets	1,785	1,168	980	874	829	786	691	520	465	451
Debt	130	42.0	71.3	77.2	89.6	85.0	82.0	93.0	102	97.0
Common Eqty.	732	411	352	303	292	284	217	138	146	147
Prop. & Cas. Loss Ratio	NA	NA	NA	NA	9.0	10.1	9.8	10.3	11.3	9.4
Prop. & Cas. Expense Ratio	NA	NA	NA	NA	99.7	92.2	93.4	90.2	91.1	89.0
Prop. & Cas. Combined Ratio	NA	NA	NA	NA	108.7	102.3	103.2	100.5	102.4	98.4
% Return On Revs.	6.9	3.4	3.4	0.6	1.4	4.4	3.9	0.4	0.5	1.9
% Ret. on Equity	34.7	16.9	16.4	2.6	6.6	24.8	24.4	2.1	2.3	9.7

Data as orig reptd.; bef. results of disc opers/spec. items. Per share data adj. for stk. divs. Bold denotes diluted EPS (FASB 128)-prior periods restated. E-Estimated. NA-Not Available. NM-Not Meaningful. NR-Not Ranked.

Office—114 East 5th St., Santa Ana, CA 92701-4699. **Tel**—(714) 558-3211. **Website**—http://www.firstam.com **Chrmn**—D. P. Kennedy. **Pres**—P. S. Kennedy. **EVP & CFO**—T. A. Klemens. **VP & Secy**—M. R. Arnesen. **Investor Contact**—Denise M. Warren (800-854-3643). **Dirs**—G. L. Argyros, G. J. Beban, J. D. Chatham, W. G. Davis, J. L. Doti, L. W. Douglas, Jr., P. B. Fay, Jr., D. P. Kennedy, P. S. Kennedy, A. R. Moiso, F. E. O'Bryan, R. B. Payne, D. V. Skilling, V. M. Ueberroth. **Transfer Agent & Registrar**—First American Trust Co., Santa Ana. **Incorporated**—in California in 1894. **Empl**— 19,669. **S&P Analyst:** Markos N. Kaminis

STANDARD
&POOR'S
STOCK REPORTS

First BanCorp

NYSE Symbol **FBP**

In S&P SmallCap 600

09-OCT-99 **Industry:** Banks (Regional)

Summary: FBP owns Firstbank Puerto Rico, the second largest independently owned commercial bank in Puerto Rico with assets of about $4 billion.

Quantitative Evaluations

Outlook
(1 Lowest—5 Highest)
• **NA**

Fair Value
• **NA**

Risk
• **Low**

Earn./Div. Rank
• **B**

Technical Eval.
• **Bearish** since 7/99

Rel. Strength Rank
(1 Lowest—99 Highest)
• **33**

Insider Activity
• **NA**

Recent Price • 20
52 Wk Range • 30½-19¾
Yield • 1.8%
12-Mo. P/E • 10.7

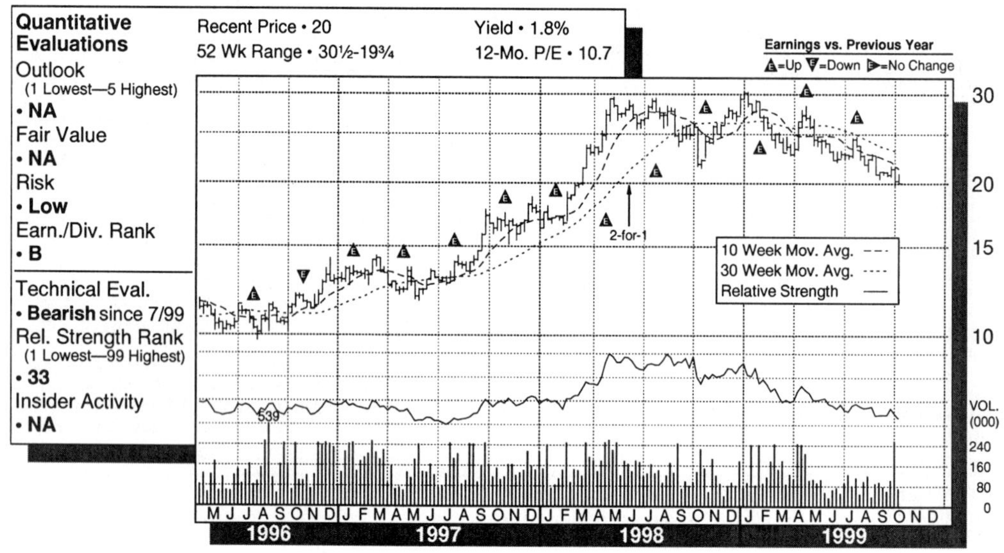

Business Profile - 10-SEP-99

Loans receivable increased to $2.32 billion at June 30, 1999, from $2.10 billion at December 31, 1998. In March 1999, the company announced plans to simplify and streamline its operations in order to make the bank more efficient, responsive and convenient in servicing customers. The bank recently announced the acquisition of Royal Bank of Canada operations in Puerto Rico and the acquisition of the credit card portfolio of Western Auto. Western Auto is the largest automotive retailer with 38 locations throughout Puerto Rico.

Operational Review - 10-SEP-99

Net interest income in the six months ended June 30, 1999, rose 11%, year to year, aided by growth in the level of interest-earning assets. The provision for loan losses decreased to $26.7 million from $35.7 million due to an improvement in the credit quality of the loan portfolio. Noninterest income was down 39% and noninterest expense rose 8.9%, and after taxes at 7.7%, versus 9.8%, net income advanced 18%, to $29,534,729 ($0.97 a share) from $25,061,405 ($0.84). The interest rate spread and net interest margin, on a taxable equivalent basis, amounted to 4.54% and 5.08%, respectively, for the six months ended June 30, 1999, compared to 5.02% and 5.53% for the six months ended June 30, 1998.

Stock Performance - 08-OCT-99

In the past 30 trading days, FBP's shares have declined 4%, compared to a 0.91% fall in the S&P 500. Average trading volume for the past five days was 13,980 shares, compared with the 40-day moving average of 24,795 shares.

Key Stock Statistics

Dividend Rate/Share	0.36	Shareholders	674
Shs. outstg. (M)	29.0	Market cap. (B)	$0.582
Avg. daily vol. (M)	0.034	Inst. holdings	21%
Tang. Bk. Value/Share	9.15		
Beta	0.78		

Value of $10,000 invested 5 years ago: $ 38,427

Fiscal Year Ending Dec. 31

	1999	1998	1997	1996	1995	1994
Revenues (Million $)						
1Q	95.30	94.15	76.77	65.21	—	45.50
2Q	94.79	—	—	68.23	—	47.94
3Q	—	—	—	74.02	—	50.94
4Q	—	58.26	—	47.94	—	54.10
Yr.	—	224.4	325.0	286.1	256.8	198.5
Earnings Per Share ($)						
1Q	**0.48**	**0.41**	0.39	0.34	0.37	0.23
2Q	**0.49**	**0.43**	0.39	0.35	0.30	0.25
3Q	—	**0.44**	0.40	0.15	0.58	0.26
4Q	—	**0.46**	**0.41**	0.38	0.33	0.27
Yr.	—	**1.74**	**1.57**	**1.22**	**1.58**	1.00

Next earnings report expected: mid October

Dividend Data (Dividends have been paid since 1995.)

Amount ($)	Date Decl.	Ex-Div. Date	Stock of Record	Payment Date
0.075	Nov. 24	Dec. 11	Dec. 15	Dec. 31 '98
0.090	Feb. 16	Mar. 11	Mar. 15	Mar. 31 '99
0.090	May. 18	Jun. 11	Jun. 15	Jun. 30 '99
0.090	Aug. 25	Sep. 13	Sep. 15	Sep. 30 '99

A Division of The McGraw-Hill Companies

First BanCorp

Business Summary - 10-SEP-99

First BanCorp (FBP) is the holding company for FirstBank Puerto Rico, the second largest locally owned commercial bank in Puerto Rico, and the third largest depository institution, with total assets of $4.0 billion as of December 31, 1998. The bank specializes in consumer lending in the Puerto Rican market, offering an array of financial services to a growing number of consumer and commercial customers.

At December 31, 1998, the loan portfolio of $2.1 billion was divided as follows: real estate (residential, commercial, construction, land acquisition and other) 33%, commercial 20%, auto 20%, personal 20%, credit card 6%, boat 1%, and other nil. The weighted average interest rates by loan type was: real estate 9.54%, commercial 9.03%, auto 12.56%, personal 16.92%, credit card 15.50%, and boat 10.91%.

In 1998, the company originated $806.2 million of new loans, up from $827.5 million in 1997.

The bank conducts business through 38 full-service branches in Puerto Rico, and two branches in the U.S. Virgin Islands of St. Thomas and St. Croix. It also has nine loan origination offices focusing on personal loans and credit cards, and four loan origination offices focusing on auto loans. FBP has two subsidiaries, First Leasing and Rental Corp., a vehicle leasing and daily rental company with six offices; and First Federal Finance Corp (Money Express), a small loan company with 26 offices.

At the end of 1998, nonperforming assets totaled $77,987,000 (1.94% of total assets), versus $74,317,000 (2.23%) a year earlier. As of December 31, 1998, the allowance for loan losses totaled $67,854,000 (94.2% of total non-performing loans), versus $57,712,000 (89.5%) a year earlier.

Deposits of $1.8 billion at year-end 1998 were apportioned as follows: non-interest bearing checking 10%, savings accounts 24%, interest bearing checking 7%, and certificate accounts of various maturities 59%.

The bank is committed to continue providing the most efficient and cost effective banking services possible in selected products niches. Management's long-term goal is to transform FBP into a conservatively managed, diversified financial institution in order to position itself to deliver superior financial performance. Historically, FBP has distinguished itself by providing innovative marketing strategies and novel products, being the first bank in Puerto Rico to accept loan applications by fax, to offer a telephone information service (in 1983), to establish a presence on the Internet, to open on weekends, and to offer in-store branches to clients.

Per Share Data ($) (Year Ended Dec. 31)	1998	1997	1996	1995	1994	1993	1992	1991	1990	1989
Tangible Bk. Val.	9.15	7.91	6.30	5.49	3.98	3.02	1.80	1.26	0.89	1.52
Earnings	1.74	1.57	1.22	1.58	1.00	0.63	0.37	0.28	-0.72	0.30
Dividends	0.23	0.24	0.20	0.08	Nil	Nil	Nil	Nil	0.02	0.07
Payout Ratio	13%	15%	16%	5%	Nil	Nil	Nil	Nil	NM	23%
Prices - High	30 1/2	18 7/8	14 1/4	12 1/4	6 3/8	5 3/4	2 5/16	1	1 3/8	1 9/16
- Low	16 1/2	11 3/4	9 3/4	5 1/2	4 1/2	2 1/4	15/16	3/4	11/16	1 1/8
P/E Ratio - High	18	12	12	8	6	9	6	4	NM	5
- Low	9	7	8	3	4	4	2	3	NM	4
Income Statement Analysis (Million $)										
Net Int. Inc.	166	155	143	112	104	87.0	73.0	61.8	59.5	58.8
Tax Equiv. Adj.	13.3	9.7	4.9	7.8	5.4	NA	NA	NA	NA	NA
Non Int. Inc.	31.4	28.5	24.8	25.2	18.2	17.1	13.6	18.9	12.6	13.2
Loan Loss Prov.	76.0	55.7	31.6	30.9	17.7	18.7	13.6	16.4	32.0	11.3
Exp./Op. Revs.	44%	45%	48%	48%	50%	NA	NA	NA	NA	NA
Pretax Inc.	56.6	55.7	49.9	63.4	43.4	28.5	18.3	12.9	-17.6	12.5
Eff. Tax Rate	8.48%	15%	25%	23%	29%	23%	16%	11%	NM	6.40%
Net Inc.	51.8	47.5	37.6	49.1	31.0	22.0	15.3	11.5	-17.7	11.7
% Net Int. Marg.	5.27	5.83	6.03	5.59	5.65	4.81	4.04	3.39	3.20	3.20
Balance Sheet & Other Fin. Data (Million $)										
Money Mkt. Assets	0.5	0.5	126	Nil	18.9	NA	NA	NA	NA	NA
Inv. Securities	1,800	1,266	694	766	563	NA	NA	NA	NA	NA
Com'l Loans	747	278	233	189	127	NA	NA	NA	NA	NA
Other Loans	1,352	1,681	1,663	1,367	1,374	NA	NA	NA	NA	NA
Total Assets	4,017	3,327	2,822	2,433	2,175	1,914	1,889	1,898	1,908	1,928
Demand Deposits	304	140	136	129	127	NA	NA	NA	NA	NA
Time Deposits	1,471	1,455	1,568	1,389	1,367	NA	NA	NA	NA	NA
LT Debt	155	142	286	218	155	NA	NA	NA	NA	NA
Common Eqty.	270	236	191	171	120	NA	NA	NA	NA	NA
% Ret. on Assets	1.4	1.5	1.4	2.2	1.5	1.1	0.8	0.6	NM	0.6
% Ret. on Equity	20.4	22.2	20.8	33.2	29.1	29.8	26.9	24.6	NM	19.1
% Loan Loss Resv.	3.2	3.0	2.9	3.5	2.5	2.5	2.7	2.3	2.0	0.5
% Loans/Deposits	118.3	116.9	107.1	102.5	100.5	NA	NA	NA	NA	NA
% Equity to Assets	6.9	7.0	6.9	6.7	5.3	5.1	2.5	1.8	2.1	2.4

Data as orig reptd.; bef. results of disc opers/spec. items. Per share data adj. for stk. divs. Bold denotes diluted EPS (FASB 128)-prior periods restated. E-Estimated. NA-Not Available. NM-Not Meaningful. NR-Not Ranked.

Organized—in Puerto Rico in 1948. **Office**—1519 Ponce de Leon Ave., Stop 23-1/2, Santurce, PR 00908. **Tel**—(787) 729-8200. **Website**—http://www.1bankpr.com **Chrmn, Pres & CEO**—A. Alvarez-Perez. **EVP, CFO & Investor Contact**—Annie Astor de Carbonell (787-729-8200). **Dirs**—A. Alvarez-Perez, J. J. Alvarez, R. Bouet, A. A. de Carbonell, F. D. Fernandez, A. Lopez, G. E. Malaret, H. M. Nevares, A. Pavia-Villamil, J. Teixidor, A. L. Umpierre. **Transfer Agent & Registrar**—Bank of New York, NYC. **Empl**— 1,750. **S&P Analyst:** C.C.P.

STANDARD
&POOR'S
STOCK REPORTS

First Midwest Bancorp

NASDAQ Symbol **FMBI**

In S&P SmallCap 600

09-OCT-99

Industry:
Banks (Regional)

Summary: This company engages in commercial banking, trust, investment management and mortgage activities primarily in the suburban Chicago area.

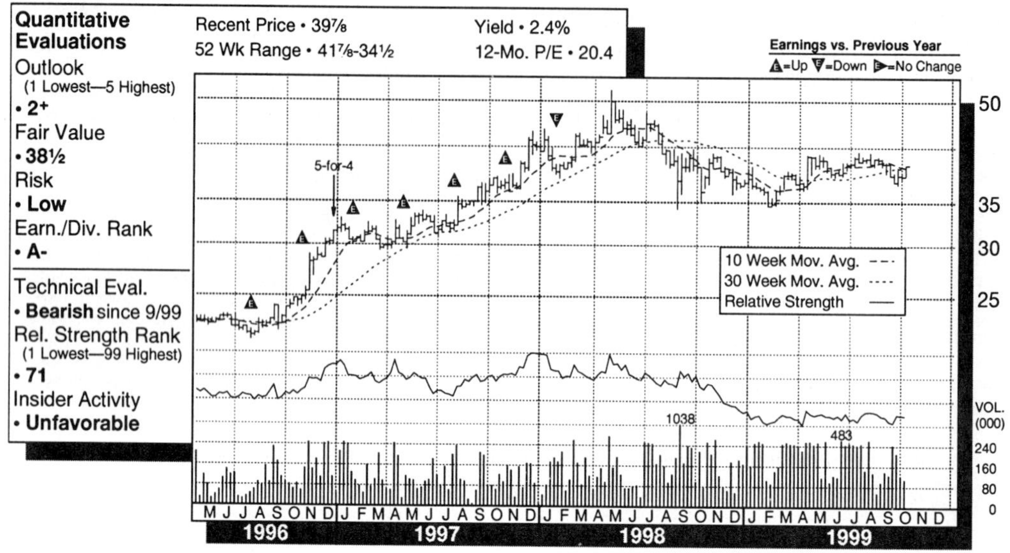

Business Profile - 03-SEP-99

First Midwest anticipates that the integration of Heritage Financial Services, Inc., acquired in mid-1998, will provide revenue enhancements over the balance of 1999. As of early 1999, the projected post-acquisition cost savings had been substantially achieved. Following the company's February 1999 stock buyback announcement, FMBI repurchased, through June 30, 1999, 881,000 common shares of the 2 million shares authorized, or approximately 7% of the total outstanding. Directors and officers own 5% of the common stock.

Operational Review - 03-SEP-99

Net interest income for the six months ended June 30, 1999, rose 1.3%, year to year, reflecting a slight rise in the level of average interest earning assets. The net interest margin inched up to 4.34%, compared with 4.33%. The provision for loan losses increased to $2.5 million, from $2.1 million. Noninterest income was 9.6% higher, due to improvement in all categories, especially corporate owned life insurance. Total noninterest expense rose 4.3%, resulting from general increases in most line items. After taxes at 26.7%, versus 30.6%, net income increased 6.3%, to $34,775,000 ($1.21 a share), from $32,727,000 ($1.09).

Stock Performance - 08-OCT-99

In the past 30 trading days, FMBI's shares have declined 0.47%, compared to a 0.91% fall in the S&P 500. Average trading volume for the past five days was 21,320 shares, compared with the 40-day moving average of 28,262 shares.

Key Stock Statistics

Dividend Rate/Share	0.96	Shareholders	3,500
Shs. outstg. (M)	27.8	Market cap. (B)	$ 1.1
Avg. daily vol. (M)	0.035	Inst. holdings	26%
Tang. Bk. Value/Share	14.35		
Beta	0.65		

Value of $10,000 invested 5 years ago: $ 22,697

Fiscal Year Ending Dec. 31

	1999	1998	1997	1996	1995	1994
Revenues (Million $)						
1Q	133.9	—	75.10	74.70	—	—
2Q	101.7	—	74.70	75.00	—	—
3Q	—	—	79.10	75.60	—	—
4Q	—	104.6	78.84	77.80	—	—
Yr.	—	420.1	307.7	303.1	309.4	265.4
Earnings Per Share ($)						
1Q	**0.58**	—	**0.51**	**0.45**	0.39	0.36
2Q	**0.63**	—	**0.52**	**0.48**	0.42	0.37
3Q	—	—	**0.56**	**0.50**	0.45	0.38
4Q	—	**0.59**	**0.33**	**0.52**	0.26	0.23
Yr.	—	**1.84**	**1.92**	**1.95**	**1.53**	**1.46**

Next earnings report expected: mid October

Dividend Data (Dividends have been paid since 1983.)

Amount ($)	Date Decl.	Ex-Div. Date	Stock of Record	Payment Date
0.240	Nov. 18	Dec. 22	Dec. 25	Jan. 25 '99
0.240	Feb. 17	Mar. 24	Mar. 26	Apr. 26 '99
0.240	May. 19	Jun. 23	Jun. 25	Jul. 26 '99
0.240	Aug. 18	Sep. 22	Sep. 24	Oct. 25 '99

First Midwest Bancorp, Inc.

Business Summary - 03-SEP-99

FMBI, with over $5.2 billion in assets at year end 1998, is the largest independent bank in the suburban Chicago area. First Midwest provides commercial banking, trust, investment management, mortgage and related financial services to a broad array of customers located in more than 40 communities primarily in the northern Illinois area. As of 1998 year-end, FMBI was operating 76 banking offices in northern Illinois and eastern Iowa. Approximately 85% of the bank's assets are located in suburban Chicago. FMBI ranks number one in Will County, IL, with a 19% share of deposits, and number two in Lake County, IL (10% share), and McHenry County, IL (14% share). The company has about 11% of its assets in the Quad Cities area of Moline and Rock Island, IL, and Davenport and Bettendorf, IA. The remaining 4% of the company's assets are in the downstate Illinois counties of Vermilion and Champaign.

The company operates four nonbank affiliates that provide trust (Heritage Bank), insurance (First Midwest Insurance Company), investment advisory (First Midwest Trust Company, N.A.), and mortgage-related services (First Midwest Mortgage Corporation). At 1998 year-end, the trust subsidiary had $2.2 billion in assets under management.

FMBI increased its total assets to $5.2 billion at December 31, 1998, from $3.6 billion at 1997 year-end, largely as a result of the acquisition of Heritage Financial Services (assets $1.4 billion) in July 1998.

The bank serves a diverse customer base, focusing its lending activities on the consumer market and small to mid-sized businesses within its geographic territory. FMBI's gross loans outstanding at the end of 1998 totaled $2.7 billion, 12.5% lower than last year, and were distributed as follows: commercial real estate 29%, commercial and industrial 27%, consumer 26%, residential real estate 10%, construction real estate 5%, agricultural 2%, and other 1%.

FMBI's credit quality weakened in 1998 primarily due to two loan customers who each accounted for half of the increase in nonperforming loans. Nonperforming assets surged to $21.7 million (0.81% of loans plus foreclosed real estate), up from $17.0 million (0.56%) a year earlier. The reserve for loan losses at year end 1998 was $43.3 million (1.62% of loans outstanding), versus $47.0 million (1.54%) a year earlier. Net charge-offs in 1998 more than doubled to $9.2 million.

First Midwest's efficiency ratio in 1998 remained relatively stable at 56.1%, compared with 56.2% a year earlier, despite the recognition of a $16 million acquisition expense related to the Heritage transaction. Excluding the acquisition charges in both 1998 and 1997, the efficiency ratio was 50.4% in 1998 and 54.1%, in 1997.

Per Share Data ($) (Year Ended Dec. 31)	1998	1997	1996	1995	1994	1993	1992	1991	1990	1989
Tangible Bk. Val.	15.60	16.82	16.08	14.58	11.17	11.97	12.12	11.38	10.60	9.74
Earnings	1.84	1.92	1.97	1.51	1.34	1.34	1.14	1.14	1.44	1.60
Dividends	0.90	0.82	0.70	0.61	0.54	0.48	0.42	0.42	0.42	0.38
Payout Ratio	49%	43%	36%	40%	41%	36%	36%	37%	29%	24%
Prices - High	52	45¼	33	23¾	23	22⅝	16¼	16	18⅜	20
- Low	34⅛	29⅜	21⅜	18⅝	17⅝	15⅜	11⅜	10⅜	9⅜	13⅛
P/E Ratio - High	28	24	17	16	17	17	14	14	13	13
- Low	19	15	11	12	13	11	10	9	7	8
Income Statement Analysis (Million $)										
Net Int. Inc.	188	145	123	119	108	104	97.6	94.3	88.3	83.2
Tax Equiv. Adj.	11.1	5.0	2.2	1.2	1.4	1.6	2.3	2.8	3.0	3.1
Non Int. Inc.	53.8	36.2	30.8	27.9	25.2	27.9	23.4	20.4	14.6	19.1
Loan Loss Prov.	5.5	8.8	7.5	11.3	8.5	11.4	15.4	15.5	8.5	6.0
Exp./Op. Revs.	66%	63%	61%	64%	70%	84%	88%	90%	87%	83%
Pretax Inc.	78.7	59.4	53.4	40.5	32.1	31.4	25.5	23.6	30.7	34.7
Eff. Tax Rate	30%	35%	36%	37%	37%	34%	30%	25%	26%	32%
Net Inc.	54.7	38.8	33.7	25.7	20.4	20.8	17.9	17.8	22.6	23.5
% Net Int. Marg.	4.21	4.54	4.33	4.04	4.24	4.60	4.80	4.50	4.60	4.80
Balance Sheet & Other Fin. Data (Million $)										
Money Mkt. Assets	100	31.1	23.1	7.9	NA	2.3	Nil	Nil	35.1	28.6
Inv. Securities	2,028	995	792	859	865	893	640	704	749	578
Com'l Loans	722	1,273	571	657	548	516	540	543	626	587
Other Loans	1,943	1,061	1,514	1,449	1,237	1,073	917	848	745	614
Total Assets	5,193	3,614	3,119	3,207	2,875	2,687	2,297	2,311	2,368	2,082
Demand Deposits	696	473	350	361	347	331	305	269	254	255
Time Deposits	3,355	2,323	1,911	1,911	1,648	1,603	1,577	1,547	1,683	1,298
LT Debt	Nil	Nil	Nil	Nil	Nil	Nil	Nil	Nil	Nil	12.1
Common Eqty.	453	338	262	249	186	200	189	178	166	143
% Ret. on Assets	1.2	1.2	1.1	0.8	0.7	0.8	0.8	0.8	1.0	1.2
% Ret. on Equity	13.8	12.9	13.2	11.2	10.6	10.8	9.8	10.3	14.3	17.5
% Loan Loss Resv.	1.6	1.6	1.4	1.4	1.4	1.4	1.5	1.5	1.3	1.3
% Loans/Deposits	NA	83.5	92.2	92.7	89.5	82.2	77.4	74.6	70.8	76.6
% Equity to Assets	9.0	8.9	8.1	7.3	6.9	7.8	8.0	7.4	7.3	6.7

Data as orig reptd.; bef. results of disc opers/spec. items. Per share data adj. for stk. divs. Bold denotes diluted EPS (FASB 128)-prior periods restated. E-Estimated. NA-Not Available. NM-Not Meaningful. NR-Not Ranked.

Office—300 Park Blvd., Suite 405, P.O. Box 459, Itasca, IL 60143-0459. **Tel**—(630) 875-7450. **Chrmn & CEO**—R. P. O'Meara. **Pres & COO**—J. M. O'Meara. **EVP & CFO**—D. J. Swistowicz. **Investor Contact**—James M. Roolf (630-875-7452). **Dirs**—V. A. Brunner, B. S. Chelberg, W. J. Cowlin, O. R. Edwards, J. W. England, J. Gafney, T. M. Garvin, J. M. O'Meara, R. P. O'Meara, J. Payan, J. L. Sterling, J. S. Vanderwoude, R. T. Wojcik. **Transfer Agent**—American Securities Transfer, Lakewood, Colorado. **Incorporated**—in Delaware in 1982. **Empl**— 1,700. **S&P Analyst:** V.G.P.

STANDARD
&POOR'S
STOCK REPORTS

FirstMerit Corp.

NASDAQ Symbol **FMER**

In S&P SmallCap 600

09-OCT-99

Industry: Banks (Regional)

Summary: This bank holding company, with about $9 billion in assets, operates approximately 170 offices, primarily in northeastern Ohio, and western Pennsylvania.

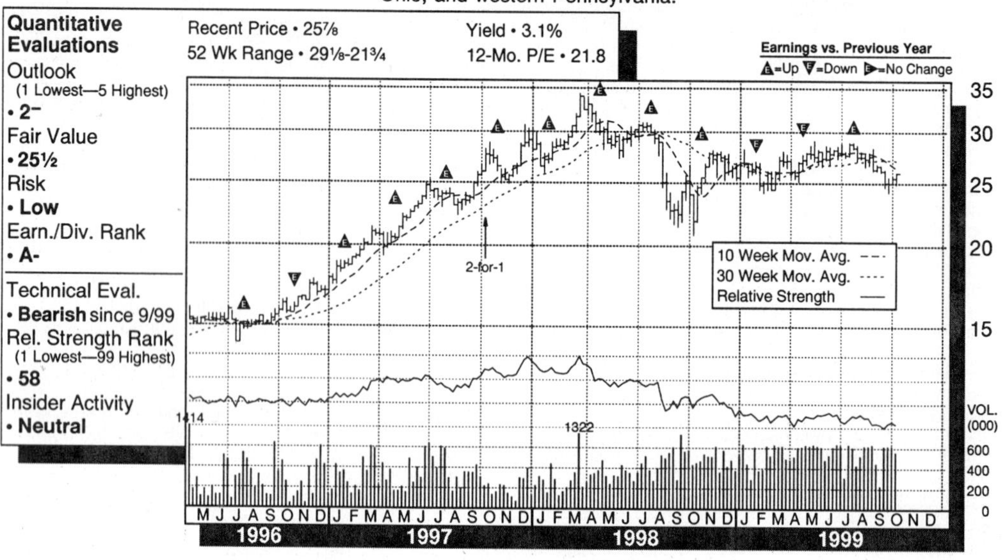

Business Profile - 12-JUL-99

In February 1999, FMER reiterated its goals for 1999, which included: double-digit EPS growth, a return on equity in the 16-18% range, core revenue growth of 6-8%, and an efficiency ratio of 50% or less by year end. Also, in February, FMER acquired Signal Corp., a $1.9 billion Ohio-based bank holding company for approximately $436 million in stock. As a result, FMER took a charge of $32.3 million related to the acquisition and a $5.8 million extraordinary charge for the early retirement of Signal debt in the first quarter of 1999. In April 1999, FMER's board approved a new stock repurchase program, authorizing the repurchase of up to 1.65 million shares (approximately 1.8%) of common stock.

Operational Review - 12-JUL-99

Net interest income in the three months ended March 31, 1999, increased 13%, year to year, primarily due to growth in earning assets from recent acquisitions. Noninterest income advanced 17%, reflecting higher gains from the sale of securities and growth in trust services, credit card fees, and other service fees. Other expenses rose 58%, mainly due to the charge related to the Signal acquisition. After taxes at 50.0%, versus 31.4%, income from operations declined 82%, to $5.3 million ($0.06 per share), from $29.4 million ($0.35). Results in 1999 exclude an after-tax extraordinary charge of $5.8 million ($0.06 a share) related to the extinguishment of debt from the Signal acquisition.

Stock Performance - 08-OCT-99

In the past 30 trading days, FMER's shares have declined 1%, compared to a 0.91% fall in the S&P 500. Average trading volume for the past five days was 111,360 shares, compared with the 40-day moving average of 133,464 shares.

Key Stock Statistics

Dividend Rate/Share	0.80	Shareholders	6,978
Shs. outstg. (M)	90.4	Market cap. (B)	$ 2.3
Avg. daily vol. (M)	0.142	Inst. holdings	25%
Tang. Bk. Value/Share	7.74		
Beta	0.96		

Value of $10,000 invested 5 years ago: $ 23,645

Fiscal Year Ending Dec. 31

	1999	1998	1997	1996	1995	1994
Revenues (Million $)						
1Q	203.3	125.8	118.1	121.3	120.9	80.64
2Q	206.7	136.1	122.0	121.1	121.5	88.86
3Q	—	144.3	125.0	122.2	122.8	95.32
4Q	—	207.4	70.33	129.7	119.9	108.9
Yr.	—	613.6	435.6	494.2	485.1	373.7
Earnings Per Share ($)						
1Q	**0.06**	**0.35**	**0.32**	**0.29**	-0.02	0.28
2Q	**0.42**	**0.38**	**0.33**	**0.29**	0.19	0.28
3Q	—	**0.39**	**0.35**	**0.21**	0.25	0.28
4Q	—	**0.23**	**0.36**	**0.29**	-0.04	0.28
Yr.	—	**1.34**	**1.36**	**1.09**	**0.38**	1.11

Next earnings report expected: mid October

Dividend Data (Dividends have been paid since 1939.)

Amount ($)	Date Decl.	Ex-Div. Date	Stock of Record	Payment Date
0.180	Nov. 19	Nov. 25	Nov. 30	Dec. 21 '98
0.180	Feb. 18	Feb. 25	Mar. 01	Mar. 15 '99
0.180	May. 20	May. 27	Jun. 01	Jun. 21 '99
0.200	Aug. 19	Aug. 26	Aug. 30	Sep. 20 '99

A Division of The McGraw-Hill Companies

FirstMerit Corporation

Business Summary - 12-JUL-99

FirstMerit Corporation (FMER), an Akron, Ohio-based bank holding company, focused on applying its leverage in 1998, moving throughout the year to build market share where the company had an existing presence, and to expand its franchise to strategically-selected neighboring markets.

In 1998, FMER acquired CoBancorp, headquartered in Elyria, Ohio, which had assets of $666 million, for about $174 million in cash and stock, and Security First Corp., a $678 million holding company based in Mayfield Heights, Ohio, for about $199 million in stock. In February 1999, FMER acquired Signal Corp., a $1.9 billion bank based in Wooster, Ohio, for $421 million in stock, extending its reach into Pennsylvania.

At March 31, 1999, FirstMerit had assets of $9.2 billion and operated 177 offices throughout 22 counties in Ohio and western Pennsylvania. In 1998, FMER consolidated administrative and processing functions, cut staff levels, implemented a $9.5 million platform/teller technology, and completed consolidation into a single national charter.

FMER aims to capitalize on its community banking orientation by adhering to high customer service standards in its banking network. Its principal subsidiary is FirstMerit Bank, N.A., which has over 150 offices. Other units include FirstMerit Credit Life Insurance Co., First Merit Community Development Corp., FirstMerit Mortgage Corp., Abell & Associates, Inc., FirstMerit Insurance Agency Inc., and FirstMerit Securities, Inc.

One of the company's more important recent undertakings was the shifting of its loan portfolio toward higher yielding commercial and consumer loans (which also have higher loss ratios), away from the traditional residential portfolio. Total loans, which grew to $5.0 billion at December 31, 1998, were divided in recent years: commercial, financial & agricultural 24% (20% in 1997), real estate 55% (58%), consumer/installment 18% (19%), and lease financing 3% (3%).

FMER earned higher net interest income in 1998, as a higher level of earning assets was partially offset by a lower net interest margin (5.04%, versus 5.11% in 1997). Net charge-offs (amount of loans written off as uncollectible) decreased to 0.35% of average loans in 1998, from 0.39% in 1997, while nonperforming assets declined to 0.33% of total loans, from 0.37% a year earlier.

After spending almost two years streamlining its operations to increase productivity and profitability, FMER re-entered the consolidation market in May 1997, with the acquisition of Abell & Associates, a nationally known life insurance and financial consulting firm. Subsequently, the company purchased three branches from First Western Bank.

Per Share Data ($) (Year Ended Dec. 31)	1998	1997	1996	1995	1994	1993	1992	1991	1990	1989
Tangible Bk. Val.	10.39	8.56	8.20	8.11	7.95	7.75	6.67	6.01	6.13	6.13
Earnings	1.34	1.36	1.09	0.39	1.11	1.09	1.01	0.79	0.69	0.80
Dividends	0.66	0.61	0.55	0.51	0.49	0.45	0.41	0.40	0.38	0.37
Payout Ratio	49%	44%	50%	132%	44%	41%	41%	51%	55%	46%
Prices - High	34 3/8	30 3/4	18	15 1/4	13 7/8	15 3/8	11 3/4	9 1/2	7 1/2	8 5/8
- Low	20 3/4	17 3/8	13 7/8	10 3/4	10 7/8	10 3/8	9	5 1/8	4 1/8	6 5/8
P/E Ratio - High	26	23	17	40	13	14	12	12	11	11
- Low	15	13	13	28	10	9	9	7	6	8
Income Statement Analysis (Million $)										
Net Int. Inc.	305	255	251	236	201	184	180	152	141	129
Tax Equiv. Adj.	5.5	3.2	3.0	3.8	4.6	5.3	5.6	6.9	9.1	10.2
Non Int. Inc.	104	81.6	84.3	68.0	56.9	54.3	49.2	44.1	37.9	34.2
Loan Loss Prov.	28.4	21.6	17.8	19.8	4.5	6.6	17.4	11.4	11.7	7.1
Exp./Op. Revs.	59%	57%	62%	74%	64%	62%	60%	64%	65%	62%
Pretax Inc.	145	126	106	56.7	86.4	80.7	73.1	55.0	46.1	50.0
Eff. Tax Rate	33%	32%	33%	55%	30%	32%	31%	28%	24%	23%
Net Inc.	97.5	86.3	70.9	25.7	60.3	55.2	50.7	39.6	34.9	38.6
% Net Int. Marg.	5.04	5.25	4.98	4.56	4.85	5.28	5.37	4.68	4.53	4.71
Balance Sheet & Other Fin. Data (Million $)										
Money Mkt. Assets	12.5	33.1	15.6	12.6	4.0	59.0	95.0	82.0	NA	NA
Inv. Securities	1,552	1,117	1,188	1,403	1,378	1,210	1,167	1,119	1,046	914
Com'l Loans	2,374	1,020	908	769	626	487	442	419	422	546
Other Loans	2,623	2,815	2,748	3,001	2,554	1,909	1,881	1,832	1,739	1,406
Total Assets	7,127	5,307	5,228	5,597	4,924	3,997	3,916	3,766	3,722	3,334
Demand Deposits	1,602	1,240	1,250	1,243	1,080	688	639	531	529	500
Time Deposits	3,820	3,015	2,955	3,259	2,783	2,739	2,745	2,737	2,700	2,344
LT Debt	Nil	Nil	Nil	Nil	Nil	Nil	Nil	Nil	Nil	16.9
Common Eqty.	768	530	524	543	432	392	358	327	308	297
% Ret. on Assets	1.5	1.6	1.3	0.5	1.3	1.4	1.3	1.1	1.0	1.2
% Ret. on Equity	14.3	16.4	13.3	4.8	14.1	14.7	14.8	12.5	11.7	13.6
% Loan Loss Resv.	1.6	1.4	1.3	1.2	1.2	1.3	1.3	1.1	1.1	1.0
% Loans/Deposits	92.5	90.1	85.3	83.8	82.3	69.9	68.6	68.8	66.7	68.4
% Equity to Assets	10.4	10.0	9.9	9.4	9.3	9.5	9.1	8.6	8.3	8.8

Data as orig reptd.; bef. results of disc opers/spec. items. Per share data adj. for stk. divs. Bold denotes diluted EPS (FASB 128)-prior periods restated. E-Estimated. NA-Not Available. NM-Not Meaningful. NR-Not Ranked.

Office—III Cascade Plaza, 7th Floor, Akron, OH 44308-1103. **Tel**—(330) 996-6300. **Website**—http://www.firstmerit.com **Chrm & CEO**—J. R. Cochran. **Pres & COO**—S. A. Bostic. **SVP & Investor Contact**—Gary J. Elek. **SVP, Fin & Admn**—A. J. Mulhern. **SVP & Secy**—T. E. Patton. **Dirs**—K. S. Belden, R. C. Blair, J. C. Blickle, S. A. Bostic, R. W. Briggs, J. R. Cochran, R. Collela, E. A. Dalton, T. L. Haines, C. J. Isroff, P. A. Lloyd II, R. G. Merzweiler, S. E. Myers, R. T. Read, J. T. Rogers, Jr., R. N. Seaman. **Transfer Agent**—FirstMerit Bank, Akron. **Incorporated**—in Ohio in 1962. **Empl**— 2,430. **S&P Analyst:** J. Rudy

STANDARD
&POOR'S
STOCK REPORTS

Fleming Cos.

NYSE Symbol **FLM**

In S&P SmallCap 600

09-OCT-99

Industry: Distributors (Food & Health)

Summary: One of the largest food wholesalers in the U.S., FLM supplies food and related products and services to some 3,000 supermarkets in 42 states, including 260 company-owned stores.

S&P Opinion: Accumulate (★★★★)

Recent Price • 9¾

52 Wk Range • 12⅝-7⅛

Yield • 0.8%

12-Mo. P/E • NM

Quantitative Evaluations

Outlook
(1 Lowest—5 Highest)
• **3**

Fair Value
• **11½**

Risk
• **Average**

Earn./Div. Rank
• **B-**

Technical Eval.
• **Bearish** since 9/99

Rel. Strength Rank
(1 Lowest—99 Highest)
• **22**

Insider Activity
• **Favorable**

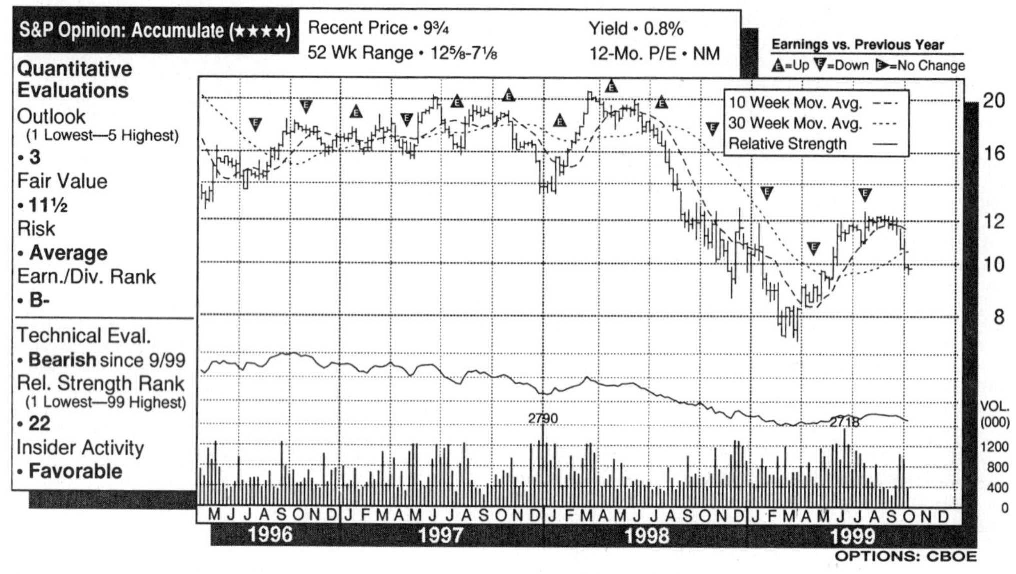

Overview - 02-AUG-99

We expect revenues to fall approximately 2.0% in 1999, reflecting the loss of business from Furr's and Randall's as well as customer losses from the consolidation of FLM's distribution centers. However, the recent addition of business from Kmart should help boost revenues starting in the fourth quarter of 1999. In addition, FLM has been aggressive in signing new food distribution business from a variety of new customers. Retail sales should get a boost from the opening and acquisition of just over 30 stores in 1999 and the remodel of another 20 units. Operating margins should improve as the year unfolds due to higher utilization rates in FLM's distribution facilities and the closure of underperforming retail units. However, operating margins at retail may suffer from strong promotions to remain competitive. We expect 1999 EBITDA to approximate $380 million, translating to approximately $1.02 in operating earnings per share.

Valuation - 02-AUG-99

We recently upgraded FLM to accumulate from hold, due to the recent acquisition of Kmart as a customer, which we expect should help boost revenues by approximately $1.4 billion annually. In addition, FLM has hired several key personnel at its retail operation, which we believe could help improve what has been a lackluster division over the past few years. The consolidation of five distribution centers in the first half of the year should help improve operating efficiency in the second half of 1999. We also expect retail operations to improve, due to the pending divestiture of some underperforming units. Recently trading at 12X our 1999 operating EPS forecast, the shares are attractive for accumulation given likely operating improvements to be made over the next few years.

Key Stock Statistics

S&P EPS Est. 1999	1.02	Tang. Bk. Value/Share	NM
P/E on S&P Est. 1999	9.6	Beta	0.34
S&P EPS Est. 2000	1.20	Shareholders	12,000
Dividend Rate/Share	0.08	Market cap. (B)	$0.381
Shs. outstg. (M)	38.8	Inst. holdings	66%
Avg. daily vol. (M)	0.139		

Value of $10,000 invested 5 years ago: $ 4,602

Fiscal Year Ending Dec. 31

	1999	1998	1997	1996	1995	1994
Revenues (Million $)						
1Q	4,465	4,567	4,752	5,168	5,459	4,032
2Q	3,349	3,506	3,551	3,742	4,000	2,884
3Q	—	3,439	3,453	3,706	3,898	4,142
4Q	—	3,558	3,617	3,870	4,144	4,696
Yr.	—	15,069	15,373	16,487	17,502	15,753
Earnings Per Share ($)						
1Q	**-0.64**	**0.40**	**0.14**	**0.16**	0.52	0.66
2Q	**-0.06**	**0.36**	**0.34**	**0.25**	0.39	0.50
3Q	—	**-0.06**	**0.26**	**0.03**	0.10	0.07
4Q	—	**-14.11**	**0.29**	**0.27**	0.11	0.28
Yr.	—	**-13.48**	**1.02**	**0.71**	**1.12**	1.51

Next earnings report expected: late October

Dividend Data (Dividends have been paid since 1927.)

Amount ($)	Date Decl.	Ex-Div. Date	Stock of Record	Payment Date
0.020	Jan. 19	Feb. 17	Feb. 19	Mar. 10 '99
0.020	Mar. 02	May. 18	May. 20	Jun. 10 '99
0.020	Jul. 20	Aug. 18	Aug. 20	Sep. 10 '99
0.020	Sep. 22	Nov. 18	Nov. 22	Dec. 10 '99

Fleming Companies, Inc.

Business Summary - 02-AUG-99

From humble beginnings in 1915 as a small food wholesaler in Topeka, KA, Fleming has grown to become one of the largest food and general merchandise distributors in the U.S., supplying supermarkets and smaller grocery stores in 42 states. In addition, the company operates a retail food division with some 270 stores in 15 states.

After growing primarily through acquisitions, at the end of 1998, the company announced a strategic restructuring plan. The plan is to be implemented over the next two years and focuses on three key initiatives to restore sales and earnings growth: focus resources to improve performance; grow sales more aggressively in wholesale and retail operations; and reduce overhead and operating costs to improve overall operating profitability.

A key element in this plan is the consolidation of food distribution operations through the divestiture of seven units. FLM believes that the divestiture of these units may optimize other food distribution operations and more efficiently support FLM's retail customers. In conjunction with this consolidation, the company plans to implement an aggressive strategy to develop new business that leverages Fleming's consolidated food distribution operations to earn a greater share of business from existing customers as well as attract new customers. To improve operations at retail, FLM plans to divest certain underperforming chains to more fully develop its better-performing chains. To improve its better performing retail stores, FLM plans to spend additional capital for new store development and remodels. Lastly, the company expects to lower overhead expenses to more properly reflect the expected configuration of the food distribution and retail divisions.

Fleming's food distribution segment sells food and non-food products to retail grocers and offers a variety of retail support to independently owned and company-owned retail food stores. During 1998, the average number of SKUs carried in full-line food distribution centers was about 14,200, including about 2,300 perishable products, while general merchandise and specialty food operating distribution centers carried approximately 19,500 SKUs. The division serves customers operating as conventional supermarkets, superstores, supercenters, warehouse stores, combination stores and convenience stores. During 1998, FLM's top 10 external customers accounted for approximately 17% of sales, with no single customer representing more than 3.6% of total net sales. The food distribution division also offers retail services to its customers such as consulting advice, and administration and information technology services to its food distribution customers and others.

The retail food division consists of 14 distinct local chains or groups in 15 states, operating under 13 banners. At year-end 1998, the retail food segment owned and operated over 280 supermarkets with an aggregate of approximately 11.5 million sq. ft. of retail space.

Per Share Data ($) (Year Ended Dec. 31)	1998	1997	1996	1995	1994	1993	1992	1991	1990	1989
Tangible Bk. Val.	NM	3.29	2.10	1.65	2.42	15.93	16.19	14.44	9.98	7.18
Cash Flow	-8.58	5.79	5.66	5.87	5.42	3.77	5.33	4.22	5.78	4.78
Earnings	-13.48	1.02	0.71	1.12	1.51	1.02	3.33	2.06	3.06	2.54
Dividends	0.08	0.08	0.36	1.20	1.20	1.20	1.20	1.14	1.03	1.00
Payout Ratio	NM	8%	51%	107%	79%	118%	37%	58%	34%	40%
Prices - High	20¾	20⅜	20⅞	29⅞	30	34⅜	35⅛	40⅝	37⅝	40
- Low	8⅝	13⅜	11½	19⅛	22⅝	23¾	27¼	29⅞	28	27½
P/E Ratio - High	NM	20	29	27	20	34	11	20	12	16
- Low	NM	13	16	17	15	23	8	15	9	11
Income Statement Analysis (Million $)										
Revs.	15,069	15,373	16,487	17,502	15,753	13,092	12,938	12,902	11,933	12,045
Oper. Inc.	384	418	396	402	329	293	348	350	325	302
Depr.	185	181	188	181	146	101	71.8	72.7	66.9	65.8
Int. Exp.	161	163	163	176	121	78.0	81.1	93.5	93.8	97.4
Pretax Inc.	-598	83.0	54.6	85.9	112	72.0	195	117	165	139
Eff. Tax Rate	NM	53%	51%	51%	50%	48%	39%	38%	41%	43%
Net Inc.	-510	39.0	26.7	42.0	56.0	37.0	119	72.3	97.3	80.1
Balance Sheet & Other Fin. Data (Million $)										
Cash	6.0	30.0	63.7	4.4	28.4	1.6	4.7	21.1	21.3	37.2
Curr. Assets	1,588	1,495	1,564	1,651	1,820	1,361	1,403	1,343	1,208	1,141
Total Assets	3,491	3,924	4,055	4,297	4,608	3,103	3,118	2,956	2,768	2,689
Curr. Liab.	1,281	1,155	1,343	1,286	1,324	919	875	915	830	778
LT Debt	1,503	1,494	1,453	1,717	1,995	1,004	1,038	952	981	692
Common Eqty.	571	1,094	1,076	1,083	1,079	1,060	1,060	957	764	692
Total Cap.	2,073	2,649	2,567	2,840	3,125	2,092	2,138	1,935	1,839	1,774
Cap. Exp.	200	129	129	117	150	56.0	114	82.0	69.0	137
Cash Flow	-325	220	215	223	202	139	191	142	160	140
Curr. Ratio	1.2	1.3	1.2	1.3	1.4	1.5	1.6	1.5	1.5	1.5
% LT Debt of Cap.	72.5	56.4	56.6	60.5	63.8	48.0	48.6	49.2	53.4	55.8
% Net Inc.of Revs.	NM	0.3	0.2	0.2	0.4	0.3	0.9	0.6	0.8	0.7
% Ret. on Assets	NM	1.0	0.6	0.9	1.4	1.2	3.8	2.3	3.5	3.0
% Ret. on Equity	NM	3.6	2.5	3.9	5.2	3.5	11.6	7.5	12.7	11.1

Data as orig reptd.; bef. results of disc opers/spec. items. Per share data adj. for stk. divs. Bold denotes diluted EPS (FASB 128)-prior periods restated. E-Estimated. NA-Not Available. NM-Not Meaningful. NR-Not Ranked.

Office—6301 Waterford Blvd., P.O. Box 26647, Oklahoma City, OK 73126. **Tel**—(405) 841-8122. **Fax**—(405) 841-8158. **Website**—www.fleming.com **Chrmn & CEO**—R. E. Stauth. **Pres & COO**—W. Dowd. **EVP & CFO**—H. L. Winn, Jr. **VP-Treas & Investor Contact**—J. M. Thompson (405-841-8170). **SVP & Secy**—D. R. Almond. **Dirs**—J. W. Baker, A. R. Dykes, C. B. Hallett, J. G. Harlow, Jr., L. M. Jones, E. C. Joullian, III, G. A. Osborn, A. Peterson, R. E. Stauth, E. D. Werries. **Transfer Agent & Registrar**—Liberty National Bank & Trust Co., Oklahoma City. **Incorporated**—in Kansas in 1915; reincorporated in Oklahoma in 1981. **Empl**— 39,700. **S&P Analyst:** Robert J. Izmirlian

STANDARD
&POOR'S
STOCK REPORTS

Florida Rock Industries

NYSE Symbol **FRK**

In S&P SmallCap 600

09-OCT-99

Industry: Construction (Cement & Aggregates)

Summary: FRK is a major provider of construction aggregates and concrete and concrete products in the southeastern and mid-Atlantic states.

Quantitative Evaluations

Outlook (1 Lowest—5 Highest) • **3**

Fair Value • **40¾**

Risk • **Average**

Earn./Div. Rank • **B+**

Technical Eval. • **Bearish** since 9/99

Rel. Strength Rank (1 Lowest—99 Highest) • **25**

Insider Activity • **NA**

Recent Price • 34 | Yield • 0.7%

52 Wk Range • 45½-22⅝ | 12-Mo. P/E • 14.6

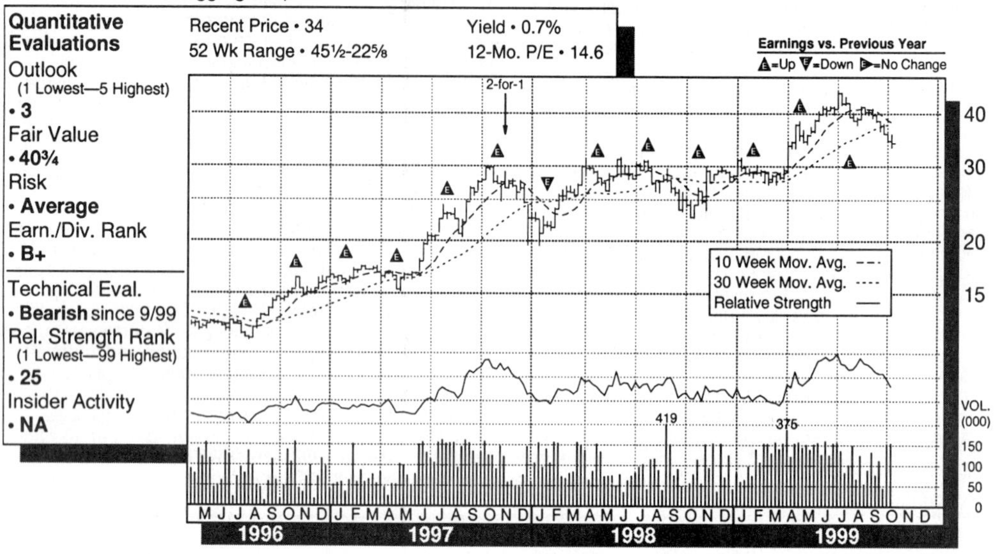

Business Profile - 22-JUL-99

For the remainder of 1999, FRK remains positive in its outlook for the construction industry and general economic conditions. The view for residential construction remains favorable in the company's markets, with the level of activity continuing to vary by region. Non-residential construction is moving with local supply and demand, with evidence that more speculative construction is under way. Public spending on infrastructure will increase as a result of the Transportation Equity Act for the 21st Century (TEA 21), which is projected to raise the amount of federal highway spending by an average of 57% in FRK's markets over previous years' funding levels.

Operational Review - 22-JUL-99

Net sales in the six months ended March 31, 1999, rose 26%, year to year, reflecting strong demand for construction products coupled with favorable weather in the company's markets. Sales were also up as a result of modest price increases in core products. Gross margins widened on the improved sales and lower maintenance and other quarry costs, and with well controlled SG&A expenses, partially offset by a $3.4 million charge for system upgrades and year 2000 costs, operating income gained 46%. Following a $4.2 million charge for settlement of interest rate hedge agreements and after taxes at 35.2% in both periods, net income advanced 35%, to $19,779,000 ($1.03 a share), from $14,690,000 ($0.77).

Stock Performance - 08-OCT-99

In the past 30 trading days, FRK's shares have declined 16%, compared to a 0.91% fall in the S&P 500. Average trading volume for the past five days was 39,180 shares, compared with the 40-day moving average of 22,459 shares.

Key Stock Statistics

Dividend Rate/Share	0.25	Shareholders	1,125
Shs. outstg. (M)	18.9	Market cap. (B)	$0.644
Avg. daily vol. (M)	0.026	Inst. holdings	49%
Tang. Bk. Value/Share	14.70		
Beta	0.61		

Value of $10,000 invested 5 years ago: $ 24,823

Fiscal Year Ending Sep. 30

	1999	1998	1997	1996	1995	1994
Revenues (Million $)						
1Q	143.1	111.6	106.4	92.27	89.61	75.91
2Q	138.1	107.7	101.6	85.80	84.68	67.00
3Q	152.3	132.0	123.9	110.3	98.26	95.60
4Q	—	141.1	124.9	110.3	96.41	98.03
Yr.	—	492.5	456.8	398.7	369.0	336.5
Earnings Per Share ($)						
1Q	**0.52**	**0.38**	0.43	0.29	0.33	0.15
2Q	**0.50**	**0.38**	0.35	0.14	0.17	0.01
3Q	**0.72**	**0.66**	0.65	0.48	0.37	0.37
4Q	—	**0.60**	0.55	0.52	0.39	0.37
Yr.	—	**2.02**	**1.99**	1.43	1.25	0.91

Next earnings report expected: early December

Dividend Data (Dividends have been paid since 1978.)

Amount ($)	Date Decl.	Ex-Div. Date	Stock of Record	Payment Date
0.125	Dec. 02	Dec. 11	Dec. 15	Jan. 04 '99
0.125	May. 05	Jun. 09	Jun. 11	Jul. 01 '99

Florida Rock Industries, Inc.

Business Summary - 22-JUL-99

Florida Rock Industries (FRK) produces and sells ready mixed concrete and mines, processes and sells sand, gravel and crushed stone (construction aggregates). The company also produces and sells concrete block and prestressed concrete and sells other building materials. Substantially all operations are conducted in the Southeast, primarily in Florida, Georgia, Virginia, Maryland, Washington, DC, and North Carolina.

In recent fiscal years (Sep.), ready mixed concrete has accounted for about 60% of sales, with most of the remainder from construction aggregates.

The estimated contribution to revenues from the sale of construction materials by major markets in FY 98 was: commercial and industrial 47%; residential 33%; and highway and government 20%.

At the end of FY 98, FRK was operating 88 ready mixed concrete plants, 10 concrete block plants, and a delivery fleet of 1,036 ready mix and block trucks.

Ready mixed concrete is produced and sold throughout peninsula Florida; southern Georgia; central Maryland; Richmond, Norfolk-Virginia Beach and northeastern Virginia; and Washington, DC.

Since ready mixed concrete hardens rapidly, delivery is generally confined to a radius of about 20 miles to 25 miles from the producing plant. The bulk weight of concrete block limits its delivery to approximately 40 miles from the plant.

During FY 98, 49% of the coarse aggregates and 64% of the sand used in concrete operations were produced by the company. Remaining aggregates were purchased from other suppliers.

FRK has received all necessary building, zoning and environmental permits for construction of a $100 million, 750,000 ton capacity cement plant near Newberry, FL; construction began in April 1997, with the plant expected to be operational by the fourth quarter of FY 99. An aggregate plant in Paulding County, GA, is being constructed to serve customers in northwest Georgia.

The company expects capital expenditures for FY 99 to total $106 million, with $50 million slated for the new cement plant. Expenditures in FY 98 were $95 million.

During the winter months, sales in the Maryland, Virginia, North Carolina, Washington, DC, and Georgia operations are adversely affected by the impact of inclement weather on the construction industry.

Per Share Data ($) (Year Ended Sep. 30)	1998	1997	1996	1995	1994	1993	1992	1991	1990	1989
Tangible Bk. Val.	15.41	13.49	11.77	10.60	9.57	8.74	8.55	8.58	8.70	8.01
Cash Flow	3.76	3.61	2.96	2.65	2.25	1.31	1.66	1.75	2.58	2.85
Earnings	2.02	1.98	1.43	1.25	0.91	0.42	0.21	0.11	0.93	1.26
Dividends	0.25	0.25	0.25	0.25	0.25	0.25	0.25	0.25	0.25	0.25
Payout Ratio	12%	13%	17%	20%	27%	59%	119%	225%	27%	20%
Prices - High	31½	30	16⅞	15	17¼	15⅜	14⅜	14⅝	16⅜	20⅞
- Low	19⅜	15⅛	11⅝	13⅛	11⅞	11⅞	10¼	9⅛	8¼	14⅞
P/E Ratio - High	16	15	12	12	19	36	68	NM	18	17
- Low	10	8	8	10	13	28	49	NM	9	12
Income Statement Analysis (Million $)										
Revs.	492	457	399	368	337	294	272	296	391	420
Oper. Inc.	94.3	86.8	71.1	65.7	52.9	36.9	33.2	35.5	63.6	71.8
Depr.	33.4	30.7	28.8	26.5	25.4	25.5	26.7	30.2	29.9	29.4
Int. Exp.	0.6	0.9	2.0	2.1	2.3	3.0	3.3	4.8	5.8	8.0
Pretax Inc.	60.0	56.4	41.1	36.4	25.5	12.2	4.3	1.7	25.1	34.9
Eff. Tax Rate	35%	34%	34%	34%	33%	36%	11%	NM	32%	33%
Net Inc.	38.9	37.1	27.0	23.9	17.2	7.8	3.9	2.0	17.1	23.3
Balance Sheet & Other Fin. Data (Million $)										
Cash	4.5	18.4	5.0	0.9	0.8	4.1	1.2	1.7	1.5	1.8
Curr. Assets	101	104	87.1	78.8	75.7	73.0	65.9	62.6	71.2	79.0
Total Assets	452	383	347	326	311	312	297	300	305	318
Curr. Liab.	74.8	55.7	51.9	57.6	49.3	52.0	46.6	47.7	48.6	55.0
LT Debt	23.9	10.9	16.9	9.7	23.1	43.9	39.4	41.4	41.7	60.2
Common Eqty.	300	265	228	211	192	172	168	170	172	160
Total Cap.	352	304	275	252	246	246	239	242	247	255
Cap. Exp.	95.3	46.5	44.9	40.2	23.0	34.0	27.0	24.0	27.0	44.0
Cash Flow	72.3	67.8	55.8	50.4	42.6	33.3	30.5	32.3	47.0	52.7
Curr. Ratio	1.3	1.9	1.7	1.4	1.5	1.4	1.4	1.3	1.5	1.4
% LT Debt of Cap.	6.8	3.6	6.1	3.8	9.4	17.8	16.4	17.1	16.9	23.6
% Net Inc.of Revs.	7.9	8.1	6.8	6.5	5.1	2.6	1.4	0.7	4.4	5.5
% Ret. on Assets	9.3	10.2	8.0	7.5	5.4	2.6	1.3	0.7	5.5	7.4
% Ret. on Equity	13.8	15.1	12.3	11.8	9.3	4.6	2.3	1.2	10.3	15.5

Data as orig reptd.; bef. results of disc opers/spec. items. Per share data adj. for stk. divs. Bold denotes diluted EPS (FASB 128)-prior periods restated. E-Estimated. NA-Not Available. NM-Not Meaningful. NR-Not Ranked.

Office—155 E. 21st St., Jacksonville, FL 32206; P.O. Box 4667, Jacksonville 32201. **Tel**—(904) 355-1781. **Chrmn**—E. L. Baker. **Pres & CEO**—J. D. Baker II. **VP, Treas & CFO**—J. J. Gilstrap. **Secy**—D. D. Frick. **Dirs**—E. L. Baker, J. D. Baker II, T. S. Baker II, A. R. Carpenter, C. H. Denny III, A. D. Ernest Jr., L. E. Fichthorn III, G. K. Thompson, F. X. Knott, R. D. Lovett, C. J. Shepherdson. **Transfer Agent & Registrar**—First Union National Bank of North Carolina, Charlotte. **Incorporated**—in Florida in 1945. **Empl**— 2,635. **S&P Analyst:** C.C.P.

STANDARD
&POOR'S
STOCK REPORTS

Flow International

NASDAQ Symbol **FLOW**

In S&P SmallCap 600

09-OCT-99

Industry:
Manufacturing (Specialized)

Summary: Flow is the world's leading manufacturer of ultrahigh-pressure waterjet technology for advanced commercial applications, and a leading provider of robotics and assembly equipment.

Quantitative Evaluations

Outlook
(1 Lowest—5 Highest)
• **3+**

Fair Value
• **12½**

Risk
• **Average**

Earn./Div. Rank
• **B**

Technical Eval.
• **Neutral** since 9/99

Rel. Strength Rank
(1 Lowest—99 Highest)
• **90**

Insider Activity
• **NA**

Recent Price • 12
52 Wk Range • 13¼-8¼

Yield • Nil
12-Mo. P/E • 28.5

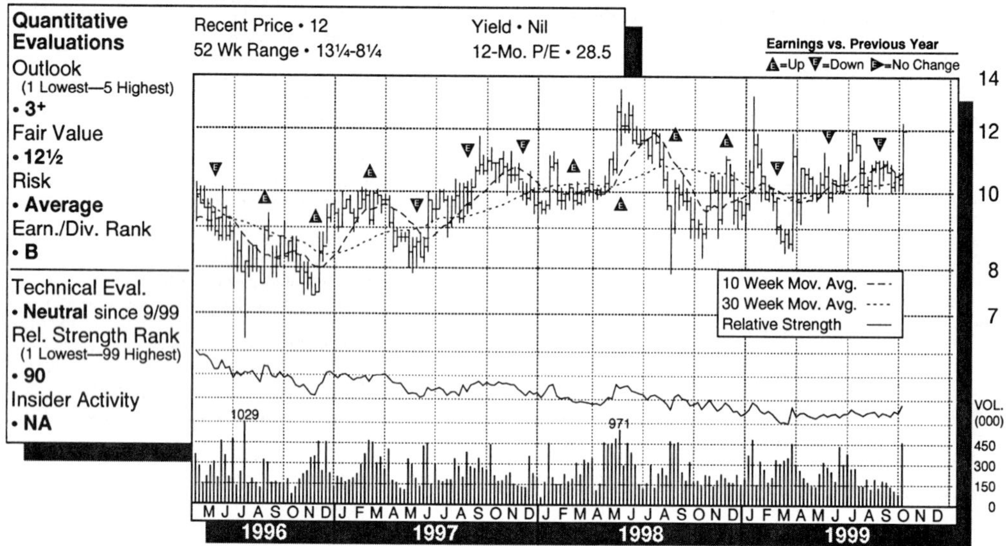

Business Profile - 23-JUN-99

In April 1999, FLOW reported that it is expanding its investment in continuous-flow food processing Fresher Under Pressure technology. The company noted that a high level of interest from major food processors points to the food purification market's potential for growth. FLOW stated that it has received equipment orders for use in purifying juice, baby food, guacamole, salsa and oysters. The company expects FY 00 (Apr.) food purification revenues to be between $7 and $10 million, and that the food purification market will double each year for the next three years.

Operational Review - 23-JUN-99

Based on a preliminary report, sales for FY 99 (Apr.) decreased 7.1%. The gross margin widened, and profit comparisons were aided by the absence of a $4.9 million restructuring charge in FY 98, which was related to the divestiture of two business units. Income from operations advanced 29%. Following well controlled interest and other expense (net), and taxes at 28.0% against 26.2%, net income rose 40%, to $6.7 million ($0.45 a share), from $4.8 million ($0.32).

Stock Performance - 08-OCT-99

In the past 30 trading days, FLOW's shares have increased 17%, compared to a 0.91% fall in the S&P 500. Average trading volume for the past five days was 117,900 shares, compared with the 40-day moving average of 40,426 shares.

Key Stock Statistics

Dividend Rate/Share	Nil	Shareholders	1,258
Shs. outstg. (M)	14.7	Market cap. (B)	$0.176
Avg. daily vol. (M)	0.046	Inst. holdings	50%
Tang. Bk. Value/Share	1.90		
Beta	0.28		

Value of $10,000 invested 5 years ago: $ 14,846

Fiscal Year Ending Apr. 30

	2000	1999	1998	1997	1996	1995
Revenues (Million $)						
1Q	41.26	36.42	47.51	40.93	33.01	24.51
2Q	—	38.38	35.16	41.32	35.62	26.76
3Q	—	33.55	34.46	39.66	35.64	27.19
4Q	—	39.84	42.34	46.28	40.63	31.56
Yr.	—	148.2	159.5	168.2	144.9	110.0
Earnings Per Share ($)						
1Q	**0.09**	**0.12**	**-0.07**	**0.15**	**0.14**	0.12
2Q	—	**0.15**	**0.12**	**0.16**	**0.12**	0.15
3Q	—	**0.10**	**0.12**	**0.09**	**0.08**	0.11
4Q	—	**0.09**	**0.14**	**-0.36**	**0.14**	0.15
Yr.	—	**0.45**	**0.32**	**0.05**	**0.47**	0.53

Next earnings report expected: NA

Dividend Data

No cash dividends have been paid. A "poison pill" stock purchase rights plan was adopted in 1990.

A Division of The McGraw-Hill Companies

Business Summary - 23-JUN-99

Tracing its roots to 1974, when a former research scientist at Boeing began a company at home, today's Flow International Corp. is a leader in developing and manufacturing ultrahigh pressure (UHP) waterjet technology and also provides robotics and assembly systems. The basic technology behind Flow's products is to pressurize water up to 60,000 pounds per square inch (ppi) and then to force it through a tiny opening. Under such conditions, the water can cut soft materials, such as rubber, food, paper and diapers. When small amounts of an abrasive, such as garnet, are added, the water can cut virtually any material, such as stone, glass, composites and metal. The pressurized water can also be used to clean ship hulls and painting equipment.

A more recent product development involves applying the UHP technology to pumpable foods, such as juice, salad dressing, and salsa. By pressuring foods from 50,000 to 100,000 ppi for up to two minutes, the effects of pasteurization can be achieved without heat. Harmful pathogens can be eliminated without removing or reducing beneficial nutritional qualities. In 1998, the company signed an agreement with the Minute Maid Co. to commercialize its technology for use in fruit juice production. Flow expects that because food companies traditionally lease processing equipment, revenues from its food preparation equipment will be modest in 1999.

In addition to its waterjet technology sales, Flow offers aftermarket consumable parts and service. Sales of consumable parts and service accounted for 34% of FY 98 (Apr.) UHP revenues, and overall UHP sales accounted for 90% of Flow's total revenue in FY 98.

In February 1999, Flow noted that year-to-date it had expensed $1.6 million in marketing research and engineering and interest expense on its Fresher Under Pressure technology. Flow has also added over $4 million to fixed assets and inventory to support the Fresher Under Pressure business.

In April 1999, FLOW reported that it had completed the acquisition of ABB Pressure Systems AB, a Swedish supplier of large, bulk ultrahigh-pressure systems to the food industry and a maker of press systems for the automotive and aerospace industries. FLOW expects AB Pressure Systems to add about $20 million to revenues in FY 00 and to be accretive to earnings in FY 00. FLOW also noted in June 1999 that the acquisition establishes it as the only supplier of both bulk and pumpable ultrahigh-pressure food processing systems in the world.

FLOW also noted in April that it is gaining market share for its waterjet technology, despite a 27% decline in the U.S. metal cutting machine tool market in FY 99.

Per Share Data ($) (Year Ended Apr. 30)	1999	1998	1997	1996	1995	1994	1993	1992	1991	1990
Tangible Bk. Val.	1.90	3.01	3.03	2.89	2.54	2.58	2.43	2.30	2.11	2.20
Cash Flow	0.77	0.61	0.54	0.93	0.89	0.45	0.54	0.47	0.14	0.44
Earnings	0.45	0.32	0.05	0.47	0.53	0.18	0.30	0.23	-0.08	0.20
Dividends	Nil	Nil	Nil	Nil	Nil	Nil	Nil	Nil	Nil	Nil
Payout Ratio	Nil	Nil	Nil	Nil	Nil	Nil	Nil	Nil	Nil	Nil
Cal. Yrs.	1998	1997	1996	1995	1994	1993	1992	1991	1990	1989
Prices - High	13 1/2	11 3/4	10 7/8	13 1/4	8 1/2	8 3/4	7 1/4	4 1/8	5	4 3/8
- Low	7 7/8	7 7/8	6 1/2	6 1/2	4 5/8	5	3	1 3/8	1 1/8	2 3/4
P/E Ratio - High	30	37	NM	28	16	49	24	18	NM	22
- Low	17	25	NM	14	9	28	10	6	NM	14
Income Statement Analysis (Million $)										
Revs.	148	159	168	145	110	88.6	79.1	48.4	41.5	46.1
Oper. Inc.	18.0	19.5	21.3	18.6	16.9	7.9	10.3	7.5	3.8	8.5
Depr.	4.9	4.4	7.5	6.9	5.2	3.9	3.4	2.7	2.5	3.0
Int. Exp.	3.2	3.2	3.8	3.5	2.4	1.8	1.4	1.0	1.8	1.7
Pretax Inc.	9.3	6.5	1.0	8.9	9.3	3.1	5.8	4.1	-0.4	3.7
Eff. Tax Rate	28%	26%	25%	20%	17%	18%	28%	25%	NM	33%
Net Inc.	6.7	4.8	0.7	7.1	7.7	2.5	4.2	3.1	-0.5	2.5
Balance Sheet & Other Fin. Data (Million $)										
Cash	10.4	3.0	2.5	3.9	1.1	1.4	0.1	0.8	1.5	0.7
Curr. Assets	120	87.7	90.7	80.8	66.0	55.1	47.4	28.2	28.5	33.8
Total Assets	179	121	133	127	106	78.2	69.3	43.7	41.0	48.4
Curr. Liab.	40.5	27.8	22.6	23.0	21.4	29.7	22.3	12.5	13.2	13.2
LT Debt	64.6	32.1	53.6	45.6	33.4	10.6	12.5	4.4	4.6	10.4
Common Eqty.	64.0	61.2	56.8	57.1	49.8	35.4	31.7	26.6	22.7	23.8
Total Cap.	130	93.4	112	104	84.1	48.5	46.9	31.2	27.7	35.2
Cap. Exp.	8.2	6.6	9.2	8.8	5.6	6.2	7.8	3.9	2.3	4.0
Cash Flow	11.6	9.2	8.2	13.9	12.9	6.4	7.3	5.4	1.6	5.4
Curr. Ratio	3.0	3.2	4.0	3.5	3.1	1.9	2.1	2.3	2.2	2.6
% LT Debt of Cap.	49.8	34.4	47.9	44.0	39.7	21.8	26.7	14.1	16.7	29.6
% Net Inc.of Revs.	4.5	3.0	0.4	4.9	7.0	2.9	5.3	6.4	NM	5.4
% Ret. on Assets	4.5	3.8	0.6	6.1	8.4	3.4	7.1	7.0	NM	6.0
% Ret. on Equity	10.7	8.1	1.3	13.3	17.6	7.3	13.6	10.5	NM	10.9

Data as orig reptd.; bef. results of disc opers/spec. items. Per share data adj. for stk. divs. Bold denotes diluted EPS (FASB 128)-prior periods restated. E-Estimated. NA-Not Available. NM-Not Meaningful. NR-Not Ranked.

Office—23500-64th Ave. South, Kent, WA 98032. **Tel**—(253) 813-3286. **Fax**—(253) 813-3311. **Website**—http://www.flowcorp.com. **Chrmn, Pres, CEO & Investor Contact**—Ronald W. Tarrant (253-850-3500). **EVP & COO**—R. B. Lawrence. **CFO**—S. D. Reichenbach. **Secy**—J. S. Leness. **Dirs**—R. D. Barbaro, D. J. Evans, K. L. Munro, A. I. Prentice, J. M. Ribaudo, K. M. Roberts, S. F. Rorem, R. W. Tarrant, D. D. Thornton. **Transfer Agent & Registrar**—ChaseMellon Shareholder Services LLC, NYC. **Incorporated**—in Washington in 1980; reincorporated in Delaware in 1983. **Empl**— 805. **S&P Analyst:** J.Friendly

STANDARD
&POOR'S
STOCK REPORTS

Footstar, Inc.

NYSE Symbol **FTS**

In S&P SmallCap 600

09-OCT-99 **Industry:** Retail (Specialty)

Summary: This company is a leading retailer of discount footwear and branded athletic footwear and apparel.

S&P Opinion: Hold (★★★)

Recent Price • 32½ | 52 Wk Range • 42⅛-19¼ | Yield • Nil | 12-Mo. P/E • 19.7

Quantitative Evaluations

Outlook (1 Lowest—5 Highest) • **4+**

Fair Value • **54⅛**

Risk • **NA**

Earn./Div. Rank • **NR**

Technical Eval. • **Neutral** since 9/99

Rel. Strength Rank (1 Lowest—99 Highest) • **33**

Insider Activity • **NA**

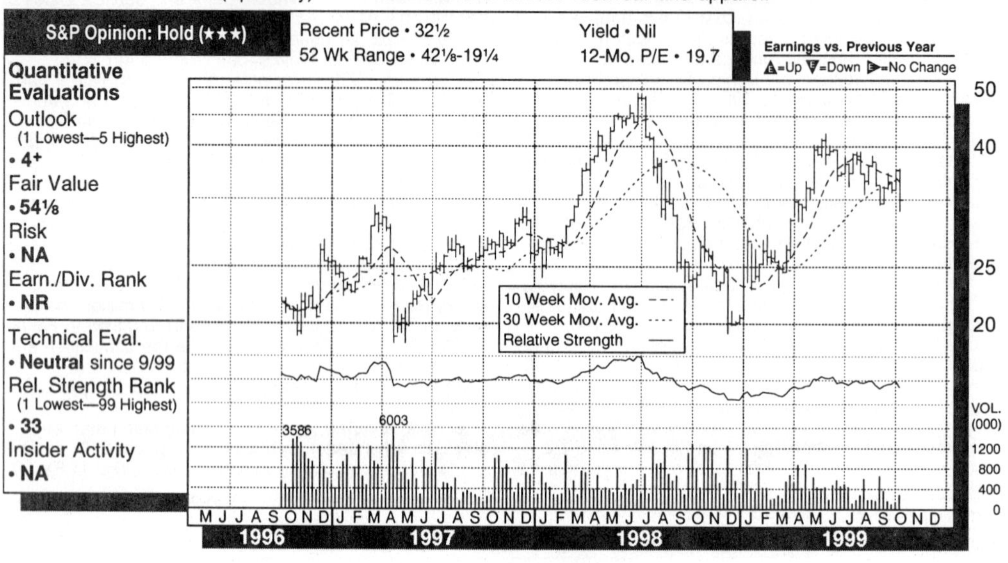

Overview - 12-AUG-99

Due mainly to the strength of the Meldisco division, we expect sales of FTS to grow about 3% in 1999. Meldisco, the company's discount retailer, continues to enjoy strong demand for its Cobbie Cuddlers and Tom McAn brands. Sales should also benefit from the expansion of leased selling space in Kmart stores and stepped-up advertising. The company's Footaction stores, however, have performed poorly along with the rest of the athletic footwear and apparel industry. With no near-term signs of a turnaround in athletic footwear and apparel sales, we expect Footaction sales to be flat to slightly negative in 1999. Margins should widen slightly, as Meldisco leverages its expense base, more than offsetting weakness at Footaction. Continued repurchases of stock should also aid EPS comparisons. Due to a stronger than expected first half of 1999, we are raising our 1999 EPS estimate $0.19 to $2.72 for 1999. Results in 1998 included a $22.7 million (after tax) nonrecurring charge.

Valuation - 12-AUG-99

We attribute the year-to-date 36% rise in FTS's stock price to investor confidence in the Meldisco division and speculation that apparel footwear sales have bottomed. However, the athletic footwear and apparel industry still suffers from too much supply, resulting in severe competition and much promotional activity. Furthermore, the industry suffers from the fashion preference of youngsters for brown shoes over sneakers. We therefore remain cautious about FTS's long-term sales outlook until Footaction reflects some positive trends. While the current P/E ratio of 13x our 1999 EPS estimate is low relative to the broad market, we believe the shares are fairly valued when considering the weak Footaction component. We therefore see no near-term impetus to spark investor interest and are maintaining our hold recommendation.

Key Stock Statistics

S&P EPS Est. 1999	2.72	Tang. Bk. Value/Share	11.43
P/E on S&P Est. 1999	11.9	Beta	NA
S&P EPS Est. 2000	2.99	Shareholders	4,613
Dividend Rate/Share	Nil	Market cap. (B)	$0.696
Shs. outstg. (M)	21.4	Inst. holdings	72%
Avg. daily vol. (M)	0.033		

Value of $10,000 invested 5 years ago: NA

Fiscal Year Ending Dec. 31

	1999	1998	1997	1996	1995	1994
Revenues (Million $)						
1Q	439.1	400.9	376.9	336.9	—	—
2Q	479.0	462.6	426.0	419.0	—	—
3Q	—	472.6	464.0	432.7	—	—
4Q	—	493.0	528.0	483.7	—	—
Yr.	—	1,829	1,795	1,672	1,615	1,613
Earnings Per Share ($)						
1Q	**0.38**	**0.20**	**0.16**	—	—	—
2Q	**0.83**	**0.69**	**0.50**	—	—	—
3Q	—	**0.74**	**0.66**	—	—	—
4Q	—	**-0.31**	**0.70**	—	—	—
Yr.	—	**1.32**	**1.99**	1.90	1.42	—

Next earnings report expected: late October

Dividend Data

The company anticipates that future earnings will be used principally to support operations and finance growth of its business. It does not intend to pay cash dividends on its common shares for the foreseeable future.

Footstar, Inc.

Business Summary - 12-AUG-99

Spun off by Melville Corp. in October 1996, Footstar is a leading retailer of discount footwear and branded athletic footwear and apparel. The company has two principal businesses: Meldisco and Footaction.

Meldisco, which has operated leased footwear departments in discount chains since 1961, is the leading operator of leased footwear departments in the U.S. In 1998, Meldisco accounted for 64% of FTS's net sales and 72% of operating profit. As of January 2, 1999, the company operated 2,538 leased footwear departments in 2,161 Kmart department stores, 357 Rite Aid (formerly Payless Drug Stores and Thrifty Drug Stores), and 20 Tesco department stores (in the Czech Republic, Slovakia and Hungary). In January 1999, the company announced that it will exit its European business operations in conjunction with a company-wide restructuring effort.

In its Kmart departments, Meldisco sells a wide variety of family footwear, including men's, women's and children's dress, casual and athletic footwear, workshoes and slippers. Most of the shoes offered are private label brands, although some brand-name merchandise is sold at discount prices. In its Rite Aid operations, Meldisco leases approximately 100 ft. of selling space to display merchandise.

In 1998, Kmart operations accounted for 97% of Meldisco's net sales and 62% of Footstar's combined net sales. The company stated in February 1999 that it believes Kmart sales will grow in 1999 due to overall improvement in store operations and the relocation of leased shoe space to better store locations.

Footaction, a mall-based specialty retailer with operations dating back to 1976, is a leading retailer of branded athletic footwear, apparel and related accessories. In 1998, Footaction accounted for 36% of FTS's net sales and 28% of the operating profit. As of January 2, 1999, it operated 572 stores in 45 states and the Caribbean. In 1998, the company opened 42 new Footaction stores and remodeled, relocated or expanded 66 existing Footaction stores. It offers the latest and most popular products and uses celebrity endorsements to appeal to its 12 to 24-year old target customers. The stores, which are located in enclosed regional malls, offer a wide variety of footwear including Nike, Reebok, Fila, Adidas, Converse, New Balance, Asics, and outdoor brands such as Timberland. In 1998 footwear, apparel, and accessories accounted for 79%, 16% and 5% respectively of Footaction's net sales.

Footaction attempts to differentiate itself from its competitors by marketing itself as the footwear retailer that is first to offer the latest styles. Working with its primary vendors, the company designs and develops exclusive product lines for its stores. Footaction also attempts to cultivate customer loyalty by offering preferred customer cards which provide customers with individualized mailings and allow Footaction to collect and monitor customer data.

Per Share Data ($) (Year Ended Dec. 31)	1998	1997	1996	1995	1994	1993	1992	1991	1990	1989
Tangible Bk. Val.	11.76	13.45	11.63	NA	NA	NA	NA	NA	NA	NA
Cash Flow	2.64	3.13	2.71	NA	NA	NA	NA	NA	NA	NA
Earnings	1.32	1.99	1.90	1.42	NA	NA	NA	NA	NA	NA
Dividends	Nil	Nil	Nil	Nil	NA	NA	NA	NA	NA	NA
Payout Ratio	Nil	Nil	Nil	Nil	NA	NA	NA	NA	NA	NA
Prices - High	49¼	31¾	27¾	NA	NA	NA	NA	NA	NA	NA
- Low	19¼	18½	19	NA	NA	NA	NA	NA	NA	NA
P/E Ratio - High	37	16	15	NA	NA	NA	NA	NA	NA	NA
- Low	15	9	10	NA	NA	NA	NA	NA	NA	NA
Income Statement Analysis (Million $)										
Revs.	1,829	1,795	NA	NA	NA	NA	NA	NA	NA	NA
Oper. Inc.	165	183	NA	NA	NA	NA	NA	NA	NA	NA
Depr.	33.5	33.5	NA	NA	NA	NA	NA	NA	NA	NA
Int. Exp.	0.6	Nil	NA	NA	NA	NA	NA	NA	NA	NA
Pretax Inc.	104	136	NA	NA	NA	NA	NA	NA	NA	NA
Eff. Tax Rate	31%	30%	NA	NA	NA	NA	NA	NA	NA	NA
Net Inc.	33.5	58.6	58.2	43.5	NA	NA	NA	NA	NA	NA
Balance Sheet & Other Fin. Data (Million $)										
Cash	49.1	152	165	NA	NA	NA	NA	NA	NA	NA
Curr. Assets	431	529	584	NA	NA	NA	NA	NA	NA	NA
Total Assets	685	771	832	NA	NA	NA	NA	NA	NA	NA
Curr. Liab.	269	244	325	NA	NA	NA	NA	NA	NA	NA
LT Debt	Nil	Nil	0.2	NA	NA	NA	NA	NA	NA	NA
Common Eqty.	303	403	384	NA	NA	NA	NA	NA	NA	NA
Total Cap.	371	468	449	NA	NA	NA	NA	NA	NA	NA
Cap. Exp.	58.6	59.1	68.3	NA	NA	NA	NA	NA	NA	NA
Cash Flow	67.0	92.1	83.0	NA	NA	NA	NA	NA	NA	NA
Curr. Ratio	1.6	2.2	1.8	NA	NA	NA	NA	NA	NA	NA
% LT Debt of Cap.	Nil	Nil	0.0	NA	NA	NA	NA	NA	NA	NA
% Net Inc.of Revs.	1.8	3.3	NA	NA	NA	NA	NA	NA	NA	NA
% Ret. on Assets	4.6	7.3	NA	NA	NA	NA	NA	NA	NA	NA
% Ret. on Equity	9.5	14.9	NA	NA	NA	NA	NA	NA	NA	NA

Data as orig reptd.; bef. results of disc opers/spec. items. Per share data adj. for stk. divs. Bold denotes diluted EPS (FASB 128)-prior periods restated. E-Estimated. NA-Not Available. NM-Not Meaningful. NR-Not Ranked.

Office—933 MacArthur Boulevard, Mahwah, NJ 07430. **Tel**—(201) 934-2000. **Website**—http://www.footstar.com **Chrmn & CEO**—J. M. Robinson. **Secy**—M. Richards. **SVP-CFO & Investor Contact**—Carlos E. Alberini (201-760-4008). **Dirs**—R. A. Davies III,.G. S. Day, S. P. Goldstein, T. R. Lautenbach, B. M. Musham, K. S. Olshan, J. M. Robinson. **Transfer Agent**—ChaseMellon Shareholder Services, Ridgefield Park, NJ. **Incorporated**—in Delaware in 1996. **Empl**— 14,979. **S&P Analyst:** Howard Choe

STANDARD
&POOR'S
STOCK REPORTS

Fossil Inc.

NASDAQ Symbol **FOSL**

In S&P SmallCap 600

09-OCT-99

Industry: Consumer (Jewelry, Novelties & Gifts)

Summary: Fossil designs and distributes fashion watches and other accessories. Its products are sold mainly through department stores and other major retailers worldwide.

Quantitative Evaluations

Outlook
(1 Lowest—5 Highest)
• **3-**

Fair Value
• **32¼**

Risk
• **High**

Earn./Div. Rank
• **NR**

Technical Eval.
• **Bearish** since 9/99

Rel. Strength Rank
(1 Lowest—99 Highest)
• **46**

Insider Activity
• **NA**

Recent Price • 28⅛
52 Wk Range • 36⅝-9⅜
Yield • Nil
12-Mo. P/E • 22.0

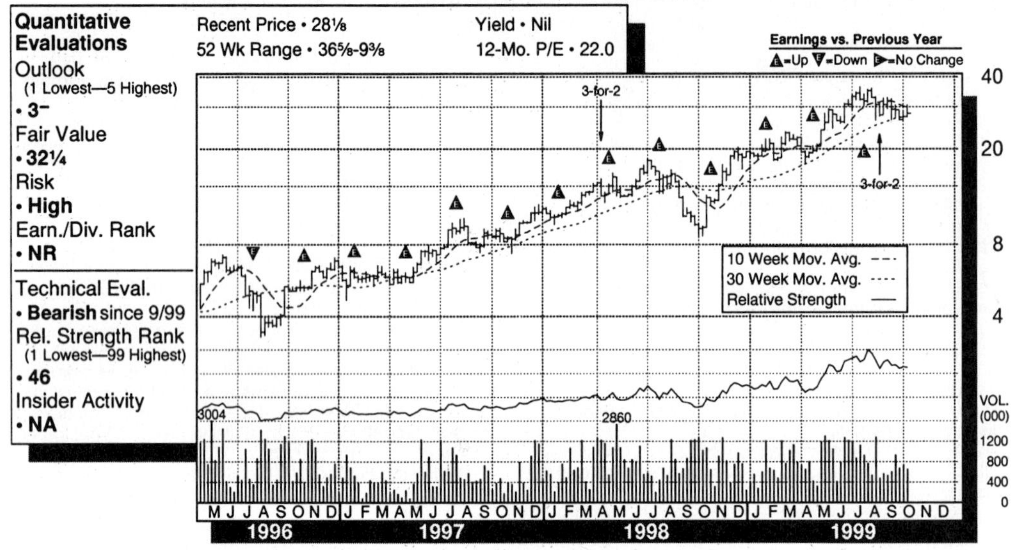

Business Profile - 19-JUL-99

Following a successful holiday season, inventory on hand of FOSSIL brand watches at many of the company's retail customers was below target levels in 1999's first quarter. This allowed the company to ship higher volumes of its watch products than normal retail demand would have warranted. In 1999's second quarter, Fossil expects to record an international-based sale totaling about $7 million of nonbranded watches used as a premium incentive. This sale will inflate the percentage year-to-year sales gain but management believes the sales gains will average closer to 20% in the later half of 1999.

Operational Review - 19-JUL-99

Net sales for the 13 weeks ended April 3, 1999, advanced 46%, year to year. Over one-half of the gain came from FOSSIL brand watches, reflecting increased sales from the core FOSSIL brand watch assortments, sales from the newly introduced BIG TIC line of watches, and from certain refilling of retailers' watch inventories. Double-digit sales growth was recorded in the company's other accessory product line and in certain private label and licensing watch lines. Profitability benefited from a shift in the sales mix toward FOSSIL brand watches and sunglasses and European-based sales, which have higher margins. Pretax income was up 125%. After taxes at 41.1%, versus 40.8%, net income rose 124%, to $10,430,556 ($0.47 a share) from $4,665,982 ($0.22).

Stock Performance - 08-OCT-99

In the past 30 trading days, FOSL's shares have declined 8%, compared to a 0.91% fall in the S&P 500. Average trading volume for the past five days was 129,580 shares, compared with the 40-day moving average of 131,424 shares.

Key Stock Statistics

Dividend Rate/Share	Nil	Shareholders	1,800
Shs. outstg. (M)	31.9	Market cap. (B)	$0.900
Avg. daily vol. (M)	0.149	Inst. holdings	48%
Tang. Bk. Value/Share	4.81		
Beta	2.04		

Value of $10,000 invested 5 years ago: $ 33,379

Fiscal Year Ending Dec. 31

	1999	1998	1997	1996	1995	1994
Revenues (Million $)						
1Q	83.28	56.89	47.45	42.91	35.50	25.43
2Q	90.27	64.36	56.93	45.24	43.34	34.34
3Q	—	82.39	61.01	52.82	43.55	44.53
4Q	—	101.1	79.40	64.93	58.73	57.59
Yr.	—	304.7	244.8	205.9	181.1	161.9
Earnings Per Share ($)						
1Q	**0.31**	**0.15**	**0.10**	**0.08**	0.08	0.07
2Q	**0.29**	**0.17**	**0.12**	**0.09**	0.10	0.08
3Q	—	**0.27**	**0.17**	**0.13**	0.09	0.15
4Q	—	**0.39**	**0.21**	**0.16**	0.13	0.20
Yr.	—	**0.99**	**0.61**	**0.45**	**0.40**	**0.51**

Next earnings report expected: early November

Dividend Data

Amount ($)	Date Decl.	Ex-Div. Date	Stock of Record	Payment Date
3-for-2	Jul. 21	Aug. 18	Aug. 03	Aug. 17 '99

Fossil Inc.

Business Summary - 19-JUL-99

Fossil, Inc. is a leading designer and distributor of contemporary, high quality fashion watches and accessories. The company developed the FOSSIL brand name to convey a distinctive fashion, quality and value message and a brand image reminiscent of "America in the 1950s" that suggests a time of fun, fashion and humor.

Since its inception in 1984, FOSL has evolved from its original flagship FOSSIL watch product into a diversified company offering an extensive line of fashion watches that includes its RELIC and FSL brands, as well as complementary lines of small leather goods, belts, handbags and sunglasses under certain of the company's brands.

The company's watch brands have suggested price point ranges of: $55 - $120 for FOSSIL, $45 - $75 for RELIC, and $30 - $150 for FSL. Fossil believes that one reason for the growth of the moderately priced watch sector has been that fashion-conscious consumers have increasingly come to regard branded fashion watches not only as time pieces but also as fashion accessories. This trend has resulted in consumers owning multiple watches that may differ significantly in terms of style, features and cost.

FOSL has capitalized on the growing awareness of the FOSSIL brand name by entering into various license agreements for other categories of fashion accessories and apparel, such as men's underwear and lounge wear and more recently, outerwear and optical frames under the FOSSIL brand. In addition, the company licenses the brands of other companies in order to further leverage its infrastructure.

Recent new product introductions include: the FOSSIL BLUE line of watches in mid-1996, the BLUE TEQ line in late 1997 and the BIG TIC brand in the fall of 1998. In addition, the company introduced its line of RELIC leather goods in 1997, a line of nylon bags and FSL sport bags in early 1998, and FOSSIL STEEL and FOSSIL BLUE sunwear in 1998.

The company sells its products in approximately 15,000 retail locations in the United States through a diversified distribution network that includes approximately 2,000 department store doors, such as Federated/Macy's, May Department Stores and Dillard's for its FOSSIL brand and JCPenney and Sears for its RELIC brand, as well as approximately 13,000 specialty retail locations. Fossil also sells its products through a network of 37 company-owned stores within the U.S., with nine retail stores located in premier retail malls and 28 outlet stores located in major outlet malls.

Fossil's products are sold to department stores and specialty retail stores in over 80 countries worldwide through company-owned foreign sales subsidiaries and through a network of approximately 50 independently distributors. International and export sales accounted for about 29% of sales in 1998.

Per Share Data ($) (Year Ended Dec. 31)	1998	1997	1996	1995	1994	1993	1992	1991	1990	1989
Tangible Bk. Val.	4.32	3.13	2.33	1.94	1.59	1.06	0.72	NA	NA	NA
Cash Flow	1.12	0.70	0.56	0.49	0.56	0.44	0.16	NA	NA	NA
Earnings	0.99	0.61	0.45	0.40	0.51	0.40	NA	NA	NA	NA
Dividends	Nil	Nil	NA	Nil	Nil	Nil	NA	NA	NA	NA
Payout Ratio	Nil	Nil	Nil	Nil	NA	Nil	NA	NA	NA	NA
Prices - High	20 3/8	11 3/4	7 1/4	11 5/8	13 1/8	9 3/8	NA	NA	NA	NA
- Low	8 5/8	4 5/8	2 7/8	3 1/8	5 1/2	3 3/8	NA	NA	NA	NA
P/E Ratio - High	21	19	16	28	25	23	NA	NA	NA	NA
- Low	9	8	6	7	10	8	NA	NA	NA	NA
Income Statement Analysis (Million $)										
Revs.	305	245	206	181	162	105	73.8	NA	NA	NA
Oper. Inc.	59.8	37.7	27.5	22.9	27.7	17.5	11.6	NA	NA	NA
Depr.	4.4	3.0	3.1	2.5	1.5	0.9	0.4	NA	NA	NA
Int. Exp.	0.2	1.0	1.2	1.1	0.6	0.2	0.6	NA	NA	NA
Pretax Inc.	54.7	32.2	23.0	20.1	24.9	16.7	10.7	NA	NA	NA
Eff. Tax Rate	41%	41%	41%	40%	38%	31%	34%	NA	NA	NA
Net Inc.	32.2	18.9	13.6	12.1	15.3	11.5	7.0	NA	NA	NA
Balance Sheet & Other Fin. Data (Million $)										
Cash	57.3	21.1	12.0	6.0	2.3	6.8	1.9	NA	NA	NA
Curr. Assets	166	114	97.6	78.1	66.5	39.6	23.7	NA	NA	NA
Total Assets	194	140	119	97.0	80.4	46.5	27.6	NA	NA	NA
Curr. Liab.	57.3	43.1	37.8	28.9	25.1	11.9	11.7	NA	NA	NA
LT Debt	Nil	Nil	4.4	NA	NA	NA	NA	NA	NA	NA
Common Eqty.	135	95.3	74.6	61.3	48.9	33.0	15.0	NA	NA	NA
Total Cap.	137	96.5	81.3	NA	NA	NA	NA	NA	NA	NA
Cap. Exp.	6.3	7.4	4.3	6.2	NA	NA	NA	NA	NA	NA
Cash Flow	36.6	22.0	16.7	14.5	16.8	12.4	7.5	NA	NA	NA
Curr. Ratio	2.9	2.6	2.6	2.7	2.7	3.3	2.0	NA	NA	NA
% LT Debt of Cap.	Nil	NA	5.5	NA	NA	NA	NA	NA	NA	NA
% Net Inc.of Revs.	10.6	7.7	6.6	6.7	9.5	10.9	9.5	NA	NA	NA
% Ret. on Assets	19.3	14.7	12.6	13.6	24.2	31.0	NA	NA	NA	NA
% Ret. on Equity	27.9	22.3	20.0	21.9	37.5	47.8	NA	NA	NA	NA

Data as orig reptd.; bef. results of disc opers/spec. items. Per share data adj. for stk. divs. Bold denotes diluted EPS (FASB 128)-prior periods restated. E-Estimated. NA-Not Available. NM-Not Meaningful. NR-Not Ranked.

Office—2280 N. Greenville Ave., Richardson, TX 75082. **Tel**—(972) 234-2525. **Website**—http://www.FOSSIL.com **Chrmn & CEO**—T. Kartsotis. **Pres & COO**—K. N. Kartsotis. **SVP-Secy**—T. R. Tunnlell. **EVP-CFO, Treas & Investor Contact**—Randy S. Kercho (972 699-6811). **Dirs**—K. W. Anderson, M. W. Barnes, A. J. Gold, T. Kartsotis, K. N. Kartsotis, J. S. Shroff, D. J. Stone. **Transfer Agent & Registrar**—ChaseMellon Shareholder Services, Ridgefield Park, NJ. **Incorporated**—in Delaware in 1991. **Empl**— 535. **S&P Analyst:** J. J. Schemitsch

Franklin Covey

NYSE Symbol **FC**

In S&P SmallCap 600

09-OCT-99

Industry:
Consumer (Jewelry, Novelties & Gifts)

Summary: This company (formerly Franklin Quest) provides time management products and training seminars for corporations, government agencies and the general public.

Quantitative Evaluations

Outlook
(1 Lowest—5 Highest)
• **NA**

Fair Value
• **NA**

Risk
• **NA**

Earn./Div. Rank
• **B**

Technical Eval.
• **Bearish** since 9/99

Rel. Strength Rank
(1 Lowest—99 Highest)
• **40**

Insider Activity
• **Favorable**

Recent Price • 7¼
52 Wk Range • 19⅞-5⅞
Yield • Nil
12-Mo. P/E • 5.8

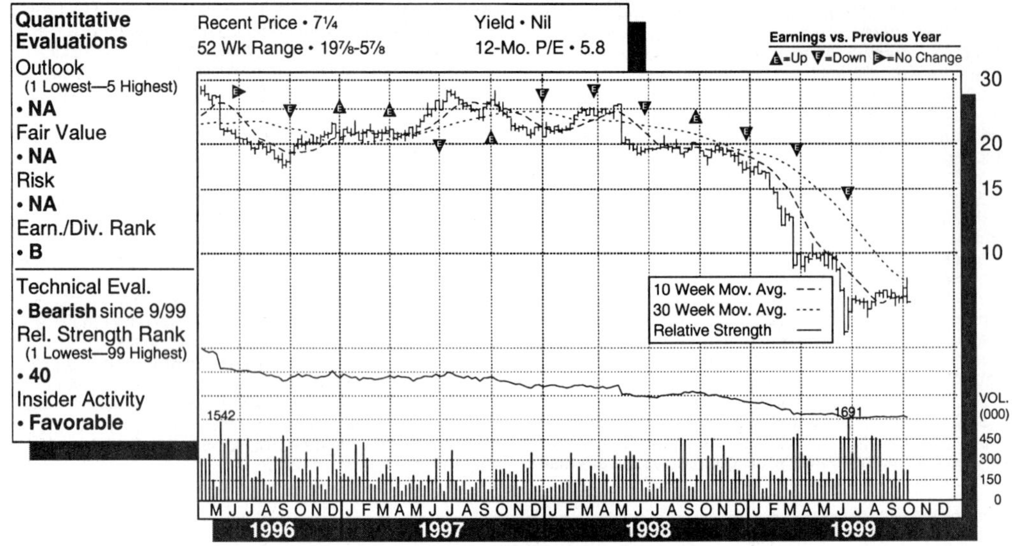

Business Profile - 28-JUN-99

Consumer product sales improved in the third quarter of FY 99 (Apr.) on a 6% increase in same retail store sales. The sales increase was led primarily by the Palm electronic planner, manufactured by 3COM, and bundled with the Franklin Planner Software. In June 1999, FC completed the placement of $75 million of 10% preferred stock with Knowledge Capital Investment Group, a private investment firm. The preferred stock is convertible into common stock at $14 per share. FC intends to offer existing shareholders the opportunity to purchase up to $75 million of convertible preferred having the same terms as the preferred stock purchased by Knowledge Capital later in 1999.

Operational Review - 28-JUN-99

Sales in the nine months ended May 29, 1999, fell 0.8%, year to year, as a decrease in training and education revenues outweighed strength in international and consumer product sales. Profitability declined on higher operating expenses and an inventory write-off; operating income declined 23%. Restricted by higher depreciation and amortization charges, greater interest expense and taxes at 42.0%, versus 41.5%, income before the cumulative effect of an accounting change plunged 51%, to $12.9 million ($0.60 a share, on 15% fewer shares), from $26.5 million ($1.05). Results in the FY 98 period exclude a charge of $0.08 a share related to a change in accounting methods.

Stock Performance - 08-OCT-99

In the past 30 trading days, FC's shares have declined 7%, compared to a 0.91% fall in the S&P 500. Average trading volume for the past five days was 43,640 shares, compared with the 40-day moving average of 45,672 shares.

Key Stock Statistics

Dividend Rate/Share	Nil	Shareholders	360
Shs. outstg. (M)	20.4	Market cap. (B)	$0.149
Avg. daily vol. (M)	0.039	Inst. holdings	52%
Tang. Bk. Value/Share	2.93		
Beta	0.57		

Value of $10,000 invested 5 years ago: $ 2,089

Fiscal Year Ending Aug. 31

	1999	1998	1997	1996	1995	1994
Revenues (Million $)						
1Q	140.4	143.9	102.4	91.85	71.06	56.44
2Q	137.1	138.6	106.0	93.60	74.67	56.17
3Q	109.3	107.5	79.80	72.47	59.38	48.91
4Q	—	156.6	145.1	74.07	72.01	54.42
Yr.	—	546.6	433.3	332.0	277.1	215.9
Earnings Per Share ($)						
1Q	**0.50**	0.53	0.62	0.57	0.56	0.46
2Q	**0.31**	**0.49**	0.63	0.57	0.53	0.41
3Q	**-0.22**	**0.02**	0.15	0.28	0.28	0.24
4Q	—	**0.67**	0.37	0.10	0.35	0.30
Yr.	—	**1.70**	**1.76**	1.53	1.71	1.40

Next earnings report expected: NA

Dividend Data

No cash dividends have been paid.

Franklin Covey Co.

Business Summary - 28-JUN-99

Franklin Covey Co. (formerly Franklin Quest Co.) is the world's leading productivity and time management training company. In FY 98 (Aug.), FC provided products and services to 80 of the Fortune 100 companies and to over 75% of Fortune 500 firms. In addition, the company serves both the governmental and educational markets. Franklin Covey also offers its products and services in 34 countries through company-owned or licensed operations.

On May 30, 1997, Franklin Quest acquired for about 5,000,000 common shares Covey Leadership Center, whose products include books, seminars, videos, corporate consulting and training programs. In conjunction with the acquisition, the name of the company was changed to Franklin Covey Co. The merger broadened the range of products and services to include Covey's leadership programs, "The 7 Habits of Highly Effective People" and "Principle-Centered Leadership."

FC's seminars and products are based upon its proprietary time management system, which it believes enables individuals to better manage their time by identifying goals and prioritizing tasks. The linchpin of this system is the Franklin Day Planner. In 1991, FC developed its Ascend software product, which can be used by itself or in conjunction with the Day Planner. Historically, a large portion of the users of FC's products repurchase the planner each year, generating substantial recurring sales. Sales of the planner and related accessories accounted for 63% of FC's total revenues in FY 98.

FC also provides training, consulting services and products designed to improve written and oral business communication skills. Through 144 domestic and 39 international training consultants, FC offers a range of workshops that trained more than 750,000 individuals in FY 98. These services comprised 32% of total revenues in FY 98.

Through the acquisition of Publishers Press in 1994, FC acquired greater control over printing of the materials for the Franklin Planner and of other related products. Publishers Press also provides book and commercial printing services to clients in the western United States and generated 5% of FY 98 sales.

Beginning in late 1985, FC began opening retail stores in areas of high client density. As of August 31, 1998, FC had 120 domestic locations in 36 states and the District of Columbia. The stores average approximately 2,000 square feet and are stocked almost entirely with Franklin Covey products.

In November 1998, FC completed an agreement to expand its retail distribution by selling selected planners and binders through Office Depot (about 580 retail stores). Management believes that increased revenues from this channel will more than offset anticipated lower margins.

Per Share Data ($)

(Year Ended Aug. 31)	1998	1997	1996	1995	1994	1993	1992	1991	1990	1989
Tangible Bk. Val.	3.21	13.49	8.80	8.11	6.61	5.55	4.15	3.64	NA	NA
Cash Flow	3.27	2.82	2.26	2.22	1.64	1.30	1.08	0.70	0.25	0.12
Earnings	1.70	1.76	1.53	1.71	1.40	1.10	0.93	0.61	0.18	0.09
Dividends	Nil	Nil	Nil	Nil	Nil	Nil	Nil	NA	NA	NA
Payout Ratio	Nil	Nil	Nil	Nil	Nil	Nil	Nil	NA	NA	NA
Prices - High	$25\frac{3}{4}$	$28\frac{1}{4}$	$29\frac{1}{8}$	$35\frac{7}{8}$	$40\frac{1}{2}$	$35\frac{1}{4}$	$21\frac{7}{8}$	NA	NA	NA
- Low	$16\frac{1}{4}$	$20\frac{1}{8}$	$17\frac{1}{8}$	$17\frac{7}{8}$	$27\frac{1}{4}$	$19\frac{1}{8}$	$14\frac{5}{8}$	NA	NA	NA
P/E Ratio - High	15	16	19	21	29	32	24	NA	NA	NA
- Low	10	11	11	10	19	17	16	NA	NA	NA

Income Statement Analysis (Million $)

	1998	1997	1996	1995	1994	1993	1992	1991	1990	1989
Revs.	547	433	332	277	216	165	121	82.0	53.0	31.0
Oper. Inc.	117	96.4	72.9	73.6	54.9	41.9	30.5	18.7	8.2	3.9
Depr.	38.6	23.6	16.2	11.7	5.3	4.3	2.7	1.5	1.3	0.6
Int. Exp.	8.3	2.3	0.6	0.6	0.9	1.1	1.3	1.2	1.4	0.6
Pretax Inc.	72.0	66.4	58.2	64.2	51.0	38.7	27.4	16.6	5.7	2.9
Eff. Tax Rate	42%	41%	41%	40%	39%	40%	39%	35%	39%	39%
Net Inc.	42.1	38.9	34.2	38.7	30.9	23.4	16.6	10.8	3.5	1.8

Balance Sheet & Other Fin. Data (Million $)

	1998	1997	1996	1995	1994	1993	1992	1991	1990	1989
Cash	27.8	20.4	24.0	35.0	49.7	63.5	58.2	53.0	NA	NA
Curr. Assets	175	170	113	120	113	108	89.4	NA	NA	NA
Total Assets	597	572	268	263	198	145	114	102	NA	NA
Curr. Liab.	93.4	86.9	28.6	32.2	28.0	23.5	20.6	NA	NA	NA
LT Debt	126	94.1	5.5	4.5	7.6	8.2	10.6	8.0	NA	NA
Common Eqty.	342	355	232	224	162	113	82.4	71.1	NA	NA
Total Cap.	504	485	240	231	170	121	93.1	79.1	NA	NA
Cap. Exp.	39.2	20.2	19.4	32.7	24.6	13.0	16.3	4.4	4.0	4.9
Cash Flow	80.8	62.4	50.4	50.4	36.2	27.7	19.3	12.4	4.8	2.3
Curr. Ratio	1.9	2.0	4.0	3.7	4.0	4.6	4.3	NA	NA	NA
% LT Debt of Cap.	25.0	19.4	2.3	1.9	4.5	6.8	11.4	10.1	NA	NA
% Net Inc.of Revs.	7.7	9.0	10.3	14.0	14.3	14.2	13.7	13.2	6.6	5.7
% Ret. on Assets	7.2	9.2	12.9	16.8	17.9	17.9	20.1	NA	NA	NA
% Ret. on Equity	12.1	13.2	15.0	20.0	22.3	23.7	32.3	NA	NA	NA

Data as orig reptd.; bef. results of disc opers/spec. items. Per share data adj. for stk. divs. Bold denotes diluted EPS (FASB 128)-prior periods restated. E-Estimated. NA-Not Available. NM-Not Meaningful. NR-Not Ranked.

Office—2200 West Parkway Blvd., Salt Lake City, UT 84119-2331. **Tel**—(801) 975-1776. **Website**—http://www.franklincovey.com **Chrmn**—H. W. Smith. **Co-Chrmn**—S. R. Covey. **CEO, Pres & COO**—J. Rowberry. **CFO**—J. L. Theler. **Secy**—V. J. Christensen. **Investor Contact**—Richard Putnam. **Dirs**—R. F. Bennett, B. B. Campbell, S. M. R. Covey, S. R. Covey, R. H. Daines, E. J. Garn, D. G. Heiner, T. H. Lenagh, J. C. Peterson, J. H. Rowberry, H. W. Smith, E. Kay Stepp, S. Wheelwright, R. A. Whitman. **Transfer Agent & Registrar**—Zions First National Bank, Salt Lake City. **Incorporated**—In Utah in 1983. **Empl**— 4,247. **S&P Analyst:** Jordan Horoschak

STANDARD
&POOR'S
STOCK REPORTS

Fremont General

NYSE Symbol **FMT**
In S&P SmallCap 600

09-OCT-99

Industry:
Insurance (Property-Casualty)

Summary: Through subsidiaries, this company provides insurance and financial services, including workers' compensation, malpractice and life insurance and asset-based lending.

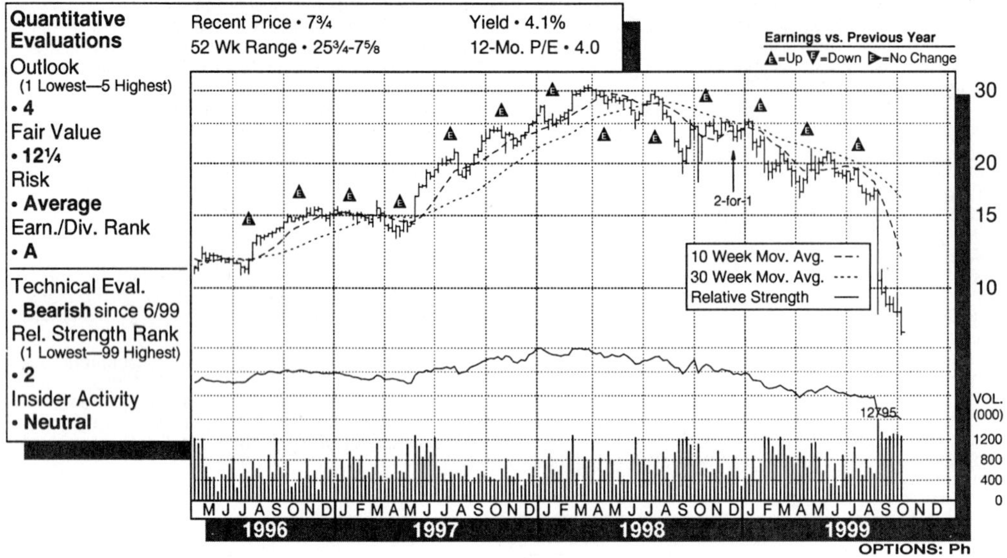

Business Profile - 14-MAY-99

In February 1999, Fremont stated that its business strategy includes achieving income balance and geographic diversity among its business units in order to limit its exposure to industry, market and regional concentrations. The strategy also includes growing its business through new business development and acquisitions. Consistent with this strategy, Fremont General acquired UNICARE Specialty Services, Inc. ($425 million in assets), for $110 million in cash in September 1998. During the first three months of 1999, the combined ratio improved slightly to 96.3%, from 96.9% a year earlier. The company also stated in February 1999 that it had observed a moderation of price competition in California and Illinois, but was uncertain whether this moderation will continue.

Operational Review - 14-MAY-99

Total revenues advanced 14% in the first three months of 1999, year to year, largely on higher loan interest resulting from the growth in the average loan portfolio, as well as an increase in premiums earned. Property and casualty income rose 3.0% to $42.3 million, while financial services income increased 26% to $16.4 million. Other interest and corporate expenses rose 7.3%. After taxes at 33.0%, versus 32.8%, net income increased 8.4%, to $34.3 million ($0.49 per share), from $31.7 million ($0.45).

Stock Performance - 08-OCT-99

In the past 30 trading days, FMT's shares have declined 25%, compared to a 0.91% fall in the S&P 500. Average trading volume for the past five days was 392,100 shares, compared with the 40-day moving average of 693,900 shares.

Key Stock Statistics

Dividend Rate/Share	0.32	Shareholders	1,454
Shs. outstg. (M)	70.1	Market cap. (B)	$0.547
Avg. daily vol. (M)	0.433	Inst. holdings	55%
Tang. Bk. Value/Share	13.69		
Beta	1.20		

Value of $10,000 invested 5 years ago: $ 11,831

Fiscal Year Ending Dec. 31

	1999	1998	1997	1996	1995	1994
Revenues (Million $)						
1Q	298.8	263.3	194.7	203.6	199.2	156.1
2Q	336.1	238.3	206.2	199.7	253.0	158.0
3Q	—	253.1	267.3	197.4	238.5	173.8
4Q	—	282.8	306.1	195.1	233.2	165.3
Yr.	—	1,038	974.3	795.8	923.8	653.1
Earnings Per Share ($)						
1Q	**0.49**	**0.46**	0.38	**0.30**	0.28	0.26
2Q	**0.50**	**0.47**	0.38	**0.35**	0.33	0.27
3Q	—	**0.49**	0.42	**0.35**	0.35	0.27
4Q	—	**0.49**	**0.44**	0.36	0.35	0.28
Yr.	—	**1.90**	**1.61**	**1.36**	**1.09**	**0.91**

Next earnings report expected: early November

Dividend Data (Dividends have been paid since 1977.)

Amount ($)	Date Decl.	Ex-Div. Date	Stock of Record	Payment Date
2-for-1	Nov. 12	Dec. 11	Nov. 20	Dec. 10 '98
0.080	Feb. 11	Mar. 29	Mar. 31	Apr. 30 '99
0.080	May. 18	Jun. 28	Jun. 30	Jul. 30 '99
0.080	Aug. 12	Sep. 28	Sep. 30	Oct. 29 '99

Fremont General Corporation

Business Summary - 14-MAY-99

Fremont General Corp. (FMT) began the 1990s as an underwriter of workers' compensation insurance operating almost exclusively in California. However, through acquisitions, it has become one of the largest underwriters of workers' compensation in the nation, and, since 1990, it has also built a complementary financial services business that contributed about one-quarter of its income in 1998. Although operations in California and Illinois remain significant (65% of total inforce premiums in 1998), the addition of Industrial Indemnity in 1997 further diversified the company geographically. This product and market diversification served the company well in 1998. Despite California's abandonment at the start of 1995 of minimum rates for workers' compensation premiums, a legislative move that precipitated severe price competition among carriers, FMT achieved a 17% increase in property and casualty pretax income in 1998.

Workers' compensation is a statutory system requiring employers to buy insurance or self-insure in order to provide workers with medical care and other benefits for work-related injuries or illnesses. Generally, employers provide for this potential liability by purchasing workers' compensation insurance from insurance carriers such as the company. Since the adoption of an "open" rating system in California in 1995, insurance companies there have set significantly lower premium rates, hurting profitability on the company's California policies, and causing it to withdraw from this market in 1995 and 1996. In 1997, FMT saw an emerging trend toward a more orderly market. Determined to survive recent consolidation in the workers' compensation industry as it pursues its key geographical diversification strategy, FMT acquired two workers' compensation providers in the summer of 1997. Industrial Indemnity Holdings, Inc., the larger of the two companies acquired, was purchased for $365 million in cash and the assumption of $79 million of debt.

Real estate lending operations began in 1990, with the acquisition of a California thrift and loan and now serve more than 53,000 deposit accounts through 14 branch offices. The loan portfolio of the real estate lending operation has grown from $807.5 million at the end of 1994 to $2.1 billion at the end of 1998, due primarily to increased loan originations, and, to a lesser extent, the purchase of loan portfolios from other financial institutions. FMT originates real estate loans nationwide through independent loan brokers, through its own marketing representatives and through bulk purchase.

In September 1998, Fremont General acquired UNICARE Specialty Services, Inc. ($425 million in assets), the workers' compensation unit of Wellpoint Health Networks Inc., one of the nation's largest publicly traded managed care companies, for $110 million in cash.

Per Share Data ($) (Year Ended Dec. 31)	1998	1997	1996	1995	1994	1993	1992	1991	1990	1989
Tangible Bk. Val.	11.24	9.88	8.76	8.41	6.35	6.67	6.92	5.18	4.57	4.11
Oper. Earnings	NA	NA	NA	NA	NA	NA	NA	NA	NA	NA
Earnings	1.90	1.61	1.63	1.30	1.08	0.93	0.86	0.78	0.64	0.44
Dividends	0.30	0.30	0.30	0.26	0.23	0.22	0.20	0.17	0.16	0.14
Payout Ratio	16%	19%	18%	20%	21%	24%	23%	22%	25%	32%
Prices - High	31 1/8	27 5/8	15 3/4	12 3/8	7 7/8	8 3/4	7	5 1/8	4 1/2	4 1/8
- Low	18	13 1/4	10 3/4	5 3/4	6 1/2	6 3/8	3 3/8	2 3/4	2 1/16	2 7/16
P/E Ratio - High	16	17	10	10	7	9	8	7	7	9
- Low	9	8	7	4	6	7	4	4	3	6

Income Statement Analysis (Million $)	1998	1997	1996	1995	1994	1993	1992	1991	1990	1989
Premium Inc.	552	601	487	607	448	470	429	434	430	350
Net Invest. Inc.	193	150	124	120	77.0	77.0	71.0	74.0	83.0	80.0
Oth. Revs.	293	223	185	197	128	104	99	73.3	60.7	40.5
Total Revs.	1,038	974	796	924	653	651	599	581	573	467
Pretax Inc.	197	159	128	100	81.6	64.3	48.6	41.0	39.0	22.2
Net Oper. Inc.	NA	NA	NA	NA	NA	NA	NA	NA	NA	NA
Net Inc.	133	108	87.3	68.0	55.8	42.7	35.2	32.1	26.1	17.7

Balance Sheet & Other Fin. Data (Million $)	1998	1997	1996	1995	1994	1993	1992	1991	1990	1989
Cash & Equiv.	124	65.0	82.2	70.0	44.7	48.6	62.6	41.8	47.7	64.6
Premiums Due	184	146	99	108	48.6	76.7	64.8	62.0	64.0	71.0
Invest. Assets: Bonds	1,647	2,059	1,124	1,659	697	996	780	770	761	994
Invest. Assets: Stocks	500	379	355	277	190	57.0	Nil	Nil	Nil	Nil
Invest. Assets: Loans	2,958	1,984	1,688	1,499	1,441	846	689	520	432	188
Invest. Assets: Total	5,345	2,443	3,172	3,437	2,330	1,902	1,472	1,293	1,205	1,195
Deferred Policy Costs	45.0	38.0	25.6	76.6	59.3	55.2	57.5	60.7	59.6	54.9
Total Assets	7,370	6,091	4,308	4,477	3,067	2,601	2,080	1,964	1,982	1,489
Debt	1,013	717	653	765	645	530	309	249	187	214
Common Eqty.	951	833	559	498	351	369	281	210	187	165
Prop. & Cas. Loss Ratio	60.8	64.7	68.9	76.0	63.1	70.0	80.4	72.7	73.7	64.6
Prop. & Cas. Expense Ratio	34.5	27.5	25.9	24.5	23.4	21.3	22.5	24.5	24.4	24.4
Prop. & Cas. Combined Ratio	96.2	93.0	94.8	100.0	86.5	91.3	102.9	97.2	98.1	89.0
% Return On Revs.	12.8	11.1	11.0	7.4	8.5	6.6	5.9	5.5	4.6	3.8
% Ret. on Equity	14.9	15.6	16.5	16.1	15.5	13.3	14.3	16.2	14.8	11.0

Data as orig reptd.; bef. results of disc opers/spec. items. Per share data adj. for stk. divs. Bold denotes diluted EPS (FASB 128)-prior periods restated. E-Estimated. NA-Not Available. NM-Not Meaningful. NR-Not Ranked.

Office—2020 Santa Monica Blvd., Suite 600, Santa Monica, CA 90404. **Tel**—(310) 315-5500. **Chrmn & CEO**—J. A. McIntyre. **Pres & COO**—L. J. Rampino. **EVP, Treas, CFO & Investor Contact**—Wayne R. Bailey. **Secy**—A. W. Faigin. **Dirs**—W. R. Bailey, H. I. Flournoy, C. D. Kranwinkle, J. A. McIntyre, D. W. Morrisroe, L. J. Rampino, D. C. Ross. **Transfer Agent & Registrar**—ChaseMellon Shareholder Services, Ridgefield Park, NJ. **Incorporated**—in Nevada in 1972. **Empl**— 3,320. **S&P Analyst:** J. Rudy

STANDARD
&POOR'S
STOCK REPORTS

Fritz Companies

NASDAQ Symbol **FRTZ**

In S&P SmallCap 600

09-OCT-99

Industry:
Air Freight

Summary: This company provides integrated global transportation and distribution services encompassing ocean and air freight forwarding, customs brokerage and warehousing.

Quantitative Evaluations

Outlook
(1 Lowest—5 Highest)
• **4-**

Fair Value
• **15⅞**

Risk
• **High**

Earn./Div. Rank
• **NR**

Technical Eval.
• **Bearish** since 9/99

Rel. Strength Rank
(1 Lowest—99 Highest)
• **39**

Insider Activity
• **Neutral**

Recent Price • 10¼
52 Wk Range • 13-6¼
Yield • Nil
12-Mo. P/E • 30.1

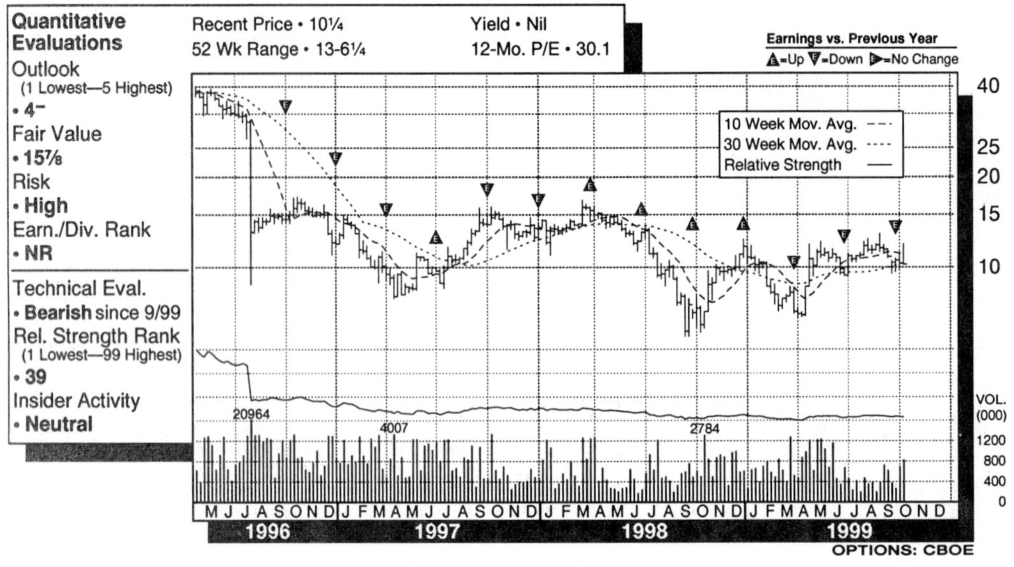

Business Profile - 16-AUG-99

This leading transportation and logistics services provider has spent the past several years restructuring its operations. FRTZ has deliberately slowed its acquisition pace while it reins in its costs and tightens controls over credit management and collection procedures. FRTZ also is vigorously pursuing a new pricing strategy to better match costs with revenues. Though profitability has improved since 1997, earnings in FY 99 (May) were restrained by costs related to Year 2000 compliance and its new global transportation system. As of April 1999, FRTZ's chairman and CEO, Lynn C. Fritz, owned 35.8% of the common shares.

Operational Review - 16-AUG-99

For the year ended May 31, 1999, net revenues advanced 3.5%. Improvement was recorded in ocean and air freight forwarding and warehousing operations, partly offset by lower customs brokerage revenues due to a large reduction in export shipments. Margins narrowed as a result of higher labor costs associated with Y2K compliance and the company's new global transportation and financial systems; operating income increased fractionally. Following a foreign exchange loss of $6.1 million, reversing a $1.9 million gain, net income declined 26%, to $13.5 million ($0.37 a share) from $18.1 million ($0.50).

Stock Performance - 08-OCT-99

In the past 30 trading days, FRTZ's shares have declined 12%, compared to a 0.91% fall in the S&P 500. Average trading volume for the past five days was 164,000 shares, compared with the 40-day moving average of 103,377 shares.

Key Stock Statistics

Dividend Rate/Share	Nil	Shareholders	615
Shs. outstg. (M)	36.4	Market cap. (B)	$0.372
Avg. daily vol. (M)	0.107	Inst. holdings	54%
Tang. Bk. Value/Share	4.16		
Beta	1.25		

Value of $10,000 invested 5 years ago: $ 7,676

Fiscal Year Ending May 31

	2000	1999	1998	1997	1996	1995
Revenues (Million $)						
1Q	150.7	145.2	139.2	129.7	115.7	–
2Q	—	153.7	145.2	130.8	119.0	—
3Q	—	134.9	132.3	118.0	103.8	—
4Q	—	144.2	141.6	130.9	119.1	—
Yr.	—	578.0	558.3	509.4	457.6	165.7
Earnings Per Share ($)						
1Q	**0.16**	**0.19**	0.11	0.22	0.36	–
2Q	—	**0.24**	0.19	0.26	0.36	—
3Q	—	**-0.08**	**0.07**	-0.48	0.09	—
4Q	—	**0.03**	**0.13**	Nil	-0.10	—
Yr.	—	**0.37**	**0.50**	**0.01**	**0.71**	-0.26

Next earnings report expected: late December

Dividend Data

No cash dividends have been paid to the public. A two-for-one common stock split was effected in 1995.

A Division of The McGraw-Hill Companies

Fritz Companies, Inc.

Business Summary - 16-AUG-99

A third-party provider of transportation and logistics services, Fritz Companies (FRTZ) is a technology and communications-driven company, having no assets in transportation equipment. FRTZ embarked on a major acquisition binge during the early 1990s, resulting in a network of 480 offices in 115 countries. Its focus now is to reclaim its leadership in technology and build the business of its existing network. Nearly 50% of FRTZ's revenues in FY 99 (May) were derived from international operations.

FRTZ is the largest customs broker in the U.S. (accounting for 28% of revenues in FY 99). Customs brokerage services also are provided in Australia, Canada, the U.K., Mexico and other parts of Latin America. As a customs broker, FRTZ coordinates all steps in the movement of imported goods via ocean or air modes. Its services include the preparation of all documentation required for the import of merchandise, obtaining customs bonds, arranging payment of collect freight charges and depositing import duties with the U.S. Customs Service. FRTZ also helps customers obtain refunds, known as drawback, when their products are re-exported. Through its "Automated Broker Interface," clients can monitor their shipments and electronically interact on-line with FRTZ.

FRTZ is one of the largest U.S. forwarders of international ocean and air freight (22% and 29%, respectively, of net revenue in FY 99). A forwarder consolidates many small shipments bound for a single destination, procuring transportation at a discount to the fee per pound charged to its clients. Fritz operates both as an agent and an indirect air carrier or non-vessel operating common carrier.

FRTZ established its network of forwarders in recent years through acquisitions. The acquisition pace has slowed as FRTZ's global network is essentially complete. FRTZ's shares fell sharply in 1996 when it developed a severe case of indigestion accompanying the acquisition of Intertrans in May 1995.

The company invested heavily in software development in preparing for the integration of several domestic and international systems into one integrated system called Global Business System (GBS). GBS is essentially an expanded version of the Fritz Logistics Expediting System, which enables customers to track the flow of goods throughout the transportation process.

FRTZ also provides a wide variety of warehousing, logistics and distribution services (21% of revenues) for import and export customers utilizing some 7.3 million sq. ft. of primarily leased space. FRTZ's warehouses are a mixture of multi-client and dedicated facilities. Some of the services offered include receiving, packaging, deconsolidation, cargo loading and unloading, and inventory management.

Per Share Data ($) (Year Ended May 31)	1999	1998	1997	1996	1995	1994	1993	1992	1991	1990
Tangible Bk. Val.	4.16	3.83	3.50	4.07	3.34	2.76	1.48	0.90	-1.24	-1.36
Cash Flow	1.13	1.23	0.70	1.26	-0.06	1.25	0.86	1.01	0.70	0.52
Earnings	0.37	0.50	0.01	0.70	-0.26	0.86	0.66	0.64	0.35	0.29
Dividends	Nil	Nil	Nil	Nil	Nil	Nil	Nil	Nil	Nil	Nil
Payout Ratio	Nil	Nil	Nil	Nil	Nil	Nil	Nil	Nil	Nil	Nil
Cal. Yrs.	1998	1997	1996	1995	1994	1993	1992	1991	1990	1989
Prices - High	16 3/4	16	42 1/4	23 5/8	23 5/8	15 1/4	13 3/8	NA	NA	NA
- Low	5 7/8	7 7/8	8 3/4	13	13	10 1/4	7 1/2	NA	NA	NA
P/E Ratio - High	45	32	NM	34	NM	18	20	NA	NA	NA
- Low	16	16	NM	19	NM	12	11	NA	NA	NA
Income Statement Analysis (Million $)										
Revs.	578	558	509	458	165	516	342	249	121	108
Oper. Inc.	52.6	52.2	27.5	73.4	24.2	40.3	25.3	20.7	17.8	13.7
Depr.	27.5	26.4	24.6	20.2	6.5	8.9	4.2	3.7	5.4	3.6
Int. Exp.	Nil	Nil	Nil	NA	NA	2.2	0.3	0.9	3.2	2.6
Pretax Inc.	19.8	26.6	0.5	38.4	-12.5	30.1	21.6	16.2	9.1	7.5
Eff. Tax Rate	32%	32%	35%	35%	NM	35%	35%	14%	40%	40%
Net Inc.	13.5	18.1	0.3	25.0	-8.3	19.6	14.0	13.1	5.4	4.5
Balance Sheet & Other Fin. Data (Million $)										
Cash	50.6	53.9	43.4	86.4	74.3	39.8	8.3	19.8	14.9	13.5
Curr. Assets	482	500	496	520	422	291	152	136	121	103
Total Assets	727	722	724	733	577	400	191	157	136	114
Curr. Liab.	363	359	394	408	361	252	143	131	132	110
LT Debt	89.6	101	84.9	89.5	33.6	33.0	2.2	Nil	17.3	19.7
Common Eqty.	264	250	235	231	174	107	39.1	21.1	-17.4	-19.6
Total Cap.	354	353	321	322	210	143	43.6	22.1	-0.1	-0.2
Cap. Exp.	35.7	21.8	42.5	42.6	13.1	35.5	15.2	7.5	6.0	2.9
Cash Flow	41.0	44.5	24.9	45.2	-1.8	28.5	18.2	16.8	10.8	8.1
Curr. Ratio	1.3	1.4	1.3	1.3	1.2	1.2	1.1	1.0	0.9	0.9
% LT Debt of Cap.	25.3	28.7	26.4	27.8	16.0	23.0	5.1	Nil	NM	NM
% Net Inc.of Revs.	2.3	3.2	0.1	5.5	NM	3.8	4.1	5.3	4.5	4.1
% Ret. on Assets	1.9	2.5	0.0	3.8	NM	6.3	8.0	7.6	4.3	3.9
% Ret. on Equity	5.2	7.5	0.1	12.3	NM	25.7	46.5	NM	NM	NM

Data as orig reptd.; bef. results of disc opers/spec. items. Per share data adj. for stk. divs. Bold denotes diluted EPS (FASB 128)-prior periods restated. E-Estimated. NA-Not Available. NM-Not Meaningful. NR-Not Ranked.

Office—706 Mission St., Suite 900, San Francisco, CA 94103. **Tel**—(415) 904-8360. **Website**—www.fritz.com **Chrmn & CEO**—L. C. Fritz. **Pres**—D. L. Pelino. **EVP-CFO**—R. F. Dutt. **SVP & Secy**—J. H. Raymond. **Investor Contact**—Graeme Stewart (415-538-0444). **Dirs**—L. C. Fritz, J. Gilleran, P. Martin, P. Otellini, D. L. Pelino, W. J. Razzouk. **Transfer Agent & Registrar**—ChaseMellon Shareholder Services, Ridgefield Park, NJ. **Incorporated**—in Delaware in 1988. **Empl**— 10,000. **S&P Analyst:** John A. Massey

Frontier Insurance Group

NYSE Symbol **FTR**

In S&P SmallCap 600

09-OCT-99

Industry: Insurance (Property-Casualty)

Summary: FTR is a specialty property and casualty insurer and reinsurer.

Quantitative Evaluations

Outlook
(1 Lowest—5 Highest)
• **3+**

Fair Value
• **9½**

Risk
• **Low**

Earn./Div. Rank
• **B**

Technical Eval.
• **Bearish** since 7/99

Rel. Strength Rank
(1 Lowest—99 Highest)
• **5**

Insider Activity
• **Neutral**

Recent Price • 8⅜
52 Wk Range • 18¾-7½
Yield • 3.3%
12-Mo. P/E • NM

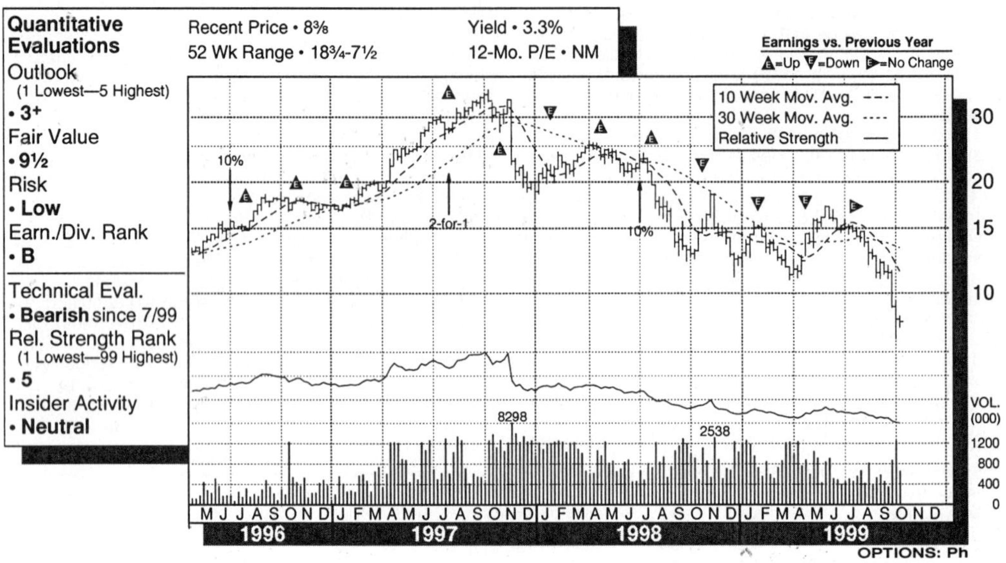

Business Profile - 02-SEP-99

Frontier Insurance Group is one of the country's leading providers of services to specialty insurance producers. By focusing on niche insurance markets that are generally perceived as unattractive by competitors, the company aims to develop expertise in areas that may offer above average profit opportunities. This strategy has succeeded in producing rapid revenue gains in recent years. However, 1998 proved to be a difficult year, with a change in management following the death of the founder and a need to increase reserves that resulted in a net loss for the year. So far in 1999, the company has increased revenues, stabilized earnings, and acquired several small insurance agencies specializing in surety insurance at a combined cost of about $12.3 million. Effective December 31, 1998, the company ended its reinsurance agreement with Zurich N.A.

Operational Review - 02-SEP-99

In the first six months of 1999, total revenues increased 13%, year to year, reflecting growth in the majority of core and new program business. Expenses rose 15%, led by higher insurance losses and loss adjustment expenses, leading to a fractional pretax gain. After taxes at 30.9%, against 25.4%, net income decreased 6.9% to $32,776,000 ($0.83 a share, on 4.5% fewer shares), from $35,208,000 ($0.85, as adjusted).

Stock Performance - 08-OCT-99

In the past 30 trading days, FTR's shares have declined 26%, compared to a 0.91% fall in the S&P 500. Average trading volume for the past five days was 129,400 shares, compared with the 40-day moving average of 139,597 shares.

Key Stock Statistics

Dividend Rate/Share	0.28	Shareholders	1,406
Shs. outstg. (M)	34.7	Market cap. (B)	$0.291
Avg. daily vol. (M)	0.177	Inst. holdings	54%
Tang. Bk. Value/Share	10.66		
Beta	0.92		

Value of $10,000 invested 5 years ago: $ 7,597

Fiscal Year Ending Dec. 31

	1999	1998	1997	1996	1995	1994
Revenues (Million $)						
1Q	161.2	142.5	90.44	66.80	51.77	41.16
2Q	159.4	143.3	89.32	75.30	53.91	37.95
3Q	—	143.5	118.0	79.77	58.07	46.44
4Q	—	144.8	128.7	83.05	62.65	54.43
Yr.	—	574.0	426.4	305.0	226.4	180.0
Earnings Per Share ($)						
1Q	**0.41**	**0.43**	**0.34**	—	0.22	0.21
2Q	**0.42**	**0.42**	**0.42**	**0.31**	0.25	0.24
3Q	—	**0.35**	**0.38**	**0.30**	0.26	-0.16
4Q	—	**-2.17**	**-0.18**	**0.34**	0.26	0.25
Yr.	—	**-1.34**	**0.92**	**1.23**	**0.98**	**0.54**

Next earnings report expected: mid November

Dividend Data (Dividends have been paid since 1992.)

Amount ($)	Date Decl.	Ex-Div. Date	Stock of Record	Payment Date
0.070	Dec. 15	Dec. 29	Dec. 31	Jan. 20 '99
0.070	Mar. 23	Mar. 29	Mar. 31	Apr. 20 '99
0.070	Jun. 18	Jun. 28	Jun. 30	Jul. 20 '99
0.070	Aug. 27	Sep. 28	Sep. 30	Oct. 20 '99

Frontier Insurance Group, Inc.

Business Summary - 02-SEP-99

Frontier Insurance Group, Inc., through its Frontier Insurance Company and other subsidiaries, is one of the country's leading providers of specialty insurance and reinsurance. It has operations in all 50 states, as well as in Washington, D.C., Puerto Rico, Mexico, Greece, Guam and the Virgin Islands. The company's strategy is to identify niche insurance markets and specialty insurance programs where it may have favorable opportunities for profitability as a result of limited competition and the company's expertise in underwriting and offering value added services (such as coverage enhancements, risk management, loss control, and specialized claims management) for the particular market.

In 1998, gross and net premiums written rose to $833.2 million and $527.0 million, respectively, from $587.6 million and $389.0 million in 1997. Growth came both from stronger core and new program business, and from the company's ongoing acquisition campaign.

The company's segments contributed to net written premiums in 1998 as follows: personal and credit-related $126.3 million (22%), health and human services $107.5 million (19%), surety $83.8 million (15%), physicians $76.9 (13%), specialty programs $67.6 (12%), environmental, excess and surplus lines $64.4 million (11%), alternative risk $34.6 million (6%), and dentists, chiropractors and other $12.8 million (2%). These amounts are prior to the ceding of $46.8 million in premiums to Zurich Reinsurance N.A. under stop loss agreements. Effective December 31, 1998, the company terminated its 1998-99 stop loss agreement with Zurich as it relates to the 1999 accident year.

FTR markets its products directly and through independent agents. In 1998, 12.6% of FTR's gross premiums were generated directly, and 87.4% came through independent insurance agencies and brokerage firms.

Total net investment income accounted for 13% of FTR's total revenues in 1998. At December 31, 1998, the company's invested assets were valued at $1.26 billion, up from $1.10 billion a year earlier.

The company made six major acquisitions in recent years, including Acceleration Life in 1998; Lyndon Property, Western Indemnity, and Environmental and Commercial in 1997; and United Capitol Holding, and Regency and Emrol in 1996.

In January 1998, FTR's founder and longtime CEO Walter Rhulen passed away after a five-month battle with leukemia. His son, Harry Rhulen, was named chairman and CEO in February 1998. Directors and officers of the company and members of the Rhulen family owned about 25% of the outstanding common shares as of March 1999.

Per Share Data ($)										
(Year Ended Dec. 31)	1998	1997	1996	1995	1994	1993	1992	1991	1990	1989
Tangible Bk. Val.	9.22	11.35	7.97	7.29	6.05	5.93	4.09	3.52	2.42	1.90
Oper. Earnings	-1.39	0.86	1.23	0.99	0.57	0.84	0.72	0.61	0.52	0.44
Earnings	-1.34	0.92	1.26	0.99	0.54	0.84	0.73	0.63	0.53	0.46
Dividends	0.26	0.25	0.23	0.20	0.19	0.16	0.15	Nil	Nil	Nil
Payout Ratio	NM	0%	18%	20%	35%	19%	20%	Nil	Nil	Nil
Prices - High	25 5/8	35 5/8	18 3/4	14	15 1/2	13 3/4	11	6 5/8	7 1/8	4 1/4
- Low	11	16 5/8	11 5/8	8 3/8	6 7/8	10 1/8	6 1/8	3 7/8	3 1/8	2 3/16
P/E Ratio - High	NM	39	15	14	29	16	15	11	14	9
- Low	NM	18	9	8	13	12	8	6	6	5
Income Statement Analysis (Million $)										
Premium Inc.	493	367	266	196	157	116	105	78.0	72.3	55.0
Net Invest. Inc.	73.5	56.1	37.2	30.0	24.5	22.5	19.9	15.9	12.1	8.6
Oth. Revs.	7.4	4.2	0.1	0.1	-1.2	0.3	1.7	2.4	1.6	Nil
Total Revs.	574	427	305	226	180	139	127	96.3	86.0	63.6
Pretax Inc.	-79.9	56.9	56.5	43.3	21.3	30.3	25.2	20.1	14.7	12.8
Net Oper. Inc.	NA	NA	NA	31.2	17.9	23.0	NA	NA	10.4	9.2
Net Inc.	-50.0	32.3	40.0	31.2	17.0	23.2	19.0	15.0	10.8	9.4
Balance Sheet & Other Fin. Data (Million $)										
Cash & Equiv.	44.9	11.8	8.3	12.6	11.4	17.8	5.0	14.4	4.1	3.8
Premiums Due	114	95.2	76.6	50.0	41.1	28.4	28.2	24.7	26.6	18.0
Invest. Assets: Bonds	1,199	1,080	685	521	346	276	242	208	153	114
Invest. Assets: Stocks	57.3	20.3	16.2	21.0	48.6	7.5	9.9	1.1	3.8	4.9
Invest. Assets: Loans	9.1	Nil	Nil	Nil	Nil	Nil	Nil	Nil	Nil	Nil
Invest. Assets: Total	1,459	1,249	702	553	408	344	262	235	165	131
Deferred Policy Costs	96.6	55.6	32.8	18.8	13.2	6.8	6.0	3.2	2.2	Nil
Total Assets	2,554	1,976	1,246	773	599	522	341	300	215	170
Debt	259	167	NM	25.0	Nil	Nil	Nil	Nil	Nil	Nil
Common Eqty.	394	454	269	230	190	186	107	91.2	49.7	39.0
Prop. & Cas. Loss Ratio	95.0	65.2	58.7	NA	70.8	66.7	71.2	69.7	73.7	75.1
Prop. & Cas. Expense Ratio	38.2	35.7	32.2	NA	27.0	26.5	25.6	26.3	24.0	23.7
Prop. & Cas. Combined Ratio	133.2	100.9	90.9	91.5	97.8	93.3	96.8	96.0	97.7	98.8
% Return On Revs.	NM	7.6	13.1	13.8	9.4	16.7	15.0	15.6	12.5	14.8
% Ret. on Equity	NM	8.9	16.1	14.9	9.1	15.8	19.2	21.3	24.3	27.5

Data as orig reptd.; bef. results of disc opers/spec. items. Per share data adj. for stk. divs. Bold denotes diluted EPS (FASB 128)-prior periods restated. E-Estimated. NA-Not Available. NM-Not Meaningful. NR-Not Ranked.

Office—195 Lake Louise Marie Rd., Rock Hill, NY 12775-8000. **Tel**—(914) 796-2100. **Website**—http://www.ftr.com **Chrmn, CEO & Pres**—H. W. Rhulen. **VP-CFO & Treas**—M. H. Mishler. **Secy**—J. P. Loughlin. **Investor Contact**—J. R. Billig (800-836-2100, ext. 5355). **Dirs**—A. Gerry, P. B. Guenther, S. Rhulen Loughlin, D. C. Moat, L. E. O'Brien, H. W. Rhulen, P. L. Rhulen. **Transfer Agent & Registrar**—American Stock Transfer & Trust Co., NYC. **Incorporated**—in Delaware in 1986. **Empl**— 1,250. **S&P Analyst:** T. W. Smith, CFA

STANDARD
&POOR'S
STOCK REPORTS

Frozen Food Express

NASDAQ Symbol **FFEX**

In S&P SmallCap 600

09-OCT-99 **Industry:** Truckers

Summary: FFEX is the largest publicly owned, full-service motor carrier of perishable commodities in North America.

Quantitative Evaluations

Outlook (1 Lowest—5 Highest) • **3+**

Fair Value • **7⅛**

Risk • **Low**

Earn./Div. Rank • **A-**

Technical Eval. • **Bearish** since 8/99

Rel. Strength Rank (1 Lowest—99 Highest) • **15**

Insider Activity • **NA**

Recent Price • 5⅜

52 Wk Range • 9¾-4⅞

Yield • 2.2%

12-Mo. P/E • 11.1

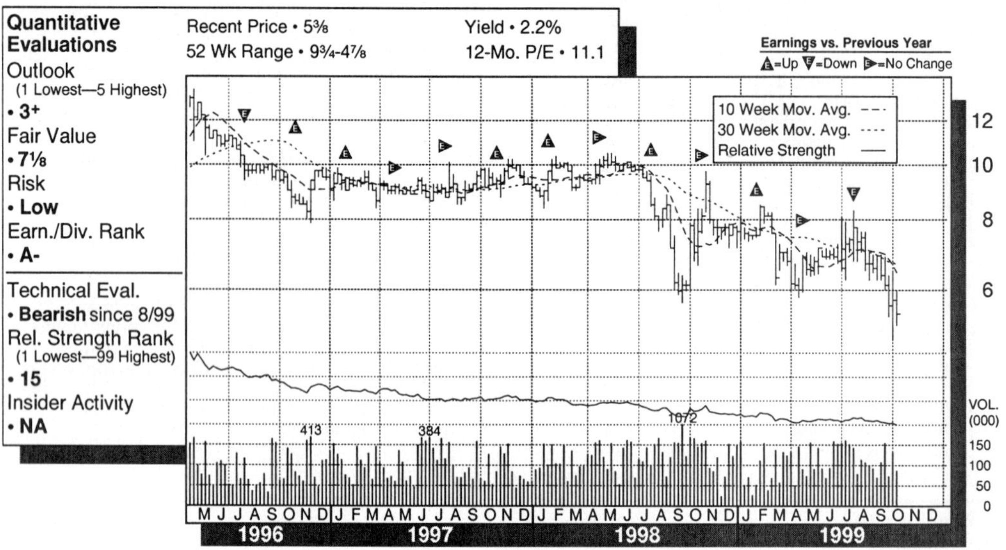

Business Profile - 04-OCT-99

Frozen Food Express Industries has been increasing its efforts to improve efficiency in moving freight in light of recent larger than expected insurance expenses coupled with the costs of implementing its new computer-based management information system (MIS), and the impact of an industrywide shortage of drivers. In July 1999, FFEX said that although it knows the costs of recruiting new drivers, it is harder to measure the opportunity cost of having a tractorunused due to the lack of a qualified driver. Costs related to the trucking industry's driver shortage were said to be increasing.

Operational Review - 04-OCT-99

Revenues for the first half of 1999 advanced 11%, year to year, reflecting gains of 3.3% for freight operations and 69% for non-freight. Although freight operating expenses were well controlled, a 70% jump in non-freight costs & operating expenses led to a drop in overall operating profit of 31%. After a more than doubling of interest & other expense (net), pretax income was down 41%. Following taxes at 37.0%, versus 35.9%, net income decreased 42%, to $2.6 million ($0.16 a share, on 4.1% fewer average shares) from $4.4 million ($0.26).

Stock Performance - 08-OCT-99

In the past 30 trading days, FFEX's shares have declined 17%, compared to a 0.91% fall in the S&P 500. Average trading volume for the past five days was 17,100 shares, compared with the 40-day moving average of 21,538 shares.

Key Stock Statistics

Dividend Rate/Share	0.12	Shareholders	7,000
Shs. outstg. (M)	16.3	Market cap. (B)	$0.089
Avg. daily vol. (M)	0.024	Inst. holdings	28%
Tang. Bk. Value/Share	6.04		
Beta	0.64		

Value of $10,000 invested 5 years ago: $ 4,031

Fiscal Year Ending Dec. 31

	1999	1998	1997	1996	1995	1994
Revenues (Million $)						
1Q	88.26	77.51	72.69	74.17	66.98	60.30
2Q	96.82	88.42	81.26	79.41	73.84	70.30
3Q	—	93.53	82.98	80.82	75.78	72.54
4Q	—	89.48	79.65	77.02	75.75	71.48
Yr.	—	349.9	316.6	311.4	292.4	274.6
Earnings Per Share ($)						
1Q	**0.08**	**0.08**	**0.08**	**0.08**	0.11	0.10
2Q	**0.08**	**0.18**	**0.16**	**0.16**	0.23	0.23
3Q	—	**0.17**	**0.17**	**0.15**	0.13	0.21
4Q	—	**0.16**	**0.15**	**0.12**	0.10	0.18
Yr.	—	**0.59**	**0.57**	**0.51**	**0.56**	0.72

Next earnings report expected: late October

Dividend Data (Dividends have been paid since 1971.)

Amount ($)	Date Decl.	Ex-Div. Date	Stock of Record	Payment Date
0.030	Nov. 11	Nov. 23	Nov. 25	Dec. 04 '98
0.030	Feb. 10	Feb. 23	Feb. 25	Mar. 04 '99
0.030	May. 14	May. 20	May. 20	May. 27 '99
0.030	Aug. 11	Aug. 23	Aug. 25	Sep. 03 '99

A Division of The McGraw-Hill Companies

Frozen Food Express Industries, Inc.

Business Summary - 04-OCT-99

In late 1946, two World War II veterans scraped up enough money to buy two used trucks. From this beginning, Frozen Food Express Industries has grown to become the largest temperature-controlled trucking company in North America.

The company is also the only nationwide, full-service, temperature-controlled trucking company in the United States offering all of the following services: full-truckload (typically weighing 20,000 to 40,000 pounds and usually from a single shipper, filling the trailer), dedicated fleets (assignment of specific trucks and drivers to handle certain of a customer's transportation needs), less-than-truckload (LTL; a load, typically 18 to 30 shipments, each weighing from 50 pounds to 20,000 pounds), and distribution (the delivery of cargo within a 50-to-75-mile radius of a company terminal).

Freight revenue from motor carrier operations accounted for more than 90% of total operating revenue during each of the five years through 1998. In 1998, full-truckload operations accounted for 67% of total freight revenue, and LTL operations the balance.

The company offers nationwide "one call does all" services to about 7,000 customers, none of which accounted for more than 10% of total revenue during any of the five years through 1998.

More than 80% of the cargo transported by FFEX is temperature-sensitive. Such cargo consists primarily of meat, poultry, seafood, processed foods, candy and other confectioneries, dairy products, pharmaceuticals, medical supplies, fruits and vegetables, cosmetics, film and heat-sensitive aerospace manufacturing materials.

FFEX has pursued a growth strategy that combines both internal growth and acquisitions. From the beginning of 1994 through 1998, the company-operated, full-truckload tractor fleet increased from about 846 units to 1,233 units. During the same period, FFEX has emphasized expansion of its fleet of independent contractor (owner-operator) provided full-truckload tractors. As of December 31, 1998, the full-truckload fleet consisted of 432 tractors provided by owner-operators, versus 233 at the beginning of 1994.

The company believes that its one call does all full-service capability, combined with the service-oriented corporate culture it gained from its many years as a successful LTL carrier, enables it to compete on the basis of service, rather than solely on price. Management also believes that major shippers will require increasing levels of service and that they will rely on their core carriers to provide transportation and logistics solutions, such as providing the shipper real-time information about the movement and condition of any shipment.

The use of a satellite-based communications system, in conjunction with computers, provides the company with automatic hourly position updates of each full-truckload tractor.

Per Share Data ($) (Year Ended Dec. 31)	1998	1997	1996	1995	1994	1993	1992	1991	1990	1989
Tangible Bk. Val.	5.96	5.53	5.04	4.59	4.03	3.31	2.72	2.03	2.06	1.88
Cash Flow	1.14	1.13	1.09	1.24	1.31	1.19	0.95	0.89	0.82	0.69
Earnings	0.59	0.57	0.52	0.57	0.72	0.58	0.45	0.34	0.25	0.26
Dividends	0.12	0.12	0.12	0.12	0.10	0.10	0.08	0.06	0.06	0.05
Payout Ratio	20%	21%	23%	21%	14%	16%	17%	20%	24%	18%
Prices - High	10 1/2	10 1/4	13 7/8	13 7/8	15	15	11 1/2	4 1/8	2 3/4	3 1/2
- Low	5 5/8	8 3/8	7 7/8	8 1/2	11	7 1/4	4	1 13/16	1 13/16	2 1/8
P/E Ratio - High	18	18	27	24	21	26	26	12	11	13
- Low	10	15	15	15	15	12	9	5	7	8
Income Statement Analysis (Million $)										
Revs.	350	317	311	292	275	227	195	177	160	122
Oper. Inc.	25.3	23.6	48.9	25.5	28.5	24.7	19.6	17.6	15.7	11.8
Depr.	9.4	9.6	9.5	10.7	9.8	9.9	8.0	8.3	8.2	6.2
Int. Exp.	Nil	NM	3.4	NA	NA	0.8	0.4	1.3	1.9	1.2
Pretax Inc.	15.7	13.8	11.7	13.2	17.8	14.4	11.2	8.6	5.8	5.5
Eff. Tax Rate	37%	30%	28%	30%	33%	35%	36%	39%	38%	31%
Net Inc.	10.0	9.7	8.5	9.3	11.9	9.4	7.1	5.2	3.6	3.8
Balance Sheet & Other Fin. Data (Million $)										
Cash	6.0	23.3	6.7	7.5	4.4	3.8	3.7	3.2	0.5	1.6
Curr. Assets	70.9	77.0	65.4	61.6	57.1	48.1	37.4	29.9	26.9	18.9
Total Assets	150	143	130	124	117	109	86.0	66.9	74.3	58.8
Curr. Liab.	31.6	32.0	31.3	36.6	31.4	27.2	20.4	14.3	13.8	9.3
LT Debt	Nil	Nil	NM	NM	9.0	17.0	12.0	7.1	21.3	14.0
Common Eqty.	98.3	93.1	83.9	75.0	64.3	52.0	41.8	35.1	30.0	27.3
Total Cap.	107	101	90.8	75.0	77.8	72.5	58.2	47.4	56.5	46.5
Cap. Exp.	27.7	14.7	13.7	10.7	13.6	23.6	20.3	2.2	17.7	13.5
Cash Flow	19.4	19.3	18.0	19.9	21.6	19.4	15.2	13.5	11.9	10.0
Curr. Ratio	2.2	2.4	2.1	1.7	1.8	1.8	1.8	2.1	1.9	2.0
% LT Debt of Cap.	Nil	NM	NM	NM	11.6	23.4	20.6	15.0	37.8	30.2
% Net Inc.of Revs.	2.9	3.1	2.7	3.2	4.3	4.2	3.7	2.9	2.3	3.1
% Ret. on Assets	6.8	7.1	6.7	7.7	10.5	9.6	9.8	6.6	5.4	7.0
% Ret. on Equity	10.4	10.9	10.7	12.1	20.3	19.9	19.6	14.5	12.5	14.5

Data as orig reptd.; bef. results of disc opers/spec. items. Per share data adj. for stk. divs. Bold denotes diluted EPS (FASB 128)-prior periods restated. E-Estimated. NA-Not Available. NM-Not Meaningful. NR-Not Ranked.

Office—1145 Empire Central Place, Dallas, TX 75247-4309. **Tel**—(214) 630-8090. **Chrmn & Pres**—S. M. Stubbs Jr. **Vice Chrmn**—E. O. Weller. **SVP & CFO**—F. D. McElwee, Jr. **Secy**—L. W. Bartholomew. **Dirs**—W. M. Baggett, B. R. Blackmarr, L. Hallman, W. G. Lord, F. D. McElwee, Jr., T. M. O'Connor, C. G. Robertson, S. M. Stubbs Jr., E. O. Weller. **Transfer Agent**—First National Bank of Boston. **Incorporated**—in Texas in 1969. **Empl**— 2,634. **S&P Analyst:** NJD

STANDARD
&POOR'S
STOCK REPORTS

G & K Services

NASDAQ Symbol **GKSRA**

In S&P SmallCap 600

09-OCT-99 **Industry:** Services (Commercial & Consumer)

Summary: This company is one of the leading U.S. suppliers of uniforms and related textile products used in a wide range of businesses and institutions.

Quantitative Evaluations
Outlook
(1 Lowest—5 Highest)
• **4**
Fair Value
• **62¼**
Risk
• **Average**
Earn./Div. Rank
• **A**

Technical Eval.
• **Bearish** since 8/99
Rel. Strength Rank
(1 Lowest—99 Highest)
• **44**
Insider Activity
• **Neutral**

Recent Price • 41¾
52 Wk Range • 56¼-37¾
Yield • 0.2%
12-Mo. P/E • 23.1

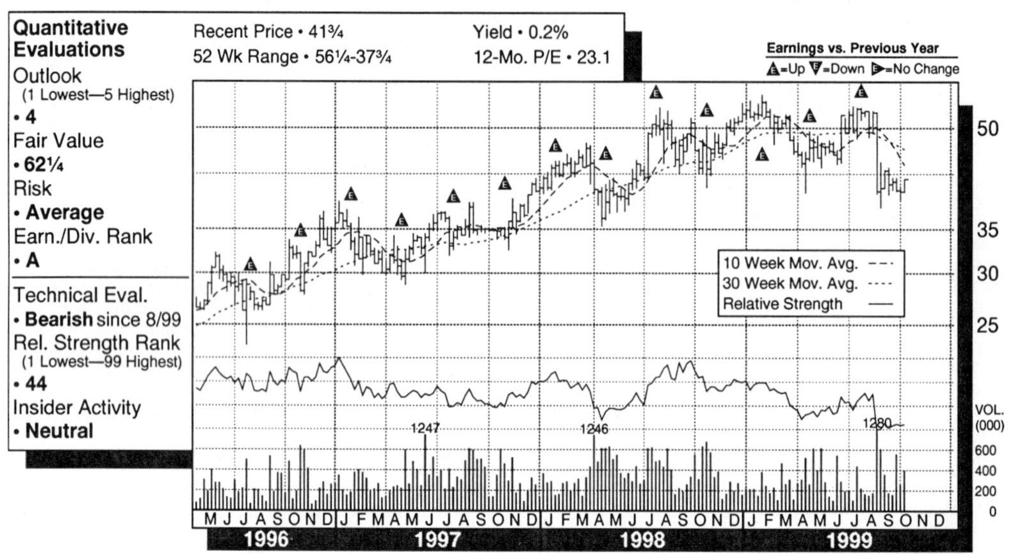

Business Profile - 19-AUG-99

The company's cost structure continued to improve in the fourth quarter of FY 99 (Jun.) as further progress was made integrating the National Linen Service (NLS) acquisition. However, SG&A expenses rose on investments in additional sales personnel, new senior management positions, and expenses related to Y2K systems compliance. GKSRA added 30 people to the sales force during FY 99 and Y2K compliance expenses equated to $0.02 per share in the fourth quarter. Looking forward, management believes FY 2000 growth rates will improve in both revenues and earnings, with revenues reaching double-digit levels by year end and net income moving closer to the company's 18% long-term goal.

Operational Review - 19-AUG-99

Based on a preliminary report, total revenues rose 3.5% in the fiscal year ended June 26, 1999, as an increase in rental operations outweighed a decline in direct sales. Despite higher selling and administrative expenses, profitability improved on wider gross margins; operating income climbed 5.0%. Comparisons were further aided by lower depreciation and amortization charges and reduced interest expense. After taxes at 39.5%, versus 39.2%, net income grew 16%, to $37.0 million ($1.81 a share), from $32.1 million ($1.57).

Stock Performance - 08-OCT-99

In the past 30 trading days, GKSRA's shares have increased 3%, compared to a 0.91% fall in the S&P 500. Average trading volume for the past five days was 79,240 shares, compared with the 40-day moving average of 97,205 shares.

Key Stock Statistics

Dividend Rate/Share	0.07	Shareholders	600
Shs. outstg. (M)	20.5	Market cap. (B)	$0.795
Avg. daily vol. (M)	0.068	Inst. holdings	62%
Tang. Bk. Value/Share	1.17		
Beta	0.71		

Value of $10,000 invested 5 years ago: $ 27,007

Fiscal Year Ending Jun. 30

	1999	1998	1997	1996	1995	1994
Revenues (Million $)						
1Q	126.1	118.4	83.31	70.95	60.53	53.35
2Q	129.9	128.3	87.44	75.09	65.55	55.53
3Q	131.2	127.5	88.47	77.48	66.72	57.13
4Q	132.8	128.4	91.69	81.89	69.67	59.22
Yr.	520.0	502.6	350.9	305.4	262.5	225.2
Earnings Per Share ($)						
1Q	**0.42**	0.36	0.34	0.25	0.21	0.17
2Q	**0.45**	**0.38**	**0.35**	0.27	0.23	0.18
3Q	**0.46**	**0.39**	0.36	0.28	0.22	0.18
4Q	**0.47**	**0.43**	0.37	0.31	0.24	0.20
Yr.	**1.81**	**1.57**	**1.42**	1.11	0.90	0.73

Next earnings report expected: late October

Dividend Data (Dividends have been paid since 1968.)

Amount ($)	Date Decl.	Ex-Div. Date	Stock of Record	Payment Date
0.018	Oct. 30	Dec. 04	Dec. 08	Dec. 29 '98
0.018	Feb. 25	Mar. 23	Mar. 25	Apr. 08 '99
0.018	May. 20	Jun. 01	Jun. 03	Jun. 17 '99
0.018	Aug. 26	Sep. 14	Sep. 16	Sep. 30 '99

A Division of The McGraw-Hill Companies

G & K Services, Inc.

Business Summary - 19-AUG-99

G&K Services believes that its uniform program can help improve a company's image, promote teamwork among workers, provide protection from wear and tear on employees' clothing, create walking advertising, and increase company morale. Across America, over 90,000 small businesses and more than half of all Fortune 100 companies have chosen G&K for their uniform service needs. By having such a large customer base, G&K accounts are well diversified, with no one client accounting for more than 1% of total revenues.

The company has expanded its operations steadily over the years to include approximately 125 locations in 28 U.S. states and the Canadian provinces of Quebec and Ontario. By comparison, G&K operated from approximately 40 locations in 21 states in 1988. Today, G&K is the third largest competitor in the estimated $5.5 billion uniform leasing industry.

Among the key elements of the company's strategy for continued revenue and earnings growth is entering new markets through acquisitions. In July 1997, G&K acquired for approximately $280 million uniform rental assets and selected linen rental assets of National Linen Service, a division of National Service Industries (NYSE: NSI). National Linen Service consisted of 20 industrial facilities and nine linen facilities. As of September 1998, GKSRA had divested eight of the linen facilities and three of the industrial facilities that were not compatible with the company's strategic goals.

G&K also hopes to improve performance through start-ups, adding customers that currently do not have uniform programs, and reducing costs through technology and innovation. The company targets its marketing efforts to focus on customers, industries and geographic locations that are expanding. G&K believes that its existing and potential customers are willing to pay a premium price for its services.

The company's full-service rental program supplies a broad range of work garments, specialized uniforms for corporate identity programs, anti-static garments, ultra-clean particle-free garments, and dress clothing for supervisors and sales personnel. Assistance is provided in selecting fabrics, styles and colors. Professional cleaning, finishing, repair and replacement are provided as part of the normal service.

GKSRA believes that uniform leasing provides customers with significant advantages over ownership. Leasing eliminates investment in uniforms and offers flexibility in styles, colors and quantities as customer requirements change. Furthermore, leasing assures professional cleaning, repair and replacement of items.

In addition to uniforms, many of the company's customers lease other items, including floor mats, dust mops and linens.

Per Share Data ($) (Year Ended Jun. 30)	1999	1998	1997	1996	1995	1994	1993	1992	1991	1990
Tangible Bk. Val.	NA	1.17	6.31	5.19	3.65	2.76	1.97	1.29	0.75	3.04
Cash Flow	NA	3.31	2.49	2.11	1.75	1.50	1.26	1.12	0.91	0.83
Earnings	1.81	1.57	1.42	1.11	0.90	0.73	0.55	0.43	0.35	0.51
Dividends	0.07	0.07	0.07	0.07	0.09	0.07	0.07	0.07	0.07	0.07
Payout Ratio	4%	4%	5%	6%	10%	10%	12%	16%	19%	13%
Prices - High	56 1/4	54 5/8	42 1/4	38 5/8	26	17 1/4	16	13 3/8	12 3/8	11
- Low	37 3/4	35 3/8	28 3/4	21 7/8	15	12 1/2	10 7/8	8 5/8	7 1/8	5 7/8
P/E Ratio - High	31	35	30	35	29	24	29	31	35	22
- Low	21	23	20	20	17	17	20	20	20	12
Income Statement Analysis (Million $)										
Revs.	NA	503	350	305	262	225	208	195	176	119
Oper. Inc.	NA	108	74.7	65.6	53.5	45.5	39.5	35.6	28.0	24.7
Depr.	NA	35.6	22.0	20.4	17.4	15.8	14.5	14.0	11.3	7.8
Int. Exp.	NA	21.8	6.8	8.0	7.1	5.8	7.3	8.5	8.3	0.5
Pretax Inc.	NA	52.7	47.9	37.2	30.3	25.3	19.1	14.1	12.3	16.5
Eff. Tax Rate	NA	39%	39%	39%	40%	42%	42%	39%	43%	38%
Net Inc.	NA	32.1	29.0	22.7	18.3	14.8	11.1	8.6	7.1	10.2
Balance Sheet & Other Fin. Data (Million $)										
Cash	NA	12.0	6.9	6.9	3.0	5.1	4.6	2.1	2.2	0.6
Curr. Assets	NA	153	113	100	87.3	63.5	59.0	52.3	56.7	32.5
Total Assets	NA	532	312	282	253	205	202	200	206	101
Curr. Liab.	NA	80.1	72.3	49.8	42.4	34.2	36.4	33.9	28.7	16.1
LT Debt	NA	235	54.3	75.1	76.5	54.7	59.8	68.4	85.9	9.1
Common Eqty.	NA	198	168	141	119	101	90.2	82.4	76.8	69.9
Total Cap.	NA	442	222	226	206	167	162	164	175	84.0
Cap. Exp.	NA	37.4	35.6	36.2	36.5	17.6	14.4	16.3	18.4	21.8
Cash Flow	NA	67.7	51.0	43.1	35.7	30.6	25.6	22.6	18.4	18.0
Curr. Ratio	NA	1.9	1.6	2.0	2.1	1.9	1.6	1.5	2.0	2.0
% LT Debt of Cap.	NA	53.1	24.5	33.3	37.2	32.8	36.9	41.8	49.1	10.8
% Net Inc.of Revs.	NA	6.4	8.3	7.4	7.0	6.6	5.4	4.4	4.0	8.6
% Ret. on Assets	NA	7.6	9.7	8.5	8.0	7.3	5.5	4.2	4.6	11.1
% Ret. on Equity	NA	17.6	18.9	17.5	16.7	15.5	12.9	10.8	9.6	15.6

Data as orig reptd.; bef. results of disc opers/spec. items. Per share data adj. for stk. divs. Bold denotes diluted EPS (FASB 128)-prior periods restated. E-Estimated. NA-Not Available. NM-Not Meaningful. NR-Not Ranked.

Office—5995 Opus Parkway, Suite 500, Minnetonka, MN 55343. **Tel**—(612) 912-5500. **Website**—http://www.gkcares.com **Chrmn**—R. M. Fink. **CEO**—T. Moberly. **Pres & COO**—J. Rotunda. **CFO & Investor Contact**—J. L. Wright. **Dirs**—B. G. Allbright, P. Baszucki, R. Fink, W. Fortun, D. Goldfus, W. Hope, T. Moberly, B. Sweet. **Transfer Agent & Registrar**—Norwest Bank, Minneapolis. **Incorporated**—in Minnesota in 1934. **Empl**—7,390. **S&P Analyst:** Jordan Horoschak

STANDARD
&POOR'S
STOCK REPORTS

Gallagher (Arthur J.)

NYSE Symbol **AJG**

In S&P SmallCap 600

09-OCT-99

Industry:
Insurance Brokers

Summary: This company provides insurance brokerage, risk management and other insurance-related services for commercial, industrial, individual and other clients.

Quantitative Evaluations

Outlook
(1 Lowest—5 Highest)
• **2−**

Fair Value
• **52⅞**

Risk
• **Low**

Earn./Div. Rank
• **A**

Technical Eval.
• **Bullish** since 8/99

Rel. Strength Rank
(1 Lowest—99 Highest)
• **60**

Insider Activity
• **Neutral**

Recent Price • 51⅞
52 Wk Range • 56½-34⅞

Yield • 3.1%
12-Mo. P/E • 15.8

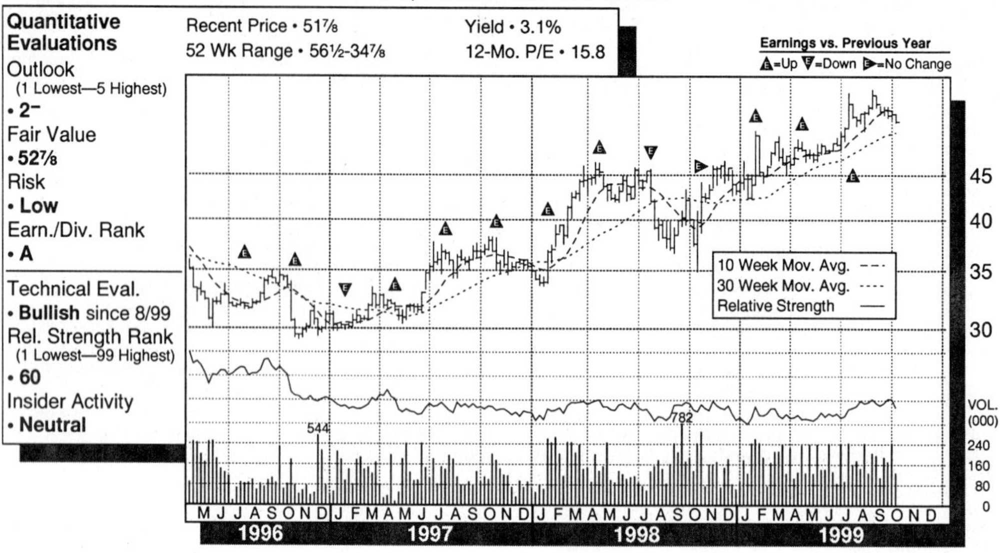

Business Profile - 25-AUG-99

In August 1999, AJG stated that the extremely competitive environment continues in the insurance marketplace and the company does not anticipate any change in these conditions in the near future. In April 1999, AJG agreed to sell a substantial portion of its investments in landfill gas collection partnerships. The company expects the proceeds from the sale of $50 million and the gain of approximately $36 million will be recognized over a period of nine years beginning in 1999. AJG also agreed to sell most of its investment in real estate partnership interests for proceeds of $6.5 million, and gain of about $3 million. During the first six months of 1999, AJG acquired the Goodman Insurance Agency, Inc., of Southern California, Associated Risk Managers of California, and Dodson-Bateman & Co., a regional retail insurance agency of Dallas, Texas.

Operational Review - 25-AUG-99

Total revenues in the six months ended June 30, 1999, rose 7.6%, year to year, mainly reflecting 11% higher fee revenue generated by AJG's Risk Management Services subsidiary, and 12% higher investment income due to a $1.5 million pretax gain from the first installment of the company's sale of its real estate partnership interests. Total expenses rose 5.5%, primarily due to a 6.7% increase in salary and benefit costs. After taxes at 35.0%, versus 32.8%, net income increased 18%, to $25.8 million ($1.36 a share), from $21.9 million ($1.17, restated).

Stock Performance - 08-OCT-99

In the past 30 trading days, AJG's shares have declined 7%, compared to a 0.91% fall in the S&P 500. Average trading volume for the past five days was 25,180 shares, compared with the 40-day moving average of 35,349 shares.

Key Stock Statistics

Dividend Rate/Share	1.60	Shareholders	650
Shs. outstg. (M)	18.2	Market cap. (B)	$0.944
Avg. daily vol. (M)	0.037	Inst. holdings	51%
Tang. Bk. Value/Share	11.20		
Beta	0.39		

Value of $10,000 invested 5 years ago: $ 17,162

Fiscal Year Ending Dec. 31

	1999	1998	1997	1996	1995	1994
Revenues (Million $)						
1Q	135.1	123.7	111.5	106.8	95.61	82.95
2Q	140.3	124.4	116.6	108.6	94.89	80.94
3Q	—	143.5	130.4	121.7	110.6	97.65
4Q	—	149.0	129.6	119.5	110.9	94.83
Yr.	—	540.7	488.0	456.7	412.0	356.4
Earnings Per Share ($)						
1Q	**0.70**	**0.65**	**0.54**	**0.49**	0.41	0.32
2Q	**0.66**	**0.54**	**0.76**	**0.41**	0.36	0.28
3Q	—	**1.08**	**1.08**	**1.04**	0.94	0.81
4Q	—	**0.83**	**0.74**	**0.59**	0.83	0.77
Yr.	—	**3.10**	**3.13**	**2.52**	**2.43**	2.17

Next earnings report expected: mid October

Dividend Data (Dividends have been paid since 1985.)

Amount ($)	Date Decl.	Ex-Div. Date	Stock of Record	Payment Date
0.350	Nov. 19	Dec. 29	Dec. 31	Jan. 15 '99
0.400	Jan. 21	Mar. 29	Mar. 31	Apr. 15 '99
0.400	May. 18	Jun. 28	Jun. 30	Jul. 15 '99
0.400	Sep. 17	Sep. 28	Sep. 30	Oct. 15 '99

Arthur J. Gallagher & Co.

Business Summary - 25-AUG-99

An insurance brokerage and risk management firm, Arthur J. Gallagher & Co. continues to look for growth opportunities in the core segments of insurance brokerage and risk management services and also in the alternative insurance and financial and related investment services areas. AJG believes that these areas continue to hold opportunities for diversification and growth. The company provides insurance brokerage, risk management, employee benefit and other related services in the U.S. and abroad.

AJG operates through a network of approximately 200 offices located throughout the United States and six countries abroad, and through a network of correspondent brokers and consultants in more than 100 countries around the world. The company has three operating segments: Insurance Brokerage Services, Risk Management Services, and Financial Services.

Its two major sources of operating revenues are commissions from brokerage and risk management operations, and service fees from risk management operations. Total revenues in 1998 were derived as follows: commissions 58% (up from 57% in 1997), fees 39% (36%), and investment income 3% (5%). Revenues in 1997 included a nonrecurring gain of $9 million, which was 2% of the total. Revenues by line of business in 1998 were: insurance brokerage services 67% (67% in 1997), risk management services 31% (28%), and financial services 2% (5%).

The company's principal activity is the negotiation and placement of insurance for its clients (corporations, organizations and individuals). It acts as an agent in soliciting, negotiating and effecting contracts of insurance through insurance companies worldwide and also as a broker in procuring contracts of insurance on behalf of insureds. Through its subsidiary, Gallagher Bassett Services, Inc., the company provides professional consulting services to assist clients.

Financial Services is responsible for all of the company's investment operations and certain non-recurring events. The company's comprehensive and diversified portfolio includes investment strategies, marketable securities, tax advantaged investments, equity investments, real estate partnerships and notes receivable from investees.

AJG aims to be at the forefront of the global claims and risk control service market. The company's international operations are principally comprised of a Lloyd's broker and risk management services company in London, a management services company in Australia and Papua New Guinea, and an insurance brokerage operation and rent-a-captive facility in Bermuda.

In April 1999, AJG entered into two agreements to sell a substantial portion of its investment in landfill gas collection partnerships and a substantial portion of its investment in real estate partnership interests. The proceeds of $50 million and $6.5 million, respectively, are expected to be received beginning in 1999.

Per Share Data ($) (Year Ended Dec. 31)	1998	1997	1996	1995	1994	1993	1992	1991	1990	1989
Tangible Bk. Val.	10.77	9.25	7.58	7.17	6.01	7.49	5.88	5.72	6.35	5.88
Cash Flow	3.75	3.78	3.13	3.03	2.63	2.42	1.99	1.72	1.86	1.70
Earnings	3.10	3.13	2.63	2.54	2.17	2.02	1.57	1.31	1.42	1.42
Dividends	1.36	1.24	1.16	1.00	0.88	0.72	0.64	0.64	0.60	0.52
Payout Ratio	44%	40%	44%	39%	41%	36%	39%	46%	40%	35%
Prices - High	46¾	38¼	39½	38	36⅜	37⅜	29¼	28⅜	25	26½
- Low	33½	29¾	29⅛	30⅛	28⅛	25½	21	19	19¾	16⅛
P/E Ratio - High	15	12	15	15	17	19	19	22	18	19
- Low	11	10	11	12	13	13	13	15	14	11
Income Statement Analysis (Million $)										
Revs.	541	488	457	412	356	318	272	232	198	173
Oper. Inc.	96.3	91.8	79.2	70.9	62.3	59.2	43.7	35.6	34.8	32.0
Depr.	11.7	11.1	9.8	8.0	7.4	6.4	6.2	5.9	5.5	3.5
Int. Exp.	Nil	Nil	Nil	NA	1.7	1.9	2.4	2.3	2.0	2.0
Pretax Inc.	84.5	80.8	69.4	62.9	53.2	51.2	36.1	26.5	27.2	26.5
Eff. Tax Rate	33%	34%	34%	34%	35%	37%	35%	29%	35%	35%
Net Inc.	56.5	53.3	45.8	41.5	34.5	32.3	23.5	18.8	17.7	17.3
Balance Sheet & Other Fin. Data (Million $)										
Cash	168	148	144	167	151	130	112	116	112	69.0
Curr. Assets	531	469	464	382	351	364	274	257	227	195
Total Assets	746	642	590	496	451	464	401	376	320	294
Curr. Liab.	531	466	445	364	342	306	275	256	206	190
LT Debt	Nil	Nil	1.1	2.3	3.4	24.5	20.0	20.0	20.0	20.0
Common Eqty.	202	164	135	118	97.0	121	91.2	85.8	81.9	74.2
Total Cap.	202	164	136	120	100	146	111	106	102	94.0
Cap. Exp.	14.0	11.3	10.1	9.4	7.4	7.0	5.8	7.7	7.2	4.7
Cash Flow	68.2	64.4	55.6	49.5	41.9	38.7	29.7	24.7	23.2	20.7
Curr. Ratio	1.0	1.0	1.0	1.0	1.0	1.2	1.0	1.0	1.1	1.0
% LT Debt of Cap.	Nil	Nil	0.8	1.9	3.4	16.8	18.0	18.9	19.6	21.2
% Net Inc.of Revs.	24.8	10.9	10.1	10.1	9.7	10.2	8.6	8.1	8.9	10.0
% Ret. on Assets	8.1	8.7	8.0	8.7	7.7	7.4	5.9	5.1	5.7	6.0
% Ret. on Equity	30.8	35.7	35.3	38.7	32.1	30.1	26.1	20.9	22.3	24.3

Data as orig reptd.; bef. results of disc opers/spec. items. Per share data adj. for stk. divs. Bold denotes diluted EPS (FASB 128)-prior periods restated. E-Estimated. NA-Not Available. NM-Not Meaningful. NR-Not Ranked.

Office—Two Pierce Place, Itasca, IL 60143-3141. **Founded**—in 1927; reincorporated in Delaware in 1972. **Tel**—(630) 773-3800. **Fax**—(630) 285-4000. **Website**—http://www.ajg.com **Chrmn**—R. E. Gallagher. **Pres & CEO**—J. P. Gallagher Jr. **VP-Fin, Secy, CFO & Investor Contact**—Michael J. Cloherty. **Dirs**—T. K. Brooker, M. J. Cloherty, P. J. Durkalski, J. P. Gallagher Jr., R. E. Gallagher, I. S. Gordon, J. M. Greenberg, F. M. Heffernan, P. A. Marineau, W. F. McClure, J. R. Wimmer. **Transfer Agent & Registrar**—Harris Trust & Savings Bank, Chicago. **Empl**— 4,300. **S&P Analyst:** J. Rudy

GC Companies

NYSE Symbol **GCX**

In S&P SmallCap 600

09-OCT-99 **Industry:** Entertainment

Summary: GCX operates General Cinema motion picture theatres in the U.S., as well as theatres in Mexico and South America. It also has a large investment portfolio.

Quantitative Evaluations

Outlook (1 Lowest—5 Highest)
• **NA**

Fair Value
• **NA**

Risk
• **Low**

Earn./Div. Rank
• **NR**

Technical Eval.
• **Bearish** since 8/99

Rel. Strength Rank (1 Lowest—99 Highest)
• **20**

Insider Activity
• **NA**

Recent Price • 28¾
52 Wk Range • 42-28¾
Yield • Nil
12-Mo. P/E • NM

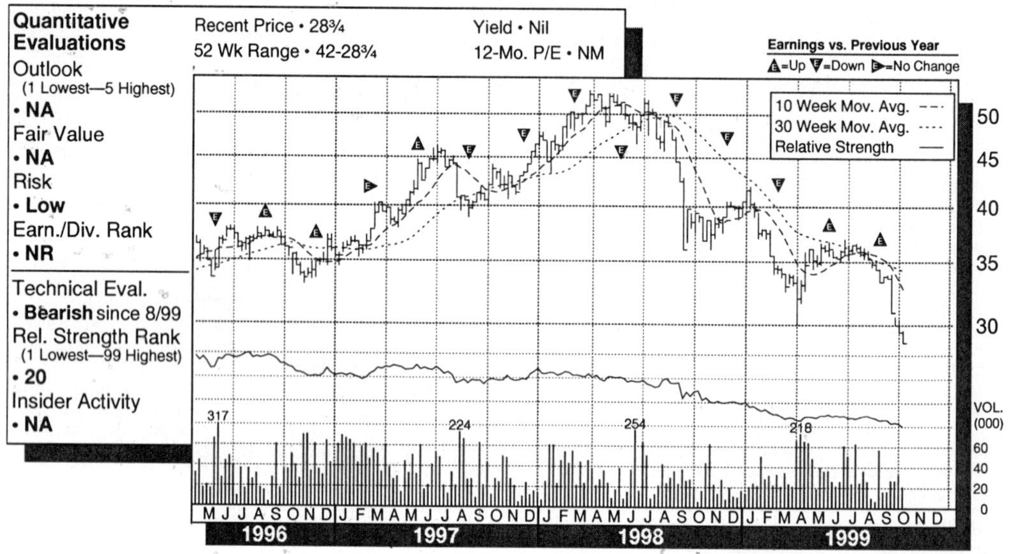

Business Profile - 14-JUN-99

GC Companies said that during the FY 99 (Oct.) second quarter it opened a 16-screen megaplex in Clifton Commons, NJ; three premium screens in Owings Mills, MD; and an additional managed unit. It also sold four units with 24 screens and closed three units with 11 screens. Going forward, the company said in May 1999 that it believed that it was well positioned to benefit from the excitement generated from release of the "Star Wars" prequel. GCX said in its first quarter FY 99 10-Q report that it expected the opening of megaplexes by competitors to continue to draw audiences away from certain of its older multiplex theater locations. Officers and directors own more than 20% of GCX.

Operational Review - 14-JUN-99

Revenues for the first half of FY 99 (Oct.) fell 14%, year to year, reflecting competitor impacts in certain markets (the opening of megaplexes by competitors has drawn audiences away from certain of GCX's older multiplex theater locations); the absence of product that was as strong as the motion picture, Titanic; and the absence of theaters that were closed in the 1998 fourth quarter. The lower revenues and a 62% rise in expenses led to a widening of the operating loss to $11.4 million from $1.6 million. After other income (net) of $8.9 million, versus nominal other income (net), and tax benefits in both periods, the net loss increased to $1.5 million ($0.20 a share), from $940,000 ($0.12).

Stock Performance - 08-OCT-99

In the past 30 trading days, GCX's shares have declined 14%, compared to a 0.91% fall in the S&P 500. Average trading volume for the past five days was 4,100 shares, compared with the 40-day moving average of 5,118 shares.

Key Stock Statistics

Dividend Rate/Share	Nil	Shareholders	7,705
Shs. outstg. (M)	7.8	Market cap. (B)	$0.224
Avg. daily vol. (M)	0.005	Inst. holdings	64%
Tang. Bk. Value/Share	24.33		
Beta	0.33		

Value of $10,000 invested 5 years ago: $ 8,303

Fiscal Year Ending Oct. 31

	1999	1998	1997	1996	1995	1994
Revenues (Million $)						
1Q	104.4	121.1	126.2	126.5	124.2	116.2
2Q	74.22	85.47	108.8	95.57	86.88	92.02
3Q	115.1	114.6	123.1	137.3	138.8	138.3
4Q	—	86.20	89.02	86.65	101.4	106.1
Yr.	—	407.4	447.1	446.0	451.3	452.6
Earnings Per Share ($)						
1Q	**0.18**	**0.40**	0.72	0.72	0.50	0.71
2Q	**-0.38**	**-0.52**	0.20	-0.18	-0.12	0.05
3Q	**0.49**	**0.26**	0.50	1.07	1.02	0.92
4Q	—	**-5.53**	0.48	0.58	-0.30	0.06
Yr.	—	**-5.39**	**1.90**	**2.19**	1.11	1.73

Next earnings report expected: early December

Dividend Data

No cash dividends have been paid. The company has said it does not contemplate paying cash dividends on its common stock in the foreseeable future.

GC Companies, Inc.

Business Summary - 14-JUN-99

As an outgrowth of a motion picture exhibition business credited with opening two of the first drive-in movies in 1938 and one of the first indoor shopping center movie theatres in 1951, GC Companies has a long tradition of providing entertainment to moviegoers.

GC Companies operates a motion picture exhibition circuit in the United States under the name, General Cinema Theatres. In addition, it operates through joint ventures motion picture theatres in South America and Mexico, and also manages a pool of its own capital for investments. Through its investment operations, GCX invests in businesses that have been, and that may continue to be, unrelated to the company's theatre business and the broader entertainment industry.

GCX was operating, as of year-end FY 98 (Oct.), 150 theatres with a total of 1,045 screens in 24 states. The company believes it provides convenient and comfortable theatres offering a popular selection of films. GCX also believes that substantially all its theatres are state-of-the-art facilities, equipped with high-quality sound and projection equipment, exhibiting films on a "first run" basis.

As of year-end FY 98, approximately 83% of the theatres and approximately 88% of the screens were located in 30 of the 50 largest areas of dominant influence (television market areas as defined by Arbitron Company) in the United States, with approximately 36% of the theatres and approximately 31% of the screens located in California, Florida, and Texas.

During FY 98, the company increased the average number of screens per theatre from 4.3 to 6.9. Multi-screen theatres enable GCX to present a variety of films appealing to diverse segments of the movie-going public while serving patrons from common support facilities such as concession stands, box offices and sales outlets.

Distributors generally license films to exhibitors on a screen-by-screen basis. Film licenses are obtained bynegotiating directly with film distributors. Fees payable to distributors are based upon several factors, including theatre location, film supply, competition, season, and film content.

GCX owns and operates the concession stands in all of its theatres. Concession sales are the second largest source of revenue after box office receipts and contribute significantly to earnings.

Effective July 1, 1998, GCX entered into an agreement to form a 50/50 joint venture with Hoyts Cinema Group creating Hoyts General Cinema South America (HGCSA). HGCSA is a stand-alone theatre circuit that will pursue theatre opportunities in South America. As of year-end FY 98, HGCSA was operating three theatre units with 34 screens in Argentina, four theatres with 25 screens in Chile, and a joint venture operating one theatre unit with six screens in Uruguay.

Per Share Data ($) (Year Ended Oct. 31)	1998	1997	1996	1995	1994	1993	1992	1991	1990	1989
Tangible Bk. Val.	21.57	24.23	22.52	20.32	19.16	NA	16.56	NA	NA	NA
Cash Flow	-2.90	4.38	4.66	3.60	4.24	NA	3.29	NA	NA	NA
Earnings	-5.39	1.90	2.20	1.11	1.73	NA	0.56	NA	NA	NA
Dividends	Nil	Nil	Nil	Nil	Nil	NA	NA	NA	NA	NA
Payout Ratio	Nil	Nil	Nil	Nil	Nil	NA	NA	NA	NA	NA
Prices - High	53	47 7/8	38	35 1/4	38 1/2	40	NA	NA	NA	NA
- Low	36	34 5/8	32 5/8	26	24 3/4	32	NA	NA	NA	NA
P/E Ratio - High	NM	25	17	32	22	NA	NA	NA	NA	NA
- Low	NM	18	15	23	14	NA	NA	NA	NA	NA
Income Statement Analysis (Million $)										
Revs.	407	447	446	451	453	495	457	NA	NA	NA
Oper. Inc.	9.1	27.5	40.1	37.5	36.5	40.3	28.1	NA	NA	NA
Depr.	19.2	19.2	19.4	19.4	19.6	22.0	20.9	NA	NA	NA
Int. Exp.	1.0	0.6	0.6	0.6	0.7	0.6	0.7	NA	NA	NA
Pretax Inc.	-69.3	25.0	29.2	14.8	23.0	17.2	7.0	NA	NA	NA
Eff. Tax Rate	NM	41%	41%	41%	41%	39%	38%	NA	NA	NA
Net Inc.	-41.6	14.8	17.2	8.7	13.6	10.5	4.3	NA	NA	NA
Balance Sheet & Other Fin. Data (Million $)										
Cash	93.6	30.0	73.3	71.3	85.0	7.8	64.0	NA	NA	NA
Curr. Assets	136	62.4	97.1	79.8	92.8	10.4	66.9	NA	NA	NA
Total Assets	390	340	314	300	297	211	267	NA	NA	NA
Curr. Liab.	172	113	93.7	95.5	100	88.6	85.8	NA	NA	NA
LT Debt	Nil	2.3	3.1	3.6	4.2	5.3	5.5	NA	NA	NA
Common Eqty.	166	187	176	159	150	NA	128	NA	NA	NA
Total Cap.	166	196	192	176	169	NA	152	NA	NA	NA
Cap. Exp.	19.7	18.7	10.8	17.3	9.5	19.3	12.7	NA	NA	NA
Cash Flow	-22.4	34.0	36.6	28.1	33.2	32.5	25.2	NA	NA	NA
Curr. Ratio	0.8	0.6	1.0	0.8	0.9	0.1	0.8	NA	NA	NA
% LT Debt of Cap.	Nil	1.2	1.6	2.0	2.5	NA	3.6	NA	NA	NA
% Net Inc.of Revs.	NM	3.3	3.9	1.9	3.0	2.1	0.9	NA	NA	NA
% Ret. on Assets	NM	4.5	5.6	2.9	4.5	NA	NA	NA	NA	NA
% Ret. on Equity	NM	8.1	10.3	5.6	9.1	NA	NA	NA	NA	NA

Data as orig reptd.; bef. results of disc opers/spec. items. Per share data adj. for stk. divs. Bold denotes diluted EPS (FASB 128)-prior periods restated. E-Estimated. NA-Not Available. NM-Not Meaningful. NR-Not Ranked.

Office—27 Boylston St., Chestnut Hill, MA, 02167.**Tel**—(617) 278-5600. **Chrmn & CEO**—Richard A. Smith. **Pres**—Robert A. Smith. **VP, Treas & CFO**—G. G. Edwards. **VP & Secy**—P. J. Szabla.**Dirs**—W. L. Brown, P. C. Read, L. A. Schlesinger, Richard A. Smith, F. E. Sutherby. **Transfer Agent & Registrar**—First National Bank of Boston. **Incorporated**—in Delaware in 1993. **Empl**— 988. **S&P Analyst:** N.J.D.

Galey & Lord

NYSE Symbol **GNL**

In S&P SmallCap 600

23-OCT-99 **Industry:** Textiles (Specialty)

Summary: This company is a leading global manufacturer of textiles.

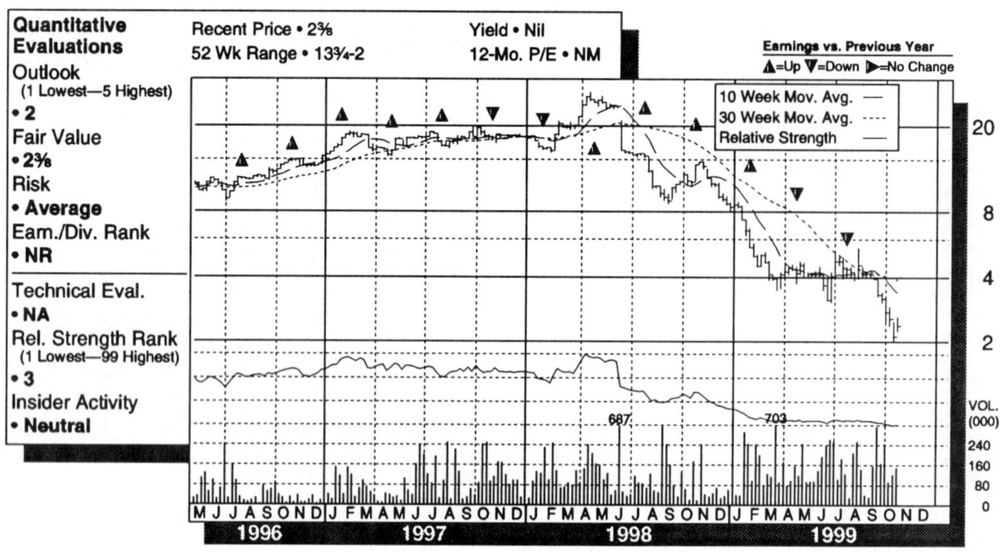

Business Profile - 19-OCT-99

As of July 3, 1999, the company was experiencing lower demand for denim, corduroy and home fashion products, as well as lower selling prices for denim. Backlog at July 3, 1999, was $164 million, down 33% from the level a year earlier. GNL has been experiencing a change in customer purchasing procedures; customers are shortening the lead times from order to delivery. If this trend continues, the company believes order backlogs will decline, and may not offer as meaningful information with regard to future sales as they formerly provided.

Operational Review - 19-OCT-99

Sales in the nine months ending July 3, 1999, advanced 15%, year to year, reflecting the addition of Swift Denim and, to a lesser extent, gains in woven sportswear. Operating income fell 33%; with higher interest expense, despite the absence of bridge financing interest expense and a loss on foreign exchange hedges, a pretax loss of $7.3 million contrasted with pretax income of $14.8 million. After tax credits of $2.6 million, versus taxes at 41.3%, a loss of $4,744,000 ($0.40 a share) contrasted with income of $8,707,000 ($0.71). Results in the FY 98 period exclude a charge of $0.04 a share for early extinguishment of debt.

Stock Performance - 22-OCT-99

In the past 30 trading days, GNL's shares have declined 46%, compared to a 4% fall in the S&P 500. Average trading volume for the past five days was 18,640 shares, compared with the 40-day moving average of 40,895 shares.

Key Stock Statistics

Dividend Rate/Share	Nil	Shareholders	1,750
Shs. outstg. (M)	11.9	Market cap. (B)	$0.025
Avg. daily vol. (M)	0.032	Inst. holdings	71%
Tang. Bk. Value/Share	NM		
Beta	0.83		

Value of $10,000 invested 5 years ago: $ 1,517

Fiscal Year Ending Sep. 30

	1999	1998	1997	1996	1995	1994
Revenues (Million $)						
1Q	246.0	127.2	110.9	85.13	127.2	99.1
2Q	237.7	237.7	129.4	100.4	133.3	111.5
3Q	249.5	275.3	135.1	115.4	127.2	120.8
4Q	—	262.6	117.9	110.5	114.4	119.8
Yr.	—	902.6	493.4	411.5	502.2	451.1
Earnings Per Share ($)						
1Q	**0.19**	**-0.01**	0.30	-0.06	0.40	0.36
2Q	**-0.09**	**0.34**	0.32	0.22	0.34	0.38
3Q	**-0.49**	**0.38**	0.35	0.34	0.17	0.42
4Q	—	**0.26**	0.18	0.30	-0.46	0.41
Yr.	—	**0.97**	**1.14**	**0.80**	0.44	1.56

Next earnings report expected: early November

Dividend Data

The company has never paid dividends on its common stock and it intends to retain earnings for the operation and expansion of its business.

Galey & Lord, Inc.

Business Summary - 19-OCT-99

Galey & Lord, Inc. (GNL), is a leading global manufacturer of textiles for sportswear, including cotton casuals, denim and corduroy, as well as a major international manufacturer of workwear fabrics. The company is also a maker of dyed and printed fabrics for use in home fashions. The apparel and home fabrics divisions accounted for 95% and 5% of total sales in 1998, respectively.

The company is the largest domestic producer by capacity of cotton and cotton blended fabrics used in apparel, with about 35% of U.S. production. These fabrics are primarily used for the production of men's and women's pants and shorts. Because of its capital investment in sophisticated dyeing and finishing equipment, GNL is able to weave a limited number of substrates, which it can finish into a variety of esthetics.

Customers include such widely recognized apparel makers as Levi Strauss, Polo Ralph Lauren, Tommy Hilfiger, Calvin Klein, and Liz Claiborne.

In January 1998, the company acquired certain subsidiaries and joint interests that comprise the Swift Denim, Klopman and Swift Europe division, for $457 million. Swift is the worlds second largest producer of denim; Klopman is one of Europe's largest suppliers of uniform fabrics; and Swift Europe is a major international supplier of denim. Swift's products are made in a full range of colors, weights, and finishes.

The company is the only vertically integrated U.S. maker of corduroy, and the largest domestic manufacturer. It makes fabrics in a variety of wale and weights. In addition to traditional corduroy fabrics, the company uses its finishing expertise to differentiate its products and produce new corduroy fabrics, including corduroy that stretches. In its uniform fabric product line, GNL stresses durability, fitness for use, continuity of color and customer service. The company also sells chemically treated fabrics, including a fire-retardant finish and an antibacterial finish. Uniform fabrics are distributed to the industrial laundry, hospitality and health care markets.

The home fashions unit makes dyed and printed fabrics for use in bedspreads, comforters, curtains and accessories. The company also makes greige fabrics (undyed and unfinished) which it sends to independent contractors for dyeing and finishing.

GNL aims to be first or second in each product category it offers; to make products that can be distinguished from those of its competitors; to continue to modernize its facilities, in order to maintain its competitive position; and to further integrate the manufacture of garments with the manufacture of fabrics, in order to increase strategic relationships with customers and boost market share.

Per Share Data ($) (Year Ended Sep. 30)	1998	1997	1996	1995	1994	1993	1992	1991	1990	1989
Tangible Bk. Val.	NM	5.69	4.34	4.45	4.02	4.98	3.80	0.26	NA	NA
Cash Flow	0.42	2.40	1.80	1.37	2.27	1.69	2.01	1.08	NA	NA
Earnings	0.97	1.14	0.80	0.44	1.56	1.12	1.30	0.26	NA	NA
Dividends	Nil	Nil	Nil	Nil	Nil	Nil	Nil	Nil	NA	NA
Payout Ratio	Nil	Nil	Nil	Nil	Nil	Nil	Nil	Nil	NA	NA
Prices - High	28⅞	20	15	16	23½	15	14¾	NA	NA	NA
- Low	8	14½	8⅞	9½	12¾	8½	9½	NA	NA	NA
P/E Ratio - High	30	18	19	36	15	13	11	NA	NA	NA
- Low	8	13	11	22	8	8	7	NA	NA	NA
Income Statement Analysis (Million $)										
Revs.	903	493	411	502	451	386	353	329	NA	NA
Oper. Inc.	107	49.5	40.0	45.0	47.5	34.7	36.3	25.5	NA	NA
Depr.	35.3	15.2	11.6	11.0	8.5	6.8	6.8	6.5	NA	NA
Int. Exp.	51.5	12.3	11.6	13.1	8.4	6.5	9.7	14.3	NA	NA
Pretax Inc.	20.5	22.0	15.5	8.7	30.7	21.4	19.9	4.7	NA	NA
Eff. Tax Rate	42%	38%	39%	39%	39%	37%	34%	36%	NA	NA
Net Inc.	11.8	13.7	9.5	5.4	18.9	13.4	13.1	3.0	NA	NA
Balance Sheet & Other Fin. Data (Million $)										
Cash	19.9	2.3	3.8	4.4	6.0	2.7	3.5	5.2	NA	NA
Curr. Assets	421	181	157	182	173	141	116	105	NA	NA
Total Assets	1,038	349	305	305	299	202	173	164	NA	NA
Curr. Liab.	139	50.4	49.7	46.8	58.3	42.2	45.0	42.7	NA	NA
LT Debt	683	177	149	162	150	95.0	80.0	106	NA	NA
Common Eqty.	128	104	89.6	81.9	77.7	59.1	45.2	4.4	NA	NA
Total Cap.	873	299	255	258	24.0	160	127	121	NA	NA
Cap. Exp.	33.8	36.6	13.5	15.0	22.4	11.7	7.3	4.3	NA	NA
Cash Flow	47.1	28.9	21.1	16.4	27.4	20.2	19.2	8.4	NA	NA
Curr. Ratio	3.0	3.6	3.2	3.9	3.0	3.3	2.6	2.5	NA	NA
% LT Debt of Cap.	78.3	59.2	58.4	62.8	62.4	59.6	63.0	88.1	NA	NA
% Net Inc.of Revs.	1.3	2.8	2.3	1.1	4.2	3.5	3.7	0.9	NA	NA
% Ret. on Assets	1.7	4.2	3.1	1.8	7.5	7.1	6.4	NA	NA	NA
% Ret. on Equity	10.2	14.1	11.1	6.8	27.3	25.6	48.2	NA	NA	NA

Data as orig reptd.; bef. results of disc opers/spec. items. Per share data adj. for stk. divs. Bold denotes diluted EPS (FASB 128)-prior periods restated. E-Estimated. NA-Not Available. NM-Not Meaningful. NR-Not Ranked.

Office—980 Ave. of the Americas, New York, NY 10018. **Tel**—(212) 465-3000. **Chrmn, Pres & CEO**—A. C. Wiener. **EVP, CFO, Secy, Treas & Investor Contact**—Michael R. Harmon (910-665-3037). **Dirs**—L. Abraham, M. T. Bradely, P. G. Gillease, W. deR. Holt, H. S. Jacobs, W. M. R. Mapel, S. C. Sherrill, D. F. Thomas. **Transfer Agent & Registrar**—First Union National Bank of North Carolina, Charlotte. **Incorporated**—in Delaware in 1987. **Empl**— 6,251. **S&P Analyst:** Howard Choe

STANDARD & POOR'S
STOCK REPORTS

Gardner Denver

NYSE Symbol **GDI**

In S&P SmallCap 600

23-OCT-99

Industry:
Machinery (Diversified)

Summary: GDI manufactures air compressors and blowers for industrial use. It also makes pumps for oil and gas production, well servicing, and drilling.

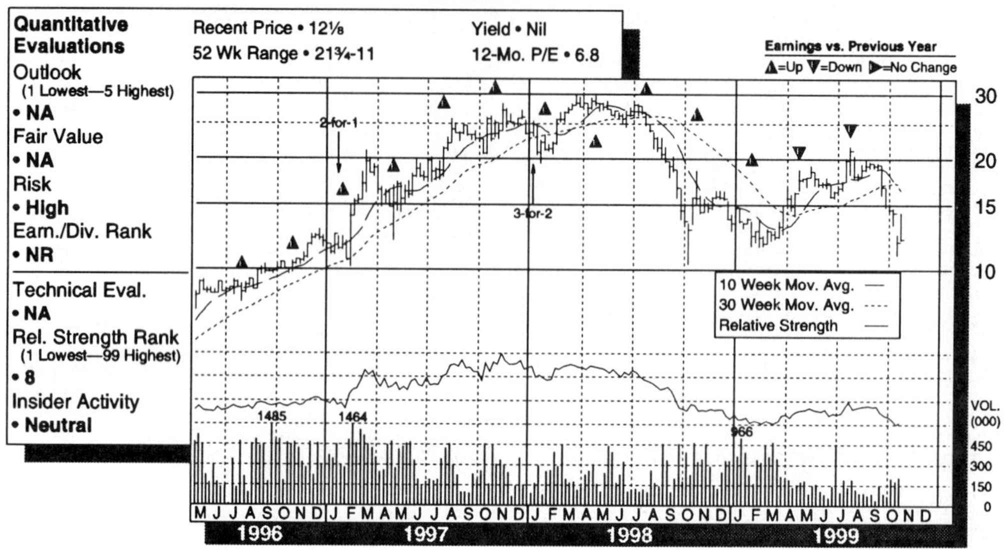

Business Profile - 21-OCT-99

In October 1999, GDI noted that while the level of order inquiries for its products has been good, increased demand for compressors typically lags other industrial goods, and it appears that order and revenue growth will be delayed until 2000. On the petroleum side of the business, GDI noted some improvement in orders for well servicing pumps, which it believes may result in a modest increase in petroleum revenues in the fourth quarter and a more significant improvement in 2000, if oil and natural gas prices remain at current levels and the rig count continues to increase. Also in October, GDI acquired Mayfield, KY based Air Relief, Inc., an independent provider of replacement parts and service for centrifugal compressors in a cash for stock transaction. Air Relief posted revenues of about $11 million in the year ended June 30, 1999.

Operational Review - 21-OCT-99

Revenues in the nine months ended September 30, 1999, fell 20%, year to year, on lower orders for petroleum products and standard industrial compressors and replacement parts. Revenues for petroleum products declined 71%, while compressor products revenues, excluding acquisitions, slid 12%. Margins narowed on the lower volume, and pretax income was down 49%. With taxes at 38.6% in both periods, net income also dropped 49%, to $13,191,000 ($0.86 a share, on 7.7% fewer shares) from $26,029,000 ($1.56).

Stock Performance - 22-OCT-99

In the past 30 trading days, GDI's shares have declined 38%, compared to a 4% fall in the S&P 500. Average trading volume for the past five days was 39,860 shares, compared with the 40-day moving average of 20,528 shares.

Key Stock Statistics

Dividend Rate/Share	Nil	Shareholders	9,500
Shs. outstg. (M)	14.9	Market cap. (B)	$0.178
Avg. daily vol. (M)	0.033	Inst. holdings	58%
Tang. Bk. Value/Share	1.41		
Beta	0.74		

Value of $10,000 invested 5 years ago: NA

Fiscal Year Ending Dec. 31

	1999	1998	1997	1996	1995	1994
Revenues (Million $)						
1Q	70.22	89.79	66.08	48.57	49.97	39.16
2Q	85.41	103.5	69.45	48.91	49.21	42.41
3Q	77.10	96.61	76.45	56.52	44.89	44.63
4Q	—	95.09	79.57	64.00	47.46	49.64
Yr.	—	385.0	291.6	218.0	191.5	175.8
Earnings Per Share ($)						
1Q	**0.21**	**0.49**	**0.34**	0.26	0.20	0.01
2Q	**0.39**	**0.55**	**0.43**	0.24	0.17	0.03
3Q	—	**0.52**	**0.44**	0.24	0.13	0.06
4Q	—	**0.66**	**0.53**	0.36	0.30	-6.46
Yr.	—	**2.22**	**1.74**	**1.11**	**0.79**	**-6.39**

Next earnings report expected: late October

Dividend Data

No cash dividends have been paid.

A Division of The McGraw-Hill Companies

Gardner Denver, Inc.

23-OCT-99

Business Summary - 21-OCT-99

From its humble beginnings in 1859, when Robert W. Gardner redesigned the fly-ball governor to provide speed control for steam engines, Gardner Denver, Inc. (GDI) has evolved into a designer, manufacturer and marketer of compressed air products and petroleum products.

The company believes that it is one of the leading manufacturers of stationary air compressors and blowers for industrial applications, based on total sales in the U.S. Stationary air compressors are used in manufacturing, process applications and materials handling, and to power air tools and equipment. Blowers are used primarily in the pneumatic conveying of dry bulk materials, wastewater aeration and vacuum systems. GDI also believes it is one of the leading manufacturers of petroleum pumps used in oil and gas production and drilling, well servicing and well stimulation. In 1998, compressed air products provided 78% of revenues (78% in 1997), and petroleum products 22% (22%).

Sales outside the U.S. accounted for 28% of 1998 revenues. Of total foreign sales, 50% was derived from Europe, 20% from Canada, 10% from Latin America, 6% from Asia, and the remainder from Africa, the Middle East and Australia.

Compressed air products consist of a broad line of reciprocating compressors, rotary screw compressors, positive displacement blowers, and centrifugal blowers that are produced for all aspects of the industrial market.

Reciprocating compressors range from 0.5 to 900 horsepower and are sold under the Gardner Denver trademark. Rotary screw compressors range from 5 to 680 horsepower and are sold under the Gardner Denver, Electra-Screw, Electra-Saver, Twistair, Tamrotor and Tempest trademarks. Blowers are used to produce a high volume of air at low pressures and vacuums.

Centrifugal blowers produce a constant level of pressure and varying volumes of air flow. Positive displacement blowers provide a constant volume of air flow at varying levels of pressure. Positive displacement blowers range from 0 to 50 pounds per square inch gauge (PSIG) and 0 to 35,000 cubic feet per minute (CFM), and are sold under the trademarks Gardner Denver, Sutorbilt, DuroFlow and CycloBlower. Multistage centrifugal blowers are sold under the trade name Lamson and range from 0.5 to 22 PSIG and 100 to 50,000 CFM.

Petroleum products consist of a diverse group of pumps for oil and gas production, well servicing, well stimulation and oil and gas drilling markets. Positive displacement reciprocating pumps are marketed under the Gardner Denver, Ajax and OPI trademarks.

Typical applications for these pumps in oil and gas production are oil transfer, salt water disposal, ammine pumping for gas processing, repressurizing, enhanced oil recovery, hydraulic power and other liquid transfer applications.

Per Share Data ($) (Year Ended Dec. 31)	1998	1997	1996	1995	1994	1993	1992	1991	1990	1989
Tangible Bk. Val.	1.93	1.17	0.26	0.84	NA	NA	NA	NA	NA	NA
Cash Flow	3.00	2.35	1.46	1.35	-5.48	NA	NA	NA	NA	NA
Earnings	2.22	1.74	1.11	0.78	-6.40	NA	NA	NA	NA	NA
Dividends	Nil	Nil	Nil	Nil	Nil	NA	NA	NA	NA	NA
Payout Ratio	Nil	Nil	Nil	Nil	Nil	NA	NA	NA	NA	NA
Prices - High	30 3/8	28 3/8	12 7/8	6 3/8	3 5/8	NA	NA	NA	NA	NA
- Low	10 3/8	10 1/8	5 7/8	3 3/8	2 1/2	NA	NA	NA	NA	NA
P/E Ratio - High	14	16	11	8	d	NA	NA	NA	NA	NA
- Low	5	6	5	4	d	NA	NA	NA	NA	NA
Income Statement Analysis (Million $)										
Revs.	385	292	218	192	176	158	NA	NA	NA	NA
Oper. Inc.	78.4	60.0	37.0	33.0	23.1	NA	NA	NA	NA	NA
Depr.	13.0	9.7	5.4	8.3	12.9	NA	NA	NA	NA	NA
Int. Exp.	4.8	3.9	3.1	5.0	4.7	NA	NA	NA	NA	NA
Pretax Inc.	59.9	46.2	28.4	19.8	-94.2	NA	NA	NA	NA	NA
Eff. Tax Rate	39%	40%	41%	42%	NM	NA	NA	NA	NA	NA
Net Inc.	36.8	27.7	16.9	11.6	-89.6	1.8	NA	NA	NA	NA
Balance Sheet & Other Fin. Data (Million $)										
Cash	24.5	8.8	8.6	1.9	NA	NA	NA	NA	NA	NA
Curr. Assets	152	125	109	90.3	NA	NA	NA	NA	NA	NA
Total Assets	342	269	236	184	23.3	NA	NA	NA	NA	NA
Curr. Liab.	63.3	58.9	49.3	31.6	NA	NA	NA	NA	NA	NA
LT Debt	81.1	51.2	55.1	36.7	56.1	NA	NA	NA	NA	NA
Common Eqty.	143	104	74.1	55.2	42.3	NA	NA	NA	NA	NA
Total Cap.	224	155	129	91.9	98.4	NA	NA	NA	NA	NA
Cap. Exp.	19.7	9.8	4.2	3.3	4.3	NA	NA	NA	NA	NA
Cash Flow	49.8	37.3	22.4	19.9	-6.7	NA	NA	NA	NA	NA
Curr. Ratio	2.4	2.1	2.2	2.9	NA	NA	NA	NA	NA	NA
% LT Debt of Cap.	36.2	33.0	42.7	39.9	57.0	NA	NA	NA	NA	NA
% Net Inc.of Revs.	9.6	9.5	7.8	6.1	NM	1.1	NA	NA	NA	NA
% Ret. on Assets	12.0	11.0	NM	6.0	NM	NA	NA	NA	NA	NA
% Ret. on Equity	29.9	31.0	26.1	23.8	NM	NA	NA	NA	NA	NA

Data as orig reptd.; bef. results of disc opers/spec. items. Per share data adj. for stk. divs. Bold denotes diluted EPS (FASB 128)-prior periods restated. E-Estimated. NA-Not Available. NM-Not Meaningful. NR-Not Ranked.

Office—1800 Gardner Expressway, Quincy, IL 62301. **Tel**—(217) 222-5400. **Fax**—(217) 228-8260. **Website**—http://www.gardnerdenver.com **Chrmn, Pres & CEO**—R. J. Centanni. **VP-Fin & CFO**—P. R. Roth. **VP, Treas, Secy & Investor Contact** —Helen W. Cornell (217) 228-8209. **Dirs**—D. G. Barger Jr., R. J. Centanni, F. J. Hansen, R. R. Hipp, T. M. McKenna, A. E. Riedel, M. J. Sebastian, R. L. Thompson. **Transfer Agent & Registrar**—First Chicago Trust Co. of New York, Jersey City, NJ. **Incorporated**—in Delaware in 1993. **Empl**— 1,600. **S&P Analyst:** M.I.

STANDARD
&POOR'S
STOCK REPORTS

GenCorp Inc.

NYSE Symbol **GY**

In S&P SmallCap 600

09-OCT-99

Industry: Manufacturing (Diversified)

Summary: GenCorp manufactures defense systems and automotive products; it recently spun off its performance chemcals, and decorative and building products businesses.

Quantitative Evaluations

Outlook (1 Lowest—5 Highest)
• **4**

Fair Value
• **23¼**

Risk
• **Average**

Earn./Div. Rank
• **B**

Technical Eval.
• **Bearish** since 8/99

Rel. Strength Rank (1 Lowest—99 Highest)
• **1**

Insider Activity
• **NA**

Recent Price • 11⅜
52 Wk Range • 27⅞-9⅝
Yield • 5.2%
12-Mo. P/E • 4.7

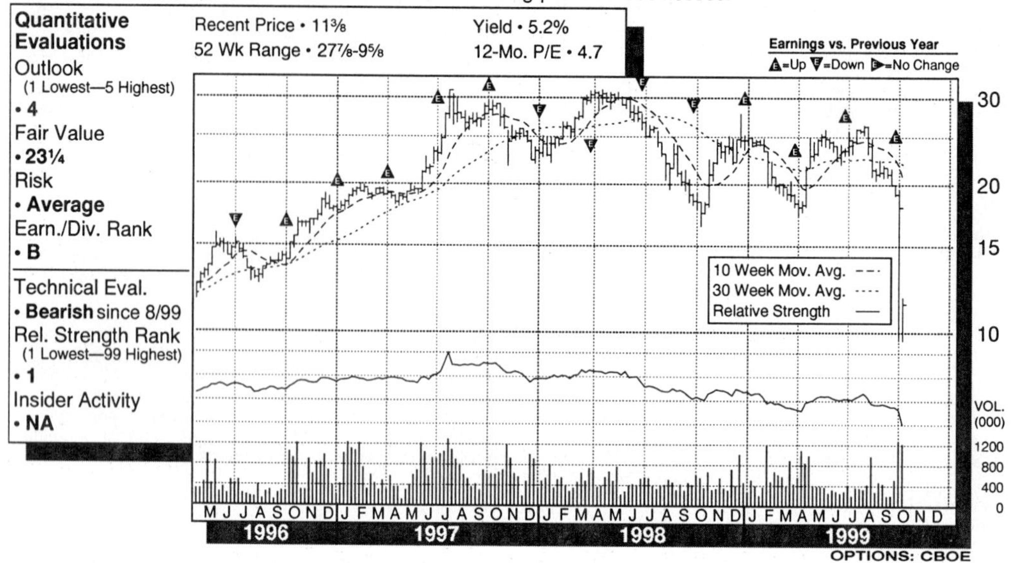

Business Profile - 04-OCT-99

The company spun off its performance chemicals (formerly specialty polymers) and decorative and building products businesses to its shareholders on October 1, 1999, distributing one OMNOVA Solutions share for each GY share. OMNOVA was listed on the NYSE under the symbol OMN. GY's chairman and CEO, John Yasinsky, moved to the spun-off unit in the same capacity. GY, which will relocate its headquarters to Sacramento, CA, will continue to operate Aerojet and its vehicle sealing unit. It expects to save $8 million annually through divestitures of non-strategic assets. In April 1999, GY acquired Morton International's global latex floor care business.

Operational Review - 04-OCT-99

Net sales from continuing operations in the nine months ended August 31, 1999, advanced 16%, year to year, as strong vehicle sealing sales, as well as higher polymer products sales, outweighed lower aerospace and defense sales. Profitability benefited from strong volume and wider margins at the Aerojet and automotive divisions, outweighing narrower polymer product margins due to lower pricing and new product development costs; operating income climbed 30%. Despite higher depreciation charges and interest expense, and spinoff-related costs, with a $15.2 million pretax gain on the sale of GY's tennis and racquet ball division, net income soared 36%, to $70.1 million ($1.66 a share, diluted), from $51.5 million ($1.22).

Stock Performance - 08-OCT-99

In the past 30 trading days, GY's shares have declined 46%, compared to a 0.91% fall in the S&P 500. Average trading volume for the past five days was 274,760 shares, compared with the 40-day moving average of 139,274 shares.

Key Stock Statistics

Dividend Rate/Share	0.60	Shareholders	12,400
Shs. outstg. (M)	41.8	Market cap. (B)	$0.478
Avg. daily vol. (M)	0.204	Inst. holdings	69%
Tang. Bk. Value/Share	2.22		
Beta	1.27		

Value of $10,000 invested 5 years ago: NA

Fiscal Year Ending Nov. 30

	1999	1998	1997	1996	1995	1994
Revenues (Million $)						
1Q	439.6	365.5	328.0	368.3	428.1	401.7
2Q	514.9	431.9	403.5	378.0	461.9	467.7
3Q	459.4	461.4	393.5	360.9	431.4	374.4
4Q	—	478.7	443.2	407.4	450.1	495.7
Yr.	—	1,737	1,568	1,515	1,772	1,740
Earnings Per Share ($)						
1Q	**0.41**	**0.31**	0.32	-0.35	0.22	-0.10
2Q	**0.77**	**0.51**	2.45	0.42	0.50	0.45
3Q	**0.48**	**0.41**	0.50	0.47	0.24	0.20
4Q	—	**0.77**	0.52	0.69	0.21	-0.95
Yr.	—	**1.99**	**3.40**	1.24	1.17	-0.41

Next earnings report expected: mid December

Dividend Data (Dividends have been paid since 1937.)

Amount ($)	Date Decl.	Ex-Div. Date	Stock of Record	Payment Date
0.150	Mar. 31	Apr. 29	May. 03	May. 28 '99
0.150	Jul. 09	Jul. 29	Aug. 02	Aug. 31 '99
Stk.	Sep. 08	Oct. 04	Sep. 27	Oct. 01 '99

GenCorp Inc.

Business Summary - 04-OCT-99

GenCorp (GY) has improved its operating margins in recent periods, and has strengthened its portfolio of businesses operationally and strategically. The company continues to build momentum through aggressive product development and marketing, combined with cost reductions, acquisitions and process improvement initiatives, and expected the October 1999 spinoff of its performance chemicals and decorative and buildings products divisions to further enhance shareholder value. GY believes the spinoff will create two better aligned and more efficient companies, where capital investments can be more easily focused on earnings and sales growth strategies.

GY produces aerospace and defense systems, which accounted for 39% of sales and 43% of operating profits in FY 98 (Nov.); polymer products (40% and 55%); and automotive parts (21% and 2%).

Aerojet General is in the aerospace and defense business, selling primarily to the U.S. government and its contractors. Aerojet has a mix of propulsion and defense electronics products and commercial chemicals. Its backlog at May 31, 1999, totaled $1.7 billion, reflecting large awards for Space Based Infrared Systems (SBIRS) and solid rocket motors.

The Vehicle Sealing division produces extruded rubber vehicle sealing and molded rubber products for domestic and European automotive original equipment manufacturers. These products prevent air, moisture and noise from penetrating vehicle windows and doors. GY sold its plastic extrusions appliance gasket business in June 1998.

The recently spun off Decorative & Building Products division has polymer-based product lines that include vinyl coated fabrics, single-ply roofing membrane wallcovering, film and laminate. The spun-off Performance Chemicals unit (formerly Specialty Polymers) produces latex used as a coating for paper, binding agents for carpets and nonwoven fabrics, and tire cord adhesives. In late 1998, the division acquired the PolymerLatex acrylics plant in Fitchburg, MA. In May 1999, GY divested its Penn Racquet Sports division, recording a pretax gain of $15.7 million. In late 1998, GY sold its residential wallcoverings business.

In 1997, GY formed a joint venture with Italy-based Saiag SpA and Japan-based Tokai Kogyo to pursue global opportunities.

The company has been acquiring polymer products businesses, including Walker Greenbank plc's commercial wallcoverings business ($70 million in revenues) in August 1998. In May 1998, GY acquired Printworld from Technographics, Inc., for $47 million. In March 1998, the company acquired Goodyear Tire & Rubber Co.'s latex manufacturing facility in Calhoun, GA, adding over $50 million in sales from the production of latex products, and expanding specialty polymers emulsion polymer production capacity by nearly 30%.

Per Share Data ($) (Year Ended Nov. 30)	1998	1997	1996	1995	1994	1993	1992	1991	1990	1989
Tangible Bk. Val.	2.22	5.57	1.67	1.05	-0.22	7.41	6.71	6.71	6.30	4.88
Cash Flow	3.31	4.77	3.19	3.53	1.89	3.69	3.18	3.44	3.94	2.46
Earnings	1.99	3.63	1.24	1.17	-0.41	1.35	0.70	1.00	1.60	0.25
Dividends	0.60	0.60	0.60	0.60	0.60	0.60	0.60	0.60	0.60	0.60
Payout Ratio	30%	17%	48%	51%	NM	44%	86%	59%	37%	238%
Prices - High	31 1/8	31	19 1/8	14 1/8	16 3/8	17 3/8	15 5/8	12 3/4	12 7/8	19 1/8
- Low	16 3/8	17 5/8	11 1/2	10	9 7/8	11 1/4	8 7/8	5 5/8	5	10 7/8
P/E Ratio - High	16	9	15	12	NM	13	22	13	8	77
- Low	8	5	9	9	NM	8	13	6	3	44
Income Statement Analysis (Million $)										
Revs.	1,737	1,568	1,515	1,772	1,740	1,905	1,937	1,993	1,775	1,938
Oper. Inc.	202	182	179	174	170	175	188	168	173	170
Depr.	55.0	60.0	65.0	76.0	73.0	74.0	79.0	77.0	74.0	70.0
Int. Exp.	14.0	16.0	27.0	34.0	32.0	36.0	46.0	52.0	62.0	67.0
Pretax Inc.	136	118	42.0	64.0	-22.0	70.0	37.0	49.0	82.0	8.0
Eff. Tax Rate	38%	NM	NM	41%	NM	39%	41%	35%	38%	Nil
Net Inc.	84.0	137	42.0	38.0	-13.0	43.0	22.0	32.0	51.0	8.0
Balance Sheet & Other Fin. Data (Million $)										
Cash	29.0	18.0	22.0	17.0	30.0	23.0	34.0	41.0	31.0	45.0
Curr. Assets	529	484	452	465	421	430	437	436	415	584
Total Assets	1,743	1,432	1,330	1,458	1,455	1,164	1,131	1,113	1,078	1,270
Curr. Liab.	430	390	370	376	367	341	408	379	365	448
LT Debt	356	84.0	263	383	378	416	344	355	345	496
Common Eqty.	344	281	56.0	35.0	-7.0	235	213	213	200	155
Total Cap.	700	365	319	418	371	651	557	582	559	652
Cap. Exp.	88.0	58.0	47.0	63.0	63.0	67.0	96.0	93.0	79.0	111
Cash Flow	139	197	107	114	60.0	117	101	109	125	78.0
Curr. Ratio	1.2	1.2	1.2	1.2	1.1	1.3	1.1	1.2	1.1	1.3
% LT Debt of Cap.	50.9	23.0	82.4	91.6	101.9	63.9	61.8	61.0	61.7	76.1
% Net Inc.of Revs.	4.8	8.7	2.8	2.1	NM	2.3	1.1	1.6	2.9	0.4
% Ret. on Assets	5.3	9.9	3.0	2.6	NM	3.7	2.0	2.9	4.3	0.6
% Ret. on Equity	26.9	81.3	92.3	NM	NM	19.2	10.3	15.5	28.7	13.4

Data as orig reptd.; bef. results of disc opers/spec. items. Per share data adj. for stk. divs. Bold denotes diluted EPS (FASB 128)-prior periods restated. E-Estimated. NA-Not Available. NM-Not Meaningful. NR-Not Ranked.

Office—175 Ghent Rd., Fairlawn, OH 44333-3300. **Registrars**—First Chicago Trust Co., NYC; First National Bank of Ohio, Akron. **Registrar**—Bank of New York Co., NYC.**Tel**—(330) 869-4200. **Website**—http://www.gencorp.com **Chrmn, Pres & CEO**—R. Wolfe. **Secy**—E. R. Dye. **SVP, CFO & Investor Contact**—Michael Hicks.**Dirs**—E. P. Campbell, A. J. G. Cooper, C. A. Corry, W. K. Hall, R. K. Jaedicke, P. X. Kelly, R. D. Kunisch, D. E. McGarry, J. M. Osterhoff, S. W. Percy, R. B. Pipes, D. M. Steuert, R. Wolfe, J. B. Yasinsky. **Transfer Agents**—First Chicago Trust Co., NYC; Co.'s office. **Incorporated**—in Ohio in 1915. **Empl**— 8,170. **S&P Analyst:** Stewart Scharf

STANDARD
&POOR'S
STOCK REPORTS

General Communication

NASDAQ Symbol **GNCMA**

In S&P SmallCap 600

09-OCT-99

Industry:
Telecommunications (Long Distance)

Summary: Through subsidiaries, this MCI affiliate provides long-distance and other telecommunications services, including cable television, to the state of Alaska.

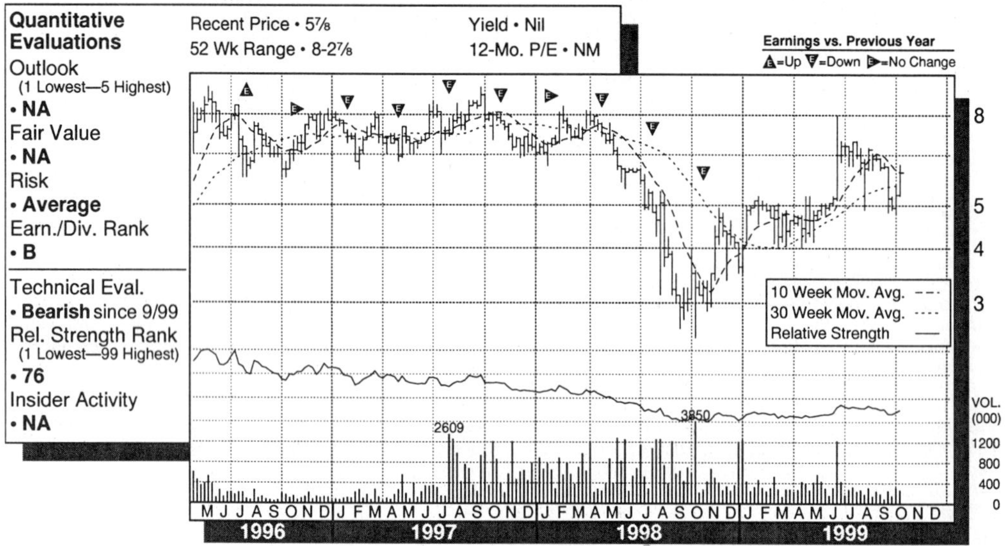

Business Profile - 03-AUG-99

The company aims to be a one-stop provider of voice, video and data transmission services. GNCMA has a leading position in facilities-based long-distance service in the state of Alaska, and is that state's largest cable operator, with more than 110,000 subscribers. The company began offering retail Internet services in 1998; as of March 31, 1999, it provided service to over 20,000 retail dial-up subscribers. In mid-1999, the company sold fiber capacity over its long haul fiber optic network to Alaska Communications Systems, for $19.5 million in cash. GNCMA began carrying commercial traffic over its newly constructed fiber optic network in February 1999.

Operational Review - 03-AUG-99

Revenues rose 5.3%, year to year, in the three months ended March 31, 1999, as higher cable, local access and Internet service revenues outweighed reduced revenues from long distance operations, reflecting competitive pressures. Results benefited from a more favorable product mix and transmission of long distance services over the company's own network, as opposed to paying other carriers for transmission. However, with continued expenditures on business growth and new products, and after sharply higher interest expense and depreciation and amortization charges, the loss widened to $4,865,000 ($0.10 a share), from $1,616,000 ($0.03).

Stock Performance - 08-OCT-99

In the past 30 trading days, GNCMA's shares have declined 7%, compared to a 0.91% fall in the S&P 500. Average trading volume for the past five days was 51,680 shares, compared with the 40-day moving average of 40,456 shares.

Key Stock Statistics

Dividend Rate/Share	Nil	Shareholders	2,500
Shs. outstg. (M)	50.3	Market cap. (B)	$0.274
Avg. daily vol. (M)	0.047	Inst. holdings	37%
Tang. Bk. Value/Share	NM		
Beta	1.18		

Value of $10,000 invested 5 years ago: $ 12,498

Fiscal Year Ending Dec. 31

	1999	1998	1997	1996	1995	1994
Revenues (Million $)						
1Q	61.30	58.15	52.88	37.97	29.69	28.19
2Q	83.66	62.94	56.19	37.20	31.86	28.97
3Q	—	62.77	57.96	38.66	33.36	30.68
4Q	—	—	56.78	51.06	34.37	28.93
Yr.	—	246.8	223.8	164.9	129.3	117.0
Earnings Per Share ($)						
1Q	**-0.10**	**-0.03**	**-0.01**	0.09	0.07	0.07
2Q	**0.04**	**-0.04**	**-0.02**	0.09	0.08	0.09
3Q	—	**-0.04**	**-0.01**	0.09	0.09	0.08
4Q	—	—	Nil	Nil	0.07	0.06
Yr.	—	**-0.14**	**-0.04**	**0.28**	**0.32**	0.30

Next earnings report expected: mid November

Dividend Data

No cash dividends have been paid.

A Division of The McGraw-Hill Companies

General Communication, Inc.

Business Summary - 03-AUG-99

Alaska-based General Communication, Inc. (GNCMA) supplies common-carrier long distance and other telecommunication products and services to residential, commercial and government users. Following the October 1996 acquisition of the three leading Alaskan cable operators, the company provides video broadcast services to about 77% of Alaskan households. Competition for GNCMA is restricted, due to its location in Alaska. Major competitors include AT&T Alascom, a subsidiary of AT&T; Anchorage Telephone Utility; and Pacific Telecom, Inc.

GNCMA offers a broad spectrum of telecommunication services to customers primarily throughout Alaska. Long distance consists of switched message and data transmission (MTS) services on both an interstate and intrastate level in Alaska and with the rest of the U.S. and foreign countries. The MTS business generated about 65% of 1998 revenue, down from 70% in 1997. Private line and private network communication services are provided between major cities. In addition, the unit sells data communication equipment and provides technical support, consulting and outsourcing services (5% of 1998 revenues). Its two largest customers, MCI and Sprint, accounted for 15% and 10% of 1998 sales, respectively. GNCMA's MTS subscribers decreased 7.8%, to about 82,000 at December 31, 1998. Systemwide minutes of use increased 5.0% in 1998, to 791,897 minutes.

Cable services are offered to 26 communities and areas in Alaska, including the three largest urban areas, Anchorage, Fairbanks and Juneau. The cable system passed approximately 171,000 homes and served approximately 112,000 subscribers, implying a 61% penetration rate. The system consisted of about 1,806 miles of installed cable plant having 300 to 550 MHz of channel capacity. Cable services provided 25% of total revenues in 1998.

Other communications offerings include wireless services provided through a cellular reseller agreement, satellite earth stations that operate in rural, hard-to-reach areas, and from an as yet to be developed PCS network, the license for which was purchased from the FCC in 1995 for $1.7 million. GNCMA also entered the local services market in Anchorage in 1997, and can access 93% of Anchorage area local loops from its facilities. The company resells its competitors' local service where GNCMA does not have access to loop facilities.

The company completed construction and placed into service in February 1999 a fiber optic cable connecting Anchorage, Whittier, Valdez, Fairbanks and Juneau, AL, and Seattle, WA, with the lower 48 states. GNCMA will use half the capacity of the cable for its own traffic. In June 1999, the company sold fiber capacity along its fiber optic network to Alaska Communications Systems, for $19.5 million in cash.

Per Share Data ($) (Year Ended Dec. 31)	1998	1997	1996	1995	1994	1993	1992	1991	1990	1989
Tangible Bk. Val.	NM	NM	NM	1.76	1.42	1.12	0.65	0.58	0.64	0.57
Cash Flow	0.51	0.49	0.61	0.56	0.58	0.47	0.43	0.28	0.33	0.35
Earnings	-0.14	-0.05	0.27	0.31	0.30	0.17	0.02	-0.12	0.04	0.08
Dividends	Nil	Nil	Nil	Nil	Nil	Nil	Nil	Nil	Nil	Nil
Payout Ratio	Nil	Nil	Nil	Nil	Nil	Nil	Nil	Nil	Nil	Nil
Prices - High	8 3/8	9 1/4	9 1/4	5 1/8	5 7/8	5 1/2	2 5/8	3 1/4	3	3 5/8
- Low	2 1/2	6	4 1/2	3 1/4	3 1/8	2 1/4	1 5/16	1 5/8	1 5/8	1 1/2
P/E Ratio - High	NM	NM	34	17	20	32	NM	NM	75	45
- Low	NM	NM	17	10	10	13	NM	NM	41	19
Income Statement Analysis (Million $)										
Revs.	247	224	165	129	117	102	96.5	75.5	63.4	52.1
Oper. Inc.	40.9	39.1	25.9	19.7	19.7	15.5	12.3	7.4	8.3	10.1
Depr.	32.0	23.8	9.5	6.2	6.7	6.7	7.0	5.8	5.0	4.7
Int. Exp.	19.8	17.6	4.8	1.0	1.5	2.3	4.0	3.2	2.6	3.5
Pretax Inc.	-10.9	-2.2	12.7	12.6	11.7	6.7	1.5	-1.4	1.0	1.9
Eff. Tax Rate	NM	NM	41%	41%	39%	41%	42%	NM	44%	34%
Net Inc.	-6.8	-1.7	7.5	7.5	7.1	4.0	0.9	-1.1	0.5	1.3
Balance Sheet & Other Fin. Data (Million $)										
Cash	12.0	42.5	13.3	4.0	1.6	2.6	3.0	0.9	0.8	1.8
Curr. Assets	61.3	44.2	47.1	29.2	21.5	23.4	20.8	19.5	13.6	11.0
Total Assets	646	545	447	84.8	74.2	71.6	72.4	70.2	54.4	47.8
Curr. Liab.	53.0	49.2	69.9	24.1	19.8	17.6	38.0	38.7	16.5	9.8
LT Debt	352	249	192	9.1	12.0	19.8	14.9	12.7	21.8	23.3
Common Eqty.	200	204	150	43.0	35.1	27.2	11.6	10.3	10.3	9.3
Total Cap.	590	492	375	59.1	53.6	53.4	33.9	30.8	37.2	37.0
Cap. Exp.	149	64.6	38.6	8.9	10.6	5.7	4.8	16.1	8.5	3.4
Cash Flow	25.2	22.1	16.9	13.7	13.9	10.5	7.3	4.1	5.5	5.9
Curr. Ratio	1.2	0.9	0.7	1.2	1.1	1.3	0.5	0.5	0.8	1.1
% LT Debt of Cap.	59.6	50.5	51.0	15.3	22.4	37.0	43.9	41.3	58.5	62.9
% Net Inc.of Revs.	NM	NM	4.5	5.8	6.1	3.9	0.9	NM	0.9	2.4
% Ret. on Assets	NM	NM	2.8	9.4	9.6	4.4	1.2	NM	1.0	2.4
% Ret. on Equity	NM	NM	7.7	19.2	22.6	17.1	2.4	NM	5.4	15.6

Data as orig reptd.; bef. results of disc opers/spec. items. Per share data adj. for stk. divs. Bold denotes diluted EPS (FASB 128)-prior periods restated. E-Estimated. NA-Not Available. NM-Not Meaningful. NR-Not Ranked.

Office—2550 Denali St., Suite 1000, Anchorage, AK 99503. **Tel**—(907) 265-5600. **Chrmn**—C. F. Page. **Vice Chrmn**—R. M. Walp. **Pres & CEO**—R. A. Duncan. **SVP, CFO, Secy, Treas & Investor Contact**—J. M. Lowber. **Dirs**—R. R. Beaumont, R. A. Duncan, D. F. Fisher, W. P. Glasgow, S. R. Mooney, C. F. Page, L. E. Romrell, J. M. Schneider, C. Shipman, R. M. Walp. **Transfer Agent**—ChaseMellon Shareholder Services, SF. **Incorporated**—in Alaska in 1979. **Empl**— 972. **S&P Analyst:** S.A.H.

STANDARD
&POOR'S
STOCK REPORTS

General Semiconductor

NYSE Symbol **SEM**

In S&P SmallCap 600

09-OCT-99

Industry:
Electronics (Semiconductors)

Summary: This company, the successor to General Instrument's semiconductor business, is a leading manufacturer of discrete semiconductors.

Quantitative Evaluations

Outlook
(1 Lowest—5 Highest)
• **NA**

Fair Value
• **NA**

Risk
• **NA**

Earn./Div. Rank
• **NR**

Technical Eval.
• **Bullish** since 8/99

Rel. Strength Rank
(1 Lowest—99 Highest)
• **21**

Insider Activity
• **NA**

Recent Price • 9 | Yield • Nil
52 Wk Range • 12⅝-5¾ | 12-Mo. P/E • 29.0

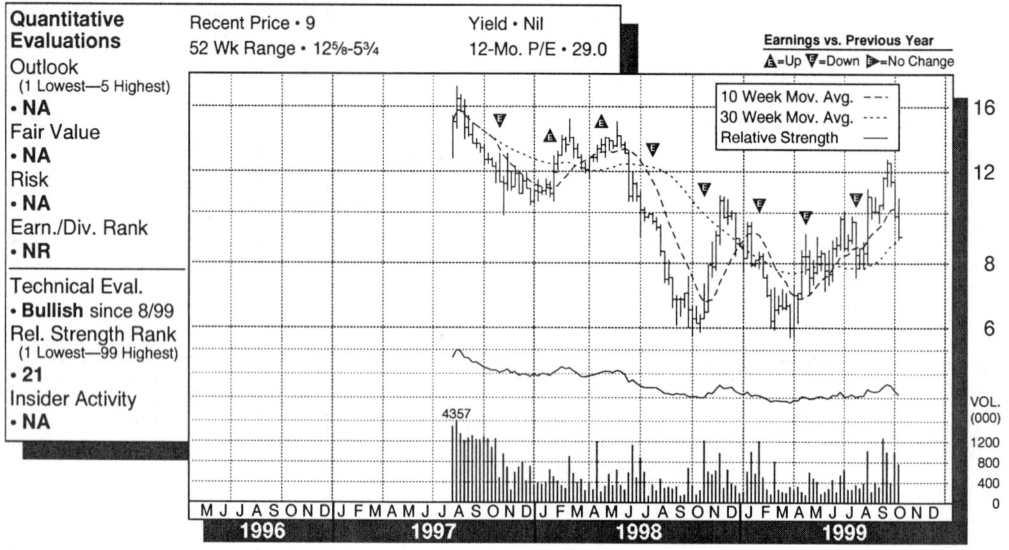

Business Profile - 08-SEP-99

As a leading manufacturer of discrete semiconductors, SEM is seeking to increase its share of the $12 billion discrete semiconductor market by focusing on value-added investment and manufacturing, introducing new products and increasing the breadth of the product portfolio, and capitalizing on its global sales and distribution capabilities. In June 1999, SEM amended its credit agreement, which will result in additional interest charges of $0.03 a share per quarter and bring earnings for 1999 (before restructuring charges) below last year's $0.74 a share; SEM expects earnings to improve sequentially. The company plans to issue senior subordinated notes, with proceeds expected to be used to repay debt.

Operational Review - 08-SEP-99

Net sales in the first half of 1999 fell 3.3%, year to year, reflecting lower average selling prices and soft demand in Europe, partially offset by increased volume in the Asia/Pacific region and favorable foreign exchange rates; sales in the second quarter edged up 2.8%. Gross margins narrowed due to the erosion of average selling prices worldwide, and although SG&A expenses were well controlled, following higher interest expense, and after taxes at 25.0%, versus 35.0% (reflecting greater income from foreign subsidiaries taxed at lower rates than in the U.S.), net income declined 43%, to $9,360,000 ($0.25 a share), from $16,311,000 ($0.44).

Stock Performance - 08-OCT-99

In the past 30 trading days, SEM's shares have declined 11%, compared to a 0.91% fall in the S&P 500. Average trading volume for the past five days was 151,560 shares, compared with the 40-day moving average of 154,300 shares.

Key Stock Statistics

Dividend Rate/Share	Nil	Shareholders	738
Shs. outstg. (M)	36.8	Market cap. (B)	$0.331
Avg. daily vol. (M)	0.156	Inst. holdings	0%
Tang. Bk. Value/Share	NM		
Beta	NA		

Value of $10,000 invested 5 years ago: NA

Fiscal Year Ending Dec. 31

	1999	1998	1997	1996	1995	1994
Revenues (Million $)						
1Q	96.96	106.4	85.37	97.90	90.00	67.76
2Q	101.6	98.76	95.51	100.0	111.5	77.26
3Q	—	97.22	95.57	84.70	109.7	83.50
4Q	—	98.76	103.6	79.34	103.1	87.17
Yr.	—	401.1	380.0	361.9	414.3	315.7
Earnings Per Share ($)						
1Q	**0.12**	**0.26**	0.14	0.29	—	—
2Q	**0.14**	**0.19**	0.24	0.36	—	—
3Q	—	**0.16**	0.22	0.25	—	—
4Q	—	**-0.10**	0.25	0.02	—	—
Yr.	—	**0.50**	0.84	0.93	1.41	0.43

Next earnings report expected: late October

Dividend Data

No dividends have been paid, and the company does not anticipate paying any in the foreseeable future. A "poison pill" shareholder rights plan was adopted in 1997.

General Semiconductor, Inc.

Business Summary - 08-SEP-99

General Semiconductor Inc. (SEM) became a stand-alone company in July 1997 with the restructuring of General Instrument Corp. At that time, NextLevel Systems Inc. and CommScope Inc. were spun off from General Instrument, and the remaining business was renamed General Semiconductor. The company is a world leader in the design, manufacture and sale of low- to medium-power rectifiers and transient voltage suppression components. It produces some 10 billion discrete semiconductors annually in manufacturing facilities located in China, Europe, Taiwan and the U.S. More than two-thirds of the company's sales are derived from outside North America.

SEM's products are used throughout the electrical and electronics industries to condition current and voltage, protect electrical circuits from power surges, amplify and switch small electrical signals and regulate voltage levels in circuits. Applications for General Semiconductor's products include consumer electronics, telecommunications, computers, lighting, and automotive products.

On October 1, 1997, the company purchased certain assets and assumed certain liabilities related to the discrete semiconductor business of ITT Industries, Inc. for $8.0 million. The acquisition was accounted for as a purchase transaction. By broadening the company's served market to include small signal transistors and zener diodes, this acquisition enabled the company to participate in approximately 50% of the worldwide discrete semiconductor market compared to the 17% in which the company participated prior to the acquisition.

The company believes that the demand for discrete semiconductors will be driven by several factors including (i) increased electronic content in a broad range of products, devices and systems, including automotive, consumer products and industrial equipment; (ii) greater demand for voice and data communications products; (iii) growth in personal computers and peripheral products; (iv) the rapid replacement of heavier and less efficient magnetic lighting ballasts with electronic ballasts; and (v) increasing international demand for all discrete products.

Research and development expenditures amounted to $6.1 million in 1998, compared to $6.0 million the year before. R&D spending reflects continued development and the advancement of new product and packaging technologies targeted for the automotive, telecommunications and computer end-market applications.

In late 1998, SEM announced a restructuring designed to enhance the interface of operations and customers, improve its cost structure, efficiency and competitive position and accelerate growth. Implementation of the plan involves a workforce reduction associated with the decentralization of certain operational functions, the closing of two sales offices and the write-off of assets related to an unprofitable product that will no longer be manufactured. A $12 million pretax restructuring charge was recorded in the 1998 fou rth quarter.

Per Share Data ($) (Year Ended Dec. 31)	1998	1997	1996	1995	1994	1993	1992	1991	1990	1989
Tangible Bk. Val.	NM	NM	NA	NA	NA	NA	NA	NA	NA	NA
Cash Flow	1.18	0.93	1.89	2.55	NA	NA	NA	NA	NA	NA
Earnings	0.50	0.84	0.93	1.41	NA	NA	NA	NA	NA	NA
Dividends	Nil	Nil	NA	NA	NA	NA	NA	NA	NA	NA
Payout Ratio	Nil	Nil	NA	NA	NA	NA	NA	NA	NA	NA
Prices - High	15$^{1}/_{8}$	17$^{1}/_{2}$	NA	NA	NA	NA	NA	NA	NA	NA
- Low	5$^{3}/_{4}$	9$^{7}/_{8}$	NA	NA	NA	NA	NA	NA	NA	NA
P/E Ratio - High	30	21	NA	NA	NA	NA	NA	NA	NA	NA
- Low	12	12	NA	NA	NA	NA	NA	NA	NA	NA
Income Statement Analysis (Million $)										
Revs.	401	380	362	414	NA	NA	NA	NA	NA	NA
Oper. Inc.	84.5	68.7	77.6	97.8	NA	NA	NA	NA	NA	NA
Depr.	25.0	24.2	22.6	21.3	NA	NA	NA	NA	NA	NA
Int. Exp.	20.0	19.6	19.6	19.6	NA	NA	NA	NA	NA	NA
Pretax Inc.	2.1	49.1	57.9	77.9	NA	NA	NA	NA	NA	NA
Eff. Tax Rate	32%	37%	41%	35%	NA	NA	NA	NA	NA	NA
Net Inc.	18.5	31.0	34.0	50.6	NA	NA	NA	NA	NA	NA
Balance Sheet & Other Fin. Data (Million $)										
Cash	3.2	5.2	20.2	36.4	NA	NA	NA	NA	NA	NA
Curr. Assets	128	118	169	156	NA	NA	NA	NA	NA	NA
Total Assets	563	550	2,057	1,799	NA	NA	NA	NA	NA	NA
Curr. Liab.	76.5	101	100	88.6	NA	NA	NA	NA	NA	NA
LT Debt	286	264	688	728	NA	NA	NA	NA	NA	NA
Common Eqty.	105	93.7	1,181	924	NA	NA	NA	NA	NA	NA
Total Cap.	391	358	1,869	1,652	NA	NA	NA	NA	NA	NA
Cap. Exp.	26.9	29.2	60.3	34.9	NA	NA	NA	NA	NA	NA
Cash Flow	43.5	55.2	56.7	71.9	NA	NA	NA	NA	NA	NA
Curr. Ratio	1.7	1.2	1.7	1.8	NA	NA	NA	NA	NA	NA
% LT Debt of Cap.	73.1	74.4	36.9	44.0	NA	NA	NA	NA	NA	NA
% Net Inc.of Revs.	4.6	8.2	9.4	12.2	NA	NA	NA	NA	NA	NA
% Ret. on Assets	3.3	3.3	2.4	NA	NA	NA	NA	NA	NA	NA
% Ret. on Equity	18.6	1.4	NA	NA	NA	NA	NA	NA	NA	NA

Data as orig reptd.; bef. results of disc opers/spec. items. Per share data adj. for stk. divs. Bold denotes diluted EPS (FASB 128)-prior periods restated. E-Estimated. NA-Not Available. NM-Not Meaningful. NR-Not Ranked.

Office—10 Melville Park Road, Melville, NY 11747. **Tel**—(516) 847-3000. **Fax**—(516) 847-3236. **Website**—http://www.gensemi.com **Chrmn, Pres & CEO**—R. A. Ostertag. **SVP & CFO**—A. M. Caggia. **SVP & Secy**—S. B. Paige. **VP-Investor Contact**—Pamela A. Jameson (516-847-3169). **Dirs**—C. S. Kulicke, R. A. Ostertag, R. Rosenzweig, P. Schwartz, S. L. Simmons, G. T. Wrixon. **Transfer Agent & Registrar**—ChaseMellon Shareholder Services, South Hackensack, NJ**Incorporated**—in Delaware. **Empl**— 5,000. **S&P Analyst:** S.S.

Genesis Health Ventures

NYSE Symbol **GHV**

In S&P SmallCap 600

23-OCT-99

Industry: Health Care (Long-Term Care)

Summary: This company provides basic and specialty health care services to the elderly through health care networks serving five geographic markets in the eastern U.S.

Quantitative Evaluations

Outlook (1 Lowest—5 Highest)
• **NA**

Fair Value
• **NA**

Risk
• **Average**

Earn./Div. Rank
• **NR**

Technical Eval.
• **NA**

Rel. Strength Rank (1 Lowest—99 Highest)
• **12**

Insider Activity
• **Neutral**

Recent Price • 2⅛ | Yield • Nil
52 Wk Range • 15-1⅞ | 12-Mo. P/E • NM

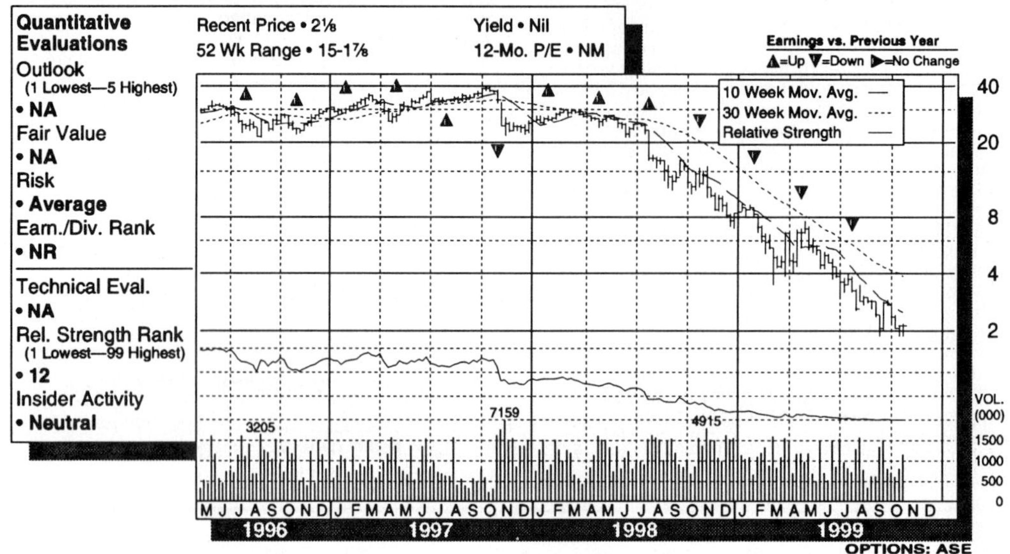

Business Profile - 18-OCT-99

Operating results in the third quarter of FY 99 (Sep.) reflected weakness in the company's pharmacy business compared with the second quarter, primarily due to the increasing reluctance by other skilled nursing facilities to admit Medicare residents in light of concerns relating to the adequacy of reimbursement under the Medicare Prospective Payment System. GHV noted that these reimbursement concerns have resulted in an industry-wide decline in occupancy levels and have caused many providers to admit customers funded by other payor sources. GHV's occupancy levels remained above 90%, but increases in staffing costs hurt operating results.

Operational Review - 18-OCT-99

Net revenues in the nine months ended June 30, 1999, climbed 41%, year to year, paced by a 159% increase in pharmacy and medical supply services. However, with increases of 51% in operating expenses and 45% in interest expense, pretax income fell 64%, to $23.4 million, from $65.0 million. After taxes at 46.4%, versus 36.5%, and a loss from unconsolidated affiliates of $8.6 million, versus income of $2.1 million, income plunged 91%, to $3,928,000 ($0.26 a share loss after preferred dividends), from $43,381,000 ($1.22). Results exclude extraordinary losses of $0.06 a share in each period.

Stock Performance - 22-OCT-99

In the past 30 trading days, GHV's shares have increased 3%, compared to a 4% fall in the S&P 500. Average trading volume for the past five days was 121,060 shares, compared with the 40-day moving average of 169,395 shares.

Key Stock Statistics

Dividend Rate/Share	Nil	Shareholders	677
Shs. outstg. (M)	36.1	Market cap. (B)	$0.077
Avg. daily vol. (M)	0.165	Inst. holdings	32%
Tang. Bk. Value/Share	NM		
Beta	1.62		

Value of $10,000 invested 5 years ago: $ 1,356

Fiscal Year Ending Sep. 30

	1999	1998	1997	1996	1995	1994
Revenues (Million $)						
1Q	479.2	302.6	258.5	132.8	111.5	71.91
2Q	464.6	344.3	273.3	154.7	117.0	98.64
3Q	465.1	352.5	284.5	172.8	126.0	105.4
4Q	—	405.9	283.6	211.1	131.9	112.7
Yr.	—	1,405	1,100	671.5	486.4	388.6
Earnings Per Share ($)						
1Q	**0.20**	**0.36**	0.34	0.25	0.21	0.15
2Q	**-0.31**	**0.41**	0.37	0.30	0.25	0.19
3Q	**-0.15**	**0.45**	0.43	0.37	0.28	0.23
4Q	—	**-1.92**	0.21	0.43	0.31	0.27
Yr.	—	**-0.68**	**1.34**	1.35	1.13	0.89

Next earnings report expected: late November

Dividend Data

No cash dividends have been paid. A "poison pill" stock purchase rights plan was adopted in April 1995.

A Division of The McGraw-Hill Companies

Genesis Health Ventures, Inc.

Business Summary - 18-OCT-99

In FY 96 (Sep.), Genesis Health Ventures consolidated its core business under the name Genesis ElderCare. The company offers an integrated health care network that provides cost-effective health care and support services to the elderly. The company's long-term growth strategy is to enhance its existing eldercare networks and establish new health networks and markets through internal development and acquisitions.

Genesis provides basic and specialty health care services to more than 175,000 customers, including 40,000 who reside in eldercare facilities. The company operates primarily in five regional markets in the eastern U.S. (New England; Mid-Atlantic; Chesapeake; Southern; and Allegheny), in which more than 6 million people over the age of 65 reside.

Consistent with its growth strategy, in October 1997, the company, in collaboration with the Cypress Group, LLC, and the Texas Pacific Group (TPG), acquired Multicare Companies, Inc. (MUL), a New Jersey-based long-term care concern, in a transaction valued at about $1.4 billion, and formed a new company, Genesis ElderCare Acquisition Corp. (GEAC).

In August 1998, the company acquired Vitalink Pharmacy Services, Inc., for approximately $680 million, including $80 million of assumed debt. GHV now has more than 100 institutional and community-based pharmacies throughout the U.S., with annual revenues of about $900 million

As of September 1998, GHV's networks included 326 eldercare centers with approximately 42,200 beds, nine primary physician clinics, approximately 85 physicians, physician assistants and nurse practitioners and 11 medical supply distribution centers. The company also operates an integrated Neighborhood pharmacy with about $900 million in annualized revenues, including 34 community based pharmacies, 79 long-term care pharmacies, infusion therapy services and certified rehabilitation agencies.

Revenue contributions in FY 98 were derived from basic health care (39% and 50% in FY 97), specialty medical (52%; 46%), and management services and other products and services (8%; 4%). The payor mix of basic and specialty medical services revenue in FY 98 was 45% private pay and other, 20% Medicare, and 35% Medicaid.

Basic health care services are offered at three levels: skilled care (provides 24-hour per day professional services of a registered nurse), intermediate care (provides less intensive nursing care), and personal care (provides for the needs of customers requiring minimal supervision and assistance). Specialty medical services provided by the company include pharmacy and medical supply, rehabilitation, subacute care, physician services, home health care, and other services.

Per Share Data ($) (Year Ended Sep. 30)	1998	1997	1996	1995	1994	1993	1992	1991	1990	1989
Tangible Bk. Val.	NM	7.07	8.29	4.84	4.15	5.78	4.19	2.57	-0.61	NA
Cash Flow	0.86	2.53	2.27	1.96	1.43	0.99	1.03	0.95	0.86	NA
Earnings	-0.68	1.35	1.35	1.13	0.89	0.67	0.53	0.37	0.08	NA
Dividends	Nil	Nil	Nil	Nil	Nil	Nil	Nil	Nil	Nil	NA
Payout Ratio	Nil	Nil	Nil	Nil	Nil	Nil	Nil	Nil	Nil	NA
Prices - High	30½	39¾	33¾	25	21⅜	16⅛	11⅜	8½	NA	NA
- Low	7	21¾	21¼	16⅞	14½	7⅝	4⅛	4½	NA	NA
P/E Ratio - High	NM	29	25	22	24	24	21	23	NA	NA
- Low	NM	16	16	15	16	12	8	12	NA	NA
Income Statement Analysis (Million $)										
Revs.	1,405	1,100	671	486	389	220	196	171	144	NA
Oper. Inc.	229	200	128	93.2	53.9	29.7	28.4	21.8	18.0	NA
Depr.	52.4	41.9	254	18.8	10.9	5.8	7.2	4.9	4.4	NA
Int. Exp.	82.1	39.1	24.9	20.4	15.7	5.1	8.8	11.1	11.4	NA
Pretax Inc.	-30.5	75.2	58.1	40.2	27.7	18.9	12.4	5.8	1.1	NA
Eff. Tax Rate	NM	36%	36%	37%	36%	37%	38%	38%	37%	NA
Net Inc.	-22.3	48.1	37.2	25.5	17.7	11.9	7.7	3.6	0.7	NA
Balance Sheet & Other Fin. Data (Million $)										
Cash	4.9	11.7	18.3	10.3	4.3	4.0	1.3	1.3	1.1	NA
Curr. Assets	574	352	233	191	120	69.7	51.9	40.7	32.8	NA
Total Assets	2,627	1,434	951	600	512	237	189	173	150	NA
Curr. Liab.	268	126	77.2	56.9	53.3	19.6	19.9	26.0	25.6	NA
LT Debt	1,359	652	339	308	251	83.8	80.2	89.8	97.7	NA
Common Eqty.	875	608	515	222	195	125	82.7	37.7	12.1	NA
Total Cap.	2,307	1,297	867	544	456	216	167	145	122	NA
Cap. Exp.	56.7	61.1	38.6	24.7	26.6	23.5	7.3	18.2	16.9	NA
Cash Flow	30.1	90.1	62.5	44.3	28.6	17.7	14.9	8.0	4.9	NA
Curr. Ratio	2.1	2.8	3.0	3.4	2.3	3.6	2.6	1.6	1.3	NA
% LT Debt of Cap.	58.9	50.3	39.1	56.6	55.1	38.9	48.1	61.8	80.1	NA
% Net Inc.of Revs.	NM	4.4	5.5	5.2	4.6	5.4	3.9	2.1	0.5	NA
% Ret. on Assets	NM	4.0	4.8	4.6	4.5	5.1	3.3	1.1	NA	NA
% Ret. on Equity	NM	8.6	10.1	12.2	10.3	10.6	10.8	8.5	NA	NA

Data as orig reptd.; bef. results of disc opers/spec. items. Per share data adj. for stk. divs. Bold denotes diluted EPS (FASB 128)-prior periods restated. E-Estimated. NA-Not Available. NM-Not Meaningful. NR-Not Ranked.

Office—148 West State St., Kennett Square, PA 19348. **Tel**—(610) 444-6350. **Website**—http://www.ghv.com **Chrmn & CEO**—M. R. Walker. **Vice Chrmn & Pres**—R. R. Howard. **EVP & COO**—D. C. Barr. **SVP, CFO & Investor Contact**—G. V. Hager Jr. **VP & Treas**—G. K. Kuhnle. **Secy**—I. C. Gubernick. **Dirs**—J. R. Anderson, R. R. Howard, S. H. Howard, R. C. Lipitz, S. E. Luongo, A. B. Miller, M. R. Walker. **Transfer Agent**—ChaseMellon Shareholder Services, NYC. **Incorporated**—in Pennsylvania in 1985. **Empl**— 45,000. **S&P Analyst:** John J. Arege

STANDARD
&POOR'S
STOCK REPORTS

Gentex Corp.

NASDAQ Symbol **GNTX**

In S&P SmallCap 600

09-OCT-99 **Industry:** Auto Parts & Equipment

Summary: Gentex manufactures automatic-dimming rearview mirrors for the automotive industry and fire protection products for commercial applications.

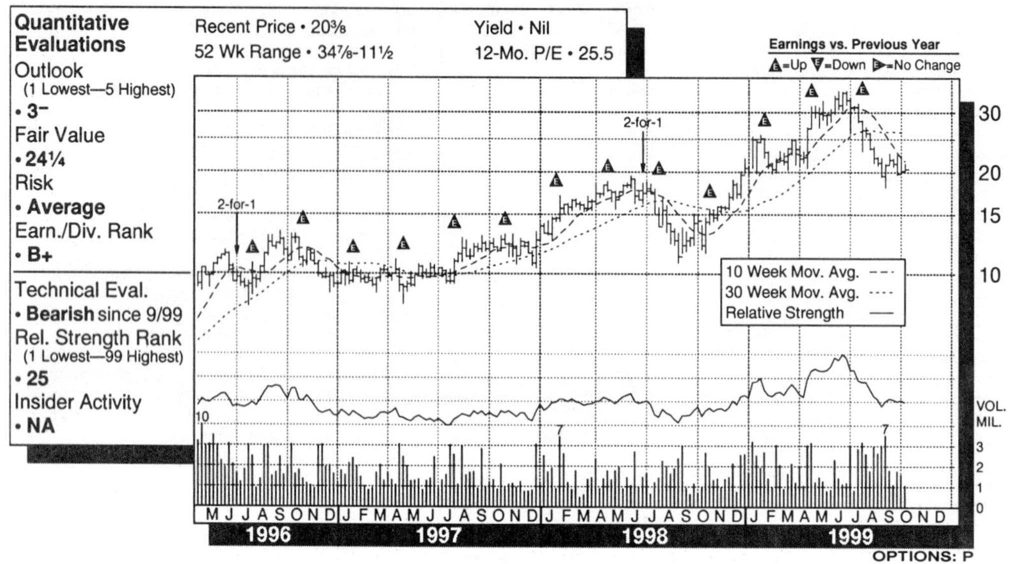

Business Profile - 17-SEP-99

Spurred by strong demand for and production of light vehicles in North America and Europe, GNTX continues to enjoy strong demand for its rearview mirror products. In the 1999 first half, unit shipments increased 25%, to three million, as auto production rose 10%. In the second half of 1999, the company has introduced two new integrated mirrors, one with an information display and another with a Homelink unit (developed in conjunction with Johnson Controls). GNTX also began shipping mirrors for the 2000 Lincoln Continental and Land Rover Discovery.

Operational Review - 17-SEP-99

Net sales in the six months ended June 30, 1999, advanced 22%, year to year, reflecting strong automatic mirror sales, and comparisons with lower shipments in 1998 due to the GM strike. Shipments to customers in and out of North America rose 30% and 14%, respectively. Gross margins widened, on higher yields on certain mirror products as a result of new coating equipment and higher unit shipments. Profitability also benefited from well controlled selling, general and administrative expense, and a 62% increase in other income. Net income climbed 43%, to $33,246,416 ($0.44 a share), from $23,265,801 ($0.32).

Stock Performance - 08-OCT-99

In the past 30 trading days, GNTX's shares have increased 5%, compared to a 0.91% fall in the S&P 500. Average trading volume for the past five days was 210,860 shares, compared with the 40-day moving average of 519,564 shares.

Key Stock Statistics

Dividend Rate/Share	Nil	Shareholders	2,273
Shs. outstg. (M)	73.2	Market cap. (B)	$ 1.5
Avg. daily vol. (M)	0.272	Inst. holdings	70%
Tang. Bk. Value/Share	3.86		
Beta	0.87		

Value of $10,000 invested 5 years ago: $ 23,190

Fiscal Year Ending Dec. 31

	1999	1998	1997	1996	1995	1994
Revenues (Million $)						
1Q	65.62	56.98	41.90	35.91	26.04	21.16
2Q	66.89	51.37	44.87	38.67	26.02	20.71
3Q	—	49.60	46.97	36.80	26.80	23.09
4Q	—	64.35	52.58	37.33	32.70	24.80
Yr.	—	222.3	186.3	148.7	111.6	89.76
Earnings Per Share ($)						
1Q	**0.22**	**0.17**	0.10	0.05	0.07	0.06
2Q	**0.22**	**0.15**	0.11	0.10	0.06	0.06
3Q	—	**0.13**	0.12	0.09	0.07	0.06
4Q	—	**0.23**	**0.15**	0.10	0.08	0.07
Yr.	—	**0.68**	**0.49**	**0.34**	**0.28**	0.24

Next earnings report expected: mid October

Dividend Data

The company has never paid cash dividends. Two-for-one stock splits were effected in 1996 and 1998.

Gentex Corporation

Business Summary - 17-SEP-99

Gentex, which was organized in 1974 to manufacture smoke detectors, now derives over 90% of its revenues from its automatic-dimming rearview mirrors business, started in 1982. In 1987, GNTX was the first company to introduce a commercial automatic-dimming mirror to the worldwide auto industry; as of December 31, 1998, it was the dominant supplier of these mirrors, with an 87% market share.

The company's Night Vision Safety (NVS) mirrors are active, crash-avoidance safety features, the same designation given to anti-lock brake systems (ABS). These mirrors use electrochromic technology and sophisticated electronic circuitry and sensors to automatically vary the reflectance of interior and exterior rearview mirrors in proportion to the amount of glare from the headlights of following vehicles. Driver safety is enhanced, because glare from following vehicles is eliminated, while optimum driver vision is preserved.

Advanced-feature NVS mirrors developed by the company include automatic-dimming mirrors with various features, including an electric compass, map lights, remote keyless entry control, and electronics to turn a vehicle's head- and tail-lamps on and off at dusk and dawn.

During 1998, GNTX sold 3.3 million interior NVS mirrors, up from 2.8 million in 1997 and 2.4 million in 1996. Sales of exterior NVS mirror subassemblies rose to 1,582,000 units in 1998, from 1,079,000 in 1997. Unit growth was attributed to the strength of light vehicle demand in the U.S. and Europe. The company markets its rearview mirror products through direct sales forces in the U.S. and Germany, and through agents in Japan.

GNTX currently supplies NVS mirrors to GM, Daimler-Chrysler, Ford, Toyota, Mercedes-Benz, BMW, Toyota/Lexus, Nissan/Infiniti, Opel, Fiat, Audi, Bentley, Rolls Royce, Honda, Hyundai, Daewoo, Kia Motors, Porsche and Samsung.

The company has derived about 10% of net sales in recent years from its line of fire protection products, which consist of more than 60 different models of smoke detectors and more than 160 different models of signaling devices. During 1996, GNTX made several revisions to its products, including weather-proofing the mechanical horn and strobe for outdoor use, increasing the power taps on the speaker series, adding three new candela ratings to the visual signals, and adding terminal blocks to the remote signaling appliances, to meet new code requirements. In 1997, the company launched a new visual and audible signaling product line. GNTX was also the first company in the fire alarm market to implement the temporal code 3 pattern on fire alarm products.

Per Share Data ($) (Year Ended Dec. 31)	1998	1997	1996	1995	1994	1993	1992	1991	1990	1989
Tangible Bk. Val.	3.28	2.44	1.84	1.40	1.08	0.76	0.52	0.45	0.42	0.40
Cash Flow	0.79	0.58	0.40	0.32	0.28	0.18	0.10	0.05	0.04	0.05
Earnings	0.68	0.49	0.34	0.28	0.24	0.15	0.08	0.03	0.02	0.04
Dividends	Nil	Nil	Nil	Nil	Nil	Nil	Nil	Nil	Nil	Nil
Payout Ratio	Nil	Nil	Nil	Nil	Nil	Nil	Nil	Nil	Nil	Nil
Prices - High	22	14 1/8	13 3/8	6 7/8	8 7/8	8 7/8	3 1/4	1 11/16	1 13/16	1 13/16
- Low	10 3/4	8 1/8	5 1/4	4	4 1/2	2 1/2	1 5/8	5/8	5/8	9/16
P/E Ratio - High	32	29	40	25	36	60	41	56	95	47
- Low	16	17	16	14	19	17	21	20	34	15
Income Statement Analysis (Million $)										
Revs.	222	186	149	112	89.8	63.7	45.1	26.9	21.2	23.8
Oper. Inc.	74.9	53.9	39.8	28.1	26.0	16.0	8.5	3.1	1.6	3.5
Depr.	7.5	6.4	3.9	3.2	3.0	2.1	1.6	1.3	1.0	0.8
Int. Exp.	Nil	Nil	Nil	Nil	Nil	0.0	0.2	0.5	0.5	0.3
Pretax Inc.	74.7	52.2	35.5	27.9	24.7	14.7	7.6	2.7	1.2	3.1
Eff. Tax Rate	33%	33%	33%	32%	33%	33%	33%	30%	5.50%	32%
Net Inc.	50.3	35.2	24.0	18.9	16.5	9.8	5.1	1.9	1.1	2.1
Balance Sheet & Other Fin. Data (Million $)										
Cash	50.0	41.1	48.5	34.2	19.3	13.3	7.8	14.3	10.9	14.1
Curr. Assets	115	75.9	72.7	56.0	36.4	27.1	17.8	20.8	15.6	20.1
Total Assets	255	190	140	109	80.5	55.2	40.3	37.2	33.9	32.5
Curr. Liab.	14.8	14.6	11.4	14.0	8.7	5.5	4.0	8.6	1.7	1.9
LT Debt	Nil	Nil	Nil	Nil	Nil	Nil	Nil	0.1	6.1	6.1
Common Eqty.	237	173	128	94.7	71.4	49.5	35.5	28.2	25.9	24.2
Total Cap.	240	175	129	95.2	71.8	49.7	36.2	28.6	32.2	30.7
Cap. Exp.	24.6	16.4	16.4	4.9	6.2	3.4	4.2	2.2	2.4	4.1
Cash Flow	57.8	41.6	27.9	22.1	19.5	12.0	6.7	3.1	2.2	2.9
Curr. Ratio	7.8	5.2	6.4	4.0	4.2	4.9	4.4	2.4	9.3	10.9
% LT Debt of Cap.	Nil	Nil	Nil	Nil	Nil	Nil	Nil	0.3	18.9	19.9
% Net Inc.of Revs.	22.6	18.9	16.1	16.9	18.3	15.5	11.2	6.9	5.3	8.8
% Ret. on Assets	22.6	21.3	19.2	19.9	24.1	20.4	12.9	5.2	3.3	9.1
% Ret. on Equity	24.5	23.4	21.5	22.8	27.0	23.0	15.8	6.8	4.5	12.2

Data as orig reptd.; bef. results of disc opers/spec. items. Per share data adj. for stk. divs. Bold denotes diluted EPS (FASB 128)-prior periods restated. E-Estimated. NA-Not Available. NM-Not Meaningful. NR-Not Ranked.

Office—600 N. Centennial, Zeeland, MI 49464. **Tel**—(616) 772-1800. **Fax**—(616) 772-7348. **Website**—http://www.gentex.com **Chrmn & CEO**—F. Bauer. **EVP**—K. LaGrand. **VP-Fin & Treas**—E. Jen. **Secy & Investor Contact**—Connie Hamblin. **Dirs**—F. Bauer, M. E. Fouts, K. LaGrand, A. Lanting, J. Mulder, T. Thompson, L. L. Weber. **Transfer Agent**—American Stock Transfer & Trust Co., NYC. **Incorporated**—in Michigan in 1974. **Empl**— 1,342. **S&P Analyst:** Howard Choe

STANDARD
&POOR'S
STOCK REPORTS

Geon Co.

NYSE Symbol **GON**

In S&P SmallCap 600

09-OCT-99

Industry: Chemicals

Summary: This company, the world's largest supplier of PVC compounds, recently joint ventured its PVC resins business with Occidental Petroleum.

S&P Opinion: Hold (★★★) Recent Price • 27⅞ 52 Wk Range • 37-16¼ Yield • 1.8% 12-Mo. P/E • 8.2

Quantitative Evaluations

Outlook (1 Lowest—5 Highest) • **4-**

Fair Value • **34¾**

Risk • **Low**

Earn./Div. Rank • **NR**

Technical Eval. • **Bearish** since 8/99

Rel. Strength Rank (1 Lowest—99 Highest) • **39**

Insider Activity • **NA**

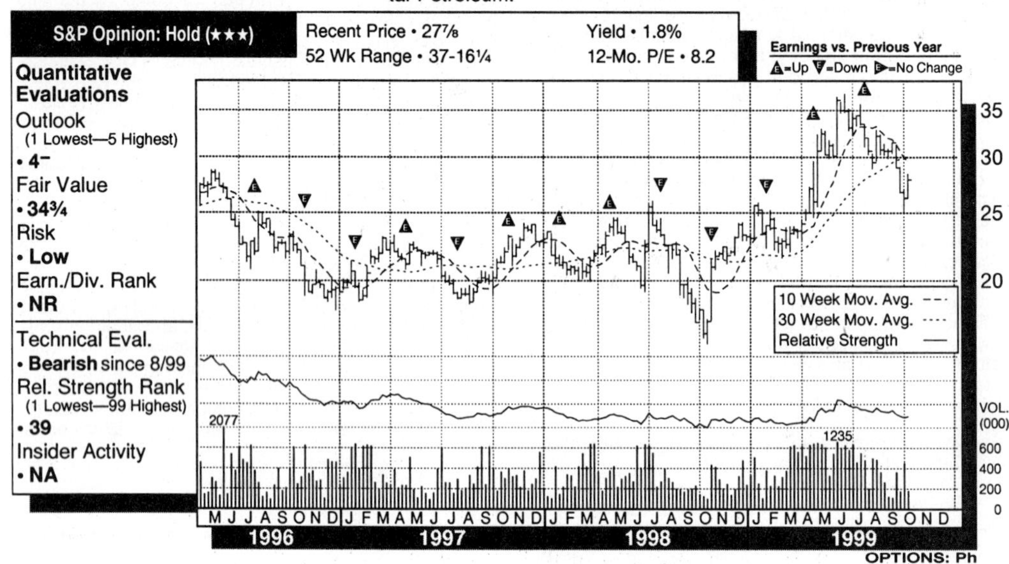

Overview - 07-OCT-99

The company will now focus solely on its compound and specialty resins businesses, which provided 65% of sales and more than 100% of 1998 operating income. In May 1999, GON and Occidental Petroleum merged their PVC suspension resins operations, forming OxyVinyls, LP. The venture, 24% owned by GON, is the largest PVC resin producer; it expects to cut annual costs by $80 million. GON acquired OXY's vinyl compound unit (annual sales of nearly $200 million), and received $110 million. We see GON with 2000 revenues of at least $1.4 billion, provided by vinyl compounds and dispersion resins, and by non-vinyl plastic compounds. Operating income as a percentage of sales for these businesses, at nearly 11%, is at the top end of the industry range. The July 1999 purchase of O'Sullivan Corp., a maker of vinyl films (annual sales of $180 million), is expected to be immediately accretive to EPS by about $0.20 annually. Several recent smaller acquisitions are projected to add a total of about $0.10 to annual EPS. EPS in the 1999 second quarter included a gain of $2.33 from the Oxy Vinyls formation; charges of $0.09, associated with consolidation of compounding operations, were recorded in the first half of 1999.

Valuation - 07-OCT-99

The shares, although up nearly 20% year to date, have recently given up some of their second quarter gains. Investors have warmed to GON's strategy of focusing solely on its performance polymers business, which offers consistent earnings growth and margins, in light of the poor conditions prevailing for commodity PVC. After the rapid run-up, we continue to recommend that investors not add to existing positions, although the shares were recently trading at a P/E multiple below that of other chemical companies.

Key Stock Statistics

S&P EPS Est. 1999	2.10	Tang. Bk. Value/Share	9.25
P/E on S&P Est. 1999	13.3	Beta	0.43
S&P EPS Est. 2000	2.50	Shareholders	7,000
Dividend Rate/Share	0.50	Market cap. (B)	$0.661
Shs. outstg. (M)	23.7	Inst. holdings	93%
Avg. daily vol. (M)	0.058		

Value of $10,000 invested 5 years ago: $ 13,297

Fiscal Year Ending Dec. 31

	1999	1998	1997	1996	1995	1994
Revenues (Million $)						
1Q	325.8	324.5	301.0	245.7	336.2	261.3
2Q	296.9	330.7	333.0	311.8	357.6	284.5
3Q	—	328.0	303.7	307.8	310.2	312.3
4Q	—	301.2	312.3	279.1	263.8	350.5
Yr.	—	1,284	1,250	1,144	1,268	1,209
Earnings Per Share ($)						
1Q	**0.46**	**0.25**	**0.10**	**-0.23**	0.80	0.25
2Q	**2.81**	**0.20**	**0.26**	**0.40**	-0.31	0.45
3Q	—	**0.26**	**0.45**	**0.25**	0.56	0.71
4Q	—	**-0.13**	**0.15**	**0.07**	0.18	0.65
Yr.	—	**0.58**	**0.95**	**0.50**	**1.24**	**2.08**

Next earnings report expected: late October

Dividend Data (Dividends have been paid since 1993.)

Amount ($)	Date Decl.	Ex-Div. Date	Stock of Record	Payment Date
0.125	Nov. 04	Nov. 27	Dec. 01	Dec. 15 '98
0.125	Feb. 12	Feb. 25	Mar. 01	Mar. 15 '99
0.125	May. 06	May. 27	Jun. 01	Jun. 15 '99
0.125	Aug. 05	Aug. 30	Sep. 01	Sep. 15 '99

A Division of The McGraw-Hill Companies

The Geon Company

Business Summary - 07-OCT-99

Geon Co. (GON) recently made another transformation. The company, part of B.F. Goodrich until the 1993 IPO, primarily makes one of the world's most widely used plastics: polyvinyl chloride, popularly known as PVC. GON is the world's largest producer of PVC compounds. Until May 1999, it was also a leading North American producer of PVC resins and the intermediate precursor to PVC: vinyl chloride monomer (VCM). In 1998, the Performance Polymers & Services segment (59% of sales and profits of $79.2 million in 1998) consisted of PVC compounds, specialty resins and plastisol formulations. The Resins and Intermediates segment (41% and a operating loss of $36.4 million) included GON's PVC and VCM operations, a 37.4% holding in Australian Vinyl Corp., and a 50% interest in the Sunbelt chlor-alkali joint venture with Olin Corp.

GON will now focus on its more profitable compound and specialty businesses, which accounted for 65% of sales in 1998, and all operating profits. As part of its strategy, in May 1999, the company merged its PVC suspension resin and VCM operations with those of Occidental Petroleum. The new venture, Oxy Vinyls, LP, is 24% owned by GON. The two partners expect the venture to reduce annual costs by $80 million, including overhead, energy, logistics, product line consolidation and purchasing. GON also acquired OXY's vinyl compound and engineered film unit (annual sales of nearly $200 million), and received $110 million. The company retained its 50% interest in the Sunbelt chlor-alkali joint venture.

Annual revenues are now about $1.2 billion, provided by vinyl compounds and dispersion resins, plastisol formulations, films, non-vinyl plastic compounds, and a technical testing service. Since late 1997, GON has built its existing PVC compound and specialty plastics businesses through acquisitions. Its first major acquisition was in October 1997, with the purchase of Synergistics Industries, a major plastics compounder with sales of $240 million in 1997. GON has also acquired five plastisol formulators since mid-1998, with total annual sales of about $165 million.

In August 1999, GON purchased O'Sullivan Corp., for a total of about $191 million. O'Sullivan is a maker of vinyl films, with 1998 sales of $163 million, and net income of $11.6 million. It is an excellent fit with GON's recently acquired calendered film business. About 60% of O'Sullivan's sales are to the automotive industry. The purchase was expected to be immediately accretive to EPS by about $0.20 annually.

Oxy Vinyls, LP is North America's largest and the world's third largest producer of PVC resins. Oxy Vinyls has manufacturing capacity totaling 4.2 billion lbs. of PVC, 4.8 billion lbs. of VCM, and chlor-alkali capacity of 900,000 electrochemical units (equivalent to 1.8 billion lbs. of chlorine and 2.0 billion lbs. of caustic soda).

Per Share Data ($) (Year Ended Dec. 31)	1998	1997	1996	1995	1994	1993	1992	1991	1990	1989
Tangible Bk. Val.	5.67	9.65	9.55	8.46	9.13	7.64	6.14	NA	NA	NA
Cash Flow	3.04	3.21	2.70	3.43	4.13	2.43	NA	NA	NA	NA
Earnings	0.58	0.95	0.50	1.24	2.06	0.08	-0.92	NA	NA	NA
Dividends	0.50	0.50	0.50	0.50	0.50	0.38	NA	NA	NA	NA
Payout Ratio	86%	53%	100%	40%	24%	NM	NA	NA	NA	NA
Prices - High	26	24 1/8	28 3/4	31 3/8	31 5/8	24 3/8	NA	NA	NA	NA
- Low	16 1/4	18 1/2	18 1/8	23 3/8	23 1/4	17 3/4	NA	NA	NA	NA
P/E Ratio - High	45	25	57	25	15	NM	NA	NA	NA	NA
- Low	28	19	36	19	11	NM	NA	NA	NA	NA
Income Statement Analysis (Million $)										
Revs.	1,284	1,250	1,144	1,268	1,209	983	894	NA	NA	NA
Oper. Inc.	110	120	84.0	184	160	87.1	NA	NA	NA	NA
Depr.	57.9	53.3	54.1	56.6	58.2	58.8	NA	NA	NA	NA
Int. Exp.	16.0	11.9	10.8	6.2	8.2	7.4	11.1	NA	NA	NA
Pretax Inc.	23.6	34.6	20.7	52.4	94.8	9.9	-36.6	NA	NA	NA
Eff. Tax Rate	42%	35%	41%	39%	39%	39%	NM	NA	NA	NA
Net Inc.	13.8	22.5	12.2	32.2	57.9	6.0	-24.2	NA	NA	NA
Balance Sheet & Other Fin. Data (Million $)										
Cash	14.4	49.1	17.9	61.1	47.5	20.0	5.0	NA	NA	NA
Curr. Assets	235	314	234	283	295	214	157	NA	NA	NA
Total Assets	802	873	737	752	792	721	697	NA	NA	NA
Curr. Liab.	257	314	204	193	247	189	175	NA	NA	NA
LT Debt	135	136	137	138	93.0	88.3	119	NA	NA	NA
Common Eqty.	214	224	222	209	240	230	181	NA	NA	NA
Total Cap.	382	356	393	384	380	343	340	NA	NA	NA
Cap. Exp.	40.7	50.9	73.4	70.0	61.5	44.1	NA	NA	NA	NA
Cash Flow	71.7	75.8	66.3	88.8	116	64.8	NA	NA	NA	NA
Curr. Ratio	0.9	1.0	1.1	1.5	1.2	1.1	0.9	NA	NA	NA
% LT Debt of Cap.	35.4	34.4	34.9	35.9	24.5	25.7	35.0	NA	NA	NA
% Net Inc.of Revs.	1.1	1.8	1.1	2.5	4.8	0.6	NM	NA	NA	NA
% Ret. on Assets	1.6	2.8	1.6	4.2	7.8	NM	NA	NA	NA	NA
% Ret. on Equity	6.3	10.1	5.6	7.2	25.2	NM	NA	NA	NA	NA

Data as orig reptd.; bef. results of disc opers/spec. items. Per share data adj. for stk. divs. Bold denotes diluted EPS (FASB 128)-prior periods restated. E-Estimated. NA-Not Available. NM-Not Meaningful. NR-Not Ranked.

Office—One Geon Center, Avon Lake, OH 44012. **Tel**—(440) 930-1000. **Website**—http://www.geon.com **Chrmn, Pres & CEO**—T. A. Waltermire. **VP & Secy**—G. L. Rutman. **VP & CFO**—W. D. Wilson. **VP & Investor Contact**—Dennis Cocco. **Dirs**—J. K. Baker, J. D. Campbell, G. Duff-Bloom, D. L. Moore, W. F. Patient, R. G. P. Styles, T. A. Waltermire, F. M. Walters. **Transfer Agent & Registrar**—Bank of New York, NYC. **Incorporated**—in Delaware in 1993. **Empl**— 3,100. **S&P Analyst:** Richard O'Reilly, CFA

STANDARD &POOR'S
STOCK REPORTS

Gerber Scientific

NYSE Symbol **GRB**

In S&P SmallCap 600

23-OCT-99

Industry: Services (Computer Systems)

Summary: This company manufactures and services computer-aided design and computer-aided manufacturing systems that automate design and production processes in a broad range of industries.

Quantitative Evaluations

Outlook (1 Lowest—5 Highest) • 4+
Fair Value • 30
Risk • Low
Earn./Div. Rank • B

Technical Eval. • NA
Rel. Strength Rank (1 Lowest—99 Highest) • 35
Insider Activity • Neutral

Recent Price • 20¼
52 Wk Range • 26-17⅜
Yield • 1.6%
12-Mo. P/E • 15.1

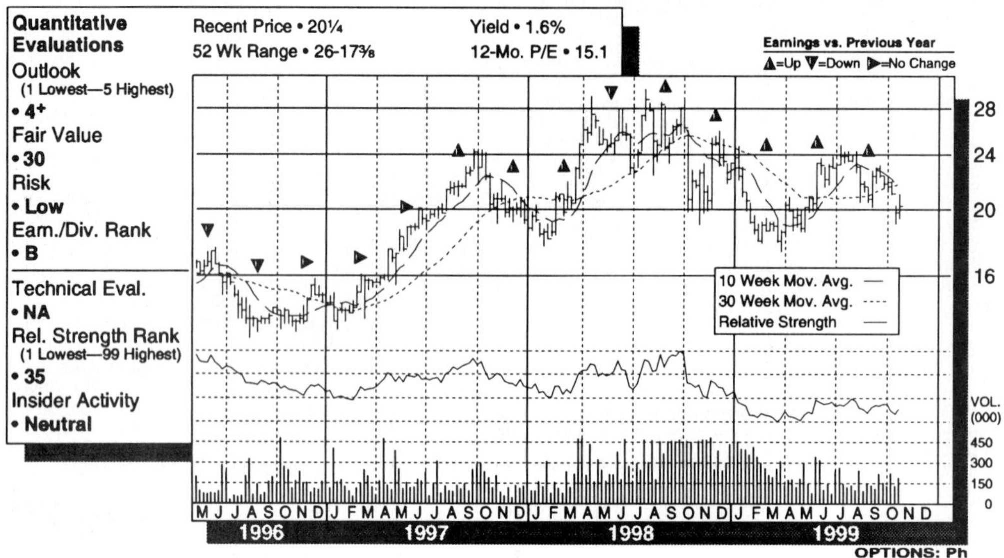

Business Profile - 21-OCT-99

In September 1999, GRB noted that strong demand for its new product introductions -- the Edge2 and Maxx thermal imaging systems, the Odyssey and Infinity plotters, the Taurus leather cutting system, and the Kappa lens finishing system -- helped increase backlog to $63.9 million as of July 31, 1999, from $46.6 million a year earlier and $50.8 million as of May 1, 1999. The company expects the large increase in backlog to drive revenue up from first quarter levels and enable it to sustain strong earnings growth. Also in September, as part of its effort to continue its expansion on a global scale, GRB acquired the assets of the Graphic-Cal Group, Australia's largest sign making supplies distributor with $12 million in annual revenues. Terms were not disclosed.

Operational Review - 21-OCT-99

Revenues in the three months ended July 31, 1999, fell 9.2%, year to year, reflecting lower optical equipment revenues, the disposition of certain distribution operations in the second quarter of FY 99 (Apr.), and less favorable translation rates for foreign currency revenue. Margins widened on a more favorable product mix, and with SG&A expenses down 11%, operating income edged up 2.3%. With lower interest expense, pretax income advanced 7.7%. After taxes at 35.2%, versus 37.9%, net income was up 12% to $7,553,000 ($0.34 per share), from $6,722,000 ($0.29).

Stock Performance - 22-OCT-99

In the past 30 trading days, GRB's shares have declined 14%, compared to a 4% fall in the S&P 500. Average trading volume for the past five days was 44,960 shares, compared with the 40-day moving average of 31,356 shares.

Key Stock Statistics

Dividend Rate/Share	0.32	Shareholders	1,471
Shs. outstg. (M)	22.2	Market cap. (B)	$0.439
Avg. daily vol. (M)	0.034	Inst. holdings	66%
Tang. Bk. Value/Share	1.02		
Beta	0.57		

Value of $10,000 invested 5 years ago: $ 15,837

Fiscal Year Ending Apr. 30

	2000	1999	1998	1997	1996	1995
Revenues (Million $)						
1Q	139.5	153.7	98.96	85.81	88.19	70.03
2Q	—	150.6	106.4	94.95	90.16	72.94
3Q	—	140.8	104.8	94.59	86.88	82.81
4Q	—	149.6	120.3	105.6	93.89	96.92
Yr.	—	594.6	430.5	380.9	359.1	322.7
Earnings Per Share ($)						
1Q	**0.34**	**0.29**	**0.19**	0.07	**0.17**	0.13
2Q	—	**0.33**	**0.24**	0.22	**0.22**	0.17
3Q	—	**0.31**	**0.27**	0.18	**0.18**	0.20
4Q	—	**0.36**	**-0.38**	0.22	**0.22**	0.26
Yr.	—	**1.29**	**0.32**	**0.69**	**0.84**	0.76

Next earnings report expected: mid November

Dividend Data (Dividends have been paid since 1978.)

Amount ($)	Date Decl.	Ex-Div. Date	Stock of Record	Payment Date
0.080	Nov. 06	Nov. 16	Nov. 18	Nov. 30 '98
0.080	Feb. 01	Feb. 10	Feb. 15	Feb. 26 '99
0.080	May. 06	May. 13	May. 17	May. 28 '99
0.080	Aug. 03	Aug. 12	Aug. 16	Aug. 31 '99

A Division of The McGraw-Hill Companies

Gerber Scientific, Inc.

Business Summary - 21-OCT-99

What do the sign making and specialty graphics, apparel and flexible materials and ophthalmic lens processing industries have in common? They all use Gerber Scientific's (GRB) computer-aided design and computer-aided manufacturing (CAD/CAM) systems to automate design and production processes. Connecticut-based GRB operates mainly through three principal operating segments.

Gerber Scientific Products (GSP) and Spandex comprise the company's sign making and specialty graphics operating segment. GSP develops and manufactures computerized sign making and specialty graphics systems, software, materials, and accessories. Digital design, printing, and production products are integrated to provide customers with comprehensive engineered solutions for color printing and dimensional signage. In addition to GSP products, Spandex PLC offers a broad inventory of specialty sign making materials. These include self-adhesive vinyl, banner materials, specialist sign making films, application tapes, and sign blanks and substrates, as well as extruded aluminum sign systems and plastic components.

Gerber Garment Technology (GT) comprises the company's apparel and flexible materials operating segment, providing advanced computer-aided design and manufacturing systems for producing sewn goods. GT produces computer-aided design, pattern-making, and marker-making systems; computer-controlled material spreading and cutting systems; and several related hardware and software systems. GT also provides maintenance services for a substantial portion of the systems it produces. These integrated hardware and software systems improve the efficiency of information data management, product and pattern design, grading and marker making, fabric spreading and cutting, and material handling processes. They also are used to manufacture products formed by flexible materials, such as luggage, toys, marine products, and composites.

Gerber Coburn Optical, Inc. (GC) comprises GRB's ophthalmic lens processing operating segment. The company's equipment, software, systems, and accessories are utilized in all aspects of surfacing and coating prescription eyewear lenses, and in the machining of eyeglass lens blanks to fit patient frames. GC develops, manufactures and distributes a wide range of fully integrated, computer-based laboratory production solutions to ophthalmic professionals around the world.

As part of its effort to continue its expansion on a global scale, GRB acquired the assets of the Graphic-Cal Group, Australia's largest sign making supplies distributor ($12 million in annual revenues) in September 1999.

Per Share Data ($) (Year Ended Apr. 30)	1999	1998	1997	1996	1995	1994	1993	1992	1991	1990
Tangible Bk. Val.	1.02	6.17	8.67	8.62	8.32	8.38	8.33	8.35	8.26	8.24
Cash Flow	2.34	0.90	1.19	1.29	1.23	1.01	0.77	0.69	0.69	1.71
Earnings	1.29	0.32	0.69	0.84	0.76	0.61	0.35	0.31	0.34	1.36
Dividends	0.32	0.32	0.32	0.32	0.30	0.23	0.20	0.20	0.20	0.16
Payout Ratio	25%	100%	46%	38%	39%	38%	57%	64%	59%	12%
Cal. Yrs.	1998	1997	1996	1995	1994	1993	1992	1991	1990	1989
Prices - High	29 7/8	24 1/2	17 3/4	19 1/2	16 3/8	14 3/4	15 1/4	14 3/4	15 7/8	21
- Low	17 5/8	13 3/8	13	12 5/8	11 7/8	10 3/4	9 3/4	8	7	14 1/8
P/E Ratio - High	23	77	26	23	22	24	44	48	47	15
- Low	14	42	19	15	16	18	28	26	21	10
Income Statement Analysis (Million $)										
Revs.	595	430	381	359	323	261	254	250	268	307
Oper. Inc.	79.6	45.0	29.7	34.1	31.0	20.6	18.0	16.2	16.1	53.6
Depr.	24.2	13.6	11.7	10.8	11.4	9.7	10.1	9.1	8.3	8.3
Int. Exp.	11.5	0.7	0.3	0.4	0.5	0.3	0.5	1.8	1.9	1.7
Pretax Inc.	46.1	9.9	22.2	27.8	25.1	21.4	12.2	11.3	12.3	49.8
Eff. Tax Rate	36%	25%	28%	29%	28%	32%	32%	34%	35%	35%
Net Inc.	29.6	7.4	16.0	19.9	18.1	14.5	8.3	7.4	8.0	32.4
Balance Sheet & Other Fin. Data (Million $)										
Cash	26.5	27.0	9.5	8.7	10.2	15.6	17.3	50.6	48.8	29.7
Curr. Assets	226	185	178	158	147	130	121	186	197	197
Total Assets	542	339	325	313	324	286	270	277	288	277
Curr. Liab.	116	90.7	58.9	56.2	68.4	41.9	38.1	42.9	55.0	51.5
LT Debt	173	7.0	7.2	7.3	7.5	7.7	7.9	8.1	9.2	9.5
Common Eqty.	243	231	248	239	237	225	215	214	210	205
Total Cap.	426	248	266	257	254	244	232	231	228	224
Cap. Exp.	22.6	15.9	13.1	12.6	12.5	4.6	6.5	8.8	6.3	6.9
Cash Flow	53.8	21.0	27.7	30.7	29.5	24.2	18.4	16.5	16.2	40.8
Curr. Ratio	1.9	2.0	3.0	2.8	2.1	3.1	3.2	4.3	3.6	3.8
% LT Debt of Cap.	40.7	2.8	2.7	2.9	3.0	3.2	3.4	3.5	4.0	4.2
% Net Inc.of Revs.	5.0	1.7	4.2	5.5	5.6	5.6	3.3	3.0	3.0	10.6
% Ret. on Assets	6.7	2.2	5.0	6.2	5.9	5.2	3.0	2.6	2.8	12.3
% Ret. on Equity	12.5	3.1	27.8	8.3	7.8	6.6	3.9	3.5	3.8	16.9

Data as orig reptd.; bef. results of disc opers/spec. items. Per share data adj. for stk. divs. Bold denotes diluted EPS (FASB 128)-prior periods restated. E-Estimated. NA-Not Available. NM-Not Meaningful. NR-Not Ranked.

Office—83 Gerber Rd. West, South Windsor, CT 06074. **Tel**—(860) 644-1551. **Fax**—(860) 643-7039. **Website**—www.gerberscientific.com **Chrmn, Pres & CEO**—M. J. Cheshire. **SVP-Fin & CFO**—G. K. Bennett. **SVP & Secy**—R. F. Treacy. **Investor Contact**—Robert Goehring (860) 648-8041. **Dirs**—D. P. Aiken, M. J. Cheshire, G. M. Gentile, D. J. Gerber, E. E. Hood, D. J. Logan, C. F. St. Mark, A. R. Towbin, W. J. Vereen. **Transfer Agent & Registrar**—ChaseMellon Shareholder Services, East Hartford, CT. **Incorporated**—in Connecticut in 1948. **Empl**— 2,700. **S&P Analyst:** M.I.

STANDARD
&POOR'S
STOCK REPORTS

Gibson Greetings

NASDAQ Symbol **GIBG**

In S&P SmallCap 600

09-OCT-99

Industry: Consumer (Jewelry, Novelties & Gifts)

Summary: Gibson Greetings makes Christmas, Valentines and other greeting cards and related products.

Quantitative Evaluations
Outlook
(1 Lowest—5 Highest)
• **3+**
Fair Value
• **5⅝**
Risk
• **Average**
Earn./Div. Rank
• **B-**

Technical Eval.
• **Bearish** since 6/99
Rel. Strength Rank
(1 Lowest—99 Highest)
• **89**
Insider Activity
• **NA**

Recent Price • 5½
52 Wk Range • 13-3¾
Yield • Nil
12-Mo. P/E • NM

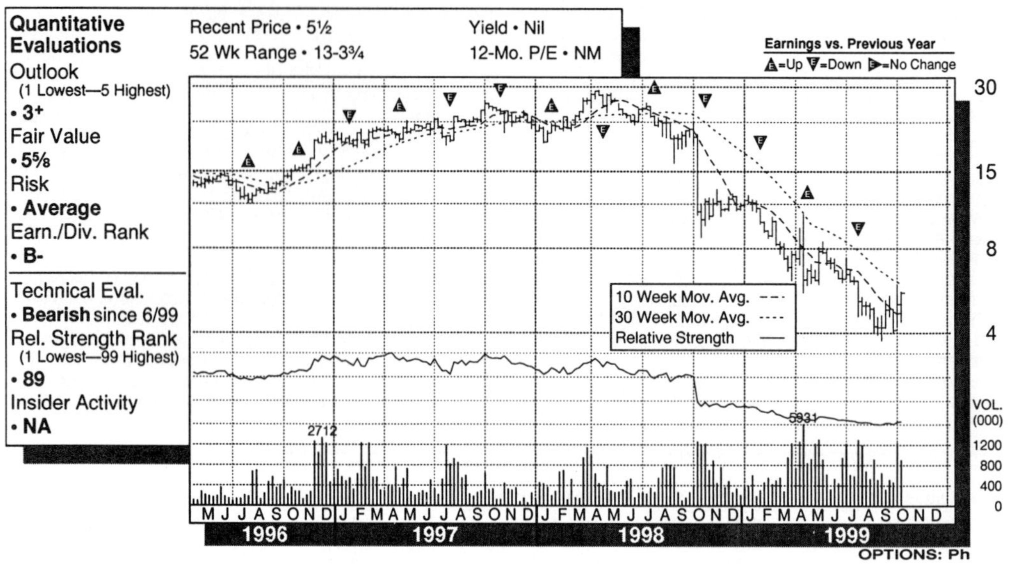

Business Profile - 30-JUN-99

Gibson operates in a highly competitive industry dominated by two companies. The company's mass-merchandiser customer base, which typically operates on low margins, is particularly susceptible to financial constraints, and to offers of more favorable terms from competitors with significantly greater financial resources. As a result, GIBG has for some time faced strong competitive pressures with regard both to price and to terms of sale. It anticipates that these pressures will continue, and expects 1999 results to be considerably below 1998 earnings of $0.97 per diluted share (excluding a restructuring charge).

Operational Review - 30-JUN-99

Revenues in the three months ended March 31, 1999, fell 18%, year to year, reflecting lower revenues in the card division, and the sale of The Paper Factory. In the absence of a pretax restructuring charge of $26.1 million, the loss narrowed, although results were still hurt by lower than anticipated everyday product sales, higher returns and allowances, increased business acquisition costs, a continued shift in product mix, and expenses associated with setting up previously announced new accounts. The net loss was cut to $3,407,000 ($0.22 a share), from $8,915,000 ($0.54).

Stock Performance - 08-OCT-99

In the past 30 trading days, GIBG's shares have increased 33%, compared to a 0.91% fall in the S&P 500. Average trading volume for the past five days was 179,360 shares, compared with the 40-day moving average of 148,733 shares.

Key Stock Statistics

Dividend Rate/Share	Nil	Shareholders	5,100
Shs. outstg. (M)	15.8	Market cap. (B)	$0.088
Avg. daily vol. (M)	0.172	Inst. holdings	40%
Tang. Bk. Value/Share	15.38		
Beta	0.60		

Value of $10,000 invested 5 years ago: $ 2,704

Fiscal Year Ending Dec. 31

	1999	1998	1997	1996	1995	1994
Revenues (Million $)						
1Q	83.47	101.6	99.6	97.78	100.3	93.43
2Q	61.03	104.8	92.66	88.59	97.47	90.65
3Q	—	86.80	92.15	92.55	144.3	153.0
4Q	—	114.8	113.3	111.3	198.7	211.5
Yr.	—	407.9	397.7	390.3	540.8	548.8
Earnings Per Share ($)						
1Q	**-0.22**	**-0.54**	**0.36**	**0.34**	0.02	-1.13
2Q	**-1.54**	**0.33**	**0.32**	**0.36**	0.04	-0.85
3Q	—	**-0.06**	**0.15**	**0.25**	-3.41	0.02
4Q	—	**0.41**	**0.44**	**0.39**	0.49	0.39
Yr.	—	**0.13**	**1.27**	**1.34**	-2.86	-1.77

Next earnings report expected: early November

Dividend Data

Dividends, paid since 1983, were omitted in February 1995.

Gibson Greetings, Inc.

Business Summary - 30-JUN-99

Gibson Greetings, Inc. is a company one tends to think of around holidays and at other special times. The company, with predecessors dating back to 1850, designs, and sells greeting cards, paper partywares, gift wraps, and related specialty relationship fostering products.

The company's major products are extensive lines of greeting cards (both everyday and seasonal). Everyday cards are categorized as conventional greeting cards and alternative market cards. Seasonal cards are devoted to holiday seasons, including, in declining order of net sales, Christmas, Valentine's Day, Mothers' Day, Easter, Fathers's Day, Graduation, and Thanksgiving. In 1998, 67% of net sales of greeting cards were derived from everyday cards, and 33% from seasonal greeting cards.

Products also include a line of talking beanbag toys, marketed under the Silly Slammers trademark; and other products, such as paper partywares, gift warp, candles, calendars, gift and plush items, and holiday decorations.

Sales by product area in 1998 were: greeting cards 56%, Silly Slammers 12%, partywares 10%, gift wrap 7%, and other products 15%.

Products are sold through more than 50,000 retail outlets worldwide, primarily supermarkets, deep discounters, mass merchandisers, card and specialty shops and variety stores. To market effectively through these outlets, the company has developed specific product programs and new product lines and introduced new in-store displays. In 1998, the five largest customers accounted for 29% of net sales, and the largest customer, Winn-Dixie Stores, accounted for 13%. Overseas sales provided 11% of the total.

Among new retail programs introduced in 1998 was Relativity, under which the company supplies retailers a broad selection of popular alternative greeting cards, including cards produced both by GIBG and by third parties. The company believes Relativity, which is marketed to non-discount retailers without payment of up-front fees, will help it break through traditional exclusivity agreements between retailers and other greeting card suppliers.

The company maintains an extensive worldwide freelance pool and a full-time staff of artists, writers, art directors and creative planners who design the majority of the company's products. Design of everyday greeting cards generally begins about six months in advance of shipment. The company's seasonal greeting cards and other items are designed and produced over longer periods than everyday cards.

Per Share Data ($) **(Year Ended Dec. 31)**	**1998**	**1997**	**1996**	**1995**	**1994**	**1993**	**1992**	**1991**	**1990**	**1989**
Tangible Bk. Val.	17.15	15.89	15.81	14.31	17.24	20.15	18.92	18.86	16.58	14.15
Cash Flow	1.48	2.63	2.72	-1.21	NM	NM	NM	3.76	3.46	3.54
Earnings	0.13	1.27	1.34	-2.86	-1.77	1.61	0.50	2.61	2.51	2.68
Dividends	Nil	Nil	Nil	Nil	Nil	0.40	0.39	0.35	0.34	0.33
Payout Ratio	Nil	Nil	Nil	Nil	Nil	25%	78%	14%	13%	12%
Prices - High	29¼	26¾	20¾	16⅛	23⅝	22¾	32	29½	26⅞	28¾
- Low	8¾	18	11½	8	11¾	17¾	15⅝	21⅜	19⅞	21
P/E Ratio - High	NM	21	15	NM	NM	14	64	11	11	11
- Low	NM	14	9	NM	NM	11	32	8	8	8
Income Statement Analysis (Million $)										
Revs.	408	397	389	540	549	547	502	524	513	465
Oper. Inc.	47.7	58.3	60.5	58.4	NA	NA	NA	95.7	86.7	80.8
Depr.	22.1	22.9	22.8	26.9	NA	NA	NA	18.5	15.0	13.6
Int. Exp.	3.4	5.4	8.8	13.2	10.6	7.7	7.9	10.6	10.2	3.9
Pretax Inc.	4.6	36.3	33.1	-63.1	-45.6	44.0	13.1	68.2	63.9	65.7
Eff. Tax Rate	52%	41%	34%	NM	NM	41%	39%	39%	38%	36%
Net Inc.	2.2	21.6	22.0	-46.5	-28.6	25.9	8.0	41.9	39.8	42.4
Balance Sheet & Other Fin. Data (Million $)										
Cash	44.3	114	98.0	16.0	2.0	9.5	9.5	9.8	25.0	5.5
Curr. Assets	245	250	253	215	382	377	334	368	379	311
Total Assets	437	443	452	426	612	580	501	544	553	439
Curr. Liab.	108	103	119	109	231	163	110	153	250	164
LT Debt	10.4	24.2	40.9	46.5	63.2	74.4	70.2	71.1	21.8	30.4
Common Eqty.	271	282	256	230	278	324	303	301	261	226
Total Cap.	282	306	297	277	341	397	376	383	295	265
Cap. Exp.	38.4	17.7	26.5	19.9	35.4	31.0	31.0	31.7	42.7	32.0
Cash Flow	24.3	44.5	44.7	-19.6	NM	NM	NM	60.4	54.8	55.9
Curr. Ratio	2.3	2.4	2.1	2.0	1.7	2.3	3.0	2.4	1.5	1.9
% LT Debt of Cap.	3.7	7.9	13.8	16.9	18.6	18.7	18.7	18.5	7.4	11.5
% Net Inc.of Revs.	0.5	5.4	5.6	NM	NM	4.7	1.6	8.0	7.8	9.1
% Ret. on Assets	0.5	4.8	5.0	NM	NM	4.8	1.5	7.6	8.0	11.0
% Ret. on Equity	0.8	8.0	9.0	NM	NM	8.2	2.6	14.8	16.3	20.5

Data as orig. reptd.; bef. results of disc. opers. and/or spec. items. Per share data adj. for stk. divs. as of ex-div. date. Bold denotes diluted EPS (FASB 128). E-Estimated. NA-Not Available. NM-Not Meaningful. NR-Not Ranked.

Office—2100 Section Rd., Cincinnati, OH 45237. **Tel**—(513) 841-6600. **Chrmn, Pres & CEO**—F. J. O'Connell. **EVP-Fin, CFO & Investor Contact**—James T. Wilson. **Secy**—H. L. Caldwell. **Dirs**—G. M. Gibson, R. P. Kirby, C. D. Lindberg, F. J. O'Connell, A. R. Pezzillo, C. A. St. Martin, C. A. Wainwright. **Transfer Agent & Registrar**—Bank of New York, NYC. **Incorporated**—in Delaware in 1982. **Empl**— 1,800. **S&P Analyst:** P.L.H.

STANDARD
&POOR'S
STOCK REPORTS

Global Industrial Technologies

NYSE Symbol **GIX**

In S&P SmallCap 600

09-OCT-99

Industry:
Machinery (Diversified)

Summary: This manufacturer of industrial products has agreed to be acquired by RHI AG for $13 a share in cash.

Quantitative Evaluations

Outlook
(1 Lowest—5 Highest)
• **NA**

Fair Value
• **NA**

Risk
• **Average**

Earn./Div. Rank
• **NR**

Technical Eval.
• **Neutral** since 9/99

Rel. Strength Rank
(1 Lowest—99 Highest)
• **74**

Insider Activity
• **Neutral**

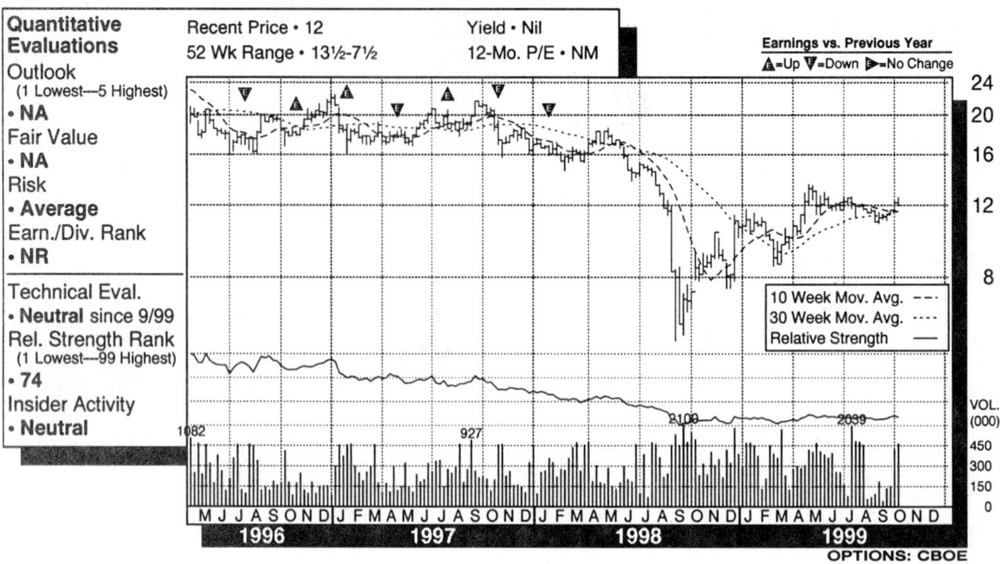

Business Profile - 26-JUL-99

In July 1999, the company and RHI AG, headquartered in Vienna, Austria, announced a definitive agreement for a subsidiary of RHI to make a $13 a share cash tender offer for GIX. The total value of the transaction, including GIX debt, will exceed $500 million. The agreement has been approved by directors of each company. Completion of the tender offer is conditioned on the tendering of a majority of GIX shares outstanding, RHI's receipt of financing, and regulatory and other conditions. In light of the definitive agreement, WHX Corp. decided to discontinue a hostile offer of $11.50 a share in cash for GIX.

Operational Review - 26-JUL-99

Total revenues in the first half of 1999 advanced 34%, year to year. Results benefited from a near-doubling of operating profits from the refractory products and minerals segment, and a return to profitability for the shredding and recycling businesses and Corrosion Technology unit. Income from continuing operations of $8.2 million ($0.36 a share) contrasted with a loss of $1.3 million ($0.06). Results exclude a loss from discontinued operations of $0.51 a share, versus income of $4.15, in the respective periods. In August 1998, the company changed its fiscal year end to December 31, from October 31.

Stock Performance - 08-OCT-99

In the past 30 trading days, GIX's shares have increased 10%, compared to a 0.91% fall in the S&P 500. Average trading volume for the past five days was 119,180 shares, compared with the 40-day moving average of 42,997 shares.

Key Stock Statistics

Dividend Rate/Share	Nil	Shareholders	7,434
Shs. outstg. (M)	22.4	Market cap. (B)	$0.269
Avg. daily vol. (M)	0.065	Inst. holdings	56%
Tang. Bk. Value/Share	9.52		
Beta	1.64		

Value of $10,000 invested 5 years ago: $ 7,741

Fiscal Year Ending Dec. 31

	1999	1998	1997	1996	1995	1994
Revenues (Million $)						
1Q	142.1	—	132.3	149.9	126.3	99.9
2Q	131.6	—	153.6	155.2	142.0	106.3
3Q	—	141.9	155.1	171.1	155.0	108.4
4Q	—	135.5	161.4	171.7	173.8	126.2
Yr.	—	496.0	602.4	647.9	597.1	440.8
Earnings Per Share ($)						
1Q	**0.15**	—	**-0.50**	0.25	0.14	0.04
2Q	**0.21**	—	0.45	**0.21**	0.43	0.21
3Q	—	**-1.88**	-0.64	0.58	0.50	0.35
4Q	—	**-0.80**	0.51	0.73	0.63	0.42
Yr.	—	**-2.32**	-0.20	2.01	1.70	1.02

Next earnings report expected: late October

Dividend Data

No cash dividends have been paid. Poison pill stock purchase rights were distributed with the company's common stock in 1992.

Business Summary - 26-JUL-99

In July 1999, Global Industrial Technologies (formerly INDRESCO, Inc.) and RHI AG signed a definitive agreement under which a subsidiary of RHI AG will make a $13 a share cash tender offer to acquire GIX. The total value of the transaction, including assumption of debt, will exceed $500 million. The agreement has been approved by directors of each company. The completion of the tender offer is conditioned on the tendering of a majority of GIX shares, RHI's obtaining financing, and regulatory and other conditions. In light of the definitive agreement, WHX Corp. decided to discontinue a hostile offer of $11.50 a share for GIX.

As of 1998 year-end, the company was operating in two segments: refractory products and minerals, and all other. Throughout 1998, GIX took steps in line with its long-term strategic plan to divest noncore businesses and focus on growth in the refractory products and minerals business. The effects of these strategic initiatives were reflected in 1998 results: primarily a gain of $81.7 million on the sale of INTOOL operations, and charges of $103.3 million related to other discontinued operations, asset impairments, and restructuring of the refractory products and minerals segment.

A significant step in GIX's growth strategy for refractory products was taken on July 1, 1998, when it acquired A.P. Green Industries, Inc. for about $200 million in cash. The purpose of the acquisition was to consolidate the refractories operations of Green and Harbison-Walker, and to realize planned annual synergies of at least $22 million. As of February 28, 1999, GIX had already realized annual synergies of about $30 million.

Harbison-Walker Refractories manufactures more than 200 refractory products in various shapes, sizes and forms. Refractories, which are made from magnesite, graphite, bauxite, quartzite and fire clays, are used in virtually every industrial process requiring heating or containment of a solid, liquid or gas at a high temperature. Iron and steel producers accounted for 40% of 1998 refractory sales.

The company's all other business segment represents its remaining continuing operations which are conducted through its Corrosion Technology International (CTI), Shred Tech, and Jeffrey businesses which manufacture a variety of products for various industrial applications. The primary products are a patent-protected polymer concrete cell used in the refining of nonferrous metals, primarily the copper refining market (CTI); shredders, crushers, vibrating feeders and coal jigs that are sold to the general processing and recycling, forest products, quarrying, coal and waste processing markets (Jeffrey); and shredding products used for reducing tires, glass, auto bodies, paper, carpet, computer scrap and other bulk materials for disposal and recycling (Shred-Tech).

Per Share Data ($) (Year Ended Dec. 31)	1998	1997	1996	1995	1994	1993	1992	1991	1990	1989
Tangible Bk. Val.	9.52	9.26	9.60	10.60	11.81	11.15	12.70	NA	NA	NA
Cash Flow	-1.26	0.80	2.84	2.33	1.41	1.29	-1.40	0.24	NA	NA
Earnings	-2.32	-0.20	2.01	1.70	1.02	0.78	-1.84	-0.18	NA	NA
Dividends	Nil	Nil	Nil	Nil	Nil	Nil	Nil	NA	NA	NA
Payout Ratio	Nil	Nil	Nil	Nil	Nil	Nil	Nil	NA	NA	NA
Prices - High	18⅝	22	25	19⅝	15½	15½	10⅛	NA	NA	NA
- Low	5½	15⅝	16	10⅞	10¼	9	6⅜	NA	NA	NA
P/E Ratio - High	NM	NM	12	12	15	20	NM	NA	NA	NA
- Low	NM	NM	8	6	10	12	NA	NA	NA	NA
Income Statement Analysis (Million $)										
Revs.	496	602	648	597	437	538	559	618	NA	NA
Oper. Inc.	16.4	71.0	72.2	56.0	27.7	32.3	21.2	-2.3	NA	NA
Depr.	23.2	22.3	18.7	16.1	9.3	13.7	12.2	11.0	NA	NA
Int. Exp.	11.0	10.1	7.0	NM	NM	Nil	Nil	NA	NA	NA
Pretax Inc.	-88.0	-6.7	55.4	42.5	24.6	11.1	-50.8	3.5	NA	NA
Eff. Tax Rate	NM	NM	18%	8.90%	Nil	NM	NM	234%	NA	NA
Net Inc.	-51.0	-4.4	45.4	38.7	24.6	21.4	-50.1	-4.7	NA	NA
Balance Sheet & Other Fin. Data (Million $)										
Cash	8.4	14.9	11.5	21.1	27.0	116	32.4	8.0	NA	NA
Curr. Assets	691	356	376	319	277	307	249	234	NA	NA
Total Assets	1,266	807	753	584	478	461	491	516	NA	NA
Curr. Liab.	534	245	207	218	130	110	131	115	NA	NA
LT Debt	203	152	137	2.3	2.0	Nil	1.9	2.7	NA	NA
Common Eqty.	235	284	300	262	274	288	352	396	NA	NA
Total Cap.	493	453	444	269	289	288	355	401	NA	NA
Cap. Exp.	200	64.4	53.7	34.8	13.0	10.4	15.3	NA	NA	NA
Cash Flow	-27.8	17.9	64.1	54.8	33.9	35.1	-37.9	6.3	NA	NA
Curr. Ratio	1.3	1.5	1.8	1.5	2.1	2.8	1.9	2.0	NA	NA
% LT Debt of Cap.	41.1	33.6	30.8	1.0	0.7	Nil	0.5	0.7	NA	NA
% Net Inc.of Revs.	NM	NM	7.0	6.5	5.6	4.0	NM	NM	NA	NA
% Ret. on Assets	NM	NM	6.8	7.3	5.6	4.7	NM	NA	NA	NA
% Ret. on Equity	NM	NM	16.2	14.5	9.4	6.9	NM	NA	NA	NA

Data as orig reptd.; bef. results of disc opers/spec. items. Per share data adj. for stk. divs. Prior to 1998 yrs. ended Oct. 31. Bold denotes diluted EPS (FASB 128)-prior periods restated. E-Estimated. NA-Not Available. NM-Not Meaningful. NR-Not Ranked.

Office—2121 San Jacinto St., Suite 2500, Dallas, TX 75201. **Tel**—(214) 953-4500. **Chrmn & CEO**—R. Fulgham. **Pres & COO**—G. L. Adelman. **VP-Fin Treas & CFO**—G. G. Garrison. **SVP & CFO**—A. L. Williams. **VP & Secy**—J. H. Quay. **Investor Contact**—George Pasley (214 953-4510).**Dirs**—G. L. Adelman, D. H. Blake, S. R. Erikson, R. Fulgham, R. LaBow, R. W. Vieser. **Transfer Agent & Registrar**—Bank of New York, NYC. **Incorporated**—in Delaware in 1995. **Empl**— 4,778. **S&P Analyst:** J.J.S.

STANDARD &POOR'S

STOCK REPORTS

Goody's Family Clothing

NASDAQ Symbol **GDYS**

In S&P SmallCap 600

09-OCT-99

Industry: Retail (Specialty-Apparel)

Summary: This retailer of moderately priced apparel for women, men and children has more than 270 stores in 16 states in the Southeast and Midwest.

Quantitative Evaluations

Outlook (1 Lowest—5 Highest)
• **5**

Fair Value
• **18¼**

Risk
• **High**

Earn./Div. Rank
• **B**

Technical Eval.
• **Bearish** since 7/99

Rel. Strength Rank (1 Lowest—99 Highest)
• **75**

Insider Activity
• **NA**

Recent Price • 9½
52 Wk Range • 15-7⅞
Yield • Nil
12-Mo. P/E • 11.0

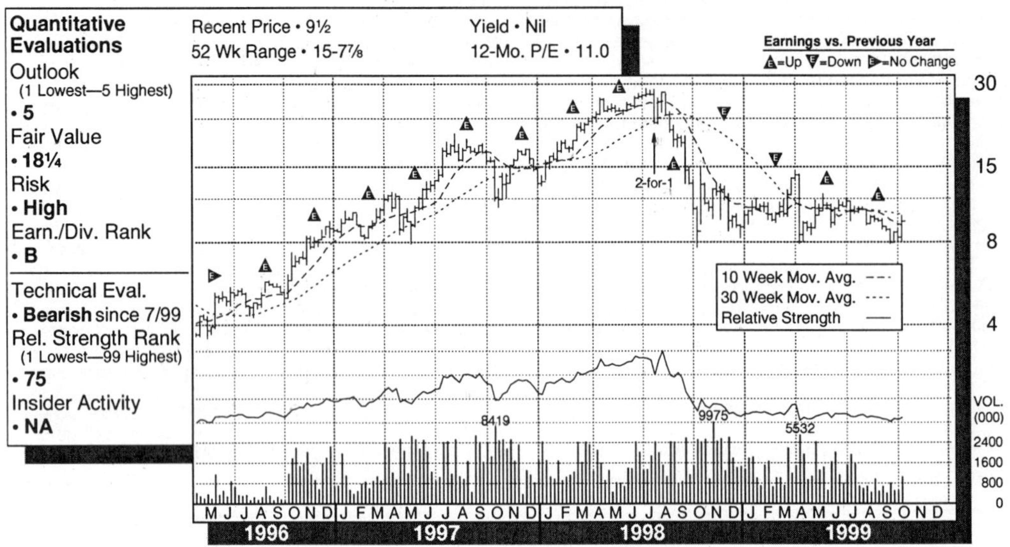

Business Profile - 09-SEP-99

In August 1999, GDYS noted that Shoe Corp. of America, Inc. (SCOA), which operates licensed shoe departments in most of the company's stores, is currently under Chapter 11 bankruptcy protection. As a result of SCOA's financial difficulties, the company's licensed shoe department sales fell about 28% year to year in the second quarter of FY 00 (Jan.), and were down about 41% on a comparable-store basis. Under a tentative agreement with SCOA, GDYS began stocking its own shoe departments on August 9, 1999; however, the company does not expect to reach an appropriate shoe inventory mix until February 2000, when the SCOA agreement was originally set to expire. In FY 00, through September 2, 1999, the company opened 15 new stores, relocated 13, and remodeled four. During the second quarter of FY 00, GDYS repurchased 100,000 of its common shares, for about $1.1 million.

Operational Review - 09-SEP-99

Sales in the first half of FY 00 advanced 13%, year to year, aided by the opening of new stores; same-store sales were down 1.2%. Gross margins narrowed slightly; with a 13% increase in SG&A expense, the gain in pretax income was held to 6.8%. After taxes at 37.5%, versus 37.7%, net income increased 7.1%, to $17,590,000 ($0.52 a share, on 2.7% fewer shares), from $16,426,000 ($0.47, adjusted).

Stock Performance - 08-OCT-99

In the past 30 trading days, GDYS's shares have declined 0.65%, compared to a 0.91% fall in the S&P 500. Average trading volume for the past five days was 208,800 shares, compared with the 40-day moving average of 136,049 shares.

Key Stock Statistics

Dividend Rate/Share	Nil	Shareholders	380
Shs. outstg. (M)	33.2	Market cap. (B)	$0.315
Avg. daily vol. (M)	0.142	Inst. holdings	34%
Tang. Bk. Value/Share	6.38		
Beta	1.20		

Value of $10,000 invested 5 years ago: $ 15,217

Fiscal Year Ending Jan. 31

	2000	1999	1998	1997	1996	1995
Revenues (Million $)						
1Q	259.9	226.7	190.1	150.8	144.9	—
2Q	277.3	249.5	212.2	183.4	155.1	132.4
3Q	—	251.3	234.9	211.4	168.1	147.4
4Q	—	363.6	33.75	273.5	228.7	209.6
Yr.	—	1,091	971.9	819.1	696.9	613.7
Earnings Per Share ($)						
1Q	**0.23**	**0.23**	0.15	0.07	0.07	0.09
2Q	**0.29**	**0.25**	0.16	0.04	0.03	0.01
3Q	—	**0.10**	0.17	0.10	0.07	-0.07
4Q	—	**0.24**	**0.51**	0.31	0.16	0.18
Yr.	—	**0.81**	**0.99**	**0.53**	**0.32**	0.21

Next earnings report expected: mid November

Dividend Data

No cash dividends have been paid. A two-for-one stock split was effected in July 1998.

A Division of The McGraw-Hill Companies

Goody's Family Clothing, Inc.

Business Summary - 09-SEP-99

Goody's Family Clothing, a retailer of moderately priced apparel for women, men and children, operated 272 stores in 16 states in the Southeast and Midwest as of September 2, 1999. To meet the changing tastes and lifestyles of its customer base, the company continually develops and refines its merchandising strategy. Its stores are generally located in strip shopping centers in small to midsize markets.

The company has experienced strong growth in recent years, due to an aggressive new store opening strategy that has increased the number of stores from 146 in FY 94 (Jan.). Stores are now located in Alabama, Arkansas, Florida, Georgia, Illinois, Indiana, Kentucky, Mississippi, Missouri, North Carolina, Ohio, South Carolina, Tennessee, Texas, Virginia, and West Virginia.

GDYS offers merchandise at prices targeted 10% to 30% below those of traditional department stores. Stores are segmented into departments including women's (juniors, misses, intimate apparel, swimwear and outerwear; 42% of sales in FY 99), denim (23%), men's (sportswear, activewear, young men's and men's furnishings; 20%), children's (infants and toddlers, boys and girls; 6.4%), accessories (jewelry, handbags, belts and gift items; 4.7%) and shoes (3.7%). The company also offers tuxedo rentals (less than 1%).

The company sells products with key brand names including Adidas, Alfred Dunner, Bugle Boy, Dockers, Lee, Leslie Fay, Levi's, Nike, Reebok, Requirements, Mickey & Co., Winnie the Pooh, and Sag Harbor. It also offers products under its own private label names such as Chandler Hill, Electro Sport, GFC Trading Co., Intimate Classics, Montana Blue Jean Company, and Mountain Lake for women; Authentic GFC, Bobby by Ivy Crew, GFC, Ivy Crew, Old College Inn and OCI -- Quality Clothing for men; and GoodKidz for children.

GDYS's aims to expand its store base approximately 12% a year over the next several years, in small and midsize markets. As opportunities present themselves, the company will also expand into suburban growth areas of metropolitan markets, opening several stores simultaneously. GDYS believes opportunities exist to expand its presence within current markets, and in new markets such as Louisiana, Oklahoma, and additional states in the Midwest. The company planned to open about 30 to 35 new stores in FY 00, and to relocate or remodel approximately 24 stores.

Per Share Data ($)										
(Year Ended Jan. 31)	**1999**	**1998**	**1997**	**1996**	**1995**	**1994**	**1993**	**1992**	**1991**	**1990**
Tangible Bk. Val.	5.87	4.37	3.83	3.29	2.96	2.75	2.37	1.86	NA	NA
Cash Flow	1.21	1.34	0.84	0.61	0.41	0.60	NA	1.04	0.42	NA
Earnings	0.81	0.99	0.52	0.33	0.21	0.43	0.50	NA	NA	NA
Dividends	Nil	Nil	NA	NA	0.01	NA	NA	NA	NA	NA
Payout Ratio	Nil	Nil	NA	NA	0%	NA	NA	NA	NA	NA
Cal. Yrs.	1998	1997	1996	1995	1994	1993	1992	1991	1990	1989
Prices - High	29	19⅞	9⅝	7⅜	10	12½	12½	8⅞	NA	NA
- Low	7⅝	7⅞	3⅜	4⅛	3¾	5⅞	7⅝	5	NA	NA
P/E Ratio - High	36	20	18	22	46	29	25	22	NA	NA
- Low	9	8	6	12	17	13	15	13	NA	NA
Income Statement Analysis (Million $)										
Revs.	1,091	972	821	697	614	505	NA	362	273	NA
Oper. Inc.	56.3	63.7	37.3	25.0	24.4	25.1	NA	22.1	11.7	NA
Depr.	13.9	11.6	10.6	9.1	6.2	5.6	NA	4.6	4.3	NA
Int. Exp.	0.5	0.5	0.8	0.6	1.2	1.5	NA	2.4	3.3	NA
Pretax Inc.	44.2	53.4	27.4	16.5	10.8	21.2	NA	17.0	5.7	NA
Eff. Tax Rate	37%	38%	38%	37%	36%	35%	NA	12%	40%	NA
Net Inc.	27.7	33.3	17.2	10.5	6.9	13.8	NA	15.0	3.4	NA
Balance Sheet & Other Fin. Data (Million $)										
Cash	89.3	64.2	43.3	33.0	23.1	18.1	NA	31.4	23.2	NA
Curr. Assets	269	228	162	119	97.6	108	NA	73.4	58.2	NA
Total Assets	377	328	254	208	186	164	NA	115	96.2	NA
Curr. Liab.	167	154	118	91.5	82.5	68.4	NA	50.3	39.3	NA
LT Debt	0.3	0.6	0.9	NA	NA	NA	NA	NA	NA	NA
Common Eqty.	195	160	124	106	95.4	88.4	NA	60.4	26.6	NA
Total Cap.	207	171	135	NA	NA	NA	NA	NA	NA	NA
Cap. Exp.	22.9	21.2	16.1	NA	NA	NA	NA	NA	NA	NA
Cash Flow	41.5	44.9	27.7	19.6	13.1	19.4	NA	19.5	7.6	NA
Curr. Ratio	1.6	1.5	1.4	1.3	1.2	1.6	NA	1.5	1.5	NA
% LT Debt of Cap.	0.2	0.4	0.6	NA	NA	NA	NA	NA	NA	NA
% Net Inc.of Revs.	2.5	3.4	2.1	1.5	1.1	2.7	NA	4.1	1.2	NA
% Ret. on Assets	7.8	11.4	7.4	5.3	3.9	NA	NA	14.2	NA	NA
% Ret. on Equity	15.6	7.7	14.9	10.4	7.5	NA	NA	34.4	NA	NA

Data as orig reptd.; bef. results of disc opers/spec. items. Per share data adj. for stk. divs. Bold denotes diluted EPS (FASB 128)-prior periods restated. E-Estimated. NA-Not Available. NM-Not Meaningful. NR-Not Ranked.

Office—400 Goody's Lane, Knoxville, TN 37922. **Tel**—(423) 966-2000. **Website**—http://www.goodysonline.com **Chrmn & CEO**—R. M. Goodfriend. **Pres & COO**—H. M. Call. **EVP, CFO & Secy**—E. R. Carlin. **Dirs**—H. M. Call, S. J. Furrow, R. M. Goodfriend, R. F. Koppel, I. L. Lowenstein, C. L. Turnbull. **Transfer Agent & Registrar**—Wachovia Bank of North Carolina, Winston-Salem, NC. **Incorporated**—in Tennessee in 1954. **Empl**—8,250. **S&P Analyst:** M.I.

STANDARD
&POOR'S
STOCK REPORTS

Gottschalks Inc.

NYSE Symbol **GOT**

In S&P SmallCap 600

09-OCT-99

Industry:
Retail (Department Stores)

Summary: This company operates 40 department stores and 20 specialty stores in non-major metropolitan areas in California, Washington, Oregon and Nevada.

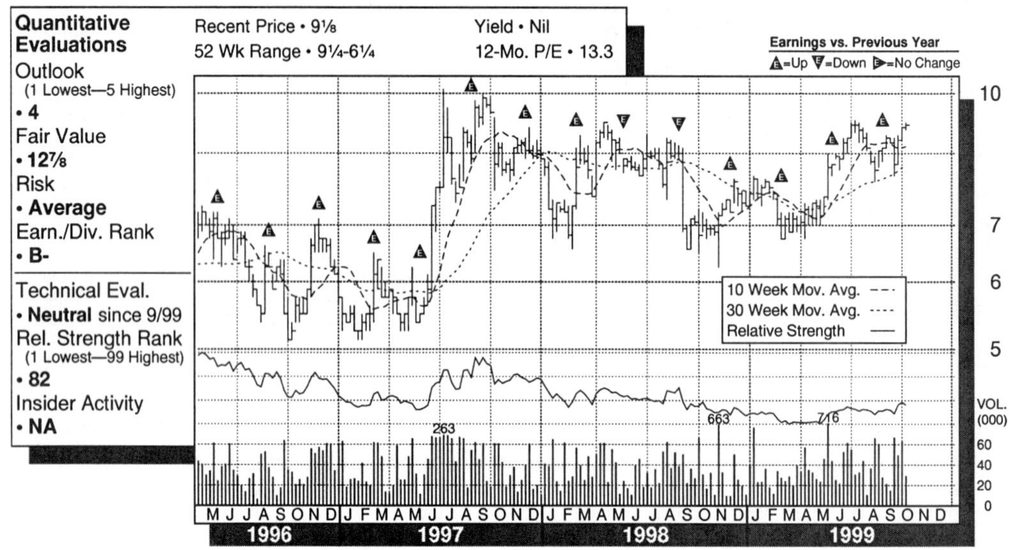

Business Profile - 09-SEP-99

This regional department store chain derives most of its revenues from Gottschalks stores, which are located mainly in smaller California cities. It offers moderate to upper moderate priced brand-name fashion apparel, cosmetics, shoes, accessories and home merchandise. GOT acquired nine stores from The Harris Co. of San Bernardino, CA, in August 1998. The company assumed the shoe operation in its stores from the former lessee on August 1, 1999, and double-digit sales increases were reported for the first month of company operations.

Operational Review - 09-SEP-99

Net sales in the first half of FY 00 (Jan.) advanced 23%, year to year; same-store sales were up 6.2%. Net credit revenues rose 36%. Gross margins widened, and with SG&A expenses and interest, depreciation and other charges well controlled, the seasonal net loss narrowed to $1,184,000 ($0.09 a share, on 20% more shares), from $3,346,000 ($0.32).

Stock Performance - 08-OCT-99

In the past 30 trading days, GOT's shares have increased 7%, compared to a 0.91% fall in the S&P 500. Average trading volume for the past five days was 5,740 shares, compared with the 40-day moving average of 11,644 shares.

Key Stock Statistics

Dividend Rate/Share	Nil	Shareholders	894
Shs. outstg. (M)	12.6	Market cap. (B)	$0.116
Avg. daily vol. (M)	0.016	Inst. holdings	29%
Tang. Bk. Value/Share	7.49		
Beta	0.32		

Value of $10,000 invested 5 years ago: $ 11,483

Fiscal Year Ending Jan. 31

	2000	1999	1998	1997	1996	1995
Revenues (Million $)						
1Q	121.4	95.47	90.51	85.56	77.93	72.50
2Q	126.5	104.1	100.0	95.68	91.88	80.52
3Q	—	124.8	101.5	95.68	86.07	78.84
4Q	—	194.4	156.2	145.3	145.2	134.0
Yr.	—	517.1	448.2	422.2	401.0	363.6
Earnings Per Share ($)						
1Q	**-0.09**	**-0.19**	**-0.09**	**-0.13**	-0.30	-0.22
2Q	**-0.01**	**-0.13**	**-0.02**	**-0.07**	-0.19	-0.38
3Q	—	**0.03**	**-0.14**	**-0.15**	-0.30	-0.05
4Q	—	**0.66**	**0.62**	**0.52**	0.25	0.81
Yr.	—	**0.46**	**0.36**	**0.18**	**-0.54**	**0.15**

Next earnings report expected: mid November

Dividend Data

No cash dividends have been paid. A two-for-one stock split was effected in April 1987.

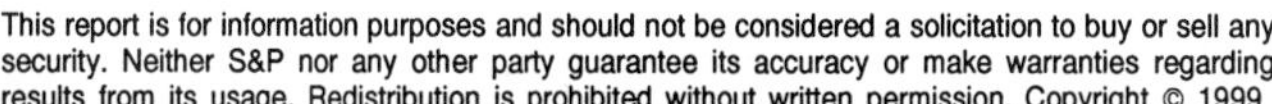

Gottschalks Inc.

Business Summary - 09-SEP-99

Fresno, CA-based Gottschalks (currently the largest independent department store chain based in California) and its predecessor, E. Gottschalk & Co., have operated continuously for more than 94 years, since their founding by Emil Gottschalk in 1904. Most of the company's growth has taken place since the initial public stock offering in 1986. As of early 1999, the company was operating 40 full-line department stores, including 30 Gottschalks stores located throughout California, and in Oregon, Washington and Nevada, and 10 Harris/Gottschalks stores located in Southern California. The company also operated 22 Gottschalks and Village East specialty stores, which carry a limited selection of merchandise. On August 20, 1998, the company acquired nine of the stores now operated under the Harris/Gottschalks nameplate (closing one of the acquired stores on January 31, 1999, as planned) from The Harris Company of San Bernardino, CA.

Gottschalks and Harris/Gottschalks department stores typically offer a wide range of brand-name and private-label merchandise, including men's, women's, junior's and children's apparel; cosmetics and accessories; shoes and jewelry; home furnishings including china, housewares, electronics (in 10 stores) and small electric appliances; and other consumer goods. Village East specialty stores offer apparel for larger women. Gottschalks stores are generally anchor tenants of regional shopping malls, with Village East specialty stores generally located in the regional malls in which a Gottschalks department store is located or as a separate department within some of the company's larger Gottschalks stores. The company's stores carry primarily moderately priced brand-name merchandise, complemented with private-label merchandise and a mix of higher and budget-priced merchandise.

Stores are located primarily in diverse, growing, non-major metropolitan areas. GOT believes it has a competitive advantage in offering brand-name merchandise and a high level of service to customers in secondary markets in the western U.S., where there is a strong demand for nationally advertised, brand-name merchandise and fewer competitors offering such merchandise. Some stores are located in agricultural areas, and cater to mature customers with above average levels of disposable income. Gottschalks strives to be the "hometown store" in each of the communities it serves.

The company services all of its stores, including its storelocations outside California, from a 420,000 sq. ft. distribution facility centrally located in Madera, CA.

Wholly owned Gottschalks Credit Receivables Corp. (GCRC) is a qualified special purpose entity formed in 1994 in connection witha receivables securitization program.

Per Share Data ($) (Year Ended Jan. 31)	1999	1998	1997	1996	1995	1994	1993	1992	1991	1990
Tangible Bk. Val.	7.49	7.90	7.53	7.35	7.90	7.73	7.98	9.02	7.01	6.29
Cash Flow	1.20	0.99	0.83	0.24	0.71	0.33	-0.19	0.94	1.34	0.88
Earnings	0.46	0.36	0.18	-0.54	0.15	-0.26	-0.77	0.44	0.80	0.46
Dividends	Nil	Nil	Nil	Nil	Nil	Nil	Nil	Nil	Nil	Nil
Payout Ratio	Nil	Nil	Nil	Nil	Nil	Nil	Nil	Nil	Nil	Nil
Cal. Yrs.	1998	1997	1996	1995	1994	1993	1992	1991	1990	1989
Prices - High	9 1/4	10 1/8	7 3/8	8 3/8	13	10 5/8	22 1/2	26 3/8	15	13 3/8
- Low	6 1/4	5 1/8	4 3/4	5 1/8	7	6 1/8	7 1/2	11 5/8	8 5/8	8
P/E Ratio - High	20	28	41	NM	87	NM	NM	60	19	29
- Low	14	14	26	NM	47	NM	NM	26	11	17
Income Statement Analysis (Million $)										
Revs.	524	455	422	401	373	351	340	324	295	243
Oper. Inc.	25.8	19.1	8.4	-0.9	21.5	13.3	7.9	16.9	21.4	15.9
Depr.	8.5	6.7	6.9	8.1	5.9	6.1	6.0	4.9	4.3	3.5
Int. Exp.	9.5	7.3	11.7	11.3	10.3	8.6	7.0	7.0	9.8	8.4
Pretax Inc.	9.0	6.4	3.1	-8.6	2.3	-3.9	-12.0	7.0	10.4	5.7
Eff. Tax Rate	41%	42%	41%	NM	35%	NM	NM	39%	38%	35%
Net Inc.	5.3	3.7	1.8	-5.6	1.5	-2.7	-8.0	4.3	6.4	3.7
Balance Sheet & Other Fin. Data (Million $)										
Cash	1.7	1.6	6.7	7.4	5.5	1.2	1.1	3.3	1.4	2.8
Curr. Assets	194	135	134	139	127	140	131	131	121	99
Total Assets	324	242	233	239	253	248	240	234	208	166
Curr. Liab.	97.8	67.1	64.0	96.0	89.0	108	114	62.6	84.9	60.8
LT Debt	94.7	62.4	60.2	34.9	33.7	31.5	15.0	50.3	41.6	44.8
Common Eqty.	103	83.9	80.1	77.9	83.6	82.1	84.5	95.7	58.7	51.8
Total Cap.	202	150	143	117	123	120	106	152	106	99
Cap. Exp.	16.8	15.0	6.8	12.8	4.5	6.5	12.1	15.0	25.8	38.0
Cash Flow	13.7	10.4	8.7	2.5	7.4	3.4	-2.0	9.2	10.8	7.1
Curr. Ratio	2.0	2.0	2.1	1.4	1.4	1.3	1.1	2.1	1.4	1.6
% LT Debt of Cap.	46.8	41.6	42.0	29.9	27.3	26.3	14.2	33.2	39.3	45.3
% Net Inc.of Revs.	1.0	0.8	0.4	NM	0.4	NM	NM	1.3	2.2	1.5
% Ret. on Assets	1.9	1.6	0.8	NM	0.6	NM	NM	1.7	3.4	2.4
% Ret. on Equity	5.6	4.5	2.3	NM	1.8	NM	NM	5.0	11.6	7.3

Data as orig reptd.; bef. results of disc opers/spec. items. Per share data adj. for stk. divs. Bold denotes diluted EPS (FASB 128)-prior periods restated. E-Estimated. NA-Not Available. NM-Not Meaningful. NR-Not Ranked.

Office—7 River Park Place East, Fresno, CA 93720. **Registrar & Transfer Agent**—ChaseMellon Shareholder Services, SF. **Tel**—(559) 434-8000. **Website**—www.gottschalks.com **Chrmn & CEO**—J. W. Levy. **Pres & COO**—J. Famalette. **SVP & CFO**—M. Geele. **Dirs**—I. Alvarez, J. R. Famalette, M. Gutmann, B. W. Levy, J. W. Levy, S. Levy, J. J. Penbera, F. R. Ruiz, J. P. Sanchez, W. Smith, O. J. Woodward III. **Transfer Agent & Registrar**—ChaseMellon Shareholder Services, SF. **Incorporated**—in California in 1912; reincorporated in Delaware in 1986. **Empl**— 6,600. **S&P Analyst:** C.F.B.

STANDARD
&POOR'S
STOCK REPORTS

Graco Inc.

NYSE Symbol **GGG**

In S&P SmallCap 600

09-OCT-99

Industry: Manufacturing (Diversified)

Summary: This company is a U.S.-based global producer of industrial pumps, valves, meters and accessories.

Quantitative Evaluations

Outlook (1 Lowest—5 Highest) • 3-

Fair Value • 40⅛

Risk • Average

Earn./Div. Rank • A-

Technical Eval. • Bullish since 7/99

Rel. Strength Rank (1 Lowest—99 Highest) • 70

Insider Activity • NA

Recent Price • 32⅞

52 Wk Range • 34⅞-19⅞

Yield • 1.3%

12-Mo. P/E • 12.7

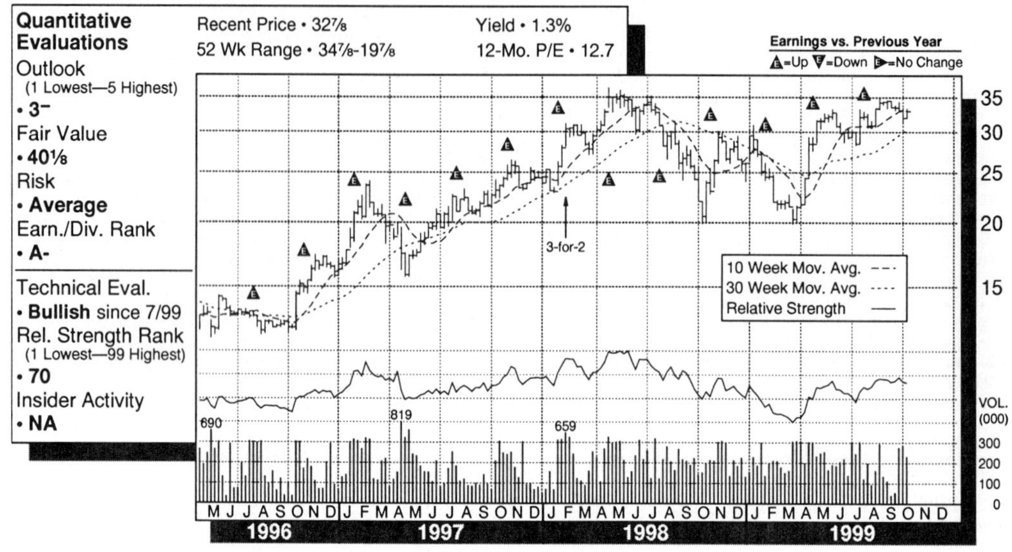

Business Profile - 06-AUG-99

Despite the recent pick up in order trends from Europe and Asia, Graco remains cautious regarding events outside North America for the remainder of 1999. However, management is confident that it can post better earnings this year. The company is determined to improve earnings through more effective business processes and higher operating margins and net profits. Management is aggressively pursuing its strategies of investing in new products (with a goal of generating 30% of sales from products introduced in the prior three years), certifying and training distributors, upgrading its marketing organization, and expanding sales coverage.

Operational Review - 06-AUG-99

Based on a brief report, revenues in the first half of 1999 declined 1.3%, year to year, due to slowing Industrial/Automotive equipment and Lubrication equipment sales, and weak European results partly offset by a double-digit rise in Contractor equipment sales. Margins widened on an improvement in product packaging and Asia Pacific restructuring activities; operating profit climbed 34%. Following a $3.2 million gain from the sale of real estate, net income increased 34%, to $29.2 million ($1.41 a share, on 22% fewer shares), from $21.7 million ($0.82).

Stock Performance - 08-OCT-99

In the past 30 trading days, GGG's shares have declined 4%, compared to a 0.91% fall in the S&P 500. Average trading volume for the past five days was 45,840 shares, compared with the 40-day moving average of 36,200 shares.

Key Stock Statistics

Dividend Rate/Share	0.44	Shareholders	6,376
Shs. outstg. (M)	20.3	Market cap. (B)	$0.670
Avg. daily vol. (M)	0.042	Inst. holdings	59%
Tang. Bk. Value/Share	1.88		
Beta	0.88		

Value of $10,000 invested 5 years ago: $ 38,187

Fiscal Year Ending Dec. 31

	1999	1998	1997	1996	1995	1994
Revenues (Million $)						
1Q	103.2	105.7	92.10	90.15	95.53	80.93
2Q	114.7	115.2	111.7	97.10	103.4	94.18
3Q	—	106.2	101.9	97.68	94.80	89.05
4Q	—	105.1	108.2	106.8	92.59	95.87
Yr.	—	432.2	413.9	391.8	386.3	360.0
Earnings Per Share ($)						
1Q	**0.54**	**0.34**	**0.24**	**0.21**	0.21	0.07
2Q	**0.86**	**0.48**	**0.40**	**0.38**	0.32	0.16
3Q	—	**0.53**	**0.49**	**0.39**	0.25	0.16
4Q	—	**0.70**	**0.59**	**0.40**	0.27	0.20
Yr.	—	**2.01**	**1.71**	**1.38**	**1.06**	**0.59**

Next earnings report expected: mid October

Dividend Data (Dividends have been paid since 1970.)

Amount ($)	Date Decl.	Ex-Div. Date	Stock of Record	Payment Date
0.110	Dec. 11	Jan. 13	Jan. 18	Feb. 03 '99
0.110	Feb. 19	Apr. 15	Apr. 19	May. 05 '99
0.110	Jun. 18	Jul. 15	Jul. 19	Aug. 04 '99
0.110	Sep. 14	Oct. 14	Oct. 18	Nov. 03 '99

A Division of The McGraw-Hill Companies

Graco Inc.

Business Summary - 06-AUG-99

This Minneapolis-based company is the successor to Gray Company, Inc., which was incorporated in 1926 as a maker of auto lubrication equipment, and became public in 1969. Graco manufactures and markets fluid dispensing equipment (industrial and commercial pumps, valves, meters and related accessories) for a variety of applications and industries. The company's products are sold to the manufacturing, processing, construction and maintenance industries through its three segments: Industrial/Automotive Equipment, Contractor Equipment, and Lubrication Equipment.

In 1998, the Americas accounted for 69% of revenues and $300 million in operating profit (67% and $276 million in 1997), Europe 22% and $93 million (20% and $82 million), and Asia/Pacific 9% and $39 million (13% and $55 million). International sales contributed 39% of total revenues in 1998.

The Industrial/Automotive equipment segment markets pumps (pressure hydraulic, electric and air-powered) for fluid application systems (primarily paints, coatings, sealants and adhesives) to automotive assembly and component plants, wood products, rail, marine, aerospace, farm and construction equipment, truck, bus and recreational vehicle markets. In 1998, GGG introduced PrecisionFlo, an electronic control device for use in sealant and adhesive dispensing systems. This segment accounted for 54%, 55% and 57% of total revenues in 1998, 1997 and 1996, respectively.

The Contractor equipment segment supplies airless sprayers for applying paint and other architectural coatings, and for high pressure cleaning of equipment and structures. In 1999, a new line of stripping equipment, LineLazer II, will be offered with higher pressure and better flow capabilities. This segment contributed 36%, 34% and 32% of total revenues in 1998, 1997 and 1996, respectively.

The Lubrication equipment segment sells products (pumps, meters, fluid and air pressure gauges, fluid management systems, hose reels and dispense valves) for the lubrication and maintenance of vehicles and other equipment. In addition, equipment that dispenses, recycles and recovers lubricants are offered. The markets for these products include fast oil change facilities, fleet service centers, automobile dealerships and the mining industry. The purchase of vehicle lubrication equipment is often funded by major oil companies for their lubrication product customers as a marketing tool. Lubrication equipment sales represented 10%, 11% and 11% of total sales in 1998, 1997 and 1996, respectively.

Per Share Data ($) (Year Ended Dec. 31)	1998	1997	1996	1995	1994	1993	1992	1991	1990	1989
Tangible Bk. Val.	0.46	6.17	4.93	4.00	3.09	2.82	3.86	3.82	3.72	3.12
Cash Flow	2.59	2.22	1.86	1.49	0.99	0.72	0.74	0.67	1.04	0.89
Earnings	2.01	1.71	1.38	1.06	0.59	0.36	0.43	0.35	0.72	0.60
Dividends	0.44	0.39	0.33	0.27	1.46	0.32	0.27	0.20	0.18	0.16
Payout Ratio	22%	23%	24%	25%	NM	87%	62%	58%	25%	27%
Prices - High	36½	26½	17⅜	17	11	10¾	8¾	9⅛	7½	6⅛
- Low	19⅞	15⅝	11⅞	8¾	7½	6⅞	6⅞	5⅞	4⅝	4½
P/E Ratio - High	18	15	13	16	19	30	20	26	10	10
- Low	10	9	9	8	13	19	16	17	6	8
Income Statement Analysis (Million $)										
Revs.	432	414	392	386	360	323	320	312	321	298
Oper. Inc.	90.6	79.0	65.7	56.3	36.8	27.9	27.4	29.8	41.9	37.1
Depr.	13.7	13.5	12.6	11.0	10.4	9.3	7.9	8.0	7.7	7.0
Int. Exp.	5.3	0.9	0.8	2.3	1.9	2.3	2.7	3.7	3.5	4.5
Pretax Inc.	71.4	63.5	52.7	43.5	23.4	13.8	18.0	15.3	29.0	24.5
Eff. Tax Rate	34%	30%	31%	37%	35%	31%	38%	42%	39%	41%
Net Inc.	47.3	44.7	36.1	27.7	15.3	9.5	11.1	8.9	17.7	14.5
Balance Sheet & Other Fin. Data (Million $)										
Cash	3.6	13.5	6.5	1.6	2.4	37.4	38.2	24.0	6.0	4.5
Curr. Assets	131	156	144	128	144	147	162	150	151	133
Total Assets	234	265	248	218	228	216	220	206	209	182
Curr. Liab.	83.0	69.0	80.6	71.5	89.5	100	77.1	74.9	84.0	69.9
LT Debt	113	6.2	8.1	10.0	26.8	13.9	17.8	19.6	23.9	28.5
Common Eqty.	9.3	158	126	104	80.4	73.2	99	96.0	90.3	74.7
Total Cap.	122	164	134	114	109	89.0	118	119	117	108
Cap. Exp.	12.0	20.1	30.0	19.8	23.1	16.2	10.2	8.4	14.7	12.3
Cash Flow	61.0	58.2	48.8	38.8	25.7	18.7	19.0	16.9	25.4	21.5
Curr. Ratio	1.6	2.3	1.8	1.8	1.6	1.5	2.1	2.0	1.8	1.9
% LT Debt of Cap.	92.4	3.8	6.0	8.8	24.7	15.7	15.1	16.4	20.4	26.4
% Net Inc.of Revs.	10.9	10.8	9.2	7.2	4.3	2.9	3.5	2.9	5.5	4.9
% Ret. on Assets	19.0	17.5	15.4	12.4	6.9	4.3	5.2	4.2	9.0	8.1
% Ret. on Equity	47.6	25.7	31.5	NA	19.9	10.9	11.3	9.4	21.3	21.0

Data as orig reptd.; bef. results of disc opers/spec. items. Per share data adj. for stk. divs. Bold denotes diluted EPS (FASB 128)-prior periods restated. E-Estimated. NA-Not Available. NM-Not Meaningful. NR-Not Ranked.

Office—4050 Olson Memorial Highway, Golden Valley, MN 55422-2332. **Tel**—(612) 623-6000. **Website**—www.graco.com **Chrmn**—D. A. Koch. **Pres & CEO**—J. A. Earnshaw. **VP, Treas & Inv Contact**—M. W. Sheahan (612-623-6656). **VP & Secy**—R. M. Mattison. **Dirs**—G. Aristides, R. O. Baukol, R. G. Bohn, W. J. Carroll, D. A. Koch, R. D. McFarland, L. R. Mitau, M. Morfitt, D. R. Olseth, J. L. Scott, W. G. Van Dyke. **Transfer Agent & Registrar**—Norwest Bank Minnesota, St. Paul. **Incorporated**—in Minnesota in 1947. **Empl**— 1,864. **S&P Analyst:** John A. Massey

STANDARD &POOR'S STOCK REPORTS

Green Mountain Power

NYSE Symbol **GMP**

In S&P SmallCap 600

09-OCT-99 **Industry:** Electric Companies

Summary: This small electric utility provides service to more than 80,000 customers in north central Vermont.

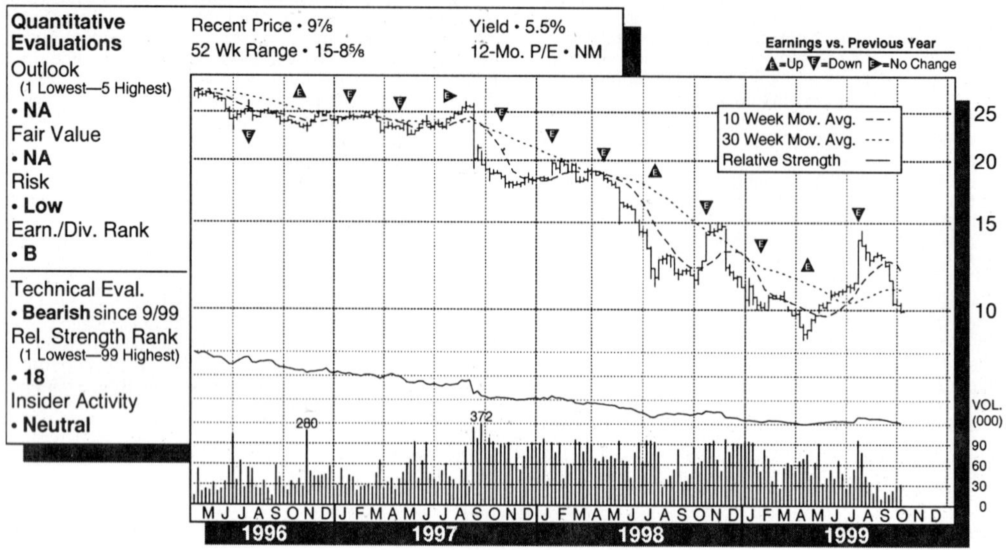

Business Profile - 30-AUG-99

In August 1999, the company said it expects substantial cost savings in future years from a reduction in its labor force (to 225 employees, from 288 at 1998 year-end), as well as other initiatives it has put in place. GMP added that it has taken a number of steps to protect itself from increasing power costs, including negotiating with additional providers to secure alternative sources during peak periods, and continuing to renegotiate its contract with Hydro-Quebec. In addition, the company has joined 17 other Vermont utilities in petitioning the Vermont Public Service Board for relief from the high cost of power from small, in-state power producers.

Operational Review - 30-AUG-99

Operating revenues in the six months ended June 30, 1999, climbed 31%, year to year, reflecting a temporary retail rate increase effective December 1998, and a new power purchase and supply agreement. Despite increased costs resulting from the unavailability of several nuclear generation facilities in New England, and the use of high-cost generating facilities, in the absence of a $4.6 million loss, related to a long-term power contract, income of $2,757,000 ($0.51 a share, after preferred dividends) contrasted with a loss of $1,363,000 ($0.27, also after preferred dividends). Results exclude losses from discontinued operations of $0.11 and $0.21 a share in the respective periods.

Stock Performance - 08-OCT-99

In the past 30 trading days, GMP's shares have declined 23%, compared to a 0.91% fall in the S&P 500. Average trading volume for the past five days was 6,120 shares, compared with the 40-day moving average of 4,503 shares.

Key Stock Statistics

Dividend Rate/Share	0.55	Shareholders	6,500
Shs. outstg. (M)	5.3	Market cap. (B)	$0.053
Avg. daily vol. (M)	0.005	Inst. holdings	14%
Tang. Bk. Value/Share	20.27		
Beta	0.12		

Value of $10,000 invested 5 years ago: $ 5,000

Fiscal Year Ending Dec. 31

	1999	1998	1997	1996	1995	1994
Revenues (Million $)						
1Q	59.02	46.93	47.20	48.42	40.02	40.61
2Q	59.54	43.73	42.68	40.47	37.13	33.60
3Q	—	47.98	43.57	44.42	39.78	36.68
4Q	—	45.66	45.86	45.70	44.61	37.30
Yr.	—	184.3	179.3	179.0	161.5	148.2
Earnings Per Share ($)						
1Q	**0.50**	**-0.66**	**0.58**	**0.80**	0.65	0.85
2Q	**-0.10**	**0.18**	**0.17**	**0.17**	0.38	0.23
3Q	—	**0.31**	**0.59**	**0.67**	0.60	0.54
4Q	—	**-0.63**	**0.23**	**0.58**	0.63	0.61
Yr.	—	**-0.80**	**1.57**	**2.22**	**2.26**	**2.23**

Next earnings report expected: mid November

Dividend Data (Dividends have been paid since 1951.)

Amount ($)	Date Decl.	Ex-Div. Date	Stock of Record	Payment Date
0.138	Nov. 23	Dec. 14	Dec. 16	Dec. 31 '98
0.138	Feb. 08	Mar. 15	Mar. 17	Mar. 31 '99
0.138	May. 20	Jun. 15	Jun. 17	Jun. 30 '99
0.138	Aug. 19	Sep. 14	Sep. 16	Sep. 30 '99

Green Mountain Power Corporation

09-OCT-99

Business Summary - 30-AUG-99

Green Mountain Power, a public utility operating company in business for more than 100 years, supplies electrical energy in Vermont in a territory with approximately one quarter of the state's population. It serves about 83,500 customers, ranging from large and sophisticated manufacturing facilities, like the IBM plant in Essex Junction (6,000 employees), to small entrepreneurial businesses like Firerobin, which employs five people to produce hand-crafted puppets.

Residential customers accounted for 33.5% of revenues in 1998, small commercial and industrial customers 33.5%, large commercial and industrial customers 21.8%, other utilities 9.0%, and other sources 2.2%.

Energy sales to IBM, GMP's largest customer, accounted for 15% of operating revenues in 1998, versus 14% in 1997. No other retail customer accounted for over 1% of revenues. Under the current regulatory system, the loss of IBM as a customer would require the company to seek rate relief to recover revenues previously paid by IBM from other customers in an amount sufficient to offset the fixed costs that IBM had been covering through its payments.

The company's energy resources for retail and wholesale sales of electricity were obtained in 1998 as follows: 44.0% from hydroelectric sources (32.8% Hydro-Quebec), 27.5% from a nuclear generating source (the Vermont Yankee nuclear plant), 2.0% from coal sources, 3.5% from wood, 2.4% from natural gas, 1.5% from oil, and 0.6% from wind. The remaining 18.5% was purchased on a short-term basis from other utilities through the New England Power Pool (NEPOOL).

A major source of power supply is GMP's entitlement to a share of the power generated by the 531mw Vermont Yankee nuclear generating plant owned and operated by Vermont Yankee Nuclear Power Corp. GMP has a 17.9% equity interest in Vermont Yankee.

The company participates in NEPOOL, a regional bulk power transmission organization established to assure reliable and economical power supply in the Northeast. Its representative to NEPOOL is Vermont Electric Power company, Inc., a transmission consortium owned by GMP and other Vermont utilities; the company holds a 30% equity interest.

Certain decisions by the Vermont Public Service Board, if not changed, could have a significant negative impact on GMP's reported financial condition, and could affect its credit rating, dividend policy, and financial viability.

Per Share Data ($) (Year Ended Dec. 31)	1998	1997	1996	1995	1994	1993	1992	1991	1990	1989
Tangible Bk. Val.	19.84	21.68	21.71	21.48	21.01	20.65	20.15	19.38	19.10	18.79
Earnings	-0.80	1.57	2.22	2.26	2.23	2.20	2.54	2.45	2.29	2.36
Dividends	0.96	1.61	2.12	2.12	2.12	2.11	2.08	2.04	2.00	1.95
Payout Ratio	NM	103%	95%	94%	95%	96%	82%	83%	87%	83%
Prices - High	20	26¼	29⅛	28⅝	31¼	36⅝	33⅝	30¼	27⅞	27⅞
- Low	10	17½	22¾	23⅞	23⅜	30¾	29	22	21¼	22⅛
P/E Ratio - High	NM	17	14	13	14	17	13	12	12	12
- Low	NM	11	11	11	10	14	11	9	9	9
Income Statement Analysis (Million $)										
Revs.	184	179	179	162	148	147	145	144	148	144
Depr.	16.1	16.3	16.3	14.1	10.7	8.6	8.1	7.0	6.8	5.9
Maint.	5.2	4.9	4.5	4.2	4.5	4.3	4.7	4.3	4.4	4.8
Fxd. Chgs. Cov.	NA	2.5	2.6	2.6	3.0	3.1	3.3	3.0	2.9	3.4
Constr. Credits	0.2	0.7	0.6	0.6	0.8	0.6	0.4	0.4	0.5	0.5
Eff. Tax Rate	NM	43%	27%	25%	33%	29%	29%	29%	28%	28%
Net Inc.	-2.9	9.4	12.0	11.5	11.0	10.6	11.8	10.5	9.0	9.0
Balance Sheet & Other Fin. Data (Million $)										
Gross Prop.	290	284	271	258	245	236	223	215	204	179
Cap. Exp.	10.9	16.4	17.5	15.3	13.5	15.9	15.3	14.8	14.3	20.2
Net Prop.	196	197	190	182	176	171	165	160	152	132
Capitalization:										
LT Debt	96.2	102	104	101	85.2	90.8	79.6	68.9	73.4	57.0
% LT Debt	44	44	44	47	44	46	44	42	47	44
Pfd.	16.1	17.7	19.3	8.9	9.1	9.4	9.6	9.8	10.1	3.4
% Pfd.	7.34	7.60	8.20	4.10	4.70	4.80	5.30	5.90	6.50	2.60
Common	107	114	112	106	101	97.1	92.6	87.5	71.9	69.5
% Common	49	49	48	49	52	49	51	53	46	54
Total Cap.	247	261	266	246	223	224	203	185	173	145
% Oper. Ratio	97.0	90.9	91.0	90.6	90.2	89.9	88.7	89.9	90.7	91.5
% Earn. on Net Prop.	2.8	8.0	8.7	8.6	8.4	8.8	10.1	9.3	9.6	9.8
% Return On Revs.	NM	5.3	6.7	7.1	7.4	7.2	8.2	7.3	6.1	6.3
% Return On Invest. Capital	2.7	6.5	7.5	3.4	8.1	8.2	9.6	9.7	9.9	10.6
% Return On Com. Equity	NM	7.1	10.0	10.4	10.3	10.3	12.2	12.5	12.0	12.5

Data as orig reptd.; bef. results of disc opers/spec. items. Per share data adj. for stk. divs. Bold denotes diluted EPS (FASB 128)-prior periods restated. E-Estimated. NA-Not Available. NM-Not Meaningful. NR-Not Ranked.

Office—25 Green Mountain Dr., South Burlington, VT 05403. **Tel**—(802) 864-5731. **Website**—http://www.gmpvt.com **Pres & CEO**—C. L. Dutton. **Secy**—D. S. Laffan. **VP, CFO & Treas**—N. R. Brock. **Investor Contact**—Bonnie V. Fairbanks (802-660-5787). **Dirs**—, N. L. Brue, W. B. Bruett, M. O.Burns, L. E. Chickering, J. V. Cleary, D. R. Coats, C. L. Dutton, E. A. Irving, M. L. Johnson, R. W. Page, T. P. Salmon (Chrmn). **Transfer Agent & Registrar**—ChaseMellon Shareholder Services, Ridgefield Park, NJ. **Incorporated**—in Vermont in 1893. **Empl**— 225. **S&P Analyst:** P.L.H.

STANDARD
&POOR'S
STOCK REPORTS

Griffon Corp.

NYSE Symbol **GFF**

In S&P SmallCap 600

09-OCT-99

Industry:
Manufacturing (Diversified)

Summary: Griffon is a diversified manufacturer of building products, electronic information and communication systems and specialty plastic films.

Quantitative Evaluations

Outlook
(1 Lowest—5 Highest)
• **NA**

Fair Value
• **NA**

Risk
• **Average**

Earn./Div. Rank
• **B**

Technical Eval.
• **Neutral** since 9/99

Rel. Strength Rank
(1 Lowest—99 Highest)
• **64**

Insider Activity
• **NA**

Recent Price • 7⅜
52 Wk Range • 11¼-6¼

Yield • Nil
12-Mo. P/E • 10.7

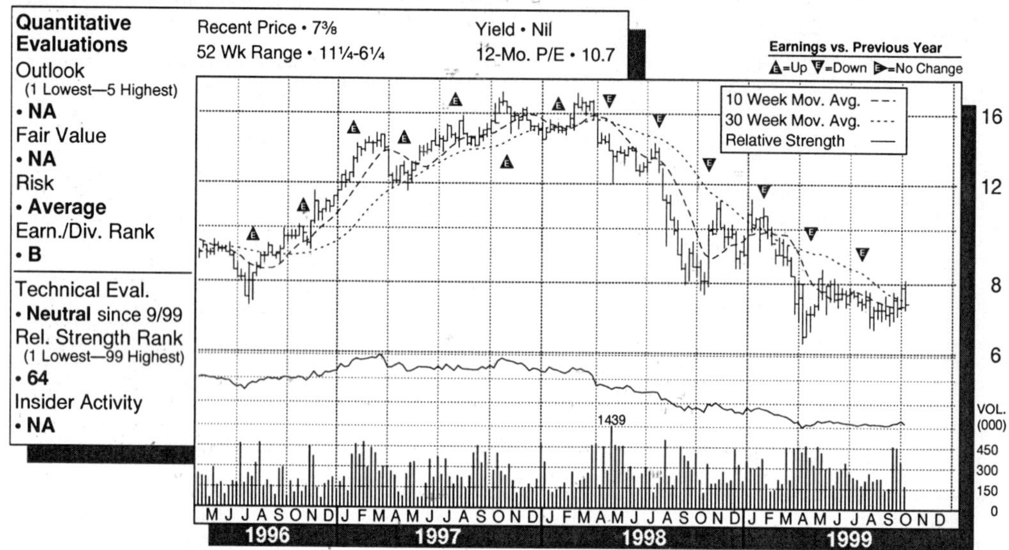

Business Profile - 23-JUN-99

Since the last half of FY 98 (Sep.) and into FY 99, the building products operation has consolidated or closed several facilities. In March 1999, the company recorded a $3.5 million restructuring charge related to the closing of a manufacturing facility to streamline operations and improve efficiency. Separately, a product line was sold that was operating at a loss. These actions will result in a 10% workforce reduction and generate annual cost savings of $2 million. During the second quarter of FY 99, GFF acquired a seller and installer of specialty products for the new residential construction market in Phoenix and Las Vegas. The operation has annual sales of $50 million and was acquired for $20 million in cash.

Operational Review - 23-JUN-99

Net sales in the six months ended March 31, 1999, rose 15%, year to year, reflecting internal growth and acquisitions. Profitability declined on pricing pressures, manufacturing inefficiencies and higher selling, general and administrative expenses; operating income fell 9.6%. Comparisons suffered further from a $3.5 million restructuring charge and substantially higher net interest expense and depreciation and amortization charges. After taxes at 37.0% in each period, net income fell 60%, to $4,691,000 ($0.15 a share), from $11,633,000 ($0.37).

Stock Performance - 08-OCT-99

In the past 30 trading days, GFF's shares have increased 3%, compared to a 0.91% fall in the S&P 500. Average trading volume for the past five days was 33,880 shares, compared with the 40-day moving average of 57,662 shares.

Key Stock Statistics

Dividend Rate/Share	Nil	Shareholders	16,000
Shs. outstg. (M)	30.4	Market cap. (B)	$0.224
Avg. daily vol. (M)	0.076	Inst. holdings	74%
Tang. Bk. Value/Share	6.30		
Beta	0.94		

Value of $10,000 invested 5 years ago: $ 8,309

Fiscal Year Ending Sep. 30

	1999	1998	1997	1996	1995	1994
Revenues (Million $)						
1Q	258.6	229.0	181.7	153.4	133.6	116.2
2Q	236.4	199.9	160.8	139.1	120.2	105.9
3Q	262.4	229.4	193.1	168.9	135.2	125.3
4Q	—	256.6	234.6	193.7	157.4	141.7
Yr.	—	914.9	770.2	655.1	546.4	489.0
Earnings Per Share ($)						
1Q	**0.23**	**0.27**	**0.24**	0.18	0.22	0.18
2Q	**-0.08**	**0.10**	0.14	0.12	0.10	0.13
3Q	**0.19**	**0.22**	0.29	0.25	0.15	0.20
4Q	—	**0.35**	0.40	0.34	0.24	0.29
Yr.	—	**0.94**	**1.06**	**0.88**	0.71	0.80

Next earnings report expected: early November

Dividend Data

No dividends have been paid on the common stock. A "poison pill" stock purchase rights plan was adopted in 1986.

Griffon Corporation

Business Summary - 23-JUN-99

In 1995, this company (formerly Instrument Systems Corp.) adopted the name Griffon Corp., after the composite beast of mythology (half eagle and half lion), to symbolize the combined strength of its diverse operations. No longer primarily a manufacturer of electronic information and communication systems, Griffon (GFF) is also a leading provider of building products and specialty plastic films.

GFF's building products unit, Clopay, accounted for 65% of FY 98 (Sep.) revenues. The company believes that Clopay is the largest manufacturer and marketer of residential garage doors and among the largest manufacturers of commercial garage doors in the United States. Clopay is focusing on increasing its market share in the $1.4 billion garage door market by expanding its dealer network, increasing brand awareness, selling additional products, and through strategic acquisitions. The company has completed three acquisitions of garage door manufacturing and installation companies as well as eight stand-alone installation companies since 1992. Clopay also operates a service company that installs and services garage doors and openers, fireplaces and a range of related products.

GFF is a leader in the development of specialty plastic films and laminates (18% of FY 98 sales) used in moisture barriers in disposable infant diapers, adult incontinence products and feminine hygiene products, and the health care market. Its strategy is to offer technologically advanced products for use in niche markets to major consumer and health care product companies. A substantial portion of the unit's sales over the past five years has been to Procter & Gamble Co.

Through its electronics information and communication systems unit (17% of FY 98 sales), GFF manufactures a variety of electronic systems used in commercial and government markets worldwide. The division, known as Telephonics, also provides audio and communication systems for use on aircraft and trains and produces custom large-scale integrated circuits. In recent years, GFF has expanded its presence in non-military government, commercial and international markets. As a result, approximately 50% of the segment's FY 98 revenues were to customers other than the United States government and its prime contractors and subcontractors on defense programs, as compared to approximately 30% in FY 92. At September 30, 1998, the unit's backlog was $189 million, up from $182 million a year earlier.

Per Share Data ($) (Year Ended Sep. 30)	1998	1997	1996	1995	1994	1993	1992	1991	1990	1989
Tangible Bk. Val.	6.30	5.41	5.18	4.33	4.17	3.56	3.06	1.52	0.90	0.31
Cash Flow	1.46	1.43	1.19	0.97	1.06	0.95	0.97	0.88	0.65	0.38
Earnings	0.94	1.06	0.88	0.71	0.80	0.70	0.66	0.51	0.32	0.13
Dividends	Nil	Nil	Nil	Nil	Nil	Nil	Nil	Nil	Nil	Nil
Payout Ratio	Nil	Nil	Nil	Nil	Nil	Nil	Nil	Nil	Nil	Nil
Prices - High	17 3/8	17 1/2	12 1/4	9 1/2	9 3/4	9 1/8	8 1/4	6 3/8	2 3/8	2
- Low	7 5/8	11 5/8	7 1/4	7 3/8	6 5/8	6	4 1/8	1 3/8	1 1/4	1
P/E Ratio - High	19	17	14	13	12	13	13	13	7	15
- Low	8	11	8	10	8	9	6	3	4	8
Income Statement Analysis (Million $)										
Revs.	915	770	655	546	489	437	500	494	459	405
Oper. Inc.	65.7	65.9	57.8	48.3	59.7	53.7	58.1	50.1	42.6	31.7
Depr.	16.3	11.5	10.3	8.7	9.8	9.5	11.1	11.2	9.8	7.3
Int. Exp.	3.9	3.5	3.4	2.2	1.8	1.9	7.0	13.5	14.8	14.3
Pretax Inc.	46.5	53.0	45.9	39.0	50.3	44.3	42.9	28.8	21.5	10.7
Eff. Tax Rate	37%	37%	39%	39%	41%	40%	40%	40%	42%	43%
Net Inc.	29.3	33.2	28.1	23.8	29.7	26.6	24.1	15.4	9.5	4.8
Balance Sheet & Other Fin. Data (Million $)										
Cash	19.3	15.4	22.1	21.9	58.4	37.6	24.4	23.5	27.5	33.4
Curr. Assets	307	264	229	212	223	200	152	202	193	185
Total Assets	488	385	311	286	293	270	247	304	295	271
Curr. Liab.	138	129	106	97.8	102	82.8	74.0	78.1	79.4	71.6
LT Debt	107	53.9	32.5	16.2	16.0	25.0	25.0	105	119	123
Common Eqty.	230	202	172	155	159	145	128	66.0	49.0	33.0
Total Cap.	350	256	205	188	192	186	170	224	214	198
Cap. Exp.	48.0	25.8	9.4	8.1	9.2	8.4	13.4	15.2	19.5	25.4
Cash Flow	45.6	44.6	37.9	32.5	39.5	36.0	35.1	26.6	19.3	11.2
Curr. Ratio	2.2	2.0	2.2	2.2	2.2	2.4	2.1	2.6	2.4	2.6
% LT Debt of Cap.	30.7	21.1	15.8	8.6	8.1	13.2	14.9	47.1	55.6	62.3
% Net Inc.of Revs.	3.2	4.3	4.3	4.4	6.1	6.1	4.8	3.1	2.1	1.2
% Ret. on Assets	6.7	9.5	9.3	8.2	10.8	10.3	7.7	5.1	3.3	1.9
% Ret. on Equity	13.6	17.7	16.1	15.1	20.0	19.5	22.9	26.7	23.2	9.7

Data as orig reptd.; bef. results of disc opers/spec. items. Per share data adj. for stk. divs. Bold denotes diluted EPS (FASB 128)-prior periods restated. E-Estimated. NA-Not Available. NM-Not Meaningful. NR-Not Ranked.

Office—100 Jericho Quadrangle, Jericho, NY 11753. **Reincorporated**—in Delaware in 1970. **Tel**—(516) 938-5544. **Website**—http://www.telephonics.com **Chrmn & CEO**—H. R. Blau. **Pres & CFO**—R. Balemian. **Secy**—S. E. Rowland. **VP, Treas & Investor Contact**—Patrick L. Alesia. **Dirs**—H.A. Alpert, R. Balemian, B. M. Bell, H. R. Blau, R. Bradley, A. M. Buchman, C. A. Hill Jr., R. J. Kramer, J. W. Stansberry, M. S. Sussman, W. H. Waldorf, L. L. Wolff. **Transfer Agent & Registrar**—American Stock Transfer & Trust Co., NYC. **Empl**— 5,400. **S&P Analyst:** Jordan Horoschak

STANDARD
&POOR'S
STOCK REPORTS

Group 1 Automotive

NYSE Symbol **GPI**

In S&P SmallCap 600

09-OCT-99

Industry: Retail (Specialty)

Summary: Group 1 owns car dealerships and collision service centers in six states.

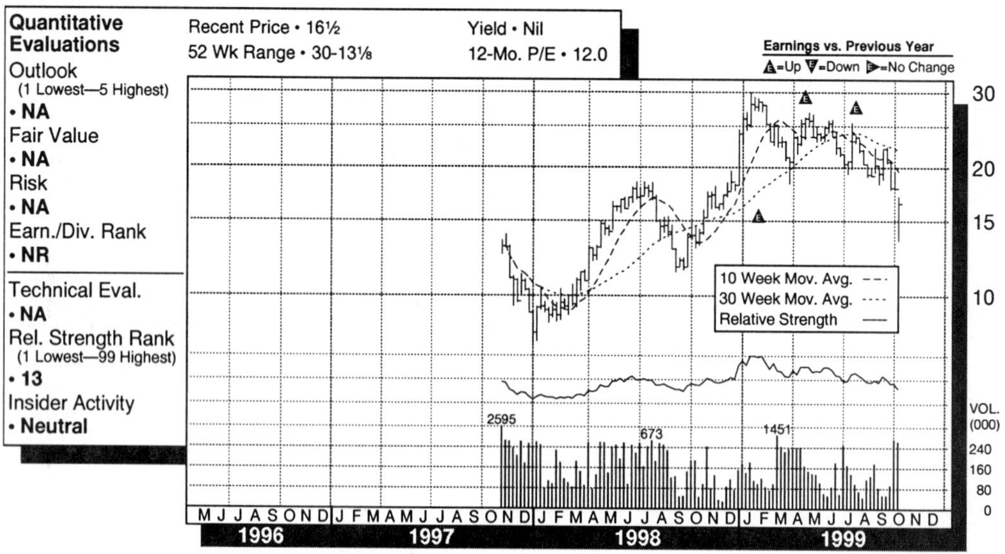

Business Profile - 13-JUL-99

The company was founded to become a leading operator and consolidator in the highly fragmented automotive retailing industry. Through July 9, the company had acquired 22 automobile franchises in 1999, with aggregate revenues of over $520 million. Upon the completion of all announced acquisitions, GPI will own 79 dealership franchises comprised of 26 different brands, and 15 collision service centers located in Texas, Oklahoma, Florida, New Mexico, Colorado and Georgia. In March 1999, GPI sold 2 million shares of common stock and $100 million of 10-year senior subordinated notes. A portion of the net proceeds of $140 million was earmarked for acquisitions.

Operational Review - 13-JUL-99

Revenues in the three months ended March 31, 1999, climbed 93%, year to year, reflecting contributions from acquisitions, and higher revenues from sales of new and used vehicles and parts and services. Gross margins widened on operating efficiencies and a more favorable product mix. With a 110% spurt in SG&A expenses and much higher interest expense, pretax income was up 93%. After taxes at 39.8%, versus 41.3%, net income nearly doubled, to $6,157,000 ($0.31 a share, on 28% more shares), from $3,114,000 ($0.20).

Stock Performance - 08-OCT-99

In the past 30 trading days, GPI's shares have declined 19%, compared to a 0.91% fall in the S&P 500. Average trading volume for the past five days was 113,800 shares, compared with the 40-day moving average of 51,997 shares.

Key Stock Statistics

Dividend Rate/Share	Nil	Shareholders	3,352
Shs. outstg. (M)	21.2	Market cap. (B)	$0.350
Avg. daily vol. (M)	0.080	Inst. holdings	21%
Tang. Bk. Value/Share	0.59		
Beta	NA		

Value of $10,000 invested 5 years ago: NA

Fiscal Year Ending Dec. 31

	1999	1998	1997	1996	1995	1994
Revenues (Million $)						
1Q	484.4	253.9	—	—	—	—
2Q	625.4	431.5	—	—	—	—
3Q	—	472.1	—	—	—	—
4Q	—	472.5	213.3	—	—	—
Yr.	—	1,630	902.3	825.6	—	—
Earnings Per Share ($)						
1Q	**0.31**	**0.20**	—	—	—	—
2Q	**0.42**	**0.31**	—	—	—	—
3Q	—	**0.35**	—	—	—	—
4Q	—	**0.29**	**0.15**	—	—	—
Yr.	—	**1.16**	**0.76**	**0.63**	—	—

Next earnings report expected: late October

Dividend Data

The company intends to retain all of its earnings to finance the growth and development of its business, including future acquisitions, and does not anticipate paying any cash dividends on its common stock for the foreseeable future.

Group 1 Automotive, Inc.

Business Summary - 13-JUL-99

With more than $600 billion in sales, automotive retailing is the largest retail trade sector in the U.S. The industry is highly fragmented and largely privately held, with approximately 22,000 automobile dealership locations representing more than 49,000 franchised dealerships. It is estimated that sales by franchised automobile dealers account for one-fifth of total U.S. retail sales of all products and merchandise. Group 1 Automotive was founded to become a leading operator and consolidator in this highly fragmented industry.

Simultaneously with the closing of its initial public offering in November 1997, GPI acquired four automobile dealerships representing 30 automobile franchises, known as its founding groups. During 1998, GPI acquired 33 additional dealership franchises.

During 1999, GPI had acquired 22 dealership franchises through July 9. Once all pending acquisitions are completed, the company will have a total of 79 dealer franchises comprised of 26 different brands and 15 collision service centers, in Texas, Oklahoma, New Mexico, Colorado, Florida and Georgia, selling new and used cars and light trucks, providing maintenance and repair services, selling replacement parts, and providing related financing, insurance and service contracts.

GPI is focusing on expanding higher-margin businesses such as used vehicle retail sales, parts and service, and finance and insurance. It sells used vehicles at each of its franchised dealerships. Profits from sales of used vehicles depend primarily on the ability of the dealerships to obtain a high quality supply of used vehicles and effectively manage that inventory.

The company currently represents 22 American, Asian andEuropean brands of economy, family, sports and luxury cars, light trucks and sport utility vehicles. In 1998, 46,099 new vehicles were sold (pro forma).

GPI believes that its structural, managerial and operational strengths include: (i) brand and geographic diversity; (ii) the ability to capitalize on regional economies of scale; (iii) cost savings derived from nationally centralized financing and administrative functions; (iv) the experience of senior management in successfully consolidating and operating in highly fragmented industries; (v) the reputations, experience and performance of the founding groups' management and principals as leaders in the automotive retailing industry; (vi) the established customer base and local name recognition of the founding groups' dealerships; (vii) the founding groups' proven ability to source high quality used vehicles cost-effectively through trade-ins and off-lease programs; and (viii) access to equity incentives to attract and retain high quality personnel.

Per Share Data ($) (Year Ended Dec. 31)	1998	1997	1996	1995	1994	1993	1992	1991	1990	1989
Tangible Bk. Val.	0.69	4.25	4.30	NA	NA	NA	NA	NA	NA	NA
Cash Flow	1.52	0.47	-0.21	NA	NA	NA	NA	NA	NA	NA
Earnings	1.16	0.76	0.63	NA	NA	NA	NA	NA	NA	NA
Dividends	Nil	Nil	NA	NA	NA	NA	NA	NA	NA	NA
Payout Ratio	Nil	Nil	NA	NA	NA	NA	NA	NA	NA	NA
Prices - High	26	13 7/8	NA	NA	NA	NA	NA	NA	NA	NA
- Low	8 5/8	7 3/4	NA	NA	NA	NA	NA	NA	NA	NA
P/E Ratio - High	22	18	NA	NA	NA	NA	NA	NA	NA	NA
- Low	7	10	NA	NA	NA	NA	NA	NA	NA	NA
Income Statement Analysis (Million $)										
Revs.	1,630	404	826	NA	NA	NA	NA	NA	NA	NA
Oper. Inc.	58.5	11.2	NA	NA	NA	NA	NA	NA	NA	NA
Depr.	6.4	1.0	NA	NA	NA	NA	NA	NA	NA	NA
Int. Exp.	16.9	4.0	3.3	NA	NA	NA	NA	NA	NA	NA
Pretax Inc.	35.2	6.4	-0.1	NA	NA	NA	NA	NA	NA	NA
Eff. Tax Rate	41%	8.98%	42%	NA	NA	NA	NA	NA	NA	NA
Net Inc.	20.7	5.8	-0.1	NA	NA	NA	NA	NA	NA	NA
Balance Sheet & Other Fin. Data (Million $)										
Cash	66.4	35.1	0.0	NA	NA	NA	NA	NA	NA	NA
Curr. Assets	327	162	0.0	NA	NA	NA	NA	NA	NA	NA
Total Assets	478	213	0.8	NA	NA	NA	NA	NA	NA	NA
Curr. Liab.	279	111	0.9	NA	NA	NA	NA	NA	NA	NA
LT Debt	42.8	7.0	8.2	NA	NA	NA	NA	NA	NA	NA
Common Eqty.	136	89.4	-0.1	NA	NA	NA	NA	NA	NA	NA
Total Cap.	179	100	101	NA	NA	NA	NA	NA	NA	NA
Cap. Exp.	9.7	2.2	NA	NA	NA	NA	NA	NA	NA	NA
Cash Flow	27.1	6.8	-0.1	NA	NA	NA	NA	NA	NA	NA
Curr. Ratio	1.2	1.5	0.0	NA	NA	NA	NA	NA	NA	NA
% LT Debt of Cap.	23.9	0.7	8.2	NA	NA	NA	NA	NA	NA	NA
% Net Inc.of Revs.	1.3	1.4	1.1	NA	NA	NA	NA	NA	NA	NA
% Ret. on Assets	6.0	5.4	NA	NA	NA	NA	NA	NA	NA	NA
% Ret. on Equity	18.4	13.0	NA	NA	NA	NA	NA	NA	NA	NA

Data as orig reptd.; bef. results of disc opers/spec. items. Per share data adj. for stk. divs. Bold denotes diluted EPS (FASB 128)-prior periods restated. E-Estimated. NA-Not Available. NM-Not Meaningful. NR-Not Ranked.

Office— 950 Echo Lane, Suite 350, Houston, TX 77024. **Tel**—(713) 467-6268. **Website**—http://www.group1auto.com **Chrmn, Pres & CEO**—B. B. Hollingsworth Jr. **SVP, CFO & Treas**—S. L. Thompson. **Secy**—J.S. Watson. **Dirs**—B. E. Bidwell, J. H. Duncan, B. B. Hollingsworth Jr., R. E. Howard II, S. B. McCall Jr., C. M. Smith. **Transfer Agent & Registrar**—ChaseMellon Shareholder Services, Dallas. **Incorporated**—in Delaware in 1995. **Empl**— 3,101. **S&P Analyst:** J.J.A.

STANDARD &POOR'S
STOCK REPORTS

Guilford Mills

NYSE Symbol **GFD**

In S&P SmallCap 600

09-OCT-99

Industry:
Textiles (Specialty)

Summary: This producer of various fabrics for home furnishings, apparel, auto and industrial customers is the world's largest warp knitter.

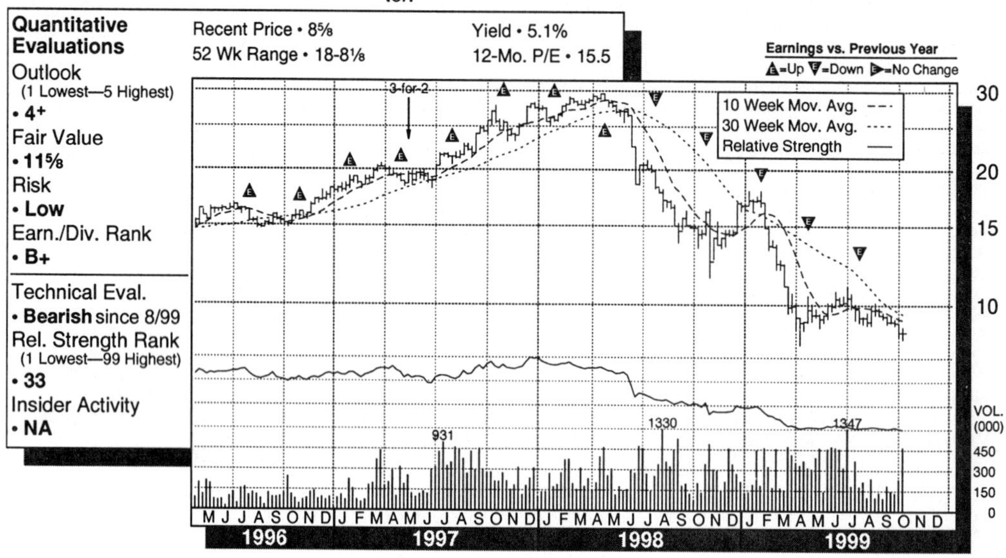

Business Profile - 31-AUG-99

In announcing results for the FY 99 (Sep.) third quarter, management said that while a strong performance in GFD's U.S. automotive group drove growth in the company's global automotive business, its home fashions business performed below expectations, as the expected shift in mix toward more value-added product had not occurred due to competitive import pricing and delays in certain programs with retailers. GFD's apparel segment continued to show mixed results as the impact from the Asian financial crisis continued to affect pricing and volumes on certain lines. In mid-August, GFD purchased about 14% of its common stock in a private deal with its largest individual shareholder. This follows the nearly completed 3.5 million share repurchase program authorized by the company in 1998.

Operational Review - 31-AUG-99

Net sales in the 40 weeks ended July 4, 1999, fell 3.5% from those of the prior year's first 39 weeks, as an increase in the automotive fabrics line was outweighed by declines in the home fashions and industrial/specialty product lines. Apparel sector sales were flat. Gross margins narrowed on the lower volume, and with higher selling and administrative expenses, operating income declined 52%. Interest expense increased 42%, and after other expense, against other income, and despite taxes at only 21.6%, versus 33.5%, net income was down 72%, to $8,049,000 ($0.36 a share) from $28,590,000 ($1.10).

Stock Performance - 08-OCT-99

In the past 30 trading days, GFD's shares have declined 9%, compared to a 0.91% fall in the S&P 500. Average trading volume for the past five days was 127,080 shares, compared with the 40-day moving average of 42,305 shares.

Key Stock Statistics

Dividend Rate/Share	0.44	Shareholders	435
Shs. outstg. (M)	22.2	Market cap. (B)	$0.193
Avg. daily vol. (M)	0.057	Inst. holdings	53%
Tang. Bk. Value/Share	16.63		
Beta	0.81		

Value of $10,000 invested 5 years ago: $ 6,486

Fiscal Year Ending Sep. 30

	1999	1998	1997	1996	1995	1994
Revenues (Million $)						
1Q	214.9	213.4	210.9	174.2	182.0	158.0
2Q	218.3	228.4	219.1	207.1	202.0	156.0
3Q	217.9	232.8	238.4	232.2	210.8	183.0
4Q	—	219.9	226.3	216.8	187.4	207.0
Yr.	—	894.5	894.7	830.3	782.5	704.0
Earnings Per Share ($)						
1Q	**0.10**	**0.25**	**0.24**	0.13	0.29	0.19
2Q	**0.21**	**0.36**	0.34	0.27	0.45	0.19
3Q	**0.04**	**0.49**	0.66	0.58	0.53	0.43
4Q	—	**0.19**	0.66	0.60	0.33	0.41
Yr.	—	**1.30**	**1.78**	**1.47**	1.61	1.21

Next earnings report expected: late November

Dividend Data (Dividends have been paid since 1973.)

Amount ($)	Date Decl.	Ex-Div. Date	Stock of Record	Payment Date
0.110	Nov. 05	Nov. 12	Nov. 16	Nov. 30 '98
0.110	Jan. 25	Feb. 03	Feb. 05	Feb. 17 '99
0.110	Apr. 26	May. 05	May. 07	May. 19 '99
0.110	Jul. 26	Aug. 04	Aug. 06	Aug. 18 '99

A Division of The McGraw-Hill Companies

Guilford Mills, Inc.

Business Summary - 31-AUG-99

In 1946, the year that James M. Hornaday founded Guilford Mills (GFD) with two warp knitting machines in the warehouse of his Hornaday Feed and Seed Store in Greensboro, NC, the company racked up sales of $90,000. More than five decades later, in FY 98 (Sep.), its sales had reached $895 million. This strong growth was achieved by a combination of internal expansion and acquisitions that led the company into various areas of the warp knitting business. GFD is a fabric producer that processes and sells warp knit, circular knit, flat woven and woven velour fabrics as well as lace. The company knits synthetic yarn, primarily nylon, acetate and polyester, on warp knitting machinery into warp knit fabrics, which it then dyes and finishes. Finished fabrics are sold to customers for use in a broad range of apparel, automotive, industrial and home fashions products. The company also designs, knits, dyes, prints and finishes elastomeric and circular knit fabrics for sale primarily to swimwear, dress and sportswear manufacturers. In addition, GFD produces flat wovens and woven velour fabrics for use in automotive products.

In January 1996, the company acquired Hofmann Laces, Ltd., Raschel Fashion Interknitting, Ltd. and Curtains and Fabrics, Inc., makers of knitted lace fabrics for the apparel, intimate apparel and home furnishings market. The purchase price consisted of $22 million in cash, 300,000 (adjusted) common shares, and a contingent payment, based on a formula, for a five-year period ending December 31, 2000.

U. S. export sales were 5.4% of total worldwide sales in FY 98.

In FY 98 (Sep.), apparel acounted for 38% of sales (39% in FY 97), automotive for 38% (37%), home fashions for 18% (15%), and specialty for 6% (9%).

GFD works closely with customers to develop patterns and create new fabrics and styles. R & D outlays totaled $19.6 million in FY 98, up from $14.9 million in FY 97.

The company owns 95% (increased from 75% in mid-1997) of Grupo Ambar, S.A. de C.V., a leading manufacturer of knit textile fabrics in Mexico, and 100% of Guilford Europe in the U.K.

In the U. S., the company has five major warp knit competitors and many other smaller competitors in the apparel and home fashions markets. GFD also competes with some apparel makers that have warp knit equipment to make their own fabrics. Some of these companies are divisions of large, well-capitalized companies while others are small manufacturers. In circular knits, the company has four major competitors and numerous smaller competitors.

Per Share Data ($) (Year Ended Sep. 30)	1998	1997	1996	1995	1994	1993	1992	1991	1990	1989
Tangible Bk. Val.	14.33	15.88	14.57	12.64	11.63	10.59	10.05	8.85	8.75	9.41
Cash Flow	3.81	4.54	4.18	3.83	3.12	2.74	2.56	1.99	0.89	2.21
Earnings	1.30	1.91	1.59	1.61	1.21	1.41	1.23	0.68	-0.38	1.19
Dividends	0.44	0.42	0.40	0.40	0.40	0.40	0.38	0.36	0.36	0.36
Payout Ratio	34%	22%	25%	25%	33%	28%	31%	53%	NM	30%
Prices - High	29 5/8	28 1/4	18 1/8	18 7/8	16 1/8	18 5/8	19	14 7/8	11 1/4	15 1/4
- Low	11 1/2	17 3/4	13	13 3/8	12 3/8	12 5/8	11 7/8	7 5/8	6 1/8	10 3/8
P/E Ratio - High	23	15	11	12	13	13	15	22	NM	13
- Low	9	9	8	8	10	9	10	11	NM	9
Income Statement Analysis (Million $)										
Revs.	895	895	830	783	704	654	615	529	544	620
Oper. Inc.	134	146	127	115	91.2	79.8	76.2	56.8	57.1	69.0
Depr.	64.0	59.6	55.4	46.7	39.3	27.4	26.8	26.4	26.9	22.8
Int. Exp.	12.4	16.2	17.0	14.1	12.4	8.2	7.0	8.4	8.4	8.6
Pretax Inc.	49.1	65.8	50.9	50.2	38.9	43.9	34.1	20.1	-15.5	41.7
Eff. Tax Rate	33%	34%	33%	33%	35%	34%	27%	32%	NM	37%
Net Inc.	33.1	43.2	34.0	33.6	25.1	28.9	24.9	13.6	-8.0	26.3
Balance Sheet & Other Fin. Data (Million $)										
Cash	30.4	24.3	31.0	18.0	6.1	17.9	15.9	14.3	25.4	40.2
Curr. Assets	362	349	352	286	264	249	227	204	227	255
Total Assets	789	730	729	586	565	507	414	375	390	410
Curr. Liab.	151	135	174	108	111	96.6	87.5	80.0	88.9	76.8
LT Debt	177	135	209	166	165	147	77.0	80.0	92.0	96.0
Common Eqty.	385	409	298	268	244	220	206	178	176	208
Total Cap.	593	566	530	454	429	386	301	278	287	319
Cap. Exp.	84.0	57.6	65.0	58.0	48.0	102	35.8	26.6	31.3	46.6
Cash Flow	97.1	103	89.4	80.3	64.5	56.2	51.7	39.9	18.9	49.1
Curr. Ratio	2.4	2.6	2.0	2.7	2.4	2.6	2.6	2.6	2.6	3.3
% LT Debt of Cap.	29.8	23.9	39.5	36.7	38.4	38.2	25.5	28.8	32.1	30.1
% Net Inc.of Revs.	3.7	4.8	4.1	4.3	3.6	4.4	4.0	2.6	NM	4.2
% Ret. on Assets	4.4	5.9	5.2	5.8	4.7	6.2	6.2	3.5	NM	6.7
% Ret. on Equity	8.3	12.1	12.1	13.1	10.8	13.5	12.8	7.7	NM	13.2

Data as orig. reptd.; bef. results of disc. opers. and/or spec. items. Fiscal yr. ended Jun. 30 prior to 1994. Per share data adj. for stk. divs. as of ex-div. date. Bold denotes diluted EPS (FASB 128). E-Estimated. NA-Not Available. NM-Not Meaningful. NR-Not Ranked.

Reincorporated—in Delaware in 1971. **Office**—4925 W. Market St., Greensboro, NC 27407. **Tel**—(910) 316-4000. **Website**—http://www.guilfordmills.com **Chrmn & CEO**—C. A. Hayes. **Pres & COO**—J. Emrich. **EVP & CFO**—T. E. Geremski. **Treas**—M. E. Cook. **Investor Contact**—Jaime Vasquez. **Dirs**—T. Adachi, D. B. Dixon, J. Emrich, M. Fishman, T. E. Geremski, P. G. Gillease, G. Greenberg, S. C. Hassenfelt, C. A. Hayes, B. Hofmann, S. R. Jacobs, S. R. Kry, G. M. Wilson, J. Zaidenweber. **Transfer Agent & Registrar**—Wachovia Bank of North Carolina, Winston-Salem. **Empl**— 6,836. **S&P Analyst:** C.C.P.

STANDARD
&POOR'S
STOCK REPORTS

Gymboree Corp.

Nasdaq Symbol **GYMB**

In S&P SmallCap 600

09-OCT-99 **Industry:** Retail (Specialty-Apparel)

Summary: This company sells apparel and accessories for children, and operates and franchises directed parent-child developmental play programs.

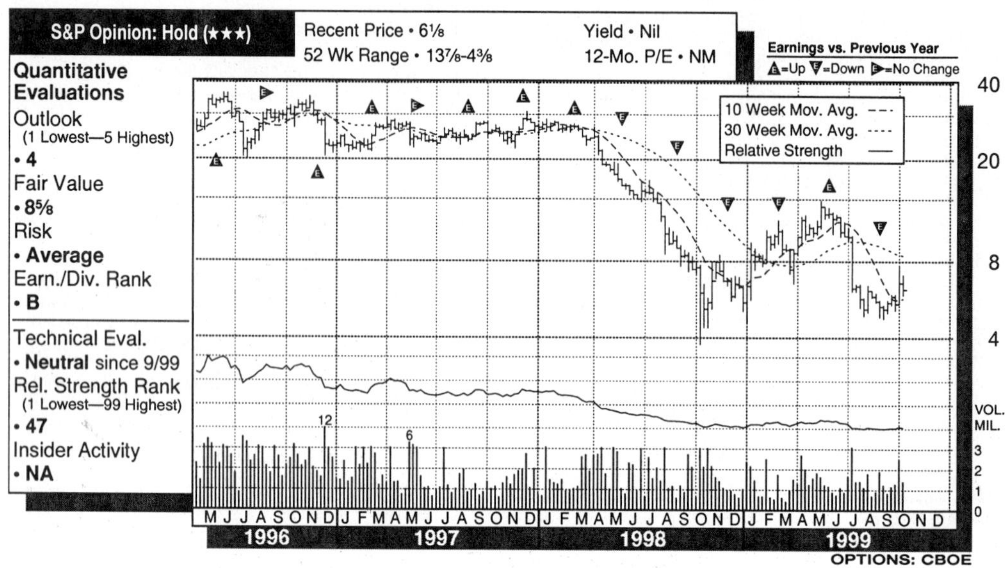

Overview - 21-SEP-99

As a result of weak demand and a deterioration in profitability, Gymboree recently initiated a comprehensive brand remerchandising program. Revenues in the second half of FY 00 (Jan.) will drop significantly, as the company focuses on full price sales and improving margins against comparisons of large clearance sales in the prior year. We expect sales growth to be in the low single digits, with a double-digit forecasted decline in comparable store sales. Gross margin improvement will be dependent on how well the company executes its pricing policy of reduced markdowns and promotional discounting. Several growth initiatives, including improvements to the website, expansion of the European business and the launching of Zutopia, will increase expenses. Overall, we anticipate EPS of $0.14 per share for FY 00.

Valuation - 21-SEP-99

Shares of this specialty apparel retailer fell over 25% after it announced a larger than expected second quarter loss and a major brand remerchandising strategy. The company is in the process of modifying its store layouts and launching new product lines. With a fiercely competitive children's apparel market, repositioning GYMB's brand will present a significant challenge. The launch of the new retail concept, Zutopia, is poorly timed, as the company needs to focus completely on refining the core business. The share price should remain at the mid-single-digit level until after the fourth quarter when the initial reaction to the new product line can be assessed. Management has decided to maintain lower inventories to keep merchandise offerings current. Although the brand repositioning presents various challenges and risks, we believe the remerchandising uncertainties are reflected in the current stock price.

Key Stock Statistics

S&P EPS Est. 2000	0.14	Tang. Bk. Value/Share	6.58
P/E on S&P Est. 2000	44.2	Beta	0.64
S&P EPS Est. 2001	0.40	Shareholders	764
Dividend Rate/Share	Nil	Market cap. (B)	$0.151
Shs. outstg. (M)	24.3	Inst. holdings	73%
Avg. daily vol. (M)	0.314		

Value of $10,000 invested 5 years ago: $ 2,780

Fiscal Year Ending Jan. 31

	2000	1999	1998	1997	1996	1995
Revenues (Million $)						
1Q	125.7	103.1	85.24	69.10	55.08	—
2Q	99.9	99.8	71.68	57.90	49.39	34.86
3Q	—	114.0	101.1	84.69	66.23	51.46
4Q	—	140.3	115.4	91.42	88.69	62.77
Yr.	—	457.2	373.4	303.1	259.4	188.4
Earnings Per Share ($)						
1Q	**0.20**	**0.17**	0.34	0.34	0.25	0.17
2Q	**-0.56**	**-0.03**	0.19	0.17	0.17	0.10
3Q	**E-0.01**	**-0.01**	0.44	0.35	0.28	0.27
4Q	**E0.16**	**0.13**	**0.46**	0.39	0.35	0.33
Yr.	**E0.14**	**0.26**	**1.41**	**1.24**	**1.04**	0.88

Next earnings report expected: mid November

Dividend Data

The company has never paid cash dividends on its common stock and anticipates that all future earnings will be retained for development of its business.

The Gymboree Corporation

Business Summary - 21-SEP-99

In an effort to revitalize its brand and broaden its appeal, Gymboree Corp. initiated a comprehensive remerchandising program in July 1999. The company plans on expanding and enhancing its fashion offerings to create a more innovative and diversified merchandise selection. The new brand strategy will also provide greater flexibility to help integrate fashion and marketplace trends into its products.

Key elements of the brand remerchandising strategy include improving apparel fashion appeal, diversifying the product line, modifying store interiors, shortening lead times and reorder processes and redesigning a new trademark. The company expects the full rollout of new product lines by the middle of the FY 00 (Jan.) fourth quarter and a new logo after the holiday season.

Gymboree operates 588 stores, including 542 stores in the U.S., 18 in Canada and 28 in Europe. It is investigating the most efficient ways to expand internationally.

In FY 99, the company opened a new distribution center in Dixon, CA, enabling it to manage product flow efficiently for all the U.S. stores. On the product mix side, the company expanded its successful layette line and began selling shoes as a stand-alone product.

During the first quarter of FY 00, Gymboree unveiled a new retail concept catering to the clothing needs of children ages 6 to 12 called Zutopia. The line features a blend of designer, street and alternative gear styled for older children. This concept represents a significant shift in theory, design and target market demographics from the company's traditional products.

In an effort to strengthen its management team, Gymboree appointed a new president and a new head designer during the fourth quarter of FY 99. Management will seek to refine its base business with better pricing policies and an improved product mix. Store expansions were slowed down to a planned opening of 40-50 new stores in FY 00 (including the opening of 15 to 20 Zutopia stores), compared with a total of 129 stores opened in FY 99.

Play & Music Programs entail parents playing with their children under the direction of an instructor. At the end of July 1999, there were 406 franchised and company-operated centers in the U.S and nine foreign countries. The company believes that its program centers provide attractive cross-marketing opportunities for its stores, and strengthen the Gymboree brand.

Gymboree is in the process of networking its retail stores to help control inventory and cut new product development time. The company is also upgrading its website to enhance its e-commerce capability. Currently, the website has only a small array of gift items from which to choose.

Per Share Data ($) (Year Ended Jan. 31)	1999	1998	1997	1996	1995	1994	1993	1992	1991	1990
Tangible Bk. Val.	6.95	6.57	6.39	4.96	3.77	2.64	1.95	NA	NA	NA
Cash Flow	1.03	2.00	1.59	1.25	1.01	0.68	0.39	NA	NA	NA
Earnings	0.26	1.41	1.24	1.04	0.88	0.57	0.31	0.13	NA	NA
Dividends	Nil	Nil	Nil	Nil	Nil	Nil	Nil	Nil	NA	NA
Payout Ratio	Nil	Nil	Nil	Nil	Nil	Nil	Nil	Nil	NA	NA
Cal. Yrs.	1998	1997	1996	1995	1994	1993	1992	1991	1990	1989
Prices - High	28 7/8	30 7/8	36 3/8	37 1/4	33	26 1/4	NA	NA	NA	NA
- Low	3 3/4	21 1/8	14 3/8	18	17 3/8	10	NA	NA	NA	NA
P/E Ratio - High	NM	22	29	36	38	46	NA	NA	NA	NA
- Low	NM	15	12	17	20	18	NA	NA	NA	NA
Income Statement Analysis (Million $)										
Revs.	457	373	303	259	188	130	86.0	NA	NA	NA
Oper. Inc.	26.2	66.9	56.4	45.5	38.6	25.5	12.9	NA	NA	NA
Depr.	18.8	13.5	8.9	5.4	3.3	2.5	1.6	NA	NA	NA
Int. Exp.	Nil	Nil	Nil	Nil	Nil	Nil	Nil	NA	NA	NA
Pretax Inc.	9.9	55.8	51.2	43.2	37.0	23.9	11.6	NA	NA	NA
Eff. Tax Rate	37%	37%	38%	39%	40%	41%	40%	NA	NA	NA
Net Inc.	6.2	35.2	31.7	26.4	22.2	14.1	6.9	NA	NA	NA
Balance Sheet & Other Fin. Data (Million $)										
Cash	27.8	17.9	90.3	73.6	63.1	46.8	NA	NA	NA	NA
Curr. Assets	118	121	146	116	101	71.0	NA	NA	NA	NA
Total Assets	257	229	217	160	127	88.0	NA	NA	NA	NA
Curr. Liab.	41.8	49.9	40.4	26.6	27.5	20.8	NA	NA	NA	NA
LT Debt	11.5	Nil	Nil	Nil	Nil	Nil	NA	NA	NA	NA
Common Eqty.	168	158	162	124	92.6	63.3	NA	NA	NA	NA
Total Cap.	180	158	162	124	92.6	63.3	NA	NA	NA	NA
Cap. Exp.	50.7	NA	37.0	Nil	11.6	6.9	5.3	NA	NA	NA
Cash Flow	25.0	48.7	40.6	31.7	25.5	16.6	8.5	NA	NA	NA
Curr. Ratio	2.8	2.4	3.6	4.4	3.7	3.4	NA	NA	NA	NA
% LT Debt of Cap.	6.4	Nil	Nil	Nil	Nil	Nil	NA	NA	NA	NA
% Net Inc.of Revs.	1.4	9.4	10.5	10.2	11.8	10.9	8.0	NA	NA	NA
% Ret. on Assets	2.6	15.8	16.8	18.4	20.6	16.0	NA	NA	NA	NA
% Ret. on Equity	3.8	22.0	22.2	24.4	28.5	35.8	NA	NA	NA	NA

Data as orig reptd.; bef. results of disc opers/spec. items. Per share data adj. for stk. divs. Bold denotes diluted EPS (FASB 128)-prior periods restated. E-Estimated. NA-Not Available. NM-Not Meaningful. NR-Not Ranked.

Office—700 Airport Blvd., Suite 200, Burlingame, CA 94010-1912. **Tel**—(650) 579-0600. **Website**—http://www.gymboree.com. **Chrmn**—S. G. Moldaw. **Vice Chrmn & CEO**—G. White. **Pres**—M. B. Cox.**SVP & CFO**—L. H. Meyer. **VP-Treas**—F. M. Petrocco. **Secy**—J. P. Saper. **Dirs**—W. F. Loeb, S. G. Moldaw, B. L. Rambo, D. A. Sorondo, W. U. Westerfield, C. J. Whitacre, G. White. **Transfer Agent & Registrar**—BankBoston. **Incorporated**—in California in 1979; reincorporated in Delaware in 1992. **Empl**— 6,500. **S&P Analyst:** A. Bensinger

STANDARD
&POOR'S
STOCK REPORTS

HA-LO Industries

NYSE Symbol **HMK**

In S&P SmallCap 600

09-OCT-99

Industry:
Services (Advertising & Marketing)

Summary: This leading marketer and distributor of advertising specialty and promotional products also provides telemarketing services to large corporations.

Quantitative Evaluations

Outlook
(1 Lowest—5 Highest)
• **5**

Fair Value
• **11¼**

Risk
• **NA**

Earn./Div. Rank
• **B**

Technical Eval.
• **Bearish** since 6/99

Rel. Strength Rank
(1 Lowest—99 Highest)
• **6**

Insider Activity
• **Favorable**

Recent Price • 5⅛
52 Wk Range • 25⅝-4⅞

Yield • Nil
12-Mo. P/E • 11.4

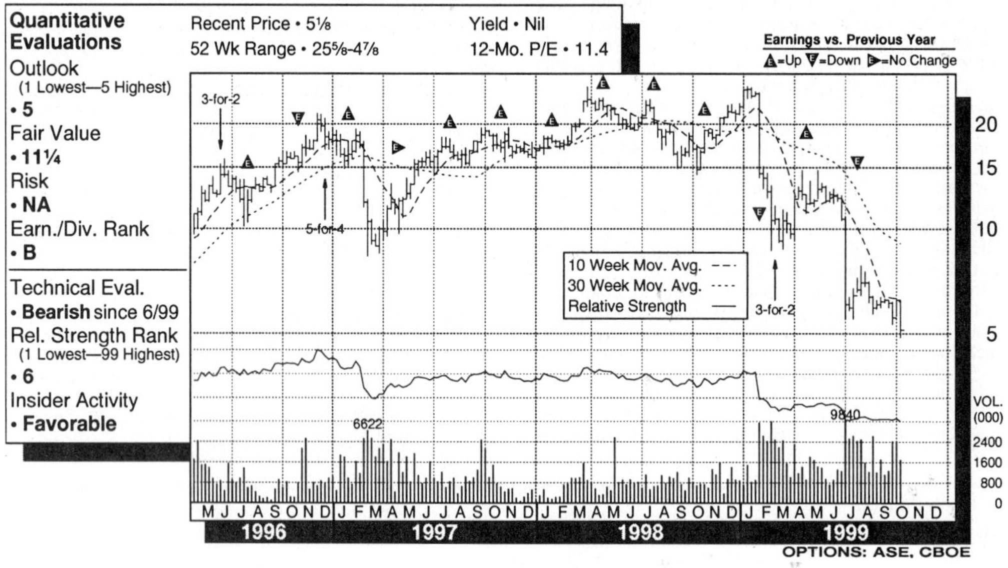

OPTIONS: ASE, CBOE

Business Profile - 12-JUL-99

In July 1999, HMK announced that 1999 second quarter revenues and EPS would be lower than expected. The company anticipated that revenues would approximate $160 million, with diluted EPS of $0.02. HMK attributed the anticipated shortfall to customer deferral of marketing programs, due to local economic conditions in Europe and South America. In addition, the company said it was experiencing a deceleration in the growth rate of promotional products sales in some markets. HMK believes revenues and EPS in 2000 will also be affected by these market forces, and estimated EPS in 2000 at about $0.55. The company also said it would incur a restructuring charge of $25 million to $30 million in the 1999 third quarter, related to streamlining back office operations and information systems.

Operational Review - 12-JUL-99

Net sales in the three months ended March 31, 1999, advanced 26%, year to year, due to acquisitions and internal growth. Despite wider gross margins and well controlled selling expenses, after costs of investment to support the marketing services business, operating income rose only 7.4%. In the absence of a $1.5 million non-recurring charge, and with interest income, versus expense, after taxes at 40.0% versus 42.8%, net income climbed 66%, to $4,199,000 ($0.09 a share, on 16% more shares), from $2,530,000 ($0.06, as adjusted).

Stock Performance - 08-OCT-99

In the past 30 trading days, HMK's shares have declined 15%, compared to a 0.91% fall in the S&P 500. Average trading volume for the past five days was 336,800 shares, compared with the 40-day moving average of 433,726 shares.

Key Stock Statistics

Dividend Rate/Share	Nil	Shareholders	250
Shs. outstg. (M)	49.7	Market cap. (B)	$0.255
Avg. daily vol. (M)	0.398	Inst. holdings	51%
Tang. Bk. Value/Share	3.74		
Beta	1.66		

Value of $10,000 invested 5 years ago: $ 26,207

Fiscal Year Ending Dec. 31

	1999	1998	1997	1996	1995	1994
Revenues (Million $)						
1Q	157.0	124.8	78.59	49.91	20.80	12.60
2Q	160.3	138.2	90.95	60.79	25.40	15.50
3Q	—	150.7	98.30	65.11	36.70	16.90
4Q	—	175.9	135.7	79.07	58.60	23.70
Yr.	—	589.7	413.8	254.9	172.9	68.60
Earnings Per Share ($)						
1Q	**0.09**	**0.06**	**0.02**	**0.02**	0.01	0.01
2Q	**0.02**	**0.10**	**0.08**	**0.05**	0.02	0.01
3Q	—	**0.13**	**0.11**	**0.05**	0.06	0.03
4Q	—	**0.20**	**0.21**	**0.13**	0.07	0.06
Yr.	—	**0.53**	**0.43**	**0.26**	**0.15**	0.11

Next earnings report expected: late October

Dividend Data

Amount ($)	Date Decl.	Ex-Div. Date	Stock of Record	Payment Date
3-for-2	Jan. 26	Feb. 22	Feb. 05	Feb. 19 '99

A Division of The McGraw-Hill Companies

HA-LO Industries, Inc.

Business Summary - 12-JUL-99

HA-LO Industries is a full service, innovative brand marketing organization with three operating segments: promotional products, marketing services and telemarketing. The company utilizes a system of 50 showrooms throughout the U.S., Canada and Europe. It displays more than 300,000 products provided by its network of more than 2,500 vendors.

The promotional products division develops customized products, generally articles of merchandise with a customer's name, logo or message, for marketing, sales incentives and awards and development of goodwill for a targeted audience. Products include: (i) apparel items such as jackets, sweaters, hats and golf shirts; (ii) business accessories such as clocks, portfolios, briefcases, blotters, and pen and pencil sets; (iii) recognition awards such as trophies and plaques; and (iv) other miscellaneous items such as etched crystalware, calendars, golf accessories, key chains, watches and mugs. According to Promotional Products Association International, the U.S. market for promotional products has grown from $4.5 billion in 1989 to $11.9 billion in 1997. The industry is highly fragmented, with more than 15,000 distributors. At the end of 1998, HMK had an industry market share of approximately 4%.

The company's clients include AlliedSignal, Ameritech, Ford Motor, GE, Seagram and Sony. In 1998, no single customer accounted for over 10% of total revenues.

The company's marketing services include promotional marketing by UPSHOT, brand strategy and identity by LAGA, and presence marketing by Events by HA-LO. UPSHOT provides promotions marketing associated with new product launches, rejuvenating brands, promotional advertising, merchandising, and event marketing. LAGA provides brand strategy in connecting a company product, service or image with a target audience. Events by HA-LO is a corporate event production company specializing in orchestrating corporate meetings, seminar events and incentive programs.

The telemarketing division creates, manages and conducts outbound and inbound telemarketing programs for large corporate clients, primarily in the insurance and financial service industries. The segment provides script development, telephone-based direct sales, database analysis and management, consultation and program design, as well as customer lead acquisition services.

Per Share Data ($) (Year Ended Dec. 31)	1998	1997	1996	1995	1994	1993	1992	1991	1990	1989
Tangible Bk. Val.	4.37	1.86	2.01	1.62	0.27	0.31	0.57	NA	NA	NA
Cash Flow	0.72	0.61	0.51	0.33	0.19	0.06	0.09	NA	NA	NA
Earnings	0.53	0.43	0.35	0.19	0.11	0.02	0.06	0.11	-0.01	NA
Dividends	Nil	Nil	Nil	Nil	Nil	Nil	Nil	Nil	Nil	NA
Payout Ratio	Nil	Nil	Nil	Nil	Nil	Nil	Nil	Nil	Nil	NA
Prices - High	$25\frac{5}{8}$	$19\frac{5}{8}$	$21\frac{1}{2}$	$10\frac{7}{8}$	$2\frac{3}{4}$	$2\frac{1}{2}$	$2\frac{5}{8}$	NA	NA	NA
- Low	$14\frac{1}{4}$	$8\frac{3}{8}$	$7\frac{1}{4}$	$2\frac{1}{8}$	$1\frac{3}{4}$	$1\frac{5}{16}$	$1\frac{15}{16}$	NA	NA	NA
P/E Ratio - High	48	46	61	57	26	NM	47	NA	NA	NA
- Low	27	20	20	11	17	NM	34	NA	NA	NA
Income Statement Analysis (Million $)										
Revs.	590	414	255	173	68.6	35.7	23.5	NA	NA	NA
Oper. Inc.	59.0	34.7	19.1	8.4	3.9	0.9	1.2	NA	NA	NA
Depr.	9.5	5.8	3.9	2.1	1.0	0.5	0.3	NA	NA	NA
Int. Exp.	1.2	1.9	0.2	1.3	0.7	0.0	0.3	NA	NA	NA
Pretax Inc.	40.9	23.1	15.6	5.0	2.1	0.4	0.8	NA	NA	NA
Eff. Tax Rate	39%	40%	40%	40%	40%	40%	37%	NA	NA	NA
Net Inc.	24.8	13.9	9.4	3.0	1.3	0.2	0.5	NA	NA	NA
Balance Sheet & Other Fin. Data (Million $)										
Cash	58.2	2.7	6.8	1.5	0.0	0.1	NA	NA	NA	NA
Curr. Assets	272	162	68.0	54.7	27.2	15.5	NA	NA	NA	NA
Total Assets	347	211	88.0	68.8	36.1	22.0	NA	NA	NA	NA
Curr. Liab.	109	84.2	26.0	27.2	13.5	7.8	NA	NA	NA	NA
LT Debt	Nil	43.6	2.9	Nil	12.0	5.5	NA	NA	NA	NA
Common Eqty.	235	81.4	57.2	39.6	8.9	7.3	NA	NA	NA	NA
Total Cap.	235	125	60.1	39.6	21.2	13.7	NA	NA	NA	NA
Cap. Exp.	NA	8.2	5.0	2.2	0.5	1.0	0.1	NA	NA	NA
Cash Flow	34.2	19.7	13.3	5.1	2.3	0.7	0.8	NA	NA	NA
Curr. Ratio	2.5	1.9	2.6	2.0	2.0	2.0	NA	NA	NA	NA
% LT Debt of Cap.	Nil	34.8	4.8	Nil	56.5	40.2	NA	NA	NA	NA
% Net Inc.of Revs.	4.2	3.4	3.7	1.7	1.9	0.6	2.0	NA	NA	NA
% Ret. on Assets	8.9	9.3	11.2	5.3	4.4	1.4	NA	NA	NA	NA
% Ret. on Equity	15.6	20.0	18.4	12.1	15.9	3.2	NA	NA	NA	NA

Data as orig reptd.; bef. results of disc opers/spec. items. Per share data adj. for stk. divs. Bold denotes diluted EPS (FASB 128)-prior periods restated. E-Estimated. NA-Not Available. NM-Not Meaningful. NR-Not Ranked.

Office—5980 W. Touhy Ave., Niles, IL 60714. **Tel**—(847) 647-2300. **Website**—http://www.ha-lo.com **Chrmn, Pres & CEO**—L. Weisbach. **Treas & COO**—R. A. Magid. **CFO**—G. J. Kilrea. **VP & Secy**—B. G. Berman. **VP-Fin**—B. T. Margolin. **VP & Investor Contact**—Michael P. Nemlich. **Dirs**—T. Herskovits, J. R. Katz, M. J. Katz, R. A. Magid, L. D. Nelson, S. N. Okner, N. A. Ramo, D. C. Robbins, R. Sosnick, L. Weisbach. **Transfer Agent & Registrar**—Harris Trust & Savings Bank, Chicago. **Incorporated**—in Illinois in 1986. **Empl**— 1,500. **S&P Analyst:** Jordan Horoschak

STANDARD
&POOR'S
STOCK REPORTS

HADCO Corp.

NASDAQ Symbol **HDCO**

In S&P SmallCap 600

09-OCT-99 **Industry:** Electrical Equipment

Summary: This company is a leading supplier of electronic interconnect products and services.

Quantitative Evaluations

Outlook (1 Lowest—5 Highest)
• **4-**

Fair Value
• **60⅛**

Risk
• **High**

Earn./Div. Rank
• **C**

Technical Eval.
• **Bullish** since 8/99

Rel. Strength Rank (1 Lowest—99 Highest)
• **60**

Insider Activity
• **NA**

Recent Price • 40⅝
52 Wk Range • 47⅝-21¼

Yield • Nil
12-Mo. P/E • 40.2

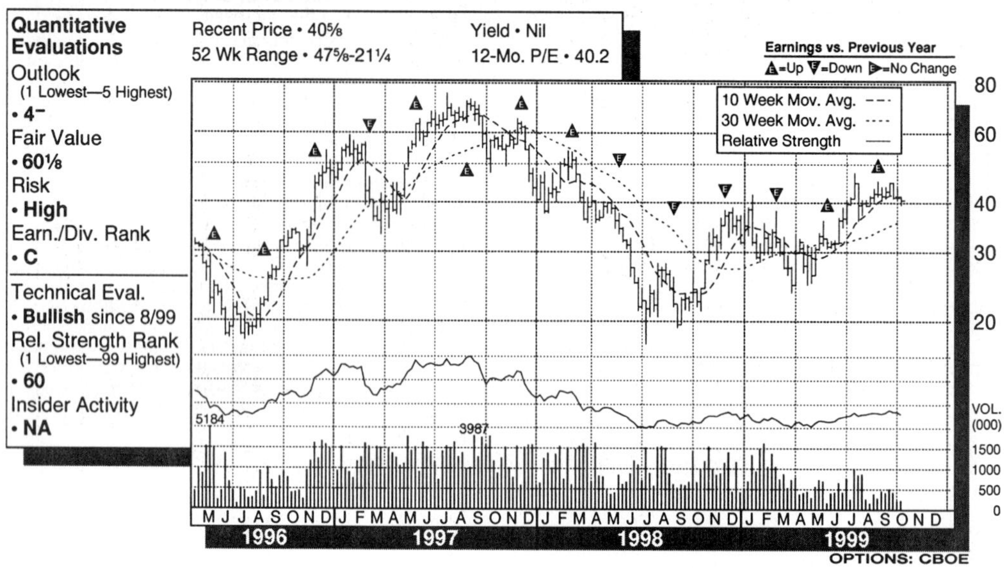

Business Profile - 30-AUG-99

In announcing results for the FY 99 (Oct.) third quarter, management noted that financial results in the prior year's third quarter had been affected by the Asian economic crisis and a general slowdown in the broad electronics industry. The company added that since then, it has experienced increased demand, and has continued to reduce production costs, resulting in dramatically improved financial results. Bookings for the quarter were $255.7 million, resulting in a book-to-bill ratio for the quarter of 1.01. Backlog at the end of the FY 99 third quarter was $148.1 million, versus $144.3 million at the end of the preceding quarter.

Operational Review - 30-AUG-99

Net sales for the nine months ended July 31, 1999, increased 22%, year to year. Gross margins narrowed somewhat; however, operating expenses were well controlled, and in the absence of $7.1 million of restructuring and other non-recurring charges and a $63.1 million write-off of R & D expenses, operating income of $44.6 million contrasted with an operating loss of $36.4 million. Interest expense was up sharply, and after taxes at 39.7%, versus taxes of $5.6 million, net income was $13,222,000 ($0.96 a share), against a net loss of $54,493,000 ($4.14).

Stock Performance - 08-OCT-99

In the past 30 trading days, HDCO's shares have declined 4%, compared to a 0.91% fall in the S&P 500. Average trading volume for the past five days was 44,400 shares, compared with the 40-day moving average of 72,697 shares.

Key Stock Statistics

Dividend Rate/Share	Nil	Shareholders	340
Shs. outstg. (M)	13.6	Market cap. (B)	$0.554
Avg. daily vol. (M)	0.067	Inst. holdings	77%
Tang. Bk. Value/Share	2.03		
Beta	1.49		

Value of $10,000 invested 5 years ago: $ 49,242

Fiscal Year Ending Oct. 31

	1999	1998	1997	1996	1995	1994
Revenues (Million $)						
1Q	236.0	198.3	111.5	76.48	56.83	46.46
2Q	255.6	209.6	180.7	88.10	67.64	56.20
3Q	252.4	201.4	183.3	88.23	67.75	59.27
4Q	—	217.1	173.2	97.89	72.95	59.64
Yr.	—	826.4	648.7	350.7	265.2	221.6
Earnings Per Share ($)						
1Q	**0.15**	**0.90**	**-6.64**	0.65	0.29	0.10
2Q	**0.34**	**-4.54**	0.91	0.71	0.49	0.22
3Q	**0.48**	**-0.52**	0.93	0.72	0.56	0.27
4Q	—	**0.03**	0.84	0.81	0.63	0.34
Yr.	—	**-4.09**	**-3.18**	2.89	1.98	0.93

Next earnings report expected: late November

Dividend Data

No cash dividends have been paid. The company plans to continue to retain earnings for use in its business. A stockholder rights plan was adopted in August 1995.

HADCO Corporation

Business Summary - 30-AUG-99

With the January 1997 acquisition of Zycon (valued at $212 million), a manufacturer of electronic interconnect products, HADCO became the largest publicly owned electronic interconnect supplier in North America. In order to solidify its position, the company in March 1998 acquired Continental Circuits Corp. (Nasdaq: CCIR) for approximately $185 million in cash, plus the assumption of approximately $33 million in debt. Continental is a leading manufacturer of complex multilayer printed circuits and will improve HADCO's position in the complex multilayer circuit board segment, one of the fastest growing segments of the interconnect industry.

HADCO offers a wide array of sophisticated manufacturing, engineering and systems integration services to meet its customers' electronic interconnect needs. The company's principal products are complex multilayer rigid printed circuits and backplane assemblies. Printed circuits are the basic platforms used to interconnect microprocessors, integrated circuits and other components essential to the functioning of electronic products. Backplane assemblies are generally larger and thicker printed circuits on which connectors are mounted to interconnect printed circuits, integrated circuits and other electronic components. Net sales of backplane assemblies accounted for 11% and 17% of the total company net sales in FY 97 (Oct.) and FY 96, respectively, and for 10% on a pro forma basis including Zycon during FY 97.

In keeping with its strategy of developing and commercializing technologies that increase density and improve electrical performance, HADCO has focused its efforts in four key areas: high-density interconnect solutions; high-performance materials; buried passive components; and emerging technologies. HADCO's customers are OEMs and contract manufacturers in the computing (mainly workstations, servers, mainframes, storage and notebooks), data communications/telecommunications and industrial automation industries, including process controls, automotive, medical and instrumentation. HADCO's largest customers during FY 97 included leading companies in the electronics industry, such as Cabletron systems, Compaq Computer, Lucent Technologies, Solectron and Sun Microsystems.

In response to a slowdown in sales in the third quarter of FY 98, HADCO announced in July 1998 a 3% overall reduction in the workforce. Management attributes the slowdown to several factors, including the general slowdown in the broad electronics industry, customer product transitions, customer inventory adjustments and the economic situation in Asia.

Per Share Data ($) (Year Ended Oct. 31)	1998	1997	1996	1995	1994	1993	1992	1991	1990	1989
Tangible Bk. Val.	0.01	10.61	13.37	10.14	7.95	7.03	6.13	5.33	4.74	4.01
Cash Flow	-3.82	-2.24	4.45	3.20	2.25	1.98	1.92	1.52	1.50	1.29
Earnings	-4.09	-3.18	2.89	1.98	0.93	0.76	0.75	0.52	0.65	0.40
Dividends	Nil	Nil	Nil	Nil	Nil	Nil	Nil	Nil	Nil	Nil
Payout Ratio	Nil	Nil	Nil	Nil	Nil	Nil	Nil	Nil	Nil	Nil
Prices - High	54	75 5/8	54	35 7/8	9 1/4	10 1/2	11	6 1/2	6 1/8	7
- Low	17 1/2	33 1/8	17 7/8	8 3/8	5 7/8	7 1/4	5 1/8	3 3/8	3 5/8	3 3/8
P/E Ratio - High	NM	NM	19	18	10	14	15	13	9	18
- Low	NM	NM	6	4	6	10	7	6	6	8
Income Statement Analysis (Million $)										
Revs.	826	649	351	265	222	189	183	153	161	156
Oper. Inc.	45.6	88.0	68.9	47.1	30.7	26.9	26.1	20.5	23.9	20.9
Depr.	3.6	11.2	17.3	13.2	14.2	13.2	12.7	10.9	10.1	10.7
Int. Exp.	22.5	10.9	0.3	0.5	0.9	1.4	2.0	2.1	2.5	2.7
Pretax Inc.	-48.2	-9.2	52.5	35.0	16.4	12.9	12.2	8.6	12.4	8.0
Eff. Tax Rate	NM	NM	39%	39%	40%	36%	34%	35%	38%	40%
Net Inc.	-54.1	-36.9	32.0	21.4	9.9	8.2	8.1	5.6	7.7	4.8
Balance Sheet & Other Fin. Data (Million $)										
Cash	7.2	12.2	42.2	36.5	31.6	27.4	25.9	23.3	20.7	19.6
Curr. Assets	221	167	114	93.6	71.6	60.7	55.6	51.3	48.3	47.1
Total Assets	744	503	220	163	126	111	104	99	92.0	90.0
Curr. Liab.	129	113	70.0	52.5	39.8	30.1	32.4	29.7	27.9	26.2
LT Debt	354	110	1.5	2.4	4.5	9.4	11.0	17.4	13.8	17.8
Common Eqty.	192	240	139	101	77.4	68.4	59.4	50.6	48.2	44.1
Total Cap.	605	380	140	103	82.0	77.8	71.1	69.5	64.0	63.4
Cap. Exp.	83.5	70.0	54.0	28.9	19.5	14.3	13.0	15.1	11.4	12.7
Cash Flow	-50.5	-25.7	49.3	34.5	24.2	21.4	20.8	16.5	17.8	15.5
Curr. Ratio	1.7	1.5	1.6	1.8	1.8	2.0	1.7	1.7	1.7	1.8
% LT Debt of Cap.	58.5	28.8	1.1	2.3	5.5	12.1	15.5	25.0	21.6	28.1
% Net Inc.of Revs.	NM	NM	9.1	8.1	4.5	4.3	4.4	3.7	4.8	3.1
% Ret. on Assets	NM	NM	16.7	14.8	8.4	7.6	7.9	6.1	8.8	5.7
% Ret. on Equity	NM	NM	26.7	24.0	13.6	12.8	14.5	11.7	17.3	11.6

Data as orig reptd.; bef. results of disc opers/spec. items. Per share data adj. for stk. divs. Bold denotes diluted EPS (FASB 128)-prior periods restated. E-Estimated. NA-Not Available. NM-Not Meaningful. NR-Not Ranked.

Office—12A Manor Pkwy., Salem, NH 03079. **Organized**—in Massachusetts in 1966. **Tel**—(603) 898-8000. **Website**—http://www.hadco.com **Chrmn**—H. H. Irvine II. **Pres & CEO**—A. E. Lietz. **VP, CFO, Treas & Investor Contact**—F.G. Bitter **Clerk**—J. C. Hamilton. **Dirs**—L. Coolidge, J. S. Hill, H. H. Irvine II, A. E. Lietz, J. E. Pomeroy, J. F. Smith, P. Sweeney, J. C. Taylor, O. O. Ward. **Transfer Agent**—BankBoston, N.A., Boston. **Empl**— 6,142. **S&P Analyst:** C.C.P.

STANDARD
&POOR'S
STOCK REPORTS

Haggar Corp.

NASDAQ Symbol **HGGR**

In S&P SmallCap 600

09-OCT-99

Industry:
Textiles (Apparel)

Summary: This company designs, makes, imports and markets men's casual and dress apparel primarily under its own name.

Quantitative Evaluations

Outlook
(1 Lowest—5 Highest)
• **NA**

Fair Value
• **NA**

Risk
• **Average**

Earn./Div. Rank
• **NR**

Technical Eval.
• **Neutral** since 9/99

Rel. Strength Rank
(1 Lowest—99 Highest)
• **56**

Insider Activity
• **NA**

Recent Price • 12½
52 Wk Range • 15⅛-9½

Yield • 1.6%
12-Mo. P/E • 11.5

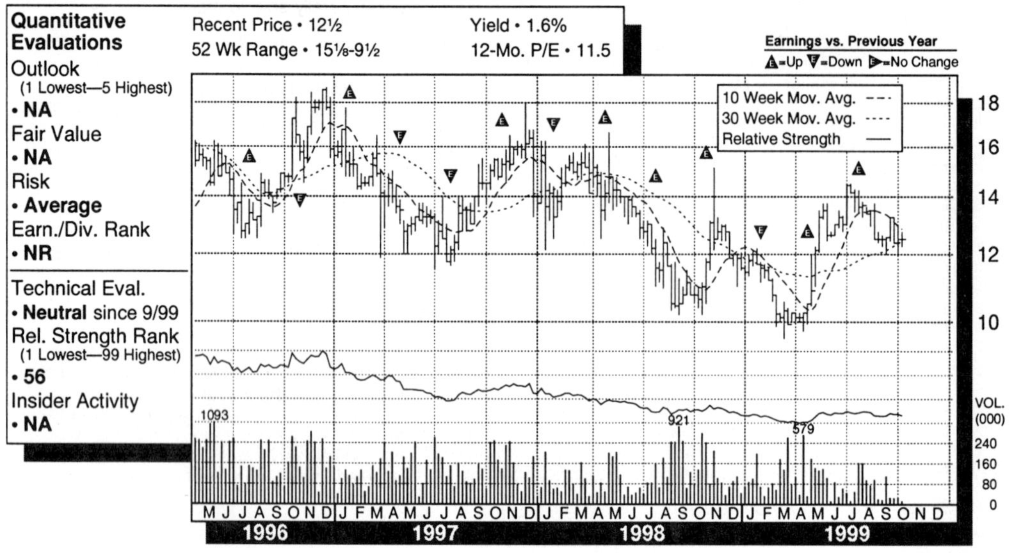

Business Profile - 04-OCT-99

In August 1999, the company established its first Canadian subsidiary, Haggar Canada, which will take on the company's women's wear business from a licensee. Jerell, Inc., acquired by HGGR in January 1999, is expected to play an instrumental role in the operation of Haggar Canada. A women's line, by Jerell, is to be launched in the U.S. in the spring of 2000. In March 1999, the company said it would introduce a new branding and communications strategy in the spring of 2000 to reach out to consumers seeking stylish clothes for business and pleasure. The company was also in the process of constructing a website for e-commerce. Subsequent to September 30, 1998, the company repurchased 1,382,000 shares under a 2 million share authorization.

Operational Review - 04-OCT-99

Net sales in the nine months ended June 30, 1999, advanced 8.7%, year to year, reflecting higher unit sales and additional sales from recently acquired Jerell's, Inc. Gross margins widened due to an improved manufacturing mix and fewer inventory markdowns. Although SG&A expenses rose 16% on higher advertising costs and expenses related to the acquisition and new stores, pretax income climbed 20%. After taxes at 38.8%, versus 38.5%, net income advanced 19%, to $4,213,000 ($0.56 a share, on 12% fewer shares) from $3,535,000 ($0.41).

Stock Performance - 08-OCT-99

In the past 30 trading days, HGGR's shares were unchanged, compared to a 0.91% fall in the S&P 500. Average trading volume for the past five days was 2,280 shares, compared with the 40-day moving average of 8,131 shares.

Key Stock Statistics

Dividend Rate/Share	0.20	Shareholders	3,003
Shs. outstg. (M)	7.2	Market cap. (B)	$0.090
Avg. daily vol. (M)	0.004	Inst. holdings	57%
Tang. Bk. Value/Share	18.31		
Beta	0.58		

Value of $10,000 invested 5 years ago: $ 5,274

Fiscal Year Ending Sep. 30

	1999	1998	1997	1996	1995	1994
Revenues (Million $)						
1Q	84.80	102.5	104.2	98.42	121.0	110.2
2Q	120.3	94.68	98.61	110.8	121.1	118.3
3Q	107.2	90.19	88.00	103.8	85.18	120.2
4Q	—	115.1	115.3	124.9	121.2	142.5
Yr.	—	402.5	406.0	437.9	448.5	491.2
Earnings Per Share ($)						
1Q	**0.06**	**0.13**	**0.16**	0.12	0.62	0.51
2Q	**0.25**	**0.14**	0.06	0.19	0.25	0.92
3Q	**0.25**	**0.14**	-0.23	0.13	-2.30	0.65
4Q	—	**0.53**	0.45	-0.71	2.57	0.86
Yr.	—	**0.94**	**0.44**	-0.28	1.14	2.95

Next earnings report expected: early November

Dividend Data (Dividends have been paid since 1993.)

Amount ($)	Date Decl.	Ex-Div. Date	Stock of Record	Payment Date
0.050	Oct. 22	Oct. 30	Nov. 03	Nov. 17 '98
0.050	Jan. 20	Jan. 28	Feb. 01	Feb. 15 '99
0.050	Apr. 27	May. 06	May. 10	May. 24 '99
0.050	Jul. 20	Jul. 29	Aug. 02	Aug. 16 '99

Haggar Corp.

Business Summary - 04-OCT-99

Haggar Corp. introduced its wrinkle-free, 100% cotton pants in FY 93 (Sep.), helping to midwife the phenomenon known worldwide as "Casual Friday." The company designs, manufacturers, imports and markets casual and dress men's apparel products, including pants, shorts, suits, sportcoats and shirts. Products are offered in wide variety of styles, fabrics, colors and sizes.

The company is well known for its use of "performance fabrics" that maintain a fresh, neat appearance. Its product lines are dominated by natural fiber (wool or cotton) and blended (polyester/wool or polyester/rayon) fabrics, although HGGR also makes some apparel using a single synthetic fabric. The company's apparel lines are focused on basic, recurring styles that are less susceptible to fashion obsolescence. Thus, while the company strives to offer current fashions and styles, the bulk of its product lines change relatively little from year to year. This consistency enables Haggar to operate on a cost-efficient basis and to more accurately forecast the demand for particular products.

Haggar-brand products, which accounted for 77% of apparel sales in FY 98, are sold nationwide mainly to major department stores and include dress and casual pants, sportcoats, suits, shirts and shorts. Haggar has developed specific product lines (such as Haggar Wrinkle-Free Cottons and Haggar City Casuals) intended to keep it in the forefront of the trend among men toward more casual clothing, while maintaining its traditional strength in men's dress apparel.

The company's mass retailer division, The Horizon Group, markets products including dress pants, casual pants, shorts, suits, sportcoats and shirts. These products, offered at lower price points than Haggar brand products, are generally sold to mass market retailers such as Wal-Mart.

During FY 98, about 12% of the company's products (measured in units) were produced in the U.S., with the balance manufactured in foreign countries.

The company's five largest customers accounted for 57.4% of sales in FY 98. Its largest customer, J. C. Penney Co., was responsible for 27.9% of sales, and Kohl's Department Stores Inc. 10.4%.

In 1995, as part of its strategic growth objectives, the company began opening and operating retail stores located in outlet malls throughout the U.S. As of September 30, 1998, it had opened 53 such stores, which market first quality company products to the general public. These stores also serve as a retail-marketing laboratory for the company.

In January 1999, the company acquired Jerell, Inc., a Texas-based women's apparel manufacturer for approximately $37 million. A women's line, by Jerell, is to be launched in the U.S. in the spring of 2000.

In August 1999, the company established its first Canadian subsidiary, Haggar Canada, which will take on the company's women's wear business from a licensee. Recently acquired Jerrell Inc. is planned to play an instrumental role in the ope ration of Haggar Canada.

Per Share Data ($) (Year Ended Sep. 30)	1998	1997	1996	1995	1994	1993	1992	1991	1990	1989
Tangible Bk. Val.	20.55	19.24	19.00	19.46	18.51	15.70	11.15	NA	NA	NA
Cash Flow	2.44	1.78	0.52	1.52	3.31	2.28	2.26	NA	NA	NA
Earnings	0.94	0.44	-0.28	1.14	2.95	1.88	1.70	NA	NA	NA
Dividends	0.20	0.20	0.20	0.20	0.20	0.10	Nil	NA	NA	NA
Payout Ratio	21%	45%	NM	18%	7%	6%	Nil	NA	NA	NA
Prices - High	16⅝	18	19	26¼	40½	25½	21½	NA	NA	NA
- Low	10⅛	11½	11½	15¾	20½	15½	16½	NA	NA	NA
P/E Ratio - High	18	40	NM	23	14	14	13	NA	NA	NA
- Low	11	26	NM	14	7	8	10	NA	NA	NA
Income Statement Analysis (Million $)										
Revs.	402	406	438	449	491	394	381	NA	NA	NA
Oper. Inc.	25.3	17.0	16.3	15.4	42.3	24.2	24.1	NA	NA	NA
Depr.	12.9	11.4	6.8	3.3	3.2	3.1	3.7	NA	NA	NA
Int. Exp.	3.5	3.5	4.3	5.0	1.3	1.5	4.0	NA	NA	NA
Pretax Inc.	13.0	6.0	-3.4	15.8	42.0	23.3	19.5	NA	NA	NA
Eff. Tax Rate	38%	38%	NM	38%	39%	36%	36%	NA	NA	NA
Net Inc.	8.0	3.7	-2.4	9.8	25.7	15.0	12.4	NA	NA	NA
Balance Sheet & Other Fin. Data (Million $)										
Cash	20.3	2.2	2.9	2.2	2.6	17.9	0.4	NA	NA	NA
Curr. Assets	185	192	210	249	215	179	146	NA	NA	NA
Total Assets	252	262	278	315	257	206	170	NA	NA	NA
Curr. Liab.	61.6	65.7	73.7	70.4	84.3	67.4	49.3	NA	NA	NA
LT Debt	24.9	31.8	42.1	78.6	15.0	5.5	28.2	NA	NA	NA
Common Eqty.	165	165	162	166	158	133	93.0	NA	NA	NA
Total Cap.	190	196	205	245	173	139	121	NA	NA	NA
Cap. Exp.	10.2	15.0	16.0	30.6	15.4	6.5	NA	NA	NA	NA
Cash Flow	20.9	15.2	4.4	13.1	28.8	18.1	15.1	NA	NA	NA
Curr. Ratio	3.0	2.9	2.9	3.5	2.6	2.7	3.0	NA	NA	NA
% LT Debt of Cap.	13.1	16.2	20.5	32.1	8.7	3.9	23.2	NA	NA	NA
% Net Inc.of Revs.	2.0	0.9	NM	2.2	5.2	3.8	3.3	NA	NA	NA
% Ret. on Assets	3.1	1.4	NM	3.4	11.1	7.9	NA	NA	NA	NA
% Ret. on Equity	4.9	2.3	NM	6.0	17.6	13.2	NA	NA	NA	NA

Data as orig reptd.; bef. results of disc opers/spec. items. Per share data adj. for stk. divs. Bold denotes diluted EPS (FASB 128)-prior periods restated. E-Estimated. NA-Not Available. NM-Not Meaningful. NR-Not Ranked.

Office—6113 Lemmon Ave., Dallas, TX 75209. **Tel**—(214) 352-8481. **Website**—http://www.haggar.com. **Chrmn & CEO**—J. M. Haggar III. **Pres & COO**—F. D. Bracken. **SVP & CFO**—D. Tehle. **Dirs**—F. D. Bracken, N. E. Brinker, R. F. Evans, J. M. Haggar III, R. W. Heath, J. C. Tolleson. **Transfer Agent & Registrar**—ChaseMellon Shareholder Services, Ridgefield Park, NJ. **Incorporated**—in Nevada in 1989. **Empl**— 3,975. **S&P Analyst:** Howard Choe

STANDARD
&POOR'S
STOCK REPORTS

Halter Marine Group

ASE Symbol **HLX**

In S&P SmallCap 600

09-OCT-99

Industry: Manufacturing (Specialized)

Summary: This company, which specializes in the construction, repair and conversion of oceangoing and inland waterway vessels, has agreed to merge with Friede Goldman International.

Quantitative Evaluations

Outlook (1 Lowest—5 Highest) • **1**

Fair Value • **5**

Risk • **Average**

Earn./Div. Rank • **NR**

Technical Eval. • **Neutral** since 9/99

Rel. Strength Rank (1 Lowest—99 Highest) • **41**

Insider Activity • **NA**

Recent Price • 5¼

52 Wk Range • 9¼-3⅝

Yield • Nil

12-Mo. P/E • 16.6

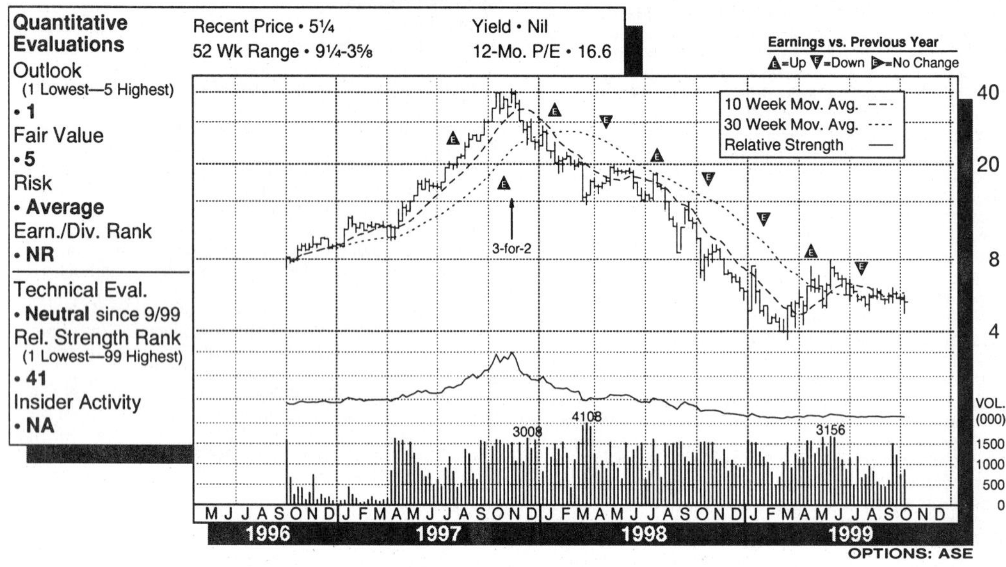

Business Profile - 22-SEP-99

In June 1999, the company definitively agreed to merge with Friede Goldman International plc (FGI; NYSE), a leading provider of offshore drilling services. In September 1999, the two companies amended the merger terms due to developments related to a contract dispute with a customer. Under the new agreement, each HLX share will be exchanged for 0.57 of a share of FGI, versus 0.4614 under the original plan. The combined company will be called Friede Goldman Halter, Inc., and will have a backlog exceeding $1 billion. Closing is seen early in the fourth quarter of calendar 1999. Recently, the company initiated cost reduction measures in its vessels and rigs segments, which is expected to lead to a minimum of $10 million in savings during FY 00 (Mar.).

Operational Review - 22-SEP-99

Contract revenues in the three months ended June 30, 1999, declined 8.4%, year to year, as lower vessels and engineered products revenues outweighed gains in the rigs segment. Gross margins narrowed, mainly due to soft margins in the rigs segment and, to a lesser extent, weakness in the engineered products area. Profitability was hurt by the lower volume and, following a rise in interest expense, net income fell 69%, to $1,923,000 ($0.07 a share, diluted, on 2.0% fewer shares), from $6,128,000 ($0.21).

Stock Performance - 08-OCT-99

In the past 30 trading days, HLX's shares have declined 2%, compared to a 0.91% fall in the S&P 500. Average trading volume for the past five days was 172,180 shares, compared with the 40-day moving average of 165,987 shares.

Key Stock Statistics

Dividend Rate/Share	Nil	Shareholders	NA
Shs. outstg. (M)	28.9	Market cap. (B)	$0.153
Avg. daily vol. (M)	0.219	Inst. holdings	31%
Tang. Bk. Value/Share	2.37		
Beta	NA		

Value of $10,000 invested 5 years ago: NA

Fiscal Year Ending Mar. 31

	2000	1999	1998	1997	1996	1995
Revenues (Million $)						
1Q	192.1	209.8	149.1	85.98	—	—
2Q	—	270.8	151.2	94.50	—	—
3Q	—	279.3	180.6	112.5	—	—
4Q	—	238.3	189.4	113.9	—	—
Yr.	—	998.1	670.2	406.8	254.3	—
Earnings Per Share ($)						
1Q	**0.07**	**0.21**	0.19	0.13	—	—
2Q	—	**0.23**	0.27	0.15	—	—
3Q	—	**-0.03**	**0.29**	0.15	—	—
4Q	—	**0.05**	**0.02**	0.17	—	—
Yr.	—	**0.46**	**0.78**	**0.59**	0.47	—

Next earnings report expected: mid October

Dividend Data

No cash dividends have been paid. A three-for-two common stock split was effected in October 1997.

Halter Marine Group, Inc.

Business Summary - 22-SEP-99

Halter Marine Group (HLX) will merge with Friede Goldman International plc (FGI; NYSE), a leading provider of offshore drilling services, in the 1999 fourth quarter. The combined company will be called Friede Goldman Halter, Inc., and will have a backlog exceeding $1 billion. In May 1997, shortly after completing its first fiscal year as a public company, HLX acquired Texas Drydock, Inc. (TDI), launching the shipbuilder into the related, and promising, business of building, converting and mending offshore drilling rigs. HLX's new capabilities complement its existing energy-related activities, including the construction of offshore support vessels and oceangoing fuel barges.

Ranked fourth among U.S. shipbuilders, HLX is the leader in the construction of small- to medium-sized oceangoing vessels in the U.S. ranging in length from 50 ft. to 400 ft. The vessels segment operates eight shipyards mainly dedicated to the construction of marine vessels. All of the company's new vessel construction yards are strategically located along the Gulf Coast in Florida, Mississippi and Louisiana. During FY 99 (Mar.), the company spent $45 million on capital improvements for its existing shipyard facilities, and has budgeted $20 million for improvements in FY 00.

In FY 98 (Mar.), HLX entered the engineered products market through the acquisition of four companies (AmClyde Engineered Products, Inc. of St. Paul, MN; Utility Steel Fabrication, Inc. of Slidell, LA; Fritz Culver, Inc. of Covington, LA; and McElroy Machine & Manufacturing Co.) that manufacture market cranes, derricks, winches, hoists, control systems and other related products.

Sales to government customers accounted for 15% of total revenues in FY 99, versus 26% in FY 98 and 53% in FY 97.

Customers in the energy industry accounted for 59% of FY 99 revenues, up from 51% in FY 98, reflecting a 12% gain in the rigs segment. Products sold to this market include offshore supply vessels and large anchor handling tug/supply vessels, tug boats and double hull oceangoing fuel barges.

In May 1998, HLX formed a joint venture to build marine vessels in China. Separately, it acquired from Trinity Industries that company's Orange, TX, shipyard, significantly increasing HLX's rig building capability. In early 1999, HLX received a $57 million U.S. Navy contract to build an oceanographic research ship.

Backlog at March 31, 1999, totaled $656 million, down 16% from a year earlier. At June 30, 1999, backlog totaled $535 million, down 46% from a year earlier.

Per Share Data ($)										
(Year Ended Mar. 31)	**1999**	**1998**	**1997**	**1996**	**1995**	**1994**	**1993**	**1992**	**1991**	**1990**
Tangible Bk. Val.	2.25	2.05	5.06	2.98	NA	NA	NA	NA	NA	NA
Cash Flow	1.31	1.30	1.32	0.71	NA	NA	NA	NA	NA	NA
Earnings	0.46	0.78	0.59	0.47	NA	NA	NA	NA	NA	NA
Dividends	Nil	Nil	Nil	Nil	NA	NA	NA	NA	NA	NA
Payout Ratio	Nil	Nil	Nil	Nil	NA	NA	NA	NA	NA	NA
Cal. Yrs.	1998	1997	1996	1995	1994	1993	1992	1991	1990	1989
Prices - High	29	41½	10	NA	NA	NA	NA	NA	NA	NA
- Low	4⅛	9	7⅜	NA	NA	NA	NA	NA	NA	NA
P/E Ratio - High	63	53	17	NA	NA	NA	NA	NA	NA	NA
- Low	9	12	12	NA	NA	NA	NA	NA	NA	NA
Income Statement Analysis (Million $)										
Revs.	998	670	407	254	NA	NA	NA	NA	NA	NA
Oper. Inc.	44.3	54.5	38.1	30.6	NA	NA	NA	NA	NA	NA
Depr.	24.6	15.2	7.9	6.7	NA	NA	NA	NA	NA	NA
Int. Exp.	8.1	6.6	3.2	3.3	NA	NA	NA	NA	NA	NA
Pretax Inc.	12.3	31.7	27.0	20.6	NA	NA	NA	NA	NA	NA
Eff. Tax Rate	NM	29%	40%	39%	NA	NA	NA	NA	NA	NA
Net Inc.	13.3	22.5	16.1	12.5	NA	NA	NA	NA	NA	NA
Balance Sheet & Other Fin. Data (Million $)										
Cash	3.9	51.1	7.1	0.7	NA	NA	NA	NA	NA	NA
Curr. Assets	313	273	148	102	NA	NA	NA	NA	NA	NA
Total Assets	592	500	209	158	NA	NA	NA	NA	NA	NA
Curr. Liab.	178	122	62.1	62.7	NA	NA	NA	NA	NA	NA
LT Debt	240	218	52.0	31.1	NA	NA	NA	NA	NA	NA
Common Eqty.	165	151	93.3	80.4	NA	NA	NA	NA	NA	NA
Total Cap.	414	369	145	112	NA	NA	NA	NA	NA	NA
Cap. Exp.	47.9	40.9	14.5	5.6	NA	NA	NA	NA	NA	NA
Cash Flow	37.9	37.7	24.0	19.2	NA	NA	NA	NA	NA	NA
Curr. Ratio	1.8	2.2	2.4	1.6	NA	NA	NA	NA	NA	NA
% LT Debt of Cap.	57.9	57.9	35.8	27.9	NA	NA	NA	NA	NA	NA
% Net Inc.of Revs.	1.3	3.4	4.0	4.9	NA	NA	NA	NA	NA	NA
% Ret. on Assets	2.4	6.4	9.2	NA	NA	NA	NA	NA	NA	NA
% Ret. on Equity	8.4	18.4	20.1	NA	NA	NA	NA	NA	NA	NA

Data as orig reptd.; bef. results of disc opers/spec. items. Per share data adj. for stk. divs. Bold denotes diluted EPS (FASB 128)-prior periods restated. E-Estimated. NA-Not Available. NM-Not Meaningful. NR-Not Ranked.

Office—13085 Industrial Seaway Rd., Gulfport, MS 39503. **Tel**—(601) 896-0029. **Website**—http://www.haltermarine.com **Chrmn, Pres & CEO**—J. Dane III. **EVP, CFO & Investor Contact**—Rick S. Rees. **SVP & Secy**—M. O'Connor Sullivan. **Dirs**—A. R. Cooper, J. Dane III, B. J. Galt, B. H. Keenan, K. W. Lewis, R. S. Rees. **Transfer Agent & Registrar**—Bank of New York, NYC. **Incorporated**—in Delaware in 1996. **Empl**— 7,296. **S&P Analyst:** Stewart Scharf

STANDARD
&POOR'S
STOCK REPORTS

Hambrecht & Quist

NYSE Symbol **HQ**

In S&P SmallCap 600

09-OCT-99

Industry:
Investment Banking/ Brokerage

Summary: HQ provides companies and investors with a full range of investment banking and brokerage services. It also invests its own capital in emerging growth companies.

Quantitative Evaluations

Outlook (1 Lowest—5 Highest)
• **2**

Fair Value
• **48**

Risk
• **High**

Earn./Div. Rank
• **NR**

Technical Eval.
• **Bullish** since 8/99

Rel. Strength Rank (1 Lowest—99 Highest)
• **93**

Insider Activity
• **Neutral**

Recent Price • 49
52 Wk Range • 49⅛-13
Yield • Nil
12-Mo. P/E • 16.5

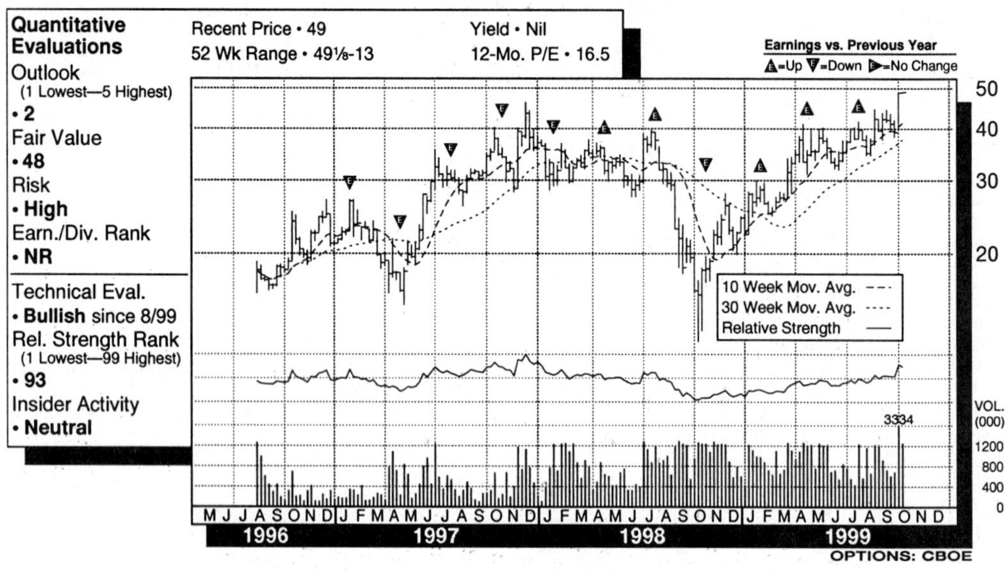

OPTIONS: CBOE

Business Profile - 06-JUL-99

This leading independent investment banker serves companies in four growth sectors of the economy: technology, health care, services, and branded consumer. In the second quarter of FY 99 (Sep.), the company posted record revenues in its principal transactions, commissions and investment banking segments. Issuance activity picked up during the quarter, and HQ completed 33 underwritten public offerings as lead or co-manager, up from 22 in the FY 98 period. In May 1999, the company issued a report anticipating a surge in mergers in the technology sector, prior to a change in pooling accounting rules expected to occur in 2000 or later, followed by a temporary lull in merger activity. HQ had no long term debt as of March 31, 1999.

Operational Review - 06-JUL-99

In the first half of FY 99, total revenues climbed 27%, year to year, as higher principal transactions, commissions, investment banking fees, and net investment gains outweighed lower corporate finance fees. Total expenses were up 17%, as higher expenses for compensation, brokerage and clearance, and communications outweighed reductions in occupancy and equipment, interest, and other expenses. After taxes at 43.0% in each period, net income soared 68%, to $37,887,830 ($1.45 a share, on 1.3% fewer shares), from $22,615,763 ($0.85).

Stock Performance - 08-OCT-99

In the past 30 trading days, HQ's shares have increased 24%, compared to a 0.91% fall in the S&P 500. Average trading volume for the past five days was 342,880 shares, compared with the 40-day moving average of 269,518 shares.

Key Stock Statistics

Dividend Rate/Share	Nil	Shareholders	305
Shs. outstg. (M)	24.4	Market cap. (B)	$ 1.2
Avg. daily vol. (M)	0.316	Inst. holdings	41%
Tang. Bk. Value/Share	17.31		
Beta	NA		

Value of $10,000 invested 5 years ago: NA

Fiscal Year Ending Sep. 30

	1999	1998	1997	1996	1995	1994
Revenues (Million $)						
1Q	99.9	91.62	94.90	107.7	–	—
2Q	153.2	107.4	74.65	96.85	–	—
3Q	178.1	102.8	82.30	107.9	–	—
4Q	—	71.32	94.38	77.47	–	—
Yr.	—	373.1	346.2	389.8	212.3	—
Earnings Per Share ($)						
1Q	**0.47**	**0.25**	**0.62**	1.11	–	—
2Q	**0.98**	**0.60**	0.29	0.86	–	—
3Q	**1.39**	**0.52**	0.40	0.94	–	—
4Q	—	**0.14**	0.37	0.47	–	—
Yr.	—	**1.51**	**1.68**	3.27	1.83	—

Next earnings report expected: late October

Dividend Data

No cash dividends have been paid on the common stock, and the company has said it has no intention of paying any in the future.

Hambrecht & Quist Group

Business Summary - 06-JUL-99

Hambrecht & Quist Group is an investment bank that focuses on emerging growth companies and growth-oriented investors. The company believes its core strength has been the early identification and sponsorship of leading growth companies in its chosen areas of focus through analysis of industry and technology trends. HQ seeks to leverage its industry expertise by providing growth companies and growth investors with a full range of investment banking and brokerage services, and by investing its own capital in emerging growth companies. The company is based in San Francisco, has principal offices in New York and Boston, and maintains offices in Europe, Japan, and Southern California.

Revenue sources in FY 98 (Sep.) were:principal transactions 28% (versus 35% in FY 97); investment banking 25% (26%); corporate finance fees 20% (16%); commissions 13% (11%); interest and dividends 7% (7%); and other 7% (5%).

The company has expanded its business by widening the range of services provided to growth companies and investors, serving the needs of larger size companies, and developing expertise in new industries and markets. HQ combines equity underwriting and brokerage services for emerging growth companies with venture capital investing. From its early concentration on the technology and healthcare industries, HQ has broadened its focus to encompass branded consumer companies and companies providing business information, outsourcing, and healthcare services.

The company is committed to working closely with entrepreneurial companies and investors interested in such companies. HQ believes it has developed a strong internal culture that emphasizes a long-term investment outlook. The company also believes that its focus on rapidly growing entrepreneurial companies and growth-oriented investors, and its tradition of principal investing, along with its broad internal distribution of equity ownership, have combined to sustain this culture.

HQ's research and investment banking professionals are organized into industry teams. Each team, often working with HQ's venture capital professionals, endeavors to develop and maintain an in-depth understanding of the secular and cyclical trends driving that particular industry sector. In addition, each team of professionals seeks to maintain close relationships not only with private and public growth companies, but also with venture capital and institutional investors, technical experts, and professional service providers. Through these relationships, HQ believes it gains the opportunity to participate actively in the growth of promising entrepreneurial companies.

Per Share Data ($) (Year Ended Sep. 30)	1998	1997	1996	1995	1994	1993	1992	1991	1990	1989
Tangible Bk. Val.	14.28	12.51	9.99	9.34	NA	NA	NA	NA	NA	NA
Cash Flow	1.51	1.68	3.70	2.11	NA	NA	NA	NA	NA	NA
Earnings	1.51	1.68	3.27	1.83	NA	NA	NA	NA	NA	NA
Dividends	Nil	Nil	Nil	Nil	NA	NA	NA	NA	NA	NA
Payout Ratio	Nil	Nil	Nil	Nil	NA	NA	NA	NA	NA	NA
Prices - High	39¾	46¼	27	NA	NA	NA	NA	NA	NA	NA
- Low	12¼	15	16	NA	NA	NA	NA	NA	NA	NA
P/E Ratio - High	26	28	8	NA	NA	NA	NA	NA	NA	NA
- Low	8	9	5	NA	NA	NA	NA	NA	NA	NA
Income Statement Analysis (Million $)										
Commissions	156	162	138	78.0	NA	NA	NA	NA	NA	NA
Int. Inc.	27.2	22.6	11.8	Nil	NA	NA	NA	NA	NA	NA
Total Revs.	323	280	390	212	NA	NA	NA	NA	NA	NA
Int. Exp.	3.6	4.5	1.4	1.3	NA	NA	NA	NA	NA	NA
Pretax Inc.	70.5	77.1	88.6	64.6	NA	NA	NA	NA	NA	NA
Eff. Tax Rate	43%	44%	20%	44%	NA	NA	NA	NA	NA	NA
Net Inc.	40.2	43.2	71.2	36.2	NA	NA	NA	NA	NA	NA
Balance Sheet & Other Fin. Data (Million $)										
Total Assets	607	679	538	515	NA	NA	NA	NA	NA	NA
Cash Items	67.0	42.6	117	NA	NA	NA	NA	NA	NA	NA
Receivables	282	408	297	NA	NA	NA	NA	NA	NA	NA
Secs. Owned	115	102	69.9	NA	NA	NA	NA	NA	NA	NA
Sec. Borrowed	18.1	11.8	16.1	NA	NA	NA	NA	NA	NA	NA
Due Brokers & Cust.	293	36.1	25.4	NA	NA	NA	NA	NA	NA	NA
Other Liabs.	175	324	261	NA	NA	NA	NA	NA	NA	NA
Capitalization:										
Debt	Nil	2.7	8.4	Nil	NA	NA	NA	NA	NA	NA
Equity	337	297	227	207	NA	NA	NA	NA	NA	NA
Total	337	300	235	207	NA	NA	NA	NA	NA	NA
% Return On Revs.	12.4	15.4	18.2	17.1	NA	NA	NA	NA	NA	NA
% Ret. on Assets	6.3	7.1	13.2	NA	NA	NA	NA	NA	NA	NA
% Ret. on Equity	12.7	16.5	31.3	NA	NA	NA	NA	NA	NA	NA

Data as orig. reptd.; bef. results of disc opers. and/or spec. items. Per share data adj. for stk. divs. as of ex-div. date. Net Inc. & EPS for 1996 are pro forma. Bold denotes diluted EPS (FASB 128). E-Estimated. NA-Not Available. NM-Not Meaningful. NR-Not Ranked.

Office—One Bush St., San Francisco, CA 94104. **Tel**—(415) 439-3000. **Website**—http://www.hamquist.com **Chrmn & CEO**—D. H. Case III. **COO**—D. M. McAuliffe. **CFO & Investor Contact**—Patrick J. Allen. **Secy**—S. N. Machtinger. **Dirs**—D. H. Case III, D. A. Coulter, H. B. Hillman, W. E. Mayer, W. J. Perry, E. H. Shea Jr., W. R. Timken. **Transfer Agent & Registrar**—American Stock Transfer & Trust Co., NYC. **Incorporated**—in Delaware in 1996. **Empl**— 827. **S&P Analyst:** T. W. Smith, CFA

STANDARD
&POOR'S
STOCK REPORTS

Hancock Fabrics

NYSE Symbol **HKF**

In S&P SmallCap 600

09-OCT-99

Industry:
Retail (Specialty)

Summary: This company, which sells fabrics and related items primarily at retail to the home sewing market, operates 457 stores in 40 states.

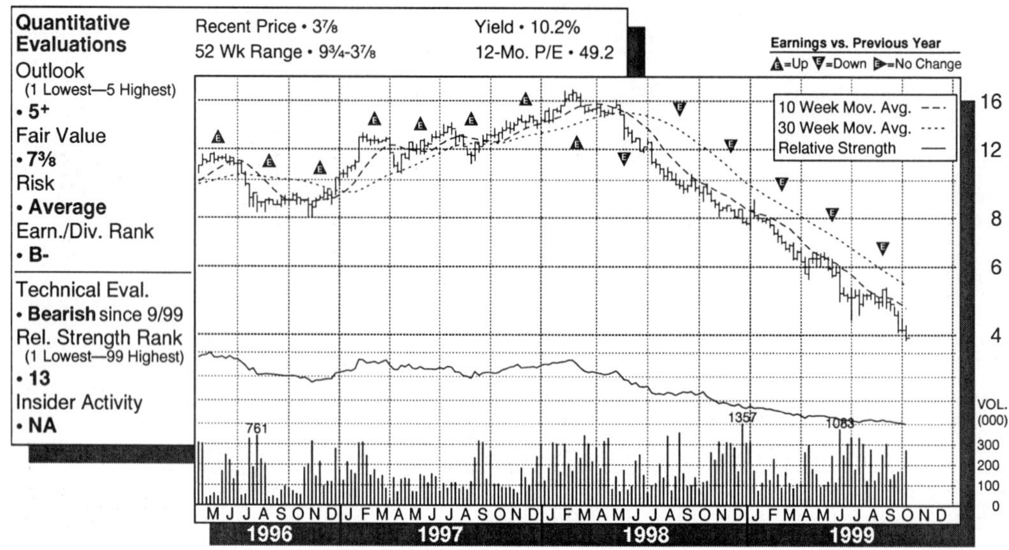

Business Profile - 07-JUL-99

New store growth is gaining momentum and HKF expects to enter at least two new markets during 1999. The company is also interested in making acquisitions that make strategic and financial sense. In line with this strategy, in April 1999 the company agreed to acquire certain of Mae's Fabric's leases for stores operating in nine Mid-Atlantic states. The company will continue its efforts to reposition its stores as large-format stores by closing underperforming stores and expanding those that have high potential. In 1999, 130 stores are scheduled for remodeling. The company will also continue to repurchase shares as market and financial conditions allow. As of January 31, 1999, the company had repurchased 10 million out of 11.5 million shares authorized.

Operational Review - 07-JUL-99

Sales in the 13 weeks ended May 2, 1999, declined 1.5%, year to year, reflecting store closings and pricing pressures. Gross margins narrowed, due to increased promotional activity. Although SG&A expenses declined slightly, higher depreciation and amortization and interest expenses hurt profitability. After taxes at 36.1%, versus 36.3%, net income fell 48%, to $1,104,000 ($0.06 a share, on 14% fewer shares), from $2,107,000 ($0.10).

Stock Performance - 08-OCT-99

In the past 30 trading days, HKF's shares have declined 25%, compared to a 0.91% fall in the S&P 500. Average trading volume for the past five days was 54,200 shares, compared with the 40-day moving average of 41,346 shares.

Key Stock Statistics

Dividend Rate/Share	0.40	Shareholders	9,365
Shs. outstg. (M)	19.1	Market cap. (B)	$0.075
Avg. daily vol. (M)	0.038	Inst. holdings	43%
Tang. Bk. Value/Share	4.15		
Beta	0.61		

Value of $10,000 invested 5 years ago: $ 5,435

Fiscal Year Ending Jan. 31

	2000	1999	1998	1997	1996	1995
Revenues (Million $)						
1Q	96.37	97.80	92.00	91.63	90.10	92.90
2Q	82.85	85.37	79.95	82.78	81.60	81.80
3Q	—	103.1	96.46	94.37	95.90	96.50
4Q	—	106.1	113.5	109.4	96.70	95.60
Yr.	—	392.3	381.9	378.2	364.2	366.8
Earnings Per Share ($)						
1Q	**0.06**	**0.10**	0.11	0.08	0.06	0.05
2Q	**-0.04**	**0.02**	0.08	0.06	0.04	0.04
3Q	—	**0.18**	0.23	0.18	0.16	0.18
4Q	—	**-0.14**	**0.30**	0.26	0.16	0.21
Yr.	—	**0.18**	**0.72**	**0.58**	0.42	0.48

Next earnings report expected: mid November

Dividend Data (Dividends have been paid since 1987.)

Amount ($)	Date Decl.	Ex-Div. Date	Stock of Record	Payment Date
0.100	Dec. 11	Dec. 29	Jan. 01	Jan. 15 '99
0.100	Feb. 28	Mar. 30	Apr. 01	Apr. 15 '99
0.100	Jun. 07	Jun. 29	Jul. 01	Jul. 15 '99
0.100	Sep. 21	Sep. 29	Oct. 01	Oct. 15 '99

Hancock Fabrics, Inc.

Business Summary - 07-JUL-99

A home fabrics maker, Hancock Fabrics is undergoing a major renovation and wants to be known as "America's Fabric Store". The company caters to the woman who makes clothing for her family and decorations for her home. HKF sells fabrics and related items at retail to the home sewing and home decorating markets and wholesale to independent retailers. Wholesale operations accounted for approximately 2% of sales in FY 99 (Jan.). As of January 31, 1999, the company operated 462 fabric stores in 40 states and supplied approximately 100 independent wholesale customers through its distribution facility in Mississippi.

Retail stores are usually located in neighborhood shopping centers and offer a wide selection of clothing fabrics. Each store maintains an inventory of cotton, wool and synthetic fabrics such as broadcloth, poplin, gabardine, unbleached muslin and corduroy, as well as seasonal and current fashions. Notions (including sewing aids and accessories such as zippers, buttons, threads and ornamentation), patterns, quilting materials and supplies, decorative fabrics (including drapery and upholstery), craft items and related supplies are also available. The company's business is slightly seasonal. Peak sale periods occur during the fall and pre-Easter weeks, while the lowest sales periods occur during the summer and January.

HKF targets its customers primarily through promotional advertising in newspapers, direct mail and television. Typically 6 to 10 direct mail pieces are circulated to approximately 1.2 million households annually. The direct mailer includes the company's magazine Directions, which offers discount coupons, sewing instructions and fashion ideas. Since 1994, the Home and Garden Television Network has sponsored a weekly sewing show called Sew Perfect. The program, which reaches 50 million U.S. households, is designed for the beginning and intermediate seamstress.

In 1996, HKF embarked on a strategy to improve profitability. One of the steps was to reposition its stores with a larger format. The company closed 40 stores and opened 21 new stores in FY 99. In connection with HKF's desire for a larger format, it acquired Northwest Fabrics & Crafts, a large-format chain located in the Plains and Upper Midwest for $20.9 million in November 1997. Another phase of the new strategy was to remodel the existing stores by adjusting and adding to the product mix. Since the plan began in 1996, almost 200 stores have been remodeled and 130 stores are scheduled for remodeling in 1999. In 1998 the company consolidated its four brands into one brand name, Hancock Fabrics, which will allow the company to market the brand as "America's Fabric Store" and advertise more effectively on a national scale.

Per Share Data ($) (Year Ended Jan. 31)	1999	1998	1997	1996	1995	1994	1993	1992	1991	1990
Tangible Bk. Val.	4.15	5.05	4.94	4.67	4.54	4.37	4.44	4.41	4.18	3.71
Cash Flow	0.38	0.87	0.75	0.61	0.68	0.46	0.77	1.21	1.40	1.20
Earnings	0.18	0.72	0.58	0.42	0.48	0.26	0.57	1.03	1.23	1.06
Dividends	0.40	0.46	0.32	0.32	0.32	0.32	0.32	0.32	0.28	0.24
Payout Ratio	222%	64%	55%	76%	67%	123%	56%	31%	22%	21%
Cal. Yrs.	1998	1997	1996	1995	1994	1993	1992	1991	1990	1989
Prices - High	17 1/8	15	11 3/4	11 3/4	10	14 1/2	19	27 3/4	20 5/8	17 1/8
- Low	7 1/2	10 1/8	8	7 3/4	6 1/2	8	9	14 1/4	15 1/2	9
P/E Ratio - High	95	21	20	28	21	56	33	27	17	16
- Low	42	14	14	18	14	31	16	14	13	9
Income Statement Analysis (Million $)										
Revs.	392	382	378	364	367	368	380	388	387	346
Oper. Inc.	11.0	28.3	25.0	20.6	23.2	15.0	25.8	42.6	51.2	46.5
Depr.	4.1	3.3	3.7	3.9	4.2	4.2	4.3	4.0	3.8	3.7
Int. Exp.	1.5	0.4	1.2	2.3	2.4	2.3	2.6	2.8	3.8	2.9
Pretax Inc.	5.6	24.8	20.3	14.7	16.8	8.7	19.1	36.6	44.5	41.3
Eff. Tax Rate	36%	38%	39%	39%	40%	37%	37%	37%	37%	37%
Net Inc.	3.6	15.3	12.5	9.0	10.1	5.4	12.1	23.0	28.1	26.0
Balance Sheet & Other Fin. Data (Million $)										
Cash	7.0	7.1	6.9	5.0	3.9	4.3	9.0	4.1	8.8	7.0
Curr. Assets	155	165	161	174	180	180	185	189	173	154
Total Assets	192	196	188	202	209	209	214	218	196	176
Curr. Liab.	55.9	55.9	57.8	51.5	56.0	53.3	47.4	58.5	64.4	51.6
LT Debt	29.0	10.0	3.0	30.0	37.0	45.0	58.0	50.3	35.5	35.8
Common Eqty.	77.2	107	105	100	97.0	94.0	95.0	97.0	93.0	86.0
Total Cap.	106	117	108	130	131	139	153	148	131	124
Cap. Exp.	NA	2.7	2.3	1.9	4.0	2.8	4.2	6.3	4.9	5.0
Cash Flow	7.7	18.6	16.2	12.9	14.3	9.7	16.4	26.9	31.9	29.6
Curr. Ratio	2.8	2.9	2.8	3.4	3.2	3.4	3.9	3.2	2.7	3.0
% LT Debt of Cap.	27.3	8.6	2.8	23.0	27.0	32.5	38.0	34.1	27.1	29.0
% Net Inc.of Revs.	0.9	4.0	3.3	2.5	2.8	1.5	3.2	5.9	7.3	7.5
% Ret. on Assets	1.8	8.0	6.4	4.4	4.9	2.6	5.7	11.2	15.4	15.8
% Ret. on Equity	3.9	14.5	12.1	9.1	10.6	5.8	12.9	24.3	31.9	28.6

Data as orig reptd.; bef. results of disc opers/spec. items. Per share data adj. for stk. divs. Bold denotes diluted EPS (FASB 128)-prior periods restated. E-Estimated. NA-Not Available. NM-Not Meaningful. NR-Not Ranked.

Office—3406 W. Main St., Tupelo, MS 38803. **Tel**—(601) 842-2834. **Website**—http://www.hancockfabrics.com. **Chrmn & CEO**—L. G. Kirk. **Pres & COO**—J. W. Busby Jr. **SVP, CFO & Investor Contact**—Bruce D. Smith (601-842-2834 Ext. 112). **Secy**—E. J. Kennedy. **Dirs**—J. W. Busby Jr., R. R. Devening, D. L. Fruge, L. G. Kirk, R. T. Knox, D. L. Weaver. **Transfer Agent & Registrar**—Continental Stock Transfer & Trust Co., NYC. **Incorporated**—in Delaware in 1987. **Empl**— 6,500. **S&P Analyst:** Howard Choe

STANDARD
&POOR'S
STOCK REPORTS

Hanger Orthopedic

NYSE Symbol **HGR**

In S&P SmallCap 600

09-OCT-99

Industry:
Health Care (Specialized Services)

Summary: HGR provides orthotic and prosthetic (O&P) services through patient care centers. It is also the largest U.S. distributor of O&P supplies and components.

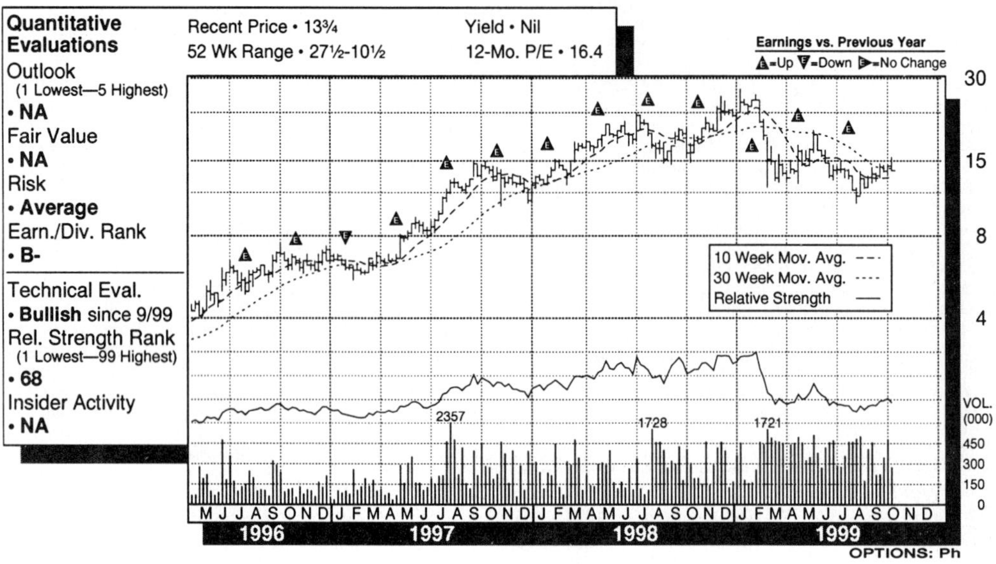

Business Profile - 13-AUG-99

HGR sees growth in the U.S. orthotic and prosthetic (O&P) market, as a result of demographic, economic, and technological trends. The company seeks to expand through acquisitions and internal growth. On July 1, 1999, HGR acquired NovaCare Orthotics & Prosthetics, Inc. from NovaCare, Inc. The acquisition made HGR the world's largest provider of O&P patient care services. The combined revenues of the two companies as of March 31, 1999, were $492 million. HGR now operates 649 patient care facilities in 42 states and the District of Columbia, and makes, and distributes O&P devices. In December 1998, trading in the shares shifted to the NYSE, from the ASE.

Operational Review - 13-AUG-99

Net sales in the first half of 1999 climbed 20%, year to year, paced by acquisitions and 6.0% higher revenue from existing patient care centers. Gross margins widened, and with well controlled SG&A expense, operating income soared 41%. With 18% lower interest expense, after taxes at 41.0%, versus 39.9%, net income surged 50%, to $5,314,000 ($0.40 a share, on 17% more shares), from $7,996,000 ($0.31).

Stock Performance - 08-OCT-99

In the past 30 trading days, HGR's shares have increased 6%, compared to a 0.91% fall in the S&P 500. Average trading volume for the past five days was 54,140 shares, compared with the 40-day moving average of 74,469 shares.

Key Stock Statistics

Dividend Rate/Share	Nil	Shareholders	821
Shs. outstg. (M)	18.9	Market cap. (B)	$0.260
Avg. daily vol. (M)	0.080	Inst. holdings	77%
Tang. Bk. Value/Share	1.69		
Beta	1.42		

Value of $10,000 invested 5 years ago: $ 22,099

Fiscal Year Ending Dec. 31

	1999	1998	1997	1996	1995	1994
Revenues (Million $)						
1Q	49.14	40.75	30.95	12.23	12.21	10.11
2Q	56.42	46.90	36.65	14.02	13.35	12.84
3Q	—	48.78	38.84	14.53	13.55	13.73
4Q	—	51.44	39.16	26.03	13.36	13.63
Yr.	—	187.9	145.6	66.81	52.47	50.30
Earnings Per Share ($)						
1Q	**0.15**	**0.10**	**0.06**	**0.02**	0.03	-0.06
2Q	**0.24**	**0.21**	**0.18**	**0.09**	0.08	0.08
3Q	—	**0.22**	**0.15**	**0.10**	0.08	0.03
4Q	—	**0.22**	**0.17**	**-0.07**	0.07	-0.36
Yr.	—	**0.75**	**0.58**	**0.12**	**0.25**	**-0.28**

Next earnings report expected: late October

Dividend Data

No dividends have been paid, and Hanger does not expect to pay any in the foreseeable future. Bank and other agreements prohibit payments.

Hanger Orthopedic Group, Inc.

Business Summary - 13-AUG-99

Hanger Orthopedic Group believes the U.S. orthotic and prosthetic (O&P) market, estimated at $2.3 billion in 1997, will expand, due to an aging population, improving technology, and efforts to decrease hospitalization expenses. As the largest company in the O&P industry, Hanger plans to build a major national rehabilitation company focused on the acquisition and operation of O&P practices and the manufacture and distribution of O&P products. Revenues from operations in 1998 were divided as follows: Practice Management & Patient Care 81%; Manufacturing 5%; and Distribution 14%.

The O&P industry is highly fragmented, and HGR believes a number of economic and logistical forces will compel the industry to consolidate. During 1998, the company acquired 17 O&P companies and a prosthetic component manufacturer, for a total of approximately $39 million. As of the end of 1998, HGR continued to engage in discussions with several O&P companies for the possible acquisition of their patient care practices.

As of December 31, 1998, HGR operated 256 O&P centers in 30 states and the District of Columbia. The company has developed OPNET, a national preferred O&P provider network serving managed care organizations. As of the end of 1998, OPNET had a network of 390 patient-care centers (which includes all 256 HGR centers) serving 353 managed care plans. Hanger intends to extend the network's reach nationwide through acquisitions and marketing. Incentives are given to independent OPNET O&P members to purchase their O&P products from the company.

Orthotics is the design, fabrication, fitting and supervised use of custom-made braces and other devices, such as knee, spinal, neck and cervical braces and foot orthoses, that provide external support to treat musculoskeletal disorders (ailments of the back, extremities or joints). Prosthetics is the design, fabrication and fitting of custom-made artificial limbs for patients who have lost limbs as a result of traumatic injuries, vascular diseases, diabetes, cancer or congenital disorders.

In February 1999, the U.S. Health Care Financing Administration proposed cutbacks in Medicare spending, including limitations on reimbursements for O&P expenditures. The proposed legislation had not been officially introduced as of late March 1999, and it is uncertain as to whether the proposed FY 2000 medicare budget would have any material impact on the company. As of year end 1998, 53.7% of revenue was derived from Medicare, Medicaid, and VA benefit programs. In July 1998, HGR sold 3,300,000 common shares (including 900,000 for shareholders) at $17 each.

Per Share Data ($) (Year Ended Dec. 31)	1998	1997	1996	1995	1994	1993	1992	1991	1990	1989
Tangible Bk. Val.	2.92	1.88	-2.72	0.55	0.20	0.61	0.38	2.30	-6.04	-3.34
Cash Flow	1.06	0.94	0.45	0.58	0.10	0.51	0.31	0.14	-0.16	-0.09
Earnings	0.75	0.58	0.12	0.26	-0.28	0.19	0.03	-0.03	-0.73	-0.40
Dividends	Nil	Nil	Nil	Nil	Nil	Nil	Nil	Nil	Nil	Nil
Payout Ratio	Nil	Nil	Nil	Nil	Nil	Nil	Nil	Nil	Nil	Nil
Prices - High	25 7/8	15	7 1/2	3 7/8	6 7/8	8 5/8	13 7/8	10 1/2	8 1/2	4
- Low	12 1/4	5 1/2	2 5/8	2 3/16	2 1/2	5 1/2	6 3/8	3 3/4	1 1/8	1 3/4
P/E Ratio - High	34	26	62	15	NM	46	NM	NM	NM	NM
- Low	16	9	22	8	NM	30	NM	NA	NA	NA
Income Statement Analysis (Million $)										
Revs.	188	146	66.8	52.5	50.3	43.9	33.5	23.6	19.3	10.4
Oper. Inc.	31.5	23.0	10.0	8.5	5.8	7.1	4.2	4.0	2.3	1.4
Depr.	5.8	4.7	2.9	2.7	3.1	2.7	2.2	1.6	1.3	0.7
Int. Exp.	1.9	4.9	2.5	2.1	1.8	1.2	1.3	2.1	2.4	1.6
Pretax Inc.	23.5	13.2	2.0	3.7	-1.9	3.2	0.8	0.3	-1.5	-0.9
Eff. Tax Rate	41%	42%	45%	42%	NM	51%	62%	80%	NM	NM
Net Inc.	13.8	7.6	1.1	2.1	-2.3	1.6	0.3	0.1	-1.5	-0.9
Balance Sheet & Other Fin. Data (Million $)										
Cash	9.7	6.6	6.6	1.5	1.1	1.4	1.4	0.5	1.1	0.7
Curr. Assets	74.3	61.5	51.5	26.9	25.3	20.7	16.0	9.9	7.3	5.2
Total Assets	206	158	135	61.8	61.5	57.4	48.0	30.3	26.4	18.5
Curr. Liab.	24.7	22.5	26.0	6.3	6.9	5.0	4.1	5.2	4.3	2.2
LT Debt	11.2	23.2	64.2	22.9	24.3	19.2	15.0	10.1	19.8	14.0
Common Eqty.	163	106	39.7	31.3	29.3	31.7	28.3	12.1	NM	1.6
Total Cap.	179	133	107	55.2	54.3	52.3	43.7	25.1	21.8	16.8
Cap. Exp.	2.9	2.6	1.2	0.7	1.1	0.7	0.8	0.5	0.3	0.6
Cash Flow	19.6	12.3	3.9	4.8	0.8	4.2	2.4	0.7	-0.4	-0.2
Curr. Ratio	3.0	2.7	2.0	4.3	3.7	4.2	3.9	1.9	1.7	2.3
% LT Debt of Cap.	6.2	17.4	60.0	41.6	44.8	36.6	34.2	40.2	90.9	86.2
% Net Inc.of Revs.	7.4	5.2	1.6	4.1	NM	3.6	0.9	NM	NM	NM
% Ret. on Assets	7.6	5.2	1.1	3.5	NM	3.0	0.6	NM	NM	NM
% Ret. on Equity	10.3	10.5	3.0	7.1	NM	5.2	0.9	NM	NM	NM

Data as orig reptd.; bef. results of disc opers/spec. items. Per share data adj. for stk. divs. Bold denotes diluted EPS (FASB 128)-prior periods restated. E-Estimated. NA-Not Available. NM-Not Meaningful. NR-Not Ranked.

Office—7700 Old Georgetown Rd., Bethesda, MD 20814. **Tel**—(301) 986-0701. **Fax**—(301) 986-0702. **Website**—http://www.hanger.com **Chrmn, Pres & CEO**—I. R. Sabel. **VP-Fin, Secy & Treas**—R. A. Stein. **Dirs**—M. J. Blutt, E. E. Charrette, T. P. Cooper, R. J. Glaser, J. G. Hellmuth, R. J. Lavizzo-Mourey, W. L. McCulloch, I. R. Sabel, H. E. Thranhardt. **Transfer Agent & Registrar**—ChaseMellon Shareholder Services, NYC. **Incorporated**—in Colorado in 1983; reincorporated in Delaware in 1988. **Empl**— 1,213. **S&P Analyst:** C.C.P.

STANDARD
&POOR'S
STOCK REPORTS

Harbinger Corp.

Nasdaq Symbol **HRBC**

In S&P SmallCap 600

09-OCT-99

Industry:
Computer (Software & Services)

Summary: HRBC produces software and provides computer communications network and consulting services designed to enable businesses to engage in electronic commerce.

S&P Opinion: Accumulate (★★★★) Recent Price • 21⅝ 52 Wk Range • 22¾-4¼ Yield • Nil 12-Mo. P/E • NM

Quantitative Evaluations

Outlook (1 Lowest—5 Highest) • **NA**

Fair Value • **NA**

Risk • **High**

Earn./Div. Rank • **NR**

Technical Eval. • **Bullish** since 9/99

Rel. Strength Rank (1 Lowest—99 Highest) • **99**

Insider Activity • **NA**

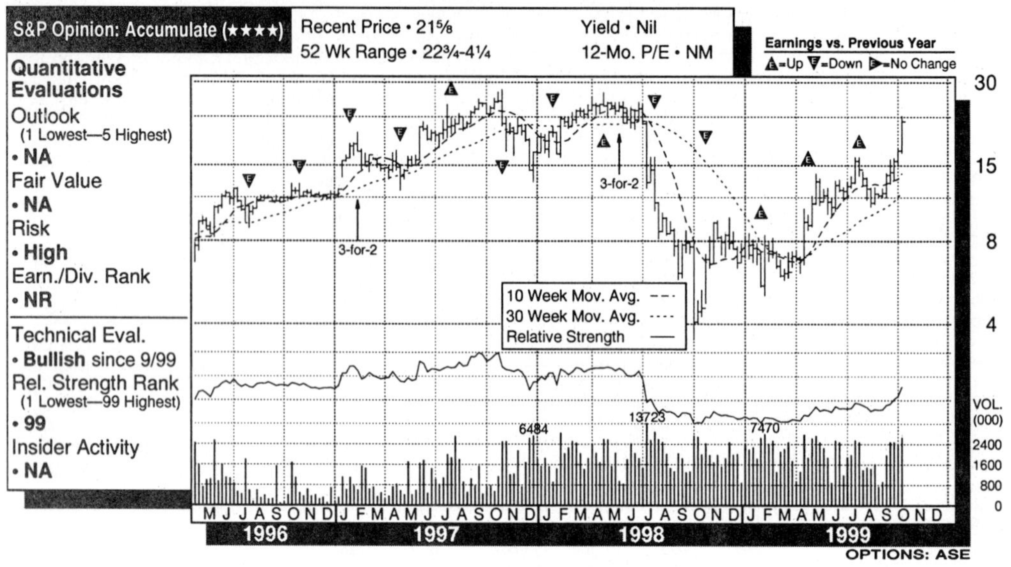

Overview - 27-SEP-99

Revenues from continuing core operations will rise 35% to 40% in 1999. This range represents a boost from the 30%-35% we had been projecting. Revenue growth in the final quarter of 1999 will be healthier than we had conservatively assumed, as it now appears that there will be only a minimal effect from businesses "locking down" their e-commerce systems in preparation for the year 2000. Margins should improve, as software gradually gains as a percentage of revenue (software carries wider gross margins than services). Restructuring efforts that began in 1998 to transition from legacy e-commerce products to web-based solutions, will result in additional cost savings and further boost profitability. We estimate earnings for the year at $0.42 a share, in comparison to a loss of $0.20 reported for 1998 (as restated for discontinued operations). In 2000, we look for revenues and earnings to grow 30%-35%.

Valuation - 27-SEP-99

HRBC is rated accumulate. The future of e-commerce is huge, with many projections placing the size of the market at well over $1 trillion within five years. We think the company will emerge as a strong participant in this growth industry. In 1999, our growth expectations have consistently exceed the consensus. This optimism was borne out in the second quarter when earnings even surpassed our expectations. In mid-September, the company revealed that the third quarter would exceed the consensus view, as well, and it posed a favorable outlook for the fourth quarter also. The current valuation affords an opportunity for long-term investors to participate in the growth of the Internet and e-commerce through purchase of HRBC at a discount to nearly every other e-commerce concern.

Key Stock Statistics

S&P EPS Est. 1999	0.42	Tang. Bk. Value/Share	2.51
P/E on S&P Est. 1999	51.6	Beta	NA
S&P EPS Est. 2000	0.56	Shareholders	7,200
Dividend Rate/Share	Nil	Market cap. (B)	$0.836
Shs. outstg. (M)	38.5	Inst. holdings	37%
Avg. daily vol. (M)	0.713		

Value of $10,000 invested 5 years ago: NA

Fiscal Year Ending Dec. 31

	1999	1998	1997	1996	1995	1994
Revenues (Million $)						
1Q	33.50	30.05	24.32	7.16	4.54	—
2Q	38.73	33.18	28.42	10.08	5.29	—
3Q	—	35.42	30.24	11.15	6.10	—
4Q	—	36.50	37.70	13.33	7.19	—
Yr.	—	135.2	120.7	41.73	23.12	13.65
Earnings Per Share ($)						
1Q	**0.06**	**-0.23**	-0.39	-0.36	0.01	—
2Q	**0.13**	**0.04**	0.07	0.00	0.01	—
3Q	**E0.11**	**-0.39**	-0.23	-0.01	0.01	—
4Q	**E0.13**	**0.14**	**-0.31**	0.01	0.02	—
Yr.	**E0.42**	**-0.20**	**-0.85**	**-0.46**	0.05	-0.14

Next earnings report expected: late October

Dividend Data

No cash dividends have been paid. A three-for-two stock split was effected in 1997.

Harbinger Corporation

Business Summary - 27-SEP-99

Harbinger Corp. (HRBC) is a leading worldwide provider of Internet Protocol (IP) products, services and solutions to the rapidly expanding business-to-business electronic commerce market. HRBC offers solutions that enable businesses of all sizes to move goods and services along their supply chain. These electronic commerce solutions are provided using standard web-based technologies over the Internet, extranets, intranets, websites, or e-mail, or over standard telephone lines and with non-IP standards.

The strategy to achieve this objective includes the following key elements: focusing on marketing to trading communities; providing a comprehensive range of integrated products and services; delivering superior customer support services; capitalizing on electronic commerce on the Internet; pursuing strategic acquisitions and alliances; and penetrating international markets. Products and services fall into three categories: telecommunications, e-commerce software, and services.

At the center of this strategy is the company's transaction portal website, harbinger.net. Harbinger is aggressively migrating customers from legacy, non-IP e-commerce solutions to harbinger.net, a process which began in late 1998. The harbinger.net portal site offers a variety of services, including online customer care, subscription-based vertical market trading communities, electronic storefronts, an e-commerce resource center, a commerce directory, and interconnections to legacy private e-commerce networks.

In addition to harbinger.net and related services, Harbinger offers Express e-commerce software and solutions for business-to-business trading communities. On August 30, 1999, the company made available Express 4.0, which incorporates a server application that allows Express to be used with a standard web browser or with a desktop application for smaller suppliers and distributors that are as yet not e-commerce capable. This allows companies' to extend their trading communities to add their partners.

The company also offers content and data management software, web site creation and management software, and a variety of professional and management services. These services are offered in several vertical markets in which Harbinger has developed particular expertise, including aerospace, automotive, electronics, financial services, food and beverage, government, healthcare, heavy manufacturing, petroleum/chemicals, retail, and utilities.

On September 13, 1999, HRBC won a contract with IBM, under which IBM will market and support Harbinger's TrustedLink e-commerce software for the IBM AS/400 UNIX, and NT platforms, with future access to additional e-commerce technologies from Harbinger. IBM Global Services division will initially market TrustedLink in North America and Europe, with Latin America and Asia/Pacific to follow.

Per Share Data ($) (Year Ended Dec. 31)	1998	1997	1996	1995	1994	1993	1992	1991	1990	1989
Tangible Bk. Val.	2.53	2.75	0.81	0.93	0.30	0.28	NM	NM	NA	NA
Cash Flow	0.06	-0.57	-0.19	0.13	-0.08	0.25	0.01	NA	NA	NA
Earnings	-0.20	-0.85	-0.35	0.05	-0.14	0.21	-0.04	-0.01	NA	NA
Dividends	Nil	Nil	Nil	Nil	Nil	Nil	Nil	Nil	NA	NA
Payout Ratio	Nil	Nil	Nil	Nil	Nil	Nil	Nil	Nil	NA	NA
Prices - High	27 5/8	28 3/8	12 7/8	13 1/8	NA	NA	NA	NA	NA	NA
- Low	3 1/2	11 1/2	6 5/8	5 3/8	NA	NA	NA	NA	NA	NA
P/E Ratio - High	NM	NM	NM	NM	NM	NA	NA	NA	NA	NA
- Low	NM	NM	NM	NM	NM	NA	NA	NA	NA	NA
Income Statement Analysis (Million $)										
Revs.	135	121	41.7	23.1	13.7	10.5	6.7	NA	NA	NA
Oper. Inc.	25.2	29.6	11.4	4.8	2.5	1.8	0.6	NA	NA	NA
Depr.	10.8	10.9	3.8	1.7	0.9	0.6	0.4	NA	NA	NA
Int. Exp.	Nil	Nil	Nil	0.1	0.1	0.2	0.1	NA	NA	NA
Pretax Inc.	-7.8	-29.4	-8.4	1.9	-3.0	1.0	-0.1	NA	NA	NA
Eff. Tax Rate	NM	NM	NM	36%	NM	NM	Nil	NA	NA	NA
Net Inc.	-8.5	-32.5	-8.2	1.3	-1.9	3.6	-0.1	NA	NA	NA
Balance Sheet & Other Fin. Data (Million $)										
Cash	92.3	69.8	8.4	11.9	4.6	0.8	NA	NA	NA	NA
Curr. Assets	138	148	22.5	20.8	10.0	6.7	NA	NA	NA	NA
Total Assets	178	184	184	40.3	15.7	12.2	4.8	NA	NA	NA
Curr. Liab.	58.4	53.5	11.2	6.5	7.3	2.9	NA	NA	NA	NA
LT Debt	Nil	Nil	Nil	Nil	Nil	2.0	4.2	NA	NA	NA
Common Eqty.	120	130	31.3	29.1	5.4	4.2	-4.5	NA	NA	NA
Total Cap.	120	130	31.3	29.1	8.3	9.2	2.7	NA	NA	NA
Cap. Exp.	12.9	8.6	6.0	3.3	1.3	1.7	NA	NA	NA	NA
Cash Flow	2.3	-21.6	-4.5	2.7	-1.2	3.9	0.1	NA	NA	NA
Curr. Ratio	2.4	2.8	2.0	3.2	1.4	2.3	NA	NA	NA	NA
% LT Debt of Cap.	Nil	Nil	Nil	Nil	Nil	21.6	154.0	NA	NA	NA
% Net Inc.of Revs.	NM	NM	NM	5.4	NM	33.9	NM	NA	NA	NA
% Ret. on Assets	NM	NM	NM	4.5	NM	13.8	NM	NA	NA	NA
% Ret. on Equity	NM	NM	NM	6.1	NM	NM	NM	NA	NA	NA

Data as orig reptd.; bef. results of disc opers/spec. items. Per share data adj. for stk. divs. Bold denotes diluted EPS (FASB 128)-prior periods restated. E-Estimated. NA-Not Available. NM-Not Meaningful. NR-Not Ranked.

Organized—in Georgia in 1994. **Office**—1277 Lenox Park Blvd., Atlanta, GA 30319. **Tel**—(404) 467-3000. **Website**—http://www.harbinger.com **Chrmn & CEO**—C. T. Howle. **Pres**—D. T. Leach. **VP-Fin, Secy & Investor Contact**—Joel G. Katz. **Dirs**—S. L. Bell, J. C. Davis, D. Hildes, C. T. Howle, W. B. King, B. R. Konsynski, T. Leach, J. Lowenberg, A. Nederlof, K. Neugebauer, W. D. Savoy. **Transfer Agent & Registrar**—First Union National Bank of North Carolina, Charlotte. **Empl**— 975. **S&P Analyst:** Mark S. Basham

STANDARD &POOR'S
STOCK REPORTS

Harland (John H.)

NYSE Symbol **JH**

In S&P SmallCap 600

09-OCT-99 **Industry:** Specialty Printing

Summary: This leading supplier of bank checks, business documents and forms also produces optical mark reading and optical character recognition forms and equipment.

S&P Opinion: Hold (★★★)

Recent Price • 19½
52 Wk Range • 21¼-12¼
Yield • 1.5%
12-Mo. P/E • NM

Quantitative Evaluations

Outlook (1 Lowest—5 Highest) • **3**

Fair Value • **24⅞**

Risk • **Average**

Earn./Div. Rank • **B**

Technical Eval. • **Bearish** since 9/99

Rel. Strength Rank (1 Lowest—99 Highest) • **63**

Insider Activity • **NA**

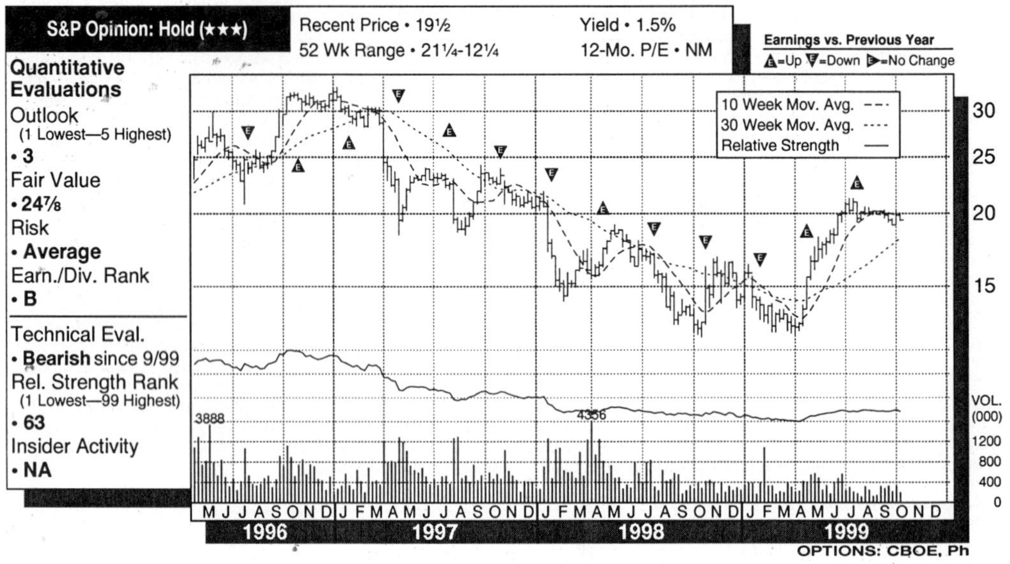

OPTIONS: CBOE, Ph

Overview - 10-SEP-99

Revenues are projected to rise roughly 5% in 2000, after a gain of about 4% expected in 1999. Profitability will continue to benefit from recent restructuring measures. The rebuilding of JH's manufacturing operations continues as planned. The majority of plant consolidations are completed, and the regional printing network was recently producing 75% of all orders. The network has successfully implemented more than $40 million in new check business. Progress also continues to be made in other areas, including marketing services, systems and work process. The new strategies are designed to improve competitiveness and boost profitability by consolidating printing facilities and combining various sales and marketing functions into a single, multi-product organization focused on serving the needs of financial institutions. We expect EPS of $1.20 in 1999 and $1.40 in 2000.

Valuation - 10-SEP-99

JH stock peaked in December 1996 at 33, and has been depressed since then by investors' ongoing disappointment with the company's operating performance and impatience with a series of restructurings that have been ongoing since 1991. JH's shares, on a downturn through the first quarter of 1999, have been recovering since April, and were recently selling within 5% of their 52-week high. Management's deliberate moves appear to be paying off, as evidenced by recovering earnings and improving cash flow. The company is investing excess cash in the repurchase of its shares. Assuming no negative surprises, the downside appears limited on the shares, which are reasonably valued at 16X our $1.20 1999 EPS estimate, which is in line with the valuations of its peer group.

Key Stock Statistics

S&P EPS Est. 1999	1.20	Tang. Bk. Value/Share	4.10
P/E on S&P Est. 1999	16.3	Beta	0.64
S&P EPS Est. 2000	1.40	Shareholders	6,618
Dividend Rate/Share	0.30	Market cap. (B)	$0.605
Shs. outstg. (M)	31.0	Inst. holdings	68%
Avg. daily vol. (M)	0.052		

Value of $10,000 invested 5 years ago: $ 10,692

Fiscal Year Ending Dec. 31

	1999	1998	1997	1996	1995	1994
Revenues (Million $)						
1Q	146.0	143.5	139.3	152.3	138.3	131.0
2Q	145.0	135.3	139.7	149.7	136.1	130.8
3Q	—	147.4	142.1	155.9	141.3	129.2
4Q	—	140.6	141.7	151.6	145.9	130.3
Yr.	—	566.7	562.7	609.4	561.6	521.3
Earnings Per Share ($)						
1Q	**0.32**	**0.20**	**0.16**	0.28	0.42	0.43
2Q	**0.32**	**0.13**	**0.21**	-1.66	0.41	0.42
3Q	**E0.28**	**0.13**	**0.16**	0.45	0.36	0.43
4Q	**E0.30**	**-1.12**	**0.03**	0.47	0.32	0.40
Yr.	**E1.20**	**-0.66**	**0.56**	**-0.45**	**1.50**	1.68

Next earnings report expected: late October

Dividend Data (Dividends have been paid since 1932.)

Amount ($)	Date Decl.	Ex-Div. Date	Stock of Record	Payment Date
0.075	Oct. 26	Nov. 17	Nov. 19	Dec. 03 '98
0.075	Jan. 25	Feb. 16	Feb. 18	Mar. 04 '99
0.075	Apr. 22	May. 18	May. 20	Jun. 03 '99
0.075	Jul. 23	Aug. 17	Aug. 19	Sep. 02 '99

A Division of The McGraw-Hill Companies

John H. Harland Company

Business Summary - 10-SEP-99

John H. Harland is mainly a financial stationer, engaged primarily in printing checks and related items. With about 30% of the market, it is among the three largest U.S. printers of personalized checks. The company, which has been involved in restructuring activities since 1991, announced in April 1996 its most recent strategic plan. Checks will continue to generate significant cash flow, and will be linked to JH's marketing services, but the company is transforming itself from a checks and forms printer into a financial marketing services company.

As part of its strategy to restore double-digit revenue and earnings growth, JH is taking measures to improve service and increase profitability of its check printing business by standardizing products and pricing and consolidating and restructuring manufacturing operations. It is completing the consolidation of its 40 core printing plants into a network of seven regional facilities incorporating advanced manufacturing technology and systems. This strategy includes creating a communications network linking the check printing business with marketing services. It also requires the development of additional marketing services to enhance JH's database management capabilities.

In order to more closely align the company's dividend payout with its overall business strategy, in February 1997, directors reduced the dividend to $0.30 a share annually, from $1.02. In 1998, JH recognized restructuring charges and software development costs aggregating $1.41 a share. JH's 1997 operating results included $0.15 of severance-related and equipment development costs. In 1996, JH incurred a second quarter restructuring charge of $92.5 million ($1.80), and an $8.0 million ($0.26) charge related to an acquisition.

The company's principal products are MICR encoded checks designed to be processed on automatic sorting and posting equipment, deposit tickets and related forms for financial institutions and their customers. JH also produces customer-designed printed, lithographed and engraved business forms and other stationery items for banks and other accounts. JH also markets checks directly to consumers through a subsidiary as a means of augmenting financial institution sales. The direct check market is growing 10% to 12% annually.

Scantron Corp. (acquired in 1988) designs, develops and produces optical mark reading (OMR) equipment and scannable forms used to score tests and tabulate data. Datascan, headquartered in Switzerland, is a leading producer of OMR equipment and optical character recognition (OCR) check reader equipment.

JH entered a third line of business with the 1994 purchase of Marketing Profiles, a database marketing and consulting firm that provides software products and related marketing services to the financial industry.

Per Share Data ($) (Year Ended Dec. 31)	1998	1997	1996	1995	1994	1993	1992	1991	1990	1989
Tangible Bk. Val.	3.03	2.49	1.78	2.91	3.34	4.25	6.42	7.99	7.92	7.26
Cash Flow	0.70	1.80	0.93	3.09	3.04	2.70	2.42	1.94	2.08	2.01
Earnings	-0.66	0.56	-0.45	1.51	1.68	1.62	1.59	1.33	1.52	1.54
Dividends	0.30	0.30	1.02	1.02	0.98	0.94	0.90	0.86	0.78	0.68
Payout Ratio	NM	54%	NM	68%	58%	58%	57%	65%	51%	44%
Prices - High	21⅞	32⅞	33	23⅝	24¾	28⅛	27¼	24⅜	26⅛	25
- Low	12¼	18⅜	20¾	19⅛	19⅜	20⅞	20½	17⅞	17⅞	19½
P/E Ratio - High	NM	59	NM	16	15	17	17	18	17	16
- Low	NM	33	NM	13	12	13	13	13	12	13
Income Statement Analysis (Million $)										
Revs.	567	563	609	562	521	519	445	379	371	345
Oper. Inc.	85.6	77.7	129	132	134	122	113	109	106	104
Depr.	42.4	39.3	42.7	48.3	41.5	35.1	29.7	22.6	20.9	18.0
Int. Exp.	7.5	8.4	10.3	8.7	7.8	NA	NA	NA	NA	NA
Pretax Inc.	-11.0	29.6	-15.5	76.9	85.1	85.7	88.3	79.7	90.6	91.8
Eff. Tax Rate	NM	42%	NM	40%	40%	39%	36%	38%	37%	37%
Net Inc.	-20.6	17.3	-13.9	46.0	51.2	52.5	56.6	49.8	57.2	58.1
Balance Sheet & Other Fin. Data (Million $)										
Cash	42.5	9.8	22.7	13.2	15.3	28.1	19.3	71.4	44.6	78.9
Curr. Assets	159	148	148	144	117	135	111	150	138	163
Total Assets	392	426	455	475	414	356	340	352	357	321
Curr. Liab.	106	110	145	121	79.3	44.0	59.5	35.1	28.4	24.0
LT Debt	107	109	114	115	115	112	12.6	11.7	12.6	11.3
Common Eqty.	162	193	182	222	203	184	256	292	296	273
Total Cap.	269	302	296	342	323	302	271	308	323	294
Cap. Exp.	33.5	45.4	28.9	33.4	37.5	27.1	18.7	17.5	29.0	28.7
Cash Flow	21.8	56.6	28.9	94.3	92.8	87.6	86.3	72.4	78.0	76.0
Curr. Ratio	1.5	1.4	1.0	1.2	1.5	3.1	1.9	4.3	4.9	6.8
% LT Debt of Cap.	39.7	36.2	38.5	33.6	35.6	37.0	4.7	3.8	3.9	3.8
% Net Inc.of Revs.	NM	3.1	NM	8.2	9.8	10.1	12.7	13.2	15.4	16.8
% Ret. on Assets	NM	3.9	NM	10.3	13.3	15.9	17.0	14.2	16.9	18.9
% Ret. on Equity	NM	9.2	NM	21.6	26.5	25.4	21.4	17.1	20.2	22.5

Data as orig reptd.; bef. results of disc opers/spec. items. Per share data adj. for stk. divs. Bold denotes diluted EPS (FASB 128)-prior periods restated. E-Estimated. NA-Not Available. NM-Not Meaningful. NR-Not Ranked.

Office—2939 Miller Rd. (P.O. Box 105250), Decatur, GA 30035 (30348). **Tel**—(800) 723-3690. **Website**—http://www.harland.net. **Chrmn**—J. H. Weitnauer. **Pres, CEO**—T. C. Tuff.**VP, CFO**—C. Carden.**VP, Secy & Investor Contact**—Victoria P. Weyand (770-593-5128). **Dirs**—J. P. Baranco, E. J. Hawie, R. K. Lochridge, J. J. McMahon, G. H. Northrop, L. L. Prince, T. C. Tuff, J. H. Weitnauer, Jr., R. A. Yellowlees. **Transfer Agent & Registrar**—First Chicago Trust Co. of New York.**Incorporated**—in Georgia in 1923. **Empl**— 5,997. **S&P Analyst:** William H. Donald

STANDARD
&POOR'S
STOCK REPORTS

Harman Int'l Industries

NYSE Symbol **HAR**

In S&P SmallCap 600

09-OCT-99

Industry:
Electrical Equipment

Summary: This company manufactures and markets high-fidelity audio products targeted primarily at the OEM (original equipment manufacturer), consumer, and professional markets.

Quantitative Evaluations

Outlook
(1 Lowest—5 Highest)
• **5+**

Fair Value
• **69⅛**

Risk
• **Average**

Earn./Div. Rank
• **B**

Technical Eval.
• **Bullish** since 9/99

Rel. Strength Rank
(1 Lowest—99 Highest)
• **37**

Insider Activity
• **NA**

Recent Price • 40½
52 Wk Range • 47½-31½
Yield • 0.5%
12-Mo. P/E • 62.4

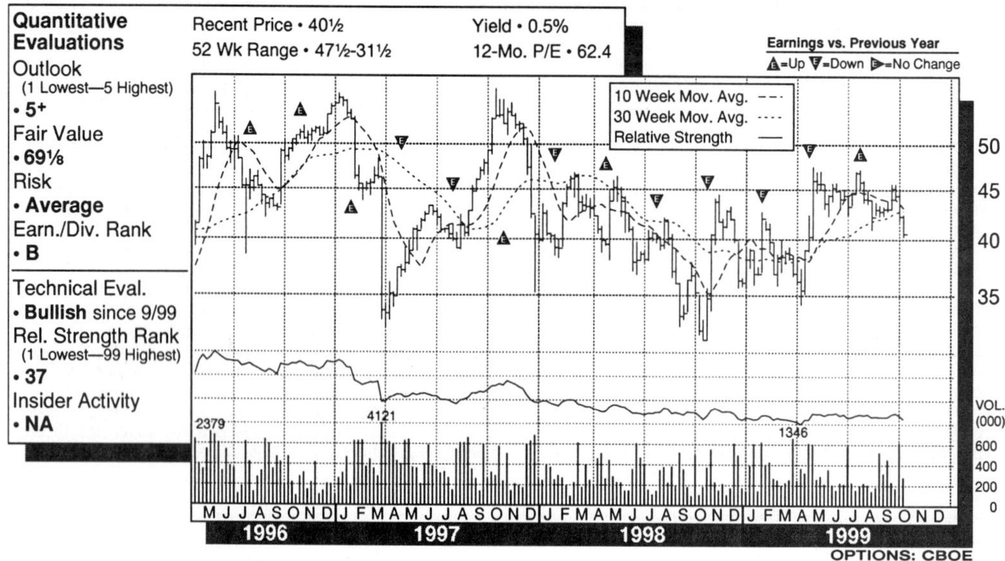

Business Profile - 13-SEP-99

In April 1999, the company said its North American Consumer Group had completed distribution changes, targets for margin improvement and overhead reduction had been achieved, and new products were on schedule for introduction in FY 00 (Jun.). The European Consumer Group launched an aggressive program to enhance margins and reduce overhead and working capital; full implementation would require about 12 months. HAR believes prospects beginning in FY 00 will be enhanced by new contracts from automobile companies for FY 01 and beyond, and from PC manufacturers for FY 00. In September 1999, the company completed the repurchase of approximately 1.5 million common shares, under a stock buyback program announced in June 1998.

Operational Review - 13-SEP-99

Based on a preliminary report, net sales declined fractionally in FY 99, as the impact of the sale of certain wholly owned international distributors, and of a reduction of consumer product inventories by independent dealers and distributors, was offset by strong sales growth to OEM customers. Gross margins narrowed, and with 5.3% higher SG&A expenses and $37 million of plant closure and asset impairment, income plunged 78%, to $11,723,000 ($0.65 a share, on 4.2% fewer shares), from $53,826,000 ($2.86, before an extraordinary charge of $0.19).

Stock Performance - 08-OCT-99

In the past 30 trading days, HAR's shares have declined 5%, compared to a 0.91% fall in the S&P 500. Average trading volume for the past five days was 55,280 shares, compared with the 40-day moving average of 73,967 shares.

Key Stock Statistics

Dividend Rate/Share	0.20	Shareholders	202
Shs. outstg. (M)	17.7	Market cap. (B)	$0.719
Avg. daily vol. (M)	0.071	Inst. holdings	84%
Tang. Bk. Value/Share	18.79		
Beta	0.53		

Value of $10,000 invested 5 years ago: $ 15,154

Fiscal Year Ending Jun. 30

	1999	1998	1997	1996	1995	1994
Revenues (Million $)						
1Q	315.9	329.3	338.0	300.5	228.6	163.7
2Q	387.5	403.0	401.3	348.7	288.7	222.7
3Q	374.9	391.9	358.1	339.3	310.5	222.9
4Q	421.8	389.1	376.6	373.1	342.4	252.8
Yr.	1,500	1,513	1,474	1,362	1,170	862.1
Earnings Per Share ($)						
1Q	**0.45**	0.46	0.41	0.36	0.28	0.10
2Q	**-1.73**	**0.84**	1.05	0.95	0.80	0.56
3Q	**0.72**	**0.80**	0.56	0.86	0.75	0.52
4Q	**1.17**	**0.76**	0.94	0.97	0.88	0.61
Yr.	**0.65**	**2.86**	**2.90**	3.16	2.72	1.89

Next earnings report expected: late October

Dividend Data (Dividends have been paid since 1994.)

Amount ($)	Date Decl.	Ex-Div. Date	Stock of Record	Payment Date
0.050	Nov. 03	Nov. 06	Nov. 11	Nov. 25 '98
0.050	Feb. 03	Feb. 08	Feb. 10	Feb. 24 '99
0.050	May. 05	May. 10	May. 12	May. 26 '99
0.050	Aug. 04	Aug. 09	Aug. 11	Aug. 25 '99

Harman International Industries, Incorporated

Business Summary - 13-SEP-99

Harman International Industries dates back to 1953, when Dr. Sidney Harman co-founded Harman/Kardon, the first domestic company to design and manufacture the high-fidelity receiver. The company currently designs, manufactures, and markets high-fidelity audio products targeted primarily at the OEM, consumer, and professional markets.

The company has developed, internally and through a series of strategic acquisitions, a broad range of product offerings sold under renowned brand names in each of its three major markets. HAR's development efforts aim to secure engineering, manufacturing and marketing leadership in its three major markets, and to strengthen its ability to provide total audio system solutions to its customers.

HAR serves three major audio markets: consumer, professional and OEM. In the consumer audio market, its range of product offerings has grown from the traditional base of two-channel stereo loudspeakers and electronics to include multi-channel, surround-sound electronics and loudspeaker systems, powered loudspeakers, mini-systems and audio systems for computers. In the professional audio market, the company offers a complete range of audio products for the sound reinforcement, broadcast and recording, and music instrument segments. In the OEM audio market, HAR offers branded and non-branded audio systems for installation as original equipment in automobiles and computers.

In FY 98 (Jun.), the Consumer Group accounted for 32% of sales, with 76% attributable to home loudspeaker and automotive aftermarket systems, 21% from home electronic components, and 3% from audio systems for computer manufacturers. The Professional Group contributed 30% of FY 98 sales, with 45% from sound reinforcement, 25% from broadcast and recording, and 30% from musical instrument support. OEM Group sales to the automakers produced 38% of FY 98 sales.

Based on its experience in, and knowledge of, the audio industry, HAR believes the consumer, professional and OEM markets, both domestic and international, have grown in recent years. In 1997 and 1998, consumer and professional audio markets slowed somewhat, due to uncertainty associated with technology transitions. The transition from analog to digital audio technology has transformed music recording and reproduction and has led to the development of a new generation of consumer and professional audio products. Although this transition has created near-term market weakness due to customer confusion and hesitancy, HAR believes the evolution of digital audio will fuel long-term growth in the consumer and professional audio markets.

Per Share Data ($) (Year Ended Jun. 30)	1999	1998	1997	1996	1995	1994	1993	1992	1991	1990
Tangible Bk. Val.	NA	18.79	19.35	16.46	10.80	12.50	7.10	6.82	5.60	7.79
Cash Flow	NA	6.16	5.82	6.32	5.73	4.28	3.13	2.88	0.08	3.73
Earnings	0.65	2.86	2.96	3.16	2.72	1.89	0.99	0.37	-2.15	1.53
Dividends	0.20	0.20	0.20	0.20	0.17	Nil	Nil	Nil	Nil	Nil
Payout Ratio	31%	7%	7%	6%	6%	Nil	Nil	Nil	Nil	Nil
Prices - High	47 1/2	46 3/4	57	56 1/2	49 3/4	36 1/4	27 7/8	14 5/8	10 5/8	19 3/4
- Low	34 1/4	31 1/2	32 3/8	32	32 3/8	23 3/8	13 3/4	8 1/2	4 1/4	6
P/E Ratio - High	73	16	19	18	18	19	28	39	NM	13
- Low	53	11	11	10	12	12	14	23	NM	4
Income Statement Analysis (Million $)										
Revs.	NA	1,513	1,474	1,362	1,170	862	665	604	587	557
Oper. Inc.	NA	163	155	157	133	100	65.3	50.9	24.1	63.0
Depr.	NA	62.5	53.1	52.0	45.7	33.6	24.4	23.4	20.5	20.1
Int. Exp.	NA	24.9	23.6	27.5	25.3	22.1	23.6	21.1	23.9	20.3
Pretax Inc.	NA	75.7	77.9	75.0	61.2	42.7	18.6	5.9	-20.6	23.0
Eff. Tax Rate	NA	29%	30%	32%	32%	38%	39%	41%	NM	39%
Net Inc.	NA	53.8	54.8	52.0	41.4	26.4	11.2	3.5	-19.8	14.1
Balance Sheet & Other Fin. Data (Million $)										
Cash	NA	16.2	4.2	0.3	11.3	9.7	2.2	2.8	3.8	2.9
Curr. Assets	NA	695	679	652	553	490	289	269	220	256
Total Assets	NA	1,131	1,014	996	887	681	432	416	359	393
Curr. Liab.	NA	327	251	275	295	274	141	167	139	148
LT Debt	NA	260	266	255	266	157	176	133	133	133
Common Eqty.	NA	512	467	436	289	232	111	111	81.0	102
Total Cap.	NA	772	734	692	560	389	287	244	214	235
Cap. Exp.	NA	57.5	68.4	80.6	54.7	40.7	25.6	21.0	24.6	40.7
Cash Flow	NA	116	108	104	87.1	60.0	35.6	26.9	0.7	34.1
Curr. Ratio	NA	2.1	2.7	2.4	1.9	1.8	2.0	1.6	1.6	1.7
% LT Debt of Cap.	NA	33.6	36.2	36.8	47.5	40.3	61.2	54.4	62.2	56.7
% Net Inc.of Revs.	NA	3.6	3.7	3.8	3.5	3.0	1.7	0.6	NM	2.5
% Ret. on Assets	NA	5.0	5.5	5.5	5.3	4.7	2.6	0.8	NM	4.0
% Ret. on Equity	NA	11.0	12.1	14.3	15.9	15.3	10.1	3.3	NM	15.0

Data as orig reptd.; bef. results of disc opers/spec. items. Per share data adj. for stk. divs. Bold denotes diluted EPS (FASB 128)-prior periods restated. E-Estimated. NA-Not Available. NM-Not Meaningful. NR-Not Ranked.

Office—1101 Pennsylvania Ave. N.W., Suite 1010, Washington, DC 20004. **Tel**—(202) 393-1101. **Website**—http://www.harman.com **Chrmn & CEO**—S. Harman. **Pres, COO & Secy**—B. A. Girod. **VP & CFO**—F. Meredith. **Investor Contact**—Sandra Robinson. **Dirs**—B. A. Girod, S. Harman, S. M. Hufstedler, A. McLaughlin, E. H. Meyer, G. P. Stapleton, S. A. Weiss. **Transfer Agent & Registrar**—ChaseMellon Shareholder Services, Encino, CA. **Incorporated**—in Delaware in 1980. **Empl**— 10,010. **S&P Analyst:** C.C.P.

STANDARD
&POOR'S
STOCK REPORTS

Harmon Industries

NASDAQ Symbol **HRMN**

In S&P SmallCap 600

09-OCT-99 **Industry:** Electrical Equipment

Summary: This company is a leading supplier of signal, inspection and control products for the rail freight and transit industries.

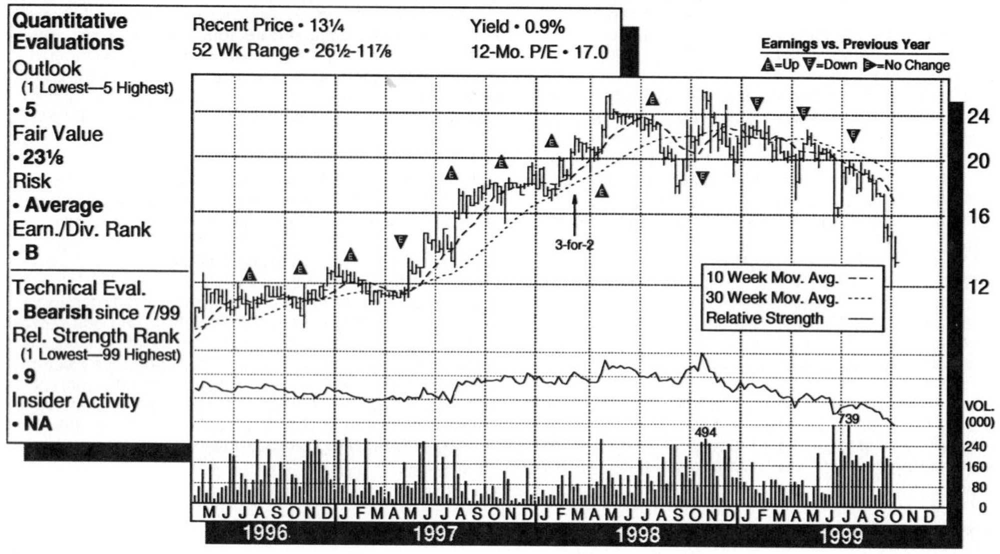

Business Profile - 14-JUL-99

In recent years, the company has expanded into commuter and urban transit markets, and has established international operations. Internationally, HRMN is targeting those countries that are privatizing railroads and share common standards with U.S. railroads. HRMN is benefiting from a long-term trend for railroads to outsource their engineering and maintenance tasks, and from the creation of new short-line railroads from major trunk systems. Harmon indicated that 1999 results would suffer from problems related to a major transit project, causing delays and rework, and a general slowdown in Harmon's largest market, the North American freight railroads.

Operational Review - 14-JUL-99

Net sales in the first quarter of 1999 declined 2.7%, year to year, due to lower sales in the international segment, reflecting lower shipments to a major customer in the United Kingdom. Margins narrowed with a larger proportion of sales from services, systems and pass-through sales; operating income fell 23%. Following a significant rise in interest expense, and after taxes at 40.5%, versus 36.1%, net income slumped 57%, to $1,203,000 ($0.11 a share, on 2.4% more shares), from $2,812,000 ($0.27). Backlog stood at $188 million at March 31, 1999, up from $132 million at year-end 1998.

Stock Performance - 08-OCT-99

In the past 30 trading days, HRMN's shares have declined 27%, compared to a 0.91% fall in the S&P 500. Average trading volume for the past five days was 10,780 shares, compared with the 40-day moving average of 29,597 shares.

Key Stock Statistics

Dividend Rate/Share	0.12	Shareholders	608
Shs. outstg. (M)	11.1	Market cap. (B)	$0.147
Avg. daily vol. (M)	0.033	Inst. holdings	53%
Tang. Bk. Value/Share	4.93		
Beta	0.84		

Value of $10,000 invested 5 years ago: $ 8,992

Fiscal Year Ending Dec. 31

	1999	1998	1997	1996	1995	1994
Revenues (Million $)						
1Q	58.95	60.56	35.99	38.40	29.42	25.90
2Q	79.78	73.71	47.62	39.11	32.85	32.17
3Q	—	57.80	56.13	41.96	38.03	29.45
4Q	—	73.20	73.80	55.98	36.49	32.19
Yr.	—	265.2	213.5	175.4	136.8	119.7
Earnings Per Share ($)						
1Q	**0.11**	**0.27**	0.14	0.20	0.07	0.15
2Q	**0.12**	**0.43**	0.29	0.26	0.20	0.24
3Q	—	**0.23**	0.25	0.24	0.22	0.22
4Q	—	**0.33**	**0.37**	0.21	0.18	0.17
Yr.	—	**1.25**	**1.06**	**0.91**	**0.67**	**0.79**

Next earnings report expected: early November

Dividend Data (Dividends have been paid since 1994.)

Amount ($)	Date Decl.	Ex-Div. Date	Stock of Record	Payment Date
0.055	Nov. 23	Nov. 24	Nov. 27	Dec. 11 '98
0.060	May. 11	May. 26	May. 28	Jun. 18 '99

A Division of The McGraw-Hill Companies

Harmon Industries, Inc.

Business Summary - 14-JUL-99

Harmon Industries is a leading supplier of signal, inspection, train control and communication products, systems and services to railroads primarily in North America. HRMN sells its products and services to major freight railroads, short-lines, commuter and urban mass transit operators. Harmon's products are used principally to increase asset utilization, enhance safety and improve communications. The company has recently begun to focus on shifting its revenue mix from sales generated strictly from individual products, to complete systems tailored to the specific needs of individual customers.

Harmon's future growth may be rooted in its international expansion. HRMN estimates that the international market is roughly eight times as large as the current domestic market. Its Mexican subsidiary was awarded an $8 million contract in July 1998, for centralized traffic control systems. In April 1999, HRMN acquired majority control of Angiolo Siliani and Siliani Elettronica ed Impianti, the largest independent signal supplier in Italy. Renamed Siliani Harmon, the company has annual sales of $30 million. Siliani is expected to participate in Italy's 10-year railroad investment programproposed by the Italian government, expected to cost U.S.$44 billion.

Harmon's largest product line (51% of 1998 revenue) is its Train Control Systems. These include signal control track circuits, interlocking control equipment, and computer-based dispatch and traffic control equipment. Railroads use HRMN products to direct the movement of trains over vast distances, allow remote switching of trains to other tracks and permit communication and remote control of locomotives.

Crossing Systems (20%) includes rail/highway cross warning systems, motion detectors, flashing lights and cantilevers. Asset Management Services (13%) involves the rapid delivery of packaged rail components. One of HRMN's most popular offerings is a containerized construction kit containing all the materials needed by a railroad for a signal installation project.

Train Inspection Systems (6%) include products that monitor trains as they pass by inspection sites. Harmon's hot-bearing detector helps railroads avoid costly and lethal train derailments. Other business segments include the production of custom designed printed wiring boards and communication systems.

Harmon has benefited from cost reduction measures adopted by large Class I railroads. As the big companies cut employment, HRMN provided products to monitor the condition of moving trains, help ensure safe switching and passage of trains, and facilitate better communication among crew members and moving trains. A reduction in cars in service prompted HRMN to make products that permit railroads to track the location and performance of a particular train.

Per Share Data ($) (Year Ended Dec. 31)	1998	1997	1996	1995	1994	1993	1992	1991	1990	1989
Tangible Bk. Val.	6.34	5.84	4.91	4.07	3.48	3.48	1.85	0.94	0.73	1.81
Cash Flow	1.93	1.67	1.39	1.05	1.04	0.97	0.82	0.65	0.93	0.63
Earnings	1.25	1.06	0.91	0.67	0.77	0.74	0.58	0.38	0.43	0.17
Dividends	0.11	0.10	0.10	0.10	0.10	Nil	Nil	Nil	0.04	0.08
Payout Ratio	9%	10%	11%	15%	13%	Nil	Nil	Nil	10%	50%
Prices - High	26 1/2	19 5/8	13	13 5/8	16 1/8	15 1/2	8 3/8	4 7/8	4 7/8	5 7/8
- Low	16 7/8	11	8	8 7/8	11	7 3/4	2 1/4	2 5/16	2 5/16	3 7/8
P/E Ratio - High	21	19	14	20	21	21	15	13	11	36
- Low	13	10	9	13	14	10	4	6	5	23
Income Statement Analysis (Million $)										
Revs.	265	214	175	137	120	99	81.9	70.9	72.7	73.3
Oper. Inc.	29.0	25.0	21.1	16.1	15.5	13.6	10.2	9.7	10.8	6.1
Depr.	7.2	6.3	5.0	3.9	2.6	2.1	1.9	2.0	3.5	3.2
Int. Exp.	1.6	1.2	0.7	0.7	0.3	0.4	1.3	2.2	1.5	2.5
Pretax Inc.	21.0	17.6	15.1	11.1	12.7	11.1	7.1	4.6	5.1	1.3
Eff. Tax Rate	36%	38%	38%	38%	40%	38%	35%	37%	40%	48%
Net Inc.	13.4	11.0	9.3	6.9	7.6	6.9	4.6	2.9	3.1	1.2
Balance Sheet & Other Fin. Data (Million $)										
Cash	1.7	6.7	Nil	Nil	0.3	3.1	0.4	0.4	0.5	0.4
Curr. Assets	109	96.4	73.0	56.8	42.7	37.0	25.6	23.3	24.3	27.9
Total Assets	163	136	105	86.8	68.4	53.0	38.5	36.6	41.4	50.4
Curr. Liab.	53.2	46.0	39.4	21.8	21.1	16.2	14.8	13.7	16.4	13.4
LT Debt	19.5	15.5	3.4	12.0	0.7	0.4	4.9	11.9	17.2	19.9
Common Eqty.	85.0	69.8	57.9	49.2	43.1	33.1	15.2	7.4	5.7	14.8
Total Cap.	104	85.3	61.3	61.3	43.8	33.5	20.1	19.3	23.0	35.3
Cap. Exp.	8.3	10.5	6.4	5.5	3.2	3.6	2.1	1.1	2.2	5.9
Cash Flow	20.6	17.3	14.3	10.8	10.3	9.0	6.5	4.9	6.6	4.3
Curr. Ratio	2.1	2.1	1.9	2.6	2.0	2.3	1.7	1.7	1.5	2.1
% LT Debt of Cap.	18.7	18.2	5.6	19.6	1.7	1.3	24.4	61.8	75.0	56.4
% Net Inc.of Revs.	5.1	5.1	5.3	5.0	6.4	6.9	5.6	4.1	4.3	1.6
% Ret. on Assets	9.0	9.1	9.7	8.9	12.2	14.0	11.8	7.3	6.6	2.4
% Ret. on Equity	17.3	17.2	17.4	8.9	19.5	27.0	39.6	43.7	29.5	8.1

Data as orig reptd.; bef. results of disc opers/spec. items. Per share data adj. for stk. divs. Bold denotes diluted EPS (FASB 128)-prior periods restated. E-Estimated. NA-Not Available. NM-Not Meaningful. NR-Not Ranked.

Office—1600 NE Coronado Drive, Blue Springs, MO 64014. **Tel**—(816) 229-3345. **Website**—www.harmonind.com**Chrmn**—R. E. Harmon. **Pres & CEO**—B. E. Olsson. **EVP-Fin, CFO, Treas, Secy & Investor Contact**—S. L Schmitz. **Dirs**—B. M. Flohr, C. M. Foudree, R. L. Gray, R. E. Harmon, H. M. Kohn, D. W. List, G. E. Myers, B. E. Olsson, S. A. Sprague, J. C. Whittaker. **Transfer Agent & Registrar**—United Missouri Bank, Kansas City. **Incorporated**—in Missouri in 1961. **Empl**— 1,662. **S&P Analyst:** John A. Massey

STANDARD
&POOR'S
STOCK REPORTS

Hartmarx Corp.

NYSE Symbol **HMX**

In S&P SmallCap 600

09-OCT-99 **Industry:** Textiles (Apparel)

Summary: This company manufactures and markets men's and women's business, casual and golfing apparel under a number of leading brand names.

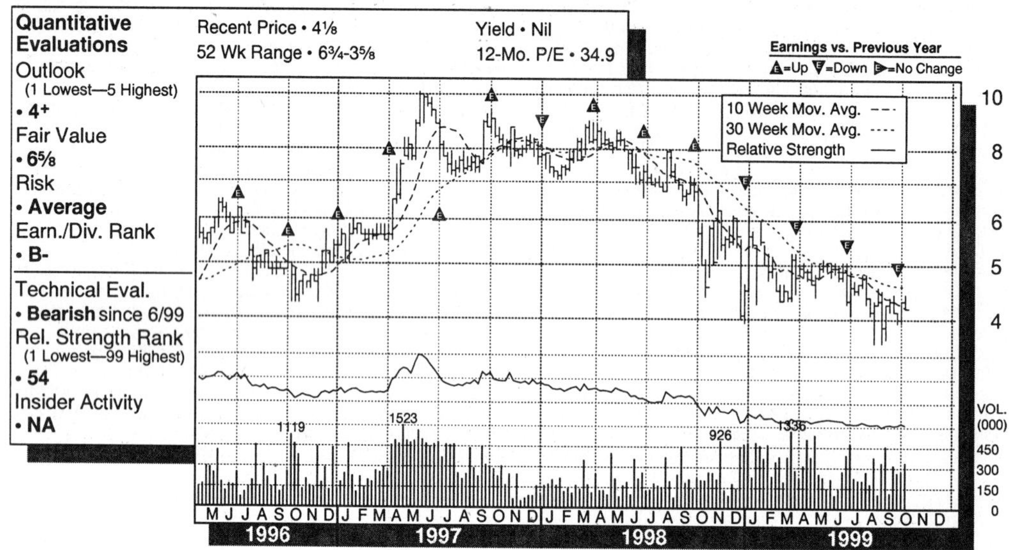

Business Profile - 27-SEP-99

Results in recent quarters have been restricted by poor sales trends at some of HMX's major retail customers, although HMX noted that more recent results were somewhat more encouraging. HMX added that its cash flow situation was healthy and that its outlook for FY 00 was positive. In August 1999, the company made its second Canadian acquisition with the purchase of the Royal Shirt Company, a manufacturer of dress and sport shirts. As of September 1999, the company had repurchased over 5 million shares of its common stock.

Operational Review - 27-SEP-99

Total sales for the nine months ended August 31, 1999, declined 1.4%, year to year, reflecting lower orders from retailers and reduced offerings of moderate tailored clothing lines. Profitability was hurt by the lower volume and an $11.2 million pretax charge, related to the termination of a systems project; a pretax loss contrasted with pretax income. After a tax benefit of $1,095,000 versus taxes at 38.0%, the net loss was $1,775,000 ($0.05 a share), compared with net income of $8,765,000 ($0.25).

Stock Performance - 08-OCT-99

In the past 30 trading days, HMX's shares have increased 8%, compared to a 0.91% fall in the S&P 500. Average trading volume for the past five days was 67,520 shares, compared with the 40-day moving average of 57,941 shares.

Key Stock Statistics

Dividend Rate/Share	Nil	Shareholders	5,915
Shs. outstg. (M)	32.4	Market cap. (B)	$0.136
Avg. daily vol. (M)	0.059	Inst. holdings	48%
Tang. Bk. Value/Share	6.21		
Beta	0.39		

Value of $10,000 invested 5 years ago: $ 5,981

Fiscal Year Ending Nov. 30

	1999	1998	1997	1996	1995	1994
Revenues (Million $)						
1Q	176.4	179.3	177.1	150.9	149.3	177.9
2Q	172.7	167.5	169.7	134.3	135.0	164.0
3Q	185.6	195.2	185.9	164.9	166.7	196.1
4Q	—	183.0	185.4	160.2	144.3	179.7
Yr.	—	725.0	718.1	610.2	595.3	717.7
Earnings Per Share ($)						
1Q	**0.04**	**0.07**	0.04	-0.05	Nil	-0.02
2Q	**-0.17**	**0.03**	0.01	-0.05	-0.09	-0.10
3Q	**0.08**	**0.15**	0.12	0.09	0.07	0.11
4Q	—	**0.17**	0.57	0.73	0.68	0.63
Yr.	—	**0.42**	**0.74**	0.72	0.66	0.62

Next earnings report expected: mid January

Dividend Data

Dividends, paid since 1939, were omitted in 1992. A poison pill stock purchase rights plan was adopted in 1986.

A Division of The McGraw-Hill Companies

Hartmarx Corporation

Business Summary - 27-SEP-99

For more than 100 years, Hartmarx Corp. (HMX) has been outfitting American men. The company, which was established in 1872, believes itself to be the largest U.S. maker and marketer of men's suits, sportcoats, and slacks. It also manufactures men's and women's sportswear, including golfwear, dress furnishings (shirts and ties), and women's career apparel. In FY 98 (Nov.), tailored clothing accounted for 65% of sales, sportswear slacks, dress furnishings and other apparel 27%, and women's apparel 8%.

As an integrated apparel company, HMX must design, manufacture, and source all its apparel. The majority of its men's tailored clothing and slacks are manufactured in fifteen company operated facilities in the U.S., three in Canada, one in Costa Rica, and one in Mexico. However, contract manufacturers are utilized to produce the company's remaining products, mainly men's and women's sportswear.

In FY 98, Hartmarx's business consisted of two groups. The larger, the Men's Apparel group (92% of total sales), designs, manufactures and markets well-known, prestigious brands of men's tailored clothing, slacks and sportswear. The Women's Apparel group (8%) consists of International Women's Apparel (IWA), which designs and markets women's career apparel to department and specialty stores under owned and licensed brand names, and Barrie Pace, a direct-mail catalog company that offers a wide range of apparel and accessories to the business and professional woman.

Hartmarx owns two of the most recognized brands in men's tailored clothing: Hart Schaffner & Marx and Hickey-Freeman. The company also offers its products under other brands it owns, such as Sansabelt, Racquet Club, Barrie Pace, Hawksley & Wight, and Desert Classic; and under exclusive license agreements for specified product lines, including Tommy Hilfiger, Jack Nicklaus, Bobby Jones, Austin Reed, Perry Ellis, Kenneth Cole, Daniel Hechter, Robert Comstock, Gieves & Hawkes, KM by Krizia and Pierre Cardin.

HMX has expanded its product offerings through acquisitions in the last three years. In November 1996, the company acquired substantially all the rights to manufacture and market under the Burberry, Claiborne, and Evan-Picone brands. HMX also took ownership of the Palm Beach and Brannoch names, as well as Plaid Clothing Group (now PCG Corp. I). In November 1998, the company acquired the wholesale apparel business of Pusser's, a West Indian company. In December 1998, HMX acquired Coppley, Noyes, and Randall Ltd., a leading Canadian men's apparel company.

HMX's long term objective is to increase revenues and improve gross and operating margins. In regards to product, the company expects to sustain its strong position in tailored clothing, broaden product offerings, and maintain its focus on womenswear.

Per Share Data ($) (Year Ended Nov. 30)	1998	1997	1996	1995	1994	1993	1992	1991	1990	1989
Tangible Bk. Val.	6.06	5.62	4.85	4.11	3.95	3.41	2.72	11.32	14.60	18.37
Cash Flow	0.65	0.99	1.00	0.96	1.05	0.65	-7.54	-0.21	-1.33	2.48
Earnings	0.42	0.74	0.72	0.66	0.62	0.20	-8.59	-1.74	-3.11	0.89
Dividends	Nil	Nil	Nil	Nil	Nil	Nil	Nil	0.60	0.90	1.18
Payout Ratio	Nil	Nil	Nil	Nil	Nil	Nil	Nil	NM	NM	132%
Prices - High	9	10 1/8	6 1/2	6 7/8	7 3/8	8 1/4	8 5/8	13 1/4	19 7/8	28 1/8
- Low	3 7/8	5	3 3/4	4 1/4	5	5 1/8	3	6 7/8	5 1/2	18 3/4
P/E Ratio - High	21	14	9	10	12	41	NM	NM	NM	32
- Low	9	7	5	6	8	26	NM	NM	NM	21
Income Statement Analysis (Million $)										
Revs.	725	718	610	595	718	732	1,054	1,215	1,296	1,297
Oper. Inc.	48.3	39.3	28.2	25.0	38.1	37.4	2.5	0.3	32.7	72.3
Depr.	8.0	8.6	9.3	10.0	13.8	14.1	26.9	33.8	35.2	31.0
Int. Exp.	18.6	17.5	16.7	19.9	21.2	22.9	21.1	23.8	29.0	28.4
Pretax Inc.	23.6	16.5	6.5	1.6	11.0	6.0	-226	-60.0	-95.0	28.0
Eff. Tax Rate	38%	NM	NM	NM	NM	3.00%	NM	NM	NM	37%
Net Inc.	14.6	25.2	23.8	21.4	20.0	6.0	-219	-38.0	-62.0	17.0
Balance Sheet & Other Fin. Data (Million $)										
Cash	5.3	1.6	2.8	5.7	2.8	1.5	22.4	6.6	2.7	2.9
Curr. Assets	363	357	320	279	312	338	430	579	578	698
Total Assets	485	470	430	377	392	405	512	740	762	908
Curr. Liab.	104	120	120	89.4	97.0	89.0	193	347	243	277
LT Debt	170	158	148	153	167	207	249	105	227	271
Common Eqty.	211	192	162	134	128	109	70.0	287	293	360
Total Cap.	381	350	310	287	295	316	319	393	519	631
Cap. Exp.	12.8	10.1	8.2	8.4	7.1	6.0	9.5	15.2	16.1	52.3
Cash Flow	22.6	33.9	33.1	31.4	34.0	20.0	-192	-5.0	-26.0	48.0
Curr. Ratio	3.5	3.0	2.7	3.1	3.2	3.8	2.2	1.7	2.4	2.5
% LT Debt of Cap.	44.6	45.1	47.7	53.2	56.6	65.6	77.9	26.9	43.7	42.9
% Net Inc.of Revs.	2.0	3.5	3.9	3.6	2.8	0.8	NM	NM	NM	1.3
% Ret. on Assets	3.1	5.6	5.9	5.6	5.0	1.2	NM	NM	NM	2.1
% Ret. on Equity	7.3	14.2	16.1	16.3	16.7	6.4	NM	NM	NM	4.7

Data as orig reptd.; bef. results of disc opers/spec. items. Per share data adj. for stk. divs. Bold denotes diluted EPS (FASB 128)-prior periods restated. E-Estimated. NA-Not Available. NM-Not Meaningful. NR-Not Ranked.

Office—101 N. Wacker Dr., Chicago, IL 60606. **Tel**—(312) 372-6300. **Chrmn & CEO**—E. O. Hand. **Pres**—H. B. Patel. **EVP & CFO**—G. R. Morgan. **SVP & Secy**—F. G. Wohlschlaeger **VP & Treas**—James E. Condon. **Investor Contact**—Adriana Schmeling (212-840-4772). **Dirs**—A. R. Abboud, S. A. Bakhsh, J. A. Cole, R. F. Farley, E. O. Hand, D. P. Jacobs, C. Marshall, H. B. Patel, M. B. Rohlfs, S. L. Scott, E. D. Strubel. **Transfer Agents & Registrars**—First National Bank of Chicago, Chicago, IL; First Chicago Trust Co. of New York, Jersey City, NJ. **Incorporated**—in New York in 1911; reincorporated in Delaware in 1983. **Empl**— 9,200. **S&P Analyst:** Howard Choe

STANDARD
&POOR'S
STOCK REPORTS

Heartland Express

NASDAQ Symbol **HTLD**

In S&P SmallCap 600

09-OCT-99 **Industry:** Truckers

Summary: This company is a short-to-medium haul truckload carrier based near Iowa City, IA.

Quantitative Evaluations

Outlook
(1 Lowest—5 Highest)
• **4**

Fair Value
• **19¼**

Risk
• **Average**

Earn./Div. Rank
• **B+**

Technical Eval.
• **Bearish** since 9/99

Rel. Strength Rank
(1 Lowest—99 Highest)
• **26**

Insider Activity
• **NA**

Recent Price • 13½ Yield • Nil
52 Wk Range • 20¼-13 12-Mo. P/E • 12.3

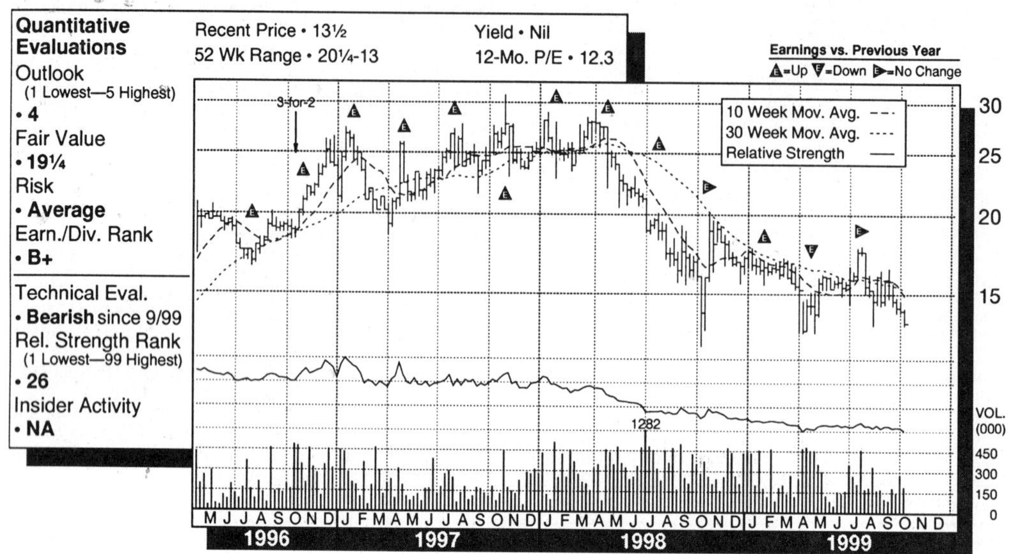

Business Profile - 03-SEP-99

Heartland Express' strategy includes focusing on satisfying customers through on-time performance, the use of dependable late-model equipment, and consistent equipment availability to serve large customers' volume requirements. The company also maintains a high trailer to tractor ratio, which facilitates the stationing of trailers at customer locations for convenient loading and unloading. This minimizes waiting time, which increases tractor utilization and assists with driver retention. Historically, Heartland Express has been debt-free, financing equipment through cash flow from operations. The company strengthened its balance sheet during 1998, ending the year with $143 million in cash, cash equivalents and municipal bonds.

Operational Review - 03-SEP-99

Operating revenue for the first half of 1999 declined 5.1% year to year, reflecting an industry-wide shortage of experienced employee drivers and independent contractors. Salaries, wages, and benefits increased 6.9%, due primarily to the impact of an increase in the percentage of employee drivers operating the company tractor fleet and a rise in employee driver pay of about 10% (to enhance recruitment and retention of qualified drivers). Operating profit was down 5.6%. After 37% higher interest income, net income decreased 1.5%, to $16.1 million from $16.3 million. Share earnings were unchanged at $0.54.

Stock Performance - 08-OCT-99

In the past 30 trading days, HTLD's shares have declined 8%, compared to a 0.91% fall in the S&P 500. Average trading volume for the past five days was 37,200 shares, compared with the 40-day moving average of 33,223 shares.

Key Stock Statistics

Dividend Rate/Share	Nil	Shareholders	270
Shs. outstg. (M)	30.0	Market cap. (B)	$0.405
Avg. daily vol. (M)	0.039	Inst. holdings	42%
Tang. Bk. Value/Share	6.76		
Beta	0.84		

Value of $10,000 invested 5 years ago: $ 12,600

Fiscal Year Ending Dec. 31

	1999	1998	1997	1996	1995	1994
Revenues (Million $)						
1Q	63.10	66.84	59.89	54.36	47.58	61.35
2Q	66.09	69.22	65.38	59.38	46.97	59.30
3Q	—	65.02	70.18	58.18	47.53	53.88
4Q	—	62.41	67.06	57.09	49.42	49.69
Yr.	—	263.5	262.5	229.0	191.5	224.3
Earnings Per Share ($)						
1Q	**0.25**	**0.26**	**0.22**	**0.19**	0.15	-0.06
2Q	**0.28**	**0.28**	**0.26**	**0.21**	0.17	0.14
3Q	—	**0.28**	**0.28**	**0.22**	0.19	0.15
4Q	—	**0.28**	**0.24**	**0.21**	0.17	0.10
Yr.	—	**1.10**	**1.00**	**0.83**	**0.69**	**0.34**

Next earnings report expected: mid October

Dividend Data

No cash has been paid. A three-for-two common stock split was effected in October 1996.

A Division of The McGraw-Hill Companies

Heartland Express, Inc.

Business Summary - 03-SEP-99

Founded by Russell A. Gerdin in 1978, Heartland Express has grown over the years, due primarily to expanding service for existing customers, acquiring new customers, and continued expansion of the company's operating regions. Heartland Express is a short-to medium haul truckload carrier based near Iowa City, Iowa.

The company provides nationwide transportation service to major shippers, using late-model equipment and a balanced fleet of company-owned and owner-operator tractors. Primary traffic lanes are between customer locations east of the Rocky Mountains, with selected service to the West. Heartland Express believes that its service standards and equipment accessibility have made it a core carrier to many of its major customers.

Serving the short to medium haul market (592-mile average length of haul in 1998) permits the company to use primarily single, rather than team drivers and dispatch most trailers directly from origin to destination without an intermediate equipment change other than for driver scheduling purposes.

In addition to its own operations department, the company operates three specialized regional distribution operations for major customers near Atlanta, GA; Columbus, OH; and Iowa City, IA. These short-haul operations concentrate on freight movements generally within a 400-mile radius of the regional terminal, and are designed to meet the needs of significant customers in those regions.

The company targets customers in its operating area that require multiple, time-sensitive shipments, including those employing "just-in-time" manufacturing and inventory management. In seeking these customers, Heartland has positioned itself as a provider of premium service at compensatory rates, rather than competing solely on the basis of price. Freight transported for the most part is non-perishable and predominantly does not require driver handling. Heartland believes that its reputation for quality service, reliable equipment, and equipment availability makes it a core carrier to many of its customers.

Heartland seeks to transport freight that will complement traffic in its existing service areas and remain consistent with the company's focus on short-to-medium haul and regional distribution markets. Management believes that building additional service in the company's primary traffic lanes will assist in controlling empty miles and enhancing driver "home time."

Primary customers are retailers, manufacturers, and third party logistics providers. Sears Logistics Services accounted for 14% of revenue in 1998.

Management believes that competition for thefreight targeted by the company is based primarily upon service and efficiency and less on freight rates.

Per Share Data ($) (Year Ended Dec. 31)	1998	1997	1996	1995	1994	1993	1992	1991	1990	1989
Tangible Bk. Val.	6.23	5.13	4.12	3.29	2.59	2.32	1.81	1.60	1.38	NA
Cash Flow	1.74	1.59	1.30	1.19	1.00	1.10	1.01	0.85	0.77	NA
Earnings	1.10	1.00	0.83	0.69	0.33	0.48	0.33	0.24	0.21	NA
Dividends	Nil	Nil	Nil	Nil	Nil	Nil	Nil	Nil	Nil	NA
Payout Ratio	Nil	Nil	Nil	Nil	Nil	Nil	Nil	Nil	Nil	NA
Prices - High	29¼	30⅞	26½	14⅜	15⅞	13	12⅛	11½	7⅛	NA
- Low	12⅜	18½	13⅛	10¾	10½	8⅝	6¼	5⅞	4⅛	NA
P/E Ratio - High	27	31	32	21	48	27	37	48	34	NA
- Low	11	18	16	16	31	18	19	24	20	NA
Income Statement Analysis (Million $)										
Revs.	263	263	229	192	224	116	97.0	74.0	NA	NA
Oper. Inc.	64.9	60.6	50.7	46.1	47.2	45.5	40.3	34.8	NA	NA
Depr.	19.2	17.5	14.0	15.1	20.1	22.8	20.7	18.5	NA	NA
Int. Exp.	Nil	0.1	0.0	Nil	2.2	5.3	5.4	4.7	NA	NA
Pretax Inc.	50.9	47.0	39.7	32.7	21.8	18.3	15.6	12.2	NA	NA
Eff. Tax Rate	35%	36%	37%	37%	54%	44%	40%	42%	NA	NA
Net Inc.	33.1	30.1	25.0	20.6	10.1	10.2	9.4	7.1	NA	NA
Balance Sheet & Other Fin. Data (Million $)										
Cash	143	76.2	59.6	46.6	10.2	9.4	NA	NA	NA	NA
Curr. Assets	182	138	121	83.9	44.4	57.9	NA	NA	NA	NA
Total Assets	257	225	191	158	136	169	150	135	NA	NA
Curr. Liab.	54.3	55.8	51.6	42.1	41.6	69.0	NA	NA	NA	NA
LT Debt	Nil	Nil	Nil	Nil	0.7	21.4	NA	NA	NA	NA
Common Eqty.	187	154	124	99	78.1	68.0	57.0	48.0	NA	NA
Total Cap.	203	170	140	116	94.8	100	NA	NA	NA	NA
Cap. Exp.	5.5	22.4	7.5	NA	3.7	28.0	32.0	NA	NA	NA
Cash Flow	52.3	47.6	39.0	35.7	30.1	33.1	30.1	25.7	NA	NA
Curr. Ratio	3.4	2.5	2.4	2.0	1.1	0.8	NA	NA	NA	NA
% LT Debt of Cap.	Nil	Nil	Nil	Nil	0.7	21.4	NA	NA	NA	NA
% Net Inc.of Revs.	12.6	11.5	10.9	10.7	4.5	4.3	4.6	4.0	NA	NA
% Ret. on Assets	13.7	14.4	14.3	14.0	6.6	6.4	6.6	5.7	NA	NA
% Ret. on Equity	19.3	21.5	22.5	23.3	13.8	16.4	17.9	15.9	NA	NA

Data as orig reptd.; bef. results of disc opers/spec. items. Per share data adj. for stk. divs. Bold denotes diluted EPS (FASB 128)-prior periods restated. E-Estimated. NA-Not Available. NM-Not Meaningful. NR-Not Ranked.

Office—2777 Heartland Drive, Coralville, IA 52241. **Tel**—(319) 645-2728. **Website**—http://www.heartlandexpress.com **Chrmn, Pres & Secy**—R. A. Gerdin. **EVP-Fin & Treas**—J. P. Cosaert. **Dirs**—B. J. Allen, L. D. Crouse, M. J. Gerdin, R. A. Gerdin, R. O. Jacobson. **Transfer Agent & Registrar**—Boatmen's Trust Co., St. Louis. **Incorporated**—in Nevada in 1978. **Empl**— 1,213. **S&P Analyst:** N.J.D.

Hecla Mining

NYSE Symbol **HL**

In S&P SmallCap 600

09-OCT-99

Industry:
Gold & Precious Metals Mining

Summary: This company produces gold, silver, lead and zinc from properties in the U.S. and Mexico. It also produces kaolin, ball clay and other industrial minerals.

S&P Opinion: Accumulate (★★★★)

Recent Price • 2⅞
52 Wk Range • 4⅞-1¹⁵⁄₁₆
Yield • Nil
12-Mo. P/E • NM

Quantitative Evaluations

Outlook
(1 Lowest—5 Highest)
• **NA**

Fair Value
• **NA**

Risk
• **Average**

Earn./Div. Rank
• **C**

Technical Eval.
• **Neutral** since 9/99

Rel. Strength Rank
(1 Lowest—99 Highest)
• **91**

Insider Activity
• **NA**

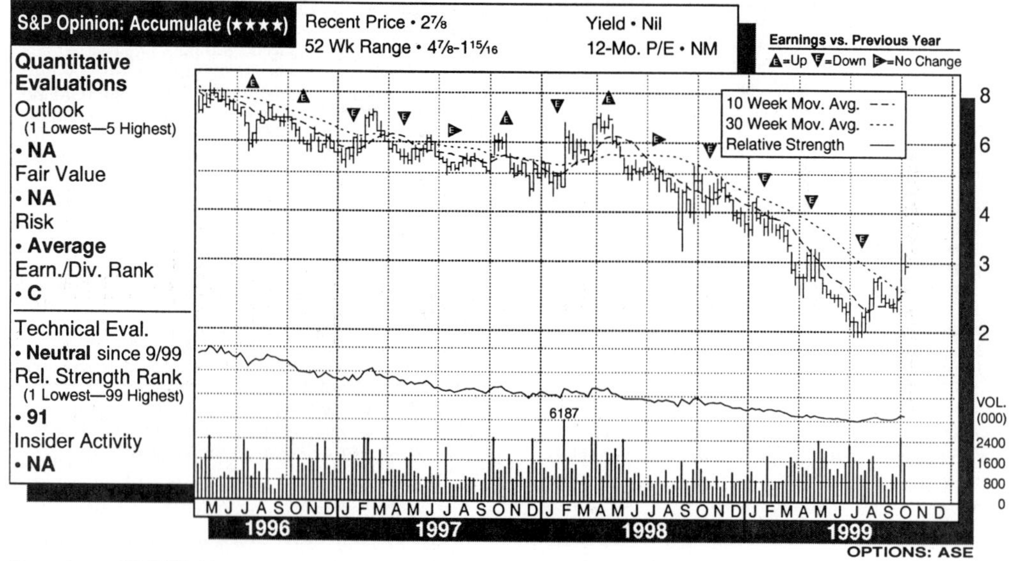

Overview - 05-AUG-99

HL expects to produce 7.2 million to 7.5 million oz. of silver in 1999, at a cash cost of $3.75/oz. to $4.00/oz., as increased output at Lucky Friday outweighs an anticipated drop at Green's Creek. Assuming some recovery in lead and zinc prices, cash costs should decline from 1998's $3.96 level, as by product credits rise. Gold production will decline in 1999, reflecting the cessation of mine production at La Choya. On June 28, 1999 HL announced that it had acquired the La Camorra gold mine in Venezuela and a silver exploration property in Mexico from Monarch Resources Limited of Bermuda. The purchase price of $25 million was comprised of $9 million in cash and 6.7 million HL common shares. La Camorra is expected to contribute 19,000 oz. of gold to HL in 1999 and achieve production of 80,000 oz. annually by 2001.

Valuation - 05-AUG-99

Although HL's reserve and production profile will stagnate in 1999, we continue to rate the shares accumulate, based on our positive outlook for silver. Silver market fundamentals have been favorable for some time, as fabrication demand has exceeded mine production and scrap recovery since 1989. The gap has been made up by liquidation of above ground supplies. Since 1993, the metal has been in an erratic uptrend. Silver declined 15% in 1998, to $5.02 an oz., from $5.99 at 1997 year end. However, the metal averaged $5.54 an oz. in 1998, versus $4.88 in 1997 and $5.18 in 1996. In contrast to gold, silver remained well above its 21-year closing low of $3.51 an oz., recorded in 1991. In addition, the 1998 average price held comfortably above the 1992 average price of $3.93 an oz., the lowest average price for silver in 21 years. Despite the volatility, favorable silver market fundamentals will lift the metal and HL shares.

Key Stock Statistics

S&P EPS Est. 1999	-0.01	Tang. Bk. Value/Share	0.63
P/E on S&P Est. 1999	NM	Beta	1.14
S&P EPS Est. 2000	0.05	Shareholders	10,162
Dividend Rate/Share	Nil	Market cap. (B)	$0.196
Shs. outstg. (M)	66.7	Inst. holdings	19%
Avg. daily vol. (M)	0.404		

Value of $10,000 invested 5 years ago: $ 2,526

Fiscal Year Ending Dec. 31

	1999	1998	1997	1996	1995	1994
Revenues (Million $)						
1Q	41.66	40.13	42.46	42.95	35.71	26.34
2Q	46.06	45.66	46.07	40.52	42.24	38.00
3Q	—	38.61	41.20	37.66	41.20	35.28
4Q	—	34.84	34.22	37.12	36.73	29.08
Yr.	—	159.2	163.9	158.3	155.9	128.8
Earnings Per Share ($)						
1Q	**-0.04**	**0.02**	**-0.03**	**-0.01**	-0.09	-0.19
2Q	**0.01**	**0.02**	**0.02**	**0.02**	0.01	-0.03
3Q	**E0.01**	**-0.05**	**-0.02**	**-0.76**	-2.17	-0.03
4Q	**E0.01**	**-0.15**	**-0.13**	**-0.04**	-0.02	-0.47
Yr.	**E-0.01**	**-0.15**	**-0.16**	**-0.79**	**-2.28**	**-0.74**

Next earnings report expected: early November

Dividend Data

Common dividends were omitted in 1991.

A Division of The McGraw-Hill Companies

Hecla Mining Company

Business Summary - 05-AUG-99

Hecla produces gold, silver, lead and zinc from properties in the U.S. and Mexico, and also produces kaolin clay and other industrial minerals. In 1998, gold accounted for 20% of sales (34% in 1997) and $3.9 million of gross profit ($15 million), silver 27% of sales (20%) and $800,000 in losses ($3.8 million of losses), and industrial minerals 53% of sales (46%) and $5.9 million of profit ($5.0 million).

The company's main business strategy is to increase its precious metals production and reserves. Its strategy also entails using the industrial minerals segment to offset the earnings and cash flow volatility of the precious metals business.

HL's strategy for reserve replacement is to concentrate on existing operations where an infrastructure already exists. In addition, it will focus on advanced-stage exploration properties that have been identified as having potential for additional discoveries. HL is currently concentrating its exploration activities at the Lucky Friday and Greens Creek silver mines, the 50%-owned Rosebud gold mine, the La Choya mine, and gold properties in Mexico, including the Pinos, La Jojoba and Porvenir properties.

On June 28, 1999 HL announced that it had acquired the La Camorra gold mine in Venezuela and a silver exploration property in Mexico from Monarch Resources Limited of Bermuda. The purchase price of $25 million was comprised of $9 million in cash and 6.7 million HL common shares. La Camorra is expected to contribute 19,000 oz. of gold to HL in 1999 and achieve production of 80,000 oz. annually by 2001.

The industrial minerals segment produces ball clay, kaolin and sodium feldspar, three of the four ingredients needed to produce ceramic products. HL plans to sell the segment's lawn and garden subsidiary in 1999. Proceeds will be used for precious metals acquisitions, expansion of the segment's remaining business, and debt repayment. Shipments in this segment totaled 1,114,987 tons in 1998, versus 1,025,993 tons in 1997.

Silver production totaled 7,244,657 oz. in 1998, versus 5,147,009 oz. in 1997. Cash cost of production were $3.96/oz. in 1998, versus $3.58/oz. in 1997. Total costs were $5.37/oz. in 1998, versus $5.42/oz, in 1997. At year end 1998, silver reserves totaled 64,629,363 oz., versus 68,378,168 oz. at year end 1997. Gold production totaled 127,433 oz. in 1998, versus 174,164 oz. in 1997. Cash costs were $189/oz. in 1998, versus $173/oz. in 1997. Total costs were $262/oz. in 1998, versus $239/oz. in 1997. Gold reserves at year end 1998 totaled 506,754 oz., versus 613,538 oz. in 1997. Lead production was 34,455 tons in 1998, versus 24,995 tons in 1997. Lead reserves were 259,584 tons in 1998, versus 253,704 tons in 1997. Zinc production was 20,155 tons in 1998, versus 16,830 tons in 1997. Zinc reserves were 379,372 tons in 1998, versus 343,200 tons in 1997.

Per Share Data ($) (Year Ended Dec. 31)	1998	1997	1996	1995	1994	1993	1992	1991	1990	1989
Tangible Bk. Val.	0.63	0.79	0.56	0.98	3.34	3.56	3.60	4.95	4.95	4.79
Cash Flow	0.26	0.23	-0.23	-1.62	-0.39	-0.11	-1.14	0.17	0.84	-0.17
Earnings	-0.15	-0.16	-0.79	-2.28	-0.74	-0.48	-1.59	-0.51	0.19	-0.83
Dividends	Nil	Nil	Nil	Nil	Nil	Nil	Nil	Nil	0.05	0.05
Payout Ratio	Nil	Nil	Nil	Nil	Nil	Nil	Nil	Nil	26%	NM
Prices - High	7 1/8	7 1/4	9 1/2	13	15	15 1/4	12 1/4	12 5/8	16 3/8	16 1/8
- Low	3 1/8	4 3/8	5 1/2	6 5/8	9 1/4	7 3/8	7 1/4	6 5/8	6 5/8	11 1/2
P/E Ratio - High	NM	NM	NM	NM	NM	NM	NM	NM	86	NM
- Low	NM	NM	NM	NM	NM	NM	NM	NM	35	NM
Income Statement Analysis (Million $)										
Revs.	159	164	158	156	129	82.0	101	118	133	99
Oper. Inc.	18.8	20.2	17.2	13.6	-3.3	0.4	-28.5	10.1	16.8	4.2
Depr.	22.6	21.3	20.8	23.8	14.8	12.2	13.9	20.5	17.6	17.9
Int. Exp.	2.3	1.7	3.1	2.0	2.6	5.0	6.9	7.0	5.8	4.7
Pretax Inc.	-1.2	1.4	-31.7	-100	-24.2	-12.7	-49.6	-18.5	2.3	-25.9
Eff. Tax Rate	NM	NM	NM	NM	NM	NM	NM	NM	NM	NM
Net Inc.	-0.3	-0.5	-32.4	-101	-23.8	-11.7	-49.2	-15.4	5.1	-22.4
Balance Sheet & Other Fin. Data (Million $)										
Cash	2.5	3.8	8.3	4.0	7.3	65.4	3.3	5.6	16.4	15.5
Curr. Assets	53.5	52.6	58.8	53.3	51.3	97.2	33.0	46.9	48.4	49.2
Total Assets	252	251	268	258	335	333	222	258	232	222
Curr. Liab.	24.3	25.0	32.7	26.0	23.5	19.6	12.7	12.6	11.7	14.4
LT Debt	42.9	22.1	38.2	36.1	2.0	49.5	70.4	76.9	70.2	65.0
Common Eqty.	151	160	145	164	161	123	114	150	134	129
Total Cap.	195	183	184	201	280	290	186	232	210	198
Cap. Exp.	22.5	24.8	33.7	45.3	66.6	58.7	23.2	19.5	29.9	40.6
Cash Flow	14.2	12.8	-11.6	-77.9	-17.1	-3.6	-35.3	5.1	22.7	-4.5
Curr. Ratio	2.2	2.1	1.8	2.0	2.2	5.0	2.6	3.7	4.1	3.4
% LT Debt of Cap.	22.0	12.1	20.8	18.0	0.7	17.1	37.9	33.2	33.4	32.8
% Net Inc.of Revs.	NM	NM	NM	NM	NM	NM	NM	NM	3.9	NM
% Ret. on Assets	NM	NM	NA	NM	NM	NM	NM	NM	2.3	NM
% Ret. on Equity	NM	NM	NM	NM	NM	NM	NM	NM	3.9	NM

Data as orig. reptd.; bef. results of disc. opers. and/or spec. items. Per share data adj. for stk. divs. as of ex-div. date. Bold denotes diluted EPS (FASB 128). E-Estimated. NA-Not Available. NM-Not Meaningful. NR-Not Ranked.

Office—6500 Mineral Dr., Coeur d'Alene, ID 83814-8788. **Tel**—(208) 769-4100. **Fax**—(208) 769-4107. **Website**—http://www.hecla-mining.com **Chrmn, Pres & CEO**—A. Brown. **VP & Secy**—M. B. White. **VP-CFO & Treas**—J. P. Stilwell. **VP & Investor Contact**—William B. Booth. **Dirs**—A. Brown, J. E. Clute, J. Coors Jr., T. Crumley, L. O. Erdahl, C. L. McAlpine, T. J. O'Neil, J. E. Ordonez, P. A. Redmond. **Transfer Agent & Registrar**—American Stock Transfer & Trust Co., NYC. **Incorporated**—in Washington in 1898; reincorporated in Delaware in 1983. **Empl**— 1,184. **S&P Analyst:** Leo J. Larkin

STANDARD
&POOR'S
STOCK REPORTS

Helix Technology

Nasdaq Symbol **HELX**

In S&P SmallCap 600

09-OCT-99

Industry:
Equipment (Semiconductor)

Summary: This company makes, sells and services products based on cryogenic and vacuum technology.

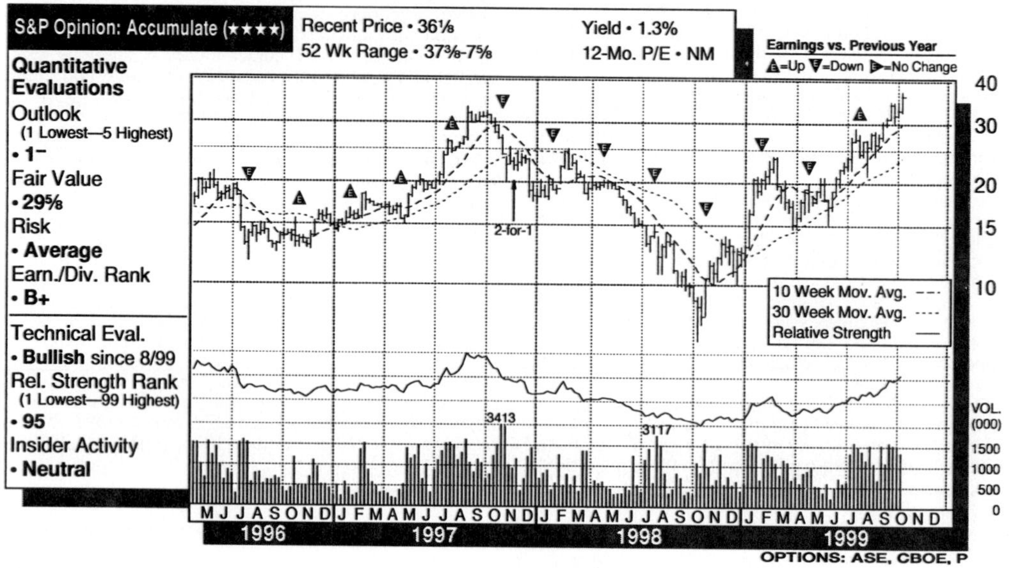

Overview - 22-SEP-99

We expect sales to rise more than 40% in 1999, reflecting a sharp recovery in the semiconductor capital equipment market and easy second half comparisons. In 1998, spending was restrained by the impact of the Asian financial crisis and by persistent overcapacity in the market for dynamic random access memory (DRAM) and other semiconductors. In light of recent positive trends in chip pricing and revenues, however, we expect market conditions to improve, allowing HELX to post relatively strong sequential sales growth over the next few quarters. Through the down cycle, the company demonstrated an impressive ability to maintain profit margins. Through the remainder of 1999 and into 2000, profit margins should improve, as fixed costs are spread over a larger sales base. As a result, we expect EPS to rebound to $0.52 in 1999, from 1998's $0.09 (excluding charges, and pro forma to include the May 1998 acquisition of Granville-Phillips Co.).

Valuation - 22-SEP-99

The shares have recovered dramatically since late 1998, reflecting improving semiconductor industry fundamentals. However, we are maintaining our accumulate recommendation, as we believe there is further upside potential. Following a sharp decline in semiconductor capital spending in 1998, supply/demand dynamics have improved, setting the stage for a prolonged industry recovery. HELX continues to command a dominant position in the market for cryogenic vacuum pumps, and is well positioned to benefit from renewed semiconductor industry growth. We believe that the shares, recently trading at 32X our 2000 EPS estimate of $1.10, remain attractively valued for purchase by aggressive investors.

Key Stock Statistics

S&P EPS Est. 1999	0.52	Tang. Bk. Value/Share	2.83
P/E on S&P Est. 1999	69.5	Beta	1.48
S&P EPS Est. 2000	1.10	Shareholders	854
Dividend Rate/Share	0.48	Market cap. (B)	$0.807
Shs. outstg. (M)	22.3	Inst. holdings	60%
Avg. daily vol. (M)	0.365		

Value of $10,000 invested 5 years ago: $ 123,366

Fiscal Year Ending Dec. 31

	1999	1998	1997	1996	1995	1994
Revenues (Million $)						
1Q	25.90	31.49	29.02	40.21	27.15	18.79
2Q	32.53	25.71	32.93	39.35	29.03	21.25
3Q	—	18.55	35.62	25.12	32.25	22.36
4Q	—	19.60	33.94	23.70	35.23	24.37
Yr.	—	95.35	131.5	128.4	123.7	86.76
Earnings Per Share ($)						
1Q	**0.06**	**0.08**	**0.21**	**0.16**	0.21	0.09
2Q	**0.13**	**-0.02**	**0.26**	**0.19**	0.25	0.13
3Q	—	**-0.15**	**0.30**	**0.38**	0.28	0.14
4Q	—	**Nil**	**0.30**	**0.37**	0.31	0.17
Yr.	—	**-0.09**	**1.07**	**1.10**	**1.05**	**0.54**

Next earnings report expected: late October

Dividend Data (Dividends have been paid since 1987.)

Amount ($)	Date Decl.	Ex-Div. Date	Stock of Record	Payment Date
0.120	Oct. 23	Nov. 03	Nov. 05	Nov. 19 '98
0.120	Feb. 11	Feb. 23	Feb. 25	Mar. 11 '99
0.120	Apr. 20	May. 03	May. 05	May. 19 '99
0.120	Jul. 19	Jul. 27	Jul. 29	Aug. 06 '99

A Division of The McGraw-Hill Companies

Helix Technology Corporation

Business Summary - 22-SEP-99

Helix Technology Corp. is a leader in the development and application of cyrogenic (low-temperature) and vacuum technology. Using proprietary engineering and unique manufacturing competence, the company delivers innovative solutions to meet customer requirements, primarily in the semiconductor, disk drive, and flat panel display markets. Helix believes it is the world's leading producer of cryogenic vacuum pumping systems.

Thin film deposition and ion implantation systems are dependent on Helix's vacuum products. These systems in turn are used in the production of rapidly growing high-technology products, including semiconductors, flat panel displays, magnetic recording heads, and optics. The company's cryogenic systems are are also facilitating the commercialization of emerging applications for superconducting electronics in the growing wireless telecommunications market.

CTI's On-Board pumping systems incorporate built-in microprocessor capabilities to provide online performance monitoring and diagnostics to enhance vacuum processing system uptime. The On-Board system allows users to set and control all key parameters of pump status, such as temperature or pumping speed, and it provides comprehensive, real time parameter monitoring with programmable alarms. This substantially increases control over the process environment, and gives the user the ability to optimize system performance for specific applications. The On-Board product line includes On-Board Cryopumps, On-Board Waterpumps, an increasing range of computer networking products and an expanding set of innovative, user friendly software offerings.

Cryopumps are designed to pump various gases from a vacuum chamber by freezing the gases onto refrigerated surfaces. These captured gases are periodically vented by shutting down the chamber and warming the condensed gases, allowing them to escape into the atmosphere. Waterpumps are high-performance cryo pumps which increase water vapor pumping speed in the vacuum process, providing improved throughput and better process results.

Helix also applies its talents to provide specialized solutions to customer requirements for low-temperature refrigeration applications, including the cooling of infrared detectors and of advanced electronic circuits and superconducting materials.

Helix's GUTS rapid-response, global customer support network ensures customers direct, 24-hour-a-day access to customer support resources.

In May 1998, HELX acquired, in exchange for 2.38 million common shares, Granville-Phillips Co., a Boulder, CO-based company that develops and manufactures instrumentation for vacuum measurement and control. Granville-Phillips had total sales in 1997 of $25.6 million.

Per Share Data ($) **(Year Ended Dec. 31)**	**1998**	**1997**	**1996**	**1995**	**1994**	**1993**	**1992**	**1991**	**1990**	**1989**
Tangible Bk. Val.	2.84	3.38	3.04	2.63	1.77	1.31	1.15	1.08	1.01	1.06
Cash Flow	0.09	1.23	1.26	1.18	0.64	0.35	0.24	0.25	0.14	0.22
Earnings	-0.09	1.07	1.10	1.05	0.54	0.26	0.15	0.16	0.06	0.13
Dividends	0.75	0.73	0.65	0.29	0.14	0.10	0.10	0.10	0.10	0.09
Payout Ratio	NM	68%	59%	27%	26%	67%	63%	58%	158%	67%
Prices - High	25 1/8	33 3/8	21 1/2	27 7/8	9 1/2	4 3/8	3 7/8	2 3/4	1 13/16	2 7/16
- Low	6 3/4	14 1/8	11 5/8	7 3/8	3 3/8	2 1/8	1 7/8	15/16	7/8	1 9/16
P/E Ratio - High	NM	31	19	27	18	17	26	17	30	18
- Low	NM	13	11	7	6	8	12	6	15	11
Income Statement Analysis (Million $)										
Revs.	95.0	132	128	124	86.8	63.9	50.8	55.8	52.4	54.6
Oper. Inc.	5.3	32.4	34.9	34.4	17.7	9.0	5.8	6.1	3.5	5.3
Depr.	4.0	3.2	3.2	2.6	2.0	1.8	1.7	1.6	1.7	1.7
Int. Exp.	Nil	Nil	Nil	Nil	Nil	0.1	0.2	0.3	0.6	0.5
Pretax Inc.	-2.6	32.5	34.4	33.7	16.4	7.4	4.1	4.8	1.9	4.1
Eff. Tax Rate	NM	34%	36%	38%	36%	34%	30%	36%	36%	35%
Net Inc.	-1.9	21.3	22.0	21.0	10.6	4.9	2.9	3.1	1.2	2.7
Balance Sheet & Other Fin. Data (Million $)										
Cash	8.8	33.4	29.4	21.7	8.1	1.7	1.6	1.2	2.2	1.3
Curr. Assets	57.9	65.3	57.5	55.4	32.9	21.0	20.5	19.6	22.0	22.3
Total Assets	75.7	81.7	71.8	69.1	45.4	32.7	32.0	29.1	30.7	31.1
Curr. Liab.	12.3	14.6	11.9	17.1	10.4	7.0	9.4	7.8	10.8	8.9
LT Debt	Nil	Nil	Nil	Nil	0.0	0.1	0.1	0.2	0.2	0.4
Common Eqty.	63.3	67.0	59.8	51.6	34.3	25.0	21.8	20.5	19.1	21.1
Total Cap.	63.3	67.0	59.8	51.9	34.9	25.7	22.6	21.3	19.9	22.3
Cap. Exp.	2.6	4.5	3.3	3.0	2.2	1.7	3.4	1.8	1.1	1.4
Cash Flow	2.1	24.5	25.2	23.6	12.7	6.7	4.6	4.7	2.9	4.3
Curr. Ratio	4.7	4.5	4.8	3.2	3.1	3.0	2.2	2.5	2.0	2.5
% LT Debt of Cap.	Nil	Nil	NM	NM	0.1	0.3	0.5	0.8	1.0	1.7
% Net Inc.of Revs.	NM	16.2	17.1	17.0	12.2	7.7	5.6	5.5	2.3	4.9
% Ret. on Assets	NM	27.8	31.2	36.7	27.0	15.2	9.4	10.3	3.9	8.6
% Ret. on Equity	NM	33.6	39.4	48.9	25.5	20.9	13.6	15.6	6.0	13.0

Data as orig reptd.; bef. results of disc opers/spec. items. Per share data adj. for stk. divs. Bold denotes diluted EPS (FASB 128)-prior periods restated. E-Estimated. NA-Not Available. NM-Not Meaningful. NR-Not Ranked.

Office—Mansfield Corporate Center, 9 Hampshire St., Mansfield, MA 02048-9171. **Tel**—(508) 337-5500. **Chrmn**—M. G. Schorr. **Pres & CEO**—R. J. Lepofsky. **SVP & CFO**—M. El-Hillow. **Treas**—L. G. Greenberg. **Secy & Investor Contact**—Beverly L. Armell. **Dirs**—A. R. Buckland, M. O. Diggs, Jr., F. Gabron, R. J. Lepofsky, M.G. Schorr, W. Skinner, M. S. Wrighton. **Transfer Agent & Registrar**—BankBoston, N.A. **Incorporated**—in Delaware in 1967. **Empl**— 457. **S&P Analyst:** T. W. Smith, CFA

STANDARD
&POOR'S
STOCK REPORTS

Henry (Jack) & Associates

NASDAQ Symbol **JKHY**

In S&P SmallCap 600

09-OCT-99

Industry:
Computer (Software & Services)

Summary: This company provides integrated computer systems for in-house data processing, as well as ATM networking products, to banks and other financial institutions.

Quantitative Evaluations

Outlook
(1 Lowest—5 Highest)
• **4-**

Fair Value
• **56½**

Risk
• **Average**

Earn./Div. Rank
• **A-**

Technical Eval.
• **Bearish** since 8/99

Rel. Strength Rank
(1 Lowest—99 Highest)
• **84**

Insider Activity
• **NA**

Recent Price • 39⅝
52 Wk Range • 55-26⅜
Yield • 0.8%
12-Mo. P/E • 26.4

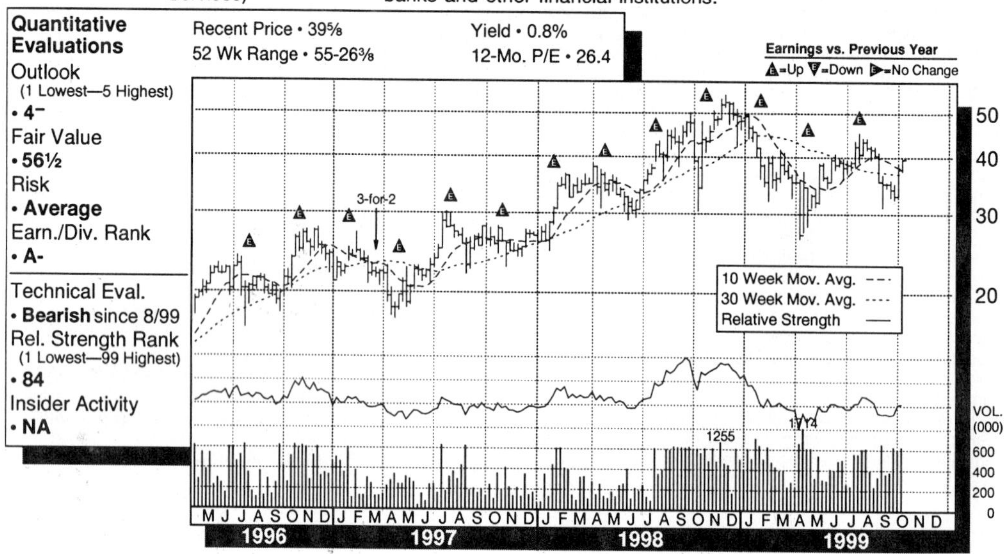

Business Profile - 23-JUL-99

The company, one of the largest providers of computer systems that perform data processing for banks and other financial institutions, believes it compares favorably with competitors with regard to comprehensiveness of applications, features and functions, flexibility and ease of use, customer support, references of existing customers, hardware preferences and pricing. In July 1999, JKHY agreed to acquire the community banking and data center operations of BancTec, Inc., for about $50 million in cash, plus the assumption of certain liabilities. In December 1998, the company acquired Peerless Group for $40 million in stock. In November 1998, JKHY purchased Digital Data Services, for $2.75 million in cash.

Operational Review - 23-JUL-99

Based on a preliminary report, revenues advanced 30% in FY 99 (Jun.) from those of FY 98, as restated, on 10% higher software licensing and installation revenues, a 53% rise in maintenance/support and service revenues, and 27% growth in hardware sales and commissions. Gross margins narrowed to 46.1% of revenues, from 47.2%. With well controlled operating expenses, despite $2 million in transaction costs related to the Peerless Group acquisition, income from continuing operations climbed 36%, to $32,526,000 ($1.54 a share, on 2.6% more shares), from $23,950,000 ($1.16). Results exclude losses from discontinued operations of $0.04 and $0.03 a share in the respective years.

Stock Performance - 08-OCT-99

In the past 30 trading days, JKHY's shares have increased 12%, compared to a 0.91% fall in the S&P 500. Average trading volume for the past five days was 171,260 shares, compared with the 40-day moving average of 123,159 shares.

Key Stock Statistics

Dividend Rate/Share	0.32	Shareholders	7,262
Shs. outstg. (M)	20.1	Market cap. (B)	$0.796
Avg. daily vol. (M)	0.135	Inst. holdings	38%
Tang. Bk. Value/Share	3.07		
Beta	0.33		

Value of $10,000 invested 5 years ago: $ 54,516

Fiscal Year Ending Jun. 30

	1999	1998	1997	1996	1995	1994
Revenues (Million $)						
1Q	40.73	20.06	18.35	16.15	9.65	9.22
2Q	47.33	27.38	21.35	16.52	11.41	10.14
3Q	43.55	27.25	22.06	16.56	10.41	8.85
4Q	42.09	38.73	20.84	18.33	14.66	10.18
Yr.	184.5	113.4	82.60	67.56	46.12	38.39
Earnings Per Share ($)						
1Q	**0.41**	0.23	0.20	0.17	0.10	0.08
2Q	**0.34**	**0.26**	0.20	0.15	0.11	0.09
3Q	**0.37**	**0.27**	0.20	0.15	0.10	0.07
4Q	**0.40**	**0.37**	0.23	0.19	0.13	0.10
Yr.	**1.50**	**1.13**	**0.83**	0.65	0.44	0.35

Next earnings report expected: mid October

Dividend Data (Dividends have been paid since 1990.)

Amount ($)	Date Decl.	Ex-Div. Date	Stock of Record	Payment Date
0.065	Oct. 29	Nov. 17	Nov. 19	Dec. 10 '98
0.080	Feb. 01	Feb. 12	Feb. 17	Mar. 10 '99
0.080	Apr. 28	May. 03	May. 05	May. 20 '99
0.080	Aug. 25	Sep. 02	Sep. 07	Sep. 23 '99

A Division of The McGraw-Hill Companies

Jack Henry & Associates, Inc.

Business Summary - 23-JUL-99

Jack Henry & Associates (JKHY), founded in 1976 by John W. Henry (currently vice chairman), and headed since October 1994 by his son Michael E. Henry, is a computer software company that has developed several banking software systems. Revenues are earned by marketing these systems, together with the computer equipment (hardware), to financial institutions nationwide, and by providing conversion and software customization services necessary for a financial institution to install a JKHY software system. The company also provides continuing support and maintenance services to customers using the system.

Software licensing and intallation accounted for 26% of total revenues in FY 99 (Jun.), versus 30% in FY 98; 37% of revenues came from maintenance, support and services (32%), and the remaining 37% came from hardware sales (38%).

Software includes development and licensing of applications software and conversion, installation and customization services. Maintenance/support consists of ongoing services to operate the systems and to modify and update software. Hardware relates to the sale of computer equipment and maintenance.

The company's primary systems are CIF 20/20 and Silverlake. Each has several fully integrated applications software modules that can interface with peripherals used in banks. CIF 20/20 is designed for community banks, savings banks and thrifts with up to $300 million in assets and runs on IBM AS/400 and IBM System 36 computers. Silverlake is aimed at larger banks, with assets of $100 million to $10 billion, and is designed to take advantage of the relational database capabilities of the IBM System 38 and AS/400.

JKHY licenses its systems under agreements that provide the customer with a fully paid, nontransferable right to use the software for 25 years on one computer at one location.

The company also provides outsourcing solutions to customers including data and item processing; offers automated teller machine software; provides regional and national switching services for various electronic fund transactions; and offers emergency facilities backup to its CIF 20/20 and Silverlake System customers through six strategic locations.

JKHY's primary market is commercial banks. The company has some savings and loan and savings bank customers, but most of them operate more like a commercial bank than a traditional thrift institution. Most of the company's sales efforts and success has been with banks that have from $2 million to $2 billion in total assets.

Per Share Data ($) (Year Ended Jun. 30)	1999	1998	1997	1996	1995	1994	1993	1992	1991	1990
Tangible Bk. Val.	NA	3.07	2.02	1.16	0.67	1.17	0.90	0.66	0.47	0.40
Cash Flow	NA	1.38	1.04	0.85	0.55	0.45	0.39	0.31	0.21	0.13
Earnings	1.50	1.13	0.83	0.65	0.44	0.35	0.30	0.24	0.14	0.06
Dividends	0.33	0.24	0.20	0.17	0.14	0.12	0.13	0.09	0.10	Nil
Payout Ratio	22%	21%	24%	26%	33%	36%	41%	38%	71%	Nil
Prices - High	50 1/8	55	30 1/4	27	17	7 7/8	8 1/2	6 1/2	2 1/2	13/16
- Low	26 3/8	24 3/4	17 1/2	13 5/8	5 7/8	4 3/8	5 1/8	2 5/16	7/16	5/16
P/E Ratio - High	33	49	36	41	39	23	28	27	19	13
- Low	18	22	21	21	13	13	17	10	3	6
Income Statement Analysis (Million $)										
Revs.	NA	113	82.6	67.6	46.1	38.4	32.6	23.5	20.7	15.2
Oper. Inc.	NA	38.9	28.3	22.8	14.0	10.7	8.8	6.1	4.3	2.6
Depr.	NA	5.1	4.1	3.6	2.0	1.8	1.5	1.2	1.2	1.2
Int. Exp.	NA	Nil	Nil	Nil	Nil	0.0	0.0	Nil	0.0	0.0
Pretax Inc.	NA	35.4	25.1	19.9	12.6	9.8	7.9	6.1	3.5	1.6
Eff. Tax Rate	NA	37%	37%	38%	37%	36%	33%	36%	38%	40%
Net Inc.	NA	22.2	15.8	12.3	8.0	6.3	5.3	3.9	2.2	0.9
Balance Sheet & Other Fin. Data (Million $)										
Cash	NA	23.3	13.9	8.1	8.0	11.7	9.4	8.8	5.7	2.7
Curr. Assets	NA	69.1	42.7	28.1	27.4	25.2	19.4	15.6	11.6	7.1
Total Assets	NA	115	82.1	60.4	58.7	38.3	29.9	22.1	17.6	14.4
Curr. Liab.	NA	39.3	27.2	21.3	28.1	14.0	12.0	9.4	8.2	5.1
LT Debt	NA	Nil	Nil	Nil	Nil	Nil	Nil	Nil	Nil	0.1
Common Eqty.	NA	73.5	52.8	37.4	29.4	23.7	17.6	12.4	9.2	8.5
Total Cap.	NA	76.0	54.8	39.2	30.5	24.3	17.9	12.7	9.5	9.3
Cap. Exp.	NA	7.8	10.3	5.0	2.6	2.4	3.7	0.6	0.2	0.7
Cash Flow	NA	27.3	19.8	15.8	10.0	8.1	6.8	5.1	3.4	2.1
Curr. Ratio	NA	1.8	1.6	1.3	1.0	1.8	1.6	1.7	1.4	1.4
% LT Debt of Cap.	NA	Nil	Nil	Nil	Nil	Nil	Nil	Nil	Nil	1.6
% Net Inc.of Revs.	NA	19.6	19.1	18.2	17.3	16.3	16.2	16.5	10.5	6.2
% Ret. on Assets	NA	22.5	22.1	20.6	16.4	18.3	20.0	19.3	13.6	7.0
% Ret. on Equity	NA	35.2	34.9	36.7	30.1	30.3	34.7	35.6	24.6	10.7

Data as orig reptd.; bef. results of disc opers/spec. items. Per share data adj. for stk. divs. Bold denotes diluted EPS (FASB 128)-prior periods restated. E-Estimated. NA-Not Available. NM-Not Meaningful. NR-Not Ranked.

Office—663 West Highway 60, P.O. Box 807, Monett, MO 65708. **Tel**—(417) 235-6652. **Fax**—(417) 235-4281. **Website**—http://www.jackhenry.com **Chrmn & CEO**—M. E. Henry. **Vice Chrmn & SVP**—J. W. Henry. **Pres & COO**—M. R. Wallace. **VP, CFO, Treas & Investor Contact**—Terry W. Thompson. **Dirs**—G. R. Curry, J. J. Ellis, B. O. George, J. D. Hall, J. W. Henry, M. E. Henry, M. R. Wallace. **Transfer Agent & Registrar**—UMB Bank, N.A., Kansas City. **Incorporated**—in Missouri in 1977; reincorporated in Delaware in 1985. **Empl**— 982. **S&P Analyst:** Jim Corridore

STANDARD & POOR'S STOCK REPORTS

Hilb, Rogal and Hamilton

NYSE Symbol **HRH**

In S&P SmallCap 600

09-OCT-99

Industry: Insurance Brokers

Summary: This company is ranked the seventh largest insurance agency in the U.S.

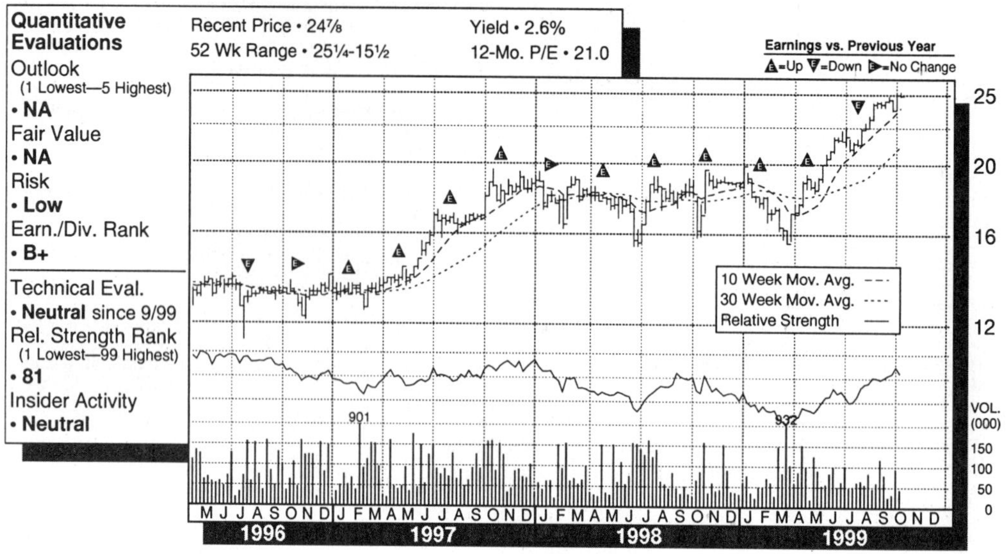

Business Profile - 16-JUL-99

Hilb, Rogal and Hamilton has been implementing a strategy of strengthening its relationships with its largest insurance carriers. The company believes that its reinforced regional organizations and intensified focus on specialty lines have enhanced its capabilities as an independent distributor to small and mid-sized corporations. In June 1999, the company acquired Phoenix Home Life Mutual Insurance Co., the fourteenth largest property and casualty insurance brokerage firm in the U.S., with revenues of $73 million in 1998. The purchase price consisted of $49.2 million in cash, a total of 1,000,000 common shares and $32 million of 5.25% convertible subordinated notes due 2014. HRH expected the acquisition to improve its middle market distribution capabilities.

Operational Review - 16-JUL-99

Total revenues in the three months ended March 31, 1999, advanced 6.3%, year to year, as a steep rise in other income reflecting gains on sales of insurance accounts and other assets outweighed reduced commission and fee revenues as a result of the sales and due to changes in the amount and timing of payments from selected carriers. Total costs and expenses increased only 1.3%, and pretax income climbed 25%. After taxes at 40.7%, versus 41.0%, net income also rose 25%, to $7.5 million ($0.60 a share, on 5% fewer shares), from $5.9 million ($0.46).

Stock Performance - 08-OCT-99

In the past 30 trading days, HRH's shares have increased 2%, compared to a 0.91% fall in the S&P 500. Average trading volume for the past five days was 8,560 shares, compared with the 40-day moving average of 12,541 shares.

Key Stock Statistics

Dividend Rate/Share	0.66	Shareholders	610
Shs. outstg. (M)	13.1	Market cap. (B)	$0.327
Avg. daily vol. (M)	0.010	Inst. holdings	73%
Tang. Bk. Value/Share	NM		
Beta	0.31		

Value of $10,000 invested 5 years ago: $ 24,350

Fiscal Year Ending Dec. 31

	1999	1998	1997	1996	1995	1994
Revenues (Million $)						
1Q	50.25	48.70	47.91	43.07	39.46	39.33
2Q	54.89	45.92	44.32	37.94	36.57	35.19
3Q	—	44.00	41.85	38.31	36.39	34.13
4Q	—	42.43	39.62	38.92	35.72	32.16
Yr.	—	181.1	173.7	158.2	148.2	140.8
Earnings Per Share ($)						
1Q	**0.60**	**0.46**	**0.40**	**0.38**	0.33	0.32
2Q	**0.23**	**0.35**	**0.27**	**0.20**	0.23	0.20
3Q	—	**0.25**	**0.19**	**0.17**	0.17	0.17
4Q	—	**0.12**	**0.10**	**0.10**	0.09	0.09
Yr.	—	**1.18**	**0.97**	**0.84**	**0.82**	**0.77**

Next earnings report expected: mid October

Dividend Data (Dividends have been paid since 1987.)

Amount ($)	Date Decl.	Ex-Div. Date	Stock of Record	Payment Date
0.160	Nov. 09	Dec. 11	Dec. 15	Dec. 31 '98
0.160	Feb. 02	Mar. 15	Mar. 17	Mar. 31 '99
0.165	Jun. 08	Jun. 14	Jun. 16	Jun. 30 '99
0.165	Aug. 03	Sep. 14	Sep. 16	Sep. 30 '99

A Division of The McGraw-Hill Companies

Hilb, Rogal and Hamilton Company

Business Summary - 16-JUL-99

In June 1999, HRH acquired Phoenix Home Life Mutual Insurance Co., the fourteenth largest property and casualty insurance brokerage firm in the U.S. Hilb, Rogal and Hamilton's growth has been aided by a merger and acquisition strategy which has added more than 170 independent agencies since the company's founding in 1982. The company has consolidated the majority of its dozens of decentralized independent agencies into six regional operating units. Each unit developed its own strategic plan, suited to the local marketplace environment, and designed to coordinate and objectify all sales and service activities.

By creating these regional operating units, HRH believes it has been able to better respond to the needs of clients and deal more effectively with trading partners. Additionally, the company has been able to streamline operations by merging multiple agency locations in the same city into a single profit center and converting smaller locations into sales offices of a larger profit center in the same region. HRH completed the divestiture of its Canadian operations near the end of 1998's fourth quarter.

HRH primarily places insurance, such as property, casualty, marine, aviation and employee benefits, with insurance carriers and underwriters on behalf of its clients. Although the company's client base ranges from personal to large national accounts, it primarily targets medium-size commercial and industrial accounts. Revenues derived from the sale of insurance products to clients, typically coming in the form of commissions paid by insurance carriers with which clients' insurance is placed, accounted for 90% of total revenues in 1998.

HRH also advises clients on risk management and employee benefits and provides claims administration and loss control consulting services to clients, which contributed about 7% of revenues in 1998. Investment and other income, including the sale of certain insurance accounts and other assets, made up the remaining 3% of sales in 1998.

In the foreign arena, HRH has been able to establish direct access to certain overseas insurance markets without the need to share commissions with excess and surplus lines brokers. This direct access has allowed the company to enhance revenues from insurance products written by foreign insurers and provide a broader array of insurance products to clients.

While HRH's acquisition strategy has slowed, it has not stopped altogether. In 1998, the company acquired a total of six agencies, each deemed a fit into the new regional infrastructure. More acquisitions are expected, though they will be less frequent and more selective than in the past.

Per Share Data ($) **(Year Ended Dec. 31)**	**1998**	**1997**	**1996**	**1995**	**1994**	**1993**	**1992**	**1991**	**1990**	**1989**
Tangible Bk. Val.	NM	NM	NM	NM	1.21	1.05	NM	NM	NM	NM
Cash Flow	2.08	1.85	1.65	1.49	1.40	1.29	1.48	1.37	1.40	1.55
Earnings	1.18	0.97	0.85	0.82	0.77	0.61	0.71	0.57	0.65	0.76
Dividends	0.64	0.62	0.60	0.57	0.50	0.45	0.41	0.37	0.30	0.19
Payout Ratio	54%	64%	71%	70%	65%	74%	58%	65%	47%	25%
Prices - High	19⅞	19⅝	14	14⅜	13⅜	16⅞	15⅝	17½	19	20⅝
- Low	15⅜	12½	11⅜	10½	11	11⅜	11	11¼	11¼	10¾
P/E Ratio - High	17	20	16	18	17	28	22	31	29	27
- Low	13	13	13	13	14	19	15	20	17	14
Income Statement Analysis (Million $)										
Revs.	181	174	158	148	141	135	126	115	97.0	78.0
Oper. Inc.	39.2	43.7	31.1	29.9	29.4	24.4	24.5	21.2	19.4	17.8
Depr.	11.5	11.7	3.3	2.8	9.3	9.5	9.2	8.8	7.2	6.0
Int. Exp.	2.3	2.0	1.3	0.6	0.8	1.2	1.7	2.1	2.7	2.4
Pretax Inc.	25.4	21.8	19.0	19.6	18.8	13.2	13.1	9.6	8.8	8.5
Eff. Tax Rate	41%	42%	40%	40%	39%	36%	36%	35%	31%	32%
Net Inc.	14.9	12.8	11.4	11.8	11.4	8.4	8.4	6.2	6.1	5.8
Balance Sheet & Other Fin. Data (Million $)										
Cash	19.4	26.2	24.9	28.1	35.7	12.1	26.6	23.2	23.7	24.4
Curr. Assets	78.2	76.8	76.3	78.6	84.9	81.1	76.9	72.2	73.5	66.0
Total Assets	188	182	182	163	159	156	139	132	133	113
Curr. Liab.	88.5	88.3	89.1	87.3	87.1	81.9	85.2	77.5	79.0	63.8
LT Debt	43.7	32.5	27.2	11.8	3.2	7.0	13.0	14.7	18.1	22.3
Common Eqty.	45.7	51.3	55.3	56.6	66.4	64.3	38.8	37.1	33.7	25.6
Total Cap.	89.4	83.8	84.5	68.4	69.6	71.3	53.8	51.8	51.8	48.5
Cap. Exp.	5.0	2.1	5.0	4.0	2.2	3.0	2.4	2.2	2.9	6.7
Cash Flow	26.5	24.5	22.3	21.6	20.7	17.9	17.6	15.0	13.3	11.8
Curr. Ratio	0.9	0.9	0.9	0.9	1.0	1.0	0.9	0.9	0.9	1.0
% LT Debt of Cap.	48.9	38.8	32.1	17.3	4.6	9.9	24.2	28.4	34.9	46.1
% Net Inc.of Revs.	8.3	7.4	7.2	8.0	8.1	6.2	6.7	5.4	6.3	7.4
% Ret. on Assets	8.1	7.0	6.6	7.3	7.1	5.5	5.9	4.4	4.4	4.9
% Ret. on Equity	30.8	24.0	20.4	19.2	17.4	16.5	21.2	16.5	18.5	21.8

Data as orig reptd.; bef. results of disc opers/spec. items. Per share data adj. for stk. divs. Bold denotes diluted EPS (FASB 128)-prior periods restated. E-Estimated. NA-Not Available. NM-Not Meaningful. NR-Not Ranked.

Office—4235 Innslake Drive, P. O. Box 1220, Glen Allen, VA 23060-1220. **Tel**—(804) 747-6500. **Fax**—(804) 747-6046. **Website**—http://www.hrh.com **Chrmn**—R. H. Hilb. **Pres & CEO**—A. L. Rogal. **SVP, CFO, Treas & Investor Contact**—Carolyn Jones. **EVP-Fin**—T. J. Korman. **VP-Secy**—W. L. Smith. **Dirs**—T. L. Chandler, Jr., N. H. Davis, Jr., P. J. Faccenda, R. W. Fiondella, J. S. M. French, R. H. Hilb, T. J. Korman, A. F. Markel, T. H. O'Brien, A. L. Rogal, D. W. Searfoss, R. S. Ukrop, M. L. Vaughan. **Transfer Agent & Registrar**—ChaseMellon Shareholder Services, Ridgefield Park, NJ. **Incorporated**—in Virginia in 1982. **Empl**— 1,610. **S&P Analyst:** S.A.H.

STANDARD & POOR'S

STOCK REPORTS

HNC Software

NASDAQ Symbol **HNCS**

In S&P SmallCap 600

09-OCT-99

Industry: Computer (Software & Services)

Summary: HNCS develops, markets and supports advanced decision software based on computational intelligence.

Quantitative Evaluations

Outlook (1 Lowest—5 Highest) • **5+**

Fair Value • **65¾**

Risk • **High**

Earn./Div. Rank • **NR**

Technical Eval. • **Bullish** since 5/99

Rel. Strength Rank (1 Lowest—99 Highest) • **88**

Insider Activity • **Neutral**

Recent Price • 40⅜ | Yield • Nil

52 Wk Range • 41½-13¾ | 12-Mo. P/E • 82.4

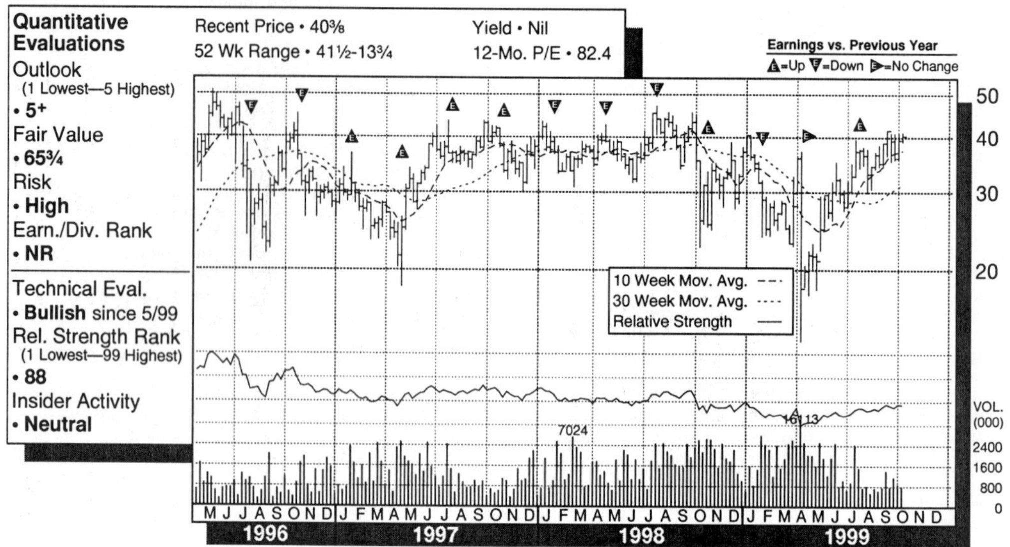

Business Profile - 05-AUG-99

HNCS seeks to: obtain recurring revenues through long-term contracts; broaden its product line into new applications and markets, such as medical payments, Internet commerce and database marketing; leverage its database to provide complete industry-specific modeling solutions; expand its worldwide distribution; and commit resources to maintain technology leadership in developed solutions. In July 1999, eHNC (HNC's e-commerce division) and QPass (in which HNCS acquired a minority interest in March 1999) announced PowerWallet, a service that fills in any form on the Internet, manages on-line receipts and manages site-specific user names, secure passwords and other shopping preferences.

Operational Review - 05-AUG-99

For the six months ended June 30, 1999, revenues advanced 34%, year to year, reflecting gains in both license and maintenance revenues, and services and other revenues. Gross margins narrowed, hurt by higher staffing and associated costs in client services to support increased volume in the retail solutions segment, and despite the absence of $6.8 million in acquisition related costs, pretax income was up 16%. After taxes at 45.1%, versus 66.3%, net income rose 89%, to $5,469,000 ($0.21 a share, on 2.8% fewer shares), from $2,895,000 ($0.11).

Stock Performance - 08-OCT-99

In the past 30 trading days, HNCS's shares have increased 16%, compared to a 0.91% fall in the S&P 500. Average trading volume for the past five days was 153,440 shares, compared with the 40-day moving average of 178,372 shares.

Key Stock Statistics

Dividend Rate/Share	Nil	Shareholders	230
Shs. outstg. (M)	24.2	Market cap. (B)	$0.976
Avg. daily vol. (M)	0.175	Inst. holdings	93%
Tang. Bk. Value/Share	3.79		
Beta	NA		

Value of $10,000 invested 5 years ago: NA

Fiscal Year Ending Dec. 31

	1999	1998	1997	1996	1995	1994
Revenues (Million $)						
1Q	49.19	35.08	24.07	9.90	5.09	—
2Q	55.93	43.14	27.59	12.56	5.92	—
3Q	—	47.75	29.99	14.60	6.91	—
4Q	—	52.64	32.08	16.78	7.25	—
Yr.	—	178.6	113.7	53.83	25.17	16.47
Earnings Per Share ($)						
1Q	**0.08**	**0.08**	**0.17**	-0.04	0.03	—
2Q	**0.13**	**-0.50**	**0.20**	0.02	0.04	—
3Q	—	**0.24**	**0.21**	0.07	0.18	—
4Q	—	**0.09**	**0.13**	0.26	0.06	—
Yr.	—	**0.39**	**0.68**	**0.47**	**0.28**	**0.17**

Next earnings report expected: NA

Dividend Data

No cash dividends have been paid. A two-for-one stock split was effected in April 1996.

A Division of The McGraw-Hill Companies

HNC Software Inc.

Business Summary - 05-AUG-99

HNC Software Inc.'s objective is to be the leading supplier of predictive software solutions by leveraging its computational intelligence technology across a series of product families targeted at specific service industries. The company's strategy for achieving this objective contains the following key elements: maintaining and strengthening its position at the core of its customers' applications infrastructure; leveraging its predictive technologies to enter new market segments; earning recurring revenues through long-term contracts; using strategic relationships to support direct distribution; and growing via acquisitions.

HNCS enables customers to optimize revenues and profits, cut costs, and provide protection against business risk and fraud by offering intelligent software solutions for decision applications in real-time environments. It also performs contract research and development using neural networks and other computational intelligence models.

In 1998 and 1997, HNCS derived nearly all of its revenues from three business segments: the Financial Solutions Group, (32% and 31%, respectively), the Retail Solutions Group, (32% and 27%) and the Insurance Solutions Group (29% and 34%).

The Financial Solutions Group caters to the financial service industry, and HNCS's products are used to detect, predict and prevent credit card fraud, and manage credit card portfolios and automate the selection of new customers.

The company's Retail Solutions Group serves the retail industry, with products used in inventory control, merchandise management and financial control management. The target market for these products are department stores, mass merchandisers and specialty retail chains in multi-store and multi-warehouse environments with gross sales in excess of $200 million.

HNCS's Insurance Solutions Group offers products used to address the containment of the medical costs of workers' compensation and automobile accident insurance claims, workers' compensation loss reserving, workers' compensation fraud, managed care effectiveness and provider effectiveness.

In March 1998, HNCS acquired Practical Control Systems, a supplier of fully integrated distribution center management software, for some $5.4 million in common stock. In April 1998, the company acquired Financial Technology Inc., a provider of profitability measurement and decision-support software to the financial services industry, for some $15.2 million in common stock and $1.5 million in cash. In June 1998, HNCS acquired the Advanced Telecommunications Abuse Control Systems product line, a fraud-management software solution for wireline, wireless and Internet telecommunication service providers for $4.75 million in cash. In December 1998, HNCS acquired the minority interest in Aptex Software Inc. that it did not already own for $5.3 million. Aptex develops, markets and supports electronic text analysis technology.

Per Share Data ($) (Year Ended Dec. 31)	1998	1997	1996	1995	1994	1993	1992	1991	1990	1989
Tangible Bk. Val.	4.94	4.23	4.31	3.28	NM	NA	NA	NA	NA	NA
Cash Flow	0.92	0.87	0.48	0.39	0.18	NA	NA	NA	NA	NA
Earnings	0.39	0.68	0.31	0.31	0.16	NA	NA	NA	NA	NA
Dividends	Nil	Nil	Nil	Nil	Nil	NA	NA	NA	NA	NA
Payout Ratio	Nil	Nil	Nil	Nil	Nil	NA	NA	NA	NA	NA
Prices - High	47 1/8	43 5/8	51	24 1/2	NA	NA	NA	NA	NA	NA
- Low	22 1/2	18 1/4	18 1/4	7	NA	NA	NA	NA	NA	NA
P/E Ratio - High	NM	64	NM	79	NA	NA	NA	NA	NA	NA
- Low	NM	27	NM	23	NA	NA	NA	NA	NA	NA
Income Statement Analysis (Million $)										
Revs.	179	114	53.8	25.2	16.5	NA	NA	NA	NA	NA
Oper. Inc.	35.1	27.9	7.5	4.2	1.7	NA	NA	NA	NA	NA
Depr.	14.0	4.8	3.3	1.1	0.3	NA	NA	NA	NA	NA
Int. Exp.	4.5	0.1	0.5	0.0	0.1	NA	NA	NA	NA	NA
Pretax Inc.	23.3	25.0	0.1	3.9	1.5	NA	NA	NA	NA	NA
Eff. Tax Rate	55%	29%	NM	15%	31%	NA	NA	NA	NA	NA
Net Inc.	10.5	17.6	6.3	4.5	1.9	NA	NA	NA	NA	NA
Balance Sheet & Other Fin. Data (Million $)										
Cash	54.3	18.1	14.9	34.5	6.0	NA	NA	NA	NA	NA
Curr. Assets	169	90.0	42.6	42.0	10.0	NA	NA	NA	NA	NA
Total Assets	284	120	94.2	53.4	12.2	NA	NA	NA	NA	NA
Curr. Liab.	29.9	15.7	11.1	5.2	2.6	NA	NA	NA	NA	NA
LT Debt	100	Nil	Nil	Nil	0.4	NA	NA	NA	NA	NA
Common Eqty.	153	104	82.4	48.3	-4.0	NA	NA	NA	NA	NA
Total Cap.	253	104	82.4	48.3	9.6	NA	NA	NA	NA	NA
Cap. Exp.	8.1	9.6	3.9	1.8	1.4	NA	NA	NA	NA	NA
Cash Flow	24.5	22.4	9.7	5.6	2.2	NA	NA	NA	NA	NA
Curr. Ratio	5.7	5.7	3.8	8.1	3.8	NA	NA	NA	NA	NA
% LT Debt of Cap.	39.5	Nil	Nil	Nil	4.2	NA	NA	NA	NA	NA
% Net Inc.of Revs.	5.9	15.4	11.8	17.7	11.7	NA	NA	NA	NA	NA
% Ret. on Assets	5.2	16.4	8.3	13.6	22.6	NA	NA	NA	NA	NA
% Ret. on Equity	8.1	18.9	9.8	10.1	NM	NA	NA	NA	NA	NA

Data as orig reptd.; bef. results of disc opers/spec. items. Per share data adj. for stk. divs. Bold denotes diluted EPS (FASB 128)-prior periods restated. E-Estimated. NA-Not Available. NM-Not Meaningful. NR-Not Ranked.

Office—5930 Cornerstone Court West, San Diego, CA 92121. **Tel**—(619) 546-8877. **Website**—http://www.hnc.com. **Pres & CEO**—R. L. North. **VP-Fin, CFO & Secy**—R. V. Thomas. **Dirs**—E. K. Chandler, T. F. Farb, C. H. Gaylord, Jr., A W. Hart, R. L. North. **Transfer Agent & Registrar**—First National Bank of Boston. **Incorporated**—in Delaware in 1995. **Empl**— 910. **S&P Analyst:** Scott H. Kessler

STANDARD & POOR'S STOCK REPORTS

Hollywood Park

NYSE Symbol **HPK**

In S&P SmallCap 600

09-OCT-99 **Industry:** Gaming, Lottery & Pari-mutuel Cos.

Summary: Hollywood Park is a leading diversified gaming, sports and entertainment holding company.

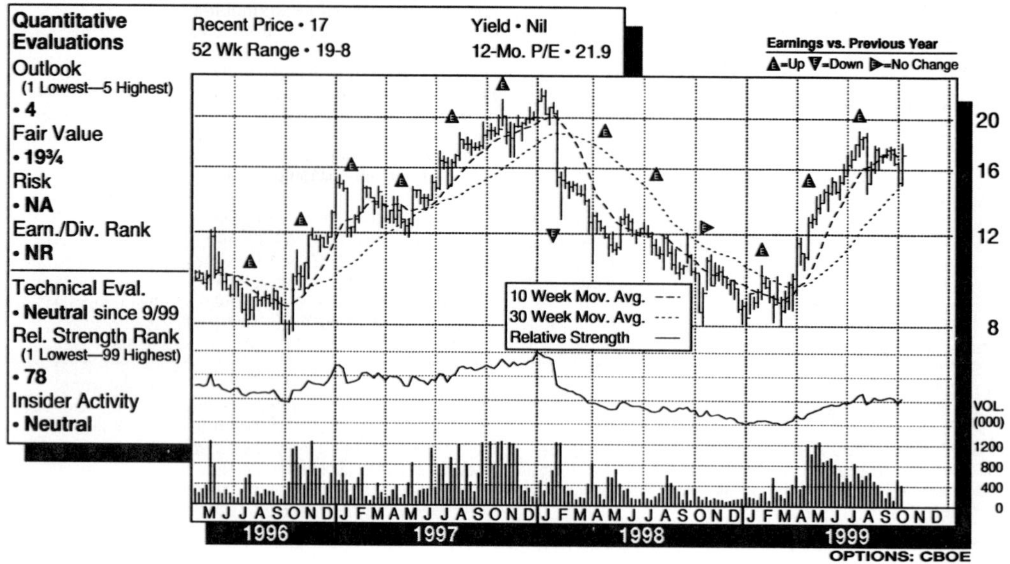

Business Profile - 31-AUG-99

As of early August 1999, HPK owned and operated eight casinos, owned two card club casinos in California, owned and operated two pari-mutuel race tracks, and had total assets in excess of $1 billion. In July 1999, HPK exercised an option to purchase 225 acres in Lake Charles, LA, in connection with the 15th and final gaming license the Louisiana Gaming Control Board has indicated it will accept applications for. The company intends to propose a project similar in scope and size to its recently commenced Switzerland County, Indiana, project. The acquisition of the company's Hollywood Park Race Track and Hollywood Park-Casino by Churchill Downs, Inc. (Nasdaq: CHDN) is on target to close August 31, 1999. Under terms of the deal, Churchill Downs will acquire the racetrack, related real estate, and the Hollywood Park casino for $140 million in cash.

Operational Review - 31-AUG-99

Revenues in the six months ended June 30, 1999, more than doubled, year to year, boosted chiefly by the October 1998 purchase of Casino Magic. Total expenses grew at a slower rate than revenues, and operating income soared to $55.0 million, from $19.3 million. After sharply higher interest expense, and taxes at 41.9%, versus 40.3%, net income soared 101%, to $13,844,000 ($0.54 a share, on 3.5% fewer shares), from $6,895,000 ($0.26).

Stock Performance - 08-OCT-99

In the past 30 trading days, HPK's shares have increased 0.36%, compared to a 0.91% fall in the S&P 500. Average trading volume for the past five days was 83,940 shares, compared with the 40-day moving average of 70,331 shares.

Key Stock Statistics

Dividend Rate/Share	Nil	Shareholders	3,600
Shs. outstg. (M)	26.1	Market cap. (B)	$0.445
Avg. daily vol. (M)	0.067	Inst. holdings	51%
Tang. Bk. Value/Share	3.48		
Beta	0.68		

Value of $10,000 invested 5 years ago: $ 5,687

Fiscal Year Ending Dec. 31

	1999	1998	1997	1996	1995	1994
Revenues (Million $)						
1Q	172.0	78.16	26.82	27.85	24.46	12.91
2Q	199.5	103.1	46.32	46.43	42.83	35.98
3Q	—	87.47	85.21	30.25	26.59	30.10
4Q	—	158.2	89.78	38.70	36.69	38.34
Yr.	—	408.0	236.0	143.2	130.6	117.3
Earnings Per Share ($)						
1Q	**0.16**	**-0.05**	-0.07	-0.74	-0.06	-0.10
2Q	**0.37**	**0.31**	0.28	0.26	0.24	0.24
3Q	—	**0.08**	0.08	0.01	-0.33	-0.16
4Q	—	**0.17**	**0.05**	0.15	-0.01	0.12
Yr.	—	**0.50**	**0.32**	**-0.33**	**-0.17**	0.10

Next earnings report expected: early November

Dividend Data

The most recent cash dividend on the common stock was paid in 1992. The company does not anticipate paying cash dividends on its common stock in the near future.

Hollywood Park, Inc.

Business Summary - 31-AUG-99

Hollywood Park, Inc. (HPK), the successor to the Hollywood Park Turf Club, organized in 1938, is a diversified gaming company that owns and/or operates eight casinos, two pari-mutuel horse racing facilities, and two card club casinos at locations in Nevada, Mississippi, Louisiana, California, Arizona and Argentina. In October 1998, HPK acquired Casino Magic Corp. (Nasdaq: CMAG) for cash and assumed debt with an aggregate value of $340 million. CMAG operated gaming casinos in Bay Saint Louis and Biloxi, MS, Bossier City, LA, and Neuquen City and San Martin de los Andes, Argentina.

The company's strategic plan is to develop a broad base of regionally diversified casino entertainment facilities by making selected acquisitions in the non-Las Vegas, non-Atlantic City gaming markets and achieving economies of scale. In pursuit of this strategy, it acquired Boomtown in June 1997, and Casino Magic in October 1998. Management seeks to develop its casinos and maximize profitability by refinancing expensive debt; fostering customer loyalty by offering a value oriented, quality customer service gaming experience; providing gaming and entertainment facilities uniquely designed for each property and targeted customer base; and using focused direct marketing incentives.

In September 1998, the Indiana Gaming Commission awarded HPK the last remaining riverboat gaming license for the Ohio River. Construction and development of HPK's Indiana Casino and Hotel Resort is progressing on schedule. Groundbreaking for the hotel/resort casino, located on the banks of the Ohio River and named Belterra Resort and Casino, occurred on July 14, 1999. The Switzerland County, Indiana, development will consist of a cruising riverboat containing over 1,800 gaming positions, a 300 plus room hotel, several restaurants, retail areas, a 1,000-seat entertainment facility, structured parking and a complete spa facility, as well as a championship golf course. The project is scheduled to open in late summer 2000.

The acquisition of the company's Hollywood Park Race Track and Hollywood Park-Casino by Churchill Downs, Inc. (Nasdaq: CHDN) is on target to close August 31, 1999. In the deal, announced in April 1999, Churchill Downs will acquire the racetrack, related real estate and the Hollywood Park casino for $140 million in cash. HPK will lease back the casino and sub-lease it to an unaffiliated third-party operator. HPK will retain 138 acres of land. The company recently announced that 42 of the 138 acres will be sold for about $13 per sq. ft. in a transaction scheduled to close in late 1999 or early 2000.

Per Share Data ($) (Year Ended Dec. 31)	1998	1997	1996	1995	1994	1993	1992	1991	1990	1989
Tangible Bk. Val.	3.48	7.18	7.50	7.48	8.79	8.65	NA	NA	NA	NA
Cash Flow	1.73	1.13	0.24	0.45	0.63	0.73	0.72	NA	NA	NA
Earnings	0.50	0.33	-0.33	-0.17	0.10	0.30	0.27	NA	NA	NA
Dividends	Nil	Nil	Nil	Nil	Nil	Nil	0.04	NA	NA	NA
Payout Ratio	Nil	Nil	Nil	Nil	Nil	Nil	15%	NA	NA	NA
Prices - High	22 5/8	22 3/4	15 1/2	15	30 3/4	35	11 7/8	NA	NA	NA
- Low	8	11 3/4	7 1/2	9	9 1/4	8 5/8	5 5/8	NA	NA	NA
P/E Ratio - High	45	69	NM	NM	NM	117	44	NA	NA	NA
- Low	16	36	NM	NM	NM	29	21	NA	NA	NA
Income Statement Analysis (Million $)										
Revs.	408	236	136	123	111	75.0	78.0	NA	NA	NA
Oper. Inc.	60.3	27.8	15.0	13.8	14.6	12.0	14.4	NA	NA	NA
Depr.	32.1	18.2	10.7	11.4	9.6	6.4	5.9	NA	NA	NA
Int. Exp.	22.5	7.3	0.9	3.9	3.1	1.5	4.9	NA	NA	NA
Pretax Inc.	22.0	14.5	-0.8	-0.5	5.3	7.4	6.7	NA	NA	NA
Eff. Tax Rate	38%	40%	NM	NM	29%	14%	47%	NA	NA	NA
Net Inc.	13.2	8.7	-4.2	-1.2	3.8	6.4	3.5	NA	NA	NA
Balance Sheet & Other Fin. Data (Million $)										
Cash	44.2	24.2	21.2	32.0	37.8	80.6	NA	NA	NA	NA
Curr. Assets	100	60.2	41.0	48.6	66.0	87.7	NA	NA	NA	NA
Total Assets	891	419	206	287	247	176	NA	NA	NA	NA
Curr. Liab.	125	57.3	35.3	75.2	26.1	17.7	NA	NA	NA	NA
LT Debt	528	132	0.3	15.6	42.8	0.3	NA	NA	NA	NA
Common Eqty.	231	221	158	166	167	154	NA	NA	NA	NA
Total Cap.	763	361	171	195	221	164	NA	NA	NA	NA
Cap. Exp.	NA	32.5	23.8	NA	27.6	12.9	5.3	NA	NA	NA
Cash Flow	45.3	25.3	4.5	8.3	11.4	11.3	9.4	NA	NA	NA
Curr. Ratio	0.8	1.1	1.2	0.6	2.5	5.0	NA	NA	NA	NA
% LT Debt of Cap.	69.2	36.6	0.2	8.0	19.4	0.2	NA	NA	NA	NA
% Net Inc.of Revs.	3.2	3.7	NM	NM	3.4	8.5	4.5	NA	NA	NA
% Ret. on Assets	2.0	2.8	NM	NM	1.8	4.8	NA	NA	NA	NA
% Ret. on Equity	5.8	3.8	NM	NM	2.4	7.8	NA	NA	NA	NA

Data as orig reptd.; bef. results of disc opers/spec. items. Per share data adj. for stk. divs. Bold denotes diluted EPS (FASB 128)-prior periods restated. E-Estimated. NA-Not Available. NM-Not Meaningful. NR-Not Ranked.

Office—1050 South Prairie Ave., Inglewood, CA 90301. **Tel**—(310) 419-1500. **Website**—http://www.hollywoodpark.com **Chrmn & CEO**—R. D. Hubbard. **Pres & COO**—P. Alanis. **EVP, CFO & Treas**—G. M. Finnigan. **Dirs**—R. D. Hubbard, J. R. Johnson, R. T. Manfuso, M. Ornest, T. J. Parrott, L. P. Reitnouer, H. Sarkowsky, M. F. Torguson, W. B. Williamson. **Transfer Agent & Registrar**—ChaseMellon Shareholder Services, NYC.**Incorporated**—in Delaware in 1981. **Empl**— 9,000. **S&P Analyst:** M.I.

STANDARD
&POOR'S
STOCK REPORTS

Hologic, Inc.

NASDAQ Symbol **HOLX**

In S&P SmallCap 600

09-OCT-99

Industry:
Health Care (Medical Products & Supplies)

Summary: This company makes and distributes proprietary X-ray bone densitometer systems to diagnose and monitor osteoporosis and other metabolic bone diseases.

Quantitative Evaluations

Outlook
(1 Lowest—5 Highest)
• **NA**

Fair Value
• **NA**

Risk
• **High**

Earn./Div. Rank
• **B-**

Technical Eval.
• **Bearish** since 6/99

Rel. Strength Rank
(1 Lowest—99 Highest)
• **12**

Insider Activity
• **NA**

Recent Price • 4

52 Wk Range • 16⅜-3⅝

Yield • Nil

12-Mo. P/E • 80.0

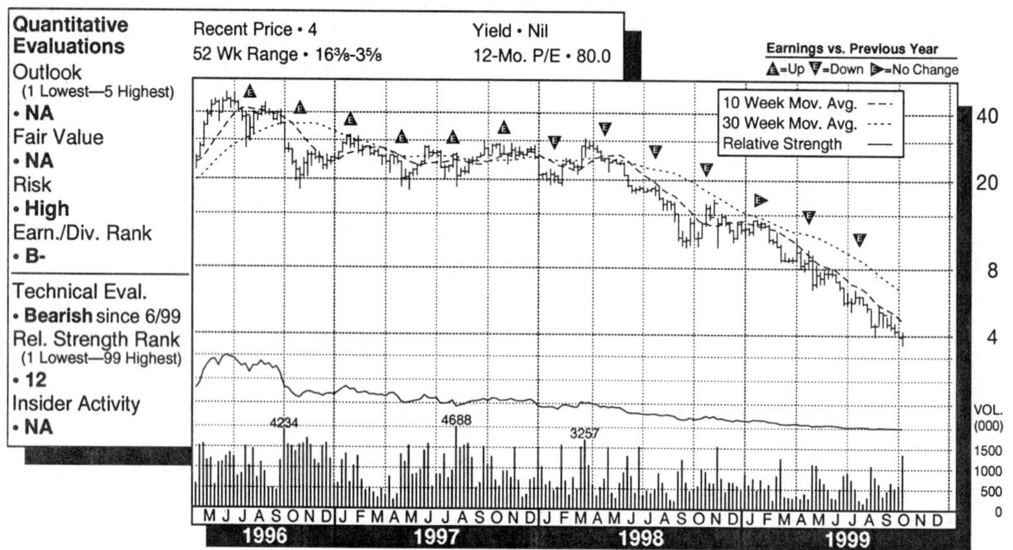

Business Profile - 26-JUL-99

Domestic sales in the first half of FY 99 (Sep.) were lower, year to year, due to slower than expected sales of bone densitometers in the primary care segment of the market. The company's efforts to accelerate sales to office based physicians include increasing the involvement of its direct sales people who have experience in the bone densitometry field. In light of its second quarter results, HOLX implemented a cost reduction strategy, including a 10% work force reduction though attrition and corporate down-sizing. In June 1999, the company acquired Direct Radiography Corp., for $7 million in cash and about 1.9 million common shares. Direct Radiography is a manufacturer of digital X-ray systems for medical imaging and non-destructive testing applications.

Operational Review - 26-JUL-99

Total revenues in the six months ended March 27, 1999, fell 22%, year to year, as lower DXA bone densitometer sales outweighed increased mini C-arm sales and higher sales of the Sahara ultrasound bone sonometer. Gross margins narrowed, on the lower volume and lower product selling prices; despite a 14% drop in costs and expenses, operating income plunged 86%, to $802,000, from $5.7 million. After taxes at 35.4%, versus 36.1%, net income was down 80%, to $949,000 ($0.07 a share), from $4.8 million ($0.35).

Stock Performance - 08-OCT-99

In the past 30 trading days, HOLX's shares have declined 22%, compared to a 0.91% fall in the S&P 500. Average trading volume for the past five days was 269,920 shares, compared with the 40-day moving average of 136,410 shares.

Key Stock Statistics

Dividend Rate/Share	Nil	Shareholders	386
Shs. outstg. (M)	13.4	Market cap. (B)	$0.054
Avg. daily vol. (M)	0.156	Inst. holdings	60%
Tang. Bk. Value/Share	10.07		
Beta	0.86		

Value of $10,000 invested 5 years ago: $ 18,285

Fiscal Year Ending Sep. 30

	1999	1998	1997	1996	1995	1994
Revenues (Million $)						
1Q	24.63	26.12	27.11	14.76	10.20	7.65
2Q	19.36	30.20	28.00	18.76	9.03	9.91
3Q	20.00	34.43	26.95	22.83	11.30	10.95
4Q	—	24.82	24.63	24.37	12.87	9.98
Yr.	—	115.6	106.7	91.59	43.40	38.48
Earnings Per Share ($)						
1Q	**0.15**	**0.15**	0.32	0.14	0.08	0.05
2Q	**-0.08**	**0.20**	0.34	0.27	0.02	0.10
3Q	**-0.11**	**0.31**	0.35	0.32	0.06	0.14
4Q	—	**0.09**	0.29	0.15	0.07	0.06
Yr.	—	**0.75**	**1.30**	0.91	0.21	0.35

Next earnings report expected: early November

Dividend Data

No cash dividends have been paid, and HOLX does not expect to pay any in the foreseeable future. A poison pill stock purchase rights plan was adopted in 1992.

A Division of The McGraw-Hill Companies

Hologic, Inc.

Business Summary - 26-JUL-99

Hologic Inc., the pioneer of the dual energy X-ray densitometer (DXA), develops, makes and markets proprietary X-ray systems. With more than 5,100 installations worldwide, the company's Quantitative Digital Radiography (QDR) and ultrasound bone densitometers are used for precise measurement of bone density to assist in diagnosing and monitoring osteoporosis and other metabolic bone diseases. Since its introduction, the DXA system has become the standard in measuring bone density.

In March 1998, HOLX became the first U.S. company to receive FDA approval for its Sahara Clinical Bone Sonometer, an ultrasound bone sonometer that estimates bone density of the heel. The Sahara aides physicians in diagnosing osteoporosis and estimating the risk of future fractures.

Osteoporosis, characterized by decreased bone density and increased risk of fractures, occurs mainly in older women. The National Osteoporosis Foundation estimates that osteoporosis afflicts more than 25 million people in the U.S., and a much larger number worldwide. Prior to 1995, there were only two drug treatments for osteoporosis in the U.S.: hormone replacement therapy and calcitonin. However, these were not proven to restore bone mass. In September 1995, the FDA approved Merck's Fosamax drug to treat established osteoporosis in post-menopausal women; Fosamax can restore bone mass.

In August 1997, the Medicare Bone Mass Measurement Coverage Standardization Act was approved, requiring Medicare to cover bone density diagnostic tests, effective July 1998. With the establishment of U.S. reimbursement levels, and FDA approval of additional osteoporosis drug therapies, HOLX believes the U.S. market for bone densitometers and other methods of bone mineral assessment will expand to the larger potential market of primary care providers.

The QDR 4500 ACCLAIM series has replaced the company's QDR 1500, QDR 2000 and QDR 2000-plus products. The ACCLAIM series integrates HOLX's most advanced technology into a compact package that facilitates installation in a standard examination room. An important feature of the QDR 4500A and QDR 4500SL is the ability to perform lateral scans of the lower spine without turning patients on their sides, in addition to posterior-anterior measurements.

In FY 98 (Sep.), 72% of product sales were generated in the U.S., 18% in Europe, 4% in Asia, and 6% in other international markets.

HOLX entered the mini C-arm market in 1996, by acquiring FluoroScan Imaging Systems, Inc., a maker of mini C-arm imaging systems for minimally invasive surgery. FluoroScan's systems are primarily used by orthopedic surgeons to perform minimally invasive surgical procedures on extremities at a cost well below that of conventional X-ray and fluoroscopic equipment.

Per Share Data ($) (Year Ended Sep. 30)	1998	1997	1996	1995	1994	1993	1992	1991	1990	1989
Tangible Bk. Val.	10.53	9.67	8.33	2.75	2.47	2.06	2.32	2.15	2.04	-0.38
Cash Flow	0.89	1.39	0.98	0.28	0.43	-0.17	0.22	0.12	0.41	0.28
Earnings	0.75	1.30	0.92	0.21	0.35	-0.23	0.18	0.09	0.37	0.26
Dividends	Nil	Nil	Nil	Nil	Nil	Nil	Nil	Nil	Nil	Nil
Payout Ratio	Nil	Nil	Nil	Nil	Nil	Nil	Nil	Nil	Nil	Nil
Prices - High	30¾	31¾	49½	22¾	9⅛	3⅛	7⅛	6⅛	15½	NA
- Low	9⅞	17⅞	17¼	4½	2	1 11/16	2 3/16	2⅜	3⅝	NA
P/E Ratio - High	41	24	54	NM	26	NM	39	72	42	NA
- Low	13	14	19	NM	6	NM	12	28	10	NA
Income Statement Analysis (Million $)										
Revs.	116	107	91.6	43.4	38.5	24.8	26.2	17.1	19.8	11.4
Oper. Inc.	12.7	23.6	18.4	5.3	4.7	-0.6	1.6	1.7	3.4	2.0
Depr.	1.9	1.3	0.9	0.6	0.6	0.4	0.3	0.3	0.2	0.1
Int. Exp.	Nil	Nil	Nil	Nil	0.1	Nil	Nil	Nil	0.0	0.1
Pretax Inc.	16.2	27.6	17.1	2.5	4.3	-2.1	2.1	1.0	3.8	1.7
Eff. Tax Rate	36%	36%	33%	26%	31%	NM	30%	31%	30%	17%
Net Inc.	10.4	17.7	11.4	1.9	3.0	-1.8	1.5	0.7	2.6	1.4
Balance Sheet & Other Fin. Data (Million $)										
Cash	48.4	28.1	75.6	9.9	9.4	10.1	10.5	11.9	13.4	2.0
Curr. Assets	132	131	113	30.6	26.3	20.4	21.0	18.6	19.2	5.1
Total Assets	173	145	123	33.9	28.5	22.2	22.7	19.8	20.3	5.4
Curr. Liab.	32.2	17.9	15.8	11.2	8.6	5.8	4.6	3.1	4.6	2.7
LT Debt	Nil	Nil	Nil	Nil	Nil	Nil	Nil	Nil	Nil	1.0
Common Eqty.	140	127	107	22.7	19.9	16.3	18.1	16.7	15.7	-0.8
Total Cap.	140	127	107	22.7	19.9	16.3	18.1	16.7	15.7	2.7
Cap. Exp.	22.6	2.1	0.9	0.2	0.5	0.2	0.6	0.4	0.9	0.3
Cash Flow	12.2	19.0	12.3	2.4	3.6	-1.4	1.8	1.0	2.9	1.5
Curr. Ratio	4.1	7.3	7.2	2.7	3.1	3.5	4.6	5.9	4.1	1.9
% LT Debt of Cap.	NA	Nil	Nil	Nil	Nil	Nil	Nil	Nil	Nil	37.5
% Net Inc.of Revs.	9.0	16.6	12.4	4.5	7.8	NM	5.6	4.1	13.2	12.3
% Ret. on Assets	6.5	13.2	13.7	6.0	11.7	NM	6.9	3.5	13.4	36.3
% Ret. on Equity	7.8	15.2	16.5	8.8	16.4	NM	8.5	4.3	35.4	NM

Data as orig reptd.; bef. results of disc opers/spec. items. Per share data adj. for stk. divs. Bold denotes diluted EPS (FASB 128)-prior periods restated. E-Estimated. NA-Not Available. NM-Not Meaningful. NR-Not Ranked.

Office—590 Lincoln St., Waltham, MA 02154. **Tel**—(617) 890-2300. **Chrmn & CEO**—S. D. Ellenbogen. **Pres & COO**—S. L. Nakashige. **Secy**—L. M. Levy. **VP-Fin & Treas**—G. P. Muir. **Dirs**—S. D. Ellenbogen, I. Jacobs, S. L. Nakashige, W. A. Peck, G. Segel, J. A. Stein, E. Ullian. **Transfer Agent & Registrar**—American Stock Transfer & Trust Co., NYC. **Incorporated**—in Massachusetts in 1985; reincorporated in Delaware in 1990. **Empl**— 396. **S&P Analyst:** John J. Arege

STANDARD
&POOR'S
STOCK REPORTS

Hooper Holmes

ASE Symbol **HH**

In S&P SmallCap 600

09-OCT-99

Industry:
Health Care (Specialized Services)

Summary: This company provides medical and other underwriting information on insurance policy applicants to major health and insurance companies via 200 branch offices throughout the U.S.

Quantitative Evaluations

Outlook
(1 Lowest—5 Highest)
• **2**⁻

Fair Value
• **26¼**

Risk
• **Average**

Earn./Div. Rank
• **B+**

Technical Eval.
• **Neutral** since 9/99

Rel. Strength Rank
(1 Lowest—99 Highest)
• **92**

Insider Activity
• **Neutral**

Recent Price • 25¾
52 Wk Range • 26⅜-9½
Yield • 0.2%
12-Mo. P/E • 49.5

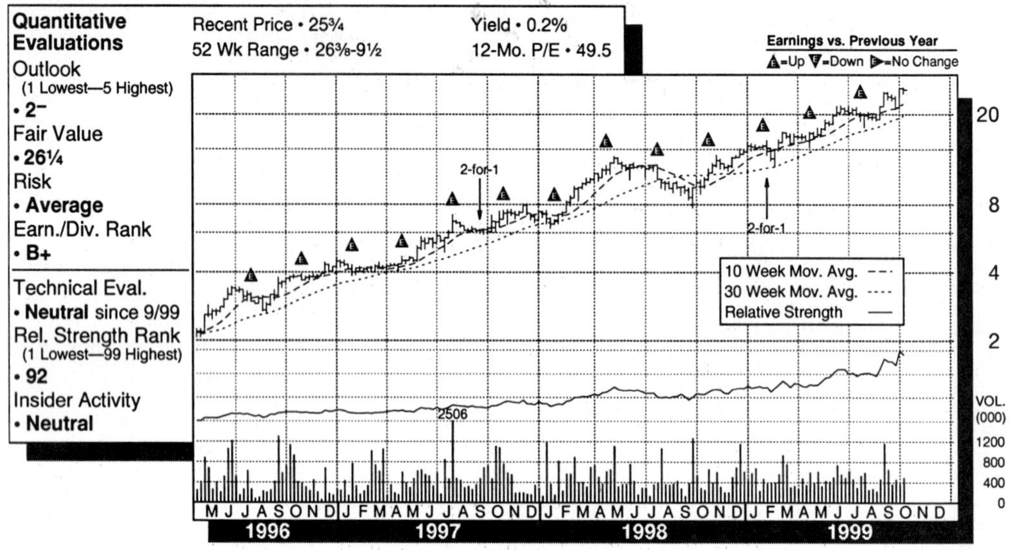

Business Profile - 14-SEP-99

In August 1999, HH agreed to acquire the assets of Paramedical Services of America, Inc. (PSA), the Atlanta-based paramedical examination subsidiary of Pediatric Services of America, Inc., for a price expected to range from $85 million to $95 million. The acquisition of PSA is in line with the company's strategy of expanding its existing capabilities of providing outsourced health information services for the life and health insurance industries on a nationwide basis. In the fiscal year ended September 30,1998, PSA generated revenue of about $90 million. The transaction, expected to close in late 1999, should be accretive to HH's earnings in 2000.

Operational Review - 14-SEP-99

Revenues in the six months ended June 30, 1999, rose 17%, year to year, reflecting a 7% increase in exams performed, as well as higher revenues per unit of service. Profitability improved, on wider gross margins and well controlled selling, general and administrative expenses; operating profit climbed 31%. After higher net interest income, and taxes at 44.9%, versus 46.7%, net income soared 45%, to $9,571,864 ($0.31 a share, on 2.5% more shares), from $6,578,642 ($0.22, as adjusted).

Stock Performance - 08-OCT-99

In the past 30 trading days, HH's shares have increased 18%, compared to a 0.91% fall in the S&P 500. Average trading volume for the past five days was 97,040 shares, compared with the 40-day moving average of 105,933 shares.

Key Stock Statistics

Dividend Rate/Share	0.05	Shareholders	833
Shs. outstg. (M)	28.8	Market cap. (B)	$0.742
Avg. daily vol. (M)	0.083	Inst. holdings	70%
Tang. Bk. Value/Share	1.87		
Beta	1.06		

Value of $10,000 invested 5 years ago: $ 92,397

Fiscal Year Ending Dec. 31

	1999	1998	1997	1996	1995	1994
Revenues (Million $)						
1Q	52.94	46.11	40.71	38.61	24.00	61.92
2Q	54.47	45.57	41.40	39.81	24.40	62.81
3Q	—	45.38	40.70	37.91	23.18	62.36
4Q	—	48.15	42.54	39.92	39.74	64.70
Yr.	—	185.2	165.3	156.3	111.3	251.8
Earnings Per Share ($)						
1Q	**0.16**	**0.11**	0.06	0.02	0.02	0.05
2Q	**0.16**	**0.12**	0.08	0.04	0.02	0.02
3Q	—	**0.12**	0.08	0.04	0.02	0.01
4Q	—	**0.14**	**0.10**	0.06	0.02	0.03
Yr.	—	**0.48**	**0.30**	**0.15**	**0.06**	0.10

Next earnings report expected: late October

Dividend Data (Dividends have been paid since 1974.)

Amount ($)	Date Decl.	Ex-Div. Date	Stock of Record	Payment Date
2-for-1	Dec. 23	Feb. 01	Jan. 08	Jan. 29 '99
0.013	Jan. 27	Feb. 10	Feb. 12	Feb. 26 '99
0.013	Apr. 23	May. 12	May. 14	May. 28 '99
0.013	Jul. 28	Aug. 11	Aug. 13	Aug. 27 '99

A Division of The McGraw-Hill Companies

Hooper Holmes, Inc.

Business Summary - 14-SEP-99

Hooper Holmes provides medical and other underwriting information on insurance policy applicants to the major companies in the health and life insurance industry, via more than 200 branch offices throughout the U.S. Contributions to revenues in 1998 were: Medical and Paramedical Examinations (92%) and Infolink Services Group (8%).

In 1998, the company performed more than 2.5 million medical and paramedical examinations for applicants seeking insurance coverage from life and health insurers. Since nearly all HH examiners are nurses and other medically trained professionals, the company can provide clients with a full range of medical and paramedical examination services, including sophisticated procedures requested by insurance underwriters, such as electrocardiograms, lung capacity measurements and blood sample collections (which are sent to independent laboratories for testing for AIDS and other life-threatening diseases). HH believes it is the leader in the $750 million industry, with a market share of about 27%. Services provided also include Infolink reports, which assist insurance underwriters in developing a more comprehensive profile of an insurance applicant, including information relating to an applicant's lifestyle, employment history and financial status. During 1998, the company provided more than 303,000 Infolink reports.

HH believes it is well positioned to continue to capitalize on favorable trends currently affecting the alternate site health information industry. Development of electronic exam technology via laptops has led to the introduction of its Teledex automated exam and application services. These services have been widely accepted as a solution to many clients' needs for accurate and timely health information.

The formation of partnerships in 1996 and 1997 with clients, using direct response to sell policies, show the result of the company's investment in technology over the past three years.

In December 1998, HH acquired a majority interest in Heritage Labs International, a provider of a wide range of laboratory testing services, primarily to insurance companies for the purpose of underwriting life and health insurance policies. It expected the acquisition to be modestly accretive to earnings in 1999.

In 1998, the company expanded its Portamedic/Infolink website, where customers can place an order, check the status of orders, and determine that the case is complete.

Per Share Data ($) (Year Ended Dec. 31)	1998	1997	1996	1995	1994	1993	1992	1991	1990	1989
Tangible Bk. Val.	1.39	0.93	0.46	0.22	0.78	0.68	1.33	1.27	0.59	0.65
Cash Flow	0.63	0.48	0.34	0.15	0.23	0.21	0.24	0.24	0.23	0.18
Earnings	0.48	0.30	0.15	0.06	0.10	0.14	0.18	0.17	0.16	0.14
Dividends	0.04	0.03	0.02	0.02	0.08	0.08	0.06	0.06	0.06	0.05
Payout Ratio	7%	8%	10%	24%	75%	56%	34%	45%	35%	36%
Prices - High	15¼	8⅛	4⅝	2¾	3¾	4½	4⅛	3¾	2⅜	1 13/16
- Low	6¼	3⅞	2	1⅝	1 7/16	2¼	2¾	2⅛	1 7/16	1⅜
P/E Ratio - High	32	26	30	43	37	34	23	21	15	13
- Low	13	13	13	26	14	17	15	12	9	10
Income Statement Analysis (Million $)										
Revs.	185	165	156	111	252	187	155	132	108	77.0
Oper. Inc.	30.3	21.4	13.7	6.5	10.6	8.9	9.9	8.6	7.0	4.6
Depr.	4.7	5.0	5.1	2.5	3.5	2.1	1.7	1.5	1.2	0.8
Int. Exp.	0.0	0.2	1.4	1.7	2.7	0.5	0.3	0.9	0.8	0.3
Pretax Inc.	26.3	16.9	7.9	3.0	5.1	6.4	8.5	6.3	5.3	4.2
Eff. Tax Rate	46%	48%	48%	45%	48%	44%	43%	44%	44%	40%
Net Inc.	14.2	8.8	4.1	1.7	2.7	3.6	4.9	3.6	3.0	2.5
Balance Sheet & Other Fin. Data (Million $)										
Cash	29.8	13.2	2.9	1.1	117	1.6	6.9	11.0	0.3	4.7
Curr. Assets	53.3	34.2	25.8	54.4	71.6	55.0	40.4	38.6	20.9	16.9
Total Assets	85.0	65.9	61.3	94.0	108	43.5	56.7	52.2	35.0	26.3
Curr. Liab.	19.8	13.8	14.0	29.6	15.5	17.6	9.3	7.9	6.2	6.1
LT Debt	Nil	Nil	5.3	26.3	46.3	30.0	3.0	3.1	10.0	3.3
Common Eqty.	62.3	48.5	37.7	33.1	46.5	45.9	44.4	41.2	18.8	17.0
Total Cap.	65.2	52.2	47.3	64.4	92.8	75.9	47.4	44.2	28.8	20.2
Cap. Exp.	1.8	1.4	1.1	0.9	1.3	1.1	1.6	1.1	1.0	0.8
Cash Flow	18.9	13.8	9.1	4.1	6.2	5.8	6.6	5.0	4.2	3.3
Curr. Ratio	2.7	2.5	1.9	1.8	4.6	3.1	4.3	4.9	3.3	2.8
% LT Debt of Cap.	Nil	Nil	11.2	40.8	49.9	39.5	6.3	7.0	34.6	16.1
% Net Inc.of Revs.	7.7	5.3	2.6	1.5	1.1	1.9	3.2	2.7	2.8	3.3
% Ret. on Assets	18.8	13.8	5.3	1.7	2.6	4.8	8.9	6.9	9.7	9.9
% Ret. on Equity	25.6	20.3	11.5	4.2	5.8	8.0	11.4	10.4	16.7	15.6

Data as orig reptd.; bef. results of disc opers/spec. items. Per share data adj. for stk. divs. Bold denotes diluted EPS (FASB 128)-prior periods restated. E-Estimated. NA-Not Available. NM-Not Meaningful. NR-Not Ranked.

Office—170 Mt. Airy Rd., Basking Ridge, NJ 07920. **Tel**—(908) 766-5000. **Website**—http://www.hooperholmes.com **Chrmn, Pres & CEO**—J. M. McNamee. **EVP & COO**—P. W. Kolacki. **SVP & Secy**—R. W. Jewett. **SVP, CFO, Treas & Investor Contact**—F. Lash. **Dirs**—B. A. Currier, Q. J. Kennedy, J. M. McNamee, J. E. Nolan, Jr., E. L. Rigolosi, K. R. Rossano, G. E. Wight. **Transfer Agent & Registrar**—First City Transfer Co., Iselin, NJ. **Incorporated**—in New York in 1906. **Empl**— 1,091. **S&P Analyst:** J.W.H.

STANDARD
&POOR'S
STOCK REPORTS

HS Resources

NYSE Symbol **HSE**

In S&P SmallCap 600

09-OCT-99

Industry:
Oil & Gas (Exploration & Production)

Summary: This independent oil and gas exploration and production company focuses on the DJ Basin and Gulf Coast regions.

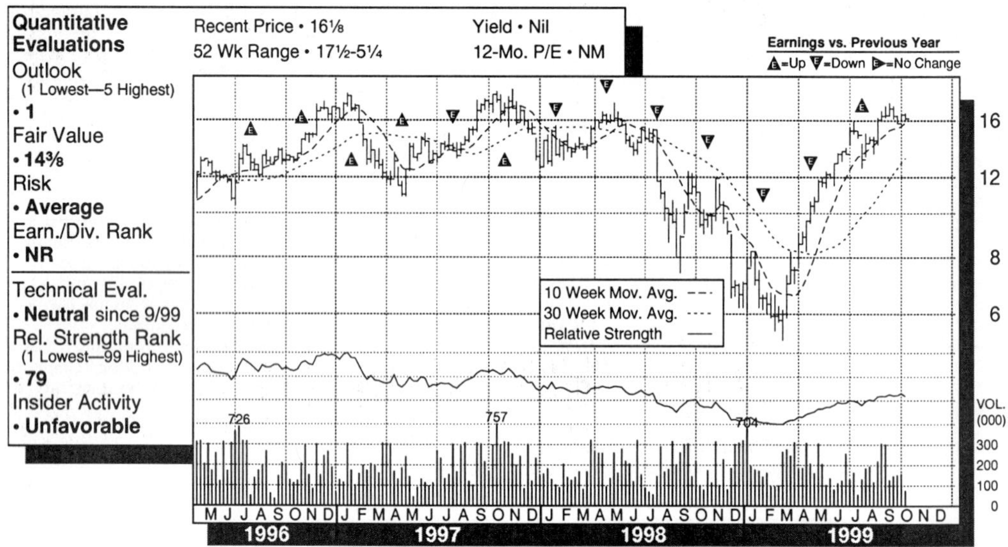

Business Profile - 27-SEP-99

Following HSE's December 1997 purchase of Amoco properties and September 1998 sale of its remaining Mid-Continent properties, this independent oil and gas exploration and production company's activities are concentrated primarily in the DJ Basin. In September 1999, HS Resources sold noncore properties in the DJ Basin; the transaction will result in a pretax gain of $3.4 million in the third quarter In addition, HSE exchanged certain properties in that region. The transactions are expected to generate operating efficiencies, cost savings and debt repayment. The company anticipates total 1999 capital spending of about $70 million, down from 1998's $118 million. In December 1998, directors authorized a $5 million stock repurchase program. Effective as of the 1998 fourth quarter, HSE adopted the more conservative successful efforts method of accounting, which led to significant downward revisions of net income and retained earnings.

Operational Review - 27-SEP-99

Revenues in the six months ended June 30, 1999, fell 14%, year to year, due to a 5% decline in production related to the Mid-Continent property sale, an 8% decrease in price realizations, and lower trading and transportation revenues. Total expenses decreased 14%, reflecting reduced per unit costs. Nevertheless, net income was down 73%, to $225,215 ($0.01 a share, diluted), from $823,857 ($0.04).

Stock Performance - 08-OCT-99

In the past 30 trading days, HSE's shares have declined 1%, compared to a 0.91% fall in the S&P 500. Average trading volume for the past five days was 14,660 shares, compared with the 40-day moving average of 38,933 shares.

Key Stock Statistics

Dividend Rate/Share	Nil	Shareholders	422
Shs. outstg. (M)	18.8	Market cap. (B)	$0.304
Avg. daily vol. (M)	0.026	Inst. holdings	54%
Tang. Bk. Value/Share	7.92		
Beta	1.18		

Value of $10,000 invested 5 years ago: $ 7,708

Fiscal Year Ending Dec. 31

	1999	1998	1997	1996	1995	1994
Revenues (Million $)						
1Q	48.07	63.77	70.16	14.19	15.75	14.09
2Q	51.33	52.20	55.16	26.83	14.84	15.01
3Q	—	49.29	54.37	47.74	11.98	15.79
4Q	—	48.94	67.47	68.20	12.77	15.51
Yr.	—	214.2	233.7	157.0	55.34	60.40
Earnings Per Share ($)						
1Q	**0.01**	**0.22**	0.25	0.02	0.06	0.15
2Q	**0.01**	**-0.16**	0.07	0.14	0.02	0.14
3Q	—	**-0.44**	0.09	0.08	-0.03	0.14
4Q	—	**-0.61**	**0.24**	0.37	-0.01	0.11
Yr.	—	**-1.00**	**0.64**	**0.61**	**0.02**	**0.53**

Next earnings report expected: early November

Dividend Data

Dividends have never been paid on the common stock. The company does not intend to declare cash dividends on its common stock for the foreseeable future and will retain earnings to support the growth of its business.

A Division of The McGraw-Hill Companies

HS Resources, Inc.

Business Summary - 27-SEP-99

HS Resources is an independent energy company that acquires, develops, exploits, explores for, produces and markets oil and natural gas. The December 1997 purchase of Amoco's properties in the Denver-Julesberg (DJ) Basin culminated the company's efforts to consolidate properties in that region. HSE pursued a consolidation strategy in that region in order to realize operating efficiencies from contiguous properties. The company paid $290 million in cash, issued 1.2 million common shares to Amoco, and transferred to Amoco certain Mid-Continent properties. Following the September 1998 sale of most remaining Mid-Continent properties for $157.5 million, HSE operates in three core areas: the DJ Basin, the Gulf Coast, and the Northern Rockies.

In addition to consolidation, HSE pursues several other strategies in an effort to maximize shareholder value. First, the company plans to increase production and reserves through the exploitation of existing wells via methods such as recompletions, as well as the drilling of new wells. Second, it will continue with an aggressive exploration program of high-potential prospects. Third, by investing in technology, primarily 3-D seismic data, HSE reduces exploratory risk, thereby enhancing economic results.

HS operates more than 40% of the production from the DJ Basin, which is equivalent to about 25% of the gas consumed annually in Colorado. The company operates nearly 3,000 wells, and owns 813,000 acres of mineral rights in that area.

At December 31, 1998 (1997), estimated proved reserves totaled 37,443.7 (45,358.1) MBbls. of oil and 797,048.8 (879,854.1) MMcf of natural gas. The standardized measure of discounted future net cash flows was $435.9 ($629.5) million. The company owned interests in 592,386 gross (457,226 net) developed acres and 919,869 gross (589,732 net) undeveloped acres. During 1998 (1997), HSE drilled 59.4 (70.6) net development wells, 59.4 (65.3) of which were productive. Net exploratory wells drilled totaled 14.4 (23.9), of which 7.3 (14.2) were productive. At year-end 1998, the company had interests in 2,891 gross (2,717.8 net) operated wells and 494 gross (115.8 net) non-operated wells.

Production in 1998 (1997) totaled 72,750 (55,524) million cubic feet of gas equivalent (MMcfe). Natural gas accounted for 78% (74%) of production. Average price realizations were $14.48 ($19.71) per bbl and $1.96 ($2.19) per Mcf of natural gas. Lease operating expenses averaged $0.42 ($0.45) per Mcfe of gas. The DJ Basin accounted for more than 97% of 1998 production and year-end reserves.

In December 1998, HSE sold $85 million of senior subordinated notes, extending the average maturity of its debt structure to better match the long-lived nature of the Amoco properties.

Per Share Data ($) (Year Ended Dec. 31)	1998	1997	1996	1995	1994	1993	1992	1991	1990	1989
Tangible Bk. Val.	7.92	12.04	11.26	10.92	10.94	10.38	8.31	10.30	NA	NA
Cash Flow	2.29	3.67	3.51	2.35	2.68	2.34	2.00	1.35	NA	NA
Earnings	-1.00	0.64	0.61	0.02	0.53	0.93	0.69	0.16	NA	NA
Dividends	Nil	Nil	Nil	Nil	Nil	Nil	Nil	Nil	NA	NA
Payout Ratio	Nil	Nil	Nil	Nil	Nil	Nil	Nil	Nil	NA	NA
Prices - High	17½	18¾	17⅝	17½	24¾	29	14¾	NA	NA	NA
- Low	6⅛	10⅞	9¼	12⅝	17⅛	13¾	12¾	NA	NA	NA
P/E Ratio - High	NM	29	29	NM	47	31	21	NA	NA	NA
- Low	NM	17	15	NM	32	15	18	NA	NA	NA
Income Statement Analysis (Million $)										
Revs.	214	234	157	55.2	60.2	47.3	27.4	12.8	NA	NA
Oper. Inc.	73.1	103	79.7	37.1	42.5	34.5	20.2	8.0	NA	NA
Depr. Depl. & Amort.	61.2	53.2	42.3	26.6	25.1	15.3	8.8	4.4	NA	NA
Int. Exp.	42.0	31.2	26.2	12.2	9.4	3.7	5.5	4.7	NA	NA
Pretax Inc.	-30.1	18.3	14.5	12.2	10.1	16.2	7.6	1.0	NA	NA
Eff. Tax Rate	NM	38%	38%	39%	38%	38%	38%	40%	NA	NA
Net Inc.	-18.6	11.3	8.9	0.3	6.3	10.1	4.7	0.6	NA	NA
Balance Sheet & Other Fin. Data (Million $)										
Cash	10.3	6.9	9.3	0.1	0.7	21.1	7.1	7.4	NA	NA
Curr. Assets	60.3	54.7	59.8	11.2	13.4	32.4	12.3	11.3	NA	NA
Total Assets	832	1,035	731	302	269	228	120	83.0	NA	NA
Curr. Liab.	79.2	63.7	46.1	27.2	15.8	16.2	8.7	9.0	NA	NA
LT Debt	535	637	400	126	103	74.4	20.6	36.3	NA	NA
Common Eqty.	153	224	193	119	119	113	79.0	28.0	NA	NA
Total Cap.	732	951	678	269	246	207	109	73.0	NA	NA
Cap. Exp.	0.9	1.9	182	62.9	86.0	100	45.0	19.0	NA	NA
Cash Flow	42.6	64.6	51.2	26.9	31.3	25.4	13.5	5.0	NA	NA
Curr. Ratio	0.8	0.9	1.3	40.8	0.8	2.0	1.4	1.3	NA	NA
% LT Debt of Cap.	73.1	66.9	59.0	46.8	42.0	35.9	18.9	50.0	NA	NA
% Ret. on Assets	NM	1.3	1.7	0.2	2.5	5.5	2.3	NA	NA	NA
% Ret. on Equity	NM	5.4	5.7	0.2	5.4	9.9	5.3	NA	NA	NA

Data as orig reptd.; bef. results of disc opers/spec. items. Per share data adj. for stk. divs. Bold denotes diluted EPS (FASB 128)-prior periods restated. E-Estimated. NA-Not Available. NM-Not Meaningful. NR-Not Ranked.

Office—One Maritime Plaza, 15th Fl., San Francisco CA 94111. **Tel**—(415) 433-5795. **Website**—http://www.hsresources.com **Chrmn & CEO**—N. J. Sutton. **Pres**—P. M. Highum. **VP-Fin & CFO**—J. E. Duffy. **VP & Secy**—J. M. Piccone. **Investor Contact**—Theodore Gazulis. **Dirs**—J. E. Duffy, K. A. Hersh, P. M. Highum, M. J. Savage, P. B. Smith, N. J. Sutton. **Transfer Agent & Registrar**—Harris Trust Co. of California, LA. **Incorporated**—in Delaware in 1987. **Empl**— 275. **S&P Analyst:** Ephraim Juskowicz

STANDARD &POOR'S
STOCK REPORTS

Hudson United Bancorp

NYSE Symbol **HU**

In S&P SmallCap 600

09-OCT-99

Industry: Banks (Regional)

Summary: This bank holding company, with operations in New Jersey, New York and Connecticut, agreed in September 1999 to merge with Dime Bancorp, Inc., a New York-based thrift.

Quantitative Evaluations

Outlook
(1 Lowest—5 Highest)
• **2+**

Fair Value
• **31⅛**

Risk
• **Low**

Earn./Div. Rank
• **B+**

Technical Eval.
• **Bearish** since 9/99

Rel. Strength Rank
(1 Lowest—99 Highest)
• **50**

Insider Activity
• **NA**

Recent Price • 30⅛
52 Wk Range • 36⅜-21½
Yield • 3.3%
12-Mo. P/E • 22.5

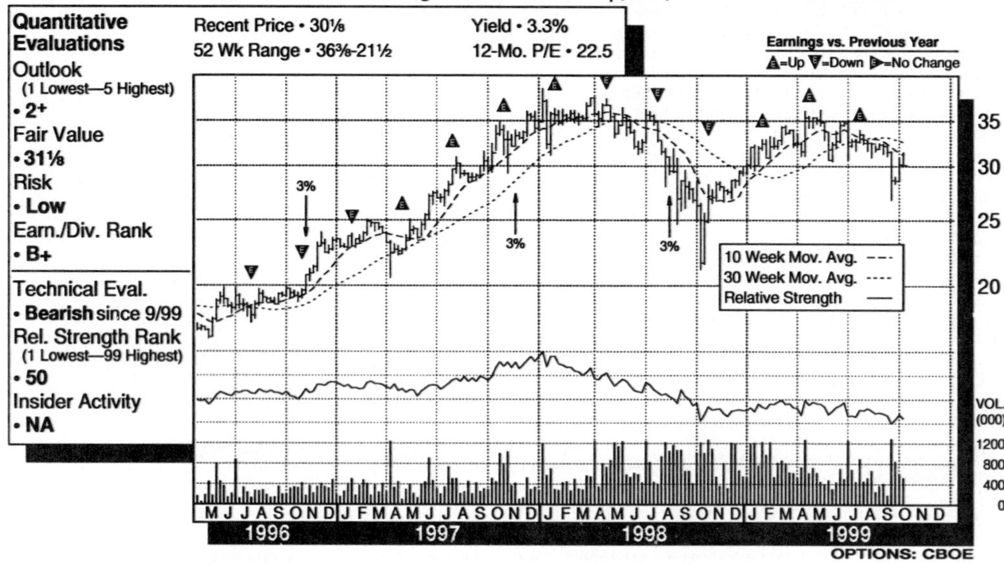

OPTIONS: CBOE

Business Profile - 20-SEP-99

In September 1999, Hudson agreed to merge with Dime Bancorp, Inc. (NYSE: DME), the parent company of the largest thrift on the East Coast. The agreement calls for Hudson shareholders to receive one share of the new Dime United Bancorp, Inc. for each share of HU held. The companies expect to incur a $136 million charge upon completion of the merger. The combined company is expected to have assets of more than $32 billion, operating through over 330 branches in New York, New Jersey, Connecticut and Pennsylvania. Also in September, HU purchased for an undisclosed amount Lyon Credit Corp., the U.S. commercial finance unit of the French bank Credit Lyonnais. Lyon Credit, with a loan portfolio of $350 million, specializes in financing small energy projects.

Operational Review - 20-SEP-99

Net interest income in the six months ended June 30, 1999, rose 3.1%, year to year, as a more favorable deposit mix offset a reduction in interest earned on loans. The provision for loan losses was down 45%, to $5,000,000, from $9,099,000, reflecting a 1998 realignment of the provision for an acquired company. Noninterest income grew 19%, but noninterest expense fell 27%, in the absence of $27.8 million of merger-related expenses and restructuring charges in 1998; pretax income rose sharply. After taxes at 35.0%, versus 39.6%, net income nearly tripled, to $50,063,000 ($1.24 a share), from $19,484,000 ($0.46).

Stock Performance - 08-OCT-99

In the past 30 trading days, HU's shares have declined 7%, compared to a 0.91% fall in the S&P 500. Average trading volume for the past five days was 104,120 shares, compared with the 40-day moving average of 136,905 shares.

Key Stock Statistics

Dividend Rate/Share	1.00	Shareholders	8,000
Shs. outstg. (M)	38.9	Market cap. (B)	$ 1.2
Avg. daily vol. (M)	0.208	Inst. holdings	44%
Tang. Bk. Value/Share	8.15		
Beta	0.96		

Value of $10,000 invested 5 years ago: $ 25,521

Fiscal Year Ending Dec. 31

	1999	1998	1997	1996	1995	1994
Revenues (Million $)						
1Q	128.6	94.64	63.05	53.25	24.20	–
2Q	138.3	133.5	66.15	63.32	24.45	36.10
3Q	—	—	65.04	50.72	24.93	23.40
4Q	—	—	64.86	67.17	64.92	—
Yr.	—	525.1	259.1	234.5	65.04	93.89
Earnings Per Share ($)						
1Q	**0.61**	**0.35**	**0.47**	**0.33**	0.38	0.35
2Q	**0.63**	**0.11**	**0.50**	**0.31**	0.42	0.37
3Q	—	**-0.50**	**0.52**	**0.08**	0.42	0.40
4Q	—	**0.58**	**0.55**	**0.14**	0.44	0.41
Yr.	—	**0.56**	**2.04**	**0.85**	**1.39**	**0.99**

Next earnings report expected: mid October

Dividend Data (Dividends have been paid since 1952.)

Amount ($)	Date Decl.	Ex-Div. Date	Stock of Record	Payment Date
0.250	Nov. 04	Nov. 10	Nov. 13	Dec. 01 '98
0.250	Jan. 28	Feb. 11	Feb. 16	Mar. 01 '99
0.250	Apr. 22	May. 13	May. 17	Jun. 01 '99
0.250	Aug. 02	Aug. 12	Aug. 16	Sep. 01 '99

Hudson United Bancorp

Business Summary - 20-SEP-99

Upon completion of its proposed merger (announced in September 1999) with Dime Bancorp Inc., the holding company for the largest thrift on the East Coast, Hudson United (to be named Dime United Bancorp after the merger) will become the Mid-Atlantic's largest independent regional banking company. The pact, subject to shareholder and regulatory approval, is expected to close in the first quarter of 2000.

Hudson United is the holding company for Hudson United Bank, which operates offices throughout northern New Jersey, Lafayette American Bank and Trust, with offices in southwestern Connecticut, and Bank of the Hudson, which operates in New York State. HU also owns MSB Travel, Inc. In addition, the company is the indirect owner, through its banks, of 13 investment subsidiaries, and owns a 50% interest in a data processing and imaged check processing company.

Acquisitions have played a key role in the bank's development. HU follows a philosophy of seeking intramarket and contiguous market opportunities that can be accomplished with little or no dilution to earnings. From October 1990 to December 1998, Hudson acquired 25 institutions, adding approximately $6.3 billion to assets and expanding its branch network from 15 to 165.

In June 1999, HU agreed to acquire Southern Jersey Bancorp, a $470 million asset bank holding company with 17 branches in Southern New Jersey. Also in June, HU agreed to acquire JeffBanks, Inc., a $1.7 billion holding company with 32 branches in the greater Philadelphia area of Pennsylvania and South Jersey. Following the acquisitions, Hudson announced plans to combine Southern Jersey Bancorp, JeffBanks and HU's existing South Jersey branches and lending businesses into a $3.3 billion Jefferson Bank division.

Interest income declined 0.6% in 1998, to $468.5 million, and accounted for 93% of total revenues. Average earning assets, from which interest income is derived, increased 3.3% in 1998, and was comprised mainly of loans (57%) and taxable securities (41%). The net interest margin (the ratio of net interest income to average earning assets) is a key measure of profitability of the bank's lending operations. In 1998, the net interest margin narrowed 15 basis points, to 4.10%. This margin contraction offset the growth in earning assets, leading to a slight decrease in net interest income.

Noninterest income fell 39% in 1998, to $33.3 million, and accounted for 6.6% of total income (10% in 1997). This decrease was largely the result of sharply lower securities gains in 1998 and a $23.3 million loss on assets held for sale in the 1999 period.

At year-end 1998, HU's loan portfolio consisted mainly of residential mortgages (47%), commercial mortgages (20%), and commercial & industrial loans (19%).

Per Share Data ($)

(Year Ended Dec. 31)	1998	1997	1996	1995	1994	1993	1992	1991	1990	1989
Tangible Bk. Val.	9.35	7.17	7.55	8.55	7.60	7.16	5.48	4.53	4.22	4.13
Earnings	0.56	2.04	0.85	1.67	1.55	1.26	0.97	0.61	0.27	0.37
Dividends	0.88	0.73	0.68	0.55	0.33	0.29	0.24	0.21	0.20	0.18
Payout Ratio	157%	36%	80%	33%	21%	23%	25%	34%	73%	49%
Prices - High	38 1/8	39 1/8	24	20 1/4	14 1/2	15 3/8	9 1/2	4 7/8	4 3/8	6 1/4
- Low	21 1/8	20 1/2	16 3/4	13 3/8	11 1/2	9 3/4	4 5/8	2 3/16	2 1/8	4
P/E Ratio - High	68	19	28	12	9	12	10	8	16	17
- Low	38	10	20	8	7	8	5	4	8	11

Income Statement Analysis (Million $)

	1998	1997	1996	1995	1994	1993	1992	1991	1990	1989
Net Int. Inc.	254	140	131	81.1	58.0	47.0	41.0	26.5	23.0	23.3
Tax Equiv. Adj.	0.7	0.5	0.3	0.7	0.9	0.8	0.7	1.0	0.9	0.7
Non Int. Inc.	33.3	32.6	29.3	16.8	10.0	8.6	7.7	5.4	4.6	4.1
Loan Loss Prov.	14.4	7.3	12.3	4.2	3.0	3.6	4.1	2.3	4.2	1.9
Exp./Op. Revs.	81%	54%	72%	61%	55%	53%	70%	68%	70%	71%
Pretax Inc.	41.0	80.4	33.1	34.5	27.0	22.1	10.2	7.4	3.4	5.8
Eff. Tax Rate	44%	39%	35%	31%	37%	36%	5.50%	32%	34%	43%
Net Inc.	23.2	49.3	21.5	23.7	16.9	14.2	9.6	5.0	2.2	3.3
% Net Int. Marg.	4.10	5.20	5.05	5.46	5.09	5.20	4.97	4.94	4.55	4.77

Balance Sheet & Other Fin. Data (Million $)

	1998	1997	1996	1995	1994	1993	1992	1991	1990	1989
Money Mkt. Assets	17.7	218	24.2	46.7	Nil	9.8	23.3	6.0	11.9	40.1
Inv. Securities	2,896	778	936	566	537	427	323	139	151	89.0
Com'l Loans	1,332	496	482	245	188	179	154	159	144	134
Other Loans	2,055	1,278	1,402	609	545	356	367	317	370	363
Total Assets	6,779	3,047	3,116	1,613	1,377	1,042	932	673	595	548
Demand Deposits	941	622	623	311	210	205	171	128	103	102
Time Deposits	4,110	1,692	1,969	1,114	990	730	672	481	410	382
LT Debt	314	100	100	25.0	25.0	Nil	Nil	0.8	0.8	0.8
Common Eqty.	457	186	203	130	100	79.0	68.3	41.1	37.6	37.4
% Ret. on Assets	0.3	1.6	0.7	1.4	1.4	1.4	1.1	0.8	0.4	0.6
% Ret. on Equity	7.2	25.1	9.8	20.6	19.4	19.3	17.4	12.8	5.9	8.9
% Loan Loss Resv.	1.6	2.1	1.9	1.9	2.3	2.0	1.5	1.4	1.4	0.8
% Loans/Deposits	67.1	74.6	70.2	59.9	61.1	56.6	60.9	78.2	72.5	76.3
% Equity to Assets	1.2	6.3	7.2	6.0	6.9	7.4	6.0	6.5	6.3	7.0

Data as orig reptd.; bef. results of disc opers/spec. items. Per share data adj. for stk. divs. Bold denotes diluted EPS (FASB 128)-prior periods restated. E-Estimated. NA-Not Available. NM-Not Meaningful. NR-Not Ranked.

Office—1000 MacArthur Blvd., Mahwah, NJ 07430. **Organized**—in New Jersey in 1982. **Tel**—(201) 236-2600. **Website**—http://www.hudsonunitedbancorp.com **Chrmn, Pres & CEO**—K. T. Neilson. **EVP & CFO**—J. F. Hurley. **EVP & Secy**—D. L. Van Borkulo-Nuzzo. **Investor Contact**—Chris A. Witkowski (201 236-6144). **Dirs**—R. J. Burke, D. P. Calcagnini, N. deCordova, Jr., J. David, T. R. Farley, B. Malcolm, W. P. McBride, K. T. Neilson, C. F. X. Poggi, D. A. Rosow, J. E. Schierloh, G. F. Strauber, J. H. Tatigian, Jr. **Transfer Agent**—American Stock Transfer & Trust Co., NYC. **Empl**— 2,002. **S&P Analyst:** Markos N. Kaminis

STANDARD & POOR'S
STOCK REPORTS

Huffy Corp.

NYSE Symbol **HUF**
In S&P SmallCap 600

09-OCT-99

Industry: Leisure Time (Products)

Summary: This leading manufacturer of bicycles also makes basketball backboards and lawn and garden tools, and provides inventory, assembly and supplier services.

Quantitative Evaluations

Outlook
(1 Lowest—5 Highest)
• **2+**

Fair Value
• **9½**

Risk
• **Low**

Earn./Div. Rank
• **B-**

Technical Eval.
• **Bearish** since 7/99

Rel. Strength Rank
(1 Lowest—99 Highest)
• **31**

Insider Activity
• **NA**

Recent Price • 10¼
52 Wk Range • 16¾-8⅛
Yield • 3.3%
12-Mo. P/E • 33.1

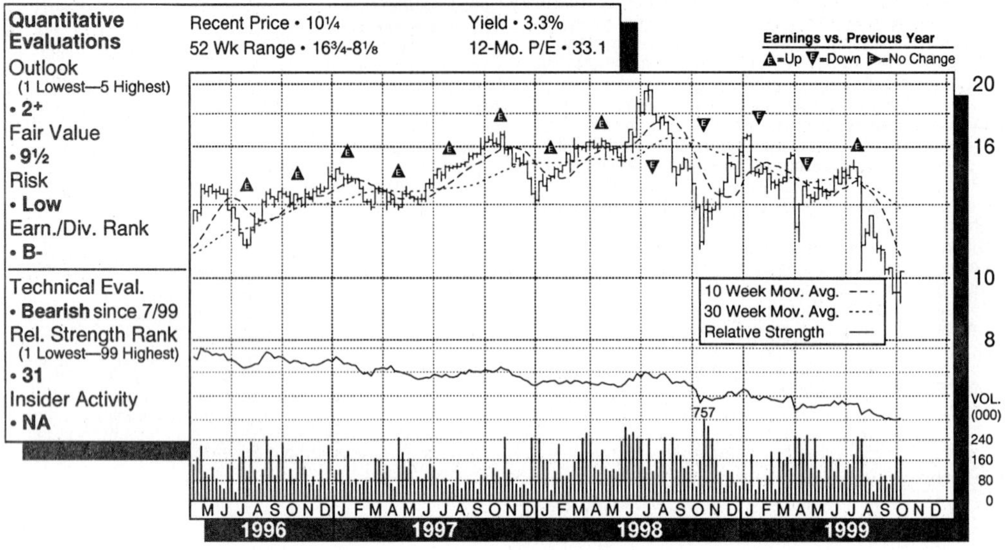

Business Profile - 12-JUL-99

In the second quarter of 1999, HUF anticipates solid volume increases at each of its operating companies, with bicycles and inventory services leading the way. Earnings for the second quarter should benefit as the company's bicycle reconfiguration plan is implemented and the excess inventory at its Celina, OH factory is eliminated. HUF completed its reconfiguration plan in the first quarter of 1999, which was aimed at improving operating efficiency. In connection with this plan, the company recognized $1.3 million in after tax charges against earnings.

Operational Review - 12-JUL-99

Net sales for the quarter ending March 31, 1999, rose 3.8%, year to year, the result of higher sales at the Retail Services segment, partially offset by lower bicycle sales. Gross margins narrowed, due to a less favorable product mix. Results were negatively impacted by a $2.1 million one-time plant closing charge and 25% higher interest expense, leading to a pretax loss of $898,000, compared with pretax income of $4.1 million. After a tax benefit of $444,000, versus taxes at 38.3%, a loss from continuing operations of $565,000 ($0.05 a share, on 6.4% fewer shares), contrasted with income from continuing operations of $1,569,000 ($0.20). Results for both periods exclude income from discontinued operations of $0.23 and $0.10 per share from the sale of True Temper.

Stock Performance - 08-OCT-99

In the past 30 trading days, HUF's shares have declined 8%, compared to a 0.91% fall in the S&P 500. Average trading volume for the past five days was 35,020 shares, compared with the 40-day moving average of 20,867 shares.

Key Stock Statistics

Dividend Rate/Share	0.34	Shareholders	3,100
Shs. outstg. (M)	10.2	Market cap. (B)	$0.104
Avg. daily vol. (M)	0.026	Inst. holdings	60%
Tang. Bk. Value/Share	4.71		
Beta	0.71		

Value of $10,000 invested 5 years ago: $ 6,480

Fiscal Year Ending Dec. 31

	1999	1998	1997	1996	1995	1994
Revenues (Million $)						
1Q	149.3	182.3	171.9	186.5	200.7	189.2
2Q	172.1	220.3	213.1	199.6	200.4	214.9
3Q	—	140.1	150.0	151.6	148.9	153.3
4Q	—	164.8	159.5	164.2	134.8	162.0
Yr.	—	707.6	694.5	701.9	684.8	719.5
Earnings Per Share ($)						
1Q	**-0.05**	**0.30**	**0.22**	**0.16**	0.33	0.33
2Q	**0.50**	Nil	**0.49**	**0.33**	0.03	0.53
3Q	—	**-0.06**	**0.08**	**-0.02**	-0.33	0.18
4Q	—	**-0.31**	**0.02**	**-0.01**	-0.80	0.14
Yr.	—	**-0.05**	**0.80**	**0.51**	**-0.70**	**0.90**

Next earnings report expected: mid October

Dividend Data (Dividends have been paid since 1950.)

Amount ($)	Date Decl.	Ex-Div. Date	Stock of Record	Payment Date
0.085	Dec. 10	Jan. 13	Jan. 15	Feb. 01 '99
0.085	Feb. 11	Apr. 13	Apr. 15	May. 03 '99
0.085	Apr. 22	Jul. 13	Jul. 15	Aug. 02 '99
0.085	Jul. 23	Oct. 13	Oct. 15	Nov. 01 '99

Business Summary - 12-JUL-99

In the first quarter of 1999, Huffy Corp. (HUF) completed the final phase of a reconfiguration plan initiated in May 1998. The plan was designed to improve operational efficiency by eliminating excess production capacity and reducing annual operating expenses at the Huffy Bicycle Company. The plan included the closing of its Celina, OH manufacturing facility to reduce capacity, the leasing of a parts fabrication facility to support other plants, and continuing to import lower priced bicycles.

HUF has classified its operations into two business segments: Sporting Goods, which include bicycles, backboards and related products; and Services for Retail, such as in-store product assembly, repair, display services, and inventory counting services.

Huffy Bicycle Company, Huffy Sports Company, and the Royce Union Bicycle Company comprise the its consumer products segment. In 1998, sales of bicycles represented 42.7% of sales (44.4% in 1997), sales of basketball backboards, poles, goals, and related products accounted for 12.1% (13.2% in 1997), and sales of lawn and garden tools accounted for 17.4% (16.4% in 1997).

In March 1999, HUF sold the assets of its Harrisburg, PA based lawn and garden tools and wheelbarrows business, including its True Temper Hardware Company, to U.S. Industries, Inc. for $100 million. Results for 1999 classify True Temper Hardware Company as a discontinued operation.

To date, HUF has not experienced significant revenues from its export business. However, the companies in the Consumer Products segment participate in various foreign markets and are actively involved in expanding the level of export business.

Huffy Bicycle Company is the largest seller of bicycles in the U.S., with a full line of adult bicycles and children's bicycles and tricycles. The company estimates that about 90% of the divisions' sales are sold under the Huffy brand name, with the balance sold under private label brands. Huffy bicycles are extensively advertised and sold primarily through high volume retailers, comprising a network representing about 75% of all bicycles sold in the U.S.

Huffy Sports Company is the leading supplier of basketball backboards, poles, goals, and related products. The company's promotional campaign highlights its connection with the National Basketball Association. The NBA logo adorns many of Huffy Sports' products.

Huffy's retail services divisions include Huffy Service First, Inc. and Washington Inventory Service. Both divisions provide services to retailers, including, assembly, repair, in-store display, merchandising services, and physical inventory services to help customers meet financial reporting requirements. The combined revenues of both divisions represented about 27.8% of net sales in 1998 (26.0% in 1997).

Per Share Data ($) (Year Ended Dec. 31)	1998	1997	1996	1995	1994	1993	1992	1991	1990	1989
Tangible Bk. Val.	5.12	7.19	6.87	6.78	7.94	7.46	6.78	7.17	5.89	5.23
Cash Flow	1.42	2.15	2.18	0.89	2.59	1.26	2.31	2.76	2.26	1.96
Earnings	-0.05	0.80	0.48	-0.78	1.20	-0.30	0.92	1.52	1.37	1.17
Dividends	0.34	0.34	0.34	0.34	0.34	0.30	0.30	0.28	0.27	0.23
Payout Ratio	NM	42%	71%	NM	28%	NM	32%	18%	19%	19%
Prices - High	19⅞	16⅞	14⅞	15⅞	19½	20⅝	24⅜	22¼	17⅛	15⅜
- Low	11	12¾	10¼	10	14	14⅝	12	9⅞	8½	8¾
P/E Ratio - High	NM	21	31	NM	16	NM	26	15	13	13
- Low	NM	16	21	NM	12	NM	13	7	6	7
Income Statement Analysis (Million $)										
Revs.	708	694	702	685	719	758	703	679	517	449
Oper. Inc.	47.1	38.7	38.5	20.5	52.1	56.1	45.4	56.2	43.2	36.9
Depr.	18.1	17.7	22.9	22.4	20.2	20.3	18.0	16.2	11.8	10.3
Int. Exp.	9.1	5.7	7.3	8.0	6.4	8.7	9.6	9.0	6.7	6.6
Pretax Inc.	-1.1	14.5	8.9	-15.0	27.6	-3.1	18.6	31.5	28.6	23.8
Eff. Tax Rate	NM	28%	27%	NM	37%	NM	36%	37%	37%	37%
Net Inc.	-0.7	10.4	6.5	-10.5	17.4	-3.8	11.8	19.8	18.0	15.0
Balance Sheet & Other Fin. Data (Million $)										
Cash	17.9	2.1	2.1	2.6	1.6	4.1	3.5	8.5	21.9	51.9
Curr. Assets	217	213	186	163	189	197	207	197	177	153
Total Assets	344	323	316	299	322	319	335	317	292	235
Curr. Liab.	189	140	121	100	99	104	116	98.0	90.0	73.0
LT Debt	29.8	36.2	43.9	51.2	58.6	43.2	74.9	80.2	84.3	57.5
Common Eqty.	93.2	117	116	116	133	136	118	125	107	96.0
Total Cap.	123	149	160	167	192	179	193	205	191	153
Cap. Exp.	23.0	17.5	17.7	24.4	35.7	21.3	23.9	21.1	9.5	13.8
Cash Flow	17.4	28.1	29.4	12.0	37.6	16.4	29.8	36.0	29.8	25.2
Curr. Ratio	1.1	1.5	1.5	1.6	1.9	1.9	1.8	2.0	2.0	2.1
% LT Debt of Cap.	24.2	24.3	27.5	30.6	30.5	24.1	38.9	39.1	44.1	37.6
% Net Inc.of Revs.	NM	1.5	0.9	NM	2.4	NM	1.7	2.9	3.5	3.3
% Ret. on Assets	NM	3.3	2.1	NM	5.7	NM	3.7	6.5	6.9	7.1
% Ret. on Equity	NM	8.8	5.6	NM	13.5	NM	9.9	17.0	17.9	16.7

Data as orig reptd.; bef. results of disc opers/spec. items. Per share data adj. for stk. divs. Bold denotes diluted EPS (FASB 128)-prior periods restated. E-Estimated. NA-Not Available. NM-Not Meaningful. NR-Not Ranked.

Office—225 Byers Rd., Miamisburg, OH 45342. **Tel**—(937) 866-6251. **Website**—http://www.huffy.com**Chrmn, Pres & CEO**—D. R. Graber. **VP-Fin & CFO**—T. A. Frederick. **VP & Secy**—N. A. Michaud. **Investor Contact**—Paul Fisher (937-865-2867). **Dirs**—D. R. Graber, W. A. Huffman, L. B. Keene, J. D. Michaels, D. K. Miller, J. F. Robeson, P. W. Rooney, T. C. Sullivan, J. P. Viviano. **Transfer Agent & Registrar**—Harris Trust & Savings Bank, Chicago.**Incorporated**—in Ohio in 1928. **Empl**— 4,000. **S&P Analyst:** Matthew C. Hershberg

STANDARD
&POOR'S
STOCK REPORTS

Hughes Supply

NYSE Symbol **HUG**

In S&P SmallCap 600

09-OCT-99

Industry: Retail (Building Supplies)

Summary: HUG is one of the largest U.S. diversified wholesale distributors of materials, equipment and supplies to construction and industrial markets.

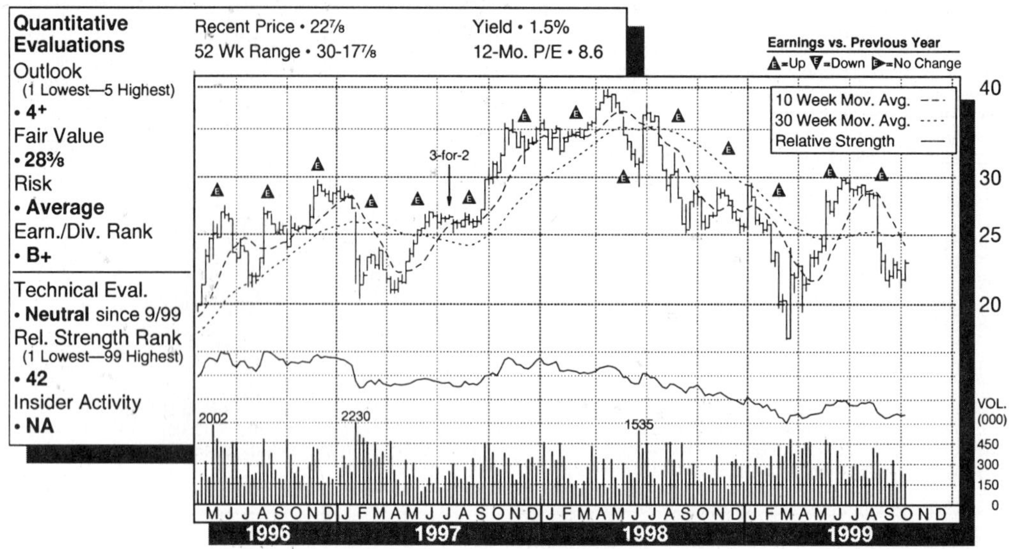

Business Profile - 23-JUN-99

HUG has pursued an active acquisition program in an effort to capitalize on opportunities presented by its industry's substantial size and highly fragmented ownership structure. In May 1999, the company said that, in coming months, it would focus on internal growth and integration of past acquisitions, with a goal of realizing additional operating synergies, partly through upgrading its information technology system to gain more administrative savings from acquisitions. In March 1999, directors authorized the repurchase of 2.5 million shares; 723,900 shares were acquired in the quarter ended April 30, 1999.

Operational Review - 23-JUN-99

Net sales in the three months ended April 30, 1999, advanced 18%, year to year, reflecting higher same-store sales and branches acquired or opened after January 31, 1998. Gross margins widened, aided by a more favorable product mix, efficiencies created by central distribution centers, and enhanced purchased power. Total operating expenses increased 22%, in part due to higher personnel and transportation costs associated with same-store sales growth, and an increase in technology costs. With lower net interest costs, pretax income climbed 20%. After taxes at 40.5%, versus 37.9%, net income was up 15%, to $13,355,000 ($0.55 a share), from $11,603,000 ($0.49).

Stock Performance - 08-OCT-99

In the past 30 trading days, HUG's shares have declined 0.54%, compared to a 0.91% fall in the S&P 500. Average trading volume for the past five days was 45,720 shares, compared with the 40-day moving average of 51,205 shares.

Key Stock Statistics

Dividend Rate/Share	0.34	Shareholders	1,179
Shs. outstg. (M)	23.4	Market cap. (B)	$0.534
Avg. daily vol. (M)	0.046	Inst. holdings	59%
Tang. Bk. Value/Share	11.53		
Beta	0.68		

Value of $10,000 invested 5 years ago: $ 18,684

Fiscal Year Ending Jan. 31

	2000	1999	1998	1997	1996	1995
Revenues (Million $)						
1Q	711.3	602.0	434.5	349.5	253.9	184.0
2Q	774.9	674.5	478.2	395.8	282.4	202.6
3Q	—	659.0	505.6	405.4	284.1	210.6
4Q	—	600.6	460.5	365.4	261.8	205.3
Yr.	—	2,536	1,879	1,516	1,082	802.5
Earnings Per Share ($)						
1Q	**0.55**	**0.49**	**0.46**	**0.40**	0.29	0.21
2Q	**0.88**	**0.82**	**0.71**	**0.66**	0.49	0.34
3Q	—	**0.79**	**0.69**	**0.60**	0.41	0.31
4Q	—	**0.45**	**0.43**	**0.42**	0.37	0.32
Yr.	—	**2.55**	**2.30**	**2.09**	**1.77**	1.19

Next earnings report expected: mid November

Dividend Data (Dividends have been paid since 1976.)

Amount ($)	Date Decl.	Ex-Div. Date	Stock of Record	Payment Date
0.085	Aug. 19	Nov. 04	Nov. 06	Nov. 20 '98
0.085	Jan. 07	Feb. 03	Feb. 05	Feb. 19 '99
0.085	Mar. 24	Apr. 29	May. 03	May. 14 '99
0.085	Jul. 20	Aug. 04	Aug. 06	Aug. 20 '99

A Division of The McGraw-Hill Companies

Hughes Supply, Inc.

Business Summary - 23-JUN-99

More than 70 years ago, Russell and Harry Hughes, and their father Clarence, started a wholesale building supply business with a single premise: "You can't do business out of an empty wagon." Since then, Hughes Supply, Inc. (HUG) has grown into one of the largest U.S. diversified wholesale distributors of materials, equipment and supplies for construction and industrial markets. The company operates primarily in the Southeast, Southwest and Midwest.

The company distributes more than 240,000 products through 453 branches located in 29 states, Mexico, and Puerto Rico. Its principal customers are electrical, plumbing and mechanical contractors, electric utility companies, property management companies, municipalities and industrial companies. Industrial companies include companies in the petrochemical, food, and beverage, pulp and paper, mining, pharmaceutical and marine industries. HUG believes it holds a significant market share in the majority of its local markets.

HUG distributes products in the three major categories. In the fluid control area, it distributes industrial pipe, plate, valves and fittings such as mechanical and weld pipe, high density polyethylene pipe and fittings, plumbing fixtures and related fittings, water works and industrial supplies, large diameter plastic and ductile iron pipe, fire hydrants, water meters and fire line vaults, jet and submersible pumps and tanks, well liners, and environmental products.

Electrical products include wire, cable, cords, boxes, breakers, panels, fuses and transformers, conductor cable, insulators, prestressed concrete transmission and distribution poles and related hardware, accessories and tools. Specialty products include heating, ventilation and air conditioning equipment, furnaces, heaters, heat pumps, condensing units, duct, grills, freon, reinforcing wire, reinforcing steel, concrete chemicals, masonry accessories, paint, flooring, janitorial products, and above-ground and in-ground pool packages, pumps, filters, lights, diving boards, deck products and cleaning equipment.

HUG has established a growth strategy that includes acquisitions and internal growth. Since January 28, 1994, the company has completed 57 acquisitions, representing 239 branches. It has also grown internally, through increases in comparable branch net sales, 70 new branch openings, and the addition of new product groups. In recent years, the company has focused internal growth and acquisitions to a greater extent on products used in repair, maintenance, replacement and renovation applications. These products generally offer wider margins, and are less dependent on new construction.

Per Share Data ($) **(Year Ended Jan. 31)**	**1999**	**1998**	**1997**	**1996**	**1995**	**1994**	**1993**	**1992**	**1991**	**1990**
Tangible Bk. Val.	12.50	11.61	10.95	15.11	14.50	13.52	13.29	13.01	13.81	13.26
Cash Flow	3.51	3.24	2.99	2.59	2.21	1.97	1.40	0.49	1.73	2.15
Earnings	2.55	2.30	2.05	1.56	1.19	0.83	0.36	-0.65	0.33	0.89
Dividends	0.33	0.29	0.25	0.18	0.14	0.09	0.08	0.20	0.24	0.23
Payout Ratio	13%	13%	12%	12%	12%	11%	22%	NM	70%	25%
Cal. Yrs.	1998	1997	1996	1995	1994	1993	1992	1991	1990	1989
Prices - High	39¾	36⅛	29¾	19⅜	21½	13⅛	10⅞	9¼	12¼	14⅝
- Low	25⅛	20⅜	17¾	11⅞	10⅝	8⅞	7	6¾	6½	11⅝
P/E Ratio - High	16	16	14	12	18	16	30	NM	38	16
- Low	10	9	9	8	9	11	19	NM	20	13
Income Statement Analysis (Million $)										
Revs.	2,536	1,879	1,516	1,082	802	661	528	481	548	530
Oper. Inc.	140	102	74.2	40.5	28.2	19.8	11.4	6.4	16.8	24.3
Depr.	23.3	18.4	15.0	10.6	8.8	7.5	6.5	7.1	9.2	9.1
Int. Exp.	25.4	18.5	13.5	7.5	4.9	4.6	4.7	5.9	8.0	7.3
Pretax Inc.	99	70.9	51.7	27.0	17.4	10.6	3.7	-6.1	3.6	10.6
Eff. Tax Rate	38%	37%	37%	41%	41%	41%	39%	NM	41%	40%
Net Inc.	61.4	44.8	32.5	16.1	10.3	6.3	2.3	-4.0	2.1	6.4
Balance Sheet & Other Fin. Data (Million $)										
Cash	6.0	7.7	6.3	3.4	3.2	1.1	2.3	5.5	3.2	2.1
Curr. Assets	797	664	477	297	260	204	170	165	164	176
Total Assets	1,124	942	650	379	329	263	225	216	220	236
Curr. Liab.	229	190	146	117	95.1	68.6	60.3	56.9	46.1	58.5
LT Debt	402	335	222	106	101	99	79.9	76.3	85.6	82.8
Common Eqty.	484	414	279	154	131	94.4	83.3	81.5	86.5	92.7
Total Cap.	891	749	501	260	232	194	163	159	173	177
Cap. Exp.	26.9	27.7	16.1	11.9	11.8	8.3	8.5	4.9	7.2	10.7
Cash Flow	84.7	63.3	47.5	26.7	19.1	13.8	8.8	3.1	11.3	15.5
Curr. Ratio	3.5	3.5	3.3	2.5	2.7	3.0	2.8	2.9	3.6	3.0
% LT Debt of Cap.	45.1	44.7	44.4	41.7	43.5	51.2	49.0	48.1	49.4	46.8
% Net Inc.of Revs.	2.4	2.4	2.2	1.5	1.3	1.0	0.4	NM	0.4	1.2
% Ret. on Assets	5.9	5.6	6.0	4.4	3.5	2.4	1.0	NM	1.0	2.8
% Ret. on Equity	13.7	12.9	14.5	11.1	9.2	6.7	2.7	NM	2.5	7.1

Data as orig reptd.; bef. results of disc opers/spec. items. Per share data adj. for stk. divs. Bold denotes diluted EPS (FASB 128)-prior periods restated. E-Estimated. NA-Not Available. NM-Not Meaningful. NR-Not Ranked.

Office—20 N. Orange Ave., Suite 200, Orlando, FL 32801. **Tel**—(407) 841-4755. **Website**—http://www.hughessupply.com **Chrmn, CEO & Investor Contact**—David H. Hughes. **Pres & COO**—A. S. Hall Jr. **CFO & Treas**—J. S. Zepf. **Secy**—B. P. Butterfield. **Dirs**—J. D. Baker II, R. N. Blackford, H. C. Day, A. S. Hall Jr., D. H. Hughes, V. S. Hughes, W. P. Kennedy. **Transfer Agent & Registrar**—American Stock Transfer & Trust Co., NYC. **Incorporated**—in Florida in 1947. **Empl**— 7,200. **S&P Analyst:** P.L.H.

STANDARD &POOR'S
STOCK REPORTS

Hutchinson Technology

NASDAQ Symbol **HTCH**

In S&P SmallCap 600

09-OCT-99

Industry: Computers (Peripherals)

Summary: This company is the leading producer of suspension assemblies for manufacturers of rigid disk drives.

Quantitative Evaluations

Outlook
(1 Lowest—5 Highest)
• **3⁻**

Fair Value
• **29½**

Risk
• **High**

Earn./Div. Rank
• **B-**

Technical Eval.
• **Bullish** since 9/99

Rel. Strength Rank
(1 Lowest—99 Highest)
• **53**

Insider Activity
• **Unfavorable**

Recent Price • 27
52 Wk Range • 51¼-13¼
Yield • Nil
12-Mo. P/E • NM

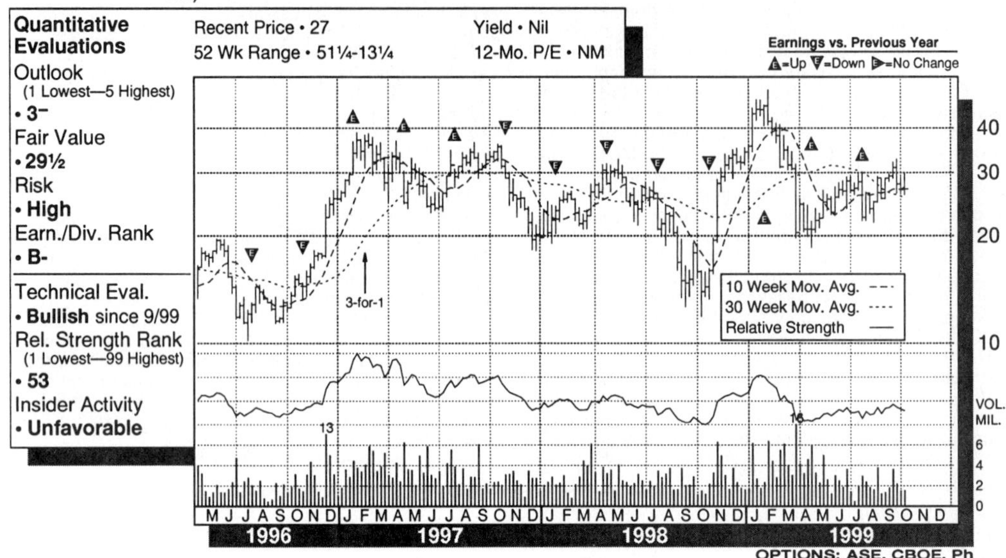

OPTIONS: ASE, CBOE, Ph

Business Profile - 07-SEP-99

In August 1999, HTCH stated that it was consolidating certain manufacturing operations to better utilize production resources and reduce costs. With resulting improvements in production capacity, the company will delay the start of production at a new manufacturing facility currently under production. A fourth quarter charge is expected for severance expenses for about 500 employees laid off as a result of the consolidation. In July, HTCH reduced planned FY 99 (Sep) capital expenditures to $150 million, from $115 million, due to productivity improvements and lower than expected demand. In February, HTCH sold publicly 4.8 million shares; proceeds of $209 million were earmarked for capital expenditures and general corporate purposes.

Operational Review - 07-SEP-99

Net sales for the 39 weeks ended June 27, 1999, rose 51%, year to year, primarily due to higher overall suspension volumes and proportionately greater sales of higher priced TSA suspension assemblies. Gross margin turned significantly positive, as improved manufacturing efficiencies on TSA production, increased TSA assembly sales and higher average TSA selling prices offset lower conventional suspension assembly sales volume. Other income (net) doubled and interest expense more than tripled. After taxes at 21.0%, versus a tax benefit, net income totaled $19,787,000 ($0.88 a share on 44% more shares), versus a net loss of $35,149,000 ($1.79).

Stock Performance - 08-OCT-99

In the past 30 trading days, HTCH's shares have increased 6%, compared to a 0.91% fall in the S&P 500. Average trading volume for the past five days was 302,860 shares, compared with the 40-day moving average of 429,731 shares.

Key Stock Statistics

Dividend Rate/Share	Nil	Shareholders	1,038
Shs. outstg. (M)	24.7	Market cap. (B)	$0.668
Avg. daily vol. (M)	0.437	Inst. holdings	64%
Tang. Bk. Value/Share	11.97		
Beta	2.08		

Value of $10,000 invested 5 years ago: $ 27,692

Fiscal Year Ending Sep. 30

	1999	1998	1997	1996	1995	1994
Revenues (Million $)						
1Q	155.3	88.98	106.9	83.33	63.50	46.96
2Q	152.4	95.13	124.3	86.55	67.89	58.64
3Q	131.3	107.1	121.7	91.42	81.89	62.79
4Q	—	116.4	100.3	91.89	86.72	70.41
Yr.	—	407.6	453.2	353.2	300.0	238.8
Earnings Per Share ($)						
1Q	**0.52**	**-0.58**	0.66	0.17	0.14	-0.15
2Q	**0.54**	**-0.73**	0.91	0.26	0.25	0.11
3Q	**-0.22**	**-0.47**	0.68	0.31	0.36	0.14
4Q	—	**-0.67**	0.02	0.08	0.52	0.25
Yr.	—	**-2.46**	**2.21**	**0.82**	1.28	0.36

Next earnings report expected: early November

Dividend Data

No cash dividends have been paid. The company does not anticipate paying cash dividends in the foreseeable future.

Hutchinson Technology Incorporated

Business Summary - 07-SEP-99

A 1998 industry report projected that total revenue for the disk drive industry would grow to over $32 billion by the year 2000, from about $27 billion in 1998. This growing demand for additional computer storage capacity is being stimulated by the increasing use of disk drives for non-computer applications such as voice mail and video data. Hutchinson Technology estimated that it produces approximately 70% (plus or minus 10%) of all suspension assemblies sold to disk drive manufacturers and their suppliers worldwide.

HTCH is the world's leading supplier of disk drive suspension assemblies, which provided 96% of the company's FY 98 (Sep) revenues. Hutchinson also produces etched and stamped components used in connection with, or related to, suspension assemblies. The company is also evaluating other product opportunities in the medical devices market but does not expect any medical related revenue in FY 99.

HTCH stated in May 1999 that it expects its new TSA suspension assembly to become a market standard platform. The TSA product incorporates thin electrical conductors in the suspension itself, which replace the wires used to connect the recording head to the drive's electronic circuitry. This permits disk drive manufacturers to increase throughput, eliminate manufacturing steps, and automate assembly processes. In FY 97 (Sep), the first fiscal year of volume manufacturing of its TSA products, the company shipped approximately 8 million TSA suspensions (about 1% of unit shipments). In FY 98 the company shipped 85 million TSA suspensions (about 16% of unit shipments).

The company's five largest customers accounted for 84%, 86% and 87% of net sales for FY 98, FY 97, and FY 96, respectively. Further, sales to recording head manufacturers are indirectly attributable to certain large disk drive manufacturers.

The company believes that the introduction of new products over time is an important factor in competitive success in the disk drive industry. Accordingly, the company devotes substantial resources to R&D. In FY 98 and FY 97, R&D spending was approximately $52 million and $48 million, respectively. As a part of its R&D efforts, the company has also been engaged in the development of products for the medical devices market. One such product development, a monitor that measures tissue oxygen saturation, received FDA clearance for marketing in the U.S. in late 1998, and is the subject of clinical trials at several hospitals.

In March 1998, the company issued $150 million of 6% convertible subordinate notes due 2005. This additional indebtedness increased Hutchinson's ratio of total debt to total capitalization to approximately 49% at the end of FY 98, from 22% at the end of FY 97.

Per Share Data ($) (Year Ended Sep. 30)	1998	1997	1996	1995	1994	1993	1992	1991	1990	1989
Tangible Bk. Val.	11.97	14.42	8.47	7.33	5.91	5.55	4.96	2.81	2.43	1.98
Cash Flow	0.13	4.23	2.82	2.99	1.83	1.50	1.82	1.31	1.25	0.54
Earnings	-2.46	2.21	0.82	1.28	0.36	0.53	0.91	0.37	0.45	-0.48
Dividends	Nil	Nil	Nil	Nil	Nil	Nil	Nil	Nil	Nil	Nil
Payout Ratio	Nil	Nil	Nil	Nil	Nil	Nil	Nil	Nil	Nil	Nil
Prices - High	36 1/8	39	26 7/8	30 3/8	13 5/8	17 1/8	15 1/8	5	4 1/2	5 1/8
- Low	11 7/8	18 1/8	10 1/8	7 7/8	7 1/8	6 3/8	4 5/8	2 3/4	1 13/16	1 11/16
P/E Ratio - High	NM	18	33	24	38	32	17	13	10	NM
- Low	NM	8	12	6	20	12	5	7	4	NM
Income Statement Analysis (Million $)										
Revs.	408	453	353	300	239	199	160	143	122	92.0
Oper. Inc.	-14.2	91.0	51.8	57.1	31.8	25.8	26.5	18.5	18.2	4.8
Depr.	50.9	38.2	33.6	28.0	24.0	15.8	12.9	11.2	9.6	12.1
Int. Exp.	4.6	3.1	2.1	2.6	2.1	0.3	1.2	1.8	2.1	2.1
Pretax Inc.	-65.4	53.7	17.3	27.7	8.0	11.1	13.8	6.0	7.3	-8.9
Eff. Tax Rate	NM	22%	20%	24%	26%	23%	7.10%	25%	27%	NM
Net Inc.	-48.4	41.9	13.8	21.1	5.9	8.6	12.8	4.5	5.3	-5.7
Balance Sheet & Other Fin. Data (Million $)										
Cash	58.9	119	26.0	31.7	18.6	8.4	33.7	6.3	8.1	0.9
Curr. Assets	194	243	109	90.5	70.8	44.1	67.3	31.4	36.7	25.0
Total Assets	549	430	239	191	151	117	109	66.0	65.0	56.0
Curr. Liab.	93.2	70.1	46.6	36.2	18.8	17.9	18.3	13.3	14.0	9.2
LT Debt	218	76.6	53.2	34.9	37.7	10.1	13.0	16.7	19.3	20.5
Common Eqty.	237	283	134	120	94.6	88.7	77.0	33.5	28.8	23.4
Total Cap.	455	360	187	155	132	99	90.8	52.7	50.7	46.5
Cap. Exp.	207	82.6	77.1	44.5	82.2	73.9	25.5	18.3	7.0	6.9
Cash Flow	2.5	80.2	47.4	49.3	29.9	24.4	25.7	15.7	15.0	6.4
Curr. Ratio	2.1	3.5	2.3	2.5	3.8	2.5	3.7	2.4	2.6	2.7
% LT Debt of Cap.	47.9	21.3	28.4	22.5	28.5	10.2	14.3	31.8	38.1	44.1
% Net Inc.of Revs.	NM	9.2	3.9	7.0	2.5	4.3	8.0	3.1	4.4	NM
% Ret. on Assets	NM	12.5	6.4	12.3	4.4	7.5	13.2	6.9	8.9	NM
% Ret. on Equity	NM	20.1	10.9	19.6	6.4	10.2	21.3	14.4	20.4	NM

Data as orig reptd.; bef. results of disc opers/spec. items. Per share data adj. for stk. divs. Bold denotes diluted EPS (FASB 128)-prior periods restated. E-Estimated. NA-Not Available. NM-Not Meaningful. NR-Not Ranked.

Office—40 W. Highland Park, Hutchinson, MN 55350. **Tel**—(320) 587-3797. **Website**—http://www.htch.com**Chrmn**—J. W. Green. **Pres & CEO**—W. M. Fortun. **VP & COO**—B. Graczyk. **VP, CFO, Secy & Investor Contact**—John A. Ingleman. **Dirs**— W. T. Brunberg, A. Cox Jr., J. E. Donaghy, H. C. Ervin Jr., W. M. Fortun, J. W. Green, S. E. Landsburg, R. B. Solum. **Transfer Agent & Registrar**—Norwest Bank Minnesota, St. Paul. **Incorporated**—in Minnesota in 1965.**Empl**— 7,764. **S&P Analyst:** Craig K. Shere, CFA

STANDARD
&POOR'S
STOCK REPORTS

Hyperion Solutions

NASDAQ Symbol **HYSL**

In S&P SmallCap 600

23-OCT-99

Industry: Computer (Software & Services)

Summary: HYSL provides analytic application software for reporting, analysis, modeling and planning.

Quantitative Evaluations

Outlook
(1 Lowest—5 Highest)
• **2−**

Fair Value
• **23⅜**

Risk
• **NA**

Earn./Div. Rank
• **NR**

Technical Eval.
• **NA**

Rel. Strength Rank
(1 Lowest—99 Highest)
• **95**

Insider Activity
• **NA**

Recent Price • 22⅞ | Yield • Nil
52 Wk Range • 36⅛-9⅞ | 12-Mo. P/E • 29.3

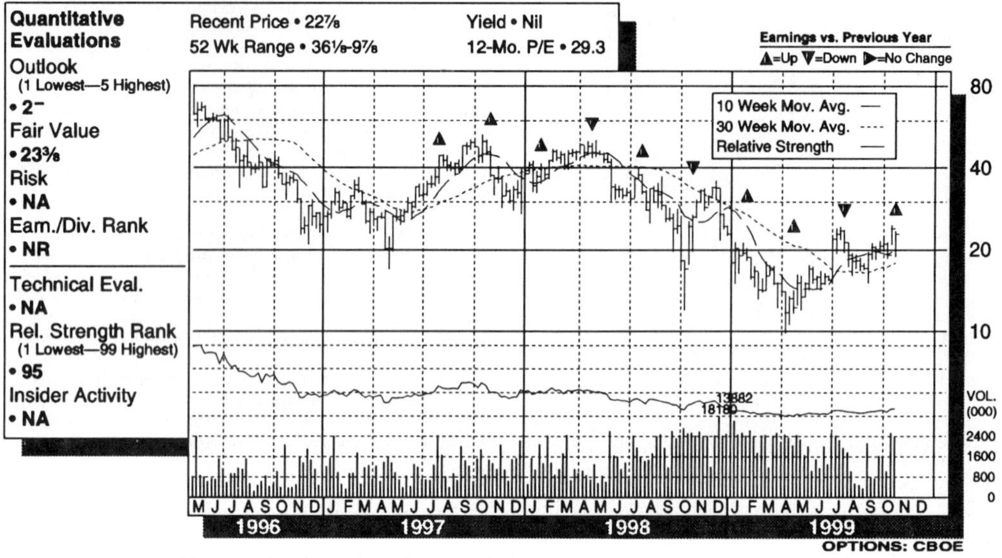

Business Profile - 21-OCT-99

In an effort to capitalize on what it perceives as a need for companies to better understand and optimize e-marketing, customer relationship and e-commerce activities, HYSL formed its e-Business division in October 1999. The division will deliver integrated analytic applications for e-marketing, website, and e-commerce analysis that transform data in e-business systems into actionable information. HYSL said analytic applications from the division will help companies improve e-marketing programs, enhance web-based customer interactions, maximize e-commerce opportunities, and significantly increase return on e-business investment. HYSL believes companies can gain a competitive advantage by applying sophisticated analytic applications to improve their performance.

Operational Review - 21-OCT-99

Total revenues in the three months ended September 30, 1999, edged up 2.3%, year to year, as a 19% gain in maintenance and services revenues was largely offset by a 14% drop in software license revenues. Margins widened fractionally; in the absence of $21.8 million of merger costs, pretax income contrasted with a pretax loss. After taxes at 37.4%, versus taxes of $2.0 million, net income of $6,025,000 ($0.19 a share, on 6.2% more shares) contrasted with a net loss of $9,933,000 ($0.33).

Stock Performance - 22-OCT-99

In the past 30 trading days, HYSL's shares have increased 17%, compared to a 4% fall in the S&P 500. Average trading volume for the past five days was 204,640 shares, compared with the 40-day moving average of 223,744 shares.

Key Stock Statistics

Dividend Rate/Share	Nil	Shareholders	274
Shs. outstg. (M)	30.7	Market cap. (B)	$0.737
Avg. daily vol. (M)	0.455	Inst. holdings	74%
Tang. Bk. Value/Share	5.05		
Beta	NA		

Value of $10,000 invested 5 years ago: NA

Fiscal Year Ending Jun. 30

	2000	1999	1998	1997	1996	1995
Revenues (Million $)						
1Q	46.40	104.9	18.01	9.27	—	—
2Q	—	107.0	21.38	10.80	—	—
3Q	—	101.6	88.80	12.47	6.76	—
4Q	—	111.4	26.74	14.84	8.23	—
Yr.	—	424.9	82.24	47.38	25.13	11.52
Earnings Per Share ($)						
1Q	**0.19**	**-0.33**	**0.15**	0.10	—	—
2Q	—	**0.28**	**0.18**	0.12	—	—
3Q	—	**0.08**	**-0.02**	0.13	—	—
4Q	—	**0.22**	0.27	0.15	0.12	—
Yr.	—	**0.26**	**0.58**	**0.50**	0.27	0.04

Next earnings report expected: late January

Dividend Data

No cash dividends have been paid.

STANDARD
&POOR'S
STOCK REPORTS

Hyperion Solutions Corporation

23-OCT-99

Business Summary - 21-OCT-99

Even as the world approaches a new millennium, some things will not change. Organizations, including corporations, government and municipal organizations and non-profit institutions, continue to generate significant amounts of data in the course of conducting ongoing business transactions in their accounting, manufacturing, human resources, and sales and marketing functions. To be useful to senior executives, managers and analysts, data must be extracted from financial and operational systems, analyzed using a range of mathematical calculations, and summarized and presented in formats ranging from spreadsheets and specific financial reports to graphical web-based presentations that are meaningful to multiple levels of business managers and knowledge workers throughout organizations. Since most organizations use multiple transactions systems throughout their global operations, integrating and delivering this enterprise data is critical.

Since 1991, Hyperion Solutions (HYSL) has been developing, marketing and supporting enterprise analytic application software that helps companies better understand, optimize and operate their businesses. Its products complement software used by companies to capture and organize data. Its products integrate with, extend and enhance transaction processing applications, enterprise resource planning and customer relationship management packaged applications, and data warehouses.

HYSL's product offerings are based on its enterprise-class analytic platform and include packaged analytic applications, OLAP (on-line analytical processing) server technology, data and application integration technologies, and a family of robust tools for client-server and web-enabled reporting, analysis, presentation and application development. The company and its partners deliver client/server and web-based products for a broad range of analytic applications including budgeting and planning, financial consolidation and reporting, activity-based management, performance management, campaign management analysis, promotional analysis, sales forecasting, demand planning, e-business analysis and industry-specific solutions. HYSL's solutions are used by more than 6,000 organizations in more than 100 countries worldwide.

The company aims to build on its position as a leading provider of analytic application software products and services. It intends to extend its leadership as a provider of cross-platform OLAP engine and tools technology by delivering increased product functionality, expanding its alliance network, and basing its analytic applications and services on its OLAP technology. In addition, HYSL intends to extend its leadership in packaged analytic applications through expanded functionality and technology, and to enter new and emerging analytic application markets, including customer relationship management and e-business markets, while maintaining a strong focus on business analysis.

Per Share Data ($) **(Year Ended Jun. 30)**	**1999**	**1998**	**1997**	**1996**	**1995**	**1994**	**1993**	**1992**	**1991**	**1990**
Tangible Bk. Val.	NA	4.67	3.83	3.16	0.97	NA	NA	NA	NA	NA
Cash Flow	NA	0.98	0.70	0.38	0.09	NA	NA	NA	NA	NA
Earnings	0.26	0.58	0.50	0.27	0.04	NA	NA	NA	NA	NA
Dividends	Nil	Nil	Nil	Nil	Nil	NA	NA	NA	NA	NA
Payout Ratio	Nil	Nil	Nil	Nil	Nil	NA	NA	NA	NA	NA
Prices - High	$24\frac{3}{4}$	$50\frac{3}{4}$	$53\frac{1}{4}$	$82\frac{3}{4}$	$48\frac{1}{2}$	NA	NA	NA	NA	NA
- Low	$9\frac{7}{8}$	12	17	21	17	NA	NA	NA	NA	NA
P/E Ratio - High	95	88	92	NM	NM	NA	NA	NA	NA	NA
- Low	38	21	29	NM	NM	NA	NA	NA	NA	NA
Income Statement Analysis (Million $)										
Revs.	NA	82.2	47.4	25.1	11.5	4.3	NA	NA	NA	NA
Oper. Inc.	NA	16.1	9.9	4.2	1.0	1.9	NA	NA	NA	NA
Depr.	NA	4.8	2.4	1.1	0.5	0.3	NA	NA	NA	NA
Int. Exp.	NA	0.3	0.2	0.3	0.2	0.1	NA	NA	NA	NA
Pretax Inc.	NA	12.7	9.0	3.6	0.4	-2.2	NA	NA	NA	NA
Eff. Tax Rate	NA	46%	35%	20%	6.10%	Nil	NA	NA	NA	NA
Net Inc.	NA	6.9	5.8	2.9	0.4	-2.2	NA	NA	NA	NA
Balance Sheet & Other Fin. Data (Million $)										
Cash	NA	138	28.9	10.7	2.7	NA	NA	NA	NA	NA
Curr. Assets	NA	166	47.0	42.6	4.9	NA	NA	NA	NA	NA
Total Assets	NA	186	59.6	45.9	6.5	NA	NA	NA	NA	NA
Curr. Liab.	NA	30.1	16.7	10.5	3.4	NA	NA	NA	NA	NA
LT Debt	NA	100	0.3	1.1	0.8	NA	NA	NA	NA	NA
Common Eqty.	NA	56.0	42.6	34.3	2.3	NA	NA	NA	NA	NA
Total Cap.	NA	156	42.9	35.4	3.1	NA	NA	NA	NA	NA
Cap. Exp.	NA	6.0	10.8	1.3	0.1	0.0	NA	NA	NA	NA
Cash Flow	NA	11.7	8.2	3.9	0.9	NA	NA	NA	NA	NA
Curr. Ratio	NA	5.5	2.8	4.1	1.4	NA	NA	NA	NA	NA
% LT Debt of Cap.	NA	64.1	0.7	3.1	26.8	NA	NA	NA	NA	NA
% Net Inc.of Revs.	NA	8.4	12.3	11.5	3.2	NA	NA	NA	NA	NA
% Ret. on Assets	NA	5.6	5.5	11.0	NA	NA	NA	NA	NA	NA
% Ret. on Equity	NA	14.0	15.2	15.7	NA	NA	NA	NA	NA	NA

Data as orig. reptd. (for Arbor Software -- yr. end. Mar. 31 -- to 1998); bef. results of disc. opers. and/or spec. items. Per share data adj. for stk. divs. as of ex-div. date. Bold denotes diluted EPS (FASB 128). E-Estimated. NA-Not Available. NM-Not Meaningful. NR-Not Ranked.

Office—1344 Crossman Ave., Sunnyvale, CA 94089. **Tel**—(408) 744-9500. **Website**—http://www.hyperion.com **Chrmn & CEO**—J. R. Rodek. **Pres & COO**—S. V. Imbler. **CFO**—M. Stemad. **Dirs**—G. G. Greenfield, H. S. Gruner, A. Papone, J. A. Perakis, J. R. Rodek. **Transfer Agent & Registrar**—Boston EquiServe, Palo Alto, CA. **Incorporated**—in Delaware in 1991. **Empl**— 2,148. **S&P Analyst:** M.I.

STANDARD &POOR'S
STOCK REPORTS

IDEC Pharmaceuticals

NASDAQ Symbol **IDPH**

In S&P SmallCap 600

09-OCT-99

Industry: Biotechnology

Summary: IDPH develops targeted therapies for the treatment of cancer and autoimmune diseases.

Quantitative Evaluations

Outlook (1 Lowest—5 Highest) • **3⁻**

Fair Value • **111**

Risk • **High**

Earn./Div. Rank • **C**

Technical Eval. • **Bearish** since 9/99

Rel. Strength Rank (1 Lowest—99 Highest) • **72**

Insider Activity • **NA**

Recent Price • 104½
52 Wk Range • 145½-20½
Yield • Nil
12-Mo. P/E • 78.6

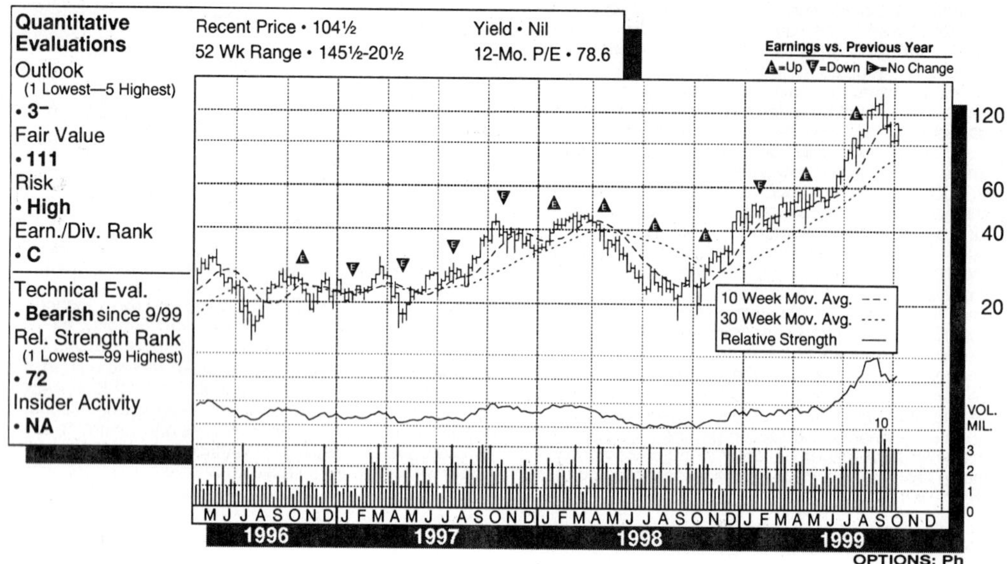

Business Profile - 04-JUN-99

The company is developing products for the long-term management of cancers and autoimmune and inflammatory diseases. IDPH has a joint venture with Genentech Inc. for the commercialization of Rituxan, used in the treatment of relapsed or refractory low grade or follicular B-cell non-Hodgkin's lymphoma. The company continued to experience strong demand for Rituxan during the 1999 first quarter. In the 1998 third quarter, IDPH and Genentech continued a transition from drop-shipment directly to end users to the more standard practice of distribution via drug wholesalers. Cash, cash equivalents and marketable securities at the end of the 1999 first quarter totaled $196 million, up from $73.5 million at 1998 year end.

Operational Review - 04-JUN-99

Total revenues in the first quarter of 1999 advanced 13%, year to year, as higher revenues from joint businesses, including an arrangement with Genentech for the sale of Rituxan, outweighed the absence of license fees; Rituxan sales climbed 48%. Operating costs and expenses were well controlled; net income gained 24%, to $4,809,000 ($0.20 a share, diluted), from $3,868,000 ($0.16). IDPH noted that it can earn a higher percentage of co-promotion profits for the balance of the year, once profits from its venture with Genetech pass a fixed level.

Stock Performance - 08-OCT-99

In the past 30 trading days, IDPH's shares have declined 20%, compared to a 0.91% fall in the S&P 500. Average trading volume for the past five days was 649,760 shares, compared with the 40-day moving average of 885,238 shares.

Key Stock Statistics

Dividend Rate/Share	Nil	Shareholders	425
Shs. outstg. (M)	20.7	Market cap. (B)	$ 2.2
Avg. daily vol. (M)	0.913	Inst. holdings	86%
Tang. Bk. Value/Share	6.60		
Beta	1.87		

Value of $10,000 invested 5 years ago: $ 181,739

Fiscal Year Ending Dec. 31

	1999	1998	1997	1996	1995	1994
Revenues (Million $)						
1Q	20.51	18.13	6.66	9.94	8.35	1.62
2Q	35.29	24.06	5.40	7.07	—	1.16
3Q	—	17.01	6.43	2.90	2.37	1.46
4Q	—	27.75	26.11	10.10	10.71	3.21
Yr.	—	86.96	44.61	30.01	23.64	7.44
Earnings Per Share ($)						
1Q	**0.20**	**0.16**	-0.12	0.10	-0.75	-0.53
2Q	**0.80**	**0.44**	-0.63	-0.22	—	-0.55
3Q	—	**0.08**	-0.51	-0.26	-0.32	-0.41
4Q	—	**0.24**	**0.35**	0.05	0.14	-0.23
Yr.	—	**0.92**	**-0.83**	**-0.34**	**-1.18**	**-1.65**

Next earnings report expected: mid October

Dividend Data

No cash dividends have been paid.

A Division of The McGraw-Hill Companies

IDEC Pharmaceuticals Corporation

Business Summary - 04-JUN-99

IDEC Pharmaceuticals Corp. (IDPH) is a biopharmaceutical company that is commercializing, researching and developing therapies to treat cancers and autoimmune and inflammatory diseases. The company's first commercial product is Rituxan, for the treatment of non-Hodgkin's B-cell lymphomas, which afflict approximately 260,000 patients in the U.S. IDPH is also developing products for the treatment of solid tumors, which afflict 1.1 million new patients each year in the U.S.; and lupus and psoriasis, which together afflict about 5.6 million people in the U.S.

Rituxan received regulatory approval in the U.S. and Switzerland in November 1997 for single agent use in relapsed or refractory, low-grade or follicular, CD20 positive, B-cell non-Hodgkin's lymphomas. Rituxan is the U.S. trade name for the compound Rituximab (formerly IDEC-C2B8). In Switzerland, Rituximab is marketed as MabThera. Rituxan is being marketed and sold in the U.S. under a co-promotion agreement with Genentech, Inc. The company's revenues depend largely on the continued U.S. sales of Rituxan. IDPH has said that 93% of U.S. oncologists surveyed have used Rituxan, and product use continues to grow, through the treatment of new patients and the re-treatment of patients who responded to Rituxan early in 1998. The company expects to transfer all manufacturing responsibilities for bulk Rituxan to Genentech at the end of the 1999 third quarter, rather than supplying it to Genentech through November 1999, as originally been planned.

The company has developed a proprietary PRIMATIZED antibody technology, designed to avoid responses in which the patient's immune system produces antibodies against the therapeutic antibodies and other immunogenicity problems by developing monoclonal antibodies from primate rather than mouse B cells.

IDPH has also discovered a proprietary antigen formulation, PROVAX, that has shown the ability to induce cellular immunity in animals immunized with protein antigens. Cellular immunity is a counterpart to antibody-based immunity, and is responsible for the direct destruction of virally infected and malignant cells. PROVAX is a combination of defined chemical entities and may provide a practical means for the development of effective immunotherapies, which the company believes may be useful for the treatment of certain cancers and viral diseases. The company intends to make PROVAX available through licenses and collaborations to interested parties for development of immunotherapeutic vaccines.

The company has entered into strategic partnering arrangements for each of its principal product development programs. Through these programs, IDPH is funding a significant portion of its product development costs, while capitalizing on the production, development, regulatory, marketing and sales capabilities of its partners.

Per Share Data ($) (Year Ended Dec. 31)	1998	1997	1996	1995	1994	1993	1992	1991	1990	1989
Tangible Bk. Val.	5.28	3.17	3.66	1.13	2.03	3.79	4.71	6.09	NA	NA
Cash Flow	1.10	-0.62	-0.14	-1.02	-1.43	-0.88	NA	NA	NA	NA
Earnings	0.92	-0.83	-0.34	-1.18	-1.65	-0.96	-1.39	-0.88	-0.86	-0.62
Dividends	Nil	Nil	Nil	Nil	Nil	Nil	NA	NA	NA	NA
Payout Ratio	Nil	Nil	Nil	Nil	Nil	Nil	NA	NA	NA	NA
Prices - High	48 1/8	46 1/4	32 5/8	23 5/8	6 3/4	9 1/4	20 1/4	21 1/4	NA	NA
- Low	17 1/4	15 3/4	13 7/8	2 1/8	2 1/8	3 3/4	5 3/4	11	NA	NA
P/E Ratio - High	52	NM	NM	NM	NM	NM	NM	NM	NA	NA
- Low	19	NM	NM	NM	NM	NM	NM	NM	NA	NA
Income Statement Analysis (Million $)										
Revs.	87.0	44.6	30.0	23.6	7.4	12.7	5.2	5.2	6.1	6.2
Oper. Inc.	23.2	-14.0	-2.8	-2.6	-16.1	-9.6	NA	-7.4	-5.2	NA
Depr.	4.3	4.0	2.6	2.4	2.4	0.7	NA	0.5	0.5	NA
Int. Exp.	0.6	0.9	2.7	2.3	0.5	0.4	NA	0.1	0.0	NA
Pretax Inc.	21.9	-15.5	-5.0	-17.3	-18.0	-8.9	-12.7	-5.8	-4.3	-3.0
Eff. Tax Rate	1.93%	NM	NM	NM	NM	NM	NM	NM	NM	NM
Net Inc.	21.5	-15.5	-5.0	-17.3	-18.0	-8.9	-12.7	-5.8	-4.3	-3.0
Balance Sheet & Other Fin. Data (Million $)										
Cash	73.5	34.8	25.3	18.8	13.7	9.7	NA	12.0	3.6	NA
Curr. Assets	101	79.2	91.6	27.4	22.6	22.7	NA	41.8	6.4	NA
Total Assets	125	106	114	47.6	45.5	50.7	52.6	58.4	8.3	NA
Curr. Liab.	14.5	19.4	13.7	8.7	9.4	11.2	NA	1.8	2.1	NA
LT Debt	2.1	2.0	5.0	6.6	7.4	3.6	0.2	NA	NA	NA
Common Eqty.	106	80.7	66.0	17.1	27.9	35.7	43.8	54.9	-15.3	NA
Total Cap.	109	84.4	71.0	23.7	35.3	39.3	43.9	NA	NA	NA
Cap. Exp.	1.7	5.9	6.3	1.3	1.6	NA	NA	NA	NA	NA
Cash Flow	25.8	-11.5	-2.3	-14.9	-15.6	-8.2	NA	-5.3	-3.8	NA
Curr. Ratio	7.0	4.1	6.7	3.1	2.4	2.0	NA	22.7	3.1	NA
% LT Debt of Cap.	1.9	2.4	7.0	27.9	20.9	9.2	Nil	NA	NA	NA
% Net Inc.of Revs.	24.7	NM	NM	NM	NM	NM	NM	NM	NM	NM
% Ret. on Assets	18.6	NM	NM	NM	NM	NM	NM	NM	NM	NM
% Ret. on Equity	23.0	NM	NM	NM	NM	NM	NM	NM	NM	NM

Data as orig reptd.; bef. results of disc opers/spec. items. Per share data adj. for stk. divs. Bold denotes diluted EPS (FASB 128)-prior periods restated. E-Estimated. NA-Not Available. NM-Not Meaningful. NR-Not Ranked.

Office—11011 Torreyana Rd., San Diego, CA 92121. **Tel**—(858) 550-8500. **Chrmn, Pres & CEO**—W. H. Rastetter. **CFO**—P. M. Schneider. **Investor Contact**—Connie Matsui (858 550-8634). **Dirs**—C. C. Edwards, A. B. Glassberg, K. Hashimoto, F. P. Johnson, R. W. Pangia, W. H. Rastetter, B. R. Ross, L. Schenk, W. D. Young. **Transfer Agent & Registrar**—First Interstate Bank, Encino, CA. **Incorporated**—in Delaware in 1985; reincorporated in Delaware in 1997. **Empl**— 400. **S&P Analyst:** S.S.

STANDARD
&POOR'S
STOCK REPORTS

IDEX Corp.

NYSE Symbol **IEX**
In S&P SmallCap 600

09-OCT-99

Industry: Manufacturing (Diversified)

Summary: This company, which designs, makes and markets a broad range of pump products and engineered equipment, serves a diverse customer base in the U.S. and internationally.

Quantitative Evaluations

Outlook (1 Lowest—5 Highest) • **1**

Fair Value • **21¼**

Risk • **Low**

Earn./Div. Rank • **B+**

Technical Eval. • **Bearish** since 9/99

Rel. Strength Rank (1 Lowest—99 Highest) • **55**

Insider Activity • **Neutral**

Recent Price • 28½
52 Wk Range • 34⅛-21⅝
Yield • 2.0%
12-Mo. P/E • 16.3

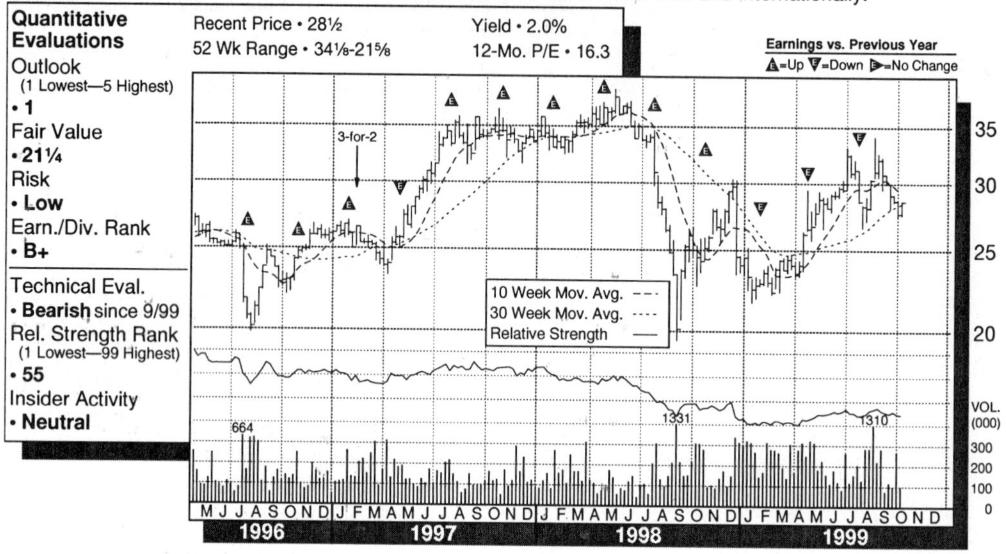

Business Profile - 08-OCT-99

In August 1998, the company sold its Strippit unit to Belgium-based LVD Co., completing a divestiture program begun in December 1997. The sale will let IEX focus on building its pump products and engineered equipment businesses. On June 4, 1999, IDEX acquired Milan, Italy-based FAST S.p.A. for approximately $61 million. FAST is a leading European manufacturer of refinishing and color-formulation equipment for a number of applications. In October 1998, directors authorized the repurchase of up to 1.5 million common shares. The dividend was raised 3.7% in January 1999.

Operational Review - 08-OCT-99

Net sales for the six months ended June 30, 1999, were down 3.2%, year to year, as a 5% decline in base business sales outweighed a 2% increase from acquisitions. While domestic sales levels equaled those of the prior year, international sales were down 9%, as weaker sales in Europe and Latin America were partially offset by slightly higher shipments to the Asia Pacific region. Gross margins narrowed and with higher SG&A expenses and goodwill amortization charges, operating income fell 14%. Interest expense decreased 26% and after taxes at 38.0% in both periods, income from continuing operations was down 10%, to $26,042,000 ($0.87 a share) from $29,033,000 ($0.96). Per share results in 1998 exclude income from discontinued operations of $0.31 and an extraordinary loss of $0.08.

Stock Performance - 08-OCT-99

In the past 30 trading days, IEX's shares have declined 11%, compared to a 0.91% fall in the S&P 500. Average trading volume for the past five days was 19,340 shares, compared with the 40-day moving average of 62,856 shares.

Key Stock Statistics

Dividend Rate/Share	0.56	Shareholders	1,268
Shs. outstg. (M)	29.6	Market cap. (B)	$0.845
Avg. daily vol. (M)	0.029	Inst. holdings	63%
Tang. Bk. Value/Share	NM		
Beta	1.21		

Value of $10,000 invested 5 years ago: $ 19,560

Fiscal Year Ending Dec. 31

	1999	1998	1997	1996	1995	1994
Revenues (Million $)						
1Q	156.5	159.1	131.4	133.9	116.6	85.90
2Q	161.5	169.5	142.0	131.2	127.2	93.50
3Q	—	159.4	141.8	140.9	116.8	107.0
4Q	—	152.2	137.0	156.6	126.7	113.1
Yr.	—	640.1	552.2	562.5	487.3	399.5
Earnings Per Share ($)						
1Q	**0.40**	**0.46**	0.41	0.41	0.37	0.25
2Q	**0.47**	**0.50**	0.44	0.43	0.42	0.28
3Q	—	**0.46**	0.45	0.40	0.36	0.30
4Q	—	**0.39**	**0.48**	0.45	0.39	0.32
Yr.	—	**1.81**	**1.78**	**1.49**	1.53	1.15

Next earnings report expected: mid October

Dividend Data (Dividends have been paid since 1995.)

Amount ($)	Date Decl.	Ex-Div. Date	Stock of Record	Payment Date
0.140	Dec. 18	Jan. 13	Jan. 15	Jan. 29 '99
0.140	Mar. 23	Apr. 13	Apr. 15	Apr. 30 '99
0.140	Jun. 29	Jul. 13	Jul. 15	Jul. 30 '99
0.140	Oct. 04	Oct. 13	Oct. 15	Oct. 29 '99

IDEX Corporation

Business Summary - 08-OCT-99

IDEX Corp. (IEX), makes a broad range of proprietary pump products and engineered equipment, serving a diverse customer base in the U.S. and internationally. Products include industrial pumps and related controls for use in a variety of process applications, and proprietary equipment that may combine pumps or other devices into products for industrial, commercial and safety applications. The company operates through three business segments: pump products, dispensing equipment, and other engineered equipment.

The pump products group (59% of sales and 61% of profits in 1998) consists of six business units that manufacture engineered industrial pumps and related controls. These products are used for a wide range of process applications, including moving paints, inks, chemicals, foods, lubricants and fuels, as well as in medical applications, water treatment and industrial production operations.

The dispensing equipment group (19% and 19%) consists of two business units that produce highly engineered equipment for dispensing, metering and mixing tints, colorants, paints, inks and dyes, and centralized lubrication systems. This equipment is used in a wide array of industries around the world, such as paints and coatings, machinery, and transportation equipment.

Other engineered products (22% and 20%) consists of two business units that manufacture proprietary equipment, including engineered banding and clamping devices, fire fighting pumps and rescue tools. These products are used in a broad range of industrial and commercial markets, including transportation equipment, oil and gas, electronics, communications, traffic and commercial signs, and fire and rescue.

IEX's growth strategy focuses on the introduction of new products, new applications for existing products, increasing market share, and international expansion. It believes that it holds the leading or second market share position in each of its business units.

Operating margins, which management feels have always been above average for an industrial company, improved somewhat, to 18.8% in 1997, from 18.5% in 1996, but narrowed to 17.1% in 1998, reflecting the inclusion of acquired companies with margins lower than the company's base businesses. IEX believes that it is well positioned, with diversity in its products and markets, and it does not produce the more cyclical capital goods. The company operates with a small backlog, and relies on daily incoming orders to meet sales and profit targets.

Per Share Data ($) (Year Ended Dec. 31)	1998	1997	1996	1995	1994	1993	1992	1991	1990	1989
Tangible Bk. Val.	NM	NM	NM	-1.16	-1.13	-0.04	-0.68	0.33	-1.00	-1.81
Cash Flow	2.93	2.59	2.17	2.09	1.61	1.26	1.05	0.89	0.88	0.83
Earnings	1.81	1.78	1.69	1.53	1.15	0.88	0.71	0.63	0.64	0.58
Dividends	0.54	0.48	0.43	0.37	Nil	Nil	Nil	Nil	Nil	Nil
Payout Ratio	30%	27%	25%	24%	Nil	Nil	Nil	Nil	Nil	Nil
Prices - High	38¾	36⅝	27⅝	29½	19½	16	10½	9	7¾	7½
- Low	19½	23¼	19⅞	18½	15	9⅝	7⅜	4¼	4½	6⅛
P/E Ratio - High	21	21	16	19	17	18	15	14	12	13
- Low	11	13	12	12	13	11	10	7	7	11
Income Statement Analysis (Million $)										
Revs.	640	552	563	487	400	309	277	228	228	221
Oper. Inc.	143	128	113	103	82.4	61.4	52.6	44.8	45.9	47.2
Depr.	33.6	24.3	14.3	16.5	13.7	11.3	9.7	6.8	5.6	5.2
Int. Exp.	22.4	18.4	18.9	15.9	13.6	11.0	12.2	12.7	15.6	17.8
Pretax Inc.	87.7	84.5	78.9	71.0	52.5	38.3	31.0	25.7	25.8	25.1
Eff. Tax Rate	38%	37%	36%	36%	36%	34%	35%	38%	39%	40%
Net Inc.	54.4	53.5	50.2	45.3	33.6	25.3	20.1	15.9	15.7	15.1
Balance Sheet & Other Fin. Data (Million $)										
Cash	2.7	11.8	5.3	5.9	6.3	3.5	2.4	1.5	0.8	3.5
Curr. Assets	196	197	201	186	151	115	117	74.0	76.0	75.0
Total Assets	696	599	584	466	371	259	253	143	134	134
Curr. Liab.	80.3	77.8	92.9	82.8	69.4	42.6	40.0	31.7	30.7	30.4
LT Debt	283	258	272	206	168	117	140	65.8	104	125
Common Eqty.	286	239	196	151	116	83.7	58.7	37.1	-4.3	-23.3
Total Cap.	569	497	468	357	284	201	199	103	100	102
Cap. Exp.	20.8	13.6	13.8	13.0	8.9	7.8	8.2	3.6	6.8	5.4
Cash Flow	88.0	77.8	64.5	61.8	47.3	36.6	29.8	22.7	21.3	17.1
Curr. Ratio	2.4	2.5	2.2	2.2	2.2	2.7	2.9	2.3	2.5	2.5
% LT Debt of Cap.	49.8	51.9	58.1	57.7	59.1	58.4	70.4	63.9	104.3	NM
% Net Inc.of Revs.	8.5	9.7	8.9	9.3	8.4	8.2	7.3	7.0	6.9	6.8
% Ret. on Assets	8.4	9.0	9.6	10.8	10.7	9.9	10.1	12.3	11.7	11.5
% Ret. on Equity	20.7	24.6	28.9	33.9	33.6	35.6	41.9	104.4	NM	NM

Data as orig reptd.; bef. results of disc opers/spec. items. Per share data adj. for stk. divs. Bold denotes diluted EPS (FASB 128)-prior periods restated. E-Estimated. NA-Not Available. NM-Not Meaningful. NR-Not Ranked.

Office—630 Dundee Road, Northbrook, IL 60062. **Tel**—(847) 498-7070. **Website**—www.idexcorp.com **Chrmn** —D. N. Boyce. **Pres & CEO**—F. J. Hansen. **SVP-Fin, CFO & Investor Contact**—Wayne P. Sayatovic. **Treas**—D. C. Lennox. **VP & Secy**—F. J. Notaro. **Dirs**—D. N. Boyce, F. J. Hansen, R. E. Heath, H. R. Kravis, W. H. Luers, P. E. Raether, C. S. Robbins, G. R. Roberts, N. A. Springer, M. T. Tokarz. **Transfer Agent & Registrar**—Harris Trust & Savings Bank, Chicago. **Incorporated**—in Delaware in 1987. **Empl**— 3,800. **S&P Analyst:** C.C.P.

IDEXX Laboratories

NASDAQ Symbol **IDXX**

In S&P SmallCap 600

09-OCT-99 **Industry:** Biotechnology

Summary: This company provides veterinary practice management software and diagnostic products for a broad range of veterinary, food and environmental testing applications.

Quantitative Evaluations

Outlook (1 Lowest—5 Highest) • **4-**

Fair Value • **22⅛**

Risk • **High**

Earn./Div. Rank • **B-**

Technical Eval. • **Bearish** since 9/99

Rel. Strength Rank (1 Lowest—99 Highest) • **32**

Insider Activity • **NA**

Recent Price • 16¾ | Yield • Nil

52 Wk Range • 28⅝-14⅜ | 12-Mo. P/E • NM

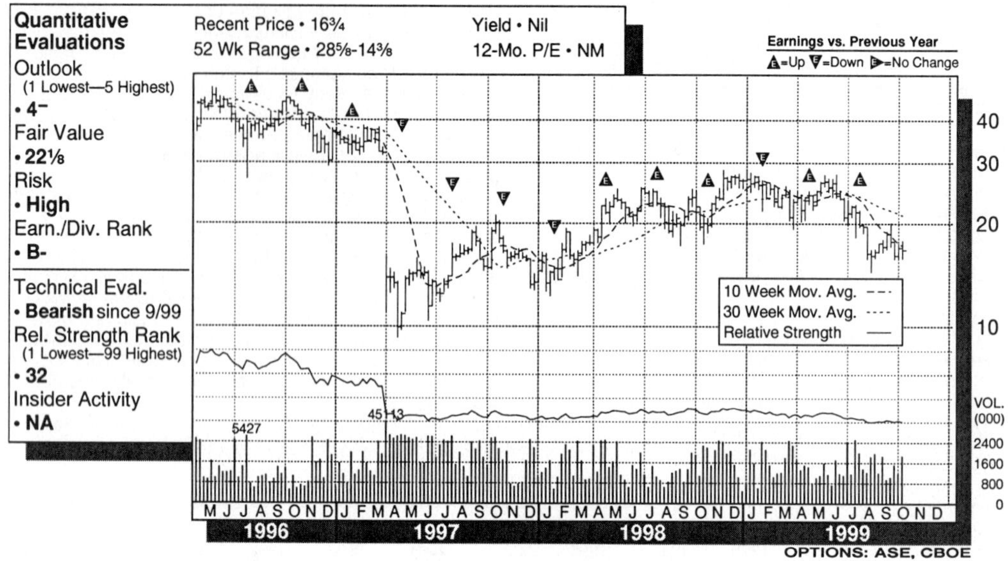

OPTIONS: ASE, CBOE

Business Profile - 31-AUG-99

In 1998, the company posted good revenue growth, on increased sales of existing and recently acquired product lines. In the 1999 second quarter, IDXX continued to see strong revenue growth, from higher sales of veterinary consumables, veterinary practice information management systems, veterinary reference laboratory services, and products for use in water testing. The company expected this momentum to continue in 1999, and planned to emphasize its key investment areas of veterinary pharmaceuticals and veterinary practice information management software. In August 1999, directors authorized the repurchase of up to 2 million common shares.

Operational Review - 31-AUG-99

Revenues in the six months ended June 30, 1999, advanced 14%, year to year, reflecting a 14% rise in companion animal group sales and a 13% increase in food and environmental division sales. Gross margins widened, on a more favorable sales mix. Sales and marketing expenses declined 8.9%; despite a 40% rise in R&D expenses, pretax income soared 70%. After taxes at 38.0%, versus 39.0%, net income surged 73%, to $15,306,000 ($0.37 a share, on 2.8% more shares), from $8,859,000 ($0.22).

Stock Performance - 08-OCT-99

In the past 30 trading days, IDXX's shares have declined 5%, compared to a 0.91% fall in the S&P 500. Average trading volume for the past five days was 370,880 shares, compared with the 40-day moving average of 293,067 shares.

Key Stock Statistics

Dividend Rate/Share	Nil	Shareholders	1,654
Shs. outstg. (M)	39.5	Market cap. (B)	$0.662
Avg. daily vol. (M)	0.277	Inst. holdings	78%
Tang. Bk. Value/Share	6.17		
Beta	1.21		

Value of $10,000 invested 5 years ago: $ 10,509

Fiscal Year Ending Dec. 31

	1999	1998	1997	1996	1995	1994
Revenues (Million $)						
1Q	89.65	77.79	60.53	57.40	39.20	27.40
2Q	91.52	80.89	58.89	65.88	46.50	31.10
3Q	—	78.49	71.73	69.84	48.70	31.90
4Q	—	82.72	71.82	74.57	54.20	35.90
Yr.	—	319.9	263.0	267.7	188.6	126.4
Earnings Per Share ($)						
1Q	**0.18**	**0.10**	**0.02**	**0.18**	0.12	0.09
2Q	**0.20**	**0.13**	**-0.05**	**0.20**	0.15	0.08
3Q	—	**0.15**	**-0.44**	**0.22**	0.16	0.11
4Q	—	**-0.78**	**-0.08**	**0.23**	0.18	0.13
Yr.	—	**-0.40**	**-0.56**	**0.83**	**0.61**	0.40

Next earnings report expected: mid October

Dividend Data

The company has never paid cash dividends on its common stock, and does not expect to pay any in the foreseeable future. The common stock was split two for one in 1993 and in 1995.

IDEXX Laboratories, Inc.

Business Summary - 31-AUG-99

IDEXX Laboratories, a world leader in diagnostic and detection systems for veterinary, food and environmental applications, offers more than 350 products to customers in more than 50 countries. The company operates in two primary business areas: veterinary products and services; and food, hygiene and environmental products and services. Products range from single-sample hand-held tests to sophisticated laboratory instrument systems to veterinary practice management software.

A majority of the company's revenues are derived from the sale of animal health diagnostic products and services. Approximately 70% and 71% of total revenues were derived from sales of veterinary diagnostic products in 1998 and 1997, respectively.

The company provides a broad range of point-of-care diagnostic products used by veterinarians in testing for a variety of companion animal disease and human conditions. IDXX also markets four instrument systems for use in veterinary clinics.

In 1997, IDXX acquired Professionals' Software, Inc. and Advanced Veterinary Systems, leaders in the veterinary practice management software business. Through these acquisitions, the company has become the leading U.S. supplier of veterinary practice management software systems. As of December 1998, IDXX software was installed in more than 8,000 U.S. clinics.

The company offers commercial veterinary laboratory and consulting services to approximately 4,500 veterinary clinics in the U.S., through facilities located in Arizona, Colorado, Illinois, California, New Jersey, Oregon and Texas. Through subsidiaries in the U.K., Japan and Australia, the company offers such services to 4,000 clinics in those countries. Veterinarians use IDXX's services by submitting samples by courier or overnight delivery to the appropriate company facility. The commercial reference laboratories offer a large selection of tests and diagnostic panels to detect a number of disease states and other conditions. Services include chemistry, hematology and pathology.

IDXX sells various detection products that help ensure the safety and wholesomeness of water and food, such as drinking water, dairy products, poultry and meat and food processing environments. Detection targets include microbial contaminants such as total coliforms, E. coli and enterococci, pathogenic bacteria such as salmonella, and other contaminants such as food antibiotic residues. The company also provides a broad range of diagnostic products to food animal producers and government customers for surveillance and eradication and health management programs. Approximately 22% and 24% of revenues were derived from sales of food and environmental products and services in 1998 and 1997, respectively.

In October 1998, the company entered the veterinary pharmaceuticals market by acquiring Blue Ridge Pharmaceuticals, an animal health drug concern, for about $50 million in cash, notes, and common stock.

Per Share Data ($) (Year Ended Dec. 31)	1998	1997	1996	1995	1994	1993	1992	1991	1990	1989
Tangible Bk. Val.	6.17	6.60	7.79	7.32	2.90	2.40	2.17	1.53	NA	NA
Cash Flow	0.02	-0.18	1.09	0.77	0.53	0.41	0.29	NA	NA	NA
Earnings	-0.40	-0.56	0.83	0.61	0.40	0.29	0.17	0.15	NA	NA
Dividends	Nil	Nil	Nil	Nil	Nil	Nil	Nil	Nil	NA	NA
Payout Ratio	Nil	Nil	Nil	Nil	Nil	Nil	Nil	Nil	NA	NA
Prices - High	28⅝	38½	53¾	47½	18⅝	16	8¼	7¼	NA	NA
- Low	12¼	9¼	26⅞	16⅞	12⅝	6⅝	4½	3⅜	NA	NA
P/E Ratio - High	NM	NM	65	78	47	55	47	48	NA	NA
- Low	NM	NM	32	28	32	23	32	22	NA	NA
Income Statement Analysis (Million $)										
Revs.	320	263	268	189	126	93.0	61.0	29.0	NA	NA
Oper. Inc.	45.0	10.0	57.4	38.7	27.2	18.4	9.6	NA	NA	NA
Depr.	15.9	14.4	10.4	5.7	4.5	3.8	3.6	NA	NA	NA
Int. Exp.	Nil	Nil	Nil	Nil	Nil	Nil	Nil	Nil	NA	NA
Pretax Inc.	-1.2	-32.3	55.3	37.0	22.8	15.0	7.0	3.3	NA	NA
Eff. Tax Rate	NM	NM	41%	42%	42%	36%	22%	10%	NA	NA
Net Inc.	-15.2	-21.1	32.6	21.5	13.3	9.7	5.4	3.0	NA	NA
Balance Sheet & Other Fin. Data (Million $)										
Cash	109	107	174	184	50.4	39.4	NA	NA	NA	NA
Curr. Assets	263	274	302	262	99	76.8	NA	NA	NA	NA
Total Assets	391	377	374	313	122	98.0	83.0	NA	NA	NA
Curr. Liab.	78.5	74.3	51.1	33.4	22.0	14.3	NA	NA	NA	NA
LT Debt	4.2	Nil	Nil	Nil	Nil	Nil	Nil	NA	NA	NA
Common Eqty.	308	303	323	279	100	83.6	71.7	NA	NA	NA
Total Cap.	312	303	323	279	100	83.6	71.7	NA	NA	NA
Cap. Exp.	9.0	12.5	11.8	15.9	4.4	2.1	2.4	NA	NA	NA
Cash Flow	0.7	-6.7	43.0	27.2	17.9	13.4	9.0	NA	NA	NA
Curr. Ratio	3.4	3.7	5.9	7.8	4.5	5.4	NA	NA	NA	NA
% LT Debt of Cap.	1.3	Nil	Nil	Nil	Nil	Nil	Nil	NA	NA	NA
% Net Inc.of Revs.	NM	NM	12.2	11.4	10.6	10.4	8.8	10.6	NA	NA
% Ret. on Assets	NM	NM	9.6	9.9	12.1	10.7	8.9	NA	NA	NA
% Ret. on Equity	NM	NM	10.9	11.3	14.5	12.4	10.4	NA	NA	NA

Data as orig. reptd.; bef. results of disc. opers. and/or spec. items. Per share data adj. for stk. divs. as of ex-div. date. Bold denotes diluted EPS (FASB 128). E-Estimated. NA-Not Available. NM-Not Meaningful. NR-Not Ranked.

Office—One IDEXX Dr., Westbrook, ME 04092. **Tel**—(207) 856-0300. **Fax**—(207) 856-0347. **Website**—http//:www.idexx.com **Chrmn**—D. E. Shaw. **Pres & CEO**—J. J. Langan. **SVP & CFO**—R. K. Carlton. **Secy**—R. B. Thorp. **VP-Fin, Treas & Investor Contact**—Merilee Raines. **Dirs**—M. L. Good, J. R. Hesse, E. R. Kinney, J. J. Langan, J. L. Moody Jr., K. Paigen, W. F. Pounds, D. E. Shaw, E. F. Workman Jr. **Transfer Agent & Registrar**—First National Bank of Boston. **Incorporated**—in Delaware in 1983. **Empl**— 2,100. **S&P Analyst:** John J. Arege

STANDARD
&POOR'S
STOCK REPORTS

IHOP Corp.

NYSE Symbol **IHP**

In S&P SmallCap 600

09-OCT-99

Industry:
Restaurants

Summary: This company develops, franchises and operates International House of Pancakes restaurants, one of the best-known national family restaurant chains in the U.S.

Quantitative Evaluations

Outlook
(1 Lowest—5 Highest)
• **5**

Fair Value
• **32¼**

Risk
• **Low**

Earn./Div. Rank
• **B+**

Technical Eval.
• **NA**

Rel. Strength Rank
(1 Lowest—99 Highest)
• **26**

Insider Activity
• **NA**

Recent Price • 20⅛
52 Wk Range • 26-14⅞
Yield • Nil
12-Mo. P/E • 13.9

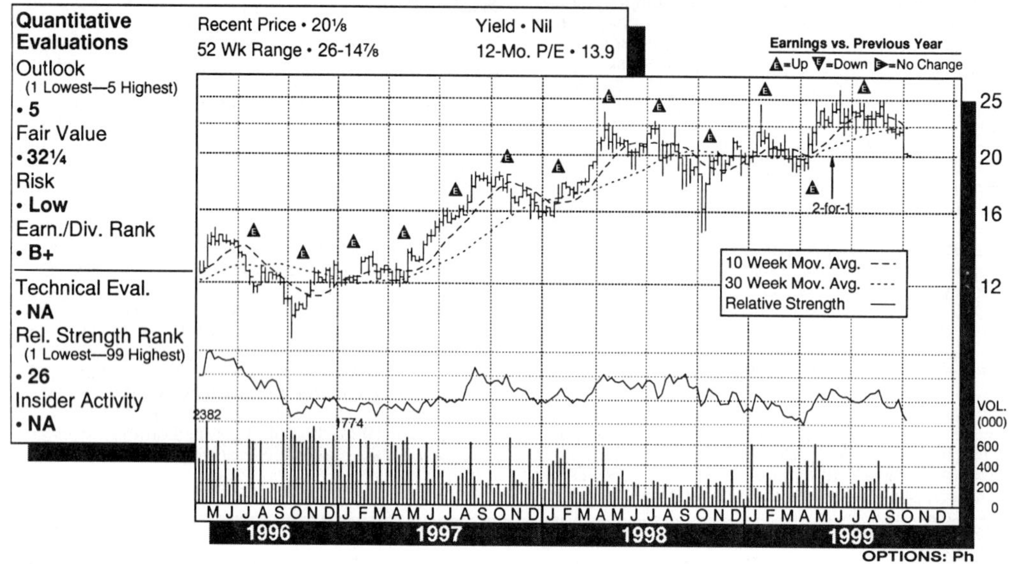

Business Profile - 20-SEP-99

IHP continues to concentrate on its long-term strategy of unit level excellence, superior service, intelligent expansion and effective marketing. In 1998, IHP decided to upgrade its lunch and dinner items by creating an "After Breakfast" menu, which has been rolled out nationally to more than 90% of the IHP chain, as of July 1999. The company opened 34 new restaurants during the first six months of 1999, bringing the total number of IHP units to 864, and has a goal of operating 1,000 restaurants within the next three years. On September 17, 1999, trading in the company's shares shifted from the Nasdaq Stock Market to the NYSE under the ticker IHP. A two-for-one stock split was effected in May 1999.

Operational Review - 20-SEP-99

Total revenues in the six months ended June 30, 1999, advanced 10%, as higher franchise operations revenue outweighed lower sale of franchises and equipment and company-operated restaurant revenue. System-wide sales, including franchisees and company-operated restaurants, rose 10%, and comparable store sales increased 0.8%. Total costs and expenses rose less rapidly than revenues, and pretax income climbed 28%. After taxes at 38.5%, versus 39.0%, net income advanced 29%, to $14.4 million ($0.71 a share), from $11.2 million ($0.56; adjusted for May 1999 two-for-one split).

Stock Performance - 08-OCT-99

In the past 30 trading days, IHP's shares have declined 12%, compared to a 0.91% fall in the S&P 500. Average trading volume for the past five days was 15,360 shares, compared with the 40-day moving average of 38,728 shares.

Key Stock Statistics

Dividend Rate/Share	Nil	Shareholders	2,500
Shs. outstg. (M)	20.0	Market cap. (B)	$0.402
Avg. daily vol. (M)	0.029	Inst. holdings	76%
Tang. Bk. Value/Share	9.69		
Beta	0.58		

Value of $10,000 invested 5 years ago: $ 13,879

Fiscal Year Ending Dec. 31

	1999	1998	1997	1996	1995	1994
Revenues (Million $)						
1Q	61.32	55.88	46.44	40.29	33.20	32.80
2Q	67.51	65.59	51.57	44.47	40.10	37.20
3Q	—	66.45	56.31	51.57	42.57	37.30
4Q	—	69.18	61.13	53.77	48.45	42.80
Yr.	—	256.2	215.5	190.1	164.3	150.0
Earnings Per Share ($)						
1Q	**0.33**	**0.23**	**0.18**	**0.16**	0.10	0.12
2Q	**0.39**	**0.32**	**0.26**	**0.23**	0.21	0.20
3Q	—	**0.36**	**0.29**	**0.28**	0.25	0.20
4Q	—	**0.39**	**0.34**	**0.30**	0.29	0.28
Yr.	—	**1.30**	**1.07**	**0.97**	**0.85**	**0.80**

Next earnings report expected: late October

Dividend Data

Amount ($)	Date Decl.	Ex-Div. Date	Stock of Record	Payment Date
2-for-1	Apr. 29	May. 28	May. 13	May. 27 '99

IHOP Corp.

Business Summary - 20-SEP-99

IHP's pancakes may be flat, but its recent growth trend is not. Systemwide sales (the retail sales of all International House of Pancakes restaurants) totaled $1.0 billion in 1998, up 15% from the 1997 level. Comparable average sales per restaurant, an important measure of operating performance trends, increased 3.7% in 1997 and 2.7% in 1998. Restaurant additions form the other part of the company's growth recipe: since the beginning of 1992, the IHP chain has added about 100 restaurants every two years; as July 1999, there were 864 IHP restaurants in 37 states, Canada, and Japan.

IHP operates fewer than 10% of the chain's restaurants, relying instead on a franchise system that stresses the active involvement of franchisees in the day-to-day management of their restaurants. IHP views franchising as a way of putting qualified, equity-involved managers in charge of a business venture. Unlike other franchisors, the company removes much of the downside risk for the franchisee by buying or leasing the site itself, building the restaurant, and then becoming the franchisee's landlord. IHP collects a hefty fee (between $200,000 and $350,000) for each newly developed restaurant it franchises, and it also receives a recurring revenue stream that includes rental income on the property and equipment it leases, as well as royalties and advertising fees.

As of July 1999, 640 of the chain's restaurants were operated by franchisees, and 148 units (located principally in Florida and Japan) were operated under area license agreements. In 1998, franchise operations (including royalties from area licensees, but excluding sales of franchises and equipment) generated revenues of $146 million, about 57% of total revenues.

IHP's marketing efforts have helped make International House of Pancakes one of the most recognizable names of any restaurant chain in the U.S. Most IHP franchisees and company-operated restaurants contribute approximately 2.0% of their revenues to local advertising cooperatives, which purchase television advertising time and place advertisements in printed media or direct mail. For many years, IHP's television advertising has featured Cliff Bemis as IHP's affable spokesman. In more recent commercials, the company has been emphasizing the appetizing appearance, quality and taste of IHP food.

In November 1998, IHP started using new Web-deployed software for managing retail franchisee contracting and billing. The company stated that the software has already increased efficiency by simplifying the financial and supply chain applications.

On September 17, 1999, trading in the company's shares shifted from the Nasdaq Stock Market to the NYSE under the ticker IHP.

Per Share Data ($) (Year Ended Dec. 31)	1998	1997	1996	1995	1994	1993	1992	1991	1990	1989
Tangible Bk. Val.	8.89	7.40	6.15	5.07	4.06	3.13	2.40	1.88	NA	NA
Cash Flow	1.87	1.59	1.41	1.22	1.14	0.89	0.77	0.72	NA	NA
Earnings	1.30	1.07	0.97	0.85	0.80	0.57	0.49	0.36	NA	NA
Dividends	Nil	Nil	Nil	Nil	Nil	Nil	Nil	Nil	NA	NA
Payout Ratio	Nil	Nil	Nil	Nil	Nil	Nil	Nil	Nil	NA	NA
Prices - High	23¾	18¾	15	15¼	16⅞	15⅝	10¾	7⅝	NA	NA
- Low	14¾	11⅞	9⅝	10¼	11¼	9¼	6	4¾	NA	NA
P/E Ratio - High	18	17	15	18	21	27	22	21	NA	NA
- Low	11	11	10	12	14	16	12	13	NA	NA
Income Statement Analysis (Million $)										
Revs.	256	216	190	164	145	139	112	103	NA	NA
Oper. Inc.	70.0	59.0	50.7	43.3	33.6	29.0	22.2	17.6	NA	NA
Depr.	11.3	10.0	8.3	6.9	6.4	5.7	5.0	4.9	NA	NA
Int. Exp.	17.4	14.6	11.7	8.9	6.8	5.6	4.8	5.7	NA	NA
Pretax Inc.	42.8	34.3	30.8	26.7	25.0	18.6	14.8	9.0	NA	NA
Eff. Tax Rate	39%	39%	40%	40%	40%	42%	41%	41%	NA	NA
Net Inc.	26.1	20.9	18.6	16.2	15.1	10.7	8.8	5.3	NA	NA
Balance Sheet & Other Fin. Data (Million $)										
Cash	8.6	6.0	8.7	3.9	2.0	1.2	5.7	2.7	NA	NA
Curr. Assets	40.8	40.8	41.3	27.5	21.2	19.9	21.7	15.9	NA	NA
Total Assets	446	383	329	252	203	180	150	113	NA	NA
Curr. Liab.	43.2	39.3	35.1	28.7	17.2	16.6	18.1	15.1	NA	NA
LT Debt	180	158	139	93.5	78.0	66.4	53.8	38.8	NA	NA
Common Eqty.	188	156	156	108	88.3	71.2	58.0	48.7	NA	NA
Total Cap.	403	343	269	223	184	162	130	97.0	NA	NA
Cap. Exp.	71.8	59.7	57.2	42.0	30.5	40.9	29.3	20.3	NA	NA
Cash Flow	37.4	30.9	26.9	23.1	21.5	16.5	13.8	10.1	NA	NA
Curr. Ratio	0.9	1.0	1.2	1.0	1.2	1.2	1.2	1.0	NA	NA
% LT Debt of Cap.	44.7	46.1	51.9	41.9	42.4	41.0	41.3	39.9	NA	NA
% Net Inc.of Revs.	10.2	9.7	9.8	9.8	10.4	7.7	7.9	5.1	NA	NA
% Ret. on Assets	6.3	5.9	6.4	7.1	7.9	6.5	6.6	4.0	NA	NA
% Ret. on Equity	15.2	14.6	15.7	16.4	18.9	16.5	16.4	14.7	NA	NA

Data as orig reptd.; bef. results of disc opers/spec. items. Per share data adj. for stk. divs. Bold denotes diluted EPS (FASB 128)-prior periods restated. E-Estimated. NA-Not Available. NM-Not Meaningful. NR-Not Ranked.

Office—525 N. Brand Blvd., Glendale, CA 91203-1903. **Tel**—(818) 240-6055. **Website**—http://www.ihop.com. **Chrmn, Pres & CEO**—R. K. Herzer. **EVP & COO**—D. M. Leifheit. **Acting CFO & Investor Contact**—Gene A. Scott. **VP & Secy**—M. D. Weisberger. **Dirs**—H. F. Christie, F. Edelstein, M. S. Gordon, R. K. Herzer, N. C. Hulsey, L. A. Kay, D. M. Leifheit, C. W. Nahas, P. W. Rose. **Transfer Agent**—ChaseMellon Shareholder Services, Ridgefield Park, NJ. **Incorporated**—in Delaware in 1976. **Empl**— 2,400. **S&P Analyst:** A. Bensinger

STANDARD
&POOR'S
STOCK REPORTS

IMCO Recycling

NYSE Symbol **IMR**

In S&P SmallCap 600

09-OCT-99 **Industry:** Iron & Steel

Summary: IMCO is the world's largest aluminum recycler, and also processes zinc and magnesium.

Quantitative Evaluations

Outlook
(1 Lowest—5 Highest)
• **5+**

Fair Value
• **24⅜**

Risk
• **Low**

Earn./Div. Rank
• **B+**

Technical Eval.
• **Bearish** since 9/99

Rel. Strength Rank
(1 Lowest—99 Highest)
• **27**

Insider Activity
• **NA**

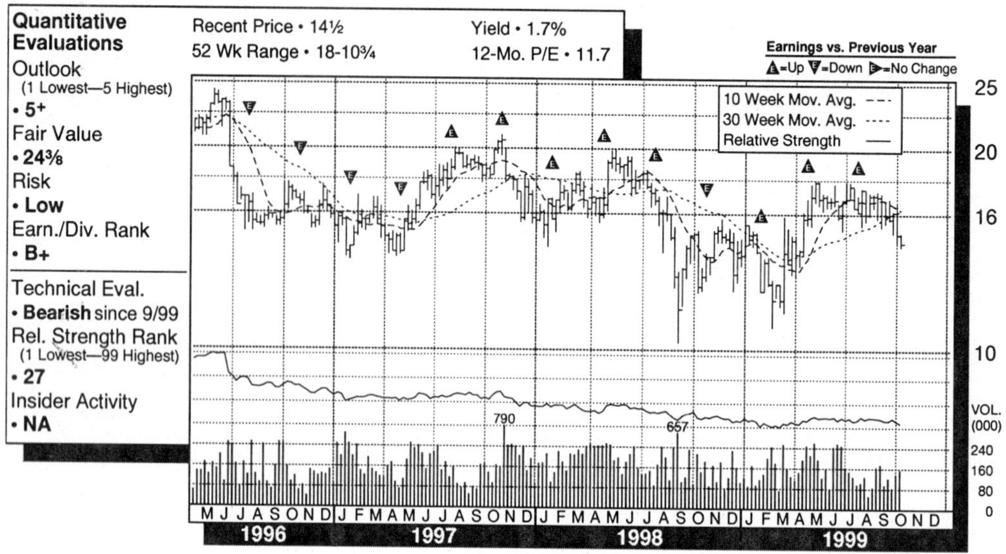

Business Profile - 03-AUG-99

In the first half of 1999, processing volume grew nearly 20%, year to year, spurred by acquisitions, new plant construction, and expansion. Tolling transactions accounted for 62% of total processing, down from 72%, reflecting IMR's acquisition of companies with buy/sell businesses. In March 1999, the company announced plans to construct an aluminum alloying facility in Saginaw, MI, to supply molten aluminum to GM under a new $1 billion contract. In February 1999, IMR acquired the Shelbyville, TN, aluminum alloys plant of Alcan Aluminium. The purchase strengthened the company's ability to serve the transportation sector.

Operational Review - 03-AUG-99

Revenues in the half of 1999 climbed 43%, year to year, reflecting the acquisition of U.S. Zinc Corp. in July 1998, and increased product sales. Gross margins narrowed, and with sharply higher SG&A expense, higher interest costs associated with increased borrowing and the operation of more production facilities, and greater amortization charges, the gain in pretax income was held to 11%. After taxes at 37.4%, versus 36.9%, net income was up 10%, to $10,614,000 ($0.64 a share), from $9,622,000 ($0.57).

Stock Performance - 08-OCT-99

In the past 30 trading days, IMR's shares have declined 15%, compared to a 0.91% fall in the S&P 500. Average trading volume for the past five days was 30,600 shares, compared with the 40-day moving average of 25,810 shares.

Key Stock Statistics

Dividend Rate/Share	0.24	Shareholders	485
Shs. outstg. (M)	16.5	Market cap. (B)	$0.239
Avg. daily vol. (M)	0.025	Inst. holdings	50%
Tang. Bk. Value/Share	4.49		
Beta	1.09		

Value of $10,000 invested 5 years ago: $ 12,700

Fiscal Year Ending Dec. 31

	1999	1998	1997	1996	1995	1994
Revenues (Million $)						
1Q	175.2	127.2	82.53	50.72	30.75	21.68
2Q	184.7	124.5	76.60	50.47	29.72	23.07
3Q	—	153.7	77.46	53.69	32.11	26.21
4Q	—	163.1	102.8	55.99	48.59	30.16
Yr.	—	568.5	339.4	210.9	141.2	101.1
Earnings Per Share ($)						
1Q	**0.31**	**0.28**	**0.18**	**0.24**	0.24	0.18
2Q	**0.33**	**0.30**	**0.28**	**0.21**	0.25	0.09
3Q	—	**0.29**	**0.32**	**-0.07**	0.27	0.22
4Q	—	**0.30**	**0.28**	**0.16**	0.27	0.24
Yr.	—	**1.17**	**1.06**	**0.55**	**1.05**	**0.74**

Next earnings report expected: late October

Dividend Data (Dividends have been paid since 1995.)

Amount ($)	Date Decl.	Ex-Div. Date	Stock of Record	Payment Date
0.060	Dec. 02	Dec. 10	Dec. 14	Dec. 31 '98
0.060	Feb. 25	Mar. 17	Mar. 19	Mar. 31 '99
0.060	May. 13	Jun. 09	Jun. 11	Jun. 30 '99
0.060	Aug. 19	Sep. 08	Sep. 10	Sep. 30 '99

A Division of The McGraw-Hill Companies

IMCO Recycling Inc.

Business Summary - 03-AUG-99

This company is not a heavy metal fan. IMCO Recycling Inc. (IMR), based in Irving, TX, is the world's largest recycler of secondary aluminum, including used aluminum beverage cans (UBCs), scrap and dross (a by-product of aluminum production). It converts UBCs, scrap and dross into molten metal, which is then delivered to customers in molten form or ingots. The company also recovers magnesium via a relatively similar process and also recycles zinc.

Recycled metal has gained a larger share of the overall U.S. aluminum market in the past two decades. Recycled aluminum, which performs as well as primary aluminum in most applications, saves the aluminum industry 95% of the energy costs and 90% of the capital and labor involved in making aluminum from bauxite.

Most of IMR's processing consists of aluminum, magnesium and zinc tolled for customers. To a lesser (but increasing) extent, the company's processing also consists of buy/sell business, which involves purchasing scrap metal and dross for processing and resale. IMR's aluminum alloying facility (acquired in November 1997) is primarily engaged in buy/sell business, as opposed to tolling; therefore, the company experienced higher levels of buy/sell business relative to tolling in 1998 and the first half of 1999. The higher level of buy/sell business has increased IMR's working capital requirements, and subjected it to greater risks associated with price fluctuations in the aluminum market. The mid-1998 acquisition of U.S. Zinc also increased the company's level of overall buy/sell business.

The company's customers include most of the major U.S. aluminum producers, aluminum diecasters, extruders, and other processors of aluminum products. Although IMR's traditional role is to be a supplier to the container and construction markets, a principal element of its strategy involves expansion into new markets, specifically the rapidly expanding aluminum automotive market. Aluminum is an attractive alternative to steel in the automobile industry because it is recyclable, corrosion-resistant, and lighter in weight.

IMR intends to continue to expand in the U.S. and abroad by establishing additional aluminum recycling facilities, expanding its existing facilities, and acquiring other recycling businesses. In early 1999, it acquired the assets of an aluminum alloying facility in Shelbyville, TN, and a zinc oxide facility in Clarksville, TN, for $11 million each. As of year-end 1998, the company had 22 domestic recycling plants, with an annual processing capacity of 2.8 billion pounds. IMR also has a 50% interest in a German joint venture that owns and operates two recycling and foundry alloy facilities mainly serving the European automotive markets, and owns an aluminum recycling plant in Swansea, Wales.

Per Share Data ($) (Year Ended Dec. 31)	1998	1997	1996	1995	1994	1993	1992	1991	1990	1989
Tangible Bk. Val.	4.53	5.72	6.64	6.13	5.38	4.50	3.83	2.92	2.34	1.84
Cash Flow	2.52	2.30	1.46	1.80	1.36	1.23	1.01	0.84	0.80	0.69
Earnings	1.17	1.06	0.55	1.03	0.73	0.70	0.67	0.52	0.53	0.54
Dividends	0.21	0.20	0.20	0.10	0.10	Nil	Nil	Nil	Nil	Nil
Payout Ratio	18%	19%	36%	10%	14%	Nil	Nil	Nil	Nil	Nil
Prices - High	20	21	24 5/8	24 1/2	16 7/8	16 3/4	15 1/8	11 3/8	6 7/8	8 1/2
- Low	10 1/4	13 5/8	14 3/8	13 3/8	12 1/8	10 7/8	6 1/2	5 3/8	4	4 3/4
P/E Ratio - High	17	20	45	24	23	24	23	22	13	16
- Low	9	13	26	13	17	16	10	10	8	9
Income Statement Analysis (Million $)										
Revs.	569	339	211	141	101	74.2	60.2	49.2	54.6	37.1
Oper. Inc.	60.6	46.8	25.1	30.3	23.6	17.9	14.2	10.7	10.9	8.6
Depr.	22.8	16.5	11.3	9.3	7.4	6.2	3.8	3.5	3.0	1.6
Int. Exp.	9.2	7.3	3.4	1.5	1.3	1.4	1.4	1.4	1.6	2.3
Pretax Inc.	31.1	23.5	10.9	20.4	13.7	11.1	9.8	6.5	7.1	5.8
Eff. Tax Rate	36%	39%	38%	39%	38%	28%	23%	15%	19%	7.30%
Net Inc.	19.6	14.1	6.7	12.5	8.5	8.0	7.5	5.6	5.7	5.4
Balance Sheet & Other Fin. Data (Million $)										
Cash	6.1	0.4	5.1	8.7	2.9	1.7	12.0	9.2	6.1	6.3
Curr. Assets	152	91.7	53.3	47.9	27.9	19.8	19.9	18.1	17.1	15.9
Total Assets	457	333	165	140	96.8	79.4	68.9	53.0	47.7	45.1
Curr. Liab.	78.9	33.8	20.7	19.9	10.6	10.7	8.6	3.4	3.8	5.9
LT Debt	169	109	48.2	29.8	11.9	8.0	10.5	13.0	13.0	13.0
Common Eqty.	187	169	88.3	83.3	68.3	57.1	48.9	35.8	29.9	25.3
Total Cap.	369	289	142	119	85.0	68.1	60.3	49.6	44.0	39.3
Cap. Exp.	35.2	37.2	16.7	15.5	6.6	11.9	16.9	7.1	4.8	8.9
Cash Flow	42.4	30.6	18.0	21.8	15.8	14.2	11.3	9.1	8.8	6.9
Curr. Ratio	1.9	2.7	2.6	2.4	2.6	1.9	2.3	5.4	4.5	2.7
% LT Debt of Cap.	45.7	37.7	33.9	25.1	14.0	11.8	17.4	26.2	29.6	33.1
% Net Inc.of Revs.	3.4	4.2	3.2	8.9	8.4	10.8	12.4	11.4	10.5	14.5
% Ret. on Assets	5.0	5.7	4.4	10.5	9.5	10.9	12.0	11.0	12.4	12.2
% Ret. on Equity	11.0	11.0	7.8	16.5	13.3	15.1	17.2	17.0	20.8	30.9

Data as orig reptd.; bef. results of disc opers/spec. items. Per share data adj. for stk. divs. Bold denotes diluted EPS (FASB 128)-prior periods restated. E-Estimated. NA-Not Available. NM-Not Meaningful. NR-Not Ranked.

Office—5215 N. O'Connor Blvd., Suite 940, Irving, TX 75039. **Tel**—(972) 401-7200. **Chrmn & CEO**—D. V. Ingram. **Pres & COO**—R. L. Kerr. **EVP, CFO, Secy & Investor Contact**—Paul V. Dufour. **Dirs**—S. Bartlett, J. J. Fleming, J. Hensarling, D. V. Ingram, D. Navarro, H. G. Robinson, W. Warshauer. **Transfer Agent & Registrar**—ChaseMellon Shareholder Services, Ridgefield Park, NJ. **Incorporated**—in 1985 in Delaware. **Empl**—1,870. **S&P Analyst:** S.A.H.

STANDARD
&POOR'S
STOCK REPORTS

Immune Response Corp.

NASDAQ Symbol **IMNR**

In S&P SmallCap 600

09-OCT-99

Industry: Biotechnology

Summary: This biopharmaceutical firm is developing immune-based therapies that induce T cell responses to treat HIV infection, autoimmune disease, and cancer.

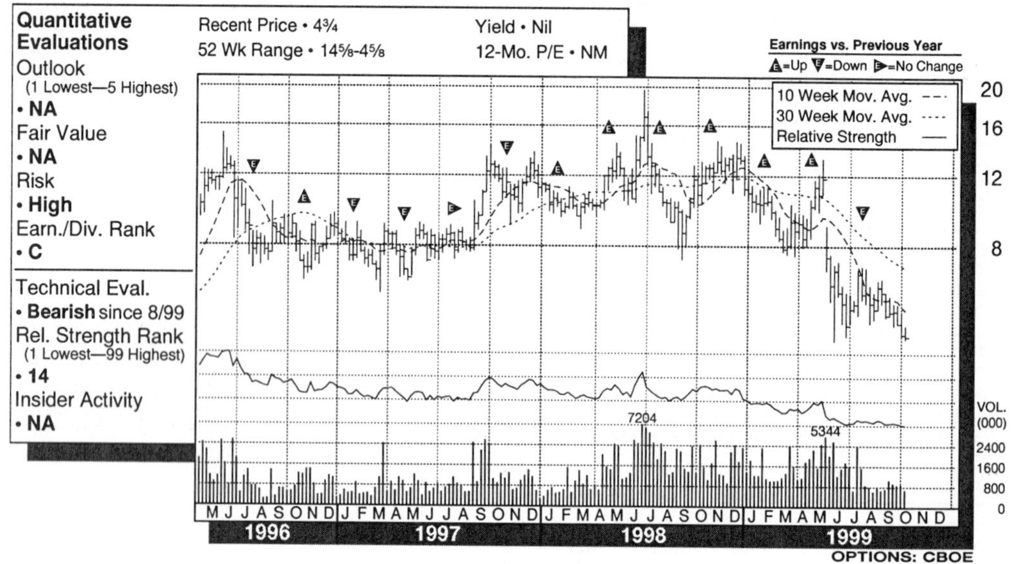

Business Profile - 11-AUG-99

In July 1999, IMNR received a $3 million payment from Agouron Pharmaceuticals for Remune development and Agouron paid $2 million for the purchase of 292,078 IMNR shares. IMNR also registered to sell an additional four million shares of common stock. In June 1999, IMNR announced plans to restructure its operations and reduce expenses by cutting its workforce by 30%. In May 1999, a Data Safety Monitoring Board recommended that a Phase III trial for Remune in treating HIV should end due to a lack of efficacy. Also in May, IMNR entered into an agreement with the University of Maryland Biotechnology Institute (UMBI), whereby IMNR would license certain technology rights to UMBI.

Operational Review - 11-AUG-99

Revenues in the six months ended June 30, 1999 advanced 12%, year to year, primarily reflecting payments from Agouron. Following 11% higher R&D spending and 31% higher G&A costs, both related to clinical development activities for Remune, and after a $650,000 restructuring charge, total operating expenses rose 16%. Following marginally higher net investment income, the net loss widened to $8.0 million ($0.33 a share, on 5.5% more shares), from $6.4 million ($0.28).

Stock Performance - 08-OCT-99

In the past 30 trading days, IMNR's shares have declined 22%, compared to a 0.91% fall in the S&P 500. Average trading volume for the past five days was 132,120 shares, compared with the 40-day moving average of 163,774 shares.

Key Stock Statistics

Dividend Rate/Share	Nil	Shareholders	889
Shs. outstg. (M)	24.9	Market cap. (B)	$0.118
Avg. daily vol. (M)	0.164	Inst. holdings	15%
Tang. Bk. Value/Share	0.74		
Beta	1.70		

Value of $10,000 invested 5 years ago: $ 4,634

Fiscal Year Ending Dec. 31

	1999	1998	1997	1996	1995	1994
Revenues (Million $)						
1Q	9.21	1.00	1.00	Nil	1.31	1.24
2Q	3.89	10.67	Nil	Nil	0.13	1.40
3Q	—	2.49	1.00	7.00	Nil	2.59
4Q	—	3.52	Nil	Nil	0.13	1.81
Yr.	—	17.67	2.00	7.00	1.56	7.03
Earnings Per Share ($)						
1Q	**-0.05**	**-0.35**	**-0.39**	**-0.33**	-0.27	-0.28
2Q	**-0.28**	**0.06**	**-0.45**	**-0.45**	-0.26	-0.32
3Q	—	**-0.24**	**-0.31**	**-0.01**	-0.31	-0.20
4Q	—	**-0.26**	**-0.38**	**-0.40**	-0.35	-0.25
Yr.	—	**-0.78**	**-1.53**	**-1.19**	**-1.19**	-1.05

Next earnings report expected: early November

Dividend Data

Cash dividends have never been paid, and the company does not expect to pay any for the foreseeable future.

The Immune Response Corporation

Business Summary - 11-AUG-99

The Immune Response Corp.'s goal is to develop and commercialize, independently and through collaborations, immunotherapeutics that act on T cells for the treatment of HIV, autoimmune diseases, and cancer. The company is also developing an intravenous delivery system designed to transport genes directly to the liver for the treatment of liver-related disorders.

IMNR's most advanced therapeutic in clinical development is Remune, an immune-based vaccine designed to prevent the onset of AIDS by stimulating natural defense mechanisms in HIV-infected individuals. Remune is designed to be taken in combination with other antiviral drugs and IMNR believes it may stimulate a broader immune response against a wider array of HIV strains in comparison to more traditional HIV vaccines.

In July 1998, IMMNR and Agouron Pharmaceuticals entered into a collaborative agreement to further develop and potentially market Remune. Agouron was granted exclusive worldwide rights for Remune, with IMNR receiving payments from Agouron, contingent upon developmental progress. In May 1999, an independent Data Safety Monitoring Board recommended that a Phase II clinical endpoint trial for Remune should conclude due to lack of evidence showing treatment efficacy. Also in May, the company announced Agouron planned to initiate new Phase III trials on Remune in order to ascertain its statistical efficacy.

IMNR is also developing immune-based treatments for autoimmune diseases that work by inhibiting abnormal T cell behavior manifested in these disorders. As of 1998 year-end, IR501 and IR703 were being developed for the treatment of rheumatoid arthritis. In December 1998, IMNR completed a Phase II trial on a vaccine for treating this disease to determine the optimal dosage and formulation to be used in future trials. Also in 1998, a Phase II clinical trial on IR502, an immunotherapeutic for treating psoriasis, was completed. In addition, IR208 was being developed for treating multiple sclerosis.

IMNR is integrating proprietary immune-based cancer vaccine technology with molecular gene therapy techniques to develop treatments that enable the immune system to recognize and control tumor growth. In late 1998, the company initiated a universal cell line vaccine trial for the treatment of colon cancer. IMNR also filed an investigational new drug application with the FDA with the goal of receiving permission to begin clinical testing on a brain cancer vaccine. Possible prostate cancer and melanoma cancer treatments were in preclinical research.

The company's novel GeneDrug products in development are based on a patented gene delivery technology, which is designed to deliver gene-based therapeutics directly to the liver. In 1996, IMNR entered into an agreement with Bayer AG to develop gene therapy products to treat hemophilia A. In July 1998, the company announced a research collaboration with Schering-Plough Corp. (SGP) to combine IMNR's gene delivery technology w ith SGP's recombinant interferon-alpha to treat hepatitis B and C.

Per Share Data ($) (Year Ended Dec. 31)	1998	1997	1996	1995	1994	1993	1992	1991	1990	1989
Tangible Bk. Val.	0.93	1.54	2.54	2.89	4.01	5.13	6.09	7.10	2.90	-1.24
Cash Flow	-0.72	-1.48	-1.14	-1.13	-0.97	-0.88	-2.15	-0.20	-0.12	-0.62
Earnings	-0.78	-1.53	-1.19	-1.19	-1.05	-0.95	-2.19	-0.23	-0.12	-0.63
Dividends	Nil	Nil	Nil	Nil	Nil	Nil	Nil	Nil	Nil	Nil
Payout Ratio	Nil	Nil	Nil	Nil	Nil	Nil	Nil	Nil	Nil	Nil
Prices - High	19 5/8	14 1/4	15 1/4	8 3/8	13 3/4	28 1/2	47 1/4	62 3/4	7 3/8	NA
- Low	7 3/8	6	4 3/4	2 5/8	5 3/8	9 1/4	12 1/4	2 7/8	2 3/4	NA
P/E Ratio - High	NM	NM	NM	NM	NM	NM	NM	NM	NM	NM
- Low	NM	NM	NM	NM	NM	NM	NM	NA	NA	NA
Income Statement Analysis (Million $)										
Revs.	17.7	2.0	7.0	1.6	7.0	4.8	4.0	4.3	4.3	3.3
Oper. Inc.	-18.2	-34.7	-22.8	-20.6	-10.8	-10.0	-6.5	-4.1	-1.7	-1.8
Depr.	1.5	1.3	0.8	1.0	1.3	1.2	0.6	0.4	0.1	0.1
Int. Exp.	Nil	Nil	Nil	Nil	NA	NA	Nil	Nil	Nil	Nil
Pretax Inc.	-18.1	-33.6	-21.0	-19.9	-17.4	-15.7	-33.8	-3.0	-1.2	-4.7
Eff. Tax Rate	NM	NM	NM	NM	NM	NM	NM	Nil	Nil	Nil
Net Inc.	-18.1	-33.6	-21.0	-19.9	-17.4	-15.7	-33.8	-3.0	-1.2	-4.7
Balance Sheet & Other Fin. Data (Million $)										
Cash	24.9	30.4	47.8	44.6	59.0	75.0	90.0	104	25.0	7.0
Curr. Assets	26.8	31.2	48.5	45.6	61.0	77.0	93.0	106	28.0	9.0
Total Assets	35.6	37.4	54.1	50.4	68.0	87.0	103	110	33.0	10.0
Curr. Liab.	4.2	2.3	2.8	2.0	1.4	1.5	2.0	1.4	0.7	0.4
LT Debt	Nil	Nil	Nil	Nil	Nil	0.3	0.5	Nil	Nil	Nil
Common Eqty.	22.1	35.1	51.3	48.4	67.0	85.0	101	108	32.0	-6.0
Total Cap.	31.4	35.1	51.3	48.4	67.0	85.0	101	108	32.0	10.0
Cap. Exp.	3.5	2.5	1.6	0.4	0.8	0.9	4.2	0.7	2.9	0.0
Cash Flow	-16.6	-32.3	-20.2	-18.9	-16.1	-14.6	-33.1	-2.6	-1.2	-4.6
Curr. Ratio	6.4	13.7	17.4	22.9	43.4	50.8	45.9	74.1	40.8	23.7
% LT Debt of Cap.	Nil	Nil	Nil	Nil	Nil	0.3	0.5	Nil	Nil	Nil
% Net Inc.of Revs.	NM	NM	NM	NM	NM	NM	NM	NM	NM	NM
% Ret. on Assets	NM	NM	NM	NM	NM	NM	NM	NM	NM	NM
% Ret. on Equity	NM	NM	NM	NM	NM	NM	NM	NM	NM	NM

Data as orig reptd.; bef. results of disc opers/spec. items. Per share data adj. for stk. divs. Bold denotes diluted EPS (FASB 128)-prior periods restated. E-Estimated. NA-Not Available. NM-Not Meaningful. NR-Not Ranked.

Office—5935 Darwin Ct., Carlsbad, CA 92008. **Tel**—(619) 431-7080. **Fax**—(619) 431-8636. **Website**—http://www.imnr.com **Chrmn**—J. B. Glavin. **Pres & CEO**—D. J. Carlo. **CFO & Treas**—H. Sampson. **COO**—S. P. Richieri. **SVP & Secy**—R.R. Mulford. **Investor Contact**—Debra L. Altman. **Dirs**—D. J. Carlo, J. B. Glavin, K. B. Kimberlin, M. Perelman, S. P. Richieri, J. Simon, W. M. Sullivan, P. M. Young. **Transfer Agent & Registrar**—First Interstate Bank, LA. **Incorporated**—in Delaware in 1986. **Empl**— 156. **S&P Analyst:** Frank DiLorenzo

STANDARD
&POOR'S
STOCK REPORTS

InaCom Corp.

NYSE Symbol **ICO**
In S&P SmallCap 600

09-OCT-99

Industry:
Services (Computer Systems)

Summary: This technology management services company provides integrated life cycle services to clients worldwide.

Quantitative Evaluations
Outlook
(1 Lowest—5 Highest)
• **5**
Fair Value
• **17⅛**
Risk
• **High**
Earn./Div. Rank
• **B**

Technical Eval.
• **Bearish** since 8/99
Rel. Strength Rank
(1 Lowest—99 Highest)
• **9**
Insider Activity
• **NA**

Recent Price • 8¼
52 Wk Range • 21⅛-7
Yield • Nil
12-Mo. P/E • NM

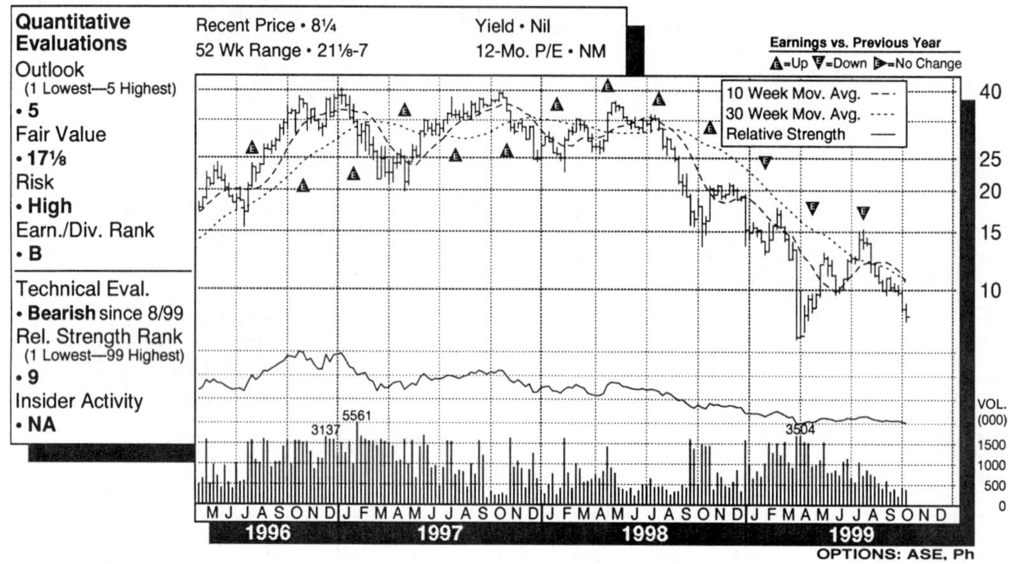

OPTIONS: ASE, Ph

Business Profile - 24-JUN-99

The February 1999 acquisition of Vanstar Corp. (in exchange for 28.2 million shares) made ICO one of the world's leading technology services companies, with nearly $7 billion in revenues, including more than $850,000 in service revenues. ICO believes the addition of Vanstar will let it better meet the distributed technology infrastructure needs of its customers. The company attributed a loss in the 1999 first quarter to weak market conditions and lost sales momentum resulting from an internal focus associated with the Vanstar merger. However, ICO expects to achieve $20 million to $25 million of cost savings from the merger in the second quarter, with sequential improvement throughout the year.

Operational Review - 24-JUN-99

Revenues in the 13 weeks ended March 27, 1999, fell 18%, year to year, on lower product and service revenues. Results were hurt by weak market conditions, and by reduced sales momentum during the pendency of the merger with Vanstar. With unusual charges in the 1999 first quarter, and $103.9 million of restructuring charges, after tax benefits of $81.6 million, versus taxes at 38.6%, a loss of $145,943,000 ($3.29 a share, after distributions on preferred securities of trust) contrasted with income of $18,966,000 ($0.37).

Stock Performance - 08-OCT-99

In the past 30 trading days, ICO's shares have declined 16%, compared to a 0.91% fall in the S&P 500. Average trading volume for the past five days was 75,340 shares, compared with the 40-day moving average of 83,718 shares.

Key Stock Statistics

Dividend Rate/Share	Nil	Shareholders	6,400
Shs. outstg. (M)	45.5	Market cap. (B)	$0.378
Avg. daily vol. (M)	0.070	Inst. holdings	45%
Tang. Bk. Value/Share	12.75		
Beta	0.75		

Value of $10,000 invested 5 years ago: $ 6,157

Fiscal Year Ending Dec. 31

	1999	1998	1997	1996	1995	1994
Revenues (Million $)						
1Q	1,366	1,000	841.7	642.1	484.0	399.3
2Q	1,456	1,139	972.2	769.9	526.9	408.6
3Q	—	1,062	1,013	769.5	533.3	459.2
4Q	—	1,057	1,069	920.7	656.2	533.0
Yr.	—	4,258	3,896	3,102	2,200	1,801
Earnings Per Share ($)						
1Q	**-3.29**	**0.54**	0.42	0.29	0.21	0.26
2Q	**0.14**	**0.62**	0.51	0.43	0.25	-0.77
3Q	—	**0.57**	0.55	0.48	0.25	0.05
4Q	—	**0.55**	**0.64**	0.56	0.43	0.24
Yr.	—	**2.26**	**2.17**	**1.66**	**1.16**	**-0.22**

Next earnings report expected: late October

Dividend Data

No cash dividends have been paid.

A Division of The McGraw-Hill Companies

InaCom Corp.

Business Summary - 24-JUN-99

The goal of InaCom Corp., a global technology services company, is to make information technology work for large and medium-sized business. Since 1982, the company has been supplying integrated services to manage the life cycle of information and telecommunications technology primarily for Fortune 1000 clients. The client portfolio includes more than 35% of Fortune 500 corporations.

Vanstar Corp. merged with the company in February 1999, making ICO one of the world's leading technology services companies, with nearly $7 billion in revenues, and more than 12,000 employees,including 7,500 technical professionals.

ICO offers a comprehensive range of services to manage the entire technology life cycle, including technology planning, technology procurement, technology integration, technology support, and technology management. Its expertise includes integration of voice and data communications. The company sells its services and products through a marketing network of approximately 90 company-owned business centers (as of December 26, 1998) throughout the U.S., focusing on serving large corporations. ICO also has a network of approximately 875 value-added independent dealers that typically have a regional, industry, or specific service focus.

The company has international locations in Central America, South America, and Mexico and international affiliations in Europe, Asia, the Caribbean, Middle East, Africa, and Canada to satisfy technology management needs of multinational clients.

ICO's expertise in procurement, customization, and deployment of personal computers, peripherals, and software from a wide range of major vendors enables the company to customize information solutions to meet specific client needs. In addition, it offers clients in-depth product knowledge and experience, competitive pricing from its purchasing arrangements, and a wide array of integration and support services supporting client needs on an on-going basis.

As a single-source provider of information technology services and products, the company seeks to help clients optimize their information technology investments and control ongoing costs throughout the entire life cycle of the clients' technology systems. ICO combines a process improvement approach along with tools and practices gained by experience and trained personnel to assist its clients in managing the entire life cycle and costs of distributed technology. The company distinguishes itself by being a client advocate, offering manufacturer-independent recommendations to clients, helping them gain more value and achieve desired return on investment from their complex and critical distributed technology infrastructure.

Per Share Data ($) (Year Ended Dec. 31)	1998	1997	1996	1995	1994	1993	1992	1991	1990	1989
Tangible Bk. Val.	12.75	15.98	11.81	12.36	11.04	11.15	9.73	8.38	9.74	8.19
Cash Flow	4.27	4.16	3.83	2.99	1.70	NA	2.31	1.36	NA	NA
Earnings	2.26	2.17	1.76	1.14	-0.22	1.23	1.25	NA	NA	NA
Dividends	Nil	Nil	Nil	Nil	Nil	Nil	Nil	Nil	Nil	Nil
Payout Ratio	Nil	Nil	Nil	Nil	Nil	Nil	Nil	Nil	Nil	Nil
Prices - High	37¼	40	40⅝	15¼	21	25½	14¾	18½	17	11¾
- Low	13½	19¾	13¼	7	6⅞	12¾	9¼	7	9¼	9⅜
P/E Ratio - High	16	18	23	13	NM	20	11	33	10	8
- Low	6	9	7	6	NM	10	7	12	5	6
Income Statement Analysis (Million $)										
Revs.	4,258	3,896	3,102	2,200	1,801	NA	1,014	680	NA	NA
Oper. Inc.	152	110	73.9	53.5	NA	NA	35.0	14.8	NA	NA
Depr.	45.8	31.3	21.8	19.1	19.8	NA	9.1	4.9	NA	NA
Int. Exp.	33.8	29.0	20.4	14.6	12.0	NA	8.0	4.1	NA	NA
Pretax Inc.	72.3	49.9	31.7	19.8	-3.7	NA	18.0	5.7	NA	NA
Eff. Tax Rate	41%	41%	41%	41%	NA	NA	40%	40%	NA	NA
Net Inc.	42.6	29.5	18.7	11.7	-2.3	NA	10.7	3.4	NA	NA
Balance Sheet & Other Fin. Data (Million $)										
Cash	54.4	52.6	31.4	20.7	10.5	NA	11.8	4.1	NA	NA
Curr. Assets	755	748	712	540	430	NA	228	245	NA	NA
Total Assets	1,104	961	848	624	520	NA	288	308	NA	NA
Curr. Liab.	474	490	612	449	351	NA	148	151	NA	NA
LT Debt	202	142	NA	NA	NA	NA	NA	NA	NA	NA
Common Eqty.	425	325	177	149	136	NA	101	89.5	NA	NA
Total Cap.	630	471	NA	NA	NA	NA	NA	NA	NA	NA
Cap. Exp.	40.2	50.7	NA	NA	NA	NA	NA	NA	NA	NA
Cash Flow	88.3	60.7	40.5	30.8	17.5	NA	19.8	8.3	NA	NA
Curr. Ratio	1.6	1.5	1.2	1.2	1.2	NA	1.5	1.6	NA	NA
% LT Debt of Cap.	32.0	30.1	NA	NA	NA	NA	NA	NA	NA	NA
% Net Inc.of Revs.	1.0	0.8	0.6	0.5	NA	NA	1.1	0.5	NA	NA
% Ret. on Assets	4.1	3.3	2.5	2.0	NA	NA	3.6	1.7	NA	NA
% Ret. on Equity	11.4	11.7	11.5	8.2	NA	NA	11.3	5.3	NA	NA

Data as orig reptd.; bef. results of disc opers/spec. items. Per share data adj. for stk. divs. Bold denotes diluted EPS (FASB 128)-prior periods restated. E-Estimated. NA-Not Available. NM-Not Meaningful. NR-Not Ranked.

Office—10810 Farnam, Omaha, NE 68154. **Tel**—(402) 392-3900. **Website**—http://www.inacom.com **Pres & CEO**—B. L. Fairfield. **EVP & CFO**—D. C. Guenther. **Secy**—M. A. Steffan.**Investor Contact**—John P. Lambrechts (402 758-3281).**Dirs**—J. Auerbach, R. H. Bard, M. C. Bay, J. Q. Crowe, B. L. Fairfield, W. G. Gregory, J. Inatome, R. Inatome, W. H. Janeway, J. R. Oltman, G. Schwendiman, W. Y. Tauscher, L. S. Wilson. **Transfer Agent & Registrar**—First Chicago Trust Co. of New York, NYC. **Incorporated**—in Delaware in 1985.**Empl**— 11,000. **S&P Analyst:** C.C.P.

STANDARD
&POOR'S
STOCK REPORTS

Incyte Pharmaceuticals

NASDAQ Symbol **INCY**

In S&P SmallCap 600

09-OCT-99

Industry:
Biotechnology

Summary: This company is a leading provider of an integrated platform of genomic technologies designed to aid in the understanding of the molecular basis of disease.

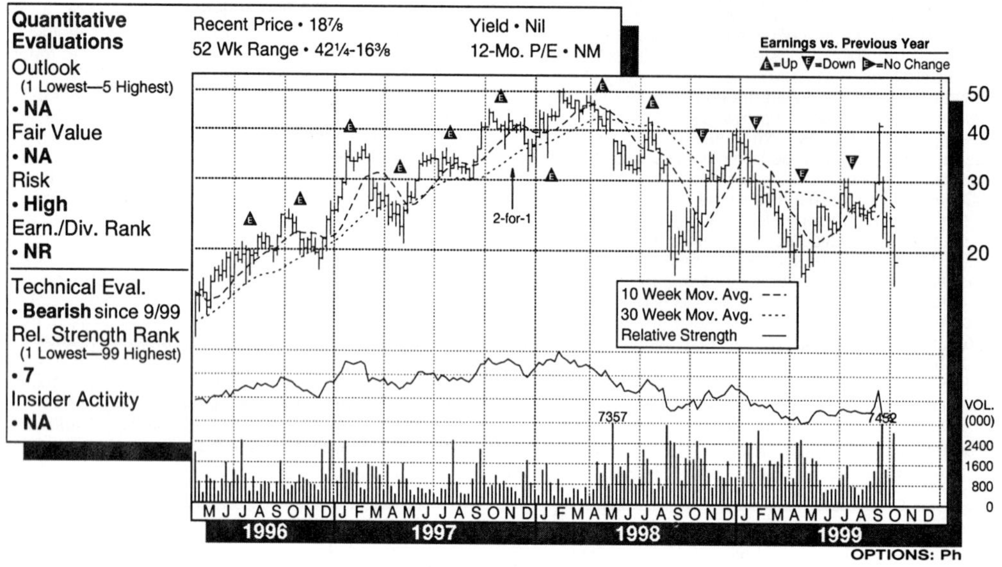

Business Profile - 18-MAY-99

The company said that during the first quarter of 1999, it experienced delays in a number of sales cycles in its microarray business. Consequently, it is revising its estimate of microarray revenue for 1999 from 15%-20% of revenue to 10% of revenue. This lowers the total 1999 revenue target from $190 million to approximately $170-$175 million. As reported earlier, the company still expects to report aloss of approximately $20 million for 1999 and anticipates a return to profitability in the second half of 2000. Plans for 1999 call for the investment of about $45 million in genomic sequencing, mapping, SNP (single nucleotide polymorphism) discovery programs, and related patent filings. In April 1999, INCY noted that its first six database collaborators have renewed their original agreements.

Operational Review - 18-MAY-99

Revenues in the first three months of 1999 advanced 24%, year to year, primarily on increased database subscription and microarray service revenues. However, total costs and expenses rose 44%, reflecting a ramp up in bioinformatics, genome sequencing and mapping programs, and higher legal expenses. A net loss of $1.9 million ($0.07 a share, on 3.6% fewer shares) contrasted with net income of $3.6 million ($0.12). Cash and equivalents were $134 million on March 31, 1999.

Stock Performance - 08-OCT-99

In the past 30 trading days, INCY's shares have declined 26%, compared to a 0.91% fall in the S&P 500. Average trading volume for the past five days was 1,171,280 shares, compared with the 40-day moving average of 580,128 shares.

Key Stock Statistics

Dividend Rate/Share	Nil	Shareholders	157
Shs. outstg. (M)	28.0	Market cap. (B)	$0.529
Avg. daily vol. (M)	0.791	Inst. holdings	60%
Tang. Bk. Value/Share	5.84		
Beta	1.33		

Value of $10,000 invested 5 years ago: $ 41,944

Fiscal Year Ending Dec. 31

	1999	1998	1997	1996	1995	1994
Revenues (Million $)						
1Q	37.63	30.38	17.86	5.58	1.48	Nil
2Q	37.89	33.09	21.19	7.63	1.95	Nil
3Q	—	34.69	22.66	12.92	2.26	Nil
4Q	—	36.60	26.64	14.18	4.21	0.24
Yr.	—	134.8	88.35	41.79	9.91	0.24
Earnings Per Share ($)						
1Q	**-0.07**	**0.12**	0.05	-0.10	-0.13	-0.17
2Q	**-0.26**	**0.18**	0.09	-0.08	-0.18	-0.20
3Q	—	**-0.25**	0.13	-0.17	-0.19	-0.21
4Q	—	**0.05**	**0.17**	0.01	-0.13	-0.26
Yr.	—	**0.12**	**0.43**	**-0.33**	**-0.59**	**-0.82**

Next earnings report expected: mid October

Dividend Data

No cash dividends have been paid, and the company does not anticipate paying any in the foreseeable future.

A Division of The McGraw-Hill Companies

Incyte Pharmaceuticals, Inc.

Business Summary - 18-MAY-99

A leading provider of an integrated platform of genomic technologies designed to aid in the understanding of the molecular basis of disease, Incyte Pharmaceuticals, Inc. designs, develops and markets genomic database products, genomic data management software tools, microarray-based gene expression services, and genomic reagents and related services to the biotechnology, pharmaceutical and agricultural industries. In building its databases, the company uses high-throughput, computer-aided gene sequencing and analysis technologies to identify and characterize the expressed genes of the human genome, as well as certain animal, plant and microbial genomes.

The company provides access to its genomic databases through collaborations with companies worldwide. By searching the genomic databases, collaborators can integrate and analyze genetic information from multiple sources in order to discover genes that may represent the basis for new biological targets, therapeutic proteins, or gene therapy, antisense or diagnostic products. The company's products and services assist with gene and target discovery, as well as with functional genomic studies, preclinical pharmacology and toxicology studies and understanding and analyzing the results of clinical development studies.

Incyte's portfolio of database modules includes the LifeSeq human gene sequence and expression database, the LifeSeq FL database of full-length human genes, the LifeSeq Atlas mapping database, the PathoSeq microbial genomic database, the ZooSeq animal genomic database, the LifeTools suite of bioinformatics software programs, LifeArray gene expression data management and analysis software, and other custom database and sequencing services.

The company also offers a variety of DNA clone and other services designed to assist its collaborators in using information from its database in internal lab-based experiments. In addition, it produces a broad line of genomic research products, such as DNA clones and insert libraries, and offers technical support services including high-throughput DNA screening, custom robotic services, contract DNA preparation, and fluorescent in-situ hybridization, to assist researchers in the identification and isolation of novel genes.

As of 1998's year-end, Incyte had entered into database collaboration agreements with 22 companies, up from 19 in 1997. Major collaborators include Abbott Laboratories, Monsanto, Bristol-Myers Squibb, Eli Lilly, Pfizer, Glaxo Wellcome, Johnson & Johnson, Pharmacia & Upjohn, Rhone-Poulenc, Schering, and SmithKline Beecham.

During 1998, Incyte signed major new multi-year microarray collaborations with Amgen, Monsanto, Novartis, Schering-Plough, and Zeneca. Only the Monsanto microarray agreement had a significant impact on 1998 revenues. Incyte expected the remaining agreements to impact 1999 revenues.

Per Share Data ($) (Year Ended Dec. 31)	1998	1997	1996	1995	1994	1993	1992	1991	1990	1989
Tangible Bk. Val.	5.84	6.07	2.16	2.39	1.51	1.26	NA	NA	NA	NA
Cash Flow	0.72	0.86	-0.01	-0.46	-0.77	-1.03	-0.23	NA	NA	NA
Earnings	0.12	0.43	-0.33	-0.62	-0.84	-1.13	-0.24	NA	NA	NA
Dividends	Nil	Nil	Nil	Nil	Nil	Nil	Nil	NA	NA	NA
Payout Ratio	Nil	Nil	Nil	Nil	Nil	Nil	Nil	NA	NA	NA
Prices - High	51	45¼	26½	12⅝	8⅛	6	NA	NA	NA	NA
- Low	17⅜	20¾	11⅝	6½	3⅜	3¾	NA	NA	NA	NA
P/E Ratio - High	NM	NM	NM	NM	NM	NM	NA	NA	NA	NA
- Low	NM	NM	NM	NM	NM	NM	NA	NA	NA	NA
Income Statement Analysis (Million $)										
Revs.	135	88.4	41.8	9.9	0.2	0.3	1.6	0.3	NA	NA
Oper. Inc.	29.5	17.7	-2.6	-8.6	-11.1	-4.5	-1.9	-1.4	NA	NA
Depr.	17.3	10.4	6.5	2.6	0.9	0.4	0.2	0.1	NA	NA
Int. Exp.	0.1	0.2	0.2	0.1	0.2	0.1	0.0	Nil	NA	NA
Pretax Inc.	5.8	11.0	-6.8	-10.1	-11.5	-4.9	-2.1	-1.4	NA	NA
Eff. Tax Rate	40%	5.00%	NM	NM	NM	NM	Nil	Nil	NA	NA
Net Inc.	3.5	10.4	-6.8	-10.1	-11.5	-4.9	-2.1	-1.4	NA	NA
Balance Sheet & Other Fin. Data (Million $)										
Cash	111	57.2	7.6	10.4	6.8	15.5	4.8	1.6	NA	NA
Curr. Assets	131	138	43.2	49.0	25.3	15.7	5.5	2.0	NA	NA
Total Assets	230	193	66.9	57.8	28.7	17.6	6.8	2.5	NA	NA
Curr. Liab.	49.9	46.6	21.1	10.4	4.6	1.0	0.6	0.5	NA	NA
LT Debt	Nil	Nil	Nil	0.0	0.1	0.5	0.4	Nil	NA	NA
Common Eqty.	180	146	45.2	46.8	24.0	16.1	5.9	2.0	NA	NA
Total Cap.	180	146	45.2	46.9	24.1	16.6	6.2	2.0	NA	NA
Cap. Exp.	30.7	26.1	20.2	7.9	2.6	0.4	0.4	0.6	NA	NA
Cash Flow	20.8	20.8	-0.3	-7.6	-10.6	-4.5	-1.9	-1.4	NA	NA
Curr. Ratio	2.6	3.0	2.0	4.7	5.5	16.2	9.2	3.8	NA	NA
% LT Debt of Cap.	Nil	Nil	Nil	0.0	0.4	3.1	6.0	Nil	NA	NA
% Net Inc.of Revs.	2.6	11.8	NM	NM	NM	NM	NM	NM	NA	NA
% Ret. on Assets	1.6	8.0	NM	NM	NM	NM	NM	NM	NA	NA
% Ret. on Equity	2.1	10.9	NM	NM	NM	NM	NM	NM	NA	NA

Data as orig. reptd.; bef. results of disc. opers. and/or spec. items. Per share data adj. for stk. divs. as of ex-div. date. Bold denotes diluted EPS (FASB 128). E-Estimated. NA-Not Available. NM-Not Meaningful. NR-Not Ranked.

Office—3174 Porter Dr., Palo Alto, CA 94304. **Tel**—(650) 855-0555. **Website**—http://www.incyte.com **Chrmn**—J. J. Collinson. **CEO**—R. A. Whitfield. **EVP-Fin & CFO**—D. M. Gilbert. **Dirs**—B. M. Bloom, J. J. Collinson, F. B. Craves, J. S. Saxe, R. W. Scott, R. A. Whitfield. **Transfer Agent & Registrar**—ChaseMellon Shareholder Services, San Francisco. **Incorporated**—in Delaware in 1991. **Empl**— 867. **S&P Analyst:** David Moskowitz

STANDARD &POOR'S
STOCK REPORTS

Information Resources

NASDAQ Symbol **IRIC**

In S&P SmallCap 600

09-OCT-99

Industry: Services (Advertising & Marketing)

Summary: This company provides information services to the consumer packaged goods industry in the U.S., and software services to a wide range of industries worldwide.

Quantitative Evaluations

Outlook (1 Lowest—5 Highest)
• **3+**

Fair Value
• **14¼**

Risk
• **Average**

Earn./Div. Rank
• **B-**

Technical Eval.
• **Bullish** since 8/99

Rel. Strength Rank (1 Lowest—99 Highest)
• **88**

Insider Activity
• **Neutral**

Recent Price • 11⅜
52 Wk Range • 12⅛-6¼
Yield • Nil
12-Mo. P/E • NM

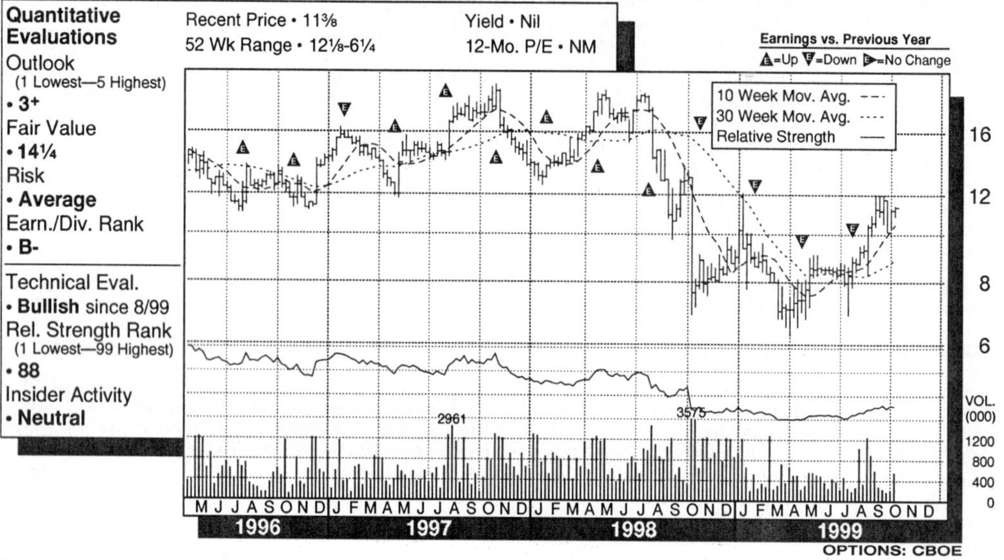

Business Profile - 21-JUN-99

In June 1999, IRIC announced a new consolidated sales data reporting service which covers multiple retail venues (food, drug and mass merchandise stores). The development of aggregated sales data across similar merchant categories, a service desired by certain customers, has increased expenses in recent periods. The company stated in May 1999 that its recent reorganization of the client service and marketing areas, improvement in data production capabilities and efficiencies, and growth in European market share should result in improved profitability in the second half of 1999. Through March 1999, Information Resources had repurchased 1,861,000 of the company's shares for an average $12.46 per share related to a 2 million share repurchase plan authorized in November 1997.

Operational Review - 21-JUN-99

Revenues for the three months ended March 31, 1999, rose 11%, year to year, with sales increases of 8% in the U.S. and 20% in Europe. Gross margin narrowed, with sharply higher U.S. employee costs, related to new product lines, offsetting improvement in international operations. Following 11% higher SG&A, a $1.8 million loss from operations contrasted with income from operations of $3.3 million. Both equity in earnings of affiliated companies and minority interests benefit were significantly higher. After a tax benefit of $310,000, versus taxes at 42.3%, a net loss of $251,000 ($0.01 a share) contrasted with net income of $1,910,000 ($0.07).

Stock Performance - 08-OCT-99

In the past 30 trading days, IRIC's shares have increased 7%, compared to a 0.91% fall in the S&P 500. Average trading volume for the past five days was 109,740 shares, compared with the 40-day moving average of 117,192 shares.

Key Stock Statistics

Dividend Rate/Share	Nil	Shareholders	1,823
Shs. outstg. (M)	28.1	Market cap. (B)	$0.319
Avg. daily vol. (M)	0.057	Inst. holdings	76%
Tang. Bk. Value/Share	7.89		
Beta	0.63		

Value of $10,000 invested 5 years ago: $ 2,946

Fiscal Year Ending Dec. 31

	1999	1998	1997	1996	1995	1994
Revenues (Million $)						
1Q	131.8	119.2	105.1	93.00	104.8	87.68
2Q	137.8	129.4	114.0	103.0	109.3	92.18
3Q	—	125.3	115.6	102.0	87.29	92.92
4Q	—	137.4	121.6	107.7	98.50	103.8
Yr.	—	511.3	456.3	405.6	399.9	376.6
Earnings Per Share ($)						
1Q	**-0.01**	**0.07**	Nil	**-0.08**	-0.12	-0.05
2Q	**0.02**	**0.12**	**0.07**	**0.01**	-0.13	Nil
3Q	—	**-0.05**	**0.07**	Nil	-0.18	-0.12
4Q	—	Nil	**0.12**	**-0.20**	Nil	-0.17
Yr.	—	**0.13**	**0.26**	**-0.27**	**-0.43**	**-0.34**

Next earnings report expected: late October

Dividend Data

No cash has been paid. In October 1990, the company distributed to shareholders one VideOcart, Inc. common share for every two IRIC shares held. VideOcart's products provide point-of-purchase advertising and promotion messages.

A Division of The McGraw-Hill Companies

Information Resources, Inc.

Business Summary - 21-JUN-99

Information Resources (IRIC) is working toward achieving profitability in Europe, while expanding its database capabilities in the United States. IRIC provides universal product code (UPC) scanner-based solutions to the consumer packaged goods (CPG) industry in the United States, Europe, and other international markets. IRIC supplies CPG manufacturers, retailers, and brokers with information and analysis for their sales, marketing, and supply chain operations.

The company's United States and international services consist of InfoScan product tracking services, related software product services and sales, consumer panel services, analytical and consulting services, the BehaviorScan product testing services and census applications. The company currently derives about 78% of its revenues from sales, and services provided in the United States.

Information Resources chief information product is the InfoScan service, which tracks client purchases of goods sold in grocerystores and other retail outlets throughout the United States. Infoscan provides subscribers with information on what quantity of products both they and their competitors sold, at what price, and under which promotional conditions. InfoScan uses data collected from UPC bar codes on CPG product packaging. IRIC provides InfoScan customers access to the company's database, which provides detailed information regarding specific product categories.

The InfoScan Census application offers retail chains product tracking based on scanner data obtained from all their stores, rather than a sample of outlets. IRIC also gathers consumer purchase information directly from individual households across the United States using consumer identification cards in stores and/or proprietary in-home scanning devices.

Information Resources' consumer panel collects information from approximately 115,000 households in the United States. About 60,000 of these households present an identification card to a participating grocery store, which enables scanners to record particular details regarding their product purchases. IRIC also gives approximately 55,000 households hand-held scanners to record their purchases.

The company's BehaviorScan service is a test marketing system available in the United States which permits CPG manufacturers to determine the impact of different marketing variables on consumer purchase behavior on new and existing products. BehaviorScan typically tests television and newspaper ads, manufacturers' coupons samples, and in-store displays, shelf price, and packaging changes.

IRIC also sells analytical software to the CPG industry for use in managing and analyzing Information Resources' data bases. Further, IRIC markets space management software, which is used to manage retail shelf space, and track manufacturers' promotional expenditures.

Per Share Data ($) **(Year Ended Dec. 31)**	**1998**	**1997**	**1996**	**1995**	**1994**	**1993**	**1992**	**1991**	**1990**	**1989**
Tangible Bk. Val.	7.89	8.41	7.62	7.84	8.05	8.36	7.35	5.12	2.78	2.88
Cash Flow	0.93	0.97	0.56	0.47	0.44	1.63	1.54	1.31	0.82	0.69
Earnings	0.13	0.26	-0.27	-0.43	-0.34	0.82	0.79	0.63	0.25	-0.17
Dividends	Nil	Nil	Nil	Nil	Nil	Nil	Nil	Nil	Nil	Nil
Payout Ratio	Nil	Nil	Nil	Nil	Nil	Nil	Nil	Nil	Nil	Nil
Prices - High	19 1/2	20	16 1/4	18 5/8	39 3/4	44 3/4	36 1/4	29 1/4	16 5/8	15 3/8
- Low	6 7/8	11 3/4	11	10	11 1/4	27	18 1/2	9 1/8	7 3/4	8 7/8
P/E Ratio - High	NM	77	NM	NM	NM	55	46	46	67	NM
- Low	NM	45	NM	NM	NM	33	23	14	31	NM
Income Statement Analysis (Million $)										
Revs.	511	456	406	400	377	335	276	208	167	136
Oper. Inc.	30.2	35.2	22.9	-7.8	27.0	62.4	56.2	38.2	24.1	20.6
Depr.	23.2	20.4	23.2	24.4	20.3	21.4	18.5	15.4	10.8	14.7
Int. Exp.	1.2	0.5	1.2	2.8	2.4	1.1	2.5	2.6	3.4	5.1
Pretax Inc.	6.2	14.7	-10.8	-16.1	-13.7	36.0	32.2	22.2	11.4	-3.8
Eff. Tax Rate	44%	46%	NM	NM	NM	43%	40%	36%	58%	NM
Net Inc.	3.8	7.7	-7.6	-11.7	-8.9	22.2	19.2	14.2	4.8	-2.9
Balance Sheet & Other Fin. Data (Million $)										
Cash	11.1	20.9	12.2	24.9	11.8	19.4	53.6	24.9	8.8	1.8
Curr. Assets	108	127	118	134	143	149	142	105	62.0	51.0
Total Assets	369	367	334	339	355	328	264	189	133	135
Curr. Liab.	103	102	83.6	89.4	73.6	57.5	53.6	52.6	38.8	47.4
LT Debt	4.6	0.6	7.9	3.8	31.5	3.1	4.7	6.6	23.5	29.4
Common Eqty.	238	242	226	230	227	229	187	117	60.0	51.0
Total Cap.	257	256	243	238	275	264	204	130	88.0	87.0
Cap. Exp.	33.7	34.4	18.8	24.5	22.8	25.9	20.0	11.6	9.2	7.6
Cash Flow	27.1	28.1	15.7	12.7	11.4	43.6	37.8	29.6	15.5	11.8
Curr. Ratio	1.1	1.2	1.4	1.5	1.9	2.6	2.6	2.0	1.6	1.1
% LT Debt of Cap.	1.8	0.2	3.7	1.6	11.4	1.2	2.3	5.1	26.8	33.9
% Net Inc.of Revs.	0.8	1.7	NM	NM	NM	6.6	7.0	6.9	2.9	NM
% Ret. on Assets	1.0	2.2	NM	NM	NM	7.4	8.0	8.3	3.4	NM
% Ret. on Equity	1.6	3.3	NM	NM	NM	10.5	12.0	15.3	8.4	NM

Data as orig reptd.; bef. results of disc opers/spec. items. Per share data adj. for stk. divs. Bold denotes diluted EPS (FASB 128)-prior periods restated. E-Estimated. NA-Not Available. NM-Not Meaningful. NR-Not Ranked.

Office—150 N. Clinton St., Chicago, IL 60661. **Tel**—(312) 726-1221. **Website**—http://www.infores.com **Chrmn, Pres & CEO**—J. P. Durrett. **EVP & CFO**—G. M. Hill. **Secy**—E. S. Berger. **Dirs**—J. G. Andress, E. E. Epstein, G. Eskin, G. M. Fulgoni, J. D. C. Little, L. M. Lodish, E. E. Lucente, E. W. Martin, J. P. Stamen, G. L. Urban, T. W. Wilson, Jr. **Transfer Agent & Registrar**—Harris Trust & Savings Bank, Chicago. **Incorporated**—in Delaware in 1982. **Empl**— 7,500. **S&P Analyst:** Craig K. Shere, CFA

STANDARD
&POOR'S
STOCK REPORTS

Innovex, Inc.

Nasdaq Symbol **INVX**

In S&P SmallCap 600

09-OCT-99

Industry:
Computers (Peripherals)

Summary: This company manufactures high precision, low cost electronic components for the computer, medical and telecommunications industries.

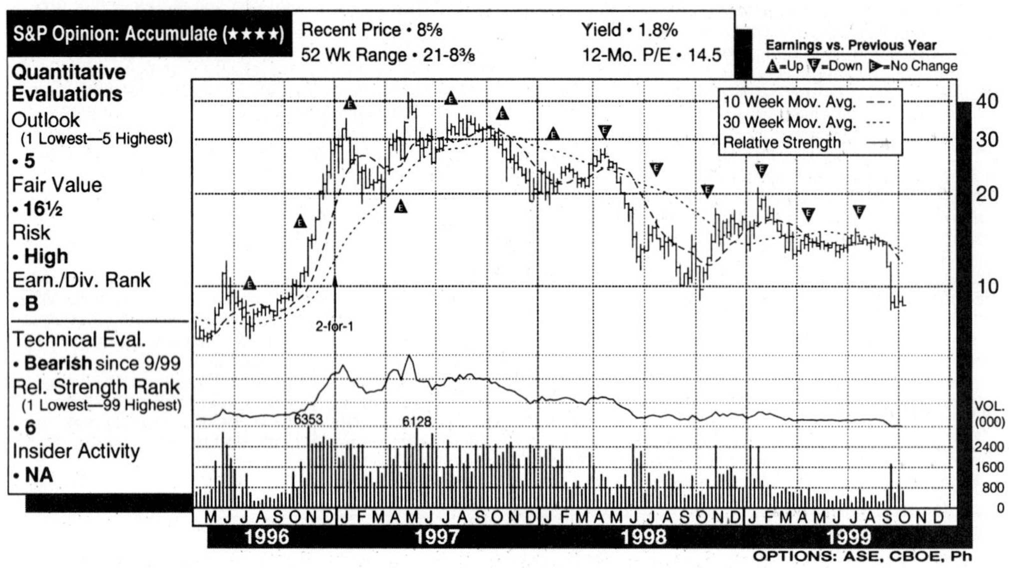

Overview - 22-SEP-99

The company is undergoing a major product transition that has seen the new FSA product supplant INVX's lead wire assembly products for disk drives as the company's primary product line. The first nine months of FY 99 (Sep.) saw a marked decline in sales of wire assemblies, as expected, and the company will exit this business at the end of September. Also as expected, volume production of flexible circuit products has been limited, because of capacity constraints. Capacity is expected to catch up with explosive growth in demand by the end of 1999. Largely because of these product transition related issues, gross margins will be negatively affected. After an $1.7 million charge for disposition of the company's former software subsidiary, Iconovex, but excluding a $2.6 million charge to write off equipment and inventory of the lead wire business, we estimate that FY 99 earnings will fall to $0.60 a share. For FY 00, we expect EPS to more than double, to $1.25.

Valuation - 22-SEP-99

We rate the shares accumulate. On September 14, 1999, the acquisition of the remaining 24% of flexible circuit maker ADFlex Solutions was completed, following the earlier tender of 76% of the shares pursuant to a cash offer of $3.80 a share. The flexible circuit business represents a potential billion dollar market opportunity in several years. In addition, INVX has targeted the chip packaging business as a large opportunity. This upside is largely unreflected in the stock's recent price, which we think is indicative of the company's historic reliance on the hard disk drive industry for a majority of its sales. Since this is no longer the case, as INVX is exiting the lead wire assembly business, we think the stock is grossly undervalued at current levels.

Key Stock Statistics

S&P EPS Est. 1999	0.60	Tang. Bk. Value/Share	6.81
P/E on S&P Est. 1999	14.5	Beta	1.23
S&P EPS Est. 2000	1.25	Shareholders	559
Dividend Rate/Share	0.16	Market cap. (B)	$0.129
Shs. outstg. (M)	14.8	Inst. holdings	36%
Avg. daily vol. (M)	0.193		

Value of $10,000 invested 5 years ago: $ 21,420

Fiscal Year Ending Sep. 30

	1999	1998	1997	1996	1995	1994
Revenues (Million $)						
1Q	22.03	33.01	29.31	13.11	9.98	5.66
2Q	20.70	25.11	38.39	14.67	11.69	6.45
3Q	20.64	20.30	41.96	19.25	14.03	8.44
4Q	—	17.85	32.34	22.53	14.50	10.01
Yr.	—	96.28	142.0	69.57	50.19	30.56
Earnings Per Share ($)						
1Q	**0.20**	**0.48**	0.42	0.19	0.12	0.04
2Q	**0.17**	**0.28**	0.66	0.20	0.15	0.04
3Q	**0.10**	**0.16**	0.72	0.24	0.20	0.07
4Q	—	**0.13**	0.51	0.27	0.23	0.11
Yr.	—	**1.05**	**2.31**	**0.91**	0.70	0.26

Next earnings report expected: early November

Dividend Data (Dividends have been paid since 1993.)

Amount ($)	Date Decl.	Ex-Div. Date	Stock of Record	Payment Date
0.035	Oct. 29	Nov. 06	Nov. 11	Nov. 25 '98
0.040	Jan. 22	Feb. 08	Feb. 10	Feb. 24 '99
0.040	Apr. 23	May. 10	May. 12	May. 26 '99
0.040	Jul. 26	Aug. 09	Aug. 11	Aug. 25 '99

A Division of The McGraw-Hill Companies

Innovex, Inc.

Business Summary - 22-SEP-99

Innovex, Inc. designs, develops and manufactures specialty components for the computer, medical, and telecommunications markets. In July 1998, the company combined its Precision Products division with its Litchfield Precision Components division, as the first step in a strategy to combine core competencies in high volume precision manufacturing, flexible circuitry and chemical etching. The union of the two businesses made sense because of a transition occurring in the computer disk drive industry from wire interconnects to flexible circuits. In addition, INVX is leveraging its expertise in flexible circuitry into substrates for integrated circuit packaging applications.

The company's historical principal products are a variety of small, thin-wire subassemblies that were used to read or write information on the head of a disk drive. Lead wire assembly sales accounted for 72% of consolidated revenues in FY 98 (Sep.), but are expected to account for less than 5% of revenue as of September 30, 1999. As part of the company's strategy to focus primarily on its rapidly growing flexible circuit business, it plans to exit this product line, and to dispose of its former software division.

Flexible circuits are the most significant line of new products that are based on the company's leading edge imaging and chemical etching technologies. Ramp-up of a newly constructed flexible circuit production facility is expected to gain momentum throughout the remainder of calendar 1999, as the disk drive industry transitions to using integrated lead suspensions.

The primary flexible circuitry product sold in FY 98 was the Head Interconnect Flex (HIF), which accounted for 10% of revenue. New products introduced included the Bridge Flex and the Flexible Suspension Assembly (FSA). The FSA is a HIF that is bonded to a suspension, while the Bridge Flex completes the connection from competitors' disk drive head interconnects to the back of the suspension. Other product opportunities in the chemical etching area include chemical machining of metals and film and optical component production.

On August 9, 1999, Innnovex completed a cash tender offer of $3.80 a share for ADFlex Solutions; 76% of ADFlex's shares were tendered. On September 14, 1999, the remaining 24% of the shares were acquired at the same price, pursuant to a merger. ADFlex is a supplier of flexible circuits for the computer, medical and telecommunications markets. Borrowings under credit facilities were used to finance the purchase.

Exports, principally to Pacific Rim customers, accounted for 83% of net sales in FY 98, down from 86% in FY 97. These accounts are often with the foreign operations of U.S.-based companies. Four customers accounted for 74% of total revenues in FY 98, nearly unchanged from 73% in FY 97.

Per Share Data ($) (Year Ended Sep. 30)	1998	1997	1996	1995	1994	1993	1992	1991	1990	1989
Tangible Bk. Val.	6.81	5.81	6.48	2.55	1.82	1.65	1.42	1.41	1.36	1.23
Cash Flow	1.51	2.66	1.94	0.92	0.40	0.37	0.96	0.14	0.20	0.14
Earnings	1.05	2.31	0.91	0.70	0.26	0.27	0.06	0.05	0.13	0.08
Dividends	0.14	0.11	0.09	0.08	0.07	0.07	Nil	Nil	Nil	Nil
Payout Ratio	13%	5%	10%	11%	28%	24%	Nil	Nil	Nil	Nil
Prices - High	28 1/8	42 7/8	30 1/4	12 3/8	5 5/8	4 1/2	1 3/4	1 13/16	1 9/16	1 5/8
- Low	9	18 1/2	5 7/8	4 3/4	2 1/2	1 11/16	15/16	13/16	1	1
P/E Ratio - High	27	19	34	18	21	16	31	37	12	19
- Low	9	8	6	7	10	6	16	17	8	12
Income Statement Analysis (Million $)										
Revs.	96.3	142	69.6	50.1	30.6	26.6	35.2	35.0	34.4	28.2
Oper. Inc.	27.5	53.5	22.0	17.4	6.9	6.7	3.4	2.0	3.7	2.2
Depr.	7.0	4.9	3.6	3.1	2.0	1.3	1.4	1.1	1.0	0.8
Int. Exp.	0.1	0.1	0.1	0.1	0.1	0.1	0.1	0.1	0.1	0.1
Pretax Inc.	22.7	50.0	18.7	14.8	5.2	5.5	1.1	0.8	2.5	1.7
Eff. Tax Rate	30%	30%	30%	32%	32%	34%	33%	18%	34%	35%
Net Inc.	15.9	35.1	13.1	10.0	3.5	3.7	0.8	0.7	1.7	1.1
Balance Sheet & Other Fin. Data (Million $)										
Cash	17.0	37.9	21.8	22.4	13.1	9.5	4.2	2.9	2.6	1.8
Curr. Assets	79.3	71.3	42.0	32.2	21.0	19.2	18.1	15.8	16.4	14.9
Total Assets	110	97.3	58.2	41.2	29.9	26.6	25.2	22.9	22.5	20.4
Curr. Liab.	6.3	9.5	8.5	3.9	3.4	2.2	5.2	3.0	3.2	3.4
LT Debt	0.8	0.9	1.1	1.2	1.5	1.9	0.9	1.0	1.1	0.6
Common Eqty.	102	86.8	48.4	36.0	24.7	22.2	18.7	18.6	17.9	16.2
Total Cap.	103	87.8	49.5	37.2	26.6	24.4	20.0	19.9	19.3	17.0
Cap. Exp.	12.7	15.6	4.2	3.0	1.8	4.0	1.9	2.3	2.0	0.9
Cash Flow	22.9	40.0	14.0	13.1	5.5	4.9	2.2	1.8	2.6	1.9
Curr. Ratio	12.7	7.5	5.0	8.3	6.2	8.7	3.5	5.2	5.1	4.4
% LT Debt of Cap.	0.7	1.1	2.2	3.1	5.8	7.7	4.5	5.2	6.0	3.6
% Net Inc.of Revs.	16.5	24.7	18.9	20.0	11.5	13.7	2.1	1.9	4.8	3.9
% Ret. on Assets	15.4	45.1	26.4	28.1	12.4	14.0	3.1	2.9	7.8	5.6
% Ret. on Equity	16.8	51.9	31.1	32.9	14.9	17.7	4.0	3.6	9.8	6.9

Data as orig reptd.; bef. results of disc opers/spec. items. Per share data adj. for stk. divs. Bold denotes diluted EPS (FASB 128)-prior periods restated. E-Estimated. NA-Not Available. NM-Not Meaningful. NR-Not Ranked.

Office—1313 S. Fifth St., Hopkins, MN 55343-9904. **Tel**—(612) 938-4155. **Website**—http://www.innovexinc.com **Chrmn & CEO**—T. W. Haley. **Pres & COO**—W. P. Murnane. **VP-Fin**—D. W. Keller. **Dirs**—G. M. Bestler, F. L. Farrar, T. W. Haley, E. E. Hawk, W. J. Miller, W. P. Murnane, M. C. Slagle, B. M. Tessem. **Transfer Agent & Registrar**—Norwest Bank Minnesota, South St. Paul. **Incorporated**—in Minnesota in 1972. **Empl**— 619. **S&P Analyst:** Mark S. Basham

STANDARD
&POOR'S
STOCK REPORTS

Input/Output, Inc.

NYSE Symbol **IO**

In S&P SmallCap 600

09-OCT-99

Industry: Oil & Gas (Drilling & Equipment)

Summary: This company designs and manufactures seismic data acquisition products used in land and marine environments.

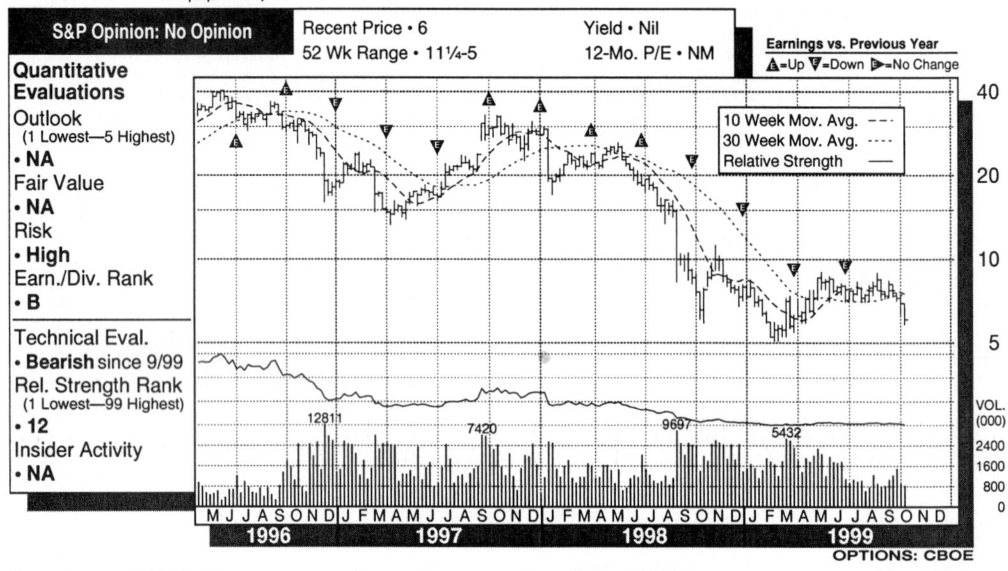

Overview - 29-MAR-99

As with much of the oil services group, seismic data firms are experiencing much lower demand for their products and services. Exploration budgets, which are crucial to IO's profitability, have been slashed 25% from 1998 levels due to worldwide commodity price declines. The company recorded pretax special charges totaling $85.7 million in the latest quarter stemming from the industry downturn. Despite a recent OPEC agreement to cut production to boost prices, the outlook for the sector remains bleak. Excess inventories must be worked off before the supply-demand balance can be restored and prices revert to normal levels. Strapped for cash, exploration and production (E&P) companies have stepped up development spending and scaled back exploration spending, waiting for prices to improve. We expect revenues in FY 2000 (May) to decline by 15%. Our reduced EPS forecasts reflect lower sales and substantial R&D expenses.

Valuation - 29-MAR-99

Shares of companies specializing in seismic data have suffered amid reduced demand, and IO is no exception; the stock was recently trading near its 52-week low. Although Input/Output is cheap relative to its peer group, the stock is trading at a significant premium to its estimated cash flow per share. It is interesting to note that shares of companies that provide services, such as drilling or seismic, often begin appreciating in anticipation of higher commodity prices, even before prices actually improve. This is even more surprising considering that E&Ps are the first to benefit from a price rebound, yet are usually the last group to trade higher. Nevertheless, trading on speculative price movements is not a basis for recommending a stock; we would not add to current positions until there is a substantial shift in the industry's fundamentals.

Key Stock Statistics

S&P EPS Est. 2000	-0.25	Tang. Bk. Value/Share	5.32
P/E on S&P Est. 2000	NM	Beta	1.55
Dividend Rate/Share	Nil	Shareholders	9,800
Shs. outstg. (M)	50.5	Market cap. (B)	$0.306
Avg. daily vol. (M)	0.220	Inst. holdings	62%

Value of $10,000 invested 5 years ago: $ 10,103

Fiscal Year Ending May 31

	1999	1998	1997	1996	1995	1994
Revenues (Million $)						
1Q	67.00	82.97	73.00	54.76	27.32	16.78
2Q	73.92	103.7	67.04	70.53	34.22	20.80
3Q	37.76	95.27	64.77	77.07	34.51	26.70
4Q	18.75	103.9	77.02	75.92	38.65	31.47
Yr.	197.4	385.9	281.9	278.3	134.7	95.75
Earnings Per Share ($)						
1Q	**0.05**	**0.26**	**0.22**	0.17	0.13	0.08
2Q	**0.08**	0.34	**0.11**	0.21	0.16	0.12
3Q	**-1.21**	**0.34**	**0.14**	0.27	0.18	0.17
4Q	**-1.00**	**0.34**	**-0.09**	0.28	0.18	0.15
Yr.	**-2.17**	**1.28**	**0.38**	**0.95**	**0.66**	**0.54**

Next earnings report expected: NA

Dividend Data

No cash has been paid, and no payments are expected in the foreseeable future.

A Division of The McGraw-Hill Companies

Input/Output, Inc.

Business Summary - 29-MAR-99

Demand for this company's seismic data acquisition products, which are crucial to the exploration activities of the oil and gas industry, is highly dependent on commodity price levels. Input/Output designs and manufacturers seismic data acquisition products used on land, in transition zones (marshes and shallow bays), and in marine environments. The company's principal customers are seismic data contractors, which collect customer-specified data. In addition, IO markets its systems to major, independent and foreign oil and gas companies. During FY 98 (May), approximately 35% of revenues were derived from foreign customers. Western Atlas International (WAI) accounted for approximately 28% of FY 98 revenues.

Companies use seismic data while mapping subsurface conditions in order to increase drilling success rates. In particular, demand for 3-D seismic data has increased substantially, as advances in technology have reduced cost requirements and improved data quality. Input/Output believes that its I/O SYSTEM product line is the most technologically advanced seismic data acquisition system. IO shipped 49 I/O SYSTEMs in FY 98. Depending on the system's configuration, the price of a land I/O SYSTEM typically ranges from $800,000 to $4.5 million.

On land, the company offers the I/O SYSTEM TWO, MRX, and RSR systems, as well as its Vibrators, a land energy source, and Geophones. Versions of the MRX and RSR systems are available for transition zones. IO's marine data acquisition systems consist primarily of marine steamers and shipboard electronics that collect seismic data in deep-water environments.

IO's growth strategy consists of technological leadership and complementary acquisitions. The company allocates approximately 8% to 10% of its revenue forecast for research and development. Most of those expenses are dedicated to I/O SYSTEM enhancements; however, IO is also investigating new technologies, such as 4-D seismic and multicomponent recording. The 4-D process, or time lapse 3-D, involves the repeated recording of 3-D image volumes at different times in the life of a producing hydrocarbon reservoir.

Input/Output has expanded its product line through several complementary acquisitions. Acquisitions in 1998 included: CompuSeis, (recording system integration); Green Mountain Geophysical (3-D survey planning software); and DigiCOURSE (designer and manufacturer of marine positioning systems). In June, IO entered into an agreement with Mitcham Industries, whereby Mitcham will purchase a minimum $90 million to $100 million of IO's products within a five year period. IO went through several organizational changes in 1998, including the appointment of new senior management and directors.

Per Share Data ($) **(Year Ended May 31)**	**1999**	**1998**	**1997**	**1996**	**1995**	**1994**	**1993**	**1992**	**1991**	**1990**
Tangible Bk. Val.	5.32	7.79	6.41	5.89	4.04	3.02	1.60	1.29	1.01	0.52
Cash Flow	-1.75	1.66	0.67	1.18	0.75	0.58	0.35	0.30	0.28	0.20
Earnings	-2.17	1.28	0.38	0.94	0.66	0.53	0.31	0.27	0.25	0.17
Dividends	Nil	Nil	Nil	Nil	Nil	Nil	Nil	Nil	Nil	Nil
Payout Ratio	Nil	Nil	Nil	Nil	Nil	Nil	Nil	Nil	Nil	Nil
Cal. Yrs.	1998	1997	1996	1995	1994	1993	1992	1991	1990	1989
Prices - High	29 5/8	33 1/8	40 1/2	28 7/8	13 5/8	6 1/8	4 1/2	3 1/2	NA	NA
- Low	5 7/8	13 1/4	16	11	6	2 7/16	2 3/8	1 3/8	NA	NA
P/E Ratio - High	NM	26	NM	31	21	12	14	13	NA	NA
- Low	NM	10	NM	12	9	5	8	5	NA	NA
Income Statement Analysis (Million $)										
Revs.	197	386	282	278	135	95.8	54.2	45.5	36.0	28.8
Oper. Inc.	-140	94.3	49.6	65.9	35.1	24.6	13.8	12.1	9.8	7.3
Depr.	20.8	16.8	12.6	10.1	3.6	1.9	1.4	1.1	0.8	0.8
Int. Exp.	897	1.1	0.8	2.5	0.0	0.2	0.2	0.3	1.0	1.1
Pretax Inc.	-154	83.7	24.3	56.3	35.4	24.0	13.3	11.9	8.7	5.5
Eff. Tax Rate	NM	32%	32%	31%	31%	31%	32%	34%	34%	34%
Net Inc.	-105	56.9	16.6	38.6	24.5	16.6	9.1	7.8	5.7	3.7
Balance Sheet & Other Fin. Data (Million $)										
Cash	75.1	72.3	2.6	34.2	57.4	58.4	4.5	9.0	6.3	1.3
Curr. Assets	259	302	203	200	121	101	40.1	29.2	26.1	16.7
Total Assets	452	490	385	355	105	132	61.5	46.3	40.8	30.9
Curr. Liab.	44.9	62.8	32.4	35.2	15.9	13.5	10.4	7.4	8.0	12.7
LT Debt	8.9	10.0	11.0	Nil	Nil	Nil	0.4	0.6	2.1	5.9
Common Eqty.	357	416	339	317	147	116	47.9	37.4	29.3	11.2
Total Cap.	406	406	350	317	147	117	49.5	38.9	32.9	18.2
Cap. Exp.	9.3	7.0	27.0	10.2	6.0	4.0	3.7	1.8	4.7	2.1
Cash Flow	-84.8	73.7	29.2	48.8	28.1	18.4	10.6	8.9	6.6	4.3
Curr. Ratio	5.8	4.8	6.3	5.7	7.6	7.5	3.8	3.9	3.3	1.3
% LT Debt of Cap.	2.2	2.4	3.1	Nil	Nil	Nil	0.9	1.4	6.3	32.3
% Net Inc.of Revs.	NM	14.7	5.9	13.9	18.2	17.3	16.9	17.2	15.9	12.7
% Ret. on Assets	NM	13.0	4.5	14.8	16.3	16.2	16.7	18.0	14.0	12.0
% Ret. on Equity	NM	15.1	5.1	16.7	18.5	19.2	21.1	23.5	25.9	37.9

Data as orig reptd.; bef. results of disc opers/spec. items. Per share data adj. for stk. divs. Bold denotes diluted EPS (FASB 128)-prior periods restated. E-Estimated. NA-Not Available. NM-Not Meaningful. NR-Not Ranked.

Office—11104 West Airport Blvd., Stafford, TX 77477. **Tel**—(281) 933-3339. **Fax**—(281) 933-9826. **Website**—http://www.i-o.com **Chrmn & CEO**—W. J. Zeringue. **Pres & COO**—A. M. Sigmar. **VP & CFO**—G. S. Mayeux. **VP & Secy**—Chris E. Wolfe. **Investor Contact**—Gregory A. Rosenstein. **Dirs**—R. P. Brindley, E. E. Cook, T. H. Elliott Jr., G. T. Graves III, A. M. Sigmar, W. F. Wallace, W. J. Zeringue. **Transfer Agent**—Harris Trust and Savings Bank, Houston, TX. **Incorporated**—in Delaware in 1979. **Empl**— 1,172. **S&P Analyst:** Ephraim Juskowicz

STANDARD &POOR'S
STOCK REPORTS

Insight Enterprises

NASDAQ Symbol **NSIT**

In S&P SmallCap 600

09-OCT-99

Industry: Retail (Home Shopping)

Summary: This company is a global direct marketer of computers, hardware and software.

Quantitative Evaluations

Outlook
(1 Lowest—5 Highest)
• **NA**

Fair Value
• **NA**

Risk
• **High**

Earn./Div. Rank
• **NR**

Technical Eval.
• **Neutral** since 9/99

Rel. Strength Rank
(1 Lowest—99 Highest)
• **75**

Insider Activity
• **NA**

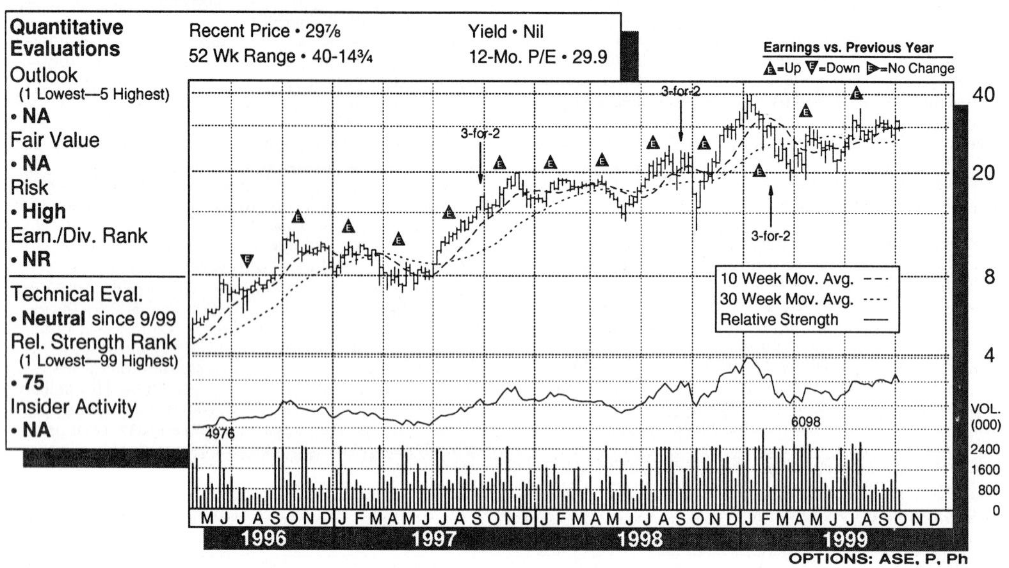

Business Profile - 21-SEP-99

Insight has agreed to acquire Action Computer Supplies Holdings plc, the leading U.K. based IT direct marketer, which offers computer products and services to small, medium and large businesses with operations in the U.K. and Spain. Terms of the transaction now call for Insight to acquire Action for about 4.23 million common shares (revised downward from about 5.64 million shares in July, 1999, due to weaker operating results recently experienced by Action). NSIT expects the acquisition to be slightly dilutive to earnings for 1999 but expects Action to enhance earnings thereafter. Management believes that Action is key to its further expansion into Europe. The combined companies have annualized sales of about $1.6 billion.

Operational Review - 21-SEP-99

Sales for the six months ended June 30, 1999, advanced 58%, year to year. Sales derived from direct marketing were up 60%, mainly reflecting increased account executive productivity, deeper account penetration, sales from three acquisitions, and a larger customer base and Internet enhancements. Margins widened, and operating income increased 67%. Following a more than doubling of depreciation and amortization charges, pretax income was up 64%. After taxes at 38.9%, versus 38.5%, net income rose 63%, to $14,694,000 ($0.55 a share, based on 7.5% more average shares) from $9,036,000 ($0.36, adjusted).

Stock Performance - 08-OCT-99

In the past 30 trading days, NSIT's shares have declined 2%, compared to a 0.91% fall in the S&P 500. Average trading volume for the past five days was 158,740 shares, compared with the 40-day moving average of 200,700 shares.

Key Stock Statistics

Dividend Rate/Share	Nil	Shareholders	80
Shs. outstg. (M)	25.7	Market cap. (B)	$0.767
Avg. daily vol. (M)	0.220	Inst. holdings	81%
Tang. Bk. Value/Share	5.66		
Beta	NA		

Value of $10,000 invested 5 years ago: NA

Fiscal Year Ending Dec. 31

	1999	1998	1997	1996	1995	1994
Revenues (Million $)						
1Q	338.1	206.8	130.8	70.78	53.73	—
2Q	365.2	237.4	139.3	76.43	66.38	—
3Q	—	261.2	171.3	94.66	64.24	—
4Q	—	297.4	186.3	101.0	60.61	—
Yr.	—	1,003	627.7	342.8	244.9	170.4
Earnings Per Share ($)						
1Q	**0.26**	**0.18**	**0.12**	0.07	0.07	—
2Q	**0.30**	**0.19**	**0.12**	0.07	0.08	—
3Q	—	**0.21**	**0.15**	0.09	0.06	—
4Q	—	**0.24**	**0.16**	0.09	0.06	—
Yr.	—	**0.81**	**0.55**	0.32	0.26	—

Next earnings report expected: late October

Dividend Data

Amount ($)	Date Decl.	Ex-Div. Date	Stock of Record	Payment Date
3-for-2	Jan. 06	Feb. 19	Jan. 25	Feb. 18 '99

Insight Enterprises, Inc.

Business Summary - 21-SEP-99

A global direct marketer of brand name computers, hardware and software, Insight Enterprises, Inc. has the following objective: to increase sales and generate improved profitability in all areas by expanding globally, increasing the penetration of its existing customer base, leveraging its existing infrastructure, expanding its product offerings and customer base, and utilizing emerging technologies. The goal of the company is to become the primary source of computer and related products to its targeted market.

Insight markets computers, hardware and software primarily to small- and medium-sized businesses consisting of 50 to 1,000 employees, through a combination of an outbound telemarketing sales force, electronic commerce, electronic marketing and direct mail catalogs.

NSIT offers an extensive assortment of more than 80,000 stock-keeping units (SKUs) of computer, hardware and software, including such popular brand names as Compaq, Hewlett-Packard, IBM, NEC, Microsoft, Seagate, Toshiba and 3COM. Notebook computers accounted for about 22% of 1998 sales, desktop computers 18%, hard disk drives 8%, memory/processors 5%, monitors/video 6%, network/connectivity products 8%, printers 9%, software 10% and miscellaneous products 14%.

The company seeks to create strong, long-term relationships with its customers through the use of a well-trained outbound sales force whose goal is to increase the depth of penetration in its existing accounts, encourage repeat buying and ensure customer satisfaction. To that end, Insight has increased its number of account executives significantly over the past five years from 129 in 1993 to 1,072 at the end of 1998, most of whom focus on outbound telemarketing.

The company's four major market segments in 1998 were: business, which contributed about 80% of sales, education institutions 7%, government organizations 3%, and home 10%.

Insight maintains a global Web site, www.insight.com, which features its current product offerings, special promotions, technical product specifications and other useful information. Unassisted Web orders - those transacted without the assistance of an Insight account executive - represented about 5% of the company's sales in 1998. NSIT believes that this percentage will increase going forward as the popularity of the Internet grows and as businesses and electronic customers increase their use of the Web to procure computing products.

The company expanded its operations outside of North America in 1998 with the acquisition of two European computer direct marketing companies. International subsidiaries, including Canadian operations established in 1997, accounted for about 8% of sales in 1998.

Per Share Data ($)										
(Year Ended Dec. 31)	**1998**	**1997**	**1996**	**1995**	**1994**	**1993**	**1992**	**1991**	**1990**	**1989**
Tangible Bk. Val.	5.00	6.58	2.29	1.28	NA	NA	NA	NA	NA	NA
Cash Flow	0.98	0.98	0.57	0.41	NA	NA	NA	NA	NA	NA
Earnings	0.81	0.55	0.32	0.26	NA	NA	NA	NA	NA	NA
Dividends	Nil	Nil	Nil	Nil	NA	NA	NA	NA	NA	NA
Payout Ratio	Nil	Nil	Nil	Nil	NA	NA	NA	NA	NA	NA
Prices - High	36 7/8	20 1/8	11 3/4	7 1/2	NA	NA	NA	NA	NA	NA
- Low	12	6 7/8	3 1/2	2 5/8	NA	NA	NA	NA	NA	NA
P/E Ratio - High	45	37	36	23	NA	NA	NA	NA	NA	NA
- Low	15	13	10	10	NA	NA	NA	NA	NA	NA
Income Statement Analysis (Million $)										
Revs.	1,003	628	343	245	170	NA	NA	NA	NA	NA
Oper. Inc.	38.2	24.7	10.7	7.4	3.4	NA	NA	NA	NA	NA
Depr.	4.3	2.5	1.1	0.8	0.5	NA	NA	NA	NA	NA
Int. Exp.	NA	NA	0.1	0.6	0.4	NA	NA	NA	NA	NA
Pretax Inc.	33.2	22.2	9.5	5.3	2.1	NA	NA	NA	NA	NA
Eff. Tax Rate	38%	40%	40%	40%	27%	NA	NA	NA	NA	NA
Net Inc.	20.5	13.2	5.7	3.2	1.5	NA	NA	NA	NA	NA
Balance Sheet & Other Fin. Data (Million $)										
Cash	13.0	7.0	5.3	7.6	2.5	NA	NA	NA	NA	NA
Curr. Assets	194	148	66.4	39.2	25.2	NA	NA	NA	NA	NA
Total Assets	251	169	73.6	42.4	27.7	NA	NA	NA	NA	NA
Curr. Liab.	92.0	33.4	31.8	17.3	23.3	NA	NA	NA	NA	NA
LT Debt	8.3	32.8	Nil	6.5	1.0	NA	NA	NA	NA	NA
Common Eqty.	151	102	41.8	18.6	3.5	NA	NA	NA	NA	NA
Total Cap.	159	135	41.8	25.1	4.5	NA	NA	NA	NA	NA
Cap. Exp.	9.7	9.4	4.9	1.3	1.2	NA	NA	NA	NA	NA
Cash Flow	24.8	15.7	6.8	4.0	2.0	NA	NA	NA	NA	NA
Curr. Ratio	2.1	4.4	2.1	2.3	1.1	NA	NA	NA	NA	NA
% LT Debt of Cap.	5.2	24.3	Nil	26.1	22.2	NA	NA	NA	NA	NA
% Net Inc.of Revs.	2.0	2.1	1.7	1.3	0.9	NA	NA	NA	NA	NA
% Ret. on Assets	9.8	10.9	9.9	9.2	NA	NA	NA	NA	NA	NA
% Ret. on Equity	16.2	18.3	19.0	29.3	NA	NA	NA	NA	NA	NA

Data as orig reptd.; bef. results of disc opers/spec. items. Per share data adj. for stk. divs. Bold denotes diluted EPS (FASB 128)-prior periods restated. E-Estimated. NA-Not Available. NM-Not Meaningful. NR-Not Ranked.

Office—6820 South Harl Avenue, Tempe, AZ 85283. **Tel**—(602) 902-1001. **Website**—http://www.insight.com **Chrmn & CEO**—E. J. Crown. **Pres**—T. A. Crown. **CFO, Treas & Secy**—S. Laybourne. **Dirs**—E. J. Crown, T. A. Crown, L. A. Gunning, R. C. Jones, S. Laybourne. **Transfer Agent & Registrar**—ChaseMellon Shareholder Services, Ridgefield Park, NJ. **Incorporated**—in Delaware in 1991. **Empl**— 2,066. **S&P Analyst:** J. J. Schemitsch

STANDARD &POOR'S STOCK REPORTS

Insituform Technologies

NASDAQ Symbol **INSUA**

In S&P SmallCap 600

09-OCT-99

Industry: Manufacturing (Specialized)

Summary: This company provides patented methods of reconstructing deteriorated pipelines and manholes with little or no excavation.

Quantitative Evaluations

Outlook (1 Lowest—5 Highest) • 2+

Fair Value • 23⅝

Risk • Average

Earn./Div. Rank • B-

Technical Eval. • **Bullish** since 8/99

Rel. Strength Rank (1 Lowest—99 Highest) • 87

Insider Activity • NA

Recent Price • 23⅞ | Yield • Nil

52 Wk Range • 25¼-9⅝ | 12-Mo. P/E • 29.9

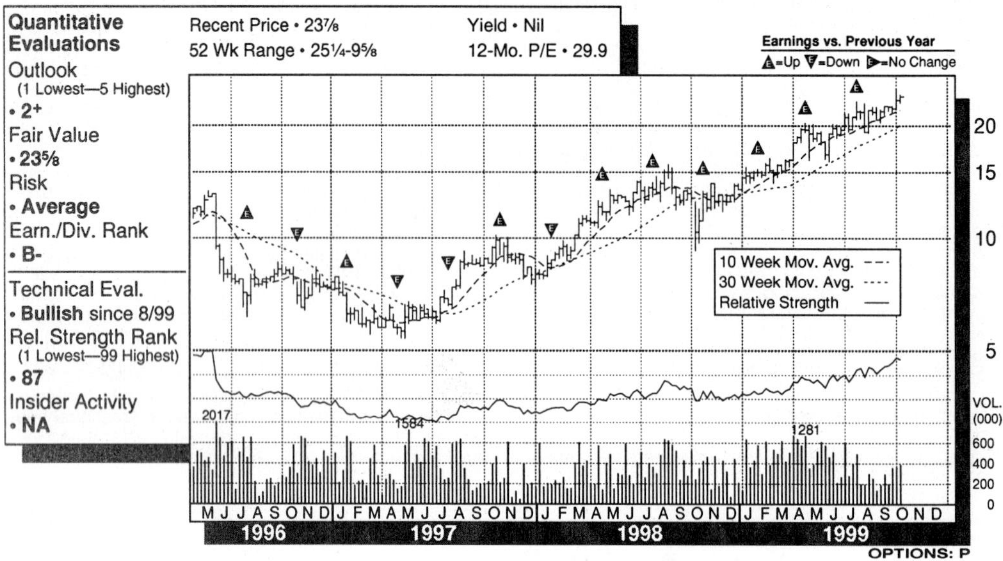

Business Profile - 05-OCT-99

The company plans to continue to develop and acquire new technologies, as it focuses on increasing productivity and decreasing costs in its core sewer rehabilitation business. The company also plans to focus on the Far East, Japan and India. In July 1999, INSUA withdrew from Midsouth Partners, a joint venture with Insituform East, due to mounting losses. East will purchase the company's 58% stake in the partnership at book value. In June 1999, the company acquired its Insituform Process licensee in the Netherlands for $11.8 million. Through June 30, 1999, INSUA had repurchased 1,895,800 of its common shares for $28.1 million under a 2.7 million share (10%) repurchase plan.

Operational Review - 05-OCT-99

Total rehabilitation revenues in the first half of 1999 advanced 13%, year to year, reflecting strength in the core sewer rehabilitation business in North America and Europe, as well as in the tunneling operations. Gross margins widened on well controlled rehabilitation costs, and with well controlled SG&A expense, pretax earnings were up 45%. After taxes at 40.8%, versus 39.7%, and minority interest and equity in earnings of affiliates, net income rose 43%, to $10,643,000 ($0.41 a share, diluted, on 3.7% fewer shares), from $7,455,000 ($0.27). INSUA plans to continue unit cost reductions while accelerating revenue growth in its core pipe rehabilitation market.

Stock Performance - 08-OCT-99

In the past 30 trading days, INSUA's shares have increased 15%, compared to a 0.91% fall in the S&P 500. Average trading volume for the past five days was 76,620 shares, compared with the 40-day moving average of 55,090 shares.

Key Stock Statistics

Dividend Rate/Share	Nil	Shareholders	2,200
Shs. outstg. (M)	25.4	Market cap. (B)	$0.608
Avg. daily vol. (M)	0.065	Inst. holdings	55%
Tang. Bk. Value/Share	2.45		
Beta	0.47		

Value of $10,000 invested 5 years ago: $ 19,540

Fiscal Year Ending Dec. 31

	1999	1998	1997	1996	1995	1994
Revenues (Million $)						
1Q	71.16	63.76	77.08	68.11	62.27	30.48
2Q	85.64	75.50	75.32	71.77	69.62	31.80
3Q	—	81.05	85.49	70.65	69.89	40.95
4Q	—	80.65	82.75	79.41	70.42	45.02
Yr.	—	301.0	320.6	289.9	272.2	148.3
Earnings Per Share ($)						
1Q	**0.16**	**0.11**	**0.05**	**0.08**	0.13	0.10
2Q	**0.25**	**0.16**	**0.01**	**0.14**	0.08	0.15
3Q	—	**0.21**	**0.16**	**0.13**	0.15	0.25
4Q	—	**0.18**	**0.14**	**0.19**	-0.40	0.18
Yr.	—	**0.66**	**0.36**	**0.17**	**-0.04**	0.68

Next earnings report expected: late October

Dividend Data

No cash has been paid.

Insituform Technologies, Inc.

Business Summary - 05-OCT-99

From a company deriving all of its revenues from royalties and product sales to its licensees just a few years ago, Insituform Technologies (INSUA) has become an integrated pipe rehabilitation company which now derives the bulk of its revenues from contracting using its non-disruptive, Insituform Process technologies. Formerly Insituform of North America, INSUA believes the domestic and international market remains strong for the trenchless rehabilitation business, as well as for the tunneling and United Pipeline companies. INSUA plans to transform the company by increasing operational efficiency and cutting fixed costs. The company has focused the marketing of its rehabilitation technologies primarily on the municipal wastewater markets worldwide, which it expects to remain the largest part of its business.

The company provides a trenchless means of rehabilitating sewers, tunnels and pipelines through its Affholder unit. INSUA's Tite Liner Process lines new and existing steel pipelines with a corrosion and abrasion resistant polyethylene pipe. It also offers the NuPipe Process in the U.S. and overseas, primarily to repair smaller or less damaged pipe. The company expanded its operations significantly through the October 1995 acquisition of Insituform Mid-America (INSMA) for 12,450,896 common shares. In March 1998, the company acquired the 40% minority interest in its Chilean unit for $2.1 million.

Pipeline technology primarily involves licensing, selling and servicing trenchless pipeline reconstruction technology and products. Construction consists mainly of the installation of trenchless pipeline reconstruction materials.

The Insituform technology utilizes the INSUA manufactured Insitutube that serves as a carrier for liquid thermosetting plastic resins. At the job site, this tube is positioned in the pipe to be reconstructed through a manhole. Once the tube is in place and positioned tightly against the inner walls of the old pipe, heated water is used to cure the resin, forming a jointless, structural, corrosion-resistant new pipe (the Insitupipe) inside the old pipe.

The NuPipe subsidiary repairs pipe by first heating material which is then pulled into the pipe to be repaired. Once in place, the NuPipe is expanded tightly against the walls of the old pipe, forming a jointless, corrosion resistant pipe-within-a-pipe.

INSUA receives royalties from a network of sublicensees that distribute and install Insituform and NuPipe in the U.S. The NuPipe Ltd. subsidiary markets and installs NuPipe in the U.K., while NuPipe International is responsible for worldwide licensing outside the U.S.

Construction backlog at 1998 year end was $109 million, up 7% from 1997 year end.

Per Share Data ($) (Year Ended Dec. 31)	1998	1997	1996	1995	1994	1993	1992	1991	1990	1989
Tangible Bk. Val.	2.70	2.37	1.99	1.69	5.15	4.45	3.91	5.74	3.77	3.58
Cash Flow	1.37	1.07	0.87	0.59	1.20	0.95	-0.15	1.97	0.35	0.55
Earnings	0.66	0.36	0.17	-0.04	0.68	0.51	-0.45	1.77	0.22	0.46
Dividends	Nil	Nil	Nil	Nil	Nil	Nil	Nil	Nil	Nil	Nil
Payout Ratio	Nil	Nil	Nil	Nil	Nil	Nil	Nil	Nil	Nil	Nil
Prices - High	15 3/4	10 1/8	13 3/8	16 5/8	15 3/8	25 3/4	26 1/2	20 5/8	8 5/8	11 1/2
- Low	7 3/4	5 3/8	6 1/8	11 1/8	10 1/2	11 1/4	14	3 1/4	2 7/16	6 7/8
P/E Ratio - High	24	28	79	NM	23	50	NM	12	39	25
- Low	12	15	36	NM	15	22	NM	2	11	15
Income Statement Analysis (Million $)										
Revs.	301	321	290	272	148	101	95.8	30.4	22.0	21.1
Oper. Inc.	57.8	48.9	40.0	43.1	26.1	16.4	12.8	5.7	2.8	3.8
Depr.	19.1	19.2	19.2	16.8	7.5	6.3	4.2	1.6	1.1	0.7
Int. Exp.	9.1	8.8	6.2	6.4	3.1	1.4	0.2	NA	NA	0.7
Pretax Inc.	31.8	17.2	9.9	4.3	16.5	11.0	-2.0	24.4	2.4	5.0
Eff. Tax Rate	41%	41%	51%	NM	37%	30%	NM	42%	29%	28%
Net Inc.	17.9	9.6	4.5	-1.0	9.8	7.3	-6.2	14.3	1.7	3.7
Balance Sheet & Other Fin. Data (Million $)										
Cash	76.9	45.7	13.5	11.4	17.7	16.1	14.3	25.9	13.9	13.0
Curr. Assets	170	161	131	121	71.7	56.3	43.7	37.8	20.7	19.5
Total Assets	305	298	268	260	162	129	87.4	58.1	41.9	40.2
Curr. Liab.	48.1	47.0	52.0	51.0	38.9	28.0	24.0	5.8	5.4	4.3
LT Debt	112	111	82.4	82.8	47.3	36.3	7.3	6.4	6.7	7.3
Common Eqty.	140	132	123	117	73.9	63.4	54.5	45.6	29.4	27.9
Total Cap.	255	250	209	208	124	101	63.4	52.2	36.5	35.6
Cap. Exp.	13.4	16.6	18.2	16.5	9.0	5.3	6.1	1.5	1.7	2.8
Cash Flow	37.0	28.9	23.7	15.8	17.3	13.6	-2.1	15.9	2.7	4.3
Curr. Ratio	3.5	3.4	2.5	2.4	1.8	2.0	1.8	6.5	3.8	4.5
% LT Debt of Cap.	43.9	44.4	39.4	39.8	38.3	35.9	11.6	12.3	18.3	20.5
% Net Inc.of Revs.	5.9	3.0	1.5	NM	6.6	7.2	NM	46.9	7.7	17.0
% Ret. on Assets	5.9	3.4	1.7	NM	6.7	6.6	NM	28.3	4.1	9.4
% Ret. on Equity	13.2	7.6	3.7	NM	14.2	12.2	NM	37.8	5.9	13.9

Data as orig reptd.; bef. results of disc opers/spec. items. Per share data adj. for stk. divs. Bold denotes diluted EPS (FASB 128)-prior periods restated. E-Estimated. NA-Not Available. NM-Not Meaningful. NR-Not Ranked.

Office—702 Spirit 40 Park Drive, Chesterfield, MO 63005. **Tel**—(314) 530-8000. **Chrmn & CEO**—A. W. Hooper. **VP & CFO**—J. A. White. **Secy**—H. Kailes. **Dirs**—R. W. Affholder, P. A. Biddelman, S. Cortinovis, A. W. Hooper, S. Spengler, T. N. Kalishman, S. Weinig, R. B. Wight, Jr., A. L. Woods. **Transfer Agent & Registrar**—American Stock Transfer & Trust Co., NYC. **Incorporated**—in Delaware in 1980. **Empl**— 1,472. **S&P Analyst:** Stewart Scharf

STANDARD
&POOR'S
STOCK REPORTS

Insteel Industries

NYSE Symbol **III**

In S&P SmallCap 600

09-OCT-99

Industry:
Manufacturing (Specialized)

Summary: This company produces concrete wire reinforcing products, industrial wire, agricultural fencing, nails, specialty wire fabrics and building panels.

Quantitative Evaluations

Outlook
(1 Lowest—5 Highest)
• **4-**

Fair Value
• **12¼**

Risk
• **Low**

Earn./Div. Rank
• **B-**

Technical Eval.
• **Bearish** since 9/99

Rel. Strength Rank
(1 Lowest—99 Highest)
• **66**

Insider Activity
• **NA**

Recent Price • 8⅞
52 Wk Range • 9⅞-3⅞
Yield • 2.7%
12-Mo. P/E • 7.7

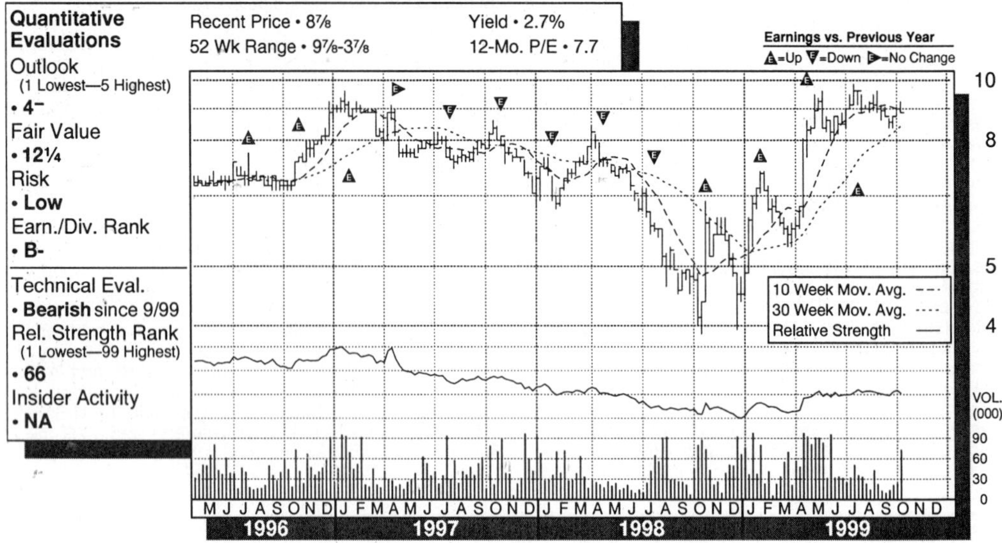

Business Profile - 28-JUN-99

Insteel is focusing on lowering its manufacturing costs in its industrial wire and nail businesses, while expanding into higher value products that offer the potential to generate significantly more attractive returns than its traditional business. Since 1994, Insteel has entered the PC strand, collated fasteners, tire bead wire and welding wire markets. The company expects sales of these new products to rise from $40 million in FY 98 (Sep.) to $100 million in 2000. In April 1999, Insteel acquired Northwestern Steel and Wire Co.'s concrete reinforcing business for $8.3 million. Insteel expects the federal TEA-21 highway spending legislation to generate additional demand for its concrete reinforcing products beginning this year.

Operational Review - 28-JUN-99

Net sales in the first half of FY 99 (Sep.) rose 4.5%, year to year, as sharply higher sales of concrete reinforcing products and nails, driven by strong construction markets, outweighed the sale of the agricultural fencing product line and lower industrial wire sales resulting from higher internal consumption. Margins widened significantly on higher shipment volumes, better operating efficiencies and increased tire bead wire and welding wire sales. Following lower interest expense related to lower inventory levels, income of $4,041,000 ($0.48 a share) contrasted with a loss of $2,474,000 ($0.24). FY 98 results exclude a loss of $0.05 a share from the early retirement of debt.

Stock Performance - 08-OCT-99

In the past 30 trading days, III's shares have declined 1%, compared to a 0.91% fall in the S&P 500. Average trading volume for the past five days was 14,480 shares, compared with the 40-day moving average of 5,513 shares.

Key Stock Statistics

Dividend Rate/Share	0.24	Shareholders	641
Shs. outstg. (M)	8.5	Market cap. (B)	$0.075
Avg. daily vol. (M)	0.007	Inst. holdings	43%
Tang. Bk. Value/Share	8.90		
Beta	0.72		

Value of $10,000 invested 5 years ago: $ 9,999

Fiscal Year Ending Sep. 30

	1999	1998	1997	1996	1995	1994
Revenues (Million $)						
1Q	62.27	59.92	58.43	57.51	58.62	50.56
2Q	66.16	63.00	65.25	63.76	66.00	56.27
3Q	72.68	69.28	68.13	72.99	69.36	71.54
4Q	—	73.96	70.52	72.51	66.36	69.30
Yr.	—	266.1	262.3	266.8	260.3	247.7
Earnings Per Share ($)						
1Q	**0.18**	**-0.20**	Nil	-0.07	0.08	Nil
2Q	**0.30**	**-0.04**	0.08	0.08	0.48	0.09
3Q	**0.40**	Nil	0.14	0.25	0.19	0.19
4Q	—	**0.28**	0.08	0.24	0.01	0.18
Yr.	—	**0.04**	**0.30**	0.50	0.76	0.45

Next earnings report expected: mid October

Dividend Data (Dividends have been paid since 1986.)

Amount ($)	Date Decl.	Ex-Div. Date	Stock of Record	Payment Date
0.060	Nov. 04	Dec. 09	Dec. 11	Jan. 04 '99
0.060	Feb. 10	Mar. 17	Mar. 19	Apr. 05 '99
0.060	Apr. 27	Jun. 16	Jun. 18	Jul. 06 '99
0.060	Aug. 31	Sep. 15	Sep. 17	Oct. 04 '99

Insteel Industries, Inc.

Business Summary - 28-JUN-99

Insteel Industries is a leading manufacturer of wire products that serve a broad range of markets (construction, industrial, appliance and home furnishings). Insteel has been making serious efforts to expand its product line to offer more profitable, value-added wire and related products. The company invested over $75 million in the past few years to expand into new products and markets, as well as upgrade existing production operations.

Insteel offers six related product lines: concrete reinforcing products, industrial wire products, bulk nails, collated fasteners, tire bead wire and welding wire. The company's concrete reinforcing products, wire and nails are sold to the construction, home furnishings and appliance markets. Management expects increased funding from federal transportation spending legislation to boost demand for welded wire fabric and PC strand (a reinforcing product used in construction of structural members, bridges, buildings, parking decks and other structural components) beginning in the second quarter of FY 99 (Sep.). The recently expanded PC strand facility will enable it to increase volume by 40%.

Consistent with its strategy of adding new business, Insteel added tire bead wire and welding wire product lines during FY 98. Tire bead wire is a bronze-plated steel wire sold to tire makers that is used to reinforce the inside diameter of a tire and hold the tire to the wheel. Welding wire is a copper-plated steel wire sold to distributors and OEMs that is used as a filler metal material in GMAW welding applications.

In February 1998, Insteel sold its money-losing agricultural fencing business to Keystone Consolidated Industries to focus on higher-margin wire and related products. Under terms of the sale, Insteel will continue producing fencing products until the equipment is relocated.

Insteel operates in a highly competitive industry. Competitors include integrated steelmakers and smaller wire mills. Most company products are commodity items, so that it competes primarily on price. Insteel believes that it is the leading low-cost producer, because of its high-tech facilities.

Sealy Corporation accounted for 11% of total sales in FY 98, and 10% in FY 97.

Per Share Data ($) (Year Ended Sep. 30)	1998	1997	1996	1995	1994	1993	1992	1991	1990	1989
Tangible Bk. Val.	8.20	8.45	8.74	8.48	7.98	7.61	7.04	6.56	6.47	6.15
Cash Flow	1.07	1.28	1.46	1.69	1.22	1.52	1.73	1.32	1.55	1.59
Earnings	0.04	0.30	0.50	0.76	0.45	0.80	0.68	0.26	0.55	1.07
Dividends	0.24	0.24	0.24	0.30	0.24	0.23	0.21	0.19	0.17	0.15
Payout Ratio	NM	80%	48%	39%	53%	29%	31%	72%	31%	14%
Prices - High	8 3/8	9 5/8	9 1/4	8 7/8	12 1/8	12 3/4	12 1/8	8 1/8	8 1/2	9 1/8
- Low	3 7/8	6 1/4	6 1/2	6 5/8	7 3/8	8 5/8	7 5/8	5 1/4	4	5 5/8
P/E Ratio - High	NM	32	19	12	27	16	18	31	15	8
- Low	NM	21	13	9	16	11	11	20	7	5
Income Statement Analysis (Million $)										
Revs.	266	262	267	260	247	245	240	240	252	197
Oper. Inc.	8.7	-14.7	17.0	16.5	13.3	13.4	13.1	10.7	13.5	13.3
Depr.	8.7	8.2	8.1	7.8	6.3	5.7	6.8	6.7	6.2	3.3
Int. Exp.	3.8	2.3	2.3	2.3	2.4	1.5	2.5	3.0	3.4	2.1
Pretax Inc.	0.5	4.0	6.6	6.3	5.3	7.1	4.8	1.6	3.6	8.7
Eff. Tax Rate	35%	36%	35%	NM	41%	19%	19%	30%	13%	23%
Net Inc.	0.3	2.5	4.2	6.3	3.8	6.3	4.3	1.7	3.5	6.7
Balance Sheet & Other Fin. Data (Million $)										
Cash	0.4	1.1	1.4	0.3	1.2	9.3	0.4	3.8	Nil	10.2
Curr. Assets	61.7	80.2	68.8	73.9	64.5	64.3	57.2	55.6	62.5	54.2
Total Assets	147	171	146	146	139	133	113	109	119	90.0
Curr. Liab.	35.4	43.5	35.2	47.8	39.3	33.9	30.0	27.1	35.6	18.9
LT Debt	35.7	49.7	29.7	22.1	26.8	29.2	30.4	32.1	33.7	27.3
Common Eqty.	69.3	71.3	73.7	71.2	66.5	62.9	44.9	41.7	41.1	38.4
Total Cap.	111	127	110	98.3	100	99	82.8	81.8	83.1	70.9
Cap. Exp.	6.7	27.1	13.2	5.5	10.7	19.7	9.8	3.4	10.9	4.5
Cash Flow	9.1	10.8	12.3	14.1	10.1	12.0	11.2	8.3	9.7	10.0
Curr. Ratio	1.7	1.8	2.0	1.5	1.6	1.9	1.9	2.1	1.8	2.9
% LT Debt of Cap.	32.1	39.1	27.1	22.5	26.9	29.5	36.8	39.3	40.5	38.5
% Net Inc.of Revs.	0.1	1.0	1.6	2.4	1.5	2.6	1.8	0.7	1.4	3.4
% Ret. on Assets	0.2	1.6	2.0	4.4	2.8	4.5	3.9	1.5	3.4	8.0
% Ret. on Equity	0.5	3.5	5.9	9.2	5.8	10.4	10.0	4.0	8.8	18.9

Data as orig reptd.; bef. results of disc opers/spec. items. Per share data adj. for stk. divs. Bold denotes diluted EPS (FASB 128)-prior periods restated. E-Estimated. NA-Not Available. NM-Not Meaningful. NR-Not Ranked.

Office—1373 Boggs Drive, Mount Airy, NC 27030. **Tel**—(910) 786-2141. **Chrmn**—H. O. Woltz Jr. **Pres & CEO**—H. O. Woltz III. **CFO & Treas**—M. C. Gazmarian. **VP & Secy**—G. D. Kniskern. **Dirs**—L. E. Hannen, F. H. Johnson, C. B. Newsome, G. L. Pechota, W. A. Rogers II, W. J. Shields, C. R. Vaughn, H. O. Woltz Jr., H. O. Woltz III. **Transfer Agent**—First Union National Bank of North Carolina, Charlotte. **Incorporated**—in North Carolina in 1953. **Empl**— 1,056. **S&P Analyst:** John A. Massey

STANDARD
&POOR'S
STOCK REPORTS

Insurance Auto Auctions

NASDAQ Symbol **IAAI**

In S&P SmallCap 600

09-OCT-99

Industry:
Services (Commercial & Consumer)

Summary: IAAI sells cars damaged in accidents or from other causes, both for itself and on behalf of insurance companies.

Quantitative Evaluations

Outlook
(1 Lowest—5 Highest)
• **5**

Fair Value
• **26¼**

Risk
• **High**

Earn./Div. Rank
• **NR**

Technical Eval.
• **Bearish** since 9/99

Rel. Strength Rank
(1 Lowest—99 Highest)
• **50**

Insider Activity
• **NA**

Recent Price • 15⅞
52 Wk Range • 19¾-10
Yield • Nil
12-Mo. P/E • 16.7

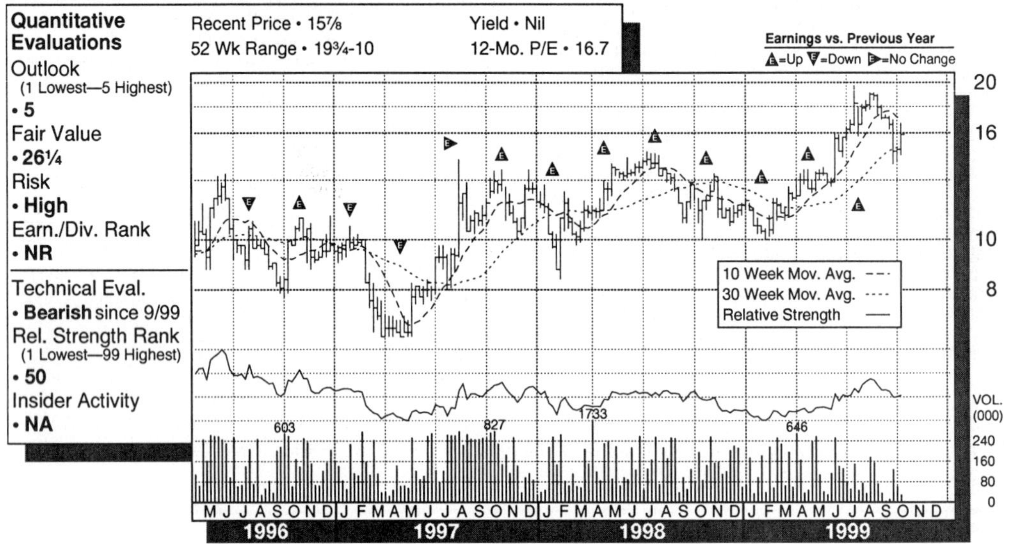

Business Profile - 27-JUL-99

In July 1999, the company announced that it had retained an investment banking firm to lead the development and structuring on a range of strategic alternatives, including acquisitions, marketing, share repurchases, or other strategic partnerships or transactions. Also in July, Insurance Auto said that it expects second quarter 1999 earnings to be at least 45%-40% above Wall Street analysts' expectations of about $0.26 a share. Management cited the following factors to explain the favorable outcome: unit volume in 1999 above original forecasts, an improvement in salvage returns, and the success of initiatives in leveraging marginal profitability per unit. Earlier in the year, directors rejected an unsolicited takeover proposal from Copart, Inc. (NASDAQ: CPRT) for about $13.27 a share.

Operational Review - 27-JUL-99

Net sales in the three months ended March 31, 1999, rose 17%, year to year, reflecting an increase in the number of units sold due to strong vehicle assignments taken in the fourth quarter of 1998 and early in the first quarter of 1999 and increased buyer fees. Comparisons benefited from initiatives to increase the number and variety of vehicle enhancement services which increase selling prices, and the absence of a $1.6 million special charge. Net income more than tripled, to $2.8 million ($0.25 a share), from $869,000 ($0.08).

Stock Performance - 08-OCT-99

In the past 30 trading days, IAAI's shares have declined 11%, compared to a 0.91% fall in the S&P 500. Average trading volume for the past five days was 5,480 shares, compared with the 40-day moving average of 12,441 shares.

Key Stock Statistics

Dividend Rate/Share	Nil	Shareholders	500
Shs. outstg. (M)	11.5	Market cap. (B)	$0.182
Avg. daily vol. (M)	0.011	Inst. holdings	78%
Tang. Bk. Value/Share	3.51		
Beta	0.54		

Value of $10,000 invested 5 years ago: $ 4,261

Fiscal Year Ending Dec. 31

	1999	1998	1997	1996	1995	1994
Revenues (Million $)						
1Q	79.88	68.56	67.89	72.82	60.24	37.63
2Q	82.53	75.40	65.98	76.04	65.19	42.37
3Q	—	70.05	61.40	68.68	64.98	41.38
4Q	—	73.06	64.06	64.36	67.59	50.75
Yr.	—	287.1	259.3	281.9	258.0	172.1
Earnings Per Share ($)						
1Q	**0.25**	**0.08**	**0.05**	**0.07**	0.24	0.18
2Q	**0.37**	**0.22**	**0.13**	**0.13**	0.17	0.27
3Q	—	**0.14**	**0.09**	**0.07**	-0.20	0.27
4Q	—	**0.20**	**0.13**	**0.01**	0.07	0.26
Yr.	—	**0.63**	**0.40**	**0.27**	**0.27**	**0.98**

Next earnings report expected: late October

Dividend Data

No dividends have been paid, and the company plans to retain all earnings to support the development and expansion of its business.

A Division of The McGraw-Hill Companies

Insurance Auto Auctions, Inc.

Business Summary - 27-JUL-99

Have you ever wondered what happens to cars that have been declared "totaled"? Many of them end up being sold by Insurance Auto Auctions, Inc., the largest vehicle salvage services company in the U.S. Insurance Auto Auctions believes it provides insurance companies with a cost-effective way to process and sell "total loss" and recovered theft vehicles. (The size of the market for the processing and sale of total loss and recovered theft vehicles in the U.S. is estimated at $3 billion a year.) The company buys such vehicles from insurance companies for resale and also sells vehicles on consignment for insurers. Vehicles are sold at live or closed bid auctions on a competitive basis. As of March 1999, the company was selling vehicles at 50 auction sites throughout the country.

Insurance Auto Auctions processes salvage vehicles under three methods: purchase agreement (30% of 1998 sales), fixed fee consignment (61%), and percentage of sale consignment (9%). In addition to fees, the company generally charges its fixed fee consignment and percentage of sale consignment vehicle suppliers for various services, including towing and storage. Under all methods of sale, the company also charges the buyer of each vehicle various buyer-related fees.

Under the purchase agreement method, IAAI generally purchases the vehicles from the insurance companies at a percentage of actual cash value (ACV) and then resells these vehicles for its own account. By assuming some of the risk in owning the salvage vehicle. the company can potentially increase profits by improving the value of the salvage vehicle prior to the sale. Under the fixed fee and percentage of sale consignment methods, the company sells vehicles on behalf of insurance companies, and costs associated with processing and sales are proportionately lower. IAAI receives agreed upon sales fees under the consignment methods and charges for other services such as towing and storage.

Vehicles processed in 1998 increased to 474,000, up from 440,000 in the previous year.

The company's BidFast service provides insurers with a binding bid for a salvage vehicle which historically may have been owner-retained. The return on such vehicles (owner-retained salvage cars) is, many times, measurably improved for the supplier using this service and enables compliance with many state department of insurance regulations. Insurance Auto also provides certain insurance company suppliers with anti-theft fraud control programs for vehicle salvage processing. Its CarCrush services helps insurance companies by ensuring that severely damaged or stripped "high profile" cars are crushed to prevent their vehicle identification numbers from being used in auto theft.

Vehicles from Insurance Auto Auctions' three largest suppliers, Allstate Insurance Co., Farmers Insurance Group and State Farm Insurance Co., accounted for 43% of unit sales in 1998.

Per Share Data ($) (Year Ended Dec. 31)	1998	1997	1996	1995	1994	1993	1992	1991	1990	1989
Tangible Bk. Val.	2.63	1.75	0.93	12.72	12.43	11.18	5.38	2.24	-0.29	0.76
Cash Flow	1.72	1.50	1.36	0.85	1.47	0.97	0.71	0.44	0.83	0.33
Earnings	0.63	0.40	0.27	0.27	0.98	0.74	0.61	-3.13	-0.19	0.21
Dividends	Nil	Nil	Nil	Nil	Nil	Nil	Nil	Nil	Nil	Nil
Payout Ratio	Nil	Nil	Nil	Nil	Nil	Nil	Nil	Nil	Nil	Nil
Prices - High	14¾	14¼	13⅜	36	38⅝	45½	23	20	NA	NA
- Low	8⅜	6½	7¾	6½	24½	17½	12⅛	11	NA	NA
P/E Ratio - High	23	36	50	NM	39	61	38	NM	NA	NA
- Low	13	16	29	NM	25	24	20	NA	NA	NA
Income Statement Analysis (Million $)										
Revs.	287	259	282	258	172	104	60.5	41.8	35.8	32.3
Oper. Inc.	28.2	23.4	21.3	21.1	24.6	12.7	6.4	3.9	3.0	1.9
Depr.	12.5	12.5	8.6	6.6	5.5	2.0	0.7	1.2	1.5	0.3
Int. Exp.	2.1	2.7	3.0	2.4	0.5	0.1	0.1	1.5	1.2	0.2
Pretax Inc.	12.8	8.3	5.4	5.5	19.1	11.0	6.3	-11.7	0.5	1.4
Eff. Tax Rate	44%	46%	43%	43%	43%	40%	31%	NM	44%	43%
Net Inc.	7.2	4.5	3.1	3.1	11.0	6.6	4.4	-11.5	0.3	0.8
Balance Sheet & Other Fin. Data (Million $)										
Cash	22.8	9.6	5.9	7.2	10.4	30.4	17.3	10.7	3.0	0.3
Curr. Assets	73.1	52.3	54.1	50.4	41.4	48.0	26.1	15.8	6.6	3.6
Total Assets	227	207	212	211	174	144	51.9	18.6	12.3	4.7
Curr. Liab.	37.8	26.5	34.4	38.2	29.3	19.2	6.5	4.9	4.7	2.5
LT Debt	20.1	20.2	26.7	24.6	0.2	1.1	0.9	Nil	6.9	0.3
Common Eqty.	159	151	147	143	140	124	44.4	13.7	-0.7	1.9
Total Cap.	186	177	173	168	140	125	45.4	13.7	6.2	2.2
Cap. Exp.	6.6	4.6	5.9	11.0	5.5	4.1	0.9	0.6	0.7	0.6
Cash Flow	19.7	17.0	15.5	9.7	16.5	8.7	5.1	1.8	3.1	1.2
Curr. Ratio	1.9	2.0	1.6	1.3	1.4	2.5	4.0	3.2	1.4	1.4
% LT Debt of Cap.	10.8	11.4	15.4	14.6	0.2	0.8	2.0	Nil	111.5	13.3
% Net Inc.of Revs.	2.5	1.7	1.1	1.2	6.4	6.4	7.2	NM	0.7	2.4
% Ret. on Assets	3.3	2.1	1.5	1.6	6.9	6.2	11.4	NM	7.9	17.0
% Ret. on Equity	4.6	3.0	2.1	2.2	8.3	7.2	13.9	NM	NA	42.3

Data as orig reptd.; bef. results of disc opers/spec. items. Per share data adj. for stk. divs. Bold denotes diluted EPS (FASB 128)-prior periods restated. E-Estimated. NA-Not Available. NM-Not Meaningful. NR-Not Ranked.

Office—850 E. Algonquin Rd., Suite 100, Schaumburg, IL 60173. **Tel**— (847) 839-3939. **Website**—http://www.iaai.com **Non-Exec Chrmn**—T. J. O'Malia. **CEO**—C. G. Knowles. **SVP, CFO & Investor Contact**—Linda C. Larrabee. **Dirs**—M. A. Cocca, S. B. Gould, P. H. Kamin, C. G. Knowles, M. R. Martin, J. F. Mazzella, T. J. O'Malia, G. E. Tullman, J. K. Wilcox. **Transfer Agent**—Bank of Boston, Boston, MA, and Palo Alto, CA. **Incorporated**—in California in 1982. **Empl**— 625. **S&P Analyst:** P.L.H.

STANDARD &POOR'S
STOCK REPORTS

Integrated Health Services

NYSE Symbol **IHS**

In S&P SmallCap 600

09-OCT-99

Industry:
Health Care
(Long-Term Care)

Summary: This company provides a broad range of medical services in medical specialty units located within nursing home facilities.

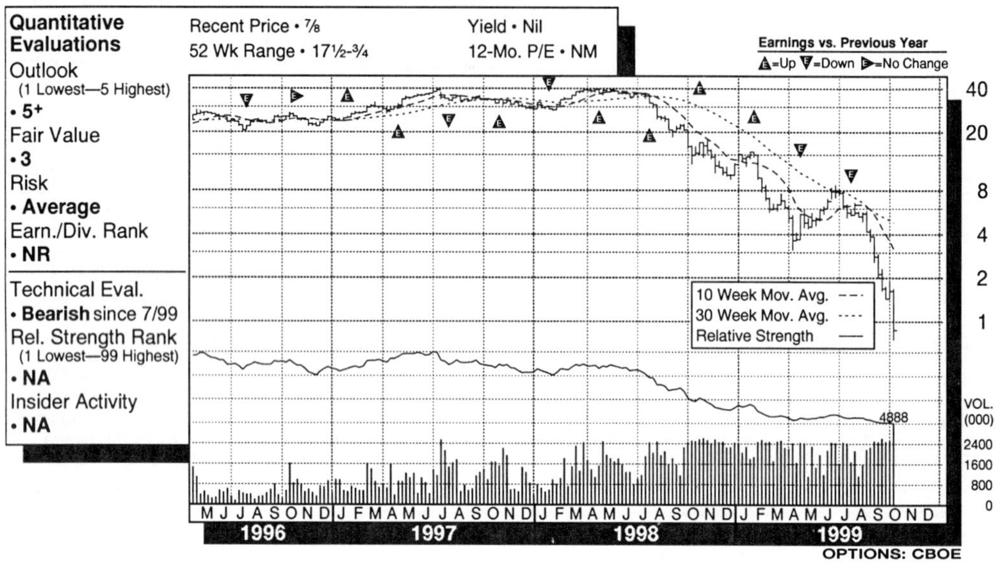

Business Profile - 06-JUL-99

Results in recent quarters have been hurt by changes in Medicare reimbursements to skilled nursing facilities (SNFs, or nursing homes) as mandated by the Balanced Budget Act (BBA) of 1997. Specifically, Medicare has implemented a prospective payment system to these facilities under which it pays a flat, per diem rate per resident regardless of the actual cost of providing services. In light of lowered revenue expectations, IHS has reduced staffing levels in its contract rehabilitation therapy division and is working with its nursing home customers to better their understanding of how to operate under the new Medicare rules. In addition, IHS sold substantially all of its home health nursing business in the 1999 first quarter.

Operational Review - 06-JUL-99

Revenues from continuing operations in the three months ended March 31, 1999, fell 19%, year to year, reflecting the sale of 37 health care facilities and lower rates for inpatient services as a result of the BBA of 1997. With only a 10% drop in operating costs and expenses, an operating loss contrasted with operating income. After taxes of $2.2 million, versus taxes at 41.0%, a loss of $6.6 million ($0.13 a share) contrasted with income of $39.3 million ($0.77). Results in the 1998 period exclude a loss from discontinued operations of $0.04.

Stock Performance - 08-OCT-99

In the past 30 trading days, IHS's shares have declined 77%, compared to a 0.91% fall in the S&P 500. Average trading volume for the past five days was 977,560 shares, compared with the 40-day moving average of 698,908 shares.

Key Stock Statistics

Dividend Rate/Share	Nil	Shareholders	1,752
Shs. outstg. (M)	52.9	Market cap. (B)	$0.046
Avg. daily vol. (M)	0.815	Inst. holdings	49%
Tang. Bk. Value/Share	NM		
Beta	1.53		

Value of $10,000 invested 5 years ago: $ 309

Fiscal Year Ending Dec. 31

	1999	1998	1997	1996	1995	1994
Revenues (Million $)						
1Q	620.4	761.7	460.9	327.3	265.4	132.3
2Q	625.5	740.5	458.0	335.8	278.1	138.7
3Q	—	750.9	472.9	360.0	299.5	177.2
4Q	—	718.9	602.2	445.7	319.2	235.4
Yr.	—	2,973	1,993	1,436	1,179	683.6
Earnings Per Share ($)						
1Q	**-0.13**	**0.77**	**0.64**	**0.54**	0.61	0.41
2Q	**-0.09**	**0.80**	**0.32**	**0.56**	0.62	0.44
3Q	—	**0.77**	**0.63**	**0.60**	0.60	0.52
4Q	—	**0.21**	**-1.55**	**0.09**	-3.03	0.59
Yr.	—	**2.56**	**-0.39**	**1.83**	**-1.21**	**1.77**

Next earnings report expected: late October

Dividend Data (Dividends have been paid since 1995.)
The most recent payment was in January 1998.

Integrated Health Services, Inc.

Business Summary - 06-JUL-99

The company ranks as one of the largest providers of "post-acute" health care services, offering a wide range of cost-effective medical and rehabilitative services more typically delivered in the acute care hospital setting and using home health care to provide those services that do not require 24-hour monitoring. IHS's post-acute care network consists of over 1,700 service locations in 47 states. The company's services include subacute care, skilled nursing facility care, contract rehabilitation and hospice services, home respiratory care, infusion and durable medical equipment, lithotripsy services and diagnostic services. The company sold most of its home health nursing business in the first quarter of 1999 and is currently exploring the sale of its home respiratory, infusion and durable medical equipment business..

The company completed several divestitures in 1998 including five long term care facilities (January 1998), the company's outpatient clinics (February 1998), five long term care facilities (June 1998) and the institutional pharmacy division (August 1998).

IHS provides subacute care through medical specialty units (MSUs), which typically have 20 to 75 beds with physical identities, specialized medical technology and staffs separate from the geriatric care facilities in which they are located. At 1998 year end, IHS operated 370 geriatric care facilities (285 owned or leased and 85 managed) and 17 specialty hospitals.

Services provided to all patients at IHS's geriatric facilities, which are licensed as skilled care nursing homes, include nursing care, room and board, special diets and other services that may be ordered by a patient's physician. Specialty medical services include complex care programs; ventilator programs; wound management programs; cardiac care programs; rehabilitative services; oncology; HIV; Alzheimer's disease programs; and hospice services.

IHS also provides contract management services to 85 geriatric care facilities in return for a management fee generally equal to 4% to 8% of gross revenues of the facility.

IHS also owns a controlling interest in 10 lithotripsy partnerships (primarily consisting of physicians), and fully owns two lithotripsy partnerships and a lithotripter maintenance company. Its lithotripsy business consists of about 35 lithotripsy machines that provide services in 170 locations in 17 states.

Patient revenues in 1998 were derived from private pay sources (38%), Medicare (40%) and Medicaid (22%).

In 1999, the company intends to focus primarily on ensuring that its core business is operating efficiently and profitably under the preferred payment system (PPS) enacted by the Balanced Budget Act of 1997. The company also intends to take advantage of attractive acquisition opportunities it expects as smaller companies have difficulty operating under PPS.

Per Share Data ($)										
(Year Ended Dec. 31)	**1998**	**1997**	**1996**	**1995**	**1994**	**1993**	**1992**	**1991**	**1990**	**1989**
Tangible Bk. Val.	NM	NM	-1.58	6.23	22.24	12.28	12.38	9.75	-149.48	NA
Cash Flow	5.67	1.40	3.79	0.65	3.41	1.71	1.28	1.13	0.94	NA
Earnings	2.56	-0.39	2.03	-1.20	1.96	1.36	1.04	0.82	0.42	NA
Dividends	Nil	0.02	0.02	0.02	0.02	Nil	Nil	Nil	Nil	NA
Payout Ratio	Nil	NM	1%	NM	1%	Nil	Nil	Nil	Nil	NA
Prices - High	39 7/8	39 1/8	28 3/4	42 1/2	41 1/8	31 3/8	29 1/4	22 1/2	NA	NA
- Low	9 1/2	23 3/4	19 5/8	19 5/8	28 1/8	19 7/8	16 3/4	13 3/4	NA	NA
P/E Ratio - High	16	NM	14	NM	21	23	28	27	NA	NA
- Low	4	NM	10	NM	14	15	16	17	NA	NA
Income Statement Analysis (Million $)										
Revs.	2,972	1,993	1,435	1,179	682	281	195	144	82.0	NA
Oper. Inc.	627	332	202	168	102	38.2	23.4	14.6	8.1	NA
Depr.	157	70.8	41.7	40.0	26.0	4.6	2.8	2.2	1.7	NA
Int. Exp.	240	123	66.3	40.8	24.7	9.8	3.6	6.1	5.7	NA
Pretax Inc.	232	13.3	111	-42.3	56.3	29.1	18.8	8.0	1.6	NA
Eff. Tax Rate	41%	183%	57%	NM	38%	39%	38%	26%	8.00%	NA
Net Inc.	137	-11.1	47.8	-26.0	35.2	17.5	11.7	5.9	1.4	NA
Balance Sheet & Other Fin. Data (Million $)										
Cash	31.4	53.0	39.0	41.3	60.0	60.0	104	16.0	2.0	NA
Curr. Assets	821	718	415	314	240	161	168	61.0	22.0	NA
Total Assets	5,393	5,063	1,993	1,434	1,238	768	312	156	102	NA
Curr. Liab.	480	654	358	177	170	100	22.7	19.1	19.7	NA
LT Debt	3,366	3,202	1,038	766	542	388	140	47.0	56.0	NA
Common Eqty.	1,332	1,088	535	432	443	209	146	87.0	-162	NA
Total Cap.	4,739	4,290	1,595	1,250	1,060	667	288	135	81.0	NA
Cap. Exp.	222	127	146	60.0	91.0	343	41.0	8.3	14.7	NA
Cash Flow	294	59.6	89.4	14.0	61.2	22.4	14.4	8.1	3.1	NA
Curr. Ratio	1.7	1.1	1.2	1.8	1.4	1.6	7.4	3.2	1.1	NA
% LT Debt of Cap.	71.0	74.6	65.1	61.3	51.1	58.2	48.8	35.0	68.9	NA
% Net Inc.of Revs.	4.6	NM	3.3	NM	5.2	6.3	6.0	4.1	1.7	NA
% Ret. on Assets	2.6	NM	2.8	NM	3.0	3.1	4.5	1.3	NA	NA
% Ret. on Equity	11.3	NM	9.9	NM	9.4	9.3	8.9	NM	NA	NA

Data as orig reptd.; bef. results of disc opers/spec. items. Per share data adj. for stk. divs. Bold denotes diluted EPS (FASB 128)-prior periods restated. E-Estimated. NA-Not Available. NM-Not Meaningful. NR-Not Ranked.

Office—10065 Red Run Blvd., Owings Mills, MD 21117. **Tel**—(410) 998-8400. **Website**—http://www.ihs-inc.com **Chrmn, Pres & CEO**—R. N. Elkins. **EVP & CFO**—C.T. Pickett. **EVP-Investor Relations & Secy**—Marc B. Levin. **Dirs**—E. M. Crawford, R. N. Elkins, K. M. Mazik, R. A. Mitchell, C. N. Newhall III, T. F. Nicholson, J. L. Silverman, G. H. Strong. **Transfer Agent & Registrar**—American Stock Transfer & Trust Co., NYC. **Incorporated**—in Delaware in 1986.**Empl**— 84,000. **S&P Analyst:** John J. Arege

STANDARD &POOR'S
STOCK REPORTS

Inter-Tel, Inc.

NASDAQ Symbol **INTL**

In S&P SmallCap 600

09-OCT-99

Industry: Communications Equipment

Summary: Inter-Tel designs, produces and markets telephone systems, applications and services to businesses requiring small to medium-size telephone system installations.

Quantitative Evaluations

Outlook (1 Lowest—5 Highest) • **5+**

Fair Value • **29**

Risk • **High**

Earn./Div. Rank • **B**

Technical Eval. • **Neutral** since 9/99

Rel. Strength Rank (1 Lowest—99 Highest) • **10**

Insider Activity • **NA**

Recent Price • 15¾

52 Wk Range • 28⅛-10

Yield • 0.3%

12-Mo. P/E • 17.5

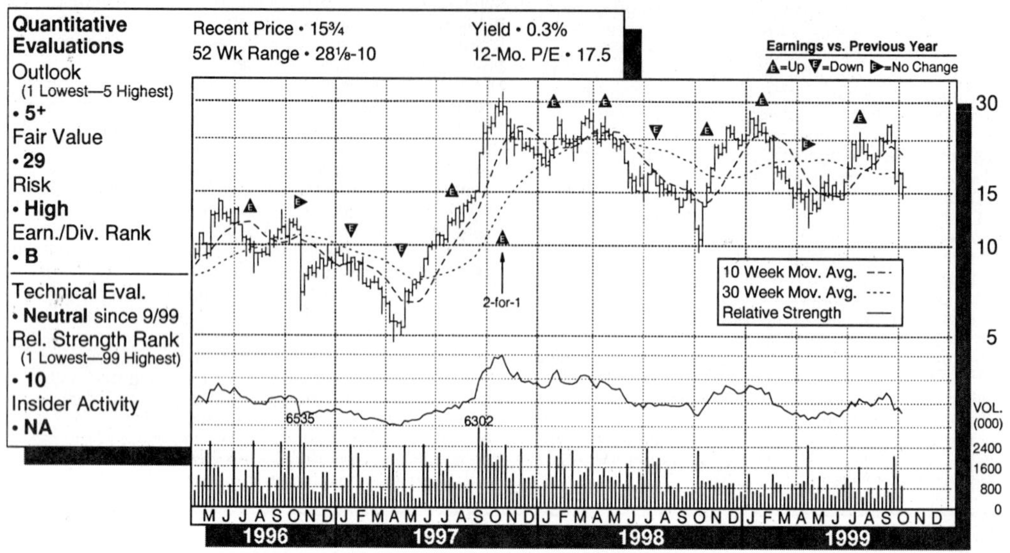

Business Profile - 21-JUN-99

The shares have fallen sharply in 1999, reflecting first quarter results that included sluggish revenue growth and a decline in net income. In April 1999, in response to the drop in the share price, directors authorized the repurchase of up to 2.5 million INTL common shares. At the time, there were still 700,000 shares authorized for purchase under an earlier buyback program. As of late April 1999, the company had about 25.6 million common shares outstanding.

Operational Review - 21-JUN-99

Net sales in the three months ended March 31, 1999, rose 2.8%, year to year, driven by increases in long distance and Internet Protocol sales. Despite a less favorable sales mix and greater R&D spending, margins widened, reflecting well controlled SG&A spending; operating income increased 5.1%. After higher depreciation and amortization charges, and a decline in other income, pretax income fell 10%. After taxes at 38.0%, versus 41.3%, net income was down 5.0%, to $5,092,000 ($0.19 a share, on 3.4% fewer shares), from $5,362,000 ($0.19).

Stock Performance - 08-OCT-99

In the past 30 trading days, INTL's shares have declined 31%, compared to a 0.91% fall in the S&P 500. Average trading volume for the past five days was 177,880 shares, compared with the 40-day moving average of 198,636 shares.

Key Stock Statistics

Dividend Rate/Share	0.04	Shareholders	6,600
Shs. outstg. (M)	25.8	Market cap. (B)	$0.407
Avg. daily vol. (M)	0.247	Inst. holdings	45%
Tang. Bk. Value/Share	5.15		
Beta	1.98		

Value of $10,000 invested 5 years ago: $ 36,153

Fiscal Year Ending Dec. 31

	1999	1998	1997	1996	1995	1994
Revenues (Million $)						
1Q	65.53	63.76	50.32	42.20	34.56	25.47
2Q	77.79	70.51	54.82	43.74	36.33	27.76
3Q	—	70.39	56.92	47.44	37.76	27.63
4Q	—	72.27	61.51	52.50	40.19	31.32
Yr.	—	274.5	223.6	185.9	148.8	112.2
Earnings Per Share ($)						
1Q	**0.19**	**0.19**	**0.10**	**0.11**	0.08	0.06
2Q	**0.27**	**-0.37**	**0.13**	**0.10**	0.06	0.08
3Q	—	**0.21**	**0.16**	**0.10**	0.10	0.07
4Q	—	**0.24**	**0.18**	**0.03**	0.11	0.10
Yr.	—	**0.32**	**0.57**	**0.34**	**0.36**	0.29

Next earnings report expected: NA

Dividend Data (Dividends have been paid since 1998.)

Amount ($)	Date Decl.	Ex-Div. Date	Stock of Record	Payment Date
0.010	Dec. 16	Dec. 29	Dec. 31	Jan. 15 '99
0.010	Mar. 18	Mar. 29	Mar. 31	Apr. 15 '99
0.010	Jun. 11	Jun. 28	Jun. 30	Jul. 15 '99
0.010	Sep. 21	Sep. 28	Sep. 30	Oct. 15 '99

A Division of The McGraw-Hill Companies

Inter-Tel, Incorporated

Business Summary - 21-JUN-99

Inter-Tel is a single point of contact, full-service provider of digital business telephone systems, call processing software, voice processing software, call accounting software, Internet Protocol (IP) telephony software, computer telephone integration applications and long distance calling services. The company also provides maintenance, leasing and support services for its products.

The company has developed a distribution network of direct sales offices, dealers and value-added resellers that sell INTL's products to small- to medium size organizations, and to divisions of larger companies, including Fortune 500 companies, large service organizations, and governmental agencies. The company has 37 sales offices in the U.S., and one each in the U.K., Japan and Singapore.

INTL offers an extensive line of digital communication systems, including hardware platforms and C++ software applications. The company's primary product, the AXXESS platform, incorporates advanced technology for computer and telephone integration providing businesses with ability to customize applications to enhance their operations and increase productivity. The AXXESS 5.1 platform, currently scheduled for release in the third quarter of 1999, is being designed to allow, through fully transparent digital networking, two or more systems to operate as one, and to increase capacity to 20,000 ports. AXXESS 5.2, currently slated for release in the 1999 fourth quarter, will add support of ISDN basic rate interfaces.

The company's gateway products are designed as transition points between two different networks, such as between a telephone network and the Internet. Gateway products convert regular voice and facsimile transmissions to or from the compressed data packets that travel over networks. The company's Vocal 'Net product is designed for carriers and services providers to bridge the traditional telephone network and IP network. Using this technology, the customers of carriers and service providers can conduct real-time, two-way voice communications over the Internet. The InterPrise product line incorporates high speed embedded DSP technology and are used primarily by business customers, carriers and service providers.

INTL's computer-telephone integration products enable users to receive phone calls through their desktop PC. The products can also manage automatic call distribution at peak efficiency, or route incoming telephone calls, based on various parameters, to a specific person. In addition, the system can collect, analyze and report real-time call processing information for staff forecasting and analysis. The company offers Visual Mail, a messaging software system that supports both voice mail and facsimile mail, providing a method to retrieve messages from a PC connected to a modem.

In June 1998, the company acquired Telecom Multimedia Systems Inc., paying $25 million in cash for the California-based provider of communications solutions.

Per Share Data ($) (Year Ended Dec. 31)	1998	1997	1996	1995	1994	1993	1992	1991	1990	1989
Tangible Bk. Val.	5.15	5.29	3.50	3.33	2.12	1.81	1.09	0.95	1.23	1.13
Cash Flow	0.57	0.74	0.49	0.45	0.36	0.30	0.29	0.20	0.21	0.14
Earnings	0.32	0.57	0.34	0.35	0.29	0.23	0.18	0.06	0.08	0.03
Dividends	0.04	0.01	Nil	Nil	Nil	Nil	Nil	Nil	Nil	Nil
Payout Ratio	12%	2%	Nil	Nil	Nil	Nil	Nil	Nil	Nil	Nil
Prices - High	28 1/2	32 3/8	14 1/4	9 7/8	6 1/8	6	2 5/8	3/4	1 1/4	1 3/8
- Low	9 1/2	4 3/4	5 3/4	3 1/2	3	2	7/16	5/16	1/2	9/16
P/E Ratio - High	89	57	42	28	21	27	14	13	16	46
- Low	30	8	17	10	10	9	3	6	6	19
Income Statement Analysis (Million $)										
Revs.	275	224	186	149	112	89.3	78.8	66.1	67.4	61.6
Oper. Inc.	42.3	27.8	22.0	15.7	10.5	7.6	6.7	4.3	5.4	4.0
Depr.	6.7	4.6	4.1	2.2	1.5	1.3	1.8	2.4	2.0	1.8
Int. Exp.	0.1	0.0	0.1	0.1	0.1	0.4	0.7	0.9	1.4	1.6
Pretax Inc.	15.8	24.6	15.3	13.7	9.8	6.1	4.9	1.5	2.5	0.8
Eff. Tax Rate	43%	40%	41%	38%	38%	38%	38%	40%	46%	39%
Net Inc.	9.0	14.7	9.0	8.4	6.1	3.8	3.0	0.9	1.3	0.5
Balance Sheet & Other Fin. Data (Million $)										
Cash	63.1	88.8	38.9	39.6	15.3	14.5	2.2	1.3	0.7	3.3
Curr. Assets	141	157	105	97.8	50.9	45.7	25.2	23.8	21.1	25.5
Total Assets	197	195	133	118	64.1	53.4	35.3	39.6	40.7	45.8
Curr. Liab.	44.3	33.6	25.8	22.3	13.3	11.6	13.0	16.0	11.3	16.8
LT Debt	Nil	Nil	Nil	Nil	Nil	Nil	1.8	5.9	7.8	8.6
Common Eqty.	143	146	94.9	85.2	45.3	38.1	19.2	16.6	20.9	20.4
Total Cap.	148	157	104	92.4	47.9	39.3	21.0	22.5	28.7	29.0
Cap. Exp.	15.2	12.5	7.0	7.9	4.1	1.4	0.6	0.9	2.0	1.6
Cash Flow	15.8	19.3	13.1	10.7	7.6	5.1	4.8	3.3	3.4	2.3
Curr. Ratio	3.2	4.7	4.1	4.4	3.8	3.9	1.9	1.5	1.9	1.5
% LT Debt of Cap.	Nil	Nil	Nil	Nil	Nil	Nil	8.8	26.1	27.0	29.5
% Net Inc.of Revs.	3.3	6.6	4.9	5.7	5.4	4.3	3.8	1.4	2.0	0.8
% Ret. on Assets	4.6	9.0	7.2	9.1	10.2	7.8	8.0	2.3	3.2	1.2
% Ret. on Equity	6.3	12.2	10.1	12.9	14.4	12.3	16.8	4.9	6.6	2.6

Data as orig reptd.; bef. results of disc opers/spec. items. Per share data adj. for stk. divs. Bold denotes diluted EPS (FASB 128)-prior periods restated. E-Estimated. NA-Not Available. NM-Not Meaningful. NR-Not Ranked.

Office—120 North 44th St., Suite 200, Phoenix, AZ 85034-1822. **Tel**—(602) 302-8900. **Website**—http://www.inter-tel.com **Chrmn, CEO & Pres**—S. G. Mihaylo. **VP, CFO, Treas & Secy**—K. R. Kneip. **Investor Contacts**—Steve Mihaylo or Tina Sargent (775 954-1288).**Dirs**—J. R. Anderson, G. D. Edens, M. S. Esperseth, C. R. Haden, S. G. Mihaylo. **Transfer Agent & Registrar**—First Interstate Bank of California, LA. **Incorporated**—in Arizona in 1969. **Empl**— 1,386. **S&P Analyst:** Stephen J. Tekirian

STANDARD
&POOR'S
STOCK REPORTS

Interface, Inc.

NASDAQ Symbol **IFSIA**

In S&P SmallCap 600

09-OCT-99

Industry:
Textiles (Home Furnishings)

Summary: The company is a leader in the worldwide commercial interiors market, offering floorcoverings, fabrics, specialty chemicals and interior architectural products.

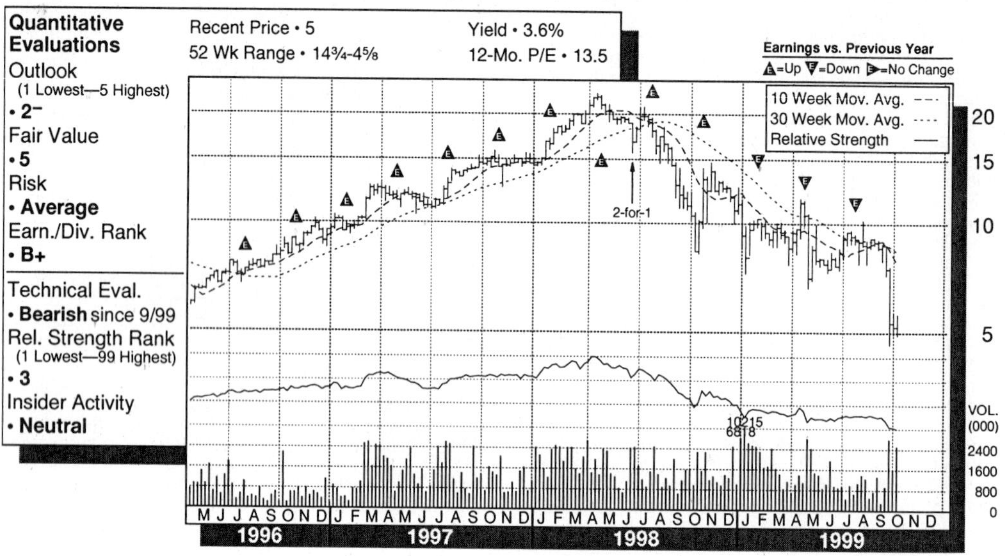

Business Profile - 24-AUG-99

During the first half of 1999, the company acquired five U.S. service companies for $2.7 million ($1.9 million in cash and $0.8 million in stock). In the first quarter of 1999, the company sold Joseph, Hamilton & Seaton Ltd., a U.K.-based contract carpet distributor for approximately $11.2 million in cash. In February 1999, the company said it was taking aggressive actions to reduce costs by implementing shared services, consolidating back office operations in Europe, and integrating manufacturing facilities in Asia, Europe and the U.S. It expects this to produce annual cost savings of about $8 million when the downsizing is completed by the end of the 1999 third quarter. Further cost improvements through another program, recent price increases, and a more favorable currency environment are also expected to enhance margins in 1999.

Operational Review - 24-AUG-99

Net sales in the six months ended July 4, 1999, declined 3.6%, year to year, primarily reflecting lower broadloom carpet sales in the U.S. and Europe and declining interior fabric sales. Gross margins narrowed, due in part to the underabsorption of overhead costs from the lower sales and shift in product mix towards lower margin service revenues. After lower SG&A expenses and higher net other income/expense, pretax income dropped 45%. After taxes, net income fell 46%, to $11,935,000 ($0.23 a share), from $21,947,000 ($0.42).

Stock Performance - 08-OCT-99

In the past 30 trading days, IFSIA's shares have declined 44%, compared to a 0.91% fall in the S&P 500. Average trading volume for the past five days was 724,920 shares, compared with the 40-day moving average of 389,521 shares.

Key Stock Statistics

Dividend Rate/Share	0.18	Shareholders	400
Shs. outstg. (M)	53.2	Market cap. (B)	$0.233
Avg. daily vol. (M)	0.620	Inst. holdings	66%
Tang. Bk. Value/Share	1.83		
Beta	0.80		

Value of $10,000 invested 5 years ago: $ 7,238

Fiscal Year Ending Dec. 31

	1999	1998	1997	1996	1995	1994
Revenues (Million $)						
1Q	307.9	318.9	257.4	205.0	191.3	160.7
2Q	305.5	316.9	271.8	237.5	202.8	181.7
3Q	—	328.3	297.4	275.0	203.3	185.0
4Q	—	317.1	308.9	284.5	204.7	196.9
Yr.	—	1,281	1,135	1,002	802.1	725.3
Earnings Per Share ($)						
1Q	**0.11**	**0.20**	0.14	0.09	0.10	0.07
2Q	**0.12**	**0.22**	0.17	0.14	0.13	0.09
3Q	—	**0.27**	0.22	0.17	0.14	0.10
4Q	—	**-0.12**	**0.26**	0.20	0.15	0.14
Yr.	—	**0.56**	**0.76**	**0.60**	**0.50**	0.41

Next earnings report expected: late October

Dividend Data (Dividends have been paid since 1977.)

Amount ($)	Date Decl.	Ex-Div. Date	Stock of Record	Payment Date
0.045	Oct. 28	Nov. 10	Nov. 13	Nov. 27 '98
0.045	Feb. 25	Mar. 10	Mar. 12	Mar. 26 '99
0.045	Apr. 29	May. 12	May. 14	May. 28 '99
0.045	Jul. 30	Aug. 11	Aug. 13	Aug. 27 '99

A Division of The McGraw-Hill Companies

Business Summary - 24-AUG-99

This company has your office covered. Interface, Inc. (formerly Interface Flooring Systems) is a leader in the worldwide commercial and institutional interiors market, providing floorcoverings, fabrics, specialty chemicals, and interior architectural products. Floorcovering & related services accounted for 79% of total sales in 1998.

The company is the world's largest manufacturer in the modular carpet segment, with a 40% market share in 1998. Marketed under the leading global brands INTERFACE and HEUGA, the company's free-lay modular carpet system utilizes carpet tiles cut in precise, dimensionally stable squares (usually 50 square centimeters) to produce a floorcovering which combines the appearance and texture of broadloom carpet with the advantages of a modular carpet system. The growing use of open plan interiors and modern office arrangements, utilizing demountable, moving partitions and modular furniture has encouraged the use of carpet tile.

Interface has obtained a significant share of the high-end, designer-oriented broadloom carpet segment by combining innovative product design and styling capabilities and short production and delivery times with a marketing strategy geared toward serving and working closely with interior designers, architects and other specifiers. The company's Prince Street design-sensitive broadloom products center around unique, multi-dimensional textured carpets with a hand-tufted look, while Bentley Mills' designs emphasize the dramatic use of color.

The company provides commercial carpet installation services through the Workplace Solutions services network, which includes about 140 owned or affiliated commercial floorcovering contractors located throughout major metropolitan areas of the U.S. The unit also provides carpet replacement services using its RENOVISIONS process, which uses patented lifting equipment and specialty tools to permit the economical replacement of existing carpet with minimal disruption.

The interior fabrics segment (17% of sales) designs, manufactures and markets specialty fabrics for use in open-plan office furniture systems and commercial interiors. Sales of panel fabrics to OEMs of movable office furniture systems constituted about 59% of total U.S. fabrics sales in FY 98. It also makes fabrics for seating, wall covering, vertical blinds in office interiors and fabrics used for cubicle curtains in health care facilities.

The Re:Source Technologies unit (4% of sales) develops specialty chemical products and an antimicrobial chemical compound called Intersept. In addition, it produces vinyl carpet tile backing and specialty mat and foam products, and offers raised/access flooring systems.

During the first half of 1999, the company acquired five U.S. service companies for $2.7 million and sold Joseph, Hamilton & Seaton Ltd., a U.K.-based carpet distributor for approximately $11.2 million in cash.

Per Share Data ($) (Year Ended Dec. 31)	1998	1997	1996	1995	1994	1993	1992	1991	1990	1989
Tangible Bk. Val.	1.83	0.78	0.56	0.35	0.31	-0.21	1.53	1.64	1.48	0.54
Cash Flow	1.35	1.54	1.50	1.30	1.19	0.96	0.75	0.90	1.19	1.14
Earnings	0.56	0.77	0.61	0.51	0.41	0.38	0.35	0.26	0.69	0.71
Dividends	0.17	0.14	0.12	0.12	0.12	0.12	0.12	0.12	0.12	0.10
Payout Ratio	29%	18%	20%	24%	29%	32%	34%	46%	18%	15%
Prices - High	22 7/8	15 7/8	10 1/4	9	8 1/2	7 3/4	8 1/4	7 1/8	9 7/8	9 3/4
- Low	8 1/4	9 1/4	5 7/8	5 7/8	4 7/8	4 7/8	4 7/8	4	3 3/8	7 3/8
P/E Ratio - High	41	21	17	18	21	21	23	27	14	14
- Low	15	12	9	11	12	13	14	15	5	10
Income Statement Analysis (Million $)										
Revs.	1,281	1,135	1,002	802	725	625	594	582	623	582
Oper. Inc.	158	136	114	90.5	79.0	66.6	54.1	59.9	76.8	78.4
Depr.	42.6	38.6	35.3	28.9	28.2	20.5	13.6	22.0	17.3	14.5
Int. Exp.	36.7	35.0	32.9	26.8	24.1	22.8	21.9	23.3	25.2	23.8
Pretax Inc.	49.1	61.3	43.4	31.7	25.7	21.3	18.6	14.3	37.7	40.6
Eff. Tax Rate	39%	39%	39%	36%	36%	35%	34%	38%	37%	40%
Net Inc.	29.8	37.5	26.4	20.3	16.5	13.8	12.3	8.9	23.6	24.5
Balance Sheet & Other Fin. Data (Million $)										
Cash	9.9	10.2	8.8	8.8	7.1	8.7	10.2	10.4	10.1	18.7
Curr. Assets	439	375	353	274	292	267	232	263	271	244
Total Assets	1,037	930	863	714	688	642	534	569	582	526
Curr. Liab.	225	192	164	115	117	126	94.0	112	114	112
LT Debt	388	390	379	324	314	292	235	240	255	244
Common Eqty.	399	316	273	232	214	182	186	199	198	157
Total Cap.	812	735	863	599	570	516	441	457	468	414
Cap. Exp.	45.2	38.7	36.4	42.1	21.3	28.7	13.7	15.9	32.8	23.0
Cash Flow	72.4	76.1	60.0	47.5	42.9	33.4	25.9	30.9	40.9	39.1
Curr. Ratio	1.9	2.0	2.2	2.4	2.5	2.1	2.5	2.3	2.4	2.2
% LT Debt of Cap.	47.8	53.1	44.0	54.1	55.0	56.5	53.5	52.5	54.4	59.0
% Net Inc.of Revs.	2.3	3.3	2.6	2.6	2.3	2.2	2.1	1.5	3.8	4.2
% Ret. on Assets	3.0	4.2	3.3	2.2	2.4	2.3	2.2	1.5	4.3	4.8
% Ret. on Equity	8.3	12.7	9.8	6.8	7.3	7.0	6.4	4.5	13.3	16.7

Data as orig reptd.; bef. results of disc opers/spec. items. Per share data adj. for stk. divs. Bold denotes diluted EPS (FASB 128)-prior periods restated. E-Estimated. NA-Not Available. NM-Not Meaningful. NR-Not Ranked.

Office—2859 Paces Ferry Rd., Suite 2000, Atlanta, GA 30339. **Tel**—(770) 437-6800. **Website**—http://www.interfaceinc.com **Chrmn & CEO**—R. C. Anderson. **Interim Pres & COO**—R. C. Anderson. **SVP-Fin, CFO, Treas & Investor Contact**—Daniel T. Hendrix. **SVP & Secy**—R. S. Willoch. **Dirs**—R. C. Anderson, B. L. DeMoura, D. Dillon-Ridgley, C. I. Gable, D. T. Hendrix, J. M. Henton, J. S. Lanier II, T. R. Oliver, L. G. Saulter, C. C. van Andel, J. H. Walker, G. D. Whitener. **Transfer Agent**—Wachovia Bank & Trust Co., Winston-Salem, NC. **Incorporated**—in Georgia in 1981. **Empl**—7,500. **S&P Analyst:** Howard Choe

STANDARD
&POOR'S
STOCK REPORTS

Interim Services

NYSE Symbol **IS**
In S&P SmallCap 600

09-OCT-99 **Industry:** Services (Employment) **Summary:** This company provides staffing solutions in technology, legal, accounting, human resources, marketing, search and outplacement, as well as clerical and light industrial.

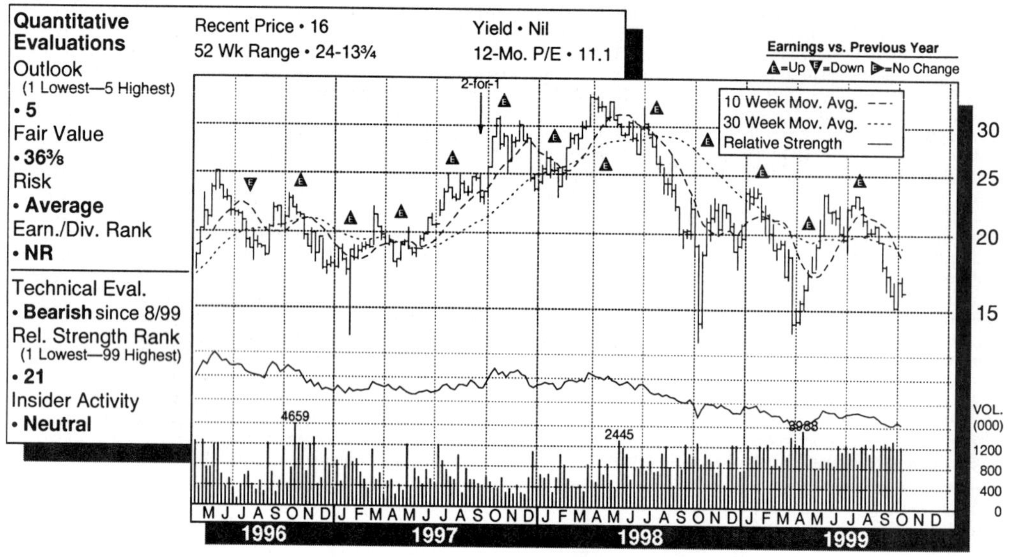

Business Profile - 29-JUN-99

After slowing to 9% in the 1998 fourth quarter, revenue growth in the administrative and light industrial staffing in North America rebounded to 13% in the first quarter of 1999. In the information technology division, IS expects total revenues to exceed $725 million in 1999. In March 1999, the company agreed to acquire Norrell Corp. (NYSE: NRL) through an exchange of stock valued at about $575 million. Norrell is a strategic work force management company with projected 1999 annualized revenues of $1.4 billion. The transaction is expected to close in July 1999. In April 1999, directors authorized the repurchase of up to 3.3 million common shares; 3.0 million shares had been purchased as of April 28, 1999.

Operational Review - 29-JUN-99

Revenues in the three months ended March 26, 1999, climbed 36%, year to year, reflecting internal growth and acquisitions. Results were restricted by a less favorable business mix, pricing pressures, and a higher selling, general and administrative expenses; the gain in operating income was held to 30%. With lower net interest expense, after taxes at 44.0%, versus 44.2%, net income soared 51%, to $15,884,000 ($0.33 a share, on 31% more shares), from $10,553,000 ($0.26).

Stock Performance - 08-OCT-99

In the past 30 trading days, IS's shares have declined 18%, compared to a 0.91% fall in the S&P 500. Average trading volume for the past five days was 262,940 shares, compared with the 40-day moving average of 355,692 shares.

Key Stock Statistics

Dividend Rate/Share	Nil	Shareholders	2,204
Shs. outstg. (M)	65.4	Market cap. (B)	$ 1.1
Avg. daily vol. (M)	0.339	Inst. holdings	61%
Tang. Bk. Value/Share	NM		
Beta	0.85		

Value of $10,000 invested 5 years ago: NA

Fiscal Year Ending Dec. 31

	1999	1998	1997	1996	1995	1994
Revenues (Million $)						
1Q	566.0	416.2	316.8	264.7	147.6	—
2Q	607.1	461.6	422.8	281.2	182.8	—
3Q	—	498.1	455.8	294.7	201.2	—
4Q	—	514.3	412.9	306.5	223.4	—
Yr.	—	1,890	1,608	1,147	780.9	634.4
Earnings Per Share ($)						
1Q	**0.33**	**0.26**	0.21	0.18	0.14	—
2Q	**0.40**	**0.31**	0.25	-0.01	0.17	—
3Q	—	**0.35**	0.30	0.25	0.20	—
4Q	—	**0.36**	0.29	0.27	0.23	—
Yr.	—	**1.29**	**1.05**	**0.69**	**0.76**	0.62

Next earnings report expected: late October

Dividend Data

No cash dividends have been paid.

Interim Services Inc.

Business Summary - 29-JUN-99

Interim Services is a $1.9 billion employment staffing and consulting company with 877 offices in 12 countries: Australia, Canada, France, Germany, Hong Kong, Italy, New Zealand, Singapore, Spain, the Netherlands, the U.K., and the U.S. The company divides its operations into three geographical segments: North America (73% of 1998 revenues), Europe (24%), and Australia/Asia (3%). IS provides four services: consulting, managed services, search/recruitment and flexible staffing.

Consulting services provided 15% of revenues in 1998. The company's primary focus in this service category is technology, outplacement, executive coaching, and human capital measurement and assessment.

Managed services accounted for 17% of 1998 revenues. Clients engage IS for its management capabilities, such as Interim On-Premise, vendor management, and functional outsourcing in such areas as help desk and data centers.

Search/recruitment (14%) services include providing full-time placement of entry-level professionals through senior executives with many types of skills.

Flexible staffing is the company's largest division, accounting for 54% of 1998 revenues. The division provides flexible staffing services at many skill levels, from light industrial and clerical to accounting, legal and technology. IS estimates that it assigned about 370,000 flexible personnel in 1998, with approximately 63,000 assigned at any given time, on average.

Interim offices are either company-owned, franchised or licensed. Approximately 84% of revenues are derived from the 543 company-owned branches. IS has been granting franchises for approximately 40 years, and currently has 18 franchisees operating 138 offices. The average tenure of franchise ownership exceeds 17 years. The company's 81 licensees operate 196 licensed offices.

Part of the company's business strategy is to grow through acquisitions. Since IS's IPO, it has acquired 26 companies with 256 offices, representing over $750 million in annualized revenues. The acquisitions included one in 1994, five in 1995, three in 1996, four in 1997, and 13 in 1998. The most significant recent acquisitions were Computer Power Group Ltd. and Crone Corkill Group PLC in 1998, and Michael Page Group PLC and Aim Executive Holdings, Inc. in 1997. In March 1999, IS agreed to acquire Norrell Corp. in a transaction valued at about $575 million. Norrell is a strategic work force management company, with 1999 annualized revenues of $1.4 billion. The transaction is expected to close in July 1999.

As part of an effort to focus on its professional and commercial staffing units, IS sold its health care business in September 1997 for $134 million in cash. Proceeds were used to reduce debt.

Per Share Data ($) (Year Ended Dec. 31)	1998	1997	1996	1995	1994	1993	1992	1991	1990	1989
Tangible Bk. Val.	NM	NM	12.33	1.08	3.78	2.48	3.74	3.29	NA	NA
Cash Flow	2.13	1.92	2.51	1.34	1.12	1.00	0.84	NA	NA	NA
Earnings	1.29	1.05	0.69	0.75	0.62	0.47	0.39	0.34	NA	NA
Dividends	Nil	Nil	Nil	Nil	Nil	Nil	Nil	Nil	NA	NA
Payout Ratio	Nil	Nil	Nil	Nil	Nil	Nil	Nil	Nil	NA	NA
Prices - High	34¼	31⅛	25⅛	17¾	14⅛	NA	NA	NA	NA	NA
- Low	13¼	13½	17	11⅜	10	NA	NA	NA	NA	NA
P/E Ratio - High	27	30	36	24	23	NA	NA	NA	NA	NA
- Low	10	13	25	15	16	NA	NA	NA	NA	NA
Income Statement Analysis (Million $)										
Revs.	1,890	1,608	1,147	781	634	515	429	382	NA	NA
Oper. Inc.	174	135	78.3	53.8	44.5	37.1	32.2	NA	NA	NA
Depr.	44.4	34.9	18.9	13.7	11.5	10.6	9.0	NA	NA	NA
Int. Exp.	30.2	24.3	5.7	1.8	0.5	0.5	Nil	NA	NA	NA
Pretax Inc.	105	81.4	45.1	31.4	26.5	18.6	16.0	14.0	NA	NA
Eff. Tax Rate	44%	48%	49%	44%	47%	50%	51%	52%	NA	NA
Net Inc.	58.6	42.5	23.0	17.5	14.2	9.4	7.8	6.8	NA	NA
Balance Sheet & Other Fin. Data (Million $)										
Cash	153	15.6	18.9	2.1	0.8	10.0	NA	NA	NA	NA
Curr. Assets	545	308	264	191	141	122	NA	NA	NA	NA
Total Assets	1,613	1,092	512	407	261	229	220	207	NA	NA
Curr. Liab.	418	235	95.0	150	82.0	62.0	NA	NA	NA	NA
LT Debt	427	379	Nil	60.0	Nil	30.0	89.1	94.3	NA	NA
Common Eqty.	738	474	415	196	179	136	75.0	66.0	NA	NA
Total Cap.	1,171	857	418	256	179	166	164	160	NA	NA
Cap. Exp.	37.5	24.9	33.0	9.9	8.4	5.0	4.0	NA	NA	NA
Cash Flow	103	77.4	41.9	31.2	25.6	20.0	16.8	NA	NA	NA
Curr. Ratio	1.3	1.3	2.8	1.3	1.7	2.0	NA	NA	NA	NA
% LT Debt of Cap.	36.4	44.2	Nil	23.4	Nil	18.1	54.3	58.9	NA	NA
% Net Inc.of Revs.	3.1	2.6	2.0	2.2	2.2	1.8	1.8	1.8	NA	NA
% Ret. on Assets	4.3	5.3	5.0	5.3	5.8	4.2	3.7	3.4	NA	NA
% Ret. on Equity	9.7	9.6	7.5	9.3	9.0	8.9	11.1	6.6	NA	NA

Data as orig reptd.; bef. results of disc opers/spec. items. Per share data adj. for stk. divs. Bold denotes diluted EPS (FASB 128)-prior periods restated. E-Estimated. NA-Not Available. NM-Not Meaningful. NR-Not Ranked.

Office—2050 Spectrum Blvd., Fort Lauderdale, FL 33309. **Tel**—(954) 938-7600. **Website**—http://www.interim.com **Chrmn, Pres & CEO**—R. Marcy. **EVP & COO**—R. E. Livonius. **EVP & CFO**—R. G. Krause. **Secry**—J. B. Smith. **Dirs**—S. S. Elbaum, W. F. Evans, J. B. Grossman, C. A. Hallman, R. Marcy, J. I. Morrison, A. M. Victory. **Transfer Agent & Registrar**—Boatmen's Trust Co., St. Louis, MO. **Incorporated**—in Delaware in 1987. **Empl**— 6,000. **S&P Analyst:** Jordan Horoschak

Intermagnetics General

ASE Symbol **IMG**
In S&P SmallCap 600

11-OCT-99

Industry:
Manufacturing (Specialized)

Summary: IMG manufactures superconducting magnet systems and superconducting wire used in medical diagnostic imaging systems; it also produces cryogenic refrigeration equipment.

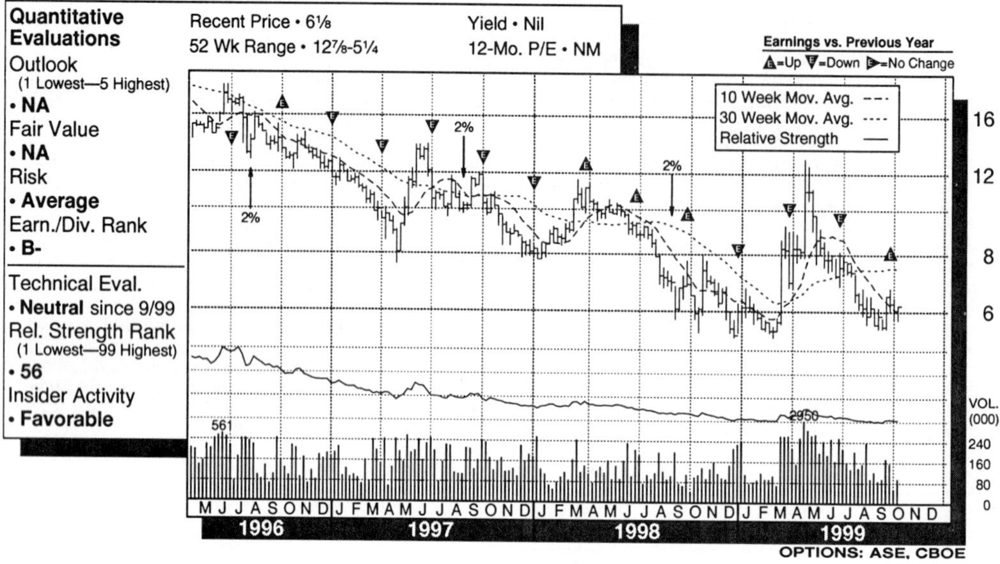

Business Profile - 11-OCT-99

Although IMG's research and development efforts over the years have yielded many innovations in high and low temperature superconductivity and related applications, the company has not always found viable commercial markets for these products. In the future, IMG will first examine market feasibility before drawing on its base of technological knowledge and innovations to develop new products. In August 1999, the company said that FRIGC FR-12 refrigerant, its proprietary alternative to Freon, had not performed up to expectations. IMG is continuing efforts to improve distribution channels for FRIGC, while determining whether the product line is compatible with its long-term objectives.

Operational Review - 11-OCT-99

Net sales in the three months ended August 29, 1999, edged up 1.3%, year to year. Gross margins narrowed, but with lower expenses and charges, operating income climbed 18%. With a sharp drop in equity in the net loss of unconsolidated affiliates, after taxes at 44.0%, versus 42.0%, net income advanced 19%, to $1,199,000 ($0.09 a share), from $1,005,000 ($0.07).

Stock Performance - 08-OCT-99

In the past 30 trading days, IMG's shares have increased 10%, compared to a 0.91% fall in the S&P 500. Average trading volume for the past five days was 18,880 shares, compared with the 40-day moving average of 22,246 shares.

Key Stock Statistics

Dividend Rate/Share	Nil	Shareholders	2,048
Shs. outstg. (M)	12.4	Market cap. (B)	$0.077
Avg. daily vol. (M)	0.024	Inst. holdings	15%
Tang. Bk. Value/Share	3.14		
Beta	1.68		

Value of $10,000 invested 5 years ago: $ 6,971

Fiscal Year Ending May 31

	2000	1999	1998	1997	1996	1995
Revenues (Million $)						
1Q	26.84	26.49	21.02	21.37	20.72	14.90
2Q	—	25.96	22.22	23.26	21.75	19.79
3Q	—	23.00	25.74	17.32	21.21	21.65
4Q	—	27.41	27.42	25.10	24.79	27.54
Yr.	—	102.9	95.89	87.05	88.47	83.88
Earnings Per Share ($)						
1Q	**0.09**	**0.07**	0.04	0.08	0.06	0.02
2Q	—	**-0.12**	0.05	0.07	0.08	0.06
3Q	—	**0.03**	**0.07**	Nil	0.06	0.09
4Q	—	**-0.57**	**0.07**	0.06	0.14	0.15
Yr.	—	**-0.57**	**0.21**	**0.21**	0.33	0.33

Next earnings report expected: late December

Dividend Data

No cash dividends have been paid. Stock dividends of 2% were paid in 1996, 1997, and 1998.

Intermagnetics General Corporation

Business Summary - 11-OCT-99

Since its inception as a spin-off from the General Electric Co. in 1971, Intermagnetics General (IMG) has been a world leader in the development and application of energy-saving products, based primarily on superconductivity, a technology that some have predicted could have an impact on the 21st century matching, or even surpassing, that of semiconductors during recent decades.

Superconductivity is a phenomenon characterized by the total loss of resistance to the flow of electric current in certain metals and alloys when cooled to near absolute zero. More recently, several ceramic materials have demonstrated similar "perfect conductivity" at much higher and more easily maintained temperatures (using liquid nitrogen, which is readily available and more cost effective than trying to reach absolute zero).

IMG is engaged in virtually all important areas of the superconductivity business: manufacture of superconducting wire, cable and tape; development and production of what are widely regarded as the world's finest superconductive magnet systems; cryogenic refrigeration systems; electronic control equipment; permanent magnet systems; and materials separation equipment. In addition, the company continues to invest in applied research studies, of which one recent result was the introduction of the FRIGC family of environmentally acceptable refrigerants as replacements for ozone-depleting chlorofluorocarbons (CFC's). In addition, the deregulation of the electric utility industry holds potential for major growth opportunities for IMG's product.

IMG's magnet products segments consists primarily of low temperature superconducting magnets, wires, cable, and radio frequency (RF) coils. These products are developed and sold through the company's IGC-Magnet Business Group (magnets), recently acquired IGC-Medical Advances Inc. (RF coils), and the IGC-Advanced Superconductors division (wire and cable). As part of the magnetic products segment, permanent magnet products and high temperature superconducting products are developed through the IGC-Technology Development division.

The company's refrigeration product segment consists of low and extremely low temperature refrigeration products, which are designed, developed, manufactured and sold through wholly owned IGC-APD Cryogenics Inc. and IGC-Polycold Systems Inc., as well as refrigerants for mobile and stationary applications, which are designed, developed and sold through wholly owned IGC-InterCool Energy Corp.

Per Share Data ($) **(Year Ended May 31)**	**1999**	**1998**	**1997**	**1996**	**1995**	**1994**	**1993**	**1992**	**1991**	**1990**
Tangible Bk. Val.	NA	4.53	4.99	5.51	4.59	4.07	3.75	3.59	3.06	2.78
Cash Flow	NA	0.61	0.52	0.60	0.59	0.38	0.54	0.64	0.49	0.27
Earnings	-0.57	0.21	0.21	0.34	0.33	0.11	0.30	0.41	0.28	0.09
Dividends	Nil	Nil	Nil	Nil	Nil	Nil	Nil	Nil	Nil	Nil
Payout Ratio	Nil	Nil	Nil	Nil	Nil	Nil	Nil	Nil	Nil	Nil
Cal. Yrs.	1998	1997	1996	1995	1994	1993	1992	1991	1990	1989
Prices - High	11 5/8	13 7/8	21	25 1/2	18 5/8	16 1/4	6 3/4	9 1/2	5	5 5/8
- Low	5 1/4	7 5/8	11 1/8	9 3/8	9	4 1/2	3 7/8	3 5/8	3	3 5/8
P/E Ratio - High	NM	66	NM	76	57	NM	23	23	18	65
- Low	NM	36	NM	28	27	NM	13	9	11	41
Income Statement Analysis (Million $)										
Revs.	NA	95.9	87.1	88.5	83.9	51.2	56.3	58.2	60.8	46.6
Oper. Inc.	NA	10.9	7.3	7.9	10.7	6.2	6.9	7.6	6.0	3.6
Depr.	NA	5.4	4.0	3.2	3.3	3.3	2.7	2.5	2.2	1.9
Int. Exp.	NA	2.1	2.1	2.6	2.8	NA	NA	NA	1.4	1.3
Pretax Inc.	NA	4.7	4.0	6.9	6.5	2.1	3.9	4.8	3.1	1.0
Eff. Tax Rate	NA	42%	35%	36%	39%	40%	20%	11%	10%	15%
Net Inc.	NA	2.8	2.6	4.4	4.0	1.3	3.1	4.3	2.8	0.8
Balance Sheet & Other Fin. Data (Million $)										
Cash	NA	3.0	12.7	18.7	13.0	13.2	1.6	1.0	0.5	0.8
Curr. Assets	NA	60.3	62.8	67.8	62.1	56.3	31.2	32.4	32.4	35.5
Total Assets	NA	128	116	112	104	93.8	58.4	53.2	49.3	50.8
Curr. Liab.	NA	14.8	13.5	14.2	9.4	7.0	11.6	7.5	9.5	13.6
LT Debt	NA	28.8	29.1	29.4	39.8	39.9	5.0	10.7	9.7	10.4
Common Eqty.	NA	76.8	73.1	67.3	53.3	46.9	41.8	35.1	30.1	26.7
Total Cap.	NA	113	103	98.2	94.3	86.8	46.8	45.7	39.8	37.2
Cap. Exp.	NA	3.1	5.5	4.1	3.9	9.4	3.1	4.9	3.9	4.3
Cash Flow	NA	8.2	6.6	7.6	7.3	4.5	5.9	6.8	5.0	2.7
Curr. Ratio	NA	4.1	4.7	4.8	6.6	8.1	2.7	4.3	3.4	2.6
% LT Debt of Cap.	NA	25.6	28.3	29.9	42.3	45.9	10.7	23.3	24.4	28.1
% Net Inc.of Revs.	NA	2.9	3.0	5.0	4.8	2.5	5.6	7.3	4.6	1.8
% Ret. on Assets	NA	2.3	2.3	4.1	4.1	1.7	5.4	8.2	5.6	1.8
% Ret. on Equity	NA	3.7	3.7	7.4	8.0	2.8	7.8	12.9	9.8	3.2

Data as orig reptd.; bef. results of disc opers/spec. items. Per share data adj. for stk. divs. Bold denotes diluted EPS (FASB 128)-prior periods restated. E-Estimated. NA-Not Available. NM-Not Meaningful. NR-Not Ranked.

Office—450 Old Niskayuna Rd., P.O. Box 461, Latham, NY 12110-0461. **Tel**—(518) 782-1122. **Website**—http://www.igc.com **Chrmn & CEO**—C. H. Rosner. **Pres & COO**—G. Epstein. **SVP & CFO**—M. C. Zeigler. **Investor Contact**—Cathy Yudzevich. **Dirs**—J. C. Abeles, J. M. Albertine, E. E. David, Jr., G. H. Epstein, J. S. Hyde, T. L. Kempner, C. H. Rosner, S. A. Shikiar, S. Weinig. **Transfer Agent & Registrar**—American Stock Transfer & Trust Co., NYC. **Incorporated**—in New York in 1971. **Empl**— 583. **S&P Analyst:** M.I.

STANDARD &POOR'S
STOCK REPORTS

Intermet Corp.

NASDAQ Symbol **INMT**

In S&P SmallCap 600

09-OCT-99 **Industry:** Auto Parts & Equipment

Summary: This company provides precision iron and aluminum parts to automotive and industrial customers in North America and Europe.

Quantitative Evaluations

Outlook (1 Lowest—5 Highest)
• **5+**

Fair Value
• **22¼**

Risk
• **Average**

Earn./Div. Rank
• **B**

Technical Eval.
• **Bearish** since 9/99

Rel. Strength Rank (1 Lowest—99 Highest)
• **19**

Insider Activity
• **NA**

Recent Price • 9⅝
52 Wk Range • 17⅛-8¼
Yield • 1.7%
12-Mo. P/E • 5.4

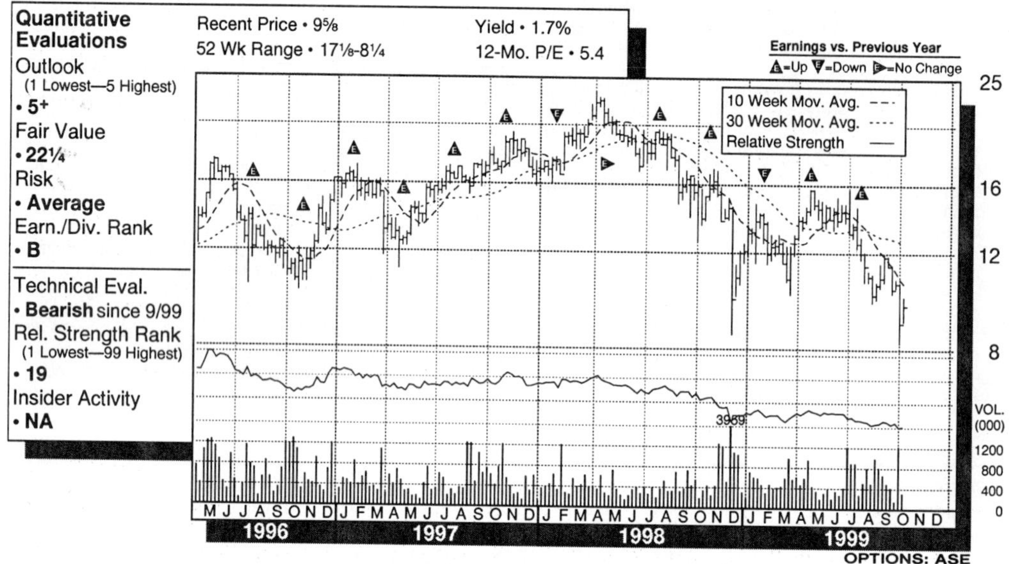

Business Profile - 25-JUN-99

The company expects its new business to continue to phase in through 2002. In late 1998, INMT acquired Quadion Corp.'s tool products division ($70 million in sales), a North American maker of aluminum die castings, for $57 million. INMT plans to continue to add capacity during 1999, and to keep its plants operating at more than 90% of capacity. In April 1999, the company noted that it is well positioned to take advantage of the long-term growth trend for ductile iron castings. In March 1999, directors authorized the repurchase of up to 10% of the company's common shares.

Operational Review - 25-JUN-99

Net sales in the first quarter of 1999 advanced 9.5%, year to year, reflecting strength in the core castings operations and demand for domestic light trucks and sport utility vehicles. Gross margins widened somewhat despite production equipment problems related to a new product launch, but following higher operating expenses due to late 1998 acquisitions, and a rise in other expenses, the gain in pretax income was held to 5.5%. After taxes at 42.1%, versus 43.3%, net income rose 7.6%, to $12,133,000 ($0.47 a share, diluted), from $11,271,000 ($0.43).

Stock Performance - 08-OCT-99

In the past 30 trading days, INMT's shares have declined 11%, compared to a 0.91% fall in the S&P 500. Average trading volume for the past five days was 60,420 shares, compared with the 40-day moving average of 132,851 shares.

Key Stock Statistics

Dividend Rate/Share	0.16	Shareholders	515
Shs. outstg. (M)	25.4	Market cap. (B)	$0.244
Avg. daily vol. (M)	0.113	Inst. holdings	74%
Tang. Bk. Value/Share	3.49		
Beta	1.11		

Value of $10,000 invested 5 years ago: $ 10,815

Fiscal Year Ending Dec. 31

	1999	1998	1997	1996	1995	1994
Revenues (Million $)						
1Q	245.2	224.0	209.5	134.2	153.3	118.9
2Q	245.7	219.9	210.9	143.8	149.0	124.6
3Q	—	188.8	189.5	130.3	117.3	121.0
4Q	—	208.9	203.8	126.3	122.1	136.8
Yr.	—	841.6	813.7	534.5	541.8	501.3
Earnings Per Share ($)						
1Q	**0.47**	**0.43**	**0.43**	**0.35**	0.26	0.07
2Q	**0.65**	**0.47**	**0.43**	**0.42**	0.39	0.10
3Q	—	**0.36**	**0.28**	**0.27**	0.14	0.02
4Q	—	**0.31**	**0.41**	**0.65**	0.24	-0.63
Yr.	—	**1.58**	**1.55**	**1.69**	**1.02**	-0.45

Next earnings report expected: mid October

Dividend Data (Dividends have been paid since 1996.)

Amount ($)	Date Decl.	Ex-Div. Date	Stock of Record	Payment Date
0.040	Oct. 15	Nov. 27	Dec. 01	Dec. 31 '98
0.040	Jan. 28	Feb. 25	Mar. 01	Mar. 31 '99
0.040	Apr. 26	May. 27	Jun. 01	Jun. 30 '99
0.040	Jul. 15	Aug. 30	Sep. 01	Sep. 30 '99

Intermet Corporation

Business Summary - 25-JUN-99

Intermet Corp. (INMT) continues to seek acquisitions that complement its existing business, to help it maintain growth and boost earnings. The company is a world leader in the manufacture of precision iron castings for automotive and industrial equipment producers, producing a wide array of ductile and gray iron castings at seven foundries in Georgia, Minnesota, Ohio, Virginia, and Portugal. In 1998, the North American passenger car and light truck market accounted for 70% of sales (66% in 1997); the North American industrial market for 14% (17%); and the European light and heavy duty vehicle market for 15% (13%).

Products manufactured for the automotive, light-truck and heavy-truck industries include brake parts, steering system components, differential cases, camshafts and crankshafts. INMT also makes products for construction equipment manufacturers, valve and air-conditioning equipment producers and farm equipment makers. The company expanded its product offerings to include aluminum castings through the November 1995 acquisition of the Bodine-Robinson aluminum foundry ($25 million annual sales) in Alexander City, AL. In early 1997, INMT acquired Sudbury, Inc. (SUDS; Nasdaq) for $156 million. Sudbury ($302 million in sales in FY 96) manufactures iron and aluminum parts for the automotive and industrial markets.

The company's marketing strategy emphasizes complex castings requiring precise metallurgical and dimensional standards. The company's six largest customers contributed 54% of 1998 sales, down from 58% in 1997, with DaimlerChrysler, Ford and GM accounting for 20%, 18% and 6%, respectively.

In May 1998, INMT formed a joint venture with an iron foundry in Portugal, adding needed capacity in Europe. In April 1998, the company terminated an agreement to purchase a 50% stake in Polcast SP, a foundry in Poland. Also in the second quarter of 1998, INMT ended a joint venture agreement with German machinery maker IWESA GmbH, and sold its industrial powder coatings unit for $22 million. INMT said the termination and the sale had a minimal impact on second quarter earnings.

In 1998, shipments of castings totaled 576,000 tons, up from 539,000 tons in 1997. INMT's foundries operated at 94% of average annual capacity. Total casting capacity at 1998 year end was 663,000 tons. Sales of ductile iron castings in 1998 accounted for 90% of total castings sales. Total castings sales in 1998 amounted to 81% of total sales, up from 76% in 1997.

Per Share Data ($) (Year Ended Dec. 31)	1998	1997	1996	1995	1994	1993	1992	1991	1990	1989
Tangible Bk. Val.	3.49	3.69	2.10	3.91	2.24	2.84	3.91	4.93	4.84	6.31
Cash Flow	2.96	2.96	2.78	2.06	0.73	0.18	0.90	1.36	0.65	1.52
Earnings	1.58	1.55	1.69	1.02	-0.45	-0.83	-0.06	0.42	-0.49	0.68
Dividends	0.16	0.16	0.08	Nil	Nil	0.12	0.16	0.14	0.20	0.20
Payout Ratio	10%	10%	5%	Nil	Nil	NM	NM	33%	NM	29%
Prices - High	23 3/4	19 7/8	17 5/8	14 1/8	10 1/2	12	13 1/4	9	9 5/8	13 1/4
- Low	8 1/2	11 1/8	9 3/4	6 1/4	4 3/4	6	7 1/4	4 1/2	3 5/8	6 7/8
P/E Ratio - High	15	13	10	14	NM	NM	NM	21	NM	19
- Low	5	7	6	6	NM	NM	NM	11	NM	10
Income Statement Analysis (Million $)										
Revs.	842	814	534	542	501	444	402	320	386	397
Oper. Inc.	111	114	83.0	81.0	41.7	25.4	27.8	27.4	37.6	46.1
Depr.	35.8	36.3	26.9	28.1	29.0	24.9	22.0	19.8	24.1	17.7
Int. Exp.	11.3	12.4	3.1	6.5	7.6	6.7	4.3	4.3	7.1	5.6
Pretax Inc.	65.2	61.4	54.3	45.5	-5.1	-29.1	2.3	11.9	-5.0	25.3
Eff. Tax Rate	37%	35%	21%	44%	NM	NM	187%	26%	NM	48%
Net Inc.	41.0	40.0	43.2	25.4	-11.0	-20.5	-1.5	8.8	-10.4	14.5
Balance Sheet & Other Fin. Data (Million $)										
Cash	5.8	7.0	23.5	11.2	13.7	11.2	6.1	8.5	7.3	6.4
Curr. Assets	197	193	189	103	123	109	89.3	76.1	81.1	96.8
Total Assets	584	539	526	274	306	307	274	214	215	277
Curr. Liab.	148	136	171	91.0	93.5	69.0	58.9	58.9	48.3	60.4
LT Debt	157	167	149	32.3	88.0	102	69.5	32.9	45.1	74.8
Common Eqty.	217	175	141	98.0	68.0	76.0	101	105	104	114
Total Cap.	376	345	293	130	159	185	174	153	165	214
Cap. Exp.	49.5	40.6	26.0	24.4	24.9	43.6	59.7	25.9	25.0	69.9
Cash Flow	76.8	76.3	70.0	53.5	18.1	4.4	20.5	28.6	13.7	32.2
Curr. Ratio	1.3	1.4	1.1	1.1	1.3	1.6	1.5	1.3	1.7	1.6
% LT Debt of Cap.	41.7	48.5	50.9	24.8	55.3	55.1	39.8	21.5	27.3	35.0
% Net Inc.of Revs.	4.9	4.9	8.1	4.7	NM	NM	NM	2.8	NM	3.7
% Ret. on Assets	7.3	7.5	10.8	8.8	NM	NM	NM	4.2	NM	5.8
% Ret. on Equity	20.9	25.3	36.1	30.6	NM	NM	NM	8.5	NM	13.3

Data as orig reptd.; bef. results of disc opers/spec. items. Per share data adj. for stk. divs. Bold denotes diluted EPS (FASB 128)-prior periods restated. E-Estimated. NA-Not Available. NM-Not Meaningful. NR-Not Ranked.

Office—5445 Corporate Dr., Suite 200, Troy, MI 48098-2683. **Tel**—(248) 952-2500. **Fax**—(248) 952-2501. **Website**—http://www.intermet.com **Chrmn & CEO**—J. Doddridge. **VP-Fin, CFO & Secy**—Doretha Christoph. **Investor Contact**—Bytha Mills. **Dirs**—J. P. Crecine, J. Doddridge, N. Ehlers, A. W. Hardy, J. R. Horne, T. H. Jeffs II, H. C. McKenzie Jr., B. O. Pond Jr., J. H. Reed. **Transfer Agent & Registrar**—SunTrust Bank, Atlanta. **Incorporated**—in Georgia in 1984. **Empl**— 7,100. **S&P Analyst:** Stewart Scharf

STANDARD
&POOR'S
STOCK REPORTS

International Rectifier

NYSE Symbol **IRF**

In S&P SmallCap 600

09-OCT-99

Industry: Electronics (Semiconductors)

Summary: This major worldwide supplier of power semiconductors is the leading producer in the power MOSFET (metal oxide semiconductor field effect transistor) market.

Quantitative Evaluations

Outlook (1 Lowest—5 Highest) • **4**

Fair Value • **20⅝**

Risk • **Average**

Earn./Div. Rank • **B-**

Technical Eval. • **Neutral** since 9/99

Rel. Strength Rank (1 Lowest—99 Highest) • **88**

Insider Activity • **Unfavorable**

Recent Price • 16¾

52 Wk Range • 17½-4⅝

Yield • Nil

12-Mo. P/E • NM

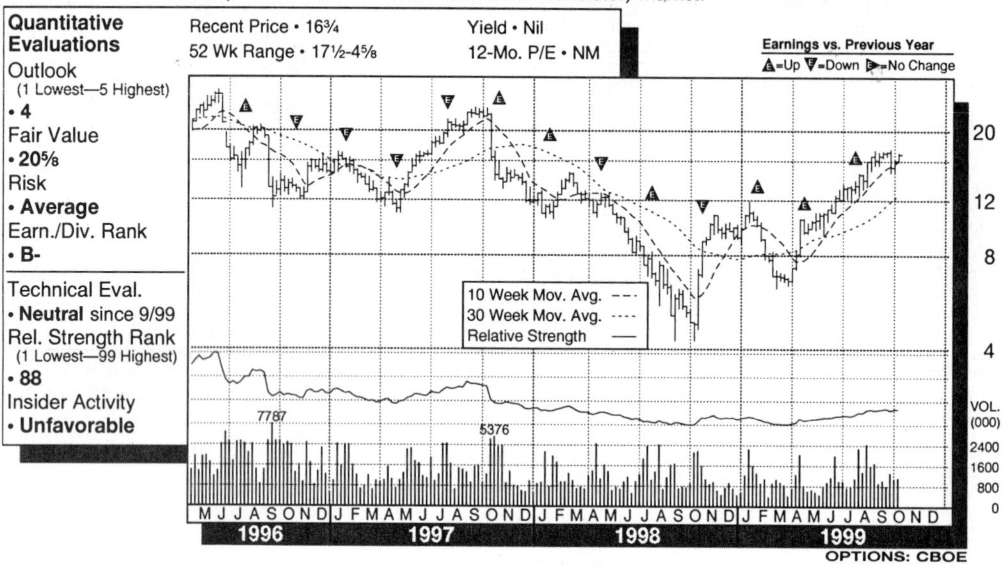

OPTIONS: CBOE

Business Profile - 16-AUG-99

During the third quarter of FY 99 (Jun.), the company began transferring high-volume assembly lines from its operation in Great Britain to its facility in Tijuana, Mexico, and streamlining its worldwide sales and service organization. In the FY 99 fourth quarter, revenues increased 10%, year to year, aided by strength in automotive applications, lighting, motor drives and telecom power supplies, as well as the distribution channel; unit shipments increased 28%. The company also reported that FY 99 fourth-quarter orders rose 27% year to year and were unchanged sequentially. The company enteredthe first quarter of FY 00 with backlog shippable in the period running 10% higher than in the FY 99 third quarter.

Operational Review - 16-AUG-99

Revenues (preliminary) in FY 99 (Jun.) slid 1.2%, with results restricted by the Asian economic crisis, excess industry capacity and sluggish global economic growth. Gross margins narrowed, and with 3.5% higher R & D expenses and after $24.5 million of restructuring and severance charges, an operating loss contrasted with operating income. However, after $53.5 million of net other income, versus $494,000 of net other expense, mostly related to a patent litigation settlement, and after taxes at 34.6%, versus 33.0%, income climbed 33%, to $10,780,000 ($0.39 a share), from $8,114,000 ($0.32). Results in FY 99 exclude a $0.50 a share charge for an accounting change.

Stock Performance - 08-OCT-99

In the past 30 trading days, IRF's shares have increased 4%, compared to a 0.91% fall in the S&P 500. Average trading volume for the past five days was 219,900 shares, compared with the 40-day moving average of 242,000 shares.

Key Stock Statistics

Dividend Rate/Share	Nil	Shareholders	1,742
Shs. outstg. (M)	51.7	Market cap. (B)	$0.869
Avg. daily vol. (M)	0.214	Inst. holdings	59%
Tang. Bk. Value/Share	7.78		
Beta	2.29		

Value of $10,000 invested 5 years ago: $ 24,017

Fiscal Year Ending Jun. 30

	1999	1998	1997	1996	1995	1994
Revenues (Million $)						
1Q	127.5	133.1	115.2	126.1	92.25	73.09
2Q	132.8	144.6	118.0	141.0	102.8	79.10
3Q	137.6	140.4	122.8	154.1	111.9	84.25
4Q	147.5	133.8	130.2	155.7	122.1	92.43
Yr.	545.4	551.9	486.1	576.9	429.0	328.9
Earnings Per Share ($)						
1Q	Nil	0.12	0.06	0.25	0.16	0.05
2Q	**0.38**	**0.13**	0.07	0.30	0.18	0.08
3Q	**0.08**	**0.06**	0.08	0.35	0.21	0.10
4Q	**0.06**	**0.01**	-1.04	0.40	0.27	0.16
Yr.	**0.12**	**0.32**	**-0.84**	**1.29**	0.84	0.39

Next earnings report expected: mid October

Dividend Data

Annual dividends, paid since 1973, were omitted in 1982. The shares were split two for one in 1995.

A Division of The McGraw-Hill Companies

International Rectifier Corporation

Business Summary - 16-AUG-99

International Rectifier Corporation is a major worldwide supplier of power semiconductors for a broad spectrum of commercial and industrial applications.

Products offered by the company include power MOSFETs (metal oxide semiconductor field effect transistors) and IGBTs (insulated gate bipolar transistors), which serve the switch function in power conversion to provide an even, usable flow of power for electronic equipment; high-voltage control ICs, which serve the control function of power conversion; and a broad line of rectifiers, diodes and thyristors that serve the output rectification and input rectification functions of power conversion.

Based on statistics from the Semiconductor Industry Association, IRF believes that it is the leader in the power MOSFET segment. Industrywide sales of power MOSFETs have grown at an average annual rate of 22% over the past five years. The company's power MOSFET and IGBT products accounted for about 70% of sales in FY 98 (Jun.)

The company's products serve all major market sectors. Applications for power semiconductors in automobiles include anti-lock braking and fuel injection systems, power accessories, air bags and electronic power steering. Computer/peripheral applications include power supplies, disk drives and printers. Office equipment applications include copiers and facsimile machines. Consumer electronics and lighting applications include home entertainment, household appliances and electronic lighting ballasts. Communications applications include portable phones, telephone networks and modems. Power semiconductors are also used widely in industrial applications such as motor-driven production lines, machine tools, fork lifts and welders. Major customers in the automotive segment include Delco, Ford, Siemens and Bosch; and major computer customers include IBM, NEC and Compaq.

Sales by region in FY 98 were: North America 47%; Europe 26%; and Asia 27%. Foreign operations accounted for 55% of sales in FY 98.

To address the fastest-growing segments of the power transistor market -- high-density MOSFETs and IGBTs -- the company installed a second wafer fabrication unit. Phase one was completed in first quarter of FY 96 and Phase two was completed in the second half of FY 97. In FY 98, the company spent about $39.1 million on R&D, up from $35.5 million in FY 97.

Per Share Data ($) (Year Ended Jun. 30)	1999	1998	1997	1996	1995	1994	1993	1992	1991	1990
Tangible Bk. Val.	NA	7.78	7.48	8.29	6.86	4.99	4.60	4.81	4.53	0.94
Cash Flow	NA	1.07	-0.12	1.88	1.33	0.78	0.28	0.61	1.08	0.58
Earnings	0.12	0.32	-0.84	1.29	0.84	0.39	-0.08	0.23	0.65	0.09
Dividends	Nil	Nil	Nil	Nil	Nil	Nil	Nil	Nil	Nil	Nil
Payout Ratio	Nil	Nil	Nil	Nil	Nil	Nil	Nil	Nil	Nil	Nil
Prices - High	17½	14¾	23¾	27	26	12¼	7½	8⅛	12⅝	6⅛
- Low	6¼	4¼	10⅞	11¼	11⅛	6½	4⅞	3¾	4⅝	2⅛
P/E Ratio - High	NM	46	NM	21	31	31	NM	35	19	67
- Low	52	13	NM	9	13	17	NM	16	7	24
Income Statement Analysis (Million $)										
Revs.	NA	552	486	577	429	329	282	265	253	230
Oper. Inc.	NA	71.3	58.7	127	71.8	39.4	16.5	26.2	38.1	31.1
Depr.	NA	38.9	37.1	30.1	23.4	15.9	14.2	15.4	11.4	11.5
Int. Exp.	NA	7.3	4.0	0.4	0.4	3.6	3.6	1.4	13.7	17.2
Pretax Inc.	NA	24.6	-52.7	95.9	47.5	18.9	-2.6	10.5	18.2	2.6
Eff. Tax Rate	NA	33%	NM	31%	17%	17%	NM	12%	6.00%	18%
Net Inc.	NA	16.5	-43.2	66.5	39.4	15.7	-3.0	9.2	17.1	2.2
Balance Sheet & Other Fin. Data (Million $)										
Cash	NA	32.3	53.4	53.8	53.8	13.1	8.5	8.5	24.3	2.4
Curr. Assets	NA	317	316	277	234	157	128	136	125	92.0
Total Assets	NA	736	680	629	496	331	278	286	250	218
Curr. Liab.	NA	154	113	125	106	89.7	69.8	68.4	49.8	66.3
LT Debt	NA	154	143	48.0	23.9	27.0	12.0	12.0	12.0	120
Common Eqty.	NA	400	382	421	345	203	186	192	180	22.0
Total Cap.	NA	365	538	488	379	230	198	204	192	143
Cap. Exp.	NA	NA	100	112	107	37.1	21.8	33.0	14.2	5.6
Cash Flow	NA	55.4	-6.1	96.6	62.8	31.6	11.1	24.6	28.6	13.6
Curr. Ratio	NA	2.1	2.8	2.2	2.2	1.7	1.8	2.0	2.5	1.4
% LT Debt of Cap.	NA	42.2	26.7	9.8	6.3	11.6	6.0	5.7	6.2	84.2
% Net Inc.of Revs.	NA	3.0	NM	11.5	9.2	4.8	NM	3.5	6.8	0.9
% Ret. on Assets	NA	2.3	NM	11.8	9.5	5.2	NM	3.4	5.5	1.0
% Ret. on Equity	NA	4.2	NM	17.3	14.4	8.1	NM	5.0	15.8	11.2

Data as orig reptd.; bef. results of disc opers/spec. items. Per share data adj. for stk. divs. Bold denotes diluted EPS (FASB 128)-prior periods restated. E-Estimated. NA-Not Available. NM-Not Meaningful. NR-Not Ranked.

Office—233 Kansas St., El Segundo, CA 90245. **Tel**—(310) 726-8000. **Fax**—(310) 322-3332. **Website**—http://www.irf.com **Chrmn**—E. Lidow. **CEO** —A. Lidow. **VP & CFO**—M. P. McGee. **Investor Contact**—Shelley Wagers (310-726-8512). **Dirs**—D. S. Burns, G. Krsek, A. Lidow, D. B. Lidow, E. Lidow, M. Matsuda, R. J. Mueller, J. D. Plummer, J. O. Vance, R. E. Vogt. **Transfer Agent & Registrar**—ChaseMellon Shareholder Services, Los Angeles. **Incorporated**—in California in 1947; reincorporated in Delaware in 1979. **Empl**— 4,395. **S&P Analyst:** C.C.P.

STANDARD
&POOR'S
STOCK REPORTS

InterVoice-Brite

NASDAQ Symbol **INTV**

In S&P SmallCap 600

09-OCT-99

Industry:
Services (Computer Systems)

Summary: This company develops, sells and services automated call processing solutions, with an emphasis on interactive voice response.

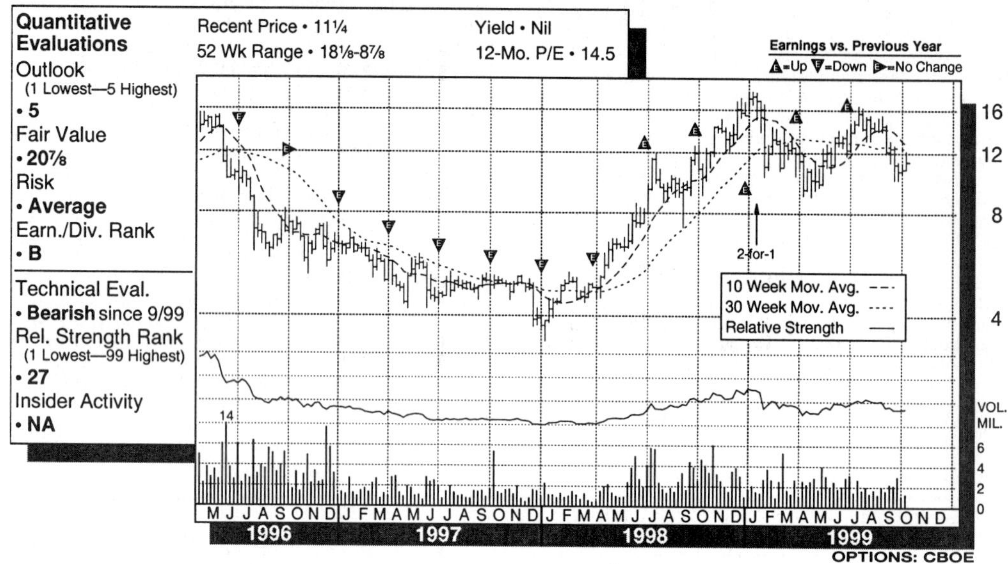

Business Profile - 08-SEP-99

In August 1999, the company changed its name from InterVoice, Inc. to InterVoice-Brite, Inc., reflecting its recent merger with Brite Voice Systems, Inc., a company that provides call automation solutions for the worldwide enterprise and telecommunications markets. As a result of the merger, the number of shares outstanding increased from about 29.1 million to about 32 million. In FY 99 (Feb.), the company had sales and income from continuing operations of approximately $135.7 million and $1.8 million, respectively.

Operational Review - 08-SEP-99

Sales in the three months ended May 31, 1999, climbed 34%, year to year, led by a 51% increase in domestic customer premises equipment sales, which accounted for 59% of total sales. Gross margins widened, on the greater volume and continued cost control efforts; operating expenses rose less rapidly than revenues; operating income more than doubled. With other income, versus expense, after taxes at 34.5%, versus 34.4%, net income climbed 109%, to $6,266,730 ($0.21 a share), from $3,002,588 ($0.11, as adjusted).

Stock Performance - 08-OCT-99

In the past 30 trading days, INTV's shares have declined 21%, compared to a 0.91% fall in the S&P 500. Average trading volume for the past five days was 247,040 shares, compared with the 40-day moving average of 363,362 shares.

Key Stock Statistics

Dividend Rate/Share	Nil	Shareholders	12,500
Shs. outstg. (M)	40.7	Market cap. (B)	$0.460
Avg. daily vol. (M)	0.365	Inst. holdings	40%
Tang. Bk. Value/Share	2.80		
Beta	1.27		

Value of $10,000 invested 5 years ago: $ 14,140

Fiscal Year Ending Feb. 28

	2000	1999	1998	1997	1996	1995
Revenues (Million $)						
1Q	40.08	30.00	24.74	25.56	22.02	16.60
2Q	—	33.07	29.28	27.30	23.68	18.00
3Q	—	35.01	25.55	24.34	25.15	20.10
4Q	—	38.82	22.74	27.65	26.26	21.60
Yr.	—	136.9	102.3	104.8	97.10	76.30
Earnings Per Share ($)						
1Q	**0.21**	**0.10**	**0.01**	**0.12**	0.13	0.08
2Q	—	**0.15**	**0.07**	**0.13**	0.13	-0.23
3Q	—	**0.18**	**0.01**	**0.04**	0.14	0.11
4Q	—	**0.24**	**-0.28**	**0.10**	0.14	0.12
Yr.	—	**0.68**	**-0.16**	**0.39**	**0.53**	**0.08**

Next earnings report expected: NA

Dividend Data

Amount ($)	Date Decl.	Ex-Div. Date	Stock of Record	Payment Date
2-for-1	Dec. 14	Jan. 12	Dec. 28	Jan. 11 '99

InterVoice-Brite, Inc.

Business Summary - 08-SEP-99

InterVoice-Brite (formerly InterVoice, Inc.) develops, sells and services call automation systems. The company's historical emphasis has been on interactive voice response systems, which allow individuals to use their telephones, personal computers, credit card terminals, or voices to access and/or provide information to computer data bases used by businesses. More recently, INTV has focused on systems for telecommunications service providers to provision a variety of automated services such as processing collect, debit and credit card calls, and advanced calling features such as prepaid calling cards, voice and text messaging, one number personal numbering plans, and voice dialing. In the last year, the company has increased its emphasis on customer relationship management systems that provide companies automated customer service, telemarketing capabilities, and the ability to generate sales without human interaction

As of May 1999, the company's systems were sold under the trade names OneVoice, AgentConnect and InControl. OneVoice systems are used by enterprises to disseminate and receive information efficiently, allowing multiple callers simultaneous access to computer data bases without the expense of maintaining a customer service representative and workstation for each telephone line. AgentConnect systems improve call center efficiency by automating routine customer service requests and providing telemarketing capabilities by automatically dialing phone numbers and only transferring a call to a live agent if the call is answered and the called party remains on the phone. OneVoice and AgentConnect applications function in a wide range of industries. InControl systems provide enhanced services for telecommunications networks by automating calls that use alternate billing methods, and provide new, revenue generating calling features and services.

In August 1999, the company changed its name, following its merger with Brite Voice Systems, Inc. earlier in the month. Brite Voice Systems designs, integrates, assembles, markets and supports voice processing and call processing systems and services which incorporate prepaid/postpaid applications, voice response, voice recognition, voice/facsimile messaging, audiotex and interactive computer applications into both standard products and customized market solutions.

The combined company, with annual revenues of about $273 million, is the world's leading supplier of call automation products and services for corporate and telecommunications markets. It is ISO 9001 certified, holds 38 patents, and has 30 satellite offices in the Americas, Europe and Asia-Pacific. Its products are installed at more than 16,000 sites in more than 65 countries.

Per Share Data ($) (Year Ended Feb. 28)	1999	1998	1997	1996	1995	1994	1993	1992	1991	1990
Tangible Bk. Val.	2.55	1.83	2.52	2.04	1.52	1.78	1.39	1.27	1.25	1.21
Cash Flow	1.05	0.15	0.54	0.66	0.14	0.36	0.27	0.10	0.10	0.19
Earnings	0.68	-0.17	0.39	0.53	0.08	0.32	0.23	0.08	0.10	0.18
Dividends	Nil	Nil	Nil	Nil	Nil	Nil	Nil	Nil	Nil	Nil
Payout Ratio	Nil	Nil	Nil	Nil	Nil	Nil	Nil	Nil	Nil	Nil
Cal. Yrs.	1998	1997	1996	1995	1994	1993	1992	1991	1990	1989
Prices - High	18 1/8	7 1/8	15 5/8	13 1/4	8 1/2	11 1/4	4 1/4	2 1/2	3 5/8	4 1/4
- Low	3 3/4	3 3/8	5 1/4	6 1/4	3	3 1/4	1 9/16	15/16	7/8	1 3/16
P/E Ratio - High	27	NM	40	25	113	35	19	32	39	23
- Low	6	NM	14	12	39	10	7	12	10	7
Income Statement Analysis (Million $)										
Revs.	137	102	105	97.1	76.3	60.9	44.6	30.2	20.6	24.4
Oper. Inc.	40.2	8.7	24.2	29.4	22.2	18.8	12.6	4.3	3.1	8.8
Depr.	11.0	9.7	5.0	4.4	2.3	1.8	1.6	0.8	0.5	0.2
Int. Exp.	Nil	Nil	Nil	Nil	Nil	Nil	Nil	Nil	Nil	Nil
Pretax Inc.	28.8	-7.6	18.2	25.6	9.7	17.7	11.5	4.3	4.6	10.1
Eff. Tax Rate	30%	NM	30%	33%	74%	34%	32%	31%	18%	31%
Net Inc.	20.2	-5.1	12.7	17.3	2.5	11.7	7.8	2.9	3.8	7.0
Balance Sheet & Other Fin. Data (Million $)										
Cash	12.2	4.2	24.1	23.6	10.3	36.2	25.0	25.9	27.9	41.9
Curr. Assets	75.0	46.4	75.0	63.8	40.0	58.7	41.1	40.1	39.5	50.4
Total Assets	111	84.9	109	90.2	62.7	74.2	52.6	49.6	46.8	56.1
Curr. Liab.	22.6	27.6	21.2	19.5	15.9	11.1	8.6	5.0	2.5	2.1
LT Debt	5.0	Nil	0.1	Nil	Nil	Nil	Nil	Nil	Nil	Nil
Common Eqty.	82.5	56.6	86.1	70.0	46.8	63.2	44.1	44.7	44.3	54.0
Total Cap.	88.9	57.3	87.8	70.7	46.8	63.2	44.1	44.7	44.3	54.0
Cap. Exp.	4.0	9.2	11.4	4.6	9.2	5.6	0.9	2.0	1.3	4.8
Cash Flow	31.2	4.6	17.7	21.7	4.8	13.5	9.5	3.7	4.3	7.2
Curr. Ratio	3.3	1.7	3.5	3.3	2.5	5.3	4.8	8.1	15.6	23.5
% LT Debt of Cap.	5.6	Nil	Nil	Nil	Nil	Nil	Nil	Nil	Nil	Nil
% Net Inc.of Revs.	14.7	NM	12.2	17.8	3.3	19.2	17.6	9.7	18.4	28.5
% Ret. on Assets	20.6	NM	12.8	22.6	4.0	17.6	16.1	6.1	8.4	18.8
% Ret. on Equity	29.0	NM	NM	29.5	5.0	20.8	18.6	6.6	8.8	20.3

Data as orig reptd.; bef. results of disc opers/spec. items. Per share data adj. for stk. divs. Bold denotes diluted EPS (FASB 128)-prior periods restated. E-Estimated. NA-Not Available. NM-Not Meaningful. NR-Not Ranked.

Office—17811 Waterview Parkway, Dallas, TX 75252. **Tel**—(214) 454-8000. **Website**—http://www.intervoice.com **Chrmn & CEO**—D. D. Hammond. **President & COO**—David A. Berger. **CFO, Secy & Investor Contact**—Rob-Roy J. Graham. **Dirs**—S. G. Brannan, D. W. Brandenburg, G A. Dove, D. D. Hammond, J. J. Pietropaolo, G. C. Platt. **Transfer Agent**—KeyCorp Shareholder Services, Dallas. **Incorporated**—in Texas in 1984. **Empl**— 1,400. **S&P Analyst:** C.C.P.

STANDARD & POOR'S
STOCK REPORTS

Invacare Corp.

NYSE Symbol **IVC**

In S&P SmallCap 600

09-OCT-99

Industry: Health Care (Medical Products & Supplies)

Summary: This company is a leading manufacturer and marketer of a broad line of health care products for the non-acute care market.

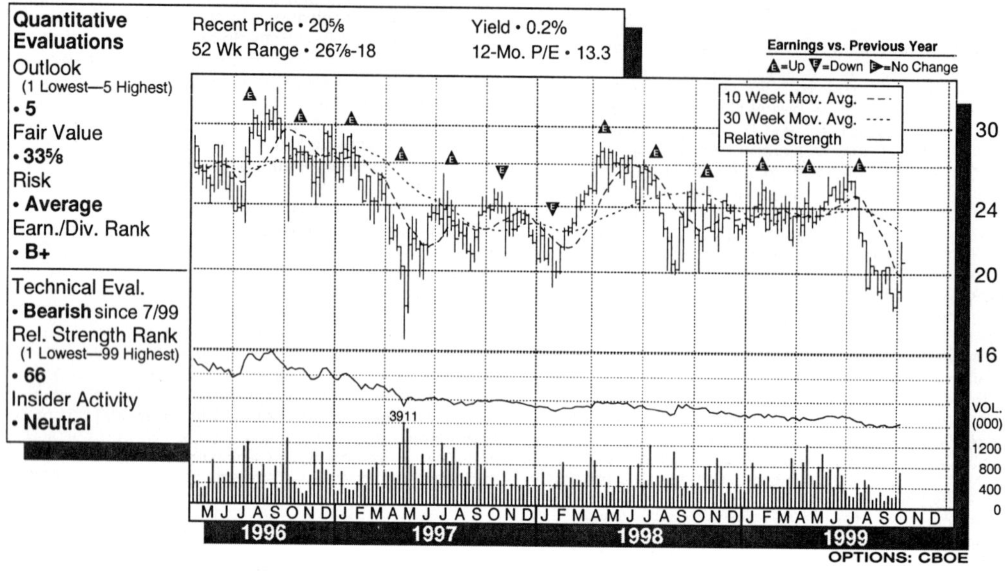

Business Profile - 02-AUG-99

IVC's 1999 second quarter results were aided by the company's focus on cost reduction, and productivity improvements that led to slightly better gross margins. European and Australian operations posted strong sales, offsetting sluggish domestic sales, which were hurt by customers continuing to reduce inventory and refurbish rental products in response to Medicare cutbacks implemented as part of the 1997 Balanced Budget Act. The company says long term demand and demographic trends remain favorable. In July 1999, IVC announced that it made a cash tender offer to acquire Scandinavian Mobility International for about $14.58 a share. The offer is open until August 11, 1999. Trading in the shares moved from the NASDAQ Stock Market to the New York Stock Exchange on June 23, 1999.

Operational Review - 02-AUG-99

Net sales in the six months ended June 30, 1999, rose 3.8%, year to year. Gross margins widened, and after a 4.2% rise in SG&A expenses, operating profit rose 9.7%, to $39.3 million, from $35.8 million. After higher interest expense, and taxes at 39.0% in both periods, net income was up 9.9% to $20.4 million ($0.67 a share), from $18.6 million ($0.61).

Stock Performance - 08-OCT-99

In the past 30 trading days, IVC's shares have increased 9%, compared to a 0.91% fall in the S&P 500. Average trading volume for the past five days was 139,180 shares, compared with the 40-day moving average of 56,305 shares.

Key Stock Statistics

Dividend Rate/Share	0.05	Shareholders	3,800
Shs. outstg. (M)	28.5	Market cap. (B)	$0.591
Avg. daily vol. (M)	0.069	Inst. holdings	64%
Tang. Bk. Value/Share	2.87		
Beta	0.53		

Value of $10,000 invested 5 years ago: $ 15,206

Fiscal Year Ending Dec. 31

	1999	1998	1997	1996	1995	1994
Revenues (Million $)						
1Q	196.1	181.1	151.5	134.5	107.7	87.90
2Q	202.2	202.8	165.0	159.2	122.3	98.89
3Q	—	203.3	166.1	158.2	130.6	109.0
4Q	—	210.3	170.8	167.7	143.5	115.3
Yr.	—	797.5	653.4	619.5	504.0	411.1
Earnings Per Share ($)						
1Q	0.28	0.25	0.24	0.20	0.16	0.13
2Q	0.39	0.36	0.33	0.32	0.26	0.21
3Q	—	0.43	-0.64	0.35	0.30	0.25
4Q	—	0.47	-0.11	0.41	0.35	0.30
Yr.	—	1.50	0.05	1.28	1.07	0.89

Next earnings report expected: late October

Dividend Data (Dividends have been paid since 1994.)

Amount ($)	Date Decl.	Ex-Div. Date	Stock of Record	Payment Date
0.013	Nov. 16	Dec. 30	Jan. 04	Jan. 15 '99
0.013	Feb. 15	Mar. 30	Apr. 01	Apr. 15 '99
0.013	May. 26	Jun. 29	Jul. 01	Jul. 15 '99
0.013	Aug. 30	Sep. 29	Oct. 01	Oct. 15 '99

A Division of The McGraw-Hill Companies

Invacare Corporation

Business Summary - 02-AUG-99

This innovative manufacturer and marketer of the broadest line of home medical equipment for the home health care, retail and extended care markets has experienced 21.6% compound average annual sales growth since inception in 1979. The company has grown from $19.5 million in sales in 1979, with a limited product line of standard wheelchairs and patient aids, to become the largest home medical equipment manufacturer, based upon its distribution channels through more than 10,000 provider locations worldwide, the breadth of its product line, and sales of $798 million in 1998.

IVC's products now include standard manual wheelchairs, motorized and lightweight prescription wheelchairs, motorized scooters, patient aids, home care beds, low air loss therapy products, home respiratory products, seating and positioning products and ambulatory infusion pumps. IVC continually revises and expands product lines to meet changing demand.

The company's complete line of wheelchairs includes standard wheelchairs, as well as prescription wheelchairs custom built for long-term use by one individual, based on specifications prescribed by a medical professional.

Invacare also makes and markets three-and four-wheeled motorized scooters; seat and positioning products such as cushions and back positioners; a wide variety of manual, semi-electric and fully electric hospital-type beds; home respiratory products; low air loss therapy products; patient transport products such as lifts, slings and multi-position recliners, and institutional and accessory products. Other products include microprocessor electronic control systems and ambulatory infusion pumps and accessories. The company also distributes medical care products made by others, including incontinence products and bedding.

Products are marketed in the U.S. primarily to home health care and medical equipment dealers, who then sell or rent directly to end-users or health care institutions. Although the primary customers are dealers, products are also marketed to medical professionals, including physical, occupational and respiratory therapists, who refer patients to dealers to purchase specific types of home medical equipment.

The company has continued to make strategic acquisitions. In 1997, IVCR made two acquisitions that extended or added new product lines and expanded distribution capabilities. In January 1998, it acquired Suburban Ostomy, a wholesaler of medical supplies and related products to the home health care industry, for about $132 million.

IVC expects sales of domestic home medical equipment products to continue to grow over the next decade. It expects sales to benefit from growth in the population over age 65, increasing trends toward home health care treatment, technological advances adapting medical equipment for home use, and continued health care cost containment efforts.

Per Share Data ($) (Year Ended Dec. 31)	1998	1997	1996	1995	1994	1993	1992	1991	1990	1989
Tangible Bk. Val.	1.81	4.38	3.91	3.38	3.13	2.59	2.21	3.17	1.81	1.43
Cash Flow	2.27	0.66	1.87	1.54	1.31	1.17	0.97	0.83	0.61	0.33
Earnings	1.50	0.05	1.28	1.07	0.89	0.75	0.63	0.53	0.33	0.12
Dividends	0.05	0.05	0.05	0.05	0.02	Nil	Nil	Nil	Nil	Nil
Payout Ratio	3%	100%	4%	5%	2%	Nil	Nil	Nil	Nil	Nil
Prices - High	28¾	29¼	33¼	29¾	18⅛	13⅞	15½	16⅛	5½	4⅜
- Low	19⅛	16½	22¾	16⅛	12⅝	10⅝	8¼	4¾	2⅛	2 3/16
P/E Ratio - High	19	NM	26	28	20	19	25	30	17	38
- Low	13	NM	18	15	14	14	13	9	7	19
Income Statement Analysis (Million $)										
Revs.	798	653	619	504	411	365	305	263	230	186
Oper. Inc.	105	56.8	83.2	68.3	56.4	49.1	37.6	31.7	24.2	13.8
Depr.	23.8	18.4	17.8	14.2	12.7	12.3	10.0	8.1	6.6	5.0
Int. Exp.	20.6	3.2	11.2	9.6	8.2	8.6	4.6	4.3	5.7	5.4
Pretax Inc.	75.1	5.2	63.7	51.8	41.9	33.5	27.6	22.9	13.9	5.0
Eff. Tax Rate	39%	70%	39%	38%	37%	34%	36%	38%	45%	48%
Net Inc.	45.8	1.6	38.9	32.2	26.4	22.1	17.7	14.1	7.6	2.6
Balance Sheet & Other Fin. Data (Million $)										
Cash	12.1	5.7	8.0	6.6	10.4	13.5	10.7	3.2	3.9	3.2
Curr. Assets	337	275	259	205	180	156	152	120	104	92.0
Total Assets	739	530	510	409	337	286	262	162	138	123
Curr. Liab.	134	110	97.7	84.9	70.4	60.9	68.2	42.1	42.8	29.7
LT Debt	311	184	173	122	103	90.4	78.6	31.8	51.5	58.8
Common Eqty.	281	236	239	201	164	135	114	86.7	41.9	32.1
Total Cap.	592	420	412	324	267	225	194	120	96.0	93.0
Cap. Exp.	29.3	38.5	22.5	11.2	10.9	12.0	14.5	12.0	8.7	10.9
Cash Flow	69.5	20.0	56.8	46.3	39.1	34.4	27.7	22.2	14.2	7.6
Curr. Ratio	2.5	2.5	2.6	2.4	2.6	2.6	2.2	2.8	2.4	3.1
% LT Debt of Cap.	52.6	43.8	41.9	37.7	38.5	40.1	40.5	26.4	53.9	63.1
% Net Inc.of Revs.	5.7	0.2	6.3	6.4	6.4	6.1	5.8	5.4	3.3	1.4
% Ret. on Assets	7.2	0.3	8.4	8.6	8.4	8.0	8.2	8.7	5.8	2.3
% Ret. on Equity	17.7	0.7	17.7	17.6	17.6	17.7	17.3	20.7	20.4	8.4

Data as orig reptd.; bef. results of disc opers/spec. items. Per share data adj. for stk. divs. Bold denotes diluted EPS (FASB 128)-prior periods restated. E-Estimated. NA-Not Available. NM-Not Meaningful. NR-Not Ranked.

Office—One Invacare Way, P.O. Box 4028, Elyria, OH 44036. **Tel**—(216) 329-6000. **Website**—http://www.invacare.com **Chrmn & CEO**—A. M. Mixon III. **Pres & COO**—B. B. Blouch. **CFO, Treas, Secy & Investor Contact**—Thomas R. Miklich. **Dirs**—G. B. Blouch, F. J. Callahan, F. B. Carr, M. F. Delaney, W. Evans, B. P. Healy, A. M. Mixon III, D. T. Moore III, E. P. Nalley, J. B. Richey II, W. M. Weber. **Transfer Agent**—National City Bank, Cleveland. **Incorporated**—in Ohio in 1971. **Empl**— 4,889. **S&P Analyst:** John J. Arege

STANDARD & POOR'S
STOCK REPORTS

Ionics, Inc.

NYSE Symbol **ION**

In S&P SmallCap 600

09-OCT-99

Industry: Manufacturing (Specialized)

Summary: Ionics manufactures and sells or leases products, systems and services for the treatment of water and other liquids. Applications include water desalination and bottled water.

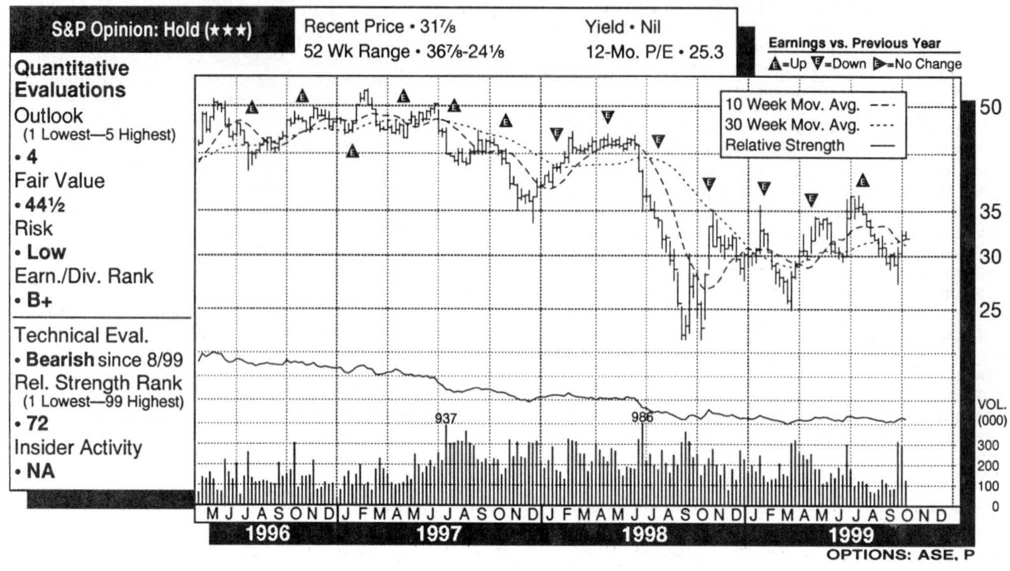

Overview - 28-JUL-99

Revenues should rise nearly 10% in 1999, and somewhat more in 2000, on gains for consumer water products in the U.S. and abroad, and more water purification projects. Gross margins should widen to about 34% in 1999, on strength in the U.S. bottled and home water treatment business, and well controlled equipment and instrument costs. Instrument sales may benefit if European regulators finally decide to enforce new water quality requirements. Capital equipment sales should benefit when the semiconductor industry returns to full capacity. Despite ION's positive long-term prospects, we recently cut our EPS estimates for 1999 and 2000 by $0.05 each, to $1.45 and $1.70, respectively. The cut reflects increased competition (including France-based Vivendi's recent acquisition of U.S. Filter), higher SG&A expense, and a rise in the effective tax rate,

Valuation - 28-JUL-99

The shares, which have traded erratically for more than a year, recently settled into a narrow range, following an uptick in June on signs of a renewed focus on the water treatment industry, as well as a rebound in semiconductors, However, we still suggest only holding ION, as we view the shares as no better than market performers over the next six to 12 months, due to competitive pricing pressures and soft instrument sales. The company's long-term prospects are positive, with new contract awards, strong backlog, and expected growth in most segments, and signs of a pick-up in bidding activity for capital projects in Latin America, the Caribbean, and the Canary Islands. However, at a P/E multiple of 23X our 1999 EPS estimate, a premium to ION's 17% projected earnings growth rate, we believe the shares are fairly valued.

Key Stock Statistics

S&P EPS Est. 1999	1.45	Tang. Bk. Value/Share	18.56
P/E on S&P Est. 1999	22.0	Beta	1.14
S&P EPS Est. 2000	1.70	Shareholders	1,700
Dividend Rate/Share	Nil	Market cap. (B)	$0.514
Shs. outstg. (M)	16.1	Inst. holdings	57%
Avg. daily vol. (M)	0.048		

Value of $10,000 invested 5 years ago: $ 12,846

Fiscal Year Ending Dec. 31

	1999	1998	1997	1996	1995	1994
Revenues (Million $)						
1Q	87.42	78.97	87.10	77.84	56.87	53.04
2Q	84.57	80.27	87.11	74.90	56.54	49.83
3Q	—	88.88	85.11	84.51	62.95	56.45
4Q	—	103.2	93.14	89.41	72.25	63.06
Yr.	—	351.3	352.5	326.7	248.6	222.4
Earnings Per Share ($)						
1Q	**0.29**	**0.37**	**0.43**	**0.38**	0.29	0.24
2Q	**0.31**	**0.28**	**0.44**	**0.40**	0.32	0.26
3Q	**E0.40**	**0.32**	**0.44**	**0.43**	0.36	0.29
4Q	**E0.45**	**0.38**	**0.42**	**0.44**	0.38	0.30
Yr.	**E1.45**	**1.31**	**1.73**	**1.65**	**1.37**	1.09

Next earnings report expected: late October

Dividend Data

No cash dividends have been paid. The shares were split two for one in January 1995. A poison pill stock purchase rights plan was adopted in 1987.

Ionics, Incorporated

Business Summary - 28-JUL-99

Ionics, a provider of water purification products and services, operates in the fragmented but consolidating $13 billion water equipment and chemicals industry. The company derives about 80% of its revenues from industrial customers and 20% from consumer markets. In 1998, ION obtained 47% of revenues from foreign sales of water-related products or operations of water treatment plants. The company is willing to sacrifice some margin improvement in order to protect its market share.

During 1998, ION restructured its business into four groups: equipment, ultrapure water, instruments, and consumer products. Consumer products include reverse-osmosis systems and instruments for monitoring and on-line detection of pollution levels. The company's products and services are used to desalt brackish water and seawater, purify and supply bottled water, treat water in the home, and recyle and reclaim process water and wastewater.

The equipment business segment accounted for 37% of revenues in 1998. The group provides treatment systems and services for seawater and brackish desalination, wastewater reuse and recycling, potable water, and high purity water. In addition, the segment includes food and chemical processing activities, and fabricated products.

The ultrapure water group (32%) includes the sale of ultrapure water equipment and systems for the semiconductor, pharmaceutical, petroleum and power generation industries. In 1998, the company commissioned a resin regeneration facility in Singapore and, in early 1999, completed a 66,000 sq. ft. facility in San Jose, CA, that contains resin regeneration, manufacturing and service facilities.

Consumer products (23%) include bottled water, over- and under-the-sink point-of-use devices and point-of-entry systems for treating the entire home water supply. ION has about 30 Aqua Cool distribution centers and nine bottling facilities in the U.S. and overseas. In early 1999, ION began to expand in Europe, acquiring Aquarelle, a French bottled water distributor.

The instrument business (8% of revenues) manufactures instruments that measure total organic carbon in everything from ultrapure water to wastewater. In 1998, the company began to market a line of instruments for the detection of thin layers of oil on water.

ION competes principally competes with U.S. Filter, the largest U.S. water treatment equipment maker, which was acquired by France's Vivendi in April 1999. A smaller competitor is Osmonics, Inc. ($165 million). The balance of the water equipment and chemicals industry consists of about 50,000 small operations around the U.S.

Backlog at June 30, 1999 totaled $189 million, down slightly from the level at the end of 1998.

Per Share Data ($) (Year Ended Dec. 31)	1998	1997	1996	1995	1994	1993	1992	1991	1990	1989
Tangible Bk. Val.	18.56	17.39	16.50	15.51	13.94	12.67	13.78	11.05	8.84	8.00
Cash Flow	2.97	3.37	3.27	2.75	2.36	2.06	1.83	1.44	1.35	1.18
Earnings	1.31	1.73	1.65	1.35	1.09	0.98	0.93	0.72	0.55	0.42
Dividends	Nil	Nil	Nil	Nil	Nil	Nil	Nil	Nil	Nil	Nil
Payout Ratio	Nil	Nil	Nil	Nil	Nil	Nil	Nil	Nil	Nil	Nil
Prices - High	45 7/8	53	51 1/4	45 1/2	31 3/8	34	34 1/4	24 1/4	16	13 3/8
- Low	22 1/2	33 1/2	38 1/8	26 1/4	21 3/8	19 1/4	21 1/8	13 1/4	9 7/8	7 3/4
P/E Ratio - High	35	31	31	34	29	35	37	33	29	31
- Low	17	19	23	19	20	20	23	18	18	18
Income Statement Analysis (Million $)										
Revs.	351	352	327	249	222	175	155	138	128	109
Oper. Inc.	58.8	69.5	64.7	48.6	39.1	32.4	27.4	18.4	16.5	14.7
Depr.	27.2	27.0	26.1	20.6	18.1	15.3	12.6	8.2	7.2	6.4
Int. Exp.	0.3	0.9	Nil	Nil	0.1	0.2	0.7	2.6	5.0	4.1
Pretax Inc.	32.9	43.2	39.5	29.6	22.7	19.7	18.2	11.6	6.4	5.3
Eff. Tax Rate	32%	33%	33%	34%	32%	30%	29%	28%	25%	27%
Net Inc.	21.4	28.3	26.5	19.7	15.4	13.8	12.8	8.3	4.7	3.6
Balance Sheet & Other Fin. Data (Million $)										
Cash	28.8	25.8	12.2	8.1	20.6	30.1	41.8	7.8	3.9	8.1
Curr. Assets	187	166	144	118	113	110	109	72.3	66.6	67.0
Total Assets	452	407	377	317	277	250	225	178	144	135
Curr. Liab.	85.9	66.0	68.1	58.1	54.9	46.1	30.5	36.5	51.7	44.8
LT Debt	1.5	0.8	2.1	0.2	0.1	0.1	0.4	5.6	8.0	14.4
Common Eqty.	346	320	292	250	219	200	190	128	76.0	68.0
Total Cap.	364	338	309	258	222	203	194	141	91.0	88.0
Cap. Exp.	42.2	33.5	46.0	49.1	38.2	30.1	24.7	36.7	8.7	13.7
Cash Flow	48.6	55.4	52.6	40.3	33.5	29.1	25.4	16.4	11.6	10.0
Curr. Ratio	2.2	2.5	2.1	2.0	2.1	2.4	3.6	2.0	1.3	1.5
% LT Debt of Cap.	0.4	0.2	0.7	Nil	Nil	0.1	0.2	4.0	8.8	16.4
% Net Inc.of Revs.	6.1	8.0	8.1	7.9	6.9	7.9	8.3	6.0	3.7	3.3
% Ret. on Assets	5.0	7.2	7.6	6.6	5.8	5.8	5.8	4.4	3.4	2.8
% Ret. on Equity	6.4	9.3	9.7	8.4	7.4	7.1	7.4	7.2	6.6	5.4

Data as orig reptd.; bef. results of disc opers/spec. items. Per share data adj. for stk. divs. Bold denotes diluted EPS (FASB 128)-prior periods restated. E-Estimated. NA-Not Available. NM-Not Meaningful. NR-Not Ranked.

Office—65 Grove St., Watertown, MA 02172. **Tel**—(617) 926-2500. **Website**—http://www.ionics.com **Chrmn, Pres & CEO**—A. L. Goldstein. **EVP**—W. E. Katz. **VP-Fin & CFO**—R. Halliday. **VP & Treas**—J.P. Bergeron. **Dirs**—D. R. Brown, W. L. Brown, A. de Vitry d'Avaucourt, K. Feldstein, A. L. Goldstein, W. E. Katz, J. J. Shields, C. S. Sloane, D. I. Wang, M. S. Wrighton, A. S. Wyett. **Transfer Agent & Registrar**—State Street Bank & Trust Co., Boston. **Incorporated**—in Massachusetts in 1948. **Empl**— 2,200. **S&P Analyst:** Stewart Scharf

Itron, Inc.

NASDAQ Symbol **ITRI**

In S&P SmallCap 600

09-OCT-99

Industry:
Electrical Equipment

Summary: Itron is a provider of integrated systems solutions for collecting, communicating, analyzing, and managing information about electric, gas and water usage.

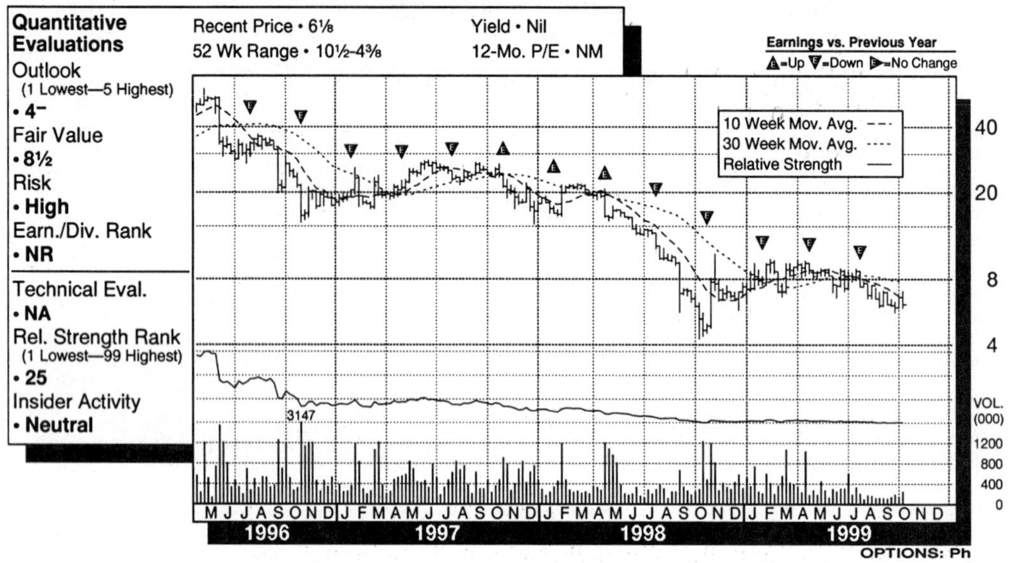

Business Profile - 07-SEP-99

Results have been erratic in recent years, with net losses in two of the three years through 1998. Losses continued in the first half of 1999, and the company anticipates that revenues in the 1999 second half will be flat relative to those of the first half. In the second half, ITRI will be defining its strategy to accelerate growth in its core market and enter sound new markets, leveraging its competencies in marketing and communications technologies. In the 1999 second quarter, the company booked an order from Southern California Edison covering about 350,000 of meters, the largest automatic meter reading (AMR) installation in California. As of June 30, 1999, ITRI had shipped 14.5 million AMR meter modules to more than 470 utilities.

Operational Review - 07-SEP-99

Total revenues in the first half of 1999 fell 17%, year to year, reflecting the completion in 1998 of meter module and fixed network product shipments under a large contract with Virginia Power Co. Gross margins widened, on improved automatic meter reading margins; operating income was up 3.2%. Results were hurt by a $4.2 million reduction on the Virginia Power contract, and a $1.1 million restructuring charge. After tax benefits of $830,000, versus $570,000, the loss widened to $1,815,000 ($0.12 a share, before a credit of $0.24 from extinguishment of debt), from $923,000 ($0.06).

Stock Performance - 08-OCT-99

In the past 30 trading days, ITRI's shares have increased 1%, compared to a 0.91% fall in the S&P 500. Average trading volume for the past five days was 48,660 shares, compared with the 40-day moving average of 29,936 shares.

Key Stock Statistics

Dividend Rate/Share	Nil	Shareholders	10,700
Shs. outstg. (M)	14.9	Market cap. (B)	$0.091
Avg. daily vol. (M)	0.036	Inst. holdings	53%
Tang. Bk. Value/Share	6.76		
Beta	0.82		

Value of $10,000 invested 5 years ago: $ 3,402

Fiscal Year Ending Dec. 31

	1999	1998	1997	1996	1995	1994
Revenues (Million $)						
1Q	51.95	63.71	40.58	48.05	36.06	25.21
2Q	51.22	60.77	52.73	48.20	37.73	28.62
3Q	—	54.84	58.43	38.74	39.33	31.95
4Q	—	62.09	64.38	42.59	42.24	34.88
Yr.	—	241.4	216.1	177.6	155.3	120.7
Earnings Per Share ($)						
1Q	**-0.02**	**0.01**	**-0.24**	**0.21**	0.18	0.11
2Q	**-0.11**	**-0.07**	**-0.05**	**0.17**	0.20	0.14
3Q	—	**-0.40**	**0.11**	**-0.34**	0.20	0.19
4Q	—	**0.04**	**0.22**	**-0.17**	0.21	0.23
Yr.	—	**-0.42**	**0.07**	**-0.11**	**0.81**	**0.80**

Next earnings report expected: mid October

Dividend Data

No cash dividends have been paid on the common stock.

Business Summary - 07-SEP-99

Itron is a global provider of integrated systems solutions forcollecting, communicating, analyzing, and managing information about electric, gas and water usage.

The company reorganized into two main divisions during 1998, Residential Systems and C&I Systems, in order to focus on the strategically different needs of each of these markets. As a result of slower activity in the residential Automatic Meter Reading (AMR) market, the company implemented restructuring measures during 1998 to reduce costs and improve operating efficiencies. These measures resulted in a $4.1 million restructuring charge in 1998. Because of the restructuring measures taken in 1998, the company was able to substantially reduce spending, and as a result, returned to profitability in the fourth quarter of the year.

Itron manufactures, installs and services hardware, software and integrated systems that enable customers to obtain, analyze and use meter data. Major product lines include Automatic Meter Reading (AMR) systems, and Electronic Meter Reading (EMR) or Handheld systems. The company sells its products and provides outsourcing services.

The AMR solutions primarily utilize radio and telephone technology to collect meter data and include Off-Site AMR, Mobile AMR and Network AMR technology reading options. Off-Site AMR utilizes a radio device attached to an Itron handheld computer that collects data from meters equipped with the company's radio meter modules. Mobile AMR uses a transceiver in a vehicle to collect data from meters equipped with ITRI's radio meter modules as thevehicle passes by.

The company offers a number of Network AMR solutions thatutilize radio, telephone, cellular or a combination of these technologies to collect and transmit meter information from a variety of fixed locations. The EMR systems product line includes the sale and service of ruggedized handheld computers and supporting products that record visually obtained meter data.

Outsourcing services typically involve the installation, operation and/or maintenance of meter reading systems to provide meter information for billing and management purposes. Outsourcing contracts usually cover long timeframes and typically involve contracts in which either a customer owns the equipment and ITRI provides meter information for a specified fee, or ITRI both owns and operates the equipment.

In March 1999, the company exchanged $22 million of its 6.75% convertible subordinated notes for $15.8 million of new notes, realizing a $5.6 million pretax gain from the exchange.

In June 1999, ITRI said a securities class action lawsuit would be settled when it makes a payment of $12 million, to be funded entirely by insurance proceeds.

Per Share Data ($) (Year Ended Dec. 31)	1998	1997	1996	1995	1994	1993	1992	1991	1990	1989
Tangible Bk. Val.	6.59	6.78	6.86	7.29	6.24	4.84	NA	NA	NA	NA
Cash Flow	0.93	1.22	0.68	1.42	1.23	1.12	0.52	NA	NA	NA
Earnings	-0.42	0.07	-0.11	0.79	0.67	0.46	0.02	NA	NA	NA
Dividends	Nil	Nil	Nil	Nil	Nil	Nil	Nil	NA	NA	NA
Payout Ratio	Nil	Nil	Nil	Nil	Nil	Nil	Nil	NA	NA	NA
Prices - High	22	28 1/8	60	34 1/2	23 1/2	18	NA	NA	NA	NA
- Low	4 1/4	14 1/4	14 1/2	18	14	13 1/2	NA	NA	NA	NA
P/E Ratio - High	NM	NM	NM	43	35	39	NA	NA	NA	NA
- Low	NM	NM	NM	23	21	29	NA	NA	NA	NA
Income Statement Analysis (Million $)										
Revs.	241	216	178	155	121	88.6	67.9	NA	NA	NA
Oper. Inc.	21.4	21.5	8.8	21.6	17.5	14.0	9.8	NA	NA	NA
Depr.	19.9	16.8	10.5	8.0	6.6	6.1	4.6	NA	NA	NA
Int. Exp.	6.5	3.9	1.2	0.2	0.1	0.7	0.5	NA	NA	NA
Pretax Inc.	-10.0	1.6	-2.1	15.3	11.9	7.4	0.9	NA	NA	NA
Eff. Tax Rate	NM	38%	NM	34%	33%	42%	NM	NA	NA	NA
Net Inc.	-6.2	1.0	-1.5	10.1	8.0	4.3	0.1	NA	NA	NA
Balance Sheet & Other Fin. Data (Million $)										
Cash	2.7	3.0	2.2	31.5	41.7	25.1	NA	NA	NA	NA
Curr. Assets	108	112	90.7	92.5	85.2	68.6	NA	NA	NA	NA
Total Assets	248	240	187	147	119	99	NA	NA	NA	NA
Curr. Liab.	54.2	44.1	64.5	28.8	22.9	25.5	NA	NA	NA	NA
LT Debt	70.8	69.8	6.4	5.6	0.1	0.3	NA	NA	NA	NA
Common Eqty.	115	120	114	109	94.0	71.0	NA	NA	NA	NA
Total Cap.	186	193	120	116	94.0	71.0	NA	NA	NA	NA
Cap. Exp.	10.7	9.3	27.5	16.5	7.3	3.8	NA	NA	NA	NA
Cash Flow	13.6	17.8	9.1	18.1	14.6	10.3	4.7	NA	NA	NA
Curr. Ratio	2.0	2.5	1.4	3.2	3.7	2.7	NA	NA	NA	NA
% LT Debt of Cap.	38.1	36.2	5.3	4.8	Nil	0.4	NA	NA	NA	NA
% Net Inc.of Revs.	NM	0.5	NM	6.5	6.6	4.8	0.2	NA	NA	NA
% Ret. on Assets	NM	0.5	NM	7.6	7.3	NA	NA	NA	NA	NA
% Ret. on Equity	NM	0.9	NM	9.9	9.6	NA	NA	NA	NA	NA

Data as orig reptd.; bef. results of disc opers/spec. items. Per share data adj. for stk. divs. Bold denotes diluted EPS (FASB 128)-prior periods restated. E-Estimated. NA-Not Available. NM-Not Meaningful. NR-Not Ranked.

Office—2818 N. Sullivan Rd., Spokane, WA 99216-1897.**Tel**—(509) 924-9900. **Website**—http://www.itron.com **Chrmn**— J. M. Humphreys. **Pres & CEO**—M. J. Chesser. **VP & CFO**—D. G. Remington. **Secy**—M. R. Blair. **Treas & Investor Contact**—Mima G. Scarpelli (509-891-3565). **Dirs**—M. B. Bracy, T. C. DeMerrit, J. E. Eliassen, J. M. Humphreys, M. A. Peters, P. A. Redmond, S. E. White, G. M. Wilson. **Transfer Agent & Registrar**—ChaseMellon Shareholder Services, SF. **Incorporated**—in Washington in 1977.**Empl**— 1,200. **S&P Analyst:** M.I.

STANDARD &POOR'S
STOCK REPORTS

J & J Snack Foods

NASDAQ Symbol **JJSF**

In S&P SmallCap 600

09-OCT-99

Industry: Foods

Summary: This company manufactures and markets snack foods and baked goods, and distributes frozen beverage products to the foodservice, retail grocery and supermarket industries.

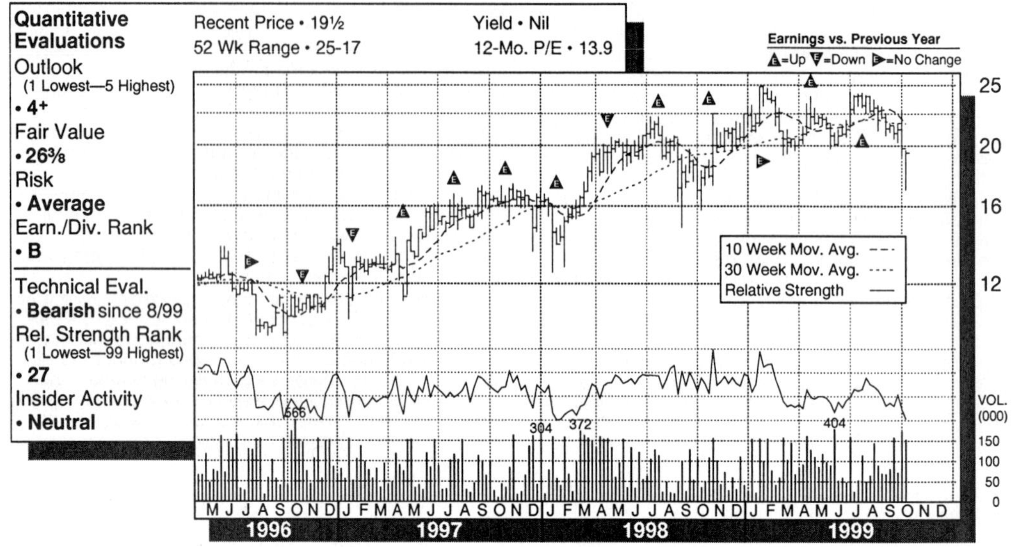

Business Profile - 07-OCT-99

In October 1999, the company said it expects to report record sales and earnings for FY 99 (Sep.), with diluted EPS seen at about $1.50. In February 1999, JJSF acquired the Camden Creek Bakery, a seller of frozen ready-to-bake cookies, from Schwan's Sales Enterprises, Inc. In December 1997, the company acquired a controlling interest in National ICEE Corp., a marketer and distributor of frozen carbonated beverages under the tradename ICEE. JJSF believed the acquisition would let it further develop the frozen beverage category and the ICEE brand on a national basis. In April 1999, the company repurchased 250,000 of its common shares from its president and CEO, for $5.6 million.

Operational Review - 07-OCT-99

Net sales in the nine months ended June 26, 1999, advanced 12%, reflecting strong performances across all the business groups, aided in part by the Camden Creek acquisition. Gross margins widened, on improved efficiencies and the effect of the National ICEE acquisition. Despite higher marketing and distribution costs, pretax income climbed 24%. After taxes at 37.0% in each period, net income was also up 24%, to $7.5 million ($0.78 a share), from $6.0 million ($0.64).

Stock Performance - 08-OCT-99

In the past 30 trading days, JJSF's shares have declined 12%, compared to a 0.91% fall in the S&P 500. Average trading volume for the past five days was 33,640 shares, compared with the 40-day moving average of 29,387 shares.

Key Stock Statistics

Dividend Rate/Share	Nil	Shareholders	2,200
Shs. outstg. (M)	9.0	Market cap. (B)	$0.175
Avg. daily vol. (M)	0.042	Inst. holdings	53%
Tang. Bk. Value/Share	8.08		
Beta	1.05		

Value of $10,000 invested 5 years ago: $ 9,454

Fiscal Year Ending Sep. 30

	1999	1998	1997	1996	1995	1994
Revenues (Million $)						
1Q	60.55	52.19	43.60	42.86	41.22	38.41
2Q	62.91	58.87	50.31	42.14	40.32	40.27
3Q	82.09	73.28	63.45	49.09	47.88	45.17
4Q	—	78.06	62.96	51.93	55.95	50.58
Yr.	—	262.4	220.3	186.0	185.4	174.4
Earnings Per Share ($)						
1Q	**0.06**	**0.06**	0.01	0.09	0.06	0.12
2Q	**0.12**	**0.08**	0.10	0.07	0.05	0.15
3Q	**0.60**	**0.50**	0.35	0.21	0.21	0.25
4Q	—	**0.62**	0.43	0.29	0.30	0.30
Yr.	—	**1.26**	**0.91**	**0.65**	0.61	0.82

Next earnings report expected: early November

Dividend Data

The company has not paid any cash dividends.

A Division of The McGraw-Hill Companies

STANDARD
&POOR'S
STOCK REPORTS

J & J Snack Foods Corporation

09-OCT-99

Business Summary - 07-OCT-99

J & J Snack Foods aims to produce niche quality products, be the low-cost producer, and develop strong marketing and distribution channels. Its principal snack food products are soft pretzels marketed primarily under the brand name Superpretzel. JJSF also manufactures frozen carbonated beverages, frozen juice treats and desserts, churros, baked goods, and other products. All products are sold to the foodservice and retail supermarkets.

Soft-pretzel products are sold under the Superpretzel, Mr. Twister, Soft Pretzel Bites, Softstix, Soft Pretzel Buns, Hot Knots, Dutch Twist, Texas Twist and Sandwich Twist brand names and, to a lesser extent, under private labels. Pretzels are sold to foodservice industry customers and to the retail grocery and supermarket industries. Pretzels are also sold direct to the public through the company's Bavarian Pretzel Bakery and Pretzel Gourmet snack food retail outlet chains. Soft pretzel sales accounted for 35% of total sales in FY 98 (Sep.), down from 40% in FY 97.

In December 1997, JJSF acquired a controlling interest in National ICEE Corp., which markets and distributes frozen carbonated beverages under the tradename ICEE in the eastern half of the U.S. The company incurred about $50 million in debt to complete the acquisition. The frozen carbonated beverage division was renamed The ICEE Company following the acquisition. Products are sold under the ICEE and ARCTIC BLAST names in the U.S., Mexico and Canada. Frozen carbonated beverages are also sold through the Bavarian Pretzel Bakery and Pretzel Gourmet snack food chains. During FY 98, JJSF entered into a long-term marketing agreement with Coca-Cola. Frozen carbonated beverage sales accounted for 29% of FY 98 revenues, up from 20% in FY 97.

Frozen juice treats and desserts are sold under the Mazzone's, Frostar, Shape-ups, Luigi's and Mama Tish's brand names. Frozen juice treat and dessert sales were 15% and 19% of total revenues in FY 98 and FY 97, respectively.

Frozen churros, sold under the Tio Pepe's brand name, are marketed primarily in the West and Southwest. Churros accounted for 4% and 5% of sales in FY 98 and FY 97, respectively.

Baked goods, such as cookies, muffins and other baked products, are sold under private labels by contract for third parties. In addition, the company markets baked goods under the Danish Mill and Pretzelcookie brand names. Baked goods sales amounted to 9% and 8% of sales in FY 98 and FY 97, respectively. JJSF also sells soft drinks and funnel cakes under the Funnel Cake Factory name, as well as popcorn under the Airport brand name. In February 1999, the company acquired the Camden Creek Bakery cookie business from Schwan's Sales Enterprises, Inc. Camden Creek, a seller of frozen ready-to-bake cookies, has annual sales of $5 million.

Per Share Data ($) (Year Ended Sep. 30)	1998	1997	1996	1995	1994	1993	1992	1991	1990	1989
Tangible Bk. Val.	7.50	9.54	9.99	9.58	9.18	8.59	7.68	7.07	4.65	4.45
Cash Flow	3.89	3.01	2.47	2.18	2.14	1.93	1.39	1.45	1.10	1.45
Earnings	1.26	0.91	0.65	0.61	0.82	0.80	0.55	0.67	0.44	0.81
Dividends	Nil	Nil	Nil	Nil	Nil	Nil	Nil	Nil	Nil	Nil
Payout Ratio	Nil	Nil	Nil	Nil	Nil	Nil	Nil	Nil	Nil	Nil
Prices - High	23	17 3/8	14 1/8	13 3/8	20 3/4	20 3/4	14 3/4	15 7/8	13 1/4	17 1/8
- Low	12 1/2	10 1/2	9 7/8	10	10 7/8	8 3/4	7 1/2	7 5/8	4 7/8	10 3/4
P/E Ratio - High	18	19	22	22	25	26	27	24	30	21
- Low	10	12	15	16	13	11	14	11	11	13
Income Statement Analysis (Million $)										
Revs.	262	220	186	185	174	147	127	110	96.0	87.0
Oper. Inc.	45.1	30.5	24.5	22.9	26.2	24.0	17.1	16.5	12.2	15.0
Depr.	24.6	18.9	16.5	15.0	13.8	11.8	9.1	7.2	5.6	4.7
Int. Exp.	3.0	0.4	0.4	0.4	0.5	0.4	0.4	0.8	0.9	1.8
Pretax Inc.	18.8	12.0	9.0	9.8	13.7	13.1	9.0	9.3	5.8	9.4
Eff. Tax Rate	37%	32%	35%	38%	38%	36%	34%	35%	36%	37%
Net Inc.	11.8	8.2	5.8	5.8	8.5	8.3	5.9	6.1	3.7	5.9
Balance Sheet & Other Fin. Data (Million $)										
Cash	3.2	1.4	11.7	14.5	11.1	15.8	15.7	23.7	2.4	6.8
Curr. Assets	55.1	41.2	44.2	44.5	41.4	43.5	41.0	46.3	22.7	24.2
Total Assets	213	137	123	123	127	121	112	104	75.0	67.0
Curr. Liab.	40.6	22.0	17.4	16.5	16.4	13.6	12.9	11.2	15.0	9.9
LT Debt	48.2	5.0	5.0	5.0	5.0	5.0	5.1	2.4	5.9	6.7
Common Eqty.	120	106	96.7	96.1	101	98.0	90.1	86.4	50.5	47.5
Total Cap.	172	114	105	106	110	108	100	93.2	60.2	56.7
Cap. Exp.	31.8	19.6	14.4	12.9	18.6	15.4	21.8	13.2	12.4	8.1
Cash Flow	36.5	27.0	22.3	20.8	22.3	20.2	15.0	13.3	9.3	10.6
Curr. Ratio	1.4	1.9	2.5	2.7	2.5	3.2	3.2	4.1	1.5	2.4
% LT Debt of Cap.	28.0	4.4	4.8	4.8	4.6	4.7	5.1	2.6	9.7	11.8
% Net Inc.of Revs.	4.5	3.7	3.1	3.2	4.9	5.7	4.7	5.5	3.8	6.8
% Ret. on Assets	6.8	6.3	4.8	4.7	7.0	7.2	5.5	6.0	5.2	7.9
% Ret. on Equity	10.5	8.1	6.1	5.9	8.8	8.9	6.8	8.0	7.6	15.3

Data as orig reptd.; bef. results of disc opers/spec. items. Per share data adj. for stk. divs. Bold denotes diluted EPS (FASB 128)-prior periods restated. E-Estimated. NA-Not Available. NM-Not Meaningful. NR-Not Ranked.

Office—6000 Central Hwy., Pennsauken, NJ 08109. **Tel**—(609) 665-9533. **Fax**—(609) 665-6718. **Website**—http://www.jjsnack.com **Chrmn, Pres & CEO**—G. B. Shreiber. **SVP & COO**—R. M. Radano. **SVP, CFO, Secy, Treas & Investor Contact**—Dennis G. Moore. **Dirs**—R.S. Cook, D. Fachner, S. N. Frankel, L. M. Lodish, D. G. Moore, R. M. Radano, G. B. Shreiber, P. G. Stanley. **Transfer Agent & Registrar**—American Stock Transfer & Trust Co., Brooklyn. **Incorporated**—in New Jersey in 1971. **Empl**— 1,900. **S&P Analyst:** A. Bensinger

STANDARD
&POOR'S
STOCK REPORTS

Jack in the Box

NYSE Symbol **JBX**

In S&P SmallCap 600

13-OCT-99

Industry: Restaurants

Summary: This company (formerly Foodmaker, Inc.) operates and franchises Jack In The Box restaurants, a leading regional fast-food chain.

Quantitative Evaluations

Outlook
(1 Lowest—5 Highest)
• **4+**

Fair Value
• **34⅝**

Risk
• **Average**

Earn./Div. Rank
• **NR**

Technical Eval.
• **Bearish** since 9/99

Rel. Strength Rank
(1 Lowest—99 Highest)
• **80**

Insider Activity
• **NA**

Recent Price • 26⅛
52 Wk Range • 29⅜-13
Yield • Nil
12-Mo. P/E • 14.6

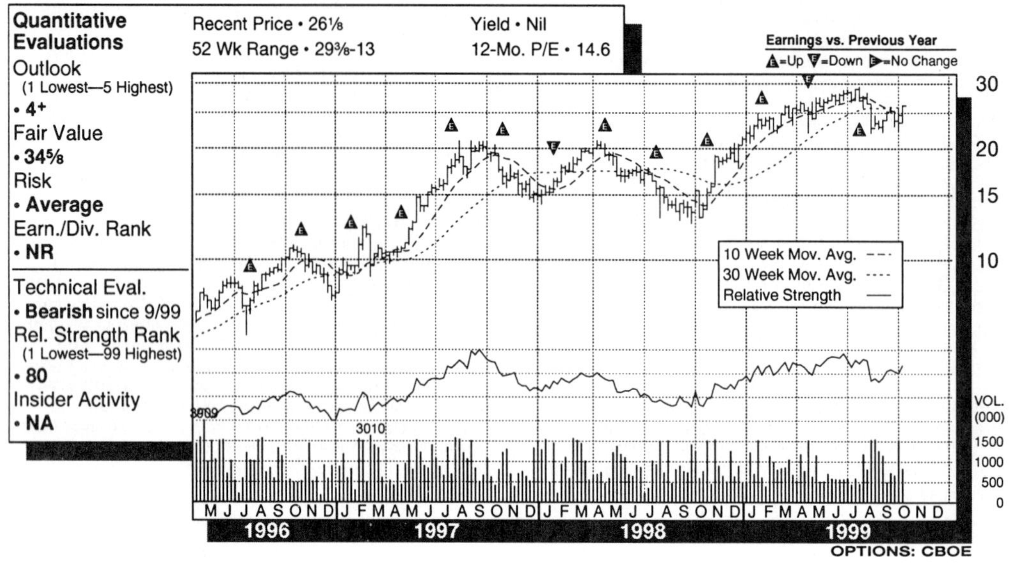

Business Profile - 13-OCT-99

Jack in the Box (formerly Foodmaker, Inc.) is benefiting from customer friendly initiatives such as an easier to read menu, an order confirmation system, and an assemble-to-order program that prepares sandwiches only after the customer orders them. The present corporate title was adopted in October, 1999. Also in October, JBX said that over 40 people became sick after eating in a Jack in the Box restaurant in Ellensburg, WA. JBX stated that the restaurant would remain closed until an investigation is complete. In July 1998, JBX completed a refinancing plan that reduced total debt by about $38 million. Also in July, directors authorized the repurchase of up to $20 million of the company's common stock.

Operational Review - 13-OCT-99

Revenues in the 40 weeks ended July 5, 1999, advanced 15%, year to year, reflecting strong restaurant sales, aided by the company's advertising and strategic initiatives, partly offset by the absence of $45.8 million in 1998 settlement income. Despite an $18 million reduction in reserves for accrued liabilities and restaurant operating costs, profitability was penalized by sharply higher restaurant cost of sales and costs of distribution and other sales. Pretax income increased 6.9%. After taxes at 37.0%, versus 32.0%, net income fell fractionally, to $58.1 million ($1.48 a share) from $58.6 million ($1.46). Results in FY 98 exclude an $0.11 a share special charge on the early extinguishment of debt.

Stock Performance - 08-OCT-99

In the past 30 trading days, JBX's shares have increased 14%, compared to a 0.91% fall in the S&P 500. Average trading volume for the past five days was 164,020 shares, compared with the 40-day moving average of 226,372 shares.

Key Stock Statistics

Dividend Rate/Share	Nil	Shareholders	600
Shs. outstg. (M)	38.3	Market cap. (B)	$0.997
Avg. daily vol. (M)	0.203	Inst. holdings	82%
Tang. Bk. Value/Share	1.69		
Beta	NA		

Value of $10,000 invested 5 years ago: $ 26,858

Fiscal Year Ending Sep. 30

	1999	1998	1997	1996	1995	1994
Revenues (Million $)						
1Q	407.1	343.8	323.5	330.6	293.7	381.6
2Q	322.0	309.9	247.0	250.0	229.7	218.7
3Q	342.4	280.6	251.7	243.2	244.1	225.8
4Q	—	289.8	249.6	239.1	251.3	227.2
Yr.	—	1,224	1,072	1,063	1,020	1,053
Earnings Per Share ($)						
1Q	**0.40**	**0.17**	0.23	0.12	-1.87	-0.11
2Q	**0.64**	**0.85**	0.17	0.10	-0.08	-0.59
3Q	**0.44**	**0.31**	0.25	0.14	0.07	-0.09
4Q	—	**0.31**	0.24	0.15	0.10	-0.14
Yr.	—	**1.77**	**0.89**	0.51	-1.77	-0.94

Next earnings report expected: early November

Dividend Data

No dividends have been paid, and the company does not intend to pay any in the foreseeable future.

A Division of The McGraw-Hill Companies

Jack in the Box, Inc.

Business Summary - 13-OCT-99

Jack in the Box (formerly Foodmaker, Inc.) credits its growing brand awareness and increased sales to its aggressive advertising campaign, which features its clown-headed "founder" Jack in television commercials for Jack in the Box restaurants. Sales rose 14% systemwide in FY 98 (Sep.) and grew over 8.0% in FY 97.

The Jack in the Box chain started in 1950 as a single drive-thru restaurant, and drive-thru sales still account for the lion's share (about 64%) of sales at company-operated restaurants. JBX currently operates about 1,500 systemwide Jack in the Box units, concentrated in the West and Southwest. Jack in the Box recently installed order confirmation systems (OCS) on all their drive through menu boards. OCS is an 8-by-6 inch liquid crystal screen that instantly displays each item a customer orders along with its price and the total cost of the order. JBX states that OCS creates improved customer service.

After growing 6.5% in FY 97, per store average sales rose 2.8% in FY 98, reflecting increases in the number of transactions and the average transaction amount. JBX uses a two-tier marketing strategy which emphasizes adult-oriented premium sandwiches and hamburgers as well as lower-priced value selections to broaden its appeal among three core customer groups: hamburger lovers, consumers who prefer higher quality levels, and individuals who shop for price. The core of the Jack in the Box menu is hamburger products, which represent about 25% of sales. JBX believes its willingness to offer certain distinctive, premium foods, such as its Chicken Teriyaki Bowl and Chicken Fajita Pita, is unique among quick-serve restaurants, and, along with its focus on the adult market, has helped Jack in the Box develop a niche in an overcrowded industry. In order to showcase value, JBX introduced its "Under a Buck" menu featuring, among other items, its Jumbo Jack hamburgers and tacos.

Over the next five years, JBX plans to open approximately 400 to 500 new restaurants. About 15% of this new development will be through meeting consumer demand for convenience by including nontraditional locations such as gas stations and supermarkets in its growth plans. JBX is also looking at dual branding, which provides consumers with two brands in a single location, and in this regard it is developing its own Mexican-brand line of foods to offer along with Jack in the Box products.

In February 1998, JBX settled the litigation it filed on February 4, 1993, against the Von Companies, Inc. and various suppliers seeking reimbursement for all damages incurred in connection with food-borne illness attributed to hamburgers served at Jack in the Box restaurants in 1993. In the second quarter of FY 98, the company received a litigation settlement of $45.8 million net after litigation costs and before income taxes.

Per Share Data ($) (Year Ended Sep. 30)	1998	1997	1996	1995	1994	1993	1992	1991	1990	1989
Tangible Bk. Val.	1.69	0.46	NM	NM	0.18	-1.49	1.24	0.83	NA	NA
Cash Flow	2.77	1.84	1.44	-0.85	-0.12	-0.05	1.83	1.87	NA	NA
Earnings	1.77	0.85	0.51	-1.77	-0.94	-1.15	0.67	0.57	NA	NA
Dividends	Nil	Nil	Nil	Nil	Nil	Nil	Nil	NA	NA	NA
Payout Ratio	Nil	Nil	Nil	Nil	Nil	NM	Nil	NA	NA	NA
Prices - High	22 3/8	21	11	7 1/4	10 3/4	14	18 1/2	NA	NA	NA
- Low	12 1/2	8 3/4	5 1/2	3 1/4	3 3/8	7 1/2	9 1/8	NA	NA	NA
P/E Ratio - High	13	21	22	NM	NM	NM	28	NA	NA	NA
- Low	7	10	11	NM	NM	NM	14	NA	NA	NA
Income Statement Analysis (Million $)										
Revs.	1,224	1,072	1,063	1,019	1,053	1,241	1,219	1,157	NA	NA
Oper. Inc.	178	123	108	73.0	57.0	86.0	149	150	NA	NA
Depr.	40.0	37.9	36.5	35.8	31.6	42.4	37.8	50.3	NA	NA
Int. Exp.	33.0	41.0	46.3	48.6	55.9	57.8	73.2	59.3	NA	NA
Pretax Inc.	104	45.2	25.4	-68.5	-33.3	-66.2	38.7	40.6	NA	NA
Eff. Tax Rate	32%	22%	21%	NM	NM	NM	43%	46%	NA	NA
Net Inc.	71.0	35.3	20.1	-69.0	-36.3	-44.1	21.9	22.0	NA	NA
Balance Sheet & Other Fin. Data (Million $)										
Cash	10.0	28.5	42.0	36.0	36.0	4.5	20.0	1.4	NA	NA
Curr. Assets	82.0	100	96.5	98.0	107	94.0	106	67.0	NA	NA
Total Assets	744	682	654	663	740	890	915	845	NA	NA
Curr. Liab.	226	193	147	132	148	203	167	159	NA	NA
LT Debt	320	346	396	440	448	500	501	505	NA	NA
Common Eqty.	137	87.9	51.4	31.3	100	139	247	182	NA	NA
Total Cap.	459	434	455	481	553	657	748	687	NA	NA
Cap. Exp.	111	59.7	33.2	27.0	92.0	59.0	77.0	NA	NA	NA
Cash Flow	111	73.2	56.5	-33.1	-4.6	-1.7	59.7	72.3	NA	NA
Curr. Ratio	0.4	0.5	0.7	0.7	0.7	0.5	0.6	0.4	NA	NA
% LT Debt of Cap.	69.7	79.7	87.0	91.6	81.0	76.2	67.0	73.5	NA	NA
% Net Inc.of Revs.	5.8	3.3	1.9	NM	NM	NM	1.8	1.9	NA	NA
% Ret. on Assets	9.9	5.3	3.0	NM	NM	NM	1.1	NA	NA	NA
% Ret. on Equity	62.8	50.7	48.5	NM	NM	NM	NM	NA	NA	NA

Data as orig reptd.; bef. results of disc opers/spec. items. Per share data adj. for stk. divs. Bold denotes diluted EPS (FASB 128)-prior periods restated. E-Estimated. NA-Not Available. NM-Not Meaningful. NR-Not Ranked.

Office—9330 Balboa Ave., San Diego, CA 92123. **Tel**—(619) 571-2121. **Website**—http://www.foodmaker.com **Chrmn**—J. W. Goodall. **CEO & Pres**—R. J. Nugent. **EVP, CFO & Investor Contact**—Charles W. Duddles. **EVP & Secy**—L. E. Schauf. **Dirs**—M. E. Alpert, J. W. Brown, P. T. Carter, C. W. Duddles, E. Gibbons, J. W. Goodall, M. H. Hutchison, R. J. Nugent, L. R. Payne. **Transfer Agent & Registrar**—ChaseMellon Shareholder Services, Ridgefield Park, NJ. **Incorporated**—in Delaware in 1971. **Empl**— 35,000. **S&P Analyst:** A. Bensinger

STANDARD &POOR'S STOCK REPORTS

Jan Bell Marketing

ASE Symbol **JBM**

In S&P SmallCap 600

09-OCT-99

Industry: Consumer (Jewelry, Novelties & Gifts)

Summary: Jan Bell markets fine jewelry, watches and other consumer products primarily through over 440 leased departments of Sam's Club stores.

Quantitative Evaluations

Outlook (1 Lowest—5 Highest) • **NA**

Fair Value • **NA**

Risk • **High**

Earn./Div. Rank • **B-**

Technical Eval. • **Bullish** since 9/99

Rel. Strength Rank (1 Lowest—99 Highest) • **33**

Insider Activity • **NA**

Recent Price • 2⅞

52 Wk Range • 7½-2$\frac{1}{16}$

Yield • Nil

12-Mo. P/E • 5.5

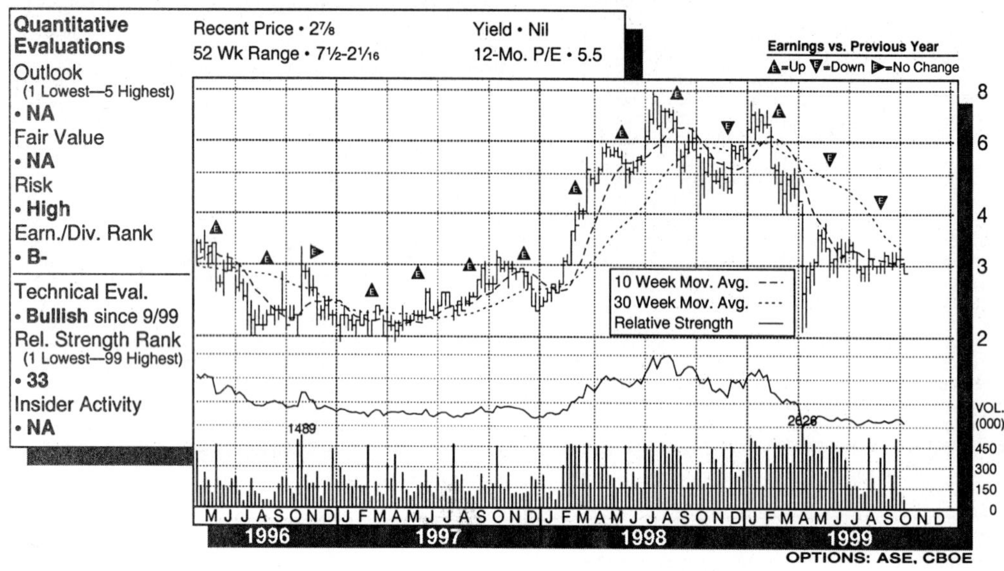

OPTIONS: ASE, CBOE

Business Profile - 07-APR-99

Results for FY 99 (Jan.) benefited from the July 1998 Mayor's Jewelers Inc. acquisition and a 13% increase in comparable store sales at Sam's Club locations. Mayor's contributed $82.5 million in sales during the last six months of the fiscal year. As of March 24, 1999, JBM operated 21 Mayor's Jewelers, Inc. stores and 452 licensed jewelry concessions in Sam's Clubs. Looking ahead to the first quarter of FY 99, sales for the four weeks ended February 27, 1999, were $11.7 million, a 63% increase over the year ago period. Comparable stores sales for Sam's Club locations in February grew 16%, while Mayor's same store sales fell 1.8%.

Operational Review - 07-APR-99

Based on a preliminary report, net sales for the fiscal year ended January 30, 1999, rose 46%, due to the Mayor's Jewelers acquisition and same-store sales increases at Sam's Club locations. Despite a 77% increase in store and warehouse operating and selling expenses, profitability improved on wider gross margins; operating income climbed 72%. Following depreciation and amortization charges, net interest expense, versus interest income, and a tax benefit of approximately $2.3 million in both years, net income grew 71% to $17,218,000 ($0.60 a share, on 11% more shares), from $10,043,000 ($0.39).

Stock Performance - 08-OCT-99

In the past 30 trading days, JBM's shares have declined 4%, compared to a 0.91% fall in the S&P 500. Average trading volume for the past five days was 13,300 shares, compared with the 40-day moving average of 78,144 shares.

Key Stock Statistics

Dividend Rate/Share	Nil	Shareholders	727
Shs. outstg. (M)	24.6	Market cap. (B)	$0.071
Avg. daily vol. (M)	0.087	Inst. holdings	45%
Tang. Bk. Value/Share	4.85		
Beta	0.91		

Value of $10,000 invested 5 years ago: $ 3,066

Fiscal Year Ending Jan. 31

	2000	1999	1998	1997	1996	1995
Revenues (Million $)						
1Q	87.66	52.49	46.98	47.45	50.02	63.01
2Q	31.99	60.35	53.31	55.15	55.45	60.08
3Q	—	79.01	45.22	44.71	46.21	68.59
4Q	—	169.2	102.4	95.77	102.3	114.0
Yr.	—	361.1	247.9	243.1	254.0	305.7
Earnings Per Share ($)						
1Q	**-0.10**	**-0.02**	**-0.09**	**-0.20**	-0.22	-0.23
2Q	**-0.16**	**0.02**	**-0.02**	**-0.05**	-0.07	-0.19
3Q	—	**-0.13**	**-0.09**	**-0.11**	-0.11	-0.18
4Q	—	**0.68**	**0.58**	**0.38**	0.28	-2.32
Yr.	—	**0.60**	**0.39**	**0.03**	**-0.13**	**-2.92**

Next earnings report expected: mid November

Dividend Data

No cash dividends have been paid on the common stock. Three-for-two stock splits were effected in 1989 and 1988.

A Division of The McGraw-Hill Companies

Jan Bell Marketing, Inc.

Business Summary - 07-APR-99

Jan Bell Marketing, Inc. markets fine jewelry, watches and other non-jewelry consumer products (including perfumes, sunglasses, writing instruments, and collectible and giftware items). The company markets its products primarily through Sam's Club, a division of Wal-Mart, pursuant to an arrangement whereby JBM operates an exclusive leased department at all Sam's domestic locations through February 1, 2001. Sales through Sam's accounted for 93% of total sales in the fiscal year ended January 31, 1998.

Each Sam's location is staffed by JBM employees, with the inventory owned by JBM. In exchange for the right to operate the department and the use of retail space, the company pays a tenancy fee of 9% of net sales. While Sam's is responsible for paying utility costs, maintenance and certain other expenses associated with operation of the departments, JBM provides and maintains all fixtures and other equipment necessary to operate the departments.

Over the last three fiscal years, the company's strategy has been to achieve cost reductions at all levels. JBM has implemented merchandise strategies that emphasize higher margin diamond, semi-precious gem, gold and watch products in place of other lower margin non-jewelry products. The company has also taken action to lower its reliance on borrowings, balance inventories, reduce discounted stock, and improve inventory returns. Management believes that additional opportunities to improve sales, gross margins, and expense savings still exist within its business with Sam's.

JBM also operates four Manhattan Diamond stores in shopping mall locations, which were acquired in September 1996. The company is presently reviewing its strategy for the stores since management believes that the four locations do not generate an acceptable rate of return on capital employed. The firm will either open additional locations to achieve economies of scale or will seek the sale of the business.

In January 1997, the company decided to close both of its Jewelry Depot stores in Massachusetts, which had been opened in FY 95, citing a lack of success.

In the second quarter of FY 99, Jan Bell consummated the acquisition of Mayor's Jewelers, Inc., a leading provider of luxury jewelry in the Southeast. Total consideration consisted of approximately $18 million in cash, 2 million shares of Jan Bell Marketing, Inc. stock and the refinancing of Mayor's outstanding debt.

Per Share Data ($) (Year Ended Jan. 31)	1999	1998	1997	1996	1995	1994	1993	1992	1991	1990
Tangible Bk. Val.	4.87	5.12	4.73	4.74	4.84	6.87	8.10	7.28	8.11	7.81
Cash Flow	0.84	0.65	0.35	0.21	-2.57	-1.14	-0.79	0.51	0.37	0.86
Earnings	0.60	0.39	0.03	-0.13	-2.92	-1.40	-0.59	0.33	0.30	0.80
Dividends	Nil	Nil	Nil	Nil	Nil	Nil	Nil	Nil	Nil	Nil
Payout Ratio	Nil	Nil	Nil	Nil	Nil	Nil	Nil	Nil	Nil	Nil
Cal. Yrs.	1998	1997	1996	1995	1994	1993	1992	1991	1990	1989
Prices - High	$7\frac{7}{8}$	$3\frac{1}{4}$	$3\frac{5}{8}$	$4\frac{1}{4}$	$20\frac{5}{8}$	23	17	$26\frac{5}{8}$	34	$13\frac{3}{8}$
- Low	$2\frac{3}{8}$	$1\frac{15}{16}$	$1\frac{3}{4}$	$2\frac{3}{16}$	$8\frac{1}{2}$	$12\frac{1}{2}$	$5\frac{3}{4}$	$6\frac{1}{4}$	$12\frac{1}{8}$	$3\frac{5}{8}$
P/E Ratio - High	13	8	NM	NM	NM	39	2	89	43	24
- Low	4	5	NM	NM	NM	21	17	20	15	6
Income Statement Analysis (Million $)										
Revs.	361	248	243	254	306	175	334	224	177	181
Oper. Inc.	23.4	13.3	14.5	7.7	-9.2	-10.9	26.9	12.3	21.0	25.0
Depr.	7.1	6.9	8.2	8.7	9.2	6.8	5.1	3.9	1.8	1.2
Int. Exp.	1.7	Nil	1.0	3.2	3.5	3.2	0.9	2.4	0.8	0.4
Pretax Inc.	15.0	7.8	0.9	-3.3	-74.7	-47.4	-21.5	11.3	13.2	25.6
Eff. Tax Rate	NM	NM	17%	NM	NM	NM	31%	27%	30%	38%
Net Inc.	17.2	10.0	0.8	-3.4	-75.1	-35.7	-14.8	7.5	6.6	16.0
Balance Sheet & Other Fin. Data (Million $)										
Cash	5.4	48.4	23.5	15.0	28.2	30.2	49.0	17.4	51.2	46.6
Curr. Assets	187	128	111	117	148	248	232	161	186	179
Total Assets	248	152	139	153	187	312	302	228	207	193
Curr. Liab.	56.2	16.1	14.0	20.4	59.4	73.4	33.9	20.4	32.9	19.8
LT Debt	26.4	Nil	Nil	7.5	Nil	33.5	33.0	Nil	Nil	Nil
Common Eqty.	164	136	125	125	127	205	235	208	172	173
Total Cap.	190	136	125	133	127	239	268	208	175	173
Cap. Exp.	6.3	1.7	2.3	1.8	6.3	12.6	6.7	4.4	5.9	10.2
Cash Flow	24.3	17.0	9.0	5.2	-65.9	-29.0	-19.9	11.4	8.4	17.2
Curr. Ratio	3.3	7.9	7.9	5.7	2.5	3.4	6.8	7.9	5.7	9.1
% LT Debt of Cap.	13.9	Nil	Nil	5.7	Nil	14.0	12.3	Nil	Nil	Nil
% Net Inc.of Revs.	4.8	4.1	0.3	NM	NM	NM	3.4	4.4	3.7	8.8
% Ret. on Assets	8.6	6.9	0.5	NM	NM	NM	5.6	3.2	3.4	11.4
% Ret. on Equity	11.5	7.7	0.6	NM	NM	NM	6.7	3.7	3.9	13.4

Data as orig. reptd.; bef. results of disc. opers. and/or spec. items. Per share data adj. for stk. divs. as of ex-div. date. Yrs. end. Dec. 31 of preceding cal yr. pr. to 1995. E-Estimated. NA-Not Available. NM-Not Meaningful. NR-Not Ranked.

Office—14051 N.W. 14th St., Sunrise, FL 33323. **Tel**—(954) 846-2718. **Chrmn & CEO**—I. Arguetty. **SEVP & Secy**—R. W. Bowers. **SVP & COO**—M. Weinstein. **SVP-Fin, CFO & Treas & Investor Contact**—D. Boudreau. **Investor Contact**—Tony Armstrong. **Dirs**—I. Arguetty, H. Bashan, G. Bedol, T. Epstein, S. A. Getz, M. Gilliam, W. Grayson, P. Offerman, R. G. Robison. **Transfer Agent & Registrar**—Sun Trust Bank, Atlanta. **Incorporated**—in Delaware in 1987. **Empl**— 3,500. **S&P Analyst:** Jordan Horoschak

STANDARD
&POOR'S
STOCK REPORTS

Jefferies Group

NYSE Symbol **JEF**

In S&P SmallCap 600

09-OCT-99

Industry: Investment Banking/ Brokerage

Summary: Jefferies Group is engaged in securities brokerage and trading, corporate finance and other financial services.

Quantitative Evaluations

Outlook (1 Lowest—5 Highest)
• **NA**

Fair Value
• **NA**

Risk
• **Average**

Earn./Div. Rank
• **A-**

Technical Eval.
• **NA**

Rel. Strength Rank (1 Lowest—99 Highest)
• **15**

Insider Activity
• **NA**

Recent Price • 20⅞
52 Wk Range • 65-19⅞

Yield • 1.0%
12-Mo. P/E • 6.9

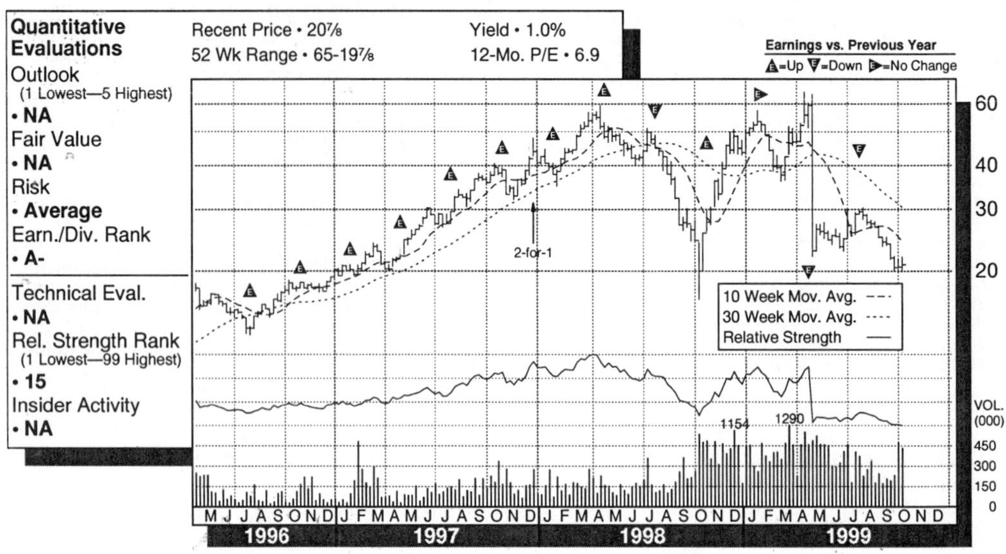

Business Profile - 03-JUN-99

Jefferies Group, Inc. (JEF) and its 81%-owned Investment Technology Group, Inc. (ITGI) subsidiary recently separated into two independent companies. In April 1999, the company completed the spinoff of Jefferies & Co., Inc. (JEFCO) and other subsidiaries, and the merger of ITG with the former Jefferies Group. The spinoff involved a tax free distribution of 100% of the shares of "New JEF," a holding company consisting of JEFCO and all direct subsidiaries of the former Jefferies Group other than ITG, to Jefferies Group shareholders. New JEF was renamed Jefferies Group, Inc. This was followed by a tax free merger of ITG and the former Jefferies Group, which was renamed Investment Technology Group, Inc.

Operational Review - 03-JUN-99

Total revenues in the first three months of 1999 declined 1.6%, year to year, as lower corporate finance revenues outweighed higher commissions, principal transactions and interest income. Interest expense increased, but non-interest expenses declined. After taxes at 48.6%, versus 41.5%, and minority interest, net income fell 6.3%, to $16,621,000 ($0.69 a share, on 2.8% more shares), from $17,476,000 ($0.75).

Stock Performance - 08-OCT-99

In the past 30 trading days, JEF's shares have declined 17%, compared to a 0.91% fall in the S&P 500. Average trading volume for the past five days was 85,980 shares, compared with the 40-day moving average of 60,336 shares.

Key Stock Statistics

Dividend Rate/Share	0.20	Shareholders	307
Shs. outstg. (M)	23.9	Market cap. (B)	$0.500
Avg. daily vol. (M)	0.078	Inst. holdings	43%
Tang. Bk. Value/Share	15.43		
Beta	1.69		

Value of $10,000 invested 5 years ago: NA

Fiscal Year Ending Dec. 31

	1999	1998	1997	1996	1995	1994
Revenues (Million $)						
1Q	200.1	203.4	153.4	126.8	95.01	75.69
2Q	175.3	198.8	209.4	127.9	108.2	67.24
3Q	—	184.3	192.0	133.4	111.0	82.17
4Q	—	212.2	240.8	152.8	105.6	91.01
Yr.	—	798.7	796.6	540.8	419.7	316.1
Earnings Per Share ($)						
1Q	**0.69**	**0.75**	0.50	0.44	0.28	0.24
2Q	**0.61**	**0.76**	0.87	0.39	0.26	0.19
3Q	—	**0.66**	0.64	0.49	0.42	0.21
4Q	—	**0.79**	**0.79**	0.54	0.23	0.17
Yr.	—	**2.96**	**2.80**	1.83	**1.19**	**0.81**

Next earnings report expected: mid October

Dividend Data (Dividends have been paid since 1988.)

Amount ($)	Date Decl.	Ex-Div. Date	Stock of Record	Payment Date
0.050	Feb. 01	Feb. 10	Feb. 15	Mar. 15 '99
Stk.	Apr. 13	Apr. 28	Apr. 20	Apr. 27 '99
0.050	May. 06	May. 13	May. 17	Jun. 17 '99
0.050	Jul. 29	Aug. 12	Aug. 16	Sep. 15 '99

A Division of The McGraw-Hill Companies

Jefferies Group, Inc.

Business Summary - 03-JUN-99

Jefferies Group, Inc. is a holding company that until April 1999 had four primary subsidiaries: Jefferies & Co., Inc., Investment Technology Group, Inc., Jefferies International Ltd. and Jefferies Pacific Ltd. The company is engaged in securities brokerage and trading, corporate finance, and other financial services. The company and its subsidiaries maintain offices in Los Angeles, New York, Short Hills and Jersey City, NJ, Chicago, Dallas, Boston, Atlanta, New Orleans, Houston, San Francisco, Stamford, London, Hong Kong, Zurich and Tokyo.

In April 1999, the company completed the spinoff of Jefferies & Co., Inc. (JEFCO) and other subsidiaries, and the merger of ITG with the former Jefferies Group. The spinoff involved a tax free distribution of 100% of the shares of "New JEF," a holding company consisting of JEFCO and all direct subsidiaries of the former Jefferies Group other than ITG, to Jefferies Group shareholders. New JEF was renamed Jefferies Group, Inc. This was followed by a tax free merger of ITG and the former Jefferies Group, which was renamed Investment Technology Group, Inc.

Jefferies & Co. is engaged in equity, convertible debt and taxable fixed-income securities brokerage and trading and corporate finance. Jefferies is one of the leading national firms engaged in the distribution and trading of blocks of equity securities and conducts such activities primarily in the third market, or trading of listed equity securities away from national securities exchanges. Revenues are derived mainly from commission revenues and market making or trading as a principal in equity, taxable fixed-income and convertible securities with or on behalf of institutional investors, with the balance generated by corporate finance and other activities.

Jefferies International Ltd. is a broker-dealer and a member of the International Stock Exchange and The Securities and Futures Authority. Jefferies Pacific Ltd. is a Hong Kong-based broker. W&D Securities, Inc. primarily provides execution services on the NYSE and other exchanges to Jefferies and ITG.

Investment Technology Group, which was spun off in April 1999, is a leading provider of technology-based equity trading services and transaction research to institutional investors and brokers. Services offered by ITG include POSIT, the world's largest intra-day electronic equity matching system, QuantEX, a fully integrated trade routing, analysis and management system, and ISIS, a set of analytical tools for systematically lowering the costs of trading.

Per Share Data ($) (Year Ended Dec. 31)	1998	1997	1996	1995	1994	1993	1992	1991	1990	1989
Tangible Bk. Val.	NA	11.76	9.43	8.28	7.28	6.34	5.21	NA	NA	NA
Cash Flow	NA	3.58	2.44	1.60	1.14	1.67	NA	NA	NA	NA
Earnings	2.96	2.80	1.83	1.20	0.81	1.34	0.95	0.43	NA	NA
Dividends	0.20	0.10	0.09	0.05	0.05	0.05	0.05	NA	NA	NA
Payout Ratio	7%	4%	5%	4%	6%	4%	5%	NA	NA	NA
Prices - High	$59\frac{1}{2}$	48	$20\frac{3}{8}$	$12\frac{1}{8}$	$11\frac{1}{2}$	$10\frac{1}{8}$	$5\frac{1}{2}$	NA	NA	NA
- Low	$16\frac{1}{2}$	$19\frac{3}{8}$	$11\frac{1}{8}$	$7\frac{1}{8}$	$7\frac{1}{8}$	$4\frac{5}{8}$	$2\frac{5}{8}$	NA	NA	NA
P/E Ratio - High	20	17	11	10	14	8	6	NA	NA	NA
- Low	6	7	6	6	9	3	3	NA	NA	NA
Income Statement Analysis (Million $)										
Commissions	395	282	240	178	155	138	107	84.0	NA	NA
Int. Inc.	90.8	70.7	47.8	65.8	51.2	21.7	16.8	23.9	NA	NA
Total Revs.	799	765	541	420	316	318	235	196	NA	NA
Int. Exp.	NA	61.5	37.9	54.4	41.6	17.5	13.3	16.0	NA	NA
Pretax Inc.	NA	116	83.2	53.2	39.0	47.3	33.7	17.8	NA	NA
Eff. Tax Rate	NA	41%	43%	41%	45%	42%	44%	45%	NA	NA
Net Inc.	NA	63.6	43.6	28.5	20.2	27.6	18.7	9.9	NA	NA
Balance Sheet & Other Fin. Data (Million $)										
Total Assets	NA	2,100	1,568	1,537	1,557	1,388	531	529	NA	NA
Cash Items	NA	140	138	68.3	71.4	NA	NA	NA	NA	NA
Receivables	NA	1,436	1,080	1,225	1,256	NA	NA	NA	NA	NA
Secs. Owned	NA	245	198	167	145	NA	NA	NA	NA	NA
Sec. Borrowed	39.6	189	Nil	Nil	19.6	NA	NA	NA	NA	NA
Due Brokers & Cust.	NA	1,270	976	1,079	1,166	NA	NA	NA	NA	NA
Other Liabs.	281	318	331	207	143	NA	NA	NA	NA	NA
Capitalization:										
Debt	NA	149	53.0	56.3	59.6	9.7	41.0	40.2	NA	NA
Equity	NA	243	195	186	163	145	97.0	78.0	NA	NA
Total	NA	392	26.0	251	229	NA	NA	NA	NA	NA
% Return On Revs.	NA	8.3	8.1	6.8	6.4	8.7	8.0	5.0	NA	NA
% Ret. on Assets	NA	3.5	5.1	1.8	1.4	2.9	3.5	NA	NA	NA
% Ret. on Equity	NA	29.0	22.8	16.3	13.1	22.8	21.4	NA	NA	NA

Data as orig reptd.; bef. results of disc opers/spec. items. Per share data adj. for stk. divs. Bold denotes diluted EPS (FASB 128)-prior periods restated. E-Estimated. NA-Not Available. NM-Not Meaningful. NR-Not Ranked.

Office—11100 Santa Monica Blvd., Los Angeles, CA 90025. **Tel**—(310) 445-1199. **Website**—http://www.jefco.com**Chrmn & CEO**—F. E. Baxter. **Pres & COO**—M. L. Klowden. **EVP & CFO**—C. T. Schmitz. **Secy**— J. M. Gluck. **Investor Contact**—Tom Tarrant (203 708-5989).**Dirs**—F. E. Baxter, R. G. Dooley, R. B. Handler, M. L. Klowden, S. B. Lubar, F. J. Macchiarola.**Transfer Agent & Registrar**—First Chicago Trust Co. of New York. **Incorporated**—in Delaware in 1983. **Empl**— 912. **S&P Analyst:** B.G.

STANDARD
&POOR'S
STOCK REPORTS

JLG Industries

NYSE Symbol **JLG**

In S&P SmallCap 600

09-OCT-99

Industry: Manufacturing (Specialized)

Summary: This company is a leading manufacturer, distributor and international marketer of mobile aerial work platforms and other equipment.

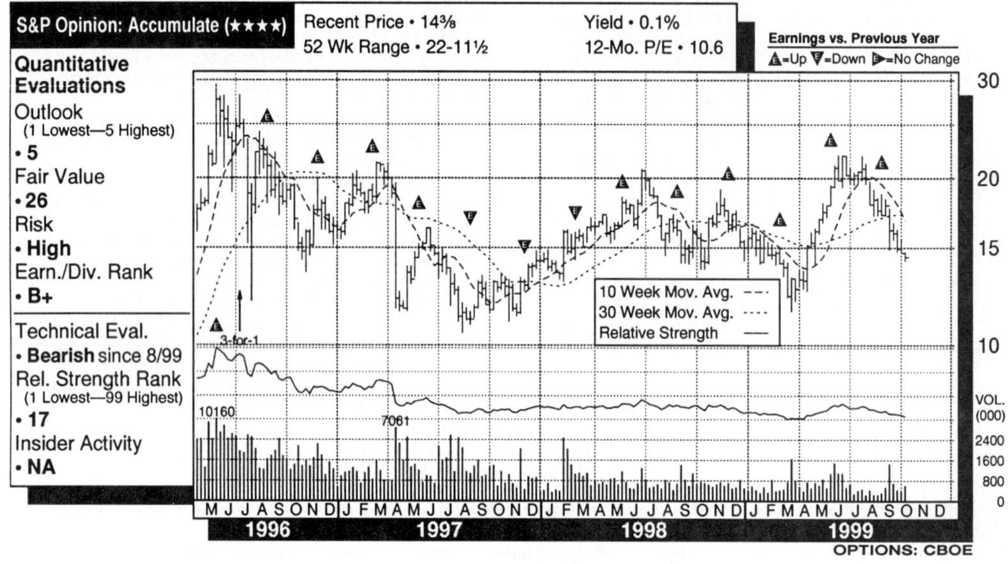

Overview - 13-SEP-99

Revenues should increase 20% to 30% in FY 00 (Jul.), primarily reflecting the Gradall acquisition, and, to a lesser extent, growth in the rental business from an expanding customer base. Gradall should help smooth sales volatility, due to high demand for excavators stemming from a federal highway spending bill. Domestically, JLG has experienced growth in orders in its core aerial lift market, including the recently introduced 450 and 800 lifts. International sales should accelerate, with Asian demand recovering and healthy demand continuing in Europe. JLG plans to build more product during the off-season, to smooth out production; we see this as potentially damaging to margins. However, JLG expects operating efficiency improvements to offset higher inventory costs associated with its plan. Overall, we expect margins to narrow slightly, on the integration of Gradall, with earnings rising about 20% in FY 00.

Valuation - 13-SEP-99

After climbing 80% from their March 1999 low, on a market shift to industrial and cyclical stocks, increased recognition of JLG's earnings prospects, and enthusiasm for the Gradall acquisition, the shares have fallen 30%, as investors, with inflation looming, have sold manufacturing stocks. We believe Gradall will enhance JLG's product offerings and solidify its standing as a preferred equipment vendor to a broader rental customer base. At less than 10X Gradall's 1998 EBIT, JLG got a leading manufacturer with healthy prospects at a bargain price. JLG shares were recently trading at about 9X our FY 00 EPS estimate, well below JLG's peer group average. JLG's core aerial platform market should continue to grow steadily at a double digit pace for the next few years. As a result, we view the stock as attractive for long-term appreciation.

Key Stock Statistics

S&P EPS Est. 2000	1.65	Tang. Bk. Value/Share	5.58
P/E on S&P Est. 2000	8.7	Beta	0.62
Dividend Rate/Share	0.02	Shareholders	20,000
Shs. outstg. (M)	44.1	Market cap. (B)	$0.637
Avg. daily vol. (M)	0.102	Inst. holdings	62%

Value of $10,000 invested 5 years ago: $ 70,623

Fiscal Year Ending Jul. 31

	1999	1998	1997	1996	1995	1994
Revenues (Million $)						
1Q	128.7	95.64	120.2	86.70	53.72	36.76
2Q	138.2	111.7	121.3	87.56	52.18	34.17
3Q	196.7	146.3	143.6	113.2	75.81	50.14
4Q	256.6	177.2	141.2	125.9	87.50	55.37
Yr.	720.2	530.9	526.3	413.4	269.2	176.4
Earnings Per Share ($)						
1Q	**0.23**	0.11	0.28	0.18	0.09	0.03
2Q	**0.25**	**0.17**	**0.25**	0.19	0.09	0.03
3Q	**0.39**	**0.32**	0.30	0.28	0.14	0.08
4Q	**0.49**	**0.46**	**0.25**	0.30	0.17	0.09
Yr.	**1.36**	**1.05**	**1.04**	0.95	0.49	0.23

Next earnings report expected: mid November

Dividend Data (Dividends have been paid since 1993.)

Amount ($)	Date Decl.	Ex-Div. Date	Stock of Record	Payment Date
0.005	Nov. 19	Dec. 11	Dec. 15	Jan. 04 '99
0.005	Feb. 22	Mar. 11	Mar. 15	Apr. 01 '99
0.005	May. 25	Jun. 11	Jun. 15	Jul. 01 '99
0.005	Sep. 08	Sep. 13	Sep. 15	Oct. 01 '99

JLG Industries, Inc.

Business Summary - 13-SEP-99

JLG Industries is the world's leading manufacturer and distributor of mobile aerial work platforms (the development of which it pioneered). These products are used primarily for construction, industrial, commercial, and institutional applications.

JLG specializes in three types of aerial work platforms: boom lifts, scissor lifts and push-around (vertical) lifts. They are powered by electric motors or gasoline, diesel, or propane engines. The self-propelled telescoping boom-lifts, which have lift capacity of up to 1,000 lbs., can reach heights of 150 ft., and may be rotated 360 degrees in either direction. Scissor-lifts, which can reach heights of 50 ft., provide larger work areas, and lift capacity of up to 2,500 lbs. Push-around units consist of an aluminum or steel base that holds a work platform up to 36 ft., with a lift capacity of up to 750 lbs.

The company believes the dramatic growth experienced by the industry over the last five years was driven by five factors: a national movement by businesses to improve productivity through the reduction of cycle times and labor costs; changes in workplace safety rules (such as an OSHA requirement for fall restraints in work done more than six ft. above the ground); growing acceptance of these machines in the developing world as a more efficient alternative to scaffolding and ladders; a strong economic environment and the growth in capital spending; and increased demand for rental equipment, along with the greater ability of rental companies to purchase equipment.

In July 1997, a slowdown in domestic orders and competitive market conditions led to the announcement of a restructuring plan aimed at improving productivity and profitability. JLG moved to reduce its exposure to the market's inherent cyclicality. Its plan included improving manufacturing efficiencies and processes, reducing costs, and shortening manufacturing lead times; accelerating new product development; expanding global distribution; enhancing customer support services; expanding its own rental fleet and used equipment business; strengthening employee involvement; and pursuing strategic acquisitions.

The company's products are sold mainly to independent distributors that rent and service the equipment. The North American distributor network consists of about 100 companies operating nearly 300 branches, while the European base includes approximately 80 locations. JLG also has a presence in the Asia/Pacific region, Australia, Japan and Latin America.

In June 1999, JLG acquired Gradall Industries, Inc., a leading U.S. manufacturer of excavating and material handling construction equipment, for about $200 million in cash. JLG expected the acquisition to increase its revenues to about $800 million, and to bring it closer to its goal of attaining $1 billion in annual revenues. It also expected the transaction to be accretive to earnings in the first full year of combined operations.

Per Share Data ($) **(Year Ended Jul. 31)**	**1999**	**1998**	**1997**	**1996**	**1995**	**1994**	**1993**	**1992**	**1991**	**1990**
Tangible Bk. Val.	NA	4.71	3.70	2.61	1.60	1.09	0.89	0.86	0.90	1.04
Cash Flow	NA	1.40	1.30	1.09	0.58	0.29	0.13	-0.01	-0.03	0.24
Earnings	1.36	1.05	1.06	0.95	0.49	0.23	0.07	-0.07	-0.08	0.20
Dividends	0.02	0.02	0.02	0.02	0.01	0.01	Nil	0.01	0.02	0.02
Payout Ratio	1%	2%	2%	2%	2%	3%	Nil	Nil	NM	8%
Prices - High	22	20 3/4	21 3/8	29 1/2	10 1/8	3 1/2	2 1/16	1	1 5/16	2 7/16
- Low	11 1/2	13	10 1/2	7 3/4	2 7/8	2	7/8	5/8	13/16	5/8
P/E Ratio - High	16	20	20	31	21	15	28	NM	NM	12
- Low	8	12	10	8	6	9	12	NM	NM	3
Income Statement Analysis (Million $)										
Revs.	NA	531	526	413	269	176	123	110	94.0	149
Oper. Inc.	NA	88.5	84.2	64.7	36.6	17.8	7.4	3.1	0.5	16.7
Depr.	NA	15.8	10.4	6.5	3.9	2.8	2.5	2.6	1.9	1.8
Int. Exp.	NA	0.3	0.4	0.3	0.4	0.4	0.5	1.2	1.5	2.3
Pretax Inc.	NA	70.5	71.2	65.7	32.7	14.6	4.6	-5.8	-6.4	13.4
Eff. Tax Rate	NA	34%	35%	36%	37%	35%	30%	NM	NM	37%
Net Inc.	NA	46.5	46.1	42.1	20.8	9.5	3.2	-3.0	-3.2	8.5
Balance Sheet & Other Fin. Data (Million $)										
Cash	NA	56.8	25.4	30.4	13.0	8.1	4.8	4.9	0.9	4.5
Curr. Assets	NA	206	156	129	84.6	62.5	49.4	53.1	58.4	70.5
Total Assets	NA	307	249	249	120	91.6	72.5	73.8	74.9	86.7
Curr. Liab.	NA	82.8	71.1	57.1	39.2	30.1	24.0	20.8	21.9	23.2
LT Debt	NA	2.5	3.7	2.0	2.3	6.3	3.2	10.2	8.8	15.5
Common Eqty.	NA	208	162	113	68.4	45.7	38.9	37.2	38.6	44.0
Total Cap.	NA	210	166	115	70.7	52.0	42.1	47.3	48.1	60.2
Cap. Exp.	NA	13.6	29.8	16.7	11.0	7.8	3.6	5.1	2.2	2.3
Cash Flow	NA	62.3	56.5	48.6	24.6	12.3	5.7	-0.5	-1.3	10.3
Curr. Ratio	NA	2.5	2.2	2.3	2.2	2.1	2.1	2.5	2.7	3.0
% LT Debt of Cap.	NA	1.2	2.2	1.7	3.2	12.1	7.5	21.4	18.4	25.8
% Net Inc.of Revs.	NA	8.8	8.8	10.2	7.7	5.4	2.6	NM	NM	5.7
% Ret. on Assets	NA	16.7	21.4	27.8	19.6	11.9	4.4	NM	NM	10.8
% Ret. on Equity	NA	25.2	33.5	46.4	36.4	23.0	8.4	NM	NM	21.4

Data as orig. reptd.; bef. results of disc. opers. and/or spec. items. Per share data adj. for stk. divs. as of ex-div. date. Bold denotes diluted EPS (FASB 128). E-Estimated. NA-Not Available. NM-Not Meaningful. NR-Not Ranked.

Office—JLG Drive, McConnellsburg, PA 17233. **Tel**—(717) 485-5161. **Website**—http://www.jlg.com **Chrmn, Pres & CEO**—L. D. Black. **EVP, CFO & Investor Contact**—Charles H. Diller Jr. **Dirs**—L. D. Black, C. H. Diller Jr., G. R. Kempton, J. A. Mezera, G. Palmer, S. Rabinowitz, T. C. Wajnert, C. O. Wood III. **Transfer Agent**—ChaseMellon Shareholder Services, Ridgefield Park, NJ. **Incorporated**—in Pennsylvania in 1969. **Empl**— 2,686. **S&P Analyst:** John A. Massey

STANDARD
&POOR'S
STOCK REPORTS

Jo-Ann Stores

NYSE Symbol **JAS.A**

In S&P SmallCap 600

23-OCT-99

Industry:
Retail (Specialty)

Summary: This leading U.S. fabric and craft retailer operates over 1,000 stores under the names Jo-Ann Fabrics and Crafts and Jo-Ann etc.

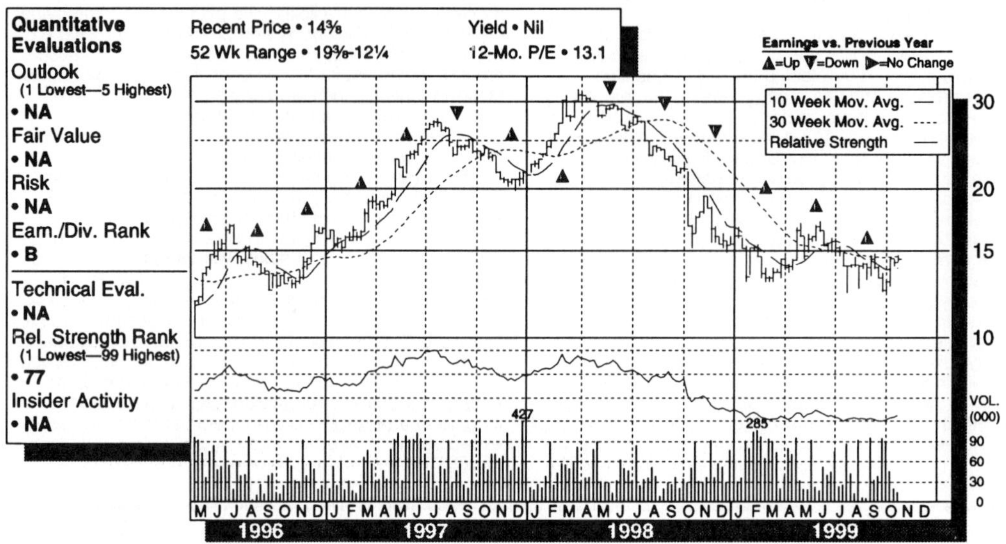

Business Profile - 14-OCT-99

In the second half of FY 00 (Jan.), Jo-Ann Stores planned to open 13 new superstores and 5 traditional stores and to relocate 9 traditional stores. The superstores, which average 46,900 square feet, are believed by management to be the future growth vehicle for the company. Management noted that its strategy of bringing seasonal products to its distribution facilities and stores at an earlier point in the season leaves the company well positioned for a strong second-half performance. In the first half of FY 00, JAS.A repurchased about 1.1 million shares of common stock for a total of $14.8 million. As of July 31, 1999, the company was authorized to repurchase up to 2 million additional shares.

Operational Review - 14-OCT-99

Net sales for the 26 weeks ended July 31, 1999, rose 15%, year to year, boosted by the acquisition of House of Fabrics and a 4.6% rise in comparable store sales. Gross margins widened on improvements in point of sale margins and shrinkage. Comparisons also benefited from the absence of a $16,700,000 non-recurring charge taken in 1998 for the House of Fabrics acquisition, and after a $1,900,000 tax benefit, versus a benefit of $7,000,000, the net loss was cut to $3,200,000 ($0.17 a share), from $10,900,000 ($0.58).

Stock Performance - 22-OCT-99

In the past 30 trading days, JAS.A's shares have increased 3%, compared to a 4% fall in the S&P 500. Average trading volume for the past five days was 9,140 shares, compared with the 40-day moving average of 13,721 shares.

Key Stock Statistics

Dividend Rate/Share	Nil	Shareholders	1,700
Shs. outstg. (M)	18.0	Market cap. (B)	$0.129
Avg. daily vol. (M)	0.009	Inst. holdings	25%
Tang. Bk. Value/Share	11.43		
Beta	0.55		

Value of $10,000 invested 5 years ago: $ 15,245

Fiscal Year Ending Jan. 31

	2000	1999	1998	1997	1996	1995
Revenues (Million $)						
1Q	295.7	252.9	218.8	203.0	183.3	132.7
2Q	282.4	251.6	197.5	188.9	168.5	112.8
3Q	—	319.7	247.2	229.6	214.4	175.4
4Q	—	418.7	311.5	307.5	268.4	256.3
Yr.	—	1,243	975.0	929.0	834.6	677.3
Earnings Per Share ($)						
1Q	0.12	-0.23	0.14	0.06	0.02	-0.07
2Q	-0.30	-0.34	-0.05	0.14	-0.17	-0.28
3Q	—	0.17	0.47	0.41	0.31	0.22
4Q	—	1.08	1.07	0.87	0.75	0.75
Yr.	—	0.69	1.60	1.26	0.90	0.63

Next earnings report expected: mid November

Dividend Data

Cash dividends were omitted in 1987, after having been paid since 1969. A "poison pill" stock purchase rights plan was adopted in 1990. A two-for-one stock split was effected in August 1995.

Jo-Ann Stores, Inc.

Business Summary - 14-OCT-99

Founded as a single store in 1943, Jo-Ann Stores Inc. (JAS.A) today is the largest retailer of fabric and crafts products in the nation operating over 1,030 traditional stores in 49 states and about 30 superstores in 12 states. The company served approximately 70% of U.S. households that engaged in crafts and hobbies in the past year. JAS.A offers a large variety of competitively priced, high quality apparel, quilting and craft fabrics and sewing-related products, home decorating fabrics, floral, craft and seasonal products, educational classes and custom services. JAS.A has approximately a 20% market share in the consolidated fabric and sewing-related products segment and about a 4% market share in the highly fragmented craft products segment.

The company's preferred mailing list includes more than 4 million customers, and management believes that there are many loyal customers who visit its stores at least every two weeks. In addition, the company's website, www.joann.com, is accessed about 100,000 times per month. Management believes that customers visit the website to obtain information on the company's products, classes and services and to communicate with other sewing and craft enthusiasts.

The company's stores mainly serve small and middle markets, and the recently developed superstores serve selected markets where store performance and area demographics are favorable. The traditional stores average 13,700 square feet, and management believes that many of these stores are located in markets that are currently underserved. Over the past five years, the company has strategically relocated certain traditional stores, increasing average square footage per store by 20% and sales per square foot by 11%. As a result, net sales per traditional store have increased 33% to $1.2 million over this period.

In November 1995, JAS.A opened its first large format "category killer" superstore which offers a more comprehensive product assortment and higher-margin custom services including framing, home decoration, and furniture and floral design. These superstores average 46,900 square feet and in FY 99 generated about five times more revenue and 40% higher sales per square foot than the traditional stores. Management believes that these superstores, which accounted for approximately 7% of FY 99 net sales, will be the vehicle for future growth.

Historically, the company has grown and increased market share mainly through existing store growth, new store openings and strategic acquisitions. In April 1998, the company acquired House of Fabrics, a chain of 261 fabric and craft stores primarily located on the West Coast. By September 1998, JAS.A successfully integrated, remerchandised and rebranded these stores.

Per Share Data ($) (Year Ended Jan. 31)	1999	1998	1997	1996	1995	1994	1993	1992	1991	1990
Tangible Bk. Val.	13.25	14.43	12.54	10.37	8.53	8.19	8.00	7.67	5.16	4.50
Cash Flow	2.08	2.61	2.45	1.87	1.31	0.96	0.73	1.27	1.03	0.86
Earnings	0.69	1.60	1.30	0.91	0.63	0.38	0.27	0.95	0.71	0.56
Dividends	Nil	Nil	Nil	Nil	Nil	Nil	Nil	Nil	Nil	Nil
Payout Ratio	Nil	Nil	Nil	Nil	Nil	Nil	Nil	Nil	Nil	Nil
Cal. Yrs.	1998	1997	1996	1995	1994	1993	1992	1991	1990	1989
Prices - High	31 7/8	27 3/4	17	16 1/8	9 3/8	9 5/8	23 5/8	23	8 5/8	4 7/8
- Low	14 7/8	14 7/8	9 7/8	7 7/8	5 7/8	6 1/4	5	7 1/2	4 5/8	3 5/8
P/E Ratio - High	46	17	13	18	15	26	88	24	12	9
- Low	22	9	8	9	9	17	19	8	6	6
Income Statement Analysis (Million $)										
Revs.	1,243	975	929	835	677	582	574	469	386	333
Oper. Inc.	87.7	78.7	71.6	58.4	40.3	27.6	22.8	36.7	26.9	23.0
Depr.	27.7	21.7	21.5	18.5	12.8	10.9	9.0	6.0	5.0	4.6
Int. Exp.	12.5	5.9	10.7	12.0	8.4	5.5	5.5	3.4	5.1	4.6
Pretax Inc.	22.4	51.2	39.4	27.9	19.1	11.1	8.3	27.4	18.0	14.1
Eff. Tax Rate	39%	38%	38%	38%	39%	38%	38%	36%	38%	38%
Net Inc.	13.6	32.0	24.6	17.5	11.7	7.0	5.2	17.5	11.2	8.8
Balance Sheet & Other Fin. Data (Million $)										
Cash	20.4	14.8	12.6	11.6	21.9	7.7	6.6	8.6	5.2	5.0
Curr. Assets	490	322	318	361	326	246	242	221	166	129
Total Assets	701	448	429	480	427	337	352	286	205	158
Curr. Liab.	209	165	141	129	127	76.6	93.6	99	72.2	58.3
LT Debt	183	24.7	72.0	155	127	103	104	40.1	52.1	28.6
Common Eqty.	259	241	199	181	162	149	148	143	77.0	68.2
Total Cap.	467	280	285	349	299	260	258	186	132	99
Cap. Exp.	75.1	36.6	13.2	34.7	11.7	8.5	32.3	19.7	15.9	9.8
Cash Flow	41.3	53.7	46.1	35.9	24.5	17.9	14.1	23.5	16.3	13.3
Curr. Ratio	2.3	2.0	2.3	2.8	2.6	3.2	2.6	2.2	2.3	2.2
% LT Debt of Cap.	39.1	8.8	25.3	44.5	42.5	39.4	40.4	21.5	39.3	28.8
% Net Inc.of Revs.	1.1	3.3	2.7	2.1	1.7	1.2	0.9	3.7	2.9	2.6
% Ret. on Assets	2.4	7.3	5.5	3.9	3.1	2.0	1.6	6.5	6.2	6.0
% Ret. on Equity	5.4	14.5	13.0	10.2	7.5	4.7	3.6	14.7	15.6	13.7

Data as orig reptd.; bef. results of disc opers/spec. items. Per share data adj. for stk. divs. Bold denotes diluted EPS (FASB 128)-prior periods restated. E-Estimated. NA-Not Available. NM-Not Meaningful. NR-Not Ranked.

Office—5555 Darrow Rd., Hudson, OH 44236. **Tel**—(216) 656-2600. **Website**—http://www.joann.com **Chrmn, Pres, CEO**—Alan Rosskamm. **EVP, CFO & Investor Contact**—Brian Carney. **SVP & Secy**—Betty Rosskamm. **Dirs**—S. S. Cowen, I. Gumberg, F. Newman, A. Rosskamm, B. Rosskamm, G. Searle, D. Walker, A. Zimmerman. **Transfer Agent & Registrar**—Harris Trust and Savings Bank, Chicago. **Incorporated**—in Ohio in 1951. **Empl**— 22,000. **S&P Analyst:** Matthew C. Hershberg

JONES PHARMA

Nasdaq Symbol **JMED**

In S&P SmallCap 600

09-OCT-99 **Industry:** Health Care (Drugs - Generic & Other)

Summary: This company offers a line of niche-oriented, specialty prescription pharmaceuticals.

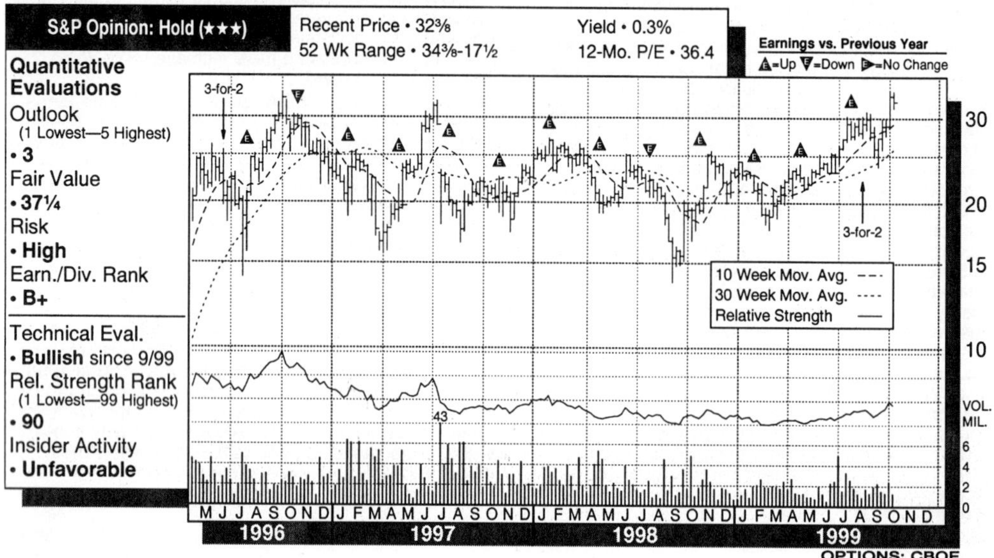

OPTIONS: CBOE

Overview - 16-AUG-99

Sales in 1999 are expected to advance about 25% from 1998's $103 million, boosted by exceptionally strong sales of critical care products and modest gains in the endocrine and veterinary product lines. Critical product sales are benefiting from the renegotiation of most hospital buying group contracts in the first quarter, which significantly reduced sales discounts on Thrombin-JMI topical hemostatic agent (sales of this product doubled in the first half). JMED is also increasing its share of the thyroid market, aided by higher sales of Levoxyl, Tapazole and Cytomel. Cytomel is benefiting from increased usage as an aid in enhancing the effectiveness of antidepressants. Margins should rise on the better volume, higher Thrombin-JMI prices and cost efficiencies. EPS are projected at $1.03, with further progress to $1.20 seen for 2000 (as adjusted for a 3-for-2 split in August 1999).

Valuation - 16-AUG-99

Despite weakness in the top-tier pharmaceutical sector, JMED shares were strong performers in recent months, buoyed by better than expected earnings in the first two quarters and prospects for improving profitability going forward. The company has chalked up a long-term record of profit growth, aided by its strategy of building a portfolio of growing products through the acquisition of under-promoted, approved products from other firms. Growth prospects are favorable for JMED's principal endocrine, critical care and veterinary drugs. The outlook for its Thombin-JMI topical hemostatic agent is especially promising, with JMED expected to become the sole supplier of this drug during the year 2000. Additional product acquisitions are expected. EPS momentum should remain strong, but JMED's relatively small size tempers the stock's overall appeal. The shares are rated a long-term hold.

Key Stock Statistics

S&P EPS Est. 1999	1.03	Tang. Bk. Value/Share	4.81
P/E on S&P Est. 1999	31.5	Beta	1.52
S&P EPS Est. 2000	1.20	Shareholders	931
Dividend Rate/Share	0.10	Market cap. (B)	$ 1.4
Shs. outstg. (M)	43.3	Inst. holdings	62%
Avg. daily vol. (M)	0.315		

Value of $10,000 invested 5 years ago: $ 83,527

Fiscal Year Ending Dec. 31

	1999	1998	1997	1996	1995	1994
Revenues (Million $)						
1Q	29.48	23.74	21.64	21.85	11.46	12.14
2Q	31.29	26.68	19.00	25.74	13.28	11.59
3Q	—	26.39	22.17	26.22	15.25	12.16
4Q	—	26.61	25.98	26.34	16.41	11.67
Yr.	—	103.4	88.78	100.2	56.40	47.55
Earnings Per Share ($)						
1Q	**0.22**	**0.17**	**0.15**	**0.05**	0.06	0.05
2Q	**0.26**	**-0.05**	**0.11**	**0.10**	0.07	0.04
3Q	**E0.27**	**0.20**	**0.15**	Nil	0.07	0.05
4Q	**E0.28**	**0.22**	**0.17**	**0.12**	0.09	0.04
Yr.	**E1.03**	**0.53**	**0.57**	**0.27**	**0.14**	**0.13**

Next earnings report expected: late October

Dividend Data (Dividends have been paid since 1989.)

Amount ($)	Date Decl.	Ex-Div. Date	Stock of Record	Payment Date
0.030	Oct. 20	Dec. 11	Dec. 15	Jan. 04 '99
0.030	Feb. 18	Mar. 17	Mar. 19	Apr. 01 '99
0.035	Jun. 01	Jun. 11	Jun. 15	Jul. 01 '99
3-for-2	Jul. 14	Aug. 09	Jul. 26	Aug. 06 '99

JONES PHARMA INCORPORATED

Business Summary - 16-AUG-99

JONES PHARMA INCORPORATED (formerly Jones Medical Industries) manufactures and distributes specialty pharmaceuticals under its own trademarks and tradenames. Approximately 60% of JMED's sales are generated from products manufactured by the company, with the remaining 40% from products manufactured for the company by third parties. In March 1998, the company's directors approved a plan to discontinue the nutritional supplements product line and contract manufacturing operations. In April 1998, the company sold its nutritional business to Twinlab Corp. for $55 million. A net gain of $17 million from the sale was recorded in 1998 second quarter results.

Since it was founded in 1981, JMED has produced a long-term record of almost uninterrupted sales and profit growth. This consistent growth has been driven by the acquisition of under-promoted, approved specialty product lines from other firms. This strategy has allowed the company to avoid the risks associated with new drug development and the lengthy and costly FDA approval process. JMED intends to leverage its existing marketing and sales capabilities through additional strategic acquisitions of complementary products and businesses, by expanding and increasing the market share for current products, and by new product introductions.

Endocrine pharmaceuticals accounted for about 56% of the company's 1998 sales. Key products include Levoxyl, a synthetic thyroid hormone used to treat hypothyroidism; Tapazole, an anti-thyroid agent for hyperthyroidism; and Cytomel, a thyroid replacement hormone in tablet form used to treat chronic thyroid disorders; and Triostat, an injectable thyroid replacement hormone for acute thyroid disorders. The latter two drugs were purchased from SmithKline Beecham in June 1997 for $22.8 million in cash. Triostat is also being studied for use with organ transplants and cardiac procedures.

Critical care pharmaceuticals (35% of sales) represent the company's second largest product category. Principal products consist of Thrombin-JMI, a topical hemostat used to arrest bleeding during surgical procedures; and Brevital Sodium, an intravenous anesthetic agent used in both minor and major surgical procedures. The company is the only manufacturer of therapeutic thrombin in the U.S. Besides marketing the compound itself, JMED is also obligated by contract to supply thrombin to Johnson & Johnson through late 2000.

Veterinary pharmaceuticals (9% of sales) include Soloxine, used to treat hypothyroidism in pets; Tussigon for pain management and kennel cough; and Pancrezyme, an animal digestive aid.

The company maintains distribution facilities in Canton, OH, and St. Louis, MO. A plant in St. Petersburg, FL, manufactures pharmaceuticals. The company makes thrombin products for itself and for Johnson & Johnson at a plant in Middleton, WI.

Per Share Data ($) (Year Ended Dec. 31)	1998	1997	1996	1995	1994	1993	1992	1991	1990	1989
Tangible Bk. Val.	3.85	2.38	2.16	0.53	0.60	0.31	0.52	0.35	0.42	0.00
Cash Flow	0.66	0.71	0.53	0.36	0.25	0.25	0.16	0.14	0.14	0.09
Earnings	0.53	0.57	0.43	0.28	0.18	0.19	0.12	0.11	0.11	0.07
Dividends	0.07	0.06	0.05	0.03	0.03	0.03	0.02	0.02	0.01	0.01
Payout Ratio	14%	12%	12%	11%	17%	14%	19%	16%	13%	17%
Prices - High	27 1/4	32 1/2	33 5/8	7 3/8	4 5/8	5 1/8	2 7/8	3 3/4	2 1/4	1 5/8
- Low	13 5/8	15 3/4	6 7/8	1 7/8	1 7/8	1 1/2	1 3/4	1 1/2	1 5/16	11/16
P/E Ratio - High	51	57	78	26	26	27	24	35	21	24
- Low	26	28	16	7	11	8	15	14	13	10
Income Statement Analysis (Million $)										
Revs.	103	88.8	100	56.4	47.5	43.2	24.1	20.5	19.7	13.3
Oper. Inc.	56.0	44.2	38.4	17.7	11.6	11.8	6.7	5.7	5.6	3.6
Depr.	5.6	6.1	4.0	2.4	2.2	1.8	1.3	0.9	0.8	0.6
Int. Exp.	0.2	0.2	0.6	0.5	0.5	0.3	0.1	0.3	0.4	0.4
Pretax Inc.	44.8	40.4	30.4	14.9	9.0	9.9	6.0	5.2	4.8	2.7
Eff. Tax Rate	47%	38%	40%	38%	37%	38%	38%	36%	41%	41%
Net Inc.	23.6	25.0	18.1	9.3	5.7	6.2	3.7	3.3	2.8	1.6
Balance Sheet & Other Fin. Data (Million $)										
Cash	123	49.9	52.2	5.4	7.2	2.3	11.8	11.1	9.5	1.3
Curr. Assets	154	85.1	81.0	25.0	20.8	18.3	19.8	18.0	15.4	5.3
Total Assets	249	204	177	74.7	54.9	51.8	35.2	33.4	26.2	16.4
Curr. Liab.	11.7	6.6	10.0	11.6	5.8	6.3	3.8	3.3	4.6	3.3
LT Debt	Nil	Nil	Nil	9.1	3.8	5.4	0.5	2.7	1.5	4.4
Common Eqty.	233	192	162	49.9	39.2	31.2	24.7	20.0	19.9	8.3
Total Cap.	237	198	167	63.1	49.1	45.5	31.4	30.1	21.5	13.1
Cap. Exp.	2.3	5.6	7.4	4.7	3.2	5.0	0.6	0.2	0.4	0.2
Cash Flow	29.2	31.2	22.1	11.7	7.9	8.0	5.0	4.2	3.6	2.2
Curr. Ratio	13.1	12.9	8.1	2.2	3.6	2.9	5.2	5.5	3.3	1.6
% LT Debt of Cap.	Nil	Nil	Nil	14.4	7.7	11.9	1.6	9.1	7.0	33.9
% Net Inc.of Revs.	22.8	28.2	18.1	16.5	12.1	14.4	15.5	16.1	14.4	12.0
% Ret. on Assets	10.4	13.1	13.8	14.4	10.6	14.2	10.8	11.0	12.2	11.9
% Ret. on Equity	11.1	14.2	167.0	20.9	16.0	21.9	16.4	16.2	18.8	20.9

Data as orig reptd.; bef. results of disc opers/spec. items. Per share data adj. for stk. divs. Bold denotes diluted EPS (FASB 128)-prior periods restated. E-Estimated. NA-Not Available. NM-Not Meaningful. NR-Not Ranked.

Office—1945 Craig Rd., St. Louis, MO 63146. **Tel**—(314) 576-6100. **Chrmn, Pres & CEO**—D. M. Jones. **EVP, Treas & Secy**—J. A. Jones. **Dirs**—M. T. Bramblett, E. A. Chod, G. A. Franz, D. M. Jones, J. A. Jones, S. L. Lopata, D. A. McLaughlin, T. F. Patton, L. J. Polite Jr. **Transfer Agent**—Mark Twain Bank, St. Louis. **Incorporated**—in Delaware in 1981. **Empl**— 562. **S&P Analyst:** Herman Saftlas

STANDARD & POOR'S
STOCK REPORTS

JSB Financial

NYSE Symbol **JSB**
In S&P SmallCap 600

09-OCT-99

Industry:
Savings & Loan Companies

Summary: JSB is the holding company for the $1.62 billion-asset Jamaica Savings Bank, which conducts business from 13 offices located mainly in the New York City borough of Queens.

Quantitative Evaluations

Outlook
(1 Lowest—5 Highest)
• **NA**

Fair Value
• **NA**

Risk
• **Low**

Earn./Div. Rank
• **NR**

Technical Eval.
• **Bullish** since 9/99

Rel. Strength Rank
(1 Lowest—99 Highest)
• **83**

Insider Activity
• **NA**

Recent Price • 59⅝
52 Wk Range • 59⅝-46⅛
Yield • 3.0%
12-Mo. P/E • 16.2

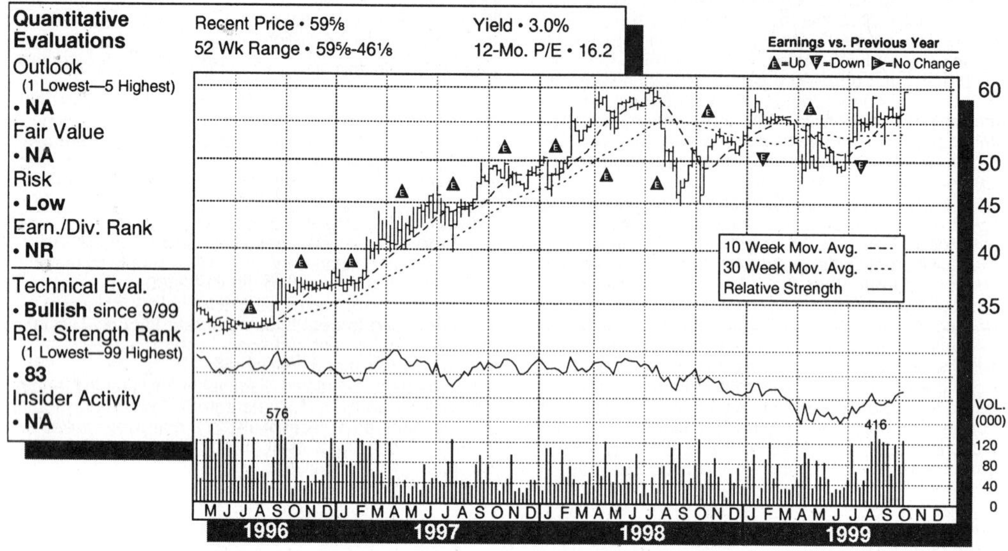

Business Profile - 06-MAY-99

In April 1999, JSB noted that by increasing emphasis on mortgage loans while reducing its investment securities portfolio, the bank, to some extent, avoided declines in net interest margin and interest rate spread during 1998 that were experienced by many of its peers. However, during the first quarter of 1999, these measures began to decline. Given the present interest rate environment, the bank expects that its net interest margin and interest rate spread could decline further, as funds from asset maturities and loan prepayments continue to be reinvested at lower market rates. The dividend was boosted 13% with the February 1999 payment.

Operational Review - 06-MAY-99

Net interest income in the three months ended March 31, 1999, rose 2.8%, year to year. The provision for possible loan losses fell 50%, and noninterest income increased to $1,979,000, from $1,656,000. With a 6.5% rise in noninterest expense, the gain in pretax income was held to 3.1%. After taxes at 42.5%, versus 39.2%, net income slipped 2.4%, to $7,479,000 ($0.78 a share, on 5.8% fewer shares), from $7,664,000 ($0.75).

Stock Performance - 08-OCT-99

In the past 30 trading days, JSB's shares have increased 7%, compared to a 0.91% fall in the S&P 500. Average trading volume for the past five days was 39,040 shares, compared with the 40-day moving average of 35,767 shares.

Key Stock Statistics

Dividend Rate/Share	1.80	Shareholders	2,143
Shs. outstg. (M)	9.3	Market cap. (B)	$0.554
Avg. daily vol. (M)	0.023	Inst. holdings	32%
Tang. Bk. Value/Share	40.43		
Beta	0.44		

Value of $10,000 invested 5 years ago: $ 30,593

Fiscal Year Ending Dec. 31

	1999	1998	1997	1996	1995	1994
Revenues (Million $)						
1Q	29.65	29.05	27.79	28.12	27.53	25.90
2Q	28.58	34.08	28.53	27.73	28.09	26.16
3Q	—	31.08	31.31	28.59	28.12	27.26
4Q	—	29.45	42.04	27.89	27.98	30.46
Yr.	—	123.7	129.7	112.7	111.7	109.8
Earnings Per Share ($)						
1Q	**0.78**	**0.75**	**0.63**	**0.56**	0.50	0.42
2Q	**0.73**	**1.49**	**0.70**	**0.64**	0.39	0.46
3Q	—	**1.13**	**0.84**	**0.65**	0.56	0.50
4Q	—	**1.03**	**1.46**	**0.72**	0.54	0.65
Yr.	—	**4.41**	**3.64**	**2.56**	**2.01**	**2.04**

Next earnings report expected: mid October

Dividend Data (Dividends have been paid since 1990.)

Amount ($)	Date Decl.	Ex-Div. Date	Stock of Record	Payment Date
0.400	Oct. 14	Nov. 02	Nov. 04	Nov. 18 '98
0.450	Jan. 06	Feb. 01	Feb. 03	Feb. 17 '99
0.450	Apr. 14	May. 03	May. 05	May. 19 '99
0.450	Jul. 21	Aug. 02	Aug. 04	Aug. 18 '99

A Division of The McGraw-Hill Companies

JSB Financial, Inc.

Business Summary - 06-MAY-99

JSB Financial, Inc. is the holding company for Jamaica Savings Bank FSB, which serves the New York City borough of Queens through 10 full service branches. The bank, which also operates one branch office in each of Manhattan and suburban Nassau (its headquarters) and Suffolk counties, NY, had assets of $1.62 billion at the end of 1998.

Founded in 1866, Jamaica Savings primarily seeks to attract deposits from the residents in the neighborhoods surrounding its branch offices and invest those deposits, together with funds generated from operations, mainly in first mortgage loans secured by real estate, CMOs, and U.S. government and agency securities. Deposits totaled $1.12 billion at the end of 1998, compared with $1.12 billion and $1.14 billion at the end of 1997 and 1996,

The bank's loan portfolio consists mainly of first mortgage loans secured by multi-family rental properties, cooperative buildings, one-to-four family residences, commercial property, and, to a lesser extent, construction loans. Other loans offered by the bank include property improvement loans, loans secured by deposit accounts, student loans, and various types of consumer loans, including auto and personal loans.

Loans receivable totaled $1.18 billion at the end of 1998, with multi-family and underlying cooperative mortgage loans comprising 61% and 26% of this total, respectively. The allowance for possible loan losses totaled $5,924,000 (0.50% of total loans) at the end of 1998, versus $5,880,000 (0.58%) a year earlier. As of December 31, 1998, the ratio of non-performing loans to total loans was 0.04%, compared with 1.32% a year earlier.

The average yield on total interest-earning assets was 7.61% in 1998 (7.51% in 1997), while the average rate paid on total interest-bearing liabilities was 3.53% (3.63%), for a net interest rate spread of 4.08% (3.88%).

During 1998, the bank continued to shift assets into fixed rate mortgage loans, which have longer maturities and produce higher yields than the short-term investments in U.S. Government and federal agency securities and CMOs they replaced. Given the combination of extended asset maturities, increased yield on assets and interest rate risk, along with the deposit trend, management decided that some degree of leveraging would be beneficial. In December 1998, the bank took a $50.0 million fixed rate advance from the Federal Home Loan Bank of New York with a balloon payment due in 10 years. By lengthening the maturity of a portion of the bank's funding liabilities at a relatively low long-term fixed rate, management believes the bank's exposure to interest rate risk is mitigated.

Per Share Data ($) (Year Ended Dec. 31)	1998	1997	1996	1995	1994	1993	1992	1991	1990	1989
Tangible Bk. Val.	40.24	37.05	34.27	32.38	30.67	27.87	25.56	23.33	21.96	NA
Earnings	4.41	3.64	2.54	1.99	2.02	1.57	1.89	1.00	0.43	NA
Dividends	1.60	1.40	1.20	1.00	0.72	0.60	0.52	0.44	0.20	NA
Payout Ratio	36%	38%	47%	50%	36%	38%	28%	44%	47%	NA
Prices - High	60	50⅝	38⅜	34¼	27½	26⅞	21⅛	19⅞	13⅝	NA
- Low	44¾	36	31½	23¾	22	20⅞	16⅛	12	10	NA
P/E Ratio - High	14	14	15	17	14	17	11	20	32	NA
- Low	10	10	12	12	11	13	9	12	23	NA
Income Statement Analysis (Million $)										
Net Int. Inc.	72.3	67.9	67.4	67.0	66.4	68.5	76.5	62.1	48.7	39.6
Loan Loss Prov.	0.1	0.6	0.6	0.6	0.6	0.6	0.6	1.7	0.6	1.0
Non Int. Inc.	12.9	14.9	5.0	4.0	6.8	2.2	4.0	NA	NA	NA
Non Int. Exp.	27.5	27.4	27.6	29.6	30.9	33.7	34.7	NA	NA	NA
Pretax Inc.	57.7	61.7	46.3	38.8	41.6	36.4	45.2	30.1	21.9	26.2
Eff. Tax Rate	23%	40%	42%	43%	43%	43%	42%	49%	47%	53%
Net Inc.	44.4	37.1	26.7	22.2	23.6	20.6	26.4	15.4	11.6	12.4
% Net Int. Marg.	4.97	4.73	4.68	4.60	4.40	4.30	4.80	4.00	NA	NA
Balance Sheet & Other Fin. Data (Million $)										
Total Assets	1,622	1,535	1,516	1,545	1,565	1,636	1,698	1,675	1,628	1,458
Loans	1,170	1,000	855	768	711	668	642	598	565	486
Deposits	1,124	1,121	1,145	1,163	1,204	1,274	1,324	1,302	1,250	1,230
Capitalization:										
Debt	NA	Nil	Nil	Nil	Nil	Nil	NA	NA	NA	NA
Equity	382	368	335	340	328	325	232	330	334	NA
Total	382	368	335	340	328	325	NA	NA	NA	NA
% Ret. on Assets	2.8	2.4	1.7	1.4	1.5	1.2	1.6	0.9	0.7	0.9
% Ret. on Equity	11.8	10.6	7.9	6.6	7.2	6.2	8.1	4.6	NA	NA
% Loan Loss Resv.	0.5	0.6	0.6	0.6	0.6	0.6	NA	0.5	0.4	NM
% Risk Based Capital	24.6	21.7	20.0	21.3	NA	NA	NA	NA	NA	NA
Price Times Book Value:										
Hi	1.5	1.4	1.1	1.1	0.9	1.0	0.8	0.9	0.6	NA
Low	1.1	1.0	0.9	0.7	0.7	0.7	0.6	0.5	0.5	NA

Data as orig reptd.; bef. results of disc opers/spec. items. Per share data adj. for stk. divs. Bold denotes diluted EPS (FASB 128)-prior periods restated. E-Estimated. NA-Not Available. NM-Not Meaningful. NR-Not Ranked.

Office—303 Merrick Rd., Lynbrook, NY 11563. **Tel**—(516) 887-7000. **Website**—http://www.jsbf.com **Chrmn & CEO**—P. T. Adikes. **Pres**—E. P. Henson. **VP, CFO & Treas**—T. R. Lehmann. **Dirs**—P. T. Adikes, J. C. Cantwell, R. M. Cummins, H. J. Dirkes Jr., C. Gibbons, J. E. Gibbons Jr., E. P. Henson, A. F. Kelly, R. W. Meyer, A. B. Pritcher.**Transfer Agent & Registrar**—ChaseMellon Shareholder Services LLC, Ridgefield, NJ. **Incorporated**—in Delaware in 1990. **Empl**— 429. **S&P Analyst:** M.I.

STANDARD
&POOR'S
STOCK REPORTS

Just For Feet

Nasdaq Symbol **FEET**

In S&P SmallCap 600

09-OCT-99 **Industry:** Retail (Specialty)

Summary: This company operates retail stores that sell brand-name athletic and outdoor footwear.

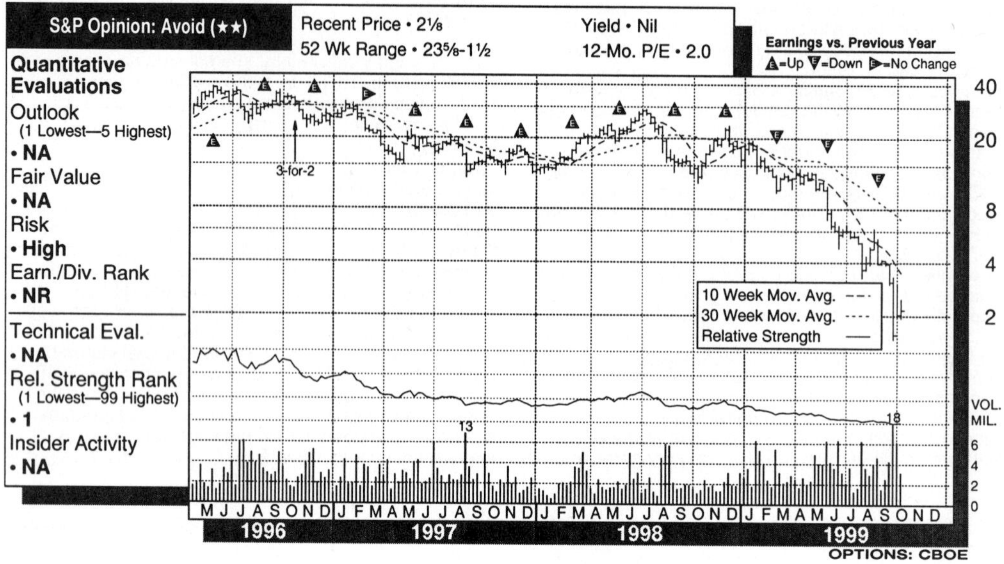

Overview - 02-SEP-99

Due to expectations of a slowdown in store expansion and continued markdown activity, we have lowered FEET's FY 00 (Jan.) sales growth projection to 21%. Suffering from an oversupply of goods, the company plans to liquidate $50 million in excess inventory by the end of October 1999. The company's cancellation of new product orders will help lower inventories but will hurt profitability. Three new superstores are planned to open in FY 00's third quarter while specialty store openings have been halted until the profitability outlook improves. We expect gross margins to narrow to about 33% of sales in FY 00, reflecting the heavy promotional activity. Higher payroll and advertising expenses, brought on by the inventory liquidation efforts, will also restrict operating margins. Due to additional borrowings, interest expense will rise significantly. With an unfavorable near to mid-term outlook, we have lowered our FY 00 EPS estimate to a loss of $2.09, from earnings of $0.60.

Valuation - 02-SEP-99

We recently downgraded our opinion of FEET to avoid from hold, reflecting the inventory problems and the challenges confronting the specialty stores. The shares are trading near their 52-week low, and well below the 1998 year end level. There have been a series of disappointing events in FY 00, with sluggish sales at the specialty stores, problems with the Sneaker Stadium conversion and an errant stock replenishment program. Management changes have been made to help resolve these problems and corrective actions have been taken. FEET has a tough road ahead with higher debt expense, weakened vendor leverage, and inroads by competitors. We believe it will be at least several quarters until the company is able to return to profitability. Thus, we recommend avoiding the stock.

Key Stock Statistics

S&P EPS Est. 2000	-2.09	Tang. Bk. Value/Share	7.46
P/E on S&P Est. 2000	NM	Beta	2.67
Dividend Rate/Share	Nil	Shareholders	15,100
Shs. outstg. (M)	31.2	Market cap. (B)	$0.067
Avg. daily vol. (M)	1.631	Inst. holdings	45%

Value of $10,000 invested 5 years ago: NA

Fiscal Year Ending Jan. 31

	2000	1999	1998	1997	1996	1995
Revenues (Million $)						
1Q	221.0	151.9	92.80	49.15	21.14	—
2Q	225.8	175.3	112.4	58.38	25.43	12.52
3Q	—	226.0	131.0	69.74	34.77	16.48
4Q	—	221.6	142.4	79.13	38.48	18.43
Yr.	—	774.9	478.6	256.4	119.8	56.36
Earnings Per Share ($)						
1Q	**0.15**	**0.19**	**0.18**	**0.11**	0.06	0.03
2Q	**-0.83**	**0.25**	**0.16**	**0.10**	0.09	0.04
3Q	**E-0.97**	**0.32**	**0.18**	**0.17**	0.11	0.06
4Q	**E-0.44**	**0.09**	**0.20**	**0.16**	0.16	0.06
Yr.	**E-2.09**	**0.84**	**0.70**	**0.55**	**0.38**	**0.18**

Next earnings report expected: late November

Dividend Data

The company has not paid any dividends on the common stock, and it does not anticipate paying cash dividends for the foreseeable future. FEET intends to retain its earnings to finance growth and development of its business.

A Division of The McGraw-Hill Companies

Just For Feet, Inc.

Business Summary - 02-SEP-99

Just For Feet is the leading operator of large format superstores specializing in brand-name athletic and outdoor footwear and apparel. The company's goal is to become the leading athletic and outdoor footwear retailer in each of its markets by offering the largest selection of brand-name shoes, superior customer service and technical sales assistance in a high-energy, entertaining store environment. As of July 31, 1999, FEET had 148 superstores in 26 states and Puerto Rico; and 211 smaller format specialty stores (including 37 franchises).

FEET's prototype superstore occupies 15,000 sq. ft. to 20,000 sq. ft., and offers approximately 2,500 to 4,500 styles of footwear, versus 200 to 700 typically offered by conventional mall-based footwear retailers, department stores and sporting goods superstores. Leading brands include Nike, Reebok, New Balance, Adidas, Fila, K-Swiss, Asics and Converse, as well as outdoor footwear brands such as Timberland and Rockport. The company seeks to carry virtually all styles in the brands it carries. The company's superstores offer shoes for practically every sport and recreational activity. The store liquidates old and slow moving inventory through its "Combat Zone", an area featuring discounted merchandise. Brand name apparel and accessories are also offered and include products such as warm-up suits, t-shirts, athletic shorts, caps, socks and shoe care products. The store layout allows the customer to locate shoes by brand or category. The stores are primarily freestanding and are typically located on outparcels of or adjacent to shopping malls.

The company tries to create an exciting, high-energy shopping experience in its superstores by using bright colors, upbeat music, an enclosed half court basketball court for use by customers, a multi-screen video bank, and appearances by sports celebrities. FEET emphasizes training and testing of its sales associates in the technology employed by manufacturers, letting it provide a higher level of customer service than that offered by most traditional footwear retailers.

Contributing to operating efficiency, vendors ship products directly to the superstores rather than a centralized distribution center. Products are warehoused in the superstores in an area behind the selling floor not visible to customers.

In July 1998 the company acquired Sneaker Stadium, a privately held athletic retailer operating 39 superstores in the Northeast and Mid-Atlantic regions. With this acquisition, FEET acquired its only likely superstore competitor and expanded into the Northeast market several years prior to plan.

FEET plans to open approximately 25 new superstores in 1999 and 2000. As of May 1999, the company decided to halt expansion of its specialty store division due to poor sales performance.

Per Share Data ($) (Year Ended Jan. 31)	1999	1998	1997	1996	1995	1994	1993	1992	1991	1990
Tangible Bk. Val.	8.16	7.64	7.56	5.55	3.01	1.38	NA	NA	NA	NA
Cash Flow	1.34	0.99	0.69	0.47	0.47	0.01	0.07	NA	NA	NA
Earnings	0.84	0.70	0.55	0.38	0.18	-0.02	0.05	-0.02	NA	NA
Dividends	Nil	Nil	Nil	Nil	Nil	Nil	Nil	Nil	NA	NA
Payout Ratio	Nil	Nil	Nil	Nil	Nil	Nil	Nil	Nil	NA	NA
Cal. Yrs.	1998	1997	1996	1995	1994	1993	1992	1991	1990	1989
Prices - High	29 1/8	32	38 1/4	24 5/8	10 3/8	NA	NA	NA	NA	NA
- Low	11 1/8	11 7/8	17 3/4	7 5/8	3 1/8	NA	NA	NA	NA	NA
P/E Ratio - High	35	46	NM	65	58	NA	NA	NA	NA	NA
- Low	13	17	NM	20	18	NA	NA	NA	NA	NA
Income Statement Analysis (Million $)										
Revs.	775	479	256	120	56.4	23.7	17.2	NA	NA	NA
Oper. Inc.	66.1	42.0	24.2	13.4	5.3	-0.2	0.9	NA	NA	NA
Depr.	16.1	8.8	4.0	2.2	0.9	0.3	0.2	NA	NA	NA
Int. Exp.	8.1	1.4	0.8	0.7	0.3	0.2	0.2	NA	NA	NA
Pretax Inc.	43.3	34.2	24.7	14.6	5.2	0.0	0.9	NA	NA	NA
Eff. Tax Rate	38%	37%	36%	33%	38%	NM	38%	NA	NA	NA
Net Inc.	26.6	21.4	16.0	9.7	3.2	-0.2	0.6	NA	NA	NA
Balance Sheet & Other Fin. Data (Million $)										
Cash	12.4	82.5	173	129	48.7	3.0	NA	NA	NA	NA
Curr. Assets	449	311	315	194	76.6	12.6	NA	NA	NA	NA
Total Assets	689	448	376	244	89.5	16.0	7.3	NA	NA	NA
Curr. Liab.	133	156	147	85.4	12.0	10.4	NA	NA	NA	NA
LT Debt	216	16.6	6.5	6.7	3.1	0.9	0.9	NA	NA	NA
Common Eqty.	326	268	219	149	73.0	1.5	0.9	NA	NA	NA
Total Cap.	544	285	226	157	77.0	4.5	1.9	NA	NA	NA
Cap. Exp.	79.0	43.4	33.7	14.2	6.0	1.9	0.7	NA	NA	NA
Cash Flow	42.8	30.2	19.9	11.9	11.9	0.1	0.7	NA	NA	NA
Curr. Ratio	3.4	2.0	2.1	2.3	6.4	1.2	NA	NA	NA	NA
% LT Debt of Cap.	39.8	5.8	2.9	4.3	4.0	20.1	48.3	NA	NA	NA
% Net Inc.of Revs.	3.4	4.5	6.2	8.1	5.7	NM	3.3	NA	NA	NA
% Ret. on Assets	4.7	5.2	5.2	5.8	6.1	NM	9.7	NA	NA	NA
% Ret. on Equity	9.0	8.8	8.7	8.8	8.6	NM	57.0	NA	NA	NA

Data as orig reptd.; bef. results of disc opers/spec. items. Per share data adj. for stk. divs. Bold denotes diluted EPS (FASB 128)-prior periods restated. E-Estimated. NA-Not Available. NM-Not Meaningful. NR-Not Ranked.

Office—7400 Cahaba Valley Rd., Birmingham, AL 35242. **Tel**—(205) 408-3000. **Website**—http://www.feet.com **Chrmn**—H. Ruttenberg. **Pres & CEO**—H. Rockey. **COO**—R. Oyster. **Treas**—B. K. Moore.**Dirs**—J. A. Berg, D. F. Bellet, E. S. Croft III, R. L. Haines, M. P. Lazarus, H. Rockey, H. Ruttenberg, W. C. Smith Jr., B. Starr Sr. **Transfer Agent**—AmSouth Bank, Birmingham. **Incorporated**—in Alabama in 1977. **Empl**— 15,000. **S&P Analyst:** Howard Choe

STANDARD
&POOR'S
STOCK REPORTS

Justin Industries

NASDAQ Symbol **JSTN**

In S&P SmallCap 600

09-OCT-99 **Industry:** Footwear

Summary: This company produces western-style footwear, face brick, concrete blocks and other building materials.

Quantitative Evaluations

Outlook
(1 Lowest—5 Highest)
• **1+**

Fair Value
• **13¾**

Risk
• **Average**

Earn./Div. Rank
• **A-**

Technical Eval.
• **Neutral** since 9/99

Rel. Strength Rank
(1 Lowest—99 Highest)
• **65**

Insider Activity
• **NA**

Recent Price • 14¼
52 Wk Range • 15⅝-9⅝
Yield • 1.4%
12-Mo. P/E • 13.4

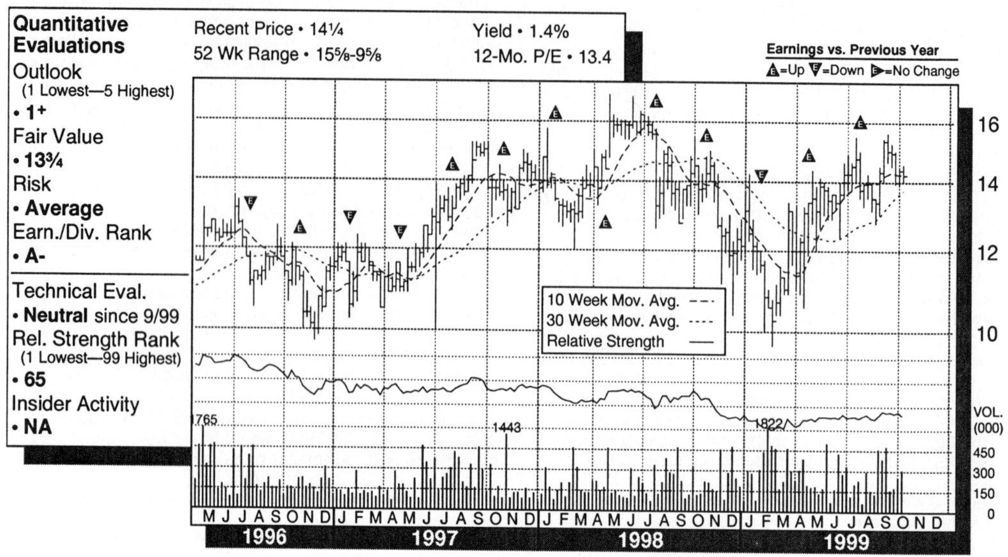

Business Profile - 20-SEP-99

In June 1999, JSTN announced that it would reorganize into two independent companies for footwear and building materials. JSTN plans to consolidate the building materials companies (Acme Brick, American Tile Supply, Featherlite Building Products, Texas Quarries, and Innovative Building Products) into one company and consolidate manufacturing, outsourcing, and administrative functions in footwear. Also in June, the company acquired Eureka Brick and Tile for approximately $7.8 million, which will add 5% to the company's production capacity. In addition, directors approved the repurchase of up to two million common shares.

Operational Review - 20-SEP-99

Net sales for the six months ended June 30, 1999, rose 7.9%, year to year, reflecting a 20% rise in building material sales, partially offset by a 4.6% decline in footwear sales. Gross margins widened, primarily due to higher unit volume and higher selling prices in the building materials division. Following slightly higher SG&A expenses (as a percentage of sales) and higher interest expense, pretax income rose 7.9%. After taxes at 36.0% versus 36.5%, net income climbed 8.7%, to $13,826,000 ($0.54 a share), from $12,719,000 ($0.48).

Stock Performance - 08-OCT-99

In the past 30 trading days, JSTN's shares have declined 0.65%, compared to a 0.91% fall in the S&P 500. Average trading volume for the past five days was 60,840 shares, compared with the 40-day moving average of 68,879 shares.

Key Stock Statistics

Dividend Rate/Share	0.20	Shareholders	1,800
Shs. outstg. (M)	25.5	Market cap. (B)	$0.362
Avg. daily vol. (M)	0.044	Inst. holdings	35%
Tang. Bk. Value/Share	11.12		
Beta	0.20		

Value of $10,000 invested 5 years ago: $ 10,475

Fiscal Year Ending Dec. 31

	1999	1998	1997	1996	1995	1994
Revenues (Million $)						
1Q	113.0	103.8	97.61	104.3	113.7	109.9
2Q	127.5	119.1	110.9	110.7	109.9	114.9
3Q	—	117.0	114.2	110.4	112.4	119.7
4Q	—	115.0	117.1	122.4	125.5	138.5
Yr.	—	454.8	439.8	447.8	461.4	483.0
Earnings Per Share ($)						
1Q	**0.22**	**0.17**	**0.12**	**0.14**	0.19	0.24
2Q	**0.32**	**0.31**	**0.28**	**0.21**	0.22	0.34
3Q	—	**0.30**	**0.27**	**0.22**	0.21	0.34
4Q	—	**0.22**	**0.32**	**0.30**	0.32	0.41
Yr.	—	**1.00**	**0.99**	**0.87**	**0.94**	**1.34**

Next earnings report expected: mid October

Dividend Data (Dividends have been paid since 1984.)

Amount ($)	Date Decl.	Ex-Div. Date	Stock of Record	Payment Date
0.050	Dec. 17	Dec. 23	Dec. 28	Jan. 05 '99
0.050	Mar. 15	Mar. 25	Mar. 29	Apr. 07 '99
0.050	Jun. 17	Jun. 24	Jun. 28	Jul. 07 '99
0.050	Sep. 16	Sep. 23	Sep. 27	Oct. 06 '99

A Division of The McGraw-Hill Companies

Justin Industries, Inc.

Business Summary - 20-SEP-99

Justin Industries, Inc., which traces its history to a company that began making boots in 1879, today operates two principal business segments: building materials (which accounted for 64% of 1998 revenue) and western-style footwear (36%).

Building materials include clay brick (primarily face brick) manufactured by Acme Brick Co. for use in residential and commercial construction; concrete building block sold under the trade name Featherlite Building Products Corp.; and cut limestone manufactured under the name Texas Quarries. The company also represents other manufacturers as a distributor of clay brick, glass block, glazed and unglazed tile and masonry units, fireplace equipment and masonry tools and related items.

Clay and shale mined from company-owned or leased properties are the principal raw materials for the building materials business. JSTN believes it has built up adequate clay reserves to supply its needs for the foreseeable future.

In the footwear segment, Justin designs, manufactures and distributes men's, women's and children's western-style safety, work and sports boots and shoes. Footwear products, made by Justin Boot Co., Nocona Boot Co. and Tony Lama Co., are sold primarily in the U.S. under the trade names Justin, Chippewa, Nocona, Tony Lama, and Sport Lace-R.

The company owns and operates footwear manufacturing plants in Texas and Missouri. Footwear products are marketed by company salesmen and independent sales representatives to a network of 6,500 retail outlets and dealers.

Justin also operates Northland Publishing Co., which publishes books about the history and art of the West. Many of the company's books have won awards in major book competitions including the Western Heritage Awards at the National Cowboy Hall of Fame.

In 1998, a strong regional economy boosted residential construction rates, giving most of JSTN's building materials businesses a sales lift. Those operations that did not perform well were American Tile Supply Co. and Tradewinds Technologies, Inc. (which was sold in the fourth quarter of 1998). The company believes that its footwear division continues to face many challenges. Demand for cowboy boots has waned, industry consolidation has put pressure on pricing and the company experienced some operational problems in 1998.

In June 1999, the company announced its plan to separate the company into two independent companies representing footwear and building materials. JSTN announced in July 1999 that it would consolidate the building materials companies (Acme Brick, American Tile Supply, Featherlite Building Products, Texas Quarries, and Innovative Building Products) into one company and consolidate manufacturing, outsourcing, and administrative functions in footwear. Also in June, the company acquired Eureka Brick and Tile for approximately $7.8 million, which will add 5% to production capacity.

Per Share Data ($) (Year Ended Dec. 31)	1998	1997	1996	1995	1994	1993	1992	1991	1990	1989
Tangible Bk. Val.	11.12	9.76	9.01	8.32	8.15	6.95	5.75	4.92	4.30	4.15
Cash Flow	1.70	1.65	1.47	1.47	1.83	1.77	1.48	0.81	0.69	0.69
Earnings	1.00	0.99	0.87	0.94	1.33	1.29	0.98	0.32	0.28	0.28
Dividends	0.20	0.18	0.16	0.16	0.16	0.16	0.14	0.13	0.13	0.10
Payout Ratio	20%	18%	18%	17%	12%	12%	14%	41%	47%	36%
Prices - High	17	15¼	13½	12⅛	16¾	25⅜	19	6⅛	6	5⅝
- Low	10⅜	10	9¾	9½	9¾	11¾	5⅝	3⅝	3¾	3⅛
P/E Ratio - High	17	15	16	13	13	20	19	19	21	20
- Low	10	10	11	10	7	9	6	11	13	11

Income Statement Analysis (Million $)	1998	1997	1996	1995	1994	1993	1992	1991	1990	1989
Revs.	455	440	448	461	483	475	453	368	315	278
Oper. Inc.	61.7	60.2	56.3	60.0	75.4	73.5	61.4	36.0	28.2	26.8
Depr.	18.8	17.7	16.3	14.7	13.9	13.5	13.8	12.8	10.7	10.5
Int. Exp.	1.8	1.8	3.4	5.0	4.1	4.0	5.2	9.5	6.6	6.0
Pretax Inc.	41.1	40.7	36.6	40.2	57.5	56.0	42.4	13.7	10.9	10.7
Eff. Tax Rate	35%	35%	36%	36%	36%	36%	36%	38%	33%	33%
Net Inc.	26.5	26.3	23.4	25.7	36.9	36.0	27.1	8.5	7.3	7.2

Balance Sheet & Other Fin. Data (Million $)	1998	1997	1996	1995	1994	1993	1992	1991	1990	1989
Cash	5.1	5.1	3.2	2.2	6.1	10.6	2.4	4.1	1.5	3.3
Curr. Assets	231	230	226	251	260	240	224	201	199	137
Total Assets	397	376	360	376	375	347	316	296	293	211
Curr. Liab.	55.5	63.9	60.9	69.2	73.8	54.9	54.1	44.9	47.9	38.9
LT Debt	30.8	23.8	32.9	57.1	65.0	89.0	100	116	125	56.0
Common Eqty.	293	273	253	236	222	189	155	128	111	106
Total Cap.	341	312	299	307	301	292	262	251	245	172
Cap. Exp.	NA	21.8	24.7	26.0	18.6	17.3	12.0	11.0	13.2	9.0
Cash Flow	45.4	44.0	39.7	40.3	50.8	49.5	40.9	21.3	18.0	17.7
Curr. Ratio	4.2	3.6	3.7	3.6	3.5	4.4	4.1	4.5	4.1	3.5
% LT Debt of Cap.	9.0	7.6	11.0	18.6	21.7	30.3	38.3	46.2	50.9	32.6
% Net Inc.of Revs.	5.8	6.0	5.2	5.5	7.6	7.6	6.0	2.3	2.3	2.6
% Ret. on Assets	6.9	7.2	6.3	6.8	10.2	10.8	8.7	2.9	2.9	3.3
% Ret. on Equity	9.4	10.0	9.5	11.2	17.9	20.9	18.8	7.1	6.7	6.9

Data as orig reptd.; bef. results of disc opers/spec. items. Per share data adj. for stk. divs. Bold denotes diluted EPS (FASB 128)-prior periods restated. E-Estimated. NA-Not Available. NM-Not Meaningful. NR-Not Ranked.

Office—2821 W. 7th St., P.O. Box 425, Fort Worth, TX 76107. **Tel**—(817) 336-5125. **Website**—http://www.justinind.com **Chrmn**—J. V. Roach. **Pres & CEO**—J. T. Dickenson. **SVP, CFO, Secy & Investor Contact**—Richard J. Savitz (817-390-2412). **Dirs**—J. T. Dickenson, M. Gearhart, R. E. Glaze, J. S. Justin, D. J. Kelly, J. R. Musolino, J. V. Roach, W. E. Tucker. **Transfer Agent**—Bank of New York, NYC. **Incorporated**—in Texas in 1916. **Empl**— 4,066. **S&P Analyst:** Howard Choe

STANDARD
&POOR'S
STOCK REPORTS

K-Swiss Inc.

NASDAQ Symbol **KSWS**

In S&P SmallCap 600

09-OCT-99 **Industry:** Footwear

Summary: KSWS designs, develops and markets high-performance and casual athletic footwear.

Quantitative Evaluations

Outlook
(1 Lowest—5 Highest)
• 3⁻

Fair Value
• 34

Risk
• Average

Earn./Div. Rank
• B

Technical Eval.
• Bearish since 9/99

Rel. Strength Rank
(1 Lowest—99 Highest)
• 1

Insider Activity
• Neutral

Recent Price • 17
52 Wk Range • 59¾-10
Yield • 0.4%
12-Mo. P/E • 7.3

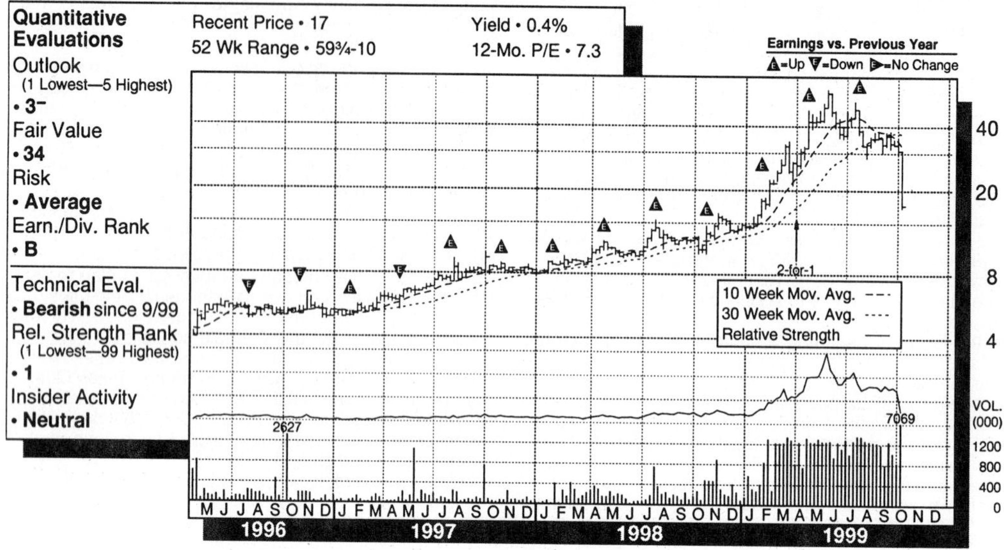

Business Profile - 10-SEP-99

K-Swiss' primary operating strategy is to design products with longer life cycles and introduce fewer new models than the competition. The company continues to focus the majority of advertising and promotion on tennis, where it is attempting to take advantage of high brand awareness. In late July 1999, K-Swiss said that domestic orders with start ship dates from July through December 1999 increased 111.5% to $115.3 million at June 30, 1999, from $54.5 million a year earlier. International orders with start ship dates from July through December 1999 increased 22% to $6.5 million from $5.3 million. A two-for-one stock split in March 1999 was accompanied by a 50% dividend hike. Biltrite Corp. holds almost 10% of KSWS shares outstanding.

Operational Review - 10-SEP-99

Revenues for the first half of 1999 soared 87%, year to year, reflecting an increase in the volume of footwear sold andhigher average wholesale prices per pair. Results benefited from a more favorable geographic and product mix and efficiencies in sourcing operations (attributed to increased contract manufacturing volume). Operating profit more than tripled. Following lower interest income (net) and taxes at 39.8%, versus 39.9%, net income advanced to $20.0 million ($1.75 a share) from $5.8 million ($0.51).

Stock Performance - 08-OCT-99

In the past 30 trading days, KSWS's shares have declined 52%, compared to a 0.91% fall in the S&P 500. Average trading volume for the past five days was 1,413,840 shares, compared with the 40-day moving average of 391,151 shares.

Key Stock Statistics

Dividend Rate/Share	0.06	Shareholders	1,350
Shs. outstg. (M)	11.3	Market cap. (B)	$0.140
Avg. daily vol. (M)	0.524	Inst. holdings	62%
Tang. Bk. Value/Share	7.34		
Beta	0.49		

Value of $10,000 invested 5 years ago: $ 15,225

Fiscal Year Ending Dec. 31

	1999	1998	1997	1996	1995	1994
Revenues (Million $)						
1Q	88.58	42.27	31.20	34.37	42.76	45.55
2Q	67.17	41.02	28.42	26.02	29.73	36.27
3Q	—	38.21	32.84	28.78	29.36	48.74
4Q	—	40.04	23.76	17.67	18.40	24.38
Yr.	—	161.5	116.2	106.8	120.3	154.9
Earnings Per Share ($)						
1Q	**1.15**	**0.31**	**0.13**	**0.16**	0.30	0.34
2Q	**0.58**	**0.20**	**-0.03**	**-0.06**	0.12	0.26
3Q	—	**0.27**	**0.14**	**0.02**	0.08	0.39
4Q	—	**0.33**	**0.11**	**-0.08**	-0.35	0.11
Yr.	—	**1.10**	**0.35**	**0.06**	**0.14**	**1.10**

Next earnings report expected: late October

Dividend Data (Dividends have been paid since 1994.)

Amount ($)	Date Decl.	Ex-Div. Date	Stock of Record	Payment Date
0.015	Feb. 08	Mar. 29	Mar. 31	Apr. 15 '99
2-for-1	Feb. 08	Mar. 29	Mar. 15	Mar. 26 '99
0.015	Jun. 02	Jun. 28	Jun. 30	Jul. 15 '99
0.015	Sep. 02	Sep. 28	Sep. 30	Oct. 15 '99

K-Swiss Inc.

Business Summary - 10-SEP-99

Tennis enthusiasts quickly recognize the name K-Swiss. As a company, KSWS develops and markets a growing array of athletic footwear for high-performance sports use and fitness activities. It was founded in 1966 by two Swiss brothers, who introduced one of the first leather tennis shoes in the U.S. The company was acquired on December 30, 1986, in a leveraged transaction by an investment group led by the current chairman and president. Subsequently, several new footwear products were introduced, and manufacturing was shifted to independent suppliers primarily in China and Indonesia.

Revenues were derived as follows in 1998: classic 61%, children's 22%, tennis/court shoes 13%, and other 4%.

K-Swiss derives the bulk of sales from its Classic leather tennis shoes. The Classic, little changed from its original design, has become popular as a casual shoe for men and women, while continuing to sell well as a tennis shoe. In recent years, the company has developed new product categories whose initial styles were extensions of the Classic. It believes that the use of classic styling reduces the effect of changes in consumer preferences.

Men's footwear accounted for 38% of revenues in 1998 (42% in 1997), while women's footwear accounted for 36% in each of 1998 and 1997.

The company sells a line of apparel and accessories manufactured by third parties. The line consists of warm-ups, skirts, shorts and shirts, fleece tops and pants, T-shirts, caps, denim shorts, bags and socks. All apparel and accessories carry the K-Swiss logo and name.

K-Swiss sells its products in the U.S. through independent sales representatives, primarily to specialty athletic footwear stores, pro shops, sporting goods stores and upscale department stores. It also sells to a number of foreign distributors. By the end of 1998, the company was working through four foreign divisions and 28 distributors to market its products in 54 countries. The Foot Locker group of stores accounted for 26% of total revenues in 1998 (17% in 1997).

Domestic backlog at December 31, 1998, was up 134%, to $131 million, up from $56 million a year earlier; international backlog was $9.0 million, up from $8.5 million.

In 1998, the company launched its largest television campaign. KSWS believes its strategy of designing products with longer life cycles and introducing fewer new models than its competition enhances the effectiveness of its advertising and promotions.

Per Share Data ($) (Year Ended Dec. 31)	1998	1997	1996	1995	1994	1993	1992	1991	1990	1989
Tangible Bk. Val.	7.34	6.36	6.13	6.00	5.88	4.75	3.70	3.00	2.32	0.45
Cash Flow	0.59	0.43	0.15	0.23	1.20	1.03	0.84	0.76	0.67	0.53
Earnings	1.10	0.35	0.06	0.14	1.10	0.94	0.74	0.67	0.61	0.46
Dividends	0.04	0.04	0.04	0.04	0.04	Nil	Nil	Nil	Nil	Nil
Payout Ratio	4%	11%	73%	29%	4%	Nil	Nil	Nil	Nil	Nil
Prices - High	15⅝	10	6½	10½	12⅞	13⅝	12⅜	14½	15⅛	NA
- Low	8	5	3⅞	4⅞	9⅛	9⅛	7⅛	5⅝	5¼	NA
P/E Ratio - High	14	28	NM	75	12	15	17	22	25	NA
- Low	7	14	NM	35	8	10	10	8	9	NA
Income Statement Analysis (Million $)										
Revs.	162	116	107	120	155	150	128	119	98.0	69.0
Oper. Inc.	20.3	6.3	2.3	7.6	25.8	21.1	18.1	17.9	17.0	12.5
Depr.	0.9	0.9	1.2	1.2	1.2	1.3	1.3	1.1	0.7	0.7
Int. Exp.	0.2	NA	NA	NA	NA	0.4	2.0	2.9	3.7	3.6
Pretax Inc.	21.2	7.2	2.6	7.2	24.8	19.4	14.8	13.9	12.6	8.2
Eff. Tax Rate	41%	42%	72%	74%	40%	36%	34%	37%	42%	42%
Net Inc.	12.5	4.2	0.7	1.9	14.9	12.5	9.8	8.8	7.2	4.8
Balance Sheet & Other Fin. Data (Million $)										
Cash	37.4	36.1	34.3	31.4	15.8	14.4	10.6	1.1	0.1	0.6
Curr. Assets	102	91.5	90.5	92.8	90.1	75.7	68.3	54.8	57.7	43.9
Total Assets	115	102	100	102	100	86.9	80.2	67.1	68.5	52.7
Curr. Liab.	18.7	16.0	11.2	9.6	12.9	15.1	23.2	10.9	17.0	26.8
LT Debt	Nil	0.1	0.2	0.5	0.5	0.6	1.4	10.9	13.8	16.3
Common Eqty.	83.3	75.9	79.6	84.1	82.8	68.0	53.7	45.0	36.1	8.5
Total Cap.	91.5	85.7	89.1	92.8	87.4	71.8	57.0	56.2	51.5	25.9
Cap. Exp.	5.7	1.6	1.0	0.4	0.7	0.8	0.7	1.6	1.0	0.4
Cash Flow	13.5	5.1	1.9	3.0	16.1	13.8	11.1	9.9	8.0	5.5
Curr. Ratio	5.5	5.7	8.1	9.7	7.0	5.0	2.9	5.0	3.4	1.6
% LT Debt of Cap.	Nil	0.2	0.2	0.5	0.6	0.9	2.5	19.5	26.7	63.0
% Net Inc.of Revs.	7.8	3.6	0.7	1.5	9.6	8.4	7.7	7.4	8.0	6.9
% Ret. on Assets	11.6	4.1	0.7	1.8	15.9	14.9	13.3	13.0	9.4	11.3
% Ret. on Equity	15.8	5.4	0.9	2.2	19.7	20.4	19.8	21.7	29.0	77.3

Data as orig reptd.; bef. results of disc opers/spec. items. Per share data adj. for stk. divs. Bold denotes diluted EPS (FASB 128)-prior periods restated. E-Estimated. NA-Not Available. NM-Not Meaningful. NR-Not Ranked.

Office—31248 Oak Crest Drive, Westlake Village, CA 91361. **Tel**—(818) 706-5100. **Website**—http://www.kswiss.com **Chrmn & Pres**—S. Nichols. **VP-Fin, CFO, Secy & Investor Contact**—George Powlick. **Dirs**—L. Feldman, J. K. Layne, S. Nichols, G. Powlick, M. Wilford. **Transfer Agent & Registrar**—Bank of New York, NYC. **Incorporated**—in Delaware in 1990. **Empl**— 160. **S&P Analyst:** N.J.D.

STANDARD
&POOR'S
STOCK REPORTS

K2 Inc.

NYSE Symbol **KTO**

In S&P SmallCap 600

09-OCT-99

Industry: Leisure Time (Products)

Summary: KTO is a leading designer, manufacturer, and marketer of brand name sporting goods and recreational and industrial products.

Quantitative Evaluations

Outlook (1 Lowest—5 Highest)
• **5**

Fair Value
• **17⅜**

Risk
• **Average**

Earn./Div. Rank
• **B+**

Technical Eval.
• **Bearish** since 8/99

Rel. Strength Rank (1 Lowest—99 Highest)
• **38**

Insider Activity
• **NA**

Recent Price • 8⅝
52 Wk Range • 14¾-7¾
Yield • Nil
12-Mo. P/E • 29.7

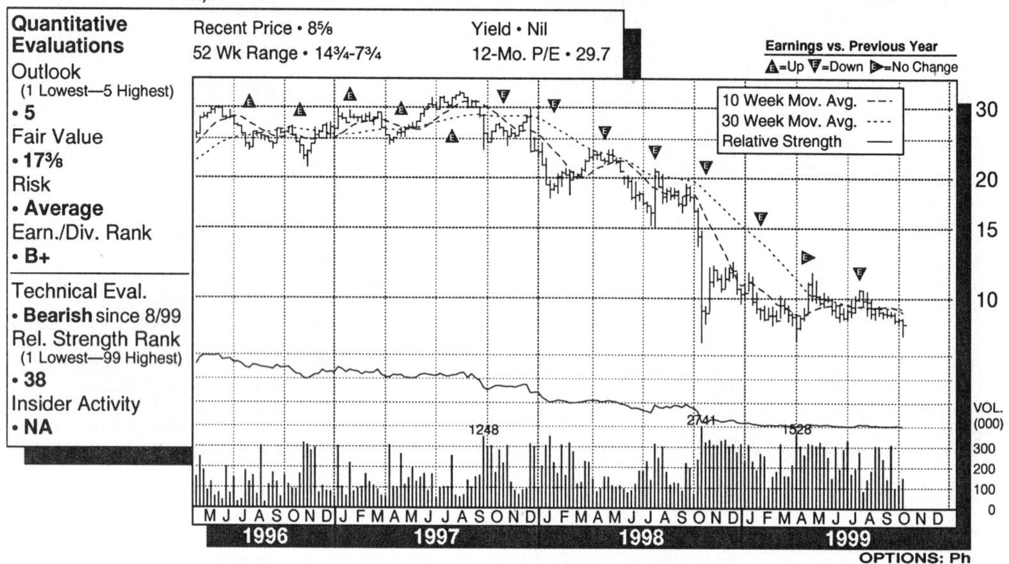

Business Profile - 07-SEP-99

K2 intends to continue to focus on adding new products and brands, and controlling costs. In August 1999, the company agreed to sell its Simplex products division to Callier Interests, a private equity group, for $32 million in cash, plus a performance-based payment of up to $3 million. The sale was expected to close within 60 days. K2 has accounted for Simplex as a discontinued operation since September 30, 1998. Separately, in July 1999, KTO agreed to acquire Ride Inc., a designer and manufacturer of snowboard equipment, apparel and accessories, for about 1.5 million common shares. KTO expected the acquisition to be accretive to its earnings during 2000, if integration can be accomplished as planned.

Operational Review - 07-SEP-99

Sales from continuing operations for the first half of 1999 rose 4.4%, year to year, reflecting a sales gain of 8.7% for sporting goods and relatively flat sales for other recreational products, partially offset by an 8.3% decline for industrial products. Slightly lower gross margins and increased selling expenses for sporting goods resulted in only a nominal rise in operating profit. After virtually flat interest expense, and taxes at 32.0% versus 32.8%, income from continuing operations was up nominally, to $10.2 million ($0.62 a share) from $10.1 million ($0.61). Results are before earnings from discontinued Simplex building products operations of $0.06 a share, versus $0.07.

Stock Performance - 08-OCT-99

In the past 30 trading days, KTO's shares have declined 7%, compared to a 0.91% fall in the S&P 500. Average trading volume for the past five days was 29,380 shares, compared with the 40-day moving average of 46,672 shares.

Key Stock Statistics

Dividend Rate/Share	Nil	Shareholders	1,662
Shs. outstg. (M)	16.5	Market cap. (B)	$0.143
Avg. daily vol. (M)	0.039	Inst. holdings	47%
Tang. Bk. Value/Share	11.36		
Beta	0.08		

Value of $10,000 invested 5 years ago: $ 6,553

Fiscal Year Ending Dec. 31

	1999	1998	1997	1996	1995	1994
Revenues (Million $)						
1Q	163.1	173.2	171.5	158.8	138.0	109.7
2Q	158.3	180.9	171.5	143.4	135.9	131.8
3Q	—	133.9	142.3	147.7	134.7	127.9
4Q	—	132.8	161.5	152.8	135.7	133.1
Yr.	—	574.5	646.9	602.7	544.3	502.4
Earnings Per Share ($)						
1Q	**0.19**	**0.19**	**0.35**	**0.29**	0.30	0.04
2Q	**0.43**	**0.49**	**0.52**	**0.42**	0.41	0.42
3Q	—	-0.48	**0.18**	**0.43**	0.36	0.38
4Q	—	**0.10**	**0.26**	**0.38**	0.29	0.25
Yr.	—	**0.23**	**1.31**	**1.51**	**1.37**	**1.15**

Next earnings report expected: late October

Dividend Data (Dividends have been paid since 1978.)

Amount ($)	Date Decl.	Ex-Div. Date	Stock of Record	Payment Date
0.110	Sep. 10	Sep. 24	Sep. 28	Oct. 06 '98
0.110	Dec. 17	Dec. 23	Dec. 28	Jan. 05 '99
0.110	Feb. 17	Mar. 09	Mar. 11	Apr. 01 '99

A Division of The McGraw-Hill Companies

K2 Inc.

Business Summary - 07-SEP-99

If you have ever gone skiing or snowboarding, you are probably familiar with some of the products of K2 Inc., most likely its K2 and Olin brands of alpine skis and its K2 brand skiboards. KTO is a designer, manufacturer and marketer of brand-name sporting goods, other recreational products, and industrial products.

Sporting goods accounted for 70% of 1998 sales, other recreational products 8%, and industrial products 22%.

Sporting goods include alpine skis (sold under the K2 and Olin brand names); snowboards and accessories (K2); in-line skates (K2); fishing rods and reels (Shakespeare, Ugly Stik, and Pfleuger); active water sports products (Stearns); mountain and BMX Bikes (K2 and Noleen); and backpacks and hydration systems (K2 and Dana Design).

KTO sells its alpine skis in the three major ski markets of the world--the United States, Europe and Japan. The company offers skis in a broad range of styles for a variety of conditions and types of skiing at mid to upper price points.

Snowboards are sold under the K2 brand, and snowboard bindings and snowboard boots under the K2 Clicker brand. Back country accessories, including day packs, high performance snowshoes integrating the Clicker bindings and backpacks for carrying snowboards and other gear when hiking into the back country have been recently introduced.

K-2 soft boot in-line skates are priced at the mid to upper end of the industry's price points. KTO sells its fishing rods, reels and fishing line in most of the world. The company believes that Shakespeare's Ugly Stik models have been the best selling fishing rods in the U.S. over the past twenty years.

Active water products include Stearns flotation vests, jackets and suits (personal flotation devices), cold water immersion products, wet suits, outdoor products, rainwear, and towables. Mountain and BMX bikes include full-suspension mountain bikes, front suspension mountain bikes, comfort bikes, and BMX bikes and components. The backpack line, which is high end, includes a series of activity specific packs marketed by K2 ski, bike and snowboard.

Other recreational products consist primarily of imprinted corporate casuals (Hilton); Skateboard apparel (Planet Earth); snowboard apparel (Planet earth), casual and surf apparel (Katin); and skateboard shoes (Adio).

Industrial products include monofilament line, composite utility and decorative light poles, and fiberglass marine radio antennas.

During the third quarter of 1998, KTO adopted a plan to dispose of its Simplex building products division. As a result, that division was classified as a discontinued operation for accounting purposes in 1998. KTO agreed to sell the division in August, 1999.

Per Share Data ($) (Year Ended Dec. 31)	1998	1997	1996	1995	1994	1993	1992	1991	1990	1989
Tangible Bk. Val.	11.02	12.21	10.43	9.75	7.02	6.19	5.84	5.61	5.33	5.79
Cash Flow	1.00	2.08	2.17	2.07	1.74	1.71	1.56	1.32	0.98	1.95
Earnings	0.23	1.31	1.51	1.37	1.09	0.94	0.73	0.57	0.24	1.23
Dividends	0.44	0.44	0.44	0.44	0.42	0.40	0.38	0.37	0.35	0.33
Payout Ratio	191%	34%	29%	32%	39%	43%	53%	64%	149%	27%
Prices - High	23 5/8	32 7/8	30 1/8	23 1/4	17 1/2	15 3/4	12 3/4	9 5/8	13 1/2	15 3/8
- Low	7 3/4	22 3/8	20 3/8	15 1/8	13 7/8	10 7/8	8 5/8	5 1/4	4 7/8	8 1/2
P/E Ratio - High	NM	25	20	17	16	17	17	17	57	13
- Low	NM	17	13	11	13	12	12	9	21	7
Income Statement Analysis (Million $)										
Revs.	575	647	603	544	502	432	402	370	377	382
Oper. Inc.	29.5	56.4	55.5	47.3	33.9	30.5	28.2	25.0	20.3	34.9
Depr.	12.7	12.9	11.2	10.2	7.7	9.1	9.7	8.7	8.4	6.8
Int. Exp.	12.2	10.6	9.3	9.9	7.5	5.8	6.8	6.9	8.8	7.9
Pretax Inc.	4.8	31.1	36.5	28.6	20.3	17.0	12.9	10.7	4.5	21.3
Eff. Tax Rate	20%	30%	31%	31%	36%	34%	34%	38%	39%	37%
Net Inc.	3.9	21.9	25.2	19.8	13.0	11.1	8.5	6.6	2.7	13.4
Balance Sheet & Other Fin. Data (Million $)										
Cash	3.4	5.9	10.9	7.4	7.7	5.9	2.1	3.1	2.6	2.8
Curr. Assets	336	330	274	300	233	188	169	152	147	144
Total Assets	453	429	368	384	304	257	236	222	221	210
Curr. Liab.	127	123	74.0	121	82.6	70.0	73.1	87.2	78.8	78.6
LT Debt	111	88.7	89.1	75.1	110	87.3	68.5	43.5	53.8	44.0
Common Eqty.	202	203	189	176	99	88.7	83.6	80.7	78.1	78.1
Total Cap.	326	307	294	264	222	187	163	134	142	131
Cap. Exp.	17.3	23.7	18.8	17.3	11.6	8.7	7.1	5.1	14.0	13.5
Cash Flow	16.6	34.8	36.4	30.0	20.7	20.2	18.2	15.3	11.1	20.3
Curr. Ratio	2.6	2.7	3.7	2.5	2.8	2.7	2.3	1.7	1.9	1.8
% LT Debt of Cap.	34.0	28.9	30.3	28.4	49.6	46.6	42.0	32.3	37.9	33.5
% Net Inc.of Revs.	0.7	3.4	4.2	3.6	2.6	2.6	2.1	1.8	0.7	3.5
% Ret. on Assets	0.9	5.5	6.7	5.8	4.6	4.5	3.7	3.0	1.2	6.6
% Ret. on Equity	1.9	11.2	13.8	14.4	13.9	12.9	10.3	8.3	3.4	18.1

Data as orig reptd.; bef. results of disc opers/spec. items. Per share data adj. for stk. divs. Bold denotes diluted EPS (FASB 128)-prior periods restated. E-Estimated. NA-Not Available. NM-Not Meaningful. NR-Not Ranked.

Office—4900 South Eastern Ave., Los Angeles, CA 90040. **Tel**—(323) 724-2800. **Website**—http://www.k2sports.com **Chrmn**—B. I. Forester. **Pres & CEO**—R. M. Rodstein. **SVP-Fin & Investor Contact**—John J. Rangel. **Secy**—Susan E. McConnell. **Dirs**—S. E. Engel, B. I. Forester, W. D. Godbold Jr., J. E. Goldress, R. J. Heckmann, S. M. Kasen, J. H. Offermans, A. E. Osborne Jr., R. M. Rodstein. **Transfer Agent & Registrar**—Harris Trust Co. of California, LA. **Incorporated**—in Delaware in 1959. **Empl**— 3,800. **S&P Analyst:** N.J.D.

STANDARD
&POOR'S
STOCK REPORTS

Kaman Corp.

NASDAQ Symbol **KAMNA**

In S&P SmallCap 600

09-OCT-99

Industry: Manufacturing (Diversified)

Summary: This company provides products and services for defense markets, and distributes industrial and commercial products.

Quantitative Evaluations

Outlook (1 Lowest—5 Highest)
• **NA**

Fair Value
• **NA**

Risk
• **Low**

Earn./Div. Rank
• **B**

Technical Eval.
• **Bearish** since 8/99

Rel. Strength Rank (1 Lowest—99 Highest)
• **51**

Insider Activity
• **NA**

Recent Price • 13
52 Wk Range • 17⅛-10¾
Yield • 3.4%
12-Mo. P/E • 10.3

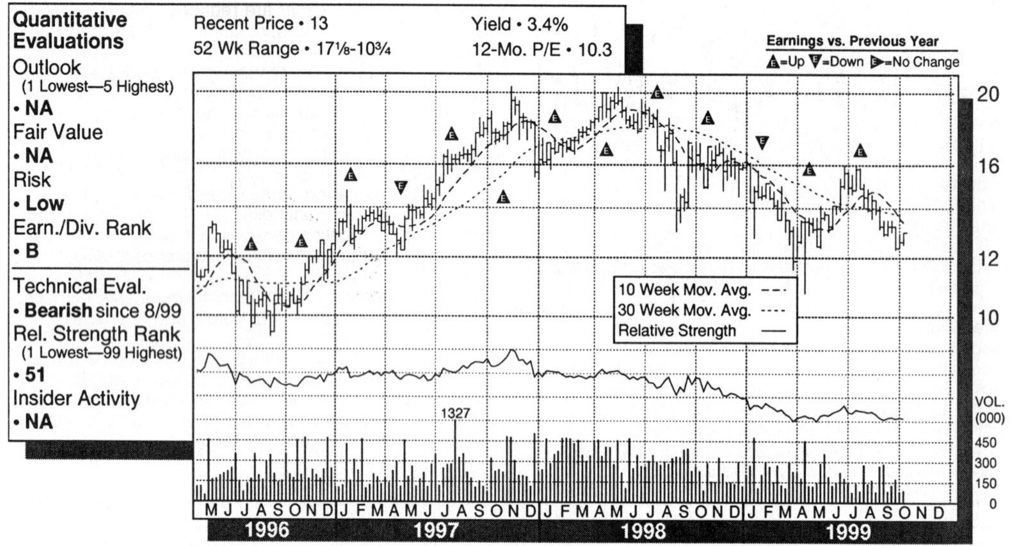

Business Profile - 07-JUL-99

The SH-2G Super Seasprite remanufacturing programs for New Zealand and Australia were significant contributors to the company's earnings in the 1999 first quarter. In April, though, management noted that the aircraft structures and components business has begun to level off, reflecting current trends in the worldwide aviation market. In the distribution area, while the overall U.S. economy has been good, there are a number of industries that are experiencing reduced international exports due to lower demand and unfavorable exchange rates. This, in turn, has slowed their production and hence requirements for the company's products and services. These industries will likely continue to feel the effects of Asian and South American economic difficulties for some time.

Operational Review - 07-JUL-99

Revenues rose 4.5%, year to year, in the first quarter of 1999, paced by an 11% increase in the aerospace operations. Pretax income was up 2.5%, as recovery in the music business and slight improvement in aerospace outweighed lower profits in industrial distribution. After taxes at 39.7% versus 40.9%, net income climbed 4.3%, to $7,273,000 ($0.30 a share, diluted), from $6,976,000 ($0.29).

Stock Performance - 08-OCT-99

In the past 30 trading days, KAMNA's shares have declined 2%, compared to a 0.91% fall in the S&P 500. Average trading volume for the past five days was 17,500 shares, compared with the 40-day moving average of 29,897 shares.

Key Stock Statistics

Dividend Rate/Share	0.44	Shareholders	7,600
Shs. outstg. (M)	23.5	Market cap. (B)	$0.297
Avg. daily vol. (M)	0.023	Inst. holdings	58%
Tang. Bk. Value/Share	13.48		
Beta	0.86		

Value of $10,000 invested 5 years ago: $ 15,652

Fiscal Year Ending Dec. 31

	1999	1998	1997	1996	1995	1994
Revenues (Million $)						
1Q	249.8	239.1	252.2	240.0	208.0	198.0
2Q	246.7	247.4	250.3	246.5	221.5	208.6
3Q	—	249.7	270.0	228.0	225.6	198.9
4Q	—	269.8	272.4	239.1	241.3	21.04
Yr.	—	1,006	1,045	953.6	896.4	820.8
Earnings Per Share ($)						
1Q	**0.30**	**0.29**	**-0.28**	**0.22**	0.25	0.18
2Q	**0.33**	**0.31**	**0.28**	**0.23**	0.20	0.20
3Q	—	**0.31**	**0.29**	**0.25**	0.20	0.22
4Q	—	**0.32**	**2.43**	**0.30**	0.21	-1.53
Yr.	—	**1.23**	**2.86**	**1.00**	**0.85**	-0.93

Next earnings report expected: mid October

Dividend Data (Dividends have been paid since 1972.)

Amount ($)	Date Decl.	Ex-Div. Date	Stock of Record	Payment Date
0.110	Nov. 17	Dec. 23	Dec. 28	Jan. 11 '99
0.110	Feb. 09	Mar. 25	Mar. 29	Apr. 12 '99
0.110	Jun. 08	Jun. 24	Jun. 28	Jul. 12 '99
0.110	Sep. 21	Sep. 30	Oct. 04	Oct. 18 '99

Kaman Corporation

Business Summary - 07-JUL-99

Kaman Corporation (KAMNA) operates in the aerospace, industrial distribution and music industries. The company was founded in 1945 by its current chairman, president and CEO Charles H. Kaman, who suffered a mild stroke following successful knee replacement surgery in August 1998. At Mr. Kaman's recommendation, a committee was established in December 1998 to seek a new CEO.

The aerospace segment (38% of 1998 sales; formerly part of the diversified technologies segment) serves commercial, U.S. defense and foreign government markets with principal programs consisting of its SH-2G maritime helicopter, K-MAX aerial truck helicopter, subcontract work involving airframe structures and the manufacture of niche market products such as self-lubricating bearings and driveline couplings for aircraft applications.

Through the industrial distribution segment (50%), Kaman serves nearly every sector of U.S. industry with industrial repair and OEM products as well as support services. A national distributor of industrial products, operating through 190 service centers in 36 states and British Columbia, it supplies a broad range of industries with original equipment, repair and replacement products needed to maintain traditional manufacturing processes and, increasingly, with products of higher technological content that are required to support automated production processes. During 1998, export demand in certain industries such as lumber, chemicals, paper and semiconductors was adversely affected by economic difficulties in Asia, which resulted in increased price pressures on this segment. In this environment, the company is working to focus sales efforts in the markets that offer the best opportunities and to carry out initiatives to enhance operating efficiencies, including consolidation and centralization of various organizational support functions.

The music distribution segment (12%) servesdomestic and foreign markets with a wide variety of musicinstruments and accessories and manufactures guitars and othermusic products for professional and amateur musicians.

Per Share Data ($) **(Year Ended Dec. 31)**	**1998**	**1997**	**1996**	**1995**	**1994**	**1993**	**1992**	**1991**	**1990**	**1989**
Tangible Bk. Val.	13.07	12.12	8.72	8.08	7.60	7.83	9.88	9.33	8.81	8.19
Cash Flow	1.63	3.84	1.72	1.54	-0.21	-0.88	1.68	1.67	1.79	1.19
Earnings	1.23	2.86	1.06	0.86	-0.93	-1.63	0.95	0.93	1.06	0.48
Dividends	0.44	0.44	0.44	0.44	0.44	0.44	0.44	0.44	0.44	0.44
Payout Ratio	36%	15%	42%	51%	NM	NM	46%	47%	42%	92%
Prices - High	20 3/8	20 3/8	13 3/8	13 3/8	11 1/8	12 1/8	10 3/4	9 5/8	9 1/2	14 7/8
- Low	13	12	9 3/8	10	8 1/2	8 5/8	7 7/8	7 3/8	6	7 5/8
P/E Ratio - High	17	7	13	16	NM	NM	11	10	9	31
- Low	11	4	9	12	NM	NM	8	8	6	16
Income Statement Analysis (Million $)										
Revs.	1,005	1,043	954	896	819	793	783	778	825	801
Oper. Inc.	61.2	58.9	58.2	51.7	46.6	44.1	48.0	48.6	56.0	41.1
Depr.	11.1	12.2	12.4	12.7	13.1	13.5	13.4	13.6	13.5	12.8
Int. Exp.	Nil	7.9	10.0	8.8	4.7	7.0	7.1	8.2	11.3	12.1
Pretax Inc.	50.4	120	40.7	32.7	-14.2	-40.5	29.0	28.3	32.8	16.6
Eff. Tax Rate	40%	41%	42%	40%	NM	NM	40%	40%	41%	48%
Net Inc.	30.0	70.5	23.6	19.6	-13.2	-28.8	17.4	17.0	19.2	8.7
Balance Sheet & Other Fin. Data (Million $)										
Cash	65.1	110	5.5	4.1	3.7	3.8	2.5	3.3	3.2	8.7
Curr. Assets	517	535	434	405	339	317	335	310	327	319
Total Assets	587	598	522	500	443	440	443	422	444	441
Curr. Liab.	229	260	196	206	193	167	122	111	117	119
LT Debt	28.2	29.9	83.9	66.4	37.0	38.0	101	102	123	131
Common Eqty.	311	253	171	157	147	171	210	202	193	183
Total Cap.	339	320	312	294	241	266	317	307	323	321
Cap. Exp.	19.2	13.7	8.0	11.5	21.6	20.4	10.6	8.6	9.6	12.4
Cash Flow	41.1	79.0	32.2	28.6	-3.8	-16.0	30.7	30.6	32.7	21.5
Curr. Ratio	2.3	2.1	2.2	2.0	1.8	1.9	2.7	2.8	2.8	2.7
% LT Debt of Cap.	8.3	9.4	26.9	22.6	15.5	14.3	31.8	33.2	38.2	40.7
% Net Inc.of Revs.	3.0	6.8	2.5	2.2	NM	NM	2.2	2.2	2.3	1.1
% Ret. on Assets	5.1	12.6	4.7	4.2	NM	NM	4.0	3.9	4.3	2.0
% Ret. on Equity	10.6	31.4	12.2	12.9	NM	NM	8.5	8.6	10.2	4.8

Data as orig reptd.; bef. results of disc opers/spec. items. Per share data adj. for stk. divs. Bold denotes diluted EPS (FASB 128)-prior periods restated. E-Estimated. NA-Not Available. NM-Not Meaningful. NR-Not Ranked.

Office—1332 Blue Hills Ave., P.O. Box 1, Bloomfield, CT 06002. **Tel**—(860) 243-7100. **Website**—http://www.kaman.com **Chrmn**—C. H. Kaman. **Pres & CEO**—P. R. Kuhn.**EVP & CFO**—R. M. Garneau. **SVP & Secy**—C. A. Clark.**Investor Contact**—Russell H. Jones (860-243-6307). **Dirs**—B. E. Barents, E. R. Callaway III, F. C. Carlucci, L. J. Chouest, J. A. DiBiaggio, H. Hardisty, C. H. Kaman, C. W. Kaman II, E. S. Kraus, P. R. Kuhn, H. Z. Lebed, W. H. Monteith Jr., W. L. Rogers. **Transfer Agent**—ChaseMellon Shareholder Services, NYC. **Incorporated**—in Connecticut in 1945. **Empl**— 4,276. **S&P Analyst:** C.F.B.

STANDARD
&POOR'S
STOCK REPORTS

Kellwood Co.

NYSE Symbol **KWD**

In S&P SmallCap 600

09-OCT-99

Industry:
Textiles (Apparel)

Summary: This global manufacturer and marketer of apparel and recreational camping products offers branded apparel, as well as private-label products.

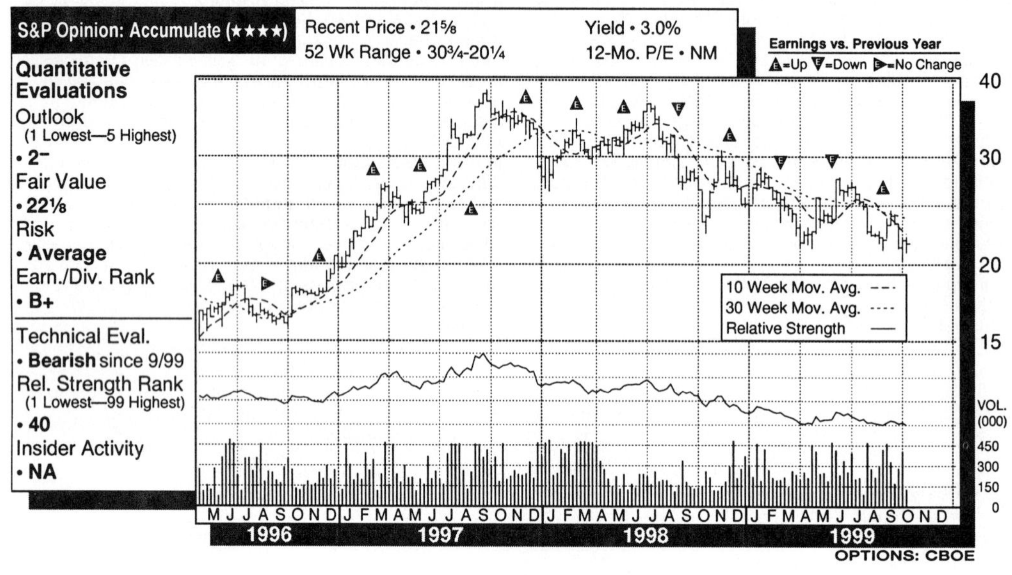

Overview - 30-AUG-99

We expect sales to grow around 5% in FY 00 (Apr.) reflecting healthy demand for the company's casual dress lines. KWD's casual divisions, most notably Sag Harbor, Fritzi California and Koret, should continue to perform well in the second half. The better-to-bridge line sales should improve in the fourth quarter of FY 00 and be bolstered in FY 01 by the addition of the new Perry Ellis lines. Gross margins should continue to widen as KWD completes its transfer of sewing operations offshore and improves sourcing. Although we expect the company to incur higher marketing costs in launching new products, operating margins should benefit from the ongoing restructuring initiatives which are expected to save $10 million in FY 00. Considering this favorable outlook, we expect FY 00 EPS to be $2.80 (excluding charges).

Valuation - 30-AUG-99

The shares have declined around 15% since the end of calendar year 1998. We attribute this to concerns over poor sales trends of certain company product lines and a possible softening of apparel sales in anticipation of higher interest rates. However, we remain optimistic that KWD should meet its objectives of moderate sales growth and a nearly 30% earnings rise (excluding restructuring charges). KWD should continue to competently meet increasing consumer demands for casual oriented apparel and make efforts to improve the underperforming sales units. In conjunction with the benefits realized from the restructuring program, KWD is expected to continue to quietly outperform its peers and the industry. Currently trading at just 8X our FY 00 EPS estimate, we believe that the shares are undervalued and recommend accumulating the stock.

Key Stock Statistics

S&P EPS Est. 2000	2.80	Tang. Bk. Value/Share	15.98
P/E on S&P Est. 2000	7.7	Beta	0.53
Dividend Rate/Share	0.64	Shareholders	1,454
Shs. outstg. (M)	27.8	Market cap. (B)	$0.602
Avg. daily vol. (M)	0.049	Inst. holdings	73%

Value of $10,000 invested 5 years ago: $ 9,493

Fiscal Year Ending Apr. 30

	2000	1999	1998	1997	1996	1995
Revenues (Million $)						
1Q	470.6	483.3	400.6	327.4	340.6	300.9
2Q	—	600.5	502.9	429.4	425.6	376.0
3Q	—	438.9	373.7	315.8	288.5	291.5
4Q	—	628.4	504.4	448.3	411.3	396.3
Yr.	—	2,151	2,094	1,521	1,466	1,365
Earnings Per Share ($)						
1Q	**0.34**	**0.32**	0.34	0.27	0.27	0.51
2Q	—	**0.82**	0.77	0.68	0.66	0.53
3Q	—	**0.07**	**0.11**	**0.09**	-0.10	-0.10
4Q	—	**-1.13**	**0.76**	0.73	0.49	-0.41
Yr.	**E2.80**	**0.07**	**1.85**	**1.75**	1.32	0.53

Next earnings report expected: late November

Dividend Data (Dividends have been paid since 1962.)

Amount ($)	Date Decl.	Ex-Div. Date	Stock of Record	Payment Date
0.160	Nov. 24	Dec. 02	Dec. 04	Dec. 18 '98
0.160	Feb. 23	Mar. 03	Mar. 05	Mar. 19 '99
0.160	May. 27	Jun. 03	Jun. 07	Jun. 18 '99
0.160	Aug. 26	Sep. 02	Sep. 07	Sep. 17 '99

Kellwood Company

Business Summary - 30-AUG-99

Kellwood Co. (KWD), which has grown through 16 acquisitions since 1985, has become one of the leading manufacturers of women's apparel. The company has expanded due to the success of its business strategy which began in the mid-1980s and which continues today. KWD's goals were to increase its branded label products, its customer base, its channels of distribution, and its global sourcing. As a result of achieving these goals, annual revenues now exceed $2.1 billion.

The company traces its origins to 1961, when it was created to manufacture clothing lines strictly for Sears. KWD has evolved into a diverse company, with 30 operating plants worldwide. By FY 99 (Apr.), Sears accounted for only 7% of total revenues, versus 50% in FY 85.

KWD's first of five segment is women's branded sportswear: popular-to-moderate (accounting for 64% of FY 99 sales) which includes labels such as Sag Harbor, Kathie Lee and Cricket Lane. Products include blazers, dresses, sweaters, blouses, vests, skirts, pants, and other items priced below $50.

The women's branded sportswear: better-to-bridge (8%) products include upper price point sportswear sold principally to small specialty stores, regional department stores, and catalog houses.

The private label apparel products segment (12%) includes intimate apparel, outerwear, activewear, pants, jeans, workwear, and sweaters.

Smart shirts (9%) is a leading manufacturer of woven dress and sport shirts in Hong Kong, China, and most recently Sri Lanka.

Recreation products (7%) makes camping products including tents, sleeping bags, backpacks and technical apparel and accessories.

In 1995, KWD embarked on a restructuring plan called Vision 2000, designed to align internal capabilities with customer needs. Under phase one of Vision 2000, which was largely completed at the end of FY 96, KWD restructured its assets and consolidated certain divisions. Phase two, which involved operational functions such as systems, logistics, warehousing, distribution and finance, began in FY 97, and was the main focus of the Vision 2000 initiative. In connection with the restructuring, the company took $56 million (pretax) in charges for impairment of goodwill and facility shutdowns in FY 99. Restructuring related spending is targeted at $25 million for FY 00.

In December 1998, the company acquired Fritzi California, which manufactures apparel for juniors and girls, for 844,000 shares and the assumption of certain liabilities. In May 1999, the company acquired Koret, Inc., a designer, manufacturer and marketer of moderately priced women's sportswear. KWD issued 5,241,000 new shares in this transaction.

Per Share Data ($) (Year Ended Apr. 30)	1999	1998	1997	1996	1995	1994	1993	1992	1991	1990
Tangible Bk. Val.	15.98	12.96	11.08	9.65	8.36	9.51	8.87	9.40	7.68	7.51
Cash Flow	1.85	3.99	3.12	2.66	1.87	2.91	2.42	2.29	1.70	1.78
Earnings	0.07	1.95	1.78	1.32	0.53	1.71	1.39	1.26	0.71	0.80
Dividends	0.64	0.64	0.60	0.60	0.60	0.55	0.53	0.53	0.53	0.53
Payout Ratio	NM	33%	34%	45%	113%	32%	38%	48%	76%	67%
Cal. Yrs.	1998	1997	1996	1995	1994	1993	1992	1991	1990	1989
Prices - High	36⁵⁄₈	38¹⁄₂	20⁷⁄₈	22⁷⁄₈	26⁷⁄₈	27¹⁄₈	22¹⁄₈	17⁷⁄₈	15¹⁄₄	23⁵⁄₈
- Low	22¹⁄₂	19⁵⁄₈	13⁵⁄₈	16¹⁄₂	19¹⁄₈	15⁷⁄₈	14¹⁄₄	6¹⁄₄	3¹⁄₂	13⁵⁄₈
P/E Ratio - High	NM	20	12	17	51	16	16	14	22	29
- Low	NM	10	8	12	36	9	10	5	5	17
Income Statement Analysis (Million $)										
Revs.	2,151	1,782	1,521	1,466	1,365	1,203	1,078	915	808	780
Oper. Inc.	184	146	128	113	87.4	96.1	80.0	66.0	48.0	47.9
Depr.	49.2	44.8	28.3	28.2	28.3	25.1	21.3	18.5	17.6	17.3
Int. Exp.	33.9	28.9	21.6	22.9	19.1	15.6	13.8	14.2	16.1	17.1
Pretax Inc.	39.2	73.9	64.8	48.5	28.5	61.0	51.9	41.5	22.6	21.6
Eff. Tax Rate	95%	42%	42%	42%	61%	42%	45%	45%	45%	35%
Net Inc.	2.0	42.7	37.6	28.0	11.1	35.6	28.7	22.8	12.4	14.0
Balance Sheet & Other Fin. Data (Million $)										
Cash	25.5	31.8	22.5	25.0	11.1	17.7	39.2	40.8	41.3	44.1
Curr. Assets	797	759	622	544	511	413	426	364	321	310
Total Assets	1,054	1,016	875	797	768	642	636	538	484	469
Curr. Liab.	332	343	374	306	274	151	228	145	143	128
LT Debt	228	243	110	125	145	153	103	111	120	128
Common Eqty.	446	384	348	325	308	307	280	260	200	197
Total Cap.	674	673	500	490	491	490	407	389	338	337
Cap. Exp.	51.5	18.4	11.6	16.4	11.7	12.5	16.8	12.6	10.4	9.7
Cash Flow	51.2	87.5	65.9	56.2	39.4	60.7	50.0	41.4	30.0	31.3
Curr. Ratio	2.4	2.2	1.7	1.8	1.9	2.7	1.9	2.5	2.2	2.4
% LT Debt of Cap.	33.8	36.1	21.9	25.6	29.5	31.2	25.3	28.4	35.5	38.0
% Net Inc.of Revs.	0.1	2.4	2.5	1.9	0.8	3.0	2.7	2.5	1.5	1.8
% Ret. on Assets	0.2	4.5	4.5	3.6	1.6	5.5	4.9	4.2	2.6	3.0
% Ret. on Equity	0.5	11.7	11.2	8.8	3.6	12.1	10.6	9.3	6.3	7.2

Data as orig reptd.; bef. results of disc opers/spec. items. Per share data adj. for stk. divs. Bold denotes diluted EPS (FASB 128)-prior periods restated. E-Estimated. NA-Not Available. NM-Not Meaningful. NR-Not Ranked.

Office—600 Kellwood Parkway, P.O. Box 14374, St. Louis, MO 63178. **Tel**—(314) 576-3100. **Website**—http://www.kellwood.com **Chrmn**—W. J. McKenna. **Vice Chrmn**—J. C. Jacobsen. **Pres & CEO**—H. J. Upbin. **VP, Finance & CFO**—Gerald M. Chaney **VP, Treas & Investor Contact**—Roger D. Joseph. **VP & Secy**—T. H. Pollihan. **Dirs**—R. F. Bentele, E. S. Bottum, K. G. Dickerson, L. A. Genovese, M. J. Granoff, J. M. Hunter, J. C. Jacobsen, J. S. Marcus, W. J. McKenna, H. J. Upbin. **Transfer Agent & Registrar**—KeyCorp Shareholder Services, Cleveland. **Incorporated**—in Delaware in 1961. **Empl**— 19,200. **S&P Analyst:** Howard Choe

STANDARD
&POOR'S
STOCK REPORTS

KEMET Corp.

Nasdaq Symbol **KMET**

In S&P SmallCap 600

09-OCT-99

Industry:
Electrical Equipment

Summary: KEMET manufactures and supplies solid tantalum capacitors and multilayer ceramic capacitors.

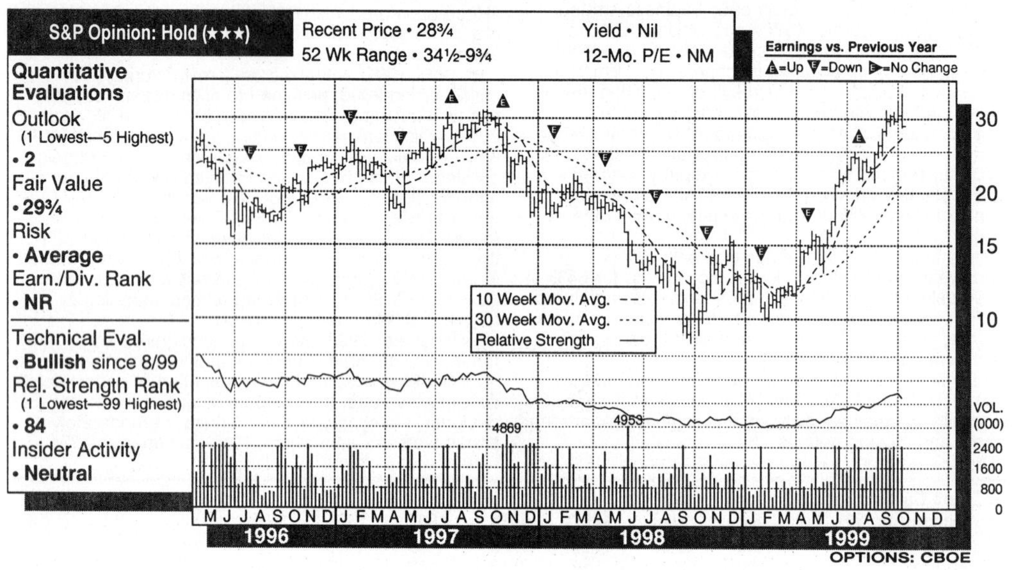

Overview - 12-AUG-99

We expect revenues to rise roughly 20% in FY 2000 (Mar.) from FY 99's depressed levels. Following a period of protracted weakness, demand for the company's tantalum and ceramic capacitors has improved significantly in the past two quarters. Capacitor prices, which generally fall throughout the product life cycle, have also improved, as strong demand has eased the effects of an oversupply condition. Given the recent strength in bookings, we expect a continuation of the positive sales trends over the next few quarters. Furthermore, margins should improve as fixed costs are spread over a larger sales base. In addition, last year's restructuring is expected to result in annual savings of $14 million. Overall, we expect EPS to rebound to $0.65 in FY 2000, from FY 99's $0.16.

Valuation - 12-AUG-99

The shares of this capacitor company have recovered significantly from this year's lows, reflecting signs of an improving operating environment. While the magnitude and duration of the recovery are difficult to assess given the somewhat commodity-type nature of the company's products, we are maintaining our hold rating on the shares. KMET's products are used in a broad base of applications related to the high growth electronics industry. In addition, the company's expansion into the organic tantalum and solid aluminum capacitor business is expected to enhance revenue opportunities. While the company's operating environment is improving, we believe that the shares are fairly valued at a recent 35X our FY 2000 EPS estimate.

Key Stock Statistics

S&P EPS Est. 2000	0.65	Tang. Bk. Value/Share	6.83
P/E on S&P Est. 2000	44.3	Beta	1.15
S&P EPS Est. 2001	1.00	Shareholders	200
Dividend Rate/Share	Nil	Market cap. (B)	$ 1.1
Shs. outstg. (M)	39.3	Inst. holdings	76%
Avg. daily vol. (M)	0.504		

Value of $10,000 invested 5 years ago: $ 37,176

Fiscal Year Ending Mar. 31

	2000	1999	1998	1997	1996	1995
Revenues (Million $)						
1Q	162.7	142.5	161.2	125.7	152.5	110.2
2Q	—	137.7	165.5	130.2	160.7	110.2
3Q	—	141.9	170.4	143.6	160.1	112.3
4Q	—	143.4	170.7	155.8	160.8	140.4
Yr.	—	565.6	667.7	555.3	634.2	473.2
Earnings Per Share ($)						
1Q	**0.12**	**0.04**	0.36	0.25	0.33	0.17
2Q	**E0.15**	**0.01**	**0.31**	0.01	0.38	0.17
3Q	**E0.17**	**0.05**	**0.19**	0.31	0.44	0.17
4Q	**E0.21**	**0.06**	**0.34**	0.38	0.52	0.29
Yr.	**E0.65**	**0.16**	**1.25**	**0.95**	1.67	0.80

Next earnings report expected: late October

Dividend Data

No cash dividends have been paid. The company has said it does not expect to pay cash dividends in the foreseeable future.

A Division of The McGraw-Hill Companies

KEMET Corporation

Business Summary - 12-AUG-99

As the world's largest manufacturer of solid tantalum capacitors and the second largest manufacturer of ceramic capacitors, KEMET is well positioned to participate in the continued rapid growth of the electronics industry. Capacitors are used in virtually all electronics applications and products to store, filter and regulate electrical energy and current flow. For example, these components are used in computers, cellular phones and watches, as well as in communications, data processing, automotive, military and aerospace systems.

FY 99 (Mar.) was a challenging year for the company, as sales fell by 15% from the prior year. During the fiscal year, a number of factors conspired to negatively impact the company's operating results. Namely, the Asian financial crisis and generally poor electronics market conditions resulted in weak product demand. This in turn exacerbated the industry's oversupply condition, causing prices to fall and customers to adjust their inventory levels. In addition, prices of palladium, a key raw material in capacitor manufacturing, rose to unprecedented levels. In the first quarter of fiscal 00, however, the company reported much improved operating results, as firmer demand and pricing resulted in solid sales growth and margin expansion.

Despite the uncertainty in the marketplace, KMET has prepared for the future over the past two years. It has spent a total of $173.5 million on capital expansion of the tantalum and ceramic business units, thereby increasing capacity to more than 26 billion units annually. The company expects to spend an additional $50 million in FY 00.

Currently, the vast majority of the company's manufacturing efforts are focused on the fastest growing segments of the capacitor industry: tantalum and ceramic capacitors. Both types of capacitors are commonly used in conjunction with integrated circuits and are best suited for applications requiring lower- to medium-capacitance values. Generally, ceramic capacitors are more cost-effective at lower capacitance values, while tantalum capacitors are more cost-effective at medium capacitance values. Demand for both products tends to reflect general demand for electronic components.

In November 1997, KMET reorganized its corporate structure into the tantalum and ceramic business units to improve its responsiveness to customer needs. Under the plan, the company reduced its U.S. workforce by 1,182 people.

Per Share Data ($)										
(Year Ended Mar. 31)	**1999**	**1998**	**1997**	**1996**	**1995**	**1994**	**1993**	**1992**	**1991**	**1990**
Tangible Bk. Val.	6.81	6.63	5.25	3.84	1.92	1.09	1.68	-2.02	NA	NA
Cash Flow	1.34	2.23	1.80	2.63	2.97	1.11	1.44	1.84	NA	NA
Earnings	0.16	1.25	0.95	1.67	0.80	0.46	0.44	-2.19	NA	NA
Dividends	Nil	Nil	Nil	Nil	Nil	Nil	Nil	Nil	NA	NA
Payout Ratio	Nil	Nil	Nil	Nil	Nil	Nil	Nil	Nil	NA	NA
Cal. Yrs.	1998	1997	1996	1995	1994	1993	1992	1991	1990	1989
Prices - High	22	31 3/8	29 1/4	36 1/8	14 7/8	10	7 1/4	NA	NA	NA
- Low	8 3/4	17 1/4	15 1/4	12 7/8	7	6 1/2	5	NA	NA	NA
P/E Ratio - High	NM	25	31	22	18	22	16	NA	NA	NA
- Low	NM	14	16	8	9	14	11	NA	NA	NA
Income Statement Analysis (Million $)										
Revs.	566	668	555	634	473	385	348	294	NA	NA
Oper. Inc.	69.5	132	111	158	89.5	61.3	62.2	45.7	NA	NA
Depr.	46.9	38.9	33.5	37.9	26.3	24.5	23.3	54.0	NA	NA
Int. Exp.	9.3	7.3	5.7	4.9	6.9	8.9	19.1	24.6	NA	NA
Pretax Inc.	9.0	70.8	54.4	105	50.3	26.4	20.9	-35.4	NA	NA
Eff. Tax Rate	32%	31%	32%	38%	39%	37%	37%	NM	NA	NA
Net Inc.	6.2	49.2	37.2	65.2	31.0	16.7	11.1	-28.2	NA	NA
Balance Sheet & Other Fin. Data (Million $)										
Cash	3.9	1.8	2.2	3.4	4.2	2.6	2.3	1.7	NA	NA
Curr. Assets	203	195	170	155	128	115	103	86.0	NA	NA
Total Assets	664	642	543	490	387	362	353	339	NA	NA
Curr. Liab.	123	146	107	122	97.7	71.2	78.2	60.8	NA	NA
LT Debt	144	104	103	78.1	77.0	107	147	188	NA	NA
Common Eqty.	314	306	252	212	139	108	52.5	-29.5	NA	NA
Total Cap.	481	426	368	318	246	250	232	229	NA	NA
Cap. Exp.	59.0	115	84.8	120	42.8	29.3	23.1	23.3	NA	NA
Cash Flow	53.0	88.0	70.7	103	57.3	41.3	33.6	24.6	NA	NA
Curr. Ratio	1.7	1.3	1.6	1.3	1.3	1.6	1.3	1.4	NA	NA
% LT Debt of Cap.	29.9	24.4	28.0	24.5	31.1	43.0	63.3	82.2	NA	NA
% Net Inc.of Revs.	1.1	7.4	6.7	10.3	6.5	4.3	3.2	NM	NA	NA
% Ret. on Assets	0.9	8.3	7.2	14.9	8.3	4.3	2.1	NM	NA	NA
% Ret. on Equity	2.0	17.6	16.0	37.2	25.1	19.5	NM	NM	NA	NA

Data as orig reptd.; bef. results of disc opers/spec. items. Per share data adj. for stk. divs. Bold denotes diluted EPS (FASB 128)-prior periods restated. E-Estimated. NA-Not Available. NM-Not Meaningful. NR-Not Ranked.

Office—2835 Kemet Way, Simpsonville, SC 29681. **Tel**—(864) 963-6300. **Website**—http://www.kemet.com **Chrmn & CEO**—D. E. Maguire. **COO**—C.E. Volpe.**SVP & Treas**—D. R. Cash. **SVP & Secy & Investor Contact**—Glenn H. Spears (864-963-6674). **Dirs**—S. A. Kohl, E. E. Maddrey II, D. E. Maguire, P. C. Schorr IV, C. E. Volpe. **Transfer Agent & Registrar**—Wachovia Corp., Winston-Salem, NC. **Incorporated**—in Delaware in 1990. **Empl**— 10,800. **S&P Analyst:** B. McGovern

STANDARD
&POOR'S
STOCK REPORTS

Kent Electronics

NYSE Symbol **KNT**
In S&P SmallCap 600

09-OCT-99

Industry: Electronics (Component Distributors)

Summary: Kent is a national specialty electronics distributor and a multi-plant custom contract manufacturer.

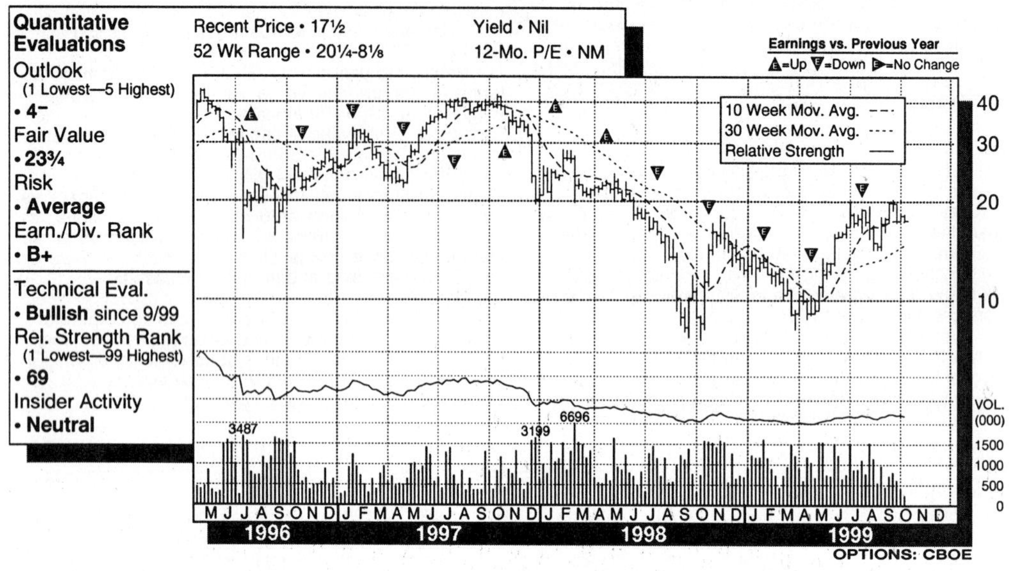

Business Profile - 24-MAY-99

In January 1999, the company said it has succeeded in diversifying its contract manufacturing base, thereby strengthening its ability to withstand the cyclicality of the personal computer and semiconductor capital equipment industries. In the fourth quarter of FY 99 (Mar.), sequential revenues grew 14% and the company achieved profitability for the first time in two quarters. In April 1999, Kent closed the acquisition, for an undisclosed amount, of SabreData Inc., a Texas-based network integrator that provides end-to-end network solutions to major corporations, governmental agencies and educational institutions. In 1998, SabreData generated approximately $37 million in revenues.

Operational Review - 24-MAY-99

Based on a preliminary report, net sales in the year ended April 3, 1999, fell 3.4%, as a result of industry-wide softness in the market for electronic components. Margins narrowed significantly, reflecting underutilization of facilities, a less favorable product mix, and pricing pressures; the loss from operations was $447,000, in contrast with income from operations of $56,399,000. Results benefited from a rise in interest income. After taxes at 38.1%, versus 39.1%, net income plunged to $182,000 ($0.01 a share), from $35,426,000 ($1.26).

Stock Performance - 08-OCT-99

In the past 30 trading days, KNT's shares have increased 2%, compared to a 0.91% fall in the S&P 500. Average trading volume for the past five days was 46,060 shares, compared with the 40-day moving average of 119,379 shares.

Key Stock Statistics

Dividend Rate/Share	Nil	Shareholders	1,361
Shs. outstg. (M)	28.0	Market cap. (B)	$0.490
Avg. daily vol. (M)	0.101	Inst. holdings	56%
Tang. Bk. Value/Share	10.93		
Beta	2.07		

Value of $10,000 invested 5 years ago: $ 18,421

Fiscal Year Ending Mar. 31

	2000	1999	1998	1997	1996	1995
Revenues (Million $)						
1Q	205.2	157.1	152.1	125.1	77.59	56.53
2Q	—	147.5	167.5	124.0	90.19	60.34
3Q	—	155.4	177.4	126.4	100.1	64.46
4Q	—	177.1	162.4	141.2	104.2	72.16
Yr.	—	637.1	659.4	516.8	372.0	253.5
Earnings Per Share ($)						
1Q	**0.07**	**0.15**	0.32	0.34	0.23	0.14
2Q	—	**-0.13**	0.34	0.25	0.28	0.16
3Q	—	**-0.03**	**0.36**	0.25	0.33	0.17
4Q	—	**0.02**	**0.25**	0.16	0.36	0.19
Yr.	—	**0.01**	**1.26**	**1.00**	1.22	0.66

Next earnings report expected: mid October

Dividend Data

The company has not paid any cash dividends.

Kent Electronics Corporation

Business Summary - 24-MAY-99

Kent Electronics is a national specialty distributor of electronic products and a manufacturer of custom-made electronic products. The company has strategically aligned its operations into four distinct, yet complementary, business units -- Kent Components, Kent Datacomm, Futronix Systems and K*TEC Electronics.

Kent Components distributes electronic connectors, wire and cable, capacitors, resistors and other passive and electromechanical components to original equipment manufacturers (OEMs) and industrial customers.

Kent Datacomm designs, delivers, installs and supports a broad range of networking products used in local area networks (LANs) and wide area networks (WANs). The unit offers a variety of voice and data communications products, such as network interface cards, switches, hubs, routers, modems, connectivity devices, fiber optics and copper cabling.

Futronix Systems is a redistributor of specialty wire and cable to electrical distributors worldwide. The unit provides just-in-time availability of exact quantities of specialty wire and cable products, as well as limited quantities of complementary products.

KNT's contract manufacturing subsidiary, K*TEC Electronics, produces a wide array of products, including electronic interconnect assemblies, printed circuit board assemblies, sheet metal fabrication, powder painting and plastic injection molding, among others.

Among the company's strategic initiatives is the provision of a continuum of services, from order fulfillment to direct distribution, to OEMs. Looking forward, KNT expects to experience a shift toward technology-based materials management services. Another part of the company's strategic plan is the pursuit of acquisitions, which will arise as a result of increasing demand on suppliers by OEMs for integrated, technology-based solutions. KNT has also expanded its professional services, which include product configuration and network monitoring, in response to greater demand for value-added services. Finally, the company believes it will be able to achieve synergies among its four operating units, including cross-selling opportunities, purchasing discounts, ease of geographic expansion and shared warehousing and materials handling capabilities.

In April 1999, Kent closed the acquisition, for an undisclosed amount, of SabreData Inc., a Texas-based network integrator that provides end-to-end network solutions to major corporations, governmental agencies and educational institutions. In 1998, SabreData generated approximately $37 million in revenues.

Per Share Data ($) (Year Ended Mar. 31)	1999	1998	1997	1996	1995	1994	1993	1992	1991	1990
Tangible Bk. Val.	10.93	10.91	9.37	8.88	4.87	4.08	3.33	2.84	1.93	1.56
Cash Flow	0.54	1.67	1.28	1.41	0.85	0.64	0.55	0.45	0.43	0.34
Earnings	0.01	1.26	1.00	1.22	0.66	0.48	0.40	0.34	0.31	0.26
Dividends	Nil	Nil	Nil	Nil	Nil	Nil	Nil	Nil	Nil	Nil
Payout Ratio	Nil	Nil	Nil	Nil	Nil	Nil	Nil	Nil	Nil	Nil
Cal. Yrs.	1998	1997	1996	1995	1994	1993	1992	1991	1990	1989
Prices - High	28¾	42⅛	43¾	30	13½	9⅝	8⅝	6¾	5	3⅛
- Low	7½	19½	15¼	12⅞	8⅞	6⅝	5⅝	3⅝	2 7/16	1⅞
P/E Ratio - High	NM	33	44	25	20	20	22	20	16	12
- Low	NM	15	15	11	13	14	14	10	8	7
Income Statement Analysis (Million $)										
Revs.	637	659	517	372	253	193	155	94.7	71.0	47.5
Oper. Inc.	14.6	68.0	54.6	47.0	24.8	17.8	14.3	9.7	7.0	4.8
Depr.	15.1	11.6	7.5	4.3	3.8	3.2	2.8	1.8	1.3	0.9
Int. Exp.	10.5	5.3	1.2	0.0	0.0	0.0	0.0	0.0	0.1	0.1
Pretax Inc.	0.3	58.2	45.1	46.9	22.1	15.4	12.2	9.2	6.0	4.6
Eff. Tax Rate	38%	39%	39%	40%	39%	38%	37%	37%	37%	35%
Net Inc.	0.2	35.4	27.6	28.0	13.4	9.5	7.7	5.8	3.8	3.0
Balance Sheet & Other Fin. Data (Million $)										
Cash	208	180	25.0	112	21.3	26.6	22.2	22.9	6.1	4.7
Curr. Assets	454	437	212	217	91.1	77.9	63.1	55.7	23.0	18.9
Total Assets	605	592	326	277	134	115	100	85.9	35.9	30.6
Curr. Liab.	68.0	70.3	61.5	51.0	24.8	22.0	16.7	13.6	6.7	5.9
LT Debt	207	209	1.7	Nil	Nil	Nil	Nil	Nil	0.7	0.8
Common Eqty.	321	313	262	225	109	92.5	81.7	71.6	28.1	23.7
Total Cap.	537	522	264	226	109	92.5	83.0	72.4	29.2	24.7
Cap. Exp.	18.9	46.9	50.8	21.0	10.0	5.8	9.2	5.7	1.9	2.0
Cash Flow	15.3	47.0	35.1	32.3	17.2	12.7	10.6	7.5	5.1	3.8
Curr. Ratio	6.7	6.2	3.5	4.2	3.7	3.5	3.8	4.1	3.4	3.2
% LT Debt of Cap.	38.6	40.0	0.6	NM	Nil	Nil	Nil	Nil	2.5	3.2
% Net Inc.of Revs.	0.0	5.4	5.3	7.5	5.3	4.9	5.0	6.1	5.3	6.2
% Ret. on Assets	0.0	7.7	8.7	13.6	10.7	8.9	8.2	8.1	11.3	10.7
% Ret. on Equity	0.1	12.3	11.1	16.8	13.2	10.9	10.0	9.9	14.4	13.4

Data as orig reptd.; bef. results of disc opers/spec. items. Per share data adj. for stk. divs. Bold denotes diluted EPS (FASB 128)-prior periods restated. E-Estimated. NA-Not Available. NM-Not Meaningful. NR-Not Ranked.

Office—1111 Gillingham Lane, Sugar Land, TX 77478. **Tel**—(281) 243-4000. **Website**—http://www.kentelec.com **Chrmn & CEO**—M. K. Abramson. **Pres & COO**—L. D. Olson. **VP, CFO, Treas, Secy & Investor Contact**—Stephen J. Chapko. **Dirs**—M. K. Abramson, T. M. Hunt, M. S. Levit, L. D. Olson, D. Siegel, R. C. Webb, A. L. Zimmerman. **Transfer Agent & Registrar**—ChaseMellon Shareholder Services, L.L.C, Ridgefield Park, NJ. **Incorporated**—in Texas in 1973. **Empl**— 1,830. **S&P Analyst:** Stephen J. Tekirian

STOCK REPORTS

Kirby Corp.

NYSE Symbol **KEX**

In S&P SmallCap 600

09-OCT-99

Industry: Shipping

Summary: Kirby is the largest domestic operator of inland tank barges transporting industrial chemicals, petroleum and other products along inland waterways.

Quantitative Evaluations

Outlook (1 Lowest—5 Highest) • **4+**

Fair Value • **26**

Risk • **Low**

Earn./Div. Rank • **B**

Technical Eval. • **Neutral** since 9/99

Rel. Strength Rank (1 Lowest—99 Highest) • **49**

Insider Activity • **NA**

Recent Price • 19⅝

52 Wk Range • 22⅜-16¾

Yield • Nil

12-Mo. P/E • 41.8

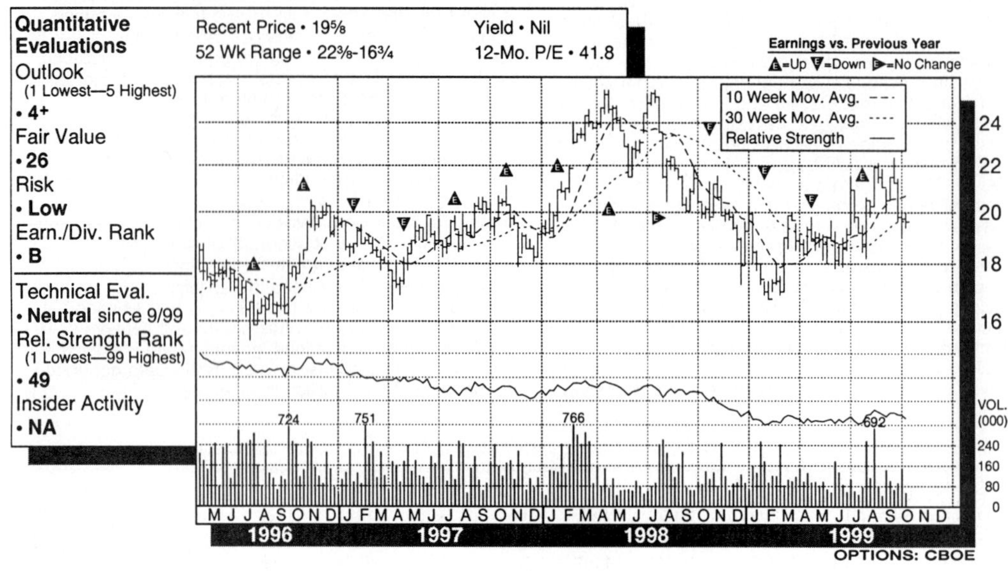

Business Profile - 25-JUN-99

Historically, the first quarter is the most difficult for the company from an operating efficiency standpoint. In the 1999 first quarter, river icing, flooding conditions, coastal fog, and lock related delays contributed to operating inefficiencies that were greater than those in the 1998 period. However, chemical and petrochemical volumes were generally higher than 1998 levels. KEX expected second quarter results to improve. In April 1999, directors increased the common stock repurchase authorization by 2 million shares, bringing the total authorization to 2.4 million shares at April 21, 1999. Officers and directors own about 20% of the shares outstanding.

Operational Review - 25-JUN-99

Revenues in the three months ended March 31, 1999, dropped 4.9%, year to year, on decreased marine transportation revenues (reflecting navigational delays), and lower diesel engine service revenue. Gross margins narrowed; despite a 3.4% decrease in costs and expenses, operating profits declined 16%, to $8.1 million, from $9.6 million. After taxes at 37.7%, in each period, net income fell 21%, to $4.0 million ($0.20 a share, on 16% fewer shares), from $5.0 million ($0.21).

Stock Performance - 08-OCT-99

In the past 30 trading days, KEX's shares have declined 7%, compared to a 0.91% fall in the S&P 500. Average trading volume for the past five days was 10,280 shares, compared with the 40-day moving average of 18,205 shares.

Key Stock Statistics

Dividend Rate/Share	Nil	Shareholders	1,600
Shs. outstg. (M)	20.1	Market cap. (B)	$0.395
Avg. daily vol. (M)	0.018	Inst. holdings	67%
Tang. Bk. Value/Share	6.53		
Beta	0.32		

Value of $10,000 invested 5 years ago: $ 9,181

Fiscal Year Ending Dec. 31

	1999	1998	1997	1996	1995	1994
Revenues (Million $)						
1Q	78.48	82.75	80.26	92.90	118.6	101.8
2Q	84.25	84.88	88.97	97.90	123.0	104.7
3Q	—	82.75	84.22	100.3	104.3	108.1
4Q	—	78.17	57.64	99.5	94.20	118.5
Yr.	—	327.1	336.5	386.8	440.1	433.1
Earnings Per Share ($)						
1Q	**0.20**	**0.21**	**0.11**	**0.14**	0.17	0.10
2Q	**0.33**	**0.31**	**0.31**	**0.26**	0.18	0.11
3Q	—	**-0.31**	**0.24**	**0.23**	-0.24	0.13
4Q	—	**0.24**	**0.46**	**0.20**	0.23	0.24
Yr.	—	**0.46**	**0.92**	**0.82**	**0.25**	**0.59**

Next earnings report expected: late October

Dividend Data

Special cash dividends of $0.10 a share were paid in 1988 and 1989.

Kirby Corporation

Business Summary - 25-JUN-99

Kirby Corp. operates in the highly competitive marine transportation market for commodities transported on the Mississippi River System, the Gulf Intracoastal Waterway and the Houston Ship Channel. The company is the leading inland tank barge carrier.

At February 25, 1999, the company had 523 inland tank barges, 128 towboats, three bowboats, six off-shore dry-cargo barges and seven offshore tugboats. Over the past five years, through consolidations within the inland barge market, KEX has expanded its distribution capabilities and achieved economies of scale to better match barges, towboats, products and destinations.

The marine transportation segment (74% of revenues in 1998) provides inland transportation of industrial chemicals, petrochemical feedstocks, agricultural chemicals and refined petroleum products by tank barges, and the offshore transportation of refined petroleum products by tanker and tank barge and dry-bulk, container and palletized cargoes by barges. The transportation segment is strictly a provider of transportation services, and does not assume ownership of any of the products that it transports.

KEX estimates that the total number of tank barges operating in U.S. inland waters has fallen from 4,200 in 1981 to 2,800 in 1998. As the supply of inland tank barges has declined, domestic production of petrochemicals (an important revenue source for the company) has risen. KEX believes a continuation of these trends will lead to higher rates.

In March 1998, the company sold its offshore tanker and harbor service operations to Hvide Marine Inc. and August Trading Co., for a total of $38.6 million in cash. The two units provided service in the transportation of refined petroleum products and chemicals primarily in domestic coastwise service.

The marine system division (25% of revenues) is engaged in the overhaul and repair of marine diesel engines, reduction gear repair, line boring, block welding services and related parts sales for customers in the marine industry. The division also services tugboats, and towboats powered by large diesel engines, as well as off-shore drilling equipment and other marine equipment.

In February 1999, KEX said it had significantly increased vessel employee compensation in 1998, including an 11% wage increase on August 1. The company added that one of it greatest challenges in the future will be to maintain a high quality labor force.

Per Share Data ($) (Year Ended Dec. 31)	1998	1997	1996	1995	1994	1993	1992	1991	1990	1989
Tangible Bk. Val.	6.53	8.71	7.97	7.63	7.41	7.04	4.96	4.99	4.31	3.65
Cash Flow	1.81	2.07	2.39	1.73	1.75	1.78	1.45	1.21	1.16	0.82
Earnings	0.46	0.92	1.05	0.34	0.58	0.86	0.60	0.61	0.60	0.39
Dividends	Nil	Nil	Nil	Nil	Nil	Nil	Nil	Nil	Nil	0.10
Payout Ratio	Nil	Nil	Nil	Nil	Nil	Nil	Nil	Nil	Nil	25%
Prices - High	25 5/8	21 1/8	20 1/2	19 3/4	23 3/8	22	15 1/2	16 1/8	11 1/8	9 3/4
- Low	17 1/4	16 3/8	15 3/8	13	15 1/2	11 3/8	10	7	6 1/8	4 3/8
P/E Ratio - High	56	23	20	58	40	26	26	26	19	25
- Low	37	18	15	38	27	13	17	11	10	11
Income Statement Analysis (Million $)										
Revs.	327	335	387	432	433	378	269	187	174	140
Oper. Inc.	67.7	69.0	81.6	59.5	74.6	69.3	46.6	34.8	36.3	26.9
Depr.	27.4	28.1	34.8	38.9	33.8	24.5	19.3	13.3	12.9	9.9
Int. Exp.	11.9	13.4	13.3	12.5	8.8	8.4	9.4	6.0	6.3	5.1
Pretax Inc.	17.0	36.5	43.4	20.6	30.3	36.9	18.7	17.8	19.1	11.3
Eff. Tax Rate	41%	38%	37%	43%	34%	34%	27%	26%	29%	21%
Net Inc.	10.1	22.7	27.2	9.4	16.7	22.8	13.6	13.3	13.5	8.9
Balance Sheet & Other Fin. Data (Million $)										
Cash	21.7	23.8	19.7	17.1	35.9	40.1	20.3	30.1	28.9	49.3
Curr. Assets	112	136	130	105	NA	NA	NA	NA	NA	NA
Total Assets	390	518	525	498	667	563	446	286	254	247
Curr. Liab.	65.9	95.6	89.7	69.4	NA	NA	NA	35.5	33.9	31.4
LT Debt	NA	149	177	174	149	110	148	80.0	67.0	76.0
Common Eqty.	141	218	206	205	223	212	123	112	97.0	88.0
Total Cap.	NA	1,272	42.0	379	432	377	309	199	169	165
Cap. Exp.	NA	24.5	37.2	49.5	31.0	71.0	128	37.2	18.1	73.9
Cash Flow	37.5	50.8	62.0	48.3	50.5	47.3	32.9	26.6	26.4	18.8
Curr. Ratio	1.7	1.4	1.4	1.5	NA	NA	NA	NA	NA	NA
% LT Debt of Cap.	NA	35.8	41.3	45.9	34.4	29.1	47.8	40.0	39.8	45.9
% Net Inc.of Revs.	3.1	6.8	7.0	2.2	3.8	6.0	5.1	7.1	7.8	6.4
% Ret. on Assets	2.2	4.4	5.3	1.6	2.7	4.1	3.7	4.9	5.5	4.3
% Ret. on Equity	5.6	10.7	13.2	3.1	7.6	12.5	11.4	12.8	14.9	10.7

Data as orig reptd.; bef. results of disc opers/spec. items. Per share data adj. for stk. divs. Bold denotes diluted EPS (FASB 128)-prior periods restated. E-Estimated. NA-Not Available. NM-Not Meaningful. NR-Not Ranked.

Office—1775 St. James Place, Suite 200, Houston, TX 77056-3453. **Tel**—(713) 435-1000. **Chrmn**—G. A. Peterkin Jr. **Pres & CEO**—J. H. Pyne. **SVP, CFO & Treas**—N. W. Nolen. **Secy**—T.G. Adler. **Investor Contact**—Steve Holcomb. **Dirs**—C. S. Day, B. G. Gower, W. M. Lamont Jr., G. A. Peterkin Jr., J. H. Pyne, R. G. Stone Jr., T. M. Taylor, J. V. Waggoner. **Transfer Agent & Registrar**—Bank of Boston. **Incorporated**—in Nevada in 1969. **Empl**— 1,570. **S&P Analyst:** J.J.A.

STANDARD &POOR'S
STOCK REPORTS

Komag, Inc.

Nasdaq Symbol **KMAG**

In S&P SmallCap 600

09-OCT-99

Industry: Computers (Peripherals)

Summary: This company is the largest independent maker of thin-film disks used in computer disk drives.

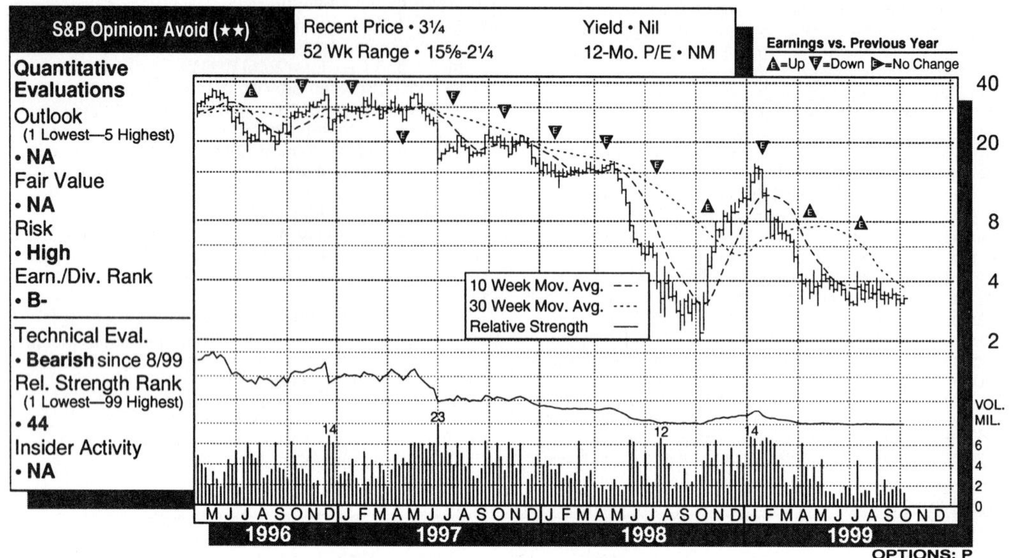

Overview - 26-JUL-99

Although we continue to expect modest revenue gains in 1999, the picture at Komag is clouded by overcapacity in the industry, and by the outlook for a decline in industry-wide unit volumes over the next couple of quarters. Revenues fell 48% in 1998. In April 1999, KMAG acquired the disk production business of Western Digital (NYSE: WDC), and signed a volume purchase agreement that will lend support to unit volumes. However, fixed costs related to the acquisition contributed to a wider loss in the second quarter. The company will incur a large charge in the third quarter, to reduce its work force, close two of the facilities acquired from WDC, and cut back U.S. capacity. In light of a difficult pricing environment, coupled with lowered unit volume expectations, we expect KMAG to post a large loss for the full year.

Valuation - 26-JUL-99

The shares have fallen sharply in recent months. KMAG is faced with a difficult competitive environment that includes pricing pressures and slowing unit volumes in the industry. With disks becoming more commoditized, cost structure is even more important to the long-term success of the company. KMAG is moving to improve its cost structure by closing facilities, reducing capacity, and cutting headcount. However, its long-term viability and ability to weather the current industry downturn are issues. In connection with KMAG's 1998 financial statements, auditors expressed concern about the company's ability to continue as a going concern, due to continued operating losses and lack of compliance with financial covenants. After a substantial net loss in 1998, we do not expect a return to profitability at least until 2000. In light of their great investment risk, we would avoid the shares.

Key Stock Statistics

S&P EPS Est. 1999	-1.30	Tang. Bk. Value/Share	6.01
P/E on S&P Est. 1999	NM	Beta	2.26
S&P EPS Est. 2000	0.10	Shareholders	476
Dividend Rate/Share	Nil	Market cap. (B)	$0.215
Shs. outstg. (M)	65.4	Inst. holdings	37%
Avg. daily vol. (M)	0.318		

Value of $10,000 invested 5 years ago: $ 3,696

Fiscal Year Ending Dec. 31

	1999	1998	1997	1996	1995	1994
Revenues (Million $)						
1Q	90.01	76.06	167.2	152.8	105.1	97.70
2Q	93.23	78.81	175.1	152.2	120.8	97.77
3Q	—	81.31	129.7	131.5	132.8	98.17
4Q	—	92.70	159.0	141.2	153.5	98.74
Yr.	—	328.9	631.1	577.8	512.3	392.4
Earnings Per Share ($)						
1Q	**-0.40**	**-1.10**	**0.33**	**0.80**	0.31	0.34
2Q	**-0.60**	**-4.95**	**0.22**	**0.80**	0.48	0.30
3Q	**E-0.25**	**-0.51**	**-1.01**	**0.31**	0.61	0.33
4Q	**E-0.10**	**-0.35**	**0.02**	**0.16**	0.72	0.30
Yr.	**E-1.30**	**-6.89**	**-0.42**	**2.07**	**2.14**	**1.27**

Next earnings report expected: mid October

Dividend Data

No cash dividends have been paid.

Komag, Incorporated

Business Summary - 26-JUL-99

Komag is the world's largest independent manufacturer of thin-film media (disks), the primary storage medium for digital data used in computer hard disk drives. The company's products are made for the high-end desktop and high-capacity/high-performance enterprise segments of the disk drive market, and are used in PCs, disk arrays, network file servers and engineering workstations. KMAG makes disk products primarily for 3.5-inch form factor hard disk drives, but also for 5.25-inch and other form factors.

International Data Corp. (IDC) forecasts that worldwide disk drive unit shipments will grow at a 15% compound annual rate from 1999 through 2002. The need for higher performance disk drives result from greater processing power, more sophisticated operating systems and application software, high-resolution graphics, larger databases and the emergence of the Internet.

Media products are the disks or platters within a disk drive onto which information is recorded and stored, and from which it is retrieved. Inside a disk drive, the media or disk rotates at speeds of up to 10,000 rpm. The head scans across the disk as it spins, magnetically recording or reading information.

The past year was a period of tremendous transition for the company, as well as for the disk drive industry. Disk drive programs using newer, more advanced, magnetoresistive (MR) media and recording heads replaced older generation programs using inductive media and heads. This led to significant increases in areal density, doubling the number of gigabits per square inch that can be stored and retrieved. KMAG largely completed its transition to MR products by the 1998 fourth quarter, and MR products, including more advanced giant magnetoresistive (GMR) disks, account for virtually all of unit sales. GMR disks accounted for 27% of units shipped in the second quarter of 1999.

Prior to 1997, market demand for thin-film media exceeded supply. In mid-1997, growth in demand slowed primarily due to rapid advances in increased storage capacity per disk achieved through the use of MR technology. As a result, drive designs incorporated fewer disks and recording heads. In addition, KMAG and its competitors began adding significant capacity. This increased supply, coupled with the improvement in storage capacity, allowed supply to catch up to, and then exceed demand. In both 1997 and 1998, the company idled certain equipment and facilities to more closely align its capacity with market demand. In the 1999 third quarter, the company will record a charge to cut additional capacity in the U.S.

In 1998, three customers accounted for 86% of total revenues: Western Digital (43%), Maxtor (25%), and IBM (18%). After spending $199 million in 1997 and $89 million in 1998, KMAG's 1999 capital expenditures were forecast at a more modest $40 million.

Per Share Data ($) (Year Ended Dec. 31)	1998	1997	1996	1995	1994	1993	1992	1991	1990	1989
Tangible Bk. Val.	6.01	13.00	13.50	11.33	7.23	5.87	5.90	4.93	3.92	2.92
Cash Flow	-4.70	2.04	3.71	3.45	2.31	0.92	1.24	1.08	1.04	0.27
Earnings	-6.89	-0.42	2.07	2.14	1.27	-0.23	0.40	0.37	0.44	-0.23
Dividends	Nil	Nil	Nil	Nil	Nil	Nil	Nil	Nil	Nil	Nil
Payout Ratio	Nil	Nil	Nil	Nil	Nil	Nil	Nil	Nil	Nil	Nil
Prices - High	16	35³/₈	37	37¹/₂	14¹/₂	12	11⁵/₈	12¹/₄	8¹/₈	5³/₄
- Low	2	13¹/₂	17⁵/₈	11¹/₈	7⁷/₈	6⁷/₈	5³/₈	5³/₈	4¹/₄	3¹/₄
P/E Ratio - High	NM	NM	18	17	11	NM	29	33	18	NM
- Low	NM	NM	9	5	6	NM	14	15	10	NM
Income Statement Analysis (Million $)										
Revs.	329	631	578	512	392	385	327	279	150	85.0
Oper. Inc.	-27.5	143	199	195	125	82.7	56.6	59.0	36.9	4.0
Depr.	117	129	86.9	65.5	47.6	49.0	36.3	29.4	18.2	13.0
Int. Exp.	19.2	9.1	0.6	1.9	2.9	5.5	3.8	5.6	3.0	3.0
Pretax Inc.	-363	-42.7	131	143	82.8	-2.5	25.8	30.7	19.2	-8.0
Eff. Tax Rate	NM	NM	16%	24%	28%	NM	71%	48%	35%	NM
Net Inc.	-365	-22.1	110	107	58.5	-9.9	16.9	15.1	13.4	-6.1
Balance Sheet & Other Fin. Data (Million $)										
Cash	64.5	134	93.2	214	93.9	91.6	89.3	91.0	45.2	37.8
Curr. Assets	219	372	251	323	172	178	153	149	82.0	64.0
Total Assets	694	1,085	938	686	424	382	356	277	163	122
Curr. Liab.	312	75.6	109	70.9	53.3	85.9	55.5	51.7	24.0	19.3
LT Debt	Nil	245	70.0	Nil	16.3	29.5	27.6	16.5	19.9	21.8
Common Eqty.	324	686	698	575	331	255	249	202	115	77.0
Total Cap.	381	1,008	829	615	370	296	300	225	138	102
Cap. Exp.	89.0	199	403	166	102	86.0	109	60.2	40.3	24.7
Cash Flow	-249	106	197	172	106	39.1	53.2	44.5	31.6	7.0
Curr. Ratio	0.7	4.9	2.3	4.6	3.2	2.1	2.8	2.9	3.4	3.3
% LT Debt of Cap.	Nil	24.3	8.4	Nil	4.4	10.0	9.2	7.3	14.4	21.4
% Net Inc.of Revs.	NM	NM	19.0	20.9	14.9	NM	5.2	5.4	8.9	NM
% Ret. on Assets	NM	NM	13.5	19.3	14.2	NM	5.3	6.0	9.0	NM
% Ret. on Equity	NM	NM	17.3	23.6	19.5	NM	7.4	8.3	13.3	NM

Data as orig reptd.; bef. results of disc opers/spec. items. Per share data adj. for stk. divs. Bold denotes diluted EPS (FASB 128)-prior periods restated. E-Estimated. NA-Not Available. NM-Not Meaningful. NR-Not Ranked.

Office—1704 Automation Parkway, San Jose, CA 95131-1873. **Tel**—(408) 576-2000. **Website**—http://www.komag.com **Pres & CEO**—S. C. Johnson. **Chrmn**—T. Chen. **SVP, CFO & Secy**—W. L. Potts, Jr. **Investor Contact**—David H. Allen. **Dirs**—T. Chen, C. A. Eyre, I. Federman, S. C. Johnson, G. A. Neil, M. Palevsky, M. R. Splinter, A. Sun, M. Takebayashi. **Transfer Agent & Registrar**—ChaseMellon Shareholder Services, SF. **Incorporated**—in Delaware in 1986. **Empl**— 4,086. **S&P Analyst:** Jim Corridore

Kroll-O'Gara Co.

NASDAQ Symbol **KROG**

In S&P SmallCap 600

09-OCT-99

Industry: Services (Commercial & Consumer)

Summary: This company is a leading global provider of a broad range of specialized products and services designed to supply solutions to a variety of security needs.

Quantitative Evaluations

Outlook (1 Lowest—5 Highest) • **NA**

Fair Value • **NA**

Risk • **NA**

Earn./Div. Rank • **NR**

Technical Eval. • **Neutral** since 9/99

Rel. Strength Rank (1 Lowest—99 Highest) • **10**

Insider Activity • **NA**

Recent Price • 16⅜

52 Wk Range • 41⅞-14

Yield • Nil

12-Mo. P/E • 34.8

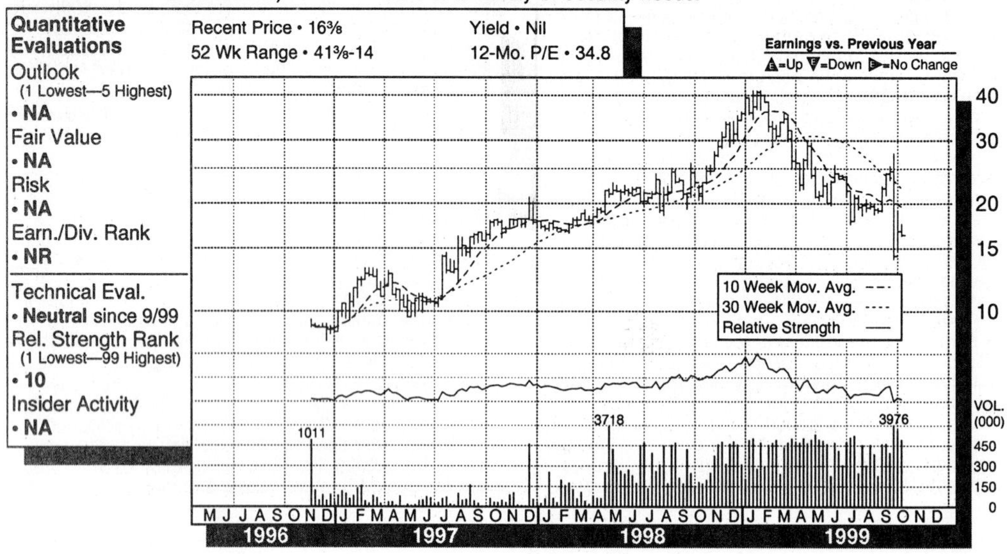

Business Profile - 08-SEP-99

KROG, based in New York City and Fairfield, OH, and with more than 60 offices and plants around the world, provides governments, businesses and individuals with information, analysis, training, advice and products to mitigate growing risks associated with fraud, electronic threats, physical threats, and uninformed decisions based upon incomplete or inaccurate information. Among many acquisitions in recent years, in June 1999, the company acquired Background America, an information technology enterprise specializing in Internet-based employment screening and compliance services. A restructuring designed to cut costs and improve efficiency was completed in mid-1999.

Operational Review - 08-SEP-99

Net sales from continuing operations in the first half of 1999, climbed 27% from those of the 1998 period, as restated for acquisitions; a 69% advance in investigations and intelligence and initial revenues from information security outweighed a 10% decline in security products and services. After $4.4 million of restructuring expenses and $3.1 million of merger-related expenses ($0.23 a share, after taxes), income from continuing operations fell 37%, to $4,078,000 ($0.18 a share, on 26% more shares), from $6,429,000 ($0.36). Per share results exclude a loss from discontinued operations and the cumulative effect of an accounting change of $0.06 in 1999, and income from discontinued operations of $0.02 in 1998.

Stock Performance - 08-OCT-99

In the past 30 trading days, KROG's shares have declined 14%, compared to a 0.91% fall in the S&P 500. Average trading volume for the past five days was 201,080 shares, compared with the 40-day moving average of 259,490 shares.

Key Stock Statistics

Dividend Rate/Share	Nil	Shareholders	94
Shs. outstg. (M)	22.2	Market cap. (B)	$0.363
Avg. daily vol. (M)	0.418	Inst. holdings	50%
Tang. Bk. Value/Share	3.43		
Beta	NA		

Value of $10,000 invested 5 years ago: NA

Fiscal Year Ending Dec. 31

	1999	1998	1997	1996	1995	1994
Revenues (Million $)						
1Q	65.57	57.20	—	—	—	—
2Q	76.51	64.56	—	—	—	—
3Q	—	72.81	—	18.80	—	—
4Q	—	70.28	54.02	—	—	—
Yr.	—	264.9	190.4	82.78	32.82	33.90
Earnings Per Share ($)						
1Q	**0.16**	**0.20**	—	—	—	—
2Q	**0.03**	**0.23**	—	—	—	—
3Q	—	**0.26**	—	—	—	—
4Q	—	**0.02**	**-0.37**	—	—	—
Yr.	—	**0.69**	**0.09**	—	—	—

Next earnings report expected: late October

Dividend Data

No cash dividends have been paid.

The Kroll-O'Gara Company

Business Summary - 08-SEP-99

Governments, businesses and individuals worldwide increasingly are recognizing the need for products and services that mitigate the growing risks associated with fraud, electronic and physical threats and uninformed decisions based on incomplete or inaccurate information. Through a network of 60 offices located in 19 countries, Kroll-O'Gara is meeting these needs by providing information, analysis, training, advice and products to its customers.

The company is organized into three primary business groups: Investigations & Intelligence, Security Products & Services, and Information Security. The Voice and Data Communications Group, which offers secure satellite communication equipment and satellite navigation systems, has been treated as a discontinued operation since April 1999, when directors approved a formal plan to discontinue its operations.

The Investigations & Intelligence Group (61% of revenues in the first half of 1999) provides financial services, including forensic accounting, business valuation, insolvency, turnaround, asset tracing and pre-acquisition due diligence. It provides business investigations and intelligence, including litigation support, monitoring and intellectual property infringement investigations. Its corporate services includepre-employment background checking, drug testing, surveillance and vendor integrity programs. It also provides clients with corporate security, including security architecture and planning, as well as computer forensics.

The Security Products & Services Group (38%) provides commercial and military armored vehicles, other armoring systems, advanced security and driver training, crisis management, and engineering services.

The Information Security Group (2%) provides network and system security services, all aspects of data security, including productevaluation assessment, security policy development, security architecture and design as well as security training.

In June 1999, the company acquired Background America, Inc., based in Nashville, TN, in exchange for 988,000 KROG common shares. Background America is an information technology enterprise specializing in Internet-based employment screening and compliance services. By focusing on innovative Internet solutions, Background America provides state-of-the-art service in theemployment-screening field. Founded in September 1995, the company employs approximately 140 people in its three operations centers and five sales offices. Background America has approximately 3,500 clients in a broad range of markets, including health care, insurance, manufacturing and retail. It has experienced rapid growth since its founding, with sales of $1.8 million, $4.2 million and $7.4 million for 1996, 1997 and 1998, respectively. The company achieved profitability in the first quarter of 1999.

Per Share Data ($) (Year Ended Dec. 31)	1998	1997	1996	1995	1994	1993	1992	1991	1990	1989
Tangible Bk. Val.	3.43	0.13	1.90	0.05	0.36	NA	NA	NA	NA	NA
Cash Flow	1.14	0.30	1.13	NA	NA	NA	NA	NA	NA	NA
Earnings	0.69	0.09	NA	NA	NA	NA	NA	NA	NA	NA
Dividends	Nil	Nil	Nil	NA	NA	NA	NA	NA	NA	NA
Payout Ratio	Nil	Nil	Nil	NA	NA	NA	NA	NA	NA	NA
Prices - High	40½	20⅞	9¾	NA	NA	NA	NA	NA	NA	NA
- Low	16½	9⅛	8¼	NA	NA	NA	NA	NA	NA	NA
P/E Ratio - High	59	NM	NA	NA	NA	NA	NA	NA	NA	NA
- Low	24	NM	NA	NA	NA	NA	NA	NA	NA	NA
Income Statement Analysis (Million $)										
Revs.	265	190	82.8	32.8	33.9	21.1	NA	NA	NA	NA
Oper. Inc.	38.4	16.9	9.4	0.3	2.7	1.6	NA	NA	NA	NA
Depr.	8.6	2.8	0.9	0.5	0.5	0.3	NA	NA	NA	NA
Int. Exp.	4.5	4.8	1.3	0.8	0.4	0.3	NA	NA	NA	NA
Pretax Inc.	20.6	3.8	7.2	-1.1	1.9	1.0	NA	NA	NA	NA
Eff. Tax Rate	36%	62%	7.22%	Nil	Nil	Nil	NA	NA	NA	NA
Net Inc.	13.1	1.3	6.7	-1.1	1.9	1.0	NA	NA	NA	NA
Balance Sheet & Other Fin. Data (Million $)										
Cash	26.1	6.9	1.5	0.3	0.6	NA	NA	NA	NA	NA
Curr. Assets	149	87.0	35.1	24.1	15.7	NA	NA	NA	NA	NA
Total Assets	249	134	43.9	27.8	19.2	NA	NA	NA	NA	NA
Curr. Liab.	65.4	55.5	30.8	27.4	17.7	NA	NA	NA	NA	NA
LT Debt	39.3	46.9	0.5	0.2	0.2	NA	NA	NA	NA	NA
Common Eqty.	141	28.0	12.7	0.2	1.3	NA	NA	NA	NA	NA
Total Cap.	182	77.1	13.2	0.5	1.5	NA	NA	NA	NA	NA
Cap. Exp.	5.5	1.1	0.8	NA	NA	NA	NA	NA	NA	NA
Cash Flow	21.7	4.1	7.5	-0.6	2.4	1.2	NA	NA	NA	NA
Curr. Ratio	2.3	1.6	1.1	0.9	0.9	NA	NA	NA	NA	NA
% LT Debt of Cap.	21.6	60.8	3.6	48.9	15.3	NA	NA	NA	NA	NA
% Net Inc.of Revs.	4.9	0.7	8.0	NA	5.5	4.5	NA	NA	NA	NA
% Ret. on Assets	6.8	1.4	18.6	NM	NA	NA	NA	NA	NA	NA
% Ret. on Equity	15.5	6.2	103.3	NM	NA	NA	NA	NA	NA	NA

Data as orig reptd.; bef. results of disc opers/spec. items. Per share data adj. for stk. divs. Bold denotes diluted EPS (FASB 128)-prior periods restated. E-Estimated. NA-Not Available. NM-Not Meaningful. NR-Not Ranked.

Office— 9113 Lesaint Drive, Fairfield, OH 45014. **Tel**—(513) 874-2112. **Website**—www.ogara.com **Chrmn & CEO**—J. B. Kroll. **Vice Chrmn**—T. M. O'Gara. **Pres & COO**—W. T. O'Gara. **VP & Secy**—A. S. Gordon. **CFO**—N. E. Paciotti. **Dirs**—M. G. Cherkasky, M. S. Cogan, J. B. Kroll, M. J. Lennon, R. E. Mabus, T. M. O'Gara, W. T. O'Gara, H. E. Price, J. E. Ritter, W. S. Sessions, H. I. Smith. **Transfer Agent & Registrar**—Fifth Third Bank, Cincinnati. **Incorporated**—in Ohio. **Empl**— 2,800. **S&P Analyst:** C.F.B.

STANDARD
&POOR'S
STOCK REPORTS

Kronos Inc.

NASDAQ Symbol **KRON**

In S&P SmallCap 600

09-OCT-99

Industry: Computer (Software & Services)

Summary: This company designs, develops, manufactures and markets integrated time accounting and other data collection systems.

Quantitative Evaluations

Outlook (1 Lowest—5 Highest) • **5**

Fair Value • **64¼**

Risk • **High**

Earn./Div. Rank • **B+**

Technical Eval. • **Bearish** since 9/99

Rel. Strength Rank (1 Lowest—99 Highest) • **25**

Insider Activity • **Unfavorable**

Recent Price • 39½
52 Wk Range • 54½-18

Yield • Nil
12-Mo. P/E • 26.2

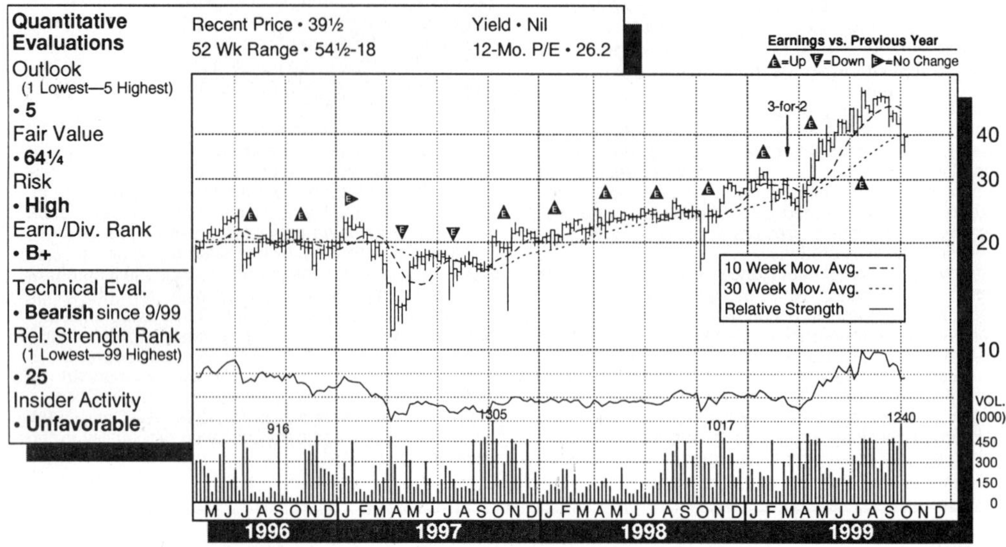

Business Profile - 15-SEP-99

KRON has completed a transition to Windows and client/server technologies, which now make up the majority of software sales. The company is attempting to expand its products into the manufacturing, retail, health care, government and education markets. KRON recently acquired Visionware labor productivity software from Cost Systems Group, part of the company's goal to provide labor management solutions in all its key markets. In May 1999, KRON acquired CrossWind Technologies, Inc., bringing additional labor tracking software to its offerings. The company recently increased its stock buyback authorization to 750,000 shares, of which, 418,600 had been repurchased as of August 6, 1999.

Operational Review - 15-SEP-99

In the first nine months of FY 99 (Sep.), revenues advanced 27%, year to year, reflecting strong growth in Windows, client/server and AS/400 software, as well as increased demand for services. Margins widened, as the benefits of higher volume and a more favorable product mix outweighed 38% higher R&D costs and 28% higher sales and marketing expense; pretax income climbed 47%. After taxes at 35.1%, versus 38.2%, net income surged 55% to $13,895,000 ($1.06 a share, on 2.2% more shares), from $8,971,000 ($0.70, as adjusted).

Stock Performance - 08-OCT-99

In the past 30 trading days, KRON's shares have declined 23%, compared to a 0.91% fall in the S&P 500. Average trading volume for the past five days was 104,080 shares, compared with the 40-day moving average of 110,426 shares.

Key Stock Statistics

Dividend Rate/Share	Nil	Shareholders	3,000
Shs. outstg. (M)	12.6	Market cap. (B)	$0.499
Avg. daily vol. (M)	0.145	Inst. holdings	69%
Tang. Bk. Value/Share	5.53		
Beta	0.53		

Value of $10,000 invested 5 years ago: $ 52,361

Fiscal Year Ending Sep. 30

	1999	1998	1997	1996	1995	1994
Revenues (Million $)						
1Q	53.12	44.57	37.11	31.47	26.15	19.02
2Q	61.69	46.47	39.40	33.10	29.21	21.05
3Q	67.22	52.68	43.30	36.25	31.07	23.49
4Q	—	58.75	50.73	42.14	33.95	29.36
Yr.	—	202.5	170.5	143.0	120.4	92.92
Earnings Per Share ($)						
1Q	**0.25**	**0.19**	0.17	0.17	0.09	0.05
2Q	**0.35**	**0.23**	0.14	0.19	0.13	0.07
3Q	**0.47**	**0.29**	0.20	0.23	0.19	0.11
4Q	—	**0.45**	0.38	0.31	0.28	0.18
Yr.	—	**1.15**	0.89	0.91	0.69	0.41

Next earnings report expected: late October

Dividend Data

Amount ($)	Date Decl.	Ex-Div. Date	Stock of Record	Payment Date
3-for-2	Feb. 08	Mar. 10	Feb. 23	Mar. 09 '99

Kronos Incorporated

Business Summary - 15-SEP-99

Kronos (Greek for time) began operations in 1977, when the company's founders saw timekeeping as an industry that could benefit from the introduction of computerized automation. The company currently designs, makes and markets time and attendance, work force management and shop floor data collection systems and application software that enhances workplace productivity. Its systems consist of fully integrated software and intelligent data collection terminals. It also maintains an extensive service and support organization that provides on-site and remote maintenance, as well as professional and educational services. Net revenues in FY 98 (Sep.) were derived from products 42% (68% in FY 97) and services 58% (32%).

Major systems include Timekeeper Central, Timekeeper/AS and Timekeeper C/S Systems, which are designed to reduce payroll preparation time, improve labor scheduling and control labor costs; ShopTrac Data Collection System, marketed primarily to manufacturing plants, which collects a wide variety of labor and material data to provide real-time information on cost, location and product completion time; Visionware, a suite of labor productivity tools that synthesize information from disparate information systems such as billing, payroll and time and attendance and accurately captures, analyzes and reports the information; and the Kronos Smart Scheduler, which can forecast the level of activity a location can expect by analyzing key business volume indicators and apply the appropriate work standards to generate the optimum level of staffing required for the expected level of business.

Optional application software includes the Kronos Archive Program, which performs long-term record keeping; the Kronos CardSaver, which records employees' in and out data for wage and hour inquiries; the Kronos Accruals Module, which calculates each employees' available benefit time; and the Kronos Attendance Tracker, which records and documents employee absences.

Other products include the Time Bank, which interfaces with commonly used payroll, human resources and scheduling software; Gatekeeper terminals, which control employee access to a facility; Kronos TeleTime System, which allows customer telephones to serve as data input devices; and ImageKeeper, which stores digital photographs and signatures of employees, and items such as badges, time cards, bar code labels and modems.

Per Share Data ($) (Year Ended Sep. 30)	**1998**	**1997**	**1996**	**1995**	**1994**	**1993**	**1992**	**1991**	**1990**	**1989**
Tangible Bk. Val.	5.92	5.28	4.42	3.43	2.58	2.68	2.28	1.11	NA	NA
Cash Flow	1.73	1.77	1.56	1.20	0.83	0.60	0.54	0.39	0.28	NA
Earnings	1.15	0.89	0.91	0.68	0.41	0.34	0.36	0.24	0.16	0.15
Dividends	Nil	Nil	Nil	Nil	Nil	Nil	Nil	Nil	Nil	Nil
Payout Ratio	Nil	Nil	Nil	Nil	Nil	Nil	Nil	Nil	Nil	Nil
Prices - High	30	23⅞	24⅝	22½	12	10⅝	10⅝	NA	NA	NA
- Low	16⅝	10⅞	16⅛	10⅞	6½	6⅛	5¼	NA	NA	NA
P/E Ratio - High	26	27	27	33	29	31	30	NA	NA	NA
- Low	14	12	18	16	16	18	15	NA	NA	NA
Income Statement Analysis (Million $)										
Revs.	202	171	143	120	92.9	67.1	58.1	47.8	39.6	32.9
Oper. Inc.	31.9	29.5	26.9	20.3	13.4	8.3	7.4	4.6	3.4	NA
Depr.	7.4	11.2	8.2	6.3	4.9	3.3	1.8	1.4	1.1	NA
Int. Exp.	Nil	Nil	Nil	Nil	0.0	0.1	0.1	0.2	0.2	NA
Pretax Inc.	24.3	18.3	18.7	13.6	7.8	6.0	5.7	3.6	2.3	NA
Eff. Tax Rate	40%	38%	39%	38%	38%	36%	38%	38%	36%	NA
Net Inc.	14.7	11.3	11.4	8.4	4.9	3.8	3.5	2.3	1.4	1.4
Balance Sheet & Other Fin. Data (Million $)										
Cash	29.9	20.7	32.8	21.4	8.7	12.2	13.8	4.1	NA	NA
Curr. Assets	109	90.2	74.4	57.2	40.7	35.0	30.3	16.9	NA	NA
Total Assets	161	128	105	77.8	59.4	46.0	37.3	22.3	17.2	15.2
Curr. Liab.	63.5	49.0	38.1	30.4	22.7	16.0	12.5	10.9	NA	NA
LT Debt	Nil	Nil	Nil	Nil	Nil	0.2	0.5	0.9	1.1	1.3
Common Eqty.	87.2	72.5	61.1	46.6	35.9	29.8	24.3	10.1	6.6	5.4
Total Cap.	88.1	75.1	63.3	46.6	35.9	30.0	24.8	11.5	10.1	9.0
Cap. Exp.	6.3	8.7	9.7	4.1	4.8	4.6	3.4	1.5	1.4	NA
Cash Flow	22.1	22.4	19.6	14.7	9.8	6.8	5.3	3.6	2.6	NA
Curr. Ratio	1.7	1.8	1.9	1.9	1.8	2.2	2.4	1.6	NA	NA
% LT Debt of Cap.	Nil	Nil	Nil	Nil	Nil	0.5	2.1	7.9	10.7	13.9
% Net Inc.of Revs.	7.3	6.6	8.0	7.0	5.3	5.7	6.1	4.7	3.7	4.3
% Ret. on Assets	10.2	9.7	12.5	12.3	9.1	9.0	10.7	11.4	8.9	9.6
% Ret. on Equity	18.4	16.9	21.3	20.4	14.6	13.9	18.8	24.4	20.5	NA

Data as orig reptd.; bef. results of disc opers/spec. items. Per share data adj. for stk. divs. Bold denotes diluted EPS (FASB 128)-prior periods restated. E-Estimated. NA-Not Available. NM-Not Meaningful. NR-Not Ranked.

Office—400 Fifth Ave., Waltham, MA 02154. **Tel**—(781) 890-3232. **Website**—http://www.kronos.com **Chrmn & CEO**—M. S. Ain. **Pres & COO**—W. P. Decker. **VP-Fin & Treas**—P. A. Lacy. **Investor Contact**—Marie Harris (617-487-4809). **Dirs**—M. S. Ain, W. P. Decker, R. J. Dumler, D. B. McWilliams, L. Portner, S. Rubinovitz. **Transfer Agent & Registrar**—State Street Bank & Trust Co., Boston. **Incorporated**—in Massachusetts in 1977. **Empl**— 1,538. **S&P Analyst:** Jim Corridore

STANDARD
&POOR'S
STOCK REPORTS

Kulicke & Soffa Industries

Nasdaq Symbol **KLIC**

In S&P SmallCap 600

09-OCT-99

Industry: Equipment (Semiconductor)

Summary: This company is the world's largest producer of semiconductor assembly equipment, including wafer dicing, die bonding and wire bonding products and systems.

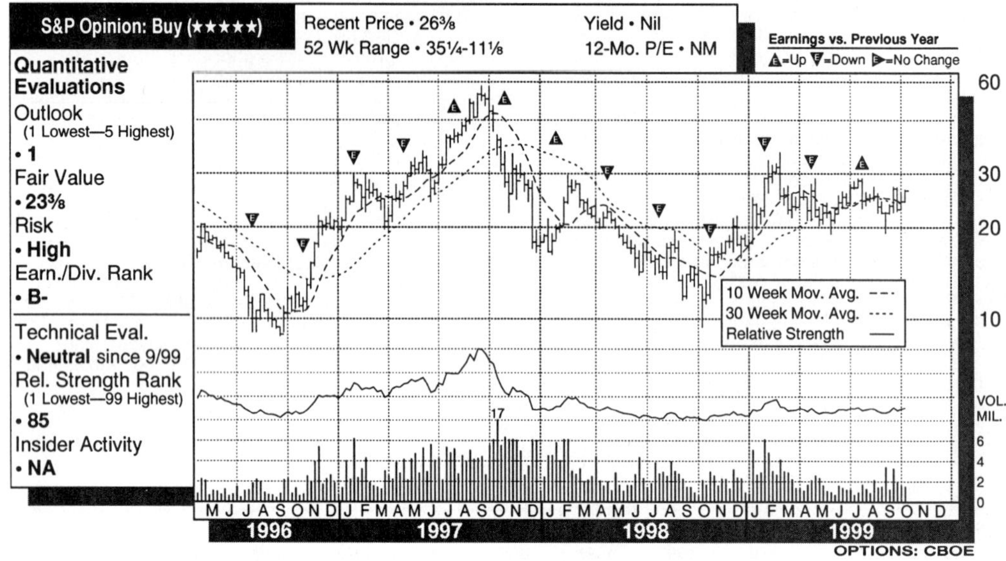

Overview - 29-SEP-99

Though sales are likely to be down for the second consecutive year in FY 99 (Sep.), the worst appears to be over for the company. Revenues have grown sharply on a sequential basis for the past two quarters, and we expect this trend to continue into FY 00, based on renewed demand for the company's wire bonders. Last year, the company's semiconductor customers canceled or deferred orders for equipment as the Asian financial crisis hurt end-market demand for chips. In the third quarter of FY 99, however, bookings were up 157% from the low point experienced in the first quarter. Gross margins should improve substantially over the course of FY 00, as costs are spread over a much larger revenue base. As a result, we expect EPS to rebound to $1.49 in FY 00, from our estimate of a $0.50 loss in FY 99 (excluding charges).

Valuation - 29-SEP-99

The company's shares have been in a trading range in the mid-20s for much of 1999. We are raising our rating on the stock to buy from hold, reflecting the company's market leading position for semiconductor assembly equipment at a time when the semiconductor industry is entering an expansionary phase that we expect to last over a year. Demand for the company's bonder products is currently strong and unaffected by the Taiwan earthquake. KLIC is gradually transitioning its business toward advanced packaging and materials, which will add new revenue streams. Although there are costs associated with the transition, operating efficiencies associated with a new plant opening in Singapore in 2000 will create some offsetting savings. Recently trading at 16X our FY 00 (Sep.) EPS estimate of $1.49, we believe the shares are undervalued and can outperform the broader market over the next six to 12 months.

Key Stock Statistics

S&P EPS Est. 1999	-0.50	Tang. Bk. Value/Share	9.33
P/E on S&P Est. 1999	NM	Beta	2.58
S&P EPS Est. 2000	1.49	Shareholders	782
Dividend Rate/Share	Nil	Market cap. (B)	$0.620
Shs. outstg. (M)	23.5	Inst. holdings	61%
Avg. daily vol. (M)	0.411		

Value of $10,000 invested 5 years ago: $ 37,767

Fiscal Year Ending Sep. 30

	1999	1998	1997	1996	1995	1994
Revenues (Million $)						
1Q	61.18	123.1	81.84	127.2	51.46	38.26
2Q	73.56	120.1	121.5	115.4	64.79	43.77
3Q	110.8	91.69	146.4	76.91	87.30	40.84
4Q	—	76.18	152.2	61.70	101.0	50.44
Yr.	—	411.0	501.9	381.2	304.5	173.3
Earnings Per Share ($)						
1Q	**-0.38**	**0.29**	**0.02**	0.82	0.22	0.14
2Q	**-0.63**	**0.39**	0.46	0.54	0.48	0.19
3Q	**-0.03**	**-0.13**	0.62	-0.13	0.76	0.07
4Q	—	**-0.79**	0.63	-0.65	0.85	0.23
Yr.	—	**-0.23**	**1.79**	0.60	2.38	0.63

Next earnings report expected: mid November

Dividend Data

Cash dividends were omitted in 1985.

A Division of The McGraw-Hill Companies

Kulicke & Soffa Industries, Inc.

Business Summary - 29-SEP-99

Founded back in 1951 to design industrial equipment, Kulicke & Soffa Industries (KLIC) is today the world's largest producer of semiconductor assembly equipment, commanding an impressive share of this critical technology market. KLIC, based in Willow Grove, PA, also supplies packaging materials used in the semiconductor assembly process. In FY 98 (Sep.), 80% of revenues were from deliveries outside the U.S., versus 85% in FY 97.

The company's sales and earnings are affected by the level of capital investment by the semiconductor (IC) industry. Demand for assembly equipment usually lags IC plant (fab) construction by 18 months to 24 months.

Principal products are computerized automatic wire bonders, which determine the location of the semiconductor devices being assembled and position the wires being attached to them automatically rather than manually. KLIC is currently the market leader in all geographic regions except Japan.

In FY 98, KLIC developed a new generation of wire bonders, the 8000 family, based on an entirely new platform; the series has required the development of new software and subassemblies. In the fourth quarter of FY 98, the model 8020 ball bonder accounted for the majority of the company's ball bonder sales, replacing the older generation 1488.

The company makes other semiconductor assembly equipment, including precision dicing saws used to cut silicon, ceramics and other materials to extremely close tolerances, and die bonders used to attach an individual semiconductor die to the package to which it is wire bonded. KLIC also offers spare parts and services for its equipment.

The company's principal strategy is to improve and broaden the range of its products. In addition to enhancing its leadership position in the wire bonder market with the development of the 8000 family of products, KLIC has been forging alliances that enable it to develop new technologies. In February 1996, the company formed a joint venture with Delco Electronics Corp. called Flip Chip Technologies, L.L.C. (FCT), which provides wafer bumping services. KLIC believes that by 2002 flip chip technologies will begin to take incremental market share from wire bonding technologies in the high end of the market. In February 1997, KLIC formed an alliance with PRI Automation Inc. to develop technology to integrate and automate semiconductor assembly equipment.

The packaging materials business was greatly expanded by the 1995 acquisition of American Fine Wire Corp., a maker of gold and aluminum bonding wire; and the 1996 acquisition of Semitec, Inc., a maker of saw blades. KLIC plans to continue to expand this business, which has a less volatile revenue pattern than the company's equipment segment.

Per Share Data ($) **(Year Ended Sep. 30)**	**1998**	**1997**	**1996**	**1995**	**1994**	**1993**	**1992**	**1991**	**1990**	**1989**
Tangible Bk. Val.	10.66	10.73	5.42	6.92	3.75	3.17	2.46	3.19	3.24	3.02
Cash Flow	0.34	2.30	1.09	2.65	0.86	0.85	-0.60	0.10	0.30	0.56
Earnings	-0.23	1.78	0.60	2.38	0.63	0.67	-0.78	-0.08	0.13	0.38
Dividends	Nil	Nil	Nil	Nil	Nil	Nil	Nil	Nil	Nil	Nil
Payout Ratio	Nil	Nil	Nil	Nil	Nil	Nil	Nil	Nil	Nil	Nil
Prices - High	29 5/8	58 3/8	25 3/4	45 3/8	11	15 5/8	4 1/4	5 1/8	6	5
- Low	9 3/8	16 1/2	8 3/4	9 1/8	4 3/4	3 1/8	1 7/8	2 5/8	2 3/16	3 1/4
P/E Ratio - High	NM	33	43	19	18	24	NM	NM	48	13
- Low	NM	9	15	4	7	5	NM	NM	18	9
Income Statement Analysis (Million $)										
Revs.	411	502	381	305	173	141	95.0	100	103	96.0
Oper. Inc.	9.1	69.0	27.1	60.4	17.9	17.3	-4.8	3.5	11.3	9.5
Depr.	13.3	11.3	9.7	5.0	3.9	3.1	2.8	2.8	2.8	2.9
Int. Exp.	0.3	2.3	3.3	1.4	2.2	2.2	2.3	2.4	2.7	3.1
Pretax Inc.	-7.4	51.8	15.6	55.6	13.0	12.1	-13.1	-1.6	2.7	5.8
Eff. Tax Rate	NM	26%	24%	23%	20%	10%	NM	NM	28%	NM
Net Inc.	-5.4	38.3	11.8	42.8	10.4	10.8	-12.3	-1.2	1.9	5.8
Balance Sheet & Other Fin. Data (Million $)										
Cash	76.5	108	45.3	38.2	21.7	22.8	22.0	21.9	22.4	22.4
Curr. Assets	234	272	163	160	91.6	84.3	63.6	71.9	77.3	76.4
Total Assets	343	377	250	191	121	105	84.0	93.0	97.0	95.0
Curr. Liab.	51.6	82.0	48.9	56.2	30.1	26.1	17.7	14.6	17.5	12.9
LT Debt	Nil	0.2	50.7	0.2	26.5	26.7	26.8	27.7	28.5	35.2
Common Eqty.	288	292	147	134	63.2	51.5	39.0	50.2	50.6	46.8
Total Cap.	288	292	198	134	90.4	78.6	65.8	77.9	79.2	82.0
Cap. Exp.	16.1	13.5	18.0	10.8	6.2	4.4	3.6	3.8	2.4	2.6
Cash Flow	7.9	49.6	21.5	47.8	14.4	13.9	-9.5	1.6	4.8	8.7
Curr. Ratio	4.5	3.3	3.3	2.9	3.0	3.2	3.6	4.9	4.4	5.9
% LT Debt of Cap.	Nil	0.1	25.6	Nil	29.3	34.0	40.7	35.6	36.0	42.9
% Net Inc.of Revs.	NM	7.6	3.1	14.1	6.0	7.7	NM	NM	1.9	6.0
% Ret. on Assets	NM	12.2	5.4	27.5	9.1	11.3	NM	NM	2.0	6.3
% Ret. on Equity	NM	17.4	8.4	43.6	18.0	23.7	NM	NM	4.0	13.3

Data as orig reptd.; bef. results of disc opers/spec. items. Per share data adj. for stk. divs. Bold denotes diluted EPS (FASB 128)-prior periods restated. E-Estimated. NA-Not Available. NM-Not Meaningful. NR-Not Ranked.

Office—2101 Blair Mill Rd., Willow Grove, PA 19090. **Tel**—(215) 784-6750. **Fax**—(215) 659-6167. **Website**—http://www.kns.com **Chrmn & CEO**—C. S. Kulicke. **SVP & CFO**—C. G. Sprague. **Investor Contact**—Jim Chiafery (215-784-6436). **Dirs**—J. W. Bagley, C. S. Kulicke, F. W. Kulicke Jr., J. A. O'Steen, A. F. Page, M. Roehm Jr., L. D. Striplin, C. W. Zadel. **Transfer Agent & Registrar**—American Stock Transfer & Trust Co., NYC. **Incorporated**—in Pennsylvania in 1956. **Empl**— 2,057. **S&P Analyst:** T. W. Smith, CFA

La-Z-Boy

NYSE Symbol **LZB**

In S&P SmallCap 600

09-OCT-99

Industry: Household Furnishings & Appliances

Summary: LZB manufactures residential and office upholstered seating products, including recliners and motion chairs, and solid-wood bedroom/dining room products.

Quantitative Evaluations

Outlook (1 Lowest—5 Highest)
• **5+**
Fair Value
• **32**
Risk
• **Low**
Earn./Div. Rank
• **A**

Technical Eval.
• **Bearish** since 9/99
Rel. Strength Rank (1 Lowest—99 Highest)
• **22**
Insider Activity
• **Neutral**

Recent Price • 19⅛
52 Wk Range • 24½-14⅝
Yield • 1.7%
12-Mo. P/E • 14.1

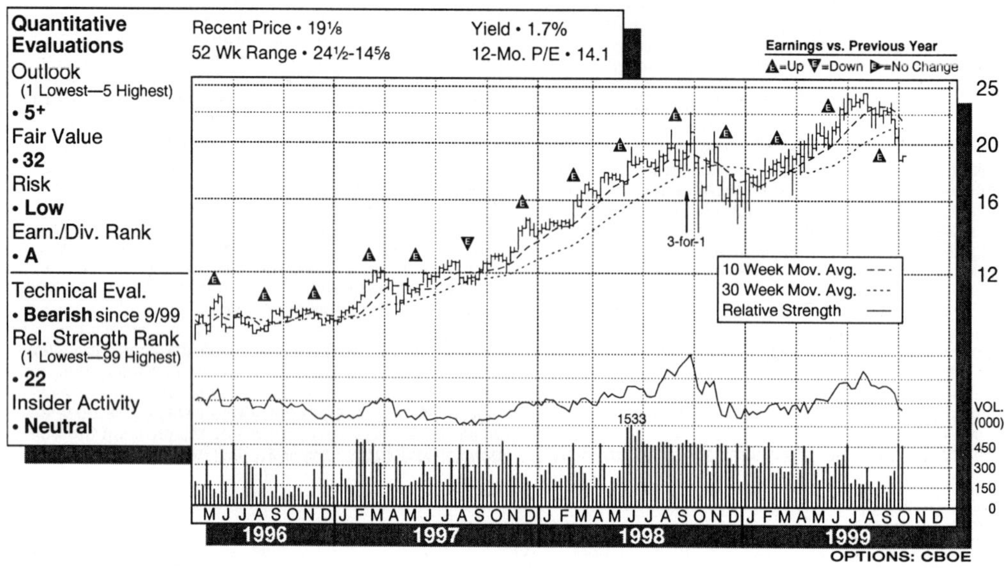

Business Profile - 16-AUG-99

The company, one of the world's largest furniture producers, continues to report record revenues and earnings. LZB aims to grow at a faster rate than the furniture industry, with a benchmark of 10% annually. Other goals include an earnings growth rate more rapid than that of sales, and a 20% return on capital. In FY 99, the company exceeded each of these goals. On June 1, 1999, the company acquired Bauhaus USA Inc., a leading designer, manufacturer and marketer of transitional upholstered furniture and convertible sofas in the medium priced segment (annual sales about $100 million).

Operational Review - 16-AUG-99

Revenues for the three months ended July 24, 1999, advanced 20%, reflecting continued strong demand for the company's products, as well as acquisitions. Profitability was aided by the higher volume, operating efficiencies, and favorable currency exchange effects; operating income gained 78%. With 21% higher interest expense, a 120% increase in other income, and after taxes at 38.4%, versus 39.7%, net income was up 85%, to $13,293,000 ($0.25 a share) from $7,184,000 ($0.13, as restated for September 1998 3-for-1 stock split).

Stock Performance - 08-OCT-99

In the past 30 trading days, LZB's shares have declined 15%, compared to a 0.91% fall in the S&P 500. Average trading volume for the past five days was 104,960 shares, compared with the 40-day moving average of 60,913 shares.

Key Stock Statistics

Dividend Rate/Share	0.32	Shareholders	13,592
Shs. outstg. (M)	52.2	Market cap. (B)	$0.999
Avg. daily vol. (M)	0.087	Inst. holdings	49%
Tang. Bk. Value/Share	7.03		
Beta	0.50		

Value of $10,000 invested 5 years ago: $ 17,217

Fiscal Year Ending Apr. 30

	2000	1999	1998	1997	1996	1995
Revenues (Million $)						
1Q	321.7	268.9	212.3	202.2	195.8	174.4
2Q	—	334.8	293.2	271.6	258.3	230.6
3Q	—	318.1	280.5	244.6	226.3	210.8
4Q	—	365.8	322.0	287.5	266.8	234.5
Yr.	—	1,288	1,108	1,006	947.3	850.3
Earnings Per Share ($)						
1Q	**0.25**	**0.13**	**0.03**	**0.08**	0.06	0.08
2Q	—	**0.35**	**0.31**	**0.28**	0.26	0.22
3Q	—	**0.33**	**0.21**	**0.18**	0.14	0.13
4Q	—	**0.43**	**0.37**	**0.29**	0.25	0.24
Yr.	—	**1.24**	**0.93**	**0.83**	**0.71**	**0.67**

Next earnings report expected: early November

Dividend Data (Dividends have been paid since 1963.)

Amount ($)	Date Decl.	Ex-Div. Date	Stock of Record	Payment Date
0.080	Nov. 20	Nov. 25	Nov. 30	Dec. 10 '98
0.080	Feb. 09	Feb. 17	Feb. 19	Mar. 10 '99
0.080	May. 04	May. 19	May. 21	Jun. 10 '99
0.080	Jul. 27	Aug. 25	Aug. 27	Sep. 10 '99

A Division of The McGraw-Hill Companies

La-Z-Boy Incorporated

Business Summary - 16-AUG-99

In 1928, Edward Knabusch and Edwin Shoemaker invented the wood slat reclining chair, enhancing the prospects of the furniture company they founded a year earlier. The 1961 introduction by the company (known since 1941 as La-Z-Boy Chair) of the three-position Reclina Rocker caused sales to explode. While reclining chairs remain an important part of its business (LZB is the world's leading producer), the company has since expanded its product line to include a full range of upholstered and wood furniture products across six operating divisions, and it believes that most of its growth opportunities lie outside the recliner market segment. In 1996, in order to better reflect the true breadth of its furniture lines, which now take LZB into every room in the home (and into offices as well), the company dropped the word Chair from its name, and is now known simply as La-Z-Boy Inc. (LZB), the third largest U.S. furniture maker.

The La-Z-Boy residential upholstery segment, which contributed 79% of sales in FY 99 (Apr.), is comprised of operating divisions that primarily manufacture and sell upholstered furniture to dealers. Upholstered furniture includes recliners, sofas, occasional chairs and reclining sofas that are mostly or fully covered with fabric, leather or vinyl. The operating divisions included in the residential upholstery segment are La-Z-Boy Residential, England/Corsair, Sam Moore, Centurion and Distincion Muebles.

The residential casegoods segment (15% of total sales) is comprised of operating divisions that primarily manufacture and sell hardwood or hardwood veneer furniture to dealers. Casegoods furniture includes dining room tables and chairs, bed frames and bed boards, dressers, coffee tables and end tables that are mostly constructed of hardwoods or veneers. The operating divisions included in the residential casegoods segment are Kincaid and Hammary.

The company distributes to over 20,000 locations, with no customer accounting for 3% of total sales in FY 99. The company's approximate dealer mix consisted of 43% proprietary, 16% to major dealers (Montgomery Ward and other department stores) and 41% to general dealers. Proprietary dealers consist of stores either dedicated to the sale of La-Z-Boy products or with a La-Z-Boy gallery within their store. The dedicated stores include La-Z-Boy Furniture Galleries stores and Showcase Shoppes.

Marketing efforts are pursued at the national, local and store level. In its national advertising campaign, the company uses the slogan "We Make the Rooms that Make a Home" to help reposition LZB as a total home furnishings resource. The company also assists dealers with local advertising and in-store promotional tools.

Per Share Data ($) (Year Ended Apr. 30)	1999	1998	1997	1996	1995	1994	1993	1992	1991	1990
Tangible Bk. Val.	7.03	6.33	5.97	5.49	5.06	4.92	4.43	4.11	3.81	3.54
Cash Flow	1.66	1.32	1.21	1.07	0.95	0.89	0.76	0.74	0.69	0.78
Earnings	1.24	0.93	0.83	0.71	0.67	0.63	0.50	0.46	0.43	0.53
Dividends	0.30	0.28	0.26	0.25	0.23	0.21	0.20	0.19	0.19	0.18
Payout Ratio	24%	30%	31%	35%	34%	34%	40%	42%	43%	34%
Cal. Yrs.	1998	1997	1996	1995	1994	1993	1992	1991	1990	1989
Prices - High	22⁵/₈	15	11³/₈	11¹/₈	13³/₈	13	9⁵/₈	8³/₈	7³/₈	7³/₄
- Low	14¹/₈	9⁷/₈	9	8¹/₂	8³/₈	8³/₈	5⁷/₈	5	4¹/₈	5⁵/₈
P/E Ratio - High	18	16	14	16	20	20	19	18	17	15
- Low	11	11	11	12	13	13	12	11	10	11
Income Statement Analysis (Million $)										
Revs.	1,288	1,108	1,006	947	850	805	684	619	608	592
Oper. Inc.	129	98.2	94.3	87.6	78.0	73.3	60.9	58.4	57.3	64.0
Depr.	22.1	21.0	20.4	20.1	15.2	14.0	14.1	14.8	14.0	13.7
Int. Exp.	4.4	4.2	4.4	5.3	3.3	2.8	3.3	5.3	6.4	7.2
Pretax Inc.	107	79.3	73.8	66.2	62.0	58.2	45.3	39.9	38.4	45.5
Eff. Tax Rate	38%	37%	39%	41%	42%	40%	40%	37%	39%	38%
Net Inc.	66.1	49.9	45.3	39.2	36.3	34.7	27.3	25.1	23.4	28.3
Balance Sheet & Other Fin. Data (Million $)										
Cash	33.5	28.7	25.0	27.0	27.0	25.9	28.8	21.7	13.0	6.7
Curr. Assets	426	383	343	337	325	296	279	254	238	240
Total Assets	630	580	528	528	504	430	401	377	363	362
Curr. Liab.	132	108	97.7	96.5	88.1	71.5	77.5	69.1	65.2	70.1
LT Debt	62.7	67.3	54.7	61.2	76.4	52.5	55.4	55.9	62.2	69.1
Common Eqty.	415	388	359	343	324	291	263	246	229	215
Total Cap.	483	461	420	411	407	350	324	308	298	292
Cap. Exp.	25.3	22.0	17.8	18.1	19.0	17.5	12.2	12.2	21.4	22.4
Cash Flow	88.2	70.9	65.7	59.4	51.5	48.7	41.3	39.9	37.4	42.0
Curr. Ratio	3.2	3.5	3.5	3.5	3.7	4.1	3.6	3.7	3.7	3.4
% LT Debt of Cap.	13.0	14.6	13.0	14.9	18.8	15.0	17.1	18.2	20.9	23.7
% Net Inc.of Revs.	5.1	4.5	4.5	4.1	4.3	4.3	4.0	4.1	3.8	4.8
% Ret. on Assets	10.9	9.0	8.7	7.7	7.8	8.3	7.0	6.8	6.4	7.9
% Ret. on Equity	16.5	13.4	12.9	11.7	11.9	12.5	10.7	10.5	10.5	13.8

Data as orig reptd.; bef. results of disc opers/spec. items. Per share data adj. for stk. divs. Bold denotes diluted EPS (FASB 128)-prior periods restated. E-Estimated. NA-Not Available. NM-Not Meaningful. NR-Not Ranked.

Office—1284 N. Telegraph Rd., Monroe, MI 48162-3390. **Tel**—(734) 242-1444. **Website**—http://www.lazboy.com **Chrmn**—P. H. Norton. **Pres**—G. L. Kiser. **EVP & CFO**—F. H. Jackson. **Secy, Treas & Investor Contact**—Gene M. Hardy. **Dirs**— G. M. Hardy, D. K. Hehl, F. H. Jackson, J. W. Johnston, G. L. Kiser, H.G. Levy, R. E. Lipford, P. H. Norton, L. G. Stevens, J. F. Weaver. **Transfer Agent & Registrar**—American Stock Transfer & Trust, NYC. **Incorporated**—in Michigan in 1941. **Empl**— 12,796. **S&P Analyst:** C.C.P.

STANDARD & POOR'S STOCK REPORTS

Labor Ready

NYSE Symbol **LRW**

In S&P SmallCap 600

09-OCT-99 **Industry:** Services (Employment) **Summary:** Labor Ready is a leading provider of temporary manual labor to the light industrial and small business markets.

Quantitative Evaluations

Outlook (1 Lowest—5 Highest) • **NA**

Fair Value • **NA**

Risk • **NA**

Earn./Div. Rank • **NR**

Technical Eval. • **Bearish** since 7/99

Rel. Strength Rank (1 Lowest—99 Highest) • **4**

Insider Activity • **Favorable**

Recent Price • 10

52 Wk Range • 28⅜-8⅞

Yield • Nil

12-Mo. P/E • 15.2

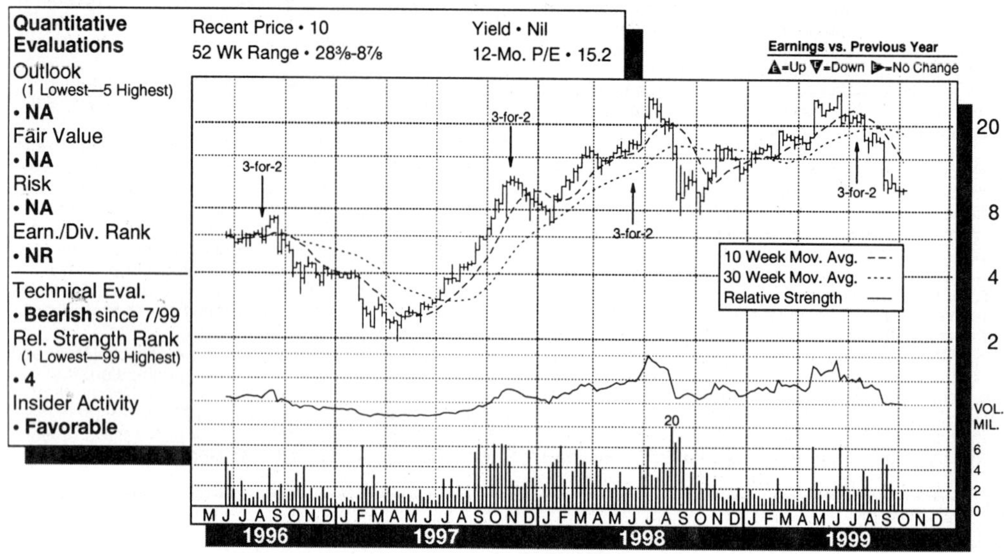

Business Profile - 22-SEP-99

In early September 1999, the company said it does not expect to meet analyst revenue and earnings estimates for the 1999 second half. However, management still expects 1999 revenue growth to exceed 40%, with earnings up over 50%. LRW also announced a stock buyback program for up to 5% of its stock (approximately 2 million shares). As of July 1999, the company had opened 201 offices in 1999, bringing the total number of offices to 687. LRW does not expect to open a material number of offices in the remainder of 1999, but it plans to open 300 more offices in 2000. The shares were split three for two in July 1999, the fifth such split in the past five years.

Operational Review - 22-SEP-99

Revenues in the six months ended July 2, 1999, climbed 54%, year to year, reflecting more offices and higher same-office growth. Results benefited from economies of scale and a rise in billing rates that was not accompanied by a rise in average wages of LRW's temporary employees; operating income soared 151%. With a sharp decline in depreciation and amortization charges, after taxes at 39.0%, versus 41.1%, income surged 259%, to $12.6 million ($0.28 a share), from $3.5 million ($0.08, as adjusted). Results in the 1999 period exclude a charge of $0.03 a share from the cumulative effect of an accounting change.

Stock Performance - 08-OCT-99

In the past 30 trading days, LRW's shares have declined 40%, compared to a 0.91% fall in the S&P 500. Average trading volume for the past five days was 369,100 shares, compared with the 40-day moving average of 490,872 shares.

Key Stock Statistics

Dividend Rate/Share	Nil	Shareholders	690
Shs. outstg. (M)	42.8	Market cap. (B)	$0.431
Avg. daily vol. (M)	0.381	Inst. holdings	46%
Tang. Bk. Value/Share	2.73		
Beta	NA		

Value of $10,000 invested 5 years ago: NA

Fiscal Year Ending Dec. 31

	1999	1998	1997	1996	1995	1994
Revenues (Million $)						
1Q	156.9	94.03	51.71	—	—	—
2Q	207.4	143.0	77.62	36.03	—	—
3Q	—	191.8	101.7	47.25	—	—
4Q	—	178.0	104.4	54.08	—	—
Yr.	—	606.9	335.4	163.4	94.36	38.95
Earnings Per Share ($)						
1Q	**0.11**	**0.00**	-0.02	—	—	—
2Q	**0.18**	**0.08**	0.03	—	—	—
3Q	—	**0.20**	0.09	0.04	—	—
4Q	—	**0.18**	**0.06**	0.00	—	—
Yr.	—	**0.46**	**0.17**	**0.05**	**0.07**	**0.04**

Next earnings report expected: late October

Dividend Data

Amount ($)	Date Decl.	Ex-Div. Date	Stock of Record	Payment Date
3-for-2	Jun. 10	Jul. 13	Jun. 24	Jul. 12 '99

A Division of The McGraw-Hill Companies

Labor Ready, Inc.

Business Summary - 22-SEP-99

The operating strategy of Labor Ready is to maintain and enhance its status as a leading national provider of temporary workers for manual labor jobs. Key elements of its strategy include aggressively opening new dispatch offices; increasing revenues from existing dispatch offices; improving operating efficiencies and reducing operating costs; providing superior service; and aggressively recruiting temporary workers.

Customers are primarily businesses in the freight handling, warehousing, landscaping, construction and light manufacturing industries. These businesses require workers for lifting, hauling, cleaning, assembling, digging, painting, and other types of manual or unskilled work. Over the past few years, the company has been diversifying its customer base to include more customers in the retail, wholesale, sanitation, printing, and hospitality industries.

LRW has grown rapidly, from eight dispatch offices in 1991 to 486 dispatch offices as of December 31, 1998. The breakdown of dispatch offices by geographic location was as follows: California 72, Central 70, Mid-Atlantic 70, Midwest 69, Southeast 66, Northwest 51, Northeast 50, Atlantic 27, and Canada 11. All of the growth in dispatch offices was achieved by opening company-owned locations, rather than through acquisitions.

Dispatch offices are locations where workers (and prospective workers) report prior to being assigned to jobs; this includes workers being called back to the same employer. Workers are required to report to the dispatch office in order to minimize "no-shows" to the customer's job site. The company pays temporary workers on a daily basis, and bills customers on a weekly basis. In 1998, LRW filled more than 4.8 million work orders, issued more than 6.5 million paychecks, and processed 533,000 W-2 forms.

LRW plans to open 300 dispatch offices in 2000; 201 were opened in 1999 through July. In 1998, the average cost to open an office was about $45,000; offices opened in 1998 typically generated revenues sufficient to cover their operating costs within six months. In 1998, average revenue per dispatch office open for more than one full year was about $1.6 million, up from $1.4 million in 1997.

The company intends to continue to focus on the short-term, light industrial manual labor niche of the temporary labor market. It believes other national and international temporary businesses have not aggressively pursued this market. LRW believes it can gain significant advantages by capturing market share, achieving economies of scale and other operating efficiencies not available to its smaller competitors, and by rapidly expanding through opening new dispatch offices and increasing revenues at existing offices.

Per Share Data ($) (Year Ended Dec. 31)	1998	1997	1996	1995	1994	1993	1992	1991	1990	1989
Tangible Bk. Val.	1.83	2.92	1.14	NA	NA	NA	NA	NA	NA	NA
Cash Flow	0.60	0.58	0.15	NA	0.15	0.05	0.06	NA	NA	NA
Earnings	0.46	0.16	0.05	NA	NA	NA	NA	NA	NA	NA
Dividends	Nil	Nil	NA	NA	NA	NA	NA	NA	NA	NA
Payout Ratio	Nil	Nil	NA	NA	NA	NA	NA	NA	NA	NA
Prices - High	27	11 1/2	7 3/8	NA	NA	NA	NA	NA	NA	NA
- Low	6 3/4	1 15/16	3 1/8	NA	NA	NA	NA	NA	NA	NA
P/E Ratio - High	59	70	151	NA	NA	NA	NA	NA	NA	NA
- Low	15	12	65	NA	NA	NA	NA	NA	NA	NA
Income Statement Analysis (Million $)										
Revs.	607	335	163	NA	39.0	15.7	8.4	NA	NA	NA
Oper. Inc.	39.7	14.7	5.2	NA	1.8	0.8	0.6	NA	NA	NA
Depr.	6.1	4.0	1.8	NA	0.2	0.1	0.0	NA	NA	NA
Int. Exp.	Nil	Nil	NA	NA	0.5	0.3	0.3	NA	NA	NA
Pretax Inc.	33.4	12.5	3.5	NA	1.2	0.3	0.2	NA	NA	NA
Eff. Tax Rate	41%	44%	45%	NA	28%	35%	8.75%	NA	NA	NA
Net Inc.	19.8	7.0	1.9	NA	0.9	0.2	0.2	NA	NA	NA
Balance Sheet & Other Fin. Data (Million $)										
Cash	26.1	22.3	19.3	NA	0.6	0.2	0.4	NA	NA	NA
Curr. Assets	106	65.6	48.7	NA	7.6	2.2	1.4	NA	NA	NA
Total Assets	131	80.4	64.3	NA	8.9	3.9	2.6	NA	NA	NA
Curr. Liab.	34.8	15.8	11.5	NA	5.6	1.7	1.2	NA	NA	NA
LT Debt	Nil	0.1	NA	NA	NA	NA	NA	NA	NA	NA
Common Eqty.	79.6	57.2	50.7	NA	2.1	0.4	-0.1	NA	NA	NA
Total Cap.	80.5	58.1	NA	NA	NA	NA	NA	NA	NA	NA
Cap. Exp.	9.5	4.0	NA	NA	NA	NA	NA	NA	NA	NA
Cash Flow	25.8	10.9	3.7	NA	1.0	0.3	0.2	NA	NA	NA
Curr. Ratio	3.0	4.2	4.2	NA	1.3	1.3	1.2	NA	NA	NA
% LT Debt of Cap.	Nil	0.1	NA	NA	NA	NA	NA	NA	NA	NA
% Net Inc.of Revs.	3.3	2.1	1.2	NA	2.2	1.4	2.6	NA	NA	NA
% Ret. on Assets	18.8	9.6	NA	NA	13.3	6.8	NA	NA	NA	NA
% Ret. on Equity	28.9	12.8	NA	NA	65.3	143.1	NA	NA	NA	NA

Data as orig reptd.; bef. results of disc opers/spec. items. Per share data adj. for stk. divs. Bold denotes diluted EPS (FASB 128)-prior periods restated. E-Estimated. NA-Not Available. NM-Not Meaningful. NR-Not Ranked.

Office—1016 S. 28th St., Tacoma, WA 98409. **Tel**—(253) 383-9101. **Website**—http://www.laborready.com **Chrmn, Pres & CEO**—G. A. Welstad. **EVP, CFO, Treas & Asst Secy**—J. P. Sambataro Jr. **Secy**—R. L. Junck. **Investor Contact**—Shannyn Roberts (800) 610-8920 (3211). **Dirs**—R. W. Gasten, R. L. Junck, T. E. McChesney, R. J. Sullivan, G. A. Welstad. **Transfer Agent & Registrar**—American Securities Transfer & Trust, Lakewood, CO**Incorporated**—in Washington in 1985. **Empl**— 2,306. **S&P Analyst:** Jordan Horoschak

STANDARD &POOR'S
STOCK REPORTS

Landry's Seafood Restaurants

Nasdaq Symbol **LDRY**

In S&P SmallCap 600

09-OCT-99 **Industry:** Restaurants

Summary: This company owns and operates full-service and take-out seafood restaurants, primarily using the Landry's Seafood House and Joe's Crab Shack names.

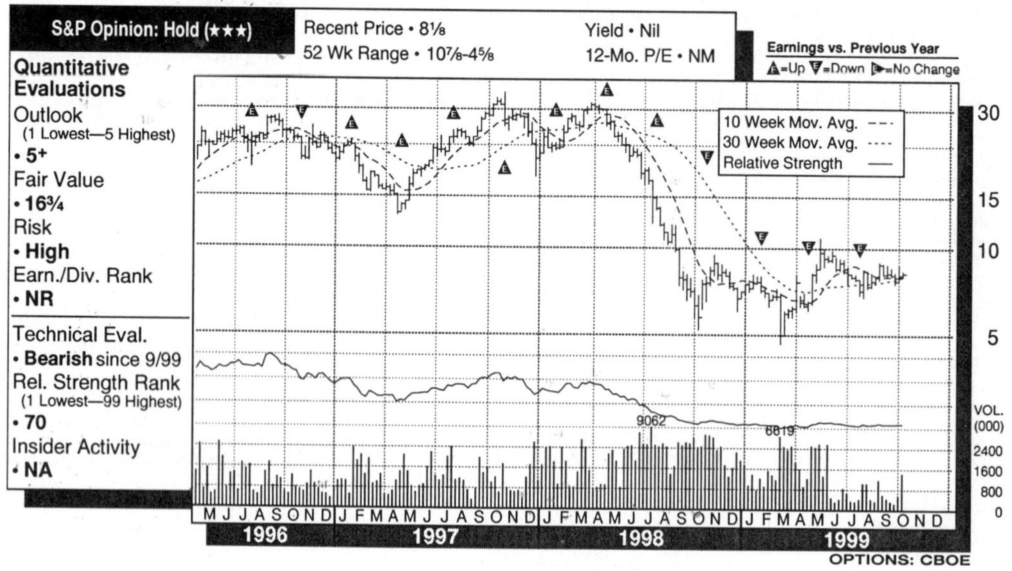

Overview - 08-SEP-99

Revenues should advance moderately in 1999, reflecting modest increases in same-store unit sales, and the addition of about 9 to 12 restaurants, mostly Joe's Crab Shack units, following the opening of 38 new units in 1998. LDRY has been focusing on its Joe's concept, because these restaurants are cheaper to build and offer better returns on investment. In addition, LDRY has been successful in converting older units to the Joe's concept, providing a 60% return on conversion investment. As the company continually strives to become more efficient, it is experimenting with opening certain restaurants only at dinner, eliminating its lunch hours. As a result, half of the units opened in 1998 will not offer lunch. LDRY began a marketing campaign in February 1999 to boost volume at its Joe's Crab Shack units. A 1998 fourth quarter charge of $50.8 million included provisions for the adoption of a new accounting standard (requiring the expensing of pre-opening costs) and for the closure of eight restaurants and other writedowns.

Valuation - 08-SEP-99

The shares have been in a fairly narrow trading range over the past few months. We are maintaining our hold rating on the shares. Unit level margins, however, continue to be hurt by lower menu prices. In addition, increased staffing, training and marketing costs will continue to keep margins from expanding. Same-store sales were up 4% in the second quarter, but operating earnings dropped 33%. Net income fell 36%, due to higher interest expense for capital expenditures and working capital. We believe 1999 will be a transitional year for LDRY. A $50 million share repurchase program gives support to the stock.

Key Stock Statistics

S&P EPS Est. 1999	0.60	Tang. Bk. Value/Share	13.42
P/E on S&P Est. 1999	13.6	Beta	1.46
S&P EPS Est. 2000	0.70	Shareholders	6,100
Dividend Rate/Share	Nil	Market cap. (B)	$0.210
Shs. outstg. (M)	25.7	Inst. holdings	39%
Avg. daily vol. (M)	0.126		

Value of $10,000 invested 5 years ago: $ 6,822

Fiscal Year Ending Dec. 31

	1999	1998	1997	1996	1995	1994
Revenues (Million $)						
1Q	101.3	90.05	64.30	53.07	20.61	11.39
2Q	123.6	111.0	81.18	66.29	27.74	15.72
3Q	—	109.3	89.81	64.39	29.01	19.69
4Q	—	89.11	76.38	52.36	26.66	15.72
Yr.	—	399.6	311.7	236.1	104.0	62.53
Earnings Per Share ($)						
1Q	**0.01**	**0.28**	**0.22**	0.17	0.12	0.08
2Q	**0.26**	**0.36**	**0.30**	0.22	0.16	0.11
3Q	**E0.21**	**0.24**	**0.32**	-0.40	0.17	0.13
4Q	**E0.12**	**-0.76**	**0.19**	0.14	0.10	0.08
Yr.	**E0.60**	**0.10**	**1.03**	**0.06**	0.55	0.40

Next earnings report expected: early November

Dividend Data

The company currently does not pay dividends. A two-for-one stock split was effected in June 1995.

Landry's Seafood Restaurants, Inc.

Business Summary - 08-SEP-99

Through an aggressive growth plan, Landry's has grown to more than 120 restaurants from the two units acquired by Tilman Fertitta, the company's chairman, in 1988. Restaurants are operated under the divisional names Joe's Crab Shack (88 units at March 12, 1999), Landry's Seafood House (41), and The Crab House (14). The 143 units are located mostly in the southern U.S.

From 1990 through the latter half of 1998, the company pursued an accelerated expansion strategy via the opening of new restaurants or the conversion of existing restaurants. Landry's opened 38 units in 1998. However, as a result of declining sales and greater management turnover, the company's per unit profitability decreased. In the fourth quarter the company announced a loss of $23.2 million and implemented a program to close a number of restaurants with marginal performance. Landry's has reduced its unit openings for 1999 to nine to twelve restaurants. Expansion efforts will primarily be focused in the South and Midwest, with selected development or acquisitions outside these areas. The primary driver of expansion will be the Joe's Crab Shack concept, based on its strong economics and customer appeal.

Landry's has always emphasized the distinctive design and locations of its units. Joe's Crab Shack units are designed to resemble an old fishing camp with a wood facade, tin roof and a raised outside deck, while Landry's Seafood Houses can typically be identified by a large theatre-style marquee over the entrance and a distinctive brick and wood facade. Crab House restaurants are highlighted by their nautical themes, many of which include a fresh seafood salad bar. Many restaurants also feature outdoor patio service for an open-air dining experience that often features waterfront views. Restaurants are generally located in markets that provide a balanced mix of tourist, convention, business and residential traffic. Factors considered in site selection include local market demographics, site visibility, aesthetics (including waterfront views), and proximity to significant generators of potential customers.

Restaurants are typically 5,000 sq. ft. to 16,000 sq. ft. in size, averaging 8,000 sq. ft., with seating capacity for approximately 215 customers, and bar seating for approximately 10 to 20 additional patrons. The menu offers a wide variety of high quality broiled, grilled and fried seafood at moderate prices; the menu includes red snapper, shrimp, crawfish, lump crabmeat, lobster, oysters, scallops, flounder, and other traditional seafood offerings. The average dinner menu main course price is $11 to $13, excluding items that are priced daily to the market. Sales of alcoholic beverages were 15% of revenues in 1998.

In November 1998, the company announced a share repurchase program of up to $50 million. Through March 29, 1999, 1.5 million shares had been purchased, at a gross price of $9.1 million.

Per Share Data ($) (Year Ended Dec. 31)	1998	1997	1996	1995	1994	1993	1992	1991	1990	1989
Tangible Bk. Val.	13.42	11.30	10.05	6.59	3.96	1.36	NA	NA	NA	NA
Cash Flow	0.73	1.67	0.60	0.87	0.61	0.40	0.30	NA	NA	NA
Earnings	0.10	1.03	0.06	0.55	0.40	0.28	0.22	NA	NA	NA
Dividends	Nil	Nil	Nil	Nil	Nil	Nil	Nil	NA	NA	NA
Payout Ratio	Nil	Nil	Nil	Nil	Nil	Nil	Nil	NA	NA	NA
Prices - High	31 5/8	34 3/8	28 3/8	22 1/4	15 3/8	12 1/8	NA	NA	NA	NA
- Low	5 1/8	12 7/8	14	12 1/2	8 5/8	6	NA	NA	NA	NA
P/E Ratio - High	NM	33	NM	40	38	43	NA	NA	NA	NA
- Low	NM	12	NM	23	22	21	NA	NA	NA	NA
Income Statement Analysis (Million $)										
Revs.	400	312	236	104	62.5	34.2	22.4	NA	NA	NA
Oper. Inc.	20.9	58.5	39.2	18.5	10.8	5.5	3.7	NA	NA	NA
Depr.	18.7	17.1	13.0	5.5	2.9	1.2	0.6	NA	NA	NA
Int. Exp.	0.0	Nil	Nil	0.1	0.1	0.3	0.2	NA	NA	NA
Pretax Inc.	4.7	42.8	2.3	14.8	8.8	4.3	3.1	NA	NA	NA
Eff. Tax Rate	34%	36%	34%	35%	36%	11%	4.40%	NA	NA	NA
Net Inc.	3.1	27.4	1.5	9.6	5.7	2.7	2.0	NA	NA	NA
Balance Sheet & Other Fin. Data (Million $)										
Cash	35.2	17.2	57.3	16.6	19.5	6.7	NA	NA	NA	NA
Curr. Assets	84.8	62.2	85.4	23.7	22.9	8.2	NA	NA	NA	NA
Total Assets	490	382	281	140	71.1	24.9	NA	NA	NA	NA
Curr. Liab.	40.9	27.1	21.0	15.2	8.1	4.5	NA	NA	NA	NA
LT Debt	35.2	50.2	0.2	0.4	0.7	1.8	NA	NA	NA	NA
Common Eqty.	409	297	256	122	62.0	18.4	NA	NA	NA	NA
Total Cap.	444	347	257	123	62.7	20.2	NA	NA	NA	NA
Cap. Exp.	138	136	64.5	71.3	32.1	9.4	2.6	NA	NA	NA
Cash Flow	21.7	44.5	14.5	15.1	8.6	3.9	2.6	NA	NA	NA
Curr. Ratio	2.1	2.3	4.1	1.6	2.8	1.8	NA	NA	NA	NA
% LT Debt of Cap.	7.9	14.5	0.1	0.3	1.2	8.9	NA	NA	NA	NA
% Net Inc.of Revs.	0.8	8.8	0.6	9.2	9.1	8.0	8.8	NA	NA	NA
% Ret. on Assets	0.7	8.3	0.6	9.1	11.8	15.5	NA	NA	NA	NA
% Ret. on Equity	0.9	9.9	0.8	10.4	14.1	25.2	NA	NA	NA	NA

Data as orig reptd.; bef. results of disc opers/spec. items. Per share data adj. for stk. divs. Bold denotes diluted EPS (FASB 128)-prior periods restated. E-Estimated. NA-Not Available. NM-Not Meaningful. NR-Not Ranked.

Office—1400 Post Oak Blvd., Suite 1010, Houston, TX 77056. **Tel**—(713) 850-1010. **Website**—http://www.landrysseafood.com/ **Chrmn, Pres & CEO**—T. J. Fertitta. **EVP & COO**—E. A. Jaksa, Jr. **VP & CFO**—P. S. West. **VP & Secy**—S. L. Scheinthal. **Dirs**—T. J. Fertitta, A. Jaska, Jr., J. E. Masucci, S. L. Scheinthal, J. M. Taylor, P. S. West. **Transfer Agent & Registrar**—American Stock Transfer & Trust Co., NYC. **Incorporated**—in Delaware in 1993. **Empl**— 14,355. **S&P Analyst:** Karen J. Sack

STANDARD
&POOR'S
STOCK REPORTS

Landstar System

Nasdaq Symbol **LSTR**

In S&P SmallCap 600

09-OCT-99 **Industry:** Truckers

Summary: Landstar is one of the largest truckload carriers in the U.S. With the sale of its Poole unit in 1998, LSTR operates entirely with independent contractors and commission agents.

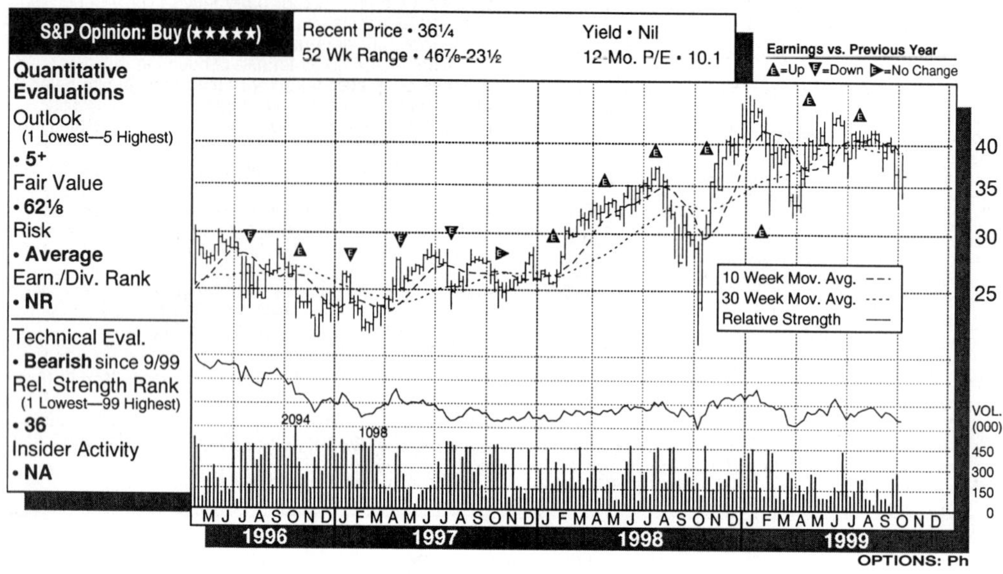

Overview - 04-AUG-99

Revenues for 1999 are projected to increase 5%, comparable to the gain from continuing operations posted in 1998. Vehicle miles logged will increase about 3%, aided by the expansion of the independent contractor base, while cargo rates increase about 2%. Limiting comparisons will be the absence of traffic gleaned from Union Pacific in 1998 when that railroad experienced service delays. Margins will widen as purchased transportation costs are rising somewhat slower than revenues, insurance and claims ease and LSTR holds the line on general and administrative costs. Agents' commissions are rising more rapidly than revenues as more agents are earning additional incentive compensation. Depreciation and amortization, although not a significant cost item, is rising faster than revenues. Interest expense will be flat. Per share earnings will benefit from some 7% fewer shares outstanding, reflecting the company's ongoing buyback program.

Valuation - 04-AUG-99

The shares of this truckload carrier were upgraded to accumulate from hold in July. We believe the shares, which have been locked in a wide trading range during 1999, are moving toward a breakout. The trading range is the result of one group of investors selling in anticipation of a recession or concern about fuel costs, while better than expected profit reports and an attractive valuation spur other investors to prop LSTR up. We side with the bulls, as we do not currently project a recession and under LSTR's business model all fuel costs are borne by its independent contractors. LSTR continues to deploy its excess cash flow to repurchase its shares - some 380,000 during 1999's first half. With its P/E, price to sales and price to growth rates below those of its peers, LSTR is a worthwhile investment.

Key Stock Statistics

S&P EPS Est. 1999	3.85	Tang. Bk. Value/Share	7.38
P/E on S&P Est. 1999	9.4	Beta	0.68
S&P EPS Est. 2000	4.05	Shareholders	86
Dividend Rate/Share	Nil	Market cap. (B)	$0.362
Shs. outstg. (M)	10.0	Inst. holdings	92%
Avg. daily vol. (M)	0.033		

Value of $10,000 invested 5 years ago: $ 16,384

Fiscal Year Ending Dec. 31

	1999	1998	1997	1996	1995	1994
Revenues (Million $)						
1Q	311.4	298.2	305.6	295.5	295.7	207.2
2Q	345.1	327.5	333.7	329.1	308.1	250.2
3Q	—	324.0	326.3	330.2	298.7	247.6
4Q	—	333.9	347.1	329.0	302.1	279.4
Yr.	—	1,284	1,313	1,284	1,205	984.4
Earnings Per Share ($)						
1Q	**0.71**	**0.42**	**0.24**	**0.25**	0.37	0.26
2Q	**1.05**	**0.79**	**0.51**	**0.54**	0.61	0.51
3Q	**E1.00**	**0.85**	**0.60**	**0.60**	0.56	0.56
4Q	**E1.09**	**1.07**	**0.62**	**0.08**	0.41	0.57
Yr.	**E3.85**	**3.10**	**1.96**	**1.47**	**1.94**	**1.89**

Next earnings report expected: mid October

Dividend Data

The company has not paid cash dividends on the common stock and does not intend to pay any for the foreseeable future.

A Division of The McGraw-Hill Companies

Landstar System, Inc.

Business Summary - 04-AUG-99

Landstar System, Inc., which operates through several major subsidiaries, is the third largest truckload carrier in North America. Truckload carriers transport large shipments from origin to destination and hence have few, if any, terminal facilities. Landstar transports a wide variety of items ranging from bulk raw materials to finished manufactured goods. LSTR's operating strategy is to limit its investment in fixed assets by harnessing the services of independent owner-operator drivers and commission sales agents. It realized its goal of a 100% variable cost operation with the sale of Landstar Poole in August 1998.

LSTR's carrier group (76% of gross revenues in 1998) consists of Landstar Ranger, Landstar Inway and Landstar Ligon. These carriers use independent contractors as drivers. The carrier group provides a variety of truckload services ranging from the movement of packaged goods to bulk goods and perishable commodities. At 1998 year end, the carrier group's fleet consisted of 7,700 dry van trailers, 3,400 flatbeds, 900 specialty trailers and 300 refrigerated vans. Independent contractors own 78% of the carrier group's trailers and 50% of its 7,900 tractors.

LSTR's multimodal group (22% of gross revenues in 1998) consists of Landstar Logistics and Landstar Express America. Logistics involves providing a single source solution for large customers for all of their transportation and distribution needs. Intermodal services involves the arrangement of transportation (both rail and truck) to provide door-to-door coverage. Landstar Express provides emergency and expedited air and ground transportation services throughout the U.S. and parts of Canada and Mexico.

LSTR now derives all of its revenues from independent drivers, with the August 1998 sale of Landstar Poole to Schneider National, Inc., for $41 million. LSTR provides its 7,900 contractors with 60% to 70% of the revenues generated per load, if they supply the tractor, and with up to 79% if a trailer is included. By using contractors, LSTR avoids investment in rolling stock, has no exposure to fuel price changes, and is relatively insulated from industry downturns.The second component of Landstar's "variable cost" strategy is to use the services of independent commission sales agents in place of salaried personnel. LSTR's 1,000 agents earn a base commission of 7% of revenues, and up to 10% after certain volume incentives have been attained.

Signature Insurance Co., established in 1997 (2% of gross revenues), cuts insurance costs for LSTR's owner-operators, and also contributes to the bottom line. Signature provides risk and claims management services for LSTR's operating companies and offers property, casualty and occupational accident coverage for its contractors.

In recent years, Landstar has generated excess cash flow, a sizable portion of which has been directed to stock buybacks. Between 1997 and June 1999, LSTR repurchased 2,861,700 (22%) of its common shares.

Per Share Data ($) (Year Ended Dec. 31)	1998	1997	1996	1995	1994	1993	1992	1991	1990	1989
Tangible Bk. Val.	7.38	8.21	7.28	5.58	5.66	3.69	2.07	NA	NA	NA
Cash Flow	4.01	3.63	3.36	3.58	2.95	2.22	0.98	NA	NA	NA
Earnings	3.10	1.96	1.48	1.95	1.90	1.14	0.67	0.22	NA	NA
Dividends	Nil	Nil	Nil	Nil	Nil	Nil	Nil	Nil	NA	NA
Payout Ratio	Nil	Nil	Nil	Nil	Nil	Nil	Nil	Nil	NA	NA
Prices - High	45⅝	29	30⅝	37¾	36	22⅛	NA	NA	NA	NA
- Low	21	21¾	21½	21¼	19¾	12¼	NA	NA	NA	NA
P/E Ratio - High	15	15	21	19	19	19	NA	NA	NA	NA
- Low	7	11	15	11	10	11	NA	NA	NA	NA
Income Statement Analysis (Million $)										
Revs.	1,284	1,313	1,284	1,205	984	781	672	NA	NA	NA
Oper. Inc.	69.9	71.3	71.2	70.8	59.3	43.0	34.7	NA	NA	NA
Depr.	10.2	20.9	24.0	20.8	13.5	12.8	11.8	NA	NA	NA
Int. Exp.	3.5	4.6	7.5	17.5	4.1	5.7	9.7	NA	NA	NA
Pretax Inc.	58.0	42.6	32.4	42.5	41.6	24.5	13.2	NA	NA	NA
Eff. Tax Rate	40%	42%	41%	41%	41%	45%	52%	NA	NA	NA
Net Inc.	34.5	24.7	19.0	25.0	24.4	13.6	6.4	NA	NA	NA
Balance Sheet & Other Fin. Data (Million $)										
Cash	26.7	18.0	4.2	3.4	17.8	15.1	NA	NA	NA	NA
Curr. Assets	219	218	201	179	155	124	NA	NA	NA	NA
Total Assets	314	357	371	353	267	219	NA	NA	NA	NA
Curr. Liab.	143	139	130	127	113	87.0	NA	NA	NA	NA
LT Debt	29.7	36.2	67.2	73.2	30.5	36.4	NA	NA	NA	NA
Common Eqty.	112	152	148	128	105	81.0	NA	NA	NA	NA
Total Cap.	142	190	215	202	136	117	NA	NA	NA	NA
Cap. Exp.	7.2	9.8	12.8	7.3	7.5	6.7	3.5	NA	NA	NA
Cash Flow	44.6	45.6	42.9	45.8	37.9	26.3	18.2	NA	NA	NA
Curr. Ratio	1.5	1.6	1.5	1.4	1.2	1.4	NA	NA	NA	NA
% LT Debt of Cap.	21.0	19.1	31.3	36.3	22.5	31.2	NA	NA	NA	NA
% Net Inc.of Revs.	2.7	1.9	1.5	2.1	2.5	1.7	0.9	NA	NA	NA
% Ret. on Assets	10.3	6.8	5.2	8.1	10.1	6.8	NA	NA	NA	NA
% Ret. on Equity	26.2	16.5	13.7	21.4	26.2	24.2	NA	NA	NA	NA

Data as orig reptd.; bef. results of disc opers/spec. items. Per share data adj. for stk. divs. Bold denotes diluted EPS (FASB 128)-prior periods restated. E-Estimated. NA-Not Available. NM-Not Meaningful. NR-Not Ranked.

Office—3410 Sutton Park Drive South, Jacksonville, FL 32224.**Tel**—(904) 390-1234. **Website**—http://www.landstar.com **Chrmn, Pres & CEO**—J. C. Crowe. **EVP & CFO**—H. H. Gerkens. **VP-Secy**—M. L. Harvey. **Investor Contact**—Pamela J. Miller (904-390-1530). **Dirs**—D. G. Bannister, J. B. Bowron, J. C. Crowe, R. W. Drucker, W. S. Elston, M. J. Mott, D. M. Murphy. **Transfer Agent**—ChaseMellon Shareholder Services, NYC. **Incorporated**—in Delaware in 1991. **Empl**— 2,050. **S&P Analyst:** Stephen R. Klein

STANDARD & POOR'S STOCK REPORTS

Laser Vision Centers

NASDAQ Symbol **LVCI**

In S&P SmallCap 600

09-OCT-99

Industry: Health Care (Medical Products & Supplies)

Summary: This company is a major provider of excimer lasers, related equipment and support services for the treatment of nearsightedness, farsightedness and astigmatism.

Quantitative Evaluations

Outlook (1 Lowest—5 Highest)
• **NA**

Fair Value
• **NA**

Risk
• **NA**

Earn./Div. Rank
• **C**

Technical Eval.
• **Bearish** since 8/99

Rel. Strength Rank (1 Lowest—99 Highest)
• **4**

Insider Activity
• **Unfavorable**

Recent Price • 15⅝
52 Wk Range • 37⅞-4⅜
Yield • Nil
12-Mo. P/E • 39.2

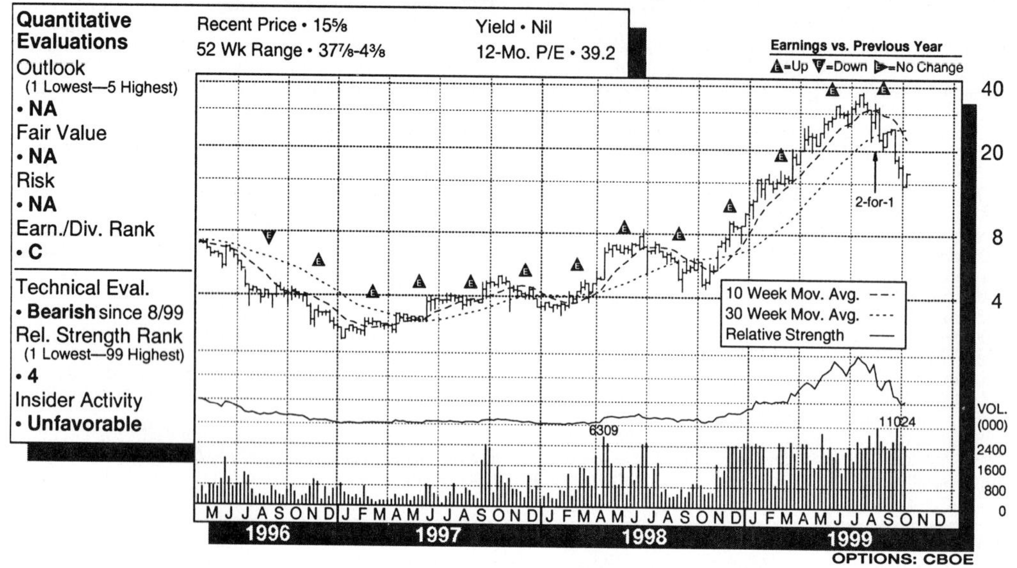

Business Profile - 28-SEP-99

Demand for LVCI's refractive laser and cataract business remains robust. In August, 1999, the company said that its pipeline remained full and it expected this trend to continue as more surgeons enter the business. LVCI planned to continue to add more excimer lasers in the second quarter of FY 00 (Apr.) to handle the growing demand. In May 1999, the company sold publicly 1,000,000 common shares (adjusted) and received net proceeds of about $43.6 million. An additional $7.7 million was received in FY 00's second quarter via the exercise of warrants and options. In September 1998, LVCI acquired for about $2.6 million in notes and cash Refractive Surgical Resources, Inc. (RSR), a provider of microkeratome access for excimer laser procedures.

Operational Review - 28-SEP-99

Revenues for the three months ended July 31, 1999, advanced 131%, year to year. The gain mainly reflected an increase both in the number of U.S. lasers in operation and the number of procedures performed by the company's eye surgeon customers on each laser in the U.S. and the acquisition of RSR. Pretax income climbed to $3,386,000 from $333,000. After tax credits of $747,000 in the FY 00 period only, net income rose to $4,133,000 ($0.14 a share, after preferred dividends and based on 32% more average shares) from $333,000 ($0.02). Per-share figures for both periods are adjusted for the August 1999 2-for-1 stock split.

Stock Performance - 08-OCT-99

In the past 30 trading days, LVCI's shares have declined 25%, compared to a 0.91% fall in the S&P 500. Average trading volume for the past five days was 716,920 shares, compared with the 40-day moving average of 1,209,846 shares.

Key Stock Statistics

Dividend Rate/Share	Nil	Shareholders	1,400
Shs. outstg. (M)	25.0	Market cap. (B)	$0.393
Avg. daily vol. (M)	1.252	Inst. holdings	71%
Tang. Bk. Value/Share	2.98		
Beta	1.44		

Value of $10,000 invested 5 years ago: $ 73,821

Fiscal Year Ending Apr. 30

	2000	1999	1998	1997	1996	1995
Revenues (Million $)						
1Q	21.00	9.11	4.10	1.50	41.19	0.84
2Q	—	10.40	5.22	1.93	0.96	0.79
3Q	—	14.06	6.35	2.01	0.85	0.87
4Q	—	18.79	7.80	2.80	1.33	0.81
Yr.	—	52.36	23.47	8.24	3.92	3.31
Earnings Per Share ($)						
1Q	**0.14**	**0.02**	-0.09	-0.16	-0.12	—
2Q	—	**0.05**	-0.07	-0.13	-0.15	—
3Q	—	**0.09**	**-0.05**	**-0.13**	-0.16	—
4Q	—	**0.12**	**0.01**	-0.30	-0.41	—
Yr.	—	**0.28**	**-0.20**	**-0.72**	-0.88	**-0.41**

Next earnings report expected: early December

Dividend Data

Amount ($)	Date Decl.	Ex-Div. Date	Stock of Record	Payment Date
2-for-1	Jul. 12	Aug. 10	Jul. 23	Aug. 09 '99

A Division of The McGraw-Hill Companies

STANDARD
&POOR'S
STOCK REPORTS

Laser Vision Centers, Inc.

09-OCT-99

Business Summary - 28-SEP-99

The business strategy of Laser Vision Centers (LVCI) is to provide eye surgeons with cost-effective access to surgical equipment used for excimer laser and cataract procedures. This strategy includes the following elements: offer a flexible delivery system, increase penetration in new and existing markets, maximize the use of its equipment, provide value-added services to eye surgeons, and expand its products and services.

LVCI is one of the nation's largest providers of excimer lasers and other equipment to eye surgeons who use them to reshape the curvature of the cornea in order to correct nearsightedness, farsightedness, astigmatism and cataracts.

Most of the company's equipment is mobile and it routinely moves from one location to another in response to customer demand. LVCI also provides its equipment at fixed locations. Its flexible delivery system enlarges the pool of potential locations, eye surgeons and patients that it can serve, and allows it to effectively respond to changing market demands.

Eye surgeons pay a fee for each procedure they perform using the company's equipment. LVCI typically provides each piece of equipment to many different eye surgeons, which allows it to more efficiently use the equipment and offer it at an affordable price. The company refers to its practice of providing equipment to multiple surgeons as "shared access."

Eye surgeons utilize LVCI's shared access and flexible delivery system to: avoid a large capital investment, eliminate the risks associated with buying high-technology equipment that may rapidly become obsolete, use the equipment without responsibility of maintenance or repair, cost effectively serve small to medium-sized markets and remote locations, and serve satellite locations even in large markets.

LVCI provides a broad range of value-added services to the eye surgeons who use its equipment, including initial training, technical support and equipment maintenance, marketing, clinical advisory services, patient financing and clinical practice satelliting.

The company provides mobile cataract equipment and services through its Midwest Surgical Services, Inc. (MSS) subsidiary, acquired in December 1998, which focuses on developing relationships between local hospitals, referring optometrists and eye surgeons in small to medium sized markets.

LVCI entered the cataract business only recently with the MSS acquisition; at that time, about 80% of the eye surgeons using MSS services were not performing excimer laser surgery. LVCI expects over time to cross market both excimer laser and cataract services to the eye surgeons it serves.

Per Share Data ($)										
(Year Ended Apr. 30)	**1999**	**1998**	**1997**	**1996**	**1995**	**1994**	**1993**	**1992**	**1991**	**1990**
Tangible Bk. Val.	0.46	0.58	NA	0.48	0.67	0.61	0.46	0.60	NA	NA
Cash Flow	0.53	0.07	-0.48	-0.63	-0.21	-0.15	-0.16	-0.10	-0.07	-0.03
Earnings	0.28	-0.20	-0.72	-0.88	-0.41	-0.33	-0.24	0.13	-0.07	-0.04
Dividends	Nil	Nil	Nil	Nil	Nil	Nil	Nil	Nil	Nil	NA
Payout Ratio	Nil	Nil	Nil	Nil	Nil	Nil	Nil	Nil	Nil	NA
Cal. Yrs.	1998	1997	1996	1995	1994	1993	1992	1991	1990	1989
Prices - High	11 1/2	5	7 5/8	8 1/2	4 1/8	3 3/4	3 3/4	3 1/2	NA	NA
- Low	3 1/4	2 1/2	2 7/16	3 1/2	2 1/8	1 3/4	2 1/2	2 5/16	NA	NA
P/E Ratio - High	42	NM	NM	NM	NM	NM	NM	NM	NA	NA
- Low	12	NM	NM	NM	NM	NM	NM	NM	NA	NA
Income Statement Analysis (Million $)										
Revs.	52.4	23.5	8.2	3.9	3.3	2.1	1.2	0.9	1.3	2.5
Oper. Inc.	12.3	2.1	-5.2	-4.0	-1.3	-0.7	-0.8	-0.5	-0.2	-0.1
Depr.	6.4	4.9	3.9	2.2	1.9	1.2	0.4	0.1	0.0	0.0
Int. Exp.	1.2	1.0	0.6	0.2	0.2	0.2	0.1	0.0	NA	NA
Pretax Inc.	5.1	-3.5	-12.2	-9.0	-3.3	-2.2	-1.2	-0.6	-0.2	-0.1
Eff. Tax Rate	NM	NM	NM	NM	NM	Nil	Nil	Nil	Nil	Nil
Net Inc.	6.5	-3.5	-12.1	-8.8	-3.3	-2.2	-1.2	-0.6	-0.2	-0.1
Balance Sheet & Other Fin. Data (Million $)										
Cash	8.7	8.9	4.3	12.7	2.1	0.7	NA	1.1	0.5	0.0
Curr. Assets	23.4	14.3	6.9	14.0	2.9	1.4	NA	1.5	2.7	0.6
Total Assets	53.2	30.8	22.9	28.9	11.3	9.1	NA	4.4	2.8	0.9
Curr. Liab.	16.3	8.7	5.2	5.2	4.2	1.6	NA	0.9	0.3	0.7
LT Debt	7.8	6.6	6.1	1.4	0.4	1.1	NA	NA	NA	NA
Common Eqty.	26.7	12.1	10.3	7.5	7.6	4.6	NA	3.0	2.5	0.2
Total Cap.	36.9	17.2	16.4	23.4	8.0	5.7	NA	NA	NA	NA
Cap. Exp.	5.3	4.1	NA	NA	NA	NA	NA	NA	NA	NA
Cash Flow	12.8	1.2	-8.2	-6.6	-1.4	-1.0	-0.8	NM	-0.2	-0.1
Curr. Ratio	1.4	1.6	1.3	2.7	0.7	0.9	NA	1.7	9.5	0.9
% LT Debt of Cap.	21.1	38.4	37.2	6.0	5.0	18.7	NA	NA	NA	NA
% Net Inc.of Revs.	12.5	NM	NM	NM	NM	NM	Nil	NA	NM	NM
% Ret. on Assets	15.6	NM	NM	NM	NM	NM	Nil	NM	NM	NM
% Ret. on Equity	32.9	NM	NM	NM	NM	NM	Nil	NM	NM	NM

Data as orig reptd.; bef. results of disc opers/spec. items. Per share data adj. for stk. divs. Bold denotes diluted EPS (FASB 128)-prior periods restated. E-Estimated. NA-Not Available. NM-Not Meaningful. NR-Not Ranked.

Office—540 Maryville Centre Drive, Suite 200, St. Louis, MO 63141. **Tel**—(314) 434-6900. **Website**—http://www.laservision.com **Chrmn & CEO**—J. J. Klobnak. **Pres & COO**—J. C. Wachtman. **EVP-CFO & Treas**—B. C. Bono III. **Vice-Chrmn & Secy**—R. W. May. **Dirs**—J. M. Garvey, J. J. Klobnak, R. L. Lindstrom, R. W. May, H. Simon,S. C. Straus, J. C. Wachtman. **Transfer Agent & Registrar**—American Stock Transfer & Trust Co., NYC. **Incorporated**—in Delaware in 1988. **Empl**— 182. **S&P Analyst:** J. J. Schemitsch

STANDARD &POOR'S
STOCK REPORTS

Lason, Inc.

NASDAQ Symbol **LSON**

In S&P SmallCap 600

09-OCT-99

Industry: Photography/Imaging

Summary: Lason provides integrated information management services for image and data capture, data management and output processing.

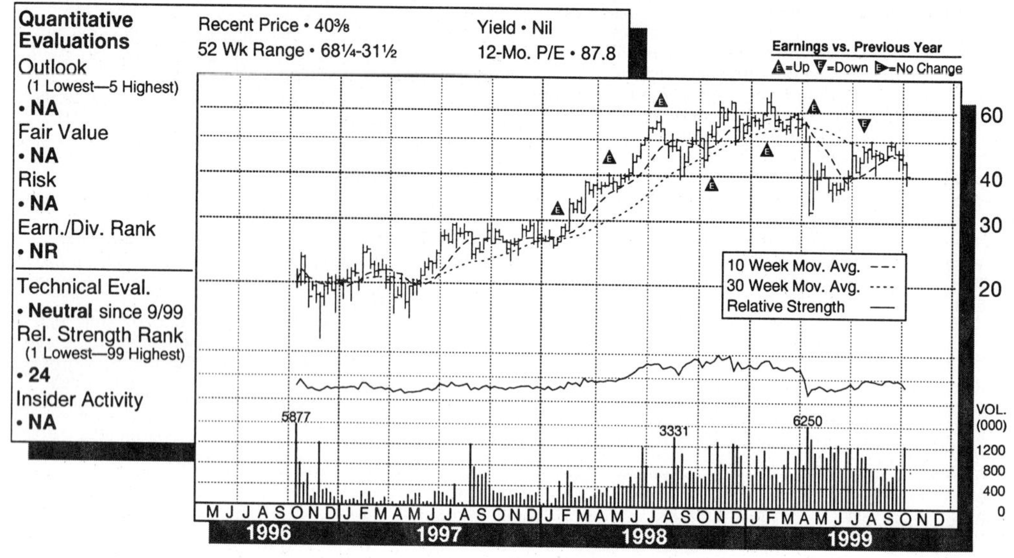

Business Profile - 22-SEP-99

Acquisitions have contributed importantly to the company's strong revenue growth in recent years. Lason acquired M-R Group plc, a major United Kingdom document and data management company, for about 3.1 million common shares in June, 1999. M-R provides various data and document management services, including scanning and conversion, electronic storage and retrieval, micrographic and data management services. The acquired company has annualized revenues of about US$90 million. Lason expects the acquisition to provide significant growth opportunities in Europe. Merger-related charges of about $30.8 million (pretax) were recorded in 1999's second quarter and included investment banking, legal, regulatory, accounting and other fees, and charges related to consolidation of facilities, severance and other expenses.

Operational Review - 22-SEP-99

Revenues for the six months ended June 30, 1999, advanced 80%, year to year, with results for both periods restated to reflect the acquisition of M-R Group plc on a pooling-of-interests basis. Income from operations improved but following merger-related charges totaling $31,088,000, a net loss of $3,240,000 ($0.18 a share, on 16% more average shares) contrasted with net income of $10,820,000 ($0.71).

Stock Performance - 08-OCT-99

In the past 30 trading days, LSON's shares have declined 10%, compared to a 0.91% fall in the S&P 500. Average trading volume for the past five days was 277,620 shares, compared with the 40-day moving average of 155,808 shares.

Key Stock Statistics

Dividend Rate/Share	Nil	Shareholders	157
Shs. outstg. (M)	18.8	Market cap. (B)	$0.758
Avg. daily vol. (M)	0.183	Inst. holdings	85%
Tang. Bk. Value/Share	0.77		
Beta	NA		

Value of $10,000 invested 5 years ago: NA

Fiscal Year Ending Dec. 31

	1999	1998	1997	1996	1995	1994
Revenues (Million $)						
1Q	131.1	46.57	26.24	—	—	—
2Q	142.1	62.64	27.42	—	—	—
3Q	—	77.93	30.61	—	—	—
4Q	—	92.62	36.07	22.19	—	—
Yr.	—	279.8	120.3	69.94	46.61	41.20
Earnings Per Share ($)						
1Q	**0.43**	**0.29**	0.21	—	—	—
2Q	**-0.59**	**0.31**	0.22	—	—	—
3Q	—	**0.35**	0.23	—	—	—
4Q	—	**0.39**	**0.25**	0.15	—	—
Yr.	—	**1.35**	**0.90**	**0.55**	**0.33**	—

Next earnings report expected: late October

Dividend Data

No cash dividends have been paid. The company intends to retain any earnings to finance operations and expansion and, therefore does not anticipate paying any cash dividends on the common stock for the foreseeable future.

A Division of The McGraw-Hill Companies

Business Summary - 22-SEP-99

A leading provider of integrated information management services, Lason, Inc. believes that significant growth opportunities have been created in Europe through its June 1999 acquisition of M-R Group plc for about 3.1 million common shares.

With annual revenues of about US$90 million, M-R is a leading United Kingdom document and data management company. It provides a variety of data and document management services, including scanning and conversion, electronic storage and retrieval, micrographic and data management services. Its services are focused on the financial telecommunications and utilities markets, in addition to government agencies. Lason believes that with the acquisition of M-R, it has a strong worldwide platform to meet the needs of its multinational customers. It incurred $30.8 million of pretax merger-related charges in 1999's second quarter.

Lason's strategy is to be able to offer a broad range of information management services across a wide variety of media types and formats, thereby permitting customers to consolidate their information management outsourcing needs with a single vendor. This broad range of information services and capabilities enables it to provide integrated solutions to its customers' complex information management needs.

The company's information management service offerings can be divided into the areas of image and data capture, data management and output processing. Image and data capture services (which accounted for about 52% of revenues in 1998) include the scanning and conversion of documents and records from various input media to a digital format. Lason also provides traditional microfilm and microfiche services, as well as on-site facility management services.

Data management services (10%) include electronic document storage and retrieval, database management and Interned-based services, as well as list manipulation, sorting services and information search solutions so that customers' data can be customized and updated for specific target market applications.

Lason's output processing services (38%) include print on demand, business communications and statement processing services. Its output processing services provide customers with rapid, reliable and cost-effective methods for making large-scale distribution of statements, reports, proxy solicitations and letters to consumers and other target audiences by fax, electronic distribution, print and mail. The company also provides print and mail services for over 500 collection agencies located throughout the United States.

The company has over 4,000 customers mainly in the commercial, healthcare, financial services and professional services industries. Historically, the majority of Lason's revenues have come from sales to the major domestic automobile manufacturers, which accounted for about 14% of revenues in 1998, versus 33% in 1997 and 57% in 1996.

Per Share Data ($) (Year Ended Dec. 31)	1998	1997	1996	1995	1994	1993	1992	1991	1990	1989
Tangible Bk. Val.	2.21	3.19	2.30	NA	NA	NA	NA	NA	NA	NA
Cash Flow	2.26	1.64	1.06	0.76	NA	NA	NA	NA	NA	NA
Earnings	1.35	0.90	0.55	0.33	NA	NA	NA	NA	NA	NA
Dividends	Nil	Nil	Nil	NA	NA	NA	NA	NA	NA	NA
Payout Ratio	Nil	Nil	Nil	NA	NA	NA	NA	NA	NA	NA
Prices - High	64⅝	30⅛	24⅛	NA	NA	NA	NA	NA	NA	NA
- Low	25⅛	16	14	NA	NA	NA	NA	NA	NA	NA
P/E Ratio - High	48	33	43	NA	NA	NA	NA	NA	NA	NA
- Low	19	18	25	NA	NA	NA	NA	NA	NA	NA
Income Statement Analysis (Million $)										
Revs.	280	120	69.9	46.6	41.2	31.2	NA	NA	NA	NA
Oper. Inc.	47.5	23.0	8.8	7.5	NA	NA	NA	NA	NA	NA
Depr.	12.4	7.4	3.4	2.6	NA	NA	NA	NA	NA	NA
Int. Exp.	4.9	1.2	1.8	1.8	NA	NA	NA	NA	NA	NA
Pretax Inc.	30.1	14.3	5.9	3.2	5.1	3.2	NA	NA	NA	NA
Eff. Tax Rate	39%	36%	36%	36%	Nil	Nil	NA	NA	NA	NA
Net Inc.	18.2	9.1	3.7	2.0	5.1	3.2	NA	NA	NA	NA
Balance Sheet & Other Fin. Data (Million $)										
Cash	1.3	2.9	0.1	0.1	NA	NA	NA	NA	NA	NA
Curr. Assets	114	59.6	31.1	14.5	NA	NA	NA	NA	NA	NA
Total Assets	432	178	78.5	37.3	15.7	13.9	NA	NA	NA	NA
Curr. Liab.	66.4	28.3	14.2	9.5	NA	NA	NA	NA	NA	NA
LT Debt	60.2	Nil	Nil	11.5	0.3	0.3	NA	NA	NA	NA
Common Eqty.	285	132	57.0	10.5	NA	NA	NA	NA	NA	NA
Total Cap.	345	132	58.1	22.0	NA	NA	NA	NA	NA	NA
Cap. Exp.	26.3	11.8	4.6	1.1	NA	NA	NA	NA	NA	NA
Cash Flow	30.6	16.5	7.2	4.6	NA	NA	NA	NA	NA	NA
Curr. Ratio	1.7	2.1	2.2	1.5	NA	NA	NA	NA	NA	NA
% LT Debt of Cap.	17.4	Nil	Nil	52.3	NA	NA	NA	NA	NA	NA
% Net Inc.of Revs.	6.5	7.5	5.3	4.3	NA	10.3	NA	NA	NA	NA
% Ret. on Assets	6.0	7.1	6.4	7.5	34.5	NA	NA	NA	NA	NA
% Ret. on Equity	8.8	9.6	11.1	NA	NA	NA	NA	NA	NA	NA

Data as orig reptd.; bef. results of disc opers/spec. items. Per share data adj. for stk. divs. Bold denotes diluted EPS (FASB 128)-prior periods restated. E-Estimated. NA-Not Available. NM-Not Meaningful. NR-Not Ranked.

Office—1305 Stephenson Highway, Troy, MI 48083. **Tel**—(248) 597-5800.**Website**—http://www.lason.com **Chrmn & CEO**—G. L. Monroe.**Pres & COO**—J. R. Messinger. **EVP-CFO, Treas & Secy**—W. J. Rauwerdink. **Dirs**—F. Ghadar, G. L. Monroe, A. J. Nesbitt, J. R. Nolan, B. V. Rauner, W. J. Rauwerdink, R. A. Yanover. **Transfer Agent & Registrar**—First Chicago Trust Co. of New York, Jersey City, NJ. **Incorporated**—in Delaware in 1995. **Empl**— 11,500. **S&P Analyst:** J. J, Schemitsch

STANDARD
&POOR'S
STOCK REPORTS

Lattice Semiconductor

NASDAQ Symbol **LSCC**

In S&P SmallCap 600

09-OCT-99

Industry: Electronics (Semiconductors)

Summary: This company designs, develops and markets both high and low performance programmable logic devices (PLDs) and related development system software.

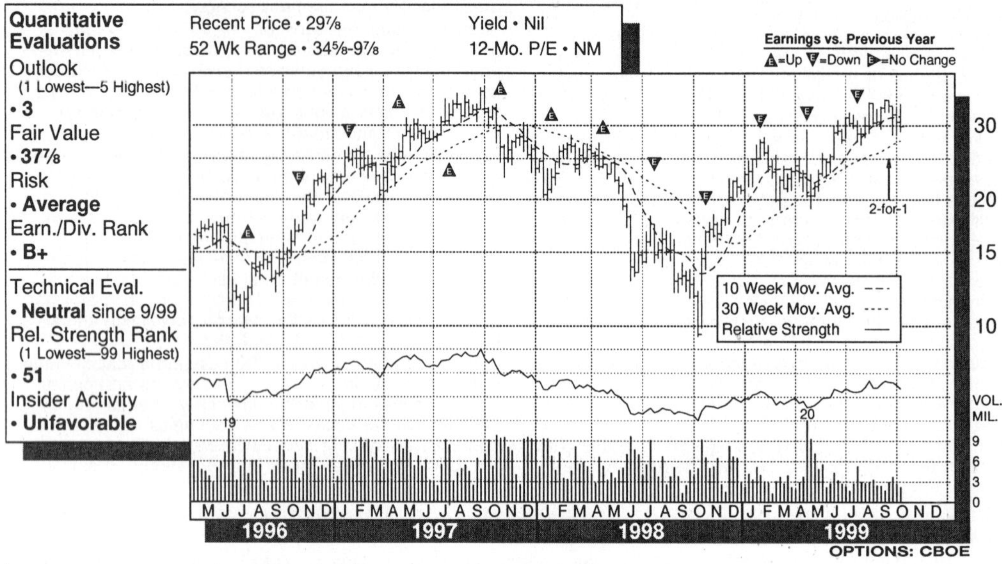

Business Profile - 24-AUG-99

The company's programmable logic devices (PLDs) shorten design cycles and reduce development costs by allowing users to quickly and efficiently incorporate different logic functions on a single device. LSCC, a fabless semiconductor company, maintains relationships with other companies to source its finished silicon wafers and assemble its products. The company's products are sold worldwide through an extensive network of independent sales representatives and distributors, primarily to original equipment manufacturers (OEMs) of communications, computing, industrial controls and military systems. In July 1999, LSCC acquired Vantis Corp., a subsidiary of Advanced Micro Devices, for $500 million in cash.

Operational Review - 24-AUG-99

In the three months ended July 3, 1999, revenues advanced 24%, year to year, aided by the inclusion of Vantis, and by a general recovery in the overall semiconductor market. Gross margins widened by 150 basis points, to 61.7%, reflecting a more favorable product mix and reductions in manufacturing costs. After an $89.0 million in-process R&D charge, and goodwill amortization of $4.2 million, a loss from operations of $77.0 million contrasted with income of $12.0 million. After a $24.1 million tax benefit, a net loss of $51.2 million ($2.16 a share) contrasted with net income of $9.8 million ($0.41, as adjusted).

Stock Performance - 08-OCT-99

In the past 30 trading days, LSCC's shares have declined 2%, compared to a 0.91% fall in the S&P 500. Average trading volume for the past five days was 436,460 shares, compared with the 40-day moving average of 539,264 shares.

Key Stock Statistics

Dividend Rate/Share	Nil	Shareholders	343
Shs. outstg. (M)	47.5	Market cap. (B)	$ 1.4
Avg. daily vol. (M)	0.570	Inst. holdings	44%
Tang. Bk. Value/Share	8.85		
Beta	1.97		

Value of $10,000 invested 5 years ago: $ 36,807

Fiscal Year Ending Mar. 31

	2000	1999	1998	1997	1996	1995
Revenues (Million $)						
1Q	59.74	48.03	61.62	48.17	45.01	32.91
2Q	—	48.09	64.07	48.64	48.61	34.56
3Q	—	50.17	60.04	51.02	51.54	36.29
4Q	—	53.79	60.17	56.26	53.01	40.32
Yr.	—	200.1	245.9	204.1	198.2	144.1
Earnings Per Share ($)						
1Q	**-1.08**	**0.20**	0.30	0.23	0.23	0.16
2Q	—	**0.21**	0.31	0.23	0.24	0.17
3Q	—	**0.23**	**0.28**	0.24	0.26	0.18
4Q	—	**0.24**	**0.29**	0.28	0.27	0.20
Yr.	—	**0.88**	**1.19**	**0.98**	0.99	0.70

Next earnings report expected: late January

Dividend Data

Amount ($)	Date Decl.	Ex-Div. Date	Stock of Record	Payment Date
2-for-1	Aug. 11	Sep. 17	Aug. 26	Sep. 16 '99

Lattice Semiconductor Corporation

Business Summary - 24-AUG-99

Lattice Semiconductor is the world's leading supplier of in-system programmable (ISP) logic devices. The company pioneered the application of electrically erasable CMOS (E2CMOS) technology to programmable logic. LSCC designs, develops and markets both high- and low-density, high performance E2CMOS programmable logic devices (PLDs) and related development system software. PLDs are standard semiconductor components that can be custom configured by the customer to perform specific logic functions. PLDs enable the customer to shorten design cycle times and reduce development costs. LSCC's proprietary generic array logic (GAL), pLSI (programmable large scale integration) and ispLSI (in-system programmable large scale integration) devices give customers quickly designed, easily configured components.

Company products are marketed worldwide through a network of independent sales representatives and indirectly through a network of distributors, primarily to original equipment manufacturers of communications, computing, industrial controls, and military systems.

As a fabless semiconductor company, Lattice does not manufacture its silicon wafers. Rather, it maintains strategic relationships with large semiconductor-makers, in order to source its finished product. This lets the company focus on product, process, and market development. The majority of LSCC's silicon wafer requirements are supplied by Seiko Epson Corp. in Japan, under an agreement with S MOS Systems, Inc., an affiliated U.S. distributor. United Microelectronics Corp. of Taiwan also provides wafers to the company. Wafer volumes, prices and terms are negotiated periodically with these suppliers. Assembly and final testing of the chips are performed by independent contractors in the Asia/Pacific region and in the U.S.

While outsourcing the chip-manufacturing process reduces the capital-intensive nature of the business and frees up resources to focus on product development and design, the strategy also adds the risk that the company will be unable to obtain wafers to meet demand.

In the in-system programmable logic device market, Lattice competes directly with Altera and Xilinx, both of which offer competing products. In July 1999, the company acquired Vantis Corp. from Advanced Micro Devices, for approximately $500 million in cash.

Per Share Data ($)										
(Year Ended Mar. 31)	1999	1998	1997	1996	1995	1994	1993	1992	1991	1990
Tangible Bk. Val.	10.25	9.28	7.88	6.75	4.29	3.40	2.75	2.22	1.90	1.04
Cash Flow	1.09	1.38	1.17	1.17	0.86	0.74	0.60	0.38	0.39	0.33
Earnings	0.89	1.19	0.98	0.99	0.70	0.59	0.47	0.30	0.31	0.26
Dividends	Nil	Nil	Nil	Nil	Nil	Nil	Nil	Nil	Nil	Nil
Payout Ratio	Nil	Nil	Nil	Nil	Nil	Nil	Nil	Nil	Nil	Nil
Cal. Yrs.	1998	1997	1996	1995	1994	1993	1992	1991	1990	1989
Prices - High	28½	37¼	23½	21½	10⅛	13⅜	8⅝	5	5¾	2 5/16
- Low	9½	19⅞	9⅞	8¼	7	6⅛	3⅝	1 13/16	1⅝	1 11/16
P/E Ratio - High	32	31	24	22	14	22	18	16	19	9
- Low	11	17	10	8	10	10	8	6	5	7
Income Statement Analysis (Million $)										
Revs.	200	246	204	198	144	126	103	71.0	64.5	38.9
Oper. Inc.	61.7	84.6	67.6	64.9	43.3	35.8	27.5	16.1	14.9	8.3
Depr.	10.1	9.6	8.6	7.1	6.0	5.8	4.7	2.8	2.8	1.8
Int. Exp.	Nil	Nil	Nil	Nil	Nil	Nil	Nil	0.1	0.2	0.3
Pretax Inc.	62.3	85.7	67.8	63.2	40.6	32.6	25.2	15.7	14.6	7.1
Eff. Tax Rate	33%	34%	34%	34%	34%	31%	31%	31%	29%	4.90%
Net Inc.	42.0	56.6	45.0	41.8	27.0	22.5	17.4	10.9	10.3	6.8
Balance Sheet & Other Fin. Data (Million $)										
Cash	79.3	60.3	229	215	88.7	93.6	80.9	63.3	51.3	23.8
Curr. Assets	381	338	311	289	141	126	110	80.1	67.1	35.1
Total Assets	541	489	403	343	193	146	129	91.7	79.1	40.8
Curr. Liab.	57.2	54.4	43.0	44.2	35.0	21.0	30.4	15.8	15.3	9.6
LT Debt	Nil	Nil	Nil	Nil	Nil	Nil	Nil	0.2	0.6	1.2
Common Eqty.	484	435	360	299	158	125	99	75.6	63.2	29.9
Total Cap.	484	435	360	299	158	125	99	75.8	63.8	31.2
Cap. Exp.	18.4	18.8	10.6	12.6	6.3	7.2	11.7	2.4	9.2	3.5
Cash Flow	52.1	66.1	53.6	48.9	33.0	28.3	22.1	13.6	13.1	8.6
Curr. Ratio	6.7	6.2	7.2	6.5	4.0	6.0	3.6	5.1	4.4	3.7
% LT Debt of Cap.	Nil	Nil	Nil	Nil	Nil	Nil	Nil	0.3	0.9	3.9
% Net Inc.of Revs.	21.0	23.0	22.1	21.1	18.8	17.8	16.8	15.3	16.0	17.5
% Ret. on Assets	8.2	12.7	12.1	15.6	15.9	16.2	15.4	12.6	16.3	5.7
% Ret. on Equity	9.2	14.2	13.7	18.3	19.1	19.9	19.5	15.5	21.0	34.1

Data as orig reptd.; bef. results of disc opers/spec. items. Per share data adj. for stk. divs. Bold denotes diluted EPS (FASB 128)-prior periods restated. E-Estimated. NA-Not Available. NM-Not Meaningful. NR-Not Ranked.

Office—5555 N.E. Moore Ct., Hillsboro, OR 97124-6421. **Tel**—(503) 681-0118. **Fax**—(503) 681-0347. **Website**—http://www.latticesemi.com **Chrmn, Pres & CEO**—C. Y. Tsui. **SVP, CFO & Secy**—S. A. Skaggs. **VP-Fin, Investor Contact**—Rodney F. Sloss. **Dirs**—M. O. Hatfield. S. Hauer, H. A. Merlo, L. W. Sonsini, D. C. Strain, C. Y. Tsui. **Transfer Agent & Registrar**—First Interstate Bank, Seattle. **Incorporated**—in Delaware in 1985. **Empl**— 546. **S&P Analyst:** B. McGovern

STANDARD &POOR'S STOCK REPORTS

Lawson Products

NASDAQ Symbol **LAWS**

In S&P SmallCap 600

09-OCT-99

Industry: Manufacturing (Diversified)

Summary: LAWS primarily distributes replacement fasteners and other parts and supplies used for the repair and maintenance of capital equipment, buildings and automobiles.

Quantitative Evaluations

Outlook (1 Lowest—5 Highest)
• **NA**

Fair Value
• **NA**

Risk
• **Low**

Earn./Div. Rank
• **B+**

Technical Eval.
• **Bearish** since 9/99

Rel. Strength Rank (1 Lowest—99 Highest)
• **56**

Insider Activity
• **NA**

Recent Price • 23 | 52 Wk Range • 28-20⅝ | Yield • 2.4% | 12-Mo. P/E • 12.0

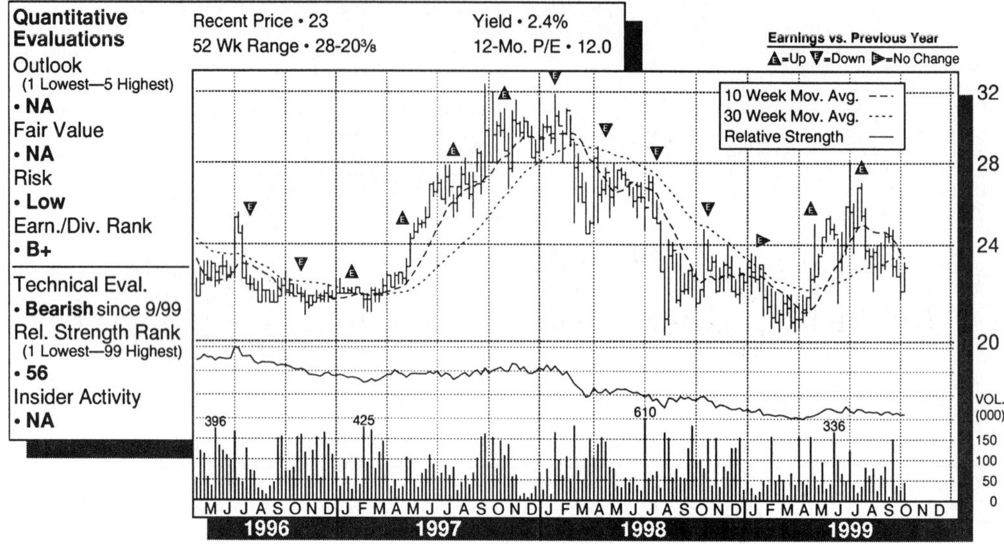

Business Profile - 05-AUG-99

Lawson Products' earnings have been somewhat erratic during the decade through 1998. The company has implemented marketing programs designed to enable it to expand into new markets and broaden existing ones with a CD-ROM catalog. LAWS expected this electronic catalog to have a positive impact on revenue growth. The balance sheet is strong, with no long term debt. Officers and directors own more than 45% of the shares outstanding, including more over 30% owned by Sidney L. Port, the company's founder and a director.

Operational Review - 05-AUG-99

Based on a brief report, net sales for the first half of 1999 advanced 6.6%, year to year. Despite an $816,000 charge for severance and early retirement expenses (related to management changes), results benefited from cost containment efforts and from a $369,000 gain from the sale of marketable securities. Net income moved ahead 12%, to $10.4 million from $9.3 million. The larger percentage gain in share earnings, to $0.98 from $0.83, reflected 5.4% fewer average diluted shares outstanding.

Stock Performance - 08-OCT-99

In the past 30 trading days, LAWS's shares have declined 0.54%, compared to a 0.91% fall in the S&P 500. Average trading volume for the past five days was 8,780 shares, compared with the 40-day moving average of 11,123 shares.

Key Stock Statistics

Dividend Rate/Share	0.56	Shareholders	1,108
Shs. outstg. (M)	10.4	Market cap. (B)	$0.238
Avg. daily vol. (M)	0.013	Inst. holdings	35%
Tang. Bk. Value/Share	13.79		
Beta	0.32		

Value of $10,000 invested 5 years ago: $ 9,011

Fiscal Year Ending Dec. 31

	1999	1998	1997	1996	1995	1994
Revenues (Million $)						
1Q	74.15	70.36	65.88	56.11	54.85	49.77
2Q	78.25	72.54	70.39	63.90	56.10	53.75
3Q	—	75.53	71.42	66.30	56.18	55.54
4Q	—	74.10	70.45	64.40	56.42	54.04
Yr.	—	292.5	278.1	250.3	223.5	213.1
Earnings Per Share ($)						
1Q	**0.50**	**0.40**	**0.42**	**0.35**	0.40	0.30
2Q	**0.49**	**0.42**	**0.51**	**0.41**	0.43	0.38
3Q	—	**0.48**	**0.53**	**0.42**	0.43	0.40
4Q	—	**0.46**	**0.46**	**0.56**	0.49	0.47
Yr.	—	**1.76**	**1.91**	**1.73**	**1.75**	**1.55**

Next earnings report expected: mid October

Dividend Data (Dividends have been paid since 1973.)

Amount ($)	Date Decl.	Ex-Div. Date	Stock of Record	Payment Date
0.140	Dec. 16	Dec. 31	Jan. 05	Jan. 19 '99
0.140	Mar. 17	Mar. 31	Apr. 05	Apr. 19 '99
0.140	May. 11	Jun. 30	Jul. 02	Jul. 16 '99
0.140	Aug. 10	Sep. 29	Oct. 01	Oct. 15 '99

A Division of The McGraw-Hill Companies

Lawson Products, Inc.

Business Summary - 05-AUG-99

Lawson Products is a distributor of fasteners, fittings and other expendable parts and supplies, serving more than 216,000 customers. The company hopes to nail down further sales with the help of a new electronic catalog that its agents now bring on sales calls. Using a laptop computer and a compact disk, agents can selectively display products relevant to a specific customer. Boasting a product line that includes 66,000 individual items, the company will be able to show more of its wares in greater detail and a shorter time, as the static printed catalog gives way to the virtual sales presentation at the dawn of the 21st century.

Lawson distributes a wide variety of maintenance, repair and replacement products and distributes (and, in some cases, makes) production components for the OEM (original equipment manufacturer) marketplace. The company's products fall into three broad categories. Fasteners, fittings and related parts (45% of 1998 net sales) include screws, nuts, rivets and other fasteners. Industrial supplies (51%) consist of hoses and hose fittings, lubricants, cleansers, adhesives and other chemicals, as well as files, drills, welding products and other shop supplies. LAWS also furnishes automotive and equipment maintenance parts (4%), such as primary wiring, connectors and other electrical supplies, exhaust and other automotive parts. About 90% of the company's products are sold under its own label. Maintenance items are purchased in bulk, and repackaged in smaller quantities.

The company's two largest markets are the heavy-duty equipment and in-plant and building maintenance markets, which accounted for 35% and 42% of 1998 sales, respectively. Customers in the heavy-duty equipment maintenance market include operators of trucks, buses, agricultural implements, construction and road building equipment, mining, logging and drilling equipment, and other off-the-road equipment. The in-plant and building maintenance market includes plants engaged in a broad range of manufacturing and processing activities as well as institutions such as hospitals, universities, school districts and governmental units. LAWS also serves the passenger car maintenance and OEM markets.

Through December 31, 1998, Lawson repurchased 951,000 common shares, under a 1996 authorization to buy back up to 1,000,000 shares. Capital spending in 1998 reflected costs for the construction of a new facility in Atlanta, and for purchases of computer related equipment. The new plant, expected to be completed during 1999 at a cost of $7 million, was expected to replace an existing facility in Norcross, GA.

Per Share Data ($) (Year Ended Dec. 31)	1998	1997	1996	1995	1994	1993	1992	1991	1990	1989
Tangible Bk. Val.	13.40	12.57	11.38	10.51	10.41	10.37	9.50	8.87	8.04	6.74
Cash Flow	2.26	2.36	2.08	1.94	1.78	1.55	1.35	1.41	1.82	1.76
Earnings	1.76	1.91	1.73	1.75	1.55	1.32	1.13	1.23	1.67	1.61
Dividends	0.56	0.54	0.52	0.51	0.48	0.44	0.40	0.40	0.37	0.33
Payout Ratio	32%	28%	30%	29%	31%	33%	35%	33%	22%	20%
Prices - High	31 7/8	32 1/2	26 1/4	28 1/2	31	30 3/4	31 3/4	35 1/4	30 1/2	26
- Low	20 1/4	21 1/8	21	23	21 3/4	23 1/4	21 1/2	22 1/2	22 3/4	18 1/2
P/E Ratio - High	18	17	15	16	20	23	28	29	18	16
- Low	12	11	12	13	14	18	19	18	14	11
Income Statement Analysis (Million $)										
Revs.	293	278	250	224	213	196	187	182	186	177
Oper. Inc.	39.0	38.9	36.1	35.5	35.4	27.8	27.5	26.7	35.7	34.9
Depr.	5.5	5.0	4.0	3.3	3.1	3.2	3.0	2.4	2.1	2.0
Int. Exp.	0.0	0.0	0.0	NM	0.1	0.0	0.0	0.1	0.0	0.0
Pretax Inc.	33.6	35.7	33.9	34.8	34.0	27.8	25.4	26.4	35.2	34.7
Eff. Tax Rate	42%	40%	41%	39%	40%	36%	40%	37%	36%	37%
Net Inc.	19.5	21.4	20.0	21.1	20.5	17.8	15.3	16.6	22.6	21.9
Balance Sheet & Other Fin. Data (Million $)										
Cash	38.7	21.9	28.8	26.5	31.7	71.9	59.6	61.3	52.3	39.1
Curr. Assets	118	104	103	88.0	92.0	127	112	110	102	86.0
Total Assets	199	189	175	161	168	171	158	150	138	119
Curr. Liab.	30.8	24.5	24.4	18.5	19.8	15.6	16.0	18.4	18.7	18.8
LT Debt	Nil	Nil	Nil	NM	Nil	Nil	Nil	Nil	Nil	Nil
Common Eqty.	143	140	129	123	131	141	129	120	109	91.0
Total Cap.	143	140	129	123	131	141	129	120	109	92.0
Cap. Exp.	5.7	5.9	4.8	3.0	6.9	1.4	8.2	4.8	6.4	7.9
Cash Flow	25.0	26.4	24.0	24.4	23.6	21.0	18.3	19.1	24.7	23.9
Curr. Ratio	3.8	4.2	4.2	4.8	4.7	8.1	7.0	6.0	5.4	4.6
% LT Debt of Cap.	Nil	Nil	Nil	NM	Nil	Nil	Nil	Nil	Nil	Nil
% Net Inc.of Revs.	6.7	7.7	8.0	9.4	9.6	9.1	8.2	9.2	12.2	12.3
% Ret. on Assets	10.0	11.8	11.9	12.8	12.5	10.8	10.0	11.6	17.6	19.7
% Ret. on Equity	13.8	15.9	15.9	16.6	15.7	13.2	12.3	14.5	22.5	25.6

Data as orig reptd.; bef. results of disc opers/spec. items. Per share data adj. for stk. divs. Bold denotes diluted EPS (FASB 128)-prior periods restated. E-Estimated. NA-Not Available. NM-Not Meaningful. NR-Not Ranked.

Office—1666 E. Touhy Ave., Des Plaines, IL 60018. **Tel**—(847) 827-9666. **Website**—http://www.lawsonprod.com **Chrmn & CEO**—B. Kalish. **EVP & COO**—J. Belford. **VP, CFO & Treas** —J. Shaffer. **Secy**—R. J. Washlow. **VP & Investor Contact**—Joseph L. Pawlick. **Dirs**—H. Allen, J. T. Brophy, B. Kalish, R. B. Port, S. L. Port, R. G. Rettig, J. Shaffer, P. G. Smith. **Transfer Agent**—First National Bank of Chicago. **Incorporated**—in Illinois in 1952; reincorporated in Delaware in 1982. **Empl**— 1,110. **S&P Analyst:** N.J.D.

STANDARD
&POOR'S
STOCK REPORTS

Legg Mason

NYSE Symbol **LM**

In S&P SmallCap 600

09-OCT-99

Industry:
Investment Banking/
Brokerage

Summary: Headquartered in Baltimore, this multi-regional broker-dealer and investment banking concern serves individual and institutional investors through offices in 22 states.

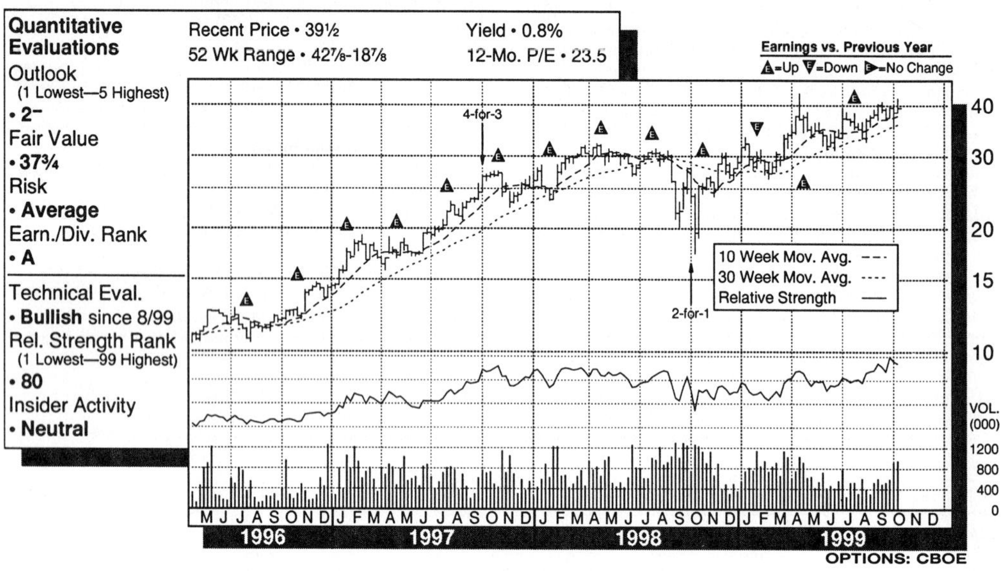

Business Profile - 12-MAY-99

In May 1999, LM stated that it is beginning to see the deal pipeline build again for middle market bankers, which is where LM focuses its corporate finance activities. The company also stated in May 1999 that fees are growing for Legg Mason thanks to good performance in its Western Asset Management and mutual fund group. At March 31, 1999, LM had $89 billion of assets under management for individual and institutional accounts and mutual funds, up from $71 billion in the prior year.

Operational Review - 12-MAY-99

Based on a preliminary report, revenues for FY 99 (Mar.) rose 18% from the prior year, reflecting solid growth in each of LM's core businesses, with the exception of investment banking, which declined 22%. Security brokerage commissions were up 16%; investment advisory revenues increased 32%; and principal transactions were up 8.5%. Total expenses rose 17%, primarily due to a 14% increase in compensation and benefits. After taxes at 40.0%, versus 40.7%, net income was up 26%, to $95.5 million ($1.62 a share), from $76.1 million ($1.31).

Stock Performance - 08-OCT-99

In the past 30 trading days, LM's shares have increased 4%, compared to a 0.91% fall in the S&P 500. Average trading volume for the past five days was 189,120 shares, compared with the 40-day moving average of 124,687 shares.

Key Stock Statistics

Dividend Rate/Share	0.32	Shareholders	1,598
Shs. outstg. (M)	56.8	Market cap. (B)	$ 2.2
Avg. daily vol. (M)	0.148	Inst. holdings	56%
Tang. Bk. Value/Share	8.83		
Beta	1.46		

Value of $10,000 invested 5 years ago: $ 45,306

Fiscal Year Ending Mar. 31

	2000	1999	1998	1997	1996	1995
Revenues (Million $)						
1Q	314.6	248.7	179.2	148.8	116.0	89.84
2Q	—	247.6	212.8	147.3	124.7	88.45
3Q	—	260.5	227.1	167.3	127.5	92.89
4Q	—	289.1	246.3	176.3	147.8	100.4
Yr.	—	1,046	889.1	639.7	516.0	371.6
Earnings Per Share ($)						
1Q	**0.54**	**0.41**	0.31	0.30	0.30	0.15
2Q	—	**0.37**	0.36	0.29	0.20	0.09
3Q	—	**0.32**	**0.39**	0.30	0.23	0.12
4Q	—	**0.43**	**0.40**	0.28	0.21	0.12
Yr.	—	**1.55**	**1.31**	**1.02**	**0.73**	**0.36**

Next earnings report expected: mid October

Dividend Data (Dividends have been paid since 1983.)

Amount ($)	Date Decl.	Ex-Div. Date	Stock of Record	Payment Date
0.065	Oct. 28	Dec. 14	Dec. 16	Jan. 11 '99
0.065	Jan. 29	Mar. 08	Mar. 10	Apr. 12 '99
0.065	Apr. 27	Jun. 11	Jun. 15	Jul. 12 '99
0.080	Jul. 27	Oct. 05	Oct. 07	Oct. 25 '99

A Division of The McGraw-Hill Companies

Legg Mason, Inc.

Business Summary - 12-MAY-99

At the start of the decade, Legg Mason, Inc. (LM), a holding company for numerous securities firms, embarked on a plan to lift the contribution of its investment management business to 25% of total revenues over a ten-year period. At the time, investment management provided only 18% of the company's revenues, and assets under management were under $10 billion. Pursuing a strategy that combined targeted acquisitions (such as the purchase of asset manager Batterymarch Financial Management, Inc. in January 1995) and the expansion of its mutual fund offerings, LM reached its goal in 1995 -- five years early. In FY 99 (Mar.), investment advisory revenues accounted for 37% of the total, and LM closed the year with $89 billion in assets under management. In May 1998, LM stated that its goal was to increase assets under management to $100 billion in two to three years, with growth coming from all market sectors (institutional accounts, high net worth individuals, and mutual funds).

LM provides securities brokerage, investment advisory, corporate and public finance and commercial mortgage banking services to individuals, institutions, corporations, and municipalities. Revenues totaled $1.05 billion in FY 99, up 18% over the previous year, and net earnings advanced 26% to $95.5 million. The company's principal broker-dealer subsidiary, Legg Mason Wood Walker, Inc., operates primarily in the eastern and mid-south regions of the U.S. Howard, Weil, Labouisse, Friedrichs Inc., another broker-dealer subsidiary, specializes in energy-related investment banking and institutional brokerage. LM's core securities brokerage business accounted for 27% of total revenues in FY 99. Investment advisory contributed 37%, investment banking 7%, and interest and other 15%.

Through its investment advisory subsidiaries, LM sponsors and serves as investment advisor and distributor for domestic and international equity, fixed-income and money market mutual funds and offshore investment funds. As of March 31, 1998, the aggregate net assets of all these funds was about $13.8 billion.

The company's securities brokerage business serves investors from 115 offices in the East, Midwest and South, as well as institutional offices in Europe. LM is placing greater emphasis on fee-based services to lessen its dependence on volume-driven commissions.

In January 1998, LM acquired Brandywine Asset Management, a value money manager that had assets under management of $7.4 billion at the time of the acquisition.

Per Share Data ($) (Year Ended Mar. 31)	1999	1998	1997	1996	1995	1994	1993	1992	1991	1990
Tangible Bk. Val.	8.83	7.97	7.33	5.64	4.71	6.01	5.04	4.06	3.39	3.30
Cash Flow	1.55	1.31	NA	NA	NA	NA	NA	NA	NA	NA
Earnings	1.62	1.31	1.17	0.93	0.49	1.12	0.98	0.70	0.46	0.41
Dividends	0.23	0.16	0.19	0.18	0.16	0.14	0.12	0.10	0.09	0.08
Payout Ratio	14%	12%	16%	19%	33%	13%	12%	15%	20%	20%
Cal. Yrs.	1998	1997	1996	1995	1994	1993	1992	1991	1990	1989
Prices - High	32¼	28⅛	14¾	11¾	9½	9½	8⅛	7⅜	5	4⅞
- Low	17¼	14⅛	10	7¾	6¾	7¼	5¾	3¾	3⅛	3⅛
P/E Ratio - High	20	21	13	13	19	8	8	11	11	12
- Low	11	11	8	8	14	7	6	5	7	8
Income Statement Analysis (Million $)										
Commissions	279	241	190	169	121	141	117	113	91.0	100
Int. Inc.	NA	127	84.1	57.1	39.3	30.0	24.0	25.6	27.8	30.8
Total Revs.	1,046	648	640	516	372	398	336	292	243	244
Int. Exp.	94.9	73.7	43.4	26.2	17.1	15.4	11.6	13.4	14.2	17.1
Pretax Inc.	149	128	95.2	63.9	27.7	59.2	49.0	35.0	21.2	19.5
Eff. Tax Rate	40%	41%	41%	41%	41%	39%	38%	40%	39%	39%
Net Inc.	89.3	76.1	56.6	37.9	16.3	36.0	30.2	21.1	12.9	11.8
Balance Sheet & Other Fin. Data (Million $)										
Total Assets	3,474	2,832	1,879	1,315	817	811	640	580	496	433
Cash Items	1,582	1,128	593	258	87.0	167	131	145	139	22.0
Receivables	921	713	527	398	371	353	305	259	216	291
Secs. Owned	144	81.5	78.9	84.2	51.9	57.6	112	94.6	64.6	53.3
Sec. Borrowed	309	448	264	197	120	96.0	90.0	100	48.0	17.0
Due Brokers & Cust.	2,181	1,568	968	569	325	310	282	243	248	212
Other Liabs.	541	85.4	57.4	50.0	58.6	64.1	56.6	53.4	39.2	52.3
Capitalization:										
Debt	100	114	100	168	103	103	34.6	35.0	35.1	35.1
Equity	554	500	419	299	226	212	177	148	126	116
Total	654	600	519	467	329	314	212	183	161	151
% Return On Revs.	12.9	11.8	8.8	7.3	4.4	9.1	9.0	7.2	5.3	4.9
% Ret. on Assets	2.8	3.2	3.5	3.5	2.0	5.0	4.9	3.9	2.8	2.8
% Ret. on Equity	16.9	16.6	15.8	14.3	7.4	18.6	18.6	15.2	10.7	10.6

Data as orig reptd.; bef. results of disc opers/spec. items. Per share data adj. for stk. divs. Bold denotes diluted EPS (FASB 128)-prior periods restated. E-Estimated. NA-Not Available. NM-Not Meaningful. NR-Not Ranked.

Office—100 Light St., Baltimore, MD 21202. **Tel**—(410) 539-0000. **Website**—http://www.leggmason.com **Chrmn, Pres & CEO**—R. A. Mason. **VP-Fin & Investor Contact**—F. B. Bilson. **SVP & Secy**—C. A. Bacigalupo. **Dirs**—H. L. Adams, C. A. Bacigalupo, J. W. Brinkley, E. J. Cashman, Jr., H. M. Ford, Jr., R. J. Himelfarb, J. E. Koerner, III, W. C. Livingston, R. A. Mason, E. I. O'Brien, P. F. O'Malley,— N. J. St. George, R. W. Schipke, M. DeB. Tutwiler, J. E. Ukrop, W. Wirth. **Transfer Agent**—First Union National Bank of North Carolina, Charlotte. **Incorporated**—in Maryland in 1981. **Empl**— 3,950. **S&P Analyst:** J. Rudy

STANDARD
&POOR'S
STOCK REPORTS

Libbey Inc.

NYSE Symbol **LBY**

In S&P SmallCap 600

09-OCT-99

Industry: Housewares

Summary: LBY is one of the largest makers of glass tableware in North America as well as a leading producer of tabletop products for the foodservice industry.

Quantitative Evaluations

Outlook
(1 Lowest—5 Highest)
• **4+**

Fair Value
• **42¾**

Risk
• **Low**

Earn./Div. Rank
• **NR**

Technical Eval.
• **Bearish** since 9/99

Rel. Strength Rank
(1 Lowest—99 Highest)
• **40**

Insider Activity
• **Neutral**

Recent Price • 28½
52 Wk Range • 33¾-24
Yield • 1.1%
12-Mo. P/E • 20.7

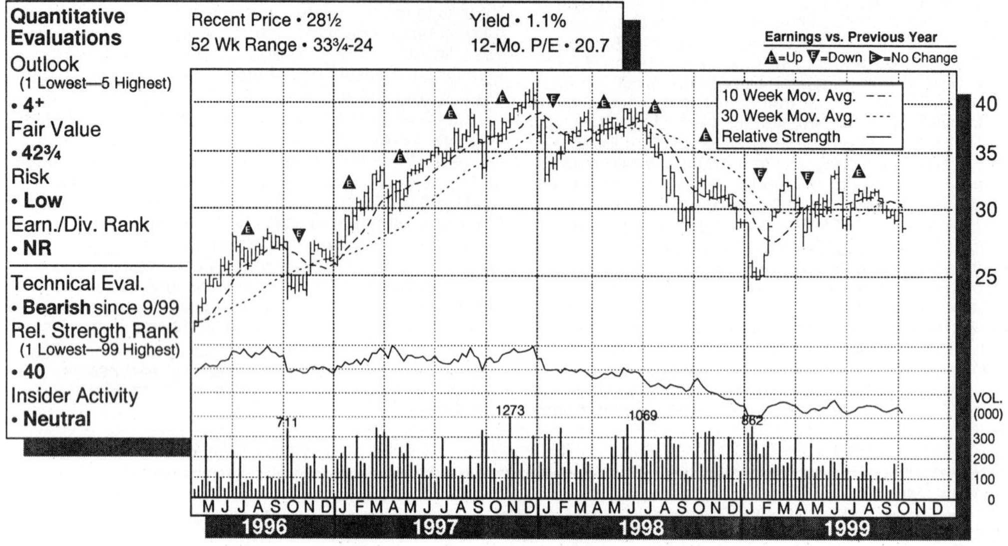

Business Profile - 21-JUN-99

Libbey said in May 1999 that it has tripled sales coverage with foodservice clients; established a distribution agreement with Luigi Bormioli for the sale of its high-end glassware; and introduced 200 new flatware, dinnerware, and glassware products in 1999, with plans to launch another 200 in the near future. LBY also said that its capacity realignment plan--involving a plant closing and reallocation of production--should increase operating profits by $4.5 million in 1999. LBY's goals for 1999 are to grow sales to $450 million and net income to $44 million, exclusive of acquisitions and restructuring charges. In April 1999, LBY made a bid to acquire Oneida Ltd., a supplier of tableware products, for $30 a share. Oneida rejected the proposal. LBY raised its offer to $37.50 a share in June, 1999.

Operational Review - 21-JUN-99

Total revenues for the first quarter of 1999 advanced 5.7%, year to year, led by strength in glassware sales to foodservice and retail customers. Including a $2.2 million capacity realignment charge (primarily related to costs associated with the closure of the company's Wallaceburg, Ontario, glassware plant, including employee severance payments and the disposition of assets), operating profit fell 17%. Excluding the capacity realignment charge, operating profit would have risen 4.1%. After sharply lower equity earnings, and taxes at 37.5%, versus 38.5%, net income was down 35%, to $4.0 million ($0.24 a share) from $6.1 million ($0.34).

Stock Performance - 08-OCT-99

In the past 30 trading days, LBY's shares have declined 8%, compared to a 0.91% fall in the S&P 500. Average trading volume for the past five days was 35,220 shares, compared with the 40-day moving average of 21,015 shares.

Key Stock Statistics

Dividend Rate/Share	0.30	Shareholders	854
Shs. outstg. (M)	16.3	Market cap. (B)	$0.463
Avg. daily vol. (M)	0.024	Inst. holdings	91%
Tang. Bk. Value/Share	2.35		
Beta	0.24		

Value of $10,000 invested 5 years ago: $ 18,332

Fiscal Year Ending Dec. 31

	1999	1998	1997	1996	1995	1994
Revenues (Million $)						
1Q	96.05	90.09	78.48	84.48	71.02	68.32
2Q	112.9	113.7	104.0	103.8	84.01	74.75
3Q	—	110.4	104.8	95.58	89.14	85.17
4Q	—	123.2	124.7	115.0	113.4	105.8
Yr.	—	440.0	415.0	397.7	360.0	336.0
Earnings Per Share ($)						
1Q	**0.24**	**0.34**	**0.30**	**0.26**	0.23	0.19
2Q	**0.82**	**0.76**	**0.65**	**0.56**	0.51	0.44
3Q	—	**0.79**	**0.74**	**0.65**	0.66	0.58
4Q	—	**-0.49**	**0.58**	**0.65**	0.60	0.57
Yr.	—	**1.42**	**2.27**	**2.12**	**1.97**	**1.76**

Next earnings report expected: late October

Dividend Data (Dividends have been paid since 1993.)

Amount ($)	Date Decl.	Ex-Div. Date	Stock of Record	Payment Date
0.075	Oct. 28	Nov. 09	Nov. 12	Dec. 02 '98
0.075	Feb. 02	Feb. 23	Feb. 25	Mar. 11 '99
0.075	Apr. 20	May. 11	May. 13	Jun. 03 '99
0.075	Jul. 22	Jul. 29	Aug. 12	Sep. 02 '99

A Division of The McGraw-Hill Companies

STANDARD
&POOR'S
STOCK REPORTS

Libbey Inc.

09-OCT-99

Business Summary - 21-JUN-99

Directors of Libbey, a major North American glass tableware maker, approved a capacity realignment plan in December 1998, which includes reallocating a portion of the current production of Libbey's Wallaceburg, Ontario, facility to its glassware facilities in the United States to improve its cost structure and more fully utilize available capacity.

A portion of Wallaceburg's production will be absorbed by a Mexican joint venture partner, Vitrocrisa. Libbey will service its Canadian glass tableware customers from its remaining manufacturing and distribution network, which includes locations in Toledo, Ohio; Shreveport, Louisiana; and City of Industry, California. Libbey also announced that it will exit the production of bottleware, a niche, low-margin business.

Libbey is a supplier of tabletop products in the U.S. and Canada. The products are also exported to more than 100 countries. Libbey designs and markets, under the LIBBEY brand name, a line of glass tableware, ceramic dinnerware, and metal flatware. Libbey alsomanufactures and markets ceramic dinnerware under the Syracuse China brand name through its subsidiary, Syracuse China. Through its World Tableware subsidiary, Libbey also imports and sells flatware, holloware and ceramic dinnerware.

Tabletop products consist of glass tableware, ceramic dinnerware, metal flatware and metal holloware. Libbey's glass tableware includes tumblers, stemware, mugs, plates, bowls, ashtrays, bud vases, salt and pepper shakers, canisters, candle holders and various other items. Vitrocrisa's product assortment includes, in addition to the product types produced by Libbey, glass bakeware and hand-made glass tableware, which are additional product categories which Libbey now offers. In addition, Vitrocrisa products include glass coffee pots, blender jars, meter covers and other industrial glassware sold principally to original equipment manufacturers.

The Syracuse China and World Tableware subsidiaries sell a wide-range of ceramic dinnerware products. These include plates, bowls, platters, cups, saucers and other tabletop accessories.

The World Tableware subsidiary sells a selection of metal flatware. These include knives, forks, spoons and serving utensils. In addition, World Tableware sells metal holloware, which includes serving trays, chafing dishes, pitchers and other metal tabletop accessories.

Export sales, which include sales to Libbey's customers in Canada, accounted for 12% of total sales in 1998. Libbey believes thatexport sales represent a growth opportunity for the future.

Due primarily to the impact of consumer buying patterns and production activity, profits tend to be strongest in the third quarter and weakest in the first quarter of each year. As a consequence, with the exception of 1998, between 37% and 42% of profits have been typically reported in the first half of each year, and 58% to 63% in the second half.

Per Share Data ($) (Year Ended Dec. 31)	1998	1997	1996	1995	1994	1993	1992	1991	1990	1989
Tangible Bk. Val.	2.20	2.91	-3.73	-5.78	-7.11	-8.65	-9.91	NA	NA	NA
Cash Flow	2.51	3.52	3.52	3.21	2.86	2.15	3.01	NA	NA	NA
Earnings	1.42	2.27	2.12	2.00	1.78	1.57	2.03	NA	NA	NA
Dividends	0.30	0.30	0.30	0.30	0.30	0.08	NA	NA	NA	NA
Payout Ratio	21%	13%	14%	15%	17%	5%	NA	NA	NA	NA
Prices - High	39 1/2	42 1/4	28 3/8	24 1/4	19 7/8	17 5/8	NA	NA	NA	NA
- Low	28 1/4	26 3/4	19 3/4	14 3/8	14	11 7/8	NA	NA	NA	NA
P/E Ratio - High	28	19	13	12	11	11	NA	NA	NA	NA
- Low	20	12	9	7	8	8	NA	NA	NA	NA
Income Statement Analysis (Million $)										
Revs.	440	415	398	360	336	305	279	NA	NA	NA
Oper. Inc.	82.9	90.4	88.7	81.3	75.5	68.2	59.8	NA	NA	NA
Depr.	19.5	19.9	21.5	18.2	16.3	14.5	14.6	NA	NA	NA
Int. Exp.	12.7	14.8	15.0	14.2	14.0	23.5	14.6	NA	NA	NA
Pretax Inc.	41.1	58.5	53.5	49.7	45.2	30.7	51.6	NA	NA	NA
Eff. Tax Rate	38%	38%	39%	40%	41%	42%	41%	NA	NA	NA
Net Inc.	25.4	36.1	32.6	30.0	26.7	17.7	30.5	NA	NA	NA
Balance Sheet & Other Fin. Data (Million $)										
Cash	3.3	2.6	2.0	2.1	3.7	1.8	Nil	NA	NA	NA
Curr. Assets	156	161	127	131	103	93.7	66.7	NA	NA	NA
Total Assets	440	450	316	322	256	249	218	NA	NA	NA
Curr. Liab.	94.6	81.9	66.0	56.0	62.1	55.1	47.2	NA	NA	NA
LT Debt	176	200	203	249	214	237	234	NA	NA	NA
Common Eqty.	94.9	100	-18.4	-47.1	-73.0	-95.0	-112	NA	NA	NA
Total Cap.	287	300	185	202	141	153	120	NA	NA	NA
Cap. Exp.	17.5	18.4	15.4	20.2	17.4	17.5	NA	NA	NA	NA
Cash Flow	44.9	56.0	54.0	48.2	43.0	32.2	45.1	NA	NA	NA
Curr. Ratio	1.6	2.0	1.9	2.3	1.7	1.7	1.4	NA	NA	NA
% LT Debt of Cap.	61.4	66.5	109.7	123.0	151.9	155.0	194.0	NA	NA	NA
% Net Inc.of Revs.	5.8	8.7	8.2	8.4	7.9	5.8	10.9	NA	NA	NA
% Ret. on Assets	5.7	9.4	10.2	10.4	10.6	NA	NA	NA	NA	NA
% Ret. on Equity	26.1	88.6	NM	NM	NM	NM	NA	NA	NA	NA

Data as orig reptd.; bef. results of disc opers/spec. items. Per share data adj. for stk. divs. Bold denotes diluted EPS (FASB 128)-prior periods restated. E-Estimated. NA-Not Available. NM-Not Meaningful. NR-Not Ranked.

Office—300 Madison Ave., Toledo, OH 43699. **Tel**—(419) 325-2100. **Website**—http://www.libbey.com **Chrmn & CEO**—J. F. Meier. **EVP & COO**—R. I. Reynolds. **VP, CFO, Treas & Investor Contact**—Kenneth G. Wilkes. **VP & Secy**—A. H. Smith. **Dirs**—W. A. Foley, P. C. M. Howell, J. F. Meier, C. B. Moerdyk, G. L. Moreau, R. I. Reynolds, T. P. Stewart. **Transfer Agent & Registrar**—Bank of New York, NYC. **Incorporated**—in Delaware in 1987. **Empl**— 3,820. **S&P Analyst:** N.J.D.

Lillian Vernon

ASE Symbol **LVC**
In S&P SmallCap 600

09-OCT-99

Industry: Retail (Home Shopping)

Summary: LVC is a direct-mail specialty catalog marketer of household, gift and other consumer products.

Quantitative Evaluations

Outlook
(1 Lowest—5 Highest)
• **NA**

Fair Value
• **NA**

Risk
• **Low**

Earn./Div. Rank
• **B**

Technical Eval.
• **Bearish** since 8/99

Rel. Strength Rank
(1 Lowest—99 Highest)
• **59**

Insider Activity
• **NA**

Recent Price • 12¾
52 Wk Range • 19¼-12
Yield • 2.5%
12-Mo. P/E • 33.6

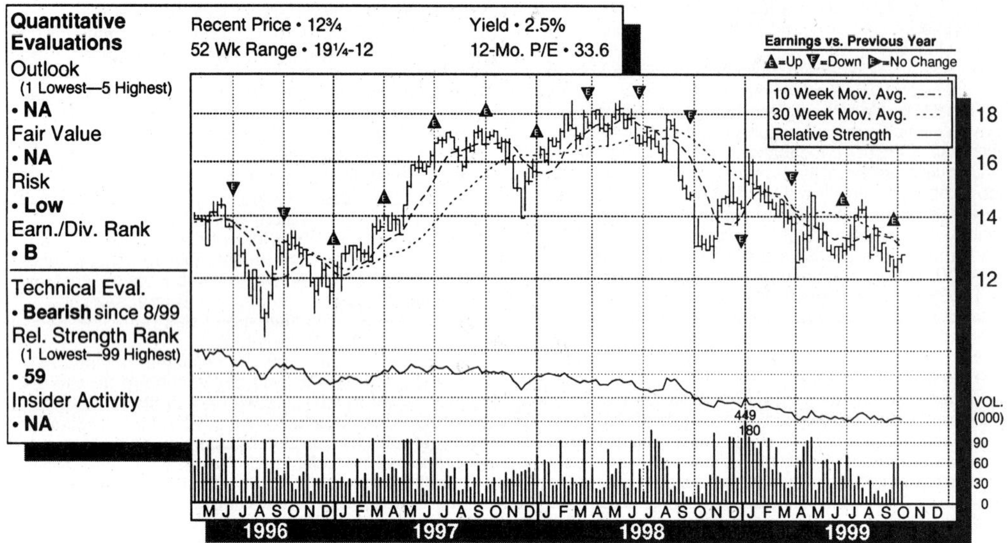

Business Profile - 07-JUL-99

In June 1999, the company said that strong cost controls and value pricing will contribute to its success as it concentrated its catalog circulation in the busy September to December holiday period. Plans are in place to offer customers new merchandise categories including teen apparel and collectibles. LVC will introduce over 1,000 new and exclusive products this fall, its most complete line ever. In addition, the company's business-to-business division will grow and contribute to fiscal 2000 results and beyond. At May 29, 1999, cash and investments were $35.0 million, stockholders' equity was $110.4 million, and there was no long term debt outstanding. In April 1999, LVC adopted a shareholder rights plan. Officers and directors own about 46% of the stock outstanding.

Operational Review - 07-JUL-99

Revenues in the three months ended May 29, 1999, fell 9.1%, year to year, reflecting the company's plan to reduce catalog circulation during its off-season; revenues per catalog were up 17%. Costs and expenses again exceeded revenues in the seasonally weak period, and the net loss narrowed slightly to $2,554.0000 ($0.28 a share), versus a deficit of $2,725,0000 ($0.29).

Stock Performance - 08-OCT-99

In the past 30 trading days, LVC's shares have declined 0.97%, compared to a 0.91% fall in the S&P 500. Average trading volume for the past five days was 6,480 shares, compared with the 40-day moving average of 5,854 shares.

Key Stock Statistics

Dividend Rate/Share	0.32	Shareholders	400
Shs. outstg. (M)	9.2	Market cap. (B)	$0.117
Avg. daily vol. (M)	0.009	Inst. holdings	41%
Tang. Bk. Value/Share	12.01		
Beta	0.17		

Value of $10,000 invested 5 years ago: $ 8,153

Fiscal Year Ending Feb. 28

	2000	1999	1998	1997	1996	1995
Revenues (Million $)						
1Q	29.12	32.01	27.75	26.31	29.61	26.00
2Q	35.50	39.39	37.26	32.97	36.92	33.66
3Q	—	107.9	106.3	100.3	97.45	91.92
4Q	—	75.95	86.92	80.43	74.21	70.63
Yr.	—	255.2	258.2	240.1	238.2	222.2
Earnings Per Share ($)						
1Q	**-0.28**	**-0.29**	**-0.24**	**-0.38**	-0.29	-0.10
2Q	**-0.19**	**-0.21**	**-0.04**	**-0.22**	-0.05	0.08
3Q	—	**0.84**	**0.99**	**0.90**	0.86	0.98
4Q	—	**0.02**	**0.23**	**0.25**	0.06	0.42
Yr.	—	**0.34**	**0.93**	**0.55**	**0.57**	**1.38**

Next earnings report expected: late December

Dividend Data (Dividends have been paid since 1992.)

Amount ($)	Date Decl.	Ex-Div. Date	Stock of Record	Payment Date
0.080	Dec. 18	Feb. 10	Feb. 15	Mar. 01 '99
0.080	Apr. 20	May. 13	May. 17	Jun. 01 '99
0.080	Jul. 21	Aug. 12	Aug. 16	Sep. 01 '99
0.080	Sep. 28	Nov. 10	Nov. 15	Dec. 01 '99

Lillian Vernon Corporation

Business Summary - 07-JUL-99

Lillian Vernon Corp. (LVC) is a direct mail specialty catalog and online company concentrating on the marketing of gift, household, gardening, kitchen, Christmas and children's products. LVC, which traces its roots back to 1951, seeks to provide customers with reasonably priced products that can be differentiated from competitive products either by design, price or personalization.

In the fiscal year ended February 27, 1999, the company mailed 188,678 catalogs (178,917 the year before), issued 34 catalog editions (34), and received 4,812,000 orders (4,936,000). The average revenue per order received in 1998 was $55.23, up from $54.13 in 1997.

LVC has developed a proprietary customer data base containing information about its customers, including such data as order frequency, size and date of last order, and type of items purchased. These and other factors are analyzed by computer to rank and segment customers to determine those most likely to purchase products offered in LVC's catalogs. The database contains information with respect to about 22 million people.

LVC's catalogs are designed to capture the reader's interest through the use of distinctive covers, colorful product presentations and product descriptions that highlight significant features. The catalogs are created and produced by LVC's in-house creative staff, which includes designers, writers and production assistants. LVC also hires free-lance designers and photographers, as needed. The combination of in-house and free-lance staff enables LVC to maintain both quality control and flexibility in the production of its catalogs.

The quantity of catalog mailings is varied based on the selling season, anticipated revenue per catalog, the price of paper and the company's capacity to process and fill orders.

Orders are executed from and products are stored in LVC's national distribution center in Virginia Beach, VA. Recently, the company established a telemarketing center in Las Vegas, NV, to supplement its Virginia Beach telemarketing facility. Products are obtained from approximately 900 suppliers, with 79% of the items sold purchased abroad, mostly in the Far East. Business is seasonal, with volume heaviest from September through February.

In the fall of 1998, the company launched a new Internet site. This new World Wide Web catalog integrates upgraded shopping capabilities and graphic enhancements to offer customers a user-friendly site featuring the company's most popular products in nine categories. Additionally, all of the company's 6,000-plus products from all of its catalog titles can be ordered online using an electronic order form.

Per Share Data ($)

(Year Ended Feb. 28)	1999	1998	1997	1996	1995	1994	1993	1992	1991	1990
Tangible Bk. Val.	NA	12.45	11.90	11.75	11.44	10.22	9.07	8.10	7.08	6.06
Cash Flow	NA	1.43	1.03	1.00	1.77	1.68	1.45	1.29	1.28	1.47
Earnings	0.34	0.93	0.55	0.59	1.38	1.35	1.15	1.02	1.00	1.17
Dividends	0.32	0.29	0.28	0.28	0.26	0.20	0.20	Nil	Nil	Nil
Payout Ratio	NM	31%	51%	47%	19%	15%	17%	Nil	Nil	Nil
Cal. Yrs.	1998	1997	1996	1995	1994	1993	1992	1991	1990	1989
Prices - High	19¼	17½	15⅜	22¼	22⅝	18⅞	17	14½	17½	17
- Low	12⅝	12	10⅜	12⅞	14½	11½	10½	7¾	6½	8⅛
P/E Ratio - High	57	19	28	38	16	14	15	14	18	15
- Low	37	13	19	22	11	9	9	8	7	7
Income Statement Analysis (Million $)										
Revs.	NA	258	240	238	222	196	173	162	160	155
Oper. Inc.	NA	19.3	12.7	12.6	22.6	22.5	18.9	16.4	16.5	20.6
Depr.	NA	4.8	4.5	4.0	3.9	3.1	2.8	2.5	2.6	2.8
Int. Exp.	NA	0.5	0.7	0.6	0.7	0.9	1.2	1.4	2.0	2.3
Pretax Inc.	NA	13.6	8.1	8.4	19.1	19.5	16.3	14.3	13.9	17.2
Eff. Tax Rate	NA	34%	34%	31%	29%	35%	34%	34%	33%	37%
Net Inc.	NA	9.0	5.3	5.7	13.6	12.8	10.8	9.5	9.3	10.8
Balance Sheet & Other Fin. Data (Million $)										
Cash	NA	25.1	22.7	25.8	38.8	52.9	51.1	43.5	35.7	36.8
Curr. Assets	NA	96.9	89.7	93.3	99	101	83.6	76.6	72.9	68.9
Total Assets	NA	144	139	136	138	131	115	105	102	99
Curr. Liab.	NA	22.5	18.9	16.6	19.4	26.6	20.7	15.9	20.9	21.8
LT Debt	NA	Nil	1.4	2.5	4.3	5.8	7.2	11.0	12.5	18.9
Common Eqty.	NA	120	114	113	110	97.3	85.1	75.5	65.8	56.2
Total Cap.	NA	118	116	116	115	104	94.3	88.7	80.9	77.6
Cap. Exp.	NA	3.1	10.3	7.7	6.3	1.8	7.5	1.8	1.5	2.3
Cash Flow	NA	13.8	9.9	9.7	17.5	15.9	13.6	12.0	11.9	13.6
Curr. Ratio	NA	4.3	4.8	5.6	5.1	3.8	4.0	4.8	3.5	3.2
% LT Debt of Cap.	NA	Nil	1.2	2.1	3.8	5.5	7.6	12.4	15.5	24.4
% Net Inc.of Revs.	NA	3.5	2.3	2.4	6.1	6.5	6.2	5.8	5.8	7.0
% Ret. on Assets	NA	6.4	3.9	4.2	10.1	10.3	9.8	9.2	9.2	11.5
% Ret. on Equity	NA	7.5	4.7	5.1	13.1	13.9	13.4	13.4	15.2	21.3

Data as orig. reptd.; bef. results of disc. opers. and/or spec. items. Per share data adj. for stk. divs. as of ex-div. date. Bold denotes diluted EPS (FASB 128). E-Estimated. NA-Not Available. NM-Not Meaningful. NR-Not Ranked.

Office—1 Theall Road, Rye, NY 10580. **Tel**—(914) 925-1200. **Website**—http://www.lillianvernon.com **Chrmn & CEO**—L. Vernon. **Interim Pres & COO**—J. Gitlitz. **SVP & CFO**—R. P. Randall.**Secy**—S. C. Handler. **Dirs**—R. A. Berman, E. M. Eveillard, J. Gitlitz, D. C. Hochberg, J. Salon, L. Vernon, B. W. Wasserman. **Transfer Agent & Registrar**—Continental Stock Transfer & Trust Co., NYC. **Incorporated**—in New York in 1965; reincorporated in Delaware in 1987. **Empl**— 1,500. **S&P Analyst:** P.L.H.

STANDARD
&POOR'S
STOCK REPORTS

Lilly Industries

NYSE Symbol **LI**

In S&P SmallCap 600

09-OCT-99

Industry:
Chemicals (Specialty)

Summary: This company is a leading producer of industrial paints and coatings for use on furniture, automotive parts, business machines, appliances and a wide variety of metal products.

Quantitative Evaluations

Outlook
(1 Lowest—5 Highest)
• **5**

Fair Value
• **22¾**

Risk
• **Low**

Earn./Div. Rank
• **B+**

Technical Eval.
• **Bearish** since 7/99

Rel. Strength Rank
(1 Lowest—99 Highest)
• **27**

Insider Activity
• **NA**

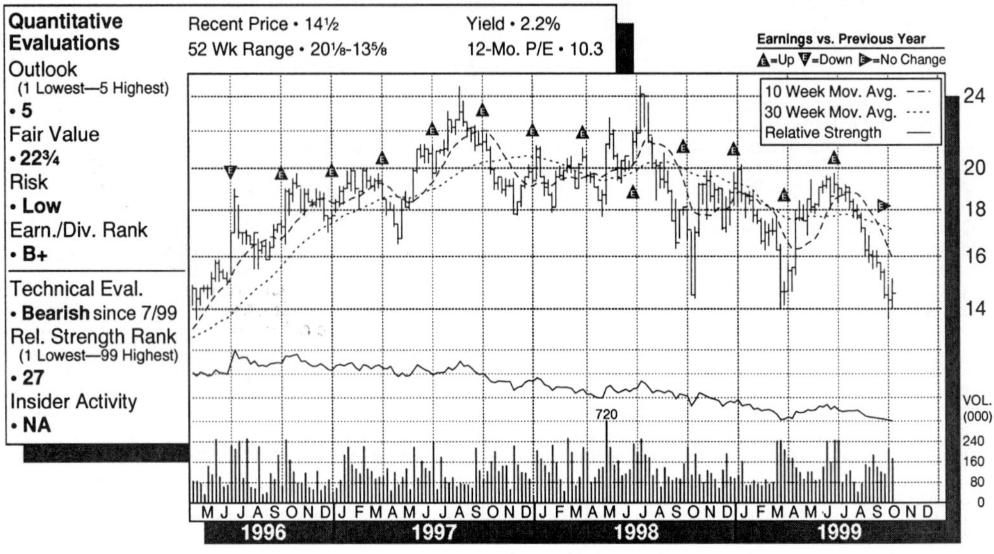

Business Profile - 08-SEP-99

In January 1999, Lilly Industries established a manufacturing presence in Mexico by acquiring an industrial coatings company, Pinturas Dygo, S.A. de C.V. LI intends to expand the Pinturas operation to support its Mexican customers and to facilitate international growth. In May 1999, LI entered into a multi-year agreement with Frigidaire Home Products for the supply of coatings to all Frigidaire North American operations. In July 1999, the company announced a $1.5 million expansion of its Wood Coatings R&D facilities. LI expects its third quarter 1999 sales to increase approximately 5.0% over the prior year's, and that EPS for the third quarter of 1999 should be about even as expenses associated with the company's growth strategy will offset the revenue gains.

Operational Review - 08-SEP-99

Net sales in the six months ended May 31, 1999, advanced 5.0%, year to year, as a result of strong powder coating sales, increases in market share, strong domestic construction and transportation markets, and improved demand in the Asia/Pacific region. Margins widened, aided by supply chain management initiatives that lowered raw material costs. Sundry expenses increased to $493,000 from $128,000, but following an 8.9% decline in interest expense, net income rose 9.8% to $15.2 million ($0.65 a share) from $13.9 million ($0.59).

Stock Performance - 08-OCT-99

In the past 30 trading days, LI's shares have declined 9%, compared to a 0.91% fall in the S&P 500. Average trading volume for the past five days was 34,380 shares, compared with the 40-day moving average of 31,359 shares.

Key Stock Statistics

Dividend Rate/Share	0.32	Shareholders	2,100
Shs. outstg. (M)	23.2	Market cap. (B)	$0.332
Avg. daily vol. (M)	0.031	Inst. holdings	47%
Tang. Bk. Value/Share	NM		
Beta	0.66		

Value of $10,000 invested 5 years ago: $ 10,193

Fiscal Year Ending Nov. 30

	1999	1998	1997	1996	1995	1994
Revenues (Million $)						
1Q	146.1	143.3	142.2	73.27	80.45	73.97
2Q	171.4	159.2	154.2	131.7	85.41	84.52
3Q	169.4	159.3	150.9	150.9	79.70	86.64
4Q	—	157.1	154.0	153.1	82.79	86.18
Yr.	—	619.0	601.3	509.0	328.4	331.3
Earnings Per Share ($)						
1Q	**0.24**	**0.22**	0.20	0.15	0.20	0.13
2Q	**0.41**	**0.37**	0.32	0.03	0.25	0.25
3Q	**0.37**	**0.37**	0.33	0.30	0.20	0.30
4Q	—	**0.39**	**0.35**	0.33	0.23	0.32
Yr.	—	**1.35**	**1.20**	**0.81**	0.88	1.00

Next earnings report expected: mid January

Dividend Data (Dividends have been paid since 1957.)

Amount ($)	Date Decl.	Ex-Div. Date	Stock of Record	Payment Date
0.080	Feb. 09	Mar. 09	Mar. 11	Apr. 01 '99
0.080	Mar. 22	Jun. 08	Jun. 10	Jul. 01 '99
0.080	Jun. 21	Sep. 08	Sep. 10	Oct. 01 '99
0.080	Sep. 27	Dec. 08	Dec. 10	Jan. 03 '00

A Division of The McGraw-Hill Companies

Lilly Industries, Inc.

Business Summary - 08-SEP-99

Lilly Industries (LI) is one of the five largest manufacturers of industrial coatings and specialty chemical products in North America, and one of the top 15 worldwide, based on annual sales. Founded as the Capital City Varnish Works in 1865 by Henry Mears, LI has increased revenues from $236 million to $619 million over the past eight years as a result of seven acquisitions, particularly Guardsman Products, Inc. which was acquired in April 1996 for $235 million.

Guardsman's strengths are in specialty coatings for appliances and furniture, and two-component coatings for construction and agricultural equipment. The combined operations and technologies will result in significant cost reductions, and access to an expanded customer base. In 1997, LI successfully reduced the combined companies' operating costs by approximately $25 million through improved raw material procurement, facility rationalization, and workforce reductions.

The company aims its products at four end use markets: metal coatings (39% of FY 98 net sales), wood coatings (38%), composites and glass (12%) and specialty (11%). The company believes that its competitive advantage is gained primarily by meeting customer-specific industrial coating demands, at a competitive price and with prompt delivery.

Principal markets for industrial coatings include wood coatings for furniture, flooring, kitchen cabinets and paneling; coil coatings for appliances, aluminum siding and components, automotive parts, doors, windows and metal buildings; and general metal coatings for a variety of metal products, including extrusions, appliances, caskets, office furniture and truck trailers.

The company's glass coatings include silver and copper plating solutions sold to mirror manufacturers, and specialty coatings, including gelcoats, mold release agents and adhesives in the fiberglass-reinforced products industry, and automotive finishes for the automotive aftermarket.

Lilly's customers are primarily in the U.S. and Canada, with the remainder in Asia and Europe. Foreign operations accounted for approximately 24% of sales in FY 98.

In January 1999, LI established a presence in Mexico by acquiring Pinturas Dygo , S.A. de C.V., an industrial coatings company. In February 1999, LI formed a strategic alliance with Dennis Chemical Company to provide plastisols to the coil coating industry, and in May 1999, the company entered into a long-term relationship with Frigidaire Home Products for the supply of coatings to all Frigidaire North American operations.

Per Share Data ($) (Year Ended Nov. 30)	1998	1997	1996	1995	1994	1993	1992	1991	1990	1989
Tangible Bk. Val.	NM	NM	NM	2.75	2.13	1.14	1.98	3.16	3.09	3.00
Cash Flow	2.21	2.14	1.48	1.23	1.39	1.01	0.86	0.44	0.57	0.64
Earnings	1.35	1.20	0.81	0.88	1.00	0.70	0.55	0.27	0.40	0.50
Dividends	0.32	0.32	0.32	0.31	0.28	0.24	0.22	0.21	0.20	0.17
Payout Ratio	24%	27%	40%	35%	28%	33%	41%	78%	47%	35%
Prices - High	24 5/8	24 5/8	19 3/4	15	18	16 1/8	10 3/4	6	7 1/4	7 3/8
- Low	14 3/8	16 1/2	12 1/8	11	11 3/4	9 1/2	5 3/4	3 7/8	3 7/8	5 1/8
P/E Ratio - High	18	21	24	17	18	23	20	22	18	15
- Low	11	14	15	12	12	14	11	14	9	10
Income Statement Analysis (Million $)										
Revs.	619	601	509	328	331	284	236	213	232	212
Oper. Inc.	92.1	92.1	73.1	43.6	51.0	36.5	29.6	16.4	21.3	23.7
Depr.	20.0	22.0	15.6	8.2	9.0	6.9	6.8	4.0	4.0	3.4
Int. Exp.	16.9	19.3	14.5	2.2	2.9	1.9	1.7	2.4	2.6	1.4
Pretax Inc.	54.4	51.2	34.1	33.8	39.7	27.9	21.9	10.8	16.9	20.7
Eff. Tax Rate	42%	45%	45%	40%	41%	42%	42%	41%	41%	41%
Net Inc.	31.6	28.1	18.8	20.3	23.3	16.2	12.7	6.4	10.0	12.6
Balance Sheet & Other Fin. Data (Million $)										
Cash	13.3	10.1	6.8	20.3	26.6	7.5	10.8	14.1	5.0	10.6
Curr. Assets	152	147	159	76.9	93.1	70.2	55.3	60.7	56.5	67.2
Total Assets	516	502	522	184	190	167	117	127	125	129
Curr. Liab.	102	94.5	108	41.4	51.5	37.0	28.2	30.3	22.0	26.8
LT Debt	204	224	245	21.2	28.0	40.6	10.4	16.6	23.0	21.1
Common Eqty.	166	142	122	109	99	81.1	70.1	74.2	73.2	74.5
Total Cap.	369	367	367	131	127	122	81.5	92.0	98.2	97.9
Cap. Exp.	17.0	12.7	19.2	15.6	6.7	7.6	3.3	1.9	4.1	2.5
Cash Flow	51.6	50.1	34.4	28.4	32.3	23.0	19.5	10.4	14.0	16.0
Curr. Ratio	1.5	1.6	1.5	1.9	1.8	1.9	2.0	2.0	2.6	2.5
% LT Debt of Cap.	55.2	61.2	66.8	16.2	22.0	33.4	12.7	18.1	23.4	21.6
% Net Inc.of Revs.	5.1	4.7	3.7	6.2	7.0	5.7	5.4	3.0	4.3	5.9
% Ret. on Assets	6.2	5.5	5.3	10.8	13.0	11.3	10.7	5.0	8.1	10.9
% Ret. on Equity	20.5	21.3	16.3	19.4	25.7	21.2	18.1	8.7	13.9	17.9

Data as orig reptd.; bef. results of disc opers/spec. items. Per share data adj. for stk. divs. Bold denotes diluted EPS (FASB 128)-prior periods restated. E-Estimated. NA-Not Available. NM-Not Meaningful. NR-Not Ranked.

Office—733 S. West St., Indianapolis, IN 46225. **Tel**—(317) 687-6700. **Website**—www.lillyindustries.com **Chrmn & CEO**—D. W. Huemme. **Pres & COO**—R.A. Taylor. **VP & CFO**—J. C. Elbin. **Dirs**— J. M. Cornelius, W. C. Dorris, J.C. Elbin, P. K. Gaston, D. W. Huemme, H. Morrison, N. J. Oman, J. D. Peterson, T. E. Reilly Jr., R. A. Taylor. **Transfer Agent & Registrar**—Harris Trust and Savings Bank, Chicago.**Incorporated**—in Indiana in 1888. **Empl**— 2,300. **S&P Analyst:** T.J. Vital

STANDARD
&POOR'S
STOCK REPORTS

Lindsay Manufacturing

NYSE Symbol **LNN**

In S&P SmallCap 600

09-OCT-99

Industry:
Manufacturing (Specialized)

Summary: Lindsay designs, manufacturers and markets center pivot and lateral move irrigation systems. It also produces diameter tubing and offers outsource manufacturing.

Quantitative Evaluations

Outlook
(1 Lowest—5 Highest)
• **1+**

Fair Value
• **16¼**

Risk
• **NA**

Earn./Div. Rank
• **B+**

Technical Eval.
• **Neutral** since 9/99

Rel. Strength Rank
(1 Lowest—99 Highest)
• **91**

Insider Activity
• **NA**

Recent Price • 20⅝
52 Wk Range • 22⅜-12⅜
Yield • 0.7%
12-Mo. P/E • 21.3

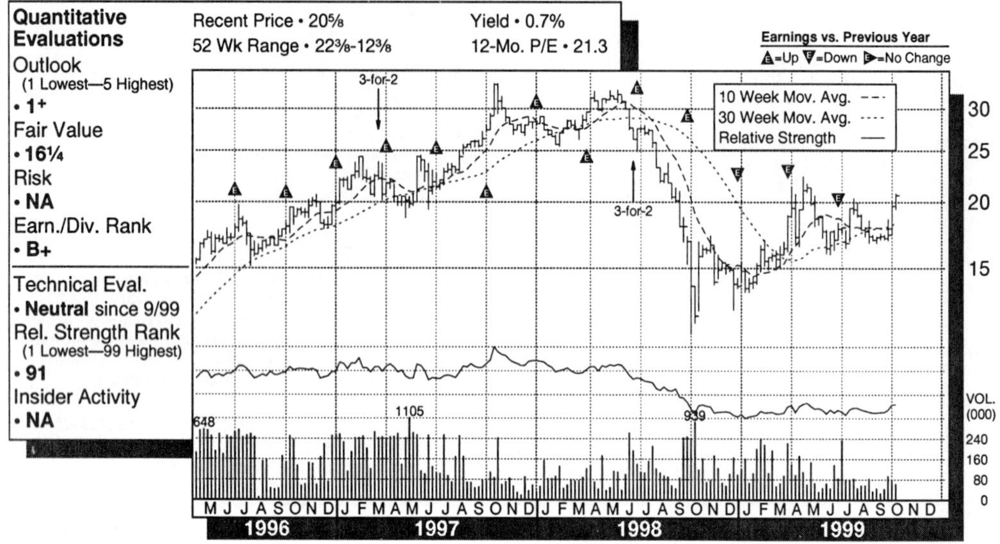

Business Profile - 23-JUL-99

In June 1999, Lindsay indicated sales have been negatively impacted by delays in capital equipment purchases by farmers concerned about weak agricultural commodity prices. Lindsay also expects continued softness in agricultural equipment manufacturing that is performed for third parties. In particular, Deere & Company has notified the company that it will now manufacture a group of products heretofore outsourced to Lindsay. The company expects performance in FY 00 (Aug.) to be similar to that of FY 99, due to anticipated flat agricultural commodity pricing. Lindsay intends to keep costs in line with lower anticipated revenues and will adjust prices as necessary to keep products competitive.

Operational Review - 23-JUL-99

Revenues for the nine months ended May 31, 1999, decreased 27%, year to year, reflecting lower revenue in domestic irrigation equipment, export irrigation equipment and diversified products. Profitability was impaired by reduced manufacturing volume. Comparisons were also hurt by the absence of a $4 million litigation settlement recorded in the prior period. Following taxes at 32.0%, versus 32.5%, net income fell 50%, to $10.3 million ($0.77 a share, based on 8.4% fewer shares), from $20.7 million ($1.41).

Stock Performance - 08-OCT-99

In the past 30 trading days, LNN's shares have increased 21%, compared to a 0.91% fall in the S&P 500. Average trading volume for the past five days was 12,460 shares, compared with the 40-day moving average of 11,774 shares.

Key Stock Statistics

Dividend Rate/Share	0.14	Shareholders	4,800
Shs. outstg. (M)	12.5	Market cap. (B)	$0.259
Avg. daily vol. (M)	0.014	Inst. holdings	53%
Tang. Bk. Value/Share	6.57		
Beta	0.31		

Value of $10,000 invested 5 years ago: $ 20,038

Fiscal Year Ending Aug. 31

	1999	1998	1997	1996	1995	1994
Revenues (Million $)						
1Q	21.64	37.45	39.47	27.33	22.14	25.57
2Q	31.09	49.71	45.69	38.14	30.35	27.56
3Q	42.99	43.90	41.66	41.14	37.45	37.72
4Q	—	24.65	31.50	29.63	21.90	21.84
Yr.	—	155.7	158.3	136.2	111.8	112.7
Earnings Per Share ($)						
1Q	**0.10**	**0.32**	0.32	0.20	0.12	0.15
2Q	**0.25**	**0.49**	0.41	0.34	0.19	0.17
3Q	**0.42**	**0.60**	0.41	0.37	0.31	0.27
4Q	—	**0.21**	0.21	0.16	0.12	0.09
Yr.	—	**1.61**	**1.34**	**1.08**	0.73	0.68

Next earnings report expected: early October

Dividend Data (Dividends have been paid since 1996.)

Amount ($)	Date Decl.	Ex-Div. Date	Stock of Record	Payment Date
0.035	Oct. 15	Nov. 10	Nov. 13	Nov. 30 '98
0.035	Jan. 27	Feb. 10	Feb. 15	Feb. 26 '99
0.035	May. 03	May. 12	May. 15	May. 28 '99
0.035	Jul. 16	Aug. 12	Aug. 16	Aug. 31 '99

A Division of The McGraw-Hill Companies

Lindsay Manufacturing Co.

Business Summary - 23-JUL-99

Founded in 1955 and headquartered in Lindsay, Nebraska, Lindsay Manufacturing Company is a leading manufacturer and marketer of center pivot and lateral move irrigation systems. The company also provides outsource manufacturing, including such services as welding, painting, machining, punching, forming, galvanizing and hydraulic, as well as electrical and mechanical assembly. Additionally, Lindsay manufactures diameter tubing, both for its own products and external sales.

The company currently distributes its products through a network of over 350 independent dealers. Lindsay feels that carefully selected and routinely reviewed dealers can offer costumers a more effective combination of product support and irrigation advice.

Center pivot irrigation systems cost approximately $65,000 and in North America typically irrigate about 130 acres. The systems are made of modular sections of pipe that are suspended from moving towers. The company provides optional electronic equipment to permit system control with a personal computer or FM radio. Lindsay believes that its irrigation systems offer the following important benefits over conventional irrigation: cutting water usage by 50%, lowering labor costs by up to 90%, increasing crop yields by making additional land economical to till, and reducing environmental contamination by using more precise chemical applications.

Outsource manufacturing and the company's sales of diameter steel tubing accounted for about 16% of total sales in FY 98. By broadening the products offered, Lindsay is endeavoring to increase this percentage to 25%. Current large customers include: Deere & Company, Caterpillar, and New Holland.

Lindsay feels that an ongoing consolidation of U.S. farms offers the company increased sales opportunities because larger, more sophisticated farming ventures are more likely to desire the efficiency and control inherent with center pivot irrigation. Of the approximately 400 million acres of cultivated farmland in the U.S., only about 4% is irrigated by central pivot systems. Lindsay estimates that an increase in usage to 20% would lead to a sale of an additional 100,000 units.

The company also notes that rapidly growing populations in Southeast Asia, India, and Latin America, and a global 1% to 2% annual decrease in farmland should benefit its products' demonstrated capacity to increase farm yields as the world seeks to feed more mouths with less cultivated land. The company feels that worldwide demand for its irrigators is largely determined by the value of crop production generated, thus the price of agricultural products has a direct correlation to irrigator sales.

In June 1999, the company noted that it repurchased 248,187 shares in the third quarter of FY 99 (Aug.), bringing its year-to-date purchases to 1.1 million. An additional 1.4 million are authorized for repurchase.

Per Share Data ($) (Year Ended Aug. 31)	1998	1997	1996	1995	1994	1993	1992	1991	1990	1989
Tangible Bk. Val.	6.69	6.16	5.39	4.66	4.28	3.51	2.82	2.09	1.53	1.02
Cash Flow	1.77	1.47	1.18	0.81	0.76	0.73	0.74	0.63	0.60	0.53
Earnings	1.61	1.34	1.08	0.73	0.68	0.65	0.68	0.57	0.54	0.47
Dividends	0.13	0.09	0.07	Nil	Nil	Nil	Nil	Nil	Nil	Nil
Payout Ratio	8%	7%	6%	Nil	Nil	Nil	Nil	Nil	Nil	Nil
Prices - High	32 5/8	33 1/2	19 3/4	11 1/2	11	10 5/8	13	9	5	3 7/8
- Low	11 1/4	18 5/8	11 1/8	8 3/8	8 1/4	8	8 1/8	3 1/4	2 3/8	2 3/8
P/E Ratio - High	20	25	18	16	16	16	19	16	9	8
- Low	7	14	10	11	12	12	12	6	4	5
Income Statement Analysis (Million $)										
Revs.	156	158	136	112	113	102	109	99	103	93.0
Oper. Inc.	29.4	28.5	20.9	15.2	15.4	14.3	13.9	12.0	15.0	11.3
Depr.	2.3	2.0	1.5	1.3	1.2	1.2	1.0	0.9	0.9	1.0
Int. Exp.	NA	NA	NA	NM	NM	Nil	Nil	Nil	Nil	Nil
Pretax Inc.	34.6	29.9	23.9	17.1	16.8	15.7	15.7	12.6	12.9	11.1
Eff. Tax Rate	32%	33%	31%	32%	33%	32%	30%	29%	35%	34%
Net Inc.	23.5	20.1	16.5	11.7	11.2	10.7	11.0	8.9	8.4	7.4
Balance Sheet & Other Fin. Data (Million $)										
Cash	3.8	4.2	26.3	23.3	13.6	15.6	18.3	18.7	16.9	12.8
Curr. Assets	50.7	49.8	57.9	43.7	36.4	39.5	35.8	39.3	38.7	27.3
Total Assets	109	108	96.8	86.1	88.4	79.9	71.4	60.4	46.9	31.7
Curr. Liab.	16.8	19.5	18.7	16.0	19.0	23.7	26.2	26.9	22.2	15.2
LT Debt	NA	0.3	Nil	Nil	Nil	Nil	Nil	Nil	Nil	Nil
Common Eqty.	90.9	87.0	76.8	68.7	68.1	55.5	44.4	32.8	24.0	16.0
Total Cap.	NA	87.2	76.8	68.7	68.1	55.5	44.4	32.8	24.0	16.0
Cap. Exp.	NA	3.3	4.0	2.8	1.3	0.9	1.7	1.7	1.2	0.8
Cash Flow	25.8	22.1	18.0	12.9	12.5	11.9	12.0	9.8	9.3	8.4
Curr. Ratio	3.0	2.6	3.1	2.8	1.9	1.7	1.4	1.5	1.7	1.8
% LT Debt of Cap.	NA	0.3	Nil	Nil	Nil	Nil	Nil	Nil	Nil	Nil
% Net Inc.of Revs.	15.1	12.7	12.1	10.0	10.0	10.5	10.1	9.0	8.2	8.0
% Ret. on Assets	21.7	19.6	18.1	13.5	13.3	14.2	16.7	16.6	21.3	26.5
% Ret. on Equity	26.4	24.5	22.7	17.1	18.1	21.4	28.5	31.3	41.9	61.5

Data as orig reptd.; bef. results of disc opers/spec. items. Per share data adj. for stk. divs. Bold denotes diluted EPS (FASB 128)-prior periods restated. E-Estimated. NA-Not Available. NM-Not Meaningful. NR-Not Ranked.

Office—E. Hwy 91, P.O. Box 156, Lindsay, NE 68644. **Tel**—(402) 428-2131. **Chrmn, Pres & CEO**—G. D. Parker. **VP-Fin, Treas, Secy & Investor Contact**—Bruce C. Karsk (402-428-7250). **Dirs**—V. L. Beals Jr., H. G. Buffett, M.N. Christodolou, J. W. Croghan, J. D. Dunn, B. C. Karsk, G. D. Parker, G. W. Plossl. **Transfer Agent & Registrar**—First National Bank of Omaha. **Incorporated**—in Nebraska in 1969; reincorporated in Delaware in 1974. **Empl**— 600. **S&P Analyst:** J. Friendly.

STANDARD &POOR'S
STOCK REPORTS

Linens 'n Things

NYSE Symbol **LIN**

In S&P SmallCap 600

09-OCT-99

Industry: Retail (Specialty)

Summary: This retailer operates a nationwide chain of superstores selling home textiles, housewares and home accessories at everyday low prices.

S&P Opinion: Accumulate (★★★★) | Recent Price • 37¾ | 52 Wk Range • 52-21¾ | Yield • Nil | 12-Mo. P/E • 36.3

Quantitative Evaluations

Outlook (1 Lowest—5 Highest) • **NA**

Fair Value • **NA**

Risk • **NA**

Earn./Div. Rank • **NR**

Technical Eval. • **Neutral** since 9/99

Rel. Strength Rank (1 Lowest—99 Highest) • **62**

Insider Activity • **NA**

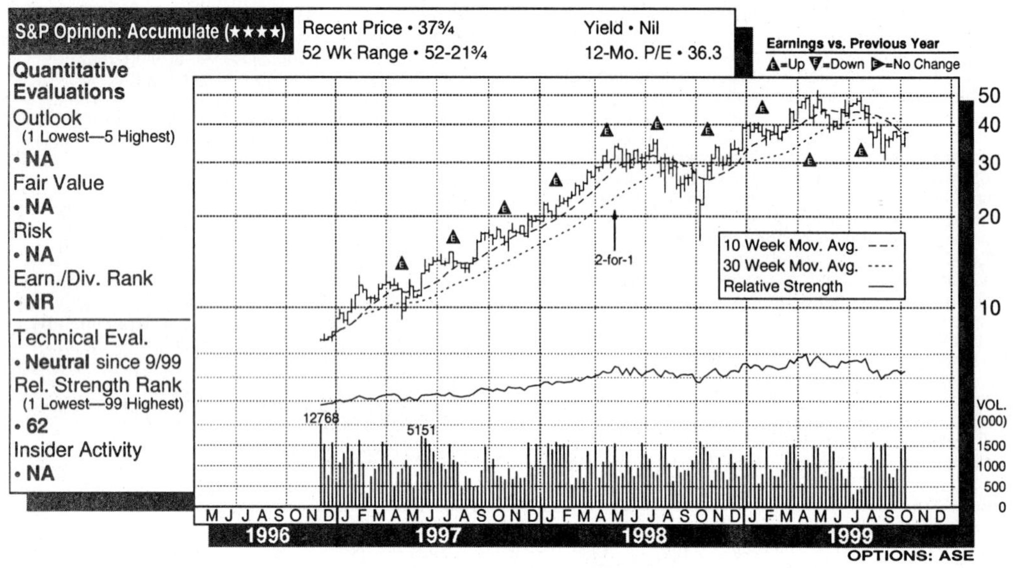

Overview - 26-JUL-99

We expect sales to continue to grow in excess of 20% during the second half of 1999, fueled by the addition of 40 to 45 new stores and comparable store increases in the mid-single digit range. At the end of June 1999, the company operated 204 stores in 38 states. With the top three superstore chains serving less than 5% of the estimated $60 billion home furnishings industry, we see continued room for expansion. Margins should continue to benefit from LIN's focus on growing the higher margin "things" portion of its business, consisting of housewares and home accessories, to 50% of its sales, from the current 38%. In addition, operating margins, which rose by almost 60 basis points in 1998, should rise another 20-40 basis points this year on improved operating leverage and a more favorable product mix. We expect earnings per share to reach $1.20 in 1999, with a further gain to $1.50 in 2000.

Valuation - 26-JUL-99

We recently upgraded LIN shares to accumulate from hold. After climbing nearly 80% in 1998, the shares have continued to outperform the broader market year-to-date in 1999. The strong performance reflects LIN's increasing ability to gain market share from department stores and weaker specialty store competitors by offering quality merchandise at low prices. We have also raised our 2000 EPS estimate, based on the company's prospects for higher than industry average same-store sales gains and margin improvement. Over the next five years, we expect the company to post 20% annual sales growth and 22%-24% earnings gains. Despite the stock recently trading at a premium to the S&P 500, and at 32X our 2000 EPS estimate of $1.50, we view the shares as attractive for long term investors.

Key Stock Statistics

S&P EPS Est. 1999	1.20	Tang. Bk. Value/Share	8.06
P/E on S&P Est. 1999	31.5	Beta	NA
S&P EPS Est. 2000	1.53	Shareholders	4,125
Dividend Rate/Share	Nil	Market cap. (B)	$ 1.5
Shs. outstg. (M)	39.5	Inst. holdings	0%
Avg. daily vol. (M)	0.230		

Value of $10,000 invested 5 years ago: NA

Fiscal Year Ending Dec. 31

	1999	1998	1997	1996	1995	1994
Revenues (Million $)						
1Q	273.5	218.0	179.9	138.1	—	—
2Q	271.6	222.1	185.2	147.7	—	—
3Q	—	278.6	225.2	180.4	—	—
4Q	—	347.4	283.4	229.8	—	—
Yr.	—	1,066	874.2	696.1	555.1	440.1
Earnings Per Share ($)						
1Q	0.09	0.04	0.01	-0.05	—	—
2Q	0.12	0.07	0.03	-0.01	—	—
3Q	E0.34	0.28	0.19	0.13	—	—
4Q	E0.65	0.56	0.42	0.32	—	—
Yr.	E1.20	0.94	0.65	0.39	Nil	0.45

Next earnings report expected: mid October

Dividend Data

The company intends to retain all its earnings for the foreseeable future for use in the operation and expansion of its business and accordingly has no plans to pay dividends on its common stock.

A Division of The McGraw-Hill Companies

Business Summary - 26-JUL-99

Founded in 1975, Linens 'n Things (LIN) was acquired by CVS Corp. (formerly Melville Corp.) in 1983 and spun off in November 1996. By the end of 1997, CVS had sold its 32.5% interest in the company. LIN's strategy is to offer a broad assortment of high-quality, brand name merchandise at everyday low prices, while providing efficient customer service and maintaining low operating costs. Prices are substantially below regular department store prices and comparable to or lower than department store sale prices. The company offers over 30,000 items across six departments: bath, home accessories, housewares, storage, bedding and window treatments.

Linens 'n Things' growth strategy includes new superstore expansion and increased productivity of the existing store base. As of April 3, 1999, the company operated 196 stores in 38 states. After opening a net of 14 new stores in 1998, the company expects to open about 30 to 35 net new stores in 1999. Since 1990, the company has replaced essentially all of its traditional stores (7,500 to 10,000 sq. ft.) with its superstore format, which has evolved from 20,000 sq. ft. to today's 30,000 to 50,000 square feet. Total square footage at April 3, 1999, was 6.5 million square feet, up from 1.2 million square feet in January 1991. Most new market opportunities exist in the western U.S., but the company will also add stores in markets in which it already has a presence.

To increase existing-store productivity, the company expects to increase sales of "things" merchandise (i.e., housewares and home accessories) to 50% of total sales (up from 10% in 1991 and 38% in 1998). These "things" carry higher margins than "linens" products (i.e., bedding, towels and pillows) and are more impulse driven. The company also sells private-label merchandise, which accounts for about 10% of sales. A 275,000 sq. ft. distribution center in Greensboro, NC, supplies approximately 85% of store merchandise. Linens 'n Things believes that this centralized infrastructure will result in lower average freight costs, more efficient scheduling of inventory shipments and improved inventory turnover. A second distribution center in Southern New Jersey is scheduled to open in mid-1999.

Total sales in the home textiles, housewares and decorative furnishings industry are estimated at over $67 billion. The industry is fragmented and highly competitive, with competition coming from department stores, mass merchandisers, specialty retailers and other stores. Specialty superstores are the fastest growing segment in the industry. However, the three largest specialty retailers (including LIN) account for less than 5% of total unit sales. Sales in the industry are highly seasonal, with most of the company's sales and earnings coming during the third and fourth quarters. Sales may also be affected by trends in the housing market.

Per Share Data ($) (Year Ended Dec. 31)	1998	1997	1996	1995	1994	1993	1992	1991	1990	1989
Tangible Bk. Val.	7.76	6.69	5.90	5.58	1.60	NA	NA	NA	NA	NA
Cash Flow	1.47	1.11	0.77	0.34	0.69	0.49	NA	NA	NA	NA
Earnings	0.94	0.65	0.39	Nil	0.45	0.30	NA	NA	NA	NA
Dividends	Nil	Nil	Nil	Nil	Nil	Nil	NA	NA	NA	NA
Payout Ratio	Nil	Nil	Nil	Nil	Nil	Nil	NA	NA	NA	NA
Prices - High	40⅝	22¼	9⅞	NA	NA	NA	NA	NA	NA	NA
- Low	16⅝	8¾	7¾	NA	NA	NA	NA	NA	NA	NA
P/E Ratio - High	43	34	25	NA	NA	NA	NA	NA	NA	NA
- Low	18	13	20	NA	NA	NA	NA	NA	NA	NA
Income Statement Analysis (Million $)										
Revs.	1,066	874	696	555	440	333	NA	NA	NA	NA
Oper. Inc.	83.3	63.5	45.2	32.0	41.8	29.1	NA	NA	NA	NA
Depr.	21.3	18.0	14.5	12.9	9.6	7.4	NA	NA	NA	NA
Int. Exp.	0.1	1.0	4.7	7.1	3.2	1.4	NA	NA	NA	NA
Pretax Inc.	61.9	44.5	25.9	1.1	29.1	20.3	NA	NA	NA	NA
Eff. Tax Rate	39%	42%	42%	103%	41%	42%	NA	NA	NA	NA
Net Inc.	38.1	25.8	15.0	0.0	17.2	11.7	NA	NA	NA	NA
Balance Sheet & Other Fin. Data (Million $)										
Cash	42.6	39.9	26.9	2.9	NA	NA	NA	NA	NA	NA
Curr. Assets	355	290	257	234	NA	NA	NA	NA	NA	NA
Total Assets	561	472	424	400	NA	NA	NA	NA	NA	NA
Curr. Liab.	201	167	146	177	NA	NA	NA	NA	NA	NA
LT Debt	Nil	Nil	13.5	13.5	NA	NA	NA	NA	NA	NA
Common Eqty.	324	280	250	237	NA	NA	NA	NA	NA	NA
Total Cap.	360	306	281	251	NA	NA	NA	NA	NA	NA
Cap. Exp.	46.3	35.3	46.4	41.3	39.1	30.6	NA	NA	NA	NA
Cash Flow	59.4	43.8	29.6	12.8	26.8	19.1	NA	NA	NA	NA
Curr. Ratio	1.8	1.7	1.8	3.0	NA	NA	NA	NA	NA	NA
% LT Debt of Cap.	Nil	Nil	4.8	5.4	NA	NA	NA	NA	NA	NA
% Net Inc.of Revs.	3.6	3.0	2.2	NM	3.9	3.5	NA	NA	NA	NA
% Ret. on Assets	7.4	5.8	3.9	NA	NA	NA	NA	NA	NA	NA
% Ret. on Equity	12.6	9.7	9.2	NA	NA	NA	NA	NA	NA	NA

Data as orig reptd.; bef. results of disc opers/spec. items. Per share data adj. for stk. divs. Bold denotes diluted EPS (FASB 128)-prior periods restated. E-Estimated. NA-Not Available. NM-Not Meaningful. NR-Not Ranked.

Office—6 Brighton Rd., Clifton, NJ 07015. **Tel**—(973) 778-1300. **Website**—http://www.linensnthings.com**Pres, Chrmn & CEO**—N. Axelrod. **CFO & Investor Contact**—William T. Giles (973-815-2929). **Dirs**—N. Axelrod, P. E. Beekman, H. F. Compton, C. C. Conaway, S. P. Goldstein. **Transfer Agent**—BankBoston, NA. **Incorporated**—in Delaware in 1996. **Empl**— 9,700. **S&P Analyst:** Maureen C. Carini

Liposome Co.

Nasdaq Symbol **LIPO**

In S&P SmallCap 600

09-OCT-99 **Industry:** Biotechnology

Summary: This company develops and makes proprietary liposome and lipid-complex based pharmaceuticals for the treatment of cancer and other life-threatening illnesses.

S&P Opinion: Accumulate (★★★★) Recent Price • 6¾ | 52 Wk Range • 28½-5⅞ | Yield • Nil | 12-Mo. P/E • 39.7

Quantitative Evaluations

Outlook (1 Lowest—5 Highest)
• 1⁻

Fair Value
• 6⅛

Risk
• **High**

Earn./Div. Rank
• **C**

Technical Eval.
• **Bearish** since 9/99

Rel. Strength Rank (1 Lowest—99 Highest)
• **NA**

Insider Activity
• **Neutral**

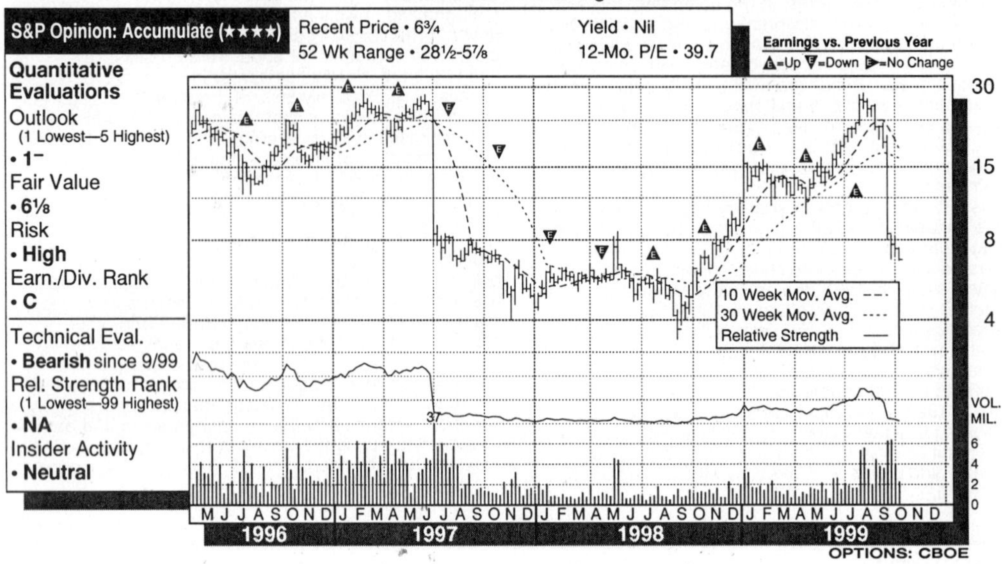

Overview - 21-SEP-99

Liposome generates the bulk of revenues from the sale of Abelcet, a potent antifungal agent used to treat systemic fungal infections in immunocompromised patients, with minimal kidney toxicity as seen with the conventional form of the drug. We expect Abelcet sales to rise 15% in 1999 to approximately $85 million, while investment and other income totals $6.0 million. The second potential product, Evacet, has been removed from our revenue assumptions for 2000 following the product's recent rejection by an FDA oncology advisory panel. As a result, we lowered our 2000 EPS estimate by $0.05 to $0.35, but still see 1999 earnings of $0.25 a share. The primary impact to our earnings targets will be felt in the year 2001, when Evacet would have generated meaningful returns. Due to the adverse FDA advisory panel decision, we now see 2001 EPS of $0.40, down from an original $0.90.

Valuation - 21-SEP-99

The stock was cut in half following the recommendation by an FDA advisory panel that Evacet not be approved as a first-line breast cancer treatment, a development that removed what was the primary near term catalyst. We believe that the panel's decision at least partially reflected concerns that Phase III clinical trials were not fully enrolled. As such, there was little confidence in data that appeared to support Evacet's efficacy and safety profile. We believe that the drug could gain FDA approval if the trial data are more fully supported, although the process of re-enrolling a clinical trial and submitting new data to the FDA is a long term proposition. Given the company's takeover appeal as a cash flow positive biotechnology entity, and the chance that a more seasoned pharmaceutical company could gain FDA approval for Evacet, we recommend that speculative investors accumulate the shares.

Key Stock Statistics

S&P EPS Est. 1999	0.25	Tang. Bk. Value/Share	1.86
P/E on S&P Est. 1999	27.0	Beta	1.33
S&P EPS Est. 2000	0.35	Shareholders	1,055
Dividend Rate/Share	Nil	Market cap. (B)	$0.263
Shs. outstg. (M)	39.0	Inst. holdings	29%
Avg. daily vol. (M)	1.819		

Value of $10,000 invested 5 years ago: $ 10,188

Fiscal Year Ending Dec. 31

	1999	1998	1997	1996	1995	1994
Revenues (Million $)						
1Q	20.73	17.09	15.85	12.41	1.85	3.04
2Q	23.70	20.23	16.65	14.40	3.72	2.94
3Q	—	18.65	16.05	14.91	3.50	2.45
4Q	—	21.90	16.54	18.21	6.65	2.02
Yr.	—	77.87	65.10	59.93	15.72	10.89
Earnings Per Share ($)						
1Q	**0.06**	**-0.13**	**-0.12**	**-0.16**	-0.49	-0.34
2Q	**0.07**	**-0.02**	**-0.23**	**-0.17**	-0.38	-0.40
3Q	**E0.04**	**-0.01**	**-0.17**	**-0.16**	-0.35	-0.42
4Q	**E0.08**	**0.04**	**-0.19**	-0.09	-0.31	-0.47
Yr.	**E0.25**	**-0.12**	**-0.71**	**-0.57**	**-1.50**	**-1.64**

Next earnings report expected: late October

Dividend Data

No cash dividends have been paid.

A Division of The McGraw-Hill Companies

The Liposome Company, Inc.

Business Summary - 21-SEP-99

Liposome (LIPO), both independently and in collaboration with others, is a leading developer of proprietary liposome and lipid-complex based pharmaceuticals for the treatment of life-threatening illnesses. LIPO's products are focused on enhanced liposomal drugs to treat cancer and severe infections.

Liposomes are microscopic synthetic spheres composed of lipids (fat molecules) that can be engineered to entrap drugs or other biologically active molecules within the lipid membranes of the spheres or in the aqueous spaces between them. The technology is used as a vehicle to deliver active therapeutic ingredients or novel bioactive lipids. In many cases, liposomal or lipid-complexed pharmaceuticals can provide less toxicity and/or better efficacy than might otherwise result from the conventional drug. Lipid technology is extremely broad and may have multiple applications in therapeutic development.

The company's first commercialized product, Abelcet (Amphotericin B lipid complex), was approved in the U.S. in November 1995. The drug is approved in 22 foreign markets including areas of Europe, with regulatory filings in several other countries. Abelcet is being used to treat refractory aspergillosis, or systemic fungal infections in immunocompromised patients. Conventional amphotericin B is very toxic, but LIPO's formulation has demonstrated lower kidney toxicity levels in patients undergoing treatment. LIPO markets the product in the U.S., Canada with its own sales force, and in other countries through marketing alliances. Currently, all product revenues are derived from sales of Abelcet.

On September 16, 1999, an FDA oncology advisory panel rejected the company's most promising new product, Evacet (liposomal doxorubicin), as a first-line treatment of metastatic breast cancer, despite clinical trials that Liposome contends showed the drug as effective as the current version of doxorubicin with significantly lower incidence of heart damage. The company may not pursue Evacet for this indication in the U.S., but awaits similar marketing approval in Europe. Evacet is involved in other clinical trials as a cancer agent used in combination with Bristol-Myers Squibb's Taxol, Rhone-Poulenc's Taxotere and Genentech's Herceptin.

Additional products include TLC ELL-12, a potential cancer treatment. This ether-lipid compound may provide advantages over existing chemotherapeutic agents, such as reduced toxicity and little or no bone marrow suppression. In February 1999, the product entered Phase I clinical trials. Other developmental products are undergoing preclinical or early research for treating various cancers or delivering genes with liposomal technology.

Per Share Data ($) (Year Ended Dec. 31)	1998	1997	1996	1995	1994	1993	1992	1991	1990	1989
Tangible Bk. Val.	1.86	1.95	2.06	0.68	0.37	4.87	3.54	2.38	0.52	0.86
Cash Flow	0.03	-0.57	-0.46	-1.29	-1.50	-1.11	-0.40	-0.19	-0.29	-0.48
Earnings	-0.12	-0.71	-0.57	-1.50	-1.64	-1.18	-0.43	-0.22	-0.35	-0.54
Dividends	Nil	Nil	Nil	Nil	Nil	Nil	Nil	Nil	Nil	Nil
Payout Ratio	Nil	Nil	Nil	Nil	Nil	Nil	Nil	Nil	Nil	Nil
Prices - High	$16\frac{7}{8}$	$29\frac{1}{2}$	$26\frac{1}{8}$	$21\frac{3}{4}$	$10\frac{3}{4}$	$12\frac{1}{2}$	$27\frac{3}{8}$	$14\frac{3}{8}$	$3\frac{1}{4}$	$3\frac{1}{2}$
- Low	$3\frac{3}{8}$	4	$11\frac{7}{8}$	$7\frac{7}{8}$	$4\frac{3}{4}$	$5\frac{1}{8}$	$7\frac{3}{8}$	$2\frac{3}{4}$	$\frac{7}{8}$	$\frac{7}{8}$
P/E Ratio - High	NM	NM	NM	NM	NM	NM	NM	NM	NM	NM
- Low	NM	NM	NM	NM	NM	NM	NM	NM	NA	NA
Income Statement Analysis (Million $)										
Revs.	73.5	60.8	56.1	12.8	5.9	5.4	6.1	6.3	3.9	2.5
Oper. Inc.	-2.6	-24.9	-17.6	-35.0	-34.8	-28.2	-13.6	-6.0	-7.0	-7.1
Depr.	5.7	5.1	3.8	3.4	3.1	1.6	0.8	0.7	0.9	0.9
Int. Exp.	0.8	0.7	0.3	0.3	0.3	0.3	0.1	0.0	0.0	0.0
Pretax Inc.	-4.7	-26.4	-17.9	-35.7	-33.7	-22.5	-9.7	-4.1	-5.0	-7.6
Eff. Tax Rate	NM	NM	NM	NM	NM	NM	NM	Nil	Nil	Nil
Net Inc.	-4.7	-26.4	-17.9	-35.7	-33.7	-22.5	-9.7	-4.1	-5.0	-7.6
Balance Sheet & Other Fin. Data (Million $)										
Cash	20.0	30.6	30.1	54.4	58.0	110	75.4	45.7	7.7	10.6
Curr. Assets	55.1	49.5	48.8	65.1	61.0	112	78.5	46.9	8.2	11.4
Total Assets	90.6	91.5	94.6	106	93.0	140	92.8	50.8	11.0	14.9
Curr. Liab.	13.7	11.0	12.1	12.0	8.9	9.6	6.6	3.3	2.9	2.0
LT Debt	5.1	17.8	19.7	4.1	5.9	7.7	2.4	Nil	0.0	0.1
Common Eqty.	71.7	73.7	74.9	89.8	9.0	115	83.2	46.9	7.4	12.2
Total Cap.	76.8	91.5	82.4	93.9	84.0	130	85.6	46.9	7.5	12.3
Cap. Exp.	1.8	1.9	9.6	8.0	2.9	7.7	9.8	1.3	0.3	0.3
Cash Flow	1.0	-21.3	-15.3	-32.3	-35.9	-26.2	-8.9	-3.4	-4.1	-6.7
Curr. Ratio	4.0	4.5	4.0	5.4	6.8	11.7	11.9	14.1	2.8	5.8
% LT Debt of Cap.	6.6	19.5	9.2	4.4	7.0	5.9	2.8	Nil	0.2	1.0
% Net Inc.of Revs.	NM	NM	NM	NM	NM	NM	NM	NM	NM	NM
% Ret. on Assets	NM	NM	NM	NM	NM	NM	NM	NM	NM	NM
% Ret. on Equity	NM	NM	NM	NM	NM	NM	NM	NM	NM	NM

Data as orig reptd.; bef. results of disc opers/spec. items. Per share data adj. for stk. divs. Rev. in Inc. tbl. excl. other income. Bold denotes diluted EPS (FASB 128)-prior periods restated. E-Estimated. NA-Not Available. NM-Not Meaningful. NR-Not Ranked.

Office—One Research Way, Princeton Forrestal Center, Princeton, NJ 08540. **Tel**—(609) 452-7060. **Website**—http://www.lipo.com **Chrmn, Pres & CEO**—C. A. Baker. **VP & CFO**—L. R. Hoffman. **VP & Secy**—C. Gillespie. **Investor Contact**—Doug Farrell (609-452-7060). **Dirs**—J. G. Andress, C. A. Baker, M. Collins, S. F. Feiner, R. F. Hendrickson, B. Samuelsson, J. T. Stewart Jr., G. Weissmann, H. Witzel. **Transfer Agent & Registrar**—American Stock Transfer & Trust, NYC. **Incorporated**—in Delaware in 1981. **Empl**— 301. **S&P Analyst:** Robert M. Gold

STANDARD
&POOR'S
STOCK REPORTS

Luby's, Inc.

NYSE Symbol **LUB**

In S&P SmallCap 600

09-OCT-99

Industry:
Restaurants

Summary: This Texas-based company (formerly Luby's Cafeterias, Inc.) owns and operates more than 220 Luby's cafeteria-style restaurants in 11 states.

Quantitative Evaluations

Outlook
(1 Lowest—5 Highest)
• **5+**

Fair Value
• **18¾**

Risk
• **Low**

Earn./Div. Rank
• **A-**

Technical Eval.
• **Bearish** since 6/99

Rel. Strength Rank
(1 Lowest—99 Highest)
• **34**

Insider Activity
• **NA**

Recent Price • 12⅝ Yield • 6.3%
52 Wk Range • 18⅝-11½ 12-Mo. P/E • 10.1

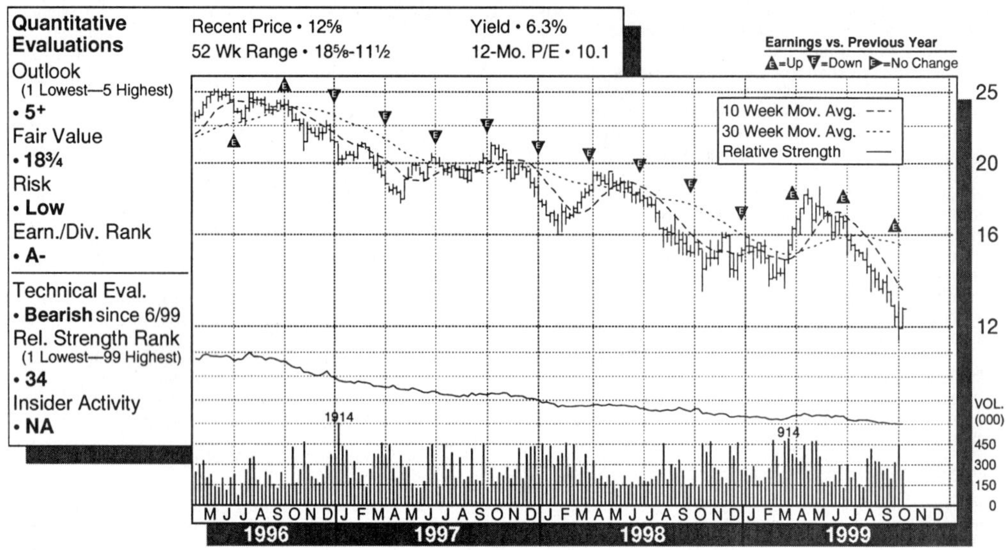

Business Profile - 18-AUG-99

The company spent this past year redesigning a prototype that it believes is more contemporary, more efficient, and will appeal to a wide range of customers. The first restaurant with this new design was scheduled to open in Georgetown, TX, and LUB plans to open additional restaurants in its Texas markets prior to the end of FY 99 (Aug.). In June 1999, management said it had six restaurants with drive-thru windows, and the food-to-go sales in these remodeled restaurants are typically increasing 30% to 50%. Also, while the company average for food-to-go sales as a percent of total sales is 12%, these restaurants are ranging from 20% to 30%. The company planned to complete several more food-to-go remodels in the Houston market prior to the end of August. In January 1999, the company changed its name to Luby's, Inc. from Luby's Cafeterias, Inc.

Operational Review - 18-AUG-99

Net sales for the nine months ended May 31, 1999, fell fractionally, year to year, primarily reflecting the closing of five restaurants in FY 98 (Aug.) and eight restaurants in FY 99. Margins remained steady as 4.3% lower food costs were offset by 1.8% higher occupancy and other operating expenses; operating income was also down fractionally. With 5.3% lower interest expense and after taxes at 34.3%, versus 35.6%, net income was up 1.7%, to $21,667,000 ($0.96 a share, on 2.5% fewer shares) from $21,295,000 ($0.92).

Stock Performance - 08-OCT-99

In the past 30 trading days, LUB's shares have declined 6%, compared to a 0.91% fall in the S&P 500. Average trading volume for the past five days was 51,360 shares, compared with the 40-day moving average of 61,362 shares.

Key Stock Statistics

Dividend Rate/Share	0.80	Shareholders	4,733
Shs. outstg. (M)	22.4	Market cap. (B)	$0.284
Avg. daily vol. (M)	0.061	Inst. holdings	43%
Tang. Bk. Value/Share	8.95		
Beta	0.51		

Value of $10,000 invested 5 years ago: $ 7,238

Fiscal Year Ending Aug. 31

	1999	1998	1997	1996	1995	1994
Revenues (Million $)						
1Q	125.7	124.7	122.3	108.3	101.5	94.17
2Q	123.8	123.2	118.8	108.8	100.6	93.72
3Q	127.1	131.2	127.6	117.1	106.9	101.1
4Q	124.9	129.8	126.7	115.8	110.1	101.8
Yr.	501.5	508.9	495.4	450.1	419.0	390.7
Earnings Per Share ($)						
1Q	**0.25**	0.27	0.35	0.37	0.35	0.32
2Q	**0.32**	**0.30**	0.36	0.40	0.36	0.33
3Q	**0.39**	**0.35**	0.41	0.46	0.42	0.40
4Q	**0.31**	**-0.70**	0.10	0.43	0.42	0.40
Yr.	—	**0.22**	**1.22**	1.66	1.55	1.45

Next earnings report expected: mid December

Dividend Data (Dividends have been paid since 1965.)

Amount ($)	Date Decl.	Ex-Div. Date	Stock of Record	Payment Date
0.200	Oct. 16	Dec. 16	Dec. 18	Jan. 04 '99
0.200	Jan. 08	Mar. 10	Mar. 12	Mar. 29 '99
0.200	May. 21	Jun. 09	Jun. 11	Jun. 28 '99
0.200	Jul. 15	Sep. 08	Sep. 10	Sep. 27 '99

Business Summary - 18-AUG-99

Demographic trends indicate that people are increasingly eating away from home and dining out. Luby's, Inc. (LUB; formerly Luby's Cafeterias, Inc.) hopes to capitalize on this development by providing freshly prepared foods in an attractive and informal environment that appeals to value-oriented consumers.

The company is one of the largest cafeteria chain companies in the U.S. As of early 1999, it was operating 222 Luby's cafeterias in 11 states, mainly in Texas, but also in Arizona, Arkansas, Florida, Kansas, Louisiana, Mississippi, Missouri, New Mexico, Oklahoma and Tennessee.

In FY 99 (Aug.), the company plans to open six new units (including one already opened) and close 12 (eight). LUB's strategic plan includes relocating several restaurants over the next few years, improving current store sales and profits, creating a more profitable business in markets outside of Texas, building new restaurants in smaller Texas markets, and building the food-to-go business. The company is testing a variety of initiatives, including expanded beverage offerings, breakfast, extended hours of operation, and the addition of drive-thru windows to selected restaurants.

A typical Luby's cafeteria seats 250 to 300 persons and contains 9,000 sq. ft. to 10,500 sq. ft. of floor space. The cafeterias cater primarily to shoppers and office or store personnel for lunch and to families for dinner. In recent years, the estimated cost of constructing, equipping and furnishing a new Luby's cafeteria in a freestanding building under normal conditions (including land acquisition costs) was $2.5 million to $2.7 million. The cost to finish out, equip and furnish a new cafeteria on a leased site has ranged from $1.2 million to $1.4 million.

Cafeterias combine the food quality and atmosphere of a good restaurant with the convenience and visual food selection of a cafeteria. Food is prepared in small quantities, offering a broad and varied menu which typically consists of 12 to 14 entrees, 12 to 14 vegetable dishes, 15 to 20 salads and 18 to 20 desserts. The cafeterias are open for lunch and dinner seven days a week and offer take-out services which accounted for 11% of sales in FY 98.

The company and a joint-venture partner, Water Street Inc., plan to open five initial Water Street Oyster Bar seafood restaurants over five years. The venture was formed in January 1996, and, after five years, LUB will have an option to buy the existing restaurants. Three units are currently in operation.

Per Share Data ($) (Year Ended Aug. 31)	1998	1997	1996	1995	1994	1993	1992	1991	1990	1989
Tangible Bk. Val.	8.83	9.41	9.41	8.27	8.50	8.78	8.01	7.40	6.68	5.95
Cash Flow	1.13	2.08	2.41	2.24	2.06	1.87	1.72	1.66	1.59	1.44
Earnings	0.22	1.22	1.66	1.55	1.45	1.31	1.19	1.18	1.17	1.08
Dividends	0.80	0.80	0.72	0.66	0.60	0.54	0.50	0.46	0.43	0.37
Payout Ratio	NM	66%	43%	43%	41%	41%	42%	39%	36%	35%
Prices - High	19½	21⅜	25¼	23¼	24⅝	25⅞	23½	20¾	21¼	18⅞
- Low	13⅜	17⅝	19⅞	18½	21⅝	19¾	14	12	15⅝	15⅜
P/E Ratio - High	89	18	15	15	17	20	20	18	18	18
- Low	61	14	12	12	15	15	12	10	13	14
Income Statement Analysis (Million $)										
Revs.	509	495	450	419	391	368	346	328	311	283
Oper. Inc.	69.2	77.3	80.7	7.3	74.8	70.1	63.7	60.3	58.3	52.2
Depr.	21.1	20.2	17.7	16.4	15.7	15.4	14.5	13.0	11.4	9.9
Int. Exp.	5.1	4.0	2.1	1.7	0.3	0.3	0.3	0.3	0.3	0.4
Pretax Inc.	7.9	42.7	62.5	58.9	60.4	56.2	50.5	48.8	48.5	44.4
Eff. Tax Rate	36%	33%	37%	37%	38%	37%	36%	34%	34%	34%
Net Inc.	5.1	28.4	39.2	37.0	37.8	35.5	32.6	32.3	32.1	29.5
Balance Sheet & Other Fin. Data (Million $)										
Cash	3.8	6.4	2.7	12.4	10.9	34.3	12.3	14.2	12.3	15.3
Curr. Assets	15.1	16.0	11.4	20.2	18.1	43.8	18.4	21.2	18.4	21.9
Total Assets	339	369	335	312	290	302	274	261	235	210
Curr. Liab.	47.4	45.7	46.5	100	56.4	43.3	38.9	40.4	32.5	28.6
LT Debt	Nil	84.0	41.0	Nil	Nil	Nil	1.4	1.9	2.3	2.8
Common Eqty.	205	219	226	193	214	239	217	203	183	163
Total Cap.	205	323	289	213	230	254	233	218	201	180
Cap. Exp.	25.1	50.8	42.8	29.7	26.3	17.8	27.1	28.8	33.7	30.0
Cash Flow	26.2	48.6	56.9	53.4	53.5	50.9	47.0	45.3	43.5	39.3
Curr. Ratio	0.3	0.3	0.2	0.2	0.3	1.0	0.5	0.5	0.6	0.8
% LT Debt of Cap.	Nil	26.0	14.2	Nil	Nil	Nil	0.6	0.8	1.2	1.6
% Net Inc.of Revs.	1.0	5.7	8.7	8.9	9.7	9.7	9.4	9.9	10.3	10.4
% Ret. on Assets	1.4	8.1	12.1	12.3	13.3	12.3	12.3	13.0	14.4	14.9
% Ret. on Equity	2.4	12.8	18.7	18.3	17.4	15.6	15.6	16.8	18.6	19.2

Data as orig reptd.; bef. results of disc opers/spec. items. Per share data adj. for stk. divs. Bold denotes diluted EPS (FASB 128)-prior periods restated. E-Estimated. NA-Not Available. NM-Not Meaningful. NR-Not Ranked.

Office—2211 Northeast Loop 410, P.O. Box 33069, San Antonio, TX 78265-3069. **Tel**—(210) 654-9000. **Chrmn**—D. B. Daviss. **CEO & Pres**—B. J. C. Parker. **SVP, CFO & Investor Contact**—Laura M. Bishop. **Secy**—J. R. Hale. **Dirs**—R. K. Calgaard, L. F. Cavazos, J.B. Craven, D. B. Daviss, A.R. Emerson, R. R. Hemminghaus, J. B. Lahourcade, B. J. C. Parker, W. J. Salmon, G. H. Wenglein, J. Winik. **Transfer Agent & Registrar**—American Stock Transfer & Trust Co. **Incorporated**—in Texas in 1959; reincorporated in Delaware in 1991. **Empl**— 12,800. **S&P Analyst:** C.C.P.

Lydall, Inc.

NYSE Symbol **LDL**

In S&P SmallCap 600

09-OCT-99

Industry:
Manufacturing (Specialized)

Summary: Lydall makes technologically advanced engineered products for demanding specialty applications primarily servicing filtration and heat management systems.

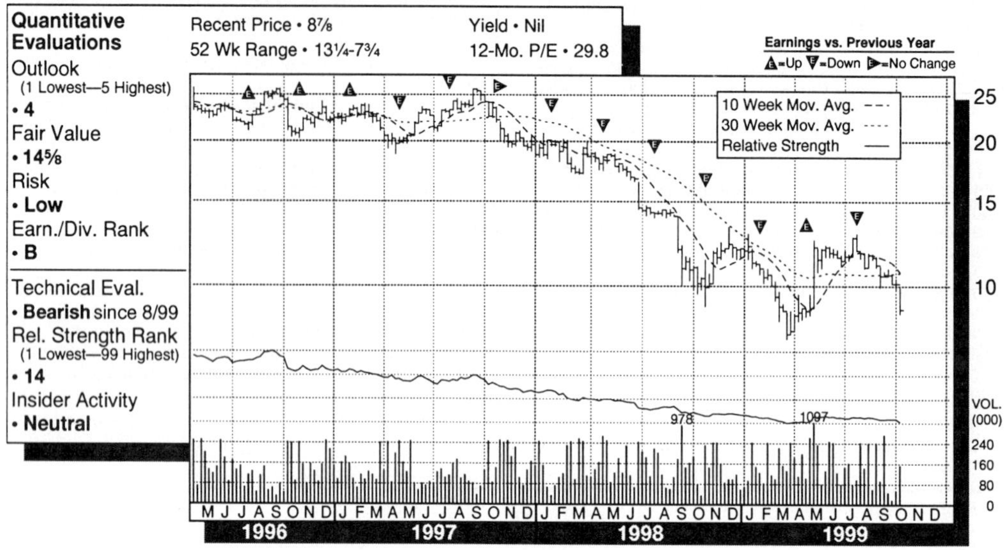

Business Profile - 13-JUL-99

Revenues for the 1999 first quarter reflect the December 1998 acquisition of Gerhardi, a German manufacturer of automotive components, which increased sales by $21 million. Excluding the impact of the Gerhardi acquisitions, revenues totaled $62.6 million and the company earned $3.6 million ($0.23 per share). The company's heat management product sales rose 136% (54% of sales), primarily due to the Gerhardi acquisition and the acquisition of Engineered Thermal Systems in April 1998. Filtration system sales were up 6% (18% of sales), while paperboard product sales rose 25% (11% of sales). The company said that the outlook for Gerhardi is very positive. Contributing to Gerhardi's long-term outlook are contracts for new business with start dates in 2000, 2001 and 2002.

Operational Review - 13-JUL-99

Net sales in the three months ended March 31, 1999, rose 48%, year to year, reflecting sales from acquisitions completed in 1998. Gross margins narrowed and after a 24% increase in SG&A expense, operating profits were up 8.7%. Results benefited from a foreign currency transaction gain versus a year earlier loss. After taxes at 33.5%, versus 33.4%, net income increased 15%, to $4,082,000 ($0.26 a share, on 4.2% fewer shares), from $3,549,000 ($0.22).

Stock Performance - 08-OCT-99

In the past 30 trading days, LDL's shares have declined 19%, compared to a 0.91% fall in the S&P 500. Average trading volume for the past five days was 30,360 shares, compared with the 40-day moving average of 32,082 shares.

Key Stock Statistics

Dividend Rate/Share	Nil	Shareholders	1,556
Shs. outstg. (M)	15.7	Market cap. (B)	$0.141
Avg. daily vol. (M)	0.013	Inst. holdings	74%
Tang. Bk. Value/Share	5.47		
Beta	0.18		

Value of $10,000 invested 5 years ago: $ 8,362

Fiscal Year Ending Dec. 31

	1999	1998	1997	1996	1995	1994
Revenues (Million $)						
1Q	83.60	56.54	61.97	65.79	62.74	48.12
2Q	84.00	59.24	64.02	67.67	65.55	53.56
3Q	—	56.50	59.38	59.71	61.49	54.45
4Q	—	57.73	58.92	59.48	62.35	56.95
Yr.	—	230.0	244.3	252.7	252.1	213.1
Earnings Per Share ($)						
1Q	**0.26**	**0.22**	0.32	0.33	0.29	0.20
2Q	**0.23**	**0.24**	0.33	0.38	0.32	0.21
3Q	—	**0.20**	0.32	0.32	0.30	0.21
4Q	—	**-0.41**	**0.30**	0.34	0.32	0.24
Yr.	—	**0.26**	**1.27**	**1.38**	**1.23**	**0.87**

Next earnings report expected: late October

Dividend Data

Cash dividends were omitted in 1982, following substantial charges related to plant closings and reorganizations.

Lydall, Inc.

Business Summary - 13-JUL-99

Lydall, Inc. manufactures technologically advanced engineered materials for demanding specialty applications. The company's long-term strategy is to emphasize two core businesses (thermal and filtration), and to return to double-digit long-term growth rates, primarily through acquisitions and new product development in core markets.

The company's products fall into four basic categories: heat-management products, filtration products, paperboard products and woven products. All other operations are aggregated in other products and services. Sales contributions by market segment in recent years were: heat management products 36% of sales in 1998, 37% in 1997 and 38% in 1996; filtration products 24%, 22% and 24%; paperboard products 14%, 13% and 13%; woven products 2%, 4% and Nil; and other products and services 24%, 25% and 25%. The woven products segment did not exist in 1996.

LDL develops and manufactures engineered fiber materials and composites in both roll and sheet form; fiber-based, metal-and-fiber, and all-metal automotive heat shields; and certain medical filtration and automotive thermal barrier components as well as wood-replacement board for pencils.

Most of the company's products are supplied to original equipment manufacturers, which convert them or incorporate them into their finished products. Using a broad spectrum of available fibers, materials, binders, resins, etc., combined with dry-laid and wet-laid nonwoven processes and specialty weaving capabilities, LDL has been able to develop a broad range of high-performance materials.

LLD serves a number of market niches. Its products are sold primarily to the customer through an internal sales force and are distributed through common carrier, ocean cargo, or its trucking operation.

LDL heat-management products include thermal barriers, heat shields, and insulating products including a range of fiber-based materials and fiber and metal combinations that protect and insulate within temperature requirements as low as -459 degrees F, up to +3,000 degrees F.

The company manufactures Lydair-registered trademark high-efficiency, glass microfiber air filtration media for rigid frame applications. The company markets six filtration classes in over 100 grades with filtering efficiencies from 10% at 0.3 micron particle size to 99.99% at 0.1 micron particle size. The company's products are used in things such as air filters, high-efficiency hydraulic oil and lubrication elements for off-road vehicles and trucks, and blood filtration devices.

The company's paperboard products include commodity paper products which are employed primarily in materials-handling and packaging applications. Lydall also produces specialty woven composites which are used in advanced structural materials sold to the aerospace, marine, and sporting goods industries.

Per Share Data ($) (Year Ended Dec. 31)	1998	1997	1996	1995	1994	1993	1992	1991	1990	1989
Tangible Bk. Val.	5.47	5.84	5.71	5.27	3.90	3.63	3.08	2.50	2.34	1.83
Cash Flow	0.93	1.82	1.87	1.70	1.28	0.91	0.82	0.68	0.65	0.61
Earnings	0.26	1.27	1.37	1.23	0.86	0.57	0.52	0.47	0.47	0.45
Dividends	Nil	Nil	Nil	Nil	Nil	Nil	Nil	Nil	Nil	Nil
Payout Ratio	Nil	Nil	Nil	Nil	Nil	Nil	Nil	Nil	Nil	Nil
Prices - High	20¾	25¾	25⅞	28½	18⅝	11¾	11⅛	8¼	5⅜	6⅛
- Low	9	18½	19¾	14¾	10⅛	9⅜	8	4⅛	3⅝	2½
P/E Ratio - High	80	20	19	23	22	21	21	17	11	14
- Low	35	15	14	12	12	16	15	9	8	6
Income Statement Analysis (Million $)										
Revs.	230	244	253	252	213	157	151	135	123	128
Oper. Inc.	25.6	42.3	48.6	45.7	36.2	23.9	22.6	19.2	18.2	18.1
Depr.	10.9	9.6	9.2	8.6	7.5	5.9	5.3	3.8	3.2	2.8
Int. Exp.	0.8	0.4	0.5	0.8	1.3	1.5	2.1	2.2	2.0	1.9
Pretax Inc.	5.4	34.5	39.9	36.9	26.5	16.9	14.6	13.3	13.2	12.6
Eff. Tax Rate	22%	36%	38%	39%	42%	41%	38%	36%	37%	37%
Net Inc.	4.2	21.9	24.7	22.4	15.5	10.0	9.0	8.5	8.3	7.9
Balance Sheet & Other Fin. Data (Million $)										
Cash	2.3	8.9	38.2	28.7	14.6	16.8	9.1	1.5	10.2	5.9
Curr. Assets	90.8	67.4	96.4	82.5	64.1	53.2	46.7	40.4	40.9	37.0
Total Assets	227	160	182	158	137	108	99	93.2	83.1	74.7
Curr. Liab.	100	28.2	43.0	29.7	33.3	21.4	22.1	20.6	14.8	15.9
LT Debt	Nil	2.1	5.0	7.8	10.6	11.2	16.2	22.7	20.4	20.6
Common Eqty.	109	117	118	102	76.2	60.1	50.1	39.1	38.5	30.1
Total Cap.	120	128	136	124	99	81.6	72.3	67.8	65.1	56.6
Cap. Exp.	17.7	17.1	10.9	12.0	8.0	6.3	6.2	4.1	8.2	6.4
Cash Flow	15.1	31.5	33.9	31.1	23.0	15.9	14.3	13.0	12.3	11.2
Curr. Ratio	0.9	2.4	2.2	2.8	1.9	2.5	2.1	2.0	2.8	2.3
% LT Debt of Cap.	Nil	1.9	3.7	6.3	10.8	13.7	22.4	33.6	31.3	36.4
% Net Inc.of Revs.	1.8	9.0	9.8	8.9	7.3	6.4	6.0	6.3	6.8	6.2
% Ret. on Assets	2.2	12.8	14.5	15.2	12.6	9.6	9.2	9.9	10.6	11.2
% Ret. on Equity	3.7	18.4	22.5	25.2	22.7	18.0	19.9	22.5	24.3	30.1

Data as orig reptd.; bef. results of disc opers/spec. items. Per share data adj. for stk. divs. Bold denotes diluted EPS (FASB 128)-prior periods restated. E-Estimated. NA-Not Available. NM-Not Meaningful. NR-Not Ranked.

Office—One Colonial Rd. (P.O. Box 151), Manchester, CT 06045-0151. **Tel**—(860) 646-1233. **Fax**—(860) 646-4917. **Website**—http://www.lydall.com **Chrmn**—R. M. Widmann. **Pres & CEO**—C. R. Skomorowski. **VP-Fin & Treas**—J. E. Hanley. **Secy**—M. A. Tremblay. **VP & Investor Contact**—Carole F. Butenas. **Dirs**—L. A. Asseo, S. P. Cooley, W. L. Duffy, D. Freeman, C. R. Skomoroski, E. F. Whitely, R. M. Widmann, A. E. Wolf. **Transfer Agent**—American Stock Transfer & Trust Co., NYC. **Incorporated**—in Connecticut in 1913; reincorporated in Delaware in 1987. **Empl**— 2,112. **S&P Analyst:** J.J.A.

STANDARD &POOR'S
STOCK REPORTS

M.D.C. Holdings

NYSE Symbol **MDC**

In S&P SmallCap 600

09-OCT-99

Industry: Homebuilding

Summary: MDC builds and sells residential housing, and also supports its building activities by originating, buying and servicing mortgages for its customers and others.

Quantitative Evaluations

Outlook (1 Lowest—5 Highest)
• **4-**

Fair Value
• **25**

Risk
• **Low**

Earn./Div. Rank
• **B**

Technical Eval.
• **Bearish** since 8/99

Rel. Strength Rank (1 Lowest—99 Highest)
• **20**

Insider Activity
• **Neutral**

Recent Price • 16¼
52 Wk Range • 22-13⅛
Yield • 1.2%
12-Mo. P/E • 5.3

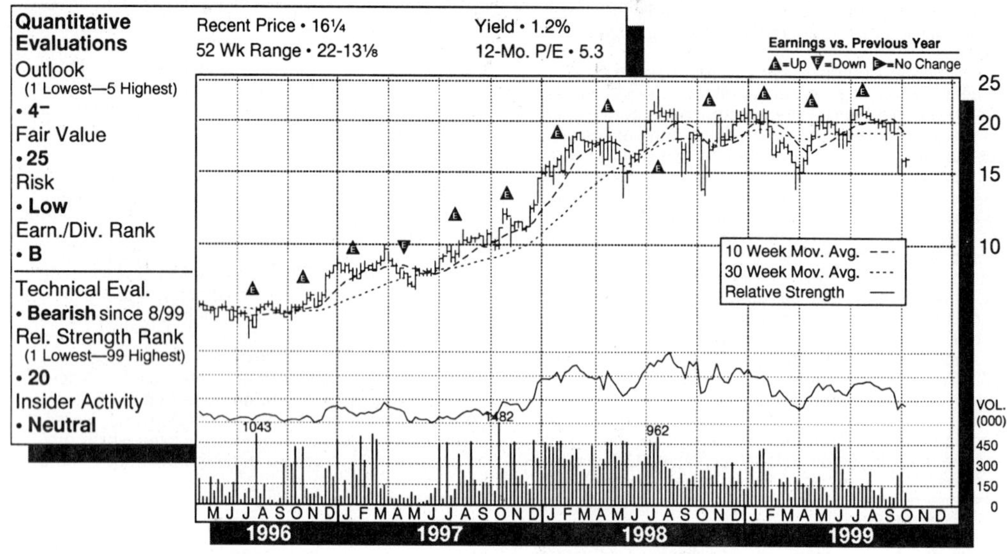

Business Profile - 23-JUN-99

MDC builds homes for first-time and move-up buyers, the largest segments of prospective home buyers. As part of its land inventory policy, the company generally limits new projects to fewer than 150 lots, avoiding overexposure to any single sub-market. MDC's priority is to acquire finished lots using rolling options and finished lots in phases for cash. If potential returns justify the risk, land is acquired for development. In the five months ended May 31, 1999, MDC received orders for 3,710 homes, up 4% from 3,556 in the 1998 period. At March 31, 1999, backlog stood at 3,729 units, valued at $750 million, versus 3,038 units ($570 million) at March 31, 1998. The IRS is currently reviewing MDC's 1996 and 1997 tax returns.

Operational Review - 23-JUN-99

Total revenues in the 1999 first quarter climbed 21%, year to year, on a 14% increase in unit closings, and higher average selling prices. Homebuilding segment gross margins widened, on higher selling prices and reduced incentives offered in Colorado, lower levels of capitalized interest, and initiatives to improve operating efficiency, control costs, and increase rates of return. After taxes at 39.5%, versus 38.5%, income soared 73%, to $13.8 million ($0.61 a share), from $7.9 million ($0.37, before charges of $0.68 for early extinguishment of debt).

Stock Performance - 08-OCT-99

In the past 30 trading days, MDC's shares have declined 17%, compared to a 0.91% fall in the S&P 500. Average trading volume for the past five days was 19,360 shares, compared with the 40-day moving average of 24,536 shares.

Key Stock Statistics

Dividend Rate/Share	0.20	Shareholders	1,503
Shs. outstg. (M)	22.3	Market cap. (B)	$0.362
Avg. daily vol. (M)	0.031	Inst. holdings	64%
Tang. Bk. Value/Share	15.27		
Beta	0.81		

Value of $10,000 invested 5 years ago: $ 29,522

Fiscal Year Ending Dec. 31

	1999	1998	1997	1996	1995	1994
Revenues (Million $)						
1Q	297.1	243.5	193.8	199.3	191.1	168.7
2Q	399.8	303.9	237.3	237.8	214.1	197.8
3Q	—	331.6	266.6	233.3	233.5	214.3
4Q	—	384.2	271.8	252.3	227.2	244.2
Yr.	—	1,263	969.6	922.6	865.9	824.9
Earnings Per Share ($)						
1Q	**0.61**	**0.37**	**0.18**	0.22	0.20	0.19
2Q	**1.10**	**0.58**	**0.26**	0.23	0.21	0.28
3Q	—	**0.65**	**0.35**	0.30	0.28	0.26
4Q	—	**0.74**	**0.39**	0.34	0.17	0.21
Yr.	—	**2.32**	**1.18**	**1.09**	0.86	0.94

Next earnings report expected: late October

Dividend Data (Dividends have been paid since 1994.)

Amount ($)	Date Decl.	Ex-Div. Date	Stock of Record	Payment Date
0.040	Oct. 28	Nov. 05	Nov. 09	Nov. 20 '98
0.050	Jan. 26	Feb. 04	Feb. 08	Feb. 19 '99
0.050	Apr. 27	Apr. 29	May. 03	May. 21 '99
0.050	Jul. 26	Jul. 28	Jul. 30	Aug. 12 '99

M.D.C. Holdings, Inc.

Business Summary - 23-JUN-99

M.D.C. Holdings, Inc. constructs and sells residential housing. The company also provides mortgage loans primarily to its home buyers.

Homebuilding operations (98% of 1998 sales) involve the design, construction and sale of single-family residential homes. The company builds homes principally on finished lots acquired using rolling options, phased acquisitions, or bulk purchases. To a lesser extent, if potential returns justify the risk, it acquires land for development for use in its homebuilding activities.

MDC is one of the largest U.S. homebuilders, building and selling homes under the name Richmond American Homes. The company is a major regional homebuilder, with a significant presence in a number of selected growth markets.

The company is the largest homebuilder in metropolitan Denver; among the five leading builders in northern Virginia, Tucson, AZ, and Colorado Springs, CO; among the 10 leading builders in Southern California, Phoenix, AZ, suburban Maryland, and Las Vegas, NV; and has a growing presence in the San Francisco Bay area. MDC believes a significant presence in its markets enables it to compete effectively for home sales, land acquisition opportunities, and subcontractor labor.

MDC builds its homes generally for first-time and move-up buyers, with base prices of $80,000 to $330,000. Approximately 74% of its homes that closed in 1998 were in subdivisions targeted to first-time and first-time move-up buyers, versus 83% and 77% in 1997 and 1996, respectively.

Financial services operations (2%) are conducted through the HomeAmerican Mortgage subsidiary, a full-service mortgage lender. HomeAmerican originates mortgage loans primarily for the company's home buyers and, to a lesser extent, for others, on a spot basis through offices located in each of MDC's markets. HomeAmerican is the principal originator of mortgage loans for MDC's home buyers.

HomeAmerican is authorized to originate Federal Housing Administration-insured (FHA), Veterans Administration-guaranteed (VA), Federal National Mortgage Association (FNMA), Federal Home Loan Mortgage Corp. (FHLMC), and conventional mortgage loans. Substantially all mortgage loans originated or purchased by HomeAmerican are sold to private investors within 40 days of origination or purchase. Through early 1999, HomeAmerican also purchased loans and the related servicing rights from unaffiliated companies; however, it does not intend to purchase third-party mortgage loans in the future.

The IRS is examining MDC's tax returns for 1996 and 1997. The company believes it has made adequate provisions for additional taxes and interest; however, it is possible that the review could result in amounts that differ materially in the near-term from amounts provided.

Per Share Data ($) (Year Ended Dec. 31)	1998	1997	1996	1995	1994	1993	1992	1991	1990	1989
Tangible Bk. Val.	13.56	12.91	11.83	10.54	10.19	9.64	8.08	8.00	8.25	7.89
Cash Flow	3.18	1.79	1.72	1.37	1.44	0.81	0.59	-0.23	-0.06	-4.68
Earnings	2.32	1.18	1.09	0.86	0.94	0.45	0.22	-0.62	-0.63	-5.66
Dividends	0.15	0.12	0.12	0.11	0.06	Nil	Nil	Nil	Nil	Nil
Payout Ratio	6%	10%	11%	13%	6%	Nil	Nil	Nil	Nil	Nil
Prices - High	24	15¼	9⅜	8⅛	7⅞	7	4½	2¼	1½	3¾
- Low	13	7¾	5⅞	4⅞	4½	3¾	1¾	¼	⅛	1
P/E Ratio - High	10	13	9	9	8	16	20	NM	NM	NM
- Low	6	7	5	6	5	8	8	NM	NM	NM
Income Statement Analysis (Million $)										
Revs.	1,263	970	923	866	825	652	517	422	507	719
Oper. Inc.	104	55.1	48.6	44.8	58.4	57.4	84.5	73.2	90.6	39.5
Depr.	20.2	15.1	12.1	10.3	10.1	8.0	8.2	8.1	10.9	15.6
Int. Exp.	26.3	0.8	44.5	48.1	44.0	45.0	77.0	103	123	170
Pretax Inc.	83.9	39.3	32.8	26.7	31.0	15.0	7.0	-14.0	-13.0	-115
Eff. Tax Rate	39%	38%	37%	35%	38%	33%	27%	NM	NM	NM
Net Inc.	51.6	24.2	20.8	17.3	19.3	10.1	4.8	-12.9	-12.0	-90.1
Balance Sheet & Other Fin. Data (Million $)										
Cash	10.1	11.7	11.3	20.8	49.0	82.0	106	91.0	83.0	91.0
Curr. Assets	NM	NA	NA	NA	NA	NA	NA	NA	NA	NA
Total Assets	714	622	617	635	725	777	859	1,316	1,477	1,664
Curr. Liab.	NA	NA	NA	NA	NA	NA	NA	NA	NA	NA
LT Debt	175	202	232	240	322	412	510	976	1,131	1,297
Common Eqty.	298	230	214	205	192	176	164	160	157	150
Total Cap.	473	431	446	445	515	587	676	1,163	1,315	1,464
Cap. Exp.	6.1	2.7	Nil	Nil	Nil	Nil	Nil	Nil	Nil	Nil
Cash Flow	71.8	39.3	32.9	27.5	29.4	18.1	12.9	-4.8	-1.1	-74.5
Curr. Ratio	NA	NA	NA	NA	NA	NA	NA	NA	NA	NA
% LT Debt of Cap.	37.0	46.9	52.1	54.0	62.6	70.1	75.4	83.9	86.0	88.6
% Net Inc.of Revs.	4.1	2.5	2.3	2.0	2.3	1.5	0.9	NM	NM	NM
% Ret. on Assets	7.7	3.9	3.3	2.7	2.5	1.3	0.4	NM	NM	NM
% Ret. on Equity	19.5	10.9	9.9	8.7	10.3	6.2	2.9	NM	NM	NM

Data as orig reptd.; bef. results of disc opers/spec. items. Per share data adj. for stk. divs. Bold denotes diluted EPS (FASB 128)-prior periods restated. E-Estimated. NA-Not Available. NM-Not Meaningful. NR-Not Ranked.

Office—3600 South Yosemite St., Suite 900, Denver, CO 80237. **Tel**—(303) 773-1100. **Website**—www.mdcholdings.com **Chrmn & CEO**—L. A. Mizel. **Pres & COO**—D. D. Mandarich. **EVP, CFO & Investor Contact**—P. G. Reece III. **Secy**—D. S. Japha. **Dirs**—S. J. Borick, H. T. Buchwald, G. Goldstein, W. B. Kemper, D. D. Mandarich, L. A. Mizel. **Transfer Agent**—Continental Stock Transfer & Trust Co., NYC. **Incorporated**—in Colorado in 1972; reincorporated in Delaware in 1985. **Empl**— 1,350. **S&P Analyst:** John A. Massey

STANDARD
&POOR'S
STOCK REPORTS

M.S. Carriers

NASDAQ Symbol **MSCA**

In S&P SmallCap 600

09-OCT-99 **Industry:** Truckers

Summary: This irregular-route truckload carrier transports a wide range of general commodities throughout the United States, and in the provinces of Quebec and Ontario, Canada.

Quantitative Evaluations

Outlook (1 Lowest—5 Highest) • **4**

Fair Value • **30¾**

Risk • **Average**

Earn./Div. Rank • **B+**

Technical Eval. • **Bearish** since 9/99

Rel. Strength Rank (1 Lowest—99 Highest) • **54**

Insider Activity • **Neutral**

Recent Price • 27⅜ | 52 Wk Range • 35-15¾ | Yield • Nil | 12-Mo. P/E • 12.4

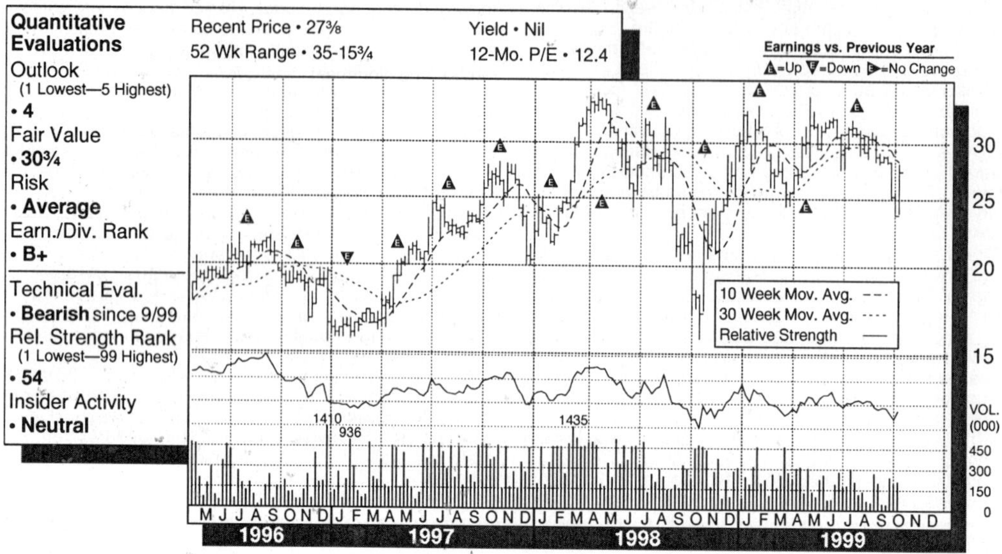

Business Profile - 26-JUL-99

M.S. Carriers' strategy includes providing premium services and charging compensating rates rather than competing solely on the basis of price. In addition, the company seeks to acquire small-to-medium trucking companies throughout the U.S. MSCA believes any acquisition should be accretive to earnings within six months and should place the company in new markets for customers and drivers or provide additional capacity for other new business opportunities. In July 1999, MSCA said that it grew by 250 units in the first half of 1999, which was on track with a previously announced growth plan of 500 trucks for the full year of 1999. The company said that its focus for the second half of 1999 will be to continue to add capacity to its network through internal growth and potential acquisitions. Officers and directors own more than 25% of the shares.

Operational Review - 26-JUL-99

Operating revenues for the first half of 1999 advanced 18%, year to year, reflecting greater demand for the company's services and more tractors in operation. The higher revenues and increased tractor utilization enabled operating profit to move ahead 23%. After 25% larger other expenses (net), pretax income was up 22%. Following taxes at an effective rate of 35.5%, compared with 36.5%, net income increased 24%, to $14.1 million ($1.10 a share), from $11.3 million ($0.89).

Stock Performance - 08-OCT-99

In the past 30 trading days, MSCA's shares have declined 5%, compared to a 0.91% fall in the S&P 500. Average trading volume for the past five days was 41,740 shares, compared with the 40-day moving average of 31,933 shares.

Key Stock Statistics

Dividend Rate/Share	Nil	Shareholders	3,000
Shs. outstg. (M)	12.3	Market cap. (B)	$0.337
Avg. daily vol. (M)	0.034	Inst. holdings	63%
Tang. Bk. Value/Share	17.74		
Beta	1.19		

Value of $10,000 invested 5 years ago: $ 12,882

Fiscal Year Ending Dec. 31

	1999	1998	1997	1996	1995	1994
Revenues (Million $)						
1Q	142.8	117.2	92.70	79.69	81.70	60.42
2Q	153.6	133.6	101.5	84.27	84.54	69.56
3Q	—	137.5	107.5	85.82	84.33	80.30
4Q	—	140.5	114.3	90.46	82.50	82.59
Yr.	—	528.8	415.9	340.2	333.1	292.9
Earnings Per Share ($)						
1Q	**0.45**	**0.35**	**0.25**	**0.15**	0.29	0.18
2Q	**0.65**	**0.54**	**0.40**	**0.34**	0.31	0.34
3Q	—	**0.56**	**0.45**	0.35	0.20	0.41
4Q	—	**0.54**	**0.44**	**0.19**	0.22	0.38
Yr.	—	**1.99**	**1.54**	**1.02**	**1.01**	1.31

Next earnings report expected: early October

Dividend Data

No cash dividends have been paid, and the company has expressed its intention to retain earnings to finance expansion of its business. Two-for-one stock splits were effected in 1992 and 1987.

A Division of The McGraw-Hill Companies

M.S. Carriers, Inc.

Business Summary - 26-JUL-99

M.S. Carriers has targeted the service-sensitive segment of the trucking market rather than the segment that uses price as its primary consideration. The company has chosen to provide premium services and charge compensating rates rather than to compete solely on the basis of price. MSCA seeks to provide on-time deliveries, dependable late-model equipment, fully integrated computer systems to monitor shipment status and variations from schedules, on-board communications systems, multiple and appointment pickups and deliveries, assistance in loading and unloading, the availability of extra trailers that can be placed for the convenience of customers and sufficient equipment to respond promptly to customers' varying requirements.

M.S. Carriers is a transportation company primarily engaged in the hauling of truckload shipments of general commodities throughout the United States and the provinces of Quebec and Ontario in Canada. The company also provides third-party logistics services.

The company has both common and contract authority to transport any type of freight (except certain types of explosives, household goods and commodities in bulk) from any point in the continental United States to any other point in any state over any route selected by MSCA. The company has authority in Canada granted by the Quebec Transport Commission and the Ontario Highway Transport Board to haul general commodities from points in the United States to points in Quebec and Ontario and from points in Quebec and Ontario into the United States. MSCA also provides interline service to and from Mexico.

M.S. Carriers' primary line-haul traffic flows are between the Middle South and the Southwest, Midwest, Central States, Southeast and Northeast. In addition, the company operates regional networks that serve the West, Southeast, Southwest, Middle South, Central States and Northeast. The average length of a trip (one-way) was approximately 689 miles in 1998 and 633 miles in 1997. The principal types of freight transported are packages, retail goods, nonperishable foodstuffs, paper and paper products, household appliances, furniture and packaged petroleum products.

The company has a policy of purchasing standardized tractors and trailers manufactured to M.S. Carriers' specifications. The company, as of year-end 1998, owned and operated 2,750 tractors; leased 739 tractors owned by traditional owner-operators; and had agreements for 264 tractors with leased owner-operators. As of the same date, MSCA owned 12,164 van trailers. All trailers are 102 inches wide with a minimum of 109.5 inches of inside height. Most of the tractors are manufactured by Freightliner and most of the trailers are manufactured by Lufkin or Great Dane.

In March 1998, M.S. Carriers acquired the U.S. operations of Challenger Motor Freight, adding 195 tractors and 481 trailers to its fleet.

Per Share Data ($) (Year Ended Dec. 31)	1998	1997	1996	1995	1994	1993	1992	1991	1990	1989
Tangible Bk. Val.	16.62	14.53	12.84	12.24	11.49	10.25	6.74	5.75	5.02	4.43
Cash Flow	5.90	4.79	4.04	4.02	3.88	3.40	2.97	2.44	2.10	1.95
Earnings	1.99	1.54	1.02	1.01	1.31	1.13	0.97	0.73	0.60	0.79
Dividends	Nil	Nil	Nil	Nil	Nil	Nil	Nil	Nil	Nil	Nil
Payout Ratio	Nil	Nil	Nil	Nil	Nil	Nil	Nil	Nil	Nil	Nil
Prices - High	35 3/8	28 1/8	22 1/8	25 1/4	28 1/2	26 1/2	22 3/4	16	10 3/4	12
- Low	15 3/4	15 3/4	15 1/4	15 1/4	17 3/4	18 1/4	12 1/2	6 3/4	4 5/8	8
P/E Ratio - High	18	18	22	25	22	23	23	22	18	15
- Low	8	10	15	15	14	16	13	9	8	10
Income Statement Analysis (Million $)										
Revs.	529	416	340	333	293	225	181	153	124	97.0
Oper. Inc.	95.5	74.5	58.4	63.8	63.4	52.4	42.2	33.6	29.0	27.7
Depr.	49.8	40.1	37.0	39.1	33.7	27.4	21.9	18.2	15.9	12.3
Int. Exp.	8.5	5.8	4.8	5.5	1.8	2.1	2.6	3.0	3.0	2.2
Pretax Inc.	39.8	29.4	19.5	20.5	28.0	23.1	18.0	13.0	10.6	13.6
Eff. Tax Rate	36%	36%	36%	36%	39%	41%	41%	40%	40%	39%
Net Inc.	25.3	19.0	12.4	13.2	17.2	13.6	10.6	7.8	6.4	8.3
Balance Sheet & Other Fin. Data (Million $)										
Cash	1.5	0.4	1.1	0.5	30.8	0.1	0.1	0.1	0.0	0.1
Curr. Assets	74.2	60.5	50.2	42.9	73.8	32.0	25.0	20.3	17.0	16.4
Total Assets	484	362	291	280	276	199	151	122	111	95.0
Curr. Liab.	79.9	46.8	43.0	42.3	44.9	22.7	24.6	16.7	17.7	17.6
LT Debt	147	80.0	45.4	47.4	51.2	18.0	32.7	26.8	25.6	18.2
Common Eqty.	204	177	154	153	148	132	72.0	61.3	53.4	46.8
Total Cap.	404	257	248	238	231	176	126	106	94.0	77.0
Cap. Exp.	75.1	96.0	57.9	76.6	100	70.1	46.5	35.3	36.9	39.9
Cash Flow	75.1	59.1	49.4	52.2	50.8	41.0	32.4	25.9	22.3	20.6
Curr. Ratio	0.9	1.3	1.2	1.0	1.6	1.4	1.0	1.2	1.0	0.9
% LT Debt of Cap.	36.3	31.1	18.3	19.9	22.1	10.2	25.9	25.4	27.4	23.6
% Net Inc.of Revs.	4.8	4.6	3.7	3.9	5.9	6.1	5.8	5.1	5.2	8.6
% Ret. on Assets	6.0	5.8	4.4	4.7	7.2	7.1	7.7	6.6	6.2	10.5
% Ret. on Equity	13.3	11.4	8.1	8.7	12.3	12.4	15.9	13.5	12.7	19.5

Data as orig reptd.; bef. results of disc opers/spec. items. Per share data adj. for stk. divs. Bold denotes diluted EPS (FASB 128)-prior periods restated. E-Estimated. NA-Not Available. NM-Not Meaningful. NR-Not Ranked.

Office—3171 Directors Row, Memphis, TN 38116. **Tel**—(901) 332-2500. **Website**—http://www.mscarriers.com **Chrmn, Pres & CEO**—M. S. Starnes. **SVP-Fin, Secy & Treas**—M. J. Barrow. **Dirs**—M. J. Barrow, M. H. Fair, J. H. Morris III, C. Mungenast, M. S. Starnes, J. W. Welch. **Transfer Agent & Registrar**—Sun Trust Bank, Atlanta. **Incorporated**—in Tennessee in 1977. **Empl**— 3,336. **S&P Analyst:** N.J.D.

STANDARD
&POOR'S
STOCK REPORTS

MacDermid, Inc.

NYSE Symbol **MRD**

In S&P SmallCap 600

23-OCT-99

Industry:
Chemicals (Specialty)

Summary: This company develops, produces and markets a broad line of specialty chemical products. It also manufactures electronic processing equipment.

Quantitative Evaluations

Outlook (1 Lowest—5 Highest)
• **4**

Fair Value
• **40¼**

Risk
• **NA**

Earn./Div. Rank
• **A**

Technical Eval.
• **NA**

Rel. Strength Rank (1 Lowest—99 Highest)
• **43**

Insider Activity
• **Unfavorable**

Recent Price • 31½
52 Wk Range • 46¾-28⅞
Yield • 0.2%
12-Mo. P/E • 21.0

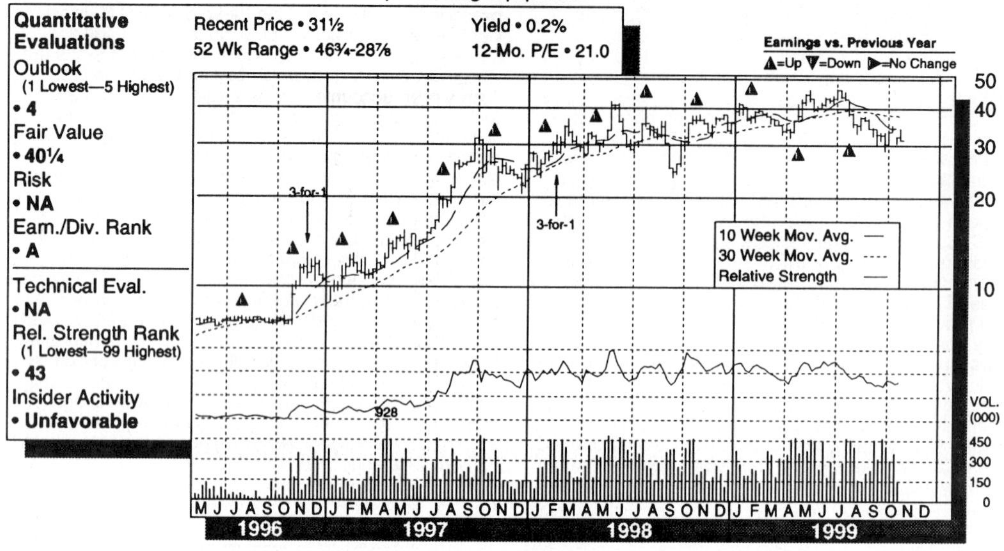

Business Profile - 22-OCT-99

In July 1999, MacDermid said it was experiencing market weakness at its printed circuit and domestic industrial products businesses. It added that while the late 1998 acquisition of Canning had been accretive to first quarter FY 00 (Mar.) earnings, many of the synergies were expected to first be realized in the second half of the fiscal year. MRD remained cautious about second quarter performance, but was more optimistic about the FY 00 second half, given expectations for improvement at the printed circuit business and in Asia in general. In February 1999, MRD agreed to acquire Polyfibron Technologies, a graphic arts company with $250 million in revenues. The transaction would transform the graphic arts business into MRD's largest operation, representing some 38% of sales. The merger was approved by shareholders of both companies in October, but was pending FTC approval.

Operational Review - 22-OCT-99

In the three months ended June 30, 1999, net sales advanced 47%, year to year, benefiting from increased net proprietary chemical sales and recent acqusitions. Gross margins widened slightly, on the higher volume and continued cost awareness initiatives. However, with selling, technical and administrative and amortization costs up 52%, primarily related to the Canning and Galvanevet acquisitions, and interest expense sharply higher, net income was up only 24%, to $9,999,000 ($0.39 a share), from $8,093,000 ($0.32).

Stock Performance - 22-OCT-99

In the past 30 trading days, MRD's shares have declined 2%, compared to a 4% fall in the S&P 500. Average trading volume for the past five days was 61,100 shares, compared with the 40-day moving average of 71,954 shares.

Key Stock Statistics

Dividend Rate/Share	0.08	Shareholders	800
Shs. outstg. (M)	25.2	Market cap. (B)	$0.813
Avg. daily vol. (M)	0.061	Inst. holdings	48%
Tang. Bk. Value/Share	NM		
Beta	1.18		

Value of $10,000 invested 5 years ago: $ 117,574

Fiscal Year Ending Mar. 31

	2000	1999	1998	1997	1996	1995
Revenues (Million $)						
1Q	119.1	81.07	74.72	72.66	48.97	42.59
2Q	—	85.86	75.00	74.04	53.36	46.50
3Q	—	96.72	83.81	74.37	58.28	44.55
4Q	—	119.0	80.53	72.66	75.29	48.47
Yr.	—	382.6	314.1	293.7	235.9	182.1
Earnings Per Share ($)						
1Q	**0.39**	**0.32**	0.29	0.17	0.11	0.10
2Q	—	**0.34**	0.29	0.20	0.12	0.09
3Q	—	**0.37**	**0.30**	0.21	0.12	0.10
4Q	—	**0.40**	**0.32**	0.27	0.15	0.10
Yr.	—	**1.43**	**1.20**	**0.85**	**0.50**	0.39

Next earnings report expected: NA

Dividend Data (Dividends have been paid since 1946.)

Amount ($)	Date Decl.	Ex-Div. Date	Stock of Record	Payment Date
0.020	Nov. 24	Dec. 11	Dec. 15	Jan. 04 '99
0.020	Feb. 01	Mar. 11	Mar. 15	Apr. 01 '99
0.020	May. 14	Jun. 11	Jun. 15	Jul. 01 '99
0.020	Jul. 22	Sep. 13	Sep. 15	Oct. 01 '99

MacDermid, Incorporated

Business Summary - 22-OCT-99

Founded in 1922 and headquartered in Waterbury Connecticut, MacDermid Inc., manufactures specialty chemical products used in the metal and plastic finishing, electronics, and graphic arts industries. Additionally, MRD produces processing equipment employed in the manufacturing of circuit boards and in chemical machining. MRD also markets chemical supplies and equipment produced by others.

In FY 99 (Mar.), proprietary chemical sales accounted for 84% of the total (88% in FY 97), resale chemicals and supplier sales 9% (7%) and equipment sales 7% (5%).

The company produces and markets more than 5,000 proprietary chemical compounds. The chemicals are used for cleaning, activating and polishing, mechanical plating, mechanical galvanizing, electroplating and phosphatizing metal surfaces, stripping of metal and final coating of metal surfaces, filtering, antitarnishing and rust retarding in the metal finishing industry, and etching, imaging, deposition of metal, and other chemical processes in the manufacture of printed circuits and other electronic parts.

MRD markets its products through some 500 sales personnel in the U.S., Europe and Asia/Pacific. It owns and operates manufacturing facilities in Australia, Great Britain, Spain and Taiwan.

In December 1998, MRD acquired Canning, a British special chemicals company, for approximately $150 million. MRD believes the addition of Canning's niche businesses will enhance the company's earnings diversity and will be additive to earnings in the first year.

In February 1999, MacDermid signed a definitive agreement to acquire PTI Inc., a holding company for Polyfibron Technologies, Inc., a graphic arts company. MRD will issue 7.7 million shares and assume approximately $150 million of debt to pay for the purchase, which will be accounted for as a pooling of interests. MRD, which expects the merger to be accretive to earnings in the first fiscal year, feels the acquisition will position the company as a leader in the supply of specialty chemicals and related materials to the graphic arts industry. MRD also noted that its graphic arts segment will now become the largest segment within the company, representing 38% of $750 million in consolidated proforma sales. Closing of the merger is contingent upon approval from the FTC.

On May 3, 1999, a subsidiary of the company acquired an additional 60% interest in Galvanevet S.P.A., an Italian specialty chemical company, bringing its total investment to 90%. The company intends to acquire the remaining 10% interest within the year.

Going forward, MRD hopes to build an industrial company will be able to deliver EPS growth of 25% compounded over 10 years. EPS growth since 1994 was 43%.

Per Share Data ($) (Year Ended Mar. 31)	1999	1998	1997	1996	1995	1994	1993	1992	1991	1990
Tangible Bk. Val.	NM	0.70	0.15	NM	2.17	2.12	2.03	1.90	1.74	1.55
Cash Flow	2.00	1.64	1.32	0.80	0.57	0.42	0.39	0.37	0.38	0.34
Earnings	1.43	1.20	0.85	0.50	0.39	0.24	0.24	0.23	0.21	0.17
Dividends	0.07	0.07	0.07	0.07	0.07	0.07	0.07	0.07	0.07	0.07
Payout Ratio	5%	6%	8%	13%	17%	28%	28%	30%	32%	40%
Cal. Yrs.	1998	1997	1996	1995	1994	1993	1992	1991	1990	1989
Prices - High	42 3/8	34	13 1/8	6 5/8	4 5/8	3 1/2	3 1/4	3	2 5/8	3 1/8
- Low	23 3/8	9 1/8	6 1/2	4	2 5/8	2 3/4	2 5/8	2 1/4	1 3/4	1 11/16
P/E Ratio - High	30	40	15	13	12	14	14	13	13	19
- Low	16	11	8	8	7	11	11	10	8	10
Income Statement Analysis (Million $)										
Revs.	383	314	294	236	182	150	156	145	151	149
Oper. Inc.	78.5	66.8	57.0	37.0	25.2	18.7	20.3	15.8	18.5	18.8
Depr.	14.6	11.2	10.2	7.8	5.0	5.6	4.8	4.8	5.3	5.7
Int. Exp.	13.7	7.8	7.3	4.4	2.0	1.4	1.9	1.6	2.0	3.1
Pretax Inc.	54.1	48.1	38.7	23.6	18.1	12.4	12.3	11.0	11.3	9.2
Eff. Tax Rate	33%	36%	38%	42%	39%	38%	38%	34%	40%	42%
Net Inc.	36.3	30.8	23.8	13.8	11.1	7.8	7.7	7.2	6.8	5.3
Balance Sheet & Other Fin. Data (Million $)										
Cash	15.5	3.5	6.5	8.8	7.6	6.5	6.3	5.1	6.0	3.9
Curr. Assets	189	132	116	119	81.2	68.4	71.5	66.1	67.8	64.0
Total Assets	506	300	261	265	123	106	107	101	103	102
Curr. Liab.	126	86.0	68.8	59.0	46.5	33.5	40.5	38.5	44.5	48.0
LT Debt	231	104	75.1	105	18.2	0.9	1.0	1.4	1.9	2.7
Common Eqty.	142	106	80.0	65.8	53.7	68.2	65.2	61.1	55.8	49.7
Total Cap.	374	210	188	202	72.9	69.2	66.7	62.7	58.8	53.7
Cap. Exp.	5.4	8.3	6.9	4.3	4.0	7.5	4.7	5.4	3.2	3.5
Cash Flow	50.9	41.7	34.0	21.0	16.2	13.4	12.4	12.0	12.1	11.0
Curr. Ratio	1.5	1.5	1.7	2.0	1.7	2.0	1.8	1.7	1.5	1.3
% LT Debt of Cap.	61.8	49.5	39.9	52.1	25.0	1.3	1.5	2.1	3.3	5.0
% Net Inc.of Revs.	9.5	9.8	8.1	5.8	6.1	5.2	4.9	5.0	4.5	3.6
% Ret. on Assets	9.0	11.0	9.0	7.1	9.7	7.3	7.4	7.1	6.6	5.3
% Ret. on Equity	29.3	32.9	32.6	22.1	18.3	11.7	12.2	12.4	12.8	11.0

Data as orig reptd.; bef. results of disc opers/spec. items. Per share data adj. for stk. divs. Bold denotes diluted EPS (FASB 128)-prior periods restated. E-Estimated. NA-Not Available. NM-Not Meaningful. NR-Not Ranked.

Office—245 Freight St., Waterbury, CT 06702-0671. **Tel**—(203) 575-5700. **Chrmn & CEO**—D. H. Leever. **Pres & COO**—R. N. Griebel. **Secy**—J. L. Cordani. **Investor Contact**—Dave Erdman (203-575-5664). **Dirs**—R. N. Griebel, D. H. Leever, H. Leever, D. G. Ogilvie, J. C. Smith, T. W. Smith. **Transfer Agent & Registrar**—Harris Trust Co. of New York, NYC. **Incorporated**—in Connecticut in 1922. **Empl**— 1,877. **S&P Analyst:** SAH

STANDARD
&POOR'S
STOCK REPORTS

Macromedia, Inc.

NASDAQ Symbol **MACR**

In S&P SmallCap 600

09-OCT-99

Industry:
Computer (Software & Services)

Summary: Macromedia is a leading provider of software tools for Web publishing, multimedia and graphics.

Quantitative Evaluations

Outlook
(1 Lowest—5 Highest)
• **3-**

Fair Value
• **48¼**

Risk
• **High**

Earn./Div. Rank
• **NR**

Technical Eval.
• **Bullish** since 8/99

Rel. Strength Rank
(1 Lowest—99 Highest)
• **96**

Insider Activity
• **Unfavorable**

Recent Price • 53⅛
52 Wk Range • 55-13¾
Yield • Nil
12-Mo. P/E • NM

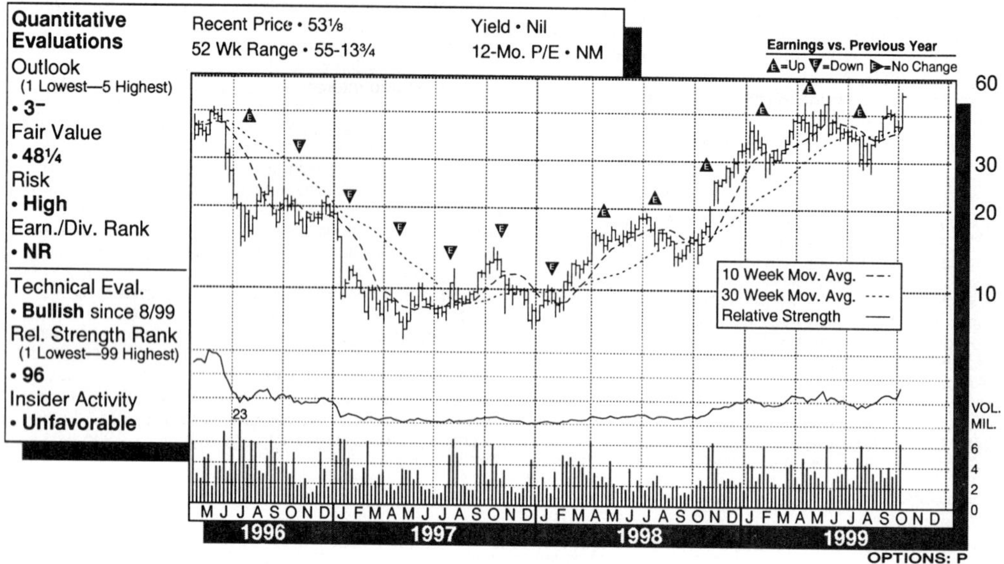

Business Profile - 21-JUL-99

In May 1999, MACR launched shockwave.com, a new personal online entertainment center, as well as Shockwave Remote and Shockmachine, which are new devices intended to enhance online entertainment for consumers. In partnership with major entertainment, Web distribution and technology leaders, shockwave.com features cartoons, music, games, and an animated greeting card creation engine. In June 1999, MACR shipped Flash 4, the new version of its Web authoring software, and announced that Sun Microsystems will integrate the Flash Player into future versions of the Java Media Framework. In May 1999, MACR announced it plans to integrate Flash 4 into a new release of RealNetworks RealSystem G2.

Operational Review - 21-JUL-99

Revenues in FY 99 (Mar.) rose 33% over those of the prior year, primarily due to sales of Dreamweaver, Fireworks and Flash, partially offset by a decline in sales of Director, due in great part to product lifecycle timing. Margins widened notably on effective cost and expense controls and improved inventory review procedures, and in the absence of $7.7 million in merger related charges, pretax income compared to a pretax loss. After a tax benefit of $7.6 million, versus $828,000, net income of $19,784,000 ($0.44 a share, on 19% more shares), contrasted with a net loss of $6,186,000 ($0.16).

Stock Performance - 08-OCT-99

In the past 30 trading days, MACR's shares have increased 34%, compared to a 0.91% fall in the S&P 500. Average trading volume for the past five days was 1,928,240 shares, compared with the 40-day moving average of 847,872 shares.

Key Stock Statistics

Dividend Rate/Share	Nil	Shareholders	483
Shs. outstg. (M)	42.9	Market cap. (B)	$ 2.3
Avg. daily vol. (M)	1.009	Inst. holdings	68%
Tang. Bk. Value/Share	3.77		
Beta	1.85		

Value of $10,000 invested 5 years ago: $ 63,506

Fiscal Year Ending Mar. 31

	2000	1999	1998	1997	1996	1995
Revenues (Million $)						
1Q	48.94	32.34	27.33	35.01	23.85	8.55
2Q	—	35.23	29.17	31.03	27.30	9.55
3Q	—	38.23	26.58	28.10	30.93	10.70
4Q	—	44.10	30.01	13.23	34.61	19.63
Yr.	—	149.9	113.1	107.4	116.7	53.70
Earnings Per Share ($)						
1Q	**0.15**	**0.07**	**-0.03**	**0.18**	0.13	0.03
2Q	—	**0.10**	**0.01**	**0.12**	0.15	0.06
3Q	—	**0.12**	**-0.19**	**-0.06**	0.18	0.05
4Q	—	**0.16**	**0.05**	**-0.41**	0.15	0.05
Yr.	—	**0.44**	**-0.16**	**-0.16**	**0.59**	**0.19**

Next earnings report expected: late October

Dividend Data

No cash dividends have been paid and the company does not plan to pay dividends for the foreseeable future.

Macromedia, Inc.

Business Summary - 21-JUL-99

Macromedia, Inc.'s new consumer business, shockwave.com, was officially announced in May 1999. This personal online entertainment center builds on MACR's investment in enabling users to experience rich multimedia experiences on the Internet. The company's aim is to become the preferred, high-volume supplier of software tools for graphics, multimedia, video and Web publishing. It develops, markets and supports an integrated line of graphics, multimedia and on-line publishing software for both Windows and Macintosh platforms.

MACR's player technologies, Shockwave and Flash, are the most widely used players for multimedia and entertainment on the Web, and are distributed with Windows 95, Windows 98, Microsoft Internet Explorer, and the Apple OS. In addition, Flash is included with every AOL client, in all Netscape browsers, in WebTV, in RealNetworks' Real Player, and was recently licensed by @Home for inclusion in its set-top boxes. Downloads of Shockwave and Flash grew steadily throughout 1998, reaching a rate of over 500,000 per day by the end of the year.

Shockwave.com builds on Shockwave's brand equity. The shockwave.com web site will aggregate multimedia content from multiple content providers, and link consumers to third-party Shockwave content on the Internet. As additional elements to its shockwave.com strategy, MACR has introduced: the Shockwave Remote, a new user interface which allows users to search, send and control Shockwave content; and Shockmachine, a $20 version of the Shockwave player with premium features.

The company has several Web development software products. Director enables developers to create visuals, animation and interactivity, all within a single working environment. Dreamweaver provides visual web page layout, HTML text editor and Dynamic HTML support capabilities to Web authors. Fireworks is a production tool for creating and optimizing Internet graphics. Flash allows users to easily create fast Web multimedia and is the Internet standard for creating vector graphics and animations. FreeHand provides a complete set of tools for graphic arts and design, enabling developers to quickly lay out concepts for web pages. As a solution for automated and personalized Web site graphics, Generator instantly builds graphics and interactive interface elements such as headlines, weather maps, calendars and charts.

International revenues represented 42% of FY 99 (Mar.) revenues, compared with 48% in FY 98. Reflecting macroeconomic and industry trends, MACR's revenues from Japan have declined from 21% of total revenues in FY 97 to just 8% in FY 99.

Per Share Data ($) (Year Ended Mar. 31)	1999	1998	1997	1996	1995	1994	1993	1992	1991	1990
Tangible Bk. Val.	3.87	3.35	3.50	3.66	1.28	NA	NA	NA	NA	NA
Cash Flow	0.62	0.04	0.05	0.69	0.25	NA	NA	NA	NA	NA
Earnings	0.44	-0.16	-0.16	0.59	0.19	0.14	-0.01	NA	NA	NA
Dividends	Nil	Nil	Nil	Nil	Nil	Nil	Nil	NA	NA	NA
Payout Ratio	Nil	Nil	Nil	Nil	Nil	Nil	Nil	NA	NA	NA
Cal. Yrs.	1998	1997	1996	1995	1994	1993	1992	1991	1990	1989
Prices - High	35¼	18¼	53¾	63¾	13⅞	8⅞	NA	NA	NA	NA
- Low	7⅞	6½	14⅛	10⅝	3¾	6⅜	NA	NA	NA	NA
P/E Ratio - High	80	NM	NM	NM	73	31	NA	NA	NA	NA
- Low	18	NM	NM	NM	20	22	NA	NA	NA	NA
Income Statement Analysis (Million $)										
Revs.	150	113	107	117	53.7	30.1	25.3	24.7	15.3	NA
Oper. Inc.	30.5	5.3	-5.9	34.3	12.4	NA	NA	NA	NA	NA
Depr.	8.1	7.7	7.8	4.1	2.1	NA	NA	NA	NA	NA
Int. Exp.	Nil	Nil	Nil	Nil	Nil	NA	NA	NA	NA	NA
Pretax Inc.	27.4	-5.4	-9.4	31.8	7.6	3.3	-0.2	-12.0	-7.6	NA
Eff. Tax Rate	28%	NM	NM	28%	14%	5.60%	NM	NM	NM	NA
Net Inc.	19.8	-6.2	-5.9	23.0	6.5	3.1	-0.2	-12.0	-7.6	NA
Balance Sheet & Other Fin. Data (Million $)										
Cash	109	10.0	15.4	117	34.0	NA	NA	NA	NA	NA
Curr. Assets	143	107	118	141	46.0	NA	NA	NA	NA	NA
Total Assets	195	154	157	155	52.0	NA	NA	NA	NA	NA
Curr. Liab.	37.7	25.1	25.0	22.0	12.6	NA	NA	NA	NA	NA
LT Debt	Nil	Nil	Nil	Nil	Nil	NA	NA	NA	NA	NA
Common Eqty.	157	128	132	133	40.0	NA	NA	NA	NA	NA
Total Cap.	157	128	132	133	40.0	NA	NA	NA	NA	NA
Cap. Exp.	11.2	12.4	27.2	9.5	4.3	NA	NA	NA	NA	NA
Cash Flow	27.9	1.5	1.8	27.1	8.6	10.4	NA	NA	NA	NA
Curr. Ratio	3.8	4.3	4.7	6.4	3.7	NA	NA	NA	NA	NA
% LT Debt of Cap.	Nil	Nil	Nil	Nil	Nil	NA	NA	NA	NA	NA
% Net Inc.of Revs.	13.2	NM	NM	19.7	12.2	10.4	NM	NM	NM	NA
% Ret. on Assets	11.3	NM	NM	22.2	NA	NA	NA	NA	NA	NA
% Ret. on Equity	13.9	NM	NM	26.6	NA	NA	NA	NA	NA	NA

Data as orig reptd.; bef. results of disc opers/spec. items. Per share data adj. for stk. divs. Bold denotes diluted EPS (FASB 128)-prior periods restated. E-Estimated. NA-Not Available. NM-Not Meaningful. NR-Not Ranked.

Office—600 Townsend St., San Francisco, CA 94103. **Tel**—(415) 252-2000. **Fax**—(415) 626-0554. **E-Mail**—ir@macromedia.com. **Website**—http://www.macromedia.com **Chmn & CEO**—R. K. Burgess. **SVP-Fin, CFO, Secy**—E. A. Nelson. **Dirs**—S. Alsop, R. K. Burgess, J. Giffen, M. D. Kvamme, D. L. Lucas, R. Siboni, W. B. Welty. **Transfer Agent**—ChaseMellon Shareholder Services, San Francisco. **Incorporated**—in Delaware in 1992. **Empl**— 553. **S&P Analyst:** Scott H. Kessler

MAF Bancorp

NASDAQ Symbol **MAFB**

In S&P SmallCap 600

09-OCT-99

Industry:
Savings & Loan Companies

Summary: MAFB is the parent company of Mid America Bank, which operates a network of retail banking offices primarily in the western suburbs of Chicago.

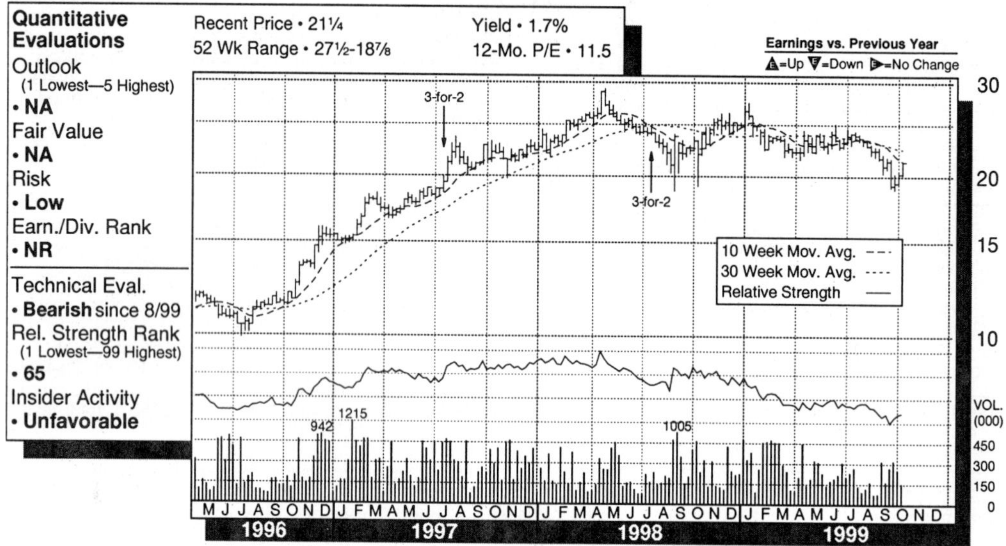

Business Profile - 29-JUL-99

MAFB offers a variety of financial services through 24 retail banking offices, mainly in the western suburbs of Chicago. On December 31, 1998, the company completed the acquisition of Westco Bancorp of Westchester, IL, in exchange for stock. The $90 million transaction added $313 million in assets, one banking office, and a drive-up facility, and made MAFB the market share leader in the Westchester-LaGrange Park area. In April 1999, MAFB told shareholders that it anticipated that strong core banking results could allow double digit earnings growth in 1999 and 2000, with diluted EPS rising to $2.00 in 2000. Also in April, the dividend was boosted 29%.

Operational Review - 29-JUL-99

In the first half of 1999, net interest income climbed 19%, year to year, reflecting the Westco acquisition and wider net interest margins (2.94%, versus 2.88%). The provision for loan losses increased 25%, to $500,000. Noninterest income grew 39%, led by higher income from real estate operations; noninterest expense and charges rose 12%, reflecting higher compensation and benefits, and higher amortization of goodwill. After taxes at 39.5%, versus 38.5%, net income soared 32%, to $24,918,000 ($0.99 a share, on 2.5% fewer shares), from $18,947,000 ($0.81, as adjusted).

Stock Performance - 08-OCT-99

In the past 30 trading days, MAFB's shares have declined 2%, compared to a 0.91% fall in the S&P 500. Average trading volume for the past five days was 30,260 shares, compared with the 40-day moving average of 41,195 shares.

Key Stock Statistics

Dividend Rate/Share	0.36	Shareholders	2,244
Shs. outstg. (M)	24.2	Market cap. (B)	$0.515
Avg. daily vol. (M)	0.049	Inst. holdings	44%
Tang. Bk. Value/Share	11.74		
Beta	0.86		

Value of $10,000 invested 5 years ago: $ 25,370

Fiscal Year Ending Dec. 31

	1999	1998	1997	1996	1995	1994
Revenues (Million $)						
1Q	74.75	66.74	62.98	—	37.36	29.92
2Q	78.53	68.67	64.25	—	38.28	33.21
3Q	—	69.11	66.56	—	38.67	32.36
4Q	—	68.30	67.85	—	45.88	36.13
Yr.	—	272.8	261.6	124.8	209.3	131.6
Earnings Per Share ($)						
1Q	**0.46**	**0.39**	0.38	—	0.32	0.21
2Q	**0.53**	**0.42**	0.43	—	0.31	0.34
3Q	—	**0.42**	0.39	—	0.33	0.25
4Q	—	**0.43**	**0.39**	—	0.31	0.33
Yr.	—	**1.67**	**1.59**	0.36	1.26	1.13

Next earnings report expected: mid October

Dividend Data (Dividends have been paid since 1994.)

Amount ($)	Date Decl.	Ex-Div. Date	Stock of Record	Payment Date
0.070	Nov. 25	Dec. 14	Dec. 16	Jan. 05 '99
0.070	Feb. 24	Mar. 08	Mar. 10	Apr. 02 '99
0.090	Apr. 28	Jun. 11	Jun. 15	Jul. 02 '99
0.090	Aug. 25	Sep. 13	Sep. 15	Oct. 04 '99

MAF Bancorp

Business Summary - 29-JUL-99

MAF Bancorp, Inc. is the parent company of Mid America Bank, fsb, a federally chartered savings bank that operates a network of retail banking offices primarily in the western suburbs of Chicago. MAFB is a leading provider of residential mortgage loans in its market. With assets of $4.1 billion and 24 branch offices (at year-end 1998), MAFB offers a wide range of personal banking services to the communities it serves. Gross loans outstanding at December 31, 1998, were $3.34 billion, up from $2.73 billion at year-end 1997.

The allowance for loan losses totaled $16,770,000 (0.52% of loans receivable) at December 31, 1998, up from $15,475,000 (0.57%) a year earlier. Net chargeoffs were $351,000 (0.01% of average loans outstanding) in 1998, versus $3,589,000 (0.14%) in 1997. Nonperforming assets were $22,406,000 (0.54% of total assets) at December 31, 1998, versus $11,144,000 (0.32%) a year earlier.

Interest on loans receivable provided 78% of total revenue in 1998, interest on mortgage-backed securities 5%, other interest 8%, income from real estate operations 2%, deposit account servicing fees 3%, and other noninterest income 4%.

Total deposits at December 31, 1998, were $2.66 billion, and were apportioned: certificate accounts 54.8%, passbook accounts 27.2%, money-market accounts 5.9%, NOW accounts 8.0%, and other accounts 5.0%.

The average yield on interest-earning assets was 7.27% in 1998, while the average rate paid on interest-bearing liabilities was 4.81%, for a net interest rate spread of 2.46%. The net interest margin narrowed to 2.85% at December 31, 1998, from 2.98% a year earlier.

MAFB also operates a real estate development unit, a full-service insurance agency, a title agency, and an investment brokerage operation through an affiliation with broker-dealer INVEST.

In December 1998, the company acquired Westco Bancorp Inc., in exchange for about $90 million in stock. In May 1996, MAFB acquired N.S. Bancorp Inc., for about $270 million in cash and stock.

Per Share Data ($) (Year Ended Dec. 31)	1998	1997	1996	1995	1994	1993	1992	1991	1990	1989
Tangible Bk. Val.	11.52	10.61	9.50	9.25	8.53	7.45	6.44	5.35	4.57	4.16
Earnings	1.67	1.59	0.36	1.26	1.13	0.99	0.98	0.67	0.37	0.37
Dividends	0.23	0.18	0.15	0.14	0.14	Nil	Nil	Nil	Nil	Nil
Payout Ratio	14%	11%	41%	11%	13%	Nil	Nil	Nil	Nil	Nil
Prices - High	29¼	24½	16	16	11⅝	9¾	9⅞	6¼	3	2 7/16
- Low	18¾	14¾	9⅞	9⅞	7⅝	7¼	5¾	2⅝	1¼	1 3/16
P/E Ratio - High	18	15	NM	13	10	10	9	9	8	7
- Low	11	9	NM	8	7	7	6	4	3	3
Income Statement Analysis (Million $)										
Net Int. Inc.	96.5	93.7	44.2	49.9	41.6	34.1	38.5	35.3	31.6	27.2
Loan Loss Prov.	0.8	1.1	0.7	0.7	0.5	1.2	2.7	4.1	1.1	0.6
Non Int. Inc.	26.0	22.3	12.0	17.1	16.7	19.6	14.3	15.8	6.0	10.1
Non Int. Exp.	60.2	54.6	26.9	37.8	33.4	31.3	28.2	29.7	28.1	29.1
Pretax Inc.	62.5	60.7	14.4	28.5	24.4	21.2	21.9	17.3	8.4	7.6
Eff. Tax Rate	38%	37%	39%	38%	38%	37%	38%	49%	41%	37%
Net Inc.	38.7	37.9	8.8	17.7	15.0	13.5	13.5	8.9	4.9	4.7
% Net Int. Marg.	2.85	2.62	2.62	2.62	2.62	2.29	2.65	2.55	2.23	1.84
Balance Sheet & Other Fin. Data (Million $)										
Total Assets	4,121	3,458	3,230	3,117	1,783	1,586	1,544	1,513	1,473	1,597
Loans	3,230	2,701	2,430	2,712	1,575	1,359	1,326	1,267	1,202	1,220
Deposits	2,657	2,337	2,262	2,254	1,313	1,293	1,290	1,269	1,237	1,208
Capitalization:										
Debt	1,035	797	660	564	327	170	138	151	153	310
Equity	345	263	251	242	105	95.2	85.0	70.2	59.8	54.4
Total	1,379	1,060	910	807	433	265	223	221	212	365
% Ret. on Assets	1.0	1.1	0.3	0.7	0.9	0.8	0.9	0.7	0.3	0.3
% Ret. on Equity	12.7	14.8	3.6	10.2	15.0	14.8	17.8	15.0	8.7	13.1
% Loan Loss Resv.	0.5	0.6	0.7	0.6	0.6	0.6	0.6	0.5	0.2	0.1
% Risk Based Capital	13.4	15.1	14.3	8.0	12.1	13.2	12.8	11.1	7.8	7.1
Price Times Book Value:										
Hi	2.5	2.3	1.7	1.3	1.2	1.3	1.4	1.2	0.6	0.6
Low	1.6	1.4	1.0	1.1	0.9	1.1	0.9	0.5	0.3	0.3

Data as orig. reptd.; bef. results of disc opers. and/or spec. items. Per share data adj. for stk. divs. as of ex-div. date. Income data for 1996 for 6 mos. ended Dec. 31, 1996. Prior to 1996, fisc. yrs. ended Jun. 30. Bold denotes diluted EPS (FASB) 128. E-Estimated. NA-Not Available. NM-Not Meaningful. NR-Not Ranked.

Office—55th St. & Holmes Ave., Clarendon Hills, IL 60514. **Tel**—(630) 325-7300. **Website**—http://www.mafbancorp.com **Chrmn & CEO**—A. H. Koranda. **Pres**—K. Koranda. **EVP & CFO**—J. A. Weberling. **VP & Secy**—C. Pihera. **SVP & Investor Contact**—Michael J. Janssen. **Dirs**—R. Bowles, D. Burba, T. Ekl, J. F. Hanauer, A. H. Koranda, K. Koranda, H. Smogolski, F. W. Trescott, L. B. Vasto, J. A. Weberling, A. J. Zych. **Transfer Agent & Registrar**—Harris Trust & Savings Bank, Chicago. **Incorporated**—in Delaware in 1989. **Empl**— 921. **S&P Analyst:** T. W. Smith, CFA

STANDARD
&POOR'S
STOCK REPORTS

Magellan Health Services

NYSE Symbol **MGL**

In S&P SmallCap 600

09-OCT-99

Industry:
Health Care (Hospital Management)

Summary: This company provides a broad range of behavioral health care services in the U.S. and Europe.

Quantitative Evaluations

Outlook
(1 Lowest—5 Highest)
• **5**

Fair Value
• **17¼**

Risk
• **Average**

Earn./Div. Rank
• **NR**

Technical Eval.
• **Bearish** since 9/99

Rel. Strength Rank
(1 Lowest—99 Highest)
• **6**

Insider Activity
• **NA**

Recent Price • 6
52 Wk Range • 11⅛-3½

Yield • Nil
12-Mo. P/E • 6.3

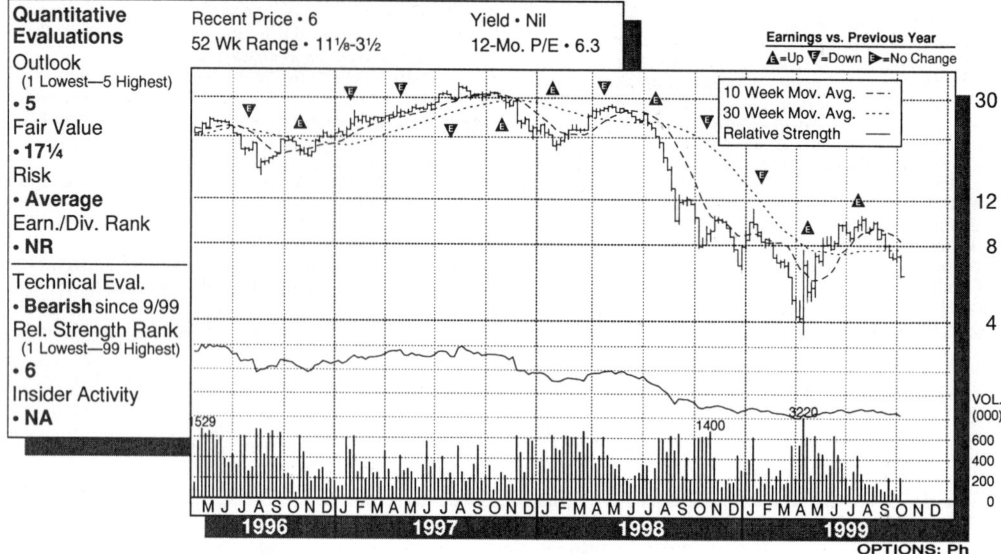

OPTIONS: Ph

Business Profile - 28-SEP-99

MGL has significantly altered its operational profile in recent years, moving from an owner/operator of inpatient psychiatric treatment facilities to a leading provider of managed behavioral care services which it offers to both private and public sector clients. In September 1999, MGL divested its hospital-based provider and franchise assets and reduced to 10% its ownership interest in Charter Behavioral Health Systems (CBHS). Under the agreement, MGL transferred all of its remaining hospital-based assets to CBHS, and it will record a primarily noncash, after-tax charge of about $42 ro $45 million in the fourth quarter of FY 99 (Sep.). In April 1999, MGL sold its European psychiatric provider operations for about $57 million. The company has used proceeds from the sale to pay down debt.

Operational Review - 28-SEP-99

Revenues in the nine months ended June 30, 1999, advanced 38%, year to year, reflecting a 60% rise in behavioral managed care revenue and a 47% increase in human services revenue. Costs and expenses rose less rapidly than revenues and after a $23.9 million gain on the sale of European hospitals, pretax income was up 76%, to $59.3 million from $33.8 million. After taxes at 49.1% versus 47.3%, and minority interest of $556,000 versus $5.1 million, income surged 133%, to $29.6 million ($0.93 a share), from $12.7 million ($0.41, before a special charge of $1.06 on the early extinguishment of debt).

Stock Performance - 08-OCT-99

In the past 30 trading days, MGL's shares have declined 29%, compared to a 0.91% fall in the S&P 500. Average trading volume for the past five days was 44,100 shares, compared with the 40-day moving average of 28,079 shares.

Key Stock Statistics

Dividend Rate/Share	Nil	Shareholders	9,597
Shs. outstg. (M)	31.8	Market cap. (B)	$0.193
Avg. daily vol. (M)	0.030	Inst. holdings	70%
Tang. Bk. Value/Share	NM		
Beta	1.33		

Value of $10,000 invested 5 years ago: $ 2,342

Fiscal Year Ending Sep. 30

	1999	1998	1997	1996	1995	1994
Revenues (Million $)						
1Q	463.1	216.1	346.8	296.0	264.0	209.0
2Q	497.3	372.2	349.9	354.9	300.0	213.0
3Q	486.7	474.8	324.9	346.4	305.0	221.0
4Q	—	457.9	189.0	348.3	283.0	262.0
Yr.	—	1,512	1,211	1,345	1,152	905.0
Earnings Per Share ($)						
1Q	**0.13**	**0.26**	**0.25**	0.35	0.01	-0.15
2Q	**0.12**	**-0.07**	0.41	0.63	-0.53	0.04
3Q	**0.67**	**0.23**	-0.85	-0.18	0.06	0.18
4Q	—	**0.03**	0.35	0.26	-1.07	-1.72
Yr.	—	**0.44**	**0.16**	**1.04**	-1.54	-1.78

Next earnings report expected: early December

Dividend Data

Cash dividend payments, suspended since 1988, are currently prohibited under terms of certain debt agreements.

Magellan Health Services, Inc.

Business Summary - 28-SEP-99

Magellan Health Services has transformed itself from the largest domestic operator of psychiatric hospitals into the leading provider of managed behavioral health care services in the U.S. Management believes that the growth of the behavioral managed care industry will continue, as payors of behavioral health care benefits attempt to reduce costs of behavioral health care while maintaining high quality care.

To facilitate the development of its managed care business, Magellan in 1997 sold substantially all of its domestic acute care psychiatric facilities and residential treatment facilities to Crescent Real Estate Equities L.P. for $417 million in cash. The two parties subsequently created an equally owned joint venture to operate the 90 facilities; original terms call for MGL to receive $78.3 million in annual franchise fees, while Crescent leases the real estate to the venture at an initial annual rate of $41.7 million.

The behavioral managed care division consists of three operating subsidiaries. Green Spring is one of the largest managed behavioral care companies in the U.S., and the largest such provider to the Blue Cross/ Blue Shield networks, covering about 21.1 million lives at the end of 1997. Human Affairs International (HAI, acquired from Aetna/U.S. Healthcare in December 1997) manages the care of more than 16 million individuals through employee assistance programs and other managed behavioral health care plans. Merit Behavioral Care Corp. (acquired in February 1998) manages health care programs covering more than 21 million people, for about 800 clients including HMOs, Blue Cross/Blue Shield organizations and other insurers, corporations and labor unions, government agencies and various state Medicaid programs.

The company's specialty managed health care business, Allied Health Group (acquired in December 1997) provides specialty risk-based products and administrative services to various insurance companies and other customers, including Prudential, CIGNA and NYLCare, through a network of over 80 physicians.

Magellan also offers specialty products related to the management of chronic medical conditions and franchises the CHARTER system of behavioral health care to the psychiatric and other facilities operated by Charter Behavioral Health System.

During FY 98 (Sep.), the company significantly expanded its operations with the acquisitions of two behavioral health care management companies. In December 1997, MGL acquired Human Affairs International Inc., from Aetna/ U.S. Healthcare for about $122 million in cash. In February 1998, MGL acquired Merit Behavioral Care Corp., for approximately $449 million plus the repayment of Merit's debt.

Per Share Data ($) (Year Ended Sep. 30)	1998	1997	1996	1995	1994	1993	1992	1991	1990	1989
Tangible Bk. Val.	NM	NM	-1.68	0.96	1.06	2.29	0.42	3.09	NA	NA
Cash Flow	2.20	1.69	2.62	0.76	-0.75	-0.53	0.05	2.08	NA	NA
Earnings	0.44	0.16	1.04	-1.54	-1.78	-1.59	-1.50	-1.43	NA	NA
Dividends	Nil	Nil	Nil	Nil	Nil	Nil	Nil	Nil	NA	NA
Payout Ratio	Nil	Nil	Nil	Nil	Nil	Nil	Nil	Nil	NA	NA
Prices - High	28 3/8	34 1/2	25	23 1/4	28 1/2	27	8 3/4	NA	NA	NA
- Low	6 3/8	20 5/8	14 3/4	13 7/8	21 1/4	8	4 5/8	NA	NA	NA
P/E Ratio - High	65	NM	24	NM	NM	NM	NM	NA	NA	NA
- Low	14	NM	14	NM	NM	NM	NM	NA	NA	NA
Income Statement Analysis (Million $)										
Revs.	1,513	1,211	1,345	1,152	905	898	1,275	1,195	NA	NA
Oper. Inc.	219	182	198	196	111	108	246	218	NA	NA
Depr.	54.9	44.9	48.9	64.1	27.2	26.4	38.6	87.2	NA	NA
Int. Exp.	87.3	55.5	58.5	58.9	44.0	78.0	88.5	98.3	NA	NA
Pretax Inc.	39.1	23.1	64.2	-54.3	-58.0	-38.0	-9.6	-27.0	NA	NA
Eff. Tax Rate	51%	40%	40%	NM	NM	NM	NM	NM	NA	NA
Net Inc.	13.7	4.8	32.3	-43.0	-47.0	-40.0	-37.7	-35.4	NA	NA
Balance Sheet & Other Fin. Data (Million $)										
Cash	181	373	121	106	130	86.0	144	117	NA	NA
Curr. Assets	400	507	338	306	325	232	355	345	NA	NA
Total Assets	1,916	896	1,140	984	961	838	1,306	1,428	NA	NA
Curr. Liab.	455	219	274	214	215	273	315	227	NA	NA
LT Debt	1,203	392	566	539	533	350	846	991	NA	NA
Common Eqty.	188	241	122	88.6	56.0	57.0	10.4	76.7	NA	NA
Total Cap.	1,418	611	753	627	602	446	877	1,068	NA	NA
Cap. Exp.	44.2	33.4	38.8	20.2	105	11.0	28.0	NA	NA	NA
Cash Flow	68.6	49.6	81.3	21.1	-20.0	-13.0	1.3	51.8	NA	NA
Curr. Ratio	0.9	2.3	1.2	1.4	1.5	0.9	1.1	1.5	NA	NA
% LT Debt of Cap.	84.8	64.1	75.2	86.0	88.6	78.5	96.5	92.8	NA	NA
% Net Inc.of Revs.	0.9	0.4	2.4	NM	NM	NM	NM	NM	NA	NA
% Ret. on Assets	1.0	0.5	3.0	NM	NM	NM	NM	NM	NA	NA
% Ret. on Equity	7.9	2.1	30.7	NM	NM	NM	NM	NM	NA	NA

Data as orig reptd.; bef. results of disc opers/spec. items. Per share data adj. for stk. divs. Bold denotes diluted EPS (FASB 128)-prior periods restated. E-Estimated. NA-Not Available. NM-Not Meaningful. NR-Not Ranked.

Office—3414 Peachtree Rd., Suite 1400, Atlanta, GA 30326. **Tel**—(410) 953-1000.**Website**—http://www.magellanhealth.com **Chrmn** —R.W. Miller. **Pres & CEO**—H.T. Harbin. **EVP & CFO**—C. W. Donnelly.**Secy**—L.C. Newlin. **Investor Contact**—Kevin Helmintoller (404-814-5742). **Dirs**—E. M. Banks, F. Dibona Jr., A. C. Dimitriadis, A. D. Frazier Jr., H.T. Harbin, R. H. Kiefer, D. S. Messina, G. L. McManis, R.W. Miller, D. D. Moore, J. A. Sonnenfeld. **Transfer Agent & Registrar**—First Union National Bank of North Carolina, Charlotte.**Incorporated**—in Delaware in 1969. **Empl**— 11,600. **S&P Analyst:** John J. Arege

STANDARD
&POOR'S
STOCK REPORTS

Manitowoc Co.

NYSE Symbol **MTW**

In S&P SmallCap 600

23-OCT-99

Industry: Machinery (Diversified)

Summary: This company manufactures cranes, excavators and ice cube machines. It also provides ship-repair services.

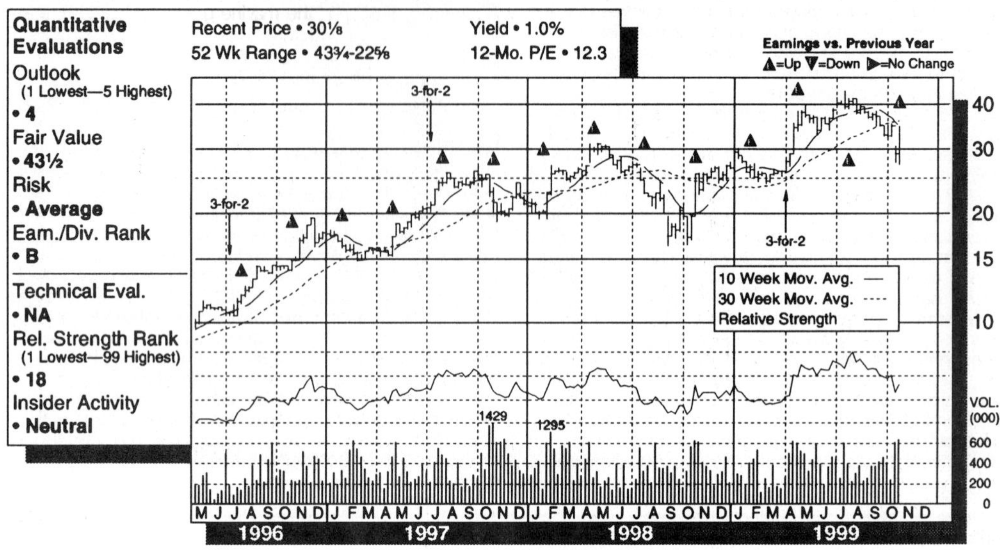

Business Profile - 22-OCT-99

In October 1999, Manitowoc said that it had reorganized its foodservice operations into two groups: Ice/Beverage, consisting of Manitowoc Ice, SerVend, Manitowoc Beverage Systems, Kyees Aluminium, and several foreign joint ventures, and Refrigeration, consisting of the Kolpak, McCall, Diversified Refrigeration and RDI operations. Management expects that the reorganization will result in lower costs, improved margins, and increased business synergies. It will also allow the company to more rapidly assimilate acquisitions. Subsequently, MTW said that it remained on track for another year of record financial performance and was eagerly anticipating similar opportunities in the new millennium.

Operational Review - 22-OCT-99

Net sales in the nine months ended September 30, 1999, rose 18%, year to year, primarily reflecting acquisitions and to a lesser extent strong demand for the company's new ice machines and cranes. Results benefited from improved operating efficiencies, continued margin expansion, and additional cost reductions in each business segment. Net income rose 32%, to $52.8 million ($2.01 a share), from $39.9 million ($1.53).

Stock Performance - 22-OCT-99

In the past 30 trading days, MTW's shares have declined 22%, compared to a 4% fall in the S&P 500. Average trading volume for the past five days was 48,020 shares, compared with the 40-day moving average of 70,959 shares.

Key Stock Statistics

Dividend Rate/Share	0.30	Shareholders	2,633
Shs. outstg. (M)	26.0	Market cap. (B)	$0.758
Avg. daily vol. (M)	0.120	Inst. holdings	63%
Tang. Bk. Value/Share	NM		
Beta	1.69		

Value of $10,000 invested 5 years ago: $ 34,705

Fiscal Year Ending Dec. 31

	1999	1998	1997	1996	1995	1994
Revenues (Million $)						
1Q	184.2	154.1	116.0	114.1	69.10	60.61
2Q	226.3	188.9	145.0	139.2	82.29	85.95
3Q	214.0	184.0	133.9	132.0	80.09	66.04
4Q	—	167.8	150.9	115.1	81.67	57.87
Yr.	—	694.8	545.9	500.5	313.1	--
Earnings Per Share ($)						
1Q	**0.47**	**0.36**	**0.25**	0.16	0.07	0.06
2Q	**0.80**	**0.59**	**0.46**	0.34	0.21	0.19
3Q	**0.74**	**0.58**	**0.37**	0.33	0.14	0.15
4Q	—	**0.44**	**0.33**	0.16	0.15	-0.34
Yr.	—	**1.97**	**1.39**	**0.99**	0.56	--

Next earnings report expected: late January

Dividend Data (Dividends have been paid since 1945.)

Amount ($)	Date Decl.	Ex-Div. Date	Stock of Record	Payment Date
3-for-2	Feb. 17	Apr. 01	Mar. 01	Mar. 31 '99
0.075	May. 04	May. 27	Jun. 01	Jun. 10 '99
0.075	Jul. 14	Aug. 30	Sep. 01	Sep. 10 '99
0.075	Oct. 19	Nov. 29	Dec. 01	Dec. 10 '99

A Division of The McGraw-Hill Companies

The Manitowoc Company, Inc.

Business Summary - 22-OCT-99

Just as three legs make a stool stable, MTW considers that three lines of business have lent it stability. In recent years, Manitowoc has transformed itself from primarily a ship services and repair company into a diversified organization with operations in foodservice equipment, construction and material-handling cranes, and ship construction and repairs.

Manitowoc hopes to achieve $1.3 billion in annual sales by 2002 and to generate 80% of revenues from new products and models introduced since 1998. The company states that it will emphasize global expansion, strategic acquisitions, and an ongoing improvement in its EVA (Economic Value Added) for all continuing operations.

The foodservice segment manufactures and sells commercial ice cube machines, ice storage bins, ice/beverage dispensers, reach-in and walk-in refrigerators and freezers, beverage dispensers and other related products. Manitowoc states that it has a leading percentage of the commercial ice cube machine market as well as the reach-in and walk-in refrigerator markets.

Manitowoc's crane division designs and manufactures a diversified line of crawler and truck-mounted lattice boom cranes, hydraulically powered telescopic boom trucks, rough terrain forklifts, and other material handling equipment. MTW also provides crane rebuilding and replacement parts for cranes and repair and refurbishment for metal-forming, scrapyard and recycling equipment.

MTW's marine division offers ship maintenance, inspections, conversions, repowering, retrofitting and other repair services. Manitowoc indicates that in order to reduce seasonality, the marine group has begun performing non-marine industrial repair in the summertime. In 1998, the company was awarded a contract to build a twin-hull tank barge for use by the Mobil Oil Corporation.

In September 1998, MTW acquired a 50% interest in an Italian ice machine maker, F.A.G., with an option to purchase an additional 30% ownership over the next five years. MTW feels the acquisition offers the company a manufacturing base in Europe and broadens its product ice maker offerings to include smaller models, which Manitowoc considers are more appropriate for European and developing markets.

In April 1999, MTW acquired Kyees Aluminum, a technology leader in making cold plate equipment, for $26 million in cash. In January 1999, MTW completed its purchase of Purchasing Support Group, a supplier of parts, components and dispenser systems to bottlers in the beverage industry, for $38 million. MTW believes the acquisition will help the company to expand the capabilities and geographic coverage of its beverage service operations and to assist MTW in achieving its goal to be a single-source solution for food and beverage cooling requirements.

Per Share Data ($) (Year Ended Dec. 31)	1998	1997	1996	1995	1994	1993	1992	1991	1990	1989
Tangible Bk. Val.	NA	NM	0.31	NM	3.26	3.77	4.65	4.79	4.62	4.60
Cash Flow	2.53	1.84	1.43	0.82	0.69	0.37	0.42	0.61	0.75	0.62
Earnings	1.97	1.41	0.99	0.56	0.48	0.19	0.24	0.44	0.60	0.49
Dividends	0.30	0.30	0.30	0.30	0.30	0.30	0.30	0.30	0.59	0.24
Payout Ratio	15%	21%	30%	53%	62%	145%	125%	67%	98%	49%
Prices - High	$31\frac{3}{8}$	$27\frac{1}{8}$	$19\frac{1}{2}$	$9\frac{1}{8}$	$9\frac{5}{8}$	$9\frac{7}{8}$	$8\frac{1}{8}$	$8\frac{3}{8}$	$6\frac{5}{8}$	$7\frac{3}{4}$
- Low	$16\frac{3}{8}$	$14\frac{7}{8}$	$8\frac{1}{8}$	$6\frac{1}{4}$	$7\frac{1}{8}$	$7\frac{1}{4}$	$5\frac{1}{2}$	$5\frac{1}{8}$	5	$5\frac{1}{8}$
P/E Ratio - High	16	19	20	16	20	51	34	19	11	16
- Low	8	11	8	11	15	38	23	12	8	11
Income Statement Analysis (Million $)										
Revs.	695	546	500	313	275	279	246	236	226	201
Oper. Inc.	107	76.7	63.7	30.0	27.4	31.5	16.8	24.0	23.2	24.4
Depr.	14.6	11.7	11.6	6.8	6.3	5.9	6.3	5.7	4.7	4.7
Int. Exp.	9.7	6.2	9.1	1.9	Nil	Nil	Nil	Nil	NA	NA
Pretax Inc.	81.4	57.8	42.5	23.1	22.6	8.9	11.6	20.5	30.4	24.2
Eff. Tax Rate	37%	37%	40%	37%	38%	29%	29%	25%	31%	30%
Net Inc.	51.4	36.4	25.6	14.6	14.0	6.3	8.3	15.4	21.0	16.9
Balance Sheet & Other Fin. Data (Million $)										
Cash	12.4	11.9	16.0	16.6	30.0	49.0	37.0	29.0	39.0	50.0
Curr. Assets	191	146	128	135	118	148	168	165	159	163
Total Assets	481	396	318	325	186	208	225	219	213	217
Curr. Liab.	198	171	110	111	63.6	58.4	43.8	42.6	41.4	36.5
LT Debt	79.8	66.4	76.5	101	Nil	Nil	Nil	Nil	Nil	Nil
Common Eqty.	173	129	100	81.6	94.0	119	166	167	162	161
Total Cap.	252	195	177	183	95.0	122	169	170	164	162
Cap. Exp.	11.7	12.0	8.4	19.2	13.9	11.2	5.1	6.3	4.3	2.7
Cash Flow	66.0	48.1	37.3	21.4	20.3	12.2	14.6	21.1	25.8	21.6
Curr. Ratio	1.0	0.9	1.2	1.2	1.8	2.5	3.8	3.9	3.9	4.5
% LT Debt of Cap.	31.6	34.1	43.3	55.6	Nil	Nil	Nil	Nil	Nil	Nil
% Net Inc.of Revs.	7.4	6.7	5.1	4.7	5.1	2.3	3.4	6.5	9.3	8.4
% Ret. on Assets	11.7	10.2	8.0	4.5	7.6	3.1	3.7	7.1	9.8	7.9
% Ret. on Equity	34.1	31.8	28.2	17.9	14.1	4.7	5.0	9.4	13.0	10.7

Data as orig reptd.; bef. results of disc opers/spec. items. Per share data adj. for stk. divs. Bold denotes diluted EPS (FASB 128)-prior periods restated. E-Estimated. NA-Not Available. NM-Not Meaningful. NR-Not Ranked.

Office—500 South 16th Street (P.O. Box 66), Manitowoc, WI 54220 (54221-0066). **Tel**—(920) 684-4410. **Website**—htt://www.manitowoc.com.**Pres & CEO**—T. D. Growcock.**VP & CFO**—G. E. Tellock.**Secy**—M. Jones. **Dirs**—D. H. Anderson, T. D. Growcock, J. P. McCann, G. T. McCoy, G. R. Rahr, Jr., G. F. Rankin, Jr., R. C. Stift, R. S. Throop. **Transfer Agent & Registrar**—First Chicago Trust Co. of New York, Jersey City, NJ. **Incorporated**—in Wisconsin in 1902. **Empl**— 3,305. **S&P Analyst:** P.L.H.

STANDARD
&POOR'S
STOCK REPORTS

Marcus Corporation

NYSE Symbol **MCS**

In S&P SmallCap 600

09-OCT-99 **Industry:** Lodging - Hotels

Summary: This company operates hotels and motels, movie theatres and restaurants, primarily in the Midwest.

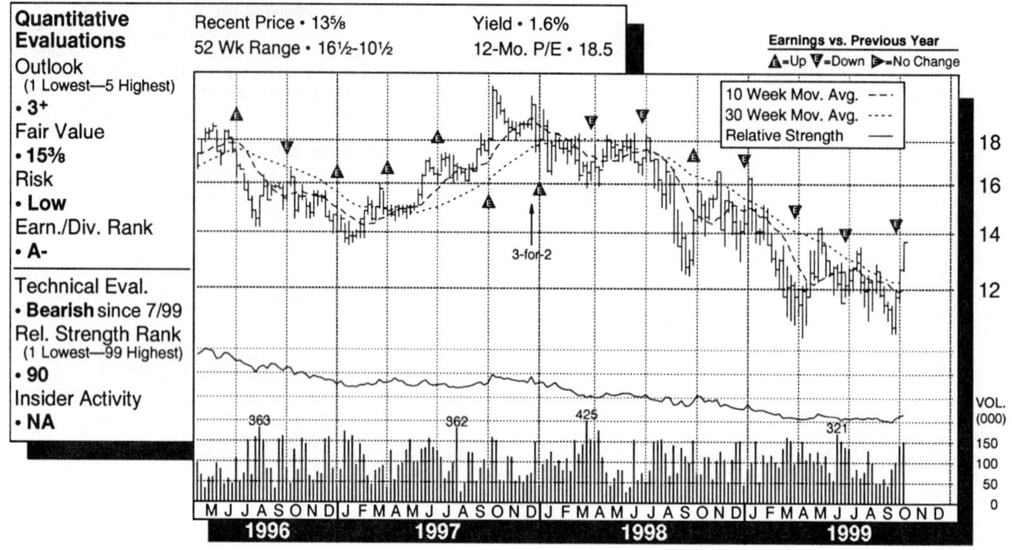

Business Profile - 04-OCT-99

In January 1999, Marcus changed the name of its Budgetel Inns to Baymont Inns & Suites. The new Baymont Inns offer a fresh, more vibrant look to better reflect the extensive amenities of the limited-service chain. An aggressive expansion program aims to increase the total number of Baymont Inns from about 170 to over 300 within the next four years, primarily through franchising. In September 1999, MCS announced an agreement to sell its 27 KFC and three 2-in-1 KFC/Taco Bell restaurants to QSR, Inc, a major operator of Taco Bell restaurants in Illinois and Wisconsin. During FY 99 (May), MCS repurchased 490,000 shares of its common stock under a 1,000,000 share repurchase plan authorized in the second quarter.

Operational Review - 04-OCT-99

Total revenues in the 13 weeks ended August 26, 1999, advanced 6.5%, year to year, as substantial gains in the theatre division, driven by a strong summer movie season, were partly offset by the sale of nine company-owned lodging properties. However, results were hurt by higher total costs and expenses, particularly in the theatre operations and concessions segments. After greater depreciation and amortization, higher interest expense and taxes at 40.5%, versus 40.0%, net income declined 7.2%, to $13.2 million ($0.44 a share), from $14.2 million ($0.47).

Stock Performance - 08-OCT-99

In the past 30 trading days, MCS's shares have increased 16%, compared to a 0.91% fall in the S&P 500. Average trading volume for the past five days was 31,180 shares, compared with the 40-day moving average of 17,387 shares.

Key Stock Statistics

Dividend Rate/Share	0.22	Shareholders	1,700
Shs. outstg. (M)	29.9	Market cap. (B)	$0.238
Avg. daily vol. (M)	0.024	Inst. holdings	40%
Tang. Bk. Value/Share	10.48		
Beta	0.79		

Value of $10,000 invested 5 years ago: $ 12,041

Fiscal Year Ending May 31

	2000	1999	1998	1997	1996	1995
Revenues (Million $)						
1Q	114.4	107.4	90.05	77.82	73.57	76.35
2Q	—	87.99	71.18	64.83	59.09	64.74
3Q	—	82.27	71.22	63.21	51.98	59.26
4Q	—	85.30	103.3	97.50	77.66	77.64
Yr.	—	362.9	335.8	303.4	244.3	278.0
Earnings Per Share ($)						
1Q	**0.44**	**0.47**	**0.44**	0.39	0.85	0.31
2Q	—	**0.20**	**0.23**	0.23	0.22	0.19
3Q	—	**0.02**	**0.10**	0.13	0.09	0.08
4Q	—	**0.09**	**0.18**	0.29	0.27	0.24
Yr.	—	**0.77**	**0.94**	**1.04**	**1.42**	0.82

Next earnings report expected: late December

Dividend Data (Dividends have been paid since 1983.)

Amount ($)	Date Decl.	Ex-Div. Date	Stock of Record	Payment Date
0.055	Dec. 17	Jan. 21	Jan. 25	Feb. 15 '99
0.055	Mar. 30	Apr. 22	Apr. 26	May. 17 '99
0.055	Jun. 30	Jul. 22	Jul. 26	Aug. 16 '99
0.055	Oct. 04	Oct. 21	Oct. 25	Nov. 15 '99

STANDARD
&POOR'S
STOCK REPORTS

The Marcus Corporation

09-OCT-99

Business Summary - 04-OCT-99

With operations in the lodging, movie theatre and restaurant fields, The Marcus Corp. is diversified yet highly focused. The company strives to bring relaxation and entertainment to patrons in a variety of settings. In each of its businesses, MCS is introducing amenities designed to further enhance the comfort or convenience of its clientele: home delivery for customers of many of its KFC restaurants, tiered stadium seating (which provides unobstructed viewing) for moviegoers, and a host of new conveniences for business travelers who stay at the company's Baymont Inns & Suites (formerly Budgetel Inns).

In the limited-service lodging division (39% of FY 99 (May) revenues), MCS changed the name of its Budgetel Inns to Baymont Inns & Suites in early January 1999. MCS operates or franchises 168 Baymont Inns in 30 states, 97 company-owned and 71 franchised, along with six all-suite hotels under the name Woodfield Suites. The company differentiates its Baymont Inn chain from other limited-service motels by providing conveniences not typically found in this segment of the lodging industry. An aggressive expansion program plans to increase the total number of Baymont Inns to over 300 within the next four years, primarily through franchising. A new Woodfield Suite is scheduled to open in Texas during FY 00.

The theatre division (31% of revenues) is the company's oldest division with 442 theatre screens at 49 locations. MCS is pursuing a growth strategy that emphasizes multi-screen theatres with 12 to 20 screens. The company is aggressively retrofitting its theatres to stadium seating. MCS currently offers stadium seating in 60% of its theatres, with a goal to have 90% stadium seating by FY 00. The company added 73 screens in FY 99, including the company's first IMAX theatre, and plans for a total of 500 of movie screens by the end of FY 00.

The hotel and resort division (22% of revenues) consists of three hotels and a resort in Wisconsin, a hotel in Minnesota, a hotel in California, and a resort in Michigan. For FY 00, MCS plans to add about 250 rooms to its 500-room Milwaukee Hilton, and construct a new 238-room Hilton hotel in Madison, Wisconsin. The company recently began construction of a vacation ownership development at its Grand Resort & Spa in Lake Geneva, WI.

The restaurant division (8% of revenues) operates 27 KFC (Kentucky Fried Chicken) restaurants and three 2-in-1 KFC/Taco Bell restaurants in Wisconsin. In September 1999, MCS announced an agreement to sell its KFC division to QSR, Inc, a major operator of Taco Bell restaurants in Ilinois and Wisconsin.

Per Share Data ($) (Year Ended May 31)	1999	1998	1997	1996	1995	1994	1993	1992	1991	1990
Tangible Bk. Val.	10.48	10.00	9.37	8.51	7.29	6.61	5.96	4.97	4.54	4.16
Cash Flow	2.04	2.03	2.01	2.27	1.62	1.40	1.32	1.21	1.06	0.98
Earnings	0.77	0.94	1.04	1.43	0.82	0.71	0.63	0.52	0.45	0.42
Dividends	0.22	0.33	0.20	0.31	0.15	0.12	0.11	0.10	0.09	0.08
Payout Ratio	29%	35%	19%	22%	18%	18%	18%	18%	20%	19%
Cal. Yrs.	1998	1997	1996	1995	1994	1993	1992	1991	1990	1989
Prices - High	19	20 7/8	18 7/8	18 1/4	13 1/8	12 1/4	9 1/8	5 1/4	5 3/8	5 7/8
- Low	12 3/8	13 1/2	13 7/8	11 3/8	10 5/8	8 3/4	4 7/8	3 3/8	2 7/8	4
P/E Ratio - High	25	22	18	13	16	17	14	10	12	14
- Low	16	14	13	8	13	12	8	7	6	10
Income Statement Analysis (Million $)										
Revs.	363	311	282	244	263	233	214	204	188	169
Oper. Inc.	90.1	69.5	68.1	58.9	55.6	48.5	42.5	43.0	36.2	32.6
Depr.	38.3	32.9	28.9	25.1	23.6	20.3	18.2	17.5	15.6	14.5
Int. Exp.	16.8	12.6	12.9	8.7	8.6	7.7	7.3	9.2	9.6	7.4
Pretax Inc.	38.9	47.4	51.2	70.1	40.2	34.7	27.0	22.0	18.9	16.4
Eff. Tax Rate	41%	40%	40%	40%	40%	39%	39%	40%	38%	34%
Net Inc.	23.1	28.4	30.9	42.3	24.1	21.0	16.5	13.3	11.6	10.8
Balance Sheet & Other Fin. Data (Million $)										
Cash	3.5	4.7	8.0	15.5	8.8	10.0	15.8	8.1	7.4	10.2
Curr. Assets	26.7	28.4	18.2	31.6	21.6	27.4	33.4	24.7	19.5	22.1
Total Assets	676	609	522	455	407	362	309	274	255	231
Curr. Liab.	59.4	66.0	46.7	50.7	52.3	40.7	37.2	34.0	29.8	24.1
LT Debt	264	206	168	127	116	108	79.0	100	96.0	86.0
Common Eqty.	314	303	277	251	214	194	174	125	115	107
Total Cap.	609	535	468	398	350	318	269	239	225	207
Cap. Exp.	112	116	108	83.7	77.0	75.8	47.2	41.8	39.9	42.4
Cash Flow	61.4	61.3	59.8	67.4	47.7	41.3	34.7	30.8	27.2	25.3
Curr. Ratio	0.5	0.4	0.4	0.6	0.4	0.7	0.9	0.7	0.7	0.9
% LT Debt of Cap.	43.3	38.5	35.9	31.9	33.1	33.9	29.4	41.8	42.8	41.4
% Net Inc.of Revs.	6.4	9.2	11.0	17.3	9.2	9.0	8.1	6.8	6.5	6.4
% Ret. on Assets	3.6	5.0	6.3	9.8	6.3	6.3	5.2	5.0	4.8	5.0
% Ret. on Equity	7.5	9.8	11.7	18.2	11.8	11.4	10.3	11.1	10.6	10.5

Data as orig reptd.; bef. results of disc opers/spec. items. Per share data adj. for stk. divs. Bold denotes diluted EPS (FASB 128)-prior periods restated. E-Estimated. NA-Not Available. NM-Not Meaningful. NR-Not Ranked.

Office—250 E. Wisconsin Ave., Suite 1700, Milwaukee, WI 53202-4200. **Reincorporated**—in Wisconsin in 1992. **Tel**—(414) 905-1000. **Website**—http://www.marcuscorp.com **Chrmn, Pres & CEO**—S. H. Marcus. **CFO, Treas & Investor Contact**—Douglas A. Neis (414-905-1100). **Secy**—T. F. Kissinger. **Dirs**—D. M. Gershowitz, B. J. Haase, T. E. Hoeksema, S. H. Marcus, P. L. Milstein, D. F. McKeithan Jr., B. J. Olson, A. H. Selig. **Transfer Agent**—Firstar Trust Co., Milwaukee. **Incorporated**—in Wisconsin in 1992; predecessor incorporated in Delaware in 1969. **Empl**—7,300. **S&P Analyst:** A. Bensinger

STANDARD
&POOR'S
STOCK REPORTS

Marshall Industries

NYSE Symbol **MI**

In S&P SmallCap 600

09-OCT-99

Industry:
Electronics (Component Distributors)

Summary: This leading U.S. distributor of electronic components and industrial production supplies has agreed to be acquired by Avnet, Inc.

Quantitative Evaluations

Outlook
(1 Lowest—5 Highest)
• **1**

Fair Value
• **32⅛**

Risk
• **Low**

Earn./Div. Rank
• **B**

Technical Eval.
• **Neutral** since 8/99

Rel. Strength Rank
(1 Lowest—99 Highest)
• **72**

Insider Activity
• **NA**

Recent Price • 35⅝
52 Wk Range • 38½-12⅜
Yield • Nil
12-Mo. P/E • NM

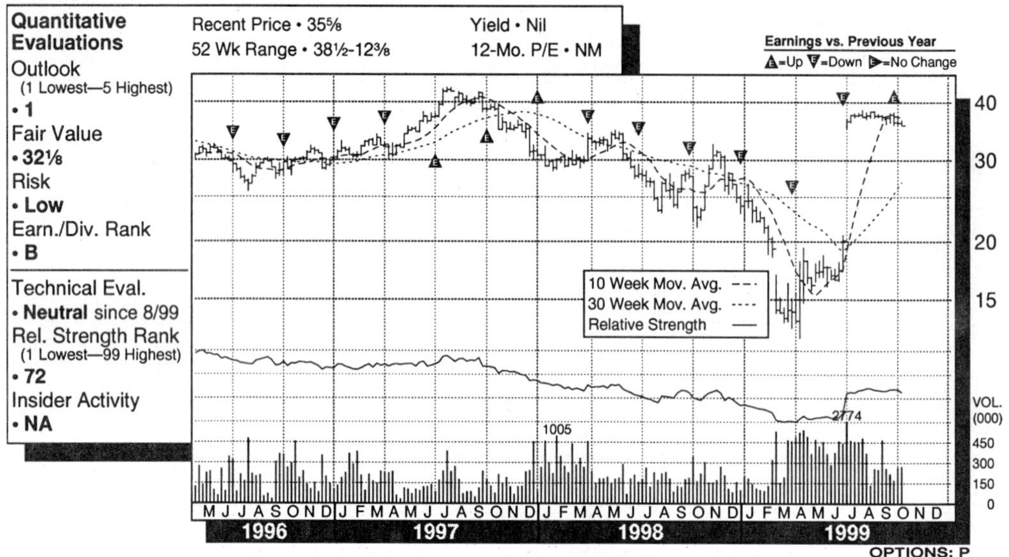

Business Profile - 22-SEP-99

On June 25, 1999, Marshall entered into a definitive agreement to merge with Avnet, Inc., one of the world's largest industrial distributors of electronic components and computer products, with net sales in FY 99 (Jul.) of $6.3 billion. Under the terms of the agreement, each outstanding common share of Marshall will be converted into the right to receive either $39.00 in cash or 0.81569 of a share of the common stock of Avnet, subject to adjustment, or a combination thereof. The proposed acquisition is subject to various regulatory approvals and approval by the shareholders of both companies. The Marshall and Avnet shareholders meetings are scheduled for October 19, 1999, and the acquisition is expected to be completed by the end of October.

Operational Review - 22-SEP-99

Net sales for the three months ended August 31, 1999, fell 3.0%, year to year. Gross margins narrowed, but with SG&A expenses down 9.4%, reflecting a reduction in staffing and operating expenses during the last half of FY 99 (May), the drop in operating income was held to 2.3%. With a 20% decrease in interest expense and after taxes at 42.9%, versus 45.4%, net income rose 7.3%, to $8,448,000 ($0.50 a share) from $7,870,000 ($0.47).

Stock Performance - 08-OCT-99

In the past 30 trading days, MI's shares have declined 5%, compared to a 0.91% fall in the S&P 500. Average trading volume for the past five days was 53,740 shares, compared with the 40-day moving average of 58,956 shares.

Key Stock Statistics

Dividend Rate/Share	Nil	Shareholders	5,000
Shs. outstg. (M)	16.6	Market cap. (B)	$0.593
Avg. daily vol. (M)	0.046	Inst. holdings	73%
Tang. Bk. Value/Share	17.63		
Beta	1.08		

Value of $10,000 invested 5 years ago: $ 14,274

Fiscal Year Ending May 31

	2000	1999	1998	1997	1996	1995
Revenues (Million $)						
1Q	446.9	460.9	324.4	269.3	275.9	223.1
2Q	—	435.5	351.2	286.4	295.5	243.8
3Q	—	393.2	368.1	304.0	288.0	261.6
4Q	—	433.1	417.6	325.0	305.4	280.8
Yr.	—	1,723	1,461	1,185	1,165	1,009
Earnings Per Share ($)						
1Q	**0.50**	**0.47**	0.55	0.51	0.70	0.50
2Q	—	**0.32**	0.56	0.55	0.78	0.54
3Q	—	**0.16**	**0.48**	0.58	0.70	0.58
4Q	—	**-0.82**	**0.40**	0.70	0.68	0.70
Yr.	—	**0.14**	**1.99**	**2.33**	2.86	2.32

Next earnings report expected: late December

Dividend Data

No cash dividends have been paid.

A Division of The McGraw-Hill Companies

Marshall Industries

Business Summary - 22-SEP-99

Marshall Industries (MI) is among the largest distributors of industrial electronic components and production supplies in North America, and also provides its customers with a variety of value-added services, such as inventory management, kitting, assembly, programming of programmable logic devices, and testing services. The company emphasizes responsive customer service through its network of sales and distribution facilities and corporate support and distribution centers in the U. S., Canada and Mexico.

The company supplies and services a broad range of products, including semiconductors, passive components, connectors and interconnect products, and computer and peripheral products, as well as production supplies. The distribution of electronic components accounted for approximately 95% and 96% of total sales in FY 98 (May) and FY 99, respectively. The distribution of industrial production supplies accounted for the balance of total sales in each of such periods. Marshall believes it is the largest domestic distributor in sales volume of industrial production supplies to customers in the electronics industry.

In January 1998, MI acquired Sterling Electronics Corp. for about $169 million in cash, plus about $55 million in debt assumption. Sterling is an international broad-line electronic parts distributor, with 39 branches in the U.S. and Canada. Since its acquisition, the company has been operating Sterling as a separate sales and marketing subsidiary but has integrated Sterling's computer, financial and administrative functions with those of the company.

In addition, Marshall has a 16% equity interest inEurotronics B.V., the holding company for the electronics distribution companies of Sonepar Electronique International, one of the largest electronic components distributors in Europe. The company also has an investment of approximately 9% as of May 31, 1999 of the common stock of Serial System Ltd., a Singapore based electronic components distributor with operations in Southeast Asia.

In 1999, Marshall developed a new website, SpotMarket.com, which includes an on-line auction connection that allows customers to negotiate for products, a discount center for the sale of aggressively priced surplus products, and a buyer-specified part and/or price locator capability.

The company's ENEN.com (Education News & Entertainment Network) subsidiary is the leading worldwide provider of business-to-business training and demand creation services over the Internet. In May 1999, it introduced several new services, including an innovative "pay for performance" pricing program that imposes no cost to electronics companies until individuals register for and attend the company's netcast.

Per Share Data ($) (Year Ended May 31)	1999	1998	1997	1996	1995	1994	1993	1992	1991	1990
Tangible Bk. Val.	NA	16.83	21.00	19.10	16.20	13.85	11.90	10.48	9.35	8.32
Cash Flow	NA	2.54	2.84	3.31	2.75	2.28	1.75	1.51	1.43	1.40
Earnings	1.31	1.99	2.32	2.86	2.32	1.91	1.38	1.13	1.01	1.13
Dividends	Nil	Nil	Nil	Nil	Nil	Nil	Nil	Nil	Nil	Nil
Payout Ratio	Nil	Nil	Nil	Nil	Nil	Nil	Nil	Nil	Nil	Nil
Cal. Yrs.	1998	1997	1996	1995	1994	1993	1992	1991	1990	1989
Prices - High	34¾	43⅛	32⅞	38¼	29½	25	21⅛	13⅜	15⅛	9¾
- Low	21½	30	25⅝	24⅜	20¼	16⅞	12¾	10	8½	7
P/E Ratio - High	27	22	14	13	13	13	15	12	15	9
- Low	16	15	11	9	9	9	9	9	8	6
Income Statement Analysis (Million $)										
Revs.	NA	1,461	1,185	1,165	1,009	823	653	575	583	544
Oper. Inc.	NA	75.0	76.1	94.2	79.0	65.4	48.0	41.2	40.1	41.6
Depr.	NA	9.2	8.8	7.9	7.6	6.3	6.5	6.6	7.0	4.9
Int. Exp.	NA	7.9	1.4	2.7	3.1	1.9	2.0	2.7	5.3	4.2
Pretax Inc.	NA	58.3	68.6	85.3	69.5	56.3	39.5	31.9	28.7	33.3
Eff. Tax Rate	NA	43%	42%	41%	42%	41%	40%	40%	40%	40%
Net Inc.	NA	33.3	39.7	50.1	40.4	33.2	23.9	19.3	17.3	20.1
Balance Sheet & Other Fin. Data (Million $)										
Cash	NA	4.8	1.7	2.2	3.5	3.7	1.6	1.8	1.9	2.0
Curr. Assets	NA	642	469	398	348	314	275	210	200	194
Total Assets	NA	854	540	473	423	364	331	268	254	250
Curr. Liab.	NA	206	138	114	93.8	84.8	67.6	53.2	48.8	57.9
LT Debt	NA	246	50.0	25.0	45.2	34.7	54.5	36.2	47.0	51.5
Common Eqty.	NA	400	349	330	279	239	203	178	158	141
Total Cap.	NA	648	402	359	329	279	263	215	205	192
Cap. Exp.	NA	12.2	2.7	5.3	2.9	1.8	3.2	6.4	7.2	16.3
Cash Flow	NA	42.5	48.5	57.9	48.0	39.5	30.3	25.9	24.3	25.0
Curr. Ratio	NA	3.1	3.4	3.5	3.7	3.7	4.1	3.9	4.1	3.4
% LT Debt of Cap.	NA	37.9	12.4	7.0	13.7	12.5	20.7	16.9	22.9	26.8
% Net Inc.of Revs.	NA	2.3	3.4	4.3	4.0	4.0	3.7	3.4	3.0	3.7
% Ret. on Assets	NA	4.8	7.8	11.2	10.3	9.5	8.0	7.4	6.8	8.8
% Ret. on Equity	NA	8.9	11.7	16.4	15.6	14.9	12.5	11.4	11.5	15.2

Data as orig reptd.; bef. results of disc opers/spec. items. Per share data adj. for stk. divs. Bold denotes diluted EPS (FASB 128)-prior periods restated. E-Estimated. NA-Not Available. NM-Not Meaningful. NR-Not Ranked.

Office—9320 Telstar Ave., El Monte, CA 91731-2895. **Tel**—(626) 307-6000. **Website**—http://www.marshall.com **Chrmn**—G. S. Marshall. **Pres & CEO**—R. Rodin. **VP-Fin, CFO, Secy & Investor Contact**—Henry W. Chin. **Dirs**—R. D. Bentley, R. C. Colyear, J. Fribourg, L. Hoffman, G. S. Marshall, J. Menendez, R. G. Rinehart, R. Rodin, H. C. White. **Transfer Agent & Registrar**—First Union National Bank, Charlotte, NC. **Incorporated**—in California in 1954. **Empl**— 2,000. **S&P Analyst:** C.C.P.

STANDARD
&POOR'S
STOCK REPORTS

MascoTech, Inc.

NYSE Symbol **MSX**

In S&P SmallCap 600

09-OCT-99

Industry: Auto Parts & Equipment

Summary: MascoTech is a diversified manufacturing company with leading metal forming process capabilities and proprietary product positions serving auto, industrial and consumer markets.

Quantitative Evaluations

Outlook
(1 Lowest—5 Highest)
• 4+

Fair Value
• 21⅝

Risk
• Low

Earn./Div. Rank
• B

Technical Eval.
• **Bearish** since 9/99

Rel. Strength Rank
(1 Lowest—99 Highest)
• 63

Insider Activity
• NA

Recent Price • 16⅜
52 Wk Range • 18¾-14
Yield • 1.9%
12-Mo. P/E • 9.8

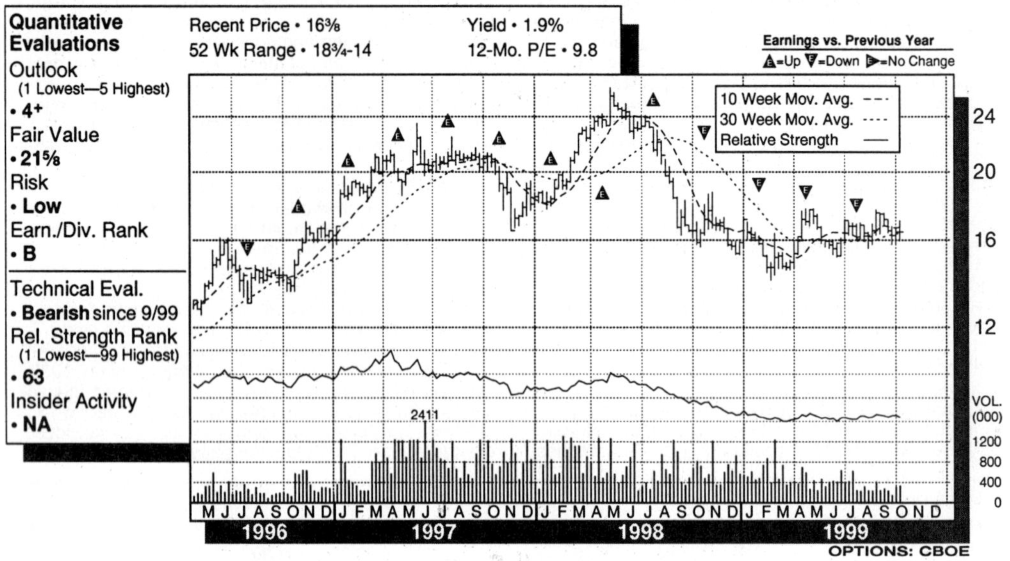

Business Profile - 19-AUG-99

The company's key strategic objectives include expanding its advanced metalworking capabilities into additional transportation-related and other markets, and creating additional value for shareholders from affiliate investments. In May 1999, MSX sold its aftermarket-related and vacuum metalizing operations for about $105 million, including $90 million in cash, which was used to reduce debt. The company expects that its ratio of debt to total debt plus equity will improve from the operating performance of its businesses and the disposition of certain businesses and financial assets.

Operational Review - 19-AUG-99

Net sales in the six months ended June 30, 1999, advanced 6.1%, year to year, reflecting gains in specialty metal formed products, new product launches and acquisitions. Operating margins were hurt by a less favorable product mix, and a gain of $16.5 million related to the sale of the company's aftermarket-related businesses was offset by $17.5 million of charges to reflect the writedown of certain assets related to the company's hydroforming process and a loss of some $3 million to reflect an equity transaction by an affiliate. Petax income was down 0.2%. After taxes at 41.5%, versus 26.9%, net income fell 20%, to $49,970,000 ($0.98 a share), from $62,560,000 ($1.14).

Stock Performance - 08-OCT-99

In the past 30 trading days, MSX's shares have declined 6%, compared to a 0.91% fall in the S&P 500. Average trading volume for the past five days was 65,620 shares, compared with the 40-day moving average of 54,464 shares.

Key Stock Statistics

Dividend Rate/Share	0.32	Shareholders	4,100
Shs. outstg. (M)	44.7	Market cap. (B)	$0.734
Avg. daily vol. (M)	0.050	Inst. holdings	31%
Tang. Bk. Value/Share	NM		
Beta	0.80		

Value of $10,000 invested 5 years ago: $ 6,393

Fiscal Year Ending Dec. 31

	1999	1998	1997	1996	1995	1994
Revenues (Million $)						
1Q	448.7	400.8	233.4	373.9	445.0	412.4
2Q	436.5	433.5	233.0	345.1	439.3	432.8
3Q	—	399.5	222.0	290.8	404.9	416.5
4Q	—	401.8	233.6	271.4	389.0	440.6
Yr.	—	1,636	922.1	1,281	1,678	1,702
Earnings Per Share ($)						
1Q	**0.47**	**0.60**	**0.59**	**0.13**	0.18	0.34
2Q	**0.51**	**0.54**	**0.46**	**-0.19**	0.21	0.39
3Q	—	**0.33**	**0.70**	**0.30**	0.22	0.21
4Q	—	**0.36**	**0.37**	**0.32**	0.20	-5.46
Yr.	—	**1.83**	**2.12**	**0.50**	**0.81**	-4.20

Next earnings report expected: early November

Dividend Data (Dividends have been paid since 1993.)

Amount ($)	Date Decl.	Ex-Div. Date	Stock of Record	Payment Date
0.070	Jan. 11	Jan. 13	Jan. 15	Feb. 15 '99
0.070	Apr. 01	Apr. 14	Apr. 16	May. 10 '99
0.080	Jul. 09	Jul. 21	Jul. 23	Aug. 16 '99
0.080	Oct. 04	Oct. 13	Oct. 15	Nov. 15 '99

A Division of The McGraw-Hill Companies

MascoTech, Inc.

Business Summary - 19-AUG-99

MascoTech, Inc. is a leading diversified industrial manufacturing company that used advanced metalworking capabilities to supply metal formed components used in vehicle engine and drivetrain applications, specialty fasteners, towing systems, packaging and sealing products and other industrial products.

Operating profits by segment in 1998 were: specialty metal formed products 42%, towing systems 13%, specialty fasteners 17%, specialty packaging and sealing products 18%, specialty industrial products 6%, and companies sold or held for sale 4%. About 11% of 1998 sales were to overseas customers.

About 83% of 1998 sales were from operations involving metalworking technologies, including cold, warm or hot metal forming, and machining and fabricating.

Specialty metal formed products for engine and drivetrain applications include semi-finished transmission shafts, drive gears, engine connecting rods, wheel spindles and front wheeldrive components.

Towing systems products include vehicle hitches, jacks, winches, couplers and related accessories for the passenger car, light truck, recreational vehicle, marine, agricultural and industrial markets. Towing systems products are sold to independent installers, distributors, manufacturers and aftermarket retailers. Specialty fastener offerings encompass standard- and customer-designed ferrous, nonferrous and special alloy fasteners for the building construction, farm implement, medium- and heavy-duty truck, appliance, aerospace, electronics and other industries. The company also provides metal treating services for makers of fasteners and similar products.

Specialty packaging and sealing products include industrial and consumer container closures and dispensing products primarily for the chemical, agricultural, refining, food, petrochemical and healthcare industries. Specialty industrial products include flame-retardant facings and jacketings used in conjunction with fiberglass insulation.

Equity investments include a 16% stake in Titan Wheel, a maker of wheels, tires and other products for agricultural, construction, and other off highway equipment; and a 17% voting interest in Delco Remy, a maker of automotive electric motors.

In January 1998, MSX acquired for about $920 million the remaining 63% of TriMas Corp. that it did not already own. TriMas makes specialty fasteners, towing systems, specialty container products and other industrial products. The acquisition expanded MSX's advanced metalworking process capabilities into additional transportation-related and other industrial markets, and helped create more value for shareholders from affiliate investments.

Per Share Data ($) (Year Ended Dec. 31)	1998	1997	1996	1995	1994	1993	1992	1991	1990	1989
Tangible Bk. Val.	NM	3.07	NM	1.50	2.92	7.46	4.64	4.19	-3.77	5.02
Cash Flow	3.09	2.59	1.57	1.63	-3.07	1.91	1.50	0.76	0.63	1.45
Earnings	1.83	2.12	0.50	0.81	-4.20	0.97	0.48	-0.31	-0.33	0.58
Dividends	0.26	0.22	0.18	0.14	0.10	0.04	Nil	Nil	Nil	Nil
Payout Ratio	14%	10%	36%	17%	NM	4%	Nil	Nil	Nil	Nil
Prices - High	26 3/8	23 1/2	17	13 3/4	27 7/8	28 1/8	13 7/8	7 3/8	8 1/2	10 5/8
- Low	15 1/4	16	10 3/8	10	11	11 3/8	4 3/4	3 7/8	3 5/8	6 3/4
P/E Ratio - High	14	11	34	17	NM	29	29	NM	NM	18
- Low	8	8	21	12	NM	12	10	NM	NM	12
Income Statement Analysis (Million $)										
Revs.	1,636	922	1,281	1,678	1,702	1,583	1,657	1,467	1,562	1,687
Oper. Inc.	306	140	145	151	189	200	177	108	162	189
Depr.	83.6	43.5	44.5	47.1	66.8	54.0	62.4	63.8	71.6	70.9
Int. Exp.	81.5	36.5	30.0	49.9	50.0	81.0	86.0	113	128	133
Pretax Inc.	145	190	77.2	100	-263	121	70.0	-10.0	-24.0	76.0
Eff. Tax Rate	33%	39%	48%	41%	NM	42%	45%	NM	NM	39%
Net Inc.	97.5	115	39.9	59.1	-233	70.9	38.4	-9.0	-24.4	46.6
Balance Sheet & Other Fin. Data (Million $)										
Cash	29.4	41.1	57.2	20.5	124	83.0	109	155	92.0	97.0
Curr. Assets	501	336	394	467	598	556	632	645	613	746
Total Assets	2,091	1,145	1,229	1,439	1,531	1,790	1,877	1,973	2,080	2,236
Curr. Liab.	250	185	158	187	188	202	285	254	222	251
LT Debt	1,388	310	752	702	868	788	1,065	1,225	1,350	1,436
Common Eqty.	269	211	-51.0	199	165	452	276	249	279	389
Total Cap.	1,745	521	917	1,117	1,249	1,456	1,478	1,632	1,769	1,902
Cap. Exp.	106	54.8	42.4	95.8	115	60.0	68.0	85.0	77.0	113
Cash Flow	181	152	84.4	93.3	-180	110	92.0	45.0	47.0	118
Curr. Ratio	2.0	1.8	2.5	2.5	3.2	2.8	2.2	2.5	2.8	3.0
% LT Debt of Cap.	79.5	59.5	82.0	62.8	69.5	54.1	72.1	75.1	76.3	75.5
% Net Inc.of Revs.	6.0	12.5	3.1	3.5	NM	4.5	2.3	NM	NM	2.8
% Ret. on Assets	6.0	9.7	3.0	4.0	NM	3.8	2.0	NM	NM	2.2
% Ret. on Equity	40.7	59.8	53.9	2.5	NM	15.3	11.1	NM	NM	12.6

Data as orig reptd.; bef. results of disc opers/spec. items. Per share data adj. for stk. divs. Bold denotes diluted EPS (FASB 128)-prior periods restated. E-Estimated. NA-Not Available. NM-Not Meaningful. NR-Not Ranked.

Office—21001 Van Born Rd., Taylor, MI 48180. **Tel**—(313) 274-7405. **Website**—www.mascotech.com **Chrmn & CEO**—R. A. Manoogian. **Pres & COO**—L. M. Gardner. **EVP-Fin** —T. Wadhams. **VP & Secy**—E. A. Gargaro, Jr. **Investor Contact**—Kenneth J. Zak. **Dirs**—P. A. Dow, R. T. Fridholm, F. M. Hennessey, W. K. Howenstein, R. A. Manoogian, J. A. Morgan, H. F. Stern. **Transfer Agent & Registrar**—Bank of New York, NYC. **Incorporated**—in Delaware in 1984. **Empl**— 9,200. **S&P Analyst:** P.L.H.

STANDARD & POOR'S
STOCK REPORTS

Material Sciences

NYSE Symbol **MSC**

In S&P SmallCap 600

09-OCT-99

Industry: Chemicals (Specialty)

Summary: MSC produces coil-coated and composite materials, electroplated sheet steel, and metallized, coated and laminated films.

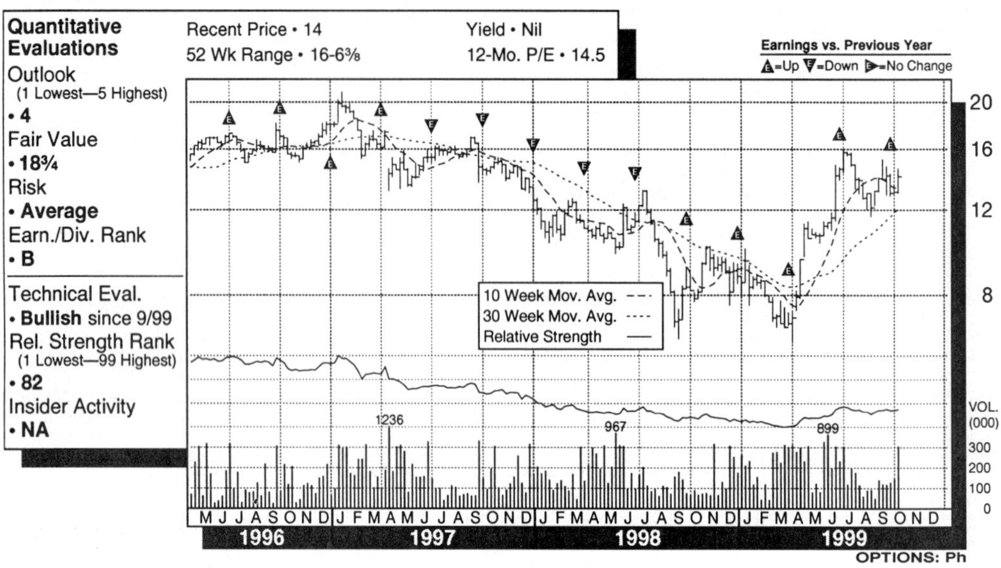

Business Profile - 30-AUG-99

In October 1998, MSC formed a 50:50 joint venture partnership with Bekaert Corp. called Innovative Specialty Films, LLC (ISF). ISF combines the sputtering operations of both companies, which the company believes makes it one of the leading sputtering companies in the world. ISF commenced operations on January 1, 1999. In December 1996, MSC authorized the repurchase of up to one million shares of its common stock, of which 523,100 shares were purchased through February 28, 1999. During the first quarter of FY 00 (Feb.), MSC repurchased 250,100 shares at an average of $9.36 per share.

Operational Review - 30-AUG-99

Net sales in the three months ended May 31, 1999, advanced 11%, year to year, reflecting gains across all business segments. Gross margins widened to 19.4% of sales, from 16.9%, reflecting the higher sales volume, lower material costs, a more favorable product mix and improved operating efficiencies; operating income was up 30%. With lower net interest expense and after taxes at 37.0%, versus 38.5%, income soared to $4,162,000 ($0.27 a share), from $1,638,000 ($0.11). Results in the 1998 period exclude a charge of $2.2 million ($0.14) for the cumulative effect of an accounting change.

Stock Performance - 08-OCT-99

In the past 30 trading days, MSC's shares have increased 7%, compared to a 0.91% fall in the S&P 500. Average trading volume for the past five days was 65,640 shares, compared with the 40-day moving average of 28,249 shares.

Key Stock Statistics

Dividend Rate/Share	Nil	Shareholders	1,140
Shs. outstg. (M)	15.3	Market cap. (B)	$0.215
Avg. daily vol. (M)	0.036	Inst. holdings	61%
Tang. Bk. Value/Share	8.37		
Beta	1.08		

Value of $10,000 invested 5 years ago: $ 9,220

Fiscal Year Ending Feb. 28

	2000	1999	1998	1997	1996	1995
Revenues (Million $)						
1Q	125.0	112.9	73.10	68.88	60.41	58.80
2Q	132.5	119.2	70.54	70.42	58.65	59.42
3Q	—	123.0	75.11	69.66	58.02	56.80
4Q	—	114.0	101.4	69.06	59.07	52.62
Yr.	—	469.1	320.2	278.0	236.2	227.7
Earnings Per Share ($)						
1Q	**0.27**	**0.11**	0.17	0.26	0.20	0.27
2Q	**0.28**	**0.13**	0.11	0.27	0.23	0.29
3Q	—	**0.17**	0.14	0.27	-0.04	0.30
4Q	—	**0.25**	Nil	0.24	0.16	0.24
Yr.	—	**0.66**	**0.42**	**1.04**	**0.55**	1.10

Next earnings report expected: mid December

Dividend Data

No cash dividends have been paid. The shares were split three for two in 1994 and 1992. A new "poison pill" shareholder rights plan was adopted in 1996.

A Division of The McGraw-Hill Companies

STANDARD
&POOR'S
STOCK REPORTS

Material Sciences Corporation

Business Summary - 30-AUG-99

Material Sciences Corp. (MSC) develops, manufactures and markets continuously processed, coated and laminated materials through three business segments: coated products and services, engineered materials and specialty films. Its materials are sold to a variety of manufacturers and distributors and used across a broad spectrum of industries and products. Founded in 1971 and headquartered near Chicago, MSC operates 11 manufacturing plants in the U.S. and Europe and sells its products around the world.

MSC's coated products and services segment includes the coil coating, hot-dip galvanizing and electrogalvanizing product groups. This segment provides galvanized and prepainted products and services primarily to the building and construction, automotive and appliance markets. The engineered materials segment includes the laminates and composites product group, which combines layers of metal and other materials designed to meet specific customer requirements for the automotive, lighting, appliance and computer disk drive markets. The specialty films segment provides solar control and safety window film, as well as industrial films used in a variety of products.

Customers generally benefit from the energy savings and environmental advantages of MSC's manufacturing processes and products. In the engineered materials, specialty films and hot-dip galvanizing portion of its business, the company is primarily a manufacturer and marketer of its own products. In the coil coating and electrogalvanizing area, MSC generally acts as a "toll coater" by processing its customers' metal for a fee, without taking ownership of the metal.

MSC believes that significant opportunities exist internationally, particularly for its disc brake noise damper products, Polycore Composites and solar control and safety window film. Direct export sales have grown each year, but at a slower rate than the consolidated net sales of the company. As a percentage of net sales, direct export sales represented 7%, 10% and 11% in FY 99 (Feb.), FY 98 and FY 97, respectively.

MSC estimates that customers in the building products market were the end-users for about 48%, 25% and 18% of its net sales in FY 99, FY 98 and FY 97, respectively. The company also estimates the original equipment and aftermarket segment of the transportation industry were the end-users for about 31%, 48% and 52% of net sales in FY 99, FY 98 and FY 97, respectively. Due to concentration in the automobile industry, sales to individual automobile companies, including indirect sales, are significant.

Per Share Data ($) (Year Ended Feb. 28)	1999	1998	1997	1996	1995	1994	1993	1992	1991	1990
Tangible Bk. Val.	8.00	7.60	7.86	7.08	6.75	5.81	5.00	3.57	2.71	2.29
Cash Flow	2.66	1.74	1.96	1.26	1.67	1.27	1.15	1.20	0.93	-2.27
Earnings	0.66	0.42	1.04	0.55	1.10	0.79	0.67	0.63	0.42	-2.71
Dividends	Nil	Nil	Nil	Nil	Nil	Nil	Nil	Nil	Nil	Nil
Payout Ratio	Nil	Nil	Nil	Nil	Nil	Nil	Nil	Nil	Nil	Nil
Cal. Yrs.	1998	1997	1996	1995	1994	1993	1992	1991	1990	1989
Prices - High	13 1/8	21	18 1/4	22 3/8	17 5/8	17 3/8	10 5/8	7 7/8	7 5/8	7 3/4
- Low	6 1/2	12	12 1/2	12 1/8	13 5/8	9 3/4	7 1/4	4 3/8	4 1/8	6 3/8
P/E Ratio - High	20	50	33	29	16	22	16	12	18	NM
- Low	10	29	23	16	13	12	11	7	10	NM
Income Statement Analysis (Million $)										
Revs.	469	320	278	236	228	188	156	143	139	153
Oper. Inc.	59.0	36.2	41.2	29.1	35.2	25.6	20.3	18.6	16.6	8.9
Depr.	30.7	20.4	14.3	11.1	8.8	7.3	6.5	6.4	5.7	4.9
Int. Exp.	11.8	6.1	2.2	0.6	0.1	0.1	0.3	1.2	2.5	2.6
Pretax Inc.	16.1	10.5	26.4	13.8	27.2	19.0	14.1	11.7	7.8	-39.0
Eff. Tax Rate	37%	39%	39%	38%	39%	38%	37%	39%	40%	NM
Net Inc.	10.2	6.5	16.2	8.5	16.7	11.8	8.9	7.1	4.7	-30.4
Balance Sheet & Other Fin. Data (Million $)										
Cash	1.2	3.6	2.1	3.4	5.8	11.9	23.5	Nil	0.9	3.5
Curr. Assets	113	126	75.0	66.7	61.8	62.3	62.1	35.1	40.5	49.4
Total Assets	395	418	254	200	172	152	129	101	104	111
Curr. Liab.	72.9	65.5	43.9	43.0	39.1	33.2	24.4	25.8	23.2	30.7
LT Debt	140	188	54.8	16.8	6.9	8.9	10.7	13.8	29.4	42.4
Common Eqty.	149	141	133	118	105	86.5	73.3	42.0	30.9	25.5
Total Cap.	307	341	200	146	123	108	96.0	69.0	73.0	78.0
Cap. Exp.	14.3	19.1	55.6	27.5	29.4	49.4	7.6	8.4	7.6	23.0
Cash Flow	40.8	26.8	30.6	19.6	25.5	19.1	15.4	13.5	10.4	-25.5
Curr. Ratio	1.6	1.9	1.7	1.6	1.6	1.9	2.5	1.4	1.7	1.6
% LT Debt of Cap.	45.5	55.1	27.4	11.5	5.6	8.2	11.2	20.1	40.4	54.6
% Net Inc.of Revs.	2.2	2.0	5.8	3.6	7.4	6.3	5.7	5.0	3.4	NM
% Ret. on Assets	2.5	1.9	7.2	4.6	10.3	8.5	7.0	6.9	4.3	NM
% Ret. on Equity	7.0	4.7	12.9	7.6	17.4	14.9	14.2	19.3	16.5	NM

Data as orig reptd.; bef. results of disc opers/spec. items. Per share data adj. for stk. divs. Bold denotes diluted EPS (FASB 128)-prior periods restated. E-Estimated. NA-Not Available. NM-Not Meaningful. NR-Not Ranked.

Office—2200 E. Pratt Blvd., Elk Grove Village, IL 60007. **Tel**—(847) 439-8270. **Website**—http://www.matsci.com **Chrmn, Pres & CEO**—G. G. Nadig. **EVP & COO**—T. E. Moore. **VP, CFO & Secy**—J. J. Waclawik Sr. **Contr**—D. J. DeNeve. **VP & Investor Contact**—Robert J. Mataya. **Dirs**—J. B. Cohen, E. W. Emmerich, G. R. Evans, E. F. Heizer Jr., G. G. Nadig, I. P. Pochter, H. B. Witt. **Transfer Agent & Registrar**—Mellon Securities Transfer Services, Ridgefield Park, NJ. **Incorporated**—in Delaware in 1983 to succeed to the business of a company founded in 1971. **Empl**— 1,206. **S&P Analyst:** M.I.

STANDARD
&POOR'S
STOCK REPORTS

MAXIMUS, Inc.

NYSE Symbol **MMS**

In S&P SmallCap 600

09-OCT-99

Industry:
Health Care (Specialized Services)

Summary: This company provides program management and consulting services to government health and human services agencies in the U.S.

Quantitative Evaluations

Outlook (1 Lowest—5 Highest) • **NA**

Fair Value • **NA**

Risk • **Average**

Earn./Div. Rank • **NR**

Technical Eval. • **Bearish** since 9/99

Rel. Strength Rank (1 Lowest—99 Highest) • **42**

Insider Activity • **Neutral**

Recent Price • 29½
52 Wk Range • 41½-21¾
Yield • Nil
12-Mo. P/E • 25.2

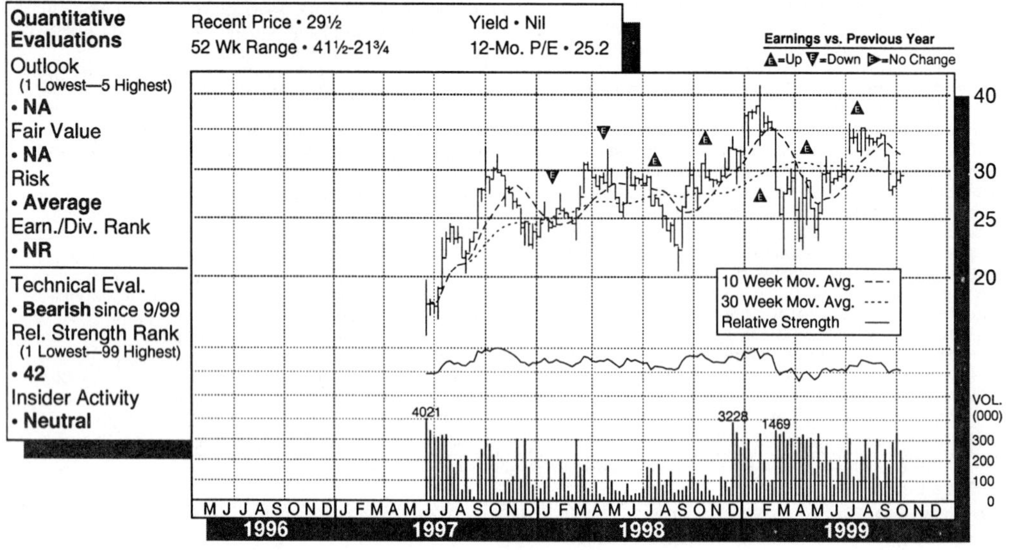

Business Profile - 04-JUN-99

MMS is seeking to become the leading provider of program management and consulting services to government health and human services agencies and is aggressively pursuing new business opportunities and acquisitions. In June 1999, MMS announced the acquisition of UNISON Consulting Group Inc., a government management consulting firm, for $7 million. In April 1999, MMS acquired Norman Roberts & Associates, an executive search firm focused on the public sector. In February, MMS acquired Control Software, Inc., a provider of fleet management software and consulting services. In December 1998, MMS completed a secondary public offering of 4.2 million common shares (including 2.2 million shares for selling shareholders), generating $61 million for the company. Officers and directors own 43% of the shares.

Operational Review - 04-JUN-99

Revenues in the six months ended March 31, 1999, advanced 40%, year to year, reflecting a 45% rise in consulting group revenue and a 36% increase in government operations revenue. Gross margins widened, and although SG&A expenses rose more rapidly than revenues, pretax income more than doubled to $20.6 million, from $10.2 million. After taxes at 40.5%, versus 37.4%, net income was up 92%, to $12.3 million ($0.60 a share, on 17% more shares), from $6.4 million ($0.37).

Stock Performance - 08-OCT-99

In the past 30 trading days, MMS's shares have declined 13%, compared to a 0.91% fall in the S&P 500. Average trading volume for the past five days was 49,600 shares, compared with the 40-day moving average of 66,038 shares.

Key Stock Statistics

Dividend Rate/Share	Nil	Shareholders	167
Shs. outstg. (M)	21.0	Market cap. (B)	$0.619
Avg. daily vol. (M)	0.087	Inst. holdings	58%
Tang. Bk. Value/Share	4.65		
Beta	NA		

Value of $10,000 invested 5 years ago: NA

Fiscal Year Ending Sep. 30

	1999	1998	1997	1996	1995	1994
Revenues (Million $)						
1Q	70.18	36.36	37.24	16.70	—	—
2Q	76.29	44.01	31.52	22.89	—	—
3Q	84.17	61.24	27.32	27.90	—	—
4Q	—	71.36	31.87	35.63	—	—
Yr.	—	233.5	128.0	103.1	—	—
Earnings Per Share ($)						
1Q	**0.29**	**0.17**	**0.18**	—	—	—
2Q	**0.31**	**0.22**	0.39	—	—	—
3Q	**0.35**	**0.22**	-0.05	—	—	—
4Q	—	**0.26**	0.19	—	—	—
Yr.	—	**0.82**	0.54	0.58	—	—

Next earnings report expected: mid November

Dividend Data

The company anticipates that it will retain all of its earnings for development of the business, and it does not expect to pay any cash dividends in the foreseeable future.

MAXIMUS, Inc.

Business Summary - 04-JUN-99

MAXIMUS, Inc. provides program management and consulting services to government health and human services agencies in the U.S. The company's services are designed to make government operations more efficient and cost effective, while improving the quality of services provided to program beneficiaries. MMS applies an entrepreneurial, private-sector approach, incorporating advanced technology, in large-scale projects in nearly every state in the U.S.

Revenues in recent fiscal years (Sep.) were derived as follows: government operations group 59.6% in FY 98 and 39.3% in FY 97; consulting group 40.4% and 41.8%; and social security contract nil and 18.9%.

The Government Operations Group specializes in administration and management of government health and human services programs. The company manages welfare-to-work programs by providing a wide range of services, including eligibility determination, emergency assistance, job referral and placement, transition services such as child care and transportation, community work training services, job readiness preparation, case management services and selected educational and training services. MMS also provides a full range of child support enforcement services. Through its disability services division, the company provides services geared to case management, client assessment, treatment and vocational rehabilitation referral, client monitoring and innovative return to work strategies.

The Consulting Group provides health and human services planning, information technology, consulting, strategic program evaluation, program improvement and revenue maximization services. It provides consulting and technical support to the federal government, as well as to state and local government agencies, in the financing, delivery and management of a range of human services programs in the areas of revenue maximization, program evaluations and program improvement.

During FY 98, MMS expanded its consulting group through acquisitions that included Carrera Consulting Group, which conducts an information technology consulting business in the human services field; Spectrum Consulting Group, a provider of information technology services to state governments; and David M. Griffith & Associates Ltd., a provider of cost accounting, human resources consulting, executive recruiting and other services to state and local governments. In December 1998, MMS purchased Interactive Web Systems Inc., an e-commerce solutions application firm.

At March 31, 1999, backlog for services was approximately $190 million, up from $103 million at December 31, 1998. The backlog represents an estimate of the remaining future revenues from existing signed contracts, and revenues from contracts that have been awarded but not yet signed.

Per Share Data ($) (Year Ended Sep. 30)	1998	1997	1996	1995	1994	1993	1992	1991	1990	1989
Tangible Bk. Val.	4.65	4.47	4.02	NA	NA	NA	NA	NA	NA	NA
Cash Flow	0.96	0.68	NA	NA	NA	NA	NA	NA	NA	NA
Earnings	0.82	0.54	0.58	NA	NA	NA	NA	NA	NA	NA
Dividends	Nil	Nil	NA	NA	NA	NA	NA	NA	NA	NA
Payout Ratio	Nil	Nil	NA	NA	NA	NA	NA	NA	NA	NA
Prices - High	37	32⅞	NA	NA	NA	NA	NA	NA	NA	NA
- Low	20⅜	16	NA	NA	NA	NA	NA	NA	NA	NA
P/E Ratio - High	45	61	NA	NA	NA	NA	NA	NA	NA	NA
- Low	25	30	NA	NA	NA	NA	NA	NA	NA	NA
Income Statement Analysis (Million $)										
Revs.	233	128	103	NA	NA	NA	NA	NA	NA	NA
Oper. Inc.	29.2	17.3	11.9	NA	NA	NA	NA	NA	NA	NA
Depr.	2.4	0.4	0.3	NA	NA	NA	NA	NA	NA	NA
Int. Exp.	Nil	Nil	Nil	NA	NA	NA	NA	NA	NA	NA
Pretax Inc.	24.9	12.0	11.8	NA	NA	NA	NA	NA	NA	NA
Eff. Tax Rate	42%	28%	40%	NA	NA	NA	NA	NA	NA	NA
Net Inc.	14.5	8.6	7.1	NA	NA	NA	NA	NA	NA	NA
Balance Sheet & Other Fin. Data (Million $)										
Cash	19.4	11.0	47.0	NA	NA	NA	NA	NA	NA	NA
Curr. Assets	112	93.1	NA	NA	NA	NA	NA	NA	NA	NA
Total Assets	121	96.8	78.6	NA	NA	NA	NA	NA	NA	NA
Curr. Liab.	35.4	30.5	NA	NA	NA	NA	NA	NA	NA	NA
LT Debt	0.5	Nil	Nil	NA	NA	NA	NA	NA	NA	NA
Common Eqty.	84.7	66.1	58.9	NA	NA	NA	NA	NA	NA	NA
Total Cap.	85.2	66.3	58.9	NA	NA	NA	NA	NA	NA	NA
Cap. Exp.	1.0	0.5	NA	NA	NA	NA	NA	NA	NA	NA
Cash Flow	16.9	9.0	NA	NA	NA	NA	NA	NA	NA	NA
Curr. Ratio	3.2	3.0	NA	NA	NA	NA	NA	NA	NA	NA
% LT Debt of Cap.	0.5	Nil	NA	NA	NA	NA	NA	NA	NA	NA
% Net Inc.of Revs.	6.2	6.7	6.9	NA	NA	NA	NA	NA	NA	NA
% Ret. on Assets	13.3	13.0	NA	NA	NA	NA	NA	NA	NA	NA
% Ret. on Equity	19.2	18.7	NA	NA	NA	NA	NA	NA	NA	NA

Data as orig. reptd.; bef. results of disc. opers. and/or spec. items. Balance Sheet data for 1996 pro forma; Bk. Val. for 1996 as of Mar. 31, 1997. Per share data adj. for stk. divs. as of ex-div. date. E-Estimated. NA-Not Available. NM-Not Meaningful. NR-Not Ranked.

Office—1356 Beverly Rd., McLean, VA 22101. **Tels**—(703) 734-4200; (800) 368-2152. **Website**—http://www.maximus-inc.com **Pres & CEO**—D. V. Mastran. **Chrmn**—R. B. Ruddy. **Treas & CFO**—F. A. Nerret. **Secy**—D. R. Francis. **Dirs**—R. A. Beliveau, J. Brown, M. Carrera, L.E. Chappuie, L. P. Davenport, D. V. Mastran, R. J. Muzzio, S. D. Pepin, P. B. Pond, R. B. Ruddy. **Transfer Agent & Registrar**—American Stock Transfer & Trust Co. **Incorporated**—in Virginia in 1975. **Empl**— 2,800. **S&P Analyst:** JJA

STANDARD
&POOR'S
STOCK REPORTS

Maxxim Medical

NYSE Symbol **MAM**

In S&P SmallCap 600

09-OCT-99

Industry:
Health Care (Medical Products & Supplies)

Summary: This company is a major manufacturer and developer of a diversified range of specialty medical products.

Quantitative Evaluations

Outlook
(1 Lowest—5 Highest)
• **5**

Fair Value
• **38¾**

Risk
• **Average**

Earn./Div. Rank
• **B+**

Technical Eval.
• **Neutral** since 9/99

Rel. Strength Rank
(1 Lowest—99 Highest)
• **64**

Insider Activity
• **NA**

Recent Price • 23¼
52 Wk Range • 30⅝-14⅞
Yield • Nil
12-Mo. P/E • 15.8

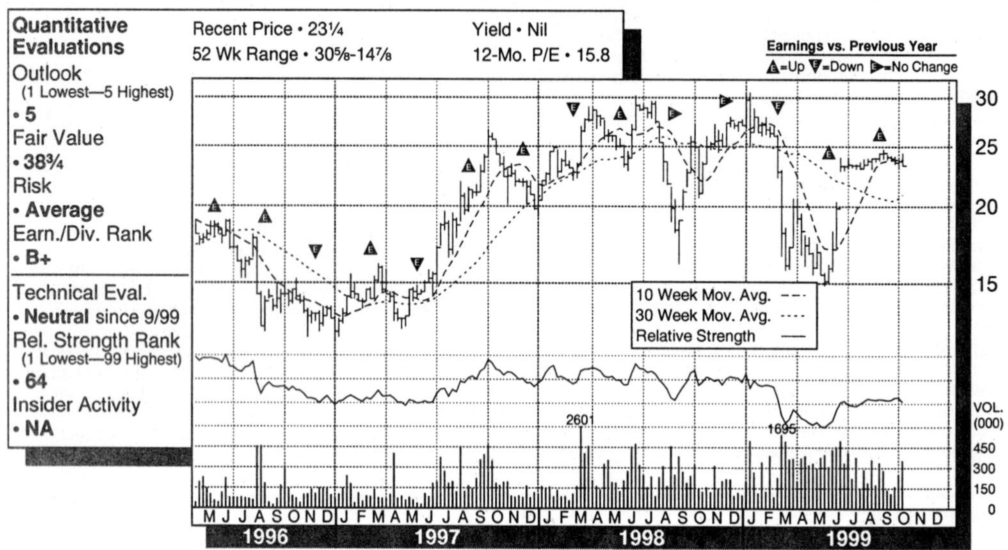

Business Profile - 08-SEP-99

The company's growth in recent years has been aided by acquisitions that expanded its market presence via vertical integration and product additions. In January 1999, MAM acquired Circon Corp., which makes endoscopy systems for diagnosis and minimally invasive surgery, for about $260 million, including the repayment of $32.5 million of Circon debt. At May 2, 1999, the company had long-term liabilities of $364 million, and shareholders' equity of $279 million.

Operational Review - 08-SEP-99

Net sales in the first nine months of FY 99 (Oct.) advanced 25%, year to year, reflecting the January 1999 Circon acquisition. Gross margins widened, due to the inclusion of Circon, which had higher margins than the company's traditional business. However, with 59% higher SG&A costs, $3.4 million of transition expenses, and a 92% rise in interest costs, the gain in pretax income was held to 16%. After taxes at 43.5%, versus 42.3%, net income rose 14%, to $15,853,000 ($1.09 a share, on 20% more shares), from $13,914,000 ($1.11).

Stock Performance - 08-OCT-99

In the past 30 trading days, MAM's shares have declined 4%, compared to a 0.91% fall in the S&P 500. Average trading volume for the past five days was 69,920 shares, compared with the 40-day moving average of 45,587 shares.

Key Stock Statistics

Dividend Rate/Share	Nil	Shareholders	237
Shs. outstg. (M)	14.3	Market cap. (B)	$0.333
Avg. daily vol. (M)	0.043	Inst. holdings	68%
Tang. Bk. Value/Share	7.65		
Beta	1.69		

Value of $10,000 invested 5 years ago: $ 11,656

Fiscal Year Ending Oct. 31

	1999	1998	1997	1996	1995	1994
Revenues (Million $)						
1Q	136.1	128.0	133.4	86.60	54.37	46.65
2Q	176.0	133.0	136.0	90.86	62.51	46.46
3Q	172.3	128.1	128.7	84.13	65.67	48.01
4Q	—	133.5	131.5	138.3	83.18	50.26
Yr.	—	522.5	529.5	399.8	265.7	191.4
Earnings Per Share ($)						
1Q	**0.26**	**0.37**	**0.39**	0.33	0.28	0.27
2Q	**0.42**	**0.37**	0.33	0.35	0.31	0.26
3Q	**0.41**	**0.37**	0.37	0.36	-0.59	0.25
4Q	—	**0.39**	0.39	0.01	0.36	0.27
Yr.	—	**1.50**	**1.42**	**1.02**	0.36	1.05

Next earnings report expected: early January

Dividend Data

Maxxim has never paid cash dividends on its common stock.

A Division of The McGraw-Hill Companies

Maxxim Medical, Inc.

Business Summary - 08-SEP-99

Maxxim Medical has grown significantly since its 1990 IPO, principally by integrating several major acquisitions of specialty medical products and custom procedure tray businesses. It aims to become a major medical company by enhancing its position as a developer, manufacturer, distributor, and marketer of a diversified range of single-use specialty medical products for use in medical treatment facilities, both domestically and abroad.

The company's objectives for FY 99 (Oct.) included: assimilating Circon Corp. (acquired in January 1999), and continuing to increase sales, improve profitability, increase shareholder value with continued improvement in share earnings, expand its European presence, and continue product line expansions.

MAM is a diversified developer, manufacturer, distributor, and marketer of disposable specialty medical products such as custom procedure trays, medical gloves, cardiology and interventional radiology products, containment products, infection control products, and electrosurgical systems primarily for use in the operating room at hospitals or surgery centers.

As of year-end 1998, the company was the second largest U.S. provider of sterilized custom procedure trays; it believes it controls about 29% of that market, as well as 58% of the rapidly growing acute care market for non-latex examination gloves. Subsequent to year-end 1998, MAM entered the endoscopy market through the January 1999 acquisition of Circon.

MAM sells more than 23,000 products to about 7,000 accounts in North America and Europe. Products are distributed through four primary channels: North American Surgical sales, North American Medical sales, European sales, and OEM/Export sales.

Products included in the Surgical distribution channel are custom procedure trays, drapes and gowns, imaging products, and electrosurgery devices. Medical distribution products consist primarily of non-latex medical examination and surgical gloves, critical care products, containment products, and IV safety devices. outside of North America and Europe.

European operations distribute all of the company's products through a direct sales force in the Benelux region and utilize distributors throughout the remainder of Europe. The European operation also manufactures and distributes Medica products, which are self-manufactured and assembled single-use hospital supply products and custom procedure kits for transfusion, infusion and patient monitoring. The company maintains an administrative staff to support sales of its products to OEM and international customers.

Per Share Data ($) **(Year Ended Oct. 31)**	**1998**	**1997**	**1996**	**1995**	**1994**	**1993**	**1992**	**1991**	**1990**	**1989**
Tangible Bk. Val.	7.65	NM	NM	9.25	11.05	8.61	10.72	5.06	4.37	2.32
Cash Flow	2.97	3.56	2.87	1.50	2.04	1.41	1.20	0.87	0.73	0.70
Earnings	1.50	1.51	1.05	0.36	1.05	0.94	0.75	0.57	0.48	0.42
Dividends	Nil	Nil	Nil	Nil	Nil	Nil	Nil	Nil	Nil	Nil
Payout Ratio	Nil	Nil	Nil	Nil	Nil	Nil	Nil	Nil	Nil	Nil
Prices - High	30⅝	26⅜	20⅜	17	20½	20⅝	24½	17⅝	8½	NA
- Low	16⅛	12⅝	12	12¼	11½	12¼	11½	4⅜	4	NA
P/E Ratio - High	20	18	19	47	20	22	32	31	18	NA
- Low	11	8	11	34	11	13	15	8	8	NA
Income Statement Analysis (Million $)										
Revs.	523	530	400	266	191	130	74.5	45.3	27.1	17.2
Oper. Inc.	65.9	59.3	43.6	29.0	20.8	11.6	8.0	4.4	2.5	1.9
Depr.	19.4	17.5	15.0	9.2	7.3	2.8	2.1	0.9	0.6	0.5
Int. Exp.	14.0	21.6	13.1	4.1	2.1	1.5	1.0	1.2	0.3	0.4
Pretax Inc.	34.1	22.4	14.5	4.8	11.8	8.1	5.3	2.5	1.8	1.1
Eff. Tax Rate	42%	42%	40%	39%	35%	32%	35%	35%	34%	36%
Net Inc.	19.6	12.9	8.7	2.9	7.7	5.5	3.5	1.6	1.2	0.7
Balance Sheet & Other Fin. Data (Million $)										
Cash	4.1	3.1	8.0	5.1	31.9	2.8	21.4	0.4	0.7	NM
Curr. Assets	173	175	205	125	107	67.5	53.0	32.1	15.1	8.8
Total Assets	468	424	467	264	165	114	70.6	48.3	21.6	10.8
Curr. Liab.	64.3	74.7	86.6	52.0	23.9	14.7	9.3	11.4	7.0	4.5
LT Debt	Nil	205	250	94.5	29.9	30.8	2.3	22.5	2.7	2.9
Common Eqty.	273	138	124	116	111	68.5	59.0	14.3	11.8	3.4
Total Cap.	273	349	380	211	141	99	61.3	36.9	14.5	6.3
Cap. Exp.	23.4	6.8	10.6	21.2	NA	1.6	2.0	0.4	NA	NA
Cash Flow	39.0	30.4	23.7	12.2	15.0	8.3	5.6	2.5	1.8	1.1
Curr. Ratio	2.7	2.3	2.4	2.4	4.5	4.6	5.7	2.8	2.2	2.0
% LT Debt of Cap.	Nil	58.7	65.8	44.8	21.2	31.1	3.8	61.1	18.8	46.0
% Net Inc.of Revs.	3.8	2.4	2.2	1.1	4.0	4.3	4.6	3.5	4.3	4.0
% Ret. on Assets	4.4	2.9	2.4	1.4	4.8	5.8	4.2	4.5	5.6	8.5
% Ret. on Equity	9.6	9.9	7.3	2.6	7.5	8.4	8.0	12.0	12.8	22.6

Data as orig reptd.; bef. results of disc opers/spec. items. Per share data adj. for stk. divs. Bold denotes diluted EPS (FASB 128)-prior periods restated. E-Estimated. NA-Not Available. NM-Not Meaningful. NR-Not Ranked.

Office—10300 49th Street North, Clearwater, FL 33762. **Tel**—(813) 561-2100. **Website**—http://www.maxximmedical.com **Chrmn, Pres & CEO**—K. W. Davidson. **SEVP-COO & Secy**—P. M. Graham. **EVP-Treas**—A. S. Blazei. **Dirs**—K. W. Davidson, D. R. DePriest, P. G. Dorflinger, M. Grabois, E. J. Henley, R. O. Martin, H. R. Wafelman. **Transfer Agent & Registrar**—KeyCorp Shareholder Services, Dallas, TX. **Incorporated**—in Texas in 1989. **Empl**— 4,068. **S&P Analyst:** P.L.H.

McWhorter Technologies

NYSE Symbol **MWT**

In S&P SmallCap 600

09-OCT-99

Industry:
Chemicals (Specialty)

Summary: This company is a leading specialty chemical manufacturer of liquid and powder resins for the coatings industry and of composite polymers for the fiberglass industry.

Quantitative Evaluations

Outlook
(1 Lowest—5 Highest)
• **3+**

Fair Value
• **17⅝**

Risk
• **Low**

Earn./Div. Rank
• **NR**

Technical Eval.
• **Bearish** since 9/99

Rel. Strength Rank
(1 Lowest—99 Highest)
• **30**

Insider Activity
• **NA**

Recent Price • 14⅜
52 Wk Range • 23¾-12⅝
Yield • Nil
12-Mo. P/E • 14.2

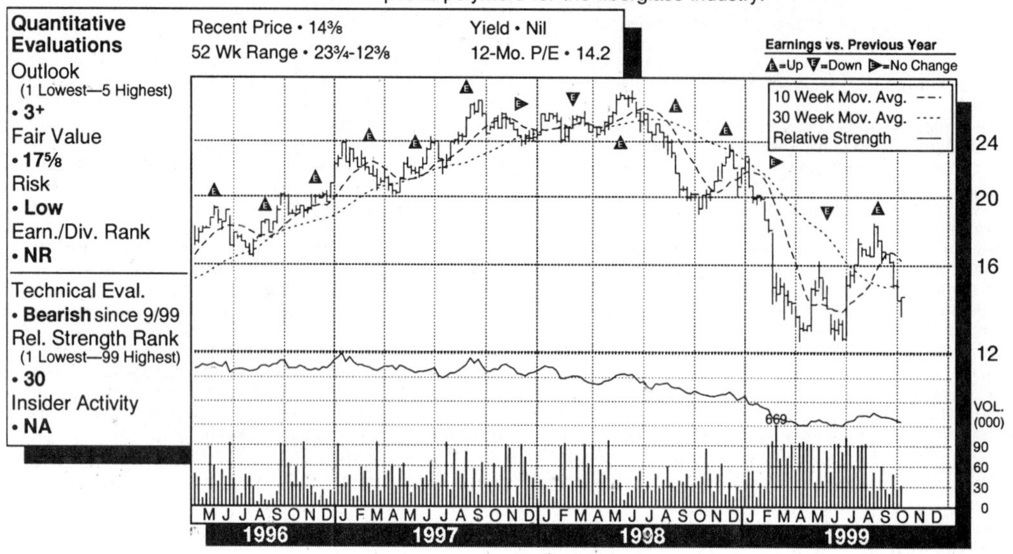

Business Profile - 22-JUN-99

For the second half of FY 99 (Oct.) MWT is projecting improved European results and continued strong performance in North American operations. The company stated that recent performance in the North American resins business has been significantly better than a year earlier. MWT noted that the European powder business performed in line with the year-earlier level. However, the company expressed disappointment with performance in the European liquid coatings and non-coating aminos businesses. In June 1999, MWT said that it expected to record an aftertax loss of about $600,000 ($0.06 a share) in 1999's third quarter on the planned sale of its 50% ownership in Syntech Far East, a Hong Kong joint venture.

Operational Review - 22-JUN-99

Net sales for the six months ended April 30, 1999, decreased 1.9%, year to year, negatively impacted by lower volumes in the European liquid coatings resins business, partially offset by the Accurate acquisition and improved volumes in the composite polymers business. Profitability was penalized by lower other income, 15% higher depreciation and amortization expense, and 17% higher interest expense. Pretax income fell 8.4%. Following taxes at 41.0%, against 15.9% (with the lower rate stemming from a $2.3 million ($0.22 a share) tax rate reduction, due to changes in Italian tax regulations) net income was down 36%, to $4.9 million ($0.47 a share), from $7.6 million ($0.73).

Stock Performance - 08-OCT-99

In the past 30 trading days, MWT's shares have declined 17%, compared to a 0.91% fall in the S&P 500. Average trading volume for the past five days was 6,320 shares, compared with the 40-day moving average of 7,328 shares.

Key Stock Statistics

Dividend Rate/Share	Nil	Shareholders	1,268
Shs. outstg. (M)	10.1	Market cap. (B)	$0.145
Avg. daily vol. (M)	0.006	Inst. holdings	49%
Tang. Bk. Value/Share	3.58		
Beta	0.32		

Value of $10,000 invested 5 years ago: NA

Fiscal Year Ending Oct. 31

	1999	1998	1997	1996	1995	1994
Revenues (Million $)						
1Q	96.24	98.12	71.53	65.24	67.31	25.39
2Q	113.5	115.6	80.88	76.92	79.12	63.11
3Q	117.9	125.8	85.58	87.14	82.97	79.24
4Q	—	115.4	93.47	86.62	82.00	74.59
Yr.	—	454.9	331.5	315.9	311.4	242.3
Earnings Per Share ($)						
1Q	**0.12**	**0.12**	0.24	0.20	0.17	-0.03
2Q	**0.36**	**0.61**	0.37	0.31	0.26	0.23
3Q	**0.50**	**0.47**	0.46	0.42	0.30	0.29
4Q	—	**1.35**	0.40	0.40	0.29	0.28
Yr.	—	**1.24**	**1.48**	**1.32**	1.02	0.78

Next earnings report expected: mid November

Dividend Data

No dividends have been paid. A "poison pill" stock purchase rights plan was adopted at the time of the company's spin-off from Valspar.

McWhorter Technologies, Inc.

Business Summary - 22-JUN-99

Headquartered in Carpentersville, Illinois, McWhorter Technologies is a leading producer of surface coating resins, colorants, as well as resins used for reinforced fiberglass plastics. Surface coating resins are a primary component of paint, colorants are used to disperse pigments in paints and plastics and reinforced fiberglass plastic is an important element in a variety of fiberglass products.

MWT believes that the paint, coatings and reinforced fiberglass plastic industries are highly fragmented with a large number of competitors. MWT notes that in the paint and coatings business there are over 800 manufacturers.

Materials used in the manufacturing of resins and colorants are procured from domestic suppliers. Most of the raw materials are derived from either petroleum or vegetable oil, and are subject to supply contracts which average one to three years in length.

McWhorter's resins include: Alkyd resins and copolymers, MWT's largest product category, which include polyurethane resins and are used for house paint, protective coatings for machinery, special-purpose coatings, such as traffic striping paints and automotive refinish coatings. Polyester resins are used for coil coated metal buildings and metal office furniture. Unsaturated polyester resins are primary ingredients in reinforced fiberglass products, with significant marine applications, such as the manufacturing of boats. Acrylic and polyvinyl acetate emulsion resins are used in consumer latex paints. While emulsions are generally employed in industrial and special purpose coatings, acrylic emulsion resins are used in trim paints and exterior applications and meet or exceed environmental regulations because of their low solvent content. Solution acrylics are necessary for applications where resistance to weathering is required. Powder resins emit no solvents, and are the fastest growing segment of the industrial coatings industry. Specialty resins include natural and synthetic adhesives and are used by the paper industry. Waterborne and solvent-based colorant systems are elements in formulated and interior and exterior paints.

In April 1998, the company acquired most of the assets of Accurate Coatings and Dispersions, Inc, (a producer of dispersed pigments for the coatings industry) for approximately $39.4 million. Also, in 1998, for a cost of $8.2 million, MWT increased its equity interest in the McWhorter Technologies Europe business to 100% from 33.3%.

In the fourth quarter of 1998, the company recorded a $2.8 million ($0.27 per share) after tax charge relating to closure of a Chicago production facility and a $1.6 million ($0.15 per share) after tax charge for a writedown of a Thailand joint venture.

In May 1999, MWT's directors authorized the repurchase of up to 500,000 shares of common stock; the authorization expires in May, 2000.

Per Share Data ($) (Year Ended Oct. 31)	1998	1997	1996	1995	1994	1993	1992	1991	1990	1989
Tangible Bk. Val.	3.04	5.36	8.00	6.66	5.72	4.94	NA	NA	NA	NA
Cash Flow	2.82	2.46	2.19	1.74	1.35	1.70	NA	NA	NA	NA
Earnings	1.24	1.47	1.32	1.02	0.78	0.93	NA	NA	NA	NA
Dividends	Nil	Nil	Nil	Nil	Nil	Nil	NA	NA	NA	NA
Payout Ratio	Nil	Nil	Nil	Nil	Nil	Nil	NA	NA	NA	NA
Prices - High	28 3/8	27 3/8	20 1/8	16 3/8	19 1/4	NA	NA	NA	NA	NA
- Low	18 7/8	20 1/8	12 7/8	14	13 1/4	NA	NA	NA	NA	NA
P/E Ratio - High	23	19	15	16	25	NA	NA	NA	NA	NA
- Low	15	14	10	14	17	NA	NA	NA	NA	NA
Income Statement Analysis (Million $)										
Revs.	455	331	316	311	242	269	NA	NA	NA	NA
Oper. Inc.	49.5	38.4	34.0	28.7	24.1	26.7	NA	NA	NA	NA
Depr.	16.4	10.4	9.1	7.9	6.2	8.3	NA	NA	NA	NA
Int. Exp.	7.7	2.2	1.6	2.3	1.1	2.0	NA	NA	NA	NA
Pretax Inc.	17.9	25.0	23.2	18.6	14.0	16.3	NA	NA	NA	NA
Eff. Tax Rate	28%	38%	41%	41%	40%	38%	NA	NA	NA	NA
Net Inc.	12.8	15.4	13.8	11.1	8.4	10.1	NA	NA	NA	NA
Balance Sheet & Other Fin. Data (Million $)										
Cash	4.1	3.9	1.0	1.9	1.4	1.6	NA	NA	NA	NA
Curr. Assets	139	107	71.4	60.5	67.1	30.7	NA	NA	NA	NA
Total Assets	362	259	153	138	139	103	NA	NA	NA	NA
Curr. Liab.	94.1	82.2	46.9	38.5	40.2	13.2	NA	NA	NA	NA
LT Debt	130	57.2	13.1	19.1	30.1	34.1	NA	NA	NA	NA
Common Eqty.	107	91.7	79.7	71.5	62.1	53.6	NA	NA	NA	NA
Total Cap.	261	171	103	97.3	95.6	88.4	NA	NA	NA	NA
Cap. Exp.	25.7	11.2	7.0	6.5	4.7	NA	NA	NA	NA	NA
Cash Flow	29.2	25.8	22.9	19.0	14.6	18.5	NA	NA	NA	NA
Curr. Ratio	1.5	1.3	1.5	1.6	1.7	2.3	NA	NA	NA	NA
% LT Debt of Cap.	49.8	33.4	13.4	19.7	31.5	38.6	NA	NA	NA	NA
% Net Inc.of Revs.	2.8	4.7	4.4	3.6	3.5	3.8	NA	NA	NA	NA
% Ret. on Assets	4.1	7.5	9.5	8.0	NA	NA	NA	NA	NA	NA
% Ret. on Equity	12.9	18.0	18.3	16.6	NA	NA	NA	NA	NA	NA

Data as orig reptd.; bef. results of disc opers/spec. items. Per share data adj. for stk. divs. Bold denotes diluted EPS (FASB 128)-prior periods restated. E-Estimated. NA-Not Available. NM-Not Meaningful. NR-Not Ranked.

Office—400 E. Cottage Place, Carpentersville, IL 60110. **Tel**—(847) 428-2657. **Fax**—(847) 428-2753. **Chrmn & CEO**—J. R. Stevenson. **Pres & COO**—Jeffrey M. Nodland. **VP & CFO & Secy**—Louise M. Tonozzi-Frederick. **Dirs**—M. L. Collins, E.M. Giles, D. G. Harris, J. G. Johnson Jr., J. M. Nodland, J. R. Stevenson, H. F. Tomfohrde III. **Transfer Agent & Registrar**—Wachovia Bank of North Carolina, Winston-Salem. **Incorporated**—in Delaware in 1993. **Empl**— 791. **S&P Analyst:** J. Friendly

STANDARD &POOR'S
STOCK REPORTS

MedQuist Inc

NASDAQ Symbol **MEDQ**

In S&P SmallCap 600

09-OCT-99

Industry: Services (Data Processing)

Summary: This company is a leading U.S. provider of electronic transcription and health care information management solutions.

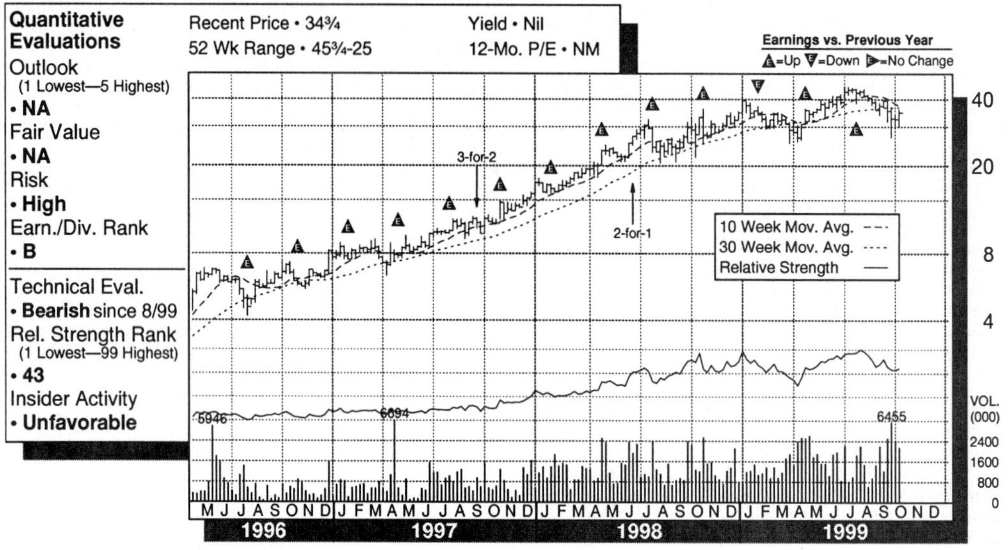

Business Profile - 07-OCT-99

In September, the company said it expected third quarter earnings to surpass analyst expectations, with revenues comfortably within the expected range. Continuing its aggressive acquisition activity, in the third quarter, MEDQ purchased Medico Transcription Service, Inc., a medical transcription firm with 1998 revenues of $2 million. In May 1999, MEDQ acquired the assets of the medical transcription unit of Lanier Professional Services, Inc. In 1998, the unit had revenues of $25 million. In April 1999, 4,493,467 MEDQ common shares (including 3,693,467 shares sold by existing shareholders) were sold in a public offering; in May, underwriters of exercised an over-allotment option to purchase an additional 505,033 shares.

Operational Review - 07-OCT-99

Revenues in the six months ended June 30, 1999, climbed 19%, year to year, driven by additional revenues generated by new and existing clients. Margins widened, reflecting cost reductions associated with recent acquisitions; operating income more than doubled. With other income of $759,000, versus $7,000, after taxes at 41.1%, versus 36.4%, net income soared 100%, to $15,932,000 ($0.44 a share), from $7,973,000 ($0.23).

Stock Performance - 08-OCT-99

In the past 30 trading days, MEDQ's shares have declined 3%, compared to a 0.91% fall in the S&P 500. Average trading volume for the past five days was 429,060 shares, compared with the 40-day moving average of 523,754 shares.

Key Stock Statistics

Dividend Rate/Share	Nil	Shareholders	1,959
Shs. outstg. (M)	35.9	Market cap. (B)	$ 1.2
Avg. daily vol. (M)	0.733	Inst. holdings	82%
Tang. Bk. Value/Share	3.25		
Beta	1.19		

Value of $10,000 invested 5 years ago: $ 213,846

Fiscal Year Ending Dec. 31

	1999	1998	1997	1996	1995	1994
Revenues (Million $)						
1Q	75.66	27.40	18.62	13.98	10.43	5.80
2Q	79.98	32.21	20.19	14.37	10.81	11.70
3Q	—	36.16	21.90	15.51	11.54	14.30
4Q	—	71.87	23.88	17.62	12.35	14.61
Yr.	—	271.7	84.59	61.48	45.13	46.35
Earnings Per Share ($)						
1Q	**0.20**	**0.12**	**0.08**	**0.05**	Nil	0.03
2Q	**0.24**	**0.12**	**0.08**	**0.06**	0.02	0.05
3Q	—	**0.11**	**0.09**	**0.06**	0.04	0.06
4Q	—	**-0.24**	**0.10**	**0.07**	0.03	0.06
Yr.	—	**0.09**	**0.34**	**0.20**	0.10	-0.19

Next earnings report expected: mid October

Dividend Data

No cash dividends have been paid. A two-for-one stock split was effected in June 1998.

A Division of The McGraw-Hill Companies

MedQuist Inc

Business Summary - 07-OCT-99

MedQuist sold its outpatient health care businesses over the past several years, and, following several acquisitions, is now a leading national provider of electronic transcription and data management services to the health care industry. Operations were considerably expanded in late 1998 through the acquisition of MRC Group, a leading national provider of medical transcription services (annual revenues of about $110 million). MEDQ issued 8.6 million common shares, and assumed employee options.

Using its proprietary software, open architecture environment and network of more than 6,000 transcriptionists, MEDQ converts free-form medical dictation into electronically formatted patient records that health care providers use in connection with patient care and for other administrative purposes. Its customized outsourcing services enable clients to improve the accuracy of transcribed medical reports, reduce report turnaround times, shorten billing cycles, and reduce overhead and other costs.

The company believes a number of factors are driving the medical transcription industry, including a need for accurate and prompt recordkeeping required for reimbursement and to avoid health care fraud and abuse penalties. In addition, consolidation in the health care industry creates larger entities that require sophisticated information management techniques. Health care providers are also increasingly outsourcing non-core functions, as part of an effort to reduce fixed costs and improve service quality.

MEDQ integrates proprietary software with digital dictation equipment, a health care provider's host system and its network of more than 2,800 transcriptionists to provide customized solutions for hospitals and other health care providers. The company captures and stores free-form medical dictation, professionally transcribes the dictation into accurate reports, and electronically receives, reviews and distributes final reports to clients by up-loading them into the client computer system for placement into patient medical records.

The company serves about 2,300 clients through 77 client service centers. In addition to hospital medical records departments, Target markets include patient care departments, such as radiology, emergency rooms, oncology, pathology, pediatrics and cardiology departments, health maintenance organizations, physician practice groups and outpatient clinics.

In the first quarter of 1999, MEDQ purchased Medico Transcription Service, Inc., a medical transcription firm with 1998 revenues of $2 million. In May 1999, the company acquired Lanier Transcription Services, which had revenues of $25 million in 1998.

Per Share Data ($) (Year Ended Dec. 31)	1998	1997	1996	1995	1994	1993	1992	1991	1990	1989
Tangible Bk. Val.	2.07	1.35	1.13	NM	NM	NM	NM	0.38	NA	NA
Cash Flow	0.56	1.13	0.65	0.69	0.56	0.51	0.67	0.52	NA	NA
Earnings	0.09	0.34	0.20	0.10	0.19	0.20	0.18	0.17	NA	NA
Dividends	Nil	Nil	Nil	Nil	Nil	Nil	Nil	Nil	NA	NA
Payout Ratio	Nil	Nil	Nil	Nil	Nil	Nil	Nil	Nil	NA	NA
Prices - High	40	17⅝	8⅜	3⅜	3	2⅝	2½	NA	NA	NA
- Low	15	6⅜	2¾	2⅛	1½	1 5/16	1½	NA	NA	NA
P/E Ratio - High	NM	52	42	34	15	12	13	NA	NA	NA
- Low	NM	19	13	21	7	6	8	NA	NA	NA
Income Statement Analysis (Million $)										
Revs.	272	84.6	61.5	45.1	46.3	29.1	27.4	22.5	NA	NA
Oper. Inc.	46.0	17.7	12.3	8.7	7.4	3.1	5.3	3.7	NA	NA
Depr.	16.5	5.1	3.6	4.0	2.3	1.9	2.1	1.2	NA	NA
Int. Exp.	Nil	0.2	1.6	3.7	2.8	1.4	0.6	0.5	NA	NA
Pretax Inc.	11.7	12.4	7.0	1.0	2.4	4.0	2.7	2.0	NA	NA
Eff. Tax Rate	73%	39%	40%	42%	40%	54%	44%	41%	NA	NA
Net Inc.	3.2	7.6	4.2	0.6	1.4	1.9	1.5	1.2	NA	NA
Balance Sheet & Other Fin. Data (Million $)										
Cash	15.9	12.3	8.9	1.8	2.4	2.5	2.2	0.9	NA	NA
Curr. Assets	75.1	33.0	23.5	13.3	14.9	9.0	10.1	5.9	NA	NA
Total Assets	187	90.8	74.3	58.1	55.1	29.6	30.6	11.1	NA	NA
Curr. Liab.	33.2	10.3	5.1	8.4	11.9	6.9	4.5	2.5	NA	NA
LT Debt	0.2	1.4	1.7	33.3	30.7	12.4	13.9	4.0	NA	NA
Common Eqty.	151	76.3	65.7	15.0	10.7	9.1	12.4	5.0	NA	NA
Total Cap.	153	80.0	68.6	48.9	42.2	21.7	25.9	8.5	NA	NA
Cap. Exp.	14.0	4.6	3.2	0.7	1.0	0.9	2.0	1.6	NA	NA
Cash Flow	19.6	12.7	7.8	4.6	3.7	3.7	3.6	2.4	NA	NA
Curr. Ratio	2.3	3.2	4.6	1.6	1.3	1.3	2.2	2.3	NA	NA
% LT Debt of Cap.	0.1	1.8	2.5	68.1	72.6	57.3	53.9	46.9	NA	NA
% Net Inc.of Revs.	1.2	9.0	6.8	1.3	3.1	6.4	5.5	5.1	NA	NA
% Ret. on Assets	2.3	9.2	6.3	1.1	3.4	6.1	7.2	NA	NA	NA
% Ret. on Equity	2.8	10.7	10.4	4.7	14.6	17.3	17.4	NA	NA	NA

Data as orig reptd.; bef. results of disc opers/spec. items. Per share data adj. for stk. divs. Bold denotes diluted EPS (FASB 128)-prior periods restated. E-Estimated. NA-Not Available. NM-Not Meaningful. NR-Not Ranked.

Office—Five Greentree Centre, Suite 311, Marlton, NJ 08053. **Tel**—(609) 596-8877. **Website**—http://www.medquist.com **Chrmn & CEO**—D. A. Cohen. **Pres & COO**—J. A. Donohoe. **VP, CFO & Treas**—J. R. Emery. **Dirs**—B. K. Anderson, W. T. Carson, Jr., J. T. Casey, R. J. Censits, D. A. Cohen, J. A. Donohoe, J. R. Emshoff, T. J. Mulligan, A. F. Ruttenberg, E. L. Samek, R. T. Stack, R. H. Stowe, J. H. Underwood. **Transfer Agent & Registrar**—American Stock Transfer & Trust Co., NYC. **Incorporated**—in New Jersey in 1987. **Empl**— 900. **S&P Analyst:** C.C.P.

STANDARD
&POOR'S
STOCK REPORTS

Men's Wearhouse

NASDAQ Symbol **SUIT**

In S&P SmallCap 600

09-OCT-99

Industry:
Retail (Specialty-Apparel)

Summary: One of the largest off-price specialty retailers of men's tailored business attire, this company operates more than 550 stores in the U.S. and Canada.

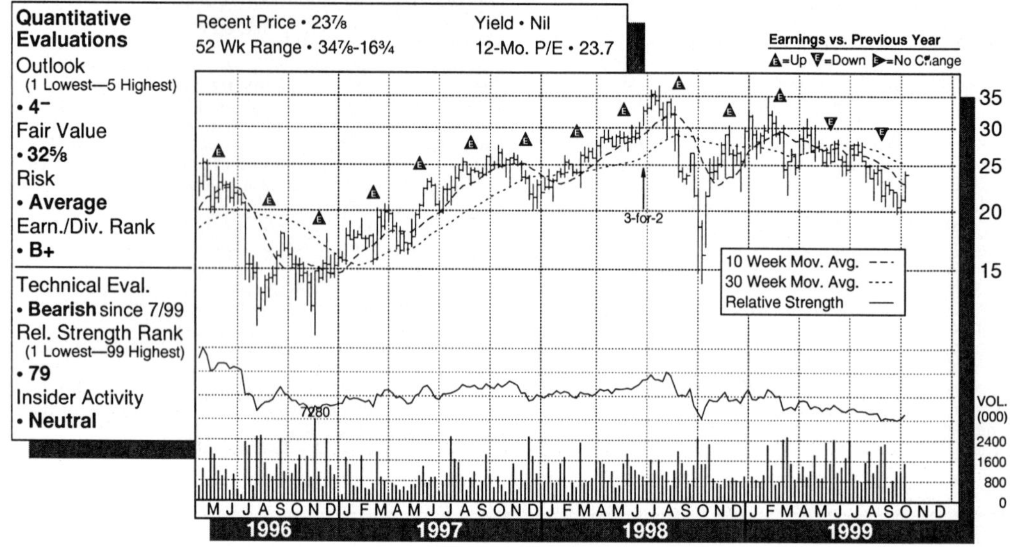

Business Profile - 23-AUG-99

This specialty retailer operates more than 550 stores, emphasizing apparel and footwear for men, at prices which the company believes are generally below the regular prices of traditional department stores. More than 400 of SUIT's stores are part of its flagship Men's Wearhouse chain, which places an emphasis on tailored business attire. The price of suits at this chain generally ranges from $199 to $599. Also, SUIT has a much smaller Value Priced Clothing (VPC) division, which addresses the market for a more price-sensitive consumer. SUIT's June 1999 acquisition of K&G Men's Center, Inc., is expected to be part of SUIT's VPC focus. Also, in February 1999, SUIT acquired Moores Retail Group, an operator of more than 100 men's apparel stores (largely in Canada) and a manufacturing facility.

Operational Review - 23-AUG-99

Net sales in the six months ended July 31, 1999, increased 13%, year to year, as restated to include a pair of pooling-of-interest acquisitions made in the first half of FY 00. Including various one-time costs, and taxes at 50.9%, versus 42.8%, income declined 32%, to $0.29 a share, from $0.45. However, excluding various costs related to acquisitions (including closing overlapping stores), pro forma income was up 28%, to $0.56 a share. Results for the FY 00 period exclude a special charge related to debt extinguishment of $0.07 a share.

Stock Performance - 08-OCT-99

In the past 30 trading days, SUIT's shares have increased 11%, compared to a 0.91% fall in the S&P 500. Average trading volume for the past five days was 297,080 shares, compared with the 40-day moving average of 283,597 shares.

Key Stock Statistics

Dividend Rate/Share	Nil	Shareholders	280
Shs. outstg. (M)	41.8	Market cap. (B)	$0.969
Avg. daily vol. (M)	0.233	Inst. holdings	57%
Tang. Bk. Value/Share	8.71		
Beta	1.44		

Value of $10,000 invested 5 years ago: $ 16,486

Fiscal Year Ending Jan. 31

	2000	1999	1998	1997	1996	1995
Revenues (Million $)						
1Q	222.2	170.9	130.6	103.7	81.36	63.93
2Q	256.6	162.9	133.9	98.89	85.71	67.20
3Q	—	170.7	146.3	110.3	92.86	73.32
4Q	—	263.5	220.2	170.7	146.4	112.7
Yr.	—	767.9	631.1	483.6	406.3	317.1
Earnings Per Share ($)						
1Q	**0.07**	**0.20**	0.13	0.10	0.07	0.06
2Q	**0.21**	**0.23**	0.17	0.13	0.10	0.08
3Q	—	**0.21**	0.17	0.12	0.10	0.08
4Q	—	**0.53**	**0.40**	0.33	0.27	0.21
Yr.	—	**1.21**	**0.87**	**0.67**	0.55	0.42

Next earnings report expected: mid November

Dividend Data

No cash dividends have been paid.

A Division of The McGraw-Hill Companies

The Men's Wearhouse, Inc.

Business Summary - 23-AUG-99

The Men's Wearhouse is one of the largest U.S. off-price retailers of men's tailored business attire. It has grown from its one store in Houston, TX, in 1973, to more than 550 stores in the U.S. and Canada. As of July 31, 1999, this included about 426 Men's Wearhouse stores, 111 stores that are related to the recently acquired Moores Retail Group business, and 52 other stores operating under various names.

In the 52 weeks ended January 30, 1999, SUIT had sales of $767.9 million, up 22% from the year before. Comparable-store sales rose 10.4%, following an 8.5% rise in the prior 52-week period. SUIT said that comparable-store sales excluded two units that were converted to a different operation, and some stores that the company has closed or was in the process of closing.

SUIT's expansion strategy includes opening traditional stores in existing and new markets, and increasing sales and profitability in existing markets. Also, in February 1999, the company acquired Moores Retail Group, which included more than 100 men's apparel stores (primarily in Canada), and a manufacturing facility in Montreal. In the transaction, SUIT issued 2.5 million common shares, and also assumed $85 million (Can.) of long-term debt. SUIT is accounting for the acquisition as a pooling of interests.

The Men's Wearhouse stores target middle- to upper-middle-income men, and offer designer brand name and private label merchandise at prices that SUIT believes are typically 20% to 30% below the regular retail prices of traditional department and specialty stores. SUIT's merchandise, which it considers conservative, includes suits, sport coats, slacks, business casual, sportswear, outerwear, dress shirts, shoes and accessories. Suits are generally offered in a price range of $199 to $599. In the fiscal year ended January 1999, 68% of SUIT's net sales were attributable to tailored apparel, down from 71% in FY 98. In FY 00, SUIT is expected to open about 40 Men's Wearhouse Stores. Also, SUIT expected that by the end of FY 00, the number of Men's Wearhouse stores offering tuxedo rentals will have increased to about 45.

SUIT launched its VPC business in late 1996 to address the market for more price-sensitive customers. The June 1, 1999, acquisition of K&G Men's Center, which operated 34 stores, is expected to be part of SUIT's VPC focus.

SUIT's advertising expenditures in the fiscal year ended January 1999 totaled $43.4 million. SUIT advertises principally on television and radio.

Starting the day after Christmas, Men's Wearhouse has a once-a-year sale that runs through January. During this period, prices on many items are reduced 20% to 50% from everyday prices. This sale reduces SUIT stock for the arrival of the new season's merchandise.

Per Share Data ($) (Year Ended Jan. 31)	1999	1998	1997	1996	1995	1994	1993	1992	1991	1990
Tangible Bk. Val.	8.55	9.97	5.07	4.39	2.97	2.13	1.54	1.34	NA	NA
Cash Flow	1.73	1.94	1.06	0.85	0.67	0.53	0.38	0.31	0.26	0.22
Earnings	1.21	0.87	0.67	0.55	0.42	0.32	0.24	0.19	0.16	0.14
Dividends	Nil	Nil	Nil	Nil	Nil	Nil	Nil	Nil	Nil	Nil
Payout Ratio	Nil	Nil	Nil	Nil	Nil	Nil	Nil	Nil	Nil	Nil
Cal. Yrs.	1998	1997	1996	1995	1994	1993	1992	1991	1990	1989
Prices - High	36 7/8	27 1/2	25 5/8	20 1/8	15 1/2	14 1/2	5 1/4	NA	NA	NA
- Low	14	15 3/8	10 7/8	8	7	4 3/4	2 1/2	NA	NA	NA
P/E Ratio - High	30	32	38	37	37	45	22	NA	NA	NA
- Low	12	18	16	15	17	15	11	NA	NA	NA
Income Statement Analysis (Million $)										
Revs.	768	631	484	406	317	240	170	133	105	80.0
Oper. Inc.	93.3	68.3	50.7	40.0	29.5	21.4	14.4	11.0	8.9	7.2
Depr.	21.6	16.8	12.6	9.4	7.1	5.6	3.6	2.6	2.1	1.5
Int. Exp.	3.0	3.6	3.4	2.5	1.8	1.1	1.0	1.5	1.4	1.0
Pretax Inc.	69.7	49.2	36.0	28.1	20.6	14.8	9.8	6.9	5.4	4.7
Eff. Tax Rate	41%	41%	41%	41%	41%	41%	40%	39%	38%	37%
Net Inc.	40.9	28.9	21.1	16.5	12.1	8.7	5.9	4.2	3.4	2.9
Balance Sheet & Other Fin. Data (Million $)										
Cash	19.7	59.9	34.1	2.5	1.2	1.6	2.4	1.1	1.8	NA
Curr. Assets	270	278	208	145	115	83.1	56.9	39.8	32.5	NA
Total Assets	404	379	295	204	160	112	78.7	54.7	43.7	30.2
Curr. Liab.	96.4	95.0	71.5	56.2	46.8	40.4	28.6	18.9	18.1	NA
LT Debt	Nil	57.5	57.5	4.7	24.6	10.8	8.9	14.8	9.8	6.5
Common Eqty.	298	220	159	137	84.9	57.9	38.4	18.3	14.1	10.8
Total Cap.	298	278	217	142	110	68.7	47.4	33.1	24.0	17.3
Cap. Exp.	46.2	27.4	26.2	22.5	23.7	12.6	10.6	5.1	3.6	3.6
Cash Flow	62.5	45.7	33.7	25.4	19.2	14.3	9.5	6.8	5.5	4.5
Curr. Ratio	2.8	2.9	2.9	2.6	2.5	2.1	2.0	2.1	1.8	NA
% LT Debt of Cap.	Nil	20.6	26.5	3.3	22.4	15.7	18.8	44.7	41.0	37.5
% Net Inc.of Revs.	5.3	4.6	4.4	4.1	3.8	3.6	3.5	3.1	3.2	3.7
% Ret. on Assets	10.5	8.6	8.5	9.1	8.7	8.8	7.9	8.5	9.1	11.2
% Ret. on Equity	15.8	15.2	14.3	14.9	16.6	27.5	18.9	25.7	26.9	31.5

Data as orig. reptd.; bef. results of disc. opers. and/or spec. items. Per share data adj. for stk. divs. as of ex-div. date. Bold denotes diluted EPS (FASB 128). E-Estimated. NA-Not Available. NM-Not Meaningful. NR-Not Ranked.

Offices—5803 Glenmont Dr., Houston, TX 77081-1701; 40650 Encyclopedia Circle, Fremont, CA 94538-2453.**Tels**—(713) 592-7200; (510) 657-9821. **Website**—http://www.menswearhouse.com **Chrmn & CEO**—G. Zimmer. **Pres**—D. H. Edwab. **COO**—E. J. Lane.**Secy**—M. W. Conlon.**Investor Contact**—Neil Davis (713 295-7200).**Dirs**—R. Brutoco, D. H. Edwab, R. E. Goldman, S. H. Greenspan, H. M. Levy, M. L. Ray, S. I. Stein, G. Zimmer, J. E. Zimmer, R. E. Zimmer. **Transfer Agent & Registrar**—American Stock Transfer & Trust Co., NYC. **Incorporated**—in Texas in 1974. **Empl**— 8,000. **S&P Analyst:** Tom Graves, CFA

STANDARD & POOR'S
STOCK REPORTS

Mentor Corp.

Nasdaq Symbol **MNTR**

In S&P SmallCap 600

09-OCT-99

Industry: Health Care (Medical Products & Supplies)

Summary: This company makes products for plastic surgery, urology and ophthalmology, including implantable devices, diagnostic and surgical instruments and disposable products.

S&P Opinion: Accumulate (★★★★)

Recent Price • 26
52 Wk Range • 28⅝-9⅞
Yield • 0.4%
12-Mo. P/E • 32.1

Quantitative Evaluations

Outlook (1 Lowest—5 Highest)
• **4+**

Fair Value
• **38⅝**

Risk
• **Average**

Earn./Div. Rank
• **B**

Technical Eval.
• **Bullish** since 6/99

Rel. Strength Rank (1 Lowest—99 Highest)
• **85**

Insider Activity
• **Neutral**

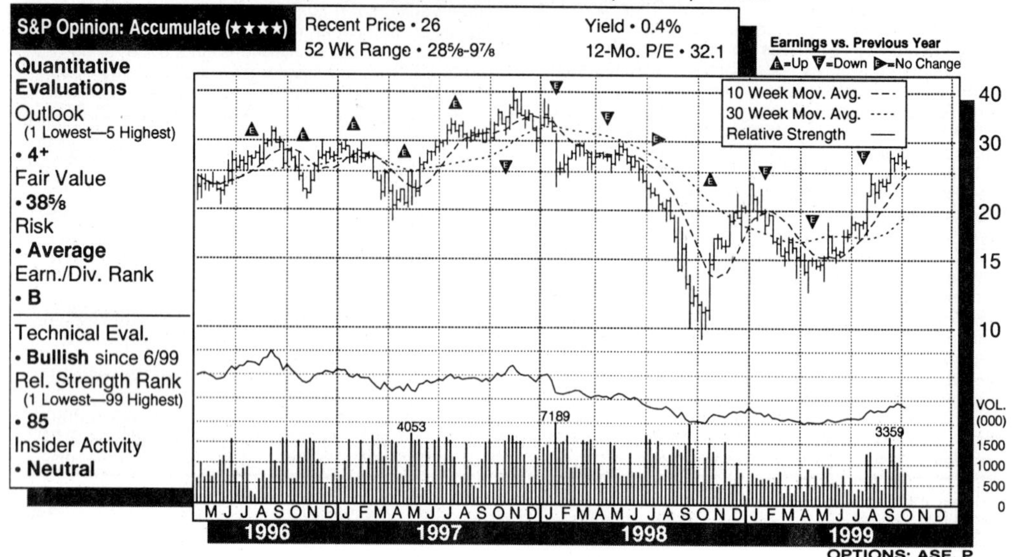

OPTIONS: ASE, P

Overview - 21-JUN-99

Excluding the ophthalmic product lines that are being sold or held for divestiture, we look for revenue growth of about 14% in FY 00 (Mar.), reflecting rising demand for prostate cancer (brachytherapy seeds) and urinary incontinence products. We do not anticipate any meaningful pickup in the penile implant segment, however, reflecting the ongoing adverse impact of drug therapy alternatives for impotence-related problems, including Pfizer's blockbuster drug Viagra. Management has agreed to sell MNTR's intraocular lens business for $38 million in cash, which should be used to enhance the urology and cosmetic surgery business lines. Margins should be enhanced by the sharpened focus on the most profitable product areas, along with recent operational restructuring initiatives, and common share earnings should benefit from stock buybacks. We look for FY 00 EPS of $1.05, and see FY 01 earnings of $1.30 a share.

Valuation - 21-JUN-99

Recent actions to improve the sustainable revenue run rate and expand operating margins are encouraging, and we look for the stock to recapture some lost value over the coming six months. Though pleased by the company's decision to exit the ophthalmic segment, we remain concerned about the chance for significant erosion in the penile implant markets. Going forward, the most promising market for MNTR appears to be within the prostate cancer area, where we look for strong demand for IoGold radioactive seeds for prostate cancer treatment, and products to treat urinary incontinence. The cosmetic surgery area should also generate steady, though not spectacular, growth. With no blockbuster products on the near term horizon, the stock appears fairly priced at recent levels, and we expect only modest P/E expansion.

Key Stock Statistics

S&P EPS Est. 2000	1.15	Tang. Bk. Value/Share	5.80
P/E on S&P Est. 2000	22.6	Beta	1.14
S&P EPS Est. 2001	1.40	Shareholders	1,800
Dividend Rate/Share	0.10	Market cap. (B)	$0.634
Shs. outstg. (M)	24.4	Inst. holdings	71%
Avg. daily vol. (M)	0.207		

Value of $10,000 invested 5 years ago: $ 40,095

Fiscal Year Ending Mar. 31

	2000	1999	1998	1997	1996	1995
Revenues (Million $)						
1Q	60.14	57.02	55.29	50.39	43.73	34.73
2Q	—	56.73	48.82	48.16	42.33	32.69
3Q	—	62.50	54.08	50.50	45.00	38.13
4Q	—	56.33	57.11	54.33	46.76	40.85
Yr.	—	202.8	215.3	203.4	177.8	146.4
Earnings Per Share ($)						
1Q	**0.28**	**0.30**	**0.30**	0.27	0.23	0.17
2Q	**E0.26**	**0.22**	**0.12**	0.24	0.21	0.15
3Q	**E0.29**	**-0.21**	**0.22**	0.27	0.23	0.19
4Q	**E0.32**	**0.19**	**0.27**	0.28	0.25	0.20
Yr.	**E1.15**	**0.80**	**0.91**	**1.06**	0.92	0.70

Next earnings report expected: mid October

Dividend Data (Dividends have been paid since 1987.)

Amount ($)	Date Decl.	Ex-Div. Date	Stock of Record	Payment Date
0.025	Dec. 14	Dec. 29	Dec. 31	Jan. 22 '99
0.025	Feb. 23	Mar. 24	Mar. 26	Apr. 16 '99
0.025	May. 18	Jun. 23	Jun. 25	Jul. 16 '99
0.025	Sep. 23	Oct. 06	Oct. 08	Oct. 29 '99

A Division of The McGraw-Hill Companies

Mentor Corporation

Business Summary - 21-JUN-99

Mentor develops, makes and markets a broad range of products for plastic and reconstructive surgery, which accounted for 50% of sales in FY 98 (Mar.); urology (32%); ophthalmology (16%); and general surgery (2%). International sales accounted for 26% of FY 98 sales.

The company makes an extensive line of implants for cosmetic and reconstructive surgery, including a line of breast implants; skin and tissue expanders, which are used to generate additional tissue for reconstruction and skin graft procedures; and facial and dermal implants, which are injected into the skin to correct scars and other skin defects. In September 1997, MNTR launched the Contour Genesis Ultrasonic Assisted Liposuction system, a liposuction surgery device.

In the area of urology, MNTR offers a line of implantable products, including penile implants for the treatment of male sexual impotence and vacuum constriction devices, used as a first-line nonsurgical treatment of male sexual impotence. Urology products also include disposable products for management of urinary incontinence or retention, and surgical products that aid in curing the problem, including Urethrin, an injectable implant currently sold outside the U.S.

In May 1997, MNTR began marketing the Suspend Sling, a surgical implant for women suffering from stress incontinence. As of October 1998, more than 3,000 women had been cured of incontinence through the procedure. In January 1998, the company launched IoGold brachytherapy seeds for the treatment of prostate cancer.

The company intends to exit the ophthalmic business during FY 00. In May 1999, an agreement was reached to sell the intraocular lens business to the eye care unit of Novartis Inc. for $48 million in cash. These products, used as replacement lenses following cataract surgery, had FY 99 sales of $15.5 million. Mentor is also seeking buyers for its ophthalmic surgical (phacoemulsifiers and hemostatic erasers) and diagnostic (tonometry, ultrasound and visual acuity testers) products; these lines had FY 99 sales of $22 million.

In May 1998, the company announced a consent agreement with the FDA. MNTR agreed to complete the revalidation of certain manufacturing processes. In connection with the project, the company has taken on about 45 additional employees; it expected to complete the process by the end of FY99.

MNTR continues to work on new and improved products in many of its principal product lines, including general surgery and ophthalmology. It is also partially funding Phase III clinical trials of the BCI-Immune Activator bladder cancer treatment.

Per Share Data ($) (Year Ended Mar. 31)	1999	1998	1997	1996	1995	1994	1993	1992	1991	1990
Tangible Bk. Val.	6.04	5.82	4.82	3.97	2.35	2.56	2.04	2.25	2.07	1.90
Cash Flow	1.14	1.26	1.35	1.20	1.04	0.80	0.13	0.42	0.45	0.51
Earnings	0.80	0.91	1.06	0.92	0.70	0.51	-0.14	0.21	0.27	0.39
Dividends	0.10	0.08	0.10	0.10	0.10	0.02	0.06	0.10	0.08	0.08
Payout Ratio	12%	8%	9%	11%	14%	4%	NM	47%	29%	20%
Cal. Yrs.	1998	1997	1996	1995	1994	1993	1992	1991	1990	1989
Prices - High	37¼	41	32½	23⅜	9⅜	8	9⅝	14⅞	10⅞	7¼
- Low	9⅜	18¾	19¼	8½	6⅜	4½	4	4¾	5	4¾
P/E Ratio - High	47	45	31	25	13	16	NM	71	40	19
- Low	12	21	18	9	9	9	NM	23	18	12
Income Statement Analysis (Million $)										
Revs.	203	215	203	178	146	124	115	89.4	73.8	50.4
Oper. Inc.	38.8	43.8	50.0	44.3	33.8	26.1	24.3	13.5	15.0	13.9
Depr.	8.6	9.1	7.8	7.2	6.8	6.2	5.6	4.7	3.9	2.4
Int. Exp.	0.3	0.0	0.6	1.1	3.1	3.7	2.5	2.3	2.2	1.8
Pretax Inc.	30.9	36.3	42.4	36.1	24.2	16.8	-4.7	6.7	8.9	12.6
Eff. Tax Rate	34%	34%	34%	34%	35%	35%	NM	33%	33%	33%
Net Inc.	20.4	23.9	27.9	23.8	15.7	11.0	-2.8	4.5	5.9	8.4
Balance Sheet & Other Fin. Data (Million $)										
Cash	21.6	27.9	27.8	18.5	11.3	10.3	8.2	6.1	9.7	31.0
Curr. Assets	142	128	116	102	81.0	70.1	61.4	47.0	42.9	50.5
Total Assets	196	201	167	150	129	121	110	90.3	84.5	74.3
Curr. Liab.	35.2	32.6	27.6	31.7	27.3	30.4	26.3	18.2	14.6	7.7
LT Debt	Nil	Nil	0.0	0.1	24.6	25.4	24.4	24.4	26.0	26.0
Common Eqty.	159	165	138	116	71.1	54.7	43.4	47.7	43.9	40.3
Total Cap.	161	169	139	118	95.8	80.0	67.8	72.1	69.9	66.6
Cap. Exp.	10.8	15.8	8.3	NA	NA	NA	7.3	NA	NA	NA
Cash Flow	29.1	33.0	35.6	31.0	22.6	17.2	2.8	9.2	9.9	10.8
Curr. Ratio	4.0	3.9	4.2	3.2	3.0	2.3	2.3	2.6	2.9	6.6
% LT Debt of Cap.	Nil	NM	–	0.1	25.7	31.7	35.9	33.8	37.1	39.0
% Net Inc.of Revs.	10.1	11.1	13.8	13.4	10.7	8.9	NM	5.0	8.0	16.7
% Ret. on Assets	NA	13.0	17.7	17.1	12.6	9.5	NM	5.2	7.5	11.9
% Ret. on Equity	NA	15.8	21.9	25.4	25.1	22.4	NM	9.8	14.1	22.7

Data as orig reptd.; bef. results of disc opers/spec. items. Per share data adj. for stk. divs. Bold denotes diluted EPS (FASB 128)-prior periods restated. E-Estimated. NA-Not Available. NM-Not Meaningful. NR-Not Ranked.

Office—5425 Hollister Ave., Santa Barbara, CA 93111. **Tel**—(805) 681-6000. **Chrmn & CEO**—C. J. Conway. **Pres, COO & Secy**—A. R. Gette. **VP-Fin, CFO & Treas**—G. E. Mistlin. **Dirs**—C. J. Conway, W. W. Faster, A. R. Gette, E. G. Glover, M. Nakonechny, B. G. Shaffer, R. W. Young. **Transfer Agent & Registrar**—American Stock Transfer & Trust Co., NYC. **Incorporated**—in Minnesota in 1969. **Empl**— 1,612. **S&P Analyst:** Robert M. Gold

Mercury Interactive

Nasdaq Symbol **MERQ**

In S&P SmallCap 600

09-OCT-99

Industry: Computer (Software & Services)

Summary: MERQ develops, markets and supports a family of automated client/server and Web-based system software tools for testing business-critical enterprise applications.

S&P Opinion: Hold (★★★)

Recent Price • 68
52 Wk Range • 72-13¾
Yield • Nil
12-Mo. P/E • 98.6

Quantitative Evaluations

Outlook
(1 Lowest—5 Highest)
• **3⁻**

Fair Value
• **77⅝**

Risk
• **High**

Earn./Div. Rank
• **NR**

Technical Eval.
• **Bullish** since 5/99

Rel. Strength Rank
(1 Lowest—99 Highest)
• **96**

Insider Activity
• **Unfavorable**

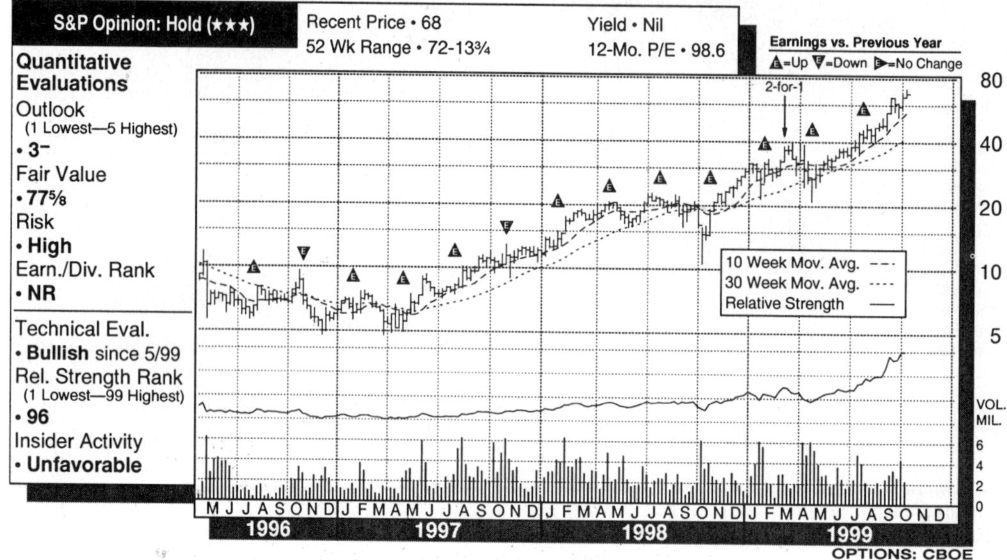

Overview - 28-SEP-99

IT spending continues to accelerate as corporations and institutions make the transition to Internet Protocol-based applications. This is driving demand for MERQ's automated software testing solutions. Along with this trend, a rush by organizations to test systems for Year 2000 compliance, have been the primary forces behind demand for MERQ's automated software testing tools; however, Y2K testing revenue by its nature is likely to trail off over the next several quarters. We forecast 40%-42% revenue growth for 1999, as a strong followup to the 57% increase in 1998. Royalty payments paid on products developed under prior research grants from Israeli government sources may inch up, as may company-funded R&D, as it expects to rely less on such grants in the future. We look for EPS to rise 40% to $0.78 in 1999, with a further 41% increase to $1.10 in 2000.

Valuation - 28-SEP-99

We rate MERQ hold on the basis of valuation. While the company is experiencing very strong growth, the shares trade at a premium to the software industry. Therefore, we think it is difficult to envision the shares outperforming from their current level. Also, we are concerned that during the latter part of 1999, sales of the company's Y2K testing solutions should wind down. This expected drop-off is the reason we forecast 40% revenue growth for all of 1999, even though revenues in the first half soared 62%. The stock price would likely crater if the company failed to meet current lofty expectations. More likely is for the company to continue to enjoy good earnings growth, but for the stock price to be range bound over the next several months. Unless the stock were to undergo an unwarranted sell-off, perhaps due to overblown Y2K fears, we would hold off making any new purchases in the short term.

Key Stock Statistics

S&P EPS Est. 1999	0.78	Tang. Bk. Value/Share	3.98
P/E on S&P Est. 1999	87.2	Beta	1.21
S&P EPS Est. 2000	1.10	Shareholders	5,500
Dividend Rate/Share	Nil	Market cap. (B)	$ 2.6
Shs. outstg. (M)	37.9	Inst. holdings	93%
Avg. daily vol. (M)	0.616		

Value of $10,000 invested 5 years ago: $ 78,840

Fiscal Year Ending Dec. 31

	1999	1998	1997	1996	1995	1994
Revenues (Million $)						
1Q	37.60	22.20	15.40	11.00	7.70	4.30
2Q	42.50	27.20	17.50	12.10	9.00	5.25
3Q	—	30.60	19.60	14.20	10.25	6.40
4Q	—	41.00	24.20	17.25	12.50	7.50
Yr.	—	121.0	76.70	54.55	39.45	23.45
Earnings Per Share ($)						
1Q	**0.14**	**0.08**	**0.06**	**-0.02**	0.04	0.03
2Q	**0.18**	**0.10**	**0.07**	**0.03**	-0.07	0.04
3Q	**E0.19**	**0.14**	**-0.07**	**0.05**	0.08	0.05
4Q	**E0.27**	**0.23**	**0.14**	**0.10**	-0.22	0.07
Yr.	**E0.78**	**0.56**	**0.20**	**0.14**	**-0.19**	**0.19**

Next earnings report expected: late October

Dividend Data

Amount ($)	Date Decl.	Ex-Div. Date	Stock of Record	Payment Date
2-for-1	Jan. 28	Mar. 01	Feb. 12	Feb. 26 '99

Mercury Interactive Corporation

Business Summary - 28-SEP-99

Mercury Interactive Corp. develops, markets and supports a family of automated client/server and Web-based (Internet and intranet) tools for testing business-critical software applications. MERQ's products allow corporate development organizations, system integrators and independent software developers to identify client/server system problems with greater accuracy, speed and efficiency than traditional methods allow. The company is committed to its research and development efforts in order to achieve its strategy of offering advanced and innovative testing solutions for evolving business needs. Research and development costs rose to $15.7 million in 1998, from $10.9 million in 1997.

Mercury's automated software quality products allow developers of client/server software to compress software development cycles, reduce costs and improve software quality throughout the development, maintenance and porting process by automating the tedious, highly structured and error-prone manual testing process.

The company's XRunner product is an automated GUI regression tool that tests X Window applications running under UNIX. XRunner makes test development easier by incorporating simplified test script management, point-and-click selection and interactive debugging. WinRunner tests client/server GUI applications on Windows 3.1, Windows 95 and Windows NT platforms. LoadRunner is an integrated client/server and Web load testing tool. It provides a scalable load testing solution for managing the risks of client/server systems. The company's TestDirector is a workgroup test management software that directs the quality assurance process for software development. WebTest is designed specifically for testing Web applications. Astra SiteManager, SiteTest, and QuickTest are used for web site management, stress testing, and functional testing, respectively.

The company markets its products primarily through its direct sales and service organization, which focuses on major accounts. Current customers include Allstate Insurance, Citibank, DHL Airways, Gap, Inc., Michelin, Nabisco, and Quebec/Hydro, among others. International sales accounted for 35%, 36%, and 33% of total revenues in 1998, 1997 and 1996, respectively.

In addition to its own sales force, MERQ has an indirect sales channel of value added resellers and major system integrators, including Andersen Consulting, Deloitte & Touche, EDS and KPMG Peat Marwick. The indirect sales channel accounted for 50%, 47%, and 43% of total license revenues in 1998, 1997 and 1996, respectively. The company believes that the indirect sales channel will account for an increasingly significant portion of total revenue in future periods.

Per Share Data ($) **(Year Ended Dec. 31)**	**1998**	**1997**	**1996**	**1995**	**1994**	**1993**	**1992**	**1991**	**1990**	**1989**
Tangible Bk. Val.	3.98	3.38	3.08	2.94	1.53	1.32	-2.19	NA	NA	NA
Cash Flow	0.66	0.31	0.24	-0.11	0.23	0.09	-0.66	NA	NA	NA
Earnings	0.56	0.20	0.14	-0.19	0.19	0.06	-0.75	NA	NA	NA
Dividends	Nil	Nil	Nil	Nil	Nil	Nil	Nil	NA	NA	NA
Payout Ratio	Nil	Nil	Nil	Nil	Nil	Nil	Nil	NA	NA	NA
Prices - High	31 5/8	14 1/8	12	14 1/2	10 7/8	11 1/2	NA	NA	NA	NA
- Low	10 5/8	4 3/4	4 3/4	5 7/8	3 1/2	6 1/2	NA	NA	NA	NA
P/E Ratio - High	56	NM	86	NM	57	NM	NA	NA	NA	NA
- Low	19	NM	34	NM	18	NA	NA	NA	NA	NA
Income Statement Analysis (Million $)										
Revs.	121	76.7	54.6	39.5	23.5	13.0	4.3	NA	NA	NA
Oper. Inc.	26.8	10.3	6.1	-4.3	5.8	1.8	-3.0	NA	NA	NA
Depr.	4.1	3.7	3.3	2.2	1.2	0.6	0.4	NA	NA	NA
Int. Exp.	Nil	Nil	Nil	Nil	0.0	0.1	0.0	NA	NA	NA
Pretax Inc.	27.3	9.6	5.8	-4.3	5.9	1.4	-3.3	NA	NA	NA
Eff. Tax Rate	20%	30%	20%	NM	15%	3.90%	Nil	NA	NA	NA
Net Inc.	21.8	6.7	4.6	-5.3	5.0	1.4	-3.3	NA	NA	NA
Balance Sheet & Other Fin. Data (Million $)										
Cash	96.1	57.2	71.0	77.8	33.3	33.7	6.3	NA	NA	NA
Curr. Assets	154	119	96.5	95.7	44.1	39.4	9.3	NA	NA	NA
Total Assets	204	143	117	113	49.6	41.7	11.1	NA	NA	NA
Curr. Liab.	58.0	30.4	18.5	20.2	10.4	8.2	4.8	NA	NA	NA
LT Debt	Nil	Nil	Nil	Nil	Nil	0.4	0.5	NA	NA	NA
Common Eqty.	146	113	99	92.6	39.2	33.0	-7.0	NA	NA	NA
Total Cap.	146	112	99	92.6	39.2	33.4	6.2	NA	NA	NA
Cap. Exp.	14.9	11.8	4.6	7.0	3.2	1.3	0.9	NA	NA	NA
Cash Flow	25.9	10.4	7.9	3.1	6.2	2.0	-2.9	NA	NA	NA
Curr. Ratio	2.6	3.9	5.2	4.7	4.2	4.8	1.9	NA	NA	NA
% LT Debt of Cap.	Nil	Nil	Nil	Nil	Nil	1.3	7.7	NA	NA	NA
% Net Inc.of Revs.	18.0	8.7	8.5	NM	21.5	10.5	NM	NA	NA	NA
% Ret. on Assets	12.6	5.1	4.0	NM	10.9	2.1	NM	NA	NA	NA
% Ret. on Equity	16.9	6.3	4.8	NM	13.8	NM	NM	NA	NA	NA

Data as orig reptd.; bef. results of disc opers/spec. items. Per share data adj. for stk. divs. Bold denotes diluted EPS (FASB 128)-prior periods restated. E-Estimated. NA-Not Available. NM-Not Meaningful. NR-Not Ranked.

Office—1325 Borregas Ave., Sunnyvale, CA 94089. **Tel**—(408) 822-5200. **Fax**—(408) 523-9911. **Website**—http://www.merc-int.com **Chrmn, Pres & CEO**—A. Landan. **VP-Fin, CFO & Secy**—S. Abrams. **Investor Contact**—Anne Marie McCauley (408-822-5359). **Dirs**—I. Kohavi, A. Landan, Y. Shamir, G. Yaron. **Transfer Agent & Registrar**—ChaseMellon Shareholder Services, SF. **Incorporated**—in Delaware in 1989. **Empl**— 621. **S&P Analyst:** Mark S. Basham

STANDARD
&POOR'S
STOCK REPORTS

Merrill Corp.

NASDAQ Symbol **MRLL**

In S&P SmallCap 600

09-OCT-99 **Industry:** Specialty Printing

Summary: This document management services company has agreed to be acquired for $22 a share in cash.

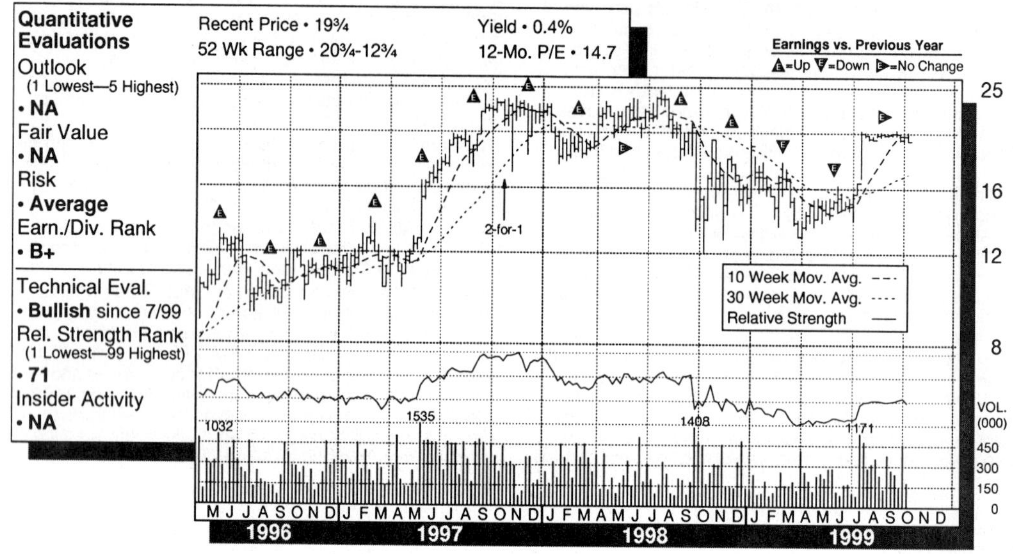

Business Profile - 15-SEP-99

In July 1999, MRLL agreed to be acquired by Viking Merger Sub, Inc., a newly formed affiliate of DLJ Merchant Banking Partners II, which in turn is a subsidiary of Donaldson, Lufkin & Jenrette Inc. MRLL shareholders will receive $22 a share in cash. After the closing, a significant amount of MRLL's outstanding stock will be owned by employees of the company, with the remainder to be owned by DLJ Merchant and affiliated entities. The transaction, valued at $500 million, will be treated as a recapitalization for accounting purposes. Revenue growth was limited and profits were hurt in the second quarter of 1999 as the number of transactions filed in the financial markets significantly lagged behind last year.

Operational Review - 15-SEP-99

Revenues in the six months ended July 31, 1999, rose 10%, year to year, as gains in other businesses offset a decline in financial transaction revenue. Despite well controlled selling, general and administrative expenses, profitability declined on fewer large, high-margin jobs in the Financial Document Services division; operating profit fell 11%. Results were further hindered by merger costs, higher net other expense, and taxes at 45.1%, versus 44.5%. Net income was down 24% to $12.7 million ($0.77 a share, on 4.2% fewer shares), from $16.7 million ($0.97).

Stock Performance - 08-OCT-99

In the past 30 trading days, MRLL's shares have declined 2%, compared to a 0.91% fall in the S&P 500. Average trading volume for the past five days was 35,260 shares, compared with the 40-day moving average of 54,097 shares.

Key Stock Statistics

Dividend Rate/Share	0.08	Shareholders	2,125
Shs. outstg. (M)	16.1	Market cap. (B)	$0.318
Avg. daily vol. (M)	0.056	Inst. holdings	63%
Tang. Bk. Value/Share	5.78		
Beta	0.74		

Value of $10,000 invested 5 years ago: $ 15,128

Fiscal Year Ending Jan. 31

	2000	1999	1998	1997	1996	1995
Revenues (Million $)						
1Q	131.8	123.5	109.9	71.20	57.43	61.46
2Q	166.2	148.5	115.6	87.57	62.70	63.68
3Q	—	119.8	112.1	93.78	62.47	57.47
4Q	—	117.8	122.0	101.2	62.70	54.26
Yr.	—	509.5	459.5	353.8	245.3	236.9
Earnings Per Share ($)						
1Q	**0.27**	**0.47**	**0.47**	**0.27**	0.13	0.29
2Q	**0.50**	**0.50**	**0.38**	**0.29**	0.17	0.28
3Q	—	**0.38**	**0.33**	**0.27**	0.19	0.14
4Q	—	**0.20**	**0.36**	**0.28**	0.18	0.05
Yr.	—	**1.55**	**1.54**	**1.11**	**0.68**	**0.77**

Next earnings report expected: early December

Dividend Data (Dividends have been paid since 1993.)

Amount ($)	Date Decl.	Ex-Div. Date	Stock of Record	Payment Date
0.020	Jan. 08	Jan. 12	Dec. 31	Jan. 15 '99
0.020	Mar. 18	Mar. 29	Mar. 31	Apr. 15 '99
0.020	Jun. 15	Jun. 28	Jun. 30	Jul. 15 '99
0.020	Sep. 16	Sep. 28	Sep. 30	Oct. 15 '99

A Division of The McGraw-Hill Companies

Merrill Corporation

Business Summary - 15-SEP-99

Merrill provides a full range of typesetting, printing, document management and reproduction, distribution and marketing services to financial, legal, investment companies and corporate markets. In July 1999, MRLL agreed to be acquired by Viking Merger Sub, Inc., a newly-formed affiliate of DLJ Merchant Banking Partners II. DLJ Merchant is a subsidiary of Donaldson, Lufkin & Jenrette Inc. (NYSE: DLJ). Under the terms of the agreement, MRLL shareholders will receive $22 a share in cash. After the closing, a significant amount of MRLL's outstanding stock will be owned by employees of the company, and the remainder will be owned by DLJ Merchant and affiliated entities. The transaction is valued at $500 million and will be treated as a recapitalization for accounting purposes.

MRLL has 36 U.S. locations, and is involved in joint ventures in Canada, Europe, Asia and Australia. Operations are in two segments: specialty communication services and document services.

The specialty communication services segment, which provided 88% of revenues in FY 99 (Jan.), consists of four units: financial document services, investment company services, managed communications programs, and the Merrill Print Group.

The financial printing operation, which accounted for 37% of revenues in FY 99, involves production and distribution of time-sensitive financial documents, such as registration statements and prospectuses. Corporate printing (31% of revenues) consists of documents that are provided at regular intervals, including annual and quarterly reports, and proxy statements. The final document is filed with the proper regulatory authorities, and then prepared for printed distribution. MRLL also offers electronic filing both with the SEC, through the EDGAR system, and in Canada, through the SEDAR system.

Commercial and other revenue (20% of revenues) provides marketing, printing and distribution services designed to promote corporate identity of large national customers with multiple franchises, members, divisions or affiliates, such as real estate companies, fast-food restaurants, and credit card companies.

The Merrill Print group was created in February 1999, to manage all of the company's printing operations. In April 1999, MRLL acquired Daniels Printing, which provides financial, corporate and commercial printing services.

Document management services (12% of revenues) provides comprehensive document management services, which can include management of the client's entire photocopying, desktop publishing, imaging, and mailroom facilities. A software product can be provided that allows customers to electronically image, code and retrieve documents for litigation management.

Per Share Data ($) (Year Ended Jan. 31)	1999	1998	1997	1996	1995	1994	1993	1992	1991	1990
Tangible Bk. Val.	5.78	4.98	3.92	4.28	4.28	2.80	2.68	2.06	1.60	1.41
Cash Flow	2.59	2.45	1.92	1.35	1.36	1.17	0.82	0.64	0.43	0.06
Earnings	1.55	1.54	1.09	0.67	0.75	0.82	0.56	0.43	0.18	-0.09
Dividends	0.08	0.07	0.06	0.06	0.06	0.05	Nil	Nil	Nil	Nil
Payout Ratio	5%	5%	5%	9%	8%	6%	Nil	Nil	Nil	Nil
Cal. Yrs.	1998	1997	1996	1995	1994	1993	1992	1991	1990	1989
Prices - High	24 3/4	24 1/4	13 1/4	10 5/8	16 1/4	14	7 7/8	6 5/8	2 3/4	2 7/8
- Low	12	10 1/4	7 1/8	7	6 7/8	6 3/4	4 1/8	1 3/4	1 3/8	1 9/16
P/E Ratio - High	16	16	12	16	22	17	14	15	15	NM
- Low	8	7	7	10	9	8	7	4	7	NM
Income Statement Analysis (Million $)										
Revs.	510	460	354	245	237	182	148	125	101	69.0
Oper. Inc.	68.8	65.4	50.0	30.3	31.5	27.5	18.2	14.2	7.6	2.6
Depr.	17.6	15.4	13.4	10.8	9.8	5.5	4.1	3.1	3.5	2.1
Int. Exp.	4.0	4.3	4.1	1.1	1.1	0.3	0.3	0.5	0.6	0.3
Pretax Inc.	47.7	46.5	32.5	18.7	21.2	22.0	14.2	10.8	4.1	-0.9
Eff. Tax Rate	45%	44%	45%	43%	43%	40%	39%	40%	38%	NM
Net Inc.	26.5	26.0	17.8	10.7	12.0	13.2	8.6	6.5	2.7	-1.2
Balance Sheet & Other Fin. Data (Million $)										
Cash	23.5	2.5	5.2	12.1	10.0	2.6	9.6	6.3	1.2	1.2
Curr. Assets	158	150	127	79.2	63.5	59.4	48.0	37.7	30.6	24.3
Total Assets	266	246	202	126	202	100	66.0	53.0	46.9	40.6
Curr. Liab.	76.7	71.1	57.4	39.9	31.9	36.9	23.3	21.0	21.2	16.4
LT Debt	39.5	40.2	40.9	6.5	7.5	8.7	2.1	2.2	2.3	2.4
Common Eqty.	141	126	96.2	77.7	66.1	53.6	39.3	29.1	22.5	20.5
Total Cap.	181	67.5	139	84.2	73.6	62.9	42.7	32.0	25.7	24.2
Cap. Exp.	16.5	17.1	9.2	12.5	10.1	7.9	7.5	2.6	2.8	5.0
Cash Flow	44.1	41.5	31.2	21.5	21.8	18.7	12.7	9.7	6.2	0.8
Curr. Ratio	2.1	2.1	2.2	2.0	2.0	1.6	2.0	1.8	1.4	1.5
% LT Debt of Cap.	21.9	24.0	29.4	7.7	10.2	13.8	5.0	7.0	9.0	9.9
% Net Inc.of Revs.	5.2	5.7	5.0	4.4	5.1	7.3	5.8	5.2	2.6	NM
% Ret. on Assets	10.3	11.6	10.9	9.2	11.5	15.7	14.2	13.0	6.2	NM
% Ret. on Equity	19.8	23.5	20.5	14.9	19.9	28.1	24.8	25.2	12.6	NM

Data as orig reptd.; bef. results of disc opers/spec. items. Per share data adj. for stk. divs. Bold denotes diluted EPS (FASB 128)-prior periods restated. E-Estimated. NA-Not Available. NM-Not Meaningful. NR-Not Ranked.

Office—One Merrill Circle, St. Paul, MN 55108. **Tel**—(612) 646-4501. **Website**—http://www.merrillcorp.com **Chrmn**—P. G. Miller. **Pres & CEO**—J. W. Castro. **VP-Fin, CFO & Treas**—K. A. Barber. **Secy**—S. J. Machov. **Dirs**—R. R. Atterbury, J. R. Campbell, J. W. Castro, R. N. Hoge, F. W. Kanner, R. G. Lareau, P. G. Miller, M. S. Morton, R. F. Nienhouse. **Transfer Agent & Registrar**—First Trust Co. Inc., St. Paul. **Incorporated**—in Minnesota in 1968. **Empl**— 3,797. **S&P Analyst:** Jordan Horoschak

STANDARD
&POOR'S
STOCK REPORTS

Mesa Air Group

NASDAQ Symbol **MESA**

In S&P SmallCap 600

09-OCT-99 **Industry:** Airlines

Summary: MESA is one of the largest independently owned regional airlines in the world, serving nearly 140 cities in the U.S., Canada and Mexico.

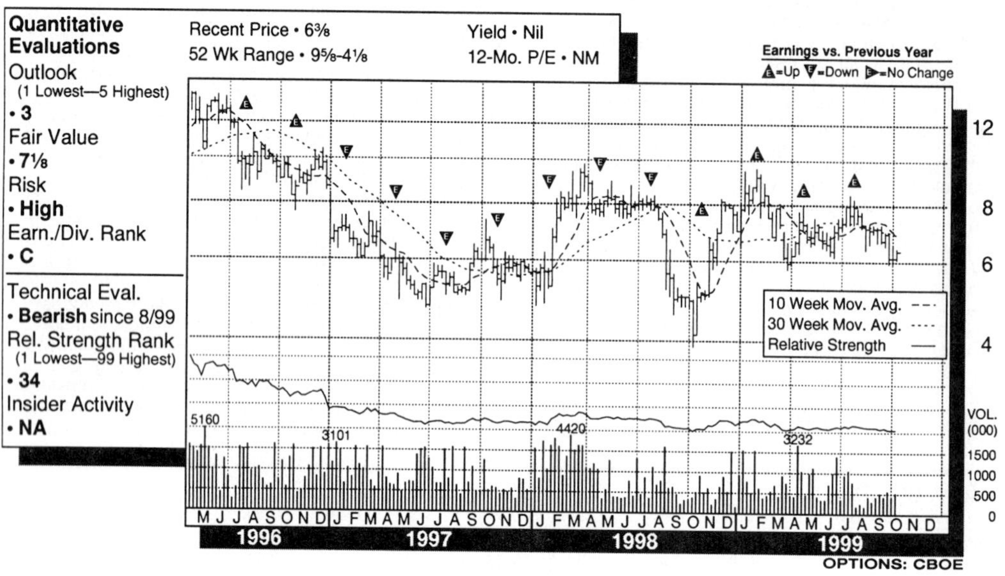

Business Profile - 05-AUG-99

In June 1999, MESA acquired CCAIR, Inc., a Charlotte, NC based regional airline operating 31 aircraft as US Airways Express, in a deal valued at about $50.7 million. Under the terms of the deal, shareholders of CCAIR received 0.6214 of a common share of MESA for each outstanding share of CCAIR common stock. While the third quarter of FY 99 (Sep.) marked MESA's fourth consecutive quarterly profit, the company expressed concern that its margins were still among the lowest in the industry, particularly in turbo prop operations. Looking forward, the company intends to expand its regional jet fleet.

Operational Review - 05-AUG-99

Total operating revenues (as restated) in the nine months ended June 30 1999, fell 24%, year to year, reflecting a 36% decrease in passengers carried, due to the discontinuation of the company's United Airlines Express (UAE) operations. Total operating expenses fell at a faster rate and operating income contrasted with an operating loss. With a 19% drop in non-operating expenses and after no taxes, versus a tax benefit of $2.5 million, net income of $10,846,000 ($0.32 a share), contrasted with a net loss of $53,220,000 ($1.57).

Stock Performance - 08-OCT-99

In the past 30 trading days, MESA's shares have declined 11%, compared to a 0.91% fall in the S&P 500. Average trading volume for the past five days was 102,080 shares, compared with the 40-day moving average of 88,449 shares.

Key Stock Statistics

Dividend Rate/Share	Nil	Shareholders	1,236
Shs. outstg. (M)	33.8	Market cap. (B)	$0.215
Avg. daily vol. (M)	0.093	Inst. holdings	57%
Tang. Bk. Value/Share	3.04		
Beta	1.88		

Value of $10,000 invested 5 years ago: $ 3,574

Fiscal Year Ending Sep. 30

	1999	1998	1997	1996	1995	1994
Revenues (Million $)						
1Q	77.12	124.6	121.4	120.0	102.0	92.00
2Q	77.94	119.6	125.4	121.0	106.0	94.00
3Q	105.3	99.5	129.4	130.3	118.0	102.0
4Q	—	79.83	134.7	129.1	128.0	108.0
Yr.	—	423.5	511.0	500.4	455.0	396.0
Earnings Per Share ($)						
1Q	**0.08**	**-1.38**	**-0.03**	0.12	0.08	0.21
2Q	**0.10**	**-0.47**	-0.03	0.39	Nil	0.17
3Q	**0.14**	**-0.15**	-0.09	0.23	0.11	0.20
4Q	—	**0.11**	-1.57	0.29	0.23	0.17
Yr.	—	**-1.89**	-1.72	—	0.42	0.75

Next earnings report expected: mid November

Dividend Data

Mesa has never paid cash dividends and does not intend to pay any in the foreseeable future. The shares were split two for one in March 1993 and three for two in August and January 1992.

A Division of The McGraw-Hill Companies

Mesa Air Group, Inc.

Business Summary - 05-AUG-99

When former Chairman and CEO Larry Risley bought one airplane and a few parts in August 1982, few would have believed that the company he started would grow up to become one of the nation's largest independently-owned regional airlines. Today, Mesa Air Group Inc. (MESA), serves 139 cities in 31 states, the District of Columbia, Toronto, Canada and Guaymas and Hermasillo, Mexico. MESA operates as America West Express in the Southwest, US Airways Express throughout the East Coast and Midwest, and independently as Mesa Airlines in New Mexico and Colorado. As of December 31, 1998, MESA operated a fleet of 107 aircraft with about 1,000 daily departures.

MESA's long-term business strategy is to operate a competitive and profitable, high-frequency, airline, primarily with a hub-and-spoke system. The strategy is implemented through a disciplined approach to the regional airline business which incorporates regional diversification; focus on profitable markets; reactions to the changing economic and competitive environment; and a modern, efficient aircraft fleet that positions the airline to be able to capitalize on future growth opportunities.

Since 1978, airlines in the U.S. have been free to set their own domestic fares without governmental regulation. MESA has increasingly relied on fee per departure contractual agreements with its two code-sharing partners to generate revenue. All of MESA's America West Express operations (except Guaymas and Hermasillo, Mexico) and all its US Airways Express jet operations are on a fee per departure basis. MESA expects the percentage of revenue generated under the fee per departure agreements to significantly increase in 1999, as the company adds additional regional jets to its America West Express and US Airways Express operations. Mesa derives the remainder of its passenger revenues from a combination of local fares, through fares, and joint fares.

In June 1999, MESA acquired CCAIR, Inc., a Charlotte, NC based regional airline operating 31 aircraft as US Airways Express, in a deal valued at about $50.7 million. Under the terms of the deal, shareholders of CCAIR received 0.6214 of a common share of MESA for each outstanding share of CCAIR common stock.

Per Share Data ($) (Year Ended Sep. 30)	1998	1997	1996	1995	1994	1993	1992	1991	1990	1989
Tangible Bk. Val.	3.54	5.48	6.06	5.84	6.43	5.74	2.81	2.25	NA	NA
Cash Flow	-0.98	-0.49	1.80	1.05	1.16	1.12	0.98	0.85	NA	NA
Earnings	-1.89	-1.72	1.00	0.42	0.75	0.73	0.50	0.39	NA	NA
Dividends	Nil	Nil	Nil	Nil	Nil	Nil	Nil	Nil	NA	NA
Payout Ratio	Nil	Nil	Nil	Nil	Nil	Nil	Nil	Nil	NA	NA
Prices - High	9 3/4	7 5/8	13 7/8	12	23	24	16 5/8	5 1/4	NA	NA
- Low	3 7/8	4 5/8	6 1/2	4 7/8	6	14	4 5/8	1 7/8	NA	NA
P/E Ratio - High	NM	NM	14	29	31	33	33	13	NA	NA
- Low	NM	NM	6	12	8	19	9	5	NA	NA
Income Statement Analysis (Million $)										
Revs.	424	511	500	455	396	354	317	NA	NA	NA
Oper. Inc.	21.4	48.3	75.3	50.5	63.5	61.2	37.5	NA	NA	NA
Depr.	25.7	34.9	24.3	20.9	15.1	13.1	11.9	NA	NA	NA
Int. Exp.	22.5	27.8	12.8	6.4	7.9	5.4	4.9	NA	NA	NA
Pretax Inc.	-61.2	-79.2	49.5	23.0	44.0	40.3	22.5	NA	NA	NA
Eff. Tax Rate	NM	NM	39%	39%	38%	38%	36%	NA	NA	NA
Net Inc.	-53.4	-48.6	30.4	14.0	27.3	25.0	14.3	NA	NA	NA
Balance Sheet & Other Fin. Data (Million $)										
Cash	35.6	57.2	60.0	109	99	135	NA	NA	NA	NA
Curr. Assets	102	167	134	176	174	186	NA	NA	NA	NA
Total Assets	471	650	678	447	420	399	NA	NA	NA	NA
Curr. Liab.	99	98.1	63.6	55.6	43.7	60.5	NA	NA	NA	NA
LT Debt	234	338	338	78.4	91.8	91.7	NA	NA	NA	NA
Common Eqty.	121	177	225	256	234	215	NA	NA	NA	NA
Total Cap.	355	517	585	363	351	323	NA	NA	NA	NA
Cap. Exp.	8.1	4.6	20.3	92.3	32.6	38.9	30.0	NA	NA	NA
Cash Flow	-27.7	-13.7	54.7	34.9	42.4	38.2	26.2	NA	NA	NA
Curr. Ratio	1.0	1.7	2.1	3.2	4.0	3.1	NA	NA	NA	NA
% LT Debt of Cap.	65.9	65.4	57.8	21.6	26.1	28.4	NA	NA	NA	NA
% Net Inc.of Revs.	NM	NM	6.1	3.1	6.9	7.1	4.5	NA	NA	NA
% Ret. on Assets	NM	NM	5.4	3.2	6.6	6.7	NA	NA	NA	NA
% Ret. on Equity	NM	NM	12.7	5.7	12.1	11.5	NA	NA	NA	NA

Data as orig reptd.; bef. results of disc opers/spec. items. Per share data adj. for stk. divs. Bold denotes diluted EPS (FASB 128)-prior periods restated. E-Estimated. NA-Not Available. NM-Not Meaningful. NR-Not Ranked.

Office—410 North 44th St.., Suite 700, Phoenix, AZ 85008. **Tel**—(602) 685-4000. **Website**—http://www.mesa-air.com **Chrmn, Pres & CEO**—J. G. Ornstein. **Vice Chrmn**—P. R. Madden. **CFO**—M. Lotz. **Dirs**—D. J. Altobello, J. Braly, H. A. Denton, R. R. Fogleman, P. R. Madden, J. Ornstein, M. Parker, L. L. Risley, J. Swigart. **Transfer Agent & Registrar**—American Securities Transfer, Denver. **Incorporated**—in Nevada in 1996; originally organized in New Mexico in 1983. **Empl**— 2,500. **S&P Analyst:** M.I.

STANDARD
&POOR'S
STOCK REPORTS

Methode Electronics

NASDAQ Symbol **METHA**

In S&P SmallCap 600

09-OCT-99

Industry:
Electronics (Instrumentation)

Summary: Methode manufactures component devices for OEMs of electronic data processing equipment, communication systems and automobiles.

Quantitative Evaluations

Outlook
(1 Lowest—5 Highest)
• 3

Fair Value
• 23⅝

Risk
• Average

Earn./Div. Rank
• B+

Technical Eval.
• **Bearish** since 9/99

Rel. Strength Rank
(1 Lowest—99 Highest)
• 63

Insider Activity
• NA

Recent Price • 19¼
52 Wk Range • 24½-10
Yield • 1.0%
12-Mo. P/E • 20.3

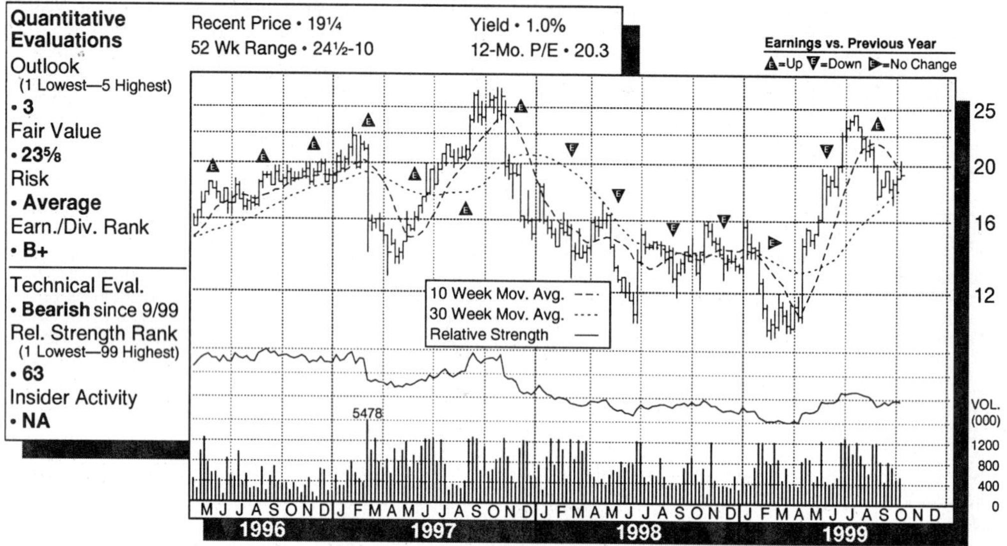

Business Profile - 12-JUL-99

The company believes it is well positioned to benefit from strong expected growth in the optoelectronics market. In addition, Methode expects the future performance of its electronics group to be positive, reflecting the launch of new programs with its automotive customers. In order to focus on higher growth businesses, the company recently decided to exit the printed circuit board business; it intends to divest its board manufacturing facilities in California and New Jersey. Through June 21, 1999, Methode had purchased 275,000 of its shares under an authorization to buy back up to $20 million of common stock. In May 1999, the company acquired Polycore Technologies, a developer of data communications modules for LAN equipment.

Operational Review - 12-JUL-99

Based on a preliminary report, revenues advanced 6.4% in FY 99 (Apr.), reflecting strong growth in optical products, as well as higher sales of automotive interconnect devices. Margins narrowed, restricted by costs of increased engineering support, new product launches, and product development. After a $3.1 million provision to exit the printed circuit business, pretax income declined 5.4%. After taxes at 35.2%, versus 34.1%, net income fell 6.9%, to $32,819,000 ($0.93 a share), from $35,266,000 ($1.00).

Stock Performance - 08-OCT-99

In the past 30 trading days, METHA's shares have increased 9%, compared to a 0.91% fall in the S&P 500. Average trading volume for the past five days was 106,300 shares, compared with the 40-day moving average of 159,577 shares.

Key Stock Statistics

Dividend Rate/Share	0.20	Shareholders	1,800
Shs. outstg. (M)	35.5	Market cap. (B)	$0.663
Avg. daily vol. (M)	0.129	Inst. holdings	67%
Tang. Bk. Value/Share	5.86		
Beta	1.15		

Value of $10,000 invested 5 years ago: $ 21,346

Fiscal Year Ending Apr. 30

	2000	1999	1998	1997	1996	1995
Revenues (Million $)						
1Q	98.61	87.96	91.90	78.97	68.22	57.76
2Q	—	107.9	99.9	85.19	78.64	66.78
3Q	—	96.39	90.74	85.94	75.73	67.39
4Q	—	111.5	96.73	92.99	84.95	78.81
Yr.	—	403.7	379.3	343.1	307.5	270.8
Earnings Per Share ($)						
1Q	**0.24**	**0.22**	**0.26**	**0.23**	0.19	0.17
2Q	—	**0.26**	**0.27**	**0.26**	0.22	0.17
3Q	—	**0.20**	**0.20**	**0.26**	0.22	0.17
4Q	—	**0.25**	**0.27**	**0.31**	0.30	0.24
Yr.	—	**0.93**	**1.00**	**1.06**	**0.92**	0.75

Next earnings report expected: late November

Dividend Data (Dividends have been paid since 1983.)

Amount ($)	Date Decl.	Ex-Div. Date	Stock of Record	Payment Date
0.050	Dec. 08	Jan. 13	Jan. 15	Jan. 29 '99
0.050	Mar. 16	Apr. 13	Apr. 15	Apr. 30 '99
0.050	Jun. 25	Jul. 16	Jul. 15	Jul. 30 '99
0.050	Sep. 14	Oct. 13	Oct. 15	Oct. 29 '99

A Division of The McGraw-Hill Companies

Methode Electronics, Inc.

Business Summary - 12-JUL-99

Methode Electronics, established in 1946, manufactures components that connect, convey and control electrical signals, digital pulses and energy. The company believes it is positioned to benefit from a continuing trend toward increased electronic content in modern products. Methode makes connectors, controls, interconnect devices, printed circuits and current-carrying distribution systems.

Company products are sold to manufacturers of electronic data processing equipment, instruments, voice and data communications, and the automotive industry.

The company's serialized optical links are becoming increasingly critical for high-speed data transfer. Power and signal busses are used in mainframe computers and in automation, robotics and cellular communications equipment. Methode's connectors contain sophisticated circuits that enhance high-speed signal transmission between computers and peripheral equipment such as printers, scanners and disc drives. Automotive components include a wide range of electromechanical and electronic controls used in both cars and trucks. Chrysler and Ford together accounted for 35%, 42% and 40% of net sales in FY 98 (Apr.), FY 97 and FY 96, respectively.

Methode's operating units specialize in segments of the interconnect and controls markets. The concept of relatively small product-oriented groupings supported by a wide range of corporate resources has proved to be a successful strategy for the company.

Products are sold through a direct sales staff, by independent manufacturers' representatives with offices throughout the world, and through a number of distributor organizations. Foreign sales accounted for 22% of the total in FY 98, up from 19% in FY 97 and 18% in FY 96.

Methode operates 20 electronic and fiber optic connector and cable assembly manufacturing plants that serve the electronics industry in the U.S., Malta, the U.K., Ireland, China and Singapore. METHA also operates five service facilities.

Recent acquisitions included AB Stratos Ltd., a developer of Fiber optic connectivity products based in England (January 1999), Adam Technologies, a broad-line supplier of connectors (May 1997), Merit Elektrik, a Maltese automotive switch manufacturer (February 1997), and 75% of Sentorque, which owns a portfolio of intellectual property covering innovative advances in circularly magnetized non-contact torque sensors (February 1997).

Per Share Data ($) (Year Ended Apr. 30)	1999	1998	1997	1996	1995	1994	1993	1992	1991	1990
Tangible Bk. Val.	6.04	5.22	4.51	4.59	3.75	2.97	2.29	1.80	1.85	1.65
Cash Flow	1.43	1.49	1.47	1.27	1.06	0.87	0.67	0.50	0.44	0.33
Earnings	0.93	1.00	1.06	0.93	0.75	0.61	0.43	0.29	0.24	0.15
Dividends	0.20	0.20	0.20	0.16	0.08	0.03	0.02	0.02	0.02	0.02
Payout Ratio	22%	20%	19%	17%	11%	5%	6%	8%	10%	15%
Cal. Yrs.	1998	1997	1996	1995	1994	1993	1992	1991	1990	1989
Prices - High	18 1/2	27 1/8	20 1/4	16 1/2	13 5/8	9 7/8	7 1/8	4 1/8	2 5/8	1 15/16
- Low	10 5/8	12 3/4	12 1/2	8 5/8	8 3/4	6 7/8	3 1/4	1 15/16	1 9/16	1 5/16
P/E Ratio - High	20	27	19	18	18	23	17	15	11	13
- Low	11	13	12	9	12	14	8	7	7	10
Income Statement Analysis (Million $)										
Revs.	404	379	343	308	271	213	172	148	149	133
Oper. Inc.	57.4	65.7	167	58.5	48.1	40.4	28.7	20.8	17.5	14.1
Depr.	17.7	17.6	14.7	12.1	10.6	9.0	7.8	7.3	6.6	5.7
Int. Exp.	0.6	0.3	0.2	0.3	0.4	0.4	0.3	0.2	0.6	0.7
Pretax Inc.	50.7	53.6	58.4	51.0	40.8	33.5	22.5	13.6	12.0	8.6
Eff. Tax Rate	35%	34%	36%	37%	36%	37%	35%	30%	34%	41%
Net Inc.	32.8	35.3	37.2	32.4	26.1	21.0	14.7	9.5	7.9	5.1
Balance Sheet & Other Fin. Data (Million $)										
Cash	22.8	24.2	23.1	50.2	40.8	26.8	21.9	19.8	11.1	9.4
Curr. Assets	171	145	123	137	120	97.0	72.0	59.6	53.9	51.4
Total Assets	317	288	254	223	191	161	129	107	90.0	84.8
Curr. Liab.	57.1	50.4	44.5	46.0	43.7	38.2	34.0	28.5	21.5	21.9
LT Debt	Nil	Nil	Nil	Nil	Nil	0.1	0.2	0.3	0.4	2.8
Common Eqty.	248	226	198	165	135	108	84.7	67.6	62.3	54.8
Total Cap.	249	226	198	165	135	108	85.3	69.0	64.6	59.6
Cap. Exp.	22.0	23.2	20.4	22.1	17.4	13.3	17.3	10.1	8.0	6.2
Cash Flow	50.6	52.9	51.9	44.5	36.7	30.0	22.6	16.8	14.5	10.8
Curr. Ratio	3.0	2.8	2.8	3.0	2.7	2.5	2.1	2.1	2.5	2.3
% LT Debt of Cap.	Nil	Nil	Nil	Nil	Nil	0.1	0.2	0.4	0.6	4.7
% Net Inc.of Revs.	8.1	9.3	10.9	10.5	9.6	9.8	8.6	6.4	5.3	3.8
% Ret. on Assets	7.2	13.0	15.7	15.6	14.8	14.4	12.4	9.6	9.1	6.4
% Ret. on Equity	9.2	16.7	20.6	21.6	21.5	21.7	19.3	14.6	13.5	9.7

Data as orig reptd.; bef. results of disc opers/spec. items. Per share data adj. for stk. divs. Bold denotes diluted EPS (FASB 128)-prior periods restated. E-Estimated. NA-Not Available. NM-Not Meaningful. NR-Not Ranked.

Office—7444 W. Wilson Ave, Harwood Heights, IL 60656. **Tel**—(708) 867-9600. **Website**—http://www.methode.com **Chrmn**—W. J. McGinley. **Pres**—J. W. McGinley. **EVP & CFO**—K. J. Hayes.**Secy**—J. W. Ashley. **Dirs**—M. G. Andre, J. W. Ashley Jr., J. R. Cannon, W. C. Croft, K. J. Hayes, J. W. McGinley, W. J. McGinley, R. J. Roberts, G. C. Wright. **Transfer Agent & Registrar**—ChaseMellon Shareholder Services, Ridgefield Park, NJ. **Incorporated**—in Illinois in 1946; reincorporated in Delaware in 1966. **Empl**— 4,000. **S&P Analyst:** J.C.

STANDARD
&POOR'S
STOCK REPORTS

Michael Foods

NASDAQ Symbol **MIKL**

In S&P SmallCap 600

09-OCT-99

Industry:
Foods

Summary: This food processor and distributor has interests in eggs and egg products, refrigerated grocery products, refrigerated potato products and specialty dairy products.

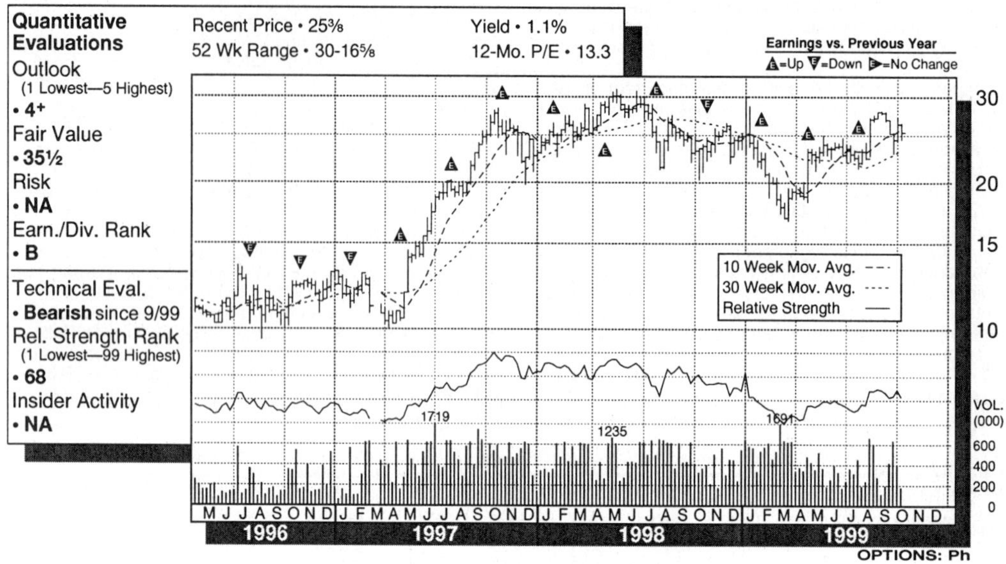

Business Profile - 04-AUG-99

MIKL's strategy focuses on creating "value-added" products, either in the product, the distribution channel or in the service provided to the customer. The company continues to spend record amounts on capital projects to expand its production capacity for value added products, particularity further-processed egg and specialty diary products. In July 1999, the company sold its Hudson, CO shell egg production facility, which did not fit into its value added strategy. MIKL expects above average operating costs to persist in its Refrigerated Distribution segment during the second half of 1999, as the division recovers from a voluntary recall of certain dairy products in February 1999.

Operational Review - 04-AUG-99

Net sales for the six months ended June 30, 1999, advanced 4.5%, reflecting volume growth in all the company's divisions. Despite wider gross margins, profitability was restrained by a 15% jump in SG&A expense and higher interest expense (net). Pretax income rose 1.3%. After taxes at 41.0%, versus 42.0%, net income increased 3.0%, to $20.2 million ($0.96 a share), from $19.6 million ($0.88).

Stock Performance - 08-OCT-99

In the past 30 trading days, MIKL's shares have declined 9%, compared to a 0.91% fall in the S&P 500. Average trading volume for the past five days was 34,940 shares, compared with the 40-day moving average of 81,110 shares.

Key Stock Statistics

Dividend Rate/Share	0.28	Shareholders	500
Shs. outstg. (M)	20.3	Market cap. (B)	$0.514
Avg. daily vol. (M)	0.098	Inst. holdings	58%
Tang. Bk. Value/Share	5.88		
Beta	0.14		

Value of $10,000 invested 5 years ago: $ 34,234

Fiscal Year Ending Dec. 31

	1999	1998	1997	1996	1995	1994
Revenues (Million $)						
1Q	253.4	245.6	195.4	143.9	126.7	121.6
2Q	258.0	243.7	237.9	151.7	130.9	125.5
3Q	—	253.8	245.9	159.9	136.3	127.9
4Q	—	277.4	277.1	160.9	142.8	130.9
Yr.	—	1,020	956.2	616.4	536.6	506.0
Earnings Per Share ($)						
1Q	**0.40**	**0.37**	**0.20**	**0.17**	0.19	0.17
2Q	**0.57**	**0.51**	**0.39**	**0.17**	0.22	0.19
3Q	—	**0.48**	**0.49**	**0.07**	0.22	0.19
4Q	—	**0.47**	**0.42**	**-0.56**	0.28	0.24
Yr.	—	**1.83**	**1.51**	**-0.16**	**0.90**	**0.78**

Next earnings report expected: NA

Dividend Data (Dividends have been paid since 1987.)

Amount ($)	Date Decl.	Ex-Div. Date	Stock of Record	Payment Date
0.060	Oct. 29	Nov. 05	Nov. 09	Nov. 23 '98
0.060	Feb. 05	Feb. 11	Feb. 16	Mar. 02 '99
0.070	Apr. 16	Apr. 29	May. 03	May. 17 '99
0.070	Jul. 19	Jul. 29	Aug. 02	Aug. 16 '99

Michael Foods, Inc.

Business Summary - 04-AUG-99

Michael Foods, a diversified food processor and distributor, continues to focus on value-added products by introducing innovative food technology and customer solutions. Food products are divided into four areas: egg products, refrigerated distribution, dairy products and potato products.

The Egg Products division (59% of net sales in 1998), comprised of M.G. Waldbaum Co. and Papetti's Hygrade Egg Products, produces, processes and distributes numerous egg products and shell eggs. The company believes the division is the largest egg products producer and the second largest egg producer in the U.S. MIKL more than doubled the division's sales base with the February 1997 acquisition of Papetti's. Since the acquisition, the company has been increasingly coordinating sales, production and distribution efforts. MIKL estimates saving approximately $12 million in pretax costs from synergies in 1998, and expects to realize another $2-to-$3 million in savings during 1999.

In an effort to enhance the company's position as the world leader in value added egg products, MIKL recently made two investments in Europe. In January 1999, MIKL purchased a 25% position in Belovo S.A., a Belgium-based egg products producer, along with a 50% interest in The Lipid Company S.A., a firm formed by Belovo for the purpose of commercializing a phospholipid extraction process.

The Refrigerated Distribution division (22%), comprised of Crystal Farms Refrigerated Distribution Co., and Wisco Farm Cooperative, distributes a wide range of cheese and other refrigerated grocery products. During the fourth quarter of 1998, Crystal Farms gained entry into a 100 plus store supermarket chain, and is seeking additional chain store growth in 1999.

The Dairy Products division (14%), comprised of Kohler Mix Specialties, processes and sells soft serve mix, ice cream mix, frozen yogurt mix, milk and specialty dairy products. In March 1999, the company acquired a Connecticut dairy mix factory from HP Hood Inc. The facility generated 1998 net sales of approximately $37 million. MIKL intends to build its Kohler Mix Specialties subsidiary into a national dairy mix and creamer supplier.

Potato products (5%) are produced and sold by Northern Star Co. and Farm Fresh Foods, Inc. With the frozen french fry business being discontinued in mid-1997, the division has been able to focus full energies on value added refrigerated potato products, mainly hash browns and mashed items.

During 1998, MIKL repurchased almost one million shares of its common stock from its two million repurchase program authorized in July 1998.

Per Share Data ($) (Year Ended Dec. 31)	1998	1997	1996	1995	1994	1993	1992	1991	1990	1989
Tangible Bk. Val.	5.88	4.84	6.19	6.32	6.14	5.50	6.22	6.13	3.49	4.47
Cash Flow	3.46	3.14	1.22	2.15	1.91	0.32	1.30	2.03	1.89	1.03
Earnings	1.83	1.51	-0.16	0.91	0.79	-0.84	0.20	1.07	1.11	0.71
Dividends	0.23	0.20	0.20	0.20	0.20	0.20	0.20	0.20	0.22	0.13
Payout Ratio	13%	13%	NM	22%	25%	NM	100%	20%	19%	19%
Prices - High	$31\frac{1}{8}$	$28\frac{3}{8}$	$13\frac{1}{2}$	$14\frac{1}{2}$	$13\frac{1}{4}$	$11\frac{1}{2}$	$20\frac{1}{2}$	$23\frac{5}{8}$	$15\frac{1}{8}$	$14\frac{5}{8}$
- Low	$20\frac{1}{4}$	10	$9\frac{1}{2}$	9	$7\frac{7}{8}$	$6\frac{1}{2}$	$7\frac{3}{4}$	$12\frac{1}{2}$	$8\frac{1}{4}$	$8\frac{1}{4}$
P/E Ratio - High	17	19	NM	16	17	NM	NM	22	14	21
- Low	11	7	NM	10	10	NM	NM	12	7	12
Income Statement Analysis (Million $)										
Revs.	1,020	956	616	537	506	475	443	455	461	255
Oper. Inc.	115	101	53.1	60.3	54.8	43.1	37.1	57.9	55.8	18.2
Depr.	35.8	35.0	26.7	24.0	21.6	22.4	21.5	17.6	13.0	5.5
Int. Exp.	NA	11.0	7.3	7.9	8.8	9.2	10.2	10.7	10.9	1.9
Pretax Inc.	69.4	55.4	-3.4	28.6	24.7	-21.6	6.0	30.7	31.0	16.3
Eff. Tax Rate	42%	42%	NM	39%	39%	NM	36%	36%	37%	26%
Net Inc.	40.3	32.4	-3.1	17.6	15.2	-16.3	3.9	19.7	18.6	12.0
Balance Sheet & Other Fin. Data (Million $)										
Cash	2.0	4.0	2.6	1.9	1.6	0.2	6.1	4.6	4.0	7.8
Curr. Assets	178	158	116	103	94.0	83.7	93.3	99	86.2	58.1
Total Assets	552	504	365	359	337	329	370	357	304	187
Curr. Liab.	117	104	59.2	60.9	60.4	61.5	38.5	39.9	72.8	29.0
LT Debt	155	138	104	89.7	89.0	94.0	129	115	99	54.6
Common Eqty.	244	229	174	180	166	155	177	176	111	95.0
Total Cap.	434	400	305	298	276	268	332	317	231	158
Cap. Exp.	64.8	38.1	30.0	23.8	23.0	12.0	32.0	48.4	40.2	35.1
Cash Flow	76.1	67.4	23.6	41.6	36.8	6.1	25.3	37.3	31.6	17.5
Curr. Ratio	1.5	3.0	2.0	1.7	1.6	1.4	2.4	2.5	1.2	2.0
% LT Debt of Cap.	85.7	34.4	34.1	30.1	32.1	35.2	38.8	36.4	42.7	34.6
% Net Inc.of Revs.	4.0	3.4	NM	3.3	3.0	NM	0.9	4.3	4.0	4.7
% Ret. on Assets	7.6	7.5	NM	5.1	4.6	NM	1.1	5.5	7.6	7.8
% Ret. on Equity	17.4	16.1	NM	10.2	9.5	NM	2.2	12.9	18.1	13.3

Data as orig reptd.; bef. results of disc opers/spec. items. Per share data adj. for stk. divs. Bold denotes diluted EPS (FASB 128)-prior periods restated. E-Estimated. NA-Not Available. NM-Not Meaningful. NR-Not Ranked.

Office—324 Park National Bank Building 5353 Wayzata Blvd., Minneapolis, MN 55416. **Tel**—(612) 546-1500. **Fax**—(612) 546-3711. **Website**—http://www.michaelfoods.com **Chrmn**—A. C. Knudston. **Pres & CEO**—G. A. Ostrander. **VP-Fin, CFO & Treas**—J. D. Reedy. **EVP & Secy**—J. M. Shapiro. **Dirs**—M. B. Bellantoni, R. A. Coonrod, D. P. Dillon, M. E. Efron, J. J. Jenko, A. C. Knudtson, J. D. Marshburn, J. J. Michael, M. D. Moore, G. A. Ostrander, A. J. Papetti, S. T. Papetti. **Transfer Agent & Registrar**—Norwest Shareowner Services, St. Paul, MN. **Incorporated**—in Delaware in 1987. **Empl**— 4,160. **S&P Analyst:** A. Bensinger

Michaels Stores

Nasdaq Symbol **MIKE**

In S&P SmallCap 600

09-OCT-99

Industry:
Retail (Specialty)

Summary: MIKE is the leading U.S. arts and crafts retailer, with a chain of more than 535 Michaels stores in 47 states, Canada and Puerto Rico, and 83 Aaron Brothers stores.

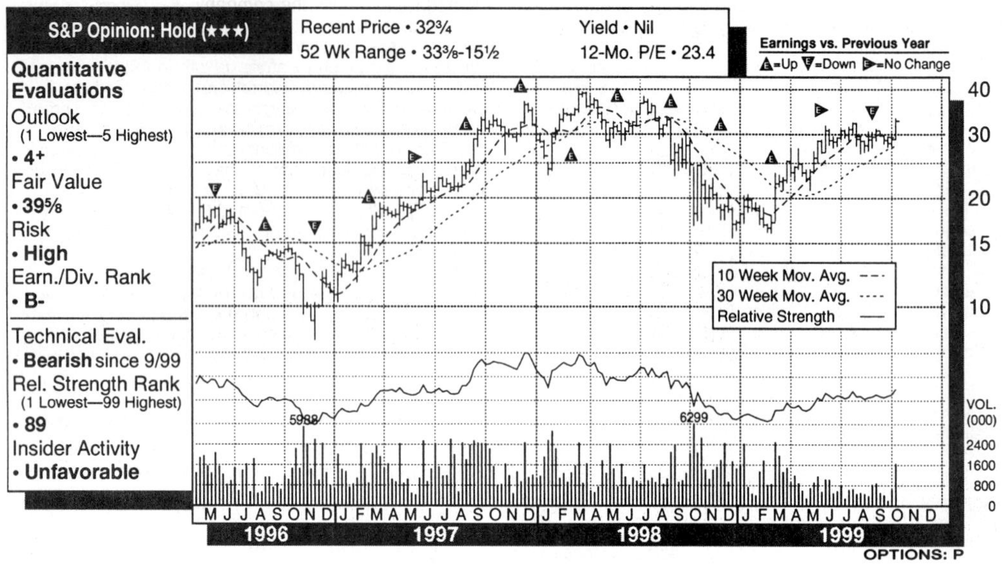

Overview - 31-AUG-99

We expect total sales to rise about 10% to 12% in the second half of FY 00 (Jan.), aided by the addition of new stores; same-stores sales should increase 3% to 5%. For the longer term, MIKE's extensive new point-of-sale (POS) system should help control inventory costs, and should also help to boost operating margins by letting stores quickly improve their in-stock position of best selling items, and more adequately react to prevailing sales trends. While its competitors are faltering, the company is aggressively expanding; it is on track to meet its goal of adding 62 Michaels locations in FY 00. MIKE is also considering a national roll-out of its 83-store Aaron Brothers custom framing and arts supplies chain. We believe this could be successful, in light of solid and improving same-store sales for the Aaron Brothers chain. We expect EPS to grow 22% in FY 00, to $1.75, and see a further rise, to $2.15, in FY 01.

Valuation - 31-AUG-99

After losing more than 60% of their value in 1998, the shares have risen more than 50% thus far in 1999. However, we are continuing our hold rating on the stock. Although the company operates the only nationwide chain of arts and crafts stores, we believe strong competition from general merchandising superstores will continue to eat away at its market share. MIKE's high inventory position and modest same-store sales increases will likely lead to increased discounting and narrower margins in coming periods. Although the stock was recently trading at a relatively modest 17X our FY 00 EPS estimate of $1.75, we would not add to holdings until comparable-store sales show sustained improvement. We expect MIKE to continue to repurchase its shares during FY 00. The company bought back approximately 1.2 million common shares during FY 99.

Key Stock Statistics

S&P EPS Est. 2000	1.75	Tang. Bk. Value/Share	12.66
P/E on S&P Est. 2000	18.7	Beta	0.82
S&P EPS Est. 2001	2.15	Shareholders	761
Dividend Rate/Share	Nil	Market cap. (B)	$0.953
Shs. outstg. (M)	29.1	Inst. holdings	79%
Avg. daily vol. (M)	0.141		

Value of $10,000 invested 5 years ago: $ 9,160

Fiscal Year Ending Jan. 31

	2000	1999	1998	1997	1996	1995
Revenues (Million $)						
1Q	388.5	335.8	321.3	301.9	265.6	159.8
2Q	359.1	314.2	278.0	260.5	259.9	174.2
3Q	—	382.8	350.1	322.2	312.7	283.1
4Q	—	541.2	507.1	493.7	456.7	377.5
Yr.	—	1,574	1,457	1,378	1,295	994.6
Earnings Per Share ($)						
1Q	**0.18**	**0.18**	**0.12**	**0.12**	0.35	0.28
2Q	Nil	**0.02**	**-0.11**	**-0.34**	-1.55	0.04
3Q	**E0.32**	**0.24**	**0.15**	**-1.45**	0.14	0.36
4Q	**E1.22**	**0.99**	**0.79**	**0.35**	0.10	1.01
Yr.	**E1.75**	**1.43**	**1.05**	**-1.35**	**-0.96**	1.77

Next earnings report expected: late November

Dividend Data

No dividends have been paid.

A Division of The McGraw-Hill Companies

Michaels Stores, Inc.

Business Summary - 31-AUG-99

Michaels Stores, Inc. is the only U.S. specialty retailer of arts, crafts, frames, floral and decorative items. Its stores offer a selection of more than 40,000 competitively priced products, including picture framing materials and services; dried flowers and other floral items; art, craft and hobby supplies; and party, holiday and seasonal merchandise. The company's primary customers are women aged 25 to 54, with above-average household incomes.

At August 25, 1999, MIKE was operating 538 Michaels outlets in 47 states, Canada, and Puerto Rico, with an average of 16,900 sq. ft. of selling space. The company expected to add 70 stores to the Michaels chain during FY 00 (Jan.), and to relocate and/or expand up to 25 stores. By the end of FY 99, MIKE had converted one-third of its stores to a new prototype format, featuring modern layouts with oval racetrack-style aisles.

Stores are located in clusters or on a single-store basis in geographic areas where rent, freight and advertising expenditures are not cost-prohibitive. Stores currently in operation are located primarily in strip shopping centers, with ample parking in areas easily accessible to customer traffic.

Substantially all products sold are manufactured in the U.S., the Far East, or Mexico. Goods manufactured in the Far East generally require long lead times, and are ordered four to six months in advance of delivery. In the past, about 40% of merchandise was shipped to the stores via the company's distribution facilities; MIKE hopes to increase this to 65%.

At August 25, 1999, the company was operating 83 Aaron Brothers stores, primarily in California, offering frames, related materials and equipment, as well as art supplies. It expected to open 15 new Aaron Brothers stores, and to relocate five additional units in FY 00. These stores average 6,100 sq. ft., and have started to feature do-it-yourself framing areas. MIKE's management has recently been considering a national roll-out of Aaron Brothers, in light of the chain's three consecutive years of improving high single-digit same-store sales growth, and the significantly fragmented nature of the custom framing market.

During FY 99, MIKE completed the implementation of an extensive point-of-sale (POS) system. The system provides Michaels outlets with full electronic inventory and merchandise management capabilities, enabling stores to quickly replenish best selling items and react to prevailing sales trends. The deployment of the POS system, and the second quarter opening of MIKE's new distribution center, should make the company's management of inventory more effective and efficient.

Per Share Data ($) **(Year Ended Jan. 31)**	**1999**	**1998**	**1997**	**1996**	**1995**	**1994**	**1993**	**1992**	**1991**	**1990**
Tangible Bk. Val.	12.34	10.51	8.11	8.94	11.17	9.70	7.96	6.90	2.39	1.70
Cash Flow	3.07	2.64	0.45	0.49	2.84	2.25	1.83	1.65	1.34	0.68
Earnings	1.43	1.05	-1.34	-0.95	1.76	1.53	1.22	0.90	0.57	Nil
Dividends	Nil	Nil	Nil	Nil	Nil	Nil	Nil	Nil	Nil	Nil
Payout Ratio	Nil	Nil	Nil	Nil	Nil	Nil	Nil	Nil	Nil	Nil
Cal. Yrs.	1998	1997	1996	1995	1994	1993	1992	1991	1990	1989
Prices - High	39 7/8	37	19 7/8	37	46 1/2	39	34	17 1/8	6 1/2	10 1/4
- Low	15 1/2	11 1/4	8	11	29 1/2	25 1/4	16	3 5/8	2 7/8	4 7/8
P/E Ratio - High	28	35	NM	NM	26	25	28	19	11	NM
- Low	11	11	NM	NM	17	17	13	4	5	NM
Income Statement Analysis (Million $)										
Revs.	1,574	1,457	1,378	1,295	995	620	493	411	362	290
Oper. Inc.	139	115	20.7	15.9	92.6	53.8	44.4	34.5	27.5	21.5
Depr.	50.3	45.6	41.7	30.9	21.5	12.5	10.2	8.9	7.8	7.2
Int. Exp.	22.7	23.4	21.0	16.8	9.1	6.4	0.3	7.0	9.7	9.9
Pretax Inc.	70.3	48.5	-41.1	-34.8	57.2	42.6	33.5	17.8	9.7	0.6
Eff. Tax Rate	38%	38%	NM	NM	38%	38%	39%	40%	40%	98%
Net Inc.	43.6	30.1	-31.2	-20.4	35.6	26.3	20.4	10.7	5.9	NM
Balance Sheet & Other Fin. Data (Million $)										
Cash	96.1	162	59.1	2.9	16.9	68.8	42.1	27.4	0.1	1.2
Curr. Assets	622	573	438	416	419	291	170	126	85.0	92.0
Total Assets	963	908	784	740	686	398	322	181	144	151
Curr. Liab.	231	214	198	187	186	109	65.6	51.1	40.5	33.5
LT Debt	222	222	222	184	138	97.8	97.8	Nil	54.2	74.2
Common Eqty.	481	442	333	336	356	185	155	126	47.0	40.0
Total Cap.	706	664	555	520	494	283	253	126	104	117
Cap. Exp.	78.0	44.0	33.6	54.9	68.1	46.8	19.8	5.5	6.8	9.5
Cash Flow	93.9	75.7	10.5	10.5	57.2	38.8	30.5	19.6	13.7	7.2
Curr. Ratio	2.7	2.7	2.2	2.2	2.2	2.7	2.6	2.5	2.1	2.8
% LT Debt of Cap.	31.5	34.8	40.0	35.4	27.9	34.5	38.6	Nil	52.2	63.3
% Net Inc.of Revs.	2.8	2.1	NM	NM	3.6	4.2	4.1	2.6	1.6	NM
% Ret. on Assets	4.7	3.6	NM	NM	6.0	7.3	7.8	5.4	4.0	NM
% Ret. on Equity	9.4	7.8	NM	NM	12.0	15.3	13.9	10.9	13.4	NM

Data as orig reptd.; bef. results of disc opers/spec. items. Per share data adj. for stk. divs. Bold denotes diluted EPS (FASB 128)-prior periods restated. E-Estimated. NA-Not Available. NM-Not Meaningful. NR-Not Ranked.

Office—8000 Brent Branch Drive, Irving, TX 75063; P.O. Box 619566, DFW, TX 75261-9566. **Tel**—(972) 409-1300. **Website**—http://www.michaels.com **Chrmn**—S. Wyly. **Vice Chrmn**—C. J. Wyly Jr. **Pres & CEO**—R. M. Rouleau. **EVP & CFO**—B. M. DeCordova. **VP-Fin**—C. J. Holland. **VP & Secy**—M. V. Beasley. **Dirs**—K. Elliot; M. C. French; R. C. Marcus; D. R. Miller, Jr.; E. A. VanStory; C. J. Wyly, Jr.; E. A. Wyly; S. Wyly. **Transfer Agent & Registrar**—Harris Trust & Savings Bank, NYC. **Incorporated**—in Delaware in 1983. **Empl**— 22,200. **S&P Analyst:** Maureen C. Carini

STANDARD
&POOR'S
STOCK REPORTS

Micrel, Inc.

NASDAQ Symbol **MCRL**

In S&P SmallCap 600

09-OCT-99

Industry: Electronics (Semiconductors)

Summary: Micrel manufactures high-performance analog power integrated circuits and mixed-signal and digital circuits which are used in a wide variety of electronic products.

Quantitative Evaluations

Outlook
(1 Lowest—5 Highest)
• **NA**

Fair Value
• **NA**

Risk
• **High**

Earn./Div. Rank
• **B**

Technical Eval.
• **Bullish** since 8/99

Rel. Strength Rank
(1 Lowest—99 Highest)
• **88**

Insider Activity
• **Unfavorable**

Recent Price • 46
52 Wk Range • 51½-12⅜
Yield • Nil
12-Mo. P/E • 97.9

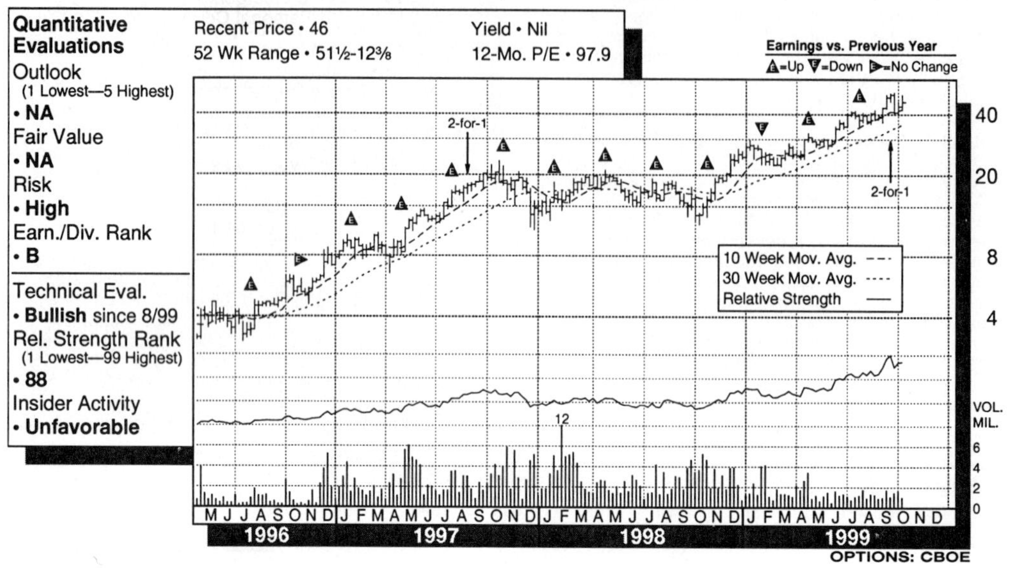

Business Profile - 24-SEP-99

Micrel reported record revenues and earnings for the second quarter of 1999, and said that demand continues to be good for its products in computer, telecommunications and industrial markets. In addition, exceptionally strong demand for its Synergy communications products led to record quarterly revenue for this portion of its businesses, and encouraged the company regarding future prospects in the fast-growing high bandwidth, high performance communications marketplace. Micrel introduced 12 new products in the 1999 second quarter, including its first 2.5 GHz products for the computing and communications markets.

Operational Review - 24-SEP-99

Net revenues in the six months ended June 30, 1999, advanced 26%, year to year, paced by a 36% gain in standard products sales, led by low dropout regulators and Synergy communications products. Custom and foundry products sales were virtually unchanged. Profitability benefited from increased manufacturing efficiency, due to greater capacity utilization and reductions in contract assembly and test units. Despite declining average selling prices and higher research and development expense, pretax income climbed 27%. After taxes at 33.0%, versus 34.0%, net income advanced 29%, to $15,498,000 ($0.35 a share, as adjusted), from $12,025,000 ($0.29).

Stock Performance - 08-OCT-99

In the past 30 trading days, MCRL's shares have increased 18%, compared to a 0.91% fall in the S&P 500. Average trading volume for the past five days was 193,580 shares, compared with the 40-day moving average of 249,718 shares.

Key Stock Statistics

Dividend Rate/Share	Nil	Shareholders	89
Shs. outstg. (M)	41.0	Market cap. (B)	$ 1.9
Avg. daily vol. (M)	0.250	Inst. holdings	33%
Tang. Bk. Value/Share	2.72		
Beta	NA		

Value of $10,000 invested 5 years ago: NA

Fiscal Year Ending Dec. 31

	1999	1998	1997	1996	1995	1994
Revenues (Million $)						
1Q	40.57	32.66	22.11	13.91	11.89	5.56
2Q	44.18	34.50	24.33	15.32	13.29	8.98
3Q	—	35.43	27.20	17.61	13.93	10.28
4Q	—	37.92	30.52	19.40	13.93	11.13
Yr.	—	140.5	104.2	66.24	53.04	35.94
Earnings Per Share ($)						
1Q	**0.17**	**0.14**	**0.08**	**0.05**	0.04	0.00
2Q	**0.18**	**0.15**	**0.09**	**0.06**	0.05	0.03
3Q	—	**0.15**	**0.10**	**0.05**	0.05	0.03
4Q	—	**-0.04**	**0.13**	**0.07**	0.05	0.04
Yr.	—	**0.40**	**0.40**	**0.23**	**0.18**	**0.10**

Next earnings report expected: late October

Dividend Data

Amount ($)	Date Decl.	Ex-Div. Date	Stock of Record	Payment Date
2-for-1	Aug. 20	Sep. 16	Aug. 30	Sep. 15 '99

A Division of The McGraw-Hill Companies

Micrel, Incorporated

Business Summary - 24-SEP-99

Micrel, Inc. (which also does business as Micrel Semiconductor) designs, manufactures and markets high-performance analog power integrated circuits and mixed signal and digital integrated circuits.

The company currently ships more than 1,000 standard products. It derived the majority of its product revenues in recent years (71% in 1998) from sales of standard analog integrated circuits for power management. These analog power circuits are used in a wide variety of electronics products, including those in the communications, computer and industrial markets.

In addition to standard products, Micrel manufactures custom analog and mixed-signal circuits, and provides wafer foundry services for a diverse range of customers who product electronic systems for communications, consumer and military applications.

Through the November 1998 acquisition of Synergy Semiconductor (its first major acquisition), the company broadened its standard product offerings to include high performance bipolar integrated circuits sold to customers within the networking telecommunications, computing and automatic test equipment/instrumentation markets. Through its Synergy division, Micrel makes more than 200 products, including communication transceivers, clock generators, distribution/clock recovery circuits, and high-speed logic and memory.

Trends in the communications and computing markets have created increased demand for power analog circuits, which control, regulate, convert and route voltage and current in electronic systems. Demand for power analog circuits has been fueled by the tremendous growth of battery powered cellular telephones and computing devices, and the emergence of lower voltage microprocessors and Personal Computer Memory Card International Association (PCMCIA) standards for peripheral devices.

Micrel's standard analog products business is focused on addressing this demand for high-performance power analog circuits. It sells various regulators, references and witches designed for cellular telephones and laptop computers. Micrel believes it was one of the first companies to offer analog products for the PCMCIA Card and universal serial bus (USB) market and that it currently provides a majority of the power analog circuits used in PC Card and USB systems. The company also offers standard analog products that address other markets, including power supplies and industrial, defense, avionics, and automotive electronics.

The company offers customers various combinations of design, process and foundry services. Through interaction with customers in its custom and foundry business, Micrel has been able to enhance its design and process technology capabilities, which in turn provides engineering and marketing benefits to its standard analog products business.

International sales accounted for 45% of net revenues in 1998, versus 50% in 1997.

Per Share Data ($) (Year Ended Dec. 31)	1998	1997	1996	1995	1994	1993	1992	1991	1990	1989
Tangible Bk. Val.	2.16	1.81	1.27	1.01	0.77	NA	NA	NA	NA	NA
Cash Flow	0.70	0.56	0.32	0.24	NA	NA	NA	NA	NA	NA
Earnings	0.41	0.40	0.23	0.18	0.10	0.01	NA	NA	NA	NA
Dividends	Nil	Nil	Nil	Nil	Nil	NA	NA	NA	NA	NA
Payout Ratio	Nil	Nil	Nil	Nil	Nil	NA	NA	NA	NA	NA
Prices - High	28 1/8	23 1/2	8 3/4	8 1/8	3 7/8	NA	NA	NA	NA	NA
- Low	11 3/8	6 1/2	3	3 1/8	2 1/4	NA	NA	NA	NA	NA
P/E Ratio - High	69	59	38	43	40	NA	NA	NA	NA	NA
- Low	28	16	13	16	23	NA	NA	NA	NA	NA
Income Statement Analysis (Million $)										
Revs.	141	104	66.0	53.0	36.0	18.0	NA	NA	NA	NA
Oper. Inc.	42.9	30.9	16.7	12.8	NA	NA	NA	NA	NA	NA
Depr.	12.3	6.5	3.4	2.2	NA	NA	NA	NA	NA	NA
Int. Exp.	0.4	0.2	0.3	0.3	NA	NA	NA	NA	NA	NA
Pretax Inc.	27.9	25.4	14.0	11.3	4.6	0.2	NA	NA	NA	NA
Eff. Tax Rate	39%	34%	34%	35%	36%	NM	NA	NA	NA	NA
Net Inc.	17.2	16.7	9.3	7.4	2.9	0.3	NA	NA	NA	NA
Balance Sheet & Other Fin. Data (Million $)										
Cash	13.4	20.1	16.6	14.1	NA	NA	NA	NA	NA	NA
Curr. Assets	81.3	52.9	42.3	37.0	NA	NA	NA	NA	NA	NA
Total Assets	145	85.5	60.0	48.3	36.5	13.0	NA	NA	NA	NA
Curr. Liab.	30.4	11.2	9.3	8.5	NA	NA	NA	NA	NA	NA
LT Debt	14.0	0.6	1.3	2.5	1.6	1.4	NA	NA	NA	NA
Common Eqty.	95.7	70.6	47.4	36.0	26.6	7.7	NA	NA	NA	NA
Total Cap.	114	73.4	49.8	39.1	NA	NA	NA	NA	NA	NA
Cap. Exp.	30.9	21.4	9.6	NA	NA	NA	NA	NA	NA	NA
Cash Flow	29.5	23.3	12.7	9.6	NA	NA	NA	NA	NA	NA
Curr. Ratio	2.7	4.7	4.5	4.4	NA	NA	NA	NA	NA	NA
% LT Debt of Cap.	12.3	0.7	2.6	6.4	NA	NA	NA	NA	NA	NA
% Net Inc.of Revs.	12.2	16.1	14.1	14.0	8.1	NA	NA	NA	NA	NA
% Ret. on Assets	14.9	23.0	17.3	17.6	NA	NA	NA	NA	NA	NA
% Ret. on Equity	20.7	28.4	22.3	23.5	NA	NA	NA	NA	NA	NA

Data as orig reptd.; bef. results of disc opers/spec. items. Per share data adj. for stk. divs. Bold denotes diluted EPS (FASB 128)-prior periods restated. E-Estimated. NA-Not Available. NM-Not Meaningful. NR-Not Ranked.

Office—1849 Fortune Drive, San Jose, CA 95131. **Tel**—(408) 944-0800. **Website**—http://www.micrel.com **Chrmn, Pres & CEO**—R. D. Zinn. **VP-Fin & CFO**—R. D. Crowley Jr. **VP & Secy**—W. H. Muller. **Dirs**—L. L. Hansen, G. Kelly, W. H. Muller, D. L. Peterson, R. D. Zinn. **Transfer Agent & Registrar**—ChaseMellon Shareholder Services, SF. **Incorporated**—in California in 1978. **Empl**— 675. **S&P Analyst:** J. J. Schemitsch

STANDARD
&POOR'S
STOCK REPORTS

MicroAge, Inc.

NASDAQ Symbol **MICA**

In S&P SmallCap 600

09-OCT-99

Industry: Retail (Computers & Electronics)

Summary: This franchisor of computer stores and distributor of microcomputer systems has an international network of outlets that sell, support and service office information products.

Quantitative Evaluations

Outlook
(1 Lowest—5 Highest)
• **5**

Fair Value
• **4⅞**

Risk
• **High**

Earn./Div. Rank
• **B**

Technical Eval.
• **Bearish** since 6/99

Rel. Strength Rank
(1 Lowest—99 Highest)
• **2**

Insider Activity
• **NA**

Recent Price • 2¹⁄₁₆
52 Wk Range • 18¾-2

Yield • Nil
12-Mo. P/E • NM

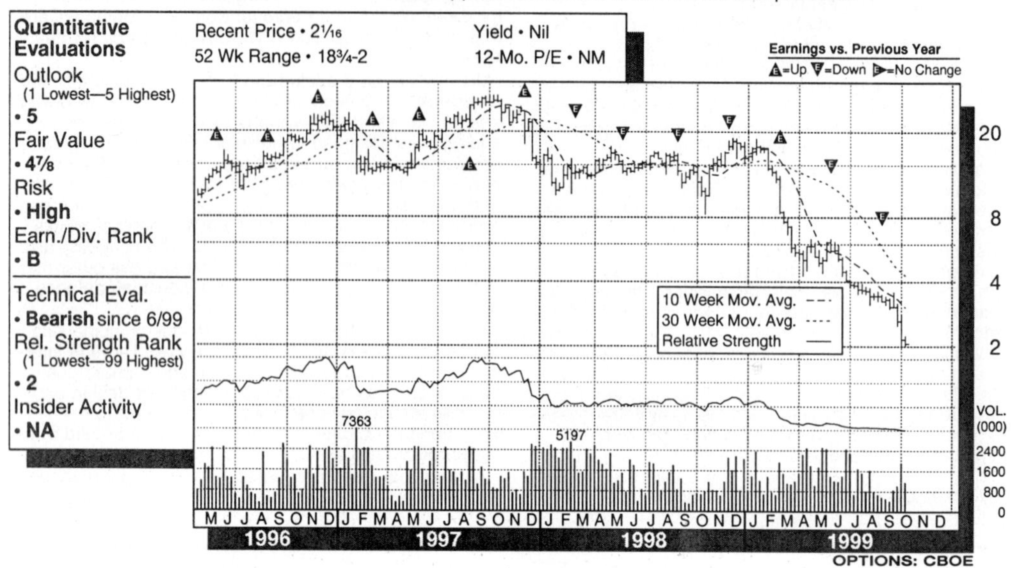

Business Profile - 09-AUG-99

After posting a large loss in the second quarter of FY 99 (Oct.), management noted that it is committed to returning to profitability in the near future, and is highly focused on expense reduction to achieve this goal. The company has eliminated several hundred positions at its Pinacor and MicroAge Technology divisions, and expects that these actions, combined with price increases and the exiting of certain businesses in an effort to improve gross margins, will increase pre-tax earnings by about $15 million per quarter. Excluding price increases associated with severance and branch closures, MICA expects that third quarter earnings will be at or near breakeven. In an effort to fully realize the value of Pinacor and MicroAge Technology Services, the company has retained the services of Salomon Smith Barney to explore possible financial options.

Operational Review - 09-AUG-99

Revenues for the six months ended May 2, 1999, rose 24%, year to year, mostly on increased sales at the Pinacor distribution business. Gross margins narrowed mainly due to pricing pressures on Pinacor products. Results were penalized by $134.1 million of restructuring and other charges related to the separation of MICA into two independent business units. After tax benefits of $15,296,000, versus $7,946,000, the net loss widened to $145,275,000 ($7.12 a share), from $12,073,000 ($0.62).

Stock Performance - 08-OCT-99

In the past 30 trading days, MICA's shares have declined 37%, compared to a 0.91% fall in the S&P 500. Average trading volume for the past five days was 226,500 shares, compared with the 40-day moving average of 178,351 shares.

Key Stock Statistics

Dividend Rate/Share	Nil	Shareholders	6,400
Shs. outstg. (M)	20.5	Market cap. (B)	$0.042
Avg. daily vol. (M)	0.243	Inst. holdings	33%
Tang. Bk. Value/Share	6.88		
Beta	1.32		

Value of $10,000 invested 5 years ago: $ 808

Fiscal Year Ending Oct. 31

	1999	1998	1997	1996	1995	1994
Revenues (Million $)						
1Q	1,445	1,179	890.8	780.3	674.3	470.4
2Q	1,657	1,327	1,086	863.6	743.5	529.6
3Q	1,514	1,441	1,148	842.7	759.1	583.4
4Q	—	1,573	1,322	1,030	764.2	637.4
Yr.	—	5,520	4,446	3,516	2,941	2,221
Earnings Per Share ($)						
1Q	**0.10**	**-0.28**	**0.28**	0.11	0.20	0.36
2Q	**-7.19**	**-0.27**	0.36	0.20	0.17	0.41
3Q	**-0.15**	**0.04**	0.37	0.24	0.05	0.23
4Q	—	**0.18**	0.40	0.34	-0.40	0.25
Yr.	—	**-0.42**	**1.43**	0.89	0.02	1.22

Next earnings report expected: mid January

Dividend Data

No cash has been paid. Under its credit agreements, the company is prohibited from paying dividends without bank consent. A three-for-two stock split was effected in January 1994.

A Division of The McGraw-Hill Companies

MicroAge, Inc.

Business Summary - 09-AUG-99

When many companies enter the information superhighway, they turn to MicroAge (MICA) for help in getting into the fast lane. The company is a global systems integrator and distributor of information technology (IT) products and services, providing an all-inclusive range of hardware and software products, along with logistics, integration and installation services.

The company markets itself as an interconnected chain, comprising products, resources and skills required to implement complex IT solutions. The various business groups of MicroAge work together to sell, ship, engineer, install and service the company's products.

MICA's computer centers distribute more than 21,000 technology hardware and software products and value-added services to reseller customers (who sell the products to others, hence the name reseller) worldwide. Resellers include franchisees, which operate under the company's proprietary name, as well as non-franchised resellers. MICA provides distribution and support services to the resellers, allowing them to realize operating efficiencies and benefit from economies of scale. Sales to value-added resellers have been one of the fastest growing segments for the company.

The integration group provides computing solutions to large corporations, government agencies and educational institutions through a network of qualified resellers (including 51 resellers owned and operated by the company).

The logistics group fulfills and ships product orders from distribution centers in Arizona, Ohio and Nevada for delivery anywhere in the continental U.S. in one to three business days. The group also provides systems set-up, local area network set-up and testing, and other installation and testing services.

The services group provides value added services to MICA's customers, allowing them to configure, place and track orders. Orders can be placed over the Internet as well as through other electronic linkages. The group's software enables users to determine product compatibility, develop custom proposals, and place orders.

MICA's distribution strategy focuses on the products of major microcomputer and peripheral manufacturers. In FY 98 (Oct.), Compaq, Hewlett-Packard and IBM together accounted for 58% of the company's product sales.

In May 1998, MicroAge completed a restructuring plan to consolidate operations into two separate units: a distribution business renamed Pinacor and an integration business. In an effort to enhance shareholder value, the company hired an investment banking firm to help explore options for Pinacor.

Per Share Data ($) **(Year Ended Oct. 31)**	**1998**	**1997**	**1996**	**1995**	**1994**	**1993**	**1992**	**1991**	**1990**	**1989**
Tangible Bk. Val.	8.11	10.93	11.56	10.96	11.11	13.48	6.32	4.87	4.27	3.66
Cash Flow	1.63	2.75	2.26	1.09	1.91	2.77	1.20	1.05	1.41	0.98
Earnings	-0.42	1.40	0.89	0.02	1.22	1.15	0.59	0.50	0.97	0.64
Dividends	Nil	Nil	Nil	Nil	Nil	Nil	Nil	Nil	Nil	Nil
Payout Ratio	Nil	Nil	Nil	Nil	Nil	Nil	Nil	Nil	Nil	Nil
Prices - High	18¾	29¾	25	15	32½	26⅝	10½	10⅛	12⅜	7⅛
- Low	8¼	12¼	7½	7¼	9¼	5⅜	3⅞	3⅞	4⅛	4⅛
P/E Ratio - High	NM	21	28	NM	27	23	18	20	13	11
- Low	NM	9	8	NM	8	5	6	8	4	6
Income Statement Analysis (Million $)										
Revs.	5,520	4,446	3,516	2,941	2,221	1,510	1,017	787	613	360
Oper. Inc.	72.2	94.7	56.8	41.1	41.8	25.1	13.4	10.0	4.7	6.2
Depr.	40.6	24.0	20.3	15.4	9.3	6.4	4.8	3.5	2.9	2.2
Int. Exp.	4.4	5.9	1.3	3.4	1.3	0.7	1.6	1.6	0.3	1.4
Pretax Inc.	-7.4	43.3	23.1	1.0	27.0	17.5	7.8	5.8	11.0	7.0
Eff. Tax Rate	NM	42%	43%	78%	39%	40%	40%	44%	41%	40%
Net Inc.	-8.3	25.0	13.3	0.2	16.3	10.5	4.7	3.2	6.5	4.2
Balance Sheet & Other Fin. Data (Million $)										
Cash	41.9	24.0	20.5	13.7	11.1	20.2	23.2	14.7	2.5	3.0
Curr. Assets	1,082	844	610	508	456	298	205	141	100	82.0
Total Assets	1,315	974	690	573	510	323	227	162	113	92.0
Curr. Liab.	1,004	701	499	400	342	214	161	117	74.0	58.0
LT Debt	5.6	35.2	3.9	4.1	2.1	1.2	9.3	11.0	8.8	6.4
Common Eqty.	290	238	186	168	166	108	56.9	33.5	29.7	27.0
Total Cap.	296	273	190	173	168	109	66.2	44.5	38.5	33.4
Cap. Exp.	42.3	36.5	24.0	22.9	17.6	7.9	4.9	8.4	4.9	1.6
Cash Flow	32.3	49.0	33.6	15.7	25.6	16.9	9.5	6.8	9.4	6.3
Curr. Ratio	1.1	1.2	1.2	1.3	1.3	1.4	1.3	1.2	1.3	1.4
% LT Debt of Cap.	1.9	12.8	2.0	2.4	1.2	1.1	14.1	24.7	22.9	19.2
% Net Inc.of Revs.	NM	0.6	0.4	NM	0.7	0.7	0.5	0.4	1.1	1.2
% Ret. on Assets	NM	3.0	2.1	0.1	3.7	3.3	2.1	2.4	6.4	5.7
% Ret. on Equity	NM	11.8	7.5	0.2	11.1	11.3	9.1	10.2	23.1	16.5

Data as orig reptd.; bef. results of disc opers/spec. items. Per share data adj. for stk. divs. Bold denotes diluted EPS (FASB 128)-prior periods restated. E-Estimated. NA-Not Available. NM-Not Meaningful. NR-Not Ranked.

Office—2400 South MicroAge Way, Tempe, AZ 85282-1896. **Tel**—(480) 366-2000. **Website**—http://www.microage.com **Chrmn & CEO**—J. D. McKeever. **Secy**—A. P. Hald. **SVP, CFO, Treas & Investor Contact**—James R. Daniel (602-929-2410). **Dirs**—L. M. Applegate, C. F. Friedheim, R. A. Herberger Jr., F. Israel, J. D. McKeever, W. H. Mallender, S. G. Mihaylo. **Transfer Agent & Registrar**—First Interstate Bank of Arizona, LA. **Incorporated**—in Delaware in 1987. **Empl**— 4,400. **S&P Analyst:** Matthew C. Hershberg

STANDARD
&POOR'S
STOCK REPORTS

MICROS Systems

NASDAQ Symbol **MCRS**

In S&P SmallCap 600

09-OCT-99

Industry:
Computers (Peripherals)

Summary: This company is a leading worldwide designer, manufacturer, supplier and servicer of restaurant point-of-sale computer systems and hotel management systems.

Quantitative Evaluations

Outlook
(1 Lowest—5 Highest)
• **5**

Fair Value
• **67⅞**

Risk
• **Average**

Earn./Div. Rank
• **B+**

Technical Eval.
• **Bullish** since 9/99

Rel. Strength Rank
(1 Lowest—99 Highest)
• **90**

Insider Activity
• **Unfavorable**

Recent Price • 41
52 Wk Range • 42¼-21½

Yield • Nil
12-Mo. P/E • 25.7

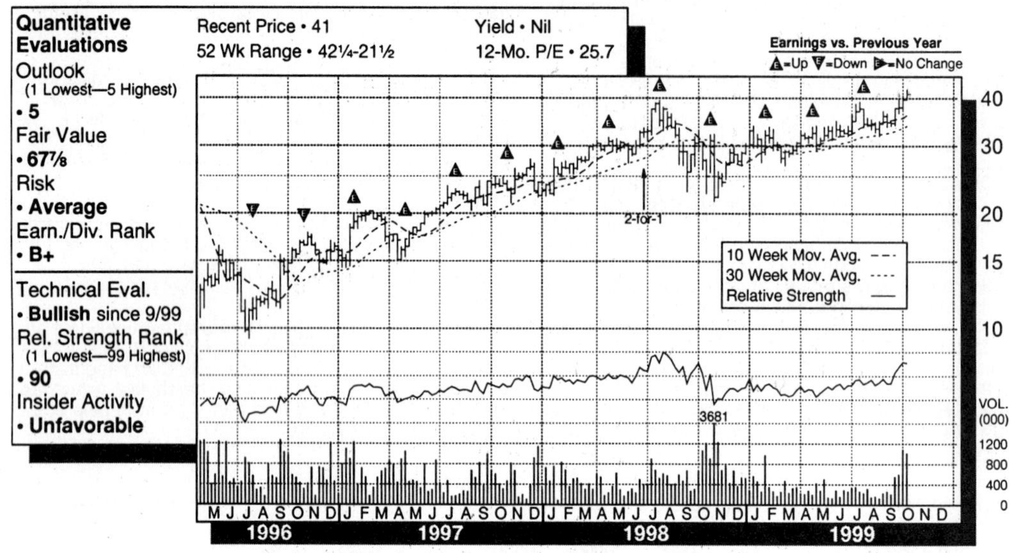

Business Profile - 13-SEP-99

MCRS said recently that its outlook for FY 00 (Jun.) is strong, due to anticipated robust demand for its point of sale and restaurant enterprise software as well as new hotel products. The company has posted revenue growth rates in recent periods in excess of the global market for point-of-sale (POS) computer systems, but does not expect to maintain growth at these levels. Increased competition is expected to put pressure on gross margins, but the company has been highly effective in achieving productivity improvements and reducing operating costs, which has aided earnings growth.

Operational Review - 13-SEP-99

Based on a preliminary report, revenues advanced 20% in FY 99, reflecting an 18% increase in hardware and software sales and a 22% gain for service revenues. Gross margins narrowed slightly, but, with well controlled SG&A expenses, operating income climbed 31%. After sharply lower office closure costs, and 13% higher depreciation and amortization charges, net income was up 36%, to $27,294,000 ($1.60 a share, on 2.1% more shares), from $20,053,000 ($1.20, as adjusted, before a charge of $0.02 for the cumulative effect of an accounting change).

Stock Performance - 08-OCT-99

In the past 30 trading days, MCRS's shares have increased 14%, compared to a 0.91% fall in the S&P 500. Average trading volume for the past five days was 201,220 shares, compared with the 40-day moving average of 102,795 shares.

Key Stock Statistics

Dividend Rate/Share	Nil	Shareholders	402
Shs. outstg. (M)	16.2	Market cap. (B)	$0.663
Avg. daily vol. (M)	0.161	Inst. holdings	84%
Tang. Bk. Value/Share	4.60		
Beta	1.15		

Value of $10,000 invested 5 years ago: $ 32,524

Fiscal Year Ending Jun. 30

	1999	1998	1997	1996	1995	1994
Revenues (Million $)						
1Q	66.64	59.59	47.51	32.36	24.47	16.40
2Q	80.59	66.27	55.96	42.89	27.12	19.32
3Q	85.12	71.08	56.71	47.31	25.19	19.28
4Q	102.7	83.31	67.99	55.50	35.24	24.27
Yr.	335.1	280.3	228.2	178.1	112.0	79.26
Earnings Per Share ($)						
1Q	**0.21**	**0.18**	**0.15**	0.20	0.19	0.13
2Q	**0.37**	**0.30**	**0.25**	-0.32	0.18	0.12
3Q	**0.45**	**0.35**	**0.27**	0.08	0.14	0.13
4Q	**0.58**	**0.36**	**0.34**	0.19	0.21	0.18
Yr.	**1.60**	**1.20**	**1.01**	**0.15**	**0.73**	**0.55**

Next earnings report expected: late October

Dividend Data

No cash dividends have been paid. The company intends to retain its earnings for use in the operation and expansion of its business and does not anticipate paying cash dividends in the foreseeable future.

A Division of The McGraw-Hill Companies

MICROS Systems, Inc.

Business Summary - 13-SEP-99

MICROS Systems, Inc. is a leading worldwide designer, manufacturer, supplier and servicer of point-of-sale (POS) computer systems for hospitality providers, primarily full service and fast food restaurants and hotels. It also markets and distributes property management information systems products and offers service and support for both systems.

The company's POS systems consist of terminals, display devices, printers, computer and software that provide transaction processing, in-store control and information management capabilities. Such systems enable users to control operations and inventory, enhance customer service efficiency, reduce labor costs, increase productivity and improve planning and reporting. POS products include the 8700 Hospitality Management System (HMS), which is designed for hotels, resorts, casinos, airports, sports arenas, theme parks and large local and chain restaurants. Features include customized workstations, flexible guest check printing, table and check tracking, automatic credit card authorization and system-wide reporting of sales mix, sales balancing, serving periods and table turns.

Other POS products include the 2700 HMS, a stand-alone intelligent terminal designed for small to large full service restaurants and certain fast food operations; 2400 HMS, a stand-alone system for the quick service restaurant sector; 3700 HMS, a PC-driven system for operations control of full service dining operations; and the Handheld Touchscreen terminal, a small remote order entry computer device that allows a server to enter a food and beverage order at the table or seat-side.

The company's property management information systems (PMS) products provide reservation, guest accounting and other information management capabilities to hotels and other lodging establishments. In addition to PMS products for the hotel industry, the company offers central reservation systems (CRS) software, which allows hotel companies to provide instantaneous updating of reservations for member hotels.

MICROS also offers service and support for its POS, PMS and CRS products, including installations, training, hardware and software maintenance, spare parts, media supplies and consulting services. Such services accounted for 35% of revenues in FY 98 (Jun.).

Products are marketed and sold through company-owned domestic and foreign sales offices as well as through international distributors. Foreign sales accounted for 54% of revenues in FY 98.

Per Share Data ($) (Year Ended Jun. 30)	1999	1998	1997	1996	1995	1994	1993	1992	1991	1990
Tangible Bk. Val.	NA	4.60	3.19	2.23	3.29	2.44	1.89	1.57	1.27	1.07
Cash Flow	NA	1.92	1.58	0.45	0.83	0.63	0.43	0.33	0.28	0.24
Earnings	1.60	1.20	1.01	0.15	0.73	0.55	0.37	0.27	0.22	0.18
Dividends	Nil	Nil	Nil	Nil	Nil	Nil	Nil	Nil	Nil	Nil
Payout Ratio	Nil	Nil	Nil	Nil	Nil	Nil	Nil	Nil	Nil	Nil
Prices - High	42¼	39½	27¾	26⅞	24⅞	20⅝	13	11⅜	3⅝	2¾
- Low	26⅝	21½	14⅜	9⅜	13⅞	11¼	5⅞	2⅞	1⅝	1⅜
P/E Ratio - High	26	33	27	179	26	38	35	43	16	15
- Low	17	18	14	63	19	21	16	10	7	8
Income Statement Analysis (Million $)										
Revs.	NA	280	228	178	112	79.0	55.3	44.3	39.6	35.2
Oper. Inc.	NA	44.8	37.0	25.1	18.2	13.6	10.3	6.8	5.6	4.8
Depr.	NA	10.7	9.2	4.8	1.6	1.2	0.9	1.0	1.0	0.9
Int. Exp.	NA	1.8	1.4	1.6	0.4	0.2	0.1	0.1	0.1	0.1
Pretax Inc.	NA	33.2	27.6	2.7	17.7	12.6	8.8	6.0	5.0	4.1
Eff. Tax Rate	NA	39%	38%	13%	35%	32%	35%	35%	34%	38%
Net Inc.	NA	20.1	16.3	2.4	11.6	8.7	5.8	4.0	3.3	2.6
Balance Sheet & Other Fin. Data (Million $)										
Cash	NA	13.6	10.9	15.2	26.4	16.3	12.8	14.0	9.7	6.7
Curr. Assets	NA	143	108	87.9	66.6	46.7	33.6	29.7	23.9	20.9
Total Assets	NA	205	164	137	89.6	66.2	48.1	37.4	30.1	26.6
Curr. Liab.	NA	97.7	79.9	67.2	29.6	19.6	15.3	11.3	9.1	8.8
LT Debt	NA	7.7	7.1	10.2	5.3	5.5	1.6	1.7	1.8	2.0
Common Eqty.	NA	91.7	71.7	56.2	53.5	39.9	30.0	23.6	19.2	15.8
Total Cap.	NA	103	83.6	69.6	60.0	46.6	32.7	26.1	21.1	17.9
Cap. Exp.	NA	9.3	8.1	4.8	2.6	1.2	0.7	0.4	1.1	0.8
Cash Flow	NA	30.7	25.5	7.2	13.2	9.9	6.7	5.0	4.3	3.5
Curr. Ratio	NA	1.5	1.3	1.3	2.3	2.3	2.2	2.6	2.6	2.4
% LT Debt of Cap.	NA	7.5	8.5	14.6	8.8	11.8	5.0	6.4	8.8	11.3
% Net Inc.of Revs.	NA	7.2	7.2	1.3	10.3	11.0	10.4	9.1	8.3	7.3
% Ret. on Assets	NA	10.9	10.9	2.1	14.9	15.2	13.5	11.8	11.6	11.8
% Ret. on Equity	NA	24.5	25.5	4.4	24.8	24.9	21.5	18.8	18.7	20.4

Data as orig reptd.; bef. results of disc opers/spec. items. Per share data adj. for stk. divs. Bold denotes diluted EPS (FASB 128)-prior periods restated. E-Estimated. NA-Not Available. NM-Not Meaningful. NR-Not Ranked.

Office—12000 Baltimore Ave., Beltsville, MD 20705-1291. **Tel**—(301) 210-6000. **Chrmn**—L. M. Brown, Jr. **Pres & CEO**—A. L. Giannopoulos. **EVP & COO**—R. J. Kolson. **SVP-Fin & CFO**—G. C. Kaufman. **Secy**—J. F. Wilbert. **Investor Contact**—Peter J. Rogers, Jr. (301 210-8059). **Dirs**—L. M. Brown, Jr., D. A. Cohen, A. L. Giannopoulos, F. S. Jenniches, J. G. Puente, D. S. Taylor. **Transfer Agent & Registrar**—Registrar and Transfer Co., Cranford, NJ. **Incorporated**—in Maryland in 1977. **Empl**— 1,754. **S&P Analyst:** Jim Corridore

STANDARD
&POOR'S
STOCK REPORTS

Midway Games

NYSE Symbol **MWY**

In S&P SmallCap 600

09-OCT-99

Industry: Leisure Time (Products)

Summary: This company designs, publishes and markets interactive entertainment software played in the coin operated and home markets.

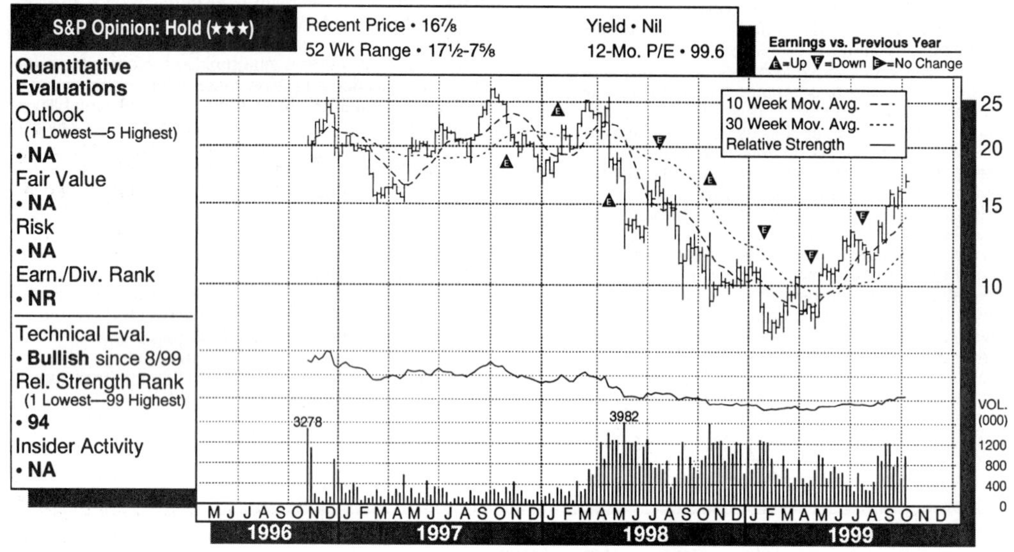

Overview - 26-AUG-99

In light of the variable nature of demand in the video game industry, it is difficult to predict revenue growth for more than a quarter or two in advance. We see the top line advancing between 20% and 30% over the next two quarters, driven by a strong pipeline of game titles in anticipation of the coming holiday season. In addition, with the termination of its relationship with GT Interactive Software, MWY will begin sales of its products in overseas markets. We expect the company to generate international sales of $60 million to $90 million in FY 00 (Jun.). Margins are likely to widen in FY 00, driven by an increased proportion of CD-ROM business, as well as the anticipated rise in revenues. We see FY 00 EPS more than doubling, to $0.94. Results in FY 99 exclude non-recurring charges related to litigation and an organizational restructuring.

Valuation - 26-AUG-99

The shares have risen sharply since April 1999, reflecting an increasingly favorable operating outlook for FY 00, and were recently trading at 14X our FY 00 EPS estimate of $0.94. While this represents a discount to the P/E of the overall market, we feel it is warranted, in light of the limited earnings visibility associated with the video game industry, as well as MWY's extremely poor performance in FY 99. As a result, we continue to recommend that investors limit themselves to holding existing positions. We are encouraged by the company's efforts to dedicate more resources to internal development of new titles, which should facilitate timely product launches and create a sizable portfolio of game offerings. In addition, the top line will be bolstered by MWY's entry into a number of foreign markets. For the long term, we also expect the company's more focused PC-based game strategy to bear fruit.

Key Stock Statistics

S&P EPS Est. 2000	0.94	Tang. Bk. Value/Share	3.46
P/E on S&P Est. 2000	18.0	Beta	NA
Dividend Rate/Share	Nil	Shareholders	1,350
Shs. outstg. (M)	38.1	Market cap. (B)	$0.644
Avg. daily vol. (M)	0.161	Inst. holdings	40%

Value of $10,000 invested 5 years ago: NA

Fiscal Year Ending Jun. 30

	1999	1998	1997	1996	1995	1994
Revenues (Million $)						
1Q	89.34	73.74	65.56	—	—	—
2Q	125.7	125.1	125.5	—	—	—
3Q	80.33	94.35	99.1	—	—	—
4Q	56.47	98.09	98.09	—	—	—
Yr.	351.8	391.2	388.2	329.4	—	—
Earnings Per Share ($)						
1Q	**0.26**	**0.19**	0.18	—	—	—
2Q	**0.29**	**0.48**	0.41	—	—	—
3Q	**0.03**	**0.18**	0.17	—	—	—
4Q	**-0.40**	**0.25**	0.29	—	—	—
Yr.	**0.17**	**1.10**	**1.06**	**0.76**	—	—

Next earnings report expected: late October

Dividend Data

MWY does not plan to pay dividends on its common stock for the foreseeable future. It intends to retain any earnings for the development and expansion of its business.

Midway Games Inc.

Business Summary - 26-AUG-99

Midway Games Inc. designs, publishes and markets interactive entertainment software played in both the coin-operated and home markets. Prior to the IPO of 5.1 million common shares in October 1996, the company was a wholly owned subsidiary of WMS Industries Inc., which continues to provide certain administrative, accounting, and information services and facilities, and acts as a contract manufacturer for MWY's coin-operated video games.

The company believes a successful video game may present the opportunity to exploit ancillary rights, such as film, television and merchandising rights.

Like coin-operated video games, interactive software programs for the home allow the consumer to participate actively in the outcome of the game. The interactive software publishing business, which provided 62% of FY 99 (Jun.) revenue, involves the creation or acquisition of titles or intellectual property rights, the development of interactive software products based on those titles or rights, and the publication, marketing, merchandising, distribution and licensing of the resulting software products. The business is depends to a high degree on consumer tastes and preferences, and on the commercial success of the hardware platform for which the software is produced. Home video games have suggested retail prices ranging from $39.95 to $59.95.

Coin-operated video games (38% of FY 99 sales), which are sold to distributors at prices ranging from $3,000 to $7,000, are made in self-contained cabinetry containing large video screens that display the game. Multiple players can play the same game simultaneously, and games are generally designed to permit players to compete with each other, in addition to being able to play against the game itself. Most coin-operated video games cost $0.50 to play a game of about two minutes in duration.

Since the late 1970s, Midway has released many of the industry's leading games, including the Mortal Kombat line (which has sold more than 15 million copies, and which accounted for 19% of revenues in FY 98), Cruis'n USA, Cruis'n World, NBA Jam, Joust, Defender, Pacman, and Space Invaders, and, through its subsidiary Atari Games Corp., such games as San Francisco Rush Extreme Racing, The NHLPA & NHL Present Wayne Gretzky's 3D Hockey, Area 51, Gauntlet, Centipede, Asteroids, and Pong. The company's games are generally available for play on all major dedicated home video game platforms, including those of Nintendo, Sony and Sega, and on personal computers.

Per Share Data ($)										
(Year Ended Jun. 30)	**1999**	**1998**	**1997**	**1996**	**1995**	**1994**	**1993**	**1992**	**1991**	**1990**
Tangible Bk. Val.	NA	3.46	2.38	1.98	NA	NA	NA	NA	NA	NA
Cash Flow	NA	1.33	1.23	0.89	NA	NA	NA	NA	NA	NA
Earnings	0.17	1.10	1.06	0.74	NA	NA	NA	NA	NA	NA
Dividends	Nil	Nil	Nil	Nil	NA	NA	NA	NA	NA	NA
Payout Ratio	Nil	Nil	Nil	Nil	NA	NA	NA	NA	NA	NA
Prices - High	17½	25⅝	26⅞	25½	NA	NA	NA	NA	NA	NA
- Low	7⅝	9	15	18⅜	NA	NA	NA	NA	NA	NA
P/E Ratio - High	NM	23	25	34	NA	NA	NA	NA	NA	NA
- Low	45	8	14	25	NA	NA	NA	NA	NA	NA
Income Statement Analysis (Million $)										
Revs.	NA	391	388	329	NA	NA	NA	NA	NA	NA
Oper. Inc.	NA	74.0	66.8	45.7	NA	NA	NA	NA	NA	NA
Depr.	NA	8.9	6.3	5.1	NA	NA	NA	NA	NA	NA
Int. Exp.	NA	Nil	2.4	0.8	NA	NA	NA	NA	NA	NA
Pretax Inc.	NA	68.0	62.7	39.9	NA	NA	NA	NA	NA	NA
Eff. Tax Rate	NA	38%	38%	38%	NA	NA	NA	NA	NA	NA
Net Inc.	NA	42.1	38.9	24.7	NA	NA	NA	NA	NA	NA
Balance Sheet & Other Fin. Data (Million $)										
Cash	NA	26.1	61.9	52.9	NA	NA	NA	NA	NA	NA
Curr. Assets	NA	162	154	NA	NA	NA	NA	NA	NA	NA
Total Assets	NA	227	214	162	NA	NA	NA	NA	NA	NA
Curr. Liab.	NA	43.9	68.1	NA	NA	NA	NA	NA	NA	NA
LT Debt	NA	Nil	Nil	7.9	NA	NA	NA	NA	NA	NA
Common Eqty.	NA	177	141	99	NA	NA	NA	NA	NA	NA
Total Cap.	NA	181	144	107	NA	NA	NA	NA	NA	NA
Cap. Exp.	NA	4.4	4.7	4.1	NA	NA	NA	NA	NA	NA
Cash Flow	NA	51.0	45.1	29.8	NA	NA	NA	NA	NA	NA
Curr. Ratio	NA	3.7	2.3	NA	NA	NA	NA	NA	NA	NA
% LT Debt of Cap.	NA	Nil	Nil	7.3	NA	NA	NA	NA	NA	NA
% Net Inc.of Revs.	NA	10.8	10.0	7.5	NA	NA	NA	NA	NA	NA
% Ret. on Assets	NA	19.1	23.4	NA	NA	NA	NA	NA	NA	NA
% Ret. on Equity	NA	26.5	32.4	NA	NA	NA	NA	NA	NA	NA

Data as orig. reptd.; bef. results of disc. opers. and/or spec. items. Per share data adj. for stk. divs. as of ex-div. date. Bold denotes diluted EPS (FASB 128). E-Estimated. NA-Not Available. NM-Not Meaningful. NR-Not Ranked.

Office—3401 North California Ave., Chicago, IL 60618. **Tel**—(773) 961-2222. **Chrmn, Pres, CEO & COO**—N. D. Nicastro. **EVP, CFO & Treas**—H. H. Bach, Jr. **VP & Secy**—O. J. Edidin. **Dirs**—H. H. Bach, Jr., W. C. Bartholomay, B. C. Cook, K. J. Fedesna, W. E. McKenna, N. J. Menell, L. J. Nicastro, N. D. Nicastro, H. Reich, I. S. Sheinfeld, G. O. Sweeney, Jr., R. D. White. **Transfer Agent & Registrar**—Bank of New York, NYC. **Incorporated**—in Delaware in 1988. **Empl**— 550. **S&P Analyst:** Stephen J. Tekirian

STANDARD
&POOR'S
STOCK REPORTS

Midwest Express Holdings

NYSE Symbol **MEH**

In S&P SmallCap 600

09-OCT-99 **Industry:** Airlines

Summary: This holding company owns Midwest Express Airlines and Skyway Airlines.

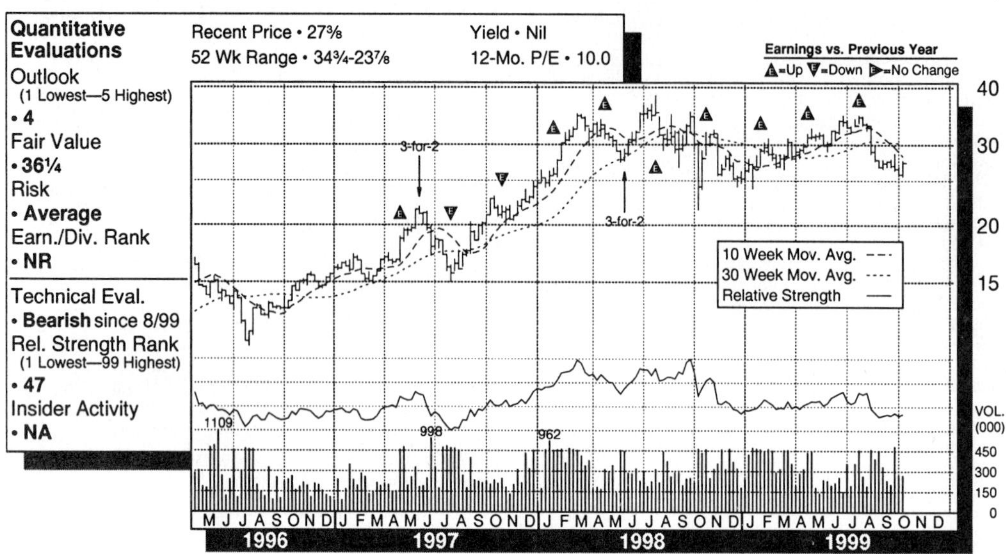

Business Profile - 12-JUL-99

Aided by healthy passenger volume, the company continues to report strong results. Earnings in recent periods benefited from lower fuel prices and a new travel agent commission structure, and from a stable economy, strong demand, and favorable pricing and competitive environments. In the 1999 first quarter, increases in passenger volume and lower unit costs outweighed the impact of lower revenue yields and increased weather-related flight cancellations. Revenue yield decreased 7.2%, primarily due to competitive pricing pressures in certain markets, and an increased proportion of passenger volume in lower-yield seasonal markets. At the same time, unit costs decreased 6.3% due to lower fuel prices and improved cost efficiency in most cost categories.

Operational Review - 12-JUL-99

Revenues in the 199 first quarter climbed 12%, year to year, reflecting increased passenger volume that resulted from strong passenger demand for air travel throughout the industry. Operating expenses rose less rapidly, reflecting a reduction in aircraft fuel and oil expenses, partly offset by higher aircraft maintenance costs; operating income advanced 20%. With lower interest income, after taxes at 37.5% in each period, net income was up 17%, to $7,103,000 ($0.50 a share), from $6,080,000 ($0.43, as adjusted).

Stock Performance - 08-OCT-99

In the past 30 trading days, MEH's shares have increased 2%, compared to a 0.91% fall in the S&P 500. Average trading volume for the past five days was 53,480 shares, compared with the 40-day moving average of 75,859 shares.

Key Stock Statistics

Dividend Rate/Share	Nil	Shareholders	612
Shs. outstg. (M)	14.2	Market cap. (B)	$0.388
Avg. daily vol. (M)	0.077	Inst. holdings	72%
Tang. Bk. Value/Share	6.59		
Beta	NA		

Value of $10,000 invested 5 years ago: NA

Fiscal Year Ending Dec. 31

	1999	1998	1997	1996	1995	1994
Revenues (Million $)						
1Q	98.88	88.41	79.92	66.61	58.54	--
2Q	117.7	100.1	83.34	76.85	69.39	--
3Q	—	103.8	89.40	83.12	67.85	--
4Q	—	96.54	91.89	78.17	63.38	--
Yr.	—	388.9	344.6	304.8	259.2	203.6
Earnings Per Share ($)						
1Q	**0.50**	**0.43**	**0.29**	**0.19**	--	--
2Q	**0.91**	**0.75**	**0.39**	**0.45**	—	--
3Q	—	**0.75**	**0.53**	**0.58**	--	--
4Q	—	**0.58**	**0.53**	**0.28**	--	--
Yr.	—	**2.51**	**1.74**	1.51	**1.23**	0.32

Next earnings report expected: mid October

Dividend Data

No cash dividends have been paid. A three-for-two stock split was effected in May 1998.

Midwest Express Holdings, Inc.

Business Summary - 12-JUL-99

Midwest Express Holdings (MEH) is the holding company for Midwest Express Airlines, which operates a single-class, premium passenger jet airline that caters to business travelers and serves selected major business destinations throughout the U.S., as well as Toronto, from operations bases in Milwaukee and Omaha.

The company also offers scheduled commuter air service under the Skyway Airlines name through Astral Aviation, Inc., a wholly owned subsidiary. Astral is a 19-seat airplane commuter service that provides connections between Milwaukee and 25 cities in seven Midwest states, feeding passenger traffic into the Midwest Express route system, and also providing point-to-point service to selected markets. Astral began operations in February 1994, taking over routes that Mesa Airlines had operated pursuant to a code-sharing agreement with Midwest Express.

Midwest Express has two bases of operations, Milwaukee and Omaha. As of December 31, 1998, Midwest Express served 26 cities from Milwaukee, and was the only carrier providing nonstop service between Milwaukee and most Midwest Express destinations. Although 10 other jet airlines serve Milwaukee's airport, these carriers generally provide nonstop flights only between Milwaukee and their respective operations' hubs.

Midwest Express primarily caters to business travelers. It provides passengers with personal attention, two-across leather seats, fine food served on china with complimentary wine or champagne, and baked on-board chocolate chip cookies on luncheon flights - all at competitive fares. Conde Nast Traveler, Travel & Leisure, and the Zagat Airline Survey have recognized Midwest Express as the best airline in the U.S., and Aviation Week &Space Technology named it the best managed national airline in the world.

Midwest Express sells approximately 70% of its tickets through travel agents. The company maintains its own reservations center at its headquarters. As with most travel agencies, MEH's reservations center obtains airline information, makes reservations and sells tickets for Midwest Express and Skyway flights through a computer reservation system. Effective September 1997, the company changed its travel agency commission rate structure to an 8% base commission rate, with no commission cap. This structure is similar to that of most other airlines.

In 1998, Midwest Express established a one-year renewable codesharing agreement with American Eagle. Under the agreement, Midwest Express provides passengers with jet service to Los Angeles or Dallas/Ft. Worth, with American Eagle providing passengers with connecting service from Los Angeles to eight cities in California, and from Dallas/Ft. Worth to 31 cities in the southern and south central U.S.

Per Share Data ($) (Year Ended Dec. 31)	1998	1997	1996	1995	1994	1993	1992	1991	1990	1989
Tangible Bk. Val.	6.59	4.14	2.46	1.08	1.10	NA	NA	NA	NA	NA
Cash Flow	3.21	2.38	2.05	1.75	0.79	NA	NA	NA	NA	NA
Earnings	2.51	1.74	1.51	1.23	0.32	NA	NA	NA	NA	NA
Dividends	Nil	Nil	Nil	Nil	NA	NA	NA	NA	NA	NA
Payout Ratio	Nil	Nil	Nil	Nil	NA	NA	NA	NA	NA	NA
Prices - High	38 3/8	26 3/8	17 1/4	13 3/4	NA	NA	NA	NA	NA	NA
- Low	21 1/2	15	10 7/8	8	NA	NA	NA	NA	NA	NA
P/E Ratio - High	15	15	11	11	NA	NA	NA	NA	NA	NA
- Low	9	9	7	6	NA	NA	NA	NA	NA	NA
Income Statement Analysis (Million $)										
Revs.	389	345	305	259	204	NA	NA	NA	NA	NA
Oper. Inc.	65.7	47.1	42.0	38.9	14.0	NA	NA	NA	NA	NA
Depr.	10.0	8.6	7.7	7.5	6.9	NA	NA	NA	NA	NA
Int. Exp.	0.3	0.1	Nil	0.0	0.3	NA	NA	NA	NA	NA
Pretax Inc.	57.0	39.6	35.2	31.5	7.4	NA	NA	NA	NA	NA
Eff. Tax Rate	37%	37%	38%	39%	39%	NA	NA	NA	NA	NA
Net Inc.	35.9	24.9	21.8	19.1	4.6	NA	NA	NA	NA	NA
Balance Sheet & Other Fin. Data (Million $)										
Cash	13.5	32.1	27.6	14.7	8.0	NA	NA	NA	NA	NA
Curr. Assets	39.6	55.6	52.6	31.1	22.2	NA	NA	NA	NA	NA
Total Assets	220	167	129	92.8	84.2	NA	NA	NA	NA	NA
Curr. Liab.	82.0	68.5	58.6	40.9	37.7	NA	NA	NA	NA	NA
LT Debt	3.2	3.3	Nil	Nil	Nil	NA	NA	NA	NA	NA
Common Eqty.	97.6	63.4	40.3	21.3	21.6	NA	NA	NA	NA	NA
Total Cap.	114	79.2	50.2	35.0	35.6	NA	NA	NA	NA	NA
Cap. Exp.	74.3	27.6	25.6	8.0	NA	NA	NA	NA	NA	NA
Cash Flow	45.9	33.6	29.5	25.3	11.5	NA	NA	NA	NA	NA
Curr. Ratio	0.5	0.8	0.9	0.8	0.6	NA	NA	NA	NA	NA
% LT Debt of Cap.	2.8	4.2	Nil	Nil	Nil	NA	NA	NA	NA	NA
% Net Inc.of Revs.	9.2	7.2	7.1	7.4	2.2	NA	NA	NA	NA	NA
% Ret. on Assets	18.5	16.9	19.7	20.3	NA	NA	NA	NA	NA	NA
% Ret. on Equity	44.5	48.1	70.8	64.7	NA	NA	NA	NA	NA	NA

Data as orig reptd.; bef. results of disc opers/spec. items. Per share data adj. for stk. divs. Bold denotes diluted EPS (FASB 128)-prior periods restated. E-Estimated. NA-Not Available. NM-Not Meaningful. NR-Not Ranked.

Office—6744 S. Howell Ave., Oak Creek, WI 53154. **Organized**—in Delaware in 1995; reincorporated in Wisconsin in 1996. **Tel**—(414) 570-4000. **Website**—http://www.midwestexpress.com**Chrmn, Pres & CEO**—T. E. Hoeksema. **SVP, CFO & Treas**—R. S. Bahlman. **Investor Contacts**—Dennis J. O'Reilly, Robert S. Bahlman. **Dirs**—J. F. Bergstrom, O. C. Boldt, J. G. Grosklaus, U. Payne, Jr., T. E. Hoeksema, B. F. Skelton, S. K. Skinner, R. H. Sonnentag, F. P. Stratton Jr., D. H. Treitel, J. W. Weekly. **Transfer Agent & Registrar**—Firstar Trust Co., Milwaukee. **Empl**—2,723. **S&P Analyst:** C.C.P.

STANDARD & POOR'S
STOCK REPORTS

Mississippi Chemical

NYSE Symbol **GRO**

In S&P SmallCap 600

09-OCT-99

Industry: Chemicals

Summary: GRO is a major manufacturer of fertilizers. It produces and markets all three primary crop nutrients: nitrogen, phosphate, and potash.

Quantitative Evaluations

Outlook (1 Lowest—5 Highest)
• 3+

Fair Value
• 8½

Risk
• **Low**

Earn./Div. Rank
• **NR**

Technical Eval.
• **Bearish** since 8/99

Rel. Strength Rank (1 Lowest—99 Highest)
• 7

Insider Activity
• **NA**

Recent Price • 6⅛
52 Wk Range • 16½-5⅞
Yield • 6.5%
12-Mo. P/E • NM

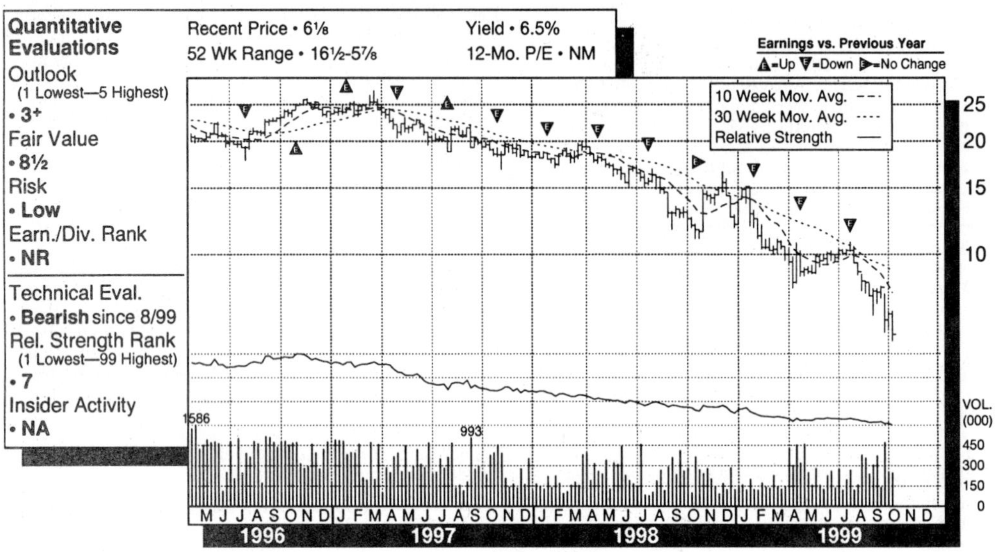

Business Profile - 11-MAY-99

A key issue for Mississippi Chemical's profitability is the direction of nitrogen pricing, which is driven by supply and demand. More specific factors that can affect pricing are Chinese purchasing practices, Russian production and pricing policies, and the impact of recent global capacity expansions. In April 1999, the company said that as it moves into the fourth quarter of FY 99 (Jun.), nitrogen market fundamentals remained relatively weak. This has resulted in a softening of nitrogen prices from those experienced in late March. GRO expected low nitrogen prices to continue to have a negative impact on results on a year-to-year basis, but the company did expect sequential improvement in performance.

Operational Review - 11-MAY-99

Revenues for the first nine months of FY 99 (Jun.) rose only nominally, year to year, as increased sales volume for most products slightly outweighed lower average selling prices. Price reductions for ammonia, ammonium nitrate, urea, and nitrogen solutions of 29%, 11%, 14%, and 16%, respectively--reflecting decreased nitrogen fertilizer prices--led to a drop in operating profit of 50%. Other expenses (net) increased 92%, exceeding operating profit, and there was a pretax loss of $4.9 million, in contrast to pretax income of $9.5 million. Following a tax credit, versus taxes at 45.7%, the net loss was $2.4 million ($0.09 a share), against net income of $5.2 million ($0.19).

Stock Performance - 08-OCT-99

In the past 30 trading days, GRO's shares have declined 21%, compared to a 0.91% fall in the S&P 500. Average trading volume for the past five days was 49,100 shares, compared with the 40-day moving average of 66,059 shares.

Key Stock Statistics

Dividend Rate/Share	0.40	Shareholders	15,048
Shs. outstg. (M)	26.1	Market cap. (B)	$0.160
Avg. daily vol. (M)	0.066	Inst. holdings	52%
Tang. Bk. Value/Share	9.99		
Beta	0.72		

Value of $10,000 invested 5 years ago: NA

Fiscal Year Ending Jun. 30

	1999	1998	1997	1996	1995	1994
Revenues (Million $)						
1Q	104.7	110.9	91.29	96.57	72.75	—
2Q	94.84	118.0	113.2	99.9	83.71	—
3Q	140.6	125.8	142.6	107.7	114.7	—
4Q	127.7	165.2	173.5	124.6	117.0	—
Yr.	467.9	519.1	520.6	428.8	388.1	309.4
Earnings Per Share ($)						
1Q	**0.16**	0.16	0.44	0.43	0.27	—
2Q	**-0.02**	**0.02**	0.56	0.53	0.46	—
3Q	**-0.23**	**0.02**	0.38	0.72	0.75	—
4Q	**-0.05**	**0.65**	0.86	0.79	0.82	—
Yr.	**-0.14**	**0.84**	**2.29**	**2.46**	2.34	—

Next earnings report expected: late October

Dividend Data (Dividends have been paid since 1995.)

Amount ($)	Date Decl.	Ex-Div. Date	Stock of Record	Payment Date
0.100	Oct. 28	Nov. 06	Nov. 11	Nov. 25 '98
0.100	Jan. 28	Feb. 09	Feb. 11	Feb. 25 '99
0.100	Apr. 22	May. 06	May. 10	May. 25 '99
0.100	Jul. 23	Aug. 09	Aug. 11	Aug. 25 '99

A Division of The McGraw-Hill Companies

Mississippi Chemical Corporation

Business Summary - 11-MAY-99

Mississippi Chemical Corp., a major manufacturer of fertilizers, produces and markets all three primary crop nutrients: nitrogen fertilizer: diammonium phosphate fertilizer; and potash fertilizer.

Sales breakdown by major product categories in FY 98 (Jun.) was as follows: nitrogen 57%, phosphate 25%, and potash 18%.

Nitrogen products were being produced, as of year-end FY 98 (Jun.), at the company's production facilities in Yazoo City, MS, and Donaldsonville, LA. The company's principal nitrogen products are: ammonia; fertilizer-grade ammonium nitrate, which is sold under the trade name Amtrate; UAN solutions, which are sold under the trade name N-Sol; urea; and nitric acid. In FY 98, the company sold approximately 2.5 million tons of nitrogen products to farmers, fertilizer dealers and distributors, and industrial users located primarily in the southern United States. These sales produced revenues of $298.6 million,

Diammonium phosphate fertilizer (DAP) was being produced, as of year-end FY 98, at the company's facility in Pascagoula, MS. In FY 98, the company sold approximately 726,000 tons of DAP, which produced revenues of $127.7 million.

DAP, which is the most common form of phosphate fertilizer, is produced by reacting phosphate rock with sulfuric acid to produce phosphoric acid, which is then combined with ammonia. DAP contains 18% nitrogen and 46% phosphate (P205) by weight. DAP is an important fertilizer product both for direct application and for use in blended fertilizers applied to all major types of row crops.

Potash was being produced, as of year-end FY 98, at two mines and related facilities near Carlsbad, NM. In FY 98, the company sold approximately 1,022,000 tons of potash, primarily in granular form, which generated revenues of $91.7 million. These sales were predominately to customers located west of the Mississippi River.

The three principal grades of potash fertilizer are granular, coarse, and standard, with granular being the largest particle size. Potash is an important fertilizer product for both direct application and for use in blended fertilizers applied to all types of crops. Granular potash is used as a direct-application fertilizer and, among the various grades, is particularly well suited for use in fertilizer blends. In addition, the company produces several grades of potash that are purchased as a raw material by industrial users.

Per Share Data ($)										
(Year Ended Jun. 30)	**1999**	**1998**	**1997**	**1996**	**1995**	**1994**	**1993**	**1992**	**1991**	**1990**
Tangible Bk. Val.	NA	9.99	9.43	11.61	10.19	7.87	NA	NA	NA	NA
Cash Flow	NA	2.20	3.32	3.28	3.10	NA	NA	NA	NA	NA
Earnings	-0.14	0.84	2.29	2.46	2.34	NA	NA	NA	NA	NA
Dividends	0.40	0.40	0.30	0.36	0.16	Nil	NA	NA	NA	NA
Payout Ratio	NM	48%	13%	15%	7%	Nil	NA	NA	NA	NA
Prices - High	15 1/8	20 1/8	27 1/4	26	25 1/4	19 1/4	NA	NA	NA	NA
- Low	5 7/8	11	16 3/4	17 3/4	15 3/8	14 3/4	NA	NA	NA	NA
P/E Ratio - High	NM	24	12	11	11	NA	NA	NA	NA	NA
- Low	NM	13	7	7	7	NA	NA	NA	NA	NA
Income Statement Analysis (Million $)										
Revs.	NA	519	521	429	388	309	289	NA	NA	NA
Oper. Inc.	NA	75.2	119	103	98.0	61.0	44.0	NA	NA	NA
Depr.	NA	37.2	28.0	17.8	17.1	17.0	14.4	NA	NA	NA
Int. Exp.	NA	12.5	8.9	0.7	2.0	4.7	6.0	NA	NA	NA
Pretax Inc.	NA	39.3	90.6	88.5	81.4	32.9	26.4	NA	NA	NA
Eff. Tax Rate	NA	42%	38%	39%	36%	18%	14%	NA	NA	NA
Net Inc.	NA	23.0	55.8	54.2	52.2	26.9	22.7	NA	NA	NA
Balance Sheet & Other Fin. Data (Million $)										
Cash	NA	3.9	8.2	60.2	29.6	23.2	NA	NA	NA	NA
Curr. Assets	NA	141	149	142	115	100	NA	NA	NA	NA
Total Assets	NA	912	859	341	302	298	NA	NA	NA	NA
Curr. Liab.	NA	76.6	95.1	60.0	44.5	64.4	NA	NA	NA	NA
LT Debt	NA	305	245	Nil	2.5	57.2	NA	NA	NA	NA
Common Eqty.	NA	449	439	248	227	90.0	NA	NA	NA	NA
Total Cap.	NA	819	743	263	243	156	NA	NA	NA	NA
Cap. Exp.	NA	96.5	93.8	NA	22.3	11.2	26.4	NA	NA	NA
Cash Flow	NA	60.2	80.8	72.0	69.3	43.9	37.1	NA	NA	NA
Curr. Ratio	NA	1.8	1.6	2.4	2.6	1.6	NA	NA	NA	NA
% LT Debt of Cap.	NA	37.2	33.0	Nil	1.0	36.7	NA	NA	NA	NA
% Net Inc.of Revs.	NA	4.4	10.7	12.6	13.5	8.7	7.9	NA	NA	NA
% Ret. on Assets	NA	2.6	9.3	16.8	17.4	NA	NA	NA	NA	NA
% Ret. on Equity	NA	5.2	16.2	22.8	32.6	NA	NA	NA	NA	NA

Data as orig reptd.; bef. results of disc opers/spec. items. Per share data adj. for stk. divs. Bold denotes diluted EPS (FASB 128)-prior periods restated. E-Estimated. NA-Not Available. NM-Not Meaningful. NR-Not Ranked.

Office—Highway 49 East, P. O. Box 388, Yazoo City, MS 39194. **Tel**—(662) 746-4131. **Website**—http://www.misschem.com **Chrmn**—C. L. Bailey. **Pres & CEO**—C. O. Dunn. **VP-Fin**—T. A. Dawson. **Secy**—R. B. Glascoe. **Investor Contact**—Keith Johnson (662 751-2203).**Dirs**—J. W. Anderson, C. L. Bailey, H. Barbour, F. R. Burnside Jr., C. O. Dunn, W. R. Dyess, W. E. Eastland, J. S. Howie, G. D. Penick Jr., W. A. Percy II, D. M. Ratcliffe, W. Thames. **Transfer Agent & Registrar**—Harris Trust & Savings Bank, Chicago. **Incorporated**—in Mississippi in 1994.**Empl**— 1,600.
S&P Analyst: N.J. DeVita

STANDARD
&POOR'S
STOCK REPORTS

Monaco Coach

NYSE Symbol **MNC**

In S&P SmallCap 600

09-OCT-99

Industry: Leisure Time (Products)

Summary: This company is a leading manufacturer of premium Class A motor coaches and towable recreational vehicles.

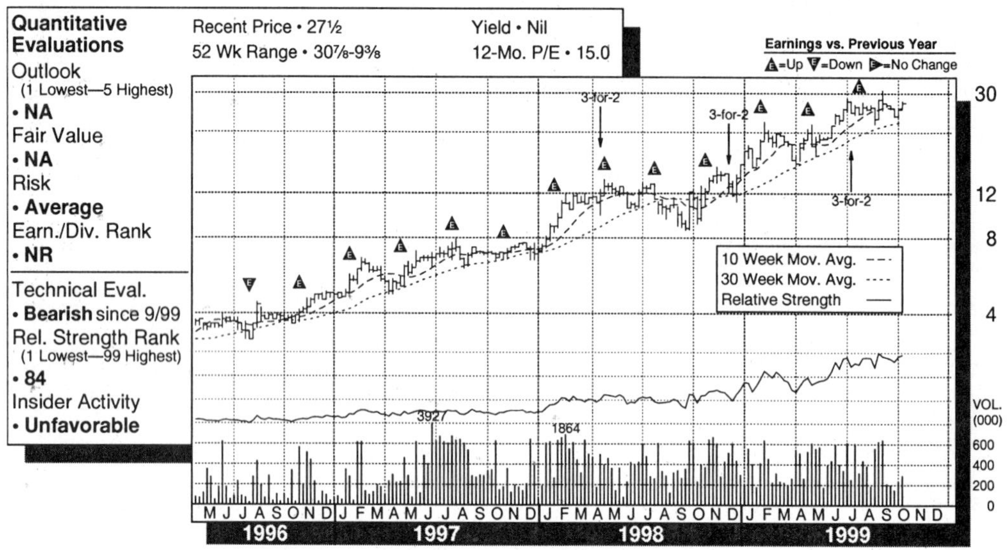

Business Profile - 08-SEP-99

In July 1999, Monaco said that its dealers have reported brisk showroom traffic and demand for its products remains strong. Construction on the company's 525,000 square foot Coburg, Oregon, facilities expansion is nearing completion. In addition, MNC recently agreed to acquire additional production space in Indiana to allow it to increase its diesel motor home production capacity. The company believes that this expansion will greatly enhance its manufacturing capabilities. The Indiana property is adjacent to Monaco's existing Elkhart operations, and includes 250,000 square feet of additional space.

Operational Review - 08-SEP-99

Net sales for the six months ended July 3, 1999, advanced 44%, year to year, as gross sales dollars on motorized and towable products were up 47% and 27%, respectively. Profitability benefited considerably from a strong mix of motorized products, and manufacturing efficiencies created from an increase in production volume in all manufacturing plants. Pretax income more than doubled, to $35,274,000 from $14,859,000. After taxes at 39.5%, versus 41.5%, net income rose to $21,331,000 ($1.10 a share) from $8,686,000 ($0.46, adjusted).

Stock Performance - 08-OCT-99

In the past 30 trading days, MNC's shares have declined 3%, compared to a 0.91% fall in the S&P 500. Average trading volume for the past five days was 57,720 shares, compared with the 40-day moving average of 89,413 shares.

Key Stock Statistics

Dividend Rate/Share	Nil	Shareholders	212
Shs. outstg. (M)	18.8	Market cap. (B)	$0.518
Avg. daily vol. (M)	0.043	Inst. holdings	53%
Tang. Bk. Value/Share	4.18		
Beta	1.20		

Value of $10,000 invested 5 years ago: $ 68,750

Fiscal Year Ending Dec. 31

	1999	1998	1997	1996	1995	1994
Revenues (Million $)						
1Q	193.2	137.2	109.0	61.96	38.02	25.84
2Q	199.2	134.7	106.0	106.7	35.08	25.79
3Q	—	153.2	105.8	102.1	36.73	26.12
4Q	—	169.7	121.1	94.88	31.79	29.56
Yr.	—	594.8	441.9	365.6	141.6	107.3
Earnings Per Share ($)						
1Q	**0.51**	**0.22**	**0.17**	**0.04**	0.11	0.10
2Q	**0.59**	**0.24**	**0.16**	**0.06**	0.11	0.10
3Q	—	**0.33**	**0.17**	**0.12**	0.05	0.09
4Q	—	**0.40**	**0.20**	**0.15**	0.06	0.09
Yr.	—	**1.19**	**0.71**	**0.38**	**0.32**	**0.39**

Next earnings report expected: late October

Dividend Data

Amount ($)	Date Decl.	Ex-Div. Date	Stock of Record	Payment Date
3-for-2	Nov. 02	Dec. 01	Nov. 16	Nov. 30 '98
3-for-2	Jun. 07	Jul. 08	Jun. 21	Jul. 07 '99

A Division of The McGraw-Hill Companies

Monaco Coach Corporation

Business Summary - 08-SEP-99

One of the nation's leading manufacturers of recreational vehicles, Monaco Coach Corp. offers customers premium Class A motor coaches and towable recreational vehicles. The company's product line consists of thirteen models of motor coaches and seven models of towable (fifth wheel trailers and travel trailers) under the Monaco, Holiday Rambler, Royale Coach and McKenzie Towables brand names.

MNC's products are typically priced at the high end of their respective product categories, and range in suggested retail price from $65,000 to $900,000 for motor coaches and from $15,000 to $70,000 for towables. Based on retail registrations, Monaco believes that it has a 23% share of the marked for diesel Class A motor coaches, a 6.3% share of the market for mid-to-high end fifth wheel trailers (units with retail prices above $24,000) and a 24.5% share of the markets for mid-to-high end travel trailers (units with retail prices above $20,000). Monaco's products are sold through an extensive network of 263 dealerships located mainly in the United States and Canada.

Monaco's operations were expanded significantly through the March 1996 acquisition of Harley-Davidson, Inc.'s, Holiday Rambler Division, a manufacturer of a full line of Class A motor coaches and towables. The acquisition more than doubled MNC's sales base; provided it with a considerably broader range of products, including complementary High-Line Class A motor coaches and the company's first product offerings of fifth wheel trailers, travel trailers and entry-level to mid-range motor coaches; and lowered the price threshold of Monaco's first-time buyers of the company's products, thus making them more affordable for a significantly larger base of potential customers.

Monaco's recreational vehicles are designed to offer all of the comforts of home within a 190 to 400 square foot area. Accordingly, the interior of the recreational vehicle is designed to maximize use of available space. Each of Monaco's recreational vehicles comes fully equipped with a wide range of kitchen and bathroom appliances, audio and visual electronics, communication devices, and other amenities, including couches, dining tables, closets and storage spaces.

In December 1997, Monaco introduced the Diplomat, a low-end diesel motor coach under the Monaco brand name and introduced two new gasoline powered models, the La Palma, under the Monaco label, and the Admiral, under the Holiday Rambler brand, in 1998. All three of these products were designed to bring customers into the company's line of products at a lower price point giving the company the opportunity to benefit as these customers trade up through its line of products.

In 1998, the average unit wholesale selling prices of the company's motor coaches, fifth wheel trailers and travel trailers were approximately $113,400, $29,900 and $22,000, respectively.

Per Share Data ($) (Year Ended Dec. 31)	1998	1997	1996	1995	1994	1993	1992	1991	1990	1989
Tangible Bk. Val.	4.13	2.85	1.54	1.26	0.89	0.45	NA	NA	NA	NA
Cash Flow	1.45	1.37	0.59	0.40	0.45	0.05	NA	NA	NA	NA
Earnings	1.19	0.71	0.38	0.32	0.39	0.26	NA	NA	NA	NA
Dividends	Nil	Nil	Nil	Nil	Nil	Nil	NA	NA	NA	NA
Payout Ratio	Nil	Nil	Nil	Nil	Nil	Nil	NA	NA	NA	NA
Prices - High	17⅝	7⅞	4⅞	5	5	4¾	NA	NA	NA	NA
- Low	7⅛	4⅝	2½	2⅜	3¾	3	NA	NA	NA	NA
P/E Ratio - High	15	11	12	15	12	18	NA	NA	NA	NA
- Low	6	6	6	7	9	11	NA	NA	NA	NA
Income Statement Analysis (Million $)										
Revs.	595	442	366	142	107	22.9	NA	NA	NA	NA
Oper. Inc.	45.0	26.3	16.7	9.4	10.4	1.5	NA	NA	NA	NA
Depr.	4.9	3.6	3.0	1.1	0.8	0.2	NA	NA	NA	NA
Int. Exp.	1.9	2.4	3.9	0.3	0.1	0.8	NA	NA	NA	NA
Pretax Inc.	38.8	21.3	10.1	8.0	9.7	0.6	NA	NA	NA	NA
Eff. Tax Rate	42%	41%	41%	39%	39%	49%	NA	NA	NA	NA
Net Inc.	22.7	12.4	5.9	4.9	5.9	0.3	NA	NA	NA	NA
Balance Sheet & Other Fin. Data (Million $)										
Cash	Nil	Nil	Nil	Nil	0.2	0.1	NA	NA	NA	NA
Curr. Assets	107	81.4	73.9	27.7	20.1	12.5	NA	NA	NA	NA
Total Assets	190	160	135	68.5	48.2	34.4	NA	NA	NA	NA
Curr. Liab.	83.2	71.0	69.4	23.9	14.2	8.0	NA	NA	NA	NA
LT Debt	5.4	11.5	16.5	5.0	Nil	NA	NA	NA	NA	NA
Common Eqty.	98.2	74.7	43.8	37.9	32.9	7.0	NA	NA	NA	NA
Total Cap.	107	88.8	65.8	42.9	34.0	NA	NA	NA	NA	NA
Cap. Exp.	10.3	19.6	7.3	13.9	NA	NA	NA	NA	NA	NA
Cash Flow	27.6	16.1	8.8	6.0	6.8	0.5	NA	NA	NA	NA
Curr. Ratio	1.3	1.1	1.1	1.2	1.4	1.6	NA	NA	NA	NA
% LT Debt of Cap.	5.1	12.9	25.0	11.7	Nil	NA	NA	NA	NA	NA
% Net Inc.of Revs.	3.8	2.8	1.6	3.5	5.5	1.2	NA	NA	NA	NA
% Ret. on Assets	13.0	8.4	5.8	8.4	14.4	NA	NA	NA	NA	NA
% Ret. on Equity	26.2	21.0	14.3	13.8	29.7	NA	NA	NA	NA	NA

Data as orig reptd.; bef. results of disc opers/spec. items. Per share data adj. for stk. divs. Bold denotes diluted EPS (FASB 128)-prior periods restated. E-Estimated. NA-Not Available. NM-Not Meaningful. NR-Not Ranked.

Office—91320 Industrial Way, Coburg, OR 97408. **Tel**—(541) 686-8011. **Website**—http://www.monaco-online.com **Chrmn, Pres & CEO**—K. L. Toolson.**VP-Fin & CFO**—J. W. Nepute.**VP-Secy**—R. E. Bond. **Dirs**—M. J. Kluger, L. Posey, C. E. Ring Jr., R. A. Rouse, K. L. Toolson, R. A. Vandenberg. **Transfer Agent & Registrar**—Norwest Bank Minnesota, St. Paul. **Incorporated**—in Delaware in 1992. **Empl**— 3,043. **S&P Analyst:** J. J. Schemitsch

STANDARD
&POOR'S
STOCK REPORTS

Morrison Knudsen

NYSE Symbol **MK**
In S&P SmallCap 600

09-OCT-99 **Industry:** Engineering & Construction

Summary: MK provides a range of engineering and construction management services.

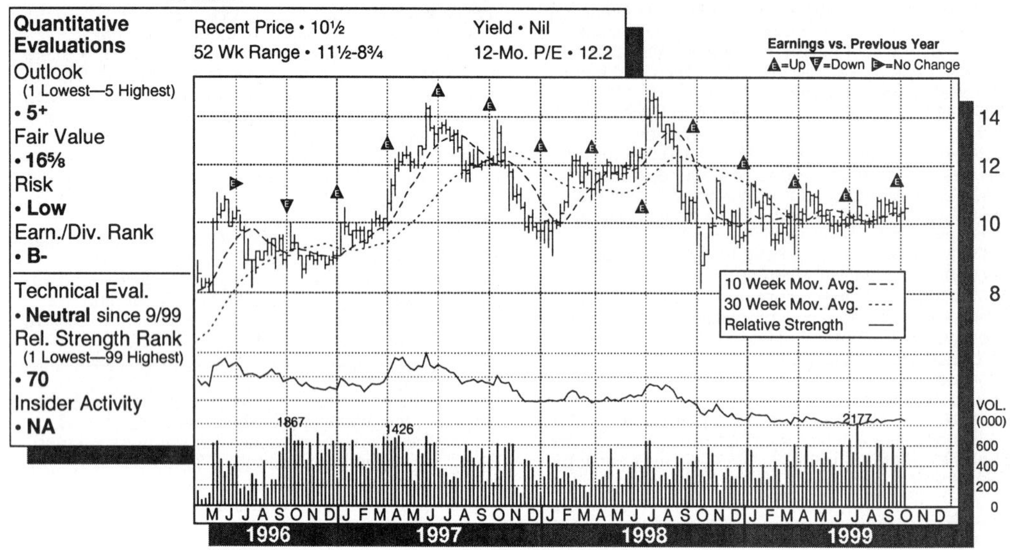

Business Profile - 10-SEP-99

On March 22, 1999, the company and British Nuclear Fuels, Ltd. acquired certain businesses from CBS Corporation (formerly Westinghouse Electric Corporation). The Westinghouse businesses provide a wide range of products, services and technologies in the government services and nuclear industries throughout the world. The acquisition is valued at approximately $1.1 billion, with MK's share at about $121 million in cash. The company 's FY 99 (Nov.) second quarter backlog of uncompleted projects was $3.1 billion, up from $2.7 billion at the end of FY 98. The company's chairman owns about 38% of the stock.

Operational Review - 10-SEP-99

Revenues for the six months ended May 28, 1999, advanced 20%, year to year, mainly reflecting the acquisition of Westinghouse Government Services Group and gains in the industrial process and energy divisions. Gross margins narrowed, hurt by a $3.2 million purchase accounting adjustment, a less favorable product mix in MK Engineers and Constructors Group, and the absence of payments for initial profit recognition on a project in 1998. Results were helped by gains of some $8.7 million from the sale of two non-core businesses, which outweighed considerably higher goodwill amortization and interest expense. Pretax income was up 20%. After taxes at 38.1%, versus 44.3%, net income was up 31%, to $22,682,000 ($0.43 a share), from $17,306,000 ($0.32).

Stock Performance - 08-OCT-99

In the past 30 trading days, MK's shares have increased 2%, compared to a 0.91% fall in the S&P 500. Average trading volume for the past five days was 117,040 shares, compared with the 40-day moving average of 107,095 shares.

Key Stock Statistics

Dividend Rate/Share	Nil	Shareholders	1,559
Shs. outstg. (M)	52.7	Market cap. (B)	$0.553
Avg. daily vol. (M)	0.102	Inst. holdings	38%
Tang. Bk. Value/Share	0.20		
Beta	0.93		

Value of $10,000 invested 5 years ago: $ 13,481

Fiscal Year Ending Nov. 30

	1999	1998	1997	1996	1995	1994
Revenues (Million $)						
1Q	421.3	385.0	389.5	62.00	36.78	50.50
2Q	567.8	436.1	414.2	82.69	51.60	63.75
3Q	595.4	497.8	434.3	97.75	71.87	78.49
4Q	—	543.3	439.3	416.6	68.28	65.96
Yr.	—	1,862	1,700	659.1	228.5	258.7
Earnings Per Share ($)						
1Q	**0.17**	**0.15**	0.13	-0.03	0.02	0.04
2Q	**0.26**	**0.17**	0.14	0.06	0.06	-0.08
3Q	**0.23**	**0.18**	0.15	-0.38	0.10	0.09
4Q	—	**0.20**	**0.17**	0.11	0.10	-0.03
Yr.	—	**0.69**	**0.59**	**-0.14**	0.28	0.02

Next earnings report expected: late January

Dividend Data

Cash distributions were omitted in 1985, resumed in 1989 on a semiannual basis, and omitted again in 1994.

Morrison Knudsen Corporation

Business Summary - 10-SEP-99

Effective September 11, 1996, the old Morrison Knudsen Corp. merged into Washington Construction Group, Inc. (WCGI), with WCGI continuing as the surviving corporation. Concurrently, Washington changed its name to Morrison Knudsen Corp. The company is an international provider of a broad range of design, engineering, construction, construction management, facilities management, environmental remediation and mining services to diverse public and private sector clients.

In providing such services, the company enters into three basic types of contracts: fixed-price or lump-sum contracts providing for a single price for the total amount of work to be performed; unit-price contracts providing for a fixed price for each unit of work performed; and cost-type contracts providing for reimbursement of costs plus a fee.

Both anticipated income and economic risk are greater under fixed-price and unit-price contracts than under cost-type contracts. Engineering, construction management and environmental and hazardous substance remediation contracts are typically awarded on a cost-plus-fee basis.

The company's operations have been conducted through three operating units: The Engineers and Constructors group based in Cleveland, OH, and the Heavy Civil Construction group and the Mining group based in Boise, ID. In January 1999, the company announced the consolidation of the Heavy Civil Construction Group and the Mining Group into the Morrison Knudsen Contractors group.

The Engineers and Constructors group provides design and construction services for new construction or renovations of plants and facilities in a wide range of markets; offers a full range of engineering and construction services to power generation utilities; provides total facilities management services to industrial clients; performs engineering and construction management of highway, bridge, railroad, airport and water resource infrastructure projects; and engages in the operation and environmental remediation of government facilities, primarily for the Department of Energy and the Department of Defense.

The Heavy Civil Construction group, one of the largest organizations of its kind in the U.S., provides services both as a general contractor and in a design-build capacity. This group targets infrastructure projects in the transportation, marine and water resources markets, and also provides site development at mine, industrial, commercial, recreational and large residential sites.

The Mining Group is an international provider of contract mining services for the fossil fuel and industrial minerals markets. In addition, this group offers a full range of technical and engineering services, including resource evaluation, geologic modeling, mine planning and development, environmental permitting, equipment selection and remediation.

Per Share Data ($) (Year Ended Nov. 30)	1998	1997	1996	1995	1994	1993	1992	1991	1990	1989
Tangible Bk. Val.	4.83	3.82	3.18	3.84	3.53	3.53	4.31	3.68	2.50	2.11
Cash Flow	1.07	1.01	0.23	0.58	0.34	0.96	0.90	0.91	0.68	0.48
Earnings	0.69	0.59	-0.14	0.28	0.02	0.39	0.65	0.61	0.39	0.18
Dividends	Nil	Nil	Nil	Nil	0.05	0.10	0.10	0.09	0.07	0.07
Payout Ratio	Nil	Nil	Nil	Nil	NM	33%	15%	16%	17%	38%
Prices - High	15¼	14⅝	11	6¾	10¾	11¼	13⅜	15½	9⅛	7½
- Low	8⅛	9	6½	4⅜	3⅞	7	6⅝	7⅜	5⅝	5
P/E Ratio - High	22	25	NM	24	NM	38	21	25	23	42
- Low	12	15	NM	16	NM	23	10	12	14	28
Income Statement Analysis (Million $)										
Revs.	1,862	1,677	659	229	259	210	162	195	153	115
Oper. Inc.	79.3	75.6	22.5	16.0	6.7	18.9	10.7	9.5	5.1	3.4
Depr.	20.5	22.8	12.9	8.9	9.2	10.1	2.5	2.8	2.2	2.3
Int. Exp.	0.9	0.9	1.0	0.2	0.1	0.1	Nil	0.3	1.1	1.4
Pretax Inc.	67.4	59.9	-5.3	12.2	1.0	11.2	9.9	8.7	4.8	2.2
Eff. Tax Rate	44%	47%	NM	33%	35%	38%	35%	35%	35%	38%
Net Inc.	37.6	32.0	-4.8	8.2	0.7	6.9	6.5	5.7	3.1	1.4
Balance Sheet & Other Fin. Data (Million $)										
Cash	67.1	53.2	48.3	30.0	44.9	53.0	45.1	47.5	44.9	33.0
Curr. Assets	428	405	459	93.7	114	118	66.4	73.9	67.9	55.3
Total Assets	788	770	840	185	182	181	78.8	85.9	79.8	65.4
Curr. Liab.	303	300	401	42.2	46.4	52.5	32.9	46.9	46.3	28.1
LT Debt	Nil	Nil	18.0	5.0	5.5	Nil	Nil	Nil	11.2	18.5
Common Eqty.	371	343	312	129	120	120	43.3	36.7	19.9	16.5
Total Cap.	371	361	330	143	136	129	45.8	39.0	33.4	37.4
Cap. Exp.	25.5	19.7	26.2	22.3	14.8	35.2	3.4	3.9	4.0	1.9
Cash Flow	58.1	54.8	8.2	17.1	9.9	17.0	9.0	8.5	5.3	3.7
Curr. Ratio	1.4	1.4	1.1	2.2	2.5	2.3	2.0	1.6	1.5	2.0
% LT Debt of Cap.	Nil	Nil	5.5	3.6	4.0	Nil	Nil	Nil	33.5	49.5
% Net Inc.of Revs.	2.0	1.9	NM	3.6	0.3	3.3	4.0	2.9	2.0	1.2
% Ret. on Assets	4.8	4.0	NM	4.5	0.4	3.4	7.8	6.1	4.2	2.3
% Ret. on Equity	10.5	9.8	NM	6.6	0.5	5.6	16.1	18.4	16.9	8.7

Data as orig reptd.; bef. results of disc opers/spec. items. Per share data adj. for stk. divs. Bold denotes diluted EPS (FASB 128)-prior periods restated. E-Estimated. NA-Not Available. NM-Not Meaningful. NR-Not Ranked.

Office—Morrison Knudsen Plaza, Boise, ID 83712. **Tel**—(208) 386-5000. **Fax**—(208) 386-5065. **Website**—http://www.mk.com **Chrmn, Pres & CEO**—D. R. Washington. **EVP & Secy**—S. G. Hanks. **EVP & CFO**—A. S. Cleberg. **Asst Treas & Investor Contact**—Lisa Ross (208-386-5120). **Dirs**—D. H. Batchelder, L. R. Judd, R. S. Miller, D. Parkinson, T. W. Payne, J. D. Roach, D. R. Washington, T. H. Zarges. **Transfer Agent & Registrar**—Norwest Bank Minnesota. **Incorporated**—in California in 1961; reincorporated in Delaware in 1993. **Empl**— 9,000. **S&P Analyst:** P.L.H.

Mueller Industries

NYSE Symbol **MLI**
In S&P SmallCap 600

09-OCT-99 **Industry:** Metal Fabricators

Summary: MLI fabricates brass, bronze, copper, plastic and aluminum products. It also owns a short-line railroad and mines gold.

Quantitative Evaluations
Outlook (1 Lowest—5 Highest) • **4**
Fair Value • **44½**
Risk • **Low**
Earn./Div. Rank • **NR**
Technical Eval. • **Bearish** since 9/99
Rel. Strength Rank (1 Lowest—99 Highest) • **47**
Insider Activity • **NA**

Recent Price • 30
52 Wk Range • 35⅝-14⅞
Yield • Nil
12-Mo. P/E • 14.2

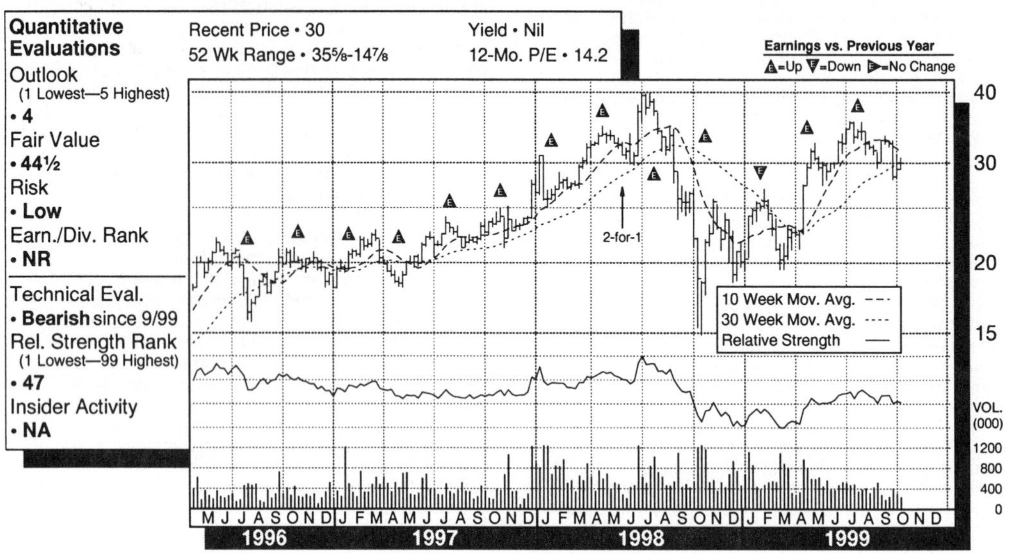

Business Profile - 10-AUG-99

Major capital investments over the past few years have resulted in expanded capacity, higher yields and improved efficiency at Mueller Industries' manufacturing operations. The company intends to continue enhancing manufacturing productivity and expects the recent strength in its business to continue, provided that interest rates do not spike upward. In February 1999, MLI said it expects European operations, which incurred losses associated with a restructuring in the 1998 fourth quarter, to break even by the second half of 1999 due to the consolidation of production facilities and, thereafter, to contribute to earnings. In November 1998, MLI acquired Halstead Industries, Inc., a manufacturer of copper tube. MLI expects the acquisition to provide economies of scale in manufacturing operations as well as reductions in overhead costs.

Operational Review - 10-AUG-99

Net sales in the six months ended June 26, 1999, advanced 28%, year to year, reflecting reflecting internal growth and acquisitions. Margins widened, and operating profit moved ahead 31%. After sharply higher depreciation and amortization charges, increased interest expense and higher other income (net), and in the absence of charges for environmental reserves, pretax income was up 19%. Following taxes at 31.2%, versus 32.3%, net income was up 21%, to $47.1 million ($1.19 a share), from $39.0 million ($0.98).

Stock Performance - 08-OCT-99

In the past 30 trading days, MLI's shares have declined 0.21%, compared to a 0.91% fall in the S&P 500. Average trading volume for the past five days was 45,280 shares, compared with the 40-day moving average of 64,405 shares.

Key Stock Statistics

Dividend Rate/Share	Nil	Shareholders	3,300
Shs. outstg. (M)	35.8	Market cap. (B)	$ 1.1
Avg. daily vol. (M)	0.057	Inst. holdings	54%
Tang. Bk. Value/Share	13.14		
Beta	1.33		

Value of $10,000 invested 5 years ago: $ 33,802

Fiscal Year Ending Dec. 31

	1999	1998	1997	1996	1995	1994
Revenues (Million $)						
1Q	287.8	226.7	201.4	180.5	171.8	120.8
2Q	293.3	225.9	215.4	189.6	181.4	136.6
3Q	—	212.8	229.1	176.0	171.6	138.0
4Q	—	264.1	243.1	172.3	154.1	154.6
Yr.	—	929.4	889.0	718.3	678.8	550.0
Earnings Per Share ($)						
1Q	**0.55**	**0.48**	**0.40**	**0.34**	0.27	0.10
2Q	**0.64**	**0.50**	**0.41**	**0.35**	0.28	0.14
3Q	—	**0.47**	**0.46**	**0.41**	0.30	0.23
4Q	—	**0.45**	**0.50**	**0.46**	0.33	0.25
Yr.	—	**1.90**	**1.78**	**1.57**	**1.17**	**0.70**

Next earnings report expected: mid October

Dividend Data

No cash dividends have been paid. The company's ability to pay dividends is limited by financial coverage covenants and restrictions. A "poison pill" stock purchase rights plan was adopted in 1994.

Mueller Industries, Inc.

Business Summary - 10-AUG-99

Since emerging from bankruptcy in 1990, Mueller Industries (MLI) has rebounded strongly. Profitability was restored in 1992, and earnings have continued to advance. In 1998, this fabricator of brass, bronze, copper, plastic and aluminum fittings, tubing and extrusions reported net income of $75.4 million, up 8% from that of 1997 and significantly above the 1992 level. Part of this recovery is attributable to the expanded capacity, higher yields and improved efficiencies of Mueller's manufacturing operations, which have benefited from a strong capital investment program.

In addition to its fabrication business (96% of net sales in 1998), MLI operates a short-line railroad in Utah and a placer mining operation in Alaska.

The fabrication business, referred to as the "manufacturing segment," produces industrial and standard products. Industrial products include brass rod, nonferrous forgings and impact extrusions, which are sold mainly to other manufacturers and distributors. Standard products include a broad line of copper tube, water tube and coils, copper and plastic fittings and related components for the plumbing and heating industry, and valves, wrot copper and brass fittings, filter driers and other related assemblies for the commercial air-conditioning and refrigeration industry. A majority of these products are ultimately used in residential and commercial construction markets and, to a lesser extent, in the on- and off-road vehicle markets.

With a significant portion of MLI's products used in the construction of single- and multi-family housing and commercial buildings, new housing starts and commercial construction are important determinants of the company's sales. Mueller remains optimistic about its sales growth prospects, due to prevailing low mortgage interest rates, which historically have stimulated the housing market.

Mueller's Utah Railway Co. subsidiary operates about 100 miles of railroad track in Utah. It serves four major customers pursuant to long-term contracts and transports between four and six million tons of coal a year. Another subsidiary, Alaska Gold, mines placer gold in Nome, AK. Mueller has agreed to sell Alaska Gold, subject to various contingencies. Mueller also holds interests in various other mineral properties in the U.S., including coal properties in Utah, but none are considered significant to its business.

Mueller's future focus is to continue with its efforts to improve its existing operations and pursue additional areas of growth. MLI intends to enhance its refining processes, thereby improving the utilization of scrap metal, broaden its plastics offering and streamline its distribution network. MLI also continues to seek external growth through acquisitions.

Per Share Data ($) (Year Ended Dec. 31)	1998	1997	1996	1995	1994	1993	1992	1991	1990	1989
Tangible Bk. Val.	11.90	11.94	9.98	8.24	6.95	5.79	5.30	3.95	5.00	5.38
Cash Flow	2.53	2.32	2.04	1.57	1.01	0.82	0.71	-0.78	NA	0.71
Earnings	1.90	1.78	1.57	1.17	0.70	0.51	0.40	-1.12	NA	0.39
Dividends	Nil	Nil	Nil	Nil	Nil	Nil	Nil	Nil	NA	NA
Payout Ratio	Nil	Nil	Nil	Nil	Nil	Nil	Nil	Nil	NA	NA
Prices - High	40	29 3/4	22 1/8	14 3/4	9 5/8	9 3/8	5 3/4	3 1/2	NA	NA
- Low	14 7/8	18 1/8	13	7 1/8	6 3/4	5	1 3/4	1 3/4	NA	NA
P/E Ratio - High	21	17	14	13	14	18	14	NM	NA	NA
- Low	8	10	8	6	10	10	4	NM	NA	NA
Income Statement Analysis (Million $)										
Revs.	929	889	718	679	550	502	517	441	505	511
Oper. Inc.	134	121	109	79.0	56.0	51.3	41.8	11.7	8.8	35.7
Depr.	24.9	21.0	18.5	15.5	12.1	13.3	12.5	13.3	13.3	13.1
Int. Exp.	5.8	5.0	5.3	4.2	6.7	5.8	5.7	6.0	5.0	2.0
Pretax Inc.	110	101	88.4	64.5	41.0	33.0	24.0	-50.0	9.0	27.0
Eff. Tax Rate	31%	31%	31%	31%	32%	37%	33%	NM	12%	43%
Net Inc.	75.4	69.8	61.2	45.0	28.0	21.0	16.0	-44.0	8.0	15.0
Balance Sheet & Other Fin. Data (Million $)										
Cash	80.6	70.0	97.0	48.4	34.5	77.3	44.0	8.0	41.0	39.0
Curr. Assets	382	309	275	211	184	194	182	152	201	229
Total Assets	875	611	509	451	431	370	373	335	416	385
Curr. Liab.	143	101	79.0	68.0	67.0	51.0	62.0	89.0	113	84.0
LT Debt	175	44.8	44.8	59.7	76.1	54.3	62.0	45.0	54.0	55.0
Common Eqty.	502	418	348	291	242	222	204	153	200	215
Total Cap.	688	466	396	353	321	280	271	211	261	269
Cap. Exp.	55.4	36.9	18.9	NA	48.2	11.1	11.0	11.8	9.9	NA
Cash Flow	100	90.8	79.6	60.3	40.0	34.0	29.0	-30.0	21.0	29.0
Curr. Ratio	2.7	3.1	3.5	3.1	2.7	3.8	3.0	1.7	1.8	2.7
% LT Debt of Cap.	25.4	9.6	11.4	16.9	23.7	19.4	23.0	21.4	20.7	20.2
% Net Inc.of Revs.	8.1	7.8	8.6	6.6	5.1	4.2	3.1	NM	1.6	3.0
% Ret. on Assets	10.2	12.5	12.8	10.2	7.3	5.7	4.6	NM	NM	NA
% Ret. on Equity	16.4	18.2	19.3	16.8	12.6	9.9	9.1	NM	NM	NA

Data as orig reptd.; bef. results of disc opers/spec. items. Per share data adj. for stk. divs. Bold denotes diluted EPS (FASB 128)-prior periods restated. E-Estimated. NA-Not Available. NM-Not Meaningful. NR-Not Ranked.

Office—6799 Great Oaks Rd., Memphis, TN 38138-2572. **Tel**—(901) 753-3200. **Chrmn**—H. L. Karp. **Pres & CEO**—W. D. O'Hagan. **Exec VP & CFO**—E. W. Bunkers. **VP & Secy**—W. H. Hensley. **VP & Investor Contact**—Kent A. McKee. **Dirs**—R. B. Hodes, H. L. Karp, G. E. Manolovici, W. D. O'Hagan, R. J. Pasquarelli. **Transfer Agent & Registrar**—Continental Stock Transfer & Trust Co., NYC. **Incorporated**—in Pennsylvania in 1900; reincorporated in Delaware in 1990. **Empl**— 4,800. **S&P Analyst:** E.P.L.

STANDARD
&POOR'S
STOCK REPORTS

Mutual Risk Management

NYSE Symbol **MM**

In S&P SmallCap 600

09-OCT-99 **Industry:** Financial (Diversified)

Summary: MM provides risk management services to clients seeking alternatives to traditional commercial insurance for certain risk exposure.

Quantitative Evaluations

Outlook (1 Lowest—5 Highest) • **5**

Fair Value • **23¾**

Risk • **Low**

Earn./Div. Rank • **A**

Technical Eval. • **Bearish** since 5/99

Rel. Strength Rank (1 Lowest—99 Highest) • **NA**

Insider Activity • **NA**

Recent Price • 11⅝ | Yield • 2.1%

52 Wk Range • 43¼-9¾ | 12-Mo. P/E • 7.6

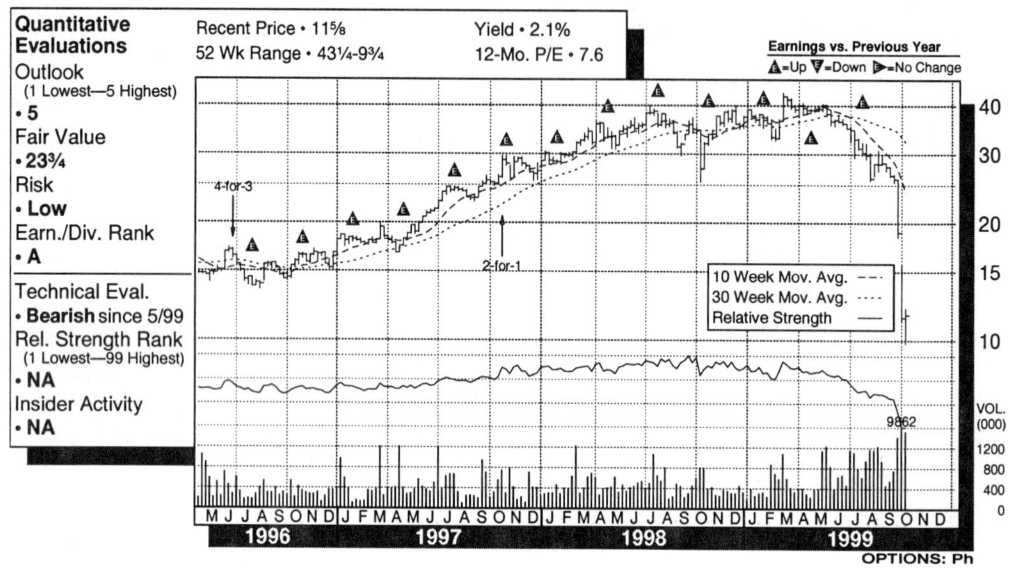

Business Profile - 07-JUL-99

MM is a leader in the fast-growing alternative insurance market, which includes self-insurance and captive insurance programs. MM's income is principally derived from fees for services provided to clients, rather than from assuming underwriting risk, which contributes to stability in revenue flows. Revenue growth has exceeded 20% in recent periods, driven by addition of new accounts and growth in existing accounts. The company has diversified its product line to include program business, financial services, and specialty brokerage for alternative risk transfer insurers and reinsurers. On March 1, 1999, the company closed its acquisition of Captive Resources, Inc., a Schaumburg, IL, provider of services to member owned captive insurance companies that generated revenues of $8 million in 1998.

Operational Review - 07-JUL-99

In the first three months of 1999, total revenues rose 27%, year to year, as restated for acquisitions, mainly reflecting higher fee income and premiums earned. Program business fees, which represent half of total fee income, climbed 41%. Total expenses were up 29%; pretax income advanced 19%. After taxes at 9.7%, versus 13.0%, net income climbed 24%, to $18,791,313 ($0.40 a share, on more shares), from $15,174,505 ($0.34).

Stock Performance - 08-OCT-99

In the past 30 trading days, MM's shares have declined 59%, compared to a 0.91% fall in the S&P 500. Average trading volume for the past five days was 1,532,420 shares, compared with the 40-day moving average of 682,956 shares.

Key Stock Statistics

Dividend Rate/Share	0.24	Shareholders	400
Shs. outstg. (M)	43.5	Market cap. (B)	$0.506
Avg. daily vol. (M)	1.162	Inst. holdings	87%
Tang. Bk. Value/Share	7.02		
Beta	0.95		

Value of $10,000 invested 5 years ago: $ 10,950

Fiscal Year Ending Dec. 31

	1999	1998	1997	1996	1995	1994
Revenues (Million $)						
1Q	91.89	68.09	47.19	36.69	28.77	29.53
2Q	103.8	59.97	48.48	40.61	32.70	30.49
3Q	—	68.91	62.21	32.78	34.78	33.61
4Q	—	74.94	56.91	47.62	26.99	35.18
Yr.	—	279.4	214.8	157.7	123.2	128.7
Earnings Per Share ($)						
1Q	**0.40**	**0.34**	**0.27**	0.24	0.19	0.17
2Q	**0.39**	**0.33**	**0.28**	0.23	0.22	0.16
3Q	—	**0.37**	**0.33**	0.24	0.21	0.18
4Q	—	**0.37**	**0.31**	0.24	0.20	0.17
Yr.	—	**1.43**	**1.16**	**0.95**	**0.81**	**0.69**

Next earnings report expected: early November

Dividend Data (Dividends have been paid since 1991.)

Amount ($)	Date Decl.	Ex-Div. Date	Stock of Record	Payment Date
0.060	Oct. 21	Nov. 04	Nov. 06	Nov. 20 '98
0.060	Jan. 21	Feb. 03	Feb. 05	Feb. 19 '99
0.060	Apr. 23	May. 05	May. 07	May. 21 '99
0.060	Jul. 22	Aug. 04	Aug. 06	Aug. 20 '99

Mutual Risk Management Ltd.

Business Summary - 07-JUL-99

Bermuda-based Mutual Risk Management provides risk management services to clients seeking alternatives to traditional commercial insurance for certain risk exposures. Risk management involves analyzing loss exposure and developing risk financing methods to reduce exposure. The use of loss financing methods in place of traditional insurance, known as the alternative market, involves client self-funding of a significant amount of loss exposure, transferring only unpredictable excess risk to insurers. By using alternative market techniques, clients typically see lower and more stable costs, greater control over their risk management programs, and greater emphasis within their organization on loss prevention and loss control.

MM's revenues in 1998 were $279.4 million, up from $223.8 million in 1997. Segment contributions to revenue in 1998 were: program business 30% (22% in 1997), corporate risk management 15% (21%), specialty brokerage 3% (4%), financial services 5% (4%), underwriting 37% (38%), and net investment income 10% (11%). Fee income, which tends to be more stable than underwriting or investment income, represented 53% of revenues in 1998 and was growing at a 30% pace. Over half of fee income stems from workers' compensation insurance.

MM's principal source of profits is fees received for services provided to clients in connection with its programs. The structure of the company's programs places most underwriting risk with the client. For regulatory and other reasons, MM is required to assume a limited amount of risk. However, the company seeks to minimize its underwriting risk, a trait that differentiates it from traditional property/casualty companies.

In connection with many programs, Legion Insurance Co., a wholly owned subsidiary admitted in 50 states, the District of Columbia and Puerto Rico, issues an insurance policy to the client and reinsures the premium and liability related to the client's chosen retention. For most programs, Legion retains only the relatively small portion of the premium associated with its retention of a portion of the specific and aggregate excess risk, ceding the majority of premiums and risk to the client's IPC (insurance profit center) program and the balance to unaffiliated excess reinsurers.

Through its subsidiaries, MM provides risk management services in the U.S., Bermuda, Barbados, the Cayman Islands and Europe. Subsidiaries besides Legion include MRM Hancock Ltd., a London-based reinsurance broker; Park International Ltd., a broker in the Bermuda market; and Commonwealth Risk Services, L.P., a marketing subsidiary based in Philadelphia.

Per Share Data ($) (Year Ended Dec. 31)	1998	1997	1996	1995	1994	1993	1992	1991	1990	1989
Tangible Bk. Val.	7.02	5.99	5.11	4.46	3.42	3.23	2.65	1.95	1.25	0.87
Oper. Earnings	1.44	1.19	1.02	0.84	0.69	0.58	0.44	0.34	NA	NA
Earnings	1.43	1.16	0.96	0.82	0.68	0.58	0.44	0.34	0.23	0.15
Dividends	0.21	0.18	0.16	0.13	0.11	0.08	0.06	0.03	Nil	Nil
Payout Ratio	15%	16%	17%	16%	16%	14%	14%	7%	Nil	Nil
Prices - High	39 7/8	29 7/8	18 5/8	17 1/8	11 1/8	12 1/4	10 1/8	8 7/8	NA	NA
- Low	25 3/8	16 3/4	13 1/2	9 3/8	7 7/8	8	6 1/2	4 1/4	NA	NA
P/E Ratio - High	28	26	19	21	17	21	23	26	NA	NA
- Low	18	14	14	11	12	14	15	12	NA	NA
Income Statement Analysis (Million $)										
Premium Inc.	102	84.2	56.4	48.2	68.2	55.2	50.4	24.4	17.5	13.4
Net Invest. Inc.	29.5	26.2	22.5	16.1	11.4	9.5	9.2	6.6	3.5	2.6
Oth. Revs.	148	104	79.1	58.9	49.0	41.4	31.7	23.3	18.1	13.2
Total Revs.	279	215	158	123	129	106	91.4	54.3	39.1	29.2
Pretax Inc.	72.0	58.5	45.6	39.3	32.3	27.2	21.7	15.6	8.2	5.6
Net Oper. Inc.	64.3	49.9	39.2	30.6	24.5	20.5	15.4	10.0	NA	NA
Net Inc.	63.6	47.9	37.2	29.9	24.0	20.7	15.6	10.3	5.5	3.9
Balance Sheet & Other Fin. Data (Million $)										
Cash & Equiv.	120	78.9	57.2	83.1	48.0	32.4	51.7	24.8	25.5	13.7
Premiums Due	206	156	73.6	39.2	19.0	15.9	10.1	6.2	3.3	2.9
Invest. Assets: Bonds	461	395	400	352	235	205	148	120	65.0	41.0
Invest. Assets: Stocks	Nil	Nil	Nil	Nil	Nil	Nil	Nil	Nil	Nil	Nil
Invest. Assets: Loans	Nil	Nil	Nil	Nil	Nil	Nil	0.6	0.6	1.2	1.5
Invest. Assets: Total	481	405	400	352	235	205	149	120	66.0	43.0
Deferred Policy Costs	27.2	29.9	20.6	19.1	9.5	8.0	6.8	3.6	1.5	1.0
Total Assets	3,041	2,147	1,639	1,374	1,018	859	499	405	310	253
Debt	125	129	122	116	3.0	6.0	8.0	9.0	10.0	4.0
Common Eqty.	1,854	1,166	208	167	122	114	95.6	62.6	34.0	23.9
Prop. & Cas. Loss Ratio	NA	NA	NA	NA	56.4	73.0	84.4	93.4	99.2	95.4
Prop. & Cas. Expense Ratio	NA	NA	NA	NA	83.9	64.7	45.7	51.6	72.7	81.4
Prop. & Cas. Combined Ratio	NA	NA	NA	NA	140.3	137.7	130.1	145.0	171.9	176.8
% Return On Revs.	22.8	22.3	23.6	24.1	18.6	19.5	17.1	19.0	14.1	13.4
% Ret. on Equity	4.2	5.1	19.9	20.3	20.2	19.8	19.6	20.9	18.2	16.5

Data as orig reptd.; bef. results of disc opers/spec. items. Per share data adj. for stk. divs. Bold denotes diluted EPS (FASB 128)-prior periods restated. E-Estimated. NA-Not Available. NM-Not Meaningful. NR-Not Ranked.

Office—44 Church St., P. O. Box HM 2064, Hamilton, Bermuda. **Tel**—(441) 295-5688. **Website**—http://www.mutrisk.com **Chrmn & CEO**—R. A. Mulderig. **Pres**—J. Kessock Jr. **Secy**—R. E. O'Brien. **SVP, CFO & Investor Contact**—James C. Kelly. **Dirs**—R. E. Dailey, D. J. Doyle, A. E. Engel, A. W. Fulkerson, W. F. Galtney Jr., J. Kessock Jr., R. A. Mulderig, G. R. Partridge, B. H. Patrick, J. S. Rosenbloom, N. L. Rosenthal, J. D. Sargent, R. G. Turner. **Transfer Agent & Registrar**—Boston EquiServe L.P., Canton, MA. **Incorporated**—in Bermuda in 1977. **Empl**— 886. **S&P Analyst:** T.W. Smith, CFA

STANDARD
&POOR'S
STOCK REPORTS

Myers Industries

ASE Symbol **MYE**
In S&P SmallCap 600

09-OCT-99

Industry: Manufacturing (Diversified)

Summary: This diversified maker of polymer and metal products is also a specialized distributor of tools, equipment and supplies for the tire service and transportation industries.

Quantitative Evaluations

Outlook (1 Lowest—5 Highest)
• **3+**

Fair Value
• **22⅝**

Risk
• **Low**

Earn./Div. Rank
• **A**

Technical Eval.
• **Bearish** since 9/99

Rel. Strength Rank (1 Lowest—99 Highest)
• **19**

Insider Activity
• **Neutral**

Recent Price • 17⅛
52 Wk Range • 27½-17
Yield • 1.4%
12-Mo. P/E • 8.4

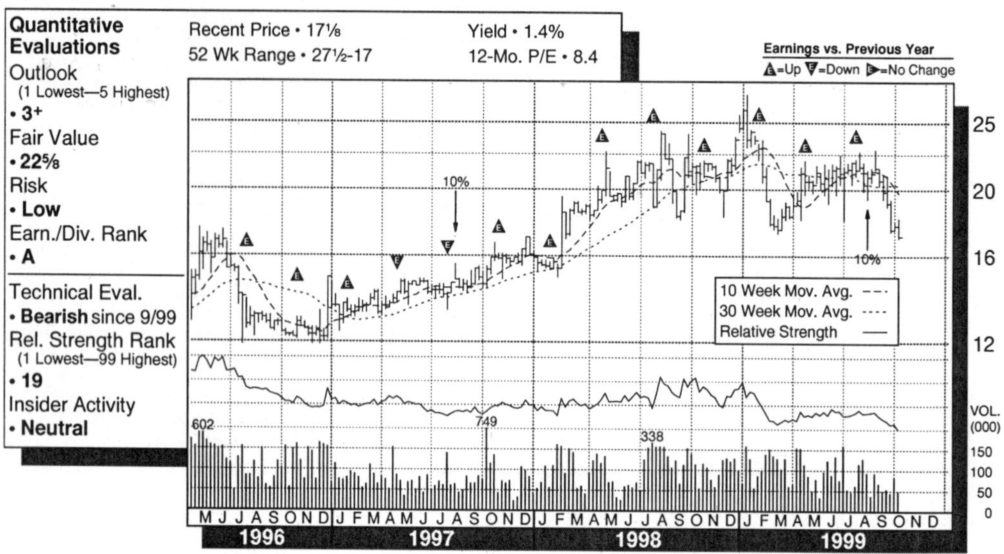

Business Profile - 20-SEP-99

In August 1999, the company acquired two manufacturers of plastic horticultural containers, Listo Products Ltd. of Canada for an undisclosed amount and Dillen Products, Inc. for approximately $50 million plus the assumption of debt. Listo and Dillen had 1998 sales of $12 million and $40 million, respectively. In February 1999, the company acquired French-based Allibert Equipement, the plastic material handling division of Sommer Allibert for approximately $150 million (excluding assumption of debt). These acquisitions reflect MYE's efforts to build on its resources to sustain long-term growth. In July 1999, the company declared a 10% stock dividend.

Operational Review - 20-SEP-99

Net sales for the six months ended June 30, 1999, advanced 45%, year to year, reflecting contributions from acquired companies (especially Allibert Equipement) and sales growth in both business segments. Gross margins widened, reflecting lower raw material costs and greater utilization of plant capacity. However, profitability was restricted by sharply higher operating and interest expenses related to acquisitions; pretax income was up 23%. After taxes at 42.6%, versus 40.9%, net income climbed 20% to $17,434,982 ($0.95 a share), from $14,587,937 ($0.80).

Stock Performance - 08-OCT-99

In the past 30 trading days, MYE's shares have declined 20%, compared to a 0.91% fall in the S&P 500. Average trading volume for the past five days was 9,640 shares, compared with the 40-day moving average of 12,077 shares.

Key Stock Statistics

Dividend Rate/Share	0.24	Shareholders	2,000
Shs. outstg. (M)	18.4	Market cap. (B)	$0.315
Avg. daily vol. (M)	0.011	Inst. holdings	51%
Tang. Bk. Value/Share	8.08		
Beta	0.69		

Value of $10,000 invested 5 years ago: $ 13,163

Fiscal Year Ending Dec. 31

	1999	1998	1997	1996	1995	1994
Revenues (Million $)						
1Q	126.8	88.19	76.80	72.55	67.50	59.69
2Q	147.6	101.1	86.18	79.95	75.58	68.44
3Q	—	92.20	81.14	77.88	74.65	66.19
4Q	—	110.5	95.51	90.56	82.96	79.73
Yr.	—	392.0	339.6	320.9	300.7	274.1
Earnings Per Share ($)						
1Q	**0.41**	**0.35**	**0.24**	**0.25**	0.18	0.17
2Q	**0.50**	**0.38**	**0.26**	**0.27**	0.21	0.25
3Q	—	**0.25**	**0.19**	**0.18**	0.17	0.19
4Q	—	**0.45**	**0.41**	**0.32**	0.22	0.26
Yr.	—	**1.43**	**1.10**	**1.03**	**0.78**	**0.87**

Next earnings report expected: mid October

Dividend Data (Dividends have been paid since 1966.)

Amount ($)	Date Decl.	Ex-Div. Date	Stock of Record	Payment Date
0.060	Jan. 25	Mar. 10	Mar. 12	Apr. 01 '99
0.060	Apr. 29	Jun. 09	Jun. 11	Jul. 01 '99
10%	Jul. 29	Aug. 11	Aug. 13	Aug. 31 '99
0.060	Jul. 29	Sep. 08	Sep. 10	Oct. 01 '99

Myers Industries, Inc.

Business Summary - 20-SEP-99

Founded in 1933, Myers Industries, Inc. (MYE) is a leading manufacturer of reusable plastic containers and distributor of equipment, tools and supplies used for tire servicing and automotive underbody repair.

The Manufacturing segment, which accounted for 60.2% of total sales in 1998 (58.1% in 1997), designs, manufactures and markets reusable plastic containers under the brand names NesTier, Akro-Bins and Buckhorn. These products are used in industrial applications including the distribution of food items, such as poultry, meat and baked goods, and the distribution of non-food items, such as apparel, electronic, automotive, and industrial components, health and beauty aids and hardware. Consumer products include the Keepbox line of household storage containers, plastic tool boxes and other products to organize the home workshop, plastic containers to facilitate consumer recycling, and a line of plastic pots, planters and urns sold to consumers through lawn and garden retailers and other similar specialty outlets.

MYE also designs, manufactures and markets molded rubber products, such as air intake hoses, rubber boots, mounts, and hood hold-down latches for diesel-powered vehicles and equipment used in the transportation, construction and agricultural industries.

The Distribution segment, which accounted for 39.8% of total sales in 1998 (41.9% in 1997), distributes equipment, tools and supplies used for tire servicing and automotive underbody repair. Its business is conducted primarily through the Myers Tire Supply division. Products distributed include air compressors, mechanic's hand tools, tire changers, tire display and storage equipment, valves, tire balancing and wheel alignment equipment, curing rims and presses, retread presses and tire repair materials for the retreading industry. The company believes that it is the only nationwide distributor supplying such products. Customers include independent tire dealers, tire retreaders, tire service centers, automotive supply chains and rubber companies.

Myers Tire Supply's domestic distribution system includes 42 owned branch warehouse distributors in 31 states. Internationally, it has two wholly owned warehouse distributors located in Canada and owns an interest in several other foreign warehouse distributors.

In 1998, MYE expanded its domestic and foreign presence with four acquisitions. The company acquired two domestic plastics manufacturers, Sherwood Plastics and Kadon, in addition to Denmark-based raaco. In the distribution segment, MYE acquired a majority interest in Myers El Salvador.

In February 1999, the company acquired French-based Allibert Equipement, a plastic material handler, for approximately $150 million (excluding the assumption of debt). In August 1999, the company acquired two manufacturers of plastic horticultural containers, Listo Products Ltd. of Canada for an undisclosed amount and Dillen Products, Inc. for approximately $50 million plu s the assumption of debt.

Per Share Data ($) (Year Ended Dec. 31)	1998	1997	1996	1995	1994	1993	1992	1991	1990	1989
Tangible Bk. Val.	8.08	7.65	7.13	6.12	5.82	5.02	3.74	3.34	2.80	2.21
Cash Flow	2.29	1.71	1.58	1.30	1.34	1.17	1.04	0.90	0.90	0.90
Earnings	1.43	1.10	1.02	0.79	0.88	0.78	0.70	0.57	0.58	0.52
Dividends	0.19	0.17	0.15	0.13	0.13	0.10	0.09	0.08	0.08	0.07
Payout Ratio	13%	16%	15%	17%	15%	13%	13%	15%	13%	13%
Prices - High	26 1/8	17	17 1/2	13 7/8	13 7/8	15 3/8	12 5/8	7 1/4	7 1/2	6 7/8
- Low	14 7/8	12 3/8	11 7/8	9 7/8	9 5/8	11 1/2	6 3/4	5	5	5 1/2
P/E Ratio - High	18	15	17	18	16	20	18	13	13	13
- Low	10	11	12	13	11	15	10	9	9	10
Income Statement Analysis (Million $)										
Revs.	392	340	321	301	274	245	229	196	202	195
Oper. Inc.	66.9	50.8	47.2	38.3	40.1	34.2	29.5	25.6	26.5	25.3
Depr.	17.5	12.5	11.3	10.5	9.4	7.6	6.3	6.0	5.7	5.4
Int. Exp.	2.4	0.6	0.6	1.0	0.8	1.2	1.5	2.0	3.1	4.2
Pretax Inc.	48.5	38.1	35.6	27.1	30.0	25.4	21.8	17.8	18.0	16.2
Eff. Tax Rate	41%	41%	41%	41%	41%	40%	40%	41%	40%	41%
Net Inc.	28.7	22.3	21.0	16.0	17.8	15.4	13.1	10.5	10.8	9.6
Balance Sheet & Other Fin. Data (Million $)										
Cash	34.8	6.3	5.6	3.4	1.8	1.7	3.4	3.2	2.5	2.5
Curr. Assets	154	107	106	101	94.7	78.9	74.9	60.7	63.3	61.5
Total Assets	307	224	207	194	172	152	142	113	116	111
Curr. Liab.	51.2	39.6	36.9	32.4	34.1	24.4	31.7	25.3	26.3	26.4
LT Debt	48.8	4.3	4.6	13.3	4.2	10.7	24.9	14.6	25.4	29.8
Common Eqty.	203	177	162	145	131	115	83.9	72.5	63.2	53.3
Total Cap.	255	181	170	161	138	128	110	88.0	90.0	85.0
Cap. Exp.	19.4	18.8	21.5	12.0	12.5	14.1	16.7	6.3	11.0	6.4
Cash Flow	46.2	34.8	32.3	26.4	27.2	23.0	19.4	16.5	16.5	15.0
Curr. Ratio	3.0	2.7	2.9	3.1	2.8	3.2	2.4	2.4	2.4	2.3
% LT Debt of Cap.	19.1	2.4	2.7	8.3	3.0	8.3	22.6	16.6	28.2	35.2
% Net Inc.of Revs.	7.3	6.6	6.5	5.3	6.5	6.3	5.7	5.4	5.3	4.9
% Ret. on Assets	10.8	10.4	10.5	8.7	11.0	10.0	10.2	9.2	9.4	8.7
% Ret. on Equity	15.1	13.2	13.7	11.6	14.5	14.9	16.7	15.5	18.5	19.6

Data as orig reptd.; bef. results of disc opers/spec. items. Per share data adj. for stk. divs. Bold denotes diluted EPS (FASB 128)-prior periods restated. E-Estimated. NA-Not Available. NM-Not Meaningful. NR-Not Ranked.

Office—1293 S. Main St., Akron, OH 44301. **Tel**—(330) 253-5592. **Pres & CEO**—S. E. Myers. **SVP & Secy**—M. I. Wiskind. **VP-Fin, CFO & Investor Contact**—Gregory J. Stodnick. **Dirs**—K. A. Brown, K. S. Hay, R. P. Johnston, S. E. Myers, R. L. Osborne, J. H. Outcalt, S. Salem, E. P. Schrank, M. I. Wiskind. **Transfer Agent & Registrar**—First Chicago Trust of New York, NYC. **Incorporated**—in Ohio in 1955. **Empl**— 2,503. **S&P Analyst:** Howard Choe

STANDARD
&POOR'S
STOCK REPORTS

Nash-Finch Co.

NASDAQ Symbol **NAFC**

In S&P SmallCap 600

09-OCT-99

Industry:
Distributors (Food & Health)

Summary: This leading food wholesaler supplies products to approximately 2,000 supermarkets, other retail outlets and institutional accounts.

Quantitative Evaluations

Outlook
(1 Lowest—5 Highest)
• **NA**

Fair Value
• **NA**

Risk
• **Low**

Earn./Div. Rank
• **B**

Technical Eval.
• **Bearish** since 9/99

Rel. Strength Rank
(1 Lowest—99 Highest)
• **13**

Insider Activity
• **Neutral**

Recent Price • 7⅛
52 Wk Range • 15½-6¼
Yield • 5.1%
12-Mo. P/E • NM

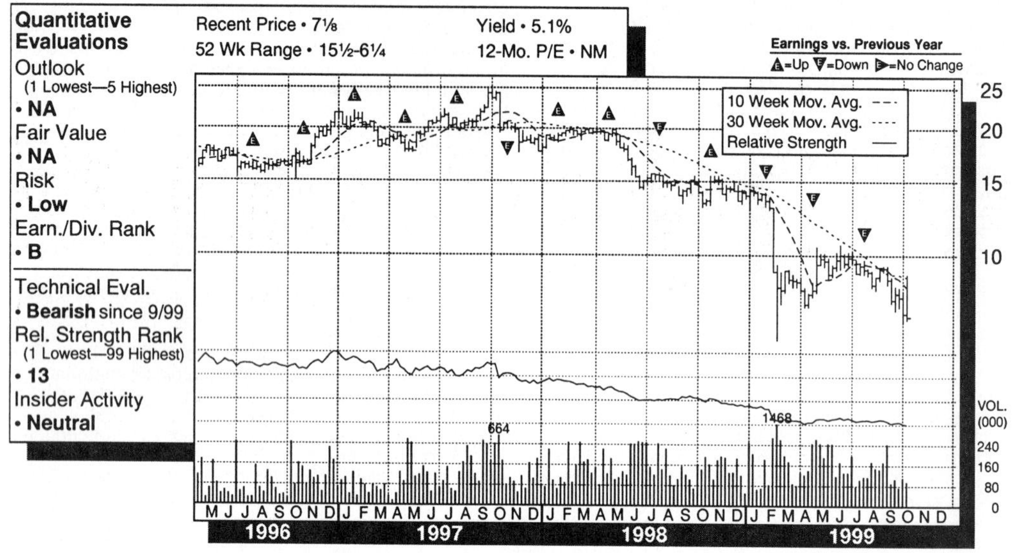

Business Profile - 30-SEP-99

Early in 1999, NAFC announced a five-year strategic revitalization plan to streamline its wholesale operation and build its retail business. As a result of the plan, the company reorganized its retail management structure and is in the process of reducing the number of its regional store names from 17 to four. During the third quarter of 1999, NAFC sold Nash-De Camp Co., a California-based produce growing and marketing subsidiary, and its majority stakes in two dairy operations. In June 1999, the company acquired 18 Erickson supermarkets in Minnesota and Wisconsin for $59 million. In July 1999, NAFC agreed to acquire certain assets of Midwest Wholesale Food, Inc., a wholesale supplier in the Detroit metro area.

Operational Review - 30-SEP-99

Total revenues in the 24 weeks ended June 19, 1999, declined 1.9%, year to year, primarily reflecting the loss of independent retail business in Nebraska and business from a national chain in Colorado. Despite wider gross margins, results were hurt by Year 2000 expenses and non-recurring closed facilities costs. Pretax income fell 50%. After taxes at 42.4%, versus 39.7%, income from continuing operations fell 53%, to $3.5 million ($0.31 a share), from $7.3 million ($0.65). Results in the 1998 period exclude an extraordinary charge of $0.49 a share and a loss from discontinued operations of $0.09.

Stock Performance - 08-OCT-99

In the past 30 trading days, NAFC's shares have declined 23%, compared to a 0.91% fall in the S&P 500. Average trading volume for the past five days was 18,820 shares, compared with the 40-day moving average of 26,669 shares.

Key Stock Statistics

Dividend Rate/Share	0.36	Shareholders	2,214
Shs. outstg. (M)	11.3	Market cap. (B)	$0.081
Avg. daily vol. (M)	0.019	Inst. holdings	42%
Tang. Bk. Value/Share	4.18		
Beta	0.63		

Value of $10,000 invested 5 years ago: $ 5,110

Fiscal Year Ending Dec. 31

	1999	1998	1997	1996	1995	1994
Revenues (Million $)						
1Q	934.8	933.0	947.8	684.5	623.6	618.2
2Q	936.0	973.1	975.5	735.2	676.5	670.4
3Q	—	1,283	1,354	1,004	918.8	887.0
4Q	—	971.4	1,114	951.9	669.9	656.5
Yr.	—	4,160	4,392	3,375	2,889	2,832
Earnings Per Share ($)						
1Q	**0.11**	**0.33**	**0.27**	**0.26**	0.25	0.24
2Q	**0.20**	**0.32**	**0.57**	**0.56**	0.54	0.48
3Q	—	**0.22**	**-0.15**	**0.61**	0.46	0.37
4Q	—	**-4.36**	**0.50**	**0.38**	0.35	0.33
Yr.	—	**-3.50**	**-0.11**	**1.82**	**1.60**	1.42

Next earnings report expected: mid November

Dividend Data (Dividends have been paid since 1926.)

Amount ($)	Date Decl.	Ex-Div. Date	Stock of Record	Payment Date
0.180	Nov. 18	Nov. 24	Nov. 27	Dec. 11 '98
0.090	Feb. 06	Feb. 24	Feb. 26	Mar. 12 '99
0.090	May. 11	May. 19	May. 21	Jun. 04 '99
0.090	Jul. 14	Aug. 18	Aug. 20	Sep. 03 '99

A Division of The McGraw-Hill Companies

Nash-Finch Company

Business Summary - 30-SEP-99

One of the largest U.S. food wholesalers, Nash-Finch Co. adopted a five-year revitalization plan in early 1999 that is designed to centralize operations, improve operational efficiency, develop a strong retail competency and enable the company to pursue aggressive growth strategies. Key initiatives of the plan include, reorganizing management, developing functional information systems, reassessing underperforming businesses, enhancing working capital and reducing cost structure.

The company's principal operations include wholesale distribution and operation of conventional and warehouse supermarkets. Wholesale operations serve primarily the Midwest and Southeast. NAFC's wholesale business serves the supermarket industry (60% of 1998 wholesale sales) and military commissaries (22%) by offering a wide array of national brand and private label products. Product offerings include dry groceries, fresh fruits and vegetables, frozen foods, fresh and processed meat products and dairy products, as well as a wide variety of non-food products including health and beauty care, tobacco, paper products, cleaning supplies and small household items. Private label products are sold primarily under the Our Family and Fame brand names.

The company's 18 distribution centers serve about 2,000 affiliated and independent supermarkets, U.S. military commissaries and other customers. Customers served by NAFC's wholesale operations range in size from small stores to large warehouse stores with over 100,000 sq. ft. of space. In an effort to increase efficiencies at its distribution centers and decrease operating costs, the company has closed four of its warehouses since 1998.

The retail segment (18%) owns and operates 93 retail outlets. During 1999, the company will reduce the number of regional store trade names under which it operates from 17 to four; Econofoods, Sunmart, Family Thrift Center and IGA. The reduction is intended to build brand equity and eliminate efficiencies.

As part of its revitalization plan, NAFC will focus on strengthening its corporate retail presence and the company plans on expanding the segment to represent as much as 50% of total company sales over the next five years.

During the third quarter of 1999, NAFC sold its wholly owned Nash-DeCamp Co., a California-based produce growing and marketing subsidiary, and sold its majority stakes in two dairy operations.

The company recorded nonrecurring pretax charges in the fourth quarter of 1998 totaling $105.6 million related to the restructuring and the reporting of its produce growing and marketing subsidiary as a discontinued operation.

Per Share Data ($) (Year Ended Dec. 31)	1998	1997	1996	1995	1994	1993	1992	1991	1990	1989
Tangible Bk. Val.	7.70	13.68	13.54	19.22	18.25	17.45	17.59	16.45	15.40	14.43
Cash Flow	0.67	4.13	4.96	4.29	4.35	4.12	4.31	4.13	4.20	3.32
Earnings	-3.50	-0.11	1.81	1.60	1.42	1.46	1.85	1.75	1.64	1.21
Dividends	0.72	0.72	0.75	0.74	0.73	0.72	0.71	0.70	0.69	0.67
Payout Ratio	NM	NM	41%	46%	51%	49%	38%	40%	42%	55%
Prices - High	20	24 7/8	22	20 3/4	18 1/2	23 1/4	19 7/8	20 1/4	25 1/4	26
- Low	12 3/4	17 1/2	15	15 1/4	15	17	16 1/4	16 1/8	15 3/4	21
P/E Ratio - High	NM	NM	12	13	13	16	11	12	15	21
- Low	NM	NM	8	10	11	12	9	9	10	17
Income Statement Analysis (Million $)										
Revs.	4,160	4,392	3,375	2,831	2,822	2,716	2,509	2,338	2,369	2,219
Oper. Inc.	86.3	112	83.3	68.8	59.3	57.9	62.7	59.9	59.6	51.4
Depr.	47.2	47.7	34.8	29.4	31.8	28.9	26.8	25.8	27.8	22.9
Int. Exp.	29.0	32.8	14.9	10.8	11.4	10.1	9.3	9.0	8.7	8.3
Pretax Inc.	-58.4	-0.2	33.7	28.6	25.8	26.7	32.6	30.8	29.0	21.2
Eff. Tax Rate	NM	NM	41%	39%	40%	41%	38%	38%	38%	38%
Net Inc.	-39.6	-1.0	20.0	17.4	15.5	15.9	20.1	19.1	17.8	13.2
Balance Sheet & Other Fin. Data (Million $)										
Cash	0.8	0.9	0.9	26.0	1.1	0.9	0.8	0.6	0.6	12.8
Curr. Assets	467	494	526	312	310	295	310	240	234	212
Total Assets	833	905	945	514	532	522	514	430	416	381
Curr. Liab.	331	294	297	208	220	215	214	155	158	128
LT Debt	328	364	404	81.1	96.0	97.9	94.1	82.5	74.3	78.0
Common Eqty.	156	226	233	215	206	199	191	179	167	157
Total Cap.	484	590	637	297	302	297	285	263	246	240
Cap. Exp.	52.7	67.7	51.3	33.2	35.0	52.0	46.3	36.8	43.8	34.6
Cash Flow	7.6	-46.7	54.8	46.8	47.3	44.8	46.8	44.9	45.6	36.1
Curr. Ratio	1.4	1.7	1.8	1.5	1.4	1.4	1.4	1.5	1.5	1.7
% LT Debt of Cap.	67.7	61.7	63.4	27.3	31.8	32.9	33.0	31.3	30.3	32.5
% Net Inc.of Revs.	NM	NM	0.6	0.6	0.5	0.6	0.8	0.8	0.8	0.6
% Ret. on Assets	NM	NM	2.7	3.3	2.9	3.1	4.3	4.5	4.5	3.4
% Ret. on Equity	NM	NM	8.9	8.2	7.6	8.1	10.8	11.0	11.0	8.5

Data as orig reptd.; bef. results of disc opers/spec. items. Per share data adj. for stk. divs. Bold denotes diluted EPS (FASB 128)-prior periods restated. E-Estimated. NA-Not Available. NM-Not Meaningful. NR-Not Ranked.

Office—7600 France Ave. South, P.O. Box 355, Minneapolis, MN 55440-0355. **Tel**—(612) 832-0534. **Fax**—(612) 844-1234. **Website**—http://www.nashfinch.com **Pres & CEO**—R. Marshall. **EVP & CFO**—J. A. Haedicke. **VP, Secy & Investor Contact**—Norman R. Soland. **VP & CFO**—J. R. Scherer. **Treas**—Suzanne S. Allen. **Dirs**—C. F. Bitter, R. A. Fisher, A. N. Flaten Jr., J. L. Ford, A. P. Graham, J. H. Grunewald, R. G. Lareau, D. E. Marsh, R. Marshall, D. R. Miller, R. F. Nash, J. O. Rodysill, W. R. Voss. **Transfer Agent & Registrar**—Norwest Bank Minnesota, St. Paul. **Incorporated**—in Delaware in 1921. **Empl**— 11,750. **S&P Analyst:** A. Bensinger

STANDARD
&POOR'S
STOCK REPORTS

Nashua Corp.

NYSE Symbol **NSH**

In S&P SmallCap 600

09-OCT-99

Industry:
Office Equipment & Supplies

Summary: This company provides a diverse mix of products including specialty coated paper products, imaging supplies and pressure-sensitive labels.

Quantitative Evaluations

Outlook
(1 Lowest—5 Highest)
• **NA**

Fair Value
• **NA**

Risk
• **Average**

Earn./Div. Rank
• **C**

Technical Eval.
• **Bearish** since 8/99

Rel. Strength Rank
(1 Lowest—99 Highest)
• **23**

Insider Activity
• **NA**

Recent Price • 8½
52 Wk Range • 16¾-8½
Yield • Nil
12-Mo. P/E • NM

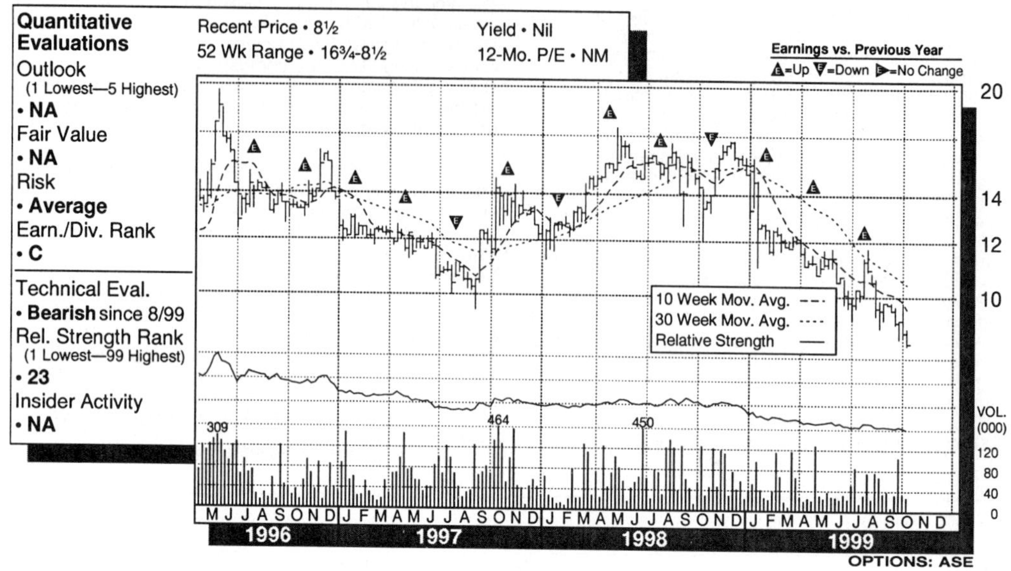

Business Profile - 21-JUN-99

In May 1999, the company unveiled plans for a $1.6 million capital improvement of the thermal coating process at its specialty coated products facility in Merrimack, NH. The project, scheduled for completion in the first quarter of 2000, will provide needed manufacturing flexibility to carry out plans for a broader range of products, and to meet growing demand for NSH's thermal paper. The initiative is part of a larger capital investment program aimed at enhancing manufacturing capacity, productivity, quality and efficiency.. The company recently concluded a stock purchase program under which it repurchased one million common shares for a total of $14.2 million.

Operational Review - 21-JUN-99

Revenues in the first quarter of 1999 fell 4.1%, year to year, as reduced orders of imaging supplies from large international customers and lower sales prices on certain items outweighed higher volume sales of thermal paper and label products. Gross margins widened, on lower manufacturing costs, efficiency improvements, and a more favorable product mix. With net interest income, versus net interest expense, after taxes at 40.4%, versus tax benefits of $356,000, income of $218,000 ($0.04 a share, on 7.3% fewer shares) contrasted with a loss of $490,000 ($0.08, before a loss of $0.04 from discontinued operations).

Stock Performance - 08-OCT-99

In the past 30 trading days, NSH's shares have declined 13%, compared to a 0.91% fall in the S&P 500. Average trading volume for the past five days was 5,300 shares, compared with the 40-day moving average of 8,623 shares.

Key Stock Statistics

Dividend Rate/Share	Nil	Shareholders	1,358
Shs. outstg. (M)	5.9	Market cap. (B)	$0.050
Avg. daily vol. (M)	0.010	Inst. holdings	73%
Tang. Bk. Value/Share	12.15		
Beta	0.57		

Value of $10,000 invested 5 years ago: $ 3,393

Fiscal Year Ending Dec. 31

	1999	1998	1997	1996	1995	1994
Revenues (Million $)						
1Q	42.65	44.49	44.40	101.5	109.6	112.8
2Q	42.57	40.08	43.20	103.6	122.2	122.7
3Q	—	42.42	42.60	100.9	121.7	127.8
4Q	—	40.84	43.00	83.71	98.74	115.2
Yr.	—	167.8	173.2	389.7	452.2	478.6
Earnings Per Share ($)						
1Q	0.04	-0.10	-0.13	-0.21	0.01	-0.18
2Q	0.09	-0.35	-0.45	3.79	0.23	0.46
3Q	—	-1.27	-0.17	-0.59	-1.14	0.37
4Q	—	0.29	-0.19	-0.08	-1.53	0.05
Yr.	—	-1.15	-0.94	3.06	-3.28	-1.33

Next earnings report expected: late October

Dividend Data

Omitted in 1983, cash dividends were resumed in 1986 and paid regularly through October 1995. Cash dividends were suspended in November 1995.

Nashua Corporation

Business Summary - 21-JUN-99

In 1998, following several years of weak results, Nashua Corp. undertook major steps in an effort to return to profitability. In March 1998, the company decided to exit the photofinishing business, and to focus on expanding niche markets where its imaging products can be differentiated, add value, and generate consistent, sustainable, profitable growth. As a result, NSH sold its international photofinishing business and its U.K.-based Microsharp imaging technology operations in April 1998. In addition, in September 1998, 37%-owned Cerion Technologies, a maker of aluminum disk substrates, announced its intention to cease operations; it is currently in the process of liquidating. NSH's continuing operations consist of two divisions: imaging supplies, and specialty coated and label products.

The imaging supplies division, which accounted for about 34% of sales from continuing operations, makes and sells consumable products used in the process of reproducing and transferring readable images. Imaging supplies include toners, developers, remanufactured laser printer cartridges and copy paper, and are marketed to national and government accounts through a network of about 150 dealers throughout the U.S.

The specialty coated and label products division (66% of sales) makes and sells thermal and non-thermal, thermosensitive label, Davac dry-gummed label paper and carbonless papers. Thermal papers develop an image upon contact with either a heated stylus or a thermal print head and are used in point of sale printers, airline and package identification systems, gaming systems, medical and industrial recording charts and for use in thermal facsimile machines. Thermosensitive label papers are coated with an adhesive that is activated when heat is applied, and are used by printers who convert the papers into labels for use primarily in the pharmaceutical industry. Davac dry-gummed label paper is coated with a moisture-activated adhesive and is sold primarily to fine paper merchants and business forms manufacturers, where it is converted into various types of labels and stamps. Carbonless paper is a coated paper used in the production of multi-part business forms which produce multiple copies without carbon paper. The division is a major supplier of labels to the supermarket industry and of labels used in the distribution and manufacture of a wide variety of other products.

Results in 1998 benefited from improved profitability at the company's continuing operations reflecting new product introductions and reduced manufacturing and procurement costs. However, after charges of $15.0 million related to a patent infringement suit with Ricoh Corp., the net loss widened to $7.2 million, from $6.2 million in 1997. NSH continues to address productivity issues, and is implementing a $30 million capital investment program designed to enhance capacity, efficiency and quality throughout its manufacturing operations.

Per Share Data ($) (Year Ended Dec. 31)	1998	1997	1996	1995	1994	1993	1992	1991	1990	1989
Tangible Bk. Val.	12.01	14.15	12.34	6.53	12.25	12.25	14.74	15.60	15.83	23.84
Cash Flow	-0.06	0.24	5.30	0.30	3.10	0.07	4.56	3.47	5.63	4.13
Earnings	-1.15	-0.94	2.58	-2.43	0.70	-3.42	0.84	0.09	2.73	1.84
Dividends	Nil	Nil	Nil	0.54	0.72	0.72	0.72	0.72	0.69	0.57
Payout Ratio	Nil	Nil	Nil	NM	103%	NM	86%	NM	21%	30%
Prices - High	17½	14¾	19⅝	21	30⅞	31¾	31¼	37	44⅞	42⅞
- Low	11½	9½	9⅛	12¼	19⅜	25¼	21	18	30½	28¾
P/E Ratio - High	NM	NM	8	NM	44	NM	37	NM	16	23
- Low	NM	NM	4	NM	28	NM	25	NM	11	16
Income Statement Analysis (Million $)										
Revs.	168	173	390	452	479	556	552	526	589	549
Oper. Inc.	7.5	1.3	16.1	18.3	27.2	41.0	33.6	26.0	58.0	53.0
Depr.	6.8	7.6	17.5	17.4	15.3	22.1	23.6	21.4	22.1	21.8
Int. Exp.	0.4	0.1	2.7	5.5	2.5	2.1	2.7	1.7	1.7	3.5
Pretax Inc.	-11.9	-10.0	28.6	-20.1	7.5	-31.4	10.5	3.5	33.9	28.5
Eff. Tax Rate	NM	NM	43%	NM	41%	NM	49%	84%	39%	38%
Net Inc.	-7.2	-6.0	16.5	-15.5	4.4	-21.7	5.3	0.6	20.8	17.6
Balance Sheet & Other Fin. Data (Million $)										
Cash	37.0	3.7	20.0	8.4	10.2	5.9	12.2	30.0	7.5	10.8
Curr. Assets	83.3	45.8	72.2	99	108	110	111	113	104	178
Total Assets	134	147	177	231	228	219	237	243	239	319
Curr. Liab.	37.5	26.9	51.0	67.0	61.0	86.0	71.0	77.0	87.0	64.0
LT Debt	1.1	3.5	2.0	68.4	49.2	20.3	27.9	25.4	10.4	19.4
Common Eqty.	75.2	95.0	102	75.0	93.0	93.0	117	130	134	236
Total Cap.	76.3	99	104	143	142	113	145	155	145	255
Cap. Exp.	6.7	4.4	12.8	13.2	16.8	35.7	23.6	33.1	49.8	36.8
Cash Flow	-0.4	1.5	34.0	1.9	19.7	0.5	28.9	22.0	42.9	39.4
Curr. Ratio	2.2	1.7	1.4	1.5	1.8	1.3	1.6	1.5	1.2	2.8
% LT Debt of Cap.	1.4	3.5	1.9	47.8	34.7	17.9	19.2	16.4	7.2	7.6
% Net Inc.of Revs.	NM	NM	4.2	NM	0.9	NM	1.0	0.1	3.5	3.2
% Ret. on Assets	NM	NM	8.1	NM	2.0	NM	2.2	0.2	9.1	4.6
% Ret. on Equity	NM	NM	18.7	NM	4.8	NM	4.3	0.4	14.1	7.7

Data as orig reptd.; bef. results of disc opers/spec. items. Per share data adj. for stk. divs. Bold denotes diluted EPS (FASB 128)-prior periods restated. E-Estimated. NA-Not Available. NM-Not Meaningful. NR-Not Ranked.

Office—44 Franklin St., P.O. Box 2002, Nashua, NH 03061-2002. **Tel**—(603) 880-2323. **Website**—http://www.nashua.com **Chrmn, Pres & CEO**—G. G. Garbacz. **VP-Fin, Treas, CFO & Investor Contact**—John L. Patenaude (603 880-2145). **VP & Gen Counsel**—P. Anastos. **Dirs**—S. A. Buckler, G. G. Garbacz, C. S. Hoppin, J. M. Kucharski, D. C. Miller, Jr., P. J. Murphy, J. F. Orr III. **Transfer Agent & Registrar**—Bank Boston, N.A. **Incorporated**—in Delaware in 1957. **Empl**— 725. **S&P Analyst:** S.A.H.

STANDARD
&POOR'S
STOCK REPORTS

National Computer Systems

NASDAQ Symbol **NLCS**

In S&P SmallCap 600

09-OCT-99

Industry: Services (Data Processing)

Summary: NLCS is the largest U.S. provider of school-based financial management, student information and instructional software and services to the K-12 market.

Quantitative Evaluations

Outlook (1 Lowest—5 Highest)
• **2⁻**

Fair Value
• **36⅛**

Risk
• **Low**

Earn./Div. Rank
• **B+**

Technical Eval.
• **Neutral** since 9/99

Rel. Strength Rank (1 Lowest—99 Highest)
• **77**

Insider Activity
• **Neutral**

Recent Price • 38
52 Wk Range • 40⅜-23
Yield • 0.5%
12-Mo. P/E • 33.3

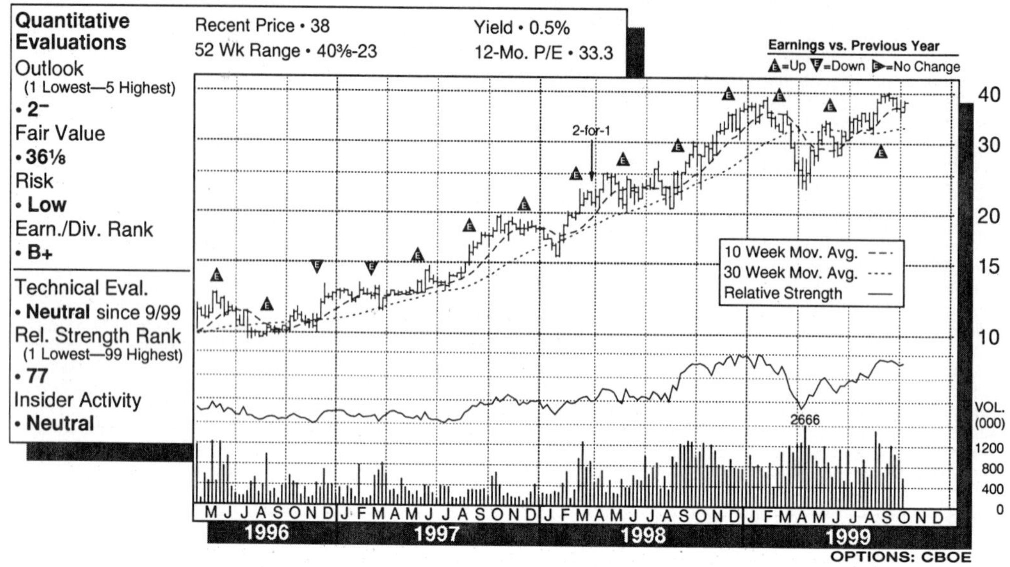

OPTIONS: CBOE

Business Profile - 30-JUL-99

The company aims to leverage its core skills of high-accuracy collection, management and interpretation of data. NLCS is increasing its capacity steadily, to keep up with additional testing contracts it has won. In June 1999, the company acquired NovaNet Learning, Inc, an interactive online curriculum content concern with revenues for 1999 expected to reach $20 million. The purchase price was about $20 million in cash. In July 1999, NLCS was awarded a contract for statewide testing and assessment services by the State of Florida Department of Education, valued at $122.5 million over the next five years.

Operational Review - 30-JUL-99

Total revenues in the first quarter of FY 2000 (Jan.) climbed 28%, year to year, spurred by gains in assessment and testing services, government and commercial outsourcing, and K-12 networking and professional services related to education software. Gross margins remained constant at 38.3%, and with relatively lower selling costs associated with the higher information services revenues, 58% greater research and development costs, and a 46% increase in general and administrative costs, pretax income soared 31%. After taxes at 40.0% in each period, net income was also up 31%, to $6,653,000 ($0.20 a share, on 1.7% more shares), from $5,095,000 ($0.16).

Stock Performance - 08-OCT-99

In the past 30 trading days, NLCS's shares have declined 4%, compared to a 0.91% fall in the S&P 500. Average trading volume for the past five days was 116,100 shares, compared with the 40-day moving average of 259,113 shares.

Key Stock Statistics

Dividend Rate/Share	0.20	Shareholders	2,100
Shs. outstg. (M)	31.9	Market cap. (B)	$ 1.2
Avg. daily vol. (M)	0.200	Inst. holdings	71%
Tang. Bk. Value/Share	5.95		
Beta	0.44		

Value of $10,000 invested 5 years ago: $ 74,684

Fiscal Year Ending Jan. 31

	2000	1999	1998	1997	1996	1995
Revenues (Million $)						
1Q	125.8	97.90	78.97	70.51	74.30	68.80
2Q	167.6	128.1	96.03	80.96	88.44	80.13
3Q	—	135.4	115.4	88.78	97.32	94.61
4Q	—	143.9	115.6	90.91	98.92	93.45
Yr.	—	505.4	406.0	331.2	359.0	336.9
Earnings Per Share ($)						
1Q	**0.20**	**0.16**	**0.13**	**0.10**	0.08	0.07
2Q	**0.40**	**0.30**	**0.22**	**0.19**	0.18	0.15
3Q	—	**0.24**	**0.19**	**0.16**	0.20	0.15
4Q	—	**0.30**	**0.26**	**-0.01**	0.26	0.07
Yr.	—	**1.00**	**0.80**	**0.44**	**0.53**	**0.37**

Next earnings report expected: mid November

Dividend Data (Dividends have been paid since 1976.)

Amount ($)	Date Decl.	Ex-Div. Date	Stock of Record	Payment Date
0.050	Mar. 04	Mar. 11	Mar. 15	Mar. 25 '99
0.050	May. 27	Jun. 10	Jun. 14	Jun. 24 '99
0.050	Aug. 25	Sep. 02	Sep. 07	Sep. 16 '99
0.050	Aug. 25	Sep. 03	Sep. 07	Sep. 16 '99

National Computer Systems, Inc.

Business Summary - 30-JUL-99

NLCS is an information services company, providing software, services and systems for the collection, management and interpretation of data. It markets these products and services mainly to the education market, but also provides large scale data collection and management services and products to business, government and other markets.

Income from operations by segment in 1998 was: assessments and testing services 34%, education software and services 16%, NCS Services 15%, data collection systems 31%, and international 4%. By major market, 75% of revenues were derived from education, and 25% from large scale data management.

The company is the largest U.S. commercial processor of academic assessment tests for grades K-12. It markets test scoring services to major test publishers, state education agencies, the federal government, local school districts and commercial customers. Offerings include program design; test item development; program management; software development; printing, packaging, distribution and collection logistics; and scoring, editing, analysis and final reporting. NLCS also publishes and distributes tests, and provides scoring services to industrial and clinical psychologists, psychiatrists, human resource professionals and educators.

NLCS's education software products include student administrative software to assist educators in student management, including applications such as academic reporting, attendance gathering and scheduling. It also offers model curriculum and test item databases to assist schools in establishing and meeting stated or mandated curriculum objectives.

NCS Service provides a comprehensive package of services and products that include: systems analysis and design; software development; comprehensive data collection technologies, including paper-based imaging and electronic; forms management; telecommunication and telephone call center support; information management and dissemination; and network support, such as internet connectivity; and training.

The company manufactures OMR scanners that can read data for specially designed forms printed by the company with specifically formulated inks. Computing capability is built into most scanners. Scanners usually incorporate, or interface with, software developed by NLCS. Optical scanning equipment is most effective for applications that require the highest accuracy, precise response definition, and cost effective data capture.

NLCS's international business strategy is to focus on certain countries with services-led applications. The applications center on testing and assessment in the education market, and on telecom deregulation for commercial or governmental clients.

Per Share Data ($) (Year Ended Jan. 31)	1999	1998	1997	1996	1995	1994	1993	1992	1991	1990
Tangible Bk. Val.	5.53	4.81	5.33	4.09	3.60	3.17	3.62	3.28	2.90	2.57
Cash Flow	1.99	1.74	1.25	1.59	0.99	0.45	1.08	1.03	1.01	0.76
Earnings	1.00	0.80	0.44	0.71	0.44	-0.08	0.52	0.48	0.41	0.23
Dividends	0.20	0.18	0.18	0.18	0.18	0.18	0.17	0.14	0.14	0.14
Payout Ratio	20%	23%	41%	25%	41%	NM	32%	30%	34%	60%
Cal. Yrs.	1998	1997	1996	1995	1994	1993	1992	1991	1990	1989
Prices - High	37 3/4	19 3/4	13 1/4	11	8 3/8	9	9 5/8	8 7/8	4 7/8	7 5/8
- Low	15 1/2	11 3/8	8 3/4	7 3/8	5 1/8	5 3/8	6 1/4	4 5/8	3	3 7/8
P/E Ratio - High	38	25	30	15	19	17	19	18	12	33
- Low	15	14	20	10	12	10	12	10	7	17
Income Statement Analysis (Million $)										
Revs.	505	406	331	359	337	305	300	303	315	284
Oper. Inc.	88.1	73.2	59.8	67.1	51.2	39.0	45.7	46.6	47.2	35.1
Depr.	32.8	30.1	25.3	27.4	16.7	16.3	18.4	17.9	19.1	11.4
Int. Exp.	0.9	1.4	1.7	3.3	3.6	2.5	2.1	4.0	7.0	6.1
Pretax Inc.	54.1	42.0	26.5	37.0	19.1	-2.9	26.6	24.2	21.0	11.5
Eff. Tax Rate	40%	40%	49%	40%	30%	NM	38%	36%	38%	37%
Net Inc.	32.5	25.2	13.7	22.2	13.4	-2.5	16.5	15.5	13.0	7.3
Balance Sheet & Other Fin. Data (Million $)										
Cash	16.3	23.3	58.1	5.2	1.2	1.7	10.8	2.4	3.3	2.8
Curr. Assets	174	147	161	115	111	104	99	96.0	104	114
Total Assets	362	315	274	235	241	220	215	218	225	250
Curr. Liab.	127	103	82.2	74.0	75.1	67.5	60.0	56.4	52.7	63.1
LT Debt	5.6	12.4	16.3	24.5	45.3	44.7	23.9	37.2	56.0	82.3
Common Eqty.	227	194	170	128	113	100	121	112	101	90.0
Total Cap.	235	213	192	161	166	153	155	161	172	187
Cap. Exp.	27.1	25.2	14.9	14.0	29.2	23.9	14.4	11.5	11.0	37.8
Cash Flow	65.3	55.3	38.9	49.7	30.1	13.8	34.9	33.3	32.1	24.3
Curr. Ratio	1.4	1.4	2.0	1.6	1.5	1.5	1.6	1.7	2.0	1.8
% LT Debt of Cap.	2.4	5.8	8.5	15.2	27.4	29.3	15.4	23.1	32.5	44.0
% Net Inc.of Revs.	6.4	6.2	4.1	6.2	4.0	NM	5.5	5.1	4.1	2.6
% Ret. on Assets	9.6	8.5	5.5	9.3	5.8	NM	7.7	7.0	5.4	3.3
% Ret. on Equity	15.4	13.8	9.2	18.4	12.4	NM	14.2	14.5	13.6	7.7

Data as orig reptd.; bef. results of disc opers/spec. items. Per share data adj. for stk. divs. Bold denotes diluted EPS (FASB 128)-prior periods restated. E-Estimated. NA-Not Available. NM-Not Meaningful. NR-Not Ranked.

Office—11000 Prairie Lakes Dr., Eden Prairie, MN 55344. **Tel**—(612) 829-3000. **Website**—http://www.ncs.com **Chrmn, Pres & CEO**—R. A. Gullotti. **VP & CFO**—J. W. Taylor. **Secy & Treas**—J. W. Fenton Jr. **Investor Contact**—Yolanda Scharton (612-829-3203). **Dirs**—W. J. Cadogan, D. C. Cox, D. M. Etter, R. A. Gullotti, M. S. Joseph, J. B. Keffeler, S. G. Shank, J. E. Steuri. **Transfer Agent & Registrar**—Norwest Bank Minnesota, Minneapolis. **Incorporated**—in Minnesota in 1962. **Empl**— 4,000. **S&P Analyst:** P.L.H.

STANDARD
&POOR'S
STOCK REPORTS

National Data Corp.

NYSE Symbol **NDC**

In S&P SmallCap 600

09-OCT-99

Industry:
Services (Data Processing)

Summary: This company is a leading provider of high-volume transaction processing services and application systems to the health care and payment systems markets.

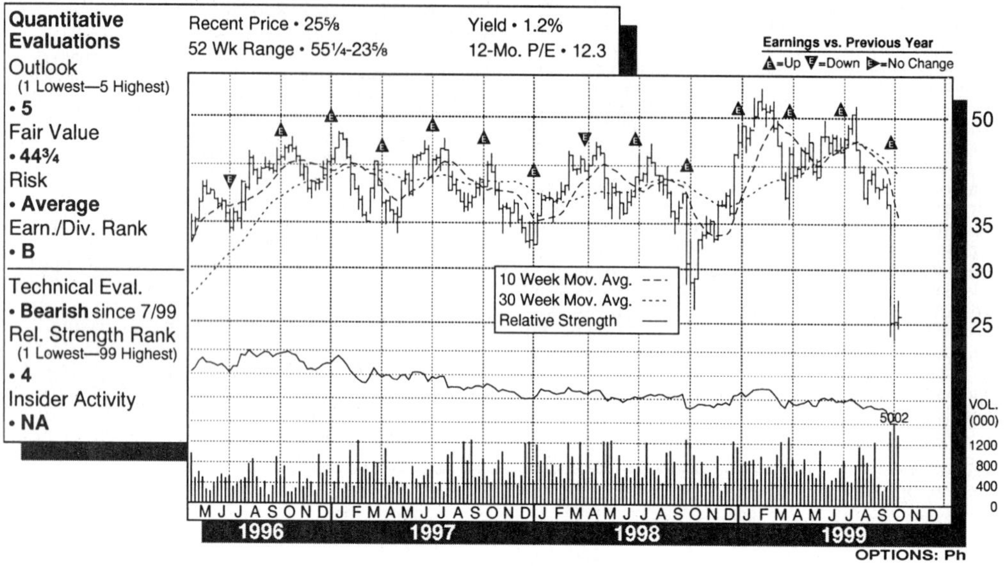

Business Profile - 04-OCT-99

NDC's priorities for FY 00 (May) are to continue the acceleration of cash earnings generation, making infrastructure enhancements and expanding distribution channels to support the next phase of revenue growth. NDC also plans to continue making investments in Internet services and partnerships. In August 1999, NDC announced the Internet Physician Suite, which facilitates the use of electronic capabilities by physicians to improve their business processes, patient relations and disease management outcomes. In September 1999, Physiciansite.com (an affiliate of HealthStar Corp.) announced a multi-year agreement to offer the NDC Internet Physician Suite through its website. Also in September, after NDC's first quarter results disappointed Wall Street and caused shares to fall, the company announced a $2 million share repurchase program.

Operational Review - 04-OCT-99

Revenues in the three months ended August 31, 1999, rose 6.5%, year to year, with 9.0% revenue growth in the electronic commerce segment. After well controlled costs of service, lower net interest and other expenses, and taxes at 38.5%, versus 39.0%, net income was up 16%, to $18,877,000 ($0.53, on 8.5% more shares), from $16,323,000 ($0.47).

Stock Performance - 08-OCT-99

In the past 30 trading days, NDC's shares have declined 35%, compared to a 0.91% fall in the S&P 500. Average trading volume for the past five days was 617,980 shares, compared with the 40-day moving average of 386,959 shares.

Key Stock Statistics

Dividend Rate/Share	0.30	Shareholders	3,663
Shs. outstg. (M)	33.8	Market cap. (B)	$0.866
Avg. daily vol. (M)	0.609	Inst. holdings	84%
Tang. Bk. Value/Share	NM		
Beta	0.58		

Value of $10,000 invested 5 years ago: $ 24,160

Fiscal Year Ending May 31

	2000	1999	1998	1997	1996	1995
Revenues (Million $)						
1Q	204.1	191.7	120.1	101.2	78.29	55.97
2Q	—	191.5	120.0	102.6	78.06	59.81
3Q	—	195.7	171.6	112.0	77.62	62.16
4Q	—	206.0	185.3	118.2	91.83	64.09
Yr.	—	784.9	649.0	433.9	325.8	242.0
Earnings Per Share ($)						
1Q	**0.53**	**0.47**	0.38	0.30	0.18	0.15
2Q	—	**0.45**	0.41	0.34	0.25	0.17
3Q	—	**0.52**	**-2.77**	0.36	0.22	0.19
4Q	—	**0.58**	**0.47**	0.38	-0.96	0.24
Yr.	—	**2.02**	**-1.90**	**0.91**	-0.31	0.76

Next earnings report expected: mid December

Dividend Data (Dividends have been paid since 1977.)

Amount ($)	Date Decl.	Ex-Div. Date	Stock of Record	Payment Date
0.075	Oct. 23	Nov. 04	Nov. 06	Nov. 30 '98
0.075	Jan. 21	Feb. 10	Feb. 12	Feb. 26 '99
0.075	May. 03	May. 13	May. 17	May. 31 '99
0.075	Aug. 03	Aug. 15	Aug. 17	Aug. 31 '99

A Division of The McGraw-Hill Companies

STANDARD
&POOR'S
STOCK REPORTS

National Data Corporation

09-OCT-99

Business Summary - 04-OCT-99

National Data Corp. believes the health care and electronic commerce markets present attractive opportunities for continued growth. The company seeks to increase its penetration of existing information processing and application systems markets. It also plans to continue identifying and creating new markets through: 1) development of value-added applications, new systems and new services; 2) enhancement of existing products; 3) expansion of distribution channels, including the Internet; and 4) acquisition of or alliance with companies with compatible products, services, and/or distribution capabilities.

The company is a leading provider of high-volume information services and systems to the health care and e-commerce markets through its Health Information Services and eCommerce business units. NDC serves a diverse customer base comprised of health care providers, hospitals, health care payers, payer plans, corporations, financial institutions, and government agencies.

NDC's offerings reduce processing costs, settlement delays, and losses from fraudulent transactions. Its computer and telecommunications network enables the company to electronically process, capture and transmit point-of-service transactions 24 hours a day, seven days a week.

NDC believes its Health Information Services unit, which accounted for 58% of FY 99 (May) revenues (55% in FY 98) is the broadest collector, processor and distributor of information to more segments of the health care industry than any other health information services provider. The unit offers products and services that serve a range of health care markets. Primary products and services include electronic eligibility, claims processing, adjudication and remittance services, practice management systems, billing services, business office management services, data warehousing/analysis, and other information-based services.

The e-commerce business segment (42%, 45%) provides services to assist customers with the movement of electronic payment and financial information. Services include mainly merchant and cardholder processing, credit and debit transaction processing, check guarantee and verification, electronic authorization and capture, terminal management services, portfolio risk management, purchase card services and financial electronic data interchange. NDC is one of the world's largest independent transaction processors of credit cards.

In July 1999, NDC announced a partnership with Medscape Inc. for the joint development and marketing of Internet-based health information offerings. Medscape operates Medscape.com, a health care website that provides medical information and interactive programs. NDC said it planned to invest $10 million in Medscape, and another $10 million in "other related considerations."

Per Share Data ($) (Year Ended May 31)	1999	1998	1997	1996	1995	1994	1993	1992	1991	1990
Tangible Bk. Val.	NM	NM	NM	0.39	2.30	3.60	3.00	2.41	2.16	2.63
Cash Flow	3.62	-0.40	1.90	0.74	1.80	1.51	1.55	1.63	0.74	2.03
Earnings	2.02	-1.90	1.38	-0.31	0.76	0.57	0.47	0.41	-0.80	0.11
Dividends	0.30	0.30	0.30	0.30	0.30	0.29	0.29	0.29	0.29	0.29
Payout Ratio	15%	NM	22%	NM	39%	51%	63%	71%	NM	263%
Cal. Yrs.	1998	1997	1996	1995	1994	1993	1992	1991	1990	1989
Prices - High	49	47 1/2	46 5/8	28	17 5/8	13	11 7/8	10	23	23 3/8
- Low	26 1/8	32 1/8	20	15 3/8	10 3/8	8 7/8	5 3/8	6 1/8	5 3/8	15 3/8
P/E Ratio - High	24	NM	34	NM	23	23	25	24	NM	NM
- Low	13	NM	14	NM	14	15	11	15	NM	NM
Income Statement Analysis (Million $)										
Revs.	785	649	434	326	242	204	205	219	230	276
Oper. Inc.	190	143	81.2	60.8	45.9	36.6	34.7	36.2	38.7	64.7
Depr.	56.7	48.4	14.5	28.6	21.0	18.2	19.7	21.6	27.2	34.0
Int. Exp.	15.4	12.9	6.8	3.8	2.5	1.5	2.2	4.2	5.6	7.4
Pretax Inc.	116	-37.1	60.6	-11.7	24.0	17.4	14.6	12.8	-23.9	6.4
Eff. Tax Rate	39%	NM	36%	NM	36%	36%	42%	42%	NM	69%
Net Inc.	71.4	-61.3	38.8	-8.5	15.4	11.2	8.5	7.4	-14.1	2.0
Balance Sheet & Other Fin. Data (Million $)										
Cash	4.3	3.2	19.2	9.8	30.8	38.0	17.8	2.9	5.4	4.0
Curr. Assets	213	172	109	81.4	98.0	100	86.0	74.0	83.0	108
Total Assets	765	731	522	368	217	183	175	195	212	277
Curr. Liab.	156	186	67.3	102	67.6	51.0	45.0	58.0	83.0	112
LT Debt	171	168	152	7.6	19.7	16.3	14.1	20.8	13.3	12.8
Common Eqty.	409	348	277	233	123	109	101	96.0	93.0	111
Total Cap.	599	535	450	241	146	127	126	128	118	145
Cap. Exp.	3.6	22.8	16.8	16.4	10.4	15.4	8.1	7.3	13.0	25.3
Cash Flow	128	-13.0	53.3	20.2	36.4	29.4	28.2	29.0	13.1	36.0
Curr. Ratio	1.4	0.9	1.6	0.8	1.5	2.0	1.9	1.3	1.0	1.0
% LT Debt of Cap.	285.0	31.4	33.8	3.1	13.5	12.8	11.2	16.3	11.3	8.8
% Net Inc.of Revs.	9.1	NM	8.9	NM	6.4	5.5	4.2	3.4	NM	0.7
% Ret. on Assets	9.5	NM	8.7	NM	7.7	6.1	4.5	3.6	NM	0.8
% Ret. on Equity	18.5	NM	15.2	NM	13.3	10.4	8.5	7.8	NM	1.8

Data as orig reptd.; bef. results of disc opers/spec. items. Per share data adj. for stk. divs. Bold denotes diluted EPS (FASB 128)-prior periods restated. E-Estimated. NA-Not Available. NM-Not Meaningful. NR-Not Ranked.

Office—National Data Plaza, Corporate Square, Atlanta, GA 30329-2010. **Tel**—(404) 728-2000. **Website**—http://www.ndcorp.com **Chrmn & CEO**—R. A. Yellowlees. **EVP & CFO**—K. C. Shea. **Dirs**—E. L. Barlow, J. V. Biggins, N. Williams, R. A. Yellowlees. **Transfer Agent**—Wachovia Bank of North Carolina, Winston-Salem. **Incorporated**—in Delaware in 1967. **Empl**— 6,000. **S&P Analyst:** Scott H. Kessler

STANDARD
&POOR'S
STOCK REPORTS

National Instruments

NASDAQ Symbol **NATI**

In S&P SmallCap 600

09-OCT-99 **Industry:** Computers (Hardware)

Summary: NATI manufactures software and hardware products that scientists and engineers use to build measurement and automation systems in various applications and industries.

Quantitative Evaluations

Outlook (1 Lowest—5 Highest) • **3-**

Fair Value • **35⅛**

Risk • **Average**

Earn./Div. Rank • **NR**

Technical Eval. • **Bullish** since 8/99

Rel. Strength Rank (1 Lowest—99 Highest) • **86**

Insider Activity • **Unfavorable**

Recent Price • 32½ | Yield • Nil

52 Wk Range • 35⅜-12⅞ | 12-Mo. P/E • 40.1

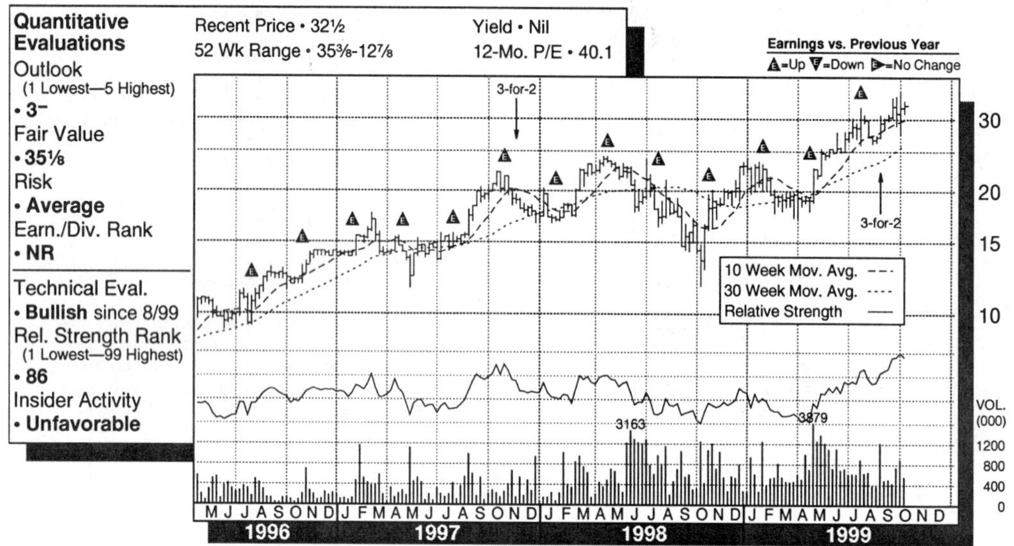

Business Profile - 01-JUL-99

In April 1999, NATI said that while the economic outlook is uncertain, the company is committed to providing the investment necessary for sustained long-term growth, noting that it generated a record $13 million in free cash in the first quarter of 1999. At March 31, 1999, assets totaled $264 million, long term debt was $4.1 million, and shareholders' equity amounted to $215 million. By region, first quarter 1999 revenues in North America were up 5% compared to the year earlier quarter, European revenues rose 24%, and Asia/Pacific revenues gained 29%.

Operational Review - 01-JUL-99

Net sales in the three months ended March 31, 1999, advanced 13%, year to year, mainly reflecting the introduction of new and upgraded products and increased marketing efforts. Gross margins widened on favorable foreign exchange rates, increased leveraging of fixed manufacturing expenses and an improved hardware product mix. With increased interest income, and despite much greater foreign exchange losses, pretax income was up 18%. After taxes at 32.0%, versus 33.0%, income rose 20%, to $10,560,000 ($0.31 a share) from $8,831,000 ($0.26). Results in the 1999 period exclude a charge of $0.02 a share reflecting the cumulative effect of an accounting change.

Stock Performance - 08-OCT-99

In the past 30 trading days, NATI's shares have increased 11%, compared to a 0.91% fall in the S&P 500. Average trading volume for the past five days was 110,340 shares, compared with the 40-day moving average of 135,559 shares.

Key Stock Statistics

Dividend Rate/Share	Nil	Shareholders	4,100
Shs. outstg. (M)	49.8	Market cap. (B)	$ 1.6
Avg. daily vol. (M)	0.130	Inst. holdings	22%
Tang. Bk. Value/Share	4.13		
Beta	NA		

Value of $10,000 invested 5 years ago: NA

Fiscal Year Ending Dec. 31

	1999	1998	1997	1996	1995	1994
Revenues (Million $)						
1Q	73.69	65.35	54.57	46.41	39.84	29.78
2Q	79.78	67.77	60.09	50.24	40.48	30.17
3Q	—	67.87	60.60	49.68	40.12	30.86
4Q	—	73.23	65.62	54.39	44.38	36.16
Yr.	—	274.2	240.9	200.7	164.8	127.0
Earnings Per Share ($)						
1Q	**0.21**	**0.17**	**0.15**	**0.11**	0.10	0.09
2Q	**0.22**	**0.18**	**0.17**	**0.11**	0.08	0.07
3Q	—	**0.17**	**0.15**	**0.13**	0.08	0.06
4Q	—	**0.21**	**0.19**	**0.17**	0.11	0.10
Yr.	—	**0.73**	**0.67**	**0.51**	**0.37**	**0.31**

Next earnings report expected: late October

Dividend Data

Amount ($)	Date Decl.	Ex-Div. Date	Stock of Record	Payment Date
3-for-2	Jul. 22	Aug. 23	Aug. 05	Aug. 20 '99

A Division of The McGraw-Hill Companies

National Instruments Corporation

Business Summary - 01-JUL-99

Using the software and hardware products manufactured by National Instruments (NATI), engineers and scientists can customize PCs to measure and automate the collection of data from the world around us, perform analysis on that data, and present it in an easy-to-understand manner.

Engineers and scientists have long used instruments to observe, better understand and manage the real-world phenomena, events and processes related to their industries or areas of expertise. NATI pioneered a new instrumentation approach called virtual instrumentation in 1986 when it introduced its LabVIEW application software, which is a graphical programming environment.

While a traditional instrument bundles the data acquisition, analysis and presentation functions in a single, stand-alone unit, a "virtual instrument" consists of an industry standard computer or workstation equipped with the company's user-friendly application software, cost-effective hardware and driver software that together perform the functions of traditional instruments.

By unbundling the key instrumentation functions, virtual instruments represent a fundamental shift from traditional hardware-centered instrumentation systems to software-centered systems that exploit the computational, display, productivity and connectivity capabilities of popular desktop computers and workstations.

NATI's virtual instrumentation application software products give users the power and flexibility to define, implement, modify and control each of the three core instrumentation functions. Users can mix and match their choice of the company's DAQ and instrument control hardware/driver software with GPIB, VXI, PXI, image acquisition, motion control or serial instruments to create virtual instrumentation systems that meet their specific instrumentation needs. Because much of the instrumentation functionality resides in the software, in a significant sense, the software is the instrument.

The objective of the company is to be a leading supplier of virtual instrumentation products and solutions to engineers and scientists in both the test and measurement (T&M) and industrial automation (IA). markets. In research and development settings, scientists and engineers use T&M instruments to collect and analyze experimental data, and IA instruments and instrumentation systems to simulate manufacturing processes or techniques. In manufacturing systems, engineers use T&M instruments to test and verify the proper operation of the products being manufactured, while IA instruments and instrumentation systems monitor and control the manufacturing machines and processes.

The company directly markets and sells its products in the United States, Canada and many European and Asia Pacific countries. International sales have accounted for over 40% of revenues in recent years. NATI expects that a significant portion of its total revenues will continue to be derived from international sales.

Per Share Data ($)										
(Year Ended Dec. 31)	**1998**	**1997**	**1996**	**1995**	**1994**	**1993**	**1992**	**1991**	**1990**	**1989**
Tangible Bk. Val.	4.13	3.30	2.61	2.05	1.51	NA	NA	NA	NA	NA
Cash Flow	0.96	0.84	0.70	0.52	0.44	NA	NA	NA	NA	NA
Earnings	0.73	0.67	0.51	0.37	0.31	NA	NA	NA	NA	NA
Dividends	Nil	Nil	Nil	Nil	Nil	Nil	NA	NA	NA	NA
Payout Ratio	Nil	Nil	Nil	Nil	Nil	Nil	NA	NA	NA	NA
Prices - High	24 3/8	22 3/8	14 1/4	10 1/8	NA	NA	NA	NA	NA	NA
- Low	11 5/8	11 1/2	7 3/8	6 1/2	NA	NA	NA	NA	NA	NA
P/E Ratio - High	33	33	27	27	NA	NA	NA	NA	NA	NA
- Low	16	17	14	17	NA	NA	NA	NA	NA	NA
Income Statement Analysis (Million $)										
Revs.	274	241	201	165	127	NA	NA	NA	NA	NA
Oper. Inc.	64.7	58.6	46.5	33.5	24.8	NA	NA	NA	NA	NA
Depr.	11.6	8.7	9.2	7.0	5.0	NA	NA	NA	NA	NA
Int. Exp.	0.5	0.5	0.8	0.9	0.3	NA	NA	NA	NA	NA
Pretax Inc.	55.8	50.2	38.0	27.4	21.1	NA	NA	NA	NA	NA
Eff. Tax Rate	33%	33%	33%	36%	39%	NA	NA	NA	NA	NA
Net Inc.	37.4	33.6	25.5	17.4	13.0	NA	NA	NA	NA	NA
Balance Sheet & Other Fin. Data (Million $)										
Cash	101	31.9	30.2	12.0	7.5	NA	NA	NA	NA	NA
Curr. Assets	174	149	132	101	45.2	NA	NA	NA	NA	NA
Total Assets	250	204	169	137	70.8	NA	NA	NA	NA	NA
Curr. Liab.	40.9	37.1	32.3	26.1	18.4	NA	NA	NA	NA	NA
LT Debt	4.4	5.2	9.2	11.6	9.1	NA	NA	NA	NA	NA
Common Eqty.	204	162	127	99	40.5	NA	NA	NA	NA	NA
Total Cap.	209	167	137	111	49.5	NA	NA	NA	NA	NA
Cap. Exp.	28.0	22.0	6.8	16.2	9.9	NA	NA	NA	NA	NA
Cash Flow	49.0	42.3	34.7	24.4	18.0	NA	NA	NA	NA	NA
Curr. Ratio	4.3	4.0	4.1	3.9	2.5	NA	NA	NA	NA	NA
% LT Debt of Cap.	2.1	3.1	6.7	10.5	18.3	NA	NA	NA	NA	NA
% Net Inc.of Revs.	13.6	14.0	12.7	10.6	10.2	NA	NA	NA	NA	NA
% Ret. on Assets	16.5	18.0	16.6	16.7	NA	NA	NA	NA	NA	NA
% Ret. on Equity	20.4	23.3	22.6	25.0	NA	NA	NA	NA	NA	NA

Data as orig reptd.; bef. results of disc opers/spec. items. Per share data adj. for stk. divs. Bold denotes diluted EPS (FASB 128)-prior periods restated. E-Estimated. NA-Not Available. NM-Not Meaningful. NR-Not Ranked.

Office—11500 N. Mopac Expwy., Building B, Austin, TX 78759-3504. **Tel**—(512) 338-9119. **Website**—http://www.natinst.com **Chrmn & Pres**—J. J. Truchard. **CFO & Treas**—A. M. Davern. **Secy**—D. G. Hugley. **Investor Contact**—Tara Mason (512-685-6873). **Dirs**—L. W. Ashby, D. M. Carlton, J. L. Kodosky, W. C. Nowlin Jr., B. G. Streetman, J. J. Truchard. **Transfer Agent & Registrar**—First National Bank of Boston, c/o Boston EquiServe. **Incorporated**—in Texas in 1976; reincorporated in Delaware in 1994. **Empl**— 1,658. **S&P Analyst:** M.I.

STANDARD
&POOR'S
STOCK REPORTS

National Presto

NYSE Symbol **NPK**

In S&P SmallCap 600

09-OCT-99

Industry:
Housewares

Summary: This company makes small electrical appliances and housewares, including comfort appliances, pressure cookers and canners, and private-label and premium sales products.

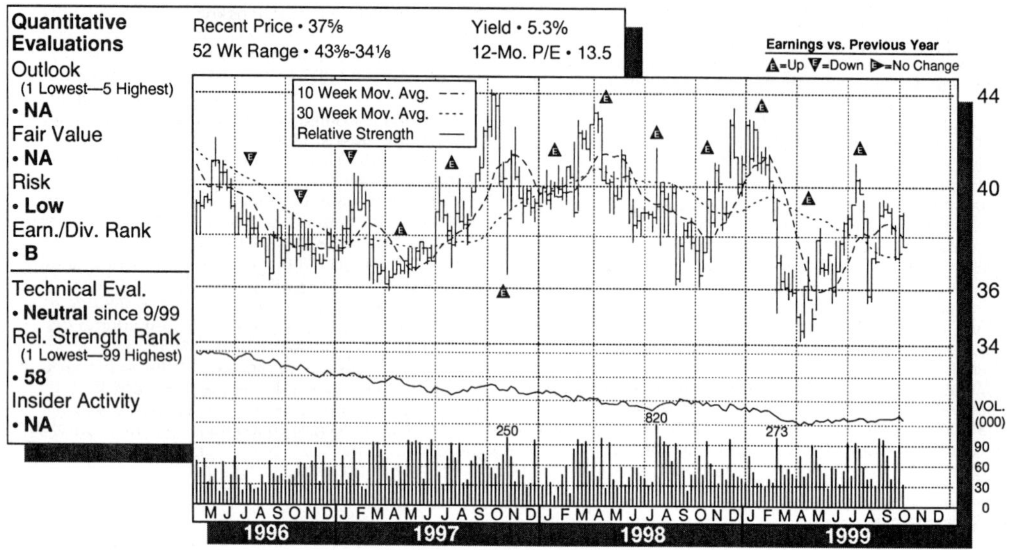

Business Profile - 25-JUN-99

This company attributed the increase in sales in the first quarter of 1999 to greater acceptance of the Presto brands amidst a generally strong retail environment. The rise in earnings for the quarter was attributed to effective cost controls. Reflecting on 1998's performance, the company stated that even though the economy was strong the housewares durable industry was more challenging than the previous year. Referring to the closing of Caldor and the difficulties at Service Merchandise stores, NPK stated that retail buying power was now more concentrated in the hands of a powerful few. As a result, manufacturers have less pricing power and so the company was quite pleased to have earnings improve during the year.

Operational Review - 25-JUN-99

Sales in the three months ended April 4, 1999, advanced 14%, year to year, reflecting higher unit volume. Gross margins widened due to a more favorable product mix and following well-controlled selling, general and administrative expenses and a decline in other income, pretax income surged 28%. After taxes at 18.8%, versus 11.0%, net income climbed advanced 17% to $3,280,000 ($0.45 a share), from $2,810,000 ($0.38).

Stock Performance - 08-OCT-99

In the past 30 trading days, NPK's shares have declined 3%, compared to a 0.91% fall in the S&P 500. Average trading volume for the past five days was 6,540 shares, compared with the 40-day moving average of 21,387 shares.

Key Stock Statistics

Dividend Rate/Share	2.00	Shareholders	1,669,664
Shs. outstg. (M)	7.3	Market cap. (B)	$0.276
Avg. daily vol. (M)	0.013	Inst. holdings	40%
Tang. Bk. Value/Share	33.38		
Beta	0.45		

Value of $10,000 invested 5 years ago: $ 10,516

Fiscal Year Ending Dec. 31

	1999	1998	1997	1996	1995	1994
Revenues (Million $)						
1Q	21.61	18.97	17.95	17.11	17.96	16.20
2Q	18.76	16.29	16.87	16.97	15.88	16.49
3Q	—	24.31	24.92	23.00	29.04	35.49
4Q	—	47.51	49.81	48.93	57.29	59.89
Yr.	—	107.1	109.5	106.0	120.2	128.1
Earnings Per Share ($)						
1Q	**0.45**	**0.38**	**0.35**	**0.26**	0.35	0.31
2Q	**0.43**	**0.38**	**0.36**	**0.31**	0.35	0.30
3Q	—	**0.50**	**0.48**	**0.38**	0.65	0.66
4Q	—	**1.42**	**1.12**	**1.05**	1.26	1.65
Yr.	—	**2.68**	**2.31**	**2.00**	**2.61**	2.92

Next earnings report expected: early November

Dividend Data (Dividends have been paid since 1994.)

Amount ($)	Date Decl.	Ex-Div. Date	Stock of Record	Payment Date
2.000	Feb. 19	Feb. 25	Mar. 01	Mar. 11 '99

A Division of The McGraw-Hill Companies

National Presto Industries, Inc.

Business Summary - 25-JUN-99

Founded in 1905 as a manufacturer of pressure canners, National Presto Industries, Inc. (NPK) is a leader in the housewares and portable electronic appliance industry. NPK's objective is to continually provide innovative and a wide variety of products to meet the needs of today's changing lifestyles.

NPK manufactures and distributes small electrical appliances and housewares under the well-known Presto name, and its offerings include pressure cookers and canners, fry pans, griddles, deep fryers, can openers, slicer/shredders, slicer/shredder/mixers, electric heaters, corn poppers, microwave bacon cookers, electronic toasters, coffee makers, electric tea kettles, electric knives, bread slicing systems, electric knife sharpeners and timers.

The company became famous in 1939 when it introduced the "Presto" stove top pressure cooker and has subsequently introduced many innovative appliances for the home. Some of those products include: the first electric steam iron (1949), the first immersible (for cleaning) electric cooking appliances (1956), the first automatic, submersible stainless steel coffee maker (1958), PrestoBurger hamburger cooker (1974), Frybaby deep fryer (1976), PopCornnow hot air corn popper (1978), Saladshooter electric slicer/shredder (1988), and the Powerpop microwave multi-popper (1994).

In 1998, 59% of consolidated net sales were provided by cast products (fry pans, griddles, deep fryers and electric multi-cookers), 13% by motorized nonthermal appliances (can openers, knife sharpeners, slicer/shredders, electric knives and bread slicing systems), and 25% by noncast/thermal appliances (stamped cookers and canners, stainless steel cookers, electronic toasters, corn poppers, coffee makers, microwave bacon cookers, tea kettles and heaters).

Products are sold directly to retailers throughout the United States and also through independent distributors. Wal-Mart accounted for 44% of consolidated net sales in 1998, versus 43% in 1997.

The company has a sales force of approximately ten employees. In selected geographic areas, manufacturers' representatives may handle sales of Presto products with other product lines. Sales promotional activities include television, radio and newspaper. The company's business is highly competitive and seasonal, with the normal peak sales period occurring in the fourth quarter of the year prior to the holiday season.

The company's products are manufactured in plants located in Mississippi and New Mexico. The company also purchases a portion (14% in 1998) of its products from nonaffiliated companies in the Pacific Rim countries. Product warehousing and distribution is handled by the company's distribution center located in Canton, Mississippi.

Per Share Data ($) (Year Ended Dec. 31)	1998	1997	1996	1995	1994	1993	1992	1991	1990	1989
Tangible Bk. Val.	34.57	33.88	33.56	33.57	33.11	32.08	29.53	29.79	27.48	27.66
Cash Flow	2.97	2.59	2.27	2.79	3.03	2.67	3.65	5.11	4.06	3.99
Earnings	2.68	2.31	2.00	2.61	2.92	2.55	3.53	4.98	3.94	3.89
Dividends	2.00	2.00	2.00	2.15	1.90	Nil	3.80	2.70	4.15	2.25
Payout Ratio	75%	87%	100%	82%	65%	Nil	108%	54%	104%	57%
Prices - High	43 1/2	44 1/8	44	48	48	60 1/8	83	62 1/4	44 1/2	40 5/8
- Low	36	35 7/8	36 1/4	38 3/4	39 1/8	45 1/2	45 1/4	39 5/8	33 1/2	32 1/2
P/E Ratio - High	16	19	22	18	16	24	24	13	11	10
- Low	13	16	18	15	13	18	13	8	9	8
Income Statement Analysis (Million $)										
Revs.	107	110	106	120	128	119	128	162	127	127
Oper. Inc.	20.4	14.3	12.3	16.6	25.4	21.8	30.7	43.8	29.4	28.0
Depr.	2.1	2.1	2.0	1.5	1.2	1.1	1.3	1.3	1.2	1.1
Int. Exp.	Nil	0.0	Nil	0.7	0.5	0.8	0.7	0.6	0.6	0.6
Pretax Inc.	27.4	22.0	19.2	25.4	30.5	26.2	36.7	52.4	39.6	39.0
Eff. Tax Rate	28%	23%	23%	25%	30%	29%	30%	30%	26%	26%
Net Inc.	19.7	17.0	15.0	19.0	21.5	18.7	25.9	36.7	29.1	28.7
Balance Sheet & Other Fin. Data (Million $)										
Cash	115	91.6	228	204	222	221	206	201	191	179
Curr. Assets	273	272	269	270	279	273	249	259	234	235
Total Assets	295	292	285	285	291	283	260	266	242	243
Curr. Liab.	40.4	42.7	38.5	38.1	43.0	42.6	38.2	43.0	35.4	34.1
LT Debt	Nil	Nil	Nil	Nil	5.1	5.1	5.1	5.1	5.1	6.0
Common Eqty.	254	249	247	247	243	235	217	218	201	203
Total Cap.	254	249	247	247	248	240	222	223	207	209
Cap. Exp.	3.7	4.0	2.0	4.5	1.7	1.0	1.5	0.8	1.2	1.4
Cash Flow	21.8	19.0	16.7	20.5	22.6	19.8	27.1	38.0	30.4	29.8
Curr. Ratio	6.8	6.4	6.9	7.1	6.5	6.4	6.5	6.0	6.6	6.9
% LT Debt of Cap.	Nil	Nil	Nil	Nil	2.1	2.1	2.3	2.3	2.5	2.9
% Net Inc.of Revs.	18.4	15.5	13.9	15.8	16.8	15.7	20.2	22.7	22.9	22.5
% Ret. on Assets	6.7	5.9	5.2	6.6	7.5	6.9	9.8	14.4	12.0	12.1
% Ret. on Equity	7.8	6.8	6.0	7.7	9.0	8.3	11.9	17.5	14.4	14.6

Data as orig reptd.; bef. results of disc opers/spec. items. Per share data adj. for stk. divs. Bold denotes diluted EPS (FASB 128)-prior periods restated. E-Estimated. NA-Not Available. NM-Not Meaningful. NR-Not Ranked.

Office—3925 North Hastings Way, Eau Claire, WI 54703-3703. **Tel**—(715) 839-2121. **Website**—http://www.presto-net.com. **Chrmn**—M. S. Cohen. **Pres, CEO, CFO & Investor Contact**—Maryjo Cohen. **Treas**—R. F. Lieble. **Secy**—J. F. Bartl. **Dirs**—J. F. Bartl, R. N. Cardozo, M. Cohen, M. S. Cohen, M. J. O'Meara, J. M. Sirianni. **Transfer Agent & Registrar**—Harris Trust & Savings Bank, Chicago. **Incorporated**—in Wisconsin in 1905. **Empl**— 628. **S&P Analyst:** Howard Choe

STANDARD
&POOR'S
STOCK REPORTS

Nature's Sunshine Products

NASDAQ Symbol **NATR**

In S&P SmallCap 600

09-OCT-99

Industry:
Personal Care

Summary: This company is a leading international manufacturer and marketer of encapsulated and tableted herbal products, high-quality natural vitamins, and other nutritional supplements.

Quantitative Evaluations

Outlook
(1 Lowest—5 Highest)
• **NA**

Fair Value
• **NA**

Risk
• **Average**

Earn./Div. Rank
• **A**

Technical Eval.
• **Bearish** since 6/99

Rel. Strength Rank
(1 Lowest—99 Highest)
• **18**

Insider Activity
• **NA**

Recent Price • 8½
52 Wk Range • 17¾-8⅛
Yield • 1.6%
12-Mo. P/E • 7.0

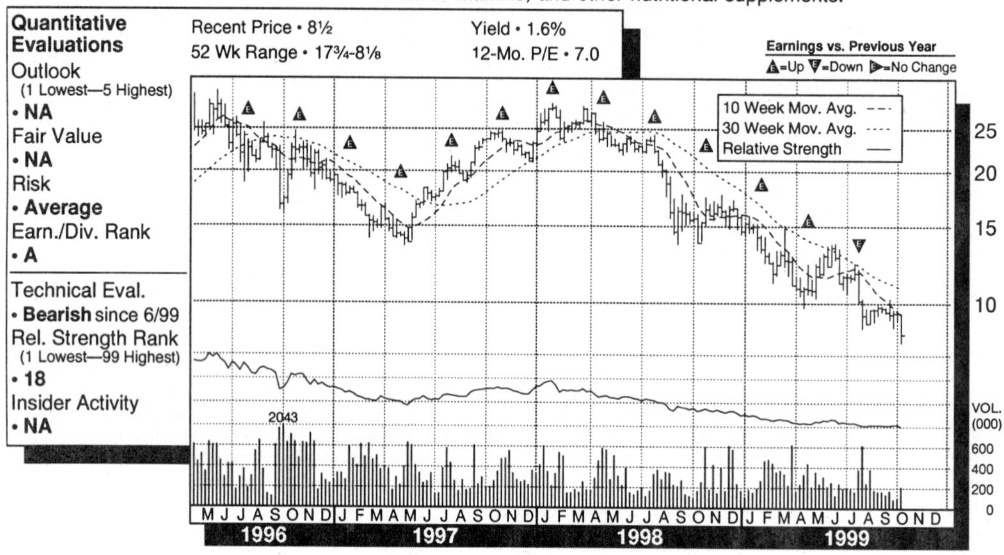

Business Profile - 27-AUG-99

In July 1999, NATR stated it remained confident in its long-term growth strategy of selling herbal products through its multi-level direct marketing program. The company also said it was focusing on revitalizing its domestic sales network through new incentive programs and marketing plans. In May 1999, directors approved a new stock repurchase plan for up to 500,000 additional shares of the company's stock. NATR also stated it had completed the repurchase of 500,000 shares previously authorized in September 1998. Also in May, the company announced results of a Norway-based clinical study showing its Fat Grabbers (FG) diet capsule produced a greater average weight loss in the FG diet pill group of patients relative to a placebo group.

Operational Review - 27-AUG-99

Sales revenue in the six months ended June 30, 1999, declined 5.7%, year to year, mainly reflecting increased product and price competition in the nutritional supplement market, as well as greater competition for new distributors and a strong U.S. dollar. Despite a 7.5% decrease in the cost of goods sold, margins were penalized by sharply lower earnings from Latin American operations and continued losses in the Asia Pacific region. Operating income fell 9.0%. Following an 11% increase in depreciation and amortization expense, and after taxes at 39.5%, versus 39.4%, net income also declined 11%, to $9.8 million ($0.54 a share, on 4.8% fewer shares), from $11.0 million ($0.58).

Stock Performance - 08-OCT-99

In the past 30 trading days, NATR's shares have declined 13%, compared to a 0.91% fall in the S&P 500. Average trading volume for the past five days was 41,160 shares, compared with the 40-day moving average of 30,133 shares.

Key Stock Statistics

Dividend Rate/Share	0.13	Shareholders	1,473
Shs. outstg. (M)	17.5	Market cap. (B)	$0.149
Avg. daily vol. (M)	0.027	Inst. holdings	40%
Tang. Bk. Value/Share	4.28		
Beta	0.79		

Value of $10,000 invested 5 years ago: $ 12,101

Fiscal Year Ending Dec. 31

	1999	1998	1997	1996	1995	1994
Revenues (Million $)						
1Q	72.18	75.28	67.83	60.11	47.06	37.34
2Q	71.64	77.20	71.41	63.18	50.73	38.31
3Q	—	73.46	71.59	63.03	53.16	41.00
4Q	—	70.11	70.08	62.72	54.62	44.25
Yr.	—	296.1	280.9	249.1	205.6	160.9
Earnings Per Share ($)						
1Q	**0.28**	**0.26**	0.21	0.17	0.11	0.09
2Q	**0.27**	**0.32**	0.28	0.22	0.16	0.12
3Q	—	**0.33**	0.29	0.23	0.17	0.12
4Q	—	**0.34**	**0.29**	0.24	0.19	0.12
Yr.	—	**1.25**	**1.06**	**0.86**	**0.63**	0.45

Next earnings report expected: mid October

Dividend Data (Dividends have been paid since 1988.)

Amount ($)	Date Decl.	Ex-Div. Date	Stock of Record	Payment Date
0.033	Oct. 29	Nov. 09	Nov. 12	Nov. 20 '98
0.033	Feb. 09	Feb. 17	Feb. 19	Feb. 26 '99
0.033	Apr. 29	May. 11	May. 13	May. 27 '99
0.033	Jul. 28	Aug. 05	Aug. 09	Aug. 19 '99

A Division of The McGraw-Hill Companies

Nature's Sunshine Products, Inc.

Business Summary - 27-AUG-99

Nature's Sunshine Products, Inc. (NATR) distributes more than 500 products. NATR primarily manufactures and sells nutritional and personal care products. Nutritional products include herbs, vitamins, mineral supplements, and homeopathic remedies. Personal care items include natural skin, hair and beauty care products.

The company's Herbal products are sold in the form of tablets, capsules or liquid extracts. Sales of herbal products accounted for about 67% of total revenues in both 1998 and 1997. NATR manufactures a wide variety of vitamin and mineral supplements, including a vitamin line containing natural antioxidants. Combined sales of vitamins and mineral supplements represented approximately 23% of total sales in 1998 and 1997. The company manufactures or contracts with independent manufacturers to supply a number of personal care products for external use including oils, lotions, aloe vera gel, herbal shampoo and skin treatments, toothpaste, and skin cleanser. Personal care products accounted for about 3% of 1998 and 1997 total sales. More than 50 distinctive homeopathic products are marketed by NATR for ailments such as allergies and other common childhood maladies. Sales of homeopathic products represented 1% of total revenues in 1998 and 1997.

NATR buys herbs and other raw materials in bulk, and, after quality control testing, encapsulates, tabulates or concentrates them, and then packages them for shipment. Most products are made at the company headquarters in Spanish Fork, UT. Certain personal care and homeopathic products are manufactured for the company by contract manufacturers in accordance with company specifications. NATR also operates regional warehouses in Columbus, OH, Dallas, TX, and Atlanta, GA.

The company sells its products primarily through an independent sales force of managers and distributors; sales managers totaled 14,000 on December 31, 1998, and distributors totaled 516,000. For domestic sales, NATR generally sells its products on a cash or credit card basis. For certain international operations, the company uses independent distribution centers, and offers credit terms consistent with industry standards. Managers resell the products to the distributors in their sales group or to consumers, or use the products themselves. Many distributors sell on a part-time basis to friends or associates, or consume the products themselves. Demand for the products is created largely by the number of active members of the independent distributor sales force.

International operations are conducted through NATR's subsidiaries in Brazil, Colombia, Mexico, Venezuela, Japan, Canada, the United Kingdom, Argentina, South Korea, Costa Rica, Chile, El Salvador, Panama, Peru, Guatemala, Nicaragua, Honduras and Ecuador. NATR also exports its products to other countries, including Australia, Malaysia, New Zealand, Norway, and Russia. International sales accounted for 36% of revenues in 1998, and 37% in 1997.

Per Share Data ($) (Year Ended Dec. 31)	1998	1997	1996	1995	1994	1993	1992	1991	1990	1989
Tangible Bk. Val.	4.10	3.60	3.30	2.26	1.81	1.58	1.32	1.07	0.90	0.79
Cash Flow	1.40	1.28	1.03	0.82	0.61	0.50	0.41	0.32	0.25	0.26
Earnings	1.25	1.06	0.86	0.63	0.45	0.40	0.32	0.25	0.19	0.21
Dividends	0.13	0.13	0.13	0.13	0.12	0.12	0.09	0.07	0.07	0.07
Payout Ratio	11%	13%	15%	21%	27%	30%	28%	28%	34%	31%
Prices - High	28 5/8	26 3/4	30 1/2	18 5/8	10 7/8	9	8 3/4	6	4 1/4	4 1/4
- Low	13 5/8	13 1/2	15 1/8	6 1/2	6 5/8	5 1/8	3 5/8	2 1/16	1 11/16	1 11/16
P/E Ratio - High	23	25	35	30	24	22	27	24	21	20
- Low	11	13	18	10	15	13	11	8	8	8
Income Statement Analysis (Million $)										
Revs.	296	281	249	206	161	127	101	72.6	60.1	52.1
Oper. Inc.	40.9	35.3	30.0	21.0	17.3	13.4	10.1	7.7	6.0	6.6
Depr.	4.8	4.3	3.4	3.5	3.1	1.9	1.6	1.1	1.0	0.8
Int. Exp.	0.0	0.2	0.1	0.2	0.1	Nil	0.1	0.0	0.0	0.1
Pretax Inc.	38.0	32.7	27.9	20.2	13.9	12.2	9.9	7.3	5.8	6.4
Eff. Tax Rate	40%	40%	40%	41%	44%	40%	40%	36%	38%	38%
Net Inc.	23.3	20.1	16.8	11.9	8.4	7.5	5.9	4.6	3.6	4.0
Balance Sheet & Other Fin. Data (Million $)										
Cash	22.1	27.8	27.9	14.2	11.2	8.7	6.3	9.2	8.5	7.3
Curr. Assets	63.0	66.0	67.1	47.2	36.6	26.5	20.5	17.8	14.6	13.0
Total Assets	104	95.8	92.0	65.2	52.5	41.5	34.0	27.4	22.0	20.1
Curr. Liab.	27.7	27.5	27.5	22.7	17.8	12.3	9.4	7.6	5.1	5.3
LT Debt	Nil	Nil	Nil	Nil	Nil	Nil	Nil	Nil	0.0	0.0
Common Eqty.	74.0	66.9	63.2	41.5	33.3	28.9	23.9	19.6	16.5	14.4
Total Cap.	76.0	68.4	64.0	42.5	34.7	29.3	24.6	19.8	16.9	14.8
Cap. Exp.	6.5	7.5	10.5	6.1	2.6	2.9	2.8	1.5	1.5	1.3
Cash Flow	28.1	24.4	20.3	15.4	11.5	9.4	7.5	5.8	4.6	4.8
Curr. Ratio	2.3	2.4	2.4	2.1	2.1	2.2	2.2	2.3	2.9	2.5
% LT Debt of Cap.	Nil	Nil	Nil	Nil	Nil	Nil	Nil	Nil	0.1	0.2
% Net Inc.of Revs.	7.9	7.2	6.7	5.8	5.3	5.9	5.9	6.4	6.0	7.6
% Ret. on Assets	23.3	21.4	21.4	20.2	18.0	19.7	19.3	18.7	17.1	21.2
% Ret. on Equity	33.0	30.9	32.2	31.9	27.2	28.2	27.2	25.6	23.3	29.3

Data as orig reptd.; bef. results of disc opers/spec. items. Per share data adj. for stk. divs. Bold denotes diluted EPS (FASB 128)-prior periods restated. E-Estimated. NA-Not Available. NM-Not Meaningful. NR-Not Ranked.

Office—75 E. 1700 S., Provo, UT 84606. **Tel**—(801) 342-4300. **Website**—http://www.nsponline.com **Chrmn**—Kristine F. Hughes. **Pres & CEO**—D. P. Howells. **COO**—D. Faggioli. **VP-Fin, Treas & CFO**—C. D. Huff. **VP & Secy**—B. F. Ashworth. **Dirs**—R. H. Daines, D. Faggioli, D. P. Howells, E. L. Hughes, K. F. Hughes, P. T. Hughes. **Transfer Agent & Registrar**—American Stock Transfer & Trust Co., NYC. **Incorporated**—in Utah in 1976. **Empl**— 971. **S&P Analyst:** Frank DiLorenzo

STANDARD
&POOR'S
STOCK REPORTS

Nautica Enterprises

Nasdaq Symbol **NAUT**

In S&P SmallCap 600

09-OCT-99

Industry:
Textiles (Apparel)

Summary: NAUT designs, sources and markets men's sportswear, outerwear and activewear apparel through retail and wholesale operations.

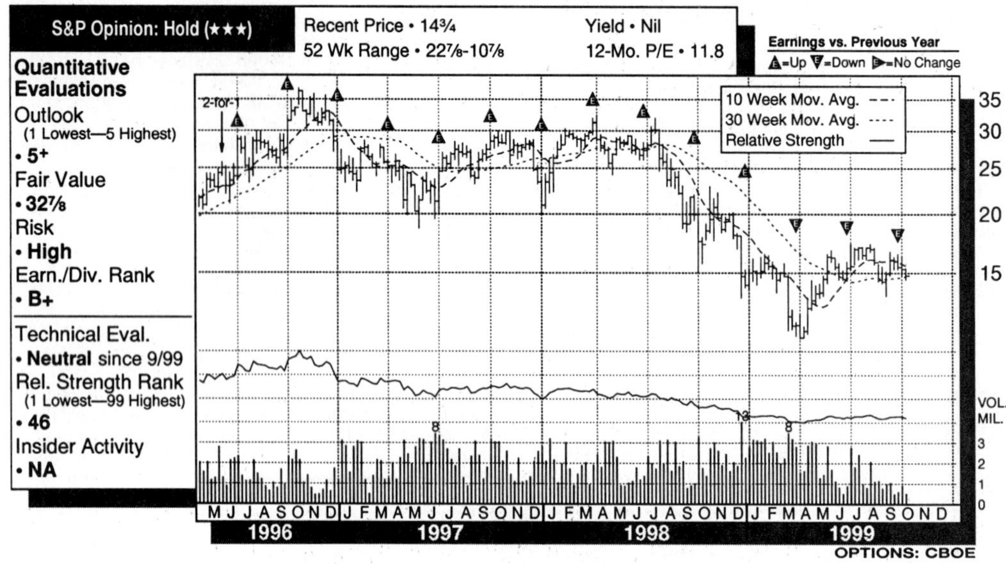

Overview - 01-OCT-99

We expect sales of this apparel maker to rise about 9% during FY 00 (Feb.), supported by revenues from new product lines and additional outlet store openings. The recently launched Nautica Jeans (men's) and women's robe and sleepwear lines have been well received by retailers and consumers. However, we remain concerned with weak outerwear sales and negative same-store (Nautica stores) sales comparisons. Depending on the success of the new women's jeanswear line next summer, NAUT will consider launching a women's sportswear line in-house. Gross margins should expand in the second half of FY 00 as markdown activity subsides. Operating margins will be under pressure from higher SG&A expenses to launch the company's new product lines. We project FY 00 and FY 01 EPS to be $1.30 and $1.46, respectively.

Valuation - 01-OCT-99

The share price is at nearly the same level as at the end of calendar 1998. Optimism for a turnaround has been tempered by investor concerns regarding near term prospects for the retail/apparel industry. Although consumer confidence and growth in spending levels are still high, they are on a downward trend. And although the company's sales outlook has moderately improved, we feel the stock is vulnerable to downside risk as investors' fears of interest rate hikes and a slowdown in consumer spending growth have hurt retail/apparel stock prices. However, the success of the newly introduced lines bodes well for the upcoming product launches and should be a catalyst for share price gains when investors become more comfortable with this sector. In light of current concerns, we feel the stock is fairly valued at 10X our $1.46 FY 01 EPS estimate.

Key Stock Statistics

S&P EPS Est. 2000	1.30	Tang. Bk. Value/Share	6.67
P/E on S&P Est. 2000	11.4	Beta	0.69
S&P EPS Est. 2001	1.46	Shareholders	403
Dividend Rate/Share	Nil	Market cap. (B)	$0.512
Shs. outstg. (M)	34.6	Inst. holdings	64%
Avg. daily vol. (M)	0.122		

Value of $10,000 invested 5 years ago: $ 16,768

Fiscal Year Ending Feb. 28

	2000	1999	1998	1997	1996	1995
Revenues (Million $)						
1Q	109.2	111.0	95.81	76.14	61.40	44.60
2Q	166.0	150.9	132.3	103.3	80.60	63.30
3Q	—	157.1	145.7	116.6	90.80	87.00
4Q	—	133.7	111.0	90.51	69.72	52.80
Yr.	—	552.6	484.8	386.6	302.5	247.7
Earnings Per Share ($)						
1Q	**0.12**	**0.23**	0.18	0.13	0.09	0.06
2Q	**0.38**	**0.46**	0.36	0.26	0.18	0.14
3Q	**E0.48**	**0.51**	0.48	0.37	0.28	0.23
4Q	**E0.31**	**0.25**	**0.33**	0.26	0.20	0.15
Yr.	**E1.30**	**1.45**	**1.35**	**1.02**	0.75	0.57

Next earnings report expected: early January

Dividend Data

No cash has been paid. Three-for-two stock splits were effected in July 1995, November 1993 and March 1992.

Nautica Enterprises, Inc.

Business Summary - 01-OCT-99

An apparel manufacturer, Nautica Enterprises, Inc. is making efforts to become a leading lifestyle brand. The company, known primarily as a designer and manufacturer of men's apparel, plans to complete its stable of product lines with the addition of womenswear in the near future.

Nautica primarily designs, manufactures and markets apparel under the following brands: Nautica. Nautica Competition, NST-Nautica Sport Tech, Nautica Jeans Company, E. Magrath, and Byron Nelson. All of the company brands are designed by an in-house design and merchandising staff.

The company was founded in 1971 as State-O-Maine, a company that offered shirts, robes, loungewear and sportswear under the Bayou Sport Label. This division operated as a subsidiary and was recently sold. The company really took off with the yachting-inspired sportswear designed by Nautica founder and principal designer David Chu; the line was so successful that the company changed its name to Nautica in 1984. The collection includes sportswear (sweaters, shirts, pants and shorts), outerwear (jackets and parkas) and activewear (tops, pants, shorts, tee shirts and swimwear). Golf apparel (E. Magrath and Byron Nelson collections) is offered through the E. Magrath Apparel subsidiary and sold to better country clubs and resorts nationwide.

The Nautica collection offers sportswear, outerwear, activewear and basics. The Nautica Competition brand offers active-inspired apparel with colorful graphics and bold logos using performance and activewear fabrics.

The company has extended its global distribution and product line through licensing of products such as fragrances for men and women, neckwear, tailored clothing, hosiery, eyewear, swimwear, watches, children's apparel, footwear, home furnishings, and accessories.

Nautica is sold at more than 1,200 in-store shops, three flagship stores, and 78 U.S. factory outlets. The factory outlet stores are used to distribute excess and out of season merchandise. The company does not own or operate any manufacturing facilities; clothing is made by contracted overseas producers.

In-store programs, whereby the company and department stores create a specific selling area and look for these brands, are an integral part of the marketing strategy for the company's wholesale business.

In 1999, the company launched the NST-Nautica Sport Tech brand, offering activewear and outerwear that combines street style and performance for young men. Through the Nautica Jeans Company brand, NAUT launched a denim-based apparel line aimed at men 16 to 35 years old. The company plans to launch a women's denim-based line for the summer of 2000. Capitalizing on the success of the men's robes and sleepwear line, NAUT introduced a women's line also in 1999.

Per Share Data ($) (Year Ended Feb. 28)	1999	1998	1997	1996	1995	1994	1993	1992	1991	1990
Tangible Bk. Val.	6.73	6.26	5.10	4.31	3.50	2.90	1.79	1.47	1.32	NA
Cash Flow	1.76	1.60	1.17	0.85	0.65	0.53	0.35	NA	NA	NA
Earnings	1.45	1.35	1.02	0.75	0.57	0.45	0.30	0.22	0.10	NA
Dividends	Nil	Nil	Nil	Nil	Nil	Nil	Nil	Nil	Nil	NA
Payout Ratio	Nil	Nil	Nil	Nil	Nil	Nil	Nil	Nil	Nil	NA
Cal. Yrs.	1998	1997	1996	1995	1994	1993	1992	1991	1990	1989
Prices - High	32½	30	37	22¾	10⅞	9⅛	4⅛	NA	NA	NA
- Low	13¼	18⅝	16¼	8⅛	6½	3¼	2$^{5}/_{16}$	NA	NA	NA
P/E Ratio - High	22	22	36	30	19	20	14	NA	NA	NA
- Low	9	14	16	11	11	7	8	NA	NA	NA
Income Statement Analysis (Million $)										
Revs.	553	485	387	303	248	193	151	NA	NA	NA
Oper. Inc.	100	93.6	71.8	52.5	39.3	27.0	19.5	NA	NA	NA
Depr.	12.6	10.5	6.3	4.3	3.1	3.0	1.8	NA	NA	NA
Int. Exp.	Nil	Nil	Nil	0.0	0.0	0.3	0.3	NA	NA	NA
Pretax Inc.	96.6	92.6	72.3	52.9	38.6	28.6	18.3	NA	NA	NA
Eff. Tax Rate	40%	40%	40%	40%	38%	41%	43%	NA	NA	NA
Net Inc.	58.7	56.4	44.0	32.0	24.0	16.8	10.5	NA	NA	NA
Balance Sheet & Other Fin. Data (Million $)										
Cash	15.5	34.6	71.9	61.0	49.2	44.9	NA	NA	NA	NA
Curr. Assets	256	246	204	170	143	118	NA	NA	NA	NA
Total Assets	332	310	251	209	168	137	NA	NA	NA	NA
Curr. Liab.	76.5	58.8	47.6	36.0	28.8	22.6	NA	NA	NA	NA
LT Debt	0.1	0.1	0.1	0.2	0.3	0.3	NA	NA	NA	NA
Common Eqty.	256	251	203	173	139	114	NA	NA	NA	NA
Total Cap.	256	252	204	173	140	114	NA	NA	NA	NA
Cap. Exp.	20.2	22.9	17.7	15.9	7.2	7.5	1.9	NA	NA	NA
Cash Flow	71.3	66.9	50.3	36.3	27.1	19.8	12.3	NA	NA	NA
Curr. Ratio	3.3	4.2	4.3	4.7	5.0	5.2	NA	NA	NA	NA
% LT Debt of Cap.	0.0	Nil	0.1	0.1	0.2	0.3	NA	NA	NA	NA
% Net Inc.of Revs.	10.6	11.6	11.4	10.6	9.7	8.7	6.9	NA	NA	NA
% Ret. on Assets	18.3	20.1	19.1	16.9	15.7	15.6	NA	NA	NA	NA
% Ret. on Equity	23.2	24.8	23.4	20.5	18.9	19.4	NA	NA	NA	NA

Data as orig. reptd.; bef. results of disc. opers. and/or spec. items. Per share data adj. for stk. divs. as of ex-div. date. Bold denotes diluted EPS (FASB 128). E-Estimated. NA-Not Available. NM-Not Meaningful. NR-Not Ranked.

Office— 40 West 57th St., New York, NY 10019. **Tel**—(212) 541-5990. **Chrmn, Pres & CEO**—H. Sanders. **EVP**—D. Chu. **CFO & Investor Contact**—Don Pennington (212-541-5757). **Dirs**—R. B. Bank, D. Chu, G. Greenberg, I. Rosenzweig, H. Sanders, C. H. Scherer, R. G. Weiner. **Transfer Agent & Registrar**—Harris Trust Co. of New York, NYC. **Incorporated**—in Delaware in 1971. **Empl**— 2,266. **S&P Analyst:** Howard Choe

NBTY, Inc.

NASDAQ Symbol **NBTY**

In S&P SmallCap 600

09-OCT-99

Industry:
Personal Care

Summary: NBTY (formerly Nature's Bounty) manufactures and distributes vitamins, food supplements, and health and beauty aids under its own and private labels.

Quantitative Evaluations

Outlook
(1 Lowest—5 Highest)
• **4-**

Fair Value
• **10½**

Risk
• **High**

Earn./Div. Rank
• **B**

Technical Eval.
• **Neutral** since 9/99

Rel. Strength Rank
(1 Lowest—99 Highest)
• **57**

Insider Activity
• **Neutral**

Recent Price • 7¼
52 Wk Range • 10-4⅜
Yield • Nil
12-Mo. P/E • 24.2

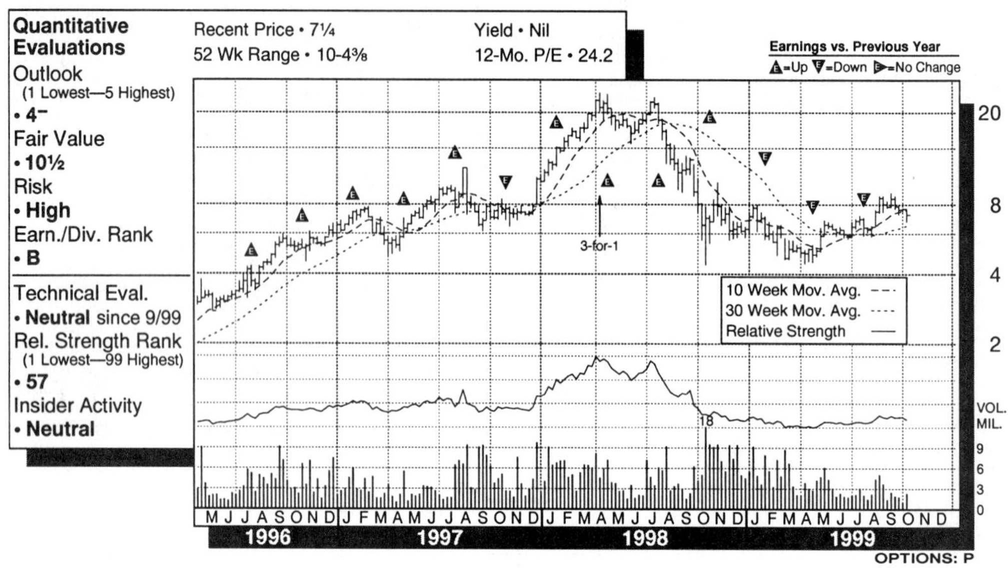

OPTIONS: P

Business Profile - 24-JUN-99

NBTY continues to increase in-house manufacturing for its Holland & Berret (H&B) business, while decreasing the use of outside suppliers. In May 1999, NBTY acquired Dynamics Essentials Inc., a Dallas based network marketer and distributor of nutritional supplements and skin products, for approximately $1 million in cash. In April 1999, the company increased its revolving credit agreement to $135 million from $60 million. In March 1999, directors authorized the repurchase of up to 20 million shares of the company's common stock.

Operational Review - 24-JUN-99

Net sales for the six months ended March 31, 1999, advanced 7.6%, reflecting a greater number of stores in the U.S. retail channel and strong results in the U.K. retail channel. Profitability was hurt by increased catalog printing, postage and promotion expense primarily associated with H&B, greater SG&A expenses related to the U.S. retail expansion program, and higher depreciation and amortization expense. Pretax income fell 49%. After taxes at 41.2%, versus 30.9%, net income declined 56%, to $10.3 million ($0.14 a share, based on 5.2% more average shares) from $23.6 million ($0.34).

Stock Performance - 08-OCT-99

In the past 30 trading days, NBTY's shares have declined 10%, compared to a 0.91% fall in the S&P 500. Average trading volume for the past five days was 453,140 shares, compared with the 40-day moving average of 494,331 shares.

Key Stock Statistics

Dividend Rate/Share	Nil	Shareholders	600
Shs. outstg. (M)	67.0	Market cap. (B)	$0.486
Avg. daily vol. (M)	0.342	Inst. holdings	24%
Tang. Bk. Value/Share	1.07		
Beta	1.14		

Value of $10,000 invested 5 years ago: $ 10,481

Fiscal Year Ending Sep. 30

	1999	1998	1997	1996	1995	1994
Revenues (Million $)						
1Q	141.0	109.4	47.33	38.59	37.48	32.74
2Q	167.7	135.0	75.02	55.61	50.95	47.00
3Q	155.1	138.9	61.76	47.90	41.65	35.86
4Q	—	146.4	97.30	52.31	48.69	40.45
Yr.	—	572.1	281.4	194.4	178.8	156.1
Earnings Per Share ($)						
1Q	**0.05**	**0.08**	0.05	0.00	0.02	0.03
2Q	**0.09**	**0.19**	0.13	0.08	0.04	0.07
3Q	**0.06**	**0.12**	0.09	0.06	0.02	0.03
4Q	—	**0.10**	0.02	0.09	0.01	Nil
Yr.	—	**0.56**	**0.42**	0.22	0.09	0.13

Next earnings report expected: late November

Dividend Data

No cash dividends have been paid. Two-for-one stock splits were effected in August 1993 and May 1992, and a three-for-one split was effected in November 1992.

NBTY, Inc.

Business Summary - 24-JUN-99

NBTY, Inc. (formerly Nature's Bounty, Inc.), a manufacturer and retailer of vitamins and nutritional supplements, emphasizes sales of its own products and, to a lesser extent, sales under private label. Products are distributed through direct mail, wholesale and retail channels. The company's retail channel include 277 stores in the U.S. and 415 stores in the U.K.

In August 1997, NBTY acquired Holland & Barrett (H&B), the largest chain of vitamin and healthfood stores in the United Kingdom for $168.8 million. The company helped finance the acquisition through a $150 million offering of senior subordinated notes due 2007. H&B classifies its products into two categories: nutritional supplement products and food products. Nutritional supplement products accounted for 60% of sales in FY 98 (Sep.), while food products accounted for 40%.

NBTY markets more than 900 products consisting of vitamins and other nutritional supplements such as minerals, amino acids, and herbs. Vitamins, minerals, and amino acids are sold as a single vitamin and in multi-vitamin combinations and in varying potency levels in powder, tablet, soft gel, chewable, and hard shell capsule form.

NBTY sells through direct mail, offering its full line of vitamins and other nutritional supplements as well as personal care items. Products are sold under its Puritan's Pride brand name at prices that are generally discounted to similar products sold in retail stores.

The Nature's Bounty line, the company's leading brand, is distributed to drug store chains and supermarkets, independent pharmacies, health food stores, health food store wholesalers, and other retailers such as mass merchandisers. Clients include Walmart, Genovese Drug Stores, Walgreens, Lucky Stores, and Bergen Brunswig. NBTY also offers private label products under the brand name Natural Wealth. In addition, a comprehensive line of over-the-counter products such as cold remedies and analgesic formulas are sold to independent pharmacies under the Hudson brand name. In March 1999, NBTY made available an extensive line of Nature's Bounty products over the internet to customers of Drugstore.com.

NBTY operates 230 Vitamin World retail stores in 40 states and the territory of Guam. The company plans to open 160 stores in FY 99. These retail stores carry a full line of NBTY's products under the Vitamin World brand name as well as products from other manufacturers.

In April 1998, NBTY merged a group of affiliated, privately held companies, known collectively as the Nutrition Headquarters Group, into the company for approximately 8.8 million shares of common stock. The company incurred merger related costs costs of about $3.3 million related to this transaction.

During FY 98, the company acquired certain assets, principally mail order data bases, of three privately held vitamin mail order companies for $7.8 million in cash.

Per Share Data ($) (Year Ended Sep. 30)	1998	1997	1996	1995	1994	1993	1992	1991	1990	1989
Tangible Bk. Val.	1.14	NM	1.67	1.44	1.38	1.21	0.33	0.31	0.25	0.19
Cash Flow	0.87	0.42	0.32	0.17	0.20	0.25	0.17	0.11	0.11	0.07
Earnings	0.56	0.29	0.22	0.09	0.13	0.18	0.09	0.03	0.02	0.01
Dividends	Nil	Nil	Nil	Nil	Nil	Nil	Nil	Nil	Nil	Nil
Payout Ratio	Nil	Nil	Nil	Nil	Nil	Nil	Nil	Nil	Nil	Nil
Prices - High	24 3/8	11 1/2	6 7/8	2 3/4	8 1/8	7 1/8	4	1/4	1/4	3/16
- Low	4 3/8	4 3/4	1 9/16	1 5/16	1 9/16	2 5/16	3/16	1/8	1/8	1/8
P/E Ratio - High	44	40	31	32	64	41	43	8	12	32
- Low	8	17	7	15	13	13	2	3	6	16
Income Statement Analysis (Million $)										
Revs.	572	281	194	179	156	138	101	74.0	71.0	63.0
Oper. Inc.	100	47.9	28.2	13.7	17.7	20.2	10.5	5.8	5.4	4.1
Depr.	22.1	8.2	5.6	4.8	4.2	4.0	3.1	2.5	3.0	2.1
Int. Exp.	16.5	6.7	1.4	1.1	0.9	1.2	1.3	1.4	1.4	1.3
Pretax Inc.	62.3	28.7	22.4	8.4	12.5	15.7	5.9	1.7	1.3	0.4
Eff. Tax Rate	38%	40%	40%	39%	38%	38%	35%	40%	42%	39%
Net Inc.	38.8	17.2	13.3	5.1	7.8	9.8	3.8	1.0	0.7	0.2
Balance Sheet & Other Fin. Data (Million $)										
Cash	14.3	26.8	20.3	10.4	5.9	10.8	2.4	2.4	0.3	0.2
Curr. Assets	174	143	78.8	67.7	66.6	63.7	32.7	24.2	17.1	20.0
Total Assets	500	543	146	124	115	102	58.3	43.5	36.3	35.8
Curr. Liab.	84.8	79.9	26.6	27.1	27.2	21.7	19.6	15.5	12.4	13.1
LT Debt	173	337	18.4	10.9	7.6	8.3	21.0	14.2	11.4	11.2
Common Eqty.	230	117	96.9	82.6	78.0	70.0	16.5	12.8	11.8	11.4
Total Cap.	412	462	118	96.3	87.5	79.2	38.0	27.6	23.8	22.7
Cap. Exp.	68.0	21.1	15.8	11.5	11.6	14.2	5.1	3.1	6.4	2.4
Cash Flow	60.9	25.4	19.0	10.0	12.0	13.7	6.9	3.6	3.7	2.4
Curr. Ratio	2.1	1.8	3.0	2.5	2.5	2.9	1.7	1.6	1.4	1.5
% LT Debt of Cap.	42.0	73.0	15.6	11.3	8.7	10.4	55.3	51.4	48.0	49.5
% Net Inc.of Revs.	6.8	6.1	6.9	2.9	5.0	7.1	3.8	1.4	1.0	0.4
% Ret. on Assets	7.4	5.0	10.0	4.3	7.2	10.0	7.5	2.6	2.1	0.7
% Ret. on Equity	22.4	16.1	14.9	6.4	10.5	20.2	26.2	8.3	6.4	2.1

Data as orig reptd.; bef. results of disc opers/spec. items. Per share data adj. for stk. divs. Bold denotes diluted EPS (FASB 128)-prior periods restated. E-Estimated. NA-Not Available. NM-Not Meaningful. NR-Not Ranked.

Office—90 Orville Dr., Bohemia, NY 11716. **Tel**—(516) 567-9500. **Website**—http://www.nbty.com. **Chrmn, Pres & CEO**—S. Rudolph. **EVP, CFO, Secy & Investor Contact**—Harvey Kamil. **Dirs**—M. Ashner, G. Cohen, M. Daly, A. Garabedian, B. G. Owen, N. Rosenblatt, A. Rudolph, S. Rudolph, A. Sacks, M. Slade, B. Solk. **Transfer Agent & Registrar**—American Stock Transfer Co., NYC. **Incorporated**—in Delaware in 1980. **Empl**— 3,670. **S&P Analyst:** A. Bensinger

NCS HealthCare

NASDAQ Symbol **NCSS**

In S&P SmallCap 600

09-OCT-99

Industry: Health Care (Specialized Services)

Summary: This company is a leading independent provider of pharmacy and related services to long-term care institutions.

Quantitative Evaluations

Outlook (1 Lowest—5 Highest) • **NA**

Fair Value • **NA**

Risk • **High**

Earn./Div. Rank • **NR**

Technical Eval. • **Bearish** since 6/99

Rel. Strength Rank (1 Lowest—99 Highest) • **3**

Insider Activity • **NA**

Recent Price • 2¾ | 52 Wk Range • 25⅛-1½ | Yield • Nil | 12-Mo. P/E • NM

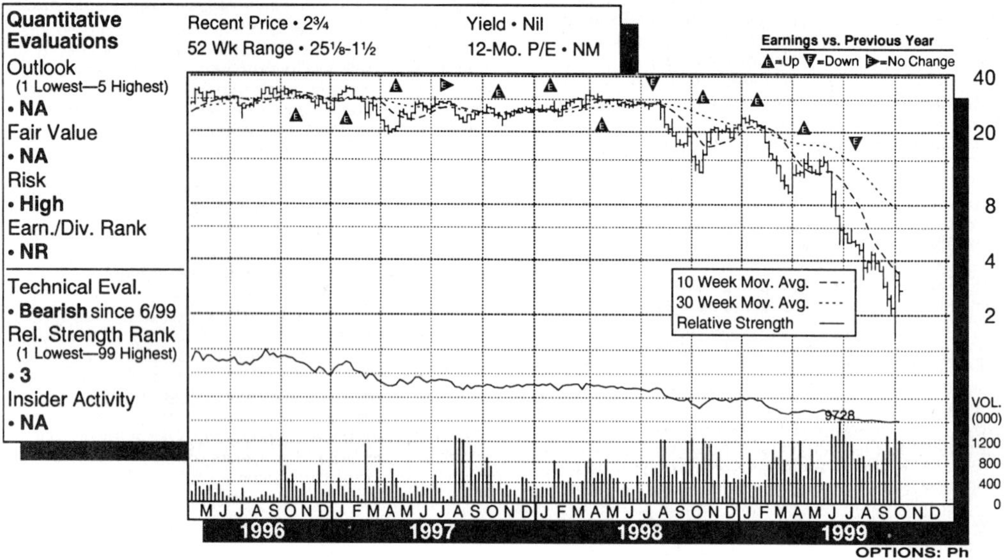

Business Profile - 19-AUG-99

In late June 1999, management said the implementation of Medicare's new Prospective Payment System (PPS) had negatively impacted NCS through pricing pressure on the company's Medicare-reimbursed business, reduced census and length of stay in client facilities and an overall lower acuity level of the residents in those facilities. It was noted that such trends are being felt throughout the long-term care industry. The company is positioning itself to succeed in the current PPS environment, by rapidly reducing operating and overhead costs and accelerating the implementation of its hub and spoke fulfillment and delivery model. Savings are expected to exceed $20 million on an annualized basis, with a large portion of these adjustments already in place.

Operational Review - 19-AUG-99

Revenues (preliminary) in FY 99 (Jun.) advanced 41%, aided by acquisitions. Gross margins narrowed; SG&A expenses grew faster than revenues, reflecting an accounting change, and with a $32.4 million charge to increase allowance for doubtful accounts, an operating loss contrasted with operating income. Interest expense more than tripled, and despite an income tax benefit of $7.6 million, versus taxes at 44.3%, the net loss was $13,404,000 ($0.67 a share, before a charge for an accounting change of $0.14), against net income of $11,331,000 ($0.58).

Stock Performance - 08-OCT-99

In the past 30 trading days, NCSS's shares have declined 30%, compared to a 0.91% fall in the S&P 500. Average trading volume for the past five days was 300,980 shares, compared with the 40-day moving average of 345,856 shares.

Key Stock Statistics

Dividend Rate/Share	Nil	Shareholders	267
Shs. outstg. (M)	20.3	Market cap. (B)	$0.038
Avg. daily vol. (M)	0.509	Inst. holdings	46%
Tang. Bk. Value/Share	NM		
Beta	NA		

Value of $10,000 invested 5 years ago: NA

Fiscal Year Ending Jun. 30

	1999	1998	1997	1996	1995	1994
Revenues (Million $)						
1Q	172.8	103.7	43.04	22.43	—	—
2Q	178.0	114.5	59.32	27.60	—	—
3Q	184.6	137.7	78.54	30.21	—	—
4Q	182.3	153.2	94.14	33.05	—	—
Yr.	717.8	509.1	275.0	113.3	65.60	48.20
Earnings Per Share ($)						
1Q	**0.24**	**0.20**	**0.15**	-0.15	—	—
2Q	**0.26**	**0.21**	**0.17**	0.10	—	—
3Q	**0.29**	**0.22**	**0.18**	0.12	—	—
4Q	**-1.23**	**-0.03**	**0.19**	0.19	—	—
Yr.	**-0.67**	**0.58**	**0.69**	**0.26**	**0.28**	**0.24**

Next earnings report expected: late October

Dividend Data

No cash dividends have been paid. The company intends to retain its earnings for use in its business and does not anticipate paying cash dividends in the foreseeable future.

NCS HealthCare, Inc.

Business Summary - 19-AUG-99

Traditionally providing institutional pharmacy and infusion products and services to long-term care facility residents, NCS HealthCare, Inc. in recent years has developed an array of services that address the needs of long-term care facilities to accommodate higher acuity admissions and manage costs. Revenues were obtained as follows in FY 98 (Jun.): Pharmacy & consultant pharmacy services, 77%; Infusion therapy, 6%; Other therapy, 3%; and Nutritional management & other, 14%.

The company's core business is providing pharmaceutical dispensing services to residents of long-term care facilities and other institutions. It purchases, repackages and dispenses prescription and non-prescription medication in accordance with physician orders and delivers the prescriptions at least daily to long-term care facilities for administration to residents by nursing home staffs. The company typically serves facilities within a two hour drive time of its distribution facility and provides 24 hour coverage 365 days per year. At FY 98 (Jun.) year end, the company provided its services from 89 sites in 34 states. It also offers services through the management of third party institutional pharmacies.

Upon receipt of a doctors' order, the information is entered into the company's management information system, which automatically reviews the order for patient-specific allergies and potentially adverse interactions. Following this analysis, a report on each order is produced for review by a company pharmacist, who may substitute generic drugs.

NCS provides consulting services that help clients comply with federal and state regulations applicable to long-term care facilities. Services include reviewing each patient's drug regimen, inspecting medication carts and storage rooms, monitoring and reporting on facility-wide drug usage and administration systems and practices, and developing and maintaining a client's pharmaceutical policy and procedure manuals.

The company also offers infusion therapy (intravenous delivery of medication) services including pain management, antibiotic therapy and chemotherapy for long-term care residents and home care patients. In 1993, it began offering physical, speech and occupational therapy services.

Nutrition management services involve assisting long-term care facilities in menu planning, purchasing and managing their dietary operations. Other services include providing long-term care facilities with assistance in complying with regulations concerning healthy and sanitary environments.

The company completed a number of acquisitions during FY 98 for an aggregate purchase price of some $188.8 million, consisting of $171.1 million in cash and the remainder in debt and stock.

Per Share Data ($) (Year Ended Jun. 30)	1999	1998	1997	1996	1995	1994	1993	1992	1991	1990
Tangible Bk. Val.	NA	NM	4.01	4.27	4.67	NA	NA	NA	NA	NA
Cash Flow	NA	1.43	1.20	0.62	0.46	NA	NA	NA	NA	NA
Earnings	-0.67	0.58	0.70	0.26	0.28	0.13	0.11	0.11	NA	NA
Dividends	Nil	Nil	Nil	Nil	Nil	NA	NA	NA	NA	NA
Payout Ratio	Nil	Nil	Nil	Nil	Nil	NA	NA	NA	NA	NA
Prices - High	24 3/4	34	35 1/4	35	NA	NA	NA	NA	NA	NA
- Low	1 1/2	11 7/8	19 1/4	16 1/2	NA	NA	NA	NA	NA	NA
P/E Ratio - High	NM	59	50	NA	NA	NA	NA	NA	NA	NA
- Low	NM	20	27	NA	NA	NA	NA	NA	NA	NA
Income Statement Analysis (Million $)										
Revs.	NA	509	275	113	65.6	48.2	33.6	28.5	NA	NA
Oper. Inc.	NA	51.4	27.2	9.0	5.7	NA	NA	NA	NA	NA
Depr.	NA	16.5	8.9	3.2	1.2	NA	NA	NA	NA	NA
Int. Exp.	NA	8.2	1.1	2.3	1.1	NA	NA	NA	NA	NA
Pretax Inc.	NA	74.2	19.9	4.2	3.4	NA	NA	NA	NA	NA
Eff. Tax Rate	NA	12%	43%	43%	45%	NA	NA	NA	NA	NA
Net Inc.	NA	65.2	11.3	2.4	1.9	1.5	0.8	0.7	NA	NA
Balance Sheet & Other Fin. Data (Million $)										
Cash	NA	21.2	8.2	21.5	0.0	NA	NA	NA	NA	NA
Curr. Assets	NA	222	107	59.2	20.4	NA	NA	NA	NA	NA
Total Assets	NA	624	321	111	38.6	NA	NA	NA	NA	NA
Curr. Liab.	NA	72.2	54.3	10.9	9.8	NA	NA	NA	NA	NA
LT Debt	NA	254	12.9	8.5	20.4	NA	NA	NA	NA	NA
Common Eqty.	NA	287	253	91.1	8.1	NA	NA	NA	NA	NA
Total Cap.	NA	551	267	100	28.7	NA	NA	NA	NA	NA
Cap. Exp.	NA	24.0	9.9	4.7	2.8	NA	NA	NA	NA	NA
Cash Flow	NA	81.6	20.2	5.6	3.1	NA	NA	NA	NA	NA
Curr. Ratio	NA	3.1	2.0	5.5	2.1	NA	NA	NA	NA	NA
% LT Debt of Cap.	NA	46.2	4.8	8.5	71.1	NA	NA	NA	NA	NA
% Net Inc.of Revs.	NA	12.8	4.1	2.1	2.9	3.1	2.4	2.5	NA	NA
% Ret. on Assets	NA	13.8	5.2	3.2	NA	NA	NA	NA	NA	NA
% Ret. on Equity	NA	24.1	6.6	4.8	NA	NA	NA	NA	NA	NA

Data as orig reptd.; bef. results of disc opers/spec. items. Per share data adj. for stk. divs. Bold denotes diluted EPS (FASB 128)-prior periods restated. E-Estimated. NA-Not Available. NM-Not Meaningful. NR-Not Ranked.

Office—3201 Enterprise Parkway, Suite 220, Beachwood, OH 44122. **Tel**—(216) 514-3350. **Website**—http://www.ncshealth.com **Chrmn**—J. H. Outcalt. **Pres & CEO**—K. B. Shaw. **CFO**—G. D. Stethem. **Dirs**—A. M. Mixon III, R. L. Osborne, J. H. Outcalt, B. A. Sells, K. B. Shaw, P. K. Wilson. **Transfer Agent & Registrar**—National City Bank, Cleveland. **Incorporated**—in Delaware. **Empl**— 3,900. **S&P Analyst:** C.C.P.

STANDARD
&POOR'S
STOCK REPORTS

Network Equipment Technologies

NYSE Symbol **NWK**

In S&P SmallCap 600

09-OCT-99

Industry: Computers (Networking)

Summary: This company is a leading designer, developer, manufacturer and supplier of WANs and associated services used by enterprises, government organizations and carriers.

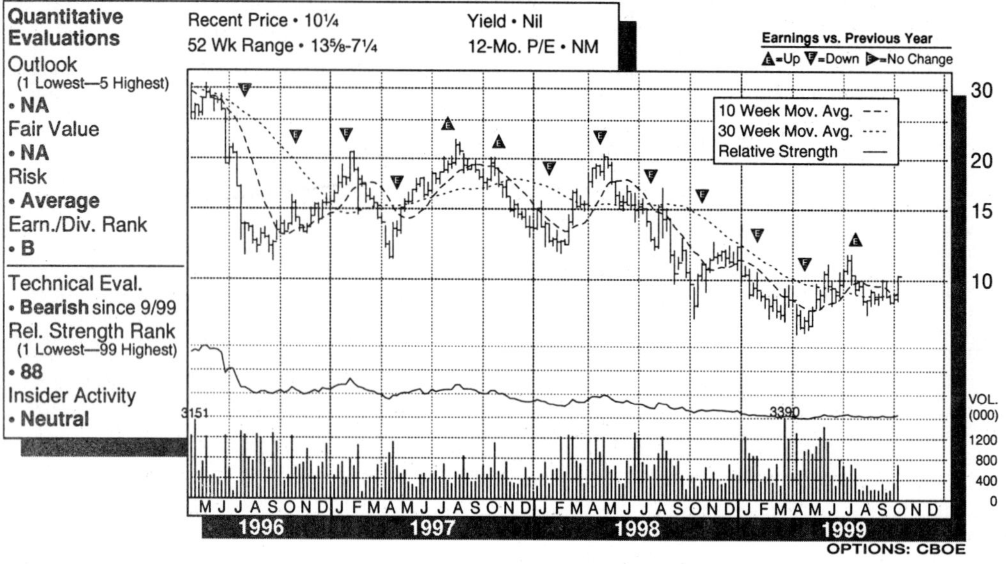

Business Profile - 22-JUN-99

In a corporate restructuring in the fourth quarter of FY 99 (Mar.), the company reduced its workforce by 10% and modified the order lead-time policy to improve internal processes. A $4.7 million resructuring charge was recorded in connection with the initiative. Also in the FY 99 fourth quarter, NWK announced availability of the Promina 4000 ATM switch, a highly efficient wide area network switch supporting traffic management for service offerings such as frame relay, ATM and circuit emulation. The PrimeVoice Secure module, which provides secure communications capabilities for compressed voice and fax traffic, meeting certain government requirements for secure communications, will be available in August 1999.

Operational Review - 22-JUN-99

Based on a preliminary report, revenues in FY 99 (Mar.) declined 15%, reflecting a 22% drop in product revenue and 2.7% lower service revenues. With greater R&D and SG&A expenses and a $4.7 million restructuring charge, and despite the absence of $3.3 million of facility relocation costs in the prior fiscal year, a loss of $7.1 million ($0.33 a share, on 2.4% more shares) contrasted with income of $14.4 million($0.65). Results exclude an extraordinary gain of $0.01 a share in FY 99.

Stock Performance - 08-OCT-99

In the past 30 trading days, NWK's shares have increased 14%, compared to a 0.91% fall in the S&P 500. Average trading volume for the past five days was 137,320 shares, compared with the 40-day moving average of 57,077 shares.

Key Stock Statistics

Dividend Rate/Share	Nil	Shareholders	723
Shs. outstg. (M)	21.3	Market cap. (B)	$0.218
Avg. daily vol. (M)	0.067	Inst. holdings	69%
Tang. Bk. Value/Share	10.67		
Beta	1.31		

Value of $10,000 invested 5 years ago: $ 11,549

Fiscal Year Ending Mar. 31

	2000	1999	1998	1997	1996	1995
Revenues (Million $)						
1Q	62.56	71.43	79.97	76.47	79.61	61.54
2Q	—	75.35	77.85	78.40	82.96	66.85
3Q	—	65.91	71.96	83.30	84.56	73.84
4Q	—	51.14	78.95	86.27	91.77	81.81
Yr.	—	263.8	308.7	324.4	338.9	284.0
Earnings Per Share ($)						
1Q	**0.16**	**0.13**	**0.26**	0.21	0.32	0.08
2Q	—	**0.16**	**0.26**	0.24	0.36	0.16
3Q	—	**-0.04**	**0.11**	0.31	0.39	0.27
4Q	—	-0.58	**0.02**	0.33	0.43	0.87
Yr.	—	**-0.33**	**0.65**	**1.08**	**1.50**	1.44

Next earnings report expected: mid October

Dividend Data

No cash has been paid. A "poison pill" stock purchase rights plan was adopted in 1989.

Network Equipment Technologies, Inc.

Business Summary - 22-JUN-99

Network Equipment Technologies offers a variety of solutions for mission-critical wide-area network (WAN) applications, primarily through sales of networking hardware and software. NWK provides expertise in systems integration, network design, installation, implementation and ongoing service and support. Products are based on a range of technologies and standards which are used throughout the industry and provide support such as switching, adaptation and aggregation for packet-, frame-, cell- and circuit-based applications. NWK allows customers to integrate diverse applications, including voice, data, video, multimedia and imaging across single network infrastructures. The company also offers efficient, cost effective and manageable backbones for wide area networks (WANs), along with a range of access capabilities. NWK allows carriers to provide a wide range of competitive service offerings such as native frame relay and Asynchronous Transfer Mode (ATM) services and enterprise customers to access those services or build their own networks.

The company competes primarily in the WAN markets. This segment provides the infrastructure and capability to link local area networks (LANs), campus networks, voice traffic, video and other applications to each other by public carrier-provided transmission facilities. In WANs, the center, or core, is the high-capacity backbone or transmission infrastructure developed and maintained by a major carrier or network service provider. Typically, these are high-speed, high-capacity links using ATM, SONET or other technology and built on switches characterized by high capacity, high reliability and other considerations. Beyond and around the core is an edge layer which defines the area at the boundary between a carrier or service provider and its enterprise customer or other user. This is the area where significant value is added by switches providing features to help manage traffic, service levels, concentration, and with capabilities such as support of traffic from multiple interfaces such as Frame Relay and native ATM.

Target markets and industries for NWK include carriers or network service providers; enterprises such as financial institutions, manufacturers, utilities and retailers; and governmental agencies.

In 1997, NWK introduced the Promina product family, delivering on its promise to bring ATM technology to its customers. NWK's ATM products include the Promina 800 Series, the Promina 2000 and the Promina 4000.

Sales to the U.S. government and agencies accounted for 33% of net sales in FY 98 (Mar.), versus 29% in the prior year. International sales accounted for 37% of net sales in FY 98, up from 35% in FY 97.

Per Share Data ($) **(Year Ended Mar. 31)**	**1999**	**1998**	**1997**	**1996**	**1995**	**1994**	**1993**	**1992**	**1991**	**1990**
Tangible Bk. Val.	10.83	11.03	10.11	8.85	5.43	3.45	3.82	4.15	4.29	7.45
Cash Flow	0.68	1.52	1.89	2.25	2.23	0.56	0.28	0.17	-2.65	1.55
Earnings	-0.33	0.65	1.08	1.50	1.44	-0.38	-0.71	-0.76	-3.47	0.93
Dividends	Nil	Nil	Nil	Nil	Nil	Nil	Nil	Nil	Nil	Nil
Payout Ratio	Nil	Nil	Nil	Nil	Nil	Nil	NA	Nil	Nil	Nil
Cal. Yrs.	1998	1997	1996	1995	1994	1993	1992	1991	1990	1989
Prices - High	20 5/8	22 3/8	36	42	24 3/4	11 1/2	18 1/4	15 7/8	34 3/8	31 7/8
- Low	8	11 1/4	11 1/8	19 3/4	7 3/8	5 3/8	8 7/8	4	5	16 1/2
P/E Ratio - High	NM	34	33	28	17	NM	NA	NM	NM	34
- Low	NM	17	10	13	5	NM	NA	NM	NM	18
Income Statement Analysis (Million $)										
Revs.	264	309	324	339	284	238	219	181	135	181
Oper. Inc.	6.7	36.3	49.8	62.9	40.8	13.5	25.4	17.4	-30.3	30.8
Depr.	21.7	19.2	17.4	15.5	14.8	15.8	15.5	13.7	11.6	9.1
Int. Exp.	2.0	2.0	2.3	4.7	5.2	5.3	5.3	5.8	6.2	6.3
Pretax Inc.	-14.7	21.1	35.8	48.2	23.3	-6.3	-11.1	-12.6	-58.8	21.4
Eff. Tax Rate	NM	32%	35%	35%	NM	NM	NM	NM	NM	37%
Net Inc.	-7.1	14.3	23.3	31.4	27.1	-6.3	-11.1	-11.2	-49.6	13.5
Balance Sheet & Other Fin. Data (Million $)										
Cash	155	59.5	139	112	86.6	41.6	52.1	44.8	49.8	66.6
Curr. Assets	232	270	258	238	190	137	132	118	111	159
Total Assets	313	335	62.9	282	232	187	187	177	170	234
Curr. Liab.	55.4	70.1	25.8	64.0	61.8	59.1	54.8	42.9	34.6	42.7
LT Debt	24.7	25.8	25.8	33.5	68.6	68.6	68.7	69.8	71.5	80.3
Common Eqty.	233	237	213	184	102	59.0	61.0	64.0	62.0	105
Total Cap.	258	265	292	218	170	128	132	134	135	191
Cap. Exp.	32.4	30.3	13.9	17.2	8.3	14.2	15.2	11.1	10.1	20.7
Cash Flow	14.6	33.6	40.7	46.8	41.9	9.4	4.4	2.4	-38.0	22.6
Curr. Ratio	4.2	3.9	4.1	3.7	3.1	2.3	2.4	2.8	3.2	3.7
% LT Debt of Cap.	9.6	9.7	10.8	15.4	40.3	53.7	52.1	52.2	52.8	42.1
% Net Inc.of Revs.	NM	4.6	7.2	9.3	9.5	NM	NM	NM	NM	7.5
% Ret. on Assets	NM	4.5	8.0	12.2	12.4	NM	NM	NM	NM	7.4
% Ret. on Equity	NM	6.4	11.7	21.9	32.6	NM	NM	NM	NM	14.0

Data as orig reptd.; bef. results of disc opers/spec. items. Per share data adj. for stk. divs. Bold denotes diluted EPS (FASB 128)-prior periods restated. E-Estimated. NA-Not Available. NM-Not Meaningful. NR-Not Ranked.

Office—6500 Paseo Padre Parkway, Fremont, CA 94555.**Tel**—(510) 713-7300. **Website**—http://www.net.com **Chrmn**—H.A. Wolf. **Pres & CEO**—J. J. Francesconi. **Investor Contact**—Billie Fagenstrom (510-574-2529). **Dirs**—D. R. Doll, J. K. Dutton, J. J. Francesconi, W. J. Gill, G. M. Scalise, H. A. Wolf. **Transfer Agent & Registrar**—First National Bank of Boston. **Incorporated**—in California in 1983; reincorporated in Delaware in 1986. **Empl**— 1,408. **S&P Analyst:** S.A.H.

STANDARD &POOR'S
STOCK REPORTS

New England Business Service

NYSE Symbol **NEB**

In S&P SmallCap 600

09-OCT-99

Industry: Office Equipment & Supplies

Summary: NEB supplies standardized business forms, software and related printed products, selling primarily by mail order to small businesses throughout the U.S., Canada and the U.K.

Quantitative Evaluations

Outlook
(1 Lowest—5 Highest)
• **2**

Fair Value
• **27**

Risk
• **Low**

Earn./Div. Rank
• **B+**

Technical Eval.
• **Neutral** since 9/99

Rel. Strength Rank
(1 Lowest—99 Highest)
• **53**

Insider Activity
• **Neutral**

Recent Price • 27¼
52 Wk Range • 39½-24
Yield • 2.9%
12-Mo. P/E • 15.1

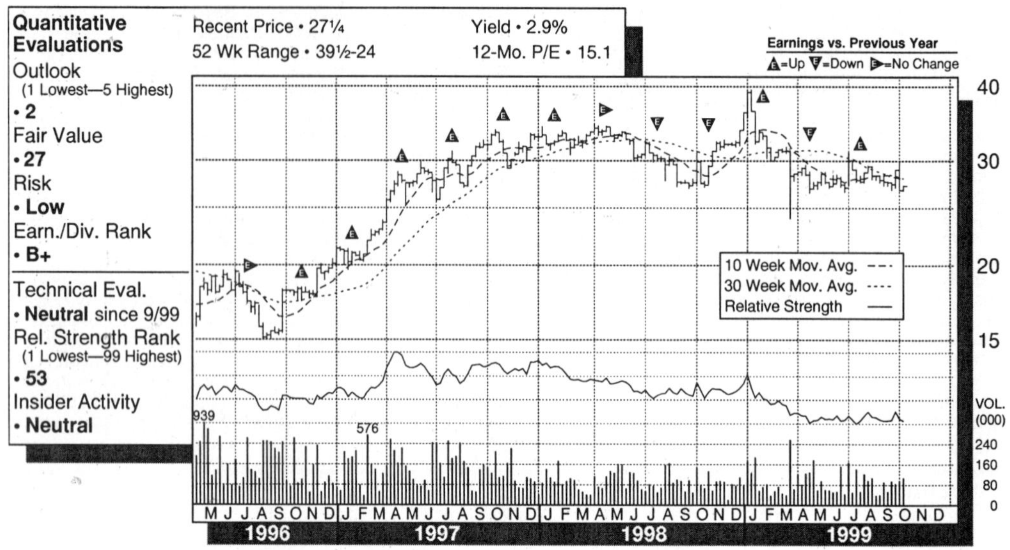

Business Profile - 02-AUG-99

The company sees revenues continuing to grow from new product lines, e-commerce, and additional small business services. Management expects FY 2000 (Jun.) EPS to grow about 10%. NEB is also targeting further penetration in the southeastern U.S. markets with an Atlanta-based warehouse. A website upgrade was recently launched by the company to provide customers with the ability to compose imprinted orders on-line with an enhanced electronic catalog and ordering system. In the second half of FY 99, NEB repurchased 515,800 of its shares and expects stock buybacks to continue to be part of its strategy to enhance shareholder value.

Operational Review - 02-AUG-99

Based on a preliminary report, net sales rose 32% in the fiscal year ended June 26, 1999, reflecting contributions from the acquisitions of Rapidforms and McBee Systems. Despite wider gross margins, profitability declined on higher selling, general and administrative costs; the gain in operating profit was held to 27%. Following a substantial increase in depreciation and amortization charges, sharply higher net interest expense, and taxes at 39.5%, versus 39.8%, net income was up 6.1%, to $26,451,000 ($1.81 a share, on 3.8% more shares), from $24,934,000 ($1.77).

Stock Performance - 08-OCT-99

In the past 30 trading days, NEB's shares have declined 2%, compared to a 0.91% fall in the S&P 500. Average trading volume for the past five days was 21,100 shares, compared with the 40-day moving average of 15,156 shares.

Key Stock Statistics

Dividend Rate/Share	0.80	Shareholders	641
Shs. outstg. (M)	14.4	Market cap. (B)	$0.391
Avg. daily vol. (M)	0.019	Inst. holdings	79%
Tang. Bk. Value/Share	2.72		
Beta	0.71		

Value of $10,000 invested 5 years ago: $ 16,102

Fiscal Year Ending Jun. 30

	1999	1998	1997	1996	1995	1994
Revenues (Million $)						
1Q	112.7	75.62	60.70	63.79	62.08	59.82
2Q	127.3	81.65	63.20	67.16	69.48	65.55
3Q	115.0	98.00	64.13	63.10	68.83	63.42
4Q	115.5	100.5	75.39	60.91	63.33	62.46
Yr.	470.5	355.8	263.4	254.9	263.7	251.3
Earnings Per Share ($)						
1Q	**0.37**	0.42	0.05	0.04	0.30	0.05
2Q	**0.53**	**0.46**	0.43	0.26	0.34	0.32
3Q	**0.42**	**0.45**	0.45	0.25	0.17	0.32
4Q	**0.47**	**0.43**	0.45	0.26	0.26	0.32
Yr.	**1.81**	**1.77**	**1.38**	0.81	1.07	1.01

Next earnings report expected: late October

Dividend Data (Dividends have been paid since 1965.)

Amount ($)	Date Decl.	Ex-Div. Date	Stock of Record	Payment Date
0.200	Oct. 23	Nov. 04	Nov. 06	Nov. 20 '98
0.200	Jan. 21	Feb. 03	Feb. 05	Feb. 19 '99
0.200	Apr. 22	May. 05	May. 07	May. 21 '99
0.200	Jul. 26	Aug. 04	Aug. 06	Aug. 20 '99

New England Business Service, Inc.

Business Summary - 02-AUG-99

New England Business Service (NEB) markets office and business products primarily by mail order to small businesses. Products include more than 1,000 standardized imprinted manual and computer business forms, check writing systems, stationery, labels, custom forms and other printed products principally designed and imprinted in-house.

The company's proprietary software consists of user-friendly forms-filling packages. The software is developed to perform a variety of tasks required to manage a small business and is compatible with all of NEB's business forms and other printed products.

NEB's standard manual business forms include billing forms, work orders, job proposals, purchase orders, invoices and personnel forms. Standard business forms provide small businesses with the financial and other business records necessary to efficiently run a business. NEB's stationery products, which include letterhead, envelopes and business cards, are available in a variety formats and colors and are designed to give small businesses a more professional image.

The company provides a broad range of printed products compatible with the software NEB distributes and with more than 3,500 other third-party small business software packages. Computer business forms include checks, billing forms and work orders, among others.

In addition, NEB offers promotional products, such as labels and pricing tags, and packaging material, including boxes and wrapping material.

The company's primary channel of distribution is mail order. Promotional materials are delivered to 1,922,000 customers and 9,400,000 prospects every year. The retail channel includes a broad network of 30,000 dealers. NEB considers its marketing database and customer/prospect list as a key competitive advantage.

NEB's growth is strongly correlated with the strength of its target small business market. The cost of paper accounts for approximately 20% of total revenues. In addition, the company relies heavily on the U.S. Postal Service for delivery of most of its promotional materials. To date, it has been able to offset increases in paper prices and postal rates through cost reduction programs and selected price increases. NEB has recently faced increasing competition from low-price, high volume office supply chain stores and smaller local printers who have access to newly available low cost, high quality printing technology.

In June 1998, the company acquired McBee Systems, Inc., for $48.5 million in cash and $12.6 million in NEB stock. McBee manufactures and markets a line of checks and related products to small business in the U.S. and Canada through a dedicated field sales force. Although it expected the acquisition to be accretive over the long term, NEB projected that it would cut FY 99 (Jun.) EPS by $0.07.

Per Share Data ($) (Year Ended Jun. 30)	1999	1998	1997	1996	1995	1994	1993	1992	1991	1990
Tangible Bk. Val.	NA	NM	3.58	5.42	6.16	6.43	6.19	6.18	6.61	6.27
Cash Flow	NA	2.85	2.03	1.51	1.90	1.77	1.58	1.63	1.73	1.81
Earnings	1.81	1.77	1.37	0.81	1.07	1.01	0.93	1.02	1.24	1.23
Dividends	0.80	0.80	0.80	0.80	0.80	0.80	0.80	0.80	0.80	0.76
Payout Ratio	44%	45%	58%	99%	75%	79%	86%	77%	64%	61%
Prices - High	39½	39⅛	34¼	22⅛	23¾	21¾	20¼	19¾	20¼	19¾
- Low	24	26⅞	19⅝	14½	16¾	17¼	14¾	13½	12¼	10½
P/E Ratio - High	22	22	25	27	22	22	22	19	16	16
- Low	13	15	14	18	16	17	16	13	10	9
Income Statement Analysis (Million $)										
Revs.	NA	356	263	255	264	251	237	232	232	233
Oper. Inc.	NA	60.1	42.2	32.8	41.8	43.4	32.8	32.2	39.8	38.9
Depr.	NA	15.2	9.1	10.3	12.7	11.6	9.9	9.5	7.9	7.6
Int. Exp.	NA	4.6	0.5	Nil	Nil	Nil	0.0	0.3	0.4	0.8
Pretax Inc.	NA	41.4	31.4	20.0	28.1	27.6	24.1	24.9	34.1	33.4
Eff. Tax Rate	NA	40%	41%	41%	42%	44%	41%	36%	40%	38%
Net Inc.	NA	24.9	18.6	11.9	16.3	15.6	14.2	15.9	20.3	20.6
Balance Sheet & Other Fin. Data (Million $)										
Cash	NA	10.8	7.8	18.4	23.0	41.0	28.1	31.6	45.2	39.1
Curr. Assets	NA	101	68.4	71.3	77.5	85.3	69.0	74.8	87.5	84.3
Total Assets	NA	308	141	104	125	132	121	121	134	130
Curr. Liab.	NA	50.7	33.3	27.3	32.2	30.1	25.3	25.6	24.1	21.6
LT Debt	NA	141	27.0	Nil	Nil	Nil	Nil	Nil	Nil	3.3
Common Eqty.	NA	115	80.6	76.0	92.0	99	95.0	94.0	108	104
Total Cap.	NA	256	108	76.0	92.0	101	95.0	95.0	109	108
Cap. Exp.	NA	13.3	9.6	9.4	10.8	6.1	6.5	9.7	9.2	8.8
Cash Flow	NA	40.2	27.7	22.3	29.0	27.2	24.2	25.5	28.2	28.2
Curr. Ratio	NA	2.0	2.0	2.6	2.4	2.8	2.7	2.9	3.6	3.9
% LT Debt of Cap.	NA	55.2	25.0	Nil	Nil	Nil	Nil	Nil	Nil	3.1
% Net Inc.of Revs.	NA	7.0	7.1	4.7	6.2	6.2	6.0	6.9	8.8	8.8
% Ret. on Assets	NA	11.1	15.2	10.5	13.0	12.3	11.7	13.0	15.5	16.0
% Ret. on Equity	NA	25.6	23.8	14.3	17.4	15.9	15.0	16.4	19.3	20.3

Data as orig reptd.; bef. results of disc opers/spec. items. Per share data adj. for stk. divs. Bold denotes diluted EPS (FASB 128)-prior periods restated. E-Estimated. NA-Not Available. NM-Not Meaningful. NR-Not Ranked.

Office—500 Main St., Groton, MA 01471. **Tel**—(978) 448-6111. **Website**—http://www.nebs.com **Chrmn, Pres & CEO**—R.J. Murray. **SVP, CFO & Treas**—D. M. Junius. **Investor Contact**—Timothy D. Althof (978-449-3425). **Dirs**—N. S. Fox, R. L. Gable, B. H. Lacy, H. W. Moller, R. J. Murray, R. H. Rhoads, M. A. Szostak, B. E. Stern. **Transfer Agent & Registrar**—BankBoston, c/o Boston EquiServe. **Incorporated**—in Massachusetts in 1955; reincorporated in Delaware in 1986. **Empl**— 3,782. **S&P Analyst:** Jordan Horoschak

STANDARD
&POOR'S
STOCK REPORTS

New Jersey Resources

NYSE Symbol **NJR**
In S&P SmallCap 600

09-OCT-99

Industry:
Natural Gas

Summary: Through New Jersey Natural Gas Co., this utility holding company supplies gas to over 391,000 customers in central and northern New Jersey.

Business Profile - 22-JUN-99

NJR's goal is to continue to grow without increasing its base rates in order to remain competitive as the utility industry transitions to a more market-based environment. In both 1999 and 2000, the company's aim is to add 11,800 to 12,000 new customers, and convert an additional 950 existing customers each year to natural gas heat. Achieving these objectives would represent a customer growth rate of more than 3% and result in a sales increase of about 1.9 billion cubic feet per year, assuming normal weather and average use, and increase gross margin under present rates by some $5.5 million per year.

Operational Review - 22-JUN-99

Revenues in the first half of FY 99 (Sep.) were up 17%, year to year, primarily reflecting growth in the customer base and higher fuel and capacity management sales. Operating expenses rose at a slightly more rapid rate, with the largest increases in gas purchases and state income taxes. Operating income was up 6.1%. With lower interest charges outweighing lower other income, net income rose 6.5%, to $45,489,000 ($2.53 a share), from $42,727,000 ($2.39).

Stock Performance - 08-OCT-99

In the past 30 trading days, NJR's shares have increased 0.95%, compared to a 0.91% fall in the S&P 500. Average trading volume for the past five days was 13,220 shares, compared with the 40-day moving average of 16,979 shares.

Key Stock Statistics

Dividend Rate/Share	1.68	Shareholders	17,735
Shs. outstg. (M)	17.8	Market cap. (B)	$0.708
Avg. daily vol. (M)	0.017	Inst. holdings	35%
Tang. Bk. Value/Share	15.46		
Beta	0.34		

Value of $10,000 invested 5 years ago: $ 20,471

Fiscal Year Ending Sep. 30

	1999	1998	1997	1996	1995	1994
Revenues (Million $)						
1Q	244.6	220.4	188.6	159.7	126.0	136.2
2Q	327.3	266.6	285.4	233.9	197.2	222.8
3Q	159.5	113.4	121.2	94.46	74.36	75.61
4Q	—	109.9	101.4	60.40	56.98	64.22
Yr.	—	710.3	696.5	548.5	454.6	498.8
Earnings Per Share ($)						
1Q	**0.84**	**0.79**	**0.71**	0.69	0.65	0.62
2Q	**1.69**	**1.60**	1.58	1.50	1.46	1.37
3Q	**0.17**	**0.16**	0.14	0.12	0.07	0.19
4Q	—	**-0.22**	-0.23	-0.25	-0.25	-0.28
Yr.	—	**2.33**	**2.21**	2.06	1.93	1.89

Next earnings report expected: late October

Dividend Data (Dividends have been paid since 1951.)

Amount ($)	Date Decl.	Ex-Div. Date	Stock of Record	Payment Date
0.420	Nov. 20	Dec. 11	Dec. 15	Jan. 04 '99
0.420	Jan. 26	Mar. 11	Mar. 15	Apr. 01 '99
0.420	May. 12	Jun. 11	Jun. 15	Jul. 01 '99
0.420	Jul. 13	Sep. 13	Sep. 15	Oct. 01 '99

A Division of The McGraw-Hill Companies

New Jersey Resources Corporation

Business Summary - 22-JUN-99

This energy services holding company provides retail and wholesale natural gas and related energy services to customers from the Gulf Coast to New England. Its principal subsidiary, New Jersey Natural Gas Co. (NJNG), provides regulated natural gas service to more than 385,000 customers in central and northern New Jersey. In FY 98 (Sep.), residential customers provided 53% of revenues; commercial & other 11%; firm transportation 3%; interruptible 2%; off-system 29%; and appliance service 2%.

New Jersey Natural Gas's service territory is primarily suburban, with a wide range of cultural and recreational activities, highlighted by about 100 miles of New Jersey seacoast. It is in proximity to New York, Philadelphia and the metropolitan areas of northern New Jersey and is accessible through a network of major roadways and mass transportation. These factors contributed to the company adding 11,819, 11,708 and 10,978 new customers in FY 98, FY 97 and FY 96, respectively. This annual growth rate of 3% is expected to continue.

NJNG also participates in "capacity release" and "off-system" sales programs whereby NJNG releases some of the capacity it has secured on interstate pipelines and sells excess gas supplies when demand is not at its peak. These programs reach wholesale customers as far away as Texas, well beyond NJNG's local franchise area. Effective October 1, 1998, through December 31, 2001, the company will retain 15% of the gross margin from off-system and capacity release sales, down from 20% prior to September 30, 1998. Off-system sales totaled 62.2 billion cubic feet and generated $2.6 million of gross margin in 1998.

The New Jersey Natural Energy Co. (NJNE) unit was formed in 1995 to participate in the unregulated marketing of natural gas and energy services. NJNE must compete for its retail gas customers against a score of other marketers; as of the end of FY 98, NJNE supplied gas to some 7,502 retail customers.

The company purchases a diverse gas supply portfolio consisting of long-term (over seven months), winter-term (for the five winter months) and short-term contracts. In 1998, the company purchased gas from 76 suppliers under contracts ranging from one month to 12 years. The company has five long-term firm gas purchase contracts and purchased about 12% of its gas in 1998 from Alberta Northeast Gas.

Per Share Data ($) (Year Ended Sep. 30)	1998	1997	1996	1995	1994	1993	1992	1991	1990	1989
Tangible Bk. Val.	15.46	15.34	15.12	14.55	14.46	14.72	14.16	12.85	13.27	13.65
Earnings	2.33	2.22	2.06	1.93	1.89	1.72	1.64	0.83	0.97	1.45
Dividends	1.64	1.60	1.55	1.52	1.52	1.52	1.52	1.50	1.44	1.36
Payout Ratio	70%	72%	75%	98%	80%	88%	93%	181%	148%	94%
Prices - High	40 1/4	42	29 7/8	30 1/2	27 3/8	29 1/2	25 1/8	21 1/8	20 7/8	21 1/2
- Low	31 1/2	28 1/8	26 5/8	21 1/2	19 3/4	24	18 1/4	17	17 1/8	17 1/8
P/E Ratio - High	17	19	15	16	14	17	15	25	22	15
- Low	14	13	13	11	10	14	11	20	18	12
Income Statement Analysis (Million $)										
Revs.	710	697	549	455	499	455	412	335	325	330
Depr.	27.8	25.8	23.2	23.0	27.6	25.4	24.3	21.7	18.3	16.1
Maint.	Nil	Nil	NA	NA	NA	NA	6.4	7.3	8.0	6.5
Fxd. Chgs. Cov.	4.3	3.8	3.7	2.8	3.0	2.8	2.5	1.7	1.9	2.3
Constr. Credits	Nil	Nil	Nil	Nil	Nil	3.2	3.3	3.6	2.6	2.2
Eff. Tax Rate	36%	34%	34%	32%	30%	30%	31%	31%	31%	32%
Net Inc.	41.8	39.9	37.1	33.9	33.9	28.5	23.5	11.3	13.0	16.4
Balance Sheet & Other Fin. Data (Million $)										
Gross Prop.	920	878	856	786	859	831	770	725	673	588
Cap. Exp.	44.5	47.0	56.1	53.8	58.6	70.4	47.6	57.4	83.2	84.8
Net Prop.	680	659	655	596	640	633	592	567	533	463
Capitalization:										
LT Debt	327	291	303	352	324	311	252	263	228	209
% LT Debt	51	49	51	57	54	54	49	55	54	52
Pfd.	20.6	20.8	21.0	21.0	22.1	22.3	32.6	32.9	13.2	13.4
% Pfd.	3.20	3.50	3.50	3.30	3.70	3.90	6.30	6.90	3.10	3.30
Common	291	278	274	259	250	248	231	179	179	180
% Common	46	47	46	41	42	43	45	38	43	45
Total Cap.	722	591	598	632	661	642	577	529	475	451
% Oper. Ratio	91.5	91.2	89.1	86.9	89.2	89.0	88.7	89.6	89.5	89.5
% Earn. on Net Prop.	9.1	9.4	9.5	9.5	8.7	8.2	8.0	6.3	6.8	8.1
% Return On Revs.	5.9	5.7	6.8	7.4	6.8	6.3	5.7	3.4	4.0	5.0
% Return On Invest. Capital	9.6	10.4	11.5	10.8	8.6	8.4	8.6	7.0	7.4	8.8
% Return On Com. Equity	14.7	14.5	13.9	13.3	13.4	11.9	11.4	6.3	7.2	10.4

Data as orig reptd.; bef. results of disc opers/spec. items. Per share data adj. for stk. divs. Bold denotes diluted EPS (FASB 128)-prior periods restated. E-Estimated. NA-Not Available. NM-Not Meaningful. NR-Not Ranked.

Office—1415 Wyckoff Road, P.O. Box 1468, Wall, NJ 07719. **Tel**—(732) 938-1480. **Website**—http://www.njresources.com **Chrmn, Pres & CEO**—L. M. Downes. **SVP & CFO**—G. C. Lockwood. **SVP & Secy**—O. J. Harden. **Investor Contact**—Dennis Puma (732-938-1229). **Dirs**—N. Aversano, B. G. Coe, L. S. Coleman, L. M. Downes, J. B. Foster, H. F. Gluck, L. D. Johnson, D. K. Light, C. G. Stalon, J. J. Unkles, Jr., G. W. Wolf, G. R. Zoffinger. **Transfer Agent & Registrar**—Bank of Boston. **Incorporated**—in New Jersey in 1922. **Empl**— 791. **S&P Analyst:** M.I.

STANDARD
&POOR'S
STOCK REPORTS

Newfield Exploration

NYSE Symbol **NFX**

In S&P SmallCap 600

09-OCT-99

Industry: Oil & Gas (Exploration & Production)

Summary: This independent oil and natural gas exploration and production company operates primarily in the Gulf of Mexico.

Quantitative Evaluations

Outlook (1 Lowest—5 Highest)
• **1⁻**

Fair Value
• **29¾**

Risk
• **Average**

Earn./Div. Rank
• **NR**

Technical Eval.
• **Neutral** since 9/99

Rel. Strength Rank (1 Lowest—99 Highest)
• **46**

Insider Activity
• **NA**

Recent Price • 28⅞
52 Wk Range • 35-14⅞
Yield • Nil
12-Mo. P/E • NM

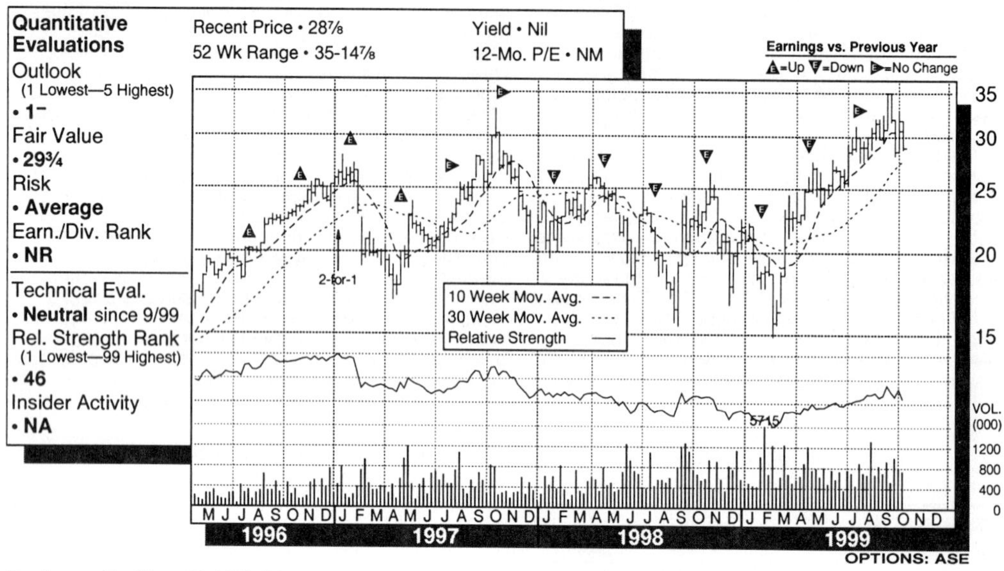

OPTIONS: ASE

Business Profile - 03-AUG-99

This independent oil and gas producer plans to continue to expand its reserve base through exploration, acquisition of proved properties, and development of its properties. Primarily as a result of significant declines in both oil and gas prices, NFX recorded a "ceiling test" writedown at December 31, 1998, leading to a large loss in 1998's fourth quarter. In July 1999, the company acquired Gulf Australia Resources Ltd., which included interests in two producing fields with identified drilling potential in the Timor Sea, for $23 million. Also in July, Newfield entered into an agreement to acquire the interests of Ocean Energy Inc. in three Gulf of Mexico oil and gas fields for about $66 million. Separately, the company announced a new production target for 1999 of 111 Bcfe, which would represent a 25% increase over 1998.

Operational Review - 03-AUG-99

Oil and gas revenues in the first half of 1999 advanced 13%, year to year, as a 26% rise in total production was offset by a decline in the average realized price for both oil and gas. Lease operating expenses and depreciation, depletion and amortization charges increased faster than revenues, and following 71% higher interest expense, pretax income fell 58%. After taxes at 37.8%, versus 35.3%, net income was down 60%, to $4,205,000 ($0.10 a share, on 9.5% more shares) from $10,484,000 ($0.27).

Stock Performance - 08-OCT-99

In the past 30 trading days, NFX's shares have declined 3%, compared to a 0.91% fall in the S&P 500. Average trading volume for the past five days was 145,620 shares, compared with the 40-day moving average of 157,049 shares.

Key Stock Statistics

Dividend Rate/Share	Nil	Shareholders	295
Shs. outstg. (M)	41.5	Market cap. (B)	$ 1.2
Avg. daily vol. (M)	0.151	Inst. holdings	79%
Tang. Bk. Value/Share	8.22		
Beta	1.22		

Value of $10,000 invested 5 years ago: $ 32,765

Fiscal Year Ending Dec. 31

	1999	1998	1997	1996	1995	1994
Revenues (Million $)						
1Q	52.91	49.98	46.93	32.96	19.03	13.86
2Q	60.07	49.90	42.35	33.01	24.81	16.40
3Q	—	45.30	49.86	35.80	24.62	18.95
4Q	—	50.51	60.26	47.48	26.14	20.53
Yr.	—	195.7	199.4	149.3	94.60	69.73
Earnings Per Share ($)						
1Q	Nil	**0.18**	**0.31**	**0.22**	0.10	0.08
2Q	**0.10**	**0.10**	**0.21**	**0.21**	0.12	0.10
3Q	—	**0.02**	**0.23**	**0.23**	0.10	0.12
4Q	—	**-1.71**	**0.32**	**0.37**	0.13	0.10
Yr.	—	**-1.55**	**1.07**	**1.03**	**0.45**	**0.40**

Next earnings report expected: late October

Dividend Data

The company does not intend to pay cash dividends on its common stock in the foreseeable future. It expects to retain any earnings for the future operation and development of the business. A shareholder rights plan was adopted in early 1999.

Newfield Exploration Company

Business Summary - 03-AUG-99

Newfield Exploration, an independent oil and gas exploration and development concern, was founded by Joe Foster (its current chairman and CEO) and 24 former employees of Tenneco Oil's Gulf of Mexico divisions in late 1988, following the sale of Tenneco Oil by its parent. Mr. Foster had been chairman of Tenneco Oil, a leading Gulf of Mexico operator. The company's concept was to use the kind of technology that had made Tenneco Oil successful (namely, major company technology with a high geophysical content), and to combine that with an independent's mindset and cost structure. Newfield went public in 1993.

Newfield's strategy has been to expand its reserve base and increase cash flow through a balanced program of exploring and developing existing properties and acquiring properties which it believes offer a significant drilling upside. Once focused solely on the Gulf of Mexico, the company now has interests in south Louisiana and South Texas, and is exploring in selected locations in China, West Africa, Australia, and the east coast of South America.

Since the company's inception in 1988, and its first discovery and acquisition of oil and gas reserves in 1990, NFX has added a total of 873 Bcfe of proved reserves (through 1998). Exploration and development activities accounted for 35% of the added reserves, while acquisitions accounted for 40%, and exploitation of acquired opportunities made up the balance. NFX had proved oil and gas reserves of 513.3 Bcfe at December 31, 1998, consisting of 15.2 MMBbls of oil and 422.3 Bcf of natural gas.

For 1999, Newfield has established a capital budget of $200 million. The company has established a production goal of 111 Bcfe, a 25% increase from the level of 1998. While the shelf of the Gulf of Mexico remains a core focus area of high potential, production growth should increasingly come from expansion onshore in south Louisiana and South Texas, where Newfield continues to expand its seismic database and opportunity set. Meanwhile, the company uses a hedging strategy to mitigate price risk, with over 50% of first half 1999 gas production locked in at prices not less than $2.20 per Mcf.

As in the past, NFX intends to develop additional exploratory drilling prospects on its existing properties through the extensive application of 3-D seismic and other advanced technologies. In concert with its balanced capital program strategy, the company will also continue to pursue proved property additions through acquisitions.

Per Share Data ($) (Year Ended Dec. 31)	1998	1997	1996	1995	1994	1993	1992	1991	1990	1989
Tangible Bk. Val.	8.01	8.12	6.81	5.63	5.08	4.62	4.29	NA	NA	NA
Cash Flow	1.75	3.54	2.75	1.83	1.35	1.36	1.57	NA	NA	NA
Earnings	-1.55	1.07	1.03	0.45	0.40	0.49	0.49	NA	NA	NA
Dividends	Nil	Nil	Nil	Nil	Nil	Nil	NA	NA	NA	NA
Payout Ratio	Nil	Nil	Nil	Nil	Nil	Nil	NA	NA	NA	NA
Prices - High	27⅝	33	26½	16⅛	13	9¼	NA	NA	NA	NA
- Low	15⅜	16⅞	12½	9	8¾	7⅞	NA	NA	NA	NA
P/E Ratio - High	NM	31	26	36	32	19	NA	NA	NA	NA
- Low	NM	16	12	20	22	16	NA	NA	NA	NA
Income Statement Analysis (Million $)										
Revs.	196	199	149	94.6	69.7	60.2	59.6	NA	NA	NA
Oper. Inc.	148	159	123	74.1	56.4	49.4	49.7	NA	NA	NA
Depr. Depl. & Amort.	123	94.0	64.0	50.0	34.1	25.1	28.6	NA	NA	NA
Int. Exp.	9.5	3.3	0.4	0.2	0.4	0.1	1.5	NA	NA	NA
Pretax Inc.	-88.4	62.4	59.3	25.0	22.5	21.8	19.7	NA	NA	NA
Eff. Tax Rate	NM	35%	35%	35%	36%	36%	34%	NA	NA	NA
Net Inc.	-57.7	40.6	38.5	16.3	14.4	14.0	13.0	NA	NA	NA
Balance Sheet & Other Fin. Data (Million $)										
Cash	0.1	8.2	13.3	12.5	18.6	65.0	NA	NA	NA	NA
Curr. Assets	45.3	64.8	61.3	42.8	35.9	88.3	NA	NA	NA	NA
Total Assets	629	554	396	227	216	184	NA	NA	NA	NA
Curr. Liab.	54.1	64.4	49.8	31.6	24.9	18.1	NA	NA	NA	NA
LT Debt	209	130	60.0	25.2	0.6	0.5	0.6	NA	NA	NA
Common Eqty.	324	292	145	194	169	153	137	NA	NA	NA
Total Cap.	564	486	249	245	190	165	NA	NA	NA	NA
Cap. Exp.	319	243	159	107	115	43.8	NA	NA	NA	NA
Cash Flow	65.4	135	103	66.3	48.6	39.1	41.6	NA	NA	NA
Curr. Ratio	0.8	1.0	1.2	1.4	1.4	4.9	NA	NA	NA	NA
% LT Debt of Cap.	NM	26.7	24.1	10.3	0.3	0.3	NA	NA	NA	NA
% Ret. on Assets	NM	8.6	11.4	6.6	7.2	9.1	NA	NA	NA	NA
% Ret. on Equity	NM	15.3	17.8	9.0	8.9	11.1	NA	NA	NA	NA

Data as orig reptd.; bef. results of disc opers/spec. items. Per share data adj. for stk. divs. Bold denotes diluted EPS (FASB 128)-prior periods restated. E-Estimated. NA-Not Available. NM-Not Meaningful. NR-Not Ranked.

Office—363 North Sam Houston Parkway East, Suite 2020, Houston, TX 77060. **Tel**—(281) 847-6000. **Fax**—(281) 847-6006. **Chrmn & CEO**—J. B. Foster. **Pres & COO**—D. A. Trice. **VP-Fin**—D. A. Trice. **VP & Secy**—T. W. Rathert. **Treas & Investor Contact**—J. P. Ulm, II. **Dirs**—P. J. Burguieres, C. W. Duncan, Jr., J. B. Foster, D. Hendrix, T. Huffington, H. H. Newman, T. G. Ricks, J. C. Sawhill, C. E. Shultz, R. W. Waldrup. **Transfer Agent & Registrar**—ChaseMellon Shareholder Services, Ridgefield Park, NJ. **Incorporated**—in Delaware in 1988. **Empl**— 96. **S&P Analyst:** SRB

STANDARD
&POOR'S
STOCK REPORTS

NFO Worldwide, Inc.

NYSE Symbol **NFO**
In S&P SmallCap 600

09-OCT-99

Industry: Services (Advertising & Marketing)

Summary: NFO provides research-based, marketing information and counsel to the worldwide business community.

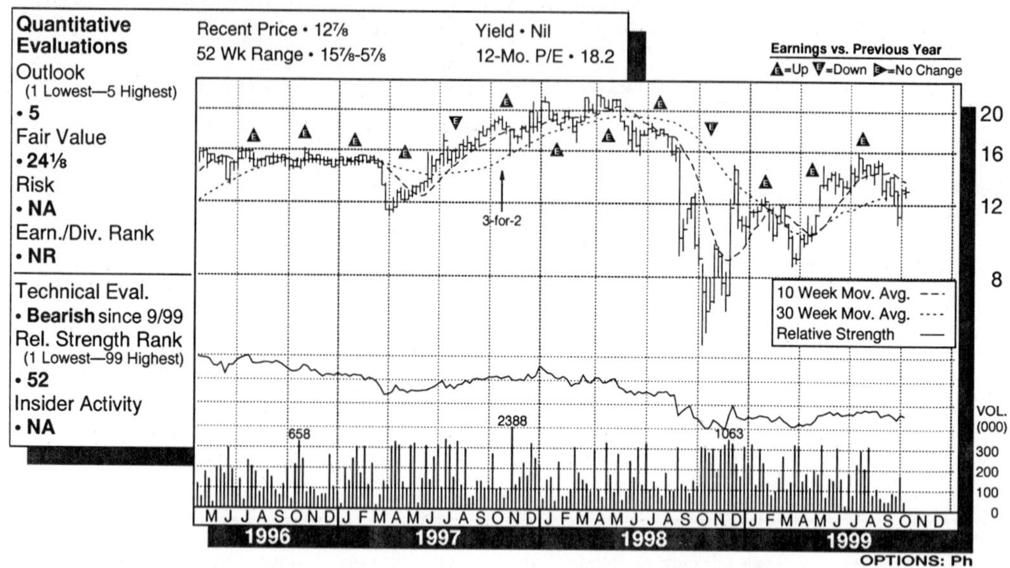

Business Profile - 24-SEP-99

In recent years, NFO Worldwide has acquired or developed a wide variety of companies with market sector expertise, proprietary products, and global scale. The company has begun shifting its focus toward organic business development, and away from acquisition-related activity. During the 1999 second quarter, NFO continued to implement its strategy of global integration and cross selling across market sectors, products, and geographies. In addition, increasing focus is being placed on the company's interactive business, where client interest has been growing.

Operational Review - 24-SEP-99

Revenues for the first half of 1999 soared 96%, year to year, due primarily to acquisitions. Internal growth amounted to about 7%. However, with increased losses in North American financialservices (due to heightened competition after recent bank mergers and consolidations), reduced profitability in Australasian operations (continued competitive and market pressures), and increased losses in Interactive operations (increased investments), the gain in operating profit was held to 55%. After a more than 6-fold increase in interest expense (net); taxes at 44.2%, compared with 39.5%; and lower minority interests deduction, net income was up 17%, to $8.0 million ($0.36 a share) from $6.8 million ($0.32).

Stock Performance - 08-OCT-99

In the past 30 trading days, NFO's shares have declined 0.48%, compared to a 0.91% fall in the S&P 500. Average trading volume for the past five days was 8,740 shares, compared with the 40-day moving average of 16,123 shares.

Key Stock Statistics

Dividend Rate/Share	Nil	Shareholders	200
Shs. outstg. (M)	22.3	Market cap. (B)	$0.288
Avg. daily vol. (M)	0.019	Inst. holdings	40%
Tang. Bk. Value/Share	NM		
Beta	1.26		

Value of $10,000 invested 5 years ago: $ 23,132

Fiscal Year Ending Dec. 31

	1999	1998	1997	1996	1995	1994
Revenues (Million $)						
1Q	106.4	50.24	30.12	24.11	16.22	14.00
2Q	119.4	65.00	35.92	25.64	17.35	15.11
3Q	—	65.49	49.34	26.84	18.56	14.96
4Q	—	94.62	51.84	32.57	20.96	17.47
Yr.	—	275.4	190.2	109.2	73.10	61.54
Earnings Per Share ($)						
1Q	**0.13**	**0.12**	**0.11**	**0.09**	0.09	0.07
2Q	**0.23**	**0.20**	**0.13**	**0.14**	0.12	0.10
3Q	—	**0.12**	**0.15**	**0.14**	0.12	0.12
4Q	—	**0.23**	**0.20**	**0.14**	0.13	0.11
Yr.	—	**0.67**	**0.60**	**0.51**	**0.48**	0.39

Next earnings report expected: early November

Dividend Data

The company has never paid any cash dividends on its capital stock. NFO has said it does not anticipate paying any cash dividends in the foreseeable future. A shareholder rights plan was adopted in October 1998.

A Division of The McGraw-Hill Companies

NFO Worldwide, Inc.

Business Summary - 24-SEP-99

NFO Worldwide, Inc. is in the business of knowing what consumers think. The company provides research-based marketing information and counsel to the worldwide business community. As of year-end 1998, the company had more than 3,000 clients globally.

The company combines knowledge of key market sectors--consumer packaged goods and foods, healthcare, financial services, travel and leisure, information technology, automotive and business-to-business--with data collection methodologies and value added products.

Key products and services include continuous brand tracking, online research, consumer panels, and multi-country research, as well as market evaluation, product development, customer satisfaction, pricing, distribution and advertising effectiveness.

NFO has three operating segments: North America, Europe and Australasia and the Middle East. Within each segment, the company has subsidiaries specializing in various market sectors and types of marketing research services.

The year 1998 was a period of unprecedented growth through acquisitions. Most significant was the November 1998 acquisition of Infratest Burke Aktiengesellschaft Holding, headquartered in Munich, Germany. Infratest Burke is a custom marketing research firm with 35 offices in 15 countries. The combination of NFO and Infratest Burke created the sixth largest marketing research firm in the world. NFO was already the largest custom marketing research firm in North America.

The company made two acquisitions in October 1998, Donovan Research Pty. Ltd. and City Research Group Plc. Donovan Research, based in Perth, Australia, is a full service custom researchagency. City Research, based in London, England, is a marketing research firm specializing in financial services.

NFO acquired Stochastic International Pty. Ltd. in August 1998; and three companies in spring of 1998, CF Group, Inc. in April; and MarketMind Technologies and Ross-Cooper-Lund both in March. Stochastic provides guidance on brand positioning to more than 60 companies in 33 countries. CF Group provides marketing, social, and business research services across a variety of industries. MarketMind uses diagnostic measures together with the analysis of multiple streams of longitudinal data. Ross-Cooper-Lund is a research-based consulting firm.

NFO's goal is to become the worldwide leader in custom marketing research. To accomplish this, the company has been pursuing a four-pronged business development strategy: broaden and expand core operations; pioneer new advances in technology to deliver services more quickly and more cost effectively; make strategic alliances and acquisitions; and expand international business.

In November 1998, the company privately placed $72 million of senior and subordinated notes.

In late March 1999, NFO privately placed $7 million of senior notes and $8 million of senior subordinated notes, with proceeds used to reduce debt.

Per Share Data ($) (Year Ended Dec. 31)	1998	1997	1996	1995	1994	1993	1992	1991	1990	1989
Tangible Bk. Val.	NM	1.08	1.13	1.24	0.26	0.26	NA	NA	NA	NA
Cash Flow	1.13	0.93	0.83	0.69	0.61	0.55	0.57	NA	NA	NA
Earnings	0.67	0.60	0.55	0.46	0.39	0.29	0.22	NA	NA	NA
Dividends	Nil	Nil	Nil	Nil	Nil	Nil	Nil	NA	NA	NA
Payout Ratio	Nil	Nil	Nil	Nil	Nil	Nil	Nil	NA	NA	NA
Prices - High	22	21⅝	17	11¾	7⅝	6⅝	NA	NA	NA	NA
- Low	5½	11⅛	11⅝	6⅜	5⅝	4¼	NA	NA	NA	NA
P/E Ratio - High	33	36	31	26	19	23	NA	NA	NA	NA
- Low	8	19	21	14	14	15	NA	NA	NA	NA
Income Statement Analysis (Million $)										
Revs.	275	190	109	73.1	61.5	51.9	47.1	NA	NA	NA
Oper. Inc.	39.0	30.2	21.6	15.2	12.4	11.0	10.0	NA	NA	NA
Depr.	10.0	6.9	4.6	3.4	3.1	3.3	3.5	NA	NA	NA
Int. Exp.	4.3	0.9	0.5	0.3	0.3	0.9	0.3	NA	NA	NA
Pretax Inc.	25.0	21.4	16.3	11.8	9.0	6.9	4.3	NA	NA	NA
Eff. Tax Rate	42%	42%	45%	43%	38%	47%	48%	NA	NA	NA
Net Inc.	14.5	12.5	9.0	6.7	5.8	3.6	2.3	NA	NA	NA
Balance Sheet & Other Fin. Data (Million $)										
Cash	17.7	8.1	4.1	5.7	6.3	5.3	NA	NA	NA	NA
Curr. Assets	154	70.8	36.1	27.2	21.0	15.7	NA	NA	NA	NA
Total Assets	452	170	102	68.2	60.2	48.8	NA	NA	NA	NA
Curr. Liab.	122	42.4	25.3	19.3	19.1	12.1	NA	NA	NA	NA
LT Debt	191	24.8	4.8	1.4	2.0	4.4	NA	NA	NA	NA
Common Eqty.	122	96.7	66.7	44.0	36.4	27.9	NA	NA	NA	NA
Total Cap.	316	124	71.6	45.4	38.4	32.3	NA	NA	NA	NA
Cap. Exp.	13.8	9.0	3.3	2.1	1.4	1.5	0.6	NA	NA	NA
Cash Flow	24.5	19.4	13.6	10.1	8.6	6.9	5.7	NA	NA	NA
Curr. Ratio	1.3	1.7	1.4	1.4	1.1	1.3	NA	NA	NA	NA
% LT Debt of Cap.	60.4	25.6	6.7	3.1	5.3	13.5	NA	NA	NA	NA
% Net Inc.of Revs.	5.3	6.6	8.3	9.2	9.4	7.0	4.8	NA	NA	NA
% Ret. on Assets	4.7	9.3	10.7	10.5	10.7	7.3	NA	NA	NA	NA
% Ret. on Equity	13.3	15.2	16.3	16.7	18.1	11.4	NA	NA	NA	NA

Data as orig reptd.; bef. results of disc opers/spec. items. Per share data adj. for stk. divs. Bold denotes diluted EPS (FASB 128)-prior periods restated. E-Estimated. NA-Not Available. NM-Not Meaningful. NR-Not Ranked.

Office—2 Pickwick Plaza, Greenwich, CT 06830. **Tel**—(203) 629-8888. **Website**—http://www.nfow.com **Chrmn, Pres & CEO**—W. E. Lipner. **CFO, Secy & Investor Contact**—Patrick G. Healy (203-618-8502). **Dirs**—W. A. Forbes, S. J. Gilbert, E. A. Hajim, W. E. Lipner, J. Sculley. **Transfer Agent & Registrar**—Fleet Bank, Providence, RI. **Incorporated**—in Delaware in 1991. **Empl**— 12,600. **S&P Analyst:** NJD.

STANDARD
&POOR'S
STOCK REPORTS

North American Vaccine

ASE Symbol **NVX**

In S&P SmallCap 600

09-OCT-99

Industry: Biotechnology

Summary: NVX is engaged in research, development and manufacture of vaccines to prevent human infectious diseases.

Quantitative Evaluations

Outlook (1 Lowest—5 Highest)
• **NA**

Fair Value
• **NA**

Risk
• **Average**

Earn./Div. Rank
• **C**

Technical Eval.
• **Bullish** since 9/99

Rel. Strength Rank (1 Lowest—99 Highest)
• **52**

Insider Activity
• **NA**

Recent Price • 6⅞
52 Wk Range • 16½-3¾

Yield • Nil
12-Mo. P/E • NM

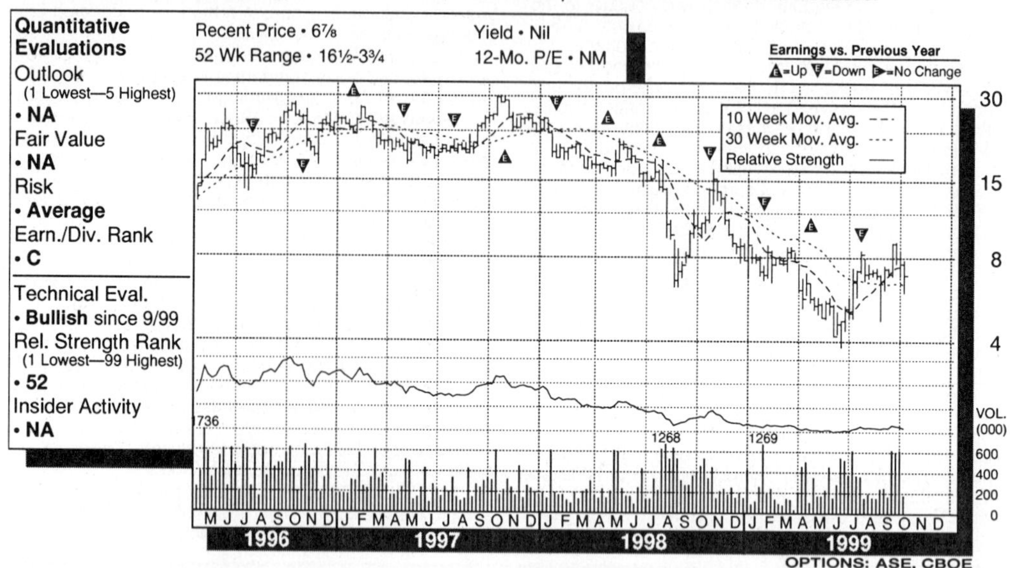

OPTIONS: ASE, CBOE

Business Profile - 07-OCT-99

In August 1999, NVX stated it intended to file for approval of its group C meningococcal vaccine in the United Kingdom during the fourth quarter of 1999. In June 1999, the company announced results of studies that showed its trivalent meningococcal A/B/C conjugate vaccine may elicit prolonged immunologic memory against meningitis. NVX also stated it expected to begin clinical trials on its group B meningococcal vaccine in the U.S. in late 1999. Also in June, the company reached an agreement to retire $8.4 million of its 6.5% convertible subordinated debt. In April 1999, NVX received German approval for its DTaP-IPV product, a combined diphtheria, tetanus, acellular pertussis and inactivated injectable polio vaccine.

Operational Review - 07-OCT-99

Total revenues in the six months ended June 30, 1999, advanced 55%, year to year, primarily from higher sales of Certiva (U.S. marketing commenced in October 1998), partially offset by lower collaborative revenues. Operating expenses were up only 2.7% (higher product, facility, and labor costs outweighed decreases in depreciation, consulting costs, and clinical trial spending) but still exceeded revenues; the operating loss was trimmed. However, following an increase in interest expense, mainly reflecting costs on conversion of debt, the net loss widened to $23.2 million ($0.72 a share), from $22.7 million ($0.71). Cash and equivalents totaled $2.1 million on June 30, 1999.

Stock Performance - 08-OCT-99

In the past 30 trading days, NVX's shares have increased 5%, compared to a 0.91% fall in the S&P 500. Average trading volume for the past five days was 34,680 shares, compared with the 40-day moving average of 79,172 shares.

Key Stock Statistics

Dividend Rate/Share	Nil	Shareholders	300
Shs. outstg. (M)	32.8	Market cap. (B)	$0.228
Avg. daily vol. (M)	0.115	Inst. holdings	22%
Tang. Bk. Value/Share	NM		
Beta	1.05		

Value of $10,000 invested 5 years ago: $ 6,306

Fiscal Year Ending Dec. 31

	1999	1998	1997	1996	1995	1994
Revenues (Million $)						
1Q	1.52	0.83	1.08	0.23	Nil	Nil
2Q	1.68	1.23	1.06	0.50	Nil	Nil
3Q	—	3.06	6.95	Nil	Nil	Nil
4Q	—	3.25	0.61	9.82	3.00	Nil
Yr.	—	8.38	9.70	10.55	3.00	—
Earnings Per Share ($)						
1Q	**-0.32**	**-0.37**	**-0.38**	-0.08	-0.12	-0.11
2Q	**-0.40**	**-0.34**	**-0.36**	-0.26	0.18	-0.13
3Q	—	**-0.32**	**-0.23**	-0.28	-0.20	-0.18
4Q	—	**-0.73**	**-0.41**	-0.01	-0.05	0.24
Yr.	—	**-1.76**	**-1.39**	**-0.63**	**-0.17**	**-0.14**

Next earnings report expected: early November

Dividend Data

No cash dividends have been paid. A two-for-one stock split was effected in 1992.

A Division of The McGraw-Hill Companies

North American Vaccine, Inc.

Business Summary - 07-OCT-99

North American Vaccine, Inc. (NVX) researches, develops, produces, and sells vaccines for the prevention of human infectious diseases. The company's first product is a patented, monocomponent acellular pertussis (aP) vaccine for the prevention of whooping cough. The aP vaccine has been combined with diphtheria and tetanus toxoids as a combined diphtheria-tetanus-acellular pertussis (DTaP) vaccine named Certiva in the U.S.

In July 1998, NVX was granted FDA approval to manufacture and market Certiva. In October 1998, marketing partner Abbott Labs (ABL) commenced U.S. sales of Certiva to private physicians and managed care markets. NVX sells Certiva directly to state governments and the Centers for Disease Control and Prevention.

Regulatory approvals were granted in 1996 in Sweden for a European formulation of Certiva and in Denmark for a DTaP-IPV vaccine, which combines the European formulation of Certiva with an enhanced, inactivated polio vaccine (IPV). Regulatory approval was also granted in Sweden in April 1997 for NVX's aPvaccine for children and young adolescents at risk for pertussis.

As of year-end 1998, the company was focused on three categories of vaccines: acellular pertussis, combination, and conjugate.

Acellular pertussis vaccines consisted of Certiva (designed to treat diphtheria, tetanus, and pertussis or whooping cough); aP (pertussis); and Amvax (tetanus, diphtheria, and pertussis).

Combination vaccines consisted of DTaP-IPV (designed to treat diphtheria, tetanus, pertussis, and polio); DTaP-HIB (diphtheria, tetanus, pertussis, and meningitis); and DTaP-IPV-HIB (diphtheria, tetanus, pertussis, polio, and meningitis).

Conjugate vaccines consisted of Group B Streptococcal (designed to treat neonatal sepsis and meningitis); Group B Meningococcal (meningitis); Group C Meningococcal (meningitis); Group A/C Meningococcal (meningitis); Group A/B/C Meningococcal (meningitis); Haemophilus Influenzae type b (meningitis); Group A Streptococcal (streptococcal pharyngitis, or strep throat, and skin infections); Pneumococcal (otitis media, or middle ear infection); and Pneumococcal (pneumococcal pneumonia).

Utilizing patented and proprietary technologies, the company is performing research on other adult and pediatric vaccines that are selected for development based on anticipated need for a particular product, the nature of the competition, and the ability of NVX to develop the product. NVX's R&D efforts are being conducted independently and in conjunction with governmental agencies, universities and corporate partners.

To maximize commercial success for its new products, NVX has been implementing a marketing strategy aimed at establishing marketing alliances in the U.S., Europe, and other territories, with well-established local partners on a country-by-country basis. The company has agreements with Abbot Laboratories, Pasteur Merieux Connaught, and BioChem Pharma.

Per Share Data ($) (Year Ended Dec. 31)	1998	1997	1996	1995	1994	1993	1992	1991	1990	1989
Tangible Bk. Val.	NM	NM	0.37	0.94	1.38	2.07	1.29	1.63	0.23	0.34
Cash Flow	-1.50	-1.04	-0.43	-0.09	-0.06	-0.36	-0.32	-0.17	0.03	-0.13
Earnings	-1.76	-1.39	-0.63	-0.17	-0.14	-0.44	-0.40	-0.26	-0.11	-0.14
Dividends	Nil	Nil	Nil	Nil	Nil	Nil	Nil	Nil	Nil	Nil
Payout Ratio	Nil	Nil	Nil	Nil	Nil	Nil	Nil	Nil	Nil	Nil
Prices - High	25	30¼	28⅜	15½	15½	12⅞	17⅛	14	3⅛	NA
- Low	6¼	17	11¾	5¼	7¾	7⅝	7	1⅛	1	NA
P/E Ratio - High	NM	NM	NM	NM	NM	NM	NM	NM	NM	NA
- Low	NM	NM	NM	NM	NM	NM	NA	NA	NA	NA
Income Statement Analysis (Million $)										
Revs.	8.4	9.7	10.5	3.0	Nil	0.1	1.5	0.9	3.7	1.9
Oper. Inc.	-31.4	-29.2	-16.4	-18.0	-12.5	-10.6	-9.7	-4.5	0.7	-1.0
Depr.	8.2	11.0	6.2	2.2	2.2	2.2	2.1	2.1	2.3	0.2
Int. Exp.	18.5	6.8	4.1	Nil	Nil	Nil	0.0	0.3	0.4	0.3
Pretax Inc.	-56.6	-43.8	-19.4	-5.0	-3.9	-12.1	-10.7	-5.8	-1.8	-2.5
Eff. Tax Rate	NM	NM	NM	NM	NM	NM	NM	NM	NM	NM
Net Inc.	-56.6	-43.8	-19.4	-5.0	-3.9	-12.1	-10.7	-5.8	-1.8	-2.5
Balance Sheet & Other Fin. Data (Million $)										
Cash	22.9	45.5	70.9	10.4	20.9	17.2	28.2	39.9	1.0	5.5
Curr. Assets	29.6	49.2	77.4	13.5	21.5	17.9	29.3	40.3	1.7	6.2
Total Assets	64.5	84.5	123	41.2	49.6	63.8	42.6	51.0	13.2	19.1
Curr. Liab.	12.3	14.0	10.9	7.8	5.4	2.1	2.5	3.1	3.4	6.0
LT Debt	111	87.8	91.9	Nil	Nil	Nil	Nil	Nil	0.5	2.0
Common Eqty.	-52.4	-23.9	14.8	28.2	40.4	57.5	35.7	43.1	4.4	6.2
Total Cap.	58.6	70.5	112	33.2	43.9	61.3	39.6	47.4	9.3	12.5
Cap. Exp.	2.3	2.1	21.1	10.3	6.4	1.6	4.7	1.6	8.5	4.8
Cash Flow	-48.4	-32.8	-13.3	-2.8	-1.7	-10.0	-8.6	-3.7	0.5	-2.3
Curr. Ratio	2.4	3.5	7.1	1.7	4.0	8.5	11.6	12.8	0.5	1.1
% LT Debt of Cap.	189.0	125.0	82.1	Nil	Nil	Nil	Nil	Nil	5.8	15.9
% Net Inc.of Revs.	NM	NM	NM	NM	NM	NM	NM	NM	NM	NM
% Ret. on Assets	NM	NM	NM	NM	NM	NM	NM	NM	NM	NM
% Ret. on Equity	NM	NM	NM	NM	NM	NM	NM	NM	NM	NM

Data as orig reptd.; bef. results of disc opers/spec. items. Per share data adj. for stk. divs. Bold denotes diluted EPS (FASB 128)-prior periods restated. E-Estimated. NA-Not Available. NM-Not Meaningful. NR-Not Ranked.

Office—10150 Old Columbia Road, Columbia, MD 21046. **Tel**—(410) 309-7100. **Website**—http://www.nava.com **Chrmn**—N. W. Flanzraich. **Co-Vice Chrmn**—F. Bellini, P. Frost. **Pres & CEO**—R. Chase. **VP-Fin**—L. J. Hineline. **Investor Contact**—Thomas Newberry (410) 309-7121. **Dirs**—F. Bellini, R. Chase, A. Cousineau, J. Deitcher, D. Dionne, G. Dionne, N. Flanzraich, P. Frost, L. Kasprick, F. Legault, R. Pfenniger. **Transfer Agent**—American Stock Transfer & Trust Co., NYC. **Incorporated**—in Canada in 1989. **Empl**— 308. **S&P Analyst:** Frank DiLorenzo

STANDARD
&POOR'S
STOCK REPORTS

Northwest Natural Gas

NASDAQ Symbol **NWNG**

In S&P SmallCap 600

09-OCT-99

Industry: Natural Gas

Summary: NWNG distributes natural gas in the Pacific Northwest and also explores for and produces natural gas.

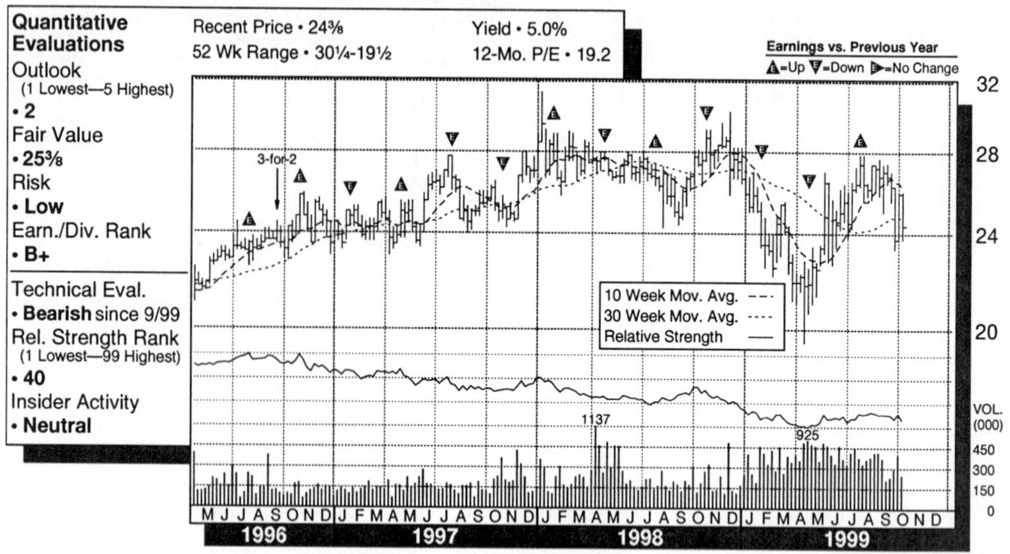

Business Profile - 20-SEP-99

Customer acquisition efforts continued to show success through the first half of 1999. New gas meter sets for residential and commercial customers, including both new construction and customer conversions, were ahead of the 1998 pace. The residential conversion market was up about 9% from 1998 levels. The company plans to continue to focus on distributing natural gas in its thriving service territory. Five-year performance goals include increasing earnings by 30%, with most of this expected to come from the core business of gas distribution. Although the sale and transportation of natural gas will remain its primary activity, NWNG hopes to sell a wider array of products and services by forming strategic alliances with other utilities.

Operational Review - 20-SEP-99

Gross operating revenues in the six months ended June 30, 1999, advanced 23%, year to year. Profitability benefited from weather in the first half of 1999 that was 14% colder than in the 1998 period, and 9% colder than average; this boosted EPS about $0.27 from the level of the 1998 first half, and $0.24 versus average weather conditions. Results included a credit of $0.09 a share from a litigation reserve; pretax climbed 37%. After taxes at 36.9%, versus 32.2%, net income was up 28%, to $34,827,000 ($1.33 a share, after preferred and preference dividends), from $27,279,000 ($1.08).

Stock Performance - 08-OCT-99

In the past 30 trading days, NWNG's shares have declined 9%, compared to a 0.91% fall in the S&P 500. Average trading volume for the past five days was 48,880 shares, compared with the 40-day moving average of 65,262 shares.

Key Stock Statistics

Dividend Rate/Share	1.22	Shareholders	12,300
Shs. outstg. (M)	25.0	Market cap. (B)	$0.609
Avg. daily vol. (M)	0.057	Inst. holdings	29%
Tang. Bk. Value/Share	16.59		
Beta	0.25		

Value of $10,000 invested 5 years ago: $ 14,295

Fiscal Year Ending Dec. 31

	1999	1998	1997	1996	1995	1994
Revenues (Million $)						
1Q	171.1	135.7	134.3	137.6	125.4	128.5
2Q	97.99	83.65	65.86	71.88	71.03	66.51
3Q	—	53.81	46.28	50.59	48.64	48.47
4Q	—	143.5	115.3	120.3	111.2	124.8
Yr.	—	416.7	361.8	380.3	356.3	368.3
Earnings Per Share ($)						
1Q	**0.93**	**0.97**	**1.04**	**1.00**	0.88	0.91
2Q	**0.40**	**0.14**	**0.07**	**0.22**	0.13	0.09
3Q	—	**-0.26**	**-0.14**	**-0.02**	-0.23	-0.23
4Q	—	**0.21**	**0.76**	**0.74**	0.86	0.86
Yr.	—	**1.02**	**1.76**	**1.94**	**1.60**	**1.61**

Next earnings report expected: early November

Dividend Data (Dividends have been paid since 1952.)

Amount ($)	Date Decl.	Ex-Div. Date	Stock of Record	Payment Date
0.305	Jan. 05	Jan. 27	Jan. 29	Feb. 12 '99
0.305	Apr. 07	Apr. 28	Apr. 30	May. 14 '99
0.305	Jul. 08	Jul. 28	Jul. 30	Aug. 13 '99
0.305	Oct. 07	Oct. 27	Oct. 29	Nov. 15 '99

Northwest Natural Gas Company

Business Summary - 20-SEP-99

Long associated with the lumber and paper industries, the Pacific Northwest is also attracting a different breed of business: companies that make computer chips instead of wood chips. These high-tech firms have brought thousands of new jobs to the region, fueling a population growth rate that exceeds the national average. With 78% of Oregon's population residing within its service area, natural gas distributor Northwest Natural Gas Co. (NWNG) is a major beneficiary of these emerging demographics. While many chipmakers have operated in the company's territories for years, the scheduled addition of billions of dollars in new semiconductor and silicon wafer plants promises to sustain the region's rapid growth in the years ahead.

NWNG distributes natural gas to about 485,000 customers (at March 31, 1999) in 16 Oregon counties and three Washington counties encompassing the Portland-Vancouver metropolitan area, the Willamette Valley, the northern Oregon coast and the Columbia River Gorge. NWNG typically derives 75% or more of its utility operating revenues from gas sales to weather-sensitive residential and commercial customers. Variations in temperature have a profound impact on sales to these customers, and in 1998 weather conditions in NWNG's service area were warmer than they were the year before. However, natural gas sales volumes to residential and commercial customers increased in 1998, largely due to new customer acquisitions.

In 1998, NWNG maintained its competitive price advantage over electricity. Throughout the year, natural gas rates continued to be substantially lower than rates for electricity provided by the investor-owned utilities. The company derived 94% of its gas deliveries and 93% of its utility operating revenues from Oregon customers, with the balance from Washington customers. In October 1998, the company filed its first general rate case in Oregon since 1989. The filing proposes a revenue increase of $14.7 million per year through rate increases averaging 3.8% to cover costs of the company's new customer information system, the Mist Storage expansion, and the Year 2000 project.

The advent of competition and customer choice is forcing electric and gas utilities alike to adopt new ways of doing business. Although the sale and transportation of natural gas will remain its primary activity, NWNG hopes to sell a wider array of products and services by forming strategic alliances with other utilities. In July 1997, NWNG announced the formation of an alliance with PacifiCorp to jointly market natural gas and electric commodity and energy services to commercial and industrial customers in Oregon and Washington.

Per Share Data ($) (Year Ended Dec. 31)	1998	1997	1996	1995	1994	1993	1992	1991	1990	1989
Tangible Bk. Val.	16.59	16.02	15.37	14.55	2.13	13.08	12.41	12.23	12.61	12.04
Earnings	1.02	1.76	1.97	1.61	1.63	1.74	0.74	0.67	1.62	1.58
Dividends	1.22	1.21	1.20	1.18	1.17	1.17	1.15	1.13	1.10	1.07
Payout Ratio	120%	68%	61%	73%	72%	67%	155%	167%	68%	68%
Prices - High	30 3/4	31 3/8	25 7/8	22 7/8	24 3/8	25 7/8	22 5/8	22 3/8	17 7/8	17 7/8
- Low	24 1/4	23	20 7/8	18 3/8	18 7/8	19	17 1/8	16 1/2	13 7/8	12 1/2
P/E Ratio - High	30	18	13	14	15	15	31	33	11	11
- Low	24	13	11	11	12	11	23	25	9	8
Income Statement Analysis (Million $)										
Revs.	417	362	380	356	368	359	274	296	296	261
Depr.	56.5	44.6	43.0	40.6	38.1	39.7	33.0	33.6	28.0	23.2
Maint.	NA	NA	NA	NA	NA	NA	NA	NA	NA	7.5
Fxd. Chgs. Cov.	2.0	2.8	3.3	3.0	2.9	3.0	1.7	1.5	2.4	2.2
Constr. Credits	1.4	1.7	0.8	0.6	0.3	0.2	NM	Nil	NM	NM
Eff. Tax Rate	31%	33%	37%	37%	37%	37%	31%	14%	31%	35%
Net Inc.	27.3	43.1	46.8	38.1	35.5	37.6	15.8	14.4	30.7	28.4
Balance Sheet & Other Fin. Data (Million $)										
Gross Prop.	1,299	1,165	1,055	969	908	840	779	722	669	623
Cap. Exp.	80.0	116	83.4	67.2	77.7	70.4	60.7	58.4	50.5	57.6
Net Prop.	895	798	719	660	629	585	546	515	485	459
Capitalization:										
LT Debt	367	344	272	280	291	273	254	253	215	221
% LT Debt	46	46	41	44	48	48	46	51	46	48
Pfd.	25.0	37.4	38.7	39.8	42.2	44.0	55.0	31.0	32.1	33.9
% Pfd.	3.11	5.00	5.90	6.20	6.90	7.60	10	6.20	6.90	7.30
Common	412	366	347	324	274	259	242	216	219	206
% Common	51	49	53	50	45	45	44	43	47	45
Total Cap.	984	900	793	775	734	694	601	552	524	519
% Oper. Ratio	84.0	81.0	32.8	85.0	85.9	82.8	84.4	86.6	81.6	82.4
% Earn. on Net Prop.	9.2	9.1	9.5	8.3	8.5	10.9	9.4	7.9	11.6	10.5
% Return On Revs.	6.6	11.9	12.3	10.7	9.6	10.5	5.7	4.9	10.4	10.9
% Return On Invest. Capital	8.6	8.3	9.4	8.5	8.5	9.7	8.6	7.6	10.5	9.7
% Return On Com. Equity	7.0	11.3	13.1	11.8	12.2	13.7	5.8	5.4	13.1	13.3

Data as orig. reptd.; bef. results of disc. opers. and/or spec. items. Per share data adj. for stk. divs. as of ex-div. date. Bold denotes diluted EPS (FASB 128). E-Estimated. NA-Not Available. NM-Not Meaningful. NR-Not Ranked.

Office—One Pacific Square, 220 N.W. Second Ave., Portland, OR 97209. **Tel**—(503) 226-4211. **Website**—http://www.nwnatural.com **Pres & CEO**—R. G. Reiten. **SVP & CFO**—B. R. De Bolt. **Treas**—S. P. Feltz. **Secy**—C. J. Rue. **Investor Contact**—James Boehlke (503-721-2451). **Dirs**—M. A. Arnstad, T. E. Dewey, Jr., T. R. Hamachek, R. B. Keller, W. D. Kuni, R. C. Pape, R. G. Reiten, R. L. Ridgley, D. A. Sangrey, M. C. Teppola, R. F. Tromley, B. R. Whiteley. **Transfer Agent & Registrar**—Co.'s office. **Incorporated**—in Oregon in 1910. **Empl**— 1,303. **S&P Analyst:** J.J.S.

STANDARD
&POOR'S
STOCK REPORTS

NorthWestern Corp.

NYSE Symbol **NOR**

In S&P SmallCap 600

09-OCT-99

Industry: Electric Companies

Summary: This company provides diversified energy, telecommunications, heating, ventilation, and air conditioning (HVAC) services, and other nonenergy related products and services.

Quantitative Evaluations

Outlook (1 Lowest—5 Highest) • **2⁻**

Fair Value • **22¾**

Risk • **NA**

Earn./Div. Rank • **A**

Technical Eval. • **Bearish** since 9/99

Rel. Strength Rank (1 Lowest—99 Highest) • **48**

Insider Activity • **Favorable**

Recent Price • 23½
52 Wk Range • 27⅛-22⅜
Yield • 4.4%
12-Mo. P/E • 15.1

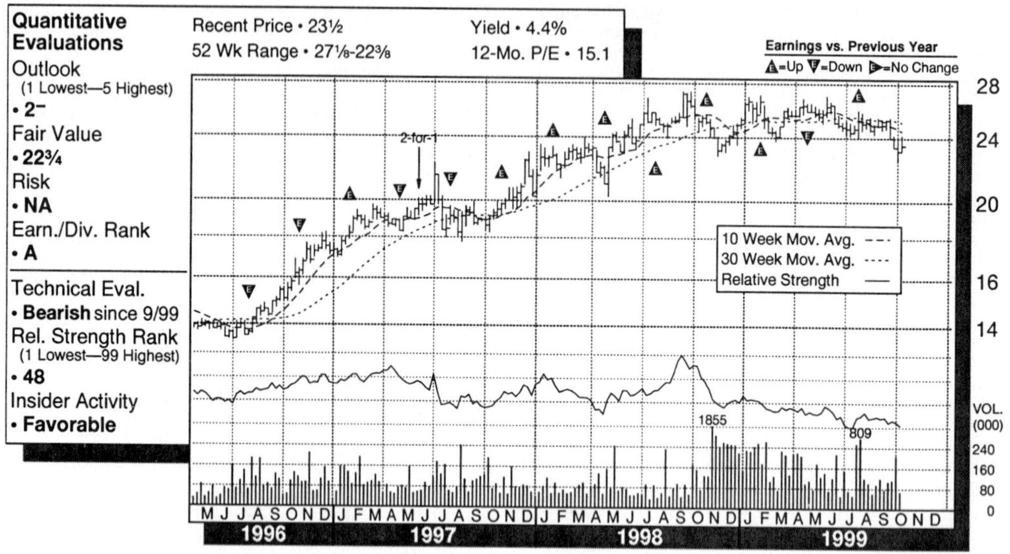

Business Profile - 03-SEP-99

In May 1999, NorthWestern said it expected another year of double-digit bottom-line growth in 1999. The company noted that its Exanets and Blue Dot business units had provided an additional $500 million in total revenue since late 1997, enabling NOR to participate in two of the fastest-growing U.S. customer service and solutions sectors. Also in May, management said that both Blue Dot and Expanets were expected to generate strong cash flow and earnings in 1999. In February 1999, the company changed the name of its Communications Systems USA unit, a national provider of integrated communication and data solutions and network services, to Expanets.

Operational Review - 03-SEP-99

Operating revenues in the six months ended June 30, 1999, advanced 108%, year to year. Profits from electric and natural gas operations and HVAC and communications operations improved, but propane operating income was penalized by the impact of a warmer heating season in the company's propane markets. Pretax income increased 38%. After taxes at 32.1%, versus 27.4%, and sharply lower minority interest, net income climbed 51%, to $21,717,000 ($0.78 a share, on 29% more shares), from $14,359,000 ($0.73).

Stock Performance - 08-OCT-99

In the past 30 trading days, NOR's shares have declined 7%, compared to a 0.91% fall in the S&P 500. Average trading volume for the past five days was 13,080 shares, compared with the 40-day moving average of 21,197 shares.

Key Stock Statistics

Dividend Rate/Share	1.03	Shareholders	8,100
Shs. outstg. (M)	23.1	Market cap. (B)	$0.543
Avg. daily vol. (M)	0.024	Inst. holdings	35%
Tang. Bk. Value/Share	NM		
Beta	0.00		

Value of $10,000 invested 5 years ago: $ 21,818

Fiscal Year Ending Dec. 31

	1999	1998	1997	1996	1995	1994
Revenues (Million $)						
1Q	509.4	284.2	284.4	97.22	50.75	55.46
2Q	595.9	184.1	165.4	56.68	40.11	33.76
3Q	—	195.6	185.1	49.71	45.55	30.20
4Q	—	378.2	283.1	140.4	68.56	37.85
Yr.	—	1,187	918.1	344.0	205.0	157.3
Earnings Per Share ($)						
1Q	**0.56**	**0.58**	0.55	0.70	0.46	0.52
2Q	**0.22**	**0.15**	0.14	0.14	0.20	0.14
3Q	—	**0.20**	0.17	0.03	0.16	0.09
4Q	—	**0.48**	**0.45**	0.41	0.29	0.25
Yr.	—	**1.44**	**1.31**	**1.28**	**1.11**	1.00

Next earnings report expected: late October

Dividend Data (Dividends have been paid since 1947.)

Amount ($)	Date Decl.	Ex-Div. Date	Stock of Record	Payment Date
0.258	Oct. 08	Nov. 10	Nov. 15	Dec. 01 '98
0.258	Feb. 04	Feb. 10	Feb. 15	Mar. 01 '99
0.258	May. 06	May. 12	May. 15	Jun. 01 '99
0.258	Aug. 05	Aug. 11	Aug. 15	Sep. 01 '99

NorthWestern Corporation

Business Summary - 03-SEP-99

NorthWestern and its partner entities provide services and solutions to more than one million customers throughout America. NOR's businesses distribute propane, sell and electric and natural gas services, provide network communication solutions and services, and offer air conditioning, heating, plumbing and related services.

Blue Dot Services (formerly ServiCenter USA) is a national provider of maintenance, repair and replacement services for heating ventilation and air conditioning (HVAC), plumbing and related systems and major appliances in homes and small businesses. The unit seeks to acquire local service providers in major markets. In each new market that it enters, Blue Dot seeks to purchase an established leading local company with a revenue mix primarily of residential and light commercial maintenance, repair and replacement sales. By the end of 1998, Blue Dot had acquired 28 companies, with 1998 revenues of $210 million, and 398,000 customers in 18 states.

CornerStone Propane Partners, L.P. is the fourth largest U.S. retail propane distributor. Cornerstone is primarily a distributor for residential, commercial, industrial, agricultural and other retail uses. Cornerstone is a wholesale marketer and distributor of propane, natural gas liquids, and crude oil. It also repairs and maintains propane heating systems. In addition, Cornerstone sells, propane-related supplies, appliances, and other equipment. At the end of 1998, it served more than 440,000 customers. Cornerstone aims to achieve balanced growth through small and large acquisitions, internal growth, and startups of new customer service centers. During 1998, 16 new companies joined CornerStone.

Expanets (formerly Communications Systems USA) provides communication solutions to businesses by offering voice and data networking solutions and network services to customers. As of the end of 1998, Expanets had acquired 18 leading private communication, data and network entities, with revenues of about $250 million. Expanets believes it can benefit from developments and technology, increased demand for complex data networking, call centers, messaging systems, and voice, data and video integration. The company aims to provide customers a single source of enterprise communications solutions.

NorthWestern Public Service provides electric and natural gas service to customers in the upper Midwest. In 1998, it sold electricity to 198 communities in South Dakota, with a population of more than 98,000. It also sells natural gas service in Nebraska and South Dakota. Gas operations cover 22 counties in South Dakota and Nebraska. The company owns and operates natural gas distribution systems serving more than 39,000 clients in eastern South Dakota. In Nebraska, it serves nearly 40,000 natural gas customers.

Per Share Data ($) (Year Ended Dec. 31)	1998	1997	1996	1995	1994	1993	1992	1991	1990	1989
Tangible Bk. Val.	NM	NM	1.88	5.81	7.47	7.14	6.97	6.89	6.71	6.34
Earnings	1.44	1.31	1.28	1.10	1.00	0.98	0.89	0.94	1.11	1.02
Dividends	1.24	1.16	0.89	0.86	0.83	0.81	0.80	0.77	0.74	0.71
Payout Ratio	86%	89%	70%	78%	84%	83%	90%	82%	66%	69%
Prices - High	27 3/8	23 1/2	18 1/4	14 1/4	14 7/8	16 3/4	14 3/8	13 1/2	10 1/4	10 1/8
- Low	20 1/4	17	13 3/8	12 1/8	12 1/4	13 1/8	11 3/4	10 1/8	8 3/8	8 1/4
P/E Ratio - High	19	18	14	13	15	17	16	14	9	10
- Low	14	13	10	11	12	13	13	11	8	8
Income Statement Analysis (Million $)										
Revs.	1,187	918	344	205	157	153	119	123	114	116
Depr.	42.6	31.2	19.4	14.6	12.4	11.6	11.1	10.5	10.2	10.0
Maint.	Nil	5.9	5.9	6.0	6.2	6.4	5.9	5.8	5.2	5.5
Fxd. Chgs. Cov.	2.2	2.2	3.1	3.3	3.4	3.5	3.9	4.7	4.9	4.7
Constr. Credits	Nil	Nil	0.2	0.5	0.1	Nil	Nil	Nil	Nil	Nil
Eff. Tax Rate	30%	28%	37%	34%	34%	31%	28%	30%	26%	27%
Net Inc.	30.4	26.3	26.1	19.3	15.4	15.2	13.7	14.8	17.5	16.1
Balance Sheet & Other Fin. Data (Million $)										
Gross Prop.	826	721	682	487	390	369	352	335	316	303
Cap. Exp.	22.6	22.4	35.2	29.6	22.7	19.7	18.5	23.0	14.9	12.4
Net Prop.	629	546	519	337	251	238	230	222	209	204
Capitalization:										
LT Debt	676	425	424	213	127	127	106	92.0	78.0	79.0
% LT Debt	70	71	52	53	52	53	49	45	42	44
Pfd.	3.8	3.8	38.8	38.0	2.6	2.7	2.3	5.6	5.8	6.0
% Pfd.	0.39	0.60	4.80	9.40	1.10	1.10	1.20	2.80	3.10	3.30
Common	282	167	164	153	115	110	107	106	103	97.0
% Common	29	28	20	38	47	46	50	52	55	53
Total Cap.	1,425	910	814	458	292	286	270	259	244	238
% Oper. Ratio	94.9	94.1	85.3	86.4	85.7	86.8	83.4	83.1	82.7	83.4
% Earn. on Net Prop.	12.6	11.1	11.8	9.5	9.2	8.7	8.7	9.6	9.6	9.5
% Return On Revs.	2.6	2.9	7.6	4.5	9.8	9.9	11.5	12.1	15.3	13.9
% Return On Invest. Capital	7.5	6.4	8.9	8.3	8.7	8.8	8.3	8.8	10.1	9.8
% Return On Com. Equity	13.5	15.8	16.2	14.2	13.1	13.7	12.8	13.7	17.0	16.2

Data as orig reptd.; bef. results of disc opers/spec. items. Per share data adj. for stk. divs. Bold denotes diluted EPS (FASB 128)-prior periods restated. E-Estimated. NA-Not Available. NM-Not Meaningful. NR-Not Ranked.

Office—125 S. Dakota Ave., Suite 1100, Sioux Falls, SD 57104. **Tel**—(605) 978-2908. **Website**—http://www.northwestern.com **Chrmn & CEO**—M. D. Lewis. **Pres & COO**—R. R. Hylland. **Treas**—D. A. Monaghan. **VP-Secy**—A. D. Dietrich. **Investor Contact**—Rogene Thaden. **Dirs**—R. G. Darcy, G. G. Drook, R. R. Hylland, J. W. Johnson, A. J. Kurtenbach, L. F. Ness, G. Olson, B. I. Smith. **Transfer Agents & Registrars**—Norwest Bank Minnesota, St. Paul; Co.'s office. **Incorporated**—in Delaware in 1923. **Empl**— 6,500. **S&P Analyst:** J.J.S.

STANDARD & POOR'S
STOCK REPORTS

Noven Pharmaceuticals

NASDAQ Symbol **NOVN**

In S&P SmallCap 600

09-OCT-99

Industry: Health Care (Drugs - Generic & Other)

Summary: This company is a leader in the development and commercialization of transdermal and transmucosal drug delivery systems.

Quantitative Evaluations

Outlook (1 Lowest—5 Highest) • **NA**

Fair Value • **NA**

Risk • **High**

Earn./Div. Rank • **C**

Technical Eval. • **Neutral** since 9/99

Rel. Strength Rank (1 Lowest—99 Highest) • **96**

Insider Activity • **Neutral**

Recent Price • 9⅜ | Yield • Nil
52 Wk Range • 9¾-4 | 12-Mo. P/E • 72.1

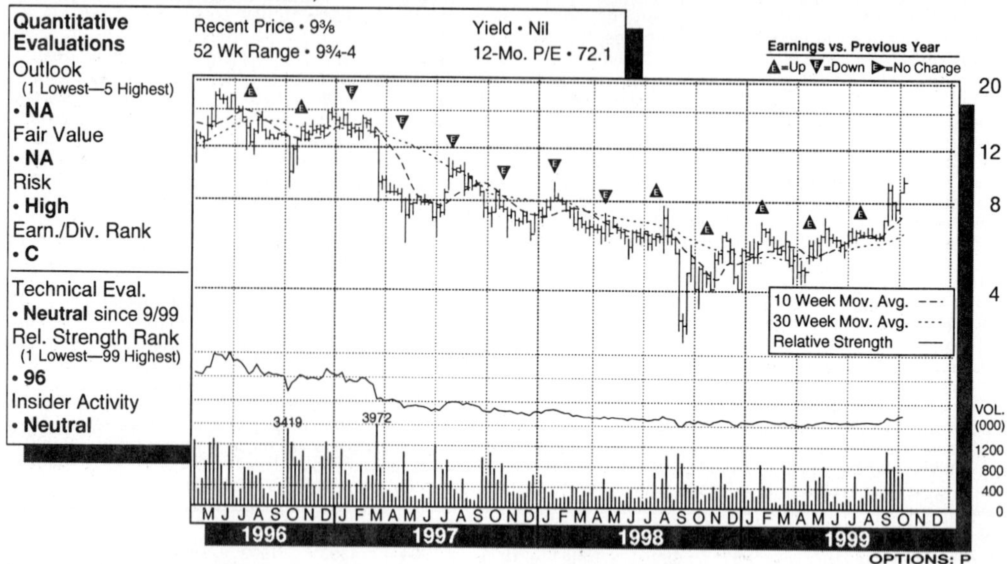

Business Profile - 09-SEP-99

In May 1999, Noven announced it was developing a transdermal patch capable of delivering a therapeutic dose of methylphenidate for up to 24 hours as a potential treatment for Attention Deficit Hyperactivity Disorder. Also in May, the company initiated the U.S. launch of Vivelle-Dot, the world's smallest transdermal estrogen delivery system, for treating symptoms of menopause. This product, approved in January 1999 by the FDA, will be marketed through Vivelle Ventures LLC (VV), a joint venture between Noven and Novartis Pharmaceuticals Corp. (NOV). In February 1999, the company announced that VV and Novartis will co-promote NOV's Miacalcin Nasal Spray in the U.S. for the treatment of osteoporosis in post menopausal women.

Operational Review - 09-SEP-99

Total revenues in the six months ended June 30, 1999, increased 67%, year to year, primarily reflecting the launch of Vivelle-Dot in May 1999, and sales of CombiPatch, which was launched by Rhone-Poulenc Rorer in September 1998. Gross margins widened, mainly due to a product mix shift and improved manufacturing efficiency. Following 21% lower R&D spending, related to fewer clinical studies, and a 38% decrease in marketing, general, and administrative expenses, principally due to lower sales and marketing costs for Dentipatch, net income of $1.7 million ($0.08, on 5.5% more shares), contrasted with a net loss of $4.8 million ($0.24).

Stock Performance - 08-OCT-99

In the past 30 trading days, NOVN's shares have increased 53%, compared to a 0.91% fall in the S&P 500. Average trading volume for the past five days was 144,560 shares, compared with the 40-day moving average of 131,269 shares.

Key Stock Statistics

Dividend Rate/Share	Nil	Shareholders	6,692
Shs. outstg. (M)	21.5	Market cap. (B)	$0.202
Avg. daily vol. (M)	0.150	Inst. holdings	23%
Tang. Bk. Value/Share	1.33		
Beta	1.44		

Value of $10,000 invested 5 years ago: $ 6,637

Fiscal Year Ending Dec. 31

	1999	1998	1997	1996	1995	1994
Revenues (Million $)						
1Q	7.48	2.55	1.68	5.56	1.24	0.95
2Q	7.49	6.40	4.16	5.75	2.04	1.17
3Q	—	5.02	5.98	5.78	3.33	1.12
4Q	—	7.88	3.37	4.58	5.53	2.80
Yr.	—	21.84	15.19	20.47	12.18	6.04
Earnings Per Share ($)						
1Q	**0.03**	**-0.16**	**-0.14**	-0.03	-0.09	-0.06
2Q	**0.05**	**-0.08**	**-0.14**	0.01	-0.11	-0.07
3Q	—	**0.01**	Nil	0.03	-0.09	-0.07
4Q	—	**0.03**	**-0.23**	-0.11	-0.05	-0.08
Yr.	—	**-0.19**	**-0.47**	**-0.10**	**-0.34**	**-0.28**

Next earnings report expected: early November

Dividend Data

No dividends have been paid.

Noven Pharmaceuticals, Inc.

Business Summary - 09-SEP-99

Noven Pharmaceutical's strategy is to become the world's premier developer, manufacturer, and marketer of proprietary transdermal and transmucosal drug delivery systems, with a therapeutic focus on treating hormone deficiencies, cardiovascular disease, central nervous system disorders, and pain-related conditions.

Noven's patented drug delivery system utilizes a thin, medicated adhesive patch that is applied to the skin or the mucosal areas of the mouth. Medication is delivered through human tissue and into the bloodstream for an extended period of time. Advantages of this delivery technology over oral or parenteral drug administration may include non-invasive administration, controlled delivery over a prolonged length of time, improved patient compliance, and an improved safety profile.

Vivelle (Menorest outside the U.S. and Canada), a prescription transdermal estrogen patch, is approved in the U.S. and 38 other countries as a treatment for menopausal symptoms. Vivelle is also approved in 36 foreign countries for the prevention of osteoporosis. In May 1998, Noven and Novartis entered into a joint venture, named Vivelle Ventures LLC (VV), to market Vivelle in the U.S. Outside the U.S. Novartis has Canadian marketing rights and Rhone-Poulenc Rorer (RPR) has rights to all other territories.

In January 1999, Noven received FDA approval to market its second-generation transdermal patch, Vivelle-Dot, for the treatment of menopause. In May 1999, VV commenced U.S. marketing of this product.

Although benefits of estrogen replacement therapy include menopausal symptom control, osteoporosis prevention, and cardiovascular protection, women who have an intact uterus may increase their risk of uterine cancer when using estrogen alone. The combination of estrogen and progestogen may reduce this risk. Realizing this, Noven developed a combination therapy for hormone replacement. In 1998, CombiPatch, a transdermal patch containing estrogen and progestogen, was approved in the U.S. and 13 other countries for treating menopausal conditions. RPR markets CombiPatch in the U.S. and under the tradename Estalis in Sweden.

A problem with orally-administered drug dosages, such as tablet and capsule formulations, is that the active therapeutic compounds are often broken down and inactivated within the stomach and intestines. Transdermal delivery may also be unsuitable since certain drug molecules are too large to effectively pass through skin tissue. Transmucosal delivery may offer a superior alternative since agents may be passed through tissue within the mouth and reach the bloodstream in a more direct manner. This delivery method may also be less invasive than injectable drug administration.

DentiPatch, Noven's first transmucosal delivery system, was approved by the FDA in May 1996 as a topical anesthetic for treating pain induced by oral injections and soft tissue dental procedures. Noven is marketing this product through its own sales fo rce in the U.S.

Per Share Data ($) (Year Ended Dec. 31)	1998	1997	1996	1995	1994	1993	1992	1991	1990	1989
Tangible Bk. Val.	1.24	1.38	1.74	1.87	2.31	1.23	1.30	NA	NA	NA
Cash Flow	-0.14	-0.42	-0.06	-0.27	-0.23	-0.16	-0.19	NA	NA	NA
Earnings	-0.19	-0.47	-0.10	-0.34	-0.28	-0.21	-0.21	-0.25	NA	NA
Dividends	Nil	Nil	Nil	Nil	Nil	Nil	Nil	Nil	NA	NA
Payout Ratio	Nil	Nil	Nil	Nil	Nil	Nil	Nil	Nil	NA	NA
Prices - High	9¼	16⅛	18¾	12⅜	19¼	15½	13½	9¼	NA	NA
- Low	2⅝	5¾	8¾	6½	10¼	10	6¾	1¾	NA	NA
P/E Ratio - High	NM	NM	NM	NM	NM	NM	NM	NM	NA	NA
- Low	NM	NM	NM	NM	NM	NM	NM	NM	NA	NA
Income Statement Analysis (Million $)										
Revs.	21.8	14.3	20.5	10.5	4.5	3.1	1.9	0.1	NA	NA
Oper. Inc.	-3.3	-9.5	-2.3	-7.0	-5.6	-3.5	-3.8	NA	NA	NA
Depr.	1.2	1.0	0.9	1.3	0.9	0.8	0.2	NA	NA	NA
Int. Exp.	Nil	NA	Nil	Nil	Nil	Nil	Nil	NA	NA	NA
Pretax Inc.	-4.1	-9.6	-2.0	-6.6	-4.9	-3.3	-3.0	-3.1	NA	NA
Eff. Tax Rate	NM	NM	NM	Nil	Nil	Nil	Nil	Nil	NA	NA
Net Inc.	-4.1	-9.6	-2.0	-6.6	-4.9	-3.3	-3.0	-3.1	NA	NA
Balance Sheet & Other Fin. Data (Million $)										
Cash	5.6	11.3	19.1	24.0	35.5	14.7	NA	NA	NA	NA
Curr. Assets	15.3	21.2	26.9	31.9	37.6	16.0	NA	NA	NA	NA
Total Assets	40.2	38.2	44.2	48.6	53.7	29.9	23.3	3.5	NA	NA
Curr. Liab.	6.2	2.5	2.1	4.3	2.6	1.1	NA	NA	NA	NA
LT Debt	Nil	Nil	Nil	Nil	Nil	Nil	Nil	Nil	NA	NA
Common Eqty.	28.3	29.9	36.1	38.0	44.5	20.7	20.7	1.6	NA	NA
Total Cap.	28.3	29.9	36.1	38.0	44.5	20.7	20.7	1.6	NA	NA
Cap. Exp.	1.5	0.6	1.1	NA	2.8	3.2	0.3	NA	NA	NA
Cash Flow	-2.9	-8.5	-1.1	-5.3	-4.0	-2.5	-2.8	NA	NA	NA
Curr. Ratio	2.5	8.6	12.8	7.4	14.7	14.0	NA	NA	NA	NA
% LT Debt of Cap.	Nil	Nil	Nil	Nil	Nil	Nil	Nil	Nil	NA	NA
% Net Inc.of Revs.	NM	NM	NM	NM	NM	NM	NM	NM	NA	NA
% Ret. on Assets	NM	NM	NM	NM	NM	NM	NM	NM	NA	NA
% Ret. on Equity	NM	NM	NM	NM	NM	NM	NM	NM	NA	NA

Data as orig reptd.; bef. results of disc opers/spec. items. Per share data adj. for stk. divs. Bold denotes diluted EPS (FASB 128)-prior periods restated. E-Estimated. NA-Not Available. NM-Not Meaningful. NR-Not Ranked.

Office—11960 S.W. 144th St., Miami, FL 33186. **Tel**—(305) 253-5099. **Website**—http://www.noven.com **Chrmn**—S. Sablotsky. **CEO & Pres**—R. C. Strauss. **VP-CFO & Investor Contact**—James B. Messiry (305) 253-1916. **Secy**—Graciela M. Lopez.**Dirs**—S. H. Becher, S. Braginsky, R. C. Bryce, L. J. Dubow, M. Goldberg, S. Sablotsky, R. C. Strauss. **Transfer Agent & Registrar**—American Stock Transfer & Trust Co., NYC. **Incorporated**—in Delaware in 1987. **Empl**— 190. **S&P Analyst:** Frank DiLorenzo

STANDARD
&POOR'S
STOCK REPORTS

O'Reilly Automotive

NASDAQ Symbol **ORLY**

In S&P SmallCap 600

23-OCT-99 **Industry:** Retail (Specialty)

Summary: This company is one the largest U.S. retailers of car parts and accessories.

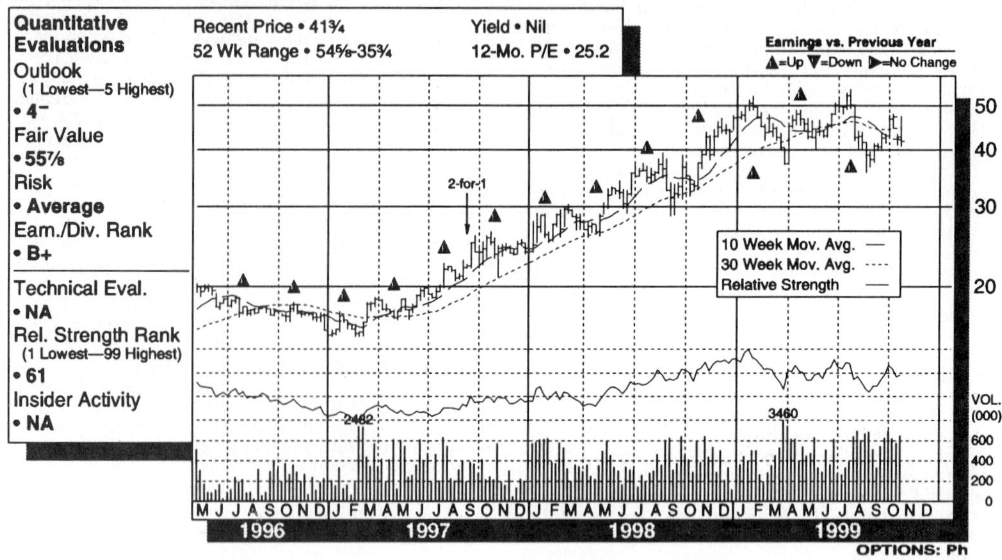

Business Profile - 13-OCT-99

The company intends to continue to aggressively open new stores, in order to achieve greater penetration of existing markets, and to expand into new, contiguous markets. In addition to 24 net new stores opened in the first half of 1999, ORLY planned to open 56 net new stores in the balance of 1999, and about 100 stores in 2000. Nearly all sites for proposed 1999 store openings, and a majority of sites for proposed 2000 openings, have been identified. The company seeks to cluster stores in geographic areas, in order to achieve economies of scale in management, advertising and distribution. In March 1999, ORLY filed with the SEC for the sale of 3,340,000 common shares (including 340,000 for selling shareholders), with company proceeds to be used to repay debt. The O'Reilly family owns about 33% of the common shares.

Operational Review - 13-OCT-99

Sales in the six months ended June 30, 1999, advanced 28%, year to year, reflecting 24 net additional stores opened during the period, and gains in same-store product sales. Margins widened, on well controlled purchasing, operating, and SG&A costs. With only slightly higher other expense, pretax income surged 52%. After taxes at 38.3%, versus 38.0%, net income was up 51%, to $20,372,000 ($0.86 a share, on 9.5% more shares), from $13,491,000 ($0.62).

Stock Performance - 22-OCT-99

In the past 30 trading days, ORLY's shares have increased 5%, compared to a 4% fall in the S&P 500. Average trading volume for the past five days was 173,400 shares, compared with the 40-day moving average of 211,559 shares.

Key Stock Statistics

Dividend Rate/Share	Nil	Shareholders	10,000
Shs. outstg. (M)	25.3	Market cap. (B)	$ 1.1
Avg. daily vol. (M)	0.223	Inst. holdings	58%
Tang. Bk. Value/Share	10.23		
Beta	0.78		

Value of $10,000 invested 5 years ago: $ 29,482

Fiscal Year Ending Dec. 31

	1999	1998	1997	1996	1995	1994
Revenues (Million $)						
1Q	166.4	118.3	68.47	55.32	42.77	36.70
2Q	196.1	165.2	82.45	68.78	50.64	43.30
3Q	—	172.8	87.52	70.43	57.18	44.69
4Q	—	160.0	77.96	64.71	50.90	42.36
Yr.	—	616.3	316.4	259.2	201.5	167.1
Earnings Per Share ($)						
1Q	**0.39**	**0.27**	**0.24**	**0.20**	0.17	0.14
2Q	**0.46**	**0.35**	**0.29**	**0.24**	0.20	0.17
3Q	—	**0.38**	**0.31**	**0.26**	0.23	0.18
4Q	—	**0.42**	**0.25**	**0.21**	0.19	0.14
Yr.	—	**1.42**	**1.09**	**0.90**	**0.79**	**0.64**

Next earnings report expected: late October

Dividend Data

No cash dividends have been paid. A two-for-one common stock split was effected in September 1997.

A Division of The McGraw-Hill Companies

O'Reilly Automotive, Inc.

Business Summary - 13-OCT-99

O'Reilly Automotive, Inc. (ORLY), founded in 1957 by Charles F. O'Reilly and his son, Charles H. "Chub" O'Reilly, Sr., began as a single store in Springfield, MO. The company has since become one of the largest U.S. specialty retailers of automotive aftermarket parts, tools, supplies, equipment and accessories. At December 31, 1998, ORLY operated 491 stores (259 a year earlier), in Texas (174), Missouri (113), Oklahoma (87), Kansas (47), Iowa (22), Arkansas (17), Louisiana (17), Nebraska (13) and Illinois (1).

In 1998, 57% of sales were to the do-it-yourself market and 43% to professional installers.

The stores carry an extensive product line of new and remanufactured automotive hard parts (alternators, starters, fuel pumps, water pumps, brake shoes and pads), maintenance items (oil, antifreeze, fluids, engine additives, appearance products), accessories (floor mats, seat covers), and a complete line of autobody paint, automotive tools and professional service equipment. Merchandise consists of nationally recognized brands: A.C. Delco, Prestone, Quaker State, STP and Turtle Wax. ORLY also carries a wide variety of private label products under the O'Reilly Auto Parts, Super-Start, BrakeBest, and other brands. ORLY offers engine machining services through its O'Reilly stores, but does not sell tires or perform automotive repairs or installations.

In 1998, the weighted average product sales per stores amounted to $1,368,000, up from $1,306,000 in 1997. Sales per sq. ft. were $238, versus $236 in 1997.

The company believes most of its stores are destination stores that generate their own traffic, rather than relying on traffic created by the presence of other stores in the immediate vicinity. Consequently, most stores are free-standing buildings situated on or near major traffic thoroughfares, and offer ample parking and easy customer access.

In January 1998, ORLY acquired Hi-Lo Automotive, Inc., for about $49.3 million in cash. The acquisition added 182 stores in Texas, Louisiana and California to ORLY's base of retail stores.

The company believes that, because it aggressively pursues both the do-it-yourself consumer and the professional installer, it can target a larger base of consumers of automotive aftermarket parts; capitalize on existing retail and distribution infrastructure; profitably operate not only in large metropolitan markets, but also in less densely populated areas which typically attract fewer competitors; and enhance service levels to its do-it-yourself market by offering a broad selection of stock keeping units and extensive product knowledge required by professional installers.

Per Share Data ($) (Year Ended Dec. 31)	1998	1997	1996	1995	1994	1993	1992	1991	1990	1989
Tangible Bk. Val.	10.23	8.62	7.44	6.46	4.04	3.35	1.99	NA	NA	NA
Cash Flow	1.99	1.48	1.20	1.01	0.82	0.68	0.62	NA	NA	NA
Earnings	1.42	1.09	0.91	0.79	0.64	0.50	0.43	NA	NA	NA
Dividends	Nil	Nil	Nil	Nil	Nil	Nil	Nil	NA	NA	NA
Payout Ratio	Nil	Nil	Nil	Nil	Nil	Nil	Nil	NA	NA	NA
Prices - High	$48\frac{3}{8}$	28	$20\frac{3}{8}$	$16\frac{7}{8}$	$17\frac{5}{8}$	$16\frac{1}{4}$	NA	NA	NA	NA
- Low	$24\frac{5}{8}$	$15\frac{1}{2}$	$14\frac{3}{8}$	$11\frac{1}{2}$	$11\frac{5}{8}$	$8\frac{3}{4}$	NA	NA	NA	NA
P/E Ratio - High	34	26	22	21	28	33	NA	NA	NA	NA
- Low	17	14	16	15	18	18	NA	NA	NA	NA
Income Statement Analysis (Million $)										
Revs.	616	316	259	201	167	137	110	NA	NA	NA
Oper. Inc.	69.1	45.4	35.0	26.1	20.4	15.4	12.6	NA	NA	NA
Depr.	12.2	8.3	6.1	4.0	3.3	2.9	2.7	NA	NA	NA
Int. Exp.	8.1	0.1	0.0	0.3	0.1	0.2	0.4	NA	NA	NA
Pretax Inc.	49.9	37.6	30.0	22.3	17.5	12.8	10.1	NA	NA	NA
Eff. Tax Rate	38%	38%	37%	37%	37%	36%	37%	NA	NA	NA
Net Inc.	30.8	23.1	19.0	14.1	11.1	8.2	6.4	NA	NA	NA
Balance Sheet & Other Fin. Data (Million $)										
Cash	1.7	2.3	2.2	26.2	5.4	12.0	1.6	NA	NA	NA
Curr. Assets	311	134	100	99	57.2	55.2	32.1	NA	NA	NA
Total Assets	493	248	184	154	87.3	73.1	58.9	NA	NA	NA
Curr. Liab.	103	40.4	26.0	18.2	15.8	14.0	16.5	NA	NA	NA
LT Debt	170	22.6	0.2	0.4	0.5	0.7	2.7	NA	NA	NA
Common Eqty.	218	182	156	134	70.2	57.8	29.3	NA	NA	NA
Total Cap.	389	207	156	135	71.1	58.7	32.1	NA	NA	NA
Cap. Exp.	57.7	37.2	34.5	28.6	13.7	8.5	4.5	NA	NA	NA
Cash Flow	42.9	31.4	25.1	18.1	14.3	11.1	9.1	NA	NA	NA
Curr. Ratio	3.0	3.3	3.8	5.4	3.6	3.9	1.9	NA	NA	NA
% LT Debt of Cap.	43.8	10.9	0.2	0.3	0.6	1.2	8.3	NA	NA	NA
% Net Inc.of Revs.	5.0	7.3	7.3	7.0	6.6	6.0	5.8	NA	NA	NA
% Ret. on Assets	8.3	10.7	11.3	11.7	13.8	11.6	11.8	NA	NA	NA
% Ret. on Equity	15.4	13.7	13.1	13.8	17.2	17.9	24.5	NA	NA	NA

Data as orig reptd.; bef. results of disc opers/spec. items. Per share data adj. for stk. divs. Bold denotes diluted EPS (FASB 128)-prior periods restated. E-Estimated. NA-Not Available. NM-Not Meaningful. NR-Not Ranked.

Office—233 S. Patterson, Springfield, MO 65801. **Tel**—(417) 862-6708. **Website**—www.oreillyauto.com **Co-Chrmn**—L. P. O'Reilly. **Co-Pres**—G. Henslee. **CFO & Investor Contact**—James R. Batten. **Secy**—A. Drennan. **Dirs**—J. D. Burchfield, J. C. Greene, C. H. O'Reilly Jr., C. H. O'Reilly Sr., D. E. O'Reilly, L. P. O'Reilly, R. O'Reilly Wooten. **Transfer Agent & Registrar**—Boatmen's Trust Co., St. Louis. **Incorporated**—in Missouri in 1957. **Empl**— 6,330. **S&P Analyst:** Howard choe

STANDARD
&POOR'S
STOCK REPORTS

Oak Industries

NYSE Symbol **OAK**

In S&P SmallCap 600

09-OCT-99 **Industry:** Electrical Equipment

Summary: This company is a leading supplier of components to manufacturers and service providers in the communications industry.

S&P Opinion: Hold (★★★) Recent Price • 32 52 Wk Range • 53¼-22 Yield • Nil 12-Mo. P/E • 21.4

Quantitative Evaluations

Outlook (1 Lowest—5 Highest) • **3-**

Fair Value • **38¼**

Risk • **Average**

Earn./Div. Rank • **B-**

Technical Eval. • **Neutral** since 9/99

Rel. Strength Rank (1 Lowest—99 Highest) • **28**

Insider Activity • **NA**

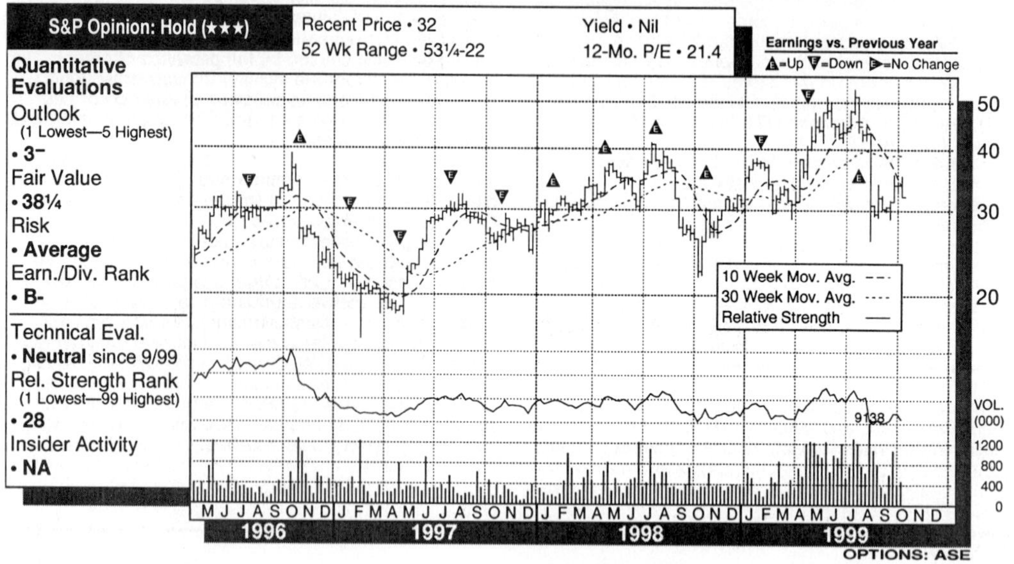

Overview - 23-SEP-99

OAK's 28% year-over-year sales increase in the first half of 1999 was well above our target, due to acquisitions and better sales in foreign markets, but we expect revenues for all of 1999 to increase only about 14%. Revenue growth in the second half may be subpar because one of the largest customers of the company's Lasertron unit stopped taking shipments of 980nm pump lasers (used in fiber optic networks) at the end of the second quarter. Lasertron is uncertain when this customer will resume purchases of pump lasers. Because of the revenue shortfall, third quarter earnings are likely to be well below prior expectations. We think fourth quarter results could be affected as well. As a result, we have cut our EPS forecasts to $0.41 for the third quarter, $0.45 for the fourth quarter and $1.66 for all of 1999. Despite this setback, we project 2000 revenues up 18% and EPS ahead 33% on improving margins to $2.20.

Valuation - 23-SEP-99

We rate OAK shares hold. The difficulty it is having with the one large customer of its Lasertron subsidiary is in sharp contrast to the bullish outlook for the communications equipment sector as a whole. Communications service providers are accelerating capital spending in anticipation of huge increases in the amount of traffic that flows over their networks, as the Internet spurs demand for new data, video, and other types of services. Nevertheless, the mid-August earnings warning for the third quarter sent the stock plummeting. The shares have subsequently traded at a large discount to their historic relative valuation, as the market's view of the company's growth prospects has been temporarily impaired. We think it will take some time for the company to mend perceptions, and expect the shares to perform in line with the market for now.

Key Stock Statistics

S&P EPS Est. 1999	1.66	Tang. Bk. Value/Share	1.81
P/E on S&P Est. 1999	19.3	Beta	0.89
S&P EPS Est. 2000	2.20	Shareholders	5,700
Dividend Rate/Share	Nil	Market cap. (B)	$0.585
Shs. outstg. (M)	18.3	Inst. holdings	97%
Avg. daily vol. (M)	0.124		

Value of $10,000 invested 5 years ago: $ 19,285

Fiscal Year Ending Dec. 31

	1999	1998	1997	1996	1995	1994
Revenues (Million $)						
1Q	104.8	79.21	73.04	78.74	71.60	61.79
2Q	109.7	88.66	80.31	80.59	66.93	65.68
3Q	—	81.63	76.98	74.09	65.04	58.40
4Q	—	98.36	84.07	70.12	73.01	63.14
Yr.	—	347.9	314.4	303.5	276.6	249.0
Earnings Per Share ($)						
1Q	**0.33**	**0.35**	**0.22**	0.92	0.58	0.40
2Q	**0.47**	**0.41**	**0.30**	0.34	0.58	0.56
3Q	**E0.41**	**0.39**	**0.32**	0.39	-4.08	0.40
4Q	**E0.45**	**0.31**	**0.36**	0.06	0.23	0.94
Yr.	**E1.66**	**1.46**	**1.20**	**1.71**	**-3.02**	**2.23**

Next earnings report expected: late October

Dividend Data

Cash dividends, paid since 1934, were omitted in 1983. A one-for-five reverse stock split was effected in 1993. A "poison pill" stock purchase rights plan was adopted in 1995.

A Division of The **McGraw-Hill** *Companies*

Oak Industries Inc.

Business Summary - 23-SEP-99

Oak Industries Inc., through its family of companies, is a leading supplier of highly engineered components to the telecommunications and selected other industries. The company also manufactures controls components for the gas appliance industry and switches and encoders for use in commercial, medical and military applications.

The cable broadband products segment is a leading manufacturer of coaxial connector products used primarily in the CATV industry. Operations are centered in the Gilbert Engineering subsidiary; on October 30, 1998, OAK purchased the remaining 3.75% interest in Gilbert. In 1998, cable broadband accounted for 36% of total sales.

The frequency controls products segment manufactures quartz-based crystals and oscillators for wireless communications base stations and other telecommunications applications. Operations were expanded into Europe through the October 1998 acquisition of Tele Quarz GmbH, Europe's largest maker of frequency control products. In 1998, frequency control products provided 22% of total sales.

The fiber-optic products segment, consisting primarily of OAK's Lasertron subsidiary, makes pump lasers and other transmission products for use in fiber optic telecommunications networks. Certain wholly-owned and joint venture operations in China in this segment also make products for the fiber optic and wireless telecommunications markets. This segment accounted for 15% of 1998 sales.

Within the controls components group, Harper-Wyman Co. is a leading supplier of components to original equipment manufacturers of gas range appliances and also supplies components for outdoor grills. OakGrigsby Inc. manufactures optical, rotary and appliance switches and encoders for applications in the test and measurement, communications, medical and other markets. Controls components, the slowest growing of the company's four segments, accounted for 28% of 1998 revenues.

A key aspect of the company's business strategy is to develop new products and increase market share. To support these initiatives, Lasertron has introduced advanced transmission products that will be marketed to the same customer base that purchases Lasertron's pump lasers for amplification of fiber-optic signals; and OFCG has introduced a voltage controlled oscillator product line, expanding its customer base to include manufacturers of switching and transmission equipment.

A second key growth strategy is acquisitions. OAK has made many acquisitions in the past decade in addition to the 1998 purchase of Tele Quarz, including a majority stake in Gilbert in 1992, Cabel-Con A/S in 1994, Lasertron in 1995, and Piezo Crystal Co. in 1997. The company has also divested non-strategic businesses, in order to make more effective use of available capital.

Per Share Data ($) (Year Ended Dec. 31)	1998	1997	1996	1995	1994	1993	1992	1991	1990	1989
Tangible Bk. Val.	0.25	0.16	0.28	2.24	5.23	3.25	1.55	5.10	4.75	4.05
Cash Flow	2.40	2.33	2.08	2.11	2.89	2.04	0.95	0.60	0.35	-0.85
Earnings	1.46	1.20	1.71	-2.74	2.31	1.47	0.60	0.35	0.10	-1.15
Dividends	Nil	Nil	Nil	Nil	Nil	Nil	Nil	Nil	Nil	Nil
Payout Ratio	Nil	Nil	Nil	Nil	Nil	Nil	Nil	Nil	Nil	Nil
Prices - High	41¼	32¼	39	32	29⅞	29	14⅜	5⅝	6⅞	8¾
- Low	21¾	16¼	18¾	16½	15⅝	10⅝	4⅜	3⅛	1¼	3¾
P/E Ratio - High	28	27	23	NM	13	20	24	16	69	NM
- Low	15	14	11	NM	7	7	7	9	16	NM
Income Statement Analysis (Million $)										
Revs.	348	314	304	277	249	220	143	124	139	160
Oper. Inc.	73.2	66.3	54.3	-13.1	61.0	47.0	10.1	6.7	4.4	0.6
Depr.	22.1	19.1	7.3	11.7	10.6	10.3	5.3	4.6	5.2	5.0
Int. Exp.	10.1	11.0	5.8	6.3	6.6	7.8	1.4	1.8	2.1	4.6
Pretax Inc.	44.7	36.7	62.0	-27.8	43.4	26.3	9.0	2.0	2.0	-19.0
Eff. Tax Rate	37%	38%	37%	NM	NM	NM	NM	NM	23%	NM
Net Inc.	27.3	21.7	32.0	-50.5	42.4	26.7	10.0	5.0	1.0	-19.0
Balance Sheet & Other Fin. Data (Million $)										
Cash	13.8	8.6	6.1	16.9	37.6	27.4	24.9	37.6	44.5	21.8
Curr. Assets	165	126	125	134	120	96.0	90.0	82.0	93.0	82.0
Total Assets	482	388	374	313	282	238	229	125	131	131
Curr. Liab.	53.3	40.8	45.5	53.7	47.5	27.0	35.0	20.0	29.0	33.0
LT Debt	220	151	138	91.6	34.0	62.0	77.0	11.0	11.0	17.0
Common Eqty.	201	188	172	119	167	127	98.1	84.0	78.0	67.0
Total Cap.	421	339	321	247	228	203	182	95.0	90.0	84.0
Cap. Exp.	16.8	14.6	23.2	17.5	6.8	7.0	4.1	4.7	6.5	5.4
Cash Flow	49.4	40.8	39.3	-38.8	53.1	37.0	16.0	10.0	6.0	-14.0
Curr. Ratio	3.1	3.1	2.7	2.5	2.5	3.6	2.6	4.0	3.2	2.5
% LT Debt of Cap.	52.2	44.7	43.0	37.1	15.1	30.3	42.2	11.8	12.6	20.7
% Net Inc.of Revs.	7.9	6.9	NM	NM	17.0	12.1	7.3	4.2	1.0	NM
% Ret. on Assets	6.3	5.7	9.3	NM	16.2	11.2	5.9	4.1	1.1	NM
% Ret. on Equity	13.8	11.9	22.0	NM	28.7	23.3	11.4	6.5	1.9	NM

Data as orig. reptd.; bef. results of disc. opers. and/or spec. items. Per share data adj. for stk. divs. as of ex-div. date. Bold denotes diluted EPS (FASB 128). E-Estimated. NA-Not Available. NM-Not Meaningful. NR-Not Ranked.

Office—1000 Winter St., Waltham, MA 02154. **Tel**—(617) 890-0400. **Website**—http://www.oakind.com **Chrmn, Pres & CEO**—W. S Antle III. **Vice Chrmn**—R. M. Hills. **SVP & CFO** —C. S. Hicks. **VP & Secy**—M. Lew. **Dirs**—W. S. Antle III, B. L. Bronner, D. W. Derbes, R. M. Hills, G. E. Matthews, C. H. B. Mills, E. L. Richardson. **Transfer Agent & Registrar**—BankBoston. **Incorporated**—in Delaware in 1960. **Empl**— 3,373. **S&P Analyst:** Mark S. Basham

STANDARD
&POOR'S
STOCK REPORTS

Oakwood Homes

NYSE Symbol **OH**
In S&P SmallCap 600

09-OCT-99 **Industry:** Homebuilding

Summary: This vertically integrated producer and retailer of manufactured homes also derives substantial profits from related financial services.

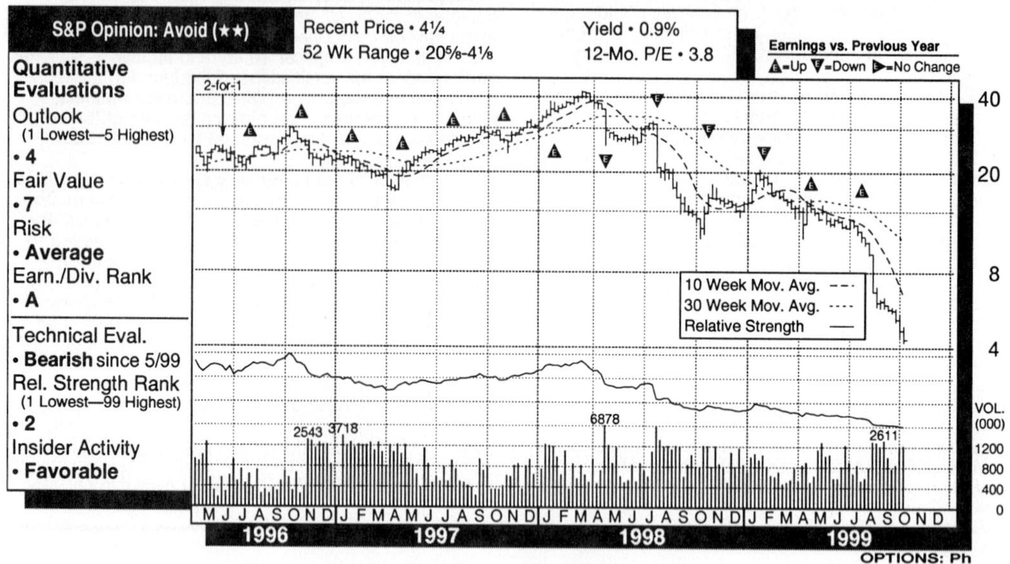

Overview - 12-AUG-99

We expect lackluster sales from comparable operations in coming periods. OH has maintained an aggressive retail network expansion, and has also realigned capacity toward higher-priced multi-section homes. However, with retail expansion in the industry going on at a feverish pace, extreme competitive pressures have surfaced, and OH has encountered sales difficulties. With management also possibly losing some focus, as it had also needed to tend to troubles in the financial services business, OH posted a 27% drop in same-store retail unit sales in the third quarter of FY 99 (Sep.), with a 40% fall in June alone. We see the challenging industry conditions and OH's disappointing recent response limiting earnings prospects for some time to come. Comparisons will be distorted by $0.67 a share of one-time charges in FY 98.

Valuation - 12-AUG-99

The shares have fallen sharply since the spring of 1998, on OH's disappointing performance. Shortfalls initially stemmed largely from troubles in financial services, on a sloppy lending program between 1994 and 1996, and excess loan prepayments, driven by lower interest rates. Management began to lose credibility when troubles kept recurring despite guidance that they had been effectively dealt with; some executive changes later took place. The situation worsened in mid-1999, when OH pre-announced a severe FY 99 third quarter EPS shortfall, related to very slow home sales; housing operations had been solid until calendar 1999. In making the last announcement, directors also reported that they would explore options to boost shareholder value, including a possible sale of the company. However, in August 1999, OH decided against seeking a buyer. We thus see no factors to support the shares in coming periods, and would steer clear of OH.

Key Stock Statistics

S&P EPS Est. 1999	-0.75	Tang. Bk. Value/Share	12.31
P/E on S&P Est. 1999	NM	Beta	1.57
S&P EPS Est. 2000	0.50	Shareholders	27,000
Dividend Rate/Share	0.04	Market cap. (B)	$0.203
Shs. outstg. (M)	47.1	Inst. holdings	64%
Avg. daily vol. (M)	0.215		

Value of $10,000 invested 5 years ago: $ 3,251

Fiscal Year Ending Sep. 30

	1999	1998	1997	1996	1995	1994
Revenues (Million $)						
1Q	359.8	221.9	207.2	204.4	167.1	113.0
2Q	396.4	264.9	220.3	221.2	187.1	129.7
3Q	441.3	440.5	292.4	263.5	226.1	164.2
4Q	—	522.5	350.1	284.8	241.1	172.1
Yr.	—	1,483	1,070	973.9	821.4	579.1
Earnings Per Share ($)						
1Q	**0.24**	**0.38**	**0.33**	0.30	0.18	0.15
2Q	**0.21**	**0.16**	0.38	0.35	0.21	0.17
3Q	**0.17**	**0.10**	0.48	0.38	0.27	0.23
4Q	**E-1.37**	**0.53**	0.56	0.44	0.33	0.23
Yr.	**E-0.75**	**1.17**	**1.75**	1.47	0.98	0.77

Next earnings report expected: early November

Dividend Data (Dividends have been paid since 1976.)

Amount ($)	Date Decl.	Ex-Div. Date	Stock of Record	Payment Date
0.010	Oct. 21	Nov. 06	Nov. 10	Nov. 25 '98
0.010	Jan. 20	Feb. 05	Feb. 09	Feb. 24 '99
0.010	Apr. 22	May. 07	May. 11	May. 26 '99
0.010	Jul. 21	Aug. 06	Aug. 10	Aug. 25 '99

Oakwood Homes Corporation

Business Summary - 12-AUG-99

Oakwood Homes produces and sells manufactured homes (95% of revenues and 71% of operating profits in FY 98 (Sep.), before one-time charges), and provides financing and insurance services (5% of revenues and 29% of profits). Oakwood's retail home sales expanded three times as fast as the industry growth rate over the five years through FY 98. However, despite this strong growth, Oakwood's business has struggled since early FY 98. Most of the problems centered around the company's financial services operations. However, when soft manufactured home sales caused OH to pre-announce a huge third quarter FY 99 EPS shortfall, the company also said directors would explore options such as a merger, sale or management buyout of Oakwood. In August 1999, OH said it had terminated its exploration of these options, as it had decided that shareholders would be best served if management focused on challenges facing the company. At that time, it was reported that N.J. St. George would retire as chairman and CEO on September 30. W.G. Edwards, the current president, will assume these positions.

OH's homes are constructed and furnished at its factories and transported by truck to the homesite. OH makes single- and multi-section homes, with retail prices ranging from $15,000 to $135,000 in FY 98. Oakwood sold 33,842 new homes in FY 98 (26,059 at its own retailers), and made 96% of the homes it sold at retail. OH has boosted its emphasis on multi-section homes, whose larger living area is attractive to consumers. Multi-sections provided 52% of retail unit sales in FY 98, up from 47% in FY 97 and 32% in FY 96.

Oakwood sells its homes through company-owned dealers (81% of manufactured housing sales in FY 98) and other channels (mainly independent dealers; 19%). OH's retail network about tripled in size in the four years through FY 98 year-end, through both expansion and acquisitions. After adding 59 net centers in FY 98, Oakwood was operating 359 company-owned retail centers at FY 98 year-end, spanning 28 states; there were 400 centers at June 30, 1999.

Oakwood also sold homes through 713 independent dealers at FY 98 year-end. It obtained most of those operations through the $101 million April 1998 purchase of Schult Homes (annual sales of $348 million), which produces manufactured and modular homes in the Midwest. However, OH believes it is better served to be vertically integrated and control its retail distribution, and will strive to establish centers to sell the homes manufactured at the Schult plants. Nonetheless, Oakwood intends to continue selling to key and exclusive independent dealers.

Most of OH's home sales are now financed through installment contracts with its finance unit. The division allows full-service, one-stop shopping.

Oakwood recorded a total of $0.67 a share of charges in the FY 98 second and third quarters, mostly stemming from problems in the financial services business.

Per Share Data ($) (Year Ended Sep. 30)	1998	1997	1996	1995	1994	1993	1992	1991	1990	1989
Tangible Bk. Val.	11.74	10.45	8.74	7.18	6.42	5.63	3.96	3.50	2.96	2.70
Cash Flow	1.69	2.06	1.70	1.20	0.86	0.70	0.64	0.53	0.43	0.27
Earnings	1.17	1.75	1.47	0.98	0.77	0.63	0.50	0.39	0.28	0.14
Dividends	0.04	0.04	0.04	0.04	0.04	0.04	0.03	0.02	0.02	0.02
Payout Ratio	3%	2%	3%	4%	5%	7%	6%	7%	8%	15%
Prices - High	42¼	33⅝	30¼	21¼	15	14⅜	10¾	5½	3¼	2⅜
- Low	10⅞	16⅝	18¼	10⅞	9⅝	8⅝	5⅛	2⅞	1$^{11}/_{16}$	1⅝
P/E Ratio - High	36	19	21	22	19	23	21	14	11	17
- Low	9	9	12	11	13	14	10	7	6	11
Income Statement Analysis (Million $)										
Revs.	1,472	1,055	954	804	575	317	228	160	134	100
Oper. Inc.	129	153	125	88.3	56.1	37.4	47.2	35.0	25.0	14.8
Depr.	24.9	14.3	10.4	8.3	4.3	2.9	3.7	3.1	3.0	2.6
Int. Exp.	24.5	19.8	22.4	24.9	24.3	26.1	25.3	20.3	16.2	14.6
Pretax Inc.	90.1	133	111	73.0	53.9	38.9	21.4	14.3	8.8	4.0
Eff. Tax Rate	39%	39%	38%	36%	37%	37%	34%	38%	38%	29%
Net Inc.	55.4	81.9	68.3	46.6	33.9	24.5	14.0	8.9	5.5	2.8
Balance Sheet & Other Fin. Data (Million $)										
Cash	29.0	28.7	28.6	6.2	12.6	23.9	17.2	16.3	12.8	14.8
Curr. Assets	NA	NA	NA	NA	NA	NA	NA	NA	NA	NA
Total Assets	1,283	905	842	783	575	557	432	345	275	229
Curr. Liab.	NA	NA	NA	NA	NA	NA	NA	NA	NA	NA
LT Debt	227	78.8	134	199	173	223	258	182	169	122
Common Eqty.	548	484	392	318	271	229	104	89.7	57.9	52.7
Total Cap.	775	563	526	517	444	452	364	274	232	179
Cap. Exp.	51.4	38.4	41.3	41.9	27.2	13.0	5.3	2.3	3.4	6.3
Cash Flow	80.3	96.2	78.8	54.9	38.2	27.4	17.7	12.0	8.5	5.3
Curr. Ratio	NA	NA	NA	NA	NA	NA	NA	NA	NA	NA
% LT Debt of Cap.	29.3	14.0	25.5	38.5	39.0	49.3	70.8	66.3	73.1	68.1
% Net Inc.of Revs.	3.8	7.8	7.2	5.8	5.9	7.7	6.1	5.5	4.1	2.8
% Ret. on Assets	5.1	9.4	8.4	6.8	5.9	4.0	3.6	2.5	2.2	1.6
% Ret. on Equity	10.7	18.7	19.2	15.7	13.3	12.6	14.3	10.7	9.9	5.5

Data as orig. reptd.; bef. results of disc. opers. and/or spec. items. Per share data adj. for stk. divs. as of ex-div. date. Bold denotes diluted EPS (FASB 128). Revs. in Inc. Statement excl. certain oth. inc. E-Estimated. NA-Not Available. NM-Not Meaningful. NR-Not Ranked.

Mailing Address—P.O. Box 27081, Greensboro, NC 27425-7081. **Tel**—(336) 664-2400. **Website**—http://www.oakwoodhomes.com **Chrmn & CEO**—N. J. St. George. **Pres & COO**—W. G. Edwards. **EVP & CFO**—R. A. Smith. **Dirs**—W. G. Edwards, D. I. Meyer, K. G. Phillips II, N. J. St. George, R. W. Schipke, L. L. Smith, S. C. Streeter, F. T. Vincent Jr., C. W. Walker, H. M. Weaver. **Transfer Agent & Registrar**—First Union National Bank of North Carolina, Charlotte. **Incorporated**—in North Carolina in 1971. **Empl**— 11,604. **S&P Analyst:** Michael W. Jaffe

STANDARD
&POOR'S
STOCK REPORTS

Oceaneering International

NYSE Symbol **OII**

In S&P SmallCap 600

23-OCT-99

Industry: Oil & Gas (Drilling & Equipment)

Summary: This company provides offshore services to the oil and gas industries, as well as services to companies that operate in other harsh environments.

Quantitative Evaluations
Outlook
(1 Lowest—5 Highest)
• **4+**
Fair Value
• **20⅛**
Risk
• **Average**
Earn./Div. Rank
• **B-**

Technical Eval.
• **NA**
Rel. Strength Rank
(1 Lowest—99 Highest)
• **16**
Insider Activity
• **Unfavorable**

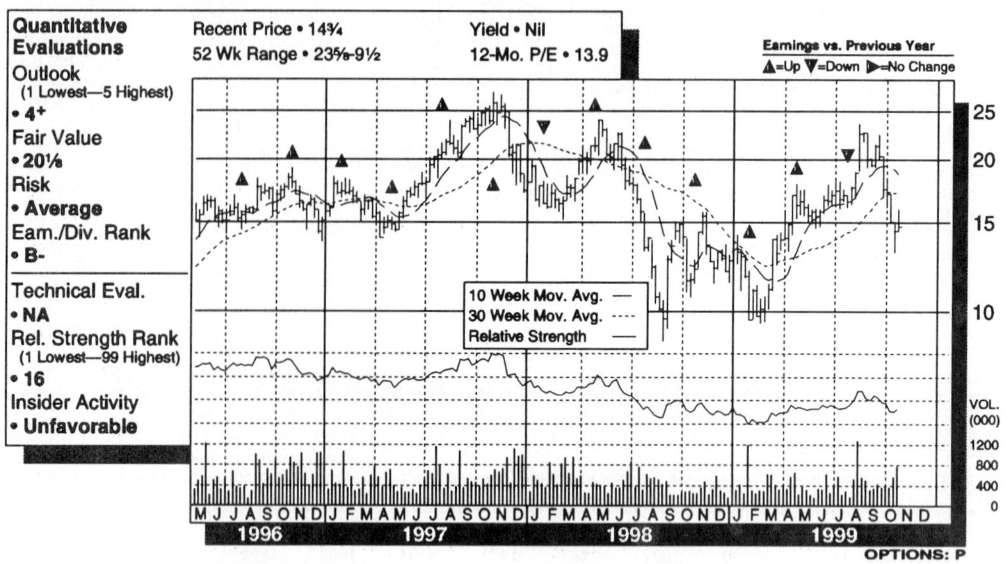

Business Profile - 14-OCT-99

This provider of hardware and engineered services operates in 27 countries; international operations accounted for 48% of FY 99 (Mar.) revenues. Offices were recently opened to service offshore development activities in Angola and Latin America. In July 1999, OII provided the first commercial logistics cargo container system for the re-supply of the International Space Station. In April, the company repaired a subsea pipeline system in a water depth of about 1,000 ft.; this was believed to be the deepest flowline repair ever attempted on the sea floor.

Operational Review - 14-OCT-99

Revenues in the three months ended June 30, 1999, were flat, year to year; worldwide demand for oilfield services decreased due to a reduction in customer capital spending, while the Advanced Technology segment benefitted from increased activity. Gross and operating margin narrowed slightly, to 19% and 9%, respectively. OII has reduced the seasonality of its business by exiting the diving sector in the North Sea, and by entering a number of new contracts. After higher interest expense, net income fell 23%, to $5.0 million ($0.22 a share, diluted, on 2.6% fewer shares), from $6.6 million ($0.28).

Stock Performance - 22-OCT-99

In the past 30 trading days, OII's shares have declined 32%, compared to a 4% fall in the S&P 500. Average trading volume for the past five days was 72,600 shares, compared with the 40-day moving average of 83,969 shares.

Key Stock Statistics

Dividend Rate/Share	Nil	Shareholders	575
Shs. outstg. (M)	22.5	Market cap. (B)	$0.325
Avg. daily vol. (M)	0.105	Inst. holdings	75%
Tang. Bk. Value/Share	7.75		
Beta	1.13		

Value of $10,000 invested 5 years ago: $ 10,595

Fiscal Year Ending Mar. 31

	2000	1999	1998	1997	1996	1995
Revenues (Million $)						
1Q	98.60	98.91	95.16	80.54	71.54	63.37
2Q	—	110.0	90.58	96.76	77.09	66.90
3Q	—	98.28	86.23	94.12	74.24	55.20
4Q	—	93.09	86.15	97.36	66.64	54.47
Yr.	—	400.3	358.1	368.8	289.5	239.9
Earnings Per Share ($)						
1Q	**0.22**	**0.28**	0.25	0.16	0.12	0.15
2Q	—	**0.34**	0.28	0.21	0.20	0.18
3Q	—	**0.28**	**0.21**	0.28	0.15	-0.12
4Q	—	**0.22**	**0.19**	0.16	0.06	0.02
Yr.	—	**1.12**	**0.93**	**0.81**	**0.53**	**0.23**

Next earnings report expected: early November

Dividend Data

No dividends have been paid since 1977. A poison pill stock purchase rights plan was adopted in November 1992.

A Division of The McGraw-Hill Companies

Oceaneering International, Inc.

Business Summary - 14-OCT-99

Oceaneering International is an advanced applied technology company that provides engineered services and hardware to customers who operate in marine, space and other harsh environments. The company's services and products are marketed worldwide to oil and gas companies, government agencies and firms in telecommunications, aerospace and civil engineering and construction industries.

Most of the company's services are provided to the oil and gas industry. Services include subsea construction, drilling support, design, lease and and operation of production systems, facilities maintenance and repair, survey and positioning, and specialized onshore and offshore engineering and inspection. OII breaks its business structure into three segments: Oilfield Marine Services, Offshore Field Developments, and Advanced Technologies.

Oilfield Marine Services consists of underwater intervention, maintenance and repair, and above-water inspection. Underwater intervention support is provided for all phases of offshore oil and gas operations. During exploration, the company provides positioning, placement and monitoring of subsea exploration equipment, collects data on seafloor characteristics at proposed drilling sites, and assists with navigational placements of drilling rigs. For development, OII aids in installing production platforms and connecting pipelines. In the production phase, OII inspects, maintains, and repairs offshore platforms, pipelines and equipment. These services are performed by divers or remotely operated vehicles (ROV's) The company believes it operates the world's most technically advanced fleet of work class ROV's, holding a 25% market share. OII also supplies the oil and gas industry with survey and navigational positioning services, as well as ocean search and recovery projects. Above-water inspection services are provided for customers required to obtain third party inspections.

The Offshore Field Development segment provides engineering, procurement, construction, installation and operation of mobile offshore production systems (MOPS). Through its Advanced Technologies (AdTech) segment, OII provides underwater intervention, topside inspection and engineering services to meet a variety of non-oilfield industrial requirements, including ship husbandry, search and recovery, subsea telecommunications cable installation, maintenance and repair, civil work projects, and commercial theme park animation. AdTech customers include the U.S. Navy and NASA.

Per Share Data ($)										
(Year Ended Mar. 31)	1999	1998	1997	1996	1995	1994	1993	1992	1991	1990
Tangible Bk. Val.	7.60	6.54	6.06	4.95	4.43	4.14	4.17	3.78	3.08	2.23
Cash Flow	2.43	1.92	1.84	1.42	0.90	1.13	1.30	1.01	1.00	0.76
Earnings	1.12	0.93	0.81	0.53	0.23	0.62	0.82	0.70	0.72	0.47
Dividends	Nil	Nil	Nil	Nil	Nil	Nil	Nil	Nil	Nil	Nil
Payout Ratio	Nil	Nil	Nil	Nil	Nil	Nil	Nil	Nil	Nil	Nil
Cal. Yrs.	1998	1997	1996	1995	1994	1993	1992	1991	1990	1989
Prices - High	24	27¼	19¼	13	14⅝	18½	18⅛	14⅛	18⅞	11⅜
- Low	8¾	14	10¾	7¾	9¾	10¾	8⅞	8½	8¾	2½
P/E Ratio - High	21	29	24	25	64	30	22	20	26	24
- Low	8	15	13	15	42	17	11	12	12	5
Income Statement Analysis (Million $)										
Revs.	400	358	369	290	240	230	216	168	147	183
Oper. Inc.	74.3	59.5	57.2	40.8	29.0	33.1	38.4	26.7	23.5	21.0
Depr.	30.0	23.2	24.7	20.6	16.2	12.2	11.5	7.2	6.3	6.5
Int. Exp.	3.4	0.6	2.0	2.3	0.7	0.9	1.4	NM	NM	NM
Pretax Inc.	41.7	35.6	41.3	19.9	12.5	20.8	25.4	22.0	22.3	15.0
Eff. Tax Rate	38%	38%	53%	38%	56%	28%	23%	26%	26%	30%
Net Inc.	25.7	22.0	19.4	12.4	5.5	14.9	19.4	15.9	16.3	10.2
Balance Sheet & Other Fin. Data (Million $)										
Cash	8.4	9.1	23.0	9.3	12.9	26.5	34.0	23.3	40.1	37.8
Curr. Assets	129	131	149	110	75.8	80.8	88.8	66.9	72.1	71.6
Total Assets	387	317	268	256	188	172	155	136	113	96.0
Curr. Liab.	87.7	86.2	95.8	68.0	52.7	46.4	46.3	38.3	30.3	32.5
LT Debt	100	54.6	Nil	48.0	9.5	0.2	0.2	0.3	0.4	Nil
Common Eqty.	179	160	156	127	115	113	98.3	85.2	68.9	49.6
Total Cap.	280	215	157	176	126	115	101	89.5	73.2	52.6
Cap. Exp.	102	94.4	79.6	57.2	32.1	36.7	12.0	34.6	19.9	11.5
Cash Flow	55.7	45.2	44.2	32.9	21.7	27.1	30.9	23.1	22.6	16.7
Curr. Ratio	1.5	1.5	1.6	1.6	1.4	1.7	1.9	1.7	2.4	2.2
% LT Debt of Cap.	35.9	25.4	Nil	27.3	7.5	0.1	0.2	0.4	0.6	Nil
% Net Inc.of Revs.	6.4	6.1	5.3	4.3	2.3	6.5	9.0	9.5	11.1	5.6
% Ret. on Assets	7.3	7.5	7.4	5.6	3.1	9.1	13.1	12.7	15.5	11.6
% Ret. on Equity	15.1	13.9	13.7	10.2	4.8	14.1	20.7	20.6	27.4	24.9

Data as orig reptd.; bef. results of disc opers/spec. items. Per share data adj. for stk. divs. Bold denotes diluted EPS (FASB 128)-prior periods restated. E-Estimated. NA-Not Available. NM-Not Meaningful. NR-Not Ranked.

Office—11911 F.M. 529, Houston, TX 77041. **Tel**—(713) 329-4500. **Website**—http://www.oceaneering.com **Chrmn & CEO**—J. R. Huff. **Pres & COO**—T. J. Collins. **SVP & CFO**—M. J. Migura. **VP & Secy**—G. R. Haubenreich, Jr. **Investor Contact**—Jack Jurkoshek, (713-329-4670). **Dirs**—C. B. Evans, D. S. Hooker, J. R. Huff, D. M. Hughes, H. J. Pappas. **Transfer Agent & Registrar**—First Chicago Trust Co. of New York, Jersey City, NJ. **Incorporated**—in Delaware in 1969. **Empl**— 2,600. **S&P Analyst:** Ephraim Juskowicz.

STANDARD
&POOR'S
STOCK REPORTS

Offshore Logistics

NASDAQ Symbol **OLOG**

In S&P SmallCap 600

09-OCT-99

Industry:
Oil & Gas (Drilling & Equipment)

Summary: This company provides helicopter transportation services to the worldwide offshore oil and gas industry.

Quantitative Evaluations

Outlook
(1 Lowest—5 Highest)
• **4+**

Fair Value
• **13⅝**

Risk
• **Average**

Earn./Div. Rank
• **B-**

Technical Eval.
• **Bearish** since 9/99

Rel. Strength Rank
(1 Lowest—99 Highest)
• **23**

Insider Activity
• **NA**

Recent Price • 10
52 Wk Range • 18-8½
Yield • Nil
12-Mo. P/E • 12.1

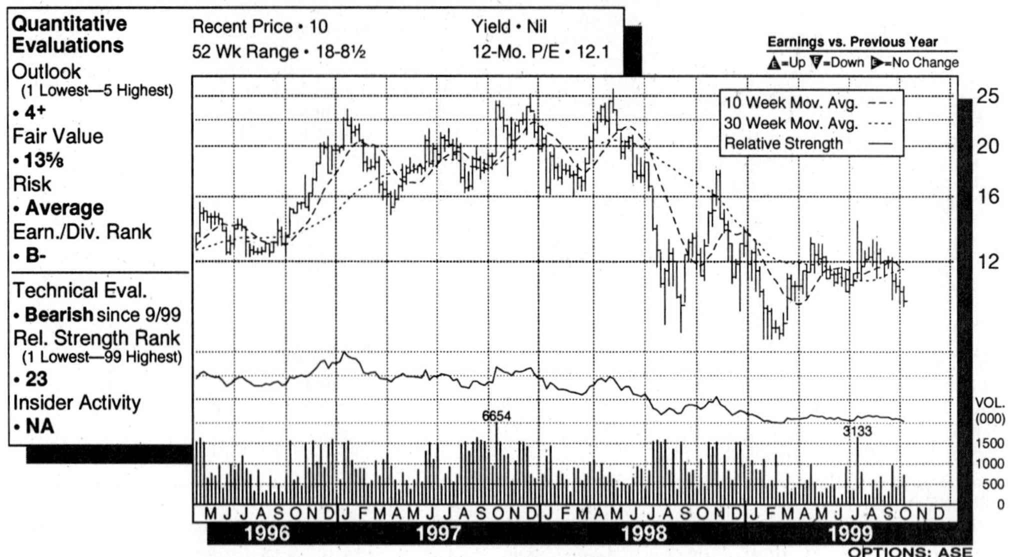

Business Profile - 23-JUN-99

During the FY 99 (Mar.) fourth quarter, industrywide exploration budget cuts, reflecting weak commodity prices, resulted in decreased demand for OLOG's services. The Bristow Aviation subsidiary, which provides helicopter transportation services to the North Sea, experienced an operating loss, as reduced pricing and utilization outweighed revenue from the commencement of a contract with Shell Exploration in July. Despite a 13% drop in flight hours from the third quarter, operating margins at Air Logistics, the Gulf of Mexico subsidiary, were positive, due to static pricing and well-contained costs. In July 1998, directors reaffirmed an earlier authorization to buy back up to one million common shares; 763,500 shares were repurchased in FY 99, together with $7.1 million of convertible debt.

Operational Review - 23-JUN-99

Based on a preliminary report, revenues in FY 99, increased 9.9%. However, following a 15% rise in operating expenses, primarily reflecting significantly higher direct costs, operating income fell 24%. Income from continuing operations declined 33%, to $20.9 million ($0.97 a share, diluted), from $31.4 million ($1.35, excluding income from discontinued operations of $0.01). Fourth quarter flight revenues at the Air Logistics and Bristow subsidiaries fell more than 13% from the third quarter due the reduced flight activity. Management has initiated a strategic review of Bristow's cost structure.

Stock Performance - 08-OCT-99

In the past 30 trading days, OLOG's shares have declined 16%, compared to a 0.91% fall in the S&P 500. Average trading volume for the past five days was 143,080 shares, compared with the 40-day moving average of 107,700 shares.

Key Stock Statistics

Dividend Rate/Share	Nil	Shareholders	2,000
Shs. outstg. (M)	21.1	Market cap. (B)	$0.212
Avg. daily vol. (M)	0.130	Inst. holdings	67%
Tang. Bk. Value/Share	12.65		
Beta	1.31		

Value of $10,000 invested 5 years ago: $ 7,317

Fiscal Year Ending Mar. 31

	2000	1999	1998	1997	1996	1995
Revenues (Million $)						
1Q	107.4	117.5	100.0	NA	38.77	26.23
2Q	—	129.2	107.6	42.22	39.94	41.70
3Q	—	116.2	113.0	32.90	37.80	36.51
4Q	—	105.9	106.2	94.02	39.72	39.80
Yr.	—	468.8	426.7	167.1	156.2	144.2
Earnings Per Share ($)						
1Q	**0.15**	**0.29**	**0.30**	NA	0.19	0.28
2Q	—	**0.43**	**0.35**	0.29	0.18	0.27
3Q	—	**0.20**	**0.34**	0.28	0.21	0.20
4Q	—	Nil	**0.37**	0.30	0.20	0.22
Yr.	—	**0.97**	**1.35**	**1.05**	0.77	0.96

Next earnings report expected: late October

Dividend Data

No cash dividends have been paid on the common shares since 1984.

Offshore Logistics, Inc.

Business Summary - 23-JUN-99

Through its Air Logistics (Air Log) subsidiaries and its investment in Bristow Aviation Holdings Ltd., Offshore Logistics is a major supplier of helicopter transportation services to the worldwide offshore oil and gas industry. At March 31, 1998, Air Log and Bristow operated a total of 379 aircraft (including 78 through unconsolidated entities).

Helicopters are chartered for varying periods of time for use in transporting personnel and time-sensitive equipment from onshore bases to offshore drilling rigs, platforms and other installations. Helicopter activities are seasonal in nature, influenced by weather conditions, length of daylight hours, and level of offshore production, exploration and construction activity. However, a secondary market for OLOG's fleet, including emergency medical transportation, agricultural and forestry support and general aviation activities, makes the company less vulnerable to oil and gas industry downturns than other oilfield equipment and services companies.

Air Log conducts helicopter activities primarily in the Gulf of Mexico, where 142 aircraft were being operated at the end of FY 98 (Mar). Air Log was also operating 12 aircraft in Alaska, providing services related to the Alyeska Pipeline. Bristow operated 73 aircraft in the U.K. and Europe, mainly in the offshore North Sea. Following the purchase in June 1998 for $2.8 million of an additional 17% interest, Bristow has an indirect 50% interest in a 15-year contract to provide pilot training and maintenance services to the British military. Internationally, Air Log operated 19 helicopters in several countries, including Brazil, Colombia, Egypt and Mexico, while Bristow operated 26 aircraft in Africa, and 29 aircraft elsewhere throughout the world.

Wholly owned Grasso Production Management, Inc. (GPM) is the leading independent contract operator of oil and gas production facilities in the Gulf of Mexico; customers include major and smaller independent oil and gas companies. GPM also provides services for certain onshore facilities. It places experienced crews employed by GPM to operate the facilities and to provide personnel, engineering, paramedic, transportation, regulatory and other services. When servicing offshore oil and gas production facilities, GPM employees normally live on the facility for a seven day rotation.

Per Share Data ($) (Year Ended Mar. 31)	1999	1998	1997	1996	1995	1994	1993	1992	1991	1990
Tangible Bk. Val.	12.65	11.97	10.09	10.24	8.13	8.04	7.06	6.09	5.10	3.81
Cash Flow	2.08	2.43	1.51	1.26	1.46	1.38	1.27	1.36	1.31	1.34
Earnings	0.97	1.35	0.86	0.77	0.96	0.96	0.90	1.00	0.97	0.98
Dividends	Nil	Nil	Nil	Nil	Nil	Nil	Nil	Nil	Nil	Nil
Payout Ratio	Nil	Nil	Nil	Nil	Nil	Nil	Nil	Nil	Nil	Nil
Cal. Yrs.	1998	1997	1996	1995	1994	1993	1992	1991	1990	1989
Prices - High	$25\frac{3}{4}$	$25\frac{1}{4}$	$20\frac{7}{8}$	$20\frac{7}{8}$	$15\frac{1}{8}$	$16\frac{1}{8}$	$19\frac{1}{4}$	$12\frac{1}{8}$	$10\frac{3}{4}$	$14\frac{3}{4}$
- Low	$8\frac{3}{4}$	$14\frac{3}{4}$	$11\frac{3}{4}$	$11\frac{3}{4}$	$12\frac{1}{4}$	$11\frac{5}{8}$	$10\frac{3}{8}$	7	$6\frac{3}{8}$	$6\frac{5}{8}$
P/E Ratio - High	27	19	NM	27	16	17	21	12	11	15
- Low	9	11	NM	15	11	12	12	7	7	7

Income Statement Analysis (Million $)	1999	1998	1997	1996	1995	1994	1993	1992	1991	1990
Revs.	466	427	167	157	144	92.0	80.0	82.0	95.0	98.0
Oper. Inc.	73.3	88.9	37.2	23.9	28.4	25.5	24.1	25.9	25.4	22.1
Depr.	32.7	32.2	13.2	9.2	9.7	7.5	6.5	6.4	6.1	6.3
Int. Exp.	19.8	20.5	5.5	0.8	0.9	1.1	1.5	1.9	2.1	2.6
Pretax Inc.	31.7	46.1	25.6	21.5	25.4	23.6	21.5	24.3	21.3	20.1
Eff. Tax Rate	30%	30%	30%	29%	29%	27%	25%	28%	20%	14%
Net Inc.	20.9	31.3	17.6	15.3	18.5	17.2	16.0	17.5	17.0	17.2

Balance Sheet & Other Fin. Data (Million $)	1999	1998	1997	1996	1995	1994	1993	1992	1991	1990
Cash	70.6	56.1	29.8	77.0	68.0	47.2	46.9	40.7	30.2	16.1
Curr. Assets	249	223	196	134	125	87.3	82.2	72.3	64.7	54.7
Total Assets	732	736	674	242	229	174	164	145	138	112
Curr. Liab.	106	101	139	18.0	18.0	10.0	16.0	19.0	27.0	17.0
LT Debt	234	252	200	0.8	5.6	2.0	9.3	10.0	19.0	25.0
Common Eqty.	284	280	235	200	184	142	124	107	88.9	66.4
Total Cap.	623	635	535	220	209	162	146	123	112	93.0
Cap. Exp.	19.2	70.5	10.1	12.5	3.0	12.0	7.9	9.2	33.4	11.8
Cash Flow	53.7	63.5	30.8	24.5	28.1	24.8	22.0	24.0	23.1	23.5
Curr. Ratio	2.4	2.2	1.4	7.4	6.8	8.6	5.2	3.8	2.4	3.2
% LT Debt of Cap.	37.5	39.7	37.4	1.0	2.7	1.2	6.4	8.2	17.0	26.4
% Net Inc.of Revs.	4.5	7.3	10.5	9.8	12.9	18.8	20.0	21.4	17.9	17.6
% Ret. on Assets	2.9	4.4	NM	6.5	9.2	10.2	10.4	12.4	13.6	14.9
% Ret. on Equity	7.4	12.1	NM	8.0	11.4	13.0	13.9	17.9	21.9	38.9

Data as orig. reptd.; bef. results of disc. opers. and/or spec. items. Yrs. ended Jun. 30 prior to 1997 (9 mos.). Per share data adj. for stk. divs. as of ex-div. date. Bold denotes diluted EPS (FASB 128). E-Estimated. NA-Not Available. NM-Not Meaningful. NR-Not Ranked.

Reincorporated—in Delaware in 1988. **Office**—224 Rue de Jean, P.O. Box 5C, Lafayette, LA 70505. **Tel**—(318) 233-1221. **Chrmn**—L. F. Crane. **Pres**—G. M. Small. **VP, CFO & Secy**—D. A. Milke. **Investor Contact**—Ann Alesi. **Dirs**— P. N. Buckley, J. H. Cartwright, L. F. Crane, D. M. Johnson, K. M. Jones, H. C. Sager, G. M. Small, H. Wolf. **Transfer Agent & Registrar**—ChaseMellon Shareholder Services, NYC. **Empl**— 3,165.
S&P Analyst: Ephraim Juskowicz

STANDARD
&POOR'S
STOCK REPORTS

OM Group

NYSE Symbol **OMP**

In S&P SmallCap 600

09-OCT-99

Industry: Chemicals (Specialty)

Summary: This company is a leading producer and international marketer of value-added metal-based specialty chemicals.

Quantitative Evaluations

Outlook (1 Lowest—5 Highest)
• **3-**

Fair Value
• **48¼**

Risk
• **Low**

Earn./Div. Rank
• **NR**

Technical Eval.
• **Bearish** since 9/99

Rel. Strength Rank (1 Lowest—99 Highest)
• **82**

Insider Activity
• **Neutral**

Recent Price • 40⅛
52 Wk Range • 42½-26
Yield • 1.0%
12-Mo. P/E • 18.6

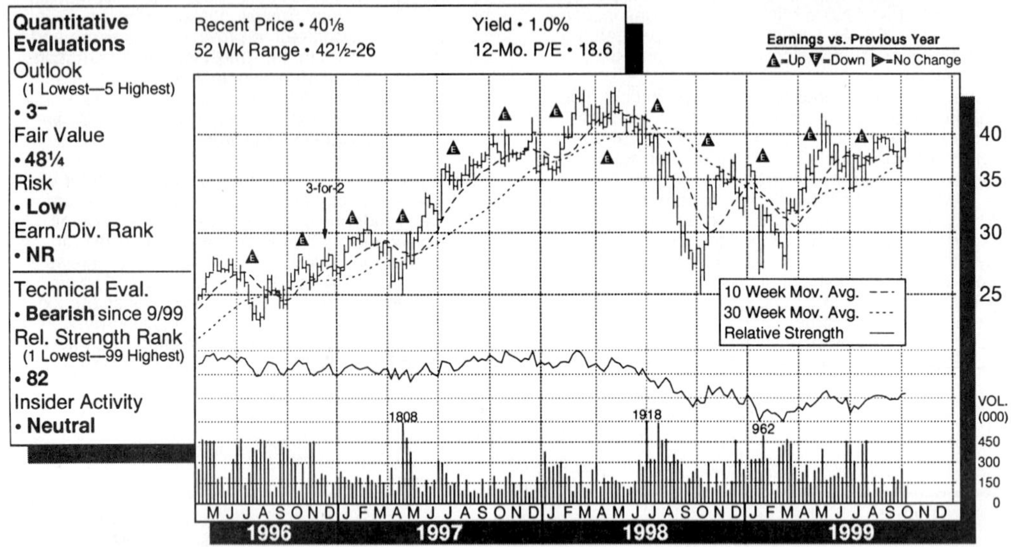

Business Profile - 25-MAY-99

In April 1999, OM Group reported that for the first quarter of 1999, the company enjoyed increased market demand and market share in the hard metal and diamond tool, memory disk and PVC additives markets. Also in April 1999, OM Group noted that it expects to enhance shareholder value in 1999 by utilizing expanded production capabilities and capacity. In January 1999, OMP announced the acquisition of Thai Oleochemicals Co., based in Thailand. OMP noted that it is the first major carboxylate and PVC additive producer to move into the Asia Pacific region, which the company expects to grow at a faster rate than western markets.

Operational Review - 25-MAY-99

For the three months ended March 31, 1999, net sales decreased 17%, year to year, primarily reflecting lower product selling prices which stemmed from a decline in cobalt, nickel and copper raw material prices. Profitability improved, reflecting an increase in physical volume of products sold and a favorable change in the product mix. The hard metal and diamond tool, memory disk and PVC additives product areas were particularly strong, due to improvements in market demand and market share. Pretax income was up 11%. Following taxes at 30.9%, against 33.7%, net income rose 16%, to $13.0 million ($0.54 a share, based on 6.2% more average shares), from $11.2 million ($0.49).

Stock Performance - 08-OCT-99

In the past 30 trading days, OMP's shares have increased 1%, compared to a 0.91% fall in the S&P 500. Average trading volume for the past five days was 24,180 shares, compared with the 40-day moving average of 30,149 shares.

Key Stock Statistics

Dividend Rate/Share	0.40	Shareholders	16,000
Shs. outstg. (M)	23.8	Market cap. (B)	$0.956
Avg. daily vol. (M)	0.036	Inst. holdings	92%
Tang. Bk. Value/Share	10.08		
Beta	0.91		

Value of $10,000 invested 5 years ago: $ 31,008

Fiscal Year Ending Dec. 31

	1999	1998	1997	1996	1995	1994
Revenues (Million $)						
1Q	114.1	138.1	110.1	102.8	89.43	54.86
2Q	123.7	139.2	124.3	101.5	84.97	59.06
3Q	—	124.7	126.3	89.07	80.97	59.52
4Q	—	119.3	126.6	94.59	105.6	77.84
Yr.	—	521.2	487.3	388.0	361.0	251.3
Earnings Per Share ($)						
1Q	**0.54**	**0.49**	0.43	**0.37**	**0.32**	0.23
2Q	**0.58**	**0.51**	0.44	**0.39**	**0.35**	0.28
3Q	—	**0.53**	0.45	**0.40**	**0.35**	0.29
4Q	—	**0.53**	**0.46**	**0.40**	**0.34**	0.29
Yr.	—	**2.05**	**1.78**	**1.56**	**1.36**	**1.09**

Next earnings report expected: mid October

Dividend Data (Dividends have been paid since 1994.)

Amount ($)	Date Decl.	Ex-Div. Date	Stock of Record	Payment Date
0.090	Nov. 09	Nov. 18	Nov. 20	Nov. 30 '98
0.100	Feb. 04	Feb. 10	Feb. 12	Feb. 26 '99
0.100	Apr. 19	May. 12	May. 14	May. 28 '99
0.100	Aug. 02	Aug. 11	Aug. 13	Aug. 31 '99

A Division of The McGraw-Hill Companies

OM Group, Inc.

Business Summary - 25-MAY-99

OM Group, a leading international producer and marketer of value-added metal based specialty chemicals and powders, believes that its focus on metal-based speciality chemicals as a core business is an important competitive advantage. In addition, OMP believes it is the only producer that manufactures and markets three categories of metal-based speciality chemicals: carboxylates, inorganic salts and powders. The company believes it is the world's leading producer of cobalt carboxylates and cobalt as well as nickel specialty inorganic salts and copper powders, and the world's second largest producer of cobalt extra fine powders.

The company serves more than 1,500 customers, with no single customer accounting for 10% or more of net sales. During 1998, approximately 52% of net sales were to customers in the Americas, 32% to European customers, and 16% to customers in the Asia-Pacific region.

The company supplies more than 400 different product offerings for diverse applications in more than 25 industries. Metal carboxylates are essential components in numerous complex chemical and industrial processes and are used in many end markets, including coatings, custom catalysts, liquid detergents, lubricants, fuel additives, plastic stabilizers and polyester and adhesion promoters. Metal salts are used in catalysts, colorants, rechargeable batteries, petroleum additives, magnetic media and finishing agents. Metal powders are components of cemented carbides for mining and machine tools, diamond tools, rechargeable batteries and in alloyed materials for a variety of applications.

OMP noted in March 1999 that its degree of profitability depends, in part, upon its ability to maintain a differential between raw material prices and product prices. Its flexibility in adjusting prices is greater with carboxylates than with inorganic salts and powders, which respond almost immediately to changes in raw material prices.

Research and development efforts are focused on adapting proprietary technologies to develop new products and working with customers to meet their specific requirements. New products under development include new chemical formulations, concentrations of various components, product forms and packaging methods.

In October 1998, OMP announced the purchase of 20,000 metric tons of cobalt-copper concentrate. The company reports that the additional concentrate will enhance OMP's ability to produce and supply cobalt for its worldwide customers. In addition, OMP said that a smelter in the Republic of Congo is scheduled for completion by the year 2000.

Per Share Data ($) (Year Ended Dec. 31)	1998	1997	1996	1995	1994	1993	1992	1991	1990	1989
Tangible Bk. Val.	9.06	8.36	8.71	7.39	6.50	5.55	NA	NA	NA	NA
Cash Flow	3.13	2.76	2.44	2.07	1.65	1.55	NA	NA	NA	NA
Earnings	2.05	1.78	1.56	1.35	1.09	0.95	0.77	NA	NA	NA
Dividends	0.36	0.32	0.29	0.24	0.19	Nil	Nil	NA	NA	NA
Payout Ratio	18%	18%	19%	18%	17%	Nil	Nil	NA	NA	NA
Prices - High	46	42	28¾	22⅜	16½	14	NA	NA	NA	NA
- Low	25	25	21⅝	14½	12½	9⅜	NA	NA	NA	NA
P/E Ratio - High	22	24	18	17	15	15	NA	NA	NA	NA
- Low	12	14	14	11	12	10	NA	NA	NA	NA
Income Statement Analysis (Million $)										
Revs.	521	487	388	361	251	180	201	NA	NA	NA
Oper. Inc.	112	91.8	67.2	57.7	45.9	34.8	NA	NA	NA	NA
Depr.	25.4	21.2	15.8	13.7	10.7	9.6	NA	NA	NA	NA
Int. Exp.	15.6	13.4	7.5	5.5	3.1	3.9	NA	NA	NA	NA
Pretax Inc.	71.3	58.0	44.4	38.5	31.0	23.1	18.8	NA	NA	NA
Eff. Tax Rate	32%	34%	32%	33%	33%	34%	36%	NA	NA	NA
Net Inc.	48.4	38.4	30.0	25.9	20.7	15.4	12.0	NA	NA	NA
Balance Sheet & Other Fin. Data (Million $)										
Cash	7.8	13.2	7.8	9.1	8.6	NA	NA	NA	NA	NA
Curr. Assets	420	325	271	234	157	110	89.0	NA	NA	NA
Total Assets	871	601	439	358	278	217	173	NA	NA	NA
Curr. Liab.	120	101	97.0	86.9	74.5	35.4	36.6	NA	NA	NA
LT Debt	310	170	109	89.8	46.6	30.6	48.5	NA	NA	NA
Common Eqty.	404	301	185	161	141	125	80.0	NA	NA	NA
Total Cap.	744	492	312	270	202	156	129	NA	NA	NA
Cap. Exp.	91.9	34.4	28.1	31.2	19.7	8.7	NA	NA	NA	NA
Cash Flow	73.8	59.7	45.9	39.7	31.4	25.0	NA	NA	NA	NA
Curr. Ratio	3.5	3.2	2.8	2.7	2.1	3.1	2.4	NA	NA	NA
% LT Debt of Cap.	41.7	34.6	34.9	33.3	23.0	19.6	37.6	NA	NA	NA
% Net Inc.of Revs.	9.3	7.9	7.7	7.2	8.3	8.6	6.0	NA	NA	NA
% Ret. on Assets	6.6	7.4	7.5	8.2	8.4	7.9	6.9	NA	NA	NA
% Ret. on Equity	13.7	15.8	17.3	13.7	15.6	15.0	15.7	NA	NA	NA

Data as orig reptd.; bef. results of disc opers/spec. items. Per share data adj. for stk. divs. Bold denotes diluted EPS (FASB 128)-prior periods restated. E-Estimated. NA-Not Available. NM-Not Meaningful. NR-Not Ranked.

Office—3500 Terminal Tower, 50 Public Square, Cleveland, OH 44113-2204. **Tel**—(216) 781-0083. **Chrmn & CEO**—J. P. Mooney. **Pres & COO**—E. W. Kissel.**CFO**—J. M. Materna. **VP & Secy**—M. J. Scott. **Investor Contact**—Kristine A. Marks. **Dirs**—E. Bak, L. R. Brodeur, F. Butler, T. R. Miklich, J. E. Mooney, J. P. Mooney, M. Toivanen. **Transfer Agent & Registrar**—National City Bank, Cleveland. **Incorporated**—in Delaware in 1991.**Empl**— 988. **S&P Analyst:** J. Friendly

STANDARD
&POOR'S
STOCK REPORTS

Omnova Solutions

NYSE Symbol **OMN**

In S&P SmallCap 600

26-OCT-99 **Industry:** Chemicals (Specialty)

Summary: Spun off by GenCorp in October 1999, OMN makes emulsion polymers, specialty chemicals and decorative and building products for industrial, commercial and consumer markets.

Quantitative Evaluations

Outlook
(1 Lowest—5 Highest)
• **NA**

Fair Value
• **NA**

Risk
• **NA**

Earn./Div. Rank
• **NR**

Technical Eval.
• **NA**

Rel. Strength Rank
(1 Lowest—99 Highest)
• **NA**

Insider Activity
• **NA**

Recent Price • 8⅛
52 Wk Range • 11⅛-7¾
Yield • Nil
12-Mo. P/E • NM

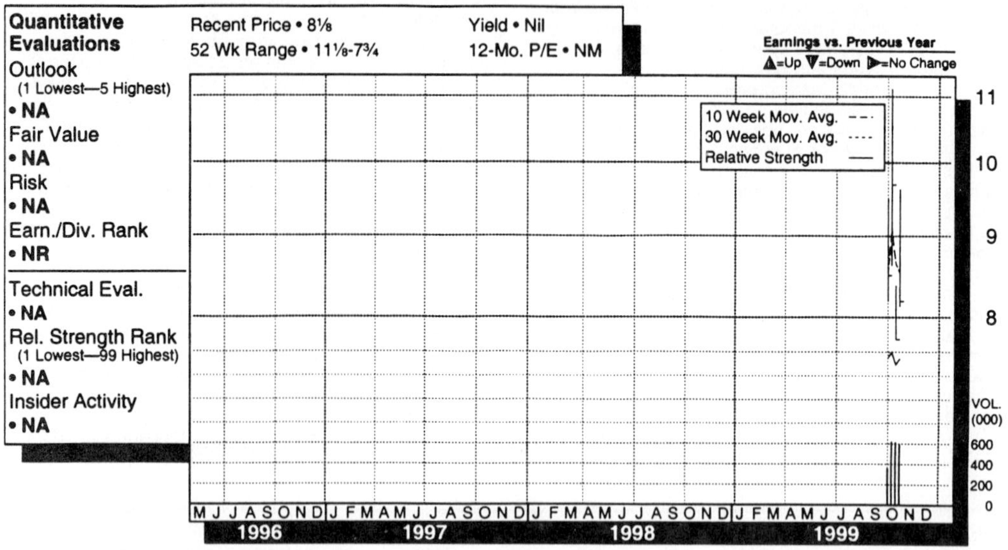

Business Profile - 15-OCT-99

Formerly a wholly owned subsidiary of GenCorp, Omnova Solutions was spun off by that company to its shareholders on October 1, 1999, with GenCorp. shareholders receiving one OMN common share for each GenCorp common share held. As part of the spinoff, GenCorp transferred its decorative and building products and performance chemicals businesses to Omnova. OMN's common shares were listed on the New York Stock Exchange concurrent with the spinoff.

Operational Review - 15-OCT-99

Based on a brief report, net sales for the three months ended February 28, 1999, rose 28%, year to year, mainly reflecting the impact of acquisitions. Performance chemicals revenues were up 57%, while decorative and building products revenues rose 12%. Net income was down 13%, to $7 million from $8 million. Earnings per share were equal to $0.21 for the first quarter of FY 99 (Nov.) and were based on 42.0 million average shares outstanding.

Stock Performance - 22-OCT-99

Stock Performance is not available because the company's shares have not been trading for all of the past 30 trading days.

Key Stock Statistics

Dividend Rate/Share	Nil	Shareholders	NA
Shs. outstg. (M)	41.8	Market cap. (B)	$0.314
Avg. daily vol. (M)	0.123	Inst. holdings	0%
Tang. Bk. Value/Share	NM		
Beta	NA		

Value of $10,000 invested 5 years ago: NA

Fiscal Year Ending Nov. 30

	1999	1998	1997	1996	1995	1994
Revenues (Million $)						
1Q	171.0	—	—	—	—	—
2Q	—	—	—	—	—	—
3Q	—	—	—	—	—	—
4Q	—	—	—	—	—	—
Yr.	—	766.0	—	—	—	—
Earnings Per Share ($)						
1Q	**0.21**	—	—	—	—	—
2Q	—	—	—	—	—	—
3Q	—	—	—	—	—	—
4Q	—	—	—	—	—	—
Yr.	—	**1.09**	—	—	—	—

Next earnings report expected: NA

Dividend Data

No cash dividends have been paid.

Omnova Solutions Inc.

Business Summary - 15-OCT-99

Engaged in the decorative and building products and performance chemicals businesses, Omnova Solutions Inc. has a comprehensive business strategy which includes: organic growth by providing total solutions, pursue growth through strategic acquisitions, leverage core competencies across businesses, expand research and design capabilities, increase technology linkages, and broaden international operations. OMN was spun off by GenCorp. to its shareholders on October 1, 1999.

The company derived about 64% of its historical revenues in FY 98 (Nov.) from its decorative and building products business, and 36% from its performance chemicals business.

The decorative and building products segment manufactures a comprehensive line of polyvinyl chloride and paper-based decorative and performance-enhancing surface products, including wallcovering, coated fabrics, vinyl woodgrain and paper laminates and graphic arts and industrial films, as well as membrane systems for roofing. Markets served include furniture, transportation, construction, remodeling, interior decorating and graphic arts.

OMN's decorative and building products business has established leading market positions in all of its product categories by using its core competencies in design, compounding, calendering, printing, embossing and coating. Given similar core competencies and base technology requirements, the business is able to leverage its investments in manufacturing, process and design improvement across this broad set of product lines and benefit from economies of scale. In addition, its broad offerings of decorative and building products uniquely positions it to provide integrated decorative solutions for its customers.

The performance chemicals segment manufactures a broad line of emulsion polymers and specialty chemicals used in the paper, carpet, textile, nonwoven, construction, coatings, adhesive and tire cord industries. Its product portfolio includes a growing specialty segment which provides resins, binders, coatings, adhesives and saturants to a broad variety of markets that include nonwoven, graphic arts, industrial coatings and construction. These products provide greater strength, improved processing ability and enhanced appearance for customer products.

With its strong number two position in the latex industry, the performance chemicals business is recognized in all of its markets for its core capabilities in polymer technology, its ability to rapidly develop highly customized products, and its ability to provide innovative, cost effective customer solutions.

The company's profits in recent years have benefited from acquisitions, operational improvement initiatives, aggressive cost containment, and a general shift toward higher-margin products.

Per Share Data ($) (Year Ended Nov. 30)	1998	1997	1996	1995	1994	1993	1992	1991	1990	1989
Tangible Bk. Val.	NA	NA	NA	NA	NA	NA	NA	NA	NA	NA
Cash Flow	1.71	NA	NA	NA	NA	NA	NA	NA	NA	NA
Earnings	1.09	NA	NA	NA	NA	NA	NA	NA	NA	NA
Dividends	NA	NA	NA	NA	NA	NA	NA	NA	NA	NA
Payout Ratio	NA	NA	NA	NA	NA	NA	NA	NA	NA	NA
Prices - High	NA	NA	NA	NA	NA	NA	NA	NA	NA	NA
- Low	NA	NA	NA	NA	NA	NA	NA	NA	NA	NA
P/E Ratio - High	NA	NA	NA	NA	NA	NA	NA	NA	NA	NA
- Low	NA	NA	NA	NA	NA	NA	NA	NA	NA	NA
Income Statement Analysis (Million $)										
Revs.	766	NA	NA	NA	NA	NA	NA	NA	NA	NA
Oper. Inc.	118	NA	NA	NA	NA	NA	NA	NA	NA	NA
Depr.	26.0	NA	NA	NA	NA	NA	NA	NA	NA	NA
Int. Exp.	11.0	NA	NA	NA	NA	NA	NA	NA	NA	NA
Pretax Inc.	77.0	NA	NA	NA	NA	NA	NA	NA	NA	NA
Eff. Tax Rate	40%	NA	NA	NA	NA	NA	NA	NA	NA	NA
Net Inc.	46.0	NA	NA	NA	NA	NA	NA	NA	NA	NA
Balance Sheet & Other Fin. Data (Million $)										
Cash	6.0	NA	NA	NA	NA	NA	NA	NA	NA	NA
Curr. Assets	190	NA	NA	NA	NA	NA	NA	NA	NA	NA
Total Assets	680	NA	NA	NA	NA	NA	NA	NA	NA	NA
Curr. Liab.	96.0	NA	NA	NA	NA	NA	NA	NA	NA	NA
LT Debt	188	NA	NA	NA	NA	NA	NA	NA	NA	NA
Common Eqty.	302	NA	NA	NA	NA	NA	NA	NA	NA	NA
Total Cap.	504	NA	NA	NA	NA	NA	NA	NA	NA	NA
Cap. Exp.	NA	NA	NA	NA	NA	NA	NA	NA	NA	NA
Cash Flow	72.0	NA	NA	NA	NA	NA	NA	NA	NA	NA
Curr. Ratio	2.0	NA	NA	NA	NA	NA	NA	NA	NA	NA
% LT Debt of Cap.	37.3	NA	NA	NA	NA	NA	NA	NA	NA	NA
% Net Inc.of Revs.	6.0	NA	NA	NA	NA	NA	NA	NA	NA	NA
% Ret. on Assets	NA	NA	NA	NA	NA	NA	NA	NA	NA	NA
% Ret. on Equity	NA	NA	NA	NA	NA	NA	NA	NA	NA	NA

Data as orig reptd.; bef. results of disc opers/spec. items. Data for 1998 is pro forma; bal. sheet data as of Feb. 28, 1999. Per share data adj. for stk. divs. Bold denotes diluted EPS (FASB 128)-prior periods restated. E-Estimated. NA-Not Available. NM-Not Meaningful. NR-Not Ranked.

Office—175 Ghent Rd., Fairlawn, OH 44333. **Tel**—(330) 869-4200. **Chrmn & CEO**—J. B. Yasinsky. **SVP-CFO**—M. E. Hicks. **Secy**—C. A. Slack. **Dirs**—E. P. Campbell, C. A. Corry, D. E. McGarry, S. W. Percy, R. B. Pipes, J. B. Yasinsky. **Transfer Agent** —Bank of New York. **Incorporated**—in Ohio in 1999. **Empl**— 2,600. **S&P Analyst:** J. J. Schemitsch

STANDARD
&POOR'S
STOCK REPORTS

Orbital Sciences

NYSE Symbol **ORB**

In S&P SmallCap 600

09-OCT-99

Industry: Aerospace/Defense

Summary: This leading maker of small satellites is expanding into various satellite service businesses.

S&P Opinion: Hold (★★★)

Recent Price • 17¾

52 Wk Range • 45¼-16¼

Yield • Nil

12-Mo. P/E • NM

Quantitative Evaluations

Outlook (1 Lowest—5 Highest) • 3⁻

Fair Value • **20¾**

Risk • **NA**

Earn./Div. Rank • **B-**

Technical Eval. • **Bearish** since 8/99

Rel. Strength Rank (1 Lowest—99 Highest) • **14**

Insider Activity • **Neutral**

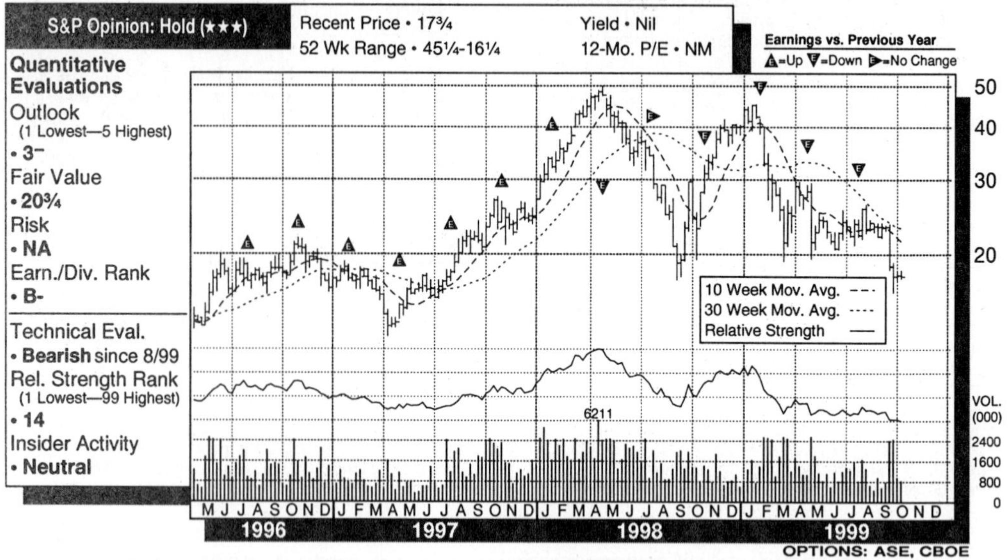

OPTIONS: ASE, CBOE

Overview - 09-JUN-99

Continuing losses in ORB's GPS receiver equipment segment continue to hurt the company's earnings and investment returns. In light of the mediocre fundamentals of the volatile satellite industry, as well as ORB's past performance, we are skeptical about ORB's ability to post outsized sustainable earnings and investment returns in future periods. Congress recently sharply curtailed the ability of U.S. satellite companies to arrange foreign launches of their satellites (the action was related to allegations that Hughes Electronics and Loral Space & Communications illegally passed sensitive rocket technology to China). It also remains to be seen whether ORB's fledgling satellite services business will be able to materially boost earnings and investment returns. Although potential demand for satellite services is enormous, actual demand does not seem to meet expectations, as shown by the troubled Iridium satellite telephone venture.

Valuation - 09-JUN-99

From 1991 through 1998, ORB slightly outpaced the S&P 500, rising at an 18% annual rate, versus 17% for the broader market. However, we must point out that ORB's performance was skewed by initially strong 1998 earnings results, which were subsequently found to be overstated by over 70% (due to overstatement of revenues from timing-related recognition of certain long-term contracts and license fees, and understatement of product improvement costs). In addition to our caution regarding ORB's financials, we're also chary about its chances of dramatically boosting investment returns, as measured by ROE. ORB's 7-year average ROE stands at a low 3%. Even if ORB could boost ROE to 10%, on increased sales of higher margin satellite services, our valuation models (which use, in part, projected ROE) still indicate that the shares are, at best, fully valued at recent levels.

Key Stock Statistics

S&P EPS Est. 1999	-1.00	Tang. Bk. Value/Share	5.62
P/E on S&P Est. 1999	NM	Beta	1.83
S&P EPS Est. 2000	1.05	Shareholders	1,325
Dividend Rate/Share	Nil	Market cap. (B)	$0.664
Shs. outstg. (M)	37.4	Inst. holdings	41%
Avg. daily vol. (M)	0.361		

Value of $10,000 invested 5 years ago: $ 8,658

Fiscal Year Ending Dec. 31

	1999	1998	1997	1996	1995	1994
Revenues (Million $)						
1Q	204.3	186.2	122.1	104.9	89.00	50.30
2Q	232.3	184.5	142.2	116.5	81.80	48.40
3Q	—	187.7	164.7	119.6	95.80	58.20
4Q	—	175.9	177.0	120.5	97.80	65.10
Yr.	—	734.3	606.0	461.4	364.3	221.9
Earnings Per Share ($)						
1Q	-0.43	0.13	0.16	0.12	-0.05	0.12
2Q	-0.27	0.17	0.17	0.14	-0.07	0.03
3Q	—	0.06	0.18	0.15	0.06	0.08
4Q	—	-0.53	0.18	0.14	-0.14	0.06
Yr.	E-1.00	-0.18	0.69	0.55	-0.03	0.32

Next earnings report expected: mid October

Dividend Data

The company has not paid dividends.

A Division of The McGraw-Hill Companies

Orbital Sciences Corporation

Business Summary - 09-JUN-99

Orbital Science is in the process of shifting its portfolio of satellite businesses. The company currently generates 95% of revenues from its satellite and satellite equipment businesses, and 5% of revenues from burgeoning satellite service businesses. Management aims ultimately to derive 50% of revenues from satellite making, and 50% of revenues from higher margin satellite services.

The Space & Ground Infrastructure Systems segment (84% of 1998 revenues) makes satellites, satellite-launching rockets, satellite ground systems, and electronics and cockpit controls equipment. ORB specializes in making small and medium-sized satellites used in low-Earth orbit (LEO) and geosynchronous orbit (GEO). The company sells its satellites to commercial and military customers for communications, broadcasting, scientific and military purposes. ORB sells its satellite ground stations, which receive and process data signals, to U.S., European and Canadian space agencies, as well commercial customers around the world. The Fairchild Defense division (10% of 1998 revenues) makes sophisticated electronics and cockpit controls equipment for use in military aircraft, helicopter and land vehicles. Latest three-year average segment profits and capital expenditures, as a percentage of segment revenues, stand at 8% and 7%, respectively.

The Satellite Access Products segment (15% of revenues) makes satellite-based navigation, positioning and communications equipment. ORB's devices receive signals from the U.S. Global Positioning System (GPS), a constellation of satellites initially used by the U.S. military. Civilians are now allowed to access GPS signals, to navigate or monitor boats and planes. The company sees growth opportunities in providing GPS-tracking devices for cars. Principal competitors include Trimble Navigation (Nasdaq: TRMB). Latest three-year average capital expenditures, as a percentage of segment revenues, stand at 4%; the segment has posted operating losses in two of the last three years.

The burgeoning Satellite Services segment (1% of revenues) consists of the majority-owned ORBCOMM and ORBIMAGE units. ORCOMM provides various satellite-delivered communications services, via ORB's recently completed constellation of 28 small LEO satellites. ORBCOMM's offerings include global monitoring, tracking and messaging services. ORBIMAGE provides color images of the Earth's surface. ORBIMAGE's imaging is used by commercial fishermen, to locate fishing beds; farmers, to improve crop yield; and meteorologists, to monitor the effects of hurricanes. In the last three years, the segment has incurred large capital expenses from installing ORBCOMM's 28-satellite constellation, and posted operating losses (as the segment had not begun operations during this time period).

Per Share Data ($) (Year Ended Dec. 31)	1998	1997	1996	1995	1994	1993	1992	1991	1990	1989
Tangible Bk. Val.	7.62	5.33	8.12	6.74	6.60	7.94	NA	NA	NA	NA
Cash Flow	0.75	1.38	1.41	0.72	1.03	0.96	0.81	NA	NA	NA
Earnings	-0.18	0.69	0.55	-0.03	0.28	0.43	0.27	0.13	-0.21	NA
Dividends	Nil	Nil	Nil	Nil	Nil	Nil	Nil	Nil	Nil	NA
Payout Ratio	Nil	Nil	Nil	Nil	Nil	Nil	Nil	Nil	Nil	NA
Prices - High	50	30¾	21⅞	22	26½	23½	19	NA	NA	NA
- Low	17⅜	12¾	11¾	12⅛	14	9½	10¾	NA	NA	NA
P/E Ratio - High	NM	45	40	NM	95	55	70	NA	NA	NA
- Low	NM	18	21	NM	50	22	40	NA	NA	NA
Income Statement Analysis (Million $)										
Revs.	734	606	461	364	222	223	204	162	123	NA
Oper. Inc.	61.9	53.3	48.9	19.9	22.9	18.4	12.5	NA	NA	NA
Depr.	36.6	23.9	25.1	22.2	14.3	7.9	7.7	NA	NA	NA
Int. Exp.	4.0	0.4	2.5	3.8	1.5	1.0	0.1	NA	NA	NA
Pretax Inc.	-12.4	22.4	17.7	-2.0	7.5	8.5	5.6	4.1	-2.2	NA
Eff. Tax Rate	NM	9.08%	10%	NM	28%	27%	29%	56%	NM	NA
Net Inc.	-6.4	23.0	15.9	-0.7	5.4	6.2	3.9	1.8	-2.4	NA
Balance Sheet & Other Fin. Data (Million $)										
Cash	25.7	12.6	32.7	15.3	33.6	76.7	15.0	38.7	12.7	NA
Curr. Assets	304	264	211	199	160	179	NA	NA	NA	NA
Total Assets	963	772	505	467	403	322	176	169	103	NA
Curr. Liab.	251	212	127	112	108	91.0	NA	NA	NA	NA
LT Debt	181	198	33.1	96.7	81.2	61.6	0.6	0.2	2.7	NA
Common Eqty.	511	355	331	239	202	166	108	103	57.0	NA
Total Cap.	709	557	362	335	283	227	109	103	59.0	NA
Cap. Exp.	48.3	45.0	43.5	17.2	27.1	35.6	41.7	NA	NA	NA
Cash Flow	30.2	46.9	41.0	21.5	19.6	14.1	11.6	NA	NA	NA
Curr. Ratio	1.2	1.2	1.7	1.8	1.5	2.0	NA	NA	NA	NA
% LT Debt of Cap.	25.6	35.5	9.1	28.9	28.7	27.1	0.5	0.2	4.6	NA
% Net Inc.of Revs.	NM	3.8	3.4	NM	2.4	2.8	1.9	1.1	NM	NA
% Ret. on Assets	NM	3.6	3.3	NM	1.5	2.5	2.3	1.3	NA	NA
% Ret. on Equity	NM	6.7	5.6	NM	2.9	4.5	3.7	2.3	NA	NA

Data as orig reptd.; bef. results of disc opers/spec. items. Per share data adj. for stk. divs. Bold denotes diluted EPS (FASB 128)-prior periods restated. E-Estimated. NA-Not Available. NM-Not Meaningful. NR-Not Ranked.

Office—21700 Atlantic Boulevard, Dulles, VA 20166. **Tel**—(703) 406-5000. **Website**—http://www.orbital.com **Chrmn, Pres & CEO**—D. W. Thompson. **CFO**—J. V. Pirone. **Secy**—L. C. Seeman. **Investor Contact**—Angela Dettwiler (703) 406-5583. **Dirs**—F. C. Alcorn, K. H. Burke, B. W. Ferguson, D. J. Fink, L. A. Fisk, J. L. Kerrebrock, D. S. Luke, J. L. McLucas, J. Obuchowski, F. L. Salizzoni, H. H. Schmitt, J. R. Thompson, S. L. Webster. **Transfer Agent & Registrar**—First National Bank of Boston. **Incorporated**—in Delaware in 1987. **Empl**— 5,200. **S&P Analyst:** Robert E. Friedman, CPA

STANDARD
&POOR'S
STOCK REPORTS

Organogenesis Inc.

ASE Symbol **ORG**

In S&P SmallCap 600

23-OCT-99 **Industry:** Biotechnology

Summary: ORG designs, develops, and manufactures medical therapeutics using living cells and natural connective tissue components.

S&P Opinion: Hold (★★★)

Recent Price • 8⅜
52 Wk Range • 18¼-6½
Yield • Nil
12-Mo. P/E • NM

Quantitative Evaluations

Outlook (1 Lowest—5 Highest)
• **NA**

Fair Value
• **NA**

Risk
• **Average**

Earn./Div. Rank
• **C**

Technical Eval.
• **NA**

Rel. Strength Rank (1 Lowest—99 Highest)
• **29**

Insider Activity
• **Neutral**

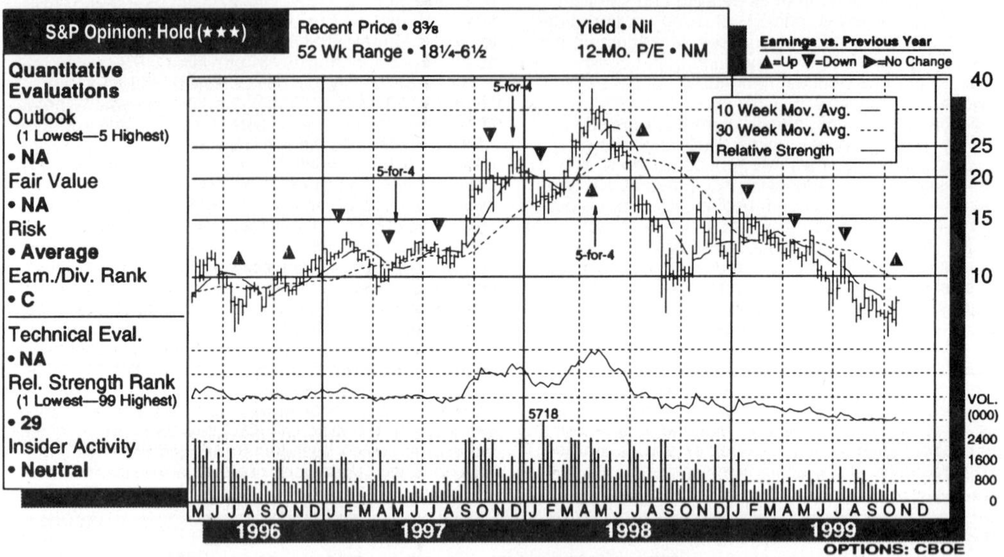

Overview - 20-APR-99

In 1998, end sales of ORG's lead product, Apligraf, totaled roughly $1.6 million. A human skin equivalent for treating venous leg ulcers, Apligraf, received FDA approval in May 1998 and is now sold in the U.S. and Canada by marketing partner, Novartis Pharma AG. ORG receives royalty and manufacturing revenues from Novartis reflecting between 20%-30% of total end sales of Apligraf. Thus far, sales of the product have fallen way short of initial expectations. Possible reasons are: the cost ($975 per application) and slow insurance reimbursement due to product coding issues. Currently, we expect ORG's product revenue to reach about $13 million in 1999 (on total Apligraf sales of $54 million), as the product continues to demonstrate favorable medical results and gain acceptance in wound care clinics. Reimbursement obstacles are anticipated to be resolved in 1999's fourth quarter. We estimate losses of $0.37 a share in 1999, and $0.15 in 2000.

Valuation - 18-AUG-99

Shares of ORG have underperformed the market in 1999, reflecting disappointing total revenues generated by Apligraf since its approval in May 1998. Sales of this product have fallen short of expectations, reflecting a lack of standardized insurance reimbursement and concerns over product cost ($975 per unit). The company and Novartis are working to gain insurance acceptance of Apligraf by emphasizing its cost-effectiveness relative to standard treatments and its therapeutic value. Through 2000, stock performance will depend on gaining reimbursement acceptance for Apligraf, a limited European introduction for Apligraf by year-end 1999, and possible approval for Apligraf in treating diabetic ulcers in 2000. Although these events are probable, the timing and impact may offer limited upside potential in the near-term.

Key Stock Statistics

S&P EPS Est. 1999	-0.79	Tang. Bk. Value/Share	0.41
P/E on S&P Est. 1999	NM	Beta	2.13
S&P EPS Est. 2000	-0.50	Shareholders	638
Dividend Rate/Share	Nil	Market cap. (B)	$0.225
Shs. outstg. (M)	30.5	Inst. holdings	30%
Avg. daily vol. (M)	0.106		

Value of $10,000 invested 5 years ago: $ 20,005

Fiscal Year Ending Dec. 31

	1999	1998	1997	1996	1995	1994
Revenues (Million $)						
1Q	0.68	2.27	0.26	2.09	0.16	0.24
2Q	0.94	5.38	2.81	2.43	0.10	0.24
3Q	—	0.74	0.27	2.78	0.16	0.22
4Q	—	0.61	0.19	0.23	0.22	0.30
Yr.	—	9.00	3.53	7.53	0.63	1.00
Earnings Per Share ($)						
1Q	**-0.19**	**-0.10**	**-0.13**	-0.07	-0.13	-0.11
2Q	**-0.25**	**0.01**	**-0.24**	-0.04	-0.14	-0.12
3Q	**E-0.17**	**-0.19**	**-0.15**	-0.03	-0.13	-0.12
4Q	**E-0.18**	**-0.19**	**-0.16**	-0.14	-0.13	-0.11
Yr.	**E-0.79**	**-0.48**	**-0.70**	**-0.27**	**-0.52**	-0.47

Next earnings report expected: mid November

Dividend Data

No cash dividends have been paid to date on the common stock, and the company does not anticipate paying cash dividends in the foreseeable future.

A Division of The McGraw-Hill Companies

Organogenesis Inc.

Business Summary - 18-AUG-99

This biotechnology concern was created to apply the emerging field of tissue engineering to major medical needs, with a focus on living tissue replacements, cell-based organ assist devices, and other tissue-engineered products. ORG's commercialization strategy is to market its products independently or through collaborative agreements with established health care firms.

ORG's most advanced product, Apligraf, is a living, all natural, and bi-layered skin substitute designed to promote the establishment and growth of new tissues that maintain, restore, or improve biological function. In April 1997 and May 1998, Apligraf received marketing approval for treating venous leg ulcers in Canada and the U.S., respectively. ORG planned to receive EU approval sometime in 1999. Novartis Pharma AG has exclusive global marketing rights to Apligraf, with ORG receiving royalties and a per unit manufacturing payment of 20-30% of aggregate volume sales of Apligraf, which is currently priced at $975 per unit.

Apligraf is also in clinical studies for the treatment of diabetic foot ulcers, with a premarketing approval application planned for the first quarter of 2000. In addition, Apilgraf is under development for the treatment of other wound conditions, including burns, epidermolysis bullosa, and wounds occurring from skin surgery.

ORG expects to advance its Vitrix product, a soft tissue replacement designed to be used as a dermal replacement in wound care, reconstructive surgery, and periodontal indications, into clinical trials in 1999.

The company is also developing a bioartificial liver product that contains healthy, highly functional liver cells. This external device is being designed to provide temporary liver function to patients with liver disorders until either a transplant becomes available or the patient's own liver recovers. In April 1999, ORG purchased intellectual property and equipment for use in the development of its bioartificial liver device from Baxter Healthcare Corp. for 50,000 common shares and contingent cash considerations.

Other products in development include a vascular graft to be used as a saphenous vein substitute in cardiovascular surgery, and injectable collagen fibrils to potentially be used in treating female urinary incontinence and to soften wrinkles.

As of 1998 year-end, the company intended to out-license its Graftpatch product (for the reinforcement of soft tissue in general surgical procedures) to a marketing partner. In December 1998, ORG began selling TestSkin II, a skin-like product for in vitro use by pharmaceutical, cosmetic, and drug delivery firms for product development and testing.

In March 1999, ORG raised $20 million through a private placement of five year 7% convertible debentures and 400,000 warrants. Interest obligations on these debentures are payable in either cash or common stock, or a combination of cash and stock.

Per Share Data ($)										
(Year Ended Dec. 31)	**1998**	**1997**	**1996**	**1995**	**1994**	**1993**	**1992**	**1991**	**1990**	**1989**
Tangible Bk. Val.	0.76	0.50	0.83	0.83	0.52	0.93	1.38	1.65	0.26	0.35
Cash Flow	-0.43	-0.80	-0.28	-0.60	-0.42	-0.40	-0.25	-0.28	-0.31	-0.23
Earnings	-0.48	-0.70	-0.34	-0.65	-0.47	-0.45	-0.28	-0.32	-0.36	-0.28
Dividends	Nil	Nil	Nil	Nil	Nil	Nil	Nil	Nil	Nil	Nil
Payout Ratio	Nil	Nil	Nil	Nil	Nil	Nil	Nil	Nil	Nil	Nil
Prices - High	$37\frac{3}{4}$	$25\frac{1}{4}$	$12\frac{7}{8}$	$11\frac{1}{2}$	$8\frac{1}{4}$	$4\frac{1}{2}$	$10\frac{5}{8}$	$10\frac{1}{2}$	$5\frac{5}{8}$	$7\frac{1}{4}$
- Low	$7\frac{3}{4}$	$8\frac{7}{8}$	$6\frac{7}{8}$	$3\frac{7}{8}$	$3\frac{1}{2}$	$2\frac{9}{16}$	3	$2\frac{7}{16}$	$1\frac{7}{8}$	$3\frac{7}{8}$
P/E Ratio - High	NM	NM	NM	NM	NM	NM	NM	NM	NM	NM
- Low	NM	NM	NM	NM	NM	NM	NM	NA	NA	NA
Income Statement Analysis (Million $)										
Revs.	7.9	3.0	6.5	0.0	0.3	0.5	3.2	3.8	3.2	3.1
Oper. Inc.	-13.6	-13.1	-7.4	-12.3	-10.1	-10.1	-7.0	-5.5	-5.8	-4.2
Depr.	1.5	1.7	1.1	1.0	0.9	1.0	0.7	0.7	0.8	0.7
Int. Exp.	Nil	Nil	Nil	Nil	Nil	Nil	Nil	Nil	Nil	Nil
Pretax Inc.	-14.0	-19.8	-7.5	-12.7	-10.4	-9.9	-6.2	-5.8	-6.1	-4.3
Eff. Tax Rate	NM	NM	NM	NM	NM	NM	NM	NM	NM	NM
Net Inc.	-14.0	-19.8	-7.5	-12.7	-10.4	-9.9	-6.2	-5.8	-6.1	-4.3
Balance Sheet & Other Fin. Data (Million $)										
Cash	5.1	0.3	14.4	13.7	8.9	11.6	14.5	16.8	2.9	3.4
Curr. Assets	19.0	7.1	15.1	14.3	9.4	12.3	15.3	17.9	3.9	4.1
Total Assets	26.7	13.8	22.4	19.3	15.1	24.0	34.5	40.2	5.9	6.4
Curr. Liab.	3.5	2.2	3.9	1.4	1.0	0.9	1.5	1.2	0.9	0.7
LT Debt	Nil	Nil	Nil	Nil	Nil	Nil	Nil	Nil	Nil	Nil
Common Eqty.	23.2	11.5	18.5	17.8	11.9	20.8	30.6	36.5	4.5	5.5
Total Cap.	23.2	11.5	18.5	17.8	13.9	22.8	32.6	38.5	4.5	5.5
Cap. Exp.	2.5	1.1	3.3	0.3	0.5	0.4	6.1	0.3	0.5	0.8
Cash Flow	-12.6	-18.1	-6.5	-11.7	-9.5	-9.0	-5.5	-5.1	-5.3	-3.6
Curr. Ratio	5.5	3.2	3.9	10.3	9.4	13.3	10.0	14.5	4.2	5.5
% LT Debt of Cap.	Nil	Nil	Nil	Nil	Nil	Nil	Nil	Nil	Nil	Nil
% Net Inc.of Revs.	NM	NM	NM	NM	NM	NM	NM	NM	NM	NM
% Ret. on Assets	NM	NM	NM	NM	NM	NM	NM	NM	NM	NM
% Ret. on Equity	NM	NM	NM	NM	NM	NM	NM	NM	NM	NM

Data as orig reptd.; bef. results of disc opers/spec. items. Per share data adj. for stk. divs. Bold denotes diluted EPS (FASB 128)-prior periods restated. E-Estimated. NA-Not Available. NM-Not Meaningful. NR-Not Ranked.

Office—150 Dan Rd., Canton, MA 02021. **Tel**—(781) 575-0775. **Website**—http://www.organogenesis.com **Chrmn & CEO**—H. M. Stein. **Pres & COO**—D. T. Rovee. **VP, CFO, Treas & Secy**—D. A. Lopolito. **Investor Contact**—Carol Hausner. **Dirs**—R. S. Cresse, A. Erani, B. Marden, K. J. Novack, B. Olsen, M. A. Piret, D. T. Rovee, A. E. Schrafl, H. M. Stein. **Transfer Agent & Registrar**—American Stock Transfer & Trust Co., NYC. **Incorporated**—in Delaware in 1985. **Empl**— 194. **S&P Analyst:** Frank DiLorenzo

STANDARD
&POOR'S
STOCK REPORTS

Orion Capital

NYSE Symbol **OC**

In S&P SmallCap 600

23-OCT-99

Industry: Insurance (Property-Casualty)

Summary: This insurance holding company, which is engaged in the specialty property and casualty insurance business, has agreed to be acquired by Royal & Sun Alliance Insurance Group plc.

Quantitative Evaluations

Outlook (1 Lowest—5 Highest) • 1

Fair Value • 45¾

Risk • Low

Earn./Div. Rank • A

Technical Eval. • NA

Rel. Strength Rank (1 Lowest—99 Highest) • 82

Insider Activity • NA

Recent Price • 48 | 52 Wk Range • 48¾-27½ | Yield • 1.5% | 12-Mo. P/E • NM

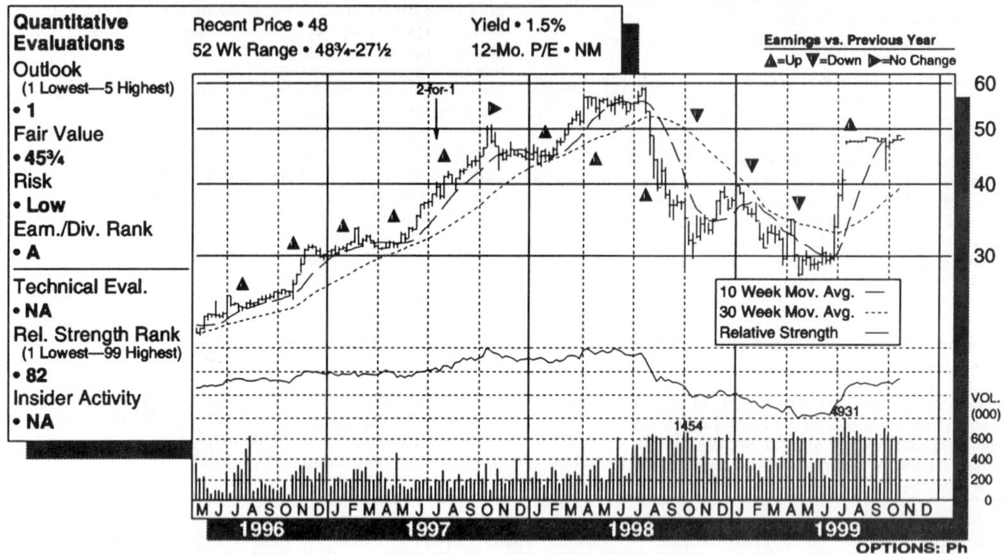

Business Profile - 20-OCT-99

In July 1999, Orion agreed to be acquired by London-based Royal & Sun Alliance Insurance Group plc. In October 1999, Royal & Sun extended the expiration date of its $50 a share cash tender offer for all Orion shares to November 5, 1999, to accommodate the insurance regulatory process, with many states still required to authorize the deal. As of October 15, 1999, approximately 15 million shares of OC common stock had been validly tendered and not withdrawn pursuant to the tender offer.

Operational Review - 20-OCT-99

Total revenues in the six months ended June 30, 1999, declined 17%, year to year, as 11% lower premiums earned reflected the effects of statutory rate decreases in workers' compensation and OC's exit of certain unprofitable commodity business in its property and casualty division. In addition, realized investment gains were sharply lower. Total expenses increased 5.4%, principally due to higher losses incurred and loss adjustment expenses reflecting a significant strengthening of the company's reserve position. After a tax benefit of $30.8 million, versus taxes at 27.5%, a loss of $45.4 million ($1.68 a share) contrasted with income of $80.3 million ($2.85). Results exclude a charge of $0.17 in 1999 due to the adoption of a new accounting principle.

Stock Performance - 22-OCT-99

In the past 30 trading days, OC's shares have increased 2%, compared to a 4% fall in the S&P 500. Average trading volume for the past five days was 119,840 shares, compared with the 40-day moving average of 181,610 shares.

Key Stock Statistics

Dividend Rate/Share	0.72	Shareholders	1,900
Shs. outstg. (M)	27.4	Market cap. (B)	$ 1.3
Avg. daily vol. (M)	0.147	Inst. holdings	67%
Tang. Bk. Value/Share	17.77		
Beta	0.82		

Value of $10,000 invested 5 years ago: $ 33,811

Fiscal Year Ending Dec. 31

	1999	1998	1997	1996	1995	1994
Revenues (Million $)						
1Q	336.3	424.8	384.9	347.8	201.8	188.7
2Q	382.0	442.6	390.1	367.2	212.1	183.6
3Q	—	421.4	398.4	380.4	222.2	204.8
4Q	—	428.0	417.2	398.1	238.2	203.8
Yr.	—	1,717	1,591	1,493	874.3	781.0
Earnings Per Share ($)						
1Q	**-3.26**	**1.50**	**1.06**	**0.64**	0.60	0.46
2Q	**1.56**	**1.36**	**0.91**	**0.74**	0.56	0.40
3Q	—	**0.08**	**0.88**	**0.88**	0.60	0.54
4Q	—	**0.75**	**1.30**	**0.86**	0.61	0.54
Yr.	—	**3.69**	**4.15**	**3.12**	**1.93**	1.93

Next earnings report expected: late October

Dividend Data (Dividends have been paid since 1978.)

Amount ($)	Date Decl.	Ex-Div. Date	Stock of Record	Payment Date
0.180	Oct. 23	Dec. 11	Dec. 15	Jan. 02 '99
0.180	Feb. 01	Mar. 12	Mar. 16	Apr. 01 '99
0.180	May. 25	Jun. 11	Jun. 15	Jul. 01 '99
0.180	Aug. 11	Sep. 13	Sep. 15	Oct. 01 '99

A Division of The McGraw-Hill Companies

Orion Capital Corporation

Business Summary - 20-OCT-99

Orion Capital Corporation agreed in July 1999 to be acquired by Royal & Sun Alliance Insurance Group plc, a global insurance provider. Orion shareholders have been offered $50 a share, and pending regulatory approval, the deal is expected to be completed in the fourth quarter of 1999. Orion has the ability to provide almost any type of property and casualty insurance nationwide and in Canada. However, Orion seeks to distinguish itself from its many competitors in the property and casualty insurance business by focusing on niche markets with high potential. Through its 19 wholly-owned insurance subsidiaries, Orion operates in three different segments: workers' compensation, nonstandard automobile and specialty commercial.

The workers' compensation segment is comprised of the EBI Companies, which provide workers' compensation insurance and accident prevention and cost containment services. Operating through more than 1,000 independent agents, EBI is the 11th largest writer of workers' compensation insurance in the U.S. EBI contributed 29% of total net premiums written in 1998. The segment targets five core business classes with high frequency of loss patterns where it believes the ability to successfully implement its "Zero Accident Culture" has been proven. Those five segments include health care, manufacturing, schools, hospitality and the service sector. The segment grew net premiums at a rate of 20% in 1998, and incurred a sustained outstanding combined ratio of 92.6%.

The nonstandard automobile segment consists of wholly owned OrionAuto (formerly Guaranty National), which is one of the top 10 nonstandard writers in the U.S. OrionAuto writes traditional nonstandard coverage and less common one-month coverage. The company operates through 12,000 independent agents in 35 states. The segment grew net written premiums 29% in 1998 (9% excluding the impact of acquisitions), and accounted for 28% of total net written premiums. The segment posted a combined operating ratio of 94.3% in 1998.

The company's specialty commercial segment concentrates on highly specialized, client-focused lines of business in the property and casualty insurance field. At year-end 1998, the segment marketed various specialty commercial products and services including professional liability insurance through DPIC Companies; client-focused specialty insurance programs through Orion Specialty; underwriting management specializing in ocean marine, inland marine and commercial property insurance through Wm. H. McGee; insurance for international trade through the company's 26% interest in Intercargo Corporation; and also includes the run-off operations of the company's assumed reinsurance business, SecurityRe, which was sold in 1996. Net written premiums in this segment grew 1.1% in 1998, and accounted for 43% of total net written premiums.

Per Share Data ($) **(Year Ended Dec. 31)**	**1998**	**1997**	**1996**	**1995**	**1994**	**1993**	**1992**	**1991**	**1990**	**1989**
Tangible Bk. Val.	20.60	21.12	17.89	15.79	11.96	12.64	9.58	7.84	3.69	4.06
Oper. Earnings	NA	3.07	2.63	2.11	1.84	1.61	1.66	2.06	1.26	1.06
Earnings	3.69	4.15	3.12	2.38	1.93	1.94	1.80	1.88	0.89	1.11
Dividends	0.68	0.92	0.52	0.43	0.38	0.34	0.30	0.29	0.29	0.26
Payout Ratio	18%	22%	17%	18%	20%	18%	17%	16%	32%	24%
Prices - High	59¼	51	31½	22⅝	17⅝	18¾	14⅜	10¾	7¾	9⅛
- Low	28	30	21¼	17⅛	14⅛	13⅝	9¼	5¼	4⅛	4⅞
P/E Ratio - High	16	12	10	9	9	10	8	6	9	8
- Low	8	7	7	7	7	7	5	3	5	4
Income Statement Analysis (Million $)										
Premium Inc.	1,503	1,358	1,301	749	691	617	560	701	688	719
Net Invest. Inc.	143	165	145	99	84.9	91.8	82.5	100	96.9	95.4
Oth. Revs.	70.5	68.0	47.0	26.0	4.8	10.9	5.5	35.8	-1.0	7.8
Total Revs.	1,717	1,426	1,493	874	781	720	648	837	784	822
Pretax Inc.	157	176	127	88.0	71.5	72.5	46.7	46.1	26.8	32.8
Net Oper. Inc.	68.6	85.7	72.9	59.9	52.8	47.5	42.7	46.5	32.8	29.5
Net Inc.	103	116	86.6	67.6	55.2	57.0	45.8	44.7	25.5	30.3
Balance Sheet & Other Fin. Data (Million $)										
Cash & Equiv.	45.0	9.3	37.3	22.9	23.6	24.1	30.9	29.3	30.7	29.5
Premiums Due	NA	189	181	137	125	111	102	96.0	113	114
Invest. Assets: Bonds	1,611	1,783	1,532	1,235	1,002	1,029	934	915	1,005	970
Invest. Assets: Stocks	511	439	362	305	264	243	186	130	105	104
Invest. Assets: Loans	NA	Nil	Nil	Nil	Nil	Nil	Nil	2.0	4.0	4.0
Invest. Assets: Total	2,704	2,733	2,310	1,603	1,319	1,322	1,157	1,075	1,134	1,102
Deferred Policy Costs	156	147	136	77.7	70.1	57.5	56.1	58.9	64.9	70.3
Total Assets	4,164	3,884	3,464	2,474	2,113	2,117	1,554	1,455	1,500	1,471
Debt	467	435	311	209	152	160	130	142	175	175
Common Eqty.	727	723	577	491	365	394	283	188	130	141
Prop. & Cas. Loss Ratio	67.9	66.7	67.9	68.4	72.1	74.4	75.7	79.1	77.0	77.8
Prop. & Cas. Expense Ratio	31.0	31.2	30.1	29.0	27.0	26.8	27.3	30.2	28.7	28.1
Prop. & Cas. Combined Ratio	98.9	97.9	98.0	97.4	99.1	101.2	103.0	109.3	105.7	105.9
% Return On Revs.	6.0	8.1	5.8	7.7	7.1	7.9	7.1	5.3	3.2	3.7
% Ret. on Equity	14.2	17.8	16.2	15.8	14.5	16.8	19.7	20.2	12.9	15.6

Data as orig reptd.; bef. results of disc opers/spec. items. Per share data adj. for stk. divs. Bold denotes diluted EPS (FASB 128)-prior periods restated. E-Estimated. NA-Not Available. NM-Not Meaningful. NR-Not Ranked.

Office—9 Farm Springs Road, Farmington, CT 06032.**Tel**—(860) 674-6600. **Website**—http://www.orioncapital.com **Chrmn & CEO**—W. M. Becker. **SVP & CFO**—M. L. Pautler. **EVP & Secy**—J. J. McCann. **VP & Treas**—C. A. Nyman. **Investor Contact**—Jeanne S. Hotchkiss (860) 674-6754. **Dirs**—W. M. Becker, G. F. Cheesbrough, D. H. Elliott, V. R. Fash, R. H. Jeffrey, W. R. Lyons, J. K. McWilliams, R. W. Moore, W. B. Weaver. **Transfer Agent & Registrar**—First Chicago Trust Co. of NY. **Incorporated**—in Delaware. **Empl**— 4,100. **S&P Analyst:** Markos N. Kaminis

STANDARD
&POOR'S
STOCK REPORTS

Orthodontic Centers of America

NYSE Symbol **OCA**

In S&P SmallCap 600

09-OCT-99

Industry: Health Care (Specialized Services)

Summary: This company develops and manages orthodontic practices on a national basis pursuant to long-term agreements.

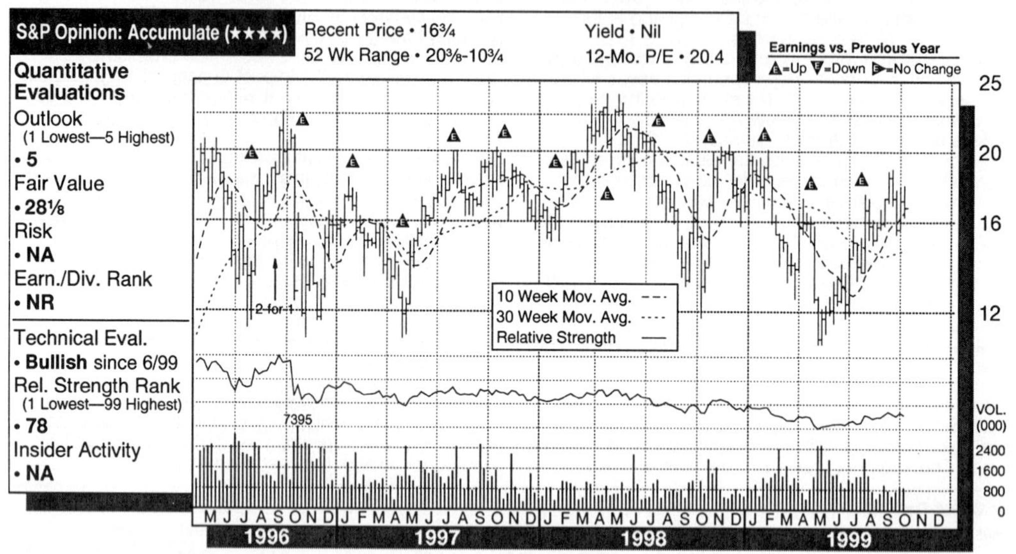

Overview - 02-AUG-99

OCA should generate 1999 revenue growth in excess of 20%, reflecting strong same-facility growth, new center openings and expanded orthodontist affiliations. Same-store growth decelerated from 13.0% in 1994 to 10.5% in 1996 and 9.1% in 1998, but we look for this negative trend to subside in coming quarters and for full 1999 comparable-store growth of about 10%. Any slowdown would materially alter our revenue growth assumptions, and could result in some operating margin deterioration. On the margin front, we look for earnings before interest, taxes, depreciation and amortization (EBITDA) to approximate 37% of revenues in 1999. Strong cash flow and significant borrowing capacity provides OCA with the ability to finance acquisitions and invest in existing facilities and operations. EPS for 1999 and 2000 are seen at $1.00 and $1.30, respectively.

Valuation - 02-AUG-99

We recently upgraded the stock to outperform from neutral to reflect our belief that earnings visibility has improved while the valuation remains depressed. Earnings in the second quarter of 1999 were ahead of our projection, as better-than-expected same-facility trends joined with cost controls. Our prior concerns revolved around eroding same-store revenue growth, and second quarter performance greatly increased the level of confidence in our 1999 EPS estimate. The shares have suffered from widespread weakness in the physician practice management (PPM) industry. However, we believe that the model can be effective within single-specialty areas such as orthodontics. With the stock trading at a 50% discount to our three-year EPS growth rate forecast, we believe investors should take advantage of the stock's 1999 weakness to add to positions.

Key Stock Statistics

S&P EPS Est. 1999	1.00	Tang. Bk. Value/Share	1.94
P/E on S&P Est. 1999	16.8	Beta	NA
S&P EPS Est. 2000	1.30	Shareholders	263
Dividend Rate/Share	Nil	Market cap. (B)	$0.805
Shs. outstg. (M)	48.1	Inst. holdings	73%
Avg. daily vol. (M)	0.150		

Value of $10,000 invested 5 years ago: NA

Fiscal Year Ending Dec. 31

	1999	1998	1997	1996	1995	1994
Revenues (Million $)						
1Q	49.05	37.69	24.90	13.72	8.46	—
2Q	55.40	41.53	27.48	15.51	9.24	—
3Q	—	44.70	31.44	18.88	11.49	—
4Q	—	47.38	33.51	23.16	12.37	—
Yr.	—	171.3	117.3	71.27	41.56	25.36
Earnings Per Share ($)						
1Q	**0.21**	**0.16**	**0.11**	**0.07**	0.06	—
2Q	**0.24**	**0.17**	**0.12**	**0.07**	0.05	—
3Q	**E0.26**	**0.18**	**0.13**	**0.09**	0.06	—
4Q	**E0.29**	**0.19**	**0.14**	**0.10**	0.07	—
Yr.	**E1.00**	**0.70**	**0.50**	**0.33**	0.24	0.11

Next earnings report expected: early November

Dividend Data

No cash dividends have been paid.

A Division of The McGraw-Hill Companies

Orthodontic Centers of America, Inc.

Business Summary - 02-AUG-99

Orthodontic Centers of America Inc. (OCA) develops, acquires and manages orthodontic practices on a national basis pursuant to long-term agreements. Since inception in 1985, OCA has grown to manage 469 orthodontic centers located in 31 states, Puerto Rico, Japan and Mexico, with a total of 275 affiliated orthodontists at the end of 1998. Of these centers, 252 were developed internally and 217 (net of 67 that were consolidated) were practices acquired by the company. OCA provides capital for the development and growth of orthodontic centers and manages the business and marketing aspects of the practices, allowing affiliated orthodontists to focus on delivering quality patient care.

The company generally manages all operations of its orthodontic centers, other than the provision of orthodontic services. It provides financial, accounting, billing and collection services and employs the orthodontic center's business personnel. OCA provides advertising and marketing services, personnel recruiting and training services, management and financial information systems, and purchasing and distribution services. During 1998, OCA spent an average of about $75,353 per affiliated orthodontist on direct marketing and advertising activities.

Comprehensive management and marketing services are provided to affiliated orthodontists pursuant to service or consulting agreements. Under these agreements, OCA manages the business and marketing sides of orthodontic centers, provides capital, facilities and equipment (including utilities, maintenance and rental), implements marketing programs, prepares budgets and financial statements, orders and purchases inventory and supplies, provides patient scheduling systems and staff, bills and collects patient fees, maintains files and records, and arranges for certain legal and accounting services.

The orthodontic centers are generally located either in shopping centers or in professional office buildings, and substantially all include private treatment rooms and large patient waiting areas, allowing the centers to locate in a broader range of office space than a traditional orthodontic practice. The centers typically include up to six treatment rooms, and range in size from about 2,000 sq. ft. to 2,500 sq. ft.

OCA believes the average cost of developing a new orthodontic center is about $250,000, including the cost of equipment, leasehold improvements, working capital and funding of losses with the initial operation of the orthodontic center.

During 1998, the company moved toward expansion in markets outside of the U.S., opening orthodontic centers for affiliated orthodontists in Mexico and Japan. It also opened centers in San Juan, Puerto Rico. In addition, OCA has been approached by orthodontists and others in Australia, Canada and Europe about expanding into these regions.

Per Share Data ($) (Year Ended Dec. 31)	1998	1997	1996	1995	1994	1993	1992	1991	1990	1989
Tangible Bk. Val.	1.65	1.91	1.42	1.71	0.78	NA	NA	NA	NA	NA
Cash Flow	0.89	0.62	0.41	0.27	0.12	NA	NA	NA	NA	NA
Earnings	0.70	0.50	0.34	0.24	0.11	NA	NA	NA	NA	NA
Dividends	Nil	Nil	Nil	Nil	Nil	NA	NA	NA	NA	NA
Payout Ratio	Nil	Nil	Nil	Nil	Nil	NA	NA	NA	NA	NA
Prices - High	24	20¼	22⅝	12	3⅛	NA	NA	NA	NA	NA
- Low	11¾	11	10⅜	2⅞	2¾	NA	NA	NA	NA	NA
P/E Ratio - High	34	40	67	50	28	NA	NA	NA	NA	NA
- Low	17	22	31	12	25	NA	NA	NA	NA	NA
Income Statement Analysis (Million $)										
Revs.	171	117	71.3	41.6	25.4	18.8	14.5	NA	NA	NA
Oper. Inc.	63.4	41.6	24.5	13.7	9.7	7.8	6.4	NA	NA	NA
Depr.	9.1	5.6	2.8	1.4	0.9	1.1	1.2	NA	NA	NA
Int. Exp.	0.3	0.2	0.4	0.5	0.3	0.2	0.2	NA	NA	NA
Pretax Inc.	54.6	37.1	23.6	14.2	4.7	6.4	5.1	NA	NA	NA
Eff. Tax Rate	38%	39%	39%	36%	57%	5.10%	11%	NA	NA	NA
Net Inc.	33.8	22.6	14.4	9.0	2.0	6.1	4.5	NA	NA	NA
Balance Sheet & Other Fin. Data (Million $)										
Cash	1.6	9.9	24.4	33.6	17.1	1.5	0.8	NA	NA	NA
Curr. Assets	87.0	84.9	56.1	54.4	28.9	9.3	5.7	NA	NA	NA
Total Assets	297	229	145	92.6	37.5	12.5	7.2	NA	NA	NA
Curr. Liab.	27.4	16.7	15.9	10.7	8.0	3.4	2.6	NA	NA	NA
LT Debt	22.7	6.5	2.5	3.4	3.7	1.5	1.2	NA	NA	NA
Common Eqty.	231	191	115	77.3	25.7	7.6	3.4	NA	NA	NA
Total Cap.	269	212	129	81.9	29.5	9.1	4.6	NA	NA	NA
Cap. Exp.	17.6	15.0	12.3	8.2	4.7	1.8	0.3	NA	NA	NA
Cash Flow	42.9	28.3	17.2	10.5	3.0	7.2	5.7	NA	NA	NA
Curr. Ratio	3.2	5.1	3.5	5.1	3.6	2.7	2.2	NA	NA	NA
% LT Debt of Cap.	8.4	3.1	1.9	4.1	12.6	16.1	26.2	NA	NA	NA
% Net Inc.of Revs.	19.7	19.3	20.2	21.7	8.0	32.5	31.1	NA	NA	NA
% Ret. on Assets	12.9	12.1	12.1	13.9	8.1	62.1	NA	NA	NA	NA
% Ret. on Equity	16.0	14.8	15.0	17.5	12.2	111.0	NA	NA	NA	NA

Data as orig reptd.; bef. results of disc opers/spec. items. Per share data adj. for stk. divs. Bold denotes diluted EPS (FASB 128)-prior periods restated. E-Estimated. NA-Not Available. NM-Not Meaningful. NR-Not Ranked.

Office—5000 Sawgrass Village, Suite 25, Ponte Vedra Beach, FL 32082. **Tel**—(904) 280-6285. **Chrmn & Co-CEO**—G. Lazzara Jr. **Co-CEO & Treas**—B. F. Palmisano Sr. **CFO & Secy**—B. F. Palmisano Jr. **Pres**—G. L. Faux. **VP & Investor Contact**—John Glover. **Dirs**—G. L. Faux, M. C. Johnsen, G. Lazzara Jr., B. F. Palmisano Sr., A. J. Ryan Jr., A. G. Tunstall, E. J. Walters Jr. **Transfer Agent**—First Union National Bank of North Carolina, Charlotte. **Incorporated**—in Delaware in 1994. **Empl**— 2,072. **S&P Analyst:** Robert M. Gold

STANDARD
&POOR'S
STOCK REPORTS

Oshkosh B'Gosh

NASDAQ Symbol **GOSHA**

In S&P SmallCap 600

09-OCT-99

Industry:
Textiles (Apparel)

Summary: This company designs, makes, sources and markets apparel for children, youth, and men.

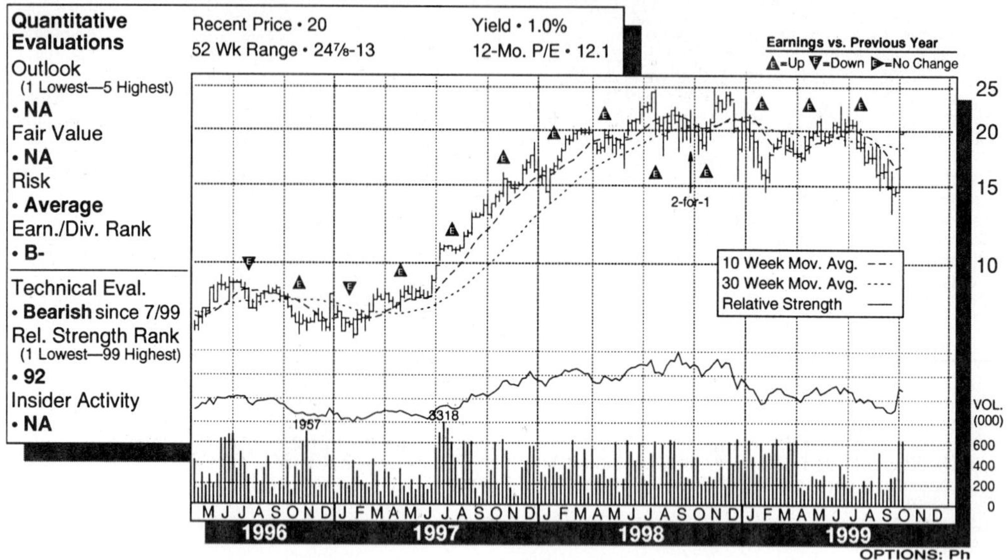

Business Profile - 05-AUG-99

Oshkosh remains committed to its strategy of focusing on product design and development activities, further development and execution of its sourcing strategy, exploring further brand extension possibilities, and continued share repurchases under its stock repurchase program. In July 1999, the company said that it remained optimistic with the prospects of further earnings growth along with an increase in net sales. GOSHA continued to focus on responding to all aspects of the total experience that consumers have with its brands by seeking to market high quality, fashion right products at competitive prices.

Operational Review - 05-AUG-99

Net sales for the first half of 1999 declined nominally, year to year. Margins widened, and operating profit moved ahead 12%. After higher interest expense, pretax income rose 10%. Following taxes at 39.0%, versus 41.0%, net income was up 14%, to $9.3 million ($0.54 a share, on 13% fewer shares) from $8.2 million ($0.41). Share earnings benefited from improved gross profit margins and continuing share repurchases. Gross margins continued to be favorably impacted through continued implementation of a global sourcing strategy. During the first six months of 1999, GOSHA repurchased 1,723,300 of its Class A Common shares for $32.0 million.

Stock Performance - 08-OCT-99

In the past 30 trading days, GOSHA's shares have increased 24%, compared to a 0.91% fall in the S&P 500. Average trading volume for the past five days was 191,080 shares, compared with the 40-day moving average of 87,546 shares.

Key Stock Statistics

Dividend Rate/Share	0.20	Shareholders	1,500
Shs. outstg. (M)	16.3	Market cap. (B)	$0.281
Avg. daily vol. (M)	0.124	Inst. holdings	56%
Tang. Bk. Value/Share	5.75		
Beta	0.38		

Value of $10,000 invested 5 years ago: $ 22,297

Fiscal Year Ending Dec. 31

	1999	1998	1997	1996	1995	1994
Revenues (Million $)						
1Q	101.9	102.5	97.36	120.9	108.5	87.39
2Q	82.52	82.29	71.14	82.58	74.93	66.16
3Q	—	131.1	124.9	136.7	142.9	118.4
4Q	—	107.4	101.8	104.6	105.9	91.41
Yr.	—	423.2	395.2	444.8	432.3	363.4
Earnings Per Share ($)						
1Q	**0.36**	**0.27**	0.17	0.14	0.10	0.03
2Q	**0.17**	**0.14**	**-0.02**	-0.40	-0.07	-0.03
3Q	—	**0.70**	**0.57**	0.41	0.33	0.19
4Q	—	**0.41**	**0.32**	-0.11	0.07	0.06
Yr.	—	**1.52**	**1.01**	**0.05**	**0.42**	**0.25**

Next earnings report expected: late October

Dividend Data (Dividends have been paid since 1985.)

Amount ($)	Date Decl.	Ex-Div. Date	Stock of Record	Payment Date
0.050	Nov. 03	Nov. 12	Nov. 16	Dec. 01 '98
0.050	Jan. 29	Feb. 10	Feb. 15	Mar. 01 '99
0.050	May. 07	May. 24	May. 21	Jun. 04 '99
0.050	Aug. 09	Aug. 19	Aug. 23	Sep. 07 '99

A Division of The McGraw-Hill Companies

Oshkosh B'Gosh, Inc.

Business Summary - 05-AUG-99

Formed in 1895, Wisconsin-based Oshkosh B'Gosh designs, manufactures, sources, and markets apparel primarily for the children's wear and youth wear markets, and also offers a children's footwear collection. While its heritage began in the men's work wear market, the company is best known for its line of high quality children's wear. It is GOSHA's vision to become the dominant global marketer of branded products for children ages newborn to 10 through leverage of the existing brand franchise and utilization of its core competencies.

The children's wear and youth wear business is targeted to reach the middle to upper middle segment of the sportswear market through the use of innovative designs, quality fabrics and classic styling. GOSHA believes that its trade name is a valuable asset in the marketing of its apparel, signifying apparel that is classic in design and of high quality construction. The tradename and trademarks are generally displayed prominently on company products.

In addition to its wholesale business, GOSHA was also operating, as of year-end 1998, a chain of 122 domestic branded stores, including 117 factory outlet stores and five specialty stores. The showcase store in New York City is designed to reinforce brand awareness among consumers. During 1997, the retail product line was expanded by offering youth wear sizes for girls and boys under the trade name Genuine Girl. Based on the sales performance of the Genuine Girl line, the distribution of this product line was expanded to wholesale customers beginning with the Spring 1998 season.

The company completed a comprehensive strategic planning initiative in 1996. As part of this initiative and combined with a commitment to more efficient utilization of working capital, GOSHA has continued to seek to improve product marketability, streamline operations, reduce the capital base and cost structure, and improve delivery performance. Actions already taken have included an analysis of product extensions, commitment to wholesale customer base, periodic review of significant licensee arrangements, and development of an effective sourcing strategy, which has resulted in the closing of certain domestic manufacturing facilities.

In 1998, 42% of the product line (excluding footwear) was produced at company-owned facilities, with the remainder produced by numerous third party contractors throughout the world. In 1997 and 1998, as part of the company's review of manufacturing capacity and utilization, the company completed the closure of certain domestic manufacturing facilities and continued to expand its use of offshore manufacturing capabilities.

Business is seasonal, with sales and income likely to be highest in the third quarter, the peak wholesale shipping period and a major retail selling season at GOSHA's retail outlet stores.

Per Share Data ($) (Year Ended Dec. 31)	1998	1997	1996	1995	1994	1993	1992	1991	1990	1989
Tangible Bk. Val.	5.75	11.48	5.86	6.03	5.88	5.89	6.00	5.74	5.18	4.41
Cash Flow	2.00	3.21	0.52	0.86	0.63	0.45	0.81	1.02	1.19	1.44
Earnings	1.52	1.01	0.05	0.42	0.25	0.15	0.54	0.81	1.01	1.29
Dividends	0.17	0.14	0.14	0.14	0.19	0.26	0.26	0.26	0.24	0.21
Payout Ratio	11%	14%	NM	33%	75%	165%	48%	32%	24%	17%
Prices - High	24 7/8	18 3/4	9 3/8	9	10 7/8	11 1/4	15 3/8	21 1/8	21 3/4	22
- Low	13 5/8	6 3/4	6 7/8	5 3/4	6 1/8	6 3/4	9 5/8	11 1/4	8 1/2	10
P/E Ratio - High	16	18	NM	21	43	73	28	26	21	17
- Low	9	7	NM	14	24	44	18	14	8	8
Income Statement Analysis (Million $)										
Revs.	423	395	445	432	363	340	346	365	323	315
Oper. Inc.	50.1	42.0	33.9	30.0	19.7	25.2	28.2	47.0	51.1	66.9
Depr.	9.4	13.0	11.7	11.4	10.7	8.4	7.9	6.1	5.0	4.3
Int. Exp.	0.4	0.3	1.1	1.8	1.3	0.6	0.8	1.1	1.8	3.0
Pretax Inc.	49.3	38.2	-4.1	20.2	13.0	9.3	26.5	39.1	48.1	61.4
Eff. Tax Rate	41%	41%	NM	46%	46%	51%	41%	41%	40%	39%
Net Inc.	29.3	22.6	1.1	10.9	7.0	4.5	15.7	23.6	29.6	37.6
Balance Sheet & Other Fin. Data (Million $)										
Cash	14.3	13.8	41.2	2.4	10.5	17.9	21.1	14.4	6.8	3.3
Curr. Assets	124	131	149	137	142	152	146	141	129	116
Total Assets	163	175	196	209	217	229	226	215	189	163
Curr. Liab.	47.1	48.3	44.3	42.0	39.8	40.1	35.2	33.9	28.7	27.2
LT Debt	Nil	Nil	Nil	Nil	0.5	0.8	1.3	2.4	3.5	4.5
Common Eqty.	103	113	138	150	159	172	175	167	151	129
Total Cap.	103	113	138	153	162	176	180	174	155	134
Cap. Exp.	11.4	6.6	7.3	9.7	9.9	9.0	14.4	19.6	15.5	7.3
Cash Flow	38.7	35.6	12.8	22.3	17.7	12.9	23.6	29.7	34.5	41.9
Curr. Ratio	2.6	2.7	3.4	3.3	3.6	3.8	4.2	4.1	4.5	4.3
% LT Debt of Cap.	Nil	Nil	Nil	Nil	0.3	0.4	0.7	1.4	2.2	3.4
% Net Inc.of Revs.	6.9	5.7	0.3	2.5	1.9	1.3	4.5	6.5	9.1	11.9
% Ret. on Assets	17.4	12.2	0.6	5.1	3.3	2.0	7.1	11.7	16.8	24.9
% Ret. on Equity	27.1	18.0	0.8	7.1	4.4	2.6	9.2	14.8	21.1	33.3

Data as orig reptd.; bef. results of disc opers/spec. items. Per share data adj. for stk. divs. Bold denotes diluted EPS (FASB 128)-prior periods restated. E-Estimated. NA-Not Available. NM-Not Meaningful. NR-Not Ranked.

Office—112 Otter Ave., Oshkosh, WI 54901. **Tel**—(920) 231-8800. **Website**—http://www.oshkoshbgosh.com **Chrmn, Pres & CEO**—D. W. Hyde. **EVP & COO**—M. D. Wachtel. **VP-Fin, Treas & CFO**—D. L. Omachinski. **Secy**—S. R. Duback. **Dirs**—O. J. Bradley, S. A. Dawe, S. R. Duback, J. M. Hiegel, D. W. Hyde, S. A. Kry, D. L. Omachinski, M. D. Wachtel, W. F. Wyman. **Transfer Agent**—Harris Trust & Savings Bank, Chicago. **Incorporated**—in Delaware in 1929. **Empl**— 3,800. **S&P Analyst:** N.J.D.

Osteotech, Inc.

NASDAQ Symbol **OSTE**

In S&P SmallCap 600

09-OCT-99

Industry: Health Care (Medical Products & Supplies)

Summary: Osteotech provides human bone and bone connective tissue for transplantation and develops and markets biomaterial and implant products for musculoskeletal surgery.

Quantitative Evaluations

Outlook (1 Lowest—5 Highest) • **NA**

Fair Value • **NA**

Risk • **Average**

Earn./Div. Rank • **B-**

Technical Eval. • **Bearish** since 6/99

Rel. Strength Rank (1 Lowest—99 Highest) • **6**

Insider Activity • **NA**

Recent Price • 15
52 Wk Range • 41⅛-12½
Yield • Nil
12-Mo. P/E • 17.6

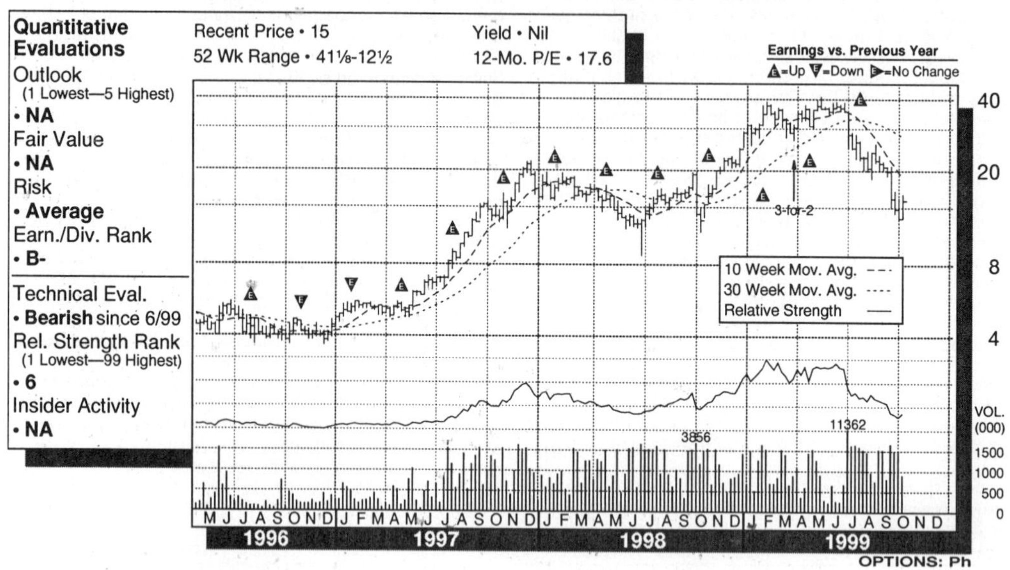

Business Profile - 31-AUG-99

In June 1999, Osteotech acquired, for $600,000 plus the cost of related inventory, the Versalok Low Back Fixation system, an easy-to-implant lumbo-sacral spine fixation system in which all components are snap-on, top-loading and top-tightening. With the acquisition, the company said it was continuing to implement its spinal product line strategy of providing surgeons with a full line of biologic and metal stabilization systems. In addition, Osteotech is implementing plans to expand its allograft tissue business in Europe in the 1999 second half. In January 1999, OSTE acquired a 90% interest in OST Developpement SA, a processor of bovine bone grafts for orthopaedic and dental use, for 9,000,000 French Francs (about $1.6 million).

Operational Review - 31-AUG-99

Revenues in the six months ended June 30, 1999, advanced 34%, year to year, mainly reflecting gains in the Grafton Demineralized Bone Matrix segment and the Base Allograft Bone Tissue segment. Domestic revenues were up 32%, and foreign revenues climbed 76%. Profitability improved in both major business segments; pretax income soared 42%. After taxes at 40.1%, versus 40.9%, net income surged 43%, to $6,502,000 ($0.44 a share), from $4,535,000 ($0.32, as adjusted).

Stock Performance - 08-OCT-99

In the past 30 trading days, OSTE's shares have declined 30%, compared to a 0.91% fall in the S&P 500. Average trading volume for the past five days was 179,460 shares, compared with the 40-day moving average of 317,044 shares.

Key Stock Statistics

Dividend Rate/Share	Nil	Shareholders	214
Shs. outstg. (M)	14.2	Market cap. (B)	$0.213
Avg. daily vol. (M)	0.373	Inst. holdings	62%
Tang. Bk. Value/Share	4.19		
Beta	0.56		

Value of $10,000 invested 5 years ago: $ 46,153

Fiscal Year Ending Dec. 31

	1999	1998	1997	1996	1995	1994
Revenues (Million $)						
1Q	18.69	13.48	10.08	8.41	6.25	5.77
2Q	19.72	15.25	10.70	8.38	6.63	5.71
3Q	—	14.28	11.93	9.01	6.98	6.18
4Q	—	16.19	12.21	9.10	7.35	6.91
Yr.	—	59.20	44.93	34.90	27.93	24.57
Earnings Per Share ($)						
1Q	0.22	0.15	0.07	0.01	—	—
2Q	0.23	0.17	0.11	0.01	-0.07	—
3Q	—	0.19	0.12	0.02	0.39	—
4Q	—	0.22	0.13	-0.08	0.05	—
Yr.	—	0.73	0.43	-0.03	0.38	0.15

Next earnings report expected: mid October

Dividend Data

Amount ($)	Date Decl.	Ex-Div. Date	Stock of Record	Payment Date
3-for-2	Feb. 18	Mar. 22	Mar. 05	Mar. 19 '99

Osteotech, Inc.

Business Summary - 31-AUG-99

Osteotech, Inc. provides services and products principally focused in the repair and healing of the musculoskeletal system. These products and services are marketed to the orthopaedic, neurological, oral/maxillofacial, dental and general surgery markets in the U.S. and Europe.

The company believes it is the world's largest processor and developer of human bone and bone connective tissue (allograft bond tissue) products. The allograft bone tissue processed by OSTE is procured by independent tissue banks mainly through the donation of tissue from deceased human donors and is used for transplantation.

OSTE has two primary operating segments: the Grafton Demineralized Bone Matrix (DBM) segment (which provided 66% of revenues and an operating profit of $13.4 million in 1998), and the Base Allograft Bone Tissue segment (29% and $4.2 million, respectively). The company's other business units (5% of revenues and an operating loss of $1.3 million) engage in providing ceramic and titanium plasma spray coating services to orthopaedic and dental implant manufacturers and marketing and distributing non-allograft bone tissue spinal implant products.

The company processes Grafton DBM using its advanced proprietary demineralization process. When applied to cortical bone, this process yields allograft bone tissue which has osteoinductive (the process by which bone is induced to grow) and osteoconductive (the matrix provided by allograft bone tissue into which the host bone can grow) capabilities greater than currently available forms of mineralized allograft bone tissue.

In the Base Tissue segment, Osteotech processes primarily mineralized weight-bearing allograft bone tissue which is generally marketed and distributed by its clients. The company recently introduced the bio-d threaded cortical bone dowel for spinal fusion which is processed in the Base Tissue segment. The bone dowel is distributed by its clients, but, unlike other tissue processed in this segment, OSTE markets the bio-d threaded cortical bone dowel.

Osteotech has leveraged its expertise in musculoskeletal tissue technology to develop innovative processes and proprietary products which are widely used by orthopaedic, spinal, neurological and oral/maxillofacial surgeons for spinal fusion procedures, to repair and replace bone loss caused by trauma or certain disease states, to augment prosthetic implant procedures and to replace damaged ligaments and tendons.

The company estimates that it processes between 40% and 50% of the allograft bone tissue donors in the U.S. OSTE believes its strong market position is attributable to its proprietary product line, its clients' national donor recovery programs, its large national sales and marketing organization and the substantial investment it has made in processing technology to ensure stringent standards and high quality control which, combined with extensive donor screening and testing performed by its clients, has virtuall y eliminated the risk of transmission of infectious agents.

Per Share Data ($) (Year Ended Dec. 31)	1998	1997	1996	1995	1994	1993	1992	1991	1990	1989
Tangible Bk. Val.	3.28	2.47	1.72	1.78	1.33	1.17	1.03	1.29	NA	NA
Cash Flow	0.90	0.63	0.20	0.52	0.26	0.20	0.12	0.11	-0.06	NA
Earnings	0.73	0.43	-0.03	0.38	0.15	0.09	NA	NA	NA	NA
Dividends	Nil	Nil	Nil	Nil	Nil	NA	Nil	NA	NA	NA
Payout Ratio	Nil	Nil	Nil	Nil	Nil	Nil	Nil	NA	NA	NA
Prices - High	$31\frac{3}{8}$	$21\frac{7}{8}$	$5\frac{5}{8}$	$6\frac{1}{8}$	$3\frac{5}{8}$	$5\frac{1}{2}$	$11\frac{5}{8}$	$12\frac{1}{8}$	NA	NA
- Low	$8\frac{3}{4}$	$4\frac{5}{8}$	$3\frac{5}{8}$	$2\frac{1}{2}$	$2\frac{9}{16}$	$2\frac{7}{8}$	$3\frac{5}{8}$	$4\frac{5}{8}$	NA	NA
P/E Ratio - High	43	50	NM	16	25	58	d	202	NA	NA
- Low	12	11	NM	6	14	31	d	77	NA	NA
Income Statement Analysis (Million $)										
Revs.	59.2	44.9	34.9	27.9	24.6	19.1	14.7	9.7	7.5	NA
Oper. Inc.	18.7	11.1	4.4	2.9	2.0	-0.4	-0.7	0.2	-0.3	NA
Depr.	2.4	2.1	2.7	1.7	1.4	1.3	1.1	0.6	0.5	NA
Int. Exp.	0.1	0.1	0.2	0.3	0.1	0.1	0.1	0.2	0.1	NA
Pretax Inc.	17.4	9.6	2.0	4.8	1.2	1.2	0.4	0.6	-0.6	NA
Eff. Tax Rate	41%	41%	NM	4.94%	NM	10%	9.73%	2.42%	NA	NA
Net Inc.	10.3	5.7	-0.3	4.6	1.7	1.1	0.4	0.6	-0.6	NA
Balance Sheet & Other Fin. Data (Million $)										
Cash	15.1	13.9	7.3	2.8	3.8	4.1	5.4	2.5	1.4	NA
Curr. Assets	37.1	28.1	19.9	17.7	13.4	11.1	10.0	12.4	3.2	NA
Total Assets	57.1	43.1	31.5	30.2	22.5	19.7	18.4	15.5	5.6	NA
Curr. Liab.	10.7	8.2	7.7	5.5	4.4	3.9	3.9	2.6	2.6	NA
LT Debt	Nil	0.2	0.8	1.6	NA	NA	NA	NA	NA	NA
Common Eqty.	45.9	34.3	22.7	22.6	18.1	15.4	14.2	12.4	2.2	NA
Total Cap.	45.9	34.5	23.5	24.2	NA	NA	NA	NA	NA	NA
Cap. Exp.	5.5	5.3	2.2	4.1	NA	NA	NA	NA	NA	NA
Cash Flow	12.7	7.8	2.4	6.3	3.1	2.4	1.5	1.2	-0.1	NA
Curr. Ratio	3.5	3.4	2.6	3.2	3.1	2.9	2.6	4.9	1.2	NA
% LT Debt of Cap.	Nil	0.1	3.6	6.6	NA	NA	NA	NA	NA	NA
% Net Inc.of Revs.	17.4	12.7	NM	16.4	7.1	5.8	2.7	6.3	NA	NA
% Ret. on Assets	20.6	15.3	NM	17.4	8.3	5.8	2.4	5.8	NA	NA
% Ret. on Equity	25.7	19.9	NM	22.5	10.4	7.5	3.0	8.3	NA	NA

Data as orig reptd.; bef. results of disc opers/spec. items. Per share data adj. for stk. divs. Bold denotes diluted EPS (FASB 128)-prior periods restated. E-Estimated. NA-Not Available. NM-Not Meaningful. NR-Not Ranked.

Office—51 James Way, Eatontown, NJ 07724. **Tel**—(732) 542-2800. **Chrmn**—D. D. Johnston. **Pres & CEO**—R. W. Bauer. **EVP, COO, CFO & Secy**—M. J. Jeffries. **Dirs**—R. W. Bauer, K. P. Fallon III, M. J. Jeffries, D. D. Johnston, J. P. Kostuik, S. J. Sogin. **Transfer Agent & Registrar**—Registrar & Transfer Co., Cranford, NJ. **Incorporated**—in Delaware in 1986. **Empl**— 290. **S&P Analyst:** J. J. Schemitsch

STANDARD
&POOR'S
STOCK REPORTS

Owens & Minor

NYSE Symbol **OMI**

In S&P SmallCap 600

09-OCT-99 **Industry:** Distributors (Food & Health)

Summary: This company is a nationwide wholesale distributor of medical and surgical supplies.

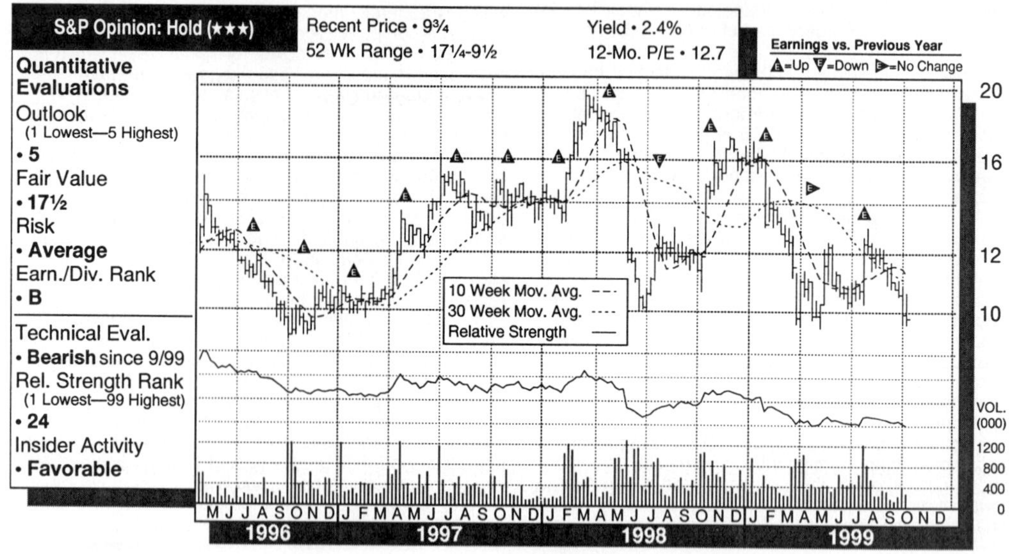

Overview - 25-MAY-99

Modest revenue growth is seen for 1999, as the commencement of a new distribution pact with Tenet Healthcare System, expansion of existing agreements and the inclusion of several other new surgicenter and nursing home contracts help moderate the negative impact of the terminated distribution pact with Columbia/HCA. That relationship accounted for about 11% of sales. The company's efforts to improve operating and gross margins were set back by the Columbia/HCA development in the second half of 1998, but we look for sequential improvements in upcoming quarters as the revenue line recovers lost momentum. Gross margins are expected to approach 11% for the full year, while lower SG&A spending allows for operating margins of approximately 6%. With lower interest costs, we see EPS of $0.85 in 1999 and $1.00 in 2000.

Valuation - 25-MAY-99

The stock has suffered from lingering concerns over the 1998 earnings shortfall and general weakness throughout the medical product/supply distribution group. However, we remain convinced that an earnings recovery is under way, and look for improvements in inventory turns and days sales outstanding as the new contracts are fully brought on line. As the earnings outlook becomes more certain, there should be a restoration of investor confidence in OMI, and we would expect the stock to outperform over the coming six to nine months. On a fundamental basis, the stock is extremely attractive, trading at only 13 times our 1999 estimate and 11 times our 2000 forecast, particularly in light of the anticipated earnings recovery. In addition, we would not be surprised to see a suitor emerge for OMI. In such a scenario, a takeover price of $18 per share, or only four times estimated 1999 EBITDA, looks extremely reasonable.

Key Stock Statistics

S&P EPS Est. 1999	0.82	Tang. Bk. Value/Share	0.43
P/E on S&P Est. 1999	12.0	Beta	0.45
S&P EPS Est. 2000	0.95	Shareholders	17,000
Dividend Rate/Share	0.24	Market cap. (B)	$0.321
Shs. outstg. (M)	32.7	Inst. holdings	82%
Avg. daily vol. (M)	0.048		

Value of $10,000 invested 5 years ago: $ 6,969

Fiscal Year Ending Dec. 31

	1999	1998	1997	1996	1995	1994
Revenues (Million $)						
1Q	751.1	798.0	749.6	771.3	747.1	390.8
2Q	772.4	799.0	776.7	749.9	743.7	581.8
3Q	—	768.4	785.8	744.1	739.0	693.0
4Q	—	716.8	804.7	753.6	746.6	730.2
Yr.	—	3,082	3,117	3,019	2,976	2,396
Earnings Per Share ($)						
1Q	**0.17**	**0.17**	**0.12**	**0.01**	0.11	0.15
2Q	**0.19**	**-0.01**	**0.14**	**0.05**	0.01	-0.19
3Q	**E0.22**	**0.20**	**0.16**	**0.08**	-0.32	0.01
4Q	**E0.24**	**0.20**	**0.18**	**0.11**	-0.33	0.18
Yr.	**E0.82**	**0.56**	**0.60**	**0.25**	**-0.53**	**0.15**

Next earnings report expected: mid October

Dividend Data (Dividends have been paid since 1926.)

Amount ($)	Date Decl.	Ex-Div. Date	Stock of Record	Payment Date
0.050	Oct. 26	Dec. 10	Dec. 14	Dec. 31 '98
0.050	Feb. 24	Mar. 11	Mar. 15	Mar. 31 '99
0.060	Apr. 28	Jun. 10	Jun. 14	Jun. 30 '99
0.060	Jul. 19	Sep. 09	Sep. 13	Sep. 30 '99

A Division of The McGraw-Hill Companies

Owens & Minor, Inc.

Business Summary - 25-MAY-99

Founded in 1882 as a wholesale drug company, Owens & Minor Inc. has become one of the largest distributors of medical/surgical supplies in the U.S. The company distributes about 140,000 finished medical and surgical products produced by 1,200 suppliers to 4,000 customers nationwide. Acute care hospitals and hospital-based systems account for over 90% of net sales. Other customers include nursing homes, clinics, surgery centers, rehabilitation facilities, physicians' offices and home health care centers.

The majority of sales consist of disposable gloves, dressings, endoscopic products, intravenous products, needles and syringes, sterile procedure trays, surgical products and gowns, urological products and wound closure products.

Aside from its core distribution services, OMI offers flexible delivery alternatives that are supported by inventory management services to meet the widely varied needs of its customers. The company's information technology systems allow it to offer customers several services to minimize their inventory holding requirements. These include PANDAC, a wound closure management system that provides customers with an accurate evaluation of their current wound closure inventories and usage levels in order to reduce costs for these products; CostTrack, an activity-based costing and pricing model that allows management to identify the cost drivers in specific distribution activities; the FOCUS program, which helps customers standardize and consolidate their purchasing decisions to gain efficiencies from volume purchases; and DSS, a database used to help customers standardize the inventory management decisions within all of the facilities in an integrated network.

The medical/surgical supply distribution industry in the U.S. is highly competitive and consists of three major nationwide distributors: Owens & Minor, Allegiance Corp. (a subsidiary of Cardinal Health) and McKesson General Medical Corp. (a division of McKesson HBOC).

In May 1998, hospital giant Columbia/HCA terminated its distribution agreement with Owens & Minor, effective October 1; Columbia/HCA accounted for 11% of 1997 sales. The company has since negotiated and signed new agreements to compensate for this lost business. Effective February 1, 1999, OMI began an eight-year contract with Tenet HealthSystems Inc. with estimated annual sales volume of $250 million. Other notable contracts included the doubling of a relationship with Sutter Health, to about $60 million annually; and an estimated $20 million annually with the University of Maryland Medical System.

OMI formed a strategic relationship with Perot Systems in late 1998, whereby Perot will manage the company's information services function and assist in the creation of new and more effective supply chain solutions for its customers. With Perot Systems, OMI hopes to expand its Internet capabilities to create a digital (e-commerce) order fulfillment system and enhance its exi sting technology.

Per Share Data ($) (Year Ended Dec. 31)	1998	1997	1996	1995	1994	1993	1992	1991	1990	1989
Tangible Bk. Val.	0.09	NA	NM	-1.67	-1.13	3.93	3.46	2.87	2.62	2.34
Cash Flow	1.12	1.15	0.75	0.13	0.57	0.84	0.72	0.50	0.49	0.22
Earnings	0.56	0.60	0.25	-0.53	0.15	0.60	0.52	0.33	0.31	0.09
Dividends	0.20	0.18	0.18	0.18	0.19	0.14	0.11	0.09	0.08	0.08
Payout Ratio	36%	30%	72%	NM	125%	23%	21%	26%	25%	87%
Prices - High	19 7/8	16 1/4	15 1/8	14 7/8	18 1/8	15 5/8	10 1/8	10 3/4	4 1/2	4 3/4
- Low	10	9 3/4	9 1/8	11 5/8	13 1/4	8 3/8	7 3/8	4 1/8	3 1/8	3 3/8
P/E Ratio - High	35	27	60	NM	NM	26	19	32	15	53
- Low	18	16	36	NM	NM	14	14	12	10	38
Income Statement Analysis (Million $)										
Revs.	3,082	3,117	3,019	2,976	2,396	1,397	1,177	1,027	1,220	953
Oper. Inc.	87.4	81.9	64.7	41.9	68.7	40.9	34.3	25.9	27.1	17.5
Depr.	18.3	17.7	16.1	15.4	13.0	7.6	5.9	5.0	5.3	3.6
Int. Exp.	17.1	18.8	23.7	29.3	12.1	2.9	2.5	4.5	7.6	6.7
Pretax Inc.	34.7	41.9	23.1	-16.4	14.0	30.4	25.9	16.5	14.2	4.7
Eff. Tax Rate	42%	42%	44%	NM	43%	39%	41%	41%	38%	47%
Net Inc.	20.1	24.3	13.0	-11.3	7.9	18.5	15.4	9.8	8.8	2.5
Balance Sheet & Other Fin. Data (Million $)										
Cash	0.5	0.6	0.7	0.2	0.5	2.0	7.1	0.8	3.3	3.3
Curr. Assets	504	499	456	624	641	282	229	267	249	226
Total Assets	718	713	680	858	869	334	275	312	290	259
Curr. Liab.	269	265	263	292	359	143	129	144	131	93.0
LT Debt	282	183	168	323	248	50.8	25.0	67.7	71.3	85.3
Common Eqty.	161	144	127	120	141	137	117	97.1	85.0	77.6
Total Cap.	443	442	410	558	505	188	142	165	156	163
Cap. Exp.	8.1	7.5	6.2	13.9	6.6	6.3	5.0	6.0	4.8	5.3
Cash Flow	36.5	36.8	23.9	4.1	17.6	26.1	21.3	14.7	14.1	6.1
Curr. Ratio	1.9	1.9	1.7	2.1	1.8	2.0	1.8	1.9	1.9	2.4
% LT Debt of Cap.	63.6	41.4	40.9	57.9	49.2	27.0	17.6	41.1	45.6	52.4
% Net Inc.of Revs.	0.7	0.8	0.4	NM	0.3	1.3	1.3	0.9	0.7	0.3
% Ret. on Assets	2.8	3.5	1.7	NM	1.3	6.0	5.2	3.2	3.2	1.1
% Ret. on Equity	11.9	14.1	6.3	NM	3.3	14.4	14.4	10.6	10.8	3.2

Data as orig reptd.; bef. results of disc opers/spec. items. Per share data adj. for stk. divs. Bold denotes diluted EPS (FASB 128)-prior periods restated. E-Estimated. NA-Not Available. NM-Not Meaningful. NR-Not Ranked.

Office—4800 Cox Rd., Glen Allen, VA 23060. **Tel**—(804) 747-9794. **Website**—http://www.owens-minor.com **Chrmn & CEO**—G. G. Minor III. **SVP & Secy**—D. St. J. Carneal. **EVP-Pres & COO**—C. R. Smith. **VP-Treas & Interm CFO**—R. F. Bozard. **Investor Contact**—Elizabeth A. Hamilton (804-967-2848). **Dirs**—H. A. Berling, J. Bunting III, J. B. Farinholt Jr., V. W. Henley, E. M. Massey, G. G. Minor III, J. E. Rogers, J. E. Ukrop, A. M. Whittemore. **Transfer Agent**—The Bank of New York, NYC. **Incorporated**—in Virginia in 1926. **Empl**— 2,898. **S&P Analyst:** Robert M. Gold

STANDARD
&POOR'S
STOCK REPORTS

Oxford Industries

NYSE Symbol **OXM**
In S&P SmallCap 600

09-OCT-99 **Industry:** Textiles (Apparel)

Summary: OXM manufactures and distributes brand-name and private-label apparel for men and women in the medium-to-higher-price range.

Quantitative Evaluations
Outlook
(1 Lowest—5 Highest)
• **NA**
Fair Value
• **NA**
Risk
• **Average**
Earn./Div. Rank
• **B+**

Technical Eval.
• **Bearish** since 9/99
Rel. Strength Rank
(1 Lowest—99 Highest)
• **38**
Insider Activity
• **NA**

Recent Price • 22
52 Wk Range • 30½-21¼
Yield • 3.8%
12-Mo. P/E • 7.2

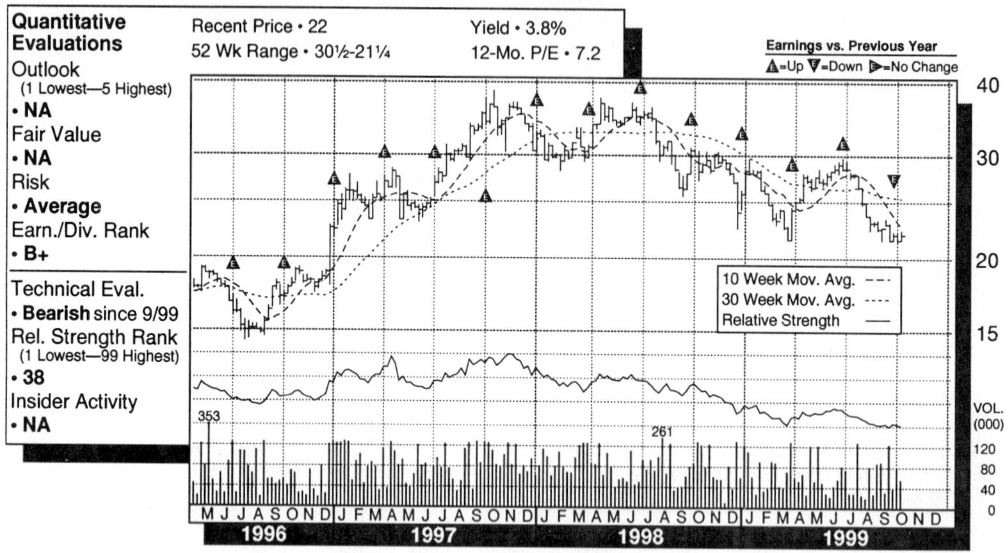

Business Profile - 02-JUL-99

OXM's strategy for dealing with a highly competitive apparel market environment includes reducing the cost of goods by shifting to global manufacturing and sourcing; cutting expenses as a percentage of sales; pursuing higher profit margin opportunities through licensing or acquisition of important brand or designer names; and focusing on asset management. In September 1998, OXM acquired Next Day Apparel, Inc., a manufacturer and marketer of private label womenswear for mass-market retailers. Next Day, headquartered in Walhalla, SC, with marketing offices in New York City and manufacturing plants in Honduras, has annual sales in excess of $100 million. The company expects continued challenging apparel market conditions and a highly promotional environment to keep pressure on operating margins.

Operational Review - 02-JUL-99

Net sales for the nine months ended February 26, 1999, rose 9.9%, year to year, aided by the acquisition of Next Day Apparel. Gross margins narrowed slightly, impacted by costs for new sewing operations and the Next Day acquisition. With interest costs up 32%, and after taxes at 39.0% in both periods, net income was up 9.4%, to $20,335,000 ($2.37 a share, on 4.4% fewer shares) from $18,582,000 ($2.07).

Stock Performance - 08-OCT-99

In the past 30 trading days, OXM's shares have declined 2%, compared to a 0.91% fall in the S&P 500. Average trading volume for the past five days was 10,920 shares, compared with the 40-day moving average of 14,331 shares.

Key Stock Statistics

Dividend Rate/Share	0.84	Shareholders	718
Shs. outstg. (M)	7.8	Market cap. (B)	$0.171
Avg. daily vol. (M)	0.016	Inst. holdings	57%
Tang. Bk. Value/Share	19.46		
Beta	0.34		

Value of $10,000 invested 5 years ago: $ 10,764

Fiscal Year Ending May 31

	2000	1999	1998	1997	1996	1995
Revenues (Million $)						
1Q	185.7	198.6	193.2	172.5	189.3	165.3
2Q	—	232.5	208.1	203.2	187.1	192.2
3Q	—	206.0	178.7	167.5	138.6	153.1
4Q	—	225.3	194.5	160.0	149.5	146.4
Yr.	—	862.4	774.5	703.2	664.4	657.0
Earnings Per Share ($)						
1Q	**0.60**	**0.67**	0.61	**0.40**	**0.03**	0.56
2Q	—	**0.94**	**0.87**	**0.75**	**0.30**	0.70
3Q	—	**0.76**	**0.60**	**0.50**	**-0.23**	0.21
4Q	—	**0.74**	**0.67**	**0.58**	**0.15**	-0.25
Yr.	—	**3.11**	**2.75**	**2.23**	**0.25**	1.22

Next earnings report expected: mid January

Dividend Data (Dividends have been paid since 1960.)

Amount ($)	Date Decl.	Ex-Div. Date	Stock of Record	Payment Date
0.210	Jan. 04	Feb. 10	Feb. 12	Feb. 27 '99
0.210	Apr. 05	May. 12	May. 14	May. 29 '99
0.210	Jul. 12	Aug. 11	Aug. 13	Aug. 28 '99
0.210	Oct. 04	Nov. 10	Nov. 15	Nov. 27 '99

Oxford Industries, Inc.

Business Summary - 02-JUL-99

Oxford Industries, a diversified manufacturer and wholesale marketer of apparel for men, women and children, reported record results for FY 98 (May), with net sales up 10% and net income advancing 25%.

A number of factors were responsible for OXM's strong performance, including growth in the company's higher-margin designer licensed businesses, a significant increase in manufacturing efficiency, and lower weighted average borrowings, which led to a 17% decrease in interest expense.

The largest sales gain in FY 98 (15%) was recorded at the Shirt Group, whose products encompass not only men's shirts but also a broad range of men's and boys' sportswear. The group's Tommy Hilfiger Dress Shirts, Tommy Hilfiger Golf, Polo/Ralph Lauren for Boys, and OxSport, the private label shirt division, had double-digit increases. Sales were down at Oxford Shirtings, OXM's private label dress shirt division, and at Ely & Walker, the western shirt division.

Lanier Clothes, a leading producer of suits, sportcoats, suit separates and dress slacks, achieved a 9.8% sales increase in FY 98 in a declining market for men's suits. All of the gain came from the licensed designer divisions, which include Oscar de la Renta, Nautica and Geoffrey Beene. OXM's new Nautica tailored clothing division completed its first full year of shipping in FY 98. OXM began initial shipments of Geoffrey Beene, but those shipments were not material in FY 98. Private label shipments were down marginally.

The company's Oxford Womenswear Group, a leading supplier of private label womenswear to major national retailers, achieved a 12% sales gain in FY 98. The Collections division posted a strong sales gain. The Womens Catalog & Special Markets division posted a solid sales gain. The Separates division experienced a decline in sales.

OXM has developed a number of operating strategies in the face of tough competition in its apparel markets. As part of an effort to lower product costs through global sourcing, the company invested in new and expanded production facilities in Mexico and the Philippines in FY 97. In FY 98, Lanier Clothes increased its offshore manufacturing base with the construction of a new facility in Honduras and an expansion of its existing facility in Mexico. OXM will also continue to pursue higher profit margin opportunities through licensing or acquisition of important brand or designer names.

The company's ten largest customers accounted for about 70% of net sales in FY 98, with JCPenney Co., Inc. and Lands' End contributing 15% and 12%, respectively.

Per Share Data ($) (Year Ended May 31)	1999	1998	1997	1996	1995	1994	1993	1992	1991	1990
Tangible Bk. Val.	NA	18.11	16.12	14.65	15.25	14.79	13.28	12.28	11.43	11.19
Cash Flow	NA	3.71	3.28	1.26	2.12	3.05	2.45	2.13	1.30	1.50
Earnings	3.11	2.75	2.25	0.25	1.22	2.23	1.70	1.42	0.62	0.82
Dividends	0.80	0.80	0.80	0.80	0.76	0.69	0.63	0.55	0.50	0.50
Payout Ratio	26%	29%	36%	NM	62%	31%	37%	39%	80%	58%
Cal. Yrs.	1998	1997	1996	1995	1994	1993	1992	1991	1990	1989
Prices - High	37 5/8	38 3/4	24 3/8	22	34 3/4	25 3/8	27 1/8	18 3/8	13	13 3/8
- Low	22 1/2	23	14 3/8	16	21 7/8	15	14 3/8	6 7/8	6 1/2	10 1/2
P/E Ratio - High	12	14	11	88	28	11	16	13	21	16
- Low	7	8	6	64	18	7	8	5	10	13

Income Statement Analysis (Million $)										
Revs.	NA	775	703	664	657	625	573	528	506	550
Oper. Inc.	NA	51.9	45.4	23.0	29.6	23.0	33.3	28.5	18.2	23.0
Depr.	NA	8.1	9.1	8.9	7.8	7.0	6.5	6.3	6.2	6.6
Int. Exp.	NA	3.4	4.1	6.1	4.1	2.3	2.3	1.7	3.0	3.5
Pretax Inc.	NA	40.4	32.2	3.7	17.6	32.3	24.5	20.5	9.0	12.8
Eff. Tax Rate	NA	39%	39%	40%	40%	41%	40%	39%	38%	38%
Net Inc.	NA	24.6	19.6	2.2	10.6	19.2	14.8	12.5	5.5	7.9

Balance Sheet & Other Fin. Data (Million $)										
Cash	NA	10.1	3.3	1.0	2.2	3.2	3.3	8.4	19.2	2.5
Curr. Assets	NA	271	247	236	269	205	186	167	154	175
Total Assets	NA	311	287	279	309	240	218	199	187	208
Curr. Liab.	NA	102	96.3	99	126	96.1	81.8	66.2	56.8	70.0
LT Debt	NA	41.4	41.8	45.0	47.0	12.4	17.8	22.7	27.3	32.0
Common Eqty.	NA	160	142	129	133	128	115	108	101	104
Total Cap.	NA	205	187	176	183	144	136	133	130	138
Cap. Exp.	NA	8.8	7.6	7.6	14.8	9.4	8.1	5.4	6.4	5.8
Cash Flow	NA	32.7	28.7	11.1	18.4	26.2	21.2	18.8	11.7	14.5
Curr. Ratio	NA	2.7	2.6	2.4	2.1	2.1	2.3	2.5	2.7	2.5
% LT Debt of Cap.	NA	20.1	27.9	25.6	25.7	8.6	13.0	17.1	20.9	23.1
% Net Inc.of Revs.	NA	3.2	2.8	0.3	1.6	3.1	2.6	2.4	1.1	1.4
% Ret. on Assets	NA	8.2	6.9	0.7	3.9	8.4	7.1	6.5	2.9	3.9
% Ret. on Equity	NA	16.3	14.5	1.7	8.1	15.8	13.3	12.0	5.5	7.8

Data as orig reptd.; bef. results of disc opers/spec. items. Per share data adj. for stk. divs. Bold denotes diluted EPS (FASB 128)-prior periods restated. E-Estimated. NA-Not Available. NM-Not Meaningful. NR-Not Ranked.

Office—222 Piedmont Ave. N.E., Atlanta, GA 30308. **Tel**—(404) 659-2424. **Chrmn, Pres & CEO**—J. H. Lanier. **VP & Secy**—D. K. Ginn. **EVP-Fin & CFO**—B. B. Blount Jr. **Investor Contact**—J. Reese Lanier, Jr. **Dirs**—B. B. Blount Jr., C. D. Conlee, T. Gallagher, J. H. Lanier, J. R. Lanier, K. J. O'Reilly, C. B. Rogers Jr., R. E. Shaw, H. B. Weeks, E. J. Wood. **Transfer Agent & Registrar**—SunTrust Bank, Atlanta. **Incorporated**—in Georgia in 1960. **Empl**— 8,802. **S&P Analyst:** C.C.P.

STANDARD & POOR'S
STOCK REPORTS

P-Com, Inc.

NASDAQ Symbol **PCMS**

In S&P SmallCap 600

09-OCT-99

Industry: Communications Equipment

Summary: PCMS develops, manufactures, and markets network access systems for the worldwide wireless telecommunications market.

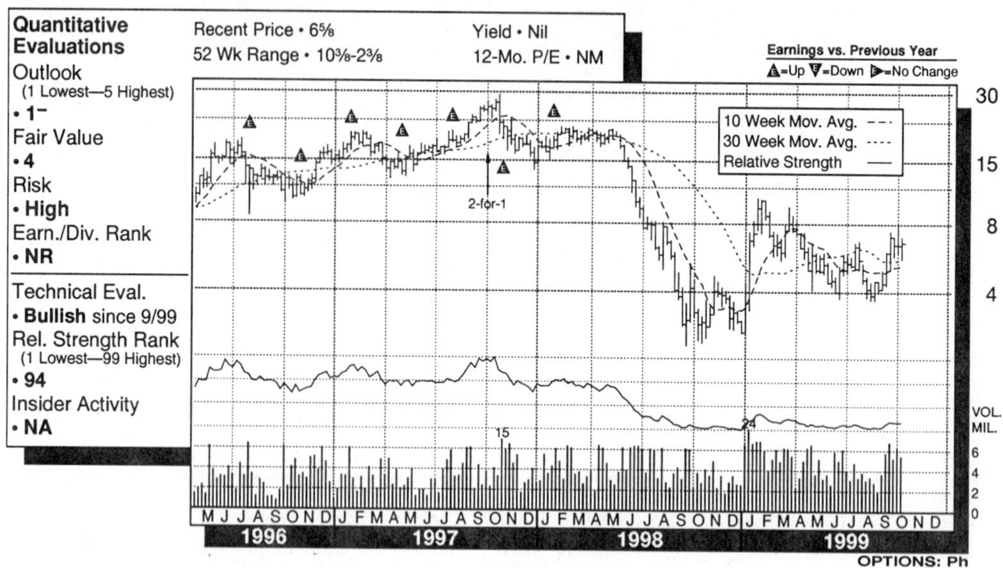

Business Profile - 13-SEP-99

The company, which has been expanding through acquisitions, posted a loss in 1998, and losses continued in the first half of 1999. PCMS said it was evaluating alternatives that included the possible sale of its Control Resources Corp. and Technosystem SpA business units, as it attempts to streamline the company, concentrate on core businesses, and focus resources on new product development and improved financial performance. PCMS recently raised $40 million through the sale of 10.1 million common shares, and eliminated all outstanding Series B preferred stock by exchanging it for common stock.

Operational Review - 13-SEP-99

Sales in the first half of 1999 fell 39%, year to year, reflecting a slowdown for the Tel-Link product line. Despite the absence of a nonrecurring $15.4 million charge for acquired in-process research and development, results were penalized by the lower sales, narrower gross margins, and higher expenses in all remaining categories; the loss from operations grew to $63.1 million, from $5.7 million. After higher interest expense, the loss widened to $67,691,000 ($1.64 a share, on 13% more shares), from $5,307,000 ($0.12). Results in the 1999 interim exclude a gain of $0.15 a share from retirement of debt.

Stock Performance - 08-OCT-99

In the past 30 trading days, PCMS's shares have increased 61%, compared to a 0.91% fall in the S&P 500. Average trading volume for the past five days was 1,077,620 shares, compared with the 40-day moving average of 1,196,790 shares.

Key Stock Statistics

Dividend Rate/Share	Nil	Shareholders	550
Shs. outstg. (M)	64.3	Market cap. (B)	$0.427
Avg. daily vol. (M)	1.633	Inst. holdings	36%
Tang. Bk. Value/Share	0.48		
Beta	NA		

Value of $10,000 invested 5 years ago: NA

Fiscal Year Ending Dec. 31

	1999	1998	1997	1996	1995	1994
Revenues (Million $)						
1Q	38.05	58.64	38.14	17.55	4.35	—
2Q	36.04	63.46	48.91	19.79	8.55	—
3Q	—	30.24	51.47	26.43	13.49	—
4Q	—	42.61	64.23	33.74	16.42	—
Yr.	—	194.9	220.7	97.52	42.81	9.24
Earnings Per Share ($)						
1Q	**-0.27**	—	**0.07**	**0.04**	-0.05	—
2Q	**-1.29**	—	**0.10**	**0.06**	Nil	—
3Q	—	—	**0.12**	**0.10**	0.05	—
4Q	—	**-0.30**	**0.18**	**0.15**	0.07	—
Yr.	—	**-1.44**	**0.43**	**0.22**	**0.11**	**-1.08**

Next earnings report expected: late October

Dividend Data

No cash dividends have been paid.

P-Com, Inc.

Business Summary - 13-SEP-99

P-Com's goal is to become a leading supplier of high performance radio systems operating in millimeter wave and spread spectrum microwave frequency bands, as well as related service offerings such as microwave relocation. Key elements of its strategy are to focus on the millimeter wave and spread spectrum microwave market, provide ancillary services in RF (radio frequency) engineering and system construction, continue to expand its worldwide presence, build and sustain a manufacturing cost advantage, leverage and maintain software leadership, position the company for emerging applications and markets, acquire companies with complementary products and services, and maintain ongoing development of point-to-multipoint systems.

The company supplies equipment and services for access to worldwide telecommunications and broadcast networks. PCMS's Tel-Link systems are used as wireless digital links in applications that include interconnecting base stations and mobile switching centers in microcellular and personal communications services (PCN/PCS) networks and for providing local telephone company connectivity in the local loop. The integrated architecture and high software content of the company's systems are designed to offer cost-effective, high-performance products with a high degree of flexibility and functionality.

PCMS also offers turnkey microwave relocation services, engineering, program management, installation and maintenance of communication systems to new licensees of radio spectrum who first remove existing users from the frequencies before implementing new systems and provides equipment for wireless network access applications. As of year-end 1998, the company field testing and further developing a range of point-to-multipoint radio systems for use in both the telecommunications and broadcast industries.

Tel-Link wireless radios use a common architecture for systems in multiple millimeter wave and spread spectrum microwave frequencies including 2.4 GHz, 5.7 GHz, 7 GHz, 13 GHz, 14 GHz, 15 GHz, 18 GHz, 23 GHz, 24 GHz, 26 GHz, 38 GHz and 50 GHz. The company's systems are designed to be highly reliable, cost effective and simple to install and maintain. PCMS believes the software embedded in its systems lets the user easily configure and adjust system settings such as frequency, power and capacity with minimal manual tuning and mechanical adjustments.

The company also markets a full line of Windows and other software products that are complementary to its systems as sophisticated diagnostic, maintenance and system configuration tools.

In the 1999 first quarter, PCMS exchanged 2,792,257 common shares for $25.5 million of 4.25% convertible subordinated notes due 2002, resulting in an extraordinary gain of $7.3 million.

Per Share Data ($) (Year Ended Dec. 31)	1998	1997	1996	1995	1994	1993	1992	1991	1990	1989
Tangible Bk. Val.	0.83	2.58	2.92	1.26	NA	NA	NA	NA	NA	NA
Cash Flow	-0.98	0.61	0.49	0.12	-0.27	NA	NA	NA	NA	NA
Earnings	-1.44	0.43	0.37	0.08	-0.29	NA	NA	NA	NA	NA
Dividends	Nil	Nil	Nil	Nil	NA	NA	NA	NA	NA	NA
Payout Ratio	Nil	Nil	Nil	Nil	NA	NA	NA	NA	NA	NA
Prices - High	21 1/4	29 3/8	18 1/2	11 3/8	NA	NA	NA	NA	NA	NA
- Low	2 5/16	12 3/8	6 3/4	3 3/4	NA	NA	NA	NA	NA	NA
P/E Ratio - High	NM	68	50	NM	NA	NA	NA	NA	NA	NA
- Low	NM	29	18	NM	NA	NA	NA	NA	NA	NA
Income Statement Analysis (Million $)										
Revs.	195	221	97.5	42.8	9.2	0.7	Nil	NA	NA	NA
Oper. Inc.	-26.1	37.9	18.7	3.5	-6.1	NA	NA	NA	NA	NA
Depr.	18.4	8.2	4.8	1.1	0.5	NA	NA	NA	NA	NA
Int. Exp.	9.0	Nil	0.1	0.3	0.2	NA	NA	NA	NA	NA
Pretax Inc.	-72.2	29.9	15.1	2.7	-6.7	-6.4	-2.3	NA	NA	NA
Eff. Tax Rate	NM	37%	7.00%	5.10%	Nil	Nil	Nil	NA	NA	NA
Net Inc.	-60.7	18.9	14.1	2.6	-6.7	-6.4	-2.3	NA	NA	NA
Balance Sheet & Other Fin. Data (Million $)										
Cash	29.2	88.1	41.9	7.7	1.3	3.6	1.0	NA	NA	NA
Curr. Assets	181	230	119	46.6	NA	NA	NA	NA	NA	NA
Total Assets	314	306	140	54.0	9.5	5.5	2.6	NA	NA	NA
Curr. Liab.	100	54.9	27.4	12.3	NA	NA	NA	NA	NA	NA
LT Debt	92.8	102	Nil	Nil	3.4	0.6	0.2	NA	NA	NA
Common Eqty.	108	148	112	41.8	1.7	3.4	2.0	NA	NA	NA
Total Cap.	215	251	113	41.8	NA	NA	NA	NA	NA	NA
Cap. Exp.	29.2	16.9	13.6	6.8	0.2	NA	NA	NA	NA	NA
Cash Flow	-42.3	27.1	18.8	3.7	-6.2	NA	NA	NA	NA	NA
Curr. Ratio	1.8	4.2	4.3	3.8	NA	NA	NA	NA	NA	NA
% LT Debt of Cap.	43.2	40.6	Nil	Nil	NA	NA	NA	NA	NA	NA
% Net Inc.of Revs.	NM	8.6	14.4	6.0	NM	NM	NM	NA	NA	NA
% Ret. on Assets	NM	8.5	14.5	8.1	NM	NM	NM	NA	NA	NA
% Ret. on Equity	NM	14.5	3.4	11.9	NM	NM	NM	NA	NA	NA

Data as orig reptd.; bef. results of disc opers/spec. items. Per share data adj. for stk. divs. Bold denotes diluted EPS (FASB 128)-prior periods restated. E-Estimated. NA-Not Available. NM-Not Meaningful. NR-Not Ranked.

Office—3175 S. Winchester Blvd., Campbell, CA 95008. **Tel**—(408) 866-3666. **Website**—http://www.p-com.com **Chrmn & CEO**—G. P. Roberts. **Pres & COO**—J. Sobczak. **VP-Fin, CFO & Investor Contact**—Robert E. Collins. **Dirs**—G. Cogan, J. A. Hawkins, M. B. Puckett, G. P. Roberts, J. J. Sobczak. **Transfer Agent & Registrar**—U.S. Stock Transfer Corp., Glendale, CA. **Incorporated**—in Delaware in 1991. **Empl**— 754. **S&P Analyst:** C.C.P.

STANDARD
&POOR'S
STOCK REPORTS

Pacific Sunwear of California

NASDAQ Symbol **PSUN**

In S&P SmallCap 600

09-OCT-99

Industry: Retail (Specialty-Apparel)

Summary: This company is a leading mall-based specialty retailer of everyday casual apparel, accessories and footwear designed for active teens and young adults.

Quantitative Evaluations

Outlook (1 Lowest—5 Highest)
• **4**

Fair Value
• **35⅞**

Risk
• **Average**

Earn./Div. Rank
• **NR**

Technical Eval.
• **Bearish** since 9/99

Rel. Strength Rank (1 Lowest—99 Highest)
• **94**

Insider Activity
• **Unfavorable**

Recent Price • 30⅜
52 Wk Range • 33⅛-8

Yield • Nil
12-Mo. P/E • 35.8

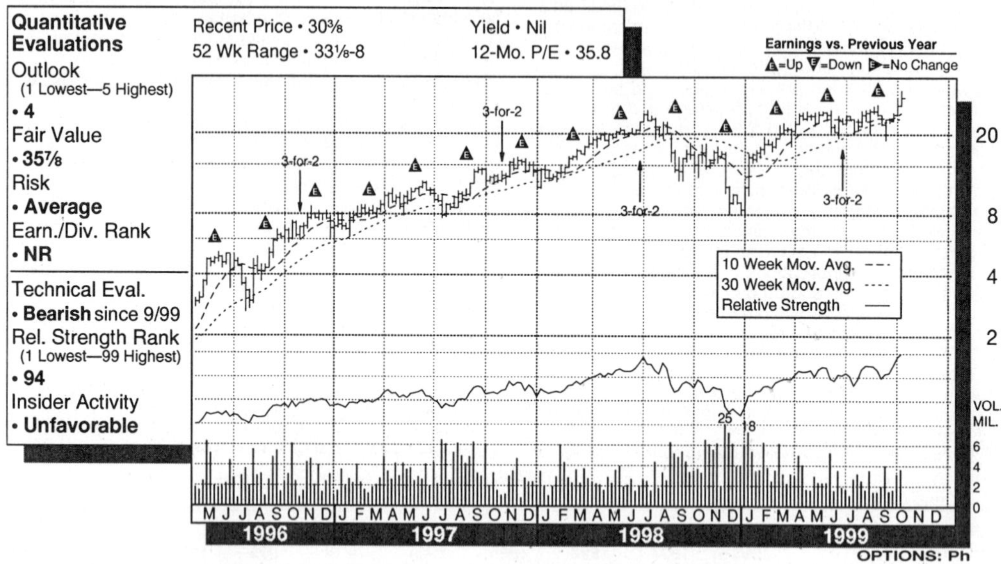

Business Profile - 24-JUN-99

In May 1999, PSUN said it planned to open about 83 new stores, including 52 Pacific Sunwear stores, 13 Pacific Sunwear outlet stores, and 18 d.e.m.o. stores in the remainder of FY 2000 (Jan.). In March 1999, the company formed wholly owned Pacific Sunwear.com Corp., in order to sell merchandise over the Internet. PSUN expects to begin selling over the Internet in the summer of 1999. The shares were split three for two in October 1997, June 1998, and June 1999.

Operational Review - 24-JUN-99

Net sales in the 13 weeks ended May 2, 1999, climbed 33%, year to year, reflecting new stores opened or converted in FY 98 and FY 99, and, to a lesser extent, a 7.2% increase in comparable-store sales. SG&A expense rose less; operating income soared 45%. With 65% lower interest income, after taxes at 38.5%, versus 39.6%, net income was up 40%, to $4,043,069 ($0.13 a share, as adjusted), from $2,886,914 ($0.09).

Stock Performance - 08-OCT-99

In the past 30 trading days, PSUN's shares have increased 21%, compared to a 0.91% fall in the S&P 500. Average trading volume for the past five days was 720,800 shares, compared with the 40-day moving average of 471,369 shares.

Key Stock Statistics

Dividend Rate/Share	Nil	Shareholders	100
Shs. outstg. (M)	31.2	Market cap. (B)	$0.948
Avg. daily vol. (M)	0.488	Inst. holdings	0%
Tang. Bk. Value/Share	4.03		
Beta	1.15		

Value of $10,000 invested 5 years ago: $ 186,772

Fiscal Year Ending Jan. 31

	2000	1999	1998	1997	1996	1995
Revenues (Million $)						
1Q	81.44	61.16	38.93	27.64	19.48	—
2Q	100.5	73.20	48.33	34.57	25.67	20.66
3Q	—	91.78	65.31	43.25	31.37	23.94
4Q	—	94.98	74.56	49.81	36.40	25.43
Yr.	—	321.1	227.1	155.3	112.9	85.32
Earnings Per Share ($)						
1Q	**0.13**	**0.09**	**0.04**	**0.00**	-0.02	0.01
2Q	**0.23**	**0.15**	**0.09**	**0.05**	0.01	0.03
3Q	—	**0.25**	**0.18**	**0.10**	0.05	0.05
4Q	—	**0.24**	**0.20**	**0.12**	0.06	0.06
Yr.	—	**0.73**	**0.53**	**0.26**	**0.10**	0.14

Next earnings report expected: mid November

Dividend Data

Amount ($)	Date Decl.	Ex-Div. Date	Stock of Record	Payment Date
3-for-2	May. 26	Jun. 21	Jun. 08	Jun. 18 '99

A Division of The McGraw-Hill Companies

Pacific Sunwear of California, Inc.

Business Summary - 24-JUN-99

Pacific Sunwear of California has grown since 1980 from a Newport Beach, CA, surf shop selling surfboards and wax, to become a leading mall-based specialty retailer of everyday casual apparel, accessories and footwear designed to meet the needs of active teens and young adults.

At June 10, 1999, the company was operating 386 stores, primarily in regional shopping malls, in 45 states. There were 343 Pacific Sunwear stores, 14 Pacific Sunwear outlet stores, and 27 d.e.m.o. stores. The stores were concentrated in the Northeast (27%), Midwest (23%), Southeast (21%), and California (14%).

Customers are primarily young men aged 12 to 24, as well as young women of the same age, who generally prefer a casual look. PSUN believes its stores are differentiated by a carefully edited selection of popular and emerging brands, offered together with its own private brands.

Pacific Sunwear stores, the company's original and primary store format (also referred to as PacSun), offer a complete selection of shirts, shorts, pants, overshirts, sweatshirts, outerwear, footwear and accessories in order to satisfy the casual wardrobe needs of its customers. In each merchandise classification, Pacific Sunwear stores offer a broad selection, with the goal of being viewed by customers as the dominant retailer in their niche. Pacific Sunwear stores are located primarily in enclosed regional shopping malls.

The company's Pacific Sunwear outlet stores average approximately 4,000 sq. ft., and are located in value-oriented outlet malls, both open-air and enclosed. The stores offer a selection similar to that of the Pacific Sunwear mall stores, with emphasis on value pricing. Merchandise at Pacific Sunwear Outlets consists primarily of off-price brand merchandise, private-brand merchandise, and a smaller selection of full-priced branded merchandise.

In FY 98, PSUN introduced a new store concept, d.e.m.o. The company opened 15 d.e.m.o. stores during FY 98 (Jan.); five were new stores, and 10 were existing Pacific Sunwear stores converted to the new format. d.e.m.o. stores offer a broad assortment of popular and emerging cross-cultural brands that primarily target young men aged 16 to 24, and, to a lesser extent, young women. There is no merchandise overlap with Pacific Sunwear stores or Pacific Sunwear Outlet stores.

The company's goal is to be the dominant nationwide specialty retailer of everyday casual apparel, footwear and accessories catering to the teen market. Its strategy includes offering a broad assortment, creating a Pacific Sunwear brand image, actively managing merchandise trends, maintaining strong vendor relationships, and providing attentive customer service.

Per Share Data ($)										
(Year Ended Jan. 31)	**1999**	**1998**	**1997**	**1996**	**1995**	**1994**	**1993**	**1992**	**1991**	**1990**
Tangible Bk. Val.	3.55	2.87	1.71	1.40	1.32	1.20	1.16	NA	NA	NA
Cash Flow	1.05	0.76	0.45	0.38	0.37	0.25	0.34	NA	NA	NA
Earnings	0.73	0.53	0.26	0.10	0.14	0.10	0.17	NA	NA	NA
Dividends	Nil	Nil	Nil	Nil	Nil	Nil	Nil	NA	NA	NA
Payout Ratio	Nil	Nil	Nil	Nil	Nil	Nil	Nil	NA	NA	NA
Cal. Yrs.	1998	1997	1996	1995	1994	1993	1992	1991	1990	1989
Prices - High	$26\frac{1}{4}$	$15\frac{3}{8}$	$8\frac{3}{4}$	3	$3\frac{1}{2}$	$3\frac{1}{2}$	NA	NA	NA	NA
- Low	8	$6\frac{1}{8}$	$1\frac{3}{8}$	$1\frac{1}{16}$	$1\frac{7}{16}$	$1\frac{1}{8}$	NA	NA	NA	NA
P/E Ratio - High	36	29	33	31	24	34	NA	NA	NA	NA
- Low	11	12	5	11	10	10	NA	NA	NA	NA
Income Statement Analysis (Million $)										
Revs.	321	227	155	113	85.3	54.9	45.8	NA	NA	NA
Oper. Inc.	48.3	32.7	17.3	8.4	8.7	5.7	5.9	NA	NA	NA
Depr.	10.4	6.9	5.3	4.3	2.9	1.7	1.3	NA	NA	NA
Int. Exp.	Nil	Nil	Nil	Nil	0.1	-0.4	0.1	NA	NA	NA
Pretax Inc.	38.9	27.1	12.2	4.2	6.1	4.3	3.9	NA	NA	NA
Eff. Tax Rate	40%	40%	39%	38%	37%	37%	22%	NA	NA	NA
Net Inc.	23.5	16.4	7.4	2.6	3.9	2.7	3.0	NA	NA	NA
Balance Sheet & Other Fin. Data (Million $)										
Cash	19.0	14.8	10.0	4.3	2.0	0.7	2.7	NA	NA	NA
Curr. Assets	70.1	66.9	34.9	23.7	23.3	23.1	8.2	NA	NA	NA
Total Assets	148	122	65.7	51.5	45.3	36.7	15.9	NA	NA	NA
Curr. Liab.	22.6	18.8	13.2	8.9	6.8	4.1	3.6	NA	NA	NA
LT Debt	Nil	Nil	Nil	0.4	0.8	Nil	NA	NA	NA	NA
Common Eqty.	117	97.7	47.9	38.5	35.6	31.2	1.0	NA	NA	NA
Total Cap.	118	99	49.4	38.8	36.4	31.2	NA	NA	NA	NA
Cap. Exp.	31.6	21.0	8.1	9.8	11.5	7.8	NA	NA	NA	NA
Cash Flow	34.0	23.3	12.7	6.9	6.7	4.3	4.2	NA	NA	NA
Curr. Ratio	3.1	3.6	2.6	2.7	3.4	5.6	2.3	NA	NA	NA
% LT Debt of Cap.	Nil	Nil	Nil	1.0	2.1	Nil	NA	NA	NA	NA
% Net Inc.of Revs.	7.3	7.2	4.8	2.3	4.5	4.9	6.6	NA	NA	NA
% Ret. on Assets	17.4	17.5	12.7	5.4	9.4	10.3	NA	NA	NA	NA
% Ret. on Equity	21.9	22.5	17.2	7.1	11.5	16.5	NA	NA	NA	NA

Data as orig reptd.; bef. results of disc opers/spec. items. Per share data adj. for stk. divs. Bold denotes diluted EPS (FASB 128)-prior periods restated. E-Estimated. NA-Not Available. NM-Not Meaningful. NR-Not Ranked.

Office—5200 East La Palma Ave., Anaheim, CA 92807. **Tel**—(714) 693-8066. **Website**—http://www.pacificsunwear.com **Chrmn & CEO**—G. H. Weaver. **Pres**—T. M. Harmon. **SVP, CFO & Secy**—C. W. Womack. **Dirs**—P. C. Cummin III, S. F. Kasaks, P. L. Harris, J. Jensen III, R. Lyons, G. H. Weaver. **Transfer Agent & Registrar**—U.S. Stock Transfer Corp., Glendale, CA. **Incorporated**—in California in 1982. **Empl**— 4,058. **S&P Analyst:** C.C.P.

Panera Bread

NASDAQ Symbol **PNRA**

In S&P SmallCap 600

09-OCT-99

Industry:
Restaurants

Summary: This company (formerly Au Bon Pain) sold its Au Bon Pain operations in May 1999, in order to concentrate on its Saint Louis Bread bakery cafe business.

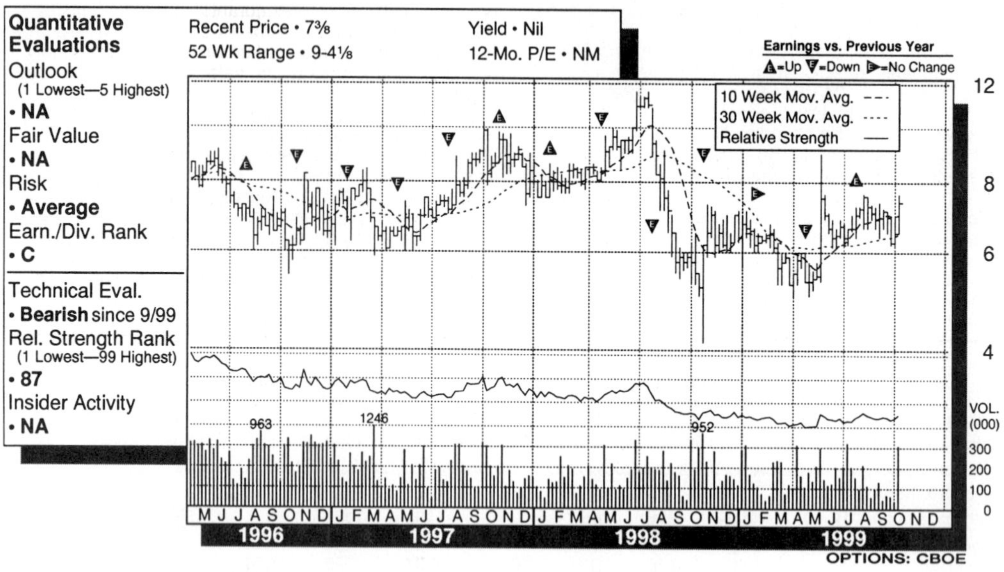

Business Profile - 11-JUN-99

In May 1999, the company sold its Au Bon Pain division to ABP Corp. for $73 million in cash, before contractual purchase price adjustments estimated at $1 million. Proceeds were earmarked to pay off outstanding debt and provide cash for growth. The company adopted its new name with the sale of the division. PNRA is focusing on plans to expand on a national basis. In 1999, it plans to add a total of 15 company-owned and 55 franchised bakery cafes, a 61% unit increase. Franchise commitments are in place for the development of an additional 546 bakery cafes.

Operational Review - 11-JUN-99

Revenues in the 16 weeks ended April 17, 1999, rose 4.0%, year to year, as higher restaurant sales outweighed lower franchise sales and other revenues. Results include the Au Bon Pain division, which was divested in May 1999. Results were penalized by a $5,545,000 loss stemming from the sale of the division, partly offset by a $3,756,000 reduction in depreciation and amortization stemming from the writedown of the book value of the division's assets in the 1998 third quarter. The net loss widened to $4,625,309 ($0.38 a share), from $2,961,644 ($0.25).

Stock Performance - 08-OCT-99

In the past 30 trading days, PNRA's shares have increased 7%, compared to a 0.91% fall in the S&P 500. Average trading volume for the past five days was 74,100 shares, compared with the 40-day moving average of 21,815 shares.

Key Stock Statistics

Dividend Rate/Share	Nil	Shareholders	1,600
Shs. outstg. (M)	12.2	Market cap. (B)	$0.078
Avg. daily vol. (M)	0.027	Inst. holdings	48%
Tang. Bk. Value/Share	4.37		
Beta	0.79		

Value of $10,000 invested 5 years ago: $ 3,241

Fiscal Year Ending Dec. 31

	1999	1998	1997	1996	1995	1994
Revenues (Million $)						
1Q	77.93	74.96	71.51	69.44	62.99	46.73
2Q	36.88	57.25	58.82	54.43	51.49	40.88
3Q	—	58.15	60.17	54.97	54.92	44.11
4Q	—	60.41	60.39	58.09	57.07	51.16
Yr.	—	249.7	250.9	236.9	226.5	182.9
Earnings Per Share ($)						
1Q	**-0.38**	**-0.16**	Nil	0.07	0.14	0.16
2Q	**0.06**	**-0.07**	-0.01	0.05	0.03	0.14
3Q	—	**-0.04**	0.12	-0.51	-0.39	0.18
4Q	—	**0.04**	**0.04**	0.02	0.09	0.20
Yr.	—	**-1.72**	**0.15**	**-0.37**	**-0.14**	**0.59**

Next earnings report expected: early November

Dividend Data

The company has never paid dividends on its capital stock and has no intention of paying cash dividends in the foreseeable future.

A Division of The McGraw-Hill Companies

Panera Bread Company

Business Summary - 11-JUN-99

On May 17, 1999, Panera Bread Co. (formerly Au Bon Pain Co., Inc.), an operator of bakery cafes, underwent a major transformation of its operations. On that day, the company announced the sale of its Au Bon Pain division to ABP Corp., an affiliate of Bruckmann, Rosser, Sherrill & Co., L.P., for $73 million in cash, before contractual purchase price adjustments estimated at $1 million. Proceeds from the sale were earmarked to pay off all outstanding debt and to provide cash for growth. The company adopted its current name concurrent with the sale of the Au Bon Pain division.

The company now consists of the Panera Bread/Saint Louis Bread Co. business unit. It has 75 company-owned bakery cafes and 63 franchised bakery cafes operating in 18 states. The cafes specialize in high-quality food for breakfast and lunch, including fresh baked goods, made-to-order sandwiches on freshly baked breads, soups, salads, custom-roasted coffees and other cafe beverages.

A total of 14 company-owned and 16 franchised bakery cafes were opened in the 1999 first quarter. For the full year, PNRA expects to open a total of 15 company-owned and 55 franchised bakery cafes, a 61% unit count increase. Franchise commitments are in place for the development of an additional 546 bakery cafes.

PNRA's target customers include urban office employees, suburban dwellers, shoppers, travelers, students and other adults who are time sensitive, yet want a higher-quality breakfast and lunch experience than is typical at quick-service restaurants. The company's menu focuses on foods in the following categories: fresh baked goods, made-to-order sandwiches on freshly baked breads, soups, salads, custom roasted coffees, and cafe beverages.

The company's strategy is to create distinctive food offerings at reasonable prices within these categories that are fresher, of higher quality and of greater variety than those offered by its competitors. In addition, PNRA believes its operational excellence, speed of service, and convenient locations further differentiate it from its competitors. Average revenue per company-operated bakery cafe open for all of 1998 was approximately $1,045,000 for the Au Bon Pain concept, and approximately $1,265,000 for the Saint Louis Bread (SLB) concept.

The average customer purchase was about $3.21 at Au Bon Pain and $5.09 at SLB. Breakfast and lunch checks averaged $2.20 and $4.36, respectively at Au Bon Pain, and $3.66 and $6.09, respectively, at SLB.

Per Share Data ($) (Year Ended Dec. 31)	1998	1997	1996	1995	1994	1993	1992	1991	1990	1989
Tangible Bk. Val.	4.37	5.06	4.78	4.95	4.92	4.24	5.70	4.06	NA	NA
Cash Flow	-0.66	1.57	1.01	1.14	1.70	1.30	1.08	0.88	NA	NA
Earnings	-1.72	0.15	-0.37	-0.14	0.67	0.60	0.48	0.30	NA	NA
Dividends	Nil	Nil	Nil	Nil	Nil	Nil	Nil	Nil	NA	NA
Payout Ratio	Nil	Nil	Nil	Nil	Nil	Nil	Nil	Nil	NA	NA
Prices - High	11 5/8	10 1/4	9 3/8	17 1/4	26 1/2	28 1/4	29	17	NA	NA
- Low	4 1/8	5 7/8	5 3/8	5 7/8	14 3/8	18	13 1/2	9	NA	NA
P/E Ratio - High	NM	68	NM	NM	40	47	60	57	NA	NA
- Low	NM	39	NM	NM	21	30	28	30	NA	NA
Income Statement Analysis (Million $)										
Revs.	250	251	237	226	183	123	97.0	68.0	NA	NA
Oper. Inc.	20.6	24.6	21.0	24.2	27.1	19.8	15.4	11.1	NA	NA
Depr.	12.7	16.9	16.2	14.9	11.9	8.0	6.6	5.2	NA	NA
Int. Exp.	6.4	7.2	5.1	3.4	1.7	0.1	0.2	1.0	NA	NA
Pretax Inc.	-26.2	0.3	-7.3	-4.4	13.3	11.7	8.9	4.3	NA	NA
Eff. Tax Rate	NM	NM	NM	NM	41%	42%	41%	40%	NA	NA
Net Inc.	-20.5	1.8	-4.4	-1.6	7.8	6.8	5.3	2.6	NA	NA
Balance Sheet & Other Fin. Data (Million $)										
Cash	1.9	0.9	2.6	6.4	1.0	4.9	4.7	NA	NA	NA
Curr. Assets	8.2	21.4	27.9	27.1	17.4	17.6	13.4	NA	NA	NA
Total Assets	154	187	196	193	166	120	77.0	NA	NA	NA
Curr. Liab.	16.5	21.4	25.2	26.3	20.9	12.4	6.7	NA	NA	NA
LT Debt	64.1	72.5	79.7	72.5	49.1	30.2	0.3	NA	NA	NA
Common Eqty.	73.3	92.3	90.1	93.2	94.2	68.3	NA	NA	NA	NA
Total Cap.	137	165	170	167	145	108	70.0	NA	NA	NA
Cap. Exp.	21.7	14.7	17.0	38.7	39.4	19.1	20.4	NA	NA	NA
Cash Flow	-7.8	18.7	11.8	13.3	19.7	14.8	11.9	7.8	NA	NA
Curr. Ratio	0.5	1.0	1.1	1.0	0.8	1.4	2.0	NA	NA	NA
% LT Debt of Cap.	46.7	44.0	46.8	43.5	33.5	28.0	1.0	NA	NA	NA
% Net Inc.of Revs.	NM	0.7	NM	NM	4.3	5.5	5.4	3.8	NA	NA
% Ret. on Assets	NM	0.9	NM	NM	5.5	6.8	7.0	NA	NA	NA
% Ret. on Equity	NM	2.0	NM	NM	9.2	9.4	8.0	NA	NA	NA

Data as orig reptd.; bef. results of disc opers/spec. items. Per share data adj. for stk. divs. Bold denotes diluted EPS (FASB 128)-prior periods restated. E-Estimated. NA-Not Available. NM-Not Meaningful. NR-Not Ranked.

Office—7930 Big Bend Blvd., Webster Groves, MO 63119. **Tel**—(314) 918-7779. **Website**—http://www.panerabread.com **Chrmn & CEO**—R. M. Shaich. **Pres & COO**—R. Postle. **CFO**—W. W. Moreton. **Dirs**—F. W. Hatch, G. E. Kane, L. I. Kane, J. R. McManus, H. J. Nasella, R. M. Shaich. **Transfer Agent & Registrar**—Boston Financial Data Services, Quincy, MA. **Incorporated**—in Delaware in 1988. **Empl**— 712. **S&P Analyst:** J.J.S.

STANDARD
&POOR'S
STOCK REPORTS

PAREXEL International

NASDAQ Symbol **PRXL**

In S&P SmallCap 600

09-OCT-99

Industry:
Health Care (Specialized Services)

Summary: In June 1999, the company terminated a merger agreement with Covance, Inc.

Quantitative Evaluations

Outlook
(1 Lowest—5 Highest)
• **5**

Fair Value
• **19¾**

Risk
• **High**

Earn./Div. Rank
• **NR**

Technical Eval.
• **Bearish** since 9/99

Rel. Strength Rank
(1 Lowest—99 Highest)
• **8**

Insider Activity
• **Favorable**

Recent Price • 8⅜
52 Wk Range • 45½-8
Yield • Nil
12-Mo. P/E • 13.6

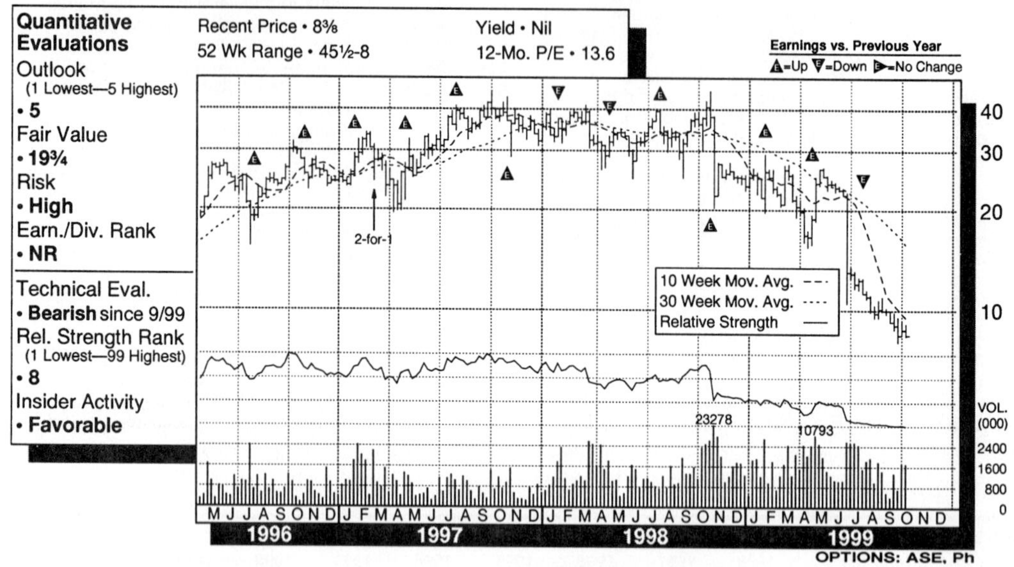

Business Profile - 25-JUN-99

In June 1999, PAREXEL terminated an agreement to merge with Covance, Inc. for some $800 million. Management said that integration planning clearly demonstrated that the merger would not produce the accelerated growth it had initially expected. In addition, PRXL announced that, based on an interim assessment of its results for the fiscal fourth quarter ended June 30, 1999, net revenues are estimated to range between $90 and $93 million; pro forma earnings per share, exclusive of merger-related and other charges, are estimated to be in the range of $0.18 to $0.20; and new business authorizations are anticipated to show sequential growth over the third quarter.

Operational Review - 25-JUN-99

Net revenue for the nine months ended March 31, 1999, rose 28%, year to year, primarily due to an increase in the volume of projects serviced. Direct costs increased 29%, and SG&A expenses were up 20%, largely due to increased expenditures for personnel, facilities and information systems to support increased operating levels. Following 20% higher depreciation and amortization charges, and in the absence of a $10.3 million acquisition related charge, pretax income nearly tripled, to $25,041,000 from $8,707,000. After taxes at 34.8%, versus 55.4%, net income improved to $16,331,000 ($0.65 a share), from $3,880,000 ($0.16).

Stock Performance - 08-OCT-99

In the past 30 trading days, PRXL's shares have declined 16%, compared to a 0.91% fall in the S&P 500. Average trading volume for the past five days was 339,700 shares, compared with the 40-day moving average of 245,395 shares.

Key Stock Statistics

Dividend Rate/Share	Nil	Shareholders	7,400
Shs. outstg. (M)	25.1	Market cap. (B)	$0.212
Avg. daily vol. (M)	0.272	Inst. holdings	70%
Tang. Bk. Value/Share	6.84		
Beta	NA		

Value of $10,000 invested 5 years ago: NA

Fiscal Year Ending Jun. 30

	1999	1998	1997	1996	1995	1994
Revenues (Million $)						
1Q	82.84	62.99	33.03	—	13.20	12.90
2Q	87.86	67.99	37.17	20.62	14.30	14.90
3Q	90.03	73.07	42.26	22.51	14.80	15.00
4Q	87.76	81.39	47.22	26.91	16.30	15.60
Yr.	348.5	285.4	159.7	88.01	58.57	58.00
Earnings Per Share ($)						
1Q	**0.22**	**0.18**	0.11	0.07	-0.58	—
2Q	**0.21**	**0.08**	0.13	0.08	0.03	—
3Q	**0.23**	**-0.10**	0.15	0.09	-0.30	—
4Q	**-0.03**	**0.22**	0.17	0.10	0.07	—
Yr.	**0.62**	**0.38**	**0.56**	**0.39**	-6.31	—

Next earnings report expected: late October

Dividend Data

No cash dividends have been paid.

PAREXEL International Corporation

Business Summary - 25-JUN-99

PAREXEL believes that it is the world's third largest contract pharmaceutical outsourcing organization, providing a wide range of knowledge-based contract research, medical marketing and consulting services worldwide to the pharmaceutical, biotechnology and medical device industries. It aims to help clients obtain necessary regulatory approvals of their products and optimize the market penetration of those products.

In FY 98 (Jun.), operating profits by region were derived as follows: North America $6,334,000, Europe $7,266,000, and Asia/Pacific -$299,000.

The company's service offerings include clinical trials management, data management, biostatistical analysis, medical marketing, clinical pharmacology, regulatory and medical consulting, performance improvement, industry training and publishing, and other drug development consulting services. Operations are largely divided into three business units: drug development, medical marketing, and consulting services.

PRXL's drug development unit (accounting for 65% of revenues) offers complete services for the design, initiation and management of clinical trial programs, a critical element in obtaining regulatory approval for drugs. The company has performed services in connection with trials in most therapeutic areas. PRXL can manage all aspects of clinical trials, including study and protocol design, placement, initiation, monitoring, report preparation and strategy development. The company also offers data management services, which include designing case report forms and training manuals for investigators to ensure that data are collected in an organized and consistent format, and biostatistical services aimed at helping clients with all phases of drug development, including biostatistical consulting, database design, data analysis and statistical reporting.

Medical marketing services include market planning and analysis, strategic consulting, product profiling and positioning, branding, pricing and reimbursement consulting, patient studies, health economics, scientific writing and publishing of medical texts and journals, and promotional material production.

PRXL's consulting unit provides comprehensive regulatory product registration services for pharmaceutical and biotechnology products in North America, Europe and Japan, including regulatory strategy formulation, document preparation and review, quality assurance, and liaison with the FDA and other regulatory agencies.

During FY 98, the company significantly enhanced its global competitive position through a number of acquisitions in Europe, including PPS Europe Ltd. and Genesis Pharma Strategies Ltd., leading marketing and clinical communications firms; MIRAI, B.V., a full service contract research organization; and LOGOS GmbH, a regulatory affairs consulting firm.

Per Share Data ($) (Year Ended Jun. 30)	1999	1998	1997	1996	1995	1994	1993	1992	1991	1990
Tangible Bk. Val.	NA	6.84	6.88	3.93	NA	NA	NA	NA	NA	NA
Cash Flow	NA	0.98	0.84	0.51	-4.97	NA	NA	NA	NA	NA
Earnings	0.62	0.38	0.57	0.34	-6.31	NA	NA	NA	NA	NA
Dividends	Nil	Nil	Nil	Nil	Nil	NA	NA	NA	NA	NA
Payout Ratio	Nil	Nil	Nil	Nil	Nil	NA	NA	NA	NA	NA
Prices - High	29$^3/_8$	45$^1/_2$	44$^3/_4$	31$^7/_8$	18	NA	NA	NA	NA	NA
- Low	8	20$^1/_4$	19$^1/_2$	13	9$^3/_8$	NA	NA	NA	NA	NA
P/E Ratio - High	47	NM	71	84	NM	NA	NA	NA	NA	NA
- Low	13	53	34	38	NM	NA	NA	NA	NA	NA
Income Statement Analysis (Million $)										
Revs.	NA	285	160	88.0	58.6	NA	NA	NA	NA	NA
Oper. Inc.	NA	38.7	18.7	8.8	3.1	NA	NA	NA	NA	NA
Depr.	NA	15.1	5.0	2.3	2.3	NA	NA	NA	NA	NA
Int. Exp.	NA	0.2	0.2	0.2	0.2	NA	NA	NA	NA	NA
Pretax Inc.	NA	17.0	16.9	7.7	-10.3	NA	NA	NA	NA	NA
Eff. Tax Rate	NA	45%	36%	40%	NM	NA	NA	NA	NA	NA
Net Inc.	NA	9.3	10.8	4.6	-10.6	2.4	-2.2	1.5	NA	NA
Balance Sheet & Other Fin. Data (Million $)										
Cash	NA	39.9	30.3	17.1	6.7	NA	NA	NA	NA	NA
Curr. Assets	NA	210	172	92.6	36.9	NA	NA	NA	NA	NA
Total Assets	NA	262	201	102	43.3	NA	NA	NA	NA	NA
Curr. Liab.	NA	90.8	61.4	39.2	25.3	NA	NA	NA	NA	NA
LT Debt	NA	Nil	Nil	0.0	0.1	NA	NA	NA	NA	NA
Common Eqty.	NA	168	138	61.2	15.5	NA	NA	NA	NA	NA
Total Cap.	NA	168	138	61.2	15.6	NA	NA	NA	NA	NA
Cap. Exp.	NA	27.7	22.0	5.0	1.5	NA	NA	NA	NA	NA
Cash Flow	NA	24.4	15.9	6.9	-8.4	NA	NA	NA	NA	NA
Curr. Ratio	NA	2.3	2.8	2.4	1.5	NA	NA	NA	NA	NA
% LT Debt of Cap.	NA	Nil	Nil	Nil	Nil	NA	NA	NA	NA	NA
% Net Inc.of Revs.	NA	3.3	6.8	5.2	NM	NA	NA	NA	NA	NA
% Ret. on Assets	NA	4.0	7.2	6.3	NM	NA	NA	NA	NA	NA
% Ret. on Equity	NA	6.1	10.9	17.3	NM	NA	NA	NA	NA	NA

Data as orig reptd.; bef. results of disc opers/spec. items. Per share data adj. for stk. divs. Bold denotes diluted EPS (FASB 128)-prior periods restated. E-Estimated. NA-Not Available. NM-Not Meaningful. NR-Not Ranked.

Office—195 West St., Waltham, MA 02154. **Tel**—(781) 487-9900. **Chrmn, Pres & CEO**—J. H. von Rickenbach. **SVP, CFO, Treas & Investor Contact**—W. T. Sobo.**Dirs**—A. D. Callow, Jr., A. J. Eagle, P. J. Fortune, W. M. Herrmann, S. Okun, J. A. Saafield, J. H. Von Rickenbach. **Transfer Agent & Registrar**—First National Bank of Boston. **Incorporated**—in Massachusetts in 1983. **Empl**— 4,300. **S&P Analyst:** P.L.H.

Park Electrochemical

NYSE Symbol **PKE**

In S&P SmallCap 600

09-OCT-99

Industry:
Electrical Equipment

Summary: This company primarily manufactures advanced electronic materials used in the production of multilayer printed circuit boards and interconnection systems.

Quantitative Evaluations

Outlook
(1 Lowest—5 Highest)
• **3**

Fair Value
• **41½**

Risk
• **Average**

Earn./Div. Rank
• **B**

Technical Eval.
• **Bearish** since 9/99

Rel. Strength Rank
(1 Lowest—99 Highest)
• **95**

Insider Activity
• **NA**

Recent Price • 37½ Yield • 0.9%
52 Wk Range • 38-14⅞ 12-Mo. P/E • 19.4

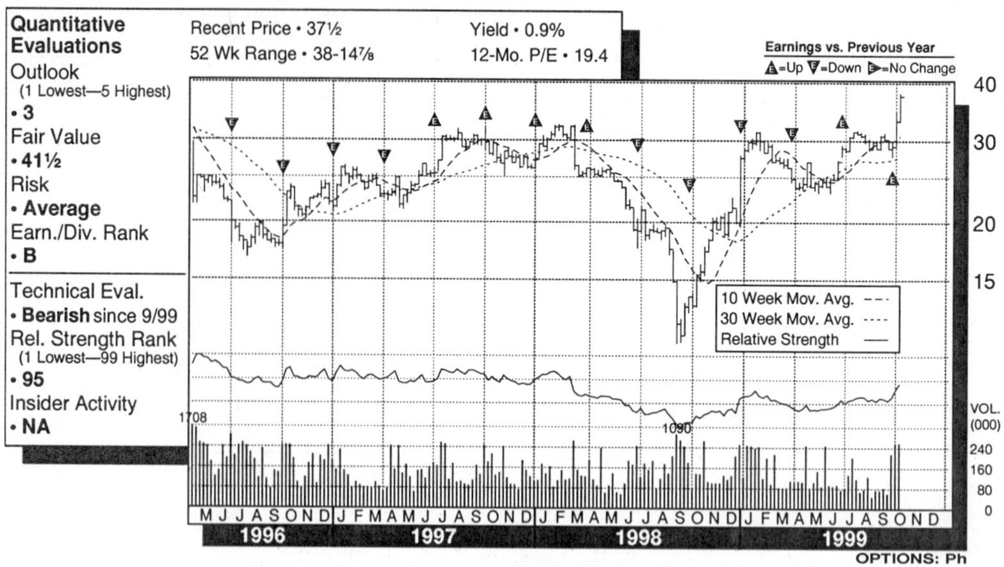

OPTIONS: Ph

Business Profile - 03-JUN-99

The loss of Delco Electronics as a customer had a material adverse effect on the business of the company's electronic materials segment in FY 99 (Feb.), and PKE is continuing to pursue a lawsuit against Delco. As of late April 1999, the company said that, while its business remained strong in Asia and North America, the European market had weakened in the past six months, and it was making adjustments there in response to that weakness. PKE planned to add significant capacity at its Singapore operation over the next few months, and also planned major expansions of its U.S. laminate operations. Although the U.S. expansions will take approximately two years to complete, they will enable the company to continue to aggressively expand its business in North America.

Operational Review - 03-JUN-99

Net sales rose 3.0% in FY 99, aided by the full-year inclusion of Dielektra (acquired in October 1997), partly offset by the loss of sales to Delco Electronics. Margins narrowed, on inefficiencies caused by operating at lower than designed levels, pricing pressures, and the loss of sales to Delco. Net income fell 39%, to $15,376,000 ($1.38 a share, on fewer shares), from $25,250,000 ($2.07).

Stock Performance - 08-OCT-99

In the past 30 trading days, PKE's shares have increased 30%, compared to a 0.91% fall in the S&P 500. Average trading volume for the past five days was 87,220 shares, compared with the 40-day moving average of 36,318 shares.

Key Stock Statistics

Dividend Rate/Share	0.32	Shareholders	2,318
Shs. outstg. (M)	10.4	Market cap. (B)	$0.389
Avg. daily vol. (M)	0.057	Inst. holdings	59%
Tang. Bk. Value/Share	16.25		
Beta	1.58		

Value of $10,000 invested 5 years ago: $ 34,229

Fiscal Year Ending Feb. 28

	2000	1999	1998	1997	1996	1995
Revenues (Million $)						
1Q	104.5	99.9	91.63	75.41	75.41	62.80
2Q	107.7	86.35	83.09	81.97	69.94	58.80
3Q	—	103.3	97.63	88.97	81.87	64.83
4Q	—	98.14	103.8	88.14	85.75	66.62
Yr.	—	387.6	376.2	334.5	313.0	253.0
Earnings Per Share ($)						
1Q	**0.51**	**0.46**	**0.51**	**0.26**	0.52	0.39
2Q	**0.53**	**0.02**	**0.41**	**0.40**	0.45	0.33
3Q	—	**0.40**	**0.56**	**0.42**	0.55	0.42
4Q	—	**0.47**	**0.59**	**0.49**	0.59	0.45
Yr.	—	**1.38**	**2.07**	**1.58**	**2.11**	**1.51**

Next earnings report expected: late December

Dividend Data (Dividends have been paid since 1985.)

Amount ($)	Date Decl.	Ex-Div. Date	Stock of Record	Payment Date
0.080	Dec. 08	Dec. 31	Jan. 05	Feb. 02 '99
0.080	Mar. 18	Apr. 09	Apr. 13	May. 11 '99
0.080	Jun. 09	Jul. 01	Jul. 06	Aug. 03 '99
0.080	Oct. 07	Oct. 14	Oct. 18	Nov. 09 '99

Park Electrochemical Corporation

Business Summary - 03-JUN-99

Park Electrochemical Corp. (PKE) is a leading global designer and producer of advanced electronic materials used to fabricate complex multilayer printed circuit boards, semiconductor packages and other electronic interconnection systems.

Park founded the modern day printed circuit industry in 1957 byinventing a composite material consisting of an epoxy resin substratereinforced with fiberglass cloth that was laminated together with sheets of thin copper foil. This epoxy-glass copper-clad laminate system is still used to construct the large majority of advanced printed circuit products. In 1962, the company invented the first multilayer printed circuit materials system, used to construct multilayer printed circuit boards. PKE also pioneered vacuum lamination and many other manufacturing technologies used in the industry today. In addition, Dielektra GmbH in Germany (acquired in October 1997) owns a patented process for continuously producing thin copper-clad laminates for printed circuit board applications.

Customers for PKE's advanced printed circuit materials include leading independent circuit board fabricators and large electronic equipment manufacturers in the computer, telecommunications, transportation, aerospace and instrumentation industries. The company's electronic materials operations, conducted by its Nelco group of companies, accounted for 90% of net sales worldwide in FY 99 (Feb.), up from 89% of net sales worldwide in FY 98. Foreign electronic materials operations accounted for 39% of total net sales worldwide in FY 99, and for 31% in FY 98.

The company also operates in the engineered materials business, which consists of the specialty adhesive tape business and advanced composite business, both of which operate as independent business units. In addition, PKE operates a plumbing hardware business. The engineered material and plumbing hardware businesses accounted for 10% of net sales worldwide in FY 99, and 11% in FY 98.

As a result of its leading edge products, extensive technical andengineering service support and responsive manufacturing capabilities, PKE expects to continue to take advantage of several industry trends. These include increasing global demand for electronic products and technology, increasing complexity of electronic products, increasingly advanced electronic materials required for interconnect performance and manufacturability, consolidation of the printed circuit board fabrication industry, and time to market and time to volumepressures that require closer collaboration with materials suppliers.

Per Share Data ($) (Year Ended Feb. 28)	1999	1998	1997	1996	1995	1994	1993	1992	1991	1990
Tangible Bk. Val.	15.95	14.60	12.72	11.64	9.75	7.58	6.75	6.93	7.08	6.62
Cash Flow	2.66	2.76	2.61	2.95	2.42	2.04	1.06	0.94	0.85	0.90
Earnings	1.38	2.07	1.61	2.11	1.59	1.01	0.27	0.19	0.24	0.40
Dividends	0.32	0.32	0.32	0.28	0.20	0.16	0.16	0.16	0.16	0.16
Payout Ratio	23%	15%	20%	13%	13%	16%	59%	84%	61%	39%
Cal. Yrs.	1998	1997	1996	1995	1994	1993	1992	1991	1990	1989
Prices - High	32 1/2	31 3/4	37 7/8	34 1/8	17 7/8	12 1/8	7 1/8	6 1/2	7 7/8	8 7/8
- Low	10 7/8	21 1/4	16 3/4	14	11 1/2	5 3/4	6 3/8	5	5 1/4	6 1/8
P/E Ratio - High	24	15	24	16	11	12	26	34	33	22
- Low	8	10	10	7	7	6	23	26	22	15
Income Statement Analysis (Million $)										
Revs.	388	376	334	313	253	208	176	165	164	148
Oper. Inc.	31.8	48.0	36.3	44.9	34.6	22.5	10.6	9.8	8.1	9.9
Depr.	14.3	13.2	11.6	9.8	8.5	8.2	7.2	6.8	6.0	5.1
Int. Exp.	5.4	5.5	5.5	0.1	0.4	2.5	2.6	2.9	3.0	2.9
Pretax Inc.	19.7	37.7	26.9	37.3	27.5	12.8	3.4	2.5	3.6	7.0
Eff. Tax Rate	22%	33%	31%	33%	37%	37%	27%	32%	35%	41%
Net Inc.	15.4	25.3	18.6	24.9	17.3	8.1	2.5	1.7	2.4	4.1
Balance Sheet & Other Fin. Data (Million $)										
Cash	140	45.1	145	143	45.9	38.1	32.9	36.9	42.8	55.0
Curr. Assets	230	247	220	218	98.3	85.8	75.9	81.2	89.1	97.0
Total Assets	352	359	308	299	162	141	130	131	136	135
Curr. Liab.	63.4	70.8	55.4	56.8	43.3	40.0	29.0	28.6	31.9	26.4
LT Debt	Nil	100	100	100	Nil	32.9	34.0	33.4	33.4	35.1
Common Eqty.	165	166	143	134	112	61.5	61.8	63.2	64.1	66.9
Total Cap.	165	275	251	241	117	99	100	102	103	108
Cap. Exp.	24.4	18.3	18.7	24.5	17.5	9.5	10.3	10.9	14.0	6.3
Cash Flow	29.7	38.5	30.1	34.7	26.3	25.8	9.6	8.6	8.4	9.2
Curr. Ratio	3.6	3.5	4.0	3.8	2.3	2.1	2.6	2.8	2.8	3.7
% LT Debt of Cap.	Nil	36.3	39.9	41.5	Nil	33.2	33.9	32.8	32.3	32.6
% Net Inc.of Revs.	4.0	6.7	5.6	8.0	6.9	3.9	1.4	1.0	1.4	2.8
% Ret. on Assets	4.3	7.6	6.2	10.8	9.6	6.3	1.9	1.3	1.8	3.1
% Ret. on Equity	9.3	16.3	13.4	20.2	17.4	13.9	3.9	2.7	3.8	6.3

Data as orig. reptd.; bef. results of disc. opers. and/or spec. items. Per share data adj. for stk. divs. as of ex-div. date. Bold denotes diluted EPS (FASB 128). E-Estimated. NA-Not Available. NM-Not Meaningful. NR-Not Ranked.

Office—5 Dakota Drive, Lake Success, NY 11042. **Tel**—(516) 354-4100. **Website**—http://www.parkelectro.com **Chrmn**—J. Shore. **Pres & CEO**—B. E. Shore. **Treas**—M. O. Stamer. **Dirs**—M. S. Ain, A. Chiesa, L. Frank, B. E. Shore, J. Shore. **Transfer Agent & Registrar**—Registrar & Transfer Co., Cranford, NJ. **Incorporated**—in New York in 1954. **Empl**— 2,680. **S&P Analyst:** C.F.B.

STANDARD &POOR'S
STOCK REPORTS

Patterson Dental

NASDAQ Symbol **PDCO**

In S&P SmallCap 600

09-OCT-99

Industry: Distributors (Food & Health)

Summary: PDCO is the largest distributor of dental products in North America, supplying more than 82,500 products to dentists and related markets. Office paper products are also sold.

Quantitative Evaluations
Outlook (1 Lowest—5 Highest) • 3
Fair Value • 52
Risk • Low
Earn./Div. Rank • B+

Technical Eval. • **Bullish** since 9/99
Rel. Strength Rank (1 Lowest—99 Highest) • 89
Insider Activity • **Unfavorable**

Recent Price • 47½
52 Wk Range • 50⅛-33⅛
Yield • Nil
12-Mo. P/E • 29.5

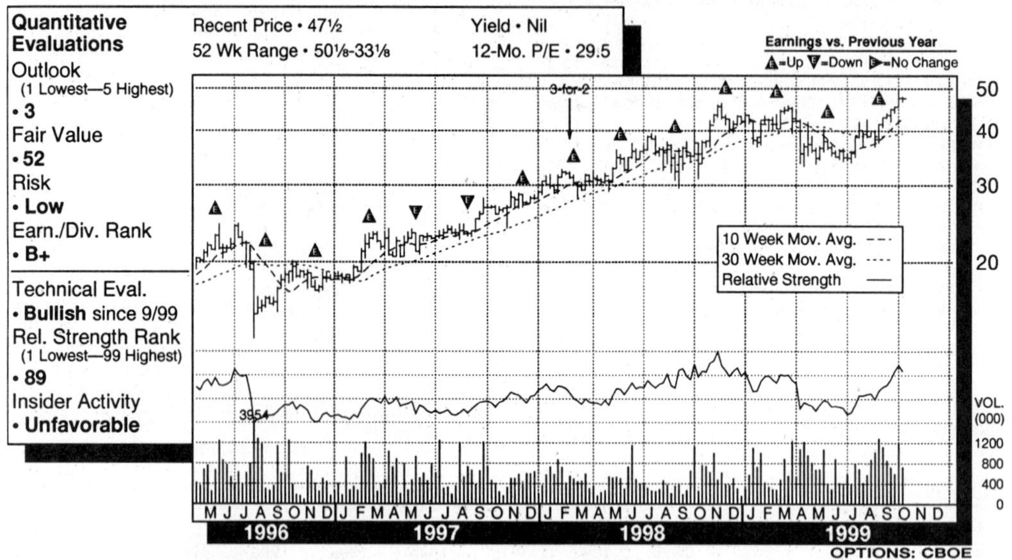

Business Profile - 04-OCT-99

In the FY 00 (Apr.) first quarter, PDCO exceeded its stated financial goals of 20% earnings growth and 10% revenue growth. The company expects that the dental supply industry will grow 7% to 9% annually, up from its previous estimate of 5% to 7%, as a result of dentists' increased productivity gained through high technology products and services as well as favorable demographics and new procedures. The company believes that its broad product coverage and its national position in a consolidating industry represent additional avenues for continued double-digit growth. PDCO's long term goal is for sales to grow 4% faster than the industry average. However, given its FY 00 first quarter results, it expects to grow 6% faster than the industry in FY 00. Officers and directors hold about 19% of the common shares. A 1 million share stock buyback plan was announced in September.

Operational Review - 04-OCT-99

Net sales in the three months ended July 31, 1999 increased 27%, year to year, reflecting increased sales of equipment and consumables. The current quarter included 14 weeks, versus 13 weeks last year. Gross margins narrowed slightly, but operating expenses decreased as a percentage of sales, and operating profits rose 36%. After taxes at 37.4%, versus 38.6%, net income climbed 42%, to $14.5 million ($0.43 a share), from $10.2 million ($0.31, as adjusted).

Stock Performance - 08-OCT-99

In the past 30 trading days, PDCO's shares have increased 15%, compared to a 0.91% fall in the S&P 500. Average trading volume for the past five days was 144,640 shares, compared with the 40-day moving average of 214,895 shares.

Key Stock Statistics

Dividend Rate/Share	Nil	Shareholders	1,876
Shs. outstg. (M)	33.7	Market cap. (B)	$ 1.6
Avg. daily vol. (M)	0.166	Inst. holdings	59%
Tang. Bk. Value/Share	6.49		
Beta	0.59		

Value of $10,000 invested 5 years ago: $ 32,927

Fiscal Year Ending Apr. 30

	2000	1999	1998	1997	1996	1995
Revenues (Million $)						
1Q	254.6	200.1	180.0	142.2	134.3	123.6
2Q	—	213.3	191.6	161.9	143.7	131.9
3Q	—	230.2	195.5	176.1	148.7	136.5
4Q	—	235.2	211.0	181.4	155.2	140.5
Yr.	—	878.8	778.2	661.5	581.9	532.6
Earnings Per Share ($)						
1Q	**0.43**	**0.31**	**0.25**	**0.28**	0.19	0.16
2Q	—	**0.36**	0.30	**0.28**	0.21	0.18
3Q	—	**0.41**	**0.33**	**0.28**	0.21	0.18
4Q	—	**0.42**	**0.35**	**0.19**	0.25	0.21
Yr.	—	**1.49**	**1.23**	**1.00**	**0.86**	**0.75**

Next earnings report expected: mid November

Dividend Data

No cash dividends have been paid. A three-for-two stock split was effected in February 1998.

A Division of The McGraw-Hill Companies

Patterson Dental Company

Business Summary - 04-OCT-99

Patterson Dental Co. provides the supplies and equipment dentists need to treat their patients. The company's broad range of consumables, such as X-ray film and impression and restorative materials, and its varied equipment lines (sterilizers, dental lights, and X-ray machines) are found in thousands of dental practices across the U.S. and Canada. Even the dreaded dental chair can be sourced at PDCO. PDCO offers about 82,500 products to dentists, dental laboratories and institutions.

In October 1996, the company acquired Colwell Systems, which provides office stationery and health care forms to medical and dental practices. Colwell strengthened PDCO's position as a single-source supplier, and allowed the company to leverage its direct sales force to pursue this new business with existing customers.

The company's consumable goods and office supplies accounted for 64% of net sales in FY 99 (Apr.). Demand for protective clothing and gloves has been boosted by heightened public concern over communicable diseases such as AIDS. In addition to its infection control products, PDCO also distributes X-ray film and solutions, hand instruments, toothbrushes, and materials and accessories used by dentists.

PDCO offers a wide range of dental equipment (27% of FY 99 sales), including X-ray machines, sterilizers, and diagnostic equipment. FY 99 revenues received a lift from sales of the CEREC 2, a chair-side laboratory that produces inlays, onlays, and full crown restorations in a single visit. Other products include the KCP 1000, a high-speed air abrasion cavity preparation device that allows the dentist to work without a traditional drill.

In an effort to increase market share, the company has made several acquisitions, introduced new products, and expanded its sales force. In February 1999, PDCO acquired Professional Business Systems Inc., (PBS), a manufacturer and distributor of filing systems and other practice management systems. Recent acquisitions also included Hill Dental Company, Inc. (February 1998), a full-service dental products distributor with 1997 sales of $29 million; Canadian Dental Supply Ltd. (CDS; August 1997), a leading Canadian dental products distributor; and EagleSoft (July 1997), a leading provider of dental practice management systems.

Total expenditures for U.S. dental services reached about $53 billion in 1998. HCFA projects that these expenditures will grow 6% annually, reaching $95 billion by 2007. The company believes it can remain a leading national distributor of dental supplies by emphasizing its full-service capabilities, using technology to enhance customer service, and through internal expansion and acquisitions.

Per Share Data ($) **(Year Ended Apr. 30)**	**1999**	**1998**	**1997**	**1996**	**1995**	**1994**	**1993**	**1992**	**1991**	**1990**
Tangible Bk. Val.	6.49	4.88	3.65	3.29	2.17	NA	NA	NA	NA	NA
Cash Flow	1.73	1.45	1.19	0.99	0.83	0.66	NA	NA	NA	NA
Earnings	1.49	1.23	1.00	0.87	0.73	0.58	0.41	0.25	0.21	NA
Dividends	Nil	Nil	Nil	Nil	Nil	Nil	Nil	Nil	NA	NA
Payout Ratio	Nil	Nil	Nil	Nil	Nil	Nil	Nil	Nil	NA	NA
Cal. Yrs.	1998	1997	1996	1995	1994	1993	1992	1991	1990	1989
Prices - High	46 3/8	30 1/2	24 5/8	19 5/8	16 1/4	14 1/2	11 3/8	NA	NA	NA
- Low	28 1/8	17 7/8	13 3/8	13 3/8	10 1/2	7	7 1/8	NA	NA	NA
P/E Ratio - High	31	25	25	23	22	25	27	NA	NA	NA
- Low	19	14	13	15	14	12	17	NA	NA	NA
Income Statement Analysis (Million $)										
Revs.	879	778	662	582	533	467	343	277	243	NA
Oper. Inc.	85.7	72.7	56.8	47.5	41.4	33.8	NA	NA	NA	NA
Depr.	8.2	7.5	6.2	3.8	3.3	2.5	NA	NA	NA	NA
Int. Exp.	0.5	0.7	0.6	0.4	0.5	0.5	NA	NA	NA	NA
Pretax Inc.	79.7	65.7	52.0	45.7	39.1	32.0	20.4	12.6	10.5	NA
Eff. Tax Rate	37%	38%	38%	37%	38%	40%	35%	32%	30%	NA
Net Inc.	49.9	40.8	32.4	28.7	24.2	19.3	13.2	8.5	7.3	NA
Balance Sheet & Other Fin. Data (Million $)										
Cash	78.7	35.6	9.1	46.1	13.6	NA	NA	NA	NA	NA
Curr. Assets	287	228	164	175	147	NA	NA	NA	NA	NA
Total Assets	373	316	244	203	171	136	105	75.0	NA	NA
Curr. Liab.	99	94.4	69.8	62.8	60.2	NA	NA	NA	NA	NA
LT Debt	1.7	2.7	2.8	3.0	3.2	NA	NA	NA	NA	NA
Common Eqty.	265	210	163	87.3	57.3	72.2	53.1	10.7	NA	NA
Total Cap.	269	215	167	131	101	NA	NA	NA	NA	NA
Cap. Exp.	7.1	6.0	4.9	6.9	6.2	8.9	NA	NA	NA	NA
Cash Flow	58.1	48.2	38.6	31.9	26.9	21.2	NA	NA	NA	NA
Curr. Ratio	2.9	2.4	2.4	2.8	2.4	NA	NA	NA	NA	NA
% LT Debt of Cap.	0.6	1.2	1.7	2.3	3.2	NA	NA	NA	NA	NA
% Net Inc.of Revs.	5.7	5.2	4.9	4.9	4.5	4.1	3.8	3.1	3.0	NA
% Ret. on Assets	14.5	14.5	14.5	15.3	12.9	16.0	14.7	12.1	NA	NA
% Ret. on Equity	21.0	21.9	24.2	38.9	37.5	30.9	41.3	130.7	NA	NA

Data as orig. reptd.; bef. results of disc. opers. and/or spec. items. Per share data adj. for stk. divs. as of ex-div. date. Bold denotes diluted EPS (FASB 128). E-Estimated. NA-Not Available. NM-Not Meaningful. NR-Not Ranked.

Office—1031 Mendota Heights Rd., St. Paul, MN 55120. **Tel**—(612) 686-1600. **Website**—http://www.pattersondental.com **Chrmn, Pres & CEO**—P. L. Frechette. **VP**—J. W. Wiltz. **EVP & CFO**—R.S. Armstrong. **Secy**—M.L. Levitt. **Dirs**—D. K. Beecken, R. E. Ezerski, P. L. Frechette, A. B. Lacy, B. E. Swanson. **Transfer Agent & Registrar**—Norwest Bank Minnesota, Minneapolis. **Incorporated**—in Minnesota in 1992. **Empl**— 3,623.
S&P Analyst: John J. Arege

STANDARD &POOR'S
STOCK REPORTS

PAXAR Corp.

NYSE Symbol **PXR**
In S&P SmallCap 600

09-OCT-99

Industry: Manufacturing (Specialized)

Summary: PAXAR manufactures bar-code tag and labeling systems, as well as printed labels, woven labels and merchandise tags, for the apparel and textile industries.

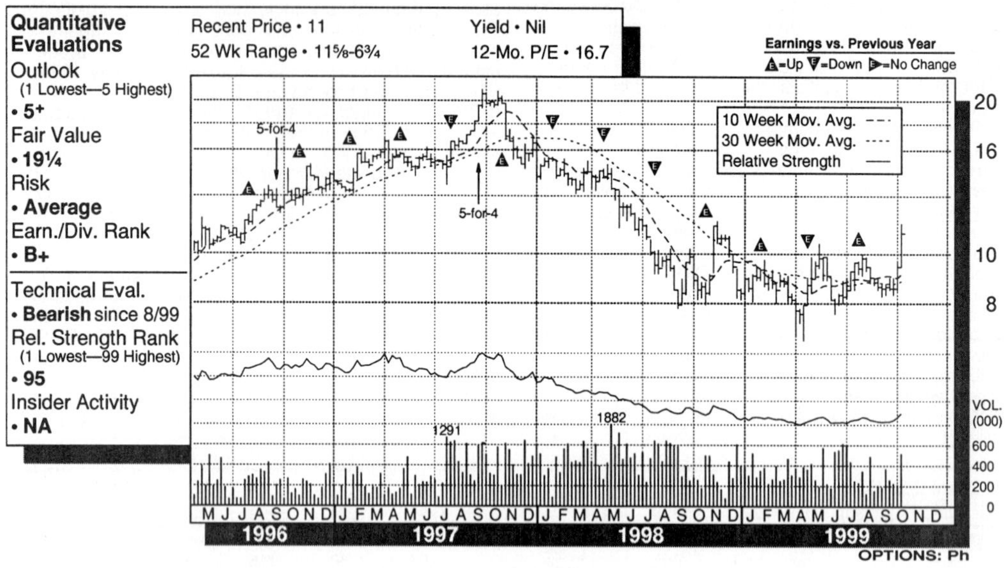

Business Profile - 25-AUG-99

In July 1999, the company said the integration of Ferguson International, acquired in February 1999, was ahead of schedule. It also said results in the second quarter benefited from improvement in the apparel ID business, and from margin improvement across all major business segments. PXR recently closed two manufacturing facilities, in order to more closely align manufacturing capacity with customer demand. In February 1999, directors increased to $40 million the size its stock repurchase program; 3.3 million common shares had been purchased through June 30, 1999, including 1.8 million shares in the first half of 1999.

Operational Review - 25-AUG-99

Net sales in the first half of 1999 advanced 5.1%, year to year, as international growth, due to the acquisition of Ferguson International, outweighed a slight decline in the identification and bar code solutions and thermal transfer ribbons business segments. Gross margins narrowed, and results were restricted by higher SG&A expense and $5.0 million in restructuring and other special charges to streamline the U.S. and U.K. business segments; net income fell 13%, to $12,600,000 ($0.27 a share, on 4.8% fewer shares), from $14,500,000 ($0.29).

Stock Performance - 08-OCT-99

In the past 30 trading days, PXR's shares have increased 28%, compared to a 0.91% fall in the S&P 500. Average trading volume for the past five days was 102,900 shares, compared with the 40-day moving average of 53,603 shares.

Key Stock Statistics

Dividend Rate/Share	Nil	Shareholders	1,300
Shs. outstg. (M)	46.5	Market cap. (B)	$0.512
Avg. daily vol. (M)	0.060	Inst. holdings	45%
Tang. Bk. Value/Share	2.34		
Beta	0.58		

Value of $10,000 invested 5 years ago: $ 17,755

Fiscal Year Ending Dec. 31

	1999	1998	1997	1996	1995	1994
Revenues (Million $)						
1Q	154.2	149.4	105.9	52.75	50.52	35.98
2Q	167.6	156.9	158.9	57.55	52.90	42.46
3Q	—	153.8	148.8	51.94	49.31	41.01
4Q	—	151.5	153.6	57.58	48.71	47.16
Yr.	—	611.6	567.2	219.8	201.4	166.6
Earnings Per Share ($)						
1Q	**0.07**	**0.15**	**0.17**	**0.15**	0.11	0.06
2Q	**0.20**	**0.15**	**0.16**	**0.18**	0.13	0.10
3Q	—	**0.22**	**0.19**	**0.17**	0.10	0.08
4Q	—	**0.17**	**-0.03**	**0.18**	0.11	0.10
Yr.	—	**0.68**	**0.49**	**0.68**	**0.52**	**0.45**

Next earnings report expected: late October

Dividend Data

No cash dividends have been paid.

PAXAR Corporation

Business Summary - 25-AUG-99

To broaden its product line and enhance its market position PAXAR has developed new products and completed several acquisitions since 1986. The company is a fully integrated manufacturer and distributor of label systems, bar-code systems, labels, tags and related supplies and services for apparel manufacturers and retailers.

In 1995, the company acquired a 49.5% interest in Monarch Marking Systems, a manufacturer of bar code systems and supplies; it purchased the remaining interest in March 1997. In January 1996, PAXAR purchased Brian Pulfrey, Ltd., a manufacturer of printed labels and tags in Nottingham, England. In 1997, the company acquired a 70% interest in a Brazilian label system manufacturer and a 50% interest in a Columbian distributor, and in February 1998, acquired a 70% interest in a Turkish maker of apparel identification systems.

In July 1997, PAXAR acquired International Imaging Materials, Inc., the largest manufacturer in North America of thermal transfer ribbons used in thermal printers and other applications, in exchange for about 12.5 million common shares valued at about $200 million. In February 1999, the company acquired the apparel identification business of Ferguson International for $24 million in cash. The acquisition of Ferguson should add about $66 million to annual sales.

The company's apparel identification products include bar-code tag systems and hot-stamp label printers. These systems let customers print, cut and batch large volumes of tags and labels in their own plants. PAXAR's bar-code tag systems include personal computers, electronic bar-code printers, thermal ink, pre-printed tag stock and supporting software. Hot-stamp printing systems include hot-stamp printers, fabrics, inks and printing accessories, which are used by manufacturers for in-house printing of care labels and labels that carry brand logo, size and other information for the retail customer. The company also designs and produces tags and woven and printed labels. Tag and label systems and supplies accounted for 34% of net sales in 1998.

Printing solutions (42% of 1998 sales) consist of identification and pricing system labelers, which print one to three lines of alphanumeric information in a variety of print sizes and types; automated identification system printers and related supplies, which consist of tabletop, handheld and portable thermal transfer and direct thermal printers; and thermal transfer ribbons, an essential consumable in the thermal transfer printing process. The International segment sells the company's apparel identification products and printing solutions, and made up the remaining 24% of net sales in 1998.

The company has more than 10,000 customers, including major retailers and apparel manufacturers such as Levi Strauss, Sears, J.C. Penney, The Limited, Liz Claiborne, Sara Lee, Land's End, and L.L. Bean.

Per Share Data ($) (Year Ended Dec. 31)	1998	1997	1996	1995	1994	1993	1992	1991	1990	1989
Tangible Bk. Val.	2.41	1.62	2.90	2.29	1.86	1.84	1.55	0.91	0.79	0.72
Cash Flow	1.45	1.16	0.89	0.68	0.54	0.41	0.38	0.24	0.15	0.27
Earnings	0.68	0.49	0.62	0.45	0.34	0.27	0.27	0.13	0.04	0.15
Dividends	Nil	Nil	Nil	Nil	Nil	Nil	Nil	Nil	Nil	Nil
Payout Ratio	Nil	Nil	Nil	Nil	Nil	Nil	Nil	Nil	Nil	Nil
Prices - High	15 1/2	21	15	10 1/4	6 1/2	6 3/4	7 1/4	2 3/8	1 9/16	2
- Low	7 3/4	13 1/8	7 1/8	4 7/8	4 7/8	4 1/4	2 5/16	15/16	7/8	7/8
P/E Ratio - High	23	43	24	23	19	24	28	19	36	13
- Low	11	27	12	11	14	16	9	7	20	6
Income Statement Analysis (Million $)										
Revs.	612	567	220	201	167	139	133	88.9	72.9	73.8
Oper. Inc.	101	100	36.1	31.3	24.8	19.6	18.3	9.9	6.0	8.6
Depr.	38.1	32.8	9.7	8.1	6.8	4.7	3.6	2.8	2.7	2.3
Int. Exp.	14.6	13.8	1.4	1.6	0.9	0.5	0.8	1.1	1.5	1.9
Pretax Inc.	48.0	37.9	29.1	22.1	17.1	14.5	13.9	6.0	1.8	6.7
Eff. Tax Rate	30%	36%	25%	29%	32%	35%	40%	42%	36%	38%
Net Inc.	33.6	24.4	21.8	15.7	11.6	9.4	8.4	3.4	1.1	4.2
Balance Sheet & Other Fin. Data (Million $)										
Cash	14.8	13.7	6.7	6.7	4.5	0.7	0.3	0.3	1.2	0.3
Curr. Assets	229	234	78.3	70.9	64.0	47.8	42.4	30.3	26.6	27.3
Total Assets	593	598	182	157	129	85.5	72.8	51.1	43.0	44.3
Curr. Liab.	89.9	113	28.9	24.3	25.0	17.6	14.1	13.1	9.1	10.2
LT Debt	205	211	19.9	23.1	13.8	0.7	2.1	10.2	10.9	13.0
Common Eqty.	273	244	120	95.2	77.9	62.5	52.8	25.0	20.8	19.2
Total Cap.	498	479	152	129	102	67.9	58.6	38.0	34.0	34.1
Cap. Exp.	35.7	30.3	13.8	12.3	11.2	12.6	8.5	6.6	3.2	1.5
Cash Flow	71.7	57.2	31.5	23.8	18.4	14.0	12.0	6.3	3.9	6.4
Curr. Ratio	2.5	2.1	2.7	2.9	2.6	2.7	3.0	2.3	2.9	2.7
% LT Debt of Cap.	41.1	44.1	13.1	17.9	13.5	1.1	3.6	27.0	32.1	38.0
% Net Inc.of Revs.	5.5	4.3	9.9	7.8	7.0	6.7	6.3	3.9	1.6	5.6
% Ret. on Assets	5.6	6.3	12.9	11.0	10.7	11.8	12.2	7.2	2.6	9.4
% Ret. on Equity	13.0	13.4	20.3	18.2	16.4	16.2	19.9	14.8	5.7	24.2

Data as orig reptd.; bef. results of disc opers/spec. items. Per share data adj. for stk. divs. Bold denotes diluted EPS (FASB 128)-prior periods restated. E-Estimated. NA-Not Available. NM-Not Meaningful. NR-Not Ranked.

Office—105 Corporate Park Drive, White Plains, NY 10604-3814. **Tel**—(914) 697-6800. **Fax**—(914) 697-6893. **Website**—http://www.paxar.com **Chrmn, Pres, CEO & COO**—A. Hershaft. **SVP & CFO**—J. R. Plaxe. **VP & Treas**—J. P. Jordan. **VP & Contr**—J. J. Fitzgerald. **VP & Secy**—D. S. Bishop. **VP & Investor Contact**—Jay M. Green (914- 697-6814). **Dirs**—J. Becker, L. Benatar, A. Hershaft, V. Hershaft, T. R. Loemker, J. C. McGroddy, C. O. Morrision, D. E. McKinney, W. W. Williams. **Transfer Agent & Registrar**—ChaseMellon Shareholder Services, S. Hackensack, NJ. **Incorporated**—in New York in 1946. **Empl**— 6,000. **S&P Analyst:** Jim Corridore

STANDARD &POOR'S
STOCK REPORTS

Pediatrix Medical Group

NYSE Symbol **PDX**

In S&P SmallCap 600

09-OCT-99

Industry: Health Care (Specialized Services)

Summary: This company provides physician management services to hospitals for the care of newborn infants.

Quantitative Evaluations
Outlook
(1 Lowest—5 Highest)
• **5**
Fair Value
• **34¼**
Risk
• **Average**
Earn./Div. Rank
• **NR**

Technical Eval.
• **Bearish** since 9/99
Rel. Strength Rank
(1 Lowest—99 Highest)
• **2**
Insider Activity
• **Neutral**

Recent Price • 9¼
52 Wk Range • 65½-8⅜
Yield • Nil
12-Mo. P/E • 4.8

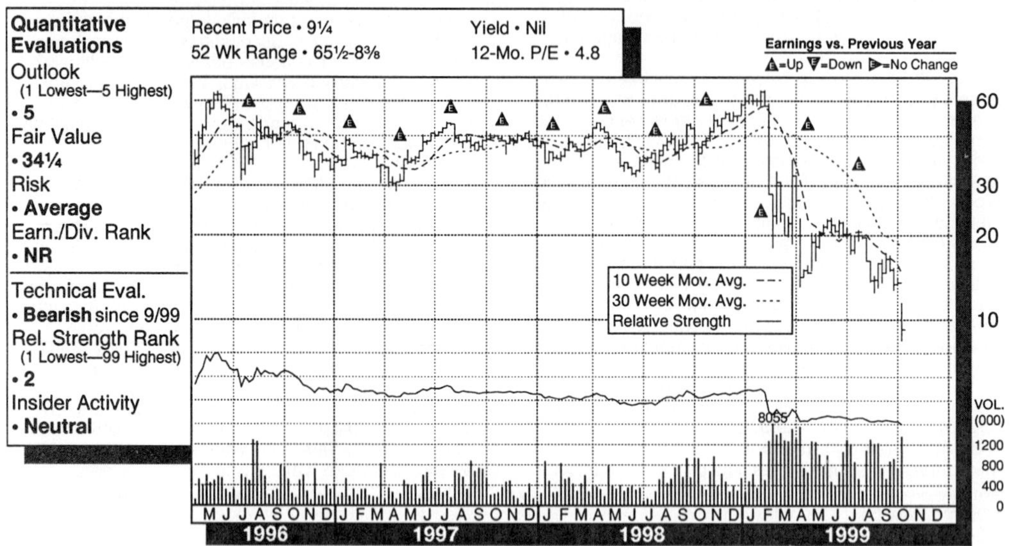

Business Profile - 13-JUL-99

The company continues to add new units and increase same-unit growth through a focus on neonatology, perinatology and pediatrics; the continued acquisition of neonatal and perinatal physician group practices; the development of regional networks; helping hospitals control costs; and addressing challenges of the managed care environment. PDX was required to perform a concurrent audit of its 1998 financial statements, after it learned that its accounting firm of record, PricewaterhouseCoopers, had violated auditor independence rules. The concurrent audit, performed by KMPG, found that the company's financial statements were fairly stated.

Operational Review - 13-JUL-99

Revenues in the three months ended March 31, 1999, climbed 42%, year to year, reflecting acquisitions, as well as gains in same-unit patient service revenues. Results were penalized by costs of hiring new physicians to support unit growth, expensing of acquisition costs that had historically been capitalized, and $500,000 of additional audit fees related to the company's 1998 concurrent audit; the gain in pretax income was held to 18%. After taxes at 40.0% in each period, net income was also up 18%, to $7,250,000 ($0.45 a share), from $6,119,000 ($0.39).

Stock Performance - 08-OCT-99

In the past 30 trading days, PDX's shares have declined 42%, compared to a 0.91% fall in the S&P 500. Average trading volume for the past five days was 667,220 shares, compared with the 40-day moving average of 250,282 shares.

Key Stock Statistics

Dividend Rate/Share	Nil	Shareholders	87
Shs. outstg. (M)	15.5	Market cap. (B)	$0.143
Avg. daily vol. (M)	0.292	Inst. holdings	0%
Tang. Bk. Value/Share	0.54		
Beta	NA		

Value of $10,000 invested 5 years ago: NA

Fiscal Year Ending Dec. 31

	1999	1998	1997	1996	1995	1994
Revenues (Million $)						
1Q	53.83	37.81	27.01	16.13	8.89	—
2Q	56.77	46.14	30.60	17.81	9.13	—
3Q	—	49.35	34.44	22.40	12.48	—
4Q	—	52.12	36.79	24.49	13.36	—
Yr.	—	185.4	128.8	80.83	43.86	32.78
Earnings Per Share ($)						
1Q	**0.45**	**0.39**	**0.28**	**0.19**	0.12	—
2Q	**0.50**	**0.45**	**0.30**	**0.22**	0.12	—
3Q	—	**0.48**	**0.35**	**0.24**	0.22	—
4Q	—	**0.51**	**0.40**	**0.25**	0.17	—
Yr.	—	**1.82**	**1.33**	**0.90**	**0.57**	**0.49**

Next earnings report expected: early November

Dividend Data

No cash dividends have been paid, and the company does not intend to pay any for the foreseeable future. In March 1999, the company adopted a shareholder rights plan.

A Division of The McGraw-Hill Companies

STANDARD &POOR'S
STOCK REPORTS

Pediatrix Medical Group, Inc.

09-OCT-99

Business Summary - 13-JUL-99

Pediatrix Medical Group is the leading U.S. provider of physician management services to hospital-based neonatal intensive care units (NICUs). NICUs provide medical care to newborn infants with low birth weight and other medical complications, and are staffed with specialized pediatric physicians, known as neonatologists. The company also provides physician management services to (i) hospital-based pediatric intensive care units (PICUs) which provide medical care to critically ill children and are staffed with specially-trained pediatricians; and (ii) pediatrics departments (PEDs) in hospitals. In addition, PDX began providing inpatient and outpatient perinatal service during 1997. Perinatology is a subspecialty of obstetrical medicine that focuses on the diagnostics, management and care of high-risk and/or complicated pregnancies. As of December 31, 1998, PDX provided services in 20 states and Puerto Rico and employed or contracted 350 physicians.

The company staffs and manages NICUs and PICUs in hospitals, providing the physicians, professional management and administrative support, including physician billing and reimbursement expertise and services.

PDX's policy is to provide 24-hour coverage at its NICUs and PICUs with on-site or on-call physicians. As a result of this policy, physicians are available to provide continuous pediatric support to other areas of the hospital on an as-needed basis, especially in the obstetrics, nursery and pediatrics departments, where immediate accessibility to specialized care is critical.

NICU patient days in 1998 totaled 450,225, up from 325,199 the year before. The number of births in 1998 was 268,923, versus 200,616 in 1997.

Of the approximately 4 million babies born in the U.S. annually, about 10% to 15% require neonatal treatment. Demand for neonatal services is primarily due to premature births, and to infants having difficulty making the transition to extrauterine life. A majority of high-risk mothers whose births require neonatal treatment are not identified until the time of delivery, thus heightening the need for continuous coverage. NICUs are important to hospitals since obstetrics generates one of the highest volumes of admissions, and obstetricians generally prefer to perform deliveries at hospital with NICUs.

Services provided to patients covered under government programs accounted for about 42% of the company's total gross patient service revenue in 1998.

Per Share Data ($) (Year Ended Dec. 31)	1998	1997	1996	1995	1994	1993	1992	1991	1990	1989
Tangible Bk. Val.	0.54	4.06	6.00	4.52	0.06	NA	NA	NA	NA	NA
Cash Flow	2.36	1.62	1.03	0.58	0.50	0.38	NA	NA	NA	NA
Earnings	1.82	1.33	0.90	0.55	0.47	0.36	NA	NA	NA	NA
Dividends	Nil	Nil	Nil	Nil	Nil	Nil	NA	NA	NA	NA
Payout Ratio	Nil	Nil	Nil	Nil	Nil	Nil	NA	NA	NA	NA
Prices - High	60 7/8	50 3/8	64 3/4	28 1/2	NA	NA	NA	NA	NA	NA
- Low	32 1/8	28 5/8	22 1/2	18 1/2	NA	NA	NA	NA	NA	NA
P/E Ratio - High	33	38	72	52	NA	NA	NA	NA	NA	NA
- Low	18	22	25	34	NA	NA	NA	NA	NA	NA
Income Statement Analysis (Million $)										
Revs.	185	129	80.8	43.9	32.8	23.6	NA	NA	NA	NA
Oper. Inc.	57.6	37.6	21.8	10.9	9.3	17.1	NA	NA	NA	NA
Depr.	8.7	4.5	1.8	0.4	0.2	0.1	NA	NA	NA	NA
Int. Exp.	1.0	0.3	0.2	0.1	0.1	0.1	NA	NA	NA	NA
Pretax Inc.	48.5	34.9	22.0	11.2	9.2	6.3	NA	NA	NA	NA
Eff. Tax Rate	40%	40%	40%	40%	41%	34%	NA	NA	NA	NA
Net Inc.	29.1	20.9	13.1	6.7	5.4	4.2	NA	NA	NA	NA
Balance Sheet & Other Fin. Data (Million $)										
Cash	0.7	18.6	75.7	46.2	7.4	NA	NA	NA	NA	NA
Curr. Assets	63.7	82.0	101	59.8	17.2	NA	NA	NA	NA	NA
Total Assets	271	197	159	69.9	20.3	14.2	NA	NA	NA	NA
Curr. Liab.	48.8	28.1	19.7	6.3	3.4	NA	NA	NA	NA	NA
LT Debt	10.2	2.5	2.8	0.8	0.8	1.0	NA	NA	NA	NA
Common Eqty.	201	164	136	62.8	0.4	-3.9	NA	NA	NA	NA
Total Cap.	221	169	139	63.6	17.9	11.5	NA	NA	NA	NA
Cap. Exp.	3.3	2.2	4.7	1.9	0.6	1.9	NA	NA	NA	NA
Cash Flow	37.8	25.4	14.9	7.1	5.7	4.3	NA	NA	NA	NA
Curr. Ratio	1.3	2.9	5.1	9.5	5.1	NA	NA	NA	NA	NA
% LT Debt of Cap.	4.6	1.5	0.2	1.2	4.5	8.4	NA	NA	NA	NA
% Net Inc.of Revs.	15.7	16.2	16.3	15.3	16.5	17.6	NA	NA	NA	NA
% Ret. on Assets	12.4	11.8	11.5	14.9	31.3	29.6	NA	NA	NA	NA
% Ret. on Equity	15.9	13.9	13.2	21.2	NM	NM	NA	NA	NA	NA

Data as orig reptd.; bef. results of disc opers/spec. items. Per share data adj. for stk. divs. Bold denotes diluted EPS (FASB 128)-prior periods restated. E-Estimated. NA-Not Available. NM-Not Meaningful. NR-Not Ranked.

Office—1455 N. Park Dr., Ft. Lauderdale, FL 33326. **Tel**—(954) 384-0175. **Website**—http://www.pediatrix.com **Pres & CEO**—R. J. Medel. **CFO**—K. B. Wagner. **VP & Secy**—B. A. Jordan. **Investor Contact**—Bob Kneeley, Jr. (800-243-3839). **Dirs**—C. L. Alvarez, W. A. Carlo, M. D. Cunningham, M. Fernandez, R. J. Medel.**Transfer Agent & Registrar**—Boston EquiServe. **Incorporated**—in Florida in 1980. **Empl**— 939. **S&P Analyst:** P.L.H.

STANDARD &POOR'S
STOCK REPORTS

Penford Corp.

NASDAQ Symbol **PENX**

In S&P SmallCap 600

23-OCT-99

Industry: Chemicals (Diversified)

Summary: This company makes and sells carbohydrate-based specialty chemicals for papermaking, food ingredients and specialty textiles.

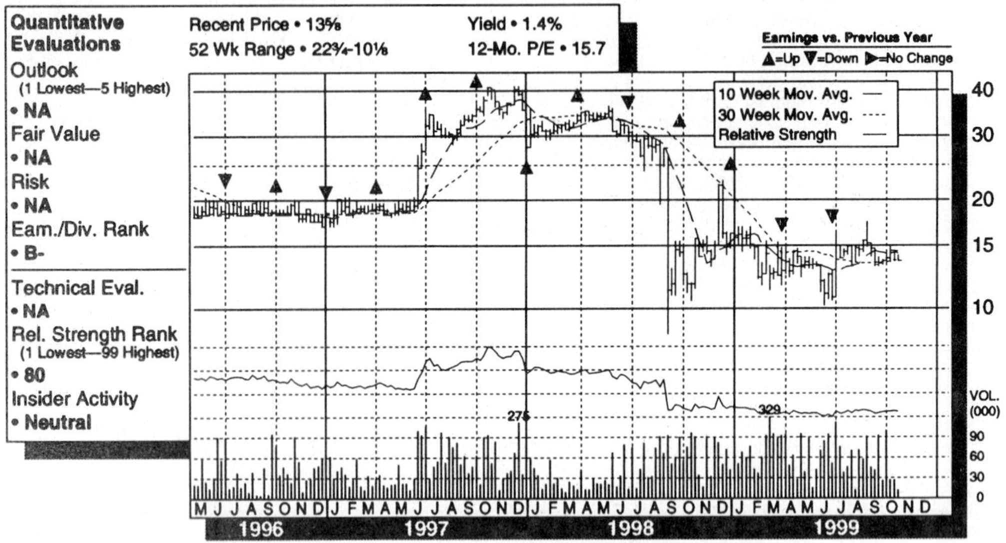

Business Profile - 22-OCT-99

In June 1999, PENX reported an improvement in its overall operating performance from the second quarter. This quarter reflected a more stable environment in certain North American paper markets served by the Penford Products Co. unit, which saw a modest improvement in operating rates and had increasingly shifted towards higher value-added products. Also, earnings and volume growth in the Penford Food Ingredients Co. unit reflected continued market share penetration in its specialty coatings and processed meats products. In the third quarter of 1999, PENX reduced its administrative workforce at Penford Products Co. by 15% (20 employees) in an effort to align operating costs with current market conditions.

Operational Review - 22-OCT-99

Sales in the nine months ended May 31, 1999, declined 6.3%, year to year, which were negatively impacted by difficult Asian and worldwide economic conditions affecting the North American paper market. Gross margins narrowed on lower volumes and an unfavorable product mix. Following workforce restructuring charges of $1.6 million versus $1.9 million, income from continuing operations fell 23%, to $4.3 million ($0.55 per share), from $5.5 million ($0.74). Results for 1998 exclude a $8.6 million ($1.14) loss from the discontinued Penwest Pharmaceuticals Co. operations.

Stock Performance - 22-OCT-99

In the past 30 trading days, PENX's shares have increased 9%, compared to a 4% fall in the S&P 500. Average trading volume for the past five days was 5,400 shares, compared with the 40-day moving average of 15,985 shares.

Key Stock Statistics

Dividend Rate/Share	0.20	Shareholders	1,100
Shs. outstg. (M)	7.4	Market cap. (B)	$0.108
Avg. daily vol. (M)	0.013	Inst. holdings	33%
Tang. Bk. Value/Share	7.83		
Beta	0.29		

Value of $10,000 invested 5 years ago: $ 6,775

Fiscal Year Ending Aug. 31

	1999	1998	1997	1996	1995	1994
Revenues (Million $)						
1Q	38.72	41.82	49.31	45.62	42.77	37.82
2Q	37.16	40.72	48.33	46.31	42.43	35.84
3Q	39.23	40.31	49.99	49.11	43.62	41.35
4Q	—	40.2[illegible]	49.00	53.43	45.38	43.79
Yr.	—	16[illegible].1	196.6	194.5	174.2	158.8
Earnings Per Share ($)						
1Q	**0.30**	**0.28**	0.20	0.25	0.25	0.25
2Q	**0.16**	**0.30**	0.18	0.13	0.31	0.12
3Q	**0.09**	**0.16**	0.26	0.15	0.29	0.25
4Q	—	**0.34**	0.29	0.20	0.19	0.24
Yr.	—	**1.08**	**1.25**	0.72	1.03	0.86

Next earnings report expected: late October

Dividend Data (Dividends have been paid since 1992.)

Amount ($)	Date Decl.	Ex-Div. Date	Stock of Record	Payment Date
0.050	Jan. 26	Feb. 17	Feb. 19	Mar. 05 '99
0.050	Apr. 22	May. 12	May. 14	Jun. 04 '99
0.050	Jun. 25	Aug. 11	Aug. 13	Sep. 03 '99
0.050	Oct. 21	Nov. 17	Nov. 19	Dec. 03 '99

A Division of The McGraw-Hill Companies

Penford Corporation

Business Summary - 22-OCT-99

PENX (formerly PENWEST Ltd.) develops, manufactures and markets specialty carbohydrate-based chemicals for papermaking and specialty food ingredients through its Penford Products Co. (Penford Products) and Penford Food Ingredient Co. (PFI) units. In August 1999 the company spun off to its shareholders ts pharmaceutical unit, Penwest Pharmaceuticals Co.

PENX competes with approximately five other companies that manufacture specialty starches for the papermaking industry; none of which is dominant in the ethylated starch business. Although PENX is one of the smaller industrial starch producers, it is one of the major producers of specialty ethylated starches. The company also competes with five other companies that manufacture specialty food ingredients; all of whom have larger market shares.

The company sells to approximately 90 major customers. Georgia-Pacific and Mead Paper accounted for 16% and 10% of FY 98 (Aug.) sales, respectively. Export sales accounted for approximately 11% of total sales in FY 98 and less than 10% in FY 97 and 96.

Penford Products makes and sells carbohydrate-based specialty chemical starches for the papermaking and textiles industries. The history of Penford Products can be traced to 1894. Starches produced by Penford Products are designed to improve the strength, quality and runnability of coated and uncoated paper. The starches are principally ethylated (chemically modified with ethylene oxide) and cationic (carrying a positive electrical charge). Ethylated starches are used in coatings and as binders, providing strength and printability to fine white, magazine and catalog paper. Cationic starches are generally used at the "wet-end" of the paper machine, providing strong internal bonding of paper fibers. In addition, Penford Products' starch copolymers, a patented combination of synthetic and natural carbohydrate chemistry, are used in coating and binder applications in various segments of the paper industry.

PFI was established in 1991 as a division of Penford Products to manufacture and market specialty carbohydrate-based ingredients to the food and confectionery industries. These ingredients include food grade potato and tapioca starch products as well as dextrose-based products including specialty dried corn syrup. PFI's modified starches are used in coatings to provide crispness, improved taste and texture and increased product life. Starch products are also used as moisture binders to reduce fat levels, modify texture and improve color and consistency in a variety of food applications. The company's potato starch products are used as coatings for french fries sold in fast-food restaurants. Its products also bind water in low-fat processed meats and improve the texture of soups, sauces and gravies. PFI is the only North American producer of food grade potato and tapioca starches.

Per Share Data ($)										
(Year Ended Aug. 31)	**1998**	**1997**	**1996**	**1995**	**1994**	**1993**	**1992**	**1991**	**1990**	**1989**
Tangible Bk. Val.	7.34	12.27	11.42	10.65	9.86	9.18	8.70	8.47	7.20	7.02
Cash Flow	2.68	2.67	2.40	2.51	2.32	2.19	2.08	2.09	1.79	1.92
Earnings	1.08	0.93	0.72	1.03	0.86	0.88	1.01	1.17	1.06	0.68
Dividends	0.20	0.20	0.20	0.20	0.20	0.20	0.20	Nil	Nil	Nil
Payout Ratio	19%	22%	28%	19%	23%	23%	20%	Nil	Nil	Nil
Prices - High	36½	41½	24¾	27	26½	23½	36¼	37¼	35½	18½
- Low	8½	17	16	18¼	17½	16	16½	19¼	17	11⅝
P/E Ratio - High	34	44	34	25	30	26	35	31	32	4
- Low	8	18	22	17	20	18	16	16	15	2
Income Statement Analysis (Million $)										
Revs.	163	197	195	175	159	136	128	113	94.9	83.3
Oper. Inc.	32.2	26.4	24.0	25.3	21.2	18.5	18.5	19.5	15.4	12.3
Depr.	12.1	12.4	11.7	10.4	10.3	9.4	8.0	7.0	5.5	4.9
Int. Exp.	5.8	5.3	5.1	5.2	3.4	2.5	2.3	2.5	2.2	2.9
Pretax Inc.	12.5	9.9	7.5	11.1	8.1	7.6	10.1	12.5	10.6	7.9
Eff. Tax Rate	35%	33%	32%	35%	24%	17%	26%	30%	25%	30%
Net Inc.	8.1	6.6	5.1	7.2	6.1	6.3	7.5	8.8	8.0	5.6
Balance Sheet & Other Fin. Data (Million $)										
Cash	3.2	0.2	--	5.3	Nil	5.5	0.2	1.0	0.3	0.6
Curr. Assets	45.7	54.4	52.7	48.9	42.1	41.5	44.1	52.1	48.0	53.6
Total Assets	183	216	203	187	164	156	131	121	102	96.0
Curr. Liab.	29.6	24.2	23.3	19.7	20.7	20.1	15.3	17.7	15.7	13.0
LT Debt	60.2	61.8	62.6	58.6	42.9	47.0	30.9	31.6	23.1	23.7
Common Eqty.	54.0	89.1	78.1	72.0	67.2	63.0	61.6	60.1	51.1	49.6
Total Cap.	136	173	169	131	110	110	93.0	92.0	74.0	73.0
Cap. Exp.	10.8	21.5	21.5	23.0	14.3	42.1	20.2	14.0	13.5	7.6
Cash Flow	20.2	19.1	16.8	17.6	16.5	15.7	15.5	15.8	13.5	10.5
Curr. Ratio	1.5	2.2	2.3	2.5	2.0	2.1	2.9	2.9	3.1	4.1
% LT Debt of Cap.	44.2	35.7	37.1	44.7	39.0	42.7	33.4	34.4	31.1	32.3
% Net Inc.of Revs.	5.0	3.4	2.6	4.1	3.8	4.7	5.9	7.8	8.4	6.7
% Ret. on Assets	4.1	3.2	2.6	4.1	3.8	4.4	6.0	7.9	8.0	4.7
% Ret. on Equity	11.3	7.9	6.7	10.4	9.4	10.1	12.3	15.8	15.8	13.0

Data as orig reptd.; bef. results of disc opers/spec. items. Per share data adj. for stk. divs. Bold denotes diluted EPS (FASB 128)-prior periods restated. E-Estimated. NA-Not Available. NM-Not Meaningful. NR-Not Ranked.

Office—777 108th Ave., NE, Suite 2390, Bellevue, WA 98004-5193. **Tel**—(425) 462-6000. **Website**—http://www.penx.com **Chrmn**—N.S. Rogers. **Pres & CEO**—J.T. Cook. **VP-Fin & CFO**—V.W. Breed. **Investor Relations**—Kekst & Co., Incorporated (212) 521-4800. **Dirs**—J.T. Cook, R.E. Engebrecht, P.E. Freiman, P.H. Hatfield, C.P. Lindley, S.G. Narodick, W.G. Parzybok Jr., N.S. Rogers, W.K. Street. **Transfer Agent & Registrar**—ChaseMellon Shareholder Services, Seattle, WA. **Incorporated**—in Delaware in 1983. **Empl**— 398. **S&P Analyst:** T.J. Vital

STANDARD & POOR'S
STOCK REPORTS

Pennsylvania Enterprises

NYSE Symbol **PNT**

In S&P SmallCap 600

09-OCT-99

Industry: Natural Gas

Summary: PNT, which provides natural gas to about 150,000 customers in 13 counties in northeastern and central Pennsylvania, has agreed to be acquired by Southern Union Co.

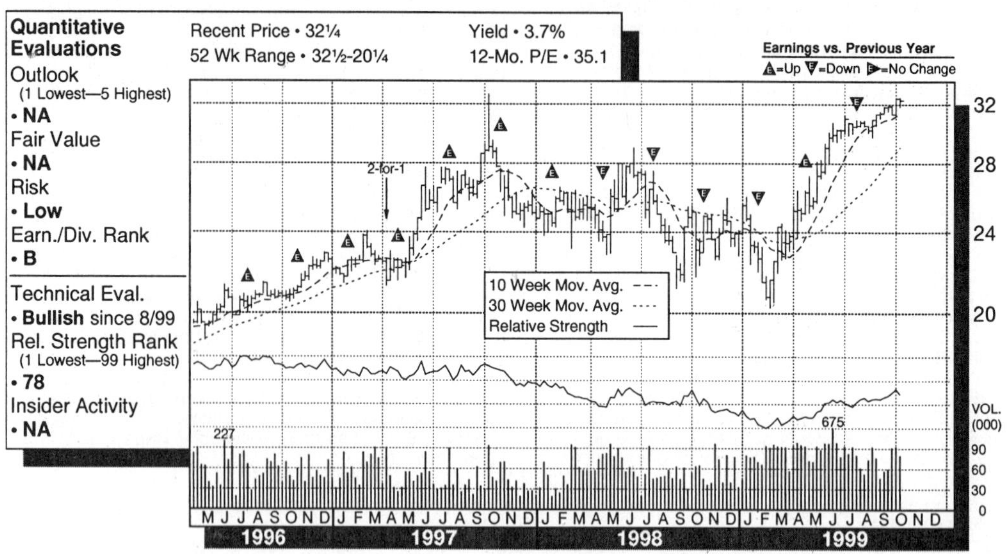

Business Profile - 07-SEP-99

In June 1999, directors approved the company's acquisition by Southern Union Co., an international energy company headquartered in Austin, TX. Under terms of the agreement, which is subject to shareholder and regulatory approval, each PNT share will be exchanged for $32 of Southern Union common stock, plus $3 in cash, subject to adjustment for market fluctuations in the price of Southern Union common stock. The transaction is expected to close in the fourth quarter of 1999.

Operational Review - 07-SEP-99

Total revenues in the first six months of 1999 climbed 34% from those of the 1998 period, as restated, reflecting a 25% increase in revenues from regulated energy products and services, and a 94% advance for revenues from nonregulated energy products and services. Operating expenses were up 33%; operating income soared 40%. Net other income fell sharply, but with only 4.4% higher interest charges and preferred dividends of subsidiaries, net income surged 66%, to $8,557,000 ($0.79 a share), from $5,148,000 ($0.52).

Stock Performance - 08-OCT-99

In the past 30 trading days, PNT's shares have increased 3%, compared to a 0.91% fall in the S&P 500. Average trading volume for the past five days was 15,820 shares, compared with the 40-day moving average of 16,449 shares.

Key Stock Statistics

Dividend Rate/Share	1.20	Shareholders	6,400
Shs. outstg. (M)	10.9	Market cap. (B)	$0.351
Avg. daily vol. (M)	0.018	Inst. holdings	19%
Tang. Bk. Value/Share	12.62		
Beta	0.56		

Value of $10,000 invested 5 years ago: $ 28,663

Fiscal Year Ending Dec. 31

	1999	1998	1997	1996	1995	1994
Revenues (Million $)						
1Q	104.3	76.89	89.49	74.09	68.24	96.29
2Q	46.64	35.87	41.86	30.26	25.18	43.48
3Q	—	26.90	24.21	19.35	12.12	31.86
4Q	—	67.67	72.48	60.78	47.22	63.09
Yr.	—	207.3	228.1	184.5	152.8	234.7
Earnings Per Share ($)						
1Q	**0.93**	**0.56**	**0.83**	**0.63**	0.50	0.79
2Q	**-0.12**	**-0.04**	**0.02**	**-0.05**	-0.18	-0.01
3Q	—	**-0.27**	**-0.24**	**-0.30**	-0.36	-0.10
4Q	—	**0.39**	**0.61**	**0.43**	0.33	0.41
Yr.	—	**0.65**	**1.30**	**0.66**	**0.27**	**0.21**

Next earnings report expected: early November

Dividend Data (Dividends have been paid since 1946.)

Amount ($)	Date Decl.	Ex-Div. Date	Stock of Record	Payment Date
0.300	Oct. 28	Nov. 27	Dec. 01	Dec. 15 '98
0.300	Jan. 20	Feb. 25	Mar. 01	Mar. 15 '99
0.300	May. 05	May. 27	Jun. 01	Jun. 15 '99
0.300	Aug. 04	Aug. 30	Sep. 01	Sep. 15 '99

Pennsylvania Enterprises, Inc.

Business Summary - 07-SEP-99

In a bid to strengthen its position in an increasingly competitive marketplace, Pennsylvania Enterprises (PNT) refocused on the energy industry in early 1996, selling its water utility business. That move has been complemented by acquisitions and other initiatives intended to hasten PNT's transformation from a traditional regulated gas utility into a total energy provider. In June 1999, directors approved a definitive agreement for the company to be acquired by Southern Union Co., with each PNT share to be exchanged for $32 of Southern Union common stock, plus $3 in cash. The transaction is expected to close in the fourth quarter of 1999.

PNT's principal business is conducted through PG Energy Inc. (PGE), a regulated public utility originally incorporated in 1867 as Dunmore Gas & Water Co., and Honesdale Gas Co., which was acquired in February 1997. Together, PG Energy and Honesdale distribute natural gas to a 13-county area in northeastern Pennsylvania, including the cities of Scranton, Wilkes-Barre and Williamsport. In 1998, PG Energy and Honesdale collectively accounted for approximately 77% of the company's operating revenues. As of December 31, 1998, PG Energy provided service to approximately 148,900 natural gas customers, and Honesdale provided service to approximately 3,300 customers.

Through its other subsidiaries -- PG Energy Services Inc., PEI Power Corp. (formed in October 1997), Theta Land Corp. and Keystone Pipeline Services, Inc. -- the company is engaged in various nonregulated activities. These activities include the sale of natural gas, propane, electricity and other energy-related products and services; the construction, maintenance and rehabilitation of utility facilities, primarily natural gas distribution pipelines; and the sale of property for residential, commercial and other development. In the fourth quarter of 1997, PG Energy Services began marketing electricity and other products and services, under the name PG Energy PowerPlus, principally in northeastern and central Pennsylvania. PEI Power Corp., an exempt wholesale generator, began generating and selling electricity in July 1998, upon completion of modifications to its cogeneration facility that enable it to burn both natural gas and methane. In 1998, the revenues of the nonregulated subsidiaries accounted for 23% of the company's operating revenues and 37% of capital expenditures.

The company believes Pennsylvania may enact legislation in 1999 with respect to the natural gas industry similar to that enacted governing the electric utility industry in 1996. Essentially, the legislation would extend the transportation service now available to a limited number of PG Energy's customers to all its customers, and customers could choose to have their natural gas provided by a supplier other than PG Energy, based on nonregulated market prices and other considerations.

Per Share Data ($) (Year Ended Dec. 31)	1998	1997	1996	1995	1994	1993	1992	1991	1990	1989
Tangible Bk. Val.	12.62	12.39	12.09	13.84	15.48	15.30	16.48	20.05	20.42	21.42
Cash Flow	1.78	2.19	1.56	0.79	2.49	2.31	2.16	2.55	1.57	2.59
Earnings	0.65	1.30	0.33	0.28	1.08	0.91	0.81	0.77	0.13	1.34
Dividends	1.20	1.19	1.10	1.10	1.10	1.10	1.10	1.10	1.10	1.10
Payout Ratio	185%	92%	NM	NM	101%	121%	137%	144%	880%	82%
Prices - High	29	32 3/4	23	19 1/8	16 1/2	16 1/8	16	18 5/8	23 1/2	29 1/4
- Low	21 1/8	21 1/4	18 3/8	13 5/8	13 1/2	13	11	11 1/8	15	21 3/4
P/E Ratio - High	45	25	70	69	15	18	20	24	NM	22
- Low	32	16	55	49	12	14	14	15	NM	16
Income Statement Analysis (Million $)										
Revs.	207	228	184	153	235	207	192	183	167	184
Oper. Inc.	18.2	21.6	31.9	20.5	69.2	57.4	53.1	46.8	34.6	38.0
Depr.	10.4	9.5	7.9	7.0	14.3	12.3	10.9	9.8	7.9	6.8
Int. Exp.	12.4	11.2	10.4	15.5	26.7	26.2	25.6	26.6	22.3	18.6
Pretax Inc.	11.9	19.2	13.9	5.6	29.1	22.5	18.9	12.5	6.4	17.3
Eff. Tax Rate	37%	39%	42%	63%	40%	36%	39%	33%	21%	32%
Net Inc.	7.5	11.8	8.1	2.0	17.5	14.4	11.5	8.4	5.0	11.8
Balance Sheet & Other Fin. Data (Million $)										
Cash	1.3	2.2	1.1	0.6	2.9	2.8	1.1	0.7	2.2	0.7
Curr. Assets	75.7	75.5	82.3	58.2	75.0	85.6	62.7	58.3	59.8	61.8
Total Assets	426	389	367	524	735	719	633	543	518	488
Curr. Liab.	115	57.6	92.9	155	39.0	79.0	78.0	129	125	91.0
LT Debt	98.0	127	75.0	107	362	296	276	195	178	181
Common Eqty.	132	122	118	163	172	166	135	110	111	116
Total Cap.	301	323	266	359	675	623	530	398	380	387
Cap. Exp.	29.0	31.0	29.3	20.6	36.8	45.9	57.1	28.5	36.4	70.5
Cash Flow	18.0	21.3	16.0	9.0	27.2	20.3	17.3	14.0	8.5	14.0
Curr. Ratio	0.7	1.3	0.8	0.4	1.9	1.1	0.8	0.5	0.5	0.7
% LT Debt of Cap.	32.6	39.4	28.2	29.8	53.6	47.5	52.1	48.9	46.8	46.9
% Net Inc.of Revs.	3.6	5.2	4.4	1.3	7.4	7.0	6.0	4.6	3.0	6.4
% Ret. on Assets	1.8	3.6	1.7	0.4	2.4	1.9	1.9	1.6	1.0	2.6
% Ret. on Equity	5.9	9.9	5.7	1.2	7.5	4.7	5.3	3.8	0.6	6.3

Data as orig reptd.; bef. results of disc opers/spec. items. Per share data adj. for stk. divs. Bold denotes diluted EPS (FASB 128)-prior periods restated. E-Estimated. NA-Not Available. NM-Not Meaningful. NR-Not Ranked.

Office—One PEI Center, Wilkes-Barre, PA 18711-0601. **Tel**—(717) 829-8843. **Website**—http://www.pnt.com **Chrmn**—R. W. Simms. **Vice Chrmn**—W. D. Davis. **Pres & CEO**—T. F. Karam. **Treas**—R. N. Marshall. **Secy**—D. M. Abdalla. **Dirs**—W. D. Davis, T. F. Karam, R. J. Keating, J. D. McCarthy, J. D. McCarthy Jr., K. M. Pollock, R. A. Rose Jr., J. A. Ross, R. W. Simms. **Transfer Agent & Registrar**—ChaseMellon Shareholder Services, L.L.C., Ridgefield Park, NJ. **Incorporated**—in Pennsylvania in 1974. **Empl**— 825. **S&P Analyst:** C.C.P.

STANDARD
&POOR'S
STOCK REPORTS

Performance Food Group

NASDAQ Symbol **PFGC**

In S&P SmallCap 600

09-OCT-99

Industry: Distributors (Food & Health)

Summary: PFGC markets and distributes more than 25,000 national and private label food and food-related products to 20,000 restaurants, hotels, cafeterias, schools and other institutions.

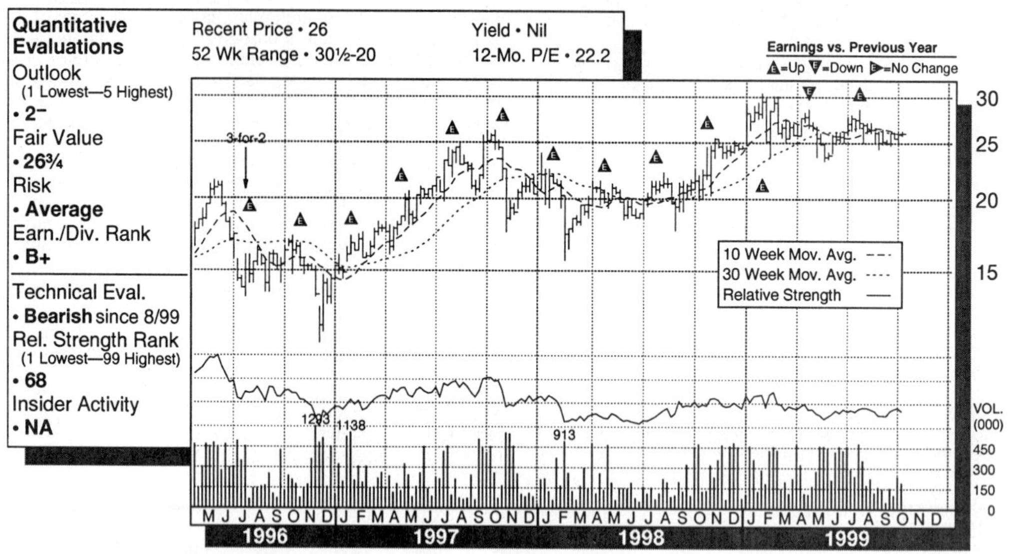

Business Profile - 23-AUG-99

In August 1999, the company signed a definitive agreement to acquire Dixon Tom-A-Toe Companies, Inc., a privately held, Atlanta-based processor of fresh-cut produce, with annual sales of over $60 million. Terms were not disclosed. PFGC believes its broadline business is continuing to expand at a rate well above that of the industry. It is continuing to focus on increasing sales with existing customers by offering more value and enhanced services. The company is increasing its penetration in fresh-cut produce operations with current accounts.

Operational Review - 23-AUG-99

Net sales in the six months ended July 3, 1999, advanced 23%, year to year, with sales from existing operations up 18% Margins benefited from the acquisition of three broadline distribution and merchandising companies with wider gross margins than the company's customized distribution operations; operating income climbed 25%. However, after $3,812,000 of nonrecurring expenses related to the NCF acquisition, a 27% rise in depreciation and amortization charges, and 28% higher interest expense, pretax income dropped 10%. After taxes at 39.2%, versus 37.9%, net income fell 12%, to $6,081,000 ($0.43 a share), from $6,933,000 ($0.50), as restated.

Stock Performance - 08-OCT-99

In the past 30 trading days, PFGC's shares have increased 4%, compared to a 0.91% fall in the S&P 500. Average trading volume for the past five days was 38,260 shares, compared with the 40-day moving average of 29,387 shares.

Key Stock Statistics

Dividend Rate/Share	Nil	Shareholders	4,900
Shs. outstg. (M)	13.8	Market cap. (B)	$0.358
Avg. daily vol. (M)	0.034	Inst. holdings	67%
Tang. Bk. Value/Share	5.91		
Beta	1.29		

Value of $10,000 invested 5 years ago: $ 15,918

Fiscal Year Ending Dec. 31

	1999	1998	1997	1996	1995	1994
Revenues (Million $)						
1Q	466.4	353.5	268.5	173.1	151.8	106.8
2Q	502.0	388.7	292.8	192.4	170.0	117.0
3Q	—	415.3	336.4	202.4	169.5	121.0
4Q	—	465.4	332.4	216.3	172.9	128.7
Yr.	—	1,623	1,230	784.2	664.1	473.4
Earnings Per Share ($)						
1Q	**0.05**	**0.20**	**0.19**	**0.16**	0.13	0.12
2Q	**0.39**	**0.32**	**0.31**	**0.26**	0.23	0.18
3Q	—	**0.36**	**0.30**	**0.26**	0.23	0.07
4Q	—	**0.36**	**0.27**	**0.25**	0.23	0.11
Yr.	—	**1.24**	**1.06**	**0.94**	**0.82**	**0.47**

Next earnings report expected: late October

Dividend Data

No cash dividends have been paid. The policy of the company's directors is to retain all earnings to support operations and to finance expansion.

A Division of The McGraw-Hill Companies

Performance Food Group Company

Business Summary - 23-AUG-99

Performance Food Group, which distributes more than 25,000 food and food-related products, plans to expand its foodservice distribution business through internal growth and acquisitions. The company's internal growth strategy is to increase sales to existing customers, and to identify new customers for which it can act as the principal supplier. PFGC also plans to consider, from time to time, strategic acquisitions of other foodservice distribution companies, both to further penetrate existing markets, and to expand into new markets. It also strives to achieve higher productivity in its existing operations.

The company markets and distributes a wide variety of food and food-related products to the foodservice, or away from home eating, industry. The foodservice industry consists of two major customer types: traditional foodservice customers, consisting of independent restaurants, hotels, cafeterias, schools, healthcare facilities and other institutional customers, and multi-unit chain customers, consisting of regional and national quick-service restaurants and casual dining restaurants. Sales to Cracker Barrel Old Country Stores accounted for 19% of the 1998 total, and sales to Outback Steakhouse contributed 16%.

Products and services provided to PFGC's traditional and multi-unit chain customers are supported by identical physical facilities, vehicles, equipment and personnel. The company's customers are located primarily in the South, Southwest, Midwest and Northeast. PFGC operates through several subsidiaries, each of which focuses on specific regional markets or sectors of the foodservice distribution industry.

The company distributes more than 25,000 national brand and private label food and food-related products to more than 20,000 foodservice customers. Items distributed include a broad selection of center-of-the-plate or entree items (such as meats, seafood and poultry), which accounted for 29% of 1998 sales; canned and dry groceries 23%; frozen foods 17%; refrigerated and dairy products 12%; paper products and cleaning supplies 7%; fresh-cut produce 4%; other produce 3%; vending 2%; procurement, merchandising and other services 2%; and equipment and supplies 1%.

PFGC procures its products from independent suppliers, food brokers and merchandisers, including its wholly owned subsidiary, Pocahontas Foods, USA, Inc. It is not dependent on a single source for any significant items, and no third-party supplier accounts for over 4% of total product purchases.

Distribution operations are conducted from 16 distribution centers, located in Tennessee, New Jersey, Maryland, Georgia, Florida, Virginia, Louisiana and Texas.

In February 1999, the company acquired, for about 850,000 common shares, NorthCenter Foodservice Corp. (NCF), an Augusta, ME-based, privately owned foodservice distributor, with 1998 sales of about $98 million.

Per Share Data ($) **(Year Ended Dec. 31)**	**1998**	**1997**	**1996**	**1995**	**1994**	**1993**	**1992**	**1991**	**1990**	**1989**
Tangible Bk. Val.	5.94	6.27	7.58	4.58	4.97	4.48	NA	NA	NA	NA
Cash Flow	2.07	1.69	1.41	2.06	1.25	1.48	1.06	NA	NA	NA
Earnings	1.24	1.06	0.94	0.82	0.47	0.60	NA	NA	NA	NA
Dividends	Nil	Nil	Nil	Nil	Nil	NA	NA	NA	NA	NA
Payout Ratio	Nil	Nil	Nil	Nil	Nil	NA	NA	NA	NA	NA
Prices - High	29⅛	26¼	21½	17	16⅛	16½	NA	NA	NA	NA
- Low	15⅝	14½	11¼	8⅛	6½	9⅜	NA	NA	NA	NA
P/E Ratio - High	23	25	22	20	34	27	NA	NA	NA	NA
- Low	13	14	12	10	13	15	NA	NA	NA	NA
Income Statement Analysis (Million $)										
Revs.	1,623	1,230	784	664	473	379	326	NA	NA	NA
Oper. Inc.	40.3	31.3	24.1	21.0	11.7	11.7	8.4	NA	NA	NA
Depr.	10.8	7.8	5.5	5.3	3.5	2.9	2.3	NA	NA	NA
Int. Exp.	3.5	2.0	0.6	2.7	0.4	1.3	2.0	NA	NA	NA
Pretax Inc.	26.1	21.5	18.1	13.0	7.5	7.6	4.1	NA	NA	NA
Eff. Tax Rate	38%	39%	39%	39%	40%	41%	42%	NA	NA	NA
Net Inc.	16.2	13.2	11.0	7.9	4.5	4.5	2.4	NA	NA	NA
Balance Sheet & Other Fin. Data (Million $)										
Cash	7.4	3.7	5.6	4.2	1.6	0.2	0.5	NA	NA	NA
Curr. Assets	200	160	113	89.5	62.1	54.3	41.8	NA	NA	NA
Total Assets	366	289	183	155	99	83.5	63.8	NA	NA	NA
Curr. Liab.	144	107	70.5	59.2	45.7	35.1	35.9	NA	NA	NA
LT Debt	64.9	44.6	NA	NA	NA	NA	NA	NA	NA	NA
Common Eqty.	152	134	101	55.8	46.3	40.6	11.4	NA	NA	NA
Total Cap.	217	182	NA	NA	NA	NA	NA	NA	NA	NA
Cap. Exp.	26.2	8.3	9.1	13.9	NA	NA	NA	NA	NA	NA
Cash Flow	27.0	21.1	16.5	13.2	8.0	7.4	4.7	NA	NA	NA
Curr. Ratio	1.4	1.5	1.6	1.5	1.4	1.5	1.2	NA	NA	NA
% LT Debt of Cap.	29.9	24.5	NA	NA	NA	NA	NA	NA	NA	NA
% Net Inc.of Revs.	1.0	1.1	1.4	1.2	1.0	1.2	0.7	NA	NA	NA
% Ret. on Assets	4.9	5.6	6.5	6.2	5.0	6.1	NA	NA	NA	NA
% Ret. on Equity	11.3	11.3	14.0	15.5	10.4	17.4	NA	NA	NA	NA

Data as orig reptd.; bef. results of disc opers/spec. items. Per share data adj. for stk. divs. Bold denotes diluted EPS (FASB 128)-prior periods restated. E-Estimated. NA-Not Available. NM-Not Meaningful. NR-Not Ranked.

Office—6800 Paragon Place, Suite 500, Richmond, VA 23230. **Tel**—(804) 285-7340. **Website**—http://www.pfgc.com **Chrmn & CEO**—R. C. Sledd. **Pres & COO**—C. M. Gray. **EVP & CFO**—R. L. Boeve. **VP & Secy**—D. W. Sober. **Dirs**—C. E. Adair, F. C. Goad Jr., T. M. Graven, C. M. Gray, R. C. Sledd, J. E. Stokely. **Transfer Agent & Registrar**—First Union National Bank of North Carolina, Charlotte. **Incorporated**—in Tennessee in 1988. **Empl**— 3,200. **S&P Analyst:** J. J. Schemitsch

STANDARD
&POOR'S
STOCK REPORTS

Pharmaceutical Product Development

NASDAQ Symbol **PPDI**

In S&P SmallCap 600

09-OCT-99

Industry:
Health Care (Specialized Services)

Summary: PPDI provides contract and consulting research and development services for pharmaceuticaland biotechnology companies.

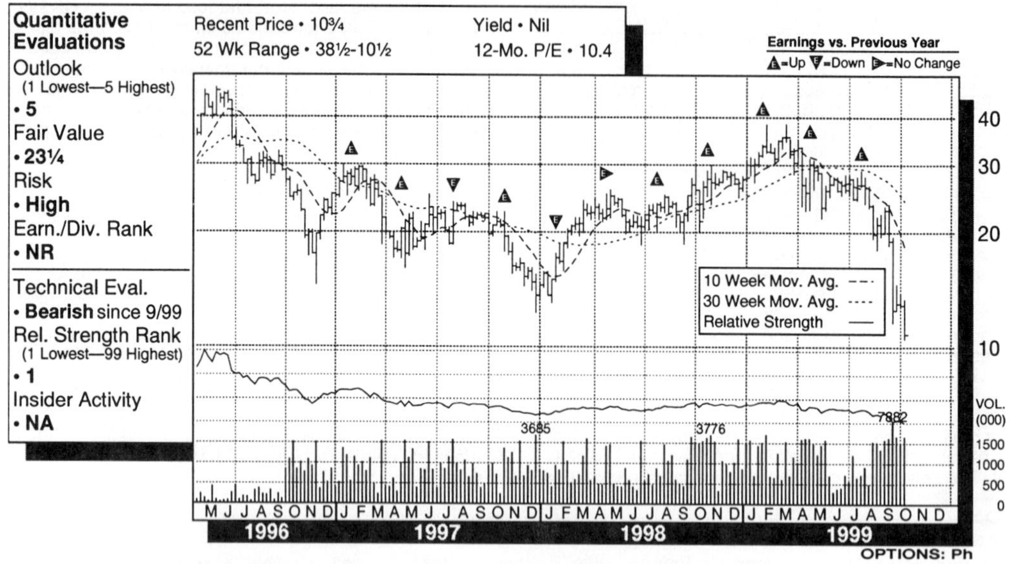

Business Profile - 19-JUL-99

Pharmaceutical Product Development said in April 1999 that as it adds to its backlog, it is investing in the necessary infrastructure to support planned growth by adding new locations, new construction at existing locations, and new technologies. In March 1999, the company acquired ATP, Inc., a health information services company, for 876,000 common shares. Effective January 31, 1999, PPDI sold its environmental sciences segment to Environ Holdings, Inc., a new company formed by the management of the segment, for $26.2 million in notes and cash. The sale resulted in no gain or loss becausethe sales price was equal to the book value of the net assets sold .

Operational Review - 19-JUL-99

Net revenues for the first quarter of 1999 advanced 33%, year to year, reflecting an increase in the size, scope and number of contracts in the global CRO (contract research organization) Phase II-IV division, as well as the March 1999 acquisition of ATP, Inc. Margins widened on the higher sales, and operating profit more than doubled. After 27% lower total other income (net), pretax income was up 82%. Following taxes at 38.8% in both periods, income from continuing operations was also up 82%, to $6.3 million ($0.25 a share), from $3.4 million ($0.15). Results were before a loss from discontinued environmental sciences operations of $0.01 a share, versus a profit of $0.05, respectively.

Stock Performance - 08-OCT-99

In the past 30 trading days, PPDI's shares have declined 46%, compared to a 0.91% fall in the S&P 500. Average trading volume for the past five days was 661,960 shares, compared with the 40-day moving average of 622,474 shares.

Key Stock Statistics

Dividend Rate/Share	Nil	Shareholders	8,450
Shs. outstg. (M)	24.6	Market cap. (B)	$0.266
Avg. daily vol. (M)	0.806	Inst. holdings	64%
Tang. Bk. Value/Share	6.72		
Beta	NA		

Value of $10,000 invested 5 years ago: NA

Fiscal Year Ending Dec. 31

	1999	1998	1997	1996	1995	1994
Revenues (Million $)						
1Q	69.61	52.15	57.67	47.08	—	—
2Q	76.25	57.47	60.07	49.47	—	—
3Q	—	61.45	58.27	49.50	—	—
4Q	—	64.48	59.20	51.75	10.97	—
Yr.	—	235.6	235.3	197.8	54.40	28.86
Earnings Per Share ($)						
1Q	**0.25**	**0.15**	**0.15**	**0.10**	—	—
2Q	**0.27**	**0.12**	**-0.06**	**0.11**	—	—
3Q	—	**0.19**	**0.18**	**-0.56**	—	—
4Q	—	**0.24**	**0.15**	**0.18**	0.10	—
Yr.	—	**0.65**	**0.42**	**-0.17**	**-0.15**	**0.26**

Next earnings report expected: late October

Dividend Data

No cash dividends have been paid. The company intends to retain its earnings for use in its business and does not anticipate paying cash dividends in the foreseeable future.

A Division of The McGraw-Hill Companies

Pharmaceutical Product Development, Inc.

Business Summary - 19-JUL-99

A provider of a broad range of research and development and consulting services in the life and discovery sciences, Pharmaceutical Product Development intends to continue to expand the depth and breadth of its services by (i) capitalizing on its managerial and operational strengths, (ii) focusing on hiring and training its staff, (iii) focusing on its strategic marketing initiatives, (iv) developing its services in healthcare economics and communications consulting, (v) pursuing strategic acquisitions to enhance discovery and development services, (vi) expanding geographically, (vii) pursuing opportunities provided by technological advances, and (viii) expanding on its vertical expertise in five core therapeutic areas.

PPDI believes that PPD Development, its life sciences subsidiary, is the fourth largest contract research organization in the world, providing integrated product development resources on a global basis to complement the research and development activities of companies in the pharmaceutical and biotechnology industries. PPDI's discovery sciences subsidiary, PPD Discovery, focuses on the discovery segment of the research and development outsourcing market. PPDI sold its environmental sciences segment, effective January 31, 1999. for about $26 million.

The Life Sciences Group provides services through PPDDevelopment in the Americas (United States, Canada, South America), Africa, Asia, Europe and the Pacific Rim. PPD Informatics, a division of PPD Development, provides software development and system integration services to the pharmaceutical and biotechnology industries.

PPD Development provides its clients with services designed to reduce drug development time. Reduced development time allows the client to get its products into the market faster and to maximize the period of marketing exclusivity and the economic return for such products. In addition, PPD Development's integrated services offer its clients a variable cost alternative to the fixed costs associated with internal drug development.

PPD Discovery was established in June 1997 whenPPDI acquired SARCO, Inc., a combinational chemistry company,and the GSX System, a functional genomics platform technology. PPD Discovery focuses on the discovery research segment of the research and development outsourcing market. In May 1998, PPDI created GenuPro, Inc., a wholly owned subsidiary, which holds licenses to a number of compounds in the genitourinary field. GenuPro manages the research and development of thesecompounds.

PPDI's fundamental strategy is to distinguish its services on the basis of superior performance to maximize its clients' return on their investments. The company strives to deliver to its clients efficient and innovative services that accelerate the rate of new product development.

Per Share Data ($) (Year Ended Dec. 31)	1998	1997	1996	1995	1994	1993	1992	1991	1990	1989
Tangible Bk. Val.	6.00	4.77	4.48	0.95	NA	NA	NA	NA	NA	NA
Cash Flow	1.26	0.96	0.33	0.84	NA	NA	NA	NA	NA	NA
Earnings	0.65	0.42	-0.17	0.35	NA	NA	NA	NA	NA	NA
Dividends	Nil	Nil	Nil	NA	NA	NA	NA	NA	NA	NA
Payout Ratio	Nil	Nil	Nil	NA	NA	NA	NA	NA	NA	NA
Prices - High	30⅝	30	47¾	NA	NA	NA	NA	NA	NA	NA
- Low	13	12¼	14½	NA	NA	NA	NA	NA	NA	NA
P/E Ratio - High	47	71	NM	NA	NA	NA	NA	NA	NA	NA
- Low	20	29	NM	NA	NA	NA	NA	NA	NA	NA
Income Statement Analysis (Million $)										
Revs.	236	235	198	54.4	NA	NA	NA	NA	NA	NA
Oper. Inc.	38.4	36.3	25.4	5.6	NA	NA	NA	NA	NA	NA
Depr.	14.2	12.4	10.4	1.5	NA	NA	NA	NA	NA	NA
Int. Exp.	0.4	0.5	0.4	NA	NA	NA	NA	NA	NA	NA
Pretax Inc.	24.6	15.7	0.6	4.3	NA	NA	NA	NA	NA	NA
Eff. Tax Rate	38%	39%	659%	NA	NA	NA	NA	NA	NA	NA
Net Inc.	15.2	9.6	-3.5	4.3	NA	NA	NA	NA	NA	NA
Balance Sheet & Other Fin. Data (Million $)										
Cash	34.1	15.9	36.0	2.3	NA	NA	NA	NA	NA	NA
Curr. Assets	173	136	128	19.1	NA	NA	NA	NA	NA	NA
Total Assets	237	197	181	27.5	NA	NA	NA	NA	NA	NA
Curr. Liab.	79.0	66.5	61.7	15.2	NA	NA	NA	NA	NA	NA
LT Debt	0.2	0.3	1.4	NA	NA	NA	NA	NA	NA	NA
Common Eqty.	155	128	115	9.4	NA	NA	NA	NA	NA	NA
Total Cap.	155	128	117	NA	NA	NA	NA	NA	NA	NA
Cap. Exp.	19.3	13.6	11.2	NA	NA	NA	NA	NA	NA	NA
Cash Flow	29.4	22.0	6.9	5.8	NA	NA	NA	NA	NA	NA
Curr. Ratio	2.2	2.1	2.1	1.3	NA	NA	NA	NA	NA	NA
% LT Debt of Cap.	0.1	0.3	0.1	NA	NA	NA	NA	NA	NA	NA
% Net Inc.of Revs.	6.4	4.1	NM	7.9	NA	NA	NA	NA	NA	NA
% Ret. on Assets	7.0	5.1	NM	17.7	NA	NA	NA	NA	NA	NA
% Ret. on Equity	10.7	7.9	NM	57.8	NA	NA	NA	NA	NA	NA

Data as orig reptd.; bef. results of disc opers/spec. items. Per share data adj. for stk. divs. Bold denotes diluted EPS (FASB 128)-prior periods restated. E-Estimated. NA-Not Available. NM-Not Meaningful. NR-Not Ranked.

Office—3151 South Seventeenth Street, Wilmington, NC 28412. **Tel**—(910) 251-0081. **Website**—http://www.ppdi.com **Chrmn**—E. Mario. **Vice-Chrmn & CEO**—F. N. Eshelman. **Pres & COO**—T. D'Alonzo. **VP-Fin, CFO & Treas**—R. C. Howard. **Dirs**—S. Bondurant, A. E. Cohen, T. D'Alonzo, F. N. Eshelman, F. Frank, D. C. Harrison, E. Mario, J. A. McNeill, Jr, P. J. Rizzo. **Transfer Agent & Registrar**—Wachovia Bank of North Carolina, Winston-Salem. **Incorporated**—in North Carolina in 1989. **Empl**— 2,470. **S&P Analyst:** N.J.D.

STANDARD
&POOR'S
STOCK REPORTS

Philadelphia Suburban

NYSE Symbol **PSC**
In S&P SmallCap 600

23-OCT-99

Industry: Water Utilities

Summary: PSC, the holding company for Philadelphia Suburban Water and Consumers Water Co., owns and operates water and wastewater utilities that serve 1.8 million customers.

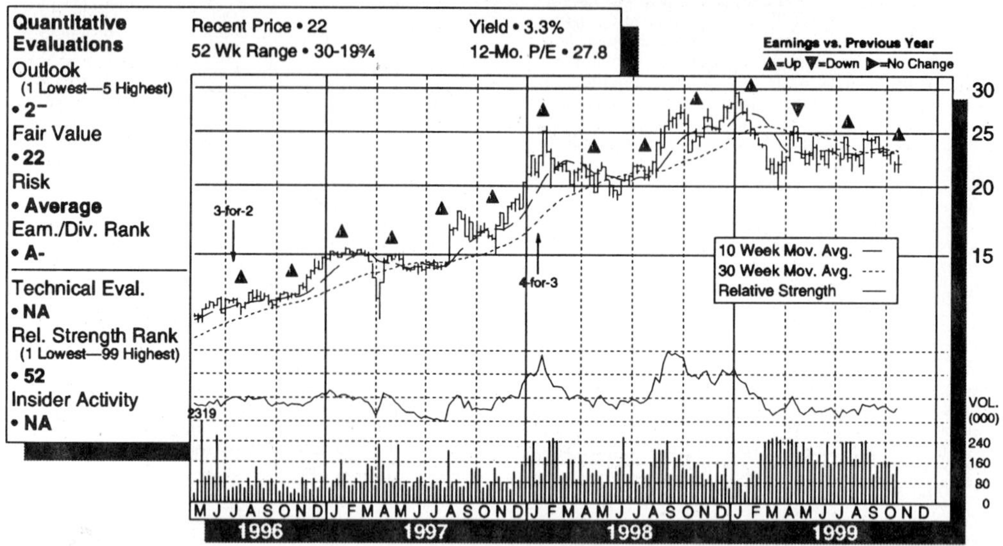

Business Profile - 20-OCT-99

In August 1999, PSC offered to acquire the water utility assets of Bensalem Township for approximately $36.5 million. While general principles of the offer have been agreed to, a final sale agreement is still being negotiated. In July 1999, management stated that it expected annual cost savings of over $2 million from PSC's March acquisition of Consumers Water for $463 million. In May, the company's Illinois subsidiary filed for a $558,000 annual rate increase. A decision on the Illinois case is expected in the first quarter of 2000. Directors raised the quarterly cash dividend 5.9%, to $0.18 a share from $0.17, with the September 1, 1999, payment.

Operational Review - 20-OCT-99

Operating revenues for the six months ended June 30, 1999, rose 4.2%, year to year, due mainly to increased water sales which stemmed from customer growth, increased weather-related demand, and rate increases. Profit comparisons were hurt by a $3.8 million restructuring charge pertaining to the Consumers Water merger, $6.3 million in merger transaction costs, and the absence of $6.7 million of prior-year gains on sales of properties. Pretax income fell 34%. After taxes at 50.2%, due to the non-deductibility of certain merger costs, versus 40.0%, net income declined 45%, to $12,418,000 ($0.30 a share after preferred dividends), from $22,527,000 ($0.55).

Stock Performance - 22-OCT-99

In the past 30 trading days, PSC's shares have declined 11%, compared to a 4% fall in the S&P 500. Average trading volume for the past five days was 32,740 shares, compared with the 40-day moving average of 39,979 shares.

Key Stock Statistics

Dividend Rate/Share	0.72	Shareholders	14,170
Shs. outstg. (M)	40.9	Market cap. (B)	$0.899
Avg. daily vol. (M)	0.030	Inst. holdings	20%
Tang. Bk. Value/Share	9.30		
Beta	-0.10		

Value of $10,000 invested 5 years ago: $ 29,926

Fiscal Year Ending Dec. 31

	1999	1998	1997	1996	1995	1994
Revenues (Million $)						
1Q	58.60	34.28	31.02	29.29	25.71	24.85
2Q	66.16	37.34	33.32	30.68	28.83	26.73
3Q	69.34	41.66	36.75	30.83	32.36	28.85
4Q	—	37.70	35.08	31.70	30.15	28.21
Yr.	—	151.0	136.2	122.5	117.0	108.6
Earnings Per Share ($)						
1Q	**0.01**	**0.21**	**0.17**	**0.16**	0.14	0.13
2Q	**0.29**	**0.27**	**0.22**	**0.21**	0.20	0.17
3Q	**0.35**	**0.32**	**0.28**	**0.25**	0.24	0.21
4Q	—	**0.23**	**0.21**	**0.20**	0.17	0.16
Yr.	—	**1.03**	**0.88**	**0.78**	**0.77**	0.68

Next earnings report expected: late October

Dividend Data (Dividends have been paid since 1939.)

Amount ($)	Date Decl.	Ex-Div. Date	Stock of Record	Payment Date
0.170	Jan. 27	Feb. 08	Feb. 10	Mar. 01 '99
0.170	Apr. 28	May. 10	May. 12	Jun. 01 '99
0.180	Aug. 03	Aug. 13	Aug. 17	Sep. 01 '99
0.180	Oct. 05	Nov. 09	Nov. 12	Dec. 01 '99

A Division of The McGraw-Hill Companies

Philadelphia Suburban Corporation

Business Summary - 20-OCT-99

Philadelphia Suburban's strategy is to pursue growth through regional acquisitions. PSC conducts business primarily through its subsidiary, Philadelphia Suburban Water. This business unit supplies water to about 300,000 residential, commercial, industrial, and public customers in 96 municipalities. Philadelphia Suburban Water's service territory encompasses 481 square miles, including a large portion of the Philadelphia suburbs. The company estimates that it serves approximately 1,000,000 people. The service area consists primarily of residential customers and is almost entirely metered for water service except for fire hydrant service. Philadelphia Suburban also provides water service to about 6,600 customers as a result of an operating and maintenance contract with a municipal authority near its service territory. PSC's customer base has grown by a compound annual growth rate of 4.3% during the past three years due mainly to acquisitions.

In March 1999, Philadelphia Suburban and Consumers Water merged in a transaction valued at $463 million in stock and assumed debt. Consumers Water became a wholly owned subsidiary of the company. Based on market capitalization, PSC will be the second largest water utility in the U.S. Philadelphia Suburban exchanged 1.432 of its shares for each share of Consumers Water. The merged company now serves 1.8 million residents in Pennsylvania, Ohio, Illinois, New Jersey, and Maine.

In 1998, Philadelphia Suburban exchanged over 42,000 shares of PSC stock for and spent more than $24 million on acquisitions and related service territory rights. In January, PSC bought the water system assets of West Chester Area Municipal Authority. During April 1998, the company purchased the water system assets of Brandywine Hospital. In June 1998, PSC bought Flying Hills Water Co. In November 1998, the company acquired the water system assets of the Greenhills Corporate Center. These systems constitute 17 square miles of service area near the company's existing service territory. Including water sale agreements, the company should gain over $5 million in revenues from these transactions.

In March 1999, PSC received approval for its Consumer New Jersey Water division to expand its water and wastewater services in Woolwich Township, NJ. In early 1999, PSC announced the purchase of the Brandywine River Estates wastewater system. The company announced a 4.2 square mile service territory expansion in a rapidly growing area of Pennsylvania. PSC has also agreed to buy a three million gallon a day supply site, which serves a 25 acre commercial office park.

Per Share Data ($) (Year Ended Dec. 31)	1998	1997	1996	1995	1994	1993	1992	1991	1990	1989
Tangible Bk. Val.	9.30	8.26	7.84	7.37	6.12	5.95	5.44	5.33	6.53	6.23
Earnings	1.03	0.88	0.78	0.75	0.68	0.64	0.61	0.65	0.64	0.53
Dividends	0.67	0.62	0.59	0.57	0.55	0.54	0.52	0.50	0.50	0.47
Payout Ratio	65%	71%	76%	76%	81%	84%	85%	78%	79%	90%
Prices - High	30	22 1/8	14 7/8	10 3/4	9 7/8	10 3/8	8 3/8	8 1/4	7 1/2	7 1/4
- Low	18 7/8	11 1/2	10 1/4	8 3/4	8 5/8	7 7/8	6 7/8	5 7/8	5 1/4	6 3/8
P/E Ratio - High	29	25	19	14	15	16	14	13	12	14
- Low	18	13	13	12	13	12	11	9	8	12
Income Statement Analysis (Million $)										
Revs.	151	136	123	117	109	101	93.0	89.0	82.0	134
Depr.	16.1	14.6	13.3	11.6	10.5	9.9	8.6	7.6	7.0	11.3
Maint.	NA	NA	NA	NA	NA	NA	NA	NA	NA	NA
Fxd. Chgs. Cov.	3.5	3.1	3.1	3.0	3.0	2.7	2.1	2.0	1.3	1.9
Constr. Credits	0.7	0.5	0.3	0.3	0.1	0.8	0.3	1.2	NA	NA
Eff. Tax Rate	40%	41%	41%	42%	43%	43%	43%	41%	38%	39%
Net Inc.	28.8	23.2	20.7	18.0	15.6	13.8	10.6	10.2	9.7	7.8
Balance Sheet & Other Fin. Data (Million $)										
Gross Prop.	746	656	613	529	463	433	402	371	350	332
Cap. Exp.	58.9	39.0	31.4	33.0	28.0	29.3	30.8	22.3	30.8	33.8
Net Prop.	610	534	503	437	386	366	346	321	307	288
Capitalization:										
LT Debt	262	232	218	175	152	145	154	168	176	163
% LT Debt	53	54	54	52	50	50	57	64	67	66
Pfd.	3.2	3.2	7.4	6.0	7.1	10.0	10.0	10.0	Nil	Nil
% Pfd.	0.65	0.80	1.90	1.80	2.30	3.40	3.70	3.80	Nil	Nil
Common	232	192	177	157	144	136	107	85.6	85.5	85.9
% Common	47	45	44	46	48	47	40	33	33	35
Total Cap.	588	535	502	409	371	382	291	283	279	266
% Oper. Ratio	68.8	69.9	59.8	60.6	73.1	73.4	71.8	72.3	88.2	83.9
% Earn. on Net Prop.	11.7	10.9	10.5	11.2	7.8	7.6	7.9	7.8	7.4	7.8
% Return On Revs.	19.1	17.0	16.1	15.4	14.4	13.7	11.4	11.5	11.8	5.8
% Return On Invest. Capital	12.2	11.0	12.5	11.8	10.9	12.4	12.0	11.3	8.0	8.6
% Return On Com. Equity	13.5	12.5	11.8	12.0	11.2	11.4	11.0	11.9	4.8	9.3

Data as orig reptd.; bef. results of disc opers/spec. items. Per share data adj. for stk. divs. Bold denotes diluted EPS (FASB 128)-prior periods restated. E-Estimated. NA-Not Available. NM-Not Meaningful. NR-Not Ranked.

Office—762 W. Lancaster Ave., Bryn Mawr, PA 19010-3489. **Tel**—(610) 527-8000. **Website**—http://www.suburbanwater.com **Chrmn, Pres & CEO**—N. DeBenedictis. **VP & Treas**—K. Pape. **Secy**—P. M. Mycek. **Investor Contact**—Idalia Rodriguez (610-645-1084). **Dirs**— M. C. Carroll, N. DeBenedictis, G. F. DiBona, Jr., R. H. Glanton, A. Hirsig, J. F. McCaughan, R. L. Smoot, H. J. Wilson. **Transfer Agent & Registrar**—ChaseMellon Shareholder Services, Ridgefield Park, NJ. **Incorporated**—in Pennsylvania in 1968. **Empl**— 542. **S&P Analyst:** Craig K. Shere, CFA

STANDARD
&POOR'S
STOCK REPORTS

Phillips-Van Heusen

NYSE Symbol **PVH**

In S&P SmallCap 600

09-OCT-99

Industry:
Textiles (Apparel)

Summary: PVH is a leading marketer of men's, women's, and children's apparel and footwear, sold under nationally recognized brand names.

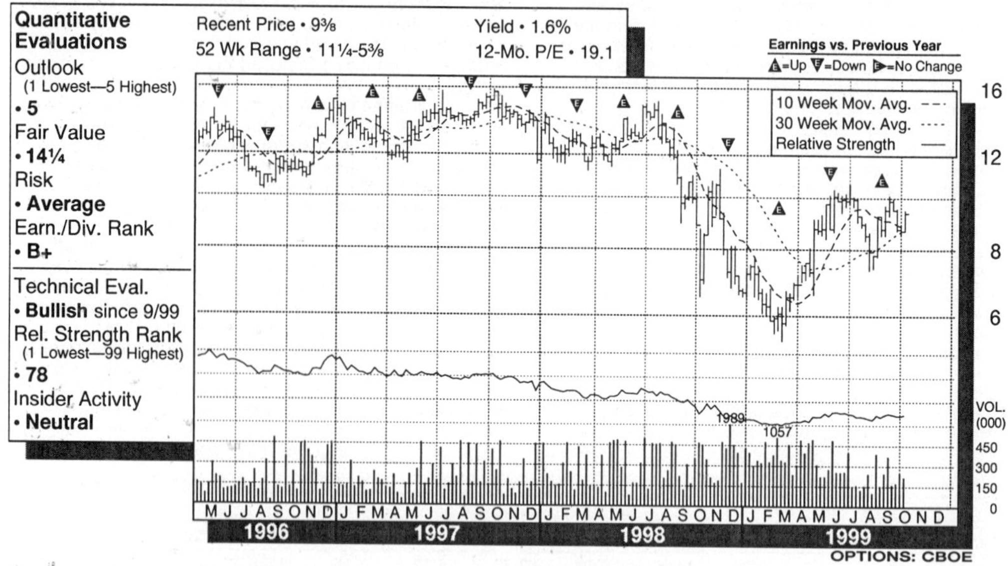

Business Profile - 11-AUG-99

Phillips-Van Heusen said in May 1999 that the launch of DKNY has proceeded better than planned. The company also said that it had integrated the John Henry and Manhattan brands into its Dress Shirt operations. In addition, PVH was pleased that sell-thrus at Izod improved in the Spring season. In February 1999, the company completed the sale of Gant to Pyramid Sportswear for $71 million. PVH believes that this both strengthens its financial position and allows the company to concentrate on its moderate to upper-moderate sportswear brands: Van Heusen, Izod and Geoffrey Beene. In March 1999, PVH entered into a license agreement to market dress shirts under the John Henry and Manhattan brands.

Operational Review - 11-AUG-99

Sales for the first quarter of FY 99 (Jan.) declined 2.1%, year to year, reflecting sales decreases of 1.6% for apparel and 3.1% for footwear and related products. The operating loss narrowed sharply, to $26,000 from $1.4 million, aided by reduced goodwill amortization and operating expenses relating to the sale of Gant, a reduction in promotional selling in footwear, and a significant drop in year 2000 computer conversion costs. Following 12% heavier interest charges and tax credits in both periods, the net loss rose to $4.6 million ($0.17 a share) from $4.5 million ($0.16, before $0.04 extraordinary loss on early retirement of debt).

Stock Performance - 08-OCT-99

In the past 30 trading days, PVH's shares have increased 7%, compared to a 0.91% fall in the S&P 500. Average trading volume for the past five days was 42,740 shares, compared with the 40-day moving average of 49,649 shares.

Key Stock Statistics

Dividend Rate/Share	0.15	Shareholders	1,540
Shs. outstg. (M)	27.3	Market cap. (B)	$0.256
Avg. daily vol. (M)	0.039	Inst. holdings	49%
Tang. Bk. Value/Share	4.23		
Beta	0.97		

Value of $10,000 invested 5 years ago: $ 2,713

Fiscal Year Ending Jan. 31

	2000	1999	1998	1997	1996	1995
Revenues (Million $)						
1Q	289.7	295.8	285.9	273.7	283.0	239.0
2Q	316.8	306.4	313.5	313.8	349.5	283.8
3Q	—	374.4	413.6	391.3	448.0	379.4
4Q	—	326.6	337.0	380.9	383.6	353.4
Yr.	—	1,303	1,350	1,360	1,464	1,255
Earnings Per Share ($)						
1Q	**-0.17**	**-0.16**	**-0.17**	**-0.24**	-0.13	-0.13
2Q	**0.13**	**0.10**	**-1.23**	**0.08**	0.15	0.21
3Q	—	**0.51**	**0.53**	**0.55**	-0.16	0.66
4Q	—	**0.02**	**-1.59**	**0.29**	0.15	0.37
Yr.	—	**0.47**	**-2.46**	**0.68**	**0.01**	**1.11**

Next earnings report expected: NA

Dividend Data (Dividends have been paid since 1970.)

Amount ($)	Date Decl.	Ex-Div. Date	Stock of Record	Payment Date
0.038	Oct. 23	Nov. 18	Nov. 20	Dec. 11 '98
0.038	Mar. 04	Mar. 11	Mar. 15	Mar. 30 '99
0.038	Apr. 22	Jun. 02	Jun. 04	Jun. 21 '99
0.038	Jul. 23	Aug. 23	Aug. 25	Sep. 10 '99

A Division of The McGraw-Hill Companies

Phillips-Van Heusen Corporation

Business Summary - 11-AUG-99

Incorporated in 1976 as the successor to a business begun in 1881, Phillips-Van Heusen is a marketer of men's, women's and children's apparel and footwear. As of year-end FY 99 (Jan.), these products were being sold under five nationally recognized brand names--Van Heusen, Bass, Izod, Geoffrey Beene, and Gant-- in the dress shirt, casual footwear, and sportswear categories. In late February 1999, PVH sold the Gant trademark and related assets.

The company is brand focused and manages the design, sourcing, and manufacturing of substantially all of its products on a brand by brand basis. Products include both dress and sport shirts and casual shoes and, to a lesser extent, sweaters, neckwear, furnishings, bottoms, outerwear, and leather and canvas accessories. Excluding Gant, 20% of FY 99 sales was derived from dress shirts, 33% from footwear and related products, and 47% from branded sportswear and other apparel.

Products are marketed at wholesale through national and regional department store chains and also directly to consumers through PVH's own retail stores, generally in factory outlet retail malls. PVH views its retail business as a complement to its strong branded positions in the wholesale market.

Excluding Gant sales, the Van Heusen, Bass, Iz and Geoffrey Beene brands accounted for 93% of s in FY 99. PVH owns three of the four brands, with sales of the fourth -- Geoffrey Beene -- being under licensing agreements with the designer. In FY 99, PVH began marketing DKNY brand men's dress shirts under a licensing agreement with Donna Karan. In March 1999, PVH entered into a licensing agreement to market dress shirts under the John Henry and Manhattan brands.

In the U.S., Van Heusen is the best selling men'sdress shirt brand, the best selling men's woven sport shirt brand and the best selling men's sweater brand. Geoffrey Beene is the best selling men's designer dress shirt brand in the U.S. The company believes that its overall share of the U.S. men's dress shirt market, including its branded, designer and private label offerings, is the largest of any company.

The Van Heusen brand, in the moderate price range, appeals to a fashion sensitive consumer. The typical Bass consumer is fashion conscious with a sense of individuality and a youthful point of view. The Izod brand is 'active inspired', designed to sell on the main floor of department stores in the moderate to upper moderate price range. Geoffrey Beene is targeted to a more fashion-forward consumer who is prepared to purchase apparel in the upper moderate price range.

Per Share Data ($) (Year Ended Jan. 31)	1999	1998	1997	1996	1995	1994	1993	1992	1991	1990
Tangible Bk. Val.	4.23	3.82	6.28	5.76	9.69	8.64	7.42	3.50	2.32	2.35
Cash Flow	1.40	-1.52	1.78	1.27	2.00	2.30	2.01	1.76	1.47	1.22
Earnings	0.47	-2.46	0.69	0.01	1.11	1.60	1.42	1.15	0.95	0.84
Dividends	0.15	0.15	0.15	0.15	0.15	0.15	0.15	0.14	0.14	0.14
Payout Ratio	32%	NM	22%	NM	14%	9%	11%	12%	14%	16%
Cal. Yrs.	1998	1997	1996	1995	1994	1993	1992	1991	1990	1989
Prices - High	15 1/8	15 7/8	15 1/8	18	39	37 1/2	29 1/4	21	11 5/8	12 1/2
- Low	6 1/2	11 1/2	9 1/2	9 1/8	14	25 3/4	16 1/2	7	5 1/4	6 7/8
P/E Ratio - High	32	NM	22	NM	35	23	21	18	12	15
- Low	14	NM	14	NM	13	16	12	6	5	8
Income Statement Analysis (Million $)										
Revs.	1,303	1,350	1,360	1,464	1,255	1,152	1,043	904	806	733
Oper. Inc.	68.9	24.8	77.2	81.3	81.0	99	88.1	74.1	66.0	59.6
Depr.	25.4	25.3	29.4	33.7	24.3	19.1	15.0	12.1	9.8	7.3
Int. Exp.	26.1	20.7	23.2	23.2	12.8	16.7	16.8	17.8	20.4	19.1
Pretax Inc.	17.4	-107	24.6	-2.6	36.9	63.6	54.5	44.0	35.2	32.7
Eff. Tax Rate	26%	NM	25%	NM	19%	32%	31%	29%	25%	26%
Net Inc.	12.9	-66.6	18.5	0.3	30.0	43.3	37.9	31.1	26.4	24.2
Balance Sheet & Other Fin. Data (Million $)										
Cash	11.0	11.7	11.6	17.5	80.5	68.1	77.1	7.0	5.8	6.6
Curr. Assets	368	385	363	445	430	419	411	303	285	267
Total Assets	674	660	657	749	596	555	517	399	377	333
Curr. Liab.	133	274	122	183	114	109	115	105	90.7	84.2
LT Debt	249	100	189	230	170	170	170	121	140	119
Common Eqty.	229	220	290	275	275	247	211	85.0	62.0	46.0
Total Cap.	478	320	480	505	445	417	382	280	275	238
Cap. Exp.	38.2	17.9	22.6	39.8	53.1	47.9	36.8	21.1	22.2	12.8
Cash Flow	38.3	-41.3	48.0	34.0	54.3	62.4	50.8	35.1	28.0	23.3
Curr. Ratio	2.8	1.4	3.0	2.4	3.8	3.8	3.6	2.9	3.1	3.2
% LT Debt of Cap.	52.1	31.2	39.5	45.5	38.1	40.8	44.6	43.4	50.9	50.0
% Net Inc.of Revs.	1.0	NM	1.4	Nil	2.4	3.8	3.6	3.4	3.3	3.3
% Ret. on Assets	1.9	NM	2.6	Nil	5.2	8.0	7.1	8.0	7.4	7.4
% Ret. on Equity	5.7	NM	6.6	Nil	11.5	18.7	21.7	30.9	33.4	40.7

Data as orig reptd.; bef. results of disc opers/spec. items. Per share data adj. for stk. divs. Bold denotes diluted EPS (FASB 128)-prior periods restated. E-Estimated. NA-Not Available. NM-Not Meaningful. NR-Not Ranked.

Office—200 Madison Ave., New York, NY 10016. **Tel**—(212) 381-3500. **Chrmn & CEO**—B. J. Klatsky. **Pres & COO**—M. Weber. **EVP, CFO & Investor Contact**—Emanuel Chirico. **Dirs**—E. H. Cohen, J. B. Fuller, J. H. Goldberg, M. Grosman, D. F. Hightower, B. J. Klatsky, M. E. Lagomasino, H. N. S. Lee, B. Maggin, S. M. Rhone, P. J. Solomon, M. Weber. **Transfer Agent & Registrar**—Bank of New York, NYC. **Incorporated**—in New York in 1919; reincorporated in Delaware in 1976. **Empl**— 7,550. **S&P Analyst:** N.J.D.

Photronics, Inc.

Nasdaq Symbol **PLAB**

In S&P SmallCap 600

Summary: PLAB is a leading manufacturer of high-precision photomasks, which contain microscopic images of electronic circuits and are used in the fabrication of semiconductors.

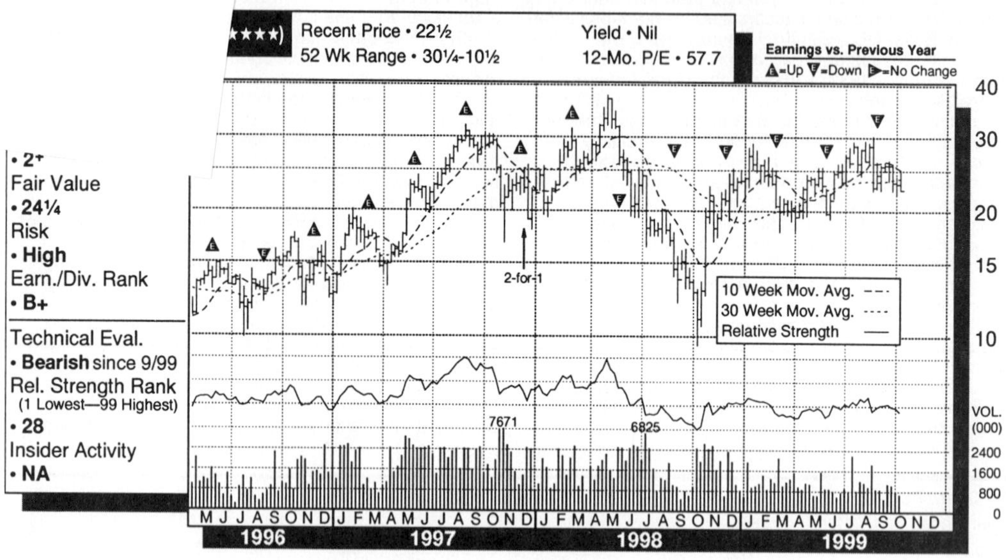

Overview - 23-AUG-99

While FY 99 (Oct.) revenues are likely to be little changed from those of FY 98, we expect sales to rise nearly 22% in FY 00, reflecting a recovery in photomask demand and an improved pricing environment. The company's fortunes are tied to growth and acceleration of integrated circuit (IC) design activity. With semiconductor manufacturers gravitating toward production of devices with linewidths of 0.25 micron and below, we expect continued strong demand for high-end photomasks that enable this technology. In FY 99, a slowdown in the overall semiconductor market and the resultant disruption to PLAB's customers led to curtailed design activity, depressing unit volumes and pricing. We expect these pressures to abate, resulting in stronger volumes, better capacity utilization, and a richer product mix. As a result, we believe EPS can improve to $0.95 in FY 00, from our estimate of $0.45 for FY 99.

Valuation - 23-AUG-99

The shares of this leading photomask manufacturer have been volatile thus far in 1999, reflecting difficult photomask industry conditions. We are maintaining our accumulate recommendation on the shares, however, as we believe revenue and earnings prospects for next year are strong. Chipmakers are moving rapidly toward chip design rules of 0.25 micron and below. This trend should fuel demand for high-end photomasks, which carry very healthy profit margins. In light of PLAB's strong level of investment in leading edge capacity over the last few years, the company is well positioned to capture this demand, and to increase its business. The shares, recently trading at 25X our FY 00 EPS estimate, are attractively valued for aggressive investors.

Key Stock Statistics

S&P EPS Est. 1999	0.45	Tang. Bk. Value/Share	7.45
P/E on S&P Est. 1999	50.0	Beta	2.71
S&P EPS Est. 2000	0.95	Shareholders	5,000
Dividend Rate/Share	Nil	Market cap. (B)	$0.536
Shs. outstg. (M)	23.8	Inst. holdings	56%
Avg. daily vol. (M)	0.177		

Value of $10,000 invested 5 years ago: $ 42,187

Fiscal Year Ending Oct. 31

	1999	1998	1997	1996	1995	1994
Revenues (Million $)						
1Q	47.82	50.93	40.03	34.67	26.18	18.86
2Q	53.83	61.31	49.03	40.51	30.04	18.65
3Q	59.03	57.68	53.08	42.68	32.85	21.31
4Q	—	52.65	55.31	42.21	36.23	21.89
Yr.	—	222.6	197.4	160.1	125.3	80.70
Earnings Per Share ($)						
1Q	**0.03**	**0.25**	0.22	0.20	0.16	0.10
2Q	**0.09**	**0.22**	0.25	0.22	0.18	0.11
3Q	**0.14**	**0.24**	0.28	0.23	0.27	0.14
4Q	—	**0.13**	0.29	0.23	0.21	0.16
Yr.	—	**0.84**	**1.03**	0.87	0.83	0.51

Next earnings report expected: early December

Dividend Data

No cash dividends have been paid. A two-for-one stock split was effected in December 1997.

Photronics, Inc.

Business Summary - 23-AUG-99

As a leading manufacturer of photomasks used in the fabrication of semiconductors, Photronics (PLAB) provides critical enabling technology necessary to advance the information age. In the struggle to make chips smaller, cheaper and faster, semiconductor makers rely heavily on PLAB's ability to manufacture high-end photomasks in a timely and accurate manner.

Photomasks are high-precision photographic quartz plates that contain microscopic images of electronic circuits. These products are used as masters to transfer circuit patterns onto semiconductor wafers during the fabrication of integrated circuits and, to a lesser extent, other types of electrical components, such as diodes and transistors. The customer base for photomasks consists primarily of semiconductor manufacturers. PLAB believes it is the largest independent U.S. photomask maker.

PLAB's photomasks are made in accordance with circuit designs provided by its customers. Photronics uses electron-beam and laser-based systems in the manufacture of its photomasks, as this technique reduces the number of steps required to manufacture a photomask and makes it possible to obtain finer line resolution, tighter overlay and larger die size for the larger and more complex circuits currently being designed. PLAB also uses the optical method, which is less precise but also less expensive, in competitive pricing situations.

Photronics is often grouped together with other well known semiconductor capital equipment companies, such as Applied Materials and Lam Research. The dynamics of the photomask market, however, are much different from those of the wafer processing equipment market. Demand for photomasks is largely dependent on the increasing complexity and accelerated design activity of semiconductors, not manufacturing capacity expansion or semiconductor sales volume. As a result, the photomask market is somewhat insulated from the boom and bust cycles of the semiconductor market.

While advanced photomasks generally have an indefinite life span, and are not customarily consumed in the semiconductor fabrication process, the demand for them has increased with the growth in the number of chip designs. For example, the manufacture of a 16 Mb DRAM requires 16 photomasks. As chip-makers migrate toward next generation 64 Mb devices, this figure increases sharply, to 23.

PLAB also manufactures semiconductor wafer plasma etching systems and sells refurbished semiconductor manufacturing equipment and replacement parts and field service for such equipment on a third-party basis. These activities accounted for a small portion of total sales during FY 98 (Oct.).

Per Share Data ($) (Year Ended Oct. 31)	1998	1997	1996	1995	1994	1993	1992	1991	1990	1989
Tangible Bk. Val.	7.48	7.65	6.21	5.30	3.80	2.96	2.77	2.50	1.74	0.92
Cash Flow	1.79	1.82	1.41	1.22	0.93	0.63	0.60	0.71	0.62	0.35
Earnings	0.84	1.03	0.87	0.83	0.50	0.29	0.27	0.45	0.35	0.09
Dividends	Nil	Nil	Nil	Nil	Nil	Nil	Nil	Nil	Nil	Nil
Payout Ratio	Nil	Nil	Nil	Nil	Nil	Nil	Nil	Nil	Nil	Nil
Prices - High	37⅞	32⅛	17⅝	20⅝	10	5⅝	5⅜	6	4	2 1/16
- Low	9½	13⅛	9⅛	8⅞	4⅞	3¼	2½	2 7/16	1⅝	5/16
P/E Ratio - High	45	31	20	25	20	19	20	13	12	23
- Low	11	13	10	11	10	11	9	6	5	4
Income Statement Analysis (Million $)										
Revs.	223	197	160	126	80.7	48.4	41.3	42.2	37.4	27.7
Oper. Inc.	70.7	60.2	44.4	32.3	22.9	12.6	11.1	12.7	9.2	4.1
Depr.	31.5	19.8	12.1	8.7	8.7	5.6	5.2	4.0	3.1	2.5
Int. Exp.	6.1	2.2	0.2	0.1	0.1	0.1	0.1	0.2	0.6	0.8
Pretax Inc.	33.1	41.4	33.9	29.8	15.3	7.4	6.7	10.9	6.3	1.3
Eff. Tax Rate	38%	38%	38%	38%	34%	34%	35%	38%	37%	32%
Net Inc.	20.5	25.6	21.0	18.6	10.1	4.9	4.4	6.8	4.0	0.9
Balance Sheet & Other Fin. Data (Million $)										
Cash	23.8	57.8	18.8	51.8	27.6	11.7	16.7	19.9	9.1	3.0
Curr. Assets	87.4	139	65.6	79.4	42.5	25.6	24.7	27.9	16.8	9.2
Total Assets	372	365	212	174	98.3	74.4	52.0	47.9	32.6	21.7
Curr. Liab.	50.5	57.5	44.0	29.8	10.1	8.0	3.9	4.4	5.7	5.4
LT Debt	104	106	2.0	1.8	0.5	1.1	1.7	1.8	2.5	7.0
Common Eqty.	201	186	156	134	80.4	62.6	44.0	39.4	22.5	8.8
Total Cap.	315	303	158	144	88.0	66.2	47.9	43.3	26.8	16.2
Cap. Exp.	66.4	96.3	55.8	35.5	4.1	21.9	11.7	6.4	6.4	3.0
Cash Flow	51.9	45.5	33.1	27.3	18.7	10.5	9.5	10.8	7.1	3.4
Curr. Ratio	1.7	2.4	1.5	2.7	4.2	3.2	6.3	6.4	3.0	1.7
% LT Debt of Cap.	32.9	35.7	1.3	1.3	0.6	1.6	3.5	4.1	9.2	43.1
% Net Inc.of Revs.	9.2	13.0	13.1	14.8	12.5	10.1	10.6	16.1	10.6	3.1
% Ret. on Assets	5.6	8.9	10.8	13.7	11.6	7.1	8.7	15.5	12.8	4.2
% Ret. on Equity	10.6	15.0	14.5	17.4	14.0	8.5	10.4	20.3	23.0	10.3

Data as orig reptd.; bef. results of disc opers/spec. items. Per share data adj. for stk. divs. Bold denotes diluted EPS (FASB 128)-prior periods restated. E-Estimated. NA-Not Available. NM-Not Meaningful. NR-Not Ranked.

Organized—in Connecticut in 1969. **Office**—15 Secor Rd., P.O. Box 5226, Brookfield, CT 06804. **Tel**—(203) 775-9000. **Website**—http://www.photronics.com **Chrmn**—C. S. Macricostas. **Pres** —J.R. Northup. **CFO**—R. Bollo. **Investor Contact**—Michael McCarthy (E-mail: mccarthy@brk.photronics.com). **Dirs**—W. M. Fiederowicz, J. A. Fiorita, Jr., C. S. Macricostas, M. J. Yomazzo. **Transfer Agent & Registrar**—Registrar & Transfer Co., Cranford, NJ. **Empl**— 1,180. **S&P Analyst:** B. McGovern

STANDARD
&POOR'S
STOCK REPORTS

PhyCor, Inc.

NASDAQ Symbol **PHYC**

In S&P SmallCap 600

09-OCT-99

Industry: Health Care (Managed Care)

Summary: PhyCor acquires and operates multi-specialty medical clinics and develops and manages independent practice associations.

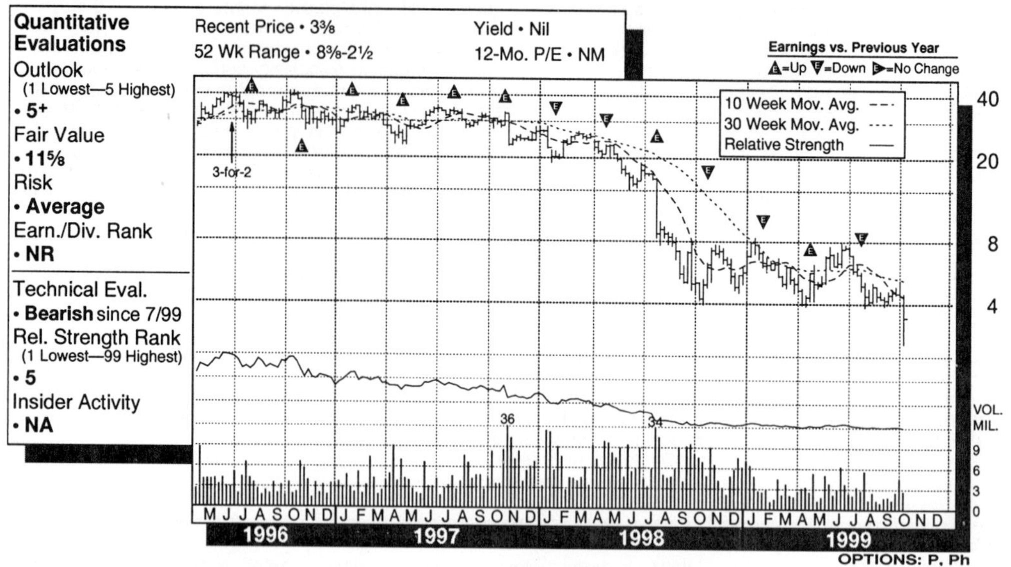

Business Profile - 17-AUG-99

As part of an effort to stabilize the company's operations and balance sheet, PhyCor has been selling clinics and using the proceeds to retire debt. However, ongoing payment pressures on both physicians and hospitals have created a difficult operating environment for the physician practice management industry, and management has lowered its 1999 EPS guidance to the $0.45 to $0.50 range, before charges. PHYC has agreed to sell $127.5 million of zero coupon subordinated notes, convertible into about 15.2 million common shares, to E.M. Warburg, Pincus & Co. LLC. Warburg also intends to buy up to $72.5 million of PHYC common in the open market.

Operational Review - 17-AUG-99

Net revenue in the six months ended June 30, 1999, rose 17%, year to year, as the inclusion of recent clinic and IPA acquisitions outweighed the absence of fees from divested clinics. Same-clinic revenues grew 7.5% in the second quarter and 8.6% in the first half. Operating expenses increased more rapidly than revenues, and the provision for asset revaluation and clinic restructurings rose to $23.9 million from $22.0 million. Despite the absence of merger expenses totaling $14.2 million, and after higher net interest expense, taxes at 32.5% versus 28.3%, and greater minority interest, net earnings plunged 53%, to $3,711,000 ($0.05 a share, on 11% more shares) from $7,815,000 ($0.11).

Stock Performance - 08-OCT-99

In the past 30 trading days, PHYC's shares have declined 19%, compared to a 0.91% fall in the S&P 500. Average trading volume for the past five days was 522,560 shares, compared with the 40-day moving average of 417,444 shares.

Key Stock Statistics

Dividend Rate/Share	Nil	Shareholders	28,000
Shs. outstg. (M)	76.1	Market cap. (B)	$0.261
Avg. daily vol. (M)	0.535	Inst. holdings	43%
Tang. Bk. Value/Share	NM		
Beta	1.73		

Value of $10,000 invested 5 years ago: $ 4,034

Fiscal Year Ending Dec. 31

	1999	1998	1997	1996	1995	1994
Revenues (Million $)						
1Q	416.5	322.7	250.7	162.5	92.76	49.77
2Q	393.5	371.4	267.4	176.6	99.2	50.46
3Q	—	408.5	284.3	196.4	114.0	63.18
4Q	—	409.9	317.3	230.8	135.7	79.08
Yr.	—	1,513	1,120	766.3	441.6	242.5
Earnings Per Share ($)						
1Q	**0.04**	**-0.12**	**0.19**	0.13	0.09	0.08
2Q	**0.01**	**0.22**	**0.20**	0.14	0.09	0.09
3Q	—	**-0.66**	**0.22**	0.15	0.11	0.07
4Q	—	**-0.90**	**-0.59**	0.18	0.12	0.08
Yr.	—	**-1.55**	**0.05**	**0.60**	**0.41**	**0.32**

Next earnings report expected: late October

Dividend Data

No cash dividends have been paid.

A Division of The McGraw-Hill Companies

PhyCor, Inc.

Business Summary - 17-AUG-99

PhyCor Inc. operates multi-specialty medical clinics, develops and manages independent practice associations (IPAs), operates two hospitals, and manages four health maintenance organizations (HMOs). As of June 30, 1999, the company operated 52 multi-specialty clinics with 3,308 physicians in 25 states, and managed IPAs with approximately 26,000 physicians in 34 markets.

By organizing previously unaffiliated physicians into professionally managed networks, the company seeks to let physicians focus on providing health care services, rather than on administrative duties. Programs and services include strategic planning and budgeting that focus, among other things, on cost containment and expense reduction. PhyCor negotiates managed care contracts, enters into national purchasing agreements, conducts productivity and procedure coding and charge capturing studies and assists the clinics in physician recruitment efforts.

PhyCor's long-term service agreements are for terms of up to 40 years, and provide that they may not be terminated by either party without cause, which includes material default or bankruptcy. Under virtually all of company service agreements, PHYC receives a service fee equal to the clinic expenses incurred plus a percentage of operating income of the clinic (net clinic revenue less certain clinic expenses before physician distributions) and, under nearly all other agreements, PHYC receives a percentage of net clinic revenue. In 1998, 92% of service revenue was derived from contracts in which the service fee was based on a percentage (11% to 18%) of clinic operating income plus reimbursement of clinic expenses.

The company's clinics also offer ancillary services, which accounted for 24% of gross clinic revenues in 1998. Most provide imaging services, including CAT scanning, mammography, nuclear medicine, ultrasound, and X-ray. Many also have clinical labs and pharmacies. Ambulatory surgery units and rehabilitation services are in place or are being planned in most clinics, while several offer diabetes centers, renal dialysis and home infusion therapy.

During 1998, managed care accounted for 51% of net clinic revenue, Medicare for 19%, private payor and insurance for 27% and Medicaid for 3%.

PhyCor recorded pretax asset revaluation and restructuring charges associated with clinic operations totaling $193.3 million in 1998, related to the sale of seven clinics and the revaluation of assets related to certain underperforming clinics. Another $8.1 million pretax charge was incurred in the first quarter of 1999, related to severance and other exit costs associated with operations that are being restructured or sold.

Per Share Data ($) (Year Ended Dec. 31)	1998	1997	1996	1995	1994	1993	1992	1991	1990	1989
Tangible Bk. Val.	NM	NM	NM	1.49	4.86	2.89	2.44	1.84	NM	NA
Cash Flow	-0.30	0.98	1.25	0.81	0.66	0.51	-0.39	0.25	0.21	-0.11
Earnings	-1.55	0.05	0.60	0.41	0.32	0.28	-0.32	0.05	0.00	-0.23
Dividends	Nil	Nil	Nil	Nil	Nil	Nil	Nil	Nil	Nil	Nil
Payout Ratio	Nil	Nil	Nil	Nil	Nil	Nil	Nil	Nil	Nil	Nil
Prices - High	28 1/2	35 1/2	41 3/4	34	12 1/2	9 1/8	5 1/4	NA	NA	NA
- Low	3 7/8	22 3/4	25 1/2	10 7/8	7 1/2	4	2 1/4	NA	NA	NA
P/E Ratio - High	NM	NM	70	84	39	46	NM	NA	NA	NA
- Low	NM	NM	42	27	23	20	NM	NA	NA	NA
Income Statement Analysis (Million $)										
Revs.	1,512	1,120	766	442	242	167	136	90.0	64.0	24.0
Oper. Inc.	225	187	122	67.5	31.4	17.9	13.6	7.6	4.9	1.2
Depr.	90.2	62.5	40.2	21.4	12.2	6.1	4.5	2.7	2.7	0.8
Int. Exp.	36.3	23.5	16.0	5.2	4.0	3.9	4.5	3.8	3.0	2.2
Pretax Inc.	-137	21.0	59.2	35.8	16.5	8.2	-13.3	1.3	0.2	-1.6
Eff. Tax Rate	NM	29%	39%	39%	29%	13%	NM	43%	67%	Nil
Net Inc.	-110	3.2	36.4	21.8	11.7	7.1	-13.7	0.8	0.1	-1.6
Balance Sheet & Other Fin. Data (Million $)										
Cash	74.3	38.2	30.5	18.8	6.5	3.2	9.2	2.6	3.6	2.1
Curr. Assets	570	497	383	218	145	77.5	69.4	39.6	33.5	13.4
Total Assets	1,847	1,563	1,119	644	351	171	141	93.0	79.0	34.0
Curr. Liab.	382	293	170	106	64.3	30.5	33.5	17.7	15.5	6.0
LT Debt	643	478	409	127	84.9	66.8	51.2	49.3	38.9	20.0
Common Eqty.	804	710	452	389	184	70.0	53.9	2.4	1.3	NA
Total Cap.	1,447	1,188	860	516	269	137	105	75.0	63.0	28.0
Cap. Exp.	67.6	66.5	50.1	29.2	17.5	13.9	13.6	6.3	4.3	0.5
Cash Flow	-21.2	65.7	76.6	43.3	23.9	13.3	-9.3	3.5	2.8	-0.8
Curr. Ratio	1.5	1.7	2.3	2.0	2.3	2.5	2.1	2.2	2.2	2.2
% LT Debt of Cap.	44.4	40.2	47.5	24.6	31.6	48.8	48.7	66.0	61.5	71.0
% Net Inc.of Revs.	NM	0.3	4.7	4.9	4.8	4.3	NM	0.8	0.1	NM
% Ret. on Assets	NM	0.2	4.1	4.4	3.8	4.4	NM	0.9	1.0	NM
% Ret. on Equity	NM	0.6	8.7	7.6	7.9	11.1	NM	41.4	3.6	NM

Data as orig. reptd.; bef. results of disc. opers. and/or spec. items. Per share data adj. for stk. divs. as of ex-div. date. Bold denotes diluted EPS (FASB 128). E-Estimated. NA-Not Available. NM-Not Meaningful. NR-Not Ranked.

Office—30 Burton Hills Blvd., Suite 400, Nashville, TN 37215. **Tel**—(615) 665-9066. **Website**—http://www.phycor.com **Chrmn, Pres & CEO**—J. C. Hutts. **EVP & Secy**—T. S. Dent. **VP, Treas & CFO**—J. K. Crawford. **Dirs**—R. B. Ashworth, S. A. Brooks Jr., T. S. Dent, W. C. Dunn, C. S. Givens, J. A. Hill, J. C. Hutts, K. C. James, J. A. Moncrief, D. W. Reeves, R. D. Wright. **Transfer Agent**—First Union National Bank of North Carolina, Charlotte. **Incorporated**—in Tennessee in 1988. **Empl**— 21,700. **S&P Analyst:** Robert Gold

STANDARD
&POOR'S
STOCK REPORTS

PictureTel Corp.

NASDAQ Symbol **PCTL**

In S&P SmallCap 600

09-OCT-99

Industry: Communications Equipment

Summary: This company develops, manufactures, markets and services visual communication systems that serve videoconferencing needs.

Quantitative Evaluations

Outlook
(1 Lowest—5 Highest)
• **1⁻**

Fair Value
• **2½**

Risk
• **High**

Earn./Div. Rank
• **B**

Technical Eval.
• **Bearish** since 6/99

Rel. Strength Rank
(1 Lowest—99 Highest)
• **11**

Insider Activity
• **NA**

Recent Price • 4¼
52 Wk Range • 11-3⅝
Yield • Nil
12-Mo. P/E • NM

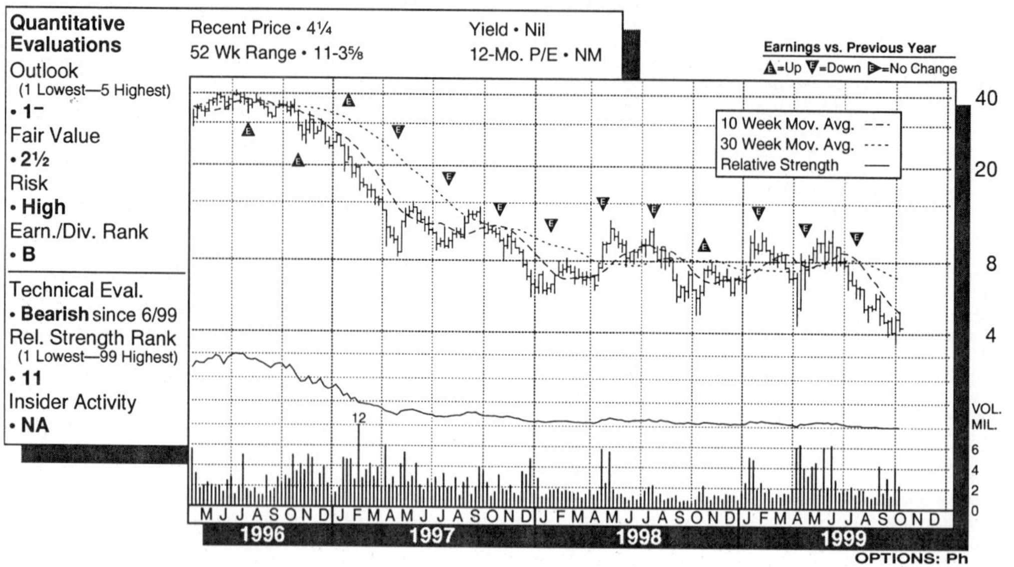

Business Profile - 03-SEP-99

The company began shipping its new compact videoconferencing systems in the 1999 second quarter, after resolving software-performance issues. PCTL is currently undergoing a restructuring designed to reduce its expense base to better match current low sales levels. In September 1999, Bruce Bond resigned as president and CEO, and was replaced by Dr. Norman Gaut. In January 1999, the company entered into an agreement with Intel, designed to accelerate the growth of videoconferencing. Intel has invested $30.5 million in PCTL, in return for convertible preferred stock.

Operational Review - 03-SEP-99

Revenues in the first half of 1999 fell 21%, year to year, reflecting delays in the release of a new compact videoconferencing system, as well as weakness in sales of the company's traditional systems. Gross margins narrowed substantially, on the lower volume; with higher operating expenses, the pretax loss widened to $55,745,000, from $13,021,000. After taxes, versus tax benefits and a preferred stock accretion of $4,271,000 in the 1999 period only, the net loss increased to $62,073,000 ($1.54 a share), from $8,854,000 ($0.23).

Stock Performance - 08-OCT-99

In the past 30 trading days, PCTL's shares have declined 25%, compared to a 0.91% fall in the S&P 500. Average trading volume for the past five days was 449,820 shares, compared with the 40-day moving average of 476,077 shares.

Key Stock Statistics

Dividend Rate/Share	Nil	Shareholders	1,907
Shs. outstg. (M)	40.4	Market cap. (B)	$0.172
Avg. daily vol. (M)	0.530	Inst. holdings	43%
Tang. Bk. Value/Share	4.62		
Beta	0.64		

Value of $10,000 invested 5 years ago: $ 4,533

Fiscal Year Ending Dec. 31

	1999	1998	1997	1996	1995	1994
Revenues (Million $)						
1Q	76.19	101.0	121.9	105.0	74.16	53.70
2Q	85.86	104.6	118.0	116.1	80.49	64.00
3Q	—	102.1	109.7	121.3	90.10	63.30
4Q	—	98.47	116.8	140.2	102.0	74.10
Yr.	—	406.1	466.4	482.5	346.7	255.2
Earnings Per Share ($)						
1Q	**-0.68**	**-0.06**	**0.05**	**0.17**	0.10	0.02
2Q	**-0.86**	**-0.17**	**-0.13**	**0.24**	0.12	0.02
3Q	—	**0.04**	**-0.44**	**0.17**	0.15	0.03
4Q	—	**-1.23**	**-0.52**	**0.22**	0.20	0.08
Yr.	—	**-1.45**	**-1.04**	**0.81**	**0.57**	**0.29**

Next earnings report expected: late October

Dividend Data

No cash dividends have been paid. A two-for-one stock split was effected in 1995.

PictureTel Corporation

Business Summary - 03-SEP-99

PictureTel's products serve videoconferencing needs from the desktop to the boardroom, eliminating the barrier of distance by providing face-to-face contact between people anywhere in the world. PCTL is the market share leader in the videoconferencing market. The company's systems use advanced video and audio compression technology that permits the transmission of full-motion color video with integrated full-duplex audio at data rates as low as 56 Kbps. By operating at such low speeds, PCTL's systems have substantially reduced the cost and increased the flexibility of videoconferencing. The company operates in three distinct business segments: videoconferencing products, services and audioconferencing.

Videoconferencing products (80% of 1998 sales) range in use from high-end group systems to personal systems for one-on-one videoconferencing. The company's group videoconferencing systems are dedicated conference-room systems that deliver high-quality video and audio performance at a variety of price points. PCTL created the compact category of videoconferencing in 1996 with the introduction of SwiftSite. The system is optimized for use in smaller offices.

The company also has a complete line of personal or desktop videoconferencing systems. These systems, which add videoconferencing capabilities to standard personal computers, are suited for use by individuals. The personal systems run on the most popular Microsoft operating systems. All of PCTL's videoconferencing systems operate deliver 15 frames per second of video performance at 128 Kbps over ISDN lines.

PCTL's service business (14%) assists customers in implementing and managing technology on a global basis. Services provided include consulting, design and project management.

The MultiLink subsidiary is a leading provider of audioconferencing solutions (6%). Audioconferencing systems allow multiple parties to participate in a telephone call simultaneously.

PictureTel uses both direct and indirect channels of distribution. In 1998, the company derived 25% of product revenue from direct selling activities, and 75% from indirect channels.

In October 1998, PCTL acquired Starlight Networks, a provider of streaming-media solutions for enterprise communications. The first new product resulting from the acquisition is expected in the second half of 1999. In January 1999, the company entered into a distribution and product development agreement with Intel to accelerate growth of videoconferencing worldwide. The two companies agreed to begln joint development of videconferencing and collaboration products based on a common PC-based technology platform. The common platform will be the foundation for future products that feature communication and multimedia capabilities such as streaming audio and video, and real-time conferencing.

Per Share Data ($) **(Year Ended Dec. 31)**	**1998**	**1997**	**1996**	**1995**	**1994**	**1993**	**1992**	**1991**	**1990**	**1989**
Tangible Bk. Val.	4.62	5.99	7.61	6.14	4.99	4.85	4.40	4.06	NA	NA
Cash Flow	-0.71	-0.11	1.56	1.07	0.73	0.62	0.52	NA	NA	NA
Earnings	-1.45	-1.04	0.96	0.56	0.15	0.24	0.27	0.15	-0.07	NA
Dividends	Nil	Nil	Nil	Nil	Nil	Nil	Nil	Nil	Nil	NA
Payout Ratio	Nil	Nil	Nil	Nil	Nil	Nil	Nil	Nil	Nil	NA
Prices - High	11 7/8	26 7/8	44 3/4	43 7/8	12 1/4	15 1/4	26 1/2	25 3/8	NA	NA
- Low	4 3/4	5 5/8	23 3/8	11 1/8	5	7 1/4	5 1/8	5 1/2	NA	NA
P/E Ratio - High	NM	NM	47	78	84	65	NM	NM	NA	NA
- Low	NM	NM	24	20	34	31	NM	NM	NA	NA
Income Statement Analysis (Million $)										
Revs.	406	466	483	347	255	176	141	78.0	37.0	NA
Oper. Inc.	4.5	-21.6	65.6	42.2	23.6	20.9	17.4	NA	NA	NA
Depr.	28.2	35.2	21.5	17.9	18.3	12.2	8.3	NA	NA	NA
Int. Exp.	2.9	1.8	0.9	1.0	1.0	1.0	1.2	NA	NA	NA
Pretax Inc.	-19.9	-55.5	51.7	27.5	6.9	11.4	13.3	NA	NA	NA
Eff. Tax Rate	NM	NM	33%	29%	34%	35%	37%	NA	NA	NA
Net Inc.	-55.7	-39.4	34.7	19.6	4.6	7.4	8.4	4.0	-0.2	NA
Balance Sheet & Other Fin. Data (Million $)										
Cash	101	49.9	102	59.9	74.7	9.1	NA	NA	NA	NA
Curr. Assets	219	258	304	214	179	85.0	NA	NA	NA	NA
Total Assets	353	355	376	288	217	187	166	145	NA	NA
Curr. Liab.	106	105	103	74.5	60.4	36.1	NA	NA	NA	NA
LT Debt	56.4	22.0	13.9	12.8	2.9	4.4	4.7	3.9	NA	NA
Common Eqty.	190	228	259	201	153	147	132	120	NA	NA
Total Cap.	247	250	273	214	156	151	137	124	NA	NA
Cap. Exp.	19.4	21.6	38.5	11.1	14.3	11.1	12.5	NA	NA	NA
Cash Flow	-27.5	-4.2	56.2	37.5	22.9	19.6	16.6	NA	NA	NA
Curr. Ratio	2.1	2.5	3.0	2.9	3.0	2.4	NA	NA	NA	NA
% LT Debt of Cap.	22.9	8.8	5.1	6.0	1.8	2.9	3.4	3.2	NA	NA
% Net Inc.of Revs.	NM	NM	7.2	5.7	1.8	4.2	6.0	5.2	NM	NA
% Ret. on Assets	NM	NM	10.5	7.8	2.3	4.2	5.4	3.0	NA	NA
% Ret. on Equity	NM	NM	15.1	11.1	3.1	5.3	6.7	4.0	NA	NA

Data as orig reptd.; bef. results of disc opers/spec. items. Per share data adj. for stk. divs. Bold denotes diluted EPS (FASB 128)-prior periods restated. E-Estimated. NA-Not Available. NM-Not Meaningful. NR-Not Ranked.

Office—222 Rosewood Dr., Danvers, MA 01923. **Tel**—(978) 292-5000. **Website**—http://www.picturetel.com **Chrmn, Pres & CEO**—N. E. Gaut. **VP & CFO**—A. Fatum. **Investor Contact**—Kevin Flanagan. **Dirs**—N. E. Gaut, R. T. Knight, D. B. Levi, E. Torresi. **Transfer Agent & Registrar**—BankBoston. **Incorporated**—in Delaware in 1984. **Empl**— 1,466. **S&P Analyst:** Mark Cavallone

STANDARD
&POOR'S
STOCK REPORTS

Piedmont Natural Gas

NYSE Symbol **PNY**

In S&P SmallCap 600

09-OCT-99

Industry:
Natural Gas

Summary: This company is primarily engaged in the transportation and sale of natural gas to customers in North Carolina, South Carolina and Tennessee.

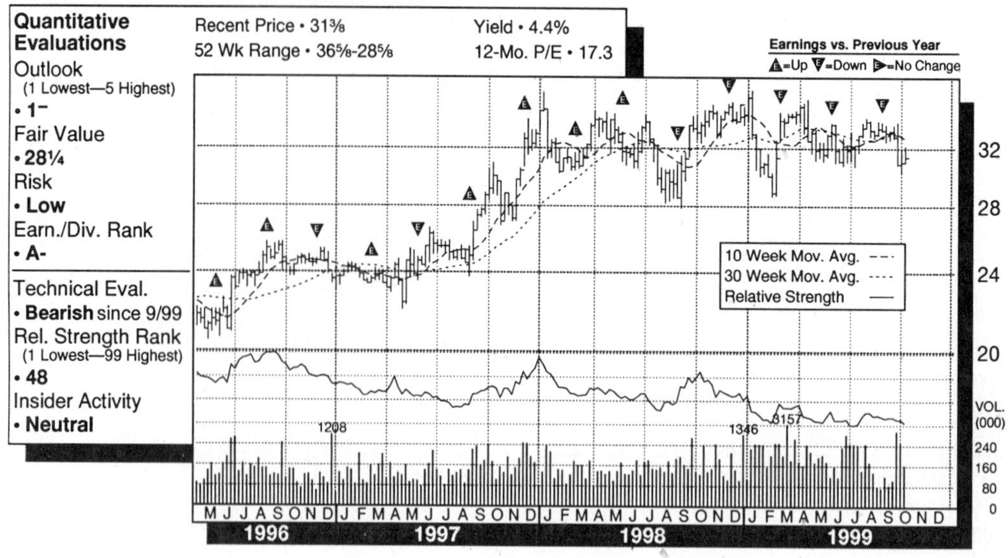

Business Profile - 18-AUG-99

Piedmont is the second largest gas utility in the Southeast. With its 5%-6% annual customer growth rate, the company continues to be one of the fastest-growing natural gas distributors in the U.S., adding customers at a rate three times the industry average. PNY kept pace in FY 98 (Oct.) by adding 31,400 natural gas customers. However, natural gas and propane sales have been soft in recent periods, reflecting warmer than normal weather. In May 1999, the company and its joint venture partners dedicated one of the largest natural gas peak-demand facilities in the U. S.

Operational Review - 18-AUG-99

Operating revenues in the first half of FY 99 (Oct.) fell 14%, year to year, primarily reflecting weather that was 14% warmer than normal and 10% warmer than the similar prior year period; total system throughput was 87.8 million dekatherms, down from 94.1 million dekatherms. Operating expenses were well controlled, but with a sharp drop in other income, net income slipped 1.9%, to $75,231,000 ($2.42 a share, based on 1.6% more shares) from $76,712,000 ($2.50).

Stock Performance - 08-OCT-99

In the past 30 trading days, PNY's shares have declined 6%, compared to a 0.91% fall in the S&P 500. Average trading volume for the past five days was 32,320 shares, compared with the 40-day moving average of 74,979 shares.

Key Stock Statistics

Dividend Rate/Share	1.38	Shareholders	19,147
Shs. outstg. (M)	31.2	Market cap. (B)	$0.978
Avg. daily vol. (M)	0.129	Inst. holdings	25%
Tang. Bk. Value/Share	16.27		
Beta	0.25		

Value of $10,000 invested 5 years ago: $ 20,164

Fiscal Year Ending Oct. 31

	1999	1998	1997	1996	1995	1994
Revenues (Million $)						
1Q	255.7	313.3	312.5	239.2	202.5	233.1
2Q	239.3	261.5	259.3	259.5	179.4	204.8
3Q	96.73	103.0	104.0	95.74	61.65	70.64
4Q	—	87.52	99.7	90.68	61.71	66.80
Yr.	—	765.3	775.5	685.1	505.2	575.4
Earnings Per Share ($)						
1Q	**1.31**	**1.35**	**1.26**	1.18	1.13	1.06
2Q	**1.11**	**1.16**	1.08	1.12	0.87	0.87
3Q	**-0.26**	**-0.20**	-0.19	-0.28	-0.31	-0.27
4Q	—	**-0.33**	-0.32	-0.33	-0.18	-0.30
Yr.	—	**1.96**	**1.79**	**1.66**	1.45	1.35

Next earnings report expected: early December

Dividend Data (Dividends have been paid since 1956.)

Amount ($)	Date Decl.	Ex-Div. Date	Stock of Record	Payment Date
0.325	Dec. 04	Dec. 21	Dec. 23	Jan. 15 '99
0.345	Feb. 26	Mar. 23	Mar. 25	Apr. 15 '99
0.345	Jun. 04	Jun. 22	Jun. 24	Jul. 15 '99
0.345	Aug. 27	Sep. 22	Sep. 24	Oct. 15 '99

Piedmont Natural Gas Company, Inc.

Business Summary - 18-AUG-99

This gas utility's growth has been fueled by the economic vibrancy of its service area, one of the fastest growing regions in the U.S. Piedmont Natural Gas (PNY), the second largest gas utility in the Southeast, transports and sells natural gas to more than 625,000 customers in the Piedmont region of the Carolinas (including Charlotte, Salisbury, Greensboro, Burlington, Winston-Salem, High Point and the Hickory area in NC, and Anderson, Greenville and Spartanburg, SC) and the metropolitan Nashville, TN, area. The company's propane market is in and adjacent to its natural gas market in all three states served.

Revenues by customer class in the fiscal year ended October 31, 1998, were obtained as follows: residential 42%, commercial 25%, industrial 21%, and other 12%.

About 90% of new single family homes built in PNY's service area use natural gas, when available. The number of customers billed averaged 589,530 in FY 98 (560,694 in FY 97). Gas volumes delivered in FY 98 totaled 143.0 million dekatherms, versus 135.1 million dekatherms in FY 97.

PNY purchases or transports gas from eight interstate pipeline suppliers. At November 1, 1998, suppliers had contracted to provide a total of 604,600 dekatherms per day to PNY, with additional daily peaking capacity available.

The company's principal non-utility business is the sale of propane to 48,000 customers in its three state service region. Other non-utility operations include acquiring, marketing and arranging for the transportation of natural gas to large-volume purchasers. Non-utility activities accounted for 5% of revenues in FY 98 and 1% of total net income.

To meet demand of its expanding customer base, PNY has budgeted capital expenditures totaling $106.8 million for utility expansion and construction projects for FY 99, not including $2.3 million slated for non-utility projects. In addition, an estimated equity contribution of $18.7 million is required in mid-1999 in connection with the construction of a liquefied natural gas peak-demand facility in which the company has a stake. PNY also is seeking new markets for natural gas including a heating and cooling unit for residential and small business applications and natural gas powered vehicles (NGVs).

In September 1997, PNY acquired two independent propane companies: Lincoln Moore County Propane in Lynchburg, TN; and McCombs Propane Co. in Morganton, NC. The acquisitions added about 1.2 million gallons and 1,650 customers to the company's sales and customer base.

Per Share Data ($) (Year Ended Oct. 31)	1998	1997	1996	1995	1994	1993	1992	1991	1990	1989
Tangible Bk. Val.	14.83	13.81	12.96	12.20	11.36	10.79	10.24	9.62	9.10	8.67
Earnings	1.96	1.81	1.67	1.45	1.35	1.45	1.40	0.89	1.22	1.21
Dividends	1.28	1.21	1.15	1.08	1.02	0.96	0.91	0.87	0.83	0.79
Payout Ratio	65%	67%	69%	75%	76%	67%	65%	98%	68%	65%
Prices - High	36 1/8	36 1/2	25 3/4	24 7/8	23 3/8	26 3/8	20 1/2	16 7/8	14 7/8	14 3/4
- Low	27 7/8	22	20 1/2	18 1/4	18	18 3/4	15 1/2	13	12 3/4	11 1/2
P/E Ratio - High	18	20	15	17	17	18	15	19	12	12
- Low	14	12	12	13	13	13	11	15	10	10
Income Statement Analysis (Million $)										
Revs.	765	776	685	505	575	553	460	412	404	421
Depr.	42.2	39.2	36.0	31.9	24.6	22.2	20.1	18.0	15.8	14.9
Maint.	14.7	16.2	15.8	16.4	15.5	15.0	13.3	13.1	11.6	10.1
Fxd. Chgs. Cov.	3.8	3.5	3.5	3.1	3.2	3.7	3.5	2.4	2.8	2.9
Constr. Credits	1.2	0.7	0.8	1.1	1.3	1.1	0.8	0.8	0.8	0.7
Eff. Tax Rate	39%	39%	39%	39%	36%	38%	38%	36%	37%	37%
Net Inc.	60.3	54.1	48.6	40.3	35.5	37.5	35.3	20.6	25.7	24.9
Balance Sheet & Other Fin. Data (Million $)										
Gross Prop.	1,372	1,284	1,168	1,075	978	877	796	723	658	591
Cap. Exp.	90.9	92.1	96.8	99	106	84.0	74.0	69.1	71.0	65.9
Net Prop.	991	942	862	801	735	655	593	538	488	434
Capitalization:										
LT Debt	371	381	391	361	313	278	231	221	174	186
% LT Debt	45	48	50	50	51	49	47	48	47	51
Pfd.	Nil	Nil	Nil	Nil	Nil	Nil	Nil	Nil	Nil	Nil
% Pfd.	Nil	Nil	Nil	Nil	Nil	Nil	Nil	Nil	Nil	Nil
Common	458	420	386	355	302	285	265	239	196	181
% Common	55	52	50	50	49	51	53	52	53	49
Total Cap.	948	914	880	810	697	653	576	534	442	437
% Oper. Ratio	86.4	89.5	89.1	87.1	90.3	89.8	88.4	90.3	89.1	90.2
% Earn. on Net Prop.	9.4	9.2	9.0	5.2	8.0	9.1	9.4	7.8	9.5	10.1
% Return On Revs.	7.9	7.0	7.1	8.0	6.2	6.8	7.7	5.0	6.4	5.9
% Return On Invest. Capital	10.0	10.3	9.4	12.6	8.9	9.7	10.2	8.8	10.8	10.9
% Return On Com. Equity	13.7	13.4	13.1	12.3	12.1	13.7	14.0	9.5	13.6	14.2

Data as orig reptd.; bef. results of disc opers/spec. items. Per share data adj. for stk. divs. Bold denotes diluted EPS (FASB 128)-prior periods restated. E-Estimated. NA-Not Available. NM-Not Meaningful. NR-Not Ranked.

Office—1915 Rexford Rd., Charlotte, NC 28211; P.O. Box 33068, Charlotte, NC 28233. **Tel**—(704) 364-3120. **Website**—www.piedmontng.com **Chrmn & CEO**—J. H. Maxheim. **Pres & COO**—W. F. Schiefer. **SVP-Fin**—D. J. Dzuricky. **VP, Treas & Investor Contact**—Ted C. Coble. **VP & Secy**—M. C. Ruegsegger. **Dirs**—J. W. Amos, C. M. Butler III, S. J. DiGiovanni, J. W. Harris, M. W. Helms, J. H. Maxheim, J. F. McNair III, N. R.McWherter, W. S. Montgomery Jr., D. S. Russell Jr., W. F. Schiefer, J. E. Simkins Jr. **Transfer Agent & Registrar**—Wachovia Bank of North Carolina, Winston-Salem. **Incorporated**—in North Carolina in 1994; previously incorporated in New York in 1950. **Empl**— 1,841. **S&P Analyst:** M.I.

STANDARD
&POOR'S
STOCK REPORTS

Pier 1 Imports

NYSE Symbol **PIR**
In S&P SmallCap 600

09-OCT-99 **Industry:** Retail (Specialty)

Summary: This company is North America's largest specialty retailer of imported decorative home furnishings, gifts and related items, with more than 800 stores.

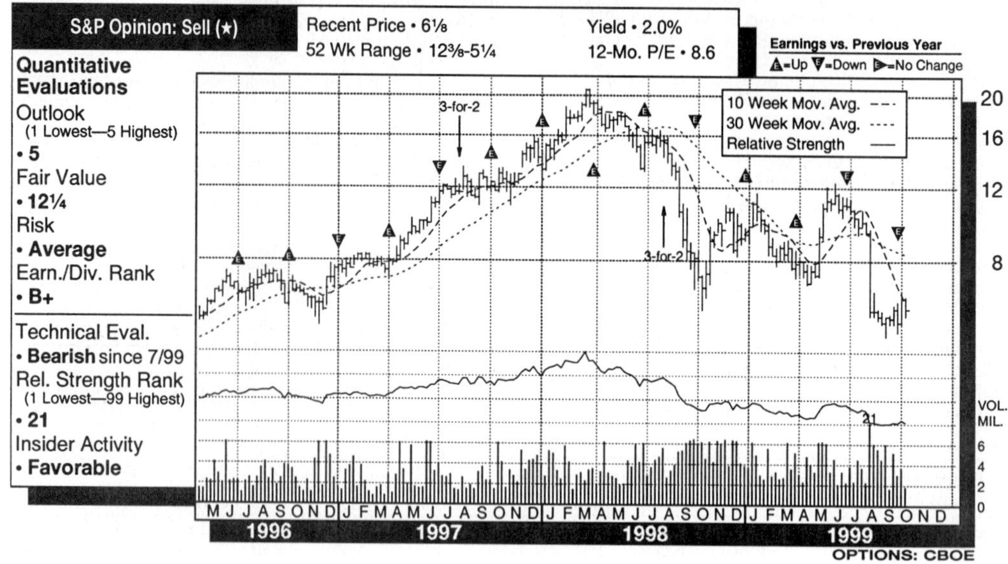

Overview - 01-OCT-99

We expect total sales in the second half of FY 00 (Feb.) to rise 3% to 5%, mainly reflecting contributions from new stores. Same-store sales should rise only about 1%. Margins will continue to be hurt by the company's new value pricing strategy, which has resulted in lower prices on more than 600 stock keeping units in its stores. Despite this lower pricing strategy, same-store sales have remained sluggish in recent months. We expect EPS to fall about 16%, to $0.65, in FY 00. Despite the negative outlook for FY 00, we continue to be optimistic about Pier 1's long term revenue growth strategy, which includes aggressive store openings, extensive store remodeling and merchandising, new product introductions, and other marketing initiatives. The company will also continue to pursue a possible acquisition that would complement its existing business.

Valuation - 01-OCT-99

We continue to rate PIR shares as sell. Although the shares are trading at only 10X our EPS estimate of $0.65 for FY 00 (Feb.), we believe they are still at risk for further decline. This negative outlook reflects our concern that PIR's strategy to attract sales by lowering prices on a good portion of its merchandise has not translated into the desired increases in same-store sales. The lower prices have also hurt margins and operating profits. The announcement of the sudden departure of PIR's chief financial officer and the news that acquisition talks with a potential suitor had broken down are further indications of a company in financial distress. Higher interest rates could also dampen enthusiasm for shares of home furnishings companies. With no near term catalyst to propel either sales or earnings, we believe PIR's share price remains vulnerable to further erosion.

Key Stock Statistics

S&P EPS Est. 2000	0.65	Tang. Bk. Value/Share	4.19
P/E on S&P Est. 2000	9.4	Beta	0.99
S&P EPS Est. 2001	0.75	Shareholders	16,000
Dividend Rate/Share	0.12	Market cap. (B)	$0.592
Shs. outstg. (M)	96.6	Inst. holdings	73%
Avg. daily vol. (M)	0.674		

Value of $10,000 invested 5 years ago: $ 15,784

Fiscal Year Ending Feb. 28

	2000	1999	1998	1997	1996	1995
Revenues (Million $)						
1Q	261.0	250.5	Nil	205.3	176.8	161.0
2Q	291.8	281.5	258.1	231.1	199.5	185.4
3Q	—	274.6	262.8	225.6	190.2	165.8
4Q	—	332.0	325.3	285.1	244.2	199.3
Yr.	—	1,139	1,075	947.1	810.7	712.0
Earnings Per Share ($)						
1Q	**0.13**	**0.15**	**-0.92**	**0.09**	-0.20	0.06
2Q	**0.12**	**0.17**	**0.20**	**0.11**	0.10	0.10
3Q	**E0.15**	**0.19**	**0.15**	**0.07**	0.08	0.00
4Q	**E0.25**	**0.27**	**0.24**	**0.17**	0.14	0.12
Yr.	**E0.65**	**0.77**	**0.72**	**0.47**	**0.11**	0.28

Next earnings report expected: early December

Dividend Data (Dividends have been paid since 1986.)

Amount ($)	Date Decl.	Ex-Div. Date	Stock of Record	Payment Date
0.030	Dec. 17	Feb. 08	Feb. 10	Feb. 24 '99
0.030	Mar. 25	May. 03	May. 05	May. 19 '99
0.030	Jun. 24	Aug. 02	Aug. 04	Aug. 18 '99
0.030	Sep. 30	Nov. 01	Nov. 03	Nov. 17 '99

Business Summary - 01-OCT-99

Pier 1 Imports, Inc. provides shoppers with a passport for finding unique, fashionable, and decorative home furnishings, gifts and related items from more than 50 countries around the world. PIR opened 63 new stores, and closed 30 locations during FY 99 (Feb.), continuing the rapid expansion pace which saw the number of stores increase from 588 at the end of FY 94 to 751 at the end of FY 98. The company expects to open approximately 60 new stores and close some 25 stores in FY 00.

PIR believes in a trend toward the renewal of the neighborhood store. With this in mind, the company generally opens its prototype 8,000 sq. ft. stores in neighborhood locations, as free-standing units near popular regional malls or in high-end strip centers. To make its stores more customer friendly, throughout FY 99 the company continued its program to remodel and remerchandise its stores. Stores were upgraded to include wider aisles, lower interior shelf displays and better lighting. The company is also expanding its use of "lifestyle merchandising", which involves placing items in home-use settings, to help the buyer envision how products can be integrated into their homes. This program, which will upgrade more than 700stores by the end of FY 01, was about 80% complete at the end of FY 99.

The stores choose their offerings very carefully, employing a well-seasoned merchandising staff that develops a clear concept of what they believe tomorrow's shoppers will find appealing. Merchandise is introduced in a carefully timed manner, so that over 40% of the offerings are new and different from those of the preceding year. PIR also emphasizes the uniqueness of its products, and ensures that more than half of its merchandise is exclusive to its stores.

PIR's offers five broad categories of products, including furniture (representing 35% of FY 99 sales), decorative home furnishings (23%), kitchen decor and housewares (13%), bed and bath products (19%) and seasonal offerings (10%). Merchandise is generally handcrafted, and is imported primarily from abroad. During FY 99, 27% of the company's offerings were imported from China, 13% from India, and 18% from Indonesia, Japan, Thailand, the Philippines and Italy. The remaining 42% was produced in various Asian, European, Central American, South American and African countries, or obtained from U.S. manufacturers.

PIR has been making noteworthy information technology investments. It is currently implementing system updates to avoid the year 2000 problem. The company will also deploy technology enhancements to its bridal and gift registry program, as well as new smart point-of-sale terminals; this is expected to improve PIR's ability to manage its inventory.

Per Share Data ($) **(Year Ended Feb. 28)**	**1999**	**1998**	**1997**	**1996**	**1995**	**1994**	**1993**	**1992**	**1991**	**1990**
Tangible Bk. Val.	4.14	5.80	3.19	2.53	2.53	2.27	2.27	2.04	1.53	2.06
Cash Flow	1.02	1.51	0.69	0.31	0.44	0.26	0.43	0.47	0.28	0.46
Earnings	0.77	0.72	0.49	0.11	0.28	0.07	0.26	0.30	0.07	0.29
Dividends	0.11	0.09	0.07	0.06	0.05	0.04	0.03	Nil	0.06	0.05
Payout Ratio	14%	12%	15%	52%	16%	59%	11%	Nil	88%	18%
Cal. Yrs.	1998	1997	1996	1995	1994	1993	1992	1991	1990	1989
Prices - High	20¾	16	8	5½	4½	5½	5½	4⅛	5¼	5¾
- Low	6	7¼	4⅝	3½	3	3½	2¾	1¾	1 5/16	3⅞
P/E Ratio - High	27	22	16	49	16	82	21	14	73	20
- Low	8	10	9	31	11	52	11	6	17	13
Income Statement Analysis (Million $)										
Revs.	1,139	1,075	947	811	712	685	629	587	609	517
Oper. Inc.	166	146	110	89.9	71.6	65.9	66.0	56.0	44.6	63.3
Depr.	31.1	23.9	19.8	17.2	16.0	17.6	15.1	15.0	18.1	15.2
Int. Exp.	7.9	8.7	12.6	14.7	14.2	16.8	15.0	16.6	14.1	9.7
Pretax Inc.	130	124	80.3	28.4	36.0	8.4	32.3	35.0	10.6	38.5
Eff. Tax Rate	38%	37%	40%	65%	31%	29%	29%	25%	47%	34%
Net Inc.	80.4	78.0	48.2	10.1	24.9	5.9	23.0	26.3	6.6	25.5
Balance Sheet & Other Fin. Data (Million $)										
Cash	41.9	80.7	32.3	13.5	54.2	17.1	73.6	9.0	18.8	16.3
Curr. Assets	382	402	285	348	353	321	318	240	270	210
Total Assets	654	653	570	531	489	463	460	386	454	350
Curr. Liab.	130	122	110	101	85.0	92.0	93.0	80.0	141	72.0
LT Debt	96.0	114	111	180	154	145	147	107	142	93.0
Common Eqty.	404	393	323	227	225	201	200	177	155	180
Total Cap.	500	508	434	408	382	350	348	289	301	279
Cap. Exp.	78.1	50.1	36.8	22.1	17.5	21.7	12.6	6.2	62.2	32.6
Cash Flow	111	102	68.0	27.3	40.8	23.5	38.1	41.3	24.4	40.5
Curr. Ratio	2.9	3.3	2.6	3.5	4.1	3.5	3.4	3.0	1.9	2.9
% LT Debt of Cap.	19.2	22.4	25.6	44.1	40.4	41.5	42.3	37.0	47.3	33.2
% Net Inc.of Revs.	7.1	7.3	5.1	1.2	3.5	0.9	3.7	4.5	1.1	4.9
% Ret. on Assets	12.3	12.8	8.8	2.0	5.2	1.3	5.4	6.2	1.6	7.3
% Ret. on Equity	20.2	21.8	17.5	4.5	11.6	2.9	12.1	15.8	3.8	16.2

Data as orig. reptd.; bef. results of disc. opers. and/or spec. items. Per share data adj. for stk. divs. as of ex-div. date. Bold denotes diluted EPS (FASB 128). E-Estimated. NA-Not Available. NM-Not Meaningful. NR-Not Ranked.

Office—301 Commerce St.; Suite 600; Fort Worth, TX 76102. **Tel**—(817) 878-8000. **Website**—http://www.pier1.com **Chrmn & CEO**—M. J. Girouard. **VP & CFO**—C. Turner. **SVP & Secy**—J. R. Lawrence. **Dirs**—J. H. Burgoyne, M. R. Ferrari, M. J. Girouard, C. G. Gordon, J. M. Hoak, Jr., S. F. McKenzie, T. Thomas. **Transfer Agent**—Chase Mellon Shareholder Services LLC, New Jersey. **Incorporated**—in Georgia in 1978; reincorporated in Delaware in 1986. **Empl**— 12,600. **S&P Analyst:** Maureen C. Carini

STANDARD
&POOR'S
STOCK REPORTS

Pillowtex Corp.

NYSE Symbol **PTX**

In S&P SmallCap 600

23-OCT-99

Industry:
Textiles (Home Furnishings)

Summary: Pillowtex is a leading manufacturer and marketer of bed pillows, blankets, mattress pads, down comforters, comforter covers and other bedroom textile furnishings.

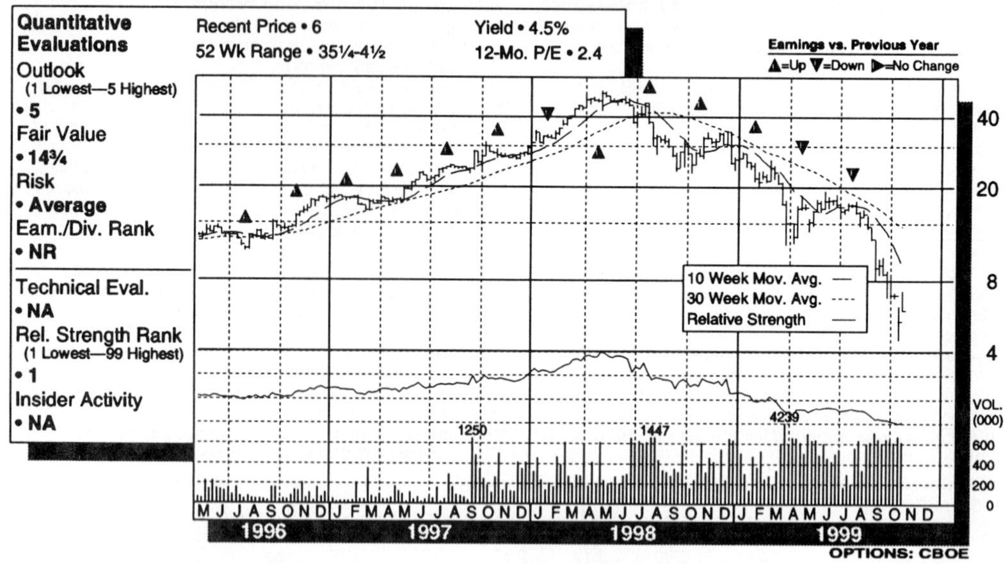

Business Profile - 14-OCT-99

In early September 1999, PTX announced that it expected to report lower than projected earnings for the second half of 1999, due to manufacturing disruptions from plant upgrades and system installations, lower gross margins, and higher sales and marketing expenses. As a result of lower projected earnings the company received a temporary waiver from its senior lending group for a potential covenant violation under its senior secured credit agreements in October 1999. The company believes that investments being made to improve its plant infrastructure will have a positive impact on profitability in 2000. PTX is also focused on improving its balance sheet by reducing inventory

Operational Review - 14-OCT-99

Sales in the six months ended July 3, 1999, advanced 4.7%, year to year, primarily reflecting the July 1998 acquisition of Leshner and higher sales of bath and bedding products. Gross margins narrowed on higher costs and unabsorbed overhead expenses related to system installations. Lower SG&A expenses and the absence of a $1.5 million restructuring charge in 1998 were more than offset by higher interest expense as pretax income dropped 8.1%. After taxes at 37.8% versus 39.5%, net income declined 5.5% to $12,026,000 ($0.71 a share, after preferred dividends), from $12,727,000 ($0.75).

Stock Performance - 22-OCT-99

In the past 30 trading days, PTX's shares have declined 43%, compared to a 4% fall in the S&P 500. Average trading volume for the past five days was 153,220 shares, compared with the 40-day moving average of 221,338 shares.

Key Stock Statistics

Dividend Rate/Share	0.24	Shareholders	300
Shs. outstg. (M)	14.2	Market cap. (B)	$0.076
Avg. daily vol. (M)	0.213	Inst. holdings	38%
Tang. Bk. Value/Share	NM		
Beta	1.17		

Value of $10,000 invested 5 years ago: $ 2,829

Fiscal Year Ending Dec. 31

	1999	1998	1997	1996	1995	1994
Revenues (Million $)						
1Q	368.5	366.4	113.8	100.8	94.74	71.82
2Q	362.5	332.1	104.9	91.19	90.79	66.58
3Q	—	419.8	152.0	143.8	146.8	102.0
4Q	—	391.6	209.4	154.9	142.6	111.5
Yr.	—	1,510	580.0	490.7	474.9	351.9
Earnings Per Share ($)						
1Q	**0.31**	**0.33**	**0.15**	**0.09**	0.11	0.20
2Q	**0.40**	**0.42**	**0.17**	**0.14**	0.10	0.12
3Q	—	**0.87**	**0.65**	**0.58**	0.45	0.32
4Q	—	**0.89**	**-0.22**	**0.52**	0.42	0.09
Yr.	—	**2.52**	**0.74**	**1.39**	**1.08**	**0.72**

Next earnings report expected: late October

Dividend Data (Dividends have been paid since 1995.)

Amount ($)	Date Decl.	Ex-Div. Date	Stock of Record	Payment Date
0.060	Nov. 10	Dec. 16	Dec. 18	Dec. 31 '98
0.060	Feb. 15	Mar. 10	Mar. 12	Mar. 31 '99
0.060	May. 05	Jun. 16	Jun. 18	Jun. 30 '99
0.060	Aug. 09	Sep. 15	Sep. 17	Sep. 30 '99

A Division of The McGraw-Hill Companies

Pillowtex Corporation

Business Summary - 14-OCT-99

Founded in 1954, Pillowtex Corporation (PTX) is one of the largest North American designers, manufacturers, and marketers of home textile products. In late 1997, the company acquired Fieldcrest Cannon (which was about twice the size of Pillowtex) for about $700 million in cash, stock, and assumed debt. Fieldcrest Cannon was one of the largest U.S. manufacturers of bath products and the third-largest U.S. producer of bedding products. The acquisition provided PTX with broader product lines that cover a wide range of price points and distribution channels, further enhancing its "one-stop-shopping" strategy to leading retail customers in the U.S. and Canada.

PTX has leading market positions in its four core product lines: blankets, bed pillows, down comforters and bath towels and a significant market share in each of the sheet, pillowcase, mattress pad, fashion bedding, bath rug and kitchen textile product segments. Its products are marketed to department and specialty stores, mass merchants, wholesale clubs, catalog retailers and institutions. The company's top ten customers accounted for approximately 61% of its total net sales in 1998. Wal-Mart Stores, Inc. accounted for approximately 24% of PTX's total net sales in 1998.

PTX manufactures and markets its products utilizing established and well-recognized company-owned brand names, including Royal Velvet, Cannon, Fieldcrest, Royal Family, Charisma, St. Mary's, Touch of Class, Royal Velvet Big & Soft, and Beacon. The company also currently has rights to make and, in some instances, market certain bedding products under the Ralph Lauren, Comforel, and Waverly brand names.

The company also operates retail outlet stores that sell certain PTX products directly to customers as a supplement to its primary distribution channels. These stores sell both first quality merchandise and seconds or "off-goods" at competitive retail prices.

PTX manufactures and distributes its products through an extensive network of facilities in Texas, Alabama, California, Georgia, Illinois, Mississippi, New York, North Carolina, Pennsylvania, South Carolina, Virginia and Toronto, Canada. This nationwide network enables the company to ship its products cost effectively to all major cities in North America.

In March 1998, PTX sold certain assets of Sure Fit, formerly Fieldcrest Cannon's ready-made furniture covering operation. The division was sold for $14 million plus the assumption of $3 million of trade payables. In July 1998, the company expanded its towels and kitchen terry products line with the acquisition of Leshner Corp., a marketer and manufacturer of bath and kitchen terry products.

In March 1999, PTX's board approved the repurchase of up to 1 million common shares.

Per Share Data ($) **(Year Ended Dec. 31)**	**1998**	**1997**	**1996**	**1995**	**1994**	**1993**	**1992**	**1991**	**1990**	**1989**
Tangible Bk. Val.	NM	4.45	4.04	3.41	2.43	5.11	5.00	NA	NA	NA
Cash Flow	5.37	2.18	2.59	2.21	1.33	1.69	1.15	NA	NA	NA
Earnings	2.52	0.74	1.39	1.08	0.73	1.32	0.84	NA	NA	NA
Dividends	0.24	0.24	0.20	0.05	Nil	Nil	NA	NA	NA	NA
Payout Ratio	10%	32%	14%	5%	Nil	Nil	NA	NA	NA	NA
Prices - High	52	35¼	18½	13⅛	21¼	20⅝	NA	NA	NA	NA
- Low	23⅛	15⅞	10⅝	8	8⅞	9	NA	NA	NA	NA
P/E Ratio - High	21	48	13	12	29	16	NA	NA	NA	NA
- Low	9	21	7	7	12	7	NA	NA	NA	NA
Income Statement Analysis (Million $)										
Revs.	1,510	580	491	475	352	292	273	NA	NA	NA
Oper. Inc.	198	58.3	50.9	48.5	24.8	27.9	20.6	NA	NA	NA
Depr.	54.0	16.1	12.8	12.0	6.4	3.6	3.1	NA	NA	NA
Int. Exp.	72.3	22.5	14.0	17.5	6.4	3.0	NA	NA	NA	NA
Pretax Inc.	70.2	13.8	24.2	19.0	12.4	21.2	NA	NA	NA	NA
Eff. Tax Rate	39%	40%	39%	40%	38%	39%	NA	NA	NA	NA
Net Inc.	42.9	8.2	14.7	11.5	7.7	12.9	8.4	NA	NA	NA
Balance Sheet & Other Fin. Data (Million $)										
Cash	5.6	4.6	0.0	0.4	0.6	2.6	NA	NA	NA	NA
Curr. Assets	707	641	222	186	185	124	NA	NA	NA	NA
Total Assets	1,654	1,410	376	325	320	181	130	NA	NA	NA
Curr. Liab.	259	246	71.2	75.7	62.3	45.6	NA	NA	NA	NA
LT Debt	944	785	195	153	177	63.7	52.4	NA	NA	NA
Common Eqty.	238	197	100	88.0	76.5	69.3	48.5	NA	NA	NA
Total Cap.	1,341	1,112	305	249	257	135	102	NA	NA	NA
Cap. Exp.	134	20.6	21.0	12.4	10.5	15.1	5.9	NA	NA	NA
Cash Flow	94.8	24.2	27.5	23.5	14.1	16.5	11.5	NA	NA	NA
Curr. Ratio	2.7	2.6	3.1	2.5	3.0	2.7	NA	NA	NA	NA
% LT Debt of Cap.	70.4	70.6	63.9	61.7	68.9	47.1	51.5	NA	NA	NA
% Net Inc.of Revs.	2.8	1.4	3.0	2.5	2.2	4.4	3.1	NA	NA	NA
% Ret. on Assets	2.8	0.9	4.2	3.6	3.1	6.5	NA	NA	NA	NA
% Ret. on Equity	18.8	5.5	15.6	14.0	10.5	31.6	NA	NA	NA	NA

Data as orig reptd.; bef. results of disc opers/spec. items. Per share data adj. for stk. divs. Bold denotes diluted EPS (FASB 128)-prior periods restated. E-Estimated. NA-Not Available. NM-Not Meaningful. NR-Not Ranked.

Office—4111 Mint Way, Dallas, TX 75237. **Tel**—(214) 333-3225. **Website**—http://www.pillowtex.com **Chrmn, Pres, COO & CEO**—C. M. Hansen Jr. **SVP Fin.**—J. Macaulay. **Investor Contact**—Katharine W. Kenny. **Dirs**—K.M. Finlay, P. G. Gillease, C. M. Hansen Jr., R. W. La Rovere, W. B. Madden, M. J. McHugh, M. A. Petricoff, M. R. Silverthorne, S. E. Shimizu. **Transfer Agent & Registrar**—ChaseMellon Shareholder Services, Ridgefield Park, NJ. **Incorporated**—in Illinois in 1954; reincorporated in Texas in 1986. **Empl**— 14,000. **S&P Analyst:** Howard Choe

STANDARD
&POOR'S
STOCK REPORTS

Pioneer Group

NASDAQ Symbol **PIOG**

In S&P SmallCap 600

09-OCT-99

Industry:
Financial (Diversified)

Summary: The Pioneer Group is engaged in global asset management, mutual fund distribution and servicing, and natural resources operations.

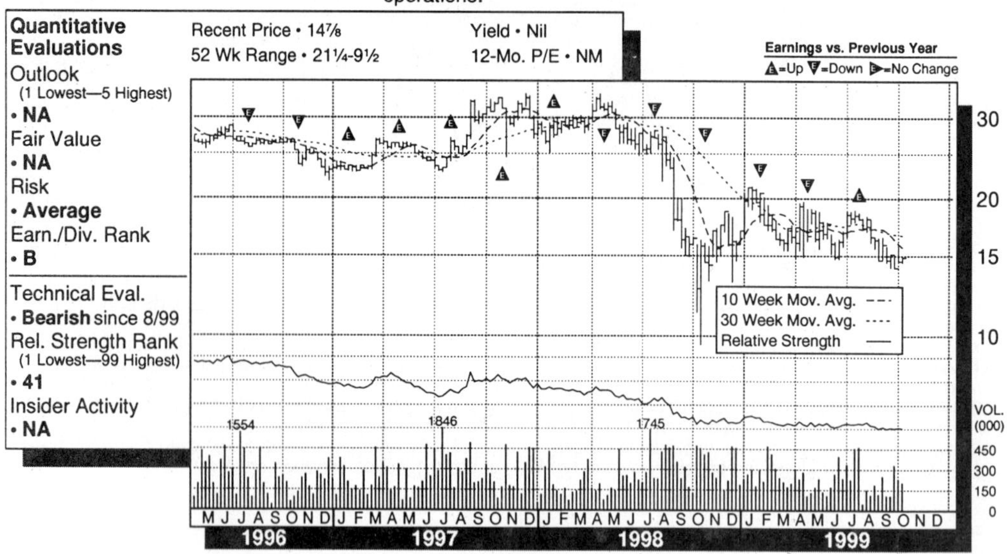

Business Profile - 08-OCT-99

In 1998, the company underwent a strategic review and restructuring program, and decided to reposition its assets and re-focus on its core capabilities of investment management and asset development. As a result, in March 1999, PIOG sold its domestic venture capital business for $34.9 million. In April 1999, it sold a 30% interest in its Polish pension company subsidiary to Nationwide Global Holdings, Inc., recognizing a gain of $12 million. In December 1998, the company sold its Russian banking operations, and it planned to close its brokerage in 1999. Finally, PIOG is preparing to divest its Ghanaian gold mine and powdered metals segment.

Operational Review - 08-OCT-99

Total income in the six months ended June 30, 1999, rose 2.1%, year to year, as higher shareholder services fees outweighed lower underwriting commissions and distribution fees. Costs and expenses declined 4.4%, on sharply reduced timber costs and expenses. Losses on venture capital and marketable securities investments, and substantial equity in losses of affiliated companies, contrasted with gains and income in 1998. After taxes at 164%, versus 54.3%, and minority interest, a loss of $2,781,000 ($0.11 a share) contrasted with income of $5,999,000 ($0.24). Per share results exclude losses from discontinued operations of $1.19 and $0.51 in the respective periods, and a charge of $0.47 in 1999 from the cumulative effect of an accounting change.

Stock Performance - 08-OCT-99

In the past 30 trading days, PIOG's shares have increased 1%, compared to a 0.91% fall in the S&P 500. Average trading volume for the past five days was 40,240 shares, compared with the 40-day moving average of 38,759 shares.

Key Stock Statistics

Dividend Rate/Share	Nil	Shareholders	5,000
Shs. outstg. (M)	26.4	Market cap. (B)	$0.393
Avg. daily vol. (M)	0.043	Inst. holdings	61%
Tang. Bk. Value/Share	4.09		
Beta	0.78		

Value of $10,000 invested 5 years ago: $ 12,387

Fiscal Year Ending Dec. 31

	1999	1998	1997	1996	1995	1994
Revenues (Million $)						
1Q	78.30	77.89	70.11	56.48	45.68	42.60
2Q	63.63	81.58	80.03	56.92	46.55	39.82
3Q	—	83.72	98.82	62.50	51.24	45.31
4Q	—	81.68	93.88	63.21	55.25	44.02
Yr.	—	324.9	343.0	239.1	198.7	171.7
Earnings Per Share ($)						
1Q	**-0.33**	**0.21**	**0.29**	**0.20**	0.23	0.31
2Q	**-0.01**	**-0.25**	**0.19**	**0.14**	0.29	0.27
3Q	—	**-0.63**	**0.37**	**0.20**	0.25	0.33
4Q	—	**-0.40**	**0.29**	**0.20**	0.13	0.25
Yr.	—	**-1.07**	**1.14**	**0.74**	**0.90**	1.16

Next earnings report expected: mid November

Dividend Data (Dividends have been paid since 1979.)

The company discontinued its dividend after the June 1998 payment of $0.10 a share.

The Pioneer Group, Inc.

Business Summary - 08-OCT-99

True to its name, The Pioneer Group has broken new ground with business ventures in many world regions. With interests ranging from mutual fund operations in Boston to asset management in the Czech Republic and timber harvesting and development in the Far East and Russia, PIOG is a global company, engaged in a wide variety of financial services and natural resource ventures.

The company offers investment management through 24 open-end mutual funds (comprised of 36 investment portfolios) and one close-end mutual fund, based in the U.S. PIOG also offers seven offshore open-end investment funds based in Ireland, available to non-U.S. investors. In addition, the company provides distribution and servicing for its mutual funds. PIOG also provides separate account management services for institutional investors. A bullish stock market and strong sales in the mutual fund industry boosted total assets under management to $23.4 billion at December 31, 1998, from $21.0 billion at year-end 1997. With management fees tied to the level of assets under management, the influx of funds helped investment management revenues increase 19% in 1998.

In international financial services, PIOG has distinguished itself by committing capital to international frontiers where it sees opportunity for growth. Such businesses include investment management and financial services operations in Warsaw, Poland, where the company manages four mutual funds, owns a majority interest in a brokerage operation, 100% of a unitholder servicing agent, and a private pension fund management company. In Prague, the Czech Republic, the company manages and distributes an open-end mutual fund. In Moscow, Russia, PIOG provides financial services, including transfer agency services, the management, servicing and distribution of shares of two open-end mutual funds, and also manages and owns 51% of the Pioneer First Investment Fund, a closed-end fund.

Asian operations include the 48%-ownership of an Indian investment advisor, distributor and shareholder servicing agent to 18 private sector mutual funds. The company also has a 10% interest in an investment management operation in Taiwan.

The global investment business unit includes PIOG's diversified businesses of timber, international venture capital and global real estate management and advisory services. A net loss in 1998, versus net income in 1997, reflected poor performance of emerging markets financial services operations. In response, the company has moved to divest some of its businesses, such as its Russian banking operations, a Ghanaian gold mine, and its interest in its domestic venture capital business.

Per Share Data ($) (Year Ended Dec. 31)	1998	1997	1996	1995	1994	1993	1992	1991	1990	1989
Tangible Bk. Val.	5.45	6.48	5.79	5.06	4.43	3.25	3.69	3.31	2.91	2.59
Earnings	-1.07	1.14	0.74	0.90	1.16	0.72	0.59	0.58	0.50	0.58
Dividends	0.20	0.40	0.40	0.40	0.32	0.23	0.21	0.20	0.20	0.20
Payout Ratio	NM	35%	54%	44%	27%	31%	36%	35%	40%	34%
Prices - High	33 7/8	33 7/8	30 1/2	29 5/8	25 3/8	13 1/2	7 3/8	6 3/8	7 1/8	6 1/4
- Low	9 1/2	22 3/4	21 3/4	17 3/4	12 3/8	7 1/8	5 1/8	4	3 3/4	4 1/2
P/E Ratio - High	NM	30	41	33	22	19	12	11	14	11
- Low	NM	20	29	20	11	10	9	7	7	8
Income Statement Analysis (Million $)										
Mgt. Fees	142	121	87.8	64.6	64.3	39.5	32.2	30.3	30.4	31.9
Gold Sales	77.3	89.5	78.3	90.2	67.6	59.2	43.8	23.2	Nil	Nil
Total Revs.	315	343	239	199	172	129	102	81.0	60.0	61.0
Int. Exp.	16.3	19.1	9.4	1.0	1.3	2.4	1.4	1.6	NA	NA
Net Bef. Taxes	-31.7	56.7	30.4	39.4	47.6	34.5	27.5	25.4	20.6	24.1
Eff. Tax Rate	NM	49%	38%	42%	30%	47%	47%	43%	41%	41%
Net Inc.	-27.0	29.2	18.8	22.8	29.0	18.1	14.6	14.4	12.3	14.1
Balance Sheet & Other Fin. Data (Million $)										
Total Assets	499	604	493	319	203	172	135	124	109	100
Cash Items	56.0	67.2	32.5	27.8	23.1	21.5	47.8	46.9	38.5	44.2
Rec.	51.2	56.8	43.2	31.9	22.0	20.2	9.2	8.4	4.5	8.8
Secs. Owned	Nil	38.3	27.5	7.6	6.5	15.8	9.2	5.4	4.9	1.3
Sec. Borrowed	Nil	Nil	15.6	56.1	13.6	6.0	4.5	4.8	4.3	1.8
Due Brokers & Cust.	Nil	Nil	9.0	12.4	7.1	7.9	2.8	3.2	1.3	5.0
Other Liabs.	39.4	Nil	78.4	44.5	33.2	35.0	21.0	13.3	8.2	8.8
Capitalization:										
Debt	133	168	150	11.0	9.1	13.3	12.0	17.1	20.3	17.3
Equity	155	184	162	150	134	107	93.0	85.0	75.0	67.0
Total	398	468	399	206	148	123	106	103	95.0	84.0
% Exp./Op. Revs.	119.6	84.4	88.7	80.5	72.3	73.1	74.4	73.4	67.0	59.9
% Return On Revs.	NA	8.5	7.9	11.5	16.9	14.0	14.3	17.8	20.4	23.3
% Ret. on Assets	NA	5.3	4.7	8.7	15.5	11.8	11.3	12.4	11.7	16.8
% Ret. on Equity	NA	16.9	12.0	16.0	24.1	18.1	16.4	18.1	17.3	22.9

Data as orig reptd.; bef. results of disc opers/spec. items. Per share data adj. for stk. divs. Bold denotes diluted EPS (FASB 128)-prior periods restated. E-Estimated. NA-Not Available. NM-Not Meaningful. NR-Not Ranked.

Office—60 State St., Boston, MA 02109. **Tel**—(617) 742-7825. **Website**—http://www.pioneerfunds.com **Chrmn & Pres**—J. F. Cogan, Jr. **Vice Chrmn**—A. J. Strassman. **EVP, CFO & Treas**—E. W. Reckard. **Secy**—J. P. Barri. **Dirs**—R. L. Butler, J. F. Cogan, Jr., M. Engleman, A. J. Strassman, J. S. Teja, D. D. Tripple, J. H. Valentine. **Transfer Agent**—State Street Bank and Trust Co., Boston. **Incorporated**—in Delaware in 1956. **Empl**— 3,300. **S&P Analyst:** Markos N. Kaminis

STANDARD
&POOR'S
STOCK REPORTS

Pioneer-Standard Electronics

NASDAQ Symbol **PIOS**

In S&P SmallCap 600

09-OCT-99 **Industry:** Electronics (Component Distributors)

Summary: Pioneer-Standard is one of the largest distributors of industrial and end-user electronic products in the U.S.

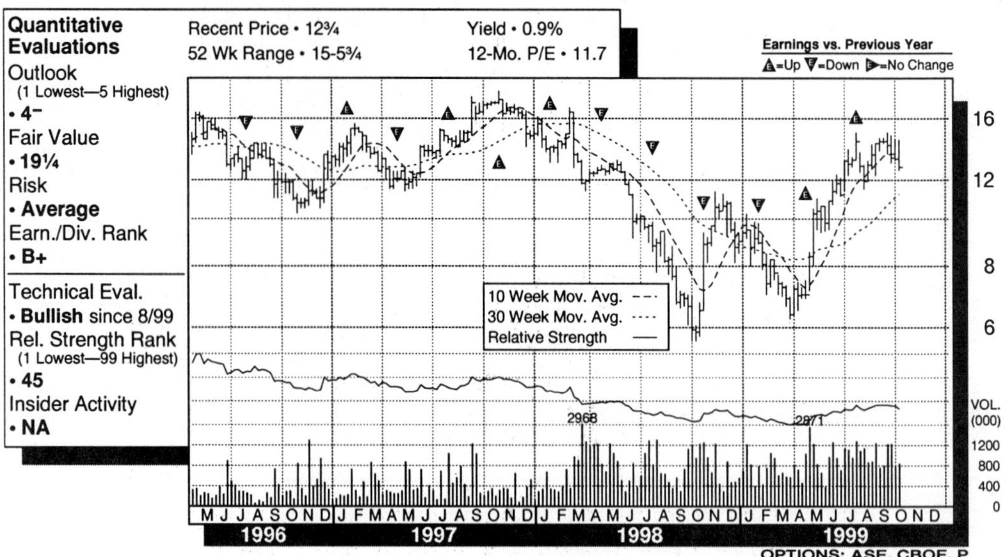

Business Profile - 03-AUG-99

Although it expects pressure on gross margins to continue throughout FY 00 (Mar.), PIOS believes that the semiconductor market is on the rebound. The company is starting to see extended lead times in several product categories, which is indicative that supply and demand are returning to more normal levels. PIOS is optimistic about the semiconductor market's recovery, as well as the outlook for the mid-range computer market. The company's goals include expanding its supplier and customer base, achieving further productivity gains, containing costs and delivering value-added services.

Operational Review - 03-AUG-99

In the first quarter of FY 00 (Mar.), revenues advanced 5.8%, year to year, reflecting increased demand in the communications and contract manufacturing market segments. Gross margins narrowed due to continued pricing pressures. However, operating expenses declined 2.1%, benefiting from tight cost controls; operating profit climbed 24%. After lower interest expense and following distributions on preferred securities, net income grew 38%, to $7,709,000 ($0.26 a share) from $5,579,000 ($0.20).

Stock Performance - 08-OCT-99

In the past 30 trading days, PIOS's shares have declined 11%, compared to a 0.91% fall in the S&P 500. Average trading volume for the past five days was 166,340 shares, compared with the 40-day moving average of 215,792 shares.

Key Stock Statistics

Dividend Rate/Share	0.12	Shareholders	2,962
Shs. outstg. (M)	27.1	Market cap. (B)	$0.345
Avg. daily vol. (M)	0.219	Inst. holdings	74%
Tang. Bk. Value/Share	3.76		
Beta	0.80		

Value of $10,000 invested 5 years ago: $ 16,133

Fiscal Year Ending Mar. 31

	2000	1999	1998	1997	1996	1995
Revenues (Million $)						
1Q	576.0	544.3	396.3	375.2	224.7	183.8
2Q	—	559.5	431.3	357.7	234.9	194.4
3Q	—	596.0	424.1	384.4	263.9	212.4
4Q	—	559.3	433.6	391.5	381.7	241.5
Yr.	—	2,259	1,685	1,509	1,105	832.1
Earnings Per Share ($)						
1Q	**0.26**	**0.20**	0.28	0.27	0.29	0.26
2Q	—	**0.22**	0.28	0.20	0.29	0.25
3Q	—	**0.30**	**0.31**	**0.24**	0.18	0.27
4Q	—	**0.31**	**0.27**	0.29	0.33	0.32
Yr.	—	**1.03**	**1.14**	**1.00**	1.09	1.09

Next earnings report expected: late October

Dividend Data (Dividends have been paid since 1965.)

Amount ($)	Date Decl.	Ex-Div. Date	Stock of Record	Payment Date
0.030	Dec. 23	Jan. 04	Jan. 06	Feb. 01 '99
0.030	Mar. 23	Apr. 06	Apr. 08	May. 01 '99
0.030	Jun. 23	Jul. 06	Jul. 08	Aug. 02 '99
0.030	Sep. 22	Oct. 04	Oct. 06	Nov. 01 '99

A Division of The McGraw-Hill Companies

STANDARD
&POOR'S
STOCK REPORTS

Pioneer-Standard Electronics, Inc.

09-OCT-99

Business Summary - 03-AUG-99

By aligning itself with some of the biggest names in the electronics and computer industries, Pioneer-Standard Electronics, Inc. (PIOS) has become one of the largest electronics distributors in North America. The company distributes a wide range of electronic components and computer products manufactured by other firms. The products are sold to value-added resellers, research laboratories, government agencies, and end users such as manufacturing companies.

The products the company offers are grouped into two categories: computer systems and industrial electronics. Computer systems accounted for 50% of sales in FY 99 (Mar.), versus 40% in FY 98 and 31% in FY 97. This category includes a wide variety of mid-range computer systems and high-end platforms, storage subsystems, software, servers, computers, display terminals and networking products. As a complement to this business, the company also provides value-added services including systems integration, enterprise resource planning, systems design and network consulting.

The industrial electronics segment accounted for 50% of total sales in FY 99, versus 60% in FY 98 and 69% in FY 97. This segment includes semiconductor products such as microprocessors, memory devices, programmable logic devices and analog and digital integrated circuits; and passive, interconnect and electromechanical products, which include capacitors, resistors, connectors, switches and power conditioning equipment. This segment also provides value-added services such as point of use inventory management, just-in-time kitting operations, turnkey assembly, memory and logic device programming, connector and cable assemblies to specifications and power products integration.

Pioneer distributes products supplied by over 100 manufacturers, including such well known companies as Compaq, Intel, IBM, Cisco Systems, Lucent Technologies, Micron Technology and 3Com Corp. However, products purchased from a relatively small number of suppliers account for a majority of Pioneer's sales. IBM, Compaq and Intel are the company's three largest suppliers, accounting for 25%, 29% and 19%, respectively, of total sales in FY 99.

In April 1998, the company acquired Dickens Data Systems for about $121 million, making the company a leading distributor of IBM computer systems, peripherals and services in North America. In April 1998, the company also purchased a minority interest in Eurodia Electron PLC, a European distributor of electronic components. In the third quarter of FY 98, the company purchased a minority interest in World Peace Industrial Co. Ltd. of Taiwan, an Asia-Pacific distributor of industrial electronic components.

Per Share Data ($) (Year Ended Mar. 31)	1999	1998	1997	1996	1995	1994	1993	1992	1991	1990
Tangible Bk. Val.	3.76	2.89	5.63	4.81	5.65	4.60	3.82	3.11	2.87	2.46
Cash Flow	1.51	1.69	1.63	1.48	1.37	1.10	0.85	0.51	0.64	0.47
Earnings	1.03	1.14	1.00	1.09	1.09	0.87	0.63	0.29	0.45	0.31
Dividends	0.12	0.12	0.12	0.11	0.08	0.07	0.05	0.05	0.04	0.04
Payout Ratio	12%	11%	12%	10%	7%	8%	8%	16%	10%	13%
Cal. Yrs.	1998	1997	1996	1995	1994	1993	1992	1991	1990	1989
Prices - High	16 7/8	18 1/4	16 1/2	19 1/4	13 1/8	11	8 1/8	5 1/4	4 1/2	3 3/8
- Low	5 5/8	11 3/8	10 1/4	10 5/8	8 1/4	5 3/8	3 1/8	2 5/8	2 1/8	2 1/8
P/E Ratio - High	16	16	16	18	12	13	13	18	10	11
- Low	5	10	10	10	8	6	5	9	5	7
Income Statement Analysis (Million $)										
Revs.	2,259	1,685	1,509	1,105	832	581	430	362	345	320
Oper. Inc.	108	87.9	72.0	61.0	50.0	36.7	25.7	16.5	20.9	16.8
Depr.	23.0	15.0	14.6	9.0	6.2	5.3	4.7	4.1	3.5	2.8
Int. Exp.	24.3	20.7	17.1	8.1	4.0	2.7	3.6	4.5	4.8	5.2
Pretax Inc.	54.8	52.1	40.3	43.6	42.2	31.7	20.0	8.5	13.4	9.5
Eff. Tax Rate	44%	41%	42%	42%	41%	38%	35%	38%	38%	40%
Net Inc.	30.8	30.5	23.3	25.3	25.0	19.7	12.9	5.3	8.3	5.7
Balance Sheet & Other Fin. Data (Million $)										
Cash	28.9	32.0	28.1	24.4	9.6	6.0	1.9	1.9	2.5	3.5
Curr. Assets	677	701	498	466	274	178	136	116	114	114
Total Assets	944	958	593	559	327	220	172	151	146	145
Curr. Liab.	201	239	200	185	142	93.0	64.8	47.1	47.8	49.7
LT Debt	313	336	174	164	56.3	22.3	21.3	44.7	44.3	49.4
Common Eqty.	272	245	214	151	126	105	84.1	57.5	52.9	44.8
Total Cap.	744	591	393	318	185	127	107	104	99	95.0
Cap. Exp.	22.1	44.2	20.0	21.0	11.3	7.6	4.2	5.1	4.1	10.3
Cash Flow	53.8	45.5	37.8	34.3	31.2	29.9	17.6	9.5	11.8	8.6
Curr. Ratio	3.4	2.9	2.5	2.5	1.9	1.9	2.1	2.5	2.4	2.3
% LT Debt of Cap.	42.1	56.9	44.2	51.8	30.4	17.5	19.9	43.1	45.0	51.8
% Net Inc.of Revs.	1.4	1.8	1.5	2.3	3.0	3.4	3.0	1.5	2.4	1.8
% Ret. on Assets	3.2	3.9	4.0	5.7	9.1	10.0	7.3	3.6	5.7	4.1
% Ret. on Equity	11.9	13.3	12.8	18.2	21.8	20.9	16.9	9.6	16.9	13.6

Data as orig reptd.; bef. results of disc opers/spec. items. Per share data adj. for stk. divs. Bold denotes diluted EPS (FASB 128)-prior periods restated. E-Estimated. NA-Not Available. NM-Not Meaningful. NR-Not Ranked.

Office—4800 East 131st St., Cleveland, OH 44105. **Tel**—(216) 587-3600. **Website**—http://www.pios.com **Chrmn & CEO**—J. L. Bayman. **Pres & COO**—A. Rhein. **SVP & CFO**—G. T. Geswein. **Secy**—W. A. Papenbrock. **VP, Treas, Asst Secy & Investor Contact**—John V. Goodger. **Dirs**—J. L. Bayman, C. F. Christ, F. A. Downey, V. Gelb, G. E. Heffern, A. Rhein, E. Z. Singer, T. C. Sullivan, K. E. Ware. **Transfer Agent & Registrar**—National City Bank, Cleveland. **Incorporated**—in Ohio in 1963. **Empl**— 2,440. **S&P Analyst:** Jim Corridore

Pittston BAX Group

NYSE Symbol **PZX**

In S&P SmallCap 600

09-OCT-99 **Industry:** Air Freight

Summary: Pittston BAX Group (formerly Pittston Burlington Group) Common Stock tracks Pittston Co.'s BAX Global unit, which provides air and ocean freight forwarding and logistics services.

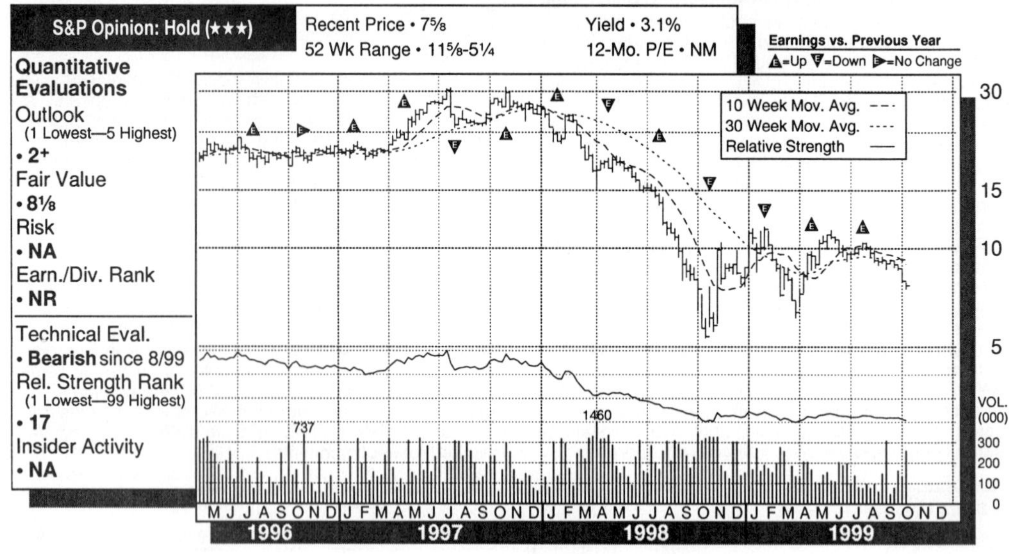

Overview - 01-SEP-99

Revenues could increase 12% in 1999, up from a 6.9% gain posted in 1998. Comparisons will benefit from the acquisition of Air Transport International, and the conversion of Asia offices from agency to company-owned status. Volume could increase 6%, versus a 3.8% gain in 1998. The strongest volume growth will be on the international side, as the high-tech sector boosts shipments from Asia, and PZX garners a larger share of the aerospace and automotive market in Europe. Buoying growth will be new contracts with Harris Semiconductor and Motorola. In North America, volumes could slip, despite new contracts with Amdahl Corp. and Philips Electronics, as PZX loses business to truckers. North American yields will rise, as the company emphasizes premium, overnight services. Comparisons will benefit from the absence of a 1998 charge of $1.47 a share to write off software costs and bad debts, and add to employee severance reserves.

Valuation - 01-SEP-99

The shares of this air freight company have been building a base since late 1998. PZX looks to be on the right track, after costs spun out of control in 1998. A new management team that was installed in the second half of 1998 chopped back an aggressive information technology upgrade program; this was accompanied by a charge of $1.47 a share. Management is shifting the company's focus to international markets, where volume growth remains healthy, and is trying to lift margins in North America by pursuing higher yielding overnight shipments. The stock, trading recently at P/E ratio 35% below that of its peers, and at a price to EBITDA ratio half that of other air freight companies, is undeniably cheap. However, we are maintaining a neutral position, since investors will continue to avoid PZX until it can deliver consistent profit performance.

Key Stock Statistics

S&P EPS Est. 1999	0.95	Tang. Bk. Value/Share	5.87
P/E on S&P Est. 1999	8.1	Beta	NA
S&P EPS Est. 2000	1.20	Shareholders	5,400
Dividend Rate/Share	0.24	Market cap. (B)	$0.160
Shs. outstg. (M)	20.8	Inst. holdings	69%
Avg. daily vol. (M)	0.031		

Value of $10,000 invested 5 years ago: NA

Fiscal Year Ending Dec. 31

	1999	1998	1997	1996	1995	1994
Revenues (Million $)						
1Q	460.3	402.4	371.4	351.9	323.9	261.5
2Q	419.7	432.9	399.6	363.4	342.0	302.3
3Q	—	460.9	439.4	377.7	365.8	311.9
4Q	—	480.8	448.0	407.3	383.1	339.6
Yr.	—	1,777	1,662	1,500	1,415	1,215
Earnings Per Share ($)						
1Q	**0.02**	**-0.15**	0.26	0.20	0.21	0.18
2Q	**0.16**	**0.05**	-0.10	0.46	0.42	0.61
3Q	**E0.40**	**-1.13**	0.82	0.56	0.56	0.71
4Q	**E0.37**	0.56	**0.66**	0.55	0.54	0.53
Yr.	**E0.95**	**-0.68**	**1.62**	**1.76**	**1.68**	2.03

Next earnings report expected: late October

Dividend Data (Dividends have been paid since 1996.)

Amount ($)	Date Decl.	Ex-Div. Date	Stock of Record	Payment Date
0.060	Nov. 06	Nov. 12	Nov. 16	Dec. 01 '98
0.060	Feb. 05	Feb. 11	Feb. 16	Mar. 01 '99
0.060	May. 07	May. 13	May. 17	Jun. 01 '99
0.060	Jul. 08	Aug. 12	Aug. 16	Sep. 01 '99

A Division of The McGraw-Hill Companies

Pittston BAX Group Common Stock

Business Summary - 01-SEP-99

Pittston BAX Group Common Stock (formerly Pittston Burlington Group Common Stock) was created in January 1996 to track the results of Pittston Co.'s BAX Global unit. It specializes in the movement of heavy air cargo (over 70 lbs.), using an integrated network of aircraft and ground vehicles. In recent years, international operations have grown faster than its domestic business, and now account for 35% of revenues. PZX's profit performance has been erratic in recent years, in part because of lack of control over its aircraft fleet. The company addressed this issue through the purchase of Air Transport International in April 1998, for $29 million.

In 1998, BAX Global moved 5,238,000 shipments weighing 1.62 billion lbs. The average yield per lb. in 1998 was 94.1 cents. In 1997, it moved 5,798,000 shipments, weighing 1.56 billion lbs. and yielding 95.7 cents per pound.

BAX Global offers one of the few fully integrated networks of air and ground transportation. In North America, it controls a fleet of 43 aircraft. Internationally, it buys space on commercial passenger airlines and is considered an air forwarder. In both markets, it consolidates the freight of various customers into shipments for common destinations, and arranges for door-to-door transportation of the freight.

In North American air freight markets (65% of total revenues in 1998), the company's fleet of 36 leased and seven owned aircraft gives it a competitive edge over several thousand domestic air forwarders. Pickup and delivery is carried out primarily by independent contractors. Until 1998, PZX did not operate any aircraft directly. Consequently, it was unable to deliver consistent service. To correct this problem, PZX acquired Air Transport International (ATI) in 1998, for $29 million.

In recent years, shippers have diverted heavy domestic, non-expedited business from PZX to lower-cost motor carriers. PZX typically charged a premium for deferred delivery, although these shipments primarily moved by ground. The company is now targeting higher value overnight freight. In mid-1998, it introduced Emergency Response, a guaranteed, overnight delivery service.

International markets accounted for 35% of revenues in 1998, with Europe providing 51% and Asia 49%. PZX, which has 500 offices in 121 nations, has started to convert its agencies to company-owned stations. In early 1999, it bought control of its Taiwanese agent; terms were not disclosed.

In 1998, PZX incurred $36 million of unusual costs, including $16 million to terminate or rescope certain information technology projects; $13 million to increase provisions on existing accounts receivable and $7 million of severance costs. In 1997, it incurred $12.5 million pretax of consulting costs related to the redesign of its organizational structure.

Per Share Data ($) (Year Ended Dec. 31)	1998	1997	1996	1995	1994	1993	1992	1991	1990	1989
Tangible Bk. Val.	5.87	7.31	6.14	3.84	2.89	0.83	NA	NA	NA	NA
Cash Flow	1.16	3.11	2.98	2.78	2.94	1.63	0.96	NA	NA	NA
Earnings	-0.68	1.62	1.76	1.73	2.03	0.84	0.18	NA	NA	NA
Dividends	0.24	0.24	0.24	NA	NA	NA	NA	NA	NA	NA
Payout Ratio	NM	15%	14%	NA	NA	NA	NA	NA	NA	NA
Prices - High	25 7/8	31	21 5/8	NA	NA	NA	NA	NA	NA	NA
- Low	5 1/4	18 1/2	17	NA	NA	NA	NA	NA	NA	NA
P/E Ratio - High	NM	19	12	NA	NA	NA	NA	NA	NA	NA
- Low	NM	11	10	NA	NA	NA	NA	NA	NA	NA
Income Statement Analysis (Million $)										
Revs.	1,777	1,662	1,500	1,415	1,215	998	900	NA	NA	NA
Oper. Inc.	40.6	83.8	79.1	71.1	81.9	48.6	26.1	NA	NA	NA
Depr.	35.5	29.9	23.4	20.0	17.3	15.4	14.5	NA	NA	NA
Int. Exp.	8.2	5.2	4.1	5.1	3.9	6.1	3.5	NA	NA	NA
Pretax Inc.	-16.4	51.3	53.5	51.6	61.2	27.9	8.6	NA	NA	NA
Eff. Tax Rate	NM	37%	37%	36%	37%	45%	61%	NA	NA	NA
Net Inc.	-13.1	32.3	33.8	32.9	38.4	15.5	3.3	NA	NA	NA
Balance Sheet & Other Fin. Data (Million $)										
Cash	30.7	28.8	17.8	25.8	18.4	13.3	NA	NA	NA	NA
Curr. Assets	338	355	283	278	251	176	NA	NA	NA	NA
Total Assets	775	701	616	572	522	432	NA	NA	NA	NA
Curr. Liab.	346	312	259	254	219	172	NA	NA	NA	NA
LT Debt	98.2	37.0	28.7	26.7	41.9	45.5	NA	NA	NA	NA
Common Eqty.	300	324	305	272	241	203	NA	NA	NA	NA
Total Cap.	400	362	349	309	284	250	NA	NA	NA	NA
Cap. Exp.	75.8	31.1	61.3	32.4	24.0	28.4	6.7	NA	NA	NA
Cash Flow	22.4	62.3	57.2	52.8	55.7	30.9	17.8	NA	NA	NA
Curr. Ratio	1.0	1.1	1.1	1.1	1.1	1.0	NA	NA	NA	NA
% LT Debt of Cap.	24.5	10.2	8.2	8.7	14.7	18.2	NA	NA	NA	NA
% Net Inc.of Revs.	NM	1.9	2.3	2.3	3.2	1.6	0.4	NA	NA	NA
% Ret. on Assets	NM	4.8	5.7	6.0	8.0	3.6	NA	NA	NA	NA
% Ret. on Equity	NM	6.3	11.7	12.8	17.3	8.1	NA	NA	NA	NA

Data as orig reptd.; bef. results of disc opers/spec. items. Per share data adj. for stk. divs. Bold denotes diluted EPS (FASB 128)-prior periods restated. E-Estimated. NA-Not Available. NM-Not Meaningful. NR-Not Ranked.

Office—1000 Virginia Center Parkway, P.O. Box 4229, Glen Allen, VA 23058-4229. **Tel**—(804) 553-3600. **Fax**—(804) 553-3753. **Website**—http://www.baxglobal.com **Chrmn**—M. T. Dan. **Pres & CEO**—C. R. Campbell. **Vice Chrmn**—D. L. Marshall. **VP & Secy**—A. F. Reed. **VP & CFO** —D. Crowley. **Investor Contact** —Burt Traub. **Dirs**—R. G. Ackerman, J. R. Barker, M. C. Breslawsky, J. L. Broadhead, W. F. Craig, M. T. Dan, G. Grinstein, R. M. Gross, R. H. Spilman, A. H. Zimmerman. **Transfer Agent & Registrar**—BankBoston NA. **Incorporated**—in Delaware in 1930; reincorporated in Virginia in 1986. **Empl**— 7,600. **S&P Analyst:** Stephen R. Klein

STANDARD
&POOR'S
STOCK REPORTS

Plains Resources

ASE Symbol **PLX**

In S&P SmallCap 600

09-OCT-99

Industry: Oil & Gas (Exploration & Production)

Summary: This exploration and production company is also engaged in midstream activities through majority-owned Plains All American Pipeline, L.P.

Quantitative Evaluations

Outlook (1 Lowest—5 Highest)
• **NA**

Fair Value
• **NA**

Risk
• **Average**

Earn./Div. Rank
• **C**

Technical Eval.
• **Bearish** since 9/99

Rel. Strength Rank (1 Lowest—99 Highest)
• **33**

Insider Activity
• **NA**

Recent Price • 17
52 Wk Range • 20⅛-8⅛
Yield • Nil
12-Mo. P/E • NM

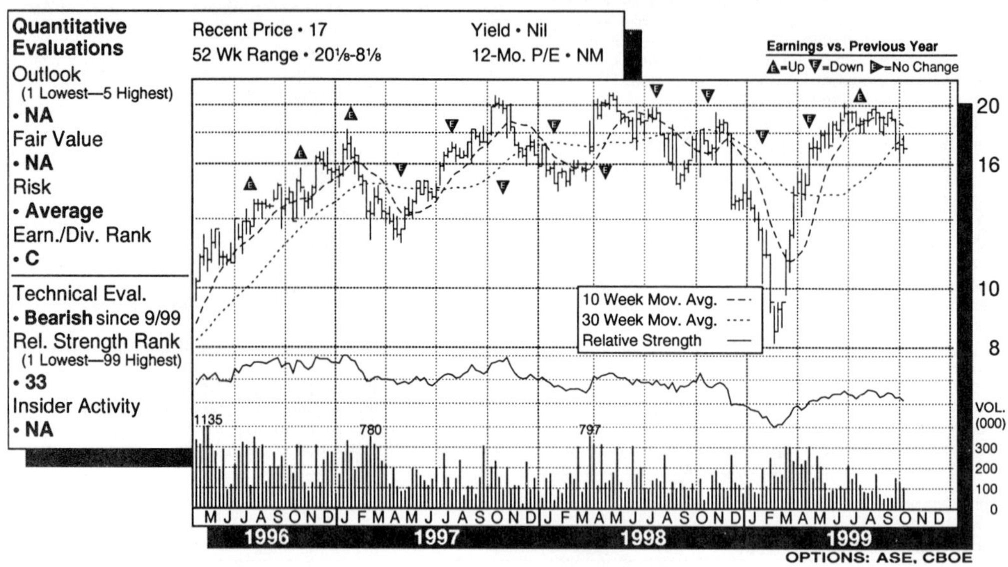

OPTIONS: ASE, CBOE

Business Profile - 07-OCT-99

In May 1999, majority-owned Plains All American Pipeline, L.P., which owns and operates a 1,233 mile crude oil pipeline, acquired Scurlock Permian LLC for $141 million in cash. Scurlock is one of the largest U.S. gatherers and marketers of crude oil. The transaction was accretive to cash flow and earnings in the second quarter, and is expected to continue to provide significant economic synergies, both in terms of cost savings and in value creation. In September, the company sold $75 million of senior subordinated notes due 2006; proceeds were to be used to reduce the balance outstanding under a revolving credit facility. In October, Plains All American signed an underwriting agreement for the issuance of 2.6 million common units at $18 per unit; proceeds would be used to repay $44 million of debt.

Operational Review - 07-OCT-99

Total revenues and expenses in the six months ended June 30, 1999, advanced 255%, year to year, reflecting marketing, transportation, storage and terminalling activities, due to the inclusion of Scurlock Permian and Plains All American Pipeline (both acquired subsequent to the 1998 period). After taxes at 39.0% versus 37.8%, and significantly higher cumulative preferred stock dividends, the gain in net income was held to 3.4%, to $2.3 million ($0.13 a share, diluted), from $2.2 million ($0.12).

Stock Performance - 08-OCT-99

In the past 30 trading days, PLX's shares have declined 6%, compared to a 0.91% fall in the S&P 500. Average trading volume for the past five days was 20,480 shares, compared with the 40-day moving average of 19,954 shares.

Key Stock Statistics

Dividend Rate/Share	Nil	Shareholders	1,409
Shs. outstg. (M)	17.0	Market cap. (B)	$0.288
Avg. daily vol. (M)	0.022	Inst. holdings	82%
Tang. Bk. Value/Share	6.98		
Beta	0.66		

Value of $10,000 invested 5 years ago: $ 26,153

Fiscal Year Ending Dec. 31

	1999	1998	1997	1996	1995	1994
Revenues (Million $)						
1Q	477.0	193.6	207.1	123.5	93.65	50.58
2Q	887.3	189.4	188.6	155.9	95.26	67.20
3Q	—	393.7	220.7	169.3	103.6	66.22
4Q	—	517.4	245.9	180.9	111.7	72.69
Yr.	—	1,294	862.2	629.6	404.2	256.7
Earnings Per Share ($)						
1Q	**0.01**	**0.06**	**0.22**	**0.54**	0.03	-0.10
2Q	**0.11**	**0.06**	**0.18**	**0.26**	0.03	0.06
3Q	—	**0.10**	**0.15**	**0.20**	0.03	0.02
4Q	—	**-4.00**	**0.23**	**0.24**	0.06	0.07
Yr.	—	**-3.77**	**0.77**	**1.23**	**0.16**	**0.04**

Next earnings report expected: late October

Dividend Data

No cash has been paid on the common. A one-for-five reverse stock split was effected in 1990.

A Division of The McGraw-Hill Companies

Plains Resources Inc.

Business Summary - 07-OCT-99

Plains Resources (PLX) acquires, exploits, develops, explores for and produces (upstream activities) crude oil and natural gas. Majority-owned Plains All American Pipeline, L.P. (PAA) is engaged in the midstream activities of marketing, pipeline transportation, terminalling and storage of crude oil. Upstream operations contributed 58% of 1998 operating income, with midstream contributing the remaining 42%.

At December 31, 1998, proved reserves consisted of 134,674 barrels of oil equivalent (BOE), versus 161,685 BOE a year earlier. The decrease reflected downward revisions related to much lower oil prices. The present value of proved reserves fell from $511 million to $227 million. Average daily production in 1998 rose to 22,100 BOE, from 20,200 BOE in 1997. Oil accounts for about 90% of the company's reserves and production. The average sales price in 1998 was $12.73 per BOE, versus $14.83 per BOE; production costs increased from $6.16, to $6.29. Upstream operations are concentrated in California, Florida and Illinois.

PAA owns and operates the All American Pipeline, a 1,233 mile common carrier crude oil pipeline extending from California to West Texas, and also owns a 45 mile crude oil gathering system in the San Joaquin Valley of California. As a common carrier, All American offers transportation services to shippers of crude oil pursuant to tariff rates established by the Federal Energy Regulatory Commission. In a November 1998 IPO, PAA sold 13.1 million shares. Plains All American Pipeline Inc., a wholly owned subsidiary of PLX, and PAA's general partner, holds a 57% interest in PAA.

Production transported on the All American Pipeline originates from the Exxon-operated Santa Ynez field, the Chevron-operated Point Arguello field, both offshore California, and the San Joaquin Valley. Deliveries from the pipeline are made to refineries located along the Gulf Coast and to the Cushing Interchange, the largest crude oil trading hub in the U.S. and the designated delivery point for NYMEX crude oil futures contracts. All American has currently configured throughput capacity of 216,000 bbl. per day of heavy crude oil; average daily deliveries during the second half of 1998 were 163,000 bbl. Unlike the All American Pipeline, PAA's San Joaquin Valley gathering system transports only oil purchased by entities owned by PAA, and does not transport for third parties.

In May 1999, PAA acquired Scurlock Permian LLC for $141 million in cash. Scurlock is one of the largest U.S. gatherers and marketers of crude oil, operating in 14 states via 2,400 miles of active pipelines, numerous storage terminals, and a fleet of 225 trucks. In July, a West Texas oil pipeline was acquired for $37 million. In addition, PLX acquired Chevron's 26% interest in the Point Arguello field for an undisclosed amount.

Per Share Data ($) (Year Ended Dec. 31)	1998	1997	1996	1995	1994	1993	1992	1991	1990	1989
Tangible Bk. Val.	3.02	6.73	5.79	4.76	3.97	3.83	5.58	3.67	4.54	4.49
Cash Flow	-1.92	2.08	2.46	1.42	1.45	-0.38	0.78	-0.71	0.85	1.25
Earnings	-3.77	0.77	1.22	0.16	0.04	-1.77	-0.32	-1.59	-0.36	-0.10
Dividends	Nil	Nil	Nil	Nil	Nil	Nil	Nil	Nil	Nil	Nil
Payout Ratio	Nil	Nil	Nil	Nil	Nil	Nil	Nil	Nil	Nil	Nil
Prices - High	21	20 3/4	17	11	8	13 1/8	21 3/4	30 3/4	8 3/8	7 3/4
- Low	13 3/8	11 7/8	7 3/8	5 1/2	5 3/8	6 3/8	7 1/2	4 7/8	5 3/8	3 1/8
P/E Ratio - High	NM	27	14	69	NM	NM	NM	NM	NM	NM
- Low	NM	15	6	34	NM	NM	NM	NM	NM	NM
Income Statement Analysis (Million $)										
Revs.	1,232	862	629	404	256	186	132	79.3	44.0	17.4
Oper. Inc.	79.5	68.1	60.7	33.0	29.2	4.4	13.6	-2.6	8.8	7.4
Depr. Depl. & Amort.	31.0	23.8	21.9	17.0	16.3	16.1	11.6	7.2	7.7	5.8
Int. Exp.	35.7	22.0	17.3	13.6	15.3	11.5	5.0	3.8	4.0	3.9
Pretax Inc.	-99.5	22.6	17.8	2.7	0.6	-20.2	-3.3	-12.8	-2.2	0.4
Eff. Tax Rate	NM	37%	NM	Nil	Nil	NM	NM	NM	NM	48%
Net Inc.	-58.6	14.3	21.7	2.7	0.6	-20.2	-3.3	-12.9	-2.2	0.2
Balance Sheet & Other Fin. Data (Million $)										
Cash	6.5	3.7	2.5	6.1	2.8	4.9	25.1	3.4	2.4	2.4
Curr. Assets	179	127	102	63.6	41.7	35.1	46.3	16.7	11.8	6.6
Total Assets	974	557	430	352	267	237	199	96.8	94.8	69.3
Curr. Liab.	193	133	107	68.3	46.2	49.1	33.3	20.1	22.4	12.4
LT Debt	432	283	225	205	145	136	100	42.2	36.5	28.8
Common Eqty.	51.0	113	95.6	77.0	46.0	44.3	62.6	33.3	33.0	22.4
Total Cap.	767	396	321	282	212	181	163	76.3	70.8	52.9
Cap. Exp.	NA	110	55.6	72.3	41.7	84.1	78.4	33.9	29.2	22.3
Cash Flow	-32.3	37.9	43.6	19.7	16.9	-4.3	8.2	-5.8	5.4	5.3
Curr. Ratio	0.9	1.0	1.0	0.9	0.9	0.7	1.4	0.8	0.5	0.5
% LT Debt of Cap.	56.3	71.5	70.1	72.7	68.3	75.1	61.2	55.3	51.5	54.5
% Ret. on Assets	NM	2.9	5.5	1.0	0.2	NM	NM	NM	NM	0.2
% Ret. on Equity	NM	13.5	25.1	4.4	1.3	NM	NM	NM	NM	NM

Data as orig. reptd.; bef. results of disc. opers. and/or spec. items. Per share data adj. for stk. divs. as of ex-div. date. Bold denotes diluted EPS (FASB 128). E-Estimated. NA-Not Available. NM-Not Meaningful. NR-Not Ranked.

Office—500 Dallas St., Suite 1500, Houston, TX 77002. **Tel**—(713) 654-1414. **Chrmn**—D. M. Krausse. **Pres & CEO**—G. L. Armstrong. **EVP, CFO, Treas & Investor Contact**—Phillip D. Kramer. **VP & Secy**—M. R. Patterson. **Dirs**—G. L. Armstrong, J. L. Dees, T. H. Delimitros, W. M. Hitchcock, D. M. Krausse, J. H. Lollar, R. V. Sinnott, J. T. Symonds. **Transfer Agent & Registrar**—American Stock Transfer & Trust, NYC. **Incorporated**—in Delaware in 1976. **Empl**— 370. **S&P Analyst:** Ephraim Juskowicz

STANDARD
&POOR'S
STOCK REPORTS

Plantronics, Inc.

NYSE Symbol **PLT**

In S&P SmallCap 600

09-OCT-99

Industry:
Communications Equipment

Summary: PLT, the world's largest manufacturer of lightweight telephone headsets, also supplies lightweight telephone headset accessories and services.

S&P Opinion: Hold (★★★)

Recent Price • 50⅞
52 Wk Range • 87½-43⅛
Yield • Nil
12-Mo. P/E • 16.0

Quantitative Evaluations

Outlook
(1 Lowest—5 Highest)
• **3⁻**

Fair Value
• **61¼**

Risk
• **Average**

Earn./Div. Rank
• **NR**

Technical Eval.
• **Neutral** since 9/99

Rel. Strength Rank
(1 Lowest—99 Highest)
• **25**

Insider Activity
• **Neutral**

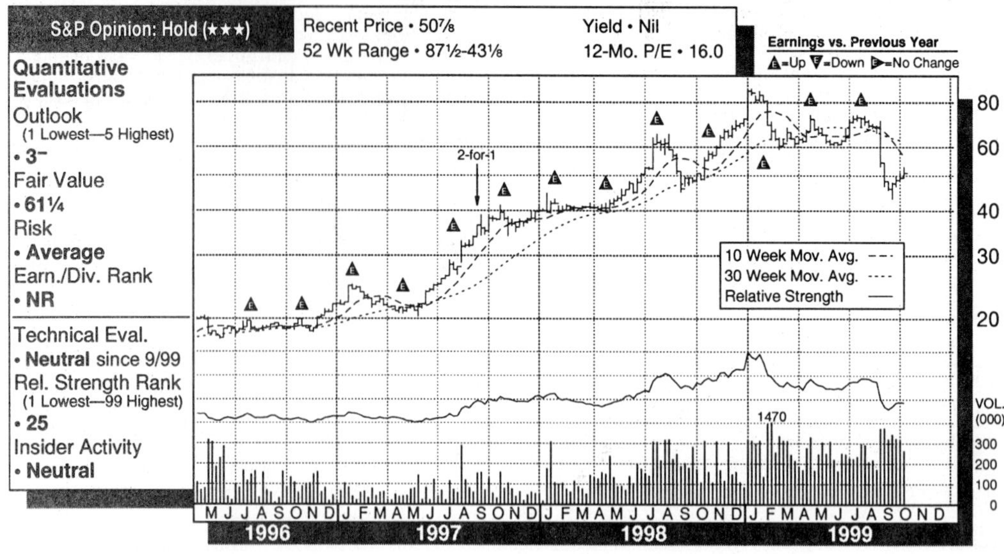

Overview - 20-SEP-99

We expect revenues to grow about 5% in FY 2000 (Mar.), well below the 20% top line growth experienced in recent years. We attribute the deceleration in sales growth to a dramatic change in buying patterns at PLT's largest original equipment manufacturer (OEM) customer, as well as to difficult comparisons in the call center division. We expect these challenges to persist over the next six months, followed by revenue growth of nearly 15% in FY 01. Despite the disappointing near-term sales outlook, long-term trends are solid, as demand for headsets will be driven by the expanding office market and rapid growth in the mobile/cellular unit. We expect margins to continue to widen for the foreseeable future, reflecting component cost savings. In addition, the bottom line will be aided by continuing share repurchases. We currently see FY 2000 EPS rising 19%, to $3.59, and forecast FY 01 EPS of $4.34.

Valuation - 20-SEP-99

The shares plunged in late August 1999, when management said the company would not meet analyst expectations for FY 2000. The shares were recently trading at 11X our calendar 2000 EPS estimate of $4.15, representing a discount both to the company's long-term growth rate and to the P/E of the overall market. Nevertheless, we believe this seemingly attractive valuation is justified, as the near-term revenue outlook is uncertain. As a result, we have initiated coverage of the stock with a hold recommendation. Although PLT's long-term outlook is favorable, we would like to see management deliver on its forecasts before we consider upgrading the shares. For the near-term, we believe the stock will be supported by share repurchases and PLT's clean balance sheet. In the future, we believe the company will benefit from its industry-leading position and solid growth prospects in several business units.

Key Stock Statistics

S&P EPS Est. 2000	3.59	Tang. Bk. Value/Share	5.91
P/E on S&P Est. 2000	14.2	Beta	0.86
S&P EPS Est. 2001	4.34	Shareholders	80
Dividend Rate/Share	Nil	Market cap. (B)	$0.850
Shs. outstg. (M)	16.7	Inst. holdings	91%
Avg. daily vol. (M)	0.106		

Value of $10,000 invested 5 years ago: NA

Fiscal Year Ending Mar. 31

	2000	1999	1998	1997	1996	1995
Revenues (Million $)						
1Q	74.72	70.06	54.02	45.58	44.11	43.69
2Q	—	71.15	56.54	47.12	45.18	42.03
3Q	—	72.04	62.02	50.31	46.57	42.09
4Q	—	73.01	63.53	52.29	47.11	42.11
Yr.	—	286.3	236.1	195.3	183.0	169.9
Earnings Per Share ($)						
1Q	**0.85**	**0.68**	0.47	0.36	0.32	0.30
2Q	**E0.83**	**0.74**	0.51	0.41	0.35	0.32
3Q	**E0.90**	**0.79**	**0.57**	0.45	0.37	0.30
4Q	**E1.01**	**0.81**	**0.61**	0.46	0.38	0.27
Yr.	**E3.59**	**3.02**	**2.15**	**1.67**	**1.42**	1.19

Next earnings report expected: mid October

Dividend Data

No cash dividends have been paid.

A Division of The McGraw-Hill Companies

Plantronics, Inc.

Business Summary - 20-SEP-99

Plantronics is a leading designer, manufacturer and marketer of lightweight communications headsets and headset accessories and services. In addition, the company manufactures and markets specialty telephone products, such as amplified telephone handsets and specialty telephones for hearing-impaired users, and noise-canceling handsets for use in high-noise environments.

PLT believes its headsets, which can be worn over the head, in the ear, or on either ear, are recognized in the industry for their safety, quality, and reliability. PLT headset products are used worldwide by call center users, such as telemarketing personnel, reservation agents, telephone operators and air traffic controllers, whose occupations involve the constant use of a telephone or communications console.

In North America and Europe, the number of call center users has grown significantly over the 10 years through FY 99 (Mar.). The use of headsets by call center users has become an industry standard. While PLT believes the number of call center users in these geographic markets will continue to grow, it expect the primary source of future sales in this market segment to be repeat sales to existing customers, including the replacement of products presently in use with new and improved products.

The company has well developed distribution channels in North America and Europe, where growth of telemarketing activities and deregulation of the telephone companies have led to more widespread use of telephone headsets. PLT headsets are also becoming more widely used in the Middle East, Africa, Australia, the Far East, and Latin America. The potential for growth in the foreign market segments is the result of such developments as the rapid expansion of the telecommunications infrastructure and increasing worldwide use of telemarketing techniques.

PLT also sells headsets in the business and home office user market segment, which it has identified as an area of long-term growth potential. Users in this market segment consist of business executives, agents, brokers, lawyers, accountants, home office business people and other professionals whose occupations may require intensive, but not constant, use of a telephone.

The business and home office user market segment can be divided into users who attach their headsets to telephones, cellular telephones or to computers. The use of headsets for mobile communications and as computer peripherals is a significant growth area for headset sales. Potential applications in this market segment include mobile communications, voice recognition, personal computer conferencing, computer telephony integration, and multimedia applications.

Per Share Data ($)										
(Year Ended Mar. 31)	**1999**	**1998**	**1997**	**1996**	**1995**	**1994**	**1993**	**1992**	**1991**	**1990**
Tangible Bk. Val.	5.91	3.45	1.33	0.09	-1.50	-2.84	-3.58	NA	NA	NA
Cash Flow	3.28	2.38	1.83	1.55	1.29	-3.12	0.51	NA	NA	NA
Earnings	3.02	2.15	1.67	1.42	1.19	-3.27	0.24	NA	NA	NA
Dividends	Nil	Nil	Nil	Nil	Nil	Nil	NA	NA	NA	NA
Payout Ratio	Nil	Nil	Nil	Nil	Nil	Nil	NA	NA	NA	NA
Cal. Yrs.	1998	1997	1996	1995	1994	1993	1992	1991	1990	1989
Prices - High	87	41 3/8	22 1/2	19	16 1/8	4 5/8	NA	NA	NA	NA
- Low	39 1/4	20 1/4	15 1/2	11	7 1/4	2 3/8	NA	NA	NA	NA
P/E Ratio - High	29	19	13	13	14	NM	NA	NA	NA	NA
- Low	13	9	9	8	6	NM	NA	NA	NA	NA
Income Statement Analysis (Million $)										
Revs.	286	236	195	183	170	134	112	NA	NA	NA
Oper. Inc.	88.3	66.0	53.3	50.0	44.9	34.7	25.6	NA	NA	NA
Depr.	4.7	3.6	2.9	2.4	1.8	1.9	4.8	NA	NA	NA
Int. Exp.	5.8	7.0	7.1	7.1	8.0	22.4	9.7	NA	NA	NA
Pretax Inc.	81.3	57.6	45.0	41.8	35.3	-37.7	7.9	NA	NA	NA
Eff. Tax Rate	32%	32%	34%	39%	41%	NM	46%	NA	NA	NA
Net Inc.	55.3	39.2	29.7	25.5	20.8	-40.7	4.3	NA	NA	NA
Balance Sheet & Other Fin. Data (Million $)										
Cash	43.0	64.9	42.3	26.8	3.4	8.5	4.0	NA	NA	NA
Curr. Assets	120	140	103	89.7	56.4	49.0	42.5	NA	NA	NA
Total Assets	143	165	127	109	75.0	67.0	61.2	NA	NA	NA
Curr. Liab.	43.4	41.3	39.7	41.1	33.2	27.4	28.8	NA	NA	NA
LT Debt	Nil	65.1	65.1	65.0	65.0	85.0	85.0	NA	NA	NA
Common Eqty.	89.4	53.4	20.9	1.4	-24.7	-46.5	-53.7	NA	NA	NA
Total Cap.	99	124	87.5	66.5	41.6	39.7	32.4	NA	NA	NA
Cap. Exp.	3.8	NA	8.2	3.9	3.6	2.2	NA	NA	NA	NA
Cash Flow	60.0	42.8	32.6	27.8	22.6	-40.0	9.1	NA	NA	NA
Curr. Ratio	2.8	3.4	2.6	2.2	1.7	1.8	1.5	NA	NA	NA
% LT Debt of Cap.	Nil	52.4	74.4	97.9	156.3	214.3	262.6	NA	NA	NA
% Net Inc.of Revs.	19.3	16.6	15.3	13.9	12.2	NM	3.8	NA	NA	NA
% Ret. on Assets	35.8	26.8	25.2	27.8	29.3	NM	NA	NA	NA	NA
% Ret. on Equity	77.4	105.5	NM	NM	NM	NM	NA	NA	NA	NA

Data as orig reptd.; bef. results of disc opers/spec. items. Per share data adj. for stk. divs. Bold denotes diluted EPS (FASB 128)-prior periods restated. E-Estimated. NA-Not Available. NM-Not Meaningful. NR-Not Ranked.

Office—345 Encinal St., Santa Cruz, CA 95060. **Tel**—(831) 426-5858. **Fax**—(831) 426-6098. **Website**—http://www.plantronics.com **Chrmn**—M. Tseu. **Pres & CEO**—S. K. Kannappan. **SVP-Fin & CFO**—B. V. Scherer. **VP-Secy**—J. A. Knutson. **Investor Relations**—(800-544-4660). **Dirs**—S. K. Kannappan, R. F. B. Logan, M. S. Muqaddam, J. M. O'Mara, T. C. Taylor, M. Tseu, D. A. Wegmann. **Transfer Agent & Registrar**—First National Bank of Boston. **Incorporated**—in Delaware in 1988. **Empl**— 1,824. **S&P Analyst:** Stephen J. Tekirian

STANDARD &POOR'S STOCK REPORTS

Players International

NASDAQ Symbol **PLAY**

In S&P SmallCap 600

09-OCT-99

Industry: Gaming, Lottery & Pari-mutuel Cos.

Summary: Directors of this casino operator have approved a merger with Jackpot Enterprises Inc., under which PLAY shareholders would receive $8.25 per share in cash and common stock.

Quantitative Evaluations

Outlook (1 Lowest—5 Highest) • **3**

Fair Value • **8**

Risk • **High**

Earn./Div. Rank • **B-**

Technical Eval. • **Neutral** since 9/99

Rel. Strength Rank (1 Lowest—99 Highest) • **72**

Insider Activity • **NA**

Recent Price • 7⅜

52 Wk Range • 8-3¼

Yield • Nil

12-Mo. P/E • NM

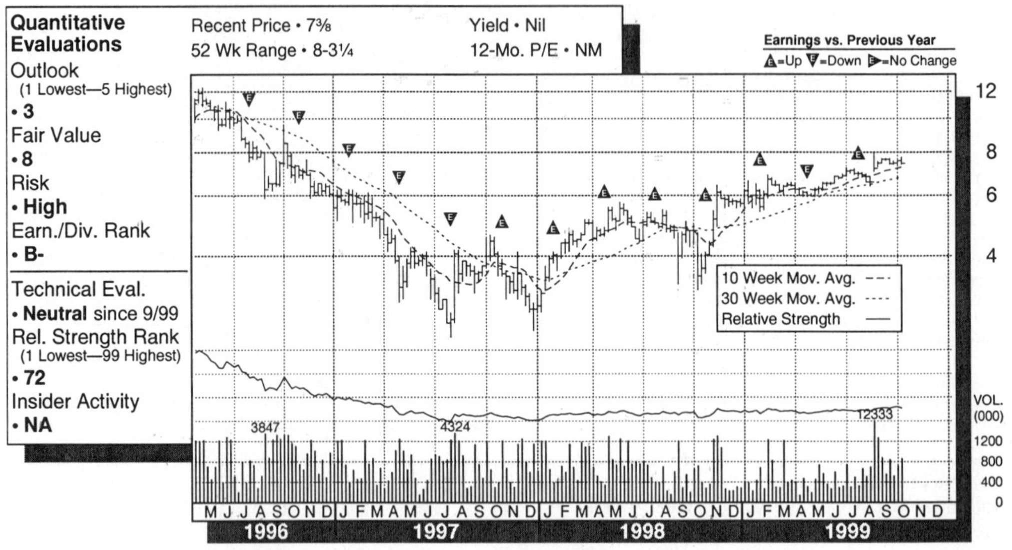

Business Profile - 04-MAY-99

In February 1999, the company agreed to be acquired by Jackpot Enterprises Inc. (NYSE: J) for $8.25 per share, consisting of $6.75 per share in cash and $1.50 in Jackpot common stock for each share of PLAY common stock. Closure of the merger, which has been approved by directors of both companies, is subject to approval by shareholders as well as all necessary regulatory approvals and financing. The merger is expected to be completed in the second half of 1999.

Operational Review - 04-MAY-99

Revenues in the nine months ended December 31, 1998, rose 3.2%, year to year, primarily reflecting gains at the Maryland Heights facility (opened March 11, 1997), which outweighed decreased revenue from the Lake Charles facility. Corporate development and other expenses fell 57%, reflecting the absence of legal and consulting costs incurred in the year-earlier period. With profitable operations at the Maryland Heights facility, in contrast to losses experienced in the 1997 period, and cost reductions at the Lake Charles facility, net income surged 172%, to $7,008,000, ($0.22 a share, on 2.5% more shares), from $2,579,000 ($0.08).

Stock Performance - 08-OCT-99

In the past 30 trading days, PLAY's shares have declined 0.20%, compared to a 0.91% fall in the S&P 500. Average trading volume for the past five days was 170,740 shares, compared with the 40-day moving average of 478,074 shares.

Key Stock Statistics

Dividend Rate/Share	Nil	Shareholders	549
Shs. outstg. (M)	32.0	Market cap. (B)	$0.238
Avg. daily vol. (M)	0.146	Inst. holdings	41%
Tang. Bk. Value/Share	4.01		
Beta	1.06		

Value of $10,000 invested 5 years ago: $ 4,498

Fiscal Year Ending Mar. 31

	2000	1999	1998	1997	1996	1995
Revenues (Million $)						
1Q	84.05	81.57	84.18	79.61	65.61	48.33
2Q	—	87.25	82.56	74.41	80.30	58.86
3Q	—	81.77	75.97	64.85	72.73	58.67
4Q	—	80.49	80.51	72.34	72.76	57.85
Yr.	—	331.1	323.2	291.2	291.4	223.7
Earnings Per Share ($)						
1Q	**0.10**	**0.08**	0.01	0.15	0.25	0.34
2Q	—	**0.11**	0.07	-0.12	0.22	0.43
3Q	—	**0.04**	**0.01**	-0.05	0.10	0.37
4Q	—	**-0.17**	**-0.02**	-1.49	0.13	0.33
Yr.	—	**0.05**	**0.06**	**-1.56**	0.70	1.47

Next earnings report expected: late October

Dividend Data

No cash dividends have been paid. The company intends to retain earnings to finance the operation and expansion of its business. A three-for-two stock split was effected in May 1995. A shareholder rights plan was adopted in January 1997.

Players International, Inc.

Business Summary - 04-MAY-99

Players International, Inc. (PLAY) owns and operates riverboat gaming and entertainment facilities. These include one riverboat casino in Metropolis, IL, two riverboat casinos in Lake Charles, LA, and two contiguous, permanently moored, dockside riverboat casinos in Maryland Heights, MO. The company operated a land-based casino in Mesquite, NV, until June 30, 1997. PLAY also owns and operates racetrack in Paducah, KY, which it plans to operate as a harness racetrack beginning in FY 99 (Mar.). In early 1999, the company agreed to be acquired by Jackpot Enterprises for $8.25 a share in cash and stock.

PLAY's marketing strategy focuses on middle-income patrons who live within a 150 mile radius of each of its facilities. The company employs database and on-site marketing, and bus programs. PLAY targets gaming customers through frequent mailings promoting visits to its casino facilities. In addition, it employs on-site marketing techniques, including the use of player tracking systems, slot clubs, and preferred player hosts to identify and service patrons.

The Metropolis, IL, riverboat facility, which began operations in February 1993, is the only riverboat casino operating in southern Illinois. The facility offers a four deck historical replica of a paddlewheel riverboat, and features a fully equipped, Las Vegas style casino that offers about 22,000 sq. ft. of gaming space. The casino is equipped with 900 slot machines and 50 table games, for a total of about 1,200 gaming positions.

The Lake Charles facility includes the Players Lake Charles Riverboat and the Star Riverboat, two riverboat casinos that share a common docking site. The riverboats operate staggered three-hour cruises up to 24 hours a day. The facility features the Players Hotel, a company owned land based 134-room hotel with meeting and entertainment space. In January 1998, the company acquired a 269 room hotel formerly operated as the Lake Charles Holiday Inn, for $19.2 million.

In March 1997, the company and Harrah's opened a riverboat casino entertainment facility in Maryland Heights, MO, offering four permanently moored, dockside riverboat casinos totaling approximately 120,000 sq. ft. of gaming space. The Maryland Heights casinos feature a topical island theme with lush foliage, waterfalls and rockscape.

Per Share Data ($) (Year Ended Mar. 31)	1999	1998	1997	1996	1995	1994	1993	1992	1991	1990
Tangible Bk. Val.	3.84	3.84	3.75	5.36	4.62	4.26	NA	NA	NA	NA
Cash Flow	0.66	0.71	-0.82	1.24	1.67	0.73	-0.30	NA	NA	NA
Earnings	0.05	0.06	-1.56	0.70	1.47	0.60	-0.32	-0.35	NA	NA
Dividends	Nil	Nil	Nil	Nil	Nil	Nil	Nil	Nil	NA	NA
Payout Ratio	Nil	Nil	Nil	Nil	Nil	Nil	Nil	Nil	NA	NA
Cal. Yrs.	1998	1997	1996	1995	1994	1993	1992	1991	1990	1989
Prices - High	6³/₈	6¹/₄	12³/₈	23	19⁷/₈	18³/₈	4³/₈	3¹/₄	NA	NA
- Low	3	2⁵/₁₆	5	10³/₈	9⁵/₈	4¹/₈	1¹/₄	1¹/₄	NA	NA
P/E Ratio - High	NM	NM	NM	33	14	30	NM	NM	NA	NA
- Low	NM	NM	NM	15	7	7	NM	NM	NA	NA
Income Statement Analysis (Million $)										
Revs.	331	323	291	291	224	107	5.7	NA	NA	NA
Oper. Inc.	54.8	57.8	41.2	61.1	77.6	30.6	-3.7	NA	NA	NA
Depr.	19.7	20.8	21.8	17.2	7.1	3.7	0.2	NA	NA	NA
Int. Exp.	21.6	24.1	16.0	14.7	0.7	0.9	0.3	NA	NA	NA
Pretax Inc.	3.1	3.1	-71.8	36.6	73.5	27.7	-4.1	NA	NA	NA
Eff. Tax Rate	50%	38%	NM	39%	38%	37%	NM	NA	NA	NA
Net Inc.	1.6	2.0	-46.3	22.3	45.8	17.5	-4.1	NA	NA	NA
Balance Sheet & Other Fin. Data (Million $)										
Cash	25.7	17.2	20.6	23.2	50.3	77.5	NA	NA	NA	NA
Curr. Assets	36.2	33.1	67.6	41.6	61.6	83.5	NA	NA	NA	NA
Total Assets	389	410	421	413	224	139	NA	NA	NA	NA
Curr. Liab.	54.9	39.2	51.9	39.7	39.3	16.1	NA	NA	NA	NA
LT Debt	155	181	188	153	5.5	5.7	NA	NA	NA	NA
Common Eqty.	160	158	156	194	176	116	NA	NA	NA	NA
Total Cap.	318	342	343	347	182	122	NA	NA	NA	NA
Cap. Exp.	9.4	40.2	46.5	147	62.4	33.8	5.2	NA	NA	NA
Cash Flow	21.3	22.8	-24.5	39.6	52.8	21.2	-3.9	NA	NA	NA
Curr. Ratio	0.7	0.8	1.3	1.1	1.6	5.2	NA	NA	NA	NA
% LT Debt of Cap.	48.8	52.9	54.8	44.1	3.0	4.7	NA	NA	NA	NA
% Net Inc.of Revs.	0.1	0.6	NM	7.7	20.5	16.3	NM	NA	NA	NA
% Ret. on Assets	0.0	0.5	NM	7.0	25.1	12.6	NA	NA	NA	NA
% Ret. on Equity	1.0	1.2	NM	12.1	31.3	15.1	NA	NA	NA	NA

Data as orig reptd.; bef. results of disc opers/spec. items. Per share data adj. for stk. divs. Bold denotes diluted EPS (FASB 128)-prior periods restated. E-Estimated. NA-Not Available. NM-Not Meaningful. NR-Not Ranked.

Office—1300 Atlantic Ave., Suite 800, Atlantic City, NJ 08401. **Tel**—(609) 449-7777. **Chrmn**—E. Fishman. **Pres & CEO**—H. Goldberg. **EVP & COO**—J. F. Groom. **CFO**—R. A. Spera. **Dirs**— A. R. Buggy, L. Cohen, E. Fishman, M. S. Geller, H. Goldberg, J. Groom, C. M. Masson, V. J. Naimoli, L. Seidler, E. E. Webb. **Transfer Agent & Registrar**—Interwest Transfer, Salt Lake City, UT. **Incorporated**—in Nevada in 1985. **Empl**—3,700. **S&P Analyst:** J.J.A.

STANDARD
&POOR'S
STOCK REPORTS

Plexus Corp.

NASDAQ Symbol **PLXS**

In S&P SmallCap 600

09-OCT-99 **Industry:** Electrical Equipment

Summary: This company provides contract design, manufacturing and testing of electronic products.

Quantitative Evaluations

Outlook (1 Lowest—5 Highest) • **4−**

Fair Value • **44**

Risk • **High**

Earn./Div. Rank • **B+**

Technical Eval. • **Bearish** since 9/99

Rel. Strength Rank (1 Lowest—99 Highest) • **28**

Insider Activity • **NA**

Recent Price • 27⅞
52 Wk Range • 40¼-18¼
Yield • Nil
12-Mo. P/E • 18.6

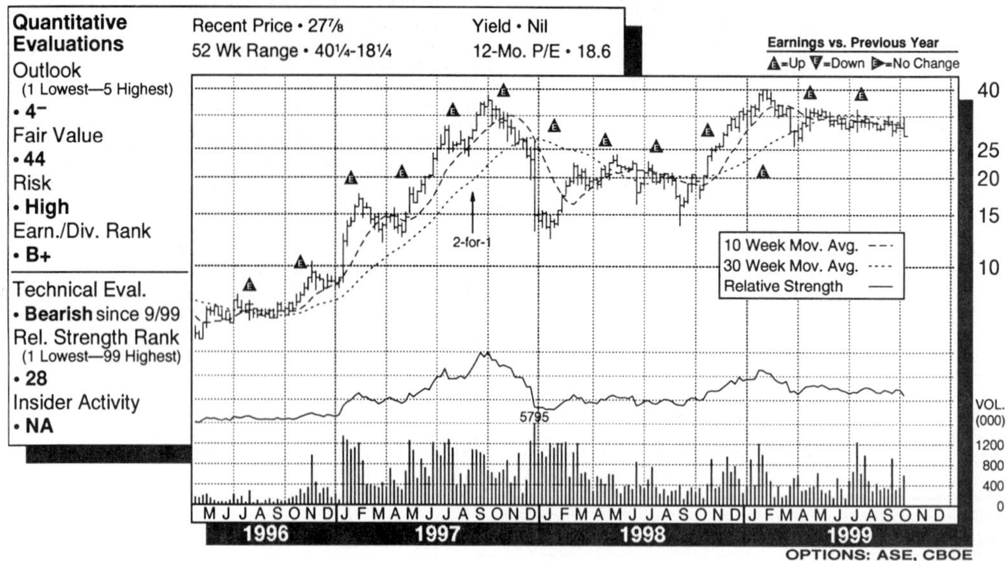

Business Profile - 25-AUG-99

Plexus expects accelerated top line growth to result from its July 1999 acquisition of SeaMED Corp., a manufacturer of durable electronic medical instruments. In July 1999, the company agreed to acquire a manufacturing facility from Shure, Inc., and will take over production of circuit boards for that company. PLXS is focusing on expanding its engineering activities, to enhance its product development and manufacturing pipelines. This should help shift the company's business mix toward more complex products. The strategy worked in the first nine months of FY 99 (Sep.), contributing to wider gross margins. Margin improvement in recent quarters was also aided by initiatives undertaken to enhance profitability, including work force and fixed cost reductions.

Operational Review - 25-AUG-99

In the first nine months of FY 99, sales advanced 6.4%, year to year, as strong unit volume growth outweighed the impact of industry-wide pressure on selling prices, higher component prices, and a company decision to move toward higher technology business. Gross margins widened to 14.5% of sales, from 12.1%, on improved operating efficiencies, lower fixed costs, higher capacity utilization, an improved product mix, and a more aggressive procurement program. Despite 20% higher SG&A expense, net income soared 37%, to $18,228,000 ($1.12 a share), from $13,285,000 ($0.83).

Stock Performance - 08-OCT-99

In the past 30 trading days, PLXS's shares have declined 6%, compared to a 0.91% fall in the S&P 500. Average trading volume for the past five days was 117,500 shares, compared with the 40-day moving average of 91,508 shares.

Key Stock Statistics

Dividend Rate/Share	Nil	Shareholders	900
Shs. outstg. (M)	17.5	Market cap. (B)	$0.488
Avg. daily vol. (M)	0.108	Inst. holdings	41%
Tang. Bk. Value/Share	7.50		
Beta	2.13		

Value of $10,000 invested 5 years ago: $ 36,557

Fiscal Year Ending Sep. 30

	1999	1998	1997	1996	1995	1994
Revenues (Million $)						
1Q	101.7	95.91	87.37	71.31	65.34	55.94
2Q	103.4	97.69	96.75	75.29	69.38	61.32
3Q	105.6	98.56	99.1	86.07	72.35	55.00
4Q	—	104.7	103.2	83.46	76.06	70.21
Yr.	—	396.8	386.4	316.1	283.1	242.5
Earnings Per Share ($)						
1Q	**0.36**	**0.23**	**0.19**	0.06	0.07	0.06
2Q	**0.38**	**0.28**	0.24	0.06	0.10	0.08
3Q	**0.39**	**0.33**	0.28	0.18	0.13	0.03
4Q	—	**0.38**	0.34	0.23	0.15	0.08
Yr.	—	**1.21**	**1.05**	0.52	0.45	0.23

Next earnings report expected: late October

Dividend Data

No cash dividends have been paid. A poison pill shareholder rights plan was adopted in August 1998.

A Division of The McGraw-Hill Companies 

Plexus Corp.

Business Summary - 25-AUG-99

Plexus Corp., a contract provider of design, manufacturing and testing services to the electronics industry, believes its growth in recent years has been significantly aided by its approach to partnering with customers through product design and development services. It plans to continue to leverage this part of its services, to achieve continued sales growth. The company is also focusing on maintaining and expanding its gross margins.

Plexus offers a full range of services including product development, design, material procurement and management, functional and in-circuit testing, incorporating the system into a final product housing, and distribution for printed circuit boards as well as full box-build. It also makes test equipment used for testing customers' products. Services are provided to OEMs in the computer (primarily high-end server and peripheral products), medical, industrial, telecommunications and transportation/automotive electronics industries.

The Technology Group, Inc. subsidiary designs electronic systems, including printed circuit boards and the arrangement of electronic components, and the development and/or programming of the application software necessary to control the functions of those components.

Manufacturing of electronic products and assemblies is offered through the Electronics Assembly Corp. subsidiary. Contract manufacturing services are provided on either a turnkey basis, where the company procures certain or all of the materials required for production, or on a consignment basis, where the customer supplies some or all of the materials. Turnkey manufacturing currently account for almost all sales. Variations in the mix between turnkey and consignment causes fluctuations in gross margins.

For the assembly process, Plexus purchases electronic components such as memory chips, microprocessing units, integrated circuits, resistors, capacitors, and related items from various manufacturers and distributors. Any shortages or delays in component procurement have a serious negative impact on revenues and earnings.

During FY 98 (Sep.), services were sold to about 120 customers, including GE, which accounted for 11% of total sales (GE was the only customer that provided over 10% of sales).

In July 1999, PLXS acquired SeaMED Corp., a leading designer and manufacturer of advanced durable electronic medical equipment, in exchange for about 2.4 million common shares. The company said the acquisition significantly increased its overall engineering capabilities, and strengthened its presence in the medical market.

Per Share Data ($) (Year Ended Sep. 30)	1998	1997	1996	1995	1994	1993	1992	1991	1990	1989
Tangible Bk. Val.	6.04	4.59	3.15	2.63	2.69	1.93	1.79	1.33	1.04	0.92
Cash Flow	1.63	1.37	0.80	0.63	0.46	0.40	0.59	0.46	0.28	0.41
Earnings	1.21	1.08	0.52	0.45	0.23	0.20	0.40	0.29	0.13	0.23
Dividends	Nil	Nil	Nil	Nil	Nil	Nil	Nil	Nil	Nil	Nil
Payout Ratio	Nil	Nil	Nil	Nil	Nil	Nil	Nil	Nil	Nil	Nil
Prices - High	34 3/4	38 1/4	10 3/8	9 1/2	9	9 3/8	11 1/8	6 5/8	2 5/8	3 1/4
- Low	12 3/8	8 3/8	5 5/8	4 1/4	4	5 1/4	6 1/8	1 3/8	1 7/16	1 1/2
P/E Ratio - High	29	35	20	21	39	47	28	23	21	14
- Low	10	8	11	10	17	26	15	5	12	6
Income Statement Analysis (Million $)										
Revs.	397	386	316	283	242	160	157	120	79.0	78.0
Oper. Inc.	37.5	31.3	17.7	15.6	11.0	8.9	11.9	9.5	5.7	8.1
Depr.	6.6	4.5	3.6	3.3	3.1	2.6	2.4	2.0	1.8	2.1
Int. Exp.	0.0	0.8	1.9	2.5	3.1	1.8	1.4	1.9	1.6	1.6
Pretax Inc.	31.7	27.1	12.3	10.2	4.9	4.1	8.2	5.8	2.5	4.7
Eff. Tax Rate	39%	39%	40%	39%	38%	38%	39%	37%	38%	38%
Net Inc.	19.2	16.4	7.4	6.3	3.1	2.6	5.0	3.6	1.6	2.9
Balance Sheet & Other Fin. Data (Million $)										
Cash	23.2	3.7	1.9	3.6	1.1	0.8	0.9	0.3	1.3	0.8
Curr. Assets	121	103	94.8	103	109	74.9	49.8	41.3	31.2	25.2
Total Assets	144	122	107	115	122	95.1	62.7	54.5	43.4	36.5
Curr. Liab.	53.0	49.5	43.3	31.6	46.0	29.7	18.5	17.9	13.7	10.2
LT Debt	0.2	3.5	15.3	41.7	40.7	40.1	20.5	19.7	16.4	14.5
Common Eqty.	89.3	67.6	48.0	41.0	34.8	24.8	23.1	16.6	13.0	11.3
Total Cap.	90.2	72.1	64.0	83.4	76.0	65.5	44.2	36.7	29.7	26.3
Cap. Exp.	9.4	10.7	4.1	2.1	5.3	8.2	2.0	3.4	2.7	1.2
Cash Flow	25.8	20.5	11.1	9.0	6.1	5.1	7.5	5.7	3.4	5.0
Curr. Ratio	2.3	2.1	2.2	3.3	2.4	2.5	2.7	2.3	2.3	2.5
% LT Debt of Cap.	0.2	4.8	23.9	50.0	53.5	61.2	46.3	53.8	55.1	55.1
% Net Inc.of Revs.	4.8	4.2	2.4	2.2	1.3	1.6	3.2	3.0	2.0	3.7
% Ret. on Assets	14.5	14.3	6.7	5.4	2.8	3.3	8.5	7.4	3.9	8.4
% Ret. on Equity	24.5	27.8	16.7	16.7	10.1	10.7	25.0	24.6	12.9	27.6

Data as orig reptd.; bef. results of disc opers/spec. items. Per share data adj. for stk. divs. Bold denotes diluted EPS (FASB 128)-prior periods restated. E-Estimated. NA-Not Available. NM-Not Meaningful. NR-Not Ranked.

Office—55 Jewelers Park Dr., Neenah, WI 54957-0156. **Tel**—(920) 722-3451. **Website**—http://www.plexus.com **Chrmn & CEO**—P. Strandwitz. **Pres & COO**—J. L. Nussbaum. **VP, CFO & Investor Contact**—Thomas B. Sabol. **VP & Secy**—J. D. Kaufman. **VP & Treas**—W. F. Denney. **Dirs**—D. J. Drury, H. R. Miller, J. L. Nussbaum, G. A. Pitner, T. J. Prosser, P. Strandwitz, J. K. Ver Hagen. **Transfer Agent & Registrar**—Firstar Trust Co., Milwaukee. **Incorporated**—in Wisconsin in 1979. **Empl**— 2,345. **S&P Analyst:** Jim Corridore

STANDARD
&POOR'S
STOCK REPORTS

Pogo Producing

NYSE Symbol **PPP**

In S&P SmallCap 600

09-OCT-99

Industry:
Oil & Gas (Exploration & Production)

Summary: This independent oil and gas company explores for, develops and produces oil and gas onshore and offshore the U.S. and offshore Thailand.

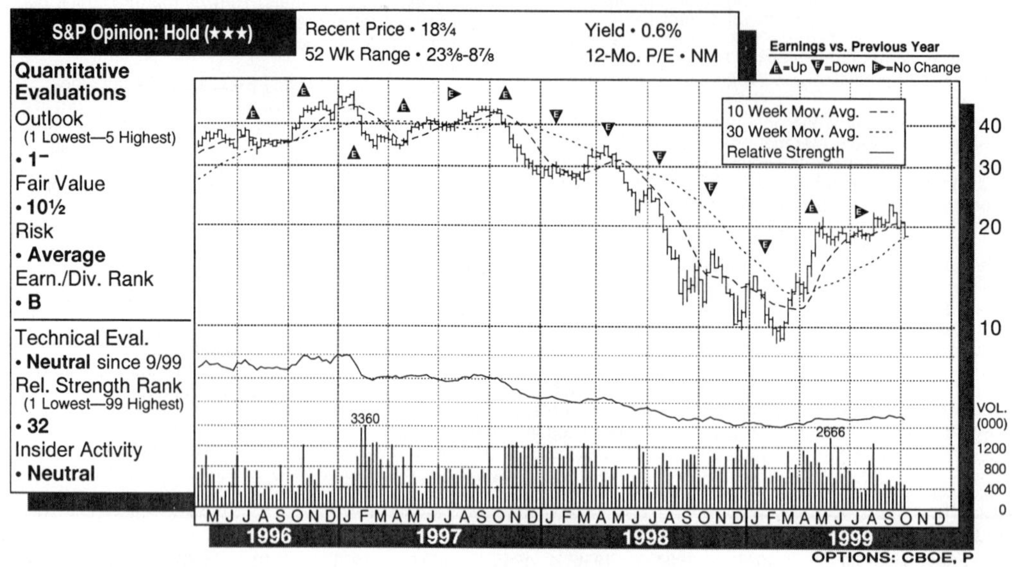

Overview - 19-AUG-99

Second quarter results reflect a significant decline in company-wide production. Year-to-date, the company has focused on lower-cost development projects. With the recent resurgence of world oil prices, Pogo expects to aggressively step up drilling of its higher quality prospects. The 1999 capital spending budget was recently increased by 15% to $195 million. Production through the remainder of the year and into 2000 will be further enhanced by the onset of production from the large Benchamas field in the Gulf of Thailand and an accelerated exploration program. We have revised our 1999 and 2000 EPS estimates, as the increased production will benefit from higher commodity prices. The 1999 estimate excludes a gain from first quarter property sales.

Valuation - 19-AUG-99

Shares of independent oil and gas companies have rebounded, reflecting improved oil prices. PPP is no exception; the shares were recently trading near their 52-week high. We are impressed with Pogo's balanced mix of gas and oil reserves (52% and 48%, respectively, of 1998 year-end reserves). Also, as the Benchamas field becomes commercial, production should become more evenly distributed between North America and Thailand, where price realizations will be stronger. Nevertheless, with the recent price run-up, we would not recommend adding to positions. In addition, the company's reserve replacement ratio and reserve life index are lower than the peer group average. Longer term, the company may prove of interest if it can maintain a low cost structure.

Key Stock Statistics

S&P EPS Est. 1999	-0.50	Tang. Bk. Value/Share	6.03
P/E on S&P Est. 1999	NM	Beta	1.38
S&P EPS Est. 2000	0.15	Shareholders	3,287
Dividend Rate/Share	0.12	Market cap. (B)	$0.753
Shs. outstg. (M)	40.1	Inst. holdings	83%
Avg. daily vol. (M)	0.099		

Value of $10,000 invested 5 years ago: $ 11,514

Fiscal Year Ending Dec. 31

	1999	1998	1997	1996	1995	1994
Revenues (Million $)						
1Q	76.05	60.73	61.31	48.05	41.81	37.89
2Q	44.83	52.66	76.74	51.54	41.74	49.73
3Q	—	46.18	77.18	48.23	36.97	46.45
4Q	—	43.23	71.07	56.15	37.04	39.53
Yr.	—	202.8	286.3	204.0	157.6	173.6
Earnings Per Share ($)						
1Q	**0.36**	**0.01**	**0.30**	**0.19**	0.10	0.22
2Q	**-0.07**	**-0.07**	**0.26**	**0.26**	0.13	0.30
3Q	—	**-0.26**	**0.21**	**0.20**	0.02	0.22
4Q	—	**-0.80**	**0.22**	**0.32**	0.02	0.08
Yr.	**E-0.50**	**-1.14**	**1.06**	**0.97**	**0.28**	**0.82**

Next earnings report expected: late October

Dividend Data (Dividends have been paid since 1994.)

Amount ($)	Date Decl.	Ex-Div. Date	Stock of Record	Payment Date
0.030	Oct. 27	Nov. 10	Nov. 13	Nov. 27 '98
0.030	Jan. 26	Feb. 10	Feb. 12	Feb. 26 '99
0.030	Apr. 27	May. 12	May. 14	May. 28 '99
0.030	Jul. 27	Aug. 11	Aug. 13	Aug. 27 '99

A Division of The **McGraw-Hill** *Companies*

Pogo Producing Company

Business Summary - 19-AUG-99

Pogo Producing Company is engaged in oil and gas exploration, development and production in the offshore Gulf of Mexico (GOM), onshore in New Mexico (NM), Texas and Louisiana, and internationally primarily in the Gulf of Thailand and Canada. As of December 31, 1998, PPP had interests in 105 lease blocks offshore Louisiana and Texas, approximately 419,000 gross acres onshore in the U.S. and Canada, about 847,000 gross acres offshore in the Kingdom of Thailand, and approximately 113,000 gross acres in the British North Sea. Most of Pogo's reserves and production come from four core operating areas: the Outer Continental Shelf area of the GOM in water depths less than 600 feet; 600 feet to 4,500 feet; the Permian Basin area in NM; and a block in the Kingdom of Thailand.

At December 31, 1998 (1997), proved reserves totaled 440.2 (401.5) Bcf of natural gas and 67.5 (58.2) MMBbls of oil, condensate and natural gas liquids (NGLs). The standardized measure of discounted future net cash flows relating to proved oil and gas reserves was $422.7 ($349.5) million. During 1998 (1997), natural gas, oil and NGL production averaged 159.0 (181.7) MMcf, 15.8 (15.9) MBbls and 2.4 (2.9) MBbls per day, respectively. The respective average sales prices were $2.00 ($2.39) per Mcf, $12.97 ($19.37) per bbl and $10.52 ($12.89) per bbl.

Pogo Producing owns interests in eight pipelines through which offshore hydrocarbon production is transported. In addition, the company has a 19% interest in a cryogenic gas processing plant near Erath, Louisiana, which entitles it to produce up to 186 MMcf of gas and 5,478 bbl. of NGLs per day. The plant is not currently operating at full capacity.

In June 1999, PPP issued three million 6.50% cumulative quarterly income preferred securities. Proceeds totaling $150 million will be used to repay outstanding indebtedness, for working capital and general corporate purposes. In January, the company completed a private placement of $150 million of senior subordinated notes, to repay outstanding debt.

In August 1998, Pogo Producing acquired Arch Petroleum in a stock transaction that provided for a fixed exchange ratio of one share of Pogo common stock for 10.4 shares of Arch common stock. The acquisition significantly increased Pogo's gross domestic acreage and provided it with new Canadian prospects, diversifying PPP's international exposure. In March, substantially all of PPP's 5.5% notes due 2004 were converted, resulting in an additional 3.9 million shares outstanding.

Per Share Data ($) (Year Ended Dec. 31)	1998	1997	1996	1995	1994	1993	1992	1991	1990	1989
Tangible Bk. Val.	6.03	4.36	3.22	2.17	1.95	1.04	0.18	-2.06	1.90	0.58
Cash Flow	1.79	3.69	2.80	2.32	2.72	2.00	2.18	1.90	3.26	2.51
Earnings	-1.14	1.06	0.98	0.28	0.82	0.76	0.66	0.37	0.70	-0.23
Dividends	0.15	0.12	0.12	0.12	0.06	Nil	Nil	Nil	Nil	Nil
Payout Ratio	NM	11%	12%	43%	7%	Nil	Nil	Nil	Nil	Nil
Prices - High	34 5/8	49 7/8	48 3/8	29	24 1/4	21	13 7/8	8 1/4	10 1/8	10 1/4
- Low	9 3/4	27	24 3/8	16	15 5/8	9 3/4	5 1/8	4 5/8	5 3/4	4
P/E Ratio - High	NM	47	49	NM	30	28	21	22	14	NM
- Low	NM	25	25	NM	19	13	8	13	8	NM
Income Statement Analysis (Million $)										
Revs.	203	285	204	157	174	137	137	121	132	121
Oper. Inc.	53.7	180	123	91.8	115	89.0	86.0	76.0	97.0	90.0
Depr. Depl. & Amort.	111	103	61.8	68.0	63.0	41.0	42.0	42.0	67.0	66.0
Int. Exp.	15.3	15.7	13.2	11.2	10.1	11.0	19.0	24.9	31.4	37.5
Pretax Inc.	-70.8	55.2	52.3	14.0	43.0	40.0	29.0	15.0	25.0	-9.0
Eff. Tax Rate	NM	33%	36%	35%	36%	37%	36%	29%	28%	NM
Net Inc.	-43.1	37.1	33.5	9.2	27.4	25.1	18.5	10.3	18.2	-5.6
Balance Sheet & Other Fin. Data (Million $)										
Cash	8.0	19.6	3.0	4.5	2.9	6.7	5.0	5.2	7.1	17.3
Curr. Assets	85.4	119	74.9	64.0	49.7	40.5	33.6	30.6	66.2	43.4
Total Assets	862	677	479	338	299	240	206	214	425	421
Curr. Liab.	107	110	68.2	51.3	38.7	37.6	32.2	30.1	37.1	41.8
LT Debt	435	348	246	163	149	131	144	222	260	311
Common Eqty.	250	146	107	71.7	64.0	34.0	6.0	-57.0	52.0	14.0
Total Cap.	738	552	353	276	250	194	167	174	380	372
Cap. Exp.	202	197	172	108	118	73.0	39.0	51.0	45.0	32.0
Cash Flow	67.8	140	95.4	77.7	90.7	66.0	61.0	52.0	85.0	60.0
Curr. Ratio	0.8	1.1	1.1	1.2	1.3	1.1	1.0	1.0	1.8	1.0
% LT Debt of Cap.	58.4	63.0	69.7	59.1	59.8	67.3	86.2	127.3	68.5	83.6
% Ret. on Assets	NM	6.4	8.2	2.9	10.1	11.2	8.1	3.2	4.0	NM
% Ret. on Equity	NM	29.3	37.5	13.6	55.7	126.9	NM	NM	53.3	NM

Data as orig reptd.; bef. results of disc opers/spec. items. Per share data adj. for stk. divs. Bold denotes diluted EPS (FASB 128)-prior periods restated. E-Estimated. NA-Not Available. NM-Not Meaningful. NR-Not Ranked.

Office—5 Greenway Plaza, Suite 2700, P.O. Box 2504, Houston, TX 77252-2504. **Tel**—(713) 297-5000. **Chrmn, Pres & CEO**—Paul G. Van Wagenen. **VP & CFO**—J. W. Elsenhans. **VP & Secy**—G. A. Morton. **Investor Contact**—Tony Van Slyke (713-297-5151). **Dirs**—T. Armstrong, J. S. Blanton, W. M. Brumley Jr., R. H. Campbell, J. B. Carter Jr., W. L. Fisher, G. W. Gong, J. S. Hunt, F. A. Klingenstein, P. G. Van Wagenen, J. A. Vickers. **Transfer Agents & Registrars**—Harris Trust Co. of New York, NYC. **Incorporated**—in Delaware in 1970. **Empl**— 185. **S&P Analyst:** Ephraim Juskowicz

STANDARD &POOR'S
STOCK REPORTS

Polaris Industries

NYSE Symbol **PII**
In S&P SmallCap 600

09-OCT-99

Industry: Leisure Time (Products)

Summary: This company manufactures snowmobiles, all-terrain vehicles, personal watercraft, and motorcycles for recreational and/or utility use.

Quantitative Evaluations

Outlook (1 Lowest—5 Highest)
• **4+**
Fair Value
• **48¾**
Risk
• **Low**
Earn./Div. Rank
• **A-**

Technical Eval.
• **Bearish** since 7/99
Rel. Strength Rank (1 Lowest—99 Highest)
• **58**
Insider Activity
• **NA**

Recent Price • 36¼
52 Wk Range • 45⅝-24⅝
Yield • 2.2%
12-Mo. P/E • 28.3

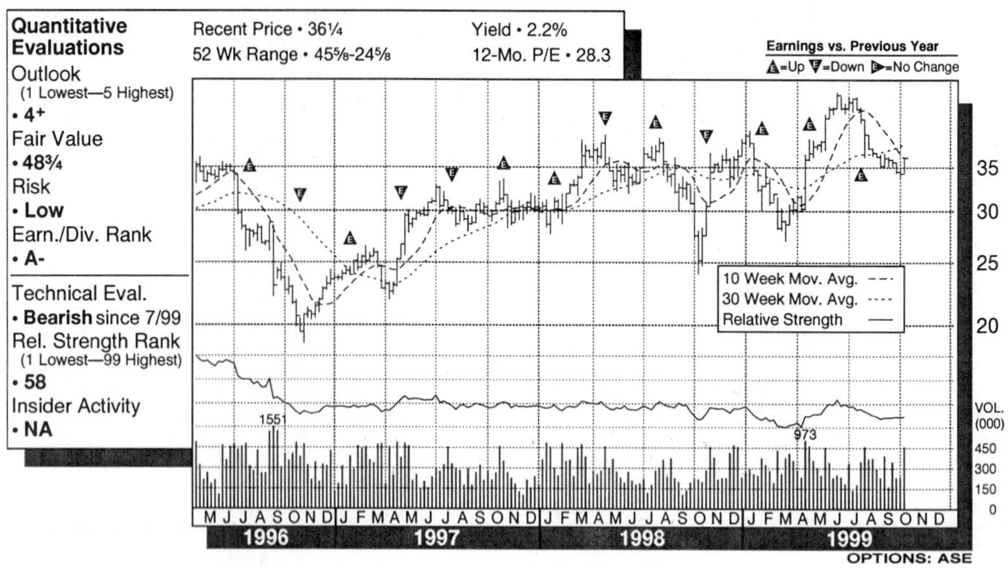

Business Profile - 07-JUN-99

This company makes a variety of recreational and utility vehicles, and also offers related accessories, clothing, and replacement parts. During the first quarter of 1999, Polaris introduced its first manual transmission ATV, the Xpedition 425. The response to this product has been enthusiastic, and the company expects it to help sustain growth in the ATV market. The company expects its new Victory motorcycle line to make a significant revenue contribution in 1999. Management also expects a modest increase in PWC sales for the year. PII continues to aggressively repurchase its common shares under an authorization for the repurchase of up to 5.0 million shares. Through March 31, 1999, the company had repurchased about 3.5 million shares.

Operational Review - 07-JUN-99

Sales in the first quarter of 1999 advanced 13%, year to year, reflecting strong international and all-terrain vehicle (ATV) sales, as well as the inclusion of Victory motorcycle sales. These gains offset lower North American snowmobile sales. Gross margins widened on lower warranty expenses and increased sales of high margin parts, garments and accessories. Total operating expenses rose 26%, and operating income increased only 5.9%. Following 7.6% higher net interest expense, and taxes at 35.5%, versus 36.0%, net income was up 8.4%, to $9,067,000 ($0.36 a share, based on 4.2% fewer shares), $8,361,000 ($0.32).

Stock Performance - 08-OCT-99

In the past 30 trading days, PII's shares have increased 3%, compared to a 0.91% fall in the S&P 500. Average trading volume for the past five days was 102,980 shares, compared with the 40-day moving average of 61,279 shares.

Key Stock Statistics

Dividend Rate/Share	0.80	Shareholders	3,306
Shs. outstg. (M)	25.0	Market cap. (B)	$0.906
Avg. daily vol. (M)	0.066	Inst. holdings	43%
Tang. Bk. Value/Share	5.14		
Beta	0.89		

Value of $10,000 invested 5 years ago: $ 20,969

Fiscal Year Ending Dec. 31

	1999	1998	1997	1996	1995	1994
Revenues (Million $)						
1Q	237.8	210.0	224.6	278.0	254.8	145.5
2Q	324.3	274.7	249.9	317.1	285.4	180.9
3Q	—	359.9	293.4	299.1	291.4	258.4
4Q	—	330.9	280.4	297.7	282.3	241.6
Yr.	—	1,176	1,048	1,192	1,114	826.3
Earnings Per Share ($)						
1Q	**0.36**	**0.32**	0.44	0.48	0.47	0.22
2Q	**0.60**	**0.55**	0.49	0.58	0.45	0.27
3Q	—	**-0.56**	0.81	0.57	0.67	0.79
4Q	—	**0.88**	**0.70**	0.61	0.60	0.71
Yr.	—	**1.19**	**2.45**	**2.24**	**2.19**	**1.98**

Next earnings report expected: mid October

Dividend Data (Dividends have been paid since 1987.)

Amount ($)	Date Decl.	Ex-Div. Date	Stock of Record	Payment Date
0.180	Oct. 22	Oct. 29	Nov. 02	Nov. 16 '98
0.200	Jan. 21	Jan. 28	Feb. 01	Feb. 15 '99
0.200	Apr. 23	Apr. 29	May. 03	May. 17 '99
0.200	Jul. 22	Jul. 29	Aug. 02	Aug. 16 '99

Polaris Industries Inc.

Business Summary - 07-JUN-99

Polaris Industries Inc. (formerly Polaris Industries Partners L.P.) engineers and makes snowmobiles, all-terrain recreational and utility vehicles (ATVs), personal watercraft (PWC), and motorcycles. It markets these products, together with related accessories, clothing and replacement parts, through a network of close to 2,000 dealers in North America, and 44 distributors in 116 countries. Sales of snowmobiles were 32% of total sales in 1998 (42% in 1997); ATVs made up 57% (45%).

Polaris produces a full line of snowmobiles, consisting of33 models, ranging from utility and economy models to performance and competition models, with 1999 suggested United States retail prices ranging from approximately $3,000 to $8,500. The company's snowmobiles are sold principally in the United States, Canada and Europe. Polaris believes it is the worldwide market share leader.

ATVs are typically four-wheel vehicles with balloon-style tires, and are designed for off-road use and traveling through rough terrain, swamps and marshland. ATVs are used for recreation in such sports as fishing and hunting, and also for utility purposes on farms, ranches and construction sites. As of early 1999, PII's line of ATVs included 14 models, with 1999 suggested retail prices ranging from about $3,000 to $7,500. In 1998, Polaris introduced a diesel powered ATV and, in early 1999, it introduced its first manual transmission ATV. In addition, this segment includes some six-wheel off-road vehicles.

In 1992, PII began shipments of a line of personal watercraft -- sit-down versions of water scooter vehicles designed principally for recreational use on lakes, rivers, bays and oceans. As of early 1999, PII had six PWC models. The 1999 suggested retail prices for PII's PWC ranged from about $5,900 to $9,500.

In 1998, PII started manufacturing a cruiser motorcycle known as the Victory V92C. Polaris estimates that approximately 152,000 cruiser motorcycles were sold in the U.S. market in 1998, with Polaris accounting for about 3,000. The 1998 Victory V92Cmotorcycle suggested retail price was $12,995.

PII's sales to customers outside of North America include snowmobiles, ATVs, PWC and related products. Polaris currently markets its products through 44 distributors in 116 countries. In 1998, international sales accounted for 6% of Polaris's sales.

Polaris also offers a full line of recreational clothing designed to its specifications, including suits, helmets, gloves, boots, hats, sweaters and jackets.

Per Share Data ($) (Year Ended Dec. 31)	1998	1997	1996	1995	1994	1993	1992	1991	1990	1989
Tangible Bk. Val.	5.14	5.60	4.85	3.42	5.29	2.29	1.81	1.84	1.92	1.88
Cash Flow	2.59	3.69	3.33	3.01	5.52	2.71	2.18	2.00	1.95	1.68
Earnings	1.19	2.45	2.24	2.19	1.98	1.50	1.15	1.10	1.10	1.08
Dividends	0.72	0.64	0.60	4.27	1.68	1.67	1.67	1.67	1.67	1.51
Payout Ratio	61%	26%	27%	195%	85%	111%	104%	107%	108%	117%
Prices - High	39 3/8	33 5/8	36 1/4	34 3/8	34 7/8	25 5/8	16 3/8	13 1/2	12 7/8	9 1/8
- Low	24	21 7/8	18 3/4	25	19 3/8	14 1/2	12	8 1/8	8	5
P/E Ratio - High	33	14	16	16	18	17	14	12	12	8
- Low	20	9	8	11	10	8	10	7	7	5
Income Statement Analysis (Million $)										
Revs.	1,176	1,048	1,192	1,114	826	528	384	298	296	243
Oper. Inc.	136	126	128	124	112	72.8	64.3	52.7	52.8	44.0
Depr.	36.2	33.2	30.6	22.7	23.7	19.6	17.3	13.8	12.6	11.5
Int. Exp.	3.0	2.8	4.3	1.7	NA	NA	6.8	7.2	9.4	6.4
Pretax Inc.	48.4	102	97.3	99	75.9	53.3	39.7	33.4	33.0	26.9
Eff. Tax Rate	36%	36%	36%	39%	NM	14%	13%	5.90%	5.00%	2.50%
Net Inc.	31.0	65.4	62.3	61.0	129	45.8	34.7	31.5	31.4	26.2
Balance Sheet & Other Fin. Data (Million $)										
Cash	1.5	1.2	5.8	3.5	62.9	33.8	19.1	20.1	32.0	27.9
Curr. Assets	184	217	193	176	206	110	75.0	59.2	66.9	60.3
Total Assets	379	385	352	314	331	181	147	136	139	138
Curr. Liab.	205	191	161	196	161	98.1	69.1	52.6	46.6	38.9
LT Debt	20.5	24.0	35.0	Nil	Nil	Nil	Nil	Nil	Nil	Nil
Common Eqty.	153	169	155	119	170	82.5	77.6	82.9	92.1	99
Total Cap.	174	194	190	119	170	82.5	77.6	82.9	92.1	99
Cap. Exp.	61.5	36.7	44.9	46.7	32.5	18.1	12.3	16.0	7.2	7.1
Cash Flow	67.2	99	93.0	83.0	153	65.4	52.0	45.3	44.0	37.7
Curr. Ratio	0.9	1.1	1.2	0.9	1.3	1.1	1.1	1.1	1.4	1.6
% LT Debt of Cap.	11.8	12.3	18.4	Nil	Nil	Nil	Nil	Nil	Nil	Nil
% Net Inc.of Revs.	2.6	6.2	5.2	5.5	15.6	8.7	9.0	10.6	10.6	10.8
% Ret. on Assets	8.1	17.8	18.7	18.9	46.9	27.6	23.7	22.9	22.7	20.5
% Ret. on Equity	19.2	40.3	45.5	42.2	95.6	56.4	41.6	36.0	32.9	26.8

Data as orig. reptd.; bef. results of disc. opers. and/or spec. items. Per share data adj. for stk. divs. as of ex-div. date; per unit data prior to 1994. Bold denotes diluted EPS (FASB 128). E-Estimated. NA-Not Available. NM-Not Meaningful. NR-Not Ranked.

Office—1225 Highway 169 North, Minneapolis, MN 55441. **Organized**—in Delaware in 1987; incorporated in Minnesota in 1994. **Website**—http://www.polarisindustries.com **Tel**—(612) 542-0500. **Chrmn**—W. H. Wendel Jr. **Pres & CEO**—T. C. Tiller. **VP-Fin, CFO & Secy**—M. W. Malone. **Investor Contact**—Nancy Moe (612-542-0573). **Dirs**—A. A. Baltins, R. J. Biggs, B. F. Dolan, S. Moe, G. R. Palen, S. G. Shank, T. C. Tiller, B. A. Thomson, W. H. Wendel Jr. **Transfer Agent**—Norwest Bank Minnesota, South St. Paul. **Empl**— 3,050. **S&P Analyst:** P.D.W.

STANDARD &POOR'S
STOCK REPORTS

Pool Energy Services

NASDAQ Symbol **PESC**

In S&P SmallCap 600

09-OCT-99

Industry: Oil & Gas (Drilling & Equipment)

Summary: In January 1999, this well-servicing firm agreed to be acquired by Nabors Industries for stock.

Quantitative Evaluations

Outlook (1 Lowest—5 Highest)
• **1-**

Fair Value
• **18**

Risk
• **Average**

Earn./Div. Rank
• **NR**

Technical Eval.
• **Neutral** since 9/99

Rel. Strength Rank (1 Lowest—99 Highest)
• **11**

Insider Activity
• **NA**

Recent Price • 19¾
52 Wk Range • 29½-6¾
Yield • Nil
12-Mo. P/E • 73.1

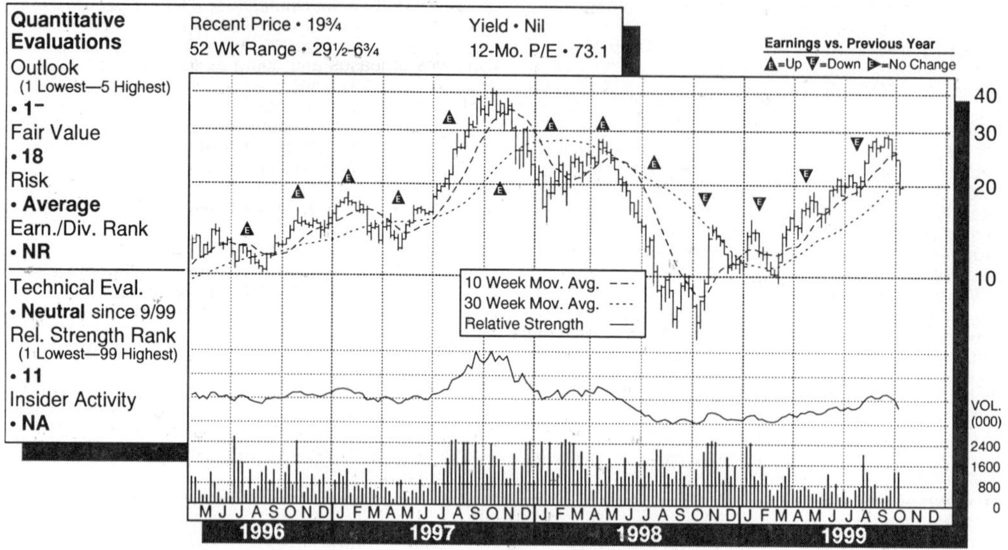

Business Profile - 22-JUN-99

In January 1999, the company agreed to be acquired by Nabors Industries (ASE; NBR), an oil and gas drilling company. Terms call for Pool shareholders to receive 1.025 Nabors shares for each Pool share held, and for Nabors to assume $144 million of Pool debt. Management expects the transaction to close during the third quarter of 1999, subject to the approval of Pool shareholders and the customary regulatory approvals. Pool had previously rejected a cash-and-stock takeover offer from Nabors.

Operational Review - 22-JUN-99

Revenues for the three months ended March 31, 1999, fell 31%, year to year, reflecting lower overall utilization of land well-servicing rigs located in Texas, New Mexico and California, reduced offshore rig activity, and lower land drilling activity in Ecuador. Results benefited from $3.7 million of earnings attributed to affiliates, against a loss of $71,000, but with costs and expenses down only 22% and sharply higher interest expense, a pretax loss contrasted with income. With an income tax credit of $927,000, versus taxes at 39.1%, net income plunged 93%, to $535,000 ($0.03 a share) from $7,453,000 ($0.38).

Stock Performance - 08-OCT-99

In the past 30 trading days, PESC's shares have declined 26%, compared to a 0.91% fall in the S&P 500. Average trading volume for the past five days was 268,800 shares, compared with the 40-day moving average of 154,508 shares.

Key Stock Statistics

Dividend Rate/Share	Nil	Shareholders	2,168
Shs. outstg. (M)	21.3	Market cap. (B)	$0.420
Avg. daily vol. (M)	0.188	Inst. holdings	45%
Tang. Bk. Value/Share	10.98		
Beta	1.48		

Value of $10,000 invested 5 years ago: $ 25,901

Fiscal Year Ending Dec. 31

	1999	1998	1997	1996	1995	1994
Revenues (Million $)						
1Q	81.03	117.7	98.38	81.68	62.85	55.98
2Q	73.08	128.0	109.8	82.99	63.80	54.26
3Q	—	115.2	118.6	83.98	75.52	56.17
4Q	—	96.43	125.2	99.9	75.13	62.77
Yr.	—	455.7	451.9	348.6	277.3	229.2
Earnings Per Share ($)						
1Q	**0.03**	**0.38**	**0.20**	**0.10**	0.02	0.05
2Q	**-0.09**	**0.36**	**0.31**	**0.13**	0.04	0.06
3Q	—	**0.25**	**0.43**	**0.14**	0.05	0.04
4Q	—	**0.07**	**0.43**	**0.20**	0.12	-1.09
Yr.	—	**1.06**	**1.36**	**0.58**	**0.23**	**-0.94**

Next earnings report expected: late October

Dividend Data

No cash dividends have been paid, and terms of Pool's credit line preclude such payments. A shareholder rights plan was adopted in 1994.

A Division of The McGraw-Hill Companies

Pool Energy Services Co.

Business Summary - 22-JUN-99

Pool Energy Services Co. (PESC) is the world's largest well-servicing and workover firm, providing services for onshore and offshore oil and gas wells, both domestically and internationally.

After reducing personnel levels in the past 10 years, PESC's customers, the oil and gas producers, are now outsourcing more and more of the services the company provides. PESC provides the maintenance services on the apparatus used to pump or lift oil from producing wells, supplying the rigs, equipment and crews needed to repair and replace pumps, sucker rods and tubing. Most of PESC's well-servicing rigs are also designed for major repairs or modifications on oil and gas wells, called "workovers." Completion services are performed when a well is first drilled.

The company operates both domestically and internationally. In the United States, the company operates in several oil and natural gas producing states, and offshore in the Gulf of Mexico, offshore California and in the Cook Inlet of Alaska. International markets where the company has an established presence include land operations in Argentina, Ecuador, Guatemala, Oman, Pakistan and Saudi Arabia and offshore operations in Australia, Malaysia and Saudi Arabia.

Domestic onshore activities (56% of revenues in 1998) are conducted in 11 states, with PESC operating the largest fleet of land well-servicing rigs in Texas, the Midcontinent area and California. PESC also operates one of the three largest offshore workover rig fleets in the Gulf of Mexico (16%) and provides marine transportation of drilling materials, supplies and crews for offshore rig operations and support for other offshore facilities (8%). International operations (13%) are conducted in nine countries.

As of December 31, 1998, the company's worldwide fleet included 783 land well-servicing/workover rigs, 29 land drilling rigs and 27 offshore rigs. The company also owns or leases and operates 337 fluid hauling trucks, 971 fluid storage tanks, 15 salt water disposal wells and other auxiliary equipment used in its domestic operations. PESC also operates a fleet of 24 support vessels to complement its offshore rig fleet.

Historically, the demand for the company's services has had a strong correlation with the fluctuations in oil and natural gas prices. During 1998, crude oil prices decreased from an average of approximately $16.67 per barrel in January to an average of approximately $11.07 per barrel in December. Thesedeclines were attributed to, among other things, an excess supply of oil in the world markets, reduced domestic demand associated with an unseasonably warm winter, and lower worldwide demand due to the impact of the economic downturn in Asia. As a result, Pool Energy has experienced a decline in overall demand and rates for its services. These market conditions negatively affected activity levels and financial results in 1998 and are expected to continue to do so until commodity prices increase to higher levels.

Per Share Data ($) (Year Ended Dec. 31)	1998	1997	1996	1995	1994	1993	1992	1991	1990	1989
Tangible Bk. Val.	10.99	9.84	9.65	8.88	9.49	10.43	9.99	10.13	9.94	10.33
Cash Flow	2.96	2.64	1.71	1.31	0.08	1.66	1.11	1.55	1.74	1.37
Earnings	1.05	1.36	0.58	0.23	-0.94	0.46	-0.22	0.19	0.44	-0.21
Dividends	Nil	Nil	Nil	Nil	Nil	Nil	Nil	Nil	Nil	Nil
Payout Ratio	Nil	Nil	Nil	Nil	Nil	Nil	Nil	Nil	Nil	Nil
Prices - High	28¼	41½	16⅝	9⅞	10½	11⅞	9	13⅛	18⅛	NA
- Low	6⅛	12	8⅝	6⅝	6¼	6⅛	5¾	5¼	8⅝	NA
P/E Ratio - High	27	31	29	43	NM	26	NM	69	41	NM
- Low	6	9	15	29	NM	13	NM	28	20	NM
Income Statement Analysis (Million $)										
Revs.	456	452	348	277	229	237	213	225	235	238
Oper. Inc.	83.8	64.0	34.1	18.3	10.2	15.3	7.9	15.1	20.7	8.5
Depr.	39.8	25.0	18.5	15.0	13.8	16.3	18.0	18.3	17.5	19.8
Int. Exp.	14.7	4.3	2.8	1.8	0.3	0.5	0.9	0.7	1.0	2.2
Pretax Inc.	35.3	42.3	17.1	5.1	-21.1	7.6	-6.7	1.8	7.1	-1.0
Eff. Tax Rate	38%	37%	44%	35%	NM	18%	NM	NM	15%	NM
Net Inc.	21.8	26.7	9.6	3.1	-12.7	6.2	-3.0	2.5	6.0	-2.7
Balance Sheet & Other Fin. Data (Million $)										
Cash	34.8	19.0	22.0	5.7	2.7	4.7	3.2	8.1	30.4	10.8
Curr. Assets	140	153	114	78.1	68.5	69.7	65.9	62.0	89.5	87.5
Total Assets	664	479	341	248	208	193	196	198	214	238
Curr. Liab.	89.8	93.6	66.7	51.2	36.1	29.2	37.6	31.9	47.1	74.6
LT Debt	173	79.3	23.1	15.8	0.4	Nil	Nil	Nil	Nil	Nil
Common Eqty.	291	234	197	136	129	141	135	137	134	129
Total Cap.	1,126	339	228	154	131	144	138	141	138	130
Cap. Exp.	91.4	60.4	30.7	23.4	11.4	20.4	12.7	26.1	11.9	NA
Cash Flow	61.6	51.7	28.2	18.1	1.0	22.5	15.1	20.9	23.5	17.1
Curr. Ratio	1.6	1.6	1.7	1.5	1.9	2.4	1.8	1.9	1.9	1.2
% LT Debt of Cap.	15.4	23.3	10.1	12.2	0.3	Nil	Nil	Nil	Nil	Nil
% Net Inc.of Revs.	4.8	5.9	2.8	1.1	NM	2.6	NM	1.1	2.6	NM
% Ret. on Assets	3.8	6.5	3.3	1.4	NM	3.2	NM	1.2	2.7	NM
% Ret. on Equity	8.3	12.4	5.8	2.4	NM	4.5	NM	1.9	4.6	NM

Data as orig reptd.; bef. results of disc opers/spec. items. Per share data adj. for stk. divs. Bold denotes diluted EPS (FASB 128)-prior periods restated. E-Estimated. NA-Not Available. NM-Not Meaningful. NR-Not Ranked.

Office—10375 Richmond Ave., P.O. Box 4271, Houston, TX 77210. **Tel**—(713) 954-3000. **Fax**—(713) 954-3326. **Chrmn, Pres & CEO**—J. T. Jongebloed. **SVP-Fin**—E. J. Spillard. **VP & Secy**—G. G. Arms. **VP & Investor Contact**—David C. Oatman (713-954-3316). **Dirs**—D. R. Hendrix, J. T. Jongebloed, J. F. Lavletta, W. H. Mobley, J. R. Musolino, J. L. Payne. **Transfer Agent & Registrar**—BankBoston. **Incorporated**—in Texas in 1988. **Empl**— 5,422. **S&P Analyst:** C.C.P.

STANDARD
&POOR'S
STOCK REPORTS

Pope & Talbot

NYSE Symbol **POP**

In S&P SmallCap 600

09-OCT-99

Industry:
Paper & Forest Products

Summary: This company produces market pulp and softwood lumber at mills the U.S. and Canada.

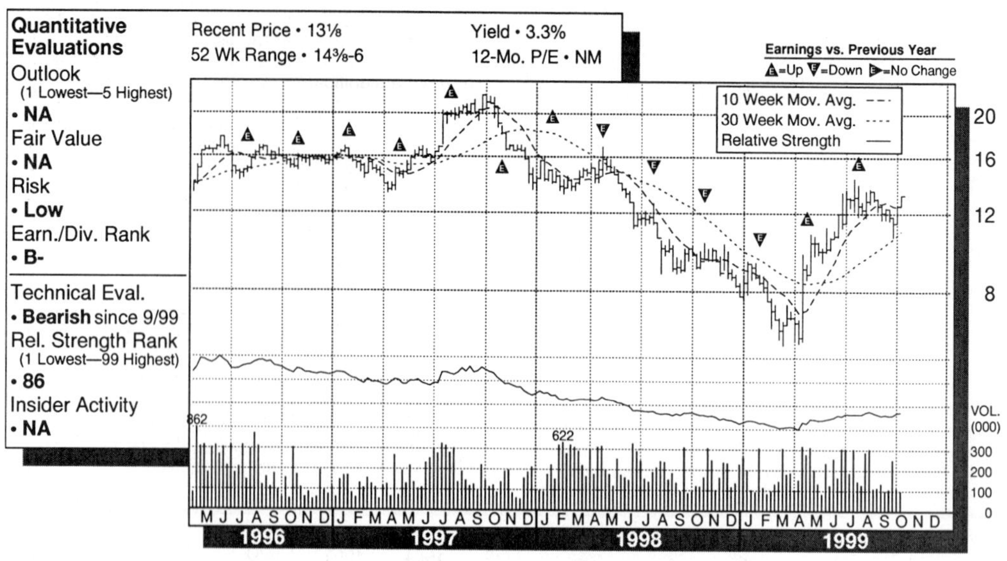

Business Profile - 03-JUN-99

In line with its strategy of narrowing its business focus to pulp and lumber, POP increased its presence in the northern bleached softwood kraft (NBSK) pulp market with the acquisition of a controlling interest in Harmac in February 1998. Pulp products contributed 48% of total revenues in 1998, up from 25% in 1997. POP is now the world's ninth largest producer of NBSK pulp, with about 460,000 metric tons of capacity. The company also has 100,000 metric tons of short-fiber (sawdust) pulp producing capacity. Peter T. Pope will step down from his position as the company's CEO effective August 1, 1999. Michael Flannery, currently president and COO, will become CEO. Mr. Pope will remain as POP's chairman during a one-year transition period.

Operational Review - 03-JUN-99

Total revenues in the three months ended March 31, 1999, advanced 5.5%, year to year, as a 14% increase in pulp products revenues outweighed a 1.3% decline in wood products sales. With higher lumber selling prices, a 13% drop in SG&A expense, and a 5.0% rise in net interest expense, the loss from continuing operations narrowed to $2,276,000 ($0.17 a share), from $6,593,000 ($0.49). Results exclude income from discontinued operations of $2.00 a share in the 1998 period.

Stock Performance - 08-OCT-99

In the past 30 trading days, POP's shares have increased 5%, compared to a 0.91% fall in the S&P 500. Average trading volume for the past five days was 19,320 shares, compared with the 40-day moving average of 25,887 shares.

Key Stock Statistics

Dividend Rate/Share	0.44	Shareholders	952
Shs. outstg. (M)	13.5	Market cap. (B)	$0.178
Avg. daily vol. (M)	0.028	Inst. holdings	47%
Tang. Bk. Value/Share	11.03		
Beta	1.13		

Value of $10,000 invested 5 years ago: $ 6,291

Fiscal Year Ending Dec. 31

	1999	1998	1997	1996	1995	1994
Revenues (Million $)						
1Q	109.2	103.5	84.09	110.7	133.8	168.7
2Q	120.3	106.5	88.34	110.6	124.5	157.9
3Q	—	104.3	80.68	112.4	131.8	171.3
4Q	—	106.5	76.79	113.9	134.3	162.0
Yr.	—	420.8	329.9	447.5	524.4	659.9
Earnings Per Share ($)						
1Q	**-0.17**	**-0.49**	**0.02**	**-0.18**	-0.08	0.70
2Q	**0.22**	**-0.53**	**0.18**	**0.01**	-0.48	0.21
3Q	—	**-0.50**	**0.11**	**0.05**	-0.25	0.07
4Q	—	**-0.22**	**0.03**	**0.01**	-0.22	0.27
Yr.	—	**-1.74**	**0.33**	**-0.10**	**-0.37**	**1.99**

Next earnings report expected: mid October

Dividend Data (Dividends have been paid since 1948.)

Amount ($)	Date Decl.	Ex-Div. Date	Stock of Record	Payment Date
0.190	Oct. 16	Oct. 30	Nov. 03	Nov. 12 '98
0.190	Jan. 28	Feb. 04	Feb. 08	Feb. 19 '99
0.110	Feb. 04	Apr. 29	May. 03	May. 14 '99
0.110	Jul. 15	Jul. 29	Aug. 02	Aug. 13 '99

A Division of The McGraw-Hill Companies

STANDARD
&POOR'S
STOCK REPORTS

Pope & Talbot, Inc.

09-OCT-99

Business Summary - 03-JUN-99

Pope & Talbot (POP), an integrated wood-fiber products company, recently sold its tissue business to focus on its core pulp and lumber operations. POP's two distinct yet integrated market segments (wood products and pulp products) are designed to counteract the unavoidable cyclical nature of the forest products industry.

The company's wood products business involves the manufacture and sale of boards and dimension lumber, some of which are specialty items, such as stress-rated lumber. Wood chips and other similar materials obtained as a by-product of lumber operations are also sold. During the last three years, revenues from lumber sales contributed 85% or more of total wood products revenues, with the balance of revenues from the sale of logs and wood chips.

POP owns a pulp mill located in Halsey, OR, and holds a 60% interest in Harmac Pacific Inc., which owns a pulp mill in Nanaimo, BC. The Halsey mill produces bleached kraft pulp, sold in various forms to writing paper, tissue and newsprint manufacturers in the Pacific Northwest and on the open market. In conjunction with its fiber acquisition program for the Halsey pulp mill, the company brokers wood chips for sale primarily into the export market. The Harmac mill supplies pulp to all sectors of the paper market, for products ranging from newsprint and tissue to high-grade coated and uncoated paper.

The company has an agreement with Grays Harbor Paper L.P. under which the Halsey mill supplies pulp to the Grays Harbor writing grade paper mill. Grays Harbor purchased about 60,000 metric tons, 89,000 metric tons and 100,000 metric tons of pulp from POP in 1998, 1997 and 1996, respectively. All output from the paper mill is sold to a single customer. In the event that the paper mill's sales to this customer are adversely affected for any reason, sales of the company's pulp may be significantly affected.

With an annual capacity of 380,000 metric tons, POP's Harmac pulp mill is one of the largest producers of market pulp in Canada. Harmac produced 354,000 metric tons of pulp in 1998, with 335,000 metric tons produced subsequent to February 2, 1998.

Since the mid-1980s, the company has reduced its dependency on timber from the Pacific Northwest, where environmental concerns have sharply restricted the availability of timber, while also increasing the cost. At the same time, POP has increased its operations in regions that currently offer more stable timber supplies, including British Columbia and the Black Hills region of South Dakota and Wyoming.

Firm backlog at December 31, 1998, totaled $37.9 million, up from $18.0 million a year earlier. In 1998, sales to Grays Harbor accounted for 13% of the company's pulp revenues, and the remaining nine largest customers accounted for an additional 40% of pulp revenues.

Per Share Data ($) (Year Ended Dec. 31)	1998	1997	1996	1995	1994	1993	1992	1991	1990	1989
Tangible Bk. Val.	11.03	13.31	13.42	13.89	16.76	15.36	14.46	15.68	17.42	16.48
Cash Flow	0.48	2.57	2.41	2.34	4.19	4.35	2.27	1.97	3.95	5.74
Earnings	-1.74	0.33	0.06	-1.03	1.21	1.85	-0.19	-0.44	1.70	3.70
Dividends	0.76	0.76	0.76	0.76	0.76	0.76	0.76	0.76	0.72	0.60
Payout Ratio	NM	NM	NM	NM	63%	41%	NM	NM	42%	16%
Prices - High	16⅞	22⅛	17⅝	17⅞	32⅝	29⅞	19¾	19	27½	29¾
- Low	7⅝	13¼	13⅛	12½	15¼	16	13⅜	12¾	10¼	17⅞
P/E Ratio - High	NM	67	NM	NM	27	16	NM	NM	16	8
- Low	NM	40	NM	NM	13	9	NM	NM	6	5
Income Statement Analysis (Million $)										
Revs.	421	330	447	524	660	629	544	502	562	619
Oper. Inc.	-2.5	44.8	40.9	37.5	61.2	74.4	33.3	26.7	60.4	93.3
Depr.	29.9	30.1	31.4	45.1	39.1	29.3	28.6	27.9	26.4	25.5
Int. Exp.	11.4	7.9	10.2	15.5	12.0	10.4	6.0	4.4	4.7	5.2
Pretax Inc.	-40.4	8.8	2.5	-21.3	26.7	36.4	-2.5	-7.1	31.0	69.2
Eff. Tax Rate	NM	49%	68%	NM	40%	41%	NM	NM	36%	37%
Net Inc.	-23.5	4.4	0.8	-13.8	15.9	21.6	-2.3	-5.1	19.8	43.6
Balance Sheet & Other Fin. Data (Million $)										
Cash	27.5	31.9	32.2	13.8	6.8	3.8	4.3	3.8	9.0	2.1
Curr. Assets	188	211	165	207	223	170	138	122	132	130
Total Assets	450	376	408	472	539	456	370	347	354	355
Curr. Liab.	85.0	84.8	87.0	113	104	101	79.7	64.5	53.8	68.5
LT Debt	138	88.7	108	139	177	135	89.5	69.0	77.5	67.6
Common Eqty.	158	179	183	190	228	184	172	187	207	199
Total Cap.	336	268	291	328	407	327	266	266	300	287
Cap. Exp.	27.6	13.1	7.2	27.8	55.6	82.6	32.3	37.3	41.9	52.1
Cash Flow	6.5	34.5	32.2	31.3	55.0	50.9	26.3	22.9	46.2	67.7
Curr. Ratio	2.2	2.5	1.9	1.8	2.2	1.7	1.7	1.9	2.4	1.9
% LT Debt of Cap.	41.1	33.0	37.1	42.2	43.6	41.2	33.7	26.0	25.8	23.5
% Net Inc.of Revs.	NM	1.3	0.2	NM	2.4	3.4	NM	NM	3.5	7.1
% Ret. on Assets	NM	1.1	0.2	NM	3.0	5.2	NM	NM	5.6	12.9
% Ret. on Equity	NM	2.4	0.0	NM	7.3	12.0	NM	NM	9.9	24.1

Data as orig reptd.; bef. results of disc opers/spec. items. Per share data adj. for stk. divs. Bold denotes diluted EPS (FASB 128)-prior periods restated. E-Estimated. NA-Not Available. NM-Not Meaningful. NR-Not Ranked.

Office—1500 S.W. First Ave., Portland, OR 97201. **Tel**—(503) 228-9161. **Website**—http://www.poptal.com **Chrmn & CEO**—P. T. Pope. **Pres & COO**—M. Flannery. **SVP & CFO**—R.J. Day. **Investor Contact**—Bob Wulf. **Dirs**—G. P. Andrews, H. W. Budge, C. Crocker, M. Flannery, K. G. Hanna, R. S. Miller Jr., P. T. Pope, H. G. L. Powell, B. Walker Jr. **Transfer Agent & Registrar**—ChaseMellon Shareholder Services, SF. **Incorporated**—in California in 1940; reincorporated in Delaware in 1979. **Empl**— 2,117. **S&P Analyst:** M.I.

STANDARD
&POOR'S
STOCK REPORTS

Powerwave Technologies

NASDAQ Symbol **PWAV**

In S&P SmallCap 600

09-OCT-99 **Industry:** Telecommunications (Cellular/Wireless)

Summary: This company is a leading supplier of high performance RF power amplifiers for use in wireless communications networks.

Quantitative Evaluations

Outlook
(1 Lowest—5 Highest)
• **NA**
Fair Value
• **NA**
Risk
• **NA**
Earn./Div. Rank
• **NR**

Technical Eval.
• **Bullish** since 6/99
Rel. Strength Rank
(1 Lowest—99 Highest)
• **96**
Insider Activity
• **Unfavorable**

Recent Price • 51⅞
52 Wk Range • 52¼-6
Yield • Nil
12-Mo. P/E • NM

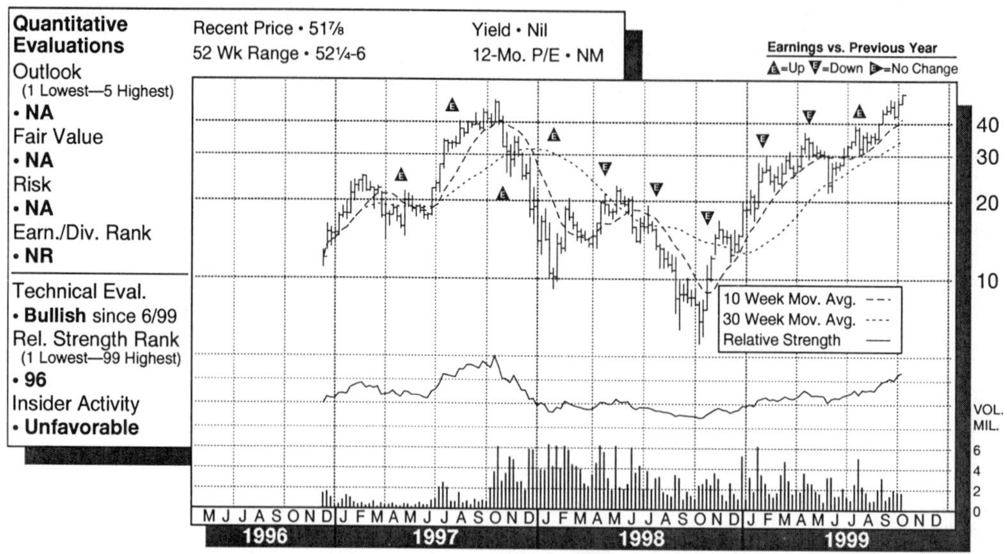

Business Profile - 08-SEP-99

The company's strategy is to become the leading supplier of high performance RF power amplifiers used in digital and analog wireless networks worldwide. During the 1999 second quarter, it continued its focus on integrating the October 1998 acquisition of Hewlett-Packard's RF power amplifier business, while operating the acquired manufacturing facility in Northern California at a higher rate than originally anticipated. The company used $22.8 million of the $57.8 million proceeds of a March 1999 stock offering to repay all of the bank debt incurred in connection with the HP acquisition.

Operational Review - 08-SEP-99

Revenues climbed 185% year to year in the first half of 1999, largely reflecting the inclusion of revenues from the sale of products acquired in the HP acquisition in October 1998. Gross margins narrowed on increased labor and overhead costs associated with operating theFolsom manufacturing facility acquired in the HP acquisition, inefficiencies in the ramp-up of increased production in the company's Irvine facility, and a significant increase in single carrier amplifiers. Other income was down sharply, and net income was up 56%, to $6,254,000 ($0.31 a share, diluted, on 12% more shares), from $4,086,000 ($0.24).

Stock Performance - 08-OCT-99

In the past 30 trading days, PWAV's shares have increased 30%, compared to a 0.91% fall in the S&P 500. Average trading volume for the past five days was 326,120 shares, compared with the 40-day moving average of 347,974 shares.

Key Stock Statistics

Dividend Rate/Share	Nil	Shareholders	2,000
Shs. outstg. (M)	20.0	Market cap. (B)	$ 1.0
Avg. daily vol. (M)	0.332	Inst. holdings	65%
Tang. Bk. Value/Share	6.29		
Beta	NA		

Value of $10,000 invested 5 years ago: NA

Fiscal Year Ending Dec. 31

	1999	1998	1997	1996	1995	1994
Revenues (Million $)						
1Q	56.02	22.65	20.24	—	—	—
2Q	68.49	21.10	27.36	—	—	—
3Q	—	16.46	34.35	—	—	—
4Q	—	40.03	37.76	—	—	—
Yr.	—	100.2	119.7	60.33	36.04	—
Earnings Per Share ($)						
1Q	**0.11**	**0.13**	**0.17**	**0.12**	—	—
2Q	**0.20**	**0.11**	**0.20**	**0.13**	—	—
3Q	—	**0.01**	**0.26**	**0.12**	—	—
4Q	—	**-0.42**	**0.29**	**0.15**	—	—
Yr.	—	**-0.17**	**0.92**	**0.52**	—	—

Next earnings report expected: mid October

Dividend Data

No dividends have been paid.

Powerwave Technologies Inc.

Business Summary - 08-SEP-99

Powerwave Technologies (formerly Milcom International) manufactures and markets ultra-linear radio frequency (RF) poweramplifiers for use in the wireless communications market. The company's RF power amplifiers, which are key components of wireless communications networks, increase the signal strength of wireless transmissions from the base station to a handset while reducing interference, or "noise." Less noise enables wireless service providers to deliver clearer call connections. Stronger signals reduce the number of interrupted or dropped calls.

The company manufactures both single and multi-carrier RF power amplifiers for a variety of frequency ranges and transmission protocols. Single carrier RF power amplifiers typically amplify a specific call channel. Multi-carrier RF power amplifiers are capable of amplifying several call channels at one time and integrate the functions of several RF power amplifiers and cavity filterswithin a single unit. The company's products are currently being utilized in both cellular and personal communications services (PCS) base stations in digital and analog-based networks.

The company sells most of its products to a small number of customers, and expects that this will continue. It believes that its future success depends upon its ability to broaden its customer base and maintain relationships with major wireless original equipment manufacturers, or OEMs, such as Hyundai, LGIC, Ericsson, Lucent, Nokia, Nortel and Samsung, as well as major operators of wireless networks, such as AT&T Wireless Services&T;, GTE Wireless and BellSouth.

In October 1998, PWAV acquired Hewlett-Packard's RF power amplifier business for about $65.9 million. As part of this acquisition, it acquired HP's manufacturing and research and development facility in Folsom, CA, and its production equipment and manufacturing lines in Malaysia. Subsequently, the company closed the Malaysian manufacturing operations and relocated the production equipment to its existing manufacturing facility in Irvine, CA. In addition, it is currently consolidating the Folsom manufacturing facility into its Irvine manufacturing facility. PWAV intends to maintain a research and development location in the Folsom area.

Per Share Data ($) (Year Ended Dec. 31)	1998	1997	1996	1995	1994	1993	1992	1991	1990	1989
Tangible Bk. Val.	4.36	6.46	2.32	NA	NA	NA	NA	NA	NA	NA
Cash Flow	0.07	1.03	0.77	NA	NA	NA	NA	NA	NA	NA
Earnings	-0.17	0.92	0.52	NA	NA	NA	NA	NA	NA	NA
Dividends	Nil	Nil	Nil	NA	NA	NA	NA	NA	NA	NA
Payout Ratio	Nil	Nil	Nil	NA	NA	NA	NA	NA	NA	NA
Prices - High	22⅞	49	16¼	NA	NA	NA	NA	NA	NA	NA
- Low	5⅝	12⅜	11	NA	NA	NA	NA	NA	NA	NA
P/E Ratio - High	NM	53	31	NA	NA	NA	NA	NA	NA	NA
- Low	NM	13	21	NA	NA	NA	NA	NA	NA	NA
Income Statement Analysis (Million $)										
Revs.	100	120	60.3	36.0	NA	NA	NA	NA	NA	NA
Oper. Inc.	9.5	24.9	13.1	7.9	NA	NA	NA	NA	NA	NA
Depr.	4.1	1.7	0.7	0.4	NA	NA	NA	NA	NA	NA
Int. Exp.	Nil	Nil	Nil	NA	NA	NA	NA	NA	NA	NA
Pretax Inc.	-4.7	25.9	12.9	7.6	NA	NA	NA	NA	NA	NA
Eff. Tax Rate	NM	37%	41%	41%	NA	NA	NA	NA	NA	NA
Net Inc.	-3.0	16.2	7.6	4.5	NA	NA	NA	NA	NA	NA
Balance Sheet & Other Fin. Data (Million $)										
Cash	13.3	67.4	32.4	5.9	NA	NA	NA	NA	NA	NA
Curr. Assets	78.0	92.5	42.6	15.3	NA	NA	NA	NA	NA	NA
Total Assets	132	102	46.9	16.5	NA	NA	NA	NA	NA	NA
Curr. Liab.	42.8	25.0	9.4	5.7	NA	NA	NA	NA	NA	NA
LT Debt	17.6	0.7	0.5	NA	NA	NA	NA	NA	NA	NA
Common Eqty.	71.1	75.5	36.8	-3.9	NA	NA	NA	NA	NA	NA
Total Cap.	88.6	76.5	37.5	NA	NA	NA	NA	NA	NA	NA
Cap. Exp.	4.9	6.9	3.8	2.3	NA	NA	NA	NA	NA	NA
Cash Flow	1.1	17.9	8.3	4.8	NA	NA	NA	NA	NA	NA
Curr. Ratio	1.8	3.7	4.5	2.7	NA	NA	NA	NA	NA	NA
% LT Debt of Cap.	19.9	0.1	1.4	NA	NA	NA	NA	NA	NA	NA
% Net Inc.of Revs.	NM	13.5	12.6	12.4	NA	NA	NA	NA	NA	NA
% Ret. on Assets	NM	21.8	24.0	NA	NA	NA	NA	NA	NA	NA
% Ret. on Equity	NM	28.8	46.2	NA	NA	NA	NA	NA	NA	NA

Data as orig reptd.; bef. results of disc opers/spec. items. Per share data adj. for stk. divs. Bold denotes diluted EPS (FASB 128)-prior periods restated. E-Estimated. NA-Not Available. NM-Not Meaningful. NR-Not Ranked.

Office— 2026 McGaw Ave., Irvine, CA 92614. **Tel**—(949) 757-0530. **Website**—www.powerwave.com **Chrmn**—J. L. Clendenin. **Pres & CEO**—B. C. Edwards. **VP, CFO & Secy**—K. T. Michaels. **Dirs**—G. M. Avis, J. L. Clendenin, A. G. Cordero, B. C. Edwards, D. L. George, E. L. Goda, A. J. Sukawaty. **Transfer Agent & Registrar**—U.S. Stock Transfer Corp., Glendale, CA. **Incorporated**—in Delaware in 1985. **Empl**— 461. **S&P Analyst:** C.F.B.

STANDARD
&POOR'S
STOCK REPORTS

Pre-Paid Legal Services

NYSE Symbol **PPD**

In S&P SmallCap 600

09-OCT-99

Industry: Services (Commercial & Consumer)

Summary: This company designs, underwrites and markets pre-paid legal expense plans, covering various legal services, throughout the U.S.

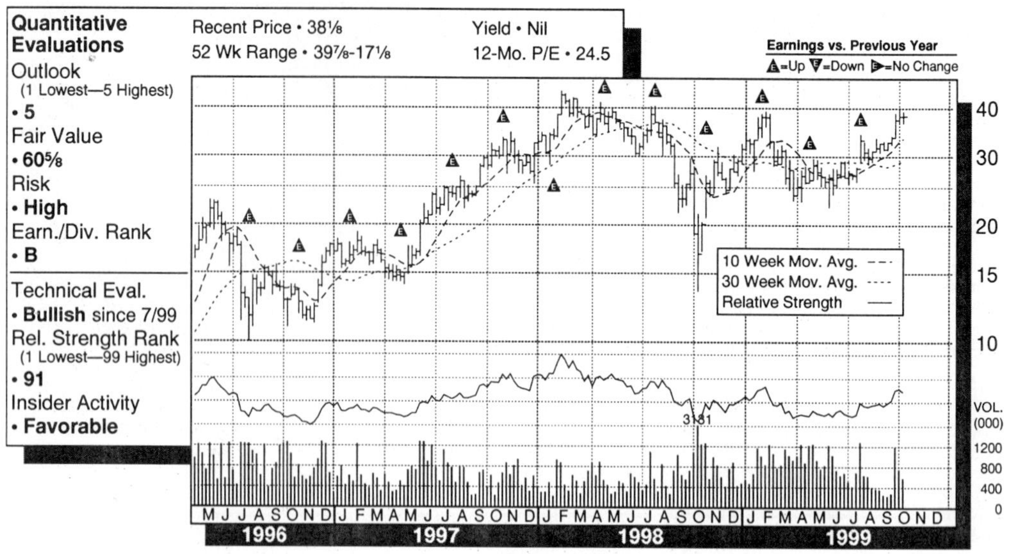

Business Profile - 21-JUL-99

In the 1999 second quarter, the company added 122,885 new members, bringing to 700,659 the number of active memberships, a 33% rise from the level a year earlier. In addition, 45,542 new sales associates were recruited during the first half of 1999. In July 1999, PPD began writing business in Ontario, Canada, through wholly owned PPL Legal Care of Canada Corp. In late July, the company expected to begin writing business in British Columbia. As of July 7, 1999, more than 5,000 Canadian sales associates had signed up to sell PPD memberships. In June 1999, directors authorized the repurchase of 250,000 common shares, following the completion of an earlier 750,000 share authorization. In May 1999, trading in the shares moved to the NYSE, from the ASE.

Operational Review - 21-JUL-99

Total revenues in the six months ended June 30, 1999, advanced 19%, year to year, as an increase in new membership premiums outweighed a decline in product sales. Profitability improved, on reduced general and administrative expenses; operating income climbed 76%. After $2.9 million in other expenses in the 1999 period, and taxes at 35.5%, versus 33.9%, the gain in net income was held to 60%, to $18,649,000 ($0.79 a share, after preferred dividends), from $11,680,000 ($0.49).

Stock Performance - 08-OCT-99

In the past 30 trading days, PPD's shares have increased 17%, compared to a 0.91% fall in the S&P 500. Average trading volume for the past five days was 114,700 shares, compared with the 40-day moving average of 100,908 shares.

Key Stock Statistics

Dividend Rate/Share	Nil	Shareholders	6,100
Shs. outstg. (M)	22.9	Market cap. (B)	$0.876
Avg. daily vol. (M)	0.138	Inst. holdings	53%
Tang. Bk. Value/Share	4.41		
Beta	1.48		

Value of $10,000 invested 5 years ago: $ 226,360

Fiscal Year Ending Dec. 31

	1999	1998	1997	1996	1995	1994
Revenues (Million $)						
1Q	44.58	37.88	19.73	12.35	7.63	5.73
2Q	47.96	39.81	22.20	14.80	8.97	6.23
3Q	—	39.81	24.20	15.76	9.82	6.41
4Q	—	42.95	26.35	17.04	11.02	6.75
Yr.	—	160.4	92.47	59.95	37.48	25.11
Earnings Per Share ($)						
1Q	**0.37**	**0.22**	**0.18**	**0.12**	0.08	0.07
2Q	**0.42**	**0.27**	**0.19**	**0.14**	0.09	0.07
3Q	—	**0.28**	**0.22**	**0.15**	0.09	0.06
4Q	—	**0.50**	**0.24**	**0.16**	0.10	0.06
Yr.	—	**1.26**	**0.83**	**0.56**	**0.34**	**0.24**

Next earnings report expected: mid October

Dividend Data

No cash has been paid on the common stock.

A Division of The McGraw-Hill Companies

Pre-Paid Legal Services, Inc.

Business Summary - 21-JUL-99

Pre-Paid Legal Services (PPD) was one of the first U.S. companies organized solely to design, underwrite and market legal expense plans. The company's plans (referred to as contracts) provide for or reimburse a portion of fees associated with a variety of legal services in a manner similar to that of medical reimbursement plans.

Contracts are offered both on an "open panel" basis, under which members may use attorneys of their choice, and on a "closed panel" basis, where members receive services from designated firms of independent provider attorneys who have contractually agreed with the company to provide scheduled benefits to members. At year-end 1998, closed-panel contracts accounted for 94% of active memberships.

The basic legal service contract, the family plan, consists of five separate benefits: (1) a preventive legal service that permits unlimited toll-free telephone access to a provider firm of attorneys and permits consultations for personal legal matters; (2) automobile legal protection, providing legal services in connection with certain licensed motor vehicle or boat-related matters; (3) a trial defense fund that provides up to 60 hours of attorneys' services available for the defense of civil or job-related criminal charges; (4) IRS audit protection service, providing up to 50 hours a year in legal assistance; and (5) the right to a 25% discount on any legal services not stipulated in the plan. About 94% of PPD's contracts outstanding are family plan contracts.

Legal service plans, while used in Europe for many years, were first developed in the U.S. in the late 1960s. Since then, there has been substantial growth in the number of Americans entitled to receive various forms of legal services through legal service plans. According to estimates developed by the National Resource Center for Consumers of Legal Services (NRC), there were 105 million Americans entitled to service through at least one legal service plan in 1997, up from 4 million in 1981, 15 million in 1985, 58 million in 1990, and 98 million in 1996. At December 31, 1998, PPD had 603,017 members in force in all 50 states and the District of Columbia. At 1998 year end, the company had 36 provider attorney firms.

In October 1998, the company acquired TPN (The Peoples Network), a marketer of personal and home care products. The acquisition was expected to significantly increase the size and effectiveness of PPD's sales force. Approximately 12,000 of TPN's 30,000 distributors were added to PPD's sales force following the acquisition. PPD, which uses a multi-level marketing approach, had 51,026 sales associates who sold at least one membership in 1998. As a result of concentrating on membership sales, the company expects product revenues to continue to decrease as a percentage of total sales.

Per Share Data ($) (Year Ended Dec. 31)	1998	1997	1996	1995	1994	1993	1992	1991	1990	1989
Tangible Bk. Val.	4.02	3.13	2.07	1.40	0.57	2.11	2.09	2.05	2.02	2.25
Cash Flow	1.38	0.86	0.58	0.37	0.29	0.07	0.08	0.08	-0.16	-0.14
Earnings	1.26	0.83	0.56	0.35	0.26	0.02	0.04	0.02	-0.23	-0.22
Dividends	Nil	Nil	Nil	Nil	Nil	Nil	Nil	Nil	Nil	Nil
Payout Ratio	Nil	Nil	Nil	Nil	Nil	Nil	Nil	Nil	Nil	Nil
Prices - High	44 1/8	34 5/8	23 1/8	10 7/8	2 3/8	2 1/2	1 7/8	1 7/8	7/8	2 1/4
- Low	13 1/2	14	9 1/8	1 11/16	1 1/4	1 1/16	3/4	3/8	1/4	3/8
P/E Ratio - High	35	42	41	31	9	NM	47	94	NM	NM
- Low	11	17	16	5	5	NM	19	19	NM	NM
Income Statement Analysis (Million $)										
Revs.	160	90.8	59.9	37.5	23.8	19.6	19.1	20.8	23.8	32.1
Oper. Inc.	44.0	29.6	19.7	11.7	3.3	1.7	1.6	1.6	0.6	-0.8
Depr.	2.9	0.7	0.5	0.5	0.4	0.5	0.6	0.6	0.7	0.8
Int. Exp.	Nil	Nil	Nil	0.0	0.3	0.5	0.8	1.2	1.5	1.7
Pretax Inc.	41.3	28.9	19.2	11.2	3.4	0.5	0.8	0.4	-3.0	-3.5
Eff. Tax Rate	27%	35%	35%	35%	NM	41%	36%	39%	NM	NM
Net Inc.	30.2	18.8	12.5	7.3	3.7	0.3	0.5	0.3	-2.4	-2.4
Balance Sheet & Other Fin. Data (Million $)										
Cash	8.6	21.8	15.3	15.0	9.5	5.3	6.0	6.7	4.7	4.5
Curr. Assets	52.3	44.1	26.1	20.0	12.6	NA	NA	NA	NA	NA
Total Assets	168	91.9	57.5	35.6	18.2	35.4	34.8	36.9	38.9	47.9
Curr. Liab.	31.1	4.9	2.8	2.3	2.4	NA	NA	NA	NA	NA
LT Debt	0.7	Nil	Nil	Nil	Nil	0.1	3.0	5.2	7.0	9.4
Common Eqty.	101	70.5	45.4	29.7	7.7	22.8	22.1	21.6	21.2	23.5
Total Cap.	129	87.0	54.7	33.3	15.8	26.9	29.2	30.7	32.1	37.6
Cap. Exp.	4.9	1.3	1.3	0.6	0.5	0.2	0.3	0.1	0.2	0.6
Cash Flow	33.1	19.5	13.0	7.7	3.7	0.8	1.1	0.8	-1.8	-1.6
Curr. Ratio	1.7	9.0	9.3	8.6	5.4	NA	NA	NA	NA	NA
% LT Debt of Cap.	0.1	Nil	Nil	Nil	Nil	0.5	10.2	16.8	21.7	25.0
% Net Inc.of Revs.	18.9	20.7	20.9	19.5	15.6	1.6	2.6	1.3	NM	NM
% Ret. on Assets	23.2	25.1	26.9	27.2	23.2	0.9	1.4	0.7	NM	NM
% Ret. on Equity	27.0	32.4	33.3	31.6	53.5	1.3	2.2	1.2	NM	NM

Data as orig reptd.; bef. results of disc opers/spec. items. Per share data adj. for stk. divs. Bold denotes diluted EPS (FASB 128)-prior periods restated. E-Estimated. NA-Not Available. NM-Not Meaningful. NR-Not Ranked.

Office—321 E. Main St., Ada, OK 74820. **Tel**—(405) 436-1234. **Fax**—(405) 436-7565. **Website**—http://www.pplsi.com **Chrmn & CEO**—H. C. Stonecipher. **Pres**—W. L. Smith. **CFO & COO**—R. Harp. **Investor Contact**—Melanie Lawson. **Dirs**—M. H. Belsky, P. K. Grunebaum, R. Harp, J. W. Hail, K. S. Pinson, D. A. Savula, W. L. Smith, H. C. Stonecipher, S. A. Stonecipher. **Transfer Agent & Registrar**—Liberty National Bank & Trust Co., Oklahoma City (NYC drop: Registrar & Transfer Co.). **Incorporated**—in Oklahoma in 1976. **Empl**— 480. **S&P Analyst:** Jordan Horoschak

STANDARD
&POOR'S
STOCK REPORTS

Premier Bancshares

NYSE Symbol **PMB**

In S&P SmallCap 600

09-OCT-99 **Industry:** Banks (Regional)

Summary: PMB is the third largest Georgia-based, independent bank holding company in the Atlanta and North Georgia markets, with assets of $1.5 billion.

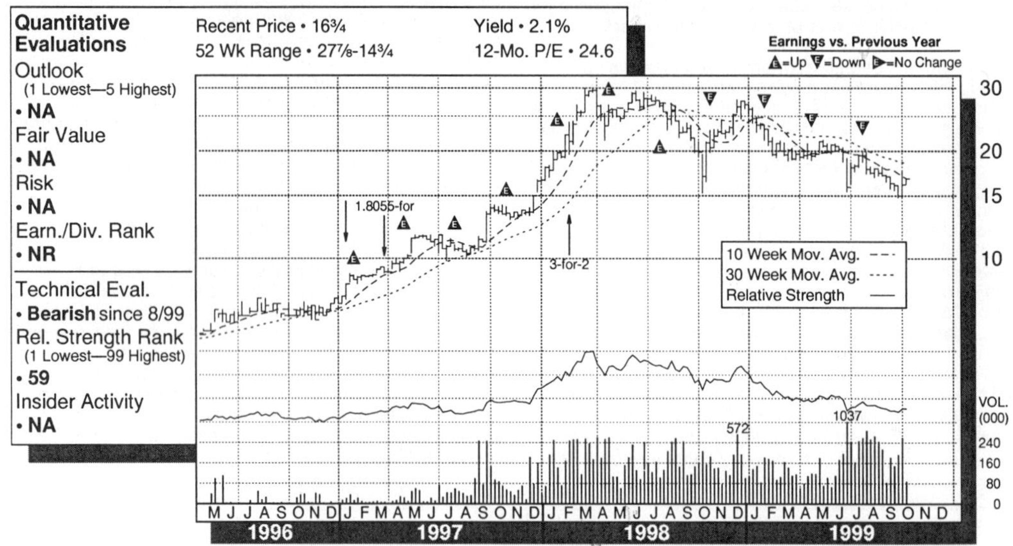

Business Profile - 26-JUL-99

Upon completion of pending acquisitions, the company and its subsidiaries will have assets of $1.9 billion (versus $1.5 billion at June 30, 1999), and will be operating 40 offices. In the 1999 second quarter, PMB completed the consolidation of all its banks into a single charter, as well as a conversion to a single operating system. The Federal Reserve's action increasing short-term interest rates on June 30 will have an immediate positive corresponding impact on over $600 million on the company's interest sensitive earning assets. Management added that it anticipated that mortgage volume would continue to grow, since the Fed's action and current neutral posture lowered long-term interest rate inflationary fears. On June 1, 1999, trading in the shares moved to the NYSE, from the ASE.

Operational Review - 26-JUL-99

Net income in the six months ended June 30, 1999, fell 20%, year to year, to $9,667,000 ($0.37 a share), from $12,132,000 ($0.47). The decline reflected a shortfall in mortgage banking operations, lower than expected earnings in commercial banking, and non-recurring expenses related in part to the consolidation of operations and systems.

Stock Performance - 08-OCT-99

In the past 30 trading days, PMB's shares have declined 2%, compared to a 0.91% fall in the S&P 500. Average trading volume for the past five days was 17,260 shares, compared with the 40-day moving average of 41,574 shares.

Key Stock Statistics

Dividend Rate/Share	0.36	Shareholders	2,400
Shs. outstg. (M)	26.2	Market cap. (B)	$0.438
Avg. daily vol. (M)	0.044	Inst. holdings	9%
Tang. Bk. Value/Share	5.12		
Beta	NA		

Value of $10,000 invested 5 years ago: NA

Fiscal Year Ending Dec. 31

	1999	1998	1997	1996	1995	1994
Revenues (Million $)						
1Q	39.20	24.62	—	8.25	3.21	—
2Q	39.34	28.77	—	8.55	3.46	—
3Q	—	38.73	—	8.31	3.55	—
4Q	—	—	—	9.77	4.02	—
Yr.	—	154.7	84.22	34.88	14.24	11.99
Earnings Per Share ($)						
1Q	0.22	0.23	0.16	0.11	—	—
2Q	0.15	0.24	0.19	0.12	—	—
3Q	—	0.18	0.21	0.08	—	—
4Q	—	0.14	0.19	0.15	0.12	—
Yr.	—	0.78	0.73	0.47	0.37	0.21

Next earnings report expected: mid October

Dividend Data (Dividends have been paid since 1996.)

Amount ($)	Date Decl.	Ex-Div. Date	Stock of Record	Payment Date
0.090	Oct. 23	Oct. 29	Nov. 02	Nov. 12 '98
0.090	Jan. 21	Feb. 10	Feb. 12	Feb. 26 '99
0.090	Apr. 13	Apr. 23	Apr. 27	May. 10 '99
0.090	Jul. 22	Aug. 03	Aug. 05	Aug. 19 '99

A Division of The McGraw-Hill Companies

Premier Bancshares, Inc.

Business Summary - 26-JUL-99

Premier Bancshares, Inc. is a locally focused, community-oriented bank holding company that at December 31, 1998 owned six subsidiary banks (subsequently consolidated into a single charter). The company operates more than 36 banking offices, in the Atlanta metropolitan area and in northern, central and coastal Georgia. In these markets, PMB provides a broad array of community banking services, including loans to small and medium-sized businesses; residential, construction and development loans; commercial real estate loans; consumer loans, and a commercial and consumer deposit accounts. In addition, through its mortgage banking unit, Premier Lending, the company operates 10 mortgage loan production offices.

The company makes both secured and unsecured loans to individuals, firms and corporations, and both consumer and commercial lending operations include various types of credit for customers. Secured loans include first and second real estate mortgage loans. PMB also makes direct installment loans to consumers on both a secured and unsecured basis. Loans totaled $1,035 million at the end of 1998, versus $852 million a year earlier, and were divided as follows: commercial, financial and agricultural 25%, real estate-construction 19%, real estate-mortgage 48%, and consumer and other 8%.

Nonperforming assets (loans past due 90 days or more, non-accrual loans and other real estate) amounted to $5.7 million (0.38% of loans) at December 31, 1998, up from $5.5 million (0.43%) a year earlier. The allowance for loan losses, the set aside for possible loan defaults, was $14.1 million (1.36% of net loans) at the end of 1998, up from $13.8 million (1.62%). Net chargeoffs were $307,0000 (0.03% of average loans) in 1998, versus net recoveries of $212,000 (0.03%) in 1997.

Revenues were obtained as follows in 1998: interest and fees on loans 64%, mortgage banking activities 17%, interest on taxable investment securities 6%, other service charges, commissions and fees 3%, and the balance of 10% from other sources.

Total deposits of $1.1 billion at 1998 year end were divided: noninterest-bearing demand deposits 16%, interest-bearing demand, savings and money market deposits 34%, and time deposits 50%.

The average yield on interest-earning assets was 8.87% in 1998 (9.23% in 1997), while the average rate paid on interest-bearing liabilities was 5.11% (5.09%), for a net interest spread of 3.76% (4.14%).

Acquisitions of financial institutions during the past two years have been a principal source of growth. In 1998, the company acquired Frederica Bank & Trust, The Bank Holding Co., Button Gwinnett Financial Corp., and Lanier Bank & Trust Co., in exchange for a total of 10,460,000 common shares.

Per Share Data ($) (Year Ended Dec. 31)	1998	1997	1996	1995	1994	1993	1992	1991	1990	1989
Tangible Bk. Val.	5.06	4.34	3.29	3.26	NA	NA	NA	NA	NA	NA
Earnings	0.79	0.73	0.39	0.32	0.05	0.07	0.04	NA	NA	NA
Dividends	0.33	0.39	0.18	Nil	NA	NA	NA	NA	NA	NA
Payout Ratio	42%	53%	46%	Nil	NA	NA	NA	NA	NA	NA
Prices - High	30	17 7/8	7 7/8	6 1/8	NA	NA	NA	NA	NA	NA
- Low	15 1/4	7 5/8	5 7/8	4 3/4	NA	NA	NA	NA	NA	NA
P/E Ratio - High	38	24	20	19	NA	NA	NA	NA	NA	NA
- Low	19	10	15	15	NA	NA	NA	NA	NA	NA
Income Statement Analysis (Million $)										
Net Int. Inc.	60.2	33.0	11.7	9.0	6.8	6.4	5.4	NA	NA	NA
Tax Equiv. Adj.	0.6	7.0	Nil	Nil	Nil	Nil	NA	NA	NA	NA
Non Int. Inc.	37.3	21.2	11.7	8.1	3.0	NA	NA	NA	NA	NA
Loan Loss Prov.	0.6	0.6	0.6	0.3	0.3	1.0	0.4	NA	NA	NA
Exp./Op. Revs.	67%	68%	83%	80%	88%	NA	NA	NA	NA	NA
Pretax Inc.	33.0	16.6	3.6	3.1	0.9	0.4	0.1	NA	NA	NA
Eff. Tax Rate	37%	33%	30%	36%	66%	24%	3.10%	NA	NA	NA
Net Inc.	20.9	11.2	2.5	2.0	0.3	0.3	0.1	NA	NA	NA
% Net Int. Marg.	4.65	4.91	4.91	4.79	NA	NA	NA	NA	NA	NA
Balance Sheet & Other Fin. Data (Million $)										
Money Mkt. Assets	132	24.3	23.1	12.5	19.1	11.6	NA	NA	NA	NA
Inv. Securities	133	116	35.1	45.8	11.6	26.4	NA	NA	NA	NA
Com'l Loans	256	90.7	28.6	22.2	NA	NA	NA	NA	NA	NA
Other Loans	777	439	183	137	NA	NA	NA	NA	NA	NA
Total Assets	1,521	794	294	238	152	140	130	NA	NA	NA
Demand Deposits	188	177	30.2	29.3	NA	NA	NA	NA	NA	NA
Time Deposits	992	376	207	149	NA	NA	NA	NA	NA	NA
LT Debt	Nil	1.8	4.0	3.0	NA	NA	NA	NA	NA	NA
Common Eqty.	136	68.9	23.8	23.4	17.6	17.9	14.0	NA	NA	NA
% Ret. on Assets	1.8	2.1	1.0	1.0	0.2	0.2	NA	NA	NA	NA
% Ret. on Equity	20.2	24.3	10.9	9.7	1.6	1.9	NA	NA	NA	NA
% Loan Loss Resv.	NA	1.6	1.3	1.4	NA	NA	NA	NA	NA	NA
% Loans/Deposits	NA	82.5	78.9	74.5	NA	NA	NA	NA	NA	NA
% Equity to Assets	8.9	8.5	8.8	10.5	12.1	11.8	NA	NA	NA	NA

Data as orig reptd.; bef. results of disc opers/spec. items. Per share data adj. for stk. divs. Bold denotes diluted EPS (FASB 128)-prior periods restated. E-Estimated. NA-Not Available. NM-Not Meaningful. NR-Not Ranked.

Office—2180 Atlanta Plaza, 950 East Paces Ferry Rd., Atlanta, GA 30326. **Tel**—(404) 814-3090. **Chrmn & CEO**—D. D. Pittard. **Pres & COO**—R. C. Oliver. **EVP & CFO**—M. E. Ricketson. **Dirs**—N. M. Anderson, G. S. Carpenter, J. L. Coxwell, Sr., D. N. Ellis, W. M. Evans, Jr., J. H. Ferguson, R. E. Flournoy III, J. E. Freeman, A. F. Gandy, R. R. Howell, B. H. Martin, C. S. McQuaig, R. C. Oliver, T. E. Owen, Jr., D. D. Pittard, J. D. Stephens, J. E. Sutherland. **Transfer Agent & Registrar**—SunTrust Bank, Atlanta. **Incorporated**—in Georgia in 1988. **Empl**— 693. **S&P Analyst:** P.L.H.

Pride International

NYSE Symbol **PDE**
In S&P SmallCap 600

09-OCT-99

Industry:
Oil & Gas (Drilling & Equipment)

Summary: This company is a leading provider of contract drilling and related services in the U.S. Gulf of Mexico, and onshore and offshore in numerous foreign countries.

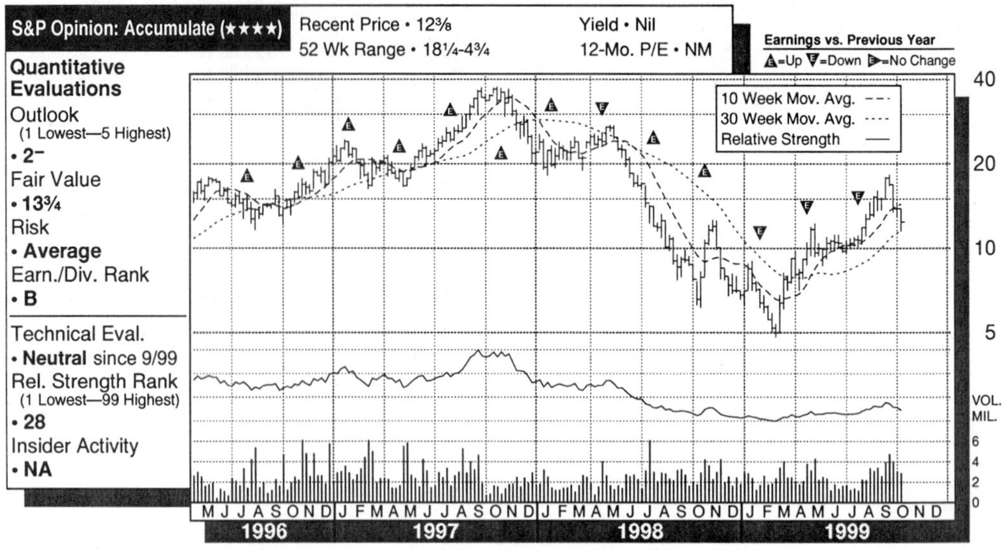

Overview - 07-JUN-99

Revenues may fall as much as 30% in 1999, in a sign of the global retrenchment in the oil and gas drilling industry. Energy companies have sharply curtailed their drilling budgets this year. While the company side-stepped the severe pullback in U.S. onshore drilling by selling its assets there back in 1997, it has not been able to avoid a slowdown in shallow water activity in the Gulf of Mexico. Drilling activity in South America, particularly Venezuela, was also weak in early 1999. Of course, pricing has declined precipitously as drillers compete for what business there is. Apart from a net restructuring charge of about $29 million recorded in the first quarter for facility consolidations and personnel reductions, we expect PDE to be modestly profitable in 1999. Although earnings from operations can be expected to drop more than 80% this year to $0.25 from 1998's $1.39, we see hope of a modest recovery in 2000, with EPS of $0.50.

Valuation - 07-JUN-99

We rate PDE accumulate. The shares have recouped some of 1998's decline, as has the entire drilling group, as recent OPEC production cuts have resulted in improved sentiment for the energy sector, and hopes that the economic recovery in Asia is taking hold have propped up forecasts for a recovery in demand for fossil fuels. The long term trend of gradual increases in global petroleum consumption bodes well for drilling contractors that can quickly deploy rigs wherever they are needed around the world. PDE has positioned itself to benefit from this trend.

Key Stock Statistics

S&P EPS Est. 1999	-0.25	Tang. Bk. Value/Share	13.99
P/E on S&P Est. 1999	NM	Beta	0.98
S&P EPS Est. 2000	0.50	Shareholders	2,004
Dividend Rate/Share	Nil	Market cap. (B)	$0.698
Shs. outstg. (M)	56.2	Inst. holdings	46%
Avg. daily vol. (M)	0.729		

Value of $10,000 invested 5 years ago: $ 24,267

Fiscal Year Ending Dec. 31

	1999	1998	1997	1996	1995	1994
Revenues (Million $)						
1Q	153.8	213.7	131.4	66.24	62.51	36.81
2Q	168.1	219.2	174.5	102.0	68.86	40.26
3Q	—	210.0	182.9	115.4	67.14	50.97
4Q	—	194.3	211.0	123.6	65.09	54.30
Yr.	—	837.2	699.8	407.2	263.6	182.3
Earnings Per Share ($)						
1Q	**-0.78**	**0.40**	**1.49**	**0.11**	0.12	0.06
2Q	**-0.13**	**0.43**	**0.27**	**0.17**	0.14	0.06
3Q	—	**0.37**	**0.28**	**0.25**	0.18	0.08
4Q	—	**0.21**	**0.37**	0.27	0.16	0.10
Yr.	—	**1.39**	**2.16**	**0.77**	**0.61**	**0.30**

Next earnings report expected: late October

Dividend Data

No cash dividends have been paid.

Pride International, Inc.

Business Summary - 07-JUN-99

Pride International, Inc. (PDE) is a leading global provider of onshore and offshore drilling, workover and related services to oil and gas exploration and production companies in more than 20 countries. In recent years, the company has focused its growth strategy on the higher-margin offshore and international drilling and workover markets. Since the beginning of 1997, it has divested its U.S. land-based operations, expanded its international operations significantly via the purchase of the operating subsidiaries of Forasol-Foramer N.V., purchased through several transactions 15 offshore rigs of various types, and acquired a 60% interest in a joint venture with the Bolivian national oil company.

As of December 31, 1998, PDE operated a fleet of 308 rigs, including 251 land-based drilling and workover rigs, 23 offshore platform rigs, 17 jackup rigs, nine tender-assisted rigs, five barge rigs, and three semisubmersible rigs. The company has also committed to invest in a 51% interest in joint ventures to build, own and operate two ultra-deepwater drillships to be deployed in 1999 and 2000 in the Atlantic off the coast of Angola in western Africa. It also has a 30% joint venture interest in a company that will construct, own, and operate four Amethyst-class semisubmersible rigs to be operated in Brazilian waters.

With these transactions, international operations have become an increasingly important source of revenues for the company, comprising over 81% of total revenues in 1998, up from 57% in 1996. In a similar trend, offshore activities grew to 52% of revenues in 1998 from just 18% in 1996. Two customers accounted for 14% and 11%, respectively, of PDE's revenues in 1998.

The company's diversification into international markets should enable it to provide services in a diverse number of geographic locations, allowing it to take advantage of market upturns while reducing its exposure to sharp downturns in any particular market sector or geographic region. Of course, along with the benefits of expanded international operations come additional risks, including foreign exchange restrictions and currency fluctuations, changes in foreign tax rates and monetary policies, and political or military instability. In extreme circumstances, foreign assets may be subject to expropriation or nationalization.

Capital expenditures, which totaled $657 million in 1998, are expected to be substantially lower in 1999 in response to the petroleum industry's sharp curtailment of exploration activities. Projected specific new construction and refurbishment expenditures, including those of joint ventures, are estimated at $270 million. Significant recent financings include the April 1998 issuance of zero coupon, 20 year convertible subordinated debentures, which will have a value of $588 million at maturity.

Per Share Data ($) (Year Ended Dec. 31)	1998	1997	1996	1995	1994	1993	1992	1991	1990	1989
Tangible Bk. Val.	15.08	13.62	6.97	5.14	4.49	4.24	3.85	3.92	3.69	3.36
Cash Flow	2.59	3.31	1.84	1.26	0.76	0.49	0.27	0.55	0.56	0.29
Earnings	1.39	2.16	0.81	0.60	0.30	0.13	-0.05	0.22	0.29	0.05
Dividends	Nil	Nil	Nil	Nil	Nil	Nil	Nil	Nil	Nil	Nil
Payout Ratio	Nil	Nil	Nil	Nil	Nil	Nil	Nil	Nil	Nil	Nil
Prices - High	27 1/2	37 3/4	23 1/4	11	6 1/4	7 1/2	5 3/8	7	8 5/8	6 5/8
- Low	6 1/8	16 1/4	9 1/8	4 3/4	4 5/8	3 1/2	3 3/8	3 5/8	4	2 5/8
P/E Ratio - High	20	17	29	18	21	58	NM	32	30	NM
- Low	4	8	11	8	15	27	NM	16	14	NM
Income Statement Analysis (Million $)										
Revs.	836	700	407	264	182	127	101	112	102	66.0
Oper. Inc.	221	167	69.2	42.9	17.6	8.8	3.0	10.3	11.3	4.8
Depr.	79.9	58.7	29.1	16.7	9.6	6.0	5.2	5.5	4.5	2.9
Int. Exp.	45.8	34.4	13.6	6.3	0.2	0.0	Nil	0.0	0.1	0.4
Pretax Inc.	102	156	30.8	22.4	8.1	3.3	-1.4	5.7	7.6	0.9
Eff. Tax Rate	24%	33%	26%	32%	23%	37%	NM	39%	39%	42%
Net Inc.	77.5	104	22.7	15.4	6.2	2.1	-0.8	3.5	4.7	0.5
Balance Sheet & Other Fin. Data (Million $)										
Cash	86.5	73.5	10.8	11.9	9.0	15.2	24.1	17.0	8.9	21.8
Curr. Assets	370	334	156	73.1	60.3	46.0	43.5	35.4	29.6	35.6
Total Assets	2,192	1,542	542	258	205	110	94.8	89.8	85.6	72.5
Curr. Liab.	285	230	93.7	41.9	33.6	24.3	18.4	12.1	10.0	8.3
LT Debt	970	524	187	61.1	42.1	0.2	3.6	4.9	5.9	2.0
Common Eqty.	763	685	202	131	111	69.1	61.8	62.4	58.9	53.1
Total Cap.	1,858	1,256	436	212	166	80.6	76.4	77.7	75.6	64.1
Cap. Exp.	574	268	61.7	40.6	59.2	23.8	4.1	5.9	14.7	4.6
Cash Flow	157	163	51.8	32.0	15.8	8.1	4.4	9.0	9.1	3.4
Curr. Ratio	1.3	1.5	1.7	1.7	1.8	1.9	2.4	2.9	2.9	4.3
% LT Debt of Cap.	52.2	41.7	42.9	28.8	25.3	0.2	4.8	6.3	7.9	3.0
% Net Inc.of Revs.	9.3	14.9	5.6	5.8	3.4	1.7	NM	3.1	4.6	0.8
% Ret. on Assets	4.2	10.0	5.7	6.6	3.4	2.0	NM	4.0	5.9	0.8
% Ret. on Equity	10.7	23.4	13.6	12.7	5.8	3.2	NM	5.8	8.3	1.1

Data as orig reptd.; bef. results of disc opers/spec. items. Per share data adj. for stk. divs. Bold denotes diluted EPS (FASB 128)-prior periods restated. E-Estimated. NA-Not Available. NM-Not Meaningful. NR-Not Ranked.

Office—1500 City West Blvd., Suite 400, Houston, TX 77042.**Tel**—(713) 789-1400.**Website**—www.pride.com **CEO, Pres & COO**—P. A Bragg. **VP & CFO**—E. W. McNiel. **VP & Secy**—R. W. Randall. **Dirs**—P. A. Bragg, J. B. Clement, J. E. Estrada M., R. D. McBride, T. H. Roberts Jr., J. T. Sneed. **Transfer Agent & Registrar**—American Stock Transfer & Trust Co., NYC.**Incorporated**—in Louisiana in 1988. **Empl**— 7,500. **S&P Analyst:** Mark S. Basham

STANDARD
&POOR'S
STOCK REPORTS

Primark Corp.

NYSE Symbol **PMK**

In S&P SmallCap 600

23-OCT-99

Industry:
Services (Commercial & Consumer)

Summary: Primark is a global information services organization supplying financial, economic and market research information to financial, corporate and government markets.

Quantitative Evaluations

Outlook
(1 Lowest—5 Highest)
• **2+**

Fair Value
• **25¾**

Risk
• **Average**

Earn./Div. Rank
• **B**

Technical Eval.
• **NA**

Rel. Strength Rank
(1 Lowest—99 Highest)
• **47**

Insider Activity
• **NA**

Recent Price • 26
52 Wk Range • 30⅝-18⅞
Yield • Nil
12-Mo. P/E • 13.1

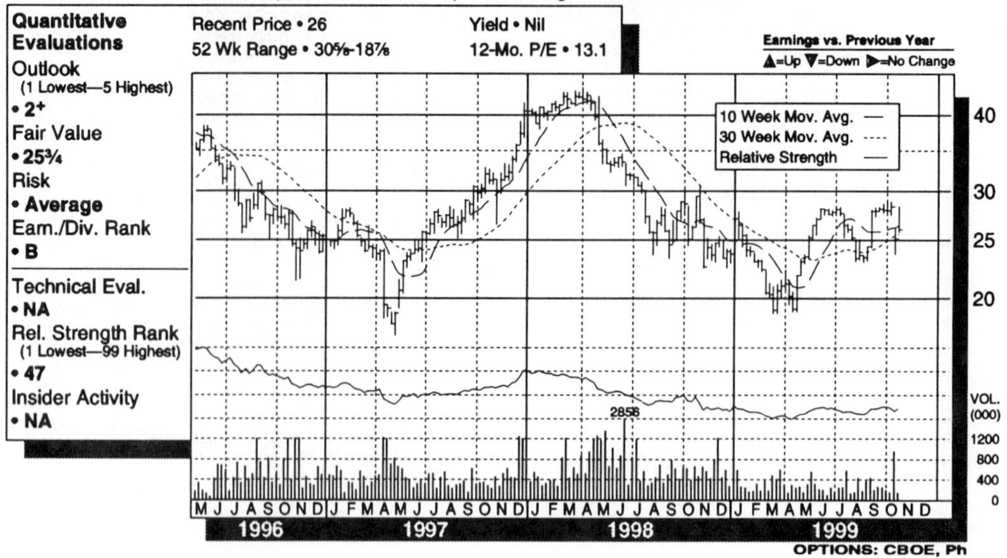

Business Profile - 19-OCT-99

In October 1999, PMK replaced its Laser Disclosure product with the launching of Global Access PRO version 1.1, a Y2K-ready document fulfillment workstation. In August 1999, PMK launched EuroTOPIC, a flexible international equities information product. In June 1999, PMK paid $16 million to acquire the remaining 20% interest in Worldscope, a producer of a global company financial information database. In February 1999, PMK purchased the Company Fundamental Data business and Extel brand name from The Financial Times Group for $31.9 million. From July 1998 through June 1999, PMK repurchased 2.6 million shares, with nearly 1.4 million more still authorized for repurchase.

Operational Review - 19-OCT-99

Operating revenues in the six months ended June 30, 1999, rose 12%, year to year, led by increased sales at PMK's financial information division, and strong revenue growth at the financial analytics division. Operating income, versus a loss in 1998, principally reflected the absence of a $68.7 million restructuring charge in 1998. After higher net interest expense and taxes at 48.8%, versus a tax benefit of $4,782,000 in 1998, income from continuing operations of $6,879,000 ($0.33 a share, on 22% fewer shares) contrasted with a loss of $44,355,000 ($1.64). Results exclude income from discontinued operations of $6.64 and an extraordinary loss of $0.19 in 1998, and a charge of $0.01 in 1999 for a change in accounting principle.

Stock Performance - 22-OCT-99

In the past 30 trading days, PMK's shares have declined 10%, compared to a 4% fall in the S&P 500. Average trading volume for the past five days was 32,260 shares, compared with the 40-day moving average of 53,577 shares.

Key Stock Statistics

Dividend Rate/Share	Nil	Shareholders	8,286
Shs. outstg. (M)	20.4	Market cap. (B)	$0.514
Avg. daily vol. (M)	0.074	Inst. holdings	52%
Tang. Bk. Value/Share	NM		
Beta	0.76		

Value of $10,000 invested 5 years ago: $ 22,333

Fiscal Year Ending Dec. 31

	1999	1998	1997	1996	1995	1994
Revenues (Million $)						
1Q	117.3	104.4	94.68	180.7	135.9	112.4
2Q	122.2	108.9	100.9	187.7	143.0	119.0
3Q	—	108.5	79.11	194.0	168.7	121.0
4Q	—	112.7	103.2	204.7	169.7	124.6
Yr.	—	434.5	397.9	767.1	617.3	477.0
Earnings Per Share ($)						
1Q	**0.13**	**0.13**	NA	NA	0.20	0.14
2Q	**0.20**	**-1.71**	NA	NA	0.21	0.16
3Q	—	**0.26**	NA	NA	0.21	0.15
4Q	—	**0.23**	NA	NA	0.22	0.17
Yr.	—	**-1.37**	**0.25**	**0.46**	**0.19**	**0.01**

Next earnings report expected: early November

Dividend Data

Dividends, which were initiated in 1982, ceased following PMK's spinoff to shareholders of Michigan Consolidated Gas in 1988. A "poison pill" stock purchase rights plan was adopted in 1988.

Primark Corporation

Business Summary - 19-OCT-99

Primark is a leading global information service provider of comprehensive financial, economic and market research information. PMK serves customers spanning the fields of investment, legal, accounting, banking, corporate and government. PMK develops and markets "value-added" database and information products that cover established and emerging markets worldwide. The company uses its proprietary analytical software applications to provide its analysis and presentation of financial, economic and market research information.

PMK serves customers in the U.S., Europe and the Pacific Rim. The company owns and maintains large-scale databases, which are accessed through its on-line distribution systems, the Internet and third-party distributors. PMK's databases are used by more than 5,000 organizations worldwide.

Primark grew primarily through acquisitions over the past six years. To capitalize on the integration of the acquired businesses, in June 1998, PMK reorganized its 12 operating units into three divisions focusing on common customer groups. Management expects to benefit from combined marketing, sales and administrative operations and the elimination of redundant production and delivery platforms. PMK also expected to provide broader access to its customer base, and to improve the speed and efficiency of product delivery.

Primark Financial Information division (PFID) develops "enterprise-wide" products and services for financial institutions on a global basis. It also includes transactional products, both historical and real-time, as well as products supporting large-scale investment accounting functions, the individual investor and the referential needs of large financial market customers. PFID includes: Datastream, a provider of global historical and fundamental real-time securities data and news; ICV, a U.K. provider of on-line equity trading products; Primark Investment Management Services, a provider of computer-based accounting and other investment fund services; Disclosure/Worldscope, providers of "as reported" and abstracted financial information; A-T Financial Information, a provider of Windows-compatible financial market data and software to institutional investors; and Extel, a provider of summarized financial statements to the investment industry worldwide.

Primark Financial Analytics division (PFAD) develops and markets a variety of analytical products for money managers, fund sponsors and other investors. PFAD includes: I/B/E/S, a provider of global earnings expectations, historical data on earnings surprises and research reports from analysts; Baseline, offering a stock and portfolio analysis and selection system designed for institutional portfolio managers; and Vestek, an international provider of portfolio information, analytics and consulting support to investment professionals.

Primark Decision Information division includes WEFA, an international provider of economic research, analysis and forecasts, and Primark Decision Economics, a disseminator of economic forecasts, analyses and commentaries, in which PMK has a 20% equity interest.

Per Share Data ($) (Year Ended Dec. 31)	1998	1997	1996	1995	1994	1993	1992	1991	1990	1989
Tangible Bk. Val.	NM	NA	-5.70	-4.77	-3.29	-4.42	-5.83	4.68	10.66	10.34
Cash Flow	0.64	2.05	3.02	2.61	2.00	1.84	0.98	0.23	0.10	0.41
Earnings	6.66	0.25	1.04	0.85	0.62	0.52	0.40	0.02	0.03	0.23
Dividends	Nil	Nil	Nil	Nil	Nil	Nil	Nil	Nil	Nil	Nil
Payout Ratio	Nil	Nil	Nil	Nil	Nil	Nil	Nil	Nil	Nil	Nil
Prices - High	44½	42	40	30¼	15	16⅜	14¾	14¾	9½	10¼
- Low	22½	17⅜	21⅜	12¾	11	10½	9	6	5⅝	6½
P/E Ratio - High	7	NM	38	36	24	31	37	NM	NM	45
- Low	3	NM	21	15	18	20	23	NM	NM	28
Income Statement Analysis (Million $)										
Revs.	435	398	767	617	477	444	310	153	27.0	39.0
Oper. Inc.	93.8	89.0	110	93.3	65.6	63.5	32.3	1.6	-5.3	-2.3
Depr.	48.8	50.2	43.4	36.4	27.5	26.2	11.3	4.3	1.3	3.6
Int. Exp.	9.5	16.0	20.2	20.4	14.2	14.6	5.9	3.0	1.0	1.1
Pretax Inc.	-30.8	20.0	49.2	34.0	23.5	21.3	16.2	1.3	-1.5	0.9
Eff. Tax Rate	NM	65%	43%	45%	42%	45%	44%	30%	NM	NM
Net Inc.	-33.4	7.0	28.0	18.9	13.8	11.7	9.0	0.9	0.7	4.5
Balance Sheet & Other Fin. Data (Million $)										
Cash	51.6	12.8	25.7	62.3	20.0	18.0	23.1	48.0	115	112
Curr. Assets	178	335	234	220	135	125	142	153	157	170
Total Assets	843	1,044	979	802	508	497	523	335	219	254
Curr. Liab.	226	202	224	139	97.0	102	109	83.0	13.6	27.8
LT Debt	151	331	242	266	146	148	171	31.5	1.0	0.5
Common Eqty.	440	471	476	354	225	208	202	195	193	205
Total Cap.	601	824	730	650	401	386	403	249	201	216
Cap. Exp.	22.8	23.9	26.3	22.7	22.6	12.7	6.9	NA	NA	NA
Cash Flow	15.4	57.2	71.0	53.8	39.9	36.5	18.9	4.6	1.9	8.1
Curr. Ratio	0.8	1.7	1.0	1.6	1.4	1.2	1.3	1.8	11.5	6.1
% LT Debt of Cap.	25.2	40.2	33.2	40.9	36.4	38.3	42.5	12.6	0.5	0.2
% Net Inc.of Revs.	NM	1.8	3.6	3.1	2.9	2.6	2.9	0.6	2.4	11.6
% Ret. on Assets	NM	0.7	3.1	2.9	2.7	2.3	1.9	0.3	0.3	1.7
% Ret. on Equity	NM	1.5	6.6	6.0	5.7	5.0	3.6	0.2	0.3	2.2

Data as orig reptd.; bef. results of disc opers/spec. items. Per share data adj. for stk. divs. Bold denotes diluted EPS (FASB 128)-prior periods restated. E-Estimated. NA-Not Available. NM-Not Meaningful. NR-Not Ranked.

Office—1000 Winter St., Suite 4300N, Waltham, MA 02451.**Tel**—(781) 466-6611. **Website**—http://www.primark.com **Chrmn, Pres & CEO**—J. E. Kasputys. **EVP & CFO**—S. H. Curran. **EVP & Secy**—M. R. Kargula. **VP & Treas**—P. Sandford. **Investor Contacts**—A. McGillicuddy & D. Kawiecki (781) 487-2124.**Dirs**—K. J. Bradley, J. C. Holt, J. E. Kasputys, S. Lazarus, P. G. McGinnis, J. Newcomb, D. Taylor, C. K. Weaver. **Transfer Agent & Registrar**—BankBoston EquiServe. **Incorporated**—in Michigan in 1981. **Empl**— 2,900. **S&P Analyst:** Markos N. Kaminis

STANDARD & POOR'S
STOCK REPORTS

Prime Hospitality

NYSE Symbol **PDQ**

In S&P SmallCap 600

09-OCT-99

Industry: Lodging - Hotels

Summary: This company owns, manages and franchises nearly 200 hotels across the United States and in the U.S. Virgin Islands.

Quantitative Evaluations

Outlook (1 Lowest—5 Highest) • 5+

Fair Value • 25⅝

Risk • Average

Earn./Div. Rank • NR

Technical Eval. • Bearish since 7/99

Rel. Strength Rank (1 Lowest—99 Highest) • 11

Insider Activity • NA

Recent Price • 7¾
52 Wk Range • 12⅞-5
Yield • Nil
12-Mo. P/E • 8.7

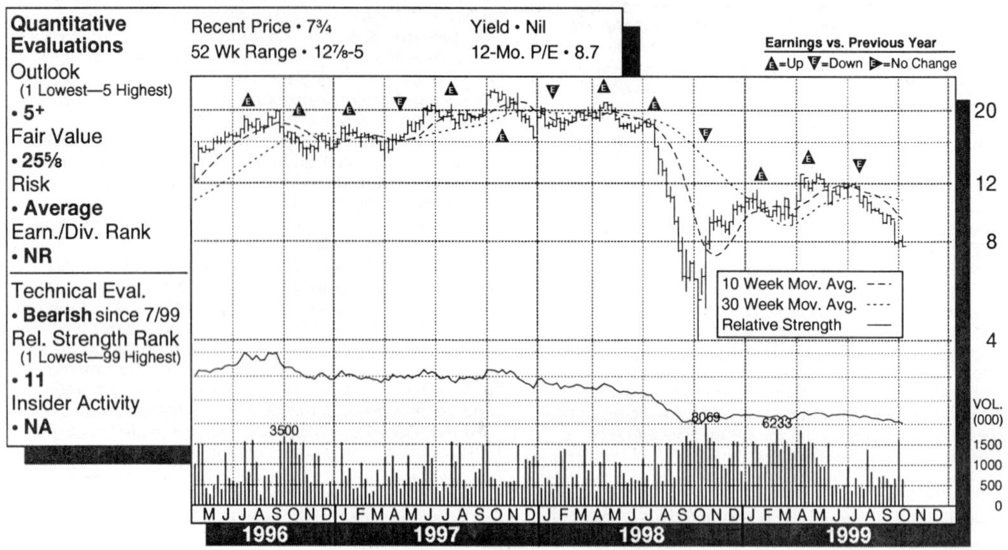

Business Profile - 22-JUN-99

PDQ is focusing on franchising opportunities to further accelerate the growth of its brands. The company intends to convert 38 of its extended-stay HomeGate hotels into its limited-service Wellesley Inns by the end of 1999. In February 1999, Meristar Hospitality Corp. (MHX) announced that it will be unable to fulfill its contract obligation to purchase nine full-service hotels from PDQ. Consequently, the company received a $4 million contract termination fee, and has decided to continue to operate these nine hotels. PDQ has generated $40 million from asset sales, and has utilized part of those proceeds to repurchase $25 million of its common stock.

Operational Review - 22-JUN-99

Total revenues for the three months ended March 31, 1999, climbed 29%, primarily reflecting additional revenues from new hotels and improved results at the company-owned Marriott's Frenchman's Reef in St. Thomas. Total costs and expenses rose more rapidly on the addition of new hotels, and operating income increased 17%. After higher interest expense and taxes at 39.0%, versus 38.0%, net income advanced 12%, to $11.5 million ($0.22 a share, based on 12% more shares), from $10.3 million ($0.20). Results in 1999 exclude a charge of $0.10 a share related to an accounting change

Stock Performance - 08-OCT-99

In the past 30 trading days, PDQ's shares have declined 21%, compared to a 0.91% fall in the S&P 500. Average trading volume for the past five days was 129,620 shares, compared with the 40-day moving average of 185,344 shares.

Key Stock Statistics

Dividend Rate/Share	Nil	Shareholders	2,022
Shs. outstg. (M)	51.7	Market cap. (B)	$0.401
Avg. daily vol. (M)	0.234	Inst. holdings	75%
Tang. Bk. Value/Share	12.48		
Beta	1.42		

Value of $10,000 invested 5 years ago: $ 12,156

Fiscal Year Ending Dec. 31

	1999	1998	1997	1996	1995	1994
Revenues (Million $)						
1Q	133.3	103.3	78.05	58.61	48.24	28.08
2Q	146.0	123.0	85.56	69.89	51.70	33.19
3Q	—	121.0	87.80	87.80	52.70	36.06
4Q	—	122.1	89.54	71.52	52.98	36.97
Yr.	—	469.4	341.0	268.9	205.6	134.3
Earnings Per Share ($)						
1Q	**0.22**	**0.20**	**0.17**	**0.19**	0.13	0.08
2Q	**0.31**	**0.43**	**0.26**	**0.17**	0.15	0.22
3Q	—	**0.17**	**0.22**	**0.17**	0.13	0.13
4Q	—	**0.20**	**-0.11**	**0.15**	0.13	0.14
Yr.	—	**1.00**	**0.54**	**0.68**	**0.54**	0.57

Next earnings report expected: late October

Dividend Data

No cash dividends have been paid, and PDQ does not expect to pay any in the foreseeable future.

A Division of The McGraw-Hill Companies

Prime Hospitality Corp.

Business Summary - 22-JUN-99

Prime Hospitality (formerly Prime Motor Inns, Inc.) is transforming itself from a hotel owner and operator into a franchisor and manager of hotels. Over the past years, PDQ invested its own capital to grow AmeriSuites into a national chain with strong recognition. Now, the company intends to expand with minimal capital investment through franchising opportunities. PDQ believes that franchising will be a major growth vehicle for the company in the coming years.

As of February 28, 1999, PDQ owned or operated 193 hotels in four major lodging industry segments: the all-suites segment with its AmeriSuites brand; the extended stay segment with its HomeGate Studios & Suites brand; the limited-service segment with its Wellesley brand; and the full-service segment under major national franchises.

AmeriSuites are upscale, all-suite hotels containing approximately 128 suites and located primarily near suburban commercial centers. As of February 28, 1999, PDQ owned or operated 94 AmeriSuites units. In addition, the company has signed 10 new AmeriSuites franchise agreements, with 22 additional AmeriSuites franchise applications pending.

Within the full-service hotel segment, PDQ operated 28 upscale hotels with food service and banquet facilities under franchise agreements with national hotel brands. As part of the company's strategic initiative to reduce its investment in real estate, PDQ sold and leased back eight full service hotels to Meristar Hospitality Group. The company intends to divest certain hotels from its remaining 13 owned full-service hotels that are not consistent with the majority of PDQ's portfolio.

Acquired in December 1997, the HomeGate brand consists of mid-priced, extended-stay hotels that typically contain between 120 to 140 suites. PDQ operated 38 Homegate hotels, with an additional six under construction.

PDQ operated 28 limited-service hotels under the Wellesley Inns brand name. In addition, the company manages another five limited-service units under franchise agreements with national chains. PDQ intends to convert its extended-stay HomeGate hotels into its limited-service Wellesley Inns in 1999. The company believes that the conversion will help improve franchising prospects for the Wellesley Inns.

At the end of 1998, PDQ had 13 land sites available for development and intends to develop AmeriSuites hotels on six of the sites. Construction on several of the properties is expected to commence around mid-1999.

PDQ's expansion strategy is to open between five and ten AmeriSuites hotels per year with additional development coming from franchisees. The company does not intend to develop additional HomeGate and Wellesley hotels in the short term, and will rely on franchising to grow these brands.

The company emerged from bankruptcy proceedings in 1992.

Per Share Data ($) (Year Ended Dec. 31)	1998	1997	1996	1995	1994	1993	1992	1991	1990	1989
Tangible Bk. Val.	11.93	11.13	10.55	7.66	6.71	5.18	NM	NA	NA	12.59
Cash Flow	1.75	1.24	1.56	1.03	0.86	0.45	NM	NA	NA	2.67
Earnings	1.00	0.54	0.80	0.54	0.57	0.24	NM	NA	NA	2.35
Dividends	Nil	Nil	Nil	Nil	Nil	Nil	Nil	Nil	0.08	0.08
Payout Ratio	Nil	Nil	Nil	Nil	Nil	Nil	Nil	Nil	NA	3%
Prices - High	21¼	23⅛	20	11	9	6⅜	2¼	2	23¾	37½
- Low	4	14⅛	9⅝	7¼	5⅜	2	1½	3/16	⅜	21⅝
P/E Ratio - High	21	43	25	20	16	27	NM	NA	NA	16
- Low	4	26	12	13	9	8	NM	NA	NA	9
Income Statement Analysis (Million $)										
Revs.	469	335	269	206	134	109	109	171	NA	315
Oper. Inc.	148	125	88.9	61.8	42.7	31.9	3.9	-20.6	NA	77.8
Depr.	42.0	34.2	25.8	16.0	9.3	7.0	6.9	7.9	NA	10.6
Int. Exp.	23.9	33.0	20.3	21.6	14.8	16.1	8.4	20.3	NA	39.4
Pretax Inc.	86.7	50.7	51.5	29.1	30.0	14.0	-71.0	-259	NA	125
Eff. Tax Rate	38%	49%	40%	40%	40%	41%	NM	NM	NA	38%
Net Inc.	53.8	25.9	30.9	17.5	18.0	8.0	-72.0	-245	NA	77.4
Balance Sheet & Other Fin. Data (Million $)										
Cash	25.0	5.0	16.2	70.4	22.0	53.0	60.0	61.0	NA	40.0
Curr. Assets	75.4	61.1	44.0	93.2	39.0	68.0	134	115	NA	270
Total Assets	1,408	1,197	786	573	435	411	554	680	NA	1,144
Curr. Liab.	99	80.8	49.3	44.7	29.0	42.0	32.0	33.0	NA	196
LT Debt	582	555	299	277	179	169	9.0	3.0	NA	423
Common Eqty.	641	524	420	233	204	171	-228	-156	NA	452
Total Cap.	1,223	1,079	719	510	383	340	-219	-153	NA	922
Cap. Exp.	28.5	108	102	14.3	63.4	23.4	14.1	21.9	NA	73.0
Cash Flow	95.8	60.1	56.7	33.4	28.0	15.0	-65.0	-237	NA	88.0
Curr. Ratio	0.8	0.8	0.9	2.1	1.3	1.6	4.2	3.5	NA	1.4
% LT Debt of Cap.	47.6	51.4	41.6	54.3	46.7	49.6	NM	NM	NA	45.8
% Net Inc.of Revs.	11.5	7.7	11.5	8.5	13.6	7.5	NM	NM	NA	24.6
% Ret. on Assets	4.1	2.6	4.5	3.5	4.5	1.7	NM	NA	NA	7.5
% Ret. on Equity	9.2	5.5	9.5	8.0	10.1	NM	NM	NA	NA	18.7

Data as orig reptd.; bef. results of disc opers/spec. items. Per share data adj. for stk. divs. Bold denotes diluted EPS (FASB 128)-prior periods restated. E-Estimated. NA-Not Available. NM-Not Meaningful. NR-Not Ranked.

Office—700 Route 46 East, Fairfield, NJ 07004. **Tel**—(973) 882-1010. **Fax**—(973) 882-8577. **Website**—http://www.primehospitality.com. **Chrmn, Pres & CEO**—A. F. Petrocelli. **SVP & CFO**—D. W. Vicari. **SVP & Secy**—J. Bernadino. **Dirs**—L. Friedland, H. M. Lorber, H. Lust II, J. H. Nusbaum, A. F. Petrocelli, D. W. Vicari. **Transfer Agent & Registrar**—Continental Stock Transfer & Trust Co., NYC.**Incorporated**—in Delaware in 1985. **Empl**— 6,800. **S&P Analyst:** A. Bensinger

STANDARD
&POOR'S
STOCK REPORTS

Priority Healthcare

NASDAQ Symbol **PHCC**

In S&P SmallCap 600

09-OCT-99

Industry: Distributors (Food & Health)

Summary: PHCC distributes specialty pharmaceuticals to the alternate healthcare market, and provides biopharmaceuticals and disease treatment programs to individuals with chronic diseases.

Quantitative Evaluations

Outlook
(1 Lowest—5 Highest)
• **NA**

Fair Value
• **NA**

Risk
• **NA**

Earn./Div. Rank
• **NR**

Technical Eval.
• **NA**

Rel. Strength Rank
(1 Lowest—99 Highest)
• **6**

Insider Activity
• **Favorable**

Recent Price • 22⅞
52 Wk Range • 48¾-14⅛

Yield • Nil
12-Mo. P/E • 31.3

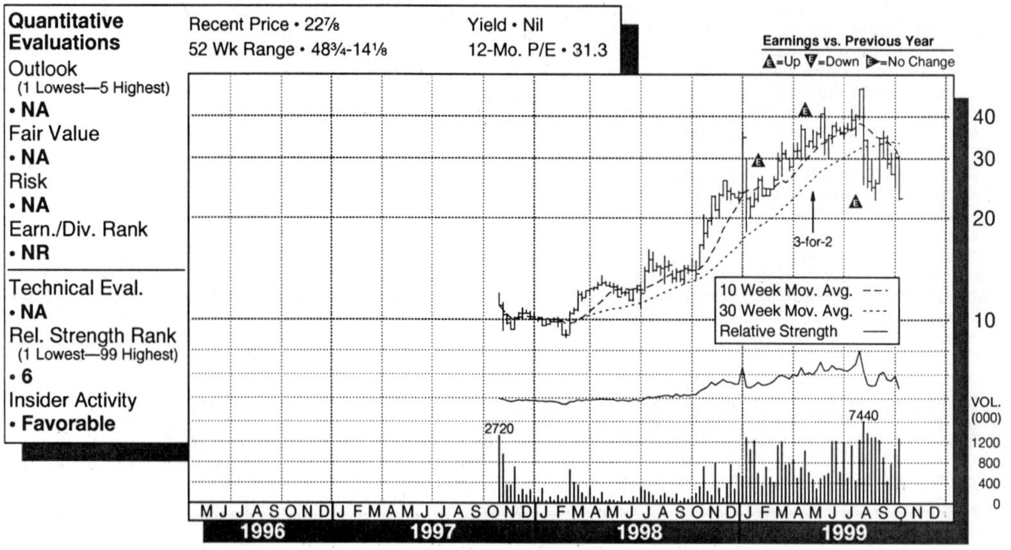

Business Profile - 24-SEP-99

The company has said it is encouraged by several new agreements it recently signed to distribute its services to various organizations, and by strong sales momentum carried into the 1999 third quarter. In April 1999, PHCC acquired Pharmacy Plus, Ltd., a specialty pharmacy that provides injectable biopharmaceuticals, for about $3.5 million. In July 1999, the company completed a public offering of 2,990,000 Class B common shares at $32.30 each. Net proceeds totaling about $96.6 million were earmarked for working capital and general corporate purposes, including potential acquisitions. In August, PHCC announced a stock repurchase program covering up to 2,000,000 shares.

Operational Review - 24-SEP-99

Net sales in the six months ended June 30, 1999, advanced 52%, year to year. The gain mainly reflected the addition of new customers, new product introductions (including the new Rebetron treatment for Hepatitis-C), additional sales to existing customers, the acquisition of Pharmacy Plus Ltd., and inflationary price increases. Margins widened; operating income soared 75%. With sharply higher net interest income and slightly lower depreciation and amortization charges, after taxes at 39.7%, versus 39.8%, net income surged 89%, to $8,224,000 ($0.42 a share) from $4,347,000 ($0.23, as adjusted).

Stock Performance - 08-OCT-99

In the past 30 trading days, PHCC's shares have declined 10%, compared to a 0.91% fall in the S&P 500. Average trading volume for the past five days was 410,360 shares, compared with the 40-day moving average of 295,215 shares.

Key Stock Statistics

Dividend Rate/Share	Nil	Shareholders	NA
Shs. outstg. (M)	21.9	Market cap. (B)	$0.358
Avg. daily vol. (M)	0.216	Inst. holdings	66%
Tang. Bk. Value/Share	7.18		
Beta	NA		

Value of $10,000 invested 5 years ago: NA

Fiscal Year Ending Dec. 31

	1999	1998	1997	1996	1995	1994
Revenues (Million $)						
1Q	83.16	58.13	—	—	—	—
2Q	102.0	63.92	—	—	—	—
3Q	—	71.72	60.70	—	—	—
4Q	—	81.85	61.68	—	—	—
Yr.	—	275.6	231.0	158.3	124.0	107.0
Earnings Per Share ($)						
1Q	**0.19**	**0.11**	—	—	—	—
2Q	**0.23**	**0.12**	—	—	—	—
3Q	—	**0.14**	—	—	—	—
4Q	—	**0.17**	**0.09**	—	—	—
Yr.	—	**0.54**	**0.39**	**0.29**	**0.12**	**0.08**

Next earnings report expected: late October

Dividend Data

Amount ($)	Date Decl.	Ex-Div. Date	Stock of Record	Payment Date
3-for-2	Apr. 07	May. 05	Apr. 20	May. 04 '99

Priority Healthcare Corporation

Business Summary - 24-SEP-99

Priority Healthcare Corp. was formed in mid-1994 to focus on distributing products and providing services to the alternate site segment of the healthcare industry

PHCC aims to continue to grow rapidly, and to enhance its market position as a leading healthcare company by capitalizing on its business strengths. It plans to pursue the following strategy: to continue to penetrate the alternate site market; enter new markets by distributing new product categories and patient-specific biopharmaceuticals; accelerate growth of its higher margin, patient-specific pharmacy business by leveraging relationships with existing distribution customers; maintain intense cost control, while investing in infrastructure; seek acquisitions to complement existing product offerings and further penetrate markets; and continue to develop physician and patient networks that enhance its alliance capabilities with manufacturers.

Through the Priority Distribution division, the company provides a broad range of services and supplies to meet the needs of the alternate site market, including the outpatient renal care market, office-based oncology market and other physician office specialty markets that are high users of vaccines. The division offers value-added services to meet the specialized needs of these markets by shipping refrigerated pharmaceuticals overnight in special packaging to maintain appropriate temperatures and offering automated order entry services and customized group account distribution. PHCC sells more than 3,500 SKUs of pharmaceuticals, such as EPO, Neupogen, Calcijex and INFeD and related medical supplies such as dialyzers, blood tubing, fistula needles, IV sets, transducers, tape and sponges.

About 27% of PHCC's 1998 revenues were attributable to sales of EPO to the renal care market. Priority Distribution serves more than 2,000 customers in all 50 states and Puerto Rico, including about 600 office-based oncologists and 800 renal dialysis clinics.

The Priority Pharmacy division provides patient-specific, self-injectable biopharmaceuticals and related disease treatment programs to individuals with chronic disease. It fills patient-specific prescriptions and ships them via overnight delivery in special shipping containers to maintain appropriate temperatures. These services are provided in combination with PHCC's disease treatment programs.

Disease treatment programs are provided for diseases that include hepatitis and cancer, with biopharmaceuticals that primarily consist of Interferon, a synthetic biopharmaceutical used to treat hepatitis B and C, Rebetron, an oral antiviral and a synthetic biopharmaceutical used to treat hepatitis C, Octreotide, a synthetic hormone used to treat diarrhea related to intestinal peptide tumors, and Epoetin Alfa, a synthetic biopharmaceutical used to treat anemia.

During 1998, the 20 largest customers accounted for 38% of revenues; a single customer, Everest Healthcare Services Corp., accoun ted for 12%.

Per Share Data ($) (Year Ended Dec. 31)	1998	1997	1996	1995	1994	1993	1992	1991	1990	1989
Tangible Bk. Val.	5.07	2.80	1.40	NA	NA	NA	NA	NA	NA	NA
Cash Flow	0.91	0.46	0.35	0.19	0.11	0.09	NA	NA	NA	NA
Earnings	0.54	0.39	0.29	0.12	0.08	0.07	NA	NA	NA	NA
Dividends	Nil	Nil	NA	NA	NA	NA	NA	NA	NA	NA
Payout Ratio	Nil	Nil	NA	NA	NA	NA	NA	NA	NA	NA
Prices - High	36	12	NA	NA	NA	NA	NA	NA	NA	NA
- Low	8⅞	9¼	NA	NA	NA	NA	NA	NA	NA	NA
P/E Ratio - High	67	31	NA	NA	NA	NA	NA	NA	NA	NA
- Low	16	24	NA	NA	NA	NA	NA	NA	NA	NA
Income Statement Analysis (Million $)										
Revs.	276	231	158	124	107	68.0	NA	NA	NA	NA
Oper. Inc.	17.2	12.6	8.7	4.7	2.8	2.2	NA	NA	NA	NA
Depr.	1.2	1.2	1.0	1.0	0.5	0.3	NA	NA	NA	NA
Int. Exp.	Nil	0.9	0.4	NA	NA	NA	NA	NA	NA	NA
Pretax Inc.	16.8	10.2	7.3	3.2	2.1	1.9	NA	NA	NA	NA
Eff. Tax Rate	40%	40%	40%	41%	40%	40%	NA	NA	NA	NA
Net Inc.	10.1	6.2	4.4	1.9	1.3	1.1	NA	NA	NA	NA
Balance Sheet & Other Fin. Data (Million $)										
Cash	0.0	9.5	1.7	NA	NA	NA	NA	NA	NA	NA
Curr. Assets	99	84.5	47.9	NA	NA	NA	NA	NA	NA	NA
Total Assets	108	93.3	57.2	41.6	36.8	26.7	NA	NA	NA	NA
Curr. Liab.	37.3	27.0	27.1	NA	NA	NA	NA	NA	NA	NA
LT Debt	Nil	6.3	0.6	0.8	0.1	Nil	NA	NA	NA	NA
Common Eqty.	70.0	59.9	29.4	25.0	20.2	17.9	NA	NA	NA	NA
Total Cap.	70.2	66.3	30.1	NA	NA	NA	NA	NA	NA	NA
Cap. Exp.	0.8	0.7	0.4	0.5	NA	NA	NA	NA	NA	NA
Cash Flow	11.4	7.3	5.4	2.9	1.8	1.4	NA	NA	NA	NA
Curr. Ratio	2.7	3.1	1.8	NA	NA	NA	NA	NA	NA	NA
% LT Debt of Cap.	Nil	9.5	1.9	NA	NA	NA	NA	NA	NA	NA
% Net Inc.of Revs.	3.7	2.7	2.8	1.5	1.2	1.6	NA	NA	NA	NA
% Ret. on Assets	10.1	8.2	8.9	4.8	3.9	NA	NA	NA	NA	NA
% Ret. on Equity	15.6	13.8	16.1	8.4	6.6	NA	NA	NA	NA	NA

Data as orig reptd.; bef. results of disc opers/spec. items. Per share data adj. for stk. divs. Bold denotes diluted EPS (FASB 128)-prior periods restated. E-Estimated. NA-Not Available. NM-Not Meaningful. NR-Not Ranked.

Office—285 West Central Parkway, Suite 1704, Altamonte Springs, FL 32714. **Tel**—(407) 869-7001. **Website**—http://www.priorityhealthcare.com **Pres & CEO**—R. L. Meyers. **EVP, CFO & Treas**—D. J. Perfetto. **Secy**—B. J. Luttrell. **Dirs**—W. E. Bindley, M. D. McCormick, R. L. Myers, D. J. Perfetto, R. W. Roberson, T. J. Salentine, R. M. Shanahan. **Transfer Agent & Registrar**—Harris Trust & Savings Bank, Chicago. **Incorporated**—in Indiana in 1994. **Empl**— 145. **S&P Analyst:** J. J. Schemitsch

STANDARD
&POOR'S
STOCK REPORTS

Profit Recovery Group

NASDAQ Symbol **PRGX**

In S&P SmallCap 600

09-OCT-99

Industry:
Services (Commercial & Consumer)

Summary: Operating in more than 25 countries, this company is a leading worldwide provider of accounts payable and other recovery audit services.

Quantitative Evaluations

Outlook
(1 Lowest—5 Highest)
• **4-**

Fair Value
• **65¼**

Risk
• **NA**

Earn./Div. Rank
• **NR**

Technical Eval.
• **Bullish** since 7/99

Rel. Strength Rank
(1 Lowest—99 Highest)
• **91**

Insider Activity
• **Neutral**

Recent Price • 42¾
52 Wk Range • 47½-13⅜
Yield • Nil
12-Mo. P/E • 69.0

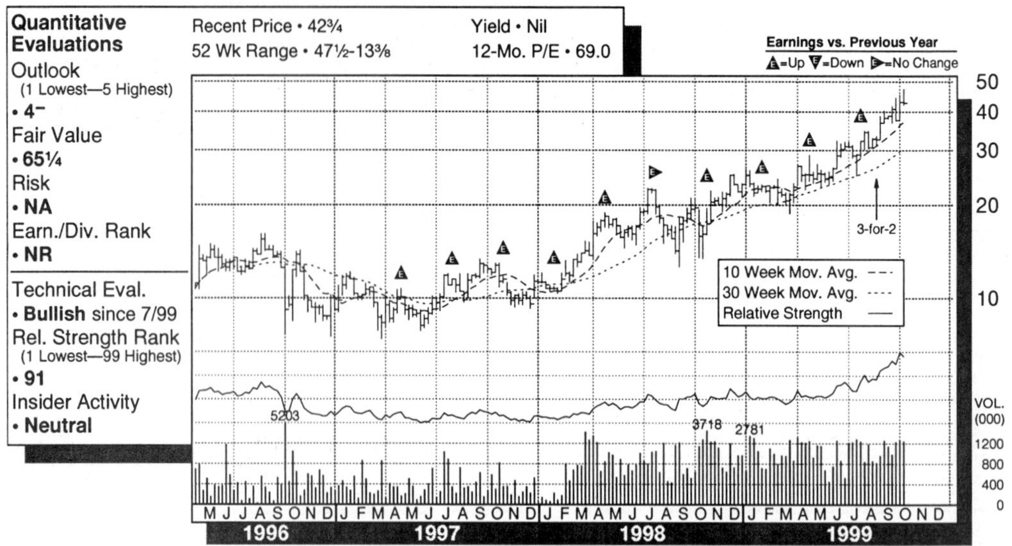

Business Profile - 19-AUG-99

In July 1999, the company agreed to acquire PRS International, Ltd. which specializes in providing accounts payable recovery audit services primarily to middle clients in various nonretail industry sectors. The acquisition is expected to be completed by the end of August 1999 and will involve the issuance of about 1.4 million (adjusted) common shares. In June 1999, PRG acquired for about $11 million and about 355,000 (adjusted) unregistered and restricted common shares Tariff Management Group, LLC, which specializes mainly in telecommunications recovery auditing and negotiating integrated services contracts with its clients' telecom suppliers on a gain-share basis.

Operational Review - 19-AUG-99

Revenues for the six months ended June 30, 1999, advanced 78%, year to year, with domestic revenues more than doubling and international revenues up 25%; domestic revenues were bolstered by companies acquired in new areas of audit emphasis. Net income more than doubled, to $9,237,000 ($0.22 a share, based on 31% more average shares) from $4,039,000 ($0.13). Results for the 1999 period are before a special charge of $0.70 a share from the cumulative effect of a change in accounting for certain aspects of revenue recognition. Per-share figures for both periods are adjusted for the August 1999 three-for-two stock split.

Stock Performance - 08-OCT-99

In the past 30 trading days, PRGX's shares have increased 16%, compared to a 0.91% fall in the S&P 500. Average trading volume for the past five days was 333,220 shares, compared with the 40-day moving average of 274,803 shares.

Key Stock Statistics

Dividend Rate/Share	Nil	Shareholders	2,500
Shs. outstg. (M)	41.3	Market cap. (B)	$ 1.8
Avg. daily vol. (M)	0.301	Inst. holdings	59%
Tang. Bk. Value/Share	0.22		
Beta	NA		

Value of $10,000 invested 5 years ago: NA

Fiscal Year Ending Dec. 31

	1999	1998	1997	1996	1995	1994
Revenues (Million $)						
1Q	58.02	33.14	20.96	15.62	—	—
2Q	71.73	38.93	25.86	17.96	—	—
3Q	—	61.80	29.63	21.96	—	—
4Q	—	68.95	35.92	21.79	—	—
Yr.	—	202.8	112.4	77.33	56.03	—
Earnings Per Share ($)						
1Q	**0.06**	**0.04**	0.03	0.02	—	—
2Q	**0.17**	**0.09**	0.09	0.06	—	—
3Q	—	**0.19**	0.13	0.10	—	—
4Q	—	**0.20**	**0.09**	0.08	—	—
Yr.	—	**0.53**	**0.34**	**0.26**	**0.14**	—

Next earnings report expected: mid October

Dividend Data

Amount ($)	Date Decl.	Ex-Div. Date	Stock of Record	Payment Date
3-for-2	Jul. 23	Aug. 18	Aug. 02	Aug. 17 '99

A Division of The McGraw-Hill Companies

The Profit Recovery Group International, Inc.

Business Summary - 19-AUG-99

The Profit Recovery Group International, Inc. is a leading provider of accounts payable and other recovery audit services to large businesses and certain governmental agencies having numerous payment transactions with many vendors. These businesses include: retailers; manufacturers of pharmaceuticals, consumer electronics, chemicals and aerospace and medical products; wholesale distributors of computer components, food products and pharmaceuticals; technology companies; and healthcare providers such as hospitals and health maintenance organizations.

In businesses with large purchase volumes and continuously fluctuating prices, some small percentage of erroneous overpayments to vendors is inevitable. In addition, the complexity of various tax laws results in overpayments to governmental agencies. Services such as freight, telecommunications and utilities provided to businesses under complex pricing arrangements also can result in overpayments. All of these overpayments result in "lost profits." PRGX's trained, experienced audit specialists use sophisticated proprietary techniques to identify overpayments to vendors and tax authorities. The company receives a contractual percentage of overpayments it identifies and its clients recover.

PRGX continuously updates and refines its proprietary databases that serve as a central repository reflecting its auditors' experiences, vendor practices and knowledge of regional and national pricing information, including seasonal allowances, discounts and rebates, but excluding confidential client data.

The company conducts its business in over 25 countries through three operating segments: accounts payable services (which provided 84% of revenues and 68% of operating profits in 1998), freight services (3% and 12%, respectively), and tax services (13% and 20%). International operations accounted for about 29% of revenues in 1998.

Accounts payable services consist of the review of client accounts payable disbursements to identify and recover overpayments. This segment includes accounts payable services provided to retailers, wholesale distributors and governmental agencies (PRGX's historical client base) and accounts payable services provided to various other types of entities by the company's Loder Drew & Associates division.

Freight services consist mainly of various businesses acquired in 1998 and 1997 which audit freight-related disbursements to identify and recover overpayments. Areas of current specialization include ocean freight, ground freight and overnight freight.

Tax services consist mainly of European businesses acquired by PRGX in 1998 and 1997 which audit tax-related disbursements to identify and recover overpayments (primarily in France) and assist businesses throughout Europe in securing available grants.

Per Share Data ($) (Year Ended Dec. 31)	1998	1997	1996	1995	1994	1993	1992	1991	1990	1989
Tangible Bk. Val.	NM	0.69	1.35	1.05	NA	NA	NA	NA	NA	NA
Cash Flow	0.86	0.51	0.21	0.73	NA	NA	NA	NA	NA	NA
Earnings	0.53	0.34	0.26	NA	NA	NA	NA	NA	NA	NA
Dividends	Nil	Nil	NA	NA	NA	NA	NA	NA	NA	NA
Payout Ratio	Nil	Nil	NA	NA	NA	NA	NA	NA	NA	NA
Prices - High	26 1/8	13 3/8	16 1/8	NA	NA	NA	NA	NA	NA	NA
- Low	10 3/8	7 3/8	7 3/8	NA	NA	NA	NA	NA	NA	NA
P/E Ratio - High	49	39	62	NA	NA	NA	NA	NA	NA	NA
- Low	19	22	28	NA	NA	NA	NA	NA	NA	NA
Income Statement Analysis (Million $)										
Revs.	203	112	77.3	56.0	NA	NA	NA	NA	NA	NA
Oper. Inc.	44.7	22.1	13.5	8.3	NA	NA	NA	NA	NA	NA
Depr.	11.4	4.8	2.5	1.8	NA	NA	NA	NA	NA	NA
Int. Exp.	3.5	0.4	0.1	1.6	NA	NA	NA	NA	NA	NA
Pretax Inc.	29.9	15.8	10.9	4.8	NA	NA	NA	NA	NA	NA
Eff. Tax Rate	39%	39%	71%	6.34%	NA	NA	NA	NA	NA	NA
Net Inc.	18.1	9.6	3.1	4.5	NA	NA	NA	NA	NA	NA
Balance Sheet & Other Fin. Data (Million $)										
Cash	28.3	19.4	16.9	0.6	NA	NA	NA	NA	NA	NA
Curr. Assets	132	78.0	55.4	20.7	NA	NA	NA	NA	NA	NA
Total Assets	387	134	68.3	30.3	NA	NA	NA	NA	NA	NA
Curr. Liab.	103	43.4	25.4	13.6	NA	NA	NA	NA	NA	NA
LT Debt	Nil	NA	NA	NA	NA	NA	NA	NA	NA	NA
Common Eqty.	166	66.7	42.2	-2.4	NA	NA	NA	NA	NA	NA
Total Cap.	166	NA	NA	NA	NA	NA	NA	NA	NA	NA
Cap. Exp.	17.9	NA	NA	NA	NA	NA	NA	NA	NA	NA
Cash Flow	29.5	14.4	5.6	6.3	NA	NA	NA	NA	NA	NA
Curr. Ratio	1.3	1.8	2.2	1.5	NA	NA	NA	NA	NA	NA
% LT Debt of Cap.	Nil	NA	NA	NA	NA	NA	NA	NA	NA	NA
% Net Inc.of Revs.	8.9	8.6	4.1	8.0	NA	NA	NA	NA	NA	NA
% Ret. on Assets	7.0	9.5	6.4	NA	NA	NA	NA	NA	NA	NA
% Ret. on Equity	15.6	17.7	15.8	NA	NA	NA	NA	NA	NA	NA

Data as orig reptd.; bef. results of disc opers/spec. items. Per share data adj. for stk. divs. Bold denotes diluted EPS (FASB 128)-prior periods restated. E-Estimated. NA-Not Available. NM-Not Meaningful. NR-Not Ranked.

Office—2300 Windy Ridge Parkway, Suite 100 North, Atlanta, GA 30339-8426. **Tel**—(770) 779-3900. **Website**—http://www.prgx.com **Chrmn & CEO**—J. M. Cook. **EVP-CFO**—S. L. Colabuono. **Investor Contact**—Scott L. Colabuono (770-779-3142). **Dirs**—S. B. Cohen, J. M. Cook, M. Eisenberg, J. Golden, G. H. Greimann, F. W. I. Lachotzki, R. K. Loder, E. J. Lowrey, M. A. Lustig, T. S. Robertson, J. M. Toma, J. M. Ward. **Transfer Agent & Registrar**—First National Bank of North Carolina, Charlotte. **Incorporated**—in Georgia in 1996. **Empl**— 1,880. **S&P Analyst:** J. J. Schemitsch

Progress Software

NASDAQ Symbol **PRGS**

In S&P SmallCap 600

23-OCT-99 **Industry:** Computer (Software & Services)

Summary: This company supplies application development and database software.

Quantitative Evaluations

Outlook (1 Lowest—5 Highest)
• **3+**

Fair Value
• **35¼**

Risk
• **Average**

Earn./Div. Rank
• **B**

Technical Eval.
• **NA**

Rel. Strength Rank (1 Lowest—99 Highest)
• **88**

Insider Activity
• **Unfavorable**

Recent Price • 32⅝
52 Wk Range • 38⅜-19⅞

Yield • Nil
12-Mo. P/E • 20.2

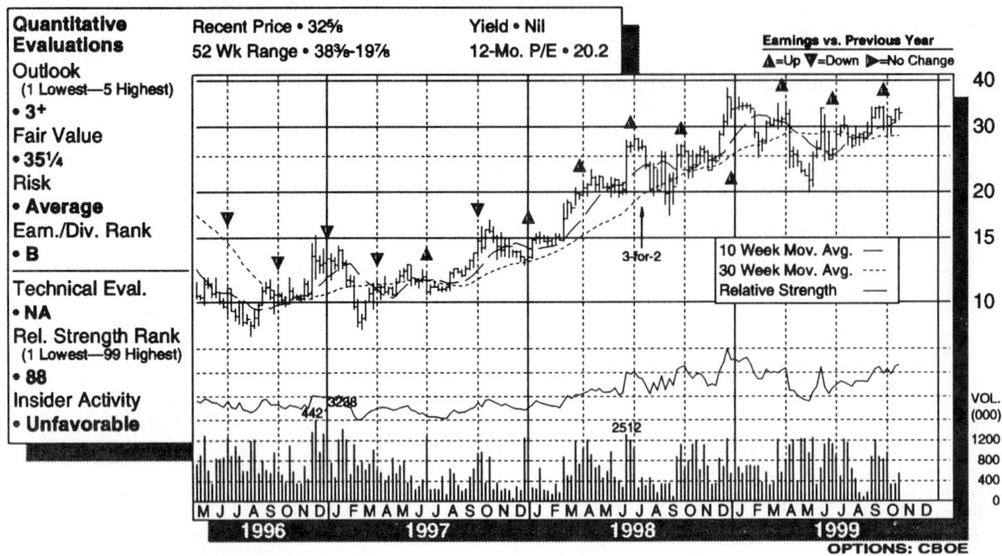

Business Profile - 19-OCT-99

In the third quarter of FY 99 (Nov.), the company moved to strengthen its position in the rapidly emerging application service provider (ASP) market by forming a new business unit to provide a combination of technology, professional services and partnerships to independent software vendors (ISVs) that want to move applications to the ASP distribution model. The ASP distribution model lets ISVs rent their business applications to end-user organizations over the Internet or through other technologies. In the first nine months of FY 99, PRGS repurchased 988,236 common shares, for $23.8 million. In September 1999, directors authorized the purchase of up to 5,000,000 additional shares through September 30, 2000.

Operational Review - 19-OCT-99

Total revenues in the nine months ended August 31, 1999, advanced 22%, year to year, reflecting gains of 17% and 26% for software license revenues and maintenance and service revenues, respectively. Total costs and expenses rose less rapidly, reflecting well controlled sales and marketing, and general and administrative expenses. With higher greater other income, after taxes at 32.0%, versus 33.0%, net income surged 61%, to $23,214,000 ($1.19 a share), from $14,381,000 ($0.75).

Stock Performance - 22-OCT-99

In the past 30 trading days, PRGS's shares have declined 1%, compared to a 4% fall in the S&P 500. Average trading volume for the past five days was 66,360 shares, compared with the 40-day moving average of 141,213 shares.

Key Stock Statistics

Dividend Rate/Share	Nil	Shareholders	4,000
Shs. outstg. (M)	17.5	Market cap. (B)	$0.583
Avg. daily vol. (M)	0.109	Inst. holdings	74%
Tang. Bk. Value/Share	6.87		
Beta	0.92		

Value of $10,000 invested 5 years ago: $ 22,885

Fiscal Year Ending Nov. 30

	1999	1998	1997	1996	1995	1994
Revenues (Million $)						
1Q	67.15	54.15	45.34	48.38	39.42	31.06
2Q	70.75	57.11	44.83	41.66	42.76	33.96
3Q	70.16	59.48	45.88	41.41	44.96	33.92
4Q	—	69.16	52.26	45.24	53.00	40.29
Yr.	—	239.9	188.3	176.7	180.1	139.2
Earnings Per Share ($)						
1Q	**0.35**	**0.19**	**0.10**	0.21	0.08	0.16
2Q	**0.40**	**0.24**	0.10	0.01	0.23	0.18
3Q	**0.43**	**0.31**	-0.53	0.01	0.21	0.16
4Q	—	**0.43**	0.20	0.03	0.30	0.24
Yr.	—	**1.18**	**-0.09**	**0.28**	0.82	0.74

Next earnings report expected: late December

Dividend Data

The company has not paid cash dividends on its common stock and does not plan to pay cash dividends in the near future. A three-for-two stock split was effected in 1998.

A Division of The McGraw-Hill Companies

Progress Software Corporation

Business Summary - 19-OCT-99

Progress Software was founded in 1981 to develop and market application development software. The company derived 57% of its FY 98 (Nov.) revenues from international sales. Changes in the value of foreign currencies relative to the U.S. dollar may significantly affect results of operations and PRGS's financial position. The company's products and services are designed to enable organizations throughout the world to rapidly and cost-effectively develop, deploy and maintain computer software applications. Principal product lines are PROGRESS, an integrated environment for developing and deploying mission-critical applications; WebSpeed, designed for Internet transaction processing applications; ProVision Plus, a programming environment for developing and deploying complex enterprise applications; and Progress Apptivity, for developing distributed, multi-tier Java-based business applications.

The company's long-term strategy is to introduce new products and product enhancements that will enable professional developers to create completely open, standard-based applications for mission-critical business environments. PGRS believes these initiatives will enhance the future adaptability of its products by providing deployment across all major computing configurations (i.e., Internet/Web, client/server, and host/terminal).

PRGS sells its products worldwide to organizations that develop and deploy major business applications. More than 50% of worldwide revenue is derived from serving more than 2,000 application partners that market applications use company technology. Remaining revenues come from serving the needs of information technology organizations of businesses and governments.

In July 1997, the company acquired Apptivity Corp., a developer of Java-based application development tools, for $3.8 million in cash, $5.4 million of stock, and the assumption of $1.4 million of liabilities.

Since beginning a share buyback program three years ago, PRGS has repurchased more than 5 million shares, including 988,236 shares, purchased for $23.8 million, in the nine months ended August 31, 1999.

Per Share Data ($) (Year Ended Nov. 30)	1998	1997	1996	1995	1994	1993	1992	1991	1990	1989
Tangible Bk. Val.	6.01	8.16	6.01	5.86	4.77	3.81	2.98	2.26	NA	NA
Cash Flow	1.79	0.74	0.75	0.83	1.03	0.87	0.64	0.47	NA	NA
Earnings	1.18	-0.09	0.27	0.81	0.75	0.67	0.51	0.35	NA	NA
Dividends	Nil	Nil	Nil	Nil	Nil	Nil	Nil	Nil	NA	NA
Payout Ratio	Nil	Nil	Nil	Nil	Nil	Nil	Nil	Nil	NA	NA
Prices - High	38 3/8	16 7/8	25 1/8	25 3/8	18 7/8	20 1/8	20 1/2	15	NA	NA
- Low	14 1/8	8 3/8	8 1/8	12 3/8	9	10 3/4	9 5/8	8 3/8	NA	NA
P/E Ratio - High	33	NM	92	31	25	30	41	42	NA	NA
- Low	12	NM	30	15	12	16	19	24	NA	NA
Income Statement Analysis (Million $)										
Revs.	240	188	177	180	139	112	85.0	NA	NA	NA
Oper. Inc.	41.8	19.9	14.0	31.9	25.3	21.3	15.6	NA	NA	NA
Depr.	11.8	10.6	9.5	7.6	5.5	3.8	2.5	NA	NA	NA
Int. Exp.	Nil	0.0	0.0	0.0	0.0	0.1	0.1	NA	NA	NA
Pretax Inc.	33.9	2.6	7.9	26.1	22.0	19.8	15.0	NA	NA	NA
Eff. Tax Rate	33%	184%	36%	38%	35%	35%	36%	NA	NA	NA
Net Inc.	22.8	-1.6	5.5	16.7	14.4	12.9	9.6	NA	NA	NA
Balance Sheet & Other Fin. Data (Million $)										
Cash	50.2	39.5	96.5	92.3	74.3	61.3	54.6	NA	NA	NA
Curr. Assets	173	142	141	144	111	90.0	NA	NA	NA	NA
Total Assets	207	172	172	176	135	108	81.0	NA	NA	NA
Curr. Liab.	104	74.0	57.0	58.8	44.5	36.5	NA	NA	NA	NA
LT Debt	Nil	Nil	0.1	0.1	0.1	0.2	0.2	NA	NA	NA
Common Eqty.	103	96.4	114	113	88.5	69.9	53.2	NA	NA	NA
Total Cap.	103	97.7	117	116	90.0	71.3	54.6	NA	NA	NA
Cap. Exp.	NA	10.1	9.6	13.4	8.0	10.5	5.6	NA	NA	NA
Cash Flow	34.5	9.0	15.0	16.9	19.9	16.7	12.2	NA	NA	NA
Curr. Ratio	1.7	1.9	2.5	2.5	2.5	2.5	NA	NA	NA	NA
% LT Debt of Cap.	Nil	Nil	Nil	Nil	0.1	0.2	0.4	NA	NA	NA
% Net Inc.of Revs.	9.5	NM	3.1	9.3	10.4	11.5	11.3	NA	NA	NA
% Ret. on Assets	12.0	NM	3.2	10.7	11.8	13.6	13.5	NA	NA	NA
% Ret. on Equity	22.9	NM	4.8	16.6	18.2	20.9	20.8	NA	NA	NA

Data as orig reptd.; bef. results of disc opers/spec. items. Per share data adj. for stk. divs. Bold denotes diluted EPS (FASB 128)-prior periods restated. E-Estimated. NA-Not Available. NM-Not Meaningful. NR-Not Ranked.

Office—14 Oak Park, Bedford, MA 01730. **Tel**—(781) 280-4000. **Fax**—(781) 280-4095. **E-mail**—finance-info@progress.com **Website**—http://www.progress.com **Pres & Treas**—J. W. Alsop. **VP-Fin & CFO**—N. R. Robertson. **Investor Contact**—Margot Carlson Delogne (781 280-4144). **Dirs**—J. W. Alsop, L. R. Harris, R. J. Heinen, Jr., S. A. McGregor, M. L. Mark, A. J. Marks, A. Rasiel. **Transfer Agent & Registrar**—Boston EquiServe, Canton, MA. **Incorporated**—in Massachusetts in 1981. **Empl**— 1,201. **S&P Analyst:** M.I.

STANDARD
&POOR'S
STOCK REPORTS

Protein Design Labs

NASDAQ Symbol **PDLI**

In S&P SmallCap 600

09-OCT-99 **Industry:** Biotechnology

Summary: PDLI develops human and humanized antibodies and other potential drugs to prevent or treat certain disease conditions.

Quantitative Evaluations

Outlook
(1 Lowest—5 Highest)
• **1**

Fair Value
• **17¼**

Risk
• **High**

Earn./Div. Rank
• **C**

Technical Eval.
• **Bullish** since 8/99

Rel. Strength Rank
(1 Lowest—99 Highest)
• **95**

Insider Activity
• **NA**

Recent Price • 34¾
52 Wk Range • 39-13⅜
Yield • Nil
12-Mo. P/E • NM

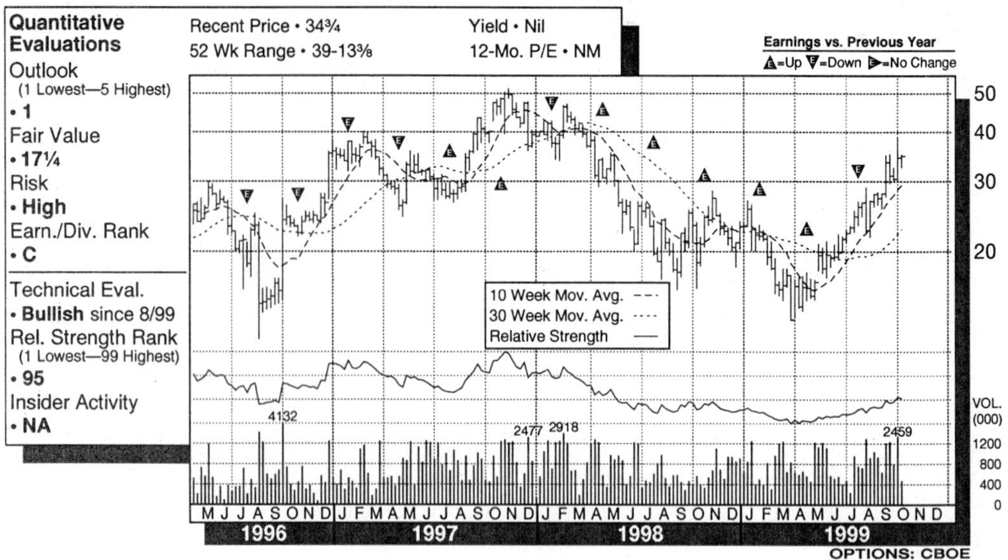

Business Profile - 13-AUG-99

In August 1999, PDLI initiated a Phase I clinical trial to evaluate the safety of its SMART 1D10 Antibody in patients with relapsed non-Hodgkin's lymphoma. In July 1999, PDLI formed a research agreement with Fujisawa Pharmaceutical Co., Ltd. to engineer antibodies to treat inflammatory and immunological diseases. In June 1999, the company announced the publication of successful Phase I/II results for Zenapax in treating uveitis. In May, PDLI announced favorable Phase I results for SMART Anti-CD3 Antibody in kidney transplantation. Also in May, PDLI licensed the European rights for its SMART Anti-L-Selectin to BioNet Pharma Gmbh. In April 1999, PDLI initiated a PhaseI/II trial for SMART Anti-CD3 in psoriasis patients. In March 1999, the company announced that Zenapax was approved for marketing in the European Union.

Operational Review - 13-AUG-99

Total revenues in the six months ended June 30, 1999 rose 36%, primarily related to a sharp rise in revenues from collaborative agreements, slightly offset by lower interest and other income. Following 22% higher R&D expenditures and 29% greater G&A costs, both reflecting increased staffing and expanded operations, total operating expenses were up 24%. The net loss narrowed to $4.6 million ($0.25 a share), from $4.9 million ($0.27). Cash, cash equivalents, and investments totaled $140.0 million at June 30, 1999.

Stock Performance - 08-OCT-99

In the past 30 trading days, PDLI's shares have increased 28%, compared to a 0.91% fall in the S&P 500. Average trading volume for the past five days was 92,700 shares, compared with the 40-day moving average of 230,595 shares.

Key Stock Statistics

Dividend Rate/Share	Nil	Shareholders	190
Shs. outstg. (M)	18.6	Market cap. (B)	$0.648
Avg. daily vol. (M)	0.259	Inst. holdings	49%
Tang. Bk. Value/Share	8.74		
Beta	0.69		

Value of $10,000 invested 5 years ago: $ 14,329

Fiscal Year Ending Dec. 31

	1999	1998	1997	1996	1995	1994
Revenues (Million $)						
1Q	8.84	4.24	3.88	5.55	4.10	3.10
2Q	8.29	8.36	5.03	5.03	4.10	4.60
3Q	—	11.88	7.04	5.55	4.10	3.00
4Q	—	6.36	4.31	6.47	5.40	4.60
Yr.	—	30.83	20.26	22.60	17.60	15.20
Earnings Per Share ($)						
1Q	**-0.10**	**-0.22**	-0.26	-0.14	-0.10	-0.09
2Q	**-0.14**	**-0.05**	-0.16	-0.22	-0.16	-0.18
3Q	—	**0.04**	-0.05	-0.28	-0.17	-0.01
4Q	—	**-0.28**	**-0.88**	-0.12	-0.11	-0.09
Yr.	—	**-0.51**	**-1.35**	**-0.76**	**-0.54**	-0.37

Next earnings report expected: late October

Dividend Data

PDLI has never paid a cash dividend on its common stock and does not expect to make any payments in the foreseeable future.

A Division of The McGraw-Hill Companies

Protein Design Labs, Inc.

Business Summary - 13-AUG-99

Protein Design Labs' strategy is to leverage its technology base and intellectual property to become a profitable pharmaceutical concern that manufactures innovative products to meet important medical needs. With the support of collaborative alliances, the company is focusing its efforts on the development of its SMART humanized antibodies for the treatment of autoimmune and inflammatory disorders, organ transplantation, cancer, and viral infections.

SMART is a humanized monoclonal antibody technology designed with the aid of proprietary software-based algorithms. Unlike mouse antibodies, which are often rejected by the immune system as a foreign substance, PDLI believes its humanized antibodies are well tolerated by the human system. SMART antibodies are humanized by combining the minimum number of mouse amino acids (about 10%) necessary to bind to a target molecule with human amino acids (about 90%).

PDLI has several potential products in human clinical trials and additional products in preclinical development. Zenapax humanized antibody has been approved in the U.S. and the European Union for the prevention of acute organ rejection in patients receiving kidney transplants. Zenapax is the first humanized monoclonal antibody to be approved for marketing by the FDA. An application for marketing approval is pending for Canada and other key markets. The company receives royalties on sales of Zenapax, which is marketed by Hoffman-La Roche, Inc. As of mid-1999, Zennapex was also in Phase I/II trials for a number of other disorders, including the treatment of graft versus host disease, liver transplantation, uveitis (an autoimmune disease inflicting the eye), and pediatric kidney transplant rejection.

As of mid-1999, PDLI's SMART M195 Antibody was in a Phase II trial for the treatment of patients with relapsed or treatment refractory acute myeloid leukemia (AML). A Phase II trial to evaluate the safety and efficacy of SMART M195 in the treatment of myelodyspastic syndrome, a condition that can lead to AML, was also underway.

As of mid-1999, the company was conducting separate Phase I/II trials of its SMART Anti-CD3 Antibody for the treatment of kidney transplant rejection and psoriasis. PDLI believes CD3 is potentially less toxic than alternative treatments for kidney rejection.

As of 1998 year-end, Ostavir (OST 577), a human anti-hepatitis B antibody, was in Phase II trails in Europe for the treatment of chronic hepatitis B in combination with the drug lamivudine. Ostavir was licensed by PDLI from Novartis Pharmaceuticals Corp., who has certain rights to co-market or co-promote these antibodies in North America or to receive royalties (if approved).

In August 1999, PDLI announced the start of a Phase I clinical trial for SMART 1d10, a humanized antibody, in the treatment of patients with relapsed non-Hodgkin's lymphoma. This study was being sponsored by the National Cancer institute.

Per Share Data ($) (Year Ended Dec. 31)	1998	1997	1996	1995	1994	1993	1992	1991	1990	1989
Tangible Bk. Val.	8.74	9.18	16.67	-0.54	7.72	5.60	4.21	1.84	NA	NA
Cash Flow	-0.31	-1.16	-0.55	-0.38	-0.22	-0.30	0.06	NA	NA	NA
Earnings	-0.51	-1.35	-0.76	-0.54	-0.37	-0.47	-0.07	0.03	NA	NA
Dividends	Nil	Nil	Nil	Nil	Nil	Nil	Nil	Nil	Nil	NA
Payout Ratio	Nil	Nil	Nil	Nil	Nil	Nil	Nil	Nil	Nil	NA
Prices - High	47 1/8	51 1/2	38 3/8	26 3/4	29 7/8	26 5/8	18 3/4	NA	NA	NA
- Low	16	24 3/8	12	13 1/8	13 3/4	6 1/2	5 7/8	NA	NA	NA
P/E Ratio - High	NM	NM	NM	NM	NM	NM	NM	NA	NA	NA
- Low	NM	NM	NM	NM	NA	NA	NA	NA	NA	NA
Income Statement Analysis (Million $)										
Revs.	21.3	11.1	16.5	11.4	11.9	14.7	6.1	4.4	3.4	NA
Oper. Inc.	-15.3	-17.9	-14.6	-12.0	-8.6	-8.0	-3.1	0.0	-0.4	NA
Depr.	3.7	3.2	3.2	2.5	2.2	2.1	1.6	NA	NA	NA
Int. Exp.	Nil	Nil	Nil	Nil	0.0	0.0	0.0	0.1	0.0	NA
Pretax Inc.	-9.5	-23.7	-11.7	-8.4	-5.2	-5.9	-0.9	0.3	0.0	NA
Eff. Tax Rate	NM	NM	NM	NM	Nil	Nil	Nil	Nil	Nil	NA
Net Inc.	-9.5	-23.7	-11.7	-8.4	-5.2	-5.9	-0.9	0.3	0.0	NA
Balance Sheet & Other Fin. Data (Million $)										
Cash	27.9	9.3	78.1	46.4	97.7	60.8	NA	NA	NA	NA
Curr. Assets	91.7	73.0	79.4	47.1	99	32.2	NA	NA	NA	NA
Total Assets	172	175	110	116	121	80.0	56.0	7.0	7.0	NA
Curr. Liab.	9.4	6.6	5.2	3.6	3.3	2.4	NA	NA	NA	NA
LT Debt	Nil	Nil	Nil	Nil	Nil	0.0	0.1	0.2	0.3	NA
Common Eqty.	162	168	105	113	118	78.0	54.0	6.0	6.0	NA
Total Cap.	162	169	105	113	118	78.0	54.0	6.0	6.0	NA
Cap. Exp.	16.8	4.6	3.7	3.6	2.4	2.8	4.1	NA	NA	NA
Cash Flow	-5.8	-20.4	-8.6	-5.8	-3.0	-3.9	0.7	NA	NA	NA
Curr. Ratio	9.8	11.1	15.2	13.1	30.2	13.7	NA	NA	NA	NA
% LT Debt of Cap.	Nil	Nil	Nil	Nil	Nil	Nil	0.2	3.5	4.2	NA
% Net Inc.of Revs.	NM	NM	NM	NM	NM	NM	NM	6.9	NM	NA
% Ret. on Assets	NM	NM	NM	NM	NM	NM	NM	4.5	NM	NA
% Ret. on Equity	NM	NM	NM	NM	NM	NM	NM	5.1	NM	NA

Data as orig reptd.; bef. results of disc opers/spec. items. Per share data adj. for stk. divs. Bold denotes diluted EPS (FASB 128)-prior periods restated. E-Estimated. NA-Not Available. NM-Not Meaningful. NR-Not Ranked.

Office—2375 Garcia Ave., Mountain View, CA 94043. **Tel**—(415) 903-3730. **Fax**—(415) 903-3700. **Website**—http://www.pdl.com **Email**—cc@pdl.com **Chrmn & CEO**—L. J. Korn. **Pres**—J. S. Saxe. **VP & CFO**—F. Kurland. **VP & Secy**—D. O. Ebersole. **Dirs**—J. Drews, G. M. Gould, L. J. Korn, M. Link, C. L. Queen, J. S. Saxe. **Transfer Agent & Registrar**—ChaseMellon Shareholder Services, SF. **Incorporated**—in Delaware in 1986. **Empl**— 256. **S&P Analyst:** Frank DiLorenzo

STANDARD &POOR'S
STOCK REPORTS

Provident Bankshares

NASDAQ Symbol **PBKS**

In S&P SmallCap 600

09-OCT-99

Industry: Banks (Regional)

Summary: This Baltimore-based bank holding company and parent of Provident Bank of Maryland, has $4.9 billion in assets and operates 69 branches, including 20 in-store locations.

Quantitative Evaluations

Outlook (1 Lowest—5 Highest)
• **3**

Fair Value
• **22⅛**

Risk
• **Low**

Earn./Div. Rank
• **A-**

Technical Eval.
• **Bearish** since 9/99

Rel. Strength Rank (1 Lowest—99 Highest)
• **54**

Insider Activity
• **NA**

Recent Price • 21⅞
52 Wk Range • 28⅝-19⅜
Yield • 2.8%
12-Mo. P/E • 14.0

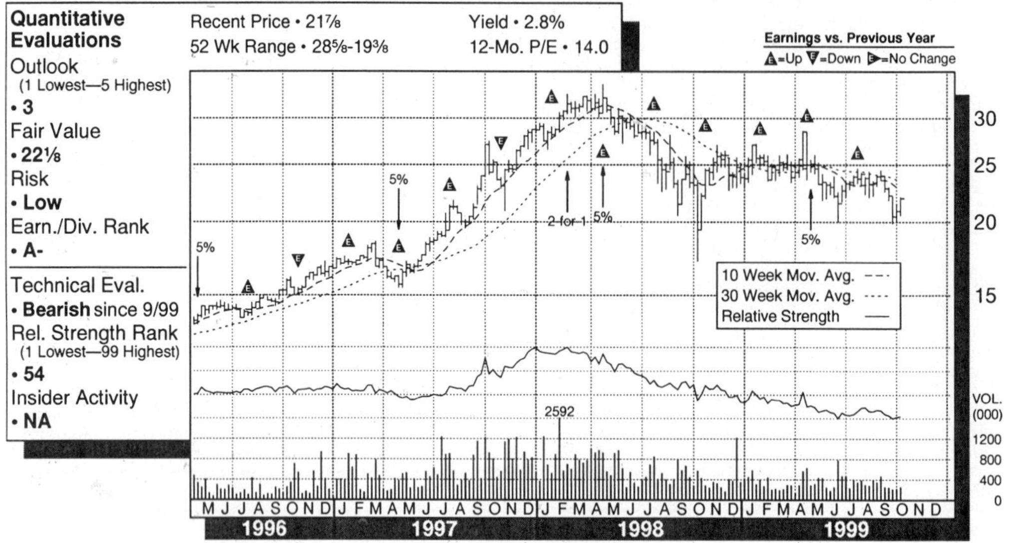

Business Profile - 08-JUL-99

In June 1999, Provident Bankshares announced that it had finalized an agreement with Virginia-based Richfood Holdings, Inc. (NYSE: RFH) to open 16 full-service branches inside Shoppers Food Warehouse supermarkets throughout the Washington, D.C. metropolitan area. This agreement will further the companies' existing relationship, which involves PBKS's operation of branches in 11 of Richfood's stores in the Baltimore metropolitan area. In May 1999, Provident announced that shareholders rejected a proposal which called for the sale of the company. During the first quarter of 1999, the bank continued its network expansion by opening its twentieth total in-store office with its seventh in-store partner, BJ's Wholesale Club.

Operational Review - 08-JUL-99

Net interest income in the three months ended March 31, 1999, rose 6.3%, year to year, mainly reflecting growth in earning assets. The provision for loan losses declined 34%, to $1,961,000, from $2,975,000. Noninterest income increased 21%, due to improved mortgage banking activity and increased deposit accounts. Noninterest expense rose 17%, reflecting higher merit increases and incentives associated with greater mortgage origination volume. After taxes at 31.5%, versus 33.1%, net income was up 11%, to $10,325,000 ($0.41 a share) from $9,305,000 ($0.37).

Stock Performance - 08-OCT-99

In the past 30 trading days, PBKS's shares have declined 8%, compared to a 0.91% fall in the S&P 500. Average trading volume for the past five days was 49,840 shares, compared with the 40-day moving average of 60,259 shares.

Key Stock Statistics

Dividend Rate/Share	0.62	Shareholders	3,300
Shs. outstg. (M)	25.5	Market cap. (B)	$0.560
Avg. daily vol. (M)	0.045	Inst. holdings	37%
Tang. Bk. Value/Share	11.10		
Beta	1.06		

Value of $10,000 invested 5 years ago: $ 32,487

Fiscal Year Ending Dec. 31

	1999	1998	1997	1996	1995	1994
Revenues (Million $)						
1Q	96.85	86.46	63.17	60.84	47.28	37.06
2Q	101.7	93.28	79.70	58.47	51.27	38.54
3Q	—	99.4	82.18	62.76	53.50	40.46
4Q	—	101.7	82.37	62.80	57.20	45.55
Yr.	—	380.9	321.8	244.9	209.1	161.5
Earnings Per Share ($)						
1Q	**0.41**	**0.36**	**0.31**	**0.25**	0.19	0.15
2Q	**0.42**	**0.36**	**0.31**	**0.26**	0.22	0.17
3Q	—	**0.37**	Nil	**0.21**	0.24	0.20
4Q	—	**0.38**	**0.34**	**0.30**	0.25	0.19
Yr.	—	**1.47**	**0.95**	**1.02**	**0.88**	**0.70**

Next earnings report expected: late October

Dividend Data (Dividends have been paid since 1988.)

Amount ($)	Date Decl.	Ex-Div. Date	Stock of Record	Payment Date
0.140	Oct. 21	Oct. 29	Nov. 02	Nov. 13 '98
0.145	Jan. 20	Jan. 28	Feb. 01	Feb. 12 '99
0.150	Apr. 21	Apr. 29	May. 03	May. 14 '99
0.155	Jul. 21	Jul. 29	Aug. 02	Aug. 13 '99

A Division of The McGraw-Hill Companies

Provident Bankshares Corporation

Business Summary - 08-JUL-99

Baltimore-based Provident Bankshares, which converted from a Maryland chartered mutual savings bank to a Maryland chartered stock commercial bank in late 1987, is now the second largest commercial bank chartered in the state. At March 31, 1999, the bank had nearly $4.9 billion in assets and operations in seven Maryland counties, and Baltimore City and York County, Pennsylvania. The bank's subsidiaries can also be found in Florida, Illinois and Virginia.

Provident, through its wholly owned subsidiary, Provident Bank of Maryland, offers consumer and commercial banking services. The company also offers related financial services, including mortgages, mutual funds, leases, annuities and insurance products.

As of June 1999, Provident's branch network included 69 full-service branches, including 20 in-store locations inside supermarkets and national retail superstores. The corporation has an agreement with Richfood Holdings, Inc. to operate branches in their Metro and Basic and Shoppers Food Warehouse supermarkets located in the Baltimore and Washington, D.C. areas. In 1999, the bank plans to open five additional in-store branches and one new traditional branch. The company's in-store branches can be found in seven various supermarket chain and retail store operators including Rich Food Corp.'s markets, Wal-Mart Stores, Rite Aid Stores and BJ's Wholesale Club.

The bank also operates seven Fast 'n Friendly Check Cashing centers. Provident operates the check cashing centers in order to offer alternative banking services to a segment of its market place that does not utilize traditional banking services. PBKS has one new center planned for 1999.

Interest income accounted for 84% of total revenues in 1998. Average earning assets, from which interest income is derived, grew 19% in 1998, to $4.2 billion. There was a decrease in the net yield on earning assets (to 3.12% from 3.49%). Net interest income for 1998 rose 6.7%. Loans accounted for the largest portion of average earning assets (68%), with mortgage backed securities making up most of the remainder (26%).

The majority of 1998's loan portfolio was made up of consumer loans (69%). The remainder of the loan portfolio included commercial business loans (12%), residential mortgage (8%), commercial mortgage (7%), and residential and commercial construction (4%).

Noninterest income advanced 43% in 1998, to $62.7 million. Service charges on deposit accounts made up 47% of noninterest income, mortgage banking activities 18%, net securities gains 11%, commissions and fees 7%, and other 17%.

Per Share Data ($) (Year Ended Dec. 31)	1998	1997	1996	1995	1994	1993	1992	1991	1990	1989
Tangible Bk. Val.	11.61	10.63	10.05	9.61	8.08	8.41	7.42	7.30	7.16	7.31
Earnings	1.33	0.96	1.13	0.91	0.71	0.53	0.26	0.19	-0.25	0.22
Dividends	0.49	0.39	0.31	0.24	0.16	0.11	0.08	0.06	0.16	0.16
Payout Ratio	37%	41%	28%	1%	23%	21%	30%	31%	NM	70%
Prices - High	$34\frac{1}{4}$	$29\frac{3}{8}$	$17\frac{1}{8}$	$14\frac{1}{2}$	$10\frac{7}{8}$	$5\frac{5}{8}$	$5\frac{5}{8}$	$3\frac{3}{8}$	5	$5\frac{1}{2}$
- Low	$17\frac{1}{8}$	$15\frac{3}{8}$	11	$8\frac{1}{2}$	$7\frac{1}{8}$	$2\frac{1}{2}$	$2\frac{1}{2}$	$1\frac{1}{16}$	$1\frac{1}{2}$	$3\frac{7}{8}$
P/E Ratio - High	26	31	15	16	15	11	22	17	NM	25
- Low	13	16	10	9	10	5	10	6	NM	17
Income Statement Analysis (Million $)										
Net Int. Inc.	131	122	91.3	82.9	72.2	64.1	54.3	44.2	44.1	47.3
Tax Equiv. Adj.	1.1	1.1	0.8	0.8	0.4	0.3	0.3	0.6	0.9	1.4
Non Int. Inc.	56.0	41.7	40.0	32.0	27.3	23.8	13.6	11.8	8.7	6.7
Loan Loss Prov.	12.0	10.0	9.9	1.6	0.5	1.5	9.2	20.3	13.1	8.5
Exp./Op. Revs.	66%	72%	38%	74%	79%	86%	84%	90%	92%	76%
Pretax Inc.	58.4	38.6	35.1	27.5	19.7	13.9	5.1	1.0	-9.9	3.9
Eff. Tax Rate	33%	35%	34%	35%	36%	36%	17%	NM	NM	11%
Net Inc.	39.0	25.0	23.0	18.0	12.5	8.9	4.2	2.9	-3.9	3.5
% Net Int. Marg.	3.12	3.49	3.57	3.64	3.99	3.92	3.62	3.07	3.32	3.98
Balance Sheet & Other Fin. Data (Million $)										
Money Mkt. Assets	40.5	31.0	65.2	52.6	47.4	42.5	32.2	24.6	67.7	NA
Inv. Securities	1,199	983	30.2	31.4	442	29.0	663	763	541	324
Com'l Loans	376	289	250	206	179	134	279	263	364	351
Other Loans	2,681	2,376	1,489	1,127	1,093	1,011	432	351	470	538
Total Assets	4,676	3,927	2,799	2,563	2,284	1,844	1,634	1,547	1,494	1,326
Demand Deposits	252	196	150	132	105	105	100	67.4	69.1	62.8
Time Deposits	3,168	2,558	1,616	1,437	1,343	1,178	1,120	1,104	1,077	1,054
LT Debt	735	469	256	268	187	104	2.2	2.8	3.4	4.4
Common Eqty.	296	270	197	184	150	134	116	112	110	116
% Ret. on Assets	0.9	0.7	0.9	0.8	0.7	0.5	0.3	0.2	NM	0.3
% Ret. on Equity	13.8	10.7	12.2	10.8	9.2	6.7	3.7	2.6	NM	3.0
% Loan Loss Resv.	1.4	1.4	1.4	1.6	1.6	1.8	2.8	3.2	1.6	1.6
% Loans/Deposits	NA	98.2	98.4	85.0	87.8	89.2	58.2	52.4	72.8	79.7
% Equity to Assets	6.6	6.9	7.0	6.9	7.2	7.2	7.1	7.3	7.3	8.7

Data as orig reptd.; bef. results of disc opers/spec. items. Per share data adj. for stk. divs. Bold denotes diluted EPS (FASB 128)-prior periods restated. E-Estimated. NA-Not Available. NM-Not Meaningful. NR-Not Ranked.

Office—114 E. Lexington St., Baltimore, MD 21202. **Tel**—(410) 277-7000. **Website**—http://www.providentbankmd.com. **Chrmn, Pres & CEO**—P. M. Martin. **EVP & CFO**—J. R. Wallis. **Secy**—R. L. Davis. **Treas**—R. W. Hall. **Investor Contact**—Lillian Kilroy (410-277-2833). **Dirs**—R. B. Barnhill, Jr., M. A. Bilal, T. S. Bozzuto, C. W. Burnett, W. B. Coe, III, C. W. Cole, Jr., P. B. Dunn, E. K. Fry, H. W. Jorgensen, M. K. Joseph, B.B. Lucas, P. M. Martin, F. W. Meier, Jr., R. Nassif, F. G. Riggs, S. K. Riggs, C. W. Stearn, J. R. Wallis. **Transfer Agent & Registrar**—Boston EquiServe, Boston. **Incorporated**—in Maryland in 1987. **Empl**— 1,414. **S&P Analyst:** Markos N. Kaminis

STANDARD &POOR'S
STOCK REPORTS

Public Service of North Carolina

NYSE Symbol **PGS**

In S&P SmallCap 600

23-OCT-99

Industry: Natural Gas

Summary: Public Service of North Carolina has agreed to be acquired by SCANA, a natural gas utility in South Carolina.

Quantitative Evaluations

Outlook (1 Lowest—5 Highest)
• **2⁻**

Fair Value
• **32⅛**

Risk
• **Low**

Earn./Div. Rank
• **B+**

Technical Eval.
• **NA**

Rel. Strength Rank (1 Lowest—99 Highest)
• **77**

Insider Activity
• **Neutral**

Recent Price • 31⅞
52 Wk Range • 31⅞-21½
Yield • 3.1%
12-Mo. P/E • 30.4

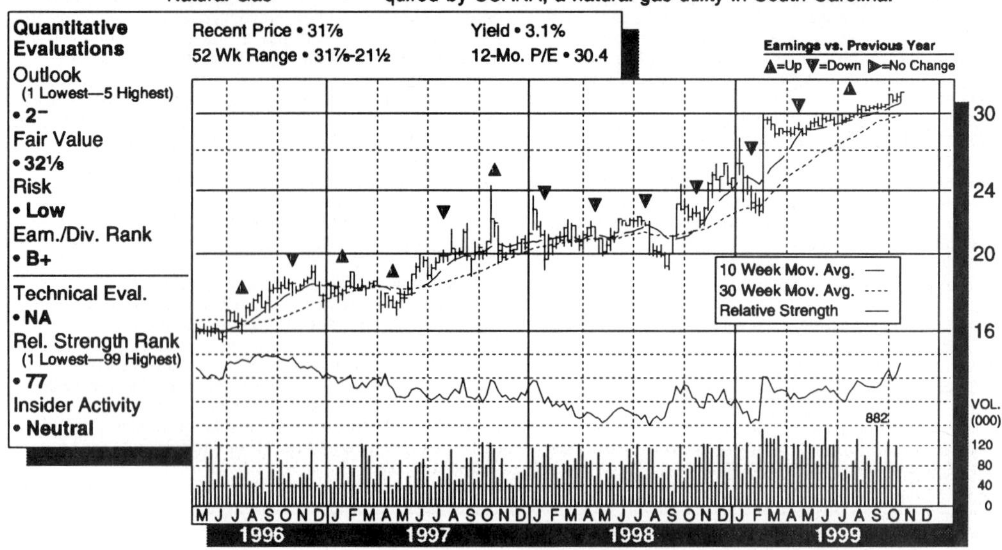

Business Profile - 26-APR-99

In February 1999, PGS agreed to be acquired by SCANA Corp. (SCG). SCANA will pay $900 million for PGS, including the assumption of debt. PGS shareholders will receive $33 a share from SCANA. It is anticipated that the approval process will be completed by the end of 1999. In February 1999, SCANA's board revised the dividend policy to reflect a dividend payout ratio of between 50% and 55%, to be in line with growth-oriented utilities as opposed to the current payout ratio of 70% to 75%. In the first quarter of FY 99 (Sep.), PGS recorded a $4,027,000 million restructuring charge associated with the company's three-year operating strategy, Plan 2001, in which PGS directors chose to eliminate 200 jobs by August 1999. PGS believes that the plan will translate to $6,000,000 in cost savings in FY 00 and FY 01 and $9,800,000 in cost savings and incremental margin in FY 99.

Operational Review - 26-APR-99

For the three months ended December 31, 1998, operating revenues declined 29%, year to year. Operating expenses and taxes were up 6.8%, primarily reflecting 30% higher operating and maintenance costs due to a $4,027,000 restructuring charge associated with severance benefits, and 10% greater depreciation, partially offset by a 49% decrease in income taxes. Operating profits decreased 27%. Following 30% lower other income, net, and a 3.2% increase in interest deductions, net income dropped 48% to $3,766,000 ($0.18 a share, on 2.7% more shares), from $7,193,000 ($0.36).

Stock Performance - 22-OCT-99

In the past 30 trading days, PGS's shares have increased 3%, compared to a 4% fall in the S&P 500. Average trading volume for the past five days was 15,980 shares, compared with the 40-day moving average of 41,592 shares.

Key Stock Statistics

Dividend Rate/Share	0.99	Shareholders	12,700
Shs. outstg. (M)	20.6	Market cap. (B)	$0.648
Avg. daily vol. (M)	0.025	Inst. holdings	30%
Tang. Bk. Value/Share	10.91		
Beta	0.09		

Value of $10,000 invested 5 years ago: $ 24,924

Fiscal Year Ending Sep. 30

	1999	1998	1997	1996	1995	1994
Revenues (Million $)						
1Q	73.20	103.8	93.65	74.92	66.80	71.40
2Q	134.3	140.2	150.2	142.1	112.7	123.2
3Q	54.06	54.53	60.11	58.81	41.65	48.20
4Q	—	32.15	34.02	33.10	26.72	30.90
Yr.	—	330.7	337.9	308.9	247.9	273.7
Earnings Per Share ($)						
1Q	**0.18**	**0.36**	0.41	0.38	0.36	0.31
2Q	**1.06**	**1.11**	1.15	1.09	1.00	1.04
3Q	**0.08**	**0.04**	0.07	0.08	0.03	0.10
4Q	—	**-0.28**	-0.26	-0.27	-0.23	-0.20
Yr.	—	**1.23**	**1.34**	1.26	1.16	1.17

Next earnings report expected: late October

Dividend Data (Dividends have been paid since 1958.)

Amount ($)	Date Decl.	Ex-Div. Date	Stock of Record	Payment Date
0.240	Nov. 18	Dec. 08	Dec. 10	Jan. 01 '99
0.240	Jan. 29	Mar. 08	Mar. 10	Apr. 01 '99
0.247	May. 10	Jun. 08	Jun. 10	Jul. 01 '99
0.247	Jul. 29	Sep. 08	Sep. 10	Oct. 01 '99

A Division of The McGraw-Hill Companies

Public Service Company of North Carolina, Inc.

Business Summary - 26-APR-99

Public Service of North Carolina (PGS) has agreed to be acquired by SCANA (SCG), a natural gas company located in South Carolina in February 1999. SCG will pay $900 million, including the assumption of debt, for PGS in February 1999. The approval process for the merger is anticipated to be completed by the end of 1999.

PGS is expanding its transmission and distribution systems to deliver higher volumes of natural gas across its service territory. The company plans to increase sales to current clients by replacing their old appliances with new gas equipment. PGS also intends to spur natural gas demand by marketing more natural gas equipment to its existing customers. Further, the company believes that continued strong growth in its service territory will lead to new accounts.

PGS transports, distributes, and sells natural gas to about 338,000 residential, commercial, and industrial customers in North Carolina. In addition to the company's natural gas distribution unit, PGS markets, sells, and installs both new and replacement cooking, water heating, laundry, space heating, cooling and humidity control natural gas appliances and equipment. PGS' nonregulated subsidiary provides conversion and maintenance services for natural gas fueled vehicles in certain cities. Through a subsidiary and a multi-state joint venture with Sonat Marketing L.P., the company participates in such unregulated businesses as natural gas brokering and supply services.

PGS serves a 31-county territory, including Raleigh, Durham, and the Research Triangle Park area in the north central part of North Carolina. These locations provide about 61% of the company's customers and 52% of its throughput. More than 2.5 million people live in the company's franchised service area. The company's central area includes the cities of Gastonia, Concord, and Statesville, which are located in the Charlotte metropolitan area. This territory accounts for 27% of customers and 33% of throughput. PGS' western area includes Asheville, Hendersonville, and Brevard, and comprises the remaining 12% of customers and 15% of throughput. Over the past three years, PGS has added 45,000 new customers to its natural gas transmission and distribution systems. These additional customers consisted of 39,000 residential, 5000 commercial, and 100 industrial clients. PGS' 5.2% annual growth rate is almost three times higher than the national average of 1.8%.

In July 1998, the company filed an application with the North Carolina Utilities Commission to extend service into Alexander County. Most of Alexander County lies within PSNC's service territory, but is not currently offered natural gas service. In October 1998, the NCUC issued an order that granted the company a $12,400,000 rate increase. Further, the NCUC allowed PGS a 9.8% return on net utility investment.

Per Share Data ($) (Year Ended Sep. 30)	1998	1997	1996	1995	1994	1993	1992	1991	1990	1989
Tangible Bk. Val.	10.91	10.40	9.75	9.28	8.82	7.73	7.40	6.92	6.87	6.66
Earnings	1.23	1.35	1.26	1.16	1.17	0.90	1.08	0.70	0.84	0.93
Dividends	0.94	0.90	0.86	0.84	0.81	0.78	0.75	0.73	0.72	0.69
Payout Ratio	76%	67%	69%	72%	69%	86%	69%	105%	86%	74%
Prices - High	26	24⅜	19⅝	18¾	17¾	19¾	20⅛	12¼	11½	11⅛
- Low	19⅛	16¾	15⅛	13¾	13½	15¼	11¼	10⅛	9¾	9½
P/E Ratio - High	21	18	15	16	15	22	19	17	14	12
- Low	16	12	12	12	12	17	10	14	12	10
Income Statement Analysis (Million $)										
Revs.	331	338	309	248	274	280	240	193	202	214
Depr.	25.0	22.6	19.7	18.2	15.2	14.1	13.1	12.2	10.9	9.9
Maint.	5.2	6.0	5.1	4.3	4.7	4.9	5.2	4.3	4.4	3.9
Fxd. Chgs. Cov.	3.1	3.4	2.6	2.7	2.5	2.0	2.2	1.8	1.9	2.3
Constr. Credits	0.6	0.3	0.3	0.3	0.1	0.1	0.1	0.3	0.6	0.3
Eff. Tax Rate	38%	37%	38%	39%	34%	35%	38%	36%	35%	36%
Net Inc.	24.8	26.3	23.9	21.4	20.0	14.2	16.8	10.6	12.3	13.3
Balance Sheet & Other Fin. Data (Million $)										
Gross Prop.	744	685	629	574	520	478	442	414	380	351
Cap. Exp.	65.3	60.3	60.4	61.1	45.5	40.1	31.1	36.5	32.3	42.9
Net Prop.	520	482	445	407	367	338	310	293	271	250
Capitalization:										
LT Debt	172	181	140	101	114	125	130	104	109	85.0
% LT Debt	44	47	43	37	42	50	53	50	51	47
Pfd.	Nil	Nil	Nil	Nil	Nil	Nil	Nil	1.7	2.0	2.2
% Pfd.	Nil	Nil	Nil	Nil	Nil	Nil	Nil	0.80	0.90	1.20
Common	223	207	189	173	161	124	115	104	101	95.0
% Common	57	53	57	63	59	50	47	50	48	52
Total Cap.	394	388	389	331	328	300	296	257	255	224
% Oper. Ratio	88.1	88.3	88.6	86.3	89.5	89.9	87.3	87.5	88.5	89.3
% Earn. on Net Prop.	7.8	8.6	4.2	9.0	8.1	8.7	10.1	8.6	8.9	9.8
% Return On Revs.	7.5	7.8	7.8	8.6	7.3	5.1	7.0	5.5	6.1	6.2
% Return On Invest. Capital	14.8	14.1	12.2	14.4	10.6	9.4	10.9	9.4	10.6	10.5
% Return On Com. Equity	11.5	13.3	13.2	12.8	14.1	11.9	15.2	10.2	12.5	14.4

Data as orig reptd.; bef. results of disc opers/spec. items. Per share data adj. for stk. divs. Bold denotes diluted EPS (FASB 128)-prior periods restated. E-Estimated. NA-Not Available. NM-Not Meaningful. NR-Not Ranked.

Office—400 Cox Rd., P.O. Box 1398, Gastonia, NC 28053-1398. **Tel**—(704) 864-6731. **Chrmn, Pres & CEO**—C. E. Zeigler Jr. **VP, Treas & CFO**—J. G. Mason. **Investor Contact**—Freida Pendleton. **VP & Secy**—J. P. Douglas. **Dirs**—W. C. Burkhardt, W. A. V. Cecil, B. Collins, J. W. Copeland, V. E. Eure, W. L. O'Brien Jr., D. W. Peterson, B. R. Rudisill II, G. S. York, C. E. Zeigler Jr. **Transfer Agent & Registrar**—First Union National Bank of North Carolina, Charlotte. **Incorporated**—in North Carolina in 1938. **Empl**— 1,047. **S&P Analyst:** John Staszak.

STANDARD
&POOR'S
STOCK REPORTS

QRS Corp.

NASDAQ Symbol **QRSI**

In S&P SmallCap 600

09-OCT-99

Industry:
Computer (Software & Services)

Summary: This company provides electronic commerce merchandise and logistics solutions throughout the retail demand chain.

Quantitative Evaluations

Outlook
(1 Lowest—5 Highest)
• 3⁻

Fair Value
• 69⅜

Risk
• Average

Earn./Div. Rank
• NR

Technical Eval.
• Bullish since 9/99

Rel. Strength Rank
(1 Lowest—99 Highest)
• 91

Insider Activity
• Unfavorable

Recent Price • 61⅜
52 Wk Range • 64¾-15⅝

Yield • Nil
12-Mo. P/E • 61.4

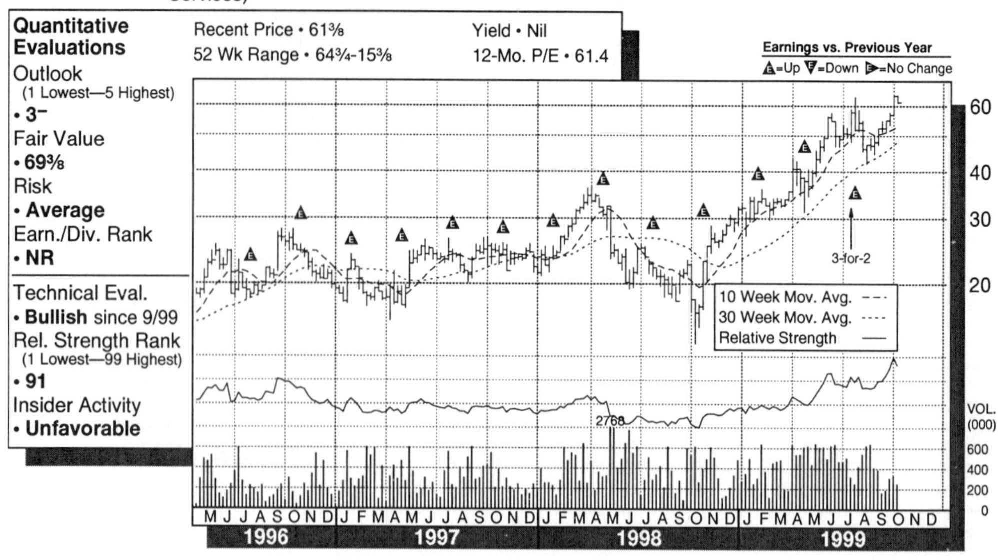

Business Profile - 27-SEP-99

In July 1999, QRS stated that its core products continue to perform well and that efforts in Korea and Shinsegae point to progress in its international efforts. The company also announced the acquisition of Retail Data Services, Inc., a provider of competitive pricing information mainly to grocery retailers, for $17.8 million in cash and stock. QRS believes the acquisition will provide it with further strength in expanding within the retail grocery segment. The number of QRS customers increased to 8,034 (270 retailers and 7,764 vendors and carriers) as of June 30, 1999, from 6,331 (226; 6,105) a year earlier. The company effected a three-for-two stock split in July 1999.

Operational Review - 27-SEP-99

In the first half of 1999, revenues rose 44%, year to year, reflecting an increased number of customers, higher network and catalog services use, additional primetime usage and product improvements. Margins widened, due to greater yield improvements and improved pricing on purchased network services, partially offset by expansion and product development costs. Following lower interest income, pretax income was up 42%. After taxes at 38.0%, versus 40.0%, net income advanced 47%, to $7,542,000 ($0.54 a share) from $5,122,000 ($0.38). Results in the 1998 period exclude a $0.07 a share gain related to the sale of the software and services business. Per-share figures are adjusted for the July 1999 3-for-2 stock split.

Stock Performance - 08-OCT-99

In the past 30 trading days, QRSI's shares have increased 28%, compared to a 0.91% fall in the S&P 500. Average trading volume for the past five days was 49,520 shares, compared with the 40-day moving average of 78,090 shares.

Key Stock Statistics

Dividend Rate/Share	Nil	Shareholders	68
Shs. outstg. (M)	13.4	Market cap. (B)	$0.823
Avg. daily vol. (M)	0.053	Inst. holdings	90%
Tang. Bk. Value/Share	6.32		
Beta	1.27		

Value of $10,000 invested 5 years ago: $ 41,846

Fiscal Year Ending Dec. 31

	1999	1998	1997	1996	1995	1994
Revenues (Million $)						
1Q	29.34	20.03	16.35	12.72	9.52	6.66
2Q	29.54	20.83	17.00	13.61	9.91	7.27
3Q	—	23.62	18.25	14.70	10.93	8.41
4Q	—	27.44	20.02	15.77	11.77	9.05
Yr.	—	91.93	71.63	56.75	42.13	31.38
Earnings Per Share ($)						
1Q	**0.27**	**0.19**	**0.15**	**0.11**	0.08	0.09
2Q	**0.28**	**0.20**	**0.16**	**0.12**	0.09	0.10
3Q	—	**0.19**	**0.17**	**0.13**	0.10	0.13
4Q	—	**0.27**	**0.19**	**0.15**	-0.08	0.80
Yr.	—	**0.84**	**0.67**	**0.51**	**0.19**	**1.11**

Next earnings report expected: late October

Dividend Data

Amount ($)	Date Decl.	Ex-Div. Date	Stock of Record	Payment Date
3-for-2	Jun. 10	Jul. 13	Jun. 21	Jul. 12 '99

QRS Corporation

Business Summary - 27-SEP-99

Formerly named QuickResponse Services, Inc., QRS Corp. provides e-commerce (electronic commerce) merchandising and logistics solutions throughout the retail demand chain. The company supplies its retailer, vendor and carrier customers with a single source for implementing network-centric demand chain management solutions.

With heightened competitive pressures within the general merchandise retail industry, retailers have increasingly focused on managing merchandise to improve financial performance. Failure to manage merchandise to meet customer demand results in lost sales. In recent years, retailers and vendors have sought to develop strategies for optimizing selection, availability and flow of information and merchandise while minimizing absolute inventory levels. QRS provides solutions to improve the efficiencies throughout the retail demand chain.

The company's products and services -Catalog Services, Network Services, Inventory Management Services (IMS), Logistics Management Services (LMS) and Professional Services- are organized and managed as a single product family. QRS derives revenues from five main and related sources: monthly charges for accessing Catalog Services, fees for use of network services including the transmission of standard business documents over a network, IMS-related fees based on negotiated monthly service charges, LMS fees, and consulting fees. Network Services pricing is based primarily on the volume of characters transmitted and the type of network access utilized, and incorporates volume discounts.

Catalog Services products and services include QRS Keystone, a product information database using the industry standard Universal Product Code (U.P.C.) numbering system. QRS Keystone is the retail industry's largest U.P.C. database, containing over 67 million U.P.C. entries as of December 31, 1998.

Network Services includes QRS Concourse, a connecting service that provides two-way electronic transmission of business data, while its partner service, QRS Alliance permits any size manufacturer, retailer or vendor to exchange business documents with its partners electronically.

The company's IMS product family includes QRS Catalyst, a management tool that enables users to track which products are selling by U.P.C. and store location; QRS Mariner, which uses a stock of models and daily sales information to determine recommended order quantity and track the flow of reordered items; and QRS Horizon, a forecasting tool to project consumer demand.

QRS LMS provides logistics information to improve merchandise movement and inventory management, allowing retailers and vendors to tender and track freight shipments to carriers and provide delivery performance reporting. The company's Professional Services engages in education and consulting services using strategic tools and industry expertise.

Per Share Data ($) (Year Ended Dec. 31)	1998	1997	1996	1995	1994	1993	1992	1991	1990	1989
Tangible Bk. Val.	5.07	4.28	3.45	2.84	2.58	1.29	NA	NA	NA	NA
Cash Flow	1.09	0.80	0.60	0.24	1.14	0.26	NA	NA	NA	NA
Earnings	0.84	0.67	0.51	0.19	1.11	0.31	NA	NA	NA	NA
Dividends	Nil	Nil	Nil	Nil	Nil	NM	NA	NA	NA	NA
Payout Ratio	Nil	Nil	Nil	Nil	Nil	Nil	NA	NA	NA	NA
Prices - High	36 5/8	26 5/8	28	18	17 1/8	21 3/8	NA	NA	NA	NA
- Low	13 7/8	15 7/8	11 7/8	7 3/8	6 1/8	8	NA	NA	NA	NA
P/E Ratio - High	44	40	54	96	15	56	NA	NA	NA	NA
- Low	16	24	23	39	5	21	NA	NA	NA	NA
Income Statement Analysis (Million $)										
Revs.	91.9	71.6	56.7	42.1	31.4	22.5	13.3	NA	NA	NA
Oper. Inc.	20.5	14.4	10.6	7.4	5.7	3.4	4.5	NA	NA	NA
Depr.	3.4	1.7	1.2	0.6	0.4	0.3	3.0	NA	NA	NA
Int. Exp.	Nil	Nil	Nil	Nil	0.1	1.4	1.5	NA	NA	NA
Pretax Inc.	18.3	14.6	11.0	4.0	6.0	1.9	-0.1	NA	NA	NA
Eff. Tax Rate	39%	40%	40%	40%	NM	Nil	NA	NA	NA	NA
Net Inc.	11.2	8.8	6.6	2.4	14.0	1.9	-0.1	NA	NA	NA
Balance Sheet & Other Fin. Data (Million $)										
Cash	36.6	16.1	16.0	6.5	8.6	8.2	2.5	NA	NA	NA
Curr. Assets	64.7	50.5	39.2	33.3	26.6	21.4	9.9	NA	NA	NA
Total Assets	83.0	64.0	55.9	46.6	39.9	23.1	12.6	NA	NA	NA
Curr. Liab.	13.8	8.1	9.8	7.9	3.6	3.5	29.2	NA	NA	NA
LT Debt	Nil	Nil	Nil	Nil	Nil	0.5	0.8	NA	NA	NA
Common Eqty.	67.9	54.7	43.6	35.4	31.4	15.5	-25.3	NA	NA	NA
Total Cap.	67.9	54.7	43.6	-24.5	31.4	16.0	NA	NA	NA	NA
Cap. Exp.	3.2	5.9	NA	NA	NA	NA	NA	NA	NA	NA
Cash Flow	14.5	10.5	7.8	3.0	14.4	2.2	2.6	NA	NA	NA
Curr. Ratio	4.7	6.2	4.0	4.2	7.5	6.2	0.3	NA	NA	NA
% LT Debt of Cap.	Nil	Nil	Nil	Nil	Nil	3.1	NM	NA	NA	NA
% Net Inc.of Revs.	12.1	12.3	11.7	5.7	44.5	8.5	NM	NA	NA	NA
% Ret. on Assets	15.2	14.6	12.9	5.5	44.3	10.7	NM	NA	NA	NA
% Ret. on Equity	18.2	17.9	16.7	7.1	59.5	NM	NM	NA	NA	NA

Data as orig reptd.; bef. results of disc opers/spec. items. Per share data adj. for stk. divs. Bold denotes diluted EPS (FASB 128)-prior periods restated. E-Estimated. NA-Not Available. NM-Not Meaningful. NR-Not Ranked.

Office—1400 Marina Way South, Richmond, CA 94804. **Tel**—(510) 215-5000. **Website**—http://www.qrsi.com **Chrmn**—P. R. Johnson. **CEO**—J. S. Simon. **Pres & COO**—S. M. O'Connor. **VP, CFO & Secy**—P. Papano. **Dirs**—T. Amochaev, S. D. Brooks, J. P. Dougall, H. L. Hazlett, P. R. Johnson, G. Saloner, P. Schlein, J. S. Simon, G. K. Staglin. **Transfer Agent & Registrar**—First Interstate Bank, Los Angeles. **Incorporated**—in Delaware in 1997; originally incorporated in California in 1985. **Empl**— 292. **S&P Analyst:** P.T.W.

STANDARD
&POOR'S
STOCK REPORTS

Quaker Chemical

NYSE Symbol **KWR**

In S&P SmallCap 600

23-OCT-99

Industry:
Chemicals (Specialty)

Summary: This company produces and markets worldwide a broad range of specialty chemical products for heavy industrial, institutional and manufacturing applications.

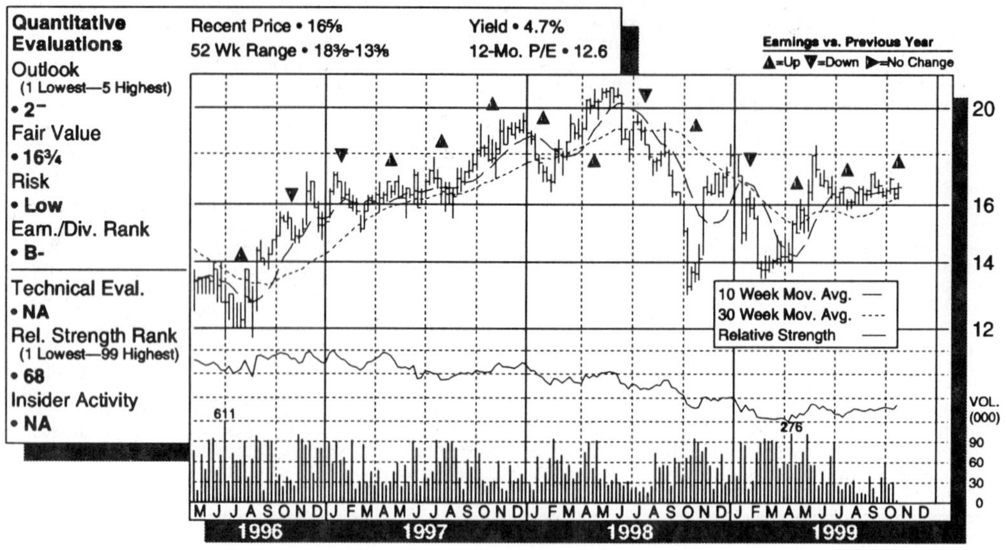

Business Profile - 21-OCT-99

In October 1999, KWR reported that third quarter results reflected higher sales on a constant currency basis in all major business segments. In addition, all geographical regions provided revenue growth on a constant currency basis with the exception of Europe, which was flat. In July 1999, the company implemented a new organizational structure, reorganized along global business lines rather than its historical regional orientation, to focus the company on its worldwide markets. KWR will now have three business units: two major commercial units, responsible for the financial performance and market share growth; and a third unit called Worldwide Operations, responsible for logistical and manufacturing activities.

Operational Review - 21-OCT-99

Net sales in the nine months ended September 30, 1999, declined fractionally, year to year, on the negative impact of the stronger dollar on translated earnings. Gross margins widened on the implementation of cost reduction initiatives and lower raw material costs. Following lower share of net income of equity companies and higher minority interest expense, net income rose 12%, to $11.1 million ($1.24 per share), versus $9.9 million ($1.12). The negative effect of the stronger dollar on translated earnings in the first nine months of 1999 was $0.06 per share.

Stock Performance - 22-OCT-99

In the past 30 trading days, KWR's shares have declined 1%, compared to a 4% fall in the S&P 500. Average trading volume for the past five days was 5,680 shares, compared with the 40-day moving average of 5,808 shares.

Key Stock Statistics

Dividend Rate/Share	0.78	Shareholders	1,007
Shs. outstg. (M)	8.9	Market cap. (B)	$0.147
Avg. daily vol. (M)	0.006	Inst. holdings	39%
Tang. Bk. Value/Share	6.41		
Beta	0.23		

Value of $10,000 invested 5 years ago: $ 13,117

Fiscal Year Ending Dec. 31

	1999	1998	1997	1996	1995	1994
Revenues (Million $)						
1Q	60.90	62.24	58.54	58.20	54.53	45.09
2Q	64.03	65.36	60.31	59.79	59.78	47.35
3Q	67.80	65.99	58.69	61.83	57.87	50.12
4Q	—	63.52	63.99	60.45	55.60	52.12
Yr.	—	257.1	241.5	240.3	227.0	194.7
Earnings Per Share ($)						
1Q	**0.34**	**0.33**	**0.30**	**0.19**	0.22	0.24
2Q	**0.42**	**0.39**	**0.54**	**0.31**	0.28	0.24
3Q	**0.48**	**0.40**	**0.38**	**-0.68**	0.24	0.26
4Q	—	**0.08**	**0.23**	**-0.70**	0.02	0.29
Yr.	—	**1.20**	**1.45**	**-0.88**	**0.76**	1.03

Next earnings report expected: early February

Dividend Data (Dividends have been paid since 1954.)

Amount ($)	Date Decl.	Ex-Div. Date	Stock of Record	Payment Date
0.190	Nov. 18	Jan. 13	Jan. 15	Jan. 29 '99
0.190	Mar. 17	Apr. 14	Apr. 16	Apr. 30 '99
0.190	May. 12	Jul. 14	Jul. 16	Jul. 30 '99
0.195	Sep. 15	Oct. 13	Oct. 15	Oct. 29 '99

A Division of The McGraw-Hill Companies

Quaker Chemical Corporation

Business Summary - 21-OCT-99

In July 1999, Quaker Chemical Corporation shifted to a global corporate structure, organized along global business lines rather than its historical regional orientation, in order to compete more effectively in the 21st century. KWR will now have three units: two major commercial business units that will be responsible for financial performance and market share growth; and one major unit to be called Worldwide Operations, responsible for logistical and manufacturing activities.

KWR develops and produces a broad range of specialty chemicals for various heavy industrial and manufacturing applications, and offers and markets chemical management services, including recycling services. In 1998, the company acquired a 60% interest in a joint venture in Brazil with Siderquimica Ltda., the leading process chemical supplier to the Brazilian steel industry.

As of December 31, 1998, the company operated in three business segments: metal working process chemicals (88% of 1998 net sales); coatings (7%); and other chemical products (5%). The metalworking process chemicals segment manufactured lubricants for various heavy industrial and manufacturing applications. The coatings segment produced coatings for metal products and chemical milling maskants. And the other chemical products segment included chemicals used in the manufacturing of paper as well as other various chemical products. The company believes that it has a dominant position in the market for process fluids used in the production of hot and cold rolling of steel. Competition in this industry sector is based on the ability to provide products which meet the needs of its customers and render technical services and laboratory assistance to customers, and to a lesser extent, on price.

KWR's products include (1) rolling lubricants; (2) corrosion preventatives; (3) metal finishing compounds; (4) machining and grinding compounds; (5) forming compounds; (6) paper production products; (7) hydraulic fluids; (8) products for the removal of hydrogen sulfide; (9) chemical milling maskants and coatings for metal products; (10) construction products, such as flexible sealants and protective coatings; and (9) programs to provide recycling and chemical management services.

During 1998, KWR's five largest customers accounted for approximately 14% of its net sales. With a significant portion of its net sales derived from sale of process fluids to manufacturers of steel, automotive, appliances, and durable goods, the company is therefore subject to the same business cycles as its customers. KWR serves customers in the United States (47% of 1998 net sales), Europe (36%), Asia/Pacific (10%) and South America (7%).

KWR uses over 500 raw materials in its processes. As of 1998, only one raw material accounted for as much as 10% of the total cost of KWR's raw material purchases. Many of the raw materials used by KWR are commodity chemicals, and therefore its earnings may be affected by ma rket changes in commodity chemical prices.

Per Share Data ($) (Year Ended Dec. 31)	1998	1997	1996	1995	1994	1993	1992	1991	1990	1989
Tangible Bk. Val.	7.01	7.01	6.73	8.66	9.23	8.32	10.03	10.05	10.14	8.64
Cash Flow	2.00	2.28	0.13	1.79	1.74	0.52	2.03	1.78	2.01	1.75
Earnings	1.20	1.45	-0.88	0.76	1.03	-0.19	1.33	1.20	1.51	1.35
Dividends	0.73	0.70	0.69	0.68	0.62	0.60	0.56	0.52	0.46	0.40
Payout Ratio	61%	49%	NM	89%	60%	NM	43%	44%	29%	30%
Prices - High	21	19¾	17¼	19	19½	24⅝	26	22¼	19¼	15⅝
- Low	13	15	11¾	11	14¾	14¼	18¾	15	12	12½
P/E Ratio - High	17	14	NM	25	19	NM	20	19	13	12
- Low	11	10	NM	14	14	NM	14	13	8	9
Income Statement Analysis (Million $)										
Revs.	257	242	240	227	195	195	212	191	201	182
Oper. Inc.	29.6	25.8	23.9	20.1	19.5	14.9	23.6	19.2	22.6	19.0
Depr.	7.1	7.3	8.7	8.7	6.5	6.5	6.4	5.2	4.7	3.9
Int. Exp.	2.2	1.5	1.9	1.7	1.3	1.5	1.5	1.8	NA	1.2
Pretax Inc.	17.8	20.9	-7.0	12.1	15.7	-1.2	19.5	17.3	23.0	20.1
Eff. Tax Rate	38%	38%	NM	40%	38%	NM	36%	35%	37%	34%
Net Inc.	10.7	12.6	-7.6	6.7	9.4	-1.8	12.1	10.8	14.1	12.8
Balance Sheet & Other Fin. Data (Million $)										
Cash	10.2	18.4	8.5	7.2	11.3	20.3	24.5	23.8	26.4	22.6
Curr. Assets	96.1	98.1	86.6	86.7	83.4	84.4	85.6	82.7	84.8	75.4
Total Assets	190	171	166	185	170	171	167	156	152	131
Curr. Liab.	50.4	47.8	64.0	60.9	43.4	42.6	28.1	36.6	40.3	27.8
LT Debt	25.3	25.2	5.2	9.3	12.2	16.1	18.6	5.2	5.5	5.7
Common Eqty.	83.7	75.6	74.3	94.0	94.0	91.0	102	99	99	90.4
Total Cap.	121	108	86.4	109	112	113	125	106	108	99
Cap. Exp.	8.1	5.6	NA	NA	NA	9.0	7.2	8.4	12.7	7.6
Cash Flow	17.8	19.9	1.1	15.8	15.9	4.8	18.5	16.0	18.8	16.7
Curr. Ratio	1.9	2.1	1.4	1.4	1.9	2.0	3.0	2.3	2.1	2.7
% LT Debt of Cap.	20.9	23.3	6.0	8.5	10.9	14.3	14.9	4.9	5.1	5.7
% Net Inc.of Revs.	4.1	5.2	NM	2.9	4.8	NM	5.7	5.6	7.0	7.1
% Ret. on Assets	5.9	7.5	NM	37.7	5.6	NM	7.4	7.0	10.2	10.3
% Ret. on Equity	13.4	16.8	NM	7.1	10.4	NM	12.0	10.8	15.3	15.0

Data as orig reptd.; bef. results of disc opers/spec. items. Per share data adj. for stk. divs. Bold denotes diluted EPS (FASB 128)-prior periods restated. E-Estimated. NA-Not Available. NM-Not Meaningful. NR-Not Ranked.

Office—Elm and Lee Streets, Conshohocken, PA 19428. **Tel**—(610) 832-4000. **Website**—http://www.quakerchem.com **Chrmn & CEO**—R.J. Naples. **Pres & COO**—J.W. Bauer. **VP & CFO**—M.F. Barry. **Investor Contact**—Irene M. Kisleiko (610) 832-4119. **Dirs**—J.B. Anderson Jr., P.C. Barron, P.A. Benoliel, L.K. Black, D.R. Caldwell, R.E. Chappell, E.J. Delattre, R.P. Hauptfuhrer, R.J. Naples, R.H. Rock. **Transfer Agent & Registrar**—American Stock Transfer & Trust Co., NYC. **Incorporated**—in Pennsylvania in 1930. **Empl**— 923. **S&P Analyst:** T.J. Vital

STANDARD &POOR'S
STOCK REPORTS

Quanex Corp.

NYSE Symbol **NX**
In S&P SmallCap 600

09-OCT-99

Industry: Iron & Steel

Summary: Quanex produces hot rolled special bar quality carbon and alloy steel bars, air-bag components and aluminum building products.

S&P Opinion: Accumulate (★★★★)

Recent Price • 24½
52 Wk Range • 29-15⅜
Yield • 2.6%
12-Mo. P/E • NM

Quantitative Evaluations

Outlook (1 Lowest—5 Highest)
• **4**

Fair Value
• **37⅛**

Risk
• **Low**

Earn./Div. Rank
• **B**

Technical Eval.
• **Neutral** since 9/99

Rel. Strength Rank (1 Lowest—99 Highest)
• **43**

Insider Activity
• **NA**

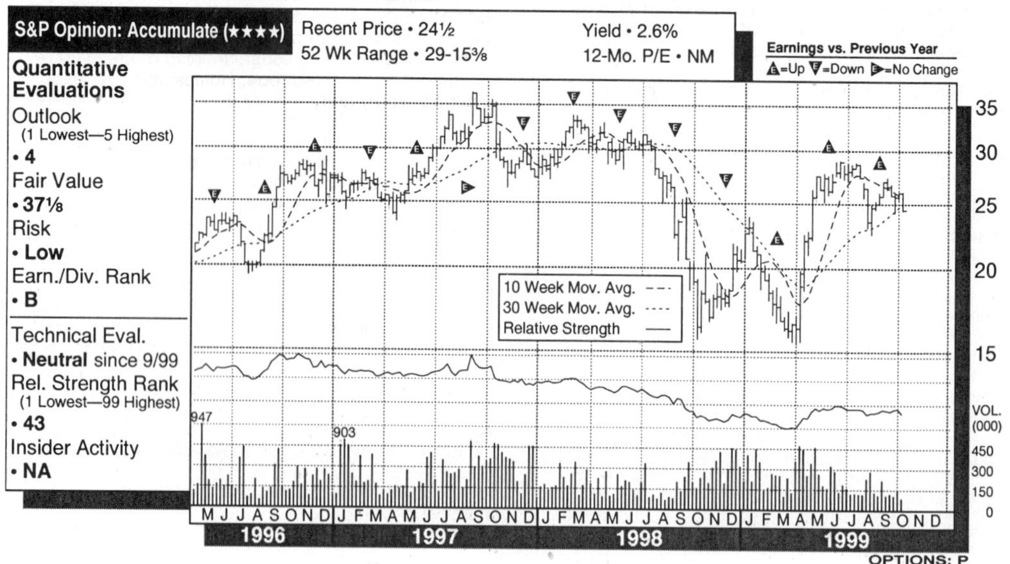

Overview - 03-SEP-99

Assuming continued strong demand from durable goods manufacturers, we project 9% sales growth for NX in FY 2000 (Oct.). The anticipated gain reflects assumed higher sales at all units. Sales at MacSteel should exceed FY 99 levels, on greater sales of premium products. Higher overall volume will also result from an expected rebound in demand from capital goods manufacturers, and continued steady demand from the auto industry. We anticipate another strong year for aluminum, based on higher volume, an improved product mix resulting from the addition of more contract business, and the inclusion of Decatur Aluminum for a full year. Finally, new markets for Piper's products and firm demand from existing customers should permit higher sales. With lower interest expense and a return to the black for Piper, EPS should rise again in FY 2000.

Valuation - 03-SEP-99

Following release of FY 99 third quarter results, and a conference call, we are maintaining our accumulate rating on NX. Earlier, in April, we upgraded NX to accumulate, from hold, based on valuation. Although the shares have since risen 39%, we believe NX remains undervalued, based on its EPS prospects for FY 2000. NX was recently trading at about 9.5X our EPS estimate, versus a P/E of 10.8X for integrated steel companies we follow. NX is very undervalued. Its steel business is far more profitable than that of any of the integrated steel makers or minimills we cover, and its EPS in general are far more consistent. Its balance sheet is also far stronger than that of most steel producers we follow. Finally, capital expenditure needs are far lower than those of most steel or aluminum companies. We expect NX's free cash flow to rise significantly in the future. Consequently, we believe NX deserves a higher multiple.

Key Stock Statistics

S&P EPS Est. 1999	2.55	Tang. Bk. Value/Share	16.96
P/E on S&P Est. 1999	9.6	Beta	0.92
S&P EPS Est. 2000	2.75	Shareholders	5,632
Dividend Rate/Share	0.64	Market cap. (B)	$0.350
Shs. outstg. (M)	14.3	Inst. holdings	80%
Avg. daily vol. (M)	0.022		

Value of $10,000 invested 5 years ago: $ 16,309

Fiscal Year Ending Oct. 31

	1999	1998	1997	1996	1995	1994
Revenues (Million $)						
1Q	183.1	181.0	194.9	188.8	199.9	149.6
2Q	202.9	203.4	217.1	218.3	234.3	172.2
3Q	206.6	204.8	225.1	225.5	228.2	181.1
4Q	—	208.2	195.6	263.1	228.8	196.5
Yr.	—	797.5	746.1	895.7	891.2	699.3
Earnings Per Share ($)						
1Q	**0.27**	**0.16**	0.23	0.30	0.23	0.02
2Q	**0.64**	**0.51**	0.61	0.60	0.62	0.17
3Q	**0.79**	**0.66**	0.67	0.67	0.63	0.32
4Q	**E0.85**	**-1.71**	0.59	0.84	0.72	0.45
Yr.	**E2.55**	**-0.27**	**1.90**	**1.60**	**1.43**	0.96

Next earnings report expected: mid December

Dividend Data (Dividends have been paid since 1988.)

Amount ($)	Date Decl.	Ex-Div. Date	Stock of Record	Payment Date
0.160	Dec. 10	Dec. 17	Dec. 21	Dec. 31 '98
0.160	Feb. 26	Mar. 12	Mar. 16	Mar. 31 '99
0.160	May. 27	Jun. 11	Jun. 15	Jun. 30 '99
0.160	Aug. 27	Sep. 14	Sep. 16	Sep. 30 '99

Quanex Corporation

Business Summary - 03-SEP-99

Quanex produces hot rolled special bar quality carbon and alloy steel bars, and aluminum building products. In August 1996, NX entered the market for impact extruded aluminum and steel products with the acquisition of Piper Impact. Sales and operating profits in FY 98 (Oct.) were:

	Sales	Profits
Engineered steel products	40%	81%
Aluminum mill sheet products	32%	11%
Engineered products	28%	8%

Engineered steel products include steel bar operations, steel bar and tube heat treating services, and steelbar and tube wear and corrosion resistant finishing services. Steel bar operations, which account for the bulk of this segment, are conducted by MacSteel at two plants. MacSteel makes hot rolled bars, including hot rolled steel bar quality carbon and steel bars used for camshafts, transmission gears, bearing cages, steering components, hydraulic mechanisms, seamless tube production, and track components for military vehicles. In recent years, NX has made incremental capacity additions to MacSteel's plants that have improved product quality as well as add volume. Operating income totaled $59.9 million in FY 98, versus $50.8 million in FY 97.

The aluminum mill sheet products segment consists of Nichols-Homeshield (NH). NH uses state of the art aluminum minimill casting equipment to make coiled aluminum sheet from scrap and operates two finishing mills to supply a diverse mix of external customers in the construction, transportation and service centers markets. Operating profit in this segment increased to $7.8 million in FY 98, from $1.8 million in FY 97.

The Engineered products segment consists of Piper Impact, Piper Impact-Europe, Homeshield Fabricated Products (HFP) and AMSCO. Piper manufactures impact extruded aluminum and steel parts for the transportation, electronics and defense markets. The majority of Piper's sales are to Autoliv (formerly Morton International) in the form of air-bag components. This includes passenger and side impact air bags, "smart" bags with adjustable inflation speed, and those with alternative inflation technologies.

Homeshield Fabricated Products (HFP) makes a wide range of residential building products that are sold through distributors, as well as engineered products for OEMs. AMSCO manufactures aluminum window and patio door screens, window frames and related accessories.

Engineered products incurred $58.5 million in charges in FY 98 to write down goodwill and provide for restructuring of operations at Piper Impact. Excluding the charges, segment operating income totaled $5.9 million in FY 98, versus $15.4 million in FY 97.

Per Share Data ($) (Year Ended Oct. 31)	1998	1997	1996	1995	1994	1993	1992	1991	1990	1989
Tangible Bk. Val.	15.50	12.62	7.66	10.27	8.12	7.76	8.54	9.94	9.24	8.56
Cash Flow	2.68	4.63	5.22	4.91	3.01	2.23	2.36	3.17	3.88	3.51
Earnings	-0.27	1.98	2.41	2.20	0.96	0.18	0.28	1.02	2.03	2.11
Dividends	0.64	0.61	0.60	0.59	0.56	0.56	0.52	0.48	0.40	0.30
Payout Ratio	NM	31%	25%	27%	58%	NM	200%	47%	19%	14%
Prices - High	33 3/4	36 1/2	29 1/8	26 5/8	27 1/4	21 1/4	31 3/4	23 1/8	18 1/2	19
- Low	15 5/8	23 3/8	18 3/4	18	17	14	15 1/2	11 3/8	9 1/8	13 1/8
P/E Ratio - High	NM	18	12	12	28	NM	NM	23	9	9
- Low	NM	12	8	8	18	NM	NM	11	4	6
Income Statement Analysis (Million $)										
Revs.	797	746	896	891	699	616	572	589	650	502
Oper. Inc.	103	92.3	105	99	69.2	50.9	52.5	60.2	79.7	70.6
Depr.	41.8	37.3	38.4	32.4	27.8	27.7	26.4	25.1	22.6	17.4
Int. Exp.	10.5	14.0	11.4	10.7	13.9	15.1	15.5	17.7	10.9	6.8
Pretax Inc.	-6.0	42.6	56.7	58.4	32.5	14.5	10.7	21.4	45.2	47.1
Eff. Tax Rate	NM	35%	42%	42%	42%	42%	42%	42%	38%	38%
Net Inc.	-3.9	27.7	32.9	33.9	18.9	8.4	6.2	12.4	28.0	29.3
Balance Sheet & Other Fin. Data (Million $)										
Cash	26.3	26.9	36.0	45.2	88.1	89.9	96.9	31.1	24.1	24.8
Curr. Assets	210	187	263	242	259	243	250	164	170	166
Total Assets	674	686	718	547	564	529	535	446	451	400
Curr. Liab.	147	134	153	165	135	95.1	96.0	95.0	96.0	90.0
LT Debt	188	202	254	112	107	128	129	156	131	93.0
Common Eqty.	272	269	195	171	146	140	151	152	147	133
Total Cap.	494	519	473	312	363	372	383	341	344	298
Cap. Exp.	58.5	72.8	44.2	26.6	44.6	37.0	52.5	57.0	31.9	13.8
Cash Flow	38.0	65.0	71.3	66.3	40.7	30.2	30.0	37.0	47.4	43.5
Curr. Ratio	1.4	1.4	1.7	1.5	1.9	2.6	2.6	1.7	1.8	1.8
% LT Debt of Cap.	38.1	38.9	53.7	35.9	29.6	34.5	33.6	45.8	38.2	31.3
% Net Inc.of Revs.	NM	3.7	3.7	3.8	2.7	1.4	1.1	2.1	4.3	5.8
% Ret. on Assets	NM	3.9	5.2	6.1	3.4	1.6	1.2	2.8	6.7	8.3
% Ret. on Equity	NM	12.0	18.0	16.8	9.0	1.7	2.2	8.0	18.0	21.3

Data as orig reptd.; bef. results of disc opers/spec. items. Per share data adj. for stk. divs. Bold denotes diluted EPS (FASB 128)-prior periods restated. E-Estimated. NA-Not Available. NM-Not Meaningful. NR-Not Ranked.

Office—1900 West Loop South, Suite 1500, Houston, TX 77027. **Tel**—(713) 961-4600. **Website**—http://www.quanex.com **Chrmn, Pres & CEO**—V. E. Oechsle. **VP & CFO**—W. M. Rose. **Secy**—M. W. Conlon. **Investor Contact**—Jeff Galow (800-231-8176). **Dirs**—D. J. Barger Jr., S. F. Davis, R. M. Flaum, D. O'Connell, V. E. Oechsle, C. E. Pfeiffer, V. R. Scorsone, M. J. Sebastian. **Transfer Agent & Registrar**—American Stock Transfer & Trust, NYC. **Incorporated**—in Michigan in 1927; reincorporated in Delaware in 1968. **Empl**— 3,261. **S&P Analyst:** Leo Larkin

STANDARD
&POOR'S
STOCK REPORTS

Queens County Bancorp

NASDAQ Symbol **QCSB**

In S&P SmallCap 600

08-OCT-99

Industry:
Savings & Loan Companies

Summary: Queens County Bancorp is the holding company for Queens County Savings Bank, the first savings bank chartered by the State of New York in the New York City Borough of Queens.

Quantitative Evaluations

Outlook
(1 Lowest—5 Highest)
• **1+**

Fair Value
• **26½**

Risk
• **Low**

Earn./Div. Rank
• **NR**

Technical Eval.
• **Bearish** since 8/99

Rel. Strength Rank
(1 Lowest—99 Highest)
• **40**

Insider Activity
• **Favorable**

Recent Price • 27⅜
52 Wk Range • 36⅛-22¾
Yield • 3.6%
12-Mo. P/E • 17.9

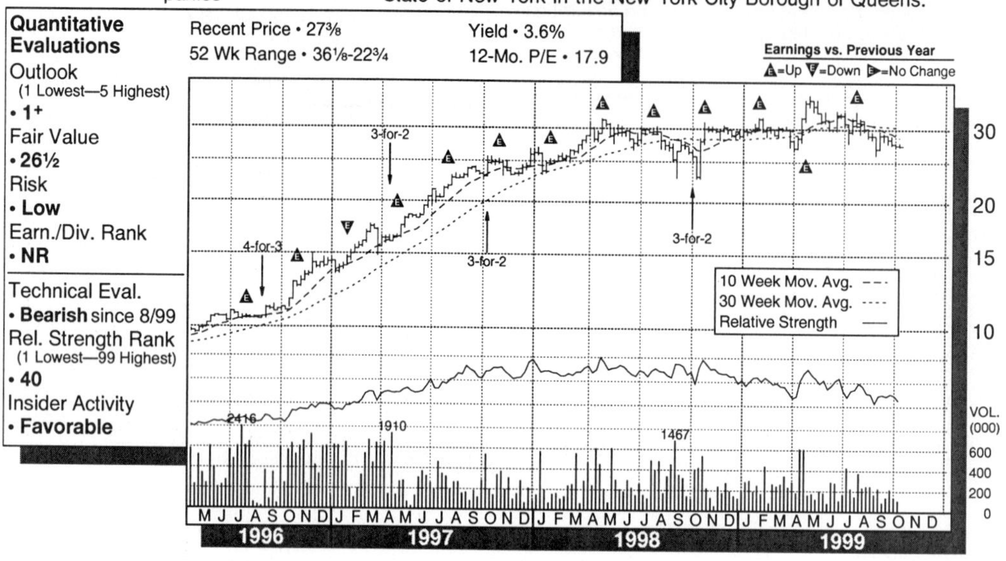

Business Profile - 11-OCT-99

The bank's primary business is gathering deposits from its customers in Queens and Nassau counties, and investing these funds in the origination of residential mortgage loans throughout metropolitan New York. QCSB has had 19 consecutive quarters without net chargeoffs, and non-performing assets, at June 30, 1999, represented 0.30% of total assets, down from 0.38% at December 31, 1998. On July 28, 1999, QCSB said it completed the share repurchase program authorized December 15, 1998. Under the authorization, the company repurchased 500,000 shares, bringing to 12,161,933 the total number of shares repurchased since 1994. The average price of the repurchased shares was $15.37. The company opened a Woodside, Queens branch July 31, 1999.

Operational Review - 11-OCT-99

Net interest income in the six months ended June 30, 1999, was up slightly, year to year, although QCSB's interest rate spread and net interest margin were below 1998 levels. The average balance of interest-earning assets was up, reaching $1.75 billion. Results benefited from a $2 million reversal of provision for loan losses in the 1999 period. Other income fell 20%, and operating expense was down 15%, led by lower compensation and benefit expenses; pretax income advanced 17%. After taxes at 39.1%, versus 41.5%; net income was up 22%, to $15,686,000 ($0.82 a share), from $12,878,000 ($0.63, adjusted).

Stock Performance - 01-OCT-99

In the past 30 trading days, QCSB's shares have declined 5%, compared to a 4% fall in the S&P 500. Average trading volume for the past five days was 26,760 shares, compared with the 40-day moving average of 36,933 shares.

Key Stock Statistics

Dividend Rate/Share	1.00	Shareholders	700
Shs. outstg. (M)	21.4	Market cap. (B)	$0.591
Avg. daily vol. (M)	0.029	Inst. holdings	33%
Tang. Bk. Value/Share	6.72		
Beta	1.00		

Value of $10,000 invested 5 years ago: $ 63,652

Fiscal Year Ending Dec. 31

	1999	1998	1997	1996	1995	1994
Revenues (Million $)						
1Q	34.00	33.04	27.41	25.00	23.02	20.23
2Q	34.68	34.03	28.96	25.54	24.29	21.00
3Q	—	34.76	30.74	25.99	23.36	21.42
4Q	—	35.00	32.93	26.62	23.91	22.40
Yr.	—	136.8	120.0	104.8	94.57	85.04
Earnings Per Share ($)						
1Q	**0.43**	**0.31**	**0.30**	0.20	0.18	0.15
2Q	**0.39**	**0.32**	**0.25**	0.24	0.19	0.17
3Q	—	**0.34**	**0.26**	0.23	0.20	0.16
4Q	—	**0.37**	**0.26**	0.16	0.20	0.19
Yr.	—	**1.34**	**1.07**	**0.85**	**0.77**	0.67

Next earnings report expected: mid October

Dividend Data (Dividends have been paid since 1994.)

Amount ($)	Date Decl.	Ex-Div. Date	Stock of Record	Payment Date
0.200	Oct. 21	Oct. 29	Nov. 02	Nov. 16 '98
0.250	Jan. 20	Jan. 28	Feb. 01	Feb. 16 '99
0.250	Apr. 21	Apr. 29	May. 03	May. 17 '99
0.250	Jul. 21	Jul. 29	Aug. 02	Aug. 16 '99

A Division of The McGraw-Hill Companies

Queens County Bancorp, Inc.

Business Summary - 11-OCT-99

Queens County Bancorp, Inc. was formed in 1993 to serve as the holding company for Queens County Savings Bank. The company acquired all of the stock of the bank upon its conversion from a New York State-chartered mutual savings bank to a New York State-chartered stock savings bank in November 1993. Queens County Savings Bank was organized in 1859 as a New York State-chartered mutual savings bank, and was the first savings bank chartered in the New York City Borough of Queens.

The bank's principal business is attracting retail deposits from the general public and investing those deposits, together with funds generated from operations, into the origination of mortgage loans on multi-family properties and one-to-four family homes. To a lesser extent, the bank also originates loans on commercial real estate, construction loans, home equity loans, and other consumer loans.

The bank is a community-oriented financial institution offering a wide variety of financial products and services to meet the needs of the communities it serves. Headquartered in the heart of Flushing, Queens, the bank operates nine branch offices and three customer service centers in Queens, and a 10th branch office in Nassau County. The bank's deposit gathering base is concentrated in the communities surrounding its offices, while its primary lending area extends throughout the greater New York metropolitan area. Most of the bank's mortgage loans are secured by properties located in the New York City Boroughs of Queens, Brooklyn and Manhattan, and in Nassau County.

As of December 31, 1998, QCSB had $1.5 billion of mortgage loans outstanding, of which $1.2 billion were multi-family mortgage loans. Another $0.2 billion was 1-to-4 family mortgage loans, and the remainder related to commercial real estate, or construction. QCSB's multi-family mortgage loans are typically originated for terms of 10 years at a rate of interest that adjusts to the prime rate of interest, as reported in The New York Times, plus a margin of 100 basis points, in each of years six through ten. In 1998, the majority of the bank's multi-family mortgage loan originations featured a fixed rate for the first five years of the credit; prepayment penalties range from five points to two over the first five years of the loan. At year-end 1998, 95.3% of the bank's multi-family mortgage loans were adjustable rate credits, including $195.9 million that are due to step upward in 1999.

To enhance its funding, QCSB has initiated a Mobile Teller program in cooperation with Queens College in Fresh Meadows. Under this program, a branch manager and a customer service representative are to visit the college on a regular basis, and QCSB planned to install an ATM at the college.

Per Share Data ($) (Year Ended Dec. 31)	1998	1997	1996	1995	1994	1993	1992	1991	1990	1989
Tangible Bk. Val.	7.03	11.43	8.21	7.68	7.23	6.22	NA	NA	NA	NA
Earnings	1.34	1.07	0.85	0.77	0.67	0.45	0.39	NA	NA	NA
Dividends	0.47	0.41	0.25	0.07	0.02	Nil	NA	NA	NA	NA
Payout Ratio	35%	38%	0%	0%	0%	Nil	NA	NA	NA	NA
Prices - High	31⅝	27	15	9½	7⅛	5⅛	NA	NA	NA	NA
- Low	22¾	13⅜	8½	5⅜	4⅞	3¾	NA	NA	NA	NA
P/E Ratio - High	24	25	18	12	10	11	NA	NA	NA	NA
- Low	17	13	10	7	7	8	NA	NA	NA	NA
Income Statement Analysis (Million $)										
Net Int. Inc.	68.5	62.4	57.5	51.9	54.6	46.4	38.8	NA	NA	NA
Loan Loss Prov.	NA	Nil	NM	0.1	1.2	4.7	3.2	NA	NA	NA
Non Int. Inc.	2.6	2.3	2.4	3.0	2.0	1.9	2.0	NA	NA	NA
Non Int. Exp.	26.0	27.1	23.3	22.9	23.0	21.4	18.0	NA	NA	NA
Pretax Inc.	45.1	37.6	38.7	31.9	32.3	22.2	-19.7	NA	NA	NA
Eff. Tax Rate	40%	38%	46%	37%	42%	45%	42%	NA	NA	NA
Net Inc.	26.9	23.3	20.9	20.2	18.8	12.1	-11.4	NA	NA	NA
% Net Int. Marg.	4.24	4.50	4.60	4.60	5.10	NA	NA	NA	NA	NA
Balance Sheet & Other Fin. Data (Million $)										
Total Assets	1,747	1,603	1,359	1,241	1,171	1,090	951	NA	NA	NA
Loans	1,487	1,395	1,146	995	938	779	685	NA	NA	NA
Deposits	1,102	1,069	1,024	932	840	827	824	NA	NA	NA
Capitalization:										
Debt	NA	Nil	Nil	Nil	Nil	Nil	Nil	NA	NA	NA
Equity	149	171	211	218	205	193	-92.4	NA	NA	NA
Total	156	171	219	218	205	193	-92.4	NA	NA	NA
% Ret. on Assets	1.6	1.6	1.6	1.7	NA	1.2	NA	NA	NA	NA
% Ret. on Equity	16.8	12.2	9.8	9.5	NA	24.0	NA	NA	NA	NA
% Loan Loss Resv.	0.6	0.9	0.8	1.1	1.2	1.3	0.9	NA	NA	NA
% Risk Based Capital	16.1	15.3	17.4	NA	NA	NA	NA	NA	NA	NA
Price Times Book Value:										
Hi	NA	3.5	1.8	1.2	1.0	NA	NA	NA	NA	NA
Low	NA	1.8	1.0	0.7	0.7	0.6	NA	NA	NA	NA

Data as orig reptd.; bef. results of disc opers/spec. items. Per share data adj. for stk. divs. Bold denotes diluted EPS (FASB 128)-prior periods restated. E-Estimated. NA-Not Available. NM-Not Meaningful. NR-Not Ranked.

Office—38-25 Main St., Flushing, NY 11354. **Tel**—(718) 359-6400. **Website**—http://www.qcsb.com **Chrmn, Pres & CEO**—J. R. Ficalora. **EVP & Secy**—M. J. Lincks. **CFO**—R. Wann. **VP & Investor Contact**—Ilene A. Angarola (Ext. 275). **Dirs**—D. M. Blake, J. G. Chisholm, D. Ciampa, J. R. Ficalora, H. E. Froebel, H. E. Johnson, M. L. Kupferberg, L. D. Lynch, H. C. Miller, R. H. O'Neill. **Transfer Agent & Registrar**—ChaseMellon Shareholder Services, Ridgefield Park, NJ. **Incorporated**—in Delaware in 1993. **Empl**— 275. **S&P Analyst:** C.C.P.

STANDARD
&POOR'S
STOCK REPORTS

Quiksilver, Inc.

NYSE Symbol **ZQK**
In S&P SmallCap 600

09-OCT-99

Industry:
Textiles (Apparel)

Summary: This company designs and makes casualwear, snowboardwear and swimwear for young men and boys under the Quiksilver label, and junior apparel under the Roxy and Raisins labels.

S&P Opinion: Hold (★★★)

Recent Price • 17⅜
52 Wk Range • 30⅞-11⅝
Yield • Nil
12-Mo. P/E • 16.1

Quantitative Evaluations
Outlook
(1 Lowest—5 Highest)
• 4-
Fair Value
• 24¾
Risk
• NA
Earn./Div. Rank
• B

Technical Eval.
• **Bearish** since 6/99
Rel. Strength Rank
(1 Lowest—99 Highest)
• 26
Insider Activity
• NA

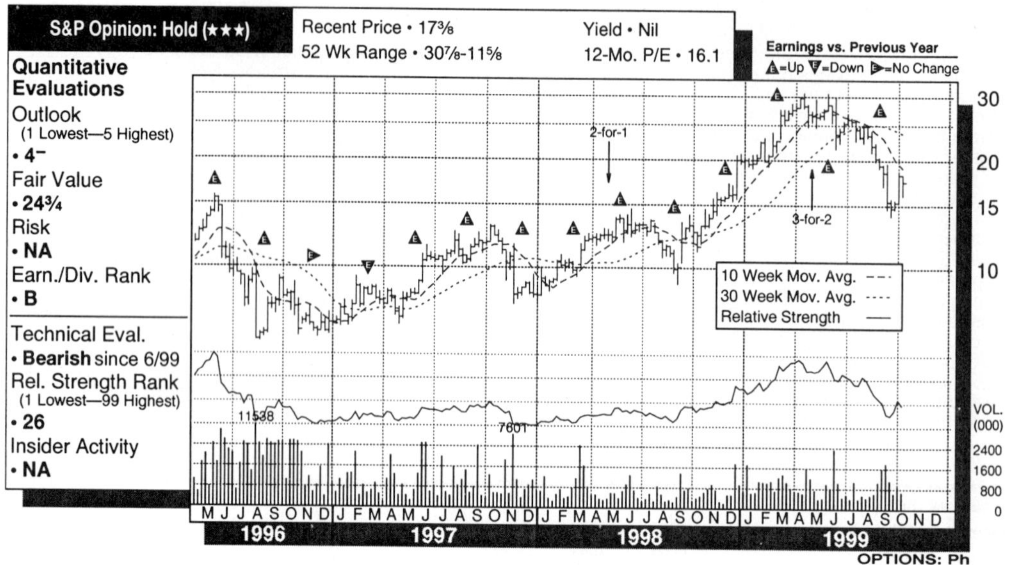

OPTIONS: Ph

Overview - 14-SEP-99

Quicksilver's improved product design and national marketing have fueled growing demand among the young and active crowd who relate to the lifestyle ZQK represents. Sales in the first nine months of FY 99 (Oct.) rose a torrid 51%. However, sales growth for the remainder of the fiscal year will likely slow to about 20%, reflecting increased retail competition and more difficult comparisons. Gross margins should remain stagnant on lower price points, limited by the increased competition. SG&A as a percentage of sales should decline slightly on the higher sales volume. Net income will be moderately hampered by higher interest expense on increased debt, which has risen to support the company's growth. Despite additional stock dilution, FY 99 EPS should rise about 38%.

Valuation - 14-SEP-99

We recently downgraded the shares from accumulate to hold. ZQK shares have fallen about 50% over the past four months, despite beating estimates in the past two quarters. We believe the drop is related to concerns about the company's ability to maintain its robust sales growth rate. Sales growth is expected to cool off from the 50% range to about 20% in FY 00. Gross margin improvement will also slow, as increased competition has forced ZQK to lower its price points. Moreover, the company recently closed several domestic accounts connected with diverting products from the U.S. to Japan. Although ZQK is currently trading at only 12X our lowered FY 00 estimate of $1.35, we expect investor concern about the slower growth rate to limit the share price. A three-for-two stock split was effected in April 1999.

Key Stock Statistics

S&P EPS Est. 1999	1.13	Tang. Bk. Value/Share	5.39
P/E on S&P Est. 1999	15.4	Beta	1.40
S&P EPS Est. 2000	1.35	Shareholders	380
Dividend Rate/Share	Nil	Market cap. (B)	$0.396
Shs. outstg. (M)	22.7	Inst. holdings	85%
Avg. daily vol. (M)	0.161		

Value of $10,000 invested 5 years ago: $ 37,034

Fiscal Year Ending Oct. 31

	1999	1998	1997	1996	1995	1994
Revenues (Million $)						
1Q	85.95	55.25	45.94	40.49	33.66	24.29
2Q	128.1	78.19	60.78	54.51	47.31	36.47
3Q	104.2	78.27	58.54	49.01	42.74	29.17
4Q	—	104.4	66.52	49.47	49.08	36.24
Yr.	—	316.1	231.8	193.5	172.8	126.2
Earnings Per Share ($)						
1Q	**0.15**	**0.10**	0.08	0.10	0.08	0.05
2Q	**0.41**	**0.25**	0.23	0.20	0.17	0.14
3Q	**0.24**	**0.19**	0.14	0.12	0.11	0.08
4Q	**E0.33**	**0.29**	0.15	0.12	0.12	0.10
Yr.	**E1.13**	**0.82**	**0.60**	**0.54**	**0.48**	0.36

Next earnings report expected: mid December

Dividend Data

Amount ($)	Date Decl.	Ex-Div. Date	Stock of Record	Payment Date
3-for-2	Mar. 19	Apr. 26	Apr. 15	Apr. 23 '99

STANDARD
&POOR'S
STOCK REPORTS

Quiksilver, Inc.

09-OCT-99

Business Summary - 14-SEP-99

Riding the wave of surfing and other sports popularity, Quiksilver (ZQK) was originally formed for the purpose of selling swimwear or boardshorts. It subsequently expanded its product lines from apparel for surfing to snowboarding, skating and other active sports. For more than 20 years, the company has promoted the strong Quiksilver brand, with an image of a cool, active lifestyle. ZQK's target market is young people, 8 to 20 years old, and older people, 20 - 50 years old. Due to the growing popularity of active sports among young people in the U.S. and in Europe, ZQK has positioned its brand to take advantage of the market expansion.

ZQK's diversified product offerings include T-shirts, shorts, pants, jackets, fleece, snowboardwear and skiwear. In July 1997, the company acquired Mervin Manufacturing Inc., a maker of snowboards and snowboard bindings.

In addition to its flagship Quiksilver brand, the company markets its products under various other labels, including: Roxy, which targets 14- to 25-year-old girls with active lifestyles and interests; Que, targeting the 20- to 45-year-old outdoor, healthy, sports-minded male; and Raisins, selling predominantly girls' swimwear.

Quiksilver sells its apparel in approximately 15,000 locations worldwide, including 3,300 sites in Europe. In FY 98 (Oct.), about 85% of ZQK's sales were derived from surf shops, specialty stores and national specialty chains, while department stores accounted for 15%. Geographically, 44% of U.S. sales in FY 98 were derived from the West Coast, 22% from the East Coast, 5% from Hawaii, and 29% from the rest of the continental U.S.

The company advertises its products through popular media such as Rolling Stone, Seventeen, MTV and ESPN. Additional marketing comes from sponsorship of surfers. Another method of brand development stems from Boardriders Clubs and Quiksvilles. Boardriders Clubs are independent stores that sell predominantly Quiksilver merchandise in an environment promoting the history and culture of surfing, snowboarding and other extreme sports. At the end of FY 98, there were a total of 60 Boardriders Clubs, including one Roxy store. The Quiksvilles are smaller, in-store shops located both in specialty and in department stores. The Quiksville concept has grown rapidly; at the end of FY 98, there were 477 locations worldwide, up from 355 at the end of FY 97. Plans call for 10 to 15 new Boardriders Clubs and 75 Quiksvilles in FY 99.

In March 1999, ZQK launched QuickJean/RoxyJean, which marks the first time the company's Young Mens and Quicksilver Roxy divisions have joined forces to design, merchandise and market a product.

Per Share Data ($) (Year Ended Oct. 31)	1998	1997	1996	1995	1994	1993	1992	1991	1990	1989
Tangible Bk. Val.	4.61	3.57	3.28	2.54	1.89	1.58	1.44	1.52	1.58	1.04
Cash Flow	1.08	0.77	0.67	0.39	0.47	0.32	0.11	0.42	0.54	0.40
Earnings	0.82	0.60	0.54	0.48	0.36	0.23	0.02	0.34	0.50	0.37
Dividends	Nil	Nil	Nil	Nil	Nil	Nil	Nil	Nil	Nil	Nil
Payout Ratio	Nil	Nil	Nil	Nil	Nil	Nil	Nil	Nil	Nil	Nil
Prices - High	20 7/8	13 1/8	15 3/4	12	6	5	3 3/8	5 1/8	10	8 1/2
- Low	8 5/8	6 7/8	6 1/4	4 5/8	3 1/4	1 7/8	1 7/16	2	3 1/4	2 1/2
P/E Ratio - High	25	22	29	25	17	22	NM	15	20	23
- Low	10	11	11	10	9	8	NM	6	6	7
Income Statement Analysis (Million $)										
Revs.	316	232	193	173	126	95.2	89.3	97.1	91.2	70.7
Oper. Inc.	37.0	25.7	21.9	19.4	14.7	9.2	3.1	12.9	16.6	12.8
Depr.	5.6	3.7	2.7	2.3	2.3	1.8	1.9	1.6	0.7	0.6
Int. Exp.	2.7	1.8	0.8	1.1	0.7	0.3	0.5	0.7	0.0	0.3
Pretax Inc.	30.8	21.3	19.3	16.8	11.8	7.6	0.9	10.9	16.2	12.1
Eff. Tax Rate	42%	41%	40%	41%	39%	42%	58%	41%	41%	42%
Net Inc.	18.0	12.6	11.7	10.0	7.1	4.4	0.4	6.4	9.5	7.0
Balance Sheet & Other Fin. Data (Million $)										
Cash	3.0	4.1	3.4	3.5	0.7	3.4	4.6	3.1	7.5	3.1
Curr. Assets	160	112	87.9	73.8	54.7	38.3	34.4	33.2	30.3	21.7
Total Assets	213	150	116	46.9	80.5	58.6	53.2	51.2	35.8	26.5
Curr. Liab.	67.7	44.5	32.2	26.9	23.1	11.5	9.9	8.7	4.2	4.9
LT Debt	27.7	10.2	2.6	3.3	2.5	2.1	2.5	2.5	Nil	Nil
Common Eqty.	118	95.0	80.7	68.9	54.9	45.0	40.8	40.1	31.6	21.5
Total Cap.	145	105	83.4	72.2	57.4	47.1	43.3	42.6	31.6	21.5
Cap. Exp.	19.8	10.3	4.9	2.6	2.9	0.8	0.6	1.0	1.1	0.5
Cash Flow	23.6	16.4	14.4	8.1	9.4	6.2	2.3	8.0	10.3	7.6
Curr. Ratio	2.4	2.5	2.7	2.7	2.4	3.3	3.5	3.8	7.3	4.4
% LT Debt of Cap.	19.0	9.7	3.1	4.6	4.3	4.4	5.7	5.9	Nil	Nil
% Net Inc.of Revs.	5.7	5.5	6.1	5.8	5.6	4.7	0.4	6.6	10.4	9.9
% Ret. on Assets	9.9	9.5	10.9	15.7	10.2	7.9	0.7	14.7	30.3	29.4
% Ret. on Equity	16.9	14.4	15.6	16.2	14.2	10.3	0.9	17.9	35.6	39.0

Data as orig reptd.; bef. results of disc opers/spec. items. Per share data adj. for stk. divs. Bold denotes diluted EPS (FASB 128)-prior periods restated. E-Estimated. NA-Not Available. NM-Not Meaningful. NR-Not Ranked.

Office—1740 Monrovia Ave., Costa Mesa, CA 92627. **Tel**—(949) 645-1395. **Website**—http://www.quiksilver.com. **Chrmn & CEO**—R. B. McKnight Jr. **CFO, Treas, Secy & Investor Contact**—Steven L. Brink. **Dirs**—W. M. Barnum Jr., C. E. Crowe, M. H. Gray, H. Hodge, R. G. Kirby, R. B. McKnight Jr., T. Roach. **Transfer Agent & Registrar**—American Stock Transfer & Trust Co., NYC. **Incorporated**—in Delaware in 1986. **Empl**—990. **S&P Analyst:** A. Bensinger

STANDARD
&POOR'S
STOCK REPORTS

Radian Group

NYSE Symbol **RDN**

In S&P SmallCap 600

09-OCT-99

Industry:
Insurance (Property-Casualty)

Summary: Radian, formed through the merger of CMAC Investment and Amerin Corp., provides private mortgage insurance and risk management services to residential mortgage lenders nationwide.

S&P Opinion: Accumulate (★★★★)

Recent Price • 46⅝
52 Wk Range • 55⅞-32
Yield • 0.3%
12-Mo. P/E • 13.0

Quantitative Evaluations

Outlook
(1 Lowest—5 Highest)
• **5**

Fair Value
• **65¾**

Risk
• **Low**

Earn./Div. Rank
• **B+**

Technical Eval.
• **Bearish** since 8/99

Rel. Strength Rank
(1 Lowest—99 Highest)
• **72**

Insider Activity
• **NA**

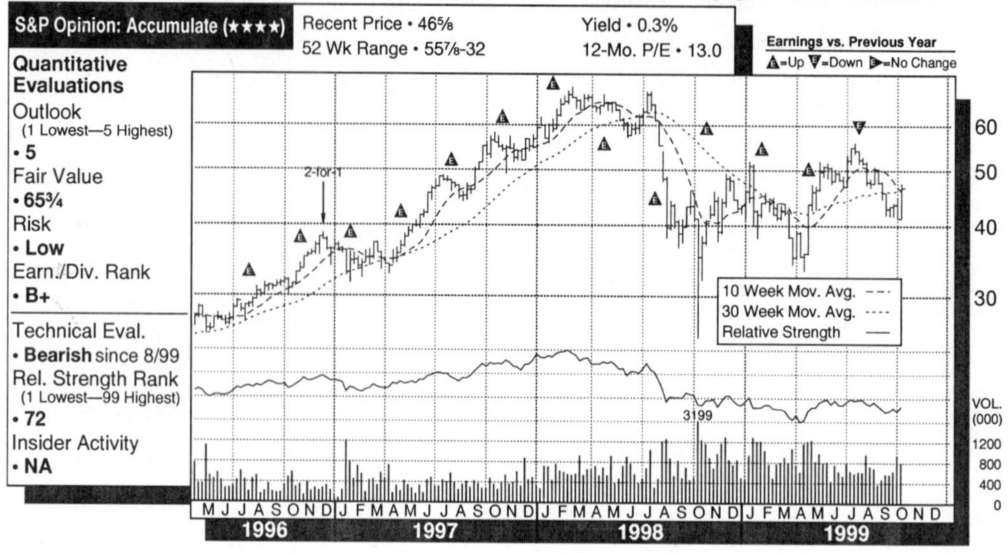

Overview - 01-SEP-99

Following the merger of two of the fastest growing private mortgage insurance (PMI) providers in CMAC Investment and Amerin Corp., Radian Group should maintain a superior rate of earned premium growth. During the second quarter of 1999, RDN experienced a 0.5% loss of market share, but with little overlapping business between the two companies, significant further attrition is unlikely. As a result of the recent interest rate hikes by the Federal Reserve, long-term mortgage rates are likely to remain conducive to new loan origination. With a great deal of new policies written at attractive rates, and the low occurrence of default typical in the early years of policy life, an improving loss environment is likely to expand RDN's profit margin. Merger-related annualized cost savings of $15.0 million should aid operating EPS growth of 21% through 2000.

Valuation - 01-SEP-99

RDN shares have risen 3.3% year to date, versus a 3.2% gain in the S&P Financial Index, as rising mortgage rates held back the shares. A few obstacles lie ahead of the PMI industry, including the influential buyer power exhibited by Fannie Mae and Freddie Mac (purchasers and securitizers of residential mortgages), increasing bargaining leverage among consolidating banks, and the effects of new legislation allowing automatic cancellation of PMI at certain threshold equity ownership levels. However, the healthy housing market should persist, fueled by attractive mortgage rates, low unemployment, increasing levels of immigrant home ownership, and government sponsored housing initiatives for the less fortunate. Given RDN's ability to achieve exceptional EPS growth in a competitive environment, and the shares' compelling valuation, trading at a significant discount to their long-term growth rate, we recommend accumulation.

Key Stock Statistics

S&P EPS Est. 1999	4.52	Tang. Bk. Value/Share	23.03
P/E on S&P Est. 1999	10.3	Beta	1.14
S&P EPS Est. 2000	5.47	Shareholders	6,800
Dividend Rate/Share	0.12	Market cap. (B)	$ 1.7
Shs. outstg. (M)	37.0	Inst. holdings	89%
Avg. daily vol. (M)	0.145		

Value of $10,000 invested 5 years ago: $ 34,355

Fiscal Year Ending Dec. 31

	1999	1998	1997	1996	1995	1994
Revenues (Million $)						
1Q	89.79	79.04	63.60	50.53	36.93	30.10
2Q	136.9	81.30	67.70	54.48	39.69	32.33
3Q	—	84.36	71.36	57.22	43.04	33.24
4Q	—	88.28	74.66	60.36	45.98	34.87
Yr.	—	333.0	277.3	222.6	165.6	130.5
Earnings Per Share ($)						
1Q	**0.94**	**0.86**	**0.71**	**0.59**	0.47	0.38
2Q	**0.64**	**0.91**	**0.76**	**0.63**	0.52	0.42
3Q	—	**0.96**	**0.78**	**0.65**	0.54	0.44
4Q	—	**1.00**	**0.81**	**0.68**	0.57	0.47
Yr.	—	**3.72**	**3.06**	**2.55**	**2.09**	1.71

Next earnings report expected: mid October

Dividend Data (Dividends have been paid since 1993.)

Amount ($)	Date Decl.	Ex-Div. Date	Stock of Record	Payment Date
0.030	Oct. 13	Nov. 04	Nov. 06	Dec. 01 '98
0.030	Jan. 19	Jan. 29	Feb. 02	Mar. 02 '99
0.030	Apr. 13	May. 03	May. 05	Jun. 02 '99
0.030	Jul. 13	Aug. 03	Aug. 05	Sep. 03 '99

A Division of The McGraw-Hill Companies

Radian Group Inc.

Business Summary - 01-SEP-99

Radian Group was formed through the June 1999 merger of CMAC Investment Corp. and Amerin Corp. Radian Group is the parent company of Radian Guaranty Inc., which provides private mortgage insurance and risk management services to residential mortgage lenders, including mortgage bankers, mortgage brokers, commercial banks and savings institutions. Private mortgage insurance (also called mortgage guarantee insurance) protects lenders from default-related losses on residential first mortgage loans made to home buyers who make down payments of less than 20% of a home's purchase price.

By enabling would-be homeowners to purchase homes with low down payments, RDN greatly increases the homeownership opportunities of many first-time homebuyers such as low and middle income families, minorities, and immigrants. Private mortgage insurance also facilitates the sale of mortgage loans in the secondary mortgage market.

The company's main product, primary mortgage insurance, provides mortgage default protection on individual loans at a specified coverage percentage which is applied to the unpaid loan principal and interest upon default. RDN has the option of paying the entire claim amount and taking title to the mortgaged property, or paying the coverage percentage. RDN also offers pool insurance on a selective basis to various mortgage pools, but plans to reduce underwriting through 2000 to decrease risk in the area. Additionally, RDN offers captive reinsurance, which allows the lender to share in the risk and rewards of coverage.

The merger of CMAC and Amerin created the second largest mortgage insurer with over 19% market share, based on 1998 pro forma data. The combined company has approximately $85 billion of insurance in force. The terms of the deal called for Amerin shareholders to receive 0.5333 of a share of CMAC for each share of Amerin they possessed.

In Amerin, CMAC found a partner with little business overlap, allowing it to diversify geographic risk and gain leverage in dealings with ever larger lenders. Radian's management believes the combined entity will have the scale and efficiencies necessary to compete effectively. Additionally, Radian should be better positioned to compete in the industry through greater capital and marketing resources. The company serves 3,500 mortgage lender clients, including 26 of the top 30 mortgage lenders. Radian's top ten lenders were responsible for 48.9% of the company's combined risk in force at December 31, 1998.

Radian had particularly high concentrations of 1998 year-end combined risk in force in California (18.6%), Florida (7.4%), New York (6.5%), Texas (5.7%), New Jersey (4.0%), Georgia (3.9%), Pennsylvania (3.8%), Arizona (3.6%), Illinois (3.5%) and Colorado (2.8%).

Per Share Data ($) (Year Ended Dec. 31)	1998	1997	1996	1995	1994	1993	1992	1991	1990	1989
Tangible Bk. Val.	23.03	19.08	15.91	13.42	10.91	9.71	8.25	7.76	NA	NA
Oper. Earnings	NA	NA	NA	NA	NA	NA	NA	NA	NA	NA
Earnings	3.72	3.06	2.55	2.09	1.71	1.39	1.40	0.91	0.65	-0.16
Dividends	0.12	0.12	0.11	0.10	0.10	0.10	Nil	NA	NA	NA
Payout Ratio	3%	4%	4%	5%	6%	7%	Nil	NA	NA	NA
Prices - High	70	61⅞	38¾	27⅞	15½	17⅝	13¼	NA	NA	NA
- Low	25⅜	31⅝	22	14⅜	11⅝	11½	9	NA	NA	NA
P/E Ratio - High	19	20	15	13	9	13	9	NA	NA	NA
- Low	7	10	9	7	7	8	6	NA	NA	NA
Income Statement Analysis (Million $)										
Premium Inc.	282	238	188	137	106	81.6	67.1	61.7	53.2	54.7
Net Invest. Inc.	38.5	33.8	30.0	25.9	22.6	20.9	13.9	12.3	12.0	11.9
Oth. Revs.	12.3	5.8	4.7	2.6	1.8	4.6	2.5	-2.6	0.2	0.2
Total Revs.	333	277	223	166	131	107	83.5	71.4	65.4	66.8
Pretax Inc.	126	102	82.6	68.2	56.4	48.2	32.4	17.8	14.4	1.4
Net Oper. Inc.	NA	NA	NA	NA	NA	NA	20.8	13.9	9.5	-0.1
Net Inc.	91.1	75.0	62.2	50.8	41.1	34.1	21.8	12.7	9.1	-2.2
Balance Sheet & Other Fin. Data (Million $)										
Cash & Equiv.	2.2	2.4	3.2	3.6	3.9	7.6	2.3	NA	NA	NA
Premiums Due	NA	NA	NA	NA	NA	NA	NA	NA	NA	NA
Invest. Assets: Bonds	690	586	508	433	359	327	304	NA	NA	NA
Invest. Assets: Stocks	27.4	Nil	Nil	Nil	Nil	Nil	Nil	NA	NA	NA
Invest. Assets: Loans	Nil	Nil	Nil	Nil	Nil	Nil	Nil	NA	NA	NA
Invest. Assets: Total	736	597	513	438	359	327	304	NA	NA	NA
Deferred Policy Costs	32.1	25.0	23.9	21.4	16.9	16.2	NA	NA	NA	NA
Total Assets	968	705	593	499	410	375	335	NA	NA	NA
Debt	Nil	Nil	Nil	Nil	Nil	Nil	Nil	Nil	NA	NA
Common Eqty.	523	430	356	299	240	213	181	170	NA	NA
Prop. & Cas. Loss Ratio	47.7	50.6	50.6	44.3	37.7	38.6	47.0	59.8	65.3	NA
Prop. & Cas. Expense Ratio	24.2	21.2	23.2	28.5	27.6	27.6	27.6	30.6	32.8	NA
Prop. & Cas. Combined Ratio	71.9	71.8	73.8	72.8	65.3	66.2	74.6	90.4	98.1	NA
% Return On Revs.	27.3	27.0	27.9	30.6	31.5	31.8	26.0	17.8	14.0	NM
% Ret. on Equity	18.4	19.1	18.9	18.9	18.2	15.7	15.9	NM	NM	NM

Data as orig reptd.; bef. results of disc opers/spec. items. Per share data adj. for stk. divs. Bold denotes diluted EPS (FASB 128)-prior periods restated. E-Estimated. NA-Not Available. NM-Not Meaningful. NR-Not Ranked.

Office—1601 Market St., Philadelphia, PA 19103.**Tel**—(215) 564-6600. **Website**—http://www.radianmi.com. **Chrmn & CEO**—F. P. Filipps. **Pres & COO**—R. J. Kasmar. **SVP & Secy**—H. S. Yaruss. **SVP & CFO**—C. R. Quint. **Dirs**—D. C. Carney, H. B. Culang, C. M. Fagin, F. P. Filipps, R. B. Greco, S. T. Hopkins, J. W. Jennings, R. J. Kasmar, J. C. Miller, R. W. Moore, R. W. Richards, A. W. Schweiger, L. E. Swedroe, H. Wender. **Transfer Agent & Registrar**—Bank of New York, NYC. **Incorporated**—in Delaware in 1991. **Empl**— 838. **S&P Analyst:** Markos N. Kaminis

RailTex, Inc.

NASDAQ Symbol **RTEX**

In S&P SmallCap 600

09-OCT-99 **Industry:** Railroads

Summary: RTEX is a short-line railroad organization providing freight service in the U.S., Canada and Mexico.

Quantitative Evaluations

Outlook (1 Lowest—5 Highest) • **4−**

Fair Value • **23⅜**

Risk • **Average**

Earn./Div. Rank • **B+**

Technical Eval. • **Bearish** since 9/99

Rel. Strength Rank (1 Lowest—99 Highest) • **85**

Insider Activity • **Neutral**

Recent Price • 15¾

52 Wk Range • 17¼-8¾

Yield • Nil

12-Mo. P/E • 10.2

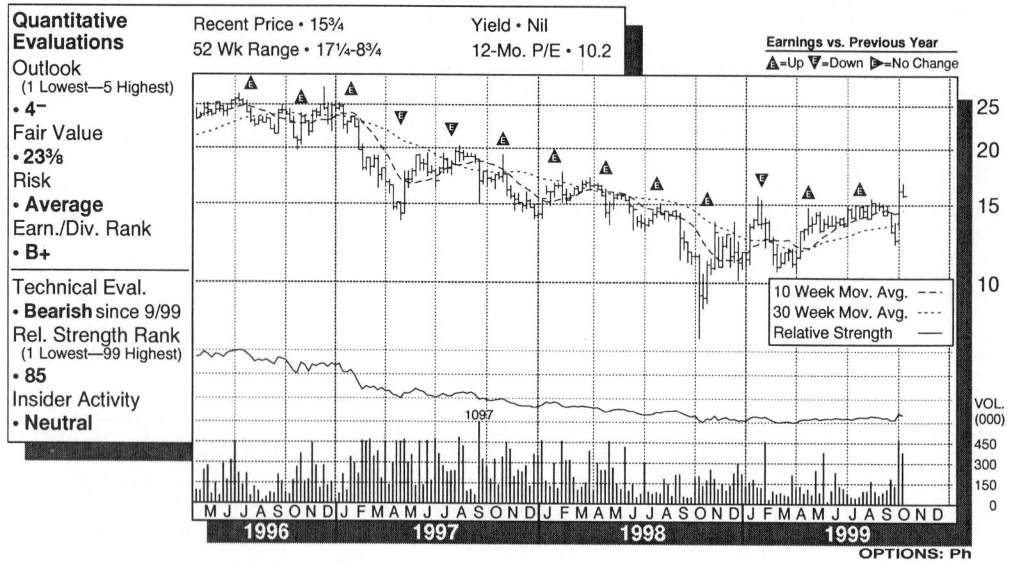

Business Profile - 04-OCT-99

RailTex's strategy is to grow through creating new business, improving the operating performance of newly added and existing properties, acquiring Class I railroad branch lines or short line properties, and divesting non-strategic lines. RTEX believes it can effectively implement its strategy because of its focus on customer service, its ability to offer multiple Class I connections to customers, its operating expertise, and its expertise in acquiring railroad properties that generate returns in excess of cost of capital. In April 1999, RTEX said it had sold the assets of its New Orleans Lower Coast Railroad, transferred the operations of its Northeast Kansas and Missouri Railroad to the Union Pacific, and entered into an agreement to assume operating responsibility for the Cornerstone Intermodal Center.

Operational Review - 04-OCT-99

Revenues in the first half of 1999 advanced 17%, year to year, reflecting higher freight revenues and carloadings due to increases in railroad equipment, and higher non-freight revenues. Transportation, equipment and maintenance of way expenses were well controlled, and pretax income rose 36%. After taxes at 40.5% versus 37.7%, income was up 30%, to $6,861,000 ($0.74 a share), from $5,266,000 ($0.57, before an $0.18 special charge from the cumulative effect of an accounting change). Prior-period figures were restated.

Stock Performance - 08-OCT-99

In the past 30 trading days, RTEX's shares have increased 5%, compared to a 0.91% fall in the S&P 500. Average trading volume for the past five days was 75,440 shares, compared with the 40-day moving average of 41,895 shares.

Key Stock Statistics

Dividend Rate/Share	Nil	Shareholders	385
Shs. outstg. (M)	9.3	Market cap. (B)	$0.146
Avg. daily vol. (M)	0.065	Inst. holdings	58%
Tang. Bk. Value/Share	16.37		
Beta	0.42		

Value of $10,000 invested 5 years ago: $ 5,675

Fiscal Year Ending Dec. 31

	1999	1998	1997	1996	1995	1994
Revenues (Million $)						
1Q	45.51	38.41	34.18	28.61	25.14	17.80
2Q	44.92	39.14	37.37	30.15	27.30	18.41
3Q	—	40.03	37.97	29.86	27.50	19.18
4Q	—	43.45	39.28	32.49	27.90	19.14
Yr.	—	161.0	148.8	121.1	107.8	74.53
Earnings Per Share ($)						
1Q	**0.36**	**0.27**	**0.17**	0.24	0.22	0.15
2Q	**0.37**	**0.27**	**0.26**	0.28	0.07	0.26
3Q	—	**0.32**	**0.31**	0.25	0.22	0.22
4Q	—	**-0.48**	**0.41**	0.31	0.27	0.25
Yr.	—	**1.38**	**1.15**	**1.08**	**0.78**	**0.88**

Next earnings report expected: mid October

Dividend Data

No cash dividends have been paid.

RailTex, Inc.

Business Summary - 04-OCT-99

RailTex, Inc., which believes it is the leading operator of short-line freight railroads in North America, began operating its first railroad in 1984. The company built its portfolio of railroads through purchase, lease or contract to operate.

RailTex's holdings include short line railroads concentrated in the Southeastern and Midwestern United States, in the Great Lakes and New England regions of the United States, and in Eastern Canada. The company also owns investments in two Brazilian railroads and provides management consulting services in Kazakhstan. In 1998, RailTex railroads transported almost 550,000 carloads of freight for more than 1,100 customers. Traffic that originated or terminated on RailTex's lines generated 86% of total freight revenues in 1998.

RailTex's strategy is to grow through the creation of new business and improvement in operating performance of newly added and currently operated properties and additions to and divestitures from its portfolio of short line railroad properties, primarily through strategic acquisitions of Class I railroad branch lines or existing short line properties, and divestiture of non-strategic lines. RTEX believes its focus on customer service, ability to offer multiple Class I connections to its customers, its operating expertise, and its expertise in acquiring railroad properties that generate financial returns in excess of its cost of capital, position it to effectively implement its strategy.

RailTex believes that the majority of its acquisition opportunities will be in the U.S. and Canada. However international rail privatization may offer additional long-term opportunities as certain governments privatize their country's rail systems. RTEX's strategy regarding international acquisitions includes analyzing the country's political and economic environment, identifying potential country risks and attracting strong local investment partners.

Commodities transported consist primarily of the following: lumber and forest products, which accounted for 19% of 1998 freight revenues, coal 13%, chemicals 12%, scrap paper and paper products 8%, farm products 8%, scrap metal and metal products 8%, railroad equipment 6%, food products 5%, non-metallic cores 5%, minerals and stone 4%, and autos and auto parts 4%.

Rolling stock consisted of 258 locomotives (232 owned and 26 leased) and 3,329 freight cars, as of March 1, 1999.

Effective January 31, 1999, RTEX's Dallas, Garland and Northeastern Railroad subsidiary began operations on an additional 89 miles of rail line north of Dallas, Texas, acquired from the Union Pacific Railroad.

In April 1999, RTEX sold the Northeast Kansas & Missouri Railroad to Union Pacific for $3.2 million. The sale was consistent with RTEX's strategy of divesting non-core assets. Also in April, RTEX said that it sold the New Orleans Lower Coast Railroad for $5.2 million.

Per Share Data ($) (Year Ended Dec. 31)	1998	1997	1996	1995	1994	1993	1992	1991	1990	1989
Tangible Bk. Val.	15.54	14.55	13.45	12.36	10.11	9.18	NA	NA	NA	NA
Cash Flow	2.92	2.56	2.18	1.70	1.55	1.41	1.05	NA	NA	NA
Earnings	1.38	1.15	1.08	0.78	0.88	0.65	0.52	0.39	0.38	NA
Dividends	Nil	Nil	Nil	Nil	Nil	Nil	Nil	Nil	Nil	NA
Payout Ratio	Nil	Nil	Nil	Nil	Nil	Nil	Nil	Nil	Nil	NA
Prices - High	17¾	25¼	27⅜	29½	31½	28¼	NA	NA	NA	NA
- Low	7½	13¾	19¾	17¼	15⅝	16½	NA	NA	NA	NA
P/E Ratio - High	13	22	25	38	36	43	NA	NA	NA	NA
- Low	5	12	18	22	18	25	NA	NA	NA	NA
Income Statement Analysis (Million $)										
Revs.	161	149	121	108	74.5	59.8	39.3	27.6	21.4	NA
Oper. Inc.	41.9	35.9	32.2	26.0	18.4	14.5	9.9	NA	NA	NA
Depr.	14.3	12.9	10.1	8.2	5.2	4.2	2.8	NA	NA	NA
Int. Exp.	11.2	10.5	6.9	5.7	2.9	4.7	2.8	1.5	1.0	NA
Pretax Inc.	20.6	16.7	16.7	11.7	11.5	6.1	4.5	2.9	2.4	NA
Eff. Tax Rate	38%	36%	40%	41%	40%	40%	40%	37%	35%	NA
Net Inc.	12.8	10.6	10.0	6.9	6.9	3.6	2.7	1.8	1.6	NA
Balance Sheet & Other Fin. Data (Million $)										
Cash	1.2	0.6	2.1	2.1	2.2	6.9	NA	NA	NA	NA
Curr. Assets	41.9	37.0	32.6	26.0	17.0	18.8	NA	NA	NA	NA
Total Assets	362	320	269	205	140	113	81.0	45.0	34.0	NA
Curr. Liab.	47.1	44.4	32.8	21.0	16.9	11.3	NA	NA	NA	NA
LT Debt	123	118	92.3	57.2	38.9	27.0	NA	NA	NA	NA
Common Eqty.	144	133	123	113	72.4	65.7	25.0	22.2	13.6	NA
Total Cap.	308	272	233	181	120	100	NA	NA	NA	NA
Cap. Exp.	30.3	35.5	28.0	63.6	31.5	27.6	35.8	NA	NA	NA
Cash Flow	27.0	23.6	20.1	15.1	12.1	7.9	5.5	NA	NA	NA
Curr. Ratio	0.9	0.8	1.0	1.2	1.0	1.7	NA	NA	NA	NA
% LT Debt of Cap.	39.9	43.4	39.7	31.6	32.5	27.1	NA	NA	NA	NA
% Net Inc.of Revs.	7.9	7.1	8.2	6.4	9.2	6.1	6.9	6.5	7.3	NA
% Ret. on Assets	3.7	3.6	4.2	4.0	5.4	3.7	4.3	4.5	NA	NA
% Ret. on Equity	9.2	8.3	8.5	7.5	10.0	8.0	11.4	10.0	NA	NA

Data as orig reptd.; bef. results of disc opers/spec. items. Per share data adj. for stk. divs. Bold denotes diluted EPS (FASB 128)-prior periods restated. E-Estimated. NA-Not Available. NM-Not Meaningful. NR-Not Ranked.

Office—4040 Broadway, Suite 200, San Antonio, TX 78209. **Tel**—(210) 841-7600. **Website**—http://www.railtex.com **Chrmn, Pres & CEO**—R. A. Rittenmeyer. **VP-Fin & CFO**—J.P. Jahnke. **Treas**—C. Wydra. **Dirs**—R. M. Ayres Jr., L. D. Davies, B. M. Flohr, H. J. Gradison, R. R. Lende, F. C. Meyer Jr., P. L. Moe, W. G. Pagonis, R. A. Rittenmeyer. **Transfer Agent & Registrar**—ChaseMellon Shareholder Services, Ridgefield Park, NJ. **Incorporated**—in Texas in 1977. **Empl**— 950. **S&P Analyst:** S.S.

Ralcorp Holdings

NYSE Symbol **RAH**

In S&P SmallCap 600

09-OCT-99 **Industry:** Foods

Summary: Ralcorp produces and sells private label cereals, as well as crackers, cookies and snack nuts.

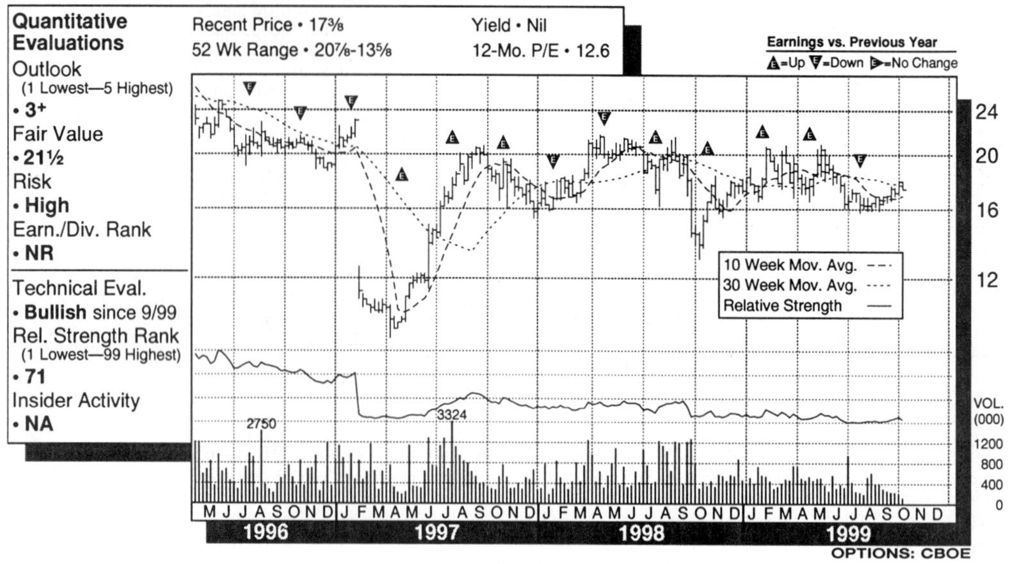

Business Profile - 12-MAY-99

It continues to be the company's goal to be the premier private label manufacturer in the country. Recent acquisitions include the March 1999 purchase of Southern Roasted Nuts of Georgia, a private label and value brand snack nut operation with estimated annual sales of some $30 million. Also in March 1999, Ralcorp purchased Martin Gillet & Co., a leading private label maker of mayonnaise and pourable, shelf-stable salad dressings with annual sales of about $70 million. During FY 98 (Sep.), RAH acquired Nutcracker Brands, Inc., a producer of snack nut products with annual estimated sales of $42 million, and sold its Beech-Nut Nutrition baby food unit to the Milnot Co. for $68 million.

Operational Review - 12-MAY-99

Net sales in the first half of FY 99 (Sep.) rose 39% from FY 98's pro forma total, and net earnings were $17.2 million ($0.54 per diluted share, on 4.2% fewer shares), versus $15.5 million ($0.47) in FY 98. Results benefited from hot cereal and co-packing volume gains, a more favorable product mix, and acquisitions, including Sugar Kake, which more than offset lower equity earnings from the company's interest in Vail Resorts. FY 98 pro forma results assume the sale of Beech-Nut had been completed as of the beginning of the prior fiscal year.

Stock Performance - 08-OCT-99

In the past 30 trading days, RAH's shares have increased 6%, compared to a 0.91% fall in the S&P 500. Average trading volume for the past five days was 22,660 shares, compared with the 40-day moving average of 52,749 shares.

Key Stock Statistics

Dividend Rate/Share	Nil	Shareholders	16,464
Shs. outstg. (M)	30.6	Market cap. (B)	$0.532
Avg. daily vol. (M)	0.037	Inst. holdings	68%
Tang. Bk. Value/Share	7.32		
Beta	0.29		

Value of $10,000 invested 5 years ago: NA

Fiscal Year Ending Sep. 30

	1999	1998	1997	1996	1995	1994
Revenues (Million $)						
1Q	154.9	137.2	292.9	295.3	278.4	267.1
2Q	150.3	147.1	161.4	277.4	258.3	262.7
3Q	154.4	143.3	140.7	230.1	231.5	220.5
4Q	—	155.3	144.7	224.6	245.2	236.7
Yr.	—	582.9	739.7	1,027	1,013	987.0
Earnings Per Share ($)						
1Q	**0.20**	**0.14**	0.40	0.44	0.51	0.49
2Q	**0.34**	**0.32**	15.47	0.64	0.65	0.71
3Q	**0.38**	**0.40**	0.09	-0.50	0.15	0.28
4Q	—	**0.46**	0.15	-2.02	-0.32	0.11
Yr.	—	**1.32**	**16.01**	**-1.42**	1.00	1.59

Next earnings report expected: early November

Dividend Data

The company does not anticipate paying cash dividends on its common stock in the near future.

Ralcorp Holdings, Inc.

Business Summary - 12-MAY-99

After the dust settled from a corporate restructuring by the company's former parent, Ralcorp Holdings, Inc. (Old Ralcorp), that included the formation of the company (Ralcorp Holdings, Inc.) to facilitate Old Ralcorp's divestiture of its branded cereal and snack business, RAH was left with operations consisting of Beech-Nut baby foods (subsequently sold in September 1998), private-label cereals, and private label crackers and cookies. In January 1997, as part of the restructuring, the company sold its branded cereal and snack business to General Mills, Inc., for $570 million in stock and debt. Also in January, RAH sold its resort operations and related ski resort properties to Vail Resorts, Inc., in exchange for the assumption of $165 million of debt and an approximate 22% equity interest in Vail Resorts, Inc.

The private label cereal business accounts for about half of Ralcorp's sales. Ready-to-eat cereals consist of 24 different types of private label cereals, manufactured for approximately 275 customers. The hot cereal products include old fashioned oatmeal, quick oats, plain instant oatmeal, flavored instant oatmeal, farina and instant Ralston, a branded hot wheat cereal. The private label cereal business also sells hot cereal under the brand Three Minute Oats.

RAH believes that its cracker and cookie business is currently the largest private label cracker manufacturer and producer of private label cookies for sale in the U.S. This business also produces Ry Krisp branded crackers. In April 1997, the company acquired Wortz Co., one of the largest U.S. makers of private label crackers and cookies, in order to expand its private label food business. Wortz, with annual sales of about $70 million, was added to Bremner, Inc., RAH's private label cracker and cookie unit. Wortz sells mainly to grocery wholesalers, while Bremner focuses on selling directly to supermarket chains. Sugar Kake Cookie Inc. ($29 million annual sales) was acquired by Bremner in August 1998.

The snack nuts segment is comprised of Flavor House Products, Inc. and Nutcracker Brands, Inc. which were acquired during FY 98 (Sep.).

Resort operations included the operation of the Keystone, Arapahoe Basin and Breckenridge ski resorts located in Summit County, CO. Vail Resorts, Inc., through the transaction in January 1997, became the world's largest skiing company, based both on revenues and on skier days.

Per Share Data ($) (Year Ended Sep. 30)	1998	1997	1996	1995	1994	1993	1992	1991	1990	1989
Tangible Bk. Val.	9.69	8.69	3.26	4.88	2.65	NA	NA	NA	NA	NA
Cash Flow	1.87	16.84	NA	2.36	3.39	2.22	NA	NA	NA	NA
Earnings	1.32	16.11	-1.42	1.00	1.59	1.20	NA	NA	NA	NA
Dividends	Nil	Nil	Nil	Nil	Nil	NA	NA	NA	NA	NA
Payout Ratio	Nil	Nil	Nil	Nil	Nil	NA	NA	NA	NA	NA
Prices - High	21⅝	23⅛	28⅝	28	24⅛	NA	NA	NA	NA	NA
- Low	13	9⅜	18⅝	21⅜	13½	NA	NA	NA	NA	NA
P/E Ratio - High	16	1	NM	28	15	NA	NA	NA	NA	NA
- Low	10	1	NM	21	8	NA	NA	NA	NA	NA
Income Statement Analysis (Million $)										
Revs.	583	740	1,027	1,013	987	903	NA	NA	NA	NA
Oper. Inc.	59.0	73.8	126	152	161	131	NA	NA	NA	NA
Depr.	18.0	24.4	46.4	46.7	60.6	35.3	NA	NA	NA	NA
Int. Exp.	Nil	7.9	26.8	28.2	12.3	27.2	NA	NA	NA	NA
Pretax Inc.	60.0	542	-73.1	54.8	87.9	67.8	NA	NA	NA	NA
Eff. Tax Rate	44%	1.90%	NM	39%	39%	39%	NA	NA	NA	NA
Net Inc.	44.0	532	-46.8	33.4	53.6	41.2	NA	NA	NA	NA
Balance Sheet & Other Fin. Data (Million $)										
Cash	12.3	8.4	Nil	Nil	Nil	4.2	NA	NA	NA	NA
Curr. Assets	127	143	193	208	184	166	NA	NA	NA	NA
Total Assets	418	400	627	716	700	685	NA	NA	NA	NA
Curr. Liab.	81.0	78.2	102	105	112	123	NA	NA	NA	NA
LT Debt	Nil	Nil	377	395	389	383	NA	NA	NA	NA
Common Eqty.	307	287	107	162	141	130	NA	NA	NA	NA
Total Cap.	307	287	484	578	560	53.8	NA	NA	NA	NA
Cap. Exp.	24.6	41.6	66.7	66.1	84.4	NA	NA	NA	NA	NA
Cash Flow	62.0	556	0.4	80.1	114	76.5	NA	NA	NA	NA
Curr. Ratio	1.6	1.8	1.9	2.0	1.6	1.4	NA	NA	NA	NA
% LT Debt of Cap.	Nil	Nil	77.8	68.4	69.6	71.1	NA	NA	NA	NA
% Net Inc.of Revs.	7.5	71.9	NM	3.3	5.4	4.4	NA	NA	NA	NA
% Ret. on Assets	10.7	270.0	NM	4.8	NA	NA	NA	NA	NA	NA
% Ret. on Equity	14.8	104.0	NM	22.0	NA	NA	NA	NA	NA	NA

Data as orig reptd.; bef. results of disc opers/spec. items. Per share data adj. for stk. divs. Bold denotes diluted EPS (FASB 128)-prior periods restated. E-Estimated. NA-Not Available. NM-Not Meaningful. NR-Not Ranked.

Office—800 Market Street, Suite 2900, St. Louis, MO 63101.**Tel**—(314) 877-7000. **Website**—http://www.ralcorp.com **Chrmn**—W. P. Stiritz. **Pres, CEO & CFO**—J. R. Micheletto. **VP & Secy**—R. W. Lockwood. **Investor Contact**—Daniel P. Zoellner (314-877-7052). **Dirs**—W. D. George, Jr., J. W. Goodall, D. W. Kemper, J. R. Micheletto, W. P. Stiritz. **Transfer Agent & Registrar**—First Chicago Trust Co. of New York, Jersey City, NJ. **Incorporated**—in Missouri in 1994. **Empl**— 2,400. **S&P Analyst:** P.L.H.

STANDARD
&POOR'S
STOCK REPORTS

Raymond James Financial

NYSE Symbol **RJF**

In S&P SmallCap 600

09-OCT-99

Industry:
Investment Banking/ Brokerage

Summary: This holding company is engaged, through subsidiaries, in securities brokerage, investment banking, financial planning, and investment advisory and related financial services.

Quantitative Evaluations

Outlook
(1 Lowest—5 Highest)
• **NA**

Fair Value
• **NA**

Risk
• **Average**

Earn./Div. Rank
• **A-**

Technical Eval.
• **Bearish** since 8/99

Rel. Strength Rank
(1 Lowest—99 Highest)
• **37**

Insider Activity
• **Neutral**

Recent Price • 19
52 Wk Range • 26¼-17¼

Yield • 1.5%
12-Mo. P/E • 10.9

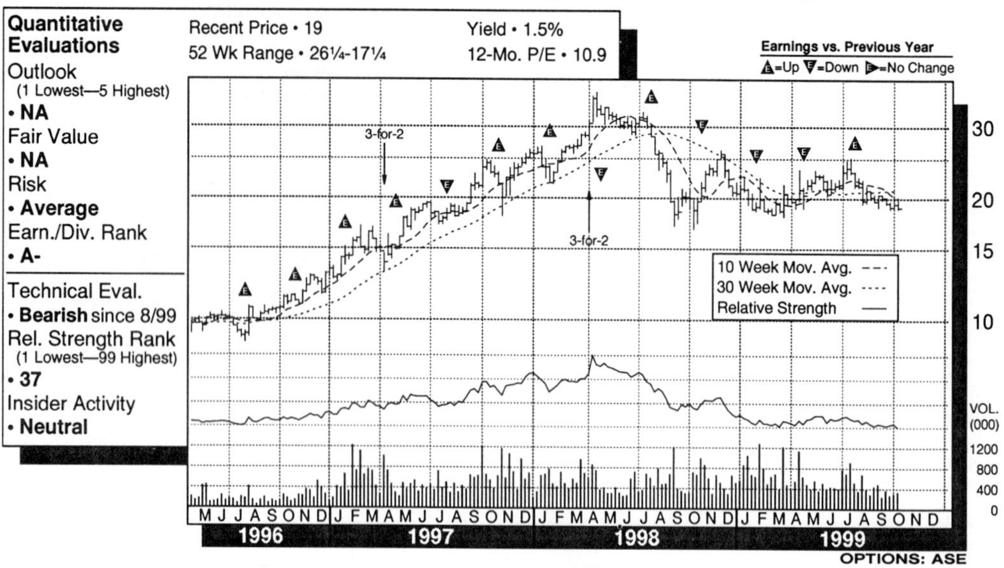

Business Profile - 30-JUN-99

This Florida-based regional broker and investment banking company, with 3,300 financial advisors in 1,400 locations throughout the U.S. and internationally, has benefited from robust activity in the securities markets over the past decade. Results for the first half of FY 99 (Sep.) saw strong growth in commissions and trading revenues; however, the new-issue market for non-technology small capitalization stocks was weak, leading to lower results in the investment banking segment. Expenses have risen recently, reflecting corporate expansion, efforts to build brand identity, and one-time costs associated with consolidation of two contractor broker-dealer units. The company continues to expand retail operations and, in early June 1999, acquired Roney & Co., a Detroit-based brokerage, for $80 million. The transaction adds 28 branches in Michigan, Ohio and Indiana; the company anticipates additional growth in the Midwest.

Operational Review - 30-JUN-99

Total revenues in the first six months of FY 99 (Sep.) rose 8.4%, year to year, as a 16% increase in commissions and gains in most other revenue categories outweighed lower investment banking revenue. Total expenses increased 13%, reflecting higher compensation and benefits. After taxes at 38.2%, against 38.7%, net income fell 17%, to $39,348,000 ($0.81 a share), from $47,445,000 ($0.96, as adjusted).

Stock Performance - 08-OCT-99

In the past 30 trading days, RJF's shares have declined 3%, compared to a 0.91% fall in the S&P 500. Average trading volume for the past five days was 65,060 shares, compared with the 40-day moving average of 68,121 shares.

Key Stock Statistics

Dividend Rate/Share	0.28	Shareholders	10,000
Shs. outstg. (M)	47.3	Market cap. (B)	$0.899
Avg. daily vol. (M)	0.062	Inst. holdings	34%
Tang. Bk. Value/Share	10.56		
Beta	1.72		

Value of $10,000 invested 5 years ago: $ 27,903

Fiscal Year Ending Sep. 30

	1999	1998	1997	1996	1995	1994
Revenues (Million $)						
1Q	264.5	252.3	194.8	152.0	115.7	134.4
2Q	299.2	267.5	250.0	178.7	125.7	130.1
3Q	324.4	275.8	210.1	198.2	148.9	117.7
4Q	—	287.3	272.7	192.8	163.7	124.9
Yr.	—	1,083	927.6	721.8	554.1	507.1
Earnings Per Share ($)						
1Q	**0.36**	**0.45**	0.36	0.27	0.17	0.28
2Q	**0.45**	**0.50**	0.79	0.32	0.22	0.25
3Q	**0.49**	**0.46**	0.35	0.39	0.30	0.16
4Q	—	**0.45**	0.54	0.41	0.31	0.19
Yr.	—	**1.86**	**2.04**	1.40	0.99	0.88

Next earnings report expected: late October

Dividend Data (Dividends have been paid since 1985.)

Amount ($)	Date Decl.	Ex-Div. Date	Stock of Record	Payment Date
0.070	Nov. 20	Dec. 08	Dec. 10	Jan. 05 '99
0.070	Feb. 16	Mar. 12	Mar. 16	Apr. 01 '99
0.070	May. 21	Jun. 14	Jun. 16	Jul. 01 '99
0.070	Aug. 26	Sep. 14	Sep. 16	Oct. 05 '99

A Division of The McGraw-Hill Companies

Raymond James Financial, Inc.

09-OCT-99

Business Summary - 30-JUN-99

Raymond James Financial is a financial services holding company that, through operating subsidiaries, is engaged in securities brokerage, investment banking, investment advisory services, financial planning and management of limited partnerships.

Segment contributions to revenues in FY 98 (Sep.) and the prior fiscal year were: securities commissions 58.4% (57.4% in FY 97 Sep.), interest 18.6% (17.4%), investment banking 10.0% (12.2%), investment advisory 7.3% (6.2%), financial services fees 2.7% (2.7%), and other 3.0% (4.1%).

The company's principal subsidiary, Raymond James & Associates, Inc. (RJA), is the largest brokerage headquartered in Florida. As of September 1998, it had 57 retail offices located primarily in the Southeast, with 578 full-time retail financial advisors. In addition, 2,540 financial advisors were affiliated as independent contractors. RJA also operates institutional offices, with six in Europe and two in Canada. Activities include trading of securities; sales of mutual funds; institutional sales and research; corporate finance; origination, syndication and marketing of limited partnerships (primarily in the real estate and equipment leasing industries); and distribution and underwriting of municipal securities.

Operating subsidiaries also include Investment Management & Research Inc., which participates in the distribution of securities offered by RJA to its retail customers via 1,336 independent contractor financial advisors in 561 offices, and 91 satellite offices in all 50 states; and Robert Thomas Securities Inc., which has 1,204 independent contractor financial advisors in a network of 434 branch offices and 164 satellite offices in all 50 states. In January 1999, the company merged these two independent contractor broker-dealers into Raymond James Financial Services, where they will operate as separate divisions.

RJF's asset management subsidiaries include Eagle Asset Management Inc., which provides investment advisory services and had $5.5 billion under management at December 24, 1998, up 33% from the year-earlier level; and Heritage Asset Management Inc., which manages 14 RJF-sponsored mutual funds with assets of about $3.9 billion at December 24, 1998, up 19%, year to year.

The investment banking group is involved in public and private debt and equity financing for corporate clients, as well as merger and acquisition consulting services. In May 1994, the company formed Raymond James Bank, FSB, from assets purchased from the Resolution Trust Corp. At the end of FY 98, the bank's total assets exceeded $500 million.

RJF has recently established joint ventures in Argentina, India and Turkey to serve institutional clients.

In June 1999, the company completed its acquisition of Roney & Co., a Detroit-based brokerage with 28 branches in Michigan, Ohio and Indiana.

Per Share Data ($) (Year Ended Sep. 30)	1998	1997	1996	1995	1994	1993	1992	1991	1990	1989
Tangible Bk. Val.	10.56	8.87	6.95	5.74	4.93	4.28	3.37	2.60	2.04	1.63
Cash Flow	2.18	2.32	NA	NA	NA	NA	NA	NA	NA	NA
Earnings	1.86	2.04	1.40	0.99	0.88	1.01	0.84	0.56	0.41	0.29
Dividends	0.24	0.18	0.17	0.20	0.14	0.09	0.07	0.04	0.03	0.03
Payout Ratio	13%	9%	12%	20%	16%	9%	8%	8%	8%	9%
Prices - High	$36\frac{1}{2}$	$26\frac{5}{8}$	$11\frac{1}{2}$	$11\frac{1}{4}$	$8\frac{3}{8}$	9	$8\frac{3}{4}$	$6\frac{3}{8}$	3	$2\frac{1}{2}$
- Low	$16\frac{3}{4}$	$12\frac{1}{2}$	$8\frac{1}{2}$	$6\frac{1}{8}$	$5\frac{7}{8}$	6	$4\frac{1}{2}$	$2\frac{1}{8}$	$1\frac{7}{8}$	$1\frac{3}{8}$
P/E Ratio - High	20	13	8	11	10	9	10	11	7	9
- Low	9	6	6	6	7	6	5	4	5	5
Income Statement Analysis (Million $)										
Commissions	632	515	422	328	303	276	204	150	126	116
Int. Inc.	202	156	126	97.2	58.5	33.6	36.4	55.0	61.3	55.8
Total Revs.	1,083	928	722	554	507	452	361	286	257	226
Int. Exp.	131	101	83.5	64.8	36.2	17.2	21.4	40.3	48.6	44.7
Pretax Inc.	150	161	109	74.5	67.2	80.3	65.8	43.5	29.2	20.5
Eff. Tax Rate	38%	38%	39%	38%	37%	39%	38%	39%	39%	40%
Net Inc.	92.7	99	66.0	46.1	42.1	49.3	41.0	26.7	17.9	12.4
Balance Sheet & Other Fin. Data (Million $)										
Total Assets	3,853	3,279	2,566	2,013	1,698	1,448	806	1,060	948	830
Cash Items	297	197	735	454	296	208	231	334	275	251
Receivables	1,922	1,933	1,377	1,247	1,124	1,088	482	655	608	522
Secs. Owned	492	411	333	201	179	72.1	33.5	31.8	32.5	26.5
Sec. Borrowed	Nil	Nil	Nil	Nil	Nil	Nil	Nil	Nil	Nil	Nil
Due Brokers & Cust.	3,098	2,628	2,047	1,637	1,359	1,142	573	869	810	709
Other Liabs.	200	213	168	96.9	99	86.8	58.6	54.6	27.9	21.9
Capitalization:										
Debt	44.8	14.2	24.7	13.1	13.2	13.4	13.5	13.6	13.7	27.8
Equity	510	423	327	266	227	206	161	122	97.0	72.0
Total	555	437	352	279	240	219	174	136	111	99
% Return On Revs.	8.6	10.8	9.1	8.3	8.3	10.9	11.4	9.3	7.0	5.5
% Ret. on Assets	2.6	3.4	2.9	2.5	2.7	4.4	4.4	2.7	2.0	1.8
% Ret. on Equity	19.9	26.4	22.3	18.7	19.4	26.9	29.0	24.4	21.3	19.0

Data as orig reptd.; bef. results of disc opers/spec. items. Per share data adj. for stk. divs. Bold denotes diluted EPS (FASB 128)-prior periods restated. E-Estimated. NA-Not Available. NM-Not Meaningful. NR-Not Ranked.

Office—880 Carillon Parkway, St. Petersburg, FL 33716. **Tel**—(727) 573-3800. **Website**—http://www.rjf.com **Chrmn & CEO**—T. A. James. **Pres**—F. S. Godbold. **Treas**—L. Pippenger. **VP-Fin & CFO**—J. P. Julien. **SVP & Secy**—B. S. Augenbraun. **VP & Investor Contact**—Lawrence A. Silver. **Dirs**—A. M. Biever, J. A. Bulkley, E. L. Chao, T. S. Franke, F. S. Godbold, M. A. Greene, H. H. Hill Jr., H.A. James, T. A. James, P. W. Marshall, J. S. Putnam, R. F. Shuck, D. W. Zank. **Transfer Agent & Registrar**—ChaseMellon Shareholder Services, Ridgefield, NJ. **Incorporated**—in Florida in 1974. **Empl**— 3,790. **S&P Analyst:** Thomas W. Smith, CFA

STANDARD
&POOR'S
STOCK REPORTS

Read-Rite Corp.

Nasdaq Symbol **RDRT**

In S&P SmallCap 600

09-OCT-99

Industry:
Computers (Peripherals)

Summary: This company is the leading independent supplier of magnetic recording heads for rigid disk drives.

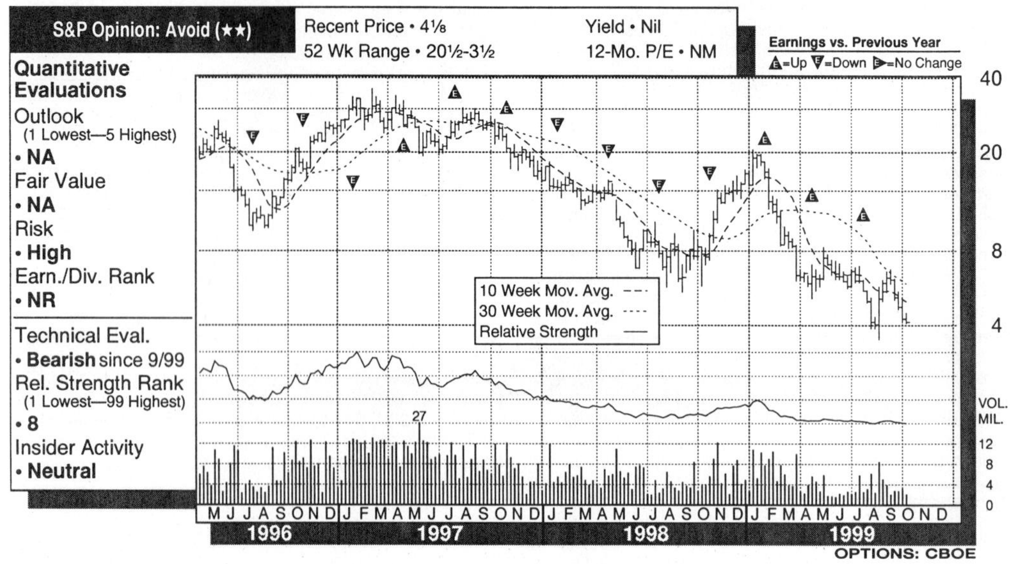

Overview - 20-JUL-99

Revenues are expected to decline for the full-year of FY 99 (Sep.), after a 30% decline in FY 98. Pricing pressures and slower demand for recording heads has led to a tough time for the industry as a whole, and Read-Rite has not been immune to these troubles. In addition, a continued trend toward fewer heads per drive, resulting from lower PC prices has also had an impact on the top-line. Visibility in the industry is very limited at this point, making it extremely difficult to forecast revenues into FY 00, as it remains to be seen when the downward spiral in pricing will lessen. Third quarter FY 99 revenues fell 15% sequentially from the March quarter, and gross margin was negative. RDRT took a $22 million charge in the third quarter to cut headcount by about 14% of its total workforce.

Valuation - 20-JUL-99

The shares have been in a steady downtrend in calendar 1999, the result of revenue and margin declines, continued EPS misses and a poor outlook for the disk drive industry as a whole. The company said in July that the short-term environment was not getting any easier, and that it expects revenues to decline further in the fourth quarter of FY 99. This should lead to a large loss for the quarter and the full year. RDRT is forecasting a rebound beginning in the first quarter of FY 00, but with the extreme price pressure the industry is seeing coupled with unit declines and limited visibility going forward, it is hard to endorse that optimistic view. The trend toward fewer recording heads per drive will make it even harder for the company to get the unit growth it needs to offset price declines. Given the difficult operating environment and lack of visibility, we would avoid the shares.

Key Stock Statistics

S&P EPS Est. 1999	-2.12	Tang. Bk. Value/Share	4.64
P/E on S&P Est. 1999	NM	Beta	2.09
S&P EPS Est. 2000	-0.30	Shareholders	42,000
Dividend Rate/Share	Nil	Market cap. (B)	$0.205
Shs. outstg. (M)	49.7	Inst. holdings	39%
Avg. daily vol. (M)	0.525		

Value of $10,000 invested 5 years ago: $ 2,750

Fiscal Year Ending Sep. 30

	1999	1998	1997	1996	1995	1994
Revenues (Million $)						
1Q	230.2	261.4	251.6	299.2	219.5	132.0
2Q	206.2	187.1	282.1	258.2	241.8	139.5
3Q	174.8	184.3	310.2	238.3	253.1	170.1
4Q	—	175.9	318.2	195.4	288.7	197.0
Yr.	—	808.6	1,162	991.1	1,003	638.6
Earnings Per Share ($)						
1Q	**0.02**	**-1.88**	0.12	0.88	0.42	-0.05
2Q	**-0.39**	**-1.29**	0.48	0.03	0.53	-0.10
3Q	**-1.16**	**-2.82**	0.64	-0.49	0.68	0.24
4Q	**E-0.55**	**-0.61**	0.32	-1.37	0.95	0.33
Yr.	**E-2.12**	**-6.59**	**1.56**	-0.92	2.60	0.43

Next earnings report expected: late October

Dividend Data

No cash dividends have been paid.

Read-Rite Corporation

Business Summary - 20-JUL-99

Read-Rite Corporation is the world's largest independent supplier of magnetic recording heads for rigid disk drives. It designs and manufactures magnetic recording heads as head gimbal assemblies (HGAs), and incorporates multiple HGAs into head stack assemblies (HSAs). Products are sold primarily to independent manufacturers of 3.5-inch form factor rigid disk drives. The company also supplies magnetoresistive (MR) heads for quarter-inch cartridge (QIC) tape drives.

The principal components of rigid disk drives are HGAs, disks, an actuator for positioning HGAs, a motor/spindle assembly to rotate the disk, control electronics and software. An HGA consists of a magnetic recording head attached to a flexure, or suspension arm, and a wire/tubing assembly. Several HGAs can be combined with other components to form an HSA. One or more rigid disks coated with a thin layer of magnetic material are attached to the motor/spindle assembly, which rotates the disks at high speed within a sealed enclosure. The heads record or retrieve data from tracks pre-formatted in the magnetic layer of each disk.

The company's goal is to be the clear technology leader through significant investments in research and development, intensified efforts on Giant MR (GMR) platforms, and efforts to attract, develop and retain high quality technical and management talent. R&D spending totaled $92,265,000 (11.4% of sales) in FY 98 (Sep.), up from $64,995,000 (5.6%) in FY 97.

During FY 98, the company supplied HGAs in volume for 24 different disk drive products to six customers, and supplied HSAs in volume for 50 different disk drive products to four customers. Read-Rite sold 68.2 million HGAs and 14.6 million HSAs, down from 106.8 million HGAs and 16.4 million HSAs in FY 97. In FY 98, Western Digital, Maxtor and Samsung accounted for 49%, 25% and 15% of net sales, respectively.

The company supplied QIC tape heads in volume for eight different tape drive products to six customers, which accounted for 2% of sales in FY 98.

In the third quarter of FY 99, RDRT took a $22.1 million restructuring charge in order to cut costs and reduce headcount by about 2,200. In the third quarter of FY 98, RDRT recorded restructuring charges of $93.7 million, or $1.93 per share.

In the third quarter of FY 99, the company shipped 16.1 million recording heads, versus 19.3 million in the second quarter, a 17% decline, following a 15% sequential decline in the second quarter. MR recording heads now account for 100% of revenues. The company began production of its new GMR heads in the second quarter of FY 99 and it expects to begin shipping volume during the second half of the fiscal year.

Per Share Data ($) (Year Ended Sep. 30)	1998	1997	1996	1995	1994	1993	1992	1991	1990	1989
Tangible Bk. Val.	4.64	11.15	9.46	11.03	8.45	10.02	6.84	2.47	-4.22	NA
Cash Flow	-1.87	5.01	1.80	4.22	1.48	0.99	2.25	1.34	0.52	NA
Earnings	-6.59	1.56	-0.92	2.60	0.43	0.02	1.59	1.04	0.33	NA
Dividends	Nil	Nil	Nil	Nil	Nil	Nil	Nil	Nil	Nil	NA
Payout Ratio	Nil	Nil	Nil	Nil	Nil	Nil	Nil	Nil	Nil	NA
Prices - High	18 3/8	36 1/4	26 7/8	49 1/2	19 7/8	31 1/4	32	15 7/8	NA	NA
- Low	5 3/8	15 1/8	9 5/8	14	10 7/8	8 5/8	14 1/8	11 3/4	NA	NA
P/E Ratio - High	NM	23	NM	19	46	NM	20	15	NA	NA
- Low	NM	10	NM	5	25	NM	9	11	NA	NA
Income Statement Analysis (Million $)										
Revs.	809	1,162	991	1,003	639	482	389	177	74.0	NA
Oper. Inc.	-30.1	288	135	251	82.9	60.2	76.6	40.5	12.4	NA
Depr.	229	168	127	73.5	48.7	34.1	19.4	6.6	3.7	NA
Int. Exp.	29.6	15.7	12.9	5.6	4.8	1.2	1.8	1.8	1.5	NA
Pretax Inc.	-374	113	3.9	178	28.8	-1.9	58.8	28.2	6.8	NA
Eff. Tax Rate	NM	26%	NM	24%	16%	NM	20%	17%	3.70%	NA
Net Inc.	-319	76.2	-43.0	124	19.7	0.9	47.0	23.1	6.6	NA
Balance Sheet & Other Fin. Data (Million $)										
Cash	62.4	119	148	169	111	124	50.8	63.2	3.0	NA
Curr. Assets	281	583	310	476	260	228	174	99	17.0	NA
Total Assets	880	1,301	909	940	631	516	345	154	36.0	NA
Curr. Liab.	184	240	196	189	130	84.6	85.5	49.9	21.6	NA
LT Debt	388	404	172	137	52.4	46.5	28.7	26.7	5.8	NA
Common Eqty.	234	546	454	538	397	350	195	13.0	-24.0	NA
Total Cap.	664	1,023	697	675	500	431	259	104	14.0	NA
Cap. Exp.	186	273	266	185	113	170	112	42.0	8.0	NA
Cash Flow	-90.7	245	84.0	197	68.4	35.0	66.4	29.7	10.3	NA
Curr. Ratio	1.5	2.4	1.6	2.5	2.0	2.7	2.0	2.0	0.8	NA
% LT Debt of Cap.	58.5	39.5	24.7	20.3	10.5	10.8	11.1	25.7	41.4	NA
% Net Inc.of Revs.	NM	6.6	NM	12.3	3.1	0.2	12.1	13.0	8.9	NA
% Ret. on Assets	NM	6.9	NM	15.7	3.0	0.2	7.8	24.9	21.3	NA
% Ret. on Equity	NM	15.2	NM	26.4	4.6	0.3	35.4	NM	NM	NA

Data as orig reptd.; bef. results of disc opers/spec. items. Per share data adj. for stk. divs. Bold denotes diluted EPS (FASB 128)-prior periods restated. E-Estimated. NA-Not Available. NM-Not Meaningful. NR-Not Ranked.

Office—345 Los Coches St., Milpitas, CA 95035. **Tel**—(408) 262-6700. **Fax**—(408) 956-3205. **Website**—http://www.readrite.com **Chrmn & CEO**—C. J. Yansouni. **Pres & COO**—A. S. Lowe. **VP-Fin & CFO**—J. T. Kurtzweil. **VP & Secy**—R. S. Jackson. **Dirs**—W. J. Almon, M. L. Hackworth, J. G. Linvill, M. J. O'Rourke, C. J. Yansouni. **Transfer Agent & Registrar**—ChaseMellon Shareholder Services, SF. **Incorporated**—in California in 1981; reincorporated in Delaware in 1985. **Empl**— 18,000. **S&P Analyst:** Jim Corridore

STANDARD &POOR'S
STOCK REPORTS

Regal-Beloit Corp.

ASE Symbol **RBC**
In S&P SmallCap 600

09-OCT-99 **Industry:** Manufacturing (Specialized) **Summary:** This company is a leading U.S. manufacturer of mechanical motion control products and electric motors and generators.

Quantitative Evaluations
Outlook (1 Lowest—5 Highest) • **5**
Fair Value • **33⅞**
Risk • **Low**
Earn./Div. Rank • **A-**

Technical Eval. • **Bearish** since 9/99
Rel. Strength Rank (1 Lowest—99 Highest) • **45**
Insider Activity • **Neutral**

Recent Price • 20⅞ | Yield • 2.3%
52 Wk Range • 26⅞-15½ | 12-Mo. P/E • 11.2

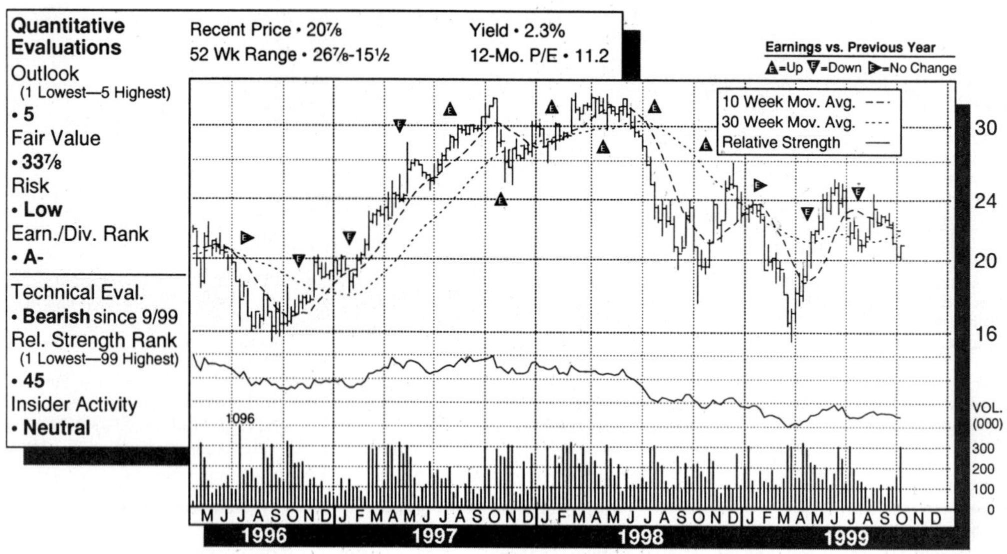

Business Profile - 02-JUN-99

Although economic uncertainties worldwide have caused its customers to be more conservative in their business dealings, the company believes that its track record for controlling costs and improving productivity will provide it with a competitive edge. In early May 1999, the company signed a definitive agreement to acquire Cleveland-based Lincoln Electric's motor business, which manufactures premium quality industrial electric motors, for an undisclosed amount. In March 1997, RBC more than doubled its size, as a result of the purchase of Marathon Electric, a manufacturer of electric motors, generators and other products.

Operational Review - 02-JUN-99

In the first three months of 1999, net sales declined 7.7%, year to year, reflecting slowing demand for the company's mechanical products, and to a lesser extent, its electrical products. Profitability was penalized by the lower volume and despite significantly lower interest expense, pretax income dropped 11%. After taxes at 40.1%, versus 38.8%, net income was down 13%, to $9,078,000 ($0.43 a share), from $10,414,000 ($0.49).

Stock Performance - 08-OCT-99

In the past 30 trading days, RBC's shares have declined 6%, compared to a 0.91% fall in the S&P 500. Average trading volume for the past five days was 67,680 shares, compared with the 40-day moving average of 27,992 shares.

Key Stock Statistics

Dividend Rate/Share	0.48	Shareholders	1,170
Shs. outstg. (M)	21.0	Market cap. (B)	$0.439
Avg. daily vol. (M)	0.036	Inst. holdings	59%
Tang. Bk. Value/Share	4.42		
Beta	0.81		

Value of $10,000 invested 5 years ago: $ 17,916

Fiscal Year Ending Dec. 31

	1999	1998	1997	1996	1995	1994
Revenues (Million $)						
1Q	127.3	137.8	70.57	75.12	74.34	58.85
2Q	137.1	139.0	143.6	71.82	76.27	60.04
3Q	—	138.0	138.4	68.15	71.55	61.19
4Q	—	128.7	134.4	66.42	73.74	62.57
Yr.	—	543.5	487.0	281.5	295.9	242.7
Earnings Per Share ($)						
1Q	**0.43**	**0.49**	**0.36**	**0.42**	0.36	0.23
2Q	**0.46**	**0.55**	**0.51**	**0.41**	0.41	0.27
3Q	—	**0.49**	**0.47**	**0.35**	0.41	0.30
4Q	—	**0.49**	**0.49**	**0.35**	0.42	0.33
Yr.	—	**2.02**	**1.83**	**1.53**	**1.57**	**1.11**

Next earnings report expected: mid October

Dividend Data (Dividends have been paid since 1961.)

Amount ($)	Date Decl.	Ex-Div. Date	Stock of Record	Payment Date
0.120	Oct. 30	Dec. 29	Dec. 31	Jan. 15 '99
0.120	Jan. 22	Mar. 29	Mar. 31	Apr. 15 '99
0.120	Apr. 21	Jun. 28	Jun. 30	Jul. 15 '99
0.120	Jul. 27	Sep. 28	Sep. 30	Oct. 15 '99

A Division of The McGraw-Hill Companies

Business Summary - 02-JUN-99

Regal-Beloit's (RBC) initial business was the production of special metalworking taps. After 34 acquisitions and internal growth, the company has become a prominent manufacturer and worldwide supplier of a diversified line of mechanical products to control motion and torque, and electrical products such as motors and generators.

The company believes that its ability to provide products on a shorter delivery schedule than other manufacturers gives it a competitive selling advantage. Also, the company credits continuous redesign of products, effective plant layout, and modern equipment for producing significant cost advantages. RBC states that its core competencies include the engineering, manufacturing, and assembly of high quality, low cost products, and the capability to acquire products or companies and develop them to their full potential.

Exports accounted for approximately 6% of company sales in 1998 and 7% in 1997.

The company's Mechanical Group (52% of net sales and 56% of operating income in 1998) makes standard and custom worm gear, bevel gear, helical gear and concentric shaft gearboxes; marine and high-performance after-market automotive transmissions; custom gearing; gear motors; and manual valve actuators. These are used in material handling systems, farm implements, gas and liquid pipeline transmission systems, civic water and waste treatment facilities, paper making machinery and luxury inboard powered craft.

In March 1997, the company acquired Marathon Electric Manufacturing Corp., a manufacturer of electric motors, generators and related products, for about $279 million. Marathon now comprises the firm's Electrical Group. The purchase of Marathon, which had 1996 revenues of about $245 million, nearly doubled RBC's sales base.

The Electrical Group (48% of net sales and 44% of operating income) produces AC electric motors ranging in size from 1/12 horsepower to over 500 horsepower and electric generators ranging in size from 5 kilowatts to 2300 kilowatts. The company is developing larger motors of up to 800 horsepower and larger generators of up to 4,000 kilowatts, which RBC expects to begin shipping to customers in the 1999 second and third quarters, respectively.

Both the Mechanical and Electrical Group products are sold to distributors, original equipment manufacturers, and end users across many industry segments.

Per Share Data ($) (Year Ended Dec. 31)	1998	1997	1996	1995	1994	1993	1992	1991	1990	1989
Tangible Bk. Val.	3.70	1.83	7.75	6.61	5.40	4.54	4.13	4.04	3.95	3.69
Cash Flow	3.05	2.78	2.07	2.10	1.57	1.14	0.81	0.49	0.72	0.75
Earnings	2.02	1.87	1.57	1.60	1.13	0.70	0.47	0.28	0.53	0.57
Dividends	0.48	0.48	0.48	0.39	0.30	0.27	0.26	0.26	0.26	0.24
Payout Ratio	24%	26%	31%	24%	27%	38%	56%	95%	49%	42%
Prices - High	33¼	32¾	22⅜	23⅛	15½	13¼	11	7⅜	8⅜	9½
- Low	17½	18	15½	12⅛	11¼	9¼	6½	5⅝	4⅝	6½
P/E Ratio - High	16	18	14	14	14	19	24	27	16	17
- Low	9	10	10	8	10	13	14	20	9	11
Income Statement Analysis (Million $)										
Revs.	544	487	282	296	243	220	200	152	168	167
Oper. Inc.	103	93.3	61.6	63.8	48.0	33.8	23.9	14.3	21.8	23.3
Depr.	22.0	18.9	10.6	10.2	9.0	8.8	7.0	4.5	4.0	3.6
Int. Exp.	11.5	10.8	0.4	0.8	1.0	1.5	1.9	1.4	1.5	1.0
Pretax Inc.	69.9	64.4	51.8	53.1	38.2	23.7	15.2	9.0	17.2	18.9
Eff. Tax Rate	39%	40%	38%	38%	39%	39%	38%	38%	38%	39%
Net Inc.	43.0	38.9	32.2	32.8	23.1	14.4	9.5	5.5	10.7	11.5
Balance Sheet & Other Fin. Data (Million $)										
Cash	3.5	3.4	38.4	7.5	13.4	2.2	5.2	7.2	10.0	3.2
Curr. Assets	176	173	122	102	91.7	71.7	77.5	68.7	73.4	72.4
Total Assets	482	486	197	175	168	139	145	118	114	111
Curr. Liab.	58.6	71.9	29.4	32.0	36.6	22.5	24.1	19.7	14.7	17.3
LT Debt	166	192	2.2	2.9	16.0	19.6	34.4	13.8	16.6	17.3
Common Eqty.	224	189	160	136	111	92.7	83.9	81.8	80.0	74.2
Total Cap.	423	413	168	143	131	117	121	98.0	99	94.0
Cap. Exp.	14.8	16.0	11.1	13.8	7.5	8.5	6.5	7.5	7.6	13.4
Cash Flow	65.0	57.8	42.8	43.0	32.1	23.1	16.4	10.0	14.6	15.1
Curr. Ratio	3.0	2.4	4.2	3.2	2.5	3.2	3.2	3.5	5.0	4.2
% LT Debt of Cap.	39.3	46.5	1.3	2.0	12.2	16.8	28.5	14.1	16.8	18.5
% Net Inc.of Revs.	7.9	8.0	11.4	11.1	9.5	6.5	4.7	3.6	6.4	6.9
% Ret. on Assets	8.9	11.4	17.3	19.1	15.1	10.1	7.2	4.8	9.5	11.2
% Ret. on Equity	20.8	22.3	17.3	26.6	22.7	16.3	11.4	6.8	13.8	16.3

Data as orig reptd.; bef. results of disc opers/spec. items. Per share data adj. for stk. divs. Bold denotes diluted EPS (FASB 128)-prior periods restated. E-Estimated. NA-Not Available. NM-Not Meaningful. NR-Not Ranked.

Office—200 State St., Beloit, WI 53511-6254. **Tel**—(608) 364-8800. **Fax**—(608) 364-8818. **Chrmn, Pres & CEO**—J. L. Packard. **EVP**—H. W. Knueppel. **VP, CFO, Secy & Investor Contact**—K. F. Kaplan. **Dirs**—F. E. Bauchiero, J. R. Coleman, J. M. Eldred, S. N. Graff, G. F. Kasten, Jr., W. W. Keefer, H. W. Knueppel, J. A. McKay, J. L. Packard. **Transfer Agent & Registrar**—Boston EquiServe. **Incorporated**—in Delaware in 1955; reincorporated in Wisconsin in 1994. **Empl**— 4,700. **S&P Analyst:** S.A.H.

STANDARD
&POOR'S
STOCK REPORTS

Regeneron Pharmaceuticals

NASDAQ Symbol **REGN**

In S&P SmallCap 600

09-OCT-99 **Industry:** Biotechnology

Summary: This biotechnology company focuses on discovery and development of nerve growth factors to treat neurological conditions, including Lou Gehrig's disease and Alzheimer's disease.

Quantitative Evaluations
Outlook
(1 Lowest—5 Highest)
• **NA**
Fair Value
• **NA**
Risk
• **High**
Earn./Div. Rank
• **NR**

Technical Eval.
• **Bearish** since 9/99
Rel. Strength Rank
(1 Lowest—99 Highest)
• **52**
Insider Activity
• **Neutral**

Recent Price • 8
52 Wk Range • 10⅛-5⅜
Yield • Nil
12-Mo. P/E • NM

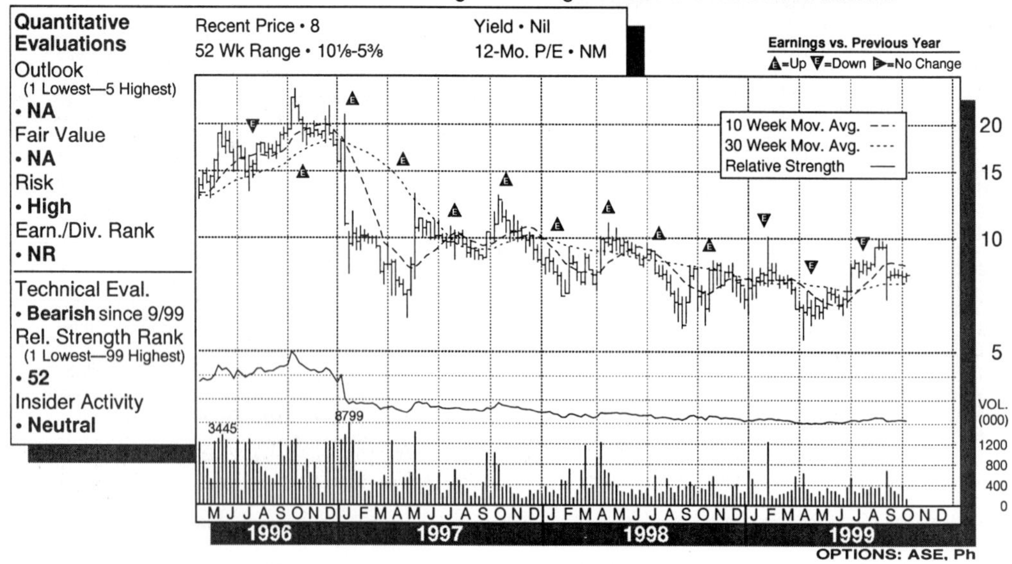

OPTIONS: ASE, Ph

Business Profile - 02-JUN-99

This development stage company has partnerships with Amgen and Sumitomo Pharmaceuticals to develop neurological treatments using brain-derived neurotrophic factor (BDNF). Amgen is currently testing BDNF intrathecally delivered (directly into the spinal fluid) to treat ALS (Lou Gehrig's disease). Despite disappointing Phase III results for BDNF subcutaneously delivered (under the skin), a review of the data indicated that a subset of ALS patients may have derived a survival benefit from the treatment. REGN and Amgen planned to begin a multicenter study in 1999 to evaluate this. In May 1999, favorable clinical results were reported for NT-3, a novel approach developed by REGN and Amgen to treat constipation in spinal cord injury patients. REGN and Procter & Gamble have a research agreement to develop Axokine to treat obesity associated with Type II diabetes. Axokine began Phase I clinical trials in the 1999 first quarter.

Operational Review - 02-JUN-99

Revenues in the first three months of 1999 fell 16%, year to year, as lower contract R&D and investment income outweighed increased contract manufacturing revenue. Total expenses were up 31%, on sharply higher R&D and contract manufacturing expenses, and a rise in G&A costs. The net loss widened to $8,930,000 ($0.29 a share), from $3,829,000 ($0.12). Cash, equivalents and marketable securities totaled $70 million at March 31, 1999.

Stock Performance - 08-OCT-99

In the past 30 trading days, REGN's shares have declined 16%, compared to a 0.91% fall in the S&P 500. Average trading volume for the past five days was 25,440 shares, compared with the 40-day moving average of 66,054 shares.

Key Stock Statistics

Dividend Rate/Share	Nil	Shareholders	900
Shs. outstg. (M)	31.3	Market cap. (B)	$0.221
Avg. daily vol. (M)	0.052	Inst. holdings	19%
Tang. Bk. Value/Share	3.69		
Beta	1.00		

Value of $10,000 invested 5 years ago: $ 5,161

Fiscal Year Ending Dec. 31

	1999	1998	1997	1996	1995	1994
Revenues (Million $)						
1Q	6.92	8.25	6.21	5.19	7.83	2.99
2Q	7.17	15.20	6.62	6.16	7.62	3.62
3Q	—	12.57	8.87	6.22	6.19	8.90
4Q	—	9.18	11.40	6.55	5.74	7.69
Yr.	—	45.19	33.10	24.11	27.38	23.19
Earnings Per Share ($)						
1Q	**-0.29**	**-0.12**	-0.23	-0.35	-0.22	-0.57
2Q	**-0.25**	**0.07**	-0.16	-0.31	-0.22	-0.54
3Q	—	**-0.04**	-0.06	-0.35	-0.37	-0.21
4Q	—	**-0.18**	**0.02**	-0.32	-0.38	-0.30
Yr.	—	**-0.28**	**-0.40**	**-1.33**	-1.19	-1.62

Next earnings report expected: late October

Dividend Data

No cash dividends have been paid.

A Division of The McGraw-Hill Companies

Regeneron Pharmaceuticals, Inc.

Business Summary - 02-JUN-99

Developing therapeutic drugs is a long and expensive process for biotechnology companies like Regeneron Pharmaceuticals, Inc. Massive spending for research, clinical trials, regulatory approvals and commercialization of products have led to collaborations with established companies in order to fund development of potential products.

REGN is developing compounds to treat neurodegenerative diseases, peripheral neuropathies and nerve injury, as well as conditions outside the nervous system, including inflammatory and muscle diseases, angiogenesis (blood vessel growth), hematopoieses, abnormal bone growth and cancer. It also earns contract revenue from a long-term manufacturing agreement with Merck & Co.

In May 1997, REGN and Procter & Gamble (P&G) signed a 10-year agreement to discover, develop and commercialize pharmaceutical products in cardiovascular, bone, muscle, arthritis and other disease areas. Over the first five years of the agreement, P&G was to provide $155 million (including $20 million from an agreement in December 1996) to support REGN and its research programs. In September 1997, the company and P&G expanded their agreement to include development of Axokine, REGN's potential neurotrophic treatment for obesity associated with Type II diabetes. P&G agreed to reimburse REGN for R&D expenses, and to pay an additional amount of up to $15 million. Phase I clinical studies for Axokine began in the 1999 first quarter. Independently of this collaboration, the company is developing Axokine to treat retinitis pigmentosa.

Neurodegenerative diseases are incurable conditions in which there is progressive loss of neurons crucial for functions such as learning and memory, sensation, control of movement, muscle strength and coordination. Such conditions include amyotrophic lateral sclerosis (ALS, or Lou Gehrig's disease), Parkinson's disease, and Alzheimer's disease.

Amgen-Regeneron Partners (equally owned by the two parties) is conducting clinical trials of brain-derived neurotrophic factor (BDNF) to treat ALS via intrathecal (infusion into the spinal fluid) and subcutaneous delivery (injection under the skin). On behalf of the partnership, REGN is conducting human clinical studies of neurotrophin-3 (NT-3) to treat enteric neuropathies. REGN is also developing BDNF in Japan, with Sumitomo Pharmaceuticals.

In January 1997, REGN and Amgen said a Phase III trial of BDNF (delivered subcutaneously) failed to demonstrate efficacy in ALS patients. Despite confirming safety and tolerability, the trial did not show a significant difference in breathing capacity or survival between treatment and placebo groups. However, a review of the data by REGN and outside experts indicated that a defined subset of ALS patients in the trial may have derived a survival benefit from BDNF treatment. Studies are underway to see if this can be confirmed.

Per Share Data ($) (Year Ended Dec. 31)	1998	1997	1996	1995	1994	1993	1992	1991	1990	1989
Tangible Bk. Val.	4.23	4.49	4.16	3.11	3.55	5.22	5.68	6.92	1.69	NA
Cash Flow	-0.18	-0.25	-1.08	-0.89	-1.42	-2.24	-1.12	-0.24	-0.29	NA
Earnings	-0.28	-0.40	-1.33	-1.19	-1.62	-2.41	-1.24	-0.29	-0.32	NA
Dividends	Nil	Nil	Nil	Nil	Nil	Nil	Nil	Nil	Nil	NA
Payout Ratio	Nil	Nil	Nil	Nil	Nil	Nil	Nil	Nil	Nil	NA
Prices - High	11	$21\frac{1}{4}$	$24\frac{7}{8}$	$16\frac{1}{2}$	$17\frac{3}{8}$	$21\frac{1}{2}$	$23\frac{1}{4}$	$23\frac{1}{4}$	NA	NA
- Low	$5\frac{3}{4}$	$6\frac{1}{8}$	$11\frac{1}{4}$	$3\frac{1}{8}$	3	$10\frac{1}{2}$	$7\frac{3}{4}$	$9\frac{3}{4}$	NA	NA
P/E Ratio - High	NM	NM	NM	NM	NM	NM	NM	NM	NM	NA
- Low	NM	NM	NM	NM	NM	NM	NM	NM	NA	NA
Income Statement Analysis (Million $)										
Revs.	45.2	33.1	19.8	24.3	20.6	6.1	6.5	7.3	3.8	0.5
Oper. Inc.	-5.2	-6.5	-29.8	-19.4	-27.5	-40.5	-21.4	-8.8	-4.1	-3.5
Depr.	3.0	4.4	6.1	5.9	3.9	2.8	2.0	0.8	0.3	0.2
Int. Exp.	0.4	0.7	0.9	1.2	1.4	1.1	0.7	0.1	0.0	0.0
Pretax Inc.	-8.6	-11.6	-32.4	-23.5	-30.7	-39.9	-19.1	-4.5	-3.3	-2.7
Eff. Tax Rate	NM	NM	NM	NM	NM	NM	NM	Nil	Nil	Nil
Net Inc.	-8.6	-11.6	-32.4	-23.5	-30.7	-39.9	-19.1	-4.5	-3.3	-2.7
Balance Sheet & Other Fin. Data (Million $)										
Cash	114	28.9	80.1	46.1	50.0	88.0	83.0	104	22.0	11.0
Curr. Assets	92.9	100	85.0	49.2	52.0	92.0	85.0	107	22.0	12.0
Total Assets	157	168	138	93.9	94.0	118	98.0	114	25.0	13.0
Curr. Liab.	9.4	10.7	12.0	12.9	17.9	13.1	4.6	3.3	1.8	0.3
LT Debt	3.1	3.8	5.2	6.0	9.3	5.9	5.8	2.4	Nil	5.0
Common Eqty.	132	139	107	67.9	67.0	98.0	87.0	106	-7.0	1.0
Total Cap.	135	143	112	73.9	76.0	104	93.0	109	19.0	13.0
Cap. Exp.	3.0	2.1	8.6	3.3	7.0	10.2	2.1	1.0	1.6	0.4
Cash Flow	-5.6	-7.2	-26.3	-17.6	-26.7	-37.0	-17.2	-3.7	-3.0	-2.5
Curr. Ratio	9.9	9.3	7.1	3.8	2.9	7.0	18.6	32.3	12.4	41.8
% LT Debt of Cap.	2.3	2.7	4.6	8.1	12.1	5.7	6.3	2.2	Nil	40.2
% Net Inc.of Revs.	NM	NM	NM	NM	NM	NM	NM	NM	NM	NM
% Ret. on Assets	NM	NM	NM	NM	NM	NM	NM	NM	NM	NM
% Ret. on Equity	NM	NM	NM	NM	NM	NM	NM	NM	NA	NM

Data as orig. reptd.; bef. results of disc. opers. and/or spec. items. Per share data adj. for stk. divs. as of ex-div. date. Rev. in Income Statement Analysis tbl. excl. investment inc. E-Estimated. NA-Not Available. NM-Not Meaningful. NR-Not Ranked.

Office—777 Old Saw Mill River Rd., Tarrytown, NY 10591-6707. **Tel**—(914) 345-7400. **Website**—http://www.regeneron.com **Chrmn**—P. R. Vagelos. **Pres & CEO**—L. S. Schleifer. **VP-Fin, CFO, Treas & Investor Contact**—Murray A. Goldberg. **VP & Secy**—P. Lubetkin. **Dirs**—C. A. Baker, M. S. Brown, A. G. Gilman, J. L. Goldstein, F. A. Middleton, L. S. Schleifer, E. M. Shooter, G. L. Sing, P. R. Vagelos. **Transfer Agent & Registrar**—American Stock Transfer & Trust Co., NYC. **Incorporated**—in New York in 1988. **Empl**— 400. **S&P Analyst:** David Moskowitz

STANDARD
&POOR'S
STOCK REPORTS

Regis Corp.

NASDAQ Symbol **RGIS**

In S&P SmallCap 600

09-OCT-99

Industry:
Services (Commercial & Consumer)

Summary: This company is the world's largest owner and operator of hair and retail product salons, with more than 3,900, following its acquisition of Supercuts, Inc.

Quantitative Evaluations

Outlook
(1 Lowest—5 Highest)
• **4-**

Fair Value
• **24¼**

Risk
• **Average**

Earn./Div. Rank
• **B**

Technical Eval.
• **Bearish** since 6/99

Rel. Strength Rank
(1 Lowest—99 Highest)
• **22**

Insider Activity
• **Neutral**

Recent Price • 17½
52 Wk Range • 28½-16¾
Yield • 0.7%
12-Mo. P/E • 23.0

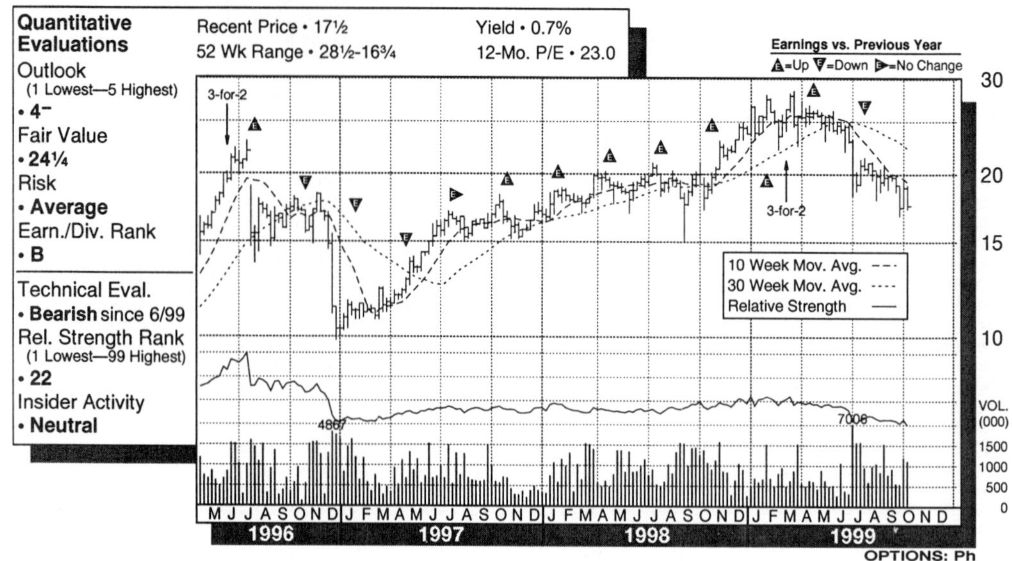

OPTIONS: Ph

Business Profile - 30-JUN-99

In April 1999, Regis announced that domestic salon operations performed better than the company's plan in the third quarter of FY 99 (Jun.), aided by about 6% higher same-store sales. Business in Europe outside of the U.K. was below plan, impacting earnings by about one cent per share. Management plans to take remedial measures to improve these results. During FY 99, RGIS will have closed or sold its unprofitable operations in Mexico, South Africa, Switzerland, Dubai, France and Ireland. The company is also downsizing and relocating its London office to a city near Birmingham, England, in order to reduce overhead costs. Due to these changes, the fourth quarter of FY 99 is expected to include a non-recurring charge of about $4-$5 million.

Operational Review - 30-JUN-99

Total revenues for the nine months ending March 31, 1999, increased 15%, year-to-year, reflecting increases in company-owned stores and in system-wide sales, resulting from acquisitions and higher same-store sales. Total operating expenses rose 14%, as higher depreciation, amortization and non-recurring charges were offset by well-contained operating expenses at company owned stores. Pretax income rose only 14%, but after taxes at 39.7%, versus 41.3%, net income rose 17%, to $24,321,000 ($0.65 a share), from $20,725,000 ($0.57).

Stock Performance - 08-OCT-99

In the past 30 trading days, RGIS's shares have declined 11%, compared to a 0.91% fall in the S&P 500. Average trading volume for the past five days was 221,080 shares, compared with the 40-day moving average of 194,882 shares.

Key Stock Statistics

Dividend Rate/Share	0.12	Shareholders	13,000
Shs. outstg. (M)	38.7	Market cap. (B)	$0.677
Avg. daily vol. (M)	0.169	Inst. holdings	69%
Tang. Bk. Value/Share	2.10		
Beta	1.27		

Value of $10,000 invested 5 years ago: $ 38,173

Fiscal Year Ending Jun. 30

	1999	1998	1997	1996	1995	1994
Revenues (Million $)						
1Q	214.5	188.7	170.6	111.7	102.4	89.50
2Q	226.8	198.9	176.5	126.6	108.4	94.50
3Q	238.3	197.3	175.5	126.2	102.7	94.90
4Q	260.8	213.2	190.7	134.9	108.8	97.70
Yr.	974.9	798.1	713.2	499.4	422.2	377.0
Earnings Per Share ($)						
1Q	**0.21**	**0.16**	0.13	0.16	0.12	0.10
2Q	**0.25**	**0.22**	**-0.26**	0.19	0.16	-0.17
3Q	**0.19**	**0.19**	0.12	0.16	0.12	0.10
4Q	**0.11**	**0.27**	0.19	0.19	0.16	0.13
Yr.	**0.76**	**0.85**	**0.19**	**0.28**	0.57	0.17

Next earnings report expected: late October

Dividend Data (Dividends have been paid since 1995.)

Amount ($)	Date Decl.	Ex-Div. Date	Stock of Record	Payment Date
0.030	Feb. 04	Feb. 10	Feb. 15	Mar. 01 '99
3-for-2	Feb. 04	Mar. 02	Feb. 15	Mar. 01 '99
0.030	May. 06	May. 13	May. 17	Jun. 01 '99
0.030	Aug. 26	Sep. 02	Sep. 07	Sep. 22 '99

A Division of The McGraw-Hill Companies

Regis Corporation

Business Summary - 30-JUN-99

RGIS is the global leader in the highly-fragmented personal hair care industry. The company has salons in all 50 states, and in Puerto Rico, Canada, Mexico, South Africa, Switzerland, the United Kingdom, and Ireland as of March 31, 1999.

Operating more than 1,000 Supercuts and 154 Wal-Mart-based salons as of mid-1999, Regis has established a presence in the hair salon industry.

As of April 1999, Regis operated and franchised about 3,900 salons in six divisions: Regis Hairstylists, Strip Center Salons (Mainly Supercuts), MasterCuts, Trade Secret, Wal-Mart/SmartStyle Family Hair salons, and an International division. As of June 30, 1998, Regis Hairstylists had 820 mall-based salons, generating 37% of company revenues, and offered a wide variety of hair care services, including $21 stylings. MasterCuts had 412 locations featuring a basic service, family-oriented environment, and generated 13.5% of Regis' revenues, with an average sale of $11. There were 273 SmartStyle salons based in Wal-Mart stores, generating 5% of Regis revenues. The Trade Secret chain included 374 hair and beauty care product-oriented stores based in malls, and accounted for 14.7% of company sales. Strip Center Salons, which is primarily comprised of Supercuts outlets, included 1,268 strip center-based, basic haircut and styling locations, and registered 16.5% of Regis' sales.

In recent years, Regis has emphasized sales of higher-margin hair care products, consisting primarily of shampoos, conditioners, and related products. Regis-label products and lines of salon-branded products, such as Joico, Paul Mitchell, Nexxus, Matrix and Sebastian, are sold only through licensed beauty salons.

Regis has continued to make acquisitions to increase its total number of salons. In May 1999, RGIS acquired The Barbers, the franchiser, owner, and operator of about 1,000 Cost Cutters Family Hair Care, City Looks Salons International, and We Care Hair Salons in a pooling of interest transaction, with each of The Barbers shareholders receiving 0.5 shares of RGIS stock for each share held. With this transaction, Regis became the sole provider of hair salons for Wal-Mart stores. The company stated that it will be operating and franchising about 5,000 salons by the end of FY 99. In March 1999, the company announced that it had acquired, for about 538,000 shares, 24 salons operating under the Heidi's trade name, which will add about $26 million in annualized revenues. Excluding this transaction, RGIS completed 111 acquisitions in the past 63 months, adding 3,095 salons.

Per Share Data ($) (Year Ended Jun. 30)	1999	1998	1997	1996	1995	1994	1993	1992	1991	1990
Tangible Bk. Val.	NA	2.10	1.41	1.39	0.99	0.47	0.09	0.05	-0.63	-3.80
Cash Flow	NA	1.83	1.11	1.39	1.16	0.70	0.70	0.67	0.56	0.94
Earnings	0.76	0.85	0.19	0.71	0.57	0.17	0.18	0.21	-0.25	0.08
Dividends	0.06	0.06	0.05	0.03	Nil	Nil	Nil	Nil	Nil	Nil
Payout Ratio	8%	7%	29%	5%	Nil	Nil	Nil	Nil	Nil	Nil
Prices - High	$28\frac{1}{2}$	$26\frac{7}{8}$	$18\frac{3}{8}$	23	$11\frac{1}{4}$	$7\frac{3}{8}$	$5\frac{7}{8}$	$4\frac{7}{8}$	$6\frac{1}{8}$	NA
- Low	$16\frac{3}{4}$	15	$10\frac{3}{8}$	$9\frac{1}{2}$	$6\frac{1}{4}$	$4\frac{3}{4}$	4	$2\frac{5}{8}$	3	NA
P/E Ratio - High	38	32	98	33	20	42	32	23	NM	NA
- Low	22	18	55	13	11	27	22	13	NM	NA
Income Statement Analysis (Million $)										
Revs.	NA	798	713	499	422	377	341	306	308	364
Oper. Inc.	NA	97.6	79.3	56.6	45.6	37.4	31.5	26.9	29.8	32.0
Depr.	NA	35.7	32.1	18.4	14.8	12.3	10.9	9.7	10.5	11.0
Int. Exp.	NA	10.1	10.3	6.1	6.5	8.2	8.5	8.5	14.3	18.7
Pretax Inc.	NA	51.0	19.7	33.0	25.3	7.1	7.0	8.3	-2.2	2.7
Eff. Tax Rate	NA	40%	67%	42%	42%	43%	45%	47%	NM	62%
Net Inc.	NA	30.5	6.6	19.1	14.7	4.0	3.9	4.4	-3.2	1.0
Balance Sheet & Other Fin. Data (Million $)										
Cash	NA	4.8	8.9	5.5	1.2	3.5	2.3	3.8	5.2	2.4
Curr. Assets	NA	81.9	77.1	49.4	35.1	38.0	28.4	22.1	28.8	26.8
Total Assets	NA	382	332	221	166	166	143	128	131	130
Curr. Liab.	NA	83.8	92.1	56.9	45.1	42.0	42.0	30.0	40.0	134
LT Debt	NA	101	82.7	50.0	38.0	54.0	52.0	55.0	61.0	4.0
Common Eqty.	NA	189	149	108	76.4	59.7	39.0	35.6	22.8	-11.9
Total Cap.	NA	290	232	158	115	117	93.0	93.0	86.0	-7.0
Cap. Exp.	NA	55.6	39.4	26.0	153	18.4	21.6	14.1	18.6	14.4
Cash Flow	NA	66.1	38.7	37.5	29.5	16.4	14.8	14.1	7.3	12.0
Curr. Ratio	NA	1.0	0.8	0.9	0.8	0.9	0.7	0.7	0.7	0.2
% LT Debt of Cap.	NA	34.8	35.6	31.5	33.0	46.6	55.4	58.8	71.4	NM
% Net Inc.of Revs.	NA	3.8	0.9	3.9	3.5	1.1	1.1	1.4	NM	0.3
% Ret. on Assets	NA	8.5	2.1	9.9	8.9	2.4	2.8	3.3	NM	0.8
% Ret. on Equity	NA	18.0	4.8	20.8	21.6	7.7	10.3	14.8	NM	NM

Data as orig reptd.; bef. results of disc opers/spec. items. Per share data adj. for stk. divs. Bold denotes diluted EPS (FASB 128)-prior periods restated. E-Estimated. NA-Not Available. NM-Not Meaningful. NR-Not Ranked.

Office—7201 Metro Blvd., Edina, MN 55439. **Tel**—(612) 947-7777. **Fax**—(612) 947-7900. **Chrmn**—M. Kunin. **Pres & CEO**—P. D. Finkelstein. **COO**—M. W. Goldstein. **SVP, CFO & Investor Contact**—Randy L. Pearce. **Dirs**—R. Bjelland, P. D. Finkelstein, C. A. Fox, T. Gregory, V. Z. Hawn, S. S. Hoyt, D. Kunin, M. Kunin. **Transfer Agent & Registrar**—Norwest Bank Minnesota, South St. Paul. **Incorporated**—in Minnesota in 1954. **Empl**— 29,000. **S&P Analyst:** Matthew C. Hershberg

STANDARD
&POOR'S
STOCK REPORTS

Reliance Steel & Aluminum

NYSE Symbol **RS**

In S&P SmallCap 600

09-OCT-99

Industry:
Manufacturing (Specialized)

Summary: This major U.S. metals service center company provides value-added metals processing services, and also distributes metal products through a network of centers.

Quantitative Evaluations

Outlook
(1 Lowest—5 Highest)
• **5+**

Fair Value
• **35¼**

Risk
• **Average**

Earn./Div. Rank
• **NR**

Technical Eval.
• **Bearish** since 9/99

Rel. Strength Rank
(1 Lowest—99 Highest)
• **40**

Insider Activity
• **NA**

Recent Price • 21⅛
52 Wk Range • 26¾-16⅞
Yield • 0.8%
12-Mo. P/E • 11.5

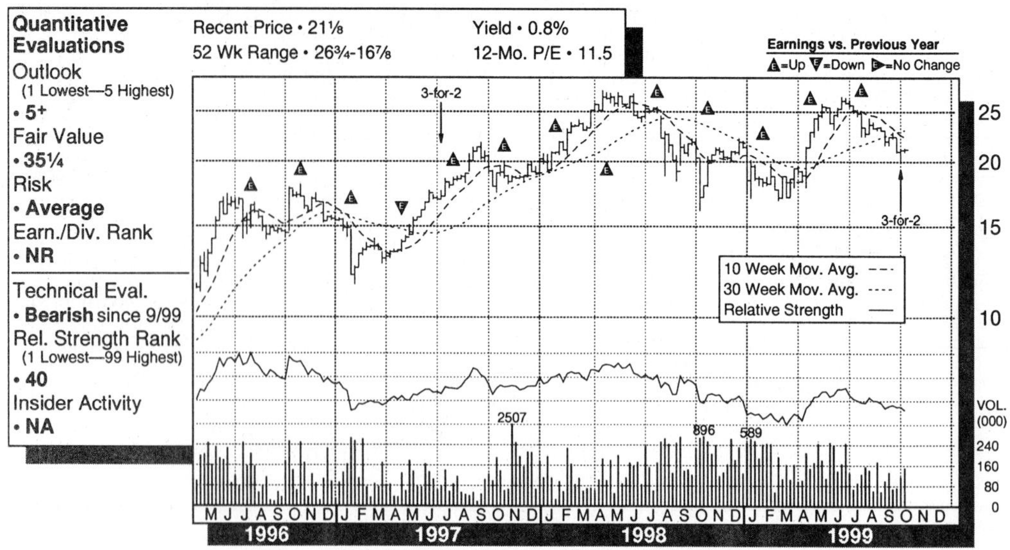

Business Profile - 11-AUG-99

In July 1999, the company said demand for its products remained healthy in most of its markets, and that the Northern California market, which is heavily dependent on the semiconductor industry, has been showing signs of improvement. The company has continued to implement an aggressive acquisition strategy. Seven privately held metals service center companies were acquired in 1998. In March 1999, RS acquired Liebovich Bros. Inc., a provider of carbon steel products, with 1998 sales of about $130 million. The acquisition marked the company's entry into the Midwest. The dividend was raised 8% in the first quarter of 1999, and will be raised another 15% in conjunction with a three-for-two stock split set for September.

Operational Review - 11-AUG-99

Sales in the first half of 1999 advanced 18%, year to year, aided by acquisitions. Costs and expenses rose more rapidly; with 24% lower equity earnings, pretax income was up 11%. After taxes at 39.5%, versus 41.0%, net income gained 14%, to $27,715,000 ($1.49 a share, on 2.5% fewer shares), from $24,263,000 ($1.27).

Stock Performance - 08-OCT-99

In the past 30 trading days, RS's shares have declined 8%, compared to a 0.91% fall in the S&P 500. Average trading volume for the past five days was 29,760 shares, compared with the 40-day moving average of 22,004 shares.

Key Stock Statistics

Dividend Rate/Share	0.17	Shareholders	298
Shs. outstg. (M)	27.8	Market cap. (B)	$0.587
Avg. daily vol. (M)	0.020	Inst. holdings	44%
Tang. Bk. Value/Share	5.73		
Beta	0.58		

Value of $10,000 invested 5 years ago: NA

Fiscal Year Ending Dec. 31

	1999	1998	1997	1996	1995	1994
Revenues (Million $)						
1Q	371.9	315.5	201.6	157.6	136.5	104.9
2Q	384.7	326.2	243.8	164.6	140.8	109.1
3Q	—	357.8	254.2	153.4	135.3	115.7
4Q	—	353.3	261.9	178.3	148.8	117.2
Yr.	—	1,353	961.5	654.0	561.3	446.9
Earnings Per Share ($)						
1Q	**0.51**	**0.41**	**0.30**	0.34	0.23	0.18
2Q	**0.49**	**0.44**	**0.37**	0.33	0.24	0.22
3Q	—	**0.42**	**0.37**	0.30	0.24	0.21
4Q	—	**0.41**	**0.40**	0.30	0.25	0.16
Yr.	—	**1.69**	**1.43**	**1.27**	**0.97**	0.76

Next earnings report expected: mid February

Dividend Data (Dividends have been paid since 1995.)

Amount ($)	Date Decl.	Ex-Div. Date	Stock of Record	Payment Date
0.065	Feb. 19	Mar. 04	Mar. 08	Mar. 31 '99
0.065	Apr. 28	May. 10	May. 12	May. 28 '99
0.065	Jul. 29	Aug. 12	Aug. 16	Sep. 01 '99
3-for-2	Jul. 29	Sep. 27	Sep. 02	Sep. 24 '99

A Division of The **McGraw-Hill** *Companies*

Reliance Steel & Aluminum Co.

Business Summary - 11-AUG-99

Reliance Steel & Aluminum started its business in 1939 fabricating steel reinforcing bar, and within 10 years had become a full-line distributor of steel and aluminum.

Processing services were added in the 1950s, expansion through acquisitions took place in the 1960s, and specialty metals service centers were started in the 1970s. RS purchased 36 companies from 1984 through year-end 1998.

RS is one of the largest U.S. metals service center companies, with a network of 20 divisions and 12 subsidiaries operating metals service centers; and 66 processing and distribution facilities (excluding American Steel, L.L.C.'s two facilities) in 22 states and France as of year-end 1998.

Through this network, the company provides value-added materials management and metals processing services and distributes a full line of more than 70,000 metal products, including carbon, alloy, stainless and specialty steel, aluminum, brass and copper products to more than 50,000 customers in a broad range of industries.

Certain metals service centers provide processing services for specialty metals only. RS's products were being delivered from facilities in Alabama, Arizona, California, Colorado, Florida, Georgia, Illinois, Kansas, Maryland, Michigan, New Jersey, New Mexico, North Carolina, Ohio, Oregon, Pennsylvania, South Carolina, Tennessee, Texas, Utah, Washington, and Wyoming as of year-end 1998.

A company subsidiary has an international unit operating a distribution center in Fuveau, France. RS also has operational control of 50%-owned American Steel, L.L.C. (ASL). ASL was operating two metals service centers in the Pacific Northwest as of year-end 1998.

Customers are served primarily through quick delivery metals processing and inventory management services. The company purchases metals from primary producers and sells these products in smaller quantities. Metals processing, or first stage processing, services are provided for about 50% of sales.

Products are distributed to manufacturers and end users, generally within 24 hours from receipt of an order, for orders that do not require extensive or customized processing. Metals processing services include leveling, slitting, blanking, shape cutting, shearing, sawing, precision plate sawing, twin milling, skin milling, tee splitting and straightening, forming, pipe threading, welding, bending, and electropolishing, all to customer specifications.

Per Share Data ($) (Year Ended Dec. 31)	1998	1997	1996	1995	1994	1993	1992	1991	1990	1989
Tangible Bk. Val.	6.10	8.71	8.29	7.09	6.13	5.80	NA	NA	NA	NA
Cash Flow	2.37	1.99	1.63	1.20	0.99	NA	NA	NA	NA	NA
Earnings	1.69	1.43	1.27	0.97	0.76	0.44	NA	NA	NA	NA
Dividends	0.14	0.09	0.05	0.04	Nil	NA	NA	NA	NA	NA
Payout Ratio	8%	7%	4%	5%	Nil	NA	NA	NA	NA	NA
Prices - High	27½	21¾	18	9¼	7¼	NA	NA	NA	NA	NA
- Low	16⅛	11½	8	5	4⅝	NA	NA	NA	NA	NA
P/E Ratio - High	16	15	14	10	10	NA	NA	NA	NA	NA
- Low	10	8	6	5	6	NA	NA	NA	NA	NA
Income Statement Analysis (Million $)										
Revs.	1,353	962	642	561	447	371	346	406	432	469
Oper. Inc.	108	72.6	52.2	39.9	28.8	19.0	14.1	17.6	23.1	24.0
Depr.	19.4	13.2	8.6	5.2	4.3	3.6	3.5	4.1	4.3	4.5
Int. Exp.	17.6	10.9	3.9	1.6	2.1	2.3	2.5	4.6	4.8	5.6
Pretax Inc.	80.3	58.0	50.6	38.6	24.3	14.9	12.9	10.1	15.0	15.2
Eff. Tax Rate	41%	41%	40%	41%	41%	38%	42%	41%	40%	40%
Net Inc.	47.7	34.2	29.8	22.7	14.4	9.2	7.6	5.9	8.9	9.1
Balance Sheet & Other Fin. Data (Million $)										
Cash	6.5	34.0	0.8	18.0	8.3	NA	NA	NA	NA	NA
Curr. Assets	420	322	211	167	125	NA	NA	NA	NA	NA
Total Assets	841	584	391	260	199	187	NA	NA	NA	NA
Curr. Liab.	129	109	74.1	66.2	40.9	NA	NA	NA	NA	NA
LT Debt	343	143	107	30.4	8.5	10.1	NA	NA	NA	NA
Common Eqty.	346	313	193	164	150	136	NA	NA	NA	NA
Total Cap.	712	475	308	194	159	146	NA	NA	NA	NA
Cap. Exp.	23.7	26.6	21.4	7.9	9.5	10.1	7.3	5.0	12.6	13.0
Cash Flow	67.1	47.3	38.4	27.9	18.7	12.9	11.1	10.0	13.2	13.5
Curr. Ratio	3.3	3.0	2.9	2.5	3.1	NA	NA	NA	NA	NA
% LT Debt of Cap.	48.2	30.2	34.7	15.7	5.4	6.9	NA	NA	NA	NA
% Net Inc.of Revs.	3.5	3.6	4.6	4.1	3.2	2.5	2.2	1.5	2.1	1.9
% Ret. on Assets	6.7	7.0	9.6	9.9	6.5	NA	NA	NA	NA	NA
% Ret. on Equity	14.5	13.5	16.7	14.5	10.2	NA	NA	NA	NA	NA

Data as orig reptd.; bef. results of disc opers/spec. items. Per share data adj. for stk. divs. Bold denotes diluted EPS (FASB 128)-prior periods restated. E-Estimated. NA-Not Available. NM-Not Meaningful. NR-Not Ranked.

Office—2550 East 25th St., Los Angeles, CA 90058. **Tel**—(323) 582-2272. **Website**—http://www.rsac.com**Chrmn**—J. D. Crider. **Pres & CEO**—D. H. Hannah. **EVP & COO**—G. J. Mollins. **VP-CFO**—Karla R. McDowell. **Secy**—Y. M. Schiotis. **Investor Contact**—David H. Hannah (323 582-2272) **Dirs**—J. D. Crider, T. W. Gimbel, D. H. Hannah, D. M. Hayes, R. Henigson, K. H. Loring, G. J. Mollins, W. I. Rumer, L. A. Waite. **Transfer Agent & Registrar**—First Chicago Trust Co. of New York, Jersey City, NJ. **Incorporated**—in California in 1939. **Empl**— 3,700. **S&P Analyst:** C.C.P.

STANDARD &POOR'S
STOCK REPORTS

Remedy Corp.

NASDAQ Symbol **RMDY**

In S&P SmallCap 600

09-OCT-99

Industry: Computer (Software & Services)

Summary: RMDY provides adaptable enterprise applications and solution deployments for service management, customer relationship management, and employee workplace automation.

Quantitative Evaluations

Outlook
(1 Lowest—5 Highest)
• **2**
Fair Value
• **29⅝**
Risk
• **High**
Earn./Div. Rank
• **NR**

Technical Eval.
• **Bullish** since 9/99
Rel. Strength Rank
(1 Lowest—99 Highest)
• **79**
Insider Activity
• **NA**

Recent Price • 26½
52 Wk Range • 29⅝-8⅝
Yield • Nil
12-Mo. P/E • 37.9

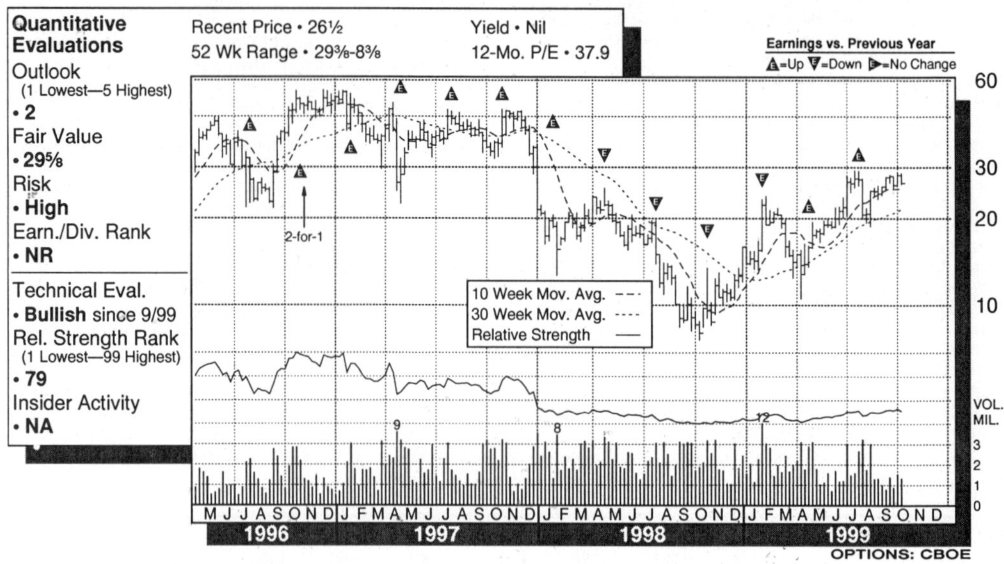

Business Profile - 27-SEP-99

Remedy said that in September 1999 it purchased privately held Fortress Technologies, Inc., the leading consulting firm focused on asset management. Using Fortress' methodology, RMDY consultants and partners will now offer a complete set of lifecycle services to analyze customers' IT (information technology) management infrastructure and identify opportunities that improve overall IT operations. RMDY said that excluding goodwill, it anticipated no material one-time charges and no dilution to 1999 share earnings. Separately, in July 1999, RMDY agreed to purchase PipestreamTechnologies, Inc., a privately held provider of modular, customer relationship management software, including sales force automation applications, for about $5 million. RMDY expected no material one-time charges.

Operational Review - 27-SEP-99

Total revenues for the first half of 1999 advanced 42%, year to year, reflecting revenue gains of 33% for products (benefiting from a growing acceptance of RMDY's software products in both U.S. and international markets) and 57% for maintenance & service (due to renewal of maintenance contracts and increased licensing activity). Margins were well maintained, and after a 21% drop in interest & other income (net), and taxes at 33.0%, versus 36.0%, net income was up 31%, to $9.4 million ($0.31 a share), from $7.2 million ($0.24).

Stock Performance - 08-OCT-99

In the past 30 trading days, RMDY's shares have increased 9%, compared to a 0.91% fall in the S&P 500. Average trading volume for the past five days was 262,720 shares, compared with the 40-day moving average of 240,544 shares.

Key Stock Statistics

Dividend Rate/Share	Nil	Shareholders	135
Shs. outstg. (M)	29.0	Market cap. (B)	$0.767
Avg. daily vol. (M)	0.253	Inst. holdings	57%
Tang. Bk. Value/Share	5.56		
Beta	NA		

Value of $10,000 invested 5 years ago: NA

Fiscal Year Ending Dec. 31

	1999	1998	1997	1996	1995	1994
Revenues (Million $)						
1Q	42.40	30.60	23.30	13.00	6.36	—
2Q	53.04	36.61	30.00	17.01	8.40	—
3Q	—	40.12	37.07	21.01	10.22	—
4Q	—	50.09	38.82	29.61	15.13	—
Yr.	—	157.4	129.2	80.64	40.12	19.75
Earnings Per Share ($)						
1Q	**0.11**	**0.08**	**0.16**	**0.08**	0.03	—
2Q	**0.21**	**0.16**	**0.20**	**0.11**	0.06	—
3Q	—	**0.21**	**0.26**	**0.15**	0.07	—
4Q	—	**0.19**	**0.27**	**0.22**	0.10	—
Yr.	—	**0.63**	**0.89**	**0.56**	**0.27**	0.14

Next earnings report expected: late October

Dividend Data

No cash dividends have been paid.

Business Summary - 27-SEP-99

Initially, Remedy Corp.'s sales and marketing strategy was to gain a significant number of Information Technology (IT) and help desk sites before broadening the product offering. With over 6,800 customer sites as of year-end 1998, Remedy has begun to broaden its product offerings and is seeking to leverage its existing customers to sell additional solutions aimed at further increasing its customers' employee productivity.

Remedy develops, markets, and supports highly adaptable, client/server applications software products and solutions that simplify employee-intensive business processes. Unlike traditional enterprise applications, the company's applications are designed to deploy in weeks, not years.

The company believes that its applications adapt quickly to the needs and changes in the customers' business, instead of requiring the customer and solutions to adapt to the software. The company also believes that these applications help organizations establish a market advantage by reacting to opportunities faster than their competitors. Remedy offers adaptable applications for IT service management, customer relationship management, and employee workplace automation.

Under the Core Product Unit, the primary product is the AR System, a foundation for automating complex business processes throughout the enterprise. Built for adaptability in a continuously changing business environment, the AR System is designed to allow for rapid prototyping and affordable applications. The Remedy Service Level Agreements (SLA) application helps managers track service quality and market their success. By automating negotiated service commitments, SLA provides for proactive alerting, notification and measurement.

The Remedy Help Desk application is a client server application used for tracking and resolving IT support requests and problems. Using simple point-and-click methods, customers adapt the application's workflow and tracking capability to the unique information, process and integration requirements of their department or enterprise.

The Customer Relationship Management (CRM) unit is focused on developing, marketing and supporting client server applications for acquisition and retention of long-term profitable customers. The company purchased BayStone Software in October 1998 to form the cornerstone of the CRM strategic marketing unit. Remedy now offers what it believes are comprehensive applications for CRM that are designed for fast deployment and easy scalability from small and mid-size companies to large enterprise use.

The Employee Workplace Automation (EWA)unit is focused on developing, marketing and supporting web-based applications that automate common tasks and approval processes to improve employee productivity by reducing workflow cycles and mundane, paper-based tasks.

Per Share Data ($) (Year Ended Dec. 31)	1998	1997	1996	1995	1994	1993	1992	1991	1990	1989
Tangible Bk. Val.	5.46	5.17	3.43	2.46	1.88	NA	NA	NA	NA	NA
Cash Flow	0.85	1.00	0.62	0.31	0.48	NA	NA	NA	NA	NA
Earnings	0.63	0.89	0.56	0.27	0.14	0.09	NA	NA	NA	NA
Dividends	Nil	Nil	Nil	Nil	NA	NA	NA	NA	NA	NA
Payout Ratio	Nil	Nil	Nil	Nil	NA	NA	NA	NA	NA	NA
Prices - High	25½	55½	55¾	23¾	NA	NA	NA	NA	NA	NA
- Low	7½	20⅜	15½	7⅝	NA	NA	NA	NA	NA	NA
P/E Ratio - High	40	62	99	88	NA	NA	NA	NA	NA	NA
- Low	12	23	27	28	NA	NA	NA	NA	NA	NA
Income Statement Analysis (Million $)										
Revs.	157	129	80.6	40.1	19.8	8.5	NA	NA	NA	NA
Oper. Inc.	33.4	41.8	25.5	11.2	5.5	NA	NA	NA	NA	NA
Depr.	6.6	3.3	1.8	1.0	0.5	NA	NA	NA	NA	NA
Int. Exp.	Nil	0.1	0.1	Nil	0.0	NA	NA	NA	NA	NA
Pretax Inc.	29.7	42.6	26.3	11.6	5.0	NA	NA	NA	NA	NA
Eff. Tax Rate	36%	36%	36%	35%	39%	NA	NA	NA	NA	NA
Net Inc.	19.0	27.3	16.8	7.6	3.1	1.7	NA	NA	NA	NA
Balance Sheet & Other Fin. Data (Million $)										
Cash	59.0	70.6	39.8	31.5	3.0	NA	NA	NA	NA	NA
Curr. Assets	189	171	114	72.0	10.3	NA	NA	NA	NA	NA
Total Assets	214	182	119	74.7	12.0	4.5	NA	NA	NA	NA
Curr. Liab.	52.7	33.0	26.4	11.3	5.9	NA	NA	NA	NA	NA
LT Debt	0.1	0.5	0.5	0.3	0.2	Nil	NA	NA	NA	NA
Common Eqty.	161	148	92.5	63.1	5.9	2.6	NA	NA	NA	NA
Total Cap.	161	149	93.0	63.4	6.1	2.6	NA	NA	NA	NA
Cap. Exp.	8.3	8.2	3.9	1.8	1.3	NA	NA	NA	NA	NA
Cash Flow	25.5	30.6	18.6	8.6	3.6	NA	NA	NA	NA	NA
Curr. Ratio	3.6	5.2	4.3	6.4	1.7	NA	NA	NA	NA	NA
% LT Debt of Cap.	0.1	0.0	0.0	0.0	3.6	NA	NA	NA	NA	NA
% Net Inc.of Revs.	12.1	21.1	20.9	18.9	15.5	20.0	NA	NA	NA	NA
% Ret. on Assets	9.6	18.1	17.3	17.5	37.1	NA	NA	NA	NA	NA
% Ret. on Equity	12.3	22.7	21.6	22.0	72.0	NA	NA	NA	NA	NA

Data as orig reptd.; bef. results of disc opers/spec. items. Per share data adj. for stk. divs. Bold denotes diluted EPS (FASB 128)-prior periods restated. E-Estimated. NA-Not Available. NM-Not Meaningful. NR-Not Ranked.

Office—1505 Salado Dr., Mountain View, CA 94043. **Registrar & Transfer Agent**—Harris Trust Co. of California, Los Angeles.**Tel**—(650) 903-5200. **Website**—http://www.remedy.com **Chrmn & CEO**—L. L. Garlick. **VP-Fin & CFO**—R. J. Fior. **Dirs**—L. L. Garlick, H. C. Jones, Jr., D. A. Mahler, J. F. Shoch, J. R. Swartz. **Transfer Agent & Registrar**—Harris Trust Co. of California, Los Angeles. **Incorporated**—in Delaware in 1990. **Empl**— 814. **S&P Analyst:** NJD.

STANDARD &POOR'S
STOCK REPORTS

Remington Oil & Gas Corp.

NASDAQ Symbol **ROIL**

In S&P SmallCap 600

09-OCT-99

Industry: Oil & Gas (Exploration & Production)

Summary: This oil and gas exploration and production company focuses on the offshore Gulf of Mexico and onshore Gulf Coast areas.

Quantitative Evaluations

Outlook (1 Lowest—5 Highest) • 1−

Fair Value • 4½

Risk • NA

Earn./Div. Rank • NR

Technical Eval. • NA

Rel. Strength Rank (1 Lowest—99 Highest) • 78

Insider Activity • NA

Recent Price • 5½ | Yield • Nil

52 Wk Range • 6⅛-2 | 12-Mo. P/E • 12.3

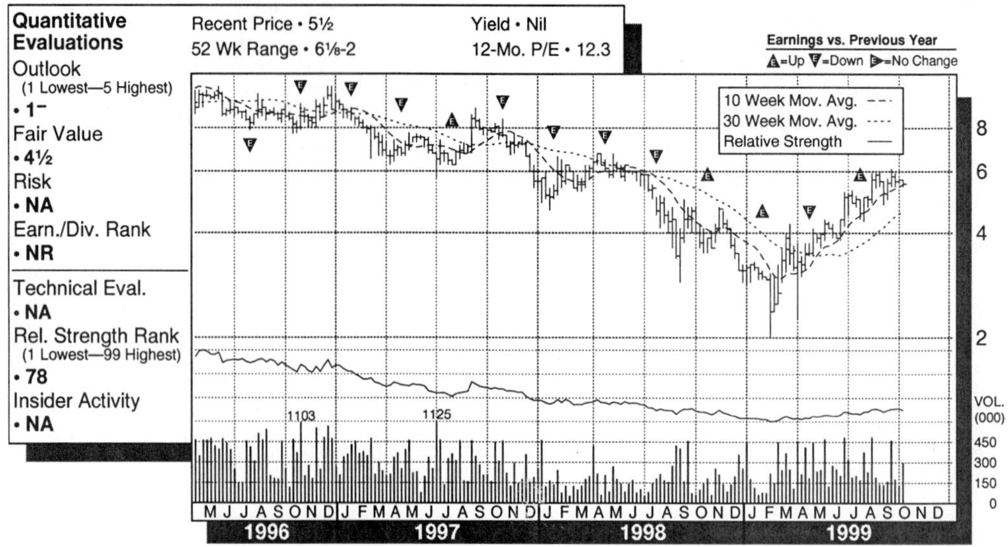

Business Profile - 13-AUG-99

In December 1998, S-Sixteen, formerly controlled by J.R. Simplot, merged into Remington Oil and Gas, and ROIL's two classes of voting and nonvoting stock were recapitalized into one single voting class. As a result of the transaction, Mr. Simplot became the company's largest shareholder, with 27% of the outstanding shares, and ROIL acquired an undivided interest in an oil pipeline that transports its oil production. An August 1998 court ruling against ROIL resulted in an $18 million judgment for Phillips Petroleum Co.; both companies have appealed. In July 1998, ROIL terminated a gas sales contract with Texas Eastern Transmission Co. (TETCO) under which TETCO was required to purchase gas from the company at fixed prices until July 2002; as a result, ROIL received approximately $50 million. Proceeds were used to reduce debt and acquire properties.

Operational Review - 13-AUG-99

Revenues in the six months ended June 30, 1999, fell 29%, year to year, due to the mid-1998 termination of a gas sales contract. Total costs and expenses decreased 9.1%, as lower operating costs and depreciation, depletion and amortization charges outweighed higher exploration, legal and interest and financing expenses. After taxes and minority interest in the 1999 period only, the net loss widened to $7.8 million ($0.36 a share), from $3.2 million ($0.15).

Stock Performance - 08-OCT-99

In the past 30 trading days, ROIL's shares have declined 2%, compared to a 0.91% fall in the S&P 500. Average trading volume for the past five days was 58,880 shares, compared with the 40-day moving average of 45,103 shares.

Key Stock Statistics

Dividend Rate/Share	Nil	Shareholders	1,370
Shs. outstg. (M)	21.3	Market cap. (B)	$0.118
Avg. daily vol. (M)	0.058	Inst. holdings	25%
Tang. Bk. Value/Share	2.45		
Beta	0.46		

Value of $10,000 invested 5 years ago: $ 4,380

Fiscal Year Ending Dec. 31

	1999	1998	1997	1996	1995	1994
Revenues (Million $)						
1Q	7.45	12.51	17.23	19.07	14.51	13.10
2Q	10.22	12.06	16.97	17.86	12.56	17.30
3Q	—	56.53	13.48	15.82	14.91	16.03
4Q	—	6.59	13.38	17.45	17.51	12.85
Yr.	—	87.69	61.05	70.21	59.49	59.24
Earnings Per Share ($)						
1Q	**-0.31**	**-0.10**	0.09	0.12	0.04	0.10
2Q	**-0.05**	**-0.06**	-0.02	-0.17	0.04	0.16
3Q	—	**1.06**	-0.37	-0.15	0.09	0.16
4Q	—	**-0.24**	**-1.01**	-0.17	0.09	0.02
Yr.	—	**0.66**	**-1.31**	**-0.37**	**0.26**	0.44

Next earnings report expected: mid November

Dividend Data

No cash dividends have been paid since 1991.

Remington Oil & Gas Corporation

Business Summary - 13-AUG-99

Remington Oil & Gas is a Dallas-based independent oil and gas exploration and production company. It focuses on the offshore shelf, onshore Texas and the Mississippi Salt Basin. At December 31, 1998, proved reserves totaled 5,519 MBbls of oil and 52.7 Bcf of natural gas, or 85.8 Bcf of natural gas equivalent (61% gas, 39% oil). This compares with 4,451 MBbls of oil and 36.5 Bcf of natural gas at the end of 1997, or 63.2 Bcfe (57% gas, 43% oil). The standardized measure of discounted future net cash flows in 1998 and 1997 was $63.5 million and $93.8 million, respectively.

Production in 1998 amounted to 1,245 MBbls of oil and 6,387 MMcf of natural gas; 1997 production totaled 1,197 MBbls of oil and 7,116 MMcf of gas. The average sales price in 1998 and 1997 was $10.99 and $17.79 per bbl. of oil, respectively, and $3.22 and $5.06 per Mcf of gas. During 1998 and 1997 operating costs per Mcfe were $0.87 and $1.06, respectively; finding and development costs were $1.05 and $2.28 per Mcfe; and average G&A costs per Mcfe were $0.39 and $0.62. Reserve replacement increased from 129% in 1997 to 263% in 1998.

At December 31, 1998, the company had interests in 74 gross (23.36 net) producing oil wells and 121 (20.01) producing gas wells. During 1998, ROIL drilled 19 gross (5.75 net) exploratory wells, of which 12 (3.62) were productive and seven (2.13) were dry holes. The company also drilled three gross (1.12 net) development wells, of which two (0.82) were productive and one (0.30) were dry holes.

In July 1998, ROIL terminated a gas sales contract with Texas Eastern Transmission Co. (TETCO) under which TETCO was to purchase gas from the company at fixed prices until July 2002. As a result, ROIL received approximately $50 million, and recorded a $2.5 million impairment charge in the 1998 third quarter, related to lost future gas revenue. ROIL used the proceeds to reduce debt and acquire properties. Gas production that would have been sold under the contract will now be sold on the spot market.

In August 1998, a Louisiana court ruled against ROIL in long-standing litigation with Phillips Petroleum Co. related to net profits interest and overriding royalty arrangements. As a result of the judgment, ROIL was required to pay $10.9 million to Phillips, plus interest totaling about $7.1 million; the total amount was expensed in the third quarter. Both companies have appealed the court decision.

Per Share Data ($) (Year Ended Dec. 31)	1998	1997	1996	1995	1994	1993	1992	1991	1990	1989
Tangible Bk. Val.	2.01	2.18	3.57	3.94	3.63	3.25	3.15	2.27	2.74	0.67
Cash Flow	NA	0.07	0.73	0.98	0.97	0.59	1.11	0.29	3.31	0.25
Earnings	0.66	-1.31	-0.37	0.26	0.44	0.10	0.92	0.13	3.05	-0.12
Dividends	Nil	Nil	Nil	Nil	Nil	Nil	Nil	0.60	1.00	0.40
Payout Ratio	Nil	Nil	Nil	Nil	Nil	Nil	Nil	446%	32%	NM
Prices - High	6¾	9⅜	11⅝	11¼	14⅛	13¼	19½	6¾	4⅝	4½
- Low	2¾	4⅞	7½	7⅝	7½	8¾	5⅞	3¼	1¾	2⅛
P/E Ratio - High	10	NM	NM	43	32	NM	21	52	2	NM
- Low	4	NM	NM	29	17	NM	6	25	1	NM
Income Statement Analysis (Million $)										
Revs.	34.3	57.3	65.6	54.4	57.0	33.5	18.7	20.6	26.1	25.9
Oper. Inc.	7.3	24.7	15.6	40.5	28.1	14.7	4.3	6.6	-0.5	10.2
Depr. Depl. & Amort.	19.9	28.3	22.8	15.0	11.1	10.1	3.9	3.2	4.6	7.7
Int. Exp.	4.3	5.3	4.9	4.8	5.1	5.0	1.1	0.2	2.5	1.8
Pretax Inc.	14.4	-12.2	-9.4	7.5	14.2	2.1	-0.5	2.7	62.9	-2.5
Eff. Tax Rate	5.20%	NM	NM	28%	36%	NM	NM	Nil	Nil	Nil
Net Inc.	13.6	-26.8	-7.7	5.4	9.2	2.2	19.2	2.7	62.9	-2.5
Balance Sheet & Other Fin. Data (Million $)										
Cash	27.8	4.6	35.7	46.4	40.5	30.6	38.2	1.1	28.3	0.2
Curr. Assets	32.8	18.9	46.2	55.7	46.2	36.0	41.5	2.3	34.5	4.8
Total Assets	130	99	137	145	135	129	129	53.0	64.0	35.0
Curr. Liab.	34.1	15.9	7.2	8.4	4.5	4.5	3.9	4.3	5.7	2.9
LT Debt	33.5	38.4	55.1	55.1	55.1	56.7	57.0	Nil	Nil	15.4
Common Eqty.	59.7	44.3	74.4	82.0	75.5	67.7	65.5	46.3	55.9	13.6
Total Cap.	93.2	82.7	129	137	131	124	123	46.0	56.0	29.0
Cap. Exp.	40.2	39.1	39.8	21.3	16.6	18.9	19.1	25.9	9.7	10.6
Cash Flow	33.5	1.5	15.1	20.4	20.2	12.3	23.1	5.9	67.5	5.2
Curr. Ratio	1.0	1.2	6.4	6.7	10.4	8.0	10.5	0.5	6.0	1.7
% LT Debt of Cap.	35.9	46.4	42.6	40.3	42.2	45.6	46.6	NM	NM	53.1
% Ret. on Assets	11.9	NM	NM	3.9	6.9	1.7	21.0	4.7	126.5	NM
% Ret. on Equity	26.1	NM	NM	6.9	12.8	3.2	34.1	5.4	180.9	NM

Data as orig reptd.; bef. results of disc opers/spec. items. Per share data adj. for stk. divs. Bold denotes diluted EPS (FASB 128)-prior periods restated. E-Estimated. NA-Not Available. NM-Not Meaningful. NR-Not Ranked.

Office—8201 Preston Rd., Suite 600, Dallas, TX 75225-6211. **Tel**—(214) 210-2650. **Chrmn**—D. H. Hawk. **CEO & Pres**—J. A. Watt. **VP-Fin & Secy**—J. B. Asher. **SVP & Investor Contact**—Steve Craig (214-210-2675). **Dirs**—D. D. Box, J. E. Goble, Jr., W. E. Greenwood, D. H. Hawk, J. A. Lyle, D. A. Preng, T. W. Rollins, A. C. Shapiro, J. A. Watt. **Transfer Agent & Registrar**—American Stock Transfer & Trust Co., NYC. **Incorporated**—in Delaware in 1991. **Empl**— 20. **S&P Analyst:** Ephraim Juskowicz

STANDARD
&POOR'S
STOCK REPORTS

Renal Care Group

NASDAQ Symbol **RCGI**

In S&P SmallCap 600

09-OCT-99

Industry:
Health Care (Specialized Services)

Summary: This nephrology services company provides care to patients with kidney disease, including patients suffering from chronic kidney failure.

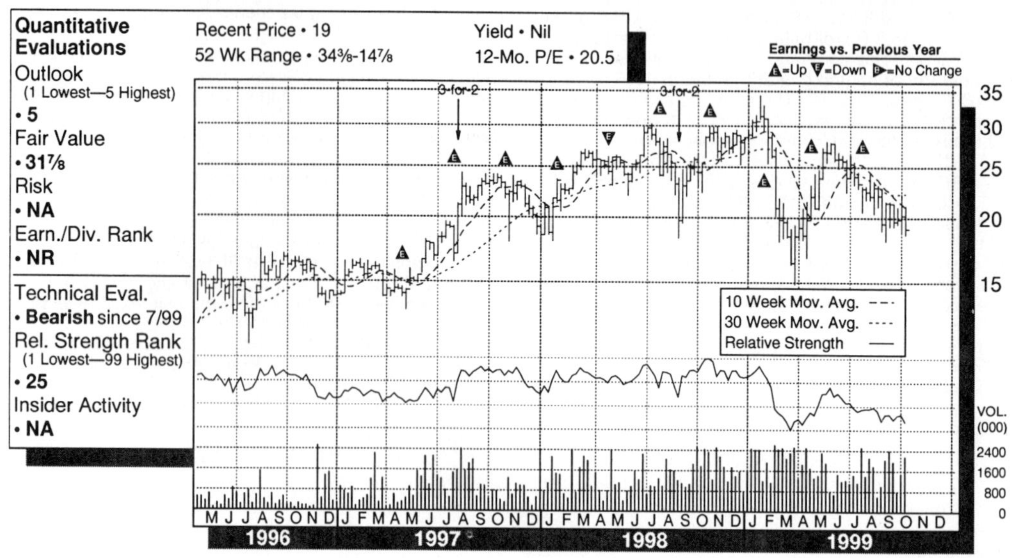

Business Profile - 25-JUN-99

Thus far in 1999, Renal Care has continued its strategy of growth through acquisitions. In January 1999, the company acquired, in exchange for 3,073,000 common shares, Dialysis Centers of America, a Chicago-based operator of 12 dialysis centers. Dialysis Centers serves about 1,700 patients, and is expected to add over $55 million to RCGI's 1999 revenues. Since the beginning of 1999, the company has also completed acquisitions in Wisconsin and Alaska, adding 350 patients to its network. As of May 3, 1999, Renal Care Group (RCGI) was providing dialysis and ancillary services to about 13,400 patients through 176 owned and managed outpatient dialysis centers in 22 states.

Operational Review - 25-JUN-99

Net revenues in the three months ended March 31, 1999, rose 32%, year to year (as restated), driven by an increase in the number of treatments, as well as a jump in average revenue per treatment. Margins widened on the increase in revenues; operating income surged 57%. Following merger costs of $4.3 million, pretax income advanced 44%. After minority interest, and taxes at 45.0%, versus 38.2%, net income advanced 22%, to $8,107,000 ($0.17 a share, based on 3.0% more shares), from $6,662,000 ($0.15).

Stock Performance - 08-OCT-99

In the past 30 trading days, RCGI's shares have declined 2%, compared to a 0.91% fall in the S&P 500. Average trading volume for the past five days was 430,020 shares, compared with the 40-day moving average of 315,310 shares.

Key Stock Statistics

Dividend Rate/Share	Nil	Shareholders	3,593
Shs. outstg. (M)	44.5	Market cap. (B)	$0.848
Avg. daily vol. (M)	0.316	Inst. holdings	71%
Tang. Bk. Value/Share	1.30		
Beta	NA		

Value of $10,000 invested 5 years ago: NA

Fiscal Year Ending Dec. 31

	1999	1998	1997	1996	1995	1994
Revenues (Million $)						
1Q	120.9	80.46	46.11	24.53	—	—
2Q	128.5	89.51	51.67	31.83	—	—
3Q	—	96.81	54.04	34.63	—	—
4Q	—	102.6	62.20	38.53	—	—
Yr.	—	369.4	214.0	129.5	42.97	41.63
Earnings Per Share ($)						
1Q	**0.17**	**0.17**	0.17	0.11	—	—
2Q	**0.28**	**0.19**	0.13	0.09	—	—
3Q	—	**0.22**	0.15	0.05	—	—
4Q	—	**0.24**	**0.16**	0.11	—	—
Yr.	—	**0.83**	**0.56**	0.37	—	—

Next earnings report expected: early November

Dividend Data

Amount ($)	Date Decl.	Ex-Div. Date	Stock of Record	Payment Date

Renal Care Group, Inc.

Business Summary - 25-JUN-99

This nephrology services company has grown substantially since it began operations in February 1996 with an aggregate of 41 dialysis centers serving about 2,663 patients in eight states. As of May 3, 1999, Renal Care Group (RCGI) was providing dialysis and ancillary services to about 13,400 patients through 176 owned and managed outpatient dialysis centers in 22 states, in addition to providing acute dialysis services in 103 hospitals.

RCGI is a provider of nephrology services, which is the specialized practice of medicine dedicated to providing care to patients with end-stage renal disease (ESRD) and other kidney-specific ailments. An essential part of the nephrologist's practice is the dialysis facility, where ESRD patients receive their dialysis treatments three times per week in a technologically advanced outpatient setting. ESRD is the state of advanced renal impairment that is irreversible and imminently lethal. Patients with ESRD eventually require dialysis or kidney transplantation to sustain life. According to industry data, the number of patients receiving chronic dialysis services in the U.S. has grown from 66,000 patients in 1982, to about 216,000 in 1996.

In addition to its dialysis business, the company offers practice management and administrative services to physician practices. At the end of 1998, RCGI served 66 physicians, including 63 of the 190 nephrologists affiliated with the company's dialysis centers. Renal Care also operates a business providing wound care and diabetic services. Because of the chronic nature of ESRD and the fact that many ESRD patients are also diabetic, many of the company's patients also require wound care services.

RCGI believes that an integrated network of nephrologist and dialysis centers, combined with its clinical expertise, management experience and access to capital, will provide significant advantages to patients and third-party payors by improving the quality of care while reducing the overall costs associated with treating patients with all forms of kidney disease, including those with ESRD.

In 1998, Medicare accounted for 60% of RCGI's net patient revenues, Medicaid for 5%, commercial and other payors 29%, and hospital inpatient dialysis services 6%.

The dialysis industry is highly fragmented and very competitive. According to industry experts, there were more than 3,000 dialysis centers in the U.S. at the end of 1996. The company believes that approximately 50% were owned by multi-center dialysis companies, 25% were owned by independent physicians and 25% were affiliated with hospitals.

Per Share Data ($) (Year Ended Dec. 31)	1998	1997	1996	1995	1994	1993	1992	1991	1990	1989
Tangible Bk. Val.	1.32	1.52	2.49	0.69	NA	NA	NA	NA	NA	NA
Cash Flow	1.26	0.81	0.53	NA	NA	NA	NA	NA	NA	NA
Earnings	0.83	0.56	0.37	NA	NA	NA	NA	NA	NA	NA
Dividends	Nil	Nil	Nil	NA	NA	NA	NA	NA	NA	NA
Payout Ratio	Nil	Nil	Nil	NA	NA	NA	NA	NA	NA	NA
Prices - High	30 3/8	24 3/8	17 3/8	NA	NA	NA	NA	NA	NA	NA
- Low	18	13 1/4	8	NA	NA	NA	NA	NA	NA	NA
P/E Ratio - High	37	43	31	NA	NA	NA	NA	NA	NA	NA
- Low	22	24	14	NA	NA	NA	NA	NA	NA	NA

Income Statement Analysis (Million $)	1998	1997	1996	1995	1994	1993	1992	1991	1990	1989
Revs.	369	214	130	43.0	41.6	18.1	8.7	NA	NA	NA
Oper. Inc.	81.8	41.5	23.6	5.0	6.5	0.9	0.6	NA	NA	NA
Depr.	18.4	9.0	4.5	1.6	1.5	0.6	0.1	NA	NA	NA
Int. Exp.	3.1	-0.6	NM	0.5	0.4	0.1	0.0	NA	NA	NA
Pretax Inc.	59.3	32.7	17.7	3.0	4.6	0.3	0.5	NA	NA	NA
Eff. Tax Rate	35%	36%	39%	Nil	Nil	50%	9.70%	NA	NA	NA
Net Inc.	35.2	20.0	10.7	3.0	4.6	0.1	0.4	NA	NA	NA

Balance Sheet & Other Fin. Data (Million $)	1998	1997	1996	1995	1994	1993	1992	1991	1990	1989
Cash	19.9	9.1	53.4	1.3	NA	NA	NA	NA	NA	NA
Curr. Assets	110	65.8	86.5	11.1	NA	NA	NA	NA	NA	NA
Total Assets	377	248	132	20.8	17.3	14.4	2.6	NA	NA	NA
Curr. Liab.	56.7	41.3	37.0	12.5	NA	NA	NA	NA	NA	NA
LT Debt	62.6	15.5	Nil	3.7	NA	NA	NA	NA	NA	NA
Common Eqty.	229	175	93.3	4.6	5.9	4.9	1.5	NA	NA	NA
Total Cap.	320	207	94.8	8.2	NA	NA	NA	NA	NA	NA
Cap. Exp.	28.8	27.4	11.4	4.8	2.4	NA	NA	NA	NA	NA
Cash Flow	53.6	29.0	15.3	4.6	6.1	0.7	0.6	NA	NA	NA
Curr. Ratio	1.9	1.6	2.3	0.9	NA	NA	NA	NA	NA	NA
% LT Debt of Cap.	19.6	7.5	Nil	44.5	NA	NA	NA	NA	NA	NA
% Net Inc.of Revs.	9.5	9.3	8.3	6.9	11.1	0.7	4.7	NA	NA	NA
% Ret. on Assets	11.3	10.5	14.1	15.6	29.3	1.5	NA	NA	NA	NA
% Ret. on Equity	17.4	14.9	22.0	56.7	85.7	4.1	NA	NA	NA	NA

Data as orig reptd.; bef. results of disc opers/spec. items. Per share data adj. for stk. divs. Bold denotes diluted EPS (FASB 128)-prior periods restated. E-Estimated. NA-Not Available. NM-Not Meaningful. NR-Not Ranked.

Office—2100 West End Ave., Suite 800, Nashville, TN 37203. **Tel**—(615) 345-5500. **Chrmn, Pres & CEO**—S. A. Brooks Jr. **EVP, CFO, Secy & Treas**—R. Hinds. **Dirs**—J. D. Bower, S. A. Brooks Jr., J. C. Hutts, H. R. Jacobson, K. Johnson, T. A. Lowrey, S. D. McMurray, T. Meredith. **Transfer Agent & Registrar**—First Union National Bank of North Carolina, Charlotte. **Incorporated**—in Delaware in 1995. **Empl**— 3,312. **S&P Analyst:** Stephen J. Tekirian

STANDARD
&POOR'S
STOCK REPORTS

Republic Group

NYSE Symbol **RGC**

In S&P SmallCap 600

09-OCT-99 **Industry:** Paper & Forest Products

Summary: Republic Group (formerly Republic Gypsum) makes paperboard and gypsum wallboard for distribution throughout the U.S.

Quantitative Evaluations
Outlook
(1 Lowest—5 Highest)
• **NA**
Fair Value
• **NA**
Risk
• **Average**
Earn./Div. Rank
• **B**

Technical Eval.
• **Bearish** since 8/99
Rel. Strength Rank
(1 Lowest—99 Highest)
• **18**
Insider Activity
• **NA**

Recent Price • 13¾
52 Wk Range • 21¼-12⅞
Yield • 2.6%
12-Mo. P/E • 10.7

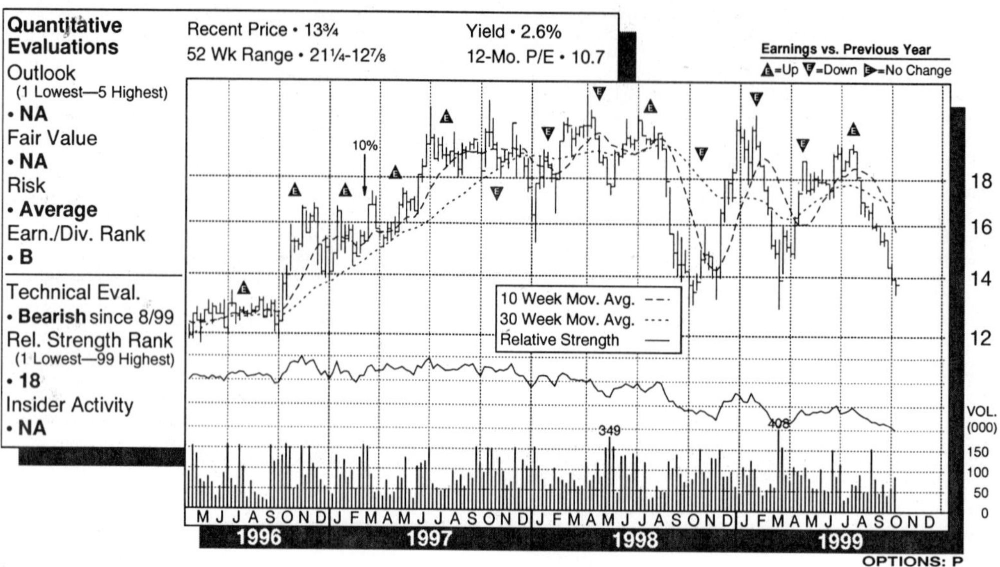

Business Profile - 15-JUL-99

Republic Group believes that various initiatives that it has implemented--including the construction of a recycled paperboard mill in Lawton, OK., and the continued expansion and incremental upgrading of its facilities--will significantly increase its overall production capabilities and enhance its competitive position in both recycled paperboard and gypsum wallboard. In April 1999, RGC said that demand for gypsum wallboard in the U.S. continued to outpace supply. A selling price increase was recently implemented; and a new record for gypsum wallboard shipments was achieved a month earlier at the Duke plant, reflecting improving production capabilities from new lines. Construction at the Lawton mill was said to be continuing on schedule.

Operational Review - 15-JUL-99

Net sales for the first nine months of FY 99 (Jun.) rose only nominally, year to year. Gypsum wallboard selling prices increased 11% and gypsum wallboard shipments declined 7%. The lower shipments and a 25% increase in gypsum wallboard per unit costs--attributed to production constraints and inefficiencies related to the start-up and longer than anticipated commissioning of newly-configured production lines--led to a drop in operating profit of 15%. After other expenses (net), versus other income (net), and taxes at 38.0% in both periods, net income fell 25%, to $9.5 million ($0.80 a share), from $12.5 million ($1.06)

Stock Performance - 08-OCT-99

In the past 30 trading days, RGC's shares have declined 14%, compared to a 0.91% fall in the S&P 500. Average trading volume for the past five days was 17,080 shares, compared with the 40-day moving average of 15,700 shares.

Key Stock Statistics

Dividend Rate/Share	0.36	Shareholders	759
Shs. outstg. (M)	11.8	Market cap. (B)	$0.162
Avg. daily vol. (M)	0.012	Inst. holdings	29%
Tang. Bk. Value/Share	7.85		
Beta	1.24		

Value of $10,000 invested 5 years ago: $ 15,865

Fiscal Year Ending Jun. 30

	1999	1998	1997	1996	1995	1994
Revenues (Million $)						
1Q	33.19	31.89	29.00	32.27	20.85	14.48
2Q	32.25	32.43	30.97	29.73	22.35	14.82
3Q	30.89	31.91	30.73	29.19	26.53	16.80
4Q	41.62	32.05	33.00	26.72	26.68	17.10
Yr.	137.9	128.3	123.7	117.9	96.41	63.20
Earnings Per Share ($)						
1Q	**0.28**	0.37	0.43	0.27	0.23	0.13
2Q	**0.32**	**0.34**	0.42	0.35	0.25	0.13
3Q	**0.20**	**0.36**	0.40	0.35	0.27	0.23
4Q	**0.49**	**0.45**	0.43	0.29	0.25	0.18
Yr.	**1.29**	**1.51**	**1.67**	1.27	1.00	0.66

Next earnings report expected: mid October

Dividend Data (Dividends have been paid since 1992.)

Amount ($)	Date Decl.	Ex-Div. Date	Stock of Record	Payment Date
0.090	Oct. 22	Nov. 25	Nov. 30	Dec. 15 '98
0.090	Jan. 26	Feb. 24	Feb. 26	Mar. 15 '99
0.090	Apr. 20	May. 26	May. 28	Jun. 15 '99
0.090	Aug. 03	Aug. 27	Aug. 31	Sep. 15 '99

A Division of The McGraw-Hill Companies

Republic Group Incorporated

Business Summary - 15-JUL-99

Founded in 1961, Republic Group Inc. is an integrated manufacturer and distributor of recycled paperboard and gypsum wallboard. RGC believes it is one of the leading producers of certain grades of recycled paperboard sold to manufacturers of consumer and industrial paperboard products such as tubes, cans, cores, spools, drums, partitions, puzzles and games as well as one of the leading suppliers of gypsum-grade recycled paperboard to independent gypsum wallboard producers. In addition, RGC sells reclaimed paper fiber for use in its recycled paperboard business as well as for sale to third parties. RGC sells its products to customers located in 43 states. In addition to its Duke, OK, gypsum wallboard plant, RGC has recycled paperboard mills in Commerce City, CO, Hutchinson, KS, and Halltown, WV, and paper fiber recycling centers in Denver, CO, Topeka, KS, and Kansas City, MO. Before intercompany eliminations, RGC's recycled paperboard (which includes reclaimed paper fiber) and gypsum wallboard businesses accounted for about 57% and 43%, respectively, of total net sales during FY 98 (Jun.).

Recently, RGC has undertaken a number of strategic initiatives designed to increase its production capabilities. RGC intends to use the proceeds from the sale of $100,000,000 of 9.50% notes, together with proceeds from borrowings under a new $85,000,000 credit facility, to construct a new recycled paperboard mill in Lawton, OK. RGC also intends to use the Lawton mill primarily for the production of gypsum-grade recycled paperboard with weight and surface characteristics superior to that currently available in the U.S. RGC believes that the operation of the Lawton mill will position the company as the largest third-party supplier of gypsum-grade recycled paperboard in the U.S. The Lawton mill is expected to have a productive capacity of about 220,000 tons per annum, which will roughly double RGC's recycled paperboard capacity. The company plans to sell about 50% of the Lawton mill's output pursuant to a recently executed long-term supply agreement with James Hardie Gypsum, Inc. and to use about 25% of the output to source its own gypsum wallboard operations. RGC estimates that the Lawton mill will begin production during the first quarter of calendar year 2000.

RGC has also completed the second phase of a two-phase expansion of the Duke plant that increased its capacity from 570 million to 1.2 billion square feet per year. In addition, RGC has recently completed an expansion of the capacity of the Commerce City mill and the Hutchinson mill by about 25% in the aggregate. The company believes that these initiatives, together with the construction of the Lawton mill and the continued expansion and incremental upgrading of its facilities, will significantly increase its overall production capabilities as well as enhance its competitive position in both the recycled paperboard and gypsum wallboard business.

Per Share Data ($) (Year Ended Jun. 30)	1999	1998	1997	1996	1995	1994	1993	1992	1991	1990
Tangible Bk. Val.	NA	7.85	6.66	5.37	4.35	3.55	3.04	2.90	0.14	2.71
Cash Flow	NA	2.16	2.27	1.80	1.31	0.90	0.48	0.35	0.17	0.45
Earnings	1.29	1.51	1.67	1.27	1.00	0.66	0.28	0.16	-0.04	0.04
Dividends	0.27	0.36	0.34	0.26	0.21	0.15	0.19	0.02	Nil	0.13
Payout Ratio	28%	24%	21%	20%	21%	23%	68%	11%	NM	376%
Prices - High	21 1/4	22 3/8	22	16 7/8	12 7/8	7	10 1/8	6 3/8	4 3/4	4 1/2
- Low	12 7/8	13	14 1/8	11 1/2	8 1/2	7 3/4	5 5/8	3 7/8	2 3/16	2 1/16
P/E Ratio - High	16	15	13	13	13	11	26	39	NM	NM
- Low	10	9	8	9	9	12	20	24	NM	NM
Income Statement Analysis (Million $)										
Revs.	NA	128	124	118	96.4	63.2	49.2	42.1	41.4	47.3
Oper. Inc.	NA	34.7	38.9	31.6	22.6	14.8	6.6	4.3	1.1	4.6
Depr.	NA	7.7	7.1	6.2	3.6	2.8	2.4	2.2	2.4	4.8
Int. Exp.	NA	Nil	1.5	1.9	0.0	0.0	0.0	Nil	0.5	0.8
Pretax Inc.	NA	28.2	31.1	24.0	19.2	12.4	4.5	2.9	-0.8	-0.1
Eff. Tax Rate	NA	37%	37%	38%	39%	38%	27%	33%	NM	NM
Net Inc.	NA	17.8	19.7	14.9	11.7	7.7	3.2	1.9	-0.4	0.4
Balance Sheet & Other Fin. Data (Million $)										
Cash	NA	1.1	2.1	14.6	6.1	1.4	5.6	6.1	1.3	8.1
Curr. Assets	NA	26.3	25.1	35.0	27.0	14.6	15.8	15.4	11.8	21.2
Total Assets	NA	125	100	106	95.4	53.0	44.1	41.3	38.9	47.9
Curr. Liab.	NA	15.3	12.1	12.8	13.5	7.3	5.2	4.5	4.6	6.1
LT Debt	NA	6.0	Nil	21.4	24.8	Nil	Nil	Nil	Nil	6.1
Common Eqty.	NA	92.2	77.9	62.7	50.6	41.2	35.1	33.6	31.8	31.6
Total Cap.	NA	110	87.7	92.7	81.2	44.9	38.3	36.5	34.4	41.9
Cap. Exp.	NA	31.2	11.6	9.1	8.8	13.3	5.6	2.7	2.3	4.2
Cash Flow	NA	25.5	26.8	21.1	15.3	10.5	5.6	4.1	2.0	5.2
Curr. Ratio	NA	1.7	2.1	2.8	2.0	2.0	3.0	3.4	2.6	3.5
% LT Debt of Cap.	NA	5.4	Nil	23.2	30.6	Nil	Nil	Nil	Nil	14.5
% Net Inc.of Revs.	NA	13.9	13.7	12.7	12.2	12.2	6.6	4.6	NM	0.9
% Ret. on Assets	NA	15.9	19.1	14.8	15.7	15.9	7.6	4.9	NM	0.8
% Ret. on Equity	NA	20.9	28.0	26.4	25.5	20.3	9.4	6.0	NM	1.3

Data as orig reptd.; bef. results of disc opers/spec. items. Per share data adj. for stk. divs. Bold denotes diluted EPS (FASB 128)-prior periods restated. E-Estimated. NA-Not Available. NM-Not Meaningful. NR-Not Ranked.

Office—811 East 30th Ave. (P.O. Box 1307, Hutchinson, KS 67504-1307), Hutchinson, KS 67502-4341.**Tel**—(316) 727-2700. **Website**—http://www.republic-group.com **Chrmn, Pres & CEO**—P. Simpson. **EVP-CFO**—D. R. Ramsey. **VP-Treas, Secy & Investor Contact**—Janey L. Rife. **Dirs**—C. W. Claypool, B. A. Nelson, T. Rain, G. L. Ray, R. F. Sexton, P. Simpson, L. L. Wallace, D. B. Yarbrough. **Transfer Agent & Registrar**—UMB Bank NA, Kansas City, MO**Incorporated**—in Delaware in 1961. **Empl**— 936. **S&P Analyst:** N.J.D.

STANDARD & POOR'S
STOCK REPORTS

Respironics, Inc.

NASDAQ Symbol **RESP**

In S&P SmallCap 600

09-OCT-99

Industry: Health Care (Medical Products & Supplies)

Summary: RESP is a leading designer, maker and marketer of technologically advanced medical devices for use in home, hospital and alternative care settings.

Quantitative Evaluations

Outlook (1 Lowest—5 Highest) • **5+**

Fair Value • **19**

Risk • **High**

Earn./Div. Rank • **B**

Technical Eval. • **Bearish** since 7/99

Rel. Strength Rank (1 Lowest—99 Highest) • **12**

Insider Activity • **NA**

Recent Price • 8⅜

52 Wk Range • 21⅜-8

Yield • Nil

12-Mo. P/E • 11.6

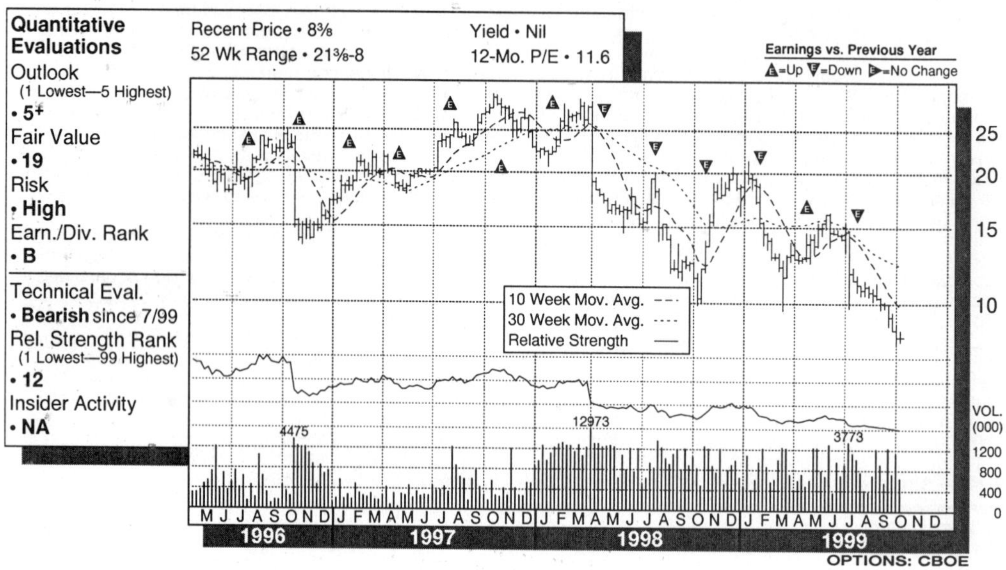

Business Profile - 25-AUG-99

In July 1999, the company announced a restructuring plan under which it would be reorganize itself into four major business units: homecare; hospital; asthma/allergy; and international. In addition, RESP said it would close or downsize a number of facilities, and position itself for a more intensive focus on research and development. The company also planned to close its Westminster, CO, manufacturing facility, and its U.S. customer satisfaction centers, and to open a centralized distribution and repair center in Youngwood, PA, in the FY 00 (Jun.) first quarter. RESP will incur a pretax restructuring charges totaling about $25 million over the next few quarters.

Operational Review - 25-AUG-99

Based on a preliminary report, net sales in FY 99 edged up 1.7%, as a 7.1% increase in sleep product sales was largely offset by a 2.6% decrease in respiratory product sales. Gross margins narrowed. However, despite a $2.4 million restructuring charge, in the absence of $40.8 million of merger related costs, net income of $23.1 million ($0.72 a share, on 3.5% fewer shares) contrasted with a net loss of $1.8 million ($0.06).

Stock Performance - 08-OCT-99

In the past 30 trading days, RESP's shares have declined 19%, compared to a 0.91% fall in the S&P 500. Average trading volume for the past five days was 127,380 shares, compared with the 40-day moving average of 189,387 shares.

Key Stock Statistics

Dividend Rate/Share	Nil	Shareholders	3,323
Shs. outstg. (M)	30.6	Market cap. (B)	$0.256
Avg. daily vol. (M)	0.197	Inst. holdings	54%
Tang. Bk. Value/Share	4.04		
Beta	1.06		

Value of $10,000 invested 5 years ago: $ 8,815

Fiscal Year Ending Jun. 30

	1999	1998	1997	1996	1995	1994
Revenues (Million $)						
1Q	86.41	90.75	34.11	26.68	21.67	18.23
2Q	90.20	95.47	43.00	30.24	23.87	18.60
3Q	90.88	80.13	47.81	32.65	25.60	19.31
4Q	90.08	85.23	53.64	36.20	28.31	22.04
Yr.	357.6	351.6	178.6	125.8	99.5	78.17
Earnings Per Share ($)						
1Q	**0.19**	**0.24**	0.22	0.18	0.14	0.05
2Q	**0.23**	**0.27**	0.24	0.20	0.15	0.12
3Q	**0.26**	**-0.69**	0.25	0.21	0.17	0.13
4Q	**0.04**	**0.11**	0.29	0.24	0.20	-0.03
Yr.	**0.72**	**-0.06**	**0.82**	**0.71**	0.67	0.27

Next earnings report expected: late October

Dividend Data

Cash dividends have never been paid. A two-for-one stock split was effected in March 1995.

Respironics, Inc.

Business Summary - 25-AUG-99

Respironics is a leading designer, manufacturer and marketer of technologically advanced medical devices for use in the home, hospital and alternative care settings. The company has employees worldwide, and has manufacturing facilities in several domestic and international locations.

In February 1998, RESP acquired Healthdyne Technologies, Inc. (HDTC), a maker of monitoring devices for newborns and products for respiratory disorders, in exchange for about 12 million common shares. The transaction formed an international respiratory products company with revenues of $350 million, nearly doubling RESP's sales volume.

In addition to monitoring devices for newborns, the company's major product lines include therapy products for obstructive sleep apnea and portable ventilation, sleep diagnostics, oxygen and a variety of products for the treatment of respiratory disorders, including asthma management devices.

Revenues by product segment in FY 99 (Jun.) were: sleep products 50%, respiratory products 41%, and asthma, allergy and OEM products 8.8%.

Product lines include continuous positive airway pressure (CPAP) devices and bi-level positive airway pressure (BiPAP) devices for the treatment of obstructive sleep apnea (OSA), a serious disorder characterized by the repeated cessation of breathing during sleep; ventilation devices, including bi-level non-invasive ventilatory support units; and patient mask products.

In February 1997, the company acquired its exclusive German distributor of therapy systems and accessories used in the treatment of obstructive sleep apnea and other respiratory disorders for $9 million in cash (with potential additional consideration of $5 million over the next four years, based on the achievement of certain financial results in Germany).

RESP markets its products through sales organizations consisting of approximately 140 direct and independent sales representatives and specialists, who sell to a network of more than 5,000 medical product dealers. In certain foreign countries, the products are sold directly to end users. International sales accounted for 22% of sales in FY 98.

The company sees long-term opportunities in the area of respiratory care, specifically obstructive sleep apnea and chronic obstructive pulmonary disease. RESP also expects that its broad respiratory product offering, combined with the strength of its enhanced infrastructure, will provide value to its customers.

Per Share Data ($) **(Year Ended Jun. 30)**	**1999**	**1998**	**1997**	**1996**	**1995**	**1994**	**1993**	**1992**	**1991**	**1990**
Tangible Bk. Val.	NA	4.04	3.72	6.21	3.38	2.71	2.41	1.95	1.61	0.77
Cash Flow	NA	0.38	1.13	1.06	0.89	0.48	0.65	0.44	0.34	0.20
Earnings	0.72	-0.06	0.82	0.84	0.67	0.28	0.42	0.32	0.26	0.15
Dividends	Nil	Nil	Nil	Nil	Nil	Nil	Nil	Nil	Nil	Nil
Payout Ratio	Nil	Nil	Nil	Nil	Nil	Nil	Nil	Nil	Nil	Nil
Prices - High	$21\frac{3}{8}$	$29\frac{5}{8}$	$30\frac{3}{8}$	25	$22\frac{1}{4}$	$12\frac{1}{4}$	$15\frac{1}{2}$	$15\frac{3}{8}$	$7\frac{1}{4}$	$5\frac{3}{8}$
- Low	8	$9\frac{7}{8}$	$16\frac{3}{4}$	$13\frac{1}{2}$	$10\frac{1}{2}$	8	$7\frac{7}{8}$	$6\frac{1}{4}$	$4\frac{1}{4}$	$2\frac{1}{8}$
P/E Ratio - High	30	NM	30	30	33	44	36	41	28	35
- Low	11	NM	17	16	16	29	19	20	17	14
Income Statement Analysis (Million $)										
Revs.	NA	352	315	126	100	78.2	69.3	49.0	36.0	23.0
Oper. Inc.	NA	62.0	57.0	27.8	21.4	17.0	14.6	9.7	6.8	3.3
Depr.	NA	14.0	10.0	4.0	3.8	3.6	3.9	2.1	1.3	0.6
Int. Exp.	NA	4.2	3.2	0.2	0.2	0.2	0.2	0.2	0.3	0.1
Pretax Inc.	NA	3.9	43.9	25.2	18.5	6.8	11.1	8.1	5.5	3.0
Eff. Tax Rate	NA	NM	40%	39%	37%	30%	34%	34%	32%	27%
Net Inc.	NA	-1.8	-26.4	15.3	11.7	4.7	7.4	5.4	3.8	2.2
Balance Sheet & Other Fin. Data (Million $)										
Cash	NA	14.9	19.0	65.3	16.1	12.4	14.6	10.2	11.3	2.2
Curr. Assets	NA	195	169	116	52.9	40.2	36.4	27.8	21.9	11.7
Total Assets	NA	328	299	144	78.0	58.9	54.6	43.5	36.1	19.8
Curr. Liab.	NA	57.1	58.0	16.5	13.5	9.2	11.2	7.8	5.8	5.9
LT Debt	NA	69.3	49.0	5.0	5.5	4.9	4.3	4.3	4.5	3.6
Common Eqty.	NA	201	192	122	58.3	44.2	39.1	31.4	25.8	10.3
Total Cap.	NA	271	241	127	64.6	49.7	43.4	35.7	30.3	13.9
Cap. Exp.	NA	20.0	4.9	6.2	6.9	8.4	6.7	3.5	3.1	5.8
Cash Flow	NA	12.2	36.4	19.3	15.5	8.3	11.2	7.5	5.1	2.7
Curr. Ratio	NA	3.4	2.9	7.0	3.9	4.4	3.2	3.6	3.8	2.0
% LT Debt of Cap.	NA	25.6	20.3	3.9	8.6	9.8	9.9	12.0	15.0	25.6
% Net Inc.of Revs.	NA	NM	8.3	0.1	11.7	6.1	10.7	11.0	10.5	9.4
% Ret. on Assets	NA	NM	11.9	13.8	17.0	8.3	15.0	13.4	12.6	14.4
% Ret. on Equity	NA	NM	16.8	17.1	22.7	11.3	20.9	18.7	19.8	23.2

Data as orig reptd.; bef. results of disc opers/spec. items. Per share data adj. for stk. divs. Bold denotes diluted EPS (FASB 128)-prior periods restated. E-Estimated. NA-Not Available. NM-Not Meaningful. NR-Not Ranked.

Office—1501 Ardmore Boulevard, Pittsburgh, PA 15221-4401. **Tel**—(412) 733-0200. **Website**—http://www.respironics.com **Chrmn**—G. E. McGinnis. **Pres & CEO**—D. S. Meteny. **EVP & COO**—C. B. Reynolds. **VP, CFO & Investor Contact** —Dan J. Bevevino (412-473-5235). **Secy**—D.A. Pishko. **Dirs**—D. P. Barry, D. A. Cotter, J. T. Dewberry, J. H. Hardie, D. H. Jones, J. C. Lawyer, G. E. McGinnis, D. S. Meteny, C.B. Reynolds. **Transfer Agent & Registrar**—ChaseMellon Shareholder Services, Pittsburgh.**Incorporated**—in Pennsylvania in 1976; reincorporated in Delaware in 1984. **Empl**— 2,045. **S&P Analyst:** John J. Arege

STANDARD
&POOR'S
STOCK REPORTS

Riggs National Corp.

NASDAQ Symbol **RIGS**

In S&P SmallCap 600

09-OCT-99

Industry:
Banks (Regional)

Summary: This bank holding company, whose principal subsidiary is Riggs Bank, has 54 branches in the Washington, D.C. metropolitan area, as well as three locations in London, England.

Quantitative Evaluations

Outlook
(1 Lowest—5 Highest)
• 3+

Fair Value
• 18⅛

Risk
• Low

Earn./Div. Rank
• B-

Technical Eval.
• **Bearish** since 8/99

Rel. Strength Rank
(1 Lowest—99 Highest)
• 60

Insider Activity
• NA

Recent Price • 18⅛
52 Wk Range • 26¼-15
Yield • 1.1%
12-Mo. P/E • 17.8

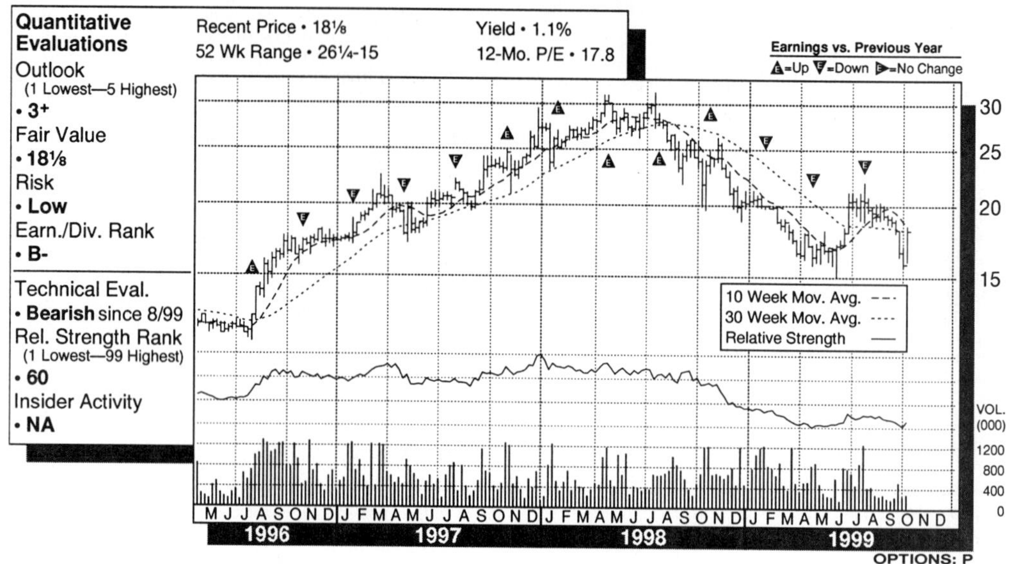

Business Profile - 30-JUN-99

In February 1999, RIGS announced the formation of Riggs Investment Corp., a full-service broker/dealer, to sell the bank's proprietary mutual funds and a variety of other investment products. In June 1999, RIGS announced plans to issue $200 million in variable rate trust preferred securities to be used to redeem $125 million in debt and up to $75 million of investments in its venture capital division. From the fourth quarter of 1998 through the first quarter of 1999, RIGS repurchased $47.6 million of common stock. In October 1998, RIGS redeemed its $100 million 10.75% noncumulative perpetual Series B preferred stock, resulting in a fourth quarter nonrecurring charge of $0.43 a share.

Operational Review - 30-JUN-99

Net interest income in the six months ended June 30, 1999, declined 3.6%, year to year. Following a 6.9% decrease in noninterest income (reflecting lower securities gains) and 6.2% higher noninterest expense, pretax income fell 24%. After taxes at 33.5% versus 25.5%, and minority interest, net income was down 43%, to $17,290,000 ($0.59 a share) from $30,181,000 ($0.78, after preferred dividends).

Stock Performance - 08-OCT-99

In the past 30 trading days, RIGS's shares have declined 6%, compared to a 0.91% fall in the S&P 500. Average trading volume for the past five days was 55,420 shares, compared with the 40-day moving average of 54,682 shares.

Key Stock Statistics

Dividend Rate/Share	0.20	Shareholders	2,457
Shs. outstg. (M)	28.3	Market cap. (B)	$0.513
Avg. daily vol. (M)	0.062	Inst. holdings	33%
Tang. Bk. Value/Share	12.47		
Beta	0.72		

Value of $10,000 invested 5 years ago: $ 21,743

Fiscal Year Ending Dec. 31

	1999	1998	1997	1996	1995	1994
Revenues (Million $)						
1Q	105.9	115.1	96.71	100.2	90.22	90.67
2Q	106.2	112.3	104.2	97.48	94.81	86.99
3Q	—	126.7	108.0	93.99	94.21	86.21
4Q	—	114.1	109.8	97.76	93.56	87.66
Yr.	—	468.1	418.7	389.4	372.8	351.5
Earnings Per Share ($)						
1Q	0.26	0.41	0.25	0.61	0.20	0.15
2Q	0.33	0.37	0.25	0.62	0.22	0.23
3Q	—	0.46	0.32	0.29	1.78	0.17
4Q	—	-0.04	0.45	0.27	0.34	0.17
Yr.	—	1.21	1.27	1.79	2.54	0.72

Next earnings report expected: mid October

Dividend Data (Dividends have been paid since 1996.)

Amount ($)	Date Decl.	Ex-Div. Date	Stock of Record	Payment Date
0.050	Oct. 14	Oct. 22	Oct. 26	Nov. 02 '98
0.050	Jan. 20	Jan. 27	Jan. 29	Feb. 05 '99
0.050	Apr. 14	Apr. 22	Apr. 26	May. 03 '99
0.050	Jul. 08	Jul. 15	Jul. 19	Aug. 02 '99

A Division of The McGraw-Hill Companies

Riggs National Corporation

Business Summary - 30-JUN-99

Riggs National Corp., the largest bank holding company headquartered in the nation's capital, provides specialized banking and financial management products and services for individuals, non-profit organizations and businesses. Specifically, RIGS's services include community banking, corporate and commercial banking, international banking, and trust and investment management services. RIGS's banking operations and separate subsidiaries are mostly located in the Washington, D.C. metropolitan area, and also include locations in New Haven, CT, Miami, FL, London, England, and Nassau Bahamas.

Riggs Bank N.A., the principal subsidiary of RIGS, was founded in 1836 and operates 54 branch offices in the Washington, D.C. metropolitan area. The bank conducts its investment advisory services through Riggs Investment Management (RIMCO) and J. Bush & Company Inc. At year-end 1998, RIGS had more than $5.8 billion in assets under management. In early 1999, RIGS formed its own broker/dealer, Riggs Investment Corp., which added a distribution channel for its proprietary mutual funds, the Riggs Funds.

RIGS strives to meet the unique requirements of Washington's dense concentration of federal agencies, high technology and government-related businesses and lobbying associations. In early 1999, the U.S. government selected RIGS to redesign and manage the U.S. Treasury's CASH-LINK cash management system, which serves 2,300 Federal agencies through linkages with 3,000 banks worldwide. The bank also serves the diplomatic community as the financial service provider of 95% of the embassies and missions in Washington.

Income earned in 1998 was comprised of interest and fees on loans (51%), interest and dividends on securities available for sale (15%), interest on money market assets (10%), trust and investment advisory income (10%), service charges and fees (8%) and other noninterest income (6%). Average earning assets, from which interest income is derived, totaled $5.1 billion in 1998 and consisted mainly of loans (60%) and securities available for sale (23%). Average sources of funds used in the lending business included interest bearing deposits (60%), demand deposits (13%), stockholders' equity (8%), short-term borrowings (8%), and long-term debt (3%).

Residential mortgage loans were 39% of loans outstanding at 1998 year end; commercial and financial 21%; foreign 16%; commercial and construction real estate 13%; home equity 9%; and consumer 2%.

At 1998 year end, the reserve for loan losses totaled $54,455,000 (equal to 1.67% of loans outstanding), versus 1.82% in 1997. Nonperforming assets were $31,431,000 (0.96% of total loans and other real estate owned), versus $8,970,000 (0.31% in 1997).

Per Share Data ($) (Year Ended Dec. 31)	1998	1997	1996	1995	1994	1993	1992	1991	1990	1989
Tangible Bk. Val.	12.47	11.31	10.58	8.50	5.53	4.81	7.58	11.99	16.58	23.79
Earnings	1.21	1.27	1.79	2.54	0.72	-3.65	-0.86	-4.79	-4.41	2.86
Dividends	0.20	0.20	0.15	Nil	Nil	Nil	Nil	0.20	1.09	1.25
Payout Ratio	17%	16%	8%	Nil	Nil	Nil	Nil	NM	NM	44%
Prices - High	31½	29½	18⅛	14⅝	11¼	11⅝	10⅛	13	22½	28
- Low	18¾	17	11½	7⅞	7½	6¼	4¼	3¾	7¾	18⅜
P/E Ratio - High	26	23	10	6	16	NM	NM	NM	NM	10
- Low	15	13	6	3	10	NM	NM	NM	NM	6
Income Statement Analysis (Million $)										
Net Int. Inc.	190	179	153	151	153	135	138	155	173	179
Tax Equiv. Adj.	3.0	3.8	4.0	3.3	3.4	4.6	6.5	7.1	7.9	9.0
Non Int. Inc.	99	84.4	89.0	73.5	85.5	88.5	96.2	92.9	78.2	65.3
Loan Loss Prov.	NA	-12.0	NM	NM	6.3	69.3	50.0	44.0	106	6.0
Exp./Op. Revs.	66%	71%	72%	86%	82%	117%	100%	114%	92%	75%
Pretax Inc.	111	93.2	72.9	88.1	33.5	-88.6	-22.1	-72.1	-90.6	57.0
Eff. Tax Rate	26%	26%	8.46%	0.39%	NM	NM	NM	NM	NM	31%
Net Inc.	61.8	50.9	65.9	87.8	34.0	-94.2	-21.1	-66.0	-61.2	39.4
% Net Int. Marg.	3.78	3.81	3.72	3.74	3.89	3.23	3.15	3.04	2.86	3.23
Balance Sheet & Other Fin. Data (Million $)										
Money Mkt. Assets	771	791	821	654	388	406	1,264	1,142	1,387	2,293
Inv. Securities	971	1,673	1,163	970	1,041	1,368	955	585	961	417
Com'l Loans	669	530	444	400	401	412	500	606	869	1,043
Other Loans	2,589	2,354	2,194	2,172	2,142	2,110	1,642	2,398	2,946	2,797
Total Assets	5,502	5,846	5,135	4,733	4,426	4,780	5,078	5,536	7,051	7,337
Demand Deposits	732	983	893	911	827	865	884	1,011	1,086	935
Time Deposits	3,413	3,315	2,686	2,063	2,276	2,909	2,670	3,902	5,025	5,042
LT Debt	542	192	192	218	218	213	213	232	246	309
Common Eqty.	393	459	426	377	268	174	245	205	278	342
% Ret. on Assets	1.1	0.9	1.3	1.9	0.8	NM	NM	NM	NM	0.6
% Ret. on Equity	12.2	9.1	16.6	28.3	12.0	NM	NM	NM	NM	11.9
% Loan Loss Resv.	1.7	1.8	2.4	2.2	3.8	3.4	3.9	3.5	2.9	1.1
% Loans/Deposits	78.6	67.1	64.1	67.9	69.8	67.0	48.3	60.9	62.0	63.7
% Equity to Assets	7.5	8.0	8.1	6.8	6.3	3.1	5.0	4.2	4.3	5.0

Data as orig reptd.; bef. results of disc opers/spec. items. Per share data adj. for stk. divs. Bold denotes diluted EPS (FASB 128)-prior periods restated. E-Estimated. NA-Not Available. NM-Not Meaningful. NR-Not Ranked.

Office—1503 Pennsylvania Ave., N.W., Washington, DC 20005. **Tel**—(301) 887-6000. **Website**—http://www.riggsbank.com. **Chrmn & CEO**—J. L. Allbritton. **Vice Chrmn** —R. L. Allbritton, R. L. Sloan. **Pres & Investor Contact**—Timothy C. Coughlin. **EVP & CFO**—J. L. Davis. **Dirs**—J. L. Allbritton, R. L. Allbritton, T. C. Coughlin, J. M. Fahey, Jr., L. I. Hebert, S. B. Pfeiffer, J. E.V. Rose, R. L. Sloan, J. Valenti, W. L. Walton, E. N. Williams.**Transfer Agent & Registrar**—The Bank of New York. **Incorporated**—in Delaware in 1980; chartered in 1896. **Empl**— 1,598. **S&P Analyst:** Markos N. Kaminis

Robbins & Myers

NYSE Symbol **RBN**

In S&P SmallCap 600

09-OCT-99

Industry: Manufacturing (Specialized)

Summary: Robbins & Myers makes industrial pumps, large glass-lined vessels and industrial mixing equipment.

Quantitative Evaluations

Outlook (1 Lowest—5 Highest)
• **4+**

Fair Value
• **21¾**

Risk
• **NA**

Earn./Div. Rank
• **A-**

Technical Eval.
• **Bearish** since 9/99

Rel. Strength Rank (1 Lowest—99 Highest)
• **18**

Insider Activity
• **NA**

Recent Price • 17¼
52 Wk Range • 25⅞-15
Yield • 1.3%
12-Mo. P/E • 16.3

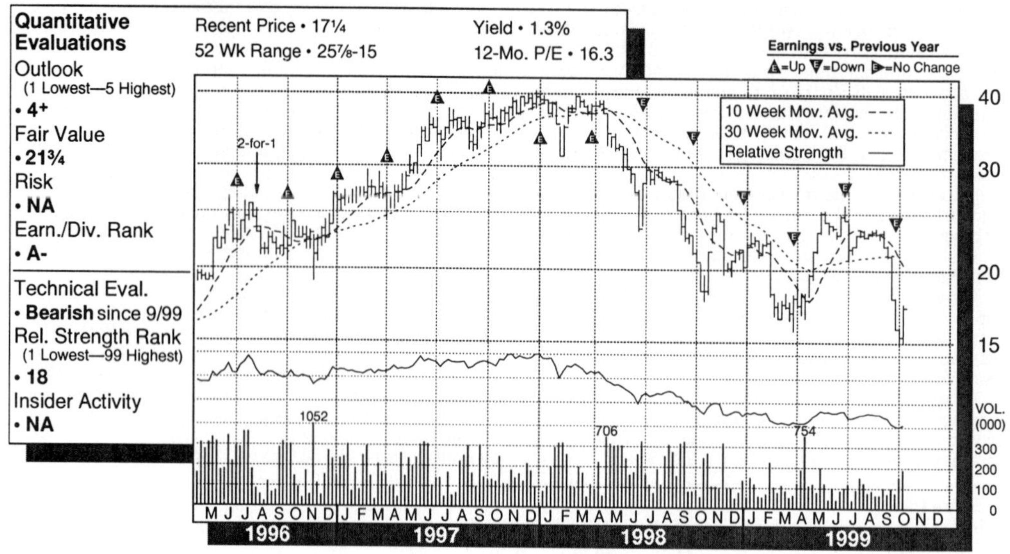

Business Profile - 06-OCT-99

As part of an effort to expand its Asian and Latin American presence, in July 1999, the company announced the completion of three transactions: (1) through a wholly owned subsidiary Pfauldler, Inc, the company increased its ownership of its Indian joint venture partner, GMM Pfaudler, to 51%, (2) acquired a controlling interest in its industrial mixing equipment licensee, Chemineer de Mexico, and (3) formed an alliance with Moyno de Mexico, its progressing cavity pump distributor. In addition, driven by weak market conditions and previously depressed oil prices, in early 1999, the company closed a manufacturing facility in Fairfield California and experienced a ten week work stoppage in its Springfield, Ohio manufacturing facility.

Operational Review - 06-OCT-99

Revenues in the nine months ended May 31, 1999, fell 8.7%, year to year, due to weak market conditions, depressed oil prices, restricted capital expenditures in the energy systems, industrial mixing and reactor systems platforms, and on the temporary work stoppage in the industrial pump platform. Margins narrowed significantly, reflecting reduced sales of higher margin products and a $5.0 million charge on the closure and relocation of the Fairfield, California manufacturing facility. Following a 4.1% rise in interest expense, and minority interest, net income fell 66%, to $8,163,000 ($0.74 a share) from $24,220,000 ($1.88).

Stock Performance - 08-OCT-99

In the past 30 trading days, RBN's shares have declined 26%, compared to a 0.91% fall in the S&P 500. Average trading volume for the past five days was 37,600 shares, compared with the 40-day moving average of 20,710 shares.

Key Stock Statistics

Dividend Rate/Share	0.22	Shareholders	3,350
Shs. outstg. (M)	11.0	Market cap. (B)	$0.189
Avg. daily vol. (M)	0.026	Inst. holdings	49%
Tang. Bk. Value/Share	NM		
Beta	0.95		

Value of $10,000 invested 5 years ago: $ 22,225

Fiscal Year Ending Aug. 31

	1999	1998	1997	1996	1995	1994
Revenues (Million $)						
1Q	98.27	104.2	93.82	81.21	68.63	21.90
2Q	94.88	108.4	93.21	84.18	70.87	22.57
3Q	103.8	112.7	97.59	89.88	79.97	25.02
4Q	103.2	111.2	101.0	95.69	83.48	52.17
Yr.	400.1	436.5	385.7	351.0	302.9	121.7
Earnings Per Share ($)						
1Q	**0.34**	0.69	0.58	0.38	0.28	0.18
2Q	**-0.03**	**0.61**	0.56	0.40	0.29	0.20
3Q	**0.37**	**0.63**	0.69	0.52	0.21	0.21
4Q	**0.32**	**0.56**	0.69	0.55	0.33	0.01
Yr.	**1.06**	**2.43**	**2.29**	1.84	1.09	0.60

Next earnings report expected: mid December

Dividend Data (Dividends have been paid since 1989.)

Amount ($)	Date Decl.	Ex-Div. Date	Stock of Record	Payment Date
0.055	Dec. 09	Jan. 13	Jan. 15	Jan. 29 '99
0.055	Mar. 24	Apr. 07	Apr. 09	Apr. 30 '99
0.055	Jun. 23	Jul. 07	Jul. 09	Jul. 30 '99
0.055	Oct. 06	Oct. 14	Oct. 18	Oct. 29 '99

Robbins & Myers, Inc.

Business Summary - 06-OCT-99

This manufacturer and marketer of fluid management products and systems markets its products globally to process industries. These include specialty chemicals, pharmaceuticals, oil and gas exploration, production and pipeline, water treatment, food and beverage, pulp and paper, and mining.

RBN seeks to continue to expand by capitalizing on the inherent growth of its end-user markets, particularly longer-term, high-growth markets, such as oil and gas exploration, production and pipeline, specialty chemical, pharmaceutical and food additives, which collectively account for over 75% of total sales.

Revenue contributions by major product category in recent fiscal years (Aug.) were: In FY 98 (Aug.), reactor systems accounted for 44% of revenues (43% in FY 97), energy systems for 19% (14%), industrial mixers for 18% (22%), industrial pump products for 15% (16%), and corrosion-resistant products for 4% (5%).

Headquartered in Dayton, Ohio, the company has facilities in the United States, Canada, Europe, Brazil, Mexico, Singapore and joint ventures in China, India, Mexico and Taiwan. The company markets its products globally to end users for which the pumping, mixing, treatment, chemical processing measurement and containment of gases, fluids and particulates are key elements in their production processes. RBN obtains approximately 47% of revenues from international markets.

The company's reactor systems business, consisting of its Pfaudler, Tycon and Technoglass business units, manufactures and sells glass-lined reactor and storage vessels, mixing systems and accessories. A reactor system performs critical functions in batch production processes by providing a temperature, agitation and pressure controlled environment for complex chemical reactions. A fully equipped reactor system can cost up to $300,000. The reactor systems business also manufacturers and sells glass-lined storage vessels with capacities up to 25,000 gallons. In July 1999, through its wholly owned subsidiary, Pfaudler, the company increased its ownership interest in its Indian joint venture, GMM Pfaudler, to 51% from 40% for $4.0 million. GMM Pfaudler is the company's largest producer of glass-lined reactor vessels with a 70% share of the market in India.

In July 1999, in order to expand its presence in Latin America, RBN acquired a controlling interest in its industrial mixing equipment licensee, Chemineer de Mexico for $1.6 million, and for a limited investment in working capital, it acquired a 51% interest in a joint venture with Moyno de Mexico, a progressing cavity pump distributor.

Per Share Data ($) (Year Ended Aug. 31)	1999	1998	1997	1996	1995	1994	1993	1992	1991	1990
Tangible Bk. Val.	NA	NM	NM	-1.58	-1.65	-1.99	4.14	4.92	4.75	3.92
Cash Flow	NA	4.97	4.10	3.09	2.33	1.01	0.85	0.98	2.12	0.96
Earnings	1.06	2.43	2.52	1.84	1.09	0.60	0.59	0.75	0.86	0.54
Dividends	0.22	0.21	0.19	0.17	0.15	0.15	0.12	0.09	0.07	0.05
Payout Ratio	21%	9%	8%	9%	14%	25%	20%	13%	8%	9%
Prices - High	25 7/8	39 3/4	40 1/2	27	17 1/2	10 1/4	10 3/4	10	10 3/4	6
- Low	15	17 5/8	24 1/4	13 5/8	8 1/2	8 1/4	7 3/4	6 1/2	4 5/8	3 7/8
P/E Ratio - High	24	16	16	15	16	17	18	13	12	11
- Low	14	7	10	7	8	14	13	9	5	7
Income Statement Analysis (Million $)										
Revs.	NA	436	386	351	303	122	85.0	76.0	79.0	109
Oper. Inc.	NA	82.9	65.0	52.6	39.5	20.6	13.4	13.2	12.9	10.6
Depr.	NA	23.5	16.0	13.9	12.4	4.3	2.8	2.4	2.0	4.3
Int. Exp.	NA	12.8	6.4	7.1	7.3	1.5	0.1	0.1	0.1	0.1
Pretax Inc.	NA	47.3	43.1	32.4	19.0	10.6	9.8	9.8	9.7	6.0
Eff. Tax Rate	NA	34%	33%	37%	38%	40%	37%	20%	11%	10%
Net Inc.	NA	31.2	28.9	20.3	11.8	6.4	6.2	7.9	8.7	5.4
Balance Sheet & Other Fin. Data (Million $)										
Cash	NA	6.8	10.3	7.1	10.2	16.1	24.5	24.1	31.4	6.6
Curr. Assets	NA	153	130	114	110	104	48.3	46.0	51.0	36.0
Total Assets	NA	501	372	372	270	258	85.0	74.0	69.0	66.0
Curr. Liab.	NA	87.8	82.7	76.4	77.7	58.5	15.0	11.7	14.7	14.6
LT Debt	NA	202	111	72.2	61.8	80.3	Nil	0.9	0.9	1.0
Common Eqty.	NA	151	124	91.4	70.0	57.0	52.3	56.3	49.2	44.6
Total Cap.	NA	356	237	164	132	137	52.3	57.0	50.0	46.0
Cap. Exp.	NA	23.0	22.1	16.5	10.1	11.4	5.3	12.4	4.2	5.4
Cash Flow	NA	54.7	44.8	34.2	24.2	10.7	9.0	10.3	10.6	9.7
Curr. Ratio	NA	1.7	1.6	1.5	1.4	1.8	3.2	3.9	3.5	2.5
% LT Debt of Cap.	NA	56.8	46.9	44.1	47.0	58.5	Nil	1.6	1.8	2.3
% Net Inc.of Revs.	NA	7.2	7.5	5.8	3.9	5.2	7.3	10.4	11.0	5.0
% Ret. on Assets	NA	7.2	8.6	7.1	4.5	3.7	7.8	10.9	12.8	8.7
% Ret. on Equity	NA	22.7	26.7	25.2	18.7	11.6	11.4	14.8	18.4	12.9

Data as orig reptd.; bef. results of disc opers/spec. items. Per share data adj. for stk. divs. Bold denotes diluted EPS (FASB 128)-prior periods restated. E-Estimated. NA-Not Available. NM-Not Meaningful. NR-Not Ranked.

Office—1400 Kettering Tower, Dayton, OH 45423. **Tel**—(937) 222-2610. **Secy**—J. M. Rigot. **Chrmn**—M. H. Murch IV. **Pres & CEO**—D. W. Duval. **VP-Fin & CFO** —S. R. Ley. **Investor Contact**—Hugh E. Becker (937-225-3335). **Dirs**—D. W. Duval, R. J. Kegerreis, T. P. Loftis, W. D. Manning, Jr., M. H. Murch IV, J. F. Tatar, J. N. Taylor, Jr. **Transfer Agent & Registrar**—KeyCorp Shareholder Services, Cleveland. **Incorporated**—in Ohio in 1928. **Empl**— 3,000. **S&P Analyst:** Sandy H. Katzler

STANDARD
&POOR'S
STOCK REPORTS

Roberts Pharmaceutical

ASE Symbol **RPC**
In S&P SmallCap 600

09-OCT-99

Industry:
Health Care (Drugs - Major Pharmaceuticals)

Summary: This international pharmaceutical company recently agreed to be acquired by Shire Pharmaceuticals in a transaction valued at about $1 billion.

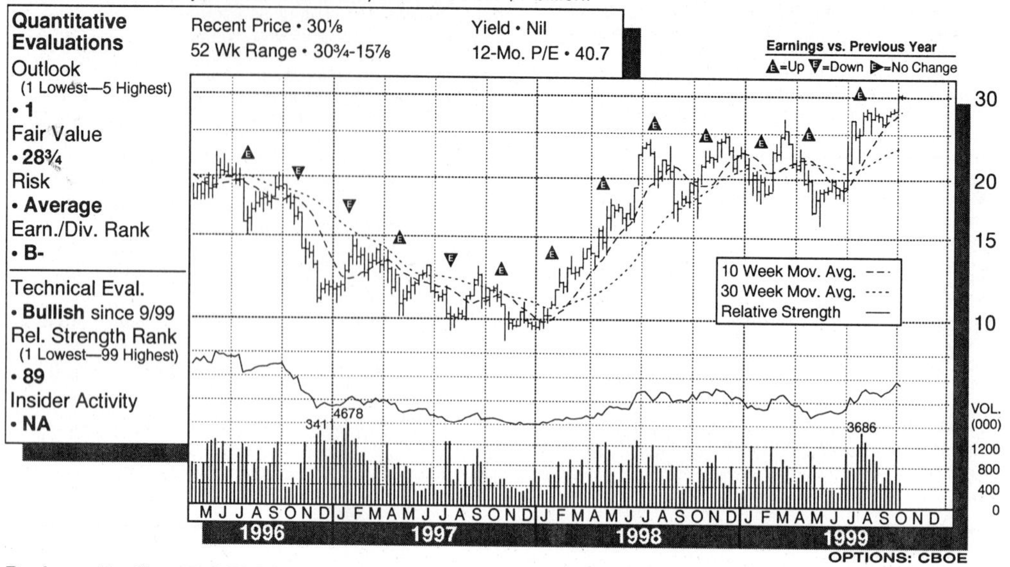

Business Profile - 06-OCT-99

In July 1999, the company agreed to merge with Shire Pharmaceuticals Group plc, a U.K.-based specialty pharmaceutical company, for about $30 a share. Shire will exchange between 1.0427 and 1.2802 ADS for each RPC share, and will own 56% of the combined company. Closing is seen in the 1999 fourth quarter. In June 1999, RPC purchased all rights to Agrylin, a drug for the treatment of high platelet levels currently marketed by the company, from Bristol-Myers Squibb. RPC expects this purchase to be accretive to earnings in 1999. Also in June, Agrylin received Orphan drug status in Japan. In March 1999, preliminary results of a Phase III clinical study for Dirame (an oral analgesic) indicated efficacy for the treatment of post-operative dental pain.

Operational Review - 06-OCT-99

Total revenues in the first half of 1999 advanced 23%, year to year, driven by the acquisition of Pentasa and growth in sales of ProAmatine and Agrylin. Gross margins widened on a more favorable product mix, sales growth in higher margin products, and a decrease in sales of lower margin drugs. Following higher marketing expenses, partly due to increased advertising, and a rise in R&D expense, which outweighed lower administrative expenses, operating profit more than tripled. After sharply higher interest expense and taxes at 35.6%, versus 39.3%, net income was up 121%, to $12,503,000 ($0.39 a share, on 5.0% more shares) from $5,531,000 ($0.18).

Stock Performance - 08-OCT-99

In the past 30 trading days, RPC's shares have increased 10%, compared to a 0.91% fall in the S&P 500. Average trading volume for the past five days was 101,480 shares, compared with the 40-day moving average of 158,344 shares.

Key Stock Statistics

Dividend Rate/Share	Nil	Shareholders	900
Shs. outstg. (M)	31.9	Market cap. (B)	$0.961
Avg. daily vol. (M)	0.153	Inst. holdings	54%
Tang. Bk. Value/Share	0.82		
Beta	0.59		

Value of $10,000 invested 5 years ago: $ 7,578

Fiscal Year Ending Dec. 31

	1999	1998	1997	1996	1995	1994
Revenues (Million $)						
1Q	44.50	32.85	26.33	17.23	16.17	25.72
2Q	50.50	44.40	30.29	26.80	30.36	25.64
3Q	—	42.70	28.60	21.69	34.32	30.77
4Q	—	55.50	37.30	32.39	32.56	30.06
Yr.	—	175.4	122.5	98.08	113.4	112.2
Earnings Per Share ($)						
1Q	**0.16**	**0.07**	0.04	-0.22	-0.06	0.23
2Q	**0.23**	**0.11**	0.04	0.10	0.06	0.24
3Q	—	**0.15**	-0.11	-0.40	0.02	0.27
4Q	—	**0.21**	**0.11**	-1.83	0.01	0.32
Yr.	—	**0.53**	**0.06**	**-2.47**	**0.15**	1.04

Next earnings report expected: late October

Dividend Data

Cash dividends have never been paid.

A Division of The McGraw-Hill Companies

Roberts Pharmaceutical Corporation

Business Summary - 06-OCT-99

This specialty pharmaceutical company's strategy is to acquire, develop, and commercialize late-stage (Phase II or Phase III) drug candidates in the therapeutic areas of cardiology, gastroenterology, neurology, oncology/hematology, and urology. Roberts Pharmaceutical also acquires and markets currently approved prescription pharmaceuticals. Major approved products include ProAmatine, Agrylin, and Pentasa.

RPC utilizes its own sales and marketing force in the United States, Canada, the United Kingdom, and Ireland. RPC products are also licensed in other countries around the world. Additionally, the company employs national account managers to target the growing market for prescription pharmaceuticals offered through managed care organizations within the United States.

RPC launched ProAmatine, its first proprietary product, in late 1996. Approved in September 1996, ProAmatine is the only FDA approved drug for the treatment of orthostatic hypotension (low blood pressure). ProAmatine has been designated as an Orphan drug by the FDA, providing seven years of market exclusivity post approval. As of year end 1998, RPC was conducting Phase II clinical trials on ProAmatine for the treatment of stress urinary incontinence.

In April 1997, the company launched Agrylin, the only FDA approved oral treatment for thrombocytosis, a blood disorder characterized by elevated blood platelet counts that can lead to heart attack or stroke. Agrylin has also been designated as an Orphan drug by the FDA, providing seven years of market exclusivity from its March 1997 approval.

In April 1998, RPC acquired the U.S. rights to Pentasa, a gastrointestinal drug indicated for the treatment of ulcerative colitis, from Hoechst Marion Roussel for approximately $130 million. Pentasa is RPC's largest revenue generator, with sales of $33.3 million for the year ended December 31, 1998.

As of year end 1998, RPC's research pipeline included: Somagard, in Phase II/III trials for the treatment of central precocious puberty, endometreosis, and prostate cancer; RL0903, in Phase III studies for treating prostate cancer; Dirame, in Phase III trials for the treatment of acute and chronic pain control; Stanate, in Phase II/III studies for treating neonatal hyperbilirubinemia, which can cause jaundice and brain damage; Sampatrilat, in Phase II trials for the treatment of essential hypertension and congestive heart failure; Emitasol, in Phase III studies for treating emesis; and Tazofelone, in Phase II trials for the treatment of inflammatory bowel diseases.

In 1998, RPC completed the divestiture of its non-core businesses in order to focus on its core business of acquiring, developing, and marketing prescription therapeutics. In 1997, the company purchased a pharmaceutical manufacturing facility in Ontario, Canada and a distribution center in suburban Chicago. The objective of these purchases is to achieve cost efficiencies.

Per Share Data ($) (Year Ended Dec. 31)	1998	1997	1996	1995	1994	1993	1992	1991	1990	1989
Tangible Bk. Val.	0.82	4.28	5.73	0.26	1.95	2.18	0.33	2.55	1.45	0.06
Cash Flow	0.89	0.32	-2.21	0.53	1.41	0.79	-0.53	-0.49	-0.82	0.01
Earnings	0.53	0.06	-2.47	0.15	1.04	0.46	-0.68	-0.58	-0.85	Nil
Dividends	Nil	Nil	Nil	Nil	Nil	Nil	Nil	Nil	Nil	Nil
Payout Ratio	Nil	Nil	Nil	Nil	Nil	Nil	Nil	Nil	Nil	Nil
Prices - High	25 1/8	15	26 1/4	46 1/2	40	42 1/2	36 3/4	33	8	NA
- Low	9 1/2	9	10 3/4	15 1/2	19 3/4	15 1/4	13 1/2	4	2 1/2	NA
P/E Ratio - High	47	NM	NM	NM	38	92	NM	NM	NM	NA
- Low	18	NM	NM	NM	19	33	NM	NA	NA	NA
Income Statement Analysis (Million $)										
Revs.	175	123	98.1	113	112	89.7	33.0	13.5	1.2	5.5
Oper. Inc.	38.2	6.2	-5.4	14.0	31.3	13.7	-8.9	-3.8	-5.0	-0.1
Depr.	11.1	6.9	7.5	7.2	7.0	5.0	2.0	0.8	0.1	0.1
Int. Exp.	6.2	0.8	1.8	3.5	4.0	3.3	1.1	1.0	0.1	0.1
Pretax Inc.	25.0	1.4	-48.9	5.5	23.3	7.2	-8.6	-4.9	-4.7	0.2
Eff. Tax Rate	33%	NM	NM	51%	17%	Nil	NM	NM	NM	46%
Net Inc.	16.8	2.5	-34.3	2.7	19.4	7.2	-9.3	-5.1	-4.7	0.1
Balance Sheet & Other Fin. Data (Million $)										
Cash	75.3	43.0	94.9	30.0	36.5	91.6	43.9	14.2	11.8	0.8
Curr. Assets	157	138	157	93.8	96.0	128	58.3	19.8	12.5	1.9
Total Assets	526	368	372	340	336	343	185	44.0	13.0	3.0
Curr. Liab.	57.7	40.0	51.5	81.7	53.9	57.7	34.0	9.8	1.0	0.6
LT Debt	127	10.3	10.6	16.1	22.4	45.7	29.0	9.2	0.4	0.5
Common Eqty.	342	317	309	235	259	239	122	25.0	10.0	Nil
Total Cap.	469	328	322	278	282	285	151	34.0	12.0	2.0
Cap. Exp.	11.1	11.9	0.7	0.2	1.0	6.6	9.4	0.3	0.0	0.1
Cash Flow	27.9	9.5	-41.4	9.9	26.5	12.3	-7.3	-4.3	-4.7	0.1
Curr. Ratio	2.7	3.5	3.0	1.1	1.8	2.2	1.7	2.0	12.7	3.4
% LT Debt of Cap.	27.0	3.1	3.2	5.8	8.0	16.0	19.2	26.9	3.6	26.3
% Net Inc.of Revs.	9.6	2.1	NM	0.4	17.3	8.1	NM	NM	NM	1.8
% Ret. on Assets	3.8	0.7	NM	0.8	5.7	2.5	NM	NM	NM	NA
% Ret. on Equity	5.1	0.8	NM	1.1	7.8	3.7	NM	NM	NM	NA

Data as orig reptd.; bef. results of disc opers/spec. items. Per share data adj. for stk. divs. Bold denotes diluted EPS (FASB 128)-prior periods restated. E-Estimated. NA-Not Available. NM-Not Meaningful. NR-Not Ranked.

Office—4 Industrial Way West, Eatontown, NJ 07724. **Tel**—(732) 676-1200. **Fax**—(732) 389-1014. **Website**—http://robertspharm.com**Chrmn**—R. A. Vukovich. **Pres & CEO**—J. T. Spitznagel. **VP, Treas & CFO**—P. M. Rogalin. **VP & Secy**—A. A. Rascio. **Dirs**—D. W. Barrios, Z. P. Horovitz, M. Lloyd, R. W. Loy, J. N. Noonburg, R. M. Nordmann, P. M. Rogalin, J. E. Smith, J. T. Spitznagel, R. A. Vukovich. **Transfer Agent & Registrar**—Continental Stock Transfer & Trust Co., NYC. **Incorporated**—in New Jersey in 1982. **Empl**— 440. **S&P Analyst:** S.S.

STANDARD &POOR'S
STOCK REPORTS

Rollins Truck Leasing

NYSE Symbol **RLC**

In S&P SmallCap 600

09-OCT-99 **Industry:** Truckers

Summary: RLC primarily leases over-the-road tractors, trucks and trailers.

Quantitative Evaluations

Outlook
(1 Lowest—5 Highest)
• **4+**

Fair Value
• **15⅛**

Risk
• **Low**

Earn./Div. Rank
• **A**

Technical Eval.
• **Bearish** since 9/99

Rel. Strength Rank
(1 Lowest—99 Highest)
• **56**

Insider Activity
• **Neutral**

Recent Price • 10⅜
52 Wk Range • 15¼-9

Yield • 1.9%
12-Mo. P/E • 11.1

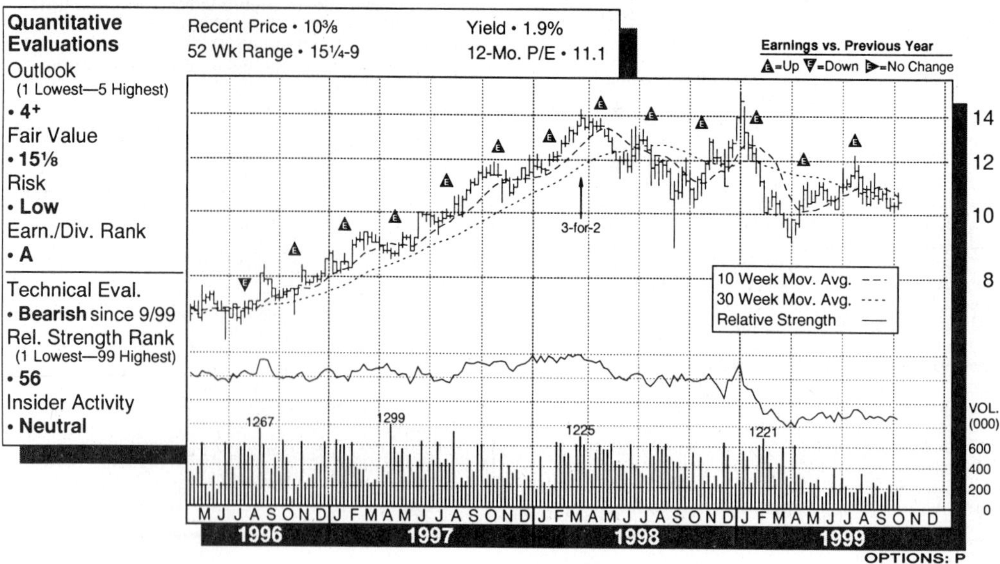

OPTIONS: P

Business Profile - 16-JUN-99

In April 1999, RLC stated that a better mix of business, lower benefit costs, decreased environmental expense and a more productive maintenance process resulted in improved margins in 1999. RLC's primary operation of full service leasing and rentals of tractors, trucks and trailers requires substantial amounts of capital. At March 31, 1999, equipment on operating leases represented 73% of the company's assets. The company's funding sources, besides its operations, are from the sale of used equipment and borrowings under the credit facility. In March 1999, the company announced that it would purchase up to 1,500,000 shares of its common stock.

Operational Review - 16-JUN-99

Total revenues for the six months ended March 31, 1999, increased 4.1%, year to year, as higher full-service lease, guaranteed maintenance and commercial rental revenues, more than offset a decline in logistics and dedicated revenues. Total expenses rose only 2.8% as higher depreciation expense, due to increased investment in revenue producing equipment and related service facilities areas, was partially offset by an 87% higher gain on sale of property and equipment. After 7.8% higher interest expense due to an increased level of borrowings, net income rose 10%, to $25.2 million ($0.43 a share, on 5.3% fewer shares), from $22.8 million ($0.37).

Stock Performance - 08-OCT-99

In the past 30 trading days, RLC's shares have declined 2%, compared to a 0.91% fall in the S&P 500. Average trading volume for the past five days was 35,540 shares, compared with the 40-day moving average of 38,995 shares.

Key Stock Statistics

Dividend Rate/Share	0.20	Shareholders	2,238
Shs. outstg. (M)	57.4	Market cap. (B)	$0.599
Avg. daily vol. (M)	0.037	Inst. holdings	57%
Tang. Bk. Value/Share	5.18		
Beta	0.60		

Value of $10,000 invested 5 years ago: $ 13,273

Fiscal Year Ending Sep. 30

	1999	1998	1997	1996	1995	1994
Revenues (Million $)						
1Q	115.3	149.0	133.7	125.0	119.1	107.4
2Q	150.9	145.1	132.4	122.2	116.7	107.1
3Q	156.6	155.2	142.1	130.7	122.7	115.8
4Q	—	160.9	148.5	135.8	124.1	120.5
Yr.	—	610.2	556.7	513.8	482.6	450.9
Earnings Per Share ($)						
1Q	**0.24**	**0.21**	0.15	0.13	0.17	0.14
2Q	**0.19**	**0.16**	0.12	0.08	0.13	0.12
3Q	**0.26**	**0.23**	0.19	0.15	0.17	0.15
4Q	—	**0.26**	0.21	0.17	0.14	0.17
Yr.	—	**0.85**	**0.68**	0.52	0.61	0.57

Next earnings report expected: late October

Dividend Data (Dividends have been paid since 1976.)

Amount ($)	Date Decl.	Ex-Div. Date	Stock of Record	Payment Date
0.050	Oct. 29	Nov. 10	Nov. 15	Dec. 15 '98
0.050	Jan. 28	Feb. 10	Feb. 15	Mar. 15 '99
0.050	Apr. 29	May. 12	May. 15	Jun. 15 '99
0.050	Jul. 29	Aug. 11	Aug. 15	Sep. 15 '99

A Division of The McGraw-Hill Companies

Rollins Truck Leasing Corp.

Business Summary - 16-JUN-99

Fiscal 1998 marked the 30th year for RLC as a publicly traded company and the 30th year of consecutive revenue growth. RLC is engaged primarily in full-service truck leasing and rentals and the provision and management of transportation and logistics systems. After Ryder System, Inc. and Penske Truck Leasing, RLC is the third largest competitor in the truck truck leasing industry. All of the company's operations currently are conducted within the United States.

Full-service leasing accounts for the major portion of Rollins' revenues. Under these leases, Rollins purchases vehicles and components that are custom-engineered to the customer's requirements. This equipment is then leased to the customer for periods usually ranging from three to eight years. Rollins provides fuel, oil, tires, washing, and regularly scheduled maintenance and repairs at its facilities. In addition, Rollins arranges for licenses and insurance, pays highway and use taxes and supplies a 24-hour-a-day emergency road service to its customers.

Through Rollins Logistics, Inc. and its subsidiaries, the Company provides and manages transportation and logistics systems for companies in a wide range of industries throughout the United States. These services are designed to meet the higher demand for the outsourcing of transportation, distribution and logistics functions. Dedicated Carriage Services analyzes a customer's specific distribution needs and then custom-designs and operates a transportation/distribution system, which can include any of the services mentioned previously plus management, drivers and other operating personnel. The Company also offers logistics management services and warehouse management to companies that desire to outsource their distribution and warehousing functions to a third-party provider. These services can range from selection and negotiation of core carrier contracts to selection of the most cost effective carrier for specific traffic lane movements.

The commercial rental fleet, which at September 30, 1998 consisted of more than 9,000 units with payload capacities ranging from 4,000 to 45,000 pounds, offers tractors, trucks and trailers to customers for short periods of time ranging from one day to several months. The Company's commercial rental fleet also provides additional vehicles to full service lease customers to handle their peak or seasonal business needs. The rental fleet's average age is approximately two years. The utilization rate of the rental fleet during fiscal year 1998 averaged in excess of 85%. Rollins does not offer services in the consumer one-way truck rental market.

Revenues grew in all areas in 1998 as a result of the stable economy and continued demand for RLC's services. However, this revenue growth was volume driven as competition limited price increases. Good cash flow (up 11% over the prior year) has enabled the company to grow without becoming over leveraged. RLC did not make any acquisitions in 1998 due to inflated selling prices.

Per Share Data ($) (Year Ended Sep. 30)	1998	1997	1996	1995	1994	1993	1992	1991	1990	1989
Tangible Bk. Val.	4.77	4.49	4.17	3.91	3.49	3.00	2.63	2.32	1.92	1.71
Cash Flow	3.86	3.36	2.94	2.77	2.33	2.05	1.90	1.83	1.71	1.63
Earnings	0.85	0.67	0.52	0.61	0.57	0.44	0.36	0.30	0.28	0.27
Dividends	15.00	0.13	0.12	0.11	0.09	0.08	0.07	0.06	0.06	0.06
Payout Ratio	18%	20%	23%	18%	15%	18%	20%	21%	21%	22%
Prices - High	15 1/4	12 1/4	8 5/8	9 5/8	9 5/8	9 3/8	7 1/8	5 1/4	2 3/4	3 3/4
- Low	8 7/8	8 1/8	6 3/8	6 1/8	7 1/4	6 1/4	4 3/4	2 1/16	1 11/16	2 3/16
P/E Ratio - High	18	18	17	16	17	21	20	17	10	14
- Low	10	12	12	10	13	14	13	7	6	8
Income Statement Analysis (Million $)										
Revs.	610	557	514	483	451	409	380	342	331	312
Oper. Inc.	311	278	254	246	225	201	183	167	161	154
Depr.	184	170	159	147	122	112	106	97.0	90.0	86.0
Int. Exp.	51.6	49.3	47.5	44.5	37.4	35.5	36.8	40.5	43.3	43.5
Pretax Inc.	85.1	70.2	56.0	67.1	66.4	54.7	40.7	31.5	29.6	27.6
Eff. Tax Rate	39%	39%	39%	39%	40%	44%	39%	40%	39%	39%
Net Inc.	52.0	42.8	34.1	41.3	39.8	30.4	24.6	19.0	18.0	16.8
Balance Sheet & Other Fin. Data (Million $)										
Cash	27.0	17.6	31.2	22.7	15.1	15.1	17.6	21.9	18.9	16.8
Curr. Assets	135	121	124	111	102	90.0	91.0	80.0	81.0	77.0
Total Assets	1,297	1,192	1,125	1,027	910	781	708	656	658	631
Curr. Liab.	65.6	62.4	53.6	51.4	78.0	68.0	72.0	73.0	91.0	84.0
LT Debt	750	672	641	553	469	404	367	351	377	376
Common Eqty.	292	289	284	276	251	217	191	169	133	120
Total Cap.	1,217	1,115	1,060	944	823	704	627	577	561	541
Cap. Exp.	333	303	297	319	297	243	203	146	170	185
Cash Flow	236	213	193	188	162	142	131	116	108	103
Curr. Ratio	2.1	1.9	2.3	2.2	1.3	1.3	1.3	1.1	0.9	0.9
% LT Debt of Cap.	61.6	60.3	60.5	58.5	57.0	57.4	58.5	60.8	67.1	69.4
% Net Inc.of Revs.	8.5	7.7	6.7	8.7	8.8	7.4	6.5	5.5	5.4	5.4
% Ret. on Assets	4.2	3.7	3.2	4.3	4.7	4.1	3.6	2.8	2.8	2.7
% Ret. on Equity	17.9	14.9	12.2	15.7	17.0	14.9	13.6	12.1	14.2	12.6

Data as orig reptd.; bef. results of disc opers/spec. items. Per share data adj. for stk. divs. Bold denotes diluted EPS (FASB 128)-prior periods restated. E-Estimated. NA-Not Available. NM-Not Meaningful. NR-Not Ranked.

Office—One Rollins Plaza, Wilmington, DE 19803. **Tel**—(302) 426-2700. **Website**—http://www.rollins.com **Chrmn & CEO**—J. W. Rollins. **Pres & COO**—J. W. Rollins Jr. **VP, Treas & Investor Contact**—Patrick J. Bagley. **VP & Secy**—K. Belohoubek. **Dirs**—W. B. Philipbar Jr., G. W. Rollins, J. W. Rollins, J. W. Rollins Jr., H. B. Tippie. **Transfer Agent & Registrar**—Registrar & Transfer Co., Cranford, NJ. **Incorporated**—in Delaware in 1954. **Empl**— 3,934. **S&P Analyst:** J. Rudy

Roper Industries

NYSE Symbol **ROP**

In S&P SmallCap 600

09-OCT-99

Industry: Manufacturing (Specialized)

Summary: This U.S.-based global concern makes hi-tech industrial equipment and analytical instruments, mostly for oil & gas producers, semiconductor equipment makers and industrial outfits.

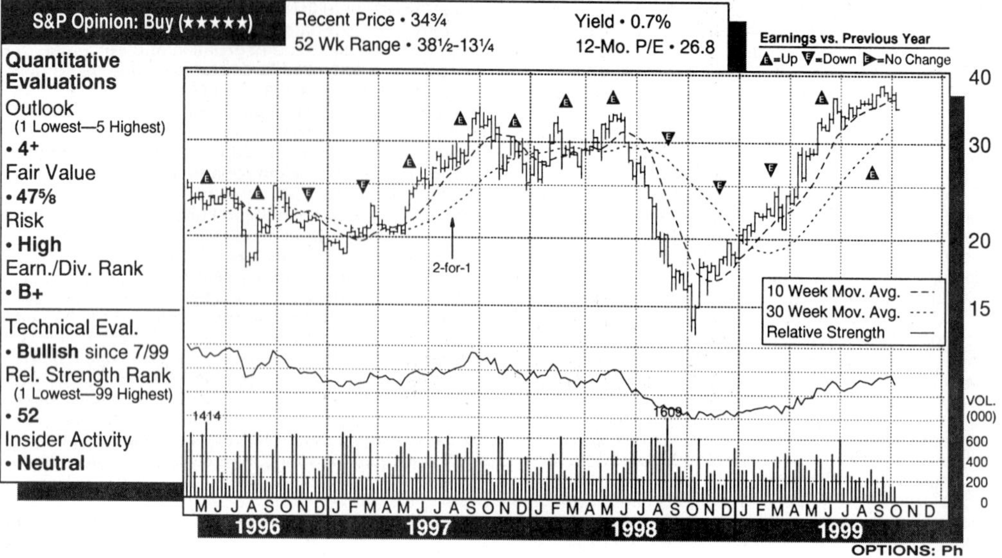

Overview - 20-AUG-99

ROP consistently posts gross profit margins of 50%, in both good and bad times. ROP can generate these margins because it sells highly sophisticated, patented components to niche markets in which it maintains a quasi-monopoly position. ROP also posts high operating margins, due to its ability to tightly control overhead costs. Although ROP believes that the volatile oil & gas and semiconductor industries (its primary markets) have solid long-term prospects, it aims to diversify into new but related growth markets (such as the health care industry), so that each market generates no more than 20% of revenues. We expect ROP to continue to enter new markets, and to bolster competitive barriers, by acquiring cheaply leading producers of complementary products. ROP typically uses debt to fund acquisitions, and then uses its strong free cash flow to quickly reduce borrowings. Overseas sales (over 45% of total revenues) play an important part in ROP's growth.

Valuation - 20-AUG-99

After six years of outperforming the S&P 500 Index, ROP shares fell dramatically in mid-1998, mostly on investor fears regarding ROP's business with RAO Gazprom (Russia's gas utility monopoly), and depressed oil and semiconductor equipment markets. We think the stock was materially oversold. We believe that investors ignored Gazprom loan guarantees, ROP's long-term record of posting annual earnings growth of 25%+, investment returns (ROE) exceeding 20%, ROP's excellent growth prospects, and highly competent management. Although it's difficult to predict when ROP's major markets will rebound, we conservatively believe ROP will be able to post sustainable earnings growth between 15%-17% and ROE in the mid-20% range. Based on these projections, our calculations value ROP 15% higher than current price levels.

Key Stock Statistics

S&P EPS Est. 1999	1.50	Tang. Bk. Value/Share	NM
P/E on S&P Est. 1999	23.2	Beta	1.04
S&P EPS Est. 2000	1.75	Shareholders	306
Dividend Rate/Share	0.26	Market cap. (B)	$ 1.1
Shs. outstg. (M)	30.3	Inst. holdings	75%
Avg. daily vol. (M)	0.031		

Value of $10,000 invested 5 years ago: $ 22,424

Fiscal Year Ending Oct. 31

	1999	1998	1997	1996	1995	1994
Revenues (Million $)						
1Q	89.08	90.10	55.11	52.90	34.41	33.50
2Q	100.5	96.00	67.02	47.11	39.82	38.40
3Q	104.1	97.41	88.52	59.95	47.10	32.70
4Q	—	105.7	87.59	65.70	54.09	43.10
Yr.	—	389.2	298.2	225.7	175.4	147.7
Earnings Per Share ($)						
1Q	**0.26**	**0.34**	**0.19**	0.29	0.11	0.13
2Q	**0.39**	**0.33**	0.33	0.18	0.14	0.22
3Q	**0.41**	**0.33**	0.37	0.23	0.22	0.10
4Q	**E0.44**	**0.24**	0.27	0.23	0.30	0.24
Yr.	**E1.50**	**1.24**	**1.16**	0.94	0.77	0.69

Next earnings report expected: early December

Dividend Data (Dividends have been paid since 1992.)

Amount ($)	Date Decl.	Ex-Div. Date	Stock of Record	Payment Date
0.065	Nov. 13	Jan. 12	Jan. 14	Jan. 29 '99
0.065	Feb. 18	Apr. 14	Apr. 16	Apr. 30 '99
0.065	May. 18	Jul. 14	Jul. 16	Jul. 31 '99
0.065	Aug. 17	Oct. 12	Oct. 14	Oct. 29 '99

STANDARD
&POOR'S
STOCK REPORTS

Roper Industries, Inc.

09-OCT-99

Business Summary - 20-AUG-99

Over the past seven fiscal years, Roper has boosted EPS at a compound annual growth rate (CAGR) of 27% and posted seven-year average ROE of 26%, at moderate debt levels. Moreover, retained earnings growth, a proxy for intrinsic value growth, expanded at an astounding CAGR of 83%. ROP's strategy has been to target high-margin industrial niche markets; increase competitive barriers through proprietary technologies and dominant market share; acquire complementary operations cheaply, and then dramatically boost their sales and profits; expand its international presence; and control operating costs. ROP's success is shown by strong operating profit margins in all three segments: Industrial Controls (21% in FY 98 (Oct.), 18% in FY 97 and 21% in FY 96), Fluid Handling (24%, 27% and 28%), and Analytical Instrumentation (18%, 23% and 15%).

The Industrial Controls unit (45% of FY 98 revenues) primarily makes high-tech industrial valves and other control equipment. IC derives 76% of its revenues from sales to the oil & gas industry. The 24% balance is divided as follows: general industrial, 10%; power utilities, 7%; petrochemical, 4%; and shipbuilding, 3%. Latest three-year IC profit margins averaged 20%.

Since FY 93, Industrial Controls has supplied Gazprom (Russia's gas utility monopoly) with over $100 million of gas pipeline flow control equipment. In late 1997, Gazprom terminated a U.S. Export-Import Bank agreement that would have guaranteed a $151 million commercial bank loan used to finance Gazprom's purchase of $151 million of ROP gas flow control equipment over a five-year period. The agreement was terminated amid U.S. government criticism of Gazprom's dealings with Iran. However in mid-1998, a Gazprom-owned Hungarian bank agreed to guarantee payment of $128 million of ROP equipment to Gazprom, using letters of credit. ROP is expected to deliver the $128 million of equipment over five years.

The Analytical Instrumentation unit (29% of FY 98 revenues) makes analytical equipment for the academic and commercial laboratory markets. Products include oil analysis equipment for the oil industry and leak-testing devices used to examine medical supplies such as rubber gloves, catheters and blood bags. In addition, AI, through its Roper Scientific division, is the world's largest maker of imaging and analytical components for electron microscopes, used commercially in such markets as the semiconductor industry (12% of AI sales). Other end-users include research labs (48% of AI sales) and general industrial (13%). Latest three-year AI profit margins averaged 19%.

The Fluid Handling unit (26% of FY 98 revenues) primarily makes high-tech industrial pumps for general industrial companies (42% of FH sales), semiconductor equipment makers (16%) and medical equipment manufacturers (9%). Latest three-year FH profit margins averaged 26%.

Per Share Data ($)										
(Year Ended Oct. 31)	**1998**	**1997**	**1996**	**1995**	**1994**	**1993**	**1992**	**1991**	**1990**	**1989**
Tangible Bk. Val.	NM	0.76	4.53	1.25	1.15	0.69	0.28	-0.07	NA	NA
Cash Flow	1.69	1.52	1.07	0.96	0.87	0.74	0.29	0.35	NA	NA
Earnings	1.24	1.16	0.94	0.77	0.69	0.65	0.18	0.23	NA	NA
Dividends	0.24	0.20	0.16	0.14	0.07	0.05	0.03	Nil	NA	NA
Payout Ratio	19%	17%	17%	18%	10%	7%	19%	Nil	NA	NA
Prices - High	34	34 7/8	26 3/8	20 1/4	17	19 1/2	5 1/4	NA	NA	NA
- Low	13 1/4	18 5/8	17 1/2	10 1/2	9	4 1/2	2 7/8	NA	NA	NA
P/E Ratio - High	27	30	28	26	24	30	28	NA	NA	NA
- Low	11	16	19	14	13	7	16	NA	NA	NA
Income Statement Analysis (Million $)										
Revs.	389	298	226	175	148	133	70.0	75.0	NA	NA
Oper. Inc.	80.5	72.3	51.4	43.4	38.3	33.4	14.3	15.2	NA	NA
Depr.	14.4	11.4	4.1	6.0	5.3	3.0	2.7	2.4	NA	NA
Int. Exp.	7.9	6.0	3.3	1.9	1.5	2.0	2.3	5.0	NA	NA
Pretax Inc.	59.6	55.1	44.2	36.0	31.6	28.4	7.5	7.9	NA	NA
Eff. Tax Rate	34%	34%	35%	35%	34%	33%	37%	37%	NA	NA
Net Inc.	39.3	36.4	28.9	23.3	20.9	19.1	4.7	4.9	NA	NA
Balance Sheet & Other Fin. Data (Million $)										
Cash	9.3	0.6	0.4	2.3	2.0	1.2	1.7	2.9	NA	NA
Curr. Assets	140	132	84.5	66.6	53.2	34.4	32.2	25.9	NA	NA
Total Assets	382	329	243	156	122	94.0	81.0	48.0	NA	NA
Curr. Liab.	57.6	44.9	39.5	27.7	20.8	20.5	10.5	11.2	NA	NA
LT Debt	120	100	63.4	20.2	16.7	9.9	28.4	31.8	NA	NA
Common Eqty.	197	178	137	106	82.9	62.4	40.5	3.7	NA	NA
Total Cap.	317	278	201	126	100	73.2	70.2	37.0	NA	NA
Cap. Exp.	5.5	5.0	5.0	3.2	4.1	3.9	0.9	4.3	NA	NA
Cash Flow	53.8	47.8	33.0	29.3	26.2	22.1	7.4	7.0	NA	NA
Curr. Ratio	2.4	2.9	2.1	2.4	2.6	1.7	3.1	2.3	NA	NA
% LT Debt of Cap.	37.9	35.9	31.6	16.0	16.8	13.5	40.4	85.9	NA	NA
% Net Inc.of Revs.	10.1	12.2	12.8	13.3	14.1	14.4	6.8	6.6	NA	NA
% Ret. on Assets	11.1	12.7	14.5	16.7	19.3	21.7	6.2	NA	NA	NA
% Ret. on Equity	21.0	23.1	23.8	24.7	28.7	36.9	20.5	NA	NA	NA

Data as orig reptd.; bef. results of disc opers/spec. items. Per share data adj. for stk. divs. Bold denotes diluted EPS (FASB 128)-prior periods restated. E-Estimated. NA-Not Available. NM-Not Meaningful. NR-Not Ranked.

Office—160 Ben Burton Rd., Bogart, GA 30622. **Tel**—(706) 369-7170. **Website**—http://www.roperind.com **Chrmn, Pres & CEO**—Derrick N. Key. **CFO**—Martin S. Headley. **Secy**—Shanler D. Cronk. **Investor Contact**—Don Templeman (706-369-7170). **Dirs**—W. L. Banks, L. von Braun, D. G. Calder, J. F. Fort III, D. N. Key, W. J. Prezzano, G. G. Schall-Riaucour, E. R. Scocimara, C. Wright. **Transfer Agent & Registrar**—SunTrust Bank, Atlanta. **Incorporated**—in Delaware in 1981. **Empl**— 2,100. **S&P Analyst:** Robert E. Friedman, CPA

STANDARD
&POOR'S
STOCK REPORTS

Royal Appliance Mfg.

NYSE Symbol **RAM**

In S&P SmallCap 600

09-OCT-99

Industry:
Housewares

Summary: This company markets plastic and metal vacuum cleaners for home and commercial use under the Dirt Devil and Royal brand names.

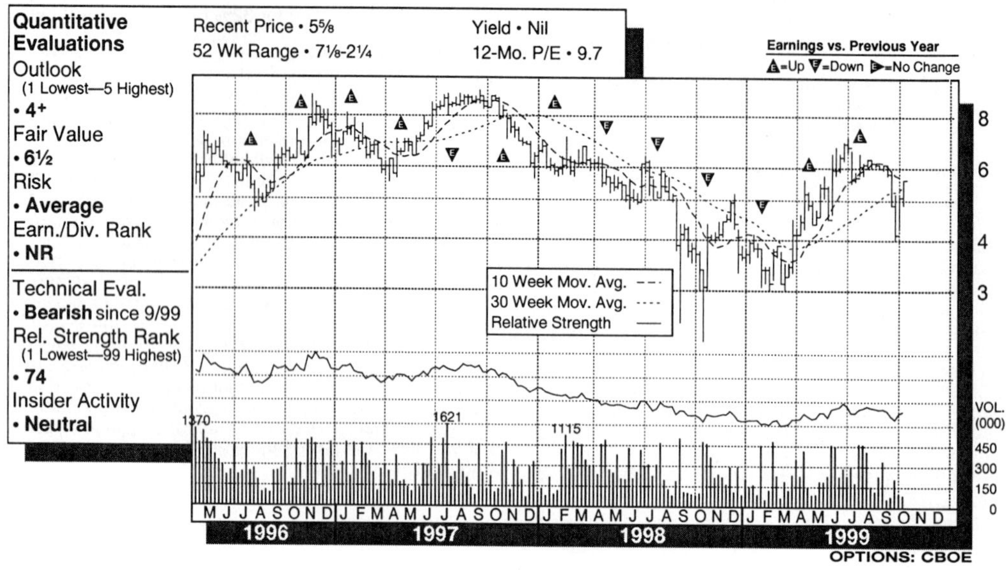

Business Profile - 12-APR-99

The company believes the domestic vacuum cleaner industry is a mature industry, with modest annual growth in many of its products but a decline in certain other products. Several major retailers have recently experienced significant financial difficulties, and some have filed for protection from creditors under bankruptcy laws. RAM sells its products to certain customers that are in bankruptcy proceedings. During the 1999 third quarter, the company will introduce the Dirt Devil Easy Steamer, a carpet extractor. At December 31, 1998, long term debt amounted to $18.4 million, and shareholders' equity was $46.7 million. Officers and directors own about 25% of the common stock outstanding.

Operational Review - 12-APR-99

Sales fell 13% in 1998, reflecting lower sales of the Dirt Devil Mop Vac and the Dirt Devil Broom Vac, partly offset by gains for upright vacuum cleaners. Gross margins narrowed, on the lower volume and a less favorable product mix; despite lower advertising and promotion and other selling costs, pretax income fell 80%. After taxes at 38.9%, versus 38.5%, net income was also down 80%, to $2,526,000 ($0.12 a share, on 9.9% fewer shares), from $12,407,000 ($0.52).

Stock Performance - 08-OCT-99

In the past 30 trading days, RAM's shares have declined 6%, compared to a 0.91% fall in the S&P 500. Average trading volume for the past five days was 17,020 shares, compared with the 40-day moving average of 30,544 shares.

Key Stock Statistics

Dividend Rate/Share	Nil	Shareholders	1,200
Shs. outstg. (M)	18.1	Market cap. (B)	$0.102
Avg. daily vol. (M)	0.023	Inst. holdings	21%
Tang. Bk. Value/Share	2.38		
Beta	2.22		

Value of $10,000 invested 5 years ago: $ 9,782

Fiscal Year Ending Dec. 31

	1999	1998	1997	1996	1995	1994
Revenues (Million $)						
1Q	89.21	51.85	58.62	52.26	49.02	59.79
2Q	80.49	51.26	61.07	62.97	58.26	55.24
3Q	—	73.61	87.38	73.69	66.99	69.06
4Q	—	106.0	118.3	97.20	96.30	96.03
Yr.	—	282.7	325.4	286.1	270.6	280.1
Earnings Per Share ($)						
1Q	**0.09**	**-0.11**	0.02	0.01	-0.10	-0.11
2Q	**0.15**	**-0.10**	0.04	0.05	-0.08	-0.05
3Q	—	**0.10**	0.17	0.13	-0.51	0.12
4Q	—	**0.26**	**0.29**	0.19	0.12	0.12
Yr.	—	**0.12**	**0.52**	**0.39**	**-0.57**	**0.08**

Next earnings report expected: mid October

Dividend Data

Royal intends to retain earnings to finance the expansion of its business. The shares were split two for one in 1992. A shareholder rights plan was adopted in 1993.

Royal Appliance Mfg. Co.

Business Summary - 12-APR-99

In 1984, the first in a long line of distinctive, red Dirt Devil hand-held vacuum cleaners appeared on store shelves. In the years since then, Royal Appliance Co. believes the Dirt Devil has become one of the largest selling line of hand-held vacuums in the U.S. The company has leveraged the well-known Dirt Devil brand name to gain market acceptance of other cleaning and floor care products. In addition, RAM markets metal vacuum cleaners for home and commercial use under the Royal brand name. Contributions by product line in recent years were:

	1998	1997	1996
Dirt Devil & plastic related products	88	90%	88%
Metal products	4%	4%	5%
Accessories & other	8%	6%	7%

The company's primary retail product lines are sold under the Dirt Devil name, and are typically intended for home use. The first product in this line was the Hand-Vac, a corded, hand-held vacuum cleaner. The line has since been expanded to include upright and canister vacuum cleaners, electric brooms and mops, and non-electric sweepers. The Dirt Devil line was expanded in 1998 by the introduction of the Dirt Devil Vision, a bagless upright, and the Scrub Devil, a cordless household scrubber.

Since the early 1900s, RAM has sold metal vacuum cleaners intended for both home and commercial use. This product line is sold exclusively through a network of independent dealers. In addition, RAM sells accessories, attachments, refurbished cleaners and replacement parts for each of its product lines. These products are available through retailers, dealers and the company..

Dirt Devil products are sold through major retailers, with Wal-Mart accounting for 32% of total sales in 1998 (36% in 1997), Target 14% (11%), and Kmart 13% (10%). Sales to the five largest customers in 1998 accounted for 64% (62%) of total sales.

The company devotes considerable attention to the design and appearance of its products and packaging to enhance their appeal to consumers and to stand out among other brands on retailers' shelves. For example, Dirt Devil products sold by mass merchants are often bright red in color. In order to increase the presence of Dirt Devil products in major retail outlets, the company provides retailers with distinct product alternatives, offering Dirt Devil product lines in a variety of styles and colors, and with various features.

Although RAM develops its products internally, it may also buy product tooling, license product designs and patents, and out-source certain products that are marketed under the Dirt Devil name.

The company's business is highly seasonal. RAM believes that a significant percentage of certain of it products, particularly the Dirt Devil Hand Vac, the Dirt Devil Broom Vac and the Dirt Devil Mop Vac, are given as gifts, and therefore sell in larger volumes during the Christmas shopping season.

Per Share Data ($) (Year Ended Dec. 31)	1998	1997	1996	1995	1994	1993	1992	1991	1990	1989
Tangible Bk. Val.	2.38	2.63	2.34	1.94	2.52	2.45	2.79	2.39	0.67	NA
Cash Flow	0.55	0.91	0.75	-0.09	0.57	0.07	1.05	1.20	0.33	NA
Earnings	0.12	0.52	0.39	-0.57	0.06	-0.35	0.81	1.09	0.27	NA
Dividends	Nil	Nil	Nil	Nil	Nil	Nil	Nil	Nil	NA	NA
Payout Ratio	Nil	Nil	Nil	Nil	Nil	Nil	Nil	Nil	NA	NA
Prices - High	7 1/8	9 1/4	9	4 5/8	6 1/4	14 1/4	31	23 7/8	NA	NA
- Low	2 1/4	5 1/2	2 5/8	2 1/2	3 1/4	4 1/2	7 5/8	7 3/4	NA	NA
P/E Ratio - High	59	18	23	NM	NM	NM	38	22	NA	NA
- Low	19	11	7	NM	NM	NM	9	7	NA	NA
Income Statement Analysis (Million $)										
Revs.	283	325	286	271	280	314	395	273	120	63.0
Oper. Inc.	14.9	32.0	26.0	11.9	19.5	4.1	42.3	51.2	15.8	6.5
Depr.	9.4	9.4	8.7	11.6	12.1	9.9	6.1	2.9	1.4	0.9
Int. Exp.	1.5	1.4	2.6	4.0	4.5	5.6	3.3	2.8	2.5	1.9
Pretax Inc.	4.1	20.2	15.3	-20.2	2.5	-13.0	33.0	45.4	11.7	3.6
Eff. Tax Rate	39%	39%	39%	NM	37%	NM	39%	40%	41%	44%
Net Inc.	2.5	12.4	9.4	-13.8	1.6	-8.3	20.2	27.4	6.9	2.0
Balance Sheet & Other Fin. Data (Million $)										
Cash	NA	1.4	1.0	Nil	Nil	Nil	Nil	Nil	1.3	0.0
Curr. Assets	77.3	89.0	83.8	84.7	86.0	93.0	134	94.3	54.2	24.7
Total Assets	117	135	126	131	142	154	188	121	62.0	30.0
Curr. Liab.	47.1	57.9	54.2	38.7	34.1	35.7	53.3	41.5	17.8	8.6
LT Debt	18.4	13.7	15.7	46.0	46.9	59.6	68.1	19.4	31.2	14.9
Common Eqty.	46.7	60.2	56.2	60.2	60.5	58.7	66.9	60.2	12.8	6.0
Total Cap.	70.4	77.1	72.0	92.6	107	118	135	79.6	43.9	20.9
Cap. Exp.	8.7	14.5	9.7	19.8	5.9	21.1	32.1	9.5	4.7	1.6
Cash Flow	11.9	21.8	18.2	-2.2	13.6	1.6	26.3	30.2	8.3	2.9
Curr. Ratio	1.6	1.5	1.5	2.2	2.5	2.6	2.5	2.3	3.0	2.9
% LT Debt of Cap.	26.2	17.7	21.9	50.0	43.7	50.4	50.4	24.4	70.9	71.2
% Net Inc.of Revs.	0.9	3.8	3.3	NM	0.6	NM	5.1	10.0	5.7	3.2
% Ret. on Assets	2.0	9.5	7.3	NM	1.1	NM	13.3	29.9	14.9	7.3
% Ret. on Equity	4.7	21.3	18.4	NM	2.6	NM	32.4	75.1	73.0	41.6

Data as orig reptd.; bef. results of disc opers/spec. items. Per share data adj. for stk. divs. Bold denotes diluted EPS (FASB 128)-prior periods restated. E-Estimated. NA-Not Available. NM-Not Meaningful. NR-Not Ranked.

Office—650 Alpha Drive, Cleveland, OH 44143. **Tel**—(216) 449-6150. **Website**—http://www.dirtdevil.com **Chrmn, Pres, CEO & Investor Contact**—Michael J. Merriman. **CFO, VP-Fin & Secy**—R. G. Vasek. **Dirs**—J. Kahl Jr., M. J. Merriman, E. P. Nalley, J. B. Richey II, J. P. Rochon, R. L. Schneeberger. **Transfer Agent**—National City Bank, Cleveland. **Incorporated**—in Ohio. **Empl**— 680. **S&P Analyst:** P.L.H.

STANDARD
&POOR'S
STOCK REPORTS

RSA Security

NASDAQ Symbol **RSAS**

In S&P SmallCap 600

13-OCT-99

Industry:
Computer (Software & Services)

Summary: This company (formerly Security Dynamics Technologies) offers security products used to protect and manage access to computer based information resources.

Quantitative Evaluations

Outlook
(1 Lowest—5 Highest)
• **4+**

Fair Value
• **43⅜**

Risk
• **High**

Earn./Div. Rank
• **NR**

Technical Eval.
• **Bullish** since 8/99

Rel. Strength Rank
(1 Lowest—99 Highest)
• **97**

Insider Activity
• **NA**

Recent Price • 32
52 Wk Range • 33-7½
Yield • Nil
12-Mo. P/E • 13.3

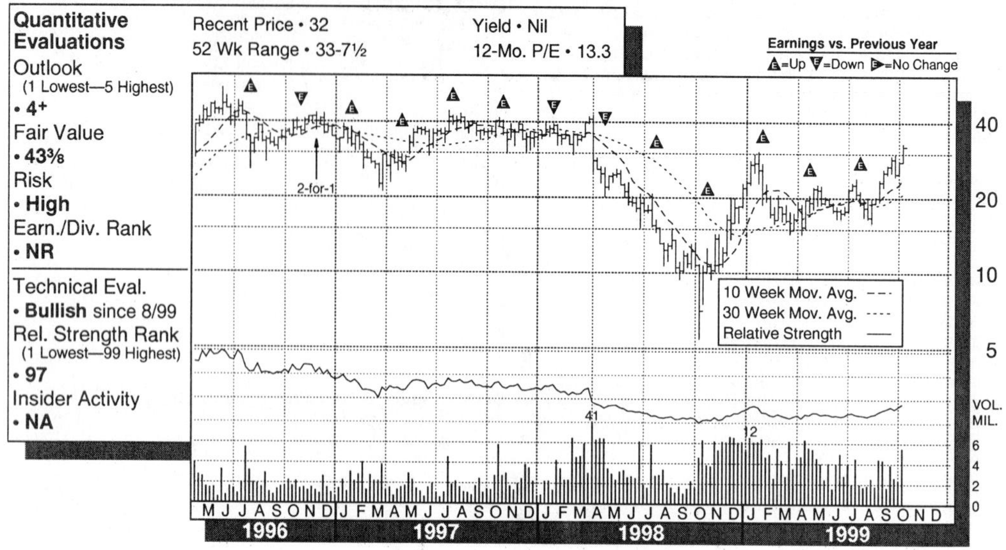

Business Profile - 17-JUN-99

Results in the first quarter of 1999 were inflated by a $74.5 million gain associated with the company's equity investment in VeriSign, Inc. RSAS expects its investment in VeriSign to result in a gain of $12.6 million in the second quarter of 1999. At March 31, 1999, RSAS owned approximately 2.6 million shares, or 11%, of VeriSign. In May 1999, RSAS said it had repurchased more than 3,000,000 shares of its common stock under a 4,000,000 share buyback program announced in October 1998. In December 1998, RSAS announced the establishment of operations to service the information security needs of companies in Latin America and the Caribbean. The present corporate title was adopted in October, 1999.

Operational Review - 17-JUN-99

Revenues in the three months ended March 31, 1999, rose 21%, year to year, on a 51% increase in OEM solutions and a 13% rise in enterprise solutions. Margins narrowed, reflecting a less favorable product mix, as well as more rapid increases in marketing costs and G&A expenditures; operating income fell 1.5%. Results benefited from a one-time gain of $74.5 million, which outweighed $6.5 million of exit costs and lower interest income. After taxes at 45.3%, versus 54.1%, and minority interest, net income jumped to $40,989,000 ($0.97 a share), from $2,964,000 ($0.07).

Stock Performance - 08-OCT-99

In the past 30 trading days, RSAS's shares have increased 38%, compared to a 0.91% fall in the S&P 500. Average trading volume for the past five days was 1,095,320 shares, compared with the 40-day moving average of 672,421 shares.

Key Stock Statistics

Dividend Rate/Share	Nil	Shareholders	319
Shs. outstg. (M)	38.9	Market cap. (B)	$ 1.2
Avg. daily vol. (M)	0.705	Inst. holdings	69%
Tang. Bk. Value/Share	7.54		
Beta	NA		

Value of $10,000 invested 5 years ago: NA

Fiscal Year Ending Dec. 31

	1999	1998	1997	1996	1995	1994
Revenues (Million $)						
1Q	48.67	40.25	26.44	12.17	6.24	—
2Q	51.81	43.37	29.66	14.07	8.17	—
3Q	—	40.80	34.83	20.36	8.77	—
4Q	—	46.92	39.73	23.50	10.62	—
Yr.	—	171.3	135.9	76.15	33.80	17.57
Earnings Per Share ($)						
1Q	**0.97**	**0.07**	0.13	0.09	0.05	—
2Q	**1.05**	**0.25**	0.15	0.10	0.06	—
3Q	—	**0.08**	0.06	0.02	0.05	—
4Q	—	**0.30**	**0.08**	0.20	0.08	—
Yr.	—	**0.69**	**0.41**	**0.36**	**0.22**	0.13

Next earnings report expected: mid October

Dividend Data

No cash dividends have been paid. Two-for-one stock splits were effected in November 1996 and October 1995.

A Division of The **McGraw-Hill** *Companies*

RSA Security Inc.

Business Summary - 17-JUN-99

In recent years, managing access to computer-based information resources has become increasingly difficult, as has guarding against unauthorized access to information. RSA Security Inc. (formerly Security Dynamics Technologies, Inc.) designs, develops, markets and supports a family of security products used to combat these two problems. The company's core product and solution offerings are continually evolving to address the following three critical areas of an information technology infrastructure: network and systems security, applications security and electronic commerce security

The company's network and systems security services and products are designed to help organizations assess, enforce and monitor security for their corporate networks and operating systems. The company provides customers with a comprehensive family of tools and services, including user authentication, intrusion detection and desktop encryption.

RSAS's application security services allow organizations to protect vital data stored across mission-critical, enterprise applications by providing a strong level of application security to protect against both internal and external threats and unauthorized access to sensitive information.

The company is also expanding into the market for software components that secure data within the fast-growing field of e-commerce. This marketplace includes the Internet, consumer and enterprise markets.

RSAS's ACE/Server and SecurID products provide centralized authentication services for enterprise networks and operating systems, ensuring that only authorized users gain access to network files, applications and communications. Utilizing smart cards and software tokens, these solutions protect network and data resources from potentially devastating accidental or malicious intrusion.

The company's Keon software enhances security for applications by providing authorized applications access and encrypted communications through the use of digital certificates. Keon technology simplifies user management and authorized applications access by providing a single administrative console for access to all public key-based applications.

The company's RSA BSAFE Encryption products are used to secure applications for electronic commerce over the Internet and intranets, enterprise security, entertainment, wireless communications and delivery of digital information over cable.

RSAS's expansion strategy includes enlarging its international presence. Sales outside North America accounted for 35% of revenues in 1998, versus 31% in 1997.

Per Share Data ($) (Year Ended Dec. 31)	1998	1997	1996	1995	1994	1993	1992	1991	1990	1989
Tangible Bk. Val.	6.00	5.02	3.53	3.53	1.29	NA	NA	NA	NA	NA
Cash Flow	0.85	0.52	0.41	0.51	0.55	0.78	NA	NA	NA	NA
Earnings	0.69	0.41	0.36	0.23	0.12	0.09	NA	NA	NA	NA
Dividends	Nil	Nil	Nil	Nil	Nil	NA	NA	NA	NA	NA
Payout Ratio	Nil	Nil	Nil	Nil	Nil	NA	NA	NA	NA	NA
Prices - High	42¾	44⅜	54½	29⅛	5⅛	NA	NA	NA	NA	NA
- Low	5⅜	21	21¼	4⅜	3½	NA	NA	NA	NA	NA
P/E Ratio - High	62	108	151	126	39	NA	NA	NA	NA	NA
- Low	8	51	59	19	27	NA	NA	NA	NA	NA
Income Statement Analysis (Million $)										
Revs.	171	136	76.1	33.8	17.6	12.1	8.9	6.1	NA	NA
Oper. Inc.	19.6	29.2	15.8	8.4	3.7	2.7	NA	NA	NA	NA
Depr.	6.8	4.4	1.8	0.7	0.3	0.1	NA	NA	NA	NA
Int. Exp.	Nil	Nil	Nil	Nil	Nil	Nil	Nil	Nil	NA	NA
Pretax Inc.	52.4	29.6	23.8	9.5	3.6	2.6	1.3	0.5	NA	NA
Eff. Tax Rate	45%	44%	45%	39%	35%	35%	39%	34%	NA	NA
Net Inc.	29.4	16.4	13.0	5.8	2.3	1.7	0.8	0.3	NA	NA
Balance Sheet & Other Fin. Data (Million $)										
Cash	158	95.7	9.5	44.6	17.5	2.8	NA	NA	NA	NA
Curr. Assets	216	206	125	98.4	31.4	6.6	NA	NA	NA	NA
Total Assets	281	232	140	102	32.6	7.3	5.5	3.7	NA	NA
Curr. Liab.	35.6	29.3	17.3	6.5	3.7	2.4	NA	NA	NA	NA
LT Debt	Nil	Nil	Nil	Nil	Nil	NA	NA	NA	NA	NA
Common Eqty.	243	199	121	95.0	28.9	-3.7	-5.4	-6.2	NA	NA
Total Cap.	245	202	123	95.0	28.9	NA	NA	NA	NA	NA
Cap. Exp.	18.9	10.9	9.2	1.5	0.8	0.2	NA	NA	NA	NA
Cash Flow	36.3	20.7	14.8	6.5	2.2	1.3	NA	NA	NA	NA
Curr. Ratio	6.1	7.0	7.2	15.1	8.5	2.8	NA	NA	NA	NA
% LT Debt of Cap.	Nil	Nil	Nil	Nil	Nil	NA	NA	NA	NA	NA
% Net Inc.of Revs.	17.2	12.0	17.1	17.2	13.2	13.8	9.0	5.3	NA	NA
% Ret. on Assets	11.5	8.8	10.8	8.7	11.6	26.3	17.5	NA	NA	NA
% Ret. on Equity	13.3	10.2	12.1	9.4	15.1	NM	NM	NA	NA	NA

Data as orig reptd.; bef. results of disc opers/spec. items. Per share data adj. for stk. divs. Bold denotes diluted EPS (FASB 128)-prior periods restated. E-Estimated. NA-Not Available. NM-Not Meaningful. NR-Not Ranked.

Office—36 Crosby Dr., Bedford, MA 01730. **Registrar & Transfer Agent**—Boston EquiServe, Boston.**Tel**—(617) 687-7000. **Website**—http://www.securitydynamics.com **Chrmn & CEO**—C. R. Stuckey, Jr. **Pres**—A. W. Coviello, Jr. **SVP-Fin, CFO & Treas**—M. G. O'Leary. **Investor Contact**—Meg O'Sullivan (781-687-7514). **Dirs**—D. J. Bidzos, A. W. Coviello, R. L. Earnest, J. B. Lassiter, III, G. M. Middlemas, J. K. Sims, C. R. Stuckey, Jr. **Transfer Agent & Registrar**—Boston EquiServe. **Incorporated**— in Massachusetts in 1984; reincorporated in Delaware in 1986. **Empl**— 764. **S&P Analyst:** Stephen J. Tekirian

STANDARD
&POOR'S
STOCK REPORTS

RTI International Metals

NYSE Symbol **RTI**
In S&P SmallCap 600

09-OCT-99

Industry:
Metal Fabricators

Summary: This holding company (formerly RMI Titanium) is a leading producer and marketer of titanium metal products used primarily in the aerospace industry.

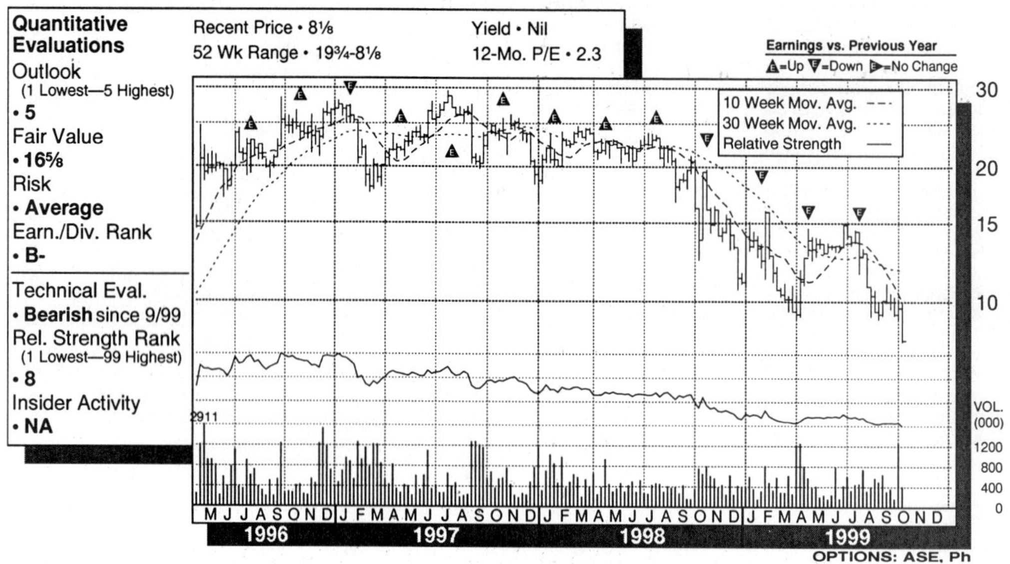

Business Profile - 01-JUL-99

During 1998, RMI Titanium became a subsidiary of this newly formed holding company. RTI has been developing new applications and markets for titanium in the energy extraction and chemical process industries, seeking to lessen its dependence on aerospace. In late 1998, it permanently closed two of its six vacuum arc furnaces, resulting in a $1 million charge in the fourth quarter. In April 1999, a new labor agreement was ratified. Results had been hurt by a labor strike at RMI Titanium's Niles, OH, plant since October 1998; the company estimated this cut earnings by $1 million to $2.5 million per month. In early 1998, RTI signed long-term aerospace supply agreements with Boeing and others.

Operational Review - 01-JUL-99

Sales in the 1999 first quarter dropped 24%, year to year, reflecting a softening commercial aerospace market, and lower shipments as a result of a strike at RMI's Niles plant. Gross margins narrowed, on the weak sales, and with higher SG&A expense and interest expense, pretax income fell 72%. After taxes at 37.0%, versus 28.8%, net income plunged 75%, to $3,742,000 ($0.18 a share, diluted), from $15,053,000 ($0.73). The company noted that, despite soft market conditions likely to continue for the balance of the year, it expects results to improve significantly following the strike settlement.

Stock Performance - 08-OCT-99

In the past 30 trading days, RTI's shares have declined 13%, compared to a 0.91% fall in the S&P 500. Average trading volume for the past five days was 80,080 shares, compared with the 40-day moving average of 119,854 shares.

Key Stock Statistics

Dividend Rate/Share	Nil	Shareholders	936
Shs. outstg. (M)	20.8	Market cap. (B)	$0.170
Avg. daily vol. (M)	0.134	Inst. holdings	66%
Tang. Bk. Value/Share	12.51		
Beta	0.76		

Value of $10,000 invested 5 years ago: $ 5,458

Fiscal Year Ending Dec. 31

	1999	1998	1997	1996	1995	1994
Revenues (Million $)						
1Q	67.45	89.04	73.71	54.60	40.10	36.36
2Q	0.76	96.54	75.03	58.31	39.62	35.34
3Q	—	81.03	86.44	64.48	42.91	32.84
4Q	—	70.87	83.35	73.97	48.53	38.85
Yr.	—	337.5	318.5	251.4	171.2	143.4
Earnings Per Share ($)						
1Q	**0.18**	**0.73**	**0.52**	**0.29**	-0.12	-1.99
2Q	**0.01**	**1.47**	**0.57**	**0.32**	-0.69	-2.05
3Q	—	**0.76**	**1.08**	**0.53**	-0.06	-0.21
4Q	—	**0.33**	**0.69**	**0.50**	0.57	-0.18
Yr.	—	**3.29**	**2.92**	**1.70**	**-0.30**	**-1.45**

Next earnings report expected: late October

Dividend Data

Dividends, paid since 1989, were omitted in 1991. A 1-for-10 reverse stock split was effected in 1994.

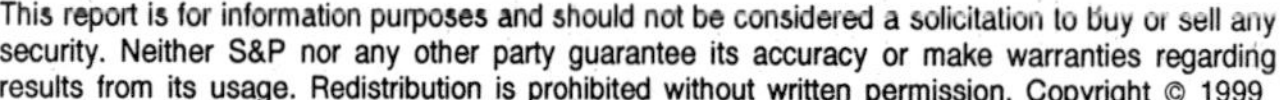

A Division of The McGraw-Hill Companies

RTI International Metals Inc.

Business Summary - 01-JUL-99

RTI International Metals (formerly RMI Titanium) is one of the world's leading producers of titanium mill and fabricated metal products. Its business was formerly conducted by a partnership equally owned by Quantum Chemical and USX Corp. Through a reorganization in late 1998, RTI formed a new holding company, consisting of RMI Titanium Co. and recently acquired New Century Metals and Weld-Tech Engineering Services, L.P. As a result of the reorganization, the company is divided into two groups: the Titanium Group, which primarily manufactures titanium mill products; and the Fabrication and Distribution Group, whose businesses manufacture and distribute other titanium products, and ferrous and non-ferrous metals. Sales and operating profits in 1998 were derived as follows: titanium accounted for 68% of revenues and 88% of operating income; fabrication and distribution 27% and 11%; and other 5% and 1%.

Titanium has physical characteristics such as high temperature performance and superior corrosion and erosion resistance. Titanium sponge is combined with alloying elements and titanium scrap for melting into ingots, which are processed into finished metal products such as bar, plate, sheet, strip, pipe and tube. About 86% of RTI's mill product sales in 1998 were aerospace related. In June 1998, the company became the sole supplier of titanium mill products for the F-22 fighter being built by Lockheed Martin and Boeing. The contract has a potential value of $340 million. In July 1997, RTI acquired a 90% stake in Galt Alloys, the largest U.S. maker of ferrotitanium, and a producer and global distributor of specialty alloys.

Major nonaerospace applications include oil and gas, and geothermal energy production industries, chemical processing and pulp and paper equipment, medical implants and high performance automotive engine parts. Golf clubs have recently emerged as an important nonaerospace application for the titanium industry.

Fabricated products include pipe and engineered tubular products, hot-formed and superplastically formed parts and cut shapes. In October 1998, RTI acquired New Century Metals, Inc., a maker of alloys ($50 million in sales), for $35 million. Separately, it acquired Weld-Tech Engineering Services, L.P., a provider of engineering and fabrication services to the oil and gas industry, for $11 million.

In November 1996, USX Corp. completed a public offering of notes exchangeable in February 2000 for up to 5,483,600 RTI common shares still owned by USX. In March 1999, USX said it had terminated its ownership position in the company by depositing the common shares with the trustee.

Exports accounted for 21% of 1998 sales.

Per Share Data ($) (Year Ended Dec. 31)	1998	1997	1996	1995	1994	1993	1992	1991	1990	1989
Tangible Bk. Val.	12.29	10.82	7.82	2.41	2.79	18.90	43.30	50.60	88.50	94.10
Cash Flow	3.56	3.17	1.99	0.12	-0.68	-3.90	-5.20	-31.70	25.70	21.10
Earnings	3.29	2.92	1.71	-0.30	-1.45	-8.10	-9.70	-39.20	18.20	14.60
Dividends	Nil	Nil	Nil	Nil	Nil	Nil	Nil	0.75	0.75	Nil
Payout Ratio	Nil	Nil	Nil	Nil	Nil	Nil	Nil	NM	4%	Nil
Prices - High	24⅝	29½	28½	10⅜	21¼	26¼	42½	80	130	NA
- Low	10⅝	16½	7⅞	3⅛	2	15	13¾	23¾	37½	NA
P/E Ratio - High	8	10	17	NM	NM	NM	NM	NM	7	NA
- Low	3	6	5	NM	NM	NM	NM	NM	2	NA
Income Statement Analysis (Million $)										
Revs.	338	319	251	171	143	127	136	166	255	242
Oper. Inc.	73.4	61.4	38.8	1.2	-1.8	-4.5	-4.9	-4.8	43.2	NA
Depr.	5.4	5.0	5.0	6.4	6.1	6.3	6.5	10.8	10.4	9.8
Int. Exp.	0.7	0.2	2.2	5.0	3.3	3.0	2.9	4.4	5.8	6.2
Pretax Inc.	70.1	57.3	31.7	-11.8	-11.6	-12.0	-14.0	-57.0	29.4	23.0
Eff. Tax Rate	2.80%	NM	NM	NM	NM	NM	NM	NM	4.30%	4.70%
Net Inc.	68.1	60.1	31.8	-4.6	-11.6	-12.0	-14.1	-57.1	28.1	22.0
Balance Sheet & Other Fin. Data (Million $)										
Cash	11.1	30.2	5.9	0.5	0.4	0.3	0.3	1.9	0.5	0.6
Curr. Assets	255	233	163	119	103	89.0	87.0	106	134	133
Total Assets	396	291	216	172	161	152	153	174	230	218
Curr. Liab.	58.7	47.7	31.0	31.8	28.7	22.9	15.2	26.6	24.6	30.2
LT Debt	20.1	Nil	3.6	64.0	54.7	66.7	62.3	58.8	61.2	68.5
Common Eqty.	293	221	159	36.9	43.0	28.0	63.0	78.0	137	111
Total Cap.	313	221	162	101	97.0	95.0	126	137	198	180
Cap. Exp.	33.1	7.9	4.2	1.6	1.1	1.0	4.2	9.0	20.4	18.0
Cash Flow	73.6	65.1	36.8	1.8	-5.4	-5.7	-7.6	-46.3	38.6	31.7
Curr. Ratio	4.3	4.9	5.3	3.7	3.6	3.9	5.8	4.0	5.4	4.4
% LT Debt of Cap.	6.4	Nil	2.2	63.4	56.2	70.5	49.6	43.1	30.9	38.1
% Net Inc.of Revs.	20.2	18.9	12.6	NM	NM	NM	NM	NM	11.0	9.1
% Ret. on Assets	19.8	23.7	16.4	NM	NM	NM	NM	NM	NA	NA
% Ret. on Equity	26.5	31.6	32.5	NM	NM	NM	NM	NM	NA	NA

Data as orig reptd.; bef. results of disc opers/spec. items. Per share data adj. for stk. divs. Bold denotes diluted EPS (FASB 128)-prior periods restated. E-Estimated. NA-Not Available. NM-Not Meaningful. NR-Not Ranked.

Office—1000 Warren Ave., Niles, OH 44446. **Tel**—(330) 544-7622. **Website**—http://www.rti-intl.com **Chrmn**—R. M. Hernandez. **Pres & CEO**—T. G. Rupert. **EVP**—J. H. Odle. **VP, CFO & Treas**—L. W. Jacobs. **Secy**—R. M. Hays. **Investor Contact**—Richard E. Leone. **Dirs**—C. R. Andersson, N. A. Armstrong, D. I. Booker, R. L. Gallatin, C. C. Gedeon, R. M. Hernandez, E. E. Holiday, J. H. Odle, T. G. Rupert, W. W. von Schack. **Transfer Agent & Registrar**—ChaseMellon Shareholder Services LLC, Ridgefield Park, NJ. **Incorporated**—in Ohio in 1975. **Empl**— 1,400. **S&P Analyst:** Stewart Scharf

STANDARD
&POOR'S
STOCK REPORTS

Ruby Tuesday

NYSE Symbol **RI**

In S&P SmallCap 600

09-OCT-99

Industry:
Restaurants

Summary: This company (formerly Morrison Restaurants) owns and operates casual dining restaurants under the names Ruby Tuesday, Mozzarella's and Tia's.

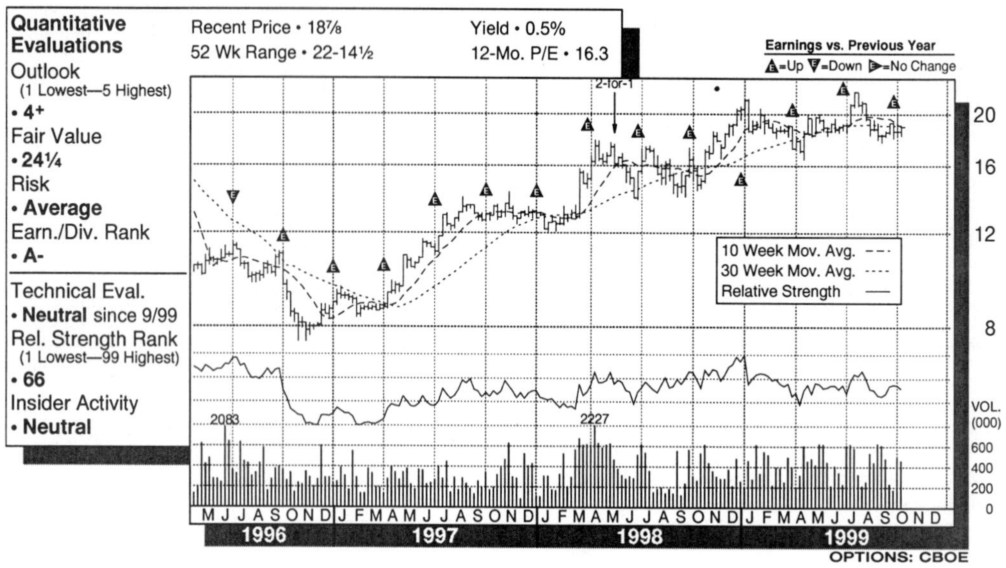

Business Profile - 07-JUL-99

A 29% EPS gain in the fiscal year ended May 31, 1999, marked the third consecutive year in which the company met or exceeded its goal of 15% to 20% EPS growth. As a result, RI has revised its goals for the coming five years: it now aims for 20% annual EPS growth, pretax margins of 10%, company-owned revenue growth of 10%, system-wide revenue growth of 15%, and return on equity of 30%. In addition, the company will continue to expand its franchising operations with the intention of achieving an equal number of company-owned and franchised restaurants. In connection with this strategy, RI has sold 65 company-owned restaurants to franchisees over the past two fiscal years.

Operational Review - 07-JUL-99

Based on a preliminary report, operating revenues increased 1.5% in FY 99; revenue gains were restricted by the sale of company-owned units to franchisees. Operating costs and expenses increased less rapidly, and with significantly lower interest expense, pretax income climbed 27%. After taxes at 36.2%, versus 35.4%, net income was up 26%, to $36,514,000 ($1.08 a share, on 2.3% fewer shares), from $29,080,000 ($0.84).

Stock Performance - 08-OCT-99

In the past 30 trading days, RI's shares have increased 4%, compared to a 0.91% fall in the S&P 500. Average trading volume for the past five days was 91,300 shares, compared with the 40-day moving average of 97,982 shares.

Key Stock Statistics

Dividend Rate/Share	0.09	Shareholders	6,220
Shs. outstg. (M)	32.0	Market cap. (B)	$0.607
Avg. daily vol. (M)	0.067	Inst. holdings	65%
Tang. Bk. Value/Share	6.38		
Beta	0.61		

Value of $10,000 invested 5 years ago: $ 7,603

Fiscal Year Ending May 31

	2000	1999	1998	1997	1996	1995
Revenues (Million $)						
1Q	195.3	178.2	174.1	157.3	146.0	241.0
2Q	—	175.8	170.3	156.3	152.0	253.0
3Q	—	184.7	181.6	172.6	164.0	272.0
4Q	—	183.7	184.6	169.2	158.2	269.0
Yr.	—	722.3	711.4	655.4	620.1	1,035
Earnings Per Share ($)						
1Q	**0.31**	**0.23**	**0.18**	0.15	0.12	0.67
2Q	—	**0.18**	**0.14**	0.11	0.07	0.34
3Q	—	**0.35**	**0.27**	0.23	-0.36	0.37
4Q	—	**0.32**	**0.26**	0.20	0.17	0.35
Yr.	—	**1.08**	**0.84**	**0.70**	-0.02	1.73

Next earnings report expected: mid January

Dividend Data (Dividends have been paid since 1998.)

Amount ($)	Date Decl.	Ex-Div. Date	Stock of Record	Payment Date
0.045	Jan. 15	Jan. 27	Jan. 29	Feb. 12 '99
0.045	Jul. 01	Jul. 14	Jul. 16	Jul. 30 '99

Ruby Tuesday Inc.

Business Summary - 07-JUL-99

Ruby Tuesday (RI) is striking out on its own as a company focused solely on the casual restaurant business. In early 1996, when it was known as Morrison Restaurants, it formed separate public companies for its family dining and health care businesses, and distributed the stock of these concerns to shareholders. This left Ruby Tuesday free from competition for corporate resources, and allowed management to focus on the restaurant business, which operates and franchises more than 480 casual dining establishments under the names Ruby Tuesday's, Mozzarella's, and Tia's. Its strategy includes improving margins and reducing costs, enhancing customer satisfaction, and adding restaurants to the system.

The first Ruby Tuesday restaurant opened in 1972 in Knoxville, TN, near the campus of the University of Tennessee. The Ruby Tuesday concept, with 16 operational units, was acquired by Morrison in 1982. During the following years, Morrison added other casual dining concepts, including the internally developed Mozzarella's American Cafe (formerly Silver Spoon). In January 1995, Morrison acquired Tia's, Inc., a chain of Tex-Mex restaurants, allowing it to enter one of the fastest growing segments of the casual dining market. The company moved into franchising in 1997, opening of one domestic franchised Ruby Tuesday restaurant and two international franchised Ruby Tuesday restaurants.

In an effort to expand its franchising operations so that it eventually achieves a mix of about the same number of company-owned and franchised restaurants, in FY 98 (May), RI sold 46 company-owned restaurants to franchise partners. It sold another 19 company-owned restaurants to franchisees in FY 99. The company had 15 franchise partners in its restaurant network as of May 31, 1999, and planned to add 20 franchise partners over the next three years.

As of June 6, 1999, RI's casual dining restaurants included 335 Ruby Tuesday's, with menu that includes fajitas, ribs, chicken, soups, and a salad bar. The company also had 45 American Cafes, including restaurants converted from the former Silver Spoon concept. In January 1995, RI acquired the Tia's Restaurants chain, featuring Mexican and southwestern U.S. food. As of June 6, 1999, there were 23 Tia's units open. In addition, at that date the company franchised 78 domestic units and seven international units. In June 1999, RI entered into an agreement to develop and operate Ruby Tuesday restaurants in Iceland.

Per Share Data ($)										
(Year Ended May 31)	**1999**	**1998**	**1997**	**1996**	**1995**	**1994**	**1993**	**1992**	**1991**	**1990**
Tangible Bk. Val.	NA	5.92	5.78	5.04	6.32	6.26	6.00	5.50	4.92	4.60
Cash Flow	NA	1.98	1.78	0.94	2.84	2.29	1.96	1.80	1.56	1.33
Earnings	1.08	0.84	0.70	-0.02	1.73	1.20	1.00	0.88	0.71	0.59
Dividends	0.09	0.05	Nil	0.14	0.35	0.33	0.32	0.29	0.28	0.28
Payout Ratio	8%	6%	Nil	NM	20%	28%	32%	34%	40%	47%
Cal. Yrs.	1998	1997	1996	1995	1994	1993	1992	1991	1990	1989
Prices - High	21¼	14⅜	17¾	27⅞	29¾	26¼	19⅞	13	12⅛	15⅛
- Low	12⅛	8⅜	7½	12½	20⅞	15⅞	11⅜	6	5⅜	10¼
P/E Ratio - High	20	17	25	NM	17	22	20	15	17	26
- Low	11	10	11	NM	12	13	11	7	8	17
Income Statement Analysis (Million $)										
Revs.	NA	711	655	620	1,033	1,210	1,098	1,039	969	898
Oper. Inc.	NA	88.3	81.3	67.6	117	108	96.1	87.5	74.9	66.7
Depr.	NA	39.5	38.6	34.1	39.9	40.8	36.5	35.1	31.7	28.7
Int. Exp.	NA	4.7	4.1	4.8	2.2	2.3	2.8	4.1	3.3	2.5
Pretax Inc.	NA	45.0	38.8	-2.3	105	71.2	60.9	51.4	42.5	35.4
Eff. Tax Rate	NA	35%	36%	NM	41%	37%	37%	37%	37%	35%
Net Inc.	NA	29.1	25.0	-0.7	62.2	44.7	38.2	32.7	26.6	23.0
Balance Sheet & Other Fin. Data (Million $)										
Cash	NA	8.3	7.6	7.1	8.3	5.0	31.4	50.1	22.5	15.5
Curr. Assets	NA	46.9	35.5	33.3	80.2	80.0	105	113	89.0	81.0
Total Assets	NA	410	419	381	484	408	398	370	331	316
Curr. Liab.	NA	84.4	69.1	66.6	125	123	103	90.4	76.8	70.2
LT Debt	NA	65.9	78.0	76.1	52.1	9.5	13.1	35.9	38.0	35.7
Common Eqty.	NA	212	224	197	245	221	220	204	181	176
Total Cap.	NA	222	315	282	309	242	256	256	241	229
Cap. Exp.	NA	65.8	74.0	109	131	90.3	63.0	37.8	43.9	55.9
Cash Flow	NA	68.6	63.6	33.5	102	85.5	74.7	67.7	58.3	51.7
Curr. Ratio	NA	0.6	0.5	0.5	0.6	0.6	1.0	1.3	1.2	1.1
% LT Debt of Cap.	NA	29.7	24.7	27.0	16.9	3.9	5.1	14.0	15.8	15.6
% Net Inc.of Revs.	NA	4.1	3.8	NM	6.0	3.7	3.5	3.1	2.7	2.6
% Ret. on Assets	NA	7.0	6.3	NM	13.9	11.3	10.0	9.3	8.2	7.7
% Ret. on Equity	NA	13.3	11.9	NM	26.6	20.6	18.1	17.0	14.9	13.3

Data as orig reptd.; bef. results of disc opers/spec. items. Per share data adj. for stk. divs. Bold denotes diluted EPS (FASB 128)-prior periods restated. E-Estimated. NA-Not Available. NM-Not Meaningful. NR-Not Ranked.

Office—150 West Church Ave., Maryville, TN 37801. **Tel**—(423) 379-5700. **Chrmn & CEO**—S. E. Beall III. **SVP, CFO & Treas**—J. R. Mothershed. **SVP & Secy**—D. T. Cronk. **Investor Contact**—Margie Naman. **Dirs**—C. L. Arnold, S. E. Beall III, J. B. McKinnon, A. R. Outlaw, B. F. Payton, D. Ratajczak, D. W. von Arx. **Transfer Agent & Registrar**—AmSouth Bank, N.A., Birmingham, AL. **Incorporated**—in Florida in 1954; reincorporated in Delaware in 1987; reincorporated in Georgia in 1996. **Empl**— 24,200. **S&P Analyst:** S.A.H.

STANDARD
&POOR'S
STOCK REPORTS

Rural/Metro Corp.

NASDAQ Symbol **RURL**

In S&P SmallCap 600

09-OCT-99

Industry:
Health Care (Specialized Services)

Summary: This company provides "911" emergency and general transport ambulance services, fire protection services and other safety and health care related services.

Quantitative Evaluations

Outlook
(1 Lowest—5 Highest)
• **5**

Fair Value
• **24½**

Risk
• **Average**

Earn./Div. Rank
• **B-**

Technical Eval.
• **Bearish** since 8/99

Rel. Strength Rank
(1 Lowest—99 Highest)
• **17**

Insider Activity
• **NA**

Recent Price • 6½
52 Wk Range • 12½-6⅛

Yield • Nil
12-Mo. P/E • 6.2

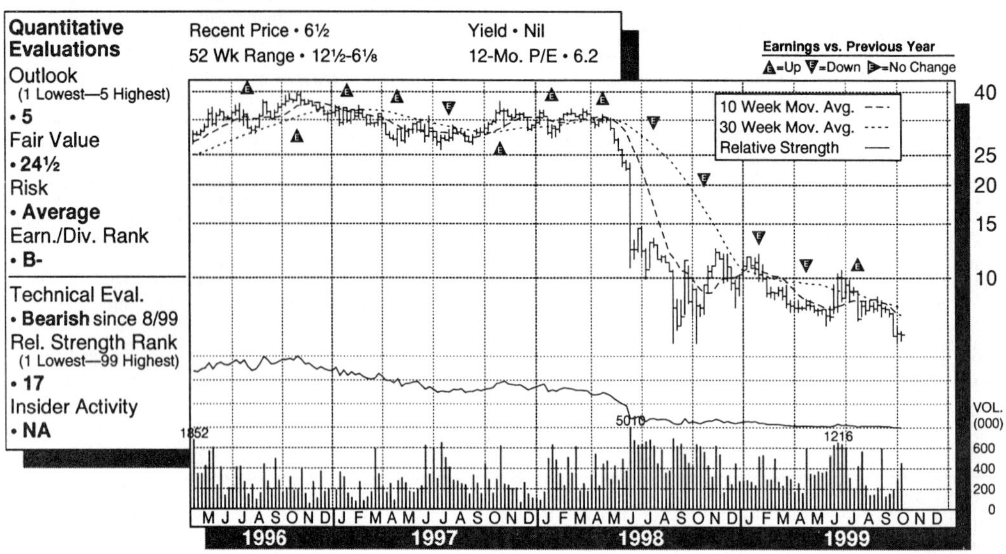

Business Profile - 16-AUG-99

Results in the first nine months of FY 99 (Jun.) reflected a restructuring charge and much higher interest expense. RURL has made moves to improve the quality of its revenue, including shifting revenue in some markets away from customers whose payors have made collection not cost effective. The company has also continued to make billing and collection a top priority, with continued investment in this area. RURL believes this helps protect the quality of its revenue and profits, and its ability to deliver consistent service quality to customers, especially in the current health care environment. If the reimbursement environment stabilizes, the company believes it will be better positioned to focus on growth opportunities it sees in the marketplace.

Operational Review - 16-AUG-99

Total revenues in the first nine months of FY 99 advanced 24%, year to year, reflecting acquisitions. Total expenses rose 27%, in part reflecting a $2.5 million restructuring charge; the gain in operating income was held to 10%. After sharply higher depreciation charges and interest expense, and taxes at 42.3%, versus 40.6%, net income fell 25%, to $12,412,000 ($0.85 a share, on 4.8% more shares), from $16,454,000 ($1.18).

Stock Performance - 08-OCT-99

In the past 30 trading days, RURL's shares have declined 20%, compared to a 0.91% fall in the S&P 500. Average trading volume for the past five days was 89,820 shares, compared with the 40-day moving average of 54,795 shares.

Key Stock Statistics

Dividend Rate/Share	Nil	Shareholders	1,005
Shs. outstg. (M)	14.5	Market cap. (B)	$0.095
Avg. daily vol. (M)	0.054	Inst. holdings	38%
Tang. Bk. Value/Share	NM		
Beta	1.58		

Value of $10,000 invested 5 years ago: $ 3,645

Fiscal Year Ending Jun. 30

	1999	1998	1997	1996	1995	1994
Revenues (Million $)						
1Q	138.8	97.77	73.99	55.76	36.27	22.87
2Q	139.6	111.3	77.53	60.84	39.96	24.12
3Q	142.9	129.8	84.92	64.98	43.79	26.40
4Q	140.1	136.7	83.36	68.68	51.57	30.97
Yr.	561.4	475.6	319.8	250.3	171.6	104.4
Earnings Per Share ($)						
1Q	**0.21**	**0.35**	**0.28**	0.23	0.18	0.11
2Q	**0.32**	**0.38**	**0.31**	0.25	0.21	0.16
3Q	**0.32**	**0.45**	**0.38**	0.31	0.25	0.21
4Q	**0.21**	**-0.64**	**0.08**	0.35	0.28	0.22
Yr.	**1.06**	**0.54**	**1.04**	**1.14**	**0.92**	**0.71**

Next earnings report expected: early November

Dividend Data

No cash dividends have been paid. The company intends to retain its earnings to finance the growth and expansion of business rather than pay cash dividends.

A Division of The McGraw-Hill Companies

Rural/Metro Corporation

Business Summary - 16-AUG-99

Two thousand sirens can make a lot of noise. Fortunately, the ambulances and fire vehicles in the Rural/Metro Corp. (RURL) fleet are spread over much of the U.S., from California to New York, from Texas up to South Dakota, and on into Canada. More than 450 communities rely on the company each day to provide ambulance or fire protection service, often, but not always, in response to a crisis. And respond RURL does: more than 1.5 million times a year.

RURL provides its core "911" emergency ambulance services under contracts with counties, fire districts and municipalities. It also furnishes general ambulance transportation for patients who require medical supervision while being ferried between residences and health care facilities. Ambulance services accounted for 81% of revenues in FY 98 (Jun.).

Several factors have led to increased demand for ambulance services in recent years, including the growth and aging of the population, and trends toward the use of outpatient services and specialized treatment facilities in an effort to contain health care costs. RURL also feels it will continue to benefit from the privatization of emergency services and the growing influence of managed care.

Fire protection services, which accounted for 10% of FY 98 revenues, consist mainly of fire prevention and fire suppression, and the company also conducts such related activities as hazardous material containment and rescue operations. RURL provides various levels of fire protection, ranging from reserve stations to fire stations that are fully staffed around the clock. For many fire departments, emergency medical response is an important part of their operation, so the company believes its ambulance and fire protection services are complementary. In addition to its contracts with municipalities and other governmental bodies, the company has arrangements with commercial establishments and large industrial complexes, such as airports.

RURL's primary growth strategy involves an aggressive campaign to acquire smaller ambulance service providers, and the company completed 11 such acquisitions in FY 98 alone. The company also entered into a few joint ventures during the fiscal year in the Baltimore, MD/Washington DC, area and San Diego, CA. Total ambulance transports rose from 915,000 in FY 97, to 1,215,000 in FY 98, with acquisitions responsible for most of the increase.

Revenues advanced 49% to $476 million in FY 98; after a $5 million pretax charge, net income fell 41%, to $7.5 million.

Per Share Data ($) (Year Ended Jun. 30)	1999	1998	1997	1996	1995	1994	1993	1992	1991	1990
Tangible Bk. Val.	NA	NM	NM	2.16	NM	NA	NA	NA	NA	NA
Cash Flow	NA	2.46	2.41	2.47	1.98	1.45	1.58	1.09	NA	NA
Earnings	1.06	0.54	1.04	1.14	0.92	0.71	0.63	0.33	NA	NA
Dividends	Nil	Nil	Nil	Nil	Nil	Nil	Nil	NA	NA	NA
Payout Ratio	Nil	Nil	Nil	Nil	Nil	Nil	Nil	NA	NA	NA
Prices - High	12	35 1/2	37 1/2	39 3/4	26 1/2	21 1/4	20 3/4	NA	NA	NA
- Low	6 1/8	6 1/8	25 7/8	22	16 3/4	13 1/4	12 1/2	NA	NA	NA
P/E Ratio - High	11	66	36	35	29	30	33	NA	NA	NA
- Low	6	11	25	19	18	19	20	NA	NA	NA
Income Statement Analysis (Million $)										
Revs.	NA	476	320	250	172	104	84.1	68.2	NA	NA
Oper. Inc.	NA	59.4	50.6	38.0	24.7	14.3	11.0	20.1	NA	NA
Depr.	NA	27.0	16.8	13.3	8.7	5.0	4.0	15.5	NA	NA
Int. Exp.	NA	14.1	5.7	5.1	3.1	1.8	2.9	2.5	NA	NA
Pretax Inc.	NA	13.5	22.1	19.6	12.9	7.6	4.2	2.0	NA	NA
Eff. Tax Rate	NA	44%	42%	41%	41%	38%	35%	35%	NA	NA
Net Inc.	NA	7.5	12.7	11.5	7.6	4.7	2.7	1.3	NA	NA
Balance Sheet & Other Fin. Data (Million $)										
Cash	NA	6.5	3.4	1.4	0.9	NA	NA	NA	NA	NA
Curr. Assets	NA	191	126	80.9	48.7	NA	NA	NA	NA	NA
Total Assets	NA	535	364	230	159	88.2	45.8	38.0	NA	NA
Curr. Liab.	NA	66.4	31.4	25.5	22.4	NA	NA	NA	NA	NA
LT Debt	NA	244	145	60.7	53.3	13.3	15.4	14.3	NA	NA
Common Eqty.	NA	178	160	120	65.6	47.3	4.1	-0.2	NA	NA
Total Cap.	NA	453	315	190	124	NA	NA	NA	NA	NA
Cap. Exp.	NA	31.0	23.9	18.2	11.5	5.3	NA	NA	NA	NA
Cash Flow	NA	34.5	29.5	24.9	16.3	9.7	6.6	4.3	NA	NA
Curr. Ratio	NA	2.9	4.0	3.2	2.2	NA	NA	NA	NA	NA
% LT Debt of Cap.	NA	53.8	45.9	32.0	43.0	NA	NA	NA	NA	NA
% Net Inc.of Revs.	NA	1.6	4.0	4.6	4.4	4.5	3.2	2.0	NA	NA
% Ret. on Assets	NA	1.7	4.3	5.9	5.6	7.1	6.4	NA	NA	NA
% Ret. on Equity	NA	4.4	9.1	12.4	13.4	18.4	120.0	NA	NA	NA

Data as orig reptd.; bef. results of disc opers/spec. items. Per share data adj. for stk. divs. Bold denotes diluted EPS (FASB 128)-prior periods restated. E-Estimated. NA-Not Available. NM-Not Meaningful. NR-Not Ranked.

Office—8401 East Indian School Rd., Scottsdale, AZ 85251. **Tel**—(602) 994-3886. **Website**—http://www.ruralmetro.com **Chrmn**—C. J. Clement. **Co-Vice Chrmn**—J. H. Bolin. **Co-Vice Chrmn & Secy**—L. G. Jekel. **Pres & CEO**—J. B. Furman. **SVP, CFO & Treas**—M. E. Liebner. **COO**—J. Brucker. **Dirs**—J. H. Bolin, M. A. Carpenter, C. J. Clement, J. Furman, L. G. Jekel, R. E. Ramsey, L. A. Witzeman. **Transfer Agent & Registrar**—American Securities Transfer, Inc. Lakewood, CO. **Incorporated**—in Arizona in 1948; reincorporated in Delaware in 1993. **Empl**— 12,250. **S&P Analyst:** C.F.B.

STANDARD
&POOR'S
STOCK REPORTS

Russ Berrie

NYSE Symbol **RUS**

In S&P SmallCap 600

09-OCT-99

Industry:
Consumer (Jewelry, Novelties & Gifts)

Summary: This company and its subsidiaries design and market a wide variety of gifts to retailers worldwide.

Quantitative Evaluations

Outlook
(1 Lowest—5 Highest)
• **NA**

Fair Value
• **NA**

Risk
• **Average**

Earn./Div. Rank
• **B+**

Technical Eval.
• **Bearish** since 8/99

Rel. Strength Rank
(1 Lowest—99 Highest)
• **36**

Insider Activity
• **NA**

Recent Price • 21¼
52 Wk Range • 27½-15¾
Yield • 3.8%
12-Mo. P/E • 11.2

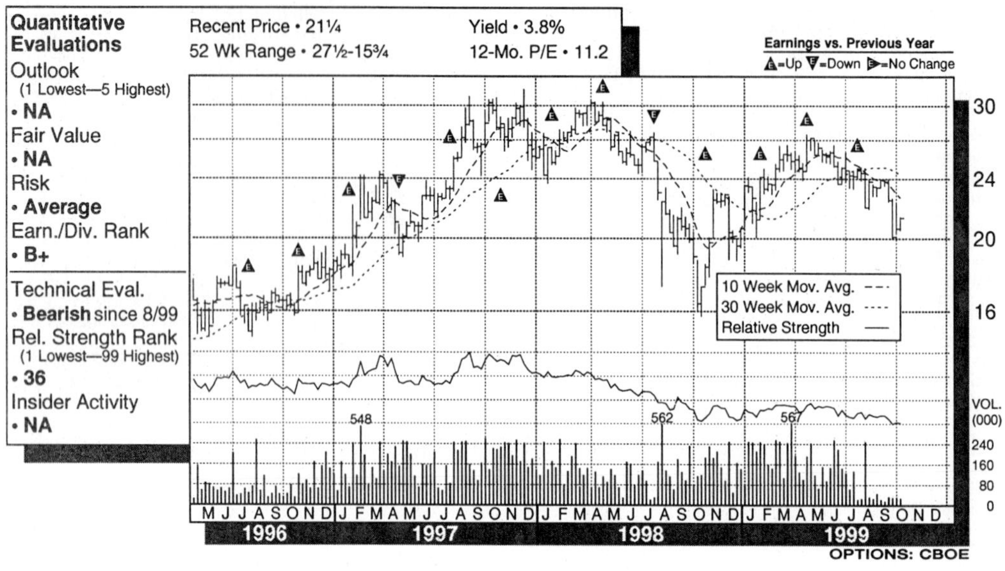

Business Profile - 01-JUL-99

Part of the earnings improvement in the first quarter of 1999 is attributable to the new Russ Marketing Plan 2000. Under the plan, RUS has become more account driven, selling products in depth to fewer customers, thereby reducing operating expenses by employing a smaller salesforce. The new telemarketing department established in 1998 has 28 full-time employees, and the company plans to continue to expand the department throughout 1999. Since expanding the authorization of its share repurchase program in January 1999, RUS has repurchased an additional 1,084,200 shares of common stock.

Operational Review - 01-JUL-99

Net sales in the three months ended March 31, 1999, rose 1.0%, year to year. Profitability improved on higher gross margins, successful inventory management, reduced salesforce costs, and savings from an office closing; operating income climbed 35%. Hindered by lower investment income and taxes at 35.6%, versus 34.7%, net income gained 19%, to $11,834,000 ($0.53 a share), from $9,933,000 ($0.44).

Stock Performance - 08-OCT-99

In the past 30 trading days, RUS's shares have declined 9%, compared to a 0.91% fall in the S&P 500. Average trading volume for the past five days was 5,120 shares, compared with the 40-day moving average of 5,615 shares.

Key Stock Statistics

Dividend Rate/Share	0.80	Shareholders	562
Shs. outstg. (M)	20.8	Market cap. (B)	$0.443
Avg. daily vol. (M)	0.006	Inst. holdings	41%
Tang. Bk. Value/Share	14.97		
Beta	0.71		

Value of $10,000 invested 5 years ago: $ 17,190

Fiscal Year Ending Dec. 31

	1999	1998	1997	1996	1995	1994
Revenues (Million $)						
1Q	75.40	74.64	62.07	56.57	80.12	64.17
2Q	47.48	50.95	58.48	41.78	74.26	57.55
3Q	—	82.97	87.53	67.90	104.0	82.85
4Q	—	61.96	63.26	60.00	90.11	73.54
Yr.	—	270.5	271.3	226.2	348.5	278.1
Earnings Per Share ($)						
1Q	**0.53**	**0.44**	**0.29**	**0.32**	0.19	0.05
2Q	**0.19**	**0.18**	**0.21**	**0.05**	0.01	-0.16
3Q	—	**0.73**	**0.72**	**0.62**	0.43	0.27
4Q	—	**0.46**	**0.45**	**0.23**	0.14	0.09
Yr.	—	**1.81**	**1.67**	**1.23**	**0.35**	**-0.13**

Next earnings report expected: late October

Dividend Data (Dividends have been paid since 1986.)

Amount ($)	Date Decl.	Ex-Div. Date	Stock of Record	Payment Date
0.190	Oct. 29	Nov. 18	Nov. 20	Dec. 04 '98
0.200	Jan. 28	Feb. 25	Mar. 01	Mar. 15 '99
0.200	Apr. 21	May. 19	May. 21	Jun. 04 '99
0.200	Jul. 29	Aug. 18	Aug. 20	Sep. 03 '99

A Division of The McGraw-Hill Companies

Russ Berrie and Company, Inc.

Business Summary - 01-JUL-99

When searching to find a gift that conveys the appropriate emotion, many people turn to Russ Berrie and Company. Under the Russ trademark, the company provides more than 6,000 gift items, priced at $3 to $50, designed to express feelings of friendship, fun or love. Products include stuffed animals, picture frames and home decor items, and revolve around a wide variety of themes, such as birthdays, anniversaries, inspirational gifts and baby products. RUS's products are sold in the U.S. and abroad to a diverse range of retailers, including gift stores, pharmacies, card shops and book stores. In 1998 and 1997, sales to foreign countries accounted for 29% and 27% of total sales, respectively.

After a lackluster performance for RUS stock in 1994 and 1995, the company decided to focus its efforts and resources on expanding its gift business, which benefits from an effective sales distribution network and the relatively low cost of purchasing products from Far East manufacturers. As part of the new strategy, in January 1996, the company sold Papel/Freelance, Inc., a subsidiary that generated 14% of 1995 gift segment revenues through the sale of ceramic products. In May 1997, RUS sold its two toy-related subsidiaries, Cap Toys and OddzOn, to a subsidiary of Hasbro Inc. (ASE: HAS), for about $167 million. The net proceeds from the sale were to be used for the acquisition of companies in the gift industry, and for general corporate purposes, including the repurchase of RUS common stock. In 1996, toy segment sales were about $151 million, or 40% of total sales.

RUS's focus on the gift business capitalizes on its utilization of low-cost independent Far East manufacturers. The company utilizes roughly 110 manufacturers in the Far East, primarily in the people's Republic of China, Taiwan, Indonesia, Philippines and Thailand. In 1998, 88% of RUS's products were produced in this region, with 12% produced in the U.S. In 1998, largest supplier to RUS accounted for 9% of all dollar volume purchases. The five largest suppliers accounted for about 32% in the aggregate.

Products are marketed primarily though RUS's own direct salesforce of 510 employees. During 1998, RUS implemented a new sales strategy, which transitioned smaller accounts from its reduced salesforce to RUS' new telemarketing department. The salesforce then can concentrate on fewer customers and sell products to larger accounts more in depth, thereby reducing operating expenses and employing a smaller salesforce. The company plans to expand the telemarketing department throughout 1999. During 1998, the company sold gift products to more than 57,000 customers, including: gift stores, pharmacies, shops, apparel stores, college and airport gift shops, hotel shops, hospitals, florists and chain stores. no single customer accounted for more than 2% of sales.

From January 1999 to April 21, 1999, RUS repurchased 1,084,200 shares of common stock.

Per Share Data ($) (Year Ended Dec. 31)	1998	1997	1996	1995	1994	1993	1992	1991	1990	1989
Tangible Bk. Val.	15.44	14.32	11.37	8.77	8.49	9.69	10.82	8.89	8.34	8.21
Cash Flow	1.93	1.80	1.39	1.10	0.58	0.91	2.99	1.27	1.06	0.76
Earnings	1.81	1.67	1.23	0.77	0.25	0.61	2.70	0.98	0.77	0.43
Dividends	0.76	0.68	0.60	0.60	0.60	0.60	0.47	0.40	0.70	0.27
Payout Ratio	42%	41%	49%	78%	NM	98%	17%	40%	91%	62%
Prices - High	30½	31½	19½	15⅞	15⅝	19⅞	24⅝	13⅛	12¼	14¼
- Low	15¾	18⅞	12¾	12	12¾	12⅜	12	8¾	9¼	9½
P/E Ratio - High	17	19	16	21	62	33	9	13	16	33
- Low	9	11	10	16	51	20	4	9	12	22
Income Statement Analysis (Million $)										
Revs.	271	271	226	348	278	279	444	268	251	246
Oper. Inc.	52.0	50.4	34.8	31.0	12.0	26.0	104	35.0	26.0	27.0
Depr.	2.6	3.0	3.4	7.2	7.0	6.4	6.6	6.5	6.5	7.4
Int. Exp.	0.1	0.2	0.1	0.2	0.2	0.6	0.5	0.8	0.5	0.9
Pretax Inc.	59.6	53.7	42.6	25.6	7.0	17.6	93.0	31.7	23.2	13.7
Eff. Tax Rate	32%	31%	37%	35%	24%	25%	35%	31%	25%	29%
Net Inc.	40.6	37.3	26.7	16.5	5.3	13.2	60.3	22.0	17.4	9.8
Balance Sheet & Other Fin. Data (Million $)										
Cash	226	93.4	52.3	36.8	48.0	82.9	92.7	51.4	38.5	78.3
Curr. Assets	334	323	216	201	189	213	264	194	178	192
Total Assets	378	353	277	265	255	259	299	226	216	217
Curr. Liab.	34.5	36.7	28.2	42.0	36.4	35.1	57.6	27.0	23.6	28.9
LT Debt	Nil	Nil	Nil	Nil	Nil	Nil	Nil	3.0	4.5	2.7
Common Eqty.	344	317	249	223	218	224	241	196	188	186
Total Cap.	344	317	249	223	218	224	241	199	193	188
Cap. Exp.	16.8	4.2	1.9	4.6	2.4	5.2	10.1	3.5	19.6	6.8
Cash Flow	43.2	40.3	30.1	23.7	12.4	19.5	66.9	28.6	23.9	17.2
Curr. Ratio	9.7	8.8	7.7	4.8	5.2	6.1	4.6	7.2	7.6	6.6
% LT Debt of Cap.	Nil	Nil	Nil	Nil	Nil	Nil	Nil	1.5	2.3	1.4
% Net Inc.of Revs.	15.0	13.7	11.8	4.7	1.9	4.7	13.6	8.2	7.0	4.0
% Ret. on Assets	11.1	11.8	10.1	6.4	2.1	4.8	22.9	10.1	8.0	4.6
% Ret. on Equity	12.3	13.2	11.3	7.5	2.4	5.8	27.5	11.6	9.3	5.3

Data as orig reptd.; bef. results of disc opers/spec. items. Per share data adj. for stk. divs. Bold denotes diluted EPS (FASB 128)-prior periods restated. E-Estimated. NA-Not Available. NM-Not Meaningful. NR-Not Ranked.

Office—111 Bauer Drive, Oakland, NJ 07436. **Tel**—(201) 337-9000. **Chrmn & CEO**—R. Berrie. **VP & Secy**—A. S. Bloom. **VP & COO**—J. Schaum. **VP, CFO & Investor Contact**—E. R. Lohwasser. **Dirs**—R. Benaroya, A. Berrie, R. Berrie, P. Cargotch, I. Kaufthal, C. Klatskin, J. Kling, W. A. Landman, S. Slauson, J.S. Weston. **Transfer Agent & Registrar**—First City Transfer Co., Iselin, NJ. **Incorporated**—in New Jersey in 1966. **Empl**—1,500. **S&P Analyst:** Jordan Horoschak

STANDARD
&POOR'S
STOCK REPORTS

Ryan's Family Steak Houses

NASDAQ Symbol **RYAN**

In S&P SmallCap 600

09-OCT-99 **Industry:** Restaurants

Summary: This company operates or franchises over 300 family-oriented restaurants, mainly in the southern and midwestern U.S.

Quantitative Evaluations

Outlook (1 Lowest—5 Highest) • **4+**

Fair Value • **14½**

Risk • **Low**

Earn./Div. Rank • **B+**

Technical Eval. • **Bearish** since 8/99

Rel. Strength Rank (1 Lowest—99 Highest) • **52**

Insider Activity • **NA**

Recent Price • 9¾ 52 Wk Range • 14-8⅝ Yield • Nil 12-Mo. P/E • 9.6

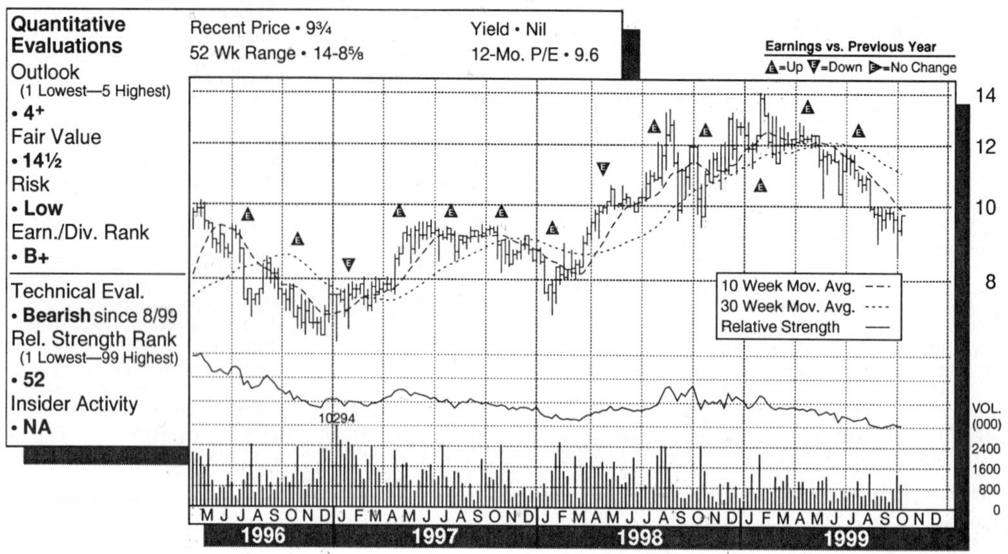

Business Profile - 16-AUG-99

Moving into the second half of 1999, RYAN has challenged itself to increase average unit sales volumes over its 1998 sales performance. RYAN's plans focus on increasing customer satisfaction through new product introductions and improved customer service. It plans to open a total of 10 new company-owned Ryan's during 1999. Target sites for these new restaurants are spread throughout the company's current 22 state operating area. The company also plans to relocate a total of six restaurants during 1999. RYAN has bought back 30% of its common shares that were outstanding at time of the buyback's inception in March 1996.

Operational Review - 16-AUG-99

Sales in the six months ended June 30, 1999, increased 4.1%, year to year, primarily due to increased same store sales, reflecting the favorable impact of the company's advertising campaign, as well as its carving program. Margins widened, aided by lower food costs, but with 24% higher general and administrative costs and 19% greater interest expense, the gain in pretax income was held to 2.4%. After taxes at 36.6%, versus 36.1%, income edged up 1.6%, to $21,478,000 ($0.55 a share, on 13% fewer shares), from $21,149,000 ($0.47).

Stock Performance - 08-OCT-99

In the past 30 trading days, RYAN's shares were unchanged, compared to a 0.91% fall in the S&P 500. Average trading volume for the past five days was 192,780 shares, compared with the 40-day moving average of 134,013 shares.

Key Stock Statistics

Dividend Rate/Share	Nil	Shareholders	20,000
Shs. outstg. (M)	37.1	Market cap. (B)	$0.362
Avg. daily vol. (M)	0.166	Inst. holdings	67%
Tang. Bk. Value/Share	7.44		
Beta	0.44		

Value of $10,000 invested 5 years ago: $ 10,833

Fiscal Year Ending Dec. 31

	1999	1998	1997	1996	1995	1994
Revenues (Million $)						
1Q	159.6	153.2	146.4	130.8	117.3	106.9
2Q	174.3	167.5	157.2	147.4	131.4	114.8
3Q	—	162.4	152.7	146.3	131.8	115.0
4Q	—	153.9	142.8	141.0	132.8	111.5
Yr.	—	637.0	599.2	565.5	513.2	448.2
Earnings Per Share ($)						
1Q	**0.26**	**0.20**	**0.21**	**0.16**	0.14	0.14
2Q	**0.29**	**0.27**	**0.24**	**0.20**	0.17	0.16
3Q	—	**0.24**	**0.20**	**0.18**	0.16	0.15
4Q	—	**0.23**	**0.17**	Nil	0.15	0.12
Yr.	—	**0.94**	**0.82**	**0.55**	0.62	**0.53**

Next earnings report expected: mid October

Dividend Data

The company does not expect to pay cash dividends in the foreseeable future. It plans to retain funds for expansion.

Ryan's Family Steak Houses, Inc.

Business Summary - 16-AUG-99

Ryan's Family Steak Houses had 283 company-owned and operated and 24 franchised family-oriented restaurants as of June 30, 1999.

Ryan's company-owned restaurants are located in freestanding masonry buildings that range in size from about 10,000 to 11,500 sq. ft. The interior of most restaurants contains two or three dining rooms, seating about 300 to 500 customers. The focal points of the main dining room are the centrally located scatter bars (referred to in the restaurants as the Mega Barr) and bakery bar. The parking lots at the restaurants can very in size with available parking ranging from 125 to 200 cars.

A Ryan's restaurant is a family-oriented restaurant serving a wide variety of foods from its Mega Barr as well as traditional grilled entrees, such as charbroiled USDA Choice steaks, hamburgers, chicken and seafood. The Mega Barr include fresh and pre-made salad items, soups, cheese, and a variety of hot meats and vegetables, and hot yeast rolls prepared and baked daily on site. All entree purchases include a trip to a bakery bar. Bakery bars feature hot and fresh-from-the-oven cookies, brownies and other bakery products as well as various dessert selections, such as ice cream, frozen yogurt, fresh fruit, cakes, cobblers and several dessert toppings.

Most Ryan's are open seven days a week. Some new restaurants are closed on Mondays for their first two to three months of operation. Typical hours of operation are 11:00 a.m to 9:30 p.m. Sunday through Thursday and 11:00 a. m. to 10:30 p.m. Friday and Saturday. The average customer count per restaurant during 1998 was about 7,000 per week. and the average meal price per person was $6.44 (including beverage.)

The company has an Operating Partner Program, providing restaurant managers with an additional career path and an opportunity to share in the profitability of their stores. After being selected and upon a $10,000 investment in the company's stock, the Operating Partners share in both the profit improvement and overall profitability of the restaurant. Operating Partners were managing 121 restaurants as of June 30, 1999. Management hopes to have 150 operating partners by the end of 1999.

At December 10, 1998, the company's sole franchise agreement was with Family Steak Houses of Florida, Inc., which, at that date, operated 26 Ryan's in central and northern Florida. The present franchise agreement expires in 2010 with a 10-year renewal option. The company has been having discussions with Family regarding Family's plans in 1999 and beyond. Such discussions may lead to a change in the number of Ryan's required to be operated by Family.

At March 3, 1999, all restaurant sites, except 13 properties under land leases, were owned by the company.

Per Share Data ($)										
(Year Ended Dec. 31)	**1998**	**1997**	**1996**	**1995**	**1994**	**1993**	**1992**	**1991**	**1990**	**1989**
Tangible Bk. Val.	7.16	6.75	6.00	5.66	5.04	4.47	3.93	3.35	2.89	2.43
Cash Flow	1.58	1.39	1.05	1.04	0.89	0.83	0.78	0.65	0.66	0.57
Earnings	0.94	0.82	0.55	0.62	0.57	0.53	0.53	0.44	0.46	0.41
Dividends	Nil	Nil	Nil	Nil	Nil	Nil	Nil	Nil	Nil	Nil
Payout Ratio	Nil	Nil	Nil	Nil	Nil	Nil	Nil	Nil	Nil	Nil
Prices - High	13 3/8	9 1/2	10 1/8	8 1/2	9 1/8	11 5/8	12 5/8	10 1/4	8 1/2	9
- Low	7 1/8	6 7/8	6 1/2	6 1/8	5 3/8	6 7/8	7 3/4	5 3/8	3 7/8	5 1/8
P/E Ratio - High	14	12	18	14	16	22	24	23	18	22
- Low	8	8	12	10	9	13	15	12	8	13
Income Statement Analysis (Million $)										
Revs.	638	600	567	515	449	396	352	299	273	241
Oper. Inc.	95.5	92.9	86.2	76.2	65.6	61.0	58.6	48.2	48.5	42.0
Depr.	27.6	27.4	25.7	22.4	17.4	16.1	13.7	11.4	10.5	8.4
Int. Exp.	6.8	5.9	6.0	4.4	2.7	1.5	1.3	1.5	1.5	1.6
Pretax Inc.	63.0	61.1	45.3	52.8	48.0	45.3	45.3	37.1	38.3	34.2
Eff. Tax Rate	36%	36%	37%	37%	36%	37%	38%	37%	37%	37%
Net Inc.	40.3	39.2	28.6	33.2	30.5	28.5	28.3	23.3	24.1	21.5
Balance Sheet & Other Fin. Data (Million $)										
Cash	1.5	0.3	0.8	1.3	0.7	1.9	1.7	2.6	2.6	0.4
Curr. Assets	13.4	12.1	11.9	11.5	9.0	9.5	6.0	6.3	6.1	3.1
Total Assets	509	496	463	431	380	334	275	238	205	165
Curr. Liab.	125	64.9	76.6	114	100	84.9	55.7	50.3	43.1	28.1
LT Debt	81.4	93.0	93.0	Nil	Nil	Nil	Nil	Nil	Nil	Nil
Common Eqty.	280	317	294	303	269	239	210	177	152	127
Total Cap.	384	431	387	317	280	249	219	187	162	137
Cap. Exp.	43.7	47.5	89.8	71.3	66.7	71.3	54.2	43.9	46.1	32.0
Cash Flow	67.9	66.6	54.3	55.6	47.9	44.6	42.0	34.7	34.6	29.9
Curr. Ratio	0.1	0.2	15.5	0.1	0.1	0.1	0.1	0.1	0.1	0.1
% LT Debt of Cap.	21.2	21.6	24.0	Nil	Nil	Nil	Nil	Nil	Nil	Nil
% Net Inc.of Revs.	6.3	6.5	5.0	6.5	6.8	7.2	8.0	7.8	8.8	8.9
% Ret. on Assets	8.0	8.1	6.3	8.2	8.6	9.4	11.0	10.5	13.0	14.0
% Ret. on Equity	13.5	12.8	9.6	11.6	12.0	12.7	14.6	14.1	17.2	18.4

Data as orig reptd.; bef. results of disc opers/spec. items. Per share data adj. for stk. divs. Bold denotes diluted EPS (FASB 128)-prior periods restated. E-Estimated. NA-Not Available. NM-Not Meaningful. NR-Not Ranked.

Office—405 Lancaster Ave., P.O. Box 100, Greer, SC 29652. **Tel**—(864) 879-1000. **Website**—http://www.ryanssteaks.com **Chrmn, Pres & CEO**—C. D. Way. **EVP**—G. E. McCranie. **VP-Fin, Treas & Investor Contact**—Fred T. Grant Jr. **Dirs**—J. D. Cockman, B. L. Edwards, B. S. MacKenzie, G. E. McCranie, H. K. Roberts Jr., J. M. Shoemaker Jr., C. D. Way. **Transfer Agent**—Wachovia Bank of North Carolina, Winston-Salem. **Incorporated**—in South Carolina in 1977. **Empl**— 18,000. **S&P Analyst:** M.I.

Ryland Group

NYSE Symbol **RYL**

In S&P SmallCap 600

09-OCT-99

Industry: Homebuilding

Summary: Ryland is one of the largest U.S. homebuilders, operating in 20 states across the nation, and also has extensive mortgage lending operations.

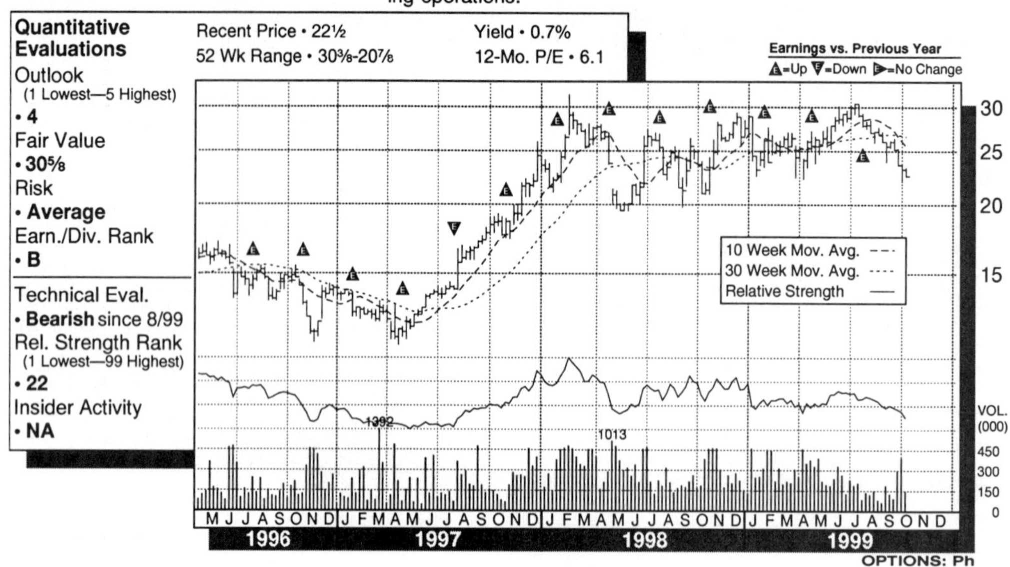

Business Profile - 13-SEP-99

Over the past few years, RYL has been repositioning its mortgage operations to take maximum advantage of the strategic relationship it has with Ryland Homes. During 1998, RYL implemented its strategy for increased market dominance by allocating additional capital to markets with the greatest potential to enhance shareholder value, including the acquisition of Regency Communities in Tampa, FL. The company also exited three smaller markets that did not meet its strategic objectives. Through the first half of 1999, RYL bought back 77,000 shares for $1.8 million under a one million (6.8%) share plan; 881,400 shares still remain available for repurchase. During 1998, RYL completed a two million share buyback plan.

Operational Review - 13-SEP-99

Revenues in the first half of 1999 advanced 19%, year to year, as higher residential homebuilding volume offset a decline in financial services and limited-purpose subsidiaries' revenues. Profitability benefited from the higher revenues and lower financial services expenses due to a reduction in RYL's loan-servicing operations; following lower interest expense, net income was up 105%, to $27,723,000 ($1.76 a diluted share, on 3.3% more shares), from $13,517,000 ($0.86). RYL believes earnings will continue to grow during 1999 as it focuses on improving its margins. New orders increased 16%, year to year, while backlog increased 19%, to $886 million.

Stock Performance - 08-OCT-99

In the past 30 trading days, RYL's shares have declined 13%, compared to a 0.91% fall in the S&P 500. Average trading volume for the past five days was 28,980 shares, compared with the 40-day moving average of 34,836 shares.

Key Stock Statistics

Dividend Rate/Share	0.16	Shareholders	3,300
Shs. outstg. (M)	14.9	Market cap. (B)	$0.336
Avg. daily vol. (M)	0.046	Inst. holdings	82%
Tang. Bk. Value/Share	23.61		
Beta	1.16		

Value of $10,000 invested 5 years ago: $ 13,144

Fiscal Year Ending Dec. 31

	1999	1998	1997	1996	1995	1994
Revenues (Million $)						
1Q	404.0	336.3	329.5	327.4	345.2	332.5
2Q	502.4	425.9	399.6	414.3	389.2	416.7
3Q	—	462.3	421.6	402.5	402.6	447.8
4Q	—	541.1	499.1	436.0	448.0	445.7
Yr.	—	1,765	1,650	1,580	1,585	1,643
Earnings Per Share ($)						
1Q	**0.65**	**0.29**	**0.08**	**0.03**	-0.13	0.23
2Q	**1.12**	**0.57**	**0.22**	**0.31**	-0.09	0.45
3Q	—	**0.81**	**0.41**	**0.25**	0.01	0.50
4Q	—	**1.12**	**0.62**	**0.28**	-1.55	0.11
Yr.	—	**2.79**	**1.32**	**0.87**	**-1.78**	1.29

Next earnings report expected: late October

Dividend Data (Dividends have been paid since 1975.)

Amount ($)	Date Decl.	Ex-Div. Date	Stock of Record	Payment Date
0.040	Oct. 28	Jan. 13	Jan. 15	Jan. 30 '99
0.040	Feb. 18	Apr. 13	Apr. 15	Apr. 30 '99
0.040	Jun. 21	Jul. 13	Jul. 15	Jul. 30 '99
0.040	Aug. 18	Oct. 13	Oct. 15	Oct. 30 '99

The Ryland Group, Inc.

Business Summary - 13-SEP-99

The Ryland Group (RYL), which constructs single-family attached and detached housing and condominiums, and also markets mortgage-related products and services, has been changing its financial strategy in an effort to enhance shareholder value. RYL has been repurchasing stock in an effort to improve its long-term prospects, which it hopes will result in a more efficient capital structure and a lower cost of capital. As of 1998 year end, the company operated in 250 communities in 21 metropolitan markets in 14 states. Homebuilding contributed 96% of revenues and 87% of operating profit from continuing operations in 1998 (excluding one-time charges). Financial services and limited-purpose subsidiaries contributed the rest.

The homebuilding segment constructs homes in five regions: Mid-Atlantic, Midwest, Southeast, Southwest and West (RYL's California region operations were consolidated into the West segment in January 1996). The company's homes vary in size and price range, but are generally marketed to customers purchasing their first home or first or second time move-up home. In 1998, RYL's average closing price was $185,000, up from $182,000 a year earlier. Substantially all construction work is performed by subcontractors monitored by company supervisors. In November 1998, RYL purchased the home building operations of Regency Communities of Tampa, FL. Regency builds single-family and age-restricted retirement communities with homes priced from $90,000 to $150,000. During 1998, the company began exiting from the Delaware Valley, Portland and Salt Lake City markets -- three smaller markets that did not meet its strategic objectives.

Financial services activities include mortgage origination, loan servicing and title and escrow services. In April 1998, RYL sold a portion of its loan servicing portfolio to PNC Mortgage Corp. of America. The company has repositioned this segment through a strategy consisting of focusing on retail mortgage loan origination and servicing activities, divesting non-core assets, leveraging its affiliation with the homebuilding segment to increase its capture rate for builder loans, and reaching mortgage customers directly through the use of technology. During 1998, RYL originated 8,412 mortgage loans, of which 30% were for buyers of homes built by other companies, purchases of existing homes, or refinancings. The company services loans that it originates, as well as loans originated by others. During 1996, RYL sold its wholesale mortgage operations, as it did not expect the unit to contribute significantly to future earnings.

In July 1998, the company redeemed $100 million of 10.5% senior subordinated notes due 2002. In April 1998, RYL had sold $100 million of 8.25% senior subordinated notes due 2008.

Per Share Data ($) (Year Ended Dec. 31)	1998	1997	1996	1995	1994	1993	1992	1991	1990	1989
Tangible Bk. Val.	21.85	19.07	18.23	17.77	18.88	17.86	18.51	16.32	15.49	16.19
Cash Flow	4.37	3.35	2.84	0.44	2.93	1.36	3.71	2.17	3.13	4.45
Earnings	2.79	1.32	0.87	-1.78	1.29	-0.34	1.66	0.53	1.53	3.25
Dividends	0.16	0.38	0.60	0.60	0.60	0.60	0.60	0.60	0.60	0.60
Payout Ratio	6%	29%	69%	NM	47%	NM	37%	111%	38%	17%
Prices - High	31 5/8	26	17 1/8	17 1/2	25 5/8	24 1/2	28	25 1/4	22	25 3/4
- Low	19 3/8	11 1/8	11 1/4	12 1/4	12 7/8	15 7/8	18 1/2	13 3/4	9 1/2	18 1/4
P/E Ratio - High	11	20	20	NM	20	NM	17	48	14	8
- Low	7	8	13	NM	10	NM	11	26	6	6
Income Statement Analysis (Million $)										
Revs.	1,765	1,650	1,580	1,585	1,643	1,474	1,442	1,214	1,313	1,402
Oper. Inc.	135	110	104	90.6	168	185	328	353	379	430
Depr.	25.6	31.4	31.4	34.5	25.6	26.1	30.6	20.5	19.9	15.9
Int. Exp.	34.3	41.9	46.5	53.6	117	167	249	302	334	362
Pretax Inc.	75.2	36.5	26.4	-42.4	37.3	-4.7	42.3	14.3	34.1	70.9
Eff. Tax Rate	42%	40%	40%	NM	40%	NM	35%	34%	36%	38%
Net Inc.	43.6	21.9	15.8	-25.5	22.4	-2.7	27.5	9.5	21.8	44.0
Balance Sheet & Other Fin. Data (Million $)										
Cash	49.8	36.1	28.7	56.0	26.8	44.3	10.4	3.5	4.5	13.3
Curr. Assets	NA	NA	NA	NA	NA	NA	NA	NA	NA	NA
Total Assets	1,215	1,283	1,339	1,581	1,704	2,316	2,897	3,559	3,860	4,212
Curr. Liab.	NA	NA	NA	NA	NA	NA	NA	NA	NA	522
LT Debt	308	310	354	397	409	352	171	NA	NA	NA
Common Eqty.	346	305	310	300	327	312	329	245	236	235
Total Cap.	654	651	665	698	737	665	501	NA	NA	NA
Cap. Exp.	22.7	47.6	19.5	30.2	19.0	12.6	14.0	3.7	10.1	9.0
Cash Flow	68.2	51.6	45.2	6.8	45.6	20.8	55.5	27.2	38.9	59.0
Curr. Ratio	NA	NA	NA	NA	NA	NA	NA	NA	NA	NA
% LT Debt of Cap.	47.0	47.6	53.2	56.9	55.5	52.9	34.1	NA	NA	NA
% Net Inc.of Revs.	2.5	1.3	1.0	NM	1.4	NM	1.9	0.8	1.7	3.1
% Ret. on Assets	3.5	1.7	1.1	NM	1.1	NM	0.8	0.3	0.5	1.1
% Ret. on Equity	13.1	6.6	4.5	NM	6.2	NM	7.8	2.8	8.2	21.6

Data as orig reptd.; bef. results of disc opers/spec. items. Per share data adj. for stk. divs. Bold denotes diluted EPS (FASB 128)-prior periods restated. E-Estimated. NA-Not Available. NM-Not Meaningful. NR-Not Ranked.

Office—11000 Broken Land Parkway, Columbia, MD 21044. **Tel**—(410) 715-7000. **Website**—http://www.ryland.com **Chrmn, Pres & CEO**—R. C. Dreier. **SVP & Treas**—B. Haase. **SVP & Secy**—T. Geckle. **Investor Contact**—Susan Cass. **Dirs**—R. C. Dreier, J. A. Flick, Jr., L. M. Frecon, R. J. Gaw, L. M. Harlan, W. L. Jews, W. G. Kagler, III, C. St. Martin, J. O. Wilson. **Transfer Agent & Registrar**—ChaseMellon Shareholder Services, Ridgefield Park, NJ. **Incorporated**—in Maryland in 1967. **Empl**— 2,119. **S&P Analyst:** Stewart Scharf

STANDARD
&POOR'S
STOCK REPORTS

S3 Incorporated

NASDAQ Symbol **SIII**

In S&P SmallCap 600

09-OCT-99

Industry: Electronics (Semiconductors)

Summary: S3 supplies high-performance accelerator solutions for the graphical user interface environments created by Microsoft Windows, IBM OS/2 and other advanced PC operating systems.

Quantitative Evaluations

Outlook (1 Lowest—5 Highest)
• **1⁻**

Fair Value
• **6⅜**

Risk
• **High**

Earn./Div. Rank
• **NR**

Technical Eval.
• **Bearish** since 9/99

Rel. Strength Rank (1 Lowest—99 Highest)
• **58**

Insider Activity
• **Unfavorable**

Recent Price • 10
52 Wk Range • 12⅞-2
Yield • Nil
12-Mo. P/E • NM

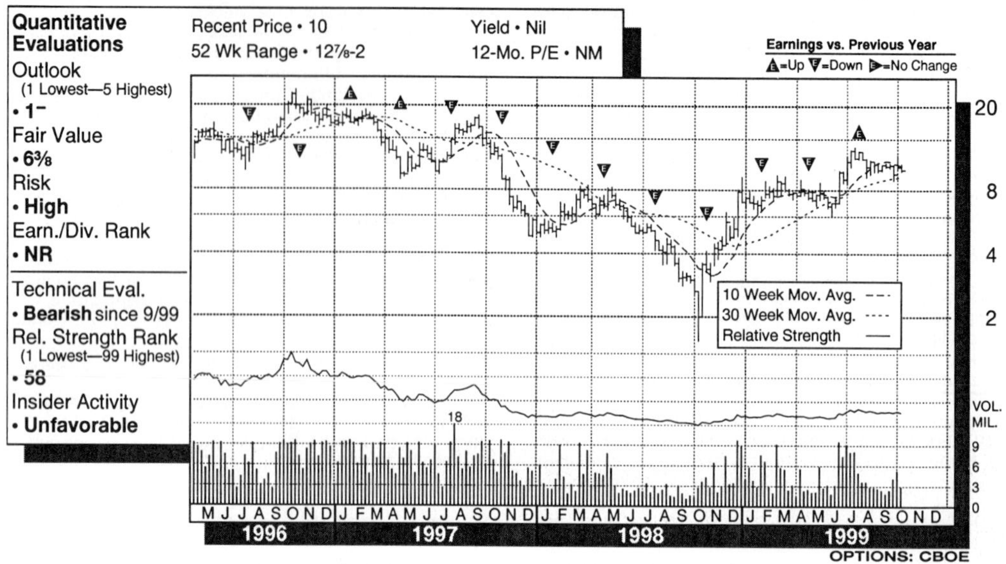

OPTIONS: CBOE

Business Profile - 30-JUL-99

S3 has said it is pleased with the widespread adoption of its Savage4D graphics accelerator product, which was introduced in the 1999 first quarter. The company's Savage3D accelerator product was introduced in the third quarter of 1998, but failed to gain market acceptance. In June 1999, S3 agreed to acquire Diamond Multimedia, a multimedia and Internet connectivity company with 1998 revenues of $600 million. The company will exchange 0.52 of an S3 common share for each of Diamond's 35.3 million shares. S3 also recently announced that it would receive $42 million in cash and 250 million common shares of United Microelectronics Corp. in connection with an earlier equity investment.

Operational Review - 30-JUL-99

Revenues in the first half of 1999 fell 25%, year to year, as a 46% drop in the first quarter outweighed 7.4% growth in the second quarter. The first quarter decline resulted from reduced unit volumes and average selling prices. Gross margins widened to 26.4% of revenues, from 16.3%. With lower operating costs, and in the absence of an $8.0 million writedown, after a gain of $7.2 million on the sale of a manufacturing joint venture, versus a gain of $26.6 million, the pretax loss narrowed. However, in the absence of a $12.0 million income tax benefit, the net loss widened to $12,779,000 ($0.24 a share, on 3.4% more shares), from $7,513,000 ($0.15).

Stock Performance - 08-OCT-99

In the past 30 trading days, SIII's shares were unchanged, compared to a 0.91% fall in the S&P 500. Average trading volume for the past five days was 570,980 shares, compared with the 40-day moving average of 613,374 shares.

Key Stock Statistics

Dividend Rate/Share	Nil	Shareholders	40,000
Shs. outstg. (M)	72.1	Market cap. (B)	$0.721
Avg. daily vol. (M)	0.721	Inst. holdings	29%
Tang. Bk. Value/Share	2.92		
Beta	1.29		

Value of $10,000 invested 5 years ago: $ 11,851

Fiscal Year Ending Dec. 31

	1999	1998	1997	1996	1995	1994
Revenues (Million $)						
1Q	44.30	82.51	130.3	110.1	57.42	37.53
2Q	57.25	53.30	84.60	103.8	70.56	27.47
3Q	—	47.29	119.6	119.4	84.79	30.89
4Q	—	41.55	101.9	132.0	103.5	44.42
Yr.	—	224.6	436.4	465.4	316.3	140.3
Earnings Per Share ($)						
1Q	**-0.27**	**0.08**	**0.27**	**0.21**	0.15	0.10
2Q	**0.02**	**-0.23**	**-0.04**	**0.15**	0.17	-0.13
3Q	—	**-0.69**	**0.08**	**0.17**	0.20	0.05
4Q	—	**-1.36**	**-0.16**	**0.27**	0.23	0.11
Yr.	—	**-2.22**	**0.17**	**0.81**	**0.75**	**0.14**

Next earnings report expected: late October

Dividend Data

Amount ($)	Date Decl.	Ex-Div. Date	Stock of Record	Payment Date

A Division of The McGraw-Hill Companies

S3 Incorporated

Business Summary - 30-JUL-99

As the personal computer (PC) continues to evolve into a graphics-oriented, interactive, real-time system, S3 believes demand for its graphics accelerators will grow. The company supplies high-performance accelerator solutions for the graphical user interface environments created by Microsoft Windows, IBM OS/2 and other advanced PC operating systems. Its integrated accelerator solutions relieve a computer's central processing unit of primary responsibility for graphics processing, and significantly improve the graphics performance of PCs.

The company was one of the pioneers in the graphics acceleration market; its first product, the 86C911 graphics accelerator chip, began shipping in volume in 1991. Since that time, it has frequently upgraded its product offerings. S3 currently offers graphics and video accelerators for desktop and mobile computers that are differentiated by a variety of features.

The desktop is the largest segment of the PC industry for the company's accelerator market, and is characterized by intense competition and rapid technological advances. In 1998, S3 introduced the Savage3D accelerator. With the Savage3D chip, the company redesigned its 3D architecture to deliver high-performance multimedia graphics using an advanced compression technology. In February 1999, S3 introduced the Savage4 accelerator, the next generation accelerator in the Savage line. The company also sells the Trio3D family of desktop accelerators.

S3's mobile strategy is to combine the same level of 2D, 3D and video capabilities found in its desktop accelerators with advanced power management and flat panel display support. Its most recent mobile product, the ViRGE/MX accelerator, brings powerful capabilities to notebook PC users.

The company also offers a broad line of software, including drivers and utilities designed to optimize the performance of its accelerators. The software is shipped as an integral part of S3's accelerator products.

In December 1998, S3 entered into a long-term strategic relationship with Intel, including a 10-year cross-license agreement for the development of future products.

R&D efforts focus on high-performance accelerator and related software products for new markets, such as real-time communications and mobile computing, and on enhanced versions of its current line of products, with an emphasis on 3D acceleration. In 1998, a total of $78.6 million (35% of net sales) was spent on R&D, versus $78.6 million (18%) in 1997. Export sales accounted for 89% of net sales in 1998, versus 70% in 1997.

Per Share Data ($) (Year Ended Dec. 31)	1998	1997	1996	1995	1994	1993	1992	1991	1990	1989
Tangible Bk. Val.	3.16	5.36	5.23	3.89	1.89	1.73	0.29	NA	NA	NA
Cash Flow	-1.68	0.53	1.16	0.90	0.24	0.45	0.19	NA	NA	NA
Earnings	-2.22	0.17	0.95	0.75	0.14	0.41	0.15	NA	NA	NA
Dividends	Nil	Nil	Nil	Nil	Nil	Nil	Nil	NA	NA	NA
Payout Ratio	Nil	Nil	Nil	Nil	Nil	Nil	Nil	NA	NA	NA
Prices - High	$9\frac{1}{4}$	$19\frac{1}{4}$	$23\frac{3}{4}$	22	$9\frac{5}{8}$	$10\frac{3}{8}$	NA	NA	NA	NA
- Low	$1\frac{1}{2}$	$4\frac{3}{4}$	$9\frac{3}{4}$	$7\frac{5}{8}$	$3\frac{1}{4}$	$3\frac{3}{4}$	NA	NA	NA	NA
P/E Ratio - High	NM	NM	25	29	69	25	NA	NA	NA	NA
- Low	NM	NM	10	10	23	9	NA	NA	NA	NA
Income Statement Analysis (Million $)										
Revs.	225	436	466	316	140	113	30.6	3.3	Nil	NA
Oper. Inc.	-136	33.0	82.9	57.8	10.1	25.0	5.7	-4.2	-6.2	NA
Depr.	27.2	18.5	10.7	6.8	4.0	1.7	0.9	0.8	0.7	NA
Int. Exp.	6.2	6.5	2.0	Nil	0.0	0.2	0.1	0.3	0.3	NA
Pretax Inc.	-124	12.3	74.4	55.4	6.9	24.4	4.7	-4.9	-6.9	NA
Eff. Tax Rate	NM	28%	35%	36%	21%	38%	4.70%	Nil	Nil	NA
Net Inc.	-112	8.9	48.4	35.4	5.5	15.1	4.5	-4.9	-6.9	NA
Balance Sheet & Other Fin. Data (Million $)										
Cash	31.0	90.5	157	93.9	34.6	44.5	5.8	5.2	NA	NA
Curr. Assets	197	301	321	236	79.5	75.3	14.2	7.5	NA	NA
Total Assets	326	493	480	322	89.5	81.7	15.8	8.3	NA	NA
Curr. Liab.	44.9	91.4	89.0	91.0	19.8	20.3	7.6	4.9	NA	NA
LT Debt	104	108	118	24.0	0.5	0.1	1.2	1.2	NA	NA
Common Eqty.	164	271	267	206	68.9	61.0	7.0	14.3	NA	NA
Total Cap.	267	379	385	230	69.7	61.4	8.2	-1.1	NA	NA
Cap. Exp.	5.9	28.1	23.4	17.6	7.6	6.3	1.7	0.1	0.1	NA
Cash Flow	-86.0	27.4	59.1	42.2	9.5	16.8	5.4	-4.1	-6.2	NA
Curr. Ratio	4.4	3.3	3.6	2.6	4.0	3.7	1.9	1.5	NA	NA
% LT Debt of Cap.	38.8	28.5	30.6	10.4	0.6	0.2	14.4	NM	NA	NA
% Net Inc.of Revs.	NM	2.0	10.4	11.2	3.9	13.4	14.5	NM	NM	NA
% Ret. on Assets	NM	1.8	12.1	17.2	6.4	14.8	36.9	NM	NA	NA
% Ret. on Equity	NM	3.3	20.5	25.7	8.5	NM	NM	NM	NA	NA

Data as orig reptd.; bef. results of disc opers/spec. items. Per share data adj. for stk. divs. Bold denotes diluted EPS (FASB 128)-prior periods restated. E-Estimated. NA-Not Available. NM-Not Meaningful. NR-Not Ranked.

Office—2801 Mission College Blvd., P.O. Box 58058, Santa Clara, CA 95052-8058. **Tel**—(408) 588-8000. **Website**—http://www.s3.com **Chrmn, Pres & CEO**—K. F. Potasher.**SVP & CFO**—W. D. Amaral. **SVP & Secy**—R. T. Yara. **Dirs**—J. C. Colligan, T. N. Holdt, R. P. Lee, K. F. Potasher, C. J. Santoro, R. T. Yara. **Transfer Agent & Registrar**—Boston EquiServe, Canton, MA. **Incorporated**—in Delaware in 1989. **Empl**— 434. **S&P Analyst:** Jim Corridore

Safeskin Corp.

Nasdaq Symbol **SFSK**

In S&P SmallCap 600

09-OCT-99

Industry:
Health Care (Medical Products & Supplies)

Summary: SFSK is the leading producer of disposable latex medical examination gloves for the U.S. market, and the world's largest maker of disposable powder-free examination gloves.

S&P Opinion: Hold (★★★)

Recent Price • 8¾
52 Wk Range • 35¼-7⅛
Yield • Nil
12-Mo. P/E • 21.9

Quantitative Evaluations

Outlook
(1 Lowest—5 Highest)
• **5**

Fair Value
• **16⅝**

Risk
• **Average**

Earn./Div. Rank
• **B**

Technical Eval.
• **Bearish** since 7/99

Rel. Strength Rank
(1 Lowest—99 Highest)
• **56**

Insider Activity
• **NA**

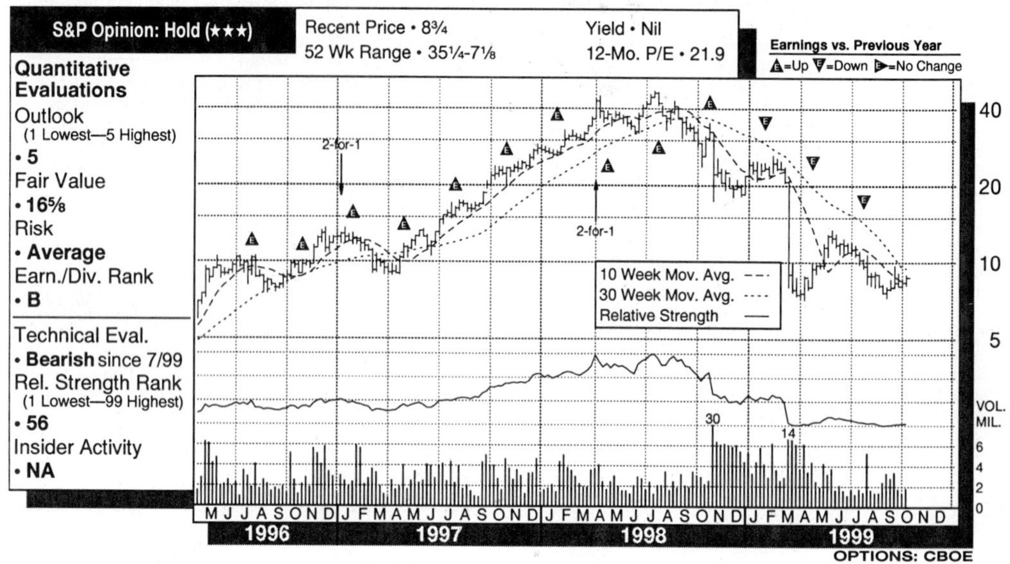

Overview - 02-AUG-99

We expect 1999 revenues of approximately $230 million, unchanged from 1998, as excess industry capacity and lower selling prices are expected to offset higher unit sales volume. SFSK expects single digit unit sales growth in the 1999 second half, although this growth will continue to be offset by lower selling prices reflecting increased capacity as a result of new manufacturers entering the market. SFSK will attempt to maintain and expand its market share and offset lower selling prices by signing contracts with large purchasing organizations, introducing new products, and expanding into new markets. Earnings will also benefit from manufacturing efficiencies due to SFSK's shift to low-cost production facilities in Thailand. However, negative foreign exchange rates and price erosion will lead to operating margin contraction. As a result, we are cutting our 1999 EPS estimate $0.10 to $0.50, and our 2000 EPS estimate $0.15 to $0.70.

Valuation - 02-AUG-99

The shares declined dramatically in early March 1999, following SFSK's warning that 1999 revenues and earnings will be significantly below expectations. Slowing demand and competitive pressures have driven down prices and reduced profitability. After five years of revenue and earnings growth in excess of 25% through the end of 1998, SFSK's sustainable growth rate is now uncertain. As the company seeks to maintain and grow its market share, gross margins will approach 45% for the 1999 second half. Sales should re-accelerate in 2000, due to stabilizing prices and demand for SFSK's high margin glove products. We recommend that investors not add to positions until the industry pricing environment stabilizes.

Key Stock Statistics

S&P EPS Est. 1999	0.50	Tang. Bk. Value/Share	2.42
P/E on S&P Est. 1999	17.5	Beta	0.93
S&P EPS Est. 2000	0.70	Shareholders	446
Dividend Rate/Share	Nil	Market cap. (B)	$0.486
Shs. outstg. (M)	55.5	Inst. holdings	26%
Avg. daily vol. (M)	0.407		

Value of $10,000 invested 5 years ago: $ 21,875

Fiscal Year Ending Dec. 31

	1999	1998	1997	1996	1995	1994
Revenues (Million $)						
1Q	41.76	53.30	41.17	33.06	22.59	17.50
2Q	59.07	58.64	44.95	35.99	29.24	20.73
3Q	—	61.57	46.90	37.49	32.44	22.66
4Q	—	59.88	49.99	39.55	32.74	23.24
Yr.	—	231.8	183.0	146.1	117.0	84.14
Earnings Per Share ($)						
1Q	**0.02**	**0.22**	**0.15**	**0.11**	0.06	—
2Q	**0.16**	**0.25**	**0.16**	**0.11**	0.06	0.08
3Q	**E0.16**	**0.27**	**0.20**	**0.13**	0.08	0.08
4Q	**E0.16**	**-0.02**	**0.20**	**0.09**	0.09	0.08
Yr.	**E0.50**	**0.70**	**0.70**	**0.42**	**0.29**	**0.29**

Next earnings report expected: late October

Dividend Data

No cash dividends have been paid.

Safeskin Corporation

Business Summary - 02-AUG-99

Since 1995, this maker of disposable medical examination gloves has been the market share leader in sales of medical examination gloves to hospitals. Safeskin is an innovator of medical exam gloves and was the first company to market a powder-free (PF) latex glove. Unlike conventional latex gloves that can produce adverse reactions when worn for long periods of time, powder free latex gloves do not produce similar side effects.

Innovations include the nitrile medical examination glove introduced in 1997. Nitrile is a synthetic co-polymer that contains no natural rubber latex, providing an alternative for individuals allergic to natural rubber latex. In 1997, SFSK acquired Tactyl Technologies, Inc., a maker of synthetic (non-latex) surgical gloves, giving SFSK a 50% share of the synthetic market. In 1999, SFSK introduced the Safeskin PFS, a PF latex surgical glove that incorporates a powder-less donning agent, to facilitate donning of the glove.

SFSK expanded into the scientific and technology glove market with the February 1998 acquisition of Absolute Quality Leadership Inc., a marketer of gloves for the high technology and scientific market.

Sales in 1998 were 61% acute care (hospitals); 26% alternate care (physician and dental offices, outpatient surgical centers and nursing homes); and 13% high technology and scientific (biotechnology and semiconductor industries).

SFSK's growth strategy includes increasing PF penetration in the acute care market, expanding its customer base at the consumer level, introducing new products, and emphasizing its high volume manufacturing capabilities.

Recent sole-source contracts include a February 1999 five-year exam glove contract with Continuum Health, valued at $20 million; and a January 1999 three-year agreement with Kaiser-Permanente, the largest non-profit health insurer in the U.S. In 1997, SFSK signed a six-year, sole-source agreement valued at $120 million with Columbia/ HCA Healthcare, to supply all latex gloves. It entered the consumer market in 1997 via a sole-source agreement with Costco Wholesale, valued at $6 million annually.

SFSK focuses on developing leading edge manufacturing facilities, using proprietary formulations and processes. Its manufacturing facility is strategically located in Thailand, near its source of materials and offering low cost labor. The company is expanding its Thailand manufacturing facilities, which is expected to boost annual production capacity to 6.5 billion gloves by the end of 1999.

In April 1999, the company signed a strategic alliance with Owens & Minor, one of SFSK's leading distributors, which establishes SFSK as Owens & Minor's glove category manager and its preferred exam glove supplier. The alliance is expected to produce approximately $9.0 million in incremental revenues.

Per Share Data ($) (Year Ended Dec. 31)	1998	1997	1996	1995	1994	1993	1992	1991	1990	1989
Tangible Bk. Val.	2.31	2.01	2.00	1.40	1.10	0.79	NA	NA	NA	NA
Cash Flow	0.91	1.65	0.54	0.36	0.33	0.32	0.20	NA	NA	NA
Earnings	0.70	0.70	0.42	0.29	0.28	0.28	0.17	0.04	NA	NA
Dividends	Nil	Nil	Nil	Nil	Nil	Nil	Nil	Nil	NA	NA
Payout Ratio	Nil	Nil	Nil	Nil	Nil	Nil	Nil	Nil	NA	NA
Prices - High	47⅞	29	13⅝	5⅛	4½	4⅛	NA	NA	NA	NA
- Low	17⅜	8⅞	4	2⅝	3⅛	3	NA	NA	NA	NA
P/E Ratio - High	67	41	32	18	16	15	NA	NA	NA	NA
- Low	25	13	10	9	11	11	NA	NA	NA	NA
Income Statement Analysis (Million $)										
Revs.	232	183	146	117	84.0	57.3	33.9	NA	NA	NA
Oper. Inc.	72.5	49.9	35.7	21.0	19.7	14.7	8.3	NA	NA	NA
Depr.	12.8	7.1	6.1	3.8	2.2	1.6	0.8	NA	NA	NA
Int. Exp.	3.0	-0.8	NM	0.2	0.0	1.4	1.5	NA	NA	NA
Pretax Inc.	45.3	46.2	26.5	17.2	18.3	11.9	6.1	NA	NA	NA
Eff. Tax Rate	7.66%	11%	11%	14%	21%	1.80%	2.10%	NA	NA	NA
Net Inc.	41.9	41.3	23.6	14.9	14.4	11.7	6.0	NA	NA	NA
Balance Sheet & Other Fin. Data (Million $)										
Cash	9.4	23.9	16.3	2.1	4.6	7.8	NA	NA	NA	NA
Curr. Assets	88.8	73.0	62.0	40.1	30.0	26.8	NA	NA	NA	NA
Total Assets	249	139	117	84.7	61.2	43.2	NA	NA	NA	NA
Curr. Liab.	37.7	29.8	13.7	12.1	7.0	4.5	NA	NA	NA	NA
LT Debt	87.7	Nil	Nil	2.8	Nil	Nil	NA	NA	NA	NA
Common Eqty.	121	107	103	69.9	54.3	38.8	NA	NA	NA	NA
Total Cap.	209	107	103	72.6	54.3	38.8	NA	NA	NA	NA
Cap. Exp.	65.4	35.2	20.2	16.5	15.4	10.2	NA	NA	NA	NA
Cash Flow	54.7	48.4	29.7	18.7	16.6	13.2	6.8	NA	NA	NA
Curr. Ratio	2.4	2.4	4.5	3.3	4.3	6.0	NA	NA	NA	NA
% LT Debt of Cap.	41.9	Nil	Nil	3.8	Nil	Nil	NA	NA	NA	NA
% Net Inc.of Revs.	18.1	22.5	16.1	12.7	17.1	20.3	17.8	NA	NA	NA
% Ret. on Assets	21.6	32.3	23.8	20.4	27.5	NA	NA	NA	NA	NA
% Ret. on Equity	36.7	39.4	27.3	23.2	32.6	NA	NA	NA	NA	NA

Data as orig reptd.; bef. results of disc opers/spec. items. Per share data adj. for stk. divs. Bold denotes diluted EPS (FASB 128)-prior periods restated. E-Estimated. NA-Not Available. NM-Not Meaningful. NR-Not Ranked.

Office—12671 High Bluff Dr., San Diego, CA 92130. **Tel**—(619) 350-6840. **Fax**—(619) 350-2380. **Website**—http://www.safeskin.com **Chrmn, Pres, CEO & COO**—R. Jaffe. **EVP & CFO**—D. L. Morash. **VP-Fin & Secy**—S. S. Goldman. **Investor Contact**—Mark Francois (619-350-6840). **Dirs**—N. K. Braverman, C. L. Garner, I. Jaffe, R. Jaffe, H. L. Shecter, J. Stemler, J.E. Stiefler. **Transfer Agent & Registrar**—American Stock Transfer & Trust Co., NYC. **Incorporated**—in Florida in 1985. **Empl**— 7,200. **S&P Analyst:** John J. Arege

STANDARD
&POOR'S
STOCK REPORTS

Schweitzer-Mauduit Int'l

NYSE Symbol **SWM**

In S&P SmallCap 600

09-OCT-99

Industry: Tobacco

Summary: This company is the world's largest supplier of fine papers to the tobacco industry. It also manufactures specialty papers for use in other industries.

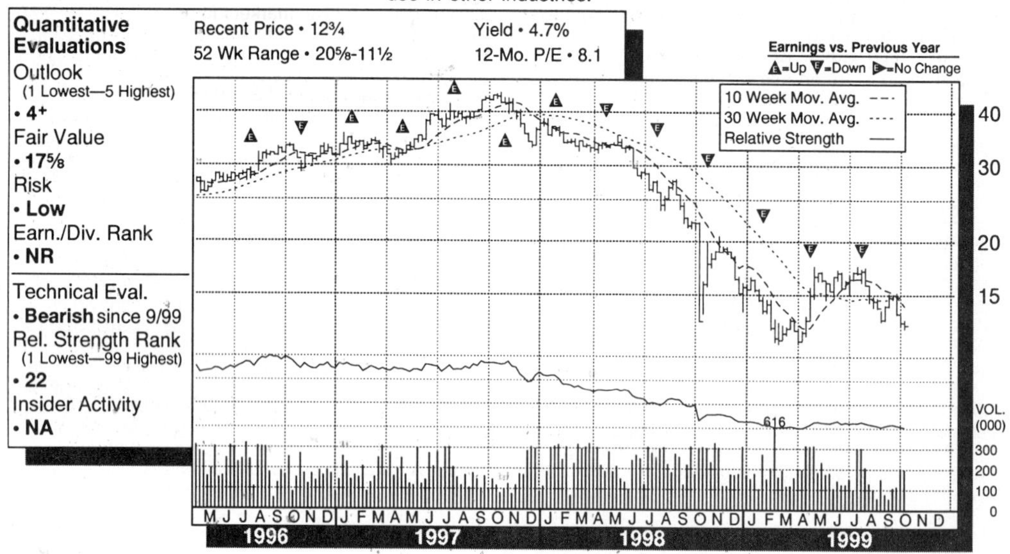

Business Profile - 02-SEP-99

Schweitzer-Mauduit International said that after taking production downtime in the 1999 second quarter to manage inventory levels, it expected further downtime to be taken during the balance of the year. Cigarette consumption and production in both the U.S. and Brazil in 1999 will be less than in the prior year, unfavorably impacting company sales. The weak pricing environment for SWM's paper products was expected to continue throughout 1999 due to adverse market conditions and global pricing negotiations with multinational cigarette manufacturers. Nevertheless, the company expected a share earnings gain for 1999, excluding one-time items, aided by anticipated cost controls and efficiency gains.

Operational Review - 02-SEP-99

Net sales for the first half of 1999 fell 11%, year to year, reflecting reduced sales volume, lower average selling prices, and unfavorable currency exchange rates. Unit sales volume decreased 6%, with declines of 9% in France and 7% in the U.S., and a 4% increase in Brazil. The lower volume and prices more than offset the benefit of improved mill operations, lower wood pulp costs, and the absence of expenses related to a one-time charge for a voluntary retirement program in 1998. Operating profit was down 13%. After much larger other income (net), but taxes at 38.2%, versus 25.8%, net income dropped 27%, to $16.2 million ($1.02 a share) from $22.2 million ($1.36).

Stock Performance - 08-OCT-99

In the past 30 trading days, SWM's shares have declined 3%, compared to a 0.91% fall in the S&P 500. Average trading volume for the past five days was 39,040 shares, compared with the 40-day moving average of 24,356 shares.

Key Stock Statistics

Dividend Rate/Share	0.60	Shareholders	7,492
Shs. outstg. (M)	15.8	Market cap. (B)	$0.201
Avg. daily vol. (M)	0.031	Inst. holdings	65%
Tang. Bk. Value/Share	11.32		
Beta	NA		

Value of $10,000 invested 5 years ago: NA

Fiscal Year Ending Dec. 31

	1999	1998	1997	1996	1995	1994
Revenues (Million $)						
1Q	128.6	134.3	113.0	119.8	109.5	—
2Q	119.7	144.0	116.3	117.5	113.4	—
3Q	—	134.4	113.4	118.5	121.5	—
4Q	—	134.0	117.9	115.5	118.5	—
Yr.	—	546.7	460.6	471.3	462.9	—
Earnings Per Share ($)						
1Q	**0.57**	**0.61**	**0.69**	**0.58**	0.49	—
2Q	**0.45**	**0.75**	**0.78**	**0.65**	0.46	—
3Q	—	**0.43**	**0.68**	**0.60**	0.75	—
4Q	—	**0.13**	**0.62**	**0.55**	0.11	—
Yr.	—	**1.92**	**2.77**	**2.38**	1.81	—

Next earnings report expected: late October

Dividend Data (Dividends have been paid since 1996.)

Amount ($)	Date Decl.	Ex-Div. Date	Stock of Record	Payment Date
0.150	Oct. 29	Nov. 05	Nov. 09	Dec. 14 '98
0.150	Jan. 28	Feb. 04	Feb. 08	Mar. 08 '99
0.150	Apr. 22	May. 06	May. 10	Jun. 14 '99
0.150	Jul. 29	Aug. 05	Aug. 09	Sep. 13 '99

A Division of The McGraw-Hill Companies

Schweitzer-Mauduit International, Inc.

Business Summary - 02-SEP-99

Schweitzer-Mauduit International, Inc. (SWM) manufactures and sells paper and reconstituted tobacco products to the tobacco industry as well as specialized paper products for use in other applications. Formerly a wholly owned subsidiary of Kimberly-Clark Corp. (KMB), SWM was spun off by that company to its shareholders in November 1995. Tobacco accounted for 90% of total sales in 1998 and nontobacco the remainder.

In 1998, about 41% of net sales were obtained in Europe, 14% in the Asia/Pacific region, and 12% in Latin America (mainly Brazil).

Tobacco industry products include cigarette, tipping and plug wrap papers (cigarette papers) used to wrap various parts of a cigarette, reconstituted tobacco wrappers and binders for cigars, and reconstituted tobacco leaf for use as filler in cigarettes and cigars. These products are sold directly to the major tobacco companies or their designated converters in North and South America, Western Europe, China and elsewhere. Sales to Phillip Morris and B.A.T. Industries accounted for 28% and 14%, respectively, of sales, in 1998.

Cigarette paper wraps the column of tobacco in a cigarette and has certain properties, such as basis weight, porosity, opacity, tensile strength, texture and whiteness, which must be closely controlled to tight tolerances. SWM believes that it has 57% of the U.S. and Canadian cigarette paper markets.

Plug wrap forms the outer layer of a cigarette filter and holds the filter material in a cylindrical form. SWM's U.S. operations are believed to have a 78% share of the U.S. and Canadian markets for plug wrap.

Tipping paper, produced in white or buff color, joins the cigarette's filter element to the tobacco section of the cigarette. SWM's U.S. operations have an estimated 59% share of the U.S. and Canadian markets for base tipping paper which is subsequently printed by converters.

Reconstituted tobacco is used by manufacturers of cigarettes, cigars and other tobacco products mainly as a filler that is blended with virgin tobacco in order to use otherwise wasted parts of the tobacco leaf.

Nontobacco related products include drinking straw wrap, lightweight printing papers, battery separator paper and other specialized papers. These products are generally sold directly to converters and other end-users.

As of year-end 1998, the company was operating eight mills (including four fiber pulping operations) in the U.S., France and Brazil that produce specialty paper and/or reconstituted tobacco products. It was also operating flax fiber processing facilities in France and Canada.

Per Share Data ($) (Year Ended Dec. 31)	1998	1997	1996	1995	1994	1993	1992	1991	1990	1989
Tangible Bk. Val.	12.37	11.17	9.72	8.09	NA	NA	NA	NA	NA	NA
Cash Flow	3.45	3.65	3.25	2.64	NA	NA	NA	NA	NA	NA
Earnings	1.92	2.77	2.41	1.81	NA	NA	NA	NA	NA	NA
Dividends	0.60	0.60	0.45	Nil	NA	NA	NA	NA	NA	NA
Payout Ratio	31%	22%	19%	Nil	NA	NA	NA	NA	NA	NA
Prices - High	38⅝	44½	33⅝	23⅝	NA	NA	NA	NA	NA	NA
- Low	13	29⅞	22¾	20⅜	NA	NA	NA	NA	NA	NA
P/E Ratio - High	20	16	14	13	NA	NA	NA	NA	NA	NA
- Low	7	11	9	11	NA	NA	NA	NA	NA	NA
Income Statement Analysis (Million $)										
Revs.	547	461	471	463	NA	NA	NA	NA	NA	NA
Oper. Inc.	83.9	96.3	87.4	74.9	NA	NA	NA	NA	NA	NA
Depr.	24.8	14.4	13.4	13.4	NA	NA	NA	NA	NA	NA
Int. Exp.	6.4	4.1	5.3	8.0	NA	NA	NA	NA	NA	NA
Pretax Inc.	53.9	79.4	69.9	45.8	NA	NA	NA	NA	NA	NA
Eff. Tax Rate	32%	36%	37%	28%	NA	NA	NA	NA	NA	NA
Net Inc.	31.0	45.3	38.7	29.0	NA	NA	NA	NA	NA	NA
Balance Sheet & Other Fin. Data (Million $)										
Cash	6.7	37.2	30.9	5.9	NA	NA	NA	NA	NA	NA
Curr. Assets	156	158	151	138	NA	NA	NA	NA	NA	NA
Total Assets	475	391	381	347	NA	NA	NA	NA	NA	NA
Curr. Liab.	125	90.5	102	94.1	NA	NA	NA	NA	NA	NA
LT Debt	108	80.8	86.6	91.6	NA	NA	NA	NA	NA	NA
Common Eqty.	197	180	156	130	NA	NA	NA	NA	NA	NA
Total Cap.	326	279	259	235	NA	NA	NA	NA	NA	NA
Cap. Exp.	36.7	35.8	51.5	22.5	NA	NA	NA	NA	NA	NA
Cash Flow	55.8	59.7	52.1	42.4	NA	NA	NA	NA	NA	NA
Curr. Ratio	1.3	1.7	1.5	1.5	NA	NA	NA	NA	NA	NA
% LT Debt of Cap.	33.2	29.0	33.4	39.0	NA	NA	NA	NA	NA	NA
% Net Inc.of Revs.	5.7	9.8	8.2	6.3	NA	NA	NA	NA	NA	NA
% Ret. on Assets	7.2	11.7	10.6	NM	NA	NA	NA	NA	NA	NA
% Ret. on Equity	16.5	26.9	27.1	NM	NA	NA	NA	NA	NA	NA

Data as orig reptd.; bef. results of disc opers/spec. items. Per share data adj. for stk. divs. Bold denotes diluted EPS (FASB 128)-prior periods restated. E-Estimated. NA-Not Available. NM-Not Meaningful. NR-Not Ranked.

Office—100 North Point Center East, Suite 600, Alpharetta, GA 30022-8246. **Tel**—1-800-514-0186. **Chrmn & CEO**—W. H. Deitrich. **CFO, Treas & Investor Contact**—Paul C. Roberts (770 569-4272). **Secy**—W. J. Sharkey. **Dirs**—C. L. Arnold, K.C. Caldabaugh, L. G. Chambaz, W. H. Deitrich, R. D. Jackson, L. J. Kujawa, J-P Le Hetet, L. B. Stillman. **Transfer Agent & Registrar**—First National Bank of Boston. **Incorporated**—in Delaware in 1995. **Empl**— 3,475. **S&P Analyst:** N.J.D.

Scott Technologies

NASDAQ Symbol **SCTT**

In S&P SmallCap 600

09-OCT-99

Industry:
Manufacturing (Diversified)

Summary: This company makes respiratory systems and other life saving products.

Quantitative Evaluations

Outlook
(1 Lowest—5 Highest)
• **1+**

Fair Value
• **17⅞**

Risk
• **NA**

Earn./Div. Rank
• **C**

Technical Eval.
• **NA**

Rel. Strength Rank
(1 Lowest—99 Highest)
• **66**

Insider Activity
• **NA**

Recent Price • 19
52 Wk Range • 20⅜-10⅝

Yield • Nil
12-Mo. P/E • 11.0

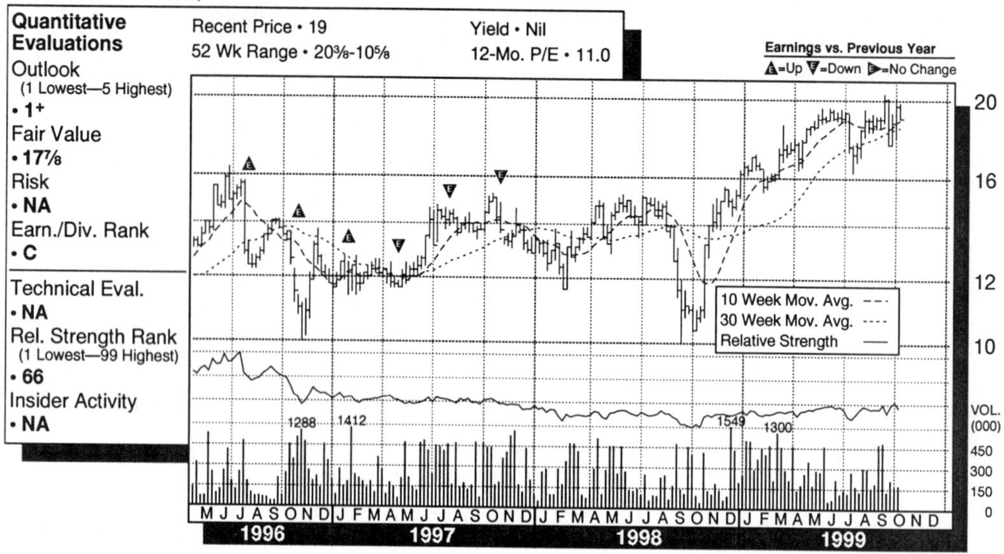

Business Profile - 02-SEP-99

Following the July 1999 sale of its Interstate Electronics Corp. unit for $60 million, the company said that its plan is to grow through strategic acquisitions, systematic market expansion, and through new and "next generation" product development. In July 1999, Scott said that bookings continue to build momentum heading into the second half of the year, primarily within the health and safety industry, and backlog remains at a comfortable level. Based on these figures, coupled with the additional revenue of about $9 million in 1999 from the Scott/Bacharach gas detection instruments joint venture, management anticipates 1999 revenues of about $200 million, up from the original projection of $190 million.

Operational Review - 02-SEP-99

Net sales from continuing operations in the six months ended June 30, 1999, rose 7.3%, year to year, due to greater shipments of Air-Paks to health and safety customers. Results benefited from the higher volume, well controlled SG&A costs, lower research and development outlays, and a 25% decline in interest costs (net). Pretax income was up 40%. After taxes at 36.9%, versus 40.1%, income from continuing operations increased to $8,883,000 ($0.48 a share), from $6,013,000 ($0.32). Results exclude income from discontinued operations of $1.87 a share in 1999, versus a loss of $0.07 in 1998, and charges of $0.01 and $0.09 for early extinguishment of debt in the respective years.

Stock Performance - 08-OCT-99

In the past 30 trading days, SCTT's shares have increased 0.33%, compared to a 0.91% fall in the S&P 500. Average trading volume for the past five days was 34,440 shares, compared with the 40-day moving average of 65,874 shares.

Key Stock Statistics

Dividend Rate/Share	Nil	Shareholders	10,900
Shs. outstg. (M)	18.2	Market cap. (B)	$0.345
Avg. daily vol. (M)	0.034	Inst. holdings	74%
Tang. Bk. Value/Share	2.94		
Beta	0.88		

Value of $10,000 invested 5 years ago: $ 13,944

Fiscal Year Ending Dec. 31

	1999	1998	1997	1996	1995	1994
Revenues (Million $)						
1Q	48.75	46.21	62.65	96.70	85.27	73.11
2Q	50.19	45.96	62.77	101.4	88.69	80.03
3Q	—	43.20	60.15	95.40	92.35	79.79
4Q	—	41.73	63.03	92.20	92.73	86.49
Yr.	—	177.1	248.6	385.7	359.0	319.4
Earnings Per Share ($)						
1Q	**0.23**	**0.13**	0.06	0.20	-0.44	-0.91
2Q	**0.25**	**0.18**	0.09	0.34	-0.32	-0.56
3Q	—	**0.11**	0.05	0.31	0.05	-0.61
4Q	—	**0.08**	—	1.84	0.13	-2.74
Yr.	—	**0.52**	**-0.08**	**1.47**	**-1.37**	-4.81

Next earnings report expected: early November

Dividend Data

Cash was paid by the company or its predecessor in each year from 1965 until payments were suspended in 1994. A shareholder rights plan was adopted in December 1998.

Scott Technologies, Inc.

Business Summary - 02-SEP-99

Following the classification of its Interstate Electronics unit as a discontinued operation in October 1998, the company's remaining business is the manufacture and sale of sophisticated, high-performance respiratory systems and other life saving products for aerospace, aviation, defense, firefighting, government and industrial markets. Scott Technologies (formerly Figgie International), operating primarily through Scott Aviation, has divested numerous businesses since 1994.

In its health and safety products division (51% of 1998 revenues, up from 49% in 1997), Scott makes the Scott Air-Pak (a self-contained breathing apparatus) and other life support products for fire fighting and personal protection against industrial contaminants; air purifying products that provide protection against environmental and safety hazards; and protective breathing equipment and oxygen masks. In addition, it manufactures instruments to detect the presence of combustible or toxic gases and the lack of oxygen.

The aviation and government products division (49%; 51%) makes protective breathing equipment, pilot and crew oxygen masks, and emergency oxygen for passengers and crew on commercial, government and private aircraft and ships.

The two units have benefited from several similarities. Scott has used its broad experience in high pressure gas regulation and distribution developed from the two product lines to provide end-users with products that are reliable, lightweight, compact and user- friendly. Each unit has been able to benefit from the common use of manufacturing cell and team technology. Aviall, Inc, a distributor of the company's aviation products, accounted for some 14% of the company's 1998 sales. The U.S. government accounted for 7.1% of sales, while 16% of sales were to overseas customers.

The Interstate Electronics unit (sold for $60 million in June 1999) makes sophisticated telemetry, instrumentation and data recording systems and position measuring systems; Global Positioning Systems (GPS) for the U.S. Navy's Polaris/Poseidon, TRIDENT and TRIDENT II ships; precise GPS for aircraft and turnkey test ranges; and GPS for commercial and business aircraft and landing systems. About 87% of Interstate's sales in 1997 were from the U.S. government, down from more than 91% in 1996. Sales from this division made up 36% of total revenues in 1997.

The company expects to continue to focus on internal growth and market expansion, and investigate acquisitions, aided by an early 1999 doubling of its credit facility to $150 million.

Per Share Data ($) (Year Ended Dec. 31)	1998	1997	1996	1995	1994	1993	1992	1991	1990	1989
Tangible Bk. Val.	2.84	3.72	0.76	1.64	2.44	7.30	16.15	15.44	14.23	12.34
Cash Flow	0.77	0.29	3.07	-0.23	-2.46	-8.74	3.53	3.95	4.08	4.32
Earnings	0.52	-0.08	2.69	-0.68	-4.81	-10.09	1.61	1.72	2.28	3.04
Dividends	Nil	Nil	Nil	Nil	Nil	0.43	0.50	0.50	0.50	0.40
Payout Ratio	Nil	Nil	Nil	Nil	Nil	NM	33%	31%	24%	13%
Prices - High	16¾	15¼	16⅜	14⅛	14½	22	26½	25	35½	32
- Low	10	11⅜	10	5⅞	4⅝	12½	17	16½	15	25⅛
P/E Ratio - High	32	NM	6	NM	NM	NM	16	15	16	11
- Low	19	NM	4	NM	NM	NM	11	10	7	8
Income Statement Analysis (Million $)										
Revs.	177	249	386	359	319	769	1,173	1,243	1,361	1,313
Oper. Inc.	32.9	29.4	47.1	29.4	27.0	-47.0	109	126	147	157
Depr.	4.6	6.9	7.2	6.3	41.6	24.0	33.6	32.8	31.5	35.1
Int. Exp.	12.6	22.2	20.2	29.7	42.9	35.6	38.3	42.7	44.6	34.9
Pretax Inc.	15.9	-1.4	22.6	-10.5	-107	-250	41.2	43.2	64.5	99
Eff. Tax Rate	40%	NM	Nil	Nil	NM	NM	31%	31%	39%	37%
Net Inc.	9.5	-1.4	50.3	-19.5	-85.0	-178	28.3	30.1	39.7	62.9
Balance Sheet & Other Fin. Data (Million $)										
Cash	39.3	104	44.4	25.9	47.0	34.0	117	110	98.0	83.0
Curr. Assets	135	182	189	179	460	534	516	NA	NA	NA
Total Assets	263	343	373	367	644	998	1,113	1,109	1,066	1,027
Curr. Liab.	75.5	55.1	67.9	88.4	316	677	282	NA	NA	NA
LT Debt	75.6	161	184	195	234	65.0	353	373	375	367
Common Eqty.	55.3	71.6	74.5	49.6	65.0	203	395	378	352	317
Total Cap.	131	233	259	245	300	289	798	804	760	714
Cap. Exp.	7.3	8.7	10.3	6.2	60.0	96.0	112	98.0	81.0	78.0
Cash Flow	14.1	5.5	57.5	-4.2	-44.0	-154	61.9	62.9	71.1	89.5
Curr. Ratio	1.8	3.3	2.8	2.0	1.5	0.8	1.8	NA	NA	NA
% LT Debt of Cap.	57.8	69.3	71.0	79.6	78.2	22.4	44.3	46.3	49.4	51.4
% Net Inc.of Revs.	5.4	NM	13.0	NM	NM	NM	2.4	2.4	2.9	4.8
% Ret. on Assets	3.2	NM	13.6	NM	NM	NM	2.6	2.8	3.8	6.6
% Ret. on Equity	14.9	NM	8.1	NM	NM	NM	7.3	8.2	11.9	20.1

Data as orig reptd.; bef. results of disc opers/spec. items. Per share data adj. for stk. divs. Bold denotes diluted EPS (FASB 128)-prior periods restated. E-Estimated. NA-Not Available. NM-Not Meaningful. NR-Not Ranked.

Office—5875 Landerbrook Dr., Suite 250, Mayfield Heights, OH 44124. **Tel**—(440) 446-1333. **Chrmn**—R. P. Collins. **Pres & CEO**—G. W. Lindemann. **SVP & CFO**—M. A. Kirk. **VP & Secy**—D. L. Kackley. **Dirs**—F. A. Breidenbach, R. P. Collins, N. C. Lind, G. W. Lindemann, F. N. Linsalata, F. R. McKnight, J. P. Reilly. **Transfer Agent & Registrar**—First National Bank of Boston. **Incorporated**—in Ohio in 1963; reincorporated in Delaware in 1983. **Empl**— 1,009. **S&P Analyst:** P.L.H.

STANDARD
&POOR'S
STOCK REPORTS

Scotts Co.

NYSE Symbol **SMG**

In S&P SmallCap 600

09-OCT-99 **Industry:** Hardware & Tools

Summary: This company is a leading U.S. and international producer of consumer lawn and garden care products and also sells consumer insecticides and herbicides.

S&P Opinion: Accumulate (★★★★)

Recent Price • 39
52 Wk Range • 48-26⅝
Yield • Nil
12-Mo. P/E • 16.7

Quantitative Evaluations

Outlook (1 Lowest—5 Highest) • **3+**

Fair Value • **37¾**

Risk • **Low**

Earn./Div. Rank • **NR**

Technical Eval. • **Bearish** since 8/99

Rel. Strength Rank (1 Lowest—99 Highest) • **65**

Insider Activity • **Neutral**

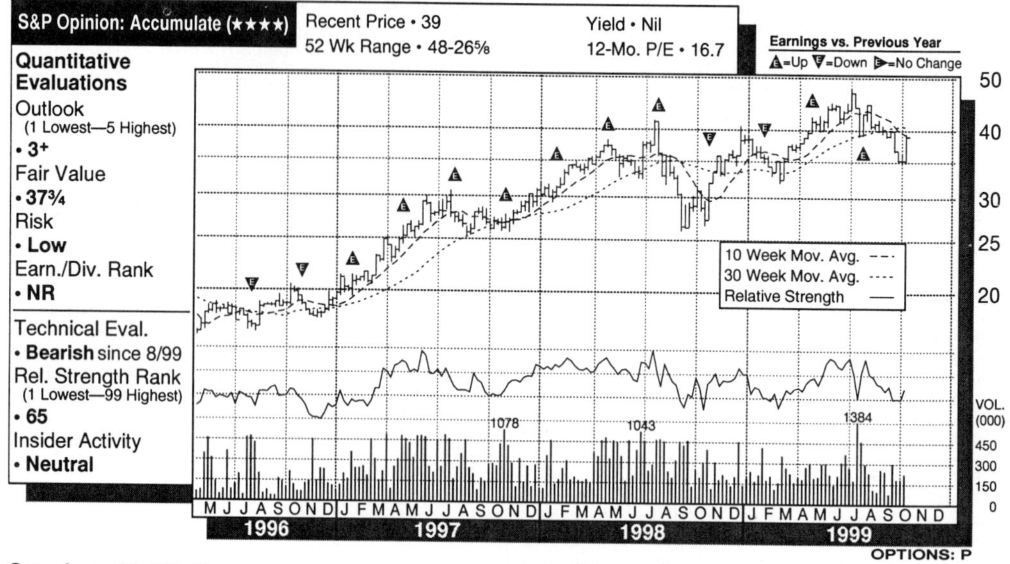

OPTIONS: P

Overview - 27-JUL-99

Revenues from continuing operations should grow about 15% in FY 00 (Sep.). Higher sales will be aided by strong growth in the lawn care business. Scotts has recently increased its already dominant market share in this segment. Most major retailers now stock only two brands of lawn care products, Scotts and a private label, with Scotts' products generate higher gross margins. SMG will also achieve significant growth in Miracle-Gro garden products. The company recently introduced Miracle-Gro potting soil, which has quickly become the number one selling potting soil in the country. International operations, especially in continental Europe, should benefit from continued distributor and retail consolidation. Sales to professional lawn care providers are likely to be flat. Margins should benefit from consolidations and layoffs at the recently acquired Ortho pesticide business, partially offset by increased marketing costs.

Valuation - 27-JUL-99

In July 1999, SMG's stock was hurt by a plan to end an exclusive distribution relationship with Central Garden & Pet Co. The relationship applies to Ortho and Roundup pesticides. We support SMG's decision and feel it will benefit shareholders in the long-run, even though in the near-term earnings may be nicked as Scotts reestablishes relationships. Having greater control over how and where its products are sold, will allow Scotts to more effectively apply its proven marketing and distribution skills. Scotts is reasonably priced at about 18X our estimated FY 00 (Sep.) EPS. In addition, Scotts has managed to improve both its gross profit margins and EBITDA margins in excess of our expectations. With good growth prospects in lawn and garden markets, both domestically and in continental Europe, Scotts is an attractive choice for capital appreciation potential.

Key Stock Statistics

S&P EPS Est. 1999	2.10	Tang. Bk. Value/Share	NM
P/E on S&P Est. 1999	18.6	Beta	0.73
S&P EPS Est. 2000	2.35	Shareholders	6,500
Dividend Rate/Share	Nil	Market cap. (B)	$0.716
Shs. outstg. (M)	18.4	Inst. holdings	75%
Avg. daily vol. (M)	0.044		

Value of $10,000 invested 5 years ago: $ 19,746

Fiscal Year Ending Sep. 30

	1999	1998	1997	1996	1995	1994
Revenues (Million $)						
1Q	184.4	125.1	100.2	117.9	98.00	68.30
2Q	631.5	430.6	346.2	251.2	236.1	207.4
3Q	586.2	367.5	299.0	248.0	229.0	200.9
4Q	—	191.1	155.4	134.8	169.7	129.7
Yr.	—	1,113	900.8	751.9	732.8	606.3
Earnings Per Share ($)						
1Q	**-0.68**	-0.42	**-0.45**	-0.51	-0.17	-0.08
2Q	**1.81**	**1.10**	0.95	0.36	0.79	0.69
3Q	**1.35**	**0.80**	0.71	0.26	0.45	0.50
4Q	**E-0.18**	**-0.96**	-0.32	-0.86	-0.10	0.16
Yr.	**E2.10**	**1.22**	**1.35**	-0.65	0.99	1.27

Next earnings report expected: late October

Dividend Data

No dividends have been paid.

The Scotts Company

Business Summary - 27-JUL-99

Scotts Company, a leading U.S. and European producer of lawn and garden care products, said in December 1998 that its recent strategy has consisted of bringing effective consumer marketing, advertising and brand prominence to the lawn and garden market. Scotts believes that its strategy has positioned it for growth. The company is also seeking long-term growth through lawn services and genetic engineering. Sales for FY 98 (Sep.) were divided as follows: North American consumer lawn care 33%, North American consumer garden care 12%, North American consumer growing media 21%, professional services 16%, and international sales 18%.

In December 1998, SMG estimated that in FY 98 it had a 58% share of the U.S. consumer lawn fertilizers market, 52% of the U.S. consumer garden fertilizers market, 47% of the U.S. consumer potting soil market, and 34% of the U.S. consumer grass seed market.

Scotts operates in three principal business segments: North American consumer business, professional business group and international business group.

North American consumer business includes lawn care products (many of which are sold under the Scotts brand name) such as fertilizers, fertilizer combination products and weed control products, consumer garden products (including a complete line of water-soluble fertilizers sold under the Miracle-Gro brand name), pesticides (sold under the Scotts, Ortho and Roundup brand names), and a variety of other tools and supplies for lawn and garden applications.

The company also has a compost division, but said in December 1998 that, due to deteriorating economics, it intends to close its composting facilities by the year 2000.

The professional business group sells its lawn products to golf courses, commercial nurseries and greenhouses, schools and sports fields, multi-family housing complexes, business and industrial sites, lawn and landscape services and specialty crop growers. The professional group's two core businesses are ProTurf, for the professionally managed turf market, and Horticulture, for the nursery and greenhouse markets.

The international business group sells lawn and garden products to consumers and professionals in over 40 countries. Markets with significant growth potential, according to Scotts, include most of Western Europe and Australia.

Scotts made 1998 a year for major acquisitions, including Rhone-Poulenc Jardin, the number one lawn and garden company in Europe, for $216 million, as well as the Ortho insecticide and herbicide business for $300 million and the exclusive international marketing and agency rights for Roundup pesticides. Under the Roundup marketing agreement, Scotts and Monsanto (which will retain ownership of Roundup) will jointly develop global consumer and trade marketing programs for Roundup.

Per Share Data ($) (Year Ended Sep. 30)	1998	1997	1996	1995	1994	1993	1992	1991	1990	1989
Tangible Bk. Val.	NM	NM	NM	NM	1.86	7.66	8.35	4.19	NA	NA
Cash Flow	2.15	2.39	0.91	2.12	2.36	1.93	1.64	1.75	NA	NA
Earnings	1.22	1.35	-0.65	0.99	1.27	1.07	0.84	0.89	-0.58	0.07
Dividends	Nil	Nil	Nil	Nil	Nil	Nil	Nil	Nil	Nil	Nil
Payout Ratio	Nil	Nil	Nil	Nil	Nil	Nil	Nil	Nil	Nil	Nil
Prices - High	41 5/8	31 3/4	21 1/2	24	20 1/4	20 1/2	24 1/2	NA	NA	NA
- Low	26	19 1/2	16 1/8	15 5/8	14 1/2	15 1/4	13 1/2	NA	NA	NA
P/E Ratio - High	34	24	NM	24	16	19	29	NA	NA	NA
- Low	21	14	NM	16	11	14	16	NA	NA	NA
Income Statement Analysis (Million $)										
Revs.	1,113	901	752	733	606	466	413	388	350	328
Oper. Inc.	151	133	86.1	88.9	82.0	61.5	56.9	55.3	51.3	49.3
Depr.	37.8	30.4	29.3	25.6	20.5	17.0	14.4	17.8	20.5	19.6
Int. Exp.	32.2	26.7	26.5	26.5	17.8	8.5	15.9	30.9	34.5	32.5
Pretax Inc.	61.9	69.6	1.3	40.7	41.8	35.4	26.2	NA	-6.8	0.9
Eff. Tax Rate	40%	43%	33%	38%	43%	41%	43%	NA	NM	NM
Net Inc.	37.0	39.5	-2.5	22.4	23.9	21.0	15.1	18.4	-6.9	-0.8
Balance Sheet & Other Fin. Data (Million $)										
Cash	10.6	13.0	10.6	7.0	10.7	2.3	0.9	2.9	NA	NA
Curr. Assets	367	286	292	349	250	144	116	110	NA	NA
Total Assets	1,035	788	732	807	529	322	269	261	NA	NA
Curr. Liab.	232	139	111	119	110	64.9	60.9	88.4	NA	NA
LT Debt	359	220	223	272	220	87.0	32.0	54.0	NA	NA
Common Eqty.	227	212	187	206	168	143	176	147	NA	NA
Total Cap.	779	609	587	505	388	230	208	201	NA	NA
Cap. Exp.	41.3	28.6	33.4	23.6	54.9	15.2	19.9	8.8	8.5	6.7
Cash Flow	65.0	60.1	17.0	48.0	44.3	38.1	29.5	36.2	13.6	20.5
Curr. Ratio	1.6	2.1	2.6	2.9	2.3	2.2	1.9	1.2	NA	NA
% LT Debt of Cap.	46.1	36.1	38.0	53.9	56.7	37.8	15.3	26.6	NA	NA
% Net Inc.of Revs.	3.3	4.4	NM	3.1	3.9	4.5	3.7	4.7	NM	NM
% Ret. on Assets	4.1	5.2	NM	3.4	5.6	7.5	3.6	6.9	NA	NA
% Ret. on Equity	12.4	14.9	NM	12.0	15.3	14.1	NM	12.5	NA	NA

Data as orig. reptd.; bef. results of disc. opers. and/or spec. items. Per share data adj. for stk. divs. as of ex-div. date. Quarterly EPS may not add bec. of changes in shs. Bold denotes diluted EPS (FASB 128). E-Estimated. NA-Not Available. NM-Not Meaningful. NR-Not Ranked.

Organized—in Delaware in 1986. **Office**—14111 Scottslawn Rd., Marysville, OH 43041. **Tel**—(937) 644-0011. **Website**—http://www.scottscompany.com **Chrmn, Pres & CEO**—C. M. Berger. **EVP & CFO**—J. H. Mordo. **SVP & Secy**—G. R. Lucas. **Investor Contact**—Rebecca J. Bruening. **Dirs**—J. B. Beard, C. M. Berger, J. P. Flannery, H. Hagedorn, J. Hagedorn, A. E. Harris, J. Kenlon, K. G. Mills, P.J. Norton, J. M. Sullivan, L. J. Van Fossen, J. Walker. **Transfer Agent & Registrar**—National City Bank, Cleveland, Ohio. **Empl**— 2,383. **S&P Analyst:** James C. Friendly

STANDARD &POOR'S
STOCK REPORTS

SEACOR SMIT

NYSE Symbol **CKH**

In S&P SmallCap 600

23-OCT-99

Industry: Oil & Gas (Drilling & Equipment)

Summary: This company is a major provider of offshore marine services to the oil and gas exploration and production industry, and a leading provider of oil spill response services.

Quantitative Evaluations

Outlook (1 Lowest—5 Highest)
• 3+

Fair Value
• 56¼

Risk
• Average

Earn./Div. Rank
• NR

Technical Eval.
• NA

Rel. Strength Rank (1 Lowest—99 Highest)
• 38

Insider Activity
• NA

Recent Price • 45¾
52 Wk Range • 57⅝-38½
Yield • Nil
12-Mo. P/E • 12.0

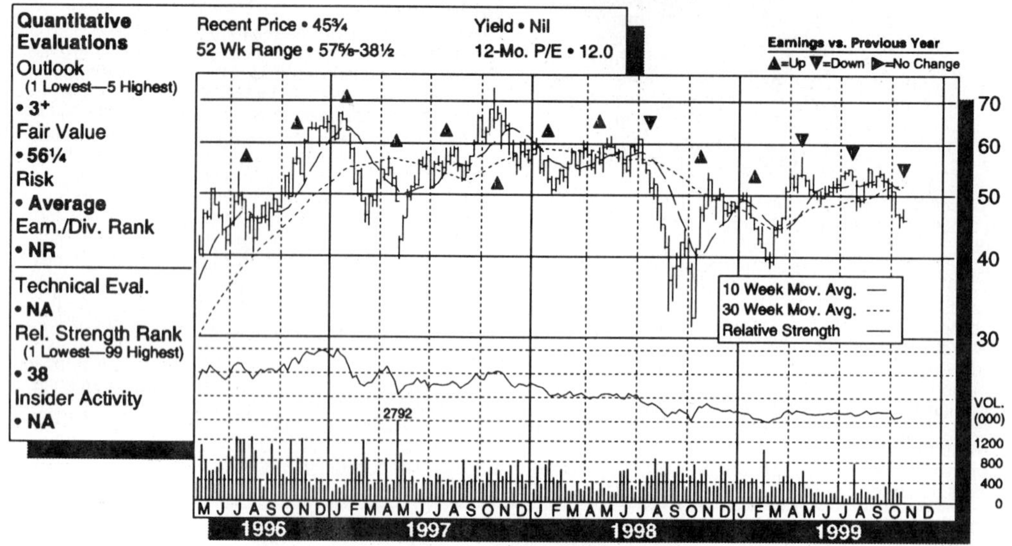

Business Profile - 20-OCT-99

A prolonged decline in oil and gas prices has resulted in reduced drilling and production support activities both domestically and internationally. As a result, revenue earned by CKH's offshore marine services fleet has declined; as of June 30, 1999, the company had 47 offshore marine vessels out of service. The decline in product prices in the oil and gas industry also led to significantly lower day rates and utilization of jackup rigs, particularly in the U.S. Gulf of Mexico shallow water market, and to excess supply in the current jackup market. In the six months ended June 30, 1999, CKH sold 11 offshore marine vessels, for a gain of about $955,000. Of the vessels sold, five were leased back by the company, and two were acquired by equity investees.

Operational Review - 20-OCT-99

Revenues in the nine months ended September 30, 1999, dropped 26%, year to year, reflecting a drop in marine revenue. Costs and expenses declined only 7.1%; operating income fell 62%. With a $1.88 million gain on the sale of equipment, versus $34.3 million, pretax income fell 73%. After taxes at 34.5%, versus 34.7%, and minority interest, income plunged 76%, to $23.6 million ($1.95 a share, on 7.4% fewer shares), from $96.7 million ($7.27). Results in the 1999 period exclude income of $0.09 a share from debt extinguishment.

Stock Performance - 22-OCT-99

In the past 30 trading days, CKH's shares have declined 14%, compared to a 4% fall in the S&P 500. Average trading volume for the past five days was 57,460 shares, compared with the 40-day moving average of 66,241 shares.

Key Stock Statistics

Dividend Rate/Share	Nil	Shareholders	117
Shs. outstg. (M)	12.1	Market cap. (B)	$0.560
Avg. daily vol. (M)	0.096	Inst. holdings	78%
Tang. Bk. Value/Share	44.71		
Beta	1.32		

Value of $10,000 invested 5 years ago: $ 19,866

Fiscal Year Ending Dec. 31

	1999	1998	1997	1996	1995	1994
Revenues (Million $)						
1Q	77.72	97.21	79.18	44.08	15.29	19.42
2Q	68.48	95.74	85.25	52.65	20.34	18.46
3Q	71.89	100.0	88.26	57.55	31.26	18.51
4Q	—	92.79	94.26	64.15	39.39	17.98
Yr.	—	385.8	346.9	224.4	106.3	74.37
Earnings Per Share ($)						
1Q	0.97	2.16	1.80	0.56	0.24	0.28
2Q	0.53	2.34	2.38	0.61	0.32	0.29
3Q	0.34	1.75	1.74	0.77	0.30	0.37
4Q	—	1.90	1.58	0.82	0.74	0.36
Yr.	—	8.17	7.50	2.80	1.37	1.22

Next earnings report expected: early February

Dividend Data

No cash dividends have been paid. The company intends to retain its earnings for working capital and to finance the expansion of its business and does not anticipate paying cash dividends in the foreseeable future.

SEACOR SMIT Inc

Business Summary - 20-OCT-99

SEACOR SMIT Inc. (formerly SEACOR Holdings, Inc.) is a major provider of offshore marine services to the oil and gas exploration and production industry (93% of revenues in 1998) and a leading provider of oil spill response services to owners of tank vessels and oil storage, processing and handling facilities (7%).

At March 1, 1999, the company operated a diversified fleet of 303 vessels dedicated mainly to servicing offshore oil and gas exploration and production facilities primarily in the U.S. Gulf of Mexico, offshore West Africa, the North Sea, the Far East, the Mediterranean and Latin America. SEACOR's offshore service vessels deliver cargo and personnel to offshore installations, handle anchors for drilling rigs and other marine equipment, support offshore construction and maintenance work, and provide standby safety support. The company also furnishes vessels for special projects such as well stimulation, seismic data gathering, freight hauling and line handling. In connection with its offshore marine services, the company, through certain joint ventures, also offers logistics services for the offshore industry.

SEACOR has formed or acquired interests in joint ventures and entered into pooling arrangements with various third parties to enter new markets, enhance its marketing capabilities and facilitate operations in certain foreign markets. Such arrangements allow the company to expand its fleet and minimize risks and capital outlays associated with independent fleet expansion.

Principal customers include major integrated oil companies and large independent oil and gas exploration and production companies. In 1998, Mobil Oil accounted for 11% of marine operating revenues.

The environmental services business mainly provides contractual oil spill response services to those who store, transport, produce or handle petroleum and certain other non-petroleum oils as required by the Oil Pollution Act of 1990 and various state regulations. Services, which are provided mainly through wholly owned National Response Corp. (NRC), include training for and supervision of activities in response to oil spill emergencies and the maintenance of specialized equipment for immediate deployment and spill response.

The company owns and maintains specialized oil spill response equipment including containment booms used to protect sensitive areas and to trap oil in areas where it can be recovered, pumps, vacuum transfer units, skimmers, portable barges, mobile command centers equipped with field communications, and utility vessels outfitted with skimming equipment to recover oil.

Environmental services are provided mainly to owners of dry cargo vessels, refineries, pipelines, exploration and production platforms and tank terminals.

Per Share Data ($) (Year Ended Dec. 31)	1998	1997	1996	1995	1994	1993	1992	1991	1990	1989
Tangible Bk. Val.	40.26	34.11	25.38	18.41	14.71	13.08	12.60	12.18	NA	NA
Cash Flow	10.02	9.27	5.20	4.32	3.41	3.19	1.88	2.80	NA	NA
Earnings	8.17	7.50	3.03	1.64	1.35	1.46	0.05	0.51	NA	NA
Dividends	Nil	Nil	Nil	Nil	Nil	Nil	Nil	Nil	NA	NA
Payout Ratio	Nil	Nil	Nil	Nil	Nil	Nil	Nil	Nil	NA	NA
Prices - High	61 7/8	73 5/8	66 3/8	28	23 1/2	28	15	NA	NA	NA
- Low	31 1/4	39 5/8	26 3/8	18	17 3/4	13	14 1/4	NA	NA	NA
P/E Ratio - High	8	10	22	17	17	19	NM	NA	NA	NA
- Low	4	5	9	11	13	9	NM	NA	NA	NA
Income Statement Analysis (Million $)										
Revs.	NA	347	224	106	74.4	73.7	57.7	47.7	NA	NA
Oper. Inc.	162	151	77.5	30.4	26.2	25.9	17.7	16.9	NA	NA
Depr.	36.4	36.5	25.0	16.7	12.0	10.0	10.7	8.1	NA	NA
Int. Exp.	22.8	14.2	5.7	6.5	5.2	4.4	6.2	5.7	NA	NA
Pretax Inc.	187	181	52.0	14.0	10.2	12.7	0.3	2.8	NA	NA
Eff. Tax Rate	32%	34%	36%	34%	34%	35%	50%	33%	NA	NA
Net Inc.	125	120	35.0	10.2	7.9	8.5	0.2	1.9	NA	NA
Balance Sheet & Other Fin. Data (Million $)										
Cash	216	175	149	24.6	41.1	31.7	15.5	6.8	NA	NA
Curr. Assets	312	296	201	58.9	55.8	NA	NA	NA	NA	NA
Total Assets	1,258	1,020	636	313	202	197	145	150	NA	NA
Curr. Liab.	71.7	59.5	29.3	16.7	12.2	NA	NA	NA	NA	NA
LT Debt	473	359	219	107	73.1	82.7	43.2	56.4	NA	NA
Common Eqty.	543	474	351	157	85.8	75.3	67.1	48.3	NA	NA
Total Cap.	662	926	605	294	190	158	100	105	NA	NA
Cap. Exp.	227	136	50.8	12.8	1.8	24.1	3.2	NA	NA	NA
Cash Flow	161	156	59.9	27.0	19.9	18.5	10.9	10.0	NA	NA
Curr. Ratio	4.4	5.0	6.9	3.5	4.0	NA	NA	NA	NA	NA
% LT Debt of Cap.	71.5	38.7	36.2	36.4	38.5	52.3	43.2	53.7	NA	NA
% Net Inc.of Revs.	32.4	34.4	15.7	9.6	10.6	11.5	3.9	3.9	NA	NA
% Ret. on Assets	11.0	14.4	7.1	4.0	4.0	5.0	0.1	1.3	NA	NA
% Ret. on Equity	24.6	28.9	13.1	8.4	9.8	11.9	0.3	3.9	NA	NA

Data as orig reptd.; bef. results of disc opers/spec. items. Per share data adj. for stk. divs. Bold denotes diluted EPS (FASB 128)-prior periods restated. E-Estimated. NA-Not Available. NM-Not Meaningful. NR-Not Ranked.

Office—11200 Westheimer, Suite 850, Houston, TX 77042. **Tel**—(713) 782-5990. **Chrmn, Pres & CEO**—C. Fabrikant. **EVP, CFO & Secy**—R. Blank. **VP & Treas**—L. P. Dantin. **Dirs**—G. E. Conway, P. de Demandolx, C. Fabrikant, R. M. Fairbanks III, M. E. Gellert,A. Kienhuis, S. Stamas. **Transfer Agent & Registrar**—Harris Trust Co. of New York, NYC. **Incorporated**—in Delaware in 1989. **Empl**— 1,787. **S&P Analyst:** M.I.

STANDARD
&POOR'S
STOCK REPORTS

SEI Investments

NASDAQ Symbol **SEIC**

In S&P SmallCap 600

09-OCT-99 **Industry:** Financial (Diversified)

Summary: This company provides global investment solutions to institutions and business solutions to investment intermediaries.

Quantitative Evaluations

Outlook (1 Lowest—5 Highest)
• **1**

Fair Value
• **82⅛**

Risk
• **Average**

Earn./Div. Rank
• **A-**

Technical Eval.
• **Bearish** since 8/99

Rel. Strength Rank (1 Lowest—99 Highest)
• **43**

Insider Activity
• **Neutral**

Recent Price • 88¾
52 Wk Range • 119¼-59½
Yield • 0.5%
12-Mo. P/E • 29.3

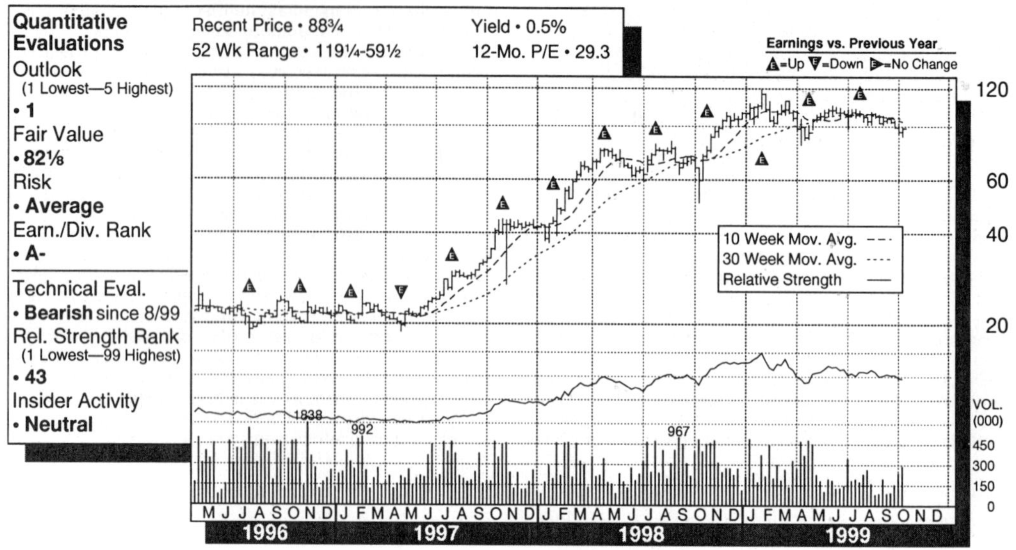

Business Profile - 03-AUG-99

In February 1999, SEI Investments (formerly SEI Corp.) said that its business growth during 1998 caused it to be optimistic that there would be continuing momentum into 1999 and beyond. The company also said that in compliance with new accounting standards, it now reports in four business segments: Technology Services, Mutual Fund Services, Asset Management, and Investments in New Business. In December 1998, SEIC signed an agreement to manage a new family of mutual funds for Mediolanum S.p.A., one of Italy's largest providers of life insurance, financial and pension products. Total assets under management for high-net-worth and institutional investors grew by 20%, to $53.9 billion in the six months ending June 30, 1999. On June 30, 1999, the company announced that it is postponing efforts to secure a listing on the New York Stock Exchange, and will remain on Nasdaq until further notice.

Operational Review - 03-AUG-99

Revenues in the first half of 1999 advanced 29%, year to year. Expenses grew less rapidly than revenues, and operating income climbed 74%. Other income (net) was up sharply, to almost $3.0 million from $535,000, and after taxes at 38.5%, versus 39.0%, net income surged 82%, to $31,323,000 ($1.64 a share) from $17,182,000 ($0.90).

Stock Performance - 08-OCT-99

In the past 30 trading days, SEIC's shares have declined 4%, compared to a 0.91% fall in the S&P 500. Average trading volume for the past five days was 57,140 shares, compared with the 40-day moving average of 31,174 shares.

Key Stock Statistics

Dividend Rate/Share	0.40	Shareholders	850
Shs. outstg. (M)	17.7	Market cap. (B)	$ 1.6
Avg. daily vol. (M)	0.038	Inst. holdings	40%
Tang. Bk. Value/Share	3.36		
Beta	0.86		

Value of $10,000 invested 5 years ago: $ 35,168

Fiscal Year Ending Dec. 31

	1999	1998	1997	1996	1995	1994
Revenues (Million $)						
1Q	104.3	81.87	63.50	63.24	53.50	63.69
2Q	111.6	85.50	70.73	61.54	55.74	64.68
3Q	—	90.49	74.28	60.17	56.48	66.11
4Q	—	108.3	84.23	62.87	60.25	69.29
Yr.	—	366.1	292.8	247.8	226.0	263.8
Earnings Per Share ($)						
1Q	**0.79**	**0.40**	**0.25**	**0.30**	0.30	0.21
2Q	**0.85**	**0.50**	**0.27**	**0.25**	0.23	0.23
3Q	—	**0.60**	**0.36**	**0.31**	0.26	0.25
4Q	—	**0.75**	**0.52**	**0.34**	0.30	0.27
Yr.	—	**2.25**	**1.40**	**1.20**	**1.08**	**0.91**

Next earnings report expected: mid October

Dividend Data (Dividends have been paid since 1988.)

Amount ($)	Date Decl.	Ex-Div. Date	Stock of Record	Payment Date
0.160	Dec. 10	Dec. 31	Jan. 05	Jan. 25 '99
0.200	May. 18	Jun. 14	Jun. 16	Jun. 30 '99

A Division of The McGraw-Hill Companies

SEI Investments Company

Business Summary - 03-AUG-99

SEI Investments Co. (formerly SEI Corp.) provides global investment solutions to institutions and business solutions to investment intermediaries. Clients include corporations, banks, insurance companies, unions, foundations, endowments and high-net-worth individuals. At December 31, 1998, total assets under administration, including assets invested in SEIC's and clients' proprietary mutual funds, were $178.4 billion, a 55% increase from year-end 1997. Assets for which SEIC provides custodial services amounted to $38.8 billion, versus $24.8 billion.

In compliance with new accounting standards, SEIC now reports in four business segments: Technology Services, Asset Management, Mutual Fund Services, and Investments in New Business.

The Technology Services segment, which accounted for 45% of revenues in 1998, consists of trust technology, trust back-office outsourcing services and liquidity products sold to bank clients. SEI's TRUST 3000 product line is a complete trust accounting and investment accounting system with integrated and automated solutions for investment managers, account administration and operations. It provides 17 months of transaction history and unlimited asset history. Customers can utilize the company's software and computer systems from the user location, or as a "total outsource," with full operation of the system by SEIC.

The Asset Management segment (25% of revenues) provides investment solutions through various investment products and services distributed directly or through professional investment advisers, financial planners and other intermediaries to institutional and high-net-worth markets. SEIC works with each client to develop investment strategies that are consistent with the client's risk tolerance, investment objectives, time horizon and investment restrictions.

The Mutual Fund Services segment (27%) provides administrative and distribution services to proprietary mutual funds created for banks, other financial institutions and money managers. Services include fund administration and accounting, legal and regulatory compliance, and shareholder record-keeping services. Distribution services range from assistance with strategic businessplanning to product development through marketing program development and execution. At the end of 1998, there were approximately 105 bank proprietary fund complexes in the U.S. As of December 31, 1998, SEIC provided fund services to 35 banks, investment management companies and insurance firms with proprietary mutual fund assets of approximately $133.4 billion.

Investments in New Business (3%) consists of the company's Canadian and international operations.

Per Share Data ($) (Year Ended Dec. 31)	1998	1997	1996	1995	1994	1993	1992	1991	1990	1989
Tangible Bk. Val.	3.34	2.44	2.93	3.04	2.34	2.21	1.97	1.75	1.79	0.97
Earnings	2.25	1.40	1.20	1.09	0.96	0.78	0.52	0.70	0.54	0.53
Dividends	0.30	0.28	0.24	0.20	0.16	0.12	0.08	0.06	0.05	0.05
Payout Ratio	13%	20%	20%	18%	17%	14%	13%	8%	9%	8%
Prices - High	100 1/2	44 1/2	26 3/8	24 1/2	28 1/2	27 1/4	16	13 3/4	11 1/8	10
- Low	37	18 3/4	17 3/4	16 3/4	16 3/4	13 3/8	11	8 7/8	7 1/4	8
P/E Ratio - High	45	32	22	22	30	35	31	20	21	19
- Low	16	13	15	15	17	17	21	13	13	15
Income Statement Analysis (Million $)										
Net Int. Inc.	NA	NA	NA	NA	NA	NA	NA	NA	NA	NA
Non Int. Inc.	NA	NA	NA	NA	NA	NA	NA	NA	NA	NA
Loan Loss Prov.	NA	NA	NA	NA	NA	NA	NA	NA	NA	NA
Non Int. Exp.	NA	NA	NA	NA	NA	NA	NA	NA	NA	NA
Exp./Op. Revs.	NA	NA	NA	NA	NA	NA	NA	NA	NA	NA
Pretax Inc.	69.9	44.0	37.9	35.6	31.6	26.0	18.3	26.0	19.5	19.1
Eff. Tax Rate	39%	39%	39%	41%	39%	38%	38%	39%	38%	37%
Net Inc.	43.0	26.8	23.1	21.1	19.3	16.1	11.3	16.0	12.1	12.1
% Net Int. Marg.	NA	NA	NA	NA	NA	NA	NA	NA	NA	NA
Balance Sheet & Other Fin. Data (Million $)										
Money Mkt. Assets	NA	NA	NA	NA	NA	NA	NA	NA	NA	NA
Inv. Securities	NA	NA	NA	NA	NA	NA	NA	NA	NA	NA
Tot. Loans	NA	NA	NA	NA	NA	NA	NA	NA	NA	NA
Total Assets	209	169	141	101	102	100	86.0	83.0	84.0	76.0
Demand Deposits	NA	NA	NA	NA	NA	NA	NA	NA	NA	NA
Time Deposits	NA	NA	NA	NA	NA	NA	NA	NA	NA	NA
LT Debt	31.0	33.0	Nil	Nil	Nil	Nil	Nil	Nil	Nil	4.1
Common Eqty.	59.7	46.4	56.1	56.0	51.3	51.5	49.4	47.9	53.1	36.5
% Ret. on Assets	NA	NA	NA	NA	NA	NA	NA	NA	NA	NA
% Ret. on Equity	NA	NA	NA	NA	NA	NA	NA	NA	NA	NA
% Loan Loss Resv.	NA	NA	NA	NA	NA	NA	NA	NA	NA	NA
% Loans/Deposits	NA	NA	NA	NA	NA	NA	NA	NA	NA	NA
% Loans/Assets	NA	NA	NA	NA	NA	NA	NA	NA	NA	NA
% Equity to Assets	NA	NA	NA	NA	NA	NA	NA	NA	NA	NA

Data as orig reptd.; bef. results of disc opers/spec. items. Per share data adj. for stk. divs. Bold denotes diluted EPS (FASB 128)-prior periods restated. E-Estimated. NA-Not Available. NM-Not Meaningful. NR-Not Ranked.

Office—1 Freedom Valley Dr., Oaks, PA 19456-1100. **Tel**—(610) 676-1000. **Website**—http://www.seic.com **Chrmn & CEO**—A. P. West Jr. **EVP**—C. V. Romeo. **Dirs**—W. M. Doran, H. H. Greer, R. B. Lieb, K. McCarthy, H. H. Porter Jr., C. V. Romeo, A. P. West Jr. **Transfer Agent & Registrar**—American Stock Transfer & Trust Co., NYC. **Incorporated**—in Pennsylvania in 1968. **Empl**— 1,309. **S&P Analyst:** C.C.P.

Seitel, Inc.

NYSE Symbol **SEI**

In S&P SmallCap 600

09-OCT-99

Industry: Oil & Gas (Drilling & Equipment)

Summary: This company owns the largest seismic data library in North America.

Quantitative Evaluations

Outlook (1 Lowest—5 Highest) • **5**

Fair Value • **19⅜**

Risk • **Average**

Earn./Div. Rank • **B**

Technical Eval. • **Bearish** since 9/99

Rel. Strength Rank (1 Lowest—99 Highest) • **9**

Insider Activity • **NA**

Recent Price • 9⅛

52 Wk Range • 18⅛-8¾

Yield • Nil

12-Mo. P/E • 11.6

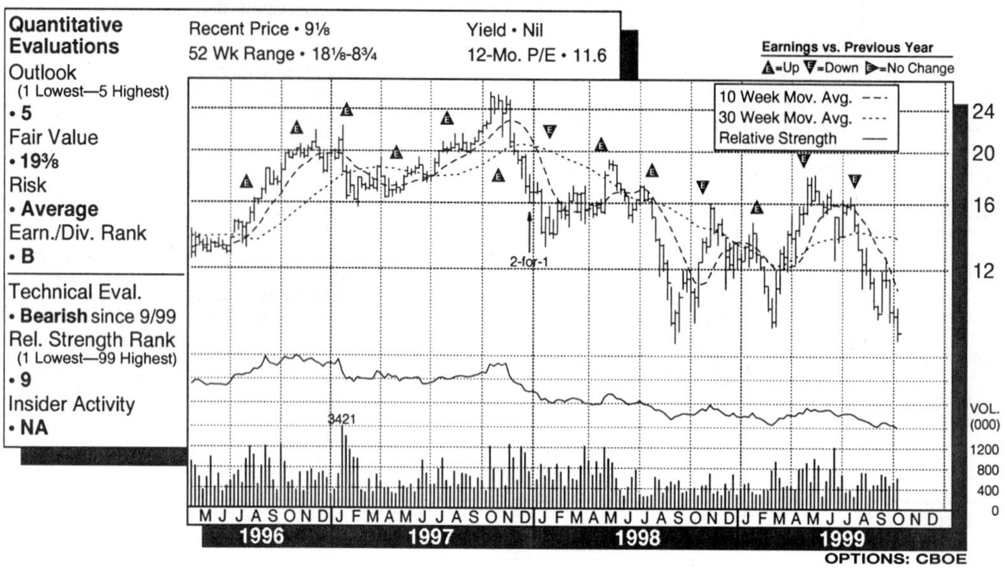

Business Profile - 03-AUG-99

In May 1999, the company signed a letter of intent to form a 50/50 joint venture with Schlumberger to perform seismic surveying work in the Gulf of Mexico in water depths up to 500 feet. In February, Olympic Seismic, Seitel's Canadian subsidiary, purchased Amoco Canada's seismic data covering the provinces of Alberta, British Columbia, the Northwest Territory and Saskatchewan. The acquisition resulted in Seitel owning 500,000 km of 2D data and 7,000 sq. km of 3D data, the largest seismic data library in North America. The company believes that the Canadian oil and gas industry will experience significant growth over the next several years similar to the U.S. in the early 1990s.

Operational Review - 03-AUG-99

Revenues in the six months ended June 30, 1999, increased 6.0%, year to year. With a 14% advance in operating expenses, operating income rose only 3.9%. After a significant hike in interest expense, taxes at 40.0% versus 37.1% and a $7.8 million impairment due to dividend distribution of affiliate stock, net income fell 50%, to $5.6 million ($0.23 a share, diluted, on 6% more shares), from $11.2 million ($0.49).

Stock Performance - 08-OCT-99

In the past 30 trading days, SEI's shares have declined 11%, compared to a 0.91% fall in the S&P 500. Average trading volume for the past five days was 122,160 shares, compared with the 40-day moving average of 109,279 shares.

Key Stock Statistics

Dividend Rate/Share	Nil	Shareholders	1,265
Shs. outstg. (M)	24.3	Market cap. (B)	$0.222
Avg. daily vol. (M)	0.113	Inst. holdings	59%
Tang. Bk. Value/Share	10.05		
Beta	1.48		

Value of $10,000 invested 5 years ago: NA

Fiscal Year Ending Dec. 31

	1999	1998	1997	1996	1995	1994
Revenues (Million $)						
1Q	37.88	30.93	27.22	20.27	16.61	12.60
2Q	34.13	36.98	34.67	27.18	22.14	16.15
3Q	—	38.33	30.79	30.31	17.87	18.79
4Q	—	38.62	34.87	28.25	17.82	26.23
Yr.	—	144.9	127.6	106.0	74.44	73.77
Earnings Per Share ($)						
1Q	**0.03**	**0.21**	**0.19**	**0.14**	0.14	0.13
2Q	**0.20**	**0.28**	**0.25**	**0.20**	0.17	0.15
3Q	—	**0.28**	**0.98**	**0.22**	0.10	0.13
4Q	—	**0.29**	**0.02**	**0.28**	0.10	0.20
Yr.	—	**1.05**	**1.43**	**0.79**	**0.49**	0.61

Next earnings report expected: early November

Dividend Data

Amount ($)	Date Decl.	Ex-Div. Date	Stock of Record	Payment Date
Stk.	May. 12	May. 14	May. 18	Jun. 10 '99

Seitel, Inc.

Business Summary - 03-AUG-99

Seitel provides proprietary seismic data and related geophysical technology used in oil and natural gas exploration and production (E&P). Its library of seismic data is owned and marketed by Seitel Data Ltd., a limited partnership of which SEI's subsidiaries constitute all of the limited and general partners, and Olympic Seismic Ltd., a wholly owned subsidiary. The data library, which consists of both two-dimensional (2D) and three-dimensional (3D) data, is marketed to more than 400 oil and gas companies under license agreements. At year-end 1998, Seitel owned about 920,000 linear mi. of 2D and 11,750 sq. mi. of 3D seismic data, which it maintained in its library, and marketed an additional 270,000 linear mi. of 2D data.

Three-dimensional seismic data provides a graphic geophysical depiction of the earth's subsurface from two horizontal dimensions and one vertical dimension, rendering a more detailed picture than 2D data, which present a cross-sectional view from one vertical and one horizontal dimension. Thus, 3D surveys enhance the interpreter's ability to predict the existence and location of subsurface hydrocarbons, increasing drilling success rates, reducing the occurrence of costly dry holes and significantly lowering exploration and development finding costs. However, the cost to create 3D seismic data is substantially greater than that of 2D seismic data, particularly for onshore data. As a result, 2D is more economical for preliminary, broad scale exploration valuation and in determining the location for 3D surveys.

Through its DDD Energy subsidiary, Seitel utilizes its seismic expertise to participate directly in petroleum exploration, development and ownership of hydrocarbon reserves via partnership relationships with over 100 oil and gas companies. DDD Energy's E&P activities are focused in the onshore Gulf Coast areas of onshore Texas, Louisiana Alabama and Mississippi, as well as California and Arkansas. At December 31, 1998, proved reserves consisted of 74.1 Bcf of natural gas and 7.3 MMBbls of oil.

In July 1999, DDD Energy and certain of its working interest partners sold their working interest in several properties, generating $13.7 million for Seitel; proceeds will be used to reduce debt. In May, the subsidiary and several partners announced six new discoveries and one development well, all located in Louisiana. In February, the company raised $138 million in a private placement of senior notes; proceeds were used to repay debt and for capital expenditures.

SEI maintains an approximate 17% equity stake in Eagle Geophysical Inc., which completed its initial public offering in August 1997.

Per Share Data ($) (Year Ended Dec. 31)	1998	1997	1996	1995	1994	1993	1992	1991	1990	1989
Tangible Bk. Val.	10.05	9.27	8.24	6.38	5.74	3.48	2.98	2.83	2.33	1.56
Cash Flow	4.08	3.68	2.69	1.88	2.36	1.85	1.56	1.43	1.43	1.21
Earnings	1.05	1.43	0.79	0.52	0.61	0.46	0.38	0.57	0.51	0.36
Dividends	Nil	Nil	Nil	Nil	Nil	Nil	0.02	0.05	0.05	Nil
Payout Ratio	Nil	Nil	Nil	Nil	Nil	Nil	7%	9%	9%	Nil
Prices - High	19 1/4	25 7/8	21 7/8	17 3/4	18 1/2	7 1/4	5 3/4	7 5/8	8	4 3/4
- Low	8 5/8	15 3/4	11 5/8	9 1/2	6 3/4	3 1/4	2 7/16	4	3 3/8	1 11/16
P/E Ratio - High	18	18	28	34	30	16	15	13	16	13
- Low	8	11	15	18	11	7	6	7	7	5
Income Statement Analysis (Million $)										
Revs.	145	128	106	74.4	73.8	43.5	31.2	27.8	25.4	17.9
Oper. Inc.	113	86.6	67.4	46.0	45.7	27.6	20.3	18.5	17.1	12.5
Depr.	69.9	49.7	39.2	26.9	27.2	19.9	13.5	9.2	9.4	7.3
Int. Exp.	6.0	4.6	4.1	3.4	3.5	2.3	1.6	0.9	0.7	0.4
Pretax Inc.	38.0	49.0	25.1	16.0	15.3	9.0	6.5	9.1	7.8	4.8
Eff. Tax Rate	36%	36%	35%	37%	37%	36%	33%	34%	34%	34%
Net Inc.	24.4	31.6	16.2	10.1	9.6	5.7	4.3	6.0	5.2	3.2
Balance Sheet & Other Fin. Data (Million $)										
Cash	3.2	4.9	3.3	6.2	1.5	1.8	3.5	1.1	1.9	1.1
Curr. Assets	NA	NA	NA	NA	NA	NA	NA	18.7	21.3	13.5
Total Assets	496	366	295	210	169	92.6	73.1	52.0	42.8	25.2
Curr. Liab.	NA	NA	NA	NA	45.6	18.4	10.5	8.0	9.8	6.4
LT Debt	151	90.0	84.0	57.6	14.6	30.7	26.2	11.5	7.4	4.5
Common Eqty.	238	208	159	120	101	41.6	35.6	31.4	24.8	13.5
Total Cap.	388	315	240	178	119	73.3	62.2	43.2	32.5	18.4
Cap. Exp.	161	141	106	82.4	52.6	22.9	22.0	20.0	0.3	0.0
Cash Flow	94.3	81.2	55.5	37.0	36.8	25.6	17.8	15.2	14.5	10.5
Curr. Ratio	NA	NA	NA	NA	NA	NA	NA	2.3	2.2	2.1
% LT Debt of Cap.	38.8	28.6	35.1	32.3	12.3	41.9	42.2	26.5	22.8	24.4
% Net Inc.of Revs.	16.8	24.7	15.3	13.6	13.0	13.2	14.4	22.0	20.8	17.6
% Ret. on Assets	5.7	9.6	6.4	5.4	6.3	6.9	6.7	12.4	14.0	13.5
% Ret. on Equity	10.9	17.2	11.5	9.1	11.8	14.8	12.5	21.0	24.9	26.5

Data as orig reptd.; bef. results of disc opers/spec. items. Per share data adj. for stk. divs. Bold denotes diluted EPS (FASB 128)-prior periods restated. E-Estimated. NA-Not Available. NM-Not Meaningful. NR-Not Ranked.

Office—50 Briar Hollow Lane, West Bldg., 7th Fl., Houston, TX 77027. **Tel**—(713) 881-8900. **Chrmn**—H. M. Pearlman. **Pres & CEO**—P. A. Frame. **EVP & COO**—H. A. Calvert. **EVP-Fin, CFO, Treas & Secy**—D. D. Valice. **Investor Contact**—Russell Hoffman (203-629-0633). **Dirs**—H. A. Calvert, W. M. Craig Jr., P. A. Frame, D. S. Lawi, W. Lerner, H. M. Pearlman, J. E. Steiglitz, D. D. Valice, F. S. Zeidman. **Transfer Agent & Registrar**—American Stock Transfer & Trust Co., NYC. **Incorporated**—in Delaware in 1982. **Empl**— 110. **S&P Analyst:** Ephraim Juskowicz

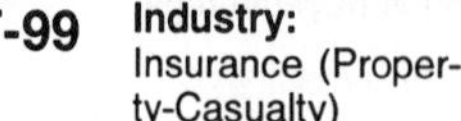

Selective Insurance Group

NASDAQ Symbol **SIGI**

In S&P SmallCap 600

09-OCT-99

Industry: Insurance (Property-Casualty)

Summary: SIGI offers a broad range of property and casualty insurance products principally to customers in suburban and rural locales.

Quantitative Evaluations

Outlook (1 Lowest—5 Highest)
• **2+**

Fair Value
• **20**

Risk
• **Low**

Earn./Div. Rank
• **B+**

Technical Eval.
• **Bearish** since 8/99

Rel. Strength Rank (1 Lowest—99 Highest)
• **62**

Insider Activity
• **NA**

Recent Price • 18½
52 Wk Range • 23-17¼
Yield • 3.2%
12-Mo. P/E • 8.2

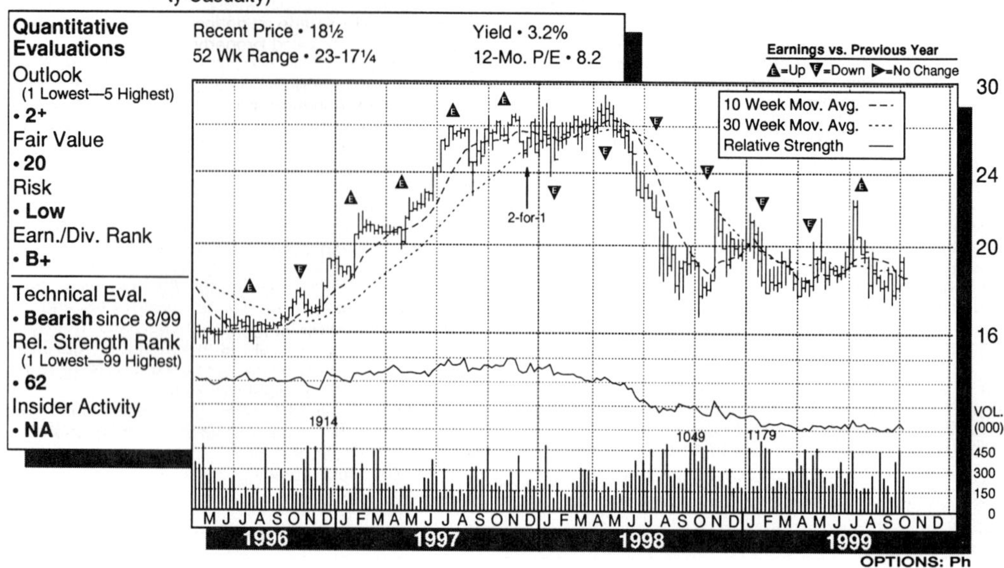

Business Profile - 17-MAY-99

As of May 1999, the company was continuing to encounter competitive conditions in commercial lines pricing; together with weather-related losses and many large property claims, this hurt results in the 1999 first quarter. SIGI believes its recent entry into the Midwest, as well as expansion of its personal insurance program, will create additional opportunities for growth; the company has recently begun to write more than 50% of its business outside its home state of New Jersey. In addition, SIGI is expanding fee service income sources. In December 1998, it purchased PDA Software Services Inc., a custom software development and processing company based in Overland Park, KS, with $13 million in annual revenues. SIGI has an ongoing share buyback program. The dividend was raised 7.1%, effective with the June 1999 payment. Directors and officers own nearly 7% of the common stock.

Operational Review - 17-MAY-99

In the first three months of 1999, net premiums written rose 10%, year to year, as strong personal lines results outweighed the impact of pricing weakness in commercial lines. Net investment revenue was lower, but fee for service revenue soared 195%, reflecting acquisitions. Catastrophe losses drove expenses up, contributing to a 45% drop in operating income. Despite after tax capital gains of $5.6 million, versus $703,000, net income fell 12%, to $14,023,000 ($0.48 a share, on 5.4% fewer shares), from $15,956,000 ($0.50).

Stock Performance - 08-OCT-99

In the past 30 trading days, SIGI's shares have increased 3%, compared to a 0.91% fall in the S&P 500. Average trading volume for the past five days was 53,940 shares, compared with the 40-day moving average of 58,182 shares.

Key Stock Statistics

Dividend Rate/Share	0.60	Shareholders	3,800
Shs. outstg. (M)	27.8	Market cap. (B)	$0.513
Avg. daily vol. (M)	0.065	Inst. holdings	41%
Tang. Bk. Value/Share	20.59		
Beta	0.48		

Value of $10,000 invested 5 years ago: $ 14,427

Fiscal Year Ending Dec. 31

	1999	1998	1997	1996	1995	1994
Revenues (Million $)						
1Q	225.4	200.9	197.2	201.9	201.0	182.7
2Q	196.4	205.6	196.0	201.6	209.0	184.4
3Q	—	212.7	198.9	196.7	216.0	200.3
4Q	—	227.1	196.3	198.7	213.1	200.8
Yr.	—	837.3	788.4	799.0	839.1	768.3
Earnings Per Share ($)						
1Q	**0.48**	**0.50**	**0.55**	0.30	0.45	0.28
2Q	**0.95**	**0.44**	**0.56**	0.51	0.43	0.34
3Q	—	**0.43**	**0.60**	0.42	0.48	0.34
4Q	—	**0.38**	**0.57**	0.62	0.49	0.42
Yr.	—	**1.74**	**2.27**	1.91	1.86	1.38

Next earnings report expected: early November

Dividend Data (Dividends have been paid since 1929.)

Amount ($)	Date Decl.	Ex-Div. Date	Stock of Record	Payment Date
0.140	Nov. 03	Nov. 12	Nov. 16	Dec. 01 '98
0.140	Feb. 02	Feb. 11	Feb. 16	Mar. 01 '99
0.150	May. 07	May. 12	May. 14	Jun. 01 '99
0.150	Aug. 03	Aug. 12	Aug. 16	Sep. 01 '99

Selective Insurance Group, Inc.

Business Summary - 17-MAY-99

Founded in 1926, Selective Insurance Group, Inc. has grown from its New Jersey base to provide property and casualty insurance through about 870 independent agents in 16 eastern and midwestern states. In 1998, the company wrote nearly half of its direct business outside New Jersey. Net premiums earned in 1998 were derived 70% from commercial lines and 30% from personal lines. A. M. Best has rated the company A+ (Superior) for 37 consecutive years. SIGI has paid dividends for 70 consecutive years.

The company has sought to increase its geographic diversification in recent years; the percentage of net written premium derived from New Jersey fell to 51% in 1998, from 60% in 1996, as the company entered six midwestern states and Rhode Island. The 1998 share for states other than New Jersey was: Pennsylvania 11%, New York 9%, Maryland 6%, South Carolina 5%, Virginia 5%, North Carolina 3%, Georgia 2%, Delaware 2%, Illinois 2%, Indiana 1%, and other states 3%. In 1999, the company planned to begin writing insurance in Connecticut, Minnesota, Missouri and Kentucky; SIGI is licensed in many additional jurisdictions.

The company's commercial insurance coverages consist of the following: workers' compensation, commercial automobile, liability, property, umbrella, and bonds.

Workers' compensation coverage insures employers against employee claims resulting from work-related injuries. Compensation is payable regardless of who was at fault.

Commercial automobile coverage insures against losses incurred from bodily injury, bodily injury to third parties, property damage to an insured's vehicle (including fire and theft) and property damage to other vehicles and property as a result of automobile accidents involving commercial vehicles.

Liability coverage insures against third party liability for bodily injury and property damage, including liability for products sold, and the defense of claims alleging such damages. The liability lines continue to reflect the potential exposure to environmental claims.

Property coverage insures policyholders against commercial property damage caused by fire, wind, hail, water, theft and vandalism, and other perils.

Personal insurance coverages include personal automobile (86% of 1998 personal lines total net premiums earned), homeowners, personal catastrophe liability, and flood. Much of the personal automobile insurance is written in New Jersey, where, beginning in mid-1999, regulatory changes are expected to cut annual earnings in this line by 15%, or about $24 million.

Investments totaled $1.8 billion at year-end 1998, and broke down as follows: taxable debt securities 36%, tax-advantaged debt securities 45%, equity securities 15%, and short-term investments/other 4%.

Per Share Data ($) (Year Ended Dec. 31)	1998	1997	1996	1995	1994	1993	1992	1991	1990	1989
Tangible Bk. Val.	20.59	18.72	15.96	14.80	11.23	11.32	11.15	10.08	9.36	9.08
Oper. Earnings	NA	2.15	1.84	1.83	1.28	0.72	0.93	0.93	0.94	1.45
Earnings	1.74	2.27	1.91	1.85	1.38	0.83	1.03	1.03	1.25	1.52
Dividends	0.56	0.56	0.56	0.56	0.56	0.56	0.55	0.52	0.51	0.46
Payout Ratio	32%	25%	29%	30%	41%	67%	53%	50%	41%	30%
Prices - High	29 1/4	28 3/8	19 3/8	19 1/4	15 3/8	15 1/2	11 3/4	9	10 1/8	10
- Low	16 5/8	18 3/8	15 1/2	12 1/4	11 1/2	10 1/4	8	6 1/2	6 1/4	7 1/4
P/E Ratio - High	17	12	10	10	11	19	11	9	8	7
- Low	10	8	8	7	8	12	8	6	5	5
Income Statement Analysis (Million $)										
Premium Inc.	723	676	695	743	680	595	536	497	464	450
Net Invest. Inc.	99	101	97.0	91.6	80.7	77.3	73.5	68.5	64.5	59.8
Oth. Revs.	12.0	11.6	7.1	4.6	7.4	7.4	6.2	5.7	12.0	6.3
Total Revs.	834	788	799	839	768	680	616	571	540	516
Pretax Inc.	63.7	91.0	69.0	65.0	43.4	21.4	31.5	31.6	35.4	46.1
Net Oper. Inc.	55.0	65.7	53.7	52.5	35.5	NA	NA	NA	NA	NA
Net Inc.	53.6	69.6	55.6	53.0	38.3	22.7	27.4	27.3	32.4	40.6
Balance Sheet & Other Fin. Data (Million $)										
Cash & Equiv.	30.5	5.0	24.2	23.6	21.8	20.7	20.3	18.4	17.0	16.7
Premiums Due	240	332	310	292	274	283	132	109	124	118
Invest. Assets: Bonds	1,434	1,455	1,418	1,389	1,170	1,053	1,034	870	786	739
Invest. Assets: Stocks	270	222	161	118	91.6	88.2	86.3	70.2	72.8	91.1
Invest. Assets: Loans	NA	20.1	10.5	10.7	10.7	10.1	10.0	8.4	3.1	3.0
Invest. Assets: Total	1,771	681	1,624	1,564	1,303	1,196	1,130	948	863	833
Deferred Policy Costs	110	98.1	83.2	82.2	81.0	78.6	76.4	53.0	53.0	49.5
Total Assets	2,432	2,306	2,184	2,113	1,867	1,739	1,479	1,211	1,139	1,074
Debt	88.8	114	104	111	111	61.3	63.7	14.5	15.2	35.8
Common Eqty.	493	476	474	437	329	323	312	270	248	230
Prop. & Cas. Loss Ratio	70.3	68.2	71.3	71.2	71.7	71.8	69.5	67.9	70.5	69.4
Prop. & Cas. Expense Ratio	33.3	32.1	31.6	30.4	32.6	36.7	37.0	38.1	35.0	32.2
Prop. & Cas. Combined Ratio	103.6	100.3	102.9	101.6	104.3	108.5	107.9	107.6	108.0	103.4
% Return On Revs.	6.4	8.8	7.0	6.3	5.0	3.3	4.5	5.5	6.0	7.9
% Ret. on Equity	11.1	15.5	12.2	13.9	11.7	7.1	9.4	10.5	13.5	18.3

Data as orig reptd.; bef. results of disc opers/spec. items. Per share data adj. for stk. divs. Bold denotes diluted EPS (FASB 128)-prior periods restated. E-Estimated. NA-Not Available. NM-Not Meaningful. NR-Not Ranked.

Office—40 Wantage Ave., Branchville, NJ 07890. **Tel**—(973) 948-3000. **Website**—http://www.selectiveinsurance.com **Chrmn**—J. W. Entringer. **Pres & CEO**—G. E. Murphy. **SVP, CFO & Investor Contact**—David B. Merclean (973-948-1776). **Dirs**—A. D. Brown, W. A. Dolan II, J. W. Entringer, W. C. Gray, C. E. Herder, F. H. Jarvis, W. M. Kearns Jr., J. Lamm-Tennant, S. G. McClellan III, G. E. Murphy, W. M. Rue, T. D. Sayles Jr., J. B. Thebault. **Transfer Agent & Registrar**—First Chicago Trust Co., Jersey City, NJ. **Incorporated**—in New Jersey in 1977. **Empl**— 1,655. **S&P Analyst:** T. W. Smith, CFA

STANDARD & POOR'S
STOCK REPORTS

Service Experts

NYSE Symbol **SVE**
In S&P SmallCap 600

09-OCT-99

Industry: Services (Commercial & Consumer)

Summary: SVE provides residential heating, ventilating and air conditioning services, as well as replacement equipment.

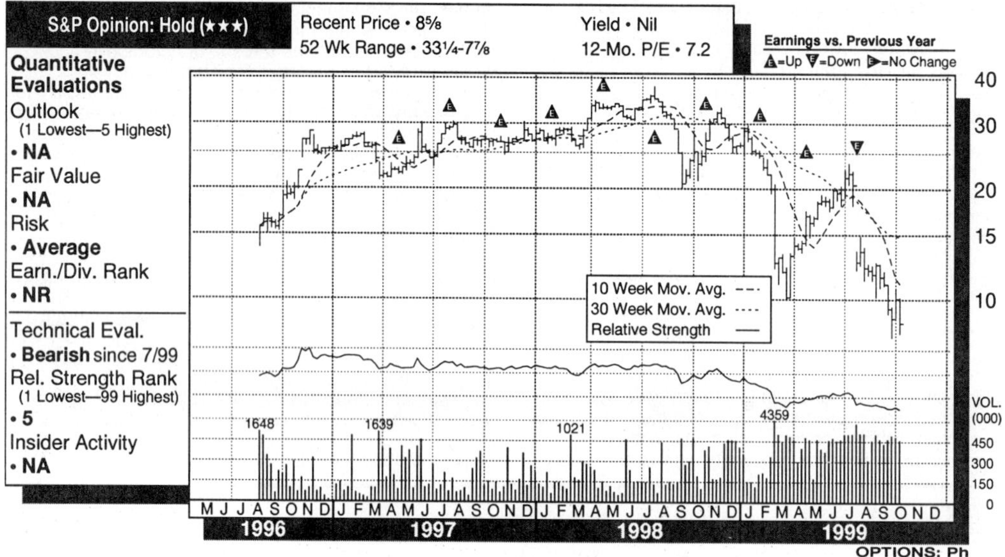

Overview - 08-OCT-99

We expect revenues to advance about 45%-50% in 1999, followed by a 25%-30% increase in 2000, driven by SVE's aggressive acquisition program, as well as solid same-store growth. The heating, ventilating and air conditioning (HVAC) market is estimated at $24 billion, with more than 30,000 participants. With less than 5% of the industry consolidated, SVE's acquisition pipeline should be full for the foreseeable future. We expect margins to narrow significantly in coming quarters, reflecting reduced profitability in the commercial business and price discounting in SVE's residential division. The bottom line will also be hurt by additional spending related to information technology and marketing initiatives. We have reduced our 1999 EPS estimate by $0.12, to $1.08, and have lowered our 2000 earnings estimate to $1.41, from $1.65.

Valuation - 08-OCT-99

Shares of SVE have fallen sharply in recent months, reflecting a deteriorating earnings outlook. As a result, the stock was recently trading at 6X our 2000 earnings estimate of $1.41, which represents a significant discount to the P/E multiple of the broader markets. Despite this seemingly attractive valuation, near term margin pressure and the possibility of an industry slowdown have tempered our enthusiasm for the stock. Consequently, we have reduced our recommendation to hold, from accumulate. In early October 1999, a major player in the industry preannounced an earnings shortfall, citing a weakening of organic growth in the HVAC market. Given this news, coupled with recent problems specific to SVE, we would not be surprised if the company failed to meet our earnings expectations for the next few quarters. However, SVE remains a leading player in a consolidating industry and is itself a takeover candidate.

Key Stock Statistics

S&P EPS Est. 1999	1.08	Tang. Bk. Value/Share	0.88
P/E on S&P Est. 1999	8.0	Beta	NA
S&P EPS Est. 2000	1.41	Shareholders	395
Dividend Rate/Share	Nil	Market cap. (B)	$0.152
Shs. outstg. (M)	17.7	Inst. holdings	45%
Avg. daily vol. (M)	0.148		

Value of $10,000 invested 5 years ago: NA

Fiscal Year Ending Dec. 31

	1999	1998	1997	1996	1995	1994
Revenues (Million $)						
1Q	116.2	70.66	33.36	—	—	—
2Q	152.8	102.9	52.35	—	—	—
3Q	—	120.0	65.65	16.25	—	—
4Q	—	114.2	71.12	20.90	—	—
Yr.	—	407.8	239.2	46.86	59.70	—
Earnings Per Share ($)						
1Q	0.23	0.19	0.18	0.11	—	—
2Q	0.23	0.44	0.32	0.20	—	—
3Q	E0.34	0.45	0.32	0.30	—	—
4Q	E0.28	0.30	0.24	0.10	—	—
Yr.	E1.08	1.37	1.06	0.74	-0.08	—

Next earnings report expected: late October

Dividend Data

No dividends have been paid, and the company has said it does not intend to pay any in the foreseeable future.

Service Experts, Inc.

Business Summary - 08-OCT-99

Service Experts provides residential heating, ventilating and air conditioning (HVAC) services and replacement equipment. As of April 1999, the company was operating 116 HVAC service and replacement businesses in 36 states. It also owns Contractor Success Group, Inc., which provides HVAC businesses with proprietary products, as well as marketing, management, educational and advisory services.

The company's service centers primarily offer the following products and services: the sale of replacement central air conditioners, furnaces and heat pumps; the maintenance and repair of HVAC units; diagnostic analysis of the condition of existing units; and the sale of ancillary products such as indoor air quality (IAQ) devices and monitors.

Most service centers employ an in-house sales force that sells replacement units, installation technicians who install replacement equipment in existing homes, service technicians who service and maintain the equipment, and an administrative staff to perform dispatching, purchasing, and other administrative functions.

Some service centers also offer plumbing services. Most service center technicians are trained to promote SVE's preventive maintenance agreements and to cross-market IAQ equipment and other ancillary services and products offered by the company.

As of year-end 1998, SVE had about 190,000 maintenance agreements with customers. These agreements are for a term of one to three years, and generally provide for two diagnostic and precision maintenance visits a year, at an average cost to the customer of about $135 per year. The sale of maintenance agreements generates recurring revenue through the payment of fees. The company believes maintenance agreements help it develop a committed, loyal customer base, and provide an opportunity for cross-marketing of other services and products.

A primary aspect of the company's strategic plan is its acquisition program, which uses a hub and spoke method of expansion into new geographic areas and further penetration into existing markets. SVE believes smaller players in the highly fragmented HVAC market will want to affiliate with the company because it provides marketing and business systems designed to improve operating efficiency, potential for national name recognition, and an opportunity to concentrate on customer service.

During 1998, the company acquired 106 HVAC businesses for total consideration of $110 million, consisting of 1.8 million common shares, $56.3 million in cash, warrants to purchase 107,500 common shares, and $6.2 million of convertible notes. In the 1999 first half, additional acquisitions were made, bringing the national service center network to 118 and annualized revenues to more than $590 million.

Per Share Data ($) (Year Ended Dec. 31)	1998	1997	1996	1995	1994	1993	1992	1991	1990	1989
Tangible Bk. Val.	0.88	2.42	1.81	1.86	NA	NA	NA	NA	NA	NA
Cash Flow	2.02	1.48	0.84	NA	NA	NA	NA	NA	NA	NA
Earnings	1.37	1.06	0.70	0.67	NA	NA	NA	NA	NA	NA
Dividends	Nil	Nil	Nil	NA	NA	NA	NA	NA	NA	NA
Payout Ratio	Nil	Nil	Nil	NA	NA	NA	NA	NA	NA	NA
Prices - High	38	30³/₈	28¹/₂	NA	NA	NA	NA	NA	NA	NA
- Low	20	21	13	NA	NA	NA	NA	NA	NA	NA
P/E Ratio - High	28	29	40	NA	NA	NA	NA	NA	NA	NA
- Low	15	20	18	NA	NA	NA	NA	NA	NA	NA
Income Statement Analysis (Million $)										
Revs.	408	239	46.9	59.7	NA	NA	NA	NA	NA	NA
Oper. Inc.	52.5	30.0	4.5	NA	NA	NA	NA	NA	NA	NA
Depr.	11.0	6.1	0.7	NA	NA	NA	NA	NA	NA	NA
Int. Exp.	3.7	0.7	0.1	Nil	NA	NA	NA	NA	NA	NA
Pretax Inc.	38.7	24.5	4.3	8.4	NA	NA	NA	NA	NA	NA
Eff. Tax Rate	39%	38%	28%	38%	NA	NA	NA	NA	NA	NA
Net Inc.	23.4	15.3	3.1	5.2	NA	NA	NA	NA	NA	NA
Balance Sheet & Other Fin. Data (Million $)										
Cash	8.4	11.2	10.7	NA	NA	NA	NA	NA	NA	NA
Curr. Assets	115	63.0	27.3	NA	NA	NA	NA	NA	NA	NA
Total Assets	357	195	68.5	26.9	NA	NA	NA	NA	NA	NA
Curr. Liab.	32.0	35.1	14.9	NA	NA	NA	NA	NA	NA	NA
LT Debt	104	15.7	0.1	Nil	NA	NA	NA	NA	NA	NA
Common Eqty.	206	142	53.1	16.2	NA	NA	NA	NA	NA	NA
Total Cap.	315	160	53.6	NA	NA	NA	NA	NA	NA	NA
Cap. Exp.	12.4	9.9	0.6	NA	NA	NA	NA	NA	NA	NA
Cash Flow	34.4	21.4	3.8	NA	NA	NA	NA	NA	NA	NA
Curr. Ratio	3.6	1.8	1.8	NA	NA	NA	NA	NA	NA	NA
% LT Debt of Cap.	33.2	9.8	0.3	Nil	NA	NA	NA	NA	NA	NA
% Net Inc.of Revs.	5.7	6.4	6.6	8.7	NA	NA	NA	NA	NA	NA
% Ret. on Assets	8.5	11.6	7.1	NA	NA	NA	NA	NA	NA	NA
% Ret. on Equity	13.4	15.6	10.3	NA	NA	NA	NA	NA	NA	NA

Data as orig. reptd. (pro forma in 1995; balance sheet data as of Jun. 30, 1996); bef. results of disc. opers. and/or spec. items. Per share data adj. for stk. divs. as of ex-div. date. Bold denotes diluted EPS (FASB 128). E-Estimated. NA-Not Available. NM-Not Meaningful. NR-Not Ranked.

Office—6 Cadillac Drive, Suite 400, Brentwood, TN 37027. **Tel**—(615) 371-9990. **Fax**—(615) 221-9881. **Website**—www.serx.com **Chrmn, Pres & CEO**—A. R. Sielbeck. **CFO, Secy & Treas**—A. M. Schofield. **Dirs**—R. J. De Riggi, A. L. Hovius, N. T. Rolf Jr., W. G. Roth, A. R. Sielbeck, T. G. Wallace. **Transfer Agent & Registrar**—SunTrust Bank, Nashville and Atlanta. **Incorporated**—in Delaware in 1996. **Empl**— 4,500. **S&P Analyst:** Stephen J. Tekirian

STANDARD &POOR'S
STOCK REPORTS

ShopKo Stores

NYSE Symbol **SKO**

In S&P SmallCap 600

09-OCT-99 **Industry:** Retail (Discounters)

Summary: This Wisconsin-based regional discount store chain operates about 158 stores in 19 states, serving small and mid-sized markets.

Quantitative Evaluations

Outlook (1 Lowest—5 Highest) • **5**

Fair Value • **48⅝**

Risk • **Average**

Earn./Div. Rank • **NR**

Technical Eval. • **Bearish** since 8/99

Rel. Strength Rank (1 Lowest—99 Highest) • **23**

Insider Activity • **NA**

Recent Price • 27 | 52 Wk Range • 40¾-24⅞ | Yield • Nil | 12-Mo. P/E • 7.6

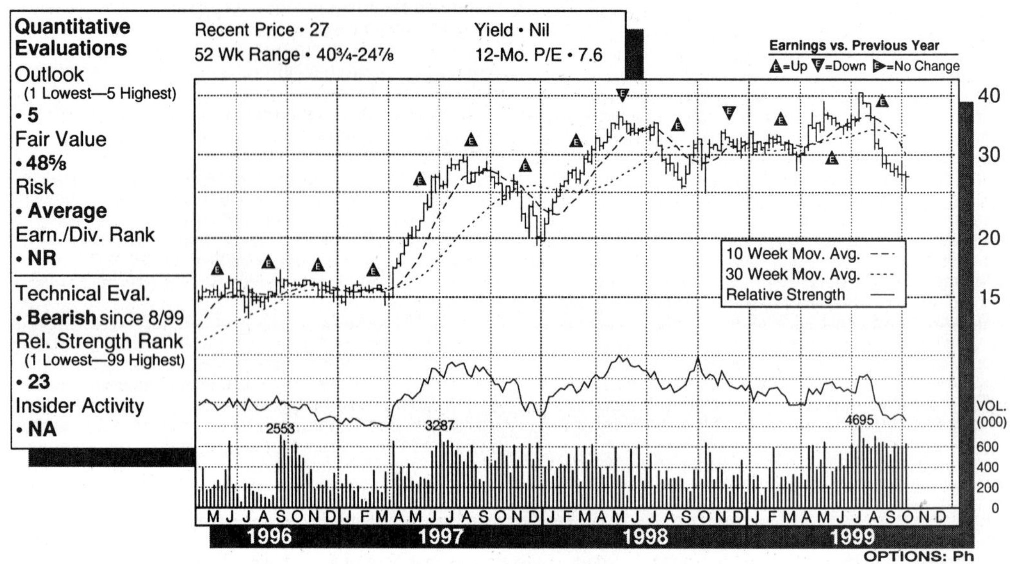

Business Profile - 27-JUL-99

SKO's current business plan is to increase the number of retail stores it operates in order to achieve economies of scale. The company believes that selective and opportunistic acquisitions of retail stores will allow it to improve its profitability and financial strength. In July 1999, SKO completed its tender offer for Pamida Holdings Corp., a Nebraska-based chain of smaller general merchandise. SKO said that about 5.9 million shares, representing about 97% of Pamida's shares outstanding, had been validly tendered. Pamida had FY 98 sales of $672 million. SKO also announced that it had filed for registration with the SEC to issue up to $500 million of common stock or senior debt securities, with proceeds expected to be used to redeem debt.

Operational Review - 27-JUL-99

Net sales for the quarter ended May 1, 1999, advanced 18%, year to year, reflecting an 8.1% increase in comparable retail store sales and a 48% gain in ProVantage sales. Gross margins narrowed, on increased promotional sales and higher third party business and prescription drug costs. In the absence of a $1.7 million non-recurring charge, net income doubled, to $4,313,000 ($0.16 a share), from $2,151,000 ($0.08). Results for the current quarter exclude an extraordinary loss of $3,776,000 ($0.14) on the early retirement of debt.

Stock Performance - 08-OCT-99

In the past 30 trading days, SKO's shares have declined 6%, compared to a 0.91% fall in the S&P 500. Average trading volume for the past five days was 185,820 shares, compared with the 40-day moving average of 168,223 shares.

Key Stock Statistics

Dividend Rate/Share	Nil	Shareholders	1,030
Shs. outstg. (M)	30.4	Market cap. (B)	$0.820
Avg. daily vol. (M)	0.144	Inst. holdings	82%
Tang. Bk. Value/Share	14.72		
Beta	0.91		

Value of $10,000 invested 5 years ago: $ 26,374

Fiscal Year Ending Jan. 31

	2000	1999	1998	1997	1996	1995
Revenues (Million $)						
1Q	759.9	645.8	720.0	610.9	560.5	514.9
2Q	871.9	681.3	546.1	498.5	418.2	381.3
3Q	—	734.4	608.4	591.2	491.0	470.9
4Q	—	925.9	573.4	632.8	498.4	485.8
Yr.	—	2,981	2,448	2,333	1,968	1,853
Earnings Per Share ($)						
1Q	**0.16**	**0.08**	**0.22**	0.18	0.17	0.16
2Q	**1.57**	**0.22**	**0.15**	0.12	0.06	0.09
3Q	—	**0.26**	**0.45**	0.34	0.32	0.35
4Q	—	**1.53**	**0.98**	0.76	0.66	0.59
Yr.	—	**2.10**	**1.71**	1.40	1.20	1.18

Next earnings report expected: mid November

Dividend Data

A dividend of $0.11 a share was last paid September 15, 1996.

ShopKo Stores, Inc.

Business Summary - 27-JUL-99

ShopKo Stores (SKO) continues to differentiate itself by meeting customer needs quickly while having more of what people expect as their life-style needs change. SKO successfully undertook a strategic repositioning under its Vision 2000 program between 1991 and 1995. The strategy combined a new, upscale image with an increased emphasis on customer service. To further build on its Vision 2000 program, SKO has developed and implemented the next step in its emphasis on improved store quality with its Beyond 2000 program. This program involves serving the changing shopping habits of time-strapped customers. The Beyond 2000 model is based on four interdependent strategic initiatives, including a differentiation strategy, an integrated business planning process, execution by a well-trained and experienced management organization, and the delivery of comprehensive value.

SKO's retail stores carry an assortment of in fashion branded and private label softline goods such as women's, men's, and children's apparel, shoes, jewelry, cosmetics, and accessories. The company also carries hardlines and homegoods including housewares, home textiles, household supplies, health and beauty aids, home entertainment products, small appliances, furniture, music and videos, and other products. SKO also provides professional health services in most of its stores.

As of January 30, 1999, SKO operated 147 stores, with virtually all stores having on-site optical and pharmacy centers. In addition to generating store traffic and building customer loyalty, these services contribute to the company's profitability and provide the opportunity for additional store growth. In FY 99 (Jan.), softlines accounted for 24% of SKO's retail store sales mix (25% in 1998), hardlines and home products represented 54% (54%), and retail health services accounted for 22% (21%).

The company's ProVantage segment provides prescription and benefit management services to health plan sponsors. As of January 1999, ProVantage provided pharmacy benefit services to about 4.5 million people and vision management services to about 500,000 people through more than 3,500 clients, typically small to mid-size employers, insurance companies, third-party administrators, HMO's, and self-funded healthplans. SKO is increasing its emphasis on marketing its pharmacy benefit management services to larger organizations based on its advanced clinical and information-based products and services.

Per Share Data ($)										
(Year Ended Jan. 31)	**1999**	**1998**	**1997**	**1996**	**1995**	**1994**	**1993**	**1992**	**1991**	**1990**
Tangible Bk. Val.	14.72	12.59	12.45	12.55	12.41	11.67	11.11	9.98	8.88	7.14
Cash Flow	4.65	3.75	3.27	2.96	2.85	2.48	2.92	2.81	2.66	2.43
Earnings	2.10	1.71	1.40	1.20	1.18	1.00	1.56	1.55	1.44	1.33
Dividends	Nil	Nil	0.22	0.44	0.44	0.44	0.44	0.11	NA	NA
Payout Ratio	Nil	Nil	16%	37%	37%	44%	28%	7%	NA	NA
Cal. Yrs.	1998	1997	1996	1995	1994	1993	1992	1991	1990	1989
Prices - High	37	29⅞	17⅛	14	12⅛	16	17¼	15⅛	NA	NA
- Low	21⅜	14⅜	10⅞	8⅝	8¾	9¾	12⅞	11¾	NA	NA
P/E Ratio - High	18	17	12	12	10	16	11	10	NA	NA
- Low	10	8	8	7	7	10	8	8	NA	NA
Income Statement Analysis (Million $)										
Revs.	2,981	2,448	2,333	1,968	1,853	1,739	1,683	1,648	1,521	1,420
Oper. Inc.	191	160	153	140	133	110	131	128	122	114
Depr.	67.6	58.3	59.8	56.4	53.5	47.3	43.0	40.4	39.1	35.2
Int. Exp.	38.3	30.6	31.8	34.3	30.3	23.5	19.4	18.3	20.0	20.1
Pretax Inc.	91.6	80.4	74.0	63.1	62.4	52.9	81.5	81.2	74.9	70.3
Eff. Tax Rate	39%	39%	39%	39%	40%	39%	39%	39%	63%	65%
Net Inc.	55.6	48.8	44.9	38.4	37.8	32.1	50.1	49.6	45.9	42.6
Balance Sheet & Other Fin. Data (Million $)										
Cash	30.2	54.3	125	89.5	12.6	2.6	2.8	2.1	2.0	1.8
Curr. Assets	588	542	565	476	469	371	296	260	273	236
Total Assets	1,374	1,251	1,234	1,118	1,110	953	792	706	705	648
Curr. Liab.	421	398	333	261	281	252	215	182	217	177
LT Debt	467	436	419	415	414	310	209	192	192	235
Common Eqty.	459	396	461	422	397	374	355	320	284	228
Total Cap.	953	853	901	857	828	701	577	524	488	471
Cap. Exp.	100	32.0	38.9	53.0	95.0	134	91.1	55.3	59.1	80.1
Cash Flow	123	107	105	94.8	91.3	79.5	93.3	90.0	85.1	77.8
Curr. Ratio	1.4	1.4	1.7	1.8	1.7	1.5	1.4	1.4	1.3	1.3
% LT Debt of Cap.	49.0	51.1	46.5	48.4	49.9	44.1	36.2	36.6	39.4	49.8
% Net Inc.of Revs.	1.9	2.0	1.9	2.0	2.0	1.8	3.0	3.0	3.0	3.0
% Ret. on Assets	4.2	3.9	3.8	3.5	3.7	3.7	6.7	7.1	6.5	7.0
% Ret. on Equity	13.0	11.4	10.2	9.4	9.8	8.8	14.8	16.7	NA	20.6

Data as orig. reptd.; bef. results of disc. opers. and/or spec. items. Per share data adj. for stk. divs. as of ex-div. date. Bold denotes diluted EPS (FASB 128). Prior to 1998, fis. yr. end. Feb. 28. E-Estimated. NA-Not Available. NM-Not Meaningful. NR-Not Ranked.

Office—700 Pilgrim Way, Green Bay, WI 54304. **Tel**—(920) 497-2211. **Website**—http://www.shopko.com **Chrmn**—D. P. Kramer. **Pres & CEO**—W. J. Podany. **SVP & CFO**—P. H. Freischlag Jr.**Investor Contact**—Vicki Shamion (920 429-7039).**Dirs**—J. W. Eugster, J. C. Girard, D. P. Kramer, W. J. Podany, J. L. Reinertsen, W. J. Tyrrell, S. E. Watson, G. H. Wolf. **Transfer Agent & Registrar**—Norwest Bank Minnesota, Minneapolis. **Incorporated**—in Wisconsin in 1961.**Empl**— 21,000. **S&P Analyst:** Matthew C. Hershberg

Shorewood Packaging

NYSE Symbol **SWD**

In S&P SmallCap 600

09-OCT-99

Industry:
Containers and Packaging (Paper)

Summary: This company prints and manufactures packaging for the cosmetics, home video, music, software, tobacco, toiletries and general consumer markets.

Quantitative Evaluations

Outlook
(1 Lowest—5 Highest)
• **2−**

Fair Value
• **13⅜**

Risk
• **NA**

Earn./Div. Rank
• **B**

Technical Eval.
• **Bearish** since 9/99

Rel. Strength Rank
(1 Lowest—99 Highest)
• **60**

Insider Activity
• **NA**

Recent Price • 15¼
52 Wk Range • 20⅝-12½

Yield • Nil
12-Mo. P/E • 11.9

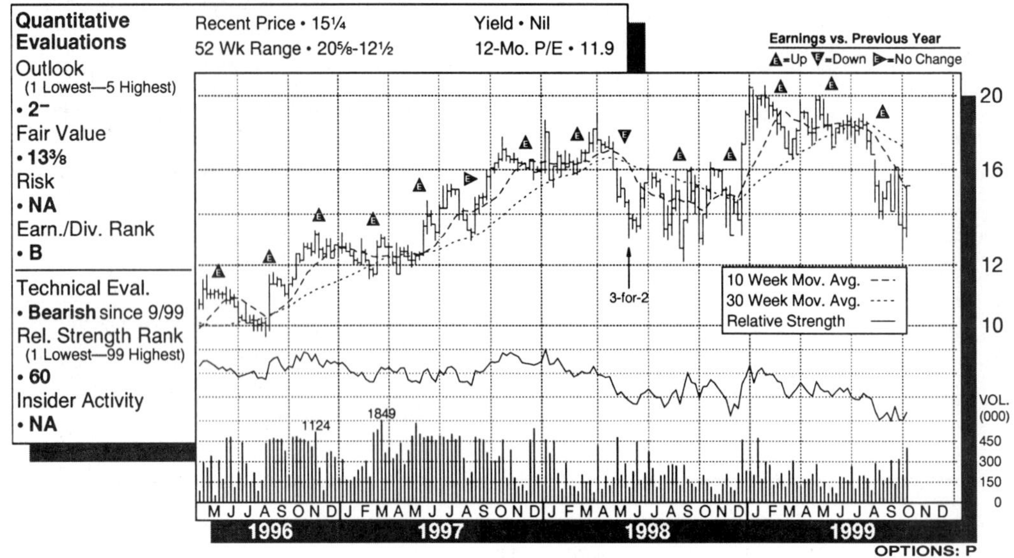

Business Profile - 23-AUG-99

In the FY 99 (Apr.) fourth quarter, the company sold a 45% stake in its new folding carton plant in China to Westvaco Corp. (NYSE: W), which paid SWD 45% of the $45 million cost of the plant, plus an additional $5 million. Proceeds totaled $23 million, resulting in a gain of $7.6 million. SWD expects increased volume and improved operating efficiencies to continue to drive cash flow and earnings growth. The company also plans to continue to pursue accretive acquisition opportunities. SWD has been expanding its market for CD-ROM products. SWD repurchased more than 300,000 shares during FY 99 and, as of May 1, 1999, had 1.6 million common shares still available for repurchase.

Operational Review - 23-AUG-99

Revenues in the fiscal year ended April 30, 1999, rose 33% from those of the preceding year, reflecting increased sales in the home entertainment and tobacco industries, and contributions from the acquired Queens facilities. Gross margins widened on a more favorable product mix, but with higher SG&A expenses, EBITDA advanced 25%. Following a $7.6 million gain on the sale of minority interest, which offset a writedown of equipment and higher interest expense, income was up 31%, to $34,344,000 ($1.25 a share, diluted), from $26,295,000 ($0.95, as adj.). Per share results in FY 99 exclude a charge of $0.11 from an accounting change and $0.01 from the early extinguishment of debt.

Stock Performance - 08-OCT-99

In the past 30 trading days, SWD's shares have increased 4%, compared to a 0.91% fall in the S&P 500. Average trading volume for the past five days was 79,640 shares, compared with the 40-day moving average of 49,487 shares.

Key Stock Statistics

Dividend Rate/Share	Nil	Shareholders	1,000
Shs. outstg. (M)	27.6	Market cap. (B)	$0.420
Avg. daily vol. (M)	0.053	Inst. holdings	62%
Tang. Bk. Value/Share	0.82		
Beta	0.62		

Value of $10,000 invested 5 years ago: $ 16,339

Fiscal Year Ending Apr. 30

	2000	1999	1998	1997	1996	1995
Revenues (Million $)						
1Q	143.7	115.4	100.6	109.8	90.70	84.77
2Q	—	145.4	114.8	117.0	105.1	97.05
3Q	—	141.4	96.63	99.3	93.11	85.65
4Q	—	150.1	103.3	104.1	105.5	89.56
Yr.	—	552.2	415.4	425.3	394.4	357.0
Earnings Per Share ($)						
1Q	**0.28**	**0.25**	**0.22**	0.22	0.20	0.20
2Q	—	**0.37**	**0.31**	0.25	0.21	0.24
3Q	—	**0.23**	**0.20**	0.17	0.13	0.19
4Q	—	**0.40**	**0.22**	0.23	0.19	0.16
Yr.	—	**1.25**	**0.95**	**0.89**	**0.73**	0.78

Next earnings report expected: mid December

Dividend Data

In July 1991, the company paid a special dividend of $3.25 a share.

Shorewood Packaging Corporation

Business Summary - 23-AUG-99

Shorewood Packaging (SWD) has been taking actions to boost its manufacturing efficiency and expects to see further improvement in operating margins. The company prints and manufactures high-quality paperboard packaging for the cosmetics, home video, music, software, tobacco, toiletries and general consumer markets in the U.S. and Canada. SWD anticipates that future sales growth will be derived from the continued penetration of its existing markets, and from the exploitation of new, emerging markets such as the expanding market for CD-ROM computer software and games packaging. SWD also plans to expand internationally.

For the music and home entertainment industry, the company's principal products are packaging for prerecorded cassettes and compact discs, and packaging for videocassettes. In addition to Sony, customers include most of the major record production and distribution companies in the U.S. For the cosmetics and toiletries and other general consumer markets, the company produces specialized packaging for customers requiring sophisticated precision graphic packaging for their products. For the tobacco industry, SWD produces the hard flip-top cigarette packages as well as the traditional slide and shell packages.

The Somerville Packaging operations (acquired in 1994) makes folding cartons for the tobacco, cosmetics and toiletries and general consumer industries. In early FY 99, the company completed a $45 million 125,000 sq. ft. facility in China to fill the demands of its multinational customers. The plant began operations in the third quarter of FY 99, and SWD subsequenty sold 45% of the plant to Westvaco. To facilitate expansion into China and other global opportunities, SWD entered into a new credit facility in May 1998, providing for up to $225 million of borrowings. In November 1998, the company acquired Queens Group ($150 million in sales), a maker of printing for music and consumer packaging, for $129 million in cash and stock. With this acquisition, SWD is the exclusive licensed supplier of the patented Q-Pack, a CD packaging alternative to the traditional plastic jewel box which autoloads on standard equipment.

Operations in Canada accounted for 32% of sales in FY 99 and 40% in FY 98. In FY 99, Philip Morris accounted for 22% of net sales.

Trading in the stock moved to the NYSE, from the Nasdaq Stock Market, in January 1998. A three-for-two stock split was effected in May 1998. In the fourth quarter of FY 97, the company discontinued its transportation division, which was subsequently sold.

Per Share Data ($)										
(Year Ended Apr. 30)	**1999**	**1998**	**1997**	**1996**	**1995**	**1994**	**1993**	**1992**	**1991**	**1990**
Tangible Bk. Val.	NA	2.71	4.16	1.87	1.82	1.01	0.95	0.61	2.43	2.15
Cash Flow	NA	1.59	2.25	1.22	1.24	0.71	0.79	0.62	0.69	0.73
Earnings	1.25	0.95	0.89	0.73	0.78	0.35	0.52	0.35	0.45	0.55
Dividends	Nil	Nil	Nil	Nil	Nil	Nil	Nil	2.17	Nil	Nil
Payout Ratio	Nil	Nil	Nil	Nil	Nil	Nil	Nil	621%	Nil	Nil
Cal. Yrs.	1998	1997	1996	1995	1994	1993	1992	1991	1990	1989
Prices - High	20½	18⅝	13⅜	13¾	15⅛	9½	8½	9¼	12⅜	12⅝
- Low	12⅛	11½	8⅝	9⅛	8⅞	4⅝	4½	4⅜	3⅞	7⅛
P/E Ratio - High	16	20	15	19	19	27	16	27	28	23
- Low	10	12	10	12	11	13	9	13	9	13
Income Statement Analysis (Million $)										
Revs.	NA	415	425	394	357	216	184	160	142	139
Oper. Inc.	NA	67.1	65.4	56.2	58.5	34.9	35.8	29.5	28.8	30.6
Depr.	NA	17.9	17.2	14.2	13.3	9.8	7.9	7.7	7.0	5.6
Int. Exp.	NA	7.6	8.9	8.3	9.0	6.9	5.5	5.5	2.1	2.3
Pretax Inc.	NA	42.3	40.2	34.4	36.2	15.8	23.4	16.2	20.5	24.2
Eff. Tax Rate	NA	38%	38%	38%	38%	41%	38%	40%	37%	33%
Net Inc.	NA	26.3	24.9	21.3	22.5	9.4	14.6	9.8	12.8	16.2
Balance Sheet & Other Fin. Data (Million $)										
Cash	NA	7.3	3.2	4.5	4.1	2.7	12.5	5.7	12.2	11.3
Curr. Assets	NA	95.8	94.5	96.2	96.9	78.2	50.8	42.3	48.1	44.5
Total Assets	NA	326	278	276	245	220	113	100	111	104
Curr. Liab.	NA	64.9	52.9	65.4	65.0	46.8	28.9	22.7	22.1	18.3
LT Debt	NA	126	107	123	100	138	49.4	52.5	13.2	15.2
Common Eqty.	NA	110	96.4	71.4	67.4	27.1	26.1	17.3	68.0	63.8
Total Cap.	NA	257	223	209	179	174	83.9	77.3	88.8	86.0
Cap. Exp.	NA	61.4	20.8	37.4	15.6	9.2	12.4	3.9	7.9	15.3
Cash Flow	NA	44.2	42.2	35.6	35.8	19.2	22.5	17.5	19.8	21.7
Curr. Ratio	NA	1.5	1.8	1.5	1.5	1.7	1.8	1.9	2.2	2.4
% LT Debt of Cap.	NA	49.0	48.0	58.9	55.8	79.5	58.9	67.9	14.9	17.7
% Net Inc.of Revs.	NA	6.3	5.9	5.4	6.3	4.3	7.9	6.1	9.0	11.6
% Ret. on Assets	NA	8.7	9.0	8.2	9.6	5.7	13.9	9.3	12.3	16.7
% Ret. on Equity	NA	25.5	29.7	30.7	47.6	35.7	68.2	22.9	20.0	29.1

Data as orig reptd.; bef. results of disc opers/spec. items. Per share data adj. for stk. divs. Bold denotes diluted EPS (FASB 128)-prior periods restated. E-Estimated. NA-Not Available. NM-Not Meaningful. NR-Not Ranked.

Office—277 Park Ave., New York, NY 10172. **Tel**—(212) 371-1500. **Website**—http://www.shorepak.com **Chrmn & CEO**—M. P. Shore. **Pres, CFO & Investor Contact**—Howard M. Liebman. **VP-Fin**—W. H. Hogan. **Secy**—Joan Matheis. **Dirs**—K. J. Bannon, M. L. Braun, F. S. Glinert, V. A. Kamsky, S. Leslie, R. T. O'Donnell, M. P. Shore, W. P. Weidner. **Transfer Agent**—Bank of New York, NYC. **Incorporated**—in Delaware in 1985. **Empl**— 3,800. **S&P Analyst:** Stewart Scharf

Sierra Health Services

NYSE Symbol **SIE**

In S&P SmallCap 600

09-OCT-99

Industry:
Health Care (Diversified)

Summary: This company provides health care services through HMOs in Nevada and Texas, and provides workers' compensation coverage in several states.

Quantitative Evaluations

Outlook
(1 Lowest—5 Highest)
• **5+**

Fair Value
• **19⅛**

Risk
• **Average**

Earn./Div. Rank
• **B**

Technical Eval.
• **Bearish** since 7/99

Rel. Strength Rank
(1 Lowest—99 Highest)
• **3**

Insider Activity
• **NA**

Recent Price • 8⅛
52 Wk Range • 24⅞-8

Yield • Nil
12-Mo. P/E • 9.8

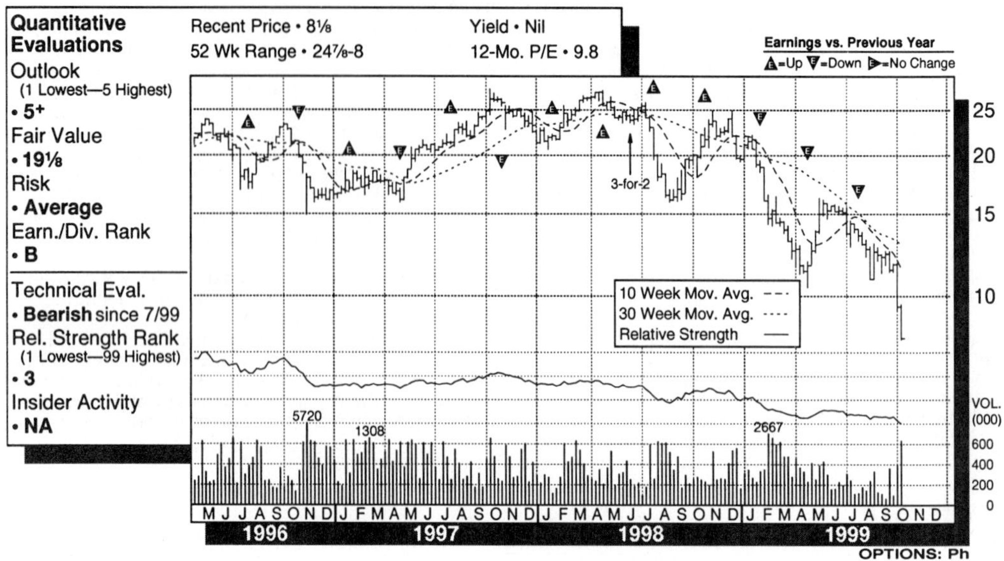

Business Profile - 02-AUG-99

In March 1999, the company closed all inpatient operations at its Mohave Valley Hospital in Arizona, and terminated about 45 employees. SIE recorded a 1999 first quarter charge of $4.3 million related to the closure. Also in the first quarter, the company incurred charges of $450,000 for certain legal and contractual settlements, as well as $400,000 to provide for SIE's portion of the writeoff of startup costs at the company's equity investee, TriWest Healthcare Alliance. In May 1999, SIE purchased the Texas operations of Exclusive Healthcare, Inc., an HMO owned by a Mutual of Omaha Insurance Co. subsidiary, operating in the Dallas-Fort Worth area.

Operational Review - 02-AUG-99

Revenues in the three months ended March 31, 1999, climbed 51%, year to year, on a 50% rise in medical premium revenues, reflecting an acquisition in the 1998 fourth quarter. Expansion into Texas, northern Nevada and Arizona, together with a higher proportion of Medicare members, pushed the medical loss ratio to 91.2%, from 82.9%. After significantly higher military contract expenses, a 34% rise in general, administrative and marketing expenses, and a $5.1 million charge, operating profits plunged 83%. With higher interest expense, after tax benefits of $354,000, versus taxes at 25.6%, a net loss of $706,000 ($0.03 a share) contrasted with net income of $12.2 million ($0.44, as adjusted).

Stock Performance - 08-OCT-99

In the past 30 trading days, SIE's shares have declined 34%, compared to a 0.91% fall in the S&P 500. Average trading volume for the past five days was 191,680 shares, compared with the 40-day moving average of 61,810 shares.

Key Stock Statistics

Dividend Rate/Share	Nil	Shareholders	254
Shs. outstg. (M)	26.8	Market cap. (B)	$0.218
Avg. daily vol. (M)	0.089	Inst. holdings	68%
Tang. Bk. Value/Share	5.22		
Beta	0.96		

Value of $10,000 invested 5 years ago: $ 5,508

Fiscal Year Ending Dec. 31

	1999	1998	1997	1996	1995	1994
Revenues (Million $)						
1Q	318.1	210.1	170.6	136.0	108.3	69.40
2Q	315.8	244.5	176.3	141.4	111.7	72.68
3Q	—	281.1	183.9	146.3	115.6	75.33
4Q	—	301.2	191.0	151.8	131.4	78.38
Yr.	—	1,037	721.7	575.4	467.1	295.8
Earnings Per Share ($)						
1Q	**-0.03**	**0.44**	**0.05**	**0.37**	0.29	0.24
2Q	**0.32**	**0.45**	**0.39**	**0.37**	0.32	0.29
3Q	—	**0.46**	**0.02**	**0.15**	0.36	0.31
4Q	—	**0.08**	**0.43**	**0.25**	0.03	0.30
Yr.	—	**1.43**	**0.89**	**1.15**	**1.05**	**1.54**

Next earnings report expected: early November

Dividend Data

No cash dividends have been paid. The shares were split three for two in 1998.

Sierra Health Services, Inc.

Business Summary - 02-AUG-99

With origins stemming from the establishment of a private medical practice in Las Vegas in 1972 by the company's chairman, Anthony Marlon, Sierra Health Services has grown into one of the largest investor-owned managed care organizations, serving approximately 1.3 million individuals through various health plan options.

Sierra's health maintenance organizations (HMOs) are a mixed group of network model HMOs in Nevada and a network model HMO in Texas. Most of the company's managed health care services in Nevada are provided through a network of more than 2,200 providers and 13 hospitals, including Sierra's multi-specialty medical group (including 170 primary care physicians), which provides medical services to 71% of its Nevada HMO members. Sierra directly provides home health care, hospice care and behavioral health care services, and operates two 24-hour urgent care centers, a radiology department, a vision department, an occupational medicine department and two freestanding surgery centers. As of December 31, 1998, HMO enrollment totaled 324,000, including commercial (277,000) and Medicare (47,000) members.

The company also operates a preferred provider organization (PPO), which offers members the option of receiving their medical care from either non-contracted or contracted providers. Members pay higher deductibles and co-payments when receiving care from non-network providers, but out-of-pocket costs are lowered by utilizing contracted providers who are part of the company's PPO network. At December 31, 1998, 41,000 members were enrolled in PPO plans.

Sierra's administrative services products provide utilization review and PPO services to large employer groups that are usually self-insured. At December 31, 1998, administrative service plans covered 318,000 individuals.

The company also writes workers' compensation insurance in California, Colorado, Kansas, Nebraska, New Mexico, Texas and Utah, primarily through independent insurance agents and brokers. The company plans to participate in the Nevada workers' compensation insurance market when the state allows private insurance companies to begin offering products on July 1, 1999.

In April 1997, Sierra began servicing a five-year contract to provide health care services to approximately 606,000 beneficiaries of the federal TriCare (formerly CHAMPUS, or Civilian Health and Medical Program of the Uniformed Services) program.

In October 1998, SIE's HMO Texas L.C. unit acquired certain assets of Kaiser Foundation Health Plan of Texas, with approximately 109,000 members, and Permanente Medical Association of Texas, a 150-physician medical group. In December 1998, the company completed the acquisition of the Nevada health care business of Mutual of Omaha Insurance Co.

Per Share Data ($) (Year Ended Dec. 31)	1998	1997	1996	1995	1994	1993	1992	1991	1990	1989
Tangible Bk. Val.	5.91	8.17	7.11	7.56	5.99	3.25	2.24	1.28	0.60	0.41
Cash Flow	2.13	1.38	1.57	1.43	1.52	1.23	1.02	0.87	0.39	0.35
Earnings	1.43	0.89	1.17	1.07	1.14	0.95	0.76	0.61	0.19	0.19
Dividends	Nil	Nil	Nil	Nil	Nil	Nil	Nil	Nil	Nil	Nil
Payout Ratio	Nil	Nil	Nil	Nil	Nil	Nil	Nil	Nil	Nil	Nil
Prices - High	27 5/8	27 3/4	24	22 3/8	22 3/8	15 1/8	14 3/8	9 7/8	4 5/8	3 1/4
- Low	15 7/8	15 7/8	14 7/8	14 3/4	14 1/8	7 5/8	5 3/8	3 3/4	1 13/16	1/2
P/E Ratio - High	19	31	20	21	20	16	19	16	25	17
- Low	11	18	13	14	12	8	7	6	10	3
Income Statement Analysis (Million $)										
Revs.	1,037	722	575	467	296	259	236	209	170	137
Oper. Inc.	93.7	74.8	67.0	65.0	43.5	31.1	25.6	21.5	14.3	6.7
Depr.	19.3	13.5	10.5	9.5	7.4	5.3	4.7	4.5	3.5	2.8
Int. Exp.	7.2	4.4	5.1	6.4	1.9	0.1	0.8	1.1	1.1	1.0
Pretax Inc.	53.4	27.5	41.6	40.1	34.2	25.9	19.5	15.1	4.7	3.3
Eff. Tax Rate	26%	12%	25%	30%	35%	32%	29%	29%	32%	1.80%
Net Inc.	37.6	24.2	31.1	27.9	22.2	17.4	13.6	10.8	3.2	3.2
Balance Sheet & Other Fin. Data (Million $)										
Cash	194	113	187	130	105	48.5	45.2	32.1	39.4	17.2
Curr. Assets	394	301	253	175	119	60.8	55.9	41.2	46.2	23.2
Total Assets	1,045	724	629	575	223	144	108	85.5	82.4	56.2
Curr. Liab.	346	212	176	157	59.1	55.0	46.7	43.3	52.0	30.2
LT Debt	242	90.8	66.2	71.3	18.4	16.0	7.7	6.3	6.1	8.4
Common Eqty.	304	266	234	208	134	62.1	42.3	24.1	11.9	8.5
Total Cap.	546	336	301	279	154	78.7	50.6	30.8	18.4	17.3
Cap. Exp.	40.7	55.7	17.9	20.5	11.2	32.0	9.3	8.5	3.1	7.7
Cash Flow	58.9	37.8	41.6	37.4	29.6	22.7	18.3	15.3	6.7	6.0
Curr. Ratio	1.1	1.4	1.4	1.1	2.0	1.1	1.2	1.0	0.9	0.8
% LT Debt of Cap.	44.3	27.0	22.0	25.6	12.0	20.3	15.1	20.5	33.2	48.5
% Net Inc.of Revs.	3.8	3.4	5.4	6.0	7.5	6.7	5.8	5.1	1.9	2.4
% Ret. on Assets	4.5	3.6	5.2	5.0	11.3	13.7	13.9	12.7	4.7	6.4
% Ret. on Equity	13.9	9.7	14.1	14.8	21.4	33.2	40.5	59.6	31.8	47.4

Data as orig reptd.; bef. results of disc opers/spec. items. Per share data adj. for stk. divs. Bold denotes diluted EPS (FASB 128)-prior periods restated. E-Estimated. NA-Not Available. NM-Not Meaningful. NR-Not Ranked.

Office—2724 N. Tenaya Way, Las Vegas, NV 89128 (P.O. Box 15645, Las Vegas 89114-5645). **Tel**—(702) 242-7000. **Website**—http://www.sierrahealth.com **Chrmn & CEO**—A. M. Marlon. **Pres & COO**— E. E. McDonald. **VP, CFO & Treas**—P. H. Palmer. **Secy**—F. E. Collins. **Investor Contact**—Ria Marie Carlson (702-242-7156). **Dirs**—T. Y. Hartley, A. M. Marlon, E. E. MacDonald, W. J. Raggio, C. L. Ruthe. **Transfer Agent & Registrar**—Continental Stock Transfer & Trust Co., NYC. **Incorporated**—in Nevada in 1984. **Empl**— 4,700. **S&P Analyst:** John J. Arege

Silicon Valley Bancshares

NASDAQ Symbol **SIVB**

In S&P SmallCap 600

09-OCT-99

Industry: Banks (Regional)

Summary: This company's Silicon Valley Bank subsidiary serves emerging growth and middle-market companies in targeted niches through banking offices in California's Silicon Valley area.

Quantitative Evaluations

Outlook (1 Lowest—5 Highest)
• **4**

Fair Value
• **34⅝**

Risk
• **Average**

Earn./Div. Rank
• **B**

Technical Eval.
• **Bearish** since 9/99

Rel. Strength Rank (1 Lowest—99 Highest)
• **82**

Insider Activity
• **NA**

Recent Price • 25
52 Wk Range • 28½-12¾
Yield • Nil
12-Mo. P/E • 17.4

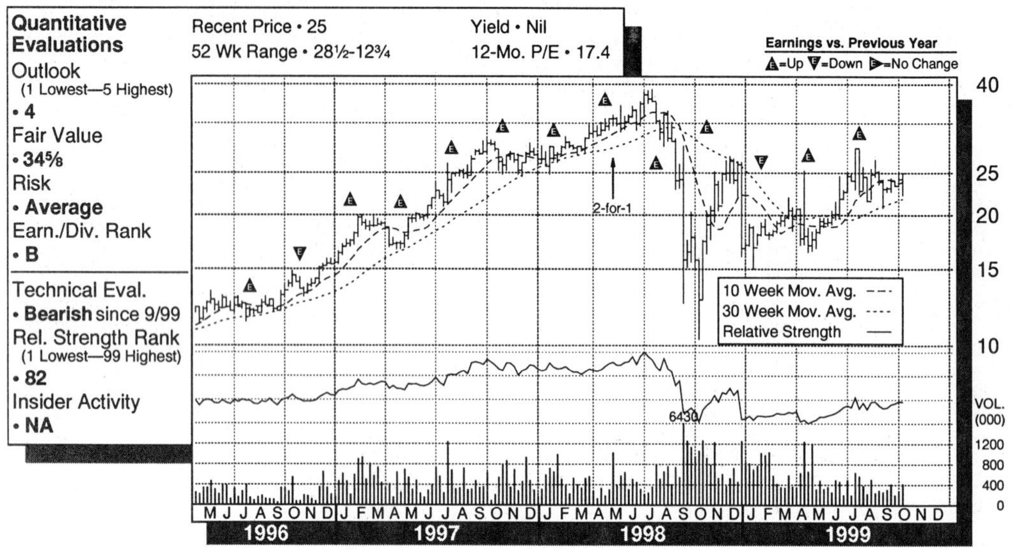

Business Profile - 08-JUL-99

The company concentrates on niche industries. It believes this strengthens its understanding of target markets, and lets it better serve clients in each category. SIVB believes this focus helps it better appreciate market dynamics faced by clients, and enhances its understanding of the unique financial characteristics of client companies. It focuses on technology, life sciences, and special industries. Technology includes communications and online services, computers and peripherals, emerging technologies, Pacific Rim, semiconductors, software, and venture capital. Life sciences consists of biotechnology, medical devices and health care services. Special industries consists of entertainment, real estate, and premium wineries.

Operational Review - 08-JUL-99

Net interest income in the first three months of 1999 advanced 30%, year to year, reflecting an increase in average earning assets, partly offset by lower average yields. The provision for loan losses rose to $7,968,000, from $5,480,000. With 2.6% lower noninterest income and a 35% increase in noninterest expense, the gain in pretax income was held to 1.6%. After taxes at 40.4%, versus 41.4%, net income was up 3.4%, to $7,836,000 ($0.38 a share), from $7,579,000 ($0.36).

Stock Performance - 08-OCT-99

In the past 30 trading days, SIVB's shares have increased 5%, compared to a 0.91% fall in the S&P 500. Average trading volume for the past five days was 81,440 shares, compared with the 40-day moving average of 59,851 shares.

Key Stock Statistics

Dividend Rate/Share	Nil	Shareholders	721
Shs. outstg. (M)	20.8	Market cap. (B)	$0.521
Avg. daily vol. (M)	0.064	Inst. holdings	60%
Tang. Bk. Value/Share	10.89		
Beta	1.01		

Value of $10,000 invested 5 years ago: $ 49,382

Fiscal Year Ending Dec. 31

	1999	1998	1997	1996	1995	1994
Revenues (Million $)						
1Q	67.61	54.93	39.72	30.04	24.99	18.95
2Q	75.18	59.17	42.70	33.57	26.78	18.60
3Q	—	67.91	46.98	35.31	30.30	19.87
4Q	—	66.39	49.84	37.76	31.75	22.60
Yr.	—	248.4	179.2	136.7	113.8	79.97
Earnings Per Share ($)						
1Q	**0.38**	**0.36**	**0.31**	0.24	0.18	0.10
2Q	**0.43**	**0.39**	**0.34**	0.29	0.22	0.13
3Q	—	**0.41**	**0.35**	0.27	0.29	0.12
4Q	—	**0.22**	**0.36**	0.30	0.29	0.17
Yr.	—	**1.38**	**1.36**	**1.10**	**0.99**	0.53

Next earnings report expected: mid October

Dividend Data

A two-for-one stock split was effected in May 1998. A shareholder rights plan was adopted in October 1998.

Silicon Valley Bancshares

Business Summary - 08-JUL-99

The founders of the Silicon Valley Bank subsidiary of Silicon Valley Bancshares (SIVB) set out in 1983 to capture a growing market in Northern California, which at that time had been greatly underserved by commercial banks: namely, the emerging growth technology companies in the Silicon Valley.

Today, SIVB is the largest independent bank holding company headquartered in Silicon Valley. It serves emerging growth and middle-market companies in specific targeted niches, focusing on the technology and life sciences industries, while also identifying and capitalizing on opportunities to serve companies in other industries whose financial services needs are underserved.

The bank's technology and life sciences niche focuses on serving companies in technology and life sciences industries and markets across the U.S., through regional banking offices in California, and loan offices in Arizona, Colorado, Georgia, Illinois, Maryland, Massachusetts, Oregon, Texas and Washington. The companies served are generally liquid, net providers of funds to the bank, and often have low utilization of their credit facilities. Lending to this niche is typically related to working capital, lines of credit, equipment financing, asset acquisition loans, and bridge financing.

Total loans of $1.61 billion (net of unearned income) outstanding at the end of 1998 were divided as follows: commercial 89%, real estate construction 4%, real estate term 4%, and consumer and other loans 3%.

At December 31, 1998, the allowance for possible loan losses totaled $46,000,000 (2.8% of total loans), versus $37,700,000 (3.2%) a year earlier. Net loan chargeoffs totaled $28,859,000 (2.2% of average loans) in 1998, versus $5,067,000 (0.5%) in 1997, and included $17.4 million of chargeoffs in the 1998 third quarter, related to five commercial credits. At the end of 1998, nonperforming assets aggregated $21,685,000 (0.6% of total assets), versus $27,350,000 (1.0%) a year earlier.

Total deposits aggregated $3.3 billion at the end of 1998, and were divided: noninterest-bearing demand 28%, NOW 1%, money market 67% and time 4%.

Interest on loans accounted for 56% of 1998 total income, interest on investment securities 26%, other interest income 8%, letter of credit and foreign exchange income 3%, and other noninterest income 6%.

In October 1998, directors adopted a shareholder rights plan that entitles shareholders to purchase Silicon Valley Bancshares common shares at a discounted price in the event that any person or group acquires 10% or more of SIVB.

Per Share Data ($) (Year Ended Dec. 31)	1998	1997	1996	1995	1994	1993	1992	1991	1990	1989
Tangible Bk. Val.	10.42	8.75	7.25	5.86	4.49	4.24	4.18	4.29	3.29	2.49
Earnings	1.38	1.36	1.10	0.99	0.53	0.10	-0.14	NA	NA	NA
Dividends	Nil	Nil	Nil	Nil	Nil	Nil	0.01	0.03	0.02	0.01
Payout Ratio	Nil	Nil	Nil	Nil	Nil	Nil	NA	NA	NA	NA
Prices - High	39	29 7/8	16 1/4	13 1/8	6 3/4	6 1/8	7 3/8	7 7/8	7 5/8	6 1/2
- Low	10 1/4	15 7/8	10 1/8	6 1/2	4 1/2	4	2 7/8	4	3 1/8	2 1/2
P/E Ratio - High	28	22	14	13	12	61	NM	9	9	11
- Low	7	12	9	6	8	39	NM	4	4	4
Income Statement Analysis (Million $)										
Net Int. Inc.	147	111	87.3	74.0	60.3	50.5	54.9	46.1	35.6	NA
Tax Equiv. Adj.	1.8	0.8	0.3	0.3	NA	NA	NA	NA	NA	NA
Non Int. Inc.	17.9	13.2	11.6	13.3	7.3	9.3	3.2	1.6	0.8	NA
Loan Loss Prov.	37.2	10.1	10.4	8.7	3.1	9.7	35.4	4.1	3.2	NA
Exp./Op. Revs.	50%	53%	53%	55%	NA	79%	45%	47%	44%	NA
Pretax Inc.	49.0	47.7	35.8	29.9	16.5	2.7	-3.7	21.2	17.2	NA
Eff. Tax Rate	41%	42%	40%	39%	45%	40%	NM	42%	41%	NA
Net Inc.	28.9	27.7	21.5	18.2	9.1	1.6	-2.2	12.3	10.1	NA
% Net Int. Marg.	5.20	5.60	6.10	7.10	7.20	6.40	6.40	NA	NA	NA
Balance Sheet & Other Fin. Data (Million $)										
Money Mkt. Assets	399	427	433	342	290	NA	NA	NA	NA	NA
Inv. Securities	1,398	1,014	625	321	156	NA	NA	NA	NA	NA
Com'l Loans	1,430	1,051	756	NA	NA	NA	NA	NA	NA	NA
Other Loans	182	123	NA	NA	NA	NA	NA	NA	NA	NA
Total Assets	3,545	2,625	1,925	1,408	1,162	992	959	869	673	NA
Demand Deposits	942	788	599	451	401	NA	NA	NA	NA	NA
Time Deposits	2,328	125	85.2	65.5	88.7	NA	NA	NA	NA	NA
LT Debt	38.5	Nil	Nil	Nil	Nil	NA	NA	NA	NA	NA
Common Eqty.	216	174	135	105	77.3	70.3	66.0	66.4	40.1	NA
% Ret. on Assets	0.9	1.2	1.3	NA	NA	0.2	NA	1.6	NA	NA
% Ret. on Equity	14.8	17.9	17.9	NA	NA	2.3	NA	23.0	NA	NA
% Loan Loss Resv.	2.9	3.2	3.8	4.0	NA	4.5	3.6	1.9	1.8	NA
% Loans/Deposits	49.3	77.3	48.7	57.2	NA	60.2	68.0	74.3	77.4	NA
% Equity to Assets	6.3	6.8	7.2	NA	NA	7.0	7.2	6.9	NA	NA

Data as orig reptd.; bef. results of disc opers/spec. items. Per share data adj. for stk. divs. Bold denotes diluted EPS (FASB 128)-prior periods restated. E-Estimated. NA-Not Available. NM-Not Meaningful. NR-Not Ranked.

Office—3003 Tasman Drive, Santa Clara, CA 95054-1191. **Tel**—(408) 654-7282. **Website**—http://www.svb.com **Chrmn**—D. J. Kelleher. **Pres & CEO**—J. C. Dean. **EVP & CFO**—C. T. Lutes. **Investor Contact**—Lisa Bertolet (408-654-7282). **Dirs**—G. K. Barr, J. F. Burns Jr., J. C. Dean, D. M. deWilde, S. E. Jackson, D. J. Kelleher, J. R. Porter, A. R. Wells. **Transfer Agent & Registrar**—Norwest Shareowner Services. **Incorporated**—in Delaware; reincorporated in Delaware in 1999. **Empl**— 625. **S&P Analyst:** S.A.H.

STANDARD
&POOR'S
STOCK REPORTS

Silicon Valley Group

Nasdaq Symbol **SVGI**

In S&P SmallCap 600

09-OCT-99

Industry: Equipment (Semiconductor)

Summary: SVGI is a leading manufacturer of automated wafer processing equipment for the semiconductor industry.

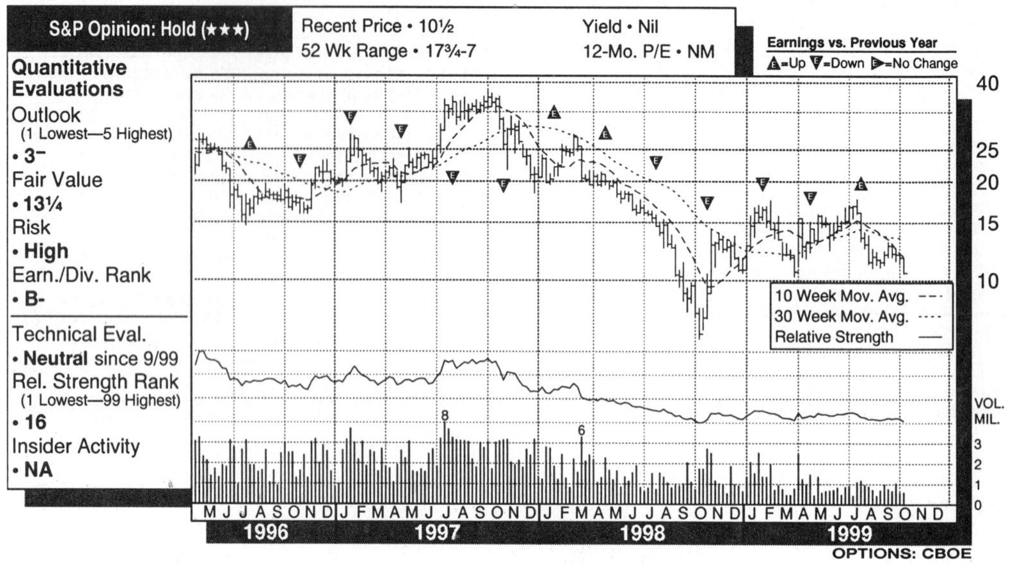

Overview - 09-AUG-99

While sales are likely to fall roughly 30% this fiscal year (Sep.), we expect a sharp recovery in FY 00 against easy comparisons. The impact of the economic crisis in Asia, coupled with chip industry oversupply, caused chip makers to cut capital spending last year. Semiconductor industry conditions have improved significantly in recent months, however, and we expect renewed investment in coming quarters. While SVGI has strong technology for deep ultraviolet (DUV) step-and-scan lithography systems, the company has had difficulty expanding its customer base. Furthermore, the Thermco and PhotoProcess divisions continue to underperform. In light of the weak near-term environment, we expect the company to post an operating loss of $0.81 a share in FY 99, but see EPS recovering to $0.60 in FY 00.

Valuation - 09-AUG-99

We are maintaining our hold rating on the shares, as we believe the company's weak near-term earnings prospects are fully reflected in the share price. While SVGI has suffered from both weak industry conditions and internal execution issues, the potential of the lithography division is compelling. This division supplies critical enabling technology to major semiconductor suppliers, such as Intel, IBM and Motorola. By establishing its ability to deliver lithography systems in volume, SVGI has an opportunity to broaden its customer base and to position itself for significant growth in the future. To date, however, the company's operating results have been highly volatile, resulting in depressed valuation multiples. The company's strong balance sheet, with over $16 a share in book value and over $4 a share in cash, offers downside protection.

Key Stock Statistics

S&P EPS Est. 1999	-0.81	Tang. Bk. Value/Share	16.64
P/E on S&P Est. 1999	NM	Beta	2.01
S&P EPS Est. 2000	0.60	Shareholders	1,269
Dividend Rate/Share	Nil	Market cap. (B)	$0.349
Shs. outstg. (M)	33.1	Inst. holdings	63%
Avg. daily vol. (M)	0.143		

Value of $10,000 invested 5 years ago: $ 10,695

Fiscal Year Ending Sep. 30

	1999	1998	1997	1996	1995	1994
Revenues (Million $)						
1Q	85.49	188.7	123.7	158.3	85.97	70.92
2Q	61.50	195.9	140.7	170.7	109.4	85.30
3Q	136.9	116.4	161.1	167.9	127.7	81.73
4Q	—	107.7	169.4	143.1	139.0	81.98
Yr.	—	608.6	595.0	639.9	462.0	319.9
Earnings Per Share ($)						
1Q	**-0.21**	**0.37**	0.11	0.54	0.25	0.15
2Q	**-0.55**	**0.29**	-0.54	0.58	0.33	0.23
3Q	**-0.06**	**-0.21**	0.20	0.58	0.45	0.21
4Q	**E0.01**	**-0.87**	0.26	0.38	0.52	0.24
Yr.	**E-0.81**	**-0.42**	**0.08**	2.07	1.57	0.84

Next earnings report expected: late October

Dividend Data

SVGI has not paid cash dividends on its common stock.

A Division of The McGraw·Hill Companies 

Silicon Valley Group, Inc.

Business Summary - 09-AUG-99

Silicon Valley Group (SVGI) makes and services semiconductor processing equipment used in the fabrication of integrated circuits.

Photolithography exposure products are manufactured through SVG Lithography Systems (SVGL); photoresist processing products through the PhotoProcess (formerly Track) division; and oxidation/diffusion and LPCVD (low-pressure chemical vapor deposition) products through the Thermco division.

SVGL has two broad product families: Micrascan step-and-scan systems and the more mature Micralign scanning projection aligners. The company believes that its Micrascan system provides the greater resolution required for the next generation of complex, fine geometry integrated circuits through its use of a deep ultraviolet (DUV) light source. The Micrascan also overcomes the throughput and yield limitations of steppers by combining the elements of both steppers and scanners into the product's step-and-scan technology. Step and scan combines the advantages of scanning projection aligners and steppers by scanning only a portion of the wafer, then stepping to another portion of the wafer and repeating the process as needed.

The company believes that its Micrascan III lithography system is the most technologically advanced product of its kind. SVGI has made significant capital investments to improve its ability to manufacture these products in volume.

SVGI has entered into agreements with Intel Corp., Motorola Inc., Texas Instruments Inc., IBM and industry consortium Sematech, pursuant to which these semiconductor makers have made equity investments in the company. Sematech has also agreed to provide certain additional funding.

PhotoProcess division products perform all steps necessary to process semiconductor wafers before and after photolithography exposure. These include wafer cleaning, adhesion promotion and photoresist coating, which are completed prior to the photolithography step. Its products also are used in steps required to treat wafers after photolithography exposure but prior to etching, including developing and baking.

Thermco division products address the oxidation/diffusion and LPCVD steps of the semiconductor fabrication process.

Since the latter part of 1997, SVGI's order trends have been negatively impacted by deteriorating semiconductor equipment industry conditions. Furthermore, since the company's primary competition is based in Japan, unfavorable dollar/yen currency fluctuations have placed the company at a competitive disadvantage from a pricing standpoint. In response to weak market conditions, SVGI has taken actions to reduce its work force by more than 20%.

Per Share Data ($) (Year Ended Sep. 30)	1998	1997	1996	1995	1994	1993	1992	1991	1990	1989
Tangible Bk. Val.	17.06	17.96	17.96	13.77	8.87	7.26	7.05	6.61	5.73	4.98
Cash Flow	0.79	0.92	2.50	1.95	1.27	0.82	0.49	0.73	0.92	1.14
Earnings	-0.42	0.05	2.07	1.57	0.84	0.22	-0.03	0.12	0.42	0.94
Dividends	Nil	Nil	Nil	Nil	Nil	Nil	Nil	Nil	Nil	Nil
Payout Ratio	Nil	Nil	Nil	Nil	Nil	Nil	Nil	Nil	Nil	Nil
Prices - High	27 7/8	38 3/8	31	49 3/8	21 1/4	12 7/8	8	11 1/4	13 3/4	9 1/2
- Low	6 5/8	17 1/8	14 5/8	18 3/8	9 1/4	6	4 1/2	5 1/8	4	5 7/8
P/E Ratio - High	NM	NM	15	31	25	59	NM	94	33	10
- Low	NM	NM	7	12	11	27	NM	43	10	6
Income Statement Analysis (Million $)										
Revs.	609	595	640	462	320	241	192	235	184	131
Oper. Inc.	40.6	52.4	99	61.9	34.5	16.4	9.3	12.7	13.7	17.5
Depr.	39.2	27.3	13.2	9.5	8.0	9.1	7.7	7.9	5.5	2.1
Int. Exp.	1.0	0.7	0.4	0.6	0.7	0.9	2.8	3.1	1.6	0.6
Pretax Inc.	-27.2	2.3	98.4	61.2	26.8	6.9	1.6	3.3	7.9	15.8
Eff. Tax Rate	NM	35%	35%	36%	38%	30%	70%	NM	39%	39%
Net Inc.	-13.6	1.5	63.0	39.0	16.8	4.5	-0.3	1.6	4.5	9.6
Balance Sheet & Other Fin. Data (Million $)										
Cash	122	207	262	181	87.8	17.6	32.7	34.1	30.7	11.8
Curr. Assets	530	589	643	466	253	188	147	154	140	66.9
Total Assets	731	741	729	499	272	212	181	192	183	84.9
Curr. Liab.	158	170	179	142	80.2	77.9	53.6	69.4	79.9	22.7
LT Debt	5.9	5.8	0.2	0.7	1.5	2.3	1.6	8.2	26.5	Nil
Common Eqty.	562	565	542	350	168	110	104	104	70.2	60.6
Total Cap.	567	569	547	355	191	133	126	122	103	61.8
Cap. Exp.	79.2	88.0	3.8	21.4	2.7	0.7	3.0	5.7	7.9	1.8
Cash Flow	25.6	28.8	76.5	48.5	23.6	12.3	7.2	9.6	9.9	11.7
Curr. Ratio	3.4	3.5	3.6	3.3	3.2	2.4	2.7	2.2	1.8	2.9
% LT Debt of Cap.	1.1	1.1	0.1	0.2	0.8	1.8	1.3	6.7	25.7	Nil
% Net Inc.of Revs.	NM	0.3	9.9	8.4	5.2	1.9	NM	0.7	2.4	7.3
% Ret. on Assets	NM	0.0	10.3	10.1	6.2	2.3	NM	0.8	3.2	12.9
% Ret. on Equity	NM	0.0	14.2	14.8	10.2	3.0	NM	1.7	6.6	17.0

Data as orig reptd.; bef. results of disc opers/spec. items. Per share data adj. for stk. divs. Bold denotes diluted EPS (FASB 128)-prior periods restated. E-Estimated. NA-Not Available. NM-Not Meaningful. NR-Not Ranked.

Office—101 Metro Dr., Suite 400, San Jose, CA 95110. **Tel**—(408) 441-6700. **Website**—http://www.svg.com **Chrmn & CEO**—P. S. Der Torossian. **Secy**—L. W. Sonsini. **VP-Fin & CFO**—R. G. Weinstock. **Investor Contact**—Nancy Szymanski (408 467-5870).**Dirs**—P. S. Der Torossian, W. A. Hightower, L. Tomlinson, K.M. Thompson, W. L. Martin, N. P. Suh. **Transfer Agent & Registrar**—ChaseMellon Shareholder Services, San Francisco. **Incorporated**—in California in 1973; reincorporated in Delaware in 1987. **Empl**— 2,616. **S&P Analyst:** B. McGovern

Simpson Industries

NASDAQ Symbol **SMPS**

In S&P SmallCap 600

23-OCT-99

Industry: Auto Parts & Equipment

Summary: SMPS makes powertrain and chassis products, primarily for auto and truck makers in the U.S. and Europe.

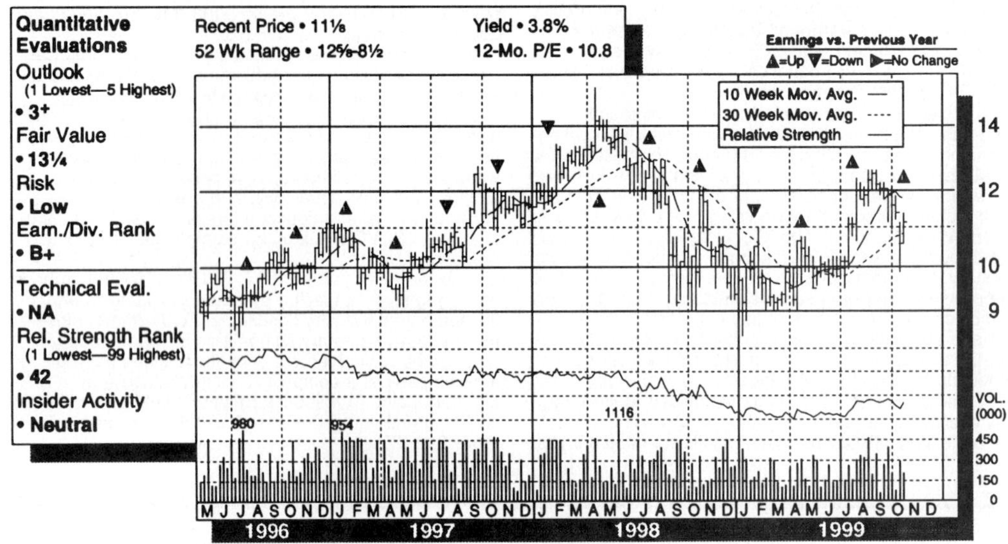

Business Profile - 19-OCT-99

In October 1999, the company said it was pleased with its third quarter financial and operating results, despite production problems caused by Hurricane Floyd at its Greenville, NC, plant. In January 1999, SMPS had said that, with recent restructuring initiatives in place and strong new business awards, it was poised to achieve strong financial results over the next several years. At September 30,1999, shareholders' equity was $130.4 million, and long term debt amounted to $106.1 million.

Operational Review - 19-OCT-99

Sales in the nine months ended September 30, 1999, advanced 8.9%, year to year. Gross margins widened, and operating and interest expenses declined; pretax income increased 38%. After taxes at 34.3%, versus 33.0%, net income was up 35%, to $15,542,000 ($0.86 a share), from $11,520,000 ($0.63).

Stock Performance - 22-OCT-99

In the past 30 trading days, SMPS's shares have declined 12%, compared to a 4% fall in the S&P 500. Average trading volume for the past five days was 16,000 shares, compared with the 40-day moving average of 55,392 shares.

Key Stock Statistics

Dividend Rate/Share	0.40	Shareholders	4,300
Shs. outstg. (M)	18.0	Market cap. (B)	$0.190
Avg. daily vol. (M)	0.040	Inst. holdings	50%
Tang. Bk. Value/Share	4.44		
Beta	0.55		

Value of $10,000 invested 5 years ago: $ 9,368

Fiscal Year Ending Dec. 31

	1999	1998	1997	1996	1995	1994
Revenues (Million $)						
1Q	133.1	125.6	105.9	101.4	107.2	82.70
2Q	139.4	128.7	110.3	110.0	103.6	91.32
3Q	124.2	110.0	112.3	98.23	86.34	85.88
4Q	—	132.1	123.0	98.30	97.89	96.75
Yr.	—	496.4	451.5	408.0	395.1	356.6
Earnings Per Share ($)						
1Q	0.32	0.27	0.24	0.22	0.31	0.23
2Q	0.38	0.31	0.30	0.33	0.27	0.25
3Q	0.16	0.05	-0.18	0.19	0.08	0.14
4Q	—	0.18	0.20	0.23	0.19	0.18
Yr.	—	0.80	0.55	0.97	0.85	0.80

Next earnings report expected: early February

Dividend Data (Dividends have been paid since 1972.)

Amount ($)	Date Decl.	Ex-Div. Date	Stock of Record	Payment Date
0.100	Nov. 18	Dec. 01	Dec. 03	Dec. 17 '98
0.100	Feb. 24	Mar. 02	Mar. 04	Mar. 25 '99
0.100	Apr. 21	Jun. 01	Jun. 03	Jun. 24 '99
0.100	Aug. 17	Aug. 31	Sep. 02	Sep. 23 '99

A Division of The McGraw-Hill Companies

Simpson Industries, Inc.

Business Summary - 19-OCT-99

Simpson Industries (SMPS) supplies powertrain and chassis products to original equipment manufacturers in the worldwide automotive and medium and heavy-duty diesel engine markets.

Net sales to the company's major customers, GM, Ford, DaimlerChrysler and consolidated Diesel, accounted respectively for 25%, 17%, 12% and 11% of 1998 sales. In 1998,13% of sales and 8.2% of operating profits were obtained in Europe.

The company makes vibration control and other products for automobile, light-truck and diesel engines, air conditioning compressor components, wheel-end and suspension components and assemblies, oil pumps, water pumps and other modular engine assemblies and transmission and driveline components that are machined from castings and forgings. These products are produced principally for original equipment manufacturers (OEMs) of automobiles, light trucks, diesel engines, and heavy-duty equipment both in North America and in Europe.

Operations are organized into three business groups: noise vibration and harshness products; wheel-end and suspension products; and modular engine products. SMPS maintains product design and process development staffs, which work with customer engineers, principally in the design, testing and development of the products, as well as in the on-going refinement of existing products to improve various performance characteristics or cost effectiveness.

The company operates 16 manufacturing plants, located in Michigan, Ohio, Indiana, North Carolina, Tennessee, Canada, Mexico, the U.K., France, Spain, and Brazil. SMPS also has interests in joint ventures in India and South Korea.

Content per North American light vehicle (the worth of SMPS parts) has been $22 for the past four years. There were 15 new program launches in 1998, up from 13 in 1997.

The basic raw materials for the company's products include aluminium and ferrous castings, steel forgings, steel bar stock and rubber, all of which are available from a large number of sources.

During 1998, SMPS invested $19.6 million in capital equipment and plant expansions, versus $29 million in 1997. Capital expenditures for 1999 were expected to be $40 million to $44 million, principally to support investment in new and replacement business both domestically and overseas.

In April 1998, the company acquired Stahl International, Inc., a closely held manufacturer of viscous dampers, with annual sales of $4.2 million.

Per Share Data ($)										
(Year Ended Dec. 31)	**1998**	**1997**	**1996**	**1995**	**1994**	**1993**	**1992**	**1991**	**1990**	**1989**
Tangible Bk. Val.	3.98	3.75	6.42	5.84	5.47	5.12	5.16	4.39	4.45	4.43
Cash Flow	2.22	1.84	2.10	1.90	1.71	1.32	1.26	1.15	1.17	1.38
Earnings	0.81	0.55	0.97	0.85	0.80	0.53	0.47	0.31	0.42	0.75
Dividends	0.40	0.40	0.40	0.40	0.39	0.37	0.37	0.37	0.37	0.37
Payout Ratio	49%	73%	41%	47%	49%	71%	83%	120%	89%	50%
Prices - High	15⅜	12¾	11⅛	12⅛	15⅝	14⅝	13⅛	9⅛	7⅝	9⅞
- Low	8¾	9⅛	8⅜	8	7⅞	10⅜	8	4⅝	4⅝	6
P/E Ratio - High	19	23	11	14	20	28	28	30	18	13
- Low	11	17	9	9	10	20	17	15	11	8
Income Statement Analysis (Million $)										
Revs.	496	452	408	395	357	262	223	192	193	197
Oper. Inc.	60.3	54.3	50.1	47.7	43.1	33.6	30.1	22.5	23.3	26.9
Depr.	26.1	23.4	20.5	18.9	16.3	14.2	13.4	12.4	10.8	9.2
Int. Exp.	9.6	7.5	5.3	5.5	4.3	3.6	3.8	2.7	2.4	2.5
Pretax Inc.	22.4	15.2	25.6	24.4	23.1	16.3	14.0	7.1	9.5	16.0
Eff. Tax Rate	34%	34%	31%	37%	38%	42%	43%	36%	36%	33%
Net Inc.	14.8	10.1	17.6	15.3	14.4	9.4	8.0	4.5	6.1	10.7
Balance Sheet & Other Fin. Data (Million $)										
Cash	6.1	8.2	28.9	13.5	4.8	18.1	43.0	21.1	8.7	8.3
Curr. Assets	115	115	94.2	82.0	70.5	70.9	76.9	51.3	38.7	41.2
Total Assets	341	342	249	324	207	187	170	138	123	124
Curr. Liab.	82.3	78.3	49.2	41.7	38.9	36.4	27.2	20.9	17.6	20.9
LT Debt	106	119	58.6	62.3	50.4	39.0	37.0	38.5	25.0	25.0
Common Eqty.	125	118	116	105	98.0	91.5	91.8	64.1	64.8	63.8
Total Cap.	241	249	186	178	158	141	141	116	104	102
Cap. Exp.	19.6	28.9	26.3	31.6	38.2	37.5	22.4	15.8	14.1	22.6
Cash Flow	40.9	33.5	38.1	34.2	30.7	23.7	21.4	16.9	17.0	19.9
Curr. Ratio	1.4	1.5	1.9	2.0	1.8	1.9	2.8	2.5	2.2	2.0
% LT Debt of Cap.	43.8	47.7	31.6	35.0	31.9	27.7	26.2	33.2	24.0	24.6
% Net Inc.of Revs.	3.0	2.2	4.3	3.9	4.0	3.6	3.6	2.4	3.2	5.4
% Ret. on Assets	4.3	3.4	7.3	5.8	7.3	5.3	4.7	3.5	4.9	8.9
% Ret. on Equity	12.2	8.6	15.9	15.1	15.1	10.3	9.4	7.0	9.5	17.6

Data as orig reptd.; bef. results of disc opers/spec. items. Per share data adj. for stk. divs. Bold denotes diluted EPS (FASB 128)-prior periods restated. E-Estimated. NA-Not Available. NM-Not Meaningful. NR-Not Ranked.

Office—47603 Halyard Dr., Plymouth, MI 48170-2429. **Tel**—(734) 207-6200. **Fax**—(734) 207-6500. **Website**—http://www.simpsonind.com **Chrmn & CEO**—R. E. Parrott. **Pres & COO**—G. A. Thomas. **VP-Fin, CFO & Investor Contact**—V. M. Khilnani. **Secy**—F. K. Zinn. **Dirs**—M. E. Batten, S. F. Haka, G. R. Kempton, W. J. Kirchberger, R. W. Navarre, R. E. Parrott, R. L. Roudebush, G. A. Thomas, F. L. Weaver, F. K. Zinn. **Transfer Agent & Registrar**—Harris Trust and Savings Bank. **Incorporated**—in Michigan in 1945. **Empl**— 2,518. **S&P Analyst:** Howard Choe

STANDARD
&POOR'S
STOCK REPORTS

Simpson Manufacturing

NYSE Symbol **SSD**

In S&P SmallCap 600

09-OCT-99

Industry:
Building Materials

Summary: This company designs, engineers and manufactures wood connector products and venting systems for gas and wood burning fire appliances.

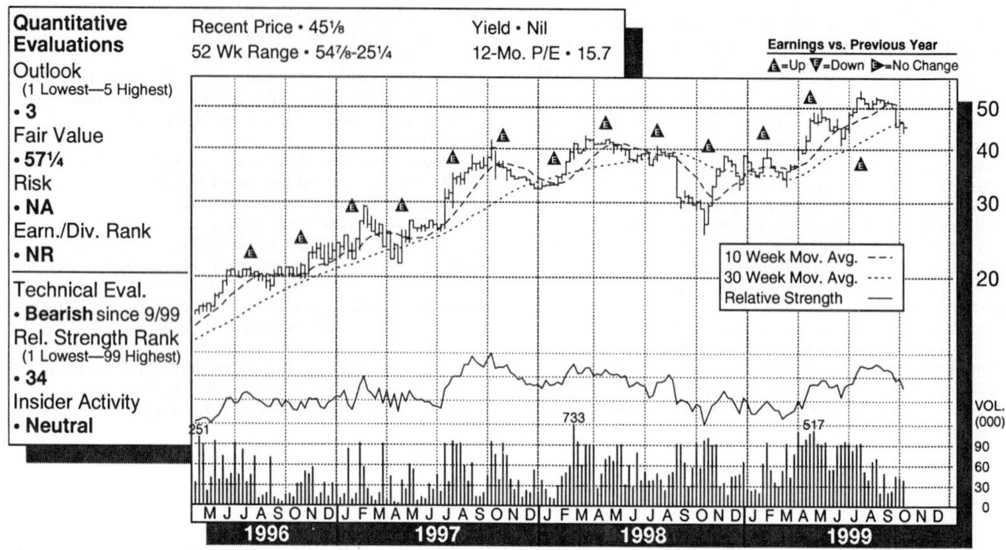

Business Profile - 10-AUG-99

Simpson's long-term strategy is to develop, acquire or invest in product lines or businesses that complement its existing product lines and that can be marketed through its existing distribution channels. The company intends to continue to purchase the capital equipment and property needed to expand its capacity through 1999, seeks to expand sales to distributors that serve building contractors, and plans to increase penetration of the do-it-yourself markets by soliciting home centers to sell its products. Sales of Simpson's major product lines of wood connector products and venting systems remain in a healthy uptrend.

Operational Review - 10-AUG-99

Net sales in the six months ended June 30, 1999, rose 22%, year to year, reflecting growth throughout the U.S., particularly in the Southeast and California. Sales also increased in most of the company's international markets. Gross margins widened on better absorption of fixed overhead costs as a result of the increased production, and with an 88% increase in net interest income, pretax income advanced more than 25%. After taxes at 40.2%, versus 40.6%, net income climbed 26%, to $17,721,159 ($1.46 a share), from $14,034,243 ($1.16).

Stock Performance - 08-OCT-99

In the past 30 trading days, SSD's shares have declined 14%, compared to a 0.91% fall in the S&P 500. Average trading volume for the past five days was 7,740 shares, compared with the 40-day moving average of 7,846 shares.

Key Stock Statistics

Dividend Rate/Share	Nil	Shareholders	2,950
Shs. outstg. (M)	11.9	Market cap. (B)	$0.538
Avg. daily vol. (M)	0.007	Inst. holdings	41%
Tang. Bk. Value/Share	15.68		
Beta	1.11		

Value of $10,000 invested 5 years ago: NA

Fiscal Year Ending Dec. 31

	1999	1998	1997	1996	1995	1994
Revenues (Million $)						
1Q	74.66	59.26	51.93	43.46	35.77	—
2Q	83.75	70.79	65.55	51.75	41.86	39.04
3Q	—	77.21	68.83	57.13	47.07	42.45
4Q	—	71.83	59.77	50.06	43.25	36.75
Yr.	—	279.1	246.1	202.4	168.0	151.3
Earnings Per Share ($)						
1Q	**0.63**	**0.47**	**0.40**	**0.28**	0.21	—
2Q	**0.82**	**0.69**	**0.59**	**0.44**	0.34	0.29
3Q	—	**0.77**	**0.68**	**0.54**	0.41	0.33
4Q	—	**0.65**	**0.50**	**0.41**	0.27	0.25
Yr.	—	**2.58**	**2.17**	**1.68**	**1.23**	**0.51**

Next earnings report expected: late October

Dividend Data

No cash dividends have been paid. The company intends to retain its earnings to finance operations and does not anticipate paying cash dividends in the foreseeable future.

Simpson Manufacturing Co., Inc.

Business Summary - 10-AUG-99

Simpson Manufacturing Co., Inc. (SSD) has been expanding its established facilities outside California in an effort to increase its sales in markets east of the Rocky Mountains. During the last five years, the company has expanded or has planned to expand nearly all of its manufacturing and warehouse facilities. Sales in the 37 states east of the Rockies accounted for 48% of SSD's 1998 domestic sales. SSD's goal is to manufacture and warehouse its products in geographic proximity to its markets.

Through its Simpson Strong-Tie Co. subsidiary, SSD designs, engineers and manufactures wood-to-wood, wood-to-concrete, and wood-to-masonry connectors, and, through its Simpson Dura-Vent Co subsidiary, designs, engineers and makes venting systems for gas and wood burning appliances. Products are marketed to the residential construction, light industrial and commercial construction, remodeling and do-it-yourself markets in all 50 states, Europe, Canada, Australia, Mexico, Chile and Japan.

Besides its three primary categories, Strong-Tie makes a line of connectors for steel frame construction and markets specialty screws and nails for proper installation of certain of its connector products. Sales and marketing activities are conducted through a branch system in Northern and Southern California, Texas, Ohio, England and France, and an extensive distribution system of dealer distributors supplying retail locations nationwide, contractor distributors, home centers, makers of engineered wood products, and specialized contractors, such as roof framers.

Simpson Dura-Vent venting systems are used to vent gas furnaces and water heaters, gas fireplaces and stoves, wood burning stoves. and pellet stoves Its metal vents, chimneys and chimney liner systems exhaust the products of combustion to the exterior of a building. Dura-Vent's objective is to expand market share in all of its distribution channels be entering markets that address energy and environmental concerns.

Simpson Dura-Vent is a leading supplier of double-wall Type B Gas Vent systems, used for venting gas furnaces, water heaters, boilers and decorative fireplaces. SSD believes there is significant potential in the gas fireplace market. It has also introduced a flexible vent connector, Dura/Connect, for use between the gas fireplace flue outlet and the connection to the Type B Gas Vent installed in the ceiling. Venting systems are marketed through wholesale distributors in the U.S., Canada and Australia to the heating, ventilating and air conditioning markets, plumbing, heating and cooling contractor markets, and to fireplace specialty shop distributors, as well as to home center and hardware store chains.

Per Share Data ($) (Year Ended Dec. 31)	1998	1997	1996	1995	1994	1993	1992	1991	1990	1989
Tangible Bk. Val.	13.93	11.20	8.93	7.18	NA	NA	NA	NA	NA	NA
Cash Flow	3.27	2.73	2.29	1.69	0.89	1.17	NA	NA	NA	NA
Earnings	2.58	2.17	1.68	1.23	0.51	0.89	NA	NA	NA	NA
Dividends	Nil	Nil	Nil	Nil	Nil	NA	NA	NA	NA	NA
Payout Ratio	Nil	Nil	Nil	Nil	Nil	NA	NA	NA	NA	NA
Prices - High	43	42	24	15⅜	12¾	NA	NA	NA	NA	NA
- Low	25¼	21½	13	9⅜	9¾	NA	NA	NA	NA	NA
P/E Ratio - High	17	19	14	13	25	NA	NA	NA	NA	NA
- Low	10	10	8	8	19	NA	NA	NA	NA	NA
Income Statement Analysis (Million $)										
Revs.	279	246	202	168	151	114	NA	NA	NA	NA
Oper. Inc.	59.5	50.0	39.9	28.2	18.0	17.2	NA	NA	NA	NA
Depr.	8.3	6.7	7.2	5.3	4.0	2.6	NA	NA	NA	NA
Int. Exp.	Nil	Nil	Nil	-0.1	0.6	1.0	NA	NA	NA	NA
Pretax Inc.	52.2	43.8	33.3	23.0	13.5	13.6	NA	NA	NA	NA
Eff. Tax Rate	40%	41%	41%	39%	60%	41%	NA	NA	NA	NA
Net Inc.	31.1	26.0	19.7	14.1	5.5	8.0	NA	NA	NA	NA
Balance Sheet & Other Fin. Data (Million $)										
Cash	37.4	19.4	19.8	7.0	5.8	1.8	NA	NA	NA	NA
Curr. Assets	133	104	90.8	66.9	57.9	43.7	NA	NA	NA	NA
Total Assets	192	151	123	96.6	80.3	58.3	NA	NA	NA	NA
Curr. Liab.	27.2	21.0	20.1	14.9	13.8	19.2	NA	NA	NA	NA
LT Debt	2.6	Nil	Nil	Nil	Nil	NA	NA	NA	NA	NA
Common Eqty.	161	129	102	81.6	66.5	32.5	NA	NA	NA	NA
Total Cap.	164	129	102	81.6	66.5	NA	NA	NA	NA	NA
Cap. Exp.	20.1	16.5	7.4	10.0	9.9	NA	NA	NA	NA	NA
Cash Flow	39.4	32.7	26.9	19.4	9.4	10.6	NA	NA	NA	NA
Curr. Ratio	4.9	5.0	4.5	4.5	4.2	2.3	NA	NA	NA	NA
% LT Debt of Cap.	1.6	Nil	Nil	Nil	Nil	NA	NA	NA	NA	NA
% Net Inc.of Revs.	11.2	10.6	9.7	8.4	3.6	7.0	NA	NA	NA	NA
% Ret. on Assets	18.2	19.0	18.0	16.0	7.9	NA	NA	NA	NA	NA
% Ret. on Equity	21.5	22.5	21.5	19.1	11.0	NA	NA	NA	NA	NA

Data as orig reptd.; bef. results of disc opers/spec. items. Per share data adj. for stk. divs. Bold denotes diluted EPS (FASB 128)-prior periods restated. E-Estimated. NA-Not Available. NM-Not Meaningful. NR-Not Ranked.

Office—4637 Chabot Dr., Suite 200, Pleasanton, CA 94588. **Tel**—(925) 460-9912. **Website**—http://www.strongtie.com **Chrmn**—B. Simpson. **Pres & CEO**—T. J. Fitzmyers. **CFO, Treas & Secy**—S. B. Lamson. **Investor Contact**—Barclay Simpson (925-738-9032).**Dirs**—E. F. Cheit, T. J. Fitzmyers, S. B. Lamson, P. N. Louras, Jr., S. W. McPeak, B. Simpson, B. L. Williams. **Transfer Agent & Registrar**—First National Bank of Boston. **Incorporated**—in California in 1994, reincorporated in Delaware in 1999. **Empl**— 1,429. **S&P Analyst:** M.I.

STANDARD
&POOR'S
STOCK REPORTS

Skyline Corp.

NYSE Symbol **SKY**

In S&P SmallCap 600

11-OCT-99 **Industry:** Homebuilding

Summary: This company produces both manufactured housing and recreational vehicles.

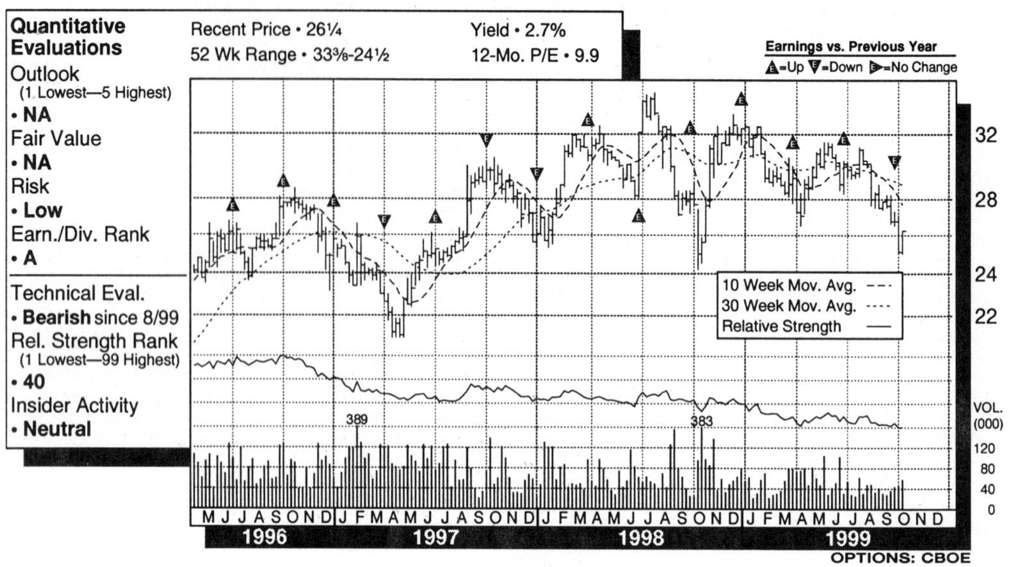

Business Profile - 11-OCT-99

This leading producer of manufactured homes and recreational vehicles has enjoyed a long earnings uptrend since profits bottomed in 1991. SKY has been profitable in each year since its founding in 1951. The balance sheet remains strong, with no long term debt. Sales of manufactured houses began an uptrend in the second half of calendar 1998, due to an increase in the sale of higher priced multi-section manufactured homes. The turnaround ended a decline in manufactured home sales that began in November 1996. In FY 99 (May), multi-section homes accounted for 68% of all homes shipped, up from 61% in FY 98. SKY spent $11.3 million to buy back 433,200 common shares during FY 99; another 1 million shares are authorized for repurchase.

Operational Review - 11-OCT-99

Sales in the three months ended August 31, 1999, declined 2.5%, year to year. After increased materials costs, particularly lumber, lumber related products and gypsum board, net income plunged 25%, to $4,895,000 ($0.54 a share, on 4.5% fewer shares), from $6,511,000 ($0.69).

Stock Performance - 08-OCT-99

In the past 30 trading days, SKY's shares have declined 5%, compared to a 0.91% fall in the S&P 500. Average trading volume for the past five days was 11,380 shares, compared with the 40-day moving average of 7,959 shares.

Key Stock Statistics

Dividend Rate/Share	0.72	Shareholders	1,700
Shs. outstg. (M)	9.0	Market cap. (B)	$0.236
Avg. daily vol. (M)	0.009	Inst. holdings	55%
Tang. Bk. Value/Share	21.30		
Beta	0.45		

Value of $10,000 invested 5 years ago: $ 15,255

Fiscal Year Ending May 31

	2000	1999	1998	1997	1996	1995
Revenues (Million $)						
1Q	166.7	171.0	161.6	171.5	163.9	155.3
2Q	—	176.4	160.3	164.4	172.5	164.5
3Q	—	145.4	131.4	118.0	138.6	150.7
4Q	—	171.9	170.1	159.3	171.1	171.7
Yr.	—	664.8	623.4	613.2	646.0	642.1
Earnings Per Share ($)						
1Q	**0.54**	**0.69**	**0.57**	0.62	0.42	0.36
2Q	—	**0.80**	0.56	0.62	0.54	0.36
3Q	—	**0.44**	**0.23**	0.18	0.30	0.23
4Q	—	**0.87**	**0.74**	0.64	0.59	0.42
Yr.	—	**2.80**	**2.10**	**2.07**	1.84	1.38

Next earnings report expected: mid December

Dividend Data (Dividends have been paid since 1960.)

Amount ($)	Date Decl.	Ex-Div. Date	Stock of Record	Payment Date
0.180	Nov. 16	Dec. 15	Dec. 17	Jan. 02 '99
0.180	Mar. 01	Mar. 15	Mar. 17	Apr. 01 '99
0.180	Jun. 01	Jun. 16	Jun. 18	Jul. 01 '99
0.180	Jul. 15	Sep. 09	Sep. 13	Oct. 01 '99

A Division of The McGraw-Hill Companies

Skyline Corporation

Business Summary - 11-OCT-99

With a business dating back to the early 1950s, Skyline Corp. (SKY) designs and produces manufactured housing (mobile homes and multi-sectional homes) and recreational vehicles (travel trailers, including park models and fifth wheels, and truck campers). Revenues contributions in FY 99 (May) were: manufactured housing 81%, and recreational vehicles 19%.

In the second half of 1998, sales began to grow again in the manufactured housing industry, after a slowdown that began in November 1996. Prior to the November 1996 slowdown, the industry had a period of sales growth extending back to 1991. The extended sales boom, which followed an even longer stretch of lean years, was made possible, in part, by the improving public image of factory-built homes. Americans have responded favorably to the industry's larger, multi-section homes, whose residential appearance often makes them difficult to distinguish from their site-built brethren. Demand for manufactured housing has also been fueled by the greater affordability of these homes. As of December 31, 1998, SKY had a 5% share of the manufactured housing market, based on number of manufactured homes produced.

The company sold 16,956 manufactured housing units in FY 99, down from 17,293 in FY 98. However, the dollar value of manufactured housing sales increased 3%, due to continued demand for multi-section homes, which have a higher selling price than single section homes. In general, demand for manufactured housing was steady in FY 99, until the fourth quarter, when the market softened temporarily.

Principal buyers for SKY's homes are young married couples and senior citizens, although the market tends to broaden when conventional housing becomes more difficult to purchase and finance. The company's manufactured homes are distributed by approximately 770 dealers, at 1,300 locations throughout the U.S.

Unit sales for the company's recreational vehicle (RV) group increased 10%, to 9,846 in FY 99. RV dollar sales were up 11%. The sales growth was attributed to continuing demand for travel trailers.

The company's RVs are distributed by approximately 330 dealers at 390 locations across the U.S.

Per Share Data ($) (Year Ended May 31)	1999	1998	1997	1996	1995	1994	1993	1992	1991	1990
Tangible Bk. Val.	NA	19.46	18.23	17.43	16.16	15.27	14.43	14.02	13.98	14.00
Cash Flow	NA	2.49	2.44	2.16	1.68	1.59	1.16	0.75	0.70	1.09
Earnings	2.80	2.10	2.07	1.84	1.38	1.34	0.92	0.52	0.47	0.87
Dividends	0.60	0.60	0.60	0.51	0.48	0.48	0.48	0.48	0.48	0.48
Payout Ratio	21%	29%	29%	28%	35%	36%	52%	92%	103%	55%
Cal. Yrs.	1998	1997	1996	1995	1994	1993	1992	1991	1990	1989
Prices - High	34 7/8	30 1/2	28 5/8	21 7/8	24 1/8	23	21 5/8	18 1/4	15 7/8	20 1/4
- Low	24 1/8	21	19 3/4	16 1/2	16 3/8	16 1/8	14	13 7/8	12 3/8	13 7/8
P/E Ratio - High	12	15	14	12	17	17	24	35	34	23
- Low	9	10	10	9	12	12	15	27	26	16
Income Statement Analysis (Million $)										
Revs.	NA	623	613	646	642	580	492	339	328	366
Oper. Inc.	NA	31.0	30.9	31.0	23.3	22.1	13.2	5.8	2.9	9.4
Depr.	NA	3.8	3.8	3.5	3.4	2.9	2.7	2.7	2.6	2.5
Int. Exp.	NA	Nil	Nil	NM	Nil	Nil	Nil	Nil	Nil	Nil
Pretax Inc.	NA	33.3	34.7	32.9	25.7	25.0	16.9	9.4	8.5	15.7
Eff. Tax Rate	NA	40%	40%	40%	40%	40%	39%	38%	38%	38%
Net Inc.	NA	19.9	20.8	19.6	15.3	15.0	10.3	5.8	5.2	9.7
Balance Sheet & Other Fin. Data (Million $)										
Cash	NA	10.7	110	55.0	40.0	17.0	14.0	17.0	111	109
Curr. Assets	NA	188	173	124	107	84.0	68.0	61.0	146	150
Total Assets	NA	233	218	230	215	209	189	180	176	179
Curr. Liab.	NA	46.3	38.6	43.1	33.2	35.8	24.7	21.3	18.1	20.7
LT Debt	NA	Nil	Nil	NM	Nil	Nil	Nil	Nil	Nil	Nil
Common Eqty.	NA	184	176	184	180	170	162	157	157	157
Total Cap.	NA	184	176	184	180	170	162	157	157	157
Cap. Exp.	NA	2.1	3.3	3.0	16.4	8.1	4.1	2.4	3.9	3.2
Cash Flow	NA	23.7	24.6	23.1	18.7	17.9	13.0	8.4	7.9	12.2
Curr. Ratio	NA	4.1	4.5	2.9	3.2	2.3	2.8	2.9	8.0	7.2
% LT Debt of Cap.	NA	Nil	Nil	NM	Nil	Nil	Nil	Nil	Nil	Nil
% Net Inc.of Revs.	NA	3.2	3.4	3.0	2.4	2.6	2.1	1.7	1.6	2.7
% Ret. on Assets	NA	8.8	9.3	8.8	7.2	7.6	5.6	3.2	2.9	5.5
% Ret. on Equity	NA	11.1	11.6	10.8	8.8	9.0	6.5	3.7	3.3	6.3

Data as orig reptd.; bef. results of disc opers/spec. items. Per share data adj. for stk. divs. Bold denotes diluted EPS (FASB 128)-prior periods restated. E-Estimated. NA-Not Available. NM-Not Meaningful. NR-Not Ranked.

Office—2520 By-Pass Rd. (P.O. Box 743), Elkhart, IN 46515. **Tel**—(219) 294-6521. **Chrmn**—A. J. Decio. **Vice Chrmn & CEO**—R. F. Kloska. **Pres & COO**—W. H. Murschel. **VP-Fin, Treas & CFO**—J. R. Weigand. **Dirs**—A. J. Decio, T. M. Decio, J. Hammes, R. F. Kloska, W. H. Lawson, D. T. Link, A. J. McKenna, W. H. Murschel, V. D. Swikert. **Transfer Agent & Registrar**—Harris Trust & Savings, Chicago. **Incorporated**—in Indiana in 1959. **Empl**— 3,500. **S&P Analyst:** S.A.H.

STANDARD
&POOR'S
STOCK REPORTS

SkyWest, Inc.

NASDAQ Symbol **SKYW**

In S&P SmallCap 600

09-OCT-99 **Industry:** Airlines

Summary: This company's SkyWest Airlines subsidiary is one of the largest U.S. regional airlines.

Quantitative Evaluations

Outlook (1 Lowest—5 Highest) • **3⁻**

Fair Value • **24¼**

Risk • **Average**

Earn./Div. Rank • **B**

Technical Eval. • **Bearish** since 8/99

Rel. Strength Rank (1 Lowest—99 Highest) • **63**

Insider Activity • **NA**

Recent Price • 22¾ Yield • 0.5%

52 Wk Range • 40½-16⅞ 12-Mo. P/E • 12.3

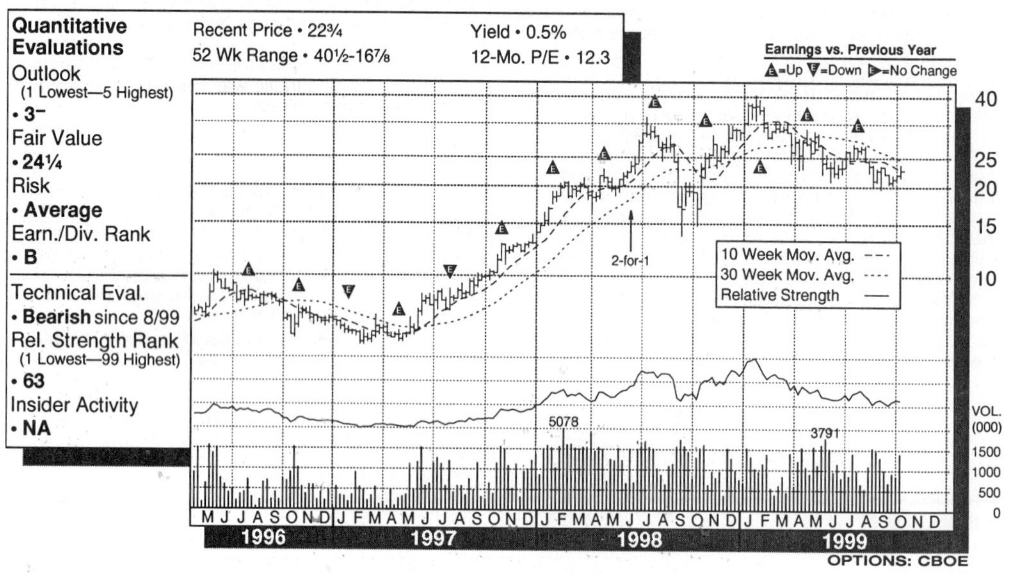

OPTIONS: CBOE

Business Profile - 29-SEP-99

This company seeks to maximize profits by entering into code-sharing and joint marketing agreements with major airlines, continually upgrading its fleet, and providing full customer service. SKYW provides service to 13 western states and Canada. During FY 99 (Mar.), SKYW took delivery of 37 Brasilia aircraft. The company had a total fleet of about 100 aircraft at June 17, 1999. SKYW also agreed to acquire 35 Canadair regional jets and related spare parts and equipment, with options for an additional 35 aircraft valued at $785 million. Delta Airlines owns 13% of the company's stock.

Operational Review - 29-SEP-99

Operating revenues in the three months ended June 30, 1999, advanced 36%, year to year, reflecting increased passenger revenues, more passengers carried and more available seat miles. Profitability benefited from the increased volume and well controlled operating expenses; pretax income rose 46%. After taxes at 38.5%, versus 35.5%, income from continuing operations rose 39%, to $13,581,000 ($0.55 a share, diluted, on 17% more shares), from $9,272,000 ($0.38). Results exclude a gain of $0.02 a share from discontinued operations in the prior year.

Stock Performance - 08-OCT-99

In the past 30 trading days, SKYW's shares have increased 0.14%, compared to a 0.91% fall in the S&P 500. Average trading volume for the past five days was 278,760 shares, compared with the 40-day moving average of 243,092 shares.

Key Stock Statistics

Dividend Rate/Share	0.12	Shareholders	1,041
Shs. outstg. (M)	24.6	Market cap. (B)	$0.558
Avg. daily vol. (M)	0.192	Inst. holdings	62%
Tang. Bk. Value/Share	10.97		
Beta	0.91		

Value of $10,000 invested 5 years ago: $ 14,117

Fiscal Year Ending Mar. 31

	2000	1999	1998	1997	1996	1995
Revenues (Million $)						
1Q	111.6	81.96	72.12	72.13	60.38	58.87
2Q	—	101.2	80.30	77.73	69.18	65.55
3Q	—	102.3	73.27	64.60	58.99	51.45
4Q	—	103.2	71.42	68.86	63.19	49.53
Yr.	—	388.6	297.1	283.3	251.7	225.4
Earnings Per Share ($)						
1Q	**0.55**	**0.40**	0.21	**0.24**	0.15	0.23
2Q	—	**0.52**	**0.37**	**0.25**	0.20	0.30
3Q	—	**0.42**	**0.26**	**-0.04**	-0.04	0.07
4Q	—	**0.45**	**0.21**	**0.06**	-0.10	0.01
Yr.	—	**1.72**	**1.04**	**0.50**	**0.21**	**0.61**

Next earnings report expected: late October

Dividend Data (Dividends have been paid since 1987.)

Amount ($)	Date Decl.	Ex-Div. Date	Stock of Record	Payment Date
0.030	Nov. 19	Dec. 29	Dec. 31	Jan. 15 '99
0.030	Feb. 09	Apr. 06	Mar. 31	Apr. 14 '99
0.030	May. 04	Jun. 28	Jun. 30	Jul. 14 '99
0.030	Aug. 10	Sep. 28	Sep. 30	Oct. 14 '99

SkyWest, Inc.

Business Summary - 29-SEP-99

SkyWest, Inc. (SKYW), which shed its remaining Metroliner aircraft in 1997 in favor of the larger, more comfortable Brasilia EMB-120s. now boasts an "all cabin-class" fleet dominated by 89 Brasilia turboprop aircraft, including 21 owned by the company. SKYW also flies 11 Canadair regional jets.

More than half of the airline's passengers are business travelers, and the balance travel for leisure purposes, lured by western ski resorts or California beaches. Through wholly owned National Parks Transportation Inc., SKYW provides car rental services at six airports through a fleet of Avis vehicles. During FY 99 (Mar.), the company sold its Scenic Airlines unit, which had provided air tours and aviation services to the scenic regions of Arizona and Utah. In August 1998, SKYW sold the unit's Las Vegas-based assets.

The company has operated as a Delta Connection throughout its markets for over a decade under a joint marketing and code-sharing agreement with Delta Air Lines, Inc. This arrangement permits SKYW to use Delta's designation code when listing flights in widely used computerized reservation systems. Under a revised agreement with Delta, SKYW coordinates its schedules with those of its code-sharing partner to maximize interline connections at hub airports in Salt Lake City and Los Angeles. In mid-1997, the company signed another code-share agreement, with United Airlines. Under this arrangement, SKYW began operating as United Express, with 288 daily flights to 15 cities in four western states. As of February 1999, United Express was operating 740 daily United Express departures on the West Coast from hubs at Los Angeles, Seattle/Tacoma, Portland and San Francisco. SKYW operates a total of 1,000 daily flights to 40 cities in 13 western states and British Columbia. As of June 1999, 47% of the company's traffic was carried under the Delta code and 53% was carried under the United code. Additionally, 23% of SKYW's flights operated under the Delta code while 77% operated under the United code.

Fleet changes in FY 99 resulted in a 26% increase in available seat miles, to 1.84 billion. Revenue passenger miles totaled 1.02 million, up from 745 million in FY 98, and passenger load factor, which measures utilization of aircraft capacity, rose slightly, to 55.1%, from 50.9%. Total passengers carried rose to 4.9 million, from 3.0 million. Yield per revenue passenger mile in FY 99 was $0.375, up from $0.348 a year earlier. Revenue per available seat mile increased to $0.21 from $0.18, while the average passenger trip length was 207 miles, down from 249 miles in FY 98.

In a February 1998 public offering, SKYW sold 2.8 million common shares at $20.25 each, plus 420,000 shares to cover over-allotments (all adjusted for the 2-for-1 split in mid-1998).

Per Share Data ($) (Year Ended Mar. 31)	1999	1998	1997	1996	1995	1994	1993	1992	1991	1990
Tangible Bk. Val.	10.47	8.79	6.13	5.76	5.71	5.37	2.65	2.24	2.14	2.06
Cash Flow	2.66	1.95	1.42	0.96	1.25	1.25	0.94	0.62	0.55	0.67
Earnings	1.72	1.04	0.50	0.21	0.61	0.73	0.42	0.13	0.13	0.30
Dividends	0.11	0.10	0.08	0.04	0.14	0.08	0.03	0.03	0.06	0.05
Payout Ratio	6%	10%	15%	19%	23%	12%	6%	22%	47%	16%
Cal. Yrs.	1998	1997	1996	1995	1994	1993	1992	1991	1990	1989
Prices - High	34 1/4	15 1/8	10 3/8	12 3/4	20 1/2	17 1/4	5	2 1/2	3	3 1/4
- Low	13 5/8	5 7/8	6 1/4	5 5/8	5 3/4	4 3/4	1 7/8	1 1/4	1 11/16	1 11/16
P/E Ratio - High	20	14	21	60	33	24	12	20	23	11
- Low	8	6	12	26	9	7	5	10	13	5
Income Statement Analysis (Million $)										
Revs.	389	297	283	252	225	188	147	125	113	100
Oper. Inc.	87.5	53.3	33.9	21.1	34.3	34.9	19.7	11.4	10.4	12.3
Depr.	23.2	19.3	18.5	15.4	14.0	10.2	8.3	7.6	6.5	5.8
Int. Exp.	2.4	2.9	2.4	2.2	1.1	2.0	1.4	1.3	1.4	1.2
Pretax Inc.	69.9	35.7	16.6	6.8	22.2	23.8	10.5	3.1	3.4	7.8
Eff. Tax Rate	39%	38%	39%	36%	38%	40%	36%	37%	40%	40%
Net Inc.	42.6	21.9	10.1	4.4	13.7	14.4	6.7	2.0	2.0	4.7
Balance Sheet & Other Fin. Data (Million $)										
Cash	162	140	55.8	43.7	48.7	68.0	12.0	10.0	9.8	13.0
Curr. Assets	217	193	90.3	76.5	71.6	87.1	28.2	24.3	24.0	25.3
Total Assets	418	330	233	228	188	184	86.9	72.4	73.3	69.2
Curr. Liab.	74.3	49.7	45.0	43.6	25.6	20.5	15.9	13.0	11.9	10.8
LT Debt	61.8	49.6	47.3	53.7	29.6	26.6	18.4	13.8	16.5	13.8
Common Eqty.	256	211	125	116	118	123	42.8	35.3	33.5	32.5
Total Cap.	343	278	188	184	160	160	67.1	54.6	55.8	51.5
Cap. Exp.	111	29.8	19.7	64.7	39.3	45.6	20.9	10.1	14.9	8.1
Cash Flow	65.9	41.2	28.6	19.8	27.7	24.6	15.0	9.6	8.6	10.5
Curr. Ratio	2.9	3.9	2.0	1.8	2.8	4.3	1.8	1.9	2.0	2.4
% LT Debt of Cap.	18.0	17.8	25.2	29.2	18.4	16.6	27.4	25.2	29.6	26.7
% Net Inc.of Revs.	11.0	7.4	3.6	1.7	6.1	7.7	4.6	1.6	1.8	4.7
% Ret. on Assets	11.4	7.8	4.4	2.1	7.7	9.4	8.3	2.7	2.8	7.0
% Ret. on Equity	18.2	13.1	8.4	3.7	12.0	15.7	17.0	5.8	6.1	15.5

Data as orig reptd.; bef. results of disc opers/spec. items. Per share data adj. for stk. divs. Bold denotes diluted EPS (FASB 128)-prior periods restated. E-Estimated. NA-Not Available. NM-Not Meaningful. NR-Not Ranked.

Office—444 S. River Rd., St. George, UT 84790. **Tel**—(801) 634-3000. **Website**—http://www.skywest.com **Chrmn, Pres & CEO**—J. C. Atkin. **Vice Chrmn**—S. J. Atkin. **EVP & COO**—R. B. Reber. **EVP-Fin, CFO, Treas & Investor Contact**—Bradford R. Rich (801-634-3300). **Dirs**—J. C. Atkin, J. R. Atkin, S. J. Atkin, M. K. Cox, I. M. Cumming, H. J. Eyring, H. W. Smith, S. F. Udvar-Hazy. **Transfer Agent & Registrar**—Zions First National Bank, Salt Lake City. **Incorporated**—in Utah in 1972. **Empl**— 3,243. **S&P Analyst:** Stewart Scharf

STANDARD
&POOR'S
STOCK REPORTS

SLI, Inc.

NYSE Symbol **SLI**

In S&P SmallCap 600

09-OCT-99 **Industry:** Electrical Equipment

Summary: This company is a leading worldwide manufacturer and supplier of lighting products.

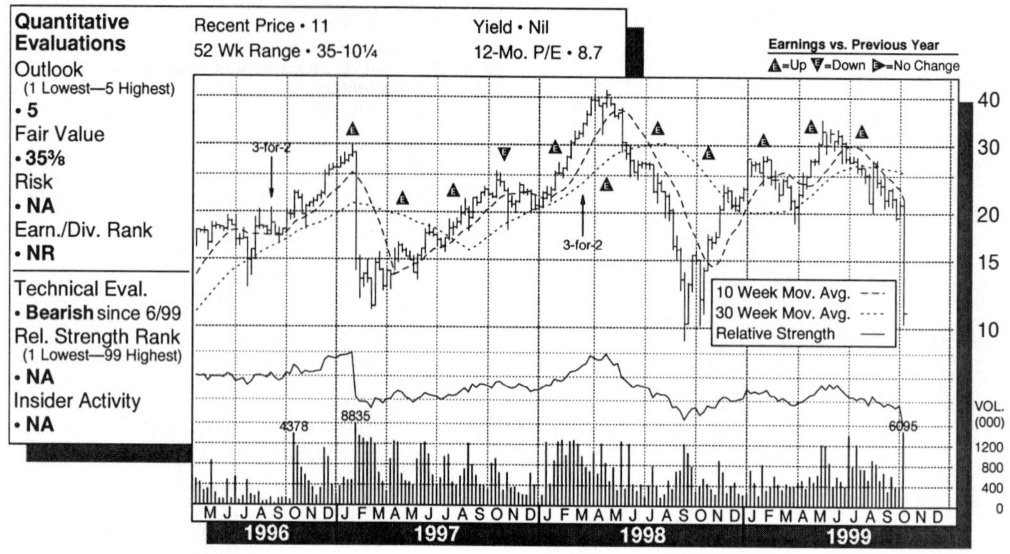

Business Profile - 22-AUG-99

In August 1999, management expressed confidence in the company's longer term fundamental growth prospects, citing SLI's financial strengths, market position, and infrastructure. Proceeds to the company from an offering of 6,000,000 shares of common stock (another 1,000,000 shares were sold for shareholders) early in 1999's third quarter at $27 a share were used for the repayment of debt. Officers and directors own about 29% of the stock outstanding.

Operational Review - 22-AUG-99

Net sales in the six months ended June 30, 1999, advanced 12%, year to year, primarily due to generic growth generated from the integration of incremental sales from 1998 acquisitions into ongoing operations, partially offset by the effect of a higher U.S. dollar. Gross margins narrowed on a less favorable product mix, but overall results benefited from the utilization of the infrastructure of recent acquisitions as a base for further sales gains, and favorable currency movements. Pretax income was up 29%. After taxes at 17.6%, versus 20.0%, net income increased 33%, to $22,132,000 ($0.72 a share), from $16,635,000 ($0.55).

Stock Performance - 08-OCT-99

In the past 30 trading days, SLI's shares have declined 53%, compared to a 0.91% fall in the S&P 500. Average trading volume for the past five days was 1,219,060 shares, compared with the 40-day moving average of 249,244 shares.

Key Stock Statistics

Dividend Rate/Share	Nil	Shareholders	4,000
Shs. outstg. (M)	29.7	Market cap. (B)	$0.327
Avg. daily vol. (M)	0.371	Inst. holdings	55%
Tang. Bk. Value/Share	5.24		
Beta	NA		

Value of $10,000 invested 5 years ago: NA

Fiscal Year Ending Dec. 31

	1999	1998	1997	1996	1995	1994
Revenues (Million $)						
1Q	218.9	192.4	34.13	19.40	—	—
2Q	206.1	185.7	51.86	22.13	—	—
3Q	—	182.0	45.83	25.09	14.59	—
4Q	—	213.0	198.1	27.55	18.41	—
Yr.	—	773.1	329.9	94.17	57.40	—
Earnings Per Share ($)						
1Q	**0.42**	**0.30**	0.17	0.11	—	—
2Q	**0.30**	**0.25**	0.17	0.12	—	—
3Q	—	**0.23**	0.11	0.13	—	—
4Q	—	**0.32**	0.28	0.19	0.18	—
Yr.	—	**1.10**	0.73	0.55	0.41	—

Next earnings report expected: NA

Dividend Data

No cash dividends have been paid. A three-for-two stock split was paid in March 1998.

A Division of The McGraw-Hill Companies

SLI, Inc.

Business Summary - 22-AUG-99

SLI, Inc. (Chicago Miniature Lamp, Inc. until April 1998) is a leading vertically integrated manufacturer and supplier of lighting systems. Through its 20 acquisitions completed since 1992, the company has grown from a specialized U.S. manufacturer and supplier of neon lamps and miniature lighting products into one of the world's largest manufacturers of lighting products to the industrial, commercial and consumer markets. The company believes it is one of the six largest global lighting companies and one of only three major international producers to offer lamps, fixtures and ballasts.

Sales by region were as follows in 1998: Europe 60%, the U.S. 21%, Central and South America 11%, Pacific Rim 6%, and Canada 2%.

The company offers a complete range of lighting products throughout the world. Lamp products produced by the company include incandescent, fluorescent, compact fluorescent, high intensity discharge (HID), halogen, and special and miniature lamps. The company's commercial and industrial fixture lines consist primarily of fluorescent ceiling mounted fixtures; its accent and decorative fixture lines range from simple downlights and spotlights to high performance lighting fixtures for art galleries and museums. Miniature lighting assemblies are used in various product applications, including automobile message centers, and aviation and telecommunications status arrays. Magnetic and electronic ballasts supply power to start and operate fluorescent and HID lamps and signage products.

Sales by product line in 1998: lamps 51%, fixtures 23%, ballasts 10%, miniature lighting assemblies 9%, and other 7%.

The company's strategy is to operate as a vertically integrated manufacturer providing "one stop" lighting solutions for its customers' lighting requirements by offering both discrete lighting components and value-added integrated products. Through its acquisition of SLI, B.V., as well as several niche businesses, the company is able to offer its global customers extensive design, engineering and manufacturing capabilities, while at the same time providing local, responsive service. At January 3, 1999, the company had 31 manufacturing facilities, as well as sales offices and distribution facilities in more than 30 countries.

In January 1997, the company significantly expanded its operations with the acquisition of Valmont Electric, Inc. (Power Lighting Products, or PLP), a manufacturer and supplier of lighting ballasts, and in September 1997, it completed the purchase of Sylvania Lighting International, B.V. (SLI, B.V.), for $161.5 million in cash. Sylvania was the third largest lighting company in Europe and a major global lighting company, selling a variety of products in its principal markets under recognized brand names including Sylvania.

Per Share Data ($) (Year Ended Dec. 31)	1998	1997	1996	1995	1994	1993	1992	1991	1990	1989
Tangible Bk. Val.	5.18	5.11	4.94	1.01	NA	NA	NA	NA	NA	NA
Cash Flow	1.67	0.98	0.68	0.74	NA	NA	NA	NA	NA	NA
Earnings	1.10	0.73	0.55	0.41	NA	NA	NA	NA	NA	NA
Dividends	Nil	Nil	Nil	Nil	NA	NA	NA	NA	NA	NA
Payout Ratio	Nil	Nil	Nil	Nil	NA	NA	NA	NA	NA	NA
Prices - High	41 7/8	29 7/8	27 7/8	11 3/8	NA	NA	NA	NA	NA	NA
- Low	9 1/4	11 1/8	9 3/4	5 1/2	NA	NA	NA	NA	NA	NA
P/E Ratio - High	38	41	50	27	NA	NA	NA	NA	NA	NA
- Low	8	15	17	13	NA	NA	NA	NA	NA	NA
Income Statement Analysis (Million $)										
Revs.	773	330	94.2	57.4	NA	NA	NA	NA	NA	NA
Oper. Inc.	78.6	39.7	21.6	14.1	NA	NA	NA	NA	NA	NA
Depr.	17.3	7.3	3.2	1.9	NA	NA	NA	NA	NA	NA
Int. Exp.	17.8	1.2	0.3	0.8	NA	NA	NA	NA	NA	NA
Pretax Inc.	41.2	28.5	19.5	11.5	NA	NA	NA	NA	NA	NA
Eff. Tax Rate	20%	27%	31%	26%	NA	NA	NA	NA	NA	NA
Net Inc.	33.0	20.9	13.4	8.5	NA	NA	NA	NA	NA	NA
Balance Sheet & Other Fin. Data (Million $)										
Cash	27.4	73.4	109	4.0	NA	NA	NA	NA	NA	NA
Curr. Assets	353	350	146	25.1	NA	NA	NA	NA	NA	NA
Total Assets	NA	652	212	59.5	NA	NA	NA	NA	NA	NA
Curr. Liab.	255	232	47.6	15.2	NA	NA	NA	NA	NA	NA
LT Debt	239	185	6.0	3.1	NA	NA	NA	NA	NA	NA
Common Eqty.	218	166	151	34.9	NA	NA	NA	NA	NA	NA
Total Cap.	467	357	157	42.8	NA	NA	NA	NA	NA	NA
Cap. Exp.	49.0	24.0	8.9	2.5	NA	NA	NA	NA	NA	NA
Cash Flow	50.3	28.2	16.6	10.4	NA	NA	NA	NA	NA	NA
Curr. Ratio	1.4	1.5	3.1	1.7	NA	NA	NA	NA	NA	NA
% LT Debt of Cap.	51.2	51.8	3.8	7.2	NA	NA	NA	NA	NA	NA
% Net Inc.of Revs.	4.3	6.3	14.3	14.7	NA	NA	NA	NA	NA	NA
% Ret. on Assets	NA	4.8	9.9	NA	NA	NA	NA	NA	NA	NA
% Ret. on Equity	17.2	13.2	14.4	NA	NA	NA	NA	NA	NA	NA

Data as orig. reptd.; bef. results of disc. opers. and/or spec. items. Per share data adj. for stk. divs. as of ex-div. date. Pr. to 1998 yrs. end Nov. Bold denotes diluted EPS (FASB 128). E-Estimated. NA-Not Available. NM-Not Meaningful. NR-Not Ranked.

Office —500 Chapman St., Canton, MA 02021. **Tel**—(781) 828-2948. **Website**—http://www.sli-lighting.com **Chrmn, Pres & CEO**—F. M. Ward. **CFO & Secy**—R. F. Parenti. **Dirs**—W. A. Arnold, D. S. Dewsnap, F. B. Howard, R. E. Ingram, F. M. Ward. **Transfer Agent & Registrar**—American Stock Transfer &Trust Co., NYC. **Incorporated**—in Oklahoma. **Empl**— 8,760. **S&P Analyst:** P.L.H.

STANDARD &POOR'S
STOCK REPORTS

Smith (A. O.)

NYSE Symbol **AOS**

In S&P SmallCap 600

09-OCT-99 **Industry:** Electrical Equipment

Summary: This company produces electric motors, water heaters, fiberglass piping systems and industrial storage tanks.

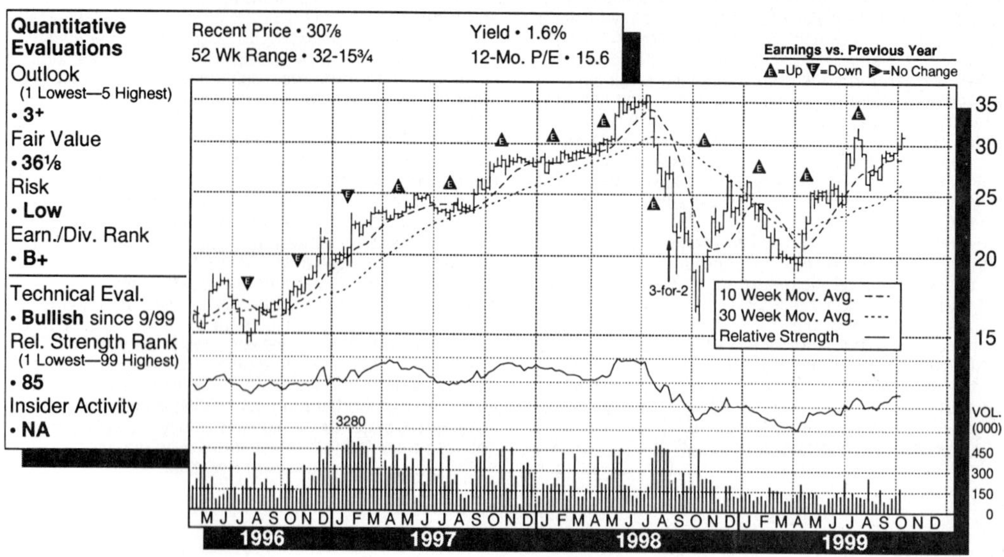

Business Profile - 01-JUL-99

The company expects difficulties at its Storage and Fluid Handling Technologies operations to persist in 1999. It remains cautiously optimistic about the Water Systems market, and believes the Electric Motors business should have another good year due to incremental business from the Scottsville acquisition and a new contract from York International. Although the company believes its 1999 earnings, excluding acquisitions, will increase from 1998 levels, accretive acquisitions will be required to reach its target of 15% annual EPS growth.

Operational Review - 01-JUL-99

Net sales in the first quarter of 1999 rose 15%, year to year, paced by a 32% gain at Electric Motors Technologies reflecting stronger air conditioning sales, a full quarter of results from the UPPCO operations, and higher hermetic motor sales; Water Systems Technology sales increased 10%, while Storage and Fluid Handling sales fell 25%, due to weakness in the petroleum production, chemical and agricultural markets. Gross margins narrowed on higher product costs, but with well controlled SG&A expenses, operating income was up 20%. Following higher interest and other expenses, the gain in net income was held to 12%, to $11,402,000 ($0.48 a share), from $10,178,000 ($0.41, as adjusted).

Stock Performance - 08-OCT-99

In the past 30 trading days, AOS's shares have increased 16%, compared to a 0.91% fall in the S&P 500. Average trading volume for the past five days was 35,180 shares, compared with the 40-day moving average of 22,497 shares.

Key Stock Statistics

Dividend Rate/Share	0.48	Shareholders	1,900
Shs. outstg. (M)	23.2	Market cap. (B)	$0.448
Avg. daily vol. (M)	0.024	Inst. holdings	40%
Tang. Bk. Value/Share	10.91		
Beta	1.42		

Value of $10,000 invested 5 years ago: $ 14,478

Fiscal Year Ending Dec. 31

	1999	1998	1997	1996	1995	1994
Revenues (Million $)						
1Q	257.3	223.0	196.3	194.8	393.0	339.8
2Q	262.0	226.7	224.9	206.5	399.8	350.2
3Q	—	243.3	206.0	188.1	354.4	332.7
4Q	—	224.7	205.8	191.8	397.6	350.8
Yr.	—	917.6	832.9	781.0	1,545	1,374
Earnings Per Share ($)						
1Q	**0.48**	**0.41**	**0.23**	**0.18**	0.59	0.51
2Q	**0.59**	**0.52**	**0.41**	**0.23**	0.64	0.57
3Q	—	**0.46**	**0.33**	**0.19**	0.24	0.32
4Q	—	**0.45**	**0.37**	**0.19**	0.49	0.43
Yr.	—	**1.84**	**1.33**	**0.81**	**0.76**	**0.54**

Next earnings report expected: NA

Dividend Data (Dividends have been paid since 1983.)

Amount ($)	Date Decl.	Ex-Div. Date	Stock of Record	Payment Date
0.120	Oct. 06	Oct. 28	Oct. 30	Nov. 16 '98
0.120	Jan. 19	Jan. 27	Jan. 29	Feb. 16 '99
0.120	Apr. 15	Apr. 28	Apr. 30	May. 17 '99
0.120	Jun. 09	Jul. 28	Jul. 30	Aug. 16 '99

A. O. Smith Corporation

Business Summary - 01-JUL-99

Reacting to the pressure of changes that have occurred in the automotive supply business over the past few years, namely the ongoing consolidation of the supply base, A. O. Smith (AOS) decided to sell its Tier I automotive products business rather than expend the vast amounts of capital it believed to be necessary to remain competitive in this market. In the largest single divestiture in its 125-year history, the company sold this business to Tower Automotive in April 1997, for about $725 million. AOS's remaining operations consist of three business segments: Electric Motor Technologies, Water Systems Technology, and Storage & Fluid Handling Technologies.

Of the three continuing businesses, Electric Motor Technologies is the largest ($480 million in net sales in 1998, representing 52% of the total). This segment produces hermetic electric motors used in refrigeration and air conditioning systems, and fractional horsepower motors used in consumer products, fan motors for furnaces, air conditioners and blowers, and jet pump motors for home water systems, swimming pools, hot tubs and spas. Sales to the heating, ventilating, air conditioning and refrigeration market account for about 60% of the segment's total sales. In April 1999, AOS definitively agreed to acquire MagneTek's motor operations ($367 million in sales) for $250 million. The company expects this acquisition to be neutral to earnings in 1999, but add $0.30 to $0.35 per share in the year 2000.

The Water Systems Technologies segment (32% of net sales) is a leading manufacturer of residential gas and electric water heaters, and commercial water heating systems used in schools, nursing homes, hospitals, prisons, hotels, laundries, restaurants, stadiums, amusement parks, car washes and other large users of hot water.

Storage & Fluid Handling Technologies (16%) provides world-wide solutions for storing liquids and a wide range of dry materials, as well as high performance piping systems that safely contain and convey corrosive, abrasive or related materials. Products include industrial, municipal and agricultural liquid and dry bulk storage systems, and reinforced thermosetting resin piping and fittings used to carry corrosive materials.

During 1998, the company repurchased 1,188,450 common shares. Since the program's inception in early 1997, AOS has bought back 8.4 million shares.

Exports accounted for 7% of the company's sales in 1998.

In March 1997, the company acquired UPPCO, Inc., a maker of sub-fractional horsepower electric motors with sales of about $57 million.

Per Share Data ($) (Year Ended Dec. 31)	1998	1997	1996	1995	1994	1993	1992	1991	1990	1989
Tangible Bk. Val.	10.91	14.24	13.52	11.87	9.27	7.90	7.14	9.95	10.92	10.28
Cash Flow	3.13	2.27	1.52	3.73	3.40	2.77	2.33	1.59	2.54	0.97
Earnings	1.84	1.33	0.81	1.96	1.83	0.24	0.93	0.07	1.13	-0.36
Dividends	0.35	0.45	0.44	0.39	0.33	0.41	0.27	0.27	0.27	0.27
Payout Ratio	19%	34%	55%	20%	18%	172%	29%	439%	24%	NM
Prices - High	35 7/8	28 7/8	22	19 1/8	26 5/8	23 7/8	12 3/4	7 1/4	6 5/8	6 1/8
- Low	15 3/4	19 1/8	13 7/8	12 3/4	14 1/8	11 5/8	5 7/8	5	3 7/8	4 1/8
P/E Ratio - High	19	22	27	10	15	99	14	NM	6	NM
- Low	9	14	17	7	8	48	6	NM	3	NM
Income Statement Analysis (Million $)										
Revs.	918	833	781	1,545	1,374	1,194	1,046	916	935	976
Oper. Inc.	112	90.0	82.0	166	152	125	96.6	61.8	87.1	61.1
Depr.	31.2	26.3	22.6	55.7	49.2	42.6	39.5	37.8	33.5	31.6
Int. Exp.	6.9	Nil	8.1	13.1	12.9	14.5	18.7	23.9	17.0	18.8
Pretax Inc.	69.8	58.9	42.3	96.9	92.1	70.8	42.3	4.0	42.1	-3.6
Eff. Tax Rate	36%	37%	41%	37%	38%	40%	36%	14%	28%	NM
Net Inc.	44.5	37.6	25.2	61.4	57.3	42.7	27.2	3.5	30.5	-5.0
Balance Sheet & Other Fin. Data (Million $)										
Cash	37.7	146	6.4	5.7	8.5	11.9	6.0	8.9	3.2	4.8
Curr. Assets	287	366	239	352	330	304	234	209	258	271
Total Assets	767	717	885	953	848	823	769	754	788	796
Curr. Liab.	132	128	138	214	216	223	172	172	206	197
LT Debt	131	101	238	191	166	191	237	249	156	155
Common Eqty.	401	400	425	372	313	270	245	265	282	269
Total Cap.	574	529	694	632	533	501	509	547	452	438
Cap. Exp.	27.9	44.9	37.8	91.0	76.1	54.7	46.9	59.3	64.9	45.9
Cash Flow	75.7	63.8	47.8	117	107	85.3	65.8	37.8	60.4	23.0
Curr. Ratio	2.2	2.9	1.7	1.6	1.5	1.4	1.4	1.2	1.3	1.4
% LT Debt of Cap.	22.8	19.9	34.3	30.2	31.1	38.0	46.4	45.5	34.5	35.3
% Net Inc.of Revs.	4.8	4.5	3.3	4.0	4.2	3.6	2.6	0.4	3.3	NM
% Ret. on Assets	6.0	4.8	3.1	6.8	6.8	5.3	3.1	0.4	3.8	NM
% Ret. on Equity	11.1	10.2	6.4	18.0	19.6	16.5	9.0	NM	9.7	NM

Data as orig reptd.; bef. results of disc opers/spec. items. Per share data adj. for stk. divs. Bold denotes diluted EPS (FASB 128)-prior periods restated. E-Estimated. NA-Not Available. NM-Not Meaningful. NR-Not Ranked.

Office—11270 W. Park Place, Milwaukee, WI 53224-3690 (P.O. Box 23972, Milwaukee 53223-0972). **Tel**—(414) 359-4000. **Fax**—(414) 359-4198. **Website**—http://www.aosmith.com **Chrmn, Pres & CEO**—R. J. O'Toole. **EVP & CFO**—G. R. Bomberger. **VP & Treas**—J. J. Kita. **VP & Secy**—W. D. Romoser. **Investor Contact**—Craig Watson (414-359-4009). **Dirs**—T. H. Barrett, G. R. Bomberger, W. F. Buehler, K. J. Hempel, R. O'Toole, R. N. Pokelwaldt, A. Pytte, A. O. Smith, B. M. Smith. **Transfer Agent & Registrar**—Firstar Trust Co., Milwaukee. **Incorporated**—in New York in 1916; reincorporated in Delaware in 1986. **Empl**— 9,700. **S&P Analyst:** S.S.

STANDARD
&POOR'S
STOCK REPORTS

Smithfield Foods

NYSE Symbol **SFD**

In S&P SmallCap 600

09-OCT-99

Industry:
Foods

Summary: This vertically integrated company is the largest producer and marketer of fresh pork and processed meats in the United States.

Quantitative Evaluations

Outlook
(1 Lowest—5 Highest)
• **5**

Fair Value
• **44⅞**

Risk
• **Average**

Earn./Div. Rank
• **B**

Technical Eval.
• **Bearish** since 8/99

Rel. Strength Rank
(1 Lowest—99 Highest)
• **18**

Insider Activity
• **Unfavorable**

Recent Price • 24½
52 Wk Range • 36⅛-14⅝

Yield • Nil
12-Mo. P/E • 9.4

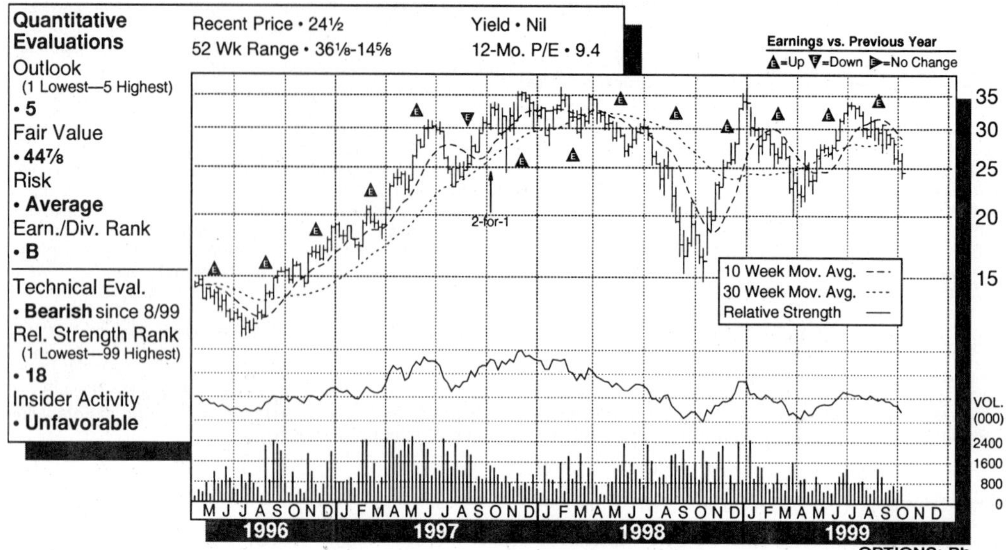

Business Profile - 30-JUL-99

SFDS's vertical integration strategy of producing hogs and selling processed meats has a counter-cyclical effect and helps stabilize earnings from cyclical swings. In May 1999, the company acquired Carroll's Foods, Inc., the second largest hog production company in the U.S., for 4.2 million shares of SFDS common stock, the assumption of $231 million in debt and liabilities. The acquisition makes SFDS the largest hog production company in the world. In March 1999, the company reached a settlement agreement with the North Carolina Department of Environment, regarding terms of a wastewater discharge permit for its North Carolina Smithfield packing plant.

Operational Review - 30-JUL-99

Based on a preliminary report, sales for the fiscal year ended May 2, 1999, decreased 2.4%, reflecting lower unit selling prices of meat products, which resulted from reduced hog prices passed through to customers. However, profitability soared, as the lower hog prices significantly improved gross margins at the Meat Processing Group. While expenses increased reflecting the newly acquired businesses, profit comparisons benefited from the absence of a $12.6 million nonrecurring charge taken in the prior year for governmental penalties. After taxes at 33.9%, versus 34.0%, net income climbed 78%, to $94.9 million ($2.32 a share), from $53.4 million ($1.34).

Stock Performance - 08-OCT-99

In the past 30 trading days, SFD's shares have declined 17%, compared to a 0.91% fall in the S&P 500. Average trading volume for the past five days was 132,180 shares, compared with the 40-day moving average of 145,441 shares.

Key Stock Statistics

Dividend Rate/Share	Nil	Shareholders	1,143
Shs. outstg. (M)	45.3	Market cap. (B)	$ 1.1
Avg. daily vol. (M)	0.116	Inst. holdings	42%
Tang. Bk. Value/Share	10.50		
Beta	0.99		

Value of $10,000 invested 5 years ago: $ 26,486

Fiscal Year Ending Apr. 30

	2000	1999	1998	1997	1996	1995
Revenues (Million $)						
1Q	1,142	865.8	915.0	892.9	367.3	331.8
2Q	—	874.4	982.7	969.2	455.8	373.8
3Q	—	1,036	1,096	1,081	687.0	439.4
4Q	—	999	873.8	927.5	873.8	381.6
Yr.	—	3,775	3,867	3,871	2,384	1,527
Earnings Per Share ($)						
1Q	**0.15**	**-0.14**	**-0.17**	0.01	-0.08	0.07
2Q	—	**0.47**	0.39	0.23	0.13	0.23
3Q	—	**1.31**	**0.60**	**0.40**	0.29	0.52
4Q	—	**0.64**	**0.52**	**0.50**	0.17	0.09
Yr.	—	**2.32**	**1.34**	**1.17**	**0.53**	0.92

Next earnings report expected: late November

Dividend Data

No cash dividends have been paid. The company does not anticipate paying cash dividends in the foreseeable future.

Smithfield Foods, Inc.

Business Summary - 30-JUL-99

Responding to strong consumer demand for leaner, more consistent pork products, Smithfield Foods, Inc. (SFDS) has spent $400 million in the past decade building what it now believes is the hog industry's most extensive vertically integrated system. SFDS also believes that it is one of the largest U.S. combined hog producer/pork slaughterers and further processors, producing a wide variety of fresh pork and processed meat products marketed in the U.S. as well as selected foreign markets that include Japan, Russia and Mexico.

Pork processing operations are conducted through five principal subsidiaries--Gwaltney of Smithfield, Ltd., The Smithfield Packing Company, Inc., John Morrell & Co., Patrick Cudahy Inc. and Lykes Meat Group, Inc. The company also conducts hog production operations through its Brown's of Carolina, Inc. subsidiary and through several joint hog production arrangements.

Fresh pork products constituted 56% of sales in FY 98 (Apr.). In an effort to provide leaner fresh pork products, as well as fat-free, lower-fat and lower-salt processed meats, SFDS has developed and markets an extremely lean line of fresh pork products under the Smithfield Lean Generation Pork label. Processed meats accounted for 40% of FY 98 sales. Processed meat products are marketed under the brand names Smithfield, Patrick Cudahy and John Morrell, among others.

SFDS sells large quantities of value-priced processed meat products as well as fresh pork to national and regional supermarket chains, wholesale distributors, the food service industry and export markets. The company's business strategy includes using the leanest genetics commercially available to enable it to market highly differentiated pork products. As consumers have become more health conscious, the company has broadened its product line to include fat-free, lower fat, and lower salt processed meats.

SFDS cites as strategic initiatives an emphasis on expansion of international markets (6% of total FY 98 sales), targeting Europe and the Pacific Rim markets, and its continued growth through acquisition of regional pork processors and brands.

SFDS continues to acquire strategically important U.S. and international companies. In September 1998, SFDS acquired Societe Bretonne De Salaisons (SBS), the largest private-label manufacturer of ham, pork shoulder, and bacon products in France, with annual sales of about $115 million. In October 1998, SFDS acquired North Side Foods Corp., a major domestic supplier of sausage to McDonald's Corp. In November 1998, SFDS acquired the Schneider Corp., the second largest meat processing company in Canada. In May 1999, SFDS acquired Carroll's Foods, Inc., the second largest hog production company in the U.S., for 4.2 million common shares and the assumption of $231 in debt, plus other liabilities.

Per Share Data ($) (Year Ended Apr. 30)	1999	1998	1997	1996	1995	1994	1993	1992	1991	1990
Tangible Bk. Val.	10.50	9.29	8.20	6.73	5.61	4.76	4.17	3.77	2.83	1.77
Cash Flow	3.99	2.50	2.21	1.34	1.50	1.22	0.65	1.09	1.39	0.57
Earnings	2.32	1.34	1.17	0.53	0.92	0.56	0.08	0.69	0.99	0.24
Dividends	Nil	Nil	Nil	Nil	Nil	Nil	Nil	Nil	Nil	Nil
Payout Ratio	Nil	Nil	Nil	Nil	Nil	Nil	Nil	Nil	Nil	Nil
Cal. Yrs.	1998	1997	1996	1995	1994	1993	1992	1991	1990	1989
Prices - High	36 3/8	35 5/8	19 3/8	17 1/8	17	9 3/4	11 1/8	12 5/8	5 1/8	4 3/4
- Low	14 5/8	16 1/4	11 3/8	9 3/4	8 7/8	6 1/4	6 7/8	4 5/8	2 1/2	2 7/8
P/E Ratio - High	16	30	14	32	19	17	NM	18	5	20
- Low	6	14	8	18	10	11	NM	7	3	12
Income Statement Analysis (Million $)										
Revs.	3,775	3,867	3,871	2,384	1,527	1,447	1,142	1,051	1,072	853
Oper. Inc.	249	171	133	79.5	84.2	69.0	34.3	47.4	51.8	24.5
Depr.	68.6	45.9	39.0	28.3	19.7	21.7	18.7	12.8	11.4	9.9
Int. Exp.	40.5	31.9	28.8	23.0	14.9	12.8	8.6	5.5	8.4	6.6
Pretax Inc.	143	81.0	67.6	30.3	50.4	35.1	5.4	33.4	43.6	10.6
Eff. Tax Rate	34%	34%	34%	35%	37%	37%	27%	35%	34%	34%
Net Inc.	94.9	53.4	44.9	19.8	31.9	19.7	2.9	21.6	28.7	7.1
Balance Sheet & Other Fin. Data (Million $)										
Cash	30.6	60.5	25.7	28.5	14.8	12.4	3.1	1.7	2.6	1.1
Curr. Assets	682	511	488	420	233	226	178	125	112	89.0
Total Assets	1,772	1,084	995	858	550	452	400	278	201	165
Curr. Liab.	466	252	324	332	172	145	113	99	77.2	74.3
LT Debt	594	407	288	189	155	119	125	49.1	37.4	28.2
Common Eqty.	542	361	307	243	184	155	136	114	71.0	45.0
Total Cap.	1,168	780	603	451	367	299	279	172	118	84.0
Cap. Exp.	95.4	92.9	69.1	74.9	91.9	28.2	88.0	75.7	26.5	19.6
Cash Flow	163	99	82.7	46.9	51.0	40.7	21.1	34.4	40.0	17.0
Curr. Ratio	1.5	2.0	1.5	1.3	1.4	1.6	1.6	1.3	1.5	1.2
% LT Debt of Cap.	50.9	52.2	47.7	41.9	42.2	39.7	44.7	28.5	31.7	33.4
% Net Inc.of Revs.	2.5	1.4	1.1	0.8	2.1	1.4	0.2	2.1	2.7	0.8
% Ret. on Assets	6.6	5.1	4.8	2.8	6.3	4.6	0.8	8.3	15.8	4.6
% Ret. on Equity	13.1	16.0	16.3	9.3	18.4	13.1	1.9	21.7	49.6	16.5

Data as orig reptd.; bef. results of disc opers/spec. items. Per share data adj. for stk. divs. Bold denotes diluted EPS (FASB 128)-prior periods restated. E-Estimated. NA-Not Available. NM-Not Meaningful. NR-Not Ranked.

Office—999 Waterside Dr., Suite 900, Norfolk, VA 23510. **Tel**—(757) 365-3000. **Chrmn & CEO**—J. W. Luter III. **Pres & COO**—L. R. Little. **VP, Secy, Treas & Investor Contact**—Aaron D. Trub. **Dirs**—R. L. Burrus, Jr., D. W. Dodds, F. J. Faison, Jr., R. A. Goldberg, J. W. Greenberg, G. E. Hamilton, Jr., R. G. Hofmann II, R. J. Holland, R. R. Kapella, L. R. Little, J. W. Luter III, W. H. Prestage, J. B. Sebring, T. A. Seeley. **Transfer Agent & Registrar**—First Union National Bank, Charlotte, NC. **Incorporated**—in Delaware in 1971. **Empl**— 19,500. **S&P Analyst:** A. Bensinger

STANDARD &POOR'S
STOCK REPORTS

Sola International

NYSE Symbol **SOL**

In S&P SmallCap 600

09-OCT-99

Industry:
Health Care (Medical Products & Supplies)

Summary: Sola designs, manufactures and distributes a broad range of eyeglass lenses, focusing primarily on the plastic lens segment of the global lens market.

Quantitative Evaluations

Outlook
(1 Lowest—5 Highest)
• **5**

Fair Value
• **29¼**

Risk
• **Average**

Earn./Div. Rank
• **NR**

Technical Eval.
• **Bearish** since 8/99

Rel. Strength Rank
(1 Lowest—99 Highest)
• **41**

Insider Activity
• **NA**

Recent Price • 15¼
52 Wk Range • 20-9⅞
Yield • Nil
12-Mo. P/E • 52.6

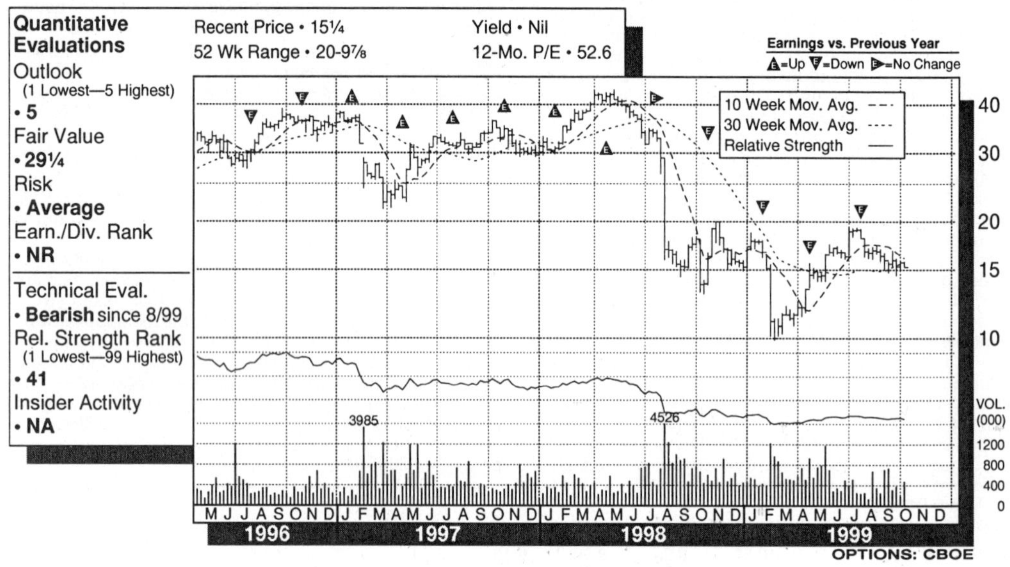

Business Profile - 13-SEP-99

Sola plans to focus on expanding its business with an emphasis on the higher value-added, faster growing product categories such as progressive lenses, lens coatings and thinner and lighter plastic lenses. The company has moved to deal with adverse economic conditions worldwide, including a reduction of manufacturing levels to work down inventory, staff cuts, and lower capital spending. Additional staff cuts and some facility consolidations led to pretax charges of $13.6 million in the FY 99 (Mar.) fourth quarter, and a $12.1 million charge was recorded due to the Brazilian currency devaluation's impact on asset realization.

Operational Review - 13-SEP-99

Net sales in the three months ended June 30, 1999, rose 3.2%, year to year, reflecting strong North American progressive lens sales resulting from new products, and improved Asian and Australian operations. Gross margins narrowed, on lower manufacturing cost absorption, due a decrease in production volumes as the company closely managed its inventory levels. With higher general and administrative expenses, and after pretax charges of $1.5 million, net income fell 48%, to $5,918,000 ($0.24 a share, diluted, on 3.1% fewer shares), from $11,297,000 ($0.44). The company expects to record additional charges of $1.0 million to $1.5 million in FY 00, related to severance costs.

Stock Performance - 08-OCT-99

In the past 30 trading days, SOL's shares have declined 7%, compared to a 0.91% fall in the S&P 500. Average trading volume for the past five days was 93,340 shares, compared with the 40-day moving average of 84,772 shares.

Key Stock Statistics

Dividend Rate/Share	Nil	Shareholders	408
Shs. outstg. (M)	24.9	Market cap. (B)	$0.379
Avg. daily vol. (M)	0.066	Inst. holdings	73%
Tang. Bk. Value/Share	5.84		
Beta	NA		

Value of $10,000 invested 5 years ago: NA

Fiscal Year Ending Mar. 31

	2000	1999	1998	1997	1996	1995
Revenues (Million $)						
1Q	133.6	129.5	137.6	109.5	95.92	83.74
2Q	—	132.7	135.7	128.2	95.87	84.42
3Q	—	126.3	129.3	119.7	91.33	82.86
4Q	—	141.3	145.1	131.2	104.6	94.62
Yr.	—	529.8	547.7	488.7	387.7	345.6
Earnings Per Share ($)						
1Q	**0.24**	**0.44**	0.44	0.09	0.32	0.14
2Q	—	**0.35**	0.46	0.27	0.39	0.25
3Q	—	**0.21**	**0.44**	0.31	0.26	0.08
4Q	—	**-0.51**	**0.66**	0.55	0.53	0.32
Yr.	—	**0.49**	**2.00**	**1.24**	1.51	0.78

Next earnings report expected: early November

Dividend Data

No cash dividends have been paid, and Sola does not intend to pay any for the foreseeable future.

A Division of The McGraw-Hill Companies

STANDARD
&POOR'S
STOCK REPORTS

Sola International Inc.

09-OCT-99

Business Summary - 13-SEP-99

Sola International (SOL) has a clear vision of the future: through plastic lenses. The company designs, makes and distributes a broad range of plastic and glass eyeglass lenses, focusing mainly on the faster growing plastic lens segment of the market. North America accounted for 50% of revenues in FY 99 (Mar.), Europe for 32%, and the rest of the world 18%.

In championing plastic lenses, SOL has proved farsighted. Its business was formed in 1960 as Scientific Optical Laboratories of Australia (SOLA), after a revolutionary new plastic lens was developed to replace glass lenses. The market for eyeglass lenses has since shifted significantly from glass to plastic, particularly in developed markets, reflecting the lighter weight, greater impact resistance, and tinting flexibility of plastic as compared with that of glass.

Plastic lenses currently account for about 90% of sales, with about 47% of sales of generated by ophthalmic plastic lenses provided by conventional hard resin plastics, with the remainder coming from advanced lens materials such as thinner and lighter plastics and plastic photochromics.

The company's lenses include single vision lenses; bifocals and progressive lenses (no-line bifocals); and plano lenses (lenses with no corrective power used primarily for sunglasses). SOL further differentiates its products from those of its competitors by lens design and coatings. Percepta, a new progressive lens, features a more customized optical design. SOL is addressing the growing market for anti-reflection (AR) coatings with its Matrix system, which delivers a finished lens with superior AR coating.

SOL also makes and sells glass lenses, mainly in North America and Europe. Its strategy for the glass lens market is to focus on high-value-added markets, such as glass progressive and higher index lenses. Glass lenses represent a decreasing portion of the company's sales. The company sells virtually no glass lenses in South America and Asia (excluding Japan), markets where glass is still the predominant material for eyeglass lenses.

The company ranks first or second in market share in North America, Europe, Australia, South America and Asia (excluding Japan). In English speaking markets (U.S., U.K. and Australia), a significant percentage of sales is to large retail chains and superoptical retail stores. In FY 99, the 10 largest customers accounted for 23% of net sales.

During FY 99, the company began marketing progressive lenses (including Visuality and AO Compact), which incorporate more complex design features than standard products, and therefore provide an above average gross profit per pair, according to SOL. In July 1998, the company acquired U.S. Coatings, Inc., an anti-reflection coating equipment maker.

Per Share Data ($) **(Year Ended Mar. 31)**	**1999**	**1998**	**1997**	**1996**	**1995**	**1994**	**1993**	**1992**	**1991**	**1990**
Tangible Bk. Val.	5.51	5.21	3.33	3.30	1.70	0.59	NA	NA	NA	NA
Cash Flow	1.48	2.87	2.11	2.26	1.98	1.11	NA	NA	NA	NA
Earnings	0.49	2.00	1.24	1.51	0.78	0.42	NA	NA	NA	NA
Dividends	Nil	Nil	Nil	Nil	Nil	NA	NA	NA	NA	NA
Payout Ratio	Nil	Nil	Nil	Nil	Nil	NA	NA	NA	NA	NA
Cal. Yrs.	1998	1997	1996	1995	1994	1993	1992	1991	1990	1989
Prices - High	43¾	38¼	39	27¾	NA	NA	NA	NA	NA	NA
- Low	13	21½	25¼	16⅜	NA	NA	NA	NA	NA	NA
P/E Ratio - High	89	19	31	18	NA	NA	NA	NA	NA	NA
- Low	27	11	20	11	NA	NA	NA	NA	NA	NA

Income Statement Analysis (Million $)										
Revs.	530	548	489	388	346	306	NA	NA	NA	NA
Oper. Inc.	90.1	115	88.4	78.0	63.7	45.8	NA	NA	NA	NA
Depr.	25.0	22.1	21.6	17.2	21.0	15.0	NA	NA	NA	NA
Int. Exp.	18.5	17.4	16.6	12.7	19.0	13.6	NA	NA	NA	NA
Pretax Inc.	20.2	76.0	41.4	48.6	21.2	16.8	NA	NA	NA	NA
Eff. Tax Rate	42%	33%	26%	28%	31%	42%	NA	NA	NA	NA
Net Inc.	12.5	51.1	30.9	34.6	13.6	9.2	NA	NA	NA	NA

Balance Sheet & Other Fin. Data (Million $)										
Cash	21.6	34.4	24.4	22.4	16.1	NA	NA	NA	NA	NA
Curr. Assets	329	342	282	207	181	NA	NA	NA	NA	NA
Total Assets	699	684	606	417	383	371	NA	NA	NA	NA
Curr. Liab.	133	142	142	111	104	NA	NA	NA	NA	NA
LT Debt	208	196	163	97.9	107	116	NA	NA	NA	NA
Common Eqty.	332	327	284	192	159	141	NA	NA	NA	NA
Total Cap.	541	523	451	295	268	NA	NA	NA	NA	NA
Cap. Exp.	30.5	39.0	30.0	17.6	11.6	NA	NA	NA	NA	NA
Cash Flow	37.6	73.2	52.5	51.8	34.6	24.1	NA	NA	NA	NA
Curr. Ratio	2.5	2.4	2.0	1.9	1.7	NA	NA	NA	NA	NA
% LT Debt of Cap.	38.5	37.5	36.2	33.2	40.1	NA	NA	NA	NA	NA
% Net Inc.of Revs.	2.4	9.3	6.4	8.9	3.9	3.0	NA	NA	NA	NA
% Ret. on Assets	1.8	7.9	6.1	8.6	Nil	NA	NA	NA	NA	NA
% Ret. on Equity	3.8	16.7	13.0	19.7	Nil	NA	NA	NA	NA	NA

Data as orig reptd.; bef. results of disc opers/spec. items. Per share data adj. for stk. divs. Bold denotes diluted EPS (FASB 128)-prior periods restated. E-Estimated. NA-Not Available. NM-Not Meaningful. NR-Not Ranked.

Office—2420 Sand Hill Rd., Menlo Park, CA 94025. **Tel**—(650) 324-6868. **Chrmn**—I. S. Shapiro. **Pres & CEO**—J. E. Heine. **EVP, CFO & Secy**—S. M. Neil. **Investor Contact**—Deborah Tuerk. **Dirs**—M. J. Cunniffe, D. D. Danforth, A. W. Hamill, J. E. Heine, H. Maxwell, J. L. Schultz, I. S. Shapiro. **Transfer Agent & Registrar**—First National Bank of Boston. **Incorporated**—in Delaware in 1993. **Empl**— 7,450. **S&P Analyst:** Stewart Scharf

STANDARD
&POOR'S
STOCK REPORTS

Sonic Corp.

NASDAQ Symbol **SONC**

In S&P SmallCap 600

09-OCT-99 **Industry:** Restaurants

Summary: Sonic operates and franchises over 1,900 drive-in restaurants that feature fast service and a limited menu of moderately priced, cooked-to-order items.

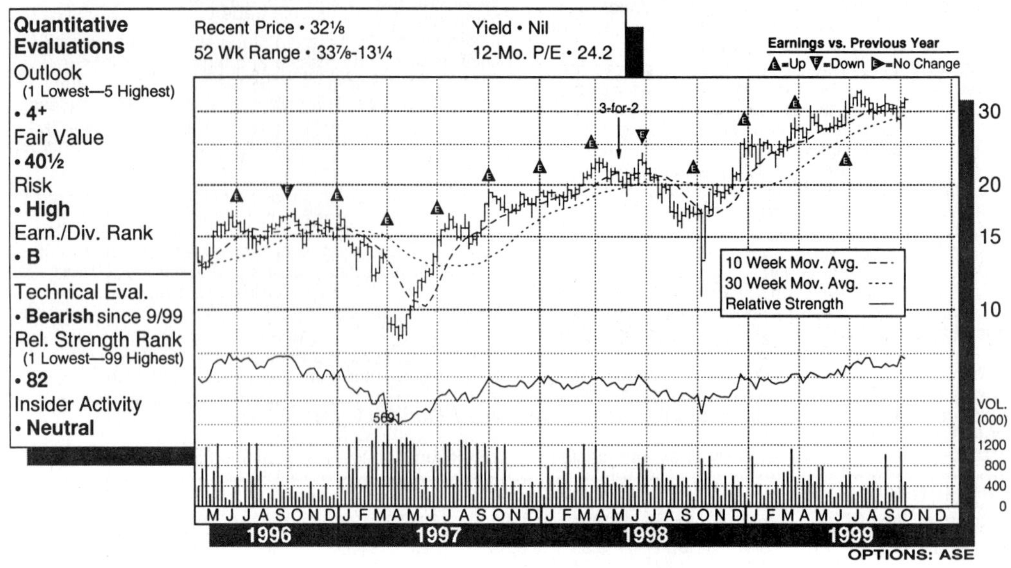

Business Profile - 06-JUL-99

Sonic continues its accelerated expansion program, under which the company has added more than 675 new drive-ins over the past five years. Results have benefited from the retrofitting of older units, with more than half of the Sonic chain remodeled under the Sonic 2000 retrofit initiative. Sonic has agreed with its franchisees on an early conversion of approximately 125 license agreements to new agreements with a higher royalty rate and a longer term. As a result, the company expects about $600,000 in additional royalties over the second half of FY 99, and about $1,000,000 during FY 00. As of June 1999, the company had purchased $8.2 million of its common stock under a $15 million share repurchase program.

Operational Review - 06-JUL-99

Revenues for the nine months ended May 31, 1999, advanced 19%, reflecting an 8.2% rise in system-wide same-store sales and increased new unit development by franchisees. Profitability was aided by successful product promotions, an expanded media program and the retrofitting of older restaurants. Income climbed 38%, to $18.1 million ($0.93 a share), from $13.1 million ($0.66, adjusted). Results for the FY 98 period exclude a special charge of $0.03 a share related to an accounting change.

Stock Performance - 08-OCT-99

In the past 30 trading days, SONC's shares have increased 7%, compared to a 0.91% fall in the S&P 500. Average trading volume for the past five days was 94,980 shares, compared with the 40-day moving average of 95,669 shares.

Key Stock Statistics

Dividend Rate/Share	Nil	Shareholders	2,600
Shs. outstg. (M)	18.7	Market cap. (B)	$0.601
Avg. daily vol. (M)	0.101	Inst. holdings	80%
Tang. Bk. Value/Share	5.90		
Beta	1.35		

Value of $10,000 invested 5 years ago: $ 28,070

Fiscal Year Ending Aug. 31

	1999	1998	1997	1996	1995	1994
Revenues (Million $)						
1Q	59.62	49.87	40.97	34.14	27.57	23.10
2Q	54.21	44.83	38.13	30.84	26.02	21.09
3Q	69.77	59.22	48.82	40.13	33.77	27.57
4Q	—	65.19	56.09	46.02	36.40	27.99
Yr.	—	219.1	184.0	151.2	123.8	99.7
Earnings Per Share ($)						
1Q	**0.31**	0.25	0.21	0.18	0.16	0.13
2Q	**0.22**	**0.18**	0.15	0.14	0.12	-0.04
3Q	**0.40**	**0.23**	0.26	0.23	0.19	0.15
4Q	—	**0.38**	0.32	0.01	0.23	0.18
Yr.	—	**1.03**	**0.95**	0.56	0.70	0.43

Next earnings report expected: mid October

Dividend Data

Sonic has not paid cash dividends on its common stock and intends to retain all earnings for working capital and general corporate purposes.

Sonic Corp.

Business Summary - 06-JUL-99

Sonic Corp. restaurants, located principally in the south central U.S., form the largest chain of quick-service, drive-in restaurants in the country. As of February 1999, there were 1,930 restaurants in the chain, with 1,624 owned by independent franchisees and 306 by the company.

The majority of revenues are derived from company-owned restaurants and royalty fees from franchisees. Average sales of company-owned units increased to $663,000 with 256 owned units in FY 98 from $649,000 and 231 owned units the year before. Franchised average unit sales increased to $775,000 with 1,424 franchised units in FY 98 from $720,000 and 1,336 franchised units in FY 97. The company also receives revenue from initial franchise fees, area development fees, the leasing of signs and real estates and from minority ownership positions in certain franchised restaurants.

Sonic aims to set itself apart from competitors by eliminating long waiting lines in the drive-through lane. At a typical Sonic restaurant, the customer drives into one of 24 to 36 covered parking spaces, orders through an intercom from a menu featuring hamburgers, hot dogs, french fries, onion rings and specialty beverages, and has the food delivered by a carhop within an average of four minutes. Since 1995, all new company-owned restaurants incorporate a drive-through window and patio seating area.

In FY 97, Sonic implemented a program to retrofit all Sonic drive-ins over the next few years. The retrofit program includes new signage, new menu and speaker housings, and considerable trade dress modifications to the exterior of each restaurant. The standard retrofit per restaurant costs an estimated $58,000 to $65,000. In addition, all new restaurants will include the new retrofit signage and trade dress style. During 1998, the company completed the retrofitting of 284 drive-ins and opened 150 new drive-ins with the retrofit image, meaning that almost one-quarter of the Sonic chain has the new retrofit look. In FY 99, Sonic plans on completing the retrofit of all company-owned restaurants, and working with the franchisees to retrofit approximately 250 additional restaurants.

The company's expansion strategy calls for the building out of existing core markets; further penetration of existing markets; and the acquisition of existing Sonic franchised restaurants. During FY 98, Sonic opened 120 franchise restaurants and 50 company-owned restaurants. In FY 99, the company plans on increasing marketing expenditures to build consumer awareness and brand loyalty and foster increased interest in franchising opportunities.

Per Share Data ($) (Year Ended Aug. 31)	1998	1997	1996	1995	1994	1993	1992	1991	1990	1989
Tangible Bk. Val.	5.86	4.99	4.33	2.69	3.06	2.63	2.05	1.66	-0.48	-1.74
Cash Flow	1.79	1.56	0.99	1.03	0.78	0.61	0.50	0.37	0.20	0.04
Earnings	1.03	0.95	0.56	0.70	0.43	0.48	0.39	0.26	0.08	-0.18
Dividends	Nil	Nil	Nil	Nil	Nil	Nil	Nil	Nil	Nil	Nil
Payout Ratio	Nil	Nil	Nil	Nil	Nil	Nil	Nil	Nil	Nil	Nil
Prices - High	$25\frac{7}{8}$	$20\frac{3}{8}$	$17\frac{5}{8}$	$16\frac{1}{4}$	$11\frac{3}{4}$	$13\frac{5}{8}$	$14\frac{5}{8}$	14	NA	NA
- Low	$10\frac{3}{4}$	$8\frac{3}{8}$	$9\frac{5}{8}$	$8\frac{3}{4}$	$7\frac{1}{2}$	$8\frac{1}{2}$	$9\frac{1}{2}$	$5\frac{1}{2}$	NA	NA
P/E Ratio - High	25	21	31	23	28	28	38	54	NA	NA
- Low	10	9	17	13	17	18	24	21	NA	NA
Income Statement Analysis (Million $)										
Revs.	219	184	151	124	100	83.8	66.7	53.9	45.9	33.9
Oper. Inc.	61.1	52.1	40.9	30.9	26.2	19.7	16.4	12.0	8.7	4.7
Depr.	14.8	12.3	8.9	5.9	6.3	2.4	2.1	1.7	1.3	1.6
Int. Exp.	3.4	2.2	1.2	1.8	1.1	0.8	0.7	2.1	3.7	3.7
Pretax Inc.	40.5	30.4	18.1	20.0	15.0	16.3	13.9	8.5	3.6	-2.6
Eff. Tax Rate	30%	37%	38%	38%	31%	31%	32%	30%	21%	NM
Net Inc.	20.5	19.1	11.2	12.5	7.6	8.6	6.8	3.7	0.9	-2.0
Balance Sheet & Other Fin. Data (Million $)										
Cash	2.6	7.3	7.7	4.0	6.0	5.4	9.0	10.3	2.5	2.8
Curr. Assets	16.5	18.7	16.2	12.7	14.1	13.6	14.2	14.7	6.5	6.4
Total Assets	233	185	147	105	77.0	63.5	50.3	41.9	31.6	31.6
Curr. Liab.	23.8	15.2	12.7	8.5	6.8	6.2	4.7	4.6	5.1	5.0
LT Debt	66.1	45.7	20.9	30.6	12.7	6.6	6.0	5.3	29.9	31.0
Common Eqty.	132	118	110	63.4	54.4	46.8	36.0	29.1	-5.2	-5.8
Total Cap.	202	165	131	93.9	69.4	56.2	44.3	36.2	26.2	25.9
Cap. Exp.	67.0	48.0	41.1	34.2	16.7	14.8	9.1	4.8	2.2	13.0
Cash Flow	35.3	31.4	20.1	18.4	13.9	11.0	8.9	5.4	2.2	-0.5
Curr. Ratio	0.7	1.2	1.3	1.5	2.1	2.2	3.0	3.2	1.3	1.3
% LT Debt of Cap.	32.7	27.7	16.0	32.6	18.3	11.7	13.5	14.7	114.1	119.8
% Net Inc.of Revs.	9.3	10.4	7.4	10.1	7.7	10.3	10.2	6.9	2.1	NM
% Ret. on Assets	9.8	11.5	8.9	13.7	10.9	15.1	14.8	8.0	NA	NM
% Ret. on Equity	16.4	16.7	12.9	21.2	15.1	20.8	20.9	NM	NA	NM

Data as orig reptd.; bef. results of disc opers/spec. items. Per share data adj. for stk. divs. Bold denotes diluted EPS (FASB 128)-prior periods restated. E-Estimated. NA-Not Available. NM-Not Meaningful. NR-Not Ranked.

Office—101 Park Ave., Oklahoma City, OK 73102. **Reincorporated**—in Delaware in 1991. **Tel**—(405) 280-7654. **Website**—http://www.sonicdrivein.com **Chrmn**—E. D. Werries. **Pres & CEO**—J. C. Hudson. **VP-Fin, Treas & CFO**—W. S. McLain. **EVP & COO**—K. L. Keymer. **VP & Secy**—R. L. Matlocks. **Dirs**—D. H. Clark, J. C. Hudson, K. L. Keymer, L. Lieberman, H. E. Rainbolt, F. E. Richardson III, R. M. Rosenberg, E. D. Werries. **Transfer Agent & Registrar**—Liberty Bank & Trust, Oklahoma City. **Empl**— 209. **S&P Analyst:** A. Bensinger

STANDARD & POOR'S
STOCK REPORTS

Southern Energy Homes

NASDAQ Symbol **SEHI**

In S&P SmallCap 600

09-OCT-99 **Industry:** Homebuilding

Summary: SEHI produces, sells and provides financing for manufactured homes primarily in the southeastern and south central U.S.

Quantitative Evaluations

Outlook (1 Lowest—5 Highest)
• **5+**

Fair Value
• **5⅞**

Risk
• **Average**

Earn./Div. Rank
• **NR**

Technical Eval.
• **Neutral** since 9/99

Rel. Strength Rank (1 Lowest—99 Highest)
• **13**

Insider Activity
• **NA**

Recent Price • 2⅞ | Yield • Nil
52 Wk Range • 7¼-2 | 12-Mo. P/E • 5.0

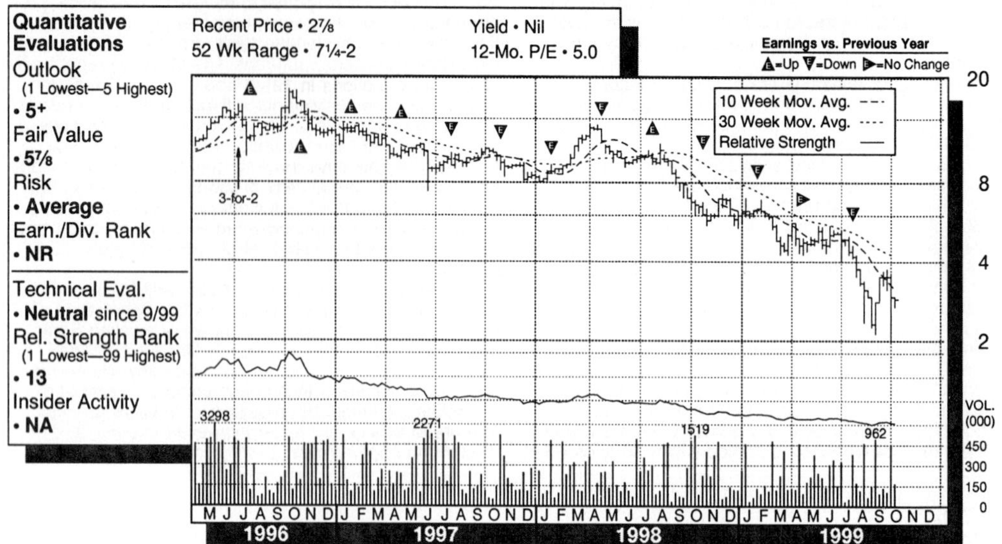

Business Profile - 12-JUL-99

The company reported in early July, that 1999 second quarter EPS could be as much as 50% lower than analyst's estimates of $0.28. Profit margins for SEHI's retail operations and manufacturing facilities have been hurt by competitive pressures due to unusually high retail inventory levels industrywide. The company said it will be taking steps to balance manufactured housing production with demand, and instituting cost controls throughout the organization. Late in 1998, directors extended the stock repurchase program for an additional 12 months, and increased the number of shares eligible for purchase to 4,000,000, from 3,000,000. SEHI repurchased 3.5 million shares through April 1, 1999, at an average cost of $8.37 a share.

Operational Review - 12-JUL-99

Net revenues in the first quarter of 1999, declined 2.0%, year to year, as reduced revenues from wholesale sales of manufactured housing and component supplies sales outweighed a small increase in revenue from retail manufactured housing sales. Gross margins widened on lower materials costs, but with significantly higher selling expenses for expansion of the retail operations, salary increases and staffing additions, operating income dropped 13%. After greater net interest expense, and taxes at 37.4%, versus 38.2%, net income was down 16%, to $2,060,000 ($0.17 a share, on 13% fewer shares), from $2,453,000 ($0.17).

Stock Performance - 08-OCT-99

In the past 30 trading days, SEHI's shares have increased 24%, compared to a 0.91% fall in the S&P 500. Average trading volume for the past five days was 32,440 shares, compared with the 40-day moving average of 54,874 shares.

Key Stock Statistics

Dividend Rate/Share	Nil	Shareholders	96
Shs. outstg. (M)	12.1	Market cap. (B)	$0.035
Avg. daily vol. (M)	0.044	Inst. holdings	52%
Tang. Bk. Value/Share	4.89		
Beta	1.17		

Value of $10,000 invested 5 years ago: $ 2,855

Fiscal Year Ending Dec. 31

	1999	1998	1997	1996	1995	1994
Revenues (Million $)						
1Q	73.55	76.11	80.12	71.11	55.57	40.98
2Q	69.75	74.15	76.88	83.92	61.22	44.99
3Q	—	82.12	76.33	77.41	58.46	47.97
4Q	—	75.62	65.21	74.40	66.02	54.82
Yr.	—	307.0	298.5	306.8	241.3	188.8
Earnings Per Share ($)						
1Q	**0.17**	**0.17**	**0.24**	**0.22**	0.16	0.13
2Q	**0.14**	**0.28**	**0.12**	**0.29**	0.23	0.17
3Q	—	**0.18**	**0.24**	**0.26**	0.21	0.18
4Q	—	**0.09**	**0.15**	**0.23**	0.19	0.16
Yr.	—	**0.72**	**0.75**	**1.00**	**0.78**	**0.72**

Next earnings report expected: late October

Dividend Data

No cash dividends have been paid.

A Division of The McGraw-Hill Companies

Southern Energy Homes, Inc.

Business Summary - 12-JUL-99

If images of unsightly trailer parks and rundown mobile homes come to mind when you hear the term manufactured home, think again. Makers of manufactured (factory-built) homes, such as Southern Energy Homes, Inc. (SEHI), have upgraded their products for an expanding market. Today, the purchase of manufactured homes is much more widespread, and many of the homes are hard to distinguish from site-built models. SEHI produces manufactured homes that are sold in 25 states, mainly in the southeastern and south central U.S., by 399 independent dealers at 565 independent dealer locations and 33 company-owned retail centers.

Company homes are designed as primary residences ready for immediate occupancy, and are customized at its nine factories to buyer specifications. SEHI designs floor plans and provides features to match homebuyer preferences, offering homes in both single and in multi-sections, which provide a larger living space. The homes, ranging in size from 640 sq. ft. to 2,417 sq. ft., sell at prices (excluding land) of $15,900 to $108,000. This provides an affordable alternative for many, including the growing number of retirees and "empty nesters" who are purchasing homes.

Homes are constructed using assembly line techniques, with seven facilities located in Alabama and one each in Texas and North Carolina. SEHI arranges, at dealer expense, for the transportation of finished homes to dealers, using its own trucking subsidiary and independent trucking companies. Dealers or other independent installers are responsible for placing the home on site, making utility hookups and providing and installing certain trim items. In 1998, SEHI sold 8,891 homes and 13,621 floor sections, down from 9,165 homes and 14,288 floor sections in 1997.

Four component divisions supply interior wall panels; windows, doors and countertops; wood moulding and trim finishing; and kitchen and dining furniture to SEHI's manufactured housing divisions and third parties.

In a quest for further vertical integration, in 1996, the company entered the retail sector of the manufactured home industry by acquiring a group of retail companies in Alabama and Mississippi. In February 1997, it formed a joint venture with 21st Century Mortgage Corp., WENCO 21, which offers, through 21st Century, consumer financing for the company's manufactured homes and other homes sold through its retail centers and independent dealers. Later in 1997, SEHI expanded the operations further with the acquisition of seven retail locations in South Carolina. During 1998, the company added 15 retail centers through acquisitions. By year-end 1998, retail operations were contributing 25% of total company sales.

Per Share Data ($) (Year Ended Dec. 31)	1998	1997	1996	1995	1994	1993	1992	1991	1990	1989
Tangible Bk. Val.	4.58	4.50	4.12	1.18	2.19	1.81	0.90	NA	NA	NA
Cash Flow	0.96	0.96	1.09	1.36	0.71	0.49	0.41	NA	NA	NA
Earnings	0.72	0.75	1.01	0.79	0.62	0.41	0.27	NA	NA	NA
Dividends	Nil	Nil	Nil	Nil	Nil	Nil	Nil	NA	NA	NA
Payout Ratio	Nil	Nil	Nil	Nil	Nil	Nil	Nil	NA	NA	NA
Prices - High	13³/₈	13³/₈	18¹/₈	12¹/₂	10¹/₈	11³/₈	NA	NA	NA	NA
- Low	5³/₈	7³/₈	9	5⁵/₈	5¹/₂	6⁷/₈	NA	NA	NA	NA
P/E Ratio - High	19	18	18	16	16	20	NA	NA	NA	NA
- Low	7	10	9	7	9	12	NA	NA	NA	NA
Income Statement Analysis (Million $)										
Revs.	307	299	307	241	189	144	83.0	NA	NA	NA
Oper. Inc.	22.4	24.7	26.0	19.1	15.1	12.2	7.7	NA	NA	NA
Depr.	3.3	3.1	1.2	1.7	1.3	1.1	1.6	NA	NA	NA
Int. Exp.	2.4	1.4	0.1	0.1	0.2	0.7	1.5	NA	NA	NA
Pretax Inc.	15.9	18.5	24.8	18.1	14.0	8.8	4.7	NA	NA	NA
Eff. Tax Rate	38%	38%	39%	38%	37%	39%	37%	NA	NA	NA
Net Inc.	9.8	11.4	15.2	11.2	8.8	5.4	2.9	NA	NA	NA
Balance Sheet & Other Fin. Data (Million $)										
Cash	4.3	17.7	5.3	18.8	11.0	12.8	NA	NA	NA	NA
Curr. Assets	67.1	71.7	53.0	53.0	36.7	32.8	NA	NA	NA	NA
Total Assets	123	123	113	75.9	54.3	43.3	26.7	NA	NA	NA
Curr. Liab.	45.8	38.8	35.3	18.7	15.2	12.1	NA	NA	NA	NA
LT Debt	3.6	4.7	Nil	0.0	0.6	1.5	12.6	NA	NA	NA
Common Eqty.	73.4	79.8	77.4	57.2	38.6	29.7	0.6	NA	NA	NA
Total Cap.	77.0	84.4	77.4	57.2	39.2	31.2	13.2	NA	NA	NA
Cap. Exp.	3.2	6.1	5.5	5.2	3.1	4.8	0.8	NA	NA	NA
Cash Flow	13.1	14.5	16.4	12.9	10.1	6.4	4.5	NA	NA	NA
Curr. Ratio	1.5	1.8	1.5	2.8	2.4	2.7	NA	NA	NA	NA
% LT Debt of Cap.	4.6	5.6	Nil	Nil	1.5	4.8	5.4	NA	NA	NA
% Net Inc.of Revs.	3.2	3.8	5.0	4.7	4.7	3.7	3.5	NA	NA	NA
% Ret. on Assets	8.0	9.6	16.2	17.3	18.1	15.3	12.3	NA	NA	NA
% Ret. on Equity	12.8	14.5	22.7	23.5	25.8	35.3	NM	NA	NA	NA

Data as orig reptd.; bef. results of disc opers/spec. items. Per share data adj. for stk. divs. Bold denotes diluted EPS (FASB 128)-prior periods restated. E-Estimated. NA-Not Available. NM-Not Meaningful. NR-Not Ranked.

Office—Highway 41 North, P. O. Box 390, Addison, AL 35540. **Tel**—(256) 747-8589. **Chrmn & CEO**—W. L. Batchelor. **Pres**—K. Holdbrooks. **EVP, CFO, Treas & Secy**—K. W. Brown. **Dirs**—W. L. Batchelor, K. W. Brown, P. J. Evanson, K. O. Holdbrooks, J. J. Incandela, J. O. Lee, J. R. Long. **Transfer Agent & Registrar**—State Street Bank & Trust Co., Quincy, MA. **Incorporated**—in Delaware in 1993. **Empl**— 2,346. **S&P Analyst:** S.A.H.

STANDARD
&POOR'S
STOCK REPORTS

Southwest Gas

NYSE Symbol **SWX**

In S&P SmallCap 600

09-OCT-99 **Industry:** Natural Gas

Summary: SWX, a natural gas distributor, agreed in December 1998 to be acquired by ONEOK, Inc.

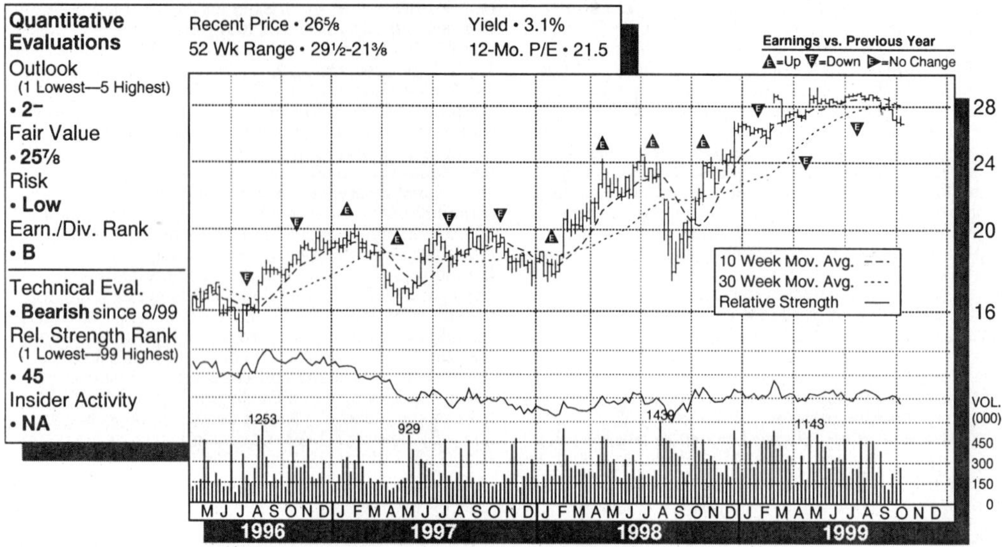

Business Profile - 15-JUL-99

In December 1998, Southwest Gas agreed to be acquired by ONEOK, Inc., an intrastate natural gas transmission, marketing and production company, for $28.50 a share and the assumption of debt. The merger will create the largest stand-alone gas distribution company in the U.S. serving 2.6 million customers in five states. Completion of the transaction, which is subject to customary conditions, including shareholder and regulatory approval, is anticipated for the fall of 1999. In June 1999, ONEOK and SWX reached agreement with the Arizona Corporation Commission Staff and the Residential Utility Consumers Office on terms and conditions governing the proposed combination of the two natural gas utilities. The ONEOK-Southwest Gas merger already has been unanimously approved by the Public Utilities Commission of Nevada.

Operational Review - 15-JUL-99

Operating revenues for the first quarter of 1999 advanced rose 5.3%, year to year. However, higher operating expenses, incurred as a result of the expansion and upgrading of the gas system to accommodate customer growth, and the absence of colder-than-normal temperatures led to a drop in operating profit of 17%. After 8.7% lower net interest deductions, pretax income was down 20%. Following taxes at 39.6%, versus 38.5%, net income decreased 21%, to $28.3 million ($0.92 a share, on 11% more shares outstanding), from $36.0 million ($1.30).

Stock Performance - 08-OCT-99

In the past 30 trading days, SWX's shares have declined 6%, compared to a 0.91% fall in the S&P 500. Average trading volume for the past five days was 52,520 shares, compared with the 40-day moving average of 52,341 shares.

Key Stock Statistics

Dividend Rate/Share	0.82	Shareholders	25,723
Shs. outstg. (M)	30.7	Market cap. (B)	$0.820
Avg. daily vol. (M)	0.037	Inst. holdings	47%
Tang. Bk. Value/Share	16.13		
Beta	0.83		

Value of $10,000 invested 5 years ago: $ 21,327

Fiscal Year Ending Dec. 31

	1999	1998	1997	1996	1995	1994
Revenues (Million $)						
1Q	308.0	292.6	235.2	188.3	238.9	239.0
2Q	200.3	192.9	136.9	123.6	158.5	140.2
3Q	—	162.5	128.7	125.3	127.4	124.3
4Q	—	269.3	231.1	206.8	146.4	224.5
Yr.	—	917.3	732.0	644.1	563.5	728.2
Earnings Per Share ($)						
1Q	**0.92**	**1.30**	**0.80**	0.60	0.68	1.07
2Q	**-0.12**	**-0.09**	**-0.47**	-0.46	-0.41	-0.47
3Q	—	**-0.38**	**-0.58**	-0.55	-0.54	-0.54
4Q	—	**0.82**	**0.85**	0.69	0.47	1.15
Yr.	—	**1.65**	**0.61**	**0.25**	**0.10**	**1.09**

Next earnings report expected: late October

Dividend Data (Dividends have been paid since 1956.)

Amount ($)	Date Decl.	Ex-Div. Date	Stock of Record	Payment Date
0.205	Jan. 19	Feb. 11	Feb. 16	Mar. 01 '99
0.205	Mar. 02	May. 13	May. 17	Jun. 01 '99
0.205	Jul. 21	Aug. 12	Aug. 16	Sep. 01 '99
0.205	Sep. 20	Nov. 12	Nov. 16	Dec. 01 '99

A Division of The McGraw-Hill Companies

Southwest Gas Corporation

Business Summary - 15-JUL-99

Incorporated in California in 1931, Southwest Gas is now based in Las Vegas, Nevada. The company purchases, transports, and distributes natural gas to, as of year-end 1998, 1,209,000 residential, commercial, and industrial customers in geographically diverse portions of Arizona, Nevada, and California. There were 58,000 customers added to the system during 1998. In December 1998, the company agreed to be acquired by ONEOK, Inc. (NYSE: OKE) for $28.50 a share and the assumption of debt.

Transportation of customer-secured gas to end-users on the Southwest system accounted for 48% of total system throughput in 1998. Although the volumes were significant, these customers provide a much smaller proportionate share of operating margin. In 1998, customers who utilized this service transported 100 million dekatherms.

Southwest Gas is subject to regulation by the Arizona Corporation Commission (ACC), the Public Utilities Commission of Nevada (PUCN), and the California Public Utilities Commission (CPUC). These commissions regulate public utility rates, practices, facilities, and service territories in their respective states. The CPUC also regulates the issuance of all securities by the company, with the exception of short-term borrowings. Certain accounting practices, transmission facilities, and rates are subject to regulation by the FederalEnergy Regulatory Commission (FERC).

Demand for natural gas is seasonal, and adverse weather conditions can affect operating results. The company believes that comparisons of earnings for interim periods do not reliably reflect overall trends and changes in its operations. In addition, earnings can be significantly affected by the timing of general rate relief. Rates charged to customers vary according to customer class and are set at levels allowing for the recovery of all incurred costs, including a return on rate base sufficient to pay interest on debt, preferred securities distributions, and a reasonable return on common equity.

Temperature can have a major impact on demand for natural gas. On cold days, use of gas by residential and commercial customers may be as much as eight times greater than on warm days because of increased use of gas for space heating. To fully satisfy this increased high-priority demand, gas is withdrawn from storage or peaking supplies are purchased from suppliers.

The Northern Pipeline Construction Co. subsidiary is a full-service underground piping contractor that provides utility companies with trenching and installation, replacement, and maintenance services for energy distribution systems. Northern contracts primarily with LDCs (local distribution companies) to install, repair, and maintain energy distribution systems from the town border station to the end-user meter. The primary focus of business operations is main and service replacement as well as new business installations. Construction work varies from relatively small projects to the piping of entir e communities. Construction activity is seasonal.

Per Share Data ($) (Year Ended Dec. 31)	**1998**	**1997**	**1996**	**1995**	**1994**	**1993**	**1992**	**1991**	**1990**	**1989**
Tangible Bk. Val.	15.67	14.09	14.60	14.55	12.85	12.87	12.14	11.83	12.89	12.14
Cash Flow	4.73	3.74	3.10	2.80	4.81	3.63	3.75	1.95	4.44	4.77
Earnings	1.65	0.61	0.25	0.10	1.22	0.56	0.81	-0.76	1.81	2.15
Dividends	0.82	0.82	0.82	0.82	0.60	0.74	0.70	1.05	1.40	1.37
Payout Ratio	50%	134%	NM	NM	50%	132%	87%	NM	77%	64%
Prices - High	26 7/8	20 1/4	19 7/8	18 3/8	19 3/8	18 1/2	15 3/8	17 1/2	18 1/2	20 3/8
- Low	17 1/4	16 1/8	14 7/8	13 5/8	13 3/4	13 3/8	10 3/8	9	11 3/4	16 5/8
P/E Ratio - High	16	33	79	NM	16	33	19	NM	10	9
- Low	10	26	59	NM	11	24	13	NM	6	8
Income Statement Analysis (Million $)										
Revs.	917	732	644	564	728	690	720	800	867	848
Oper. Inc.	154	102	145	121	168	151	249	247	367	377
Depr.	88.8	84.7	73.7	62.5	65.1	63.6	60.7	55.3	51.6	49.8
Int. Exp.	63.4	64.8	56.7	54.6	58.0	50.1	157	207	256	259
Pretax Inc.	89.4	26.8	10.4	3.5	44.0	23.6	32.1	-13.5	62.8	71.2
Eff. Tax Rate	41%	18%	37%	24%	40%	48%	45%	NM	41%	40%
Net Inc.	47.5	16.5	6.6	2.6	26.3	12.4	17.7	-14.2	37.2	42.7
Balance Sheet & Other Fin. Data (Million $)										
Cash	18.5	17.6	8.3	11.2	166	136	133	113	70.0	41.0
Curr. Assets	247	289	160	317	NA	NA	NA	NA	NA	NA
Total Assets	1,831	1,769	1,560	1,533	3,090	2,944	3,342	3,463	3,764	3,706
Curr. Liab.	251	324	261	330	NA	NA	NA	NA	NA	NA
LT Debt	873	779	665	608	786	648	614	598	817	830
Common Eqty.	476	386	380	356	339	340	329	327	353	334
Total Cap.	1,529	1,393	1,257	1,163	1,262	1,147	1,062	1,058	1,313	1,302
Cap. Exp.	195	170	219	166	145	115	105	86.0	105	114
Cash Flow	136	101	80.3	64.8	90.9	75.2	77.3	39.8	87.2	90.7
Curr. Ratio	1.0	0.9	0.6	1.0	NA	NA	NA	NA	NA	NA
% LT Debt of Cap.	57.1	55.9	52.9	52.3	62.2	56.5	57.8	56.5	62.2	63.8
% Net Inc.of Revs.	5.2	2.2	1.0	0.5	3.6	1.8	2.5	NM	4.3	5.0
% Ret. on Assets	2.6	1.0	0.4	0.2	0.9	0.4	0.5	NM	1.0	1.1
% Ret. on Equity	11.0	4.3	1.8	0.7	7.5	3.5	5.1	NM	10.2	12.5

Data as orig. reptd.; bef. results of disc. opers. and/or spec. items. Per share data adj. for stk. divs. as of ex-div. date. Bold denotes diluted EPS (FASB 128). E-Estimated. NA-Not Available. NM-Not Meaningful. NR-Not Ranked.

Office—5241 Spring Mountain Rd., P.O. Box 98510, Las Vegas, NV 89193-8510. **Tel**—(702) 876-7237. **Website**—http://www.swgas.com **Chrmn**—T. Y. Hartley. **Pres & CEO**—M. O. Maffie. **SVP, CFO & Secy**—G. C. Biehl. **Investor Contact**—Laura Hobbs. **Dirs**—G. C. Biehl, M. J. Cortez, L. T. Dyer, T. Y. Hartley, M. B. Jager, L. R. Judd, J. J. Kropid, M. O. Maffie, C. M. Sparks, R. S. Sundt, T. L. Wright. **Transfer Agent & Registrar**—Co. itself. **Incorporated**—in California in 1931. **Empl**— 3,696. **S&P Analyst:** N.J.D.

STANDARD
&POOR'S
STOCK REPORTS

Southwestern Energy

NYSE Symbol **SWN**

In S&P SmallCap 600

09-OCT-99 **Industry:** Natural Gas

Summary: SWN is an integrated natural gas company engaged in gas and oil exploration and production; and natural gas gathering, transmission, and marketing, and distribution.

Quantitative Evaluations

Outlook (1 Lowest—5 Highest) • **3**

Fair Value • **10⅜**

Risk • **Low**

Earn./Div. Rank • **B+**

Technical Eval. • **Bearish** since 9/99

Rel. Strength Rank (1 Lowest—99 Highest) • **74**

Insider Activity • **Neutral**

Recent Price • 9
52 Wk Range • 11-5⅛
Yield • 2.6%
12-Mo. P/E • 22.7

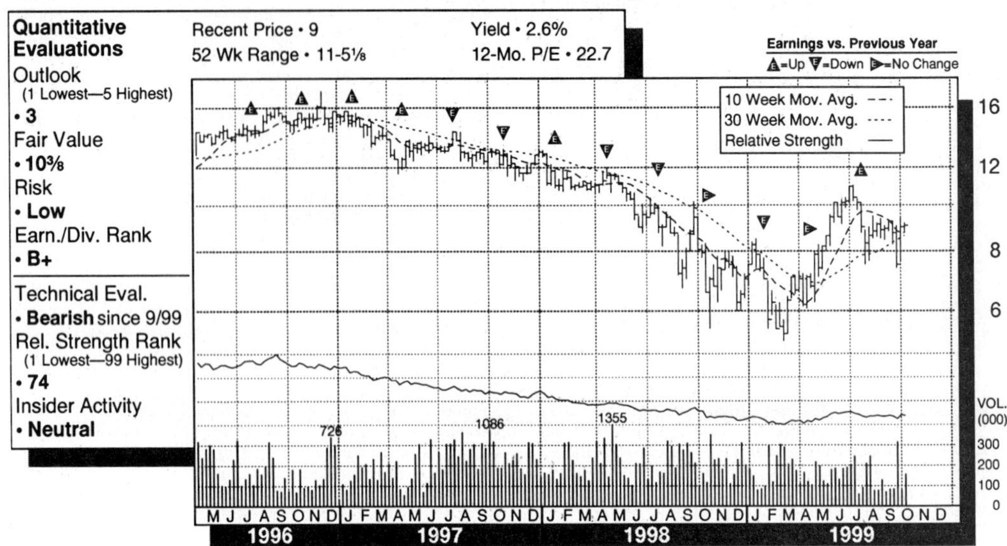

Business Profile - 18-AUG-99

Southwestern Energy said that its drilling program added an estimated 16.6 Bcf equivalent of proved oil and gas reserves during the first half of 1999, primarily through exploration and exploitation drilling activities in the Arkoma and Permian Basins. Gas and oil production for the six months ended June 30, 1999, was 16.6 Bcf equivalent, down from 19.0 Bcf equivalent for the same period of 1998. The production declines over the past six months are the result of the combined effects of lower production from the company's non-operated properties caused primarily by the industry slowdown that began last year, reduced demand from the company's utility systems due to warm weather, and greater declines than expected from some of the company's Gulf Coast properties.

Operational Review - 18-AUG-99

Total revenues for the first half of 1999 declined 3.6%, year to year, primarily reflecting a 20% drop in exploration and production revenues resulting from lower production volumes and lower gas prices. While costs and expenses were well controlled, comparisons primarily benefitted from the absence of a $66.4 million charge for the write-down of oil and gas properties. With lower other expenses and after taxes at 39.0%, versus a tax benefit of $21.1 million, net income of $7,428,000 ($0.30 a share), contrasted with a net loss of $32,986,000 ($1.33).

Stock Performance - 08-OCT-99

In the past 30 trading days, SWN's shares have increased 2%, compared to a 0.91% fall in the S&P 500. Average trading volume for the past five days was 30,920 shares, compared with the 40-day moving average of 29,215 shares.

Key Stock Statistics

Dividend Rate/Share	0.24	Shareholders	2,333
Shs. outstg. (M)	24.9	Market cap. (B)	$0.226
Avg. daily vol. (M)	0.039	Inst. holdings	61%
Tang. Bk. Value/Share	7.64		
Beta	0.96		

Value of $10,000 invested 5 years ago: $ 5,713

Fiscal Year Ending Dec. 31

	1999	1998	1997	1996	1995	1994
Revenues (Million $)						
1Q	78.20	82.96	88.92	63.86	51.75	65.40
2Q	56.04	56.33	51.24	34.30	30.64	34.60
3Q	—	53.55	48.64	30.25	25.45	27.81
4Q	—	73.46	87.38	60.81	45.26	42.34
Yr.	—	266.3	276.2	189.2	153.1	170.2
Earnings Per Share ($)						
1Q	**0.37**	**0.37**	**0.50**	**0.38**	0.28	0.51
2Q	**-0.07**	**-1.70**	Nil	**0.11**	0.02	0.18
3Q	—	**-0.05**	**-0.05**	**0.01**	-0.04	0.09
4Q	—	**0.15**	**0.31**	**0.28**	0.20	0.20
Yr.	—	**-1.23**	**0.76**	**0.78**	**0.46**	0.98

Next earnings report expected: mid November

Dividend Data (Dividends have been paid since 1939.)

Amount ($)	Date Decl.	Ex-Div. Date	Stock of Record	Payment Date
0.060	Jan. 06	Jan. 15	Jan. 20	Feb. 05 '99
0.060	Apr. 07	Apr. 16	Apr. 20	May. 05 '99
0.060	Jul. 07	Jul. 16	Jul. 20	Aug. 05 '99
0.060	Oct. 07	Oct. 18	Oct. 20	Nov. 05 '99

A Division of The McGraw-Hill Companies

Southwestern Energy Company

Business Summary - 18-AUG-99

Southwestern Energy Company's business strategy is to provide long-term growth through focused exploration and production of oil and natural gas, while creating additional value through the company's natural gas distribution, marketing and transportation activities. Southwestern Energy seeks to maximize cash flow and earnings and provide consistent growth in oil and gas production and reserves through the discovery, production and marketing of high margin reserves from a balanced portfolio of drilling opportunities. This portfolio includes low risk development drilling in the Arkoma Basin, moderate risk exploration and exploitation in the Permian Basin in New Mexico, and high potential exploration opportunities in south Louisiana and the Gulf Coast.

In addition, the company strives to operate its utility systems safely and efficiently and to position them to earn their full, authorized return. The company is also committed to enhancing shareholder value by creating and capturing additional value beyond the wellhead through its marketing and transportation activities.

Southwestern Energy is an integrated energy company primarily focused on natural gas. The company is involved in the following business segments: 1. Exploration and Production: natural gas and oil exploration, development and production, with operations principally located in Arkansas, Oklahoma, Texas, New Mexico, south Louisiana, and the Gulf Coast. 2. Natural Gas Distribution: gathering, distribution and transmission of natural gas to approximately 179,000 customers in northern Arkansas and parts of Missouri. 3. Marketing and Transportation: providing marketing and transportation services in the company's core areas of operation; owns a 25% interest in the NOARK Pipeline System, Limited partnership.

At December 31, 1998, the company had proved oil and gas reserves of 344.8 billion cubic feet (Bcf) equivalent, including proved natural gas reserves of 303.7 Bcf and proved oil reserves of 6,850 thousand barrels (MBbls). All of these reserves are located entirely within the United States.

Revenues of the exploration and production subsidiaries are predominately generated from production of natural gas. Sales of gas production accounted for 89% of total operating revenues for this segment in 1998.

During 1998, Southwestern brought in new senior operating management and replaced over 50% of its professional technical staff to refocus its exploration and production segment. In addition in 1998, the company closed its Oklahoma City office and moved these operations to its Houston office in an effort to increase future profitability. Another major part of this segment's restructuring was a reorganization into asset management teams.

Per Share Data ($) (Year Ended Dec. 31)	1998	1997	1996	1995	1994	1993	1992	1991	1990	1989
Tangible Bk. Val.	7.45	8.92	8.41	7.87	7.92	7.18	5.97	5.30	4.70	4.15
Cash Flow	0.66	2.70	2.49	1.89	2.36	2.26	1.80	1.49	1.16	1.21
Earnings	-1.23	0.76	0.78	0.46	0.98	1.05	0.87	0.78	0.57	0.56
Dividends	0.24	0.24	0.24	0.24	0.24	0.22	0.20	0.19	0.19	0.19
Payout Ratio	NM	32%	31%	52%	24%	21%	23%	24%	33%	33%
Prices - High	$12\frac{7}{8}$	$15\frac{3}{4}$	$17\frac{3}{8}$	$15\frac{1}{2}$	$18\frac{7}{8}$	$21\frac{1}{2}$	14	$12\frac{3}{4}$	$12\frac{1}{8}$	$11\frac{1}{8}$
- Low	$5\frac{1}{2}$	$11\frac{1}{4}$	$10\frac{5}{8}$	$11\frac{3}{4}$	14	$12\frac{1}{8}$	$9\frac{1}{4}$	$9\frac{1}{8}$	$9\frac{1}{2}$	$5\frac{3}{4}$
P/E Ratio - High	NM	21	22	34	19	21	16	16	21	20
- Low	NM	15	14	26	14	12	11	12	16	10
Income Statement Analysis (Million $)										
Revs.	266	276	189	153	170	175	144	136	117	126
Oper. Inc.	-29.0	51.9	48.0	31.2	52.1	57.6	46.0	42.1	33.6	32.7
Depr.	46.9	48.2	42.4	36.0	35.5	30.9	23.9	18.2	14.8	16.3
Int. Exp.	21.1	20.9	17.2	13.6	10.5	10.6	11.5	11.2	11.9	12.3
Pretax Inc.	-50.1	30.5	30.9	18.8	40.9	46.9	35.6	32.2	23.1	22.2
Eff. Tax Rate	NM	39%	38%	39%	39%	42%	37%	38%	37%	37%
Net Inc.	-30.6	18.7	19.2	11.5	25.1	27.1	22.3	20.1	14.5	14.0
Balance Sheet & Other Fin. Data (Million $)										
Cash	1.6	4.6	2.3	1.5	1.1	0.8	1.1	2.2	1.2	1.1
Curr. Assets	72.3	88.0	72.9	63.9	48.0	46.3	45.1	41.5	34.7	34.6
Total Assets	648	711	660	569	485	445	427	392	366	347
Curr. Liab.	54.8	49.0	41.8	45.4	39.0	38.7	31.3	31.4	32.7	32.5
LT Debt	282	296	275	208	136	124	143	131	123	126
Common Eqty.	186	222	208	195	203	185	153	136	121	103
Total Cap.	589	657	612	520	442	405	394	359	332	313
Cap. Exp.	64.4	89.0	125	102	76.3	59.2	49.3	38.5	36.9	39.0
Cash Flow	16.3	66.9	61.6	47.5	60.7	58.0	46.1	38.3	29.3	30.3
Curr. Ratio	1.3	1.8	1.7	1.4	1.2	1.2	1.4	1.3	1.1	1.1
% LT Debt of Cap.	47.8	45.1	44.9	40.0	30.8	30.6	36.3	36.5	36.9	40.1
% Net Inc.of Revs.	NM	6.8	10.1	7.5	14.8	15.5	15.5	14.7	12.4	11.1
% Ret. on Assets	NM	2.7	3.1	2.2	3.4	6.2	5.4	5.3	4.0	4.2
% Ret. on Equity	NM	8.7	9.5	5.8	13.0	16.0	15.4	15.6	12.8	14.2

Data as orig reptd.; bef. results of disc opers/spec. items. Per share data adj. for stk. divs. Bold denotes diluted EPS (FASB 128)-prior periods restated. 1998 cash flow refl. $40.5 million noncash writedown from oil & gas prop. E-Estimated. NA-Not Available. NM-Not Meaningful. NR-Not Ranked.

Office—1083 Sain St., P.O.Box 1408, Fayetteville, AR 72702-1408. **Tel**—(501) 521-1141. **Website**—http://www.swn.com **Chrmn**—C. E. Scharlau. **Pres, CEO & COO**—H. M. Korell. **SVP-Fin & CFO**—G. D. Kerley. **Dirs**—L. E. Epley, J. P. Hammerschmidt, R. L. Howard, H. M. Korell. K. R. Mourton, C. E. Scharlau. **Transfer Agent & Registrar**—First Chicago Trust Co. of New York, NYC. **Incorporated**—in Arkansas in 1929. **Empl**—706. **S&P Analyst:** M.I.

STANDARD
&POOR'S
STOCK REPORTS

Spacelabs Medical

NASDAQ Symbol **SLMD**

In S&P SmallCap 600

09-OCT-99 **Industry:** Health Care (Medical Products & Supplies)

Summary: This company is a leading manufacturer of clinical information systems, patient monitoring equipment and diagnostic monitoring products.

Quantitative Evaluations

Outlook
(1 Lowest—5 Highest)
• **4**

Fair Value
• **19¾**

Risk
• **Low**

Earn./Div. Rank
• **C**

Technical Eval.
• **Bearish** since 9/99

Rel. Strength Rank
(1 Lowest—99 Highest)
• **35**

Insider Activity
• **Favorable**

Recent Price • 14⅝
52 Wk Range • 23⅛-14
Yield • Nil
12-Mo. P/E • 16.8

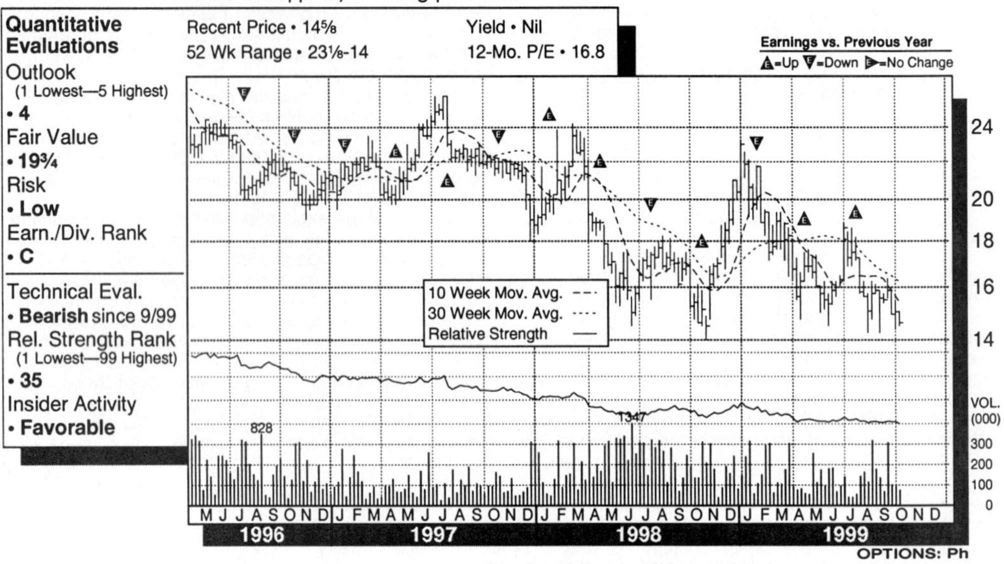

OPTIONS: Ph

Business Profile - 04-JUN-99

SLMD reported strong 1999 first quarter results in its U.S. monitoring and hospital cardiology businesses. In January 1999, the company introduced the Ultraview Web Source - Remote Connectivity System, an Internet service that allows clinicians to view comprehensive patient information through the World Wide Web. Also in January, SLMD introduced a new generation product line, the Ultraview Care Network, a premium mid-range color patient monitoring platform with expanded networking capability. The design also allows software enhancements to be incorporated more quickly. In March 1999, the company announced that its Ultraview 1030 and 1050 patient monitors were approved for use onboard all U.S. Air Force aircraft for testing during all phases of a flight.

Operational Review - 04-JUN-99

Net revenues in the three months ended March 31, 1999, increased 5.7%, year to year, as a 12% rise in U.S. revenue was partly offset by a 5.8% decline in international revenue. Gross margins widened, on a more favorable product mix. SG&A expenses rose 2.4%, but R&D expenses were down 13%, resulting in operating income, in contrast to an operating loss. After taxes at 35.6%, versus tax credits of $503,000, net income of $1,782,000 ($0.19 a share) contrasted with a net loss of $871,000 ($0.09). At March 31, 1999, cash and short term investments totaled $6.4 million, up from $1.5 million at March 31, 1998.

Stock Performance - 08-OCT-99

In the past 30 trading days, SLMD's shares have declined 8%, compared to a 0.91% fall in the S&P 500. Average trading volume for the past five days was 14,720 shares, compared with the 40-day moving average of 38,877 shares.

Key Stock Statistics

Dividend Rate/Share	Nil	Shareholders	6,621
Shs. outstg. (M)	9.4	Market cap. (B)	$0.138
Avg. daily vol. (M)	0.032	Inst. holdings	73%
Tang. Bk. Value/Share	17.37		
Beta	0.64		

Value of $10,000 invested 5 years ago: $ 6,030

Fiscal Year Ending Dec. 31

	1999	1998	1997	1996	1995	1994
Revenues (Million $)						
1Q	70.31	66.51	63.02	63.30	63.14	61.24
2Q	73.84	66.02	62.14	62.37	64.02	63.26
3Q	—	67.48	65.30	60.05	63.23	60.03
4Q	—	74.24	74.90	62.23	62.52	62.67
Yr.	—	274.2	265.3	247.9	252.9	247.2
Earnings Per Share ($)						
1Q	**0.19**	**-0.09**	**-0.34**	**-0.43**	0.41	0.26
2Q	**0.27**	**-0.03**	**0.31**	**0.17**	0.43	0.43
3Q	—	**0.18**	**-2.41**	**0.27**	0.45	0.48
4Q	—	**0.23**	**0.30**	0.25	0.44	0.51
Yr.	—	**0.29**	**-2.13**	**0.25**	**1.73**	**1.68**

Next earnings report expected: late October

Dividend Data

No cash dividends have been paid on the common shares, and no payments are expected in the foreseeable future.

A Division of The McGraw-Hill Companies

Spacelabs Medical, Inc.

Business Summary - 04-JUN-99

Spacelabs Medical develops, makes, markets and services patient monitoring and clinical information systems products for use in critical and acute care worldwide. The company's three part strategy is to continue its transition into the emerging clinical information systems (CIS) market; to enhance its position in the U.S. U.S. healthcare market through the expansion of its medical device product line; and to expand its presence in international markets (30% of 1998 sales, down from 34% in 1997).

SLMD intends to capitalize on its large installed base of patient monitoring and diagnostic cardiology systems to make a transition into the CIS market with its suite of point-of-care products. The second part of this strategy is to broaden its position through acquisitions and joint ventures. In March 1997, it acquired Advanced Medical Systems (AMS), added fetal monitoring products and an obstetrical clinical information system (CIS) to its perinatal product line. The acquisition of Ameritech Knowledge Data Inc. added both a clinical data repository and a master patient index system. The acquisition of Burdick Inc., added an electrocardiographic management system.

The company is seeking to maintain technological leadership in critical care monitoring and to expand the company's presence in the medical device marketplace. During 1998, SLMD introduced a new, technologically advanced monitoring product line, the Ultraview Care Network. Over the last two years, the company has also significantly expanded its product line and the markets in which it competes through acquisitions and agreements. In 1997, it acquired Burdick Inc., a developer and maker of diagnostic cardiology systems.

The Ultraview products, which represent SLMD's principal business, forms an advanced and comprehensive critical care patient monitoring system, and the foundation for CIS. The company sells Ultraview products as an integrated system, as stand-alone monitors, or as add-on components of its customers existing systems. Sales of these products to hospitals vary over a wide range, depending on the size and configuration of the system. A typical eight-bed, hard-wired system sells for about $170,000, while a typical 12-bed telemetry system sells for about $85,000.

The company is also seeking to further penetrate international markets. SLMD's approach incudes investment in product related requirements such as regulatory approvals, user interfaces and documentation in the local language, as well as investment in the creation and distribution channels and in the establishment of a base of satisfied customers.

In the 1998 second quarter, SLMD began several restructuring programs, including the consolidation of service operations and printed circuit board manufacturing. The company believes these programs will reduce both fixed and variable costs, and will cut its overall annual cost structure by about $5 million.

Per Share Data ($) (Year Ended Dec. 31)	1998	1997	1996	1995	1994	1993	1992	1991	1990	1989
Tangible Bk. Val.	14.33	13.76	19.26	18.77	16.89	15.26	13.68	9.98	NA	NA
Cash Flow	1.34	-1.15	1.08	2.49	2.48	2.47	2.43	2.24	1.78	NA
Earnings	0.29	-2.13	0.25	1.73	1.68	1.71	1.57	1.54	1.19	0.89
Dividends	Nil	Nil	Nil	Nil	Nil	Nil	Nil	Nil	Nil	Nil
Payout Ratio	Nil	Nil	Nil	Nil	Nil	Nil	Nil	Nil	Nil	Nil
Prices - High	24¼	26	29	29⅛	26¾	28¾	30¾	NA	NA	NA
- Low	14	18	19	22¼	19¾	16½	19¾	NA	NA	NA
P/E Ratio - High	84	NM	NM	17	16	17	20	NA	NA	NA
- Low	48	NM	NM	13	12	10	13	NA	NA	NA
Income Statement Analysis (Million $)										
Revs.	274	265	248	253	247	249	252	225	198	173
Oper. Inc.	11.4	29.7	31.0	37.0	37.7	37.6	33.0	25.4	19.9	NA
Depr.	10.0	9.4	8.6	8.3	8.6	8.4	9.4	7.2	6.0	NA
Int. Exp.	4.8	2.3	0.6	NM	NA	NA	0.9	0.9	0.2	NA
Pretax Inc.	4.4	-16.1	8.1	29.7	28.9	30.9	29.6	25.8	19.9	14.7
Eff. Tax Rate	38%	NM	68%	37%	37%	38%	42%	39%	39%	38%
Net Inc.	2.7	-20.4	2.6	18.6	18.1	19.2	17.2	15.8	12.1	9.2
Balance Sheet & Other Fin. Data (Million $)										
Cash	1.5	12.9	32.1	52.7	49.1	55.4	38.5	1.0	NA	NA
Curr. Assets	181	179	175	190	180	170	158	114	NA	NA
Total Assets	286	290	257	254	234	219	209	168	138	117
Curr. Liab.	59.9	58.5	43.1	35.0	36.3	34.9	34.0	36.9	NA	NA
LT Debt	65.1	66.8	13.5	14.3	11.2	11.9	12.6	13.3	Nil	Nil
Common Eqty.	161	165	196	204	185	171	161	116	100	88.0
Total Cap.	226	232	214	219	198	184	175	131	100	88.0
Cap. Exp.	8.3	9.6	18.3	17.2	14.9	7.2	6.7	15.7	8.1	NA
Cash Flow	12.7	-11.0	11.1	26.9	26.7	27.6	26.6	22.9	18.2	NA
Curr. Ratio	3.0	3.1	4.1	18.4	5.0	4.9	4.6	3.1	NA	NA
% LT Debt of Cap.	28.8	28.8	6.3	6.5	5.7	6.5	7.2	10.2	Nil	Nil
% Net Inc.of Revs.	1.0	NM	1.0	7.4	7.3	7.7	6.8	7.0	6.1	5.3
% Ret. on Assets	0.9	NM	1.0	7.6	8.0	9.1	9.1	10.3	9.5	8.4
% Ret. on Equity	1.7	NM	1.3	9.6	10.2	11.8	12.4	14.6	12.9	11.1

Data as orig reptd.; bef. results of disc opers/spec. items. Per share data adj. for stk. divs. Bold denotes diluted EPS (FASB 128)-prior periods restated. E-Estimated. NA-Not Available. NM-Not Meaningful. NR-Not Ranked.

Office—15220 N.E. 40th St. (P. O. Box 97013), Redmond, WA 98052. **Tel**—(206) 883-3700. **Fax**—(206) 885-4877. **Website**—http://www.spacelabs.com **Chrmn & CEO**—C. A. Lombardi. **VP & CFO**—J.A. Richman. **VP & Secy**—E. V. DeFelice. **Investor Contact**—Clark Thompson (425-867-7345). **Dirs**—G. W. Anderson, T. J. Dudley, H. Feigenbaum, C. A. Lombardi, A.R. Nara, P. M. Nudelman, P.H. vanOppen. **Transfer Agent & Registrar**—First Chicago Trust Co. of New York, NYC. **Incorporated**—in Delaware in 1958. **Empl**— 1,500. **S&P Analyst:** John J. Arege

STANDARD
&POOR'S
STOCK REPORTS

Spartan Motors

NASDAQ Symbol **SPAR**

In S&P SmallCap 600

09-OCT-99

Industry:
Trucks & Parts

Summary: Spartan makes custom-designed heavy truck chassis for motorhome, fire apparatus and utility applications and also produces vehicles for special applications.

Quantitative Evaluations

Outlook
(1 Lowest—5 Highest)
• 3

Fair Value
• 5¾

Risk
• **Average**

Earn./Div. Rank
• **B**

Technical Eval.
• **Bearish** since 9/99

Rel. Strength Rank
(1 Lowest—99 Highest)
• **15**

Insider Activity
• **NA**

Recent Price • 4⅝
52 Wk Range • 7-4
Yield • 1.5%
12-Mo. P/E • 10.6

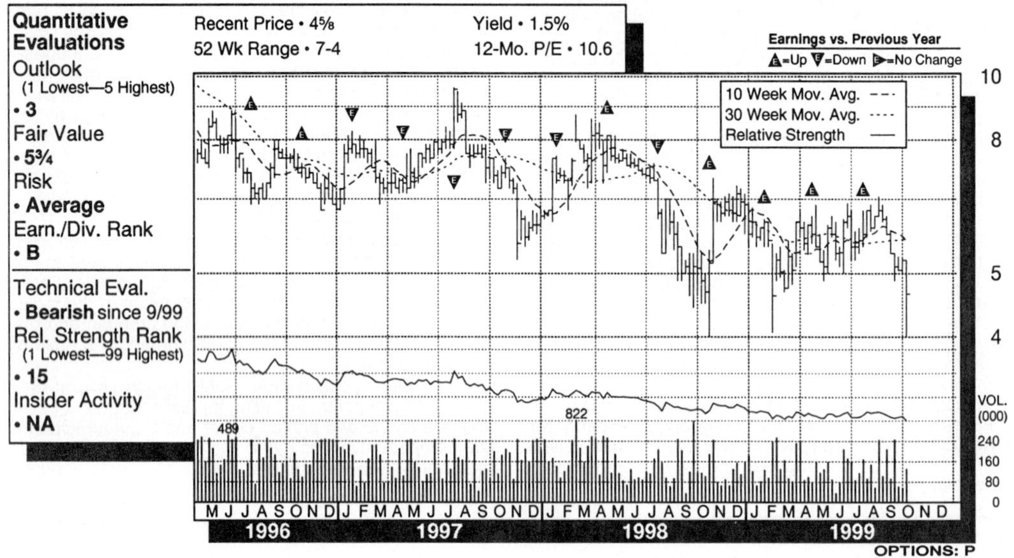

OPTIONS: P

Business Profile - 02-JUL-99

SPAR is continuing its efforts to turn around its operations through an expanded product mix featuring higher-margin products, cost controls and improved efficiencies. The company has continued to ramp up its U.S. transit bus and school bus business, and has reorganized its plant operations. In May 1999, SPAR formed a purchasing alliance with industrial products and specialized vehicles maker Federal Signal Corp. (FSS; NYSE). In October 1998, SPAR acquired a controlling interest in Carpenter Industries, further diversifying its business by offering custom chassis products to the 35,000-unit annual school bus marketplace. A special $0.07 a share dividend was paid in June 1999.

Operational Review - 02-JUL-99

Sales in the first quarter of 1999 advanced 28%, year to year, reflecting increased motorhome and fire truck chassis volume. Gross margins narrowed due to the bodies group operating at lower margins than the chassis group, and with higher SG&A and R&D expense, and a rise in interest expense, income before taxes an equity losses of affiliates fell 7.2%. In the absence of an equity loss of an affiliate, net income was up 54%, to $1,445,053 ($0.12 a share), from $938,237,000 ($0.07). Backlog at March 31, 1999 rose 53%, year to year, to $124 million. SPAR sees second quarter results down sequentially, but a breakeven performance for the second half of 1999.

Stock Performance - 08-OCT-99

In the past 30 trading days, SPAR's shares have declined 23%, compared to a 0.91% fall in the S&P 500. Average trading volume for the past five days was 25,860 shares, compared with the 40-day moving average of 31,282 shares.

Key Stock Statistics

Dividend Rate/Share	0.07	Shareholders	1,016
Shs. outstg. (M)	12.5	Market cap. (B)	$0.058
Avg. daily vol. (M)	0.027	Inst. holdings	28%
Tang. Bk. Value/Share	3.02		
Beta	0.89		

Value of $10,000 invested 5 years ago: $ 2,890

Fiscal Year Ending Dec. 31

	1999	1998	1997	1996	1995	1994
Revenues (Million $)						
1Q	75.63	59.16	45.79	47.39	44.20	54.76
2Q	75.26	55.50	39.13	44.70	28.79	46.36
3Q	—	69.63	38.33	41.32	36.03	44.77
4Q	—	71.04	55.43	42.41	45.06	45.64
Yr.	—	255.3	178.6	175.8	154.1	191.5
Earnings Per Share ($)						
1Q	**0.12**	**0.07**	**0.01**	**0.10**	0.14	0.27
2Q	**0.08**	**-0.04**	**-0.03**	**0.09**	-0.02	0.24
3Q	—	**0.16**	**-0.12**	**0.10**	0.05	0.23
4Q	—	**0.08**	**-0.91**	**0.09**	0.10	0.06
Yr.	—	**0.28**	**-1.06**	**0.18**	**0.27**	**0.80**

Next earnings report expected: late October

Dividend Data (Dividends have been paid since 1988.)

Amount ($)	Date Decl.	Ex-Div. Date	Stock of Record	Payment Date
0.070	May. 18	May. 26	May. 31	Jun. 30 '99

Spartan Motors, Inc.

Business Summary - 02-JUL-99

While it is continuing to diversify through acquisitions of fire truck apparatus and emergency vehicle manufacturers, Spartan Motors (SPAR) still derives most of its sales from its motorhome chassis segment. SPAR produces custom-designed heavy truck chassis for specialized applications, selling to four principal markets: fire truck, motorhome, school and transit bus, and step van and specialty vehicles.

The direct customers for the company's designed and manufactured chassis are OEMs that finish the building of the specialty vehicle by mounting the body or apparatus on the chassis. Spartan does not sell standard commercial truck chassis, but focuses on certain niches within its principal markets. SPAR manufactures its chassis with components purchased from outside suppliers, which allows for easier serviceability of finished products, reduces production costs, and expedites the development of new products. In 1998, sales to two major customers -- Fleetwood Motor Homes of Indiana and Newmar Corp. -- accounted for 25% and 16% of the company sales, respectively.

Spartan believes that its bus/specialty vehicles group has the strongest sales growth potential. SPAR continues to develop specialized chassis and seeks additional applications of its existing products. Its Custom Low Floor bus chassis, delivered in 1995, eliminated the need for costly mechanical wheel chair lifts through a curb height that permits the use of manually operated ramps. SPAR said the chassis continued to increase market share in 1998.

The company noted that the transit bus business continues to show encouraging growth for custom chassis manufacturing as the market recognizes the long-term cost savings related to maintenance and the extended life cycle of a custom bus.

In November 1997, SPAR acquired two fire truck apparatus manufacturers for $6.1 million in cash and stock. It expected the companies, Luverne Fire Apparatus and Quality Manufacturing, to contribute $30 million in revenues on an annual basis. In early 1997, SPAR acquired a 33% interest in Carpenter Industries, Inc., a Richmond, IN-based school bus manufacturer, for $10 million. Following a going concern opinion for Carpenter's 1997 financial statements, SPAR wrote down its investment in Carpenter to zero. In October 1998, the company announced a plan under which it increased its ownership position in Carpenter to 49.9%. SPAR also purchased 95.5% of Carpenter's non-voting stock and acquired board control. In November 1998, SPAR said that Carpenter, which had halted production since July, would resume operations.

Since April 1995, SPAR has repurchased 1,058,100 of its common shares under buyback programs totaling 1.25 million shares. Chassis backlog at December 31, 1998, exceeded $83 million, up from $71 million a year earlier.

Per Share Data ($) (Year Ended Dec. 31)	1998	1997	1996	1995	1994	1993	1992	1991	1990	1989
Tangible Bk. Val.	3.02	3.58	4.97	4.74	4.72	4.11	3.29	1.85	0.84	0.62
Cash Flow	0.48	-0.91	0.34	0.42	0.93	0.86	0.77	0.61	0.28	0.15
Earnings	0.28	-1.06	0.18	0.27	0.80	0.80	0.72	0.58	0.24	0.11
Dividends	0.07	0.07	0.05	0.05	0.05	0.05	0.03	0.02	0.02	0.02
Payout Ratio	25%	NM	28%	19%	6%	6%	5%	4%	9%	20%
Prices - High	8 3/4	9 5/8	11	14 5/8	21 3/4	25 1/4	23 1/8	16 1/2	2 5/8	3 3/8
- Low	4	5 1/4	6 1/4	8 5/8	12 3/8	12 3/4	8 5/8	1 9/16	1 7/16	1 9/16
P/E Ratio - High	31	NM	61	54	27	32	32	28	11	29
- Low	14	NM	35	32	15	16	12	3	6	13
Income Statement Analysis (Million $)										
Revs.	255	179	175	153	189	166	123	94.0	51.0	36.0
Oper. Inc.	15.2	4.7	9.5	6.0	16.5	16.0	13.8	10.5	4.8	2.8
Depr.	2.6	1.9	1.9	2.0	1.6	0.9	0.7	0.4	0.4	0.3
Int. Exp.	1.2	0.8	0.5	0.5	0.5	0.5	0.2	0.5	0.8	0.9
Pretax Inc.	7.7	-12.5	3.9	5.4	16.5	15.8	13.7	9.9	3.8	1.8
Eff. Tax Rate	55%	NM	40%	37%	36%	34%	33%	34%	34%	34%
Net Inc.	3.5	-13.1	2.3	3.4	10.6	10.5	9.2	6.5	2.5	1.2
Balance Sheet & Other Fin. Data (Million $)										
Cash	0.5	4.8	13.9	12.9	14.2	11.3	12.1	0.9	0.2	0.5
Curr. Assets	94.1	65.6	67.9	60.5	65.5	56.2	46.9	27.3	19.2	12.9
Total Assets	126	81.2	79.7	75.2	81.1	71.3	56.4	34.7	23.7	17.2
Curr. Liab.	48.9	24.2	13.1	9.6	13.2	12.8	10.8	8.7	12.5	7.2
LT Debt	30.2	9.6	5.2	5.8	6.2	4.7	2.9	3.7	2.5	3.5
Common Eqty.	45.1	47.5	61.4	59.8	61.6	53.8	42.7	22.3	8.7	6.5
Total Cap.	75.4	57.1	66.6	65.6	67.8	58.4	45.6	26.0	11.2	10.0
Cap. Exp.	1.0	1.6	1.4	1.8	4.7	4.1	4.4	1.7	0.5	2.0
Cash Flow	6.0	-11.2	4.3	5.4	12.2	11.4	9.9	7.0	2.9	1.5
Curr. Ratio	1.9	2.7	5.2	6.3	5.0	4.4	4.4	3.2	1.5	1.8
% LT Debt of Cap.	40.1	16.8	7.8	8.8	9.2	8.0	6.4	14.3	22.0	35.3
% Net Inc.of Revs.	1.4	NM	1.4	2.2	5.6	6.3	7.5	6.9	4.9	3.3
% Ret. on Assets	3.4	NM	3.0	4.4	13.9	16.4	19.7	21.0	12.2	6.9
% Ret. on Equity	7.5	NM	3.9	5.6	18.4	21.7	27.7	40.3	32.8	19.7

Data as orig reptd.; bef. results of disc opers/spec. items. Per share data adj. for stk. divs. Bold denotes diluted EPS (FASB 128)-prior periods restated. E-Estimated. NA-Not Available. NM-Not Meaningful. NR-Not Ranked.

Office—1000 Reynolds Rd., Charlotte, MI 48813. **Tel**—(517) 543-6400. **Website**—http://www.spartanmotors.com**Chrmn & CEO**—G. W. Sztykiel. **Pres & COO**—J. E. Sztykiel. **CFO, Treas & Secy**—R. J. Shalter. **Investor Contact**—John Gaedert (517 543-6400 Ext. 280).**Dirs**—W. F. Foster, C. E. Nihart, J. C. Penman, A. G. Sommer, G. W. Sztykiel, J. E. Sztykiel, G. Tesseris, D. R. Wilson. **Transfer Agent**—American Stock Transfer & Trust Co., NYC. **Incorporated**—in Michigan in 1975. **Empl**— 1,025. **S&P Analyst:** Stewart Scharf

STANDARD
&POOR'S
STOCK REPORTS

Specialty Equipment

NYSE Symbol **SEC**

In S&P SmallCap 600

09-OCT-99

Industry: Manufacturing (Specialized)

Summary: This company manufactures a broad array of commercial cooking and refrigeration equipment for the foodservice industry.

Business Profile - 15-SEP-99

SEC remains highly confident regarding its long-term growth plan, based on its global brand and market leadership, strong cash flow generation and track record of product innovation. The company believes it has grown at about 1.5X the rate of the foodservice industry as a whole, through leveraging its brands, developing new products, and strengthening its preferred supplier relationships with the major U.S. fast food chains, soft drink bottlers, and international breweries. Through July 31, 1999, SEC had purchased 755,400 of its common shares, under its second 1,000,000 share repurchase program.

Operational Review - 15-SEP-99

Revenues in the six months ended July 31, 1999, edged up 0.3%, year to year. Profitability was restricted by a softening in refrigerated equipment sales to the soft drink industry in the second quarter of FY 00 (Jan.). However, aided by a 52% drop in interest expense, pretax income advanced 10%. After taxes at 38.3% versus 36.3%, and minority interest, net income was up 6.4%, to $22,534,000 ($1.12 a share), from $21,180,000 ($1.06).

Stock Performance - 08-OCT-99

In the past 30 trading days, SEC's shares have increased 8%, compared to a 0.91% fall in the S&P 500. Average trading volume for the past five days was 45,940 shares, compared with the 40-day moving average of 23,474 shares.

Key Stock Statistics

Dividend Rate/Share	Nil	Shareholders	1,300
Shs. outstg. (M)	19.3	Market cap. (B)	$0.476
Avg. daily vol. (M)	0.024	Inst. holdings	52%
Tang. Bk. Value/Share	NM		
Beta	0.91		

Value of $10,000 invested 5 years ago: $ 36,573

Fiscal Year Ending Jan. 31

	2000	1999	1998	1997	1996	1995
Revenues (Million $)						
1Q	139.5	127.7	109.2	105.3	106.1	—
2Q	129.2	140.2	113.2	105.0	104.8	96.13
3Q	—	120.5	107.7	102.8	97.85	99.3
4Q	—	107.3	103.0	88.12	83.72	79.68
Yr.	—	495.6	433.1	401.2	392.5	371.7
Earnings Per Share ($)						
1Q	**0.59**	**0.47**	0.38	0.33	-0.34	-0.78
2Q	**0.54**	**0.58**	0.38	0.32	0.15	-0.75
3Q	—	**0.43**	0.33	0.29	0.15	-0.78
4Q	—	**0.71**	**0.70**	0.64	0.38	-0.38
Yr.	—	**2.18**	**1.86**	**1.70**	0.42	-3.29

Next earnings report expected: early December

Dividend Data

No cash dividends have been paid since 1992, and the company does not intend to pay dividends for the foreseeable future.

A Division of The McGraw-Hill Companies

Specialty Equipment Companies, Inc.

Business Summary - 15-SEP-99

Specialty Equipment Companies has as the principal goal of its business strategy to maintain and improve its position as a leader in the foodservice equipment industry. Key components of its strategy are to focus on major national chains and beverage companies; leverage the company's long-term relationships with existing major customers; and develop new products and line extensions by extending engineering expertise to standardized foodservice equipment.

The company manufactures a diversified line of highly engineered commercial and institutional foodservice equipment. Its products are used by customers in the foodservice equipment market segment, including various quick service restaurant chains, other commercial restaurants, convenience store chains, specialty chains, soft drink bottlers, brewers, and institutional foodservice operators.

SEC emphasizes the engineering and development of specially designed, state-of-the-art foodservice equipment, and sells a wide array of standardized foodservice equipment and related products. The company serves its customers through a broad-based global distribution and service network.

The company's domestic operations and some of its foreign operations are conducted by wholly owned Specialty Equipment Manufacturing. Specialty Equipment International (through wholly owned Gamko Holding) conducts a substantial portion of SEC's foreign operations. International business accounted for 28% of revenues in FY 99 (Jan.).

SEC generally markets its products through one of six global brands: Taylor, Beverage-Air, Bloomfield, Wells, World Dryer, and Gamko. Each of these brands has been a prominent brand in its specific market niche for many years. For example, Wells produced its first waffle baker in 1920. Taylor provided its first ice cream freezer to a restaurant in 1926, and has been providing shake machines to McDonald's since the 1970s. Beverage-Air started making refrigerated cabinets in 1944, and Bloomfield introduced its first coffee service products in the 1950s. World Dryer started selling warm air hand dryers in 1951, and Gemko produced its first cooler in 1965.

Sales to McDonald's restaurants (both McDonald's-owned and independently franchised) accounted for 14% of revenues in FY 99, and sales to Coca-Cola Enterprises contributed 11%.

Per Share Data ($) (Year Ended Jan. 31)	1999	1998	1997	1996	1995	1994	1993	1992	1991	1990
Tangible Bk. Val.	NM	NM	NM	NA	NM	NM	NA	NA	NA	NA
Cash Flow	2.60	2.15	1.92	2.17	1.52	1.30	NA	NA	NA	NA
Earnings	2.18	1.86	1.59	0.42	-3.29	-3.56	NA	NA	NA	NA
Dividends	Nil	Nil	Nil	Nil	Nil	Nil	NA	NA	NA	NA
Payout Ratio	Nil	Nil	Nil	Nil	Nil	Nil	NA	NA	NA	NA
Cal. Yrs.	1998	1997	1996	1995	1994	1993	1992	1991	1990	1989
Prices - High	27 1/8	17 1/2	15 3/4	14	11	7 1/4	NA	NA	NA	NA
- Low	16 3/8	12 1/8	10 1/4	9 1/4	5	4 1/2	NA	NA	NA	NA
P/E Ratio - High	12	9	9	33	NM	NM	NA	NA	NA	NA
- Low	8	7	6	22	NM	NM	NA	NA	NA	NA
Income Statement Analysis (Million $)										
Revs.	496	433	401	393	372	321	NA	NA	NA	NA
Oper. Inc.	82.5	68.9	67.3	66.1	60.5	45.8	NA	NA	NA	NA
Depr.	8.4	5.8	6.9	26.7	78.9	79.8	NA	NA	NA	NA
Int. Exp.	14.1	15.9	18.7	21.0	23.0	17.1	NA	NA	NA	NA
Pretax Inc.	60.1	47.1	42.0	18.4	-41.3	-51.3	NA	NA	NA	NA
Eff. Tax Rate	27%	20%	19%	51%	NM	NM	NA	NA	NA	NA
Net Inc.	44.0	37.5	34.1	8.9	-54.0	-58.4	NA	NA	NA	NA
Balance Sheet & Other Fin. Data (Million $)										
Cash	6.8	42.6	10.8	34.3	3.2	2.8	NA	NA	NA	NA
Curr. Assets	174	175	132	136	105	99	NA	NA	NA	NA
Total Assets	237	241	177	180	169	232	NA	NA	NA	NA
Curr. Liab.	107	119	90.3	92.9	87.9	79.3	NA	NA	NA	NA
LT Debt	129	160	155	193	199	217	NA	NA	NA	NA
Common Eqty.	0.1	-38.8	-71.2	-107	-120	-67.2	NA	NA	NA	NA
Total Cap.	129	121	84.0	85.0	78.0	NA	NA	NA	NA	NA
Cap. Exp.	7.5	4.7	9.2	5.7	6.7	NA	NA	NA	NA	NA
Cash Flow	52.4	43.4	41.0	35.6	24.9	21.3	NA	NA	NA	NA
Curr. Ratio	1.6	1.5	1.5	1.5	1.2	1.3	NA	NA	NA	NA
% LT Debt of Cap.	99.9	132.2	184.5	227.1	255.1	144.7	NA	NA	NA	NA
% Net Inc.of Revs.	8.9	8.7	8.5	2.3	NM	NM	NA	NA	NA	NA
% Ret. on Assets	18.4	17.9	19.1	5.1	NM	NM	NA	NA	NA	NA
% Ret. on Equity	NA	NM	NM	NM	NM	NM	NA	NA	NA	NA

Data as orig reptd.; bef. results of disc opers/spec. items. Per share data adj. for stk. divs. Bold denotes diluted EPS (FASB 128)-prior periods restated. E-Estimated. NA-Not Available. NM-Not Meaningful. NR-Not Ranked.

Office—1245 Corporate Blvd., Suite 401, Aurora, IL 60504. **Tel**—(630) 585-5111. **Website**—http://www.specialty-equipment.com **Pres, CEO & COO**—J. P. Rhodenbaugh. **Chrmn**—D. B. Greenwood. **EVP, CFO, Treas & Secy**—D. K. McKay. **Investor Contact**—Douglas C. Johnson (630 585-2911). **Dirs**—W. E. Dotterweich, A. A. Glazer, K. E. Glazer, M. I. Glazer, D. B..Greenwood, C. E. Hutchinson, R. A. Kent, B. L. MacLean, J. P. Rhodenbaugh. **Transfer Agent & Registrar**—LaSalle National Bank, Chicago. **Incorporated**—in Delaware in 1984. **Empl**— 2,916. **S&P Analyst:** J. J. Schemitsch

STANDARD
&POOR'S
STOCK REPORTS

SpeedFam-IPEC

NASDAQ Symbol **SFAM**

In S&P SmallCap 600

23-OCT-99

Industry:
Equipment (Semiconductor)

Summary: SFAM (formerly SpeedFam International) makes chemical mechanical planarization systems used in the fabrication of semiconductor devices and other precision processing systems.

Quantitative Evaluations

Outlook
(1 Lowest—5 Highest)
• **3-**

Fair Value
• **13⅝**

Risk
• **High**

Earn./Div. Rank
• **NR**

Technical Eval.
• **NA**

Rel. Strength Rank
(1 Lowest—99 Highest)
• **28**

Insider Activity
• **Neutral**

Recent Price • 10⅞
52 Wk Range • 21¾-8⅝
Yield • Nil
12-Mo. P/E • NM

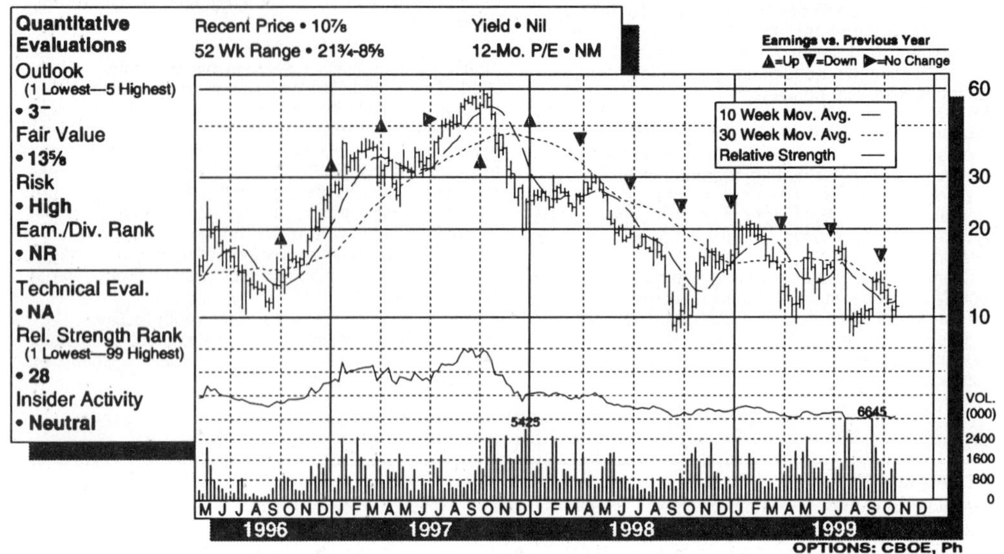

OPTIONS: CBOE, Ph

Business Profile - 20-OCT-99

In September 1999, SFAM noted that with the integration of Integrated Process Equipment Corp. (acquired in April 1999) largely completed, it will now focus on building CMP (chemical mechanical planarization) market share through the aggressive pursuit of new accounts, as well as repeat business from existing accounts, and on maintaining high levels of satisfaction in its customer base. The company's growth depends on continued and increased acceptance of CMP among semiconductor manufacturers. While CMP is used by a number of advanced logic semiconductor manufacturers, it has been used to manufacture advanced memory devices only in the past two years. Continued and increased acceptance of CMP systems is vital to SFAM's profitability going forward.

Operational Review - 20-OCT-99

Total revenues in the three months ended August 31, 1999, declined 23%, year to year, reflecting a decline in CMP equipment sales and, to a lesser extent, lower sales to the thin film memory disk market. Gross margins narrowed, and with other expense versus other income, no taxes versus a tax benefit of $1,096,000, and equity in net loss versus earnings of affiliates, the net loss widened to $10,963,000 ($0.37 a share, based on 2.5% more shares) from $7,289,000 ($0.25, after preferred dividends).

Stock Performance - 22-OCT-99

In the past 30 trading days, SFAM's shares have declined 20%, compared to a 4% fall in the S&P 500. Average trading volume for the past five days was 151,360 shares, compared with the 40-day moving average of 357,844 shares.

Key Stock Statistics

Dividend Rate/Share	Nil	Shareholders	114
Shs. outstg. (M)	29.4	Market cap. (B)	$0.311
Avg. daily vol. (M)	0.218	Inst. holdings	53%
Tang. Bk. Value/Share	8.40		
Beta	NA		

Value of $10,000 invested 5 years ago: NA

Fiscal Year Ending May 31

	2000	1999	1998	1997	1996	1995
Revenues (Million $)						
1Q	50.33	64.47	53.85	39.73	17.82	—
2Q	—	47.75	56.53	39.12	25.44	—
3Q	—	51.52	48.38	45.28	33.14	—
4Q	—	48.59	26.50	49.30	43.78	—
Yr.	—	212.3	185.3	173.4	120.2	59.78
Earnings Per Share ($)						
1Q	**-0.37**	**-0.25**	0.39	0.36	0.09	—
2Q	—	**-0.59**	0.49	0.42	0.16	—
3Q	—	**-0.54**	**0.31**	0.42	0.39	—
4Q	—	**-3.42**	**-0.34**	0.46	0.46	—
Yr.	—	**-4.84**	**0.83**	**1.67**	1.16	0.20

Next earnings report expected: late December

Dividend Data

No cash dividends have been paid, and the company has said it does not expect to pay any for the foreseeable future.

STANDARD
&POOR'S
STOCK REPORTS

SpeedFam-IPEC, Inc.

23-OCT-99

Business Summary - 20-OCT-99

SpeedFam-IPEC, Inc. (SFAM) designs, develops, manufactures, markets and supports chemical mechanical planarization (CMP) systems used in the fabrication of semiconductor devices and other high-throughput precision surface processing systems. The company's flat surface processing systems are used in the thin film memory disk media, silicon wafer and general industrial applications markets. SFAM also markets and distributes polishing liquids (slurries), parts and consumables used in its customers' manufacturing processes. The company's processing systems include polishing, grinding, lapping, and pre-deposition cleaning equipment.

SFAM offers the broadest range of CMP systems currently available to the semiconductor industry, including both rotary and orbital technology. The company's Auriga system is a five-head, two polishing table CMP system capable of processing 65-90 wafers an hour based on a two-minute polishing cycle. The Auriga system incorporates certain modifications from the original CMP-V system in the control and automation system to decrease the time interval between processes, thereby increasing production.

During FY 98 (May), SpeedFam International introduced its Auriga-C systems, its third generation five-head, semiconductor CMP system, with fully integrated, on-board dry-in/dry-out cleaning and in-situ endpoint detection capabilities.

The company offers a broad line of slurry and slurry components used in surface treatment processes as part of a total process solution. Slurries are used by manufacturers of thin-film memory disk media, semiconductor wafers and other products as part of their polishing processes. Substantially all slurries sold by the company are made by Fujimi Inc.

SFAM's research, development and engineering expenditures totaled $70.2 million in FY 99, versus $67.2 million in FY 98.

In April 1999, SFAM merged with Integrated Process Equipment Corp., another leading supplier of CMP systems to the worldwide semiconductor industry.

Per Share Data ($)										
(Year Ended May 31)	**1999**	**1998**	**1997**	**1996**	**1995**	**1994**	**1993**	**1992**	**1991**	**1990**
Tangible Bk. Val.	NA	18.10	11.75	5.71	3.09	NA	NA	NA	NA	NA
Cash Flow	NA	1.12	1.90	1.29	0.28	NA	NA	NA	NA	NA
Earnings	-4.84	0.83	1.67	1.16	0.20	0.30	-0.06	NA	NA	NA
Dividends	Nil	Nil	Nil	Nil	Nil	NA	NA	NA	NA	NA
Payout Ratio	Nil	Nil	Nil	Nil	Nil	NA	NA	NA	NA	NA
Cal. Yrs.	1998	1997	1996	1995	1994	1993	1992	1991	1990	1989
Prices - High	31¼	60⅞	29¼	19⅛	NA	NA	NA	NA	NA	NA
- Low	8⅞	19⅛	9½	10	NA	NA	NA	NA	NA	NA
P/E Ratio - High	NM	73	18	16	NA	NA	NA	NA	NA	NA
- Low	NM	23	6	9	NA	NA	NA	NA	NA	NA
Income Statement Analysis (Million $)										
Revs.	NA	176	173	120	59.8	51.4	43.3	NA	NA	NA
Oper. Inc.	NA	10.5	24.3	12.4	2.2	NA	NA	NA	NA	NA
Depr.	NA	4.5	2.9	1.3	0.6	NA	NA	NA	NA	NA
Int. Exp.	NA	0.0	0.2	0.7	1.0	NA	NA	NA	NA	NA
Pretax Inc.	NA	16.3	28.3	16.1	1.8	2.1	0.1	NA	NA	NA
Eff. Tax Rate	NA	21%	28%	27%	10%	NM	NM	NA	NA	NA
Net Inc.	NA	12.9	20.2	11.8	1.6	2.3	-0.5	NA	NA	NA
Balance Sheet & Other Fin. Data (Million $)										
Cash	NA	141	76.9	10.9	1.1	NA	NA	NA	NA	NA
Curr. Assets	NA	250	156	76.0	37.3	NA	NA	NA	NA	NA
Total Assets	NA	330	207	108	60.0	45.7	35.7	NA	NA	NA
Curr. Liab.	NA	39.9	48.9	44.8	26.2	NA	NA	NA	NA	NA
LT Debt	NA	Nil	0.3	2.6	10.4	NA	NA	NA	NA	NA
Common Eqty.	NA	289	157	60.0	23.0	18.6	15.7	NA	NA	NA
Total Cap.	NA	290	158	63.2	33.8	NA	NA	NA	NA	NA
Cap. Exp.	NA	32.1	17.4	8.1	0.7	0.4	NA	NA	NA	NA
Cash Flow	NA	17.4	23.1	13.1	2.3	NA	NA	NA	NA	NA
Curr. Ratio	NA	6.3	3.2	1.7	1.4	NA	NA	NA	NA	NA
% LT Debt of Cap.	NA	Nil	0.2	4.1	30.6	NA	NA	NA	NA	NA
% Net Inc.of Revs.	NA	7.0	11.7	9.8	2.8	4.4	NM	NA	NA	NA
% Ret. on Assets	NA	4.8	12.9	14.1	3.1	5.6	NA	NA	NA	NA
% Ret. on Equity	NA	5.8	18.7	28.5	7.9	13.3	NA	NA	NA	NA

Data as orig. reptd.; bef. results of disc. opers. and/or spec. items. Per share data adj. for stk. divs. as of ex-div. date. Bold denotes diluted EPS (FASB 128). E-Estimated. NA-Not Available. NM-Not Meaningful. NR-Not Ranked.

Office—305 N. 54th St., Chandler, AZ 85226. **Tel**—(602) 705-2100. **Website**—http://www.speedfam.com **Pres & CEO**—R. J. Faubert. **Co-Chrmn**—J. N. Farley, S. R. Chitre. **Vice Chrmn**—M. Kouzuma. **CFO & Treas**—J. M. Dodson. **Dirs**—N. R. Bonke, S. R. Chitre, J. N. Farley, R. J. Faubert, W. J. Freschi, R. S. Hill, M. Kouzuma, K. Levy, R. D. McDaniel. **Transfer Agent & Registrar**—Firstar Bank Milwaukee. **Incorporated**—in Illinois in 1959. **Empl**— 1,100. **S&P Analyst:** M.I.

Sports Authority

NYSE Symbol **TSA**

In S&P SmallCap 600

09-OCT-99 **Industry:** Retail (Specialty)

Summary: This U.S. operator of large-format sporting goods stores is the largest chain of its kind, with 200 stores in 32 U.S. states and Canada, and 13 in Japan.

S&P Opinion: Avoid (★★)

Recent Price • 2⅞ | 52 Wk Range • 8½-2¾ | Yield • Nil | 12-Mo. P/E • NM

Quantitative Evaluations

Outlook (1 Lowest—5 Highest)
• **5**

Fair Value
• **6¾**

Risk
• **Average**

Earn./Div. Rank
• **NR**

Technical Eval.
• **Neutral** since 9/99

Rel. Strength Rank (1 Lowest—99 Highest)
• **8**

Insider Activity
• **Favorable**

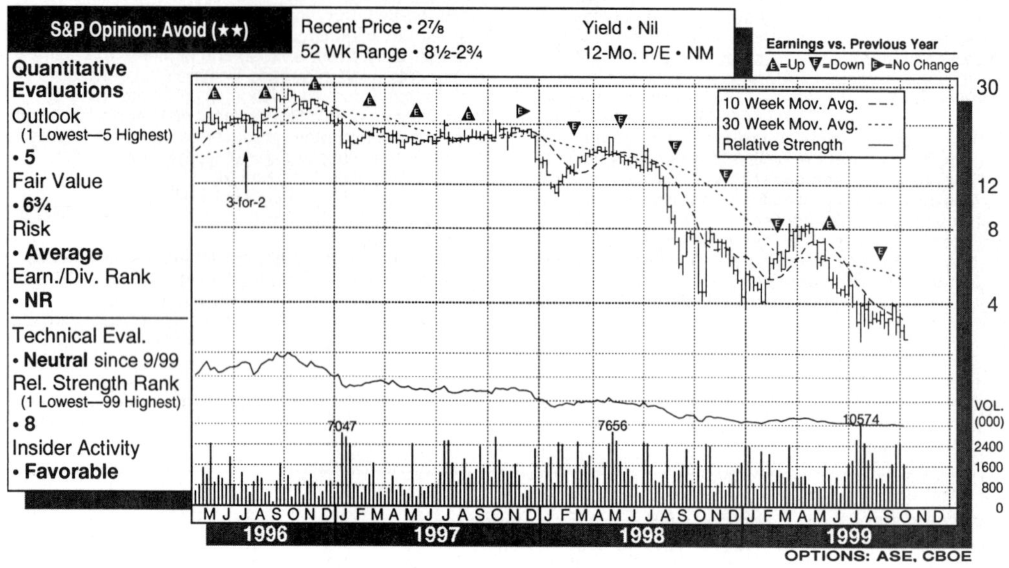

OPTIONS: ASE, CBOE

Overview - 23-AUG-99

We expect sales to advance only about 1% to 2% during the second half of FY 00 (Jan.), as a modest recovery in same-store sales is partly offset by a reduction in the number of stores. Margins will continue to be restricted by an industrywide slowdown in sales of footwear, licensed apparel for men, and golf equipment. For the longer term, management will focus on improving distribution, reducing the breadth of products offered, and closing underperforming stores. TSA will also seek to boost profit margins through a combination of lower capital spending and reduced procurement and payroll costs. The company has canceled many planned new store openings, and is instead focusing on enhancing existing stores through a combination of re-pricing store merchandise and improved marketing. We project EPS of $0.05 for FY 2000.

Valuation - 23-AUG-99

Although the shares were recently trading near their 52-week low, we continue to rate them avoid. Despite the company's commitment to improving operating earnings with cost savings initiatives such as store closings, improved shipments from TSA's distribution center, reduced markdowns, and an improved in-stock position, earnings have not yet begun to rebound. During the first quarter of FY 00, the company posted its first comparable-store sales increase in more than two years. However, sales in recent months again posted negative comparisons with year-earlier results. In addition, margins during the first half of the year were hurt by sharply higher advertising expenses to drive the sales. We believe that turning around a retailer in distress is a challenging task. We therefore expect the shares to be only weak market performers until concrete signs of a sales and earnings recovery are visible.

Key Stock Statistics

S&P EPS Est. 1999	NA	Tang. Bk. Value/Share	7.11
P/E on S&P Est. 1999	NA	Beta	NA
S&P EPS Est. 2000	0.05	Shareholders	1,243
Dividend Rate/Share	Nil	Market cap. (B)	$0.092
Shs. outstg. (M)	32.0	Inst. holdings	33%
Avg. daily vol. (M)	0.485		

Value of $10,000 invested 5 years ago: NA

Fiscal Year Ending Jan. 31

	2000	1999	1998	1997	1996	1995
Revenues (Million $)						
1Q	357.0	346.5	346.5	270.6	221.6	173.9
2Q	385.9	427.3	383.3	331.6	268.4	201.3
3Q	—	367.0	340.9	292.9	234.2	195.1
4Q	—	459.0	420.6	376.2	322.5	268.3
Yr.	—	1,600	1,465	1,271	1,047	838.5
Earnings Per Share ($)						
1Q	**-0.05**	**-0.12**	0.08	0.06	0.05	0.04
2Q	**0.07**	**0.12**	0.30	0.29	0.22	0.15
3Q	**E-0.09**	**-2.04**	0.06	0.06	0.02	Nil
4Q	**E0.12**	**0.03**	**0.25**	0.53	0.42	0.35
Yr.	**E0.05**	**-2.01**	**0.70**	**0.94**	**0.71**	**0.54**

Next earnings report expected: late November

Dividend Data

The company intends to retain earnings to finance growth and therefore does not anticipate paying any cash dividends for the foreseeable future.

The Sports Authority, Inc.

Business Summary - 23-AUG-99

The Sports Authority is the largest U.S. operator of large-format sporting goods stores, based both on sales and on the number of stores, and is also the largest full-line sporting goods retailer. The company's stores stock extensive selections of brand-name sporting equipment and athletic and active footwear and apparel, and offer everyday fair prices and premium customer service.

In May 1998, TSA agreed to be acquired by Venator Group, Inc. (formerly Woolworth Corp.) via an exchange of stock. However, the offer was ultimately rejected by TSA shareholders, as was a later bid in August 1998 by Gart's Sports to acquire the company for $14 a share, plus a 51% interest in a newly combined entity.

As of May 20, 1999, the company was operating 200 full-line sporting goods superstores, with 195 stores in 32 states across the U.S., five stores in Canada, and 13 in Japan under a license agreement with Mega Sports Co., Ltd.; virtually all stores are in excess of 40,000 gross sq. ft. The stores are located primarily in regional strip or power centers with tenants that are value-oriented, large-format retailers; some stores are located in malls, and some are stand-alones. Unlike warehouse stores, the interior of each store has features comparable to those of department stores.

Until mid-1998, TSA carried out a rapid expansion program. In 1998, it opened 30 new stores and closed three, for a total of 226 at the end of the year. In the third quarter of FY 99 (Jan.), the company said it would close 18 underperforming stores as part of a comprehensive restructuring plan; 15 stores had been closed by the FY 2000 first quarter. Expansion plans for FY 2000 call for only three to seven new stores.

The superstore format lets the company offer under one roof an extensive selection of merchandise for sports and leisure activities ordinarily associated with specialty and pro shops, such as for golf, tennis, snow skiing, cycling, hunting, fishing, bowling, archery, boating and water sports. Each superstore stocks about 45,000 SKUs across 16 major departments. TSA's merchandise assortment includes more than 900 brand names.

In each of the past three years, hard lines accounted for about 50% of total sales, apparel 22%, and footwear 28%.

TSA encountered difficulties in FY 99, reflecting the impact of a soft footwear market, combined with increased competition. As a result, it recorded special charges of approximately $1.72 a share in the third quarter, related to store exit costs, restructuring charges, and charges for impaired assets.

Per Share Data ($) (Year Ended Jan. 31)	1999	1998	1997	1996	1995	1994	1993	1992	1991	1990
Tangible Bk. Val.	7.03	8.97	8.19	7.12	6.29	4.19	NA	NA	NA	NA
Cash Flow	-0.50	1.87	1.84	1.35	1.05	0.75	NA	NA	NA	NA
Earnings	-2.01	0.70	0.94	0.71	0.54	0.41	NA	NA	NA	NA
Dividends	Nil	Nil	Nil	Nil	Nil	Nil	NA	NA	NA	NA
Payout Ratio	Nil	Nil	Nil	Nil	Nil	Nil	NA	NA	NA	NA
Cal. Yrs.	1998	1997	1996	1995	1994	1993	1992	1991	1990	1989
Prices - High	18¾	22	29	20⅛	16⅝	NA	NA	NA	NA	NA
- Low	3¾	13¾	11¼	10⅞	12⅝	NA	NA	NA	NA	NA
P/E Ratio - High	NM	31	31	28	31	NA	NA	NA	NA	NA
- Low	NM	20	12	15	23	NA	NA	NA	NA	NA
Income Statement Analysis (Million $)										
Revs.	1,600	1,465	1,271	1,047	841	607	412	241	109	53.0
Oper. Inc.	-24.5	74.7	75.6	55.4	46.1	29.4	16.5	7.3	NA	NA
Depr.	47.9	37.3	28.5	20.0	15.9	10.2	7.2	4.4	2.8	0.8
Int. Exp.	13.2	8.5	4.6	0.8	0.3	0.0	0.1	0.1	0.1	NM
Pretax Inc.	-100	34.7	48.0	37.4	29.8	20.9	10.0	37.4	-3.4	-4.3
Eff. Tax Rate	NM	42%	41%	41%	44%	39%	43%	59%	NM	NM
Net Inc.	-63.8	22.2	30.0	22.3	16.9	12.8	5.7	1.3	-3.0	-3.5
Balance Sheet & Other Fin. Data (Million $)										
Cash	22.9	20.4	110	11.8	37.1	8.2	2.2	NA	NA	NA
Curr. Assets	439	392	445	312	303	180	126	NA	NA	NA
Total Assets	902	812	754	524	460	298	236	185	121	28.0
Curr. Liab.	409	293	269	228	196	143	92.0	NA	NA	NA
LT Debt	173	157	152	Nil	Nil	Nil	Nil	NA	NA	NA
Common Eqty.	273	334	310	278	253	148	139	131	97.0	14.0
Total Cap.	442	491	462	278	253	148	139	NA	NA	NA
Cap. Exp.	84.6	114	102	55.3	51.4	23.5	25.9	15.6	4.7	3.9
Cash Flow	-15.9	59.5	58.5	42.1	32.8	22.9	12.9	5.7	-0.1	-2.7
Curr. Ratio	1.1	1.3	1.7	1.4	1.5	1.3	1.4	NA	NA	NA
% LT Debt of Cap.	39.2	32.0	32.9	Nil	Nil	Nil	Nil	NA	NA	NA
% Net Inc.of Revs.	NM	1.5	2.4	2.1	2.0	2.1	1.4	0.6	NM	NM
% Ret. on Assets	NM	2.8	4.7	4.5	Nil	4.8	2.7	0.9	NM	NA
% Ret. on Equity	NM	6.9	10.2	8.4	Nil	8.9	4.2	1.2	NM	NA

Data as orig reptd.; bef. results of disc opers/spec. items. Per share data adj. for stk. divs. Bold denotes diluted EPS (FASB 128)-prior periods restated. E-Estimated. NA-Not Available. NM-Not Meaningful. NR-Not Ranked.

Office—3383 N. State Road 7, Fort Lauderdale, FL 33319. **Tel**—(954) 735-1701. **Website**—http://www.sportsauthority.com **CEO**—M. E. Hanaka. **Chrmn**—J. A. Smith. **Pres & COO**—R. J. Lynch, Jr. **SVP & CFO**—A. F. Crudele. **VP & Secy**—F. W. Bubb, III. **VP & Treas**—A L. Stanton. **Investor Contact**—Dietta Slayton, (954-735-1701; ext 6005). **Dirs**—A. D. Brown, N. A. Buoniconti, C. R. Cohen, S. Dougherty, J. W. Erving, C. Farmer, M. E. Hanaka, J. F. Kemp, J. A. Smith. **Transfer Agent & Registrar**—First Union National Bank of North Carolina, Charlotte. **Incorporated**—in Delaware.**Empl**— 13,900. **S&P Analyst:** Maureen C. Carini

STANDARD &POOR'S
STOCK REPORTS

SPS Technologies

NYSE Symbol **ST**

In S&P SmallCap 600

09-OCT-99

Industry: Manufacturing (Specialized)

Summary: This company manufactures high-strength fastening and assembly systems, superalloys, magnetic and other specialty materials.

S&P Opinion: Accumulate (★★★★)

Recent Price • 36½
52 Wk Range • 57⅜-35
Yield • Nil
12-Mo. P/E • 9.9

Quantitative Evaluations

Outlook (1 Lowest—5 Highest)
• **4**

Fair Value
• **57⅞**

Risk
• **Low**

Earn./Div. Rank
• **B**

Technical Eval.
• **Bearish** since 9/99

Rel. Strength Rank (1 Lowest—99 Highest)
• **41**

Insider Activity
• **NA**

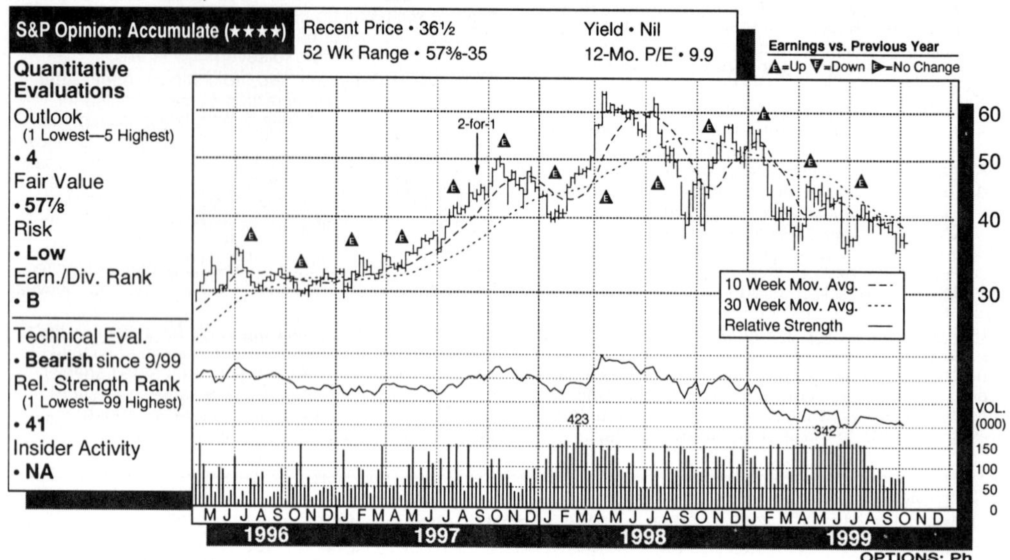

OPTIONS: Ph

Overview - 02-SEP-99

The company's strategy is to maintain its aerospace businesses at current levels, maximize free cash flow, and continue to diversify through acquisitions. Continuing its recent acquisition pace, on June 30, 1999, ST acquired National Set Screw Corp., a maker of steel components for automotive and other industrial applications, for $43.6 million. Without consideration of additional purchases, 1999 revenues are projected to grow 12% to 14%, with total fastener sales up 20% to 22%. A stronger second half in the specialty materials and alloys and magnetic materials group should offset first half softness that we attribute to a hangover from the global financial crisis in late 1998, and we think these segments are likely to be flat for the year. Cost saving measures enacted since the end of 1998 should let margins widen. We look for 1999 EPS to climb 20%, to $4.10. For 2000, we project revenue gains of 5% to 7%, with EPS increasing 10%, to $4.51.

Valuation - 02-SEP-99

The shares merit accumulation, and should do well as cyclical stock valuations improve, on continuing recovery in foreign markets and further growth in the U.S. The appeal of the company's acquisition strategy has been extended by its ability to trim costs at acquired businesses. The aerospace business should continue to generate substantial free cash flow. All in all, ST's diverse markets should generate overall growth, with strength in some groups offsetting occasional short term weakness in others. Also, while we have not incorporated any acquisitions beyond the National Set Screw purchase into our outlook, it would be surprising if ST did not make additional purchases. ST makes acquisitions that are additive to cash flow. A stock buyback of up to about 4% of the shares outstanding was authorized in July 1999.

Key Stock Statistics

S&P EPS Est. 1999	4.10	Tang. Bk. Value/Share	20.86
P/E on S&P Est. 1999	8.9	Beta	1.03
S&P EPS Est. 2000	4.51	Shareholders	985
Dividend Rate/Share	Nil	Market cap. (B)	$0.463
Shs. outstg. (M)	12.7	Inst. holdings	54%
Avg. daily vol. (M)	0.015		

Value of $10,000 invested 5 years ago: $ 40,067

Fiscal Year Ending Dec. 31

	1999	1998	1997	1996	1995	1994
Revenues (Million $)						
1Q	202.5	179.9	138.0	114.0	102.4	81.58
2Q	194.6	175.2	153.1	121.3	100.6	87.87
3Q	—	184.4	142.3	125.4	100.5	88.47
4Q	—	177.2	155.3	125.2	106.3	90.99
Yr.	—	716.6	588.6	485.9	409.8	348.9
Earnings Per Share ($)						
1Q	**1.02**	**0.85**	**0.56**	**0.41**	0.27	-0.41
2Q	**1.00**	**0.90**	**0.66**	**0.47**	0.34	0.36
3Q	**E1.03**	**0.84**	**0.66**	**0.48**	0.35	0.20
4Q	**E1.03**	**0.83**	**0.66**	**0.41**	0.30	0.16
Yr.	**E4.10**	**3.42**	**2.54**	**1.77**	**1.25**	0.31

Next earnings report expected: mid October

Dividend Data

Quarterly dividend payments were suspended in December 1993.

SPS Technologies, Inc.

Business Summary - 02-SEP-99

Despite fierce competition among major aircraft manufacturers, which has led to some shifts in market share, the overall outlook for SPS Technologies (ST) has not changed as dramatically, since it supplies both Boeing and Airbus. As a result, the company expects its aerospace fasteners business (34% of 1998 net revenues) to cruise, while it continues to expand its other business groups.

ST is organized into seven business groups, each with distinct management issues, different customers, and important differences in manufacturing processes, although for financial reporting purposes the company combines its operations into three segments. Together with the aerospace fasteners group, the automotive fasteners, industrial fasteners and tools groups (combined 64% of 1998 revenues) report as the Precision Fasteners and Components segment. The other two segments are specialty materials and alloys (16%), and magnetic materials (20%).

The aerospace fastener group develops fasteners, as well as parts, components and consumable tools, in conjunction with, and supplies them to, leading commercial and military aircraft manufacturers. The group operates manufacturing plants in the U.S., including the world's largest aerospace fastener plant in Pennsylvania, as well as facilities in England, Canada, Ireland and Brazil. Aerospace operations were expanded in October 1998 by the acquisition of Chevron Aerospace Group Ltd., Nottingham, England, for $55 million.

The automotive fastener group's goals are to further expand and broaden its product offerings through additional strategic acquisitions. It supplies fasteners and other engineered components worldwide to the auto, truck, and heavy equipment industries. On June 30, 1998, ST acquired Terry Machine, a maker of specialty cold headed fasteners for the auto industry.

The industrial fastener group was formed in 1997 to unify the marketing and manufacturing operations of business units with 11 facilities on four continents.

The precision tool group is targeting growth through acquisition. On June 30, 1998, ST acquired the operating assets of Howell Penncraft, a maker of high speed tool steel and carbide products used in metal forming.

The Specialty Materials and Alloys and Magnetic Materials segments have also rapidly expanded in recent years through acquisitions. Sales of superalloys (so called because of the materials or processes by which they are made and resulting unusual physical characteristics, such as superior strength) have been strong, because of demand from the industrial turbine and computer, telecommunications, and U.S. automotive markets.

Per Share Data ($) (Year Ended Dec. 31)	1998	1997	1996	1995	1994	1993	1992	1991	1990	1989
Tangible Bk. Val.	20.86	13.40	12.83	11.89	10.16	8.84	13.71	17.64	17.81	17.35
Cash Flow	5.68	4.34	3.27	2.48	1.58	-1.70	0.49	1.84	0.38	2.71
Earnings	3.42	2.54	1.77	1.25	0.31	-3.04	-0.69	0.55	-0.99	1.60
Dividends	Nil	Nil	Nil	Nil	Nil	0.48	0.64	0.64	0.64	0.61
Payout Ratio	Nil	Nil	Nil	Nil	Nil	NM	NM	116%	NM	38%
Prices - High	65	50½	35⅝	26⅞	13¾	15⅛	14¾	18½	22	30⅛
- Low	37	29¼	25⅝	12¾	9⅜	7⅞	9½	10⅜	10¼	20½
P/E Ratio - High	19	20	20	21	44	NM	NM	34	NM	19
- Low	11	11	14	10	30	NM	NM	19	NM	13
Income Statement Analysis (Million $)										
Revs.	717	589	486	410	349	319	321	374	441	423
Oper. Inc.	109	81.2	57.0	40.1	24.5	17.0	18.3	31.5	21.6	37.5
Depr.	29.3	23.1	18.9	14.7	13.1	13.6	12.1	13.1	13.7	11.1
Int. Exp.	10.9	9.0	8.0	6.5	6.9	5.9	5.4	7.7	10.6	8.6
Pretax Inc.	67.1	49.5	31.0	21.3	6.1	-33.6	-8.3	10.7	-4.9	22.4
Eff. Tax Rate	33%	34%	28%	30%	48%	NM	NM	48%	NM	28%
Net Inc.	44.6	32.5	22.3	14.9	3.2	-31.0	-7.0	5.6	-10.0	16.1
Balance Sheet & Other Fin. Data (Million $)										
Cash	8.4	18.7	33.3	8.1	9.5	6.8	2.9	3.8	5.2	6.8
Curr. Assets	272	227	232	179	160	161	152	157	218	195
Total Assets	607	472	428	322	289	286	290	311	369	324
Curr. Liab.	138	121	105	77.4	71.9	66.5	59.9	60.1	86.8	68.4
LT Debt	154	95.5	99	58.1	56.4	81.8	63.1	60.6	91.3	74.9
Common Eqty.	267	215	178	146	124	103	143	179	180	174
Total Cap.	444	327	297	217	191	194	215	251	282	256
Cap. Exp.	32.1	37.5	28.2	21.5	17.6	12.2	14.5	11.1	24.2	18.9
Cash Flow	73.9	55.6	41.2	29.6	16.3	-17.4	5.0	18.7	3.7	27.2
Curr. Ratio	2.0	1.9	2.2	2.3	2.2	2.4	2.5	2.6	2.5	2.9
% LT Debt of Cap.	34.7	29.2	33.2	26.8	29.5	42.2	29.4	24.2	32.4	29.3
% Net Inc.of Revs.	6.2	5.5	4.6	3.7	0.9	NM	NM	1.5	NM	3.8
% Ret. on Assets	8.3	7.2	5.9	4.9	1.1	NM	NM	1.6	NM	4.9
% Ret. on Equity	18.5	16.6	13.8	11.1	2.7	NM	NM	3.1	NM	9.3

Data as orig reptd.; bef. results of disc opers/spec. items. Per share data adj. for stk. divs. Bold denotes diluted EPS (FASB 128)-prior periods restated. E-Estimated. NA-Not Available. NM-Not Meaningful. NR-Not Ranked.

Office—101 Greenwood Ave., Suite 470, Jenkintown, PA 19046. **Tel**—(215) 517-2000. **Website**—http://www.spstech.com **Chrmn, Pres & CEO**—C. W. Grigg. **VP, CFO & Investor Contact**—William M. Shockley (215-517-2008). **VP & Secy**—J. D. Dee. **Contr**—M. B. Zminda. **Dirs**—C. W. Grigg, H. T. Hallowell III, R. W. Kelso, J. F. O'Connor, E. M. Ruttenberg, R. P. Sharpe, H. J. Wilkinson. **Transfer Agent & Registrar**—ChaseMellon Shareholder Services, Ridgefield Park, NJ. **Incorporated**—in Pennsylvania in 1903. **Empl**— 5,983. **S&P Analyst:** Mark S. Basham

STANDARD
&POOR'S
STOCK REPORTS

St. Mary Land & Exploration

NASDAQ Symbol **MARY**

In S&P SmallCap 600

09-OCT-99

Industry:
Oil & Gas (Exploration & Production)

Summary: This independent oil and gas concern has diversified exploration, development and production holdings in five core areas in the U.S.

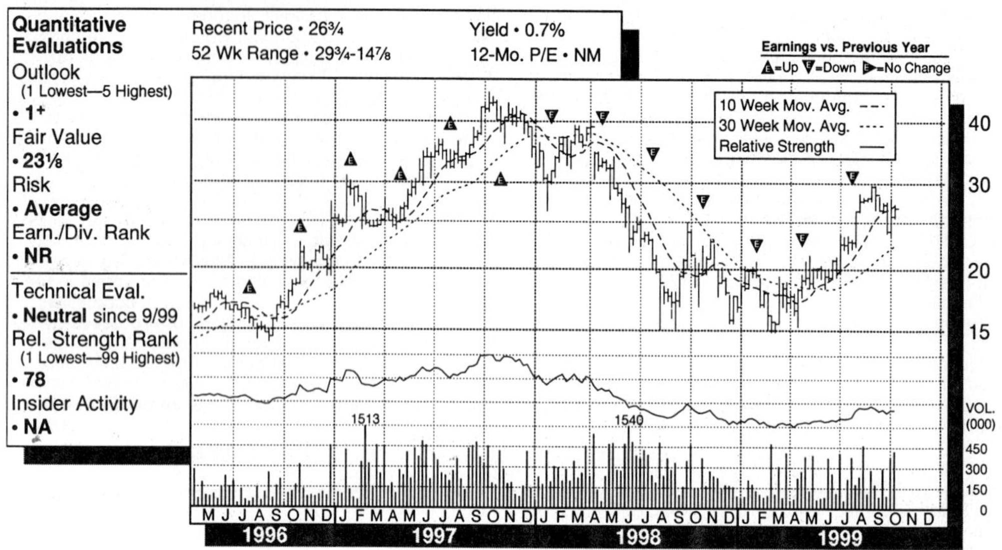

Business Profile - 23-JUL-99

The company's objective is to build value by focusing its resources within selected basins in the U.S. where management believesestablished acreage positions, long-standing industry relationships and specialized geotechnical and engineering expertise provide a significant competitive advantage. The company's ongoing development and exploration programs are complemented by less predictable opportunities to acquire producing properties having significant exploitation potential, to monetize assets at apremium, and to repurchase shares of its common stock at attractive values.

Operational Review - 23-JUL-99

Total operating revenues fell 26% year to year in the first quarter of 1999, reflecting lower production and prices. Revenues in 1998 included eight fields sold in the third quarter of 1998. Production costs and depreciation, depletion and amortization charges were slightly higher, and net income plunged 76%, to $409,000 ($0.04 a share), from $1,670,000 ($0.15).

Stock Performance - 08-OCT-99

In the past 30 trading days, MARY's shares have declined 10%, compared to a 0.91% fall in the S&P 500. Average trading volume for the past five days was 83,580 shares, compared with the 40-day moving average of 46,641 shares.

Key Stock Statistics

Dividend Rate/Share	0.20	Shareholders	164
Shs. outstg. (M)	11.1	Market cap. (B)	$0.297
Avg. daily vol. (M)	0.059	Inst. holdings	60%
Tang. Bk. Value/Share	12.51		
Beta	1.00		

Value of $10,000 invested 5 years ago: $ 22,998

Fiscal Year Ending Dec. 31

	1999	1998	1997	1996	1995	1994
Revenues (Million $)						
1Q	14.11	19.14	30.86	11.43	10.03	9.18
2Q	15.81	20.31	19.84	13.60	9.03	11.77
3Q	—	16.71	18.49	15.15	8.38	14.11
4Q	—	22.58	21.86	19.37	11.21	9.72
Yr.	—	78.74	91.05	59.55	38.65	44.79
Earnings Per Share ($)						
1Q	**0.04**	**0.15**	1.20	0.04	0.14	0.07
2Q	**0.15**	**0.18**	0.50	0.27	0.03	0.26
3Q	—	**-0.71**	0.36	0.35	0.01	0.32
4Q	—	**-0.44**	**0.12**	0.50	Nil	-0.22
Yr.	—	**-0.81**	**2.10**	**1.15**	**0.20**	0.43

Next earnings report expected: early November

Dividend Data (Dividends have been paid since 1993.)

Amount ($)	Date Decl.	Ex-Div. Date	Stock of Record	Payment Date
0.050	Oct. 19	Nov. 04	Nov. 06	Nov. 16 '98
0.050	Jan. 28	Feb. 10	Feb. 15	Feb. 25 '99
0.050	Apr. 26	May. 12	May. 14	May. 25 '99
0.050	Jul. 19	Aug. 04	Aug. 05	Aug. 16 '99

St. Mary Land & Exploration Company

Business Summary - 23-JUL-99

St. Mary Land & Exploration Co. is an independent energy company engaged in the exploration, development, acquisition and production of natural gas and crude oil. Its operations are focused in five core operating areas in the U.S.: the Mid-Continent region; theArkLaTex region; south Louisiana; the Williston Basin; and the Permian Basin.

As of December 31, 1998, the company had estimated net proved reserves of approximately 8.6 MMBbls of oil and 132.6 Bcf of natural gas, or an aggregate of 184.3 BCFE (86% proved developed, 72% gas) with a PV-10 value (present value discounted at 10%) before tax of $125.1 million.

From January 1, 1994, through December 31, 1998, the company added estimated net proved reserves of 270.0 BCFE at an average finding cost of $5.84 per BOE. Its average annual production replacement was 220% during this five-year period.

In 1998, production increased 10% to a total of 33.1 BCFE, or average daily production of 90.6 MMcf per day. The company's 1999 capital budget of approximately $71.0 million includes $37.0 million for ongoing development and exploration programs in the core operating areas, $25.0 million for niche acquisitions of oil and gas properties and $9.0 million for higher-risk, large-target exploration prospects.

St. Mary's objective is to build stockholder value through consistenteconomic growth in reserves and production and the resulting increase in net asset value per share, cash flow per share and earnings per share. A focused and balanced program of low- to medium-risk exploration and development and niche acquisitions in each of its core operating areas is designed to provide the foundation for steady growth while the company's portfolio of higher-risk, large-target exploration prospects has the potential to significantly increase the company's reserves and production. All investment decisions are measured and ranked by their risk-adjusted impact on per share value.

Per Share Data ($) (Year Ended Dec. 31)	1998	1997	1996	1995	1994	1993	1992	1991	1990	1989
Tangible Bk. Val.	12.43	13.47	8.58	7.57	7.54	7.26	7.00	4.38	3.86	NA
Cash Flow	1.47	3.81	2.61	1.33	1.58	1.39	3.02	1.26	1.11	NA
Earnings	-0.81	2.13	1.16	0.17	0.43	0.39	2.10	0.49	0.50	NA
Dividends	0.20	0.20	0.16	0.16	0.16	0.16	0.16	0.16	0.16	NA
Payout Ratio	NM	9%	14%	94%	37%	41%	8%	33%	32%	NA
Prices - High	39⅝	46	27⅜	15	14⅜	18	11½	NA	NA	NA
- Low	15	24	13½	10⅞	10⅞	18	11	NA	NA	NA
P/E Ratio - High	NM	22	24	75	33	46	6	NA	NA	NA
- Low	NM	11	12	54	25	28	5	NA	NA	NA
Income Statement Analysis (Million $)										
Revs.	78.7	81.4	59.6	38.7	44.8	38.6	50.7	27.8	27.6	NA
Oper. Inc.	20.9	44.1	28.9	11.8	14.8	14.0	30.5	12.0	12.4	NA
Depr. Depl. & Amort.	24.9	18.4	12.7	10.2	NA	8.8	6.2	5.6	4.4	NA
Int. Exp.	1.7	1.1	2.1	1.2	0.9	0.7	1.1	1.0	2.5	NA
Pretax Inc.	-14.2	34.9	15.5	0.7	4.2	4.5	22.5	5.4	5.6	NA
Eff. Tax Rate	NM	35%	34%	NM	11%	24%	33%	35%	36%	NA
Net Inc.	-8.8	22.6	10.2	1.4	3.7	3.4	15.2	3.5	3.6	NA
Balance Sheet & Other Fin. Data (Million $)										
Cash	8.5	7.1	3.3	1.7	10.0	14.8	NA	NA	NA	NA
Curr. Assets	27.1	31.9	32.1	10.8	18.9	22.6	NA	NA	NA	NA
Total Assets	184	211	144	96.1	89.4	NA	75.9	53.8	NA	NA
Curr. Liab.	17.3	22.3	18.2	7.7	9.5	7.4	NA	NA	NA	NA
LT Debt	19.4	22.6	43.6	19.6	11.1	7.4	5.0	15.8	NA	NA
Common Eqty.	136	149	75.2	66.3	66.0	63.6	61.4	31.1	NA	NA
Total Cap.	166	189	125	87.1	78.9	73.7	66.5	46.9	NA	NA
Cap. Exp.	0.1	54.2	27.5	22.7	NA	13.5	7.0	NA	NA	NA
Cash Flow	16.1	41.0	22.9	11.7	5.8	12.2	21.8	9.1	7.9	NA
Curr. Ratio	1.6	1.4	1.8	1.4	2.0	3.1	NA	NA	NA	NA
% LT Debt of Cap.	11.7	12.0	34.9	22.5	14.1	10.1	7.5	NA	NA	NA
% Ret. on Assets	NM	12.7	8.5	1.5	4.4	4.3	24.1	7.5	NA	NA
% Ret. on Equity	NM	20.0	14.4	2.0	NA	5.4	33.0	12.1	NA	NA

Data as orig reptd.; bef. results of disc opers/spec. items. Per share data adj. for stk. divs. Revs. in quarterly table for 1997 incl. gain on sale of investment of $9.67 million. Bold denotes diluted EPS (FASB 128)-prior periods restated. E-Estimated. NA-Not Available. NM-Not Meaningful. NR-Not Ranked.

Office—1776 Lincoln St., Suite 1100, Denver, CO 80203. **Tel**—(303) 861-8140. **Fax**—(303) 861-0934. **Website**—http://www.stmaryland.com **Chrmn**—T. E. Congdon. **Pres, CEO & Investor Contact**—Mark A. Hellerstein. **EVP & COO**—R. D. Boone. **VP-Fin, Treas & Secy**—R. C. Norris. **Dirs**—L. W. Bickle, R. D. Boone, T. E. Congdon, D. C. Dudley, M. A. Hellerstein, R. C. Kraus, R. J. Nicholson, A. J. Sandbulte, J. M. Seidl. **Transfer Agent**—American Securities Transfer, Inc., Lakewood, CO. **Incorporated**—in Delaware in 1915; business founded in 1908. **Empl**— 110. **S&P Analyst:** C.F.B.

STANDARD
&POOR'S
STOCK REPORTS

StaffMark, Inc.

NASDAQ Symbol **STAF**

In S&P SmallCap 600

09-OCT-99 **Industry:** Services (Employment)

Summary: StaffMark provides diversified staffing, information technology (IT), professional, consulting and solutions services to businesses, professional and service organizations.

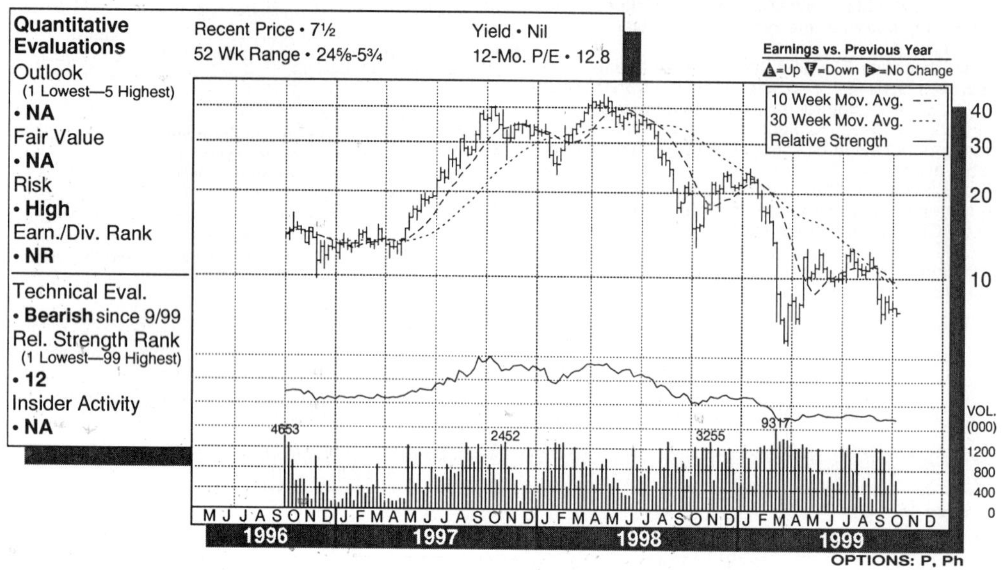

Business Profile - 13-AUG-99

StaffMark aims to increase its revenues, enhance profitability, and improve cash flow by the timely delivery of human resource and business solutions to clients through the creation of opportunities for its professionals and associates. In the 1999 second quarter, the company further diversified its Professional/IT segment by acquiring Edgewater Technology. In November 1998, StaffMark acquired for about 6.7 million common shares Robert Walters plc, a London-based international recruitment consultancy operating in 14 cities in 10 countries; this was the company's largest acquisition to date.

Operational Review - 13-AUG-99

Revenues in the six months ended June 30, 1999, advanced 28%, year to year, on gains of 19% and 38% for professional/information technology and commercial revenues, respectively. However, profitability was hurt by a shift in the revenue mix from permanent placement revenues, a 69% increase in depreciation and amortization charges, and a rise in net interest and other expense to $7.7 million, from $1.9 million; pretax income fell 10%. After taxes at 36.6%, versus 39.4%, net income was down 5.8%, to $17,166,000 ($0.58 a share), from $18,228,000 ($0.62).

Stock Performance - 08-OCT-99

In the past 30 trading days, STAF's shares have declined 32%, compared to a 0.91% fall in the S&P 500. Average trading volume for the past five days was 120,240 shares, compared with the 40-day moving average of 180,826 shares.

Key Stock Statistics

Dividend Rate/Share	Nil	Shareholders	618
Shs. outstg. (M)	29.3	Market cap. (B)	$0.222
Avg. daily vol. (M)	0.150	Inst. holdings	26%
Tang. Bk. Value/Share	NM		
Beta	NA		

Value of $10,000 invested 5 years ago: NA

Fiscal Year Ending Dec. 31

	1999	1998	1997	1996	1995	1994
Revenues (Million $)						
1Q	280.3	214.6	63.86	—	—	—
2Q	304.3	243.2	96.12	—	—	—
3Q	—	264.3	121.6	52.69	—	—
4Q	—	292.9	139.2	55.90	—	—
Yr.	—	1,015	426.5	198.4	171.5	—
Earnings Per Share ($)						
1Q	0.22	0.25	0.16	—	—	—
2Q	0.37	0.37	0.24	—	—	—
3Q	—	0.41	0.28	—	—	—
4Q	—	-0.40	0.29	0.20	—	—
Yr.	—	0.63	1.00	0.67	—	—

Next earnings report expected: mid October

Dividend Data

No cash dividends have been paid. The company intends to retain earnings to finance the expansion and operations of its business. It does not anticipate paying any cash dividends on its common stock for the foreseeable future.

StaffMark, Inc.

Business Summary - 13-AUG-99

StaffMark Inc. specializes in providing hard-to-find human resources and offers a complementary set of value-added consulting and outsourcing solutions. Customers include businesses, professional and service organizations and governmental agencies. The company offers services through more than 330 offices in 32 states and 14 countries.

STAF's overall business strategy is to increase revenues, expand profits, and bolster cash flow through the timely delivery of human resource and business solutions to customers by creating opportunities for its professionals, consultants and associates, with these opportunities being enhanced over time by training and education programs.

The company implements its business strategy by developing long-term relationships with customers, increasing operating efficiencies, providing corporate support, maintaining a decentralized and entrepreneurial environment, further developing and using the global pipeline, establishing service platforms and brand name identification, and through education, training and career management.

Operations are grouped into two segments: Professional/information technology (IT), which accounted for 52% of revenues and 56% of operating profit in 1998; and Commercial (48% and 44%, respectively). The Professional/IT segment provides staffing, consulting, technical support and solutions primarily in the areas of IT, finance, accounting and legal services. Business solutions include IT staffing, help desk and distributed services, network services development systems, integration, training, enterprise resource planning, clinical research and solutions, finance and accounting staffing and legal staffing. The Commercial segment provides clerical, administrative, outsourcing and light industrial services.

From its October 1996 IPO through the end of 1998, the company completed 40 acquisitions. It made 18 acquisitions in 1998, 11 of which were Professional/IT companies, with combined revenues of about $225 million. Seven 1998 acquisitions were Commercial companies, with revenues of about $126.4 million.

Robert Walters plc, a London-based international recruitment consultancy acquired in exchange for about 6.7 million common shares in November 1998, specializes in placing accounting, finance and IT professionals on a contract, temporary and permanent basis with customers in the finance, commercial and industrial sectors.

Through its acquisition strategy, STAF has achieved critical mass and geographic diversification, and increased its Professional/IT segment to over 50% of the revenue base. While focusing on internal growth and building infrastructure in certain of its platforms, the company has decided to slow down its acquisition program for the balance of 1999.

Foreign operations (primarily the U.K. and Australia) accounted for 26% of revenues in 1998.

Per Share Data ($) (Year Ended Dec. 31)	1998	1997	1996	1995	1994	1993	1992	1991	1990	1989
Tangible Bk. Val.	NM	1.17	2.06	NA	NA	NA	NA	NA	NA	NA
Cash Flow	1.11	1.14	0.40	NA	NA	NA	NA	NA	NA	NA
Earnings	0.63	1.00	0.67	NA	NA	NA	NA	NA	NA	NA
Dividends	Nil	Nil	Nil	NA	NA	NA	NA	NA	NA	NA
Payout Ratio	Nil	Nil	Nil	NA	NA	NA	NA	NA	NA	NA
Prices - High	44⅞	40½	16¾	NA	NA	NA	NA	NA	NA	NA
- Low	12¾	11½	9¾	NA	NA	NA	NA	NA	NA	NA
P/E Ratio - High	71	40	25	NA	NA	NA	NA	NA	NA	NA
- Low	20	11	14	NA	NA	NA	NA	NA	NA	NA
Income Statement Analysis (Million $)										
Revs.	1,015	426	104	43.9	NA	NA	NA	NA	NA	NA
Oper. Inc.	92.3	33.8	8.2	3.0	NA	NA	NA	NA	NA	NA
Depr.	14.2	5.3	1.4	0.6	NA	NA	NA	NA	NA	NA
Int. Exp.	6.8	1.3	1.4	0.8	NA	NA	NA	NA	NA	NA
Pretax Inc.	43.8	27.9	5.8	1.6	NA	NA	NA	NA	NA	NA
Eff. Tax Rate	57%	41%	31%	NA	NA	NA	NA	NA	NA	NA
Net Inc.	18.6	16.5	4.0	1.6	NA	NA	NA	NA	NA	NA
Balance Sheet & Other Fin. Data (Million $)										
Cash	12.8	0.3	13.9	0.3	NA	NA	NA	NA	NA	NA
Curr. Assets	181	62.6	36.5	5.4	NA	NA	NA	NA	NA	NA
Total Assets	581	249	71.5	21.8	NA	NA	NA	NA	NA	NA
Curr. Liab.	86.8	40.0	12.4	3.9	NA	NA	NA	NA	NA	NA
LT Debt	177	12.0	Nil	NA	NA	NA	NA	NA	NA	NA
Common Eqty.	260	195	58.1	2.8	NA	NA	NA	NA	NA	NA
Total Cap.	446	209	58.5	NA	NA	NA	NA	NA	NA	NA
Cap. Exp.	10.2	7.1	0.7	NA	NA	NA	NA	NA	NA	NA
Cash Flow	32.8	21.8	5.4	2.2	NA	NA	NA	NA	NA	NA
Curr. Ratio	2.1	1.6	2.9	1.4	NA	NA	NA	NA	NA	NA
% LT Debt of Cap.	39.6	5.7	Nil	NA	NA	NA	NA	NA	NA	NA
% Net Inc.of Revs.	1.8	3.9	3.9	3.6	NA	NA	NA	NA	NA	NA
% Ret. on Assets	4.5	10.3	8.6	NA	NA	NA	NA	NA	NA	NA
% Ret. on Equity	8.2	13.0	13.2	NA	NA	NA	NA	NA	NA	NA

Data as orig reptd.; bef. results of disc opers/spec. items. Per share data adj. for stk. divs. Bold denotes diluted EPS (FASB 128)-prior periods restated. E-Estimated. NA-Not Available. NM-Not Meaningful. NR-Not Ranked.

Office—302 East Millsap Road, Fayetteville, AR 72703. **Tel**—(501) 973-6000. **Website**—http://www.staffmark.com **Pres & CEO**—C. T. Brewer. **Chrmn**—J. T. Brewer. **Secy**—G. Y. Allison. **Dirs**—W. D. Bartholomew, J. Blethen, C. T. Brewer, J. T. Brewer, W. T. Gregory, J. H. Maxwell Jr., S. E. Schulte. **Transfer Agent & Registrar**—First Chicago Trust Co. of New York, Chicago. **Incorporated**—in Delaware in 1996. **Empl**— 2,000. **S&P Analyst:** J. J. Schemitsch

STANDARD
&POOR'S
STOCK REPORTS

Standard Microsystems

NASDAQ Symbol **SMSC**

In S&P SmallCap 600

09-OCT-99

Industry: Computers (Networking)

Summary: This leading supplier of PC LAN system products and semiconductors for PCs recently sold a majority stake in its System Products Division.

Quantitative Evaluations

Outlook (1 Lowest—5 Highest) • 2+

Fair Value • 9⅛

Risk • High

Earn./Div. Rank • C

Technical Eval. • Bullish since 8/99

Rel. Strength Rank (1 Lowest—99 Highest) • 84

Insider Activity • NA

Recent Price • 9 · Yield • Nil

52 Wk Range • 10¼-4⅞ · 12-Mo. P/E • NM

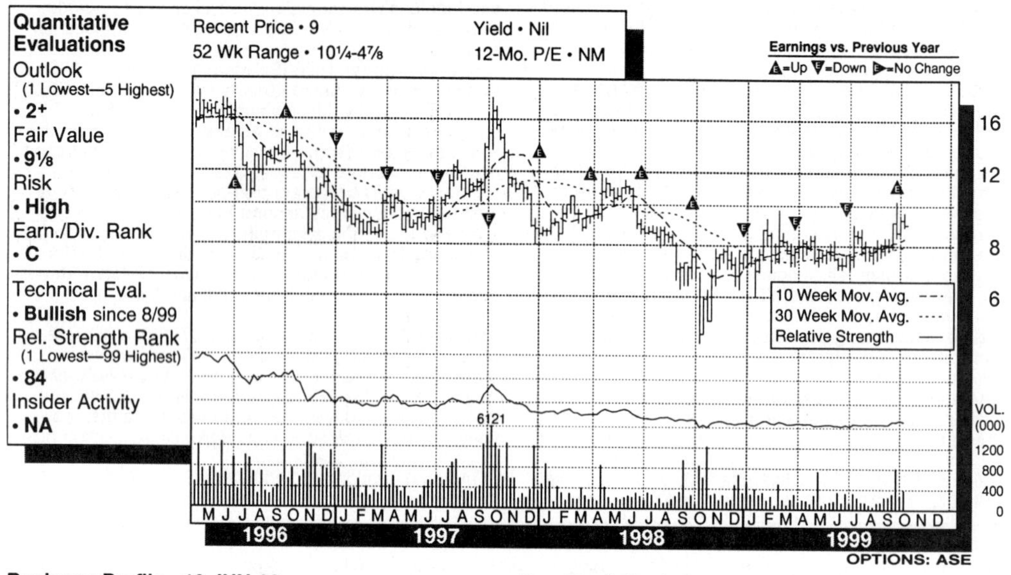

Business Profile - 16-JUN-99

With the early June 1999 divestiture of its Foundry Business Unit, which had experienced significant losses in recent years, Standard Microsystems is now exclusively a supplier of semiconductor integrated circuits. SMSC merged its Foundry operations with Inertia Optical Technology Applications (IOTA), a privately held company, in exchange for a 38% minority interest in the combined entity. SMSC has committed to reducing its minority interest to 20% within one year. Intel owns approximately 10% of SMSC's shares outstanding.

Operational Review - 16-JUN-99

Revenues for FY 99 (Feb) rose 5.1%, from the prior year, as almost a 30% increase in unit sales of I/O integrated circuits and revenues from new connectivity products offset lower average selling prices for I/O circuits. The gross margin widened significantly, with reduced product material costs and a more favorable product mix offsetting lower average selling prices. With controlled operating expenses, on higher R&D but fractionally lower SG&A, and after $2.4 million in non interest income, compared with $902,000, on higher cash balances, income from continuing operations of $6,003,000 ($0.38 a share), contrasted with a loss from continuing operations of $1,105,000 ($0.07). Results for FY 99 and FY 98 exclude net losses from the operation and sale of discontinued operations of $18,548,000 ($1.17 a share) and $17,816,000 ($1.15).

Stock Performance - 08-OCT-99

In the past 30 trading days, SMSC's shares have increased 12%, compared to a 0.91% fall in the S&P 500. Average trading volume for the past five days was 74,440 shares, compared with the 40-day moving average of 63,154 shares.

Key Stock Statistics

Dividend Rate/Share	Nil	Shareholders	1,100
Shs. outstg. (M)	15.6	Market cap. (B)	$0.141
Avg. daily vol. (M)	0.087	Inst. holdings	52%
Tang. Bk. Value/Share	9.85		
Beta	1.23		

Value of $10,000 invested 5 years ago: $ 4,186

Fiscal Year Ending Feb. 28

	2000	1999	1998	1997	1996	1995
Revenues (Million $)						
1Q	35.43	37.60	34.80	100.1	72.21	80.00
2Q	38.27	40.88	41.18	99.2	85.43	91.96
3Q	—	45.27	42.77	93.77	90.57	104.8
4Q	—	39.93	36.99	61.08	93.71	101.9
Yr.	—	155.8	155.8	354.1	341.9	378.7
Earnings Per Share ($)						
1Q	**0.01**	**0.03**	-0.22	0.14	-0.22	0.41
2Q	**0.05**	**0.04**	-0.14	0.01	-0.91	0.42
3Q	—	**0.01**	0.02	-0.28	0.02	0.51
4Q	—	**-0.93**	**0.03**	-1.40	1.94	0.55
Yr.	—	**0.38**	**-0.29**	**-0.32**	0.86	1.89

Next earnings report expected: mid December

Dividend Data

No cash has been paid. A "poison pill" stock purchase plan was adopted in 1988.

Standard Microsystems Corporation

Business Summary - 16-JUN-99

SMSC has increasingly focused on its integrated circuit products in recent years. With the mid 1999 divestiture of its Foundry Business Unit, which produces microelectromechanical systems, the company is now engaged solely in the design, development, and marketing of semiconductor integrated circuits for the personal computer and related industries. After a nearly 30% increase in unit shipments during FY 99 (Feb), Standard Microsystems Corp. believes it is now the worldwide leader in shipments of input/output (I/O) integrated circuits.

Standard Microsystems' integrated circuit products provide logic control and connectivity for personal computer (PC) systems. Products are grouped into several families, among which are PC I/O controllers, PC LAN devices, and PC connectivity products. I/O controllers, which represented about 80% of revenue in FY 99, provide control over and interfacing with various peripheral and PC communications functions, such as floppy disks, serial and parallel ports, and keyboard and mouse. PC LAN devices enable personal computers to connect to networks in order to send messages to and receive messages from other LAN users and share common resources such as printers, disk drives, files and programs.

PC connectivity products rely on the new communications standard IEEE1394 to enable enhanced communications features for both PC OEM's and PC peripheral device customers. Standard Microsystems introduced a new line of connectivity products in FY 99 based on this new communications standard. The company intends to introduce several new PC connectivity devices and expects this product family to contribute a growing portion of revenues in FY 00. Applications for some of these products relate to the convergence of the PC and entertainment media such as TV's, VCR's, and camcorders.

The company sells the largest portion of its products to OEM's, of which PC producers are the largest customer group. Products are also sold to distributors of electronic components. During FY 99, SMSC's most significant customer accounted for almost 12% of sales. International shipments accounted for 83% of FY 99 revenue, compared to 73% in FY 98. Due to the concentration of PC and PC motherboard manufacturing activity in Asia and the Pacific Rim, this region is by far the most significant international market for the company's products.

In October 1998, the SMSC approved the repurchase of up to one million shares of common stock. At the end of FY 99, the company had repurchased 521,000 shares of common stock for $2,957,000.

Per Share Data ($) (Year Ended Feb. 28)	1999	1998	1997	1996	1995	1994	1993	1992	1991	1990
Tangible Bk. Val.	9.87	10.82	11.69	13.09	11.16	11.18	6.59	4.73	7.65	7.43
Cash Flow	1.05	0.57	0.07	2.26	3.00	2.17	2.23	0.88	0.78	1.16
Earnings	0.38	-0.29	-1.54	0.86	1.89	1.52	1.27	0.05	0.10	0.41
Dividends	Nil	Nil	Nil	Nil	Nil	Nil	Nil	Nil	Nil	Nil
Payout Ratio	Nil	Nil	Nil	Nil	Nil	Nil	Nil	Nil	Nil	Nil
Cal. Yrs.	1998	1997	1996	1995	1994	1993	1992	1991	1990	1989
Prices - High	11 7/8	18 1/8	18 3/4	31 5/8	30 3/8	27	26 1/4	7 1/4	9 7/8	7 5/8
- Low	4 5/8	8	8 3/8	12 1/2	13 3/8	12 1/2	6 3/8	3 5/8	4 1/8	4 1/2
P/E Ratio - High	31	NM	NM	37	16	18	21	NM	99	19
- Low	12	NM	NM	15	7	8	5	NM	41	11
Income Statement Analysis (Million $)										
Revs.	156	156	354	342	379	323	250	133	87.0	77.0
Oper. Inc.	18.5	7.6	-6.8	-4.5	55.4	44.0	42.8	12.2	9.8	14.2
Depr.	10.5	13.4	22.2	19.0	14.8	8.5	12.0	9.6	7.8	8.6
Int. Exp.	0.3	0.2	0.6	1.1	1.3	1.6	2.3	1.2	0.3	0.5
Pretax Inc.	8.7	-6.9	-33.0	20.0	41.3	33.5	27.9	1.9	2.1	7.5
Eff. Tax Rate	30%	NM	NM	41%	39%	41%	45%	75%	56%	39%
Net Inc.	6.0	-4.5	-21.3	11.6	25.2	19.9	15.8	0.6	1.2	4.7
Balance Sheet & Other Fin. Data (Million $)										
Cash	70.1	45.2	8.4	18.5	29.5	32.1	35.9	17.9	31.1	38.9
Curr. Assets	124	109	130	149	163	140	111	79.7	75.2	76.3
Total Assets	202	211	234	261	229	206	184	154	112	113
Curr. Liab.	24.2	19.6	39.3	55.8	43.4	41.8	41.0	35.1	8.1	11.1
LT Debt	3.0	2.5	7.0	Nil	Nil	9.2	12.1	18.2	1.8	1.9
Common Eqty.	158	172	172	194	174	144	120	89.3	88.0	85.0
Total Cap.	173	186	190	205	185	164	143	119	104	102
Cap. Exp.	10.8	5.8	19.4	39.0	13.6	8.6	5.4	6.5	7.9	2.0
Cash Flow	16.5	8.9	1.0	30.6	40.0	28.4	27.8	10.2	9.0	13.2
Curr. Ratio	5.1	5.5	3.3	2.7	3.7	3.4	2.7	2.3	9.3	6.9
% LT Debt of Cap.	1.7	1.4	3.7	Nil	Nil	5.6	8.5	15.3	1.7	1.8
% Net Inc.of Revs.	3.8	NM	NM	3.4	6.6	6.2	6.3	0.4	1.4	6.1
% Ret. on Assets	2.9	NM	NM	4.7	11.4	10.1	9.4	0.4	1.1	4.2
% Ret. on Equity	3.6	NM	NM	6.3	15.6	15.0	14.8	0.7	1.4	5.6

Data as orig reptd.; bef. results of disc opers/spec. items. Per share data adj. for stk. divs. Bold denotes diluted EPS (FASB 128)-prior periods restated. E-Estimated. NA-Not Available. NM-Not Meaningful. NR-Not Ranked.

Office—80 Arkay Drive, P.O. Box 18047, Hauppauge, NY 11788-8847. **Tel**—(516) 435-6000. **Fax**—(516) 273-5550. **Website**—http://www.smc.com **Chrmn**—P. Richman. **Pres & CEO**—S. J. Bilodeau. **COO**—A. Sidorsky. **SVP & General Counsel**—G. Houseweart. **VP-Fin & CFO**—E. M. Nowling. **Secy**—D. C. Fischer. **Investor Contact**—John Tweedy (516) 434-4630. **Dirs**—E. Berezin, J. R. Berrett, R. M. Brill, P. F. Dicks, K. B. Early, H. Fialkov, I. T. Frisch, P. Richman. **Transfer Agent**—Mellon Securities Trust Co., Ridgefield, NJ. **Incorporated**—in Delaware in 1971. **Empl**— 538. **S&P Analyst:** Craig K. Shere, CFA

STANDARD
&POOR'S
STOCK REPORTS

Standard Motor Products

NYSE Symbol **SMP**

In S&P SmallCap 600

09-OCT-99 **Industry:** Auto Parts & Equipment

Summary: This company manufactures and distributes automotive replacement parts.

Quantitative Evaluations

Outlook
(1 Lowest—5 Highest)
• **4**

Fair Value
• **25¾**

Risk
• **Low**

Earn./Div. Rank
• **B-**

Technical Eval.
• **Bearish** since 9/99

Rel. Strength Rank
(1 Lowest—99 Highest)
• **6**

Insider Activity
• **Neutral**

Recent Price • 16⅝
52 Wk Range • 29⅝-16⅝
Yield • 2.2%
12-Mo. P/E • 8.3

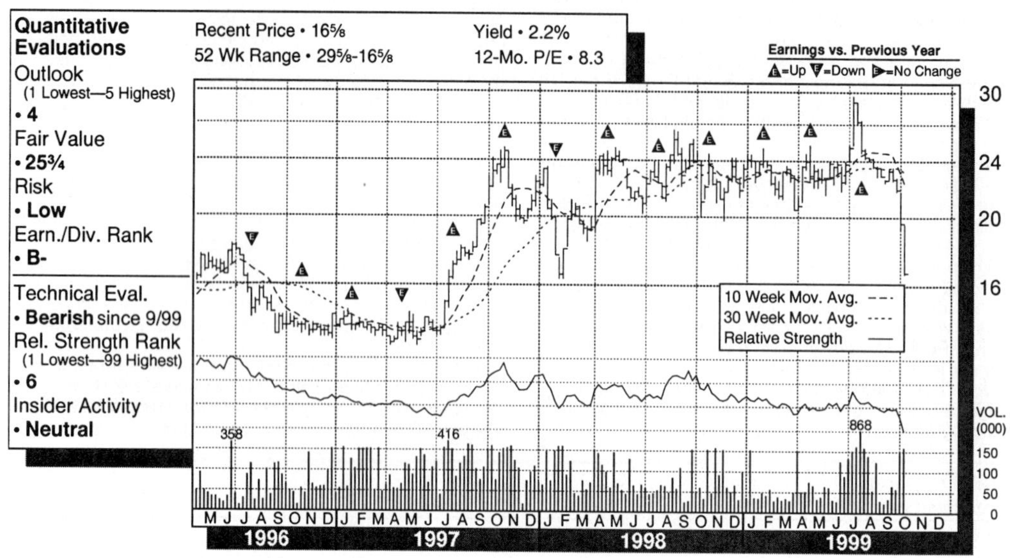

Business Profile - 20-JUL-99

In April 1999, SMP acquired Lemark Auto Accessories Ltd. a U.K. supplier of wire sets. Lemark, with annual sales of about $4.5 million, strengthens the company's engine management business in Europe, which is a continuing focus for future growth. Temperature control sales remained strong, with sales in the first half of 1999 showing double-digit growth excluding the impact of acquisitions. Sales of engine management products continue to be below 1998 levels, primarily reflecting the late 1998 sale of the company's fuel pump business and the effect on its orders from a major customer that is consolidating inventories purchased through acquisitions. In May, SMP filed a registration statement with the SEC covering the proposed offering of $75 million of convertible subordinated debentures.

Operational Review - 20-JUL-99

Net sales in the first half of 1999 rose 14%, year to year, mainly reflecting the addition of $47 million in sales from acquisitions. Gross margins narrowed, but with an 8.7% drop in SG&A expenses, operating income was up 46%. After lower interest expense and taxes at 27.5%, versus 12.4%, net income climbed 39%, to $15,681,000 ($1.19 a share), from $11,292,000 ($0.86).

Stock Performance - 08-OCT-99

In the past 30 trading days, SMP's shares have declined 27%, compared to a 0.91% fall in the S&P 500. Average trading volume for the past five days was 49,240 shares, compared with the 40-day moving average of 18,821 shares.

Key Stock Statistics

Dividend Rate/Share	0.36	Shareholders	685
Shs. outstg. (M)	13.2	Market cap. (B)	$0.220
Avg. daily vol. (M)	0.026	Inst. holdings	44%
Tang. Bk. Value/Share	12.70		
Beta	0.40		

Value of $10,000 invested 5 years ago: $ 6,961

Fiscal Year Ending Dec. 31

	1999	1998	1997	1996	1995	1994
Revenues (Million $)						
1Q	176.8	126.0	137.7	174.4	159.7	147.1
2Q	205.7	208.8	163.2	205.3	184.0	187.7
3Q	—	201.3	155.2	187.8	178.3	168.3
4Q	—	113.3	103.7	154.3	141.5	137.8
Yr.	—	649.4	559.8	721.8	663.5	640.8
Earnings Per Share ($)						
1Q	**0.28**	**0.20**	**-0.01**	**0.06**	0.30	0.21
2Q	**0.91**	**0.65**	**0.42**	**0.27**	0.63	0.62
3Q	—	**0.72**	**0.53**	**0.46**	0.24	0.59
4Q	—	**0.11**	**-1.07**	**0.33**	0.06	0.38
Yr.	—	**1.69**	**-0.12**	**1.82**	**1.28**	**1.67**

Next earnings report expected: late October

Dividend Data (Dividends have been paid since 1960.)

Amount ($)	Date Decl.	Ex-Div. Date	Stock of Record	Payment Date
0.080	Nov. 06	Nov. 10	Nov. 13	Dec. 01 '98
0.080	Mar. 03	Mar. 05	Mar. 09	Mar. 15 '99
0.080	Apr. 21	May. 12	May. 14	Jun. 01 '99
0.090	Jul. 22	Aug. 11	Aug. 13	Sep. 01 '99

A Division of The McGraw-Hill Companies

Standard Motor Products, Inc.

Business Summary - 20-JUL-99

Standard Motor Products, Inc. is an automotive replacement parts manufacturer and distributor with product offerings in the areas of engine management (ignition) and temperature control. SMP's engine management segment provides ignition and electrical parts, emission and engine controls, on-board computers, sensors, ignition wires, battery cables, and carburetor and fuel system parts. SMP's temperature control segment consists primarily of air conditioning compressors, clutches, accumulators, filter/driers, blower motors, heater valves, heater cores, evaporators, condensers, hoses and fittings.

During 1998, the company completed the sale of its service line business to R&B Inc., and exchanged its brake business for the temperature control business of Moog Automotive, Inc., a subsidiary of Cooper Industries. Completion of the smallest and final phase of the sale, for the assets of the Everco Brass and Brake Lines, was completed in the first quarter of 1999. The exchanges allow SMP to concentrate on achieving further efficiencies in its core climate control business.

SMP is pursuing a number of strategies, often with the help of acquisitions, as it seeks to prosper -- and grow -- in an industry the company itself concedes may offer limited growth. Factors aiding the outlook for the automotive aftermarket include growth in the number of vehicles on the road, an increase in the driving age population, an increase in longer duration vehicles and in the miles driven per year per vehicle, the high price of new cars, the attempt by retailers to displace traditional jobbers, and more stringent environmental laws. Conversely, the automotive aftermarket has been hurt by the broader range in prices for replacement parts, the increased complexity of vehicle systems requiring a greater specialization of parts, higher quality new cars with longer service warranties, and the effect of foreign imports and dealer versus non-dealer servicing. The net impact of these factors is a forecast for the automotive aftermarket to grow at just 1% to 2% over the next several years.

In response to competitive pricing pressures, SMP was forced to offer economy lines along with its premium products without eroding sales of higher-margin lines. SMP acquired Federal Parts Corp., a leading supplier of economy ignition wire sets, in 1996, and has made acquisitions in other product areas as well to gain access to other economy lines.

In 1996, SMP acquired a majority equity interest in Standard Motor Products Holdings Ltd., and followed this action with 1999 acquisitions of majority stakes in Webcon Ltd. and Injection Correction Ltd. These three companies, based in Great Britain, supply ignition components, fuel system components and rebuilt engine computers throughout the U.K. and Western Europe. They provide a solid base to increase sales in Europe, a market that is forecast to grow at a rate more than double that of the U.S.

Per Share Data ($) (Year Ended Dec. 31)	1998	1997	1996	1995	1994	1993	1992	1991	1990	1989
Tangible Bk. Val.	12.70	11.71	14.33	15.33	14.29	12.77	12.20	11.78	11.46	11.10
Cash Flow	3.00	1.32	2.36	2.27	2.63	2.20	1.41	1.18	1.20	1.56
Earnings	1.69	-0.12	1.12	1.23	1.80	1.41	0.68	0.51	0.59	1.00
Dividends	0.16	0.32	0.32	0.32	0.32	0.32	0.32	0.32	0.32	0.32
Payout Ratio	9%	NM	29%	26%	18%	23%	47%	63%	54%	32%
Prices - High	26½	25	18¼	20⅝	26⅞	26⅞	13⅝	13⅞	15⅝	20
- Low	16¼	13⅛	12⅝	14½	14¾	13⅛	9½	7⅜	5⅞	13¾
P/E Ratio - High	16	NM	16	17	15	19	20	27	26	20
- Low	10	NM	11	12	8	9	14	14	10	14
Income Statement Analysis (Million $)										
Revs.	649	560	722	663	641	583	536	535	508	429
Oper. Inc.	61.2	28.4	53.1	46.2	54.2	50.8	32.2	33.4	35.8	40.4
Depr.	17.3	19.0	16.3	14.0	11.0	10.5	9.7	8.9	8.0	7.3
Int. Exp.	16.4	14.2	18.7	14.6	12.3	12.3	12.3	17.2	18.9	17.4
Pretax Inc.	26.1	-3.7	19.8	20.2	35.4	26.8	10.8	7.8	9.7	17.6
Eff. Tax Rate	14%	NM	26%	29%	33%	31%	18%	15%	20%	25%
Net Inc.	22.3	-1.6	14.6	16.1	23.7	18.6	8.9	6.7	7.7	13.1
Balance Sheet & Other Fin. Data (Million $)										
Cash	30.7	16.8	4.7	17.5	8.8	12.4	17.0	24.0	15.8	13.8
Curr. Assets	343	390	418	365	329	304	265	291	321	313
Total Assets	522	577	625	512	462	423	375	393	422	406
Curr. Liab.	164	213	207	133	140	100	74.0	160	175	149
LT Debt	134	159	172	149	110	131	136	73.0	90.0	103
Common Eqty.	205	184	223	210	195	178	161	155	151	146
Total Cap.	339	346	399	365	310	312	301	232	247	257
Cap. Exp.	15.3	15.6	21.3	16.7	12.6	12.3	15.3	12.0	16.2	23.2
Cash Flow	39.5	17.4	30.9	29.8	34.7	29.1	18.6	15.5	15.8	20.5
Curr. Ratio	2.1	1.8	2.0	2.7	2.4	3.1	3.6	1.8	1.8	2.1
% LT Debt of Cap.	39.5	45.9	43.1	40.8	35.5	41.8	45.3	31.6	36.5	40.1
% Net Inc.of Revs.	3.4	NM	2.0	2.5	3.7	3.2	1.7	1.2	1.5	3.1
% Ret. on Assets	4.1	NM	2.5	3.4	5.4	4.6	2.3	1.6	1.9	3.5
% Ret. on Equity	11.4	NM	6.7	8.0	12.8	10.9	5.6	4.4	5.2	8.8

Data as orig reptd.; bef. results of disc opers/spec. items. Per share data adj. for stk. divs. Bold denotes diluted EPS (FASB 128)-prior periods restated. E-Estimated. NA-Not Available. NM-Not Meaningful. NR-Not Ranked.

Office—37-18 Northern Blvd., Long Island City, NY 11101. **Tel**—(718) 392-0200. **Website**—http://www.smpcorp.com **Chrmn & CEO**—N. L. Sills. **Pres & COO**—L. I. Sills. **SVP-Fin, CFO & Investor Contact**—Michael J. Bailey. **Dirs**—M. F. Cragin, A. D. Davis, S. F. Davis, R. M. Gerrity, J. L. Kelsey, A. M. Massimilla, A. S. Sills, L. I. Sills, N. L. Sills, R. J. Swartz, W. H. Turner. **Transfer Agent & Registrar**—Registrar & Transfer Co., Cranford, NJ. **Incorporated**—in New York in 1926. **Empl**— 3,700. **S&P Analyst:** M.I.

STANDARD
&POOR'S
STOCK REPORTS

Standard Pacific

NYSE Symbol **SPF**

In S&P SmallCap 600

09-OCT-99 **Industry:** Homebuilding

Summary: SPF is primarily a builder of medium-priced single-family homes in major metropolitan markets in California, Texas, and Arizona.

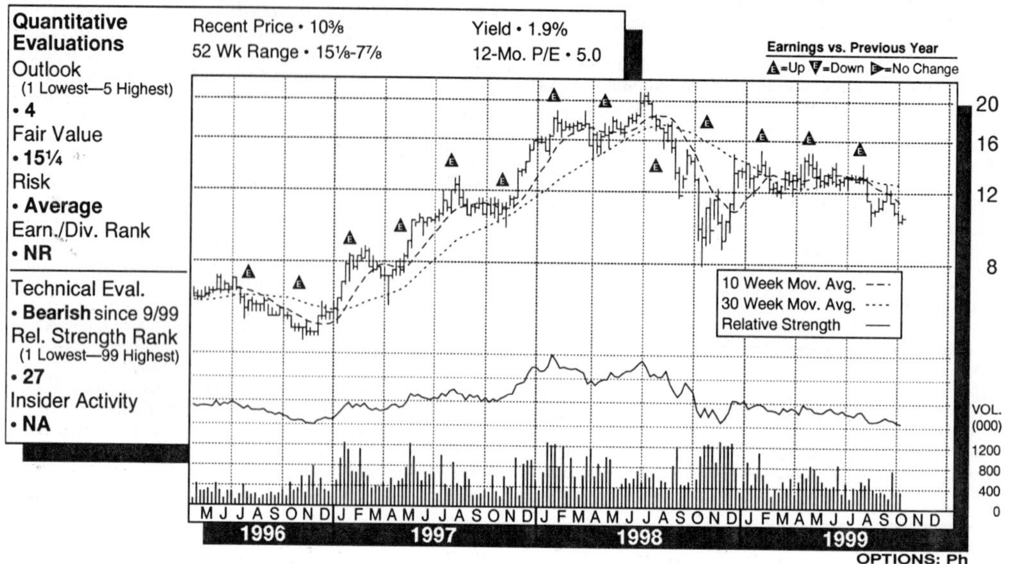

Business Profile - 29-JUL-99

Standard Pacific said in July 1999 that its backlog at June 30, 1999, amounted to 1,400 homes, with an estimated sales value of $478 million, a 15% increase from the 1998 second quarter backlog value. In addition, the company said it was planning to open 33 new communities through the balance of 1999. SPF believed that these new openings, coupled with the strong backlog at June 30,1999, should position it for continued growth in unit volume for the balance of 1999. Separately, in June 1999, the company sold its savings and loan subsidiary to American General Corp. for $8.6 million. In April 1999, SPF sold $100 million of 8.5% senior notes, with proceeds used to reduce debt under its revolving credit agreement.

Operational Review - 29-JUL-99

Total revenues from continuing operations for the first half of 1999 more than doubled to $523.7 million from $250.1 million, reflecting a strong housing market in California. Homebuilding pretax income advanced 99%. Following nominal financial services pretax income, versus a nominal loss, overall pretax income also rose 99%. With taxes at 41.1%, versus 41.5%, income from continuing operations more than doubled to $30.1 million ($1.01 a share), from $15.0 million ($0.50, before a $0.01 extraordinary charge for early extinguishment of debt). Results exclude a loss from discontinued operations of $0.01 a share, versus a gain of $0.02.

Stock Performance - 08-OCT-99

In the past 30 trading days, SPF's shares have declined 6%, compared to a 0.91% fall in the S&P 500. Average trading volume for the past five days was 66,540 shares, compared with the 40-day moving average of 77,223 shares.

Key Stock Statistics

Dividend Rate/Share	0.20	Shareholders	1,683
Shs. outstg. (M)	29.7	Market cap. (B)	$0.310
Avg. daily vol. (M)	0.082	Inst. holdings	49%
Tang. Bk. Value/Share	11.34		
Beta	1.85		

Value of $10,000 invested 5 years ago: $ 10,288

Fiscal Year Ending Dec. 31

	1999	1998	1997	1996	1995	1994
Revenues (Million $)						
1Q	214.5	96.91	121.2	70.89	77.33	78.94
2Q	309.2	153.1	140.6	112.2	89.85	107.7
3Q	—	194.1	177.2	114.7	109.6	111.5
4Q	—	315.4	155.5	141.4	110.5	122.3
Yr.	—	759.6	584.6	439.3	387.2	420.5
Earnings Per Share ($)						
1Q	**0.46**	**0.16**	0.12	0.02	0.04	0.02
2Q	**0.54**	**0.34**	0.16	0.07	0.04	0.04
3Q	—	**0.38**	0.23	0.07	-0.02	0.07
4Q	—	**0.70**	**0.31**	0.12	-0.97	0.07
Yr.	—	**1.58**	**0.81**	**0.26**	**-0.73**	**0.21**

Next earnings report expected: late October

Dividend Data (Dividends have been paid since 1976.)

Amount ($)	Date Decl.	Ex-Div. Date	Stock of Record	Payment Date
0.050	Oct. 28	Nov. 06	Nov. 10	Nov. 24 '98
0.050	Jan. 27	Feb. 10	Feb. 12	Feb. 26 '99
0.050	Apr. 28	May. 12	May. 14	May. 28 '99
0.050	Jul. 30	Aug. 11	Aug. 13	Aug. 27 '99

A Division of The McGraw-Hill Companies

Standard Pacific Corp.

Business Summary - 29-JUL-99

Through its predecessors, Standard Pacific Corp. began its homebuilding operations in 1966 with a single tract of land in Orange County, California. Since then, the company has grown considerably.

Standard Pacific operates primarily as a geographically diversified builder of single-family homes for use as primary residences. The company has operations throughout the major metropolitan markets in California, Texas, and Arizona. For the year ended December 31, 1998, 72%, 20% and 8% of home deliveries (including unconsolidated joint ventures) were in California, Texas, and Arizona, respectively.

The company also offers mortgage loans to its home buyers and others through a mortgage banking subsidiary and a joint venture with a financial institution.

Standard Pacific's strategy includes focusing on a broad move-up market and maintaining the following: high quality standards, a conservative operating approach, a strong land position, geographic diversification, control of overhead and operating expenses, and decentralized operations.

As of year-end 1998, the company was building homes in California, Texas and Arizona through a total of seven geographic divisions, with 152 projects under development or held for future development.

Substantially all homes are single-family detached dwellings, although during the past few years up to 10% have been townhouses or condominiums generally attached in varying configurations of two, three, four and six dwelling units.

The homes are designed to suit the particular area of the country in which they are located and are available in a variety of models, exterior styles and materials depending upon local preferences. The homes typically range in size from about 2,000 to 3,000 square feet and typically include three or four bedrooms, two or three baths, a living room, kitchen, dining room, family room and a two or three-car garage. SPF has also built single-family attached and detached homes ranging from 1,100 to 5,500 square feet.

In the third quarter of 1998, SPF expanded into the Phoenix, Arizona market with the acquisition of a portion of the Arizona single-family homebuilding operations of Shea Homes, Inc. In connection with this acquisition, SPF purchased, or assumed the rights to acquire, over 2,000 single-family lots in 13 communities in the Phoenix metropolitan area, and it acquired a backlog of 400 presold homes. SPF paid about $59 million for these assets, using borrowings under its revolving credit facility.

In June 1999, SPF sold its savings and loan subsidiary, Standard Pacific Savings, F.A., to American General Finance, Inc., a wholly owned subsidiary of American General Corp. Proceeds from the sale totaled $8.6 million.

Per Share Data ($) **(Year Ended Dec. 31)**	**1998**	**1997**	**1996**	**1995**	**1994**	**1993**	**1992**	**1991**	**1990**	**1989**
Tangible Bk. Val.	10.37	9.35	8.79	8.58	9.51	9.49	9.52	9.35	9.32	9.54
Cash Flow	1.65	0.83	0.31	-0.88	0.22	0.08	0.18	0.44	1.83	4.07
Earnings	1.58	0.81	0.28	-0.90	0.19	0.06	0.15	0.40	1.77	3.87
Dividends	0.17	0.14	0.12	0.12	0.12	0.12	0.09	0.30	2.00	2.10
Payout Ratio	11%	17%	43%	NM	63%	200%	61%	74%	112%	53%
Prices - High	21	16¼	7⅜	8⅜	12⅞	11⅜	14	12	16	19⅞
- Low	7⅞	5⅝	5⅛	5⅛	4⅞	6¼	4½	5⅛	4¾	11⅞
P/E Ratio - High	13	20	26	NM	68	NM	93	30	9	5
- Low	5	7	18	NM	26	NM	30	13	3	3
Income Statement Analysis (Million $)										
Revs.	760	585	439	387	416	294	305	299	383	486
Oper. Inc.	80.4	42.1	34.7	60.2	16.0	9.0	18.0	33.0	64.0	130
Depr.	2.2	0.8	0.9	0.6	0.8	0.7	0.8	1.1	1.2	4.2
Int. Exp.	1.2	5.0	16.7	19.2	28.8	26.8	34.9	41.3	45.9	45.3
Pretax Inc.	80.9	41.0	14.0	-45.9	10.0	3.0	6.0	12.0	49.0	106
Eff. Tax Rate	41%	42%	40%	NM	41%	39%	30%	4.90%	1.00%	0.10%
Net Inc.	47.4	24.0	8.4	-27.4	6.0	2.0	5.0	11.0	48.0	106
Balance Sheet & Other Fin. Data (Million $)										
Cash	15.1	8.4	21.6	43.0	16.5	18.6	82.7	56.9	26.5	25.9
Curr. Assets	NA	NA	NA	NA	NA	NA	NA	NA	NA	NA
Total Assets	866	548	695	773	923	858	953	972	934	896
Curr. Liab.	NA	NA	NA	NA	NA	NA	NA	NA	NA	NA
LT Debt	405	214	271	313	365	321	353	413	436	398
Common Eqty.	325	284	260	258	291	290	291	254	253	259
Total Cap.	729	490	531	571	656	612	644	669	689	657
Cap. Exp.	NA	1.3	0.6	0.2	0.4	NA	1.0	0.7	0.6	2.0
Cash Flow	49.6	24.8	9.3	-26.8	7.0	3.0	5.0	12.0	50.0	111
Curr. Ratio	NA	NA	NA	NA	NA	NA	NA	NA	NA	NA
% LT Debt of Cap.	55.5	43.1	51.1	54.9	55.6	52.5	54.8	61.8	63.3	60.6
% Net Inc.of Revs.	6.2	4.1	2.0	NM	1.4	0.6	1.5	3.7	12.6	21.9
% Ret. on Assets	6.7	3.9	1.2	NM	0.7	0.2	0.4	1.2	5.3	12.9
% Ret. on Equity	15.6	8.8	3.3	NM	2.0	0.6	1.6	4.3	18.9	45.3

Data as orig reptd.; bef. results of disc opers/spec. items. Per share data adj. for stk. divs. Bold denotes diluted EPS (FASB 128)-prior periods restated. E-Estimated. NA-Not Available. NM-Not Meaningful. NR-Not Ranked.

Office—1565 West MacArthur Blvd., Costa Mesa, CA 92626. **Tel**—(714) 668-4300. **Chrmn & CEO**—A. E. Svendsen. **Pres**—S. J. Scarborough. **VP, CFO & Treas**—A. H. Parnes. **VP & Secy**—C. H. Halvorsen. **Dirs**—J. L. Doti, R. R. Foell, D. C. Jacobs, K. D. Koeller, R. J. St. Lawrence, L. McNabb, S. J. Scarborough, D. H. Spengler, A. E. Svendsen. **Transfer Agent & Registrar**—First Chicago Trust Co. of New York. **Incorporated**—in California in 1961; organized in Delaware in 1986; reincorporated in Delaware in 1991. **Empl**— 625. **S&P Analyst:** N.J.D.

STANDARD &POOR'S
STOCK REPORTS

Standard Products

NYSE Symbol **SPD**

In S&P SmallCap 600

09-OCT-99

Industry: Auto Parts & Equipment

Summary: SPD produces highly engineered polymer-based products and systems on a global basis for the automotive, appliance and construction industries.

Quantitative Evaluations

Outlook
(1 Lowest—5 Highest)
• 2+

Fair Value
• 37⅛

Risk
• Low

Earn./Div. Rank
• B

Technical Eval.
• **Bullish** since 4/99

Rel. Strength Rank
(1 Lowest—99 Highest)
• 85

Insider Activity
• NA

Recent Price • 35⅝
52 Wk Range • 36-14¼
Yield • 2.0%
12-Mo. P/E • 20.0

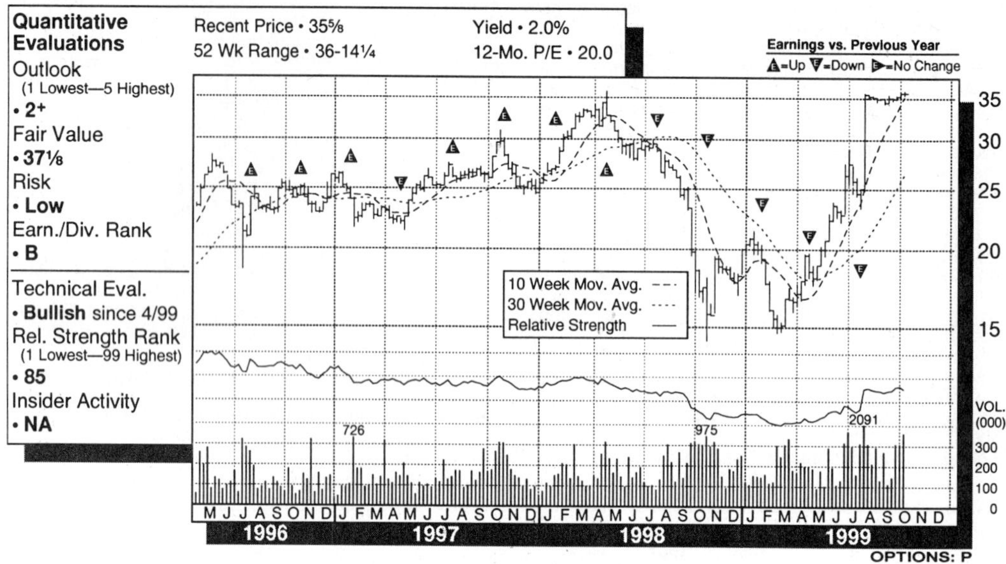

Business Profile - 19-JUL-99

Standard Products said in April 1999 that it expects fourth quarter FY 99 (Jun.) operating results to exceed third quarter levels, although they will not match year-earlier results. The company added that it was proceeding with its worldwide plant capacity study and expected to announce consolidations of certain operations in conjunction with its fiscal year results. Capital spending for the first nine months of FY 99 totaled $52.8 million, and management believes capital spending in FY 99 will approach $75 million. This includes expenditures required at SPD's Mexican facility, which is ramping up to full production for the fall of 1999, as well as the start of a new plant in Poland. In February 1999, directors authorized the repurchase of up to 5% of SPD shares outstanding over the next three years. Officers and directors own about 20% of the stock. .

Operational Review - 19-JUL-99

Net sales for the first nine months of FY 99 (Jun.) declined 3.6%, year to year. Results were adversely affected by a downturn in the economy of Brazil, operating difficulties related to product launches, manufacturing inefficiencies, the costs of a voluntary retirement program, and higher interest expense. Net income dropped 54%, to $11.6 million ($0.71 a share, on 3.8% fewer shares) from $25.1 million ($1.48).

Stock Performance - 08-OCT-99

In the past 30 trading days, SPD's shares have increased 2%, compared to a 0.91% fall in the S&P 500. Average trading volume for the past five days was 257,940 shares, compared with the 40-day moving average of 76,241 shares.

Key Stock Statistics

Dividend Rate/Share	0.72	Shareholders	921
Shs. outstg. (M)	16.1	Market cap. (B)	$0.573
Avg. daily vol. (M)	0.109	Inst. holdings	46%
Tang. Bk. Value/Share	10.95		
Beta	0.02		

Value of $10,000 invested 5 years ago: $ 12,089

Fiscal Year Ending Jun. 30

	1999	1998	1997	1996	1995	1994
Revenues (Million $)						
1Q	231.8	246.2	265.6	238.8	220.9	201.7
2Q	276.2	282.5	266.6	264.8	243.8	198.3
3Q	270.0	277.9	281.8	277.3	265.0	222.7
4Q	305.8	294.7	294.3	303.1	266.2	249.7
Yr.	1,084	1,101	1,108	1,084	995.9	872.4
Earnings Per Share ($)						
1Q	**0.03**	**0.16**	0.08	-0.58	0.17	0.29
2Q	**0.30**	**0.52**	0.38	0.09	0.32	0.37
3Q	**0.39**	**0.80**	0.03	0.43	0.41	0.49
4Q	**0.11**	**1.08**	1.15	0.93	0.30	0.83
Yr.	**1.78**	**2.56**	**1.63**	0.87	1.20	1.99

Next earnings report expected: mid October

Dividend Data (Dividends have been paid since 1949.)

Amount ($)	Date Decl.	Ex-Div. Date	Stock of Record	Payment Date
0.180	Dec. 08	Jan. 06	Jan. 08	Jan. 22 '99
0.180	Mar. 16	Apr. 07	Apr. 09	Apr. 23 '99
0.180	Jun. 29	Jul. 07	Jul. 09	Jul. 23 '99
0.180	Sep. 01	Oct. 06	Oct. 08	Oct. 22 '99

The Standard Products Company

Business Summary - 19-JUL-99

The Standard Products Company expanded its international operations during the three years through FY 98 (Jun.). In May 1995, SPD increased its interest in Brazil-based Itatiaia Standard to 100% from 20%. SPD then formed Standard Products Brasil Industria E Comercio Ltda., which took ownership of a new manufacturing facility constructed in Varginha, Brazil. All manufacturing operations at Itatiaia Standard locations were transferred to the Varginha plant.

SPD produces highly engineered polymer-based products and systems on a global basis for the automotive, appliance and construction industries.

In FY 98, transportation equipment contributed 85% of the company's profit, while tread rubber accounted for the balance of 15%.

Major customers in FY 98 included Chrysler (18% of sales), Ford (22%) and General Motors (13%).

The transportation segment consists of automotive original equipment, and sealing components for the refrigeration industry.

Rubber products supplied to the automotive manufacturing industry include flocked rubber and steel weatherstrip assemblies to seal vehicle windows; flocked rubber window channel assemblies and rubber window gaskets; and vehicle body and door dynamic sealing systems. These products form the sealing system of automotive vehicles, preventing water leakage and inhibiting windnoise from entering the vehicle. Attractiveness of design is an important feature of the sealing system.

The Holm Industries subsidiary, the largest supplier of extruded plastic gaskets and seals to the North American refrigeration and freezer market, makes custom designed extruded plastic (primarily polyvinyl chloride compounds) gaskets and seals sold as original equipment to manufacturers of residential and commercial refrigerators, dishwashers and air conditioners. These products are custom designed to enhance energy control and, in dishwashers, to prevent water leakage. Holm also makes extruded plastic parts for the residential exterior door and window industries; and extruded rubber products for the automobile restoration and truck manufacturing industries.

The Oliver Rubber subsidiary produces precure and moldcure tread rubber, bonding gum, cement, repair materials and equipment for the tire retreading industry. Custom mixed rubber is also supplied to SPD for use in automotive original equipment products and to 50%-owned NSC for the manufacture of door seals for automotive original equipment. Oliver also custom mixes rubber compounds for certain customers throughout the U.S.

In January 1999, SPD adopted a "poison pill" stock purchase rights plan.

Per Share Data ($) (Year Ended Jun. 30)	1999	1998	1997	1996	1995	1994	1993	1992	1991	1990
Tangible Bk. Val.	NA	14.02	12.03	11.15	11.68	10.80	9.82	11.24	7.29	12.05
Cash Flow	NA	5.81	4.80	4.02	4.00	4.39	4.26	3.70	0.30	2.49
Earnings	1.78	2.56	1.64	0.87	1.20	1.99	2.21	1.79	-1.65	0.93
Dividends	0.54	0.68	0.68	0.68	0.68	0.64	0.48	0.38	0.56	0.74
Payout Ratio	30%	27%	41%	78%	57%	32%	24%	25%	NM	79%
Prices - High	36	35 7/8	31	28 1/4	24 1/8	38 3/4	36 5/8	29 5/8	20 3/8	21
- Low	14 5/8	14 1/4	21 3/8	16 3/8	13 1/2	21 3/8	25 3/4	19 1/8	9 5/8	9 5/8
P/E Ratio - High	20	14	19	32	20	19	17	17	NM	23
- Low	8	6	13	19	11	11	12	11	NM	10
Income Statement Analysis (Million $)										
Revs.	NA	1,101	1,108	1,084	996	872	764	657	592	652
Oper. Inc.	NA	143	130	91.4	77.3	97.7	89.8	77.4	23.6	50.3
Depr.	NA	55.1	53.1	52.5	47.0	40.0	31.0	24.9	24.7	20.0
Int. Exp.	NA	12.4	12.9	12.8	13.0	9.0	9.7	15.0	12.6	11.1
Pretax Inc.	NA	68.5	46.5	28.5	17.3	50.2	50.2	38.8	-13.1	19.9
Eff. Tax Rate	NA	37%	41%	49%	NM	34%	34%	40%	NM	41%
Net Inc.	NA	43.4	27.5	14.6	20.0	33.0	33.4	23.3	-21.0	11.8
Balance Sheet & Other Fin. Data (Million $)										
Cash	NA	1.6	7.0	NM	19.5	Nil	5.5	44.3	19.3	15.7
Curr. Assets	NA	240	272	261	307	271	234	218	182	183
Total Assets	NA	684	692	685	702	624	565	399	368	362
Curr. Liab.	NA	216	225	207	189	183	155	121	121	93.0
LT Debt	NA	92.5	122	143	191	135	14.3	69.0	113	99
Common Eqty.	NA	300	268	259	260	243	224	178	102	153
Total Cap.	NA	444	390	402	451	378	340	247	216	252
Cap. Exp.	NA	77.3	59.0	79.7	55.0	61.0	115	19.9	21.2	39.2
Cash Flow	NA	99	80.7	67.1	66.9	73.0	64.4	48.2	3.8	31.8
Curr. Ratio	NA	1.1	1.2	1.3	1.6	1.5	1.5	1.8	1.5	2.0
% LT Debt of Cap.	NA	20.8	31.3	35.6	42.3	36.0	34.0	28.0	52.5	39.4
% Net Inc.of Revs.	NA	3.9	2.5	1.3	2.1	3.8	4.4	3.5	NM	1.8
% Ret. on Assets	NA	6.3	4.0	2.1	3.1	5.6	6.7	5.6	NM	3.4
% Ret. on Equity	NA	15.2	10.4	5.6	8.0	14.2	15.9	15.6	NM	7.7

Data as orig reptd.; bef. results of disc opers/spec. items. Per share data adj. for stk. divs. Bold denotes diluted EPS (FASB 128)-prior periods restated. E-Estimated. NA-Not Available. NM-Not Meaningful. NR-Not Ranked.

Office—2401 S. Gulley Rd., Dearborn, MI 48124. **Tel**—(313) 561-1100. **Website**—http://www.stand-prod.com **Chrmn**—J. S. Reid Jr. **Vice Chrmn & CEO**—R. L. Roudebush. **Pres & COO**—T. K. Zampetis. **VP-Fin, CFO & Investor Contact**—Donald R. Sheley Jr. **Secy**—R. N. Jacobson. **Dirs**—J. C. Baillie, E. B. Brandon, J. Doddridge, J. D. Drinko, C. E. Moll, M. R. Myers, L. H. Perkins, A. M. Rankin Jr., J. S. Reid Jr., A. E. Riedel, R. L. Roudebush, D. R. Sheley, Jr. , J. D. Sigel, W. H. Thompson, T. K. Zampetis. **Transfer Agent & Registrar**—National City Bank, Cleveland. **Incorporated**—in Ohio in 1927. **Empl**— 10,017. **S&P Analyst:** P.L.H.

STANDARD
&POOR'S
STOCK REPORTS

Standex International

NYSE Symbol **SXI**
In S&P SmallCap 600

09-OCT-99

Industry: Manufacturing (Diversified)

Summary: This diversified manufacturer operates in three broad business segments: food service, industrial products, and consumer products.

Quantitative Evaluations

Outlook (1 Lowest—5 Highest) • **2+**

Fair Value • **28¼**

Risk • **Low**

Earn./Div. Rank • **A-**

Technical Eval. • **Bearish** since 9/99

Rel. Strength Rank (1 Lowest—99 Highest) • **75**

Insider Activity • **NA**

Recent Price • 25¾
52 Wk Range • 29-19⅞
Yield • 3.0%
12-Mo. P/E • 10.7

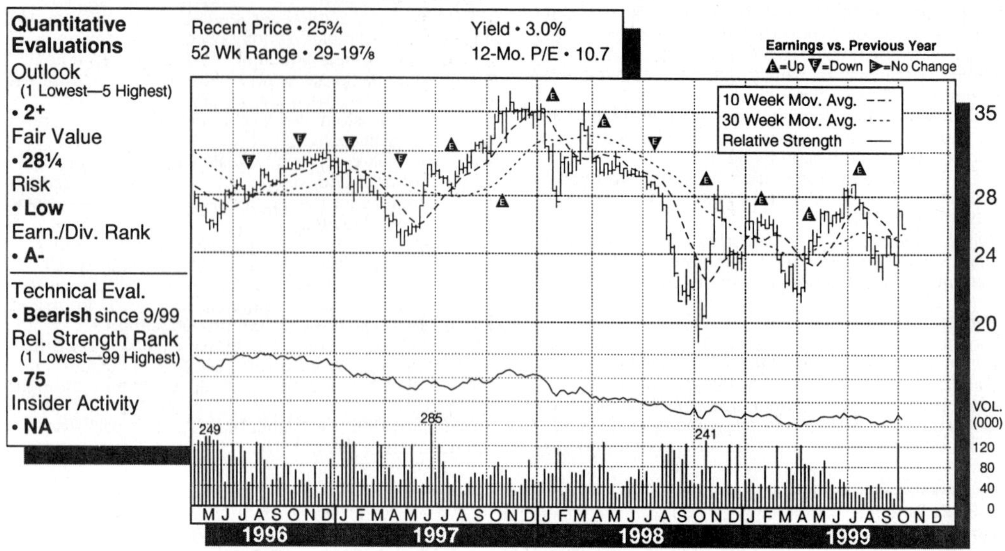

Business Profile - 30-JUL-99

In April 1999, management noted that margins have been steady to date in FY 99 (Jun.), as backlogs remain up significantly throughout the company. With the benefit of strong cash flow from operations, Standex has reduced long-term debt by approximately $7.0 million during the first three quarters of FY 99, and has repurchased more than $2.5 million of company stock. Earlier, the company stated that it is continually seeking opportunities through acquisitions that provide a synergistic impact or growth potential in its primary businesses.

Operational Review - 30-JUL-99

Net sales in the nine months ended March 31, 1999, rose 5.0%, year to year, largely due to added sales from ACME Manufacturing, acquired in early October 1997, which outweighed the absence of sales from Doubleday Bros. product lines. Gross margins were flat as increased efficiencies in food services and lower initial margins at ACME essentially offset each other. Selling, general and administrative expenses were well controlled. Despite a sharp rise in interest expense and following a $700,000 restructuring credit, pretax income was up 17%. After taxes at 39.8%, versus 38.6%, net income rose 14%, to $23,992,000 ($1.84 a share), from $20,968,000 ($1.59).

Stock Performance - 08-OCT-99

In the past 30 trading days, SXI's shares have increased 11%, compared to a 0.91% fall in the S&P 500. Average trading volume for the past five days was 7,060 shares, compared with the 40-day moving average of 10,823 shares.

Key Stock Statistics

Dividend Rate/Share	0.76	Shareholders	3,500
Shs. outstg. (M)	12.9	Market cap. (B)	$0.331
Avg. daily vol. (M)	0.014	Inst. holdings	56%
Tang. Bk. Value/Share	8.65		
Beta	0.69		

Value of $10,000 invested 5 years ago: $ 10,655

Fiscal Year Ending Jun. 30

	1999	1998	1997	1996	1995	1994
Revenues (Million $)						
1Q	157.4	141.1	140.2	142.2	140.6	127.3
2Q	171.2	168.1	152.3	154.1	143.9	133.5
3Q	152.3	148.6	130.4	130.3	141.6	130.9
4Q	160.6	158.5	141.7	136.0	143.2	137.7
Yr.	641.4	616.2	564.6	562.7	569.3	529.4
Earnings Per Share ($)						
1Q	**0.61**	0.58	0.56	0.66	0.80	0.41
2Q	**0.72**	**0.63**	**0.60**	0.65	0.62	0.46
3Q	**0.51**	**0.38**	0.31	0.41	0.56	0.41
4Q	**0.57**	**-0.07**	0.53	0.49	0.66	0.50
Yr.	**2.41**	**1.52**	**2.00**	2.21	2.64	1.78

Next earnings report expected: late October

Dividend Data (Dividends have been paid since 1964.)

Amount ($)	Date Decl.	Ex-Div. Date	Stock of Record	Payment Date
0.190	Oct. 27	Nov. 04	Nov. 06	Nov. 25 '98
0.190	Jan. 27	Feb. 04	Feb. 08	Feb. 25 '99
0.190	Apr. 28	May. 06	May. 10	May. 25 '99
0.190	Jul. 28	Aug. 05	Aug. 09	Aug. 25 '99

Standex International Corporation

Business Summary - 30-JUL-99

Salem, NH-based Standex International (SXI) offers an amazingly diverse spectrum of products and services, including Sunday school literature, grapefruit gift packages, food service equipment, electrical connectors, rotary vane pumps, casters and wheels, and Christmas tree stands. The company has a total of 92 principal plants and warehouses in the U.S., Western Europe, Canada, Australia, Singapore, and Mexico; it also operates 23 retail stores.

SXI has grouped its businesses into three different segments: food service products, industrial products, and consumer products. Segment contributions in FY 98 (Jun.) were: food service products, 25% of sales and 21% of profits; industrial products, 41% (45%); and consumer products, 34% (34%).

In the consumer products area, the company publishes and markets educational and religious literature, and provides commercial and specialized printing, binding systems and office supplies. SXI also operates a chain of 23 Berean Christian Bookstores. In addition, the segment offers by mail order Frank Lewis Grapefruit gift packages, Harry's Crestview Groves grapefruit packages, grapefruit juice, grapefruit sections, onions, melons, and roses. Among other offerings of this diversified unit are Williams chiropractic and traction tables and ultrasound equipment, Snappy metal ducting and fittings, and National Metal Christmas tree stands. In October 1997, SXI purchased Philadelphia-based ACME Manufacturing Co., a maker of heating, ventilation and air conditioning pipe, duct and fittings for the home building industry; ACME had annual sales of about $60 million.

SXI's food service segment produces USECO food service equipment and patient feeding systems, Master-Bilt beverage coolers and freezers, Barbecue King ovens, Federal Industries bakery and deli equipment, and Procon rotary vane pumps.

The industrial products division makes texturizing systems such as Roehlen embossing rolls, Mold-Tech mold engraving, Keller-Dorian print rolls, Spincraft power metal spinning and custom components, Custom Hoists telescopic and piston rod hydraulic cylinders, and Perkins converting and finishing machinery systems. The division also makes machinery and complete binding systems for printers, publishers and binders of checkbooks, calendars, diaries and cookbooks through Wire-O; makes casters and wheels, and industrial hardware; and offers electrical and electronics products, such as Standex reed switches and relays, electrical connectors, sensors, toroids and relays, fixed and variable inductors and electronic assemblies.

Backlog at June 30, 1998 (latest available), totaled $102 million, up from $81.6 million a year earlier.

Per Share Data ($) (Year Ended Jun. 30)	1999	1998	1997	1996	1995	1994	1993	1992	1991	1990
Tangible Bk. Val.	NA	8.65	9.60	8.93	8.36	7.04	6.85	7.11	6.69	6.44
Cash Flow	NA	2.57	2.94	3.10	3.49	2.54	2.25	1.90	1.62	1.62
Earnings	2.41	1.52	2.00	2.21	2.64	1.78	1.47	1.23	1.05	1.06
Dividends	0.76	0.76	0.75	0.71	0.63	0.52	0.42	0.38	0.35	0.34
Payout Ratio	32%	50%	37%	32%	24%	29%	29%	28%	32%	30%
Prices - High	29	35⅞	37	32⅞	36¾	32⅝	27¾	19	13⅝	13⅞
- Low	21⅛	19	24½	25⅜	29	24⅝	18½	11	10⅛	10⅜
P/E Ratio - High	12	24	19	15	14	18	19	15	13	13
- Low	9	13	12	11	11	14	13	9	10	10
Income Statement Analysis (Million $)										
Revs.	NA	616	565	563	569	529	506	477	482	460
Oper. Inc.	NA	68.8	62.8	69.0	72.0	58.1	55.3	49.2	51.1	50.7
Depr.	NA	13.9	12.8	12.5	12.4	11.8	12.9	11.9	12.0	11.3
Int. Exp.	NA	10.8	8.5	9.0	8.4	6.9	5.6	6.6	7.9	8.3
Pretax Inc.	NA	33.1	43.5	48.1	57.8	42.2	37.5	33.7	32.6	34.8
Eff. Tax Rate	NA	39%	38%	36%	34%	36%	36%	35%	38%	38%
Net Inc.	NA	20.1	26.9	30.7	38.3	27.1	24.0	21.9	20.2	21.7
Balance Sheet & Other Fin. Data (Million $)										
Cash	NA	9.3	6.2	5.1	9.0	5.0	7.5	10.9	7.3	8.0
Curr. Assets	NA	235	207	207	220	197	182	186	177	182
Total Assets	NA	411	341	335	343	324	309	317	297	298
Curr. Liab.	NA	86.3	70.1	68.5	77.2	70.2	73.2	74.5	72.9	66.8
LT Debt	NA	163	112	114	112	113	94.4	86.7	70.1	73.0
Common Eqty.	NA	146	141	135	132	119	122	137	139	142
Total Cap.	NA	322	267	261	256	246	229	236	220	225
Cap. Exp.	NA	19.8	16.8	15.3	12.0	13.2	10.7	15.7	13.8	12.7
Cash Flow	NA	34.0	39.7	43.2	50.7	38.9	36.9	33.8	32.2	33.1
Curr. Ratio	NA	2.7	3.0	3.0	2.8	2.8	2.5	2.5	2.4	2.7
% LT Debt of Cap.	NA	50.6	41.9	43.6	43.7	46.0	41.2	36.7	31.9	32.4
% Net Inc.of Revs.	NA	3.3	4.8	5.5	6.8	5.1	4.7	4.6	4.2	4.7
% Ret. on Assets	NA	5.4	11.3	9.1	11.5	8.8	8.0	7.4	7.0	7.8
% Ret. on Equity	NA	14.0	19.5	23.0	30.5	23.1	19.4	16.6	14.9	16.0

Data as orig reptd.; bef. results of disc opers/spec. items. Per share data adj. for stk. divs. Bold denotes diluted EPS (FASB 128)-prior periods restated. E-Estimated. NA-Not Available. NM-Not Meaningful. NR-Not Ranked.

Office—6 Manor Parkway, Salem, NH 03079. **Tel**—(603) 893-9701. **Fax**—(603) 893-7324. **Website**—http://www.standex.com **Chrmn**—T. L. King. **Pres & CEO**—E. J. Trainor. **VP, CFO & Investor Contact**—E. F. Paquette. **Secy**—D. A. Rosen. **Dirs**—J. Bolten, Jr., D. R. Crichton, S. S. Dennis III, W.R. Fenoglio, W. F. Greeley, D. B. Hogan, T. L. King, C. K. Landry, H. N. Muller III, E. J. Trainor. **Transfer Agent & Registrar**—Boston EquiServe. **Incorporated**—in Ohio in 1955; reincorporated in Delaware in 1975. **Empl**— 5,500. **S&P Analyst:** S.S.

STANDARD &POOR'S
STOCK REPORTS

Steel Technologies

NASDAQ Symbol **STTX**

In S&P SmallCap 600

09-OCT-99

Industry: Iron & Steel

Summary: This intermediate steel processor purchases flat-rolled steel produced by major steel mills and processes it to specifications required by industrial end-users.

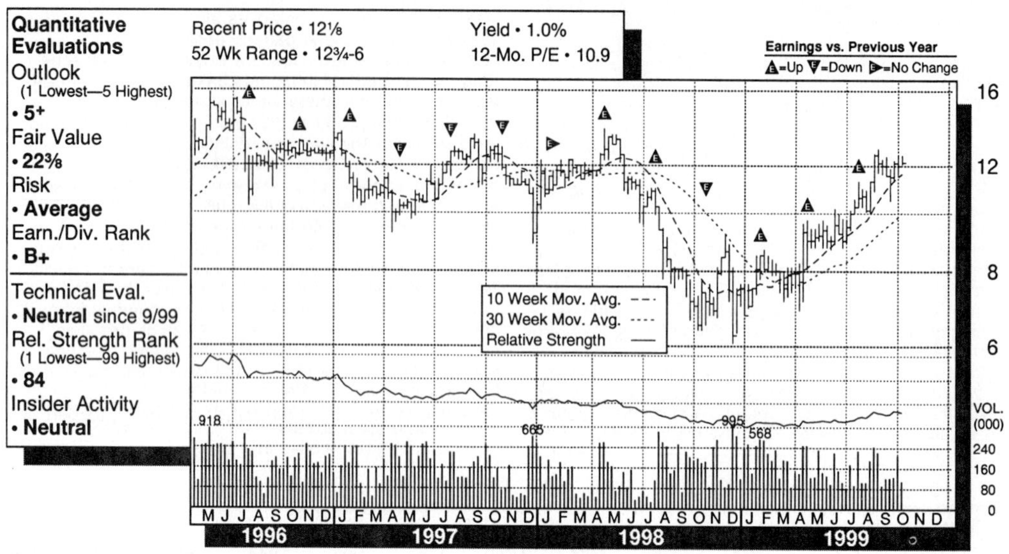

Business Profile - 23-JUL-99

In July 1999, the company reported that demand for its products and services is strong, reflecting growth and diversification initiatives of recent years. With results at record levels, management said it expects further improvement through FY 99 (Sep.) and into next year. A number of expansion projects have been announced, including a new processing facility in Matamoros, Mexico, with a scheduled start-up in the latter half of 2000. Expansion of the recently acquired steel processing facility in Willoughby, Ohio, is nearing completion, with the start-up of this phase scheduled for mid-August 1999

Operational Review - 23-JUL-99

Net sales in the first nine months of FY 99 (Sep.) rose 6.9%, year to year, aided by the acquisition of The Roberts Steel Co. in July 1998. Operating margins expanded as a result of an improved product mix and productivity gains. The successful start-up of the Berkeley, SC, facility in March contributed to earnings in the third quarter, and the Mi-Tech Steel joint venture realized improved results. Net income climbed 32%, to $11,366,000 ($1.01 a share, diluted, on fewer shares), from $8,582,000 ($0.71).

Stock Performance - 08-OCT-99

In the past 30 trading days, STTX's shares have increased 0.26%, compared to a 0.91% fall in the S&P 500. Average trading volume for the past five days was 21,200 shares, compared with the 40-day moving average of 31,887 shares.

Key Stock Statistics

Dividend Rate/Share	0.12	Shareholders	547
Shs. outstg. (M)	11.1	Market cap. (B)	$0.135
Avg. daily vol. (M)	0.028	Inst. holdings	30%
Tang. Bk. Value/Share	9.94		
Beta	0.50		

Value of $10,000 invested 5 years ago: $ 6,317

Fiscal Year Ending Sep. 30

	1999	1998	1997	1996	1995	1994
Revenues (Million $)						
1Q	98.20	96.45	78.03	65.71	64.25	54.06
2Q	106.9	101.3	79.80	76.63	71.50	62.73
3Q	109.3	96.39	101.1	76.62	60.15	63.29
4Q	—	89.78	86.71	75.20	56.84	60.67
Yr.	—	383.9	345.6	294.2	252.7	240.8
Earnings Per Share ($)						
1Q	**0.26**	**0.21**	0.21	0.18	0.17	0.20
2Q	**0.35**	**0.27**	0.15	0.28	0.22	0.24
3Q	**0.40**	**0.24**	0.23	0.28	0.17	0.26
4Q	—	**0.10**	0.13	0.24	0.06	0.17
Yr.	—	**0.82**	**0.71**	0.98	0.61	0.87

Next earnings report expected: late October

Dividend Data (Dividends have been paid since 1985.)

Amount ($)	Date Decl.	Ex-Div. Date	Stock of Record	Payment Date
0.050	Nov. 09	Nov. 18	Nov. 20	Dec. 04 '98
0.060	Apr. 26	May. 11	May. 13	May. 28 '99

A Division of The McGraw-Hill Companies

Steel Technologies Inc.

Business Summary - 23-JUL-99

As its name implies, Steel Technologies, Inc. (STTX) recognizes the impact that changing manufacturing technology can have on the steel industry. Founded in 1971, STTX is an intermediate steel processor engaged in the business of processing flat rolled steel to specified close tolerances in response to orders from industrial customers who require steel of precise thickness, width, temper, finish and shape for their manufacturing purposes. The company's principal processed products are: hot-rolled strip and sheet, high strength low alloy strip and sheet, hot-rolled pickle and oil and coated strip and sheet, pickling of hot-rolled black coils, blanking and cut-to-length processing of coil steel, cold-rolled strip and sheet, cold-rolled one-pass strip, and high carbon and alloy strip and sheet. Steel Technologies commitment to the latest technology and its investment in new equipment and facilities have been instrumental in the growth of its revenues and shipments.

In FY 98 (Sep.), sales to the automotive supply industry accounted for 50% of STTX's sales while sales directly to the automotive industry accounted for 10%.

STTX occupies a niche between the primary steel producers (major and mini mills) and end-product manufacturers. The primary producers have historically emphasized the sale of commercial tolerance steel to large volume purchasers and have viewed the intermediate processor as part of this customer base. Further, end-product manufacturers have increasingly sought steel with closer tolerances, on shorter lead times, and with more reliable and more frequent delivery than the primary producers can efficiently provide.

One of the first processing functions involves the pickling of hot rolled black coil steel. This process is a cleaning process that improves the quality of hot rolled steel by removing the scale on the surface of the steel and prepares the hot rolled steel for further refinement. Picking is performed on steel owned by customers as well as on hot rolled steel owned by the company. The next function typically involves splitting coils to specific widths subject to close tolerances. Many orders also involve a process known as cold reduction, which reduces the thickness of the steel by passing it through a set of rolls under pressure. This process significantly increases the value added by STTX to the product.

STTX has achieved high quality and productivity levels using the most advanced rolling, pickling, blanking, slitting and annealing equipment. The company has computerized all of its rolling equipment, improving its capability to deliver flat rolled steel products processed to closer than standard tolerances.

In 1997, the company formed Mi-Tech Steel, Inc., a 50% owned joint venture with Mitsui Steel Development Co., Inc. Mi-Tech was established to own and operate high-volume steel splitting facilities to serve Japanese and domestic automotive and appliance parts manufacturers located in the U. S.

Per Share Data ($) (Year Ended Sep. 30)	1998	1997	1996	1995	1994	1993	1992	1991	1990	1989
Tangible Bk. Val.	9.03	8.64	8.47	7.64	7.21	6.42	5.63	5.17	4.91	4.38
Cash Flow	1.79	1.58	1.77	1.19	1.28	1.19	0.85	0.57	0.78	0.67
Earnings	0.82	0.71	0.98	0.61	0.87	0.83	0.50	0.29	0.53	0.49
Dividends	0.10	0.10	0.09	0.08	0.07	0.05	0.04	0.03	0.03	0.02
Payout Ratio	12%	14%	9%	13%	8%	6%	8%	9%	5%	4%
Prices - High	13¾	13⅝	15⅞	13¾	21¾	23½	10⅝	9⅛	9⅞	11⅜
- Low	6	8⅞	8⅝	6¼	10⅛	10½	6⅜	6	6	6
P/E Ratio - High	17	19	16	23	25	28	21	31	18	23
- Low	7	13	9	10	12	13	13	20	11	12
Income Statement Analysis (Million $)										
Revs.	384	346	294	253	241	198	154	130	141	123
Oper. Inc.	33.5	27.6	31.0	21.5	21.5	20.8	14.5	10.2	14.4	11.7
Depr.	11.6	10.4	9.5	7.1	5.0	4.4	4.2	3.4	3.0	2.2
Int. Exp.	6.1	5.7	5.0	3.9	1.3	0.9	0.9	1.2	1.2	0.8
Pretax Inc.	16.4	13.1	18.2	11.3	16.6	15.8	9.5	5.7	10.3	9.5
Eff. Tax Rate	40%	35%	36%	34%	37%	37%	37%	38%	38%	38%
Net Inc.	9.8	8.5	11.7	7.4	10.5	9.9	6.0	3.5	6.4	5.9
Balance Sheet & Other Fin. Data (Million $)										
Cash	4.8	3.5	4.2	2.7	1.0	0.1	0.6	1.6	0.7	0.4
Curr. Assets	132	130	105	80.3	118	82.1	53.0	43.5	55.3	37.0
Total Assets	266	258	217	195	200	144	107	95.0	99	74.0
Curr. Liab.	51.3	40.0	40.1	26.9	47.3	31.9	20.7	21.0	17.8	10.8
LT Debt	88.3	97.2	67.3	68.6	60.8	30.0	15.6	8.7	18.9	8.9
Common Eqty.	114	109	101	93.0	88.0	78.0	67.8	62.3	59.2	52.8
Total Cap.	215	218	177	168	153	112	86.7	74.1	81.2	63.7
Cap. Exp.	14.2	9.5	24.5	37.9	24.5	11.5	7.0	10.1	9.0	12.5
Cash Flow	21.4	18.9	21.2	14.5	15.5	14.3	10.2	6.9	9.4	8.1
Curr. Ratio	2.6	3.3	2.6	3.0	2.5	2.6	2.6	2.1	3.1	3.4
% LT Debt of Cap.	41.1	44.7	38.0	40.8	39.7	26.8	18.0	11.7	23.3	13.9
% Net Inc.of Revs.	2.6	2.5	4.0	2.9	4.4	5.0	3.9	2.7	4.6	4.8
% Ret. on Assets	3.7	3.6	5.7	3.8	6.1	7.9	5.9	3.6	7.4	7.8
% Ret. on Equity	8.8	8.1	12.0	8.2	12.7	13.6	9.2	5.8	11.5	13.1

Data as orig reptd.; bef. results of disc opers/spec. items. Per share data adj. for stk. divs. Bold denotes diluted EPS (FASB 128)-prior periods restated. E-Estimated. NA-Not Available. NM-Not Meaningful. NR-Not Ranked.

Office—15415 Shelbyville Rd., Louisville, KY 40245. **Tel**—(502) 245-2110. **Chrmn & CEO**—M. J. Ray. **Pres & COO**—B. T. Ray. **CFO & Treas**—J. P. Bellino. **Dirs**—D. L. Armstrong, H. F. Bates, Jr., D. A. Bawel, M. J. Carroll, J. D. Conner, W. E. Hellmann, R. W. McIntyre, A. J. Payton, B. T. Ray, M. J. Ray. **Transfer Agent & Registrar**—Mid-America Bank of Louisville & Trust Co. **Incorporated**—in Kentucky in 1971. **Empl**— 904. **S&P Analyst:** C.F.B.

STANDARD
&POOR'S
STOCK REPORTS

Stein Mart

NASDAQ Symbol **SMRT**

In S&P SmallCap 600

09-OCT-99 **Industry:** Retail (Discounters)

Summary: Stein Mart operates 194 retail stores in 29 states offering moderate to designer brand-name apparel for women, men and children, as well as accessories, gifts, linens and shoes.

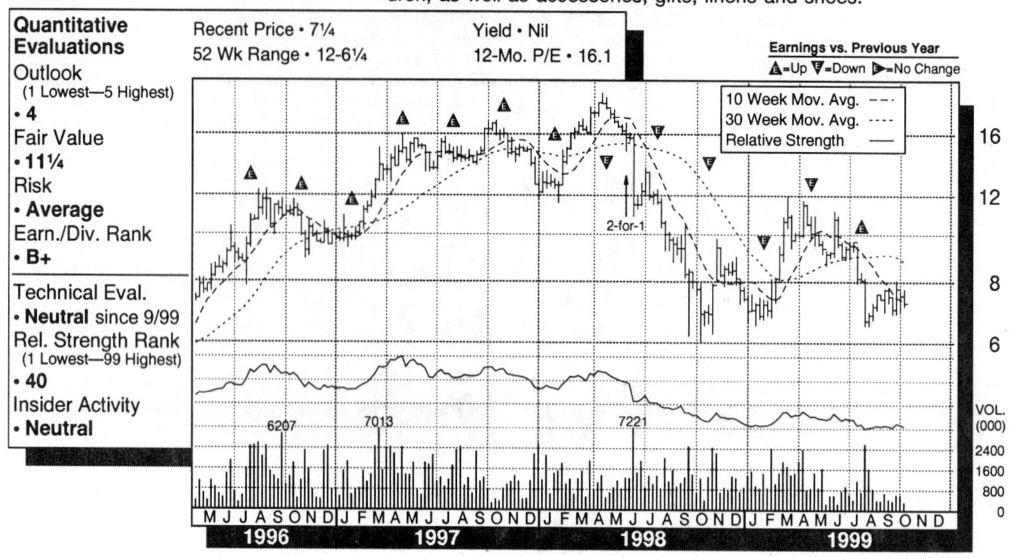

Business Profile - 06-JUL-99

In April 1999, SMRT announced that first quarter sales benefitted from the opening of nine new stores in the first quarter of 1999. Stores were opened in several markets, including Atlanta, Cleveland, Denver, Houston, Las Vegas, New Orleans, Florence and Myrtle Beach, SC, and St. Petersburg, FL. The company also noted that one store in New Orleans was to be closed by the end of April 1999. The company plans to open about 33 new stores in 1999. Management said that it was pleased with regaining its sales momentum during the first quarter, but still faces challenges with some of its newer stores, particularly in new markets. SMRT's focus in 1999 will be to elevate these stores to a more productive level that the company traditionally has enjoyed.

Operational Review - 06-JUL-99

Net sales for the three months ended April 3, 1999, rose 25%, year to year, on a higher store count, and a comparable-store sales increase of 7.9%. Gross margins narrowed, mainly from an increase in markdowns and the effect of recording the results of the company's physical inventory. SG&A expense increased 22%, primarily due to the higher store count. Other income also rose 22%, mainly on higher sales from in-store leased shoe departments, aided by the additional stores. Despite 40% higher interest expense, net income was up 33%, to $243,000 ($0.01 a share), from $183,000 ($0.01, as restated).

Stock Performance - 08-OCT-99

In the past 30 trading days, SMRT's shares have declined 2%, compared to a 0.91% fall in the S&P 500. Average trading volume for the past five days was 61,100 shares, compared with the 40-day moving average of 92,541 shares.

Key Stock Statistics

Dividend Rate/Share	Nil	Shareholders	1,099
Shs. outstg. (M)	44.8	Market cap. (B)	$0.325
Avg. daily vol. (M)	0.091	Inst. holdings	51%
Tang. Bk. Value/Share	3.92		
Beta	0.47		

Value of $10,000 invested 5 years ago: $ 7,532

Fiscal Year Ending Dec. 31

	1999	1998	1997	1996	1995	1994
Revenues (Million $)						
1Q	212.1	169.5	151.4	108.5	87.71	79.15
2Q	244.9	214.0	183.6	149.4	116.5	97.92
3Q	—	192.1	166.7	131.3	108.2	90.71
4Q	—	322.2	290.9	227.0	183.6	151.4
Yr.	—	897.8	792.7	616.1	496.0	419.2
Earnings Per Share ($)						
1Q	**0.01**	0.02	**0.03**	-0.01	-0.03	0.01
2Q	**0.21**	0.19	**0.20**	**0.17**	0.11	0.10
3Q	—	-0.10	**0.07**	**0.05**	0.04	0.04
4Q	—	0.35	**0.43**	**0.35**	0.26	0.24
Yr.	—	**0.44**	**0.73**	**0.56**	**0.39**	**0.40**

Next earnings report expected: late October

Dividend Data

No cash dividends have been paid on the common shares.

Stein Mart, Inc.

Business Summary - 06-JUL-99

Stein Mart, Inc. operated a single store in Greenville, MS, from the early 1900's until 1977, when it embarked on an ambitious expansion program. As of January 2, 1999, this retail chain operated 182 stores offering fashionable, primarily branded merchandise, comparable in quality and presentation to that of traditional department and fine specialty stores, at prices typically 25% to 60% below those charged by such stores. SMRT's merchandise assortment features moderate to designer brand-name apparel for men, women and children, as well as accessories, gifts, linens, shoes and fragrances.

SMRT's business strategy is to maintain the quality of merchandise, store appearance, merchandise presentation and customer service level of traditional department and fine quality stores and to offer value pricing to its customers through its vendor relationships, tight control over corporate and store expenses and efficient management of inventory. SMRT differentiates itself from other off-price retailers by offering a higher percentage of current-season merchandise and achieves this by buying from vendors well in advance of the selling season, rather than by buying close-out merchandise or overruns. Its merchandise presentation is also more comparable to that of traditional department and fine specialty stores.

In 1998, net sales were $898 million, versus about $793 million in 1997, a 13% increase. Comparable store net sales increased 1.2% for the year. Sales by category in 1998 were: Ladies' & Boutique Apparel (36%), Ladies' Accessories (11%), Men's & Young Men's (20%), Gifts & Linens (18%), Shoes - Leased Department (8%), Children's (6%), and Other (1%).

At the end of 1998, SMRT operated retail stores in 29 states, with the average store at 38,000 gross square feet, primarily in neighborhood shopping centers in metropolitan areas. The company's expansion strategy is to add stores in new markets, including markets with the potential for multiple stores, as well as new stores in existing markets to capture advertising and management efficiencies. The company targets metropolitan areas with populations of 125,000 or more for new store expansion.

Management believes that the company occupies a market niche closer to traditional department stores than typical off-price retail chains. SMRT feels it is well positioned to compete in the retail apparel industry in the areas of assortment, presentation, quality of merchandise, price, customer service, vendor relations and store locations.

Per Share Data ($) (Year Ended Dec. 31)	1998	1997	1996	1995	1994	1993	1992	1991	1990	1989
Tangible Bk. Val.	3.92	3.61	2.89	2.27	1.90	1.49	1.11	NA	NA	NA
Cash Flow	0.67	0.92	0.70	0.49	0.47	0.41	0.36	NA	NA	NA
Earnings	0.44	0.73	0.55	0.38	0.39	0.35	0.30	NA	NA	NA
Dividends	Nil	Nil	Nil	Nil	Nil	Nil	Nil	NA	NA	NA
Payout Ratio	Nil	Nil	Nil	Nil	Nil	Nil	Nil	NA	NA	NA
Prices - High	19½	17⅛	12⅜	7½	10¾	12⅛	10½	NA	NA	NA
- Low	6	9⅜	4¼	4⅝	6⅛	7⅜	3¾	NA	NA	NA
P/E Ratio - High	44	23	18	20	28	35	34	NA	NA	NA
- Low	14	13	6	12	16	21	12	NA	NA	NA
Income Statement Analysis (Million $)										
Revs.	898	793	616	496	419	343	278	NA	NA	NA
Oper. Inc.	35.6	57.7	43.2	29.2	30.3	27.1	21.5	NA	NA	NA
Depr.	10.5	8.8	6.7	5.2	4.1	3.1	2.4	NA	NA	NA
Int. Exp.	2.4	1.2	1.6	1.3	0.7	0.5	0.8	NA	NA	NA
Pretax Inc.	33.1	57.0	42.5	29.1	30.5	27.5	21.4	NA	NA	NA
Eff. Tax Rate	38%	39%	39%	39%	40%	39%	38%	NA	NA	NA
Net Inc.	20.5	34.8	26.0	17.8	18.4	16.7	13.4	NA	NA	NA
Balance Sheet & Other Fin. Data (Million $)										
Cash	22.3	28.0	23.6	15.1	21.3	9.9	NA	NA	NA	NA
Curr. Assets	242	208	167	131	119	89.3	NA	NA	NA	NA
Total Assets	318	271	218	174	154	116	87.0	NA	NA	NA
Curr. Liab.	131	98.0	80.3	67.7	65.4	46.8	NA	NA	NA	NA
LT Debt	Nil	Nil	Nil	Nil	Nil	Nil	Nil	NA	NA	NA
Common Eqty.	178	166	132	101	85.3	66.9	50.2	NA	NA	NA
Total Cap.	187	175	138	106	88.6	69.6	NA	NA	NA	NA
Cap. Exp.	21.5	19.7	16.1	13.8	11.5	12.2	3.8	NA	NA	NA
Cash Flow	31.1	43.5	32.7	22.9	22.5	19.9	15.8	NA	NA	NA
Curr. Ratio	1.8	2.1	2.1	1.9	1.8	1.9	NA	NA	NA	NA
% LT Debt of Cap.	Nil	Nil	Nil	Nil	Nil	Nil	NA	NA	NA	NA
% Net Inc.of Revs.	2.3	4.4	4.2	3.6	4.4	4.9	4.8	NA	NA	NA
% Ret. on Assets	7.0	12.8	17.8	10.9	13.6	16.5	NA	NA	NA	NA
% Ret. on Equity	11.9	21.0	29.9	19.0	24.2	28.5	NA	NA	NA	NA

Data as orig reptd.; bef. results of disc opers/spec. items. Per share data adj. for stk. divs. Bold denotes diluted EPS (FASB 128)-prior periods restated. E-Estimated. NA-Not Available. NM-Not Meaningful. NR-Not Ranked.

Office—1200 Riverplace Blvd., Jacksonville, FL 32207. **Tel**—(904) 346-1500. **E-mail**—SteinMrt@aol.com **Chrmn & CEO**—J. Stein. **Pres & COO**—J. H. Williams Jr. **SVP & CFO**—J. G. Delfs. **Dirs**—A. R. Carpenter, A. Ernst Jr., M. W. Legler, M. D. Rose, J. Stein, J. H. Williams, Jr., J. H. Winston. **Transfer Agent & Registrar**—ChaseMellon Shareholder Services, Ridgefield Park, NJ. **Incorporated**—in Florida in 1992. **Empl**— 10,500. **S&P Analyst:** Matthew C. Hershberg

STANDARD
&POOR'S
STOCK REPORTS

Stillwater Mining

ASE Symbol **SWC**
In S&P SmallCap 600

09-OCT-99 **Industry:** Gold & Precious Metals Mining

Summary: This company is the only US producer of platinum and palladium, and operates a mining complex in southern Montana.

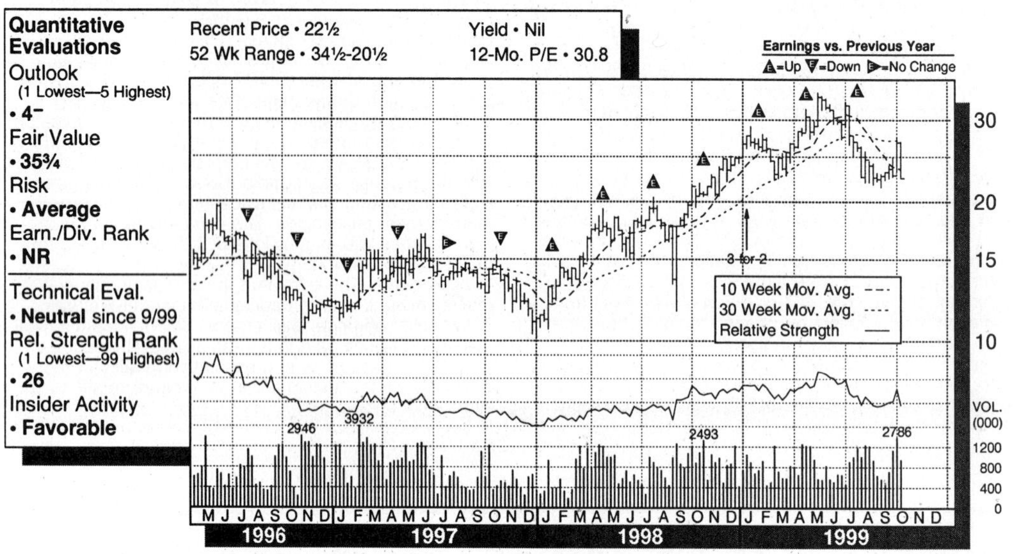

Business Profile - 09-JUL-99

In April 1999, Stillwater reported that palladium demand appears favorable in 1999, especially in the autocatalyst sector, which is benefiting from global tightening of emissions standards. SWC also noted that Russian palladium supply in 1999 is expected to be at or slightly below 1998 levels. SWC's cash production costs in the first quarter of 1999 were above its target range of $140 to $160 an ounce; the company has reorganized its mining supervision and has introduced new equipment, both of which it expects to aid productivity. SWC said it should produce between 525,000 and 575,000 ounces of metal in 1999, at a production cost between $140 and $160 an ounce.

Operational Review - 09-JUL-99

Revenues in the three months ended March 31, 1999, advanced 77%, year to year, benefiting from a 7% increase in the quantity of metal sold and a 64% gain in the average realized price per ounce of palladium and platinum. Profitability benefited from the boost in ounces shipped and higher selling prices, and following lower interest expense, due to capitalization of interest, and taxes at 33.5%, against 38.5%, net income rose to $10.6 million ($0.28 a share, on 24% more shares outstanding), from $984,000 ($0.03, adjusted for the December 1998 3-for-2 stock split).

Stock Performance - 08-OCT-99

In the past 30 trading days, SWC's shares have increased 0.56%, compared to a 0.91% fall in the S&P 500. Average trading volume for the past five days was 187,720 shares, compared with the 40-day moving average of 208,356 shares.

Key Stock Statistics

Dividend Rate/Share	Nil	Shareholders	12,481
Shs. outstg. (M)	37.8	Market cap. (B)	$0.850
Avg. daily vol. (M)	0.278	Inst. holdings	77%
Tang. Bk. Value/Share	7.94		
Beta	NA		

Value of $10,000 invested 5 years ago: NA

Fiscal Year Ending Dec. 31

	1999	1998	1997	1996	1995	1994
Revenues (Million $)						
1Q	38.03	21.51	16.00	13.65	13.26	12.50
2Q	36.85	26.52	22.29	10.65	18.87	14.91
3Q	—	28.20	17.00	16.48	10.65	12.68
4Q	—	30.49	21.58	15.43	11.29	18.51
Yr.	—	106.7	76.88	56.21	54.06	58.61
Earnings Per Share ($)						
1Q	**0.28**	**0.03**	**-0.07**	**0.46**	0.03	-0.01
2Q	**0.21**	**0.10**	**-0.03**	**-0.03**	-0.01	0.02
3Q	—	**0.12**	**-0.05**	**-0.03**	-0.02	0.05
4Q	—	**0.15**	**-0.03**	**-0.04**	0.01	0.01
Yr.	—	**0.38**	**-0.18**	**-0.09**	Nil	**0.11**

Next earnings report expected: mid October

Dividend Data

Amount ($)	Date Decl.	Ex-Div. Date	Stock of Record	Payment Date
3-for-2	Dec. 08	Jan. 04	Dec. 21	Dec. 31 '98

Stillwater Mining Company

Business Summary - 09-JUL-99

Operating from the underground Stillwater Mine in southern Montana, Stillwater Mining Co. (SWC) is engaged in the exploration, development, mining and production of platinum, palladium and associated metals. SWC is the only significant primary producer of platinum group metals (PGMs) outside of South Africa.

In March 1999, SWC reported that its growth goals include producing 1.2 million ounces of metal by the end of 2001. It feels the increased production will be facilitated by a $385 million expansion project. The project includes: increasing production at the Stillwater Mine from the current 2,000 tons of ore per day to 3,000, constructing a second mine located at East Boulder, Montana, which will be capable of processing 2,000 tons of ore per day and expanding a smelter and base metals refinery. For 1999, production is projected at between 525,000 and 575,000 ounces of metal at cash costs between $140 and $160 an ounce. SWC considers itself to be the lowest cash cost producer of palladium and platinum in the world.

In order to assure steady cash flow, SWC has entered into five year contracts with end users of palladium and platinum. The palladium contracts set a floor price averaging $225 per ounce on virtually all production. The palladium contracts also stipulate a price cap on 30% of production at $400 per ounce; the remaining 70% of production has no price cap. SWC signed contracts for 20% of platinum output with an average floor of $350 and a ceiling of $425 an ounce.

The Stillwater Mine accesses an extensive mineralized zone containing PGMs known as the J-M Reef, which is the only significant source of PGMs outside South Africa and Russia. SWC holds 995 patented and unpatented lode or millsite claims covering approximately 16,000 acres on the J-M Reef.

As of December 31, 1998, the company had proved and probable reserves of some 37.1 million tons of ore at 0.71 ounce per ton containing 26.3 million ounces of platinum and palladium. Over the past several years, SWC reports that the cut-off grade used for reserve calculation has been 0.50 to 0.40 ounce of metal per ton or ore. However, due to increasing realized prices, particularly for palladium, as well as declining operating costs, material at a grade of 0.30 ounce per ton is being processed through the company's concentrator, and SWC has lowered its reserve cut-off grade to 0.30 ounce of metal per ton of ore.

In the first quarter of 1999, SWC noted that the market outlook for palladium was positive. It expects palladium demand growth to continue, due to increased usage in auto catalysts and believes that palladium demand will outpace supply for the next several years, even if substitution to other metals occurs. SWC also expects longer term platinum demand to show higher growth, resulting from increased usage in automotive catalysts and for new applications in fuel cell technology.

Per Share Data ($) (Year Ended Dec. 31)	1998	1997	1996	1995	1994	1993	1992	1991	1990	1989
Tangible Bk. Val.	6.60	4.63	4.75	4.39	4.39	3.29	NA	NA	NA	NA
Cash Flow	0.71	0.21	0.19	Nil	0.29	0.27	NA	NA	NA	NA
Earnings	0.38	-0.18	-0.09	Nil	0.07	0.06	NA	NA	NA	NA
Dividends	Nil	Nil	Nil	Nil	Nil	Nil	NA	NA	NA	NA
Payout Ratio	Nil	Nil	Nil	Nil	Nil	Nil	NA	NA	NA	NA
Prices - High	27 3/8	17	19 3/4	19 1/8	9 1/8	NA	NA	NA	NA	NA
- Low	10 5/8	10 1/8	9 7/8	8 7/8	8 5/8	NA	NA	NA	NA	NA
P/E Ratio - High	72	NM	NM	NM	NM	NA	NA	NA	NA	NA
- Low	28	NM	NM	NM	NM	NA	NA	NA	NA	NA
Income Statement Analysis (Million $)										
Revs.	107	76.9	56.2	54.1	58.6	53.8	NA	NA	NA	NA
Oper. Inc.	34.8	5.5	4.3	3.5	8.1	7.4	NA	NA	NA	NA
Depr.	11.6	11.7	8.7	5.8	5.2	4.9	NA	NA	NA	NA
Int. Exp.	2.8	3.6	1.5	0.4	0.3	0.1	NA	NA	NA	NA
Pretax Inc.	21.8	-8.7	4.5	0.1	2.8	2.4	NA	NA	NA	NA
Eff. Tax Rate	39%	NM	NM	39%	39%	38%	NA	NA	NA	NA
Net Inc.	13.4	-5.4	-2.8	0.1	1.7	1.5	NA	NA	NA	NA
Balance Sheet & Other Fin. Data (Million $)										
Cash	49.8	4.2	33.4	24.6	57.0	2.5	NA	NA	NA	NA
Curr. Assets	85.4	35.3	49.1	45.0	77.2	22.1	NA	NA	NA	NA
Total Assets	336	229	240	162	153	92.0	NA	NA	NA	NA
Curr. Liab.	26.6	12.2	15.8	10.4	9.4	6.8	NA	NA	NA	NA
LT Debt	59.0	61.5	62.6	8.7	1.7	1.8	NA	NA	NA	NA
Common Eqty.	228	141	144	132	132	74.0	NA	NA	NA	NA
Total Cap.	306	215	222	149	143	84.0	NA	NA	NA	NA
Cap. Exp.	78.3	15.8	58.4	46.1	9.3	2.0	NA	NA	NA	NA
Cash Flow	25.0	6.3	5.9	5.8	7.0	6.4	NA	NA	NA	NA
Curr. Ratio	3.2	2.9	3.1	4.3	8.2	3.3	NA	NA	NA	NA
% LT Debt of Cap.	19.3	28.7	28.2	5.8	1.2	2.1	NA	NA	NA	NA
% Net Inc.of Revs.	12.5	NM	NM	0.1	2.9	2.7	NA	NA	NA	NA
% Ret. on Assets	4.7	NM	NM	NM	1.4	1.6	NA	NA	NA	NA
% Ret. on Equity	7.2	NM	NM	NM	1.7	1.9	NA	NA	NA	NA

Data as orig reptd.; bef. results of disc opers/spec. items. Per share data adj. for stk. divs. Bold denotes diluted EPS (FASB 128)-prior periods restated. E-Estimated. NA-Not Available. NM-Not Meaningful. NR-Not Ranked.

Office—One Tabor Center, 1200 17th Street, Suite 900, Denver, CO 80202. **Tel**—(303) 352-2060. **Fax**—(303) 352-2095. **Website**—http://www.stillwatermining.com. **Chrmn & CEO**—W. E. Nettles. **Pres & COO**—J. E. Andrews. **VP & CFO**—J. A. Sabala. **Secy**—M. A. Shea. **Investor Relations Contact**—Gina Wilson. **Dirs**—J. E. Andrews, D. D. Donald, R. E. Gilbert, L. M. Glaser, A. Guzman, W. E. Nettles, T. Schwinden, P. Steen. **Transfer Agent & Registrar**—Harris Trust & Savings Bank, Chicago, IL. **Incorporated**—in Delaware in 1992. **Empl**— 899. **S&P Analyst:** J. F.

STANDARD
&POOR'S
STOCK REPORTS

Stone & Webster

NYSE Symbol **SW**

In S&P SmallCap 600

09-OCT-99 **Industry:** Engineering & Construction

Summary: This company is a global leader in engineering, construction and consulting services for power, process, environmental/infrastructure and industrial markets.

Quantitative Evaluations

Outlook
(1 Lowest—5 Highest)
• **1-**

Fair Value
• **25⅜**

Risk
• **Low**

Earn./Div. Rank
• **B-**

Technical Eval.
• **Bullish** since 8/99

Rel. Strength Rank
(1 Lowest—99 Highest)
• **78**

Insider Activity
• **NA**

Recent Price • 28
52 Wk Range • 34⅜-19⅜
Yield • 2.1%
12-Mo. P/E • NM

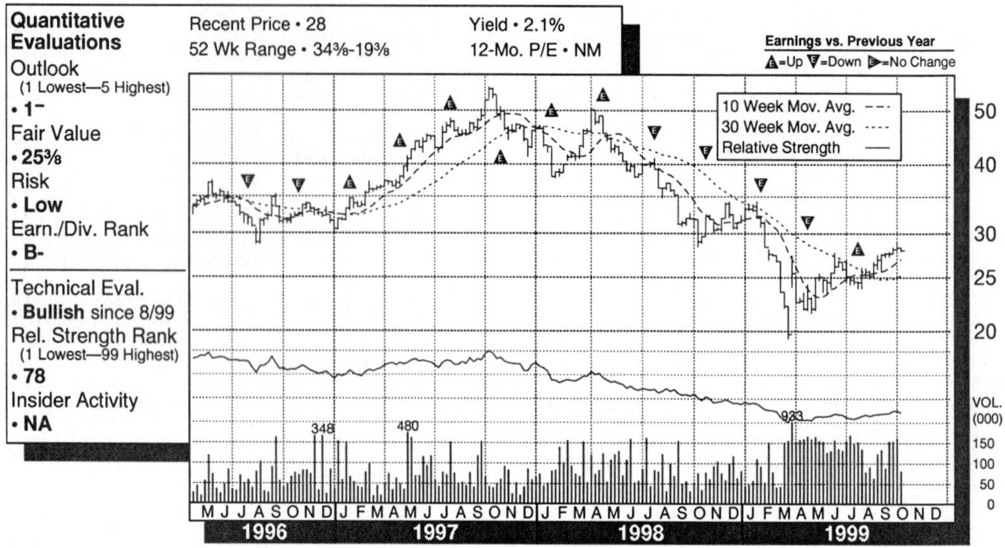

Business Profile - 19-JUL-99

The company said in April 1999 that while new orders were somewhat lower than anticipated in the first quarter, it expected to regain momentum over the next few quarters, based on projects in negotiation and the stronger trends in the power sectors as well as recent increases in crude oil and petrochemical prices. The company has also taken steps to be more selective in avoiding high risk, low margin business. SW expects that the improved margin included in its backlog, and its continuing drive to reduce costs and operating expenses, will produce improved results in the second half of the year.

Operational Review - 19-JUL-99

Revenues in the three months ended March 31, 1999, slid 9.5%, year to year, reflecting delayed or canceled power projects in Asia due to that region's economic slowdown and weak demand from petrochemical customers. Results were impaired by a provision of $74.2 million on two international projects for unanticipated cost increases. A pretax loss of $68,694,000 contrasted with pretax income of $12,420,000. After tax benefits of $10,000,000, against taxes at 38.7%, the loss was $58,694,000 ($4.50 a share), against income of $7,613,000 ($0.59).

Stock Performance - 08-OCT-99

In the past 30 trading days, SW's shares have increased 4%, compared to a 0.91% fall in the S&P 500. Average trading volume for the past five days was 15,980 shares, compared with the 40-day moving average of 29,267 shares.

Key Stock Statistics

Dividend Rate/Share	0.60	Shareholders	5,400
Shs. outstg. (M)	13.1	Market cap. (B)	$0.366
Avg. daily vol. (M)	0.037	Inst. holdings	38%
Tang. Bk. Value/Share	18.06		
Beta	0.64		

Value of $10,000 invested 5 years ago: $ 11,200

Fiscal Year Ending Dec. 31

	1999	1998	1997	1996	1995	1994
Revenues (Million $)						
1Q	266.1	294.0	349.5	305.8	222.5	192.7
2Q	310.3	317.0	286.3	268.7	230.7	190.4
3Q	—	350.4	368.2	282.2	219.2	205.4
4Q	—	287.4	318.5	308.1	330.4	229.7
Yr.	—	1,249	1,323	1,165	1,003	818.2
Earnings Per Share ($)						
1Q	**-4.50**	**0.59**	**0.43**	**0.41**	0.32	-0.86
2Q	**0.48**	**0.05**	**0.74**	**0.28**	0.55	-0.27
3Q	—	**0.17**	**0.73**	**-1.86**	0.35	0.35
4Q	—	**-4.64**	**0.69**	**0.37**	-0.18	0.26
Yr.	—	**-3.83**	**2.59**	**-1.32**	**1.04**	-0.52

Next earnings report expected: late October

Dividend Data (Dividends have been paid since 1939.)

Amount ($)	Date Decl.	Ex-Div. Date	Stock of Record	Payment Date
0.150	Oct. 27	Nov. 04	Nov. 06	Nov. 14 '98
0.150	Jan. 26	Feb. 03	Feb. 05	Feb. 13 '99
0.150	Apr. 27	May. 05	May. 07	May. 15 '99
0.150	Jul. 26	Aug. 04	Aug. 06	Aug. 14 '99

Stone & Webster Incorporated

Business Summary - 19-JUL-99

Stone & Webster provides complete engineering, design, construction and environmental services for power, process, governmental, industrial, transportation and civil works projects. The company also constructs from plans developed by others, makes engineering reports and business examinations, undertakes consulting engineering work, and offers information management and computer systems expertise to clients. SW remains active in the nuclear power business, for utility and governmental clients, and continues to engage in a significant amount of modification and maintenance work on existing nuclear power plants as well as decommissioning and decontamination projects. It also has cold storage warehousing operations.

Revenues by division in 1998 were as follows: power 50%, process 23%, environmental/infrastructure 9%, industrial 12%, and other 6%. International operations accounted for 37% of the company's revenues and generated $4.4 million in operating income.

SW's power division is a global leader in the development, engineering, design and construction of facilities supporting domestic and international power generation. It provides technical depth and offers full-service engineering, procurement and construction capabilities. The unit participates in power projects worldwide, including gas, oil-fired, simple and combined-cycle combustion turbine, hydroelectric, geothermal and nuclear.

The process division employs technology to provide cost-effective solutions for petrochemical, refining and gas processing applications for the global process engineering and construction market. Activities extend from basic laboratory and pilot plant work through construction of full-scale facilities. Capabilities include refining technologies for fluid catalytic cracking, deep catalytic cracking and hydroprocessing.

The environmental/infrastructure business provides engineering, construction and consulting services to three core markets: federal facilities/environmental remediation, water and wastewater transportation. Activities cover cleanup at former nuclear weapons production facilities and Superfund sites; state-of-the-art membrane water treatment plant services; rail, rapid transit and facility design; and selected highway, airport and bridge projects.

The industrial division applies a full range of design, engineering, construction and project finance skills as a complete service provider to the chemicals and fibers, pipeline, telecommunications energy services and manufacturing markets.

Stone & Webster Management Consultants assists clients in the deregulation and restructuring of domestic and global gas, power and water industries. It supports sellers, buyers and financiers in the emerging U.S. divestiture market for utility generation assets.

Nordic Refrigerated Services operates the largest public refrigerated warehouse system in the southeastern U.S., providing cold storage and frozen food handling services to manufacturers, distributors and wholesale and retail grocers.

Per Share Data ($) (Year Ended Dec. 31)	1998	1997	1996	1995	1994	1993	1992	1991	1990	1989
Tangible Bk. Val.	22.36	26.90	24.71	26.10	25.69	28.40	26.93	26.29	25.22	24.97
Cash Flow	-1.99	3.65	-0.04	2.37	0.80	1.32	1.96	2.34	1.64	2.57
Earnings	-3.83	2.59	-1.31	1.04	-0.52	-0.03	0.62	1.08	0.50	1.37
Dividends	0.60	0.60	0.45	0.60	0.60	0.60	0.60	0.60	1.05	1.20
Payout Ratio	NM	23%	NM	58%	NM	NM	97%	56%	210%	87%
Prices - High	50 1/2	55 1/8	37 3/8	40	34	30 1/4	31	36 1/4	41 3/4	45 3/4
- Low	28 3/8	31 1/8	28 5/8	27 1/4	27 1/4	21 1/4	23 3/4	26 1/8	25 1/8	34 1/8
P/E Ratio - High	NM	21	NM	38	NM	NM	50	34	84	33
- Low	NM	12	NM	26	NM	NM	38	24	50	25
Income Statement Analysis (Million $)										
Revs.	1,249	1,323	1,165	1,003	766	262	266	257	232	242
Oper. Inc.	-48.8	61.0	-9.0	54.3	-37.0	26.5	29.4	34.3	5.5	9.8
Depr.	23.7	13.7	16.9	19.2	19.7	20.1	20.1	18.8	17.3	18.1
Int. Exp.	4.1	1.7	6.7	9.0	5.3	3.0	3.0	3.7	4.2	6.1
Pretax Inc.	-72.9	50.8	-29.4	23.5	-8.8	8.5	23.6	28.1	14.1	27.2
Eff. Tax Rate	NM	34%	NM	37%	NM	104%	60%	42%	47%	24%
Net Inc.	-49.3	33.5	-17.4	14.9	-7.8	-0.4	9.3	16.4	7.5	20.8
Balance Sheet & Other Fin. Data (Million $)										
Cash	45.5	75.0	61.9	123	130	119	104	81.0	70.0	103
Curr. Assets	392	409	394	364	278	292	286	306	296	314
Total Assets	835	739	692	717	678	680	615	602	569	566
Curr. Liab.	473	297	286	206	141	118	116	119	126	120
LT Debt	22.2	22.5	24.3	74.7	89.6	47.7	24.8	28.0	11.4	21.6
Common Eqty.	292	345	317	362	375	425	403	395	380	378
Total Cap.	347	425	385	488	514	538	475	461	422	425
Cap. Exp.	20.3	25.9	24.4	28.0	52.3	31.7	26.9	26.6	18.4	21.7
Cash Flow	-25.6	47.2	-0.5	34.1	11.9	19.8	29.5	35.2	24.8	38.9
Curr. Ratio	0.8	1.4	1.4	1.8	2.0	2.5	2.5	2.6	2.4	2.6
% LT Debt of Cap.	6.4	5.3	6.3	15.3	17.5	8.9	5.2	6.1	2.7	5.1
% Net Inc.of Revs.	NM	2.5	NM	1.5	NM	NM	3.5	6.4	3.2	8.6
% Ret. on Assets	NM	4.7	NM	2.1	NM	NM	1.5	2.8	1.3	3.7
% Ret. on Equity	NM	10.1	NM	4.0	NM	NM	2.3	4.2	2.0	5.6

Data as orig reptd.; bef. results of disc opers/spec. items. Per share data adj. for stk. divs. Bold denotes diluted EPS (FASB 128)-prior periods restated. E-Estimated. NA-Not Available. NM-Not Meaningful. NR-Not Ranked.

Office—245 Summer Street, Boston, MA, 02210. **Tel**—(617) 589-5111. **Chrmn, Pres & CEO**—H. K. Smith. **VP & Secy**—J. P. Jones. **EVP & CFO**—T. L. Langford. **Dirs**—D. F. Bethell, F. J. A. Cilluffo, K. F. Hansen, E. R. Heiberg III, D. N. McCammon, J. A. McKee, J. P. Merrill, Jr., B. W. Reznicek, H. K. Smith, P. M. Wood. **Transfer Agent & Registrar**—ChaseMellon Shareholder Services, Ridgefield Park, NJ. **Incorporated**—in Delaware in 1929. **Empl**— 5,500. **S&P Analyst:** P.L.H.

STANDARD
&POOR'S
STOCK REPORTS

Stone Energy

NYSE Symbol **SGY**

In S&P SmallCap 600

09-OCT-99

Industry:
Oil & Gas (Exploration & Production)

Summary: This company acquires and explores for producing oil and gas properties in the Gulf Coast Basin.

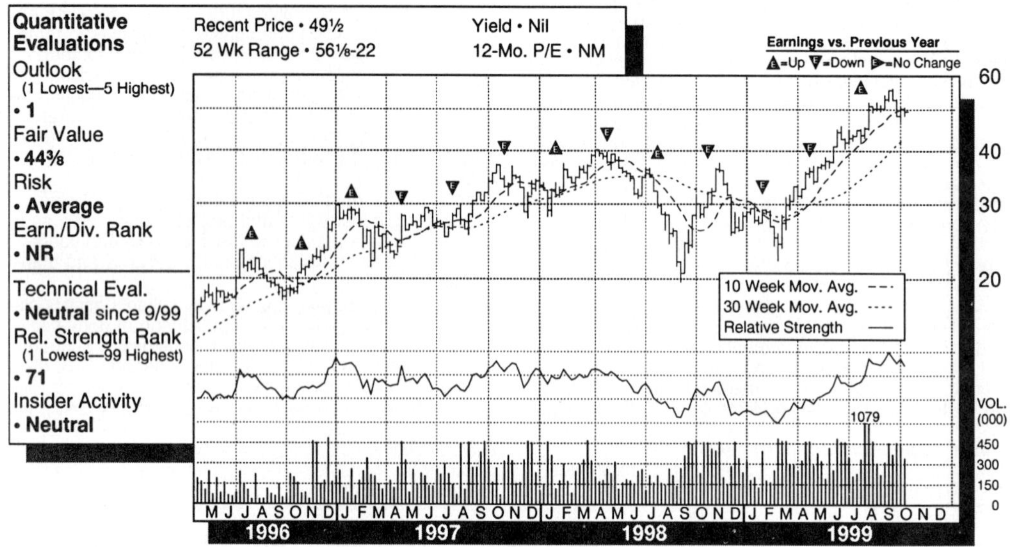

Business Profile - 12-JUL-99

SGY focuses on acquiring mature properties that have an established production history and significant exploitation and development potential. In July 1999, it acquired the 67.5% interest in the East Cameron Block 64 Field that it did not already own, in an exchange for a volumetric production payment of natural gas. In June 1999, SGY acquired a majority interest in the Lafitte Field, in Jefferson Parish, LA. The company expects the property additions to result in a 5% increase in average daily production. SGY plans to use a portion of the proceeds from an upcoming equity offering to finance the Lafitte acquisition, and the development of both fields.

Operational Review - 12-JUL-99

Total revenues in the three months ended March 31, 1999, advanced 7.4%, year to year, as higher production volumes of oil and gas outweighed lower product prices. Results were hurt by significant increases in normal lease operating expense, interest expense, and depreciation, depletion and amortization charges; pretax income plunged 47%. After taxes at 35.1%, versus 35.6%, net income was also down 47%, to $1,746,000 ($0.11 a share), from $3,298,000 ($0.22).

Stock Performance - 08-OCT-99

In the past 30 trading days, SGY's shares have declined 1%, compared to a 0.91% fall in the S&P 500. Average trading volume for the past five days was 67,900 shares, compared with the 40-day moving average of 75,756 shares.

Key Stock Statistics

Dividend Rate/Share	Nil	Shareholders	179
Shs. outstg. (M)	18.3	Market cap. (B)	$0.906
Avg. daily vol. (M)	0.083	Inst. holdings	55%
Tang. Bk. Value/Share	6.99		
Beta	0.93		

Value of $10,000 invested 5 years ago: $ 36,666

Fiscal Year Ending Dec. 31

	1999	1998	1997	1996	1995	1994
Revenues (Million $)						
1Q	30.92	28.80	16.24	15.09	8.18	7.69
2Q	36.27	28.47	13.66	14.40	10.28	8.16
3Q	—	27.42	15.96	13.25	10.66	8.59
4Q	—	31.94	25.13	15.23	11.44	8.45
Yr.	—	116.6	70.99	57.97	40.55	32.89
Earnings Per Share ($)						
1Q	**0.11**	**0.22**	**0.24**	**0.28**	0.07	0.11
2Q	**0.35**	**0.12**	**0.11**	**0.24**	0.13	0.09
3Q	—	**0.05**	**0.16**	**0.17**	0.14	0.07
4Q	—	**-3.82**	**0.28**	**0.21**	0.15	0.07
Yr.	—	**-3.43**	**0.78**	**0.90**	**0.49**	**0.34**

Next earnings report expected: early November

Dividend Data

SGY does not intend to pay cash dividends in the foreseeable future. A shareholder rights plan was adopted in October 1998.

Stone Energy Corporation

Business Summary - 12-JUL-99

Stone Energy Corp. (SGY) is an independent oil and gas company that acquires, explores, develops and operates oil and gas properties onshore and offshore in the Gulf Coast Basin. The company and its predecessors have been active in the Gulf Coast Basin since 1973; as a result, SGY has extensive geophysical, technical and operational expertise in the area. At December 31, 1998, the company had estimated proved reserves of about 243.3 Bcf of natural gas and 18,500,000 bbl. of oil, or an aggregate of about 354,100,000 Bcf of gas equivalent, with a present value of estimated pretax future net cash flow of $286.1 million (based on year-end 1998 prices and a 10% discount rate).

The company's strategy is to increase production, cash flow and reserves by acquiring and developing mature properties in the Gulf Coast Basin. SGY seeks properties with an established production history, proved undeveloped reserves, and multiple prospective reservoirs that provide significant development opportunities and an attractive price due to low current production levels, and properties in which it could control operations. Prior to acquiring a property, the company performs a thorough geological, geophysical and engineering analysis of the property to formulate a comprehensive development plan. Through development activities, SGY seeks to increase cash flow from existing proved reserves and to establish additional proved reserves. These activities typically involve the drilling of new wells, workovers and recompletions of existing wells, and the application of other techniques designed to increase production.

From 1993 through 1998, SGY increased the number of properties in which it has an interest from five to 15; it serves as operator of 14 of the properties. In addition, the company has substantially expanded its technical database, including 3-D seismic data relating to its properties and potential acquisitions. As a result, SGY has been able to significantly increase its development activities. For 1999, the company budgeted exploration and development spending of $73.3 million, including plans to drill 20 new wells and, depending upon the success of specific development activities, to install two new offshore production platforms. Capital spending in 1998 totaled $158.9 million, of which $14 million was for the acquisition of interests in producing properties.

Per Share Data ($) (Year Ended Dec. 31)	1998	1997	1996	1995	1994	1993	1992	1991	1990	1989
Tangible Bk. Val.	6.99	10.41	9.62	5.68	5.18	5.01	NA	NA	NA	NA
Cash Flow	1.10	2.71	2.47	1.82	1.32	1.64	NA	NA	NA	NA
Earnings	-3.43	0.79	0.89	0.49	0.34	0.85	NA	NA	NA	NA
Dividends	Nil	Nil	Nil	Nil	Nil	Nil	NA	NA	NA	NA
Payout Ratio	Nil	Nil	Nil	Nil	Nil	Nil	NA	NA	NA	NA
Prices - High	40¼	37⅞	30	19	19¼	16⅝	NA	NA	NA	NA
- Low	19⅝	21¼	13¼	11	9⅞	11½	NA	NA	NA	NA
P/E Ratio - High	NM	47	34	39	57	20	NA	NA	NA	NA
- Low	NM	27	15	22	29	14	NA	NA	NA	NA
Income Statement Analysis (Million $)										
Revs.	117	71.0	58.0	40.6	31.6	28.9	NA	NA	NA	NA
Oper. Inc.	90.2	52.1	41.1	27.4	17.7	19.3	NA	NA	NA	NA
Depr.	68.2	28.7	19.6	15.7	11.6	8.0	NA	NA	NA	NA
Int. Exp.	12.9	4.9	3.6	2.2	1.0	1.5	NA	NA	NA	NA
Pretax Inc.	-80.1	18.4	17.9	9.5	6.4	9.8	NA	NA	NA	NA
Eff. Tax Rate	NA	35%	39%	39%	38%	9.60%	34%	NA	NA	NA
Net Inc.	-51.6	11.9	11.0	5.8	4.0	8.8	NA	NA	NA	NA
Balance Sheet & Other Fin. Data (Million $)										
Cash	27.4	10.3	20.2	16.5	20.3	28.1	NA	NA	NA	NA
Curr. Assets	54.4	53.2	33.2	24.5	28.3	37.9	NA	NA	NA	NA
Total Assets	366	354	209	139	110	101	NA	NA	NA	NA
Curr. Liab.	44.5	44.8	26.5	19.1	23.9	19.5	NA	NA	NA	NA
LT Debt	210	132	26.2	47.8	22.7	21.6	NA	NA	NA	NA
Common Eqty.	105	157	144	66.9	61.0	59.1	NA	NA	NA	NA
Total Cap.	315	307	182	120	85.7	80.7	NA	NA	NA	NA
Cap. Exp.	164	134	72.7	48.1	41.2	18.2	NA	NA	NA	NA
Cash Flow	16.6	40.7	30.6	21.5	15.6	16.6	NA	NA	NA	NA
Curr. Ratio	1.2	1.2	1.3	1.3	1.2	1.9	NA	NA	NA	NA
% LT Debt of Cap.	66.6	42.9	14.4	39.8	26.5	26.8	NA	NA	NA	NA
% Net Inc.of Revs.	NM	16.8	19.0	14.3	12.7	30.6	NA	NA	NA	NA
% Ret. on Assets	NM	4.2	6.3	4.7	3.8	NA	NA	NA	NA	NA
% Ret. on Equity	NM	7.9	10.4	9.1	6.7	NA	NA	NA	NA	NA

Data as orig reptd.; bef. results of disc opers/spec. items. Per share data adj. for stk. divs. Bold denotes diluted EPS (FASB 128)-prior periods restated. E-Estimated. NA-Not Available. NM-Not Meaningful. NR-Not Ranked.

Office—625 E. Kaliste Saloom Rd., Lafayette, LA 70508. —**Tel**—(318) 237-0410. **Chrmn & CEO**—J. H. Stone. **Vice Chrmn**—J. R. Klutts. **Pres & COO**—D. P. Canty. **VP & Secy**—A. L. Gates III. **CFO & Investor Contact**—James H. Prince. **Dirs**—R. A. Bernhard, D. P. Canty, B. J. Duplantis, R. B. Gary, J. R. Klutts, J. P. Laborde, J. H. Stone, D. R. Voelker. **Transfer Agent & Registrar**—ChaseMellon Shareholder Services, Dallas. **Incorporated**—in Delaware in 1993. **Empl**— 115. **S&P Analyst:** S.A.H.

STANDARD
&POOR'S
STOCK REPORTS

Stride Rite

NYSE Symbol **SRR**

In S&P SmallCap 600

09-OCT-99 **Industry:** Footwear

Summary: SRR is a leading marketer of children's and adults' footwear sold under the Stride Rite, Sperry Top-Sider, Keds, Tommy Hilfiger and other names.

Quantitative Evaluations

Outlook (1 Lowest—5 Highest) • **2+**

Fair Value • **6⅞**

Risk • **Average**

Earn./Div. Rank • **B+**

Technical Eval. • **Bearish** since 7/99

Rel. Strength Rank (1 Lowest—99 Highest) • **13**

Insider Activity • **Neutral**

Recent Price • 7 | 52 Wk Range • 13⅜-6¾ | Yield • 2.9% | 12-Mo. P/E • 15.9

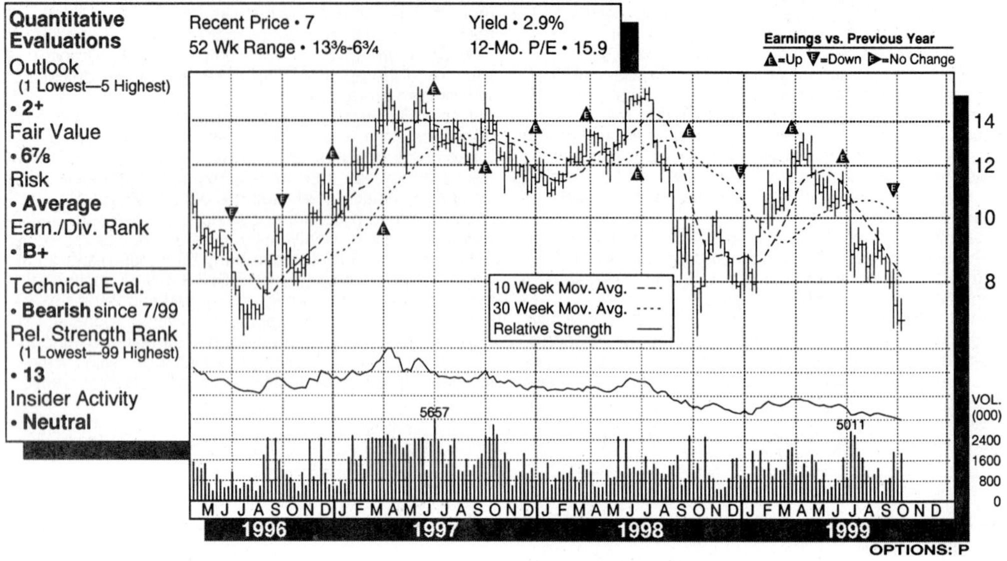

Business Profile - 23-AUG-99

In August 1999, Stride Rite said that it will streamline certain corporate and divisional operations in order to competitively position the company for future growth and increased profitability. The restructuring will include centralizing merchandising, finance, and operations functions from divisions and eliminating approximately 125 administrative positions. SRR expects to save $9 million annually and a $3 million pretax charge will be taken in the third quarter of FY 99 (Nov.). It stated that this restructuring should allow for more consistent execution of key functions and bring more focus on integrating strategic initiatives. SRR's directors also approved increasing the ongoing share repurchase program authorization by two million shares.

Operational Review - 23-AUG-99

Net sales in the six months ended May 28, 1999, rose 16%, year to year, reflecting double-digit gains in three core brands (Keds, Sperry Top-Sider, Tommy Hilfiger), improvement in the Stride Rite children's business, and a higher-priced product mix. Gross margins widened slightly, primarily due to reduction in inventory obsolescence charges and sales allowances. Operating income increased, as selling and administrative expenses were well controlled despite additional spending on advertising and Y2K compliance. Following higher interest expense, pretax income rose 16%. After taxes at 37.8%, versus 36.5%, net income was up 14%, to $15,912,000 ($0.34 a share), from $13,997,000 ($0.29).

Stock Performance - 08-OCT-99

In the past 30 trading days, SRR's shares have declined 22%, compared to a 0.91% fall in the S&P 500. Average trading volume for the past five days was 375,180 shares, compared with the 40-day moving average of 242,162 shares.

Key Stock Statistics

Dividend Rate/Share	0.20	Shareholders	5,100
Shs. outstg. (M)	46.4	Market cap. (B)	$0.325
Avg. daily vol. (M)	0.296	Inst. holdings	71%
Tang. Bk. Value/Share	5.42		
Beta	1.32		

Value of $10,000 invested 5 years ago: $ 5,007

Fiscal Year Ending Nov. 30

	1999	1998	1997	1996	1995	1994
Revenues (Million $)						
1Q	148.2	129.0	131.8	118.9	134.8	122.1
2Q	166.3	143.2	141.6	124.2	144.4	161.7
3Q	155.9	168.5	144.5	123.5	139.1	155.0
4Q	—	97.73	97.86	81.67	78.13	85.14
Yr.	—	539.4	515.7	448.3	496.4	523.9
Earnings Per Share ($)						
1Q	**0.13**	**0.09**	0.08	0.03	0.10	0.10
2Q	**0.21**	**0.20**	0.14	0.06	0.08	0.15
3Q	**0.22**	**0.27**	0.17	0.06	0.07	0.17
4Q	—	**-0.12**	0.01	-0.10	-0.42	-0.02
Yr.	—	**0.44**	**0.40**	0.05	-0.17	0.40

Next earnings report expected: early January

Dividend Data (Dividends have been paid since 1955.)

Amount ($)	Date Decl.	Ex-Div. Date	Stock of Record	Payment Date
0.050	Nov. 11	Nov. 20	Nov. 24	Dec. 15 '98
0.050	Feb. 04	Feb. 22	Feb. 24	Mar. 15 '99
0.050	Apr. 15	May. 21	May. 25	Jun. 15 '99
0.050	Aug. 19	Aug. 25	Aug. 27	Sep. 15 '99

The Stride Rite Corporation

Business Summary - 23-AUG-99

With brand names such as Munchkin, Sperry Top-Sider, Keds, Tommy Hilfiger, and Nine West, Stride Rite Corp. (SRR) is the leading marketer of children's footwear in the U.S. and a major marketer of athletic and casual footwear for children and adults. After closing manufacturing facilities in the U.S. and in the Caribbean, the company now purchases substantially all of its products overseas.

The company markets children's footwear under the trademarks Stride Rite, Munchkin, Sperry and Street Hot. Children's and adults' marine shoes and outdoor recreational and casual footwear are marketed under the Sperry Top-Sider and Sperry trademarks. Casual and athletic footwear is marketed for adults and children under the Keds, Pro-Keds and Grasshoppers trademarks.

SRR also produces and markets a line of premium dress casual, sport casual, dress and athletic shoes for men, women and children under the Tommy Hilfiger trademark.

Footwear is distributed through independent retail stores, including Stride Rite Bootery stores, department stores, sporting goods stores and marinas, and company-owned stores, including manufacturer's outlet stores, Keds concept stores, Great Feet concept stores and children's footwear departments in department stores. The company owns two distribution centers, one located in Kentucky and the other in Indiana.

At the end of FY 98 (Nov.), the company operated 111 Stride Rite children's shoe stores, four Great Feet stores, 60 leased children's shoe departments in department stores, and 24 manufacturer's outlet stores under the Stride Rite Family Footwear name. Outside the U.S., SRR uses independent distributors and licensees to market its various product lines. As of the end of FY 98, foreign licensees operated 17 Stride Retail stores in Canada, Costa Rica, El Salvador, Honduras, Mexico, and Peru. International sales accounted for 6% of sales in FY 98.

In FY 98, SRR opened four leased departments and five manufacturers' outlet stores, but closed 16 retail stores. In FY 99, the company plans to open 10 to 15 stores, and close 5 to 10 underperforming stores.

As part of the company's plan to diversify its portfolio of footwear brands, SRR introduced Tommy Hilfiger for women and Nine West Kids for girls in FY 98. The Tommy Hilfiger collection of footwear for women consists of athletic, casual and dress casual footwear. The Nine West Kids line is targeted for girls between six and ten years old. After experiencing disappointing sales, the company discontinued a Levi's line of casual footwear and boots for boys and young men in the fourth quarter of FY 98.

In August 1999, the company announced a restructuring to streamline company functions which is expected to save $9 million annually. A $3 million pretax charge will be taken in the third quarter of FY 99.

Per Share Data ($) (Year Ended Nov. 30)	1998	1997	1996	1995	1994	1993	1992	1991	1990	1989
Tangible Bk. Val.	5.25	5.09	5.24	5.37	5.74	5.81	5.12	4.64	3.54	3.09
Cash Flow	0.65	0.60	0.24	0.05	0.57	1.31	1.30	1.36	1.14	0.94
Earnings	0.44	0.40	0.05	-0.17	0.40	1.19	1.19	1.28	1.05	0.86
Dividends	0.20	0.20	0.20	0.43	0.38	0.35	0.31	0.26	0.20	0.17
Payout Ratio	45%	50%	NM	NM	95%	29%	26%	20%	18%	20%
Prices - High	$15\frac{3}{4}$	$15\frac{7}{8}$	$11\frac{7}{8}$	$13\frac{1}{4}$	$18\frac{7}{8}$	$23\frac{1}{8}$	$31\frac{7}{8}$	$30\frac{1}{4}$	$15\frac{1}{4}$	$15\frac{1}{8}$
- Low	$6\frac{5}{8}$	$9\frac{7}{8}$	6	7	$10\frac{1}{2}$	$12\frac{1}{8}$	$16\frac{3}{8}$	$13\frac{3}{8}$	$9\frac{3}{4}$	$6\frac{1}{2}$
P/E Ratio - High	36	40	NM	NM	47	19	27	24	14	18
- Low	15	25	NM	NM	26	10	14	10	9	8
Income Statement Analysis (Million $)										
Revs.	539	516	448	496	524	583	586	574	516	454
Oper. Inc.	38.9	40.9	11.0	11.0	47.0	107	122	109	94.0	83.0
Depr.	9.4	9.8	9.7	10.9	8.5	6.3	5.4	4.2	4.3	4.4
Int. Exp.	1.7	0.2	0.7	1.0	0.5	0.5	0.5	0.7	1.8	3.3
Pretax Inc.	33.2	31.9	3.0	-18.1	33.0	98.0	100	108	90.0	77.0
Eff. Tax Rate	37%	38%	17%	NA	39%	38%	39%	39%	39%	40%
Net Inc.	21.1	19.8	2.5	-8.4	19.8	60.3	61.5	66.0	55.5	46.2
Balance Sheet & Other Fin. Data (Million $)										
Cash	42.4	41.7	57.2	54.0	76.0	104	98.2	88.4	32.9	24.8
Curr. Assets	258	272	296	292	331	344	345	301	235	220
Total Assets	335	344	364	367	397	412	384	332	266	252
Curr. Liab.	84.7	95.4	94.5	88.0	94.0	100	98.3	78.0	66.7	64.4
LT Debt	Nil	Nil	Nil	0.8	1.7	2.5	3.3	4.2	5.0	5.8
Common Eqty.	245	242	262	267	293	302	272	240	181	167
Total Cap.	251	249	270	279	302	312	285	254	199	187
Cap. Exp.	17.3	14.3	7.8	22.3	8.5	33.9	3.7	3.5	2.7	4.3
Cash Flow	30.4	29.6	12.1	2.4	28.3	66.6	66.9	70.2	59.8	50.6
Curr. Ratio	3.0	2.8	3.1	3.3	3.5	3.4	3.5	3.9	3.5	3.4
% LT Debt of Cap.	Nil	Nil	Nil	0.3	0.6	0.8	1.2	1.6	2.5	3.1
% Net Inc.of Revs.	3.9	3.8	NM	NM	3.8	10.3	10.5	11.5	10.8	10.2
% Ret. on Assets	6.2	5.6	NM	NM	4.9	15.2	17.3	21.9	22.0	18.7
% Ret. on Equity	8.7	7.9	NM	NM	6.7	21.1	24.2	31.1	32.7	30.8

Data as orig reptd.; bef. results of disc opers/spec. items. Per share data adj. for stk. divs. Bold denotes diluted EPS (FASB 128)-prior periods restated. E-Estimated. NA-Not Available. NM-Not Meaningful. NR-Not Ranked.

Office—191 Spring St., P.O. Box 9191, Lexington, MA 02420-9191. **Tel**—(617) 824-6000. **Website**—http://www.striderite.com **Chrmn & CEO**—M.J. Slosberg. **Pres & COO**—D. M. Sullivan. **CFO, Treas & Investor Contact**—John M. Kelliher (617-824-6028). **Clerk**—C. W. Redepenning Jr.**Dirs**—W. Flick, D. R. Gant, J. M. Jacobson, F. R. Mori, R. L. Seelert, M. J. Slosberg, D. S. Sullivan, W. P. Tippett, Jr., B. Van Saun. **Transfer Agent & Registrar**—BankBoston, N.A. **Incorporated**—in Massachusetts in 1919. **Empl**— 2,400. **S&P Analyst:** Howard Choe

STANDARD
&POOR'S
STOCK REPORTS

Sturm, Ruger

NYSE Symbol **RGR**

In S&P SmallCap 600

09-OCT-99

Industry:
Leisure Time (Products)

Summary: This leading manufacturer of rifles and handguns for sporting and law enforcement purposes also produces ferrous and nonferrous investment castings.

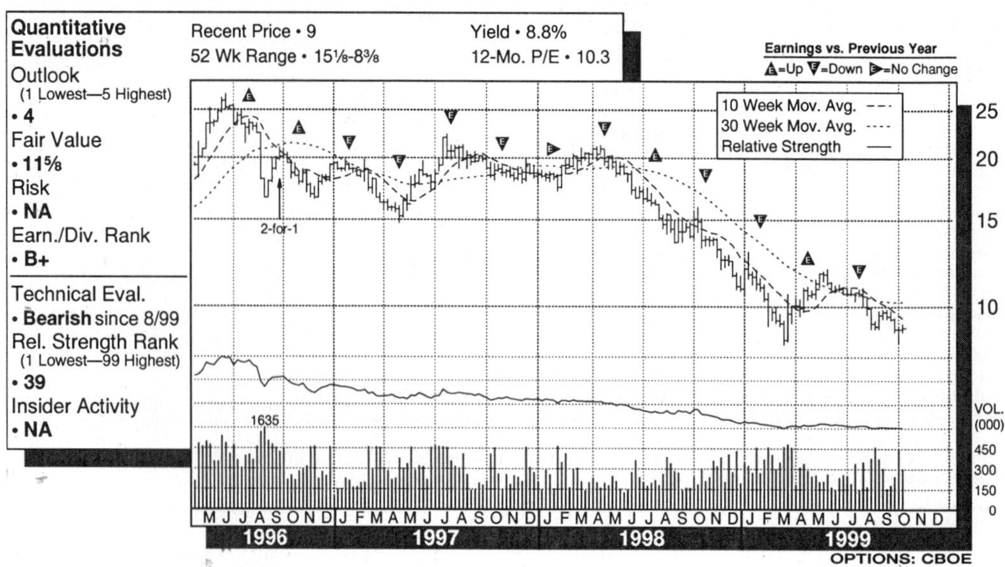

Business Profile - 26-AUG-99

With golf club head shipments to Callaway Golf Co. slipping during the second half of 1998 due to a soft market resulting from the weak Asian economy, RGR expects a recovery in casting sales during 1999 to depend on the status of the golf industry. The company continues to pursue other titanium markets as well as other golf club casting business. RGR also continues to develop new firearms products in an effort to improve this segment's performance. The company expects capital expenditures of $6.4 million in 1999 to be used to upgrade three divisions.

Operational Review - 26-AUG-99

Net sales in the first half of 1999 rose 6.2%, year to year, as strong market demand for firearms outweighed lower castings volume due to a decrease in shipments of titanium golf club heads to Callaway Golf Co. Gross margins narrowed on the lower casting sales and increased product liability expenses related to lawsuits, and despite a decrease in SG&A expenses and higher other income, net income advanced only 2.3%, to $15,920,000 ($0.59 a share, diluted), from $15,569,000 ($0.58).

Stock Performance - 08-OCT-99

In the past 30 trading days, RGR's shares have declined 6%, compared to a 0.91% fall in the S&P 500. Average trading volume for the past five days was 59,680 shares, compared with the 40-day moving average of 65,369 shares.

Key Stock Statistics

Dividend Rate/Share	0.80	Shareholders	1,968
Shs. outstg. (M)	26.9	Market cap. (B)	$0.244
Avg. daily vol. (M)	0.059	Inst. holdings	35%
Tang. Bk. Value/Share	5.94		
Beta	0.45		

Value of $10,000 invested 5 years ago: $ 9,866

Fiscal Year Ending Dec. 31

	1999	1998	1997	1996	1995	1994
Revenues (Million $)						
1Q	62.89	58.52	55.09	65.56	50.30	51.05
2Q	63.02	60.00	54.51	65.93	45.20	48.55
3Q	—	43.37	47.23	48.04	42.09	44.94
4Q	—	49.69	52.56	43.78	54.88	51.89
Yr.	—	211.6	209.4	223.3	192.5	196.4
Earnings Per Share ($)						
1Q	**0.31**	**0.27**	**0.29**	**0.41**	0.32	0.36
2Q	**0.28**	**0.31**	**0.28**	**0.43**	0.24	0.32
3Q	—	**0.09**	**0.18**	**0.21**	0.08	0.26
4Q	—	**0.20**	**0.28**	**0.28**	0.34	0.33
Yr.	—	**0.87**	**1.03**	**1.28**	**0.97**	1.26

Next earnings report expected: NA

Dividend Data (Dividends have been paid since 1955.)

Amount ($)	Date Decl.	Ex-Div. Date	Stock of Record	Payment Date
0.200	Oct. 28	Nov. 27	Dec. 01	Dec. 15 '98
0.200	Jan. 13	Feb. 25	Mar. 01	Mar. 15 '99
0.200	May. 13	May. 27	Jun. 01	Jun. 15 '99
0.200	Jul. 15	Aug. 30	Sep. 01	Sep. 15 '99

A Division of The McGraw-Hill Companies

Sturm, Ruger & Company, Inc.

Business Summary - 26-AUG-99

Founded in 1949, Sturm, Ruger & Co., Inc. (RGR) is the largest firearms manufacturer in the U.S. and the only one that makes firearms in all four industry categories - rifles, shotguns, pistols and revolvers. Southport, CT-based RGR also produces precision metal investment castings.

The company's "Ruger" firearms are made for a variety of sporting and law enforcement purposes. Targeted end-users include sportsmen, hunters, law enforcement organizations and gun collectors. As of early 1999, RGR manufactured 28 types of firearm products, with most available in several models, based upon caliber, finish, barrel length and other features.

Firearms (68% of 1998 sales) consist of .22-caliber target pistols; single-action revolvers in various calibers from .22 to .44 magnum; .22 caliber sporting carbines; single shot and bolt-action rifles; hunting rifles in .223 and 7.62 x 39mm calibers; double-action revolvers; 9mm, .40 and .45 caliber pistols; police and military automatic rifles; and over-and-under shotguns.

RGR aims to position its products at the high end of their respective markets, and emphasizes that it does not manufacture inexpensive, concealable firearms. In addition, RGR does not make any firearm classified as an assault weapon by the 1994 crime bill. In 1998, Jerry's Sport Center accounted for 15% of the company's firearms sales and 10% of net sales. As of March 1999, unfilled firearms orders totaled $128 million, up from $93 million a year earlier.

Many of the firearms introduced by RGR over the years have retained their popularity for decades, and are sought by collectors. These include the single-action Single-Six, Blackhawk and Bearcat revolvers, the double-action Redhawk revolvers, and the 10/22 and Mini-14 autoloading, M-77 and Number One Single-Shot rifles. In 1998, the company introduced several new firearms, including the new Ruger 10/22 Magnum rifle, the Ruger Super Redhawk double action revolver, and the Ruger Mark II pistol. In 1997, the company introduced the new Ruger 77/50 Muzzleloading rifle, the compact Ruger 77/44 Bolt Action rifle, and the Ruger Carbine, an autoloading rifle which uses pistol ammunition.

Ferrous, aluminum and titanium investment casting facilities (32% of 1998 sales) produce parts used in RGR's firearms, as well as for outside commercial customers in several different industries. Foremost among these in recent periods has been the sale of the popular Great Big Bertha series of titanium golf club heads for Callaway Golf Co., which accounted for 63% of castings revenues in 1998.

In June 1995, RGR and Callaway entered into an equally owned joint venture, Antelope Hills, to build and operate a foundry for the production of titanium golf club heads. The facility was completed in the first quarter of 1997. In June 1997, RGR purchased Callaway's 50% interest in Antelope Hills, and operations began.

Per Share Data ($) (Year Ended Dec. 31)	1998	1997	1996	1995	1994	1993	1992	1991	1990	1989
Tangible Bk. Val.	5.74	5.68	5.45	4.97	4.70	4.03	3.33	3.14	2.90	2.67
Cash Flow	1.25	1.37	1.56	1.23	1.46	1.40	0.97	0.71	0.66	0.83
Earnings	0.87	1.03	1.28	0.97	1.26	1.24	0.82	0.54	0.50	0.68
Dividends	0.80	0.80	0.80	0.70	0.60	0.53	0.63	0.30	0.28	0.38
Payout Ratio	92%	78%	63%	72%	47%	43%	76%	55%	55%	56%
Prices - High	21 1/4	22 3/8	27	17 7/8	16 5/8	16	10 1/4	7 3/8	7 7/8	9 1/8
- Low	10 1/2	14 3/4	13 7/8	13	12	9 5/8	6 1/2	5 1/4	5 3/8	4 7/8
P/E Ratio - High	24	22	21	18	13	13	12	14	16	14
- Low	12	14	11	13	9	8	8	10	11	7
Income Statement Analysis (Million $)										
Revs.	212	209	224	192	196	194	156	137	135	134
Oper. Inc.	45.7	54.6	61.5	47.5	59.6	58.8	40.0	30.0	29.5	32.2
Depr.	10.3	9.2	7.6	6.9	5.3	4.3	4.1	4.7	4.3	4.2
Int. Exp.	Nil	Nil	Nil	Nil	Nil	Nil	Nil	Nil	Nil	Nil
Pretax Inc.	39.4	46.6	56.8	43.8	57.0	56.0	37.1	24.3	22.3	29.5
Eff. Tax Rate	41%	41%	40%	40%	40%	41%	40%	40%	40%	39%
Net Inc.	23.4	27.8	34.4	26.2	34.0	33.2	22.2	14.6	13.5	18.1
Balance Sheet & Other Fin. Data (Million $)										
Cash	4.7	4.5	33.4	47.1	66.4	59.6	31.4	22.3	9.0	14.6
Curr. Assets	128	125	119	118	119	106	85.5	77.0	66.4	62.5
Total Assets	197	200	190	179	169	150	124	116	107	100
Curr. Liab.	25.2	27.7	23.9	25.6	24.7	24.6	18.5	16.0	13.9	12.3
LT Debt	Nil	Nil	Nil	Nil	Nil	Nil	Nil	Nil	Nil	Nil
Common Eqty.	155	153	147	134	126	108	89.7	84.4	78.0	71.6
Total Cap.	155	153	147	134	126	108	89.7	84.4	78.0	71.6
Cap. Exp.	6.0	4.5	7.6	15.7	12.4	7.3	3.5	3.0	7.1	8.2
Cash Flow	33.7	37.0	42.0	33.1	39.3	37.6	26.3	19.2	17.9	22.3
Curr. Ratio	5.1	4.5	5.0	4.6	4.8	4.3	4.6	4.8	4.8	5.1
% LT Debt of Cap.	Nil	Nil	Nil	Nil	Nil	Nil	Nil	Nil	Nil	Nil
% Net Inc.of Revs.	11.1	13.3	15.4	13.7	17.3	17.1	14.2	10.7	10.0	13.6
% Ret. on Assets	11.8	14.2	18.7	15.1	21.3	24.2	18.4	13.1	13.0	19.0
% Ret. on Equity	15.2	18.5	24.5	20.2	29.0	33.5	25.4	18.0	18.1	26.8

Data as orig reptd.; bef. results of disc opers/spec. items. Per share data adj. for stk. divs. Bold denotes diluted EPS (FASB 128)-prior periods restated. E-Estimated. NA-Not Available. NM-Not Meaningful. NR-Not Ranked.

Office—1 Lacey Place, Southport, CT 06490. **Tel**—(203) 259-7843. **Website**—http://www.ruger-firearms.com **Chrmn, CEO & Treas**—W. B. Ruger. **Vice Chrmn, Pres & COO**—W. B. Ruger, Jr. **VP & CFO**—E. G. Blanchard. **Secy**—L. M. Gasper. **Dirs**—R. T. Cunniff, T. Hornor, P. X. Kelley, J. M. Kingsley Jr., W. B. Ruger, W. B. Ruger Jr., S. L. Sanetti, J. E. Service, S. B. Terhune. **Transfer Agent & Registrar**—Harris Trust Co. of New York, NYC. **Incorporated**—in Delaware in 1969. **Empl**— 2,171. **S&P Analyst:** Stewart Scharf

STANDARD
&POOR'S
STOCK REPORTS

Summit Technology

Nasdaq Symbol **BEAM**

In S&P SmallCap 600

09-OCT-99

Industry: Health Care (Medical Products & Supplies)

Summary: This company develops, makes and sells ophthalmic laser systems used to treat common refractive vision disorders.

S&P Opinion: Accumulate (★★★★)

Recent Price • 17⅝
52 Wk Range • 29⅜-3
Yield • Nil
12-Mo. P/E • NM

Quantitative Evaluations

Outlook (1 Lowest—5 Highest)
• **1-**
Fair Value
• **13⅝**
Risk
• **High**
Earn./Div. Rank
• **B-**

Technical Eval.
• **Neutral** since 9/99
Rel. Strength Rank (1 Lowest—99 Highest)
• **61**
Insider Activity
• **NA**

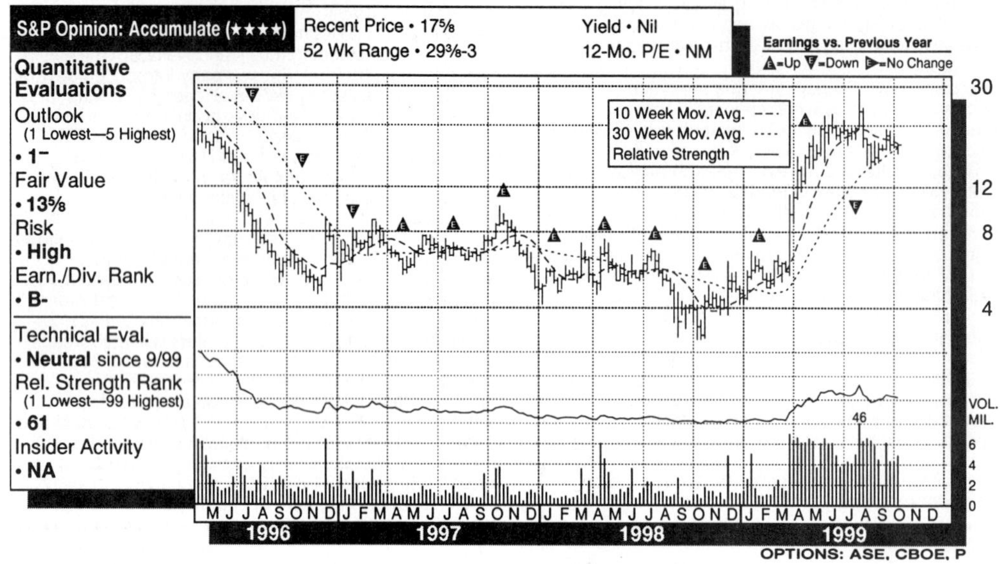

Overview - 23-AUG-99

As the second largest U.S. maker of computer controlled excimer laser systems for vision correction, the company hopes to gain market share following its April 1999 acquisition of Autonomous Technologies, maker of the new LADARVision laser system. BEAM derives revenues from the sale of laser systems, and from its contact lens business. A fast growing portion of revenues comes from a $250 per-procedure laser vision correction licensing fee. At the end of the 1999 second quarter, BEAM had an installed base of more than 300 lasers, a majority of which were in the U.S. In the first half of 1999, about 69,000 procedures were performed with a Summit laser. However, reflecting integration risks following the recent acquisition, revenue and earnings visibility is somewhat low. We expect revenues to grow approximately 22% in 1999, to $111 million. Assuming gross margins of about 46%, and after amortization of goodwill following the Autonomous acquisition, we see an operating loss per share of $0.07 for 1999, with EPS of $0.10 for 2000.

Valuation - 23-AUG-99

We are maintaining our accumulate rating on the shares, which surged from March until late July 1999, reflecting investor optimism related to the Autonomous acquisition, and to prospects for explosive growth in laser vision correction procedure volume. However, in August, concerns over pricing pressures and increased competition led to a moderate sell-off. Some uncertainty exists concerning ophthalmologist acceptance of the Autonomous lasers, which were rolled out in April 1999. However, BEAM has a large installed base of laser systems, and, based on its significant growth prospects, we recommend accumulation of the shares by aggressive investors. BEAM could also be an acquisition target in this growing market.

Key Stock Statistics

S&P EPS Est. 1999	NA	Tang. Bk. Value/Share	3.09
P/E on S&P Est. 1999	NA	Beta	1.86
S&P EPS Est. 2000	0.10	Shareholders	2,866
Dividend Rate/Share	Nil	Market cap. (B)	$0.753
Shs. outstg. (M)	42.6	Inst. holdings	23%
Avg. daily vol. (M)	1.051		

Value of $10,000 invested 5 years ago: NA

Fiscal Year Ending Dec. 31

	1999	1998	1997	1996	1995	1994
Revenues (Million $)						
1Q	25.68	21.84	20.70	12.68	7.11	3.66
2Q	27.40	23.40	23.64	17.96	9.26	5.86
3Q	—	22.28	22.90	21.01	13.81	6.50
4Q	—	11.86	21.55	17.88	14.96	8.19
Yr.	—	91.64	88.79	80.48	45.13	24.21
Earnings Per Share ($)						
1Q	**0.08**	**0.01**	-0.05	-0.11	-0.08	-0.17
2Q	**-0.61**	**0.97**	0.08	-0.39	-0.08	-0.17
3Q	**E-0.07**	**0.02**	Nil	-0.13	0.01	-0.13
4Q	**E-0.05**	**0.12**	**0.01**	-0.27	0.01	-0.15
Yr.	—	**1.17**	**0.05**	**-0.44**	**-0.06**	-0.63

Next earnings report expected: late October

Dividend Data

No cash has been paid.

A Division of The McGraw-Hill Companies

Summit Technology, Inc.

Business Summary - 23-AUG-99

Summit Technology is a leading developer, manufacturer, and worldwide marketer of ophthalmic laser systems in more than 50 countries. Its systems are designed to correct common refractive vision disorders with a procedure known as laser vision correction. The company derives revenue from system sales (15% of revenues), licensing fees (34%), and sales of contact lenses and related products (51%).

In October 1995, BEAM's Apex laser was the first excimer laser system to receive FDA commercial approval to treat nearsightedness in the U.S. In February 1997, an advanced model of the excimer system, the Apex Plus, was also approved by the FDA for mild to moderate nearsightedness with mild to moderate astigmatism. The FDA has not yet approved the excimer system to treat astigmatism and farsightedness. In July 1999, BEAM said that an FDA Advisory Panel had recommended approval of its PMA application to treat high myopia and high astigmatism with LASIK, using the Apex Plus Excimer Workstation.

BEAM estimates that 20% to 25% of the estimated 400,000 laser vision correction procedures performed in the U.S. in 1999 were done with its lasers.

Laser vision correction, also known as Photorefractive Keratectomy (PRK), is an outpatient procedure performed with the excimer laser to treat nearsightedness, farsightedness and astigmatism requiring about 150 laser pulses, and lasts about 15 to 40 seconds. Phototherapeutic Keratectomy (PTK) is an outpatient procedure performed with the excimer system to treat corneal pathologies.

Lens Express is a leading mail order distributor of contact lenses and related products in the U.S. Sales consist of new and reorders of contact lenses, program sales, sales of eye care solutions and shipping and handling fees.

In 1998, the company settled all pending litigation with its major competitor, VISX, Inc., which paid BEAM $34.4 million. The companies now cross-license certain laser vision correction patents.

In August 1997, BEAM sold its Refractive Centers International, Inc. subsidiary, which owns and operates its Vision Center business, to LCA-Vision Inc. (Nasdaq: LCAV). As part of the agreement, BEAM received about 17 million LCAV common shares. About 9 million shares were distributed to shareholders, with the remainder held by BEAM.

In April 1999, the company acquired Autonomous Technologies Corp., for about 11.2 million common shares and $46.8 million in cash. Autonomous manufacturers the LADARVision system. BEAM estimates that the integration of Autonomous and costs associated with the merger are likely to delay efforts to achieve consistent profitability at least until 2000. In an August 1999 public offering, BEAM sold 3,500,000 common shares at $16.00 each.

Per Share Data ($) (Year Ended Dec. 31)	1998	1997	1996	1995	1994	1993	1992	1991	1990	1989
Tangible Bk. Val.	3.59	2.69	3.07	4.45	1.51	1.65	1.32	1.36	0.53	0.68
Cash Flow	1.29	0.15	-0.32	-0.04	-0.53	-0.32	0.04	0.05	-0.01	-0.10
Earnings	1.17	0.05	-0.44	-0.14	-0.63	-0.39	-0.02	0.03	-0.03	-0.11
Dividends	Nil	Nil	Nil	Nil	Nil	Nil	Nil	Nil	Nil	Nil
Payout Ratio	Nil	Nil	Nil	Nil	Nil	Nil	Nil	Nil	Nil	Nil
Prices - High	7½	10⅛	35½	38¾	26⅝	20½	25⅝	19⅛	12⅜	10⅝
- Low	3	4⅛	4½	18⅜	13⅝	12	14⅛	6⅝	3⅞	1 9/16
P/E Ratio - High	6	NM	NM	NM	NM	NM	NM	NM	NM	NM
- Low	3	NM	NM	NM	NM	NM	NM	NM	NA	NA
Income Statement Analysis (Million $)										
Revs.	91.6	88.8	80.5	45.1	24.2	26.8	31.1	22.0	11.6	5.2
Oper. Inc.	5.6	2.5	-15.1	-2.5	-13.2	-7.2	1.0	1.0	-0.6	-1.6
Depr.	3.7	3.3	3.6	2.5	2.3	1.7	1.3	0.7	0.4	0.2
Int. Exp.	0.8	NA	NA	NA	NA	0.1	0.1	0.1	0.0	0.0
Pretax Inc.	41.8	1.6	-13.4	-3.5	-15.4	-9.2	-0.4	1.0	-0.6	-1.5
Eff. Tax Rate	12%	8.35%	NM	NM	NM	NM	NM	47%	Nil	Nil
Net Inc.	36.7	1.5	-13.5	-3.5	15.4	-9.2	-0.4	0.5	-0.7	-1.5
Balance Sheet & Other Fin. Data (Million $)										
Cash	31.3	35.0	64.9	95.9	17.2	10.9	8.6	17.1	5.9	7.3
Curr. Assets	101	87.7	93.3	125	35.5	36.6	32.7	31.0	11.4	10.5
Total Assets	145	115	134	157	51.2	50.5	38.8	35.5	13.7	11.5
Curr. Liab.	21.8	19.8	20.2	19.3	12.1	10.0	8.2	5.4	3.4	1.4
LT Debt	0.1	6.3	11.5	1.0	1.2	0.2	0.7	0.4	0.1	0.0
Common Eqty.	119	89.0	102	137	37.9	40.4	29.9	29.7	10.1	10.1
Total Cap.	119	95.3	113	138	39.1	40.5	30.6	30.1	10.3	10.1
Cap. Exp.	3.0	1.8	5.6	4.1	1.2	3.1	1.8	2.0	1.2	0.8
Cash Flow	40.5	4.8	-9.9	-1.0	-13.1	-7.5	0.9	1.2	-0.3	-1.3
Curr. Ratio	4.6	4.4	4.6	6.5	2.9	3.7	4.0	5.8	3.4	7.7
% LT Debt of Cap.	0.1	6.6	10.1	0.7	3.0	0.4	2.4	1.3	1.2	0.1
% Net Inc.of Revs.	40.1	1.7	NM	NM	NM	NM	NM	2.4	NM	NM
% Ret. on Assets	28.3	1.2	NM	NM	NM	NM	NM	2.0	NM	NM
% Ret. on Equity	35.3	1.6	NM	NM	NM	NM	NM	2.5	NM	NM

Data as orig reptd.; bef. results of disc opers/spec. items. Per share data adj. for stk. divs. Bold denotes diluted EPS (FASB 128)-prior periods restated. E-Estimated. NA-Not Available. NM-Not Meaningful. NR-Not Ranked.

Office—21 Hickory Drive, Waltham, MA 02154. **Tel**—(781) 890-1234. **Website**—http://www.sum-tech.com**Pres & COO** —D. V. Sharma. **CEO**—R. J. Palmisano. **Clerk**—J. A. Lightman.**VP, Treas & CFO**—R. J. Kelly. **Investor Contact**—Paula Elliott Whelan. **Dirs**—J. A. Bernfeld, C.G. Bradley, R.W. Frey, R. F. Miller, J. A. Norris, R. J. Palmisano, R. M. Traskos. **Transfer Agent & Registrar**—American Stock Transfer & Trust Co., NYC. **Incorporated**—in Massachusetts in 1985. **Empl**— 425. **S&P Analyst:** John J. Arege

STANDARD
&POOR'S
STOCK REPORTS

Sunrise Medical

NYSE Symbol **SMD**
In S&P SmallCap 600

09-OCT-99

Industry:
Health Care (Medical Products & Supplies)

Summary: This company manufactures a broad line of medical products used to address rehabilitation, recovery and home respiratory needs.

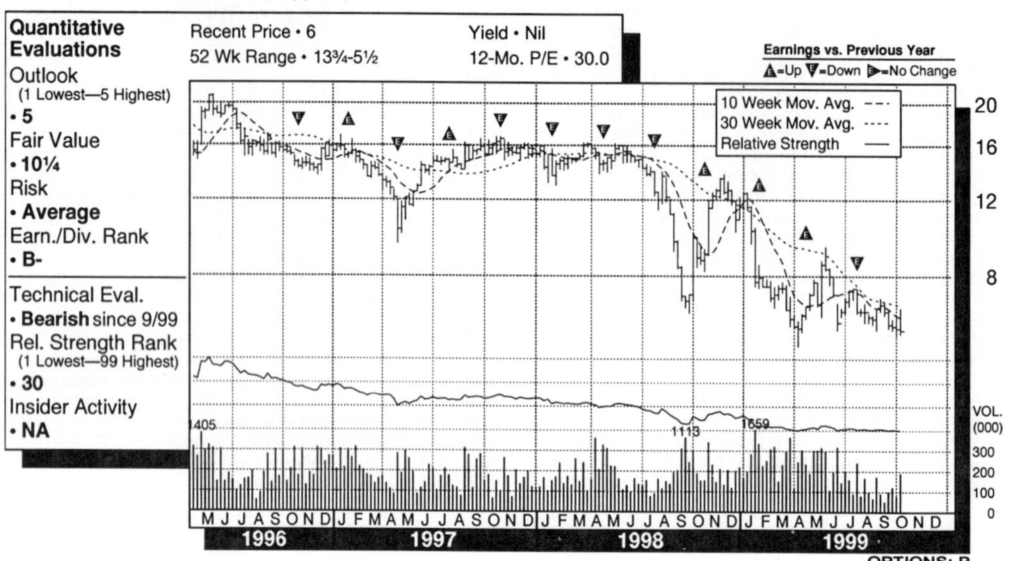

Business Profile - 14-SEP-99

In response to a difficult pricing environment in the home care industry, the company incurred a one-time pretax charge of $6.0 million ($0.16 a share) in the FY 99 (Jun.) fourth quarter, primarily relating to severance costs associated with the elimination of 600 jobs, expected to generate $18 million in annual savings, and interest rate swap termination expenses in connection with foreign debt redenomination. The financial results of the FY 99 fourth quarter resulted in the company being out of compliance with a financial covenant in its bank credit agreement. The company's banking group has waived this default until September 30, 1999. The company is negotiating an amendment to the agreement, which it expects will result in the permanent waiver of the default.

Operational Review - 14-SEP-99

Net sales in the year ended July 3, 1999, rose less than 1.0%, as increased DynaVox sales were offset by lower U.S. home health care and continuing care group sales. Gross margins narrowed. However, with lower marketing, selling and administrative expenses, and in the absence of a $29 million charge, an operating profit contrasted with an operating loss. Despite higher interest expense and lower interest income, after taxes at 45.6%, versus taxes at $208,000, net income of $4,498,000 ($0.20 a share) contrasted with a loss of $12,010,000 ($0.55).

Stock Performance - 08-OCT-99

In the past 30 trading days, SMD's shares have declined 11%, compared to a 0.91% fall in the S&P 500. Average trading volume for the past five days was 37,300 shares, compared with the 40-day moving average of 21,751 shares.

Key Stock Statistics

Dividend Rate/Share	Nil	Shareholders	6,100
Shs. outstg. (M)	22.2	Market cap. (B)	$0.133
Avg. daily vol. (M)	0.024	Inst. holdings	66%
Tang. Bk. Value/Share	0.27		
Beta	0.87		

Value of $10,000 invested 5 years ago: $ 2,000

Fiscal Year Ending Jun. 30

	1999	1998	1997	1996	1995	1994
Revenues (Million $)						
1Q	164.8	155.0	165.3	157.2	140.6	99.9
2Q	163.5	169.1	169.7	173.7	146.9	111.1
3Q	169.7	164.4	158.4	169.6	148.6	120.0
4Q	162.3	168.6	163.3	166.7	165.8	136.0
Yr.	660.3	657.2	656.7	667.1	601.9	466.9
Earnings Per Share ($)						
1Q	**0.16**	**0.04**	**0.16**	0.20	—	—
2Q	**0.08**	**0.02**	**0.14**	-1.28	—	—
3Q	**0.08**	Nil	**0.06**	0.14	—	—
4Q	**-0.12**	**0.04**	**0.19**	-1.23	—	—
Yr.	**0.20**	**-0.55**	**0.55**	**-1.89**	1.03	1.19

Next earnings report expected: late October

Dividend Data

No cash dividends have been paid. A two-for-one stock split was effected in 1992.

Sunrise Medical Inc.

Business Summary - 14-SEP-99

Sunrise Medical is a maker of medical products for the home care and extended care markets that address rehabilitation, recovery and respiratory needs. In June 1997, the company announced the launch of a new structure dividing its operations into three groups (Home Healthcare, Continuing Care, and Sunrise Medical Europe), and renamed a number of business units to reinforce its corporate identity.

A re-engineering program that spanned three fiscal years was completed during the fourth quarter of FY 98 (Jun.). The program included the July 1997 merger of SMD's five U.S. home care divisions into the Home Healthcare Group, with a single sales force; the consolidation of four U.K. manufacturing divisions into one plant; and the conversion of computer systems in North America and Europe.

In June 1999, the company announced a series of profit improvement actions including job eliminations, expense reductions, productivity enhancements and new product introductions. The profit improvement plan identified $18 million in annualized cost savings related to the job eliminations and a total of $30 million from all sources. The savings are expected to be fully phased in by the end of FY 00.

The Home Healthcare Group (52% of sales in FY 99) focuses on the outpatient equipment needs of the elderly and disabled. Products include wheelchairs (including custom, power, pediatric and standard wheelchairs) and seating and positioning systems; medical products to assist in walking, bathing, toileting and patient lifting; and respiratory products such as aerosol, oxygen and sleep therapy products.

The Continuing Care Group (12%) makes products for recovering patients and long-term residents in nursing homes, subacute facilities, hospitals and assisted living centers. Health care beds, nursing home furniture, patient support surfaces and institutional bathing systems are part of this group's product line.

Sunrise Medical Europe (33%) makes products in the U.K., Germany, Spain and France, and owns distribution companies in five other countries that market SMD's products in Europe.

During the FY 98 fourth quarter, SMD acquired Sentient Systems Technology (renamed DynaVox Systems 12%), a manufacturer of augmentative communication devices for people with speech disabilities, in exchange for 2.7 million common shares. The transaction was accounted for on a pooling-of-interests basis, and all financial data was restated. In November 1997, SMD acquired Mechanical Application Designs, a maker of modular power tilt and recline systems for power wheelchairs.

The company was founded in 1983, to take advantage of a shift in care from hospitals to alternate sites. SMD believes an aging population, increased use of lower cost, alternate-site treatment, improved outpatient care, and greater emphasis on the integration of the disabled into communities will contribute to continued growth in the home care and extended care markets.

Per Share Data ($) **(Year Ended Jun. 30)**	**1999**	**1998**	**1997**	**1996**	**1995**	**1994**	**1993**	**1992**	**1991**	**1990**
Tangible Bk. Val.	NA	0.26	0.26	0.97	1.56	3.17	6.98	1.65	2.92	0.12
Cash Flow	NA	0.54	1.48	-1.16	2.30	2.15	1.86	1.53	1.31	1.10
Earnings	0.20	-0.55	0.55	-2.17	1.03	1.19	1.21	0.94	0.79	0.58
Dividends	Nil	Nil	Nil	Nil	Nil	Nil	Nil	Nil	Nil	Nil
Payout Ratio	Nil	Nil	Nil	Nil	Nil	Nil	Nil	Nil	Nil	Nil
Prices - High	12½	16¼	16⅞	20⅞	36¾	33¼	31	31¾	19⅛	11½
- Low	5½	6½	9½	13⅝	24⅞	20	18⅜	11⅝	9	4
P/E Ratio - High	62	NM	31	NM	36	28	26	34	24	20
- Low	27	NM	17	NM	24	17	15	12	11	7
Income Statement Analysis (Million $)										
Revs.	NA	657	657	667	602	467	319	244	204	172
Oper. Inc.	NA	47.1	58.3	55.0	66.7	59.9	43.6	30.7	22.7	18.7
Depr.	NA	23.9	17.9	19.1	23.7	17.6	9.7	7.6	5.3	4.7
Int. Exp.	NA	15.2	14.8	16.7	10.4	6.1	4.3	2.9	3.7	4.8
Pretax Inc.	NA	-11.8	21.0	-52.5	33.9	36.2	29.7	20.2	13.7	9.2
Eff. Tax Rate	NA	NM	50%	NM	43%	40%	39%	41%	41%	43%
Net Inc.	NA	-12.0	10.6	-40.9	19.5	21.8	18.1	12.0	8.1	5.3
Balance Sheet & Other Fin. Data (Million $)										
Cash	NA	0.9	2.8	1.8	1.7	2.6	40.0	1.3	0.1	0.2
Curr. Assets	NA	257	238	252	237	192	146	82.9	55.6	50.3
Total Assets	NA	616	611	620	598	472	284	202	120	115
Curr. Liab.	NA	149	136	147	112	91.0	53.5	50.8	33.4	29.7
LT Debt	NA	188	188	207	182	119	32.5	56.0	16.9	48.1
Common Eqty.	NA	273	279	261	299	260	195	92.3	67.4	34.6
Total Cap.	NA	467	475	473	486	381	231	151	87.0	85.0
Cap. Exp.	NA	15.6	29.3	19.0	23.1	23.4	18.3	21.5	7.0	4.7
Cash Flow	NA	11.9	28.5	-21.8	43.2	39.4	27.8	19.6	13.4	10.0
Curr. Ratio	NA	1.7	1.8	1.7	2.1	2.1	2.7	1.6	1.7	1.7
% LT Debt of Cap.	NA	40.3	39.6	43.8	37.4	31.2	14.1	37.1	19.5	56.7
% Net Inc.of Revs.	NA	NM	1.6	NM	3.2	4.7	5.7	4.9	4.0	3.1
% Ret. on Assets	NA	NM	1.7	NM	3.6	5.8	6.7	7.3	5.9	4.6
% Ret. on Equity	NA	NM	3.9	NM	7.0	9.6	11.6	14.7	14.2	16.7

Data as orig reptd.; bef. results of disc opers/spec. items. Per share data adj. for stk. divs. Bold denotes diluted EPS (FASB 128)-prior periods restated. E-Estimated. NA-Not Available. NM-Not Meaningful. NR-Not Ranked.

Office—2382 Faraday Ave., Suite 200, Carlsbad, CA 92008. **Tel**—(619) 930-1500. **Website**—http://www.sunrisemedical.com **Chrmn & CEO**—R. H. Chandler. **SVP-Fin, CFO & Investor Contact**—Ted N. Tarbet. **SVP & Secy** —S. A. Jaye. **Dirs**—L. A. Ault III, R. H. Chandler, M. N. Hammes, M. H. Hutchison, W. L. Pierpoint, J. Stemler, J. R. Woodhull. **Transfer Agent & Registrar**—ChaseMellon Shareholder Services, Encino, CA. **Incorporated**—in Delaware in 1983. **Empl**— 4,400. **S&P Analyst:** John J. Arege

STANDARD &POOR'S STOCK REPORTS

Susquehanna Bancshares

NASDAQ Symbol **SUSQ**

In S&P SmallCap 600

23-OCT-99 **Industry:** Banks (Regional)

Summary: SUSQ is a multibank holding company whose subsidiaries operate in Pennsylvania, Maryland and southern New Jersey.

Quantitative Evaluations

Outlook (1 Lowest—5 Highest) • 1−

Fair Value • 14¾

Risk • Low

Earn./Div. Rank • A-

Technical Eval. • NA

Rel. Strength Rank (1 Lowest—99 Highest) • 86

Insider Activity • NA

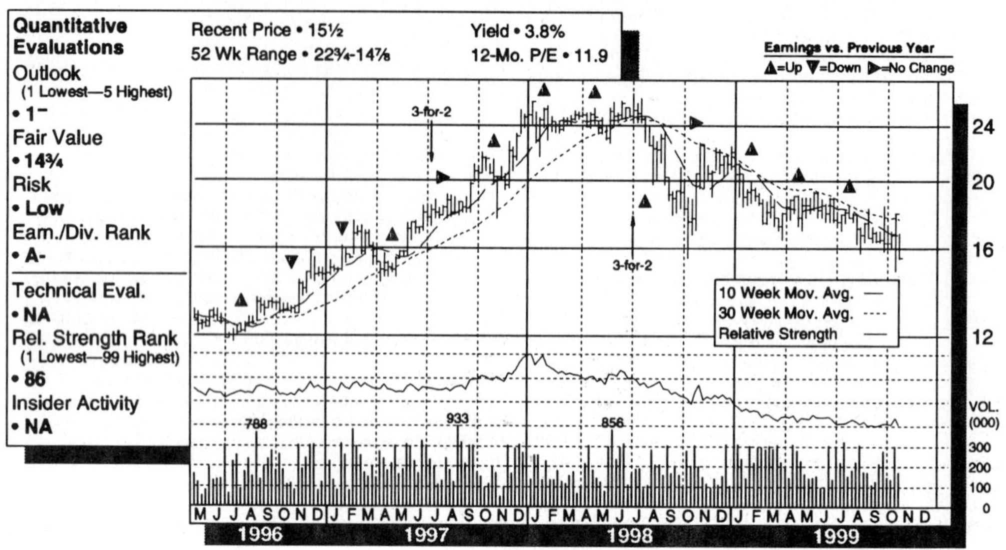

Business Profile - 19-OCT-99

Susquehanna Bancshares has been quite active in seeking and making acquisitions and, as of July 1999, had grown its branch count to 140 community banking offices throughout central Pennsylnvania, Maryland, and southern New Jersey. Total assets have grown to more than $4.2 billion, with loans receivable of $2.9 billion, and total deposits of $3.2 billion at June 30, 1999, compared with total assets of $4.0 billion, loans of $2.8 billion, and deposits of $3.1 billion at June 30, 1998. Return on tangible average equity and return on tangible average assets for the first half of 1999 were 13.93% and 1.26%, respectively. Total nonperforming assets at June 30, 1999 were $21.7 million, versus $27.6 million in the prior year.

Operational Review - 19-OCT-99

Net interest income for the six months ended June 30, 1999, rose 1.7%, reflecting higher average earning assets and a narrower net interest margin (4.33%, versus 4.44%). The loan loss provision was up 7.4% to $2,718,000 and noninterest income fell 2.2%. Noninterest expenses declined fractionally, resulting from decreased salaries and benefits expenses, which was offset by higher consulting, insurance, and delivery expenses. Following taxes at 30.5%, against 31.8%, net income advanced 5.7%, to $23,985,000 ($0.65 a share), from $22,698,000 ($0.61).

Stock Performance - 22-OCT-99

In the past 30 trading days, SUSQ's shares have increased 10%, compared to a 4% fall in the S&P 500. Average trading volume for the past five days was 27,080 shares, compared with the 40-day moving average of 34,810 shares.

Key Stock Statistics

Dividend Rate/Share	0.68	Shareholders	6,891
Shs. outstg. (M)	37.0	Market cap. (B)	$0.665
Avg. daily vol. (M)	0.038	Inst. holdings	20%
Tang. Bk. Value/Share	10.91		
Beta	0.73		

Value of $10,000 invested 5 years ago: $ 18,176

Fiscal Year Ending Dec. 31

	1999	1998	1997	1996	1995	1994
Revenues (Million $)						
1Q	80.79	78.95	63.29	60.58	44.92	34.39
2Q	82.10	81.94	70.63	64.16	51.44	34.04
3Q	—	81.71	73.41	63.93	54.38	37.88
4Q	—	81.08	75.20	64.51	55.17	38.69
Yr.	—	323.7	287.9	253.2	205.9	145.0
Earnings Per Share ($)						
1Q	**0.32**	**0.31**	**0.29**	**0.27**	0.20	0.24
2Q	**0.33**	**0.32**	**0.27**	**0.27**	0.24	0.23
3Q	—	**0.32**	**0.32**	**0.17**	0.28	0.24
4Q	—	**0.33**	**0.33**	**0.25**	0.27	0.23
Yr.	—	**1.26**	**1.20**	**0.95**	**0.95**	**0.84**

Next earnings report expected: late October

Dividend Data (Dividends have been paid since 1982.)

Amount ($)	Date Decl.	Ex-Div. Date	Stock of Record	Payment Date
0.150	Jan. 20	Jan. 28	Feb. 01	Feb. 22 '99
0.150	Apr. 21	Apr. 29	May. 03	May. 21 '99
0.150	Jul. 21	Jul. 29	Aug. 02	Aug. 20 '99
0.170	Oct. 20	Oct. 28	Nov. 01	Nov. 22 '99

A Division of The McGraw-Hill Companies

Susquehanna Bancshares, Inc.

Business Summary - 19-OCT-99

As a "super-community" bank holding company, SUSQ's strategy has been to manage its banking subsidiaries on a decentralized basis, allowing each subsidiary operating in different markets to retain its name and board of directors as well as substantial autonomy in its day to day operations. The company believes that this approach permits these institutions greater flexibility to better serve their markets, increasing responsiveness to local needs, and differentiates Susquehanna from other large competitors.

Susquehanna Bancshares, Inc. is a multi-bank financial holding company headquartered in Lititz, PA. As of December 31, 1998, SUSQ owned eight commercial banks, one federal savings bank, and two non-bank subsidiaries with total assets of $4.1 billion, loans receivable of $2.8 billion, and deposits of $3.1 billion. The subsidiaries were providing banking and banking-related services from 134 offices in central and eastern Pennsylvania, Maryland, and southern New Jersey.

Susquehanna provides a wide range of retail and commercial banking services. Its strategy for retail banking operations is to expand deposit and other product market share through a high level of customer service, new product offerings, application of new technologies and delivery systems, and selective acquisitions.

Retail banking services consist primarily of checking and savings accounts, money market accounts, certificates of deposit, individual retirement accounts, Christmas clubs, mutual funds and annuities, home equity lines of credit, residential mortgage loans, home improvement loans, student loans, automobile loans and personal loans.

Commercial lending operations are made up of commercial, financial and agricultural lending (15% of the total loan portfolio at year-end 1998), real estate construction (9%), and commercial mortgage (21%).

As of December 31, 1998, the allowance for loan and lease losses totaled $35.1 million (1.27% of loans and leases outstanding), versus $35.5 million (1.34%) a year earlier. Net loan charge-offs totaled $5.6 million (0.21% of average loans) in 1998, compared with $5.3 million (0.21%) a year earlier. At the end of 1998, nonperforming assets totaled $26.1 million (0.94% of loans, leases and other real estate owned), versus $27.8 million (1.05%) a year earlier.

In early January 1999, SUSQ completed the acquisition of First Capitol, of York, Pennsylvania. Earlier, in December 1998, SUSQ completed the acquisition of Cardinal Bancorp, Inc. of Everett, Pennsylvania, and its subsidiary, First American (assets $138 million). The Cardinal acquisition represented SUSQ's initial entry into southwestern Pennsylvania.

Per Share Data ($) (Year Ended Dec. 31)	1998	1997	1996	1995	1994	1993	1992	1991	1990	1989
Tangible Bk. Val.	10.91	10.25	9.87	9.38	8.29	8.35	7.71	7.20	NA	NA
Earnings	1.26	1.20	1.01	0.99	0.94	0.91	0.88	0.85	NA	NA
Dividends	0.57	0.55	0.52	0.49	0.45	0.41	0.39	0.37	NA	NA
Payout Ratio	45%	46%	51%	49%	48%	45%	44%	44%	NA	NA
Prices - High	26¾	25⅞	15⅞	13½	12½	12¾	10	7⅝	NA	NA
- Low	15½	14⅜	11½	9½	9½	9¾	7	5½	NA	NA
P/E Ratio - High	21	22	16	14	13	14	11	9	NA	NA
- Low	12	12	11	10	10	11	8	6	NA	NA
Income Statement Analysis (Million $)										
Net Int. Inc.	154	146	129	107	94.0	87.0	84.0	78.0	NA	NA
Tax Equiv. Adj.	NA	4.3	4.1	4.3	4.2	3.9	NA	NA	NA	NA
Non Int. Inc.	30.8	23.6	21.2	16.1	15.1	15.8	15.3	13.3	NA	NA
Loan Loss Prov.	5.2	4.6	4.6	5.0	4.0	5.1	4.7	4.9	NA	NA
Exp./Op. Revs.	61%	63%	66%	63%	64%	62%	64%	64%	NA	NA
Pretax Inc.	66.7	58.8	44.6	37.4	32.5	31.7	30.7	27.8	NA	NA
Eff. Tax Rate	32%	32%	33%	30%	30%	30%	28%	23%	NA	NA
Net Inc.	45.6	40.2	30.0	26.0	22.8	22.1	22.2	21.3	NA	NA
% Net Int. Marg.	4.37	4.73	4.78	4.89	4.94	4.94	NA	NA	NA	NA
Balance Sheet & Other Fin. Data (Million $)										
Money Mkt. Assets	NA	139	195	179	95.0	NA	NA	NA	NA	NA
Inv. Securities	1,009	657	562	610	598	563	475	441	NA	NA
Com'l Loans	289	368	255	222	202	195	NA	NA	NA	NA
Other Loans	2,485	2,202	1,918	1,491	1,264	1,115	NA	NA	NA	NA
Total Assets	4,065	3,525	3,038	2,586	2,231	2,052	1,967	1,904	NA	NA
Demand Deposits	423	352	338	270	261	250	NA	NA	NA	NA
Time Deposits	2,702	2,499	2,416	1,846	1,604	1,468	NA	NA	NA	NA
LT Debt	370	182	115	86.3	49.3	58.3	52.5	53.5	NA	NA
Common Eqty.	391	347	293	273	217	218	194	181	NA	NA
% Ret. on Assets	1.2	1.2	1.1	1.1	1.1	1.2	1.1	1.1	NA	NA
% Ret. on Equity	12.4	12.6	10.6	11.3	10.5	11.5	11.9	12.3	NA	NA
% Loan Loss Resv.	1.3	1.3	1.5	1.6	1.6	1.7	1.4	1.3	NA	NA
% Loans/Deposits	88.8	90.1	87.1	80.9	78.6	76.3	76.7	80.8	NA	NA
% Equity to Assets	9.7	9.7	10.1	9.5	10.2	10.3	9.7	9.3	NA	NA

Data as orig. reptd.; bef. results of disc. opers. and/or spec. items. Prior to 1995, per share, income statement and balance sheet data as restated for acquisitions on pooling-of-interests basis. Bold denotes diluted EPS (FASB 128). Per share data adj. for stk. divs. as of ex-div. date. E-Estimated. NA-Not Available. NM-Not Meaningful. NR-Not Ranked.

Office—26 N. Cedar St., Lititz, PA 17543. **Tel**—(717) 626-4721. **Website**—http://www.susqbanc.com **Pres & CEO**—R. S. Bolinger. **VP-CFO, Treas & Investor Contact**—Drew K. Hostetter (717 626-4721 Ext. 400). **VP-Secy**—R. M. Cloney. **Dirs**—J. G. Apple, R. S. Bolinger, R. M. Cloney, T. B. Cunningham, J. M. Denlinger, O. O. Freeman Jr., H. H. Gibbel, M. R. Gross, T. M. Hall, E. W. Helfrick, C. W. Hetzer Jr., G. W. Miller, G. J. Morgan, C. R. Morris, W. J. Reuter, R. V. Wiest. **Transfer Agent & Registrar**—The Bank of New York **Incorporated**—in Pennsylvania in 1982. **Empl**—1,866. **S&P Analyst:** V.G. Piazza

STANDARD
&POOR'S
STOCK REPORTS

Swiss Army Brands

NASDAQ Symbol **SABI**

In S&P SmallCap 600

09-OCT-99

Industry:
Consumer (Jewelry, Novelties & Gifts)

Summary: This company, the exclusive U.S. and Canadian distributor of the Victorinox Original Swiss Army Knife, also sells Victorinox cutlery and Swiss Army Brand watches and sunglasses.

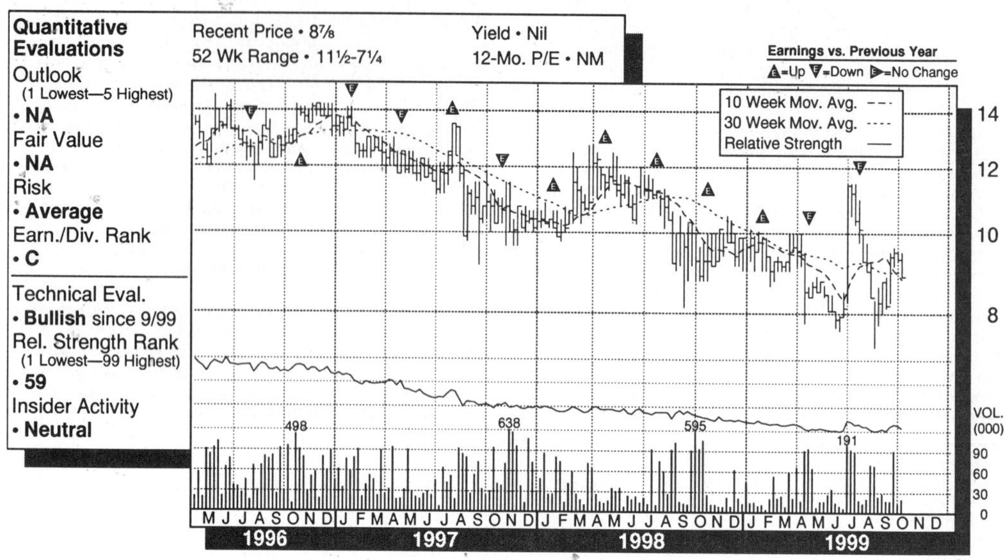

Business Profile - 20-JUL-99

An unexpected $2.4 million after-tax writedown of SABI's 1994 investment in Hudson River Capital LLC negatively affected 1999 first half results. The new management of Hudson River, a private equity company, notified SABI that it had recently written down five of its investments in conjunction with the audit of its financial statements. Detailed financial results are expected to be released on July 27, 1999. Victorinox recently raised its interest in the company to 36%, and observers have speculated that it may be seeking to buy some or all of the rest.

Operational Review - 20-JUL-99

In July 1999, SABI announced preliminary results for the six months ended June 30, 1999. Profitability improved on wider gross margins and well controlled expenses; the operating loss narrowed. However, comparisons were hurt by a $2.4 million after-tax writedown of an investment, compared to after-tax gains in 1998. A net loss of $2,453,000 ($0.31 a share) contrasted with income of $389,000 ($0.04). Excluding non-operating gains and losses in the 1999 and 1998 periods, the net loss per share narrowed to $0.03, from $0.07.

Stock Performance - 08-OCT-99

In the past 30 trading days, SABI's shares have increased 8%, compared to a 0.91% fall in the S&P 500. Average trading volume for the past five days was 3,980 shares, compared with the 40-day moving average of 7,262 shares.

Key Stock Statistics

Dividend Rate/Share	Nil	Shareholders	341
Shs. outstg. (M)	7.9	Market cap. (B)	$0.070
Avg. daily vol. (M)	0.007	Inst. holdings	27%
Tang. Bk. Value/Share	8.12		
Beta	0.44		

Value of $10,000 invested 5 years ago: $ 5,819

Fiscal Year Ending Dec. 31

	1999	1998	1997	1996	1995	1994
Revenues (Million $)						
1Q	23.57	24.61	24.21	26.08	29.37	27.05
2Q	30.40	30.19	28.86	28.68	25.92	39.94
3Q	—	31.37	27.87	34.62	30.19	37.26
4Q	—	41.68	37.80	40.66	41.21	40.19
Yr.	—	127.8	118.7	130.0	126.7	144.4
Earnings Per Share ($)						
1Q	**-0.04**	**0.03**	**-0.13**	**-0.03**	0.15	0.21
2Q	**-0.27**	**0.01**	**-0.12**	**-0.49**	0.03	0.17
3Q	—	**0.06**	**-0.09**	**0.08**	0.02	0.42
4Q	—	**0.08**	**-0.15**	**-0.20**	0.18	0.37
Yr.	—	**0.18**	**-0.49**	**-0.64**	**0.38**	**1.16**

Next earnings report expected: late October

Dividend Data

Cash dividends have never been paid.

A Division of The McGraw-Hill Companies

Swiss Army Brands Inc.

Business Summary - 20-JUL-99

Although many manufacturers produce multiblade knives under the "Swiss Army Knife" name, Swiss Army Brands Inc. (SABI) is one of only two companies that supply knives to the Swiss armed forces. SABI is the exclusive U.S., Canadian and Caribbean distributor of the Victorinox Original Swiss Army Knife, Victorinox SwissTool, Victorinox SwissCard, Victorinox cutlery and Victorinox watches. The company also sells its own line of watches, sunglasses, and other high-quality Swiss-made products under its Swiss Army Brand.

Victorinox Swiss Army Knives are multi-blade pocket knives containing implements capable of more functions than standard pocket knives. For example, the most popular Classic knife, with a suggested retail price of $16, features a knife, scissors, nail file with screwdriver tip, toothpick and tweezers. The company markets more than 70 different models of Victorinox Original Swiss Army Knives, containing up to 35 different implements, and ranging from a basic knife with a suggested retail price of $10 to the highest-priced model at about $160.

In 1997, SABI added the SwissCard and SwissTool to its product line. The SwissCard is a credit card shaped, 10-function instrument, and the SwissTool is a multi-tool with 23 features, including full size pliers. Sales of Victorinox Original Swiss Army Knives, SwissCards and SwissTools accounted for approximately 36% of 1998 sales.

SABI offers a line of Victorinox and Swiss Army Brand watches. The Victorinox line consists of 10 models with prices ranging from $60 to $175. The Swiss Army Brand line includes 25 models with price points ranging from $85 to $595. During 1997, the company introduced the Swiss Army Brand sunglass line that includes 22 models with suggested retail prices ranging from $60 to $120. Watches and other Swiss Army Brand products accounted for about 48% of 1998 sales.

The majority of the company's professional cutlery products, made of stainless steel, are manufactured by Victorinox and others in Germany, England and France. Customers for cutlery include distributors of hotel, restaurant, butcher and slaughterhouse supplies and retail cutlery stores throughout the U.S. and Canada. In 1998, sales of these products accounted for 16% of the total. In February 1997, SABI sold Cuisine de France Ltd., the exclusive North American distributor of cutlery under the Cuisine de France Sabatier trademark. During 1997, the company introduced a cut-resistant glove to be sold to its existing cutlery customers. SABI believes it has the largest market share of imported professional cutlery products sold in the United Sates.

Per Share Data ($) (Year Ended Dec. 31)	1998	1997	1996	1995	1994	1993	1992	1991	1990	1989
Tangible Bk. Val.	9.08	8.79	9.21	9.68	9.20	7.61	6.00	3.22	2.71	1.95
Cash Flow	0.52	-0.16	-0.15	0.77	1.56	1.39	0.94	0.62	0.58	0.80
Earnings	0.18	-0.49	-0.64	0.38	1.16	1.04	0.80	0.45	0.51	0.75
Dividends	Nil	Nil	Nil	Nil	Nil	Nil	Nil	Nil	Nil	Nil
Payout Ratio	Nil	Nil	Nil	Nil	Nil	Nil	Nil	Nil	Nil	Nil
Prices - High	12¾	14⅛	15	13	16¼	18¼	16	12¾	12½	14½
- Low	8⅛	9⅛	11¼	10	10¼	12	9½	5¾	4½	5
P/E Ratio - High	71	NM	NM	34	14	18	20	28	25	19
- Low	45	NM	NM	26	9	12	12	13	9	7
Income Statement Analysis (Million $)										
Revs.	128	119	130	127	144	103	74.1	60.1	50.2	43.8
Oper. Inc.	3.8	-4.2	1.1	7.2	20.2	13.8	9.6	5.2	4.5	6.4
Depr.	2.8	2.7	4.0	3.3	3.2	2.5	0.9	0.7	0.3	0.2
Int. Exp.	0.1	0.0	0.1	0.2	0.0	0.0	0.3	0.4	0.4	0.7
Pretax Inc.	2.7	-6.4	-7.6	5.6	16.0	11.5	8.9	3.5	3.9	5.6
Eff. Tax Rate	45%	NM	NM	45%	42%	37%	45%	45%	47%	46%
Net Inc.	1.5	-4.0	-5.3	3.1	9.4	7.3	4.9	2.0	2.1	3.0
Balance Sheet & Other Fin. Data (Million $)										
Cash	1.3	1.1	2.1	0.6	18.0	7.8	6.6	0.1	2.3	0.8
Curr. Assets	70.4	64.1	70.4	74.4	78.6	57.6	43.7	25.2	21.4	17.1
Total Assets	100	94.1	99	101	106	78.0	54.3	29.0	24.7	20.0
Curr. Liab.	25.8	18.3	18.8	16.3	23.9	17.7	10.8	6.8	8.3	4.6
LT Debt	Nil	Nil	Nil	Nil	Nil	Nil	Nil	8.1	4.7	7.3
Common Eqty.	74.6	75.7	79.9	84.9	82.4	60.4	43.0	13.3	11.0	7.4
Total Cap.	74.6	75.7	79.9	84.9	82.4	60.4	43.5	21.9	16.2	15.2
Cap. Exp.	1.3	1.1	1.5	1.4	1.7	2.8	1.1	0.7	0.7	0.2
Cash Flow	4.3	-1.3	-1.2	6.4	12.6	9.8	5.8	2.7	2.4	3.3
Curr. Ratio	2.7	3.5	3.7	4.6	3.3	3.3	4.1	3.7	2.6	3.7
% LT Debt of Cap.	Nil	Nil	Nil	Nil	Nil	Nil	Nil	37.2	29.3	48.3
% Net Inc.of Revs.	1.1	NM	NM	2.5	6.5	7.1	6.7	3.3	4.2	7.0
% Ret. on Assets	1.5	NM	NM	3.0	9.5	10.7	9.9	7.2	9.1	15.8
% Ret. on Equity	1.9	NM	NM	3.7	12.2	13.6	15.5	16.0	22.2	46.8

Data as orig reptd.; bef. results of disc opers/spec. items. Per share data adj. for stk. divs. Bold denotes diluted EPS (FASB 128)-prior periods restated. E-Estimated. NA-Not Available. NM-Not Meaningful. NR-Not Ranked.

Office—One Research Drive, Shelton, CT 06484. **Tel**—(203) 929-6391. **Website**—http://www.swissarmy.com **Chrmn**—P. W. Gilson. **Pres & CEO**—J. M. Taggart. **SVP, CFO, Treas & Secy**—T. M. Lupinski. **Investor Contact**—Donald Dwight (603-795-2800).**Dirs**—A. C. Allen, C. H. Bailey, T. A. Barron, V. D. Farrell, Jr., H. M. Friedman, P. W. Gilson, K. R. Lively, L. Marx, Jr., R. S. Prather, Jr., S. R. Rawn, Jr., E. M. Reynolds, J. Spencer, J. M. Taggart, J.V. Tunney. **Transfer Agent & Registrar**—Registrar & Transfer Co., Cranford, NJ. **Incorporated**—in Delaware in 1974. **Empl**— 219. **S&P Analyst:** Jordan Horoschak

STANDARD
&POOR'S
STOCK REPORTS

SymmetriCom

NASDAQ Symbol **SYMM**

In S&P SmallCap 600

09-OCT-99

Industry: Communications Equipment

Summary: SYMM manufactures specialized transmission equipment for telephone companies and private network operators.

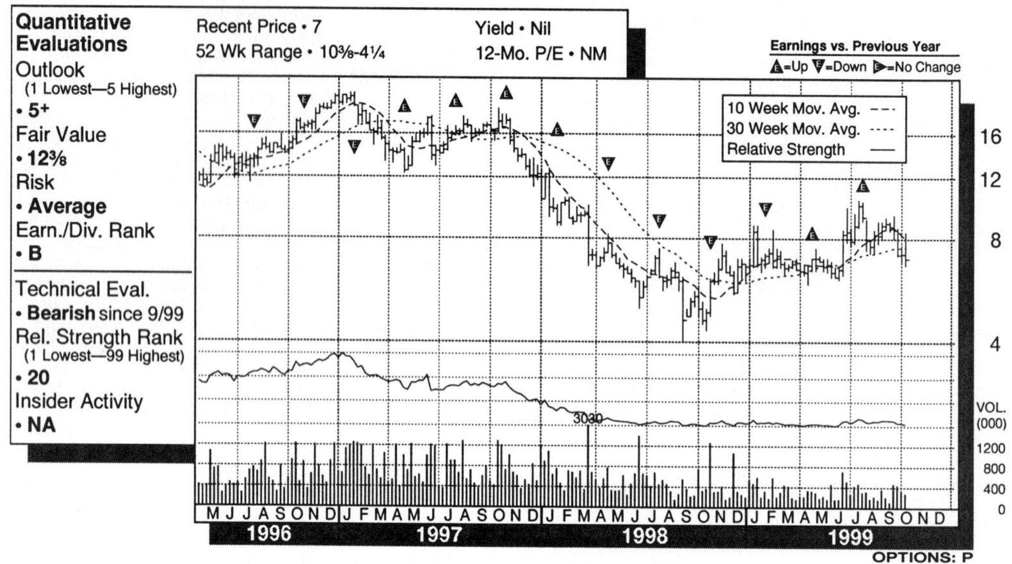

OPTIONS: P

Business Profile - 05-MAY-99

In April 1999, the company completed the sale of its Linfinity Microelectronics Inc. subsidiary, which produced power management products, to Microsemi Corp. (NASDAQ: MSCC) for approximately $24.1 million in cash, of which some $1.1 million is subject to an escrow agreement. The transaction, which concluded Symmetricom's previously announced efforts to secure a strategic partnership for Linfinity, enables the company to focus on its network synchronization, timing and location business. SYMM is continuing to introduce a steady stream of new products into new markets for its synchronization and timing technology.

Operational Review - 05-MAY-99

Net sales from continuing operations in the nine months ended March 31, 1999, rose 5.3%, year to year. Gross margins narrowed slightly, and with higher R&D and SG&A expenses, operating income was down 53%. Pretax income fell 44%. After taxes at 21.0%, versus 22.4%, income from continuing operations plunged 43%, to $1,915,000 ($0.12 a share), from $3,377,000 ($0.21). Results exclude losses from discontinued operations of $0.26 (mostly from estimated loss on disposal) and $0.30 a share in the respective periods.

Stock Performance - 08-OCT-99

In the past 30 trading days, SYMM's shares have declined 20%, compared to a 0.91% fall in the S&P 500. Average trading volume for the past five days was 53,580 shares, compared with the 40-day moving average of 58,159 shares.

Key Stock Statistics

Dividend Rate/Share	Nil	Shareholders	1,300
Shs. outstg. (M)	15.0	Market cap. (B)	$0.105
Avg. daily vol. (M)	0.074	Inst. holdings	26%
Tang. Bk. Value/Share	5.35		
Beta	0.80		

Value of $10,000 invested 5 years ago: $ 7,777

Fiscal Year Ending Jun. 30

	2000	1999	1998	1997	1996	1995
Revenues (Million $)						
1Q	19.62	29.20	33.98	32.02	27.68	24.18
2Q	—	31.00	34.34	35.45	28.43	25.59
3Q	—	19.74	24.21	37.75	22.69	26.26
4Q	—	18.99	28.05	39.13	27.24	27.08
Yr.	—	76.92	120.6	144.4	106.0	103.1
Earnings Per Share ($)						
1Q	**0.06**	**0.02**	0.17	0.14	0.17	0.13
2Q	—	**0.04**	**0.21**	0.20	0.21	0.15
3Q	—	**0.05**	**-0.47**	0.23	0.02	0.18
4Q	—	**0.06**	**-0.01**	0.26	0.07	0.20
Yr.	—	**-0.08**	**-0.10**	**0.83**	0.47	0.66

Next earnings report expected: mid October

Dividend Data

No cash dividends have been paid, and the company does not intend to pay any in the foreseeable future.

A Division of The McGraw-Hill Companies

SymmetriCom, Inc.

Business Summary - 05-MAY-99

Timing is everything. A musician, for instance, relies on the steady beat of a metronome to set the tempo for a piece of music. If the timing is off, the performance will be undermined and the music's quality compromised. Similarly, sophisticated network synchronization systems, such as those made by the Telecom Solutions division of SymmetriCom, Inc. (SYMM), provide the "beat" that telecommunications networks need to send and receive data in an orderly fashion. Bad timing leads to poor transmission quality and unwanted results, such as annoying clicks in a voice call. By coordinating the beat of internal clocks located throughout the network, SYMM's network synchronization equipment ensures error-free transmission of data at high speeds.

Serving the worldwide telecommunications industry, SYMM's Telecom Solutions unit makes intelligent access or transmission products, in addition to its broad range of network synchronization systems. The division accounted for 61% of SYMM's net sales in FY 98 (Jun.). The company's Linfinity Microelectronics Inc. subsidiary, which accounted for 39% of FY 98 net sales, was sold in April 1999. Its business was the design and production of linear (or analog) and mixed-signal integrated circuits and modules for use in power management and communication applications.

Telecom Solutions' net sales decreased by $16.4 million (18%) to $73.3 million in FY 98 as compared to FY 97 primarily due to lower sales to AT&T Corp., which decreased to $8.1 million in FY 98 from $22.5 million in FY 97, and the completion of the Secure7 contract with SBC Communications Inc., partially offset by higher sales to international accounts, particularly Italy, Germany and South Africa. SYMM expects sales to AT&T to fall further in FY 99.

In July 1998, SYMM began a process to identify alternatives to broaden Linfinity's market access for its products and to provide greater financial resources for executing Linfinity's marketing strategy. In April 1999, Linfinity was sold to Microsemi Corp. for about $24.1 million in cash, of which some $1.1 million is subject to an escrow agreement.

During the March 1999 quarter, the company booked the first orders for its new TimeSource products to competitive local exchange carrier (CLEC) and cable telephony customers.

Per Share Data ($) (Year Ended Jun. 30)	1999	1998	1997	1996	1995	1994	1993	1992	1991	1990
Tangible Bk. Val.	NA	5.35	5.52	4.52	3.98	3.32	2.78	2.35	2.18	2.04
Cash Flow	NA	0.43	1.23	0.79	0.99	0.80	0.73	0.37	0.37	0.34
Earnings	-0.08	-0.10	0.83	0.47	0.66	0.43	0.40	0.10	0.11	0.07
Dividends	Nil	Nil	Nil	Nil	Nil	Nil	Nil	Nil	Nil	Nil
Payout Ratio	Nil	Nil	Nil	Nil	Nil	Nil	Nil	Nil	Nil	Nil
Prices - High	10 3/8	12 3/4	21	21 3/8	26 5/8	13 5/8	18 1/4	10 3/8	4 1/4	3
- Low	5 7/8	4	10 1/4	8 7/8	12 7/8	6 1/2	8 7/8	3 1/8	2	1 1/4
P/E Ratio - High	NM	NM	25	45	40	32	46	NM	47	43
- Low	NM	NM	12	19	20	15	22	NM	22	18
Income Statement Analysis (Million $)										
Revs.	NA	121	144	106	103	98.4	87.9	68.8	62.0	58.2
Oper. Inc.	NA	3.3	22.5	13.4	16.1	14.1	12.9	6.8	5.9	5.7
Depr.	NA	8.4	6.5	5.2	5.3	5.8	5.0	3.7	3.4	3.4
Int. Exp.	NA	0.8	0.6	0.6	0.6	0.6	0.6	0.6	0.7	1.3
Pretax Inc.	NA	-4.1	17.3	9.5	11.6	8.1	7.7	2.8	2.1	1.1
Eff. Tax Rate	NA	NM	22%	21%	11%	19%	22%	52%	34%	24%
Net Inc.	NA	-1.5	13.5	7.5	10.3	6.5	6.0	1.3	1.4	0.9
Balance Sheet & Other Fin. Data (Million $)										
Cash	NA	34.3	41.6	34.3	33.2	21.3	18.2	10.1	7.5	1.0
Curr. Assets	NA	75.7	88.8	70.3	66.6	51.7	42.3	31.3	24.3	20.3
Total Assets	NA	115	129	93.5	85.3	69.1	59.0	48.2	43.1	41.3
Curr. Liab.	NA	20.2	30.5	14.8	15.9	13.2	12.9	10.6	8.2	9.5
LT Debt	NA	8.4	8.6	5.7	5.8	5.8	5.9	5.9	5.9	4.9
Common Eqty.	NA	84.4	87.6	70.4	60.1	46.8	38.1	30.2	27.3	25.1
Total Cap.	NA	94.7	99	78.7	69.2	55.4	45.4	36.9	34.0	30.7
Cap. Exp.	NA	6.5	15.1	9.1	6.6	3.6	4.6	1.9	1.0	1.5
Cash Flow	NA	6.9	20.0	12.6	15.6	12.3	10.9	5.1	4.7	4.3
Curr. Ratio	NA	3.8	2.9	4.8	4.2	3.9	3.3	3.0	3.0	2.1
% LT Debt of Cap.	NA	8.8	8.7	7.3	8.3	10.5	12.9	16.0	17.5	15.9
% Net Inc.of Revs.	NA	NM	9.3	7.1	10.0	6.7	6.8	2.0	2.2	1.5
% Ret. on Assets	NA	NM	12.1	8.4	13.3	10.2	10.9	2.9	3.2	2.0
% Ret. on Equity	NA	NM	17.0	11.5	19.4	15.4	17.1	4.6	5.1	3.5

Data as orig reptd.; bef. results of disc opers/spec. items. Per share data adj. for stk. divs. Bold denotes diluted EPS (FASB 128)-prior periods restated. E-Estimated. NA-Not Available. NM-Not Meaningful. NR-Not Ranked.

Office—2300 Orchard Parkway, San Jose, CA 95131-1017. **Tel**—(408) 943-9403. **Website**—www.symmetricom.com **Chrmn** —W. D. Rasdal. **CEO**—T. Steipp. **VP-Fin & Secy**—M. Rorabaugh. **Dirs**—R. H. Neumeister, R. W. Oliver, K. A. Prabhu, W. D. Rasdal, T. Steipp, R. A. Strauch, R. M. Wolfe. **Transfer Agent & Registrar**—Chase Trust Co. of California, SF. **Incorporated**—in California in 1973. **Empl**— 642. **S&P Analyst:** C.F.B.

STANDARD
&POOR'S
STOCK REPORTS

Syncor International

NASDAQ Symbol **SCOR**

In S&P SmallCap 600

09-OCT-99

Industry:
Health Care (Medical Products & Supplies)

Summary: This distributor of radiopharmaceuticals operates an international network of nuclear pharmacy centers serving hospitals, clinics, and physicians.

Quantitative Evaluations

Outlook
(1 Lowest—5 Highest)
• **4-**

Fair Value
• **53¼**

Risk
• **High**

Earn./Div. Rank
• **B**

Technical Eval.
• **Bullish** since 8/99

Rel. Strength Rank
(1 Lowest—99 Highest)
• **38**

Insider Activity
• **NA**

Recent Price • 34¼
52 Wk Range • 40⅞-14½
Yield • Nil
12-Mo. P/E • 24.0

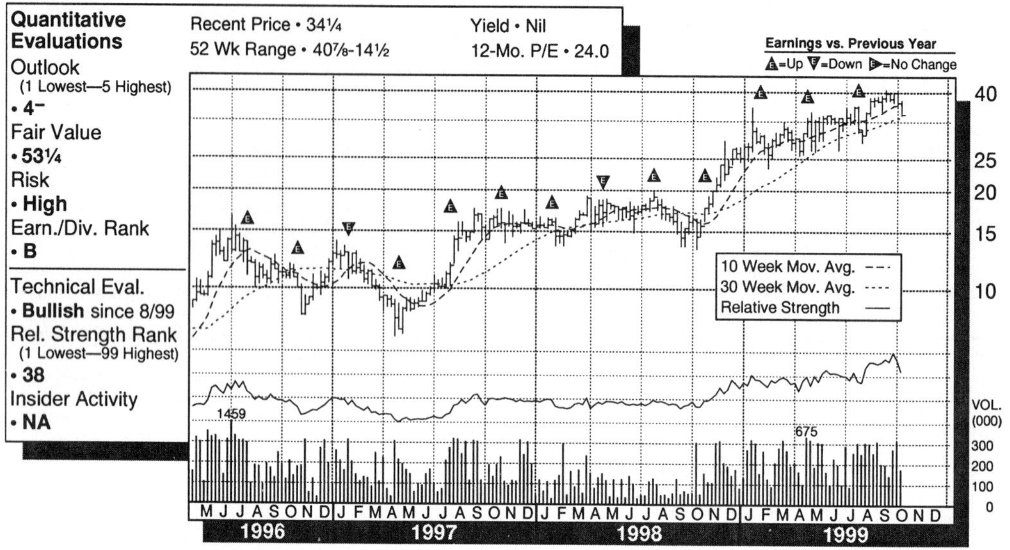

Business Profile - 07-AUG-99

In July 1999, Syncor International stated that the consistent operating performance of its radiopharmacy business segment benefited from expense controls. The company anticipated continued margin improvement and double-digit sales growth going forward. Further, in the short-term, its medical imaging subsidiary was focusing on systems integration and leveraging SCOR's internal resources. As of July 1999, the company distributed radiopharmaceuticals through a network of 120 domestic and 14 international nuclear pharmacies. During the second half of 1998, SCOR instituted a general price increase in its radiopharmacy division.

Operational Review - 07-AUG-99

Net sales in the six months ended June 30, 1999 increased 18%, year to year, attributable to sales growth in both the radiopharmacy and medical imaging business segments. Gross margins expanded primarily as a result of a more favorable product mix. Operating, selling, and administrative costs rose 28% and depreciation and amortization increased 19%, both principally due to acquisitions in the medical imaging unit. Following significantly higher net other expense, and after taxes at 41.5%, versus 42.9%, net income advanced 47% to $11.4 million ($0.91 a share, on 15.3% more shares) from $7.8 million ($0.71).

Stock Performance - 08-OCT-99

In the past 30 trading days, SCOR's shares have declined 9%, compared to a 0.91% fall in the S&P 500. Average trading volume for the past five days was 34,700 shares, compared with the 40-day moving average of 54,405 shares.

Key Stock Statistics

Dividend Rate/Share	Nil	Shareholders	3,500
Shs. outstg. (M)	11.7	Market cap. (B)	$0.402
Avg. daily vol. (M)	0.053	Inst. holdings	55%
Tang. Bk. Value/Share	3.51		
Beta	0.84		

Value of $10,000 invested 5 years ago: $ 15,307

Fiscal Year Ending Dec. 31

	1999	1998	1997	1996	1995	1994
Revenues (Million $)						
1Q	123.9	102.7	93.08	92.32	83.00	74.80
2Q	130.3	113.3	98.19	93.30	83.30	81.90
3Q	—	114.1	94.49	90.25	81.01	81.60
4Q	—	119.0	94.80	90.88	85.15	81.67
Yr.	—	449.0	380.6	366.4	332.5	320.0
Earnings Per Share ($)						
1Q	**0.41**	**0.31**	**0.32**	**0.17**	0.10	0.19
2Q	**0.50**	**0.40**	**0.33**	**0.25**	0.12	0.07
3Q	—	**0.24**	**0.17**	**0.13**	0.12	-0.10
4Q	—	**0.29**	**0.16**	**0.10**	0.11	-0.05
Yr.	—	**1.23**	**0.98**	**0.65**	**0.48**	**0.13**

Next earnings report expected: late October

Dividend Data

No cash has been paid on the common shares.

Syncor International Corporation

Business Summary - 07-AUG-99

Syncor International Corp.'s strategy is to be the worldwide leader in providing imaging, specialized pharmacy, and management services to the healthcare industry by profitably growing both its core radiopharmacy services business and its medical imaging business. SCOR is the world's leading provider of radiopharmacy services, engaged in compounding, dispensing, and distributing radiopharmaceutical products and services through an international network of nuclear pharmacy service centers. SCOR is also pursuing a leadership position through growth in its Comprehensive Medical Imaging, Inc. ("CMI") subsidiary, which provides medical imaging services.

SCOR's nuclear pharmacy network services approximately 7,000 hospitals and clinics in 48 U.S. states. The radiopharmaceutical products dispensed through this network are used by physicians in conjunction with nuclear imaging cameras and computers to obtain patient images of organs and body functions for diagnostic purposes in the monitoring and treatment of diseases. The company processes its radiopharmaceutical prescriptions in a convenient "unit dose" packaging format. SCOR also provides related services such as record-keeping (required by federal and state regulatory agencies) and radiopharmaceutical technical consulting.

The company, through its Syncor Pharmaceuticals, Inc. subsidiary, manufactures Iodine-123 capsules, a radiopharmaceutical diagnostic product used for thyroid disorders. This subsidiary allows SCOR to maintain a reliable supply of the product for its customers and their patients. As of year-end 1998, SCOR also hoped to manufacture and distribute additional pharmaceutical products in the future.

SCOR has two types of radiopharmacy customers. Corporate account customers, such as managed care providers, purchase the majority of their radiopharmaceuticals through the company. In 1998, these customers accounted for about 35% of firm-wide sales. The second client type is individual hospitals or clinics, which accounted for 63% of 1998 company sales.

SCOR, through its CMI subsidiary, expanded its role in medical imaging services by acquiring three medical imaging businesses in 1998, which include TME Inc., National Diagnostic Services Inc., and International Magnetic Imaging Inc. As of year-end 1998, the company owned or partly-owned 40 medical imaging centers. These centers provide various diagnostic imaging services to health care clients, such as X-rays, ultrasound, and mammography. The company's goal is to provide timely, accurate, and cost-effective diagnostic services to its clients.

SCOR also provides a service called IMI-Net, which is a multi-state patient referral network that contracts with insurance payers. The system arranges for patients to receive diagnostic scanning at service facilities that meet IMI-Net quality standards.

Per Share Data ($)										
(Year Ended Dec. 31)	**1998**	**1997**	**1996**	**1995**	**1994**	**1993**	**1992**	**1991**	**1990**	**1989**
Tangible Bk. Val.	3.51	7.25	6.30	6.16	5.96	5.51	5.15	3.89	2.93	2.32
Cash Flow	2.57	1.94	1.63	1.48	1.08	0.64	1.62	1.13	0.85	0.66
Earnings	1.23	0.98	0.64	0.45	0.11	0.16	0.95	0.63	0.46	0.32
Dividends	Nil	Nil	Nil	Nil	Nil	Nil	Nil	Nil	Nil	Nil
Payout Ratio	Nil	Nil	Nil	Nil	Nil	Nil	Nil	Nil	Nil	Nil
Prices - High	28 3/8	17 5/8	16 5/8	12 1/8	24 3/4	26 1/2	34 1/2	27 1/4	10 1/2	8 1/4
- Low	13 1/4	7 1/8	6 1/8	6 1/8	6 1/2	14 1/4	15	9 1/8	6 1/4	4 3/8
P/E Ratio - High	23	18	26	27	NM	NM	36	43	23	26
- Low	11	7	9	14	NM	NM	16	14	14	14
Income Statement Analysis (Million $)										
Revs.	449	381	366	332	320	142	231	210	157	130
Oper. Inc.	39.8	23.0	19.0	17.8	12.2	7.7	23.4	16.7	11.7	8.1
Depr.	15.3	9.9	10.4	10.8	10.6	5.3	7.2	5.4	3.9	3.4
Int. Exp.	5.3	1.2	0.8	0.7	0.8	0.3	0.6	0.8	1.0	0.8
Pretax Inc.	24.2	17.0	11.3	7.8	2.1	2.8	16.9	11.6	8.2	5.2
Eff. Tax Rate	42%	41%	39%	40%	42%	39%	40%	41%	42%	38%
Net Inc.	13.9	10.0	6.9	4.7	1.2	1.7	10.2	6.9	4.8	3.3
Balance Sheet & Other Fin. Data (Million $)										
Cash	13.8	25.5	25.2	23.0	18.0	18.7	20.9	10.0	9.3	9.6
Curr. Assets	119	92.6	93.0	83.6	76.3	63.7	60.7	52.0	42.8	37.7
Total Assets	257	165	146	134	129	115	104	90.8	74.6	65.7
Curr. Liab.	74.6	57.9	57.0	49.4	49.7	36.6	33.3	31.8	22.6	20.4
LT Debt	70.3	17.3	7.6	5.2	5.2	6.8	4.5	6.0	7.9	8.5
Common Eqty.	111	89.3	78.5	78.3	73.9	71.2	65.8	52.4	42.8	35.8
Total Cap.	182	107	86.1	83.5	79.0	78.0	70.7	59.7	52.0	45.3
Cap. Exp.	16.0	10.9	8.1	3.9	9.2	5.5	10.6	10.5	5.3	2.0
Cash Flow	29.2	20.0	17.3	15.5	11.8	6.9	17.3	12.3	8.7	6.7
Curr. Ratio	1.6	1.6	1.6	1.7	1.5	1.7	1.8	1.6	1.9	1.8
% LT Debt of Cap.	38.7	16.2	8.8	6.2	6.5	8.8	6.4	10.2	15.2	18.7
% Net Inc.of Revs.	3.1	2.6	1.9	14.0	0.4	1.2	4.4	3.3	3.0	2.5
% Ret. on Assets	6.6	6.5	4.9	3.6	1.0	NA	10.4	8.3	6.7	5.4
% Ret. on Equity	13.9	11.8	8.8	6.1	1.7	NA	17.1	14.4	12.0	8.6

Data as orig. reptd.; bef. results of disc. opers. and/or spec. items. Per share data adj. for stk. divs. as of ex-div. date. Bold denotes diluted EPS (FASB 128). E-Estimated. NA-Not Available. NM-Not Meaningful. NR-Not Ranked.

Office—6464 Canoga Ave., Woodland Hills, CA 91367. **Tel**—(818) 737-4000. **Website**—http://www.syncor.com **Chrmn**—M. Fu. **Pres & CEO**—R. G. Funari. **Sr VP, CFO & Investor Contact**—Michael E. Mikity (818) 737-4610. **Sr VP & Secy**—H. Bagerdjian. **Dirs**—M. Fu, R. G. Funari, S. B. Gerber, G. S. Oki, A. E. Spangler, H. N. Wagner Jr., G. R. Wilensky, R. Williams. **Transfer Agent & Registrar**—American Stock Transfer & Trust Co., NYC. **Incorporated**—in New Mexico in 1974; reincorporated in Delaware in 1985. **Empl**— 2,900. **S&P Analyst:** Frank DiLorenzo

STANDARD &POOR'S
STOCK REPORTS

TJ International

NASDAQ Symbol **TJCO**

In S&P SmallCap 600

09-OCT-99 **Industry:** Building Materials

Summary: This company makes fabricated structural lumber for the residential and light commercial building industries.

Quantitative Evaluations

Outlook (1 Lowest—5 Highest) • **3+**

Fair Value • **31¼**

Risk • **Average**

Earn./Div. Rank • **B**

Technical Eval. • **Bearish** since 8/99

Rel. Strength Rank (1 Lowest—99 Highest) • **54**

Insider Activity • **NA**

Recent Price • 27⅝
52 Wk Range • 33⅞-16½
Yield • 0.8%
12-Mo. P/E • 16.2

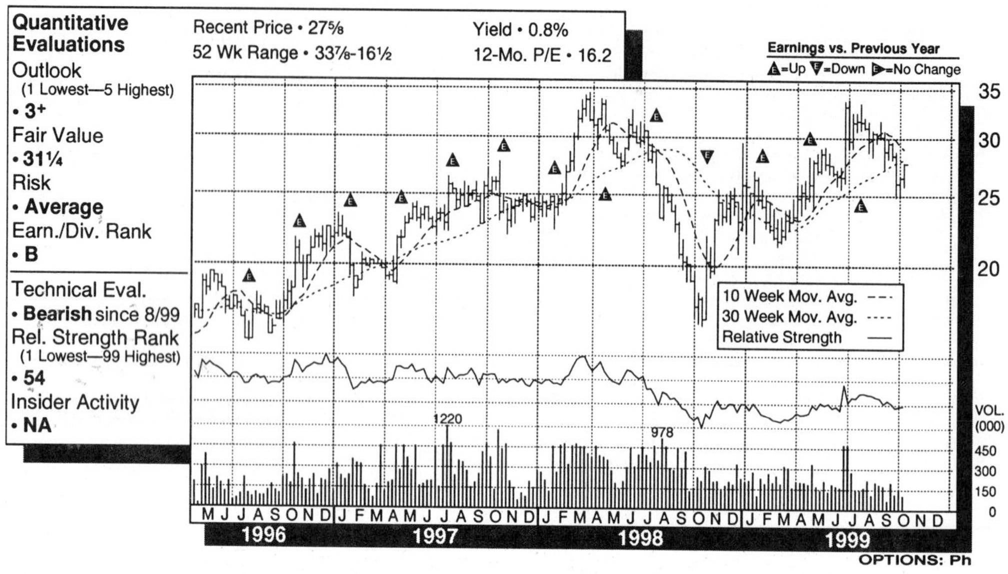

OPTIONS: Ph

Business Profile - 10-AUG-99

The company's primary aim continues to be to increase market penetration for its engineered lumber products. It believes the fundamentals that have driven its growth over the past several years remain in place, including declining availability of high-quality, large diameter timber; superior performance of engineered lumber products; and TJCO's continuing transition to proprietary, lower-cost technologies. In addition, TJCO continues to enjoy strong brand name recognition, supported by an extensive North American distribution network. The company believes there is continuing growth in market acceptance of engineered lumber products as superior alternatives to traditional solid sawn lumber. In 1998, TJCO repurchased $38.1 million of its common stock (8.2%). A further $25 million buyback was authorized in late 1998.

Operational Review - 10-AUG-99

Sales rose 18% year to year in the first half of 1999, aided by very strong demand in North American residential markets, and growth in international markets. Cost of sales increased 23%, and with much lower investment income, pretax income was up only 6.4%. After taxes at 36.5%, versus 37.5%, net income advanced 8.1%, to $16,117,000 ($0.93 a share, diluted, on 8.4% fewer shares), from $14,907,000 ($0.79).

Stock Performance - 08-OCT-99

In the past 30 trading days, TJCO's shares have declined 8%, compared to a 0.91% fall in the S&P 500. Average trading volume for the past five days was 20,360 shares, compared with the 40-day moving average of 30,295 shares.

Key Stock Statistics

Dividend Rate/Share	0.22	Shareholders	2,100
Shs. outstg. (M)	15.5	Market cap. (B)	$0.428
Avg. daily vol. (M)	0.028	Inst. holdings	37%
Tang. Bk. Value/Share	13.61		
Beta	1.11		

Value of $10,000 invested 5 years ago: $ 9,707

Fiscal Year Ending Dec. 31

	1999	1998	1997	1996	1995	1994
Revenues (Million $)						
1Q	217.0	185.8	161.3	111.2	109.9	135.1
2Q	230.9	193.4	185.7	155.1	123.9	163.5
3Q	—	222.4	185.6	179.6	137.8	171.7
4Q	—	176.4	173.8	131.4	113.3	148.6
Yr.	—	778.1	706.3	577.2	484.9	618.9
Earnings Per Share ($)						
1Q	0.42	0.36	0.28	-0.01	0.09	0.13
2Q	0.51	0.43	0.39	0.23	0.15	-0.01
3Q	—	0.43	0.45	0.40	0.21	0.23
4Q	—	0.34	0.31	0.21	0.03	-0.23
Yr.	—	1.57	1.44	0.82	0.48	0.83

Next earnings report expected: late October

Dividend Data (Dividends have been paid since 1977.)

Amount ($)	Date Decl.	Ex-Div. Date	Stock of Record	Payment Date
0.055	Dec. 18	Dec. 24	Dec. 29	Jan. 13 '99
0.055	Feb. 12	Mar. 24	Mar. 26	Apr. 14 '99
0.055	May. 26	Jun. 21	Jun. 23	Jul. 12 '99
0.055	Aug. 30	Sep. 22	Sep. 24	Oct. 13 '99

A Division of The McGraw-Hill Companies

TJ International, Inc.

Business Summary - 10-AUG-99

TJ International is the 51% owner and managing partner of Trus Joist MacMillan A L.P. (TJM), the world's leading manufacturer and marketer of engineered lumber products. Engineered lumber products are high-quality, resource-efficient alternatives for the dwindling supply of wide-dimension lumber traditionally cut from large logs. Substantially all company operating assets are held and revenue generated by TJM. MacMillan Bloedel Ltd. (MB) owns a 49% interest in TJM.

The company's primary objective remains increasing market penetration for its engineered lumber products. TJCO believes its fundamentals remain strong: builders continue to switch to engineered lumber products, which they are using in more applications on each project; consumer confidence and employment rates are high, so that housing starts should remain at favorable levels; and the company believes it is well positioned with manufacturing, sales, marketing and distribution to continue to grow its business. TJCO also believes regional fundamentals that have driven the company's growth over the past several years remain in place, including declining availability of high-quality, large diameter timber; superior performance of engineered lumber products; and the company's continuing transition to proprietary, lower-cost technologies. In addition, TJCO continues to enjoy strong brand name recognition, supported by an extensive North American distribution network. Most importantly, it believes there continues to be growth in market acceptance of engineered lumber products.

The company's primary competitors are traditional lumber mills. TJCO believes it has significant competitive advantages over traditional mills, because its proprietary technologies allow the company to use less expensive, more abundant wood by-products in the manufacture of its products.

To a lesser extent, TJCO competition from a few large wood products companies that offer a limited line of engineered lumber products. It expects increased competition from these companies. However, it believes it has competitive advantages over these concerns, due to its ability to make laminated lumber from proprietary technologies, extensive product line, greater brand name recognition, and broad North American distribution system.

Unlike its principal competitors, the company does not own any timberlands or significant amounts of timber inventory. It purchases its raw material, mostly by contract, from independent suppliers. TJCO does not expect any raw material shortages in the foreseeable future.

Per Share Data ($) (Year Ended Dec. 31)	1998	1997	1996	1995	1994	1993	1992	1991	1990	1989
Tangible Bk. Val.	13.61	12.22	11.07	10.19	11.17	12.38	7.86	6.66	5.95	6.55
Cash Flow	4.02	3.73	3.15	2.51	2.09	2.47	2.01	0.84	1.71	1.88
Earnings	1.57	1.44	0.86	0.51	0.46	0.82	0.38	-0.32	0.82	1.06
Dividends	0.22	0.22	0.22	0.22	0.22	0.21	0.21	0.21	0.21	0.20
Payout Ratio	14%	15%	26%	43%	48%	31%	54%	NM	25%	19%
Prices - High	34½	27¾	23¼	21½	32¼	33	13	15	13¼	18⅛
- Low	16½	18	14¾	15¼	14¼	11⅛	8	7¾	7⅛	11½
P/E Ratio - High	22	19	27	42	70	40	34	NM	16	17
- Low	11	12	17	30	31	14	21	NM	9	11
Income Statement Analysis (Million $)										
Revs.	778	706	577	485	619	551	400	283	327	351
Oper. Inc.	135	128	94.0	63.6	69.6	56.5	13.0	12.3	34.0	39.3
Depr.	44.5	42.9	39.5	33.2	28.3	23.6	21.8	14.9	12.6	11.9
Int. Exp.	8.8	6.9	6.3	0.6	5.3	3.4	3.5	2.4	2.8	3.1
Pretax Inc.	89.8	83.7	25.7	15.5	43.6	30.1	-11.0	-12.4	19.6	25.5
Eff. Tax Rate	19%	20%	37%	37%	18%	25%	NM	NM	39%	40%
Net Inc.	28.8	27.5	16.1	9.7	8.9	12.5	6.4	-3.2	11.9	15.3
Balance Sheet & Other Fin. Data (Million $)										
Cash	149	119	36.8	19.7	73.7	73.3	0.2	0.5	3.1	3.3
Curr. Assets	312	295	172	105	188	183	80.9	68.9	59.1	66.3
Total Assets	731	712	600	546	614	454	345	335	167	173
Curr. Liab.	70.6	75.9	60.0	57.0	62.4	57.1	56.8	54.7	27.7	35.4
LT Debt	142	142	88.1	89.4	102	30.9	33.1	26.4	28.9	30.3
Common Eqty.	220	228	214	196	238	231	127	112	78.0	92.0
Total Cap.	633	605	511	286	540	382	274	276	137	135
Cap. Exp.	47.4	42.6	19.0	106	152	34.0	27.0	145	14.0	37.0
Cash Flow	72.1	69.6	55.7	42.9	36.3	35.3	26.9	10.9	24.3	27.2
Curr. Ratio	4.4	3.9	2.9	1.8	3.0	3.2	1.4	1.3	2.1	1.9
% LT Debt of Cap.	22.5	23.5	17.2	31.2	19.0	8.1	12.1	9.6	21.1	22.4
% Net Inc.of Revs.	3.7	3.9	2.8	2.0	1.1	2.3	1.6	NM	3.6	4.3
% Ret. on Assets	4.0	4.2	2.8	1.7	1.6	2.8	1.9	NM	7.3	9.5
% Ret. on Equity	12.4	12.4	7.8	4.6	3.4	5.9	4.0	NM	14.3	17.8

Data as orig reptd.; bef. results of disc opers/spec. items. Per share data adj. for stk. divs. Bold denotes diluted EPS (FASB 128)-prior periods restated. E-Estimated. NA-Not Available. NM-Not Meaningful. NR-Not Ranked.

Office—200 E. Mallard Dr., Boise, ID 83706. **Tel**—(208) 364-3300. **Website**—http://www.tjco.com **Chrmn**—H. E. Thomas. **Pres & CEO**—T. H. Denig. **VP-Fin & CFO**—V. A. Heusinkveld. **Secy & Treas**—R. B. Drury. **Investor Contact**—Mel Landers (208 364-3000). **Dirs**—T. H. Denig, J. A. Godwin, R. L. King, J. L. Scott, H. E. Thomas, S. C. Wheelwright, W. J. White. **Transfer Agent & Registrar**—West One Bank, Boise. **Incorporated**—in Idaho in 1960; reincorporated in Nevada in 1973; reincorporated in Delaware in 1987. **Empl**— 3,735. **S&P Analyst:** C.F.B.

STANDARD
&POOR'S
STOCK REPORTS

Taco Cabana

NASDAQ Symbol **TACO**

In S&P SmallCap 600

09-OCT-99

Industry: Restaurants

Summary: Taco Cabana operates a chain of Mexican patio-style restaurants primarily in the Southwest.

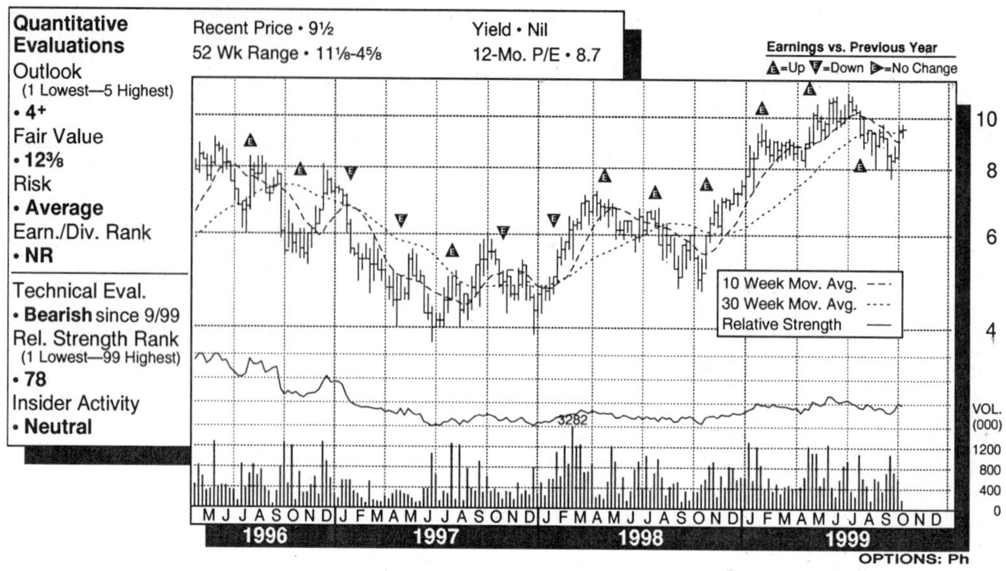

Business Profile - 10-AUG-99

The company attributed continued recent strength in its sales to a more consistent marketing program featuring a value meal message, increased staffing at existing restaurants, an ongoing re-image program, a 2% price increase at the beginning of the year, the continued opening of higher than average volume restaurants, and the closing of underperforming restaurants. In late July, TACO said it remained on target to open 10 restaurants in 1999, including two more in the Oklahoma City market, where the company opened its first restaurant in June.

Operational Review - 10-AUG-99

Total revenues advanced 14% year to year in the first half of 1999, reflecting increased sales at existing restaurants, new restaurant openings, and the effects of a restaurant re-imaging program. Despite a 22% increase in depreciation and amortization charges and restaurant opening costs, net income climbed 28%, to $6,622,000 ($0.48 a share, diluted, on 8.7% fewer shares), from $5,154,000 ($0.34). No taxes were paid in either period, as a result of the availability of tax loss carryforwards resulting from a special charge in 1997.

Stock Performance - 08-OCT-99

In the past 30 trading days, TACO's shares have increased 3%, compared to a 0.91% fall in the S&P 500. Average trading volume for the past five days was 35,220 shares, compared with the 40-day moving average of 119,938 shares.

Key Stock Statistics

Dividend Rate/Share	Nil	Shareholders	900
Shs. outstg. (M)	13.4	Market cap. (B)	$0.128
Avg. daily vol. (M)	0.125	Inst. holdings	67%
Tang. Bk. Value/Share	2.79		
Beta	1.01		

Value of $10,000 invested 5 years ago: $ 5,369

Fiscal Year Ending Dec. 31

	1999	1998	1997	1996	1995	1994
Revenues (Million $)						
1Q	36.91	32.41	30.19	31.26	32.84	27.42
2Q	41.42	36.29	34.20	35.31	36.94	32.44
3Q	—	36.27	35.05	33.81	35.67	34.67
4Q	—	37.98	32.77	31.81	33.09	32.73
Yr.	—	142.9	132.2	132.2	138.5	127.3
Earnings Per Share ($)						
1Q	**0.20**	**0.12**	**0.04**	**0.05**	0.07	0.12
2Q	**0.28**	**0.22**	**0.06**	**-0.04**	-0.39	0.17
3Q	—	**0.20**	**0.04**	**0.08**	0.05	0.15
4Q	—	**0.41**	**-5.07**	**-0.04**	0.03	0.11
Yr.	—	**0.95**	**-4.78**	**0.04**	**-0.24**	**0.55**

Next earnings report expected: late October

Dividend Data

The company has never paid cash dividends on its common stock. TACO intends to retain all earnings for the operation and development of its business and does not expect to pay cash dividends on the common in the foreseeable future. A preferred stock purchase rights plan was adopted in 1995.

Taco Cabana, Inc.

Business Summary - 10-AUG-99

While it may not have the same recognition factor as the golden arches of a McDonald's or the red roof of a Pizza Hut, the vivid pink exterior of a Taco Cabana restaurant makes for easy identification by passing motorists. This chain of Mexican patio-style restaurants serves authentic Tex-Mex and traditional Mexican-style cuisine, set to the festive backdrop of Latin music, a brightly colored interior dining area, a trellis-shaded outdoor patio area, authentic decorative artifacts, and tropical landscaping.

Taco Cabana pioneered the Mexican Patio cafe concept with the opening of its first restaurant in San Antonio in 1978. Since then, the company has expanded heavily in Texas, and has also moved into other southwestern states, as well as Georgia and Indiana. As of January 3, 1999, TACO's restaurant universe, which comprises restaurants operating under the names Taco Cabana, Two Pesos, and Sombrero Rosa, included 102 company-owned units and 10 franchised units. TACO's revenues are derived mainly from sales by company-owned units, with franchise fees and royalty income generally contributing less than 1% of total revenues in 1998.

In 1998, comparable-store sales, defined as restaurants that have been open 18 months or more at the beginning of each quarter, increased 4.7%. The company attributed the increase to several factors, including a more consistent marketing program featuring a value meal message, a commitment to increased staffing levels at existing restaurants, and an ongoing re-image program. Overall sales increased 8.1% in 1998, to $142.6 million. An extra week of operations reflecting a business year ended January 3, 1999, versus December 28 in 1997, added $2.6 million to sales. Sales from restaurants opened after year-end 1997 accounted for additional sales of $8.3 million. This was partly offset by the closure of restaurants with sales of $7.1 million in 1997. There were nine restaurant openings and five restaurant closures in 1998.

TACO's restaurants strive to offer fresh, premium-quality food at value prices. Typical menu items include flame-grilled beef and chicken fajitas served on sizzling iron skillets, a marinated rotisserie chicken, quesadillas, tortillas, traditional Mexican and American breakfasts, as well as other Tex-Mex dishes and salad entrees. A typical Taco Cabana restaurant provides seating for about 80 customers, with additional patio seating for another 50 customers. Most units provide drive-thru windows that, in the aggregate, account for 40% of total sales.

During 1997, TACO initiated a re-image program for existing restaurants, incorporating many of the features of a new prototype design. As of January 3, 1999, 41 restaurants had been re-imaged or converted to the new protoype, bringing to 57 the total number of restaurants under the new design systemwide. TACO expects to re-image 30 to 35 restaurants during 1999.

Per Share Data ($) (Year Ended Dec. 31)	1998	1997	1996	1995	1994	1993	1992	1991	1990	1989
Tangible Bk. Val.	2.25	1.69	4.32	4.16	4.33	4.64	2.21	NA	NA	NA
Cash Flow	1.50	-4.15	0.63	0.42	1.00	0.91	0.72	1.06	0.47	NA
Earnings	0.95	-4.78	0.04	-0.24	0.55	0.55	0.40	0.79	0.28	NA
Dividends	Nil	Nil	Nil	Nil	Nil	Nil	Nil	Nil	Nil	NA
Payout Ratio	Nil	Nil	Nil	Nil	Nil	Nil	Nil	Nil	Nil	NA
Prices - High	8	7 3/8	9 1/8	9 1/8	20	22 1/4	14 1/4	NA	NA	NA
- Low	4 1/2	3 3/4	4 7/8	4 3/8	7 1/4	11 1/2	9	NA	NA	NA
P/E Ratio - High	8	NM	NM	NM	36	41	35	NA	NA	NA
- Low	5	NM	NM	NM	13	21	22	NA	NA	NA
Income Statement Analysis (Million $)										
Revs.	143	132	132	139	127	97.0	59.0	34.0	32.0	NA
Oper. Inc.	21.0	14.8	18.0	17.3	20.2	15.6	8.3	4.5	3.4	NA
Depr.	8.0	9.7	9.2	10.3	7.1	4.7	2.5	1.3	0.9	NA
Int. Exp.	2.0	1.1	1.3	1.4	0.8	0.3	0.6	0.6	0.5	NA
Pretax Inc.	13.7	-74.7	13.3	-6.0	13.3	10.9	5.2	6.4	2.0	NA
Eff. Tax Rate	NA	NM	36%	NM	36%	35%	39%	39%	32%	NA
Net Inc.	13.7	-73.2	0.7	-3.8	8.5	7.1	3.2	3.9	1.3	NA
Balance Sheet & Other Fin. Data (Million $)										
Cash	0.7	0.3	0.8	2.7	7.3	26.2	NA	NA	NA	NA
Curr. Assets	6.8	4.8	7.1	11.4	15.5	34.2	NA	NA	NA	NA
Total Assets	90.2	76.3	143	149	152	119	42.0	14.0	10.0	NA
Curr. Liab.	19.9	16.5	10.4	13.5	13.5	11.3	NA	NA	NA	NA
LT Debt	21.1	13.5	10.6	15.0	11.8	4.6	1.8	3.7	6.1	NA
Common Eqty.	40.8	36.4	113	112	116	NA	35.0	5.0	1.0	NA
Total Cap.	61.8	49.9	127	129	127	106	37.0	9.0	7.0	NA
Cap. Exp.	21.3	16.8	9.2	18.7	36.6	26.5	8.5	NA	NA	NA
Cash Flow	21.7	-63.5	9.9	6.5	15.6	11.8	5.7	5.2	2.2	NA
Curr. Ratio	0.3	0.3	0.7	0.8	1.1	3.0	NA	NA	NA	NA
% LT Debt of Cap.	34.1	27.1	8.3	11.6	9.3	4.3	5.0	42.3	82.4	NA
% Net Inc.of Revs.	9.6	NM	0.0	NM	6.7	7.3	5.4	11.5	4.2	NA
% Ret. on Assets	16.5	NM	NM	NM	6.3	8.8	11.4	32.7	NA	NA
% Ret. on Equity	35.6	NM	NM	NM	79.0	10.4	15.8	123.3	NA	NA

Data as orig reptd.; bef. results of disc opers/spec. items. Per share data adj. for stk. divs. Bold denotes diluted EPS (FASB 128)-prior periods restated. E-Estimated. NA-Not Available. NM-Not Meaningful. NR-Not Ranked.

Office—8918 Tesoro Dr., Suite 200, San Antonio, TX 78217. **Tel**—(210) 804-0990. **Pres, CEO & COO**—S. V. Clark. **SVP, CFO, Secy, Treas & Investor Contact**—David G. Lloyd. **Dirs**—S. V. Clark, W. J. Nimmo, R. Sands, C. Schenker, R. Sherman, L. Sosa. **Transfer Agent & Registrar**—KeyCorp Shareholder Services, Dallas. **Incorporated**—in Delaware in 1991. **Empl**— 3,200. **S&P Analyst:** C.F.B.

TALK.com

NASDAQ Symbol **TALK**

In S&P SmallCap 600

09-OCT-99

Industry:
Telecommunications
(Long Distance)

Summary: This company (formerly Tel-Save.com, Inc.) provides long-distance telecommunication services to small and medium-size businesses in the U.S.

Quantitative Evaluations

Outlook
(1 Lowest—5 Highest)
• **4+**

Fair Value
• **19¼**

Risk
• **High**

Earn./Div. Rank
• **NR**

Technical Eval.
• **Bullish** since 9/99

Rel. Strength Rank
(1 Lowest—99 Highest)
• **88**

Insider Activity
• **NA**

Recent Price • 12⅜
52 Wk Range • 22½-5⅝
Yield • Nil
12-Mo. P/E • NM

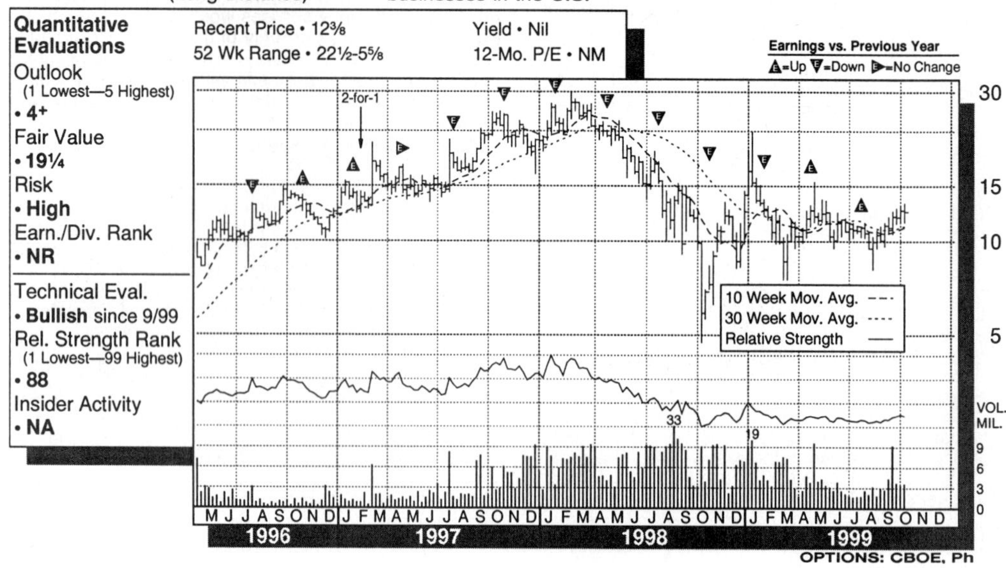

OPTIONS: CBOE, Ph

Business Profile - 21-JUL-99

The company changed its name to TALK.com from Tel-Save.com, Inc. in April 1999. An agreement with America Online (AOL) under which TALK markets telecommunications services to AOL customers has been responsible for the company's rapidly growing revenues. However, the high cost of promotions related to the agreement led to large losses in 1998. The company returned to profitability in the first quarter of 1999. In January 1999, the agreement was extended through 2003. In connection with that and other amendments to the agreement, AOL acquired 4,121,372 common shares of TALK, for $55 million in cash and the surrender of rights to acquire up to 5,076,016 common shares under various warrants.

Operational Review - 21-JUL-99

Revenues in the first quarter of 1999 advanced 21%, year to year, on increased sales under the AOL agreement. Gross margins widened, due to lower network operating costs resulting from reduced non-AOL sales. With sharply lower promotional expenditures and in the absence of $21.0 million of acquisition-related costs, operating income contrasted with an operating loss. After reduced net other expense, and no tax provision, versus a tax benefit of $26.7 million, the company recorded income of $12,334,000 ($0.20 a share, on 2.8% fewer shares), compared to a net loss of $41,795,000 ($0.65). Results exclude a special gain of $0.30 a share in 1999.

Stock Performance - 08-OCT-99

In the past 30 trading days, TALK's shares have increased 24%, compared to a 0.91% fall in the S&P 500. Average trading volume for the past five days was 709,380 shares, compared with the 40-day moving average of 833,787 shares.

Key Stock Statistics

Dividend Rate/Share	Nil	Shareholders	57
Shs. outstg. (M)	61.3	Market cap. (B)	$0.762
Avg. daily vol. (M)	1.049	Inst. holdings	49%
Tang. Bk. Value/Share	NM		
Beta	NA		

Value of $10,000 invested 5 years ago: NA

Fiscal Year Ending Dec. 31

	1999	1998	1997	1996	1995	1994
Revenues (Million $)						
1Q	110.6	91.15	71.16	51.07	36.62	14.41
2Q	117.1	111.1	75.03	57.02	44.73	14.71
3Q	—	122.5	80.31	60.08	48.37	22.52
4Q	—	123.8	78.26	64.27	50.39	31.20
Yr.	—	448.6	304.8	232.4	180.1	82.84
Earnings Per Share ($)						
1Q	**0.20**	**-0.65**	**0.08**	**0.08**	0.06	–
2Q	**0.22**	**-1.49**	**-0.09**	**0.07**	0.12	0.07
3Q	—	**-1.58**	**0.01**	**0.11**	0.08	0.06
4Q	—	**-1.56**	**-0.32**	**0.09**	0.07	0.06
Yr.	—	**-5.20**	**-0.33**	**0.35**	**0.32**	**0.18**

Next earnings report expected: mid November

Dividend Data

No cash dividends have been paid.

Business Summary - 21-JUL-99

TALK.com (formerly Tel-Save.com, Inc and, prior to that, Tel-Save Holdings, Inc.), formed in 1989 to capitalize on an FCC mandate permitting the resale of AT&T services, now provides AT&T long-distance services to more than 500,000 small and medium-sized businesses as well as residential customers, primarily through its e-commerce platform. The company believes it currently holds the largest share of the e-commerce market for long distrance telephone services.

TALK's long-distance service offerings include outbound service, inbound toll-free 800 service, and dedicated private line services for data. The company markets its services principally through its exclusive telecommunications marketing agreement with America Online Inc. (AOL) and through a company website. To reduce its dependence on contract tariffs that govern charges paid to AT&T, TALK deployed its own telecommunications network, One Better Net (OBN), in 1996. As of December 31, 1998, TALK provisioned more than 80% of the lines using its services over OBN.

The company recently said it would remain independent, following a long search for an acquirer or strategic partner. In November 1997, TALK agreed to terminate a merger agreement with Shared Technologies Fairchild Inc. in exchange for about $71 million. In November 1997, the company's bid for ACC Corp. was unsuccessful, as ACC agreed to merge with Teleport Communications.

In February 1997, the company entered into an agreement with America Online, Inc. (AOL) under which TALK's long-distance services would be marketed to AOL's subscribers. A majority of the company's customers now come from AOL's rapidly expanding subscriber base. Since beginning the relationship, TALK has negotiated a number of amendments to the agreement with AOL. The most recent amendments, made in early 1999, eliminated TALK's obligation to make profit-sharing and bounty payments to AOL and introduced fixed quarterly payments during the exclusivity period of the agreement; altered the terms of online and offline marketing arrangements between the company and AOL; and extended the term of the agreement, including the long distance and wireless exclusivity periods, until June 2003. AOL may allow others to market long distance telephone and wireless services to the AOL membership after June 2000 by foregoing the fixed quarterly payments. As part of the negotiations, AOL made a significant equity investment in the company, consisting of 4,121,372 common shares, in exchange for $55 million in cash and the surrender of rights to acquire up to 5,076,016 common shares under various warrants.

Per Share Data ($) (Year Ended Dec. 31)	1998	1997	1996	1995	1994	1993	1992	1991	1990	1989
Tangible Bk. Val.	NM	3.33	3.37	1.02	0.77	NA	NA	NA	NA	NA
Cash Flow	-5.11	-0.24	0.40	0.36	0.20	0.07	0.03	NA	NA	NA
Earnings	-5.20	-0.33	0.35	0.32	0.18	0.07	0.03	0.01	-0.01	NA
Dividends	Nil	Nil	Nil	Nil	NA	NA	NA	NA	NA	NA
Payout Ratio	Nil	Nil	Nil	Nil	NA	NA	NA	NA	NA	NA
Prices - High	30	26	15 1/8	5 1/2	NA	NA	NA	NA	NA	NA
- Low	4 3/4	12 1/4	4	4	NA	NA	NA	NA	NA	NA
P/E Ratio - High	NM	NM	42	17	NA	NA	NA	NA	NA	NA
- Low	NM	NM	11	12	NA	NA	NA	NA	NA	NA
Income Statement Analysis (Million $)										
Revs.	449	305	232	180	82.8	31.9	17.7	11.0	0.9	NA
Oper. Inc.	-159	-79.6	24.3	19.0	9.8	3.2	1.4	NA	NA	NA
Depr.	5.5	5.4	2.5	1.3	0.5	0.0	0.0	NA	NA	NA
Int. Exp.	Nil	Nil	Nil	Nil	Nil	1.7	2.0	NA	NA	NA
Pretax Inc.	-267	-34.3	32.4	18.0	9.4	3.3	1.4	0.3	-0.2	NA
Eff. Tax Rate	NM	NM	38%	40%	40%	40%	40%	40%	NM	NA
Net Inc.	-307	-20.9	20.2	10.8	5.6	2.0	0.8	0.2	-0.1	NA
Balance Sheet & Other Fin. Data (Million $)										
Cash	92.7	317	8.0	41.2	NA	NA	NA	NA	NA	NA
Curr. Assets	150	691	202	65.2	NA	NA	NA	NA	NA	NA
Total Assets	273	815	257	71.4	71.5	NA	NA	NA	NA	NA
Curr. Liab.	137	56.3	26.3	27.0	NA	NA	NA	NA	NA	NA
LT Debt	242	500	Nil	Nil	Nil	NA	NA	NA	NA	NA
Common Eqty.	-136	223	235	41.3	30.2	NA	NA	NA	NA	NA
Total Cap.	106	723	235	44.1	NA	NA	NA	NA	NA	NA
Cap. Exp.	16.9	28.8	27.6	2.3	0.3	77.0	108	NA	NA	NA
Cash Flow	-302	-15.5	22.6	12.1	6.1	2.0	0.9	NA	NA	NA
Curr. Ratio	1.1	12.3	7.7	2.4	NA	NA	NA	NA	NA	NA
% LT Debt of Cap.	229.5	69.2	Nil	Nil	NA	NA	NA	NA	NA	NA
% Net Inc.of Revs.	NM	NM	8.7	6.0	6.8	6.1	4.8	1.5	NM	NA
% Ret. on Assets	NM	NM	12.3	NA	NA	NA	NA	NA	NA	NA
% Ret. on Equity	NM	NM	14.6	NA	NA	NA	NA	NA	NA	NA

Data as orig reptd.; bef. results of disc opers/spec. items. Per share data adj. for stk. divs. Bold denotes diluted EPS (FASB 128)-prior periods restated. E-Estimated. NA-Not Available. NM-Not Meaningful. NR-Not Ranked.

Office—12020 Sunrise Valley Drive, Ste. 250, Reston, VA 20190. **Tel**—(703) 391-7500. **Website**—www.TALK.com **E-mail**—investorrelations@talk.com **Chrmn & CEO**—G. Battista. **Pres**—G. W. McCulla. **CFO & Treas**—G. P. Farley. **Secy**—A. T. Lawn IV. **Investor Contact**—Cathy Bryer (877) OUR-STOCK. **Dirs**—G. Battista, E. J. DeMaio, H. First, G. Farley, G. W. McCulla, R. R. Thoma. **Transfer Agent & Registrar**—Midlantic Bank, Edison, NJ. **Incorporated**—in Delaware in 1995. **Empl**— 525. **S&P Analyst:** S.A.H.

STANDARD
&POOR'S
STOCK REPORTS

TBC Corp.

NASDAQ Symbol **TBCC**

In S&P SmallCap 600

09-OCT-99 **Industry:** Auto Parts & Equipment

Summary: TBCC is one of the largest U.S. distributors of replacement tires.

Quantitative Evaluations

Outlook
(1 Lowest—5 Highest)
• **4+**

Fair Value
• **9½**

Risk
• **Average**

Earn./Div. Rank
• **B**

Technical Eval.
• **Neutral** since 9/99

Rel. Strength Rank
(1 Lowest—99 Highest)
• **56**

Insider Activity
• **NA**

Recent Price • 7
52 Wk Range • 8⅜-5½
Yield • Nil
12-Mo. P/E • 9.5

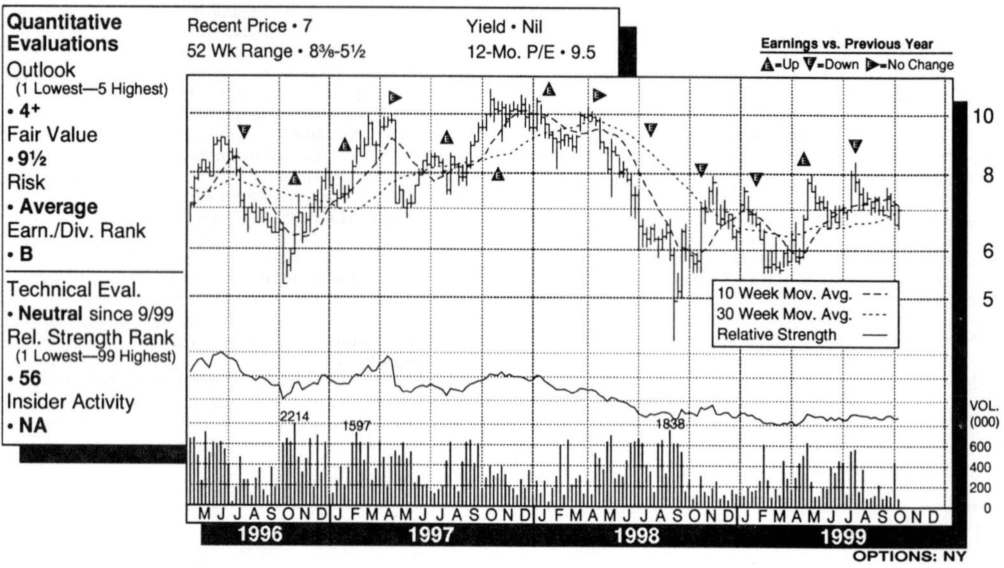

Business Profile - 22-JUN-99

The company continued its expansion efforts in 1998. In November, it acquired Carroll's, Inc., its largest customer, which serves more than 5,000 independent dealers through 15 distribution facilities. The transaction secured TBCC's control over distribution of its tires directly to independent dealers in a major portion of the Southeast and Mid-Atlantic. The company expects to realize cost savings in 1999 from the integration of the two organizations. Despite substantial challenges faced throughout the replacement tire industry, particularly pricing pressures, TBCC is encouraged by the momentum in its marketing program, and expects growth in net sales and earnings in 1999.

Operational Review - 22-JUN-99

Net sales in the 1999 first quarter advanced 15%, year to year, reflecting a 6.0% rise in tire shipments and 7.5% higher average tire prices, both due to the acquisition of Carroll's in late 1998. Gross margins widened, aided by the positive impact of Carroll's; despite 24% increases in both distribution and selling/administrative expenses, also related to Carroll's, pretax income climbed 22%. After taxes at 39.2%, versus 38.4%, net income was up 21%, to $3,806,000 ($0.18 a share), from $3,150,000 ($0.14).

Stock Performance - 08-OCT-99

In the past 30 trading days, TBCC's shares have declined 4%, compared to a 0.91% fall in the S&P 500. Average trading volume for the past five days was 15,980 shares, compared with the 40-day moving average of 31,241 shares.

Key Stock Statistics

Dividend Rate/Share	Nil	Shareholders	4,800
Shs. outstg. (M)	21.2	Market cap. (B)	$0.148
Avg. daily vol. (M)	0.036	Inst. holdings	55%
Tang. Bk. Value/Share	5.07		
Beta	1.10		

Value of $10,000 invested 5 years ago: $ 5,656

Fiscal Year Ending Dec. 31

	1999	1998	1997	1996	1995	1994
Revenues (Million $)						
1Q	162.2	140.7	144.4	121.4	130.3	133.8
2Q	187.7	161.9	163.8	134.5	132.2	132.9
3Q	—	177.7	182.7	177.3	147.2	157.5
4Q	—	165.8	152.1	165.7	126.4	127.7
Yr.	—	646.1	642.9	604.6	536.1	551.9
Earnings Per Share ($)						
1Q	**0.18**	**0.14**	**0.14**	**0.14**	0.17	0.18
2Q	**0.11**	**0.16**	**0.20**	**0.14**	0.16	0.13
3Q	—	**0.25**	**0.26**	**0.20**	0.16	0.21
4Q	—	**0.21**	**0.24**	**0.17**	0.13	0.20
Yr.	—	**0.75**	**0.84**	**0.65**	**0.62**	**0.71**

Next earnings report expected: late October

Dividend Data

No cash has been paid. A three-for-two stock split was effected in December 1992.

TBC Corporation

Business Summary - 22-JUN-99

Faced with an increasingly competitive automotive aftermarket, TBC Corp. decided in late 1996 to focus on its core replacement tire business. The company, one of the largest U.S. distributors of products to the automotive replacement market, shed its non-tire operations, which included batteries, custom wheels, shock absorbers, brake parts and filters.

Reflecting this shift in business focus, tire sales accounted for 95% of total sales in 1998, up from 88% in 1996. The company is one of the largest independent wholesale distributors of replacement tires in the U.S. Its lines of tires are made by others to company specifications, and are marketed under TBCC's own brand names. The Kelly-Springfield Tire Co. subsidiary of Goodyear Tire & Rubber Co. has manufactured more than half of the company's tires in recent years.

TBCC offers three complete lines of tires under its Cordovan, Multi-Mile and Sigma brands. Each line includes tires for passenger, truck, farm, industrial, recreational and other applications. The company also markets automotive replacement parts under the brand names Grand Prix, Grand Am, Grand Spirit, Wild Spirit, Grand Sport, Gran Esprit, Aqua-Flow, Wild Country, Wild Trac, Stampede, Power King, Harvest King, Big Foot, Legacy, Prestige and Sun Valley.

In July 1996, the company acquired Big O Tires, Inc., the largest independent U.S. tire and service franchise organization. Big O brand tires are primarily for passenger and light truck applications. As of December 31, 1998, Big O had 436 stores in the U.S. and 39 associate dealers in British Columbia, Canada.

Most products are sold through a network of distributors located throughout the U.S., Canada and Mexico, most of which act as wholesalers or operate retail outlets, with some functioning in both capacities. The retail outlets that sell TBCC products are primarily independent tire dealers. The 10 largest distributors accounted for 40% of gross sales in 1998 (44% in 1997), including 10% for Les Schwab Warehouse Center and Carroll's Inc. (prior to its acquisition by the company). TBCC has an on-line information system to permit continuous contact with distributors and facilitate just-in-time service to retail dealers.

In November 1998, TBCC acquired Carroll's Inc., a wholesale distributor of tires and automotive accessories, serving more than 5,000 independent dealers through 15 distribution facilities, for $28 million in cash. Prior to the acquisition, Carroll's was the company's largest customer.

In 1998, the company repurchased 2.1 million of its common shares. As of early February 1999, it was authorized to repurchase an additional 1.9 million shares.

Per Share Data ($) (Year Ended Dec. 31)	1998	1997	1996	1995	1994	1993	1992	1991	1990	1989
Tangible Bk. Val.	4.76	4.41	3.67	4.36	4.31	4.09	3.52	3.01	2.50	2.15
Cash Flow	1.07	1.16	0.91	0.74	0.85	0.87	0.87	0.68	0.61	0.55
Earnings	0.75	0.84	0.65	0.62	0.71	0.74	0.76	0.59	0.52	0.47
Dividends	Nil	Nil	Nil	Nil	Nil	Nil	Nil	Nil	Nil	Nil
Payout Ratio	Nil	Nil	Nil	Nil	Nil	Nil	Nil	Nil	Nil	Nil
Prices - High	10 5/8	11	9 1/8	11 3/4	13 7/8	18 1/4	16	9 1/4	6	5 7/8
- Low	4 1/4	6 3/4	5 1/4	6 5/8	8 1/2	10 1/4	9 1/8	5	3 3/8	3 7/8
P/E Ratio - High	14	13	14	19	20	25	21	16	11	12
- Low	6	8	8	11	12	14	12	8	7	8
Income Statement Analysis (Million $)										
Revs.	646	643	605	536	552	569	570	499	499	482
Oper. Inc.	39.4	41.8	33.0	29.9	33.8	37.7	37.4	30.1	28.4	21.5
Depr.	7.2	7.7	6.3	4.6	4.1	3.9	3.3	2.7	2.6	2.8
Int. Exp.	5.9	5.8	4.1	Nil	1.3	1.8	1.1	1.7	1.9	2.4
Pretax Inc.	27.8	31.6	25.4	24.8	31.4	34.6	35.6	28.1	26.1	25.8
Eff. Tax Rate	39%	38%	39%	38%	38%	38%	37%	37%	36%	37%
Net Inc.	16.9	19.7	15.5	15.2	19.5	21.4	22.5	17.7	16.6	16.2
Balance Sheet & Other Fin. Data (Million $)										
Cash	1.7	0.9	Nil	Nil	Nil	Nil	1.9	0.3	Nil	0.5
Curr. Assets	232	183	172	150	146	145	155	117	126	119
Total Assets	334	265	254	180	170	167	177	135	137	131
Curr. Liab.	126	52.8	54.0	73.6	55.0	50.2	73.9	44.7	59.9	59.6
LT Debt	59.7	67.6	70.0	0.6	Nil	Nil	Nil	Nil	Nil	Nil
Common Eqty.	138	134	120	105	114	117	103	90.0	76.7	70.8
Total Cap.	205	209	197	106	114	117	103	91.0	77.0	71.4
Cap. Exp.	12.4	9.1	21.8	9.2	3.6	3.1	6.8	10.3	1.8	2.4
Cash Flow	24.1	27.4	21.8	19.8	23.6	25.3	25.7	20.3	19.3	19.0
Curr. Ratio	1.8	3.5	3.2	2.0	2.7	2.9	2.1	2.6	2.1	2.0
% LT Debt of Cap.	29.1	32.3	35.3	1.0	Nil	Nil	Nil	Nil	Nil	Nil
% Net Inc.of Revs.	2.6	3.1	2.6	2.8	3.5	3.8	3.9	3.5	3.3	3.4
% Ret. on Assets	5.6	7.6	7.1	8.7	12.1	12.6	14.6	13.1	12.8	12.7
% Ret. on Equity	12.4	15.5	13.8	13.9	17.6	19.7	23.5	21.3	23.3	24.0

Data as orig reptd.; bef. results of disc opers/spec. items. Per share data adj. for stk. divs. Bold denotes diluted EPS (FASB 128)-prior periods restated. E-Estimated. NA-Not Available. NM-Not Meaningful. NR-Not Ranked.

Office—4770 Hickory Hill Rd., Memphis, TN 38141. **Tel**—(901) 363-8030. **Fax**—(901) 541-3639. **Chrmn**—M. E. Bruce. **Vice Chrmn & CEO**—L. S. DiPasqua. **Pres & COO**—L. Day. **EVP, CFO & Treas**—R. E. McCollough. **Secy**—S. A. Freedman. **Dirs**—M. E. Bruce, R. E. Carroll Jr., L. S. DiPasqua, R. H. Dunlap, C. A. Ledsinger, R. A. McStay, R. M. O'Hara, R. R. Schoeberl, R. E. Schultz. **Transfer Agent & Registrar**—First National Bank of Boston. **Incorporated**—in Delaware in 1970. **Empl**— 780. **S&P Analyst:** SRB

STANDARD
&POOR'S
STOCK REPORTS

TCBY Enterprises

NYSE Symbol **TBY**

In S&P SmallCap 600

09-OCT-99 **Industry:** Restaurants

Summary: This Arkansas-based company is the largest franchisor, licensor and operator of soft-serve frozen yogurt stores in the world.

Quantitative Evaluations

Outlook
(1 Lowest—5 Highest)
• **4**

Fair Value
• **6⅛**

Risk
• **Low**

Earn./Div. Rank
• **B-**

Technical Eval.
• **Bearish** since 6/99

Rel. Strength Rank
(1 Lowest—99 Highest)
• **14**

Insider Activity
• **Neutral**

Recent Price • 4¼
52 Wk Range • 7¾-4¼
Yield • 4.7%
12-Mo. P/E • 14.7

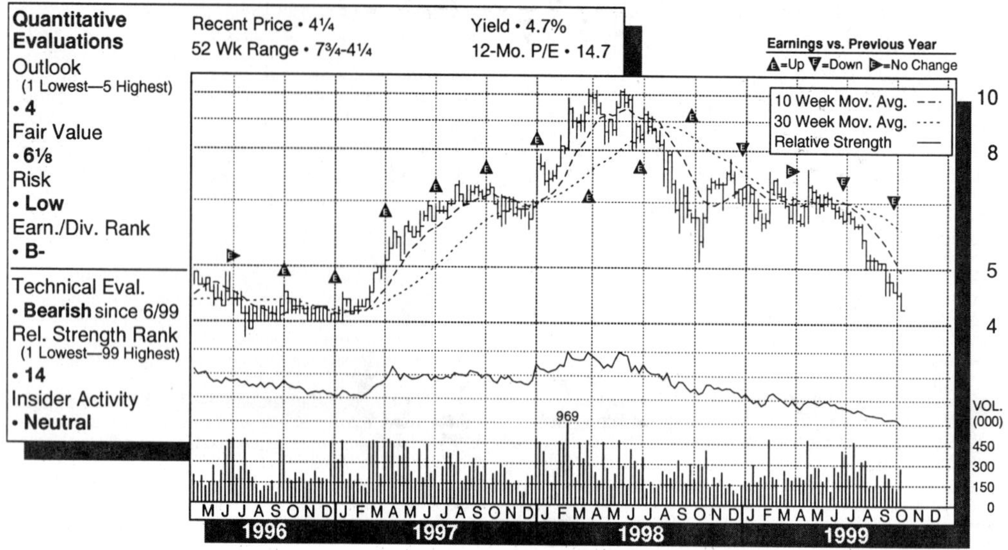

Business Profile - 30-AUG-99

TCBY operated 3,035 TCBY and Juice Works locations as of May 30, 1999, as well as several thousand retail points of sale for TBY products worldwide. The company has development agreements in over 70 foreign countries, and has approximately 300 locations under agreement for development in the U.S. Most of these stores will be co-branded locations with petroleum or other food companies. TBY continues to develop Juice Works locations in airports, travel plazas, and mall food courts with Host Marriott Services. The company said that it will continue to pursue growth opportunities through the development of new co-branded locations and private label manufacturing.

Operational Review - 30-AUG-99

Sales and franchising revenue for the six months ended May 30, 1999, rose 3.8%, year to year, reflecting the development of co-branded locations and an increase in sales of private label products. Profitability was restricted by increased sales of specialty products (which have a higher cost of sales) and 30% lower interest income. Pretax income was down 10%. After taxes at 35.0%, versus 34.0%, net income fell 12%, to $3,774,186 ($0.16 a share, on 3.7% fewer shares), from $4,268,556 ($0.18).

Stock Performance - 08-OCT-99

In the past 30 trading days, TBY's shares have declined 17%, compared to a 0.91% fall in the S&P 500. Average trading volume for the past five days was 54,320 shares, compared with the 40-day moving average of 37,410 shares.

Key Stock Statistics

Dividend Rate/Share	0.20	Shareholders	4,467
Shs. outstg. (M)	22.9	Market cap. (B)	$0.097
Avg. daily vol. (M)	0.036	Inst. holdings	19%
Tang. Bk. Value/Share	3.20		
Beta	0.91		

Value of $10,000 invested 5 years ago: $ 8,252

Fiscal Year Ending Nov. 30

	1999	1998	1997	1996	1995	1994
Revenues (Million $)						
1Q	21.01	19.21	18.47	17.28	27.95	24.26
2Q	31.01	30.90	31.18	27.94	32.78	43.30
3Q	30.02	32.87	34.14	30.22	39.24	50.67
4Q	—	24.00	20.54	20.36	21.60	34.20
Yr.	—	107.0	104.3	95.80	121.6	152.5
Earnings Per Share ($)						
1Q	**0.03**	**0.03**	0.01	-0.02	-0.17	-0.02
2Q	**0.14**	**0.15**	0.13	0.10	0.10	0.14
3Q	**0.13**	**0.24**	0.18	0.15	0.09	0.18
4Q	—	**0.01**	0.05	0.03	-0.84	0.01
Yr.	—	**0.43**	**0.36**	**0.26**	-0.83	0.30

Next earnings report expected: mid January

Dividend Data (Dividends have been paid since 1988.)

Amount ($)	Date Decl.	Ex-Div. Date	Stock of Record	Payment Date
0.050	Dec. 18	Dec. 24	Dec. 29	Jan. 08 '99
0.050	Mar. 19	Mar. 26	Mar. 30	Apr. 12 '99
0.050	Jun. 10	Jun. 18	Jun. 22	Jul. 06 '99
0.050	Sep. 17	Sep. 24	Sep. 28	Oct. 08 '99

A Division of The McGraw-Hill Companies

TCBY Enterprises, Inc.

Business Summary - 30-AUG-99

When you want ice-cream or frozen yogurt, TCBY Enterprises (TBY) may soon be the company that serves you. The company makes and serves frozen yogurt, hardpack frozen yogurt and ice cream, and novelty food products through company-owned and franchised stores, as well as in non-traditional locations such as airports, schools, hospitals, convenience stores, travel plazas, and other "co-branded" locations, in addition to grocery stores and wholesale clubs. TBY sells a variety of frozen package products and other specialty dairy products for sale to private label customers. The company also sells equipment related to the food service industry, and develops locations under the Juice Works brand in conjunction with its TCBY brand.

On November 29, 1998, the company operated 2,938 locations, including 1,027 domestic franchised stores, one company owned store, 216 international licensed stores, and 1,694 non-traditional domestic locations that combine TCBY and Juice Works products.

Franchises operate under the name TCBY -- "The Country's Best Yogurt" -- and are located in shopping malls, strip malls and free-standing locations. A typical TCBY store occupies between 800 to 1,600 square feet and accommodates both carryout and in-store business. Non-traditional outlets are located in airports, hospitals, office buildings, schools, sports arenas, theme parks and travel plazas.

The company has experienced more non-traditional than traditional store development in the last few years. TBY believes that this trend will continue in FY 99 (Nov.). The rate of development of non-traditional locations is partially determined by the co-branding partners, who must approve each location in a process not controlled by TBY.

The company sells registered TCBY brand hardpack frozen yogurt and frozen novelties for distribution to the retail grocery business for resale, mainly in grocery stores and wholesales clubs. TBY does employ a small direct sales force; however, a broker network is the primary means of the company's sales and service to the retail trade.

TBY's Juice Works stores sell fruit and vegetable juices, fresh-made fruit smoothies, and lowfat and nonfat baked goods. The company began merging the operations of its Juice Works concept into the TCBY concept in 1998. TCBY's franchisees are able to purchase an addendum to their original agreement that allows them to operate a Juice Works store within their regular TCBY store.

Per Share Data ($) (Year Ended Nov. 30)	1998	1997	1996	1995	1994	1993	1992	1991	1990	1989
Tangible Bk. Val.	3.14	3.10	3.03	3.06	3.73	3.89	3.87	3.92	4.07	3.61
Cash Flow	0.61	0.58	0.47	NM	0.67	0.57	0.50	0.62	1.00	1.28
Earnings	0.43	0.37	0.26	-0.83	0.30	0.25	0.20	0.31	0.75	1.10
Dividends	0.20	0.20	0.20	0.20	0.20	0.20	0.20	0.35	0.18	0.07
Payout Ratio	47%	54%	77%	NM	67%	80%	101%	113%	24%	6%
Prices - High	10 1/4	7 7/8	5	6 1/2	6 7/8	9 5/8	6 7/8	9 1/4	24 3/4	29
- Low	5 1/8	4	3 3/4	3 7/8	5	5 1/8	3 7/8	4 1/2	4 1/8	11 1/8
P/E Ratio - High	24	21	19	NM	23	39	34	30	33	26
- Low	12	11	14	NM	17	21	19	15	6	10
Income Statement Analysis (Million $)										
Revs.	107	104	96.0	122	152	120	119	129	151	145
Oper. Inc.	16.8	18.1	14.8	-5.6	20.6	17.5	17.2	19.2	35.0	48.2
Depr.	4.3	5.2	5.2	10.9	9.5	8.3	7.8	8.3	6.8	5.0
Int. Exp.	0.5	0.8	1.0	1.1	0.6	0.8	1.2	1.8	2.3	2.5
Pretax Inc.	15.4	13.6	10.0	-32.1	11.3	9.7	7.3	12.2	30.5	45.2
Eff. Tax Rate	34%	35%	35%	NM	33%	34%	30%	35%	35%	35%
Net Inc.	10.2	8.9	6.5	-21.4	7.6	6.4	5.1	8.0	20.0	29.5
Balance Sheet & Other Fin. Data (Million $)										
Cash	16.9	19.7	19.2	14.4	20.2	25.0	27.8	22.8	24.5	29.9
Curr. Assets	46.8	46.2	44.7	51.4	59.0	53.8	51.5	52.8	55.8	54.8
Total Assets	94.5	99	103	112	142	129	132	135	142	134
Curr. Liab.	12.0	11.7	10.8	14.7	12.5	8.8	9.3	8.1	10.3	11.9
LT Debt	3.0	6.3	9.5	12.6	15.9	11.5	14.8	17.3	19.7	21.3
Common Eqty.	76.2	77.4	79.2	82.2	108	105	105	106	109	98.0
Total Cap.	82.5	87.6	92.0	97.0	130	120	123	127	131	122
Cap. Exp.	2.0	1.9	3.4	9.9	11.4	6.5	7.6	4.2	13.4	28.1
Cash Flow	14.5	14.1	11.7	-10.5	17.0	14.7	12.9	16.3	26.7	34.5
Curr. Ratio	3.9	4.0	4.1	3.5	4.7	6.1	5.5	6.5	5.4	4.6
% LT Debt of Cap.	3.6	7.2	10.3	13.1	12.3	9.6	12.1	13.7	15.0	17.5
% Net Inc.of Revs.	9.5	8.5	6.8	NM	5.0	5.3	4.3	6.2	13.2	20.4
% Ret. on Assets	10.5	8.8	6.1	NM	5.6	4.9	3.8	5.8	14.6	26.0
% Ret. on Equity	13.3	11.3	8.1	NM	7.1	6.1	4.8	7.5	19.4	35.1

Data as orig. reptd.; bef. results of disc. opers. and/or spec. items. Per share data adj. for stk. divs. as of ex-div. date. Bold denotes diluted EPS (FASB 128). E-Estimated. NA-Not Available. NM-Not Meaningful. NR-Not Ranked.

Office—425 W. Capitol Ave., Suite 1200, Little Rock, AR 72201. **Tel**—(501) 688-8229. **Website**—http://www.tcby.com.**Chrmn & CEO**—F. D. Hickingbotham. **Pres & COO**—H. C. Hickingbotham. **EVP, Treas & CFO**—G. H. Whisenhunt. **Secy**—W. P. Creasman.**Dirs**—W. H. Bowen, D. R. Grant, F. D. Hickingbotham, F. T. Hickingbotham, H. C. Hickingbotham, D. O. Kirkpatrick, M. D. Loyd, H. H. Pollard. **Transfer Agent & Registrar**—Wachovia Bank & Trust Co., Winston-Salem, NC. **Incorporated**—in Delaware in 1984. **Empl**— 440. **S&P Analyst:** Matthew C. Hershberg

STANDARD
&POOR'S
STOCK REPORTS

Technitrol, Inc.

NYSE Symbol **TNL**

In S&P SmallCap 600

09-OCT-99

Industry:
Electrical Equipment

Summary: TNL makes electronic components, electrical contacts and assemblies, thermostatic metal products and laminated metal materials for a variety of industrial applications.

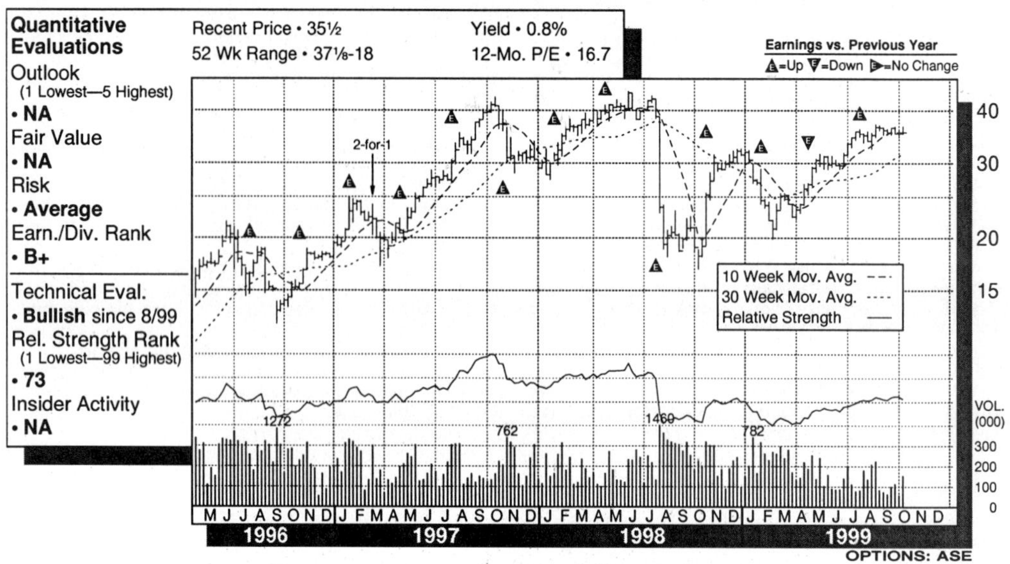

Business Profile - 30-AUG-99

Technitrol said in July 1999 that recent forecasts showed an improving outlook for the European and Asian economies, but due to the lead time to delivery in TNL's business and seasonal summer slowness, it did not foresee significant revenue improvement in European operations before the 1999 fourth quarter. Meanwhile, the automotive market for electrical contacts continued to be strong in both North American and Europe. Vehicle demand was described as robust, and the number of electrical contacts per vehicle has been growing to support increases in electronic sophistication. TNL believed that its electronics components segment was well positioned to continue capturing opportunities arising from growth of the Internet and electronic commerce, increasing demand for higher-bandwidth connections, and greater network functionality.

Operational Review - 30-AUG-99

Sales for the first half of 1999 advanced 17%, year to year, as record electronic components (ECS) sales were partially offset by lower metallurgical components sales. The addition of lower gross margin FEE and Valor businesses. expenses related to integration efforts of FEE and Valor; pricing pressures from ECS customers, and much larger interest expenses, led to a drop in pretax income of 12%. However, with taxes at 24.7%, versus 38.2%, net income increased 6.9%, to $19.0 million ($1.17 a share) from $17.8 million ($1.10).

Stock Performance - 08-OCT-99

In the past 30 trading days, TNL's shares have declined 2%, compared to a 0.91% fall in the S&P 500. Average trading volume for the past five days was 30,400 shares, compared with the 40-day moving average of 21,982 shares.

Key Stock Statistics

Dividend Rate/Share	0.27	Shareholders	900
Shs. outstg. (M)	16.2	Market cap. (B)	$0.576
Avg. daily vol. (M)	0.021	Inst. holdings	44%
Tang. Bk. Value/Share	8.38		
Beta	1.67		

Value of $10,000 invested 5 years ago: $ 75,778

Fiscal Year Ending Dec. 31

	1999	1998	1997	1996	1995	1994
Revenues (Million $)						
1Q	125.2	110.8	92.81	62.85	40.04	34.96
2Q	127.9	104.9	103.9	68.03	39.39	37.82
3Q	—	113.3	102.1	59.05	35.94	36.59
4Q	—	119.5	98.81	84.14	61.03	37.08
Yr.	—	448.5	397.1	274.1	176.4	146.4
Earnings Per Share ($)						
1Q	**0.54**	**0.58**	**0.40**	**0.29**	0.14	0.12
2Q	**0.63**	**0.52**	**0.49**	**0.30**	0.17	0.14
3Q	—	**0.46**	**0.44**	**0.22**	0.14	0.15
4Q	—	**0.50**	**0.46**	**0.31**	0.24	0.16
Yr.	—	**2.06**	**1.80**	**1.27**	**0.56**	0.57

Next earnings report expected: late October

Dividend Data (Dividends have been paid since 1975.)

Amount ($)	Date Decl.	Ex-Div. Date	Stock of Record	Payment Date
0.060	Nov. 18	Jan. 06	Jan. 08	Jan. 29 '99
0.060	Feb. 17	Apr. 07	Apr. 09	Apr. 30 '99
0.068	May. 20	Jul. 07	Jul. 09	Jul. 30 '99
0.068	Aug. 18	Oct. 06	Oct. 08	Oct. 29 '99

A Division of The McGraw·Hill Companies

Technitrol, Inc.

Business Summary - 30-AUG-99

Technitrol is s global manufacturer of electronic and metallurgical components that provides critical components to original equipment manufacturers. The two segments are relatively even in terms of revenues, with metallurgical components (MCS) providing 51% of 1998 net sales and electronic components (ECS) 49%. The company has expanded through internal growth, as well as acquisitions; its test and measurement products business (12% of sales in 1996) was sold in 1997.

The electronic components segment provides a variety of magnetics-based components, miniature chip inductors and modules. These components modify or filter electrical signals. They are used primarily in local area network, Internet connectivity, and in telecommunication and power conversion products.

The company has grown this business rapidly through acquisitions. Recent acquisitions include GTI Corp. in November 1998, FEE Technology in July 1998, the magnetic components business of Northern Telecom in November 1997 and Pulse Engineering in 1995. The acquisition of Pulse significantly increased the size of this business. After the acquisition of Pulse, the company consolidated its electronic components businesses into one unified business operating under the Pulse name.

The metallurgical components segment (MCS), which operates globally under the name AMI Doduco, makes electrical contacts (used in circuit protection), assemblies (used in high-voltage circuit breakers), thermostatic metals (bonded metal laminates that convert a change in temperature to a mechanical action) and clad metals (laminates of two or more metals bonded together for nonthermostatic applications).

In June 1997, Technitrol sold its test and measurement products business for $34 million in cash. Products included electronic force measurement products (such as hand-held digital force gauges) and materials testing systems (to determine the strength of materials such as packaging). Assets related to production of document counters and dispensers, the smallest segment of this business, were sold in March 1996, for about $3.7 million.

Sales are made to customers in North America and many other countries throughout the world. In 1998, sales in the U.S. made up 40% of total sales, Germany 19%, the rest of Europe 22%, Asia 12% and other 7%.

The company does not engage in any basic research and development activities. Engineers focus on improving existing products and developing new products related to current product lines.

Per Share Data ($) (Year Ended Dec. 31)	1998	1997	1996	1995	1994	1993	1992	1991	1990	1989
Tangible Bk. Val.	8.38	6.99	5.62	4.71	3.80	3.37	3.24	3.23	3.18	2.96
Cash Flow	3.06	2.62	1.84	1.23	1.01	0.69	0.65	0.56	0.70	0.94
Earnings	2.06	1.80	1.27	0.71	0.57	0.28	0.24	0.23	0.39	0.64
Dividends	0.23	0.21	0.20	0.20	0.19	0.19	0.19	0.19	0.19	0.15
Payout Ratio	11%	12%	16%	27%	33%	67%	79%	80%	48%	23%
Prices - High	44 3/8	43 1/8	21 7/8	11 7/8	8	5 1/8	5 1/2	5	6 7/8	7 1/8
- Low	16 7/8	17 1/8	9 5/8	6 5/8	5	3 3/4	3 3/8	4	3 3/8	4 7/8
P/E Ratio - High	22	24	17	17	14	18	23	21	18	11
- Low	8	10	8	9	9	14	14	17	9	8
Income Statement Analysis (Million $)										
Revs.	449	397	274	176	146	100	99	81.2	83.6	91.9
Oper. Inc.	69.7	58.9	39.1	21.7	17.8	10.3	9.7	8.6	11.2	15.1
Depr.	16.3	13.1	9.1	6.2	5.3	4.9	4.9	3.9	3.7	3.5
Int. Exp.	3.3	2.4	1.2	1.4	1.1	0.4	0.7	0.6	0.8	1.5
Pretax Inc.	52.3	46.8	31.0	14.5	11.4	5.2	4.3	4.7	7.6	10.6
Eff. Tax Rate	36%	38%	34%	36%	39%	35%	35%	41%	39%	28%
Net Inc.	33.3	29.1	20.4	9.3	6.9	3.4	2.8	2.8	4.6	7.6
Balance Sheet & Other Fin. Data (Million $)										
Cash	50.6	48.8	43.5	13.9	8.7	7.7	2.7	6.7	13.9	7.3
Curr. Assets	204	157	143	82.6	54.0	37.2	33.4	34.8	35.3	34.6
Total Assets	344	255	218	145	84.8	58.6	55.7	52.5	51.6	52.5
Curr. Liab.	102	74.6	67.8	39.3	23.9	13.1	10.2	11.6	9.0	9.9
LT Debt	60.7	30.9	39.7	15.1	15.1	5.1	6.9	2.6	5.0	7.3
Common Eqty.	175	142	104	84.7	45.8	40.3	38.7	38.3	37.4	35.0
Total Cap.	236	173	143	100	60.9	45.4	45.5	40.9	42.6	42.6
Cap. Exp.	20.4	20.5	11.7	5.9	4.4	2.7	8.9	4.6	2.7	2.7
Cash Flow	49.6	42.2	29.6	15.9	12.2	8.3	7.7	6.6	8.3	11.0
Curr. Ratio	2.0	2.1	2.1	2.1	2.3	2.8	3.3	3.0	3.9	3.5
% LT Debt of Cap.	25.8	17.8	27.7	15.1	24.8	11.3	15.1	6.4	11.7	17.1
% Net Inc.of Revs.	7.4	7.3	7.5	5.3	4.7	3.3	2.9	3.4	5.5	8.2
% Ret. on Assets	11.1	12.3	11.2	8.1	9.7	5.9	5.2	5.3	8.9	14.2
% Ret. on Equity	21.0	23.7	21.7	20.7	16.1	8.5	7.3	7.3	12.8	23.5

Data as orig. reptd.; bef. results of disc. opers. and/or spec. items. 1996 EPS total in quarterly table incl. disc. opers. Per share data adj. for stk. divs. as of ex-div. date. Bold denotes diluted EPS (FASB 128). E-Estimated. NA-Not Available. NM-Not Meaningful. NR-Not Ranked.

Office—1210 Northbrook Dr., Suite 385, Trevose, PA 19053. **Tel**—(215) 355-2900. **Website**—http://www.technitrol.com **Chrmn**—J. M. Papada III. **Pres & CEO**—T. J. Flakoll. **VP & CFO**—A. Thorp III. **Secy & Contr**—D. A. Moyer. **Dirs**—S. E. Basara, J. E. Burrows Jr., T. J. Flakoll, R. L. Gupta, J. B. Harrison, R. E. Hock, G. Humes, E. M. Mazze, J. M. Papada III. **Transfer Agent & Registrar**—Registrar & Transfer Co., Cranford, NJ. **Incorporated**—in Pennsylvania in 1947. **Empl**— 21,400. **S&P Analyst:** N.J.D.

STANDARD
&POOR'S
STOCK REPORTS

Technology Solutions

NASDAQ Symbol **TSCC**

In S&P SmallCap 600

09-OCT-99

Industry:
Services (Computer Systems)

Summary: This company provides strategic consulting and systems integration services to deliver business benefits to clients in a broad range of industries.

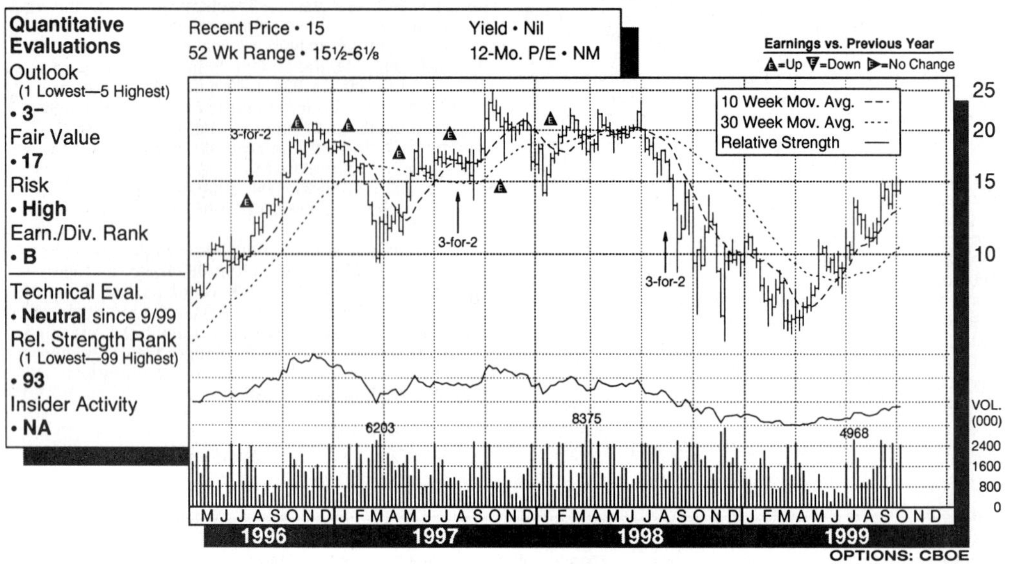

Business Profile - 21-SEP-99

During the second quarter of 1999, TSCC launched eLoyalty, formerly its Enterprise Customer Management business. eLoyalty is a global consulting and systems integration organization focused on building customer loyalty for its clients. In July 1999, TSCC said it expects to spin off eLoyalty in a tax-free distribution to shareholders following a late fall IPO. In August 1999, Sutter Hill Ventures and Technology Crossover Ventures agreed to pay some $8.4 million for approximately 5% of eLoyalty, and purchased 500,000 shares of TSCC in a private placement valued at $4.5 million.

Operational Review - 21-SEP-99

Revenues in the six months ended June 30, 1999, fell fractionally, year to year, reflecting a decrease in demand for Enterprise Solutions services attributable to companies focusing budgets on Year 2000 matters, nearly offset by an increase in demand for eLoyalty consulting offerings. Results were restricted by higher professional salaries, a $10.5 million charge to restructure the Enterprise Solutions operations, and sharply higher incentive compensation, which led to a pretax loss of $3.0 million, compared with $23.8 million in pretax income. After a tax benefit of $235,000, versus taxes at 41.7%, the net loss was $2,751,000 ($0.07 a share, on 4.81% fewer shares), in contrast to net income of $13,857,000 ($0.32).

Stock Performance - 08-OCT-99

In the past 30 trading days, TSCC's shares have increased 25%, compared to a 0.91% fall in the S&P 500. Average trading volume for the past five days was 533,820 shares, compared with the 40-day moving average of 495,977 shares.

Key Stock Statistics

Dividend Rate/Share	Nil	Shareholders	935
Shs. outstg. (M)	41.9	Market cap. (B)	$0.629
Avg. daily vol. (M)	0.430	Inst. holdings	80%
Tang. Bk. Value/Share	3.67		
Beta	1.22		

Value of $10,000 invested 5 years ago: $ 56,249

Fiscal Year Ending Dec. 31

	1999	1998	1997	1996	1995	1994
Revenues (Million $)						
1Q	76.94	—	60.41	32.16	20.73	13.44
2Q	78.41	—	63.90	39.52	23.30	15.56
3Q	—	—	67.40	42.35	25.47	17.22
4Q	—	—	80.17	51.06	28.10	19.61
Yr.	—	189.4	271.9	165.1	97.60	65.82
Earnings Per Share ($)						
1Q	**-0.16**	—	0.09	0.06	0.04	0.02
2Q	**0.09**	—	0.13	0.09	0.00	0.03
3Q	—	—	**0.13**	**0.10**	0.02	0.01
4Q	—	—	**0.15**	0.13	0.07	0.04
Yr.	—	**0.10**	**0.49**	**0.38**	0.13	0.11

Next earnings report expected: late October

Dividend Data

No cash dividends have been paid.

STANDARD
&POOR'S
STOCK REPORTS

Technology Solutions Company

09-OCT-99

Business Summary - 21-SEP-99

Technology Solutions Co. (TSCC) aims to anticipate market needs and apply leading-edge information technologies to deliver business solutions. TSCC's strategic goal is to combine current high interest areas such as enterprise customer management, e-commerce and digital customer service, knowledge management, and operations and network management with the company's more mature offerings to achieve competitive advantages in the marketplace.

TSCC offers information technology (IT) consulting services and strategic business consulting services targeting IT technology areas, specific software packages, along with specific business processes or vertical markets, in large middle-market firms located in major markets and countries around the world. TSCC's clients generally generate between $500 million and $5 billion in annual revenue.

The company is organized into two business segments, each with its own business focus and service offering expertise: Enterprise Solutions (ES) and eLoyalty (formerly Enterprise Customer Management). Each services TSCC customers in the U.S. and abroad. TSCC believes that a structure based upon these focused business segments addresses its clients' needs for specialized industry and systems knowledge, and allows its employees the flexibility and opportunity to grow and develop. For 1998, the ES and ECM businesses contributed 65% and 35%, respectively, to total revenues (70% and 30% in 1997).

The ES business segment provides IT consulting and business consulting services that help clients in implementing third-party application software packages, cost controls and related services to implement strategic change in an organization. The ES business includes the following practice groups: Enterprise Applications and Supply Chain Management, Innovation Technology Group (helps client firms utilize information technology to help transform and grow businesses), Change and Learning Technologies (assists in managing the human side of implementing strategic change), Financial Services, and OrTech Solutions (represents Oracle Corp. in the sales of Oracle applications in exclusive territories).

TSCC's eLoyalty business segment help clients optimize their customer relationships by defining a vision and implementing a solution that helps them understand their customers and how to maximize interaction with these customers. TSCC has developed methodologies, tools and software applications which it uses to reduce a project's completion time, risk and cost. TSCC has established a Relationship Architecture Design and Development Lab that focuses on the deployment of enterprise customer management solutions.

Effective January 1999, the company changed its fiscal year end from May to December.

Per Share Data ($) (Year Ended Dec. 31)	1998	1997	1996	1995	1994	1993	1992	1991	1990	1989
Tangible Bk. Val.	3.67	3.57	2.76	2.00	1.73	1.64	1.79	1.69	0.53	NA
Cash Flow	0.35	0.66	0.49	0.20	0.15	0.04	0.17	0.32	0.25	NA
Earnings	0.10	0.49	0.38	0.13	0.11	Nil	0.14	0.30	0.24	NA
Dividends	Nil	Nil	Nil	Nil	Nil	Nil	Nil	Nil	Nil	NA
Payout Ratio	Nil	Nil	Nil	Nil	Nil	Nil	Nil	Nil	Nil	NA
Prices - High	23 5/8	25	21	7 1/8	2 3/4	4 1/2	9 1/8	7 5/8	NA	NA
- Low	6 1/8	9 1/2	4 7/8	2 1/8	1 7/16	2 1/16	2	4 1/2	NA	NA
P/E Ratio - High	NM	51	55	53	26	NM	67	26	NA	NA
- Low	NM	19	13	16	14	NM	15	15	NA	NA
Income Statement Analysis (Million $)										
Revs.	189	272	165	97.6	65.8	53.2	62.5	71.0	52.4	NA
Oper. Inc.	17.5	415	27.3	10.7	6.4	7.7	18.5	24.9	15.4	NA
Depr.	10.7	7.1	4.4	2.6	2.0	1.3	1.5	0.9	0.6	NA
Int. Exp.	0.0	0.1	0.2	0.2	Nil	0.0	0.1	0.4	0.6	NA
Pretax Inc.	8.6	36.4	25.0	6.8	4.7	-0.8	9.0	19.9	13.8	NA
Eff. Tax Rate	48%	42%	40%	32%	28%	NM	36%	39%	39%	NA
Net Inc.	4.5	21.0	15.1	4.6	3.4	Nil	5.7	12.1	8.5	NA
Balance Sheet & Other Fin. Data (Million $)										
Cash	84.7	38.5	28.0	24.6	17.3	23.7	34.3	45.7	10.6	NA
Curr. Assets	183	159	108	60.6	37.8	41.8	49.6	70.1	21.2	NA
Total Assets	219	197	134	89.4	65.2	69.3	76.0	75.6	28.7	NA
Curr. Liab.	50.9	41.3	28.1	19.4	13.5	15.2	8.0	6.2	7.0	NA
LT Debt	Nil	Nil	Nil	Nil	Nil	Nil	Nil	Nil	1.4	NA
Common Eqty.	168	169	113	70.0	51.7	54.1	68.0	68.2	14.5	NA
Total Cap.	168	156	113	70.0	51.7	54.1	68.0	68.2	15.9	NA
Cap. Exp.	2.5	5.8	6.1	3.6	2.1	1.0	0.6	1.7	1.2	NA
Cash Flow	15.2	28.1	19.5	7.1	5.4	1.4	7.2	13.0	9.1	NA
Curr. Ratio	3.8	3.6	3.8	3.1	2.8	2.7	6.2	11.3	3.0	NA
% LT Debt of Cap.	Nil	Nil	Nil	Nil	Nil	Nil	Nil	Nil	8.8	NA
% Net Inc.of Revs.	2.4	7.7	9.1	4.7	5.1	0.1	9.1	17.0	16.2	NA
% Ret. on Assets	2.5	12.7	13.5	5.9	5.0	0.1	7.8	20.4	35.4	NA
% Ret. on Equity	3.2	14.1	16.3	7.5	6.4	0.1	8.6	26.9	82.8	NA

Data as orig reptd.; bef. results of disc opers/spec. items. Per share data adj. for stk. divs. Bold denotes diluted EPS (FASB 128)-prior periods restated. Prior to 1998 (seven mos.), yrs. ended May 31 of fol. cal. yr. E-Estimated. NA-Not Available. NM-Not Meaningful. NR-Not Ranked.

Office—205 N. Michigan Ave., Suite 1500, Chicago, IL 60601. **Tel**—(312) 228-4500. **Website**—http://www.techsol.com **Chrmn**—W. H. Waltrip. **Pres & CEO**—J. T. Kohler. **CFO**—T. P. Dimond. **SVP & Secy**—P. R. Peterson. **Dirs**—R. P. Caldierro, J. T. Kohler, M. J. Murray, S. B. Oresman, J. R. Purcell, W. H. Waltrip, M. R. Zucchini. **Transfer Agent & Registrar**—ChaseMellon Shareholder Services. **Incorporated**—in Delaware in 1988. **Empl**— 1,700. **S&P Analyst:** Scott H. Kessler

STANDARD &POOR'S
STOCK REPORTS

Telxon Corp.

NASDAQ Symbol **TLXN**

In S&P SmallCap 600

09-OCT-99 **Industry:** Computers (Hardware)

Summary: This company is a leading manufacturer and designer of wireless and mobile information systems for vertical markets.

Quantitative Evaluations

Outlook (1 Lowest—5 Highest) • **1**

Fair Value • **4½**

Risk • **Average**

Earn./Div. Rank • **B-**

Technical Eval. • **Bearish** since 9/99

Rel. Strength Rank (1 Lowest—99 Highest) • **93**

Insider Activity • **NA**

Recent Price • 9⅞

52 Wk Range • 30¾-5¾

Yield • 0.1%

12-Mo. P/E • NM

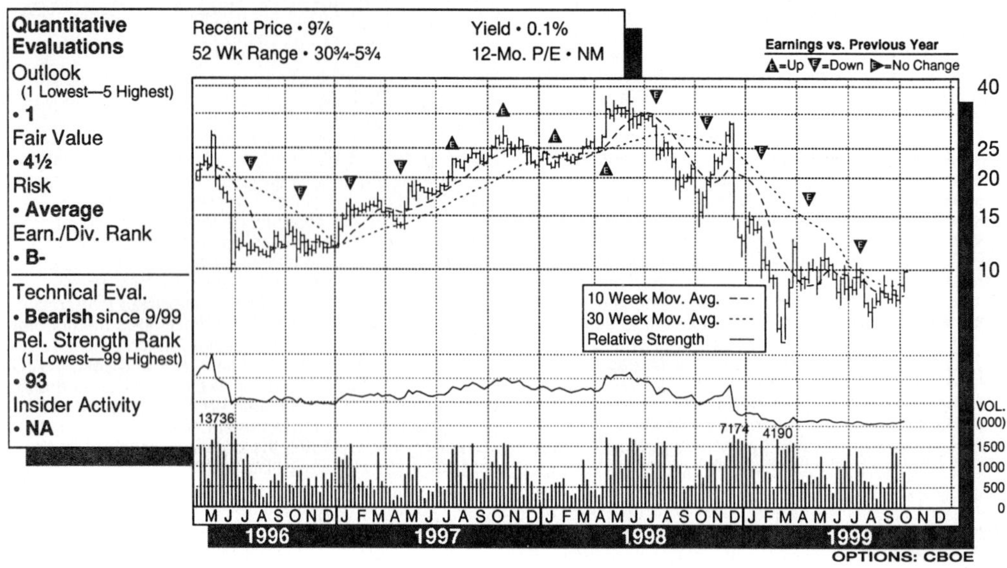

Business Profile - 27-JUL-99

Telxon has seen revenue growth in the first quarter of FY 00 (Mar.), and it expects quarter-to-quarter sequential growth for the remainder of FY 00. For the first quarter, it projected revenues in the mid $90 million area, which will include growth in both domestic and international operations. The shares plummeted in mid-December 1998 following the company's announcement that it will restate previously reported second quarter FY 99 (Mar.) results to reflect a change in the timing of recognizing revenues financed under a new floor-plan arrangement, to a segment of its Value-Add Distributor channel.

Operational Review - 27-JUL-99

Revenues for the fiscal year ended March 31, 1999 (preliminary) fell 16% from those of the prior year, partly reflecting the absence of a $30 million sale to a major domestic retail customer recorded in FY 98 as well as the December 1998 cancellation of a $13 million order by a large logistics company. Results were hurt by the lower revenues, charges of $37.4 million for inventory obsolescence, and various other charges totaling about $31 million. A net loss of $136,982,000 ($8.50 a share) contrasted with net income of $9,175,000 ($0.56, restated). Results for FY 98 exclude a $0.06 a share extraordinary charge.

Stock Performance - 08-OCT-99

In the past 30 trading days, TLXN's shares have increased 16%, compared to a 0.91% fall in the S&P 500. Average trading volume for the past five days was 174,000 shares, compared with the 40-day moving average of 157,349 shares.

Key Stock Statistics

Dividend Rate/Share	0.01	Shareholders	897
Shs. outstg. (M)	16.2	Market cap. (B)	$0.160
Avg. daily vol. (M)	0.210	Inst. holdings	37%
Tang. Bk. Value/Share	0.75		
Beta	1.38		

Value of $10,000 invested 5 years ago: $ 9,332

Fiscal Year Ending Mar. 31

	2000	1999	1998	1997	1996	1995
Revenues (Million $)						
1Q	97.32	111.2	104.9	112.4	103.5	87.43
2Q	—	103.6	110.3	108.3	107.0	91.89
3Q	—	96.41	117.3	123.6	131.0	98.20
4Q	—	77.08	133.3	121.7	144.9	102.0
Yr.	—	388.3	465.9	466.0	486.5	379.5
Earnings Per Share ($)						
1Q	**-1.03**	**-0.01**	**0.10**	**-0.30**	0.14	0.08
2Q	—	**-0.39**	**0.15**	**-0.29**	0.17	0.10
3Q	—	**-2.86**	**0.27**	**0.13**	0.25	0.16
4Q	—	**-5.27**	**0.50**	**0.02**	0.44	0.23
Yr.	—	**-8.50**	**1.01**	**-0.44**	**1.00**	**0.57**

Next earnings report expected: late October

Dividend Data (Dividends have been paid since 1988.)

Amount ($)	Date Decl.	Ex-Div. Date	Stock of Record	Payment Date
0.010	Mar. 04	Mar. 11	Mar. 15	Mar. 25 '99

Telxon Corporation

Business Summary - 27-JUL-99

Telxon designs, manufactures, sells and supports transaction-based work force automation systems. It integrates its mobile computing devices and wireless local area network products with customer host enterprise computer systems and third-party wide area networks, enabling mobile workers to process data on a real-time basis at the point of transaction. The company's products are sold for use in key supply chain vertical markets, including retail (historically accounts for over 50% of total revenues), manufacturing, warehouse/distribution, transportation/logistics and route sales, and several segments of the emerging mobile services markets, such as insurance/financial services. International sales accounted for 29% of total net revenues in FY 98 (Mar.).

TLXNE offers a broad line of handheld devices, ranging from low-end batch terminals to highly integrated mobile computers that incorporate laser bar code readers and spread spectrum radios, including a variety of pen-based and touch-screen workslate devices. It also provides wireless data communication solutions for mobile, distributed data processing application systems through computing devices equipped with radios to transfer programs or data, and from other computers or peripheral devices while remaining mobile.

The company incurred a large net loss for FY 99 (Mar.), reflecting a decline in revenues, charges of $37.4 million for inventory obsolescence, and various other charges totaling about $31 million.

During FY 97, management implemented a new, three-phase business model. The first phase consisted of improving gross margins through the implementation of programs aimed at reducing the cost of its products through new design procedures, improved sourcing and model consolidations. The second phase centered on improving operating efficiencies and lowering the overall cost of serving TLXNE's global markets. The final phase focuses on redesigning TLXNE's infrastructure and logistics system. Aided by the new business model, the company returned to profitability in FY 98.

In addition to subjecting all operations to ongoing review, the company will continue to evaluate alternative strategies for reflecting the imbedded value of its technical subsidiaries in its market value. In March 1998, Telxon sold 1.1 million shares of its Aironet subsidiary, a leading supplier of spread-spectrum radios for wireless local area networks, to third party investors, for about $3.4 million.

An important element of Telxon's approach to selling application systems is the support provided to the customer. Revenues from customer service accounted for about 15% of total revenues in each of the past three fiscal years.

Per Share Data ($)										
(Year Ended Mar. 31)	1999	1998	1997	1996	1995	1994	1993	1992	1991	1990
Tangible Bk. Val.	0.75	9.86	8.59	8.82	7.73	6.59	6.33	8.94	7.57	6.19
Cash Flow	-6.70	2.56	1.34	2.39	1.91	0.99	0.07	1.67	1.39	-0.64
Earnings	-8.50	1.01	-0.44	1.00	0.57	-0.18	-0.79	1.13	0.91	-1.09
Dividends	0.01	0.01	0.01	0.01	0.02	0.01	0.01	0.01	0.01	0.01
Payout Ratio	NM	1%	2%	1%	4%	NM	NM	1%	1%	NM
Cal. Yrs.	1998	1997	1996	1995	1994	1993	1992	1991	1990	1989
Prices - High	$38\frac{5}{8}$	$29\frac{3}{4}$	$28\frac{1}{2}$	$26\frac{1}{2}$	$18\frac{1}{4}$	$12\frac{3}{4}$	$28\frac{1}{4}$	$28\frac{1}{8}$	$15\frac{1}{2}$	$20\frac{1}{4}$
- Low	11	$12\frac{1}{4}$	$9\frac{3}{4}$	12	10	$6\frac{1}{2}$	$11\frac{1}{4}$	$13\frac{3}{8}$	$4\frac{3}{4}$	$6\frac{3}{8}$
P/E Ratio - High	NM	29	NM	26	32	NM	NM	25	17	NM
- Low	NM	12	NM	12	18	NM	NM	12	5	NM
Income Statement Analysis (Million $)										
Revs.	388	466	466	486	380	296	238	215	185	143
Oper. Inc.	-73.0	59.5	-5.3	54.3	42.3	17.9	-0.3	31.9	24.7	1.3
Depr.	29.2	25.2	28.6	22.9	21.0	18.0	12.7	7.6	6.4	6.0
Int. Exp.	9.9	7.2	8.1	6.8	4.3	2.5	2.3	2.2	2.6	3.9
Pretax Inc.	-119	28.9	-10.5	26.8	17.2	-1.9	-15.7	25.0	19.9	-25.2
Eff. Tax Rate	NM	43%	NM	38%	48%	NM	NM	37%	38%	NM
Net Inc.	-136	16.4	-7.1	16.5	9.0	-2.8	-11.6	15.9	12.3	-14.4
Balance Sheet & Other Fin. Data (Million $)										
Cash	22.5	27.5	45.4	35.7	31.4	24.8	27.2	42.3	44.7	55.5
Curr. Assets	249	296	270	300	205	186	138	162	138	140
Total Assets	349	391	362	389	276	260	213	199	167	167
Curr. Liab.	215	107	101	114	104	106	53.2	45.3	35.7	43.5
LT Debt	108	108	108	111	31.7	27.5	24.9	25.6	26.0	36.5
Common Eqty.	17.0	165	147	161	139	125	128	124	102	83.0
Total Cap.	125	276	255	272	170	152	153	151	129	122
Cap. Exp.	36.0	26.1	14.6	22.7	15.2	21.7	16.4	9.0	7.6	7.7
Cash Flow	-107	41.6	21.5	39.5	30.4	15.2	1.1	23.5	18.7	-8.4
Curr. Ratio	1.2	2.8	2.7	2.6	2.0	1.8	2.6	3.6	3.9	3.2
% LT Debt of Cap.	86.4	39.1	42.4	40.8	18.6	18.1	16.3	16.9	20.1	29.9
% Net Inc.of Revs.	NM	3.5	NM	3.4	2.4	NM	NM	7.4	6.7	NM
% Ret. on Assets	NM	4.4	NM	5.0	3.4	NM	NM	8.5	7.4	NM
% Ret. on Equity	NM	10.6	NM	11.0	6.9	NM	NM	13.8	13.3	NM

Data as orig reptd.; bef. results of disc opers/spec. items. Per share data adj. for stk. divs. Bold denotes diluted EPS (FASB 128)-prior periods restated. E-Estimated. NA-Not Available. NM-Not Meaningful. NR-Not Ranked.

Office—3330 W. Market St., Akron, OH 44333. **Tel**—(330) 664-1000. **Website**—http://www.telxon.com **Chrmn & CEO**—J. W. Paxton. **Pres & COO**—K. A. Cassady. **Vice Chrmn**—J. H. Cribb. **CFO**—W. M. McGee. **Dirs**—R. J. Bogomolny, K. A. Cassady, J. H. Cribb, R. A. Goodman, J. R. Macey, J. W. Paxton, N. W. Rose. **Transfer Agent & Registrar**—Harris Trust and Savings Bank, Chicago. **Incorporated**—in Delaware in 1969. **Empl**— 1,550. **S&P Analyst:** J.J.S.

STANDARD
&POOR'S
STOCK REPORTS

Tetra Tech

NASDAQ Symbol **WATR**

In S&P SmallCap 600

23-OCT-99 **Industry:** Services (Facilities & Environmental)

Summary: Tetra Tech provides specialized management consulting and technical services in three principal areas: resource management, infrastructure and communications.

Quantitative Evaluations

Outlook (1 Lowest—5 Highest) • **4-**

Fair Value • **23¼**

Risk • **Average**

Earn./Div. Rank • **B+**

Technical Eval. • **NA**

Rel. Strength Rank (1 Lowest—99 Highest) • **72**

Insider Activity • **NA**

Recent Price • 15⅛ Yield • Nil

52 Wk Range • 22⅜-13½ 12-Mo. P/E • 21.5

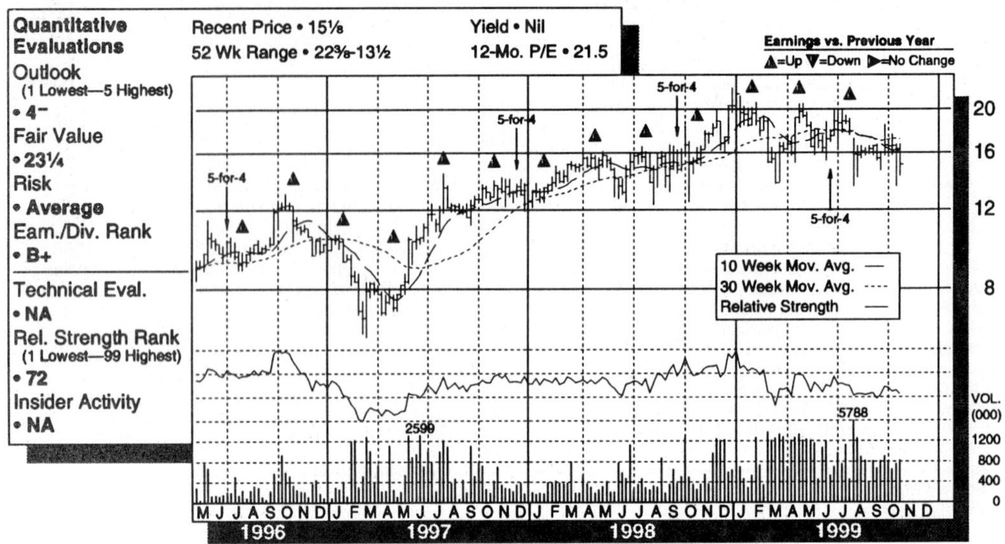

Business Profile - 23-SEP-99

A significant part of Tetra Tech's growth strategy is to acquire other companies which complement its lines of business or that broaden its geographic presence. It purchased 10 companies in five separate transactions in FY 98 (Sep.). During the first nine months of FY 99, WATR acquired seven companies. In September 1999, the company was awarded a three-year contract valued at up to $46 million by the U.S. Environmental Protection Agency (EPA) for the Office of Water's National Watershed Protection Program. Tetra Tech's shares were split 5-for-4 in each of the past seven years.

Operational Review - 23-SEP-99

Net revenues for the nine months ended July 4, 1999, advanced 53%, year to year, with all client sectors contributing to the gain. Revenue gains from commercial clients as well as revenues contributed by acquired companies bolstered 1999 revenues. Profitability was restricted by higher expenses related to acquisitions as well as a 71% increase in depreciation and amortization charges. After taxes at 43.2%, versus 43.5%, net income rose 45%, to $20,392,000 ($0.52 a share, based on 8.3% more average shares) from $14,064,000 ($0.39, adjusted).

Stock Performance - 22-OCT-99

In the past 30 trading days, WATR's shares have increased 5%, compared to a 4% fall in the S&P 500. Average trading volume for the past five days was 130,140 shares, compared with the 40-day moving average of 148,982 shares.

Key Stock Statistics

Dividend Rate/Share	Nil	Shareholders	891
Shs. outstg. (M)	38.1	Market cap. (B)	$0.622
Avg. daily vol. (M)	0.150	Inst. holdings	83%
Tang. Bk. Value/Share	1.66		
Beta	0.99		

Value of $10,000 invested 5 years ago: $ 31,910

Fiscal Year Ending Sep. 30

	1999	1998	1997	1996	1995	1994
Revenues (Million $)						
1Q	89.25	66.44	40.42	38.02	—	—
2Q	96.96	92.73	43.91	40.08	—	—
3Q	157.1	75.15	48.62	40.31	—	—
4Q	120.7	96.98	57.83	42.62	—	—
Yr.	—	297.6	190.8	161.0	87.90	67.80
Earnings Per Share ($)						
1Q	**0.14**	**0.12**	0.09	0.07	0.06	0.05
2Q	**0.17**	**0.13**	0.10	0.08	0.07	0.05
3Q	**0.21**	**0.15**	0.12	0.09	0.07	0.06
4Q	—	**0.18**	0.14	0.11	0.09	0.07
Yr.	—	**0.57**	**0.46**	0.36	0.29	0.22

Next earnings report expected: mid November

Dividend Data

Amount ($)	Date Decl.	Ex-Div. Date	Stock of Record	Payment Date
5-for-4	Apr. 21	Jun. 16	May. 14	Jun. 15 '99

A Division of The McGraw-Hill Companies

Tetra Tech, Inc.

Business Summary - 23-SEP-99

The objective of Tetra Tech Inc. is to become the leading provider of specialized management consulting and technical services in its three principal business areas: resource management, infrastructure and communications. To achieve this objective, the company plans to continue the following primary strategies: identify and expand into new business areas, expand service offerings and geographic presence through acquisitions, focus on government projects, manage internal financial controls, and leverage its existing client base.

As a specialized management consultant, WATR assists its clients in defining problems and developing innovative and cost-effective solutions. Its management consulting services are complemented by its technical services. These technical services, which implement solutions, include research and development, applied science, engineering and architectural design, construction management, and operations and maintenance.

Since its December 1991 initial public offering, the company has increased the size and scope of its business and has expanded its service offerings through acquisitions (with 10 completed in FY 98 - Sep.) and internal growth. It is currently performing services under 1,000 active contracts, ranging from small site investigations to large, complex infrastructure projects.

The company's service offerings include: management consulting, research and development, applied science, engineering and architectural design, construction management, and operations and maintenance.

One of Tetra Tech's major concentrations is water resource management, where it has a leadership position in understanding the interrelationships of water quality and human activities. The company supports high priority government programs for water quality improvement, environmental restoration, productive reuse of defense facilities and strategic environmental resource planning.

In the infrastructure area, the company focuses on the development of water resource projects, institutional facilities, commercial, recreational and leisure facilities and transportation projects.

In communications, Tetra Tech focuses on the delivery of technical solutions necessary to build and manage communications infrastructure projects. Its capabilities support a wide range of technologies, including broadband and wireless communications.

The company has developed a diverse base of over 700 clients both in the public and private sectors. In FY 98 (Sep.), the Department of Defense, Environmental Protection Agency and the Department of Energy accounted for 26%, 17% and 4%, respectively, of net revenues. Although agencies of the Federal government are among its most significant clients, WATR often supports multiple programs within a single Federal agency. Its private sector clients include companies in the chemical, mining, pharmaceutical, aerospace, automotive, petroleum, communications and utility industries. International business accounted for about 3% of net revenues in FY 98.

Per Share Data ($) (Year Ended Sep. 30)	1998	1997	1996	1995	1994	1993	1992	1991	1990	1989
Tangible Bk. Val.	1.65	1.18	1.48	1.06	1.11	1.04	0.86	0.65	NA	NA
Cash Flow	0.74	0.61	0.49	0.45	0.43	0.41	0.40	0.58	NA	NA
Earnings	0.57	0.46	0.36	0.28	0.22	0.16	0.12	NA	NA	NA
Dividends	Nil	Nil	Nil	Nil	Nil	Nil	Nil	NA	NA	NA
Payout Ratio	Nil	Nil	Nil	Nil	Nil	Nil	Nil	NA	NA	NA
Prices - High	22 3/8	14 1/2	13	9 3/4	6 5/8	5 1/8	3 5/8	2 5/8	NA	NA
- Low	12 3/8	6 1/4	8	5 1/4	4 3/8	2 3/4	2 1/16	1 3/4	NA	NA
P/E Ratio - High	39	31	36	33	30	31	28	19	NA	NA
- Low	22	13	22	18	19	17	16	12	NA	NA
Income Statement Analysis (Million $)										
Revs.	298	191	161	87.9	67.8	51.2	43.5	38.0	NA	NA
Oper. Inc.	46.4	29.1	21.3	13.7	10.5	7.9	6.0	4.5	NA	NA
Depr.	6.6	4.5	3.6	1.9	1.4	1.1	0.8	0.9	NA	NA
Int. Exp.	2.3	0.3	1.1	Nil	Nil	Nil	0.3	1.1	NA	NA
Pretax Inc.	37.9	24.6	17.0	12.6	9.5	7.1	5.1	2.6	NA	NA
Eff. Tax Rate	42%	42%	40%	40%	40%	40%	40%	11%	NA	NA
Net Inc.	20.6	14.3	10.1	7.6	5.7	4.3	3.0	2.3	NA	NA
Balance Sheet & Other Fin. Data (Million $)										
Cash	4.9	12.3	6.1	13.1	15.9	13.4	9.0	1.0	NA	NA
Curr. Assets	142	80.9	57.9	72.3	42.9	35.8	27.4	17.6	NA	NA
Total Assets	267	160	88.5	92.9	51.6	38.6	30.1	20.1	NA	NA
Curr. Liab.	65.3	38.3	25.2	32.4	18.1	12.1	8.1	8.7	NA	NA
LT Debt	NA	Nil	Nil	19.0	Nil	Nil	NA	NA	NA	NA
Common Eqty.	152	108	63.3	41.5	33.5	26.4	22.0	2.8	NA	NA
Total Cap.	NA	121	63.3	60.5	33.5	26.5	NA	NA	NA	NA
Cap. Exp.	NA	2.6	2.4	NA	NA	NA	NA	NA	NA	NA
Cash Flow	27.2	18.8	13.7	9.4	7.1	5.3	3.9	3.2	NA	NA
Curr. Ratio	2.2	2.1	2.3	2.2	2.4	3.0	3.4	2.0	NA	NA
% LT Debt of Cap.	NA	Nil	Nil	31.4	Nil	Nil	NA	NA	NA	NA
% Net Inc.of Revs.	6.9	7.5	6.3	8.6	8.4	8.4	7.0	6.2	NA	NA
% Ret. on Assets	9.7	11.5	11.1	10.5	12.7	12.5	12.1	NA	NA	NA
% Ret. on Equity	15.8	16.7	19.3	20.1	19.0	17.7	24.6	NA	NA	NA

Data as orig reptd.; bef. results of disc opers/spec. items. Per share data adj. for stk. divs. Bold denotes diluted EPS (FASB 128)-prior periods restated. E-Estimated. NA-Not Available. NM-Not Meaningful. NR-Not Ranked.

Office—670 N. Rosemead Blvd., Pasadena, CA 91107**Tel**—(626) 351-4664.**Website**—http://tetratech.com**Chrmn, Pres & CEO**—Li-San Hwang.**VP-CFO & Treas**—J. M. Jaska.**VP-Secy**—R. A. Lemmon.**Dirs**—P. C. Haden, Li-San Hwang, J. C. Lewis, J. J. Shelton, D. A. Whalen.**Transfer Agent & Registrar**—U. S. Stock Transfer Corp., Glendale, CA**Incorporated**—in Delaware in 1988.**Empl**— 3,662. **S&P Analyst:** J. J. Schemitsch

STANDARD
&POOR'S
STOCK REPORTS

TETRA Technologies

NYSE Symbol **TTI**

In S&P SmallCap 600

09-OCT-99

Industry:
Waste Management

Summary: TTI is a specialty inorganic chemical company selling products, process technologies and services to the oil and gas, agriculture and environmental markets.

Quantitative Evaluations

Outlook
(1 Lowest—5 Highest)
• **5**

Fair Value
• **18½**

Risk
• **NA**

Earn./Div. Rank
• **B**

Technical Eval.
• **Neutral** since 9/99

Rel. Strength Rank
(1 Lowest—99 Highest)
• **33**

Insider Activity
• **Neutral**

Recent Price • 9
52 Wk Range • 14-6⅛

Yield • Nil
12-Mo. P/E • 6.2

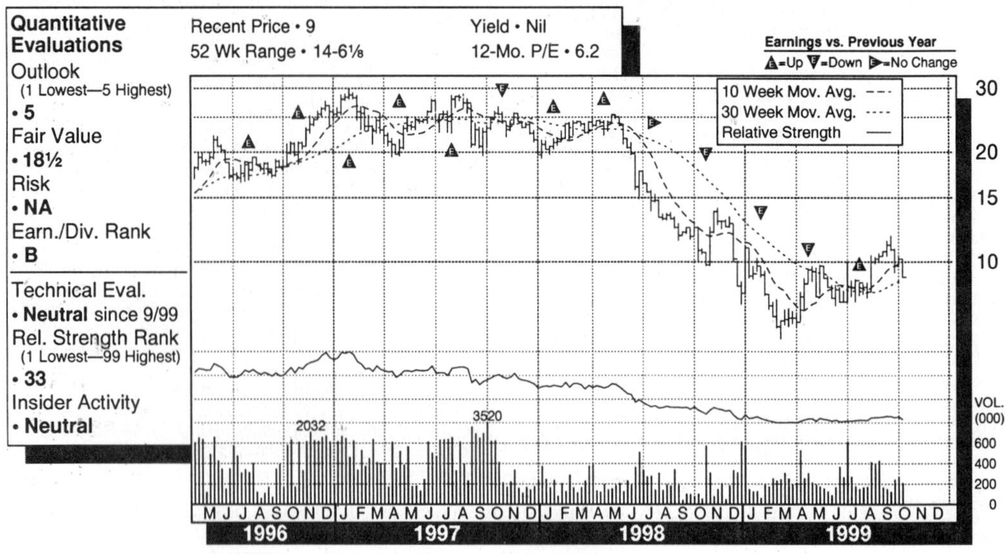

Business Profile - 25-AUG-99

TETRA Technologies is involved in an ongoing program, begun in 1998 and expanded in 1999, to enhance shareholder value and optimize profitability. The objectives of this program are tofocus on core businesses and implement a cost structure that is appropriate for the existing level of business activity. In July 1999, the company announced the sale of its noncore waste and potable water treatment business for $38.8 million, creating a $28.8 million pretax profit. Proceeds of the sale, which was effective May 1, 1999, were earmarked to reduce bank debt. The company was investigating the sale of other noncore assets.

Operational Review - 25-AUG-99

Revenues for the first half of 1999 fell 17%, year to year, reflecting a reduction in drilling activity throughout the energy industry and related pricing pressures. Gross margins declined, due primarily to the lower sales volume and the pricing pressure. Including a $4.7 million nonrecurring charge for abandoned assets, there was an operating loss of $1.2 million, in contrast to a profit of $15.5 million. However, including gains on sales of assets totaling $35.6 million, net income more than doubled to $18.6 million ($1.37 a share, on 4.9% fewer shares, before a $0.43 special charge from the cumulative effect of an accounting change), from $7.7 million ($0.54).

Stock Performance - 08-OCT-99

In the past 30 trading days, TTI's shares have declined 13%, compared to a 0.91% fall in the S&P 500. Average trading volume for the past five days was 41,440 shares, compared with the 40-day moving average of 49,818 shares.

Key Stock Statistics

Dividend Rate/Share	Nil	Shareholders	2,900
Shs. outstg. (M)	13.5	Market cap. (B)	$0.123
Avg. daily vol. (M)	0.041	Inst. holdings	81%
Tang. Bk. Value/Share	8.74		
Beta	0.99		

Value of $10,000 invested 5 years ago: $ 12,718

Fiscal Year Ending Dec. 31

	1999	1998	1997	1996	1995	1994
Revenues (Million $)						
1Q	58.00	67.34	46.87	34.19	25.27	17.91
2Q	50.31	63.79	52.40	36.71	26.08	18.93
3Q	—	52.31	60.44	45.16	28.42	23.06
4Q	—	55.03	59.71	44.73	33.70	28.60
Yr.	—	238.5	219.4	160.8	113.5	88.51
Earnings Per Share ($)						
1Q	**0.16**	**0.28**	**0.26**	**0.21**	0.15	0.08
2Q	**1.22**	**0.26**	**0.26**	**0.22**	0.15	0.10
3Q	—	**0.03**	**0.12**	**0.25**	0.19	0.10
4Q	—	**0.06**	**0.35**	**0.30**	0.23	0.20
Yr.	—	**0.64**	**0.98**	**0.97**	**0.72**	**0.48**

Next earnings report expected: late October

Dividend Data

No cash dividends have been paid on the common shares, and TTI does not expect to pay any in the foreseeable future.

A Division of The McGraw-Hill Companies

TETRA Technologies, Inc.

Business Summary - 25-AUG-99

A specialty inorganic chemical company selling products, services and process technologies to a variety of markets, TETRA Technologies' aggressive growth strategy includes both internal growth and acquisitions. In January 1999, the company acquired WyZinCo, Inc., CoZinCo Sales, Inc. and certain assets of CoZinCo, Inc. for $11.7 million in cash and notes. TETRA believes that the acquisition will significantly expand its presence in the micronutrients market.

The Specialty Chemicals Division manufactures and marketsspecialty chemicals to the energy, agriculture, water treatment, industrial, cement, food processing, ice melt and consumer products markets. This division uses proprietary technologies to convert low-cost feedstocks into high quality commercial products.

The division's Chlorides group produces liquid and dry calcium chloride and also markets hydrochloric acid. The Micronutrients groupmanufactures and distributes zinc and manganese products to the feed and fertilizer markets, as well as calcium chloride- based agricultural products. The division also markets a line of desiccant products, predominantly calcium chloride based, to the consumer products market under the trademark DampRid.

The Bromine group manufactures and distributes calcium bromide, zinc bromide and sodium bromide to the energy and water treatment markets. The division's Process Technologies group employs proprietary technologies to provide engineered systems and services that treat industrial and municipal wastewater and potablewater and, in some cases, solid waste streams, to ensure compliance with environmental effluent requirements, to achieve on-site waste minimization, and/or to recover reusable constituents. The Process Services group reduces or eliminates refinery and petrochemical waste from certain process industries.

The Oil & Gas Services Division markets chemical products,including those produced by the Specialty Chemicals Division, and systems to the oil and gas industry for use in well completion and workover operations in both domestic and international markets. It also provides associated on-site fluid engineering, fluid management and handling, and filtration services for completion and workover applications, as well as line of a specialty drilling fluids products. This division also offers oil and gas well abandonment services and production testing services.

During the third quarter of 1998, TETRA acquired from Cargill, Inc. the assets of its calcium chloride facility for $2.1 million. This business, which utilizes solar evaporation and other techniques to produce three grades of calcium chloride from underground brine reserves, is being integrated into the Specialty Chemicals Division.

Per Share Data ($) (Year Ended Dec. 31)	1998	1997	1996	1995	1994	1993	1992	1991	1990	1989
Tangible Bk. Val.	8.43	7.76	6.90	6.62	5.87	5.58	5.51	5.84	4.04	-0.35
Cash Flow	1.80	1.80	1.59	1.18	0.84	0.46	0.04	0.99	0.85	0.63
Earnings	0.64	0.98	0.97	0.72	0.48	0.07	-0.31	0.70	0.62	0.49
Dividends	Nil	Nil	Nil	Nil	Nil	Nil	Nil	Nil	Nil	Nil
Payout Ratio	Nil	Nil	Nil	Nil	Nil	Nil	Nil	Nil	Nil	Nil
Prices - High	25½	30	27¾	17⅞	12¼	9¼	15¾	21¾	16¼	NA
- Low	7⅝	19⅛	13¼	10¼	6⅝	5¾	5¾	13½	9¼	NA
P/E Ratio - High	40	31	29	25	26	NM	NM	31	26	NA
- Low	12	20	14	14	14	NM	NM	19	15	NA
Income Statement Analysis (Million $)										
Revs.	238	219	161	113	88.5	62.8	57.2	85.3	58.1	48.8
Oper. Inc.	37.6	36.6	29.1	17.4	12.6	6.1	1.2	16.2	12.4	7.1
Depr.	16.2	11.6	8.3	6.0	4.6	4.9	4.4	3.7	2.5	1.8
Int. Exp.	6.5	3.3	1.3	0.2	0.4	0.6	0.7	0.9	0.9	1.0
Pretax Inc.	14.6	23.1	20.5	14.5	9.0	1.3	-6.2	13.8	10.1	4.4
Eff. Tax Rate	39%	40%	36%	36%	33%	32%	NM	37%	34%	5.30%
Net Inc.	8.9	13.9	13.1	9.4	6.1	0.9	-3.9	8.7	6.7	4.1
Balance Sheet & Other Fin. Data (Million $)										
Cash	2.8	2.8	2.8	7.5	13.3	16.6	16.4	32.4	18.3	0.8
Curr. Assets	131	110	76.1	61.3	55.7	46.9	50.3	66.5	43.4	19.3
Total Assets	311	264	179	130	103	89.2	88.2	99	65.7	36.9
Curr. Liab.	42.6	41.8	38.7	31.2	18.4	10.8	9.7	17.2	10.5	17.1
LT Debt	110	78.5	24.7	3.9	2.3	3.2	4.7	5.8	6.9	5.8
Common Eqty.	139	130	108	89.2	77.7	71.4	70.3	73.4	45.6	13.8
Total Cap.	267	222	139	98.1	84.2	77.9	77.8	81.6	54.3	19.7
Cap. Exp.	43.2	47.4	12.1	18.0	6.0	5.3	10.2	10.4	7.0	4.2
Cash Flow	25.1	25.5	21.5	15.4	10.7	5.8	0.5	12.4	9.2	5.3
Curr. Ratio	3.1	2.6	2.0	2.0	3.0	4.3	5.2	3.9	4.1	1.1
% LT Debt of Cap.	41.3	35.4	17.7	3.9	2.7	4.1	6.0	7.2	12.8	29.9
% Net Inc.of Revs.	3.7	6.4	8.2	8.3	6.8	1.4	NM	10.2	11.5	8.5
% Ret. on Assets	3.1	6.3	8.5	8.1	6.3	1.0	NM	10.1	5.4	13.2
% Ret. on Equity	6.6	11.7	13.3	11.2	8.1	1.2	NM	14.0	22.5	16.8

Data as orig reptd.; bef. results of disc opers/spec. items. Per share data adj. for stk. divs. Bold denotes diluted EPS (FASB 128)-prior periods restated. E-Estimated. NA-Not Available. NM-Not Meaningful. NR-Not Ranked.

Office—25025 I-45 North, The Woodlands, TX 77380. **Tel**—(281) 367-1983. **Fax**—(281) 364-4306. **Website**—http://www.tetratec.com **Chrmn**—J. T. Symonds. **Pres & CEO**—A. T. McInnes. **EVP-Fin, CFO & Investor Contact**—Geoffrey M. Hertel. **Dirs**—H. Ammidon Jr, O. S. Andras, P. D. Coombs, R. S. Cunningham, T. H. Delimitros, G. M. Hertel, A. T. McInnes, K. P. Mitchell, J. T. Symonds. **Transfer Agent & Registrar**—Harris Trust & Savings Bank, NYC. **Incorporated**—in Delaware in 1981. **Empl**— 1,425. **S&P Analyst:** N.J.D.

Texas Industries

NYSE Symbol **TXI**
In S&P SmallCap 600

09-OCT-99

Industry:
Construction (Cement & Aggregates)

Summary: This company is a leading cement producer in Texas and California and also makes structural steel products.

S&P Opinion: Accumulate (★★★★)

Recent Price • 37½
52 Wk Range • 39¾-20
Yield • 0.8%
12-Mo. P/E • 10.7

Quantitative Evaluations

Outlook (1 Lowest—5 Highest)
• **4**

Fair Value
• **56¼**

Risk
• **Average**

Earn./Div. Rank
• **B**

Technical Eval.
• **Bearish** since 8/99

Rel. Strength Rank (1 Lowest—99 Highest)
• **85**

Insider Activity
• **NA**

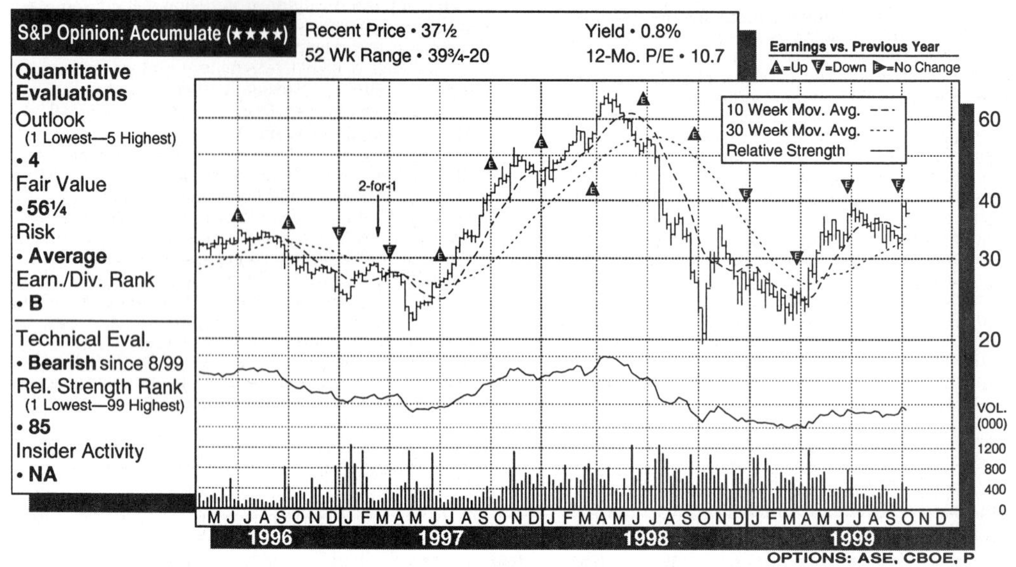

Overview - 05-OCT-99

Sales should advance at a high single-digit rate in FY 00 (May) due to the importation of cement to fill demand imbalances and the start-up of TXI's new Virginia steel mill. Despite recent slowing in residential construction spending, cement capacity continues to lag demand. While funds from the federal highway bill (TEA-21) are not likely to impact TXI until mid-2000, cement profitability remains above traditional levels due to the demand imbalance. A surge of imports from ailing Asian producers in late 1998 hurt steel operations by lowering average selling costs. However, Asia's recovery combined with a federal inquiry into dumping allegations has curtailed the importation of steel into the U.S. TXI's recently announced price hike and facility start-up should gradually lead to improved operations. The new steel facility is not expected to be accretive until FY 02.

Valuation - 05-OCT-99

TXI benefited nicely from a June pre-announcement of better than expected fiscal fourth quarter results, and more recently by structural steel price hikes. With residential and commercial building construction moderating and spending from TEA 21 nearly a year off, we believe TXI's long-term prospects in cement and aggregates remain good. However, despite near-term capacity shortages, cement prices are not expected to appreciate much due to the plentiful supply of offshore product. Furthermore, earnings will be restricted by higher depreciation and capitalized interest costs associated with a new steel plant in Virginia and expansion work on TXI's North Texas cement facility. Trading at 14X our FY 00 estimated EPS, TXI appears fairly valued near term. However, considering the long-term fundamentals, we believe the stock will outperform the market.

Key Stock Statistics

S&P EPS Est. 2000	2.70	Tang. Bk. Value/Share	22.73
P/E on S&P Est. 2000	13.9	Beta	0.50
Dividend Rate/Share	0.30	Shareholders	3,630
Shs. outstg. (M)	21.0	Market cap. (B)	$0.788
Avg. daily vol. (M)	0.073	Inst. holdings	60%

Value of $10,000 invested 5 years ago: $ 24,360

Fiscal Year Ending May 31

	2000	1999	1998	1997	1996	1995
Revenues (Million $)						
1Q	311.9	299.1	297.1	245.9	232.1	201.0
2Q	—	280.4	282.7	234.4	244.3	201.1
3Q	—	252.8	281.4	216.6	235.0	199.0
4Q	—	294.5	335.1	276.9	256.0	229.5
Yr.	—	1,127	1,196	973.8	967.4	830.5
Earnings Per Share ($)						
1Q	**0.75**	**1.17**	1.16	0.87	0.77	0.42
2Q	—	**1.01**	1.07	0.79	0.94	0.48
3Q	—	**0.48**	**0.85**	**0.47**	0.70	0.28
4Q	—	**1.25**	**1.60**	1.29	1.11	0.78
Yr.	**E2.70**	**3.92**	**4.69**	**3.42**	3.52	1.94

Next earnings report expected: mid December

Dividend Data (Dividends have been paid since 1962.)

Amount ($)	Date Decl.	Ex-Div. Date	Stock of Record	Payment Date
0.075	Oct. 20	Oct. 29	Nov. 02	Nov. 27 '98
0.075	Jan. 14	Jan. 28	Feb. 01	Feb. 26 '99
0.075	Apr. 19	Apr. 29	May. 03	May. 28 '99
0.075	Jul. 19	Jul. 29	Aug. 02	Aug. 27 '99

Texas Industries, Inc.

Business Summary - 05-OCT-99

Dallas-based Texas Industries initially operated as a cement company with the opening of its Midlothian, TX, facility in 1960, and later added steel operations in 1975.

TXI is the second largest structural steel (H-beams) supplier in North America, providing materials primarily for nonresidential construction. The company's new low-cost Richmond, VA, minimill will double structural steel capacity and produce a wider range of products. The new plant's capacity will total 1.2 million tons. However, start-up costs are expected to adversely affect results during FY 00. The Midlothian, TX, minimill (1.6 million ton capacity) produces steel beams and bar products such as rebar. The company's steel products are sold mainly to steel service centers and steel fabricators for use in the construction industry. Orders are generally filled within 45 days. Steel sales accounted for 43% of net sales and 7% of operating profit in FY 99 (May).

The largest cement producer in Texas, TXI has four production facilities in California and Texas, the two largest markets in the U.S. In March 1999, TXI began an expansion of its Midlothian, TX, cement plant, which when completed will boost the plant's construction capacity from 1.3 million to 2.8 million tons per year. TXI displaces about 35% of its fuel requirement at Midlothian by introducing alternative (waste) fuels. The unit also markets aggregates, ready-mix concrete, concrete pipe, block and brick in Texas, Louisiana, California and Colorado. As the cost of transportation limits the marketing of these products, sales are dependent on the level of construction activity near the plants. During 1999, the company sold its pipe and bridge span manufacturing facilities. Cement, aggregate and concrete product sales accounted for 57% of net sales and 93% of operating profit in FY 99.

The company is also involved in the development of surplus real estate and real estate acquired for development of high quality industrial, office and multi-use parks in Dallas/Ft. Worth, Houston, and Richmond, VA.

In February 1999, TXI announced the licensing of its patented Cemstar cement production enhancement technology to Holnam, Inc., and California Portland Cement Co. TXI noted that licensing the Cemstar technology demonstrates the viability of Cemstar as a method to increase cement production and reduce carbon emissions. Cemstar has generated average production increases of 8% in the company's Texas and California plants.

Per Share Data ($) (Year Ended May 31)	1999	1998	1997	1996	1995	1994	1993	1992	1991	1990
Tangible Bk. Val.	22.73	18.88	18.64	16.25	12.78	11.18	9.38	9.33	9.23	11.87
Cash Flow	6.64	7.54	5.82	5.68	3.92	3.06	2.15	2.23	3.04	1.65
Earnings	3.92	4.69	3.40	3.52	1.94	1.15	0.06	0.10	0.98	-0.42
Dividends	0.30	0.30	0.21	0.20	0.15	0.10	0.10	0.10	0.10	0.38
Payout Ratio	8%	6%	6%	6%	8%	9%	182%	105%	10%	NM
Cal. Yrs.	1998	1997	1996	1995	1994	1993	1992	1991	1990	1989
Prices - High	68 1/4	52	34 5/8	27 5/8	19 7/8	16 1/4	12 5/8	12 1/2	11 3/4	17 3/4
- Low	19 1/2	20 7/8	25 1/8	15 1/8	14 3/4	10 5/8	9 5/8	7	5 3/8	10 5/8
P/E Ratio - High	17	11	10	8	10	14	NM	NM	12	NM
- Low	5	4	7	4	8	9	NM	NM	5	NM
Income Statement Analysis (Million $)										
Revs.	1,127	1,196	974	967	831	716	621	606	664	659
Oper. Inc.	207	225	184	191	140	113	79.0	65.0	71.0	71.0
Depr.	74.0	62.3	53.9	49.3	49.3	43.6	46.8	47.5	45.0	43.8
Int. Exp.	11.3	20.5	18.9	20.0	20.1	26.2	32.6	34.5	34.0	31.7
Pretax Inc.	144	160	123	135	77.9	43.6	Nil	5.0	39.4	-4.4
Eff. Tax Rate	34%	33%	33%	35%	33%	36%	NM	35%	35%	NM
Net Inc.	88.7	102	75.5	80.0	48.0	25.8	1.1	1.9	22.1	-7.3
Balance Sheet & Other Fin. Data (Million $)										
Cash	17.7	16.7	19.8	28.1	26.0	31.8	33.1	20.7	23.2	42.3
Curr. Assets	310	372	344	325	293	277	261	240	227	261
Total Assets	1,531	1,186	848	801	753	749	757	777	789	703
Curr. Liab.	148	145	101	106	105	116	101	105	111	108
LT Debt	656	406	176	160	185	171	267	289	293	260
Common Eqty.	633	553	453	420	343	352	282	281	282	239
Total Cap.	1,383	1,041	747	695	567	560	645	657	661	578
Cap. Exp.	475	253	85.2	79.3	48.8	23.3	17.9	21.6	98.4	50.4
Cash Flow	163	164	129	129	97.3	69.3	47.8	49.4	67.0	36.4
Curr. Ratio	2.1	2.6	3.4	3.1	2.8	2.4	2.6	2.3	2.0	2.4
% LT Debt of Cap.	47.4	39.0	23.6	23.0	32.6	30.6	41.4	44.0	44.3	44.9
% Net Inc.of Revs.	7.7	8.5	7.8	8.3	5.8	3.6	0.2	0.3	3.3	NM
% Ret. on Assets	6.5	10.0	9.2	10.3	6.4	3.2	0.1	0.2	2.8	NM
% Ret. on Equity	15.0	20.3	17.3	21.0	13.8	7.7	0.4	0.7	8.0	NM

Data as orig reptd.; bef. results of disc opers/spec. items. Per share data adj. for stk. divs. Bold denotes diluted EPS (FASB 128)-prior periods restated. E-Estimated. NA-Not Available. NM-Not Meaningful. NR-Not Ranked.

Office—1341 W. Mockingbird Lane, Dallas, TX 75247-6913. **Tel**—(972) 647-6700. **Fax**—(972) 647-3878. **Website**—www.txi.com. **Chrmn**—G. R. Heffernan. **Pres & CEO**— R. D. Rogers. **VP-Fin & CFO**—R. M. Fowler. **VP & Secy**—R. C. Moore. **Treas & Investor Contact**—Kenneth R. Allen. **Dirs**—R. Alpert, J. M. Belk, G. E. Forward, R. I. Galland, G. R. Heffernan, J. M. Hoak, E. C. Reyes, R. D. Rogers, I. Wachtmeister, E. C. Williams. **Transfer Agent & Registrar**—ChaseMellon Shareholder Services, Ridgefield Park, NJ**Incorporated**—in Delaware in 1951. **Empl**— 4,200. **S&P Analyst:** John A. Massey

STANDARD
&POOR'S
STOCK REPORTS

Thomas Industries

NYSE Symbol **TII**

In S&P SmallCap 600

09-OCT-99

Industry:
Manufacturing (Diversified)

Summary: TII makes compressors and vacuum pumps, pneumatic construction equipment, and leakage detection systems. It also owns a minority interest in a manufacturer of lighting fixtures.

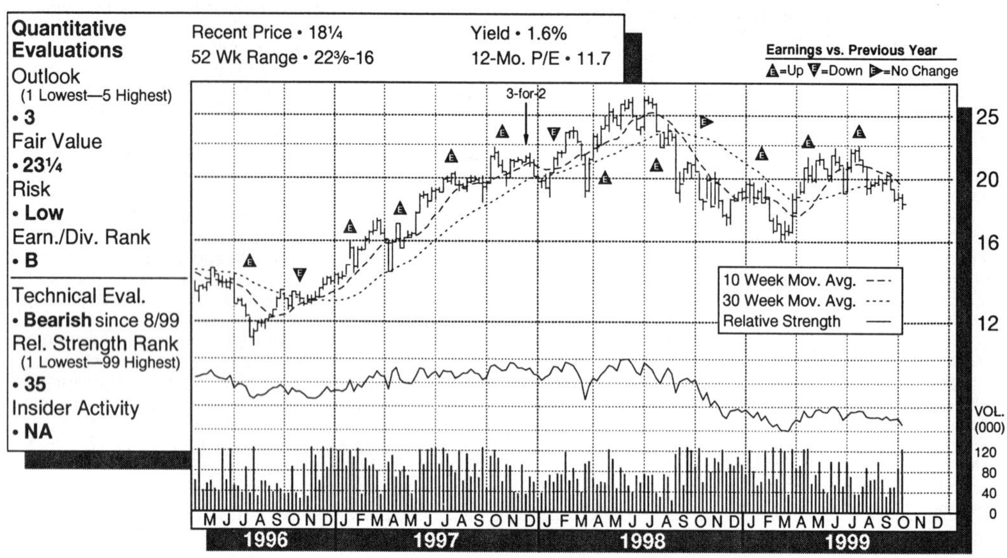

Business Profile - 01-JUL-99

Thomas Industries said in its first quarter 1999 report that its compressor and vacuum pump business was off to a slow start in 1999 as OEMs (original equipment manufacturers) and distributors adjusted inventories in 1998 and in early 1999. However, sales orders and operating profits were up since the fourth quarter of 1998. Thomas anticipated continued earnings improvements for compressors and vacuum pumps. Although it acknowledged some uncertainties in the global economy, the company expected record earnings for 1999.

Operational Review - 01-JUL-99

Net sales for the first quarter of 1999 declined 4.0%, primarily due to lower sales in the European Compressor & Vacuum Pump segment. However, 60% larger equity income from lighting (the 32%-owned Genlyte Thomas Group LLC joint venture that was formed in August 1998), enabled operating profit to increase 9.4%. After 47% lower total other expenses (net), pretax income moved ahead 18%. Following taxes at 40.4%, versus 37.0%, net income was up 12%, to $5.9 million ($0.36 a share), from $5.3 million ($0.32), restated.

Stock Performance - 08-OCT-99

In the past 30 trading days, TII's shares have declined 8%, compared to a 0.91% fall in the S&P 500. Average trading volume for the past five days was 33,580 shares, compared with the 40-day moving average of 15,662 shares.

Key Stock Statistics

Dividend Rate/Share	0.30	Shareholders	2,041
Shs. outstg. (M)	15.8	Market cap. (B)	$0.289
Avg. daily vol. (M)	0.018	Inst. holdings	69%
Tang. Bk. Value/Share	11.59		
Beta	0.77		

Value of $10,000 invested 5 years ago: $ 23,317

Fiscal Year Ending Dec. 31

	1999	1998	1997	1996	1995	1994
Revenues (Million $)						
1Q	48.21	141.9	126.4	123.5	117.6	109.4
2Q	47.47	46.33	140.0	127.9	127.4	117.3
3Q	—	43.15	141.2	129.6	128.8	119.0
4Q	—	39.53	140.2	129.1	116.8	110.8
Yr.	—	177.2	547.7	510.1	490.6	456.6
Earnings Per Share ($)						
1Q	**0.36**	**0.32**	**0.25**	**0.16**	0.11	0.07
2Q	**0.45**	**0.42**	**0.39**	**0.37**	0.25	0.33
3Q	—	**0.43**	**0.43**	**0.28**	0.31	0.19
4Q	—	**0.33**	**0.31**	**1.09**	0.17	0.11
Yr.	—	**1.50**	**1.38**	**1.09**	**0.83**	**0.25**

Next earnings report expected: late October

Dividend Data (Dividends have been paid since 1955.)

Amount ($)	Date Decl.	Ex-Div. Date	Stock of Record	Payment Date
0.075	Oct. 15	Dec. 02	Dec. 04	Jan. 01 '99
0.075	Feb. 11	Mar. 03	Mar. 05	Apr. 01 '99
0.075	Apr. 15	Jun. 02	Jun. 04	Jul. 01 '99
0.075	Jul. 15	Sep. 01	Sep. 03	Oct. 01 '99

A Division of The McGraw-Hill Companies

Thomas Industries Inc.

Business Summary - 01-JUL-99

Founded in 1928, Thomas Industries believes that research leading to new and improved products is the key to keeping one step ahead of the competition. A new strategic focus, that was finalized in 1994, led the company to divest its non-core businesses and concentrate on lighting and compressors & vacuum pumps. Significant additions to these businesses in lighting operations included the acquisitions of Lumec and Day-Brite Lighting in 1987 and 1989; and compressor & vacuum pump acquisitions, which included ASF, Pneumotive, Brey, WISA, and Welch, made from 1987 through 1996.

Thomas is the leading supplier of compressors and vacuum pumps to the original equipment manufacturer (OEM) market in such applications as medical equipment, gasoline vapor and refrigerant recovery, automotive and transportation applications, printing, tape drives, laboratory equipment, and many other applications for consumer, commercial, and industrial uses. The company manufactures and sells these products through operations that are located worldwide.

Thomas offers a wide selection of standard air compressors and vacuum pumps and will modify or design products to meet exacting OEM applications. For the OEM market, the company's compressors and vacuum pump products are manufactured under the names Thomas in the U.S. and ASF Thomas in Europe. Other vertically integrated products are marketed under the Welch (high vacuum systems for laboratory and chemical markets), Air-Pac (pneumatic construction equipment), Vakuumatic (leakage detection systems), and Medi-Pump (respiratory products) brand names.

The medical equipment market, which includes oxygen concentrators, nebulizers, aspirators, and other devices, is important to Thomas. Worldwide sales to medical equipment OEMs were $65 million in 1998. Oxygen concentrator OEMs represent about 50% of the total sales in the medical equipment market.

In August 1998, Thomas and The Genlyte Group formed a lighting joint venture that combined substantially all of the assets and liabilities of Genlyte and substantially all of the lighting assets and related liabilities of Thomas to create Genlyte Thomas Group LLC (GTG), estimated to be the third largest lighting fixture manufacturer in North America. As of year-end 1998, Thomas owned 32% of GTG, and Genlyte owned the balance.

GTG manufactures lighting fixtures for a wide variety of applications in the commercial, industrial, and residential markets. GTG operates in these three industry segments through the following divisions: Lightolier, Controls, Wide-Lite, Hadco, Diamond F, Supply (Crescent, ExceLine, and Stonco product lines), Consumer, Indoor, Accent, and Outdoor in the United States and Mexico; and Canlyte, Thomas Lighting Canada, Lumec, and ZED in Canada.

Per Share Data ($) (Year Ended Dec. 31)	1998	1997	1996	1995	1994	1993	1992	1991	1990	1989
Tangible Bk. Val.	11.59	7.38	6.27	5.39	4.71	4.06	4.19	4.58	4.60	4.56
Cash Flow	1.93	2.37	2.07	1.80	1.73	1.35	0.95	1.33	1.75	2.10
Earnings	1.50	1.38	1.09	0.83	0.70	0.25	-0.13	0.25	0.77	1.35
Dividends	0.30	0.28	0.27	0.27	0.27	0.27	0.27	0.51	0.51	0.49
Payout Ratio	20%	20%	25%	32%	38%	NM	NM	201%	65%	36%
Prices - High	26¾	22⅜	15⅞	16⅛	11	9⅜	9⅜	9⅞	13⅞	13¾
- Low	16⅞	13⅝	11	9⅛	8½	6⅛	5⅝	6⅛	6⅛	11¾
P/E Ratio - High	18	16	15	19	16	37	NM	39	18	10
- Low	11	10	10	11	12	24	NM	24	8	9
Income Statement Analysis (Million $)										
Revs.	177	548	510	491	457	450	421	408	462	437
Oper. Inc.	31.3	57.5	49.8	44.5	38.7	37.8	32.2	33.4	45.3	42.3
Depr.	7.2	16.0	15.7	14.8	15.5	16.5	16.3	16.1	15.0	11.5
Int. Exp.	6.2	6.5	7.3	8.2	9.2	10.3	10.4	11.0	12.2	10.5
Pretax Inc.	39.4	35.6	27.7	21.1	18.2	7.8	0.2	7.2	20.2	34.8
Eff. Tax Rate	38%	37%	37%	39%	42%	51%	919%	48%	42%	41%
Net Inc.	24.5	22.5	17.4	12.8	10.5	3.8	-2.0	3.8	11.7	20.6
Balance Sheet & Other Fin. Data (Million $)										
Cash	18.2	17.4	18.8	18.3	5.1	2.4	3.5	14.2	21.0	30.1
Curr. Assets	64.2	177	170	165	155	153	141	142	156	178
Total Assets	282	328	320	314	305	303	294	303	323	333
Curr. Liab.	34.4	84.4	84.5	83.9	77.8	74.4	70.1	66.3	67.5	74.5
LT Debt	48.3	55.0	62.6	70.8	80.0	88.0	90.0	93.0	109	117
Common Eqty.	191	173	158	143	134	125	130	139	142	139
Total Cap.	245	228	229	222	221	221	221	237	256	259
Cap. Exp.	7.0	17.7	15.1	12.3	16.3	13.9	13.2	11.6	21.6	15.5
Cash Flow	31.7	38.5	33.1	27.6	26.1	20.3	14.3	19.9	26.7	32.1
Curr. Ratio	1.9	2.1	2.0	2.0	2.0	2.1	2.0	2.1	2.3	2.4
% LT Debt of Cap.	19.7	24.1	27.4	31.9	36.0	39.6	40.6	39.4	42.5	45.3
% Net Inc.of Revs.	13.8	4.1	3.5	2.6	2.3	0.8	NM	0.9	2.5	4.7
% Ret. on Assets	8.0	6.9	5.5	4.1	3.5	1.3	NM	1.2	3.6	7.6
% Ret. on Equity	13.5	13.6	11.6	9.2	811.0	3.0	NM	2.7	8.4	15.6

Data as orig. reptd.; bef. results of disc. opers. and/or spec. items. Per share data adj. for stk. divs. as of ex-div. date. Bold denotes diluted EPS (FASB 128). E-Estimated. NA-Not Available. NM-Not Meaningful. NR-Not Ranked.

Office—4360 Brownsboro Rd., Louisville, KY 40207. **Tel**—(502) 893-4600. **Website**—http://www.thomasind.com **Chrmn, Pres & CEO**—T. C. Brown. **VP, CFO & Secy**—P. J. Stuecker. **Investor Contact**—Laurie Lyons. **Dirs**—T. C. Brown, W. H. Dunbar, H. J. Ferguson, G. P. Gardner, L. E. Gloyd, W. M. Jordan, F. J. Lunding Jr., A. A. Massaro. **Transfer Agent & Registrar**—Fifth Third Bank, Cincinnati.**Empl**— 1,050. **S&P Analyst:** N.J.D.

STANDARD
&POOR'S
STOCK REPORTS

Thomas Nelson, Inc.

NYSE Symbol **TNM**

In S&P SmallCap 600

23-OCT-99 **Industry:** Publishing

Summary: This company is a leading publisher, producer and distributor of books with primarily religious themes, as well as a seller of a broad line of gift and and stationery products.

Quantitative Evaluations

Outlook
(1 Lowest—5 Highest)
• 3+

Fair Value
• 10⅜

Risk
• Average

Earn./Div. Rank
• B+

Technical Eval.
• NA

Rel. Strength Rank
(1 Lowest—99 Highest)
• 49

Insider Activity
• NA

Recent Price • 9¼
52 Wk Range • 14-8
Yield • 1.7%
12-Mo. P/E • 15.4

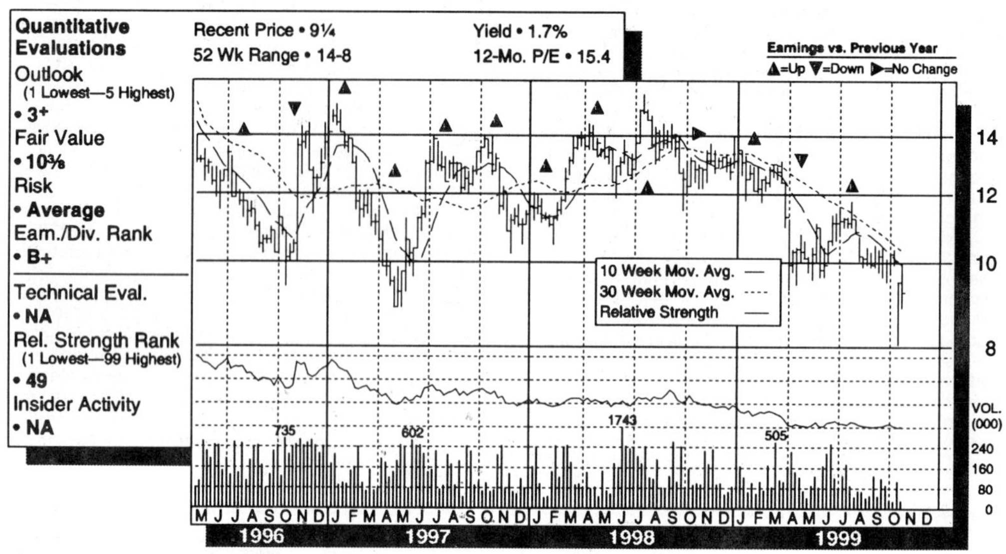

Business Profile - 22-OCT-99

Thomas Nelson announced in August 1999 that its new book release "When Christ Comes" has gotten its second quarter (FY 00 Mar.) off to a strong start, and also noted that the company's strong financial position has enabled it to redeploy its resources toward other business opportunities. The company's gift business is still adjusting to last year's restructuring, and management is refocusing the efforts of its field sales force, which it believes will likely have a positive impact on second-half performance. As of June 30, 1999, TNM had repurchased about 2.9 million shares of common stock at a total price of $39.1 million under its repurchase program over the past 12 months.

Operational Review - 22-OCT-99

Revenues for the quarter ended June 30, 1999, rose 5.6%, year to year, as higher publishing revenues outweighed a drop in gift sales due to the timing of certain new book releases. Profitability benefited from the strength in publishing revenues, a 1.7% drop in SG&A costs, and only slightly higher interest and depreciation and amortization expenses. Net income advanced 9.9%, to $1,380,000 ($0.10 a share, on 29% fewer shares), from $19,991,000 ($0.08).

Stock Performance - 22-OCT-99

In the past 30 trading days, TNM's shares have declined 7%, compared to a 4% fall in the S&P 500. Average trading volume for the past five days was 6,140 shares, compared with the 40-day moving average of 14,149 shares.

Key Stock Statistics

Dividend Rate/Share	0.16	Shareholders	2,000
Shs. outstg. (M)	14.2	Market cap. (B)	$0.125
Avg. daily vol. (M)	0.010	Inst. holdings	47%
Tang. Bk. Value/Share	4.91		
Beta	0.40		

Value of $10,000 invested 5 years ago: $ 5,258

Fiscal Year Ending Mar. 31

	2000	1999	1998	1997	1996	1995
Revenues (Million $)						
1Q	59.12	55.99	54.46	55.18	60.30	49.10
2Q	—	70.45	68.62	65.21	80.53	70.51
3Q	—	66.58	64.66	63.56	86.24	71.09
4Q	—	68.62	65.22	59.49	81.34	74.41
Yr.	—	261.6	253.0	243.4	308.4	265.1
Earnings Per Share ($)						
1Q	0.10	0.08	0.06	0.01	-0.01	-0.04
2Q	—	0.27	0.27	0.21	0.25	0.42
3Q	—	0.27	0.24	0.23	0.13	0.36
4Q	—	-0.06	0.16	0.14	-0.72	0.14
Yr.	—	0.58	0.73	0.56	-0.06	0.88

Next earnings report expected: early November

Dividend Data (Dividends have been paid since 1989.)

Amount ($)	Date Decl.	Ex-Div. Date	Stock of Record	Payment Date
0.040	Nov. 19	Jan. 28	Feb. 01	Feb. 15 '99
0.040	Feb. 18	May. 06	May. 10	May. 24 '99
0.040	May. 20	Jul. 29	Aug. 02	Aug. 16 '99
0.040	Aug. 19	Oct. 28	Nov. 01	Nov. 15 '99

A Division of The McGraw-Hill Companies

Thomas Nelson, Inc.

Business Summary - 22-OCT-99

Thomas Nelson, Inc. (TNM) is a leading publisher and distributor of books emphasizing Christian, inspirational and family value themes. TNM's publishing business accounted for about 64% of FY 99 (Mar.) revenues. The company also produces specialty gift items, including journals, photo albums, kitchen accessories and stationery, which contributed about 36% of FY 99 revenues. Over the past two years, the company began emphasizing its core book and gift businesses. Notably, TNM sold its music division in January 1997 for $120 million and discontinued the operations of its Royal Media division in the fourth quarter of 1996.

The company's books are published under imprints including Thomas Nelson, Word, J. Countryman and Tommy Nelson, and consist of inspirational, trade, gift, children's and reference books emphasizing Christian and family value themes. TNM distributes books mainly through Christian bookstores, general bookstores, mass merchandisers and and direct sales to consumers. The company also distributes books published by other companies to complement their marketing and distribution capabilities.

TNM's book publishing business is enhanced by its extensive marketing and distribution channels, which enable the company to more successfully sign and renew contracts with popular authors than its competitors because of its ability to reach a wider audience.

Virtually all Bibles and related products currently published in the U.S. are based on one of 13 major translations. Of these 13 translations, 12 are protected by copyright laws which grant the copyright owner the exclusive right to control the publication of the of such translation for a limited term. Approximately 71% of the company's FY 99 revenues were generated through sales of its proprietary Bible products.

Electronic Bibles and biblical reference books are published under the Nelson Electronic Publishing imprint. These products include electronic collections centered on Bible study; electronic libraries featuring well-known authors, such as Jack Hayford, John MacArthur, John Maxwell and Charles Stanley.

TNM's gift division more than doubled in size in FY 96, as a result of the acquisition of C.R. Gibson, and nearly doubled in size again in FY 97. In FY 98, however, gift revenues declined slightly, due to a change in product focus away from the mass merchandisers stationery category. In FY 99, gift revenues increased, primarily due to higher sales of a special selection of products, including scrapbooks, to mass merchandisers. Current lines offered through the company include journals and gift books, photo albums, baby and wedding memory books, scrapbooks, kitchen accessories and stationary.

Per Share Data ($)										
(Year Ended Mar. 31)	**1999**	**1998**	**1997**	**1996**	**1995**	**1994**	**1993**	**1992**	**1991**	**1990**
Tangible Bk. Val.	4.91	5.84	5.18	2.38	2.74	1.93	0.87	3.68	2.62	2.26
Cash Flow	1.24	1.24	1.05	0.18	1.31	0.97	0.67	0.60	0.50	0.41
Earnings	0.58	0.73	0.56	-0.39	0.88	0.66	0.49	0.48	0.42	0.32
Dividends	0.16	0.16	0.16	0.16	0.13	0.13	0.11	0.09	0.07	0.03
Payout Ratio	28%	22%	29%	NM	15%	20%	22%	19%	18%	10%
Cal. Yrs.	1998	1997	1996	1995	1994	1993	1992	1991	1990	1989
Prices - High	15⅝	15¼	16¾	26½	20¼	20¾	15¾	9½	5⅞	4¾
- Low	10½	8⅞	9⅜	12½	14¼	11⅜	8¼	5⅜	3¼	3¼
P/E Ratio - High	27	21	30	NM	23	32	32	20	14	15
- Low	18	12	17	NM	16	17	17	11	8	10
Income Statement Analysis (Million $)										
Revs.	262	253	243	308	265	228	138	93.1	73.6	59.4
Oper. Inc.	31.4	33.4	33.4	8.7	31.9	24.2	14.6	11.0	8.5	6.9
Depr.	9.0	8.6	8.4	9.0	5.9	4.2	2.4	1.5	1.0	0.9
Int. Exp.	6.7	6.1	8.4	10.7	8.6	6.9	2.9	0.9	1.3	0.9
Pretax Inc.	14.0	20.3	15.1	-10.4	18.3	13.3	9.4	9.0	6.7	5.6
Eff. Tax Rate	37%	37%	37%	NM	36%	34%	33%	35%	36%	41%
Net Inc.	8.9	12.7	9.5	-6.2	11.7	8.8	6.4	5.9	4.3	3.3
Balance Sheet & Other Fin. Data (Million $)										
Cash	0.6	39.7	43.5	0.7	0.8	0.8	0.8	0.7	1.3	0.3
Curr. Assets	163	185	197	237	184	150	119	61.7	49.7	35.1
Total Assets	255	285	302	374	250	216	192	76.8	58.4	41.6
Curr. Liab.	44.3	44.8	65.5	65.6	54.2	45.9	36.7	17.4	16.9	13.2
LT Debt	79.5	79.6	83.5	180	120	103	92.8	9.7	13.9	4.6
Common Eqty.	126	156	147	122	72.7	62.7	55.4	49.1	26.9	23.8
Total Cap.	210	239	234	306	194	167	150	59.4	41.5	28.4
Cap. Exp.	4.2	3.3	1.9	4.2	2.2	3.2	11.1	3.2	2.4	0.5
Cash Flow	17.8	21.3	18.0	2.8	17.6	12.9	8.8	7.4	5.3	4.2
Curr. Ratio	3.7	4.1	3.0	3.6	3.4	3.3	3.2	3.5	2.9	2.7
% LT Debt of Cap.	37.9	33.2	35.7	58.9	61.8	62.0	62.0	16.3	33.4	16.2
% Net Inc.of Revs.	3.4	5.0	4.0	NM	4.4	3.8	4.6	6.4	5.6	5.6
% Ret. on Assets	3.3	4.3	2.9	NM	5.0	4.3	4.7	7.9	8.7	8.3
% Ret. on Equity	6.3	8.4	7.1	NM	17.3	14.7	12.1	14.2	17.2	14.5

Data as orig. reptd.; bef. results of disc. opers. and/or spec. items. Per share data adj. for stk. divs. as of ex-div. date. Bold denotes diluted EPS (FASB 128). E-Estimated. NA-Not Available. NM-Not Meaningful. NR-Not Ranked.

Office—501 Nelson Place, Nashville, TN 37214-1000. **Tel**—(615) 889-9000. **Website**—http://www.thomasnelson.com.**Chrmn, Pres & CEO**—S. Moore. **EVP & Secy**—J. L. Powers. **Dirs**— B. O. Currey, W. L. Davis Jr., S. J. Moore, S. Moore, R. J. Neibel, M. V. Oakley, J. M. Rodgers, S. Young.**Transfer Agent**—SunTrust Co. Bank, Atlanta, GA. **Incorporated**—in Tennessee in 1961. **Empl**— 1,130. **S&P Analyst:** Matthew C. Hershberg

STANDARD
&POOR'S
STOCK REPORTS

Thor Industries

NYSE Symbol **THO**

In S&P SmallCap 600

09-OCT-99

Industry: Leisure Time (Products)

Summary: Thor is the second largest manufacturer of recreational vehicles in the U.S. and Canada and the largest producer of mid-size buses.

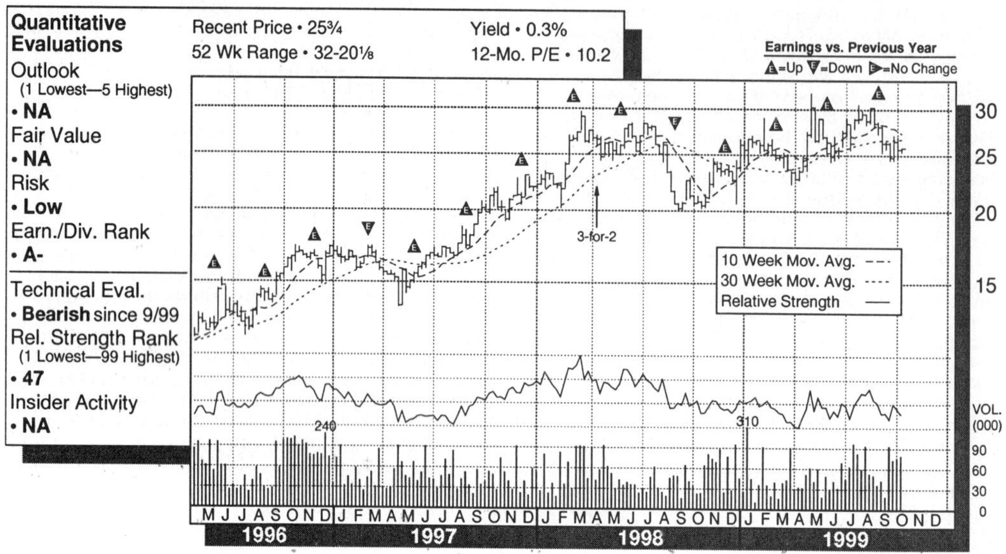

Business Profile - 23-SEP-99

In FY 99 (Jul.) recreational vehicle sales rose 8% and bus sales climbed 29%, reflecting the February 1998 acquisition of Champion Bus, Inc. Sales continued strong into August 1999, with net sales up 18% for the month, and net income up 48%. Backlog at September 1, 1999, was $230 million, up 29% from the level a year earlier. In May 1999, THO said construction of a new 165,000 sq. ft. motor plant for Four Winds was under way. At July 31, 1999, cash totaled $68.9 million, and the balance sheet showed no debt. In December 1998, THO sold its Thor West operations, which incurred an operating loss of $3.9 million on revenues of $29.2 million in FY 98.

Operational Review - 23-SEP-99

Based on a preliminary report, net sales increased 13% in the fiscal year ended July 31, 1999, reflecting increased bus sales. Gross margins widened; despite higher selling, general and administrative expenses, operating income climbed 47%. Aided by higher interest income and lower other expenses, after taxes at 41.3% in each period, net income soared 59%, to $30,766,000 ($2.53 a share), from $19,395,000 ($1.59).

Stock Performance - 08-OCT-99

In the past 30 trading days, THO's shares have declined 8%, compared to a 0.91% fall in the S&P 500. Average trading volume for the past five days was 15,740 shares, compared with the 40-day moving average of 12,792 shares.

Key Stock Statistics

Dividend Rate/Share	0.08	Shareholders	192
Shs. outstg. (M)	12.1	Market cap. (B)	$0.313
Avg. daily vol. (M)	0.018	Inst. holdings	44%
Tang. Bk. Value/Share	9.89		
Beta	0.93		

Value of $10,000 invested 5 years ago: $ 15,407

Fiscal Year Ending Jul. 31

	1999	1998	1997	1996	1995	1994
Revenues (Million $)						
1Q	189.2	165.5	150.5	151.5	139.2	128.2
2Q	165.5	134.5	123.5	119.8	114.4	90.78
3Q	223.7	206.9	169.3	169.2	163.1	129.0
4Q	227.4	208.7	181.1	161.6	146.1	143.1
Yr.	805.8	715.6	624.4	602.1	562.7	491.1
Earnings Per Share ($)						
1Q	**0.57**	**0.45**	**0.37**	0.33	0.43	0.40
2Q	**0.44**	**0.28**	**0.13**	0.15	0.17	0.15
3Q	**0.73**	**0.50**	**0.36**	0.31	0.28	0.26
4Q	**0.77**	**0.35**	**0.45**	0.43	0.15	0.39
Yr.	**2.53**	**1.58**	**1.31**	1.21	1.03	1.20

Next earnings report expected: late October

Dividend Data (Dividends have been paid since 1987.)

Amount ($)	Date Decl.	Ex-Div. Date	Stock of Record	Payment Date
0.020	Dec. 14	Dec. 21	Dec. 23	Jan. 04 '99
0.020	Feb. 16	Mar. 17	Mar. 19	Apr. 02 '99
0.020	May. 17	Jun. 15	Jun. 17	Jul. 02 '99
0.020	Sep. 03	Sep. 23	Sep. 27	Oct. 08 '99

Thor Industries, Inc.

Business Summary - 23-SEP-99

Thor Industries produces a wide range of recreation vehicles (RVs) and small and mid-size buses in the U.S. and Canada. It conducts operations through two business segments: RVs, which contributed 77% of revenues and 74% of profits in FY 98 (Jul.); and bus products, which accounted for 23% and 26%, respectively.

Principal operating subsidiaries and their products, as of year-end FY 98, were as follows.

Airstream's products are premium and medium-high priced travel trailers and motorhomes sold under the model names Airstream Classic, Land Yacht, and Cutter. Airstream Classic vehicles are distinguished by their rounded shape and bright aluminum finish and, in management's judgment, constitute the most recognized product in the industry. Responding to demands for a lighter, lower-cost product, Airstream also makes the Airstream Safari and Bambi travel trailers.

Dutchmen makes conventional travel trailers and fifth wheels, sold under the names Dutchmen and Four Winds. Aero Manufacturing's products are lightweight, European-styled travel trailers designed for towing behind cars, mini vans, and sport utility vehicles. Aero also makes folding camping trailers sold under the Dutchmen and Skamper names.

Four Winds makes conventional Class C and Class A motorhomes, sold under the Four Winds, Hurricane, Infinity, WindSport, Dutchmen and Chateau names. Thor America products are moderate and lower-priced travel trailers and fifth wheels, sold under the names Citation and Chateau.

Thor Indiana makes laminated fifth wheels and travel trailers, sold under the names Signature and Fifth Avenue. Citair is one of the largest Canadian producers of moderately priced travel trailers, fifth wheels, Class C motorhomes, and truck campers. Citair operates under the name General Coach, and sells under the names Citation and Corsair.

Komfort products are travel trailers and fifth wheels, sold primarily in the western U.S. and western Canada. Thor California's products are conventional travel trailers and fifth wheels, sold under the names Wanderer and Tahoe, primarily in the western U.S.

ElDorado National's makes small and mid-size buses for transit, airport car rental and hotel/motel shuttles, paramedical transit for hospitals and nursing homes, and tour and charter operations. Buses are built under the names Aerotech, Escort, MST, Transmark, and EZ Rider.

Champion Bus (acquired February 1998) makes small and mid-size buses, sold under the names Challenger, Contender, and SoLo. Thor Bus (ElDorado National and Champion) is believed to be the largest manufacturer of small and mid-size commercial buses in North America.

Per Share Data ($) **(Year Ended Jul. 31)**	**1999**	**1998**	**1997**	**1996**	**1995**	**1994**	**1993**	**1992**	**1991**	**1990**
Tangible Bk. Val.	NA	9.89	8.31	7.39	6.21	5.32	6.06	5.34	3.80	3.25
Cash Flow	NA	1.94	1.79	1.59	1.39	1.54	1.17	1.04	0.20	0.44
Earnings	2.53	1.58	1.43	1.21	1.03	1.20	0.85	0.77	0.05	0.31
Dividends	0.08	0.08	0.08	0.08	0.08	0.08	0.08	0.06	0.05	0.05
Payout Ratio	3%	5%	6%	7%	8%	7%	9%	10%	100%	17%
Prices - High	32	29 5/8	23 1/8	17 1/2	14 1/2	20 1/4	19 1/8	18 5/8	10 1/8	4 3/4
- Low	22 1/4	20	13 5/8	10 7/8	11 5/8	12 1/2	10	8 1/8	4 1/4	3
P/E Ratio - High	13	19	16	14	14	17	23	24	NM	15
- Low	9	13	9	9	11	10	12	11	NM	10
Income Statement Analysis (Million $)										
Revs.	NA	716	624	602	563	491	412	273	141	163
Oper. Inc.	NA	39.5	34.1	31.8	27.6	32.0	23.7	17.9	2.3	5.5
Depr.	NA	4.4	4.5	5.0	4.8	4.5	4.3	3.0	1.6	1.4
Int. Exp.	NA	0.2	0.6	0.6	0.3	0.3	1.1	1.4	0.2	Nil
Pretax Inc.	NA	33.1	30.0	27.2	22.6	26.8	18.8	14.4	0.9	5.6
Eff. Tax Rate	NA	41%	41%	41%	39%	40%	40%	42%	39%	40%
Net Inc.	NA	19.4	17.8	16.0	13.8	16.0	11.3	8.4	0.6	3.4
Balance Sheet & Other Fin. Data (Million $)										
Cash	NA	43.5	13.4	13.0	6.8	13.6	10.6	21.7	19.1	15.2
Curr. Assets	NA	174	133	130	105	102	82.9	81.6	51.4	44.1
Total Assets	NA	214	175	175	148	142	123	124	74.0	57.0
Curr. Liab.	NA	74.6	51.1	55.0	39.4	45.5	41.0	52.4	32.3	15.3
LT Debt	NA	Nil	Nil	Nil	Nil	Nil	Nil	Nil	Nil	Nil
Common Eqty.	NA	138	122	119	108	95.9	80.8	71.1	40.8	40.9
Total Cap.	NA	138	122	119	108	95.9	80.8	71.1	41.3	41.5
Cap. Exp.	NA	2.1	1.8	4.7	5.2	4.3	1.8	2.0	1.0	1.6
Cash Flow	NA	23.8	22.3	21.0	18.5	20.6	15.6	11.4	2.2	4.8
Curr. Ratio	NA	2.3	2.6	2.4	2.7	2.2	2.0	1.6	1.6	2.9
% LT Debt of Cap.	NA	Nil	Nil	Nil	Nil	Nil	Nil	Nil	Nil	Nil
% Net Inc.of Revs.	NA	2.7	2.9	2.7	2.5	3.3	2.7	3.1	0.4	2.1
% Ret. on Assets	NA	10.0	10.2	9.8	9.5	12.1	9.1	7.8	0.9	6.0
% Ret. on Equity	NA	14.9	14.8	14.0	13.5	18.1	14.8	13.8	1.4	8.5

Data as orig reptd.; bef. results of disc opers/spec. items. Per share data adj. for stk. divs. Bold denotes diluted EPS (FASB 128)-prior periods restated. E-Estimated. NA-Not Available. NM-Not Meaningful. NR-Not Ranked.

Office—419 W. Pike St., Jackson Center, OH 45334-0629. **Tel**—(937) 596-6849. **Chrmn, Pres & CEO**—W. F. B. Thompson. **Vice Chrmn & Treas**—P. B. Orthwein. **SVP-Fin & Secy**—W. L. Bennett. **Dirs**—N. D. Chrisman, P. B. Orthwein, A. Siegel, J. H. Suwinski, W. F. B. Thompson, W. C. Tomson. **Transfer Agent & Registrar**—Bank One, Indianapolis. **Incorporated**—in Delaware in 1983. **Empl**— 3,051. **S&P Analyst:** J.W.H.

STANDARD & POOR'S
STOCK REPORTS

Three-Five Systems

NYSE Symbol **TFS**

In S&P SmallCap 600

09-OCT-99

Industry: Electrical Equipment

Summary: This company makes liquid crystal display modules used in cellular telephones, office product equipment and other areas.

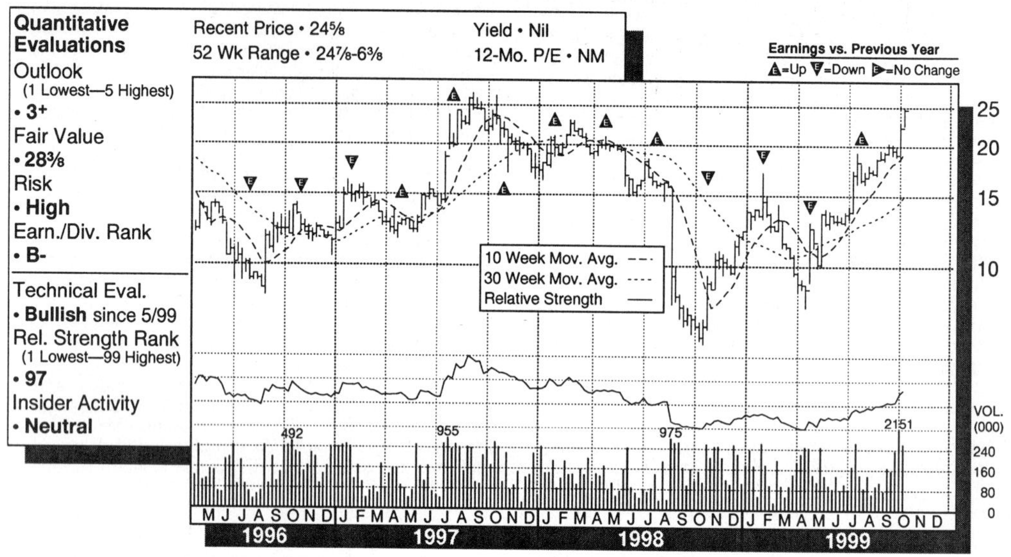

Business Profile - 07-JUN-99

The company seeks to identify industries that offer the greatest long-term potential for growth, and then to focus on technological developments to meet current and future requirements of these industries. TFS won several important design awards in the first quarter of 1999, including wins at 3Com, Sperry, and a major U.S.-based telecommunications company. These customers are new to TFS and have products in networking, marine applications, and cellular telephones. The company also received a design win at a new division of an existing customer for a telecommunications product. The company anticipates that production for these designs will commence in the second half of 1999. If all the new designs go into production, the expected sales from these products alone would exceed $30 million, equal to 32% of TFS's 1998 revenues.

Operational Review - 07-JUN-99

Net sales in the three months ended March 31, 1999, rose 25%, year to year, primarily reflecting new business in Asia for Motorola, Inc., the company's key customer. Gross margins narrowed on a less favorable product mix and under-absorption of fixed overhead; an operating loss contrasted with operating income. With net interest expense, versus income, and after a tax benefit of $960,000 versus taxes at 40.0%, a net loss of $642,000 ($0.09 a share, on 14% fewer shares) contrasted with net income of $995,000 ($0.12).

Stock Performance - 08-OCT-99

In the past 30 trading days, TFS's shares have increased 33%, compared to a 0.91% fall in the S&P 500. Average trading volume for the past five days was 95,360 shares, compared with the 40-day moving average of 88,672 shares.

Key Stock Statistics

Dividend Rate/Share	Nil	Shareholders	1,160
Shs. outstg. (M)	7.0	Market cap. (B)	$0.174
Avg. daily vol. (M)	0.151	Inst. holdings	20%
Tang. Bk. Value/Share	7.32		
Beta	1.68		

Value of $10,000 invested 5 years ago: $ 14,006

Fiscal Year Ending Dec. 31

	1999	1998	1997	1996	1995	1994
Revenues (Million $)						
1Q	23.04	18.48	16.13	18.08	24.48	16.42
2Q	31.60	22.68	18.74	14.46	22.10	21.25
3Q	—	24.57	24.07	13.12	24.22	23.67
4Q	—	29.31	25.70	15.06	20.78	24.14
Yr.	—	95.05	84.64	60.71	91.59	85.48
Earnings Per Share ($)						
1Q	**-0.09**	**0.12**	0.10	0.09	0.41	0.27
2Q	**0.15**	**0.14**	0.13	0.02	0.35	0.43
3Q	—	**-0.05**	0.19	-0.70	0.17	0.42
4Q	—	**0.12**	**0.23**	0.09	0.11	0.46
Yr.	—	**0.33**	**0.65**	**-0.49**	**1.04**	**1.59**

Next earnings report expected: mid October

Dividend Data

No cash dividend has ever been paid. A two-for-one stock split was effected in 1994.

A Division of The McGraw-Hill Companies

Three-Five Systems, Inc.

Business Summary - 07-JUN-99

Three-Five Systems is an innovator of visual communicatons technology and products. It designs and manufacturers user interface devices for operational control and information display functions in products of original equipment manufacturers. The company specializes in liquid crystal display (LCD) and light emitting diode (LED) components and technology, which account for more than 90% of its revenues, in providing its custom design and manufacturing services for customers in the communications, medical electronics, industrial process control, wireless data collection, instrumentation, consumer electronic, automotive equipment, military control and office automation marketplaces.

In 1998, the company's largest customer, Motorola Inc., accounted for 64% of net sales, compared with about 35% in 1997, while Hewlett-Packard accounted for 6.6% of net sales in 1998.

An LCD modifies light that passes through or is reflected by it, rather than emitting light like an LED. An LCD generally consists of a layer of liquid crystalline material suspended between two glass plates. The crystals align themselves in a predictable manner, and this alignment changes when stimulated electrically. The changed alignment produces a visual representation of the information desired when used in conjunction with a polarizer and either natural ambient light or an external light source. An LED chip produces light as the result of the application of direct current at a low voltage. Different wavelengths (colors) can be produced in a product depending upon the manufacturing process and the impurity added to the basic chip material.

Visible standard devices include solid-state lamps used for indicators, status lights, on-board circuit monitors and instrumentation; multi-digit numerical displays used for calculators, industrial controls, data terminals, instrumentation timers, hand-held instruments, event counters and PCB diagnostics; displays used for hand-held terminals, minicomputers, telecommunications and instrumentation word processors; bar graph displays used for power meters in stereo systems, ham and CB radio meters and other various types of meters; and multi-digit numeric displays used for industrial controls, data terminals, test equipment, point-of-sale, minicomputer readout and home consumer.

Infrared standard devices include emitters and silicon detectors used for TV remote controls, disk and tape drives, printers, encoders, solid-state relays, photoelectric controls, switches, intrusion alarms, touch screens and sensors.

TFS believes that it is positioned to continue the growth that it experienced in 1997 and 1998 as a result of its efforts in expanding its customer base and the markets it serves as well as its strength in designing, prototyping, and producing, a wide range of display modules required in the end products of OEMs. In the past few years, TFS has refocused its research and development capabilities with the intention of developing display technologies and manufacturing processes that will be useful for its current and future customers.

Per Share Data ($) (Year Ended Dec. 31)	1998	1997	1996	1995	1994	1993	1992	1991	1990	1989
Tangible Bk. Val.	7.29	7.15	6.56	7.12	6.03	1.50	0.68	-0.57	-0.73	-1.42
Cash Flow	0.93	1.16	-0.04	1.32	1.75	0.67	0.20	0.07	0.15	0.08
Earnings	0.33	0.65	-0.49	1.04	1.59	0.59	0.14	0.03	0.10	0.02
Dividends	Nil	Nil	Nil	Nil	Nil	Nil	Nil	Nil	Nil	Nil
Payout Ratio	Nil	Nil	Nil	Nil	Nil	Nil	Nil	Nil	Nil	Nil
Prices - High	23	26 7/8	22 3/4	38 7/8	50	17 5/8	2 3/8	1 7/8	9/16	NA
- Low	6 3/8	11 5/8	8 3/8	16	16 5/8	1 11/16	1	1/2	3/8	NA
P/E Ratio - High	70	41	NM	37	31	30	17	63	6	NA
- Low	19	18	NM	15	10	3	7	17	4	NA
Income Statement Analysis (Million $)										
Revs.	95.0	84.6	60.7	91.6	85.5	38.0	20.8	18.7	17.0	10.8
Oper. Inc.	9.1	12.4	-3.5	15.6	21.1	7.1	1.9	0.9	1.5	0.5
Depr.	4.7	4.1	3.5	2.3	1.2	0.6	0.4	0.3	0.4	0.3
Int. Exp.	NA	NA	3.5	NA	NA	0.1	0.2	0.2	0.2	0.1
Pretax Inc.	4.4	8.6	-6.8	14.0	20.7	6.2	1.2	0.3	0.6	0.1
Eff. Tax Rate	41%	39%	NM	40%	39%	33%	13%	7.10%	Nil	Nil
Net Inc.	2.6	5.2	-3.8	8.4	12.5	4.1	1.0	0.2	0.6	0.1
Balance Sheet & Other Fin. Data (Million $)										
Cash	4.9	16.4	12.6	4.5	27.1	0.8	0.6	0.6	0.6	0.3
Curr. Assets	41.0	42.7	31.3	29.9	47.0	14.4	7.9	6.3	7.2	3.5
Total Assets	77.9	72.8	62.6	63.8	56.3	17.5	9.8	8.4	9.2	4.6
Curr. Liab.	16.2	13.6	9.8	7.5	9.4	6.9	3.4	3.5	4.5	1.5
LT Debt	7.4	Nil	Nil	Nil	0.2	0.2	1.7	0.8	0.7	0.3
Common Eqty.	51.1	56.5	51.2	55.2	46.6	10.2	4.7	-2.2	-2.9	-4.3
Total Cap.	61.7	59.2	52.8	56.3	46.9	10.5	6.4	4.9	4.6	3.0
Cap. Exp.	8.1	3.0	0.9	27.1	7.4	1.9	0.3	0.7	0.4	0.1
Cash Flow	7.3	9.4	-0.3	10.7	13.8	4.7	1.4	0.5	1.0	0.3
Curr. Ratio	2.5	3.1	3.2	4.0	5.0	2.1	2.3	1.8	1.6	2.4
% LT Debt of Cap.	12.1	Nil	Nil	Nil	0.3	1.7	27.0	15.9	14.9	9.3
% Net Inc.of Revs.	2.7	6.2	NM	9.2	14.7	10.9	4.9	1.3	3.7	0.9
% Ret. on Assets	3.4	7.7	NM	14.1	32.8	29.9	9.3	2.7	8.0	NA
% Ret. on Equity	4.8	9.7	NM	16.6	43.0	55.0	NA	NM	NM	NA

Data as orig reptd.; bef. results of disc opers/spec. items. Per share data adj. for stk. divs. Bold denotes diluted EPS (FASB 128)-prior periods restated. E-Estimated. NA-Not Available. NM-Not Meaningful. NR-Not Ranked.

Office—1600 N. Desert Dr., Tempe, AZ 85281. **Tel**—(602) 389-8600. **Fax**—(602) 389-8836. **Website**—http://www.threefive.com **Chrmn**—D. C. Malmberg. **Pres & CEO**—D. R. Buchanan. **EVP, CFO, Treas & Secy**—J. D. Buchanan. **Dirs**—J. D. Buchanan, K. M. Julien, G. R. Long, D. C. Malmberg, T. H. Werner. **Transfer Agent & Registrar**—Bank of New York, NYC. **Incorporated**—in Delaware in 1990. **Empl**— 867. **S&P Analyst:** M.I.

Timberland Co.

NYSE Symbol **TBL**

In S&P SmallCap 600

09-OCT-99

Industry: Footwear

Summary: This company designs, engineers and markets footwear, apparel and accessories; core products consist of waterproof boots, shoes and apparel.

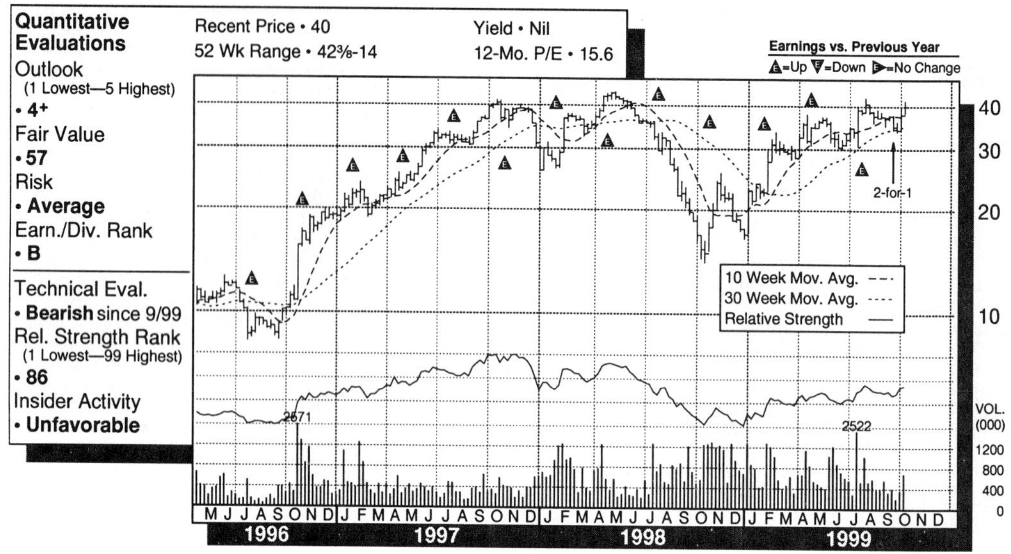

Business Profile - 29-SEP-99

In July 1998, the company introduced a line of "cooling" hiking boots, featuring ComforTemp thermal management materials from Frisby Technologies, Inc., that allow wearers to experience cooler inner temperatures in warm weather conditions. Timberland will initially use ComforTemp in three hiking boot models and trail running footwear. Also in July, directors authorized a 2-for-1 stock split of its Class A and B common shares. In the previous month, directors authorized the repurchase of up to one million additional shares of the company's Class A common stock. Timberland completed another one million share buyback program in October 1998.

Operational Review - 29-SEP-99

Revenues in the six months ended June 25, 1999, rose 7.2%, primarily due to increases in footwear, apparel, and accessories unit sales. Gross margins widened, helped by a greater proportion of higher margin retail revenue. Following well-controlled operating expenses and a reduction in interest costs, net income advanced 11%, to $10,244,000 ($0.45 a share; adjusted for September 1999 2-for-1 split), from $9,266,000 ($0.39).

Stock Performance - 08-OCT-99

In the past 30 trading days, TBL's shares have increased 7%, compared to a 0.91% fall in the S&P 500. Average trading volume for the past five days was 135,700 shares, compared with the 40-day moving average of 82,969 shares.

Key Stock Statistics

Dividend Rate/Share	Nil	Shareholders	900
Shs. outstg. (M)	21.1	Market cap. (B)	$0.658
Avg. daily vol. (M)	0.081	Inst. holdings	20%
Tang. Bk. Value/Share	11.13		
Beta	1.56		

Value of $10,000 invested 5 years ago: $ 14,988

Fiscal Year Ending Dec. 31

	1999	1998	1997	1996	1995	1994
Revenues (Million $)						
1Q	176.9	163.1	150.7	127.7	141.6	108.1
2Q	152.9	144.7	132.2	113.7	125.1	126.9
3Q	—	291.9	274.7	227.6	212.6	222.2
4Q	—	262.5	238.9	221.1	175.8	180.4
Yr.	—	862.2	796.5	690.0	655.1	637.5
Earnings Per Share ($)						
1Q	**0.34**	**0.31**	**0.18**	-0.05	0.04	-0.07
2Q	**0.10**	**0.08**	**0.03**	-0.30	-0.92	0.01
3Q	—	**1.24**	**1.05**	**0.76**	0.32	0.72
4Q	—	**0.90**	**0.74**	**0.49**	0.04	0.13
Yr.	—	**2.52**	**2.02**	**0.91**	**-0.53**	**0.79**

Next earnings report expected: mid October

Dividend Data

Amount ($)	Date Decl.	Ex-Div. Date	Stock of Record	Payment Date
2-for-1	Jul. 28	Sep. 16	Aug. 31	Sep. 15 '99

The Timberland Company

Business Summary - 29-SEP-99

Known as the "Boot Company" due to its trademark outdoor shoe, Timberland Co. designs, engineers and distributes, under the Timberland brand, premium-quality footwear, apparel and accessories products for men, women and children. The attributes of the company's products are functional performance, classic styling and lasting protection from the elements.

The company has recently benefited from a footwear fashion shift toward "brown shoes" (outdoor and sporty style footwear). Sales for the footwear and apparel & accessories divisions were 76.9% and 23.1% in 1998, versus 75.4% and 24.6% in 1997, respectively.

Sales to international markets represented 29% of sales in 1998.

Timberland products are sold primarily through independent retailers, better-grade department stores and athletic stores that reinforce the qualities of the Timberland brand. In addition, products are sold in Timberland specialty stores and Timberland factory outlet stores. As of December 31, 1998, Timberland operated a chain of 30 retail and 44 factory outlet stores throughout the world (17 retail and 37 factory outlets in the U.S.). U.S. shops accounted for 19% of 1998 total sales.

From its origins of producing a yellow "work boot," Timberland now offers a wide range of footwear in five product categories: men's footwear, women's footwear, performance footwear, boots, and kids' footwear.

Timberland's men's and women's 1998 footwear products included the Work Casual, Casual, Boat Shoes, Sandals and Rugged collections. The performance footwear line is designed for outdoor activities, and the kids' footwear is based on the models of the company's adult shoes.

To complement its footwear business, Timberland also markets apparel, which includes rugged outerwear, sweaters, shirts, pants and shorts. Although women's apparel is not currently offered, the company is evaluating alternatives for a women's line. Timberland's boy's apparel is designed, manufactured and distributed through a licensee. In 1998, the company entered into a license agreement with Paramount Headwear to design, manufacture and distribute hats and caps beginning in 1999. The company also expanded its apparel accessory offerings to include watches, men's belts, day packs and travel gear, socks and legwear, gloves and eyewear and men's small leather goods.

Timberland has two manufacturing facilities in Puerto Rico and the Dominican Republic. During 1998, the company manufactured approximately 20% of its footwear unit volume. The remaining footwear products, apparel and accessories were produced by independent manufacturers and licensees in Asia, Europe, and Latin America. The company distributes its products through three company-managed facilities in Kentucky, Ontario, California, and Holland.

Per Share Data ($) (Year Ended Dec. 31)	1998	1997	1996	1995	1994	1993	1992	1991	1990	1989
Tangible Bk. Val.	11.13	8.54	6.41	5.34	5.63	5.08	3.97	3.44	3.06	2.54
Cash Flow	3.33	2.88	1.85	0.34	1.48	1.47	0.95	0.67	0.61	0.48
Earnings	2.52	2.02	0.91	-0.52	0.79	1.00	0.59	0.38	0.36	0.30
Dividends	Nil	Nil	Nil	Nil	Nil	Nil	Nil	Nil	Nil	Nil
Payout Ratio	Nil	Nil	Nil	Nil	Nil	Nil	Nil	Nil	Nil	Nil
Prices - High	43⅞	41½	20⅛	18⅜	30½	42¾	10	5¼	6¼	7¾
- Low	14	18⅜	8¼	8¾	10	9½	4⅜	2⅞	2½	4⅜
P/E Ratio - High	17	21	22	NM	39	42	17	14	17	26
- Low	6	9	9	NM	13	9	7	8	7	15
Income Statement Analysis (Million $)										
Revs.	862	796	690	655	638	419	291	226	196	156
Oper. Inc.	114	104	72.3	28.2	58.4	50.7	33.8	23.7	21.8	17.5
Depr.	19.2	20.3	21.4	19.1	15.3	10.3	8.0	6.3	5.3	4.0
Int. Exp.	9.5	14.8	20.6	22.9	15.1	6.3	5.5	5.8	6.5	5.0
Pretax Inc.	87.0	67.6	30.9	-18.8	28.1	34.1	19.0	11.7	11.0	9.1
Eff. Tax Rate	32%	30%	34%	NM	37%	34%	32%	31%	29%	30%
Net Inc.	59.2	47.3	20.4	-11.6	17.7	22.5	12.9	8.1	7.8	6.4
Balance Sheet & Other Fin. Data (Million $)										
Cash	152	99	93.3	38.4	6.4	3.3	1.2	7.5	1.6	5.0
Curr. Assets	388	342	372	338	374	221	138	119	118	103
Total Assets	469	420	450	421	473	291	194	173	170	148
Curr. Liab.	95.7	99	102	70.0	107	65.4	43.4	26.3	29.3	17.6
LT Debt	100	100	172	199	207	90.8	41.5	44.2	46.9	46.7
Common Eqty.	266	215	165	142	149	128	105	93.4	85.7	74.9
Total Cap.	374	321	348	351	366	225	151	147	141	131
Cap. Exp.	20.7	25.7	15.1	13.5	31.5	21.6	11.8	7.5	9.1	6.9
Cash Flow	78.4	67.6	41.8	7.5	33.1	32.8	20.9	14.4	13.1	10.4
Curr. Ratio	4.0	3.5	3.6	4.8	3.5	3.4	3.2	4.5	4.0	5.8
% LT Debt of Cap.	26.8	31.2	49.4	56.7	56.5	40.3	27.6	30.1	33.3	35.7
% Net Inc.of Revs.	6.9	5.9	2.9	NM	2.8	5.4	4.4	3.6	4.0	4.1
% Ret. on Assets	13.3	10.9	4.7	NM	4.6	9.3	7.0	4.7	4.9	4.5
% Ret. on Equity	24.6	24.9	13.3	NM	12.7	19.3	13.0	9.0	9.8	8.8

Data as orig reptd.; bef. results of disc opers/spec. items. Per share data adj. for stk. divs. Bold denotes diluted EPS (FASB 128)-prior periods restated. E-Estimated. NA-Not Available. NM-Not Meaningful. NR-Not Ranked.

Office—200 Domain Dr., Stratham, NH 03885. **Tel**—(603) 772-9500. **Website**—http://www.timberland.com **Chrmn**—S. W. Swartz. **Pres & CEO**—J. B. Swartz. **SVP & CFO**—G. J. Hibner. **Dirs**—R. M. Agate, J. F. Brennan, I. W. Diery, J. A. Fitzsimmons, V. H. Kent, I. K. Nooyi, J. B. Swartz, S. W. Swartz, A. Zaleznik. **Transfer Agent & Registrar**—First National Bank of Boston. **Incorporated**—in Delaware in 1978; predecessor incorporated in 1933. **Empl**— 5,200. **S&P Analyst:** Howard Choe

STANDARD &POOR'S
STOCK REPORTS

Titan International

NYSE Symbol **TWI**
In S&P SmallCap 600

11-OCT-99 **Industry:** Trucks & Parts

Summary: This company is a leading global maker of steel wheels and rims for off-highway vehicles.

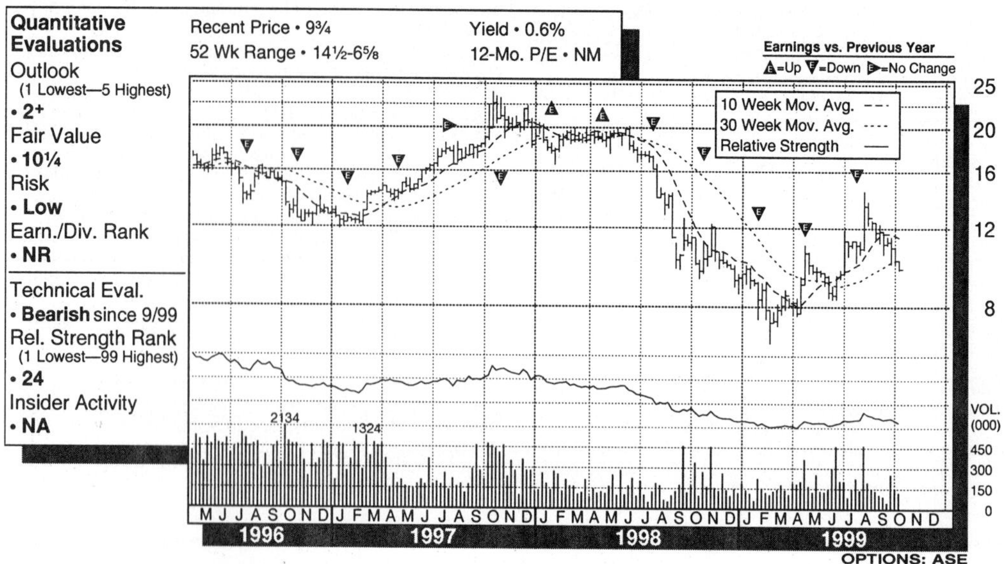

Business Profile - 11-OCT-99

In September 1999, a letter of intent for the company to merge into Carlisle Companies Inc. expired. However, TWI said it expected further discussions with Carlisle. A new plant in Texas is expected to enable TWI to offer a full line of off-highway tires. As a result, the company plans to increase its aftermarket sales to 50% of the total. In July 1999, TWI reached a new labor agreement with workers at its Walcott, IA, facility. The company projected 1999 capital expenditures at $40 million to $50 million. In mid-1998, TWI entered the South American market by purchasing an 81% interest in Uruguay-based FUNSA ($36 million), a maker of car radial and specialty tires. In the first half of 1999, the company bought back 300,000 common shares; an additional 3.1 million shares are authorized for repurchase.

Operational Review - 11-OCT-99

Net sales in the first half of 1999 declined 14%, year to year, reflecting lower production volumes in the agricultural and earthmoving/construction markets, due to the impact of strikes at the Des Moines, IA, and Natchez, MS tire plants, and facility shutdowns at several large customers; consumer market sales advanced 11%. Gross margins narrowed, on inefficiencies resulting from the strike. With higher selling, general and administrative expenses, and increased interest expense, net income plunged to $393,000 ($0.02 a share, on 4.7% fewer shares), from $13.1 million ($0.60).

Stock Performance - 08-OCT-99

In the past 30 trading days, TWI's shares have declined 17%, compared to a 0.91% fall in the S&P 500. Average trading volume for the past five days was 23,620 shares, compared with the 40-day moving average of 26,190 shares.

Key Stock Statistics

Dividend Rate/Share	0.06	Shareholders	727
Shs. outstg. (M)	20.6	Market cap. (B)	$0.201
Avg. daily vol. (M)	0.028	Inst. holdings	48%
Tang. Bk. Value/Share	9.65		
Beta	0.99		

Value of $10,000 invested 5 years ago: $ 8,819

Fiscal Year Ending Dec. 31

	1999	1998	1997	1996	1995	1994
Revenues (Million $)						
1Q	158.6	187.4	180.2	177.3	157.7	91.90
2Q	159.1	181.2	187.4	167.0	157.6	102.7
3Q	—	149.2	156.7	145.7	149.5	97.83
4Q	—	142.9	165.9	144.6	158.3	114.6
Yr.	—	660.8	690.1	634.5	623.2	407.0
Earnings Per Share ($)						
1Q	**0.01**	**0.38**	**0.36**	**0.40**	0.56	0.24
2Q	**0.01**	**0.22**	**0.38**	**0.38**	0.55	0.31
3Q	—	**0.02**	**0.17**	**0.34**	0.40	0.26
4Q	—	**-0.25**	**0.19**	**0.18**	0.43	0.33
Yr.	—	**0.38**	**1.10**	**1.30**	**1.50**	1.14

Next earnings report expected: mid October

Dividend Data (Dividends have been paid since 1993.)

Amount ($)	Date Decl.	Ex-Div. Date	Stock of Record	Payment Date
0.015	Dec. 10	Dec. 29	Dec. 31	Jan. 15 '99
0.015	Mar. 10	Mar. 29	Mar. 31	Apr. 15 '99
0.015	Jun. 10	Jun. 28	Jun. 30	Jul. 15 '99
0.015	Sep. 10	Sep. 28	Sep. 30	Oct. 15 '99

A Division of The McGraw-Hill Companies

Titan International, Inc.

Business Summary - 11-OCT-99

Titan Wheel International did not reinvent itself when it changed its name in May 1997 to Titan International (TWI); the company is still a leading global manufacturer of steel wheels and tires for off-highway equipment. TWI's Engineered Products, including Tractech and Automation International, were divested in 1996, reflecting the company's effort to focus on core business.

TWI usually makes both the wheels and the tires for vehicles, and increasingly also assembles the completed wheel-tire system. The company offers more than 25,000 different products, and continues to focus on expanding its core operations through product innovation. In 1997, TWI developed the Grizz LSW series of wheels and tires; this line is expected to considerably enhance the performance of off-highway vehicles, by providing less bounce and heat build-up, and more stability and safety for the operator.

The company plans to increase its penetration of the aftermarket for tires and wheels, expand its presence in Europe and other global markets, focus on acquisitions, and continue to improve its operating efficiencies. During 1998, TWI purchased a wheel company in Europe, a majority interest in a South American tire company, and interests in an Asian wheel maker and a North American tire company, with combined sales in excess of $145 million. The company spent $4.1 million in 1998 for equipment and construction related to the Brownsville, TX facility. In 1998, TWI generated 26% of revenues from foreign operations, in Europe and South America, and exported 16% of its sales.

In 1998, the agricultural market accounted for 50% of sales, the consumer market for 24%, and earthmoving and construction equipment 26%. Wheels, rims, and tires are sold to original equipment manufacturers (OEMs) of tractors, combines, plows, planters, and irrigation equipment; Deere and Co. accounted for 16% of 1998 sales, with the 10 largest customers providing 46% of total sales. Consumer products include wheels and tires for boat and camping trailers, lawn and garden equipment, and specialty cars and light trucks. Earthmoving and construction vehicles such as cranes, graders and levelers, scrapers, shovel and back-hoe loaders, load transporters, and haul trucks roll on Titan wheels.

In March 1997, TWI completed a tender offer for up to 5,000,000 common shares. Shareholders tendered 3,763,919 shares at $15 each, representing about 15% of the shares outstanding. The company was acquired in a 1990 management-led leveraged buyout by MascoTech, Inc. and certain investors; it went public in 1993.

Firm backlog at February 28, 1999, totaled $193 million, down from $230 million a year earlier.

Per Share Data ($) (Year Ended Dec. 31)	1998	1997	1996	1995	1994	1993	1992	1991	1990	1989
Tangible Bk. Val.	9.86	9.50	10.07	7.25	3.93	2.76	2.93	NA	NA	NA
Cash Flow	1.98	2.46	0.91	3.08	2.21	0.84	NA	NA	NA	NA
Earnings	0.38	1.10	1.57	1.91	1.14	0.46	0.41	NA	NA	NA
Dividends	0.06	0.06	0.06	0.04	0.01	0.01	NA	NA	NA	NA
Payout Ratio	16%	5%	4%	2%	1%	3%	NA	NA	NA	NA
Prices - High	20 3/8	24	18 1/8	21 1/8	13 5/8	11 1/2	NA	NA	NA	NA
- Low	8 1/2	11 7/8	12	11 5/8	9 5/8	6 5/8	NA	NA	NA	NA
P/E Ratio - High	54	22	12	11	12	25	NA	NA	NA	NA
- Low	23	11	8	6	8	15	NA	NA	NA	NA
Income Statement Analysis (Million $)										
Revs.	661	690	635	623	407	150	129	NA	NA	NA
Oper. Inc.	65.9	84.5	78.9	96.5	55.4	18.5	NA	NA	NA	NA
Depr.	34.7	30.9	28.0	23.4	17.4	5.3	NA	NA	NA	NA
Int. Exp.	18.3	15.1	10.7	12.0	8.5	3.2	1.1	NA	NA	NA
Pretax Inc.	13.1	40.5	59.1	63.3	30.1	10.1	NA	NA	NA	NA
Eff. Tax Rate	38%	38%	37%	40%	39%	37%	NA	NA	NA	NA
Net Inc.	8.2	25.1	35.0	38.0	18.5	6.4	5.1	NA	NA	NA
Balance Sheet & Other Fin. Data (Million $)										
Cash	14.1	21.2	27.4	14.2	7.3	29.3	NA	NA	NA	NA
Curr. Assets	312	299	285	265	192	142	NA	NA	NA	NA
Total Assets	678	585	559	512	400	261	89.0	NA	NA	NA
Curr. Liab.	142	115	104	114	72.4	50.9	NA	NA	NA	NA
LT Debt	248	182	113	142	178	124	15.0	NA	NA	NA
Common Eqty.	247	248	301	216	100	66.7	40.3	NA	NA	NA
Total Cap.	518	451	433	374	297	201	NA	NA	NA	NA
Cap. Exp.	64.9	38.3	36.7	20.2	15.2	5.4	NA	NA	NA	NA
Cash Flow	42.9	56.1	63.3	61.4	35.9	11.7	NA	NA	NA	NA
Curr. Ratio	2.2	2.6	2.8	2.3	2.7	2.8	NA	NA	NA	NA
% LT Debt of Cap.	47.8	40.4	26.1	38.1	60.1	61.6	NA	NA	NA	NA
% Net Inc.of Revs.	1.2	3.6	5.6	6.1	4.5	4.2	4.0	NA	NA	NA
% Ret. on Assets	1.3	4.4	6.6	8.3	5.5	3.8	NA	NA	NA	NA
% Ret. on Equity	3.3	9.2	13.7	24.0	21.8	17.3	NA	NA	NA	NA

Data as orig reptd.; bef. results of disc opers/spec. items. Per share data adj. for stk. divs. Bold denotes diluted EPS (FASB 128)-prior periods restated. E-Estimated. NA-Not Available. NM-Not Meaningful. NR-Not Ranked.

Office—2701 Spruce St., Quincy, IL 62301. **Tel**—(217) 228-6011. **Website**—http://www.titan-intl.com **Pres & CEO**—M. M. Taylor Jr. **VP & COO**—M. Samide. **VP-Fin & CFO**—K. W. Hackamack.**Secy**—C. T Holley. **Investor Contact**—Phillip Stanhope (515-265-9438). **Dirs**—E. H. Billig, E. J. Campbell, R. K. Cashin Jr., A. J. Febbo, M. I. Quain, A. I. Soave, M. M. Taylor Jr. **Transfer Agent & Registrar**—Harris Trust & Savings Bank, Chicago. **Incorporated**—in Illinois in 1983. **Empl**— 5,600. **S&P Analyst:** Stewart Scharf

STANDARD
&POOR'S
STOCK REPORTS

TNP Enterprises

NYSE Symbol **TNP**

In S&P SmallCap 600

09-OCT-99 **Industry:** Electric Companies

Summary: In late May 1999, TNP agreed to be acquired by an investor group in a transaction expected to close in the first quarter of 2000.

Quantitative Evaluations

Outlook (1 Lowest—5 Highest)
• **2**

Fair Value
• **39½**

Risk
• **Low**

Earn./Div. Rank
• **B**

Technical Eval.
• **Bullish** since 9/99

Rel. Strength Rank (1 Lowest—99 Highest)
• **77**

Insider Activity
• **NA**

Recent Price • 39
52 Wk Range • 40½-28
Yield • 3.0%
12-Mo. P/E • 18.3

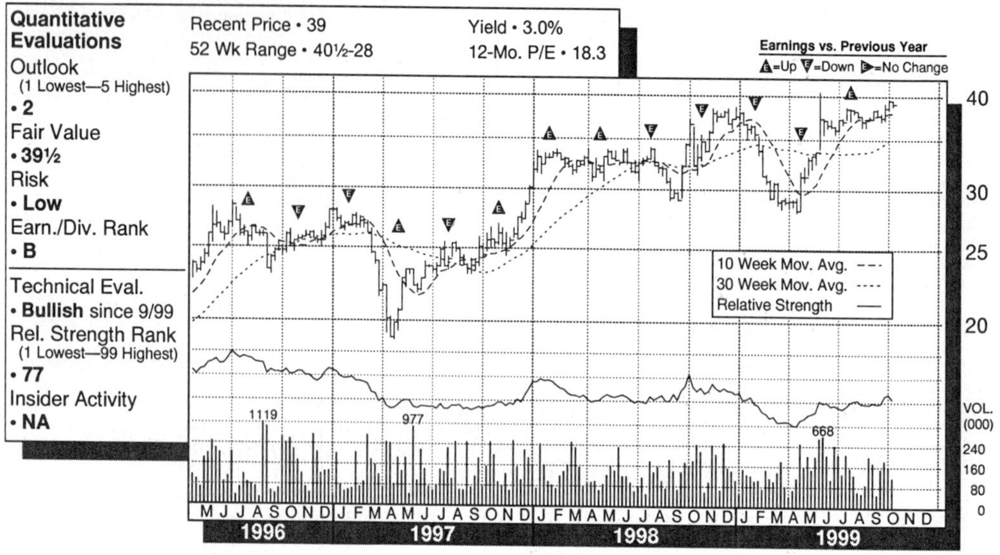

Business Profile - 07-SEP-99

In May 1999, TNP Enterprises agreed to be acquired by an investor group for approximately $1 billion, including the assumption of debt. The merger agreement, expected to close by the first quarter of 2000, calls for TNP shareholders to receive $44 a share in cash, or a 39% premium over its previous 30 day average price. The transaction is subject to the availability of financing and the approval of shareholders and various regulatory agencies. A shareholder vote is scheduled for September 22. In July, the company stated that electric utility restructuring legislation passed during 1999 in Texas and New Mexico generally confirmed or enhanced its pre-existing transition plans.

Operational Review - 07-SEP-99

Operating revenues from continuing operations for the six months ended June 30, 1999, declined 2.2%, year to year, as Texas rate reductions and the loss of certain business with industrial customers was partially offset by growth in the customer base and accounting adjustments relating to electricity deregulation. Profitability benefited from reduced purchased power and fuel expense, a doubling of net other income, and 18% lower interest charges due to debt refinancing and reduced debt levels. Income from continuing operations rose 42%, to $15,536,000 ($1.17 a share, after preferred dividends), from $10,961,000 ($0.83). Results for the 1998 period exclude a loss of $7.1 million ($0.54) from discontinued operations.

Stock Performance - 08-OCT-99

In the past 30 trading days, TNP's shares have increased 5%, compared to a 0.91% fall in the S&P 500. Average trading volume for the past five days was 23,040 shares, compared with the 40-day moving average of 28,510 shares.

Key Stock Statistics

Dividend Rate/Share	1.16	Shareholders	3,481
Shs. outstg. (M)	13.4	Market cap. (B)	$0.524
Avg. daily vol. (M)	0.030	Inst. holdings	62%
Tang. Bk. Value/Share	23.19		
Beta	0.48		

Value of $10,000 invested 5 years ago: $ 30,136

Fiscal Year Ending Dec. 31

	1999	1998	1997	1996	1995	1994
Revenues (Million $)						
1Q	118.1	124.6	128.4	99.8	105.7	107.6
2Q	144.0	143.1	136.0	122.0	121.2	111.0
3Q	—	189.4	197.6	157.4	151.6	149.9
4Q	—	129.4	135.7	123.4	107.3	109.5
Yr.	—	586.5	585.2	502.7	485.8	478.0
Earnings Per Share ($)						
1Q	**0.23**	**0.39**	**0.38**	**0.05**	-0.57	-0.29
2Q	**0.93**	**0.44**	**0.68**	**0.72**	0.54	-2.04
3Q	—	**1.58**	**1.73**	**1.37**	2.44	1.09
4Q	—	**0.02**	**0.29**	**0.19**	0.20	-0.47
Yr.	—	**2.42**	**3.08**	**2.27**	**2.98**	-1.70

Next earnings report expected: early November

Dividend Data (Dividends have been paid since 1936.)

Amount ($)	Date Decl.	Ex-Div. Date	Stock of Record	Payment Date
0.290	Feb. 16	Feb. 24	Feb. 26	Mar. 15 '99
0.250	Feb. 11	Feb. 25	Mar. 01	Mar. 15 '99
0.290	May. 03	May. 19	May. 21	Jun. 15 '99
0.290	Aug. 09	Aug. 25	Aug. 27	Sep. 15 '99

TNP Enterprises, Inc.

Business Summary - 07-SEP-99

On May 25, 1999, TNP Enterprises agreed to be acquired by an investor group for approximately $1 billion, including the assumption of debt. Expected to close by early 2000, the merger agreement calls for TNP shareholders to receive $44 a share in cash, or a 39% premium over its previous 30 day average price. The transaction is subject to the availability of financing and the approval of shareholders and various regulatory agencies. In May 1999, directors stated that this transaction will permit TNP to remain a stand alone utility and avoid being swallowed up in the current era of industry consolidation. No changes in management or employees are expected as a result of the acquisition.

TNP's business operations are primarily conducted by its utility subsidiary, Texas-New Mexico Power Co. (TNMP). TNMP provides electric service to 85 Texas and New Mexico municipalities and adjacent rural areas with more than 228,000 customers at the end of 1998. Utility operations are divided into three regions. The Gulf Coast region (50% of 1998 revenues) includes the area along the Texas Gulf Coast between Houston and Galveston. The North-Central region (28% of revenue) extends from Lewisville, TX, to municipalities along the Red River, and the Mountain region (20% of revenue) includes areas in southwest and south-central New Mexico, and far west Texas. Sales in all regions are primarily to retail customers. Total electricity sales in 1998 were 9,843 GWH, down 3% from 1997.

The company purchased 80% of its electric requirements in 1998. TNP owns one 300 MW lignite-fueled generating facility, TNP One, which provided approximately 20% of TNP's total energy requirements. Power generated at TNP One is transmitted over the company's own transmission lines to other utilities' transmission systems for delivery to TNP's Texas service area systems.

TNP has actively embraced the coming era of electricity deregulation by filing voluntary competition plans for its operations in New Mexico and Texas. The New Mexico plan, which calls for customer choice in 2000, was approved in 1997. The Texas proposal, which provides for choice of electricity suppliers in 2003, was approved in July 1998.

In the third quarter of 1998, TNP discontinued operations of its Facility Works subsidiary, which was pursuing opportunities in the unregulated facility service and construction market. In January 1999, the company issued $175 million of senior notes at a 6.25% coupon and used the proceeds to repay $130 million of 12.5% debentures and reduce borrowings under its credit line. This refinancing will reduce the company's interest expense by approximately $8 million annually.

Per Share Data ($) (Year Ended Dec. 31)	1998	1997	1996	1995	1994	1993	1992	1991	1990	1989
Tangible Bk. Val.	23.19	22.71	21.41	19.86	17.01	19.97	20.55	21.35	20.76	20.55
Earnings	2.42	3.08	1.98	2.98	-1.70	1.01	1.17	2.23	1.84	1.90
Dividends	1.10	1.00	0.93	0.82	1.22	1.63	1.63	1.63	1.63	1.55
Payout Ratio	45%	33%	47%	28%	NM	161%	139%	73%	89%	82%
Prices - High	38⅝	33¾	28⅝	19⅛	18⅞	19½	21⅝	21	22½	22⅜
- Low	29	18⅞	18½	14⅝	13⅛	14⅝	17¼	15⅞	14½	19
P/E Ratio - High	16	11	14	6	NM	19	18	9	12	12
- Low	12	6	9	5	NM	14	15	7	8	10
Income Statement Analysis (Million $)										
Revs.	586	585	503	486	478	474	444	441	397	378
Depr.	38.1	38.9	38.2	37.9	36.8	36.0	35.1	28.0	18.5	16.0
Maint.	NA	NA	10.7	11.5	12.0	11.5	11.3	11.2	8.8	8.0
Fxd. Chgs. Cov.	1.9	NA	1.4	1.5	0.6	1.2	1.2	1.6	2.0	2.5
Constr. Credits	NM	NM	NM	NM	0.3	0.3	0.1	4.6	4.6	0.5
Eff. Tax Rate	33%	33%	31%	27%	NM	30%	22%	29%	29%	31%
Net Inc.	32.1	40.4	23.1	33.1	-17.4	11.6	10.9	19.5	16.4	16.8
Balance Sheet & Other Fin. Data (Million $)										
Gross Prop.	1,267	1,243	1,216	1,197	1,196	1,209	1,189	1,162	853	475
Cap. Exp.	38.6	28.2	28.0	28.7	29.0	26.0	22.1	29.9	40.8	24.0
Net Prop.	923	929	934	944	967	1,006	1,016	1,017	729	363
Capitalization:										
LT Debt	462	478	534	612	683	679	742	525	350	135
% LT Debt	60	61	66	74	78	75	76	73	66	42
Pfd.	Nil	3.2	3.4	3.6	8.7	9.6	10.4	11.3	12.6	13.9
% Pfd.	Nil	0.40	0.40	0.40	1.00	1.10	1.10	1.60	2.40	4.40
Common	309	298	278	217	185	214	219	178	172	169
% Common	40	38	34	26	21	24	23	25	32	53
Total Cap.	889	885	911	909	940	1,007	1,085	819	630	387
% Oper. Ratio	85.4	83.6	81.4	80.1	83.7	83.5	82.7	85.8	90.7	92.5
% Earn. on Net Prop.	9.2	10.2	2.5	10.1	7.9	7.7	7.6	7.2	6.8	7.9
% Return On Revs.	5.5	6.9	4.6	6.8	NM	2.4	2.5	4.4	4.1	4.4
% Return On Invest. Capital	9.9	10.8	9.1	11.9	6.0	7.6	8.3	8.7	7.3	8.0
% Return On Com. Equity	10.2	14.0	9.3	20.3	NM	5.0	5.0	10.5	8.9	9.3

Data as orig reptd.; bef. results of disc opers/spec. items. Per share data adj. for stk. divs. Bold denotes diluted EPS (FASB 128)-prior periods restated. E-Estimated. NA-Not Available. NM-Not Meaningful. NR-Not Ranked.

Office—4100 International Plaza, P.O. Box 2943, Fort Worth, TX 76113. **Tel**—(817) 731-0099. **Website**—http://www.tnpe.com **Chrmn, Pres & CEO**—K. R. Joyce. **SVP & CFO**—Manjit S. Cheema. **Secy**—P. W. Talbot. **Investor Contact**—P. L. Bridges (817) 731-0088. **Dirs**—R. D. Alexander, J. A. Fanning, S. M. Gutierrez, K. R. Joyce, J. R. Holland Jr., H. L. Kempner Jr., C. D. Smith Surles, L. G. Wheeler, D. H. Withers. **Transfer Agent & Registrar**—Bank of New York, NYC. **Incorporated**—in Texas in 1963; reincorporated in Texas in 1984. **Empl**— 885. **S&P Analyst:** Craig K. Shere, CFA

STANDARD
&POOR'S
STOCK REPORTS

Toll Brothers

NYSE Symbol **TOL**

In S&P SmallCap 600

09-OCT-99 **Industry:** Homebuilding

Summary: This company builds luxury homes mostly in the Northeast, but increasingly in other regions of the U.S.

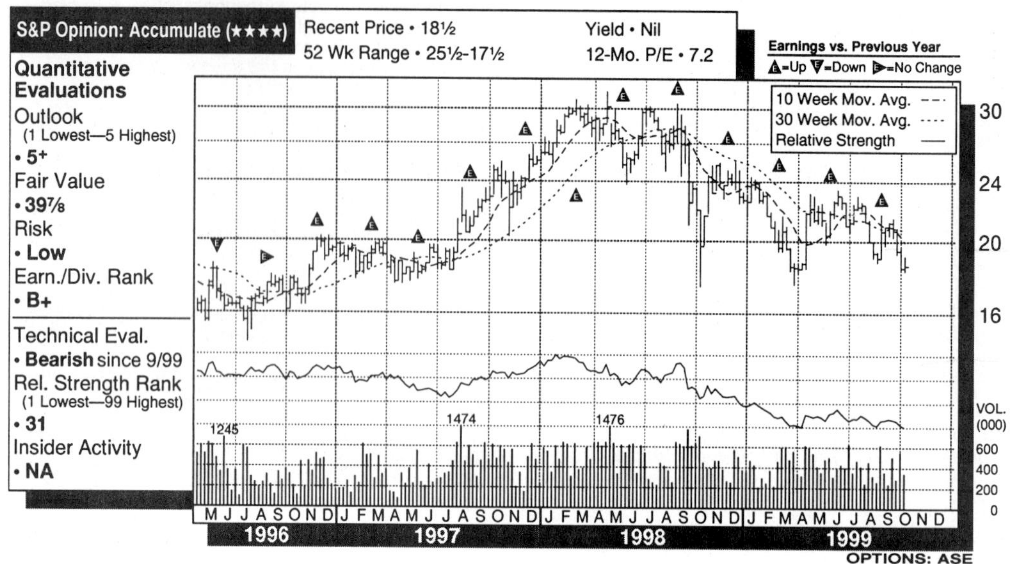

Overview - 30-JUN-99

Toll seems likely to record ongoing solid sales gains through FY 00 (Oct.), benefiting from still accommodating interest rates (despite some recent worries) and the positive demographics of its markets. TOL's focus on the upper end of the homebuilding market should pay benefits (as long as rates remain favorable), as many baby boomers entering their peak earnings years have begun to seek move-up homes. In addition, its growing concentration on the empty nester market should boost order rates, as the leading edge of the baby boom generation has now entered its 50s. We also see Toll's top line boosted by an increase in its active community count. Operating margins should widen slightly, as the negative impact from deliveries related to the Silverman Companies (bought in March 1999) should be eliminated when TOL integrates the modest-sized unit into its method of operation.

Valuation - 30-JUN-99

The shares have mostly weakened since the summer of 1998. They have been hurt by diverse factors, including economic worries and nervousness that the upturn in interest rates since late 1998 (although still at a historically modest rate) will end the housing upcycle. We believe actions to guard against possible Year 2000 interruptions, and modest growth in the global economy, will leave interest rates a friend. We also favor the demographics of TOL's customer and geographic bases, and believe that the company's expansion program leaves it better positioned. The cyclical homebuilding industry typically trades at a sizeable discount to the broad market, but TOL shares still seem undervalued in their recent trading range of seven to eight times our FY 00 forecast. However, we would still limit the aggressiveness of our purchases, as the shares could be restricted by uncertainties about the housing cycle.

Key Stock Statistics

S&P EPS Est. 1999	2.65	Tang. Bk. Value/Share	16.08
P/E on S&P Est. 1999	7.0	Beta	0.63
S&P EPS Est. 2000	3.05	Shareholders	703
Dividend Rate/Share	Nil	Market cap. (B)	$0.677
Shs. outstg. (M)	36.5	Inst. holdings	51%
Avg. daily vol. (M)	0.083		

Value of $10,000 invested 5 years ago: $ 10,839

Fiscal Year Ending Oct. 31

	1999	1998	1997	1996	1995	1994
Revenues (Million $)						
1Q	272.9	244.7	202.5	142.1	122.3	118.1
2Q	342.7	249.6	209.2	145.5	137.5	91.44
3Q	405.7	342.1	241.8	212.8	186.9	120.1
4Q	—	374.4	318.1	260.4	199.6	174.4
Yr.	—	1,211	971.7	760.7	646.3	504.1
Earnings Per Share ($)						
1Q	**0.46**	**0.44**	**0.39**	0.24	0.25	0.25
2Q	**0.59**	**0.41**	0.36	0.23	0.28	0.13
3Q	**0.80**	**0.67**	0.47	0.45	0.45	0.24
4Q	**E0.80**	**0.73**	0.70	0.64	0.47	0.46
Yr.	**E2.65**	**2.25**	**1.86**	**1.50**	1.47	1.08

Next earnings report expected: early December

Dividend Data

No cash dividends have ever been paid

Toll Brothers, Inc.

Business Summary - 30-JUN-99

The leading U.S. builder of luxury homes, Toll Brothers (TOL) caters primarily to "move-up buyers" who have previously owned a home. The company also targets the "empty nester" market (the 50 years and older buyer), which accounted for about 27% of its home sales in FY 98 (Oct.), up significantly from around 15% three years earlier. TOL builds the majority of its homes in Pennsylvania and New Jersey, but has been diversifying into new areas to take advantage of differing regional economic cycles. Since 1994, Toll has expanded into California, Arizona, Texas, Florida and North Carolina, which all rank in the top 10 in the U.S. census forecast of population growth through 2025. At FY 98 year-end, more than 33% of TOL's order backlog came from those and several other states it has entered since 1994. At April 30, 1999, Toll offered homes in 18 states.

Toll delivered 3,099 homes in FY 98, up from 2,517 in the prior year. The company's single-family detached homes generally ranged in price from $132,000 to $832,000 in FY 98, with an average base sales price of $396,000. Attached homes were offered at prices between $103,000 and $535,000, with an average base sales price of $229,000. Toll also offers hundreds of options at an additional cost, enabling buyers to create a nearly custom home. Charges for options boosted the average sales price of a home by 19% above the base in FY 98.

Toll typically locates its communities in suburban areas near highways with access to major cities. It offers at least three types of detached home plans, and two or three types of attached home floor plans.

The company attempts to reduce risk by controlling or purchasing land through options, beginning construction after sales agreements are executed, and using subcontractors to perform all construction and site improvement work on a fixed price basis.

An increasing number of households in age groups most likely to buy luxury homes (35 to 54 years of age; up 35% in the 10 years through 1995) and a growing number of affluent households currently leaves TOL with more potential buyers than at any time in its history. Moreover, with the number of households in the 55 to 64 year category projected to grow by nearly 70% through 2010, Toll has been placing greater focus on the "empty nester" market. To serve the changing housing needs of that group, TOL has developed a variety of smaller luxury homes with special features and community amenities. The company expects to open its its first age restricted community in 1999.

Toll recorded a 19% year to year gain in new home orders (on a dollar basis) in the second quarter of FY 99, to $517.3 million (1,208 homes, up 12% on a unit basis). Backlog grew to $1.1 billion (2,516 homes) at April 30, 1999, a 27% gain from a year earlier. Orders and backlog both marked record levels for TOL.

Per Share Data ($) (Year Ended Oct. 31)	1998	1997	1996	1995	1994	1993	1992	1991	1990	1989
Tangible Bk. Val.	14.22	11.24	9.28	7.63	6.11	5.01	4.12	3.59	3.19	2.85
Cash Flow	2.38	2.06	1.66	1.56	1.16	0.89	3.58	0.18	0.37	0.51
Earnings	2.25	1.94	1.56	1.47	1.08	0.82	0.52	0.12	0.30	0.44
Dividends	Nil	Nil	Nil	Nil	Nil	Nil	Nil	Nil	Nil	Nil
Payout Ratio	Nil	Nil	Nil	Nil	Nil	Nil	Nil	Nil	Nil	Nil
Prices - High	31 5/8	27 1/2	23 1/2	23	19 3/4	17 3/4	14	12 5/8	4	5 7/8
- Low	17 3/8	17 1/2	14 5/8	10	9 1/8	8 7/8	7 1/2	2 3/8	2 1/4	2 7/8
P/E Ratio - High	14	14	15	16	18	21	27	NM	13	13
- Low	8	9	9	7	8	11	14	NM	8	7
Income Statement Analysis (Million $)										
Revs.	1,206	972	761	646	504	397	285	182	205	185
Oper. Inc.	171	138	114	105	84.7	63.5	47.1	22.1	35.5	35.9
Depr.	5.6	4.1	3.3	2.9	2.7	2.5	2.3	2.1	2.2	2.2
Int. Exp.	35.9	29.4	24.2	22.2	21.7	NA	NA	16.7	17.8	24.6
Pretax Inc.	134	108	85.8	79.4	56.8	43.9	28.8	6.2	14.9	21.5
Eff. Tax Rate	36%	37%	37%	37%	36%	38%	40%	41%	41%	39%
Net Inc.	85.8	67.8	53.7	49.9	36.2	27.4	17.4	3.7	8.9	13.1
Balance Sheet & Other Fin. Data (Million $)										
Cash	80.1	148	22.9	27.8	41.7	34.3	48.9	31.5	10.4	9.2
Curr. Assets	NA	NA	NA	NA	NA	NA	NA	NA	NA	NA
Total Assets	1,254	1,119	838	692	587	476	385	312	317	348
Curr. Liab.	NA	NA	NA	NA	NA	NA	NA	NA	NA	NA
LT Debt	453	512	343	284	250	210	179	145	179	218
Common Eqty.	526	385	315	257	204	167	136	118	95.0	85.0
Total Cap.	979	942	658	541	468	391	333	278	288	315
Cap. Exp.	2.8	5.3	3.6	2.5	3.0	1.8	1.4	0.5	0.6	2.5
Cash Flow	91.4	71.9	57.3	52.9	38.9	29.9	19.6	5.8	11.1	15.4
Curr. Ratio	NA	NA	NA	NA	NA	NA	NA	NA	NA	NA
% LT Debt of Cap.	46.3	54.4	52.2	52.5	53.5	53.7	53.8	52.2	62.3	69.0
% Net Inc.of Revs.	7.1	7.0	7.1	7.7	7.2	6.9	6.1	2.0	4.3	7.1
% Ret. on Assets	7.2	6.9	7.0	7.8	6.8	6.4	5.0	1.1	2.7	4.3
% Ret. on Equity	18.8	19.4	18.8	21.7	19.5	18.0	13.6	3.3	9.9	16.6

Data as orig reptd.; bef. results of disc opers/spec. items. Per share data adj. for stk. divs. Bold denotes diluted EPS (FASB 128)-prior periods restated. E-Estimated. NA-Not Available. NM-Not Meaningful. NR-Not Ranked.

Office—3103 Philmont Ave., Huntingdon Valley, PA 19006-4298. **Tel**—(215) 938-8000. **Website**—http://www.tollbrothers.com **Chrmn & CEO**—R. I. Toll. **Pres & COO**—Z. Barzilay. **SVP, Treas, & CFO**—J. H. Rassman. **Investor Contact**—Joseph R. Sicree. **Dirs**—Z. Barzilay, R. S. Blank, R. J. Braemer, R. S. Hillas, C. B. Marbach, J. H. Rassman, P. E. Shapiro, B. E. Toll, R. I. Toll. **Transfer Agent & Registrar**—ChaseMellon Shareholder Services, Ridgefield Park, NJ. **Incorporated**—in Delaware in 1986. **Empl**— 1,583. **S&P Analyst:** Michael W. Jaffe

Toro Co.

NYSE Symbol **TTC**
In S&P SmallCap 600

09-OCT-99 **Industry:** Hardware & Tools

Summary: This company is a leading maker of consumer and commercial lawn and turf maintenance equipment, snow removal equipment and irrigation systems.

Quantitative Evaluations
Outlook
(1 Lowest—5 Highest)
• **4**
Fair Value
• **48½**
Risk
• **Low**
Earn./Div. Rank
• **B**

Technical Eval.
• **Bullish** since 8/99
Rel. Strength Rank
(1 Lowest—99 Highest)
• **57**
Insider Activity
• **Unfavorable**

Recent Price • 36
52 Wk Range • 39½-16⅞
Yield • 1.3%
12-Mo. P/E • 20.8

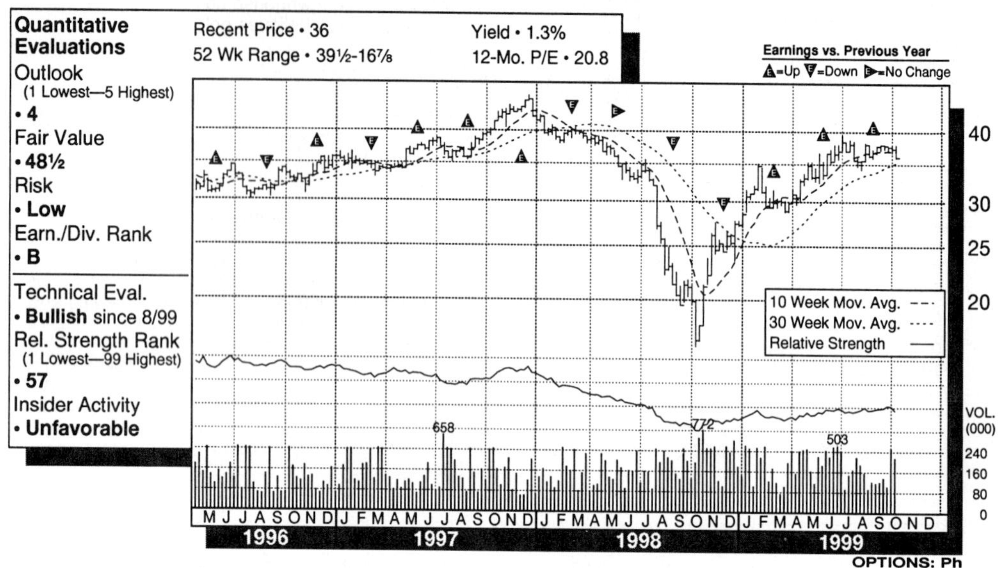

Business Profile - 22-SEP-99

Despite difficult comparisons with strong third quarter sales in FY 98 (Oct.), consumer sales increased in the third quarter of FY 99, led by continued strength for the new Toro Personal Pace lawn mower. Better results in the first nine months of FY 99 reflected the implementation of a profit improvement plan. TTC incurred related restructuring charges of $0.7 million in the third quarter. The company planned to close its plant in Murray Bridge, Australia, during the fourth quarter, resulting in an additional $0.9 million charge. During the third quarter, TTC acquired the technology and manufacturing rights for battery-operated valves and remote, hand-held controllers from a French manufacturer. The technology will be used in TTC's irrigation systems. In May 1999, the company completed the purchase of its Minnesota-based distributor.

Operational Review - 22-SEP-99

Net sales in the nine months ended July 31, 1999, advanced 15%, year to year, reflecting strength in the consumer, commercial and irrigation divisions. Aided by price increases, manufacturing efficiencies, and well controlled SG&A expense, operating income climbed 60%. After restructuring charges of $722,000, versus $10.5 million, and taxes at 39.0%, versus 39.5%, net income surged 114%, to $35.2 million ($2.66 a share), from $16.4 million ($1.24).

Stock Performance - 08-OCT-99

In the past 30 trading days, TTC's shares have declined 2%, compared to a 0.91% fall in the S&P 500. Average trading volume for the past five days was 42,680 shares, compared with the 40-day moving average of 32,077 shares.

Key Stock Statistics

Dividend Rate/Share	0.48	Shareholders	6,393
Shs. outstg. (M)	12.7	Market cap. (B)	$0.457
Avg. daily vol. (M)	0.040	Inst. holdings	55%
Tang. Bk. Value/Share	22.52		
Beta	1.05		

Value of $10,000 invested 5 years ago: $ 14,025

Fiscal Year Ending Oct. 31

	1999	1998	1997	1996	1995	1994
Revenues (Million $)						
1Q	250.8	210.1	209.0	211.5	206.0	136.0
2Q	433.1	379.7	352.2	288.6	214.0	189.0
3Q	325.3	291.0	249.3	232.6	311.0	276.0
4Q	—	229.7	240.8	198.2	203.0	193.0
Yr.	—	1,110	1,051	930.9	933.0	794.0
Earnings Per Share ($)						
1Q	**0.06**	**-0.08**	**0.20**	0.67	0.64	-0.15
2Q	**1.83**	**1.53**	1.53	1.33	0.51	0.35
3Q	**0.78**	**-0.20**	0.80	0.52	1.32	1.19
4Q	—	**-0.96**	0.40	0.37	0.32	0.31
Yr.	—	**0.31**	**2.93**	**2.90**	**2.81**	1.71

Next earnings report expected: mid December

Dividend Data (Dividends have been paid since 1984.)

Amount ($)	Date Decl.	Ex-Div. Date	Stock of Record	Payment Date
0.120	Nov. 18	Dec. 17	Dec. 21	Jan. 12 '99
0.120	Mar. 16	Mar. 25	Mar. 29	Apr. 12 '99
0.120	May. 13	Jun. 16	Jun. 18	Jul. 09 '99
0.120	Sep. 16	Sep. 23	Sep. 27	Oct. 12 '99

The Toro Company

Business Summary - 22-SEP-99

Founded in 1914 to build engines for farm tractors, Toro Co. turned away from its agricultural roots when a golf course superintendent suggested that the company design a tractor-towed mower for golf course fairways. By 1925, TTC's turf maintenance machines were in service on many major U.S. golf courses. Through internal development, acquisitions and alliances, the company has become a leading designer, manufacturer and marketer of outdoor maintenance equipment in the consumer, commercial and irrigation market.

The company was the first manufacturer to offer a consumer lawn mower with electric starting, the first to include a bagging attachment with each mower, and the first to offer a "Guaranteed To Start" in the first two pulls or your money back warranty. Today, the consumer products division offers walk power mowers, riding mowers and lawn and garden tractors, trimmers, blowers and snowthrowers.

In 1989, TTC purchased Lawn-Boy, Inc., its most formidable competitor. This gave TTC three strong brand names (Toro, Wheel Horse, and Lawn-Boy), and additional opportunities to expand its distribution channels. The company distributes its products through distributors, dealers, home centers and mass retailers.

TTC's commercial products segment consists of a broad range of products designed for large turf areas of schools, parks, cemeteries, sports fields, plant sites, apartment buildings, townhouse complexes and golf courses. Management believes golf courses will continue to be a significant market for turf maintenance equipment as new golf course construction continues throughout the world.

The company also offers a full line of irrigation products designed for residential, commercial, golf course and agricultural use. TTC's irrigation products are used by 74 of the 100 leading golf courses, as rated by Golf Digest in May 1997. The FY 98 (Oct.) acquisition of Drip In enhanced the company's product line for the agricultural microirrigation market.

In FY 98, TTC implemented a profit improvement plan to reposition the consumer business and improve profitability. The restructuring resulted in plant closings and the anticipated sale of a portion of the professional fertilizer business. Management expects significant savings from the profit improvement plan by FY 00.

Per Share Data ($) (Year Ended Oct. 31)	1998	1997	1996	1995	1994	1993	1992	1991	1990	1989
Tangible Bk. Val.	20.62	15.38	19.15	16.50	13.43	11.78	11.01	13.48	12.92	9.85
Cash Flow	3.21	5.53	4.35	4.31	3.16	2.61	-0.15	2.38	3.01	3.03
Earnings	0.31	2.93	2.90	2.81	1.71	1.05	-1.98	0.81	1.55	2.10
Dividends	0.48	0.48	0.48	0.48	0.48	0.48	0.48	0.48	0.48	0.48
Payout Ratio	155%	16%	17%	17%	28%	45%	NM	59%	35%	22%
Prices - High	42¾	46¼	36½	32⅞	30½	26¾	17½	20½	30	26
- Low	16½	33	30	25⅝	20⅞	16½	11⅜	13¼	11	18⅝
P/E Ratio - High	NM	16	13	12	18	25	NM	25	19	12
- Low	NM	11	10	9	12	16	NM	16	7	9
Income Statement Analysis (Million $)										
Revs.	1,110	1,051	931	933	794	684	635	712	751	644
Oper. Inc.	77.0	103	81.6	82.1	61.4	54.7	23.4	46.2	58.2	60.4
Depr.	38.2	30.9	18.2	17.2	18.8	19.2	22.0	18.8	15.1	9.3
Int. Exp.	25.4	19.9	13.6	11.9	13.6	17.2	18.7	19.0	23.7	17.4
Pretax Inc.	6.8	60.3	60.2	61.1	37.1	21.4	-34.9	15.3	26.3	36.9
Eff. Tax Rate	40%	40%	40%	40%	40%	39%	NM	37%	37%	40%
Net Inc.	4.1	36.5	36.4	36.7	22.2	13.0	-23.8	9.7	16.6	22.1
Balance Sheet & Other Fin. Data (Million $)										
Cash	0.1	0.0	0.1	11.9	36.2	61.8	25.5	17.0	12.3	19.7
Curr. Assets	479	472	405	382	364	344	333	319	320	266
Total Assets	724	662	497	468	444	419	421	415	424	326
Curr. Liab.	258	238	208	213	189	150	122	108	130	123
LT Debt	197	178	53.0	64.9	81.0	123	164	145	134	97.0
Common Eqty.	263	241	214	185	169	145	133	161	153	98.0
Total Cap.	360	419	267	256	250	269	299	307	293	203
Cap. Exp.	33.8	37.0	21.3	28.2	18.2	10.2	12.8	11.4	14.6	11.5
Cash Flow	42.3	67.4	54.6	53.9	4.1	32.3	-1.8	28.5	31.0	30.5
Curr. Ratio	1.9	2.0	1.9	1.8	1.9	2.3	2.7	3.0	2.5	2.2
% LT Debt of Cap.	54.7	42.4	19.9	25.4	32.5	45.7	54.8	47.3	45.9	47.7
% Net Inc.of Revs.	0.4	3.5	3.9	3.9	2.8	1.9	NM	1.4	2.2	3.4
% Ret. on Assets	0.6	6.3	7.5	7.8	5.1	3.1	NM	2.3	4.1	7.5
% Ret. on Equity	1.6	16.1	18.0	20.7	14.0	9.3	NM	6.2	11.9	23.7

Data as orig. reptd.; bef. results of disc. opers. and/or spec. items. Per share data adj. for stk. divs. as of ex-div. date. Data to 1995 for fiscal yr. ended July 31. Bold denotes diluted EPS (FASB 128). E-Estimated. NA-Not Available. NM-Not Meaningful. NR-Not Ranked.

Office—8111 Lyndale Ave. South, Bloomington, MN 55420. **Tel**—(612) 888-8801. **Website**—http://www.toro.com **Chrmn & CEO**—K. B. Melrose. **VP & Secy**—J. L. McIntyre. **VP-Fin, CFO & Treas**—S. P. Wolfe. **Asst Treas & Investor Contact**—Stephen D. Keating. **Dirs**—R. O. Baukol, R. C. Buhrmaster, W. H. Buxton, J. K. Cooper, K. B. Melrose, A. A. Meyer, R. H. Nassau, D. R. Olseth, C. A. Twomey, E. H. Wingate. **Transfer Agent & Registrar**—Norwest Bank Minnesota, South St. Paul. **Incorporated**—in Minnesota in 1935; reincorporated in Delaware in 1984. **Empl**— 4,700. **S&P Analyst:** Jordan Horoschak

STANDARD
&POOR'S
STOCK REPORTS

Tower Automotive

NYSE Symbol **TWR**

In S&P SmallCap 600

09-OCT-99

Industry:
Auto Parts & Equipment

Summary: This company designs and manufactures structural metal stampings and assemblies for use by original equipment manufacturers in the automotive industry.

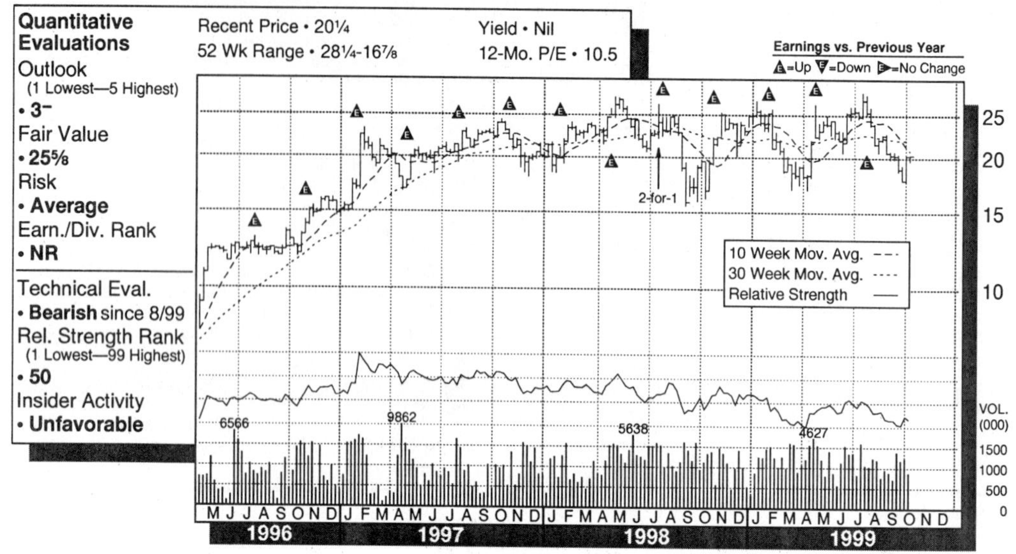

Business Profile - 23-AUG-99

This company operates in the large and highly fragmented structural segment of the automotive supply industry, which continues to undergo significant consolidation. Tower intends to capitalize on this consolidation trend with acquisitions and joint ventures. The company is also positioned to benefit from the trends toward increased outsourcing of automotive production, and greater demand for pre-manufactured modules and systems. In April, Tower said it expects continued strong domestic automotive production, although the pace of growth may slow in the second half of the year. Capital expenditures of $185 million to $200 million were planned for 1999. The company forecast depreciation and amortization charges of $110 million for the year.

Operational Review - 23-AUG-99

Revenues in the six months ended June 30, 1999, rose 12%, year to year, reflecting strong vehicle production. Gross and operating margins both widened, on increased productivity; income from operations climbed 30%. After amortization charges and lower interest expense, pretax income soared 61%. After taxes at 40.0% in each period, equity in earnings of joint ventures, and minority interest and preferred dividends, net income was up 43%, to $60,704,000 ($1.08 a share, on 14% more shares), from $42,566,000 ($0.83, as adjusted).

Stock Performance - 08-OCT-99

In the past 30 trading days, TWR's shares have declined 1%, compared to a 0.91% fall in the S&P 500. Average trading volume for the past five days was 173,860 shares, compared with the 40-day moving average of 202,941 shares.

Key Stock Statistics

Dividend Rate/Share	Nil	Shareholders	NA
Shs. outstg. (M)	46.7	Market cap. (B)	$0.949
Avg. daily vol. (M)	0.232	Inst. holdings	0%
Tang. Bk. Value/Share	4.00		
Beta	1.45		

Value of $10,000 invested 5 years ago: NA

Fiscal Year Ending Dec. 31

	1999	1998	1997	1996	1995	1994
Revenues (Million $)						
1Q	498.6	457.1	125.1	68.92	58.42	—
2Q	530.7	465.9	327.3	96.52	55.18	—
3Q	—	444.9	349.5	114.6	51.17	—
4Q	—	468.6	433.9	119.9	58.04	—
Yr.	—	1,836	1,236	399.9	222.8	165.5
Earnings Per Share ($)						
1Q	**0.51**	**0.38**	**0.23**	**0.14**	0.14	—
2Q	**0.58**	**0.46**	**0.24**	**0.22**	0.14	0.14
3Q	—	**0.36**	**0.25**	**0.18**	0.10	—
4Q	—	**0.50**	**0.34**	0.23	0.15	—
Yr.	—	**1.68**	**1.14**	**0.78**	**0.53**	0.43

Next earnings report expected: mid October

Dividend Data

No cash dividends have been paid

Tower Automotive, Inc.

Business Summary - 23-AUG-99

Tower Automotive, Inc. is a leading designer and producer of high quality body structure components and assemblies used by the major North America automotive original equipment manufacturers (Ford, DaimlerChrysler, and GM) and certain foreign manufacturers (Honda, Toyota, Nissan, Mazda, Fiat, BMW, Volkswagen and Mercedes).

The company's business strategy is to capitalize on consolidation and globalization and system/modular trends in the automotive supply industry.

Principal products range from large structural stampings and assemblies, such as body pillars, chassis, suspension and floor pan components, and major housing assemblies, to engineered mechanical parts, such as hood and deck lid hinges and brake components.

Many of the company's stamped, formed, welded and assembled metal components are critical to the structural integrity of a vehicle. The stampings and assemblies are attached directly to the frame of an automobile at the OEM assembly plant, and comprise the major structure of the vehicle. Engineered assemblies manufactured by the company, such as hood and deck lid hinges, are attached to larger structural components. These parts use various grades and thicknesses of steel, including hot and cold rolled, galvanized, organically coated, stainless and aluminized steel. Systems and assemblies produced by Tower include front and rear structural suspension systems comprised of control arms, suspension links and axle assemblies consisting of stamped metal trailing axles, assembled brake shoes, hoses and tie rods.

Tower is generally awarded contracts by OEMs for parts to be supplied for a particular model, with contracts ranging from one year to the typical three- to seven-year life of a model. The company supplies parts for a broad cross-section of both new and mature models.

The company formed several strategic international alliances in 1997, and continued to pursue global opportunities in 1998. The acquisitions and joint ventures, which substantially increased revenues, included the following: Automotive Parts Co. (APC). acquired in April 1997; Societu Industria Meccanica e Stampaggio (May 1997); and joint ventures Metalsa in October 1997 and Metalurgica Caterina S.A. in March 1998. These alliances gave Tower entry into regions such as Europe, Asia, and Latin America, and added key new clients. For example, the 1998 Brazilian joint venture with Metalurgica Caterina S.A. added Volkswagen and Mercedes as clients.

S&P is forecasting production of 16.3 million cars and light vehicles for 1999, versus 15.6 million units produced in 1998. Production of more than 15.0 million is considered strong, and bodes well for parts suppliers such as Tower.

Per Share Data ($) (Year Ended Dec. 31)	1998	1997	1996	1995	1994	1993	1992	1991	1990	1989
Tangible Bk. Val.	4.00	2.29	6.37	2.10	1.58	NA	NA	NA	NA	NA
Cash Flow	2.94	2.14	1.24	0.80	0.66	NA	NA	NA	NA	NA
Earnings	1.68	1.14	0.78	0.53	0.43	NA	NA	NA	NA	NA
Dividends	Nil	Nil	Nil	Nil	Nil	NA	NA	NA	NA	NA
Payout Ratio	Nil	Nil	Nil	Nil	Nil	NA	NA	NA	NA	NA
Prices - High	27 1/2	24 3/8	16 1/8	8 3/4	7	NA	NA	NA	NA	NA
- Low	15 1/2	14 7/8	7 1/8	3 5/8	3 5/8	NA	NA	NA	NA	NA
P/E Ratio - High	16	21	21	17	16	NA	NA	NA	NA	NA
- Low	9	13	9	7	9	NA	NA	NA	NA	NA
Income Statement Analysis (Million $)										
Revs.	1,836	1,236	400	223	166	NA	NA	NA	NA	NA
Oper. Inc.	263	158	52.2	28.5	18.4	NA	NA	NA	NA	NA
Depr.	87.4	48.0	12.8	6.5	4.1	NA	NA	NA	NA	NA
Int. Exp.	42.5	36.7	5.1	1.8	1.9	NA	NA	NA	NA	NA
Pretax Inc.	148	81.0	34.3	20.1	12.4	NA	NA	NA	NA	NA
Eff. Tax Rate	37%	40%	40%	40%	41%	NA	NA	NA	NA	NA
Net Inc.	88.0	48.7	20.6	12.1	7.4	NA	NA	NA	NA	NA
Balance Sheet & Other Fin. Data (Million $)										
Cash	6.1	7.9	50.4	15.3	6.5	NA	NA	NA	NA	NA
Curr. Assets	436	371	137	61.8	59.8	NA	NA	NA	NA	NA
Total Assets	1,936	1,680	399	209	178	NA	NA	NA	NA	NA
Curr. Liab.	329	231	55.4	29.6	26.6	NA	NA	NA	NA	NA
LT Debt	801	744	114	70.3	49.5	NA	NA	NA	NA	NA
Common Eqty.	607	515	182	85.6	73.1	NA	NA	NA	NA	NA
Total Cap.	1,428	1,259	308	157	123	NA	NA	NA	NA	NA
Cap. Exp.	185	117	16.3	26.1	28.5	NA	NA	NA	NA	NA
Cash Flow	175	96.6	33.4	18.6	11.5	NA	NA	NA	NA	NA
Curr. Ratio	1.3	1.6	2.5	2.1	2.2	NA	NA	NA	NA	NA
% LT Debt of Cap.	56.1	59.1	36.9	44.7	40.4	NA	NA	NA	NA	NA
% Net Inc.of Revs.	4.8	3.9	5.2	5.4	4.4	NA	NA	NA	NA	NA
% Ret. on Assets	4.9	4.7	6.8	6.2	NA	NA	NA	NA	NA	NA
% Ret. on Equity	15.7	14.0	15.4	15.2	NA	NA	NA	NA	NA	NA

Data as orig reptd.; bef. results of disc opers/spec. items. Per share data adj. for stk. divs. Bold denotes diluted EPS (FASB 128)-prior periods restated. E-Estimated. NA-Not Available. NM-Not Meaningful. NR-Not Ranked.

Office—4508 IDS Center, Minneapolis, MN 55402. **Tel**—(612) 342-2310. **Website**—http://www.towerautomotive.com **Chrmn**—S. A. Johnson. **Vice Chrmn**—A. V. Starre. **Pres & CEO**—D. K. Campbell. **VP & CFO**—A. A. Barone. **Investor Contact**—Patty Hoffman (612-872-3781). **Dirs**—D. K. Campbell, K. B. Clark, W. H. Clement, M. O. Diggs, Jr., S. A. Johnson, F. J. Loughrey, J. R. Lozelle, E. J. Rosen, A. V Starre, E. Zambrano. **Transfer Agent & Registrar**—American Stock Transfer & Trust Co., NYC. **Incorporated**—in Delaware in 1993. **Empl**— 8,750. **S&P Analyst:** Efraim Levy

STANDARD
&POOR'S
STOCK REPORTS

Tredegar Corp.

NYSE Symbol **TG**

In S&P SmallCap 600

09-OCT-99

Industry: Manufacturing (Diversified)

Summary: Tredegar makes plastic films and aluminum products, and has interests in various technology businesses.

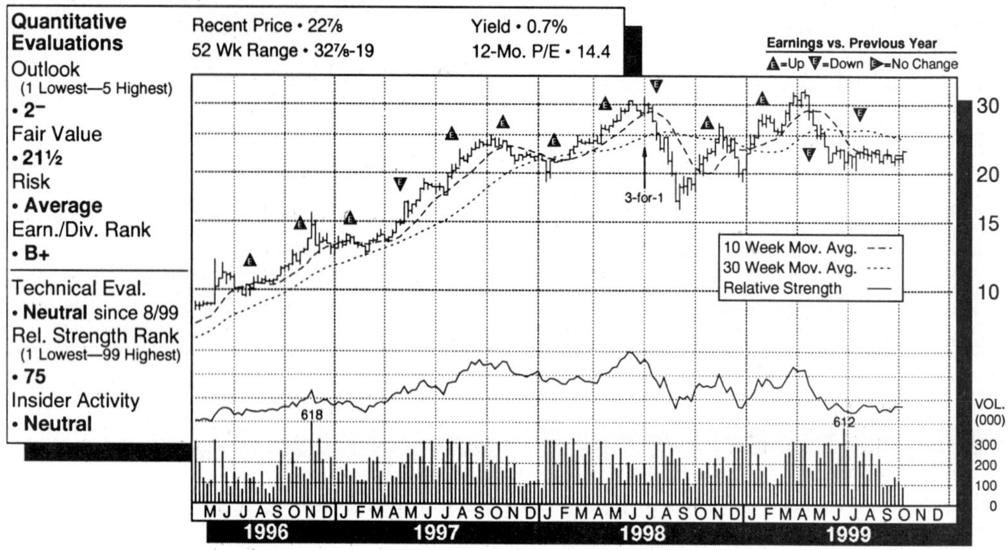

Business Profile - 07-JUN-99

Tredegar seeks to enhance shareholder value through continued global expansion, the introduction of new products, acquisitions, penetration of new markets in the U.S. and Canada, expansion of the portfolio of drug discovery collaborations, and broadening of its portfolio of investment opportunities in new technologies. In line with this strategy, the company has acquired four of its eight aluminum plants since January 1998. In May 1999, TG acquired the assets of Exxon Chemical Co.'s plastic film business for $200 million. The acquisition includes two plants in Lake Zurich, IL, and Pottsville, PA, that manufacture films used primarily in packaging, personal hygiene and medical markets. In the 12 months through March 31, the Exxon business had revenues of $111 million and generated EBITDA (earnings before interest, taxes, depreciation and amortization) of $24.6 million.

Operational Review - 07-JUN-99

Total revenues in the three months ended March 31, 1999, climbed 14%, year to year, reflecting continued volume growth and acquisitions in the aluminum extrusions business. Gross margins widened, on improved margins in the aluminum extrusions business. SG&A expenses climbed 29%, due to acquisitions as well as higher spending on new products in the film products segment. After taxes at 35.5%, versus 25.2%, net income slipped 12%, to $15,298,000 ($0.39 a share), from $17,296,000 ($0.44).

Stock Performance - 08-OCT-99

In the past 30 trading days, TG's shares have increased 6%, compared to a 0.91% fall in the S&P 500. Average trading volume for the past five days was 17,400 shares, compared with the 40-day moving average of 26,241 shares.

Key Stock Statistics

Dividend Rate/Share	0.16	Shareholders	6,402
Shs. outstg. (M)	37.2	Market cap. (B)	$0.851
Avg. daily vol. (M)	0.022	Inst. holdings	23%
Tang. Bk. Value/Share	4.92		
Beta	1.26		

Value of $10,000 invested 5 years ago: $ 71,834

Fiscal Year Ending Dec. 31

	1999	1998	1997	1996	1995	1994
Revenues (Million $)						
1Q	179.5	156.7	133.3	141.4	151.1	121.0
2Q	194.8	169.9	145.0	126.3	149.7	122.9
3Q	—	186.6	155.1	129.4	146.0	132.2
4Q	—	186.6	147.6	126.4	142.7	126.1
Yr.	—	699.8	581.0	523.5	589.5	502.2
Earnings Per Share ($)						
1Q	**0.39**	**0.44**	**0.28**	**0.42**	0.11	-0.10
2Q	**0.26**	**0.39**	**0.42**	**0.20**	0.15	0.06
3Q	—	**0.50**	**0.38**	**0.27**	0.17	0.00
4Q	—	**0.41**	**0.40**	**0.23**	0.18	0.09
Yr.	—	**1.66**	**1.48**	**1.15**	0.60	0.03

Next earnings report expected: mid October

Dividend Data (Dividends have been paid since 1989.)

Amount ($)	Date Decl.	Ex-Div. Date	Stock of Record	Payment Date
0.040	Nov. 18	Dec. 16	Dec. 18	Jan. 01 '99
0.040	Feb. 24	Mar. 17	Mar. 19	Apr. 01 '99
0.040	May. 20	Jun. 16	Jun. 28	Jul. 01 '99
0.040	Aug. 24	Sep. 15	Sep. 17	Oct. 01 '99

A Division of The McGraw-Hill Companies

STANDARD
&POOR'S
STOCK REPORTS

Tredegar Corporation

09-OCT-99

Business Summary - 07-JUN-99

Tredegar Corp. (formerly Tredegar Industries) is a manufacturer of plastic films, aluminum extrusions and vinyl extrusions. It also has interests in a variety of technology-based businesses. In 1998, 43% of sales and 56% of operating profit was obtained through film products and Fiberlux; 56% and 47% from aluminum extrusions; and 1% and -3% from technology.

Film products are produced in two major market categories: disposables and industrial. Disposable products, which accounted for more than 30% of revenues in each of the past three years, include permeable films for use as liners in feminine hygiene products and adult incontinent products. TG also supplies embossed films and nonwoven film laminates for use as backsheet in such disposable products as baby diapers, adult incontinent products and feminine hygiene products. The company's primary customer for permeable films, embossed films and nonwoven film laminates is Procter & Gamble, the leading global diaper maker. Film products for industrial markets include coextruded and monolayer permeable films used to regulate fluid and vapor transmissions. Specific examples include filter plies for surgical masks and other medical applications, permeable ground cover, natural cheese mold release cloths and rubber bale wrap.

Fiberlux is a leading U.S. producer of rigid vinyl extrusions for windows and patio doors. Its primary raw material, polyvinyl chloride resin, is purchased from producers in open market purchases and under contract.

Aluminum extrusions (metal that is heated and pushed through dies to form specific shapes) is composed of The William L. Bonnel Co., Capitol Products Corp., Bon L Campo Limited Partnership and Bon L Canada, which make plain, anodized and painted aluminum extrusions for sale directly to fabricators and distributors that use aluminum extrusions in the production of curtain walls, moldings, architectural shapes, running boards, tub and shower doors, boat windshields, window components, tractor-trailer shapes, ladders and furniture, among other products.

TG's Molecumetics, Ltd. subsidiary conducts drug design research using patented chemistry to develop new drug candidates for license to pharmaceutical and biotech companies in exchange for up-front fees, research and development support payments, milestone-driven success payments and future royalties. Tredegar Investments invests in venture capital funds and early stage technology companies.

Per Share Data ($) (Year Ended Dec. 31)	1998	1997	1996	1995	1994	1993	1992	1991	1990	1989
Tangible Bk. Val.	7.58	6.81	5.24	3.85	4.25	3.45	3.31	2.28	2.42	2.90
Cash Flow	1.26	1.94	1.66	1.10	0.54	0.55	0.80	0.80	0.07	0.83
Earnings	1.66	1.48	1.15	0.60	0.03	0.08	0.31	0.12	-0.49	0.32
Dividends	0.15	0.11	0.09	0.06	0.05	0.05	0.05	0.05	0.05	0.03
Payout Ratio	9%	8%	8%	10%	185%	70%	17%	46%	NM	8%
Prices - High	31 1/4	25	15 3/4	7 7/8	4 1/8	4	4 1/4	2 7/16	3 1/2	3 7/8
- Low	16 1/8	12 1/4	6 7/8	3 7/8	3 1/8	2 3/4	2 3/16	1 7/16	1 9/16	2 7/8
P/E Ratio - High	19	17	14	13	NM	53	13	21	NM	19
- Low	10	8	6	6	NM	36	7	12	NM	14
Income Statement Analysis (Million $)										
Revs.	700	581	524	590	502	449	479	474	547	638
Oper. Inc.	115	91.3	75.8	66.0	49.6	35.9	55.7	50.9	36.2	56.6
Depr.	22.5	18.4	20.3	23.8	23.5	23.1	23.9	33.5	28.4	27.6
Int. Exp.	1.3	2.0	2.2	3.0	4.2	5.4	6.9	9.1	9.3	4.8
Pretax Inc.	95.2	90.2	69.0	38.3	5.3	6.9	25.5	8.9	-39.8	27.7
Eff. Tax Rate	33%	35%	35%	37%	73%	46%	40%	37%	NM	38%
Net Inc.	64.2	58.4	45.0	24.1	1.4	3.7	15.3	5.6	-24.7	17.3
Balance Sheet & Other Fin. Data (Million $)										
Cash	25.4	120	101	2.1	9.0	Nil	Nil	0.5	2.3	1.7
Curr. Assets	166	223	194	126	135	117	125	119	134	127
Total Assets	457	411	341	314	318	353	359	339	342	368
Curr. Liab.	88.9	72.8	61.3	69.8	72.8	54.8	62.5	58.1	62.0	49.3
LT Debt	25.0	30.0	35.0	35.0	38.0	97.0	102	100	100	100
Common Eqty.	310	273	213	171	172	169	162	150	147	185
Total Cap.	360	325	265	228	230	289	295	280	279	317
Cap. Exp.	34.1	23.9	23.9	25.1	15.6	16.5	21.0	36.8	39.7	45.6
Cash Flow	86.6	76.9	65.3	47.9	24.9	26.8	39.2	39.1	3.7	44.9
Curr. Ratio	1.9	3.1	3.2	1.8	1.9	2.1	2.0	2.1	2.2	2.6
% LT Debt of Cap.	6.9	9.2	13.2	10.6	16.5	33.5	34.4	35.8	35.8	31.5
% Net Inc.of Revs.	9.2	10.1	8.6	4.1	0.3	0.8	3.2	1.2	NM	2.7
% Ret. on Assets	14.8	15.5	13.7	7.6	0.5	1.0	4.4	1.7	NM	NA
% Ret. on Equity	22.0	24.1	2.3	14.1	0.9	2.2	9.8	3.8	NM	NA

Data as orig reptd.; bef. results of disc opers/spec. items. Per share data adj. for stk. divs. Bold denotes diluted EPS (FASB 128)-prior periods restated. E-Estimated. NA-Not Available. NM-Not Meaningful. NR-Not Ranked.

Office—1100 Boulders Parkway, Richmond, VA 23225. **Tel**—(804) 330-1000. **Website**—http://www.tredegar.com **Pres & CEO**—J. D. Gottwald. **EVP & COO**—D. R. Monk. **EVP & CFO**—N. A. Scher. **V-P & Treas**—D. A. Edwards. **V-P & Secy**—N. M. Taylor. **Investor Contact**—Edward A. Cunningham (804-330-1598). **Dirs**—A. Brockenbrough III, P. Cothran, R. W. Goodrum, F. D. Gottwald Jr., J. D. Gottwald, Dr. W. M. Gottwald, A. B. Lacy, Dr. R. L. Morrill, E. J. Rice, N. A. Scher, T. G. Slater. **Transfer Agent & Registrar**—American Stock Transfer & Trust, NYC. **Incorporated**—in Virginia in 1988. **Empl**— 3,400. **S&P Analyst:** M.I.

STANDARD &POOR'S
STOCK REPORTS

Trenwick Group

NASDAQ Symbol **TREN**

In S&P SmallCap 600

09-OCT-99

Industry: Insurance (Property-Casualty)

Summary: TREN provides treaty and facultative reinsurance, as well as specialty insurance. It has agreed to acquire Chartwell Re, another U.S. insurer.

Quantitative Evaluations

Outlook (1 Lowest—5 Highest) • **3+**

Fair Value • **21¼**

Risk • **Low**

Earn./Div. Rank • **A-**

Technical Eval. • **Bearish** since 9/99

Rel. Strength Rank (1 Lowest—99 Highest) • **20**

Insider Activity • **Neutral**

Recent Price • 19 | Yield • 5.5%

52 Wk Range • 35¼-16½ | 12-Mo. P/E • 7.0

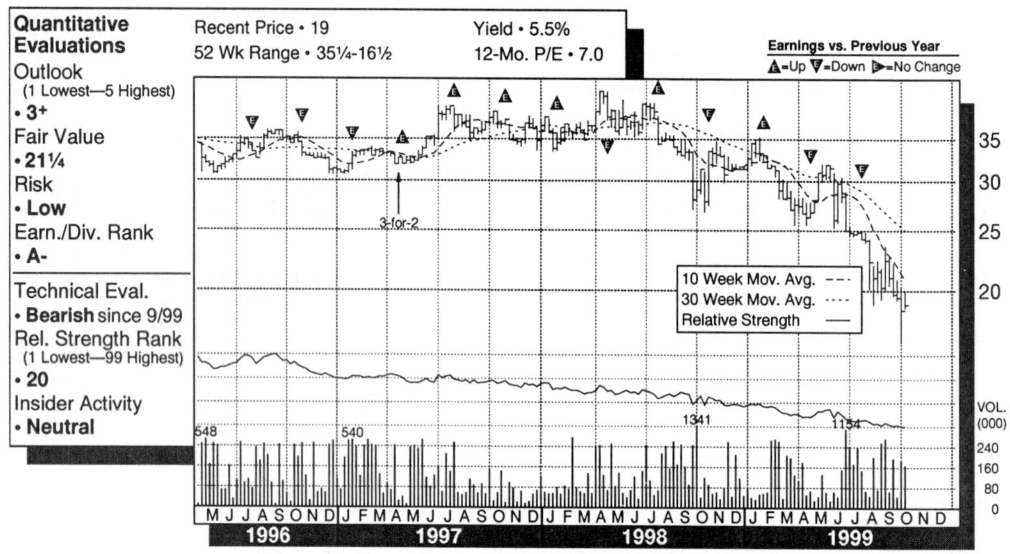

Business Profile - 08-SEP-99

In July 1999, TREN agreed to merge with Chartwell Re Corp. via the issuance of about 8 million new shares. On a combined basis, the new company would have total assets in excess of $3.0 billion, shareholders' equity of approximately $500 million, and total capitalization of approximately $800 million. The combination of the two companies is expected to provide a cost-effective means of augmenting capital, accelerating premium growth, and adding structural platforms for future expansion. The addition of Chartwell's U.S. reinsurance business, its admitted and non-admitted U.S. insurance companies, and its operations at Lloyd's will further Trenwick's strategy of entering new markets and product lines. The acquisition, which is expected to generate substantial economies, is expected to close in the fourth quarter of 1999. As of late August 1999, TREN had acquired nearly all of the 1.6 million shares authorized for repurchase, and directors authorized the purchase of another 1 million shares.

Operational Review - 08-SEP-99

Total revenues rose 6.6% year to year in the first half of 1999, mostly reflecting the impact of the February 1998 acquisition of Trenwick International Ltd. (formerly SOREMA Ltd.). Total expenses increased 12%, reflecting continued competitive conditions; net income fell 24%, to $13,770,000 ($1.28 a share, diluted, on fewer shares), from $18,220,000 ($1.51).

Stock Performance - 08-OCT-99

In the past 30 trading days, TREN's shares have declined 6%, compared to a 0.91% fall in the S&P 500. Average trading volume for the past five days was 33,180 shares, compared with the 40-day moving average of 45,059 shares.

Key Stock Statistics

Dividend Rate/Share	1.04	Shareholders	1,000
Shs. outstg. (M)	10.6	Market cap. (B)	$0.202
Avg. daily vol. (M)	0.029	Inst. holdings	65%
Tang. Bk. Value/Share	31.49		
Beta	0.35		

Value of $10,000 invested 5 years ago: $ 8,594

Fiscal Year Ending Dec. 31

	1999	1998	1997	1996	1995	1994
Revenues (Million $)						
1Q	75.55	58.94	67.56	57.61	53.11	38.50
2Q	79.77	86.80	59.24	63.55	52.94	39.88
3Q	—	79.50	55.90	65.32	52.69	41.73
4Q	—	86.07	58.17	66.12	55.86	46.31
Yr.	—	311.3	240.9	252.6	214.6	166.4
Earnings Per Share ($)						
1Q	**0.74**	**0.77**	**0.90**	**0.69**	0.65	0.11
2Q	**0.53**	**0.74**	**0.71**	**0.70**	0.73	0.61
3Q	—	**0.44**	**0.73**	**0.72**	0.79	0.64
4Q	—	**1.02**	**0.75**	**0.74**	0.79	0.67
Yr.	—	**2.95**	**3.01**	**2.85**	**2.59**	2.03

Next earnings report expected: late October

Dividend Data (Dividends have been paid since 1988.)

Amount ($)	Date Decl.	Ex-Div. Date	Stock of Record	Payment Date
0.250	Nov. 04	Dec. 11	Dec. 15	Dec. 31 '98
0.260	Mar. 03	Mar. 17	Mar. 19	Mar. 31 '99
0.260	May. 20	Jun. 11	Jun. 15	Jun. 30 '99
0.260	Aug. 11	Sep. 13	Sep. 15	Sep. 30 '99

Trenwick Group Inc.

Business Summary - 08-SEP-99

After 10 years of soft domestic property and casualty reinsurance business, Trenwick Group has sought to develop strategic alliances and diversify outside the U.S. The company has initiated strategic reinsurance alliances with other major insurers in order to facilitate entry into new lines of business. In late February 1998, TREN concluded a plan to diversify internationally, acquiring Trenwick International Ltd. London-based Trenwick International underwrites reinsurance and specialty insurance worldwide.

Trenwick Group now owns and operates two principal subsidiaries, Trenwick American Reinsurance (TAR) and Trenwick International (TI). Through TAR, the company primarily served U.S. insurers through the reinsurance of property and casualty risks. Trenwick American accounted for 68% of total net premiums written in 1998. At the end of 1998, major lines of reinsurance written by TAR included automobile liability, errors and omissions, general liability and accident and health. In 1998, domestic accident and health net premiums written increased 74%, largely due to a new strategic alliance with Duncanson and Holt. TAR's other product lines have experienced declining net premiums written since 1996.

In March 1999, the company said there were three major reasons for declines in most of its domestic insurance lines. First, competition among primary insurers caused reductions in the writing of new policies and the rate at which primary companies seek reinsurance to reduce their risks. Second, as a result of industry consolidation, many primary carriers are now larger and financially stronger, reducing their need for reinsurance to control risk. Finally, a resulting increase in competition has driven reinsurance prices on a number of accounts below pricing levels that the company is willing to accept.

At the time of its February 1998 acquisition of Trenwick International (formerly SOREMA Ltd.), the company said the new London-based subsidiary was a means of diversifying both geographically and structurally. TREN also said Trenwick International (TI) was an opportune platform for further international expansion. TI provides reinsurance and specialty insurance underwriting in both London (representing most of its business) and Paris. Its principal lines of business underwritten in 1998 include property, engineering, accident and health, professional indemnity, financial institutions, liability, extended warranty and yacht hull. In order to facilitate expansion into other markets and business lines, TREN doubled TI's capital base, to approximately $125 million, immediately following the acquisition. In September 1998, TI opened a branch office in Paris, specializing in reinsurance of large, technically complex property risks.

Per Share Data ($) (Year Ended Dec. 31)	1998	1997	1996	1995	1994	1993	1992	1991	1990	1989
Tangible Bk. Val.	31.49	29.93	26.25	24.23	19.32	20.94	17.35	15.97	14.50	NA
Oper. Earnings	NA	NA	NA	NA	NA	NA	NA	NA	NA	NA
Earnings	**2.95**	3.01	3.30	2.96	2.03	2.32	1.67	1.86	1.65	NA
Dividends	1.00	0.97	0.83	0.75	0.67	0.57	0.51	0.42	0.30	NA
Payout Ratio	34%	32%	25%	25%	33%	25%	30%	23%	18%	NA
Prices - High	41 3/4	39 5/8	37 7/8	38 3/8	29 1/4	33 1/8	28 1/8	20	16 7/8	NA
- Low	26 3/4	30 5/8	30 5/8	27 1/8	22 1/8	25 1/8	16 5/8	14 1/2	11 1/8	NA
P/E Ratio - High	14	13	11	13	14	14	17	11	10	NA
- Low	9	10	9	9	11	11	10	8	7	NA
Income Statement Analysis (Million $)										
Premium Inc.	246	190	211	177	133	93.0	82.0	85.0	94.0	NA
Net Invest. Inc.	56.3	48.4	41.2	36.8	33.9	35.0	30.9	30.4	27.0	NA
Oth. Revs.	9.4	2.3	0.3	0.4	-0.2	1.8	0.4	NA	0.3	NA
Total Revs.	311	241	253	215	166	130	113	118	122	NA
Pretax Inc.	52.7	55.9	43.8	38.4	23.0	28.0	19.5	22.0	19.8	NA
Net Oper. Inc.	NA	NA	NA	NA	NA	NA	NA	NA	NA	NA
Net Inc.	34.8	36.3	33.8	29.8	20.3	23.7	16.8	18.6	17.2	NA
Balance Sheet & Other Fin. Data (Million $)										
Cash & Equiv.	63.0	12.8	14.3	17.0	20.1	15.2	NA	NA	NA	NA
Premiums Due	139	91.8	62.7	49.0	27.8	26.6	NA	NA	NA	NA
Invest. Assets: Bonds	893	812	714	634	532	540	NA	NA	NA	NA
Invest. Assets: Stocks	49.2	39.1	26.0	13.4	9.8	Nil	NA	NA	NA	NA
Invest. Assets: Loans	Nil	Nil	Nil	Nil	Nil	Nil	NA	NA	NA	NA
Invest. Assets: Total	942	39.2	740	647	542	540	500	NA	NA	NA
Deferred Policy Costs	35.3	22.5	21.8	16.7	10.7	8.5	NA	NA	NA	NA
Total Assets	1,392	1,088	921	821	727	700	652	NA	NA	NA
Debt	185	110	104	104	104	104	104	NA	NA	NA
Common Eqty.	348	358	266	241	188	207	169	NA	NA	NA
Prop. & Cas. Loss Ratio	62.4	57.6	61.3	63.7	70.0	68.5	78.4	NA	NA	NA
Prop. & Cas. Expense Ratio	39.9	38.9	34.5	31.9	33.2	34.0	33.9	NA	NA	NA
Prop. & Cas. Combined Ratio	102.3	96.5	95.8	95.6	103.2	102.5	112.3	108.0	106.9	NA
% Return On Revs.	11.2	15.1	13.4	13.9	12.2	18.3	12.7	21.9	18.3	NA
% Ret. on Equity	9.9	11.6	13.4	13.9	10.3	12.6	10.4	12.6	12.8	NA

Data as orig reptd.; bef. results of disc opers/spec. items. Per share data adj. for stk. divs. Bold denotes diluted EPS (FASB 128)-prior periods restated. E-Estimated. NA-Not Available. NM-Not Meaningful. NR-Not Ranked.

Office—Metro Center, One Station Place, Stamford, CT 06902. **Tel**—(203) 353-5500. **Chrmn, Pres & CEO**—J. F. Billett Jr. **VP, CFO & Treas**—A. L. Hunte. **VP & Secy**—J. T. Wiznitzer. **Dirs**—W. M. Becker, J. F. Billett Jr., A. S. Brown, N. Dunn, P. A. Jacobs, H. Palmberger, J. D. Sargent, F. D. Watkins, S. R. Wilcox. **Transfer Agent**—First Chicago Trust Co. of New York, NYC. **Incorporated**—in Delaware in 1985. **Empl**— 147. **S&P Analyst:** C.F.B.

STANDARD
&POOR'S
STOCK REPORTS

Triarc Cos.

NYSE Symbol **TRY**

In S&P SmallCap 600

23-OCT-99

Industry: Beverages (Non-Alcoholic)

Summary: TRY operates in the restaurant (Arby's) and beverage (Snapple, Royal Crown, Cable Car and Mistic) sectors.

Quantitative Evaluations

Outlook
(1 Lowest—5 Highest)
• 1+

Fair Value
• 12½

Risk
• **Average**

Earn./Div. Rank
• C

Technical Eval.
• NA

Rel. Strength Rank
(1 Lowest—99 Highest)
• 51

Insider Activity
• NA

Recent Price • 19⅝
52 Wk Range • 22⅛-14¾
Yield • Nil
12-Mo. P/E • NM

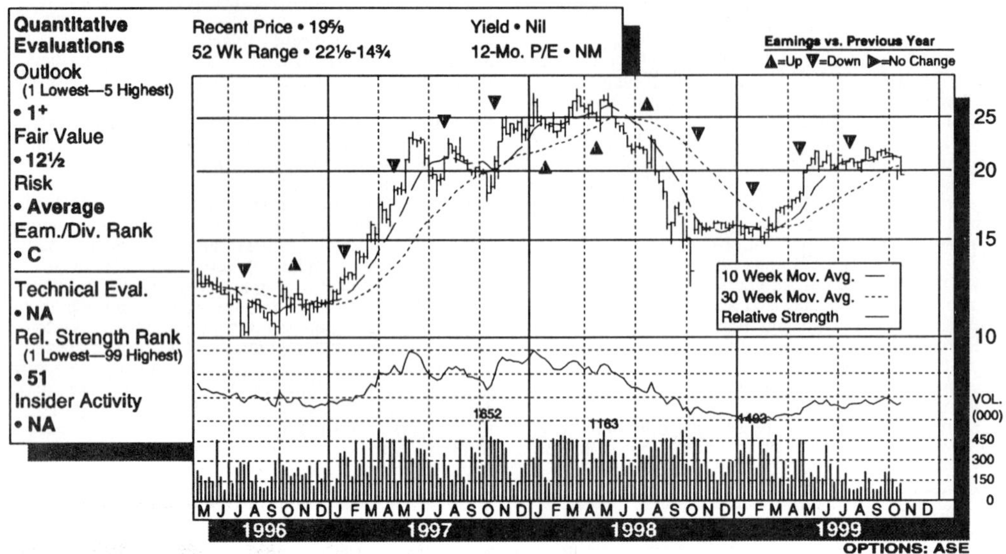

OPTIONS: ASE

Business Profile - 14-OCT-99

During the 1999 second quarter, the company introduced Elements, a new product platform of herbally enhanced drinks, to the Snapple category. Initial reaction to the new product was strong; approximately 1.4 million cases of Elements were sold in the second quarter. In July 1999, TRY sold its 42.7% interest in National Propane Partners to Columbia Propane Corp. In April 1999, the company repurchased 3.8 million common shares at $18.25 a share via a tender offer; the total cost was $70 million. In early 1999, two TRY executives withdrew an offer of $18 a share to take the company private.

Operational Review - 14-OCT-99

Revenues from continuing operations in the six months ended July 4, 1999, advanced 5.9%, year to year, reflecting higher premium beverage volume, aided by strong sales of Snapple. Despite wider gross margins, results were hurt by sharply higher interest expense, coupled with lower net investment income. After taxes at 47.1%, versus 57.0%, income from continuing operations fell 67%, to $10.5 million ($0.32 a share), from $3.5 million ($0.12). Per share results exclude income from discontinued operations of $0.02 and $0.05 in the respective periods, and a charge of $0.43 for early retirement of debt in the 1998 interim.

Stock Performance - 22-OCT-99

In the past 30 trading days, TRY's shares have declined 8%, compared to a 4% fall in the S&P 500. Average trading volume for the past five days was 31,960 shares, compared with the 40-day moving average of 31,215 shares.

Key Stock Statistics

Dividend Rate/Share	Nil	Shareholders	5,700
Shs. outstg. (M)	25.6	Market cap. (B)	$0.392
Avg. daily vol. (M)	0.030	Inst. holdings	27%
Tang. Bk. Value/Share	NM		
Beta	1.02		

Value of $10,000 invested 5 years ago: $ 8,000

Fiscal Year Ending Dec. 31

	1999	1998	1997	1996	1995	1994
Revenues (Million $)						
1Q	178.2	172.1	205.4	328.9	298.0	270.0
2Q	250.8	232.9	226.1	246.5	279.3	267.0
3Q	—	247.0	275.0	206.4	291.9	256.1
4Q	—	163.0	205.3	207.4	315.1	268.9
Yr.	—	815.0	861.3	989.3	1,184	1,063
Earnings Per Share ($)						
1Q	-0.04	0.05	-0.06	0.06	0.22	0.34
2Q	0.19	0.25	-1.07	-0.18	0.03	-0.13
3Q	—	0.07	0.33	1.54	-0.19	-0.18
4Q	—	0.01	0.09	-1.82	-1.30	-0.33
Yr.	—	0.38	-0.68	-0.46	-1.32	-0.71

Next earnings report expected: early November

Dividend Data

Cash dividends were omitted in 1974. The most recent stock payment was in 1986.

A Division of The McGraw-Hill Companies

Triarc Companies, Inc.

Business Summary - 14-OCT-99

Triarc Companies plans to achieve revenue and volume growth through its consumer product businesses: beverages and restaurants, with recognizable brand names such as Snapple and Arby's leading the way. Beverage operations are conducted through Triarc Beverage Group, which owns Snapple Beverage Corp., Mistic Brands, Inc., Cable Car Beverage Corp., and Royal Crown Co., Inc. Restaurant operations are conducted through the Triarc Restaurant Group (Arby's).

Snapple (purchased from Quaker Oats Co. in 1997) markets and distributes ready-to-drink teas, juice drinks, and juices. In 1998, Snapple sales accounted for 79% of the company's total premium beverage case sales, and the brand had the leading market share (26%) of premium beverage sales volume in grocery stores, mass merchandisers, and convenience stores. During 1998, TRY introduced WhipperSnapple, a smoothie like beverage.

In November 1997, TRY acquired Cable Car Beverage Corp., a marketer of premium soft drinks, primarily under the Stewart's brand name. The acquisitions helped the company's positioning in the premium beverage category. Stewart's case sales rose 17%, reflecting increased penetration of existing markets and continuing product innovation. In February 1999, Triarc acquired Millrose Distributors Inc., the second largest U.S. distributor of Stewarts products, for $17.3 million in cash.

The Mistic beverage business, acquired in 1995, develops and produces a wide variety of premium beverages, including fruit drinks, ready-to-drink teas, juices, and sweetened seltzers. Royal Crown produces and sells concentrates for soft drinks both domestically and internationally to licensed bottlers who distribute finished beverage products. RC Cola is the largest national brand cola available to the independent bottling system.

In May 1997, TRY sold all of the 355 company-owned Arby's restaurants to RTM Inc., the largest franchisee in the Arby's system. With the sale, Triarc Restaurant Group (TRG) became essentially a franchisor of restaurants. As of January 3, 1999, TRG franchised 3,135 single and co-branded Arby's unit. Franchisees have committed to open up to 1,011 Arby's restaurants over the next 12 years. To help develop its Arby's brand, TRG has developed a multi-branding strategy that allows a single restaurant to offer distinct but complementary brands. Currently, the company's two co-branded concepts include T.J. Cinnamons and p.t. Noodles.

In February 1999, TRY's subsidiaries sold $300 million principle amount 10.25% senior sunordinated notes due 2009, and concurrently entered into a new $535 million senior secured credit facility.

Per Share Data ($) (Year Ended Dec. 31)	1998	1997	1996	1995	1994	1993	1992	1991	1990	1989
Tangible Bk. Val.	NM	NM	NM	-1.22	-9.79	-11.82	-10.49	-3.84	-3.31	-2.86
Cash Flow	1.56	0.62	1.49	-0.26	1.40	-0.04	-0.26	1.72	1.21	1.34
Earnings	0.38	-0.68	-0.28	-1.24	-0.34	-1.62	-1.73	-0.29	-0.68	-0.51
Dividends	Nil	Nil	Nil	Nil	Nil	Nil	Nil	Nil	Nil	Nil
Payout Ratio	Nil	Nil	Nil	Nil	Nil	Nil	Nil	Nil	Nil	Nil
Prices - High	28½	27¾	14⅜	16¾	26⅛	33	15¼	4⅜	15⅝	16
- Low	12⅜	11½	10	9½	9½	14	3	1½	2¾	5⅜
P/E Ratio - High	75	NM	NM	NM	NM	NM	NM	NM	NM	NM
- Low	33	NM	NM	NM	NM	NM	NM	NM	NM	NM
Income Statement Analysis (Million $)										
Revs.	824	866	989	1,184	1,063	704	1,058	1,275	1,215	1,231
Oper. Inc.	117	105	119	98.2	118	55.0	117	111	79.0	114
Depr.	35.2	39.3	53.1	46.9	40.6	25.0	38.0	52.0	48.9	46.8
Int. Exp.	70.8	71.6	73.4	84.2	73.0	44.8	72.8	75.4	70.6	70.9
Pretax Inc.	28.6	-23.1	4.6	-38.2	0.8	-22.9	-39.3	-0.1	-33.8	-11.1
Eff. Tax Rate	58%	NM	NM	NM	199%	NM	NM	NM	NM	NM
Net Inc.	12.0	-20.6	-8.5	-30.4	-2.1	-3.0	-44.5	-7.5	-17.6	-12.9
Balance Sheet & Other Fin. Data (Million $)										
Cash	261	129	209	106	96.0	138	102	55.0	75.0	63.0
Curr. Assets	409	356	446	413	359	393	359	NA	NA	NA
Total Assets	1,020	1,005	854	1,086	922	897	911	882	917	929
Curr. Liab.	201	226	240	255	223	241	226	NA	NA	NA
LT Debt	699	605	501	763	612	575	489	308	364	425
Common Eqty.	10.9	44.0	6.8	20.7	-32.0	-76.0	-35.0	86.0	92.0	109
Total Cap.	797	741	576	808	675	572	591	468	522	605
Cap. Exp.	3.5	13.9	30.0	70.0	61.6	29.0	24.0	48.0	60.0	63.0
Cash Flow	47.3	18.8	44.6	-5.5	32.6	-9.3	-13.5	44.5	31.3	33.9
Curr. Ratio	2.0	1.6	1.9	1.6	1.6	1.6	1.6	NA	NA	NA
% LT Debt of Cap.	87.7	81.6	87.0	94.4	90.7	100.5	82.7	65.8	69.7	70.3
% Net Inc.of Revs.	1.5	NM	NM	NM	NM	NM	NM	NM	NM	NM
% Ret. on Assets	1.2	NM	NM	NM	NM	NM	NM	NM	NM	NM
% Ret. on Equity	43.8	NM	NM	NM	NM	NM	NM	NM	NM	NM

Data as orig. reptd.; bef. results of disc. opers. and/or spec. items. Per share data adj. for stk. divs. as of ex-div. date. Yrs. ended Apr. 30 of fol. cal. yr. prior to 1993. E-Estimated. NA-Not Available. NM-Not Meaningful. NR-Not Ranked.

Office—280 Park Ave., New York, NY 10017. **Tel**—(212) 451-3000. **Website**—http://www.triarc.com **Chrmn & CEO**—N. Peltz. **Pres & COO**—P. W. May. **EVP & CFO**—J. L. Barnes, Jr. **VP & Secy**—S. I. Rosen. **SVP & Investor Contact**—Anne A. Tarbell. **Dirs**—H. L Carey, C. Chajet, J. A. Levato, P. W. May, N. Peltz, D. E. Schwab II, J. S. Silverman, R. S. Troubb, G. Tsai Jr. **Transfer Agent & Registrar**—Harris Trust & Savings Bank, Chicago. **Incorporated**—in Ohio in 1929; reincorporated in Delaware in 1994. **Empl**— 1,880. **S&P Analyst:** A. Bensinger

STANDARD
&POOR'S
STOCK REPORTS

Trimble Navigation

NASDAQ Symbol **TRMB**

In S&P SmallCap 600

09-OCT-99

Industry: Electronics (Instrumentation)

Summary: Trimble makes satellite-based navigation, positioning and communication data devices.

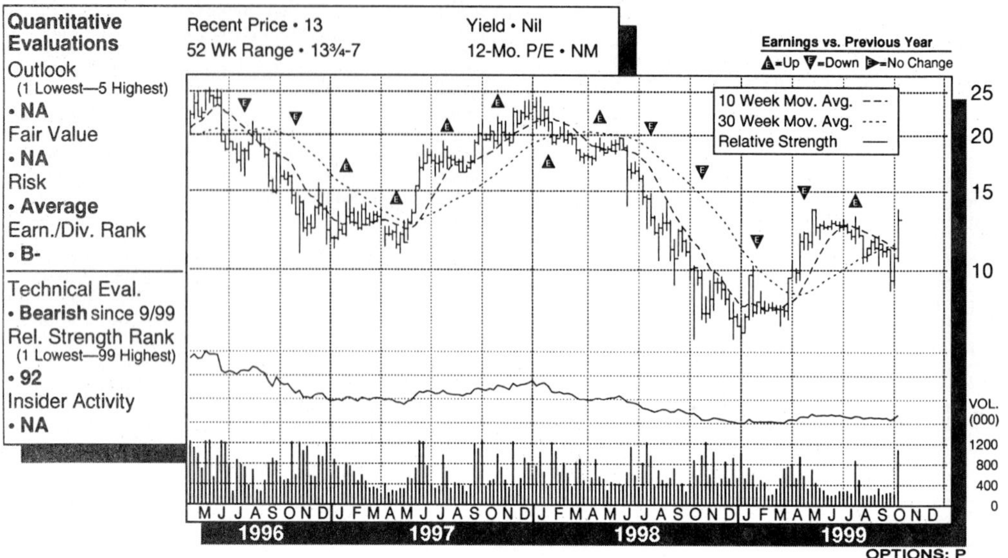

Business Profile - 30-JUN-99

TRMB's devices receive signals from the Global Positioning System (GPS) for navigation or positioning of ships, cars, and agricultural and surveying equipment. TRMB provides 30% of the GPS engines embedded in car navigation systems worldwide. In early 1999, TRMB launched a strategic alliance with Autodesk; Trimble Link software, the first collaboration, will be incorporated in the next release of Autodesk Survey software later in 1999. In April 1999, TRMB announced that it was negotiating the sale of its Sunnyvale, CA, manufacturing facility to Solectron, which would assume GPS and RF technology product production.

Operational Review - 30-JUN-99

Revenues from continuing operations in the first quarter of 1999 declined 7.3%, year to year (restated), due primarily to decreases in military, commercial marine and commercial avionics product lines. Gross margins were flat, as cost of goods sold fell along with sales; operating profit decreased 21%. Following lower interest income, and after taxes at 15.0%, versus 11.1%, income from continuing operations slumped 25%, to $3,014,000 ($0.14 a share, on 5.7% fewer shares) from $4,002,000 ($0.17). Results in the 1998 period exclude losses from discontinued operations of $0.09 a share.

Stock Performance - 08-OCT-99

In the past 30 trading days, TRMB's shares have increased 16%, compared to a 0.91% fall in the S&P 500. Average trading volume for the past five days was 214,840 shares, compared with the 40-day moving average of 69,577 shares.

Key Stock Statistics

Dividend Rate/Share	Nil	Shareholders	1,686
Shs. outstg. (M)	22.5	Market cap. (B)	$0.293
Avg. daily vol. (M)	0.089	Inst. holdings	31%
Tang. Bk. Value/Share	3.30		
Beta	0.74		

Value of $10,000 invested 5 years ago: $ 14,647

Fiscal Year Ending Dec. 31

	1999	1998	1997	1996	1995	1994
Revenues (Million $)						
1Q	68.77	71.66	60.55	56.72	49.90	37.19
2Q	70.84	71.92	68.94	58.60	59.01	44.45
3Q	—	57.42	64.72	54.09	62.83	46.70
4Q	—	59.28	78.09	64.25	63.63	47.36
Yr.	—	260.3	272.3	233.7	235.4	175.7
Earnings Per Share ($)						
1Q	**0.14**	**0.17**	**0.06**	**-0.05**	0.10	0.06
2Q	**0.20**	**0.11**	**0.17**	**-0.12**	0.21	0.13
3Q	—	**-0.68**	**0.07**	**-0.40**	0.20	0.19
4Q	—	**-0.82**	**0.10**	**0.06**	0.03	0.15
Yr.	—	**-1.19**	**0.40**	**-0.51**	**0.53**	**0.53**

Next earnings report expected: late October

Dividend Data

No cash dividends have been paid, and Trimble does not plan to pay any in the foreseeable future. Certain borrowing arrangements restrict the company's ability to pay cash dividends.

Trimble Navigation Limited

Business Summary - 30-JUN-99

California-based Trimble Navigation is a leader in emerging commercial markets for satellite-based navigation, positioning and communication data products using the NAVSTAR Global Positioning System (GPS). It designs, makes and markets electronic instruments to determine precise geographic location. The instruments, called GPS engines and systems, collect, analyze and display position data in forms optimized for a wide range of specific end-user applications. The market for GPS based products is expected to grow rapidly as new applications are developed.

TRMB follows a dual strategy to reach targeted markets. The company makes complete or partially integrated systems for high cost applications such as surveying and mapping, marine navigation and avionics. TRMB also sells GPS engines, chip sets embedded with software at the heart of the system, to makers of high volume, low cost applications, such as cellular and mobile computing platforms and car navigation systems. All products are derived from the same basic technology, but revenues are classified in two business units: Precision Positioning Group and Mobile and Timing Technologies.

The NAVSTAR system of 27 GPS satellites was established for use by the U.S. military, but is now available for use in commercial and civilian applications. TRMB's GPS engines are used in devices ranging from inexpensive hand-held receivers used by hikers, mountain climbers and boaters, to integration in complex aircraft navigation. TRMB's surveying products determine relative positions to accuracies down to one centimeter; marine, aviation and military navigation applications typically provide accuracy of a few meters.

TRMB sells to end-users through a network of dealers in more than 85 countries. Sales to unaffiliated customers in foreign locations accounted for 46% of the total in 1998; Europe and the Far East represented 25% and 13% of revenues in 1998. The company also has alliances with producers of electronic equipment that incorporate TRMB's GPS engines in their systems. Important alliances include Honeywell (commercial aircraft navigation), Pioneer, Philips, Xanavi, and GM's Delco division (in-car navigation). These alliances are becoming more important as the market for GPS devices expands from expensive devices used in commercial applications to devices for high volume consumer electronics markets. The range of possible uses for GPS continues to expand, as new ideas are pursued by independent companies.

In October 1998, TRMB decided to discontinue its General Aviation division as part of its strategy to return to profitability. However, in March 1999, the company reversed itself and decided to retain certain product lines included within this division.

Per Share Data ($) **(Year Ended Dec. 31)**	**1998**	**1997**	**1996**	**1995**	**1994**	**1993**	**1992**	**1991**	**1990**	**1989**
Tangible Bk. Val.	3.30	5.95	5.42	5.96	2.83	2.12	1.66	2.82	2.41	0.51
Cash Flow	-0.63	0.94	-0.05	0.91	0.93	0.59	-0.92	0.72	0.30	0.14
Earnings	-1.19	0.40	-0.51	0.53	0.53	0.19	-1.37	0.40	0.14	0.04
Dividends	Nil	Nil	Nil	Nil	Nil	Nil	Nil	Nil	Nil	Nil
Payout Ratio	Nil	Nil	Nil	Nil	Nil	Nil	Nil	Nil	Nil	Nil
Prices - High	24 3/8	24 1/4	26 1/4	35 3/8	16 3/4	13 1/2	18	19 1/4	11 3/4	NA
- Low	7	10 7/8	10 7/8	14 1/2	8 5/8	7 1/4	6 1/2	8 1/4	5 3/4	NA
P/E Ratio - High	NM	61	NM	67	32	71	NM	48	84	NA
- Low	NM	27	NM	27	16	38	NM	21	41	NA
Income Statement Analysis (Million $)										
Revs.	260	272	234	235	176	149	128	151	63.0	32.0
Oper. Inc.	-0.4	22.6	0.0	21.3	23.0	15.3	-7.5	15.4	5.3	2.8
Depr.	12.5	12.2	10.1	8.0	7.7	7.5	7.6	5.5	2.2	1.1
Int. Exp.	5.9	3.5	3.9	3.9	2.8	1.8	1.9	0.9	0.7	0.8
Pretax Inc.	-25.2	11.6	-11.6	14.0	12.2	4.2	-23.7	8.9	2.9	0.9
Eff. Tax Rate	NM	20%	NM	20%	18%	18%	NM	22%	25%	46%
Net Inc.	-26.6	9.3	-11.3	11.3	10.0	3.4	-23.0	7.0	2.1	0.5
Balance Sheet & Other Fin. Data (Million $)										
Cash	57.1	20.0	82.5	97.1	38.2	1.9	1.9	1.6	10.0	0.5
Curr. Assets	132	174	159	171	93.0	53.4	52.8	64.9	44.8	14.4
Total Assets	156	208	190	197	109	67.6	69.5	86.8	52.9	18.6
Curr. Liab.	49.9	37.5	34.9	35.5	22.8	NA	32.1	31.6	13.9	8.6
LT Debt	31.6	30.7	30.9	31.3	32.9	4.5	5.8	4.3	1.1	4.4
Common Eqty.	74.7	139	124	130	53.6	38.9	29.5	47.0	36.2	5.6
Total Cap.	106	170	155	161	86.5	43.4	35.3	51.2	37.3	10.0
Cap. Exp.	11.5	11.0	10.3	14.6	7.9	3.9	3.4	10.7	4.8	1.1
Cash Flow	-14.1	21.5	-1.2	19.3	17.7	10.9	-15.4	12.5	4.3	1.6
Curr. Ratio	2.6	4.6	4.6	4.8	4.1	2.2	1.6	2.1	3.2	1.7
% LT Debt of Cap.	29.8	18.1	19.9	19.4	38.1	10.5	16.6	8.3	3.0	44.1
% Net Inc.of Revs.	NM	3.4	NM	4.8	5.7	2.3	NM	4.6	3.4	1.6
% Ret. on Assets	NM	4.7	NM	7.4	11.2	4.9	NM	9.7	5.5	3.2
% Ret. on Equity	NM	7.0	NM	12.3	21.4	9.9	NM	16.3	9.8	14.5

Data as orig reptd.; bef. results of disc opers/spec. items. Per share data adj. for stk. divs. Bold denotes diluted EPS (FASB 128)-prior periods restated. E-Estimated. NA-Not Available. NM-Not Meaningful. NR-Not Ranked.

Office—645 North Mary Ave., Sunnyvale, CA 94086. **Tel**—(408) 481-8000. **Website**—www.trimble.com **Chrmn**—R. S. Cooper. **Pres & CEO**—S. W. Berglund. **VP-Fin & CFO**—M. E. Genovese. **Secy**—J. B. Goodrich. **Investor Contact**—Barbara Hall. **Dirs**—S. W. Berglund, R. S. Cooper, J. B. Goodrich, W. Hart, N. Y. Mineta, B. W. Parkinson. **Transfer Agent & Registrar**—ChaseMellon Shareholder Services, SF. **Incorporated**—in California in 1981. **Empl**— 1,291. **S&P Analyst:** John A. Massey

STANDARD
&POOR'S
STOCK REPORTS

True North Communications

NYSE Symbol **TNO**

In S&P SmallCap 600

09-OCT-99

Industry: Services (Advertising & Marketing)

Summary: TNO became the world's sixth largest advertising company through the late 1997 acquisition of Bozell, Jacobs, Kenyon and Eckhardt.

Quantitative Evaluations

Outlook
(1 Lowest—5 Highest)
• 2⁻

Fair Value
• 37⅞

Risk
• Average

Earn./Div. Rank
• B

Technical Eval.
• Bullish since 6/99

Rel. Strength Rank
(1 Lowest—99 Highest)
• 91

Insider Activity
• NA

Recent Price • 37⅝
52 Wk Range • 38¼-18¾
Yield • 1.6%
12-Mo. P/E • 41.3

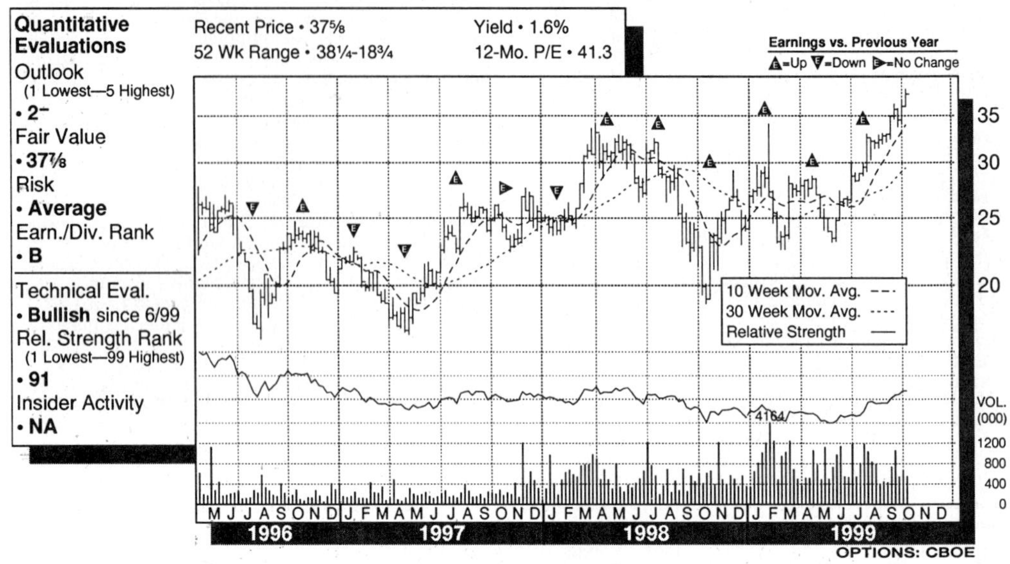

Business Profile - 27-AUG-99

The company nearly doubled in size with the late 1997 acquisition of Bozell, Jacobs, Kenyon and Eckhardt, Inc., in exchange for 18.6 million shares. It became the world's sixth largest advertising company, with more than $11.5 billion in billings, and 350 offices worldwide. In early November 1998, TNO said Bozell had been integrated successfully, with anticipated cost savings realized, as shown by strong results for 1998. With the acquisition of Bozell, the company acquired Poppe Tyson; in the 1998 third quarter, it combined Poppe Tyson with Modem Media to create one of the world's largest interactive marketing companies. Following an early February 1999 IPO, TNO retained a majority ownership interest in Modem Media.Poppe Tyson, Inc.

Operational Review - 27-AUG-99

Revenues in the first half of 1999 advanced 8.6%, year to year, reflecting acquisitions and internal growth. Operating costs and expenses were well controlled; with lower other expense, pretax income climbed 33%. After taxes at 43.5%, versus 47.1%, and lower equity income, net income was up 32%, to $28,207,000 ($0.58 a share, diluted), from $21,330,000 ($0.45). The company has said it intends to reduce staff costs to under 60% of revenues.

Stock Performance - 08-OCT-99

In the past 30 trading days, TNO's shares have increased 15%, compared to a 0.91% fall in the S&P 500. Average trading volume for the past five days was 109,180 shares, compared with the 40-day moving average of 122,467 shares.

Key Stock Statistics

Dividend Rate/Share	0.60	Shareholders	7,600
Shs. outstg. (M)	47.7	Market cap. (B)	$ 1.8
Avg. daily vol. (M)	0.140	Inst. holdings	52%
Tang. Bk. Value/Share	NM		
Beta	1.17		

Value of $10,000 invested 5 years ago: $ 18,184

Fiscal Year Ending Dec. 31

	1999	1998	1997	1996	1995	1994
Revenues (Million $)						
1Q	303.4	280.1	266.2	105.9	95.39	88.36
2Q	355.6	311.5	301.3	118.4	110.9	102.1
3Q	—	294.7	294.4	125.8	108.7	100.5
4Q	—	356.1	343.0	142.9	124.2	112.8
Yr.	—	1,242	1,205	493.1	439.1	403.7
Earnings Per Share ($)						
1Q	**0.15**	**0.08**	**-0.02**	**-0.01**	-0.49	0.09
2Q	**0.43**	**0.38**	**0.33**	**0.24**	0.51	0.46
3Q	—	**0.29**	**0.22**	**0.22**	0.19	0.18
4Q	—	**0.03**	**-1.73**	**0.43**	0.67	0.63
Yr.	—	**0.78**	**-1.17**	**0.81**	0.87	1.34

Next earnings report expected: early November

Dividend Data (Dividends have been paid since 1963.)

Amount ($)	Date Decl.	Ex-Div. Date	Stock of Record	Payment Date
0.150	Nov. 04	Dec. 16	Dec. 18	Jan. 04 '99
0.150	Mar. 03	Mar. 16	Mar. 18	Apr. 01 '99
0.150	May. 26	Jun. 15	Jun. 17	Jul. 01 '99
0.150	Aug. 04	Sep. 15	Sep. 17	Oct. 01 '99

True North Communications Inc.

Business Summary - 18-AUG-99

In December 1994, True North Communications Inc. succeeded Foote, Cone & Belding Communications, Inc. as the holding company for Foote, Cone & Belding, one of America's largest advertising agencies. In December 1997, through a merger with Bozell, Jacobs, Kenyon & Eckhardt, Inc., the company nearly doubled its size, adding Bozell Worldwide, Temerlin McClain, and other specialized communications businesses to its network. With these brands as the foundation, TNO is building a new type of architecture to offer clients leverageable marketplace advantage.

TNO offers full-service advertising through two separate, independent global agency networks: FCB Worldwide and Bozell Worldwide. The company also operates two significant independent regional full-service agencies, Temerlin McClain and Tierney & Partners. In addition, TNO owns certain marketing service and specialty advertising companies through the True North Diversified Services Companies, and certain interactive marketing companies through True North Technologies Inc.

FCB Worldwide and Bozell Worldwide, by themselves and through their respective subsidiaries and affiliates, independently operate advertising agency networks worldwide. Their primary business is to create marketing communications for their clients' goods and services across the total spectrum of advertising and promotion media. Each of the agency networks has its own clients and competes with the other in the same markets.

True North Diversified Services Companies offer a wide variety of marketing, communications and specialty advertising services. Marketing services include promotion, public relations, public affairs, direct/database marketing, branding consultancy, graphic arts, sports marketing and directory advertising. Specialty advertising includes health care and multicultural advertising. True North Diversified Services Companies have both U.S. and international operations, including BSMG Worldwide, Wahlstrom, Bozell Wellness Worldwide, Market Growth Resources, and McCracken Brooks.

Through planned acquisitions and internal growth, TNO believes it has become a communications company encompassing resources much broader in scope than other existing advertising holding companies. It considers its architecture unique, with three specialized business units: TN Technologies Inc., a leader in global interactive marketing; TN Media Inc., a global network of the company's specialists in the planning and buying of media time and space (one of the largest media buying companies in the world); and TN Services Inc., established to house all TNO's agency support services around the globe.

Per Share Data ($) (Year Ended Dec. 31)	1998	1997	1996	1995	1994	1993	1992	1991	1990	1989
Tangible Bk. Val.	NM	NM	3.79	5.87	6.65	6.46	6.24	5.44	6.13	5.69
Cash Flow	1.75	-0.06	2.01	1.66	1.99	1.81	1.46	-0.20	1.71	1.57
Earnings	0.78	-1.17	1.20	0.87	1.34	1.15	0.83	-0.91	1.05	0.97
Dividends	0.60	0.60	0.60	0.60	0.60	0.60	0.60	0.60	0.60	0.60
Payout Ratio	77%	NM	50%	69%	45%	54%	77%	NM	61%	65%
Prices - High	34	$27\frac{5}{8}$	$27\frac{3}{4}$	$21\frac{7}{8}$	24	24	$15\frac{3}{4}$	$13\frac{3}{4}$	$15\frac{1}{8}$	16
- Low	$18\frac{3}{4}$	17	$16\frac{1}{4}$	$15\frac{3}{4}$	$19\frac{7}{8}$	$14\frac{3}{4}$	$11\frac{1}{2}$	$9\frac{3}{8}$	$8\frac{7}{8}$	$11\frac{1}{4}$
P/E Ratio - High	44	NM	23	25	18	21	18	NM	14	16
- Low	24	NM	14	18	15	13	13	NM	8	12
Income Statement Analysis (Million $)										
Revs.	1,242	1,205	493	439	404	373	353	342	338	326
Oper. Inc.	163	91.9	42.7	48.0	51.9	47.9	39.9	35.4	42.8	41.4
Depr.	45.1	47.5	19.0	17.8	14.9	14.9	13.7	14.8	13.4	12.1
Int. Exp.	22.0	20.1	8.6	8.1	7.0	9.4	6.7	9.4	9.7	14.4
Pretax Inc.	96.9	-36.4	19.2	14.8	46.2	32.8	29.3	-16.5	34.4	32.9
Eff. Tax Rate	59%	NM	50%	16%	35%	20%	37%	NM	36%	38%
Net Inc.	36.1	-50.0	27.8	19.7	30.3	25.7	18.0	-19.1	21.6	19.6
Balance Sheet & Other Fin. Data (Million $)										
Cash	232	109	57.0	57.0	77.0	65.0	45.0	63.0	69.0	111
Curr. Assets	1,174	998	504	430	383	355	320	326	365	398
Total Assets	1,779	1,674	932	766	674	638	589	591	648	658
Curr. Liab.	1,335	1,232	553	476	400	341	315	326	376	394
LT Debt	15.3	35.9	31.5	5.4	5.5	35.4	31.3	37.2	43.1	43.3
Common Eqty.	307	331	241	222	208	200	183	163	191	178
Total Cap.	323	304	273	229	221	241	217	207	242	238
Cap. Exp.	40.5	42.4	17.7	9.0	9.7	9.0	8.2	9.8	14.9	20.0
Cash Flow	81.2	-2.5	46.8	37.4	45.2	40.6	31.7	-4.4	35.1	31.7
Curr. Ratio	0.9	0.8	0.9	0.9	1.0	1.0	1.0	1.0	1.0	1.0
% LT Debt of Cap.	4.7	11.8	11.5	2.4	2.5	14.7	14.4	18.0	17.8	18.1
% Net Inc.of Revs.	2.9	NM	5.6	4.5	7.5	6.9	5.1	NM	6.4	6.0
% Ret. on Assets	2.1	NM	3.3	5.2	4.7	4.2	3.0	NM	3.3	2.8
% Ret. on Equity	11.3	NM	12.0	9.1	15.0	13.4	10.3	NM	11.6	11.6

Data as orig reptd.; bef. results of disc opers/spec. items. Per share data adj. for stk. divs. Bold denotes diluted EPS (FASB 128)-prior periods restated. E-Estimated. NA-Not Available. NM-Not Meaningful. NR-Not Ranked.

Office—101 East Erie St., Chicago, IL 60611-2897. **Tel**—(312) 425-6500. **Chrmn & CEO**—D. Bell. **EVP & CFO**—D. L. Seeley. **SVP & Secy**—D. F. Perona. **Dirs**—D. A. Bell, R. W. Bess, D. M. Elliman, W. G. Gregory, L-A. Kelmenson, B. Mason, R. P. Mayer, M. E. Murphy, C. D. Peebler Jr., J. B. Ryan, M. R. Seymann, T. J. Theophilos, S. T. Vehslage. **Transfer Agent & Registrar**—First Chicago Trust Co. of New York, Jersey City, NJ. **Incorporated**—in Delaware in 1942. **Empl**— 11,448. **S&P Analyst:** S.S.

STANDARD &POOR'S
STOCK REPORTS

TrustCo Bank Corp NY

NASDAQ Symbol **TRST**

In S&P SmallCap 600

09-OCT-99 **Industry:** Banks (Regional)

Summary: Through its Trustco Bank subsidiary, this bank holding company operates more than 50 branch offices in the upstate region of New York.

Quantitative Evaluations

Outlook (1 Lowest—5 Highest) • **1**

Fair Value • **27¾**

Risk • **NA**

Earn./Div. Rank • **NR**

Technical Eval. • **Neutral** since 9/99

Rel. Strength Rank (1 Lowest—99 Highest) • **75**

Insider Activity • **Neutral**

Recent Price • 29½ Yield • 3.7%

52 Wk Range • 30½-23 12-Mo. P/E • 22.5

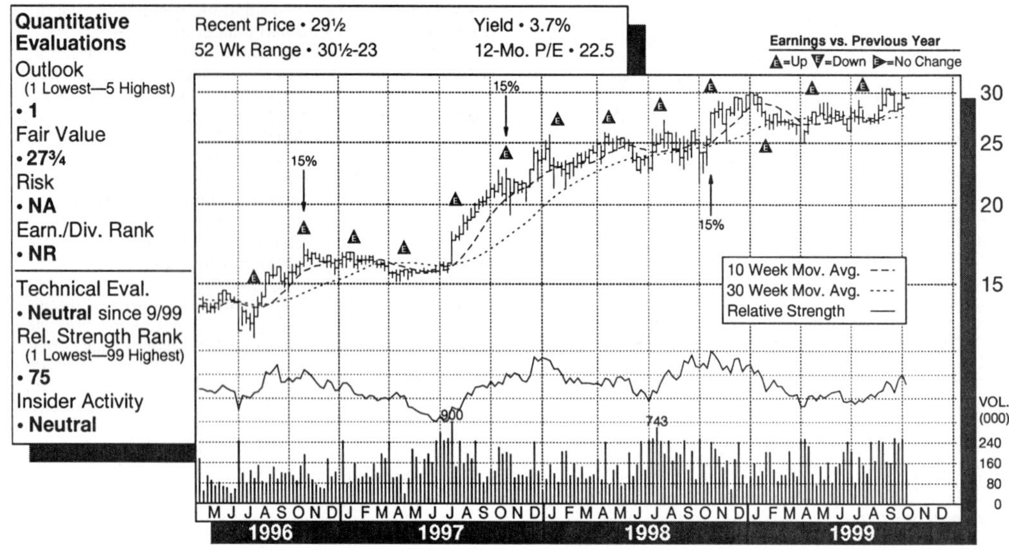

Business Profile - 08-SEP-99

The company has noted that the upstate New York region is experiencing continued consolidation of the banking industry, with two of TRST's strongest competitors acquired in 1998 by out of state banking companies. TrustCo evaluated a number of acquisition opportunities itself, but was not successful in completing any deals. During 1998, TRST opened two additional branches and plans to open two to three branches a year until the gaps in its market have been filled. Management plans on continuing an emphasis on home equity loan, home equity credit line and first mortgage products in 1999. Returns on average equity and assets for the six months ended June 30, 1999, were 22.47% and 1.56%, respectively, versus 21.37% and 1.43% in the six months ended June 30, 1998.

Operational Review - 08-SEP-99

Net interest income in the six months ended June 30, 1999, rose 5.6%, year to year, aided by an increase in earning assets. The provision for loan losses edged up 2.8%, to $3.0 million. Noninterest income was down 2.3%, and with a 3.2% rise in noninterest expense, pretax income gained 5.0%. After taxes at 34.0%, versus 37.2%, net income was up 10%, to $18,815,000 ($0.67 a share, as adjusted) from $17,044,000 ($0.61, adjusted for a 15% stock dividend). Per share amounts have not been adjusted for the 2-for-1 split payable November 12, 1999, to holders of record October 22.

Stock Performance - 08-OCT-99

In the past 30 trading days, TRST's shares have increased 3%, compared to a 0.91% fall in the S&P 500. Average trading volume for the past five days was 31,460 shares, compared with the 40-day moving average of 54,123 shares.

Key Stock Statistics

Dividend Rate/Share	1.10	Shareholders	7,309
Shs. outstg. (M)	26.9	Market cap. (B)	$0.792
Avg. daily vol. (M)	0.061	Inst. holdings	21%
Tang. Bk. Value/Share	6.94		
Beta	0.32		

Value of $10,000 invested 5 years ago: $ 35,594

Fiscal Year Ending Dec. 31

	1999	1998	1997	1996	1995	1994
Revenues (Million $)						
1Q	47.09	47.96	45.43	44.64	41.55	35.19
2Q	45.85	49.16	46.67	42.85	43.95	34.32
3Q	—	48.89	47.97	44.00	45.15	37.05
4Q	—	50.17	49.15	45.48	44.97	—
Yr.	—	196.2	189.2	177.0	175.6	144.8
Earnings Per Share ($)						
1Q	**0.33**	**0.30**	**0.27**	0.24	0.22	0.19
2Q	**0.34**	**0.31**	**0.29**	**0.24**	0.24	0.20
3Q	—	**0.33**	**0.30**	**0.27**	0.24	0.22
4Q	—	**0.31**	**0.30**	**0.28**	0.25	0.23
Yr.	—	**1.25**	**1.16**	**1.04**	**0.93**	**0.84**

Next earnings report expected: late October

Dividend Data (Dividends have been paid since 1982.)

Amount ($)	Date Decl.	Ex-Div. Date	Stock of Record	Payment Date
0.275	Feb. 16	Mar. 10	Mar. 12	Apr. 01 '99
0.275	May. 18	Jun. 09	Jun. 11	Jul. 01 '99
0.275	Aug. 17	Sep. 01	Sep. 03	Oct. 01 '99
2-for-1	Aug. 17	Nov. 15	Oct. 22	Nov. 12 '99

TrustCo Bank Corp NY

Business Summary - 08-SEP-99

TrustCo Bank Corp NY is one of only 40 (out of 16,000) U.S. companies to have delivered higher earnings per share for at least 20 consecutive years. The streak was kept alive in 1998 with an 8.7% increase in EPS. Operating mainly through its TrustCo Bank subsidiary, TRST has 53 offices and 33 automatic teller machines in Albany, Columbia, Greene, Rensselaer, Saratoga, Schenectady, Schoharie, Warren and Washington counties of New York. It also operates a full service trust department with $1.24 billion of assets under management. TrustCo Bank operates a general commercial banking business serving individuals, partnerships, corporations, municipalities and governments of New York.

Total loans of $1.32 billion at December 31, 1998, versus $1.30 billion a year earlier, consisted of 72% residential mortgage loans (70% a year earlier), 14% commercial loans (14%), 11% home equity credit lines (13%), 2% installment loans (2%), and 1% construction loans (1%).

The allowance for loan losses, which is set aside for possible loan defaults, was $54.4 million (4.11% of loans) at 1998 year end, up from $53.5 million (4.12%) a year earlier. Net chargeoffs, or the amount of loans actually written off as uncollectible, were $3.7 million (0.28% of average loans) in 1998, versus $3.5 million (0.28%) in 1997. Nonperforming assets, consisting of loans in nonaccrual status, loans past due three payments or more, restructured loans and foreclosed real estate, amounted to $17.6 million (0.71% of total assets) at the end of 1998, down from $20.0 million (0.84%) a year earlier.

Interest and fees on loans provided 56% of total income in 1998, interest and dividends on investment securities 30%, other interest income 3%, trust department income 4%, service fees 5%, and other noninterest income 2%

Deposits of $2.11 billion at the end of 1998 were divided: demand deposits 7%, savings deposits 31%, interest-bearing checking account deposits 13%, money market deposits 3%, and other time deposits 46%.

Management opened two additional branches in 1998 and plans to open two to three branches a year until the gaps in TRST's market have been filled. Approximately every seven years, each branch receives a major review and renovation.

Per Share Data ($) (Year Ended Dec. 31)	1998	1997	1996	1995	1994	1993	1992	1991	1990	1989
Tangible Bk. Val.	6.94	6.64	6.03	5.97	5.22	NA	NA	NA	NA	NA
Earnings	1.25	1.16	1.04	0.93	0.84	0.87	NA	NA	NA	NA
Dividends	0.96	0.86	0.72	0.63	0.50	0.41	NA	NA	NA	NA
Payout Ratio	77%	1%	1%	1%	1%	0%	NA	NA	NA	NA
Prices - High	30	25 1/4	17 3/8	15 1/8	11 3/4	11 3/8	NA	NA	NA	5 3/8
- Low	21 1/4	15 1/8	12 3/8	10	9 1/8	10 1/2	NA	NA	NA	4 1/4
P/E Ratio - High	24	22	16	16	14	13	NA	NA	NA	NA
- Low	17	13	11	10	10	12	NA	NA	NA	NA
Income Statement Analysis (Million $)										
Net Int. Inc.	85.7	85.5	84.3	81.4	79.6	72.0	66.9	42.6	33.1	31.5
Tax Equiv. Adj.	89.1	88.7	87.0	83.0	NA	NA	NA	NA	NA	NA
Non Int. Inc.	21.1	17.4	14.8	13.8	13.4	13.0	12.5	9.4	7.7	7.8
Loan Loss Prov.	4.6	5.4	6.6	12.7	8.1	11.6	12.7	6.5	2.7	2.1
Exp./Op. Revs.	45%	45%	42%	47%	44%	51%	54%	54%	54%	59%
Pretax Inc.	54.5	51.1	46.0	38.3	35.5	36.1	26.8	17.7	14.2	12.8
Eff. Tax Rate	36%	37%	38%	33%	36%	35%	35%	27%	26%	26%
Net Inc.	35.0	32.2	28.7	25.5	22.9	23.6	17.5	12.9	10.6	9.4
% Net Int. Marg.	3.81	4.02	4.07	4.18	4.25	NA	NA	NA	NA	NA
Balance Sheet & Other Fin. Data (Million $)										
Money Mkt. Assets	358	438	356	NA	NA	NA	NA	NA	NA	NA
Inv. Securities	742	602	619	NA	NA	NA	NA	NA	NA	NA
Com'l Loans	187	192	224	NA	NA	NA	NA	NA	NA	NA
Other Loans	1,136	1,108	1,019	NA	NA	NA	NA	NA	NA	NA
Total Assets	2,485	2,372	2,262	2,176	1,976	1,971	1,945	1,758	935	819
Demand Deposits	154	130	124	NA	NA	NA	NA	NA	NA	NA
Time Deposits	1,953	1,891	1,953	NA	NA	NA	NA	NA	NA	NA
LT Debt	Nil	Nil	Nil	NA	NA	NA	NA	NA	NA	NA
Common Eqty.	186	179	162	160	139	130	120	111	60.2	53.4
% Ret. on Assets	1.4	1.4	1.3	1.2	1.2	1.2	0.9	1.0	1.2	1.2
% Ret. on Equity	19.2	18.9	17.8	17.1	17.0	18.9	15.1	15.0	18.6	18.8
% Loan Loss Resv.	4.1	4.1	4.2	3.9	3.4	3.2	2.6	1.9	2.9	2.6
% Loans/Deposits	62.8	64.2	63.6	63.5	64.4	59.1	58.1	65.4	59.0	61.0
% Equity to Assets	7.5	7.4	7.3	7.2	6.8	6.4	6.3	6.4	6.5	6.3

Data as orig. reptd.; bef. results of disc. opers. and/or spec. items. Per share data adj. for stk. divs. as of ex-div. date. Bold denotes diluted EPS (FASB 128). E-Estimated. NA-Not Available. NM-Not Meaningful. NR-Not Ranked.

Office—320 State St., Schenectady, NY 12305. **Tel**—(518) 377-3311. **Pres & CEO**—R. A. McCormick. **VP & CFO**—R. T. Cushing. **Secy**—W. F. Terry. **Dirs**—B. A. Andreoli, L. O. Barthold, M. N. Brickman, J. A. Lucarelli, Jr., R. A. McCormick, N. A. McNamara, A. J. Marinello, J. S. Morris, J. H. Murphy, R. J. Murray, Jr., K. C. Peterson, W. D. Powers, W. J. Purdy, W. F. Terry. **Transfer Agent & Registrar**—TrustCo Bank, Schenectady. **Incorporated**—in New York in 1981. **Empl**— 480. **S&P Analyst:** M.I.

STANDARD
&POOR'S
STOCK REPORTS

Tuboscope Inc.

NYSE Symbol **TBI**

In S&P SmallCap 600

09-OCT-99

Industry: Oil & Gas (Drilling & Equipment)

Summary: TBI is the world's leading provider of oilfield tubular inspection and coating services; coiled tubing equipment; solids control services; and inspection equipment.

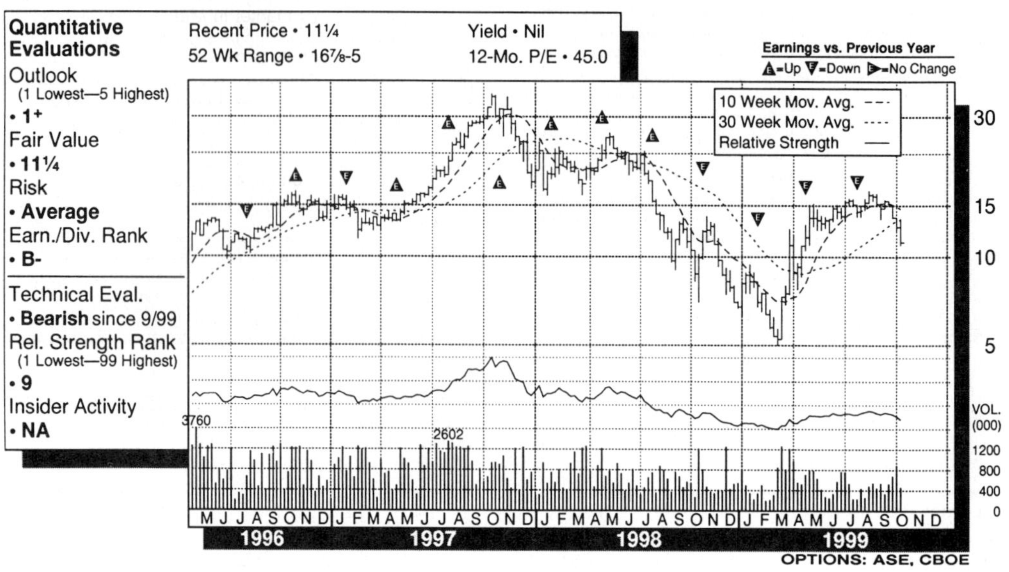

Business Profile - 12-JUL-99

In June 1999, the company agreed to merge with Newpark Resources Inc. (NYSE: NR) in a transaction valued at about $1.3 billion. The two companies had 1998 combined sales in excess of $800 million. Subject to shareholder, lender and regulatory approval, each of NR's 68.9 million common shares would be exchanged for 0.65 of a TBI common share. The combined company, which would be owned about equally by shareholders of each existing company, would combine TBI's leading position in solids control products used to separate drilling waste from drilling fluids with NR's drilling fluid and waste minimization and disposal capabilities. Although TBI will be the surviving company, its name is likely to be changed, to reflect the integrated services to be provided.

Operational Review - 12-JUL-99

Total revenues in the three months ended March 31, 1999, declined 37%, year to year, reflecting weak demand for the company's products, as a result of a 35% decrease in worldwide drilling activity. Gross profit dropped 55%, as a result of pricing pressures. Operating profit fell 86%. After taxes at 40.0%, versus 37.6%, net income plunged 98%, to $305,000 ($0.01 a share), from $14,233,000 ($0.30).

Stock Performance - 08-OCT-99

In the past 30 trading days, TBI's shares have declined 26%, compared to a 0.91% fall in the S&P 500. Average trading volume for the past five days was 89,880 shares, compared with the 40-day moving average of 110,995 shares.

Key Stock Statistics

Dividend Rate/Share	Nil	Shareholders	300
Shs. outstg. (M)	44.3	Market cap. (B)	$0.499
Avg. daily vol. (M)	0.126	Inst. holdings	31%
Tang. Bk. Value/Share	2.23		
Beta	1.15		

Value of $10,000 invested 5 years ago: $ 18,367

Fiscal Year Ending Dec. 31

	1999	1998	1997	1996	1995	1994
Revenues (Million $)						
1Q	95.21	150.2	105.5	47.02	43.69	45.53
2Q	92.71	153.5	126.0	94.64	45.65	45.24
3Q	—	139.8	141.4	94.67	47.07	49.45
4Q	—	124.2	152.3	105.1	53.61	51.95
Yr.	—	567.7	525.2	341.4	190.0	192.2
Earnings Per Share ($)						
1Q	**0.01**	**0.30**	**0.19**	**-2.97**	**0.05**	0.05
2Q	**-0.03**	**0.31**	**0.28**	**-0.02**	**0.09**	0.07
3Q	—	**0.20**	**0.32**	**0.16**	**0.10**	0.11
4Q	—	**0.08**	**0.34**	**0.01**	**0.20**	0.18
Yr.	—	**0.89**	**1.14**	**-1.17**	**0.44**	0.41

Next earnings report expected: late October

Dividend Data

No cash dividends have been paid on the common shares.

Tuboscope Inc.

Business Summary - 12-JUL-99

Serving markets in 49 countries, Tuboscope is a leading supplier of oilfield products and services to the petroleum industry and provides tubular and pipeline quality assurance and inspection services to a diverse range of industries. The company has four main product lines. Tubular services include internal coating products and services and inspection and quality assurance services for tubular goods. Solids control products and services consist of the sale and rental of technical equipment used in oil and gas drilling processes. Coiled tubing and pressure control products include highly engineered coiled tubing, pressure control, wireline and related tools to companies providing oil and gas well drilling, completion and remediation services. Pipeline and other industrial services provide technical inspection services and quality assurance for in-service pipelines used to transport oil and gas.

TBI is the successor of one of the first companies to provide tubular inspection services to the oil and gas industry, with operations dating back to 1937. The company has since expanded its product line through mergers and acquisitions. It entered the coiled tubing and pressure control products businesses in April 1996, through a merger with D.O.S., Ltd., the largest provider of solids control services and coiled tubing equipment worldwide. During 1997, TBI acquired 11 companies, and it purchased eight more in 1998.

Tubular services is the largest business line, accounting for 39% of total revenues in 1998 (43% in 1997 and 51% in 1996). The company provides tubular inspection services at drilling and workover rig locations, at pipe yards owned by its customers, at steel mills making tubular goods, and at facilities which it owns. TBI entered the fiberglass tubular market in March 1997, with the acquisition of Fiber Glass Systems, Inc. The company believes it is the world's largest provider of tubular inspection and internal tubular coating services.

The company also believes it is the world's leading maker and provider of solids control equipment and services (30% of revenues in 1998) to the oil and natural gas drilling industry. TBI believes market conditions are improving in solids control, due to strong demand by oil and gas drillers to reduce overall drilling costs and minimize environmental impact.

Coiled tubing and pressure products (21% of revenues) include capital equipment and consumables sold to oilfield coiled tubing service companies. TBI sees advances in the manufacturing process of coiled tubing, tubing fatigue protection, and the capability to make larger diameter coiled tubing strings increasing the use and application for these products.

The company sees growth opportunities in pipeline services, reflecting the aging of the worldwide pipeline network, and new pipeline construction. An extensive pipeline infrastructure in Eastern Europe is also expected to contribute to future growth in this area.

Per Share Data ($) (Year Ended Dec. 31)	1998	1997	1996	1995	1994	1993	1992	1991	1990	1989
Tangible Bk. Val.	NM	1.68	1.54	2.39	6.14	5.72	1.83	1.78	3.15	3.56
Cash Flow	1.55	1.69	-0.70	1.25	1.03	0.10	0.70	0.89	0.87	0.63
Earnings	0.89	1.14	-1.17	0.44	0.41	-0.49	0.15	0.35	0.34	0.08
Dividends	Nil	Nil	Nil	Nil	Nil	Nil	Nil	Nil	Nil	Nil
Payout Ratio	Nil	Nil	Nil	Nil	Nil	Nil	Nil	Nil	Nil	Nil
Prices - High	26 1/2	36	16 3/4	8 1/2	8	10 1/4	8 1/4	10	11 1/2	NA
- Low	6 1/4	11 1/2	5 5/8	5 5/8	4 1/2	5 3/4	4 1/2	6 3/8	6	NA
P/E Ratio - High	30	32	NM	19	20	NM	55	29	34	NA
- Low	7	10	NM	13	11	NM	30	18	18	NA
Income Statement Analysis (Million $)										
Revs.	568	525	341	190	192	183	165	152	128	108
Oper. Inc.	118	127	61.6	42.5	38.4	26.5	27.1	28.8	24.0	18.4
Depr.	30.9	26.1	17.6	15.0	11.4	10.8	9.9	6.9	5.4	6.4
Int. Exp.	18.1	14.5	13.4	12.3	12.9	11.4	12.6	11.3	12.0	9.4
Pretax Inc.	67.8	85.6	-34.9	15.0	15.0	-9.9	5.3	7.5	6.4	1.9
Eff. Tax Rate	37%	37%	NM	42%	40%	NM	19%	37%	38%	48%
Net Inc.	41.9	53.1	-43.2	8.8	8.3	-8.4	3.5	4.5	4.0	1.0
Balance Sheet & Other Fin. Data (Million $)										
Cash	8.7	12.6	10.4	9.4	8.5	2.5	5.3	32.9	4.2	7.3
Curr. Assets	230	248	166	85.0	81.0	72.3	66.3	95.1	46.8	41.9
Total Assets	712	686	505	307	317	310	300	327	191	173
Curr. Liab.	116	166	91.8	40.1	45.1	67.0	38.1	45.3	19.6	20.0
LT Debt	219	188	168	107	124	101	101	118	82.0	69.0
Common Eqty.	339	300	219	121	113	105	120	115	70.0	66.0
Total Cap.	585	510	402	255	261	229	250	268	172	153
Cap. Exp.	39.8	35.2	18.6	7.6	7.5	20.2	5.3	39.2	9.3	2.5
Cash Flow	72.8	79.2	-25.6	23.2	18.9	1.8	12.7	11.3	8.9	7.4
Curr. Ratio	2.0	1.5	1.8	2.1	1.8	1.1	1.7	2.1	2.4	2.1
% LT Debt of Cap.	37.5	36.8	41.8	42.0	47.5	44.3	40.6	44.1	47.8	44.7
% Net Inc.of Revs.	7.4	10.1	NM	4.7	4.3	NM	2.1	3.0	3.1	0.9
% Ret. on Assets	6.0	8.9	NM	2.9	2.6	NM	1.1	1.5	0.9	0.6
% Ret. on Equity	13.1	20.5	NM	7.0	6.9	NM	2.4	4.1	NM	2.9

Data as orig reptd.; bef. results of disc opers/spec. items. Per share data adj. for stk. divs. Bold denotes diluted EPS (FASB 128)-prior periods restated. E-Estimated. NA-Not Available. NM-Not Meaningful. NR-Not Ranked.

Office—2835 Holmes Rd., Houston, TX 77051; P.O. Box 808, Houston, TX 77001. **Tel**—(713) 799-5100. **Chrmn**—L. E. Simmons. **Pres & CEO**—J. Lauletta. **EVP, Treas, CFO & Investor Contact**—Joe Winkler. **Dirs**—J. R. Baier, J. F. Lauletta, E. L. Mattson, L. E. Simmons, J. Smisek, D. E. Swanson. **Transfer Agent & Registrar**—Chase Shareholder Services Group, Inc., Dallas. **Incorporated**—in Delaware in 1988. **Empl**— 3,999. **S&P Analyst:** M.C.

U.S. Bioscience

ASE Symbol **UBS**

In S&P SmallCap 600

09-OCT-99 **Industry:** Health Care (Drugs - Generic & Other)

Summary: This pharmaceutical company develops and sells products to treat cancer, AIDS and allied diseases.

Quantitative Evaluations

Outlook (1 Lowest—5 Highest)
• **1⁻**

Fair Value
• **13⅛**

Risk
• **High**

Earn./Div. Rank
• **C**

Technical Eval.
• **Bullish** since 8/99

Rel. Strength Rank (1 Lowest—99 Highest)
• **97**

Insider Activity
• **NA**

Recent Price • 15½
52 Wk Range • 15⅞-5⅛
Yield • Nil
12-Mo. P/E • NM

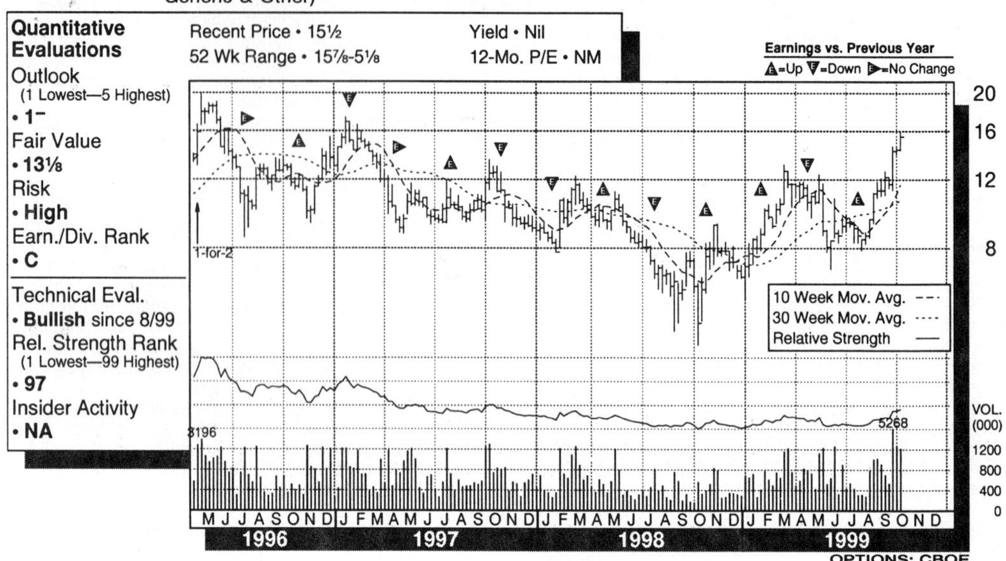

OPTIONS: CBOE

Business Profile - 29-JUN-99

UBS received FDA approval in June 1999, and EU approval in April 1999, for the use of Ethyol, a cytoprotective agent, to reduce radiation therapy-induced dry mouth in head and neck cancer patients. Ethyol, which is also used to reduce toxicity associated with chemotherapy, is marketed in the U.S. by ALZA Corp., and in Europe by Schering-Plough. ALZA also markets UBS's NeuTrexin drug (an intravenous treatment for pneumonia) and Hexalen (an oral treatment for advanced ovarian cancer). In May 1999, UBS reported that interim Phase III clinical trial results indicate that NeuTrexin may enhance the efficacy of combination drug treatments for use in colorectal cancer. Lodenosine is an HIV/AIDS inhibitor currently in Phase I/II clinical trials, and the company is also investigating the potential use of Ethyol in treating bone marrow disorders.

Operational Review - 29-JUN-99

Total revenues in the first quarter ended March 31, 1999 fell 28%, year to year, as 52% higher product sales, chiefly attributable to Ethyol sales growth, were offset by significantly lower licensing, royalty and other income, in the absence of a $5 million milestone payment for Ethyol. Following a 13% rise in R&D costs, primarily due to clinical trials, 20% higher cost of sales, and 20% lower G&A costs, total expenses were up only fractionally. The net loss was $3,122,200 ($0.12 a share) compared to $136,700 ($0.01). Cash and investments totaled $32.9 million on March 31, 1999.

Stock Performance - 08-OCT-99

In the past 30 trading days, UBS's shares have increased 38%, compared to a 0.91% fall in the S&P 500. Average trading volume for the past five days was 267,460 shares, compared with the 40-day moving average of 324,485 shares.

Key Stock Statistics

Dividend Rate/Share	Nil	Shareholders	4,669
Shs. outstg. (M)	27.4	Market cap. (B)	$0.424
Avg. daily vol. (M)	0.452	Inst. holdings	32%
Tang. Bk. Value/Share	1.99		
Beta	1.21		

Value of $10,000 invested 5 years ago: $ 9,253

Fiscal Year Ending Dec. 31

	1999	1998	1997	1996	1995	1994
Revenues (Million $)						
1Q	7.42	10.34	4.21	3.83	2.64	2.41
2Q	9.09	5.11	14.52	4.84	3.61	1.77
3Q	—	6.77	4.51	6.66	2.62	2.01
4Q	—	7.24	4.48	5.14	22.47	2.36
Yr.	—	29.47	27.72	20.46	31.35	8.55
Earnings Per Share ($)						
1Q	**-0.12**	**-0.01**	-0.16	-0.16	-0.20	-0.30
2Q	**-0.07**	**-0.13**	0.17	-0.12	-0.12	-0.36
3Q	—	**-0.10**	-0.16	0.02	-0.28	-0.28
4Q	—	**-0.14**	**-0.19**	-0.17	0.60	-0.26
Yr.	—	**-0.37**	**-0.33**	**-0.43**	**-0.01**	**-1.19**

Next earnings report expected: mid October

Dividend Data

No cash dividends have been paid. A one-for-two reverse stock split was effected in April 1996.

U.S. Bioscience, Inc.

Business Summary - 29-JUN-99

U.S. Bioscience develops and markets drugs for the treatment of patients with cancer and AIDS. The company's strategy is to acquire the rights to potential drug candidates through licensing agreements with other firms. UBS then attempts to cultivate these candidates through the clinical trial and regulatory approval processes. Three drugs (Ethyol, NeuTrexin and Hexalen) have received marketing approval in the U.S. and several major foreign markets.

Ethyol, an injectable agent used to protect healthy cells from the harmful effects of chemotherapy, has received marketing approval in 50 countries for a range of indications. In the U.S., the product is indicated for the reduction of kidney toxicity associated with the administration of cisplatin (a chemotherapeutic) in patients with advanced ovarian and non-small cell lung cancer. In April 1999, UBS received European Union approval for utilizing Ethyol as a radioprotective agent in the treatment of head and neck cancer. European marketing partner Schering-Plough paid UBS $3 million for this milestone. In June 1999, Ethyol was approved for the same indication by the FDA.

NeuTrexin is a methotrexate analog, commonly used as an intravenous anticancer agent, used to treat Pneumocystis carinii pneumonia in patients with immune system disorders. UBS is currently conducting Phase III clinical trials of NeuTrexin as a combination drug for advanced colorectal cancer. An oral formulation is under development for potentially treating psoriasis and rheumatoid arthritis.

Hexalen is a cytotoxic drug approved to treat patients with persistent or recurrent ovarian cancer following first-line combination chemotherapy. Hexalen is approved in the U.S. and 20 additional countries.

Lodenosine is an anti-HIV reverse transcriptase inhibitor currently in Phase I/II clinical trials at the National Institutes of Health (NIH). Data from a Phase I clinical trial demonstrated anti-HIV activity even in patients who had failed other anti-retroviral therapies such as AZT, 3TC, and d4T.

The company has distribution and marketing agreements with ALZA for the co-promotion of Ethyol, NeuTrexin, and Hexalen in the U.S. For territories outside the U.S., UBS has entered into distribution and licensing agreements for these products with a number of pharmaceutical companies, including Schering-Plough and Eli Lilly & Co. The company plans to solely market and distribute NeuTrexin and Hexalen after the co-promotion of these two drugs with ALZA ends in mid-1999.

In February 1999, UBS privately placed 2.7 million shares of common stock with Domain Partners IV L.P. and Proquest Investments L.P., raising $20 million. Research and development costs for the first quarter ended March 31, 1999 were $5.5 million, compared with $4.8 million in the first quarter of 1998.

Per Share Data ($)										
(Year Ended Dec. 31)	**1998**	**1997**	**1996**	**1995**	**1994**	**1993**	**1992**	**1991**	**1990**	**1989**
Tangible Bk. Val.	1.59	1.94	1.61	1.38	1.18	1.92	3.92	4.80	2.08	0.54
Cash Flow	-0.34	-0.30	-0.39	0.04	-1.14	-2.02	-1.00	-0.34	-0.30	-0.52
Earnings	-0.37	-0.33	-0.43	-0.02	-1.20	-2.06	-1.02	-0.36	-0.30	-0.52
Dividends	Nil	Nil	Nil	Nil	Nil	Nil	Nil	Nil	Nil	Nil
Payout Ratio	Nil	Nil	Nil	Nil	Nil	Nil	Nil	Nil	Nil	Nil
Prices - High	12¼	17⅜	19⅞	11½	20¾	24½	88	80¾	20⅞	14
- Low	4½	8⅜	8½	4	3¼	12½	12¼	16¾	8¾	6½
P/E Ratio - High	NM	NM	NM	NM	NM	NM	NM	NM	NM	NM
- Low	NM	NM	NM	NM	NM	NM	NM	NA	NA	NA
Income Statement Analysis (Million $)										
Revs.	20.7	12.9	10.8	8.7	7.3	4.4	4.1	3.5	0.2	Nil
Oper. Inc.	-16.8	-21.6	-8.1	1.0	-24.2	-33.4	-26.9	-13.8	-7.9	-5.7
Depr.	0.9	0.8	1.1	1.0	1.0	0.8	0.6	0.3	0.1	0.1
Int. Exp.	0.1	0.2	0.5	0.3	0.1	Nil	Nil	0.1	0.2	0.5
Pretax Inc.	-9.1	-7.9	-9.7	-0.2	-24.0	-40.6	-20.2	-6.5	-4.9	-5.7
Eff. Tax Rate	NM	NM	NM	NM	NM	NM	NM	Nil	Nil	Nil
Net Inc.	-9.1	-7.9	-9.7	-0.2	-24.0	-40.6	-20.2	-6.5	-4.9	-5.7
Balance Sheet & Other Fin. Data (Million $)										
Cash	6.8	26.6	36.7	45.6	24.4	48.4	77.2	95.5	38.0	13.0
Curr. Assets	30.2	45.2	43.0	56.0	28.0	5.9	80.0	97.5	39.0	13.6
Total Assets	52.7	62.4	49.1	61.9	34.5	57.8	83.3	99	40.2	14.1
Curr. Liab.	11.5	12.4	8.9	13.0	6.4	8.6	5.3	3.8	2.6	2.0
LT Debt	0.5	1.1	1.9	19.0	1.0	Nil	Nil	Nil	0.7	4.0
Common Eqty.	38.9	47.0	36.9	28.8	23.9	38.1	77.5	94.1	35.0	6.8
Total Cap.	39.4	48.1	38.7	47.9	24.9	38.1	77.5	94.1	35.8	10.8
Cap. Exp.	0.8	0.9	1.1	0.5	1.3	3.6	2.2	0.8	1.0	0.1
Cash Flow	-8.2	-7.1	-8.6	0.8	-23.0	-39.8	-19.6	-6.2	-4.8	-5.7
Curr. Ratio	2.6	4.6	4.8	4.3	4.3	6.1	15.0	25.4	15.2	6.6
% LT Debt of Cap.	1.3	2.3	4.8	39.9	4.0	Nil	Nil	Nil	2.0	37.3
% Net Inc.of Revs.	NM	NM	NM	NM	NM	NM	NM	NM	NM	NM
% Ret. on Assets	NM	NM	NM	NM	NM	NM	NM	NM	NM	NM
% Ret. on Equity	NM	NM	NM	NM	NM	NM	NM	NM	NM	NM

Data as orig. reptd.; bef. results of disc. opers. and/or spec. items. Per share data adj. for stk. divs. as of ex-div. date. Qtrly. rev. table incl. other income. Bold denotes diluted EPS (FASB 128). E-Estimated. NA-Not Available. NM-Not Meaningful. NR-Not Ranked.

Office—One Tower Bridge, 100 Front St., West Conshohocken, PA 19428. **Tel**—(610) 832-0570. **Website**—http://www.usbio.com **Chrmn**—A. Misher. **Pres & CEO**—C. B. Clarke. **EVP, CFO & Investor Contact**—Robert I. Kriebel. **EVP-Secy**—M.E. Manning. **Dirs**—C. B. Clarke, B. H. Dovey, R. I. Kriebel, D. J. MacMaster Jr., A. Misher, G. H. Ohye, B. Wright. **Transfer Agent & Registrar**—American Stock Transfer & Trust Co., NYC. **Incorporated**—in Delaware in 1987. **Empl**— 170. **S&P Analyst:** Frank DiLorenzo

STANDARD
&POOR'S
STOCK REPORTS

U.S. Home

NYSE Symbol **UH**

In S&P SmallCap 600

09-OCT-99 **Industry:** Homebuilding

Summary: This company, one of the largest U.S. builders of single-family homes, also provides mortgage financing.

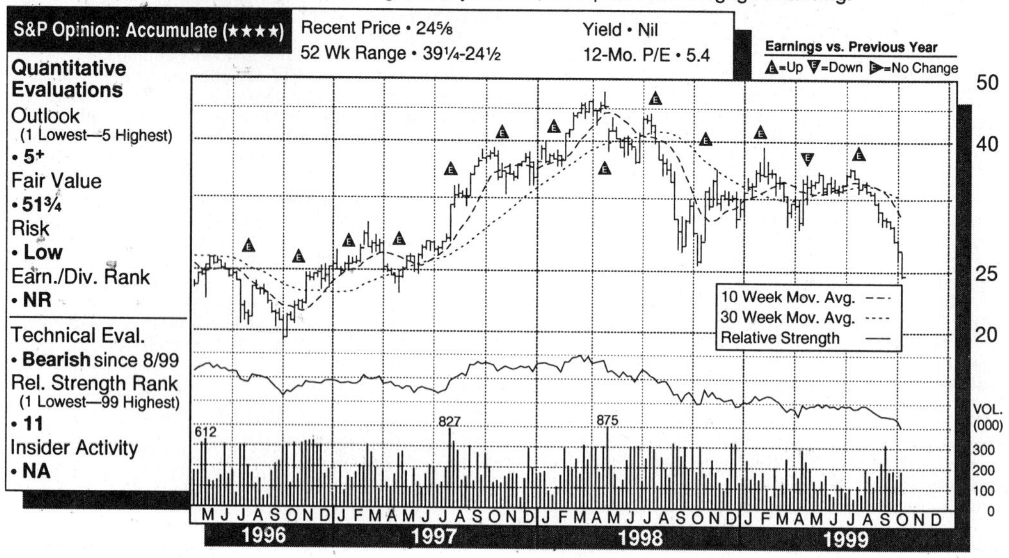

Overview - 01-SEP-99

Revenue growth should go on into 2000. Near-term gains should remain solid, as UH closes on its sizable order backlog. However, a mature housing cycle and tough comparisons could moderate the gains as we move further through 2000. Rising mortgage rates since the fall of 1998 also pose a big threat, but we expect a short Fed Funds (an overnight lending rate) tightening program and productivity gains to settle down long-term rates. Diverse home offerings, a concentration in demographically favorable regions, and a growing focus on retirement/active adult markets should also aid UH. Margins should widen a bit, on higher sales volume and a greater proportion of higher-margined California home sales. The timing of retirement community openings will also have an influence. Preselling in retirement communities (UH always presells in that sector) limits margins somewhat, as revenues lag costs, but the communities aid UH's bottom line considerably as they take on residents.

Valuation - 01-SEP-99

The shares have mostly weakened since mid-1998. The downturn has reflected capital market worries in the last half of 1998, rising mortgage rates and a mature housing cycle. We still think that a variety of factors will enable mortgage rates to grow more accommodating over the next year. Given that forecast, we also believe UH's positive market and geographic concentrations will let it record solid EPS gains through 2000. The shares have been trading at one of the lower forward earnings multiples in the industry. When combined with our generally positive outlook for UH's business prospects over the next couple of years, we find the shares undervalued. However, we would limit the aggressiveness of our purchases pending better visibility of the interest rate situation, as we feel lower rates are necessary for the housing upcycle to go on.

Key Stock Statistics

S&P EPS Est. 1999	4.95	Tang. Bk. Value/Share	41.08
P/E on S&P Est. 1999	5.0	Beta	1.21
S&P EPS Est. 2000	5.50	Shareholders	2,056
Dividend Rate/Share	Nil	Market cap. (B)	$0.330
Shs. outstg. (M)	13.4	Inst. holdings	82%
Avg. daily vol. (M)	0.035		

Value of $10,000 invested 5 years ago: $ 9,248

Fiscal Year Ending Dec. 31

	1999	1998	1997	1996	1995	1994
Revenues (Million $)						
1Q	400.6	334.5	316.0	272.8	263.2	225.3
2Q	459.9	367.5	340.5	293.3	259.3	241.1
3Q	—	382.0	337.3	317.7	286.7	255.8
4Q	—	413.6	325.9	327.8	298.8	273.1
Yr.	—	1,498	1,320	1,211	1,108	995.3
Earnings Per Share ($)						
1Q	**1.06**	**1.49**	**0.75**	**0.69**	0.70	0.60
2Q	**1.28**	**1.01**	**0.82**	**0.75**	0.67	0.63
3Q	**E1.27**	**1.00**	**0.94**	**0.91**	0.83	0.81
4Q	**E1.34**	**1.20**	**1.00**	**0.94**	0.92	0.82
Yr.	**E4.95**	**4.68**	**3.50**	**3.28**	**2.78**	**2.50**

Next earnings report expected: late October

Dividend Data

The most recent payment was in September 1984.

A Division of The McGraw-Hill Companies

U.S. Home Corporation

Business Summary - 01-SEP-99

U.S. Home Corporation has been among the 10 largest on-site homebuilders in the U.S. for more than 20 years. The company currently sells homes in more than 230 new home communities in 33 market areas in 12 different states across the nation. The greatest proportion of its sales come from Florida, Colorado, Arizona, California and Texas. The company sells homes to both first-time and move-up buyers, and in response to changing demographic trends, has become one of the largest builders in the retirement/active adult market. UH emerged from Chapter 11 bankruptcy protection in June 1993, two years after filing its petition.

U.S. Home delivered 8,258 homes in 1998, at an average price of $175,000, compared with 7,496 homes at an average price of $170,500 in the prior year. Single-family detached units accounted for 78% to 83% of unit volume over the past three years. UH seeks to generate one-third of sales through advertisements, one-third through customer referrals and one-third through realtor contacts. The homebuilding industry tends to be quite cyclical, with sales and profit performance sensitive to interest rates, fluctuations in economic activity and the level of consumer confidence.

Like most major builders, the company employs independent subcontractors to perform all land development and construction activities. This allows UH to minimize its investment in direct labor costs, equipment and facilities. To coordinate subcontractor activities and ensure that quality standards are met, U.S. Home places on-site company managers at projects.

During 1998, 35% of UH's home deliveries consisted of affordable homes, 39% move-up homes and the remaining 26% retirement and active adult homes. Recognizing the imminent graying of the nation's population, UH set a goal several years ago to boost retirement/active adult/intergenerational development sales to one-third of its home closings by the end of the decade. The company had a total of 30 such communities in operation as of July 1999, after opening seven new developments of that sort in 1999's second quarter. (UH also closed out several communities in the first half of the year.) It had 10 more planned for opening over the two years to follow.

Through U.S. Home Mortgage Corp., the company also originates mortgage loans for purchasers of UH's homes and those of third parties. It then sells the mortgages and related servicing rights to investors.

UH experienced a 17% year-to-year increase in new home unit orders (including joint venture activities) in 1999's second quarter. Following disappointing first quarter orders related to delays in community openings, orders for the first half of the year fell by 1.1%. The company also experienced a 23% rise in order backlog from a year earlier (9.2% on a unit basis), to a record $1.2 billion as of June 30, 1999.

Per Share Data ($) (Year Ended Dec. 31)	1998	1997	1996	1995	1994	1993	1992	1991	1990	1989
Tangible Bk. Val.	38.09	35.69	32.37	28.55	25.53	22.17	13.75	NA	NA	NA
Cash Flow	4.68	3.50	3.11	NA	NA	6.54	2.46	-0.10	NA	NA
Earnings	4.68	3.50	3.70	3.14	2.89	6.16	2.12	NA	NA	NA
Dividends	Nil	Nil	Nil	Nil	Nil	Nil	NA	NA	NA	NA
Payout Ratio	Nil	Nil	Nil	Nil	Nil	Nil	NA	NA	NA	NA
Prices - High	47 7/8	39 3/8	29 3/8	29 1/4	29 1/2	29	NA	NA	NA	NA
- Low	25 1/2	23	19 1/4	14 3/4	14	19	NA	NA	NA	NA
P/E Ratio - High	10	11	8	9	10	5	NA	NA	NA	NA
- Low	5	7	5	5	5	3	NA	NA	NA	NA
Income Statement Analysis (Million $)										
Revs.	1,498	1,320	1,211	1,108	995	812	690	NA	NA	NA
Oper. Inc.	130	111	106	NA	NA	50.5	32.0	NA	NA	NA
Depr.	Nil	Nil	Nil	NA	NA	4.4	3.9	NA	NA	NA
Int. Exp.	40.8	33.8	64.3	32.7	31.4	23.4	28.2	NA	NA	NA
Pretax Inc.	89.3	74.9	55.9	59.0	53.0	38.0	25.6	NA	NA	NA
Eff. Tax Rate	29%	37%	21%	38%	38%	NM	5.10%	NA	NA	NA
Net Inc.	63.7	47.2	44.2	36.9	32.8	71.7	24.3	NA	NA	NA
Balance Sheet & Other Fin. Data (Million $)										
Cash	51.0	11.8	13.2	5.1	6.7	20.9	3.5	NA	NA	NA
Curr. Assets	NA	NA	NA	NA	NA	NA	NA	NA	NA	NA
Total Assets	1,353	1,067	947	842	748	679	545	NA	NA	NA
Curr. Liab.	NA	NA	NA	NA	163	117	100	NA	NA	NA
LT Debt	425	396	363	300	294	305	237	NA	NA	NA
Common Eqty.	514	420	374	329	278	208	118	NA	NA	NA
Total Cap.	939	716	737	630	585	562	427	NA	NA	NA
Cap. Exp.	10.0	3.1	2.7	2.5	2.0	Nil	NA	NA	NA	NA
Cash Flow	63.7	47.2	44.2	NM	NM	76.1	28.2	NA	NA	NA
Curr. Ratio	NA	NA	NA	NA	NA	NA	NA	NA	NA	NA
% LT Debt of Cap.	45.3	55.3	49.3	47.8	50.2	54.3	55.5	NA	NA	NA
% Net Inc.of Revs.	4.3	3.6	3.6	3.4	3.3	8.8	3.5	NA	NA	NA
% Ret. on Assets	5.3	4.7	4.9	4.7	4.3	6.7	NA	NA	NA	NA
% Ret. on Equity	13.6	11.9	12.6	11.9	12.6	40.7	NA	NA	NA	NA

Data as orig reptd.; bef. results of disc opers/spec. items. Per share data adj. for stk. divs. Bold denotes diluted EPS (FASB 128)-prior periods restated. E-Estimated. NA-Not Available. NM-Not Meaningful. NR-Not Ranked.

Office—1800 West Loop South, Houston, TX 77027. **Tel**—(713) 877-2311. **Website**—http://www.USHOME.com **Chrmn & Co-CEO**—R. J. Strudler. **Pres, Co-CEO & COO**—I. Heimbinder. **VP & Investor Contact**—Kelly Fawcett Somoza (713-877-2391). **Dirs**—G. Adams, S. L. Gerard, K. J. Hanau, Jr., I. Heimbinder, M. T. Hopkins, C. A. McKee, G. A. Poole, Jr., H. Ripault, J. W. Sight, R. J. Strudler. **Transfer Agent & Registrar**—First Chicago Trust Co. of NY, Jersey City, NJ. **Incorporated**—in Delaware in 1959. **Empl**— 1,641. **S&P Analyst:** Michael W. Jaffe

STANDARD
&POOR'S
STOCK REPORTS

U.S. Trust Corp.

NYSE Symbol **UTC**

In S&P SmallCap 600

09-OCT-99 **Industry:** Financial (Diversified)

Summary: This company provides investment management, private banking and fiduciary services to affluent individuals, families and institutions nationwide.

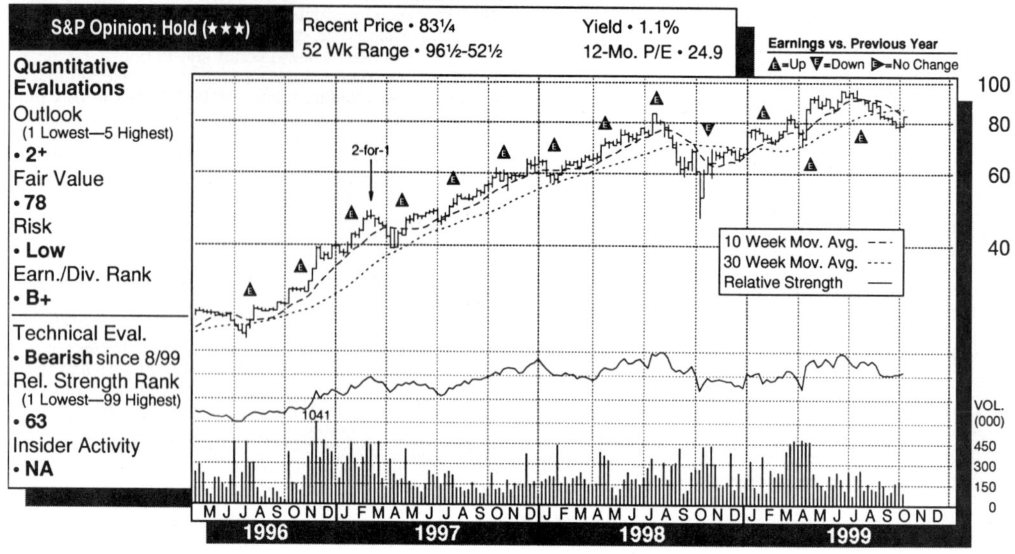

Overview - 16-AUG-99

U.S. Trust's geographic expansion and success in attracting personal wealth have driven healthy fee income growth. During the second quarter of 1999, market-related fees earned from assets under management grew 28%, year to year, generating 82% of total fee income. The anticipated fourth quarter acquisition of North Carolina Trust Co., an investment manager with $2.5 billion in managed assets, should help fuel growth. However, recent indications of a heating economy, which appears likely to bring higher interest rates, reduces the possibility of continued financial market exuberance and similar fee income growth going forward. In spite of 23% higher salaries, incentive and benefit expenses in the second quarter, the pretax operating margin expanded to 20%. As new offices are leveraged over a growing customer base, profitability should improve further, driving EPS growth of 16% through 2000.

Valuation - 16-AUG-99

UTC shares are up 13% thus far in 1999, matching the appreciation of the S&P Investment Management Index. The rise in the company's stock was attributable to an exceptional return on equity of 30% in the first half of 1999. UTC's remarkable returns were aided by the strength of the U.S. economy. Equity market prices have come under pressure of late however, raising questions about the stability of managed assets and the fee income they generate. Though this lucrative business appears to be attracting many competitors, UTC's history, experience and acquisition strategy for entering new regions give it an advantage in garnering assets. Additionally, the forward progress of Glass-Steagall reform increases the attractiveness of UTC's shares. In light of our near-term outlook for rising interest rates, and with shares trading at a premium to our long-term EPS growth estimate, they appear fairly valued.

Key Stock Statistics

S&P EPS Est. 1999	3.59	Tang. Bk. Value/Share	13.92
P/E on S&P Est. 1999	23.2	Beta	0.77
S&P EPS Est. 2000	4.18	Shareholders	1,791
Dividend Rate/Share	0.88	Market cap. (B)	$ 1.5
Shs. outstg. (M)	18.4	Inst. holdings	39%
Avg. daily vol. (M)	0.026		

Value of $10,000 invested 5 years ago: NA

Fiscal Year Ending Dec. 31

	1999	1998	1997	1996	1995	1994
Revenues (Million $)						
1Q	158.5	104.0	88.45	77.42	127.0	118.6
2Q	164.2	108.0	90.08	79.44	126.4	120.5
3Q	—	113.6	94.04	81.65	104.6	127.3
4Q	—	116.1	100.2	84.21	118.7	90.87
Yr.	—	564.4	494.4	419.6	476.8	457.3
Earnings Per Share ($)						
1Q	**0.88**	**0.70**	0.55	0.46	0.42	0.64
2Q	**0.93**	**0.73**	0.58	0.47	0.27	0.55
3Q	—	**0.76**	**0.93**	0.48	-3.80	0.66
4Q	—	**0.76**	**0.64**	0.53	0.45	-0.82
Yr.	—	**2.96**	**2.39**	**1.95**	**-2.62**	1.06

Next earnings report expected: mid October

Dividend Data (Dividends have been paid since 1854.)

Amount ($)	Date Decl.	Ex-Div. Date	Stock of Record	Payment Date
0.180	Oct. 27	Jan. 06	Jan. 08	Jan. 25 '99
0.220	Jan. 26	Apr. 07	Apr. 09	Apr. 23 '99
0.220	Apr. 27	Jul. 07	Jul. 09	Jul. 23 '99
0.220	Jul. 27	Oct. 06	Oct. 08	Oct. 25 '99

A Division of The McGraw-Hill Companies

U.S. Trust Corporation

Business Summary - 16-AUG-99

Founded in 1853, U.S. Trust Corp. is the oldest investment management and trust company in the U.S. The company was organized for and continues to focus on the purpose of helping affluent individuals and their families preserve and enhance their wealth. At year-end 1998, approximately 76%, or $46.7 billion, of UTC's investment assets under management were personal assets. In addition to its core investment management services, U.S. Trust provides financial and estate planning, fiduciary services and private banking. With $14.6 billion institutional investment assets under management, UTC is also a significant provider of trust, agency, and related services to corporations, non-profit organizations, municipalities and financial institutions.

U.S. Trust believes its history and experience in wealth management have established it with a reputation for quality, performance and integrity. UTC plans to leverage this reputation to increase its share of an individual wealth market it considers one of the most attractive for financial services, with households holding over $1 million in investable assets totaling $6.3 trillion.

UTC focuses on building business based on relationships, not transactions. By providing clients with a comprehensive array of wealth management services, UTC hopes to build relationships that span generations.

In 1998, with the philosophy that independent research is critical to investment decision making, UTC significantly enhanced its equity research capabilities. The company also established a collaboration for investment research with Lombard Odier & Cie, a private bank in Switzerland. A results-oriented culture prevails at UTC, backed by a comprehensive incentive and commission program. For instance, portfolio managers are compensated on the basis of their performance and success in meeting client objectives.

In 1998, UTC accelerated its pace of national expansion, which remains a key strategic component of growth. U.S. Trust has a network of regional offices in two-thirds of the 20 most affluent metropolitan regions of the U.S. The company intends to fill in markets where it already has a presence, and enter the remaining through acquisition wherever feasible. At year-end 1998, the company had 21 offices in eight states and Washington, D.C. During 1998 and early 1999, the company acquired the investment management firms of Wood Island Associates, Larkspur, CA, McMurrey Investment Advisors, Houston, TX, and Radnor Capital Management, Wayne, PA. UTC's goal is for regional offices such as these, which currently account for roughly 30% of fee revenue, to be contributing 50% by 2002.

U.S. Trust has set financial objectives of 8% to 12% annual revenue growth (reported over 18% in 1998), a pretax margin over 25% (23%), 15% to 20% EPS growth (24%), and ROE of over 25% (26%).

Per Share Data ($) (Year Ended Dec. 31)	1998	1997	1996	1995	1994	1993	1992	1991	1990	1989
Tangible Bk. Val.	NA	12.16	19.98	9.34	11.81	12.21	10.63	10.01	9.06	9.40
Earnings	2.96	2.39	1.92	-2.62	1.06	2.13	1.88	1.66	0.62	1.54
Dividends	0.69	0.58	0.50	0.75	0.98	0.92	0.84	0.80	0.79	0.71
Payout Ratio	23%	24%	26%	NM	94%	43%	45%	48%	127%	46%
Prices - High	84 1/8	65 3/4	40 3/8	40 3/4	33	29 7/8	25 1/2	22 1/4	19	21 5/8
- Low	46 3/4	37 1/2	23	21	24 3/4	24 5/8	21 1/8	14	13 3/8	18 1/4
P/E Ratio - High	28	28	21	NM	32	14	14	13	31	14
- Low	16	16	12	NM	24	12	11	8	22	12
Income Statement Analysis (Million $)										
Net Int. Inc.	NA	91.7	78.9	99	108	116	109	96.0	89.0	83.0
Tax Equiv. Adj.	NA	NA	NA	3.2	4.7	5.8	8.2	10.2	11.0	13.6
Non Int. Inc.	NA	282	244	284	270	276	243	212	197	194
Loan Loss Prov.	NA	0.8	1.0	1.6	2.0	4.0	6.0	6.0	8.4	1.6
Exp./Op. Revs.	NA	77%	78%	124%	81%	80%	81%	80%	87%	80%
Pretax Inc.	NA	83.7	69.3	-93.4	34.4	72.7	58.9	48.8	18.6	43.2
Eff. Tax Rate	NA	39%	41%	NM	39%	42%	38%	36%	37%	29%
Net Inc.	NA	51.0	40.9	-50.5	21.0	42.3	36.5	31.4	11.7	30.7
% Net Int. Marg.	NA	3.12	3.24	3.74	3.49	3.95	4.16	4.35	4.67	4.64
Balance Sheet & Other Fin. Data (Million $)										
Money Mkt. Assets	NA	388	286	4.9	142	298	62.0	400	400	199
Inv. Securities	NA	1,131	1,166	760	1,034	923	1,196	1,013	896	866
Com'l Loans	Nil	Nil	Nil	69.2	140	58.0	58.0	66.0	676	728
Other Loans	2,191	1,939	1,688	1,390	1,487	1,341	1,202	1,098	384	350
Total Assets	NA	3,815	3,477	2,573	3,223	3,186	2,951	2,917	2,778	2,526
Demand Deposits	NA	746	688	490	1,032	1,241	1,221	1,037	969	1,004
Time Deposits	NA	2,328	2,076	1,503	1,409	1,246	1,134	1,071	1,071	983
LT Debt	NA	22.3	26.5	29.4	60.9	65.1	65.1	68.9	70.9	75.2
Common Eqty.	NA	231	214	182	223	229	197	182	166	177
% Ret. on Assets	NA	1.4	1.4	NM	0.5	1.1	1.1	1.1	0.5	1.2
% Ret. on Equity	NA	20.6	20.7	NM	9.2	20.5	19.4	18.1	5.9	15.2
% Loan Loss Resv.	NA	0.9	1.0	1.1	1.1	1.0	0.9	0.7	0.8	0.7
% Loans/Deposits	NA	63.1	61.1	73.2	66.7	56.2	53.5	55.2	52.0	54.3
% Equity to Assets	NA	6.8	6.5	7.0	5.7	5.4	5.4	6.8	7.7	8.2

Data as orig reptd.; bef. results of disc opers/spec. items. Per share data adj. for stk. divs. Bold denotes diluted EPS (FASB 128)-prior periods restated. E-Estimated. NA-Not Available. NM-Not Meaningful. NR-Not Ranked.

Office—114 West 47th St., New York, NY 10036. **Tel**—(212) 852-1000. **Website**—http://www.ustrust.com **Chrmn & CEO**—H. M. Schwarz. **Vice Chrmn** —M. S. Rahe, F. B. Taylor. **Pres & COO**—J. S. Maurer. **EVP & CFO**—J. L. Kirby. **Dirs**—E. Baum, S. C. Butler, P. O. Crisp, P. de Montebello, R. E. Denham, A. M. Grumbach, F. C. Hamilton, P. L. Malkin, J. S. Maurer, D. A. Olsen, C. H. Pforzheimer, III, M. S. Rahe, H. M. Schwarz, P. L. Smith, J. H. Stookey, F. B. Taylor, R. N. Wilson, R. A. Wooden. **Transfer Agent & Registrar**—Co.'s office. **Incorporated**—in New York in 1877. **Empl**— 1,538. **S&P Analyst:** Markos N. Kaminis

STANDARD
&POOR'S
STOCK REPORTS

Ultratech Stepper

Nasdaq Symbol **UTEK**

In S&P SmallCap 600

09-OCT-99

Industry: Equipment (Semiconductor)

Summary: UTEK manufactures photolithography equipment designed to reduce the cost of ownership for manufacturers of integrated circuits and thin-film head magnetic recording devices.

S&P Opinion: Hold (★★★) | Recent Price • 14⅜ | 52 Wk Range • 21⅛-12⅜ | Yield • Nil | 12-Mo. P/E • NM

Quantitative Evaluations

Outlook (1 Lowest—5 Highest) • **3-**

Fair Value • **14**

Risk • **High**

Earn./Div. Rank • **NR**

Technical Eval. • **Bearish** since 8/99

Rel. Strength Rank (1 Lowest—99 Highest) • **79**

Insider Activity • **Neutral**

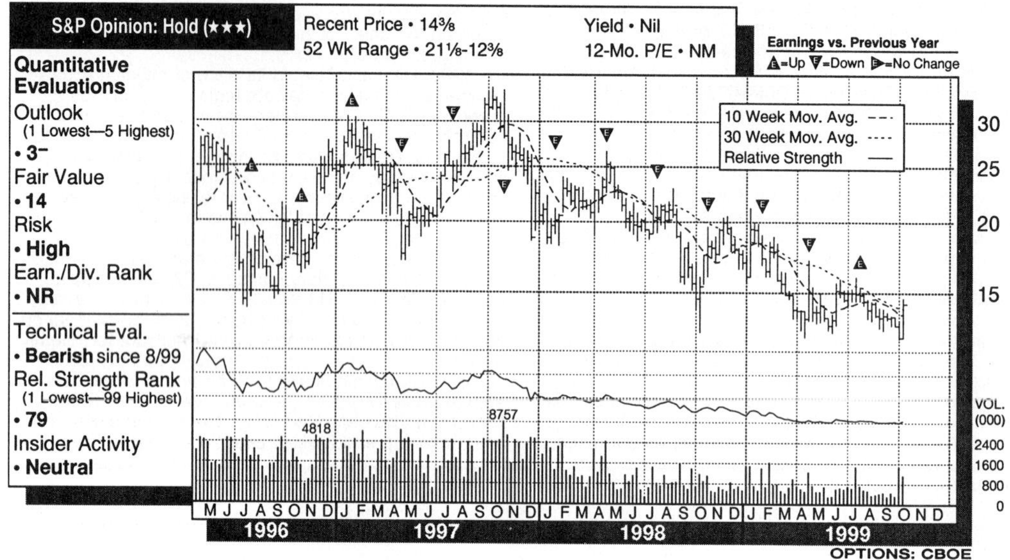

Overview - 10-AUG-99

Following a 45% decline in 1998, revenues should improve dramatically over the course of 1999, as the semiconductor and disk drive sectors recover from overcapacity. While shipment delays and weak demand have hurt recent operating results, we expect sequential gains over the next few quarters, driven by new products. Margins should begin to improve from recent depressed levels, as volume gains result in better absorption of fixed costs. In addition, the company has taken actions to reduce its expenses in light of last year's sharp decline in sales. These cost reductions, coupled with interest income from UTEK's healthy cash reserves, should enhance the company's operating performance. Overall, we expect the company to lose $0.10 a share in 1999, versus 1998's loss of $0.73 a share (before charges). Based on improving semiconductor equipment industry conditions, we look for EPS of $0.55 in 2000.

Valuation - 10-AUG-99

Although the company's operating results have been disappointing in recent quarters, we are maintaining our hold rating on the shares. UTEK holds a dominant market share of lithography equipment for disk drives, but near-term growth in this area has been restricted by weak demand for front-end processes. We expect considerable improvement in late 1999 and 2000 as both the disk drive and semiconductor sectors slowly recover from the impact of overcapacity and weak demand. At a recent level of 1.4X book value, the shares are fairly valued. With strong new product offerings and a healthy balance sheet (no long term debt, and $6.91 a share in cash), UTEK remains a worthwhile holding for aggressive investors.

Key Stock Statistics

S&P EPS Est. 1999	-0.10	Tang. Bk. Value/Share	9.22
P/E on S&P Est. 1999	NM	Beta	1.24
S&P EPS Est. 2000	0.55	Shareholders	36,300
Dividend Rate/Share	Nil	Market cap. (B)	$0.307
Shs. outstg. (M)	21.4	Inst. holdings	30%
Avg. daily vol. (M)	0.166		

Value of $10,000 invested 5 years ago: $ 15,612

Fiscal Year Ending Dec. 31

	1999	1998	1997	1996	1995	1994
Revenues (Million $)						
1Q	25.78	27.78	38.73	51.71	32.08	18.19
2Q	29.28	22.40	38.05	51.79	36.26	20.14
3Q	—	12.36	36.75	46.50	42.20	24.41
4Q	—	18.92	33.81	43.50	47.29	28.61
Yr.	—	81.46	147.3	193.5	157.8	91.34
Earnings Per Share ($)						
1Q	**-0.12**	**0.02**	**0.21**	**0.41**	0.23	0.14
2Q	**-0.05**	**-0.74**	**0.27**	**0.44**	0.27	0.14
3Q	—	**-1.34**	**0.25**	**0.42**	0.32	0.18
4Q	—	**-0.70**	**0.09**	**0.40**	0.38	0.19
Yr.	—	**-2.76**	**0.81**	**1.66**	**1.20**	**0.65**

Next earnings report expected: late October

Dividend Data

No cash dividends have been paid. The company intends to retain earnings for use in its business and does not expect to pay cash dividends in the foreseeable future.

A Division of The McGraw-Hill Companies

Ultratech Stepper, Inc.

Business Summary - 10-AUG-99

Ultratech Stepper (UTEK) manufactures photolithography equipment for use in the fabrication of integrated circuits (ICs), micromachining devices, thin film magnetic recording devices, and photomasks for the semiconductor industry. The company's strategy is to provide photolithography equipment (steppers) that reduces costs for manufacturers of ICs and TFH magnetic recording devices. Photolithography is one of the most critical and expensive steps in IC and TFH manufacturing. According to the Semiconductor Industry Association, up to 35% of the cost of processing silicon is related to photolithography.

Steppers are used to image device features on the surface of wafers by selectively exposing a light-sensitive polymer photoresist coated on a wafer surface through a photomask containing the master image of a particular device layer. Depending on design complexity, this step may be repeated up to 25 times during the production of a single chip.

UTEK's 1X steppers cost significantly less than more advanced steppers, but are less precise. The company's products specifically address non-critical layer (greater than 0.65 micron linewidths) operations. Using a strategy called mix-and-match (M&M), UTEK's steppers share the processing load with higher-priced steppers that are designed for processing critical layers. The alternative to M&M is for chip makers to use high priced systems for all layers. Usually less than 50% of an IC's layers are considered critical.

The company currently offers three different series of 1X systems for use in the semiconductor fabrication process: the model 1500 and 1500 MVS Series, which addresses the markets for scanner replacement and high volume/low cost semiconductor fabrication; the Saturn Wafer Stepper family, which address the mix and match market in advanced semiconductor fabrication; and the Titan Wafer Stepper, which addresses the market for photosensitive polyamide applications as well as the markets served by the model 1500 Series.

Ultratech also supplies photolithography systems to the thin film head (TFH) market with its model 1700 series, model 4700 series, and the model 6700 and 6800 series, which extend the model 4700 capabilities into the submicron range.

Steppers for both IC and TFH production feature size capabilities ranging from 2.0 microns to 0.65 microns and are priced from $800,000 to $2.6 million.

Ultratech also offers photolithography equipment for use in the micromachining market. In addition, in December 1997, the company shipped its first UltraBeam model V2000 electron beam pattern generation system for use in the development and production of photomasks for the IC industry. The system addresses production requirements for leading edge photomasks, and has an approximate price range of $6 million to $9 million.

Per Share Data ($) **(Year Ended Dec. 31)**	**1998**	**1997**	**1996**	**1995**	**1994**	**1993**	**1992**	**1991**	**1990**	**1989**
Tangible Bk. Val.	9.96	12.68	11.81	10.08	4.83	3.00	NA	NA	NA	NA
Cash Flow	-2.26	1.14	1.94	1.39	0.77	0.46	NA	NA	NA	NA
Earnings	-2.76	0.81	1.66	1.20	0.65	0.36	NA	NA	NA	NA
Dividends	Nil	Nil	Nil	Nil	Nil	Nil	NA	NA	NA	NA
Payout Ratio	Nil	Nil	Nil	Nil	Nil	Nil	NA	NA	NA	NA
Prices - High	26 5/8	34 1/2	31 3/4	47 1/2	20 7/8	10 1/8	NA	NA	NA	NA
- Low	12 3/4	17	14	17	8 1/4	6 1/4	NA	NA	NA	NA
P/E Ratio - High	NM	43	19	40	32	28	NA	NA	NA	NA
- Low	NM	21	8	14	13	17	NA	NA	NA	NA
Income Statement Analysis (Million $)										
Revs.	81.5	147	194	158	91.3	54.1	35.3	31.9	NA	NA
Oper. Inc.	-17.1	32.6	52.7	35.6	17.3	7.8	3.1	2.7	NA	NA
Depr.	10.6	7.2	6.1	3.9	2.0	1.0	0.8	1.1	NA	NA
Int. Exp.	0.4	0.2	0.2	Nil	0.1	0.3	0.0	0.0	NA	NA
Pretax Inc.	-64.1	24.8	52.7	36.2	16.4	6.7	2.1	1.6	NA	NA
Eff. Tax Rate	NM	29%	33%	33%	33%	38%	38%	29%	NA	NA
Net Inc.	-57.9	17.6	35.3	24.2	11.0	4.1	1.3	1.1	NA	NA
Balance Sheet & Other Fin. Data (Million $)										
Cash	54.1	43.9	47.8	161	49.7	26.1	NA	NA	NA	NA
Curr. Assets	202	257	252	221	93.1	50.5	NA	NA	NA	NA
Total Assets	246	300	281	245	105	56.4	NA	NA	NA	NA
Curr. Liab.	35.4	33.8	39.4	44.7	23.7	17.5	NA	NA	NA	NA
LT Debt	Nil	Nil	Nil	Nil	0.4	0.8	NA	NA	NA	NA
Common Eqty.	210	264	240	200	80.0	38.1	NA	NA	NA	NA
Total Cap.	210	266	241	200	80.5	38.9	NA	NA	NA	NA
Cap. Exp.	9.5	9.3	7.8	9.8	7.8	2.8	1.0	1.1	NA	NA
Cash Flow	-47.3	24.8	41.4	28.1	13.0	5.1	2.1	2.2	NA	NA
Curr. Ratio	5.7	7.6	6.4	4.9	3.9	2.9	NA	NA	NA	NA
% LT Debt of Cap.	Nil	Nil	Nil	Nil	0.5	2.1	NA	NA	NA	NA
% Net Inc.of Revs.	NM	11.9	18.2	15.3	12.1	7.6	3.7	3.6	NA	NA
% Ret. on Assets	NM	6.0	13.4	13.8	13.6	NA	NA	NA	NA	NA
% Ret. on Equity	NM	7.0	16.1	17.3	18.6	NA	NA	NA	NA	NA

Data as orig reptd.; bef. results of disc opers/spec. items. Per share data adj. for stk. divs. Bold denotes diluted EPS (FASB 128)-prior periods restated. E-Estimated. NA-Not Available. NM-Not Meaningful. NR-Not Ranked.

Office—3050 Zanker Road, San Jose, CA 95134. **Tel**—(408) 321-8835. **Chrmn, Pres & CEO**—A. W. Zafiropoulo. **VP-Fin, CFO, Secy & Treas**—W. G. Leunis III. **Dirs**—L.R. Carter, T.D. George, J. Gemunder, G. Harrison, K. A. Levy, A. W. Zafiropoulo. **Transfer Agent & Registrar**—Bank of Boston. **Incorporated**—in Delaware in 1992. **Empl**— 488. **S&P Analyst:** B. McGovern

STANDARD
&POOR'S
STOCK REPORTS

United Bankshares

NASDAQ Symbol **UBSI**

In S&P SmallCap 600

09-OCT-99 **Industry:** Banks (Regional)

Summary: This multi-bank holding company operates approximately 80 offices, primarily in West Virginia, and also in Virginia.

Quantitative Evaluations

Outlook (1 Lowest—5 Highest) • **2-**

Fair Value • **24¾**

Risk • **Low**

Earn./Div. Rank • **A-**

Technical Eval. • **Bearish** since 9/99

Rel. Strength Rank (1 Lowest—99 Highest) • **44**

Insider Activity • **Neutral**

Recent Price • 23⅞ Yield • 3.5%

52 Wk Range • 29⅞-21¾ 12-Mo. P/E • 18.4

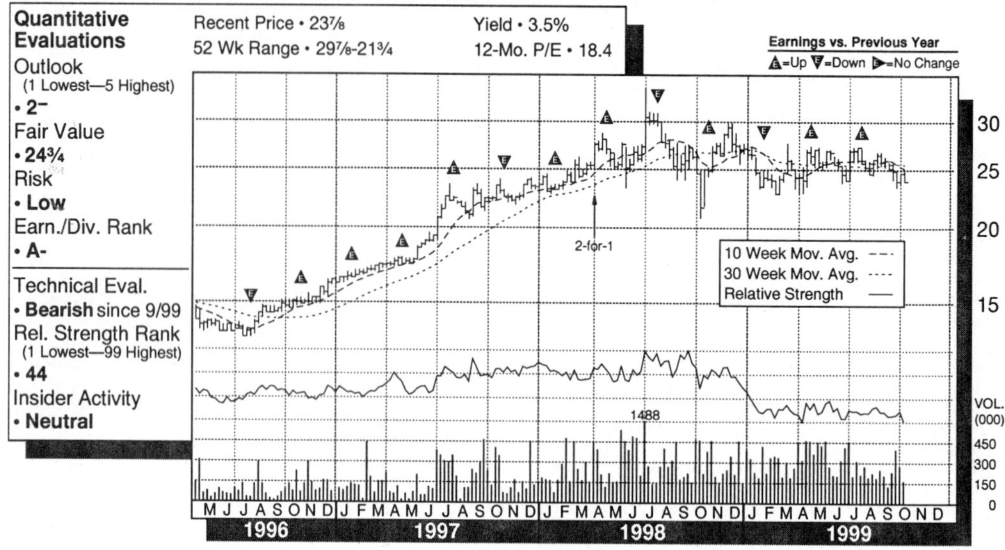

Business Profile - 11-AUG-99

In the first half of 1999, the company recorded a 1.50% return on average assets and a 16.30% return on average equity; nonperforming assets comprised 0.54% of total assets at the end of the 1999 second quarter. Through acquisitions in 1998, UBSI expanded its presence in several key banking markets, including northern Virginia and the rapidly growing eastern panhandle of West Virginia, and made its first entry into Ohio. Total deposits, as restated for acquisitions, grew 10%, on the introduction of new products, while loans, net of unearned income, decreased 1.4%, reflecting greater emphasis on secondary market lending activity. Dividends have been boosted regularly for many years.

Operational Review - 11-AUG-99

Net interest income in the six months ended June 30, 1999, rose 10%, year to year. The loan loss provision fell 66%, and noninterest expense was down 17%, in part reflecting the absence of merger-related and nonrecurring charges associated with the George Mason Bankshares acquisition. Despite lower noninterest income, pretax income soared 73%. After taxes at 34.4%, versus 28.5%, net income was up 59%, to $34,957,000 ($0.79 a share) from $21,968,000 ($0.51), as restated.

Stock Performance - 08-OCT-99

In the past 30 trading days, UBSI's shares have declined 7%, compared to a 0.91% fall in the S&P 500. Average trading volume for the past five days was 32,520 shares, compared with the 40-day moving average of 46,274 shares.

Key Stock Statistics

Dividend Rate/Share	0.84	Shareholders	5,225
Shs. outstg. (M)	43.2	Market cap. (B)	$ 1.0
Avg. daily vol. (M)	0.053	Inst. holdings	24%
Tang. Bk. Value/Share	9.19		
Beta	0.57		

Value of $10,000 invested 5 years ago: $ 22,391

Fiscal Year Ending Dec. 31

	1999	1998	1997	1996	1995	1994
Revenues (Million $)						
1Q	96.14	60.01	48.38	45.77	36.50	31.75
2Q	99.5	85.65	49.55	43.26	37.13	32.50
3Q	—	90.55	55.01	49.16	37.30	34.19
4Q	—	131.2	57.05	48.36	38.15	33.92
Yr.	—	367.4	210.0	186.6	149.1	132.4
Earnings Per Share ($)						
1Q	**0.39**	**0.36**	**0.33**	**0.27**	**0.29**	0.26
2Q	**0.40**	**0.17**	**0.34**	**0.04**	**0.29**	0.26
3Q	—	**0.39**	**0.34**	**0.37**	**0.30**	0.27
4Q	—	**0.14**	**0.34**	**0.33**	**0.29**	0.26
Yr.	—	**1.02**	**1.35**	1.00	**1.09**	**1.00**

Next earnings report expected: mid October

Dividend Data (Dividends have been paid since 1994.)

Amount ($)	Date Decl.	Ex-Div. Date	Stock of Record	Payment Date
0.200	Nov. 24	Dec. 09	Dec. 11	Jan. 02 '99
0.200	Feb. 24	Mar. 10	Mar. 12	Apr. 01 '99
0.200	May. 17	Jun. 09	Jun. 11	Jul. 01 '99
0.210	Aug. 25	Sep. 08	Sep. 10	Oct. 01 '99

United Bankshares, Inc.

Business Summary - 11-AUG-99

United Bankshares (UBSI), a multi-bank holding company headquartered in Charleston, WV, has conducted an active acquisition program since it was formed in 1982. The company began conducting business in May 1984 with the acquisition of three wholly owned subsidiaries that were merged in late 1985 and renamed United National Bank (UNB). Since that time, more than 10 banks have been acquired. In April 1998, UBSI acquired George Mason Bank (total assets of $1 billion) in exchange for 9 million common shares, and renamed it United Bank.

At the end of 1998, UNB operated 53 offices, located throughout West Virginia, as well as three offices in Ohio. It also operated a loan production offices in Bridgeport, WV. As of 1998 year-end, United Bank operated 23 offices in the northern Virginia, Maryland and Washington, DC, areas.

All of the company's subsidiary banks are full-service commercial banks and offer such banking services as accepting deposits, making and servicing of personal, commercial, floor plan and student loans, and the making of construction and real estate loans.

UBSI's total loan portfolio (net of unearned income) decreased 1.4%, to $2.65 billion in 1998, reflecting increased emphasis on originating mortgage loans for sale in the secondary market. The outstanding loan portfolio is comprised of commercial, financial and agricultural loans (19% of the total), real estate mortgages (64%), real estate construction loans (5%), and consumer loans (12%).

The commercial loan portfolio consists of loans to corporate borrowers in small to mid-size industrial and commercial companies, as well as automobile dealers, service, retail and wholesale merchants. Commercial real estate loans consist of commercial mortgages, which generally are secured by nonresidential and multi-family residential properties. Real estate mortgage loans to consumers are traditional one-to-four family residential mortgages. Consumer loans are secured by automobiles, boats, recreational vehicles, and other personal property.

At December 31, 1998, the allowance for possible loan losses totaled $39.2 million (1.48% of loans outstanding), versus $31.9 million (1.19%) a year earlier. Net chargeoffs as a percentage of average loans outstanding were 0.18% in 1998, versus 0.14% in 1997. Nonperforming loans totaled $18.67 million (0.62% of loans outstanding) at the end of 1998, versus $18.69 million (0.75%) a year earlier.

The average yield on total earning assets was 8.26% in 1998 (8.19% in 1997), while the average rate paid on total interest-bearing funds was 4.70% (4.56%), for an interest spread of 3.56% (3.63%).

Per Share Data ($) (Year Ended Dec. 31)	1998	1997	1996	1995	1994	1993	1992	1991	1990	1989
Tangible Bk. Val.	9.75	9.32	8.56	7.75	7.61	6.66	6.78	6.37	6.03	NA
Earnings	1.02	1.35	1.00	1.18	1.04	NA	NA	NA	NA	NA
Dividends	0.72	0.68	0.61	0.57	0.52	0.46	0.42	0.40	0.28	0.32
Payout Ratio	71%	50%	1%	0%	1%	NA	NA	NA	NA	NA
Prices - High	34 1/8	24 3/8	16 1/2	15 1/2	13 1/2	14 1/4	10 3/8	7 1/2	6 3/4	7 7/8
- Low	20 3/4	16 1/8	13 1/8	11 5/8	11 1/2	9 5/8	6 1/2	5 1/8	4 1/2	6 1/4
P/E Ratio - High	34	18	16	13	13	16	13	10	10	10
- Low	20	12	13	9	11	11	8	6	7	8
Income Statement Analysis (Million $)										
Net Int. Inc.	170	106	99	81.7	77.3	71.5	57.7	52.7	50.4	46.4
Tax Equiv. Adj.	3.8	2.4	2.4	NA	NA	NA	NA	NA	NA	NA
Non Int. Inc.	39.4	19.7	14.2	12.6	12.1	12.2	9.3	7.8	7.9	6.9
Loan Loss Prov.	12.2	3.1	2.6	2.1	1.8	4.3	2.9	4.9	5.9	3.0
Exp./Op. Revs.	65%	48%	56%	52%	54%	59%	62%	62%	64%	65%
Pretax Inc.	61.9	62.4	47.2	43.3	38.0	30.1	22.7	18.4	14.9	15.8
Eff. Tax Rate	28%	34%	35%	35%	34%	32%	30%	29%	28%	27%
Net Inc.	44.4	40.9	30.5	28.1	24.9	20.4	15.8	13.1	10.7	11.5
% Net Int. Marg.	4.37	4.80	4.90	NA	NA	NA	NA	NA	NA	NA
Balance Sheet & Other Fin. Data (Million $)										
Money Mkt. Assets	16.7	9.7	3.2	NA	NA	NA	NA	NA	NA	NA
Inv. Securities	927	453	332	310	361	430	NA	NA	NA	NA
Com'l Loans	509	369	249	NA	NA	NA	NA	NA	NA	NA
Other Loans	2,151	1,699	1,604	NA	NA	NA	NA	NA	NA	NA
Total Assets	4,568	2,700	2,327	1,815	1,788	1,720	1,548	1,189	1,194	1,099
Demand Deposits	543	318	261	239	245	229	NA	NA	NA	NA
Time Deposits	2,950	1,788	1,567	1,235	1,190	1,201	NA	NA	NA	NA
LT Debt	351	143	133	33.9	84.0	32.2	NA	NA	NA	NA
Common Eqty.	422	279	259	201	180	171	150	113	107	95.0
% Ret. on Assets	1.2	1.6	1.5	1.6	1.4	1.2	1.2	1.1	0.9	1.1
% Ret. on Equity	12.7	15.2	13.3	14.7	14.2	12.7	12.0	12.0	10.6	12.7
% Loan Loss Resv.	1.5	1.2	1.2	1.5	1.5	1.6	1.4	1.4	1.2	1.1
% Loans/Deposits	75.9	99.3	101.1	93.3	90.4	82.5	80.6	83.6	81.6	78.1
% Equity to Assets	9.6	10.7	11.1	10.6	10.0	9.8	9.6	9.2	8.8	8.5

Data as orig reptd.; bef. results of disc opers/spec. items. Per share data adj. for stk. divs. Bold denotes diluted EPS (FASB 128)-prior periods restated. E-Estimated. NA-Not Available. NM-Not Meaningful. NR-Not Ranked.

Office—300 United Center, 500 Virginia St., East, Charleston, WV 25301. **Tel**—(304) 424-8761. **Chrmn & CEO**—R. M. Adams. **EVP, Treas, Secy & CFO**—S. E. Wilson. **Dirs**—R. M. Adams, T. J. Blair III, H. L. Buch, R. T. Butcher, H. S. Fahlgren, T. J. Georgelas, F. T. Graff Jr., R. P. McLean, I. N. Smith Jr., C. E. Stealey, W. A. Thornhill III, W. W. Wagner, H. L. Wilkes, P. C. Winter Jr., S. E. Wilson. **Transfer Agent & Registrar**—ChaseMellon Shareholder Services, Ridgefield Park, NJ. **Incorporated**—in West Virginia in 1982. **Empl**— 1,154. **S&P Analyst:** J.J.S.

United Illuminating

NYSE Symbol **UIL**

In S&P SmallCap 600

09-OCT-99

Industry: Electric Companies

Summary: This Connecticut-based electric utility also participates in several non-regulated businesses through its United Resources subsidiary.

Quantitative Evaluations

Outlook (1 Lowest—5 Highest) • **1**

Fair Value • **44⅞**

Risk • **Low**

Earn./Div. Rank • **B**

Technical Eval. • **Neutral** since 9/99

Rel. Strength Rank (1 Lowest—99 Highest) • **71**

Insider Activity • **Neutral**

Recent Price • 48⅜ | Yield • 6.0%

52 Wk Range • 52⅞-38⅞ | 12-Mo. P/E • 13.2

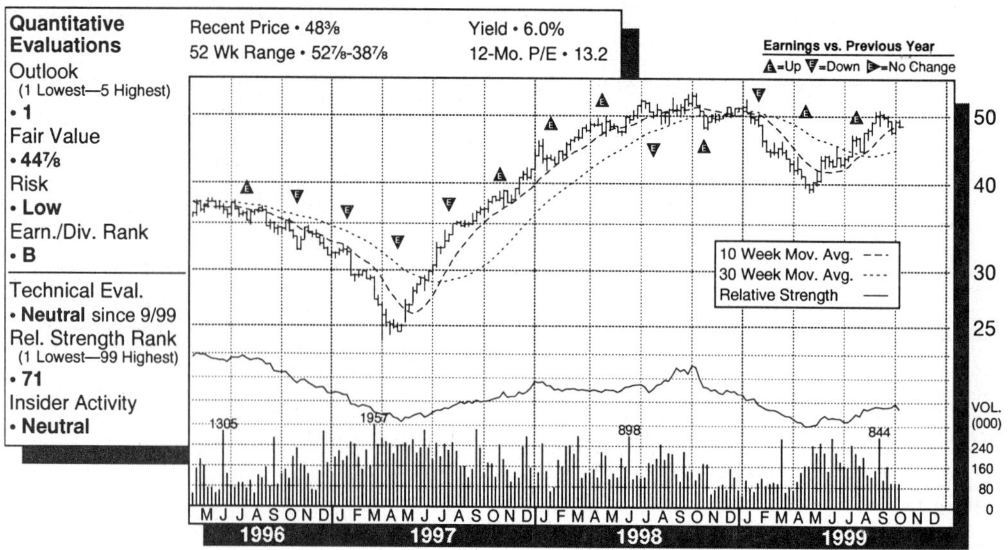

Business Profile - 19-AUG-99

In April 1999, UIL sold its fossil-fueled generation assets for $272 million, and proposed creating a holding company for its regulated electricity distribution business and its unregulated businesses, headed by United Resources. The changes were the result of legislation enacted in April 1998 intended to promote competition in Connecticut's electricity sector by allowing customers to choose alternative electricity suppliers and distributors. The laws are intended to lower rates for the state's electricity consumers, who pay among the highest in the nation. Proceeds from the sale were used to pay down debt, and will assist UIL in achieving a required 10% rate reduction from 1996 levels. In May, the company increased its investment in Bridgeport Energy from 4% to 33%. In July, Precision Power, an unregulated subsidiary, acquired Allan Electric Co., Inc.

Operational Review - 19-AUG-99

Revenues in the six months ended June 30, 1999, climbed 3.4%, year to year, primarily reflecting "real" retail sales growth and weather-related factors. Overall retail sales margin from operations rose, contributing to a 10% increase in operating income. Following a 13% decrease in interest charges, net income increased 65%, to $23.8 million ($1.69 a share, after preferred dividends), from $14.4 million ($1.03).

Stock Performance - 08-OCT-99

In the past 30 trading days, UIL's shares have declined 4%, compared to a 0.91% fall in the S&P 500. Average trading volume for the past five days was 18,980 shares, compared with the 40-day moving average of 42,818 shares.

Key Stock Statistics

Dividend Rate/Share	2.88	Shareholders	16,057
Shs. outstg. (M)	14.3	Market cap. (B)	$0.693
Avg. daily vol. (M)	0.023	Inst. holdings	31%
Tang. Bk. Value/Share	31.74		
Beta	0.28		

Value of $10,000 invested 5 years ago: $ 18,318

Fiscal Year Ending Dec. 31

	1999	1998	1997	1996	1995	1994
Revenues (Million $)						
1Q	168.7	162.5	180.3	170.9	165.4	167.6
2Q	164.5	159.8	163.8	168.8	163.4	153.4
3Q	—	198.6	196.6	209.2	200.3	184.6
4Q	—	165.3	169.6	177.2	161.3	151.1
Yr.	—	686.2	710.3	726.0	690.5	656.8
Earnings Per Share ($)						
1Q	**0.70**	**0.64**	0.54	0.82	0.62	0.86
2Q	**0.99**	**0.39**	0.61	0.75	0.67	0.40
3Q	—	**1.87**	1.68	1.27	1.89	1.78
4Q	—	**0.10**	**0.44**	0.04	0.46	0.14
Yr.	—	**3.00**	**3.26**	**2.87**	**3.63**	3.18

Next earnings report expected: late October

Dividend Data (Dividends have been paid since 1900.)

Amount ($)	Date Decl.	Ex-Div. Date	Stock of Record	Payment Date
0.720	Oct. 26	Dec. 08	Dec. 10	Jan. 01 '99
0.720	Feb. 22	Mar. 09	Mar. 11	Apr. 01 '99
0.720	May. 19	Jun. 08	Jun. 10	Jul. 01 '99
0.720	Aug. 23	Sep. 02	Sep. 07	Oct. 01 '99

A Division of The McGraw-Hill Companies

The United Illuminating Company

Business Summary - 19-AUG-99

As a result of recent legislation in Connecticut designed to promote competition in the electric industry, in April 1999, The United Illuminating Co. sold its Bridgeport Harbor Station and New Haven Harbor Station fossil-fueled generation assets for $272 million. In addition, the company's nuclear generation facilities, 17.5%-owned Seabrook and 3.7%-owned Millstone 3, must be divested by 2004. The company chose to focus on the transmission/distribution side of the business, and on expanding its unregulated businesses, rather than on electricity supply, enabling it to participate in the recovery of certain "stranded" costs. By July 2000, all customers will be able to choose an alternative power supplier. Those who do not will continue to be supplied by UIL at rates that are 10% below 1996 levels.

United Illuminating is an electric utility serving an area of about 335 sq. mi. in southwestern Connecticut, with a population of 726,000 (21% of the state's population). Its service area includes the cities of Bridgeport and New Haven; the company has about 314,000 customers. Although UIL sells electricity to other utilities (wholesale), its primary revenue source is retail customers, comprised of residential (42%), commercial (40%) and industrial (16%) customers. Retail sales are affected by local weather, economic conditions, and regulatory agencies.

Wholly owned United Resources has four of its own wholly owned subsidiaries. American Payment Systems manages a national network of agents for the processing of bill payments made by customers of UIL and other utilities. Precision Power provides power-related equipment and services to owners of commercial and government buildings and industrial facilities. Thermal Energies owns and operates heating and cooling energy centers in commercial and industrial buildings, and is participating in the development of district heating and cooling facilities in the downtown New Haven area. United Bridgeport Energy is participating in a 520-mw merchant wholesale electric generating facility being constructed on land leased from UIL at one of its generating plants.

In December 1996, the Connecticut Department of Public Utility Control (DPUC) ordered a five-year rate reduction program, based on allowed utility equity return of 11.5%, in an effort to reduce customer prices. The plan also calls for the accelerated amortization of certain regulatory assets. Earnings above the allowed equity return are to be shared one-third with customers via price reductions; the remaining two-thirds are to be split evenly between shareholders and applied amortization.

Per Share Data ($) (Year Ended Dec. 31)	1998	1997	1996	1995	1994	1993	1992	1991	1990	1989
Tangible Bk. Val.	31.74	31.56	31.20	30.67	29.97	27.24	27.61	26.20	24.56	23.72
Earnings	3.00	3.26	2.88	3.64	3.18	2.57	3.76	3.14	3.55	-5.87
Dividends	2.88	2.88	2.88	2.82	2.76	2.66	2.56	2.44	2.32	2.32
Payout Ratio	96%	88%	100%	77%	87%	104%	68%	78%	65%	NM
Prices - High	54 1/8	46	40	38 5/8	40	45 7/8	42	39 1/8	34 1/8	34 1/4
- Low	41 5/8	23 3/4	31 1/8	29 3/8	28 3/4	38 1/2	34 1/8	30	26 7/8	24 5/8
P/E Ratio - High	18	14	14	11	13	18	11	12	10	NM
- Low	14	7	11	8	9	15	9	10	8	NM
Income Statement Analysis (Million $)										
Revs.	686	710	726	690	657	653	667	673	594	531
Depr.	96.6	88.4	65.9	61.4	58.2	56.3	50.7	48.2	36.5	35.6
Maint.	42.9	42.2	37.7	36.1	41.8	41.5	38.4	41.8	40.5	39.4
Fxd. Chgs. Cov.	2.8	2.5	2.2	2.4	2.0	1.6	1.9	1.7	1.8	NM
Constr. Credits	0.5	1.6	2.4	2.8	3.5	4.1	3.2	5.2	3.4	65.4
Eff. Tax Rate	50%	43%	53%	52%	47%	40%	39%	38%	24%	41%
Net Inc.	42.2	45.8	39.1	50.4	48.1	40.5	56.8	48.0	54.0	-73.0
Balance Sheet & Other Fin. Data (Million $)										
Gross Prop.	1,979	1,951	1,908	1,878	1,851	1,808	1,744	1,712	1,670	1,726
Cap. Exp.	38.0	33.4	47.0	59.0	63.0	95.0	70.0	68.0	67.0	142
Net Prop.	1,264	1,306	1,322	1,346	1,357	1,361	1,336	1,340	1,337	1,402
Capitalization:										
LT Debt	681	662	777	863	726	895	917	1,006	998	976
% LT Debt	59	57	61	63	62	65	66	68	69	69
Pfd.	4.3	54.4	54.5	60.5	44.7	60.9	60.9	63.0	70.0	70.0
% Pfd.	4.60	4.70	4.30	4.40	3.80	4.40	4.30	4.30	4.80	5.00
Common	446	439	440	440	428	423	423	402	380	363
% Common	38	38	35	32	36	31	30	27	26	26
Total Cap.	1,501	1,456	1,625	1,790	1,646	1,824	1,710	2,069	2,036	1,959
% Oper. Ratio	78.9	84.9	85.0	81.6	80.6	82.4	83.8	84.7	83.4	82.3
% Earn. on Net Prop.	7.5	7.9	8.2	9.4	9.4	8.5	8.1	7.7	7.2	6.4
% Return On Revs.	6.1	6.4	5.4	7.3	7.3	6.2	8.5	7.2	9.1	NM
% Return On Invest. Capital	9.8	6.6	6.6	7.2	7.5	7.1	9.0	7.0	8.1	NM
% Return On Com. Equity	9.5	10.4	8.8	11.3	12.1	8.6	12.7	11.2	13.3	NM

Data as orig reptd.; bef. results of disc opers/spec. items. Per share data adj. for stk. divs. Bold denotes diluted EPS (FASB 128)-prior periods restated. E-Estimated. NA-Not Available. NM-Not Meaningful. NR-Not Ranked.

Office—157 Church St., New Haven, CT 06506. **Website**—http://www.uinet.com **Tel**—(203) 499-2000. **Chrmn, Pres & CEO**—Nathaniel D. Woodson. **Vice Chrmn & CFO**—Robert L. Fiscus. **Treas, Secy & Investor Contact**—Kurt Mohlman (203-499-2592). **Dirs**—T. R. Albright, M. C. Breslawsky, D. E. A. Carson, J. F. Croweak, R. L. Fiscus, B. Henley-Cohn, J. L. Lahey, F. P. McFadden, Jr., F. R. O'Keefe, Jr., J. A. Thomas, N. D. Woodson. **Transfer Agent & Registar**—American Stock Transfer & Trust Co., NYC. **Incorporated**—in Connecticut in 1899. **Empl**— 1,193. **S&P Analyst:** Ephraim Juskowicz

STANDARD
&POOR'S
STOCK REPORTS

United Natural Foods

NASDAQ Symbol **UNFI**

In S&P SmallCap 600

09-OCT-99

Industry: Distributors (Food & Health)

Summary: This company is the largest U.S. distributor of natural and organic foods, serving more than 6,500 customers.

Quantitative Evaluations

Outlook
(1 Lowest—5 Highest)
• **NA**

Fair Value
• **NA**

Risk
• **Average**

Earn./Div. Rank
• **NR**

Technical Eval.
• **Bearish** since 7/99

Rel. Strength Rank
(1 Lowest—99 Highest)
• **2**

Insider Activity
• **NA**

Recent Price • 8⅝
52 Wk Range • 29¾-7⅝
Yield • Nil
12-Mo. P/E • 11.8

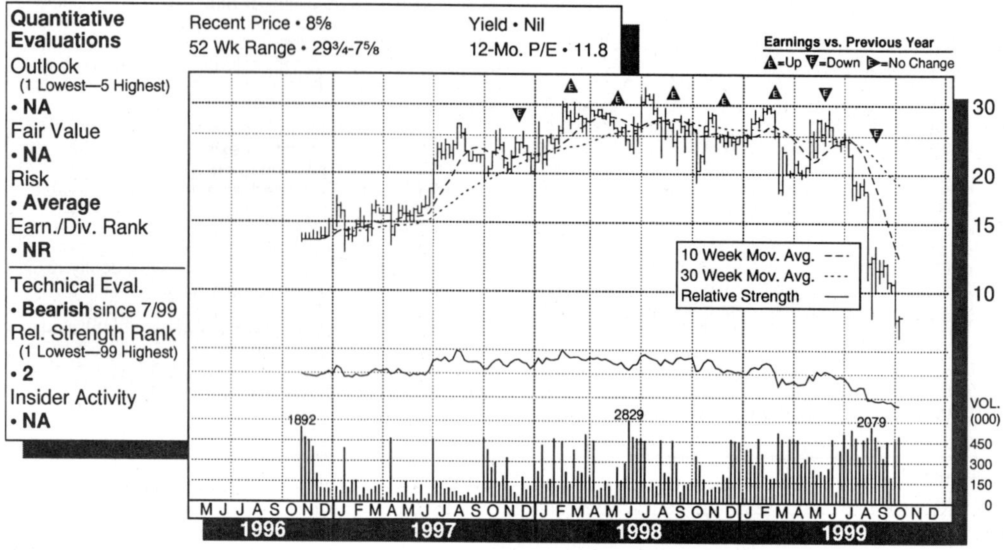

Business Profile - 14-JUL-99

The company's new conventional supermarket accounts have been major contributors to sales growth in recent periods. This has become UNFI's fastest growing sector nationwide, with many additional prospects in development. The company said that in the third quarter of FY 99 (Jul.), it made substantial progress in integrating recently acquired businesses. It expects to complete the consolidation of business from its Chesterfield, NH, facility into its Dayville, CT, facility by late August 1999; costs savings are anticipated from this consolidation.

Operational Review - 14-JUL-99

Net sales in the nine months ended April 30, 1999, advanced 19%, year to year. The gain mainly reflected increased sales to existing customers, the sale of new product offerings, and the Albert's Organics acquisition in September 1998. Margins benefited from the greater volume, increased purchasing efficiencies, and an increased proportion of higher margin business; operating income climbed 41%. With sharply higher net other income, pretax income advanced 51%. After taxes at 42.8%, versus 49.6%, net income soared 71%, to $14,814,000 ($0.80 a share), from $8,651,000 ($0.49).

Stock Performance - 08-OCT-99

In the past 30 trading days, UNFI's shares have declined 24%, compared to a 0.91% fall in the S&P 500. Average trading volume for the past five days was 188,980 shares, compared with the 40-day moving average of 152,474 shares.

Key Stock Statistics

Dividend Rate/Share	Nil	Shareholders	50
Shs. outstg. (M)	18.2	Market cap. (B)	$0.157
Avg. daily vol. (M)	0.109	Inst. holdings	45%
Tang. Bk. Value/Share	4.66		
Beta	NA		

Value of $10,000 invested 5 years ago: NA

Fiscal Year Ending Jul. 31

	1999	1998	1997	1996	1995	1994
Revenues (Million $)						
1Q	199.9	173.4	99.5	—	—	—
2Q	215.8	178.0	103.4	—	—	—
3Q	226.9	187.6	108.1	—	—	—
4Q	214.5	190.0	110.7	—	—	—
Yr.	857.0	728.9	421.7	286.0	283.3	200.6
Earnings Per Share ($)						
1Q	**0.26**	-0.04	0.14	—	—	—
2Q	**0.27**	**0.24**	0.18	—	—	—
3Q	**0.28**	**0.29**	0.23	—	—	—
4Q	**-0.07**	**0.25**	0.22	—	—	—
Yr.	**0.73**	**0.74**	**0.63**	0.40	**0.37**	—

Next earnings report expected: early December

Dividend Data

No cash dividends have been paid. The company anticipates that all of its earnings in the foreseeable future will be retained to finance the continued growth and development of its business. It has no current intention to pay cash dividends.

A Division of The McGraw-Hill Companies

United Natural Foods, Inc.

Business Summary - 14-JUL-99

United Natural Foods is the leading U.S. independent national distributor of natural foods and related products. The company has achieved a market leadership position through a combination of strong internal growth and acquisitions. Since 1985, UNFI has completed 20 acquisitions of distributors, suppliers, and retail stores.

The company's growth strategy is to maintain and enhance its position as the leading independent national distributor to the natural products industry. Key elements of its strategy include increasing its market share of the rapidly growing natural products industry; expanding its existing customer base; increasing its share of existing customer distribution needs; continuing to expand and penetrate into new distribution territories; continuing to improve efficiency of its nationwide distribution network; capitalizing on the benefits of the 1997 acquisition of Stone Mills Inc.; and continuing to provide the leading distribution solution to the natural products industry.

UNFI is the primary supplier to a majority of its customers, offering more than 26,000 high-quality natural products, consisting of groceries and general merchandise, nutritional supplements, bulk and food service products, personal care items, perishables, and frozen foods.

The company serves more than 6,500 customers in 46 states, including independent natural products retailers, super natural chains and conventional supermarkets. It is the primary distributor to the two largest super natural chains, Whole Foods Markets, Inc. and Wild Oats Markets, Inc. The company also owns and operates 16 retail natural products stores that complement its distribution business.

UNFI's extensive selection of natural products enables it to provide a primary source of supply to a diverse base of customers whose product needs vary significantly. Products distributed include national brand, regional brand, private label and master distribution products.

The company evaluates more than 10,000 potential products each year, based on existing and anticipated trends in consumer preference and buying patterns. Since 1992, it has introduced an average of 350 new products each month, while discontinuing about 150 less successful products.

UNFI maintains long-standing relationships with independent natural products retailers, including super natural chains, and has continued to emphasize its relationships with new customers, such as conventional supermarkets, Internet retailers and other mass market outlets, as well as gourmet stores. Sales in FY 98 (Jul.) by type of customers served was: independent natural products stores 56%, super natural chains 31%, conventional supermarkets 9%, and other 4%. Whole Foods Markets accounted for 16% of sales in FY 98.

Per Share Data ($) (Year Ended Jul. 31)	1999	1998	1997	1996	1995	1994	1993	1992	1991	1990
Tangible Bk. Val.	NA	4.65	4.41	3.49	NA	NA	NA	NA	NA	NA
Cash Flow	NA	1.08	1.17	0.69	NA	NA	NA	NA	NA	NA
Earnings	0.73	0.74	0.79	0.40	NA	NA	NA	NA	NA	NA
Dividends	Nil	Nil	Nil	Nil	NA	NA	NA	NA	NA	NA
Payout Ratio	Nil	Nil	Nil	Nil	NA	NA	NA	NA	NA	NA
Prices - High	29¾	33⅜	27⅛	17½	NA	NA	NA	NA	NA	NA
- Low	7⅝	19	12½	13¼	NA	NA	NA	NA	NA	NA
P/E Ratio - High	41	45	33	51	NA	NA	NA	NA	NA	NA
- Low	10	26	15	39	NA	NA	NA	NA	NA	NA
Income Statement Analysis (Million $)										
Revs.	NA	729	422	286	NA	NA	NA	NA	NA	NA
Oper. Inc.	NA	35.1	22.8	13.6	NA	NA	NA	NA	NA	NA
Depr.	NA	6.1	4.4	3.0	NA	NA	NA	NA	NA	NA
Int. Exp.	NA	5.2	3.1	3.9	NA	NA	NA	NA	NA	NA
Pretax Inc.	NA	24.7	15.7	6.8	NA	NA	NA	NA	NA	NA
Eff. Tax Rate	NA	47%	41%	41%	NA	NA	NA	NA	NA	NA
Net Inc.	NA	13.1	9.3	4.0	NA	NA	NA	NA	NA	NA
Balance Sheet & Other Fin. Data (Million $)										
Cash	NA	1.4	0.0	0.1	NA	NA	NA	NA	NA	NA
Curr. Assets	NA	146	80.5	67.2	NA	NA	NA	NA	NA	NA
Total Assets	NA	212	111	99	NA	NA	NA	NA	NA	NA
Curr. Liab.	NA	80.6	31.6	57.1	NA	NA	NA	NA	NA	NA
LT Debt	NA	25.8	16.6	22.9	NA	NA	NA	NA	NA	NA
Common Eqty.	NA	104	62.2	18.2	NA	NA	NA	NA	NA	NA
Total Cap.	NA	132	79.4	41.1	NA	NA	NA	NA	NA	NA
Cap. Exp.	NA	15.2	3.6	NA	NA	NA	NA	NA	NA	NA
Cash Flow	NA	19.2	13.7	7.0	NA	NA	NA	NA	NA	NA
Curr. Ratio	NA	1.8	2.5	1.2	NA	NA	NA	NA	NA	NA
% LT Debt of Cap.	NA	19.5	20.9	55.7	NA	NA	NA	NA	NA	NA
% Net Inc.of Revs.	NA	1.8	2.2	1.4	NA	NA	NA	NA	NA	NA
% Ret. on Assets	NA	8.1	8.8	NA	NA	NA	NA	NA	NA	NA
% Ret. on Equity	NA	15.7	23.0	NA	NA	NA	NA	NA	NA	NA

Data as orig reptd.; bef. results of disc opers/spec. items. Per share data adj. for stk. divs. Bold denotes diluted EPS (FASB 128)-prior periods restated. E-Estimated. NA-Not Available. NM-Not Meaningful. NR-Not Ranked.

Office—260 Lake Road, Dayville, CT 06241. **Tel**—(860) 779-2800. **Chrmn & CEO**—N. A. Cloutier. **Vice Chrmn & Pres**—M. S. Funk. **CFO & Treas**—R. T. Cirulnick. **Secy**—D. V. Atwood. **Dirs**—N. A. Cloutier, M. S. Funk, B. McFadden, K. T. Michel, R. B. Simone, R. J. Williams, R. S. Youngman. **Transfer Agent & Registrar**—Continental Stock Transfer & Trust Co., NYC. **Incorporated**—in Delaware in 1994. **Empl**— 2,442. **S&P Analyst:** J. J. Schemitsch

STANDARD
&POOR'S
STOCK REPORTS

United Water Resources

NYSE Symbol **UWR**

In S&P SmallCap 600

09-OCT-99

Industry:
Water Utilities

Summary: UWR, which is engaged in water-related businesses and real estate investments, has agreed to be acquired by Suez Lyonnaise des Eaux for $35 a share in cash.

Quantitative Evaluations

Outlook
(1 Lowest—5 Highest)
• 2−

Fair Value
• 33¼

Risk
• Low

Earn./Div. Rank
• B

Technical Eval.
• **Neutral** since 9/99

Rel. Strength Rank
(1 Lowest—99 Highest)
• 89

Insider Activity
• NA

Recent Price • 33
52 Wk Range • 33¾-18

Yield • 2.9%
12-Mo. P/E • 27.6

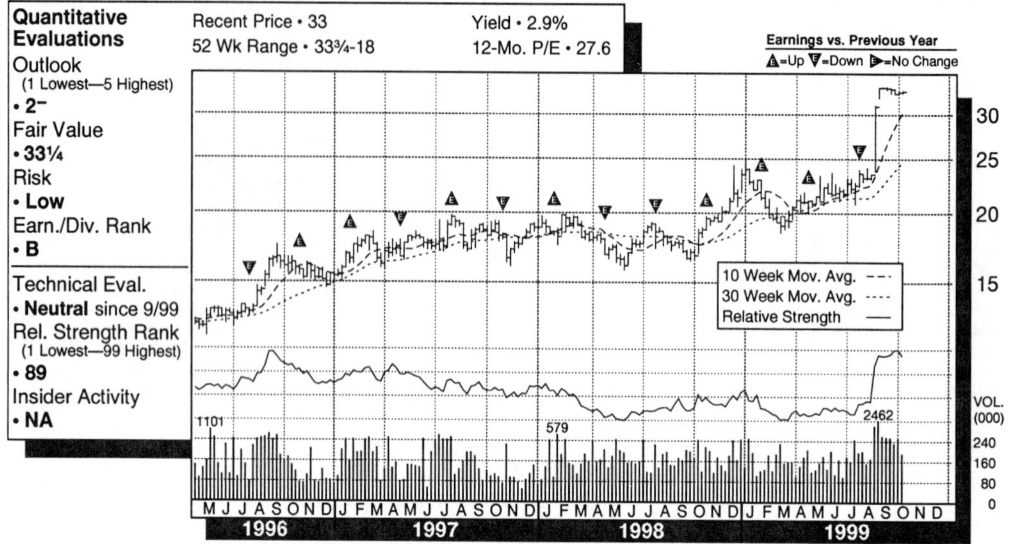

Business Profile - 26-AUG-99

In August 1999, UWR announced a definitive agreement to be acquired by Suez Lyonnaise des Eaux, a leading international provider of private infrastructure services, for $35 a share in cash. The agreement, which was approved by directors of both companies, is subject to UWR shareholder approval and regulatory approvals; the transaction is expected to be completed in the first half of 2000. Suez Lyonnaise currently owns about 30% of UWR's common shares. In July 1999, UWR agreed to sell several small utility subsidiaries to American Water Works Co., for about $49 million in cash.

Operational Review - 26-AUG-99

Operating revenues in the six months ended June 30, 1999, rose 5.8%, year to year. Despite improved domestic utility performance, profitability from operations was restricted by lower earnings from UWR's interest in Northumbrian Water Group, as a result of the effect on deferred taxes of a decrease in the U.K. corporate tax rate. However, including a $5.8 million gain on the sale of two office buildings (Harrison Plaza), pretax income advanced 25%. After taxes at 31.3%, versus 23.7%, net income was up 12%, to $18,263,000 ($0.43 a share, after preferred dividends, on 3.9% more shares), from $16,274,000 ($0.39).

Stock Performance - 08-OCT-99

In the past 30 trading days, UWR's shares have declined 1%, compared to a 0.91% fall in the S&P 500. Average trading volume for the past five days was 37,940 shares, compared with the 40-day moving average of 159,010 shares.

Key Stock Statistics

Dividend Rate/Share	0.96	Shareholders	18,700
Shs. outstg. (M)	38.8	Market cap. (B)	$ 1.3
Avg. daily vol. (M)	0.057	Inst. holdings	18%
Tang. Bk. Value/Share	14.92		
Beta	0.50		

Value of $10,000 invested 5 years ago: $ 32,402

Fiscal Year Ending Dec. 31

	1999	1998	1997	1996	1995	1994
Revenues (Million $)						
1Q	79.23	75.44	80.01	69.76	71.41	39.02
2Q	91.83	86.22	87.76	82.58	83.57	82.40
3Q	—	108.8	99.7	97.87	96.38	93.49
4Q	—	85.80	83.95	81.83	76.47	78.10
Yr.	—	356.2	351.4	332.1	327.8	293.0
Earnings Per Share ($)						
1Q	**0.13**	**0.09**	**0.12**	**0.15**	0.03	0.12
2Q	**0.29**	**0.30**	**0.32**	**0.22**	0.24	0.28
3Q	—	**0.51**	**0.18**	**0.46**	0.45	0.46
4Q	—	**0.27**	**0.21**	**0.18**	-0.17	0.12
Yr.	—	**1.17**	**0.83**	**1.01**	0.54	1.01

Next earnings report expected: mid October

Dividend Data (Dividends have been paid since 1886.)

Amount ($)	Date Decl.	Ex-Div. Date	Stock of Record	Payment Date
0.240	Mar. 18	May. 12	May. 14	Jun. 01 '99
0.240	Jul. 08	Aug. 11	Aug. 13	Sep. 01 '99
.06 Spl.	Oct. 07	Oct. 11	Oct. 15	Dec. 01 '99
0.240	Oct. 07	Nov. 10	Nov. 15	Dec. 01 '99

A Division of The McGraw-Hill Companies

United Water Resources Inc.

Business Summary - 26-AUG-99

In August 1999, United Water Resources (UWR) announced a definitive agreement to be acquired by Suez Lyonnaise des Eaux, a world leader in private infrastructure services, for $35 a share in cash. Suez Lyonnaise currently owns about 30% of UWR's common stock. The agreement permits United Water to increase its regular quarterly dividend, and to pay a special dividend at closing, for an aggregate dividend increase of $0.48 a share. The transaction is subject to approval by shareholders of UWR, and to regulatory approvals in the U.S. The acquisition is expected to close during the first half of 2000.

Only a few years ago, United Water Resources was a regional water supplier serving one million people in two states: New York and New Jersey. Today, it is the second largest U.S. investor-owned water services company (only American Water Works is larger) with a presence in 19 states across the country. UWR has interests in Canada and Mexico as well, and, across the Atlantic, its 10%-owned affiliate, Northumbrian Water Group, provides water services to four million people in the U.K.

Through its United Water New Jersey and United Water New York utilities, which serve contiguous areas of the two states, UWR furnishes water to one million people. UWR provides water and wastewater services to another million people in 13 states through its United Waterworks subsidiary. In all, the company's regulated utility operations served some 541,813 separate water customer accounts and 28,072 wastewater customers at the end of 1998. Residential customers accounted for 63% of utility revenues in 1998, commercial customers 26%, industrial 7%, and fire protection 4%.

While revenues from regulated water utilities (91% of total revenues in 1998) are expected to remain strong over the next five years, the company anticipates a dramatic increase in revenues from non-regulated water services over the same period. Through public-private partnerships, including a 1996 alliance with Jersey City, NJ, forming the largest such partnership for a U.S. municipal water operation, cities retain ownership of their water systems while, the company operates and maintains them. UWR also has a stake in JMM Operational Services, Inc., which provides contract operations and management services on behalf of municipally owned water and wastewater treatment facilities in North America. A July 1997 restructuring lifted UWR's interest in JMM, which it holds through United Water Services LLC, to 50%. UWR's various real estate activities, including property holdings in several states, constitute another non-regulated business area.

Per Share Data ($)										
(Year Ended Dec. 31)	**1998**	**1997**	**1996**	**1995**	**1994**	**1993**	**1992**	**1991**	**1990**	**1989**
Tangible Bk. Val.	14.92	14.36	14.10	14.14	14.09	9.62	9.12	8.81	8.54	8.07
Earnings	1.17	0.83	1.14	0.54	1.01	1.03	0.87	0.96	1.10	0.86
Dividends	1.17	0.92	0.92	0.92	0.92	0.92	0.92	0.91	0.88	0.88
Payout Ratio	100%	111%	81%	170%	91%	89%	106%	95%	80%	102%
Prices - High	25	19 3/4	17 1/2	14 1/8	14 3/4	15 7/8	16 5/8	16 5/8	16 1/2	17 7/8
- Low	15 3/4	15	12	11 3/4	12 1/4	14	13	10 7/8	9 7/8	15 3/4
P/E Ratio - High	21	24	15	26	15	15	19	17	15	21
- Low	13	18	11	22	12	14	15	11	9	18
Income Statement Analysis (Million $)										
Revs.	356	22.2	332	328	293	200	165	162	165	133
Depr.	40.0	34.7	30.8	30.2	25.2	14.3	14.0	13.1	11.4	9.3
Maint.	NA	NA	NA	NA	NA	0.5	0.8	NA	NA	NA
Fxd. Chgs. Cov.	1.9	1.7	2.0	1.6	2.5	2.3	2.0	2.1	2.4	2.2
Constr. Credits	4.6	3.4	3.4	1.9	1.3	0.6	0.6	0.8	1.9	3.9
Eff. Tax Rate	29%	38%	38%	39%	40%	39%	31%	31%	34%	28%
Net Inc.	48.0	33.7	43.0	22.1	31.3	20.0	15.8	16.4	18.3	14.3
Balance Sheet & Other Fin. Data (Million $)										
Gross Prop.	1,812	1,682	1,421	1,410	1,346	606	569	556	550	524
Cap. Exp.	104	83.3	74.5	70.0	58.0	16.0	14.1	16.1	27.6	30.0
Net Prop.	1,472	1,385	1,146	1,153	1,110	502	474	470	463	443
Capitalization:										
LT Debt	676	623	558	559	505	277	294	302	251	254
% LT Debt	57	55	53	55	53	54	58	62	59	60
Pfd.	57.8	95.6	117	107	107	32.8	33.1	18.4	19.9	21.5
% Pfd.	4.90	8.40	11	11	11	6.40	6.50	3.80	4.70	5.10
Common	456	419	391	358	350	202	180	164	153	146
% Common	38	37	37	35	36	40	36	34	36	35
Total Cap.	1,386	1,455	1,353	1,312	1,242	624	582	553	493	475
% Oper. Ratio	78.1	78.6	71.1	80.4	78.6	78.7	76.7	76.8	78.2	77.2
% Earn. on Net Prop.	6.8	7.1	8.3	6.9	7.8	8.9	8.1	8.0	7.9	7.1
% Return On Revs.	13.5	9.6	12.9	6.8	10.7	10.0	9.6	10.2	11.1	10.7
% Return On Invest. Capital	10.3	6.2	9.9	6.4	7.2	7.3	7.0	7.6	8.0	6.7
% Return On Com. Equity	10.0	7.2	4.1	4.9	11.3	10.5	9.2	10.4	12.3	9.7

Data as orig reptd.; bef. results of disc opers/spec. items. Per share data adj. for stk. divs. Bold denotes diluted EPS (FASB 128)-prior periods restated. E-Estimated. NA-Not Available. NM-Not Meaningful. NR-Not Ranked.

Office—200 Old Hook Rd., Harrington Park, NJ 07640. **Tel**—(201) 784-9434. **Website**—http://www.unitedwater.com **Chrmn, Pres & CEO**—D. L. Correll. **Treas**—J. J. Turner. **Investor Contact**—Nicholas P. Gicas (201-767-2887). **Secy**—D. W. Hawes. **Dirs**—E. E. Barr, F. J. Borelli, T. Bourbie, C. Chaumin, L. R. Codey, D. L. Correll, P. Del Col, R. L. Duncan, Jr., J. F. Hanson, D. W. Hawes, G. F. Keane, D. M. Newnham, M. L. Worthing. **Transfer Agent & Registrar**—ChaseMellon Shareholder Services, Ridgefield Park, NJ. **Incorporated**—in New Jersey in 1869; reincorporated in New Jersey in 1983. **Empl**— 1,400. **S&P Analyst:** J.J.S.

STANDARD & POOR'S
STOCK REPORTS

Unitrode Corp.

NYSE Symbol **UTR**

In S&P SmallCap 600

09-OCT-99

Industry: Electronics (Semiconductors)

Summary: In July 1999, Unitrode agreed to be acquired by Texas Instruments for about $39 a share in stock.

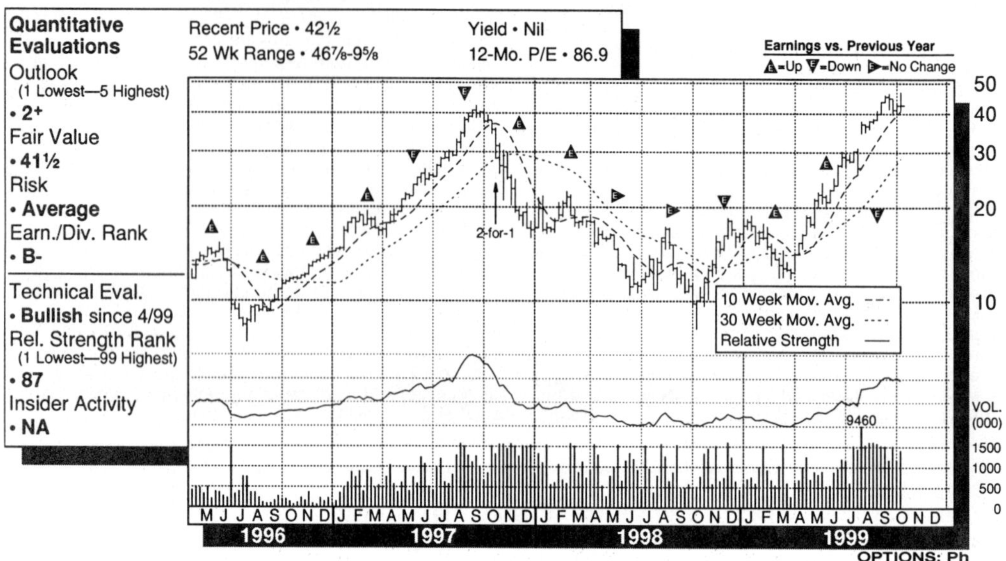

Business Profile - 06-AUG-99

In July 1999, the company agreed to be acquired by Texas Instruments for some $38.60 a share in stock, or a total of $1.2 billion at the time of announcement. The acquisition will strengthen Texas Instruments' analog catalog portfolio of standard products targeted at a breadth of customers and applications for the mass market. Completion remained subject to shareholder approval, termination of the applicable waiting period under anti-trust legislation, and other customary conditions.

Operational Review - 06-AUG-99

Net sales in the first quarter of FY 00 (Jan.) rose 20%, year to year, reflecting increased demand in the electronic data, communications, and portable PC markets as well as a general industry-wide rebound in demand for semiconductors. Gross margins widened, helped by increased factory utilization, reduced costs of wafers, and lower assembly costs from subcontractors. Results were further aided by the absence of $1.1 million of new fab pre-operating expenses, $1.4 million of merger costs, $1.3 million of restructuring and other expenses, and other non-operating costs of $2.6 million. Net income of $6,449,000 ($0.20 a share) contrasted with a net loss of $2,499,000 ($0.08).

Stock Performance - 08-OCT-99

In the past 30 trading days, UTR's shares have increased 7%, compared to a 0.91% fall in the S&P 500. Average trading volume for the past five days was 280,580 shares, compared with the 40-day moving average of 353,192 shares.

Key Stock Statistics

Dividend Rate/Share	Nil	Shareholders	521
Shs. outstg. (M)	32.5	Market cap. (B)	$ 1.4
Avg. daily vol. (M)	0.265	Inst. holdings	81%
Tang. Bk. Value/Share	6.83		
Beta	0.89		

Value of $10,000 invested 5 years ago: $ 58,706

Fiscal Year Ending Jan. 31

	2000	1999	1998	1997	1996	1995
Revenues (Million $)						
1Q	44.31	36.93	36.93	34.22	25.89	22.30
2Q	50.43	38.90	38.90	30.01	28.86	24.00
3Q	—	40.40	48.54	32.07	30.12	25.80
4Q	—	41.57	40.05	37.23	33.67	25.06
Yr.	—	157.8	177.6	133.5	118.5	97.08
Earnings Per Share ($)						
1Q	**0.20**	**-0.08**	-0.08	0.22	0.16	0.08
2Q	**0.06**	**0.11**	0.11	0.20	0.17	0.05
3Q	—	**-0.09**	0.35	0.21	0.19	0.10
4Q	—	**0.32**	**0.27**	0.24	0.21	0.15
Yr.	—	**0.27**	**1.21**	**0.87**	**0.74**	0.38

Next earnings report expected: mid November

Dividend Data

No cash dividends have been paid. A two-for-one stock split was effected in October 1997.

A Division of The McGraw-Hill Companies

Unitrode Corporation

Business Summary - 06-AUG-99

Unitrode Corp. (UTR) designs, manufacturers and sells analog/linear and mixed-signal integrated circuits, electronic modules and non-volatile products. Its offerings are used principally to address power management, portable power and interface applications. The company's products have a broad range of applications in the computer, tele- and data-communications, consumer and defense/aerospace industries.

Integrated circuits (ICs) are the building blocks of today's electronic products and may be classified as either analog or digital. Digital circuits are used mostly in computer memory or logic devices and in microprocessors. Analog circuits process "real-world" signals that measure physical conditions, such as temperature, force, speed, and pressure, the frequency and wavelength of which vary continuously. Analog circuits are used to amplify, monitor, condition, or transform these signals or to interpret these signals for use by digital logic.

Sales by product category in the fiscal year ended January 31, 1999, were as follows: power management 39%, data transmission/interface 33%, portable power 18%, and non-volatile and other 10%. About one-half of FY 99 sales were to the electronic data processing/ computer market for use in monitors, tape drives, peripherals, servers, and other areas.

Power management circuits are used in switching power supplies (either AC/DC or DC/DC) to modulate, amplify, or regulate current or voltages, or to protect other circuitry from irregular, spurious, or erroneous signals. Examples of such products are current-mode pulse-width modulators, power factor pre-regulator ICs, phase-shift resonant converters, power driver circuits, and load-share circuits. Using these advanced control ICs, a customer can design a power supply that is smaller and more efficient or can incorporate these ICs into a distributed power system that responds to instantaneous changes in current levels required during operations.

Data transmission/interface circuits transfer data signals between or within electronic systems or a single system. These circuits are used as small computer systems interface (SCI) active termination circuits and as drivers or receivers in high-speed data transmission, as well as for power interface, such as in hot swap and certain transceiver applications. The company's largest product family in this line is used mainly to provide active termination for various lines of data transmission in SCSI applications.

Portable power management circuits and modules provide charge control, capacity monitoring, conditioning and power conversion in a variety of battery-powered applications. Non-volatile circuits and modules include static random access memory and related time clock product families.

Per Share Data ($) (Year Ended Jan. 31)	1999	1998	1997	1996	1995	1994	1993	1992	1991	1990
Tangible Bk. Val.	6.49	6.49	4.88	3.93	3.46	3.35	2.71	2.23	2.85	2.88
Cash Flow	0.72	1.67	1.36	1.09	0.68	0.54	0.48	-0.20	0.35	-0.28
Earnings	0.27	1.21	0.87	0.73	0.38	0.32	0.24	-0.62	-0.07	-0.74
Dividends	Nil	Nil	Nil	Nil	Nil	Nil	Nil	Nil	Nil	Nil
Payout Ratio	Nil	Nil	Nil	Nil	Nil	Nil	Nil	Nil	Nil	Nil
Cal. Yrs.	1998	1997	1996	1995	1994	1993	1992	1991	1990	1989
Prices - High	22 1/2	42 3/8	15 3/8	16 1/4	10 1/2	7 7/8	5 3/4	3 5/8	3 1/8	4 1/4
- Low	8 1/8	14 1/2	7 3/8	8 7/8	6 3/4	4 7/8	2 7/8	1 1/2	1 1/2	2 1/16
P/E Ratio - High	83	35	18	22	28	24	24	NM	NM	NM
- Low	30	12	8	12	18	15	12	NM	NM	NM
Income Statement Analysis (Million $)										
Revs.	158	178	134	119	97.0	87.0	87.0	108	125	139
Oper. Inc.	34.9	53.2	40.8	35.4	24.3	17.5	14.4	11.9	8.5	5.7
Depr.	14.9	11.4	11.7	9.0	7.4	5.7	6.4	11.2	11.5	13.0
Int. Exp.	0.1	0.1	0.1	0.1	0.1	0.1	0.0	0.1	0.2	0.6
Pretax Inc.	15.2	47.8	33.7	28.0	12.5	12.8	9.1	-16.4	-1.2	-21.4
Eff. Tax Rate	43%	37%	39%	37%	26%	35%	32%	NM	NM	NM
Net Inc.	8.6	30.2	20.7	17.5	9.2	8.3	6.2	-16.4	-1.8	-20.6
Balance Sheet & Other Fin. Data (Million $)										
Cash	92.6	66.3	52.0	36.2	30.7	30.8	25.9	22.1	15.2	15.8
Curr. Assets	153	114	87.5	71.3	58.5	61.0	51.0	58.0	60.0	64.0
Total Assets	240	202	142	118	103	102	86.0	93.0	104	118
Curr. Liab.	27.3	39.8	24.9	24.2	20.9	17.9	18.2	28.8	20.9	32.0
LT Debt	Nil	NM	NM	NM	Nil	Nil	Nil	Nil	Nil	Nil
Common Eqty.	209	159	116	92.4	82.0	84.0	68.0	64.0	84.0	86.0
Total Cap.	209	160	117	93.8	82.0	84.0	68.0	64.0	84.0	86.0
Cap. Exp.	10.2	45.8	18.7	11.8	15.6	12.6	9.6	5.0	5.7	8.4
Cash Flow	23.6	41.6	32.4	26.5	16.7	14.0	12.6	-5.2	9.8	-7.6
Curr. Ratio	5.6	2.9	3.5	2.9	2.8	3.4	2.8	2.0	2.9	2.0
% LT Debt of Cap.	Nil	NM	NM	NM	Nil	Nil	Nil	Nil	Nil	Nil
% Net Inc.of Revs.	5.5	17.0	15.4	14.8	9.5	9.6	7.1	NM	NM	NM
% Ret. on Assets	3.9	17.6	15.9	15.8	9.3	8.9	7.1	NM	NM	NM
% Ret. on Equity	4.7	21.9	19.9	20.1	11.5	11.0	9.6	NM	NM	NM

Data as orig reptd.; bef. results of disc opers/spec. items. Per share data adj. for stk. divs. Bold denotes diluted EPS (FASB 128)-prior periods restated. E-Estimated. NA-Not Available. NM-Not Meaningful. NR-Not Ranked.

Office—7 Continental Blvd., Merrimack, NH 03054. **Tel**—(603) 424-2410. **Website**—http://www.unitrode.com **Chrmn, Pres & CEO**—R. J. Richardson. **SVP & Secy**—A. R. Campbell. **EVP & CFO**—J. L. Kokulis. **Dirs**—W. W. R. Elder, D. R. Erdmann, R. L. Gable, L. E. Lataif, R. J. Richardson, J. T. Vanderslice. **Transfer Agent & Registrar**—Boston EquiServe, Boston. **Incorporated**—in Maryland in 1960. **Empl**— 840. **S&P Analyst:** P.L.H.

STANDARD
&POOR'S
STOCK REPORTS

Universal Forest Products

NASDAQ Symbol **UFPI**

In S&P SmallCap 600

09-OCT-99

Industry:
Building Materials

Summary: This company makes, treats and distributes lumber products for the do-it-yourself, manufactured housing, wholesale lumber and industrial markets.

Quantitative Evaluations

Outlook
(1 Lowest—5 Highest)
• **4**

Fair Value
• **21**

Risk
• **Average**

Earn./Div. Rank
• **NR**

Technical Eval.
• **Bearish** since 8/99

Rel. Strength Rank
(1 Lowest—99 Highest)
• **8**

Insider Activity
• **Neutral**

Recent Price • 13
52 Wk Range • 24⅛-11⅞

Yield • 0.5%
12-Mo. P/E • 9.4

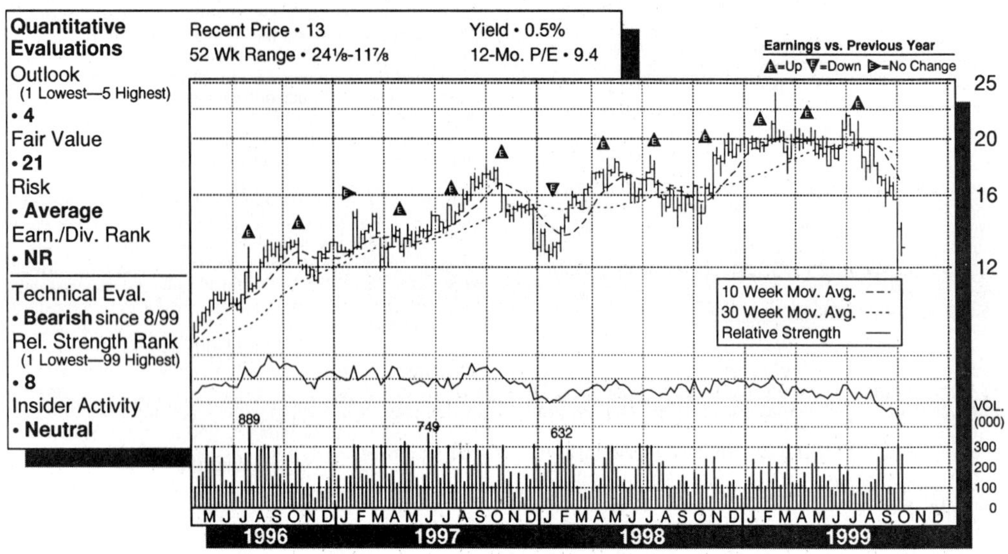

Business Profile - 16-AUG-99

UFPI believes it is the leading U.S. producer of lumber products for the do-it-yourself (DIY) retail and factory-built housing (FBH) markets. The company's Performance 2002 goals include attaining sales of $2 billion in 2002. Management is focusing on expanding the industrial and site-built markets; it wants both to grow to $250 million by 2002, from $77 million and $128 million, respectively, in 1998. In recent years, UFPI has taken steps to boost profits by attempting to expand volume growth, increase sales of more profitable value-added products, and improve manufacturing efficiency.

Operational Review - 16-AUG-99

Sales in the first half of 1999 rose 19%, year to year, due to the acquisition of several companies and higher sales to UFPI's largest DIY customer. Margins widened as a stronger lumber market outweighed higher selling, general and administrative expenses related to acquired companies; operating income climbed 28%. After higher interest expense, and taxes at 39.5%, versus 38.4%, net income increased 23%, to $18.1 million ($0.85 a share, on 7.7% more shares), from $14.7 million ($0.74). At June 26, 1999, long-term debt stood at $172 million, up 30% from 1998 year end.

Stock Performance - 08-OCT-99

In the past 30 trading days, UFPI's shares have declined 25%, compared to a 0.91% fall in the S&P 500. Average trading volume for the past five days was 52,620 shares, compared with the 40-day moving average of 43,638 shares.

Key Stock Statistics

Dividend Rate/Share	0.07	Shareholders	6,200
Shs. outstg. (M)	20.8	Market cap. (B)	$0.270
Avg. daily vol. (M)	0.046	Inst. holdings	30%
Tang. Bk. Value/Share	5.50		
Beta	0.95		

Value of $10,000 invested 5 years ago: $ 12,231

Fiscal Year Ending Dec. 31

	1999	1998	1997	1996	1995	1994
Revenues (Million $)						
1Q	300.2	238.2	214.7	159.6	175.0	178.0
2Q	446.8	388.7	341.3	275.7	235.0	283.0
3Q	—	341.1	285.0	243.9	189.0	226.0
4Q	—	271.0	209.0	188.5	140.1	180.0
Yr.	—	1,239	1,066	867.7	739.3	866.0
Earnings Per Share ($)						
1Q	**0.25**	**0.20**	0.18	0.15	0.20	0.14
2Q	**0.60**	**0.52**	0.51	0.46	0.30	0.25
3Q	—	**0.40**	0.29	0.27	0.18	0.11
4Q	—	**0.15**	**-0.09**	0.12	0.12	0.12
Yr.	—	**1.28**	**0.93**	**0.98**	**0.80**	0.61

Next earnings report expected: mid October

Dividend Data (Dividends have been paid since 1993.)

Amount ($)	Date Decl.	Ex-Div. Date	Stock of Record	Payment Date
0.035	Oct. 23	Nov. 27	Dec. 01	Dec. 15 '98
0.035	Apr. 28	Jun. 01	Jun. 01	Jun. 15 '99

A Division of The McGraw-Hill Companies

Universal Forest Products, Inc.

Business Summary - 16-AUG-99

Founded in 1955, this Michigan-based company's business originally consisted of distributing carload lots of lumber to mobile and modular home manufacturers. In the early 1970s, with its customers suffering from supply and inventory problems, Universal Forest Products added manufacturing capabilities to its distribution business. This allowed mobile and modular home builders to manage inventory better, reduce labor costs and conserve capital during a time of high interest rates. Today, UFPI makes, treats and distributes lumber products for the do-it-yourself, manufactured housing, site-built construction, industrial and wholesale lumber markets. The company is the largest U.S. producer of pressure-treated lumber.

The do-it-yourself segment (DIY; 45% of total sales) markets its products primarily to warehouse-format home improvement retailers, chain lumberyards and contractor-oriented wholesalers. In 1998, 1997 and 1996, Home Depot, Inc. accounted for 20%, 18% and 15% of DIY sales, respectively. Offerings include treated and untreated lumber, decking, fencing and a variety of related products. The company knows of no other manufacturer that competes with its DIY products on a national basis. The company also believes its full range of offerings provides significant competitive advantages in the DIY market.

The manufactured housing segment (MH; 32%) sells its products to producers of mobile, modular and prefabricated homes and recreational vehicles. Offerings include roof and floor trusses, custom-cut lumber, plywood, particle board and dimension lumber. The company believes it is the largest maker of roof trusses for manufactured housing in North America; Universal estimates that it supplies 65% of the trusses to the MH market.

The company entered the site-built construction, or residential, market (10%) through five acquisitions completed since December 1997. Customers include large-volume, multitract builders and smaller custom builders. Products sold include roof and floor trusses, wall panels and I-joints. UFPI's objective is to continue growing production capacity while developing a national presence.

The industrial segment (6%) makes pallets, crates and wooden boxes for industrial manufacturers and agricultural customers that use them for packing, shipping and material handling purposes. Many of the products sold to this market are produced from by-products of other manufactured products, thereby increasing raw material yields. UFPI plans to increase its industrial market share internally, by utilizing technology acquired from Atlantic General Packaging (AGP) in 1998, and through strategic acquisitions.

UFPI's wholesale lumber segment (6%) markets its offerings to lumber wholesalers that resell to retail outlets. Because UFPI's wholesale competitors are also DIY customers, it does not emphasize the wholesale lumber sector.

Per Share Data ($)										
(Year Ended Dec. 31)	1998	1997	1996	1995	1994	1993	1992	1991	1990	1989
Tangible Bk. Val.	4.65	6.45	5.68	4.90	4.20	3.65	2.89	2.61	2.43	NA
Cash Flow	1.89	1.45	1.47	1.23	0.93	0.94	0.54	NA	NA	NA
Earnings	1.28	0.93	1.00	0.80	0.61	0.66	0.29	0.15	0.06	NA
Dividends	0.07	0.07	0.06	0.06	0.05	0.05	0.05	0.05	0.05	NA
Payout Ratio	5%	7%	6%	7%	8%	4%	17%	33%	83%	NA
Prices - High	20 1/2	18	13 1/2	10 3/8	11	11	NA	NA	NA	NA
- Low	12 1/4	11 3/4	7 5/8	6	5 7/8	7	NA	NA	NA	NA
P/E Ratio - High	16	19	13	13	18	16	NA	NA	NA	NA
- Low	10	13	8	7	10	10	NA	NA	NA	NA
Income Statement Analysis (Million $)										
Revs.	1,239	1,066	868	739	866	644	450	NA	NA	NA
Oper. Inc.	64.7	41.5	40.8	33.9	72.5	58.3	45.0	NA	NA	NA
Depr.	12.6	9.5	8.3	7.6	5.7	4.3	3.7	NA	NA	NA
Int. Exp.	9.5	4.3	3.0	3.6	5.9	3.9	3.2	NA	NA	NA
Pretax Inc.	43.0	26.0	29.7	23.6	18.2	17.0	7.2	NA	NA	NA
Eff. Tax Rate	39%	35%	40%	41%	41%	41%	40%	NA	NA	NA
Net Inc.	26.4	17.0	17.7	14.1	10.7	10.0	4.3	NA	NA	NA
Balance Sheet & Other Fin. Data (Million $)										
Cash	0.9	3.2	1.3	21.5	0.1	1.3	NA	NA	NA	NA
Curr. Assets	182	158	127	116	114	144	NA	NA	NA	NA
Total Assets	420	229	193	176	169	186	NA	NA	NA	NA
Curr. Liab.	82.0	67.9	38.1	38.0	35.9	98.4	NA	NA	NA	NA
LT Debt	132	39.8	49.0	52.5	58.8	23.0	NA	NA	NA	NA
Common Eqty.	192	116	100	83.4	71.6	61.9	NA	NA	NA	NA
Total Cap.	332	158	151	138	132	86.0	NA	NA	NA	NA
Cap. Exp.	28.4	13.6	9.1	14.3	18.0	9.3	6.9	NA	NA	NA
Cash Flow	39.0	26.5	26.1	21.7	16.5	14.3	8.1	NA	NA	NA
Curr. Ratio	2.2	2.3	3.3	3.1	3.2	1.5	NA	NA	NA	NA
% LT Debt of Cap.	39.8	25.3	32.4	38.1	44.5	26.6	NA	NA	NA	NA
% Net Inc.of Revs.	2.1	1.6	2.0	1.9	1.2	1.6	1.0	NA	NA	NA
% Ret. on Assets	8.1	8.0	9.6	8.1	6.1	6.4	NA	NA	NA	NA
% Ret. on Equity	17.2	15.4	19.4	18.1	16.6	18.8	NA	NA	NA	NA

Data as orig reptd.; bef. results of disc opers/spec. items. Per share data adj. for stk. divs. Bold denotes diluted EPS (FASB 128)-prior periods restated. E-Estimated. NA-Not Available. NM-Not Meaningful. NR-Not Ranked.

Office—2801 E. Beltline N.E., Grand Rapids, MI 49525. **Tel**—(616) 364-6161. **Website**—http://www.ufpinc.com **Chrmn**—P. F. Secchia. **Pres & CEO**—W. G. Currie. **CFO & Treas**—E. A. Nickles. **EVP & Secy**—M. J. Missad. **Investor Contact**—Charles R. Felix (888 BUY-UFPI). **Dirs**—J. C. Canepa, W. G. Currie, R. M. DeVos, J. W. Garside, P. M. Novell, P. F. Secchia, L. A. Smith, C. M. Shoffner. **Transfer Agent & Registrar**—American Stock Transfer & Trust Co., NYC. **Incorporated**—in Michigan in 1955. **Empl**— 4,400. **S&P Analyst:** John A. Massey

STANDARD
&POOR'S
STOCK REPORTS

Universal Health Services

NYSE Symbol **UHS**

In S&P SmallCap 600

09-OCT-99 **Industry:** Health Care (Hospital Management)

Summary: This company owns and operates acute care medical/surgical/psychiatric hospitals, as well as outpatient surgery and radiation therapy centers nationwide.

S&P Opinion: Hold (★★★) | Recent Price • 24⅝ | 52 Wk Range • 55⅛-23⅛ | Yield • Nil | 12-Mo. P/E • 9.4

Quantitative Evaluations

Outlook (1 Lowest—5 Highest) • **5+**

Fair Value • **58¼**

Risk • **Low**

Earn./Div. Rank • **B+**

Technical Eval. • **Bearish** since 9/99

Rel. Strength Rank (1 Lowest—99 Highest) • **6**

Insider Activity • **Neutral**

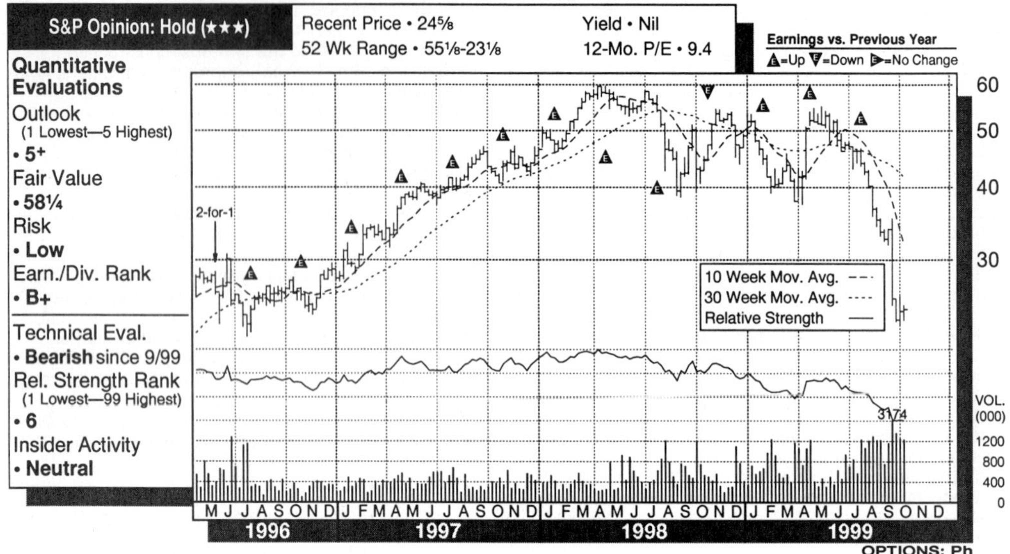

OPTIONS: Ph

Overview - 11-JUN-99

UHS is seen growing operating revenues approximately 16% in 1999, reflecting improved performance at the existing base of acute care and behavioral care facilities, both on an outpatient and inpatient basis. With UHS's strong balance sheet, acute care hospital acquisitions could provide incremental revenue growth opportunities. Despite strength in the first quarter, same-store inpatient acute care admissions in 1999 are not expected to exceed 4.0%, but pricing pressures from HMO customers should moderate during the year. On the operating margin front, we look for earnings before interest, taxes, depreciation and amortization (EBITDA) margins of about 15%, up from 14% in 1998, aided by the integration of acquired facilities into the existing hospital network. Assuming no significant changes in either interest expense or depreciation charges, and taxes at 37.0%, net margins of about 4% are anticipated, and we look for 1999 EPS of $2.90, with a rise to $3.35 in 2000.

Valuation - 11-JUN-99

Although significantly trailing the S&P 500 Index, the stock's performance in the first half of 1999 surpassed that of the average hospital stock in our analytical universe. This positive relative performance reflects the company's strong first quarter admission trends which, combined with well controlled operating costs, resulted in per-share earnings above analyst expectations. Although hospital stocks offer defensive characteristics in a highly priced stock market environment, we maintain a neutral opinion and would not add to holdings until the Medicare reimbursement outlook clarifies. Recently trading at 17 times our 1999 EPS estimate, the stock is priced somewhat above the industry average P/E multiple, and slightly ahead of our three-year EPS growth target of 15%.

Key Stock Statistics

S&P EPS Est. 1999	2.35	Tang. Bk. Value/Share	11.49
P/E on S&P Est. 1999	10.5	Beta	1.19
S&P EPS Est. 2000	3.00	Shareholders	900
Dividend Rate/Share	Nil	Market cap. (B)	$0.725
Shs. outstg. (M)	31.7	Inst. holdings	84%
Avg. daily vol. (M)	0.441		

Value of $10,000 invested 5 years ago: $ 24,382

Fiscal Year Ending Dec. 31

	1999	1998	1997	1996	1995	1994
Revenues (Million $)						
1Q	520.1	463.1	340.2	271.6	220.7	194.4
2Q	513.1	474.6	343.8	287.0	214.2	192.2
3Q	—	456.1	362.4	303.5	234.1	191.5
4Q	—	480.7	396.3	328.1	262.1	204.1
Yr.	—	1,874	1,443	1,190	931.1	782.2
Earnings Per Share ($)						
1Q	**0.92**	**0.77**	**0.65**	**0.54**	0.42	0.36
2Q	**0.71**	**0.61**	**0.51**	**0.42**	0.34	0.28
3Q	**E0.32**	**0.40**	**0.42**	**0.34**	0.26	0.20
4Q	**E0.40**	**0.61**	**0.45**	**0.36**	0.24	0.16
Yr.	**E2.35**	**2.39**	**2.03**	**1.65**	**1.26**	**1.01**

Next earnings report expected: mid October

Dividend Data

No regular dividends have been paid on the common stock. A special cash dividend of $0.10 a share was paid in 1989, as adjusted for a two-for-one stock split in 1996.

Universal Health Services, Inc.

Business Summary - 11-JUN-99

Universal Health Services (UHS) ranks as the third largest investor-owned hospital chain, with 1998 revenues of $1.9 billion. At 1998 year end, the company operated 44 health care facilities, including 21 acute care hospitals, 20 behavioral care centers and three women's centers in Arkansas, California, the District of Columbia, Florida, Georgia, Illinois, Louisiana, Massachusetts, Michigan, Missouri, Nevada, Oklahoma, Pennsylvania, Puerto Rico, South Carolina, Texas and Washington. The company also owns, outright or in partnership with physicians, and operates or manages 24 surgery and radiation oncology centers.

Services provided by the company's acute care hospitals include general surgery, internal medicine, obstetrics, emergency room care, radiology, oncology, diagnostic care, coronary care, pediatric services and psychiatric services. UHS provides capital resources as well as a variety of management services to its facilities, including central purchasing, data processing, finance and control systems, facilities planning, physician recruitment services, administrative personnel management, marketing and public relations.

UHS selectively seeks opportunities to expand its operations by acquiring, constructing or leasing additional hospital facilities. In addition, it is the company's objective to increase the operating revenues and profitability of its hospitals by the introduction of new services, improvement of existing services, physician recruitment, and the application of financial and operational controls. UHS also continues to examine its facilities and to dispose of those that do not have the potential to contribute to its growth or operating strategy.

During 1998, acute care hospitals owned by the company (including acquisitions and divestitures up to their respective dates of purchase and sale) had an average of 4,696 licensed beds (3,389 in 1997), while admissions amounted to 187,833 (128,020). The average length of stay declined to 4.7 days (4.8), patient days totaled 884,966 (616,965), and the average occupancy rate per licensed bed was 50% (50%). At the behavioral care centers, licensed beds averaged 1,782 (1,777), admissions totaled 32,400 (28,350), average length of stay was 11.3 days (11.9), patient days reached 365,935 (336,850) and average occupancy rate per licensed bed was 56% (52%).

During 1998, net patient revenues were derived from Medicare (34%), Medicaid (11%) and private/other (55%) sources.

The company serves as adviser to Universal Health Realty Income Trust (NYSE: UHT), which leases to UHS the real property of seven UHS facilities and holds interests in properties owned by unrelated companies. UHS receives a fee for its advisory services based on the value of Universal Health Realty's assets, and owns 8.0% of its outstanding shares.

Per Share Data ($)										
(Year Ended Dec. 31)	**1998**	**1997**	**1996**	**1995**	**1994**	**1993**	**1992**	**1991**	**1990**	**1989**
Tangible Bk. Val.	10.80	11.62	9.39	5.78	8.04	6.93	6.20	5.18	3.76	3.02
Cash Flow	5.56	4.47	3.97	3.08	2.47	2.15	1.85	1.84	2.17	1.68
Earnings	2.39	2.03	1.64	1.26	1.01	0.85	0.71	0.72	0.42	0.31
Dividends	Nil	Nil	Nil	Nil	Nil	Nil	Nil	Nil	Nil	0.10
Payout Ratio	Nil	Nil	Nil	Nil	Nil	Nil	Nil	Nil	Nil	31%
Prices - High	59¾	50¾	30¾	22¼	14⅞	10⅝	7⅞	9¼	5⅛	5⅞
- Low	38⅜	27¾	21⅝	11¼	9⅝	6¼	5⅝	4⅛	3¼	3⅛
P/E Ratio - High	25	25	19	18	15	12	11	13	12	19
- Low	16	14	13	9	9	7	8	6	8	10
Income Statement Analysis (Million $)										
Revs.	1,874	1,443	1,190	931	781	747	699	686	616	587
Oper. Inc.	404	315	177	127	104	81.0	69.0	68.0	78.0	79.0
Depr.	105	80.7	71.9	51.4	42.4	39.6	35.6	35.0	48.5	39.7
Int. Exp.	29.7	19.4	21.4	11.8	6.5	9.1	11.9	10.3	24.2	26.6
Pretax Inc.	132	106	80.0	53.0	46.9	35.1	41.0	30.3	18.5	14.1
Eff. Tax Rate	33%	36%	37%	33%	39%	32%	51%	33%	37%	36%
Net Inc.	79.6	67.3	50.7	35.5	28.7	24.0	20.0	20.3	11.6	9.0
Balance Sheet & Other Fin. Data (Million $)										
Cash	1.3	0.3	0.3	0.0	0.8	0.6	6.7	22.7	22.9	21.2
Curr. Assets	320	230	194	157	118	102	119	141	131	104
Total Assets	1,448	1,085	966	749	521	460	472	501	535	526
Curr. Liab.	170	160	140	135	104	86.0	85.0	127	93.0	101
LT Debt	418	272	276	237	85.0	75.0	115	127	206	206
Common Eqty.	627	527	453	298	261	224	203	184	167	158
Total Cap.	1,198	799	729	535	346	303	327	326	408	399
Cap. Exp.	96.8	129	106	60.7	59.0	59.0	44.0	55.0	34.0	35.0
Cash Flow	185	148	123	86.9	71.1	63.6	55.6	55.3	60.1	48.7
Curr. Ratio	1.9	1.4	1.4	1.2	1.1	1.2	1.4	1.1	1.4	1.0
% LT Debt of Cap.	34.9	34.0	37.8	44.3	24.6	24.7	35.2	39.0	50.4	51.5
% Net Inc.of Revs.	4.2	4.7	4.3	3.8	3.7	3.2	2.9	3.0	1.9	1.5
% Ret. on Assets	6.3	6.6	5.9	5.6	5.8	5.2	4.1	3.9	2.2	1.7
% Ret. on Equity	13.8	13.7	13.5	12.7	11.7	11.3	10.4	11.5	7.2	5.9

Data as orig reptd.; bef. results of disc opers/spec. items. Per share data adj. for stk. divs. Bold denotes diluted EPS (FASB 128)-prior periods restated. E-Estimated. NA-Not Available. NM-Not Meaningful. NR-Not Ranked.

Office—367 South Gulph Rd., P.O. Box 61558, King of Prussia, PA 19406-0958. **Tel**—(610) 768-3300. **Website**—http://www.uhsinc.com **Chrmn, Pres & CEO**—A. B. Miller. **SVP, CFO & Investor Contact**—Kirk E. Gorman. **Secy**—S. Miller. **Dirs**—J. H. Herrell, R. H. Hotz, L. Ducat, A. B. Miller, S. Miller, A. Pantaleoni, P. R. Verkuil. **Transfer Agent & Registrar**—ChaseMellon Shareholder Services, Ridgefield Park, NJ. **Incorporated**—in Delaware in 1978. **Empl**— 19,200. **S&P Analyst:** Robert M. Gold

STANDARD
&POOR'S
STOCK REPORTS

URS Corp.

NYSE Symbol **URS**

In S&P SmallCap 600

09-OCT-99

Industry: Engineering & Construction

Summary: URS is a worldwide provider of architectural and engineering services to public and private sector clients.

Business Profile - 07-AUG-99

In June 1999, URS acquired Dames & Moore Group (DM), a US-based engineering and construction services firm, for approximately $600 million. The acquisition of DM is expected to be accretive to earnings in the first full year after closing. In February 1999, URS acquired privately-held Thorburn Colquhoun Holdings plc, a UK-based civil engineering consulting firm with US$40 million in 1998 revenues, for $13.6 million. The TCH acquisition is not expected to have a material impact on URS' earnings for FY 99 (Oct.). URS' backlog on April 30, 1999 totaled $713 million, compared to $675 million on October 31, 1998.

Operational Review - 07-AUG-99

Revenues for the six months ended April 30, 1999 advanced 8.8%, year to year, reflecting strength across all business areas including increased demand for infrastructure project services. Direct operating expenses rose marginally and G&A costs were up 16%, both due to increased business activity. Following a 10% increase in net interest expense, total expenses rose only 7.7%. After taxes at 43.6%, versus 45.5%, net income increased 39%, to $12.7 million ($0.77 a share), from $9.1 million ($0.58).

Stock Performance - 08-OCT-99

In the past 30 trading days, URS's shares have declined 6%, compared to a 0.91% fall in the S&P 500. Average trading volume for the past five days was 43,460 shares, compared with the 40-day moving average of 29,026 shares.

Key Stock Statistics

Dividend Rate/Share	Nil	Shareholders	3,336
Shs. outstg. (M)	15.7	Market cap. (B)	$0.379
Avg. daily vol. (M)	0.036	Inst. holdings	73%
Tang. Bk. Value/Share	2.42		
Beta	1.15		

Value of $10,000 invested 5 years ago: $ 42,999

Fiscal Year Ending Oct. 31

	1999	1998	1997	1996	1995	1994
Revenues (Million $)						
1Q	199.1	186.2	95.54	48.50	40.31	36.76
2Q	222.2	195.2	99.8	64.86	44.81	40.52
3Q	428.5	207.5	100.2	89.73	44.46	41.33
4Q	—	217.1	111.0	102.4	50.20	45.48
Yr.	—	806.0	406.4	305.5	179.8	164.1
Earnings Per Share ($)						
1Q	**0.35**	**0.27**	**0.22**	0.11	0.11	0.10
2Q	**0.42**	**0.31**	0.24	0.18	0.15	0.14
3Q	**0.53**	**0.40**	0.28	0.22	0.18	0.14
4Q	—	**0.45**	0.32	0.29	0.24	0.23
Yr.	—	**1.43**	**1.08**	**0.81**	0.68	0.60

Next earnings report expected: mid December

Dividend Data

Cash dividends, which have not been paid since 1986, are restricted by terms of debt agreements.

A Division of The McGraw-Hill Companies

URS Corporation

Business Summary - 07-AUG-99

URS' strategy is to be a major global engineering force by utilizing its technical and professional resources in providing comprehensive engineering services to the infrastructure market, which includes surface, air and rail transportation systems, commercial/industrial and facilities projects, and environmental programs involving water/wastewater and hazardous waste management. URS provides its services to local and state agencies (43% of FY 98 revenues), federal agencies (14%), the private sector (36%), and international firms (7%), through 130 worldwide offices in four major areas: planning, design, applied sciences, and program and construction management.

Planning covers a broad range of assignments, from conceptual design and technical and economic feasibility studies to community involvement programs and archaeological investigations. In many instances, the planning process is used to develop the blueprint, or overall scheme, for the project. Planning analyses and reports are used to identify and evaluate alternatives, estimate usage levels, determine financial feasibility, assess available technology, and recommend optimal courses of action.

Design involves providing a broad range of design and design-related services, including: architectural and interior design and civil, structural, mechanical, electrical, sanitary, environmental, water resources, geotechnical/underground, dam, mining, and seismic engineering design. For each project, URS identifies the project requirements and then integrates and coordinates the various design elements. The result is a set of contract documents that may include plans, specifications, and cost estimates that are used to build a project.

Applied sciences encompass diverse services for the natural and built environment. These services are typically provided to protect or restore the environment or to plan and design underground or earth-based structures. Services include waste management and remediation engineering to characterize waste or contamination, develop alternative remedies, and design and implement optimum solutions; environmental management including the development of pollution prevention programs and environmental mitigation plans; civil and geo-engineering; and engineering geology applied to natural hazard assessment and mitigation.

Program and construction management services include master scheduling of both the design and construction phases, construction and life-cycle cost estimating, cash flow analysis, value engineering, constructability reviews, and bid management. Once construction has begun, URS oversees and coordinates the activities of construction contractors.

In June 1999, the company acquired Dames & Moore Group (DM) for $16 per share in cash, totaling about $300 million, and the assumption of approximately $300 million in debt. URS stated that the combined firms would result in a global engineering company with approximately $2 billion in revenue s. DM is the company's largest acquisition to date.

Per Share Data ($) (Year Ended Oct. 31)	1998	1997	1996	1995	1994	1993	1992	1991	1990	1989
Tangible Bk. Val.	2.42	3.23	1.48	3.89	4.16	3.45	3.21	2.48	-1.37	-28.62
Cash Flow	2.36	1.79	1.58	0.95	0.82	0.61	0.81	0.63	-0.69	-18.88
Earnings	1.43	1.06	0.80	0.68	0.60	0.18	0.55	0.40	-1.57	-23.60
Dividends	Nil	Nil	Nil	Nil	Nil	Nil	Nil	Nil	Nil	Nil
Payout Ratio	Nil	Nil	Nil	Nil	Nil	Nil	Nil	Nil	Nil	Nil
Prices - High	23 5/8	19	9 7/8	7 3/8	8	10 1/8	11 1/8	12 1/2	7 1/2	41 1/4
- Low	11 1/4	9	6 1/4	5 1/8	4 3/4	4 3/8	6 1/2	3 1/8	2 1/4	3 3/4
P/E Ratio - High	17	18	12	11	13	56	20	31	NM	NM
- Low	8	8	8	8	8	24	12	8	NM	NM
Income Statement Analysis (Million $)										
Revs.	806	406	305	180	164	146	137	123	105	99
Oper. Inc.	64.8	31.9	20.2	10.8	8.7	7.6	8.3	6.8	5.0	-6.0
Depr.	14.6	7.9	5.3	3.1	2.6	3.0	2.4	2.0	2.1	3.8
Int. Exp.	8.8	4.8	3.9	1.4	1.2	1.2	1.2	2.3	5.0	5.9
Pretax Inc.	41.5	19.2	12.1	6.4	4.9	1.4	4.7	2.5	-3.7	-18.5
Eff. Tax Rate	45%	40%	39%	21%	9.20%	9.80%	9.70%	9.80%	NM	NM
Net Inc.	22.7	11.5	7.4	5.1	4.4	1.3	4.3	2.3	-3.7	-18.9
Balance Sheet & Other Fin. Data (Million $)										
Cash	36.5	22.1	22.4	8.8	9.5	6.6	5.7	5.2	7.2	0.8
Curr. Assets	286	149	128	59.7	54.3	46.5	43.8	37.8	39.2	28.8
Total Assets	452	213	186	74.1	65.2	58.1	54.9	49.8	51.4	50.7
Curr. Liab.	95.0	86.2	70.3	23.4	20.6	18.8	17.0	15.9	24.8	32.2
LT Debt	95.0	41.4	55.4	10.0	9.3	8.3	8.7	8.3	22.3	18.8
Common Eqty.	166	77.2	56.7	39.5	34.0	29.4	27.9	23.3	1.2	-17.1
Total Cap.	267	119	112	49.5	43.2	37.7	36.6	31.6	23.5	1.7
Cap. Exp.	12.2	5.1	3.0	1.6	2.1	1.9	1.2	1.0	0.8	1.2
Cash Flow	37.3	19.4	12.7	8.2	7.0	4.3	6.7	4.3	-1.9	-15.1
Curr. Ratio	3.0	1.7	1.8	2.6	2.6	2.5	2.6	2.4	1.6	0.9
% LT Debt of Cap.	35.6	34.8	49.4	20.2	21.4	22.0	23.8	26.4	94.8	NM
% Net Inc.of Revs.	2.8	2.8	2.4	2.9	2.7	0.9	3.1	1.9	NM	NM
% Ret. on Assets	6.8	5.8	5.6	7.3	7.2	2.3	8.1	3.3	NM	NM
% Ret. on Equity	18.7	17.2	15.4	13.8	14.0	4.5	16.6	18.1	NM	NM

Data as orig reptd.; bef. results of disc opers/spec. items. Per share data adj. for stk. divs. Bold denotes diluted EPS (FASB 128)-prior periods restated. E-Estimated. NA-Not Available. NM-Not Meaningful. NR-Not Ranked.

Office—100 California St., Suite 500, San Francisco, CA 94111-4529. **Tel**—(415) 774-2700. **Website**—http://www.urscorp.com **Chrmn & CEO**—M. M. Koffel. **EVP, Secy, CFO & Investor Contact**—Kent P. Ainsworth. **Dirs**—R. C. Blum, S. R Foley Jr., R. D. Glynn, Jr., M. M. Koffel, R. B. Madden, A. Der Marderosian, Jean-Yves Perez, R. Q. Praeger, I. L. Rosenstein, W. D. Walsh. **Transfer Agent & Registrar**—First Interstate Bank of California, SF. **Incorporated**—in California in 1957; reincorporated in Delaware in 1976. **Empl**— 6,600. **S&P Analyst:** F. DiLorenzo

STANDARD
&POOR'S
STOCK REPORTS

US Oncology, Inc.

NASDAQ Symbol **USON**

In S&P SmallCap 600

09-OCT-99

Industry: Health Care (Managed Care)

Summary: This company, formed through the June 1999 merger of American Oncology and Physician Reliance Network, is the nation's leading cancer management firm.

Quantitative Evaluations

Outlook (1 Lowest—5 Highest) • **5**

Fair Value • **18⅝**

Risk • **High**

Earn./Div. Rank • **NR**

Technical Eval. • **Bearish** since 8/99

Rel. Strength Rank (1 Lowest—99 Highest) • **18**

Insider Activity • **NA**

Recent Price • 8⅞

52 Wk Range • 15½-6⅜

Yield • Nil

12-Mo. P/E • 18.9

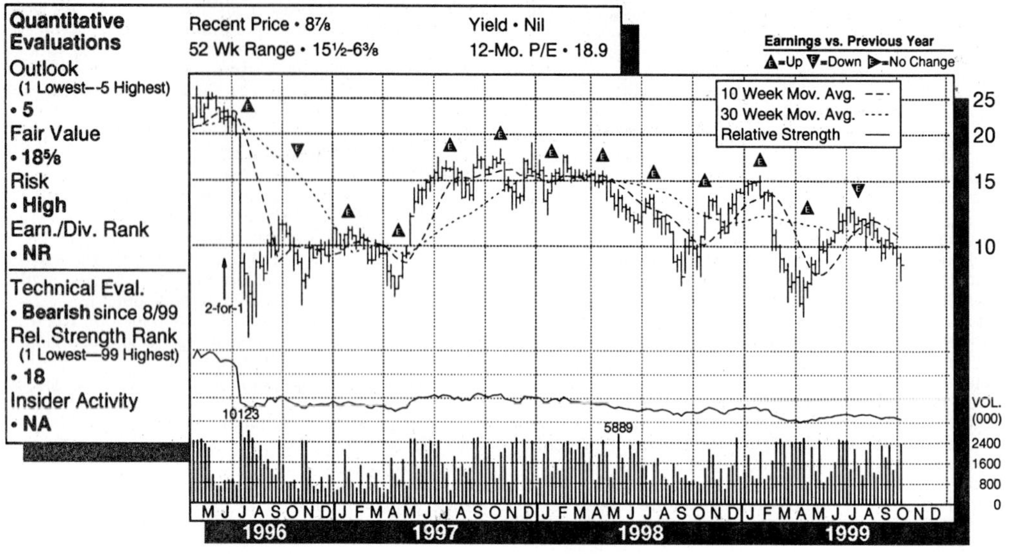

Business Profile - 26-AUG-99

In May 1999, the boards of directors of American Oncology and Physician Reliance Network estimated that, based on internal estimates of the management of both companies, the combination of the two entities should result in an additional $12.0 million of pre-tax earnings in the year 2000, without giving effect to any transaction, integration, and restructuring costs related to the merger. The expected increase in earnings anticipates that the combined company (a) will have lower general and administrative costs as a percentage of revenues, (b) will be able to obtain drugs at a lower price than either company could on its own and (c) will be able to capitalize on each company's separate strengths.

Operational Review - 26-AUG-99

Revenues in the six months ended June 30, 1999, rose 31%, year to year (1998 restated to reflect the combined company under the pooling of interest method of accounting), primarily due to expansion of services, increases in patient volume and recruitment of or affiliation with additional physicians and income of $3.2 million from the termination of a research services contract. Results were impaired by a less favorable product mix, lower reimbursement from payors, merger and integration costs of about $24.5 million, and greater interest costs, Pretax income was down 35%. After taxes at 49.8%, versus 37.6%, net income fell 47%, to $15,301,000 ($0.15 a share), from $29,093,000 ($0.29).

Stock Performance - 08-OCT-99

In the past 30 trading days, USON's shares have declined 14%, compared to a 0.91% fall in the S&P 500. Average trading volume for the past five days was 472,920 shares, compared with the 40-day moving average of 362,903 shares.

Key Stock Statistics

Dividend Rate/Share	Nil	Shareholders	5,810
Shs. outstg. (M)	85.5	Market cap. (B)	$0.761
Avg. daily vol. (M)	0.383	Inst. holdings	38%
Tang. Bk. Value/Share	9.09		
Beta	NA		

Value of $10,000 invested 5 years ago: NA

Fiscal Year Ending Dec. 31

	1999	1998	1997	1996	1995	1994
Revenues (Million $)						
1Q	139.8	101.0	70.40	40.75	14.60	2.35
2Q	266.4	111.6	79.53	47.37	24.64	4.15
3Q	—	118.3	82.29	53.70	25.50	5.94
4Q	—	125.1	89.63	63.64	34.43	7.97
Yr.	—	455.9	321.8	205.5	99.2	20.41
Earnings Per Share ($)						
1Q	**0.17**	**0.14**	**0.11**	**0.09**	0.03	-0.01
2Q	**-0.01**	**0.16**	**0.12**	**0.09**	0.06	0.01
3Q	—	**0.15**	**0.12**	**0.09**	0.10	0.02
4Q	—	**0.16**	**0.13**	**0.10**	0.09	0.03
Yr.	—	**0.61**	**0.48**	**0.37**	**0.30**	0.04

Next earnings report expected: early November

Dividend Data

No cash dividends have been paid.

US Oncology, Inc.

Business Summary - 26-AUG-99

US Oncology, Inc. (formerly American Oncology Resources) is a cancer management company which provides comprehensive management services under long-term agreements to its affiliated oncology practices, including operational and clinical research services and data management, and furnishes personnel, facilities, supplies and equipment. These affiliated practices provide a broad range of medical services to cancer patients, integrating the specialties of medical and gynecological oncology, hematology, radiation oncology, diagnostic radiology and stem cell transplantation. Substantially all of the company's revenue consists of management fees and includes all medical practice operating costs for which the company is contractually responsible. The company was formed through the June 1999 merger of American Oncology and Physician Reliance Network (PRN) in which PRN shareholder received 0.94 shares of American Oncology common stock for each PRN share held.

Management fees include all practice costs (other than amounts retained by physicians), a fixed monthly fee, an amount equal to 7% of each affiliated physicians group's net revenue (in most states) and, if certain financial criteria are satisfied, a performance fee. The management agreements permit the affiliated physician group to retain a specified percentage of the group's net revenues (generally 23%) for physician salaries, and payment of such salaries is given priority over payment of the management fee.

In 1998 (prior to the merger) the payor mix of affiliated physician groups' medical practice revenue was 34% for Medicare and Medicaid, 47% for managed care and 19% for private insurance and other payors. Texas Oncology, P. A. accounted for about 25% of total revenue in the six months ended June 30, 1999.

Physicians Reliance Network (PRN) is a leading provider of management services, facilities and equipment to (a) physicians specializing in the diagnosis and treatment of cancer and (b) radiologists. As of April 30, 1999, it provided comprehensive management services under long-term agreements to medical practices comprised of 370 physicians in 13 states. PRN's affiliated physicians provide all aspects of care related to the diagnosis and outpatient treatment of cancer, including medical oncology, radiation oncology, gynecological oncology and diagnostic radiology.

Both companies believed for some time that a combination would represent a unique strategic fit and enhance their competitive and strategic positions. First, American Oncology and Physicians' Network are the largest participants in the oncology management sector, and a combination of the two would create the leading cancer management company in the U. S. In addition, the companies shared common strategies and demonstrated an ability to execute on those strategies.

The combined company will treat about 13% of the new cancer cases in the U. S. in the year 2000.

Per Share Data ($) (Year Ended Dec. 31)	1998	1997	1996	1995	1994	1993	1992	1991	1990	1989
Tangible Bk. Val.	9.09	8.88	8.11	6.96	2.03	NA	NA	NA	NA	NA
Cash Flow	1.07	0.77	0.57	0.81	0.07	NM	-0.04	NA	NA	NA
Earnings	0.61	0.48	0.37	0.29	0.04	-0.01	-0.05	-0.01	NA	NA
Dividends	Nil	Nil	Nil	Nil	NA	NA	NA	NA	NA	NA
Payout Ratio	Nil	Nil	Nil	Nil	NA	NA	NA	NA	NA	NA
Prices - High	$17\frac{5}{8}$	19	$26\frac{7}{8}$	$24\frac{3}{4}$	NA	NA	NA	NA	NA	NA
- Low	$7\frac{3}{4}$	$7\frac{1}{4}$	$5\frac{5}{8}$	$10\frac{1}{2}$	NA	NA	NA	NA	NA	NA
P/E Ratio - High	29	40	72	85	NA	NA	NA	NA	NA	NA
- Low	13	15	15	36	NA	NA	NA	NA	NA	NA

Income Statement Analysis (Million $)	1998	1997	1996	1995	1994	1993	1992	1991	1990	1989
Revs.	456	322	205	99	20.4	7.2	4.4	NA	NA	NA
Oper. Inc.	83.9	59.4	41.3	22.2	2.2	-0.1	-0.4	NA	NA	NA
Depr.	23.3	14.2	9.3	4.7	0.8	0.2	0.0	NA	NA	NA
Int. Exp.	12.1	8.7	4.3	3.7	0.2	0.1	0.1	NA	NA	NA
Pretax Inc.	48.8	36.8	28.7	17.5	1.4	-0.3	-1.1	NA	NA	NA
Eff. Tax Rate	38%	38%	39%	33%	9.20%	NM	NM	NA	NA	NA
Net Inc.	30.2	22.9	17.6	11.6	1.2	-0.3	-1.1	NA	NA	NA

Balance Sheet & Other Fin. Data (Million $)	1998	1997	1996	1995	1994	1993	1992	1991	1990	1989
Cash	10.6	5.0	3.4	14.8	4.2	NA	NA	NA	NA	NA
Curr. Assets	172	115	75.7	95.8	12.5	NA	NA	NA	NA	NA
Total Assets	568	484	339	272	55.7	5.4	3.4	NA	NA	NA
Curr. Liab.	89.6	71.2	32.8	36.1	5.8	NA	NA	NA	NA	NA
LT Debt	173	140	81.8	44.2	18.7	0.1	1.0	NA	NA	NA
Common Eqty.	294	264	222	191	31.0	1.3	0.4	NA	NA	NA
Total Cap.	479	413	307	236	49.9	NA	NA	NA	NA	NA
Cap. Exp.	22.6	22.5	10.0	3.7	1.0	0.5	NA	NA	NA	NA
Cash Flow	53.5	37.0	27.0	16.3	2.0	-0.1	-1.1	NA	NA	NA
Curr. Ratio	1.9	1.6	2.3	2.7	2.1	NA	NA	NA	NA	NA
% LT Debt of Cap.	36.2	33.9	26.6	18.7	37.5	NA	NA	NA	NA	NA
% Net Inc.of Revs.	6.6	7.1	8.6	11.7	6.1	NM	NM	NA	NA	NA
% Ret. on Assets	5.7	5.6	5.8	7.1	4.1	NM	NM	NA	NA	NA
% Ret. on Equity	10.8	9.4	8.5	10.5	7.7	NM	NM	NA	NA	NA

Data as orig reptd.; bef. results of disc opers/spec. items. Per share data adj. for stk. divs. Bold denotes diluted EPS (FASB 128)-prior periods restated. E-Estimated. NA-Not Available. NM-Not Meaningful. NR-Not Ranked.

Office—16825 Northchase Drive, Suite 1300, Houston, TX 77060. **Tel**— (281) 873-2674. **Website**—http://www.aori.com **Chrmn & CEO**—R. D. Ross. **COO**—O. E. French. **VP & CFO**—L. F. Pounds. **Dirs**—N. G. Brinker, R. L. Carson, J. T. Casey, J. T. Crandall, J. E. Dalton, R. W. Daly, S. E. Jones, , S. A. Marks, R. B. Mayor, R. A. Ortenzio, B. Powell, Jr., E. E. Rogoff, R. D. Ross, B. S. Schwartz. **Transfer Agent & Registrar**—American Stock Transfer & Trust Co., NYC. **Incorporated**—in Delaware in 1992. **Empl**— 0. **S&P Analyst:** P.L.H.

STANDARD
&POOR'S
STOCK REPORTS

USA Detergents

NASDAQ Symbol **USAD**

In S&P SmallCap 600

09-OCT-99

Industry:
Household Products
(Nondurables)

Summary: This company is a leading manufacturer and marketer of quality nationally distributed value brand laundry and household cleaning products.

Quantitative Evaluations
Outlook
(1 Lowest—5 Highest)
• **NA**
Fair Value
• **NA**
Risk
• **NA**
Earn./Div. Rank
• **NR**

Technical Eval.
• **Bearish** since 8/99
Rel. Strength Rank
(1 Lowest—99 Highest)
• **46**
Insider Activity
• **NA**

Recent Price • 5
52 Wk Range • 10½-4¼
Yield • Nil
12-Mo. P/E • 16.1

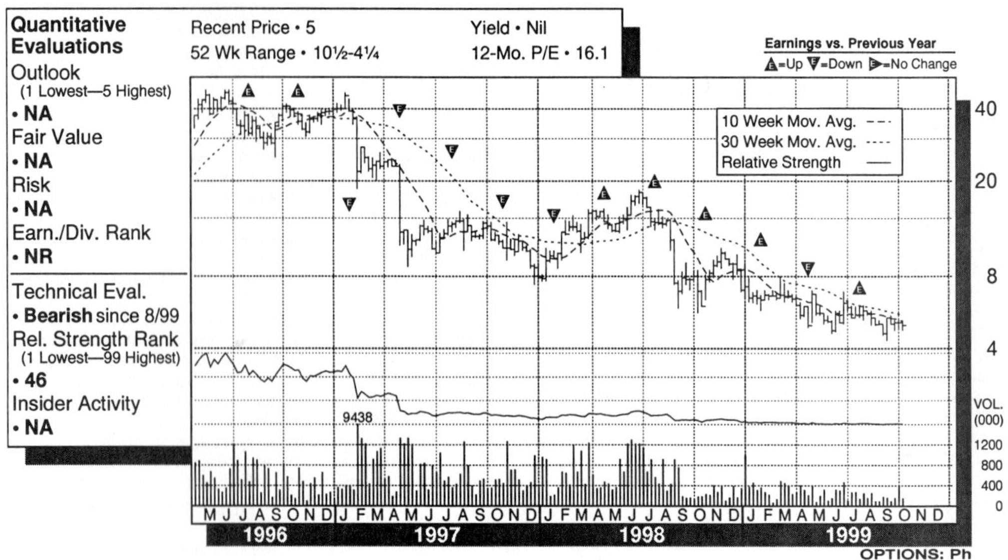

Business Profile - 30-JUN-99

In February 1999, the company refinanced its debt with FINOVA Capital, to provide for an additional $14.5 million of financing. A charge of $64,000 was incurred in the 1999 first quarter, for unamortized financing costs associated with the financing agreement with FINOVA. USAD is continuing initiatives aimed at increasing market share, including penetrating foreign markets, and emphasizing its core products, XTRA and Nice 'n FLUFFY. In the 1998 fourth quarter, the company's XTRA liquid laundry detergent improved its retail volume sales ranking to third, from fifth in 1997. The Nice'n FLUFFY liquid fabric softener brand maintained its position as third in the category.

Operational Review - 30-JUN-99

Net sales in the three months ended March 31, 1999, rose 4.8%, year to year, on an increase in unit sales of liquid laundry products. Despite lower material costs and the benefits of manufacturing efficiencies, results were restricted by higher marketing and salary expense; operating income slid 4.7%. With higher interest costs, after taxes at 4.7%, versus 1.5%, income fell 13%, to $1,166,000 ($0.08 a share), from $1,343,000 ($0.10). Results in the 1999 period exclude an extraordinary charge of $64,000 (nil per share).

Stock Performance - 08-OCT-99

In the past 30 trading days, USAD's shares have declined 1%, compared to a 0.91% fall in the S&P 500. Average trading volume for the past five days was 28,380 shares, compared with the 40-day moving average of 31,764 shares.

Key Stock Statistics

Dividend Rate/Share	Nil	Shareholders	87
Shs. outstg. (M)	13.8	Market cap. (B)	$0.069
Avg. daily vol. (M)	0.037	Inst. holdings	26%
Tang. Bk. Value/Share	1.29		
Beta	NA		

Value of $10,000 invested 5 years ago: NA

Fiscal Year Ending Dec. 31

	1999	1998	1997	1996	1995	1994
Revenues (Million $)						
1Q	59.39	56.68	60.53	34.07	23.26	17.47
2Q	58.78	54.07	54.97	42.92	25.65	17.19
3Q	—	52.71	57.35	48.11	27.12	18.52
4Q	—	56.64	54.28	48.94	28.85	15.48
Yr.	—	220.1	227.3	174.0	104.9	68.66
Earnings Per Share ($)						
1Q	**0.08**	**0.10**	-0.30	0.16	0.08	0.06
2Q	**0.08**	**-0.16**	-1.07	0.20	0.10	0.07
3Q	—	**0.05**	-0.08	0.23	0.13	0.06
4Q	—	**0.09**	**0.01**	0.07	0.13	0.03
Yr.	—	**0.08**	**-1.53**	**0.27**	**0.43**	0.22

Next earnings report expected: early November

Dividend Data

No cash dividends have been paid and the company does not anticipate paying any dividends. Certain credit facilities restrict USAD's ability to declare and pay dividends.

A Division of The McGraw-Hill Companies

USA Detergents, Inc.

Business Summary - 30-JUN-99

USA Detergents makes and markets value brand laundry and household cleaning products.

The company currently competes in eight laundry and household product categories, and offers 13 distinct value brands. USAD believes the market for household products is segmented into four types of brands: value brands, store brands, mid-priced brands, and premium priced brands. Its objective is to be the leading supplier of value brand household products. Product areas in which the company competes or intends to compete are: liquid laundry detergent, powder laundry detergent, liquid fabric softener, fabric softener sheets, household cleaners, dish detergent, personal soap products, air fresheners, bleaches, rug and upholstery cleaners, and floor cleaners.

USAD's products include XTRA liquid and powder laundry detergent, Nice 'n FLUFFY liquid and sheet fabric softener, Touch of Glass and Tile Action cleaners, Fine Care dish detergent, Country Air air fresheners, and Speedway automotive products. XTRA and Nice'n FLUFFY are the company's core brands, and rank among the five largest U.S. brands in their respective categories, in terms of total retail volume sales. Laundry detergents and fabric softeners accounted for 86% of net sales in 1998. In total, the XTRA and Nice 'n FLUFFY brands accounted for 65% and 21%, respectively, of company's net sales in 1998. According to IRI Data, in the quarter ended December 31, 1998, 67% to 68% of all food, drug and mass merchant retail outlets sold XTRA liquid laundry detergent and Nice 'n FLUFFY liquid fabric softener.

The company introduced 23 new products in 1998 (following the introduction of 65 new products in 1997), including reformulations and alternate sizes. Net sales of products introduced in 1998 were $2.6 million (1.2% of net sales).

USAD sells to both large and small retailers throughout the U.S. Customers include mass merchandisers, supermarkets, variety and dollar stores, drug stores, and small grocery stores. WalMart is the company's largest customer, accounting for 11% of net sales in 1998. No other customer accounted for over 10%. Net sales in 1998 were divided as follows: supermarkets (47%), mass merchandisers (24%), variety and dollar stores (11%), drug stores (8%), and small grocery and other (10%).

The company's strategy is to enable retailers to increase sales and realize attractive relative profit margins on its products, while providing value to consumers. USAD also seeks to develop strong brand name recognition through eye-catching packaging and a reputation for quality at a low price.

Per Share Data ($) (Year Ended Dec. 31)	1998	1997	1996	1995	1994	1993	1992	1991	1990	1989
Tangible Bk. Val.	1.15	1.13	3.00	1.51	NA	NA	NA	NA	NA	NA
Cash Flow	0.46	-1.18	0.82	0.52	0.29	0.05	NA	NA	NA	NA
Earnings	0.08	-1.53	0.65	0.43	0.22	0.02	NA	NA	NA	NA
Dividends	Nil	Nil	Nil	Nil	Nil	Nil	NA	NA	NA	NA
Payout Ratio	Nil	Nil	Nil	Nil	Nil	Nil	NA	NA	NA	NA
Prices - High	18 3/8	46 3/4	48	19	NA	NA	NA	NA	NA	NA
- Low	5 5/8	7 3/8	15 1/2	9 5/8	NA	NA	NA	NA	NA	NA
P/E Ratio - High	NM	NM	74	44	NA	NA	NA	NA	NA	NA
- Low	NM	NM	24	22	NA	NA	NA	NA	NA	NA
Income Statement Analysis (Million $)										
Revs.	220	227	174	105	69.0	47.0	NA	NA	NA	NA
Oper. Inc.	15.6	-14.6	18.0	10.7	5.7	2.0	NA	NA	NA	NA
Depr.	5.3	4.8	2.3	1.0	0.8	0.4	NA	NA	NA	NA
Int. Exp.	5.0	2.7	0.9	0.6	0.6	0.4	NA	NA	NA	NA
Pretax Inc.	1.3	-24.5	14.8	9.2	4.3	0.3	NA	NA	NA	NA
Eff. Tax Rate	11%	NM	40%	41%	39%	46%	NA	NA	NA	NA
Net Inc.	1.1	-21.1	8.9	5.4	2.7	0.2	NA	NA	NA	NA
Balance Sheet & Other Fin. Data (Million $)										
Cash	NA	1.8	2.4	0.1	0.1	NA	NA	NA	NA	NA
Curr. Assets	42.2	54.3	65.0	27.4	16.3	NA	NA	NA	NA	NA
Total Assets	90.9	103	99	40.6	24.4	NA	NA	NA	NA	NA
Curr. Liab.	39.7	47.0	24.4	16.3	11.2	NA	NA	NA	NA	NA
LT Debt	33.0	38.9	30.8	1.8	6.2	NA	NA	NA	NA	NA
Common Eqty.	17.3	15.6	41.3	20.3	5.9	NA	NA	NA	NA	NA
Total Cap.	50.3	54.6	73.2	23.1	12.1	NA	NA	NA	NA	NA
Cap. Exp.	4.8	23.7	20.5	3.9	1.6	4.6	NA	NA	NA	NA
Cash Flow	6.4	-16.3	11.2	6.4	3.4	0.6	NA	NA	NA	NA
Curr. Ratio	1.1	1.2	2.7	1.7	1.5	NA	NA	NA	NA	NA
% LT Debt of Cap.	65.6	71.2	42.1	7.9	51.2	NA	NA	NA	NA	NA
% Net Inc.of Revs.	0.5	NM	5.1	5.2	3.9	3.6	NA	NA	NA	NA
% Ret. on Assets	1.2	NM	12.7	16.7	NA	NA	NA	NA	NA	NA
% Ret. on Equity	7.0	NM	28.8	41.4	NA	NA	NA	NA	NA	NA

Data as orig reptd.; bef. results of disc opers/spec. items. Per share data adj. for stk. divs. Bold denotes diluted EPS (FASB 128)-prior periods restated. E-Estimated. NA-Not Available. NM-Not Meaningful. NR-Not Ranked.

Office—1735 Jersey Ave., North Brunswick, NJ 08902. **Tel**—(908) 828-1800. **Fax**—(908) 246-7733. **Chrmn & CEO**—U. Evan. **Vice Chrmn**—J. S. Cohen. **CFO**—R. D. Coslow. **VP & Secy**—D. Bergman. **Dirs**—F. R. Adler, D. Bergman, U. Evan, C. D. Illick, R. A. Mandell. **Transfer Agent & Registrar**—Continental Stock Transfer & Trust Co., NYC. **Incorporated**—in New Jersey in 1988; reorganized in Delaware in 1995. **Empl**— 585. **S&P Analyst:** Jordan Horoschak

STANDARD
&POOR'S
STOCK REPORTS

USFreightways

Nasdaq Symbol **USFC**

In S&P SmallCap 600

09-OCT-99 **Industry:** Truckers

Summary: This company offers a broad array of transportation services including regional less-than-truckload (LTL) and full truckload carriage, freight forwarding and logistics services.

S&P Opinion: Accumulate (★★★★) Recent Price • 46⅜ 52 Wk Range • 52-17⅝ Yield • 0.8% 12-Mo. P/E • 14.9

Quantitative Evaluations

Outlook (1 Lowest—5 Highest) • **3**

Fair Value • **57**

Risk • **Average**

Earn./Div. Rank • **B+**

Technical Eval. • **Bearish** since 9/99

Rel. Strength Rank (1 Lowest—99 Highest) • **71**

Insider Activity • **Neutral**

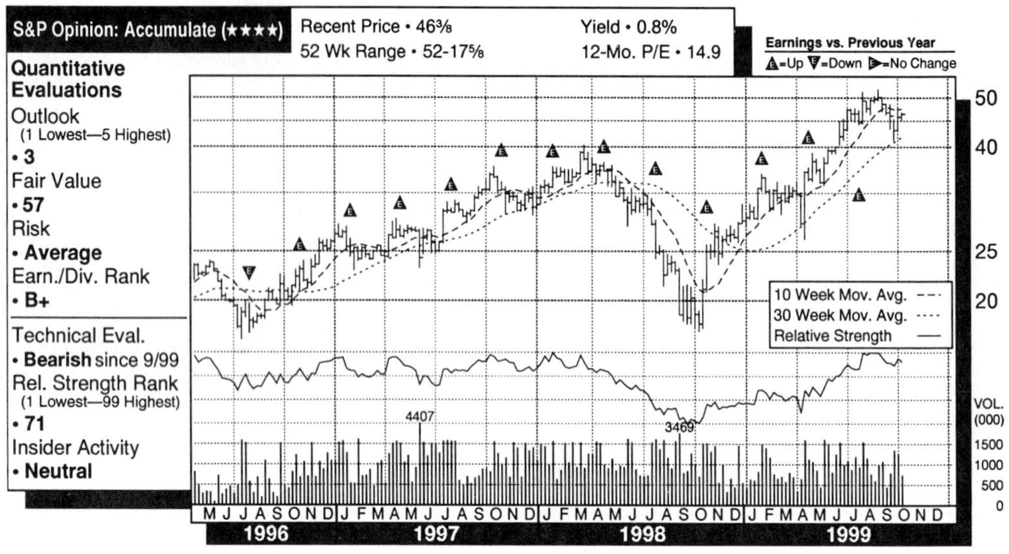

Overview - 08-OCT-99

Total revenues are projected to increase 20% in 1999, versus 17.3% in 1998 with almost half the anticipated revenue growth derived from acquisitions. We project an 8%-9% gain for LTL tonnage in 1999, and a 2.5% improvement in yields. USFC will benefit from the acquisition of CBL and the demise of competing lines. Faster transit times will also help the company boost volumes faster than other truckers and we expected its new expedited delivery service to be popular. Margins will widen, aided in part by the absence of costs related to the 1998 strike at GM. Logistics is benefiting from expanding business with existing customers and the acquisitions of Moore & Son and Processors Unlimited Co. A positive contribution is anticipated from recently acquired truckload carrier Glen Moore Transport. USF Worldwide will benefit from the inclusion of Golden Eagle Group and the buy out of several agencies. Interest charges will increase, reflecting recent acquisitions.

Valuation - 08-OCT-99

USFC has climbed steadily since late 1998 as investors tossed aside their recession concerns and focused on the company's strengthening fundamentals. Wall Street likes USFC's business model which is to provide one-stop transportation services for shippers and to grow aggressively through acquisition of smaller, typically privately-held companies. USFC began offering a synthetic long-haul LTL service in July 1999 by connecting its five regional carriers' service. Based on a static valuation method, USFC looks rich relative to its peers. It rates highly only on margins and employment of capital. Nevertheless, we think investors should continue to accumulate USFC because of its outstanding management team which has delivered consistent profit growth since going public.

Key Stock Statistics

S&P EPS Est. 1999	3.35	Tang. Bk. Value/Share	12.62
P/E on S&P Est. 1999	13.9	Beta	0.89
S&P EPS Est. 2000	3.75	Shareholders	9,000
Dividend Rate/Share	0.37	Market cap. (B)	$ 1.2
Shs. outstg. (M)	26.4	Inst. holdings	96%
Avg. daily vol. (M)	0.205		

Value of $10,000 invested 5 years ago: $ 18,566

Fiscal Year Ending Dec. 31

	1999	1998	1997	1996	1995	1994
Revenues (Million $)						
1Q	513.2	442.3	355.8	313.7	279.0	251.0
2Q	548.9	447.0	380.8	332.1	287.0	221.0
3Q	—	469.4	393.5	343.2	290.0	274.0
4Q	—	476.2	435.2	342.0	288.0	271.0
Yr.	—	1,835	1,565	1,331	1,144	1,016
Earnings Per Share ($)						
1Q	**0.65**	**0.52**	**0.40**	**0.20**	0.37	0.27
2Q	**0.96**	**0.68**	**0.56**	**0.37**	0.44	0.20
3Q	**E0.90**	**0.74**	**0.67**	**0.48**	0.40	0.57
4Q	**E0.84**	**0.76**	**0.56**	**0.35**	0.30	0.47
Yr.	**E3.35**	**2.70**	**2.19**	**1.40**	**1.51**	**1.51**

Next earnings report expected: mid October

Dividend Data (Dividends have been paid since 1992.)

Amount ($)	Date Decl.	Ex-Div. Date	Stock of Record	Payment Date
0.093	Dec. 11	Dec. 22	Dec. 24	Jan. 08 '99
0.093	Mar. 10	Mar. 24	Mar. 26	Apr. 09 '99
0.093	Jun. 08	Jun. 23	Jun. 25	Jul. 09 '99
0.093	Sep. 07	Sep. 22	Sep. 24	Oct. 08 '99

A Division of The McGraw-Hill Companies

USFreightways Corporation

Business Summary - 08-OCT-99

USFreightways (formerly TNT Freightways) has undertaken a major diversification program in recent years. Once solely a provider of regional less-than-truckload (LTL) service, USFC has emerged as a single-source provider of a broad array of transportation services. This has been accomplished through a series of acquisitions, including Seko Worldwide in 1997, which brought USFC into the freight forwarding business; and Glen Moore Transport in 1998, which brought USFC back into the truckload market. USFC also offers logistics and customs brokerage services.

USFC operates a family of five regional LTL freight carriers. Collectively, these carriers generated 83.9% of revenues in 1998, down from 90.0% in 1997. Regional LTL carriers primarily provide for the overnight or second day movement of shipments moving under 500 miles that are routed directly between origin and destination terminals. USFC introduced an expedited delivery service in July 1999 for long-haul shipments. By combining its regional carriers and harnessing sleeper teams, USFC is able to offer transit times three to four days faster than established national lines.

USFC's largest regional carrier is USF Holland, which serves the Midwest and Southeast. USF Red Star operates in the eastern U.S. and parts of Canada. Both Holland and Red Star operate with Teamster employee under contracts that expire in March 2003. USF Dugan provides service in the South and Plains states. The Northwest and Rocky Mountain states are served by USF Reddaway. USF Bestway serves the Southwest and California.

Truckload services (0.7% of revenues) reflect the September 1998 acquisition of Glen Moore Transport, Inc. a truckload carrier with annual revenue of $35 million. USFC tried unsuccessfully to develop its own truckload operations, but sold its Comet Transportation unit in late 1997. USFC expanded its truckload operations into the Midwest with the acquisition of Underwood Trucking in August 1999.

Freight forwarding (8.3% of 1998 revenues) has grown rapidly in recent years through acquisitions. USF Worldwide provides domestic and international air and ocean freight forwarding services, customs brokerage and cargo consolidation services for shipments moving between the U.S. mainland and Hawaii, Guam and Puerto Rico. USFC entered the air freight forwarding market in 1997 by acquiring SEKO Worldwide. In November 1998, USFC bought Golden Eagle Group, a freight forwarder that specializes in international movements.

Logistics services (7.1% of 1998 revenues) involve the total management of the transportation, distribution and warehousing supply chain from raw materials to finished products. In March 1999, USFC acquired Processors Unlimited Co., which handles the movement of discontinued or damaged goods returned from retailers to manufacturers.

Per Share Data ($) (Year Ended Dec. 31)	1998	1997	1996	1995	1994	1993	1992	1991	1990	1989
Tangible Bk. Val.	12.25	11.24	8.40	7.45	6.19	4.75	5.32	NA	NA	NA
Cash Flow	5.64	4.91	4.25	3.78	3.51	2.97	1.99	1.62	NA	NA
Earnings	2.70	2.19	1.41	1.51	1.51	1.25	0.78	0.59	NA	NA
Dividends	0.37	0.37	0.37	0.37	0.37	0.37	0.28	Nil	NA	NA
Payout Ratio	14%	17%	26%	25%	25%	30%	36%	Nil	NA	NA
Prices - High	40⅜	36¾	28¼	28⅝	29¾	27½	14⅜	NA	NA	NA
- Low	17⅜	22⅞	16¾	16¼	19¼	12	9⅜	NA	NA	NA
P/E Ratio - High	15	17	20	19	20	23	18	NA	NA	NA
- Low	6	10	12	11	13	10	12	NA	NA	NA
Income Statement Analysis (Million $)										
Revs.	1,835	1,565	1,331	1,144	1,016	899	775	NA	NA	NA
Oper. Inc.	207	175	131	118	114	101	72.0	NA	NA	NA
Depr.	78.0	70.1	63.9	50.3	44.3	39.4	32.8	NA	NA	NA
Int. Exp.	8.8	8.5	12.1	8.9	9.1	7.6	2.0	NA	NA	NA
Pretax Inc.	121	97.5	54.9	58.5	59.2	52.1	36.8	NA	NA	NA
Eff. Tax Rate	41%	42%	43%	43%	44%	45%	44%	NA	NA	NA
Net Inc.	71.4	56.6	31.5	33.3	33.4	28.5	20.8	NA	NA	NA
Balance Sheet & Other Fin. Data (Million $)										
Cash	5.5	6.5	4.1	1.7	2.1	2.3	NA	NA	NA	NA
Curr. Assets	280	237	204	159	145	123	NA	NA	NA	NA
Total Assets	975	800	689	578	501	461	NA	NA	NA	NA
Curr. Liab.	229	182	144	128	118	98.0	NA	NA	NA	NA
LT Debt	151	115	178	137	106	124	NA	NA	NA	NA
Common Eqty.	459	392	269	233	208	181	NA	NA	NA	NA
Total Cap.	677	560	494	411	350	334	NA	NA	NA	NA
Cap. Exp.	157	129	0.3	117	68.8	84.2	63.3	NA	NA	NA
Cash Flow	149	127	95.4	83.7	77.7	67.9	53.6	NA	NA	NA
Curr. Ratio	1.2	1.3	1.4	1.2	1.2	1.3	NA	NA	NA	NA
% LT Debt of Cap.	22.3	20.5	36.0	33.3	30.3	37.2	NA	NA	NA	NA
% Net Inc.of Revs.	3.9	3.6	2.4	2.9	3.3	3.2	2.7	NA	NA	NA
% Ret. on Assets	8.1	7.6	5.0	6.2	6.9	6.6	NA	NA	NA	NA
% Ret. on Equity	16.8	17.1	12.5	15.1	17.2	14.0	NA	NA	NA	NA

Data as orig reptd.; bef. results of disc opers/spec. items. Per share data adj. for stk. divs. Bold denotes diluted EPS (FASB 128)-prior periods restated. E-Estimated. NA-Not Available. NM-Not Meaningful. NR-Not Ranked.

Office—9700 Higgins Rd., Suite 570, Rosemont, IL 60018. **Tel**—(847) 696-0200. **Fax**—(847) 696-2080. **Website**—http://www.usfreightways.com **Chrmn & CEO**—J. C. Carruth. **SVP & CFO & Investor Contact**—C. L. Ellis.**Secy**—R. C. Pagano. **Dirs**—J. C. Carruth, R. V. Delaney, M. Koffman, R. P. Neuschel, A. J. Paoni, J. W. Puth, N. A. Springer, W. N. Weaver. **Transfer Agent & Registrar**—Harris Trust and Savings Bank, Chicago. **Incorporated**—in Delaware in 1991. **Empl**— 19,179. **S&P Analyst:** Stephen R. Klein

STANDARD &POOR'S
STOCK REPORTS

UST Corp.

NASDAQ Symbol **USTB**

In S&P SmallCap 600

09-OCT-99

Industry:
Banks (Regional)

Summary: This Boston-based bank holding company and provider of a wide range of financial services recently agreed to be acquired by Citizens Financial Group, Inc. for $32 a share in cash.

Quantitative Evaluations

Outlook
(1 Lowest—5 Highest)
• **2**

Fair Value
• **29¾**

Risk
• **Average**

Earn./Div. Rank
• **B**

Technical Eval.
• **Bullish** since 6/99

Rel. Strength Rank
(1 Lowest—99 Highest)
• **76**

Insider Activity
• **NA**

Recent Price • 30⅞
52 Wk Range • 31-19⅛
Yield • 1.9%
12-Mo. P/E • 24.8

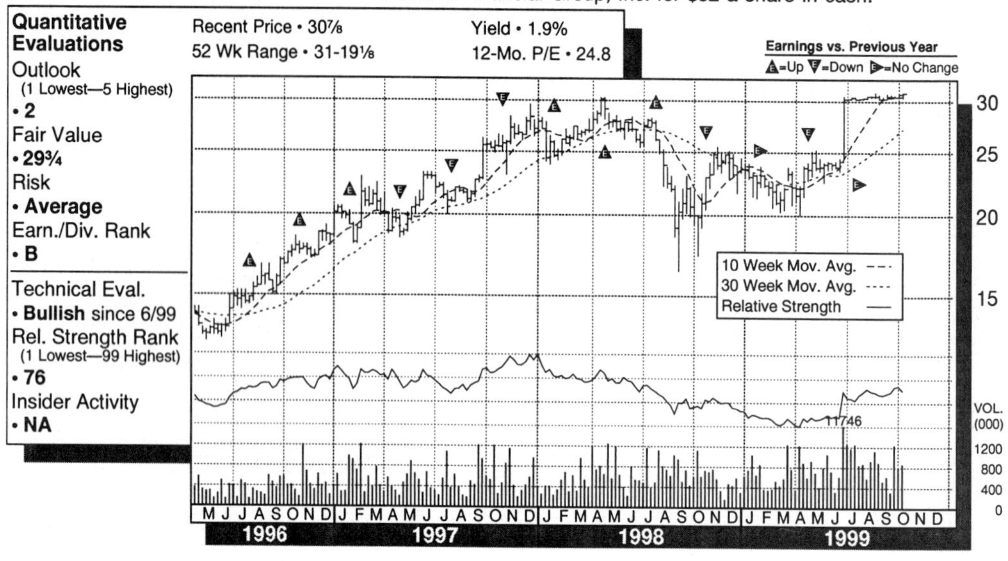

Business Profile - 08-JUL-99

In June 1999, UST Corp. announced a definitive agreement to be acquired for $32 a share in cash (for a total of $1.4 billion) by Citizens Financial Group, Inc., the New England subsidiary of Royal Bank of Scotland plc. The acquisition is subject to regulatory approval and is expected to close in early 2000 pending regulatory approval. The transaction would create the second largest bank in New England with assets of $28 billion. In June 1999, USTB completed the acquisition of Brewer & Lord, one of the largest independent insurance agencies in New England. The insurer operates independently as a wholly owned subsidiary of USTrust, a banking subsidiary of USTB.

Operational Review - 08-JUL-99

Net interest income in the three months ended March 31, 1999, advanced 5.8%, year to year, as an increase in earning assets more than offset a narrower net interest margin (4.82%, versus 4.95%). The provision for loan losses rose 9.0%. Noninterest income increased 8.4%, primarily due to higher asset management fees and deposit account service charges. Noninterest expense rose 15%, reflecting increased personnel as functions previously outsourced by newly consolidated banks were transferred internally, and on higher technology and Y2K readiness expense. After taxes at 34.8%, versus 34.3%, net income declined 7.8%, to $17,265,000 ($0.40 a share), from $18,733,000 ($0.43, as restated).

Stock Performance - 08-OCT-99

In the past 30 trading days, USTB's shares have increased 2%, compared to a 0.91% fall in the S&P 500. Average trading volume for the past five days was 170,660 shares, compared with the 40-day moving average of 169,654 shares.

Key Stock Statistics

Dividend Rate/Share	0.60	Shareholders	2,603
Shs. outstg. (M)	42.8	Market cap. (B)	$ 1.3
Avg. daily vol. (M)	0.175	Inst. holdings	53%
Tang. Bk. Value/Share	10.73		
Beta	1.23		

Value of $10,000 invested 5 years ago: $ 31,194

Fiscal Year Ending Dec. 31

	1999	1998	1997	1996	1995	1994
Revenues (Million $)						
1Q	121.2	85.44	80.93	45.14	44.63	39.79
2Q	122.5	85.19	75.16	44.65	43.47	40.33
3Q	—	119.4	82.06	47.70	44.71	41.05
4Q	—	121.5	83.74	57.46	45.12	41.48
Yr.	—	477.4	323.2	194.9	177.9	162.7
Earnings Per Share ($)						
1Q	**0.40**	**0.42**	**0.03**	**0.26**	0.16	0.06
2Q	**0.41**	**0.41**	**0.29**	**0.41**	0.20	0.07
3Q	—	**0.04**	**0.35**	**0.50**	0.23	0.06
4Q	—	**0.40**	**0.40**	**0.30**	0.25	0.08
Yr.	—	**1.28**	**1.08**	**1.53**	**0.92**	0.27

Next earnings report expected: late October

Dividend Data (Dividends have been paid since 1995.)

Amount ($)	Date Decl.	Ex-Div. Date	Stock of Record	Payment Date
0.150	Dec. 15	Dec. 29	Dec. 31	Jan. 22 '99
0.150	Mar. 12	Mar. 29	Mar. 31	Apr. 26 '99
0.150	Jun. 15	Jun. 28	Jun. 30	Jul. 26 '99
0.150	Sep. 21	Sep. 28	Sep. 30	Oct. 26 '99

A Division of The McGraw-Hill Companies

UST Corp.

Business Summary - 08-JUL-99

UST Corporation, with $5.9 billion in assets at year-end 1998, agreed in June 1999 to be acquired by Royal Bank of Scotland's Citizens Financial unit for $32 a share in cash, or a total of $1.4 billion. The transaction is subject to regulatory approval and other conditions, and is expected to be completed in early 2000.

Through its banking and nonbanking subsidiaries, Boston-based UST Corp. provides a broad range of financial services, principally to individuals and small and medium-sized companies in New England. In addition, the company provides trust and money management services to professionals, corporate executives, nonprofit organizations, labor unions, foundations, mutual funds and owners of closely-held businesses. Through the June 1999 acquisition of Brewer & Lord, USTB offers accident & health, fire & casualty, and life insurance products to consumers and medium and large-size businesses.

USTB's banking subsidiaries, USTrust and United States Trust Co., are both headquartered in Boston. In addition, USTB owns, indirectly through its subsidiary banks, eight active nonbanking subsidiaries: Firestone Financial Corp. and its Canadian subsidiary, Firestone Financial Canada, UST Leasing Corp., UST Capital Corp., UST Realty Trust, Inc., UST Auto Lease Corp., Cambridge Trade Finance Corp. and Brewer & Lord as well as seven subsidiaries which hold foreclosed real estate and six subsidiaries which are passive holders of securities.

Interest income advanced 4.9% in 1998 and accounted for 90% of USTB's total income. Average earning assets, from which interest income is derived, advanced approximately 6.2%, to $5.3 billion. Average loan growth of 10% was the largest contributor to USTB's improved net interest income over that of 1997.

Loans, which comprised the majority of average earning assets (77%), totaled $4.3 billion at December 31, 1998. Commercial and financial loans accounted for 33% of the loan portfolio at year-end 1998. The remainder of the loan portfolio was divided as follows: residential mortgage loans 25%, indirect automobile installment loans 21%, commercial real estate loans 13%, home equity loans 3% and other 5%.

The bank's net interest margin (a key measure of profitability for the bank's lending operations) widened 13 basis points in 1998, to 4.77%. The wider margin, coupled with the growth in average earning assets, led to a 9.4% gain in net interest income.

Total noninterest income amounted to $48.8 million in 1998, up 17% from a year earlier. Asset management fees made up 31% of noninterest income, deposit account service charges 25%, corporate services income 13% and other 31%.

Per Share Data ($) (Year Ended Dec. 31)	1998	1997	1996	1995	1994	1993	1992	1991	1990	1989
Tangible Bk. Val.	11.27	9.49	8.00	9.47	7.41	8.70	10.25	10.54	10.92	12.03
Earnings	1.28	1.08	1.79	0.83	0.27	-1.36	-0.34	-0.58	0.13	2.10
Dividends	0.52	0.40	0.29	0.05	Nil	Nil	Nil	0.15	0.60	0.58
Payout Ratio	41%	37%	16%	6%	Nil	Nil	Nil	NM	450%	28%
Prices - High	30 3/8	29 5/8	20 5/8	15 1/2	14 3/8	12 1/2	10 1/2	9	15 1/4	19 1/2
- Low	16 3/8	18	12 3/4	9 3/4	8 3/4	7 3/8	6 5/8	5 1/4	5 1/4	13 7/8
P/E Ratio - High	24	27	12	19	53	NM	NM	NM	NM	9
- Low	13	17	7	12	32	NM	NM	NM	NM	7
Income Statement Analysis (Million $)										
Net Int. Inc.	252	175	96.1	95.4	92.1	92.7	88.1	86.9	91.1	97.0
Tax Equiv. Adj.	1.2	0.7	0.3	0.9	1.0	1.2	1.6	2.0	2.7	4.0
Non Int. Inc.	44.9	39.5	29.4	30.0	29.2	32.3	28.6	33.1	22.6	21.6
Loan Loss Prov.	2.2	0.9	18.6	13.1	23.1	64.3	41.9	53.7	43.7	9.8
Exp./Op. Revs.	70%	75%	73%	70%	76%	77%	81%	73%	63%	55%
Pretax Inc.	89.6	55.2	53.7	24.1	6.8	-36.4	-7.7	-12.5	0.2	43.1
Eff. Tax Rate	38%	41%	39%	38%	30%	NM	NM	NM	NM	34%
Net Inc.	55.3	32.4	32.7	15.0	4.8	-20.9	-4.7	-7.9	1.9	28.3
% Net Int. Marg.	4.77	5.10	4.94	5.54	5.29	5.00	4.40	3.60	3.60	4.60
Balance Sheet & Other Fin. Data (Million $)										
Money Mkt. Assets	8.0	164	112	90.0	103	96.3	1.3	38.7	28.1	172
Inv. Securities	1,290	722	528	576	402	474	484	445	378	203
Com'l Loans	1,490	1,358	747	643	728	763	781	873	1,008	1,013
Other Loans	2,849	1,426	1,101	629	538	555	690	775	861	832
Total Assets	5,901	3,838	2,707	1,969	1,803	2,044	2,178	2,365	3,055	2,579
Demand Deposits	917	708	799	373	372	374	571	470	442	394
Time Deposits	3,317	891	1,307	1,140	1,119	1,267	1,221	1,528	1,998	1,284
LT Debt	76.0	Nil	Nil	0.1	4.1	10.0	18.6	23.4	22.0	24.5
Common Eqty.	534	340	198	174	133	153	144	146	148	160
% Ret. on Assets	1.1	1.0	1.4	0.8	0.3	NM	NM	NM	0.1	1.2
% Ret. on Equity	12.7	12.0	17.6	9.1	3.1	NM	NM	NM	1.2	18.9
% Loan Loss Resv.	1.5	1.8	2.1	4.4	4.9	4.8	3.4	3.0	1.9	1.0
% Loans/Deposits	101.5	403.0	87.8	84.1	84.9	80.3	82.1	82.5	76.6	109.9
% Equity to Assets	9.0	8.2	7.9	8.9	8.1	7.0	6.5	5.6	5.6	6.2

Data as orig reptd.; bef. results of disc opers/spec. items. Per share data adj. for stk. divs. Bold denotes diluted EPS (FASB 128)-prior periods restated. E-Estimated. NA-Not Available. NM-Not Meaningful. NR-Not Ranked.

Office—40 Court St., Boston, MA 02108. **Tel**—(617) 726-7000. **Website**—http://www.ustrustboston.com**Chrmn**—W. Schwartz. **Pres & CEO**—N. F. Finnegan. **EVP, CFO & Treas**—J. K. Hunt. **Clerk**—E. R. Fischer.**Investor Contact**—Ed Sweeney (617-726-7037). **Dirs**— C. G. Atkins, D. E. Bradbury, K. G. Bushnell, R. M. Coard, R. L. Culver, J. F. Drew, A. K. DerKazarian, D. C. Dolben, N. F. Finnegan, T. J. Hansberry, E. S. Heald, B. W. Hotarek, J. E. McCobb, Jr., F. X. Messina, S. L. Miller, V. L. Pryor, G. M. Ridge, W. Schwartz, B. C. Sidell, J. V. Sidell, P. D. Slater, G. R. Tod, M. J. Verrochi, Jr. **Transfer Agent & Registrar**—United States Trust Co., Boston. **Incorporated**—in Massachusetts in 1967. **Empl**— 2,100. **S&P Analyst:** Markos N. Kaminis

STANDARD &POOR'S
STOCK REPORTS

Valassis Communications

NYSE Symbol **VCI**
In S&P SmallCap 600

09-OCT-99 **Industry:** Specialty Printing

Summary: Valassis is one of the largest printers and publishers of cents-off coupons and other consumer purchase incentives, most of which are featured in Sunday editions of newspapers.

Quantitative Evaluations
Outlook
(1 Lowest—5 Highest)
• **2+**
Fair Value
• **42½**
Risk
• **Average**
Earn./Div. Rank
• **NR**

Technical Eval.
• **Bullish** since 8/99
Rel. Strength Rank
(1 Lowest—99 Highest)
• **74**
Insider Activity
• **Unfavorable**

Recent Price • 42⅝
52 Wk Range • 46½-19⅞
Yield • Nil
12-Mo. P/E • 24.1

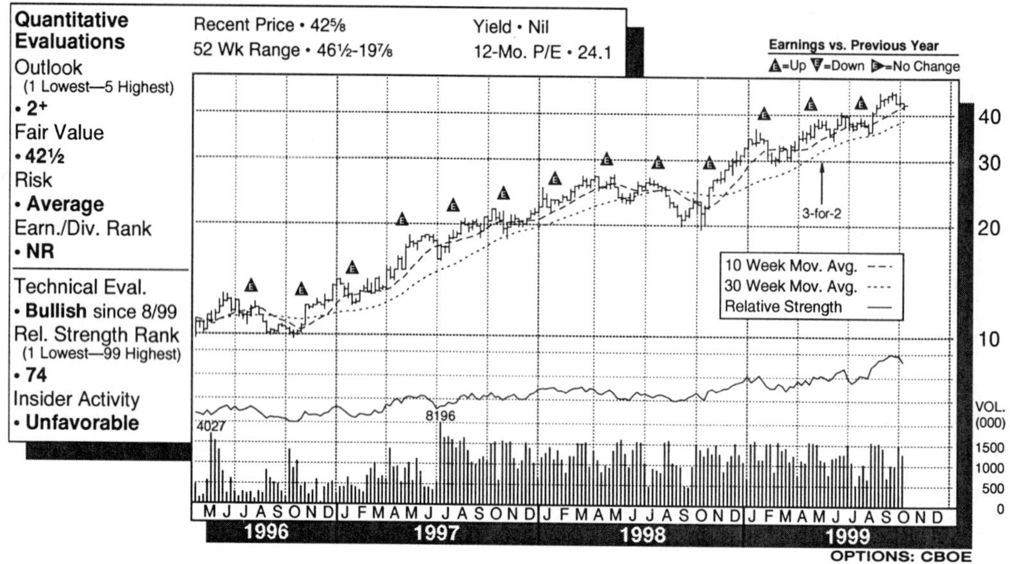

Business Profile - 26-JUL-99

Free-standing insert (FSI) revenue was up 7.9% in the 1999 second quarter, while Valassis Impact Promotion (VIP) sales rose 21%. For the full year, management expects VIP sales growth of 15%, with Valassis Target Marketing Services expected to grow 20%. Due to negotiated multi-year contracts with paper suppliers, the company is on track to realize a 6-9% reduction in paper costs in 1999. In the second quarter of 1999, VCI acquired the name Save.com for its Internet couponing venture and scheduled a test for e-commerce FSI in the fall of 1999. VCI repurchased more than 450,000 of its common shares during the second quarter, and expects to use half its future net income for additional purchases.

Operational Review - 26-JUL-99

Total revenues in the six months ended June 30, 1999, rose 8.5%, year to year, on industry page growth and moderate price increases. Profitability improved on lower costs in the free-standing insert division and lower selling, general and administrative expenses; operating income climbed 28%. With lower amortization charges and reduced interest expense, and after taxes at 38.2% in each period, net income jumped 45%, to $62.4 million ($1.07 a share, on 3.0% fewer shares), from $43.0 million ($0.72, as adjusted).

Stock Performance - 08-OCT-99

In the past 30 trading days, VCI's shares have declined 3%, compared to a 0.91% fall in the S&P 500. Average trading volume for the past five days was 253,600 shares, compared with the 40-day moving average of 265,451 shares.

Key Stock Statistics

Dividend Rate/Share	Nil	Shareholders	365
Shs. outstg. (M)	56.3	Market cap. (B)	$ 2.4
Avg. daily vol. (M)	0.236	Inst. holdings	96%
Tang. Bk. Value/Share	NM		
Beta	0.87		

Value of $10,000 invested 5 years ago: $ 47,873

Fiscal Year Ending Dec. 31

	1999	1998	1997	1996	1995	1994
Revenues (Million $)						
1Q	222.2	205.7	190.0	180.5	157.4	--
2Q	195.0	178.9	164.3	162.7	155.5	--
3Q	—	167.1	153.5	151.8	138.0	131.3
4Q	—	189.7	167.8	164.1	162.8	147.8
Yr.	—	741.4	675.5	659.1	613.8	—
Earnings Per Share ($)						
1Q	**0.58**	**0.43**	**0.35**	**0.16**	0.13	--
2Q	**0.49**	**0.29**	**0.19**	**0.15**	0.11	--
3Q	—	**0.34**	**0.29**	**0.17**	0.05	0.01
4Q	—	**0.37**	**0.31**	**0.19**	-0.15	0.01
Yr.	—	**1.42**	**1.13**	**0.67**	**0.15**	0.03

Next earnings report expected: late October

Dividend Data

Amount ($)	Date Decl.	Ex-Div. Date	Stock of Record	Payment Date
3-for-2	Apr. 05	May. 13	Apr. 16	May. 12 '99

STANDARD
&POOR'S
STOCK REPORTS

Valassis Communications, Inc.

09-OCT-99

Business Summary - 26-JUL-99

Clipping coupons is a favorite pastime of cost-conscious American consumers. Since 1972, Valassis Communications (VCI) has played an integral part in this penny-pinching process through its printing and publishing of cents-off coupons and other consumer purchase incentives.

The company's most popular product is its Free-standing inserts (FSIs), colorful booklets that arrive inside the Sunday edition of more than 500 newspapers, with an average paid circulation of 57.7 million, on 46 publishing dates. VCI offers customers more than 270 different layout versions per publication date, providing the flexibility to target specific markets with tailored promotional offers. FSIs generated 77% of 1998 total sales.

Valassis Impact Promotions (VIPs) was rolled out in 1989 to meet increasing demand for customized printed promotions for solo marketers. Because these promotions feature only a single manufacturer, VCI is able to develop a completely individualized promotion. VIPs generated 14% of 1998 sales; they generally serve packaged goods manufactures, fast-food chains, food brokers, and retailers.

Valassis Targeted Marketing (formerly Valassis Sampling) offers newspaper delivered sampling product that can reach up to 58 million households in a weekend. Revenues from this segment accounted for 3.8% of the 1998 total.

In March 1995, VCI acquired McIntyre and Dodd Marketing, which is now known as Valassis of Canada. Since 1995, when the division faced pricing pressures, a poor economy, and a mail order volume decline, the company has streamlined and repositioned the business.

Other products include Run-of-Press (ROP) promotions, which can be published in any newspaper in the U.S., on any day and in any section of the paper, and a newspaper-delivered sampling product that enables manufacturers to cost-effectively reach up to 50 million households in one day.

The average price of paper, a major cost factor for VCI, increased in 1998, but is expected to decrease in 1999. Management projects that paper costs will be 6% to 9% lower in 1999 overall. As of March 31, 1999, VCI had repurchased 3.2 million of its common shares under a 5 million share authorization. In the future, management expects to allocate approximately half the company's net income to purchasing common stock.

Per Share Data ($) (Year Ended Dec. 31)	1998	1997	1996	1995	1994	1993	1992	1991	1990	1989
Tangible Bk. Val.	NM	NM	NM	-5.75	-6.14	-6.15	-6.67	-7.81	-8.66	NA
Cash Flow	1.69	1.44	0.91	0.44	0.18	0.45	1.65	1.69	1.14	NA
Earnings	1.42	1.13	0.67	0.15	0.03	0.08	1.26	1.08	0.50	NA
Dividends	Nil	Nil	Nil	Nil	Nil	Nil	0.28	0.07	NA	NA
Payout Ratio	Nil	Nil	Nil	Nil	Nil	Nil	22%	6%	NA	NA
Prices - High	34½	25¼	14⅛	12⅜	13⅛	13⅛	16¾	15¼	NA	NA
- Low	19⅜	12	9¾	9⅛	7	7	6⅜	10⅝	NA	NA
P/E Ratio - High	29	22	21	85	NM	NM	13	14	NA	NA
- Low	16	10	15	62	NM	NM	5	10	NA	NA
Income Statement Analysis (Million $)										
Revs.	741	675	657	610	278	540	660	669	635	NA
Oper. Inc.	187	169	123	94.0	32.0	61.0	199	194	179	NA
Depr.	15.8	15.6	15.2	19.0	9.7	24.0	25.4	35.7	41.3	NA
Int. Exp.	34.5	38.3	39.6	40.5	19.6	38.2	39.9	37.7	47.4	NA
Pretax Inc.	137	115	71.1	23.0	4.0	-2.0	135	128	NA	NA
Eff. Tax Rate	38%	39%	40%	58%	56%	NM	39%	42%	NA	NA
Net Inc.	84.3	69.9	42.9	9.6	1.9	5.2	81.9	74.4	32.4	NA
Balance Sheet & Other Fin. Data (Million $)										
Cash	6.9	35.4	60.2	34.4	21.2	32.3	39.6	15.3	NA	NA
Curr. Assets	143	151	178	155	109	118	118	107	122	NA
Total Assets	232	241	274	259	234	240	275	293	323	NA
Curr. Liab.	159	148	161	149	131	133	173	207	199	NA
LT Debt	340	367	396	416	418	419	419	463	550	NA
Common Eqty.	-268	-276	-286	-308	-318	-316	-321	-385	-433	NA
Total Cap.	73.4	92.4	112	110	104	106	102	86.0	NA	NA
Cap. Exp.	13.4	13.0	7.1	6.5	9.2	4.1	4.0	4.2	8.0	NA
Cash Flow	100	85.5	58.1	28.6	12.0	29.0	107	110	74.0	NA
Curr. Ratio	0.9	1.0	1.1	1.0	0.8	0.9	0.7	0.5	0.6	NA
% LT Debt of Cap.	463.5	397.2	353.6	378.2	403.1	395.3	410.8	NM	NA	NA
% Net Inc.of Revs.	11.4	10.4	6.5	1.6	0.7	9.6	12.4	11.1	5.1	NA
% Ret. on Assets	35.6	27.2	16.1	3.9	NA	2.0	28.9	16.4	NA	NA
% Ret. on Equity	NA	NM	NM	NA	NA	NM	NM	NM	NA	NA

Data as orig. reptd.; bef. results of disc. opers. and/or spec. items. Per share data adj. for stk. divs. as of ex-div. date. Prior to 1994 (6 mos.), fiscal yrs. ended Jun. 30 of the fol. cal. yr. Bold denotes diluted EPS (FASB 128). E-Estimated. NA-Not Available. NM-Not Meaningful. NR-Not Ranked.

Office—19975 Victor Parkway, Livonia, MI 48152. **Tel**—(313) 591-3000. **Website**—http://www.valassis.com **Chrmn**—D. A. Brandon. **Pres, CEO & COO**—A. F. Schultz. **VP, CFO & Treas**—R. L. Recchia. **Secy**—B. P Hoffman. **VP & Investor Contact**—Lynn M. Liddle. **Dirs**—R. N. Anderson, P. F. Brennan, S. Goldstein, B. J. Husselbee, J. E. Laird, R. L. Recchia, M. A. Sampson, A. F. Schultz, F. R. Whittlesey. **Transfer Agent & Registrar**—Bank of New York, NYC. **Incorporated**—in Delaware in 1986. **Empl**— 1,456. **S&P Analyst:** Jordan Horoschak

STANDARD & POOR'S
STOCK REPORTS

Valence Technology

NASDAQ Symbol **VLNC**

In S&P SmallCap 600

09-OCT-99

Industry: Manufacturing (Specialized)

Summary: This company is engaged in research and development of advanced rechargeable batteries based on lithium and polymer technologies.

Quantitative Evaluations

Outlook (1 Lowest—5 Highest)
• **NA**

Fair Value
• **NA**

Risk
• **High**

Earn./Div. Rank
• **NR**

Technical Eval.
• **Bearish** since 9/99

Rel. Strength Rank (1 Lowest—99 Highest)
• **44**

Insider Activity
• **Favorable**

Recent Price • 5¼
52 Wk Range • 11¼-4
Yield • Nil
12-Mo. P/E • NM

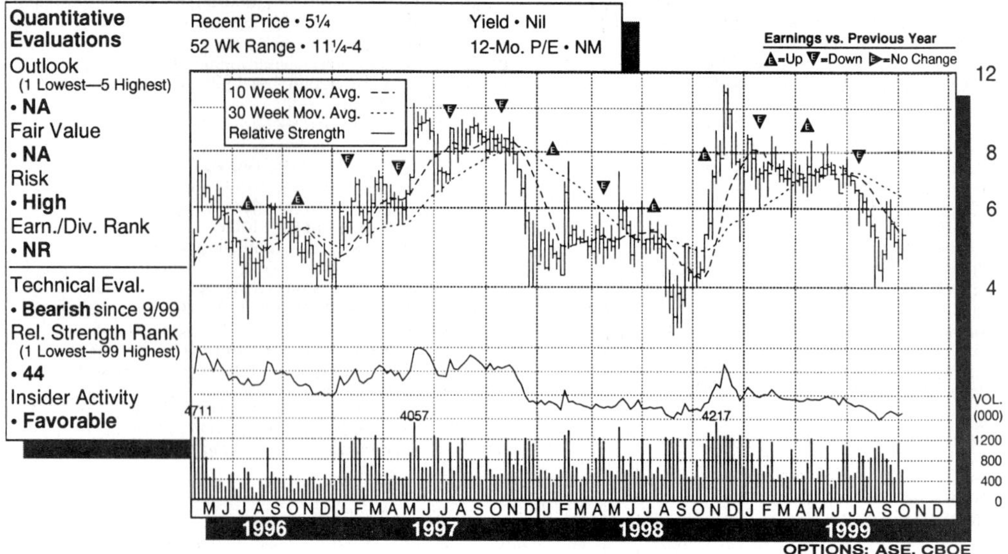

OPTIONS: ASE, CBOE

Business Profile - 28-SEP-99

In August 1999, VLNC stated that it expects to start recording revenues during the second quarter of FY 00 (Mar). In the last quarter of FY 99 and the first quarter of FY 00, the company began taking steps toward the commercialization of its battery technology, including the initiating of commercial production at its Northern Ireland plant and shipping battery components to its joint venture partners. Also in August, Valence announced that the Industrial Development Board of Northern Ireland authorized the funding of over $3 million for the company to expand its Irish manufacturing facilities. In August, VLNC stated that its existing financial resources would be insufficient to fund its operations through mid-September 1999, unless additional debt or equity financing was obtained.

Operational Review - 28-SEP-99

During the three months ended June 27, 1999, no contract revenues were recognized. Total costs and expenses were up 55%, largely due to efforts to commercialize the company's proprietary batteries, including increases in purchases, machine design engineering, testing and production raw material. Interest expense tripled. Despite equity in earnings of a South Korean joint venture versus a prior-year loss, the net loss widened to $7,709,000 ($0.30 a share, after preferred dividends, and on 5.5% more shares), from $5,315,000 ($0.21).

Stock Performance - 08-OCT-99

In the past 30 trading days, VLNC's shares have increased 20%, compared to a 0.91% fall in the S&P 500. Average trading volume for the past five days was 122,440 shares, compared with the 40-day moving average of 173,936 shares.

Key Stock Statistics

Dividend Rate/Share	Nil	Shareholders	703
Shs. outstg. (M)	27.7	Market cap. (B)	$0.146
Avg. daily vol. (M)	0.146	Inst. holdings	8%
Tang. Bk. Value/Share	0.30		
Beta	1.32		

Value of $10,000 invested 5 years ago: $ 3,442

Fiscal Year Ending Mar. 31

	2000	1999	1998	1997	1996	1995
Revenues (Million $)						
1Q	Nil	Nil	Nil	Nil	Nil	1.63
2Q	—	Nil	Nil	Nil	Nil	1.63
3Q	—	Nil	Nil	Nil	Nil	0.45
4Q	—	Nil	Nil	Nil	Nil	0.45
Yr.	—	Nil	Nil	Nil	Nil	4.15
Earnings Per Share ($)						
1Q	**-0.30**	**-0.21**	-0.24	-0.15	-0.16	-1.09
2Q	—	**-0.15**	-0.26	-0.16	-0.43	-0.21
3Q	—	**-0.44**	**-0.21**	-0.22	-0.11	-0.20
4Q	—	**-0.32**	**-0.34**	-0.31	-0.18	-0.18
Yr.	—	**-1.13**	**-1.06**	**-0.73**	-0.83	-1.68

Next earnings report expected: mid November

Dividend Data

No cash dividends have been paid, and the company does not intend to pay any in the foreseeable future.

Valence Technology, Inc.

Business Summary - 28-SEP-99

Valence Technology conducts research and development to produce advanced rechargeable batteries based upon lithium ion and polymer technologies. VLNC is a development-stage company whose primary activities to date have been obtaining and developing technology, implementing a production line, manufacturing limited quantities of prototype batteries, recruiting personnel, and raising capital. Except for a small amount of revenue from sales of prototype lithium polymer batteries, almost all of the company's revenues to date have been earned from a completed research and development contract with the Delphi Automotive Systems Group of General Motors Corp.

If R&D efforts lead to commercially viable products, Valence's strategy is to accelerate the introduction of its batteries into the portable consumer electronics and telecommunications markets through the provision of prototype batteries to a limited number of original equipment manufacturers, with the expectation that the company's batteries will be included in advanced designs.

Valence believes that its lithium polymer technology is superior to most currently available rechargeable battery technologies. In particular, VLNC's research prototype lithium polymer batteries have demonstrated energy density above that of most other rechargeable technologies. This greater energy density will lead to batteries that provide energy capacity significantly greater than that of most batteries currently in use. In addition, the company believes that its lithium polymer battery technology is much less likely to leak, because it is contained within a solid polymer matrix.

In May 1998, the company and Delphi completed their collaboration on lithium polymer battery development. The company will retain a license to use Delphi-developed lithium polymer technology in all other applications. After September 1998, Valence anticipates that it will receive no further payments as a result of the Joint Research and Development agreements with Delphi.

In the second half of 1999, VLNC obtained $25 million in private financing through the issuance of $15 million in preferred stock and arrangements for a $10 million credit line. Valence raised a total of $6 million through private equity offerings to institutional investors in June and July 1999.

In February 1999, Valence was issued a patent for a new class of cathode materials. VLNC's patented materials consist of lithium-containing phosphates, which should last longer between charges, cost less, and offer better safety than most currently available cathodes. The company expects to include the patented material in sample batteries sometime in 1999, without any adverse impact on its efforts to commercialize batteries using other cathode materials.

Per Share Data ($) (Year Ended Mar. 31)	1999	1998	1997	1996	1995	1994	1993	1992	1991	1990
Tangible Bk. Val.	0.30	0.92	1.76	2.45	3.32	4.98	4.23	3.47	NM	NM
Cash Flow	-0.89	-0.99	-0.57	-0.58	-1.45	-0.84	-0.46	-0.36	-0.51	-0.04
Earnings	-1.13	-1.06	-0.73	-0.83	-1.68	-1.08	-0.63	-0.37	-0.52	-0.04
Dividends	Nil	Nil	Nil	Nil	Nil	Nil	Nil	Nil	Nil	Nil
Payout Ratio	Nil	Nil	Nil	Nil	Nil	Nil	Nil	Nil	Nil	Nil
Cal. Yrs.	1998	1997	1996	1995	1994	1993	1992	1991	1990	1989
Prices - High	11¼	10¼	7⅝	6½	20½	26	27	NA	NA	NA
- Low	3⅛	4	3⅜	1 9/16	2⅛	11	7¼	NA	NA	NA
P/E Ratio - High	NM	NM	NM	NM	NM	NM	NM	NM	NM	NM
- Low	NM	NM	NM	NM	NM	NM	NM	NA	NA	NA
Income Statement Analysis (Million $)										
Revs.	Nil	Nil	Nil	Nil	4.2	7.3	6.4	3.8	Nil	Nil
Oper. Inc.	-25.6	-21.6	-14.1	-15.0	-13.1	-16.8	-7.3	-1.0	-1.4	-0.4
Depr.	3.4	1.8	3.5	5.2	4.5	4.2	2.3	0.1	0.1	NM
Int. Exp.	0.6	0.5	0.8	0.9	0.8	0.3	0.3	0.4	0.3	0.0
Pretax Inc.	-26.4	-24.5	-15.9	-17.5	-33.6	-18.7	-8.5	-3.8	-5.1	-0.4
Eff. Tax Rate	NM	NM	NM	Nil	Nil	NM	NM	Nil	Nil	Nil
Net Inc.	-26.4	-24.5	-15.9	-17.5	-33.6	-18.7	-8.5	-3.8	-5.1	-0.4
Balance Sheet & Other Fin. Data (Million $)										
Cash	2.5	8.4	33.4	51.0	59.6	61.0	61.8	0.8	0.1	0.0
Curr. Assets	3.8	10.7	34.1	52.3	61.4	62.4	62.4	0.9	0.1	0.0
Total Assets	38.4	42.9	55.5	70.2	92.0	121	77.2	3.3	0.4	0.1
Curr. Liab.	11.6	12.5	12.0	11.0	16.4	14.1	6.4	5.9	0.8	0.0
LT Debt	8.2	5.0	5.2	6.2	8.8	7.3	1.8	7.2	5.1	0.4
Common Eqty.	8.0	23.0	38.3	53.0	66.7	100	69.0	-9.8	-5.5	-0.4
Total Cap.	24.3	27.9	43.6	59.2	75.5	107	70.8	-2.6	-0.4	0.0
Cap. Exp.	9.6	16.3	3.4	2.3	8.8	23.5	6.0	1.7	0.5	0.0
Cash Flow	-23.0	-22.7	-12.4	-12.3	-29.1	-14.5	-6.2	-3.6	-5.0	-0.4
Curr. Ratio	0.3	0.9	2.8	4.8	3.7	4.4	9.7	0.2	0.1	1.5
% LT Debt of Cap.	33.6	17.7	12.0	10.4	11.7	6.8	2.5	NM	NM	NM
% Net Inc.of Revs.	NM	NM	NM	NM	NM	NM	NM	NM	NM	NM
% Ret. on Assets	NM	NM	NM	NM	NM	NM	NM	NM	NM	NM
% Ret. on Equity	NM	NM	NM	NM	NM	NM	NM	NM	NM	NM

Data as orig reptd.; bef. results of disc opers/spec. items. Per share data adj. for stk. divs. Bold denotes diluted EPS (FASB 128)-prior periods restated. E-Estimated. NA-Not Available. NM-Not Meaningful. NR-Not Ranked.

Office—301 Conestoga Way, Henderson, NV 89015. **Tel**—(702) 558-1000. **Website**—http://www.Valence-Tech.com **Chrmn, Pres & CEO**—L. M. Dawson. **VP & CFO**—J. L. King. **Secy**—B. A. Perkins. **Dirs**—C. E. Berg, L. M. Dawson, B. C. Roberts, Jr., A. F. Shugart. **Transfer Agent & Registrar**—First National Bank of Boston. **Incorporated**—in Delaware in 1989. **Empl**— 173. **S&P Analyst:** Craig K. Shere

STANDARD
&POOR'S
STOCK REPORTS

Valmont Industries

NASDAQ Symbol **VALM**

In S&P SmallCap 600

09-OCT-99

Industry: Manufacturing (Diversified)

Summary: Valmont is the world's largest manufacturer of mechanized agricultural irrigation equipment. It also supplies pole and tower structures for lighting and other applications.

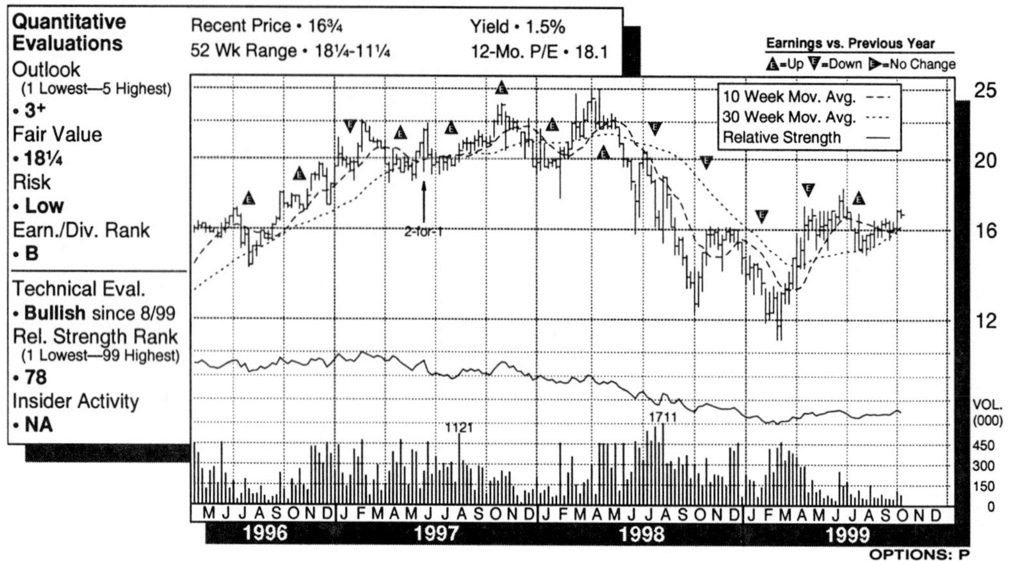

Business Profile - 04-OCT-99

In July 1999, the company reaffirmed its previous assessment of flat earnings for 1999, and has observed no changes in the long-term drivers for its businesses. This assessment is based upon continued weakness in U.S. agricultural commodity prices, which should curtail the level of sales for mechanized irrigation equipment for the balance of 1999, and overshadow the strong backlog for North American lighting, traffic and utility products, and improved order flow in Europe.

Operational Review - 04-OCT-99

Net sales in the six months ended June 26, 1999, declined 0.7%, year to year, hurt by reduced sales in the irrigation segment and other sales. Gross margins widened as a result of improvements in the infrastructure segment. SG&A grew 13% following acquisitions and investments in management information systems. Following an 89% rise in net interest expense as a result of increased borrowings for a stock repurchase plan and taxes at 36.9%, versus 36.7%, net income declined 26% to $12.7 million ($0.51 per share, on 13% fewer shares) from $17.1 million ($0.60).

Stock Performance - 08-OCT-99

In the past 30 trading days, VALM's shares have increased 5%, compared to a 0.91% fall in the S&P 500. Average trading volume for the past five days was 15,560 shares, compared with the 40-day moving average of 13,492 shares.

Key Stock Statistics

Dividend Rate/Share	0.26	Shareholders	5,500
Shs. outstg. (M)	24.2	Market cap. (B)	$0.407
Avg. daily vol. (M)	0.014	Inst. holdings	25%
Tang. Bk. Value/Share	7.12		
Beta	0.74		

Value of $10,000 invested 5 years ago: $ 18,261

Fiscal Year Ending Dec. 31

	1999	1998	1997	1996	1995	1994
Revenues (Million $)						
1Q	154.4	160.6	165.4	148.9	142.2	111.2
2Q	162.8	154.3	159.1	166.8	133.4	122.0
3Q	—	140.1	136.0	148.1	128.3	109.8
4Q	—	151.3	162.0	180.7	140.7	128.7
Yr.	—	606.3	622.5	644.5	544.6	471.8
Earnings Per Share ($)						
1Q	**0.23**	**0.34**	**0.32**	**0.25**	**0.21**	0.13
2Q	**0.28**	**0.26**	**0.35**	**0.30**	**0.25**	0.18
3Q	—	**0.18**	**0.28**	**0.24**	**0.19**	0.17
4Q	—	**0.23**	**0.38**	**-0.03**	**0.25**	0.21
Yr.	—	**1.02**	**1.33**	**0.76**	**0.90**	**0.69**

Next earnings report expected: mid October

Dividend Data (Dividends have been paid since 1980.)

Amount ($)	Date Decl.	Ex-Div. Date	Stock of Record	Payment Date
0.065	Dec. 14	Dec. 22	Dec. 24	Jan. 15 '99
0.065	Feb. 24	Mar. 24	Mar. 26	Apr. 15 '99
0.065	Apr. 26	Jun. 23	Jun. 25	Jul. 15 '99
0.065	Sep. 09	Sep. 22	Sep. 24	Oct. 15 '99

Valmont Industries, Inc.

Business Summary - 04-OCT-99

In 1946, after serving in World War II, Robert B. Daugherty purchased a small Nebraska manufacturing firm and began to build farm elevators. In 1954, Daugherty licensed a patent for an odd-looking contraption from a Nebraska inventor, which later became the standard for mechanized irrigation technology worldwide; and Daugherty's company, now called Valmont Industries, Inc., emerged as the industry leader. The need to obtain timely, cost-effective pipe led VALM to manufacture pipe for its irrigation systems. From this beginning, the company found an opportunity to develop markets for tubular products for original equipment manufacturers, steel service centers, and for both private and public projects.

Today VALM is an industry leader in two segments: Infrastructure (49% of 1998 sales) and Irrigation (36%). In addition, the company has several other businesses that do not fit within these segments, but are not individually more than 10% of combined net sales. These businesses include the Coatings Division, which provides custom coatings, and the Industrial Products Division, which manufactures steel tubing, pressure vessels, machine tool accessories and distributes industrial fasteners. The company operates 21 plants located in nine countries in North and South America, Europe and Asia, and markets its products in more than 100 countries.

The Infrastructure segment manufactures and distributes engineered metal structures and related products for the lighting, utility and wireless communications industries. VALM is a world leader in the manufacture of steel and aluminum lighting and traffic control structures. The company has focused its efforts on highly engineered poles and towers for world markets that should continue to expand as industrialized infrastructures are upgraded and emerging countries are developed. The Irrigation segment includes the manufacture and distribution of agricultural irrigation equipment and related products and services. VALM is the world leader in mechanized agricultural irrigation equipment, which provides solutions for the world's challenge of doubling its food production over the next 35 years to meet a growing global population.

VALM reported that although its long-term outlook remained positive, 1998 performance was impacted by a decline in agricultural commodity prices which dampened the market for irrigation equipment. In addition, the wireless communication industry remained weak throughout the year, and prices in the lighting and traffic business were pressured by competition. However, the company had completed a series of acquisitions which strengthened their position in the water management and coatings industries, and international development efforts led to sales growth in global markets.

Per Share Data ($) (Year Ended Dec. 31)	1998	1997	1996	1995	1994	1993	1992	1991	1990	1989
Tangible Bk. Val.	7.12	7.49	6.41	5.88	5.52	4.92	4.87	4.45	4.96	4.42
Cash Flow	1.75	1.96	1.28	1.35	1.14	0.66	1.08	0.15	1.12	1.23
Earnings	1.02	1.33	0.76	0.90	0.69	0.23	0.57	-0.34	0.67	0.89
Dividends	0.24	0.22	0.19	0.15	0.15	0.14	0.13	0.13	0.13	0.11
Payout Ratio	24%	17%	25%	17%	22%	64%	22%	NM	19%	12%
Prices - High	25	23 7/8	20 7/8	13	10 1/4	11 3/8	9 3/8	9 1/4	12 1/2	10
- Low	12 1/4	18 1/2	12 1/8	8 1/8	6 3/4	6 1/2	5 1/4	4 3/4	4 5/8	5 1/2
P/E Ratio - High	25	18	27	14	15	51	16	NM	19	11
- Low	12	14	16	9	10	29	9	NM	7	6
Income Statement Analysis (Million $)										
Revs.	606	623	645	545	472	439	425	430	874	790
Oper. Inc.	67.6	78.4	67.3	54.2	37.4	34.1	32.8	20.6	47.7	50.4
Depr.	19.8	16.4	14.8	12.4	10.4	10.0	11.8	11.6	10.5	7.9
Int. Exp.	5.9	3.7	4.0	4.3	4.7	5.9	7.5	8.6	9.1	7.3
Pretax Inc.	43.5	58.9	33.1	38.5	24.9	8.1	18.4	-12.3	26.9	36.5
Eff. Tax Rate	37%	36%	36%	36%	35%	35%	28%	NM	36%	40%
Net Inc.	27.6	37.5	21.2	24.8	16.1	5.3	13.2	-4.0	15.5	20.7
Balance Sheet & Other Fin. Data (Million $)										
Cash	7.6	11.5	9.5	17.0	29.6	14.0	12.7	7.3	12.8	20.5
Curr. Assets	220	218	211	186	171	166	153	159	254	241
Total Assets	407	368	342	309	266	247	273	281	351	322
Curr. Liab.	120	124	129	105	90.0	83.0	89.0	94.0	164	143
LT Debt	90.5	20.7	21.9	28.7	35.5	38.4	60.4	70.4	55.3	60.9
Common Eqty.	280	207	175	159	127	113	111	101	112	99
Total Cap.	387	241	209	201	173	161	182	182	187	179
Cap. Exp.	29.7	39.1	35.6	34.8	23.0	16.3	7.9	15.5	23.6	30.3
Cash Flow	47.5	54.0	36.0	37.1	26.5	15.3	25.0	3.6	26.1	28.5
Curr. Ratio	1.8	1.8	1.6	1.8	1.9	2.0	1.7	1.7	1.5	1.7
% LT Debt of Cap.	23.4	8.6	5.7	14.3	20.5	23.9	33.2	38.7	29.6	34.0
% Net Inc.of Revs.	4.6	6.0	3.3	4.5	3.4	1.2	3.1	NM	1.8	2.6
% Ret. on Assets	7.1	10.6	10.7	8.4	6.3	2.0	4.8	NM	4.6	7.1
% Ret. on Equity	11.3	19.6	12.7	16.7	13.4	4.7	12.4	NM	14.7	22.9

Data as orig reptd.; bef. results of disc opers/spec. items. Per share data adj. for stk. divs. Bold denotes diluted EPS (FASB 128)-prior periods restated. E-Estimated. NA-Not Available. NM-Not Meaningful. NR-Not Ranked.

Office—One Valmont Plaza, Omaha, NE 68154.**Tel**—(402) 963-1000. **Website**—http://www.valmont.com **Chrmn & CEO**—M.C. Bay. **SVP & COO**—V.T. Corso. **SVP & CFO**—T.J. McClain. **VP & Secy**—T.P. Egan, Jr. **Investor Contact**—Jeffrey S. Laudin (402) 963-1158. **Dirs**—M.C. Bay, R.B. Daugherty, C.M. Harper, J.E. Jones, T.F. Madison, C.D. Peebler, Jr., B. Rohde, W. Scott Jr., K.E. Stinson. **Transfer Agent & Registrar**—First National Bank of Omaha. **Incorporated**—in Delaware in 1974. **Empl**— 3,869. **S&P Analyst:** T.J. Vital

STANDARD
&POOR'S
STOCK REPORTS

Vantive Corp.

NASDAQ Symbol **VNTV**

In S&P SmallCap 600

09-OCT-99

Industry:
Computer (Software & Services)

Summary: Vantive is a worldwide leader in the front-office automation software market.

Quantitative Evaluations

Outlook
(1 Lowest—5 Highest)
• **4-**

Fair Value
• **11¾**

Risk
• **High**

Earn./Div. Rank
• **NR**

Technical Eval.
• **Bearish** since 9/99

Rel. Strength Rank
(1 Lowest—99 Highest)
• **68**

Insider Activity
• **Neutral**

Recent Price • 8⅞
52 Wk Range • 15¾-6
Yield • Nil
12-Mo. P/E • NM

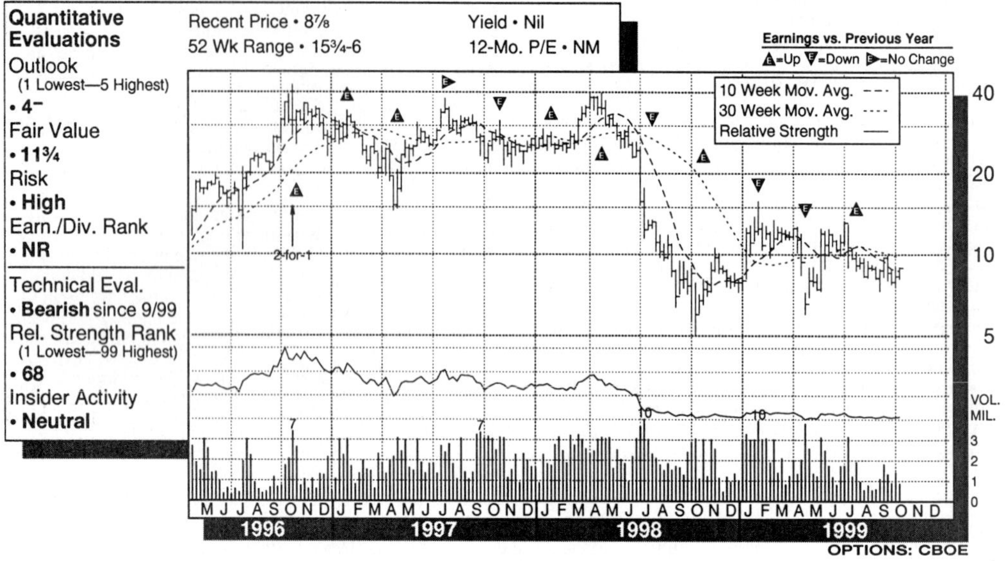

OPTIONS: CBOE

Business Profile - 17-JUN-99

In the 1999 first quarter, receivables days sales outstanding totaled 81 days, approximately the same as in the previous quarter, and cash and short-term investments on the balance sheet grew 2.0% from the level of the prior quarter, to $96.7 million. In the first quarter of 1999, 32% of revenues were generated from international operations, primarily in Europe. In April 1999, T.L. Thomas, formerly Chief Information Officer at 3Com Corp., was appointed as VNTV's chairman and CEO.

Operational Review - 17-JUN-99

Total revenues in the three months ended March 31, 1999, climbed 23%, year to year, as a 65% increase in the service segment outweighed a 1.6% decline in license revenues. Margins narrowed, reflecting larger increases in direct service costs, sales and marketing expense and R&D spending; operating income fell 71%. After taxes of $131,000, versus $2,184,000, net income plunged to $252,000 ($0.01 a share, on 4.1% more shares), from $3,719,000 ($0.14).

Stock Performance - 08-OCT-99

In the past 30 trading days, VNTV's shares have increased 9%, compared to a 0.91% fall in the S&P 500. Average trading volume for the past five days was 170,500 shares, compared with the 40-day moving average of 216,428 shares.

Key Stock Statistics

Dividend Rate/Share	Nil	Shareholders	365
Shs. outstg. (M)	27.1	Market cap. (B)	$0.242
Avg. daily vol. (M)	0.223	Inst. holdings	71%
Tang. Bk. Value/Share	2.48		
Beta	NA		

Value of $10,000 invested 5 years ago: NA

Fiscal Year Ending Dec. 31

	1999	1998	1997	1996	1995	1994
Revenues (Million $)						
1Q	44.80	36.28	22.52	10.81	4.19	—
2Q	48.52	37.74	26.01	15.20	5.52	—
3Q	—	41.68	31.09	17.25	6.61	—
4Q	—	47.40	37.23	21.01	8.72	—
Yr.	—	163.1	117.3	64.27	25.04	10.21
Earnings Per Share ($)						
1Q	0.01	0.14	0.10	0.05	—	—
2Q	-0.13	-0.31	0.13	0.13	—	—
3Q	—	0.04	-0.71	0.12	0.03	—
4Q	—	0.04	0.19	0.12	0.04	—
Yr.	—	-0.09	-0.28	0.42	0.09	-0.14

Next earnings report expected: late October

Dividend Data

No cash dividends have been paid on the public shares. A two-for-one stock split was effected in 1996.

The Vantive Corporation

Business Summary - 17-JUN-99

Vantive Corp. is a leading provider of customer asset management applications software that enables businesses to attract, acquire and retain customers by automating call center, marketing and sales, customer support, defect tracking, field service and internal help desk functions. These tightly integrated customer asset management applications, called the Vantive Enterprise, are based on a multi-tiered client/server architecture and a common data model. Vantive's customer asset management applications may also be used through a Web-based browser, thereby providing the applications directly to the end-user outside the boundaries of the business. The software can be used independently, or as part of an integrated, enterprise-wide customer asset management information system.

VNTV believes businesses implementing a customer asset management information system can better manage customer relationships by leveraging valuable customer information that is shared throughout the organization. The company's software applications have been deployed by businesses in a wide range of industries, including software, communications, consumer products, finance, outsourcing services, personal computer hardware, health care, manufacturing, medical projects, public sector/regulated industry, online services, consumer goods and retail.

Vantive Sales is a front-office software application designed to automate the sales and marketing process. It enables clients to distribute the collective knowledge, information, experience and expertise of top sales performers to the entire sales force. The product delivers up-to-the-minute sales, product and customer information and provides a single source for managing tasks, contacts and scheduling.

The company's first product, Vantive Support, is an application for automating and managing a customer support center. It supports activities such as product support, consumer affairs and complaint management. Vantive FieldService, Vantive Inventory, and Vantive Procurement are applications designed to manage the allocation, scheduling and dispatching of resources, including parts and materials, to perform services or complete work orders to solve customer problems at their site.

Vantive Quality is a front-office software solution used to collect and leverage customer feedback on products and services. This feedback can be used to design, build and deliver high-quality, customer-aligned products and services. The software also plays a key role in tracking and resolving product defects.

The company's growth strategy includes undertaking marketing initiatives designed to increase repeat business from existing customers; strengthening the functionality, scalability and customizability of VNTV's Web-based software applications; and further penetrating the call center market.

Per Share Data ($) (Year Ended Dec. 31)	1998	1997	1996	1995	1994	1993	1992	1991	1990	1989
Tangible Bk. Val.	2.61	2.21	1.63	1.12	NA	NA	NA	NA	NA	NA
Cash Flow	0.14	-0.18	0.48	0.12	NA	NA	NA	NA	NA	NA
Earnings	-0.09	-0.28	0.42	0.09	NA	NA	NA	NA	NA	NA
Dividends	Nil	Nil	Nil	Nil	NA	NA	NA	NA	NA	NA
Payout Ratio	Nil	Nil	Nil	Nil	NA	NA	NA	NA	NA	NA
Prices - High	39¾	38	42¾	14⅝	NA	NA	NA	NA	NA	NA
- Low	5	14½	8¾	6	NA	NA	NA	NA	NA	NA
P/E Ratio - High	NM	NM	NM	NM	NA	NA	NA	NA	NA	NA
- Low	NM	NM	NM	NM	NA	NA	NA	NA	NA	NA
Income Statement Analysis (Million $)										
Revs.	163	117	64.3	25.0	10.2	2.5	0.0	NA	NA	NA
Oper. Inc.	17.5	23.7	15.7	2.5	-0.2	-3.4	NA	NA	NA	NA
Depr.	6.0	2.5	1.4	0.6	0.3	0.2	NA	NA	NA	NA
Int. Exp.	4.0	1.5	0.2	0.1	0.1	0.0	NA	NA	NA	NA
Pretax Inc.	1.3	1.4	15.6	2.3	-0.6	-3.6	-2.2	NA	NA	NA
Eff. Tax Rate	NM	615%	30%	10%	NM	NM	NM	NA	NA	NA
Net Inc.	-2.3	-7.0	10.9	2.0	-0.6	-3.6	-2.2	NA	NA	NA
Balance Sheet & Other Fin. Data (Million $)										
Cash	51.6	77.6	32.9	26.4	3.1	NA	NA	NA	NA	NA
Curr. Assets	155	147	51.1	31.7	6.3	NA	NA	NA	NA	NA
Total Assets	184	163	58.4	34.6	7.5	3.4	3.1	NA	NA	NA
Curr. Liab.	45.9	37.6	18.2	7.3	2.9	NA	NA	NA	NA	NA
LT Debt	69.2	69.0	0.3	0.6	0.4	NA	NA	NA	NA	NA
Common Eqty.	69.0	55.7	39.4	26.7	-6.7	-6.2	-2.6	NA	NA	NA
Total Cap.	138	125	39.8	27.2	4.5	NA	NA	NA	NA	NA
Cap. Exp.	14.7	8.1	5.2	1.5	0.2	0.6	NA	NA	NA	NA
Cash Flow	3.7	-4.4	12.3	2.7	-0.2	-3.5	NA	NA	NA	NA
Curr. Ratio	3.4	3.9	2.8	4.4	2.2	NA	NA	NA	NA	NA
% LT Debt of Cap.	50.0	55.3	0.9	2.1	9.1	NA	NA	NA	NA	NA
% Net Inc.of Revs.	NM	NM	17.0	8.2	NM	NM	NA	NA	NA	NA
% Ret. on Assets	NM	NM	23.5	9.7	NM	NM	NA	NA	NA	NA
% Ret. on Equity	NM	NM	33.0	21.5	NM	NM	NA	NA	NA	NA

Data as orig reptd.; bef. results of disc opers/spec. items. Per share data adj. for stk. divs. Bold denotes diluted EPS (FASB 128)-prior periods restated. E-Estimated. NA-Not Available. NM-Not Meaningful. NR-Not Ranked.

Office—2455 Augustine Dr., Santa Clara, CA 95054. **Tel**—(408) 982-5700. **Website**—http://www.vantive.com **Chrmn & CEO**—T. L. Thomas. **Pres & COO**—P. M. Dunkelberger. **EVP & CFO**—L. J. LeBlanc. **Dirs**—W. R. Davidow, J. R. Luongo, P. Manuel, R. L. Ocampo Jr., P. A. Roshko, T. L. Thomas. **Transfer Agent & Registrar**—Harris Trust Co. of California, LA. **Incorporated**—in Delaware in 1995. **Empl**— 592. **S&P Analyst:** Stephen J. Tekirian

STANDARD
&POOR'S
STOCK REPORTS

Varian Medical Systems

NYSE Symbol **VAR**

In S&P SmallCap 600

09-OCT-99

Industry:
Health Care (Medical Products & Supplies)

Summary: This company (formerly Varian Associates Inc.) was reorganized in April 1999, and is the world's leading maker of integrated cancer therapy systems.

Quantitative Evaluations

Outlook
(1 Lowest—5 Highest)
• **2-**

Fair Value
• **22**

Risk
• **Low**

Earn./Div. Rank
• **B+**

Technical Eval.
• **Bearish** since 8/99

Rel. Strength Rank
(1 Lowest—99 Highest)
• **67**

Insider Activity
• **Neutral**

Recent Price • 21¾
52 Wk Range • 43-16¼
Yield • Nil
12-Mo. P/E • NM

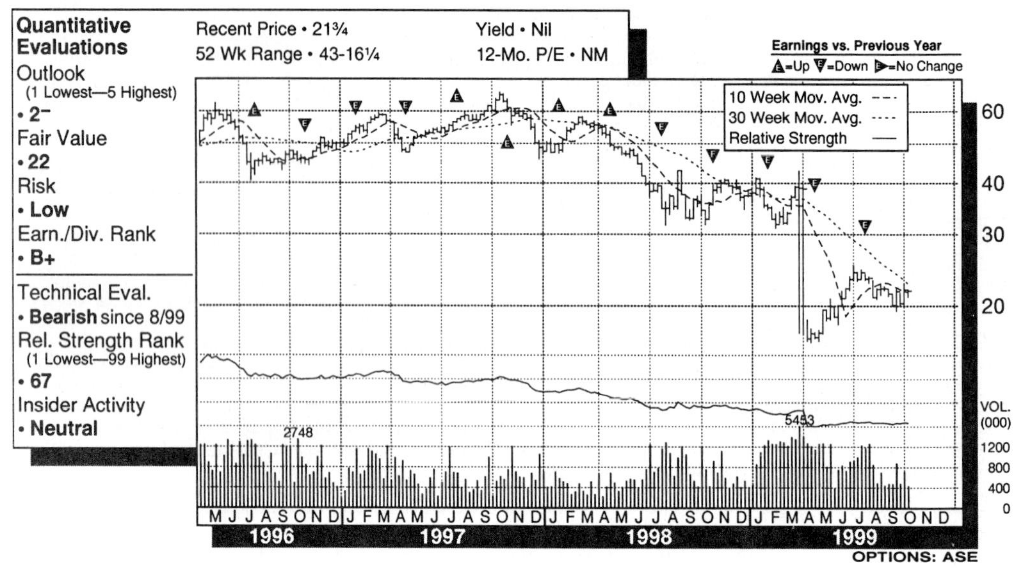

Business Profile - 31-AUG-99

On April 2, 1999, the company (formerly known as Varian Associates Inc.) reorganized into three separate publicly traded companies by spinning off, through a tax-free distribution, two of its businesses to stockholders. The distribution resulted in three companies: Varian Medical Systems Inc., Varian Inc. (NASDAQ: VARI), and Varian Semiconductor Equipment Associates Inc. (NASDAQ: VSEA). Operations retained by Varian Medical Associates include the medical systems business, principally the sale and service of oncology systems, and the sale of X-ray tubes and imaging sub-systems. Backlog at July 3, 1999, totaled $401 million, up from $358 million a year earlier.

Operational Review - 31-AUG-99

Sales (pro forma) from continuing operations in the nine months ended July 3, 1999, increased 10%, year to year, reflecting a 16% rise in oncology sales. Gross margins narrowed. Marketing expenses grew more rapidly then revenues, and after a $31.4 million reorganization charge, an operating loss contrasted with operating income. Despite a tax credit of $8.7 million, versus taxes at 27.2%, a loss of $5.7 million ($0.19 a share) contrasted with income of $9.0 million ($0.29). Results exclude a loss from discontinued operations of $1.03 and income of $1.71 in the respective periods.

Stock Performance - 08-OCT-99

In the past 30 trading days, VAR's shares have declined 1%, compared to a 0.91% fall in the S&P 500. Average trading volume for the past five days was 85,460 shares, compared with the 40-day moving average of 116,603 shares.

Key Stock Statistics

Dividend Rate/Share	Nil	Shareholders	5,992
Shs. outstg. (M)	30.5	Market cap. (B)	$0.666
Avg. daily vol. (M)	0.124	Inst. holdings	74%
Tang. Bk. Value/Share	5.46		
Beta	0.75		

Value of $10,000 invested 5 years ago: NA

Fiscal Year Ending Sep. 30

	1999	1998	1997	1996	1995	1994
Revenues (Million $)						
1Q	105.0	344.8	322.0	351.3	346.1	323.8
2Q	149.3	372.8	338.2	417.6	428.7	394.5
3Q	144.5	340.0	359.9	417.1	394.2	393.1
4Q	—	364.5	405.8	413.4	406.7	441.1
Yr.	—	1,422	1,426	1,599	1,576	1,552
Earnings Per Share ($)						
1Q	**-0.02**	**0.64**	0.41	0.79	0.51	0.33
2Q	**-0.34**	**0.75**	0.55	1.03	0.75	0.51
3Q	**0.21**	**0.61**	1.67	1.07	0.82	0.63
4Q	—	**0.42**	1.06	0.43	0.94	0.76
Yr.	—	**2.43**	**3.67**	**3.81**	3.01	2.22

Next earnings report expected: late October

Dividend Data (Dividends have been paid since 1973.)

Amount ($)	Date Decl.	Ex-Div. Date	Stock of Record	Payment Date
0.100	Nov. 30	Dec. 02	Dec. 04	Jan. 04 '99
Stk	Feb. 23	Apr. 05	Mar. 24	Apr. 02 '99

STANDARD
&POOR'S
STOCK REPORTS

Varian Medical Systems, Inc.

09-OCT-99

Business Summary - 31-AUG-99

Varian Medical Associates (formerly known as Varian Associates Inc.) reorganized into three separate publicly traded companies by spinning off, through a tax-free distribution, two of its businesses to stockholders in April 1999. The distribution resulted in three companies: Varian Medical Systems Inc., Varian Inc., and Varian Semiconductor Equipment Associates Inc. The business retained by Varian Medical Associates consists of the medical systems business, principally the sale and service of oncology systems, and the sale of X-ray tubes and imaging sub-systems. The company has been engaged in the health care business since 1959.

VAR is the worldwide leader in the design and production of equipment for treating cancer with radiation. The company also manufactures high-quality, cost effective X-ray tubes for equipment manufacturers as well as replacement tube and imaging subsystems suppliers.

The company's oncology systems group designs, manufactures, sells and services hardware and software products for cancer radiation treatment, including linear accelerators, simulators and computer systems for planning cancer treatments, high dose rate brachytherapy systems and data management systems for radiation oncology centers. The company offers an integrated system of products embracing both linear accelerators and sophisticated ancillary products and services to extend its capabilities and efficiency.

The company sells its oncology products primarily to hospitals, clinics, private and governmental institutions, health care agencies and doctors' offices. Total oncology sales were $408 million in 1998 and $347 million in 1997.

Linear accelerators are primarily used in cancer therapy. VAR's CLINAC series of products, marketed to hospitals and clinics worldwide, generates therapeutic x-rays and radiation beams for cancer treatment. VariSource, VAR's high dose brachytherapy system, treats tumors internally by delivering radiation to the tumor by means of a radioactive source on the end of a wire catheter. It is a cost-effective and efficacious adjunct to linear accelerator therapy.

VAR also designs and manufactures sub-systems for diagnostic radiology, including X-ray generating tubes and imaging sub-systems. Its tubes are a key component of X-ray imaging sub-systems, including both new system configurations and replacement tubes for the installed base. VAR manufactures tubes for four primary medical X-ray imaging applications: CT scanners; radiographic/fluoroscopic; special procedures; and mammography. Total sales for X-ray tube products were $130 million in 1998, and $129 million in 1997.

Per Share Data ($) (Year Ended Sep. 30)	1998	1997	1996	1995	1994	1993	1992	1991	1990	1989
Tangible Bk. Val.	18.75	17.42	15.27	12.72	13.23	12.16	11.79	11.36	10.38	10.74
Cash Flow	3.83	5.10	5.15	4.43	3.70	2.63	2.31	2.63	1.40	1.80
Earnings	2.43	3.66	3.81	3.01	2.22	1.26	1.02	1.48	0.32	0.77
Dividends	0.39	0.35	0.31	0.33	0.23	0.19	0.17	0.14	0.13	0.13
Payout Ratio	16%	10%	8%	11%	10%	14%	16%	10%	40%	16%
Prices - High	58 3/8	67	62 7/8	57 3/8	39 1/4	30	22 3/8	25 1/8	17 3/8	15 1/4
- Low	31 1/2	45 7/8	40 1/2	34 1/2	28 1/4	19	16 3/4	14 7/8	10	10
P/E Ratio - High	24	18	17	19	18	24	22	17	54	20
- Low	13	13	11	11	13	15	16	10	31	13
Income Statement Analysis (Million $)										
Revs.	1,422	1,426	1,599	1,576	1,552	1,311	1,288	1,378	1,265	1,344
Oper. Inc.	158	176	233	217	183	128	114	146	129	109
Depr.	42.7	45.6	42.9	50.0	52.5	49.7	48.9	45.4	42.2	42.9
Int. Exp.	8.8	7.8	6.4	6.9	6.3	6.6	5.9	8.4	13.0	10.8
Pretax Inc.	113	178	189	165	128	73.9	62.4	92.8	20.7	50.8
Eff. Tax Rate	35%	35%	36%	36%	38%	38%	38%	38%	39%	38%
Net Inc.	73.8	116	122	106	79.4	45.8	38.7	57.5	12.6	31.5
Balance Sheet & Other Fin. Data (Million $)										
Cash	150	142	83.0	123	78.9	73.3	67.0	54.0	26.0	Nil
Curr. Assets	840	813	744	758	669	605	604	595	668	643
Total Assets	1,218	1,104	1,019	1,004	962	893	893	884	924	931
Curr. Liab.	505	464	500	501	432	382	384	350	408	414
LT Debt	111	73.2	60.3	89.4	60.4	60.5	49.7	68.0	76.8	54.9
Common Eqty.	558	525	468	395	449	422	428	434	400	427
Total Cap.	669	604	540	503	531	511	509	535	516	517
Cap. Exp.	47.0	55.1	67.7	65.4	62.6	45.1	48.6	59.7	54.9	49.4
Cash Flow	117	161	165	756	132	95.0	88.0	103	55.0	74.0
Curr. Ratio	1.7	1.8	1.5	1.5	1.5	1.6	1.6	1.7	1.6	1.6
% LT Debt of Cap.	16.5	12.2	11.2	17.8	11.4	11.8	9.8	12.7	14.9	10.6
% Net Inc.of Revs.	5.2	8.1	7.6	6.7	5.1	3.5	3.0	4.2	1.0	2.3
% Ret. on Assets	6.4	10.9	12.1	10.8	8.6	5.2	4.5	6.4	1.4	3.7
% Ret. on Equity	13.6	23.3	28.3	25.1	18.4	11.0	9.2	13.8	3.1	7.5

Data as orig reptd.; bef. results of disc opers/spec. items. Pro forma data for FY 98 (Sep.). Per share data adj. for stk. divs. Bold denotes diluted EPS (FASB 128)-prior periods restated. E-Estimated. NA-Not Available. NM-Not Meaningful. NR-Not Ranked.

Office—3100 Hansen Way, Palo Alto, CA 94304-1000. **Tel**—(650) 493-4000. **Website**—http://www.varian.com/vms **Pres & CEO**—R.M. Levy. **Chrmn**—R.W. Vieser. **VP-Fin, CFO & Investor Contact**—Elisha M. Finney (650-424-6803). **Secy** —J.B. Phair. **Dirs**—J.S. Brown, S. Hellman, T. R. Lautenbach, R.M. Levy, D. W. Martin Jr., A.A. McNaughton, J.G. McDonald, W.R. Moon, B. Richter, E.E. Tallett, R.W. Vieser. **Transfer Agent & Registrar**—First Chicago Trust Co. of New York, Jersey City, NJ. **Incorporated**—in California in 1948; reincorporated in Delaware in 1976. **Empl**—2,034. **S&P Analyst:** John J. Arege

1.75

STANDARD &POOR'S
STOCK REPORTS

Vertex Pharmaceuticals

NASDAQ Symbol **VRTX**

In S&P SmallCap 600

09-OCT-99

Industry:
Biotechnology

Summary: This development-stage company utilizes structure-based drug design to discover and develop therapeutics for diseases which have limited or no effective treatments.

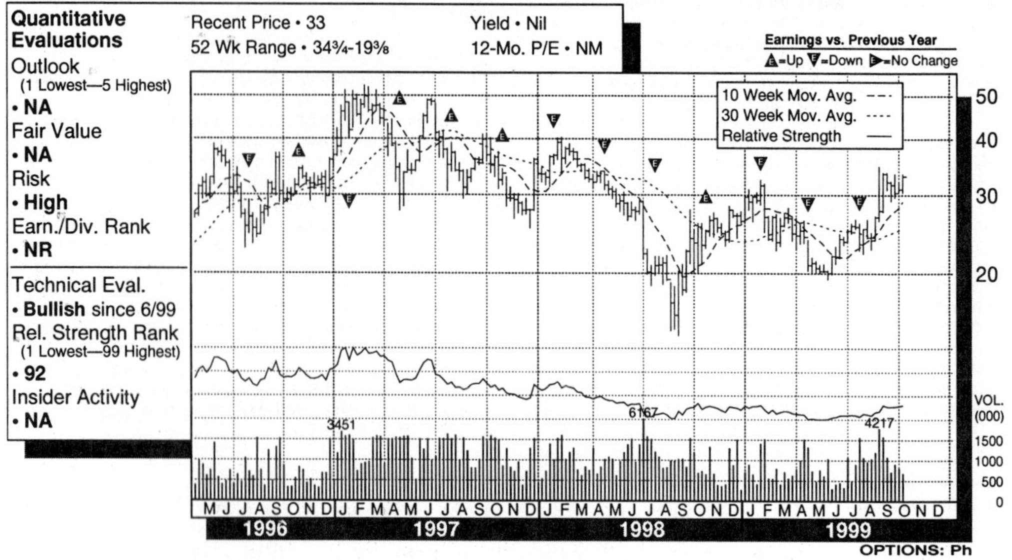

Business Profile - 09-AUG-99

In April 1999, VRTX was granted FDA approval for Agenerase for the treatment of HIV infection in combination with other HIV-related agents. The company also received a $5 million milestone payment from its marketing partner, Glaxo Welcome. In July 1999, Kissei Pharmaceutical, VRTX's marketing partner in Japan, filed for Japanese approval of Agenerase and paid VRTX a $1 million milestone award. In May 1999, the company reported Phase II clinical data on Incel for the treatment of soft tissue sarcoma patients resistant to doxorubicin-based chemotherapy. Data showed Incel to be effective for some patients who failed prior doxorubicin treatment.

Operational Review - 09-AUG-99

Total revenues in the six months ended June 30, 1999 advanced 57%, year to year, reflecting $2,874,000 in royalty and product sales from Agenerase for 1999 only and a sharp rise in collaborative research payments. R&D spending was up 52%, primarily related to development activities on new drug candidates, and SG&A expenses also rose 52%, mainly due to additional employees and co-promotion costs for Agenerase. The net loss widened to $28.4 million ($1.12 a share), from $18.2 million ($0.72). Cash and investments totaled $205.0 million on June 30, 1999.

Stock Performance - 08-OCT-99

In the past 30 trading days, VRTX's shares have increased 19%, compared to a 0.91% fall in the S&P 500. Average trading volume for the past five days was 134,260 shares, compared with the 40-day moving average of 303,649 shares.

Key Stock Statistics

Dividend Rate/Share	Nil	Shareholders	7,200
Shs. outstg. (M)	25.5	Market cap. (B)	$0.844
Avg. daily vol. (M)	0.153	Inst. holdings	56%
Tang. Bk. Value/Share	9.71		
Beta	1.30		

Value of $10,000 invested 5 years ago: $ 17,871

Fiscal Year Ending Dec. 31

	1999	1998	1997	1996	1995	1994
Revenues (Million $)						
1Q	7.13	7.17	6.92	3.75	6.33	5.63
2Q	15.33	7.15	12.16	4.15	7.95	4.78
3Q	—	18.42	13.55	4.12	3.49	6.50
4Q	—	11.66	11.18	6.58	9.76	6.24
Yr.	—	44.40	43.80	18.60	27.53	23.15
Earnings Per Share ($)						
1Q	**-0.69**	**-0.33**	-0.26	-0.43	-0.44	-0.22
2Q	**-0.43**	**-0.39**	-0.06	-1.28	-0.52	-0.35
3Q	—	**-0.09**	-0.23	-0.33	-0.40	-0.24
4Q	—	**-0.50**	**-0.27**	-0.18	-0.05	-0.30
Yr.	—	**-1.31**	**-0.82**	**-2.13**	**-1.25**	**-1.11**

Next earnings report expected: late October

Dividend Data

No dividends have been paid.

A Division of The McGraw-Hill Companies

Vertex Pharmaceuticals Incorporated

Business Summary - 09-AUG-99

This development-stage company's strategy is to discover, develop, and commercialize drugs both independently and in collaboration with partners, for the treatment of viral, autoimmune, inflammatory, neurological, and cancerous diseases. Vertex Pharmaceuticals Inc. is applying its knowledge of the atomic structure of proteins involved in the control of disease processes to a structure-based drug design ("SBDD") system.

SBDD integrates the disciplines of advanced biology, biophysics, chemistry, and information technology in determining optimal lead molecules that have the potential to treat a specific disease target. In contrast, traditional drug discovery methodologies rely on screening thousands of compounds against a predictive assay in order to determine a possible lead for a particular disease target. The company believes that, relative to the traditional drug discovery approach, application of SBDD increases the probability of discovering multiple lead compounds. As of 1998 year-end, VRTX had taken an average of 39 months from project initiation to yield a specific clinical drug candidate, which is about two times faster than the industry average.

The company's sole commercial pharmaceutical product is Agenerase (apmrenavir), an orally-administered HIV protease inhibitor designed to be used in combination with other antiviral HIV drugs. In April 1999, Agenerase received FDA approval and VRTX's worldwide (except the Far East) marketing partner, Glaxo Welcome, began sales of this therapeutic in the second quarter of 1999. In the Far East, Kissei Pharmaceutical will market Agenerase under the brand name of Prozei following proper country approval. In July 1999, Kissei filed for approval of Prozei in Japan.

VRTX's lead clinical candidate is Incel (VX-710), a multidrug resistance inhibitor (MDR), which is being tested in combination with chemotherapy agents to combat a patient's bodily resistance to cancer treatment. As of 1998 year-end, VRTX was conducting five Phase II clinical trials on Incel for treating breast cancer, ovarian cancer, soft tissue sarcoma, prostate cancer, and small cell lung cancer. In May 1999, the company reported positive results from a Phase II clinical trial for treating soft tissue sarcoma patients.

As of 1998 year-end, VRTX had numerous other compounds in development. VX-497, an orally administered IMPDH enzyme inhibitor, was in Phase II trials for treating plague-type psoriasis and hepatitis C infection. VX-740, a novel inhibitor of ICE (IL-1 beta converting enzyme), may be useful for treating inflammatory diseases such as rheumatoid arthritis and osteoarthritis. A Phase I trial on VX-740 was completed in 1998.

VRTX's Neurophilin Ligand Program was created to develop compounds for the treatment of neurologcial disorders such as diabetic neuropathy and Parkinson's disease. VX-853 (timcodar dimesylate) is designed to promote the regeneration of nerve function and growth. As of July 1999, a Phas e II clinical trial was in progress for diabetic neuropathy patients to ascertain the safety and tolerability of various dose regimens.

Per Share Data ($) (Year Ended Dec. 31)	1998	1997	1996	1995	1994	1993	1992	1991	1990	1989
Tangible Bk. Val.	9.71	10.95	6.20	4.93	6.14	3.97	3.60	NA	NA	NA
Cash Flow	-1.13	-0.67	-1.96	-1.03	-0.89	0.48	-0.47	NA	NA	NA
Earnings	-1.31	-0.82	-2.13	-1.25	-1.11	0.16	-0.70	-0.64	NA	NA
Dividends	Nil	Nil	Nil	Nil	Nil	Nil	Nil	Nil	NA	NA
Payout Ratio	Nil	Nil	Nil	Nil	Nil	Nil	Nil	Nil	NA	NA
Prices - High	40 3/8	52 3/4	42 1/4	25 1/2	20	19	17 1/2	16	NA	NA
- Low	14 1/2	25 1/4	22	12 3/8	10 1/2	6 1/2	6 5/8	8 3/8	NA	NA
P/E Ratio - High	NM	NM	NM	NM	NM	120	NM	NM	NA	NA
- Low	NM	NM	NM	NM	NM	41	NM	NM	NA	NA
Income Statement Analysis (Million $)										
Revs.	29.1	29.9	13.3	22.1	19.6	27.9	3.8	NA	NA	NA
Oper. Inc.	-43.2	-29.5	-26.6	-22.8	-17.2	6.5	-6.2	NA	NA	NA
Depr.	4.5	3.6	3.2	3.7	3.5	3.9	2.8	NA	NA	NA
Int. Exp.	0.7	0.6	0.5	0.5	0.4	0.5	0.5	NA	NA	NA
Pretax Inc.	-33.1	-19.8	-40.0	-21.5	-17.6	2.1	-8.5	NA	NA	NA
Eff. Tax Rate	NM	Nil	Nil	Nil	Nil	3.80%	Nil	NA	NA	NA
Net Inc.	-33.1	-19.8	-40.0	-21.5	-17.6	2.0	-8.5	NA	NA	NA
Balance Sheet & Other Fin. Data (Million $)										
Cash	26.5	73.8	37.2	87.0	106	52.1	43.7	NA	NA	NA
Curr. Assets	249	282	132	88.0	107	53.0	NA	NA	NA	NA
Total Assets	266	296	143	99	116	61.0	51.0	NA	NA	NA
Curr. Liab.	13.1	13.7	7.1	8.8	6.0	7.3	NA	NA	NA	NA
LT Debt	7.0	5.9	5.6	4.9	4.7	4.2	4.0	NA	NA	NA
Common Eqty.	246	276	131	85.0	105	50.0	44.0	NA	NA	NA
Total Cap.	253	282	136	90.0	110	54.0	48.0	NA	NA	NA
Cap. Exp.	7.9	6.0	4.0	NA	1.9	1.8	1.4	NA	NA	NA
Cash Flow	-28.6	-16.2	-36.8	-17.8	-14.1	6.0	-5.7	NA	NA	NA
Curr. Ratio	19.0	20.6	18.7	10.0	17.9	7.3	NA	NA	NA	NA
% LT Debt of Cap.	2.8	NA	4.1	5.5	4.3	7.8	8.3	NA	NA	NA
% Net Inc.of Revs.	NM	NM	NM	NM	NM	7.2	NM	NA	NA	NA
% Ret. on Assets	NM	NM	NM	NM	NM	3.6	NM	NA	NA	NA
% Ret. on Equity	NM	NM	NM	NM	NM	4.4	NM	NA	NA	NA

Data as orig reptd.; bef. results of disc opers/spec. items. Per share data adj. for stk. divs. Bold denotes diluted EPS (FASB 128)-prior periods restated. E-Estimated. NA-Not Available. NM-Not Meaningful. NR-Not Ranked.

Office—130 Waverly St., Cambridge, MA 02139-4242. **Tel**—(617) 577-6000. **Website**—http://www.vpharm.com **Chrmn, Pres & CEO**—J. S. Boger. **SVP & CBO**—R. H. Aldrich. **SVP & CSO**—V. L. Sato. **CFO & Treas**—T. G. Auchincloss Jr. **Investor Contact**—L. H. Brum. **Dirs**—B. M. Bloom, J. S. Boger, R. W. Brimblecombe, D. R. Conklin, W. W. Helman IV, B. I. Sachs, C. A. Sanders, E. S. Ullian. **Transfer Agent & Registrar**—Boston EquiServe. **Incorporated**—in Massachusetts in 1989. **Empl**— 304. **S&P Analyst:** Frank DiLorenzo

STANDARD
&POOR'S
STOCK REPORTS

Vicor Corp.

NASDAQ Symbol **VICR**

In S&P SmallCap 600

09-OCT-99

Industry:
Electrical Equipment

Summary: This company designs, develops, manufactures and markets modular power components and complete power systems for use in electronic products.

Quantitative Evaluations

Outlook
(1 Lowest—5 Highest)
• **5+**

Fair Value
• **46⅞**

Risk
• **Average**

Earn./Div. Rank
• **B+**

Technical Eval.
• **Neutral** since 9/99

Rel. Strength Rank
(1 Lowest—99 Highest)
• **96**

Insider Activity
• **Unfavorable**

Recent Price • 25¾
52 Wk Range • 26¼-6¾

Yield • Nil
12-Mo. P/E • 75.9

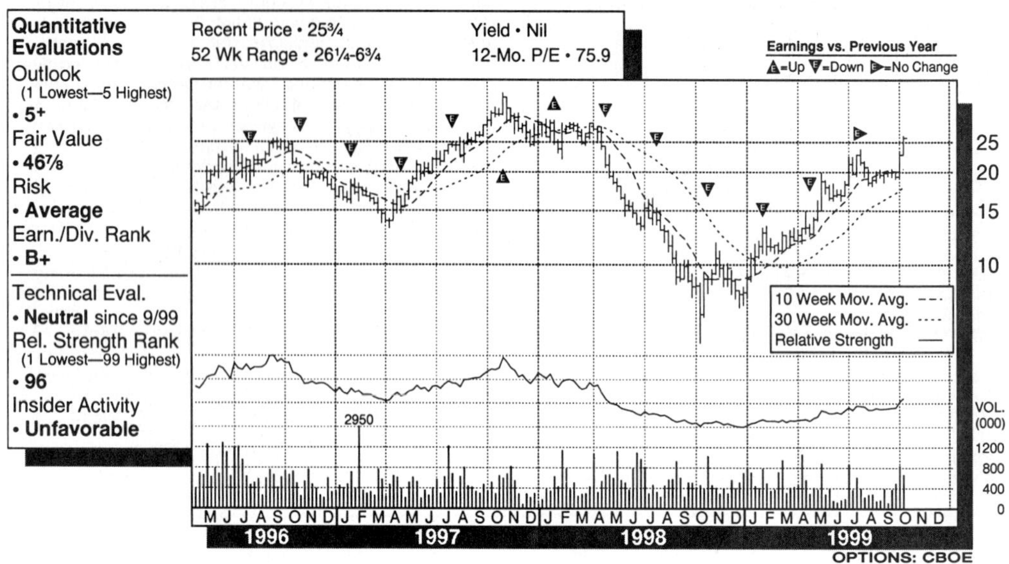

Business Profile - 09-SEP-99

During 1998, Vicor introduced the first complete family of its second-generation high power density, component-level DC-DC converters. The family operates from 48 volts input and is designed for the telecommunications market as well as distributed power systems. VICR does not expect to generate significant revenues from second-generation products for several quarters, and believes gross margins will be penalized until ramp-up costs are fully absorbed by higher production volumes. In November 1997, directors authorized the repurchase of up to $30 million of the company's common stock; VICR spent $17.6 million for repurchases under the program in 1998, and another $5.5 million in the first half of 1999.

Operational Review - 09-SEP-99

Net revenues in the first half of 1999 rose 2.2%, year to year, aided by a non-recurring license payment for past use of Vicor's intellectual property. With an increase in depreciation on the second-generation automated production line of about $1,500,000, changes in the revenue mix, and a non-recurring charge of $700,000 in the first quarter for exit costs in connection with the relocation of certain manufacturing operations, net income fell 18%, to $7,833,000 ($0.19 a share, on 3.0% fewer shares), from $9,570,000 ($0.22).

Stock Performance - 08-OCT-99

In the past 30 trading days, VICR's shares have increased 32%, compared to a 0.91% fall in the S&P 500. Average trading volume for the past five days was 131,680 shares, compared with the 40-day moving average of 80,149 shares.

Key Stock Statistics

Dividend Rate/Share	Nil	Shareholders	600
Shs. outstg. (M)	41.4	Market cap. (B)	$0.756
Avg. daily vol. (M)	0.117	Inst. holdings	23%
Tang. Bk. Value/Share	5.13		
Beta	1.83		

Value of $10,000 invested 5 years ago: $ 22,445

Fiscal Year Ending Dec. 31

	1999	1998	1997	1996	1995	1994
Revenues (Million $)						
1Q	41.96	43.19	37.94	35.81	33.79	25.76
2Q	44.81	41.72	39.72	36.70	35.12	27.68
3Q	—	39.32	41.40	35.67	37.31	30.05
4Q	—	40.41	43.19	36.80	37.80	31.95
Yr.	—	164.6	162.2	145.0	144.0	115.4
Earnings Per Share ($)						
1Q	**0.09**	**0.12**	**0.14**	**0.16**	0.16	0.11
2Q	**0.10**	**0.10**	**0.15**	**0.16**	0.17	0.12
3Q	—	**0.07**	**0.16**	**0.15**	0.18	0.14
4Q	—	**0.08**	**0.15**	**0.14**	0.17	0.15
Yr.	—	**0.37**	**0.60**	**0.60**	**0.68**	**0.52**

Next earnings report expected: mid October

Dividend Data

No cash payments have been made. For the foreseeable future, the company plans to retain earnings to finance the expansion of its business. A two-for-one stock split was effected in 1995.

A Division of The McGraw-Hill Companies

STANDARD
&POOR'S
STOCK REPORTS

Vicor Corporation

09-OCT-99

Business Summary - 09-SEP-99

This maker of power system components called the introduction during 1996 of the first models of its next generation of DC-DC power converters "a major milestone." One of these newcomers -- the first-ever "micro" sized converter -- delivers 150 watts in one-third the volume of the company's first-generation converter. Vicor Corp. (VICR) decided to introduce its next-generation products in stages to allow it to build up manufacturing capacity and its ability to support and service the new lines ahead of anticipated demand. VICR plans to make continuing investments in manufacturing equipment, much of which is built internally. At December 31, 1998, the company had approximately $3.1 million of capital expenditure commitments related to the construction of new and expanded facilities.

VICR's modular power components and complete power systems are used primarily by original equipment manufacturers in the communications, data processing, industrial control, test equipment, medical and defense electronic markets. Built into virtually all electronic products, power systems convert electric power from a primary source, such as a wall outlet, into the low, stable voltages required by electronic circuits. Since power systems are forged in a myriad of application-specific configurations, the company's basic strategy is to exploit the density and performance advantages of its core technology by offering comprehensive families of economical, component-level building blocks that can be applied by users to easily fashion a power system specific to their needs.

At the heart of VICR's product line are high-density DC-DC converters that come in thousands of combinations of input voltage, output voltage and power levels. Accessory components integrate other power system functions. Together, these products allow OEM users to meet their unique power requirements by selecting and interconnecting standard, modular parts.

The company currently offers four first generation families of component-level DC-DC power converters, including a family designed specifically to meet many of the performance and environmental requirements of the military/defense markets. In 1998, VICR introduced the first complete family of its second generation of high power density, component-level DC-DC converters. This family operates from 48 volts input and is designed for the telecommunications markets as well as distributed power systems. It consists of 26 modules with the most popular output voltages.

During 1998, the company shipped an increased volume of second-generation products, while continuing to make modifications to the designs, processes, equipment and parts associated with them. Significant revenues from these products are not expected for several quarters. VICR believes that gross margins will be negatively impacted until ramp-up and related costs are fully absorbed by higher production volumes.

Per Share Data ($) (Year Ended Dec. 31)	1998	1997	1996	1995	1994	1993	1992	1991	1990	1989
Tangible Bk. Val.	5.02	4.87	4.05	3.55	2.73	2.42	2.09	1.69	0.40	0.20
Cash Flow	0.64	0.80	0.79	0.87	0.69	0.51	0.39	0.36	0.18	0.10
Earnings	0.37	0.60	0.60	0.68	0.52	0.35	0.28	0.28	0.14	0.07
Dividends	Nil	Nil	Nil	Nil	Nil	Nil	Nil	Nil	Nil	Nil
Payout Ratio	Nil	Nil	Nil	Nil	Nil	Nil	Nil	Nil	Nil	Nil
Prices - High	$29\frac{3}{4}$	$36\frac{1}{4}$	$25\frac{3}{4}$	26	$15\frac{1}{8}$	$12\frac{3}{4}$	$22\frac{7}{8}$	$22\frac{5}{8}$	$4\frac{3}{8}$	NA
- Low	$5\frac{1}{2}$	$13\frac{1}{8}$	$12\frac{1}{2}$	$12\frac{1}{4}$	9	$6\frac{1}{2}$	$6\frac{7}{8}$	$4\frac{1}{8}$	$1\frac{3}{4}$	NA
P/E Ratio - High	80	60	43	38	29	36	83	79	33	NA
- Low	15	22	21	18	17	19	25	14	13	NA
Income Statement Analysis (Million $)										
Revs.	165	162	145	144	115	84.0	63.8	55.6	36.8	28.5
Oper. Inc.	30.0	44.2	44.9	50.9	40.9	28.3	21.7	20.3	10.1	5.4
Depr.	11.6	8.3	8.3	8.2	7.6	6.7	4.8	3.2	1.8	1.4
Int. Exp.	Nil	NA	Nil	Nil	0.0	0.1	0.1	0.3	0.5	0.6
Pretax Inc.	23.3	41.0	40.4	46.8	35.7	24.2	19.2	18.3	8.1	3.8
Eff. Tax Rate	32%	36%	37%	37%	38%	38%	38%	39%	38%	33%
Net Inc.	15.8	26.2	25.6	29.5	22.1	15.1	12.0	11.2	5.1	2.5
Balance Sheet & Other Fin. Data (Million $)										
Cash	58.9	84.9	73.6	65.2	43.2	45.2	42.9	37.4	1.8	1.2
Curr. Assets	122	147	123	111	77.1	73.4	65.5	60.5	15.7	10.6
Total Assets	250	229	186	167	126	115	97.0	77.6	27.5	18.7
Curr. Liab.	37.1	18.6	14.0	15.2	12.1	10.6	6.7	6.4	8.9	3.5
LT Debt	Nil	Nil	Nil	Nil	Nil	0.1	0.5	1.1	2.2	4.7
Common Eqty.	209	208	171	150	113	102	88.5	70.1	13.0	6.2
Total Cap.	212	210	172	152	114	104	89.6	71.2	18.6	15.2
Cap. Exp.	36.4	20.2	14.3	15.6	15.5	16.1	14.8	8.4	5.5	3.8
Cash Flow	27.4	34.5	34.0	37.7	29.7	21.8	16.8	14.4	6.9	3.9
Curr. Ratio	3.3	7.9	8.8	7.3	6.4	6.9	9.7	9.4	1.8	3.0
% LT Debt of Cap.	Nil	Nil	Nil	Nil	Nil	0.1	0.6	1.5	11.6	30.7
% Net Inc.of Revs.	9.6	16.2	17.7	20.5	19.2	18.0	18.8	20.2	13.8	8.9
% Ret. on Assets	6.6	12.6	14.5	20.1	18.5	14.3	13.6	19.9	21.7	15.2
% Ret. on Equity	7.6	13.8	16.0	22.4	20.7	15.8	15.0	25.9	52.5	26.3

Data as orig reptd.; bef. results of disc opers/spec. items. Per share data adj. for stk. divs. Bold denotes diluted EPS (FASB 128)-prior periods restated. E-Estimated. NA-Not Available. NM-Not Meaningful. NR-Not Ranked.

Office—23 Frontage Rd., Andover, MA 01810. **Tel**—(978) 470-2900. **Website**—http://www.vicr.com **Chrmn & Pres**—P. Vinciarelli. **VP-Fin, Treas, Secy & Investor Contact**—Mark A. Glazer. **Dirs**—M. M. Ansour, R. E. Beede, E. J. Eichten, J. M. Prager, D. T. Riddiford, P. Vinciarelli. **Transfer Agent**—State Street Bank & Trust Co., Boston. **Incorporated**—in Delaware in 1981. **Empl**— 1,129. **S&P Analyst:** C.F.B.

STANDARD
&POOR'S
STOCK REPORTS

Vintage Petroleum

NYSE Symbol **VPI**

In S&P SmallCap 600

09-OCT-99

Industry: Oil & Gas (Exploration & Production)

Summary: This independent oil and gas company is engaged in acquisition, exploration, and development of oil and gas properties.

Quantitative Evaluations

Outlook (1 Lowest—5 Highest) • **1⁻**

Fair Value • **11¼**

Risk • **Average**

Earn./Div. Rank • **B**

Technical Eval. • **Neutral** since 9/99

Rel. Strength Rank (1 Lowest—99 Highest) • **37**

Insider Activity • **Neutral**

Recent Price • 12
52 Wk Range • 15½-4

Yield • Nil
12-Mo. P/E • NM

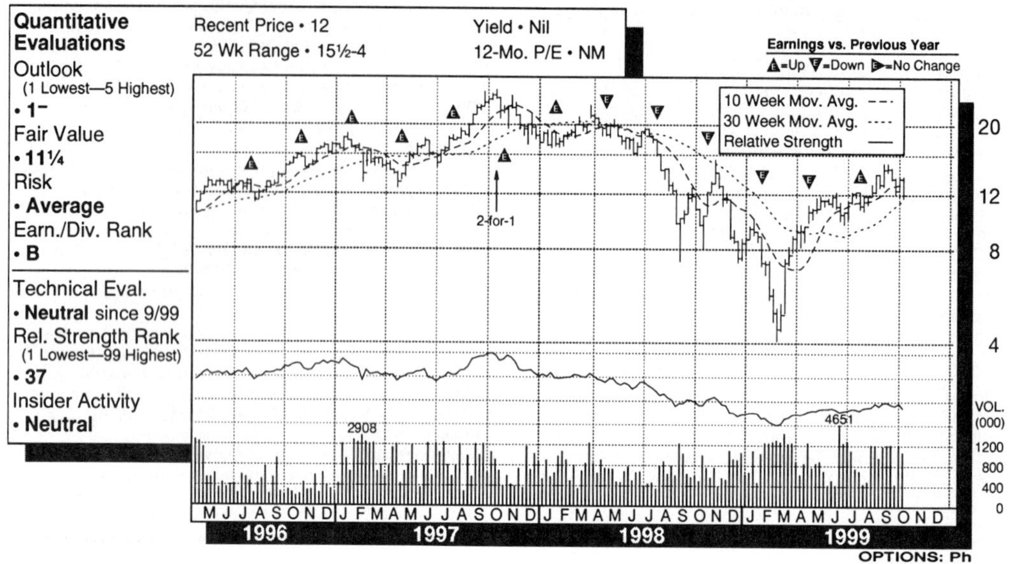

OPTIONS: Ph

Business Profile - 12-MAY-99

In mid-May 1999, VPI said that current oil and gas prices were well above their respective averages in the first quarter of 1999 when the current capital budget of $56 million was established. At these higher prices, the company has regained substantially all of the 49 million equivalent barrels of reserves temporarily lost as a result of the low oil price environment at the end of 1998. Vintage expects a sustained rebound in oil and gas prices to generate excess cash flow relative to the existing budget. With more capital directed toward increasing production as a result of continued strength in commodity prices, VPI is optimistic about its ability to improve bottom line results in the remainder of 1999. Mainly reflecting the effect of significantly lower oil and gas price expectations, VPI incurred a noncash impairment charge of $43.3 million after taxes in 1998's fourth quarter.

Operational Review - 12-MAY-99

Revenues in the three months ended March 31, 1999, fell 27%, year to year, on a 26% decrease in oil and gas sales, a 28% drop in gas marketing revenues and a 41% fall in oil and gas gathering revenues. Results were penalized by substantially lower average prices received for gas and especially oil, and by a decline in oil and gas production. The net loss widened to $18,121,000 ($0.34 a share) from $1,582,000 ($0.03). in the year-earlier period.

Stock Performance - 08-OCT-99

In the past 30 trading days, VPI's shares have declined 7%, compared to a 0.91% fall in the S&P 500. Average trading volume for the past five days was 212,840 shares, compared with the 40-day moving average of 221,259 shares.

Key Stock Statistics

Dividend Rate/Share	Nil	Shareholders	85
Shs. outstg. (M)	62.3	Market cap. (B)	$0.748
Avg. daily vol. (M)	0.205	Inst. holdings	52%
Tang. Bk. Value/Share	5.51		
Beta	1.78		

Value of $10,000 invested 5 years ago: $ 13,589

Fiscal Year Ending Dec. 31

	1999	1998	1997	1996	1995	1994
Revenues (Million $)						
1Q	66.00	89.99	99.2	71.34	41.04	44.64
2Q	92.56	84.93	99.8	76.04	45.23	48.09
3Q	—	79.29	104.4	75.95	50.10	48.25
4Q	—	74.72	113.1	88.35	58.42	44.68
Yr.	—	328.9	416.6	311.7	194.8	185.7
Earnings Per Share ($)						
1Q	**-0.34**	**-0.03**	**0.41**	0.15	0.04	0.06
2Q	**0.09**	**-0.18**	**0.27**	0.20	0.08	0.10
3Q	—	**-0.19**	**0.29**	0.20	0.07	0.10
4Q	—	**-1.27**	**0.41**	0.29	0.09	0.08
Yr.	—	**-1.69**	**1.39**	**0.85**	**0.27**	**0.33**

Next earnings report expected: mid November

Dividend Data (Dividends have been paid since 1992.)

Amount ($)	Date Decl.	Ex-Div. Date	Stock of Record	Payment Date
0.025	Dec. 07	Dec. 18	Dec. 22	Jan. 06 '99

A Division of The McGraw-Hill Companies

Vintage Petroleum, Inc.

Business Summary - 12-MAY-99

The goal of Vintage Petroleum, Inc., an independent oil and gas company, is to maximize its value through profitable growth in its oil and gas reserves and production. The company's ongoing strategy includes: acquiring producing oil and gas properties, at favorable prices, with significant upside potential; focusing on exploitation, development and exploration activities to maximize production and ultimate reserve recovery; exploring nonproducing properties; maintaining a low-cost operating structure; and maintaining financial flexibility.

Vintage focuses on acquiring producing oil and gas properties with potential for increased value through exploitation and development. VPI also purchases, gathers and markets natural gas and crude oil, and explores and develops non-producing properties.

The company seeks to acquire producing properties with significant upside potential to be realized through its exploitation and development expertise. VPI consistently attempts to purchase reserves at costs well below the industry averages. Exploitation and development activities raise the value of the acquired properties by increasing production and adding reserves at low cost.

VPI believes that its primary strengths are its ability to add reserves at attractive prices through property acquisitions and subsequent exploitation, and its low-cost operating structure. These strengths allowed it to substantially increase reserves, production and cash flow over the years. As VPI has increased its cash flow and added to its technical staff, exploration has become a greater focus for future growth.

As of December 31, 1998, VPI owned and operated producing properties in 13 states, with domestic proved reserves located primarily in four core areas: the West Coast, Gulf Coast, East Texas, and Mid-Continent areas of the U.S. In 1996 and the first half of 1997, VPI expanded its Gulf Coast presence through the acquisitions of certain oil and gas properties from Exxon, Conoco, and Burlington Resources Inc. In 1995, it established a new core area by acquiring oil concessions in the south flank of the San Jorge Basin in southern Argentina. VPI expanded its South American operations into Bolivia in 1996 through the acquisition of Shamrock Ventures Ltd., which owns and operates three blocks covering approximately 570,000 gross acres in the Chaco Plains area of southern Bolivia. In late 1998, the company purchased a subsidiary of Elf Aquitane which has producing properties in Ecuador.

As of December 31, 1998, VPI owned interests in 4,495 gross (2,398 net) producing wells in the U.S., of which about 80% are operated by VPI; 712 gross (696 net) producing wells in Argentina, of which about 97% are operated by VPI; 4 gross (3 net) producing wells in Bolivia, all of which are operated by VPI; and 5 gross (2 net) producing wells in Ecuador, all of which are operated by VPI.

Due to the current historically low oil and gas price environment, VPI has tempo rarily suspended its regular quarterly cash dividend. The most recent dividend payment was $0.025 per share on January 6, 1999.

Per Share Data ($) (Year Ended Dec. 31)	1998	1997	1996	1995	1994	1993	1992	1991	1990	1989
Tangible Bk. Val.	5.16	7.44	5.51	4.74	3.87	3.56	2.40	2.15	1.95	NA
Cash Flow	0.41	3.29	2.27	1.50	1.41	1.20	0.77	0.58	0.56	0.50
Earnings	-1.69	1.39	0.84	0.27	0.33	0.41	0.26	0.20	0.23	0.18
Dividends	0.09	0.06	0.06	0.05	0.04	0.03	0.01	Nil	Nil	Nil
Payout Ratio	NM	4%	7%	17%	11%	6%	4%	Nil	Nil	Nil
Prices - High	23 1/8	25 7/8	17 3/8	11 1/4	11 3/8	13	7	4 5/8	5 3/8	NA
- Low	7 1/4	12 1/2	9 1/2	8	7 3/8	6 1/8	2 3/4	2 3/4	3 1/2	NA
P/E Ratio - High	NM	19	21	42	34	32	27	22	24	NA
- Low	NM	9	11	30	22	15	11	13	16	NA
Income Statement Analysis (Million $)										
Revs.	329	417	312	194	183	157	100	69.9	50.7	49.1
Oper. Inc.	92.3	225	157	86.8	77.8	65.8	34.5	24.0	25.6	24.4
Depr. Depl. & Amort.	109	99	70.1	52.3	45.8	33.2	17.4	12.8	10.1	10.8
Int. Exp.	43.7	36.8	30.1	20.2	12.0	6.9	4.5	4.2	5.1	5.0
Pretax Inc.	-130	89.6	56.6	15.6	22.4	28.5	13.7	10.9	10.9	10.3
Eff. Tax Rate	NM	19%	26%	33%	38%	41%	37%	38%	38%	38%
Net Inc.	-87.7	72.2	41.2	11.4	13.9	16.8	8.7	6.8	6.8	6.4
Balance Sheet & Other Fin. Data (Million $)										
Cash	5.2	5.8	2.8	2.5	0.4	0.6	0.6	0.3	0.5	0.8
Curr. Assets	84.1	89.7	84.7	59.1	39.3	36.6	27.1	16.4	13.6	14.8
Total Assets	1,014	990	814	648	408	384	260	144	123	121
Curr. Liab.	66.9	79.7	113	59.0	34.0	42.6	34.2	23.3	20.4	24.9
LT Debt	673	451	372	316	187	174	128	36.6	27.6	28.0
Common Eqty.	274	384	265	224	156	143	78.7	69.8	62.9	57.4
Total Cap.	946	907	697	585	374	342	226	121	103	96.0
Cap. Exp.	262	268	164	145	67.0	151	120	32.3	27.6	NA
Cash Flow	21.3	171	111	63.6	59.7	49.9	26.0	19.6	16.9	17.1
Curr. Ratio	1.3	1.1	0.8	1.0	1.2	0.9	0.8	0.7	0.7	0.6
% LT Debt of Cap.	71.1	49.7	53.4	54.0	49.9	51.0	56.7	30.3	26.9	29.1
% Ret. on Assets	NM	8.0	5.7	2.2	3.5	4.8	4.3	5.1	4.7	NA
% Ret. on Equity	NM	22.3	16.9	6.0	9.3	14.0	11.6	10.2	16.3	NA

Data as orig reptd.; bef. results of disc opers/spec. items. Per share data adj. for stk. divs. Bold denotes diluted EPS (FASB 128)-prior periods restated. E-Estimated. NA-Not Available. NM-Not Meaningful. NR-Not Ranked.

Office—110 West 7th St., Tulsa, OK 74119.**Tel**—(918) 878-5745. **Fax**—(918) 584-7282. **Chrmn**—C. C. Stephenson Jr. **Vice Chrmn**—J. B. Hille. **Pres & CEO**—S. C. George. **EVP, CFO, Secy & Treas**—W. C. Barnes. **VP & Investor Contact**—Robert E. Phaneuf. **Dirs**—W. C. Barnes, S. C. George, J. B. Hille, B. H. Lawrence, J. T. McNabb, II, C. C. Stephenson Jr. **Transfer Agent & Registrar**—ChaseMellon Shareholder Services, Ridgefield Park, NJ. **Incorporated**—in Delaware in 1983. **Empl**— 580. **S&P Analyst:** J.J.S.

STANDARD & POOR'S
STOCK REPORTS

Visio Corp.

NASDAQ Symbol **VSIO**

In S&P SmallCap 600

09-OCT-99

Industry: Computer (Software & Services)

Summary: This company is a leading supplier of business diagramming and technical drawing software.

Quantitative Evaluations

Outlook (1 Lowest—5 Highest)
• **5**

Fair Value
• **66¼**

Risk
• **Average**

Earn./Div. Rank
• **NR**

Technical Eval.
• **Bullish** since 9/99

Rel. Strength Rank (1 Lowest—99 Highest)
• **92**

Insider Activity
• **NA**

Recent Price • 40½
52 Wk Range • 43½-14
Yield • Nil
12-Mo. P/E • 32.4

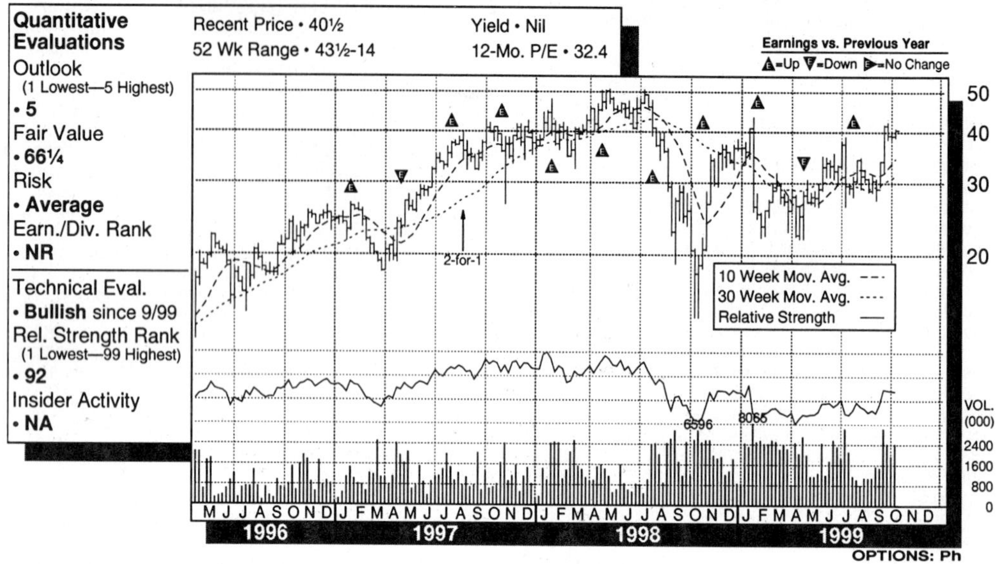

OPTIONS: Ph

Business Profile - 11-AUG-99

The company continues to focus on penetrating the corporate market, with solid growth in securing volume licensing agreements in the third quarter of FY 99 (Sep.) and strengthening of its domestic and international sales force. The company plans to launch Visio 2000, the next generation of its technology and product family in FY 99's fourth quarter and will broadly distribute the product through its sales force, online and through traditional distribution channels. Visio 2000 has new drawing, navigational and Internet enhancements, which the company believes will lead to overall ease of use and productivity. Visio repurchased 313,500 of its common shares during the third quarter under a two million share buyback program announced earlier in the year; a total of 696,500 shares have been repurchased since the start of the program.

Operational Review - 11-AUG-99

In the nine months ended June 30, 1999, revenues rose 23%, year to year, reflecting strong growth in the corporate volume licensing business and continued solid IT design and documentation group sales. Comparisons benefited from well controlled operating costs and the absence of an $8.1 million charge for acquired technology mainly related to the InfoModelers Technology acquisition. Pretax income jumped 60%. After taxes at 26.0%, versus 25.1%, net income was up 58%, to $30,304,000 ($0.96 a share) from $19,153,000 ($0.60).

Stock Performance - 08-OCT-99

In the past 30 trading days, VSIO's shares have increased 33%, compared to a 0.91% fall in the S&P 500. Average trading volume for the past five days was 495,060 shares, compared with the 40-day moving average of 486,933 shares.

Key Stock Statistics

Dividend Rate/Share	Nil	Shareholders	229
Shs. outstg. (M)	30.2	Market cap. (B)	$ 1.2
Avg. daily vol. (M)	0.694	Inst. holdings	51%
Tang. Bk. Value/Share	4.21		
Beta	NA		

Value of $10,000 invested 5 years ago: NA

Fiscal Year Ending Sep. 30

	1999	1998	1997	1996	1995	1994
Revenues (Million $)						
1Q	48.19	37.50	19.01	13.42	—	—
2Q	51.35	40.09	23.54	14.53	—	—
3Q	50.35	44.19	25.81	15.23	—	—
4Q	—	44.22	31.16	16.52	—	—
Yr.	—	166.0	99.5	59.70	34.22	—
Earnings Per Share ($)						
1Q	**0.32**	**0.24**	**0.14**	0.08	—	—
2Q	**0.01**	**0.11**	0.02	0.08	—	—
3Q	**0.31**	**0.26**	**0.10**	0.10	—	—
4Q	—	**0.28**	**0.20**	0.13	—	—
Yr.	—	**0.89**	**0.44**	0.38	—	—

Next earnings report expected: late October

Dividend Data

No cash dividends have been paid.

A Division of The McGraw-Hill Companies

Visio Corporation

Business Summary - 11-AUG-99

Founded in 1990 to bring powerful computer graphics capabilities to the desktops of mainstream computer users, Visio Corp. today is a leading supplier of enterprise-wide business diagramming and technical drawing software for businesses, governments, and other organizations.

The company's mission is to become the single worldwide standard for creating, storing and exchanging drawings and diagrams in business. By becoming the standard, Visio believes it can introduce new users to electronic drawing and diagramming and thereby expand the market for its products. As of May 1999, Visio had an installed base of over three million customers.

Visio software allows business and technical users to create drawings and diagrams using a "drag and drop" approach. The company's software is utilized for creating drawings and diagrams ranging from flowcharts, block diagrams and organizational charts to more complex technical drawings such as space plans, electrical schematics and network designs.

The company has five core software products. Four of the core products - Visio Standard, Visio Technical, Visio Professional and Visio Enterprise - are based on a common graphics " engine" that drives parametrically defined pre-drawn shapes (SmartShapes symbols), intelligent objects and connectors that maintain relationships within and between shapes as they are moved. The company's SmartShapes objects, its stencil metaphor and its drag-and-drop features allow users with no previous graphics or CAD (computer aided design) training to select shapes easily, combine them with text and manipulate them to create sophisticated drawings and diagrams.

Visio believes that its software is expanding the market for drawing and diagramming software by replacing hand-drawing and single-use products and moving drawing and diagramming out of the specialist art and drafting departments and onto the desktops of general users throughout business.

In 1998, the company released its fifth core software product, IntelliCAD, which is designed as an affordable alternative to expensive and complex CAD programs. Business diagramming products (Visio Standard, Visio Business Modeler and Visio Maps) accounted for 29% of total company sales in 1998; technical drawing products (Visio Technical and IntelliCAD) 23%; and the IT design and documentation product group (Visio Professional and Visio Network Equipment) 48%. Revenues from customers outside of North America accounted for 41% of the total.

Visio's principal product development efforts focus on continued enhancements to the graphics engines for its Visio products and IntelliCAD, development of new customer solutions and applications, including increased drawing complexity, increased number of objects, increased "smartness" of SmartShapes objects and improved database connectivity. Visio 2000, the company's next generation Visio product family, was to be launched starting in the fourth quarter of FY 99 (Sep.).>

Per Share Data ($) (Year Ended Sep. 30)	1998	1997	1996	1995	1994	1993	1992	1991	1990	1989
Tangible Bk. Val.	4.21	2.72	2.02	NA	NA	NA	NA	NA	NA	NA
Cash Flow	1.10	0.59	0.85	NA	NA	NA	NA	NA	NA	NA
Earnings	0.89	0.50	0.38	NA	NA	NA	NA	NA	NA	NA
Dividends	Nil	Nil	Nil	NA	NA	NA	NA	NA	NA	NA
Payout Ratio	Nil	Nil	Nil	NA	NA	NA	NA	NA	NA	NA
Prices - High	50⅞	42⅝	26⅜	NA	NA	NA	NA	NA	NA	NA
- Low	14	18⅛	10⅜	NA	NA	NA	NA	NA	NA	NA
P/E Ratio - High	57	85	69	NA	NA	NA	NA	NA	NA	NA
- Low	16	36	27	NA	NA	NA	NA	NA	NA	NA
Income Statement Analysis (Million $)										
Revs.	166	100	59.7	NA	NA	NA	NA	NA	NA	NA
Oper. Inc.	48.8	30.0	15.9	NA	NA	NA	NA	NA	NA	NA
Depr.	6.7	2.7	1.3	NA	NA	NA	NA	NA	NA	NA
Int. Exp.	Nil	Nil	Nil	NA	NA	NA	NA	NA	NA	NA
Pretax Inc.	37.7	20.4	16.1	NA	NA	NA	NA	NA	NA	NA
Eff. Tax Rate	25%	26%	31%	NA	NA	NA	NA	NA	NA	NA
Net Inc.	28.1	15.1	11.1	NA	NA	NA	NA	NA	NA	NA
Balance Sheet & Other Fin. Data (Million $)										
Cash	67.1	79.6	61.1	NA	NA	NA	NA	NA	NA	NA
Curr. Assets	138	98.3	68.2	NA	NA	NA	NA	NA	NA	NA
Total Assets	159	109	71.6	NA	NA	NA	NA	NA	NA	NA
Curr. Liab.	32.2	32.4	16.2	NA	NA	NA	NA	NA	NA	NA
LT Debt	Nil	Nil	0.1	NA	NA	NA	NA	NA	NA	NA
Common Eqty.	127	76.8	55.2	NA	NA	NA	NA	NA	NA	NA
Total Cap.	127	76.8	55.4	NA	NA	NA	NA	NA	NA	NA
Cap. Exp.	7.7	NA	NA	NA	NA	NA	NA	NA	NA	NA
Cash Flow	34.8	17.8	12.4	NA	NA	NA	NA	NA	NA	NA
Curr. Ratio	4.3	3.0	4.2	NA	NA	NA	NA	NA	NA	NA
% LT Debt of Cap.	Nil	Nil	0.3	NA	NA	NA	NA	NA	NA	NA
% Net Inc.of Revs.	16.9	15.2	18.6	NA	NA	NA	NA	NA	NA	NA
% Ret. on Assets	20.9	16.7	24.4	NA	NA	NA	NA	NA	NA	NA
% Ret. on Equity	27.6	22.9	40.9	NA	NA	NA	NA	NA	NA	NA

Data as orig reptd.; bef. results of disc opers/spec. items. Per share data adj. for stk. divs. Bold denotes diluted EPS (FASB 128)-prior periods restated. E-Estimated. NA-Not Available. NM-Not Meaningful. NR-Not Ranked.

Office—2211 Elliott Avenue, Seattle, WA 98121. **Tel**—(206) 956-6000. **Website**—http://www.visio.com **Pres & CEO**—J. A. Jaech. **SVP & CFO**—S. M. Gordon. **Secy**—W. K. McGraw. **Dirs**—T. A. Alberg, T. Byers, J. A. Jaech, T. C. Johnson, J. R. Johnston, D. J. Mackenzie, S. Oki. **Transfer Agent & Registrar**—ChaseMellon Shareholder Services LLC, South Hackensack, NJ. **Incorporated**—in Washington in 1989. **Empl**— 555. **S&P Analyst:** P.T.W.

STANDARD
&POOR'S
STOCK REPORTS

Vital Signs, Inc.

NASDAQ Symbol **VITL**

In S&P SmallCap 600

09-OCT-99

Industry:
Health Care (Medical Products & Supplies)

Summary: Vital Signs markets a wide variety of single-use anesthesia, respiratory and related critical care products.

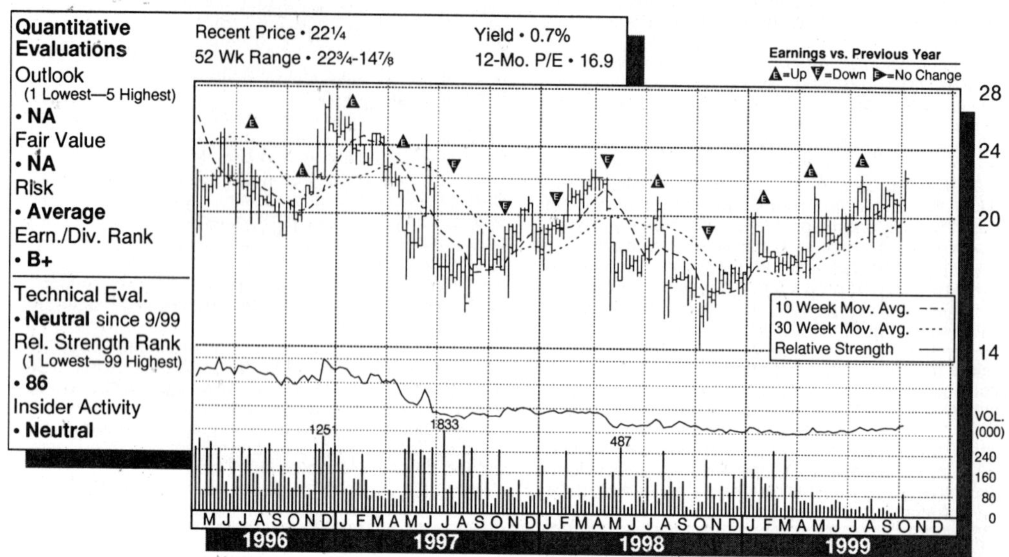

Business Profile - 28-JUL-99

The company recently cut its sales force about 50%, to approximately 90, resulting in $3 million of savings in the FY 99 (Sep.) first half. VITL also restructured its sales compensation program, providing higher commissions on incremental sales. Following the restructuring, the company's goal is to achieve double digit sales and earnings growth in FY 99. VITL has said that the reduction and consolidation of the sales force is proceeding as planned, and added that manufacturing and other efficiencies should contribute to earnings improvement over the next several quarters. In October 1998, directors authorized the repurchase of up to 1.0 million common shares. As of January 1999, officers and directors owned about 58% of the shares outstanding.

Operational Review - 28-JUL-99

Net sales in the six months ended March 31, 1999, edged up fractionally, year to year, as increased unit sales were offset by lower selling prices. Gross margins narrowed, on a less favorable product mix and lower selling prices. With a 15% decrease in SG&A expenses, reflecting a reduction in the sales force, pretax income increased 12%. After taxes at 31.5%, versus 34.5%, income climbed 22%, to $8,372,000 ($0.68 a share, on 2.9% fewer shares), from $5,325,000 ($0.54, before a charge of $0.12 for the cumulative effect of an accounting change).

Stock Performance - 08-OCT-99

In the past 30 trading days, VITL's shares have increased 7%, compared to a 0.91% fall in the S&P 500. Average trading volume for the past five days was 17,480 shares, compared with the 40-day moving average of 6,913 shares.

Key Stock Statistics

Dividend Rate/Share	0.16	Shareholders	457
Shs. outstg. (M)	12.3	Market cap. (B)	$0.273
Avg. daily vol. (M)	0.008	Inst. holdings	33%
Tang. Bk. Value/Share	7.44		
Beta	0.39		

Value of $10,000 invested 5 years ago: $ 16,170

Fiscal Year Ending Sep. 30

	1999	1998	1997	1996	1995	1994
Revenues (Million $)						
1Q	31.01	30.92	22.83	22.12	21.33	20.79
2Q	32.41	32.30	23.85	22.59	22.68	21.26
3Q	32.41	31.86	28.36	23.02	22.69	21.42
4Q	—	31.33	28.53	22.59	22.85	21.66
Yr.	—	126.5	103.6	90.73	89.55	85.12
Earnings Per Share ($)						
1Q	**0.32**	**0.27**	**0.37**	0.35	0.25	0.25
2Q	**0.36**	**0.27**	0.37	0.36	0.30	0.24
3Q	**0.36**	**0.21**	-0.16	0.37	0.34	0.21
4Q	—	**0.29**	0.30	0.37	0.35	-0.56
Yr.	—	**1.03**	**0.87**	1.44	1.24	0.13

Next earnings report expected: mid November

Dividend Data (Dividends have been paid since 1994.)

Amount ($)	Date Decl.	Ex-Div. Date	Stock of Record	Payment Date
0.040	Nov. 11	Nov. 12	Nov. 09	Nov. 16 '98
0.040	Feb. 05	Feb. 08	Feb. 01	Feb. 08 '99
0.040	May. 05	May. 07	May. 07	May. 14 '99
0.040	Aug. 05	Aug. 09	Jul. 29	Aug. 05 '99

A Division of The McGraw-Hill Companies

Vital Signs, Inc.

Business Summary - 28-JUL-99

Vital Signs is a pioneer in the introduction and development of a number of single-use products for the health care industry. Single-patient products have captured an increasing share of the medical products market because of lower cost as well as reduced risk of transmitting infection. In 1981, the Totowa, NJ-based company introduced the first clear plastic single-use air-filled cushion face mask for anesthesia delivery and resuscitation. The face mask is still the company's best-selling product.

Other single-use products introduced by VITL include a manual resuscitator (1984), a laryngoscope system (1988), a general anesthesia kit that can combine more than 20 items in one package (1989), and the first single-use infant lung resuscitation circuit capable of adjusting pressurization (1992). VITL also pioneered a special tracheal tube for use during high-risk deliveries, a pediatric emergency kit, and a device for measuring the effect of neouromuscular blockage during anesthesia. Innovative new products include the company's flexible face mask called the Flexmask; a flush device for vascular access catheters called Vasceze; and a closed suction system designed for ventilated patients, the Isocath.

In July 1997, the company acquired Marquest Medical Products, a manufacturer of respiratory products with $20 million in annual sales. It believed that Marquest would eventually attain the same status in critical care that VITL has in anesthetics, and the parent company restructured its sales force to that end. VITL divested its endoscopic products line in FY 96.

Revenues in FY 98 (Sep.) were derived from anesthesia sales (48% of total sales), respiratory sales (30%) and critical care sales (22%). International revenues accounted for about 12% of net sales.

The company's principal strategy has been to sell its anesthesia and respiratory products to U.S. hospitals through its own sales force. Sales to hospitals through national distributors accounted for 33% of the total in FY 98. VITL's sales force participates with these national distributors in making sales to hospitals. In FY 98, one large national distributor accounted for 13% of net sales.

In FY 98, the company restructured its sales compensation program, providing higher commissions on incremental sales. In addition, during the FY 98 second quarter, VITL expanded its sales force in connection with the acquisition of Marquest from 90 persons to 184. However, the sales force has since been reduced to 90.

Per Share Data ($) (Year Ended Sep. 30)	1998	1997	1996	1995	1994	1993	1992	1991	1990	1989
Tangible Bk. Val.	7.59	6.57	7.17	5.94	5.12	4.69	4.37	NA	NA	NA
Cash Flow	1.30	1.10	1.62	1.36	0.23	1.07	0.88	NA	NA	NA
Earnings	1.03	0.88	1.44	1.24	0.13	0.98	0.81	0.66	NA	NA
Dividends	0.16	0.16	0.13	0.09	0.02	Nil	Nil	Nil	NA	NA
Payout Ratio	16%	18%	9%	7%	15%	Nil	Nil	Nil	NA	NA
Prices - High	$22\frac{5}{8}$	$25\frac{7}{8}$	33	27	$15\frac{1}{4}$	$29\frac{3}{4}$	$35\frac{1}{2}$	$28\frac{1}{4}$	NA	NA
- Low	14	$15\frac{3}{8}$	$18\frac{1}{2}$	$10\frac{3}{4}$	$7\frac{3}{4}$	$13\frac{1}{2}$	$18\frac{1}{4}$	$9\frac{1}{4}$	NA	NA
P/E Ratio - High	22	29	23	19	117	30	44	43	NA	NA
- Low	14	17	13	9	60	14	23	14	NA	NA
Income Statement Analysis (Million $)										
Revs.	127	104	90.7	89.6	85.1	79.9	65.7	NA	NA	NA
Oper. Inc.	23.9	25.6	26.9	25.0	16.6	18.9	16.2	NA	NA	NA
Depr.	3.4	2.9	2.3	1.5	1.3	1.2	1.0	NA	NA	NA
Int. Exp.	0.4	0.5	0.3	0.4	0.6	0.6	0.6	NA	NA	NA
Pretax Inc.	18.9	16.9	28.4	25.3	5.8	18.6	15.2	NA	NA	NA
Eff. Tax Rate	30%	33%	34%	36%	71%	32%	32%	NA	NA	NA
Net Inc.	13.1	11.3	18.8	16.1	1.7	12.7	10.4	NA	NA	NA
Balance Sheet & Other Fin. Data (Million $)										
Cash	20.3	3.7	18.3	12.1	29.1	27.9	NA	NA	NA	NA
Curr. Assets	45.8	51.3	53.5	45.7	59.7	55.1	NA	NA	NA	NA
Total Assets	138	137	124	110	92.0	92.0	79.0	NA	NA	NA
Curr. Liab.	10.2	13.2	8.7	12.8	9.3	8.3	NA	NA	NA	NA
LT Debt	2.5	5.5	2.7	3.2	3.7	5.8	6.4	NA	NA	NA
Common Eqty.	121	112	110	92.6	77.7	76.1	63.8	NA	NA	NA
Total Cap.	124	119	114	96.8	82.0	83.4	70.2	NA	NA	NA
Cap. Exp.	10.6	10.0	8.6	2.0	2.3	1.5	0.5	NA	NA	NA
Cash Flow	16.6	14.2	21.1	17.7	3.0	13.9	11.4	NA	NA	NA
Curr. Ratio	4.5	3.9	6.2	3.6	6.4	6.7	NA	NA	NA	NA
% LT Debt of Cap.	2.0	4.6	2.4	3.3	4.5	7.0	9.2	NA	NA	NA
% Net Inc.of Revs.	10.4	10.9	20.7	18.0	2.0	15.9	15.8	NA	NA	NA
% Ret. on Assets	9.5	8.7	16.1	16.0	1.8	13.8	14.4	NA	NA	NA
% Ret. on Equity	11.2	10.1	18.6	18.9	2.2	16.7	18.1	NA	NA	NA

Data as orig reptd.; bef. results of disc opers/spec. items. Per share data adj. for stk. divs. Bold denotes diluted EPS (FASB 128)-prior periods restated. E-Estimated. NA-Not Available. NM-Not Meaningful. NR-Not Ranked.

Office—20 Campus Rd., Totowa, NJ 07512. **Tel**—(973) 790-1330. **Website**—http://www/vital-signs.com **Pres & CEO**—T. D. Wall. **EVP, CFO & Secy**—A. J. Dimun. **Dirs**—D. J. Bershad, A, J, Dimun, J. J. Thomas, J. Toedtman, T. D. Wall, B. Wicker. **Transfer Agent & Registrar**—Union National Bank, Charlotte, NC. **Incorporated**—in New York in 1972; reincorporated in New Jersey in 1988. **Empl**— 1,052. **S&P Analyst:** John J. Arege

STANDARD
&POOR'S
STOCK REPORTS

Volt Information Sciences

NYSE Symbol **VOL**

In S&P SmallCap 600

11-OCT-99

Industry:
Services (Employment)

Summary: This company operates in the areas of staffing services, telecommunications and information solutions, and prepress publishing systems.

Quantitative Evaluations

Outlook
(1 Lowest—5 Highest)
• **NA**

Fair Value
• **NA**

Risk
• **Average**

Earn./Div. Rank
• **B**

Technical Eval.
• **Bearish** since 9/99

Rel. Strength Rank
(1 Lowest—99 Highest)
• **45**

Insider Activity
• **NA**

Recent Price • 21⅞
52 Wk Range • 26⅞-15½
Yield • Nil
12-Mo. P/E • 13.3

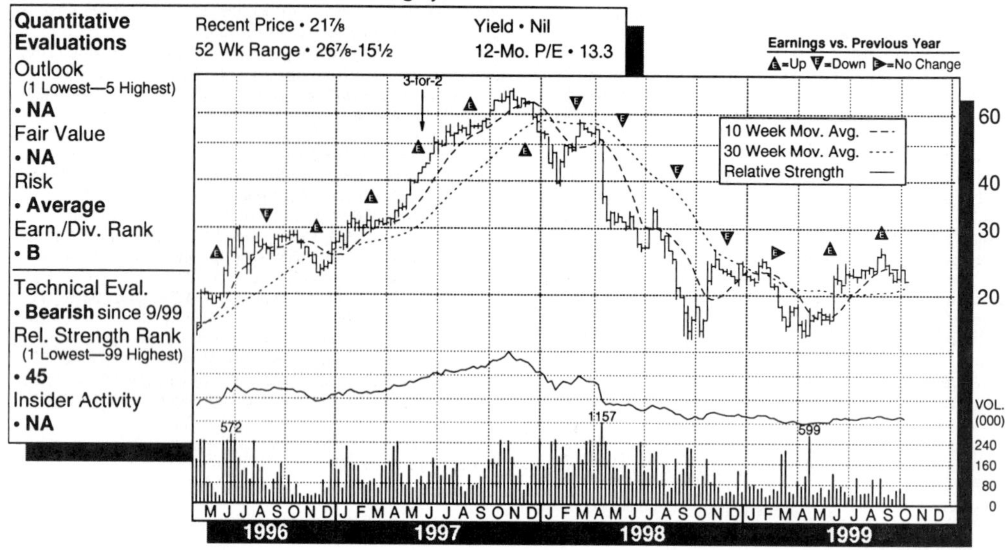

Business Profile - 11-OCT-99

Results in the first nine months of FY 99 (Oct.) include a previously deferred $2.0 million gain on sale in 1997 of the company's interest in a Brazilian joint venture. Volt has initiated an evaluation of the profitability of its commercial light and industrial branch offices and as a result closed five offices in 1999 with a possible 10 to 15 more expected. In December 1998, VOL acquired Gatton Computing Group Limited, a provider of Information Technology (IT) contractor resourcing services and IT managed services. The acquisition, along with two toll-free directories acquired in late 1998, and a network solutions company acquired in April 1999, resulted in an increase in intangible assets of $37.0 million.

Operational Review - 11-OCT-99

Net sales in the nine months ended July 30, 1999, increased 31%, year to year, as growth in the staffing services, telephone directory, telecommunications services, and computer systems segments outweighed a decline in the electronic publication and typesetting systems segment. Despite profit improvement in the staffing services, telecommunications services and computer systems division, margins narrowed in the other two business lines; the gain in operating profit was held to 16%. After a $2.0 million gain on the sale of a Brazilian joint venture, which was offset by greater interest expense, and substantially higher minority interest income, net income rose 36%, to $15,942,000 ($1.05 a share), from $11,730,000 ($0.77).

Stock Performance - 08-OCT-99

In the past 30 trading days, VOL's shares have declined 15%, compared to a 0.91% fall in the S&P 500. Average trading volume for the past five days was 9,220 shares, compared with the 40-day moving average of 10,456 shares.

Key Stock Statistics

Dividend Rate/Share	Nil	Shareholders	433
Shs. outstg. (M)	15.0	Market cap. (B)	$0.329
Avg. daily vol. (M)	0.010	Inst. holdings	34%
Tang. Bk. Value/Share	10.95		
Beta	0.96		

Value of $10,000 invested 5 years ago: $ 39,772

Fiscal Year Ending Oct. 31

	1999	1998	1997	1996	1995	1994
Revenues (Million $)						
1Q	489.9	361.5	288.8	224.8	183.3	142.6
2Q	532.3	412.6	346.9	252.3	190.6	161.7
3Q	560.0	431.8	370.7	258.9	225.9	165.9
4Q	—	502.7	410.6	312.9	307.5	250.7
Yr.	—	1,709	1,420	1,049	907.4	720.9
Earnings Per Share ($)						
1Q	**0.17**	**0.17**	**0.33**	0.15	0.14	-0.14
2Q	**0.38**	**0.28**	0.47	0.34	0.10	0.40
3Q	**0.51**	**0.32**	0.61	0.31	0.35	0.16
4Q	—	**0.61**	1.20	0.70	0.55	0.41
Yr.	—	**1.37**	**2.62**	1.51	1.13	0.84

Next earnings report expected: mid December

Dividend Data

No cash dividend has been paid since 1967. A three-for-two stock split was effected in 1997.

A Division of The McGraw-Hill Companies

Volt Information Sciences, Inc.

Business Summary - 11-OCT-99

Volt Information Sciences (VOL) operates three major businesses: staffing services, telecommunications and information solutions, and prepress publishing systems. The telecommunications and information solutions unit is further divided into three segments: telephone directory, telecommunications services, and computer systems. Revenue contributions by industry segment in FY 98 (Oct.) were: staffing services (77%), telephone directory (5%), telecommunications services (10%), computer systems (3%), electronic publication and typesetting (5%).

The staffing services segment provides a broad range of employee staffing services, including temporary help, technical personnel placement, and other contingent staffing services, employment and direct hire placement services, payroll services, employment outsourcing service and employee leasing services. As of August 1999, the company had 323 offices across the U.S. but was evaluating the possible closure of several under-performing branch offices. An insignificant loss of revenue is expected from these closings, as alternative offices will serve their markets.

The telecommunications services segment consists of three segments. The telephone directory segment publishes independent telephone directories, provides telephone directory production, commercial printing, database management, sales and marketing services, licensing of directory production and contract management software to directory publishers. During FY 98, the division added 62 new directories, bringing the total directories to 129.

The telecommunications services division provides engineering, design, construction, installation, maintenance, removals and distribution of telecommunications products. Customers include private and government entities consisting of telephone operating companies, local exchange carriers, cable television, utility companies, and state and local government units.

The computer systems segment provides directory assistance outsourcing services. The unit designs, develops and markets computer-based directory assistance systems for the telecommunications industry. Computer based service projects are also provided to public utilities and financial institutions.

The prepress publishing system division designs, develops, manufactures, markets and services computerized imagesetting and publication systems equipment and software that automates the various prepress production steps in the publishing process.

The company owns a 50% interest in westVista Advertising Services, a joint venture with a subsidiary of TELUS Corporation. The venture was formed in FY 98 for the acquisition or establishment and subsequent operation of one or more businesses engaged in the publication of telephone directories in the western U.S. During the second quarter of FY 99, the venture made its first acquisition, purchasing 11 community Yellow Pages directories.

Per Share Data ($) (Year Ended Oct. 31)	1998	1997	1996	1995	1994	1993	1992	1991	1990	1989
Tangible Bk. Val.	12.10	10.99	7.89	7.01	5.90	4.98	5.15	5.09	4.65	4.61
Cash Flow	2.73	3.98	2.67	1.97	1.58	0.45	0.85	0.80	0.66	0.96
Earnings	1.37	2.63	1.51	1.13	0.84	-0.26	0.08	0.02	-0.06	0.29
Dividends	Nil	Nil	Nil	Nil	Nil	Nil	Nil	Nil	Nil	Nil
Payout Ratio	Nil	Nil	Nil	Nil	Nil	Nil	Nil	Nil	Nil	Nil
Prices - High	58¼	70¼	30⅜	18⅛	10	6⅝	4⅛	3⅞	4¾	6
- Low	15¼	26⅛	12⅝	9	5⅛	3⅝	2 5/16	1¾	1 13/16	3⅝
P/E Ratio - High	43	27	20	16	12	NM	54	NM	NM	20
- Low	11	10	8	8	6	NM	30	NM	NM	12
Income Statement Analysis (Million $)										
Revs.	1,709	1,401	1,049	907	721	558	521	466	489	493
Oper. Inc.	60.1	69.8	51.0	45.0	24.5	15.4	14.1	5.4	10.4	17.2
Depr.	20.8	20.5	16.0	12.0	10.7	10.2	11.1	11.3	12.2	12.3
Int. Exp.	5.7	5.7	5.0	6.0	7.5	11.1	11.6	13.4	14.4	14.5
Pretax Inc.	35.8	62.4	34.9	27.3	19.8	-5.6	1.8	-1.1	-1.7	9.5
Eff. Tax Rate	41%	37%	36%	40%	39%	NM	39%	NM	NM	43%
Net Inc.	20.9	40.0	22.4	16.4	12.0	-3.7	1.1	0.3	-1.0	5.4
Balance Sheet & Other Fin. Data (Million $)										
Cash	31.6	54.2	13.3	25.4	22.0	43.3	30.0	20.0	16.0	23.0
Curr. Assets	373	336	243	182	155	159	147	121	124	140
Total Assets	469	419	337	264	227	236	227	215	232	256
Curr. Liab.	195	166	130	125	93.6	98.0	64.0	48.0	58.0	70.0
LT Debt	54.0	55.4	57.0	29.0	41.0	58.0	81.0	86.0	92.0	93.0
Common Eqty.	201	178	130	107	90.0	78.0	80.0	80.0	82.0	92.0
Total Cap.	275	252	208	139	133	138	162	166	174	186
Cap. Exp.	22.4	15.5	36.7	11.9	14.9	11.3	7.1	6.8	10.9	13.9
Cash Flow	41.7	60.5	38.7	28.4	22.8	6.5	12.2	11.6	11.2	17.7
Curr. Ratio	1.9	2.0	1.9	1.5	1.7	1.6	2.3	2.5	2.1	2.0
% LT Debt of Cap.	19.7	21.9	27.7	20.8	30.6	42.0	50.0	51.8	52.9	50.2
% Net Inc.of Revs.	1.2	2.9	2.1	1.8	1.7	NM	0.2	0.1	NM	1.1
% Ret. on Assets	4.7	10.6	7.5	6.7	5.2	NM	0.5	0.2	NM	2.1
% Ret. on Equity	11.0	26.0	18.9	16.6	14.4	NM	1.4	0.4	NM	6.0

Data as orig reptd.; bef. results of disc opers/spec. items. Per share data adj. for stk. divs. Bold denotes diluted EPS (FASB 128)-prior periods restated. E-Estimated. NA-Not Available. NM-Not Meaningful. NR-Not Ranked.

Office—1221 Ave. of the Americas, New York, NY 10020-1579. **Tel**—(212) 704-2400. **Website**—http://www.volt-tech.com **Chrmn, Pres & CEO**—W. Shaw. **EVP & Secy**—J. Shaw. **SVP, CFO & Investor Contact**—James J. Groberg. **Treas**—L. M. Guarino. **Dirs**—J. J. Groberg, M. N. Kaplan, I. B. Robins, J. Shaw, S. A. Shaw, W. Shaw, J. R. Torell III, W. H. Turner. **Transfer Agent & Registrar**—Registrar & Transfer Co., NYC. **Incorporated**—in New York in 1957. **Empl**— 38,700. **S&P Analyst:** Sandy H. Katzler

STANDARD
&POOR'S
STOCK REPORTS

WD-40 Company

Nasdaq Symbol **WDFC**

In S&P SmallCap 600

09-OCT-99 **Industry:** Hardware & Tools

Summary: This company, which is best known for its WD-40 product, also makes and markets 3-IN-ONE Oil and Lava soap.

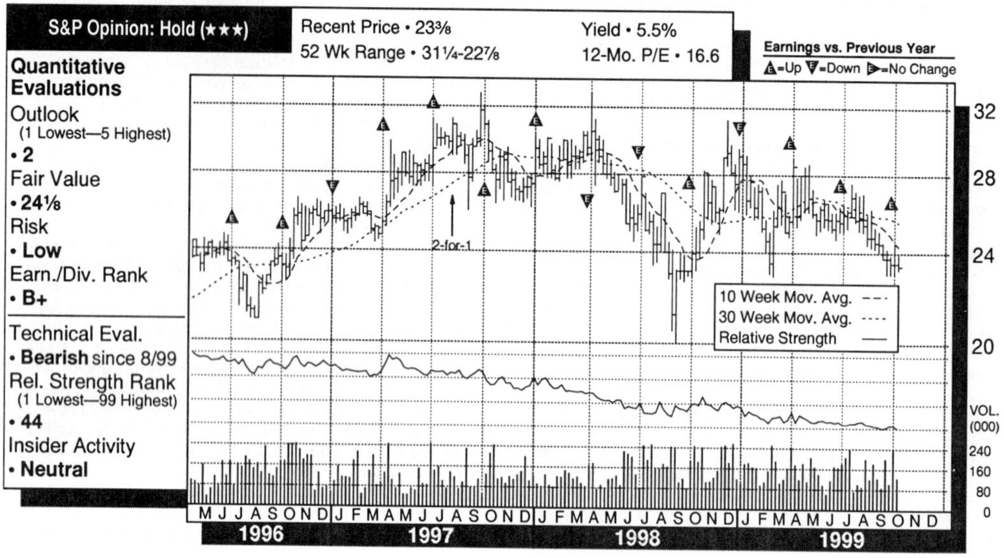

Overview - 15-JUL-99

Revenue should increase in the mid single digits in FY 99 (Aug.) and into FY 00, falling short of the company's goal of double-digit growth. Although we expect flat to down U.S. sales of the flagship WD-40 lubricant, overseas sales, particularly in Europe, should attain the double-digit growth target. The company has resisted fully leveraging the WD-40 brand name into many products in order to avoid risks to the perceived value and status of the brand. Instead, WDFC has opted to acquire or introduce selected products, such as Lava industrial soap, that would still be of interest to the core handyman and auto mechanic market. Lava should get a sales boost from product tie-ins with the WD-40 lubricant. We expect Lava sales to more than offset the announced phase out of the T.A.L. 5 lubricant. Margins will be restricted by costs associated with developing the Lava product.

Valuation - 15-JUL-99

The market has taken a wait-and-see attitude regarding the WDFC's goal to grow the business via introduction of new products related to the three major brands. Until new products are forthcoming, the main attraction of the stock is a hefty dividend yield of about 5.0%. However, the payout ratio has topped 90% of earnings for several years, leaving little money to grow the business. In fact, WDFC borrowed $16 million to acquire Lava. While the company's long-term debt to equity ratio is a reasonable 30%, we question the wisdom of maintaining such a high dividend when funds might be used to acquire a major new brand or for sizable share repurchases. Nevertheless, the company has indicated its preference to maintain the dividend. The shares, trading at about 17X our FY 00 (Aug.) EPS estimate, are a reasonable holding for yield investors, but growth investors should look elsewhere.

Key Stock Statistics

S&P EPS Est. 2000	1.50	Tang. Bk. Value/Share	1.47
P/E on S&P Est. 2000	15.6	Beta	0.89
S&P EPS Est. 2001	1.60	Shareholders	2,166
Dividend Rate/Share	1.28	Market cap. (B)	$0.365
Shs. outstg. (M)	15.6	Inst. holdings	34%
Avg. daily vol. (M)	0.033		

Value of $10,000 invested 5 years ago: $ 13,116

Fiscal Year Ending Aug. 31

	1999	1998	1997	1996	1995	1994
Revenues (Million $)						
1Q	29.62	33.60	28.27	27.61	29.77	28.88
2Q	41.71	39.17	39.81	35.08	29.39	27.56
3Q	33.47	31.83	34.53	34.23	29.92	29.46
4Q	41.55	39.80	35.30	33.99	27.70	26.27
Yr.	146.3	144.4	137.9	130.9	116.8	112.2
Earnings Per Share ($)						
1Q	**0.24**	0.34	0.28	0.34	0.36	0.34
2Q	**0.43**	**0.40**	**0.42**	0.39	0.36	-0.17
3Q	**0.30**	**0.26**	0.33	0.33	0.32	0.34
4Q	**0.44**	**0.40**	0.35	0.33	0.29	0.32
Yr.	**1.41**	**1.40**	**1.37**	**1.38**	1.33	0.82

Next earnings report expected: mid December

Dividend Data (Dividends have been paid since 1973.)

Amount ($)	Date Decl.	Ex-Div. Date	Stock of Record	Payment Date
0.320	Dec. 17	Jan. 06	Jan. 08	Jan. 29 '99
0.320	Mar. 30	Apr. 08	Apr. 12	Apr. 30 '99
0.320	Jun. 30	Jul. 08	Jul. 12	Jul. 30 '99
0.320	Sep. 28	Oct. 14	Oct. 18	Nov. 09 '99

A Division of The McGraw-Hill Companies

WD-40 Company

Business Summary - 15-JUL-99

After more than four decades of being identified with a single petroleum-based product, WD-40, this company has dramatically shifted its corporate identity and strategy.

With the acquisition of the 3-IN-ONE Oil brand in December 1995 and with the April 1999 acquisition of Lava brand heavy duty hand cleaners from Block Drug Co., WDFC has become a company identified with three products.

The company's goal is to dominate the entire category of lubrication products by combining the smaller niche markets targeted by 3-IN-ONE Oil with the broad-based market held by the WD-40 brand.

The WD-40 product is a multi-purpose product which can act as a lubricant, a rust preventative, a penetrant and a moisture displacer. It has a wide variety of uses in the home and in industrial applications, as well as in the protection of sporting goods and marine and automotive equipment. It is sold (primarily in aerosol cans) through chain stores, automotive parts outlets, hardware and sporting goods stores, and industrial distributors and suppliers.

3-IN-ONE Oil is a drip oil lubricant that is sold through the same distribution channels as the WD-40 brand. The key to its success is the lubrication control it gives consumers and industrial users, allowing precise application for small mechanisms and assemblies, tool maintenance and threads on screws and bolts. As a low-cost, entry-level lubricant, it has excellent growth potential in the developing nations of Eastern Europe, Latin America and Asia.

The new product lineup gives WD-40 Co. the opportunity to pursue a comprehensive and targeted marketing strategy. The acquisition of the 3-IN-ONE Oil brand provides WDFC with a built-in distribution network in 17 countries, including several markets in which the WD-40 product has not been sold.

In April 1999, WDFC completed the purchase of the Lava brand hand cleaner product line for $19 million, approximately two times Lava's most recent annual revenue of $9.3 million. The company noted that it does not anticipate significant changes to the bottom line from Lava sales in FY 99 (Aug.). However, WDFC expects Lava to have a positive impact on earnings in FY 00.

In June 1999, WDFC reported that it would be discontinuing its T.A.L. 5 product, which was introduced in FY 97. T.A.L. 5 (Triple Additive Lubricant/5) is an extra-strength lubricant for heavy duty applications. The company noted that T.A.L. 5 did not fit into its strategic emphasis on brands with wide appeal. WDFC intends to exit the T.A.L. 5 brand over the next few months.

Per Share Data ($) (Year Ended Aug. 31)	1999	1998	1997	1996	1995	1994	1993	1992	1991	1990
Tangible Bk. Val.	NA	2.72	2.44	2.13	2.89	2.73	2.98	2.96	2.69	2.58
Cash Flow	NA	1.54	1.52	1.50	1.40	0.88	1.30	1.23	1.04	1.05
Earnings	1.41	1.40	1.38	1.38	1.33	0.82	1.26	1.19	1.01	1.02
Dividends	1.28	1.28	1.25	1.24	1.21	1.15	1.15	1.08	0.86	1.01
Payout Ratio	91%	91%	91%	90%	91%	139%	91%	91%	85%	99%
Prices - High	29 1/8	33	32 7/8	26 5/8	22 3/4	24	24 3/8	25	17	17 1/4
- Low	22 7/8	20	24 3/8	20 1/4	19 3/8	18 7/8	21 1/2	15 1/8	11 7/8	11 3/4
P/E Ratio - High	21	24	24	19	17	29	19	21	17	17
- Low	16	14	18	15	15	23	17	13	12	11
Income Statement Analysis (Million $)										
Revs.	NA	144	138	131	117	112	109	100	89.8	91.0
Oper. Inc.	NA	36.3	36.9	34.4	32.5	33.2	33.6	28.8	24.2	23.8
Depr.	NA	2.2	2.2	1.8	1.0	0.8	0.6	0.6	0.5	0.5
Int. Exp.	NA	Nil	Nil	NA	NA	NA	Nil	Nil	Nil	Nil
Pretax Inc.	NA	34.3	33.4	33.4	32.7	20.5	31.7	29.5	25.1	25.2
Eff. Tax Rate	NA	36%	36%	36%	37%	38%	39%	39%	39%	39%
Net Inc.	NA	21.9	21.4	21.3	20.5	12.7	19.3	18.1	15.3	15.5
Balance Sheet & Other Fin. Data (Million $)										
Cash	NA	8.6	10.9	6.5	24.3	22.7	21.9	19.1	24.9	21.6
Curr. Assets	NA	49.8	42.4	37.6	49.6	45.5	43.2	41.4	43.9	43.2
Total Assets	NA	70.9	65.4	61.7	59.6	54.9	58.8	53.5	47.8	46.8
Curr. Liab.	NA	13.9	11.4	11.0	11.1	8.2	9.7	8.2	6.9	7.6
LT Debt	NA	0.9	1.7	2.4	3.1	3.8	2.6	Nil	Nil	Nil
Common Eqty.	NA	55.0	51.3	47.2	44.5	42.1	45.7	45.2	40.7	39.0
Total Cap.	NA	56.0	53.0	49.7	47.6	45.9	48.3	45.3	40.8	39.2
Cap. Exp.	NA	1.3	1.5	1.4	1.4	0.8	1.4	0.7	1.1	0.5
Cash Flow	NA	24.0	23.6	23.1	21.4	13.5	19.9	18.6	15.8	16.0
Curr. Ratio	NA	3.6	3.7	3.4	4.5	5.6	4.4	5.1	6.3	5.7
% LT Debt of Cap.	NA	1.6	3.2	5.2	6.6	8.3	5.5	Nil	Nil	Nil
% Net Inc.of Revs.	NA	15.2	15.5	16.3	17.5	11.3	17.7	18.1	17.0	17.0
% Ret. on Assets	NA	32.1	33.6	35.1	35.7	22.3	34.4	35.5	32.4	33.9
% Ret. on Equity	NA	41.2	43.4	46.5	47.2	28.9	42.5	41.8	38.4	40.4

Data as orig reptd.; bef. results of disc opers/spec. items. Per share data adj. for stk. divs. Bold denotes diluted EPS (FASB 128)-prior periods restated. E-Estimated. NA-Not Available. NM-Not Meaningful. NR-Not Ranked.

Office—1061 Cudahy Place, San Diego, CA 92110. **Tel**—(619) 275-1400. **Website**—http://www.wd40.com **Chrmn**—J. S. Barry. **Pres & CEO**—G. O. Ridge. **VP & CFO**—T. J. Tranchina. **Secy**—H. F. Harmsen. **Dirs**—J. S. Barry, M. L. Crivello, D. W. Derbes, H. F. Harmsen, J. L. Heckel, G. O. Ridge, M. L. Roulette, G. C. Schleif, C. F. Sehnert, E. J. Walsh. **Transfer Agent & Registrar**—Harris Trust Co. of California, Los Angeles. **Incorporated**—in California in 1953. **Empl**— 166. **S&P Analyst:** J. Friendly

STANDARD
&POOR'S
STOCK REPORTS

Wabash National

NYSE Symbol **WNC**

In S&P SmallCap 600

09-OCT-99 **Industry:** Trucks & Parts

Summary: This company, the largest U.S. manufacturer of truck trailers, is the leading producer of both fiberglass-reinforced plastic trailers and aluminum plate trailers.

Quantitative Evaluations

Outlook (1 Lowest—5 Highest)
• **5**

Fair Value
• **36⅛**

Risk
• **Average**

Earn./Div. Rank
• **NR**

Technical Eval.
• **Bullish** since 4/99

Rel. Strength Rank (1 Lowest—99 Highest)
• **54**

Insider Activity
• **NA**

Recent Price • 19⅞
52 Wk Range • 22½-10⅝
Yield • 0.8%
12-Mo. P/E • 18.6

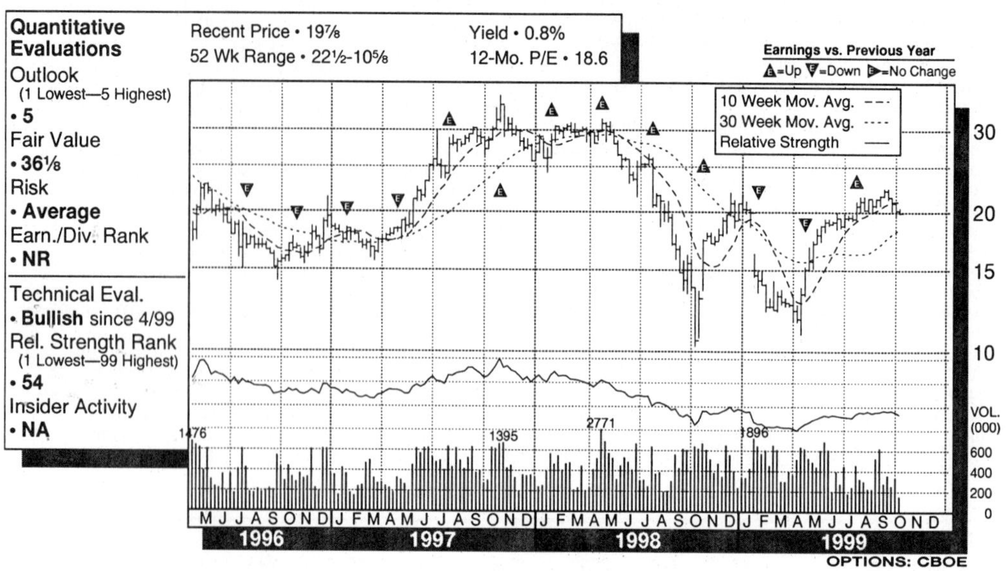

Business Profile - 30-SEP-99

The company believes it has created opportunities for growth through the startup of a composite materials plant, the acquisition of the Fruehauf retail distribution network, and expansion into the European bimodal and conventional trailer markets. WNC has been replacing its aluminum plate trailer with a new composite plate trailer made of steel and plastic. The company continues to expand its international markets, and further reduce its costs through in-house manufacturing of high value components. In August 1999, WNC projected capital expenditures of $40 million to $60 million over the next 12 to 24 months. Backlog at June 30, 1999, exceeded $1.2 billion, including $750 million from composite plate trailers.

Operational Review - 30-SEP-99

Net sales in the first half of 1999 advanced 14%, year to year, reflecting strong production of the company's new composite plate trailer, and increased leasing and finance revenues, which outweighed slower growth in the retail distribution business. Gross margins widened on the increased volume and a change in the product mix, and with well controlled SG&A expense and lower interest expense, pretax earnings were up 30%. After taxes at 41.3%, versus 39.9%, net income advanced 27%, to $16,714,000 ($0.68 a share, after preferred dividends), from $13,161,000 ($0.60).

Stock Performance - 08-OCT-99

In the past 30 trading days, WNC's shares have declined 7%, compared to a 0.91% fall in the S&P 500. Average trading volume for the past five days was 29,700 shares, compared with the 40-day moving average of 74,805 shares.

Key Stock Statistics

Dividend Rate/Share	0.15	Shareholders	1,124
Shs. outstg. (M)	23.0	Market cap. (B)	$0.458
Avg. daily vol. (M)	0.054	Inst. holdings	66%
Tang. Bk. Value/Share	14.30		
Beta	0.99		

Value of $10,000 invested 5 years ago: $ 9,079

Fiscal Year Ending Dec. 31

	1999	1998	1997	1996	1995	1994
Revenues (Million $)						
1Q	341.6	293.6	135.1	161.2	177.6	116.6
2Q	380.2	337.7	196.4	140.6	193.4	137.7
3Q	—	334.1	246.4	161.3	176.1	147.9
4Q	—	326.8	268.2	168.4	187.1	159.7
Yr.	—	1,292	846.1	631.5	734.3	561.8
Earnings Per Share ($)						
1Q	**0.26**	**0.33**	**0.05**	**0.07**	0.37	0.27
2Q	**0.42**	**0.27**	**0.13**	**0.01**	0.43	0.35
3Q	—	**0.33**	**0.24**	**0.01**	0.31	0.34
4Q	—	**0.08**	**0.31**	**0.12**	0.24	0.35
Yr.	—	**0.99**	**0.74**	**0.19**	**1.34**	**1.32**

Next earnings report expected: mid October

Dividend Data (Dividends have been paid since 1993.)

Amount ($)	Date Decl.	Ex-Div. Date	Stock of Record	Payment Date
0.038	Dec. 16	Jan. 07	Jan. 11	Jan. 25 '99
0.038	Mar. 18	Apr. 09	Apr. 13	Apr. 27 '99
0.038	May. 07	Jul. 12	Jul. 14	Jul. 28 '99
0.038	Sep. 20	Oct. 12	Oct. 14	Oct. 28 '99

A Division of The McGraw-Hill Companies

Wabash National Corporation

Business Summary - 30-SEP-99

Since inception in 1985, Wabash National Corp. (WNC) has expanded its product offerings from a single product, the aluminum plate trailer, to a broad line of transportation equipment and related items, and has grown at a compound annual rate of over 40%. The company believes it is the largest U.S. maker of truck trailers, and the leading manufacturer of both fiberglass-reinforced plastic composite trailers and aluminum plate trailers. It is also the exclusive maker of RoadRailer, a patented bimodal technology that consists of trailers and detachable rail bogies that permit a vehicle to run both on the highway and directly on railroad lines. The Wabash National Finance unit provides leasing and financing programs to customers for new and used trailers. WNC also produces aftermarket parts.

The company markets its products to truckload and less-than-truckload common carriers, household and package moving companies, leasing companies, package carriers and intermodal carriers. WNC believes customers have historically replaced trailers in cycles that run from six to eight years. Its current strategy is to produce products in the trucking and bimodal industries, generating wider profit margins than those associated with standard trailers; and to increase its share of the factory direct market, while expanding its dealer sales by attracting additional high quality regional dealers.

WNC plans to expand its retail distribution network to 50 retail outlets, from 31 outlets, by early 2000. The five largest customers accounted for 18% of total sales in 1998. Sales to leasing companies provided 10% of 1998 total new trailer sales. The company's market share in the U.S. trailer industry in 1998 was about 22%.

In July 1998, WNC acquired Cloud Corp. and Cloud Oak Flooring Co. for $10 million in cash, $13 million in convertible preferred stock, and assumption of debt. The Cloud companies ($40 million in sales) produce laminated hardwood flooring. In April 1997, WNC acquired Fruehauf Trailer Corp., for $51 million in cash and stock. Assets acquired included retail outlets in 31 major markets.

During 1998, the company established an electronics division, leading to the development of its anti-lock braking system. New products include AllRailer, a railcar designed to carry larger motor vehicles; AutoRailer, a highway trailer capable of running on rails and carrying six full-size or smaller automobiles; RefrigeRailer; ChassisRailer; and the PupRailer trailer.

In November 1997, the company bought a 25% stake in Germany-based RoadRailer for $6 million. In July 1998, it formed a joint venture to market its RoadRailer technology in South America.

In April 1998, WNC sold publicly 3,000,000 common shares at $30.75 each.

Per Share Data ($) (Year Ended Dec. 31)	1998	1997	1996	1995	1994	1993	1992	1991	1990	1989
Tangible Bk. Val.	12.33	10.50	9.46	9.39	8.14	5.03	3.73	3.21	1.28	0.89
Cash Flow	1.82	1.59	1.00	1.95	1.72	1.18	0.71	NA	0.43	NA
Earnings	0.99	0.74	0.19	1.34	1.32	0.90	0.54	0.52	0.31	NA
Dividends	0.14	0.13	0.12	0.10	0.08	0.07	Nil	Nil	NA	NA
Payout Ratio	14%	17%	63%	7%	6%	7%	Nil	Nil	NA	NA
Prices - High	31¾	35⅝	24⅞	40½	43½	23⅜	19⅝	16½	NA	NA
- Low	10¼	15⅝	14⅛	19⅜	22⅝	14⅛	8⅝	9⅜	NA	NA
P/E Ratio - High	32	48	NM	30	33	25	36	32	NA	NA
- Low	10	21	NM	14	17	15	16	18	NA	NA
Income Statement Analysis (Million $)										
Revs.	1,292	846	631	734	562	360	289	191	171	155
Oper. Inc.	75.1	57.8	30.8	57.4	48.6	31.9	18.0	14.2	9.1	10.7
Depr.	18.4	16.6	15.3	11.5	7.4	4.9	2.9	1.6	1.1	1.0
Int. Exp.	14.8	16.1	10.3	6.5	2.7	1.4	0.7	1.6	2.2	2.3
Pretax Inc.	38.5	25.8	6.0	40.3	39.6	25.9	14.5	11.1	4.8	6.9
Eff. Tax Rate	40%	41%	40%	37%	40%	40%	38%	39%	41%	38%
Net Inc.	23.3	15.2	3.6	25.4	23.9	15.6	8.9	6.8	2.8	4.3
Balance Sheet & Other Fin. Data (Million $)										
Cash	67.1	14.6	5.5	2.1	39.7	27.6	3.0	14.6	1.9	1.7
Curr. Assets	413	408	236	228	198	116	94.0	71.4	37.9	35.8
Total Assets	704	630	440	384	301	180	135	93.4	49.9	47.3
Curr. Liab.	142	128	87.0	114	108	59.3	49.9	35.1	20.7	17.0
LT Debt	165	232	151	73.7	24.9	24.4	18.1	1.9	13.3	19.6
Common Eqty.	346	227	178	178	154	87.5	62.1	53.4	15.3	10.7
Total Cap.	543	485	329	269	193	120	84.5	57.8	28.6	30.3
Cap. Exp.	31.0	20.2	11.2	37.9	32.7	20.1	16.5	6.8	1.7	2.0
Cash Flow	40.3	31.1	18.9	36.9	31.3	20.5	11.9	8.3	4.0	5.3
Curr. Ratio	2.9	3.2	2.7	2.0	1.8	2.0	1.9	2.0	1.8	2.1
% LT Debt of Cap.	30.4	47.8	45.9	27.4	12.9	20.3	21.4	3.2	68.3	64.6
% Net Inc.of Revs.	1.8	1.8	0.6	3.5	4.3	4.3	3.1	3.6	1.7	2.8
% Ret. on Assets	3.5	3.0	0.9	7.4	9.6	9.7	7.8	12.9	NM	9.4
% Ret. on Equity	7.6	7.1	2.0	15.3	19.2	20.4	15.5	28.1	NM	45.7

Data as orig reptd.; bef. results of disc opers/spec. items. Per share data adj. for stk. divs. Bold denotes diluted EPS (FASB 128)-prior periods restated. E-Estimated. NA-Not Available. NM-Not Meaningful. NR-Not Ranked.

Office—1000 Sagamore Parkway South, Lafayette, IN 47905. **Tel**—(765) 771-5300.**Website**—http://www.wncwabash.com **Chrmn, Pres & CEO**—D. J. Ehrlich. **VP & CFO**—M. R. Holden. **Investor Contact**—Connie L. Koleszar. **Secy**—J. R. Gambs. **Dirs**—R. E. Dessimoz, D. J. Ehrlich, J. T. Hackett, E. H. Harrison, M. R. Holden, L. F. Koci. **Transfer Agent & Registrar**—Harris Trust and Savings Bank, Chicago. **Incorporated**—in Delaware in 1991. **Empl**— 5,302. **S&P Analyst:** Stewart Scharf

STANDARD
&POOR'S
STOCK REPORTS

Wall Data

NASDAQ Symbol **WALL**

In S&P SmallCap 600

09-OCT-99

Industry: Computer (Software & Services)

Summary: This company primarily develops and markets software products and related services for users of personal computers in business organizations.

Quantitative Evaluations

Outlook (1 Lowest—5 Highest) • **1-**

Fair Value • **3⅜**

Risk • **High**

Earn./Div. Rank • **C**

Technical Eval. • **Bearish** since 7/99

Rel. Strength Rank (1 Lowest—99 Highest) • **11**

Insider Activity • **NA**

Recent Price • 5⅞ | Yield • Nil
52 Wk Range • 24¼-5 | 12-Mo. P/E • NM

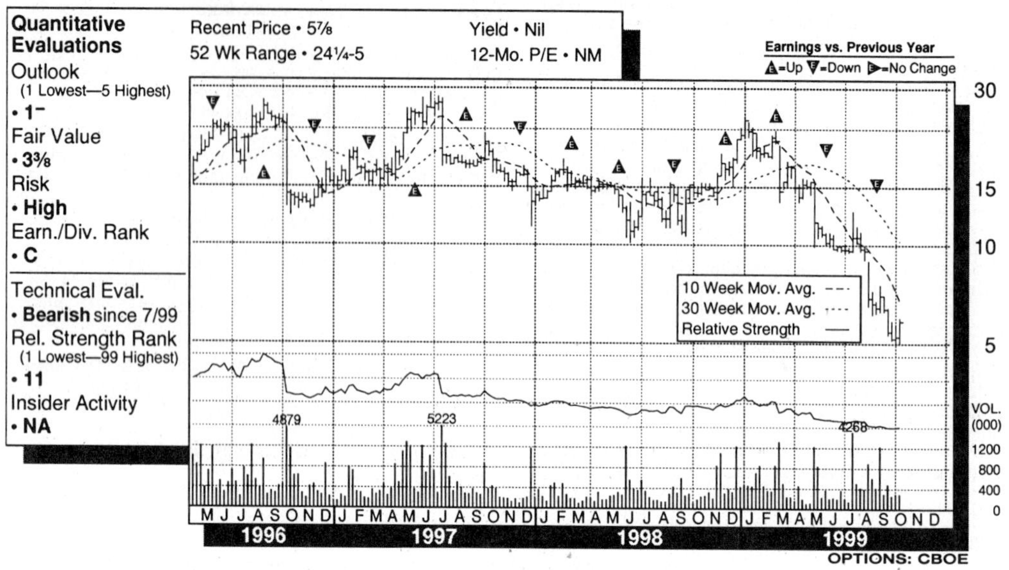

OPTIONS: CBOE

Business Profile - 29-AUG-99

In August 1999, WALL announced plans to restructure its worldwide operations around its RUMBA business and estimated that it will take a related charge of $14-16 million in the second quarter of FY 00 (Apr.). The company reduced its workforce by roughly one-third and was in the process of closing and consolidating offices and facilities. WALL will also no longer pursue the corporate information portal market. In addition, the company engaged the investment banking firm of Bear, Stearns & Co. to assist in evaluating strategic alternatives. Also in August 1999, WALL announced the sale of its 10% equity investment in DataChannel, a private Internet software company, which will result in a $2.9 million non-operating gain during the second quarter of FY 00 (Apr.).

Operational Review - 29-AUG-99

In the three months ended July 31, 1999, net revenues fell 50%, year to year, reflecting the continued effects of a salesforce reorganization during the fourth quarter of FY 99 and the slowing of the enterprise software market, caused in part by customers focusing on their Year 2000 compliance. Operating margins fell drastically, as sharply lower license fees were spread over a relatively fixed expense base. After taxes of $234,000, versus taxes at 19.9%, the net loss was $11,340,000 ($1.12 a share, on 1.9% more shares), versus net income of $2,183,000 ($0.22).

Stock Performance - 08-OCT-99

In the past 30 trading days, WALL's shares have declined 9%, compared to a 0.91% fall in the S&P 500. Average trading volume for the past five days was 56,880 shares, compared with the 40-day moving average of 103,287 shares.

Key Stock Statistics

Dividend Rate/Share	Nil	Shareholders	301
Shs. outstg. (M)	10.2	Market cap. (B)	$0.060
Avg. daily vol. (M)	0.065	Inst. holdings	56%
Tang. Bk. Value/Share	6.60		
Beta	0.67		

Value of $10,000 invested 5 years ago: $ 1,456

Fiscal Year Ending Apr. 30

	2000	1999	1998	1997	1996	1995
Revenues (Million $)						
1Q	20.07	40.41	37.02	29.86	22.10	17.16
2Q	—	37.35	35.60	34.83	24.73	23.14
3Q	—	41.82	28.56	30.83	26.15	25.01
4Q	—	20.15	39.66	43.86	37.76	35.93
Yr.	—	139.7	140.8	139.4	110.7	101.2
Earnings Per Share ($)						
1Q	**-1.12**	**0.22**	**0.35**	**0.05**	Nil	-0.04
2Q	—	**0.01**	**-0.50**	**0.17**	0.49	0.36
3Q	—	**0.30**	Nil	**-0.07**	-0.02	0.40
4Q	—	**-1.41**	**0.35**	**0.28**	0.25	0.69
Yr.	—	**-0.89**	**0.23**	**0.43**	**0.72**	**1.40**

Next earnings report expected: late November

Dividend Data

No cash dividends have been paid, and the company does not expect to pay any in the foreseeable future. A "poison pill" shareholder rights plan was adopted in 1995.

Wall Data Incorporated

Business Summary - 29-AUG-99

During the fourth quarter of FY 99 (Apr.), Wall Data Inc. restructured its RUMBA host access segment and its Cyberprise portal unit into two separate businesses, each with its own sales, service, development and marketing organizations. In August 1999, WALL announced plans to restructure its worldwide operations around its RUMBA business and said it will no longer pursue the corporate information portal market. WALL engaged the investment banking firm of Bear Stearns & Co. to evaluate strategic alternatives for the two operating segments. In addition, John Wall resigned as CEO, president and a director of the company to pursue other interests, and was replaced as president by the president of the RUMBA unit.

WALL is an enterprise software company providing products and services that allow organizations to integrate and deploy applications over intranets, extranets and the Internet. WALL's solutions allow internal users, remote users and third parties (including partners and customers) to access the information and applications of a corporate network.

WALL's flagship RUMBA software products provide users with access to information located anywhere within the corporate enterprise and beyond in the public domain. The RUMBA product line was upgraded to take advantage of the emerging Web-to-host market by allowing users to access legacy systems from Internet browser software. The RUMBA family of host connectivity products operates in Microsoft's Windows 3.x, Windows 95 and Windows NT environments and supports the exchange of information between PC applications and IBM-compatible mainframe computing platforms. RUMBA accounted for 86% of total net revenues in FY 99, down from the FY 98 contribution of 99%.

In January 1998, WALL announced a strategy known as Cyberprise, with a new line of products and services for the Web-extended enterprise. Cyberprise solutions enable companies to move existing systems and public information to the Internet, and to extend those systems to remote users, vendors and customers. WALL began rolling out a complete line of Cyberprise products in March 1998, enabling companies to develop enterprise information portals that integrate applications, data and content within a browser interface.

In March 1998, the company purchased First Service Computer Dienstleistungs-GmbH of Germany, for $11 million in cash. First Service distributes and supports a range of connectivity software solutions to major corporations throughout Germany, and has been a distributor of WALL's products for over seven years.

Per Share Data ($)										
(Year Ended Apr. 30)	**1999**	**1998**	**1997**	**1996**	**1995**	**1994**	**1993**	**1992**	**1991**	**1990**
Tangible Bk. Val.	7.05	7.09	9.66	9.34	8.79	6.99	5.55	NM	NM	NM
Cash Flow	-0.37	-0.10	1.51	1.45	1.76	1.15	0.68	0.25	-2.01	NA
Earnings	-0.89	0.23	0.44	0.74	1.40	1.00	0.58	0.19	-2.29	-2.15
Dividends	Nil	Nil	Nil	Nil	Nil	Nil	Nil	Nil	Nil	Nil
Payout Ratio	Nil	Nil	Nil	Nil	Nil	Nil	Nil	Nil	Nil	Nil
Cal. Yrs.	1998	1997	1996	1995	1994	1993	1992	1991	1990	1989
Prices - High	24¼	29⅛	27½	55½	60	42½	NA	NA	NA	NA
- Low	10⅛	11¼	12¼	14½	29¼	12¾	NA	NA	NA	NA
P/E Ratio - High	NM	NM	62	75	43	43	NA	NA	NA	NA
- Low	NM	NM	28	20	21	13	NA	NA	NA	NA
Income Statement Analysis (Million $)										
Revs.	140	39.1	139	111	101	64.6	31.8	14.6	4.4	2.4
Oper. Inc.	1.9	-2.1	18.4	8.6	28.7	19.1	8.0	2.1	-1.0	NA
Depr.	12.6	3.7	10.1	7.0	3.6	1.4	0.7	0.3	0.2	NA
Int. Exp.	Nil	Nil	Nil	Nil	0.2	0.2	0.2	0.2	0.4	NA
Pretax Inc.	-7.9	-4.5	7.2	11.7	22.8	15.3	6.8	1.7	-1.6	-1.5
Eff. Tax Rate	NM	NM	42%	38%	38%	38%	35%	37%	Nil	Nil
Net Inc.	-8.9	-4.6	4.2	7.3	14.2	9.6	4.4	1.1	-1.6	-1.5
Balance Sheet & Other Fin. Data (Million $)										
Cash	17.7	57.5	62.5	52.0	48.9	50.3	4.6	1.8	NA	NA
Curr. Assets	94.3	101	108	86.9	80.7	67.3	14.1	6.0	NA	NA
Total Assets	127	140	127	110	106	74.4	16.1	6.9	2.0	2.2
Curr. Liab.	37.8	44.0	36.4	26.1	24.4	12.0	6.1	3.6	NA	NA
LT Debt	Nil	Nil	Nil	Nil	Nil	0.1	1.0	0.6	4.5	4.2
Common Eqty.	86.4	92.8	91.0	83.7	81.2	62.3	9.0	2.7	-4.6	-3.0
Total Cap.	89.0	94.9	91.0	83.7	81.2	62.5	10.0	3.2	-0.1	1.2
Cap. Exp.	5.7	3.9	5.1	7.1	10.1	3.8	1.6	0.3	0.1	NA
Cash Flow	3.7	-0.9	14.3	14.3	17.8	11.0	5.1	1.3	-1.4	NA
Curr. Ratio	2.5	2.3	3.0	3.3	3.3	5.6	2.3	1.6	NA	NA
% LT Debt of Cap.	Nil	Nil	Nil	Nil	Nil	0.2	10.1	17.5	NM	NM
% Net Inc.of Revs.	NM	1.6	3.0	6.5	14.0	14.8	13.8	7.2	NM	NM
% Ret. on Assets	NM	1.7	3.5	6.7	15.5	10.8	38.3	23.7	NM	NM
% Ret. on Equity	NM	2.4	4.8	8.8	19.4	19.7	75.3	NM	NM	NM

Data as orig. reptd.; bef. results of disc. opers. and/or spec. items. Prior to 1998 (four mos.), yrs. ended Dec. 31 of prior cal. yr. Per share data adj. for stk. divs. as of ex-div. date. E-Estimated. NA-Not Available. NM-Not Meaningful. NR-Not Ranked. Bold denotes diluted EPS (FASB 128).

Office—11332 N.E. 122nd Way, Kirkland, WA 98034-6931. **Tel**—(425) 814-9255. **Website**—http://www.walldata.com. **Chrmn**—R. J. Frankenberg. **Pres**—K. Vitale. **VP-Fin, CFO & Treas**—R. Fox. **VP & Secy**—C. E. Shank. **Dirs**—R. J. Frankenberg, J. A. Heimbuck, H. N. Lewis, D. F. Millet, S. Sarich Jr., B. Steiger, K. Vitale. **Transfer Agent & Registrar**—ChaseMellon, Seattle. **Incorporated**—in Washington in 1982. **Empl**— 758. **S&P Analyst:** Scott H. Kessler

STANDARD
&POOR'S
STOCK REPORTS

Watkins-Johnson

NYSE Symbol **WJ**

In S&P SmallCap 600

09-OCT-99

Industry:
Equipment (Semiconductor)

Summary: WJ makes electronic products for wireless telecommunications. Directors are pursuing the sale of the company.

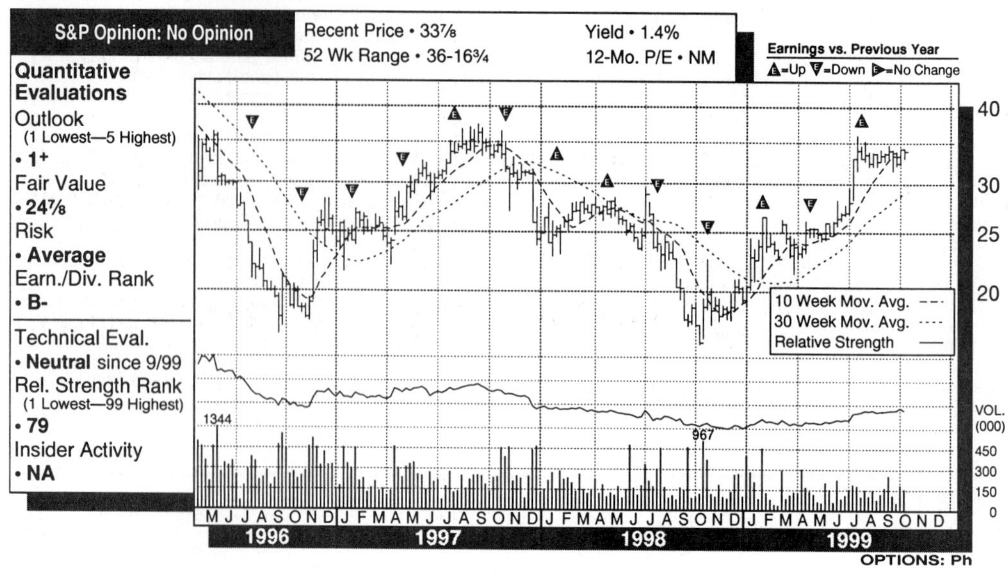

Overview - 12-AUG-99

In March 1999, directors announced their intention to pursue the sale of the company. The move, intended to maximize shareholder value, follows a protracted period of operational and share price underperformance. In May, the company agreed to sell its Semiconductor Equipment Group to Silicon Valley Group, for a total value, including retained receivables, exceeding $50 million. The value includes approximately $20 million in debt to be assumed by Silicon Valley Group. The transaction includes the business associated with the atmospheric chemical vapor deposition products, and real estate in Scotts Valley, CA, and Kawasaki, Japan. The high density chemical vapor deposition equipment and associated intellectual property rights were sold to Applied Materials in March, generating a $9 million second quarter gain.

Valuation - 12-AUG-99

While up from recent lows, the shares of this technology concern have generally lagged the market for some time, reflecting weak chip industry conditions, and limited growth in the company's wireless segment. We view favorably the company's shareholder-minded decision to sell itself, and are maintaining our hold recommendation on the shares. While the sale of the semiconductor operations realized only a modest price, we believe the company's remaining wireless operations, and its real estate holdings in Palo Alto and San Jose, CA, have considerable value. Although it may take some time for WJ to realize the value of these assets, we believe downside risk in the stock is limited, and recommend that patient investors hold the shares.

Key Stock Statistics

S&P EPS Est. 2000	NA	Tang. Bk. Value/Share	20.11
P/E on S&P Est. 2000	NA	Beta	1.57
Dividend Rate/Share	0.48	Shareholders	6,500
Shs. outstg. (M)	6.6	Market cap. (B)	$0.223
Avg. daily vol. (M)	0.025	Inst. holdings	52%

Value of $10,000 invested 5 years ago: $ 18,908

Fiscal Year Ending Dec. 31

	1999	1998	1997	1996	1995	1994
Revenues (Million $)						
1Q	65.18	68.72	67.22	122.7	92.98	80.56
2Q	34.86	53.74	72.68	126.5	102.0	87.37
3Q	—	26.26	79.17	94.96	95.55	83.17
4Q	—	63.48	72.20	94.17	96.49	81.54
Yr.	—	212.2	291.3	438.3	387.0	332.6
Earnings Per Share ($)						
1Q	**0.43**	**1.15**	**-0.04**	**0.61**	0.63	0.47
2Q	**2.03**	**-0.75**	**0.10**	**-0.09**	0.88	0.77
3Q	—	**-6.93**	**0.21**	**0.25**	0.98	0.63
4Q	—	**0.25**	**-0.76**	**-0.95**	1.04	0.77
Yr.	—	**-6.36**	**-0.48**	**0.36**	**2.49**	2.66

Next earnings report expected: mid October

Dividend Data (Dividends have been paid since 1974.)

Amount ($)	Date Decl.	Ex-Div. Date	Stock of Record	Payment Date
0.120	Nov. 23	Dec. 15	Dec. 17	Jan. 04 '99
0.120	Feb. 22	Mar. 09	Mar. 11	Mar. 25 '99
0.120	May. 24	Jun. 08	Jun. 10	Jun. 24 '99
0.120	Jul. 26	Sep. 07	Sep. 09	Sep. 23 '99

A Division of The McGraw-Hill Companies

Watkins-Johnson Company

Business Summary - 12-AUG-99

In 1998, Watkins-Johnson Co. had continuing operations in two distinct high-technology businesses: semiconductor equipment manufacturing (46% of sales and a loss of $81 million in 1998, versus 64% and a loss of $13 million in 1997) and wireless communications (54% and a loss of $14 million, versus 36% and a loss of less than $1 million).

In March 1999, directors announced their intention to pursue the sale of the company, following a strategic review of operations. In May, the company agreed to sell its semiconductor equipment operations to Silicon Valley Group.

The Semiconductor Equipment Group produces chemical vapor deposition (CVD) equipment for semiconductor manufacturing. CVD processes are used to deposit dielectric films on an integrated circuit (IC). The company's WJ-1000 product specializes in the premetal dielectric sector, applying the crucial initial layer of doped (ionized) silicon dioxide (glass) onto a silicon wafer that is the basic material used in making ICs. The WJ-2000, a high-density plasma CVD system for depositing intermetal dielectric films, was introduced in 1995. WJ's tools are used by semiconductor manufacturers worldwide for all types of ICs. A related application is in liquid crystal flat-panel display.

The wireless communications segment serves original equipment manufacturers (OEMs). Watkins-Johnson has entered two wireless communications business areas which parallel the skills it developed as a defense electronics supplier. One business involves the production of components and subassemblies for cellular, personal communication services (PCS) and space applications. The company has successfully adapted its communications-intelligence equipment technology to the design and production of low-cost, sensitive receivers and wideband transceivers for base station applications.

In October 1997, the company completed the sale of its defense electronics business to Mentmore Holdings Corp., a privately held investment company. Proceeds of approximately $103 million were expected to be used for expansion and development of WJ's remaining semiconductor equipment and wireless communications businesses.

Operating results in 1998 were hurt by a slowdown in the semiconductor equipment industry. Overcapacity in the market for dynamic random access memory (DRAM) chips, coupled with the impact of economic turmoil in Asia, caused chip makers to defer or cancel orders for semiconductor equipment. While the semiconductor equipment segment is being sold, management expects the wireless segment to post pretax profits of 3% to 4% of sales in 1999.

Per Share Data ($) (Year Ended Dec. 31)	1998	1997	1996	1995	1994	1993	1992	1991	1990	1989
Tangible Bk. Val.	20.11	26.68	23.38	23.54	19.75	17.62	16.55	15.67	19.15	17.74
Cash Flow	-4.32	1.11	1.68	4.66	3.72	2.69	2.15	-1.42	3.23	3.68
Earnings	-6.36	-0.48	0.36	3.54	2.66	1.45	0.66	-2.98	1.67	2.23
Dividends	0.48	0.48	0.48	0.48	0.48	0.48	0.48	0.48	0.48	0.46
Payout Ratio	NM	NM	133%	14%	18%	33%	73%	NM	28%	21%
Prices - High	29½	37⅜	44⅝	57	36⅝	26¼	15	19½	20⅞	27¼
- Low	16⅜	21½	17	29¾	19⅝	12	8⅝	9¼	10⅝	19
P/E Ratio - High	NM	NM	NM	16	14	18	23	NM	13	12
- Low	NM	NM	NM	8	7	8	13	NM	6	9
Income Statement Analysis (Million $)										
Revs.	212	291	438	387	333	286	264	278	312	311
Oper. Inc.	-51.6	-1.2	16.2	51.8	39.3	26.9	19.0	13.6	29.7	38.6
Depr.	15.8	13.1	11.3	9.9	8.7	10.0	11.3	11.7	12.1	12.2
Int. Exp.	1.2	1.4	1.6	0.9	1.1	1.3	1.5	1.5	1.6	1.9
Pretax Inc.	-73.0	-7.0	4.3	44.0	30.9	16.8	7.2	-28.7	18.7	28.3
Eff. Tax Rate	NM	NM	30%	29%	30%	31%	31%	NM	30%	34%
Net Inc.	-49.2	-4.0	3.0	31.4	21.7	11.6	5.0	-22.4	13.0	18.7
Balance Sheet & Other Fin. Data (Million $)										
Cash	64.6	134	15.7	34.6	34.5	45.0	49.1	40.1	17.2	26.6
Curr. Assets	172	258	204	217	179	169	153	153	159	169
Total Assets	245	358	314	288	235	221	206	213	223	227
Curr. Liab.	81.1	105	80.9	74.8	62.8	60.3	52.4	62.8	59.3	55.1
LT Debt	32.7	33.2	27.8	7.7	7.8	12.2	12.9	14.8	15.8	19.0
Common Eqty.	132	220	195	191	150	134	125	118	144	149
Total Cap.	164	253	223	199	157	146	138	133	160	168
Cap. Exp.	15.1	22.2	50.0	25.6	12.5	9.7	5.2	9.9	16.8	11.8
Cash Flow	-33.4	9.2	14.3	41.4	30.4	21.6	16.3	-10.7	25.2	30.9
Curr. Ratio	2.1	2.5	2.5	2.9	2.9	2.8	2.9	2.4	2.7	3.1
% LT Debt of Cap.	19.9	13.1	12.5	3.9	5.0	8.3	9.3	11.2	9.9	11.3
% Net Inc.of Revs.	NM	NM	0.7	8.1	6.5	4.1	1.9	NM	4.2	6.0
% Ret. on Assets	NM	NM	1.0	12.0	9.5	5.4	2.4	NM	6.1	8.6
% Ret. on Equity	NM	NM	1.6	18.4	15.3	8.9	4.1	NM	9.4	13.2

Data as orig reptd.; bef. results of disc opers/spec. items. Per share data adj. for stk. divs. Bold denotes diluted EPS (FASB 128)-prior periods restated. E-Estimated. NA-Not Available. NM-Not Meaningful. NR-Not Ranked.

Office—3333 Hillview Ave., Stanford Research Park, Palo Alto, CA 94304-1223. **Tel**—(650) 493-4141. **Fax**—(650) 813-2402. **Website**—http://www.wj.com **Chrmn**—D. A. Watkins. **Vice Chrmn**—H. R. Johnson. **Pres & CEO**—W. K. Kennedy Jr. **Secy**—C.D. Kelly. **VP & CFO**—S. G. Buchanan. **Investor Contact**—Frank E. Emery (650-813-2752). **Dirs**—G. M. Cusumano, W. R. Graham, J. J. Hartmann, H. R. Johnson, W. K. Kennedy Jr., R. F. O'Brien, R. L. Prestel, D. A. Watkins. **Transfer Agent** —ChaseMellon Shareholder Services, Ridgefield Park, NJ. **Incorporated**—in California in 1957. **Empl**— 1,520. **S&P Analyst:** B. McGovern

STANDARD
&POOR'S
STOCK REPORTS

Watsco, Inc.

NYSE Symbol **WSO**

In S&P SmallCap 600

09-OCT-99 **Industry:** Electrical Equipment

Summary: WSO is the largest U.S. distributor of air conditioning, heating and refrigeration equipment and related products.

Quantitative Evaluations

Outlook
(1 Lowest—5 Highest)
• **4-**

Fair Value
• **17½**

Risk
• **Average**

Earn./Div. Rank
• **A-**

Technical Eval.
• **Bearish** since 6/99

Rel. Strength Rank
(1 Lowest—99 Highest)
• **8**

Insider Activity
• **NA**

Recent Price • 10⅞
52 Wk Range • 20-10⅜
Yield • 0.9%
12-Mo. P/E • 10.7

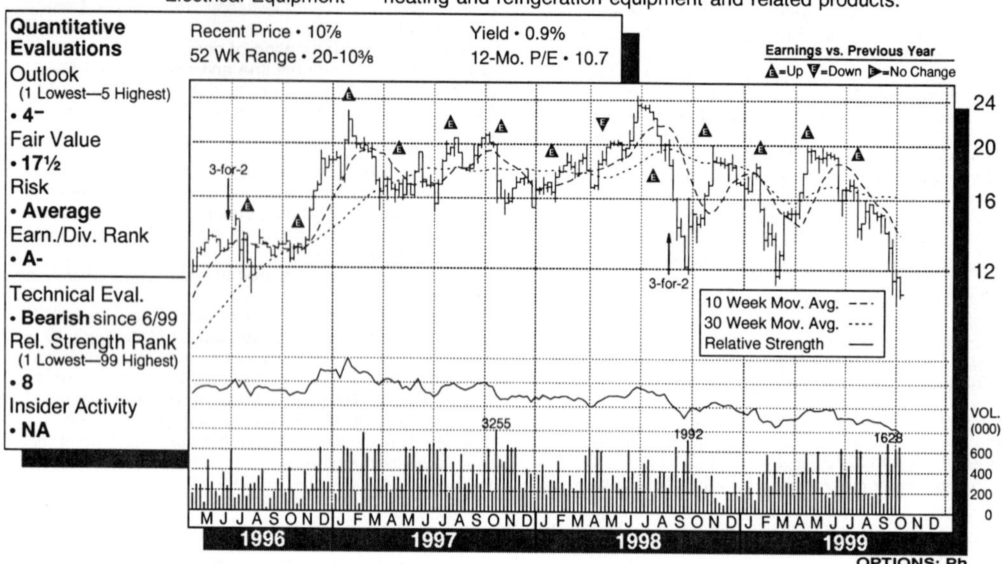

Business Profile - 22-JUN-99

The company seeks to increase its market share, and to identify, acquire and integrate other businesses in the highly fragmented air conditioning industry, in an effort to leverage operating costs. Its strategy includes expansion in the Sunbelt, where air conditioning usage is highest, the population is growing, and demand is more predictable; and a focus on the growing replacement market, where margins are wider, and sales tend to offset cyclical downturns in housing. In 1998, WSO acquired 11 distributors, adding 25 locations in 14 states, with annualized revenues of $165 million. In early 1999, the company purchased two New England-based distributors, with combined revenues of $61 million. At April 15, 1999, the company was serving 29 states from 323 locations.

Operational Review - 22-JUN-99

Total revenues in the three months ended March 31, 1999, advanced 43%, year to year, paced by acquisitions and higher same-store sales, as a result of market share gains and an expanded product line. Gross margins widened slightly, on the higher volume, but, with a sharp rise in SG&A expense and substantially greater interest expense, the gain in pretax income was held to 32%. After taxes at 37.2%, versus 37.0%, income from continuing operations was also up 32%, to $2,343,000 ($0.08 a share, on 3.9% more shares), from $1,776,000 ($0.06, as adjusted). Results exclude income of $104,000 and $149,000 from discontinued operations in the respective periods.

Stock Performance - 08-OCT-99

In the past 30 trading days, WSO's shares have declined 28%, compared to a 0.91% fall in the S&P 500. Average trading volume for the past five days was 230,840 shares, compared with the 40-day moving average of 132,572 shares.

Key Stock Statistics

Dividend Rate/Share	0.10	Shareholders	600
Shs. outstg. (M)	28.7	Market cap. (B)	$0.277
Avg. daily vol. (M)	0.206	Inst. holdings	57%
Tang. Bk. Value/Share	6.28		
Beta	1.80		

Value of $10,000 invested 5 years ago: $ 29,950

Fiscal Year Ending Dec. 31

	1999	1998	1997	1996	1995	1994
Revenues (Million $)						
1Q	247.4	172.7	96.30	77.79	60.32	55.25
2Q	331.0	270.9	164.7	118.5	91.06	75.83
3Q	—	317.0	189.5	125.3	98.81	82.81
4Q	—	248.3	184.8	103.8	80.82	69.85
Yr.	—	1,009	635.2	425.4	331.0	283.7
Earnings Per Share ($)						
1Q	**0.08**	**0.06**	**0.08**	0.08	0.06	0.05
2Q	**0.38**	**0.31**	**0.22**	0.19	0.16	0.13
3Q	—	**0.37**	**0.25**	0.23	0.19	0.16
4Q	—	**0.15**	**0.12**	0.11	0.08	0.06
Yr.	—	**0.90**	**0.68**	**0.51**	**0.36**	0.40

Next earnings report expected: mid October

Dividend Data (Dividends have been paid since 1984.)

Amount ($)	Date Decl.	Ex-Div. Date	Stock of Record	Payment Date
0.025	Jan. 06	Jan. 13	Jan. 15	Jan. 29 '99
0.025	Apr. 05	Apr. 13	Apr. 15	Apr. 30 '99
0.025	Jul. 01	Jul. 13	Jul. 15	Jul. 30 '99
0.025	Oct. 01	Oct. 13	Oct. 15	Oct. 29 '99

Business Summary - 22-JUN-99

Watsco is the largest U.S. independent distributor of residential central air conditioners and heating equipment and related parts and supplies. The company has spurred its growth through acquisitions. Since 1989, WSO has acquired more than 35 distributors of air conditioning and heating equipment; revenue from distribution operations has grown from $64 million in 1989 to $1 billion in 1998.

Residential central air conditioning and heating equipment is sold to the replacement and the homebuilding markets. The replacement market has surpassed the homebuilding market in significance, as a result of the aging of the installed base of residential air conditioners. According to the Air Conditioning and Refrigeration Institute (ARI), more than 75 million central air conditioning units have been installed in the U.S. in the past 20 years, with the majority of these units installed in the Sunbelt. The life of air conditioners can range from eight to 20 years. The company also sells products used in the refrigeration industry, including condensing units, compressors, evaporators, valves, walk-in coolers and ice machines for industrial and commercial applications.

WSO's acquisition strategy is to establish a network of distribution facilities, particularly in the Sunbelt. The Sunbelt, which has the fastest population growth in the U.S., has a historically hot weather pattern and air conditioning is considered a necessity. The company seeks to enhance the value of acquired operations by serving the one-stop shopping needs of contractors. This includes broadening product line and committing other capital resources to develop the acquired businesses, including expanding existing locations and opening new locations.

In November 1997, the company approved a plan to divest its non-distribution operations, Watsco Components, Inc. and Dunhill Staffing Systems, Inc. These operations were classified as discontinued in 1997. WSO sold Watsco Components to International Comfort Products Corp. in June 1998.

In January 1999, WSO acquired two leading distributors of heating and air conditioning products that serve the New England market, in a move designed to establish a major presence, and increase WSO's share of that market. The companies were Homans Associates, Inc., founded in 1952; and Heat, Inc., founded in 1955. Homans serves the New England market through 14 locations; Heat distributes its products from a single location. In 1998, the companies had combined revenues of $61 million.

Per Share Data ($) (Year Ended Dec. 31)	1998	1997	1996	1995	1994	1993	1992	1991	1990	1989
Tangible Bk. Val.	5.95	5.67	4.58	2.66	2.43	2.07	1.32	0.93	0.66	1.37
Cash Flow	1.19	0.86	0.83	0.69	0.56	0.52	0.51	0.42	0.45	0.46
Earnings	0.90	0.68	0.62	0.48	0.39	0.38	0.31	0.22	0.27	0.31
Dividends	0.07	0.09	0.09	0.08	0.08	0.07	0.05	0.10	0.08	0.08
Payout Ratio	8%	14%	15%	17%	19%	20%	17%	44%	31%	28%
Prices - High	24 1/2	22 7/8	19 3/8	8	5	5	3 7/8	4 1/8	3 1/8	2 7/8
- Low	11 3/4	15	7 1/2	4 5/8	3 7/8	3 3/8	2 1/16	3 1/8	2 1/4	1 13/16
P/E Ratio - High	27	34	31	17	13	13	12	19	11	9
- Low	13	22	12	10	10	9	7	14	8	6
Income Statement Analysis (Million $)										
Revs.	1,009	635	425	331	284	231	195	169	118	94.0
Oper. Inc.	60.3	37.8	28.4	21.0	17.4	13.2	11.8	10.4	8.3	7.0
Depr.	8.4	4.8	4.2	3.0	2.4	1.9	1.9	1.8	1.3	1.0
Int. Exp.	11.1	4.7	3.7	4.2	3.2	2.8	3.2	4.1	2.9	2.5
Pretax Inc.	40.8	29.8	21.2	14.1	12.0	10.1	7.1	5.0	4.2	3.7
Eff. Tax Rate	37%	39%	38%	37%	39%	38%	39%	40%	36%	33%
Net Inc.	25.7	18.3	13.0	7.3	5.6	5.0	2.9	2.0	1.9	2.0
Balance Sheet & Other Fin. Data (Million $)										
Cash	6.7	7.9	5.3	4.0	5.0	2.6	0.9	2.2	5.5	4.5
Curr. Assets	371	318	159	112	93.6	86.7	61.9	62.5	62.8	36.3
Total Assets	532	426	204	145	120	110	81.1	81.8	83.6	47.6
Curr. Liab.	81.2	60.3	29.0	71.2	53.6	47.4	17.3	16.8	17.1	11.4
LT Debt	172	137	51.7	6.3	6.7	7.8	30.3	36.8	39.7	20.7
Common Eqty.	273	226	120	53.8	46.8	41.8	25.3	20.8	18.9	12.8
Total Cap.	449	366	175	73.7	66.1	62.3	63.8	65.0	66.6	36.2
Cap. Exp.	9.7	6.6	5.4	4.3	4.2	1.9	2.0	1.1	0.9	1.0
Cash Flow	34.1	23.1	17.2	10.2	8.0	6.8	4.8	3.8	3.3	3.1
Curr. Ratio	4.6	5.3	5.5	1.6	1.7	1.8	3.6	3.7	3.7	3.2
% LT Debt of Cap.	38.3	37.7	29.6	8.6	10.2	12.6	47.5	56.6	59.6	57.2
% Net Inc.of Revs.	2.5	2.9	3.1	2.2	2.0	2.2	1.5	1.2	1.6	2.2
% Ret. on Assets	5.4	5.8	7.5	5.5	4.9	4.5	3.6	2.4	2.6	5.5
% Ret. on Equity	10.3	10.6	15.0	14.4	12.7	13.0	12.7	9.9	10.7	16.6

Data as orig reptd.; bef. results of disc opers/spec. items. Per share data adj. for stk. divs. Bold denotes diluted EPS (FASB 128)-prior periods restated. E-Estimated. NA-Not Available. NM-Not Meaningful. NR-Not Ranked.

Office—2665 South Bayshore Dr., Suite 901, Coconut Grove, FL 33133. **Tel**—(305) 714-4100. **Website**—http://www.watsco.com **Chrmn & Pres**—A. H. Nahmad. **VP-Fin, Secy & Investor Contact**—Barry S. Logan. **Dirs**—C. L. Alvarez, D. B. Fleeman, J. I. Harris, P. F. Manley, B. L. Moss, R. Motta, A. H. Nahmad, R. J. Novello, A. H. Potamkin. **Transfer Agent & Registrar**—First Union Bank, Charlotte, NC. **Incorporated**—in Florida in 1956. **Empl**— 2,900. **S&P Analyst:** M.I.

STANDARD
&POOR'S
STOCK REPORTS

Werner Enterprises

Nasdaq Symbol **WERN**

In S&P SmallCap 600

09-OCT-99 **Industry:** Truckers

Summary: This company provides a variety of truckload and logistics services throughout the U.S. The Werner family holds 40% of the shares.

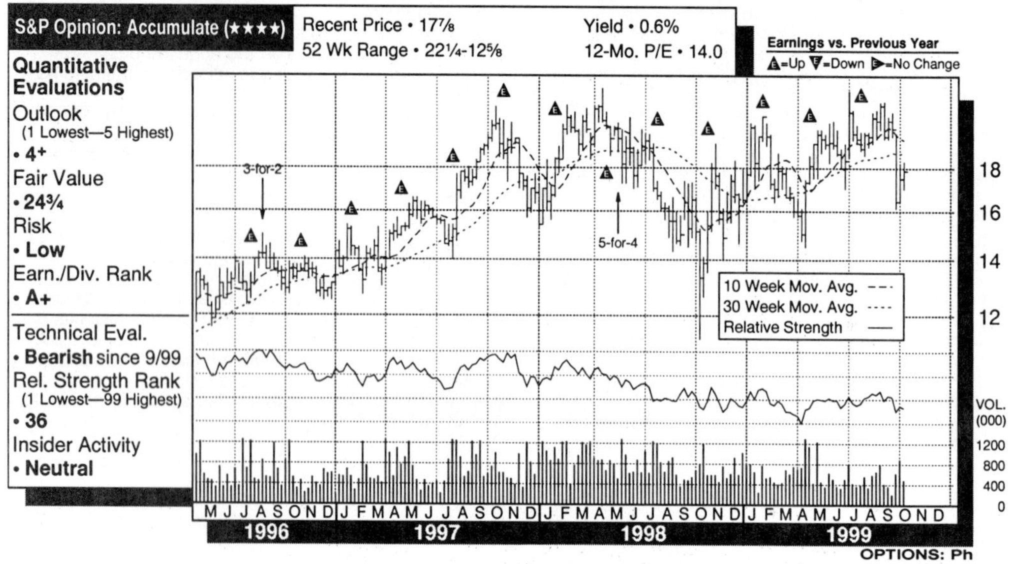

Overview - 14-JUL-99

Revenues are projected to increase about 13% in 1999, up from a 12% growth rate in 1998. WERN's fleet growth objective for 1999 is 15%, comparable to the 1998 level. However, we anticipate that average revenue generated per mile will increase somewhat more rapidly than the 1.1% seen in 1998, largely reflecting tightening industry capacity. Margins are expected to be flat. While labor costs will keep pace with revenues, and unit maintenance costs will fall, Werner faces higher fuel costs in 1999, and heavier than normal insurance and claims, due to the effects of severe weather in early 1999. In addition, depreciation charges and communications and utility expenses will increase faster than revenues. Comparisons will also be restricted by the fact that operating taxes benefited from a favorable adjustment in 1998. Interest costs will be higher.

Valuation - 14-JUL-99

In July 1999, the shares of this leading truckload carrier were closing in on highs set in early 1998. WERN's shares have rebounded sharply, as recession clouds have receded and the company has demonstrated that it is able to continue to attract enough drivers to maintain its historic 15% growth rate. WERN has demonstrated leadership over the years in the use of technology to optimize operating efficiencies, and, in the process, to improve job satisfaction for drivers. In addition, by maintaining one of the industry's youngest fleet, the company not only boosts driver satisfaction, but cuts maintenance and fuel consumption rates. Through 1998 year-end, WERN has repurchased 750,725 of its common shares, under a 2,500,000 share buyback program authorized in 1997. With the stock recently trading at a P/E to growth rate below 1.0, we advise accumulation of the shares during periods of weakness.

Key Stock Statistics

S&P EPS Est. 1999	1.35	Tang. Bk. Value/Share	9.91
P/E on S&P Est. 1999	13.2	Beta	0.54
S&P EPS Est. 2000	1.55	Shareholders	6,400
Dividend Rate/Share	0.10	Market cap. (B)	$0.848
Shs. outstg. (M)	47.4	Inst. holdings	52%
Avg. daily vol. (M)	0.108		

Value of $10,000 invested 5 years ago: $ 11,327

Fiscal Year Ending Dec. 31

	1999	1998	1997	1996	1995	1994
Revenues (Million $)						
1Q	241.0	199.7	172.1	147.9	132.4	116.0
2Q	260.6	211.7	193.6	159.6	143.3	129.6
3Q	—	219.7	200.2	167.2	150.3	134.6
4Q	—	232.3	206.2	168.6	150.0	135.8
Yr.	—	863.4	772.1	643.3	576.0	516.0
Earnings Per Share ($)						
1Q	**0.27**	**0.23**	**0.16**	**0.15**	0.16	0.15
2Q	**0.37**	**0.31**	**0.26**	**0.21**	0.18	0.20
3Q	**E0.35**	**0.33**	**0.30**	**0.25**	0.21	0.22
4Q	**E0.38**	**0.33**	**0.30**	**0.24**	0.21	0.21
Yr.	**E1.35**	**1.19**	**1.01**	**0.86**	**0.77**	**0.77**

Next earnings report expected: mid October

Dividend Data (Dividends have been paid since 1987.)

Amount ($)	Date Decl.	Ex-Div. Date	Stock of Record	Payment Date
0.025	Dec. 08	Jan. 07	Jan. 11	Jan. 26 '99
0.025	Mar. 01	Apr. 15	Apr. 19	May. 04 '99
0.025	May. 26	Jul. 01	Jul. 06	Jul. 20 '99
0.025	Sep. 07	Sep. 30	Oct. 04	Oct. 19 '99

A Division of The **McGraw-Hill** *Companies*

Werner Enterprises, Inc.

Business Summary - 14-JUL-99

Werner Enterprises is one of the five largest U.S. truckload motor carriers. It has grown faster than its peers by leading the industry in the application of technology and maintaining high driver satisfaction. In 1998, it became the first carrier to use electronic driver logs. The fastest growing segment of WERN's business is its dedicated fleet operation, in which it takes control of fleets formerly operated by private carriers. The Werner family controlled 40% of the shares as of March 1999.

WERN provides interstate and intrastate truckload services in all 48 contiguous states, 10 Canadian provinces, and to points in Mexico. It offers shippers a broad range of services, including regional and long-haul dry van, temperature-controlled, flatbed and dedicated carriage. In its dedicated fleet service, WERN assumes total responsibility for the trucking needs of specific customers. In February 1998, it took control of an additional 250 trucks for Dollar General Corp., a leading retailer.

Werner Logistics, started in 1995, is a non-asset based service that manages all of a company's transportation, distribution and warehousing requirements. It is responsible for carrier and mode selection and shipment routing. Logistic's margins are narrower than truckload carriage, but because the business requires little capital, return on investment is high.

WERN focuses on the premium end of the truckload market. Its chief selling point is its superior on-time and reliable service. Shippers also choose WERN because of its financial strength and new equipment fleet. Its use of technology has helped differentiate its product in a historically very price sensitive industry. Since 1992, all WERN trucks have been equipped with satellite communication devices. This lets WERN provide shippers with real-time update of the movement of their freight.

The company has also used technology to improve operating and safety performance. Using sophisticated software, it minimizes empty miles and helps find loads that bring drivers back to their home base. Onboard computers monitor about two dozen mechanical functions for each truck, letting WERN alert drivers to potential safety hazards. WERN has pioneered the development of the electronic driver log. Beginning in 1998, all its trucks were to use paperless logs. Instead of requiring drivers to manually record time spent driving, to comply with hours of service regulations, truck movements will be automatically monitored through a device supplied by Qualcomm Inc. WERN expected this to promote safety, help attract drivers, and aid productivity.

At December 31, 1998, WERN operated 6,150 tractors (average age 1.3 years): 5,220 company-owned and 930 owned by owner-operators. At that date, it operated 16,350 trailers (average age 3.1 years). By maintaining one of the industry's youngest fleet, WERN has been able to cut driver turnover, thereby reducing training and recruitment costs.

Per Share Data ($) (Year Ended Dec. 31)	1998	1997	1996	1995	1994	1993	1992	1991	1990	1989
Tangible Bk. Val.	9.31	8.27	7.34	6.54	5.85	5.16	3.87	NA	NA	NA
Cash Flow	2.92	3.15	2.24	2.07	1.90	1.69	1.48	NA	NA	NA
Earnings	1.19	1.01	0.86	0.77	0.77	0.68	0.57	NA	NA	NA
Dividends	0.09	0.08	0.07	0.06	0.06	0.04	0.04	NA	NA	NA
Payout Ratio	7%	8%	8%	8%	7%	6%	7%	NA	NA	NA
Prices - High	22 3/8	21 1/4	15	13 3/4	18	16 1/4	12 1/8	NA	NA	NA
- Low	11 1/4	12 3/4	10 1/4	9 3/8	11 3/8	9 7/8	7 3/8	NA	NA	NA
P/E Ratio - High	19	21	18	18	23	24	21	NA	NA	NA
- Low	9	13	12	12	15	14	13	NA	NA	NA
Income Statement Analysis (Million $)										
Revs.	863	772	643	576	516	418	362	NA	NA	NA
Oper. Inc.	178	150	131	122	114	95.0	80.0	NA	NA	NA
Depr.	82.5	72.6	65.0	61.2	53.7	44.2	39.3	NA	NA	NA
Int. Exp.	4.9	3.0	2.1	2.3	0.7	1.5	1.3	NA	NA	NA
Pretax Inc.	92.3	76.1	65.7	59.6	60.0	49.7	39.9	NA	NA	NA
Eff. Tax Rate	38%	36%	38%	39%	39%	40%	40%	NA	NA	NA
Net Inc.	57.2	48.4	40.6	36.4	36.7	30.0	24.1	NA	NA	NA
Balance Sheet & Other Fin. Data (Million $)										
Cash	15.9	22.3	23.1	16.2	11.7	9.8	NA	NA	NA	NA
Curr. Assets	145	146	116	101	88.2	75.7	NA	NA	NA	NA
Total Assets	769	668	549	508	454	373	NA	NA	NA	NA
Curr. Liab.	91.9	91.8	59.1	54.0	57.3	51.1	NA	NA	NA	NA
LT Debt	100	60.0	30.0	40.0	30.0	Nil	NA	NA	NA	NA
Common Eqty.	441	395	348	309	276	245	NA	NA	NA	NA
Total Cap.	646	547	461	425	372	299	NA	NA	NA	NA
Cap. Exp.	259	216	118	132	NA	NA	NA	NA	NA	NA
Cash Flow	140	121	106	97.6	90.4	74.1	63.5	NA	NA	NA
Curr. Ratio	1.6	1.6	2.0	1.9	1.5	1.5	NA	NA	NA	NA
% LT Debt of Cap.	15.5	11.0	6.5	9.6	8.1	Nil	NA	NA	NA	NA
% Net Inc.of Revs.	6.6	6.3	6.3	6.3	7.1	7.2	6.7	NA	NA	NA
% Ret. on Assets	8.0	8.0	7.7	7.6	8.9	8.9	NA	NA	NA	NA
% Ret. on Equity	13.7	13.0	9.2	12.4	14.1	14.4	NA	NA	NA	NA

Data as orig reptd.; bef. results of disc opers/spec. items. Per share data adj. for stk. divs. Bold denotes diluted EPS (FASB 128)-prior periods restated. E-Estimated. NA-Not Available. NM-Not Meaningful. NR-Not Ranked.

Office—14507 Frontier Rd., P.O. Box 45308, Omaha, NE 68145-0308. **Tel**—(402) 895-6640. **Website**—http://www.werner.com **Chrmn & CEO**—C. L. Werner. **Vice Chrmn**—Curtis G. Werner. **Pres**—Gregory L. Werner. **VP, CFO & Treas**—J. J. Steele. **Secy**—J. L. Johnson. **EVP & Investor Contact**—R. E. Synowicki. **Dirs**—J. G. Doll, I. B. Epstein, D. W. Rogert, M. F. Thompson, G. H. Timmerman, C. G. Werner, C. L. Werner, Gary L. Werner, Gregory L. Werner. **Transfer Agent & Registrar**—ChaseMellon Shareholder Services, Ridgefield Park, NJ. **Incorporated**—in Nebraska in 1982. **Empl**— 8,871. **S&P Analyst:** Stephen R. Klein

Wesley Jessen VisionCare

NASDAQ Symbol **WJCO**

In S&P SmallCap 600

09-OCT-99

Industry:
Health Care (Medical Products & Supplies)

Summary: This company is a worldwide developer and manufacturer of specialty soft contact lenses.

Quantitative Evaluations

Outlook
(1 Lowest—5 Highest)
• **NA**

Fair Value
• **NA**

Risk
• **Average**

Earn./Div. Rank
• **NR**

Technical Eval.
• **Bearish** since 9/99

Rel. Strength Rank
(1 Lowest—99 Highest)
• **77**

Insider Activity
• **Unfavorable**

Recent Price • 31¾
52 Wk Range • 35½-16½
Yield • Nil
12-Mo. P/E • 18.4

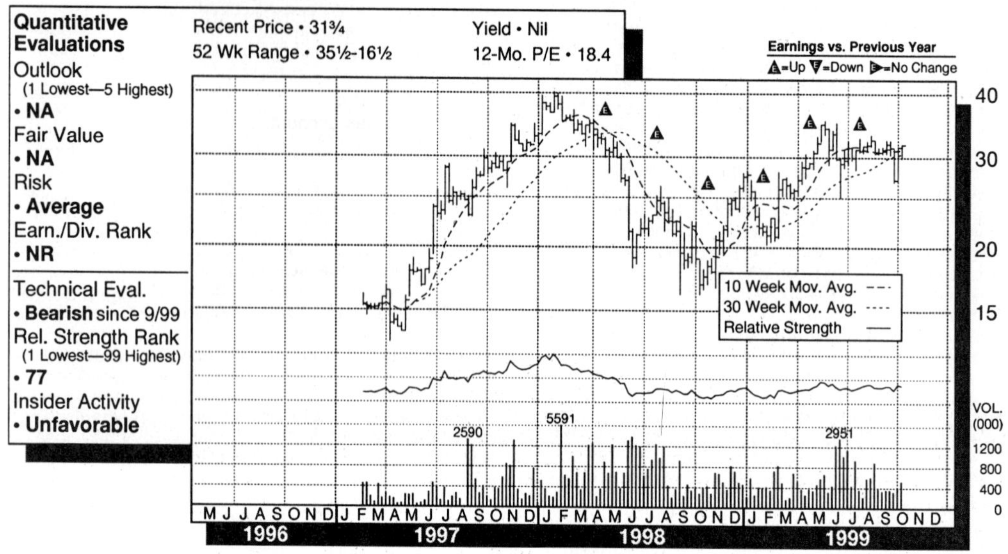

Business Profile - 27-SEP-99

In September 1999, the company launched new colored and clear lenses to correct astigmatism, designed for quarterly replacement. WJCO said that this is its first entry into the quarterly planned replacement toric lens market segment. The company announced its first diversification initiative beyond contact lenses in June 1999 with the acquisition of exclusive rights from Inoveon Corp. to market to optometrists an Internet-based system to manage diabetic retinopathy, the leading cause of preventable blindness among adults. WJCO said that its sales momentum continued to build in 1999's second quarter as it launched new products abroad and enjoyed strong growth in cosmetic and toric specialty lens products. It anticipated strong sales and earnings gains in the quarters ahead.

Operational Review - 27-SEP-99

Net sales for the six months ended July 3, 1999, rose 8.5%, year to year, mainly reflecting a 40% gain in sales of disposable and planned replacement contact lenses driven by the introduction of FreshLook ColorBlends and FreshLook Toric. Margins benefited from the higher volume, and operating income increased 18%. Following significantly higher depreciation and amortization charges, pretax income advanced 15%. After taxes at 32.0%, versus 34.0%, net income was up 18%, to $15,369,000 ($0.83 a share, based on 4.3% fewer average shares) from $12,997,000 ($0.67).

Stock Performance - 08-OCT-99

In the past 30 trading days, WJCO's shares have increased 3%, compared to a 0.91% fall in the S&P 500. Average trading volume for the past five days was 102,320 shares, compared with the 40-day moving average of 89,821 shares.

Key Stock Statistics

Dividend Rate/Share	Nil	Shareholders	2,698
Shs. outstg. (M)	17.3	Market cap. (B)	$0.550
Avg. daily vol. (M)	0.079	Inst. holdings	76%
Tang. Bk. Value/Share	3.60		
Beta	NA		

Value of $10,000 invested 5 years ago: NA

Fiscal Year Ending Dec. 31

	1999	1998	1997	1996	1995	1994
Revenues (Million $)						
1Q	76.31	70.60	64.07	—	—	—
2Q	80.01	73.42	72.08	—	—	—
3Q	—	75.25	75.24	—	—	—
4Q	—	72.99	70.79	—	—	—
Yr.	—	292.3	282.2	—	—	—
Earnings Per Share ($)						
1Q	**0.34**	**0.27**	**-0.38**	—	—	—
2Q	**0.49**	**0.40**	**-0.02**	—	—	—
3Q	—	**0.43**	**0.37**	—	—	—
4Q	—	**0.47**	**0.38**	—	—	—
Yr.	—	**1.57**	**0.45**	—	—	—

Next earnings report expected: early November

Dividend Data

No cash dividends have been paid and the company does not expect to pay dividends for the foreseeable future. It intends to retain earnings to support its growth strategy and reduce indebtedness.

Wesley Jessen VisionCare, Inc.

Business Summary - 27-SEP-99

The oldest major contact lens manufacturer in the world, Wesley Jessen VisionCare, Inc. was founded by two optometrists, Drs. Newton K. Wesley and George Jessen, in 1946. The company believes that it has been responsible for many industry firsts, including: the first commercially successful contact lens, the first soft lens to correct astigmatism, the first extended wear soft lens, the first opaque color lens, the first color disposable lens, and the first disposable lens with UV absorber.

WJCO is the leading worldwide developer, manufacturer and marketer of specialty soft contact lenses, based on its share of the specialty lens market. The company's products include cosmetic lenses (sold under the DuraSoft, Elegance, Natural Touch and Wild Eyes brand names), which change or enhance the wearer's eye color appearance; toric lenses (CSI, Optifit and Hydrocurve), which correct vision for people with astigmatism; and premium lenses (Aquaflex, CSI Clarity and Hydrocurve), which offer value-added features such as improved comfort for dry eyes and protection from UV light.

Wesley Jessen offers a broad range of both conventional contact lenses, which can typically be used for up to 24 months, and disposable contact lenses, which are intended to be replaced at least every two weeks.

The company operates mainly in the specialty segment of the soft lens market. In recent years, in both the clear and specialty lens segments, there has been a pronounced shift in consumers' preferences toward disposable lenses and away from conventional lenses, which has led to a significant increase in contact lens expenditures per wearer. WJCO estimates that more than 40% of the U.S. soft lens wearers use disposable lenses, up from 21% in 1993. The company also offers a complete line of conventional and disposable clear lenses, which are positioned as companion products to its cosmetic lenses.

Specialty lenses accounted for about 83% of the company's sales in 1998, clear lenses 14% and hard/other lenses 3%.

It is believes that over 75% of all contact lens prescribers in the U.S. offer the company's products, which permits it to rapidly launch new categories of products. WJCO develops proprietary technologies, manufacturing processes and products through a combination of its in-house staff of more than 100 engineers and scientists and company-sponsored research by third-party experts.

The company is among the largest advertisers in the industry and markets and sells its products to consumers through advertising campaigns and to eyecare practitioners through its 211 person salesforce and network of independent distributors, which together sell the company's products in more than 75 countries. International sales accounted for about 42% of the total in 1998.

Per Share Data ($) (Year Ended Dec. 31)	1998	1997	1996	1995	1994	1993	1992	1991	1990	1989
Tangible Bk. Val.	3.52	2.84	NA	NA	NA	NA	NA	NA	NA	NA
Cash Flow	1.63	0.45	NA	NA	NA	NA	NA	NA	NA	NA
Earnings	1.57	0.45	NA	NA	NA	NA	NA	NA	NA	NA
Dividends	Nil	Nil	NA	NA	NA	NA	NA	NA	NA	NA
Payout Ratio	Nil	Nil	NA	NA	NA	NA	NA	NA	NA	NA
Prices - High	40¼	39⅝	NA	NA	NA	NA	NA	NA	NA	NA
- Low	16⅛	13	NA	NA	NA	NA	NA	NA	NA	NA
P/E Ratio - High	26	88	NA	NA	NA	NA	NA	NA	NA	NA
- Low	10	29	NA	NA	NA	NA	NA	NA	NA	NA
Income Statement Analysis (Million $)										
Revs.	292	282	NA	NA	NA	NA	NA	NA	NA	NA
Oper. Inc.	49.8	18.0	NA	NA	NA	NA	NA	NA	NA	NA
Depr.	1.1	0.0	NA	NA	NA	NA	NA	NA	NA	NA
Int. Exp.	5.4	6.1	NA	NA	NA	NA	NA	NA	NA	NA
Pretax Inc.	43.8	12.4	NA	NA	NA	NA	NA	NA	NA	NA
Eff. Tax Rate	32%	34%	NA	NA	NA	NA	NA	NA	NA	NA
Net Inc.	29.6	8.2	NA	NA	NA	NA	NA	NA	NA	NA
Balance Sheet & Other Fin. Data (Million $)										
Cash	8.9	4.8	NA	NA	NA	NA	NA	NA	NA	NA
Curr. Assets	152	128	NA	NA	NA	NA	NA	NA	NA	NA
Total Assets	205	176	NA	67.3	NA	NA	NA	NA	NA	NA
Curr. Liab.	68.2	62.6	NA	NA	NA	NA	NA	NA	NA	NA
LT Debt	69.0	57.0	NA	NA	NA	NA	NA	NA	NA	NA
Common Eqty.	50.0	36.8	NA	NA	NA	NA	NA	NA	NA	NA
Total Cap.	119	94.0	NA	NA	NA	NA	NA	NA	NA	NA
Cap. Exp.	17.2	16.3	NA	NA	NA	NA	NA	NA	NA	NA
Cash Flow	30.7	8.2	NA	NA	NA	NA	NA	NA	NA	NA
Curr. Ratio	2.2	2.1	NA	NA	NA	NA	NA	NA	NA	NA
% LT Debt of Cap.	58.0	60.6	NA	NA	NA	NA	NA	NA	NA	NA
% Net Inc.of Revs.	10.1	2.9	NA	NA	NA	NA	NA	NA	NA	NA
% Ret. on Assets	15.6	4.6	NA	NA	NA	NA	NA	NA	NA	NA
% Ret. on Equity	68.2	69.6	NA	NA	NA	NA	NA	NA	NA	NA

Data as orig reptd.; bef. results of disc opers/spec. items. Per share data adj. for stk. divs. Bold denotes diluted EPS (FASB 128)-prior periods restated. Data for 1995 is from Jun. 29 to Dec. 31. E-Estimated. NA-Not Available. NM-Not Meaningful. NR-Not Ranked.

Office—333 East Howard Ave., Des Plaines, IL 60018-5903. **Tel**—(847) 294-3000. **Website**—http://www.wesley-jessen.com**Chrmn, Pres & CEO**—K. J. Ryan. **VP-Fin, CFO & Secy**—E. J. Kelley. **Dirs**—M. A. D'Amato, E. J. Kelley, A. W. Kirsch, S. Levine, J. W. Maki, J. J. O'Malley, S. G. Pagliuca, K. J. Ryan. **Transfer Agent & Registrar**—American Stock Transfer & Trust Co., NYC. **Incorporated**—in Delaware in 1995. **Empl**—2,690. **S&P Analyst:** J. J. Schemitsch

STANDARD
&POOR'S
STOCK REPORTS

Whitney Holding Corp.

NASDAQ Symbol **WTNY**

In S&P SmallCap 600

09-OCT-99

Industry:
Banks (Regional)

Summary: This New Orleans-based bank holding company operates through offices in Louisiana, Mississippi, Alabama, Florida, and a foreign branch in the West Indies.

Quantitative Evaluations

Outlook
(1 Lowest—5 Highest)
• **2⁻**

Fair Value
• **33⅞**

Risk
• **Low**

Earn./Div. Rank
• **B**

Technical Eval.
• **Bearish** since 8/99

Rel. Strength Rank
(1 Lowest—99 Highest)
• **53**

Insider Activity
• **Neutral**

Recent Price • 35⅝
52 Wk Range • 42-31¾
Yield • 3.7%
12-Mo. P/E • 16.2

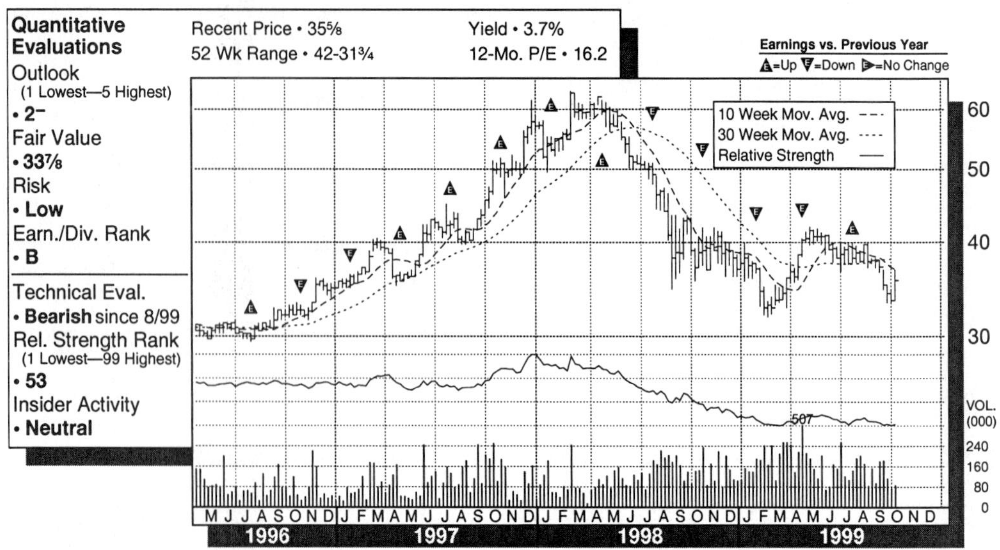

Business Profile - 30-JUL-99

In the first half of 1999, average loans increased 15% and average deposits grew 9%. The company also continued to see growth in credit card income and service charges on deposit accounts. In mid-July 1999, WTNY said that expense control programs implemented in late 1998, were showing an impact. In the second quarter of 1999, the company purchased 530,000 WTNY common shares under a stock repurchase program announced in the previous quarter.

Operational Review - 30-JUL-99

Net interest income in the six months ended June 30, 1999, advanced 4.8%, year to year, aided by continued loan growth. The provision for possible loan losses was $2,250,000, up from $73,000. After 3.5% greater noninterest income, and a 6.7% increase in noninterest expense, net income declined 3.9%, to $29,396,000 ($1.26 a share), from $30,581,000 ($1.30). As of June 30, 1999, loans approximated $3.3 billion and deposits were about $4.2 billion.

Stock Performance - 08-OCT-99

In the past 30 trading days, WTNY's shares have declined 6%, compared to a 0.91% fall in the S&P 500. Average trading volume for the past five days was 17,040 shares, compared with the 40-day moving average of 24,533 shares.

Key Stock Statistics

Dividend Rate/Share	1.32	Shareholders	3,415
Shs. outstg. (M)	22.9	Market cap. (B)	$0.816
Avg. daily vol. (M)	0.023	Inst. holdings	23%
Tang. Bk. Value/Share	23.98		
Beta	0.75		

Value of $10,000 invested 5 years ago: $ 18,442

Fiscal Year Ending Dec. 31

	1999	1998	1997	1996	1995	1994
Revenues (Million $)						
1Q	100.5	87.24	76.87	65.64	53.39	50.59
2Q	101.9	98.75	86.65	66.15	55.22	52.16
3Q	—	98.70	89.95	68.36	57.15	53.66
4Q	—	—	88.97	78.88	59.66	41.70
Yr.	—	396.9	342.4	279.0	225.4	208.1
Earnings Per Share ($)						
1Q	**0.61**	**0.67**	**0.52**	**0.46**	0.55	1.09
2Q	**0.65**	**0.63**	**0.68**	**0.56**	0.55	0.65
3Q	—	**0.45**	**0.65**	**0.58**	1.03	0.93
4Q	—	**0.49**	**0.65**	**0.57**	0.64	0.97
Yr.	—	**2.24**	**2.50**	**2.17**	**2.44**	**3.25**

Next earnings report expected: late October

Dividend Data (Dividends have been paid since 1993.)

Amount ($)	Date Decl.	Ex-Div. Date	Stock of Record	Payment Date
0.300	Nov. 18	Dec. 11	Dec. 15	Jan. 04 '99
0.330	Feb. 24	Mar. 11	Mar. 15	Apr. 01 '99
0.330	May. 26	Jun. 11	Jun. 15	Jul. 01 '99
0.330	Aug. 25	Sep. 13	Sep. 15	Oct. 01 '99

Whitney Holding Corporation

Business Summary - 30-JUL-99

This New Orleans-based bank holding company has made 11 separate banking acquisitions in the past five years, including several in 1998. By participating in a consolidation trend of the industry, WTNY has expanded its geographic reach, mostly along the coast of the Gulf of Mexico. It now operates in Louisiana, Alabama, Mississippi, Florida, and has one foreign branch, on Grand Cayman in the British West Indies.

From 1995 and through 1997, the company operated as a multi-bank holding company. In January 1998, it merged all of its banking operations into Whitney National Bank (Bank). Through the Bank, the company provides a comprehensive line of financial services to individuals, businesses and other public and private institutions.

Loan growth has been healthy, with average loans increasing 14% in 1998, primarily due to business expansion along the Gulf Coast, particularly in Southern Louisiana. Commercial and construction real estate lending in the tourism and hotel business in the New Orleans metropolitan area grew to 32% of the loan portfolio at December 31, 1998. As of the 1998 year-end, there were $3.3 billion of loans outstanding. Loan growth in 1998 was mainly funded by reductions in the securities portfolio and steady deposit growth.

Average deposits increased 7% in 1998. The most significant growth came from a new premium money market product. The Bank also continued to see growth in time deposits and non-interest-bearing demand deposits. There were total deposits of $4.3 million at December 31, 1998.

As of year-end 1998, the reserve for possible loan losses covered non-accruing loans by 4.5 times and represented 1.23% of the total loans. Non-performing assets, which includes non-accruing loans, in-substance foreclosures and other real estate, totaled $16 million, and was 0.49% of total loans plus foreclosed assets as of December 31, 1998, compared to 0.51 a year earlier.

In 1997, the company acquired two banks in exchange for an aggregate of 2.58 million shares. It acquired two more banks in the first half of 1998, for a total of $92.5 million in stock. In the second half of 1998, the company completed two additional acquisitions.

Per Share Data ($) (Year Ended Dec. 31)	1998	1997	1996	1995	1994	1993	1992	1991	1990	1989
Tangible Bk. Val.	23.98	22.10	21.35	20.61	19.38	17.36	12.68	11.50	NA	NA
Earnings	2.24	2.50	2.26	2.77	3.63	5.25	1.41	-0.33	NA	NA
Dividends	1.18	1.09	0.97	0.82	0.64	0.43	0.07	Nil	NA	NA
Payout Ratio	53%	44%	43%	30%	18%	8%	5%	Nil	NA	NA
Prices - High	63 1/2	61 3/4	35 7/8	34	28 1/2	26 1/8	17 1/4	10 1/2	NA	NA
- Low	34 5/8	34 3/4	29 1/2	22	20 3/4	15 5/8	8 3/8	5 3/4	NA	NA
P/E Ratio - High	28	25	16	12	8	5	12	NM	NA	NA
- Low	15	14	13	8	6	3	6	NM	NA	NA
Income Statement Analysis (Million $)										
Net Int. Inc.	213	184	152	129	124	121	112	99	NA	NA
Tax Equiv. Adj.	4.7	NA	4.5	3.8	3.8	3.3	NA	NA	NA	NA
Non Int. Inc.	59.9	51.0	37.3	31.3	32.4	31.0	27.2	26.9	NA	NA
Loan Loss Prov.	0.1	-2.8	5.0	10.0	26.1	60.0	3.4	45.4	NA	NA
Exp./Op. Revs.	71%	68%	69%	68%	65%	65%	NA	NA	NA	NA
Pretax Inc.	77.8	78.7	59.7	59.6	78.1	111	29.1	-6.7	NA	NA
Eff. Tax Rate	32%	34%	32%	31%	32%	32%	31%	NM	NA	NA
Net Inc.	52.7	52.2	40.6	40.9	52.8	75.8	20.2	-4.7	NA	NA
% Net Int. Marg.	4.92	4.97	4.81	5.00	4.79	4.75	4.52	3.99	NA	NA
Balance Sheet & Other Fin. Data (Million $)										
Money Mkt. Assets	152	222	234	231	215	297	NA	NA	NA	NA
Inv. Securities	1,340	1,268	1,326	1,368	1,533	1,634	1,475	1,139	NA	NA
Com'l Loans	1,242	1,192	993	1,150	868	NA	NA	NA	NA	NA
Other Loans	2,028	1,456	1,072	289	192	NA	NA	NA	NA	NA
Total Assets	5,212	4,313	3,775	3,151	2,913	3,003	2,953	2,858	NA	NA
Demand Deposits	1,240	1,061	935	852	769	784	NA	NA	NA	NA
Time Deposits	3,016	2,450	1,927	1,710	1,642	2,505	NA	NA	NA	NA
LT Debt	Nil	Nil	Nil	Nil	Nil	Nil	Nil	Nil	NA	NA
Common Eqty.	561	479	405	338	298	260	185	170	NA	NA
% Ret. on Assets	1.1	1.3	1.1	1.4	1.8	2.6	0.7	NM	NA	NA
% Ret. on Equity	10.1	11.8	10.4	13.0	19.1	34.8	11.5	NM	NA	NA
% Loan Loss Resv.	1.2	1.6	1.9	2.6	3.3	4.6	9.4	8.5	NA	NA
% Loans/Deposits	76.8	NA	72.2	56.2	44.0	39.0	41.2	51.9	NA	NA
% Equity to Assets	10.9	10.9	10.7	10.7	10.2	8.6	6.3	5.8	NA	NA

Data as orig reptd.; bef. results of disc opers/spec. items. Per share data adj. for stk. divs. Bold denotes diluted EPS (FASB 128)-prior periods restated. E-Estimated. NA-Not Available. NM-Not Meaningful. NR-Not Ranked.

Office—228 St. Charles Ave., New Orleans, LA 70130 (P. O. Box 61260, New Orleans 70161). **Tel**—(504) 586-7272. **Chrmn & CEO**—W. L. Marks. **Pres**—R. King Milling. **CFO**—T. L. Callicutt, Jr. **Dirs**—G. C. Billups, H. J. Blumenthal Jr., J. B. Bullard Jr., J. M. Cain, A. R. Cooper II, R. H. Crosby Jr., R. B. Crowell, C. A. Cutrone, W. A. Hines, R. E. Howson, J. J. Kelly, E. J. Kock Jr., A. S. Lippman, W. L. Marks, R. K. Milling, J. G. Phillips, J. K. Roberts Jr., C. W. Suggs, W. P. Snyder III, W. K. Watters. **Transfer Agent & Registrar**—Boatmen's Trust Co., St. Louis, MO. **Incorporated**—in Louisiana in 1962. **Empl**— 2,269. **S&P Analyst:** S.A.H.

STANDARD
&POOR'S
STOCK REPORTS

Whittman-Hart, Inc.

NASDAQ Symbol **WHIT**

In S&P SmallCap 600

09-OCT-99

Industry:
Services (Computer Systems)

Summary: This company provides strategic information technology business solutions designed to improve clients' productivity and competitive position.

Quantitative Evaluations

Outlook (1 Lowest—5 Highest)
• **NA**
Fair Value
• **NA**
Risk
• **High**
Earn./Div. Rank
• **NR**

Technical Eval.
• **Bullish** since 9/99
Rel. Strength Rank (1 Lowest—99 Highest)
• **95**
Insider Activity
• **NA**

Recent Price • 36⅜
52 Wk Range • 39⅝-17
Yield • Nil
12-Mo. P/E • 88.7

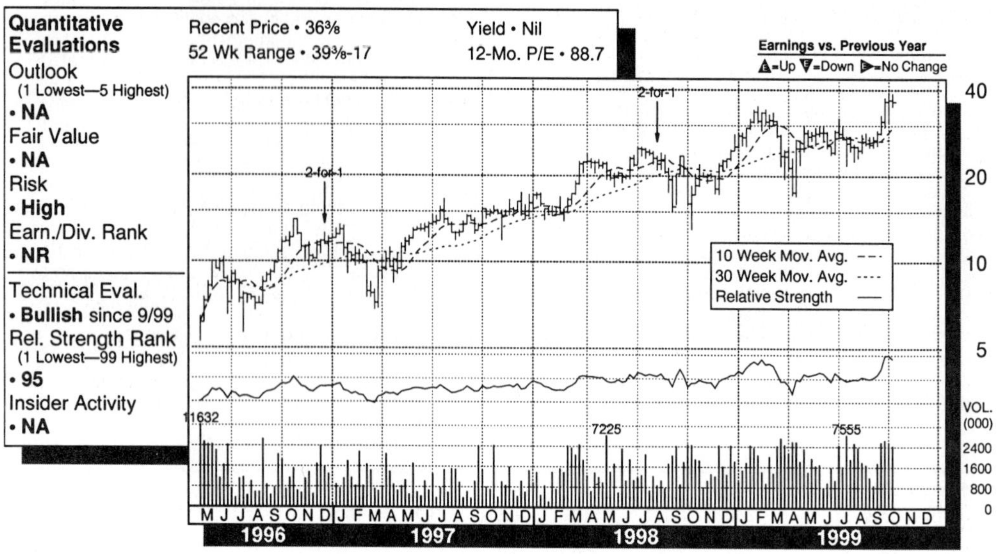

Business Profile - 11-JUN-99

Thus far in 1999, the company has aggressively pursued acquisition opportunities. In May 1999, the company announced the acquisition of POV Partners, Inc., an Ohio-based information technology services firm that provides a broad range of business strategy and IT services, including Internet-enabled application solutions and e-commerce initiatives. In March 1999, WHIT purchased, for 574,074 shares of Whittman common stock, Waterfield Technology Group, a Boston-based IT services firm focused on client server and Internet-related applications. The company expects to open a new office in Pittsburgh in July 1999.

Operational Review - 11-JUN-99

Revenues in the three months ended March 31, 1999, rose 62%, year to year, driven by the addition of new clients and growth of client relationships at existing and new branch locations. Margins widened, reflecting a more favorable sales mix, as well as less rapid increases in selling, recruiting and G&A costs; operating income surged 111%. Results were hurt by a significant jump in business combination costs, partially offset by higher other income. After taxes at 46.2%, versus 47.6%, net income advanced 88%, to $5,559,526 ($0.09 a share, on 17% more shares), from $2,962,338 ($0.06).

Stock Performance - 08-OCT-99

In the past 30 trading days, WHIT's shares have increased 41%, compared to a 0.91% fall in the S&P 500. Average trading volume for the past five days was 545,280 shares, compared with the 40-day moving average of 563,138 shares.

Key Stock Statistics

Dividend Rate/Share	Nil	Shareholders	415
Shs. outstg. (M)	54.1	Market cap. (B)	$ 2.0
Avg. daily vol. (M)	0.826	Inst. holdings	66%
Tang. Bk. Value/Share	4.57		
Beta	NA		

Value of $10,000 invested 5 years ago: NA

Fiscal Year Ending Dec. 31

	1999	1998	1997	1996	1995	1994
Revenues (Million $)						
1Q	104.1	58.66	29.05	—	—	—
2Q	111.2	68.94	34.73	—	—	—
3Q	—	82.11	39.25	—	—	—
4Q	—	92.10	51.89	—	—	—
Yr.	—	307.6	173.5	103.7	—	—
Earnings Per Share ($)						
1Q	**0.09**	**0.06**	0.05	—	—	—
2Q	**0.11**	**0.09**	0.06	—	—	—
3Q	—	**0.09**	0.07	—	—	—
4Q	—	**0.12**	**0.04**	—	—	—
Yr.	—	**0.35**	**0.22**	0.14	—	—

Next earnings report expected: mid October

Dividend Data

No cash dividends have been paid. The company intends to reinvest its earnings in future growth opportunities and does not anticipate paying cash dividends in the foreseeable future.

A Division of The McGraw-Hill Companies

Business Summary - 11-JUN-99

Providing strategic information technology business solutions to improve the productivity and competitive position of its clients, Whittman-Hart is a single source for a wide range of services required to design, develop and implement integrated solutions in the client/server, Internet and midrange computing environments. Its marketing efforts focus on middle-market companies ranging from $50 million to $500 million in revenues.

The company has five business units: Solution Strategies, Package Software Solutions, Custom Applications, Network Enabled Solutions and Interactive Solutions. The Solution Strategies unit helps clients identify their critical business objectives and formulates integrated people, process and technology solutions to improve their business. The Package Software Solutions segment uses a business-requirements and user-driven methodology for rapid package software implementation.

The Custom Applications unit develops and maintains custom business software applications, from analysis and design through software testing and quality assurance. The Network Enabled Solutions segment uses network computing strategies and technologies to develop business connectivity solutions that allow people, technology and organizations to work regardless of geographic location. The Interactive Solutions unit helps clients assess their training and education needs and develops appropriate strategies. The group provides customized, performance-based training solutions to support package and custom software system implementations in instructor-led and computer-based formats.

Services are sold and delivered through a network of 17 branch offices throughout the U.S. and in London. The company serves a wide range of industries including communications, consumer products, distribution, diversified services, financial services, insurance, manufacturing, pharmaceutical, professional services, retail and technology.

Whittman-Hart continues to aggressively pursue growth through acquisitions. In May 1999, the company announced the acquisition of POV Partners, Inc., an Ohio-based information technology services firm. POV Partners provides a broad range of business strategy and IT services, including Internet-enabled application solutions and e-commerce initiatives. In March 1999, WHIT purchased, for 574,074 shares of Whittman common stock, Waterfield Technology Group, a Boston-based IT services firm focused on client server and Internet-related applications.

Per Share Data ($) (Year Ended Dec. 31)	1998	1997	1996	1995	1994	1993	1992	1991	1990	1989
Tangible Bk. Val.	4.03	2.15	1.83	NA	NA	NA	NA	NA	NA	NA
Cash Flow	0.42	0.27	0.19	NA	NA	NA	NA	NA	NA	NA
Earnings	0.35	0.22	0.14	NA	NA	NA	NA	NA	NA	NA
Dividends	Nil	Nil	Nil	NA	NA	NA	NA	NA	NA	NA
Payout Ratio	Nil	Nil	Nil	NA	NA	NA	NA	NA	NA	NA
Prices - High	28¼	17½	14⅛	NA	NA	NA	NA	NA	NA	NA
- Low	13	6⅞	4	NA	NA	NA	NA	NA	NA	NA
P/E Ratio - High	81	80	97	NA	NA	NA	NA	NA	NA	NA
- Low	37	31	28	NA	NA	NA	NA	NA	NA	NA
Income Statement Analysis (Million $)										
Revs.	308	173	104	NA	NA	NA	NA	NA	NA	NA
Oper. Inc.	32.7	18.4	9.2	NA	NA	NA	NA	NA	NA	NA
Depr.	3.8	2.5	1.3	NA	NA	NA	NA	NA	NA	NA
Int. Exp.	0.1	0.0	0.1	NA	NA	NA	NA	NA	NA	NA
Pretax Inc.	33.7	18.1	9.2	NA	NA	NA	NA	NA	NA	NA
Eff. Tax Rate	44%	43%	37%	NA	NA	NA	NA	NA	NA	NA
Net Inc.	18.8	10.3	5.8	NA	NA	NA	NA	NA	NA	NA
Balance Sheet & Other Fin. Data (Million $)										
Cash	48.2	9.1	36.5	NA	NA	NA	NA	NA	NA	NA
Curr. Assets	178	106	87.5	NA	NA	NA	NA	NA	NA	NA
Total Assets	243	122	94.1	NA	NA	NA	NA	NA	NA	NA
Curr. Liab.	32.7	23.1	13.4	NA	NA	NA	NA	NA	NA	NA
LT Debt	Nil	Nil	Nil	NA	NA	NA	NA	NA	NA	NA
Common Eqty.	208	97.2	79.6	NA	NA	NA	NA	NA	NA	NA
Total Cap.	209	97.4	79.8	NA	NA	NA	NA	NA	NA	NA
Cap. Exp.	21.7	10.9	4.0	NA	NA	NA	NA	NA	NA	NA
Cash Flow	22.7	12.8	7.1	NA	NA	NA	NA	NA	NA	NA
Curr. Ratio	5.4	4.6	6.5	NA	NA	NA	NA	NA	NA	NA
% LT Debt of Cap.	Nil	Nil	Nil	NA	NA	NA	NA	NA	NA	NA
% Net Inc.of Revs.	6.1	5.9	5.6	NA	NA	NA	NA	NA	NA	NA
% Ret. on Assets	10.3	9.7	NA	NA	NA	NA	NA	NA	NA	NA
% Ret. on Equity	12.3	11.7	NA	NA	NA	NA	NA	NA	NA	NA

Data as orig reptd.; bef. results of disc opers/spec. items. Per share data adj. for stk. divs. Bold denotes diluted EPS (FASB 128)-prior periods restated. E-Estimated. NA-Not Available. NM-Not Meaningful. NR-Not Ranked.

Office—311 South Wacker Dr., Suite 3500, Chicago, IL 60606-6618. **Tel**—(312) 922-9200. **Chrmn & CEO**—R. F. Bernard. **Pres & Secy**—E. V. Szofer. **CFO & Investor Contact**—Kevin M. Gaskey. **COO**—M. J. Berent. **Dirs**—R. F. Bernard, P. D. Carbery, L. P. Roches, R. F. Steel, E. V. Szofer. **Transfer Agent & Registrar**—Harris Trust and Savings Bank, Chicago. **Incorporated**—in Delaware in 1991. **Empl**— 3,100. **S&P Analyst:** Stephen J. Tekirian

STANDARD &POOR'S STOCK REPORTS

Whole Foods Market

Nasdaq Symbol **WFMI**

In S&P SmallCap 600

09-OCT-99 **Industry:** Retail (Food Chains)

Summary: This company owns and operates the largest U.S. chain of natural foods supermarkets, with 96 stores in 20 states and the District of Columbia.

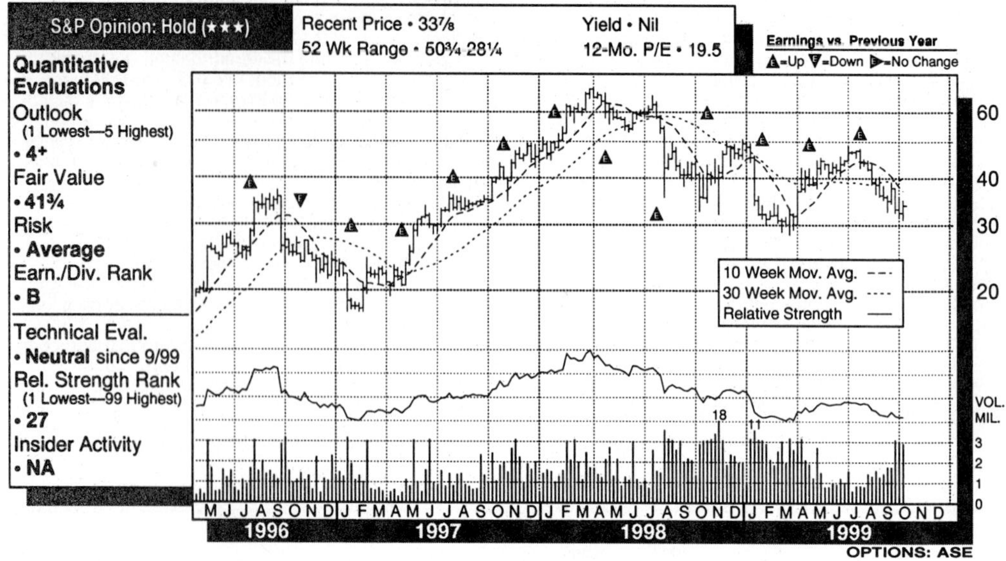

Overview - 09-AUG-99

Sales should grow nearly 20% in FY 00 (Sep.), fueled by the addition of 15 to 20 new stores, a full year's contribution from the recently acquired Nature's Heartland company (four stores), and same-store sales gains of about 8.0%. Gross margins should widen on improved purchasing, better category management and shrink improvement. However, SG&A expense may rise temporarily, reflecting Internet start-up costs, higher store development expenses, and lower leverage from weak sales at Amrion which has been hurt by industry weakness in the nutritional supplement market. However, this increase may be offset by greater store leverage from a larger store base and improved sales at recently opened units as the company's store base begins to mature. Based on these assumptions, we expect earnings to grow to $2.17, up 23% from a somewhat depressed FY 1999 EPS estimate of $1.76.

Valuation - 09-AUG-99

We recently downgraded the shares to hold, from accumulate, reflecting a recent rise in the share value. The shares recently traded at 20X our FY 00 EPS estimate which is in-line with the average P/E multiple within our supermarket universe. Due to WFMI's aggressive store opening schedule, it is likely that the company will need to increase its outside financing requirements. Additionally, it appears that SG&A expenses as a percentage of sales may increase in the near term until WFMI's store base matures and the company develops its Internet offering. Also, weakness at Amrion may slow earnings growth in the near term due to weakness in the nutritional supplement market. Thus, while we believe the shares should offer strong earnings growth for the next few years, short term problems are likely to limit near term upside momentum.

Key Stock Statistics

S&P EPS Est. 1999	1.76	Tang. Bk. Value/Share	9.63
P/E on S&P Est. 1999	19.2	Beta	1.05
S&P EPS Est. 2000	1.92	Shareholders	1,500
Dividend Rate/Share	Nil	Market cap. (B)	$0.890
Shs. outstg. (M)	26.3	Inst. holdings	73%
Avg. daily vol. (M)	0.593		

Value of $10,000 invested 5 years ago: $ 15,055

Fiscal Year Ending Sep. 30

	1999	1998	1997	1996	1995	1994
Revenues (Million $)						
1Q	456.2	407.8	312.6	245.0	139.0	116.5
2Q	358.9	324.8	259.8	203.9	117.0	92.77
3Q	377.6	331.0	274.5	213.4	119.9	97.36
4Q	—	326.2	270.4	230.8	120.5	95.10
Yr.	—	1,390	1,117	892.0	496.4	401.6
Earnings Per Share ($)						
1Q	**0.47**	**0.44**	**0.24**	Nil	0.17	0.18
2Q	**0.43**	**0.40**	0.29	0.08	0.18	0.14
3Q	**0.44**	**0.40**	0.32	0.23	0.07	0.15
4Q	**E0.42**	**0.40**	0.20	-1.22	0.16	0.14
Yr.	**E1.76**	**1.64**	**1.06**	**-0.54**	0.58	0.61

Next earnings report expected: mid November

Dividend Data

No cash dividends have been paid. WFMI intends to retain earnings for use in its business and therefore does not anticipate paying any cash dividends in the foreseeable future. A two-for-one stock split was effected in 1993.

Whole Foods Market, Inc.

Business Summary - 09-AUG-99

One-stop shopping for the health-conscious consumer of the 90s is what Whole Foods Market (WFMI) aims to provide. After a series of store openings and aggressive acquisitions, the company has grown from a single Austin, TX, store in 1981 to a chain of 96 stores in 20 states and Washington, DC. WFMI's goal continues to be to provide the highest quality foods it can find, in terms of taste, appearance and nutrition. The company attributes its success to its ability to differentiate its stores from those of its competition by tailoring its product mix, customer service attitude, and store environment to appeal to health conscious and gourmet customers.

Whole Foods stores offer organic fruits and vegetables, poultry and meats free from antibiotics and growth hormones, as well as conventionally grown, high quality foods. Hearth-baked crusty breads, a full line of natural household supplies, and body care products are also available. Stores average about 24,000 sq. ft. and offer a selection of about 10,000 to 18,000 food and non-food products, including prepared foods, vitamins and nutriceuticals, bakeries and specialty wines and cheeses. In addition, the company covers every item sold in its stores with a 100% money-back guarantee.

The company opens or acquires stores in existing regions, and in metropolitan areas where management believes WFMI can become the leading natural foods supermarket retailer. To this end, the company planned to open 10 stores in FY 99 (Sep.), and 15 to 20 units in FY 00. In developing new stores, WFMI seeks to open large format units of 30,000 sq. ft. to 50,000 sq. ft., located on premium sites, often in urban, highly populated areas.

Over the past few years, WFMI has developed two private label brands. The Whole Foods label is used to promote premium and super premium products while the 365 label is used to sell everyday value products. Products sold under private label brands include organic pasta sauces, pear and plum butters, organic kalamata olives, jams, organic olive oil, salsa, honey, organic chocolate bars, frozen vegetables and fruit, dolphin-safe tuna, spring water, dry and canned pet food, dry breakfast cereals, 100% recycled paper towels, bathroom tissue, whole bean coffees, ice cream, soft drinks, and 100% fruit juices.

Amrion Inc., acquired in September 1997, develops, produces and markets high quality nutriceuticals and nutritional supplements. Amrion currently sells more than 900 products, including nutriceuticals, herbs, herbal formulas, vitamins, minerals and homeopathic products. Coenzyme Q10, Ginko Biloba, and Bilberry account for a significant portion of Amrion's annual net sales. Amrion products are sold primarily under company-owned trademarks via direct marketing.

Per Share Data ($) (Year Ended Sep. 30)	**1998**	**1997**	**1996**	**1995**	**1994**	**1993**	**1992**	**1991**	**1990**	**1989**
Tangible Bk. Val.	8.65	6.48	5.36	4.45	4.53	3.20	4.29	1.06	NA	NA
Cash Flow	3.16	2.41	0.43	1.45	1.16	0.67	0.72	0.88	NA	NA
Earnings	1.64	1.05	-0.90	0.58	0.61	0.29	0.43	0.38	NA	NA
Dividends	Nil	Nil	Nil	Nil	Nil	Nil	Nil	Nil	NA	NA
Payout Ratio	Nil	Nil	Nil	Nil	Nil	Nil	Nil	Nil	NA	NA
Prices - High	70 1/8	51 3/8	37 1/8	16 1/4	25 3/4	23 3/8	17	NA	NA	NA
- Low	32	17 1/2	13 1/2	10 1/8	9 1/2	13 1/2	7 1/4	NA	NA	NA
P/E Ratio - High	43	49	NM	28	42	81	39	NA	NA	NA
- Low	20	17	NM	17	16	47	17	NA	NA	NA
Income Statement Analysis (Million $)										
Revs.	1,390	1,117	892	496	402	322	120	92.5	NA	NA
Oper. Inc.	125	89.5	50.0	29.7	22.8	16.4	6.7	5.1	NA	NA
Depr.	42.3	34.5	25.5	12.3	7.9	5.0	2.1	1.6	NA	NA
Int. Exp.	7.7	6.0	4.7	1.5	0.5	0.8	0.3	1.0	NA	NA
Pretax Inc.	72.1	39.4	-20.6	13.6	14.7	8.4	4.9	2.6	NA	NA
Eff. Tax Rate	37%	32%	NM	39%	41%	55%	38%	40%	NA	NA
Net Inc.	45.4	26.6	-17.2	8.2	8.6	3.8	3.1	1.6	NA	NA
Balance Sheet & Other Fin. Data (Million $)										
Cash	36.7	13.4	1.7	5.2	4.3	6.8	16.0	2.2	NA	NA
Curr. Assets	184	114	61.6	37.3	31.3	23.7	23.6	8.2	NA	NA
Total Assets	545	400	311	196	136	106	46.5	23.4	NA	NA
Curr. Liab.	91.0	77.3	56.7	35.8	26.0	22.7	7.9	8.3	NA	NA
LT Debt	159	92.7	84.3	47.0	7.2	3.2	0.3	9.3	NA	NA
Common Eqty.	277	205	146	106	97.7	75.5	36.3	5.0	NA	NA
Total Cap.	439	306	237	157	107	80.3	38.0	14.8	NA	NA
Cap. Exp.	41.2	31.1	18.2	16.0	28.9	27.8	6.7	2.8	NA	NA
Cash Flow	87.7	61.1	8.3	20.5	16.5	8.8	5.1	3.2	NA	NA
Curr. Ratio	2.0	1.5	1.1	1.0	1.2	1.0	3.0	1.0	NA	NA
% LT Debt of Cap.	36.2	30.3	35.6	30.0	6.7	4.0	0.9	62.9	NA	NA
% Net Inc.of Revs.	3.3	2.4	NM	1.7	2.2	1.2	2.6	1.7	NA	NA
% Ret. on Assets	9.6	7.5	NM	5.0	6.9	4.1	5.2	NA	NA	NA
% Ret. on Equity	18.8	15.1	NM	8.0	9.7	5.5	11.6	NA	NA	NA

Data as orig reptd.; bef. results of disc opers/spec. items. Per share data adj. for stk. divs. Bold denotes diluted EPS (FASB 128)-prior periods restated. E-Estimated. NA-Not Available. NM-Not Meaningful. NR-Not Ranked.

Office—601 N. Lamar, Suite 300, Austin, TX 78703. **Tel**—(512) 477-4455. **Website**—http://www.wholefoods.com **Chrmn & CEO**—J. Mackey. **Pres**—Chris Hitt. **VP, CFO & Investor Contact**—Glenda Flanagan. **Dirs**—D. W. Dupree, J. E. Elstrott, A. J. Goldberg, F. Lager, J. Mackey, L. A. Mason, J. Rysavy, R. Z. Sorenson. **Transfer Agent & Registrar**—Securities Transfer Corp., Dallas. **Incorporated**—in Texas in 1980. **Empl**—14,200. **S&P Analyst:** Robert J. Izmirlian

STANDARD
&POOR'S
STOCK REPORTS

WHX Corp.

NYSE Symbol **WHX**

In S&P SmallCap 600

09-OCT-99

Industry:
Iron & Steel

Summary: WHX provides specialty wire and tubing, and precious metals plating, stamping and fabrication; and makes value-added and flat rolled steel products.

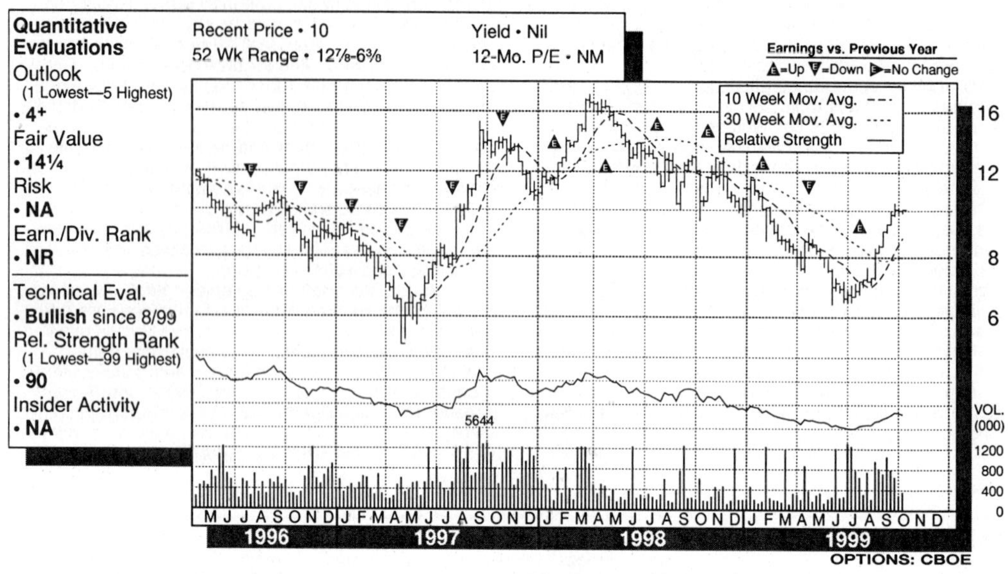

Business Profile - 24-AUG-99

This holding company has been structured to acquire and operate a diverse group of businesses on a decentralized basis. Its primary business is currently Wheeling-Pittsburgh Corp. (WPC), a vertically integrated manufacturer of value-added flat rolled steel products. Results in the 1999 first half were hurt by declining sales in the WPC business segment, reflecting continued weakness in steel prices. WHX's other principal businesses include Handy & Harman (H&H), a diversified manufacturing company acquired in April 1998. In August 1999, directors authorized the repurchase of up to 10% of the common shares (about 1.7 million shares).

Operational Review - 24-AUG-99

Net sales in the six months ended June 30, 1999, rose 5.5%, year to year, reflecting the April 1998 acquisition of H&H, partly offset by declining sales for WPC operations. Gross margins narrowed, and SG&A expense rose 43%, reflecting costs associated with H&H. With significantly higher interest expense, and lower other income, a pretax loss contrasted with pretax income. After tax credits of $8.7 million, versus taxes at 34.9%, a loss of $21,060,000 ($1.86 a share, after preferred dividends, on 8.9% fewer shares) contrasted net income of $15,155,000 ($0.25, as adjusted). Results exclude an extraordinary gain of $0.05 a share in the 1999 period.

Stock Performance - 08-OCT-99

In the past 30 trading days, WHX's shares have increased 19%, compared to a 0.91% fall in the S&P 500. Average trading volume for the past five days was 69,580 shares, compared with the 40-day moving average of 142,685 shares.

Key Stock Statistics

Dividend Rate/Share	Nil	Shareholders	12,700
Shs. outstg. (M)	16.7	Market cap. (B)	$0.168
Avg. daily vol. (M)	0.103	Inst. holdings	63%
Tang. Bk. Value/Share	NM		
Beta	0.61		

Value of $10,000 invested 5 years ago: $ 5,875

Fiscal Year Ending Dec. 31

	1999	1998	1997	1996	1995	1994
Revenues (Million $)						
1Q	396.9	304.1	113.6	315.5	324.2	253.8
2Q	413.8	464.5	128.5	357.8	366.3	300.4
3Q	—	459.6	144.6	391.9	339.4	309.8
4Q	—	417.4	255.4	167.5	334.7	329.8
Yr.	—	1,646	642.1	1,233	1,365	1,194
Earnings Per Share ($)						
1Q	**-2.45**	**-0.21**	**-1.92**	**-0.17**	0.61	1.18
2Q	**0.46**	**0.39**	**-1.58**	**0.37**	0.60	0.36
3Q	—	**0.61**	**-4.49**	**0.40**	0.52	0.55
4Q	—	**-0.15**	**-0.79**	**-1.60**	0.44	0.44
Yr.	—	**0.99**	**-8.83**	**-0.83**	**1.79**	**2.72**

Next earnings report expected: mid November

Dividend Data

Dividends were omitted in 1979.

A Division of The McGraw-Hill Companies

WHX Corporation

Business Summary - 24-AUG-99

WHX Corp. (WHX) is a holding company formed in July 1994 to acquire and operate a diverse group of businesses on a decentralized basis. The company's steel related businesses are Wheeling-Pittsburgh Corp. (WPC), a vertically integrated manufacturer of value-added flat rolled steel products; and Unimast Inc., a leading manufacturer of steel framing and other products for commercial and residential construction. WHX's other business segment is Handy & Harman, a diversified industrial manufacturing company with business units that manufacture and sell metal wire, cable and tubing products (primarily stainless steel and specialty alloys); make and sell precious metals products and precision electroplated materials and molded parts; and manufacture and sell other specialty products to the roofing, construction, do-it-yourself, natural gas, electric and water industries.

Key elements of the company's business strategy have been the expansion of downstream operations, reorganization of acquired businesses, and facilities expansion.

WPC is a vertically integrated manufacturer of predominately value-added flat rolled steel products. It sells a broad array of value-added products, including cold rolled steel, tin and zinc-coated steels and fabricated steel products. WPC's products are sold to the construction industry, steel service centers, converters, processors, and the container and appliance industries.

In March 1995, the company acquired Unimast, a leading manufacturer of steel framing and related accessories for commercial and residential building construction. Unimast uses galvanized steel to manufacture steel framing components for wall, floor and roofing systems, in addition to other roll formed expanded metal construction accessories.

In April 1998, WHX acquired Handy & Harman. Handy & Harman's business groups are manufacturing and selling of metal wire, cable and tubing products, primarily stainless steel and specialty alloy; manufacturing and selling of precious metals products and precision electroplated materials and molded parts; and manufacturing and selling of other specialty products supplied to roofing, construction, do-it-yourself, natural gas, electric, and water industries. Handy & Harman's products are sold to industrial users in a wide range of applications, including the electric, electronic, automotive original equipment, computer equipment, oil and other energy related, refrigeration, construction, utility, telecommunications, and medical industries.

Per Share Data ($) (Year Ended Dec. 31)	1998	1997	1996	1995	1994	1993	1992	1991	1990	1989
Tangible Bk. Val.	8.38	20.38	29.53	32.61	25.65	16.65	13.42	15.50	16.92	NA
Cash Flow	7.15	-6.57	1.81	5.35	4.67	3.26	1.17	2.89	NA	NA
Earnings	0.99	-8.83	-0.82	2.18	2.54	1.02	-1.85	0.27	NA	NA
Dividends	Nil	Nil	Nil	Nil	Nil	Nil	Nil	Nil	Nil	NA
Payout Ratio	Nil	Nil	Nil	Nil	Nil	Nil	Nil	Nil	Nil	NA
Prices - High	17 3/8	15 1/4	14	14 5/8	22 5/8	18 1/4	7 7/8	8 7/8	13 1/4	NA
- Low	9 1/2	5 1/4	7 3/8	9 5/8	12 7/8	4 7/8	3 1/4	5 3/4	2 3/8	NA
P/E Ratio - High	18	NM	NM	7	9	18	NM	33	NA	NA
- Low	10	NM	NM	4	5	5	NM	21	NA	NA
Income Statement Analysis (Million $)										
Revs.	1,645	642	1,233	1,365	1,194	1,047	930	957	1,103	1,147
Oper. Inc.	148	-145	141	144	141	107	47.0	58.0	131	184
Depr.	16.7	49.8	69.3	67.9	61.5	57.1	54.9	45.0	48.9	44.6
Int. Exp.	78.1	29.0	28.5	29.2	31.0	27.9	29.9	35.9	4.9	5.0
Pretax Inc.	62.8	-266	-3.5	100	111	40.0	-34.0	-3.0	-255	195
Eff. Tax Rate	37%	NM	NM	19%	22%	23%	NM	NM	NM	34%
Net Inc.	19.5	-173	0.7	81.1	86.0	31.0	-34.0	5.0	-266	129
Balance Sheet & Other Fin. Data (Million $)										
Cash	0.3	1.0	483	440	402	280	9.0	45.0	65.0	584
Curr. Assets	1,294	939	738	798	786	654	337	397	506	892
Total Assets	412	2,070	1,719	1,796	1,730	1,492	1,117	1,174	1,218	1,486
Curr. Liab.	885	610	246	257	262	272	232	248	249	176
LT Debt	893	350	268	286	290	347	214	225	302	2.0
Common Eqty.	446	466	714	768	698	442	244	281	250	-16.0
Total Cap.	1,340	817	982	1,054	989	789	458	506	552	174
Cap. Exp.	48.3	36.7	35.4	83.3	82.0	74.0	67.0	97.0	107	90.0
Cash Flow	136	-144	47.6	149	135	83.0	21.0	50.0	-224	164
Curr. Ratio	1.5	1.5	3.0	3.1	3.0	2.4	1.5	1.6	2.0	5.1
% LT Debt of Cap.	66.7	42.9	27.3	27.1	29.3	44.0	46.7	44.4	54.7	1.2
% Net Inc.of Revs.	2.4	NM	0.1	5.9	7.2	2.9	NM	0.5	NM	11.2
% Ret. on Assets	1.6	NM	NM	4.6	5.3	2.0	NM	0.4	NM	9.3
% Ret. on Equity	8.6	NM	NM	11.1	12.7	6.5	NM	1.6	NM	NM

Data as orig reptd.; bef. results of disc opers/spec. items. Per share data adj. for stk. divs. Bold denotes diluted EPS (FASB 128)-prior periods restated. E-Estimated. NA-Not Available. NM-Not Meaningful. NR-Not Ranked.

Office—110 E. 59th St., New York, NY 10022. **Tel**—(212) 355-5200. **Website**—http://www.wpsc.com **Chrmn**—R. LaBow. **Vice Chrm**—R. A. Davidow. **Secy**—M. Olshan. **Dirs**—N. D. Arnold, P. W. Bucha, R. A. Davidow, W. Goldsmith, R. LaBow, R. D. LeBlanc, M. L. Olshan, R. S. Troubh. **Transfer Agent & Registrar**—First National Bank of Boston. **Incorporated**—in Delaware in 1920. **Empl**— 7,363. **S&P Analyst:** J.J.A.

WICOR, Inc.

NYSE Symbol **WIC**

In S&P SmallCap 600

09-OCT-99 **Industry:** Natural Gas

Summary: This holding company's Wisconsin Gas subsidiary, is the largest gas distributor in Wisconsin. Other subsidiaries produce pumps and fluid processing and filtration equipment.

Quantitative Evaluations

Outlook (1 Lowest—5 Highest) • **2**

Fair Value • **29¼**

Risk • **Low**

Earn./Div. Rank • **B+**

Technical Eval. • **Neutral** since 9/99

Rel. Strength Rank (1 Lowest—99 Highest) • **72**

Insider Activity • **NA**

Recent Price • 29 Yield • 3.1%

52 Wk Range • 29⅝-18¾ 12-Mo. P/E • 22.1

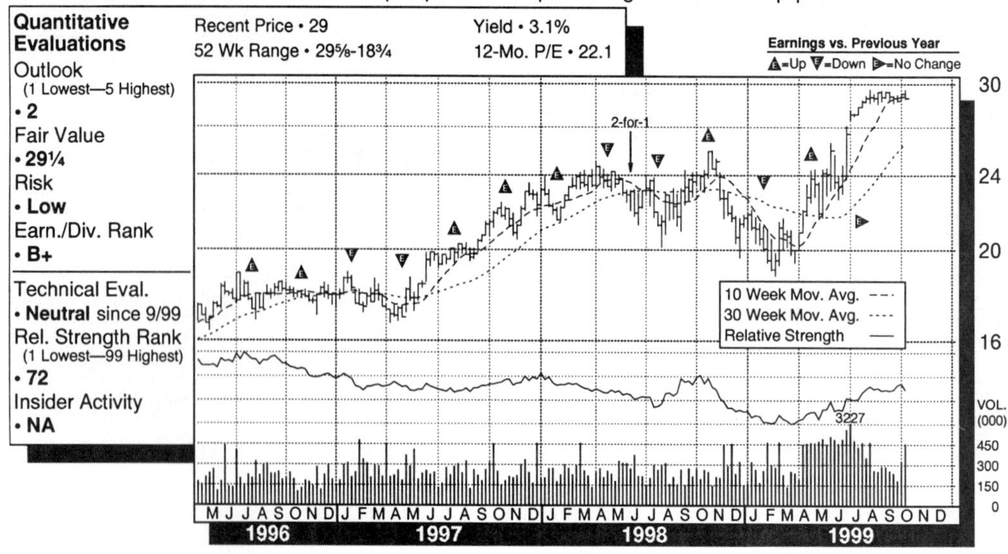

Business Profile - 09-MAR-99

This holding company has two principal businesses: natural gas distribution in Wisconsin and pump manufacturing. As a result of possible legislation designed to promote competition in the gas marketing industry among third-party providers, coupled with the fact that margins for the selling and transporting functions are about equal, WIC is pursuing a long-term strategy of no longer selling gas. The effects of recent warmer than normal weather, which adversely impact gas throughput, have been partially offset by growth in the company's pump manufacturing business. In January 1999, the gas distribution subsidiary sold $50 million of long-term notes; proceeds were used to retire debt and for general corporate purposes. A two-for-one stock split was effected in late May 1998.

Operational Review - 09-MAR-99

Based on a preliminary report, revenues in 1998 fell 7.5%, as an 8.9% increase in manufacturing revenues related to product introductions, market share gains and a strong domestic economy was outweighed by a 19% decline in energy revenues. Utility revenues were adversely impacted by weather that was 16% warmer than last year, resulting in a lower throughput. Despite a significant decrease in cost of gas sold, overall operating expenses rose, reflecting increased costs associated with the growing manufacturing business. Net income declined 8.1%, to $45.5 million ($1.21 a share, diluted), from $49.5 million ($1.33).

Stock Performance - 08-OCT-99

In the past 30 trading days, WIC's shares have declined 0.21%, compared to a 0.91% fall in the S&P 500. Average trading volume for the past five days was 94,540 shares, compared with the 40-day moving average of 58,446 shares.

Key Stock Statistics

Dividend Rate/Share	0.90	Shareholders	22,312
Shs. outstg. (M)	37.5	Market cap. (B)	$ 1.1
Avg. daily vol. (M)	0.061	Inst. holdings	36%
Tang. Bk. Value/Share	8.96		
Beta	0.33		

Value of $10,000 invested 5 years ago: $ 23,552

Fiscal Year Ending Dec. 31

	1999	1998	1997	1996	1995	1994
Revenues (Million $)						
1Q	304.2	303.3	349.1	328.8	269.3	321.0
2Q	225.3	219.9	221.6	227.6	179.2	186.1
3Q	—	172.8	173.3	175.1	162.7	151.0
4Q	—	248.2	277.0	281.1	249.3	210.0
Yr.	—	944.2	1,021	1,013	860.6	867.8
Earnings Per Share ($)						
1Q	**0.77**	**0.67**	**0.76**	0.84	0.73	0.85
2Q	**0.16**	**0.16**	**0.17**	0.15	0.08	0.03
3Q	—	**-0.03**	**-0.06**	-0.12	-0.14	-0.24
4Q	—	**0.42**	**0.47**	0.40	0.49	0.35
Yr.	—	**1.21**	**1.33**	**1.26**	1.16	0.99

Next earnings report expected: late October

Dividend Data (Dividends have been paid since 1960.)

Amount ($)	Date Decl.	Ex-Div. Date	Stock of Record	Payment Date
0.220	Oct. 28	Nov. 06	Nov. 10	Nov. 30 '98
0.220	Jan. 26	Feb. 03	Feb. 05	Feb. 26 '99
0.220	Apr. 22	May. 05	May. 07	May. 28 '99
0.225	Jul. 27	Aug. 06	Aug. 10	Aug. 31 '99

WICOR, Inc.

Business Summary - 09-MAR-99

WICOR is a holding company with six subsidiaries in two industries: energy services (Wisconsin Gas, WICOR Energy Services and FieldTech) and pump manufacturing (Sta-Rite Industries, SHURflo Pump Manufacturing and Hypro). Contributions to revenues and profits in 1997 were as follows:

	Revs.	Profits
Energy services	58%	63%
Pump manufacturing	42%	37%

Wisconsin Gas is the largest natural gas distribution public utility in Wisconsin, distributing about 40% of the state's total gas used. At December 31, 1997, Wisconsin Gas distributed gas to approximately 521,000 residential, commercial and industrial customers. Sales to residential customers, which are highly seasonal, are usually under firm (uninterruptible) rates. Lower-priced interruptible rates are offered to large commercial and industrial users; most of them are equipped to switch to alternate fuels throughout the year to take advantage of price differentials. Wisconsin Gas also transports third-party gas; sales and transportation margins are about equal. Total gas throughput in 1997 was 1.3 billion therms (67% sales, 33% transported), down from 1.4 billion therms in 1996 (80% sales, 20% transported). The subsidiary is regulated by the Public Utilities Commission of Wisconsin.

WICOR Energy, an unregulated marketing subsidiary, sells energy supply-related services, such as gas purchasing, storage, energy and risk management. FieldTech, an unregulated subsidiary, offers meter reading technology and services to gas, water and electric utilities nationwide. The results of these subsidiaries, which were formed in 1995, are not material to WIC's financial performance.

WICOR's manufacturing subsidiaries manufacture pumps and fluid processing and filtration equipment for residential, agricultural and industrial markets worldwide. The company has manufacturing and assembly plants in the U.S., Australia, Germany, India, Italy, Mexico and New Zealand. Products are sold to markets in approximately 100 countries.

Sta-Rite Industries manufactures pumps and water processing equipment for residential, industrial and agricultural markets. Major markets are water systems and pool/spa. Shurflo makes small, high-performance pumps and fluid-handling equipment. Major markets include beverage/food service, recreational vehicles, marine, industrial and water purification. Hypro manufactures pumps and fluid-handling equipment used in the agricultural spraying, high pressure cleaning, marine industrial and firefighting markets.

Per Share Data ($) (Year Ended Dec. 31)	1998	1997	1996	1995	1994	1993	1992	1991	1990	1989
Tangible Bk. Val.	8.96	8.67	8.30	7.74	8.62	8.23	7.96	8.14	8.32	8.70
Cash Flow	2.14	2.24	2.21	2.04	1.88	1.78	1.61	1.66	1.40	2.01
Earnings	1.21	1.33	1.27	1.16	0.99	0.91	0.70	0.77	0.52	1.20
Dividends	0.87	0.85	0.83	0.81	0.79	0.77	0.75	0.73	0.71	0.69
Payout Ratio	72%	64%	65%	70%	79%	85%	107%	98%	137%	57%
Prices - High	25 1/2	24	18 7/8	16 1/2	16 3/8	16 1/2	13 3/4	12 1/4	12 5/8	12 3/4
- Low	19 5/8	16 3/4	15 1/8	13 3/8	12 3/4	12 7/8	11 1/2	9 3/8	9 1/8	9 3/4
P/E Ratio - High	21	18	15	14	16	18	20	16	24	11
- Low	16	13	12	11	13	14	16	12	18	8
Income Statement Analysis (Million $)										
Revs.	944	1,021	1,013	861	868	850	705	682	660	711
Oper. Inc.	84.6	65.7	125	109	96.0	92.0	76.0	73.8	65.5	91.7
Depr.	35.0	33.2	34.4	29.7	29.4	28.0	26.7	24.8	24.0	22.0
Int. Exp.	16.7	17.4	18.3	19.3	16.7	17.4	18.0	16.6	18.1	17.4
Pretax Inc.	71.5	77.8	73.5	62.2	50.5	46.8	32.6	33.7	23.9	53.6
Eff. Tax Rate	36%	36%	36%	37%	34%	37%	37%	36%	40%	39%
Net Inc.	45.5	49.5	46.8	39.5	33.2	29.3	20.5	21.5	14.3	32.7
Balance Sheet & Other Fin. Data (Million $)										
Cash	13.4	11.8	18.8	20.4	35.1	23.0	16.5	47.6	16.0	29.7
Curr. Assets	354	385	373	329	312	315	238	242	210	259
Total Assets	1,015	1,031	1,058	1,009	931	934	810	669	638	601
Curr. Liab.	245	310	289	254	239	256	192	149	166	190
LT Debt	190	149	171	176	162	165	164	168	128	122
Common Eqty.	403	390	368	345	291	270	236	235	230	238
Total Cap.	648	539	585	567	504	490	455	489	443	388
Cap. Exp.	49.3	51.6	51.7	56.2	55.1	54.0	80.5	47.9	36.5	39.7
Cash Flow	80.5	82.7	81.1	69.2	62.6	57.4	47.1	46.3	38.4	54.7
Curr. Ratio	1.4	1.2	1.3	1.3	1.3	1.2	1.2	1.6	1.3	1.4
% LT Debt of Cap.	29.2	27.6	31.5	31.0	32.1	33.7	36.0	34.4	28.9	31.5
% Net Inc.of Revs.	4.8	4.9	4.6	4.6	3.8	3.5	2.9	3.2	2.2	4.6
% Ret. on Assets	4.4	4.7	4.5	4.1	3.5	3.2	2.8	3.2	2.3	5.7
% Ret. on Equity	11.5	13.1	13.1	12.4	11.6	11.0	8.7	9.0	6.1	14.1

Data as orig reptd.; bef. results of disc opers/spec. items. Per share data adj. for stk. divs. Bold denotes diluted EPS (FASB 128)-prior periods restated. E-Estimated. NA-Not Available. NM-Not Meaningful. NR-Not Ranked.

Office—626 E. Wisconsin Ave., P.O. Box 334, Milwaukee, WI 53201. **Tel**—(800) 236-3453. **Website**—http://www.wicor.com **Chrmn & CEO**—G. E. Wardeberg. **Pres & COO**—T. F. Schrader. **SVP, CFO, Treas & Investor Contact**—Joseph P. Wenzler. **Secy**—R. A. Nuernberg. **Dirs**—W. F. Bueche, W. D. Davis, J. D. McGaffey, D. F. McKeithan Jr., G. A. Osborn, T. F. Schrader, S. W. Tisdale, G. Wardeberg, E. M. Whitelaw, W. B. Winter. **Transfer Agent & Registrar**—ChaseMellon Shareholder Services, Ridgefield Park, NJ. **Incorporated**—in Wisconsin in 1852; reincorporated in Wisconsin in 1980. **Empl**— 3,625. **S&P Analyst:** Ephraim Juskowicz

STANDARD
&POOR'S
STOCK REPORTS

Winnebago Industries

NYSE Symbol **WGO**

In S&P SmallCap 600

09-OCT-99

Industry: Leisure Time (Products)

Summary: Winnebago primarily manufactures motor homes used in leisure travel and outdoor recreational activities.

Quantitative Evaluations

Outlook
(1 Lowest—5 Highest)
• **NA**

Fair Value
• **NA**

Risk
• **Average**

Earn./Div. Rank
• **B-**

Technical Eval.
• **Neutral** since 9/99

Rel. Strength Rank
(1 Lowest—99 Highest)
• **4**

Insider Activity
• **Neutral**

Recent Price • 16⅜
52 Wk Range • 28¾-9¼
Yield • 1.2%
12-Mo. P/E • 8.4

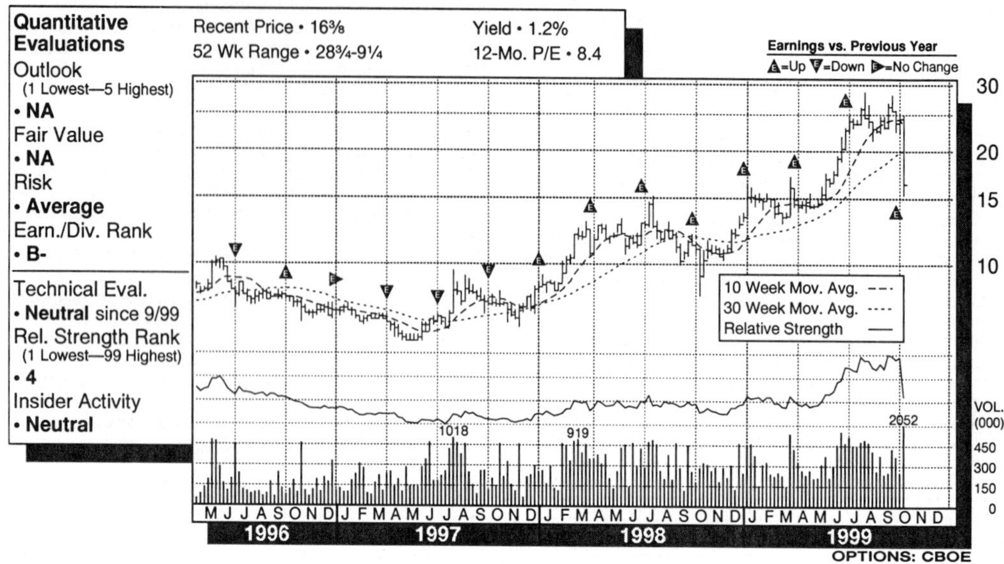

Business Profile - 27-JUL-99

In June 1999, Winnebago stated that it expected to experience continued growth due to higher discretionary income in the company's growing target market of consumers age 50 and older, as well as strength in the U.S. economy. WGO also announced plans for a $3.6 million expansion at its Forest City, IA, plant, in order to meet increased product demand. Also in June, directors announced a new stock repurchase plan authorizing a total of $15 million in common stock purchases. As of May 29, 1999, WGO's sales order backlog was 2,229 units, representing a 170% increase over the prior year period. In March 1999, WGO stated it was experiencing market share growth for newly introduced 1999 models, including the Winnebago Adventurer, Itasca Suncruiser, and the Ultimate series motor homes.

Operational Review - 27-JUL-99

Net revenues in the nine months ended May 29, 1999 increased 27%, year to year, as a strong U.S. economy aided demand for the company's motor home vehicles. Gross margins widened on the higher volume and a more favorable product mix. Selling and delivery expenses rose 14%, reflecting increased advertising and delivery costs. Following a 2.4% increase in G&A expenses and 19% lower financial income, net income doubled to $34.2 million ($1.52 a share, on 8.7% fewer shares), from $17.0 million ($0.69).

Stock Performance - 08-OCT-99

In the past 30 trading days, WGO's shares have declined 32%, compared to a 0.91% fall in the S&P 500. Average trading volume for the past five days was 410,420 shares, compared with the 40-day moving average of 107,633 shares.

Key Stock Statistics

Dividend Rate/Share	0.20	Shareholders	10,855
Shs. outstg. (M)	22.3	Market cap. (B)	$0.365
Avg. daily vol. (M)	0.154	Inst. holdings	30%
Tang. Bk. Value/Share	5.11		
Beta	0.98		

Value of $10,000 invested 5 years ago: $ 18,792

Fiscal Year Ending Aug. 31

	1999	1998	1997	1996	1995	1994
Revenues (Million $)						
1Q	157.7	125.9	113.9	113.7	130.8	104.6
2Q	154.1	118.7	105.7	106.2	115.5	99.0
3Q	191.6	150.5	117.2	144.4	125.1	129.7
4Q	164.3	130.0	101.3	120.5	113.3	118.9
Yr.	667.6	525.1	438.1	484.8	484.6	452.1
Earnings Per Share ($)						
1Q	**0.43**	0.21	0.11	0.11	0.30	0.15
2Q	**0.45**	**0.18**	-0.15	0.09	0.48	0.05
3Q	**0.65**	**0.31**	0.15	0.21	0.26	0.29
4Q	**0.44**	**0.32**	0.15	0.16	0.06	0.20
Yr.	**1.96**	**1.00**	**0.26**	0.57	1.10	0.69

Next earnings report expected: mid December

Dividend Data (Dividends have been paid since 1995.)

Amount ($)	Date Decl.	Ex-Div. Date	Stock of Record	Payment Date
0.100	Oct. 16	Dec. 09	Dec. 11	Jan. 11 '99
0.100	Mar. 18	Jun. 02	Jun. 04	Jul. 02 '99

Winnebago Industries, Inc.

09-OCT-99

Business Summary - 27-JUL-99

Winnebago Industries, Inc.'s mission is to constantly improve its products and services in order to meet or exceed customer expectations. In FY 98 (Aug.), the company's 40th anniversary, WGO refocused its strategy on its core business of producing quality motor homes, with new product development receiving top priority. Additional focal points of the company's overall strategy include expanding production capacity, increasing brand awareness, and growing shareholder value.

WGO primarily targets its self-contained, recreational motor home offerings at consumers over age 50 and the baby boomer generation, which is approaching the 50 year old age group. According to a University of Michigan study, people between the ages of 55 and 64 will grow by 8 million over the next 12 years. The company believes that motor homes are increasingly in demand as a result of these demographic trends. Over the last five fiscal years, at least 91% of WGO sales was derived from recreational vehicle products.

The company manufactures or converts three types of motor homes: Class A, B and C. Class A models are conventional motor homes constructed on medium-duty truck chassis, which include the engine and drive components. The living area and driver's compartment are designed and produced by WGO. Class B models are panel-type trucks to which sleeping, kitchen and toilet facilities are added. These models also have a top extension added to them for more head room. Class C models are mini motor homes built on van-type chassis on which the company constructs a living area with access to the driver's compartment.

Class A and Class C motor homes range in size from 22 to 40 feet. These models can accommodate four to seven people, and have kitchen, dining, sleeping and bath areas, and in some cases, a lounge. The A and C Class motor homes range in price from about $45,000 to $225,000 and are sold under the brand names Winnebago, Itasca, Vectra, Rialta, and Ultimate. Pricing depends on model size and type, optional equipment, and delivery charges.

As of August 1998, WGO offered its motor homes through a network of approximately 350 and 340 dealers in the U.S. and Canada, respectively. The company also converts Class B motor homes under the EuroVan Camper brand name, which is distributed through the Volkswagon dealer organization. Foreign sales, accounting for less than 5% of net revenues in FY 98, are handled by five distributors.

WGO also manufactures extruded aluminum commercial vehicles, and a wide range of component products for other manufacturers. In addition, the company receives finance revenues, which consist of revenues from floor plan unit financing for a limited number of company dealers.

In September 1998, WGO completed a share repurchase program of more than 3.6 million common shares for an aggregate price of about $36.5 million. In June 1999, directors authorized the repurchase of an additional $15 million of common stock.

Per Share Data ($) (Year Ended Aug. 31)	1999	1998	1997	1996	1995	1994	1993	1992	1991	1990
Tangible Bk. Val.	NA	5.11	4.86	4.15	3.96	3.16	3.26	2.88	3.30	4.49
Cash Flow	NA	1.23	0.51	0.95	1.45	1.00	0.68	0.25	-0.27	-0.21
Earnings	1.96	1.00	0.26	0.57	1.10	0.69	0.37	-0.07	-0.65	-0.72
Dividends	0.20	0.20	0.20	0.30	0.30	Nil	Nil	Nil	Nil	0.10
Payout Ratio	10%	20%	77%	53%	27%	Nil	Nil	Nil	Nil	NM
Prices - High	28 3/4	16 3/8	9 5/8	10 3/8	10 3/4	13 7/8	10 1/2	9 1/2	6 3/4	5 3/4
- Low	12 7/8	8 1/4	6 1/4	6 3/4	7 3/8	7 7/8	5 5/8	3 5/8	2 1/4	2 1/8
P/E Ratio - High	15	16	37	18	10	20	28	NM	NM	NM
- Low	7	8	24	12	7	11	15	NM	NM	NM
Income Statement Analysis (Million $)										
Revs.	NA	525	438	485	485	452	384	295	223	335
Oper. Inc.	NA	38.6	11.6	30.4	27.2	25.0	15.7	4.9	-12.1	-13.1
Depr.	NA	5.6	6.5	9.7	8.9	7.7	7.8	8.1	9.6	12.6
Int. Exp.	NA	0.4	0.7	0.8	1.8	1.4	0.6	0.4	1.4	2.3
Pretax Inc.	NA	35.9	7.0	21.1	19.8	16.3	7.7	-2.8	-22.4	-32.3
Eff. Tax Rate	NA	32%	5.95%	32%	NM	NM	NM	NM	NM	NM
Net Inc.	NA	24.4	6.6	14.4	27.8	17.4	9.3	-1.8	-16.3	-17.8
Balance Sheet & Other Fin. Data (Million $)										
Cash	NA	53.9	32.1	5.1	11.0	4.1	13.5	14.5	7.9	23.6
Curr. Assets	NA	155	141	127	121	111	94.0	82.0	77.0	129
Total Assets	NA	231	213	221	212	184	157	140	135	198
Curr. Liab.	NA	62.6	41.2	64.5	51.2	52.0	50.0	44.0	39.0	64.0
LT Debt	NA	Nil	Nil	1.7	12.7	4.1	3.2	3.1	3.9	3.5
Common Eqty.	NA	117	124	105	100	80.0	82.0	72.0	83.0	111
Total Cap.	NA	117	124	109	115	88.0	89.0	79.0	90.0	129
Cap. Exp.	NA	5.6	4.4	10.5	9.3	12.0	7.7	3.0	3.8	9.6
Cash Flow	NA	30.0	13.0	25.1	36.7	25.2	17.0	6.3	-6.7	-5.2
Curr. Ratio	NA	2.5	3.4	2.0	2.4	2.1	1.9	1.8	2.0	2.0
% LT Debt of Cap.	NA	Nil	Nil	1.6	12.7	4.7	3.6	3.9	4.4	2.8
% Net Inc.of Revs.	NA	4.6	1.5	3.0	5.7	3.9	2.4	NM	NM	NM
% Ret. on Assets	NA	11.0	3.0	6.7	14.0	10.2	6.2	NM	NM	NM
% Ret. on Equity	NA	20.3	5.7	14.1	30.9	21.6	12.1	NM	NM	NM

Data as orig reptd.; bef. results of disc opers/spec. items. Per share data adj. for stk. divs. Bold denotes diluted EPS (FASB 128)-prior periods restated. E-Estimated. NA-Not Available. NM-Not Meaningful. NR-Not Ranked.

Office—605 W. Crystal Lake Rd., P.O. Box 152, Forest City, IA 50436. **Tel**—(515) 582-3535. **Website**—http://www.winnebagoind.com **Chrmn, Pres & CEO**—B. D. Hertzke. **VP, CFO & Investor Contact**—Edwin F. Barker (515-582-6141). **VP & Secy**—R. M. Beebe. **Dirs**—G. E. Boman, J.N. Currie, F. G. Dohrmann, J. V. Hanson, B. D. Hertzke, G. C. Kitch, R. C. Scott, F. M. Zimmerman. **Transfer Agent & Registrar**—Norwest Bank Minnesota, St. Paul. **Incorporated**—in Iowa in 1958. **Empl**— 3,010. **S&P Analyst:** F. DiLorenzo

STANDARD
&POOR'S
STOCK REPORTS

Wolverine Tube

NYSE Symbol **WLV**

In S&P SmallCap 600

09-OCT-99 **Industry:** Metal Fabricators

Summary: This leading North American manufacturer and distributor of copper and copper alloy tube focuses on custom-engineered, high-value-added products.

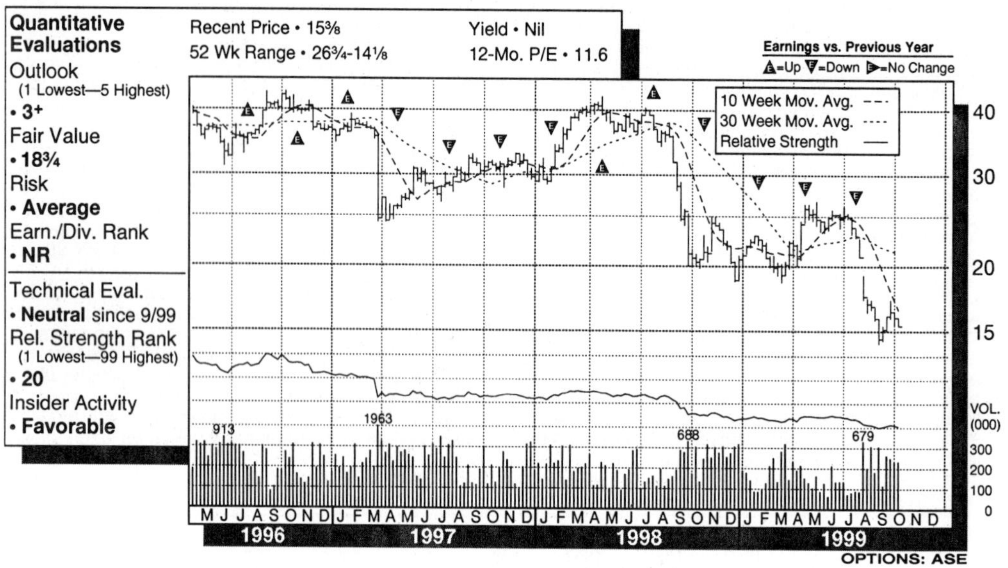

Business Profile - 27-JUL-99

In April 1999, the company said it remained cautiously optimistic that demand for technical tube in the second half of 1999 will be significantly improved over the same period in 1998. Management added that demand for industrial tube, used in unitary air conditioners, remains strong, with further strengthening expected as the cooling season accelerates. Wolverine still expects to realize about $8-10 million in annual pretax savings by the year 2000, about half of which should be realized during 1999, primarily in the second half.

Operational Review - 27-JUL-99

Net sales in the three months ended April 3, 1999, declined 5.6%, year to year, largely due to a decrease in copper prices, which are a "pass through" to a majority of WLV customers, and unit fabrication charges; total pounds shipped for the period increased to 97.5 million pounds, from 95.6 million pounds. Results were impaired by decreased shipments of technical tube, the company's highest margin product, increased salaries and benefits, marketing expenses and professional fees, and interest costs of $3.1 million, against $1.6 million. Income fell 32%, to $7,220,000 ($0.53 a share, after preferred dividends, on 5.3% fewer shares) from $10,575,000 ($0.74) Results exclude a charge of $0.43 a share in the 1999 period for an accounting change.

Stock Performance - 08-OCT-99

In the past 30 trading days, WLV's shares have declined 3%, compared to a 0.91% fall in the S&P 500. Average trading volume for the past five days was 46,180 shares, compared with the 40-day moving average of 51,000 shares.

Key Stock Statistics

Dividend Rate/Share	Nil	Shareholders	300
Shs. outstg. (M)	13.3	Market cap. (B)	$0.205
Avg. daily vol. (M)	0.048	Inst. holdings	76%
Tang. Bk. Value/Share	11.15		
Beta	0.92		

Value of $10,000 invested 5 years ago: $ 7,784

Fiscal Year Ending Dec. 31

	1999	1998	1997	1996	1995	1994
Revenues (Million $)						
1Q	160.8	170.3	173.6	179.4	179.8	129.6
2Q	164.3	169.6	178.1	180.3	164.4	128.3
3Q	—	147.9	159.4	168.7	159.9	132.4
4Q	—	129.7	156.7	171.5	160.5	135.3
Yr.	—	617.5	667.7	699.9	664.6	525.6
Earnings Per Share ($)						
1Q	**0.53**	**0.74**	**0.62**	**0.72**	0.65	0.51
2Q	**0.63**	**0.81**	**0.49**	**0.73**	0.63	0.50
3Q	—	**-0.06**	**0.51**	**0.67**	0.49	0.44
4Q	—	**0.23**	**0.51**	**0.65**	0.50	0.38
Yr.	—	**1.72**	**2.13**	**2.77**	**2.26**	**1.82**

Next earnings report expected: late October

Dividend Data

No dividends have been paid on the common stock. The company intends to retain earnings to support the growth of its business.

Wolverine Tube, Inc.

Business Summary - 27-JUL-99

Wolverine Tube (WLV) is a leading North American manufacturer and distributor of copper and copper alloy tube and other tubular products, and believes that it offers the broadest product line of any North American tube maker. The company also makes and distributes copper alloy rod, bar and strip products. Management believes that in 1998 Wolverine Tube was the largest North American producer of copper and copper alloy tube for commercial products. The unique attributes of copper (thermal conductivity, ease of bending and joining, and resistance to erosion and corrosion) allow a broad range of applications in diverse industries.

Gross profit by product segment in 1998 was obtained as follows: commercial 89%, wholesale 8%, and rod, bar and strip 3%. WLV also has substantial sales in Canada, primarily of commodity type products.

The company's wide range of commercial products includes small (down to 0.01 in.) and medium diameter copper tube supplied to residential air conditioning, appliance and refrigeration manufacturers. Technical tube is used to increase heat transfer in large commercial air conditioners, heat exchangers for power generating and chemical processing plants, water heaters, swimming pool and spa heaters, and large industrial equipment oil coolers. Copper alloy tube (copper mixed with nickel) is used for severe or corrosive environments such as condenser tubes and heat exchangers in power generating plants, chemical plants, refineries and ships.

Wholesale products include plumbing tube and refrigeration service tube, which are produced in standard sizes and lengths primarily for plumbing, air conditioning and refrigeration service applications. These are considered commodity products because price and delivery are the primary competitive factors.

Rod, bar and strip products are copper and copper alloy formed into special shapes and used in many different ways. Brass rod and bar are used by machinery manufacturers for valves, fittings and plumbing; copper bars are used in electrical distribution systems; and copper and copper alloy strip products are used for cars, hardware, electrical equipment, roofs, and for the minting of coins.

The company has benefited and expects to continue to benefit from the chlorofluorocarbons phaseout as existing large commercial air conditioners (chillers) are replaced over the next five to seven years with units utilizing alternative refrigerants. The company estimates there are approximately 130,000 large industrial chillers worldwide, including 80,000 in North America, that are affected by 1990 legislation and the Montreal Protocol.

A significant and increasing amount of the company's sales result from "partnership" relationships wherein Wolverine Tube provides a high degree of specialized service and generally becomes the largest supplier of a customer's copper tube requirements.

Per Share Data ($) (Year Ended Dec. 31)	1998	1997	1996	1995	1994	1993	1992	1991	1990	1989
Tangible Bk. Val.	11.15	10.29	8.88	7.56	9.55	7.50	4.74	NA	NA	NA
Cash Flow	2.94	3.31	3.94	3.38	2.76	2.31	2.11	1.14	NA	NA
Earnings	1.72	2.13	2.77	2.26	1.82	1.39	0.98	0.20	NA	NA
Dividends	Nil	Nil	Nil	Nil	Nil	Nil	NA	NA	NA	NA
Payout Ratio	Nil	Nil	Nil	Nil	Nil	Nil	NA	NA	NA	NA
Prices - High	42½	39¼	43⅜	43½	26⅝	19¾	NA	NA	NA	NA
- Low	18⅝	24¼	31	23¼	18⅞	15½	NA	NA	NA	NA
P/E Ratio - High	25	18	16	19	15	14	NA	NA	NA	NA
- Low	11	11	11	10	10	11	NA	NA	NA	NA
Income Statement Analysis (Million $)										
Revs.	618	668	700	665	526	469	484	418	479	542
Oper. Inc.	73.7	76.6	88.2	76.3	61.6	49.5	45.1	29.3	25.0	37.2
Depr.	17.3	16.8	16.3	15.8	12.9	10.4	11.9	10.1	8.9	8.2
Int. Exp.	9.4	7.8	10.5	10.8	10.3	9.6	9.4	10.3	9.6	10.4
Pretax Inc.	38.0	48.1	61.4	49.8	40.6	27.2	21.5	6.7	5.9	19.7
Eff. Tax Rate	35%	36%	36%	35%	38%	41%	44%	39%	12%	39%
Net Inc.	24.6	30.6	39.6	32.0	25.0	16.0	12.2	4.0	5.1	11.9
Balance Sheet & Other Fin. Data (Million $)										
Cash	78.9	15.1	3.0	5.5	0.1	55.2	NA	NA	NA	NA
Curr. Assets	254	176	156	142	126	136	NA	NA	NA	NA
Total Assets	549	425	397	357	341	276	NA	NA	NA	NA
Curr. Liab.	54.3	50.0	43.2	49.5	64.2	37.3	NA	NA	NA	NA
LT Debt	216	98.4	100	101	101	100	100	NA	NA	NA
Common Eqty.	237	233	209	165	129	97.6	92.0	NA	NA	NA
Total Cap.	481	360	338	289	255	217	NA	NA	NA	NA
Cap. Exp.	34.7	21.6	8.5	15.8	34.4	22.3	4.0	1.9	4.2	13.8
Cash Flow	41.7	47.1	55.9	47.7	37.7	26.2	22.4	12.4	12.2	20.1
Curr. Ratio	4.7	3.5	3.6	2.9	2.0	3.7	NA	NA	NA	NA
% LT Debt of Cap.	44.9	27.3	29.8	34.9	39.5	46.1	NA	NA	NA	NA
% Net Inc.of Revs.	4.0	4.6	5.7	4.9	4.8	3.4	2.5	1.0	1.1	2.2
% Ret. on Assets	5.1	7.4	10.5	9.3	8.0	5.7	NA	NA	NA	NA
% Ret. on Equity	10.4	13.7	21.2	21.8	21.6	21.0	NA	NA	NA	NA

Data as orig reptd.; bef. results of disc opers/spec. items. Per share data adj. for stk. divs. Bold denotes diluted EPS (FASB 128)-prior periods restated. E-Estimated. NA-Not Available. NM-Not Meaningful. NR-Not Ranked.

Office—1525 Perimeter Parkway, Suite 210, Huntsville, AL 35806. **Tel**—(256) 890-0460. **Website**—http://www.wlv.com **Pres & CEO**—D. Horowitz. **EVP-Fin, CFO, Secy & Investor Contact**—James E. Deason (256-890-0460). **Dirs**—C. A. Davis, J. E. Deason, J. L. Duncan, T. P. Evans, J. K. Ver Hagen, W. B. Hauptfuhrer, D. J. Horowitz, G. O. Neuman, C. E. Thompson. **Transfer Agent & Registrar**—SunTrust Bank, Atlanta.**Incorporated**—in Delaware in 1987. **Empl**— 3,316. **S&P Analyst:** P.L.H.

STANDARD
&POOR'S
STOCK REPORTS

Wolverine World Wide

NYSE Symbol **WWW**

In S&P SmallCap 600

09-OCT-99 **Industry:** Footwear

Summary: WWW makes, imports and markets casual footwear sold under the Hush Puppies, and Wolverine, and other brand names, and is the largest domestic tanner of pigskins.

Quantitative Evaluations

Outlook (1 Lowest—5 Highest)
• **5+**

Fair Value
• **19**

Risk
• **Average**

Earn./Div. Rank
• **B+**

Technical Eval.
• **Bearish** since 9/99

Rel. Strength Rank (1 Lowest—99 Highest)
• **41**

Insider Activity
• **NA**

Recent Price • 10¾
52 Wk Range • 15-8⅞
Yield • 1.1%
12-Mo. P/E • 16.3

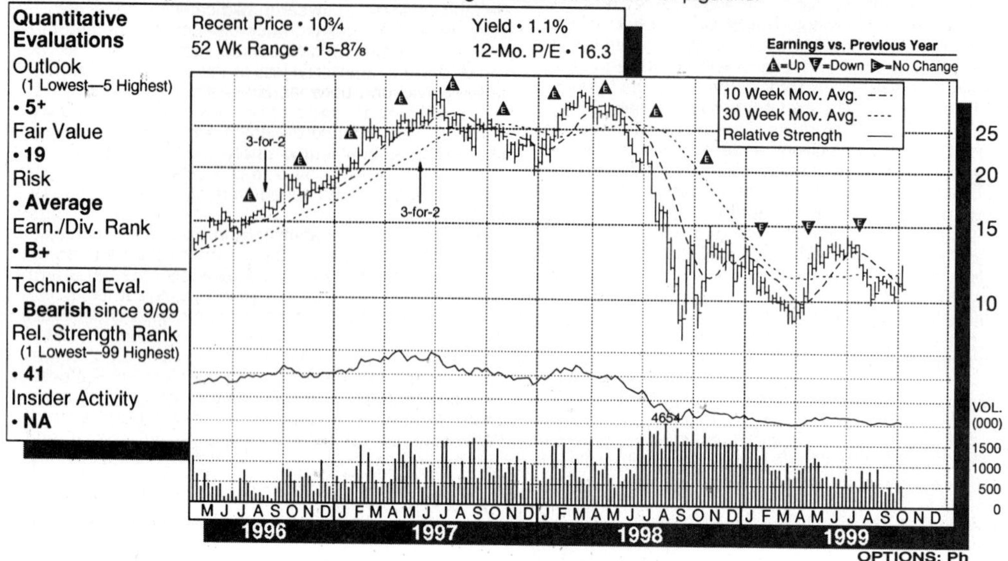

Business Profile - 30-JUN-99

Wolverine World Wide's first quarter earnings were affected by disappointing U.S. sales of Hush Puppies shoes, a reduction in U.K. sales, and the downsizing of Wolverine Russia. The company noted that the Hush Puppies brand, which accounts for about a third of WWW's global sales and operating income, was experiencing strong interest from U.S. retailers for the fall introduction of two new proprietary comfort shoe technologies, the ZeroGravity men's shoes and the Air Paradise HPO2 women's shoes. The company stated that the anticipated improvement for shoe retailing in the second half of the year, combined with its new products and marketing efforts, should offset the issues that the Hush Puppies brand faces in the first half of 1999.

Operational Review - 30-JUN-99

Net sales and other operating income for the 12 weeks ended March 27, 1999, fell 8.3%, year to year, primarily from reduced sales of the company's branded footwear, including Wolverine Footwear Group, Caterpillar Footwear Group and the Hush Puppies Company. Gross margins narrowed, due to lower margins at WWW's other non-branded business units. SG&A expense fell 1.2%, as higher depreciation and selling costs were outweighed by cost reductions. After a 37% rise in interest expense, due to borrowings used for the repurchase of common stock, net income fell 56%, to $3,603,000 ($0.09 a share, on 5.8% fewer shares), from $6,388,000 ($0.15).

Stock Performance - 08-OCT-99

In the past 30 trading days, WWW's shares have declined 4%, compared to a 0.91% fall in the S&P 500. Average trading volume for the past five days was 105,540 shares, compared with the 40-day moving average of 112,351 shares.

Key Stock Statistics

Dividend Rate/Share	0.12	Shareholders	1,992
Shs. outstg. (M)	41.3	Market cap. (B)	$0.444
Avg. daily vol. (M)	0.100	Inst. holdings	58%
Tang. Bk. Value/Share	7.28		
Beta	1.34		

Value of $10,000 invested 5 years ago: $ 18,567

Fiscal Year Ending Dec. 31

	1999	1998	1997	1996	1995	1994
Revenues (Million $)						
1Q	136.2	148.5	129.3	83.84	76.33	66.78
2Q	131.4	142.0	127.8	94.15	86.29	79.32
3Q	170.5	164.5	162.3	120.5	100.5	91.91
4Q	—	214.3	245.8	212.6	150.9	140.5
Yr.	—	669.3	665.1	511.0	414.0	378.5
Earnings Per Share ($)						
1Q	0.09	0.15	0.11	0.08	0.07	0.04
2Q	-0.07	0.21	0.17	0.12	0.10	0.07
3Q	0.28	0.25	0.21	0.17	0.14	0.10
4Q	—	0.36	0.47	0.39	0.32	0.28
Yr.	—	0.97	0.96	0.76	0.62	0.45

Next earnings report expected: early February

Dividend Data (Dividends have been paid since 1988.)

Amount ($)	Date Decl.	Ex-Div. Date	Stock of Record	Payment Date
0.028	Dec. 14	Dec. 30	Jan. 04	Feb. 01 '99
0.030	Feb. 25	Mar. 30	Apr. 01	May. 03 '99
0.030	Jun. 25	Jun. 29	Jul. 01	Aug. 02 '99
0.030	Jul. 13	Sep. 29	Oct. 01	Nov. 01 '99

A Division of The McGraw-Hill Companies

Wolverine World Wide, Inc.

Business Summary - 30-JUN-99

Walking tall as one of the world's leading footwear companies, Wolverine World Wide (WWW) sold nearly 38 million pairs of company branded footwear in 1998. WWW manufactures, imports and markets casual shoes, outdoor and work footwear, slippers and moccasins.

WWW is organized as three basic business units. First, the casual unit offers Hush Puppies, the company's principal and best known brand. The brand offers a line of casual shoes for men, women and children sold in over 80 countries. This unit also offers Wolverine Slippers and Children's Footwear. WWW believes that the 40 year heritage of the Hush Puppies brand as a pioneer of comfortable and casual shoes positions the brand to capitalize on the global trend toward more casual workplace and leisure attire. The diverse product line includes several styles for work and casual wear.

The Caterpillar Footwear Group, WWW's second business unit, began operating as a separate division in 1997. The company is capitalizing on the trend toward rugged performance products with its Wolverine work and sport footwear. Footwear with the Caterpillar and Cat trademarks are sold in the U.S. under license agreements. Caterpillar products are manufactured for leading U.S. retailers and catalogs, such as Nordstrom, J.C. Penny, L.L. Bean, Eddie Bauer, and Lands' End.

The third business unit, The Wolverine Footwear Group, is one of the world's largest work and outdoor footwear companies, offering multiple brands with performance and comfort features. The Wolverine brand, which has been in existence for 116 years, markets work and outdoor footwear in two categories: The first being work and industrial footwear, and the second rugged outdoor and sports footwear. This group also includes the Bates and Hy-Test product lines, as well as Harley-Davidson Footwear. Hy-Test was acquired in March 1996 from Florsheim Shoe Co., for $24.5 million in cash, and positioned the company as the domestic leader in occupational and safety shoes and boots.

WWW also operated 56 domestic retail footwear stores as of March 1, 1999, under two formats, consisting of factory outlet stores and one mall-based specialty store. Most of the company's 55 factory outlet stores carry a large selection of first quality branded footwear at discount prices. Sales are also made to large footwear chains (including those owned or operated by other companies in the shoe industry), catalog houses, and independently and company-owned Hush Puppies specialty stores. Other businesses owned by WWW include a pigskin tannery through its Wolverine Leathers Division, and Wolverine Procurement, Inc., which purchases and cures raw pigskins for sale to customers.

Per Share Data ($) (Year Ended Dec. 31)	1998	1997	1996	1995	1994	1993	1992	1991	1990	1989
Tangible Bk. Val.	6.88	6.20	5.74	4.98	3.64	4.88	2.96	3.32	3.24	3.40
Cash Flow	1.27	1.17	0.93	0.39	0.64	0.71	0.29	0.25	-0.02	0.36
Earnings	0.97	0.96	0.77	0.63	0.49	0.33	0.14	0.10	-0.17	0.21
Dividends	0.10	0.09	0.06	0.06	0.04	0.03	0.03	0.03	0.03	0.03
Payout Ratio	11%	9%	8%	9%	9%	10%	23%	32%	NM	15%
Prices - High	30⅞	31⅛	19¾	15⅛	8	6⅝	3	2⅝	2½	3⅛
- Low	8	18⅝	10½	6⅞	5½	2¾	1½	1½	1 3/16	2⅛
P/E Ratio - High	32	32	26	24	16	20	22	26	NM	14
- Low	8	19	14	11	11	8	11	16	NM	10
Income Statement Analysis (Million $)										
Revs.	669	665	511	414	378	333	293	314	322	324
Oper. Inc.	82.2	76.1	55.4	43.3	35.0	24.9	17.8	19.7	17.7	18.4
Depr.	13.0	9.2	7.2	5.8	5.7	5.2	5.2	5.0	5.1	4.9
Int. Exp.	8.4	5.5	3.1	4.7	4.0	5.1	3.6	5.2	5.1	5.6
Pretax Inc.	61.8	61.1	47.7	34.1	25.4	15.9	6.5	4.5	-6.2	10.3
Eff. Tax Rate	33%	32%	31%	30%	29%	28%	29%	28%	NM	29%
Net Inc.	41.7	41.5	32.9	24.1	18.1	11.5	4.6	3.3	-5.7	7.3
Balance Sheet & Other Fin. Data (Million $)										
Cash	6.2	5.8	8.5	27.1	2.9	3.7	2.4	2.2	2.5	3.2
Curr. Assets	341	304	265	215	169	150	148	155	142	142
Total Assets	521	450	362	284	230	206	204	208	190	189
Curr. Liab.	51.3	64.9	69.8	38.0	43.0	38.3	52.4	61.7	44.4	33.8
LT Debt	157	89.8	41.3	30.6	43.5	44.9	42.7	31.6	34.3	36.3
Common Eqty.	300	282	239	204	133	113	100	110	108	116
Total Cap.	463	376	283	237	178	159	144	142	142	152
Cap. Exp.	32.4	35.4	20.6	18.6	9.9	6.6	4.1	6.7	7.2	5.8
Cash Flow	54.7	50.7	40.0	14.9	23.7	16.7	9.8	8.3	-0.6	12.2
Curr. Ratio	6.7	4.7	3.8	5.7	3.9	3.9	2.8	2.5	3.2	4.2
% LT Debt of Cap.	33.9	23.9	14.6	12.9	24.4	28.2	29.6	22.3	24.2	23.8
% Net Inc.of Revs.	6.2	6.2	6.4	5.8	4.8	3.4	1.6	1.0	NM	2.3
% Ret. on Assets	8.6	10.2	10.1	9.4	8.1	5.5	2.2	1.6	NM	3.9
% Ret. on Equity	14.1	15.5	14.8	14.3	14.4	10.7	4.3	3.0	NM	6.4

Data as orig reptd.; bef. results of disc opers/spec. items. Per share data adj. for stk. divs. Bold denotes diluted EPS (FASB 128)-prior periods restated. E-Estimated. NA-Not Available. NM-Not Meaningful. NR-Not Ranked.

Office—9341 Courtland Dr., Rockford, MI 49351. **Tel**—(616) 866-5500. **Chrmn & CEO**—G. B. Bloom. **Pres & COO**—T. J. O'Donovan. **EVP, CFO & Treas**—S. L. Gulis, Jr. **Investor Contact**—Thomas Mundt (616-866-5589). **Dirs**—G. B. Bloom, D. T. Carroll, J. Deem, D. V. Fltes, A. L. Grimoldi, D. T. Kollat, P. D. Matthews, D. P. Mehney, J. A. Parini, J. Parker, E. A. Sanders, P. D. Schrage. **Transfer Agent & Registrar**—Harris Trust & Savings Bank, Chicago. **Incorporated**—in Michigan in 1906; reincorporated in Delaware in 1969. **Empl**— 6,600. **S&P Analyst:** Matthew C. Hershberg

STANDARD
&POOR'S
STOCK REPORTS

Wynn's International

NYSE Symbol **WN**

In S&P SmallCap 600

09-OCT-99

Industry:
Auto Parts & Equipment

Summary: This company manufactures automotive parts and accessories and specialty chemicals. Products include O-rings, seals and molded rubber products.

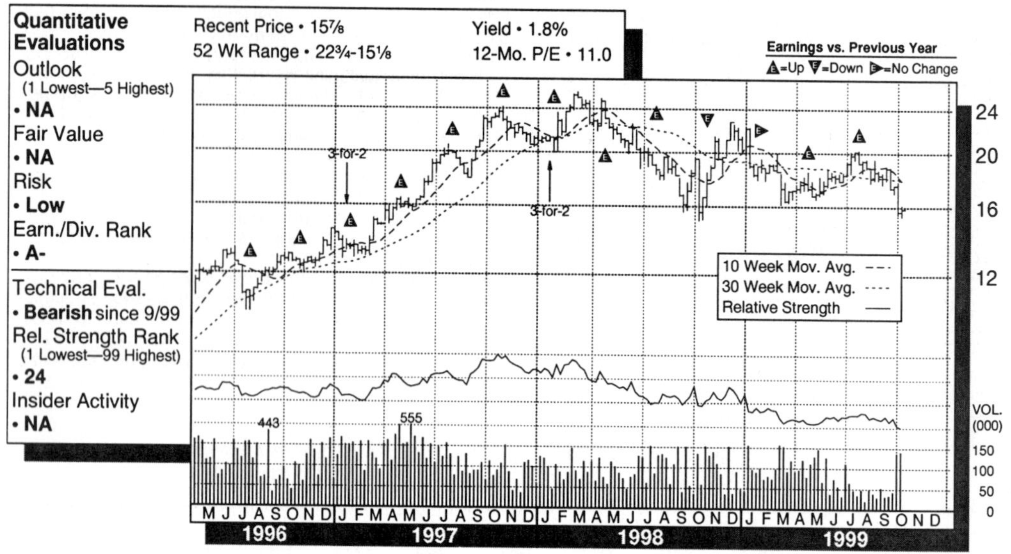

Business Profile - 01-JUN-99

The company's financial condition remained strong at March 31 1999, with cash and cash equivalents of over $46 million and no interest-bearing debt, which will allow WN to implement its three-year $15 million share repurchase program as well as to pursue sound acquisitions. The company expects capital expenditures in 1999 to total about $16 million, and continues to explore possible niche acquisitions. In 1998, Wynn began selling vehicle service contract programs for new and used automobiles and light trucks.

Operational Review - 01-JUN-99

Net sales in the first three months of 1999 advanced 3.3%, year to year, reflecting a 7.0% gain from specialty chemicals and a small increase from automotive and industrial components. Profitability benefited from improved gross margins at Wynn-Precision due to higher sales of the composite gasket line, but after greater SG&A expenses associated with costs for vehicle service contract programs at the specialty chemicals division, pretax income fell 2.4%. With taxes at 36.0%, versus 37.2%, net income was down 0.5%, at $7,453,000 ($0.39 a share, on 3.4% fewer shares), from $7,494,000 ($0.38).

Stock Performance - 08-OCT-99

In the past 30 trading days, WN's shares have declined 13%, compared to a 0.91% fall in the S&P 500. Average trading volume for the past five days was 27,980 shares, compared with the 40-day moving average of 12,759 shares.

Key Stock Statistics

Dividend Rate/Share	0.28	Shareholders	844
Shs. outstg. (M)	18.7	Market cap. (B)	$0.297
Avg. daily vol. (M)	0.017	Inst. holdings	74%
Tang. Bk. Value/Share	7.34		
Beta	0.33		

Value of $10,000 invested 5 years ago: $ 31,982

Fiscal Year Ending Dec. 31

	1999	1998	1997	1996	1995	1994
Revenues (Million $)						
1Q	88.54	85.81	77.89	71.46	78.07	76.78
2Q	93.40	85.59	81.04	71.83	78.05	76.87
3Q	—	79.84	79.36	70.61	74.61	72.22
4Q	—	85.64	82.67	74.63	73.05	66.79
Yr.	—	336.9	320.9	288.5	303.8	292.6
Earnings Per Share ($)						
1Q	**0.39**	**0.38**	**0.30**	**0.22**	0.18	0.14
2Q	**0.40**	**0.36**	**0.32**	**0.26**	0.20	0.17
3Q	—	**0.31**	**0.32**	**0.26**	0.18	0.16
4Q	—	**0.34**	**0.34**	**0.27**	0.18	0.14
Yr.	—	**1.39**	**1.28**	**1.01**	0.75	0.62

Next earnings report expected: mid October

Dividend Data (Dividends have been paid since 1975.)

Amount ($)	Date Decl.	Ex-Div. Date	Stock of Record	Payment Date
0.060	Dec. 09	Dec. 16	Dec. 18	Jan. 04 '99
0.070	Feb. 10	Mar. 09	Mar. 11	Mar. 31 '99
0.070	Apr. 28	Jun. 11	Jun. 15	Jun. 30 '99
0.070	Aug. 04	Sep. 15	Sep. 17	Sep. 30 '99

A Division of The McGraw-Hill Companies

Wynn's International, Inc.

Business Summary - 01-JUN-99

Wynn's International, Inc. (WN) had delivered consistent earnings growth and a steadily increasing return on average equity over the four years through 1995. Nevertheless, in 1996 management of this producer of automotive and industrial components and specialty chemicals believed that its stock was still undervalued, based on the fundamental strengths of its core businesses, and that poor results in its automotive air-conditioning division, Wynn's Climate Systems, Inc., were clouding the performance of its other businesses.

Consequently, WN sold its automotive air-conditioning business in May 1996 for $26.1 million in cash. The company is now focused on its two remaining core businesses, Wynn's-Precision and Wynn Oil Co.

Wynn's-Precision (Precision), together with Robert Skeels & Co., a wholesale distributor of locksets and locksmith supplies, comprises WN's Automotive and Industrial Components division (52% of net sales and 62% of pretax profits in 1998). Precision is a leading maker of O-rings, composite gaskets and other static and dynamic seals. These products, which are made from elastomeric and thermoplastic polymers, are sold mainly to customers in the automotive, aerospace, oil service and hydraulic industries. In September 1996, Precision strengthened its leadership position in the market for plastic boots and bellows, which are used for sealing rack and pinion and constant velocity joints in automobiles, with the acquisition of the Wheaton Automotive Plastics division of Lawson Mardon Wheaton.

Wynn Oil Co., which comprises the Specialty Chemicals division (48% of net sales and 38% of pretax profits in 1998), produces and markets a wide variety of car care products, including preventive or corrective maintenance, as well as industrial specialty products, such as forging compounds, coolants, lubricants and cutting fluids. It also sells a power-flush machine, which automatically cleans a vehicle's cooling system and antifreeze, and restores the antifreeze so it can be reused.

Foreign sales accounted for 38% of the total in 1998 and 1997. GM, the largest customer of automotive components, accounted for some 10.0% of consolidated sales in each year .

In April 1997, WN, via a "Dutch Auction" self-tender, purchased 2,475,000 shares (about 8%) of its common shares (adjusted for 3-for-2 stock split) at $16.17 (adj.) each. In December 1998, directors authorized the repurchase of up $15 million of additional common shares over the next three years.

Per Share Data ($) (Year Ended Dec. 31)	1998	1997	1996	1995	1994	1993	1992	1991	1990	1989
Tangible Bk. Val.	7.34	6.47	6.33	5.56	4.91	4.35	4.13	3.97	4.40	4.08
Cash Flow	1.81	1.78	1.35	1.14	0.97	0.84	0.73	-0.20	0.76	0.77
Earnings	1.39	1.28	1.00	0.75	0.62	0.48	0.40	-0.61	0.33	0.39
Dividends	0.23	0.21	0.18	0.15	0.13	0.12	0.12	0.12	0.12	0.12
Payout Ratio	17%	16%	18%	21%	21%	26%	30%	NM	34%	31%
Prices - High	$25\frac{3}{4}$	$24\frac{1}{8}$	$14\frac{1}{2}$	9	$7\frac{1}{8}$	7	$5\frac{5}{8}$	$3\frac{7}{8}$	$4\frac{3}{4}$	$5\frac{1}{2}$
- Low	15	$12\frac{3}{4}$	8	$5\frac{3}{4}$	$5\frac{3}{8}$	5	$3\frac{1}{8}$	$2\frac{7}{8}$	$2\frac{3}{4}$	$4\frac{1}{8}$
P/E Ratio - High	19	19	14	12	12	15	13	NM	15	14
- Low	11	10	8	8	9	10	7	NM	8	11
Income Statement Analysis (Million $)										
Revs.	337	321	289	304	293	285	292	274	285	284
Oper. Inc.	48.9	47.6	40.0	33.4	28.6	25.6	23.8	18.8	26.2	22.9
Depr.	8.4	8.3	7.4	8.2	6.8	6.7	6.1	7.5	8.5	7.4
Int. Exp.	0.3	0.2	0.2	1.6	3.0	3.9	5.1	5.2	5.8	5.2
Pretax Inc.	42.6	41.2	33.9	24.6	19.4	15.8	13.3	-13.9	13.0	13.0
Eff. Tax Rate	36%	37%	37%	37%	39%	43%	46%	NM	51%	42%
Net Inc.	27.3	25.9	21.3	15.4	11.8	9.0	7.3	-11.2	6.4	7.6
Balance Sheet & Other Fin. Data (Million $)										
Cash	46.5	43.3	53.3	23.1	16.4	21.4	14.7	6.1	7.7	12.4
Curr. Assets	164	148	154	127	120	118	125	118	128	129
Total Assets	226	207	205	182	176	168	171	166	188	189
Curr. Liab.	66.4	61.4	64.0	58.5	59.2	56.3	54.5	44.7	50.2	53.5
LT Debt	Nil	Nil	Nil	0.1	14.9	23.4	32.5	40.7	41.2	41.2
Common Eqty.	141	128	133	116	95.4	84.4	78.9	75.6	89.8	87.9
Total Cap.	148	135	141	123	117	112	116	121	138	135
Cap. Exp.	9.9	11.8	9.1	7.5	13.8	10.0	6.5	4.2	8.3	10.7
Cash Flow	35.7	34.2	28.7	23.6	18.6	15.6	13.4	-3.7	14.8	15.0
Curr. Ratio	2.5	2.4	2.4	2.2	2.0	2.1	2.3	2.6	2.5	2.4
% LT Debt of Cap.	Nil	Nil	Nil	0.1	12.7	21.0	28.0	33.7	29.9	30.5
% Net Inc.of Revs.	8.1	8.1	7.4	5.1	4.0	3.2	2.5	NM	2.2	2.7
% Ret. on Assets	12.6	12.6	11.1	8.7	6.8	5.2	4.3	NM	3.5	4.0
% Ret. on Equity	20.3	19.9	17.1	14.5	13.1	10.9	9.4	NM	7.4	8.9

Data as orig reptd.; bef. results of disc opers/spec. items. Per share data adj. for stk. divs. Bold denotes diluted EPS (FASB 128)-prior periods restated. E-Estimated. NA-Not Available. NM-Not Meaningful. NR-Not Ranked.

Office—500 N. State College Blvd., Suite 700, Orange, CA 92668. **Tel**—(714) 938-3700. **WebSite**—http//:www.wynns.com **Chrmn, CEO & Investor Contact**—James Carroll. **Pres & COO**—J. W. Huber. **VP-Fin & CFO**—S. A. Schlosser. **Secy**—W. K. K. Nishikawa.**VP & Gen Counsel**—G. M. Gibbons. **Dirs**—B. Beek, J. Carroll, B. L. Herrmann, R. Hood Jr., R. L. Nelson, D. C. Trauscht, J. D. Woods. **Transfer Agent & Registrar**—ChaseMellon Shareholder Services, Los Angeles. **Incorporated**—in Delaware in 1973. **Empl**— 2,121. **S&P Analyst:** S.A.H.

STANDARD
&POOR'S
STOCK REPORTS

X-Rite, Inc.

NASDAQ Symbol **XRIT**

In S&P SmallCap 600

09-OCT-99

Industry: Electronics (Instrumentation)

Summary: This company manufactures quality control products for a variety of industries.

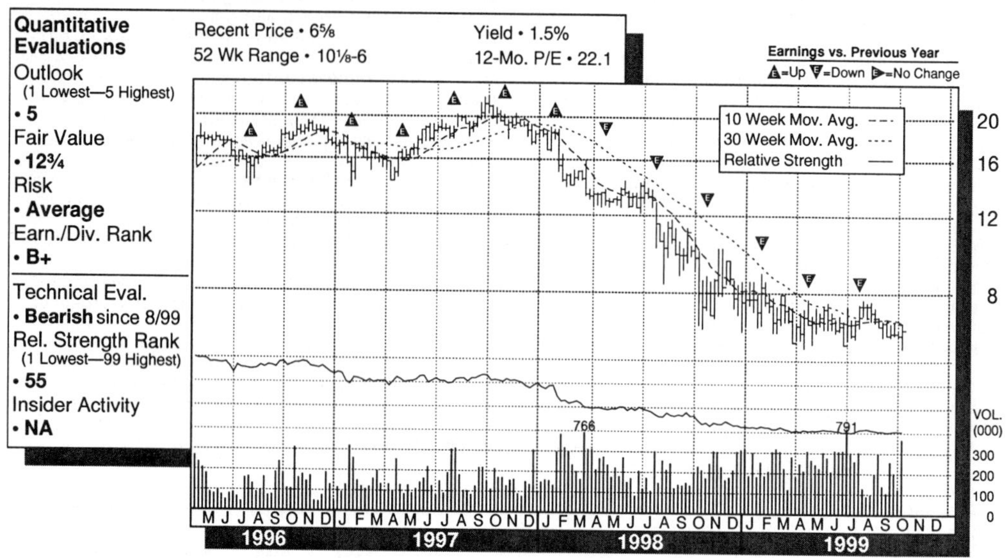

Business Profile - 19-JUL-99

The company's new strategic business units are focused on establishing relationships with companies in different industries. This diversification offers protection from a downturn in any one industry, as well as a wide base for future sales opportunities. In June 1999, XRIT introduced new portable color measurement instruments for the coatings, plastics and textile industries; QA-Master 2000, software for displaying, analyzing and storing spectral color data; and an update to its entry-level quality control software, QA-Lite.

Operational Review - 19-JUL-99

For the three months ended April 3, 1999, net sales rose fractionally, year to year. International sales accounted for a higher percentage of total sales than in the year-ago period. Despite a favorable change in the product mix, margins narrowed, primarily due to expenses related to the addition of a sales office in France and expansion of the Hong Kong and U.K. offices. Pretax income was down 2.2%. After taxes at 35.3%, versus, 34.0%, net income fell 4.1%, to $2,983,000 ($0.14 a share, on 4.0% more shares), from $3,110,000 ($0.15).

Stock Performance - 08-OCT-99

In the past 30 trading days, XRIT's shares have declined 2%, compared to a 0.91% fall in the S&P 500. Average trading volume for the past five days was 140,300 shares, compared with the 40-day moving average of 51,641 shares.

Key Stock Statistics

Dividend Rate/Share	0.10	Shareholders	1,560
Shs. outstg. (M)	21.2	Market cap. (B)	$0.141
Avg. daily vol. (M)	0.064	Inst. holdings	24%
Tang. Bk. Value/Share	2.17		
Beta	0.51		

Value of $10,000 invested 5 years ago: $ 6,334

Fiscal Year Ending Dec. 31

	1999	1998	1997	1996	1995	1994
Revenues (Million $)						
1Q	23.69	23.64	23.08	19.70	17.95	12.35
2Q	24.33	24.29	23.99	20.83	18.91	14.76
3Q	—	21.46	24.86	21.36	18.76	15.64
4Q	—	25.43	25.06	22.51	17.03	16.73
Yr.	—	94.81	96.99	84.39	72.63	59.48
Earnings Per Share ($)						
1Q	**0.14**	**0.15**	**0.20**	**0.16**	0.16	0.12
2Q	**0.15**	**0.16**	**0.22**	**0.18**	0.12	0.15
3Q	—	**-0.14**	**0.22**	**0.19**	0.12	0.16
4Q	—	**0.15**	**0.21**	**0.20**	0.07	0.17
Yr.	—	**0.32**	**0.85**	**0.73**	**0.47**	**0.60**

Next earnings report expected: late October

Dividend Data (Dividends have been paid since 1986.)

Amount ($)	Date Decl.	Ex-Div. Date	Stock of Record	Payment Date
0.025	Jan. 04	Jan. 13	Jan. 15	Feb. 12 '99
0.025	Apr. 05	Apr. 14	Apr. 16	May. 14 '99
0.025	Jul. 06	Jul. 15	Jul. 19	Aug. 16 '99
0.025	Oct. 04	Oct. 14	Oct. 18	Nov. 15 '99

X-Rite, Incorporated

Business Summary - 19-JUL-99

X-Rite, Inc. has expanded its product offerings by concentrating on its instrument technologies and developing expertise in the fields of light and color measurement. As a result, XRIT markets and develops numerous quality control instruments, software products and accessories.

XRIT primarily manufactures and sells proprietary quality control instruments which utilize advanced electronics and optics technologies. The company has two main product lines: instruments that measure color and appearance, and instruments that measure optical or photographic density. Products include densitometers, sensitometers, colorimeters, spectrophotometers, point-of-purchase paint matching systems, integrating spheres, and sphere systems. In 1998, XRIT launched its 500 series line of spectrodensitomers, the only hand-held densitometer equipped with a spectral engine.

A densitometer is an instrument that measures light, compares that measurement with a reference standard, and signals the result. Sensitometers are used to expose photographic film of various types in a very precise manner for comparison to a reference standard. X-Rite provides these instruments to the photographic, graphic arts, medical, and digital imaging industries. A colorimeter measures color much like the human eye perceives color, using red, green and blue receptors. Colorimeters are used to measure printed colors on packages, labels, textiles and other materials where appearance is critical for buyer acceptance.

XRIT has grown through internal expansion and acquisitions. The company diversified through the 1995 acquisition of Labsphere, a leading supplier of integrating spheres, sphere systems, and reflectance coatings. Integrating spheres and integrating sphere systems are used in testing incandescent and fluorescent lamp output, calibrating remote sensors, and laser power measurement. In May 1997, XRIT acquired Light Source Computer Images, Inc., a producer of high-quality, easy-to-use scanning, imaging and print optimization software.

Sales of the company's products are made by its own personnel and through independent manufacturers' representatives. Certain products not sold directly to end-users are distributed in the U.S. through a network of 1,500 independent dealers and outside the U.S. through 400 dealers in more than 50 countries. International sales and foreign subsidiary sales accounted for 34% of total sales in both 1998 and 1997.

The company's new strategic business units are focused on establishing relationships/partnering arrangements with market leaders such as Ace Hardware, Heidelberg CPS, Home Hardware Stores Ltd. and Xerox. This diversification offers protection from a downturn in any one industry, as well as a wide base for future sales opportunities.

Per Share Data ($) (Year Ended Dec. 31)	1998	1997	1996	1995	1994	1993	1992	1991	1990	1989
Tangible Bk. Val.	2.17	3.34	3.01	2.34	2.44	1.90	1.61	1.33	1.13	0.97
Cash Flow	0.60	1.10	0.93	0.63	0.66	0.41	0.39	0.28	0.23	0.21
Earnings	0.32	0.85	0.73	0.47	0.60	0.36	0.34	0.23	0.18	0.17
Dividends	0.10	0.10	0.10	0.10	0.08	0.08	0.05	0.03	0.03	0.02
Payout Ratio	31%	12%	14%	21%	13%	22%	15%	14%	15%	11%
Prices - High	19	22 3/8	19 3/4	24	21	13 1/2	16 5/8	7 1/2	3 5/8	3 1/8
- Low	6 1/2	13 3/4	12	13 3/4	10 1/2	8 3/4	5 5/8	2 3/4	2	2 1/16
P/E Ratio - High	59	26	27	51	35	38	49	33	20	18
- Low	20	16	16	29	18	24	17	12	11	12
Income Statement Analysis (Million $)										
Revs.	94.8	97.0	84.4	72.6	59.5	39.2	36.2	29.1	23.6	21.2
Oper. Inc.	22.8	32.5	27.1	18.0	19.1	11.0	10.7	7.1	5.5	5.2
Depr.	5.8	5.5	4.3	3.4	1.3	1.2	1.1	1.0	0.8	0.7
Int. Exp.	Nil	NA	Nil	NM	Nil	Nil	Nil	Nil	Nil	Nil
Pretax Inc.	10.7	27.3	23.2	14.7	18.4	10.4	10.1	6.8	5.5	5.2
Eff. Tax Rate	36%	34%	34%	33%	31%	28%	30%	30%	32%	30%
Net Inc.	6.9	18.0	15.4	9.9	12.6	7.5	7.1	4.7	3.8	3.6
Balance Sheet & Other Fin. Data (Million $)										
Cash	1.5	2.8	1.6	4.4	14.9	18.3	15.4	12.6	9.7	8.4
Curr. Assets	58.7	52.2	47.4	32.0	39.4	32.4	27.4	22.7	18.8	16.1
Total Assets	95.4	92.5	79.0	63.5	54.6	41.9	35.8	30.5	26.0	22.2
Curr. Liab.	5.3	5.7	5.3	4.0	2.9	1.7	1.7	2.3	1.9	1.5
LT Debt	Nil	Nil	Nil	NM	Nil	Nil	Nil	Nil	Nil	Nil
Common Eqty.	90.1	86.1	73.0	59.3	51.1	39.8	33.7	27.8	23.5	20.2
Total Cap.	90.1	86.1	73.6	59.9	51.7	40.2	34.1	28.2	24.0	20.6
Cap. Exp.	4.2	4.3	3.1	3.4	4.2	1.5	1.7	1.7	2.1	0.7
Cash Flow	12.7	23.5	19.6	13.3	13.9	8.7	8.2	5.7	4.6	4.3
Curr. Ratio	11.0	9.1	8.9	8.0	13.8	19.4	15.9	10.0	9.7	10.4
% LT Debt of Cap.	Nil	Nil	Nil	NM	Nil	Nil	Nil	Nil	Nil	Nil
% Net Inc.of Revs.	7.2	18.6	18.2	13.6	21.3	19.2	19.5	16.3	16.0	17.1
% Ret. on Assets	7.3	21.0	21.6	16.8	26.2	19.4	21.3	16.8	15.7	17.7
% Ret. on Equity	7.8	22.7	23.3	17.9	27.8	20.5	23.0	18.5	17.3	19.6

Data as orig reptd.; bef. results of disc opers/spec. items. Per share data adj. for stk. divs. Bold denotes diluted EPS (FASB 128)-prior periods restated. E-Estimated. NA-Not Available. NM-Not Meaningful. NR-Not Ranked.

Office—3100 44th St. SW, Grandville, MI 49418. **Tel**—(616) 534-7663. **Fax**—(616) 534-9212. **Website**—http://www.x-rite.com **Chrmn & CEO**—T. Thompson. **Pres & COO**—R. E. Cook. **VP, CFO & Investor Contact**—Duane Kluting. **Dirs**—P. M. Banks, S. W. Cheff, R. E. Cook, J.A. Knister, R. S. Teesdale, T. Thompson, C. Van Namen, R. A. VandenBerg. **Transfer Agent & Registrar**—State Street Bank & Trust Co., Boston. **Incorporated**—in Michigan in 1958. **Empl**— 662. **S&P Analyst:** Scott H. Kessler

STANDARD
&POOR'S
STOCK REPORTS

Xircom, Inc.

Nasdaq Symbol **XIRC**

In S&P SmallCap 600

09-OCT-99

Industry: Computers (Peripherals)

Summary: Xircom's principal products are local area network (LAN) adapters, which enable portable personal computers to be connected to a LAN.

S&P Opinion: Buy (★★★★★) | Recent Price • 47⅛ | 52 Wk Range • 48-15¾ | Yield • Nil | 12-Mo. P/E • 29.1

Quantitative Evaluations

Outlook (1 Lowest—5 Highest) • **2⁻**

Fair Value • **43⅞**

Risk • **High**

Earn./Div. Rank • **NR**

Technical Eval. • **Neutral** since 9/99

Rel. Strength Rank (1 Lowest—99 Highest) • **94**

Insider Activity • **Unfavorable**

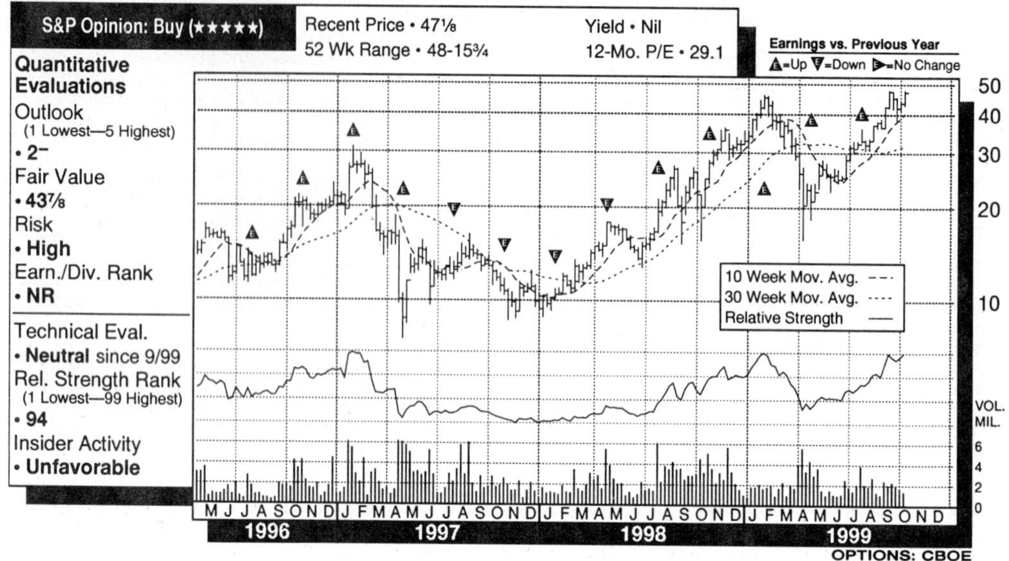

OPTIONS: CBOE

Overview - 27-JUL-99

We project revenue growth of nearly 50% for FY 99 (Sep.), and, from that higher base, we see another 25% gain in FY 2000, fueled mainly by strong demand for the company's new RealPort Integrated PC Card line. We expect gross margins to widen to approximately 43%, from FY 98's 35.4%, reflecting contributions from the RealPort product family, as well as manufacturing efficiencies. We recently raised our gross margin expectation from 39%, based on Xircom's success in reducing costs at a faster than expected rate. Meanwhile, operating expenses should grow roughly in line with revenues, and we expect operating margins to widen to 15% during FY 99, from 8% in FY 98. Finally, we expect the tax rate to decrease 200 basis points, to 28%, reflecting a change in XIRC's tax strategies related to its investments. Based on these assumptions, we estimate that FY 99 EPS should advance to $1.80, with a further gain, to $2.05, in FY 2000.

Valuation - 27-JUL-99

We continue to recommend buying the shares. Xircom's new RealPort Integrated PC card has introduced a compelling, innovative product to the company's lineup. Benefiting from patented technology, the product should enjoy strong growth over the next few years. Even without gaining market share from the RealPort product line, XIRC, as leader in PC cards for laptops, should benefit from a continuing trend toward networking mobile professionals. In addition, we are impressed with management's success in achieving manufacturing gains, better asset management, and faster time to market with new products. In many instances, XIRC has exceeded its goals. With $4.58 a share in cash, and trading at a below market P/E ratio, we believe the shares are undervalued.

Key Stock Statistics

S&P EPS Est. 1999	1.80	Tang. Bk. Value/Share	6.91
P/E on S&P Est. 1999	26.2	Beta	1.50
S&P EPS Est. 2000	2.05	Shareholders	278
Dividend Rate/Share	Nil	Market cap. (B)	$ 1.1
Shs. outstg. (M)	24.2	Inst. holdings	68%
Avg. daily vol. (M)	0.349		

Value of $10,000 invested 5 years ago: $ 27,757

Fiscal Year Ending Sep. 30

	1999	1998	1997	1996	1995	1994
Revenues (Million $)						
1Q	96.02	52.55	62.31	37.70	40.11	26.38
2Q	97.68	64.13	57.14	45.33	39.97	30.25
3Q	103.1	71.31	50.23	52.22	16.47	36.09
4Q	—	88.07	20.90	58.06	30.01	38.87
Yr.	—	276.1	184.6	193.3	126.6	131.6
Earnings Per Share ($)						
1Q	**0.39**	**0.11**	0.22	-0.04	0.27	0.21
2Q	**0.42**	**0.14**	0.22	0.07	0.15	0.23
3Q	**0.48**	**0.20**	0.02	0.13	-2.86	0.25
4Q	—	**0.33**	-0.57	0.14	-0.91	0.26
Yr.	—	**0.78**	**-0.16**	0.30	-3.44	0.95

Next earnings report expected: mid October

Dividend Data

No cash has been paid. The company intends to retain earnings for use in its business.

A Division of The McGraw-Hill Companies

Xircom, Inc.

Business Summary - 27-JUL-99

About 10 years ago, in 1988, Xircom essentially created the market for mobile networking with its Pocket LAN Adapter, the first universal solution for connecting notebook PCs (personal computers) to LANs (local area networks), and continues to lead in the competitive PC Card market today.

XIRC's products let PC users access information and resources found on local area networks (LANs), and on-line Internet services. Over the past several years, there has been a significant increase in the number of PC users accessing corporate networks or the Internet from remote locations. Increasingly, people need to communicate and share information in geographically diverse locations, and greater reliance on mobile work forces has meant that reliable mobile connectivity has become a critical business requirement.

The market for PC Cards, credit-card-size devices that slide into a slot on laptops, is expected to surge from 16 million in 1997 to more than 30 million by 2000. With Xircom's strong competitive position, it stands to benefit from this explosive growth. The company has leadership positions in the three core markets it serves. XIRC is ranked first in the combination Ethernet+Modem PC Card space; second in PC Card LAN adapters; and second in high-speed modem-only adapters. XIRC has brought high-speed communications technologies to the notebook environment with a series of products based on 100 Mbps Ethernet, 32-bit CardBus interfaces, ISDN and 56Kbps modem technology. In addition, XIRC supports Global Systems for Mobile Communications (GSM), the international standard for wireless digital cellular technology, and PCS 1900, the North American GSM wireless digital service, in its modem and multi-function PC Cards.

XIRC's newly introduced RealPort Integrated PC Card has experienced rapid growth, as its patented form factor, which features built-in connectors, resolves two problems faced by mobile workers: damaged or forgotten cables, and broken pop-out jacks. While accounting for only 5% of revenues in the June 1998 quarter, by the December quarter the RealPort product line had surged to account for 40% of total sales, and it reached 50% of the total in the March 1999 quarter.

Xircom's growth has also been fueled by the success of its speed-based processes. This model has sought to promote rapid product innovation, improve fill rates, reduce product inventory in distribution channels and increase inventory turns. The company's recent results have showed dramatic operating benefits from this effort.

In 1997, Intel purchased a 12.5% interest in Xircom, valued at approximately $52 million.

Per Share Data ($) (Year Ended Sep. 30)	1998	1997	1996	1995	1994	1993	1992	1991	1990	1989
Tangible Bk. Val.	5.92	5.02	3.32	2.81	5.10	3.99	3.42	NM	NA	NA
Cash Flow	1.13	0.15	0.72	-3.06	1.17	0.71	0.47	0.22	NA	NA
Earnings	0.78	-0.16	0.30	-3.44	0.95	0.59	0.41	0.19	NA	NA
Dividends	Nil	Nil	Nil	Nil	Nil	Nil	Nil	Nil	NA	NA
Payout Ratio	Nil	Nil	Nil	Nil	Nil	Nil	Nil	Nil	NA	NA
Prices - High	36⅛	31⅛	23¾	19	28¼	19½	22	NA	NA	NA
- Low	9¼	7½	9½	9	12¾	7¼	7	NA	NA	NA
P/E Ratio - High	46	NM	79	NM	30	33	54	NA	NA	NA
- Low	12	NM	32	NM	13	12	17	NA	NA	NA
Income Statement Analysis (Million $)										
Revs.	276	185	193	127	132	82.2	59.1	26.3	NA	NA
Oper. Inc.	29.9	0.7	19.8	-13.6	29.1	17.0	10.5	4.6	NA	NA
Depr.	8.0	6.5	8.2	6.5	3.8	2.0	1.0	0.4	NA	NA
Int. Exp.	Nil	Nil	Nil	Nil	0.2	0.2	0.4	0.1	NA	NA
Pretax Inc.	26.2	-4.8	8.8	-65.8	25.1	15.8	9.6	4.1	NA	NA
Eff. Tax Rate	30%	NM	33%	NM	37%	39%	37%	40%	NA	NA
Net Inc.	18.3	-3.3	6.0	-58.8	15.9	9.7	6.1	2.5	NA	NA
Balance Sheet & Other Fin. Data (Million $)										
Cash	106	75.1	21.5	13.7	51.5	40.4	32.7	Nil	NA	NA
Curr. Assets	168	130	84.1	63.3	91.4	69.7	53.6	12.0	NA	NA
Total Assets	195	148	109	81.0	101	75.3	57.0	13.7	NA	NA
Curr. Liab.	49.4	34.0	40.6	34.8	18.8	11.9	6.3	6.9	NA	NA
LT Debt	Nil	Nil	1.9	0.8	0.1	0.4	0.8	0.6	NA	NA
Common Eqty.	137	113	65.6	53.1	82.1	62.5	49.6	-9.0	NA	NA
Total Cap.	146	114	68.2	53.9	82.2	63.0	50.4	6.8	NA	NA
Cap. Exp.	17.9	6.4	9.5	13.6	7.4	4.0	1.9	1.4	NA	NA
Cash Flow	26.3	3.1	14.1	-52.3	19.7	11.6	7.0	2.9	NA	NA
Curr. Ratio	3.4	3.8	2.1	1.8	4.9	5.8	8.5	1.7	NA	NA
% LT Debt of Cap.	Nil	Nil	2.8	1.5	0.2	0.7	1.7	8.6	NA	NA
% Net Inc.of Revs.	6.6	NM	3.1	NM	12.1	11.7	10.3	9.4	NA	NA
% Ret. on Assets	10.7	NM	6.1	NM	17.8	14.1	NM	NA	NA	NA
% Ret. on Equity	14.6	NM	10.1	NM	21.7	16.6	NM	NA	NA	NA

Data as orig reptd.; bef. results of disc opers/spec. items. Per share data adj. for stk. divs. Bold denotes diluted EPS (FASB 128)-prior periods restated. E-Estimated. NA-Not Available. NM-Not Meaningful. NR-Not Ranked.

Office—2300 Corporate Center Dr., Thousand Oaks, CA 91320. **Tel**—(805) 376-9300. **Website**—http://www.xircom.com **Chrmn, Pres & CEO**—D. I. Gates. **VP-Fin & CFO**—S. F. DeGennaro. **Secy**—R. H. Holliday. **Investor Contact**—Kristi Cushing (805-376-6969). **Dirs**—M. F. G. Ashby, K. J. Biba, G. J. Bowen, D. I. Gates, J. K. Mathews, C. E. Russo, W. J. Schroeder. D. W. Yocam. **Transfer Agent & Registrar**—Bank of Boston. **Incorporated**—in California in 1988. **Empl**— 1,300. **S&P Analyst:** M. Graham Hackett

STANDARD
&POOR'S
STOCK REPORTS

Xomed Surgical Products

NASDAQ Symbol **XOMD**

In S&P SmallCap 600

09-OCT-99

Industry:
Health Care (Medical Products & Supplies)

Summary: A leading manufacturer of surgical products for use by ear, nose and throat surgeons, XOMD recently agreed to be acquired by Medtronic, Inc. for $60 a share in common stock.

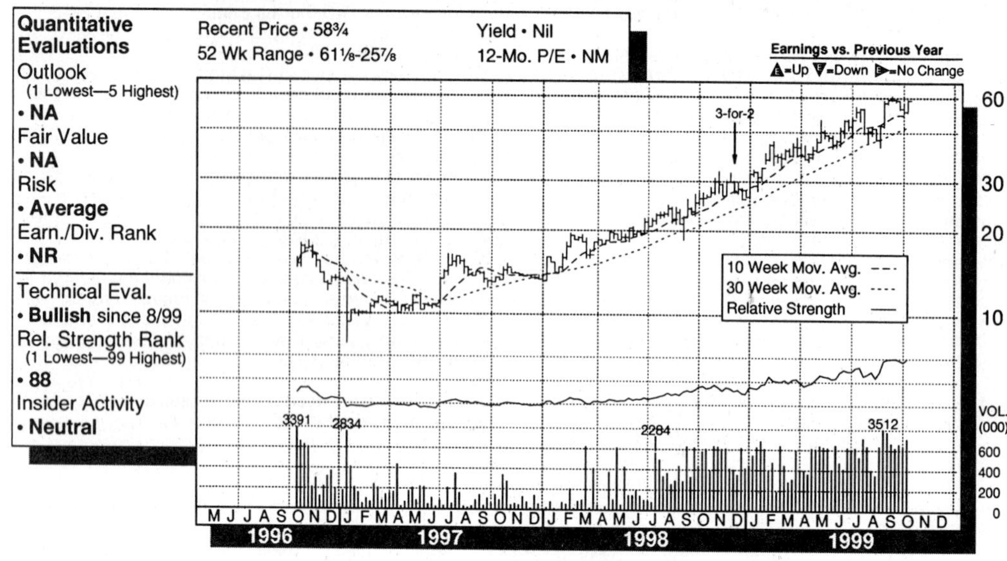

Business Profile - 29-SEP-99

On August 27, 1999, an agreement was announced under which XOMD would be acquired by Medtonic, Inc. Terms call for XOMD shareholders to receive $60 a share in Medtronic common stock for each XOMD common share held. The transaction is subject to certain collar provisions, approval by XOMD shareholders and regulatory conditions. The acquisition is expected to be completed before the end of 1999. Medtronic is a leading medical technology company, specializing in implantable and interventional therapies that restore health, extend life and alleviate pain. Medtronic believes that the acquisition of XOMD would establish it as the global leader in the market for medical problems in the ear, nose and throat.

Operational Review - 29-SEP-99

Net sales for the six months ended July 3, 1999, advanced 31%, year to year, with all major product lines recording gains. Domestic sales rose 24%, while international sales were up 47%. Profitability improved and pretax income increased 46%. After taxes at 37.8%, versus 39.5%, net income was up 50%, to $5,814,000 ($0.45 a share, based on 14% more average shares) from $3,880,000 ($0.34, adjusted).

Stock Performance - 08-OCT-99

In the past 30 trading days, XOMD's shares have increased 2%, compared to a 0.91% fall in the S&P 500. Average trading volume for the past five days was 414,160 shares, compared with the 40-day moving average of 359,654 shares.

Key Stock Statistics

Dividend Rate/Share	Nil	Shareholders	700
Shs. outstg. (M)	12.3	Market cap. (B)	$0.722
Avg. daily vol. (M)	0.256	Inst. holdings	92%
Tang. Bk. Value/Share	5.86		
Beta	NA		

Value of $10,000 invested 5 years ago: NA

Fiscal Year Ending Dec. 31

	1999	1998	1997	1996	1995	1994
Revenues (Million $)						
1Q	27.61	20.68	17.80	—	—	—
2Q	29.37	22.87	19.20	—	—	—
3Q	—	21.91	18.65	15.85	—	—
4Q	—	25.92	21.58	16.87	—	—
Yr.	—	91.38	77.24	65.66	59.87	—
Earnings Per Share ($)						
1Q	**0.20**	**0.15**	0.12	—	—	—
2Q	**0.25**	**0.19**	—	—	—	—
3Q	—	**0.18**	0.12	—	—	—
4Q	—	**0.08**	**0.21**	0.10	—	—
Yr.	—	**0.59**	**0.55**	-0.01	**-0.02**	—

Next earnings report expected: late October

Dividend Data

Amount ($)	Date Decl.	Ex-Div. Date	Stock of Record	Payment Date
3-for-2	Oct. 27	Dec. 01	Nov. 16	Nov. 30 '98

A Division of The McGraw-Hill Companies

Xomed Surgical Products, Inc.

Business Summary - 29-SEP-99

A leading manufacturer of surgical products for use by ear, nose and throat (ENT) specialists and ophthalmic surgeons, Xomed Surgical Products signed an agreement on August 27, 1999, for it to be acquired by Medtonic, Inc. (MDT), a leading medical technology company.

Terms of the acquisition agreement call for XOMD shareholders to receive $60 in MDT common stock for each XOMD common share held. The transaction is subject to certain collar provisions, approval by shareholders of XOMD, and Hart-Scott-Rodino clearance. The companies expect the transaction to be completed before the end of 1999.

Medtronic specializes in implantable and interventional therapies that restore health, extend life and alleviate pain. It believes that the acquisition of XOMD would establish it as the global leader in the market for medical problems in the ear, nose and throat. MDT believes that XOMD's market leadership, strong clinical relationships, and range of products offer it a new platform for continued growth beyond its current franchises in cardiac rhythm management, cardiac surgery, vascular and neurological and spinal.

XOMD's broad line of products includes, in its core ENT market, powered tissue-removal systems and other microendoscopy instruments, implantable devices, nerve monitoring systems, disposable fluid-control products and image guided surgery systems. The company also offers a line of ophthalmic and other products. About 77% of XOMD's revenues in 1998 were derived from disposable and implantable products.

The company's objective is to enhance its leading position in the ENT market and to enter new markets. Its strategy for achieving this objective is to: continue to focus on the ENT market, facilitate ENT market conversion to less traumatic approaches, emphasize product innovations through internal research and development and corporate alliances, maintain a broad line of ENT products with particular emphasis on disposable and implantable products, expand its global distribution network, and leverage core competencies by entering new markets.

About 43% of the company's sales in 1998 were derived from powered tissue-removal instrumentation systems, visualization products, fluid-control products and hand instruments designed for microendoscopic sinus surgery. Products and devices related to the head and neck anatomy contributed about 23% of 1998 sales, otology products announced for about 17%, and ophthalmic and other products contributed about 17%.

XOMD distributes its products through a direct sales organization of nearly 100 persons in the U.S. and selected other countries and through a network of over 130 independent distributors. The company is the only major manufacturer and marketer of ENT surgical products with a direct U.S. sales force exclusively serving ENT specialists. About 29% of XOMD's sales in 1998 were derived from international markets.

Per Share Data ($) (Year Ended Dec. 31)	1998	1997	1996	1995	1994	1993	1992	1991	1990	1989
Tangible Bk. Val.	5.33	6.01	3.23	NA	NA	NA	NA	NA	NA	NA
Cash Flow	1.00	1.50	0.34	3.31	NA	NA	NA	NA	NA	NA
Earnings	0.59	0.55	-0.01	NA	NA	NA	NA	NA	NA	NA
Dividends	Nil	Nil	Nil	NA	NA	NA	NA	NA	NA	NA
Payout Ratio	Nil	Nil	Nil	NA	NA	NA	NA	NA	NA	NA
Prices - High	32⅝	16⅜	18⅛	NA	NA	NA	NA	NA	NA	NA
- Low	14	7⅞	12	NA	NA	NA	NA	NA	NA	NA
P/E Ratio - High	55	30	NM	NA	NA	NA	NA	NA	NA	NA
- Low	24	14	NM	NA	NA	NA	NA	NA	NA	NA
Income Statement Analysis (Million $)										
Revs.	91.4	77.2	65.7	59.9	NA	NA	NA	NA	NA	NA
Oper. Inc.	19.2	15.1	11.7	9.4	NA	NA	NA	NA	NA	NA
Depr.	5.1	5.1	4.8	4.7	NA	NA	NA	NA	NA	NA
Int. Exp.	0.0	0.3	2.2	3.1	NA	NA	NA	NA	NA	NA
Pretax Inc.	11.5	10.1	-0.3	1.7	NA	NA	NA	NA	NA	NA
Eff. Tax Rate	38%	39%	NM	81%	NA	NA	NA	NA	NA	NA
Net Inc.	7.1	6.1	-1.2	0.3	NA	NA	NA	NA	NA	NA
Balance Sheet & Other Fin. Data (Million $)										
Cash	4.3	1.7	0.6	0.4	NA	NA	NA	NA	NA	NA
Curr. Assets	46.7	34.3	29.3	27.9	NA	NA	NA	NA	NA	NA
Total Assets	142	95.7	94.1	93.1	NA	NA	NA	NA	NA	NA
Curr. Liab.	14.2	8.2	10.9	15.7	NA	NA	NA	NA	NA	NA
LT Debt	13.1	Nil	3.6	32.7	NA	NA	NA	NA	NA	NA
Common Eqty.	114	86.5	79.6	-13.1	NA	NA	NA	NA	NA	NA
Total Cap.	127	86.5	83.2	77.4	NA	NA	NA	NA	NA	NA
Cap. Exp.	7.7	2.4	2.4	NA	NA	NA	NA	NA	NA	NA
Cash Flow	12.2	11.2	3.7	5.1	NA	NA	NA	NA	NA	NA
Curr. Ratio	3.3	4.2	2.7	1.8	NA	NA	NA	NA	NA	NA
% LT Debt of Cap.	10.3	Nil	4.3	42.2	NA	NA	NA	NA	NA	NA
% Net Inc.of Revs.	7.7	7.9	NM	0.5	NA	NA	NA	NA	NA	NA
% Ret. on Assets	6.0	6.5	NM	0.3	NA	NA	NA	NA	NA	NA
% Ret. on Equity	7.1	7.4	NM	NM	NA	NA	NA	NA	NA	NA

Data as orig reptd.; bef. results of disc opers/spec. items. Per share data adj. for stk. divs. Bold denotes diluted EPS (FASB 128)-prior periods restated. E-Estimated. NA-Not Available. NM-Not Meaningful. NR-Not Ranked.

Office—6743 Southport Drive N., Jacksonville, FL 32216-0980. **Tel**—(904) 296-9600. **Website**—http://www.xomed.com **Chrmn, Pres & CEO**—J. T. Treace. **VP-Fin, CFO, Secy & Investor Contact**—Thomas E. Timbie (904 279-7525). **Dirs**—R. B. Emmitt, W. R. Miller, J. E. Thomas, J. T. Treace, E. H. Weatherman. **Transfer Agent & Registrar**—First Union Bank of North Carolina, Charlotte. **Incorporated**—in Delaware in 1994.. **Empl**— 724. **S&P Analyst:** J. J. Schemitsch

STANDARD
&POOR'S
STOCK REPORTS

Yellow Corp.

Nasdaq Symbol **YELL**

In S&P SmallCap 600

09-OCT-99 **Industry:** Truckers

Summary: YELL operates the nation's largest long-haul less-than-truckload (LTL) carrier and offers regional LTL service. In July 1999 YELL bought Jevic Transportation for $200 million.

S&P Opinion: Accumulate (★★★★) Recent Price • 17 Yield • Nil 52 Wk Range • 19⅝-10⅜ 12-Mo. P/E • 11.6

Quantitative Evaluations

Outlook (1 Lowest—5 Highest) • 5+

Fair Value • 28⅛

Risk • **Average**

Earn./Div. Rank • C

Technical Eval. • **Bearish** since 8/99

Rel. Strength Rank (1 Lowest—99 Highest) • 79

Insider Activity • NA

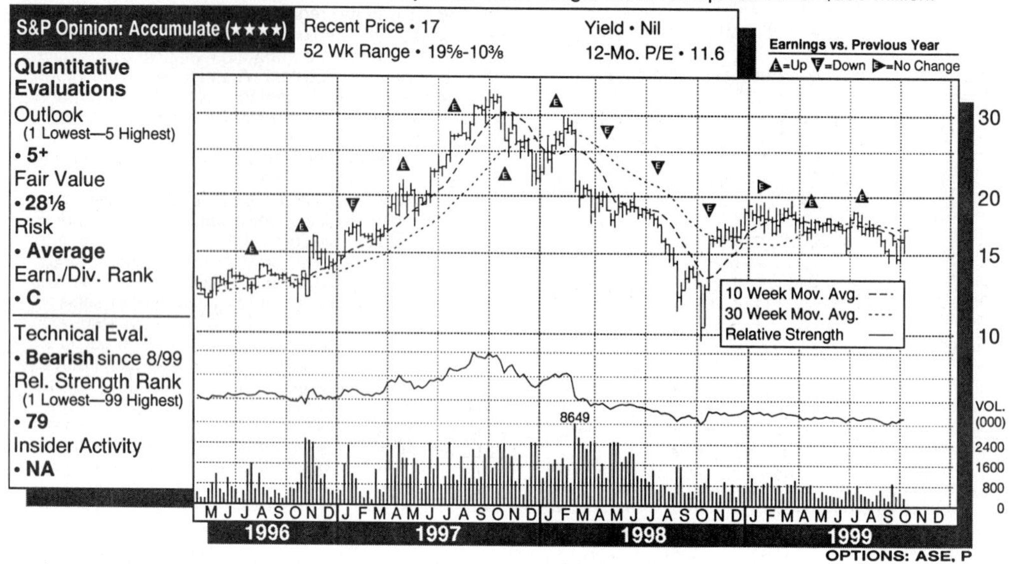

Overview - 02-AUG-99

Revenues for 1999 could increase 5.5% after a flat year in 1998, largely reflecting the acquisition of Jevic and Action Express and a rebound at Yellow Freight System. Yellow's traffic will be flat in 1999 after falling 3.6% in 1998 when shippers diverted freight away from all Teamster carriers due to strike concerns. Volumes are static because Yellow has chosen to improve is business mix; accordingly yield should rise about 3% in 1999. Margins will widen as Yellow employs technology to make process improvements and cut costs. Higher fuel costs will be recovered through a rate surcharge. Saia's profit growth will slow markedly as traffic increases just 3%. Additional volumes derived from Saia's entry into Virginia will be offset by weakness in the Gulf region. YELL will see a positive contribution from its mid-1999 acquisition of Jevic and from the inclusion of Action Express, bought in December 1998. WestEx will move into the black as it builds density and network efficiencies.

Valuation - 02-AUG-99

The shares of this trucker have yet to recover from their steep loss in 1998. Yellow slid in 1998 when shippers turned their backs on LTL carriers having Teamster exposure. Though no strike developed in 1998, the company lost some business which it is only now winning back. We endorse YELL's strategy of building a non-union regional LTL presence. Towards this end, the company dumped its Preston Trucking unit, a Teamster carrier, in mid-1998. Preston was replaced by non-union Jevic Transportation, which YELL bought in July 1999 for $162 million in cash. The company repurchased 2,900,000 of its shares in 1998 (about 10%) for $19 each. At recent prices, YELL, which was trading at a P/E, price-to-sales and price to EBITDA ratio well below that of its peer, is worth accumulating.

Key Stock Statistics

S&P EPS Est. 1999	1.85	Tang. Bk. Value/Share	13.71
P/E on S&P Est. 1999	9.2	Beta	0.86
S&P EPS Est. 2000	2.15	Shareholders	2,900
Dividend Rate/Share	Nil	Market cap. (B)	$0.423
Shs. outstg. (M)	24.9	Inst. holdings	71%
Avg. daily vol. (M)	0.106		

Value of $10,000 invested 5 years ago: $ 7,373

Fiscal Year Ending Dec. 31

	1999	1998	1997	1996	1995	1994
Revenues (Million $)						
1Q	727.5	692.5	785.1	741.7	765.0	748.2
2Q	756.1	727.4	844.4	759.3	773.8	592.2
3Q	—	744.9	882.2	790.4	772.0	769.3
4Q	—	735.8	837.1	781.1	745.9	757.9
Yr.	—	2,901	3,349	3,072	3,057	2,867
Earnings Per Share ($)						
1Q	**0.19**	**0.13**	0.23	-0.51	0.11	-0.23
2Q	**0.52**	**0.45**	0.50	0.07	0.04	-0.78
3Q	**E0.60**	**0.52**	0.71	0.32	-0.41	0.47
4Q	**E0.55**	**0.41**	**0.41**	-0.85	-0.81	0.40
Yr.	**E1.85**	**1.49**	**1.83**	**-0.97**	**-1.07**	-0.14

Next earnings report expected: mid October

Dividend Data

Cash dividends were suspended in 1995, after having been paid each year since 1958. A poison pill stock purchase right was distributed in 1986.

Yellow Corporation

Business Summary - 02-AUG-99

Yellow Corporation is a holding company for a family of motor carriers that offer long-haul and regional less-than-truckload (LTL) freight services. LTL services are tailored to the needs of shippers seeking to cut inventory levels by making more frequent shipment of smaller lots. The purchase of Jevic Transportation in July 1999 filled a hole in YELL's regional LTL system created when the firm sold its unprofitable Preston Trucking unit in 1998.

Yellow Freight System, accounting for 86% of total revenues in 1998, is the largest U.S. LTL freight motor carrier. Yellow provides direct service throughout the 50 states, Puerto Rico, Canada and Mexico and through alliances provides service to Europe, Asia/Pacific and Latin America.

Yellow's traditional market has been long-haul LTL freight. To improve its competitive position in shorter-haul markets, Yellow has reduced transit time by routing freight to bypass intermediate consolidation centers. Accordingly, Yellow cut its terminal network to 385 at 1998 year-end, from 445 in 1995. In addition, it is expediting shipments, while lowering costs, by employing more sleeper teams and expanding its use of rail intermodal, which in 1998 accounted for 27.3% of vehicle miles. In April 1999 Yellow rolled out an expedited delivery service called "EXCELeration".

Yellow Freight initiated a new time and day-definite freight service in July 1998 dubbed "Exact Express." The new premium service, covering shipments weighing over 70 lbs, allows shippers to select from a variety of time options including overnight. YELL estimates that 70% of Exact Express shipments will move on its ground system, while the rest will be moved by air.

Yellow entered the regional LTL market in 1993 with the acquisition of Preston Trucking and Saia Motor Freight Line. YELL sold Preston in July 1998 to that carrier's senior management. A $63.6 million charge ($2.36 a share) made made against 1998 net income to cover costs related to the sale of Preston. Preston, which operated with Teamster labor, had been unprofitable in recent years. In July 1999 YELL acquired Jevic Transportation, Inc., a non-union LTL carrier serving the Northeast, for $162 million in cash and the assumption of $38 million of liabilities. Jevic earned $9.3 million in 1998 on revenue of $226 million.

Saia Motor Freight Line, accounting for 12% of total revenues in 1998, is the cornerstone of Yellow Corp.'s regional LTL thrust. Saia, which specializes in overnight and second day delivery, serves 11 southeastern states In 1999 Saia launched service to Virginia.

WestEx, acquired in 1994, accounts for 2.2% of revenues. It provides regional LTL service in California, Arizona, New Mexico, Colorado, Texas and Nevada, operating through a network of 32 terminals. In late 1998, YELL acquired Action Express, Inc. an LTL carrier primarily serving the Pacific Northwest. Action has annual revenues of about $40 million.

Per Share Data ($) (Year Ended Dec. 31)	1998	1997	1996	1995	1994	1993	1992	1991	1990	1989
Tangible Bk. Val.	13.71	15.86	14.08	15.04	16.40	17.31	17.28	16.94	16.69	15.24
Cash Flow	5.35	5.97	3.70	3.73	4.63	5.38	5.68	5.39	6.83	4.93
Earnings	1.49	1.83	-0.97	-1.07	-0.14	0.67	1.46	0.95	2.31	0.65
Dividends	Nil	Nil	Nil	0.47	0.94	0.94	0.94	0.94	0.82	0.73
Payout Ratio	Nil	Nil	Nil	NM	NM	140%	64%	99%	35%	113%
Prices - High	29 7/8	34 1/8	16 3/8	24 3/8	30 1/4	29 7/8	32 3/8	33 1/2	31 1/4	32 7/8
- Low	9 5/8	14 1/8	10 1/4	11 7/8	16 3/4	16 7/8	21 3/4	23 3/4	18 3/4	23 7/8
P/E Ratio - High	20	19	NM	NM	NM	45	22	35	14	51
- Low	7	8	NM	NM	NM	25	15	25	8	37
Income Statement Analysis (Million $)										
Revs.	2,901	3,349	3,072	3,057	2,867	2,857	2,263	2,344	2,302	2,220
Oper. Inc.	187	218	163	114	145	204	201	182	248	216
Depr.	104	119	131	135	134	132	118	125	128	123
Int. Exp.	11.7	13.5	21.0	23.4	18.4	17.7	12.2	14.2	15.8	15.5
Pretax Inc.	69.5	89.2	-34.3	-45.0	-3.0	35.0	65.0	40.0	102	27.0
Eff. Tax Rate	42%	41%	NM	NM	NM	47%	37%	34%	36%	30%
Net Inc.	40.1	52.4	-27.2	-30.1	-3.8	18.8	41.0	26.7	65.3	18.6
Balance Sheet & Other Fin. Data (Million $)										
Cash	25.5	19.8	24.8	31.2	24.9	20.7	32.3	12.7	8.3	4.4
Curr. Assets	375	459	390	485	403	379	274	270	270	266
Total Assets	1,106	1,271	1,228	1,435	1,307	1,266	1,061	1,098	1,116	1,082
Curr. Liab.	416	481	424	443	376	342	255	288	290	269
LT Debt	157	163	193	342	240	214	123	146	164	187
Common Eqty.	371	446	396	423	461	486	485	476	469	439
Total Cap.	547	639	621	821	755	760	681	705	723	714
Cap. Exp.	111	118	58.0	163	183	77.0	86.0	110	169	193
Cash Flow	144	171	104	105	0.3	151	159	151	193	142
Curr. Ratio	0.9	1.0	0.9	1.1	1.1	1.1	1.1	0.9	0.9	1.0
% LT Debt of Cap.	28.7	25.5	31.1	41.7	31.8	28.2	18.1	20.7	22.6	26.1
% Net Inc.of Revs.	1.4	1.6	NM	NM	NM	0.7	1.8	1.1	2.8	0.8
% Ret. on Assets	3.4	4.2	NM	NM	NM	1.6	3.8	2.4	6.0	1.8
% Ret. on Equity	9.8	12.5	NM	NM	NM	3.9	8.5	5.6	14.6	4.4

Data as orig reptd.; bef. results of disc opers/spec. items. Per share data adj. for stk. divs. Bold denotes diluted EPS (FASB 128)-prior periods restated. E-Estimated. NA-Not Available. NM-Not Meaningful. NR-Not Ranked.

Office—10990 Roe Ave., P.O. Box 7563, Overland Park, KS 66207. **Tel**—(913) 696-6100. **Website**—http://www.yellowcorp.com **Chrmn, Pres & CEO**—A. M. Myers. **SVP & Secy**—W. F. Martin Jr. **SVP, CFO & Investor Contact**—H. A. (Bert) Trucksess III. **Dirs**—K. E. Agthe, C. C. Carr, H. M. Dean, R. T. LeMay, J. C. McKelvey, A. M. Myers, W. L. Trubeck, C. W. Vogt, W. D. Zollars. **Transfer Agent & Registrar**—ChaseMellon Shareholder Services, South Hackensack, NJ. **Incorporated**—in Indiana in 1950; reincorporated in Delaware in 1983. **Empl**— 29,700. **S&P Analyst:** Stephen R. Klein

STANDARD
&POOR'S
STOCK REPORTS

Zale Corp.

NYSE Symbol **ZLC**
In S&P SmallCap 600

09-OCT-99 **Industry:** Retail (Specialty)

Summary: Zale is the largest U.S. specialty retailer of fine jewelry, operating approximately 1,150 retail locations throughout the U.S., Guam and Puerto Rico.

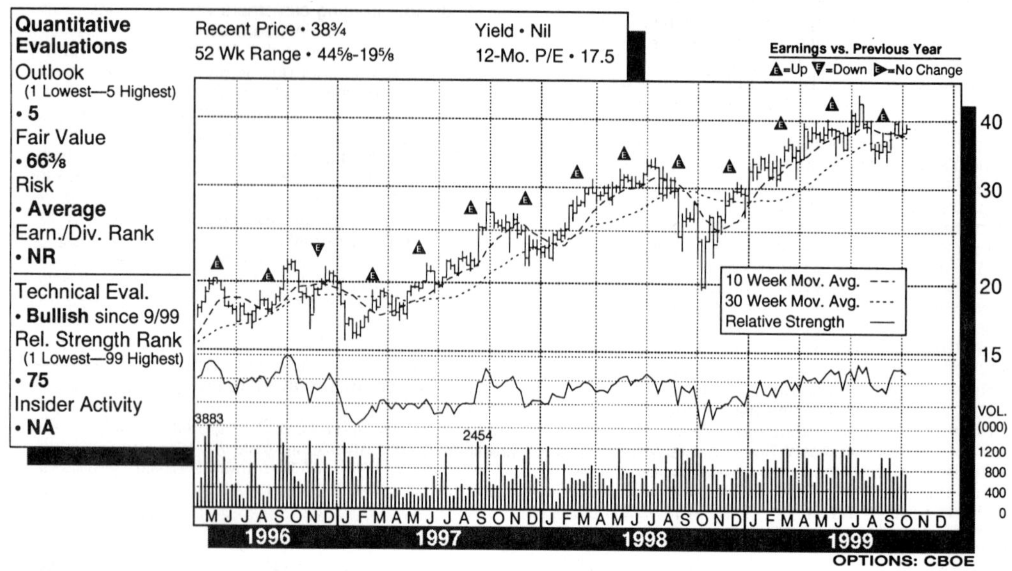

Business Profile - 09-AUG-99

ZLC plans to open approximately 156 new stores in FY 99 (Jul.) and FY 00, mainly in the Zales and Bailey, Banks & Biddle Divisions. The new stores will cost about $44 million, and will solidify its core mall businesses. In June 1999, ZLC acquired Peoples Jewellers Corp., a privately owned 177 store chain in Canada, for C$115 million, and retired C$20 million of related bank debt. ZLC said that it is pleased with its third quarter performance, and should post earnings growth for the year in excess of its stated 20% goal. The company also noted that the results of its merchandising and support strategies continue to have a positive impact on its bottom line, and should continue to drive profitability and productivity going forward.

Operational Review - 09-AUG-99

Net sales for the nine months ended April 30, 1999, rose 6.8%, year to year, on 6.2% higher comparable store sales and an increased store count. Gross margins widened on reduced markdowns resulting from more efficient purchasing. SG&A expense rose less rapidly than sales, due to store productivity efforts and the sale of Diamond Park stores. Depreciation and amortization rose 25%. In the absence of one-time gains from the sale of land and Diamond Park, net income was up 18%, to $72,390,000 ($1.98 a share), from $61,486,000 ($1.64).

Stock Performance - 08-OCT-99

In the past 30 trading days, ZLC's shares have increased 8%, compared to a 0.91% fall in the S&P 500. Average trading volume for the past five days was 146,180 shares, compared with the 40-day moving average of 164,382 shares.

Key Stock Statistics

Dividend Rate/Share	Nil	Shareholders	1,253
Shs. outstg. (M)	36.4	Market cap. (B)	$ 1.4
Avg. daily vol. (M)	0.147	Inst. holdings	91%
Tang. Bk. Value/Share	17.80		
Beta	0.84		

Value of $10,000 invested 5 years ago: $ 41,891

Fiscal Year Ending Jul. 31

	1999	1998	1997	1996	1995	1994
Revenues (Million $)						
1Q	254.2	252.5	230.8	214.3	205.5	184.8
2Q	568.0	522.0	505.1	452.0	427.2	368.6
3Q	280.7	258.3	244.4	222.3	192.1	167.1
4Q	326.0	280.9	273.6	248.9	211.4	199.9
Yr.	1,429	1,314	1,254	1,137	1,036	920.3
Earnings Per Share ($)						
1Q	**0.06**	0.03	-0.03	0.03	-0.09	-0.18
2Q	**1.75**	**1.57**	**1.41**	1.27	1.19	1.07
3Q	**0.17**	**0.04**	-0.04	-0.07	-0.11	-0.13
4Q	**0.23**	**0.20**	0.04	Nil	-0.09	-0.11
Yr.	**2.21**	**1.84**	**1.38**	**1.23**	**0.88**	**0.62**

Next earnings report expected: mid November

Dividend Data

The company currently intends to retain future earnings for use in the expansion and operation of its business. ZLC does not anticipate paying dividends on its common stock in the foreseeable future.

A Division of The McGraw-Hill Companies

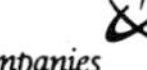

Zale Corporation

Business Summary - 09-AUG-99

Zale Corp. (ZLC) is the largest U.S. specialty retailer of fine jewelry. As of July 31, 1998, the company operated 1,125 retail jewelry stores, mainly located in shopping malls throughout the U.S., Guam, and Puerto Rico. The company operates through three distinct divisions: Zales, Gordon's and Bailey, Banks & Biddle. In September 1997, ZLC signed an agreement to sell the majority of the assets of its Diamond Park Fine Jewelers Division, which managed leased jewelry departments in major department stores. ZLC continued to operate 47 leased fine jewelry departments in Dillard's stores through January 1998, when the lease expired.

The Zales Division provides more traditional, moderately priced jewelry to a broad range of customers. The company also operates six Zales outlet stores in four states. The Gordon's Division offers contemporary merchandise that is targeted to regional preferences at somewhat higher price points than Zales. The Bailey, Banks & Biddle Division operates upscale jewelry stores.

The company believes it is well-positioned to compete in the highly fragmented retail jewelry industry, which is estimated at about $38 billion. ZLC believes it can leverage its established brand names, economies of scale, and geographic and demographic diversity. The company attributes its significant brand name recognition to its long standing presence in the industry and its national and regional advertising campaigns. ZLC believes that name recognition is an important advantage in jewelry retailing, as products are normally unbranded and customers must trust the reliability and credibility of a retailer. The Zales division is positioned as the company's flagship store, operating 695 stores as of July 31, 1998. The store offers merchandise that is generally standardized, targeting customers who represent a cross-section of the mainstream U.S. population. The average Zales store is about 1,450 square feet, and the average selling price per unit sold is $254. The division accounted for about 56% of FY 98 sales.

Gordon's differentiates itself from Zales by providing a more upscale, contemporary product mix. At July 31, 1998, Gordon's had 317 stores in 35 states and Puerto Rico, substantially all of which operate under the trade name Gordon's Jewelers. The average store size is about 1,400 sq. ft. and the average selling price per unit sold is $302. Gordon's accounted for about 24% of the company's FY 98 net sales. The Bailey, Banks & Biddle division offers higher-end merchandise, more exclusive designs and a prestigious shopping environment for the upscale costumer. At July 31, 1998, Bailey, Banks & Biddle operated 107 upscale jewelry stores in 27 states and Guam. The average store is approximately 3,200 sq. ft. The average selling price per unit sold was $528.

ZLC offers and grants credit through its private label credit card program. Approximately 50% of the company's retail sales in FY 98 through its Zale, Gord on's and Bailey, Banks & Biddle divisions were generated by credit sales on the private label credit cards.

Per Share Data ($) (Year Ended Jul. 31)	1999	1998	1997	1996	1995	1994	1993	1992	1991	1990
Tangible Bk. Val.	NA	19.42	17.48	15.54	11.20	9.80	8.89	NA	NA	NA
Cash Flow	NA	2.48	1.83	1.44	0.91	0.66	NA	NA	NA	NA
Earnings	2.21	1.84	1.38	1.23	0.88	0.66	NA	NA	NA	NA
Dividends	Nil	Nil	Nil	Nil	Nil	Nil	Nil	NA	NA	NA
Payout Ratio	Nil	Nil	Nil	Nil	Nil	Nil	Nil	NA	NA	NA
Prices - High	44 5/8	34 1/8	28 1/8	20 1/4	17	14	11 5/8	NA	NA	NA
- Low	30 1/4	19 1/2	15 5/8	13 1/4	10 1/8	8 1/4	8	NA	NA	NA
P/E Ratio - High	20	19	20	16	19	21	NA	NA	NA	NA
- Low	14	11	11	11	12	13	NA	NA	NA	NA
Income Statement Analysis (Million $)										
Revs.	NA	1,314	1,254	1,137	1,036	920	NA	NA	NA	NA
Oper. Inc.	NA	157	132	103	78.9	58.7	NA	NA	NA	NA
Depr.	NA	23.7	16.3	7.5	1.2	NM	NA	NA	NA	NA
Int. Exp.	NA	37.2	36.9	33.2	37.5	30.2	NA	NA	NA	NA
Pretax Inc.	NA	110	79.9	70.1	47.8	34.7	NA	NA	NA	NA
Eff. Tax Rate	NA	37%	37%	36%	34%	33%	NA	NA	NA	NA
Net Inc.	NA	68.9	50.6	45.0	31.5	23.1	NA	NA	NA	NA
Balance Sheet & Other Fin. Data (Million $)										
Cash	NA	179	41.6	50.0	155	154	NA	NA	NA	NA
Curr. Assets	NA	1,180	1,047	953	951	974	NA	NA	NA	NA
Total Assets	NA	1,446	1,281	1,164	1,111	1,113	NA	NA	NA	NA
Curr. Liab.	NA	208	170	178	169	211	NA	NA	NA	NA
LT Debt	NA	480	451	404	441	444	NA	NA	NA	NA
Common Eqty.	NA	707	542	476	392	343	NA	NA	NA	NA
Total Cap.	NA	1,128	993	882	833	787	NA	NA	NA	NA
Cap. Exp.	NA	63.5	54.0	48.8	42.3	27.8	NA	NA	NA	NA
Cash Flow	NA	92.6	66.8	52.5	32.7	23.1	NA	NA	NA	NA
Curr. Ratio	NA	5.7	6.2	5.4	5.6	4.5	NA	NA	NA	NA
% LT Debt of Cap.	NA	42.6	45.4	45.9	52.9	56.4	NA	NA	NA	NA
% Net Inc.of Revs.	NA	5.2	4.0	4.0	3.0	2.5	NA	NA	NA	NA
% Ret. on Assets	NA	5.1	4.1	4.0	2.8	2.2	NA	NA	NA	NA
% Ret. on Equity	NA	10.5	9.9	10.4	8.6	7.1	NA	NA	NA	NA

Data as orig reptd.; bef. results of disc opers/spec. items. Per share data adj. for stk. divs. Bold denotes diluted EPS (FASB 128)-prior periods restated. E-Estimated. NA-Not Available. NM-Not Meaningful. NR-Not Ranked.

Office—901 West Walnut Hill Lane, Irving, TX 75038-1003. **Tel**—(972) 580-4000. **Website**—http://www.zalecorp.com **Chrmn & CEO**—R. J. DiNicola. **Pres & COO**—B. Raff **EVP & CFO**—S. Gove. **Investor Contact**—Cynthia Gordon (972) 580-5047.**Dirs**—G. Adams, A. D. Brown, P. P. Copses, R. J. DiNicola, A. Jung, R. C. Marcus, C. H. Pistor, A. H. Tisch. **Transfer Agent & Registrar**—Bank of New York**Incorporated**—in Delaware in 1989; originally incorporated in Texas in 1924. **Empl**— 10,000. **S&P Analyst:** Matthew C. Hershberg

STANDARD
&POOR'S
STOCK REPORTS

Zebra Technologies

Nasdaq Symbol **ZBRA**

In S&P SmallCap 600

09-OCT-99

Industry: Photography/Imaging

Summary: Zebra Technologies is an international provider of demand label printers and supplies for users of automatic identification and data collection systems.

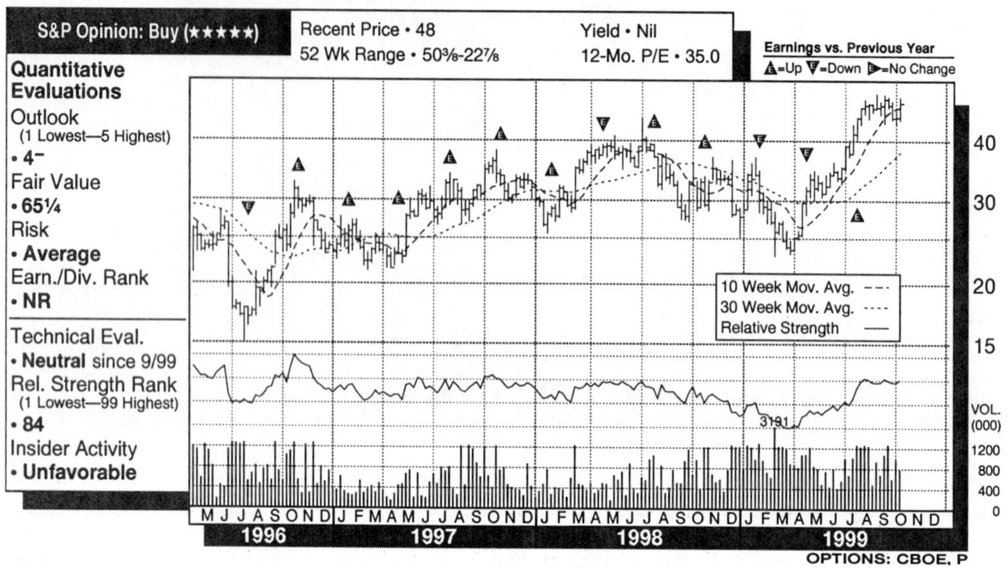

Overview - 27-JUL-99

We see revenues advancing about 15% in 1999, driven by strength across all geographies and product lines. Following stronger than anticipated results in the first two quarters of 1999, it appears that the majority of challenges associated with integration of the Eltron merger are behind the company, allowing management to focus on growing the business. In future quarters, we expect ZBRA to further penetrate promising new markets, such as the plastic card business. We expect margins to widen in 1999, reflecting increased purchasing power of the combined company, as well as the elimination of inefficiencies related to integrating the acquisition. We have raised our 1999 operating EPS estimate $0.19, to $2.18, which represents a 37% increase over 1998 EPS (excluding merger costs), and see earnings rising 19%, to $2.58 a share, in 2000.

Valuation - 27-JUL-99

Shares of ZBRA have risen sharply sharply since early April 1999, and were recently trading at 20 times our upwardly revised 1999 EPS estimate of $2.18 (17X our 2000 EPS estimate of $2.58), which represents a discount to the P/E multiple of the broader markets. We believe the disruptions associated with the Eltron merger are behind Zebra, evidenced by two consecutive quarters of earnings that beat analysts' expectations. We believe this strong operating momentum will carry into the latter half of 1999 and, consequently, continue to recommend that investors buy the shares. Our long-term revenue outlook is strong, reflecting the expectation of continued strength in North America and improving Asian economies. In addition, with about $190 million of cash on the balance sheet and no debt, an acquisition in the early part of 2000 is possible.

Key Stock Statistics

S&P EPS Est. 1999	2.18	Tang. Bk. Value/Share	9.69
P/E on S&P Est. 1999	22.0	Beta	1.12
S&P EPS Est. 2000	2.58	Shareholders	600
Dividend Rate/Share	Nil	Market cap. (B)	$ 1.2
Shs. outstg. (M)	31.3	Inst. holdings	57%
Avg. daily vol. (M)	0.212		

Value of $10,000 invested 5 years ago: $ 16,953

Fiscal Year Ending Dec. 31

	1999	1998	1997	1996	1995	1994
Revenues (Million $)						
1Q	89.82	80.80	42.42	38.35	34.39	21.98
2Q	97.32	87.04	47.84	40.49	35.49	25.89
3Q	—	88.07	49.89	43.76	37.48	28.25
4Q	—	80.08	53.33	47.12	41.23	30.99
Yr.	—	336.0	192.1	169.7	148.6	107.1
Earnings Per Share ($)						
1Q	**0.41**	**0.42**	**0.48**	**0.23**	0.27	0.17
2Q	**0.55**	**0.45**	**0.40**	**0.28**	0.29	0.21
3Q	—	**0.42**	**0.41**	**0.36**	0.04	0.23
4Q	—	**-0.01**	**0.48**	**0.40**	0.33	0.26
Yr.	—	**1.29**	**1.76**	**1.27**	**1.22**	0.87

Next earnings report expected: late October

Dividend Data

No cash dividends have been paid. A two-for-one stock split was effected in December 1995.

A Division of The McGraw-Hill Companies

Zebra Technologies Corporation

Business Summary - 27-JUL-99

Heading into 1999, Zebra Technologies' biggest challenge is the successful integration of its merger with Eltron International, previously a major competitor of ZBRA. The transaction was completed in October 1998 and called for the exchange of 0.90 shares of Zebra Class B common stock for each Eltron common share. The combined company generated pro forma sales of nearly $340 million in 1998.

ZBRA products consist of a broad line of computerized on-demand bar code label printers, print engines, plastic card printers, specialty bar code labeling materials, ink ribbons and bar code label design software. In 1998, hardware sales represented 79% of revenues, while supplies accounted for 19% of revenues. Working together, ZBRA's products provide identification labeling solutions for customers within the manufacturing, service and government sectors. Zebra's products are instrumental in many processes, including inventory control, small package delivery, baggage handling, automated warehousing, Just-In-Time (JIT) manufacturing, employee records and hospital management systems, among others.

The company believes that the advantages afforded by thermal transfer printing, including the ability to print high-resolution images on a wide variety of label materials at a lower cost than that of competing technologies, make it the technology of choice in ZBRA's target markets for the foreseeable future. The company's printers are designed to operate at the user's location to produce and dispense bar coded labels in environments ranging from fiery steel mills to the icy interiors of freezer compartments. Bar codes printed with Zebra printers are also used to control the movement of goods through warehouses.

One of the fastest growing areas in the bar code labeling industry is plastic card printers, which have the ability to produce on-site, full color, photographic quality plastic cards. These cards can typically be created in less than 30 seconds for under one dollar. The company believes that personalized card applications, such as driver's licenses, loyalty cards, school and work identification cards, and financial transaction cards, are well-suited to benefit from plastic printer card technology.

ZBRA's products are sold in over 90 countries, and in 1998 sales to foreign customers accounted for 41% of net sales. ZBRA believes that international sales growth will outpace growth in the U.S. because of the lower penetration of bar code systems in foreign markets.

In July 1997, ZBRA announced the discontinuation of its retail software business, which it had acquired two years earlier. The action resulted in a $2.4 million charge in the second quarter of 1997.

Per Share Data ($) (Year Ended Dec. 31)	1998	1997	1996	1995	1994	1993	1992	1991	1990	1989
Tangible Bk. Val.	8.67	7.39	5.79	4.47	3.41	2.53	1.76	1.28	0.58	NA
Cash Flow	0.16	1.94	1.35	1.03	0.94	0.81	0.53	0.50	0.53	NA
Earnings	1.29	1.76	1.19	0.94	0.88	0.76	0.49	0.48	0.52	NA
Dividends	Nil	Nil	Nil	Nil	Nil	Nil	Nil	Nil	Nil	NA
Payout Ratio	Nil	Nil	Nil	Nil	Nil	Nil	Nil	Nil	Nil	NA
Prices - High	44 5/8	38 1/4	35 3/4	35 1/4	28 5/8	30 3/8	12 3/8	9 1/2	NA	NA
- Low	25	21 1/4	15	18	11 3/4	10 1/8	7 1/4	7 1/4	NA	NA
P/E Ratio - High	35	22	30	37	33	40	25	20	NA	NA
- Low	19	12	13	19	13	13	15	15	NA	NA
Income Statement Analysis (Million $)										
Revs.	336	192	170	149	107	87.5	58.7	45.6	38.0	NA
Oper. Inc.	80.0	57.0	43.5	40.8	31.7	25.9	16.2	13.2	10.9	NA
Depr.	10.2	4.3	3.8	2.2	1.4	1.0	0.8	0.5	0.4	NA
Int. Exp.	0.4	0.0	0.1	0.1	0.3	0.2	0.2	0.1	0.0	NA
Pretax Inc.	65.0	66.7	44.6	38.0	32.9	28.5	17.8	13.3	10.7	NA
Eff. Tax Rate	38%	36%	35%	41%	36%	36%	34%	19%	1.60%	NA
Net Inc.	40.1	42.8	28.9	22.6	21.1	18.3	11.8	10.8	10.5	NA
Balance Sheet & Other Fin. Data (Million $)										
Cash	163	7.2	94.5	71.9	54.2	41.5	33.7	31.2	1.0	NA
Curr. Assets	266	187	149	119	88.7	71.5	51.4	46.8	14.2	NA
Total Assets	310	204	163	131	95.0	76.7	54.8	48.9	16.2	NA
Curr. Liab.	36.8	22.6	20.2	19.0	12.4	15.5	12.0	17.1	3.8	NA
LT Debt	0.0	0.3	2.2	2.2	0.2	0.3	0.3	0.4	0.5	NA
Common Eqty.	271	180	140	108	82.0	60.6	42.2	30.7	11.9	NA
Total Cap.	273	181	143	112	82.3	60.9	42.7	31.7	12.4	NA
Cap. Exp.	25.6	5.3	6.0	4.3	2.1	2.5	2.2	0.7	1.0	NA
Cash Flow	50.3	47.1	32.8	24.8	22.5	19.3	12.7	11.3	10.9	NA
Curr. Ratio	7.2	8.3	7.4	6.3	7.1	4.6	4.3	2.7	3.7	NA
% LT Debt of Cap.	0.0	0.1	1.5	2.0	0.3	0.5	0.8	1.3	3.6	NA
% Net Inc.of Revs.	11.9	22.3	17.0	15.2	19.7	20.9	20.2	23.8	27.7	NA
% Ret. on Assets	15.6	23.3	19.6	20.0	24.5	27.7	22.8	31.9	NA	NA
% Ret. on Equity	17.8	26.8	23.3	23.7	29.5	35.5	32.5	48.5	NA	NA

Data as orig reptd.; bef. results of disc opers/spec. items. Per share data adj. for stk. divs. Bold denotes diluted EPS (FASB 128)-prior periods restated. E-Estimated. NA-Not Available. NM-Not Meaningful. NR-Not Ranked.

Office—333 Corporate Woods Pkwy., Vernon Hills, IL 60061. **Reincorporated**—in Delaware in 1991. **Tel**—(847) 634-6700. **Fax**—(847) 634-1830. **Website**—http://www.zebra.com **Chrmn & CEO**—E. L. Kaplan. **Pres**—C. E. Turnbull. **SVP & Secy**—G. Cless. **CFO, Treas & Investor Contact**—Charles R. Whitchurch. **Dirs**—G. Cless, E. L. Kaplan, C. Knowles, D. R. Riley, M. A. Smith. **Transfer Agent & Registrar**—Harris Trust & Savings Bank, Chicago. **Empl**— 627. **S&P Analyst:** Stephen J. Tekirian

STANDARD
&POOR'S
STOCK REPORTS

Zenith National Insurance

NYSE Symbol **ZNT**

In S&P SmallCap 600

09-OCT-99

Industry: Insurance (Property-Casualty)

Summary: Through subsidiaries, ZNT writes workers' compensation, reinsurance, other property and casualty and health insurance primarily in California and Texas.

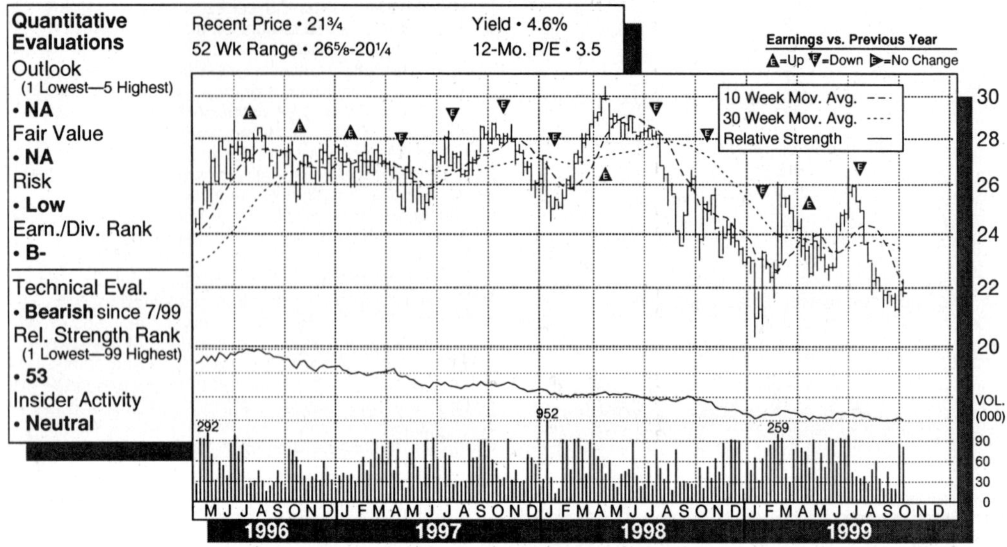

Business Profile - 21-JUN-99

In March 1999, ZNT completed the sale of CalFarm Insurance Company to Nationwide Mutual Insurance Company for approximately $273.0 million in cash, subject to post-closing adjustments in certain circumstances. The after-tax gain on the sale for Zenith was approximately $104.0 million, or $6.08 per share. In May 1999, the company stated that competition in the workers' compensation business continues to be intense, and has resulted in unsatisfactory operating results in workers' compensation. Catastrophe losses continued to take its toll on ZNT as reflected in the decline in the total combined ratio to 109.6% for the three months ended March 31, 1999, from 102.0% in the year ago period.

Operational Review - 21-JUN-99

Total revenues in the three months ended March 31, 1999, rose 12%, year to year, as premiums earned increased 14%, primarily due to the RISCORP acquisition, partially offset by a decrease in workers' compensation premiums in California. However, total expenses rose 20%, as the RISCORP acquisition and catastrophe losses contributed to increases of loss and loss adjustment expenses of 26% and policy acquisition costs of 22%, but after a $160.3 million gain on the sale of CalFarm, and taxes at 34.9%, versus 33.6%, net income increased to $104.4 million ($6.09 a share), from $7.1 million ($0.42).

Stock Performance - 08-OCT-99

In the past 30 trading days, ZNT's shares have declined 0.85%, compared to a 0.91% fall in the S&P 500. Average trading volume for the past five days was 16,180 shares, compared with the 40-day moving average of 9,310 shares.

Key Stock Statistics

Dividend Rate/Share	1.00	Shareholders	353
Shs. outstg. (M)	17.2	Market cap. (B)	$0.375
Avg. daily vol. (M)	0.010	Inst. holdings	0%
Tang. Bk. Value/Share	23.46		
Beta	0.49		

Value of $10,000 invested 5 years ago: $ 12,515

Fiscal Year Ending Dec. 31

	1999	1998	1997	1996	1995	1994
Revenues (Million $)						
1Q	162.2	145.3	146.7	134.6	127.3	138.9
2Q	106.5	165.0	152.4	133.7	130.7	151.3
3Q	—	162.1	147.1	137.1	130.3	153.2
4Q	—	164.4	154.3	151.1	130.7	151.7
Yr.	—	636.8	600.5	556.4	519.0	595.1
Earnings Per Share ($)						
1Q	**6.09**	**0.42**	**0.40**	**0.70**	0.23	0.43
2Q	**-0.20**	**0.42**	**0.44**	**0.60**	0.40	0.57
3Q	—	**0.20**	**0.45**	**0.51**	0.34	0.53
4Q	—	**0.08**	**0.28**	**0.30**	0.10	0.46
Yr.	—	**1.11**	**1.57**	**2.12**	**0.36**	**1.99**

Next earnings report expected: early November

Dividend Data (Dividends have been paid since 1978.)

Amount ($)	Date Decl.	Ex-Div. Date	Stock of Record	Payment Date
0.250	Dec. 08	Jan. 27	Jan. 29	Feb. 12 '99
0.250	Feb. 25	Apr. 28	Apr. 30	May. 14 '99
0.250	May. 20	Jul. 28	Jul. 30	Aug. 13 '99
0.250	Sep. 02	Oct. 27	Oct. 29	Nov. 15 '99

A Division of The McGraw-Hill Companies

Zenith National Insurance Corp.

Business Summary - 21-JUN-99

After the March 1999 sale of CalFarm, Zenith has focused its efforts on improving the underwriting profitability of its nationally diversified workers' compensation operations, with California premiums currently representing less than half of Zenith's workers' compensation business for the first time.

Zenith National Insurance, through its subsidiaries, is engaged in the business of writing workers' compensation insurance, reinsurance, health insurance, and commercial, auto, homeowners, farmowners and other coverages, primarily in California and Texas. Zenith also conducts real estate operations, which develops land and constructs homes in Las Vegas, Nevada. Workers' compensation insurance is written by Zenith Insurance Co. Automobile, homeowners and farmowners insurance is offered by Zenith's former subsidiary, CalFarm Insurance. Contributions to net premiums earned in recent years were: workers' compensation 53% in 1998 (up from 49% in 1997), property casualty 42% (44%), and reinsurance 5% (7%).

The company's workers' compensation business is produced by independent licensed insurance agents and brokers primarily in California and Texas. The standard policy issued by Zenith provides payments for, among other things, temporary or permanent disability benefits, death benefits, medical and hospital expenses, and expenses of vocational rehabilitation. Zenith is licensed to conduct business in 39 states and the District of Columbia. In April 1998, ZNT completed the purchase of the workers' compensation business of RISCORP Inc., for the difference in book value of RISCORP's assets and liabilities on the closing date, or a minimum of $35 million. In March 1999, ZNT paid $53.7 million to RISCORP, which was the balance of the purchase price payable including interest from April 1, 1998, less an amount for assets not transferred by RISCORP. In December 1996, the company acquired the Associated General Contractors' Self-Insurers' Fund, a Florida workers' compensation self-insurers' fund, which was merged into Zenith Insurance.

In March 1999, ZNT completed the sale of CalFarm to Nationwide Mutual Insurance Company for $273.0 million. CalFarm Insurance offers a comprehensive line of property and casualty insurance, with about 105,000 policies in-force including homeowners, automobile, commercial multiple peril and farmowners coverage. CalFarm also offers group health insurance with about 24,000 certificates in-force.

ZNT operates its reinsurance activity as a participant in contracts or treaties in which, typically, the reinsurance coverage is syndicated to a number of assuming companies.

Per Share Data ($) (Year Ended Dec. 31)	1998	1997	1996	1995	1994	1993	1992	1991	1990	1989
Tangible Bk. Val.	18.73	19.89	19.17	18.13	15.09	17.21	14.57	14.73	12.40	13.14
Oper. Earnings	0.67	1.10	1.72	0.95	1.86	1.75	1.01	1.73	2.10	2.22
Earnings	1.11	1.57	2.11	1.08	1.99	2.76	1.02	2.28	-0.47	1.98
Dividends	1.00	1.00	1.00	1.00	1.00	1.00	1.00	1.00	0.86	0.82
Payout Ratio	90%	64%	47%	93%	50%	36%	98%	44%	NM	41%
Prices - High	30½	28¾	28⅞	24⅝	27⅜	29¼	20	18½	18¾	21½
- Low	22⅞	24⅝	21⅛	19⅜	20⅝	19⅝	14½	12	9⅞	16¾
P/E Ratio - High	27	18	13	68	13	10	19	8	d	10
- Low	21	16	10	53	10	7	14	5	d	8
Income Statement Analysis (Million $)										
Premium Inc.	530	489	453	438	463	470	442	438	431	413
Net Invest. Inc.	53.6	52.3	51.2	46.2	98.0	92.5	96.6	95.7	90.0	77.9
Oth. Revs.	53.3	59.4	52.4	34.8	33.9	23.5	10.8	13.0	-53.0	-7.0
Total Revs.	637	600	556	519	595	583	549	546	468	484
Pretax Inc.	28.8	43.5	57.1	29.4	57.6	73.5	19.7	52.5	-2.7	49.0
Net Oper. Inc.	11.6	19.7	30.6	17.4	35.5	33.7	19.1	32.9	41.4	46.2
Net Inc.	19.1	28.1	37.6	19.7	37.9	53.2	19.3	43.3	-9.2	41.1
Balance Sheet & Other Fin. Data (Million $)										
Cash & Equiv.	15.6	12.5	12.1	6.9	7.1	8.6	1.9	9.6	4.6	4.5
Premiums Due	134	72.8	80.5	70.2	126	118	91.0	76.6	77.6	76.8
Invest. Assets: Bonds	770	834	815	799	1,225	1,409	1,243	987	822	655
Invest. Assets: Stocks	51.6	45.7	37.6	36.5	46.0	58.0	132	170	203	251
Invest. Assets: Loans	Nil	Nil	Nil	Nil	45.3	44.1	39.3	35.2	30.2	25.5
Invest. Assets: Total	1,049	880	853	835	1,418	1,456	1,336	1,167	1,033	913
Deferred Policy Costs	23.9	20.8	20.8	20.3	109	108	91.0	76.6	63.9	47.2
Total Assets	1,819	1,252	1,243	1,115	1,841	1,858	1,704	1,478	1,327	1,182
Debt	148	74.5	74.4	74.2	74.1	74.0	73.9	49.8	53.6	26.7
Common Eqty.	347	362	338	330	310	349	302	281	241	299
Prop. & Cas. Loss Ratio	72.4	71.3	70.1	74.4	65.6	67.8	76.8	70.4	64.1	62.7
Prop. & Cas. Expense Ratio	32.9	32.1	29.7	27.4	27.7	25.7	27.9	29.6	29.2	29.2
Prop. & Cas. Combined Ratio	105.3	103.4	99.8	101.8	93.3	93.5	104.7	100.0	93.3	91.9
% Return On Revs.	3.0	4.7	6.8	3.8	6.4	9.1	3.5	7.9	NM	8.5
% Ret. on Equity	5.4	8.0	11.3	6.2	11.5	16.3	6.6	16.6	NM	13.7

Data as orig reptd.; bef. results of disc opers/spec. items. Per share data adj. for stk. divs. Bold denotes diluted EPS (FASB 128)-prior periods restated. E-Estimated. NA-Not Available. NM-Not Meaningful. NR-Not Ranked.

Office—21255 Califa St., Woodland Hills, CA 91367-5021. **Tel**—(818) 713-1000. **Website**—www.znic.com **Chrmn & Pres**—S. R. Zax. **EVP, CFO & Investor Contact**—Fredricka Taubitz. **SVP & Secy**—J. J. Tickner. **Dirs**—G. E. Bello, M. M. Kampelman, R. J. Miller, W. S. Sessions, H. L. Silbert, R. M. Steinberg, S. P. Steinberg, G. Tsai Jr., M. W. Zavis, S. R. Zax. **Transfer Agent & Registrar**—ChaseMellon Shareholder Services, Los Angeles.**Incorporated**—in Delaware in 1971. **Empl**— 1,800. **S&P Analyst:** J. Rudy

STANDARD
&POOR'S
STOCK REPORTS

ZixIt Corp.

NASDAQ Symbol **ZIXI**

In S&P SmallCap 600

13-OCT-99

Industry:
Electrical Equipment

Summary: This development stage company recently changed its business focus and now plans to concentrate on Internet-related businesses.

Quantitative Evaluations

Outlook
(1 Lowest—5 Highest)
• **NA**

Fair Value
• **NA**

Risk
• **NA**

Earn./Div. Rank
• **C**

Technical Eval.
• **Bearish** since 9/99

Rel. Strength Rank
(1 Lowest—99 Highest)
• **4**

Insider Activity
• **Neutral**

Recent Price • 24⅜
52 Wk Range • 90-3½

Yield • Nil
12-Mo. P/E • 36.9

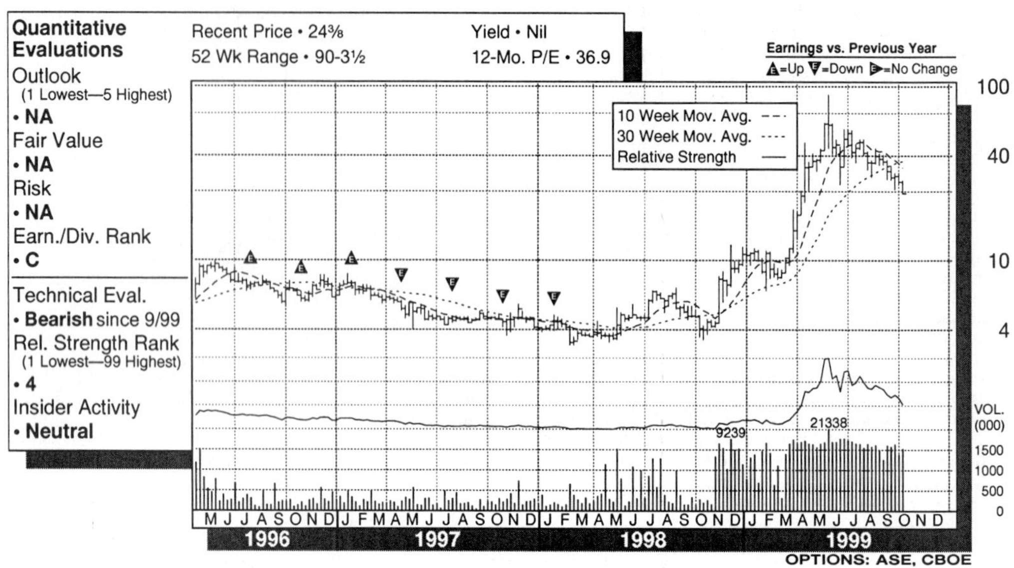

Business Profile - 22-JUL-99

During 1998, ZIXI sold all of its business units as it completely overhauled itself to focus on new opportunities. In May 1999, ZIXI announced that it expected to invest $20-$30 million during 1999 in an Internet transaction payment system, called ZixCharge, which will use ZIXI's digital signature technology to allow consumers to purchase items over the Internet without divulging personal information to merchants. ZixCharge was on track to be operational by the end of the third quarter of 1999. The company's new digital signature system, ZixMail, was expected to be released for commercial use before the end of August 1999. The present corporate title was adopted in October, 1999.

Operational Review - 22-JUL-99

For the three months ended March 31, 1999, investment income advanced to $1.1 million, from $262,000, reflecting higher cash balances. Following initial research and development expenses of $2.7 million related to the development of a new Internet transaction payment system, partially offset by lower corporate expenses, the net loss widened to $2,415,000 ($0.16 a share) from $946,000 ($0.06). Results in the 1998 period exclude income from discontinued operations of $0.08 a share.

Stock Performance - 08-OCT-99

In the past 30 trading days, ZIXI's shares have declined 36%, compared to a 0.91% fall in the S&P 500. Average trading volume for the past five days was 336,240 shares, compared with the 40-day moving average of 425,779 shares.

Key Stock Statistics

Dividend Rate/Share	Nil	Shareholders	587
Shs. outstg. (M)	15.3	Market cap. (B)	$0.428
Avg. daily vol. (M)	0.437	Inst. holdings	18%
Tang. Bk. Value/Share	4.96		
Beta	NA		

Value of $10,000 invested 5 years ago: $ 10,280

Fiscal Year Ending Dec. 31

	1999	1998	1997	1996	1995	1994
Revenues (Million $)						
1Q	1.06	—	24.15	28.28	13.94	18.96
2Q	—	—	28.88	29.87	13.00	18.51
3Q	—	—	30.19	27.97	24.53	12.21
4Q	—	—	34.49	30.39	28.61	11.77
Yr.	—	—	117.7	116.5	80.07	61.46
Earnings Per Share ($)						
1Q	**-0.16**	—	**-0.22**	**0.02**	-0.02	0.25
2Q	**-0.84**	—	**-0.46**	Nil	-0.09	0.23
3Q	—	—	**-0.11**	Nil	-0.03	0.03
4Q	—	—	**-0.37**	**-0.06**	-0.15	0.01
Yr.	—	**-0.09**	**-1.17**	**-0.04**	**-0.29**	**0.52**

Next earnings report expected: mid November

Dividend Data

Quarterly cash dividends, initiated in June 1993, were suspended in May 1995. A five-for-four stock split was effected in 1993, and a three-for-two split in 1992.

A Division of The McGraw·Hill Companies

ZixIt Corporation

Business Summary - 22-JUL-99

ZixIt Corp. (formerly CustomTracks Corp., and prior to that Amtech Corp.) had a momentous 1998. In May 1998, the company acquired Petabyte Corp., a start-up enterprise founded by David P. Cook, who thereafter became ZIXI's CEO. Although Petabyte had no operations, it owned certain intellectual property and aimed to manufacture and distribute customized digital data products. In September 1998, the company changed its name from Amtech to CustomTracks, reflecting the intended change in business focus from electronic access control and radio frequency identification to the customized compact disc business. The present corporate title was adopted in October, 1999.

In June 1998, ZIXI sold its Transportation Systems Group to UNOVA, Inc. for approximately $33.3 million in cash and stock. Included in UNOVA's purchase were ZIXI's manufacturing and technology facility in Albuquerque, NM, the company's radio frequency identification technologies and other intellectual properties, the brand name Amtech, and all current operations associated with the transportation business.

In July 1998, ZIXI sold the net assets of its Cotag International business unit to Metric Gruppen AB of Solna, Sweden, for $4.6 million. ZIXI may receive up to an estimated additional $800,000 depending on the level and mix of Cotag revenues achieved in 1999. Included in Metric's purchase is the brand name and intellectual property underlying Cotag's hands-free proximity technology, Cotag's manufacturing facility in Cambridge, England, and the ongoing business of the unit.

In November 1998, ZIXI sold its electronic security products business to Johnson Controls, Inc. The sale consisted of the company's wholly-owned subsidiaries: Cardkey Systems, Inc., Cardkey European Holdings Ltd. and Cardkey Systems Pacific Pty. Ltd. ZIXI's proceeds from sale were $44.7 million. Included in the sale were ZIXI's electronic security systems technologies, the brand name Cardkey, and all operations associated with Cardkey.

In February 1999, ZIXI announced that its directors approved a significant investment in a new business that will focus on charging and collecting transaction payments over the Internet. The system design for this business came as a by-product of the company's efforts to obtain music content rights from major record companies. In May 1999, ZIXI announced that it expected to invest $20-$30 million during 1999 in its Internet transaction payment system, called ZixCharge, which will use ZIXI's digital signature technology to allow consumers to purchase items over the Internet without divulging personal information to merchants. ZixCharge was on track to be operational by the end of the third quarter of 1999. The company's new digital signature system, ZixMail, was expected to be released for commercial use before the end of August 1999.

Per Share Data ($) (Year Ended Dec. 31)	1998	1997	1996	1995	1994	1993	1992	1991	1990	1989
Tangible Bk. Val.	5.40	3.36	4.32	4.36	5.16	4.59	3.40	1.26	1.56	2.12
Cash Flow	-0.09	-0.84	0.27	0.28	0.72	0.84	0.63	-0.28	-0.48	-0.74
Earnings	-0.09	-1.17	-0.04	-0.28	0.52	0.70	0.51	-0.40	-0.57	-0.82
Dividends	Nil	Nil	Nil	0.02	0.08	0.06	Nil	Nil	Nil	Nil
Payout Ratio	Nil	Nil	Nil	NM	15%	9%	Nil	Nil	Nil	Nil
Prices - High	12 1/4	8 3/8	9 7/8	10 5/8	33 3/4	32	23 3/4	15 5/8	11 1/4	8
- Low	3 1/4	3 5/8	5 1/8	4 5/8	7 5/8	18 1/4	11 1/4	4 3/4	4 1/8	6
P/E Ratio - High	NM	NM	NM	NM	65	46	46	NM	NM	NM
- Low	NM	NM	NM	NM	15	26	22	NM	NM	NM
Income Statement Analysis (Million $)										
Revs.	2.0	118	117	80.0	61.5	59.4	39.9	18.7	14.8	6.0
Oper. Inc.	-2.1	-10.8	1.5	-2.4	12.9	14.5	7.8	-3.9	-7.7	-7.0
Depr.	0.0	5.0	4.6	3.6	3.0	2.1	1.7	1.5	1.1	0.7
Int. Exp.	Nil	0.1	0.3	0.2	Nil	Nil	Nil	Nil	Nil	Nil
Pretax Inc.	-2.1	-14.7	-0.4	-3.9	12.1	14.1	7.4	-5.0	-7.0	-7.3
Eff. Tax Rate	NM	NM	NM	NM	57%	27%	1.80%	Nil	Nil	Nil
Net Inc.	-1.5	-17.6	-0.6	-4.1	7.7	10.4	7.3	-5.0	-7.0	-7.3
Balance Sheet & Other Fin. Data (Million $)										
Cash	81.2	15.2	17.1	27.8	49.9	36.8	31.2	12.0	7.5	19.2
Curr. Assets	86.7	60.3	62.3	68.0	67.0	54.8	42.8	17.9	16.9	22.8
Total Assets	86.9	85.5	91.0	93.3	80.6	76.7	57.4	23.0	22.3	27.2
Curr. Liab.	5.4	21.8	19.3	18.2	3.5	7.1	4.7	4.3	3.3	1.7
LT Debt	Nil	Nil	Nil	2.6	Nil	Nil	Nil	Nil	Nil	Nil
Common Eqty.	81.4	63.7	71.8	72.5	75.3	66.8	48.8	16.0	18.9	25.5
Total Cap.	81.4	63.7	71.8	75.0	75.3	66.8	48.8	16.0	18.9	25.5
Cap. Exp.	0.1	2.2	4.2	3.3	2.3	7.3	1.1	1.1	1.9	2.5
Cash Flow	-1.5	-12.6	4.0	-0.5	10.6	12.5	8.9	-3.5	-5.8	-6.6
Curr. Ratio	15.9	2.8	3.2	3.7	19.3	7.7	9.0	4.1	5.1	13.7
% LT Debt of Cap.	Nil	Nil	Nil	13.5	Nil	Nil	Nil	Nil	Nil	Nil
% Net Inc.of Revs.	NM	NM	NM	NM	12.5	17.4	18.2	NM	NM	NM
% Ret. on Assets	NM	NM	NM	NM	9.7	15.4	17.4	NM	NM	NM
% Ret. on Equity	NM	NM	NM	NM	10.8	17.8	21.7	NM	NM	NM

Data as orig reptd.; bef. results of disc opers/spec. items. Per share data adj. for stk. divs. Bold denotes diluted EPS (FASB 128)-prior periods restated. E-Estimated. NA-Not Available. NM-Not Meaningful. NR-Not Ranked.

Office—One Galleria Tower, 13355 Noel Rd., Suite 1555, Dallas, TX 75240-6604. **Tel**—(972) 702-7055. **Fax**—(972) 702-7056. **Website**—http://www.customtracks.com. **Chrmn, Pres & CEO**—D. P. Cook. **SVP, CFO & Treas**—S. M. York. **VP-Secy**—R. A. Woessner. **Investor Contact**—Beverly V. Fuortes. **Dirs**—D. P. Cook, M. E. Keane, J. S. Marston, J. L. Martin, A. R. Sanchez Jr., B. G. Streetman, M. Tebbe. **Transfer Agent**—Society National Bank, Dallas. **Incorporated**—in Texas in 1988. **Empl**— 15. **S&P Analyst:** Scott H. Kessler